WHITAKER'S ALMANACK 2000

AN

Almanack

For the Year of Our Lord

2000

ESTABLISHED 1868

BY

JOSEPH WHITAKER, FSA

CONTAINING AN ACCOUNT OF THE

ASTRONOMICAL AND OTHER PHENOMENA

AND

A vast Amount of INFORMATION respecting the

GOVERNMENT, FINANCES, POPULATION,

COMMERCE, and GENERAL STATISTICS of

the various Nations of the WORLD

with an INDEX containing

nearly 10,000

References

LONDON

OFFICE: 51 NINE ELMS LANE

LONDON SW8 5DR

The traditional design of the title page for Whitaker's Almanack which has appeared in each edition since 1868

Whitaker's Almanack

2000

LONDON:

THE STATIONERY OFFICE

The Stationery Office Ltd

51 Nine Elms Lane, London sw8 5DR

Whitaker's Almanack published annually since 1868

© 132nd edition The Stationery Office Ltd 1999

Standard edition (1,291 pages)

Cloth covers

0 11 702252 7

Leather binding

0 11 702253 5

Designed by Douglas Martin
Jacket designed by Compendium
Jacket photographs Telegraph Colour Library, PA News Ltd, Super Stock Ltd
Typeset, printed and bound in Great Britain by
William Clowes Ltd, Beccles, Suffolk

Editorial Consultants
Sally Whitaker
Gyles Brandreth
Rupert Pennant-Rea

Editorial Staff
Lauren Hill (*Editor*)
Bridie Macmahon; Neil Mackay (*Assistant Editors, UK*)
Chris Sadowski (*Assistant Editor, International*)
Arlene Zuccolo (*Database Co-ordinator*)

Published by The Stationery Office and available from:

The Publications Centre
(mail, telephone and fax orders only)
PO Box 276, London sw8 5DT
General enquiries/Telephone orders 0870-600 5522
Fax orders 0870-600 5533

The Stationery Office Bookshops
123 Kingsway, London WC2B 6PQ
020-7242 6393   Fax 020-7242 6394
16 Arthur Street, Belfast BT1 4GD
028-9023 8451   Fax 028-9023 5401
68–69 Bull Street, Birmingham B4 6AD
0121-236 9696   Fax 0121-236 9699
33 Wine Street, Bristol BS1 2BQ
0117-926 4306   Fax 0117-929 4515
The Stationery Office Oriel Bookshop
18–19 High Street, Cardiff CF1 2BZ
029-2039 5548   Fax 029-2038 4347
71 Lothian Road, Edinburgh EH3 9AZ
0870-606 5566   Fax 0870-606 5588
9–21 Princess Street, Manchester M60 8AS
0161-834 7201   Fax 0161-833 0634

The Stationery Office's Accredited Agents
(*see* Yellow Pages)
and through good booksellers

Contents

CONTENTS CONTINUED

Preface

To the 132nd Annual Volume

Welcome to *Whitaker's Almanack 2000*, the 132nd edition. As we enter a new millennium the world about us is changing ever more rapidly and the *Whitaker's Almanack* team have to work harder than ever to keep abreast of current affairs and maintain the high levels of accuracy and breadth of information that readers have come to expect.

I took over as Editor in July at the height of the researching and compilation of this edition. Developing *Whitaker's Almanack* and its associated titles presents an interesting and diverse challenge for me, and I very much hope that you enjoy this edition as much as I have enjoyed co-ordinating its production.

I would like to take this opportunity to thank the editorial team, the contributors and everyone else who works hard to ensure that *Whitaker's Almanack* is published to a consistently high standard. This preface would be incomplete without a further expression of gratitude from myself and The Stationery Office to Hilary Marsden, editor of Whitaker's Almanack for the past thirteen years, who has been most supportive during the transitional period.

I would also like to thank the many readers who take the time to contact us with comments and suggestions about the content of future editions. I hope that readers will continue to do this and contact details for the editorial department are given below.

Whitaker's Almanack now produces a quarterly newsletter, *Whit and Wisdom*, to provide readers with news, quizzes and a host of *Whitaker's Almanack*-related information throughout the year. If you would like further details of *Whit and Wisdom*, please contact Matt Brady at The Stationery Office, St Crispins, Duke Street, Norwich, NR3 1PD.

51 Nine Elms Lane, London sw8 5dr   LAUREN HILL
Tel: 0171-873 8442 (editorial); 0870-600 5522 (customer services)   *Editor*
E-mail: whitakers.almanack@theso.co.uk   October 1999
Web: www.whitakers-almanack.co.uk

NOTE – Telephone and Fax Number Changes
As you will know, telephone and fax number codes are changing in some parts of the country. These changes are not reflected in this edition; however, details of the nature and timescale of the changes are as follows:

AREA	OLD CODE	NEW CODE	NUMBER PREFIX
Cardiff	01222	029	20
Coventry	01203	024	76
London	0171	020	7
London	0181	020	8
Northern Ireland	various	028	various
Portsmouth	01705	023	92
Southampton	01703	023	80

From 1 June 1999 parallel running was established and it is possible to dial these areas using either the old dialling codes and local numbers or the new numbers. Parallel running will be phased out between August and October 2000 depending on location, after which time only the new area codes and numbers will be available for use. These changes will, of course, be reflected throughout the next edition of *Whitaker's Almanack*.

The Year 2000

CHRONOLOGICAL CYCLES AND ERAS

Dominical Letter	BA
Epact	24
Golden Number (Lunar Cycle)	VI
Julian Period	6713
Roman Indiction	8
Solar Cycle	21

	Beginning
Japanese year Heisei 12	1 January
Chinese year of the Dragon	5 February
Regnal year 49	6 February
Hindu new year	5 April
Indian (Saka) year 1922	5 April
Muslim year AH 1421	6 April
Sikh new year	13 April
Jewish year AM 5761	30 September
Roman year 2753 AUC	

RELIGIOUS CALENDARS

CHRISTIAN

Epiphany	6 January
Presentation of Christ in the Temple	2 February
Ash Wednesday	8 March
The Annunciation	25 March
Maundy Thursday	20 April
Good Friday	21 April
Easter Day (western churches)	23 April
Easter Day (Eastern Orthodox)	30 April
Rogation Sunday	28 May
Ascension Day	1 June
Pentecost (Whit Sunday)	11 June
Trinity Sunday	18 June
Corpus Christi	22 June
All Saints' Day	1 November
Advent Sunday	3 December
Christmas Day	25 December

HINDU

Makara Sankranti	15 January
Vasant Panchami (Sarasvati-puja)	10 February
Mahashivaratri	4 March
Holi	19 March
Chaitra (Hindu new year)	5 April
Ramanavami	12 April
Raksha-bandhan	15 August
Janmashtami	22 August
Ganesh Chaturthi, first day	1 September
Ganesh festival, last day	12 September
Durga-puja	28 September
Navaratri festival, first day	28 September
Sarasvati-puja	5 October
Dasara	7 October
Diwali, first day	24 October
Diwali, last day	29 October

JEWISH

Passover, first day	20 April
Feast of Weeks, first day	9 June
Jewish new year	30 September
Yom Kippur (Day of Atonement)	9 October
Feast of Tabernacles, first day	14 October
Chanucah, first day	22 December

MUSLIM

Muslim new year	6 April
Ramadan, first day	28 November

SIKH

Birthday of Guru Gobind Singh Ji	14 January
Baisakhi Mela (Sikh new year)	13 April
Martyrdom of Guru Arjan Dev Ji	5 June
Birthday of Guru Nanak Dev Ji	11 November
Martyrdom of Guru Tegh Bahadur Ji	1 December

CIVIL CALENDAR

Accession of Queen Elizabeth II	6 February
Duke of York's birthday	19 February
St David's Day	1 March
Earl of Wessex's birthday	10 March
Commonwealth Day	13 March
St Patrick's Day	17 March
Birthday of Queen Elizabeth II	21 April
St George's Day	23 April
Europe Day	9 May
Coronation of Queen Elizabeth II	2 June
Duke of Edinburgh's birthday	10 June
The Queen's Official Birthday	17 June
Queen Elizabeth the Queen Mother's birthday	4 August
Princess Royal's birthday	15 August
Princess Margaret's birthday	21 August
Lord Mayor's Day	11 November
Remembrance Sunday	12 November
Prince of Wales's birthday	14 November
Wedding Day of Queen Elizabeth II	20 November
St Andrew's Day	30 November

LEGAL CALENDAR

LAW TERMS

Hilary Term	11 January to 19 April
Easter Term	2 May to 26 May
Trinity Term	6 June to 31 July
Michaelmas Term	2 October to 21 December

QUARTER DAYS

England, Wales and Northern Ireland

Lady	25 March
Midsummer	24 June
Michaelmas	29 September
Christmas	25 December

TERM DAYS

Scotland

Candlemas	28 February
Whitsunday	28 May
Lammas	28 August
Martinmas	28 November
Removal Terms	28 May, 28 November

2000

JANUARY

Sunday	2	9	16	23	30
Monday	3	10	17	24	31
Tuesday	4	11	18	25	
Wednesday	5	12	19	26	
Thursday	6	13	20	27	
Friday	7	14	21	28	
Saturday	1	8	15	22	29

FEBRUARY

Sunday		6	13	20	27
Monday		7	14	21	28
Tuesday	1	8	15	22	29
Wednesday	2	9	16	23	
Thursday	3	10	17	24	
Friday	4	11	18	25	
Saturday	5	12	19	26	

MARCH

Sunday		5	12	19	26
Monday		6	13	20	27
Tuesday		7	14	21	28
Wednesday	1	8	15	22	29
Thursday	2	9	16	23	30
Friday	3	10	17	24	31
Saturday	4	11	18	25	

APRIL

Sunday	2	9	16	23	30
Monday	3	10	17	24	
Tuesday	4	11	18	25	
Wednesday	5	12	19	26	
Thursday	6	13	20	27	
Friday	7	14	21	28	
Saturday	1	8	15	22	29

MAY

Sunday		7	14	21	28
Monday	1	8	15	22	29
Tuesday	2	9	16	23	30
Wednesday	3	10	17	24	31
Thursday	4	11	18	25	
Friday	5	12	19	26	
Saturday	6	13	20	27	

JUNE

Sunday		4	11	18	25
Monday		5	12	19	26
Tuesday		6	13	20	27
Wednesday		7	14	21	28
Thursday	1	8	15	22	29
Friday	2	9	16	23	30
Saturday	3	10	17	24	

JULY

Sunday	2	9	16	23	30
Monday	3	10	17	24	31
Tuesday	4	11	18	25	
Wednesday	5	12	19	26	
Thursday	6	13	20	27	
Friday	7	14	21	28	
Saturday	1	8	15	22	29

AUGUST

Sunday		6	13	20	27
Monday		7	14	21	28
Tuesday	1	8	15	22	29
Wednesday	2	9	16	23	30
Thursday	3	10	17	24	31
Friday	4	11	18	25	
Saturday	5	12	19	26	

SEPTEMBER

Sunday		3	10	17	24
Monday		4	11	18	25
Tuesday		5	12	19	26
Wednesday		6	13	20	27
Thursday		7	14	21	28
Friday	1	8	15	22	29
Saturday	2	9	16	23	30

OCTOBER

Sunday	1	8	15	22	29
Monday	2	9	16	23	30
Tuesday	3	10	17	24	31
Wednesday	4	11	18	25	
Thursday	5	12	19	26	
Friday	6	13	20	27	
Saturday	7	14	21	28	

NOVEMBER

Sunday		5	12	19	26
Monday		6	13	20	27
Tuesday		7	14	21	28
Wednesday	1	8	15	22	29
Thursday	2	9	16	23	30
Friday	3	10	17	24	
Saturday	4	11	18	25	

DECEMBER

Sunday		3	10	17	24	31
Monday		4	11	18	25	
Tuesday		5	12	19	26	
Wednesday		6	13	20	27	
Thursday		7	14	21	28	
Friday	1	8	15	22	29	
Saturday	2	9	16	23	30	

PUBLIC HOLIDAYS

	England and Wales	*Scotland*	*Northern Ireland*
New Year	†3 January	3, †4 January	†3 January
St Patrick's Day	—	—	17 March
*Good Friday	21 April	21 April	21 April
Easter Monday	24 April	—	24 April
Early May	†1 May	1 May	†1 May
Spring	29 May	†29 May	29 May
Battle of the Boyne	—	—	‡12 July
Summer	28 August	7 August	28 August
*Christmas	25, 26 December	25, †26 December	25, 26 December

*In England, Wales and Northern Ireland, Christmas Day and Good Friday are common law holidays
In the Channel Islands, Liberation Day (9 May) is a bank and public holiday
†Subject to royal proclamation
‡Subject to proclamation by the Secretary of State for Northern Ireland

2001

JANUARY				
Sunday		7	14	21	28
Monday	1	8	15	22	29
Tuesday	2	9	16	23	30
Wednesday	3	10	17	24	31
Thursday	4	11	18	25	
Friday	5	12	19	26	
Saturday	6	13	20	27	

FEBRUARY				
Sunday		4	11	18	25
Monday		5	12	19	26
Tuesday		6	13	20	27
Wednesday		7	14	21	28
Thursday	1	8	15	22	
Friday	2	9	16	23	
Saturday	3	10	17	24	

MARCH				
Sunday		4	11	18	25
Monday		5	12	19	26
Tuesday		6	13	20	27
Wednesday		7	14	21	28
Thursday	1	8	15	22	29
Friday	2	9	16	23	30
Saturday	3	10	17	24	31

APRIL				
Sunday	1	8	15	22	29
Monday	2	9	16	23	30
Tuesday	3	10	17	24	
Wednesday	4	11	18	25	
Thursday	5	12	19	26	
Friday	6	13	20	27	
Saturday	7	14	21	28	

MAY				
Sunday		6	13	20	27
Monday		7	14	21	28
Tuesday	1	8	15	22	29
Wednesday	2	9	16	23	30
Thursday	3	10	17	24	31
Friday	4	11	18	25	
Saturday	5	12	19	26	

JUNE				
Sunday		3	10	17	24
Monday		4	11	18	25
Tuesday		5	12	19	26
Wednesday		6	13	20	27
Thursday		7	14	21	28
Friday	1	8	15	22	29
Saturday	2	9	16	23	30

JULY				
Sunday	1	8	15	22	29
Monday	2	9	16	23	30
Tuesday	3	10	17	24	31
Wednesday	4	11	18	25	
Thursday	5	12	19	26	
Friday	6	13	20	27	
Saturday	7	14	21	28	

AUGUST				
Sunday		5	12	19	26
Monday		6	13	20	27
Tuesday		7	14	21	28
Wednesday	1	8	15	22	29
Thursday	2	9	16	23	30
Friday	3	10	17	24	31
Saturday	4	11	18	25	

SEPTEMBER				
Sunday		2	9	16	23	30
Monday		3	10	17	24	
Tuesday		4	11	18	25	
Wednesday		5	12	19	26	
Thursday		6	13	20	27	
Friday		7	14	21	28	
Saturday	1	8	15	22	29	

OCTOBER				
Sunday		7	14	21	28
Monday	1	8	15	22	29
Tuesday	2	9	16	23	30
Wednesday	3	10	17	24	31
Thursday	4	11	18	25	
Friday	5	12	19	26	
Saturday	6	13	20	27	

NOVEMBER				
Sunday		4	11	18	25
Monday		5	12	19	26
Tuesday		6	13	20	27
Wednesday		7	14	21	28
Thursday	1	8	15	22	29
Friday	2	9	16	23	30
Saturday	3	10	17	24	

DECEMBER				
Sunday		2	9	16	23	30
Monday		3	10	17	24	31
Tuesday		4	11	18	25	
Wednesday		5	12	19	26	
Thursday		6	13	20	27	
Friday		7	14	21	28	
Saturday	1	8	15	22	29	

PUBLIC HOLIDAYS

	England and Wales	Scotland	Northern Ireland
New Year	†1 January	1, †2 January	†1 January
St Patrick's Day	—	—	‡19 March
*Good Friday	13 April	13 April	13 April
Easter Monday	16 April	—	16 April
Early May	†7 May	7 May	†7 May
Spring	28 May	†28 May	28 May
Battle of the Boyne	—	—	‡12 July
Summer	27 August	6 August	27 August
*Christmas	25, 26 December	25, †26 December	25, 26 December

FORTHCOMING EVENTS 2000

This is the UN International Year for the Culture of Peace and the Arts Council Year of the Artist
The European Cities of Culture are Avignon, France; Bologna, Italy; Prague, Czech Republic; Helsinki, Finland; Bergen, Norway; Brussels, Belgium; Reykjavik, Iceland; Santiago de Compostela, Spain; Cracow, Poland
*Provisional dates

6–16 January	London International Boat Show Earls Court, London
15 January– 3 April	The Year 1900: Art at the Crossroads Royal Academy of Arts, London
9–12 March	Cruft's Dog Show National Exhibition Centre, Birmingham
11 March–29 May	Jean-Baptiste-Simeon Chardin Royal Academy of Arts, London
16 March–9 April	Ideal Home Exhibition Earls Court, London
17–19 March	Liberal Democrat Party Spring Conference Plymouth
19–21 March	London Book Fair Olympia, London
7 April–4 June	British Art Show 5 Scottish National Gallery of Modern Art, Edinburgh
May–October	Chichester Festival Theatre season
*29 May–12 August	Royal Academy Summer Exhibition Piccadilly, London
19 May–4 June	Bath International Music Festival
22–27 May	Chelsea Flower Show Royal Hospital, Chelsea
26 May–4 June	Hay Festival of Literature Hay-on-Wye, Hereford
*9–25 June	Aldeburgh Festival of Music and Arts Suffolk
*17 June	Trooping the Colour Horse Guards Palace, London
22 June–22 July	York Millennium Mystery Plays York Minster
23 June–20 August	British Art Show 5 City Art Gallery, Southampton
27–28 June	Wisley Flower Show RHS Garden, Wisley, Surrey
3–6 July	The Royal Show Stoneleigh Park, Kenilworth, Warks
4–9 July	Hampton Court Palace Flower Show East Molesey, Surrey
7–16 July	York Early Music Festival
13–23 July	Buxton Festival Buxton, Derbyshire
14 July– 9 September	Promenade Concerts Season Royal Albert Hall, London
*20–29 July	Welsh Proms 2000 St David's Hall, Cardiff
28 July– 31 October	Pitlochry Festival Theatre season Tayside
4–26 August	Edinburgh Military Tattoo Edinburgh Castle
5–12 August	Royal National Eisteddfod of Wales Llanelli
10–11 August	Battle of the Flowers Jersey
13 August– 2 September	Edinburgh International Festival Edinburgh
19–25 August	Three Choirs Festival Gloucester

22–23 August	Wisley Flower Show RHS Garden, Wisley, Surrey
27–28 August	Notting Hill Carnival London
1 September– 5 November	Blackpool Illuminations
2 September	Braemar Royal Highland Gathering Aberdeenshire
8 September– 5 November	British Art Show 5 National Museum of Wales, Cardiff
11–14 September	TUC Annual Congress Glasgow
15–24 September	Southampton International Boat Show West Esplanade, Southampton
17–20 September	Liberal Democrat Party Autumn Conference Bournemouth
24–29 September	Labour Party Conference Brighton
2–5 October	Conservative Party Conference Blackpool
*2–19 November	London International Film Festival London
5 November	London to Brighton Veteran Car Run
11 November	Lord Mayor's Procession and Show City of London Two minute silence at 11 a.m.
15–26 November	Huddersfield Contemporary Music Festival
26–29 November	Smithfield Show Earls Court, London

SPORTS EVENTS

2–6 January	Cricket: 4th Test Match, England v. South Africa Cape Town, South Africa
14–18 January	Cricket: 5th Test Match, England v. South Africa Centurion, South Africa
17–30 January	Tennis: Australian Open Championships Melbourne, Australia
23 January	Cricket: One-day International, England v. South Africa Bloemfontein, South Africa
26 January	Cricket: One-day International, England v. South Africa Cape Town, South Africa
28 January	Cricket: One-day International, England v. Zimbabwe Paarl, South Africa
30 January	Cricket: One-day International, England v. Zimbabwe Kimberley, South Africa
4 February	Cricket: One-day International, England v. South Africa East London, South Africa
5 February	Rugby Union: England v. Ireland Twickenham, London Rugby Union: Wales v. France Cardiff Rugby Union: Italy v. Scotland Rome, Italy
16 February	Cricket: One-day International, England v. Zimbabwe Bulawayo, Zimbabwe

19 February	Rugby Union: Wales v. Italy
	Cardiff
	Rugby Union: Ireland v. Scotland
	Dublin, Republic of Ireland
	Rugby Union: France v. England
	Paris, France
	Cricket: One-day International,
	England v. Zimbabwe
	Harare, Zimbabwe
20 February	Cricket: One-day International,
	England v. Zimbabwe
	Harare, Zimbabwe
23 February	Cricket: One-day International,
	England v. Zimbabwe
	Harare, Zimbabwe
4 March	Rugby Union: England v. Wales
	Twickenham, London
	Rugby Union: Scotland v. France
	Edinburgh
	Rugby Union: Ireland v. Italy
	Dublin, Republic of Ireland
18 March	Rugby Union: Italy v. England
	Rome, Italy
	Rugby Union: Wales v. Scotland
	Cardiff
19 March	Rugby Union: France v. Ireland
	Paris, France
25 March	Rowing: Oxford and Cambridge Boat
	Race
	Putney to Mortlake, London
1 April	Rugby Union: Ireland v. Wales
	Dublin, Republic of Ireland
2 April	Rugby Union: Scotland v. England
	Edinburgh
*15 April–1 May	Snooker: World Professional
	Championship
	Crucible Theatre, Sheffield
16 April	London Marathon
29 April	Rugby League: Challenge Cup Final
	Murrayfield, Edinburgh
4 May	Badminton Horse Trials
	Badminton
7 May	Football: Welsh FA Cup Final
11–14 May	Royal Windsor Horse Show
	Home Park, Windsor
20 May	Football: FA Cup Final
	Wembley Stadium, London
	Rugby Union: Tetley's Bitter Cup
	Final
	Twickenham, London
27 May	Football: Scottish FA Cup Final
	Hampden Park, Glasgow
	Rugby Union: County Championship
	Final
	Twickenham, London
29 May–9 June	Motorcycle: TT Races
	Isle of Man
29 May–11 June	Tennis: French Open Championships
	Paris, France
24 June	Football: European Championships
	Quarter-Finals
	King Baudouin, Brussels, Belgium and
	Amsterdam, Netherlands
25 June	Football: European Championships
	Quarter-Finals
	Feijenoord, Rotterdam, Netherlands
	and Jan Breydel, Bruges, Belgium
26 June–9 July	Lawn Tennis: All-England
	Championships
	Wimbledon, London

28 June	Football: European Championships
	Semi-Final
	King Baudouin, Brussels, Belgium
28 June–2 July	Rowing: Henley Royal Regatta
	Henley-on-Thames, Oxon
29 June	Football: European Championships
	Semi-Final
	Amsterdam, Netherlands
*16 July	British Formula 1 Grand Prix
	Silverstone, Northants
2 July	Football: European Championship
	Final
	Feijenoord, Rotterdam, Netherlands
8–22 July	Shooting: NRA Imperial Meeting
	Bisley Camp, Woking, Surrey
20–23 July	Golf: The Open
	Old Course, St Andrews
29 July–5 August	Yachting: Cowes Week
	Isle of Wight
*12 August–	Yachting: Commodore Cup
19 August	Cowes, Isle of Wight
16–20 August	Golf: British Amateur Championship
	Royal Troon
28 August–	Tennis: US Open Championships
10 September	New York, USA
31 August–	Burghley Horse Trials
3 September	
September	Cricket: Natwest Trophy Final
	Lord's, London
19 September–	Summer Olympic Games
1 October	Sydney, Australia
27 September–	Horse of the Year Show
1 October	Wembley Arena, London
6–8 October	Golf: Solheim Cup
	Loch Lomond

HORSE-RACING*

*16 March	Cheltenham Gold Cup
*25 March	Lincoln Handicap
	Doncaster
*8 April	Grand National
	Aintree, Liverpool
*6 May	Two Thousand Guineas
	Newmarket
*7 May	One Thousand Guineas
	Newmarket
*9 June	The Oaks
	Epsom
*9 June	Coronation Cup
	Epsom
*10 June	The Derby
	Epsom
*20 June–23 June	Royal Ascot
*29 July	King George VI and Queen Elizabeth
	Diamond Stakes
	Ascot
*6 September	St Leger
	Doncaster
*30 September	Cambridgeshire Handicap
	Newmarket
*14 October	Cesarewitch
	Newmarket

CENTENARIES OF 2000

1400

14 February	Richard II, King 1377–99, killed
25 October	Geoffrey Chaucer, poet, died

1500

29 May	Bartolomeu Diaz, Portuguese navigator who sailed around the Cape of Good Hope, died
1 November	Benvenuto Cellini, Italian sculptor and engraver, born

1600

17 January	Pedro Calderón de la Barca, Spanish playwright, born
19 November	Charles I, King 1625–49, born

1700

1 May	John Dryden, poet, died

1800

24 January	Sir Edwin Chadwick, social reformer, born
11 February	William Fox Talbot, photography pioneer, born
25 April	William Cowper, poet, died
9 May	John Brown, American slavery abolitionist, born
14 June	Battle of Marengo
25 October	Thomas, Lord Macaulay, historian, born

1900

20 January	John Ruskin, author and art critic, died
24 January	Battle of Spion Kop, Boer War
22 February	Luis Buñuel, Spanish film director, born
27 February	Labour Party founded
28 February	Relief of Ladysmith, Boer War
2 March	Kurt Weill, German-born composer, born
2 March	Lord Cottesloe, soldier and philanthropist, born
5 April	Spencer Tracy, American actor, born
19 April	Richard Hughes, novelist, born
25 April	Gladwyn Jebb, diplomat, born
17 May	Relief of Mafeking, Boer War
28 May	Sir George Grove, musicologist, died
6 June	Arthur Askey, comedian, born
13 June	Boxer Rebellion broke out in China
25 June	Louis, Earl Mountbatten of Burma, born
2 July	Sir Tyrone Guthrie, theatre producer, born
4 July	Louis Armstrong, American trumpeter, born
10 July	Evelyn Laye, actress, born
4 August	Queen Elizabeth the Queen Mother born
25 August	Friedrich Nietzsche, philosopher, died
7 September	Joan Cross, opera singer, born
8 October	Sir Geoffrey Jellicoe, architect, born
16 October	Edward Ardizzone, illustrator, born
23 October	Douglas Jardine, cricketer, born
14 November	Aaron Copland, American composer, born
22 November	Sir Arthur Sullivan, composer, died
30 November	Oscar Wilde, novelist and playwright, died
16 December	Sir Victor Pritchett, author, born

CENTENARIES OF 2001

1501

17 January	Leonhard Fuchs, German botanist after whom the fuchsia was named, born

1701

6 September	James II and VII, King 1685–9, died
27 November	Anders Celsius, Swedish astronomer, born

1801

11 January	Domenico Cimarosa, Italian composer, died
21 February	Cardinal John Henry Newman, churchman and man of letters, born
2 April	Battle of Copenhagen
28 April	Anthony Ashley Cooper, 7th Earl of Shaftesbury, politician, reformer and philanthropist, born
14 June	Benedict Arnold, American general and turncoat, died
3 August	Sir Joseph Paxton, architect and landscape gardener, born
3 November	Karl Baedeker, German publisher and founder of Baedeker guidebooks, born
3 November	Vincenzo Bellini, Italian composer, born

1901

16 January	Laura Riding, American poet and critic, born

22 January	Victoria, Queen 1837–1901, died
27 January	Giuseppe Verdi, Italian composer, died
1 February	Clark Gable, American actor, born
22 February	Stefan Lorant, Hungarian-born British photojournalist, first editor of Picture Post, born
28 February	Linus Pauling, American chemist, born
24 March	Charlotte Yonge, novelist, died
30 March	Sir John Stainer, composer, died
3 April	Richard D'Oyly Carte, producer of Gilbert and Sullivan operas and founder of the Savoy Theatre, died
15 April	Joe Davis, snooker player, born
7 May	Gary Cooper, American actor, born
12 June	Sir Norman Hartnell, couturier, born
13 July	Sir Reginald Goodall, conductor, born
20 July	Dilys Powell, film critic and reviewer, born
9 September	Henri de Toulouse-Lautrec, French painter, died
17 September	Sir Francis Chichester, yachtsman who made a solo circumnavigation of the world in 1966–7, born
10 October	Alberto Giacometti, Swiss sculptor and painter, born
6 November	Kate Greenaway, artist and illustrator, died
5 December	Walt Disney, American artist and animated film producer, born
10 December	Nobel Prizes awarded for the first time

Astronomy

The following pages give astronomical data for each month of the year 2000. There are four pages of data for each month. All data are given for 0h Greenwich Mean Time (GMT), i.e. at the midnight at the beginning of the day named. This applies also to data for the months when British Summer Time is in operation (for dates, *see* below).

The astronomical data are given in a form suitable for observation with the naked eye or with a small telescope. These data do not attempt to replace the *Astronomical Almanac* for professional astronomers.

A fuller explanation of how to use the astronomical data is given on pages 71–3.

CALENDAR FOR EACH MONTH

The calendar for each month shows dates of religious, civil and legal significance for the year 2000.

The days in bold type are the principal holy days and the festivals and greater holy days of the Church of England as set out in the calendar authorized for use from 1997. Observance of certain festivals and greater holy days is transferred if the day falls on a principal holy day. The calendar shows the date on which holy days and festivals are to be observed in 2000.

The days in small capitals are dates of significance in the calendars of non-Anglican denominations and non-Christian religions.

The days in italic type are dates of civil and legal significance. The royal anniversaries shown in italic type are the days on which the Union flag is to be flown.

The rest of the calendar comprises days of general interest and the dates of birth or death of well-known people.

Fuller explanations of the various calendars can be found under Time Measurement and Calendars (pages 81–9).

The zodiacal signs through which the Sun is passing during each month are illustrated. The date of transition from one sign to the next, to the nearest hour, is given under Astronomical Phenomena.

JULIAN DATE

The Julian date on 2000 January 0.0 is 2451543.5. To find the Julian date for any other date in 2000 (at 0h GMT), add the day-of-the-year number on the extreme right of the calendar for each month to the Julian date for January 0.0.

SEASONS

The seasons are defined astronomically as follows:

Spring   from the vernal equinox to the summer solstice
Summer from the summer solstice to the autumnal equinox
Autumn from the autumnal equinox to the winter solstice
Winter from the winter solstice to the vernal equinox

The seasons in 2000 are:

Northern hemisphere

Vernal equinox	March 20d 08h GMT
Summer solstice	June 21d 02h GMT
Autumnal equinox	September 22d 17h GMT
Winter solstice	December 21d 14h GMT

Southern hemisphere

Autumnal equinox	March 20d 08h GMT
Winter solstice	June 21d 02h GMT
Vernal equinox	September 22d 17h GMT
Summer solstice	December 21d 14h GMT

The longest day of the year, measured from sunrise to sunset, is at the summer solstice. The longest day in the United Kingdom will fall on 21 June in 2000. *See also* page 81.

The shortest day of the year is at the winter solstice. The shortest day in the United Kingdom will fall on 21 December in 2000. *See also* page 81.

The equinox is the point at which day and night are of equal length all over the world. *See also* page 81.

In popular parlance, the seasons in the northern hemisphere comprise the following months:

Spring   March, April, May
Summer June, July, August
Autumn September, October, November
Winter December, January, February

BRITISH SUMMER TIME

British Summer Time is the legal time for general purposes during the period in which it is in operation (*see also* page 75). During this period, clocks are kept one hour ahead of Greenwich Mean Time. The hour of changeover is 01h Greenwich Mean Time. The duration of Summer Time in 2000 is from March 26 01h GMT to October 29 01h GMT.

 # January 2000

FIRST MONTH, 31 DAYS. *Janus,* god of the portal, facing two ways, past and future

1	*Saturday*	**Naming and Circumcision of Jesus**	1
2	*Sunday*	**2nd S. of Christmas.** Sir Michael Tippett b. 1905	2
3	*Monday*	*Bank Holiday in UK.* J. R. R. Tolkien b. 1892	*week 1 day 3*
4	*Tuesday*	*Bank Holiday in Scotland.* Augustus John b. 1878	4
5	*Wednesday*	Twelfth Night. Lord Frederic Leighton d. 1896	5
6	*Thursday*	**The Epiphany.** Rudolf Nureyev d. 1993	6
7	*Friday*	Glasgow University founded 1450	7
8	*Saturday*	Galileo d. 1642. Sir Laurence Alma-Tadema b. 1936	8
9	*Sunday*	**Baptism of Christ. 1st S. of Epiphany**	9
10	*Monday*	Dame Barbara Hepworth b. 1903. Coco Chanel d. 1971	*week 2 day 10*
11	*Tuesday*	*Hilary Law Sittings begin.* Girolamo Mazzola b. 1503	11
12	*Wednesday*	John Singer Sargent b. 1856. Dame Agatha Christie d. 1976	12
13	*Thursday*	Jan van Goyen b. 1596. James Joyce d. 1941	13
14	*Friday*	Henri Fantin-Latour b. 1836. Jean Ingres d. 1867	14
15	*Saturday*	British Museum opened 1759. Molière b. 1622	15
16	*Sunday*	**2nd S. of Epiphany.** Anton Chekhov b. 1860	16
17	*Monday*	Pedro Calderón de la Barca d. 1600. T. H. White d. 1964	*week 3 day 17*
18	*Tuesday*	Captain Scott reaches South Pole 1912	18
19	*Wednesday*	William Congreve d. 1729. General Robert E. Lee b. 1807	19
20	*Thursday*	George Burns b. 1896. Sir Matthew Busby d. 1994	20
21	*Friday*	Christian Dior b. 1905. Benny Hill b. 1925	21
22	*Saturday*	August Strindberg b. 1847. Walter Sickert d. 1942	22
23	*Sunday*	**3rd S. of Epiphany.** Édouard Manet b. 1832	23
24	*Monday*	**Conversion of St Paul.** Amedeo Modigliani d. 1920	*week 4 day 24*
25	*Tuesday*	Edward III acceded to throne 1327	25
26	*Wednesday*	Théodore Géricault d. 1824. Jacqueline du Pré b. 1945	26
27	*Thursday*	Samuel Palmer b. 1805. Arthur Marshall d. 1989	27
28	*Friday*	Sir Francis Drake d. 1596. Jackson Pollock b. 1912	28
29	*Saturday*	W. C. Fields b. 1880. Alfred Sisley d. 1899	29
30	*Sunday*	**4th S. of Epiphany.** Vanessa Redgrave b. 1937	30
31	*Monday*	Anna Pavlova b. 1885. John Galsworthy d. 1933	*week 5 day 31*

ASTRONOMICAL PHENOMENA

d	h	
3	05	Venus in conjunction with Moon. Venus 3° S.
3	05	Earth at perihelion (147 million km)
6	05	Mercury in conjunction with Moon. Mercury 4° S.
10	20	Mars in conjunction with Moon. Mars 2° N.
12	05	Saturn at stationary point
14	18	Jupiter in conjunction with Moon. Jupiter 4° N.
15	18	Saturn in conjunction with Moon. Saturn 3° N.
16	01	Mercury in superior conjunction
20	18	Sun's longitude 300° ≈≈
21	05	Total eclipse of Moon (*see* page 71)
24	18	Neptune in conjunction

MINIMA OF ALGOL

d	h	d	h	d	h
1	19.7	13	07.0	24	18.2
4	16.5	16	03.8	27	15.1
7	13.3	19	00.6	30	11.9
10	10.1	21	21.4		

CONSTELLATIONS

The following constellations are near the meridian at

d	h		d	h
December	1	24	January	16	21
December	16	23	February	1	20
January	1	22	February	15	19

Draco (below the Pole), Ursa Minor (below the Pole), Camelopardus, Perseus, Auriga, Taurus, Orion, Eridanus and Lepus

THE MOON

Phases, Apsides and Node	d	h	m
● New Moon	6	18	14
☽ First Quarter	14	13	34
○ Full Moon	21	04	40
☾ Last Quarter	28	07	57

	d	h	m
Apogee (406,418 km)	4	12	23
Perigee (359,361 km)	19	22	47

Mean longitude of ascending node on January 1, 125°

THE SUN   s.d. 16′.3

Day	Right Ascension	Dec. −	Equation of time	Rise 52°	Rise 56°	Transit	Set 52°	Set 56°	Sidereal time	Transit of First Point of Aries
	h m s	° ′	m s	h m	h m	h m	h m	h m	h m s	h m s
1	18 42 54	23 04	− 3 03	8 08	8 31	12 03	15 59	15 35	6 39 51	17 17 18
2	18 47 19	23 00	− 3 31	8 08	8 31	12 04	16 00	15 37	6 43 48	17 13 22
3	18 51 44	22 54	− 3 59	8 08	8 31	12 04	16 01	15 38	6 47 44	17 09 26
4	18 56 08	22 49	− 4 27	8 08	8 30	12 05	16 02	15 39	6 51 41	17 05 30
5	19 00 32	22 42	− 4 55	8 07	8 30	12 05	16 03	15 41	6 55 38	17 01 35
6	19 04 56	22 36	− 5 22	8 07	8 29	12 06	16 04	15 42	6 59 34	16 57 39
7	19 09 19	22 29	− 5 48	8 07	8 29	12 06	16 06	15 43	7 03 31	16 53 43
8	19 13 42	22 21	− 6 15	8 06	8 28	12 06	16 07	15 45	7 07 27	16 49 47
9	19 18 04	22 14	− 6 40	8 06	8 28	12 07	16 08	15 47	7 11 24	16 45 51
10	19 22 26	22 05	− 7 05	8 05	8 27	12 07	16 10	15 48	7 15 20	16 41 55
11	19 26 47	21 56	− 7 30	8 05	8 26	12 08	16 11	15 50	7 19 17	16 37 59
12	19 31 08	21 47	− 7 54	8 04	8 25	12 08	16 13	15 52	7 23 13	16 34 03
13	19 35 27	21 38	− 8 17	8 03	8 24	12 08	16 14	15 53	7 27 10	16 30 07
14	19 39 47	21 28	− 8 40	8 03	8 23	12 09	16 16	15 55	7 31 07	16 26 11
15	19 44 05	21 17	− 9 02	8 02	8 22	12 09	16 17	15 57	7 35 03	16 22 15
16	19 48 23	21 06	− 9 24	8 01	8 21	12 10	16 19	15 59	7 39 00	16 18 20
17	19 52 41	20 55	− 9 44	8 00	8 20	12 10	16 20	16 01	7 42 56	16 14 24
18	19 56 57	20 43	−10 04	7 59	8 18	12 10	16 22	16 03	7 46 53	16 10 28
19	20 01 13	20 31	−10 24	7 58	8 17	12 11	16 24	16 04	7 50 49	16 06 32
20	20 05 28	20 19	−10 42	7 57	8 16	12 11	16 25	16 06	7 54 46	16 02 36
21	20 09 43	20 06	−11 00	7 56	8 14	12 11	16 27	16 08	7 58 43	15 58 40
22	20 13 56	19 53	−11 17	7 55	8 13	12 11	16 29	16 10	8 02 39	15 54 44
23	20 18 09	19 39	−11 34	7 54	8 12	12 12	16 30	16 12	8 06 36	15 50 48
24	20 22 21	19 25	−11 49	7 52	8 10	12 12	16 32	16 15	8 10 32	15 46 52
25	20 26 33	19 11	−12 04	7 51	8 08	12 12	16 34	16 17	8 14 29	15 42 56
26	20 30 43	18 56	−12 18	7 50	8 07	12 12	16 36	16 19	8 18 25	15 39 00
27	20 34 53	18 41	−12 31	7 48	8 05	12 13	16 37	16 21	8 22 22	15 35 05
28	20 39 02	18 26	−12 44	7 47	8 03	12 13	16 39	16 23	8 26 18	15 31 09
29	20 43 10	18 10	−12 55	7 46	8 02	12 13	16 41	16 25	8 30 15	15 27 13
30	20 47 18	17 54	−13 06	7 44	8 00	12 13	16 43	16 27	8 34 12	15 23 17
31	20 51 24	17 38	−13 16	7 43	7 58	12 13	16 45	16 29	8 38 08	15 19 21

DURATION OF TWILIGHT (in minutes)

Latitude	52°	56°	52°	56°	52°	56°	52°	56°
	1 January		11 January		21 January		31 January	
Civil	41	47	40	45	38	43	37	41
Nautical	84	96	82	93	80	90	78	87
Astronomical	125	141	123	138	120	134	117	130

THE NIGHT SKY

Mercury is unsuitably placed for observation throughout the month since superior conjunction occurs on the 16th.

Venus is a brilliant object in the south-eastern sky before dawn, magnitude −4.0, though the duration of its period of visibility shortens noticeably during the month. On the morning of the 3rd the old crescent Moon passes 2° north of Venus. On the 7th Venus passes 7° north of Antares.

Mars, magnitude +1.1, is visible in the south-western sky in the evenings. Its slightly reddish appearance is an aid to its identification. Mars is in the constellation of Aquarius, and south of the Square of Pegasus. The Moon, four days old, will be seen about 3° below Mars on the evening of the 10th.

Jupiter, magnitude −2.4, is an evening object, visible in the south-western quadrant of the sky shortly after sunset. Jupiter is in the constellation of Pisces. The Moon, at First Quarter, passes nearly 5° south of Jupiter on the evening of the 14th.

Saturn, magnitude +0.2, is visible in the southern and south-western sky until after local midnight. On the early evening of the 15th the planet will be seen about 4° above the gibbous Moon. Saturn is almost stationary in the constellation of Aries.

THE MOON

Day	RA	Dec.	Hor. par.	Semi- diam.	Sun's co- long.	PA of Bright Limb	Phase	Age	Rise 52°	Rise 56°	Transit	Set 52°	Set 56°
	h m	°	'	'	°	°	%	d	h m	h m	h m	h m	h m
1	14 27	− 9.0	54.7	14.9	202	111	27	24.1	2 41	2 50	8 01	13 11	13 02
2	15 13	−12.7	54.3	14.8	214	109	19	25.1	3 47	3 59	8 45	13 35	13 22
3	16 00	−15.8	54.1	14.7	226	107	12	26.1	4 51	5 06	9 30	14 03	13 47
4	16 49	−18.3	54.0	14.7	238	104	7	27.1	5 52	6 11	10 16	14 36	14 17
5	17 38	−20.0	54.0	14.7	250	102	3	28.1	6 50	7 11	11 04	15 16	14 55
6	18 29	−20.9	54.1	14.7	263	103	1	29.1	7 42	8 04	11 52	16 03	15 41
7	19 20	−20.8	54.2	14.8	275	234	0	0.2	8 28	8 49	12 41	16 57	16 36
8	20 11	−19.8	54.5	14.8	287	256	1	1.2	9 07	9 26	13 30	17 57	17 39
9	21 01	−17.8	54.8	14.9	299	255	5	2.2	9 40	9 56	14 17	19 02	18 47
10	21 51	−15.0	55.2	15.0	311	253	10	3.2	10 08	10 20	15 04	20 09	19 58
11	22 40	−11.6	55.7	15.2	324	251	16	4.2	10 33	10 41	15 51	21 19	21 11
12	23 29	− 7.5	56.2	15.3	336	249	24	5.2	10 55	11 00	16 37	22 30	22 27
13	0 18	− 3.1	56.9	15.5	348	248	34	6.2	11 17	11 18	17 23	23 43	23 44
14	1 07	+ 1.7	57.6	15.7	0	248	44	7.2	11 39	11 36	18 11	—	—
15	1 58	+ 6.4	58.4	15.9	12	249	55	8.2	12 03	11 55	19 01	0 58	1 03
16	2 51	+10.9	59.1	16.1	24	251	66	9.2	12 30	12 19	19 55	2 15	2 25
17	3 47	+15.0	59.9	16.3	36	254	76	10.2	13 04	12 48	20 52	3 35	3 49
18	4 47	+18.2	60.5	16.5	49	259	86	11.2	13 46	13 27	21 53	4 53	5 12
19	5 49	+20.3	60.9	16.6	61	264	93	12.2	14 40	14 19	22 56	6 08	6 29
20	6 54	+20.9	61.0	16.6	73	269	98	13.2	15 45	15 24	23 59	7 12	7 34
21	7 58	+20.1	60.8	16.6	85	269	100	14.2	17 00	16 41	—	8 06	8 25
22	9 00	+17.9	60.4	16.5	97	102	99	15.2	18 19	18 04	1 00	8 48	9 03
23	10 00	+14.5	59.7	16.3	109	106	95	16.2	19 38	19 28	1 57	9 21	9 32
24	10 55	+10.4	58.8	16.0	121	108	89	17.2	20 55	20 49	2 51	9 48	9 55
25	11 48	+ 5.8	57.9	15.8	134	110	82	18.2	22 09	22 08	3 40	10 12	10 15
26	12 38	+ 1.2	56.9	15.5	146	111	73	19.2	23 20	23 23	4 27	10 33	10 33
27	13 26	− 3.4	56.1	15.3	158	110	63	20.2	—	—	5 13	10 54	10 50
28	14 13	− 7.7	55.4	15.1	170	,109	53	21.2	0 28	0 35	5 57	11 16	11 08
29	15 00	−11.6	54.8	14.9	182	107	44	22.2	1 35	1 46	6 41	11 39	11 27
30	15 47	−15.0	54.4	14.8	194	104	34	23.2	2 40	2 55	7 26	12 06	11 50
31	16 35	−17.7	54.1	14.8	206	101	26	24.2	3 43	4 01	8 12	12 37	12 18

MERCURY

Day	RA	Dec.	Diam.	Phase	Transit	5° high 52°	5° high 56°
	h m	°	"	%	h m	h m	h m
1	18 05	−24.4	5	97	11 26	8 36	9 16
3	18 19	−24.5	5	98	11 32	8 43	9 24
5	18 32	−24.5	5	99	11 38	8 49	9 30
7	18 46	−24.5	5	99	11 44	8 54	9 35
9	19 00	−24.3	5	99	11 50	8 59	9 39
11	19 14	−24.1	5	100	11 57	9 03	9 42
13	19 29	−23.8	5	100	12 03	15 01	14 23
15	19 43	−23.3	5	100	12 09	15 11	14 35
17	19 57	−22.8	5	100	12 16	15 23	14 49
19	20 11	−22.2	5	100	12 22	15 35	15 03
21	20 25	−21.4	5	99	12 28	15 47	15 17
23	20 39	−20.6	5	99	12 34	16 01	15 33
25	20 54	−19.6	5	98	12 41	16 14	15 49
27	21 08	−18.6	5	97	12 47	16 28	16 05
29	21 21	−17.4	5	96	12 53	16 43	16 21
31	21 35	−16.2	5	94	12 58	16 57	16 37

VENUS

Day	RA	Dec.	Diam.	Phase	Transit	5° high 52°	5° high 56°
	h m	°	"	%	h m	h m	h m
1	15 57	−18.3	15	76	9 18	5 38	6 02
6	16 22	−19.6	14	77	9 23	5 52	6 19
11	16 48	−20.6	14	79	9 29	6 06	6 35
16	17 14	−21.5	14	80	9 35	6 19	6 50
21	17 40	−22.0	13	81	9 42	6 30	7 02
26	18 06	−22.3	13	83	9 48	6 39	7 13
31	18 33	−22.4	13	84	9 55	6 46	7 20

MARS

Day	RA	Dec.	Diam.	Phase	Transit	5° high 52°	5° high 56°
1	22 01	−13.3	5	93	15 20	19 35	19 19
6	22 15	−11.9	5	93	15 15	19 38	19 24
11	22 30	−10.4	5	93	15 10	19 42	19 29
16	22 44	− 8.9	5	94	15 05	19 45	19 34
21	22 59	− 7.4	5	94	14 59	19 49	19 39
26	23 13	− 5.9	5	94	14 54	19 52	19 43
31	23 27	− 4.3	5	95	14 48	19 54	19 48

SUNRISE AND SUNSET

	London		Bristol		Birmingham		Manchester		Newcastle		Glasgow		Belfast	
	0°05′	51°30′	2°35′	51°28′	1°55′	52°28′	2°15′	53°28′	1°37′	54°59′	4°14′	55°52′	5°56′	54°35′
	h m	h m	h m	h m	h m	h m	h m	h m	h m	h m	h m	h m	h m	h m
1	8 06	16 01	8 16	16 12	8 18	16 04	8 25	16 00	8 31	15 48	8 47	15 53	8 46	16 08
2	8 06	16 02	8 16	16 13	8 18	16 05	8 25	16 01	8 31	15 50	8 47	15 54	8 46	16 09
3	8 06	16 04	8 16	16 14	8 18	16 06	8 25	16 02	8 31	15 51	8 47	15 56	8 46	16 10
4	8 06	16 05	8 15	16 15	8 18	16 07	8 24	16 03	8 31	15 52	8 47	15 57	8 45	16 12
5	8 05	16 06	8 15	16 16	8 17	16 08	8 24	16 04	8 30	15 53	8 46	15 58	8 45	16 13
6	8 05	16 07	8 15	16 17	8 17	16 10	8 24	16 06	8 30	15 55	8 46	16 00	8 45	16 14
7	8 05	16 08	8 15	16 18	8 17	16 11	8 23	16 07	8 29	15 56	8 45	16 01	8 44	16 16
8	8 04	16 10	8 14	16 20	8 16	16 12	8 23	16 08	8 29	15 58	8 44	16 03	8 44	16 17
9	8 04	16 11	8 14	16 21	8 16	16 14	8 22	16 10	8 28	15 59	8 44	16 04	8 43	16 19
10	8 03	16 12	8 13	16 22	8 15	16 15	8 22	16 11	8 27	16 01	8 43	16 06	8 42	16 20
11	8 03	16 14	8 13	16 24	8 15	16 17	8 21	16 13	8 26	16 02	8 42	16 08	8 42	16 22
12	8 02	16 15	8 12	16 25	8 14	16 18	8 20	16 14	8 26	16 04	8 41	16 09	8 41	16 23
13	8 01	16 17	8 11	16 27	8 13	16 20	8 19	16 16	8 25	16 06	8 40	16 11	8 40	16 25
14	8 01	16 18	8 10	16 28	8 12	16 21	8 19	16 18	8 24	16 07	8 39	16 13	8 39	16 27
15	8 00	16 20	8 10	16 30	8 12	16 23	8 18	16 19	8 23	16 09	8 38	16 15	8 38	16 28
16	7 59	16 21	8 09	16 31	8 11	16 24	8 17	16 21	8 22	16 11	8 37	16 16	8 37	16 30
17	7 58	16 23	8 08	16 33	8 10	16 26	8 16	16 23	8 21	16 13	8 36	16 18	8 36	16 32
18	7 57	16 24	8 07	16 35	8 09	16 28	8 15	16 24	8 20	16 14	8 35	16 20	8 35	16 34
19	7 56	16 26	8 06	16 36	8 08	16 29	8 14	16 26	8 18	16 16	8 33	16 22	8 34	16 36
20	7 55	16 28	8 05	16 38	8 07	16 31	8 12	16 28	8 17	16 18	8 32	16 24	8 32	16 37
21	7 54	16 29	8 04	16 39	8 05	16 33	8 11	16 30	8 16	16 20	8 31	16 26	8 31	16 39
22	7 53	16 31	8 03	16 41	8 04	16 34	8 10	16 31	8 14	16 22	8 29	16 28	8 30	16 41
23	7 52	16 33	8 02	16 43	8 03	16 36	8 09	16 33	8 13	16 24	8 28	16 30	8 28	16 43
24	7 51	16 34	8 01	16 45	8 02	16 38	8 07	16 35	8 12	16 26	8 26	16 32	8 27	16 45
25	7 49	16 36	7 59	16 46	8 01	16 40	8 06	16 37	8 10	16 28	8 25	16 34	8 26	16 47
26	7 48	16 38	7 58	16 48	7 59	16 42	8 05	16 39	8 09	16 30	8 23	16 36	8 24	16 49
27	7 47	16 40	7 57	16 50	7 58	16 43	8 03	16 41	8 07	16 32	8 21	16 38	8 22	16 51
28	7 46	16 41	7 55	16 52	7 56	16 45	8 02	16 43	8 05	16 34	8 20	16 40	8 21	16 53
29	7 44	16 43	7 54	16 53	7 55	16 47	8 00	16 45	8 04	16 36	8 18	16 43	8 19	16 55
30	7 43	16 45	7 53	16 55	7 53	16 49	7 58	16 47	8 02	16 38	8 16	16 45	8 18	16 57
31	7 41	16 47	7 51	16 57	7 52	16 51	7 57	16 48	8 00	16 40	8 14	16 47	8 16	16 59

JUPITER

Day	RA	Dec.	Transit	5° high	
				52°	56°
	h m	° ′	h m	h m	h m
1	1 35.4	+ 8 35	18 53	1 07	1 11
11	1 37.4	+ 8 50	18 15	0 31	0 35
21	1 40.6	+ 9 12	17 39	23 53	0 01
31	1 45.0	+ 9 39	17 04	23 21	23 25

Diameters – equatorial 41″ polar 38″

SATURN

Day	RA	Dec.	Transit	5° high	
				52°	56°
	h m	° ′	h m	h m	h m
1	2 35.1	+12 37	19 52	2 27	2 34
11	2 34.6	+12 38	19 12	1 48	1 55
21	2 34.8	+12 42	18 33	1 09	1 16
31	2 35.7	+12 49	17 55	0 31	0 38

Diameters – equatorial 19″ polar 17″
Rings – major axis 42″ minor axis 14″

URANUS

Day	RA	Dec.	Transit	10° high	
				52°	56°
	h m	° ′	h m	h m	h m
1	21 09.8	−17 02	14 28	17 34	17 03
11	21 11.9	−16 52	13 50	16 58	16 27
21	21 14.1	−16 42	13 13	16 22	15 52
31	21 16.4	−16 32	12 36	15 46	15 17

Diameter 4″

NEPTUNE

Day	RA	Dec.	Transit	10° high	
				52°	56°
	h m	° ′	h m	h m	h m
1	20 21.7	−19 13	13 40	16 27	15 48
11	20 23.2	−19 08	13 02	15 50	15 12
21	20 24.7	−19 03	12 24	15 13	14 35
31	20 26.3	−18 58	11 46	14 36	13 58

Diameter 2″

 # February 2000

SECOND MONTH, 28 or 29 DAYS. *Februa*, Roman festival of Purification

1	*Tuesday*	Muriel Spark b. 1918. Buster Keaton d. 1966	32
2	*Wednesday*	**Presentation of Christ in the Temple (Candlemas)**	33
3	*Thursday*	George Crabbe d. 1832. Gertrude Stein b. 1874	34
4	*Friday*	Charles Lindbergh b. 1902. Karen Carpenter d. 1983	35
5	*Saturday*	*Chinese Year of the Dragon.* Sir John Pritchard b. 1921	36
6	*Sunday*	**5th S. before Lent.** *Queen's Accession 1952*	37
7	*Monday*	Charles Dickens b. 1812. King Hussein of Jordan d. 1999	*week 6 day* 38
8	*Tuesday*	Mary, Queen of Scots executed 1587	39
9	*Wednesday*	Alban Berg b. 1885. Bill Haley d. 1981	40
10	*Thursday*	Charles Montesquieu d. 1755. Boris Pasternak b. 1890	41
11	*Friday*	Sir Vivian Fuchs b. 1908. John Buchan d. 1940	42
12	*Saturday*	Immanuel Kant d. 1804. Franco Zeffirelli b. 1923	43
13	*Sunday*	**4th S. before Lent.** Accession of William III and Mary II 1689	44
14	*Monday*	St Valentine's Day. Captain James Cook d. 1779	*week 7 day* 45
15	*Tuesday*	Galileo b. 1564. Norman Parkinson d. 1990	46
16	*Wednesday*	Sonny Bono b. 1935. Angela Carter d. 1992	47
17	*Thursday*	Geronimo d. 1909. Ruth Rendell b. 1930	48
18	*Friday*	Mary I b. 1516. Gustave Charpentier d. 1956	49
19	*Saturday*	Duke of York b. 1960. Deng Xiaoping d. 1997	50
20	*Sunday*	**3rd S. before Lent.** Enzo Ferrari b. 1898	51
21	*Monday*	W. H. Auden b. 1907. Sir Frederick Banting d. 1941	*week 8 day* 52
22	*Tuesday*	Niki Lauda b. 1949. Elizabeth Bowen d. 1973	53
23	*Wednesday*	John Keats d. 1821. George Frideric Handel b. 1685	54
24	*Thursday*	William C. Russell b. 1844. Bobby Moore d. 1993	55
25	*Friday*	Anthony Burgess b. 1917. Tennessee Williams d. 1983	56
26	*Saturday*	Sir James Goldsmith b. 1933. Sir Harry Lauder d. 1950	57
27	*Sunday*	**2nd S. before Lent.** Elizabeth Taylor b. 1932	58
28	*Monday*	Linus Pauling b. 1901. Sir Stephen Spender b. 1909	*week 9 day* 59
29	*Tuesday*	John Whitgift d. 1604. Gioacchino Rossini b. 1792	60

ASTRONOMICAL PHENOMENA

d   h
2   15   Venus in conjunction with Moon. Venus 1° S.
5   13   Partial eclipse of Sun (*see* page 71)
6   07   Uranus in conjunction
6   21   Mercury in conjunction with Moon. Mercury 2° N.
8   20   Mars in conjunction with Moon. Mars 4° N.
11 05   Jupiter in conjunction with Moon. Jupiter 4° N.
12 02   Saturn in conjunction with Moon. Saturn 3° N.
15 01   Mercury at greatest elongation E.18°
19 09   Sun's longitude 330°)(
21 13   Mercury at stationary point

MINIMA OF ALGOL

d	h	d	h	d	h
2	08.7	13	20.0	25	07.3
5	05.5	16	16.8	28	04.1
8	02.4	19	13.6		
10	23.2	22	10.5		

CONSTELLATIONS

The following constellations are near the meridian at

	d	h		d	h
January	1	24	February	15	21
January	16	23	March	1	20
February	1	22	March	16	19

Draco (below the Pole), Camelopardus, Auriga, Taurus, Gemini, Orion, Canis Minor, Monoceros, Lepus, Canis Major and Puppis

THE MOON

Phases, Apsides and Node	d	h	m
● New Moon	5	13	03
☽ First Quarter	12	23	21
○ Full Moon	19	16	27
☾ Last Quarter	27	03	53
Apogee (405,608 km)	1	01	20
Perigee (364,494 km)	17	02	32
Apogee (404,615 km)	28	20	45

Mean longitude of ascending node on February 1, 123°

THE SUN

s.d. 16′.2

Day	Right Ascension	Dec. −	Equation of time	Rise 52°	Rise 56°	Transit	Set 52°	Set 56°	Sidereal time	Transit of First Point of Aries
	h m s	° ′	m s	h m	h m	h m	h m	h m	h m s	h m s
1	20 55 30	17 21	−13 26	7 41	7 56	12 14	16 47	16 32	8 42 05	15 15 25
2	20 59 35	17 04	−13 34	7 40	7 54	12 14	16 48	16 34	8 46 01	15 11 29
3	21 03 40	16 47	−13 42	7 38	7 52	12 14	16 50	16 36	8 49 58	15 07 33
4	21 07 43	16 29	−13 49	7 36	7 50	12 14	16 52	16 38	8 53 54	15 03 37
5	21 11 46	16 12	−13 55	7 35	7 48	12 14	16 54	16 40	8 57 51	14 59 41
6	21 15 47	15 54	−14 00	7 33	7 46	12 14	16 56	16 42	9 01 47	14 55 45
7	21 19 48	15 35	−14 04	7 31	7 44	12 14	16 58	16 45	9 05 44	14 51 50
8	21 23 49	15 17	−14 08	7 29	7 42	12 14	17 00	16 47	9 09 41	14 47 54
9	21 27 48	14 58	−14 11	7 28	7 40	12 14	17 01	16 49	9 13 37	14 43 58
10	21 31 46	14 38	−14 13	7 26	7 38	12 14	17 03	16 51	9 17 34	14 40 02
11	21 35 44	14 19	−14 14	7 24	7 36	12 14	17 05	16 53	9 21 30	14 36 06
12	21 39 41	13 59	−14 15	7 22	7 34	12 14	17 07	16 56	9 25 27	14 32 10
13	21 43 37	13 40	−14 14	7 20	7 31	12 14	17 09	16 58	9 29 23	14 28 14
14	21 47 33	13 19	−14 13	7 18	7 29	12 14	17 11	17 00	9 33 20	14 24 18
15	21 51 28	12 59	−14 11	7 16	7 27	12 14	17 13	17 02	9 37 16	14 20 22
16	21 55 21	12 39	−14 08	7 15	7 25	12 14	17 14	17 04	9 41 13	14 16 26
17	21 59 15	12 18	−14 05	7 13	7 22	12 14	17 16	17 07	9 45 09	14 12 30
18	22 03 07	11 57	−14 01	7 11	7 20	12 14	17 18	17 09	9 49 06	14 08 35
19	22 06 59	11 36	−13 56	7 09	7 18	12 14	17 20	17 11	9 53 03	14 04 39
20	22 10 50	11 15	−13 51	7 07	7 15	12 14	17 22	17 13	9 56 59	14 00 43
21	22 14 40	10 53	−13 45	7 04	7 13	12 14	17 24	17 15	10 00 56	13 56 47
22	22 18 30	10 31	−13 38	7 02	7 11	12 14	17 26	17 18	10 04 52	13 52 51
23	22 22 19	10 10	−13 30	7 00	7 08	12 13	17 27	17 20	10 08 49	13 48 55
24	22 26 08	9 48	−13 22	6 58	7 06	12 13	17 29	17 22	10 12 45	13 44 59
25	22 29 55	9 26	−13 14	6 56	7 03	12 13	17 31	17 24	10 16 42	13 41 03
26	22 33 43	9 03	−13 04	6 54	7 01	12 13	17 33	17 26	10 20 38	13 37 07
27	22 37 30	8 41	−12 55	6 52	6 58	12 13	17 35	17 28	10 24 35	13 33 11
28	22 41 16	8 18	−12 44	6 50	6 56	12 13	17 37	17 30	10 28 32	13 29 15
29	22 45 01	7 56	−12 33	6 47	6 53	12 12	17 38	17 33	10 32 28	13 25 20

DURATION OF TWILIGHT (in minutes)

Latitude	52°	56°	52°	56°	52°	56°	52°	56°
	1 February		11 February		21 February		28 February	
Civil	37	41	35	39	34	38	34	38
Nautical	77	86	75	83	74	81	73	81
Astronomical	117	130	114	126	113	125	112	124

THE NIGHT SKY

Mercury is visible low in the west-south-western sky at the end of evening civil twilight during the middle two weeks of the month, its magnitude decreasing during this period from −1.0 to +1.0. For observers in the northern hemisphere this is the most favourable evening apparition of the year. While Mercury is visible there will be three other planets visible in the south-western quadrant of the sky; moving to the left observers will see Mars, then Jupiter, with Saturn near the meridian.

Venus continues to be visible as a brilliant object in the morning skies, magnitude −4.0, though it will only be seen low above the south-eastern horizon for a short period of time, just before sunrise.

Mars, magnitude +1.2, continues to be visible as an evening object in the south-western sky. Mars is close to the three-day-old crescent Moon on the evening of the 8th, the Moon passing about 4° south of the planet.

Jupiter continues to be visible in the south-western sky in the early part of the evening, magnitude −2.2. The crescent Moon is near the planet on the evenings of the 10th and 11th. On the 11th the relative positions of Jupiter, Saturn and the Moon are of some interest since the Moon is almost at its maximum distance south of the ecliptic (5.2°) and thus well below the line joining the two planets. During February Jupiter moves from Pisces into Aries.

Saturn, magnitude +0.3, continues to be visible in the south-western quadrant of the sky in the evenings but is unlikely to be visible for long after 2200 hours by the end of the month.

Zodiacal Light. The evening cone may be observed stretching up from the western horizon, along the ecliptic, after the end of twilight, from the beginning of the month to the 7th and again after the 20th. This faint phenomenon is only visible under good conditions and in the absence of both moonlight and artificial lighting.

THE MOON

Day	RA	Dec.	Hor. par.	Semi- diam.	Sun's co- long.	PA of Bright Limb	Phase	Age	Rise		Transit	Set	
									52°	56°		52°	56°
	h m	°	'	'	°	°	%	d	h m	h m	h m	h m	h m
1	17 24	−19.6	54.1	14.7	219	97	18	25.2	4 42	5 03	8 59	13 14	12 53
2	18 14	−20.7	54.1	14.7	231	92	11	26.2	5 37	5 58	9 47	13 58	13 36
3	19 05	−20.9	54.3	14.8	243	87	6	27.2	6 25	6 46	10 36	14 49	14 28
4	19 57	−20.1	54.6	14.9	255	81	2	28.2	7 07	7 26	11 25	15 48	15 29
5	20 48	−18.4	54.9	15.0	267	70	0	29.2	7 42	7 59	12 14	16 52	16 36
6	21 38	−15.8	55.3	15.1	280	269	0	0.5	8 12	8 25	13 02	17 59	17 47
7	22 28	−12.5	55.8	15.2	292	257	2	1.5	8 38	8 47	13 49	19 09	19 01
8	23 17	− 8.5	56.2	15.3	304	254	6	2.5	9 01	9 07	14 35	20 21	20 16
9	0 06	− 4.1	56.7	15.5	316	252	12	3.5	9 23	9 25	15 22	21 33	21 33
10	0 56	+ 0.6	57.2	15.6	328	251	20	4.5	9 44	9 42	16 09	22 47	22 51
11	1 46	+ 5.3	57.8	15.7	341	251	29	5.5	10 07	10 01	16 58	—	—
12	2 37	+ 9.9	58.3	15.9	353	253	39	6.5	10 33	10 23	17 49	0 02	0 11
13	3 31	+14.0	58.8	16.0	5	256	50	7.5	11 03	10 49	18 43	1 19	1 32
14	4 28	+17.4	59.3	16.2	17	260	62	8.5	11 40	11 22	19 40	2 36	2 53
15	5 27	+19.7	59.7	16.3	29	265	73	9.5	12 27	12 06	20 40	3 49	4 10
16	6 29	+20.9	60.0	16.4	41	271	82	10.5	13 25	13 03	21 41	4 56	5 18
17	7 32	+20.6	60.2	16.4	53	277	90	11.5	14 33	14 13	22 41	5 53	6 14
18	8 34	+19.0	60.1	16.4	66	285	96	12.5	15 49	15 33	23 40	6 39	6 57
19	9 33	+16.1	59.8	16.3	78	298	99	13.5	17 09	16 56	—	7 16	7 30
20	10 31	+12.3	59.2	16.1	90	79	100	14.5	18 27	18 20	0 35	7 46	7 56
21	11 25	+ 7.8	58.6	16.0	102	101	98	15.5	19 44	19 41	1 27	8 12	8 17
22	12 17	+ 3.1	57.8	15.7	114	106	93	16.5	20 58	20 59	2 16	8 35	8 36
23	13 07	− 1.7	57.0	15.5	126	107	87	17.5	22 10	22 15	3 03	8 56	8 53
24	13 55	− 6.2	56.2	15.3	138	107	79	18.5	23 19	23 29	3 49	9 18	9 11
25	14 43	−10.4	55.5	15.1	151	105	70	19.5	—	—	4 35	9 41	9 30
26	15 31	−14.0	54.9	15.0	163	103	61	20.5	0 27	0 40	5 20	10 06	9 52
27	16 19	−17.0	54.5	14.8	175	100	52	21.5	1 31	1 48	6 06	10 35	10 18
28	17 08	−19.2	54.3	14.8	187	96	42	22.5	2 32	2 52	6 53	11 10	10 50
29	17 58	−20.6	54.2	14.8	199	91	33	23.5	3 29	3 50	7 41	11 51	11 30

MERCURY

Day	RA	Dec.	Diam.	Phase	Transit	5° high	
						52°	56°
	h m	°	"	%	h m	h m	h m
1	21 42	−15.5	5	92	13 01	17 04	16 45
3	21 55	−14.2	5	89	13 06	17 18	17 01
5	22 08	−12.7	6	86	13 11	17 32	17 17
7	22 20	−11.2	6	81	13 15	17 45	17 32
9	22 31	− 9.8	6	75	13 19	17 57	17 45
11	22 42	− 8.3	6	68	13 21	18 07	17 57
13	22 51	− 6.8	7	60	13 22	18 16	18 07
15	22 59	− 5.5	7	51	13 21	18 21	18 14
17	23 04	− 4.4	8	42	13 18	18 24	18 17
19	23 08	− 3.5	8	32	13 13	18 23	18 17
21	23 09	− 2.8	9	23	13 06	18 18	18 13
23	23 08	− 2.4	9	15	12 56	18 10	18 04
25	23 04	− 2.4	10	9	12 44	17 57	17 52
27	22 59	− 2.7	10	4	12 30	17 41	17 35
29	22 52	− 3.3	10	2	12 15	17 23	17 16
31	22 44	− 4.0	11	1	12 00	17 03	16 56

VENUS

Day	RA	Dec.	Diam.	Phase	Transit	5° high	
						52°	56°
	h m	°	"	%	h m	h m	h m
1	18 38	−22.4	13	84	9 57	6 48	7 21
6	19 05	−22.1	12	85	10 03	6 52	7 24
11	19 31	−21.5	12	86	10 10	6 54	7 24
16	19 57	−20.7	12	87	10 17	6 53	7 22
21	20 23	−19.6	12	88	10 23	6 51	7 17
26	20 49	−18.3	11	89	10 29	6 47	7 11
31	21 14	−16.7	11	90	10 34	6 42	7 03

MARS

Day	RA	Dec.	Diam.	Phase	Transit	5° high	
1	23 30	− 4.0	5	95	14 47	19 55	19 48
6	23 44	− 2.4	5	95	14 41	19 58	19 52
11	23 58	− 0.8	5	95	14 36	20 00	19 56
16	0 12	+ 0.8	4	96	14 30	20 02	20 00
21	0 26	+ 2.3	4	96	14 24	20 04	20 03
26	0 39	+ 3.9	4	96	14 18	20 06	20 07
31	0 53	+ 5.4	4	96	14 12	20 08	20 10

SUNRISE AND SUNSET

	London		Bristol		Birmingham		Manchester		Newcastle		Glasgow		Belfast	
	0°05′	51°30′	2°35′	51°28′	1°55′	52°28′	2°15′	53°28′	1°37′	54°59′	4°14′	55°52′	5°56′	54°35′
	h m	h m	h m	h m	h m	h m	h m	h m	h m	h m	h m	h m	h m	h m
1	7 40	16 49	7 50	16 59	7 50	16 53	7 55	16 50	7 59	16 42	8 13	16 49	8 14	17 01
2	7 38	16 50	7 48	17 00	7 49	16 55	7 54	16 52	7 57	16 44	8 11	16 51	8 12	17 03
3	7 37	16 52	7 47	17 02	7 47	16 56	7 52	16 54	7 55	16 46	8 09	16 53	8 11	17 05
4	7 35	16 54	7 45	17 04	7 45	16 58	7 50	16 56	7 53	16 48	8 07	16 56	8 09	17 07
5	7 33	16 56	7 43	17 06	7 44	17 00	7 48	16 58	7 51	16 50	8 05	16 58	8 07	17 09
6	7 32	16 58	7 42	17 08	7 42	17 02	7 47	17 00	7 49	16 53	8 03	17 00	8 05	17 11
7	7 30	16 59	7 40	17 10	7 40	17 04	7 45	17 02	7 47	16 55	8 01	17 02	8 03	17 13
8	7 28	17 01	7 38	17 11	7 38	17 06	7 43	17 04	7 45	16 57	7 59	17 04	8 01	17 15
9	7 27	17 03	7 37	17 13	7 37	17 08	7 41	17 06	7 43	16 59	7 57	17 06	7 59	17 18
10	7 25	17 05	7 35	17 15	7 35	17 10	7 39	17 08	7 41	17 01	7 54	17 09	7 57	17 20
11	7 23	17 07	7 33	17 17	7 33	17 12	7 37	17 10	7 39	17 03	7 52	17 11	7 55	17 22
12	7 21	17 09	7 31	17 19	7 31	17 14	7 35	17 12	7 37	17 05	7 50	17 13	7 53	17 24
13	7 19	17 10	7 29	17 21	7 29	17 15	7 33	17 14	7 35	17 07	7 48	17 15	7 51	17 26
14	7 18	17 12	7 27	17 22	7 27	17 17	7 31	17 16	7 33	17 09	7 46	17 17	7 49	17 28
15	7 16	17 14	7 26	17 24	7 25	17 19	7 29	17 18	7 31	17 12	7 43	17 20	7 47	17 30
16	7 14	17 16	7 24	17 26	7 23	17 21	7 27	17 20	7 28	17 14	7 41	17 22	7 45	17 32
17	7 12	17 18	7 22	17 28	7 21	17 23	7 25	17 22	7 26	17 16	7 39	17 24	7 42	17 34
18	7 10	17 20	7 20	17 30	7 19	17 25	7 23	17 24	7 24	17 18	7 37	17 26	7 40	17 36
19	7 08	17 21	7 18	17 31	7 17	17 27	7 21	17 26	7 22	17 20	7 34	17 28	7 38	17 38
20	7 06	17 23	7 16	17 33	7 15	17 29	7 19	17 28	7 19	17 22	7 32	17 30	7 36	17 40
21	7 04	17 25	7 14	17 35	7 13	17 31	7 16	17 30	7 17	17 24	7 30	17 33	7 33	17 42
22	7 02	17 27	7 12	17 37	7 11	17 32	7 14	17 32	7 15	17 26	7 27	17 35	7 31	17 44
23	7 00	17 29	7 10	17 39	7 09	17 34	7 12	17 34	7 12	17 28	7 25	17 37	7 29	17 46
24	6 58	17 30	7 08	17 40	7 07	17 36	7 10	17 36	7 10	17 30	7 22	17 39	7 27	17 48
25	6 56	17 32	7 06	17 42	7 05	17 38	7 08	17 38	7 08	17 32	7 20	17 41	7 24	17 50
26	6 54	17 34	7 03	17 44	7 02	17 40	7 05	17 40	7 05	17 34	7 17	17 43	7 22	17 52
27	6 51	17 36	7 01	17 46	7 00	17 42	7 03	17 42	7 03	17 37	7 15	17 45	7 20	17 54
28	6 49	17 38	6 59	17 48	6 58	17 44	7 01	17 43	7 01	17 39	7 13	17 48	7 17	17 56
29	6 47	17 39	6 57	17 49	6 56	17 45	6 58	17 45	6 58	17 41	7 10	17 50	7 15	17 59

JUPITER

Day	RA	Dec.	Transit	5° high	
				52°	56°
	h m	° ′	h m	h m	h m
1	1 45.4	+ 9 42	17 01	23 18	23 22
11	1 50.8	+10 15	16 27	22 46	22 52
21	1 57.1	+10 52	15 54	22 17	22 22
31	2 04.0	+11 31	15 22	21 48	21 54

Diameters – equatorial 37″ polar 35″

SATURN

Day	RA	Dec.	Transit	5° high	
				52°	56°
	h m	° ′	h m	h m	h m
1	2 35.9	+12 50	17 51	0 27	0 35
11	2 37.6	+13 01	17 13	23 47	23 55
21	2 39.9	+13 15	16 36	23 11	23 19
31	2 42.9	+13 31	16 00	22 37	22 45

Diameters – equatorial 18″ polar 16″
Rings – major axis 40″ minor axis 13″

URANUS

Day	RA	Dec.	Transit	10° high	
				52°	56°
	h m	° ′	h m	h m	h m
1	21 16.6	−16 31	12 33	9 22	9 52
11	21 18.9	−16 21	11 56	8 44	9 13
21	21 21.2	−16 10	11 19	8 06	8 34
31	21 23.4	−16 00	10 41	7 27	7 55

Diameter 4″

NEPTUNE

Day	RA	Dec.	Transit	10° high	
				52°	56°
	h m	° ′	h m	h m	h m
1	20 26.4	−18 57	11 42	8 53	9 30
11	20 28.0	−18 52	11 05	8 14	8 51
21	20 29.4	−18 47	10 27	7 36	8 12
31	20 30.8	−18 42	9 49	6 57	7 33

Diameter 2″

March 2000

THIRD MONTH, 31 DAYS. *Mars,* Roman god of battle

1	*Wednesday*	St David's Day. Yitzhak Rabin b. 1922	61
2	*Thursday*	Cardinal Basil Hume b. 1923. Lord Lloyd Webber b. 1948	62
3	*Friday*	James Michener b. 1907. Joe DiMaggio d. 1999	63
4	*Saturday*	Forth Railway Bridge opened 1890. Patrick Moore b. 1923	64
5	*Sunday*	**S. next before Lent.** Sir Rex Harrison b. 1908	65
6	*Monday*	Battle of the Alamo ended 1836. Davy Crockett d. 1836	*week* 10 *day* 66
7	*Tuesday*	Shrove Tuesday. Stanley Kubrick d. 1999	67
8	*Wednesday*	**Ash Wednesday.** William III d. 1702	68
9	*Thursday*	Imogen Holst d. 1984. George Burns d. 1996	69
10	*Friday*	*Earl of Wessex b. 1964.* Sir Charles Groves b. 1915	70
11	*Saturday*	Sir Henry Tate b. 1819. Outbreak of Russian Revolution 1917	71
12	*Sunday*	**1st S. of Lent.** Liza Minnelli b. 1946	72
13	*Monday*	Commonwealth Day. Tsar Alexander II d. 1881	*week* 11 *day* 73
14	*Tuesday*	Johann Strauss (elder) b. 1804. Fred Zinnemann d. 1997	74
15	*Wednesday*	Julius Caesar d. 44 BC. Aristotle Onassis d. 1975	75
16	*Thursday*	Georg Ohm b. 1789. Sir Austen Chamberlain d. 1937	76
17	*Friday*	St Patrick's Day. *Bank Holiday in Northern Ireland*	77
18	*Saturday*	Rudolph Diesel b. 1858. Joan Freeman d. 1998	78
19	*Sunday*	**2nd S. of Lent. St Joseph of Nazareth**	79
20	*Monday*	Sir Isaac Newton d. 1727. Dame Vera Lynn b. 1917	*week* 12 *day* 80
21	*Tuesday*	Ayrton Senna b. 1960. Ernie Wise d. 1999	81
22	*Wednesday*	Thomas Hughes d. 1896. Marcel Marceau b. 1923	82
23	*Thursday*	Princess Eugenie of York b. 1990. Joan Crawford b. 1906	83
24	*Friday*	Elizabeth I d. 1603. Charlotte Yonge d. 1901	84
25	*Saturday*	**The Annunciation.** Treaty of Rome 1957	85
26	*Sunday*	**3rd S. of Lent.** Beethoven d. 1827	86
27	*Monday*	Yuri Gagarin d. 1968. Sir Henry Royce b. 1863	*week* 13 *day* 87
28	*Tuesday*	St Teresa of Ávila b. 1515. Virginia Woolf d. 1941	88
29	*Wednesday*	Sir William Walton b. 1902. Carl Orff d. 1982	89
30	*Thursday*	Sean O'Casey b. 1880. Russia sold Alaska to USA 1867	90
31	*Friday*	John Donne d. 1631. Jesse Owens d. 1980	91

ASTRONOMICAL PHENOMENA

d	h	
1	15	Mercury in inferior conjunction
4	01	Venus in conjunction with Moon. Venus 0.6° N.
5	13	Mercury in conjunction with Moon. Mercury 6° N.
8	17	Mars in conjunction with Moon. Mars 5° N.
9	20	Jupiter in conjunction with Moon. Jupiter 4° N.
10	11	Saturn in conjunction with Moon. Saturn 3° N.
14	21	Mercury at stationary point
15	12	Pluto at stationary point
15	18	Venus in conjunction with Mercury. Venus 2° S.
20	08	Sun's longitude 0° ♈
28	21	Mercury at greatest elongation W.28°

MINIMA OF ALGOL

d	h	d	h	d	h
2	00.9	13	12.2	24	23.5
4	21.8	16	09.0	27	20.3
7	18.6	19	05.9	30	17.1
10	15.4	22	02.7		

CONSTELLATIONS

The following constellations are near the meridian at

	d	h		d	h
February	1	24	March	16	21
February	15	23	April	1	20
March	1	22	April	15	19

Cepheus (below the Pole), Camelopardus, Lynx, Gemini, Cancer, Leo, Canis Minor, Hydra, Monoceros, Canis Major and Puppis

THE MOON

Phases, Apsides and Node	d	h	m
● New Moon	6	05	17
☽ First Quarter	13	06	59
○ Full Moon	20	04	44
☾ Last Quarter	28	00	21
Perigee (369,533 km)	14	23	39
Apogee (404,167 km)	27	17	19

Mean longitude of ascending node on March 1, 122°

THE SUN   s.d. 16′.1

Day	Right Ascension	Dec.	Equation of time	Rise 52°	Rise 56°	Transit	Set 52°	Set 56°	Sidereal time	Transit of First Point of Aries
	h m s	° ′	m s	h m	h m	h m	h m	h m	h m s	h m s
1	22 48 47	− 7 33	−12 22	6 45	6 51	12 12	17 40	17 35	10 36 25	13 21 24
2	22 52 31	− 7 10	−12 10	6 43	6 48	12 12	17 42	17 37	10 40 21	13 17 28
3	22 56 16	− 6 47	−11 58	6 41	6 46	12 12	17 44	17 39	10 44 18	13 13 32
4	22 59 59	− 6 24	−11 45	6 39	6 43	12 12	17 46	17 41	10 48 14	13 09 36
5	23 03 43	− 6 01	−11 32	6 36	6 41	12 11	17 47	17 43	10 52 11	13 05 40
6	23 07 26	− 5 38	−11 18	6 34	6 38	12 11	17 49	17 45	10 56 07	13 01 44
7	23 11 08	− 5 15	−11 04	6 32	6 36	12 11	17 51	17 47	11 00 04	12 57 48
8	23 14 50	− 4 51	−10 50	6 30	6 33	12 11	17 53	17 49	11 04 01	12 53 52
9	23 18 32	− 4 28	−10 35	6 27	6 30	12 10	17 54	17 52	11 07 57	12 49 56
10	23 22 13	− 4 04	−10 19	6 25	6 28	12 10	17 56	17 54	11 11 54	12 46 01
11	23 25 54	− 3 41	−10 04	6 23	6 25	12 10	17 58	17 56	11 15 50	12 42 05
12	23 29 35	− 3 17	− 9 48	6 21	6 23	12 10	18 00	17 58	11 19 47	12 38 09
13	23 33 15	− 2 53	− 9 32	6 18	6 20	12 09	18 01	18 00	11 23 43	12 34 13
14	23 36 55	− 2 30	− 9 15	6 16	6 17	12 09	18 03	18 02	11 27 40	12 30 17
15	23 40 35	− 2 06	− 8 59	6 14	6 15	12 09	18 05	18 04	11 31 36	12 26 21
16	23 44 15	− 1 42	− 8 42	6 11	6 12	12 09	18 07	18 06	11 35 33	12 22 25
17	23 47 54	− 1 19	− 8 24	6 09	6 10	12 08	18 08	18 08	11 39 30	12 18 29
18	23 51 33	− 0 55	− 8 07	6 07	6 07	12 08	18 10	18 10	11 43 26	12 14 33
19	23 55 12	− 0 31	− 7 49	6 04	6 04	12 08	18 12	18 12	11 47 23	12 10 37
20	23 58 51	− 0 08	− 7 32	6 02	6 02	12 07	18 14	18 14	11 51 19	12 06 41
21	0 02 29	+ 0 16	− 7 14	6 00	5 59	12 07	18 15	18 16	11 55 16	12 02 46
22	0 06 08	+ 0 40	− 6 56	5 58	5 56	12 07	18 17	18 18	11 59 12	11 58 50
23	0 09 46	+ 1 04	− 6 37	5 55	5 54	12 06	18 19	18 20	12 03 09	11 54 54
24	0 13 25	+ 1 27	− 6 19	5 53	5 51	12 06	18 20	18 22	12 07 05	11 50 58
25	0 17 03	+ 1 51	− 6 01	5 51	5 48	12 06	18 22	18 25	12 11 02	11 47 02
26	0 20 41	+ 2 14	− 5 43	5 48	5 46	12 06	18 24	18 27	12 14 58	11 43 06
27	0 24 20	+ 2 38	− 5 25	5 46	5 43	12 05	18 26	18 29	12 18 55	11 39 10
28	0 27 58	+ 3 01	− 5 07	5 44	5 41	12 05	18 27	18 31	12 22 52	11 35 14
29	0 31 37	+ 3 25	− 4 48	5 41	5 38	12 05	18 29	18 33	12 26 48	11 31 18
30	0 35 15	+ 3 48	− 4 30	5 39	5 35	12 04	18 31	18 35	12 30 45	11 27 22
31	0 38 54	+ 4 11	− 4 13	5 37	5 33	12 04	18 32	18 37	12 34 41	11 23 26

DURATION OF TWILIGHT (in minutes)

Latitude	52°	56°	52°	56°	52°	56°	52°	56°
	1 March		11 March		21 March		31 March	
Civil	34	38	34	37	34	37	34	38
Nautical	73	81	73	80	74	82	76	84
Astronomical	112	124	113	125	116	129	120	136

THE NIGHT SKY

Mercury is too close to the Sun for observation, inferior conjunction occurring on the 1st.

Venus, magnitude −3.9, is a brilliant morning object at first, but only visible low in the east-south-eastern sky for a short time before dawn. On the morning of the 4th the old crescent Moon is in the vicinity of the planet, but this will be a very difficult observation to make as Venus is only about 5° above the horizon at sunrise. Thereafter the planet is too close to the Sun for observation.

Mars continues to be visible in the south-western sky in the early evenings, until about 2000 hours. The crescent Moon will be seen passing about 5° south of the planet on the evening of the 8th. Mars, magnitude +1.4, is in the constellation of Pisces.

Jupiter, magnitude −2.1, is still visible for a short time in the south-western sky after sunset.

Saturn is still an evening object in the western sky but moving closer to the Sun and only visible for a short time after sunset. Its magnitude is +0.3. The thin crescent Moon, only three days old, is near the planet on the evening of the 10th. By the end of the month Jupiter is only about 6° west of Saturn and, although nearer to the Sun, may be used as a guide to Saturn, which is over 2 magnitudes fainter.

Zodiacal Light. The evening cone may be observed, stretching up from the western horizon, along the ecliptic, after the end of twilight, from the beginning of the month up to the 7th, and again after the 22nd.

THE MOON

Day	RA h m	Dec. °	Hor. par. ′	Semi-diam. ′	Sun's co-long. °	PA of Bright Limb °	Phase %	Age d	Rise 52° h m	Rise 56° h m	Transit h m	Set 52° h m	Set 56° h m
1	18 49	−21.0	54.3	14.8	211	86	25	24.5	4 20	4 41	8 29	12 40	12 18
2	19 40	−20.5	54.6	14.9	224	81	17	25.5	5 04	5 24	9 18	13 36	13 16
3	20 31	−19.1	54.9	15.0	236	76	10	26.5	5 41	5 59	10 07	14 38	14 21
4	21 22	−16.8	55.4	15.1	248	69	5	27.5	6 13	6 28	10 55	15 45	15 31
5	22 13	−13.6	55.9	15.2	260	60	2	28.5	6 41	6 52	11 43	16 55	16 45
6	23 03	− 9.7	56.5	15.4	272	16	0	29.5	7 05	7 12	12 31	18 07	18 02
7	23 53	− 5.3	57.0	15.5	285	270	1	0.8	7 27	7 31	13 18	19 21	19 20
8	0 42	− 0.6	57.5	15.7	297	259	4	1.8	7 49	7 48	14 06	20 36	20 39
9	1 33	+ 4.3	58.0	15.8	309	256	9	2.8	8 12	8 07	14 55	21 52	22 00
10	2 25	+ 9.0	58.4	15.9	321	256	16	3.8	8 36	8 27	15 46	23 09	23 21
11	3 19	+13.2	58.7	16.0	333	258	25	4.8	9 05	8 52	16 39	—	—
12	4 15	+16.8	59.0	16.1	346	261	36	5.8	9 39	9 22	17 35	0 26	0 43
13	5 13	+19.4	59.2	16.1	358	266	47	6.8	10 22	10 02	18 32	1 40	2 00
14	6 13	+20.9	59.3	16.2	10	271	58	7.8	11 15	10 53	19 32	2 48	3 10
15	7 14	+21.0	59.3	16.2	22	277	69	8.8	12 18	11 57	20 31	3 47	4 08
16	8 14	+19.8	59.3	16.2	34	283	79	9.8	13 29	13 11	21 28	4 35	4 54
17	9 13	+17.3	59.1	16.1	47	289	88	10.8	14 46	14 31	22 23	5 14	5 30
18	10 10	+13.8	58.8	16.0	59	295	94	11.8	16 03	15 54	23 15	5 46	5 57
19	11 04	+ 9.6	58.4	15.9	71	305	98	12.8	17 20	17 15	—	6 12	6 19
20	11 56	+ 4.9	57.9	15.8	83	353	100	13.8	18 36	18 35	0 05	6 36	6 38
21	12 47	+ 0.1	57.3	15.6	95	88	99	14.8	19 49	19 52	0 53	6 57	6 56
22	13 36	− 4.6	56.6	15.4	107	99	96	15.8	21 01	21 08	1 40	7 19	7 14
23	14 24	− 9.0	56.0	15.2	119	101	91	16.8	22 10	22 22	2 26	7 41	7 32
24	15 13	−12.9	55.4	15.1	132	101	85	17.8	23 17	23 32	3 12	8 05	7 53
25	16 02	−16.2	54.9	15.0	144	98	77	18.8	—	—	3 58	8 33	8 17
26	16 51	−18.7	54.5	14.9	156	95	69	19.8	0 21	0 39	4 45	9 06	8 46
27	17 41	−20.4	54.3	14.8	168	91	60	20.8	1 20	1 41	5 33	9 44	9 23
28	18 32	−21.2	54.3	14.8	180	87	50	21.8	2 13	2 35	6 22	10 30	10 07
29	19 23	−21.0	54.4	14.8	192	82	41	22.8	3 00	3 21	7 10	11 23	11 01
30	20 14	−19.9	54.7	14.9	205	77	32	23.8	3 40	3 59	7 59	12 22	12 03
31	21 04	−17.8	55.2	15.0	217	73	23	24.8	4 13	4 30	8 47	13 27	13 11

MERCURY

Day	RA h m	Dec. °	Diam. ″	Phase %	Transit h m	5° high 52° h m	5° high 56° h m
1	22 48	− 3.6	11	1	12 08	17 13	17 06
3	22 40	− 4.5	11	1	11 52	6 51	6 58
5	22 33	− 5.5	11	3	11 37	6 41	6 49
7	22 27	− 6.4	11	6	11 24	6 32	6 41
9	22 22	− 7.3	10	10	11 11	6 25	6 35
11	22 19	− 8.2	10	15	11 01	6 18	6 29
13	22 17	− 8.8	10	20	10 51	6 13	6 24
15	22 17	− 9.3	10	24	10 44	6 08	6 20
17	22 19	− 9.7	9	29	10 38	6 04	6 16
19	22 22	− 9.9	9	33	10 33	6 00	6 12
21	22 26	−10.0	9	38	10 30	5 57	6 09
23	22 31	− 9.9	8	41	10 27	5 53	6 06
25	22 37	− 9.7	8	45	10 26	5 50	6 03
27	22 44	− 9.3	8	48	10 25	5 48	5 59
29	22 51	− 8.9	8	52	10 25	5 45	5 56
31	23 00	− 8.3	7	55	10 25	5 42	5 53

VENUS

Day	RA h m	Dec. °	Diam. ″	Phase %	Transit h m	5° high 52° h m	5° high 56° h m
1	21 09	−17.0	11	90	10 33	6 43	7 04
6	21 34	−15.3	11	91	10 38	6 37	6 55
11	21 58	−13.5	11	92	10 43	6 29	6 45
16	22 22	−11.4	11	93	10 47	6 21	6 35
21	22 45	− 9.3	11	93	10 50	6 12	6 24
26	23 09	− 7.0	11	94	10 54	6 03	6 12
31	23 32	− 4.6	10	95	10 57	5 53	6 01

MARS

Day	RA h m	Dec. °	Diam. ″	Phase %	Transit h m	5° high 52° h m	5° high 56° h m
1	0 51	+ 5.1	4	96	14 13	20 08	20 09
6	1 04	+ 6.6	4	97	14 07	20 10	20 12
11	1 18	+ 8.1	4	97	14 02	20 11	20 15
16	1 32	+ 9.5	4	97	13 56	20 13	20 18
21	1 46	+10.9	4	97	13 50	20 14	20 20
26	2 00	+12.2	4	98	13 44	20 16	20 23
31	2 14	+13.5	4	98	13 39	20 17	20 25

SUNRISE AND SUNSET

	London		Bristol		Birmingham		Manchester		Newcastle		Glasgow		Belfast	
	0°05′	51°30′	2°35′	51°28′	1°55′	52°28′	2°15′	53°28′	1°37′	54°59′	4°14′	55°52′	5°56′	54°35′
	h m	h m	h m	h m	h m	h m	h m	h m	h m	h m	h m	h m	h m	h m
1	6 45	17 41	6 55	17 51	6 54	17 47	6 56	17 47	6 56	17 43	7 08	17 52	7 12	18 01
2	6 43	17 43	6 53	17 53	6 51	17 49	6 54	17 49	6 53	17 45	7 05	17 54	7 10	18 03
3	6 41	17 45	6 51	17 55	6 49	17 51	6 52	17 51	6 51	17 47	7 03	17 56	7 08	18 05
4	6 38	17 46	6 48	17 56	6 47	17 53	6 49	17 53	6 48	17 49	7 00	17 58	7 05	18 07
5	6 36	17 48	6 46	17 58	6 45	17 55	6 47	17 55	6 46	17 51	6 57	18 00	7 03	18 09
6	6 34	17 50	6 44	18 00	6 42	17 56	6 45	17 57	6 44	17 53	6 55	18 02	7 00	18 10
7	6 32	17 52	6 42	18 02	6 40	17 58	6 42	17 59	6 41	17 55	6 52	18 04	6 58	18 12
8	6 30	17 53	6 40	18 03	6 38	18 00	6 40	18 01	6 39	17 57	6 50	18 07	6 55	18 14
9	6 27	17 55	6 37	18 05	6 35	18 02	6 37	18 02	6 36	17 59	6 47	18 09	6 53	18 16
10	6 25	17 57	6 35	18 07	6 33	18 04	6 35	18 04	6 34	18 01	6 45	18 11	6 51	18 18
11	6 23	17 59	6 33	18 09	6 31	18 05	6 33	18 06	6 31	18 03	6 42	18 13	6 48	18 20
12	6 21	18 00	6 31	18 10	6 28	18 07	6 30	18 08	6 29	18 05	6 39	18 15	6 46	18 22
13	6 18	18 02	6 28	18 12	6 26	18 09	6 28	18 10	6 26	18 07	6 37	18 17	6 43	18 24
14	6 16	18 04	6 26	18 14	6 24	18 11	6 25	18 12	6 23	18 09	6 34	18 19	6 41	18 26
15	6 14	18 05	6 24	18 15	6 21	18 13	6 23	18 14	6 21	18 11	6 32	18 21	6 38	18 28
16	6 12	18 07	6 22	18 17	6 19	18 14	6 21	18 15	6 18	18 13	6 29	18 23	6 36	18 30
17	6 09	18 09	6 19	18 19	6 17	18 16	6 18	18 17	6 16	18 15	6 26	18 25	6 33	18 32
18	6 07	18 10	6 17	18 20	6 14	18 18	6 16	18 19	6 13	18 17	6 24	18 27	6 31	18 34
19	6 05	18 12	6 15	18 22	6 12	18 20	6 13	18 21	6 11	18 19	6 21	18 29	6 28	18 36
20	6 03	18 14	6 13	18 24	6 10	18 21	6 11	18 23	6 08	18 21	6 19	18 31	6 26	18 38
21	6 00	18 16	6 10	18 26	6 07	18 23	6 09	18 25	6 06	18 23	6 16	18 33	6 23	18 40
22	5 58	18 17	6 08	18 27	6 05	18 25	6 06	18 27	6 03	18 24	6 13	18 35	6 21	18 42
23	5 56	18 19	6 06	18 29	6 03	18 27	6 04	18 28	6 01	18 26	6 11	18 37	6 18	18 44
24	5 53	18 21	6 03	18 31	6 00	18 28	6 01	18 30	5 58	18 28	6 08	18 39	6 15	18 45
25	5 51	18 22	6 01	18 32	5 58	18 30	5 59	18 32	5 55	18 30	6 05	18 41	6 13	18 47
26	5 49	18 24	5 59	18 34	5 56	18 32	5 56	18 34	5 53	18 32	6 03	18 43	6 10	18 49
27	5 47	18 26	5 57	18 36	5 53	18 34	5 54	18 36	5 50	18 34	6 00	18 45	6 08	18 51
28	5 44	18 27	5 54	18 37	5 51	18 35	5 52	18 37	5 48	18 36	5 58	18 47	6 05	18 53
29	5 42	18 29	5 52	18 39	5 49	18 37	5 49	18 39	5 45	18 38	5 55	18 49	6 03	18 55
30	5 40	18 31	5 50	18 41	5 46	18 39	5 47	18 41	5 43	18 40	5 52	18 52	6 00	18 57
31	5 37	18 32	5 47	18 42	5 44	18 41	5 44	18 43	5 40	18 42	5 50	18 54	5 58	18 59

JUPITER

Day	RA	Dec.	Transit	5° high	
				52°	56°
	h m	° ′	h m	h m	h m
1	2 03.3	+11 27	15 25	21 51	21 57
11	2 10.8	+12 09	14 53	21 23	21 29
21	2 18.9	+12 52	14 22	20 55	21 03
31	2 27.5	+13 36	13 51	20 28	20 36

Diameters – equatorial 35″ polar 32″

SATURN

Day	RA	Dec.	Transit	5° high	
				52°	56°
	h m	° ′	h m	h m	h m
1	2 42.6	+13 30	16 04	22 40	22 48
11	2 46.0	+13 48	15 28	22 06	22 14
21	2 49.9	+14 08	14 52	21 32	21 41
31	2 54.2	+14 28	14 17	20 59	21 08

Diameters – equatorial 17″ polar 15″
Rings – major axis 38″ minor axis 13″

URANUS

Day	RA	Dec.	Transit	10° high	
				52°	56°
	h m	° ′	h m	h m	h m
1	21 23.2	−16 01	10 45	7 31	7 59
11	21 25.3	−15 51	10 08	6 53	7 21
21	21 27.3	−15 42	9 30	6 14	6 42
31	21 29.0	−15 34	8 53	5 35	6 03

Diameter 4″

NEPTUNE

Day	RA	Dec.	Transit	10° high	
				52°	56°
	h m	° ′	h m	h m	h m
1	20 30.7	−18 42	9 53	7 01	7 37
11	20 31.9	−18 38	9 15	6 22	6 58
21	20 33.0	−18 34	8 36	5 44	6 19
31	20 34.0	−18 31	7 58	5 05	5 40

Diameter 2″

April 2000

FOURTH MONTH, 30 DAYS. *Aperire,* to open; Earth opens to receive seed

1	*Saturday*	Robert III d. 1406. Royal Air Force formed 1918	92
2	*Sunday*	**4th S. of Lent.** Mothering Sunday	93

3	*Monday*	Johannes Brahms d. 1897. Doris Day b. 1924	*week* 14 *day* 94
4	*Tuesday*	Edgar Wallace b. 1875. Sir Cuthbert Whitaker d. 1950	95
5	*Wednesday*	HINDU NEW YEAR. Howard Hughes d. 1976	96
6	*Thursday*	MUSLIM NEW YEAR. Richard I d. 1199	97
7	*Friday*	St Francis Xavier b. 1506. Jim Clark d. 1968	98
8	*Saturday*	Mary Pickford b. 1893. Pablo Picasso d. 1973	99
9	*Sunday*	**5th S. of Lent.** Sir Francis Bacon d. 1626	100

10	*Monday*	Battle of Toulouse 1814. General William Booth b. 1829	*week* 15 *day* 101
11	*Tuesday*	Sir Charles Hallé b. 1819. Josephine Baker d. 1975	102
12	*Wednesday*	Joe Louis d. 1981. Sugar Ray Robinson d. 1989	103
13	*Thursday*	SIKH NEW YEAR. Seamus Heaney b. 1939	104
14	*Friday*	Arnold Toynbee b. 1889. Dorothy Squires d. 1998	105
15	*Saturday*	*Titanic* sank 1912. John Curry d. 1994	106
16	*Sunday*	**Palm Sunday.** Wilbur Wright b. 1867	107

17	*Monday*	Nikita Krushchev b. 1894. Clare Francis b. 1946	*week* 16 *day* 108
18	*Tuesday*	Leopold Stokowski b. 1882. Albert Einstein d. 1955	109
19	*Wednesday*	*Hilary Law Sittings end.* Charles Darwin d. 1882	110
20	*Thursday*	**Maundy Thursday.** PASSOVER begins	111
21	*Friday*	**Good Friday.** Bank Holiday in UK. *Queen Elizabeth II b. 1926*	112
22	*Saturday*	Easter Eve. Immanuel Kant b. 1724	113
23	*Sunday*	**Easter Day** (Western churches). **St George**	114

24	*Monday*	*Bank Holiday in England, Wales and Northern Ireland*	*week* 17 *day* 115
25	*Tuesday*	Tchaikovsky b. 1840. Anna Sewell d. 1878	116
26	*Wednesday*	**St Mark.** Jill Dando d. 1999	117
27	*Thursday*	Ferdinand Magellan d. 1521. Cecil Day-Lewis b. 1904	118
28	*Friday*	Ferruccio Lamborghini b. 1916. Richard Hughes d. 1976	119
29	*Saturday*	Frank Auerbach b. 1931. Sir Alfred Hitchcock d. 1980	120
30	*Sunday*	**2nd S. of Easter.** EASTER DAY (Eastern Orthodox)	121

ASTRONOMICAL PHENOMENA

d	h		
2	14	Mercury in conjunction with Moon. Mercury 2° N.	
3	08	Venus in conjunction with Moon. Venus 3° N.	
6	07	Jupiter in conjunction with Mars. Jupiter 1° S.	
6	13	Jupiter in conjunction with Moon. Jupiter 4° N.	
6	13	Mars in conjunction with Moon. Mars 5° N.	
6	23	Saturn in conjunction with Moon. Saturn 3° N.	
15	20	Saturn in conjunction with Mars. Saturn 2° S.	
19	19	Sun's longitude 30° ♉	
28	13	Venus in conjunction with Mercury. Venus 0.3° N.	

MINIMA OF ALGOL

d	h	d	h	d	h
2	14.0	14	01.2	25	12.5
5	10.8	16	22.1	28	09.3
8	07.6	19	18.9		
11	04.4	22	15.7		

CONSTELLATIONS

The following constellations are near the meridian at

d	h		d	h
March	1	24	April	15	21
March	16	23	May	1	20
April	1	22	May	16	19

Cepheus (below the Pole), Cassiopeia (below the Pole), Ursa Major, Leo Minor, Leo, Sextans, Hydra and Crater

THE MOON

Phases, Apsides and Node	d	h	m
● New Moon	4	18	12
☽ First Quarter	11	13	30
○ Full Moon	18	17	41
☾ Last Quarter	26	19	30
Perigee (368,258 km)	8	22	06
Apogee (404,558 km)	24	12	25

Mean longitude of ascending node on April 1, 120°

THE SUN   s.d. 16′.0

Day	Right Ascension	Dec. +	Equation of time	Rise 52°	Rise 56°	Transit	Set 52°	Set 56°	Sidereal time	Transit of First Point of Aries
	h m s	° ′	m s	h m	h m	h m	h m	h m	h m s	h m s
1	0 42 32	4 34	− 3 55	5 34	5 30	12 04	18 34	18 39	12 38 38	11 19 31
2	0 46 11	4 58	− 3 37	5 32	5 27	12 03	18 36	18 41	12 42 34	11 15 35
3	0 49 50	5 21	− 3 19	5 30	5 25	12 03	18 38	18 43	12 46 31	11 11 39
4	0 53 29	5 44	− 3 02	5 28	5 22	12 03	18 39	18 45	12 50 27	11 07 43
5	0 57 09	6 06	− 2 45	5 25	5 20	12 03	18 41	18 47	12 54 24	11 03 47
6	1 00 48	6 29	− 2 27	5 23	5 17	12 02	18 43	18 49	12 58 21	10 59 51
7	1 04 28	6 52	− 2 11	5 21	5 14	12 02	18 44	18 51	13 02 17	10 55 55
8	1 08 08	7 14	− 1 54	5 18	5 12	12 02	18 46	18 53	13 06 14	10 51 59
9	1 11 48	7 37	− 1 37	5 16	5 09	12 01	18 48	18 55	13 10 10	10 48 03
10	1 15 28	7 59	− 1 21	5 14	5 07	12 01	18 50	18 57	13 14 07	10 44 07
11	1 19 09	8 21	− 1 05	5 12	5 04	12 01	18 51	18 59	13 18 03	10 40 12
12	1 22 50	8 43	− 0 50	5 09	5 02	12 01	18 53	19 01	13 22 00	10 36 16
13	1 26 31	9 05	− 0 34	5 07	4 59	12 00	18 55	19 03	13 25 56	10 32 20
14	1 30 12	9 26	− 0 19	5 05	4 56	12 00	18 56	19 05	13 29 53	10 28 24
15	1 33 54	9 48	− 0 04	5 03	4 54	12 00	18 58	19 07	13 33 50	10 24 28
16	1 37 36	10 09	+ 0 10	5 01	4 51	12 00	19 00	19 09	13 37 46	10 20 32
17	1 41 18	10 30	+ 0 24	4 59	4 49	11 59	19 02	19 11	13 41 43	10 16 36
18	1 45 01	10 51	+ 0 38	4 56	4 46	11 59	19 03	19 13	13 45 39	10 12 40
19	1 48 45	11 12	+ 0 51	4 54	4 44	11 59	19 05	19 15	13 49 36	10 08 44
20	1 52 28	11 33	+ 1 04	4 52	4 42	11 59	19 07	19 18	13 53 32	10 04 48
21	1 56 12	11 53	+ 1 17	4 50	4 39	11 59	19 08	19 20	13 57 29	10 00 52
22	1 59 57	12 14	+ 1 29	4 48	4 37	11 58	19 10	19 22	14 01 25	9 56 57
23	2 03 42	12 34	+ 1 40	4 46	4 34	11 58	19 12	19 24	14 05 22	9 53 01
24	2 07 27	12 53	+ 1 51	4 44	4 32	11 58	19 13	19 26	14 09 19	9 49 05
25	2 11 13	13 13	+ 2 02	4 42	4 29	11 58	19 15	19 28	14 13 15	9 45 09
26	2 15 00	13 32	+ 2 12	4 40	4 27	11 58	19 17	19 30	14 17 12	9 41 13
27	2 18 47	13 52	+ 2 21	4 38	4 25	11 58	19 19	19 32	14 21 08	9 37 17
28	2 22 34	14 11	+ 2 31	4 36	4 22	11 57	19 20	19 34	14 25 05	9 33 21
29	2 26 22	14 29	+ 2 39	4 34	4 20	11 57	19 22	19 36	14 29 01	9 29 25
30	2 30 11	14 48	+ 2 47	4 32	4 18	11 57	19 24	19 38	14 32 58	9 25 29

DURATION OF TWILIGHT (in minutes)

Latitude	52°	56°	52°	56°	52°	56°	52°	56°
	1 April		11 April		21 April		30 April	
Civil	34	38	35	40	37	42	39	44
Nautical	76	85	79	90	84	96	89	105
Astronomical	121	137	128	148	138	167	152	200

THE NIGHT SKY

Mercury is unsuitably placed for observation throughout April.

Venus is unsuitably placed for observation throughout April.

Mars, magnitude +1.5, is visible for a short time, low above the western horizon in the evenings. It is coming towards the end of its evening apparition and will be lost in the lengthening evening twilight before the end of the month.

Jupiter is an evening object, magnitude −2.0, visible for a short time, low in the western sky shortly after sunset, for the first half of the month. Jupiter passes within 1° of Mars on the 5th to 6th, and could be a useful guide to locating the fainter planet. On the evening of the 5th Mars is 1.0° to the right of and 0.3° higher than Jupiter, while on the following evening Mars is 0.8° to the right and 0.8° higher than Jupiter. During these two evenings Saturn may be seen about 4° to the left and 4° above Jupiter, given good conditions. On the 6th the crescent Moon, only two days old, may be seen about 4° below and 1° to the left of Saturn. After Jupiter has disappeared from view no naked-eye planet is visible during the hours of darkness until about the last week of May.

Saturn, magnitude +0.3, is disappearing into the lengthening evening twilight in the west, and is unlikely to be seen with the naked eye after the first few days of the month. However, it may be possible to detect it with binoculars for a little longer as it remains about 4° or 5° above and to the left of Jupiter for some time.

THE MOON

Day	RA h m	Dec. °	Hor. par. ′	Semi-diam. ′	Sun's co-long. °	PA of Bright Limb °	Phase %	Age d	Rise 52° h m	Rise 56° h m	Transit h m	Set 52° h m	Set 56° h m
1	21 55	−14.9	55.7	15.2	229	68	15	25.8	4 42	4 55	9 35	14 36	14 24
2	22 45	−11.3	56.4	15.4	241	63	9	26.8	5 07	5 16	10 22	15 48	15 40
3	23 35	− 7.0	57.1	15.6	254	57	4	27.8	5 30	5 35	11 10	17 02	16 58
4	0 25	− 2.2	57.8	15.7	266	42	1	28.8	5 52	5 53	11 58	18 18	18 19
5	1 16	+ 2.7	58.4	15.9	278	305	0	0.2	6 14	6 11	12 47	19 35	19 41
6	2 09	+ 7.7	58.9	16.1	290	267	2	1.2	6 38	6 31	13 39	20 55	21 05
7	3 03	+12.3	59.3	16.1	302	262	7	2.2	7 06	6 54	14 33	22 14	22 29
8	4 00	+16.2	59.5	16.2	315	263	13	3.2	7 39	7 22	15 29	23 32	23 51
9	4 59	+19.1	59.5	16.2	327	266	22	4.2	8 19	7 59	16 27	—	—
10	5 59	+20.9	59.5	16.2	339	271	33	5.2	9 09	8 47	17 27	0 43	1 05
11	7 00	+21.3	59.3	16.2	351	276	44	6.2	10 09	9 47	18 26	1 45	2 07
12	8 01	+20.4	59.0	16.1	3	282	55	7.2	11 18	10 58	19 23	2 36	2 56
13	8 59	+18.2	58.7	16.0	16	287	66	8.2	12 32	12 16	20 18	3 17	3 33
14	9 55	+15.0	58.4	15.9	28	291	76	9.2	13 48	13 36	21 09	3 49	4 02
15	10 49	+11.0	57.9	15.8	40	295	85	10.2	15 04	14 57	21 59	4 16	4 25
16	11 41	+ 6.5	57.5	15.7	52	299	92	11.2	16 18	16 16	22 46	4 40	4 44
17	12 30	+ 1.7	57.0	15.5	64	305	97	12.2	17 31	17 33	23 33	5 01	5 02
18	13 19	− 3.0	56.5	15.4	77	321	99	13.2	18 43	18 49	—	5 22	5 18
19	14 08	− 7.6	56.0	15.3	89	52	100	14.2	19 54	20 04	0 19	5 43	5 36
20	14 56	−11.7	55.5	15.1	101	89	98	15.2	21 02	21 16	1 04	6 06	5 55
21	15 45	−15.3	55.0	15.0	113	94	95	16.2	22 08	22 26	1 51	6 32	6 17
22	16 34	−18.2	54.7	14.9	125	93	90	17.2	23 10	23 31	2 38	7 02	6 44
23	17 25	−20.2	54.4	14.8	137	91	83	18.2	—	—	3 26	7 38	7 17
24	18 15	−21.3	54.2	14.8	150	87	76	19.2	0 06	0 29	4 14	8 21	7 58
25	19 06	−21.4	54.2	14.8	162	83	67	20.2	0 56	1 18	5 03	9 11	8 48
26	19 57	−20.6	54.4	14.8	174	79	58	21.2	1 38	1 59	5 51	10 07	9 47
27	20 47	−18.9	54.7	14.9	186	75	48	22.2	2 14	2 32	6 39	11 10	10 52
28	21 37	−16.3	55.2	15.0	198	71	39	23.2	2 44	2 58	7 26	12 16	12 02
29	22 26	−12.9	55.9	15.2	211	67	29	24.2	3 10	3 20	8 13	13 26	13 16
30	23 16	− 8.9	56.6	15.4	223	64	20	25.2	3 33	3 40	9 00	14 38	14 33

MERCURY

Day	RA h m	Dec. °	Diam. ″	Phase %	Transit h m	5° high 52° h m	56° h m
1	23 04	− 8.0	7	56	10 26	5 40	5 51
3	23 13	− 7.3	7	59	10 27	5 38	5 47
5	23 22	− 6.5	7	61	10 28	5 35	5 43
7	23 32	− 5.6	7	64	10 30	5 32	5 40
9	23 42	− 4.6	6	66	10 33	5 29	5 36
11	23 53	− 3.5	6	69	10 36	5 26	5 32
13	0 04	− 2.4	6	71	10 39	5 23	5 28
15	0 15	− 1.1	6	74	10 42	5 20	5 24
17	0 27	+ 0.2	6	76	10 46	5 17	5 20
19	0 39	+ 1.5	6	79	10 50	5 14	5 16
21	0 51	+ 3.0	6	81	10 55	5 11	5 12
23	1 04	+ 4.4	5	84	11 00	5 08	5 08
25	1 17	+ 6.0	5	87	11 05	5 06	5 04
27	1 31	+ 7.6	5	89	11 11	5 03	5 00
29	1 45	+ 9.2	5	92	11 18	5 01	4 57
31	2 00	+10.8	5	94	11 25	5 00	4 54

VENUS

Day	RA h m	Dec. °	Diam. ″	Phase %	Transit h m	5° high 52° h m	56° h m
1	23 36	− 4.2	10	95	10 58	5 51	5 58
6	23 59	− 1.8	10	96	11 01	5 42	5 46
11	0 22	+ 0.7	10	96	11 04	5 32	5 35
16	0 44	+ 3.1	10	97	11 07	5 22	5 23
21	1 07	+ 5.5	10	97	11 10	5 13	5 12
26	1 30	+ 7.9	10	98	11 13	5 04	5 01
31	1 53	+10.2	10	98	11 16	4 56	4 51

MARS

Day	RA h m	Dec. °	Diam. ″	Phase %	Transit h m	5° high 52° h m	56° h m
1	2 17	+13.8	4	98	13 37	20 17	20 25
6	2 31	+15.0	4	98	13 32	20 18	20 27
11	2 45	+16.2	4	98	13 26	20 19	20 29
16	2 59	+17.2	4	99	13 21	20 19	20 31
21	3 14	+18.3	4	99	13 16	20 20	20 32
26	3 28	+19.2	4	99	13 10	20 20	20 34
31	3 43	+20.1	4	99	13 05	20 20	20 34

SUNRISE AND SUNSET

	London		Bristol		Birmingham		Manchester		Newcastle		Glasgow		Belfast	
	0°05′	51°30′	2°35′	51°28′	1°55′	52°28′	2°15′	53°28′	1°37′	54°59′	4°14′	55°52′	5°56′	54°35′
	h m	h m	h m	h m	h m	h m	h m	h m	h m	h m	h m	h m	h m	h m
1	5 35	18 34	5 45	18 44	5 42	18 42	5 42	18 45	5 38	18 44	5 47	18 56	5 55	19 01
2	5 33	18 36	5 43	18 46	5 39	18 44	5 39	18 47	5 35	18 46	5 44	18 58	5 53	19 03
3	5 31	18 37	5 41	18 47	5 37	18 46	5 37	18 48	5 33	18 48	5 42	19 00	5 50	19 05
4	5 28	18 39	5 38	18 49	5 35	18 48	5 35	18 50	5 30	18 50	5 39	19 02	5 48	19 07
5	5 26	18 41	5 36	18 51	5 32	18 49	5 32	18 52	5 28	18 52	5 37	19 04	5 45	19 08
6	5 24	18 42	5 34	18 52	5 30	18 51	5 30	18 54	5 25	18 54	5 34	19 06	5 43	19 10
7	5 22	18 44	5 32	18 54	5 28	18 53	5 28	18 56	5 23	18 56	5 32	19 08	5 40	19 12
8	5 20	18 46	5 30	18 56	5 25	18 55	5 25	18 58	5 20	18 58	5 29	19 10	5 38	19 14
9	5 17	18 47	5 27	18 57	5 23	18 56	5 23	18 59	5 18	19 00	5 26	19 12	5 36	19 16
10	5 15	18 49	5 25	18 59	5 21	18 58	5 20	19 01	5 15	19 02	5 24	19 14	5 33	19 18
11	5 13	18 51	5 23	19 01	5 19	19 00	5 18	19 03	5 13	19 03	5 21	19 16	5 31	19 20
12	5 11	18 52	5 21	19 02	5 16	19 02	5 16	19 05	5 10	19 05	5 19	19 18	5 28	19 22
13	5 09	18 54	5 19	19 04	5 14	19 03	5 13	19 07	5 08	19 07	5 16	19 20	5 26	19 24
14	5 06	18 56	5 16	19 06	5 12	19 05	5 11	19 08	5 05	19 09	5 14	19 22	5 23	19 26
15	5 04	18 57	5 14	19 07	5 10	19 07	5 09	19 10	5 03	19 11	5 11	19 24	5 21	19 28
16	5 02	18 59	5 12	19 09	5 07	19 09	5 07	19 12	5 00	19 13	5 09	19 26	5 19	19 30
17	5 00	19 01	5 10	19 11	5 05	19 10	5 04	19 14	4 58	19 15	5 06	19 28	5 16	19 31
18	4 58	19 02	5 08	19 12	5 03	19 12	5 02	19 16	4 56	19 17	5 04	19 30	5 14	19 33
19	4 56	19 04	5 06	19 14	5 01	19 14	5 00	19 18	4 53	19 19	5 01	19 32	5 12	19 35
20	4 54	19 06	5 04	19 16	4 59	19 15	4 57	19 19	4 51	19 21	4 59	19 34	5 09	19 37
21	4 52	19 07	5 02	19 17	4 57	19 17	4 55	19 21	4 49	19 23	4 56	19 36	5 07	19 39
22	4 49	19 09	5 00	19 19	4 54	19 19	4 53	19 23	4 46	19 25	4 54	19 38	5 05	19 41
23	4 47	19 11	4 58	19 21	4 52	19 21	4 51	19 25	4 44	19 27	4 52	19 40	5 02	19 43
24	4 45	19 12	4 56	19 22	4 50	19 22	4 49	19 27	4 42	19 29	4 49	19 42	5 00	19 45
25	4 43	19 14	4 54	19 24	4 48	19 24	4 47	19 28	4 39	19 31	4 47	19 44	4 58	19 47
26	4 41	19 16	4 52	19 26	4 46	19 26	4 44	19 30	4 37	19 33	4 44	19 46	4 56	19 49
27	4 39	19 17	4 50	19 27	4 44	19 28	4 42	19 32	4 35	19 35	4 42	19 48	4 53	19 51
28	4 38	19 19	4 48	19 29	4 42	19 29	4 40	19 34	4 33	19 37	4 40	19 50	4 51	19 52
29	4 36	19 21	4 46	19 31	4 40	19 31	4 38	19 36	4 30	19 38	4 38	19 52	4 49	19 54
30	4 34	19 22	4 44	19 32	4 38	19 33	4 36	19 37	4 28	19 40	4 35	19 54	4 47	19 56

JUPITER

Day	RA	Dec.	Transit	5° high	
				52°	56°
	h m	° ′	h m	h m	h m
1	2 28.3	+13 41	13 48	20 26	20 34
11	2 37.3	+14 25	13 18	19 59	20 08
21	2 46.5	+15 08	12 47	19 33	19 42
31	2 55.9	+15 50	12 17	19 07	19 17

Diameters – equatorial 33″ polar 31″

SATURN

Day	RA	Dec.	Transit	5° high	
				52°	56°
	h m	° ′	h m	h m	h m
1	2 54.6	+14 30	14 14	20 56	21 05
11	2 59.3	+14 52	13 39	20 23	20 32
21	3 04.1	+15 14	13 05	19 50	20 00
31	3 09.2	+15 35	12 30	19 18	19 28

Diameters – equatorial 16″ polar 15″
Rings – major axis 37″ minor axis 14″

URANUS

Day	RA	Dec.	Transit	10° high	
				52°	56°
	h m	° ′	h m	h m	h m
1	21 29.2	−15 33	8 49	5 32	5 59
11	21 30.7	−15 27	8 11	4 53	5 20
21	21 31.9	−15 21	7 33	4 14	4 41
31	21 32.8	−15 17	6 55	3 35	4 02

Diameter 4″

NEPTUNE

Day	RA	Dec.	Transit	10° high	
				52°	56°
	h m	° ′	h m	h m	h m
1	20 34.1	−18 30	7 54	5 01	5 36
11	20 34.8	−18 28	7 16	4 22	4 57
21	20 35.3	−18 26	6 37	3 43	4 18
31	20 35.6	−18 25	5 58	3 04	3 39

Diameter 2″

May 2000

FIFTH MONTH, 31 DAYS. *Maia*, goddess of growth and increase

1	*Monday*	**SS Philip and James.** *Bank Holiday in UK*	*week* 18 *day* 122
2	*Tuesday*	*Easter Law Sittings begin.* Dr Benjamin Spock b. 1903	123
3	*Wednesday*	Thomas Hood d. 1845. Golda Meir b. 1898	124
4	*Thursday*	Joseph Whitaker b. 1820. Sir Osbert Sitwell d. 1969	125
5	*Friday*	Søren Kierkegaard b. 1813. Karl Marx b. 1818	126
6	*Saturday*	Tony Blair b. 1953. Sigmund Freud b. 1856	127
7	*Sunday*	**3rd S. of Easter.** Johannes Brahms b. 1833	128
8	*Monday*	Antoine-Laurent Lavoisier d. 1794. Sir David Attenborough b. 1926	*week* 19 *day* 129
9	*Tuesday*	Europe Day. Channel Islands liberated 1945	130
10	*Wednesday*	Louis XV d. 1774. Karl Barth b. 1886	131
11	*Thursday*	Battle of Fontenoy 1745. Sir John Herschel d. 1871	132
12	*Friday*	Florence Nightingale b. 1820. Sir Alfred Beit d. 1894	133
13	*Saturday*	United Presbyterian Church of Scotland formed 1847	134
14	*Sunday*	**4th S. of Easter. St Matthias**	135
15	*Monday*	Edwin Muir b. 1887. Joseph Whitaker d. 1895	*week* 20 *day* 136
16	*Tuesday*	H. E. Bates b. 1905. Sammy Davis Jnr d. 1990	137
17	*Wednesday*	Edward Jenner b. 1749. Paul Dukas d. 1935	138
18	*Thursday*	Dame Margot Fonteyn b. 1919. Pope John Paul II b. 1920	139
19	*Friday*	William Gladstone d. 1898. Dr Edward de Bono b. 1933	140
20	*Saturday*	John Stuart Mill b. 1806. Gilbert Murray d. 1957	141
21	*Sunday*	**5th S. of Easter.** Christopher Columbus d. 1506	142
22	*Monday*	Sir Arthur Conan Doyle b. 1859. Lord Olivier b. 1907	*week* 21 *day* 143
23	*Tuesday*	Sir Samuel Curran b. 1912. Herbert Austin d. 1941	144
24	*Wednesday*	Nicolaus Copernicus d. 1543. Queen Victoria b. 1819	145
25	*Thursday*	The Venerable Bede d. 735. William Aitken b. 1879	146
26	*Friday*	*Easter Law Sittings end.* Queen Mary b. 1867	147
27	*Saturday*	Niccolò Paganini d. 1840. Arnold Bennett b. 1867	148
28	*Sunday*	**6th S. of Easter.** Rogation Sunday	149
29	*Monday*	*Bank Holiday in UK.* George I b. 1660	*week* 22 *day* 150
30	*Tuesday*	Joan of Arc d. 1431. Benny Goodman b. 1909	151
31	*Wednesday*	**Visit of Virgin Mary to Elizabeth.** Battle of Jutland 1916	152

ASTRONOMICAL PHENOMENA

d　h
3　10　Venus in conjunction with Moon. Venus 4° N.
3　17　Mercury in conjunction with Moon. Mercury 4° N.
4　09　Jupiter in conjunction with Moon. Jupiter 4° N.
4　13　Saturn in conjunction with Moon. Saturn 3° N.
5　08　Mars in conjunction with Moon. Mars 5° N.
8　04　Jupiter in conjunction
8　13　Neptune at stationary point
8　19　Jupiter in conjunction with Mercury. Jupiter 0.8° S.
9　04　Mercury in superior conjunction
9　20　Saturn in conjunction with Mercury. Saturn 2° S.
10　20　Saturn in conjunction
17　11　Jupiter in conjunction with Venus. Jupiter 0.01° S.
18　13　Saturn in conjunction with Venus. Saturn 1° S.
19　12　Mars in conjunction with Mercury. Mars 1° S.
20　18　Sun's longitude 60° ♊
25　08　Uranus at stationary point
28　16　Saturn in conjunction with Jupiter. Saturn 1° S.

MINIMA OF ALGOL

Algol is inconveniently situated for observation during May.

CONSTELLATIONS

The following constellations are near the meridian at

	d	h		d	h
April	1	24	May	16	21
April	15	23	June	1	20
May	1	22	June	15	19

Cepheus (below the Pole), Cassiopeia (below the Pole), Ursa Minor, Ursa Major, Canes Venatici, Coma Berenices, Bootes, Leo, Virgo, Crater, Corvus and Hydra

THE MOON

Phases, Apsides and Node	d	h	m
● New Moon	4	04	12
☽ First Quarter	10	20	00
○ Full Moon	18	07	34
☾ Last Quarter	26	11	55
Perigee (363,169 km)	6	09	06
Apogee (405,428 km)	22	03	58

Mean longitude of ascending node on May 1, 119°

THE SUN   s.d. 15′.8

Day	Right Ascension	Dec. +	Equation of time	Rise 52°	Rise 56°	Transit	Set 52°	Set 56°	Sidereal time	Transit of First Point of Aries
	h m s	° ′	m s	h m	h m	h m	h m	h m	h m s	h m s
1	2 34 00	15 06	+ 2 55	4 30	4 16	11 57	19 25	19 40	14 36 54	9 21 33
2	2 37 50	15 24	+ 3 01	4 28	4 13	11 57	19 27	19 42	14 40 51	9 17 37
3	2 41 40	15 42	+ 3 08	4 26	4 11	11 57	19 29	19 44	14 44 48	9 13 42
4	2 45 31	15 59	+ 3 14	4 24	4 09	11 57	19 30	19 46	14 48 44	9 09 46
5	2 49 22	16 17	+ 3 19	4 22	4 07	11 57	19 32	19 48	14 52 41	9 05 50
6	2 53 14	16 34	+ 3 23	4 21	4 05	11 57	19 34	19 50	14 56 37	9 01 54
7	2 57 06	16 50	+ 3 28	4 19	4 03	11 57	19 35	19 52	15 00 34	8 57 58
8	3 00 59	17 07	+ 3 31	4 17	4 00	11 56	19 37	19 54	15 04 30	8 54 02
9	3 04 53	17 23	+ 3 34	4 15	3 58	11 56	19 38	19 56	15 08 27	8 50 06
10	3 08 47	17 39	+ 3 37	4 14	3 56	11 56	19 40	19 58	15 12 23	8 46 10
11	3 12 41	17 54	+ 3 39	4 12	3 54	11 56	19 42	20 00	15 16 20	8 42 14
12	3 16 37	18 09	+ 3 40	4 10	3 52	11 56	19 43	20 02	15 20 17	8 38 18
13	3 20 32	18 24	+ 3 41	4 09	3 50	11 56	19 45	20 03	15 24 13	8 34 22
14	3 24 29	18 39	+ 3 41	4 07	3 49	11 56	19 46	20 05	15 28 10	8 30 27
15	3 28 25	18 53	+ 3 41	4 06	3 47	11 56	19 48	20 07	15 32 06	8 26 31
16	3 32 23	19 07	+ 3 40	4 04	3 45	11 56	19 49	20 09	15 36 03	8 22 35
17	3 36 21	19 21	+ 3 38	4 03	3 43	11 56	19 51	20 11	15 39 59	8 18 39
18	3 40 19	19 34	+ 3 36	4 01	3 41	11 56	19 52	20 13	15 43 56	8 14 43
19	3 44 18	19 47	+ 3 34	4 00	3 40	11 56	19 54	20 14	15 47 52	8 10 47
20	3 48 18	20 00	+ 3 31	3 59	3 38	11 57	19 55	20 16	15 51 49	8 06 51
21	3 52 18	20 12	+ 3 27	3 57	3 36	11 57	19 57	20 18	15 55 46	8 02 55
22	3 56 19	20 24	+ 3 23	3 56	3 35	11 57	19 58	20 20	15 59 42	7 58 59
23	4 00 20	20 36	+ 3 18	3 55	3 33	11 57	19 59	20 21	16 03 39	7 55 03
24	4 04 22	20 47	+ 3 13	3 54	3 32	11 57	20 01	20 23	16 07 35	7 51 07
25	4 08 24	20 58	+ 3 07	3 53	3 30	11 57	20 02	20 25	16 11 32	7 47 12
26	4 12 27	21 08	+ 3 01	3 51	3 29	11 57	20 03	20 26	16 15 28	7 43 16
27	4 16 30	21 19	+ 2 55	3 50	3 28	11 57	20 05	20 28	16 19 25	7 39 20
28	4 20 34	21 28	+ 2 47	3 49	3 26	11 57	20 06	20 29	16 23 21	7 35 24
29	4 24 38	21 38	+ 2 40	3 48	3 25	11 57	20 07	20 31	16 27 18	7 31 28
30	4 28 43	21 47	+ 2 31	3 47	3 24	11 58	20 08	20 32	16 31 15	7 27 32
31	4 32 48	21 56	+ 2 23	3 47	3 23	11 58	20 09	20 33	16 35 11	7 23 36

DURATION OF TWILIGHT (in minutes)

Latitude	52°	56°	52°	56°	52°	56°	52°	56°
	1 May		11 May		21 May		31 May	
Civil	39	45	41	49	44	53	46	57
Nautical	90	106	97	121	106	143	116	TAN
Astronomical	154	209	179	TAN	TAN	TAN	TAN	TAN

THE NIGHT SKY

Unusually, until about the last week of the month, no naked-eye planet will be visible during the hours of darkness.

Mercury is unsuitably placed for most of the month, superior conjunction occurring on the 9th. However, during the last week of May it may be glimpsed as a difficult evening object low above the north-western horizon, though the lengthening twilight hinders observation. During this period its magnitude fades from −0.8 to −0.1.

Venus is too close to the Sun for observation throughout May.

Mars is unsuitably placed for observation.

Jupiter is too close to the Sun for observation, conjunction occurring on the 8th. Keen skywatchers will have noticed that before the two giant planets, Jupiter and Saturn, were lost in the evening twilight in April, Jupiter was west of Saturn. During May Jupiter overtakes Saturn and when they emerge from the morning twilight in June, Saturn will appear to the west of Jupiter.

Saturn is unsuitably placed for observation throughout May, conjunction occurring on the 10th.

THE MOON

Day	RA h m	Dec. °	Hor. par. ′	Semi-diam. ′	Sun's co-long. °	PA of Bright Limb °	Phase %	Age d	Rise 52° h m	Rise 56° h m	Transit h m	Set 52° h m	Set 56° h m
1	0 05	− 4.3	57.4	15.7	235	62	13	26.2	3 54	3 57	9 47	15 53	15 52
2	0 56	+ 0.7	58.3	15.9	247	58	6	27.2	4 16	4 15	10 36	17 10	17 14
3	1 48	+ 5.7	59.1	16.1	260	52	2	28.2	4 39	4 33	11 27	18 30	18 39
4	2 42	+10.6	59.7	16.3	272	8	0	29.2	5 05	4 55	12 20	19 52	20 05
5	3 39	+15.0	60.1	16.4	284	278	1	0.8	5 35	5 21	13 17	21 14	21 32
6	4 39	+18.4	60.4	16.4	296	270	5	1.8	6 13	5 54	14 17	22 31	22 52
7	5 41	+20.7	60.3	16.4	308	271	11	2.8	7 01	6 39	15 18	23 39	—
8	6 44	+21.6	60.1	16.4	321	275	20	3.8	7 59	7 36	16 19	—	0 02
9	7 46	+21.0	59.7	16.3	333	280	30	4.8	9 07	8 46	17 18	0 35	0 57
10	8 46	+19.1	59.2	16.1	345	285	41	5.8	10 21	10 03	18 15	1 20	1 38
11	9 43	+16.0	58.6	16.0	357	289	52	6.8	11 37	11 24	19 07	1 55	2 09
12	10 38	+12.2	58.0	15.8	10	293	63	7.8	12 53	12 44	19 57	2 23	2 33
13	11 29	+ 7.7	57.4	15.6	22	295	73	8.8	14 07	14 03	20 44	2 47	2 52
14	12 18	+ 3.1	56.8	15.5	34	297	82	9.8	15 19	15 19	21 30	3 08	3 10
15	13 07	− 1.7	56.3	15.3	46	299	89	10.8	16 31	16 35	22 15	3 28	3 26
16	13 54	− 6.3	55.8	15.2	58	301	95	11.8	17 41	17 49	23 00	3 48	3 42
17	14 42	−10.6	55.4	15.1	71	305	98	12.8	18 49	19 02	23 46	4 10	4 00
18	15 30	−14.4	55.0	15.0	83	335	100	13.8	19 57	20 13	—	4 34	4 20
19	16 19	−17.5	54.6	14.9	95	73	99	14.8	21 00	21 20	0 32	5 02	4 45
20	17 09	−19.8	54.4	14.8	107	86	97	15.8	22 00	22 22	1 20	5 35	5 15
21	18 00	−21.2	54.2	14.8	119	86	93	16.8	22 52	23 15	2 08	6 15	5 53
22	18 51	−21.7	54.1	14.7	131	84	88	17.8	23 37	23 59	2 57	7 02	6 39
23	19 42	−21.2	54.1	14.7	144	80	81	18.8	—	—	3 45	7 56	7 35
24	20 32	−19.7	54.3	14.8	156	76	73	19.8	0 15	0 35	4 33	8 56	8 37
25	21 21	−17.4	54.7	14.9	168	73	65	20.8	0 46	1 03	5 20	10 00	9 45
26	22 10	−14.3	55.2	15.0	180	70	55	21.8	1 13	1 26	6 06	11 08	10 56
27	22 59	−10.6	55.8	15.2	192	67	45	22.8	1 37	1 45	6 52	12 17	12 10
28	23 47	− 6.2	56.6	15.4	205	65	35	23.8	1 58	2 03	7 38	13 29	13 26
29	0 36	− 1.5	57.5	15.7	217	64	25	24.8	2 19	2 20	8 25	14 44	14 45
30	1 26	+ 3.5	58.4	15.9	229	64	17	25.8	2 40	2 37	9 13	16 02	16 08
31	2 19	+ 8.5	59.3	16.2	241	64	9	26.8	3 04	2 56	10 05	17 22	17 33

MERCURY

Day	RA h m	Dec. °	Diam. ″	Phase %	Transit h m	5° high 52° h m	56° h m
1	2 00	+10.8	5	94	11 25	5 00	4 54
3	2 15	+12.5	5	96	11 32	4 58	4 51
5	2 31	+14.1	5	98	11 40	4 58	4 49
7	2 47	+15.7	5	100	11 49	4 57	4 47
9	3 04	+17.3	5	100	11 58	4 58	4 46
11	3 21	+18.8	5	100	12 07	19 19	19 32
13	3 39	+20.2	5	98	12 17	19 36	19 52
15	3 57	+21.5	5	96	12 27	19 54	20 10
17	4 14	+22.6	5	92	12 37	20 10	20 28
19	4 32	+23.5	5	88	12 47	20 25	20 44
21	4 49	+24.3	6	83	12 56	20 39	20 59
23	5 06	+24.9	6	78	13 04	20 51	21 11
25	5 22	+25.3	6	73	13 13	21 01	21 22
27	5 37	+25.5	6	68	13 20	21 09	21 31
29	5 52	+25.6	6	63	13 26	21 16	21 38
31	6 05	+25.6	7	58	13 32	21 21	21 42

VENUS

Day	RA h m	Dec. °	Diam. ″	Phase %	Transit h m	5° high 52° h m	56° h m
1	1 53	+10.2	10	98	11 16	4 56	4 51
6	2 16	+12.4	10	99	11 20	4 48	4 41
11	2 40	+14.5	10	99	11 24	4 41	4 32
16	3 04	+16.4	10	99	11 29	4 35	4 24
21	3 29	+18.2	10	100	11 34	4 30	4 18
26	3 54	+19.7	10	100	11 39	4 27	4 13
31	4 20	+21.1	10	100	11 45	4 25	4 09

MARS

Day	RA h m	Dec. °	Diam. ″	Phase %	Transit h m	5° high 52° h m	56° h m
1	3 43	+20.1	4	99	13 05	20 20	20 34
6	3 57	+20.9	4	99	13 00	20 19	20 35
11	4 12	+21.6	4	99	12 55	20 19	20 35
16	4 27	+22.2	4	99	12 50	20 17	20 34
21	4 42	+22.8	4	100	12 45	20 16	20 33
26	4 56	+23.2	4	100	12 40	20 14	20 32
31	5 11	+23.6	4	100	12 35	20 11	20 30

SUNRISE AND SUNSET

	London		Bristol		Birmingham		Manchester		Newcastle		Glasgow		Belfast	
	0°05'	51°30'	2°35'	51°28'	1°55'	52°28'	2°15'	53°28'	1°37'	54°59'	4°14'	55°52'	5°56'	54°35'
	h m	h m	h m	h m	h m	h m	h m	h m	h m	h m	h m	h m	h m	h m
1	4 32	19 24	4 42	19 34	4 36	19 34	4 34	19 39	4 26	19 42	4 33	19 56	4 45	19 58
2	4 30	19 26	4 40	19 36	4 34	19 36	4 32	19 41	4 24	19 44	4 31	19 58	4 43	20 00
3	4 28	19 27	4 38	19 37	4 32	19 38	4 30	19 43	4 22	19 46	4 29	20 00	4 41	20 02
4	4 26	19 29	4 36	19 39	4 30	19 40	4 28	19 45	4 20	19 48	4 26	20 02	4 38	20 04
5	4 25	19 31	4 35	19 40	4 28	19 41	4 26	19 46	4 18	19 50	4 24	20 04	4 36	20 06
6	4 23	19 32	4 33	19 42	4 27	19 43	4 24	19 48	4 16	19 52	4 22	20 06	4 34	20 07
7	4 21	19 34	4 31	19 44	4 25	19 45	4 22	19 50	4 13	19 54	4 20	20 08	4 32	20 09
8	4 19	19 35	4 29	19 45	4 23	19 46	4 20	19 52	4 12	19 56	4 18	20 10	4 31	20 11
9	4 18	19 37	4 28	19 47	4 21	19 48	4 19	19 53	4 10	19 57	4 16	20 12	4 29	20 13
10	4 16	19 38	4 26	19 48	4 20	19 50	4 17	19 55	4 08	19 59	4 14	20 14	4 27	20 15
11	4 14	19 40	4 24	19 50	4 18	19 51	4 15	19 57	4 06	20 01	4 12	20 16	4 25	20 17
12	4 13	19 42	4 23	19 51	4 16	19 53	4 13	19 58	4 04	20 03	4 10	20 18	4 23	20 18
13	4 11	19 43	4 21	19 53	4 15	19 54	4 12	20 00	4 02	20 05	4 08	20 20	4 21	20 20
14	4 10	19 45	4 20	19 54	4 13	19 56	4 10	20 02	4 00	20 07	4 06	20 22	4 19	20 22
15	4 08	19 46	4 18	19 56	4 11	19 58	4 08	20 03	3 58	20 08	4 04	20 23	4 18	20 24
16	4 07	19 48	4 17	19 57	4 10	19 59	4 07	20 05	3 57	20 10	4 03	20 25	4 16	20 25
17	4 05	19 49	4 15	19 59	4 08	20 01	4 05	20 07	3 55	20 12	4 01	20 27	4 14	20 27
18	4 04	19 50	4 14	20 00	4 07	20 02	4 04	20 08	3 53	20 13	3 59	20 29	4 13	20 29
19	4 03	19 52	4 13	20 02	4 06	20 04	4 02	20 10	3 52	20 15	3 57	20 31	4 11	20 30
20	4 01	19 53	4 11	20 03	4 04	20 05	4 01	20 11	3 50	20 17	3 56	20 32	4 10	20 32
21	4 00	19 55	4 10	20 05	4 03	20 07	3 59	20 13	3 49	20 18	3 54	20 34	4 08	20 34
22	3 59	19 56	4 09	20 06	4 02	20 08	3 58	20 14	3 47	20 20	3 53	20 36	4 07	20 35
23	3 58	19 57	4 08	20 07	4 00	20 09	3 57	20 16	3 46	20 22	3 51	20 37	4 05	20 37
24	3 56	19 59	4 07	20 09	3 59	20 11	3 55	20 17	3 44	20 23	3 50	20 39	4 04	20 38
25	3 55	20 00	4 05	20 10	3 58	20 12	3 54	20 19	3 43	20 25	3 48	20 41	4 03	20 40
26	3 54	20 01	4 04	20 11	3 57	20 13	3 53	20 20	3 42	20 26	3 47	20 42	4 01	20 41
27	3 53	20 03	4 03	20 12	3 56	20 15	3 52	20 21	3 40	20 28	3 45	20 44	4 00	20 43
28	3 52	20 04	4 02	20 14	3 55	20 16	3 51	20 23	3 39	20 29	3 44	20 45	3 59	20 44
29	3 51	20 05	4 01	20 15	3 54	20 17	3 50	20 24	3 38	20 31	3 43	20 47	3 58	20 45
30	3 50	20 06	4 00	20 16	3 53	20 18	3 49	20 25	3 37	20 32	3 42	20 48	3 57	20 47
31	3 49	20 07	4 00	20 17	3 52	20 20	3 48	20 27	3 36	20 33	3 41	20 50	3 56	20 48

JUPITER

Day	RA	Dec.	Transit	5° high	
				52°	56°
	h m	° '	h m	h m	h m
1	2 55.9	+15 50	12 17	5 28	5 18
11	3 05.4	+16 31	11 48	4 55	4 44
21	3 14.9	+17 10	11 18	4 21	4 10
31	3 24.4	+17 46	10 48	3 48	3 36

Diameters – equatorial 33" polar 31"

SATURN

Day	RA	Dec.	Transit	5° high	
				52°	56°
	h m	° '	h m	h m	h m
1	3 09.2	+15 35	12 30	5 43	5 33
11	3 14.3	+15 56	11 56	5 07	4 57
21	3 19.5	+16 16	11 22	4 31	4 20
31	3 24.6	+16 36	10 48	3 55	3 44

Diameters – equatorial 16" polar 15"
Rings – major axis 37" minor axis 14"

URANUS

Day	RA	Dec.	Transit	10° high	
				52°	56°
	h m	° '	h m	h m	h m
1	21 32.8	−15 17	6 55	3 35	4 02
11	21 33.5	−15 14	6 16	2 56	3 23
21	21 33.8	−15 13	5 37	2 17	2 43
31	21 33.8	−15 14	4 58	1 38	2 04

Diameter 4"

NEPTUNE

Day	RA	Dec.	Transit	10° high	
				52°	56°
	h m	° '	h m	h m	h m
1	20 35.6	−18 25	5 58	3 04	3 39
11	20 35.6	−18 25	5 18	2 24	3 00
21	20 35.4	−18 26	4 39	1 45	2 20
31	20 35.1	−18 27	3 59	1 05	1 41

Diameter 2"

June 2000

SIXTH MONTH, 30 DAYS. *Junius,* Roman *gens* (family)

1	*Thursday*	**Ascension Day.** Helen Keller d. 1968	153
2	*Friday*	*Coronation Day 1953.* Jesse Boot b. 1850	154
3	*Saturday*	Richard Cobden b. 1804. Samuel Plimsoll d. 1898	155
4	*Sunday*	**7th S. of Easter.** Battle of Magenta 1859	156
5	*Monday*	Adam Smith b. 1723. Stravinsky b. 1882	*week 23 day* 157
6	*Tuesday*	*Trinity Law Sittings begin.* Sir Isaiah Berlin d. 1997	158
7	*Wednesday*	Robert I d. 1329. Dennis Potter d. 1994	159
8	*Thursday*	Muhammad d. 632. Sir Norman Hartnell d. 1979	160
9	*Friday*	FEAST OF WEEKS begins. John Constable b. 1776	161
10	*Saturday*	*Duke of Edinburgh b. 1921. Queen's Official Birthday*	162
11	*Sunday*	**Pentecost (Whit Sunday). St Barnabas**	163
12	*Monday*	Harriet Martineau b. 1802. John Ireland d. 1962	*week 24 day* 164
13	*Tuesday*	W. B. Yeats b. 1865. Sir Eugene Goossens d. 1962	165
14	*Wednesday*	Harriet Beecher Stowe b. 1811. John Baird d. 1946	166
15	*Thursday*	Magna Carta sealed 1215. Ella Fitzgerald d. 1996	167
16	*Friday*	Stan Laurel b. 1890. Margaret Bondfield d. 1953	168
17	*Saturday*	Edward I b. 1239. Battle of Bunker Hill 1775	169
18	*Sunday*	**Trinity Sunday.** Battle of Waterloo 1815	170
19	*Monday*	Blaise Pascal b. 1623. The Duchess of Windsor b. 1896	*week 25 day* 171
20	*Tuesday*	William IV d. 1837. Dame Catherine Cookson b. 1906	172
21	*Wednesday*	Prince William of Wales b. 1982. Benazir Bhutto b. 1953	173
22	*Thursday*	**Corpus Christi.** Dame Cicely Saunders b. 1918	174
23	*Friday*	James Mill d. 1836. The Duke of Windsor b. 1894	175
24	*Saturday*	**John the Baptist.** Book of Common Prayer issued 1559	176
25	*Sunday*	**1st S. after Trinity.** Erskine Childers b. 1870	177
26	*Monday*	Joseph-Michel Montgolfier d. 1810. George IV d. 1830	*week 26 day* 178
27	*Tuesday*	Helen Keller b. 1880. Sir Alfred Ayer d. 1989	179
28	*Wednesday*	Treaty of Versailles signed 1919	180
29	*Thursday*	**SS Peter and Paul.** Lana Turner d. 1995	181
30	*Friday*	Sir Stanley Spencer b. 1891. Nancy Mitford d. 1973	182

ASTRONOMICAL PHENOMENA

d	h	
1	06	Saturn in conjunction with Moon. Saturn 3° N.
1	06	Jupiter in conjunction with Moon. Jupiter 4° N.
1	18	Pluto at opposition
2	08	Venus in conjunction with Moon. Venus 3° N.
3	02	Mars in conjunction with Moon. Mars 4° N.
4	04	Mercury in conjunction with Moon. Mercury 4° N.
9	13	Mercury at greatest elongation E.24°
11	11	Venus in superior conjunction
21	02	Sun's longitude 90° ♋
21	19	Mars in conjunction with Venus. Mars 0.3° N.
23	09	Mercury at stationary point
28	21	Saturn in conjunction with Moon. Saturn 2° N.
29	03	Jupiter in conjunction with Moon. Jupiter 3° N.

MINIMA OF ALGOL

Algol is inconveniently situated for observation during June.

CONSTELLATIONS

The following constellations are near the meridian at

	d	h		d	h
May	1	24	June	15	21
May	16	23	July	1	20
June	1	22	July	16	19

Cassiopeia (below the Pole), Ursa Minor, Draco, Ursa Major, Canes Venatici, Bootes, Corona, Serpens, Virgo and Libra

THE MOON

Phases, Apsides and Node	d	h	m
● New Moon	2	12	14
☽ First Quarter	9	03	29
○ Full Moon	16	22	27
☾ Last Quarter	25	01	00
Perigee (359,089 km)	3	13	18
Apogee (406,112 km)	18	12	57

Mean longitude of ascending node on June 1, 117°

THE SUN   s.d. 15′.8

Day	Right Ascension	Dec. +	Equation of time	Rise 52°	Rise 56°	Transit	Set 52°	Set 56°	Sidereal time	Transit of First Point of Aries
	h m s	° ′	m s	h m	h m	h m	h m	h m	h m s	h m s
1	4 36 54	22 04	+ 2 14	3 46	3 22	11 58	20 11	20 35	16 39 08	7 19 40
2	4 41 00	22 12	+ 2 04	3 45	3 21	11 58	20 12	20 36	16 43 04	7 15 44
3	4 45 06	22 19	+ 1 54	3 44	3 20	11 58	20 13	20 37	16 47 01	7 11 48
4	4 49 13	22 26	+ 1 44	3 44	3 19	11 58	20 14	20 39	16 50 57	7 07 52
5	4 53 20	22 33	+ 1 34	3 43	3 18	11 59	20 15	20 40	16 54 54	7 03 57
6	4 57 27	22 40	+ 1 23	3 42	3 17	11 59	20 16	20 41	16 58 50	7 00 01
7	5 01 35	22 46	+ 1 12	3 42	3 16	11 59	20 16	20 42	17 02 47	6 56 05
8	5 05 43	22 51	+ 1 00	3 41	3 16	11 59	20 17	20 43	17 06 44	6 52 09
9	5 09 51	22 56	+ 0 49	3 41	3 15	11 59	20 18	20 44	17 10 40	6 48 13
10	5 14 00	23 01	+ 0 37	3 40	3 15	11 59	20 19	20 45	17 14 37	6 44 17
11	5 18 08	23 05	+ 0 25	3 40	3 14	12 00	20 20	20 46	17 18 33	6 40 21
12	5 22 17	23 09	+ 0 13	3 40	3 14	12 00	20 20	20 46	17 22 30	6 36 25
13	5 26 26	23 13	0 00	3 40	3 14	12 00	20 21	20 47	17 26 26	6 32 29
14	5 30 35	23 16	− 0 12	3 39	3 13	12 00	20 21	20 48	17 30 23	6 28 33
15	5 34 44	23 19	− 0 25	3 39	3 13	12 01	20 22	20 48	17 34 19	6 24 37
16	5 38 54	23 21	− 0 38	3 39	3 13	12 01	20 22	20 49	17 38 16	6 20 41
17	5 43 03	23 23	− 0 51	3 39	3 13	12 01	20 23	20 49	17 42 13	6 16 46
18	5 47 13	23 24	− 1 03	3 39	3 13	12 01	20 23	20 50	17 46 09	6 12 50
19	5 51 22	23 25	− 1 16	3 39	3 13	12 01	20 23	20 50	17 50 06	6 08 54
20	5 55 32	23 26	− 1 29	3 40	3 13	12 02	20 24	20 50	17 54 02	6 04 58
21	5 59 41	23 26	− 1 42	3 40	3 13	12 02	20 24	20 50	17 57 59	6 01 02
22	6 03 51	23 26	− 1 55	3 40	3 13	12 02	20 24	20 51	18 01 55	5 57 06
23	6 08 00	23 26	− 2 08	3 40	3 14	12 02	20 24	20 51	18 05 52	5 53 10
24	6 12 10	23 25	− 2 21	3 41	3 14	12 02	20 24	20 51	18 09 48	5 49 14
25	6 16 19	23 23	− 2 34	3 41	3 15	12 03	20 24	20 51	18 13 45	5 45 18
26	6 20 28	23 21	− 2 47	3 41	3 15	12 03	20 24	20 50	18 17 42	5 41 22
27	6 24 37	23 19	− 2 59	3 42	3 16	12 03	20 24	20 50	18 21 38	5 37 26
28	6 28 46	23 16	− 3 12	3 43	3 16	12 03	20 24	20 50	18 25 35	5 33 31
29	6 32 55	23 13	− 3 24	3 43	3 17	12 03	20 24	20 50	18 29 31	5 29 35
30	6 37 04	23 10	− 3 36	3 44	3 18	12 04	20 23	20 49	18 33 28	5 25 39

DURATION OF TWILIGHT (in minutes)

Latitude	52°	56°	52°	56°	52°	56°	52°	56°
	1 June		11 June		21 June		30 June	
Civil	47	58	48	61	49	63	49	62
Nautical	117	TAN	125	TAN	128	TAN	125	TAN
Astronomical	TAN	TAN	TAN	TAN	TAN	TAN	TAN	TAN

THE NIGHT SKY

Mercury may be visible, though only as a difficult evening object. The long summer twilight will seriously hinder observation but under good conditions it may be possible to glimpse the planet during the first ten days of the month, very low above the north-western horizon at the end of evening civil twilight. During this period its magnitude fades from 0.0 to +1.0. Under very good conditions it may be possible to glimpse the thin crescent Moon, about 2.4 days old, about 10° to the left of the planet on the evening of the 4th.

Venus is at superior conjunction on the 11th, actually passing behind the disk of the Sun, and thus remaining too close to the Sun for observation throughout the month.

Mars is too close to the Sun for observation.

Jupiter, magnitude −2.1, becomes a morning object during the second half of the month, low in the eastern sky shortly before dawn. Both Jupiter and Saturn are moving eastwards in the western part of Taurus, with Jupiter about 3° further east. It will continue to be a useful guide to locating Saturn, which is over 2 magnitudes fainter.

Saturn is not visible for the first three weeks of June, but then begins to emerge from the long morning twilight and may be detected low above the east-north-eastern horizon before the sky gets too bright. The fact that in these latitudes even nautical twilight is continuous throughout the night means that Saturn will not be an easy object to locate. Its magnitude is +0.3.

Twilight. Reference to the section above shows that astronomical twilight lasts all night for a period around the summer solstice (i.e. in June and July), even in southern England. Under these conditions the sky never gets completely dark as the Sun is always less than 18° below the horizon.

THE MOON

Day	RA	Dec.	Hor. par.	Semi-diam.	Sun's co-long.	PA of Bright Limb	Phase	Age	Rise 52°	Rise 56°	Transit	Set 52°	Set 56°
	h m	°	'	'	°	°	%	d	h m	h m	h m	h m	h m
1	3 15	+13.2	60.1	16.4	254	63	4	27.8	3 31	3 19	11 00	18 45	19 01
2	4 14	+17.1	60.7	16.5	266	51	1	28.8	4 05	3 48	11 59	20 07	20 27
3	5 16	+20.0	61.0	16.6	278	289	0	0.5	4 48	4 28	13 01	21 22	21 45
4	6 20	+21.5	61.0	16.6	290	277	3	1.5	5 43	5 20	14 05	22 26	22 49
5	7 25	+21.5	60.8	16.6	303	279	9	2.5	6 49	6 27	15 07	23 17	23 37
6	8 28	+20.0	60.2	16.4	315	283	17	3.5	8 04	7 45	16 07	23 57	—
7	9 28	+17.2	59.5	16.2	327	287	27	4.5	9 22	9 07	17 03	—	0 13
8	10 24	+13.4	58.8	16.0	339	291	38	5.5	10 40	10 30	17 54	0 28	0 40
9	11 17	+ 9.0	58.0	15.8	352	293	49	6.5	11 56	11 50	18 43	0 53	1 01
10	12 08	+ 4.3	57.2	15.6	4	294	59	7.5	13 10	13 08	19 29	1 15	1 19
11	12 56	− 0.5	56.5	15.4	16	295	69	8.5	14 21	14 24	20 14	1 35	1 35
12	13 43	− 5.1	55.9	15.2	28	295	78	9.5	15 31	15 38	20 59	1 55	1 51
13	14 31	− 9.5	55.3	15.1	40	294	86	10.5	16 40	16 51	21 44	2 16	2 07
14	15 18	−13.4	54.9	15.0	53	292	92	11.5	17 47	18 02	22 29	2 39	2 26
15	16 07	−16.7	54.5	14.9	65	291	96	12.5	18 52	19 11	23 16	3 05	2 49
16	16 56	−19.3	54.3	14.8	77	294	99	13.5	19 53	20 14	—	3 36	3 16
17	17 46	−20.9	54.1	14.7	89	17	100	14.5	20 48	21 11	0 04	4 13	3 51
18	18 37	−21.7	54.0	14.7	101	79	99	15.5	21 36	21 58	0 53	4 57	4 34
19	19 28	−21.5	54.0	14.7	114	80	96	16.5	22 16	22 37	1 41	5 49	5 27
20	20 19	−20.3	54.1	14.7	126	78	92	17.5	22 50	23 07	2 29	6 47	6 27
21	21 08	−18.3	54.3	14.8	138	75	86	18.5	23 18	23 32	3 17	7 50	7 33
22	21 57	−15.4	54.7	14.9	150	72	79	19.5	23 42	23 52	4 03	8 55	8 42
23	22 45	−11.9	55.1	15.0	162	69	70	20.5	—	—	4 48	10 03	9 54
24	23 32	− 7.8	55.7	15.2	175	68	61	21.5	0 03	0 10	5 32	11 13	11 08
25	0 20	− 3.2	56.5	15.4	187	67	51	22.5	0 23	0 26	6 17	12 24	12 23
26	1 08	+ 1.6	57.3	15.6	199	66	40	23.5	0 44	0 42	7 04	13 38	13 42
27	1 58	+ 6.5	58.3	15.9	211	67	30	24.5	1 05	1 00	7 52	14 55	15 03
28	2 51	+11.2	59.2	16.1	224	69	20	25.5	1 30	1 20	8 44	16 15	16 28
29	3 48	+15.5	60.1	16.4	236	72	12	26.5	1 59	1 45	9 40	17 37	17 54
30	4 48	+18.9	60.8	16.6	248	76	5	27.5	2 36	2 18	10 41	18 56	19 17

MERCURY

Day	RA	Dec.	Diam.	Phase	Transit	5° high 52°	5° high 56°
	h m	°	"	%	h m	h m	h m
1	6 12	+25.6	7	56	13 34	21 23	21 44
3	6 24	+25.4	7	51	13 38	21 25	21 46
5	6 35	+25.1	7	47	13 41	21 26	21 46
7	6 46	+24.7	8	43	13 43	21 25	21 45
9	6 55	+24.2	8	39	13 44	21 22	21 42
11	7 03	+23.7	8	35	13 44	21 19	21 37
13	7 10	+23.2	9	31	13 43	21 14	21 31
15	7 15	+22.6	9	27	13 40	21 07	21 24
17	7 20	+22.0	10	24	13 36	21 00	21 16
19	7 23	+21.4	10	20	13 31	20 51	21 06
21	7 25	+20.9	10	17	13 25	20 41	20 56
23	7 25	+20.3	11	14	13 17	20 30	20 44
25	7 25	+19.8	11	10	13 08	20 18	20 31
27	7 23	+19.3	11	8	12 58	20 05	20 18
29	7 20	+18.9	12	5	12 47	19 51	20 04
31	7 16	+18.5	12	3	12 35	19 37	19 50

VENUS

Day	RA	Dec.	Diam.	Phase	Transit	5° high 52°	5° high 56°
	h m	°	"	%	h m	h m	h m
1	4 25	+21.3	10	100	11 47	19 09	19 25
6	4 51	+22.4	10	100	11 53	19 22	19 39
11	5 18	+23.2	10	100	12 00	19 34	19 52
16	5 44	+23.7	10	100	12 07	19 43	20 02
21	6 11	+23.9	10	100	12 14	19 52	20 11
26	6 38	+23.8	10	100	12 21	19 58	20 17
31	7 05	+23.4	10	100	12 28	20 02	20 21

MARS

Day	RA	Dec.	Diam.	Phase	Transit	5° high 52°	5° high 56°
1	5 14	+23.7	4	100	12 34	20 10	20 29
6	5 29	+23.9	4	100	12 30	20 07	20 26
11	5 44	+24.1	4	100	12 25	20 03	20 23
16	5 58	+24.2	4	100	12 20	19 59	20 18
21	6 13	+24.2	4	100	12 15	19 54	20 13
26	6 28	+24.1	4	100	12 10	19 48	20 07
31	6 42	+24.0	4	100	12 04	19 42	20 01

SUNRISE AND SUNSET

	London		Bristol		Birmingham		Manchester		Newcastle		Glasgow		Belfast	
	0°05′	51°30′	2°35′	51°28′	1°55′	52°28′	2°15′	53°28′	1°37′	54°59′	4°14′	55°52′	5°56′	54°35′
	h m	h m	h m	h m	h m	h m	h m	h m	h m	h m	h m	h m	h m	h m
1	3 49	20 08	3 59	20 18	3 51	20 21	3 47	20 28	3 35	20 34	3 40	20 51	3 55	20 49
2	3 48	20 09	3 58	20 19	3 50	20 22	3 46	20 29	3 34	20 36	3 39	20 52	3 54	20 50
3	3 47	20 10	3 57	20 20	3 49	20 23	3 45	20 30	3 33	20 37	3 38	20 53	3 53	20 52
4	3 47	20 11	3 57	20 21	3 49	20 24	3 44	20 31	3 32	20 38	3 37	20 55	3 52	20 53
5	3 46	20 12	3 56	20 22	3 48	20 25	3 44	20 32	3 31	20 39	3 36	20 56	3 51	20 54
6	3 45	20 13	3 56	20 23	3 47	20 26	3 43	20 33	3 31	20 40	3 35	20 57	3 51	20 55
7	3 45	20 14	3 55	20 24	3 47	20 27	3 42	20 34	3 30	20 41	3 34	20 58	3 50	20 56
8	3 44	20 15	3 55	20 25	3 46	20 28	3 42	20 35	3 29	20 42	3 34	20 59	3 49	20 57
9	3 44	20 16	3 54	20 25	3 46	20 28	3 41	20 36	3 29	20 43	3 33	21 00	3 49	20 58
10	3 44	20 16	3 54	20 26	3 45	20 29	3 41	20 37	3 28	20 44	3 33	21 01	3 48	20 58
11	3 43	20 17	3 53	20 27	3 45	20 30	3 40	20 37	3 28	20 45	3 32	21 02	3 48	20 59
12	3 43	20 18	3 53	20 28	3 45	20 31	3 40	20 38	3 28	20 45	3 32	21 02	3 48	21 00
13	3 43	20 18	3 53	20 28	3 45	20 31	3 40	20 39	3 27	20 46	3 31	21 03	3 47	21 01
14	3 43	20 19	3 53	20 29	3 44	20 32	3 40	20 39	3 27	20 47	3 31	21 04	3 47	21 01
15	3 43	20 19	3 53	20 29	3 44	20 32	3 40	20 40	3 27	20 47	3 31	21 04	3 47	21 02
16	3 42	20 20	3 53	20 30	3 44	20 33	3 39	20 40	3 27	20 48	3 31	21 05	3 47	21 02
17	3 42	20 20	3 53	20 30	3 44	20 33	3 39	20 41	3 27	20 48	3 31	21 05	3 47	21 03
18	3 43	20 21	3 53	20 30	3 44	20 33	3 39	20 41	3 27	20 49	3 31	21 06	3 47	21 03
19	3 43	20 21	3 53	20 31	3 44	20 34	3 40	20 41	3 27	20 49	3 31	21 06	3 47	21 03
20	3 43	20 21	3 53	20 31	3 45	20 34	3 40	20 42	3 27	20 49	3 31	21 06	3 47	21 04
21	3 43	20 21	3 53	20 31	3 45	20 34	3 40	20 42	3 27	20 49	3 31	21 06	3 47	21 04
22	3 43	20 21	3 53	20 31	3 45	20 34	3 40	20 42	3 27	20 50	3 31	21 07	3 47	21 04
23	3 43	20 22	3 54	20 31	3 45	20 34	3 40	20 42	3 28	20 50	3 32	21 07	3 48	21 04
24	3 44	20 22	3 54	20 31	3 46	20 35	3 41	20 42	3 28	20 50	3 32	21 07	3 48	21 04
25	3 44	20 22	3 54	20 31	3 46	20 35	3 41	20 42	3 29	20 50	3 33	21 07	3 49	21 04
26	3 45	20 22	3 55	20 31	3 46	20 34	3 42	20 42	3 29	20 49	3 33	21 06	3 49	21 04
27	3 45	20 21	3 55	20 31	3 47	20 34	3 42	20 42	3 30	20 49	3 34	21 06	3 50	21 04
28	3 46	20 21	3 56	20 31	3 48	20 34	3 43	20 42	3 30	20 49	3 34	21 06	3 50	21 04
29	3 46	20 21	3 56	20 31	3 48	20 34	3 43	20 41	3 31	20 49	3 35	21 06	3 51	21 03
30	3 47	20 21	3 57	20 31	3 49	20 34	3 44	20 41	3 32	20 48	3 36	21 05	3 52	21 03

JUPITER

Day	RA	Dec.	Transit	5° high	
				52°	56°
	h m	° ′	h m	h m	h m
1	3 25.3	+17 50	10 45	3 45	3 33
11	3 34.7	+18 23	10 15	3 12	2 59
21	3 43.8	+18 54	9 45	2 38	2 25
31	3 52.6	+19 21	9 14	2 05	1 52

Diameters – equatorial 34″ polar 32″

SATURN

Day	RA	Dec.	Transit	5° high	
				52°	56°
	h m	° ′	h m	h m	h m
1	3 25.1	+16 38	10 44	3 51	3 40
11	3 30.1	+16 55	10 10	3 15	3 04
21	3 34.8	+17 12	9 35	2 39	2 28
31	3 39.3	+17 26	9 01	2 03	1 51

Diameters – equatorial 17″ polar 15″
Rings – major axis 38″ minor axis 15″

URANUS

Day	RA	Dec.	Transit	10° high	
				52°	56°
	h m	° ′	h m	h m	h m
1	21 33.7	−15 14	4 54	1 34	2 00
11	21 33.4	−15 16	4 14	0 54	1 21
21	21 32.7	−15 19	3 34	0 15	0 42
31	21 31.8	−15 24	2 54	23 31	0 02

Diameter 4″

NEPTUNE

Day	RA	Dec.	Transit	10° high	
				52°	56°
	h m	° ′	h m	h m	h m
1	20 35.0	−18 27	3 55	1 01	1 37
11	20 34.4	−18 29	3 15	0 22	0 57
21	20 33.7	−18 32	2 35	23 38	0 18
31	20 32.8	−18 36	1 55	22 58	23 34

Diameter 2″

 # July 2000

SEVENTH MONTH, 31 DAYS. *Julius* Caesar, formerly *Quintilis*, fifth month of Roman pre-Julian calendar

1	*Saturday*	Diana, Princess of Wales b. 1961. Juan Perón d. 1974	183
2	*Sunday*	**2nd S. after Trinity.** Christoph Gluck b. 1714	184
3	*Monday*	**St Thomas.** Ken Russell b. 1927	*week* 27 *day* 185
4	*Tuesday*	Dr Thomas Barnardo b. 1845. Marie Curie d. 1934	186
5	*Wednesday*	Cecil Rhodes b. 1853. Salvation Army founded 1865	187
6	*Thursday*	Beatrix Potter b. 1866. Roy Rogers d. 1998	188
7	*Friday*	Georg Ohm d. 1854. Sir Arthur Conan Doyle d. 1930	189
8	*Saturday*	Edmund Burke d. 1797. Vivien Leigh d. 1967	190
9	*Sunday*	**3rd S. after Trinity.** Ann Radcliffe b. 1764	191
10	*Monday*	Hadrian d. 138 AD. George Stubbs d. 1806	*week* 28 *day* 192
11	*Tuesday*	Battle of Courtrai 1302. Paul Nash d. 1946	193
12	*Wednesday*	*Bank Holiday in Northern Ireland.* Julius Caesar b. 102 BC	194
13	*Thursday*	Jean-Paul Marat d. 1793. Sir George Scott b. 1811	195
14	*Friday*	Storming of the Bastille 1789. Leon Garfield b. 1921	196
15	*Saturday*	Rembrandt b. 1606. Versace d. 1997	197
16	*Sunday*	**4th S. after Trinity.** Roald Amundsen b. 1872	198
17	*Monday*	Jules-Henri Poincaré d. 1912. Juan Fangio d. 1995	*week* 29 *day* 199
18	*Tuesday*	Thomas Cook d. 1892. Spanish Civil War began 1936	200
19	*Wednesday*	A. J. Cronin b. 1896. Sir James Goldsmith d. 1997	201
20	*Thursday*	Andrew Lang d. 1912. Guglielmo Marconi d. 1937	202
21	*Friday*	Robert Burns d. 1796. Paul Reuter b. 1816	203
22	*Saturday*	**Mary Magdalene.** Battle of Falkirk 1298	204
23	*Sunday*	**5th S. after Trinity.** Haile Selassie b. 1891	205
24	*Monday*	Amelia Earhart b. 1897. Treaty of Lausanne 1923	*week* 30 *day* 206
25	*Tuesday*	**St James.** Samuel Taylor Coleridge d. 1834	207
26	*Wednesday*	Francesco Cilea b. 1866. Robert Graves b. 1895	208
27	*Thursday*	Sir Anton Dolin b. 1904. Gertrude Stein d. 1946	209
28	*Friday*	Thomas Cromwell exec. 1540. J. S. Bach d. 1750	210
29	*Saturday*	Mussolini b. 1883. Van Gogh d. 1890	211
30	*Sunday*	**6th S. after Trinity.** Henry Moore b. 1898	212
31	*Monday*	*Trinity Law Sittings end.* Sir George Allen b. 1902	*week* 31 *day* 213

ASTRONOMICAL PHENOMENA

d h
1 16 Mars in conjunction
1 19 Mars in conjunction with Moon. Mars 2° N.
1 19 Partial eclipse of Sun (*see* page 71)
2 05 Venus in conjunction with Moon. Venus 2° N.
2 06 Mercury in conjunction with Moon. Mercury 3° S.
2 18 Venus in conjunction with Mercury. Venus 5° N.
4 00 Earth at aphelion (152 million km)
6 12 Mercury in inferior conjunction
7 14 Mars in conjunction with Mercury. Mars 6° N.
16 14 Total eclipse of Moon (*see* page 71)
17 13 Mercury at stationary point
22 13 Sun's longitude 120° ♌
26 10 Saturn in conjunction with Moon. Saturn 2° N.
26 21 Jupiter in conjunction with Moon. Jupiter 3° N.
27 09 Mercury at greatest elongation W.20°
27 23 Neptune at opposition
29 17 Mercury in conjunction with Moon. Mercury 0.8° S.
30 12 Mars in conjunction with Moon. Mars 0.6° N.
31 02 Partial eclipse of Sun (*see* page 71)

MINIMA OF ALGOL

d	h	d	h	d	h
3	08.1	14	19.3	26	06.5

6	04.9	17	16.1	29	03.3
9	01.7	20	12.9		
11	22.5	23	09.7		

CONSTELLATIONS

The following constellations are near the meridian at

	d	h		d	h
June	1	24	July	16	21
June	15	23	August	1	20
July	1	22	August	16	19

Ursa Minor, Draco, Corona, Hercules, Lyra, Serpens, Ophiuchus, Libra, Scorpius and Sagittarius

THE MOON

Phases, Apsides and Node	d	h	m
● New Moon	1	19	20
☽ First Quarter	8	12	53
○ Full Moon	16	13	55
☾ Last Quarter	24	11	02
● New Moon	31	02	25
Perigee (357,362 km)	1	22	16
Apogee (406,200 km)	15	15	33
Perigee (358,375 km)	30	07	44

Mean longitude of ascending node on July 1, 115°

THE SUN

s.d. 15′.8

Day	Right Ascension	Dec. +	Equation of time	Rise 52°	Rise 56°	Transit	Set 52°	Set 56°	Sidereal time	Transit of First Point of Aries
	h m s	° ′	m s	h m	h m	h m	h m	h m	h m s	h m s
1	6 41 12	23 06	− 3 48	3 44	3 19	12 04	20 23	20 49	18 37 24	5 21 43
2	6 45 20	23 02	− 3 59	3 45	3 19	12 04	20 23	20 48	18 41 21	5 17 47
3	6 49 28	22 57	− 4 11	3 46	3 20	12 04	20 22	20 48	18 45 17	5 13 51
4	6 53 36	22 52	− 4 22	3 47	3 21	12 04	20 22	20 47	18 49 14	5 09 55
5	6 57 43	22 47	− 4 32	3 48	3 22	12 05	20 21	20 46	18 53 11	5 05 59
6	7 01 50	22 41	− 4 42	3 49	3 23	12 05	20 21	20 45	18 57 07	5 02 03
7	7 05 56	22 34	− 4 52	3 49	3 25	12 05	20 20	20 45	19 01 04	4 58 07
8	7 10 02	22 28	− 5 02	3 50	3 26	12 05	20 19	20 44	19 05 00	4 54 11
9	7 14 08	22 21	− 5 11	3 51	3 27	12 05	20 18	20 43	19 08 57	4 50 16
10	7 18 13	22 13	− 5 19	3 52	3 28	12 05	20 18	20 42	19 12 53	4 46 20
11	7 22 18	22 05	− 5 28	3 54	3 30	12 06	20 17	20 41	19 16 50	4 42 24
12	7 26 22	21 57	− 5 35	3 55	3 31	12 06	20 16	20 40	19 20 46	4 38 28
13	7 30 26	21 49	− 5 43	3 56	3 32	12 06	20 15	20 38	19 24 43	4 34 32
14	7 34 29	21 40	− 5 49	3 57	3 34	12 06	20 14	20 37	19 28 40	4 30 36
15	7 38 32	21 30	− 5 56	3 58	3 35	12 06	20 13	20 36	19 32 36	4 26 40
16	7 42 34	21 21	− 6 01	3 59	3 37	12 06	20 12	20 34	19 36 33	4 22 44
17	7 46 36	21 11	− 6 07	4 01	3 38	12 06	20 11	20 33	19 40 29	4 18 48
18	7 50 37	21 00	− 6 11	4 02	3 40	12 06	20 10	20 32	19 44 26	4 14 52
19	7 54 38	20 50	− 6 16	4 03	3 41	12 06	20 08	20 30	19 48 22	4 10 56
20	7 58 38	20 39	− 6 19	4 05	3 43	12 06	20 07	20 29	19 52 19	4 07 00
21	8 02 38	20 27	− 6 22	4 06	3 45	12 06	20 06	20 27	19 56 15	4 03 05
22	8 06 37	20 15	− 6 25	4 07	3 46	12 06	20 05	20 25	20 00 12	3 59 09
23	8 10 35	20 03	− 6 27	4 09	3 48	12 06	20 03	20 24	20 04 09	3 55 13
24	8 14 33	19 51	− 6 28	4 10	3 50	12 06	20 02	20 22	20 08 05	3 51 17
25	8 18 31	19 38	− 6 29	4 12	3 52	12 06	20 00	20 20	20 12 02	3 47 21
26	8 22 28	19 25	− 6 29	4 13	3 53	12 06	19 59	20 18	20 15 58	3 43 25
27	8 26 24	19 11	− 6 29	4 14	3 55	12 06	19 57	20 17	20 19 55	3 39 29
28	8 30 20	18 58	− 6 28	4 16	3 57	12 06	19 56	20 15	20 23 51	3 35 33
29	8 34 15	18 44	− 6 27	4 17	3 59	12 06	19 54	20 13	20 27 48	3 31 37
30	8 38 09	18 29	− 6 25	4 19	4 01	12 06	19 53	20 11	20 31 44	3 27 41
31	8 42 03	18 15	− 6 22	4 21	4 02	12 06	19 51	20 09	20 35 41	3 23 45

DURATION OF TWILIGHT (in minutes)

Latitude	52°	56°	52°	56°	52°	56°	52°	56°
	1 July		11 July		21 July		31 July	
Civil	48	61	46	58	44	53	41	49
Nautical	124	TAN	116	TAN	107	144	98	122
Astronomical	TAN	TAN	TAN	TAN	TAN	TAN	180	TAN

THE NIGHT SKY

Mercury is unsuitably placed for observation for most of the month, inferior conjunction occurring on the 6th. However, for the last few days of July it may be glimpsed as a difficult morning object, low above the east-north-eastern horizon at the beginning of morning civil twilight. During this period its magnitude brightens from +0.6 to −0.3.

Venus is too close to the Sun for observation for most of July. However, during the last week of the month it may be glimpsed with difficulty for a short time after sunset, low above the west-north-western horizon. Its magnitude is −3.9.

Mars is unsuitably placed for observation as it passes through conjunction on the 1st.

Jupiter continues to be visible as a morning object in the south-eastern sky, magnitude −2.1. It is moving eastwards between the Pleiades and the Hyades. On the morning of the 27th the old crescent Moon will be seen near the planet.

Saturn, magnitude +0.3, is a difficult morning object at first. However, it is rising earlier each night and by the end of the month it may be detected low above the eastern horizon shortly after midnight. On the morning of the 26th, the gibbous Moon will be seen approaching the planet. Saturn is in Taurus.

Neptune is at opposition on the 27th, in Capricornus. It is not visible to the naked eye since its magnitude is +7.8.

THE MOON

Day	RA h m	Dec. °	Hor. par. ′	Semi-diam. ′	Sun's co-long. °	PA of Bright Limb °	Phase %	Age d	Rise 52° h m	Rise 56° h m	Transit h m	Set 52° h m	Set 56° h m
1	5 51	+21.1	61.2	16.7	260	78	1	28.5	3 25	3 03	11 44	20 07	20 30
2	6 57	+21.7	61.4	16.7	273	296	0	0.2	4 26	4 03	12 48	21 06	21 28
3	8 02	+20.8	61.2	16.7	285	281	2	1.2	5 39	5 18	13 51	21 52	22 10
4	9 05	+18.5	60.7	16.5	297	284	7	2.2	6 58	6 41	14 51	22 28	22 42
5	10 05	+14.9	59.9	16.3	309	287	15	3.2	8 20	8 07	15 46	22 57	23 06
6	11 01	+10.6	59.1	16.1	322	290	24	4.2	9 39	9 32	16 38	23 21	23 25
7	11 53	+ 5.8	58.2	15.8	334	292	34	5.2	10 56	10 53	17 26	23 42	23 42
8	12 43	+ 0.9	57.2	15.6	346	293	44	6.2	12 10	12 11	18 12	—	23 59
9	13 32	− 3.9	56.4	15.4	358	292	55	7.2	13 21	13 27	18 57	0 02	—
10	14 19	− 8.4	55.7	15.2	11	291	65	8.2	14 30	14 40	19 42	0 22	0 15
11	15 07	−12.4	55.1	15.0	23	289	74	9.2	15 38	15 52	20 28	0 44	0 33
12	15 55	−15.9	54.7	14.9	35	286	82	10.2	16 44	17 01	21 14	1 09	0 54
13	16 44	−18.7	54.3	14.8	47	282	89	11.2	17 46	18 07	22 01	1 38	1 20
14	17 34	−20.6	54.1	14.7	59	278	94	12.2	18 43	19 06	22 49	2 13	1 52
15	18 24	−21.6	54.0	14.7	72	273	98	13.2	19 33	19 56	23 38	2 55	2 32
16	19 15	−21.6	54.0	14.7	84	269	100	14.2	20 16	20 38	—	3 44	3 21
17	20 06	−20.7	54.1	14.7	96	83	100	15.2	20 52	21 11	0 26	4 40	4 19
18	20 56	−18.9	54.2	14.8	108	79	98	16.2	21 22	21 37	1 14	5 42	5 23
19	21 45	−16.2	54.5	14.8	120	76	95	17.2	21 47	21 59	2 01	6 47	6 32
20	22 33	−12.8	54.8	14.9	133	73	90	18.2	22 09	22 17	2 46	7 54	7 43
21	23 20	− 8.9	55.3	15.1	145	71	83	19.2	22 29	22 33	3 30	9 02	8 56
22	0 07	− 4.4	55.8	15.2	157	69	75	20.2	22 49	22 49	4 15	10 12	10 10
23	0 55	+ 0.2	56.5	15.4	169	69	65	21.2	23 09	23 05	5 00	11 23	11 25
24	1 43	+ 5.0	57.2	15.6	181	69	55	22.2	23 32	23 23	5 46	12 37	12 43
25	2 34	+ 9.7	58.0	15.8	194	71	44	23.2	23 58	23 45	6 35	13 53	14 04
26	3 27	+14.0	58.9	16.0	206	74	33	24.2	—	—	7 27	15 12	15 27
27	4 24	+17.6	59.7	16.3	218	78	23	25.2	0 30	0 13	8 23	16 30	16 50
28	5 25	+20.3	60.4	16.5	230	83	14	26.2	1 11	0 51	9 24	17 44	18 06
29	6 28	+21.6	60.9	16.6	243	90	7	27.2	2 05	1 42	10 27	18 49	19 11
30	7 33	+21.4	61.2	16.7	255	98	2	28.2	3 11	2 49	11 30	19 41	20 01
31	8 37	+19.7	61.1	16.7	267	142	0	29.2	4 28	4 09	12 32	20 23	20 39

MERCURY

Day	RA h m	Dec. °	Diam. ″	Phase %	Transit h m	5° high 52° h m	5° high 56° h m
1	7 16	+18.5	12	3	12 35	19 37	19 50
3	7 11	+18.3	12	2	12 22	19 23	19 35
5	7 06	+18.1	12	1	12 09	19 09	19 21
7	7 00	+18.0	12	1	11 56	4 56	4 44
9	6 55	+18.0	12	2	11 43	4 43	4 31
11	6 51	+18.0	11	3	11 31	4 31	4 19
13	6 47	+18.2	11	5	11 20	4 18	4 06
15	6 45	+18.4	11	8	11 10	4 07	3 54
17	6 44	+18.7	10	11	11 01	3 57	3 44
19	6 44	+19.0	10	16	10 54	3 47	3 34
21	6 46	+19.4	9	20	10 49	3 40	3 26
23	6 50	+19.8	9	25	10 45	3 33	3 19
25	6 55	+20.1	8	31	10 43	3 29	3 14
27	7 02	+20.5	8	37	10 42	3 26	3 11
29	7 11	+20.7	7	44	10 44	3 25	3 10
31	7 21	+20.9	7	51	10 46	3 27	3 11

VENUS

Day	RA h m	Dec. °	Diam. ″	Phase %	Transit h m	5° high 52° h m	5° high 56° h m
1	7 05	+23.4	10	100	12 28	20 02	20 21
6	7 31	+22.8	10	99	12 35	20 05	20 22
11	7 58	+21.8	10	99	12 42	20 05	20 21
16	8 24	+20.6	10	99	12 48	20 04	20 19
21	8 49	+19.2	10	98	12 53	20 01	20 14
26	9 14	+17.5	10	98	12 58	19 56	20 08
31	9 38	+15.6	10	97	13 03	19 50	20 00

MARS

Day	RA h m	Dec. °	Diam. ″	Phase %	Transit h m	5° high 52° h m	5° high 56° h m
1	6 42	+24.0	4	100	12 04	4 27	4 08
6	6 57	+23.7	4	100	11 59	4 23	4 05
11	7 11	+23.4	4	100	11 54	4 20	4 02
16	7 25	+23.0	4	100	11 48	4 17	3 59
21	7 39	+22.5	4	100	11 42	4 14	3 57
26	7 53	+21.9	4	100	11 37	4 12	3 56
31	8 07	+21.3	4	100	11 31	4 10	3 54

SUNRISE AND SUNSET

	London		Bristol		Birmingham		Manchester		Newcastle		Glasgow		Belfast	
	0°05′	51°30′	2°35′	51°28′	1°55′	52°28′	2°15′	53°28′	1°37′	54°59′	4°14′	55°52′	5°56′	54°35′
	h m	h m	h m	h m	h m	h m	h m	h m	h m	h m	h m	h m	h m	h m
1	3 48	20 21	3 58	20 30	3 49	20 33	3 45	20 41	3 32	20 48	3 36	21 05	3 52	21 03
2	3 48	20 20	3 58	20 30	3 50	20 33	3 46	20 40	3 33	20 47	3 37	21 04	3 53	21 02
3	3 49	20 20	3 59	20 30	3 51	20 32	3 46	20 40	3 34	20 47	3 38	21 04	3 54	21 01
4	3 50	20 19	4 00	20 29	3 52	20 32	3 47	20 39	3 35	20 46	3 39	21 03	3 55	21 01
5	3 51	20 19	4 01	20 29	3 53	20 31	3 48	20 39	3 36	20 46	3 40	21 02	3 56	21 00
6	3 52	20 18	4 02	20 28	3 54	20 31	3 49	20 38	3 37	20 45	3 41	21 01	3 57	21 00
7	3 52	20 18	4 03	20 27	3 55	20 30	3 50	20 37	3 38	20 44	3 42	21 01	3 58	20 59
8	3 53	20 17	4 04	20 27	3 56	20 29	3 51	20 36	3 39	20 43	3 44	21 00	3 59	20 58
9	3 54	20 16	4 05	20 26	3 57	20 29	3 52	20 36	3 40	20 42	3 45	20 59	4 00	20 57
10	3 55	20 15	4 06	20 25	3 58	20 28	3 53	20 35	3 42	20 41	3 46	20 58	4 01	20 56
11	3 56	20 15	4 07	20 24	3 59	20 27	3 54	20 34	3 43	20 40	3 47	20 57	4 03	20 55
12	3 58	20 14	4 08	20 24	4 00	20 26	3 56	20 33	3 44	20 39	3 49	20 56	4 04	20 54
13	3 59	20 13	4 09	20 23	4 01	20 25	3 57	20 32	3 45	20 38	3 50	20 54	4 05	20 53
14	4 00	20 12	4 10	20 22	4 02	20 24	3 58	20 31	3 47	20 37	3 52	20 53	4 06	20 52
15	4 01	20 11	4 11	20 21	4 03	20 23	3 59	20 30	3 48	20 36	3 53	20 52	4 08	20 51
16	4 02	20 10	4 12	20 20	4 05	20 22	4 01	20 29	3 49	20 35	3 54	20 51	4 09	20 50
17	4 03	20 09	4 14	20 19	4 06	20 21	4 02	20 27	3 51	20 33	3 56	20 49	4 11	20 48
18	4 05	20 08	4 15	20 17	4 07	20 20	4 03	20 26	3 52	20 32	3 58	20 48	4 12	20 47
19	4 06	20 06	4 16	20 16	4 09	20 18	4 05	20 25	3 54	20 31	3 59	20 46	4 14	20 46
20	4 07	20 05	4 17	20 15	4 10	20 17	4 06	20 23	3 56	20 29	4 01	20 45	4 15	20 44
21	4 09	20 04	4 19	20 14	4 11	20 16	4 08	20 22	3 57	20 28	4 02	20 43	4 17	20 43
22	4 10	20 03	4 20	20 13	4 13	20 14	4 09	20 21	3 59	20 26	4 04	20 42	4 18	20 41
23	4 11	20 01	4 21	20 11	4 14	20 13	4 11	20 19	4 00	20 24	4 06	20 40	4 20	20 40
24	4 13	20 00	4 23	20 10	4 16	20 12	4 12	20 18	4 02	20 23	4 07	20 38	4 21	20 38
25	4 14	19 59	4 24	20 08	4 17	20 10	4 14	20 16	4 04	20 21	4 09	20 36	4 23	20 36
26	4 15	19 57	4 26	20 07	4 19	20 09	4 15	20 15	4 05	20 19	4 11	20 35	4 25	20 35
27	4 17	19 56	4 27	20 06	4 20	20 07	4 17	20 13	4 07	20 18	4 13	20 33	4 26	20 33
28	4 18	19 54	4 29	20 04	4 22	20 06	4 19	20 11	4 09	20 16	4 15	20 31	4 28	20 31
29	4 20	19 53	4 30	20 03	4 23	20 04	4 20	20 10	4 10	20 14	4 16	20 29	4 30	20 30
30	4 21	19 51	4 31	20 01	4 25	20 02	4 22	20 08	4 12	20 12	4 18	20 27	4 31	20 28
31	4 23	19 50	4 33	19 59	4 26	20 01	4 23	20 06	4 14	20 10	4 20	20 25	4 33	20 26

JUPITER

Day	RA	Dec.	Transit	5° high	
				52°	56°
	h m	° ′	h m	h m	h m
1	3 52.6	+19 21	9 14	2 05	1 52
11	4 01.0	+19 46	8 43	1 32	1 18
21	4 08.9	+20 07	8 12	0 58	0 44
31	4 16.2	+20 26	7 39	0 24	0 10

Diameters – equatorial 35″ polar 33″

SATURN

Day	RA	Dec.	Transit	5° high	
				52°	56°
	h m	° ′	h m	h m	h m
1	3 39.3	+17 26	9 01	2 03	1 51
11	3 43.5	+17 39	8 25	1 26	1 15
21	3 47.2	+17 50	7 50	0 50	0 38
31	3 50.5	+17 58	7 14	0 13	0 01

Diameters – equatorial 17″ polar 16″
Rings – major axis 39″ minor axis 16″

URANUS

Day	RA	Dec.	Transit	10° high	
				52°	56°
	h m	° ′	h m	h m	h m
1	21 31.8	−15 24	2 54	23 31	0 02
11	21 30.6	−15 30	2 13	22 51	23 19
21	21 29.3	−15 37	1 33	22 12	22 39
31	21 27.8	−15 44	0 52	21 32	22 00

Diameter 4″

NEPTUNE

Day	RA	Dec.	Transit	10° high	
				52°	56°
	h m	° ′	h m	h m	h m
1	20 32.8	−18 36	1 55	22 58	23 34
11	20 31.8	−18 39	1 15	22 19	22 55
21	20 30.7	−18 43	0 34	21 39	22 15
31	20 29.6	−18 47	23 50	20 59	21 36

Diameter 2″

August 2000

EIGHTH MONTH, 31 DAYS. *Augustus,* formerly *Sextilis,* sixth month of Roman pre-Julian calendar

1	*Tuesday*	Queen Anne d. 1714. Yves St Laurent b. 1936	214
2	*Wednesday*	John Pinkerton b. 1919. Alexander Graham Bell d. 1922	215
3	*Thursday*	James II d. 1460. Rupert Brooke b. 1887	216
4	*Friday*	*Queen Elizabeth the Queen Mother b. 1900*	217
5	*Saturday*	Thomas Newcomen d. 1729. Richard Burton d. 1984	218
6	*Sunday*	**7th S. after Trinity. The Transfiguration**	219
7	*Monday*	*Bank Holiday in Scotland.* Ossie Clark d. 1996	*week 32 day* 220
8	*Tuesday*	Princess Beatrice of York b. 1988. Sir Frank Whittle d. 1996	221
9	*Wednesday*	Thomas Telford b. 1757. Hermann Hesse d. 1962	222
10	*Thursday*	Greenwich Observatory founded 1675	223
11	*Friday*	Charlotte Yonge b. 1823. Cardinal Newman d. 1890	224
12	*Saturday*	George IV b. 1762. Viscount Stewart d. 1822	225
13	*Sunday*	**8th S. after Trinity.** Sir Alfred Hitchcock b. 1899	226
14	*Monday*	Japan surrenders 1945. Enzo Ferrari d. 1988	*week 33 day* 227
15	*Tuesday*	**Blessed Virgin Mary.** *Princess Royal b. 1950*	228
16	*Wednesday*	Robert Bunsen d. 1899. Elvis Presley d. 1977	229
17	*Thursday*	Construction of Berlin Wall began 1961	230
18	*Friday*	Genghis Khan d. 1227. Lord John Russell b. 1792	231
19	*Saturday*	Augustus d. 14 AD. Coco Chanel b. 1883	232
20	*Sunday*	**9th S. after Trinity.** Rajiv Gandhi b. 1944	233
21	*Monday*	*Princess Margaret b. 1930.* William IV b. 1765	*week 34 day* 234
22	*Tuesday*	Michael Collins d. 1922. Dr Jacob Bronowski d. 1974	235
23	*Wednesday*	Louis XVI b. 1754. Rudolf Valentino d. 1926	236
24	*Thursday*	**St Bartholomew.** First Edinburgh Festival 1947	237
25	*Friday*	David Hume d. 1776. Sir Frederick Herchel d. 1822	238
26	*Saturday*	Mother Teresa b. 1910. Sir Francis Chichester d. 1972	239
27	*Sunday*	**10th S. after Trinity.** Haile Selassie d. 1975	240
28	*Monday*	*Bank Holiday in England, Wales and Northern Ireland*	*week 35 day* 241
29	*Tuesday*	First motorcycle patented 1885. Eamon de Valera d. 1975	242
30	*Wednesday*	Maria Montessori b. 1870. Ernest Rutherford b. 1871	243
31	*Thursday*	Diana, Princess of Wales d. 1997	244

ASTRONOMICAL PHENOMENA

d	h	
1	02	Venus in conjunction with Moon. Venus 1° S.
10	13	Mars in conjunction with Mercury. Mars 0.06° N.
11	05	Uranus at opposition
20	23	Pluto at stationary point
22	01	Mercury in superior conjunction
22	20	Sun's longitude 150° ♍
22	20	Saturn in conjunction with Moon. Saturn 2° N.
23	11	Jupiter in conjunction with Moon. Jupiter 3° N.
28	03	Mars in conjunction with Moon. Mars 0.9° S.
30	00	Mercury in conjunction with Moon. Mercury 3° S.
31	01	Venus in conjunction with Moon. Venus 4° S.

MINIMA OF ALGOL

d	h	d	h	d	h
1	00.2	12	11.4	23	22.6
3	21.0	15	08.2	26	19.4
6	17.8	18	05.0	29	16.3
9	14.6	21	01.8		

CONSTELLATIONS

The following constellations are near the meridian at

d	h		d	h
July	1	24	August	16	21
July	16	23	September	1	20
August	1	22	September	15	19

Draco, Hercules, Lyra, Cygnus, Sagitta, Ophiuchus, Serpens, Aquila and Sagittarius

THE MOON

Phases, Apsides and Node	d	h	m
☽ First Quarter	7	01	02
○ Full Moon	15	05	13
☾ Last Quarter	22	18	51
● New Moon	29	10	19

Apogee (405,652 km)	11	22	24
Perigee (361,906 km)	27	13	58

Mean longitude of ascending node on August 1, 114°

THE SUN   s.d. 15′.8

Day	Right Ascension	Dec. +	Equation of time	Rise 52°	Rise 56°	Transit	Set 52°	Set 56°	Sidereal time	Transit of First Point of Aries
	h m s	° ′	m s	h m	h m	h m	h m	h m	h m s	h m s
1	8 45 56	18 00	− 6 19	4 22	4 04	12 06	19 49	20 07	20 39 38	3 19 50
2	8 49 49	17 44	− 6 15	4 24	4 06	12 06	19 48	20 05	20 43 34	3 15 54
3	8 53 41	17 29	− 6 10	4 25	4 08	12 06	19 46	20 03	20 47 31	3 11 58
4	8 57 32	17 13	− 6 05	4 27	4 10	12 06	19 44	20 01	20 51 27	3 08 02
5	9 01 23	16 57	− 5 59	4 28	4 12	12 06	19 43	19 59	20 55 24	3 04 06
6	9 05 13	16 40	− 5 53	4 30	4 14	12 06	19 41	19 57	20 59 20	3 00 10
7	9 09 03	16 24	− 5 46	4 31	4 16	12 06	19 39	19 54	21 03 17	2 56 14
8	9 12 52	16 07	− 5 38	4 33	4 18	12 06	19 37	19 52	21 07 13	2 52 18
9	9 16 40	15 50	− 5 30	4 35	4 20	12 05	19 35	19 50	21 11 10	2 48 22
10	9 20 28	15 32	− 5 21	4 36	4 22	12 05	19 33	19 48	21 15 07	2 44 26
11	9 24 15	15 14	− 5 12	4 38	4 23	12 05	19 31	19 45	21 19 03	2 40 30
12	9 28 02	14 57	− 5 02	4 39	4 25	12 05	19 29	19 43	21 23 00	2 36 35
13	9 31 48	14 38	− 4 52	4 41	4 27	12 05	19 27	19 41	21 26 56	2 32 39
14	9 35 33	14 20	− 4 41	4 43	4 29	12 05	19 25	19 38	21 30 53	2 28 43
15	9 39 18	14 01	− 4 29	4 44	4 31	12 04	19 23	19 36	21 34 49	2 24 47
16	9 43 03	13 42	− 4 17	4 46	4 33	12 04	19 21	19 34	21 38 46	2 20 51
17	9 46 47	13 23	− 4 04	4 48	4 35	12 04	19 19	19 31	21 42 42	2 16 55
18	9 50 30	13 04	− 3 51	4 49	4 37	12 04	19 17	19 29	21 46 39	2 12 59
19	9 54 13	12 45	− 3 37	4 51	4 39	12 03	19 15	19 27	21 50 36	2 09 03
20	9 57 55	12 25	− 3 23	4 52	4 41	12 03	19 13	19 24	21 54 32	2 05 07
21	10 01 37	12 05	− 3 09	4 54	4 43	12 03	19 11	19 22	21 58 29	2 01 11
22	10 05 19	11 45	− 2 54	4 56	4 45	12 03	19 09	19 19	22 02 25	1 57 15
23	10 09 00	11 25	− 2 38	4 57	4 47	12 03	19 07	19 17	22 06 22	1 53 20
24	10 12 41	11 04	− 2 22	4 59	4 49	12 02	19 04	19 14	22 10 18	1 49 24
25	10 16 21	10 44	− 2 06	5 01	4 51	12 02	19 02	19 12	22 14 15	1 45 28
26	10 20 01	10 23	− 1 49	5 02	4 53	12 02	19 00	19 09	22 18 11	1 41 32
27	10 23 40	10 02	− 1 32	5 04	4 55	12 01	18 58	19 07	22 22 08	1 37 36
28	10 27 19	9 41	− 1 15	5 06	4 57	12 01	18 56	19 04	22 26 05	1 33 40
29	10 30 58	9 20	− 0 57	5 07	4 59	12 01	18 53	19 02	22 30 01	1 29 44
30	10 34 37	8 58	− 0 39	5 09	5 01	12 00	18 51	18 59	22 33 58	1 25 48
31	10 38 15	8 37	− 0 20	5 10	5 03	12 00	18 49	18 56	22 37 54	1 21 52

DURATION OF TWILIGHT (in minutes)

Latitude	52°	56°	52°	56°	52°	56°	52°	56°
	1 August		11 August		21 August		31 August	
Civil	41	48	39	45	37	42	35	40
Nautical	97	120	89	106	83	96	79	89
Astronomical	177	TAN	153	205	138	166	127	147

THE NIGHT SKY

Mercury is a morning object during the first week of the month, low above the east-north-eastern horizon at the (time of) beginning of morning civil twilight. During this period its magnitude increases from −0.4 to −1.1. For the remainder of August it is too close to the Sun for observation, superior conjunction occurring on the 22nd.

Venus, magnitude −3.9, is visible in the evenings at sunset, though only for a short time, extremely low above the western horizon. The further north the observer is in Britain, the greater the difficulty in locating the planet.

Mars, magnitude +1.8, gradually becomes visible as a difficult morning object towards the end of the month, low above the east-north-eastern horizon, about an hour before sunrise.

Jupiter, magnitude −2.3, is still a splendid morning object in the south-eastern sky. The Moon, at Last Quarter, will be seen about 7° to the right of the planet during the early hours of the 23rd, while Saturn is on the opposite side of the Moon.

Saturn continues to be visible as a morning object, magnitude +0.2. By the end of the month the planet is visible low in the eastern sky by 2200 hours. Saturn is in Taurus.

Uranus is at opposition on the 11th, in Capricornus. Uranus is barely visible to the naked eye as its magnitude is +5.7, but it is readily located with only small optical aid.

Meteors. The maximum of the famous Perseid meteor shower occurs on the morning of the 12th. Conditions are best between moonset (shortly after 0100 hours) and the beginning of morning twilight.

THE MOON

Day	RA h m	Dec. °	Hor. par. ′	Semi- diam. ′	Sun's co- long. °	PA of Bright Limb °	Phase %	Age d	Rise 52° h m	Rise 56° h m	Transit h m	Set 52° h m	Set 56° h m
1	9 39	+16.6	60.7	16.6	279	278	1	0.9	5 51	5 36	13 31	20 55	21 07
2	10 38	+12.4	60.1	16.4	292	285	5	1.9	7 14	7 04	14 26	21 22	21 29
3	11 33	+ 7.6	59.3	16.2	304	288	12	2.9	8 34	8 29	15 17	21 45	21 47
4	12 26	+ 2.6	58.4	15.9	316	290	20	3.9	9 52	9 51	16 06	22 06	22 04
5	13 16	− 2.4	57.4	15.6	328	290	30	4.9	11 06	11 10	16 52	22 27	22 21
6	14 05	− 7.1	56.5	15.4	340	289	40	5.9	12 18	12 26	17 38	22 48	22 39
7	14 53	−11.4	55.7	15.2	353	287	50	6.9	13 27	13 40	18 24	23 12	22 59
8	15 42	−15.1	55.1	15.0	5	284	60	7.9	14 35	14 51	19 11	23 40	23 23
9	16 31	−18.0	54.6	14.9	17	280	69	8.9	15 38	15 58	19 58	—	23 52
10	17 21	−20.2	54.3	14.8	29	276	77	9.9	16 37	16 59	20 46	0 13	—
11	18 11	−21.4	54.1	14.7	42	271	85	10.9	17 30	17 53	21 34	0 52	0 30
12	19 02	−21.7	54.0	14.7	54	265	91	11.9	18 15	18 37	22 23	1 39	1 16
13	19 53	−21.1	54.1	14.7	66	259	96	12.9	18 53	19 13	23 11	2 33	2 11
14	20 43	−19.4	54.3	14.8	78	250	99	13.9	19 25	19 42	23 58	3 33	3 14
15	21 33	−16.9	54.5	14.9	90	208	100	14.9	19 52	20 05	—	4 38	4 22
16	22 21	−13.7	54.8	14.9	102	89	99	15.9	20 15	20 24	0 44	5 45	5 33
17	23 09	− 9.8	55.2	15.0	115	78	97	16.9	20 36	20 41	1 29	6 54	6 46
18	23 56	− 5.4	55.7	15.2	127	74	92	17.9	20 55	20 56	2 14	8 03	8 00
19	0 43	− 0.8	56.2	15.3	139	72	86	18.9	21 15	21 12	2 58	9 14	9 15
20	1 31	+ 4.0	56.7	15.5	151	72	78	19.9	21 36	21 29	3 44	10 27	10 32
21	2 21	+ 8.6	57.3	15.6	163	73	69	20.9	22 00	21 49	4 31	11 41	11 50
22	3 12	+13.0	58.0	15.8	176	75	59	21.9	22 29	22 13	5 21	12 57	13 11
23	4 07	+16.8	58.6	16.0	188	79	48	22.9	23 05	22 46	6 14	14 13	14 31
24	5 04	+19.7	59.3	16.1	200	84	37	23.9	23 51	23 29	7 11	15 26	15 48
25	6 05	+21.4	59.8	16.3	212	89	26	24.9	—	—	8 11	16 33	16 56
26	7 08	+21.8	60.3	16.4	225	96	16	25.9	0 50	0 27	9 12	17 30	17 51
27	8 11	+20.6	60.5	16.5	237	103	8	26.9	2 01	1 40	10 14	18 15	18 33
28	9 13	+18.1	60.6	16.5	249	112	3	27.9	3 21	3 03	11 14	18 51	19 05
29	10 13	+14.3	60.3	16.4	261	138	0	28.9	4 43	4 31	12 10	19 20	19 29
30	11 10	+ 9.7	59.8	16.3	274	266	1	0.6	6 06	5 59	13 04	19 45	19 50
31	12 04	+ 4.7	59.1	16.1	286	282	4	1.6	7 27	7 24	13 54	20 07	20 07

MERCURY

Day	RA h m	Dec. °	Diam. ″	Phase %	Transit h m	5° high 52° h m	5° high 56° h m
1	7 27	+21.0	7	54	10 48	3 28	3 13
3	7 39	+21.0	6	61	10 53	3 32	3 17
5	7 53	+20.9	6	69	10 59	3 39	3 24
7	8 07	+20.6	6	76	11 06	3 48	3 33
9	8 23	+20.2	6	82	11 14	3 58	3 44
11	8 39	+19.5	6	87	11 22	4 10	3 56
13	8 55	+18.7	5	92	11 30	4 23	4 10
15	9 12	+17.8	5	95	11 39	4 38	4 26
17	9 28	+16.7	5	98	11 47	4 52	4 42
19	9 44	+15.4	5	99	11 56	5 08	4 58
21	10 00	+14.1	5	100	12 03	18 42	18 50
23	10 15	+12.7	5	100	12 11	18 42	18 48
25	10 30	+11.2	5	99	12 17	18 41	18 46
27	10 44	+ 9.7	5	99	12 24	18 39	18 43
29	10 58	+ 8.2	5	98	12 30	18 37	18 40
31	11 12	+ 6.6	5	96	12 35	18 34	18 36

VENUS

Day	RA h m	Dec. °	Diam. ″	Phase %	Transit h m	5° high 52° h m	5° high 56° h m
1	9 43	+15.3	10	97	13 04	19 49	19 58
6	10 07	+13.2	10	96	13 08	19 42	19 49
11	10 30	+10.9	10	96	13 12	19 34	19 39
16	10 54	+ 8.6	10	95	13 15	19 25	19 28
21	11 16	+ 6.2	10	94	13 18	19 15	19 17
26	11 39	+ 3.7	11	94	13 21	19 05	19 05
31	12 01	+ 1.1	11	93	13 23	18 55	18 52

MARS

Day	RA h m	Dec. °	Diam. ″	Phase %	Transit h m	5° high 52° h m	5° high 56° h m
1	8 10	+21.2	4	100	11 29	4 09	3 54
6	8 23	+20.5	4	100	11 23	4 07	3 53
11	8 36	+19.7	4	100	11 17	4 05	3 51
16	8 50	+18.9	4	99	11 10	4 04	3 51
21	9 03	+18.0	4	99	11 03	4 02	3 50
26	9 15	+17.1	4	99	10 57	4 00	3 49
31	9 28	+16.2	4	99	10 50	3 58	3 48

SUNRISE AND SUNSET

	London		Bristol		Birmingham		Manchester		Newcastle		Glasgow		Belfast	
	0°05′	51°30′	2°35′	51°28′	1°55′	52°28′	2°15′	53°28′	1°37′	54°59′	4°14′	55°52′	5°56′	54°35′
	h m	h m	h m	h m	h m	h m	h m	h m	h m	h m	h m	h m	h m	h m
1	4 24	19 48	4 34	19 58	4 28	19 59	4 25	20 04	4 16	20 09	4 22	20 23	4 35	20 24
2	4 26	19 46	4 36	19 56	4 29	19 57	4 27	20 03	4 17	20 07	4 24	20 21	4 37	20 22
3	4 27	19 45	4 37	19 54	4 31	19 55	4 28	20 01	4 19	20 05	4 26	20 19	4 38	20 20
4	4 29	19 43	4 39	19 53	4 33	19 54	4 30	19 59	4 21	20 03	4 28	20 17	4 40	20 18
5	4 30	19 41	4 41	19 51	4 34	19 52	4 32	19 57	4 23	20 01	4 29	20 15	4 42	20 16
6	4 32	19 39	4 42	19 49	4 36	19 50	4 33	19 55	4 25	19 59	4 31	20 13	4 44	20 14
7	4 34	19 37	4 44	19 47	4 37	19 48	4 35	19 53	4 27	19 57	4 33	20 11	4 45	20 12
8	4 35	19 36	4 45	19 46	4 39	19 46	4 37	19 51	4 28	19 54	4 35	20 09	4 47	20 10
9	4 37	19 34	4 47	19 44	4 41	19 44	4 39	19 49	4 30	19 52	4 37	20 06	4 49	20 08
10	4 38	19 32	4 48	19 42	4 42	19 42	4 40	19 47	4 32	19 50	4 39	20 04	4 51	20 06
11	4 40	19 30	4 50	19 40	4 44	19 40	4 42	19 45	4 34	19 48	4 41	20 02	4 53	20 04
12	4 41	19 28	4 51	19 38	4 46	19 38	4 44	19 43	4 36	19 46	4 43	20 00	4 55	20 02
13	4 43	19 26	4 53	19 36	4 47	19 36	4 45	19 41	4 38	19 44	4 45	19 57	4 56	19 59
14	4 45	19 24	4 55	19 34	4 49	19 34	4 47	19 39	4 39	19 41	4 47	19 55	4 58	19 57
15	4 46	19 22	4 56	19 32	4 51	19 32	4 49	19 37	4 41	19 39	4 49	19 53	5 00	19 55
16	4 48	19 20	4 58	19 30	4 52	19 30	4 51	19 35	4 43	19 37	4 51	19 50	5 02	19 53
17	4 49	19 18	4 59	19 28	4 54	19 28	4 52	19 32	4 45	19 34	4 53	19 48	5 04	19 50
18	4 51	19 16	5 01	19 26	4 56	19 26	4 54	19 30	4 47	19 32	4 55	19 45	5 05	19 48
19	4 52	19 14	5 03	19 24	4 57	19 24	4 56	19 28	4 49	19 30	4 56	19 43	5 07	19 46
20	4 54	19 12	5 04	19 22	4 59	19 22	4 58	19 26	4 51	19 27	4 58	19 41	5 09	19 44
21	4 56	19 10	5 06	19 20	5 01	19 20	4 59	19 24	4 53	19 25	5 00	19 38	5 11	19 41
22	4 57	19 08	5 07	19 18	5 02	19 17	5 01	19 21	4 54	19 23	5 02	19 36	5 13	19 39
23	4 59	19 06	5 09	19 16	5 04	19 15	5 03	19 19	4 56	19 20	5 04	19 33	5 15	19 37
24	5 00	19 04	5 11	19 14	5 06	19 13	5 05	19 17	4 58	19 18	5 06	19 31	5 17	19 34
25	5 02	19 01	5 12	19 11	5 07	19 11	5 06	19 14	5 00	19 16	5 08	19 28	5 18	19 32
26	5 04	18 59	5 14	19 09	5 09	19 09	5 08	19 12	5 02	19 13	5 10	19 26	5 20	19 29
27	5 05	18 57	5 15	19 07	5 11	19 06	5 10	19 10	5 04	19 11	5 12	19 23	5 22	19 27
28	5 07	18 55	5 17	19 05	5 12	19 04	5 12	19 07	5 06	19 08	5 14	19 21	5 24	19 25
29	5 08	18 53	5 18	19 03	5 14	19 02	5 13	19 05	5 08	19 06	5 16	19 18	5 26	19 22
30	5 10	18 51	5 20	19 00	5 16	19 00	5 15	19 03	5 09	19 03	5 18	19 16	5 28	19 20
31	5 12	18 48	5 22	18 58	5 17	18 57	5 17	19 00	5 11	19 01	5 20	19 13	5 29	19 17

JUPITER

Day	RA	Dec.	Transit	5° high	
				52°	56°
	h m	° ′	h m	h m	h m
1	4 16.9	+20 27	7 36	7 36	0 06
11	4 23.3	+20 42	7 03	23 43	23 28
21	4 28.8	+20 54	6 29	23 08	22 53
31	4 33.3	+21 03	5 55	22 32	22 17

Diameters – equatorial 38″ polar 36″

SATURN

Day	RA	Dec.	Transit	5° high	
				52°	56°
	h m	° ′	h m	h m	h m
1	3 50.7	+17 59	7 10	0 09	23 53
11	3 53.4	+18 06	6 33	23 28	23 16
21	3 55.4	+18 10	5 56	22 50	22 38
31	3 56.7	+18 12	5 18	22 12	22 00

Diameters – equatorial 18″ polar 16″
Rings – major axis 41″ minor axis 17″

URANUS

Day	RA	Dec.	Transit	10° high	
				52°	56°
	h m	° ′	h m	h m	h m
1	21 27.6	−15 45	0 48	4 04	3 36
11	21 26.1	−15 52	0 07	3 22	2 54
21	21 24.5	−16 00	23 22	2 40	2 12
31	21 23.0	−16 07	22 41	1 59	1 30

Diameter 4″

NEPTUNE

Day	RA	Dec.	Transit	10° high	
				52°	56°
	h m	° ′	h m	h m	h m
1	20 29.5	−18 48	23 46	2 41	2 04
11	20 28.4	−18 52	23 05	2 00	1 23
21	20 27.3	−18 55	22 25	1 19	0 42
31	20 26.4	−18 59	21 45	0 38	0 01

Diameter 2″

September 2000

NINTH MONTH, 30 DAYS. *Septem* (seven), seventh month of Roman pre-Julian calendar

1	Friday	Pope Adrian IV d. 1159. Great Fire of London 1666	245
2	Saturday	Frederick Soddy b. 1877. Henri Rousseau d. 1910	246
3	Sunday	**11th S. after Trinity.** Ferdinand Porsche b. 1875	247
4	Monday	Albert Schweitzer d. 1965. Professor Hans Eysenck d. 1997 *week 36 day*	248
5	Tuesday	Jesse James b. 1847. Mother Teresa d. 1997	249
6	Wednesday	Henry Walford Davies b. 1869. Austin Reed b. 1873	250
7	Thursday	Elizabeth I b. 1533. Sir Leonard Hutton d. 1990	251
8	Friday	Richard I b. 1157. Peter Sellers b. 1925	252
9	Saturday	Battle of Flodden 1513. Captain William Bligh b. 1754	253
10	Sunday	**12th S. after Trinity.** Arnold Palmer b. 1929	254
11	Monday	David Ricardo d. 1823. D. H. Lawrence b. 1885 *week 37 day*	255
12	Tuesday	Cleopatra's Needle erected 1878. Steve Biko d. 1977	256
13	Wednesday	British capture Quebec 1759. Roald Dahl b. 1916	257
14	Thursday	**Holy Cross Day.** Princess Grace of Monaco d. 1982	258
15	Friday	Battle of Britain Day. Prince Henry of Wales b. 1984	259
16	Saturday	Fire of Moscow 1812. Sir Gordon Newton b. 1907	260
17	Sunday	**13th S. after Trinity.** Laura Ashley d. 1985	261
18	Monday	Dr Samuel Johnson b. 1709. Jimi Hendrix d. 1970 *week 38 day*	262
19	Tuesday	Meyer Amschel Rothschild d. 1812. Sir William Golding b. 1911	263
20	Wednesday	Mungo Park b. 1771. Jacob Grimm d. 1863	264
21	Thursday	**St Matthew.** John McAdam b. 1756	265
22	Friday	Anne of Cleves b. 1515. Coronation of George III 1761	266
23	Saturday	Augustus b. 63 BC. Aldo Moro assassinated 1916	267
24	Sunday	**14th S. after Trinity.** Horace Walpole b. 1717	268
25	Monday	Transatlantic telephone service began 1956 *week 39 day*	269
26	Tuesday	Ivan Pavlov b. 1849. Sir Barnes Wallis b. 1887	270
27	Wednesday	Sir Martin Ryle b. 1918. *Queen Elizabeth I* launched 1938	271
28	Thursday	Edwin Hubble d. 1953. Miles Davis d. 1991	272
29	Friday	**St Michael and All Angels.** Lord Nelson b. 1758	273
30	Saturday	JEWISH NEW YEAR. James Dean d. 1955	274

ASTRONOMICAL PHENOMENA

d h
12 12 Saturn at stationary point
19 02 Saturn in conjunction with Moon. Saturn 2° N.
19 20 Jupiter in conjunction with Moon. Jupiter 2° N.
22 17 Sun's longitude 180° ♎
25 18 Mars in conjunction with Moon. Mars 2° S.
29 13 Jupiter at stationary point
29 18 Mercury in conjunction with Moon. Mercury 7° S.
30 04 Venus in conjunction with Moon. Venus 5° S.

MINIMA OF ALGOL

d	h	d	h	d	h
1	13.1	13	00.3	24	11.5
4	09.9	15	21.1	27	08.4
7	06.7	18	17.9	30	05.2
10	03.5	21	14.7		

CONSTELLATIONS

The following constellations are near the meridian at

	d	h		d	h
August	1	24	September	15	21
August	16	23	October	1	20
September	1	22	October	16	19

Draco, Cepheus, Lyra, Cygnus, Vulpecula, Sagitta, Delphinus, Equuleus, Aquila, Aquarius and Capricornus

THE MOON

Phases, Apsides and Node	d	h	m
☽ First Quarter	5	16	27
○ Full Moon	13	19	37
☾ Last Quarter	21	01	28
● New Moon	27	19	53
Apogee (404,761 km)	8	12	35
Perigee (366,961 km)	24	08	21

Mean longitude of ascending node on September 1, 112°

THE SUN   s.d. 15′.9

Day	Right Ascension	Dec.	Equation of time	Rise 52°	Rise 56°	Transit	Set 52°	Set 56°	Sidereal time	Transit of First Point of Aries
	h m s	° ′	m s	h m	h m	h m	h m	h m	h m s	h m s
1	10 41 52	+ 8 15	− 0 02	5 12	5 05	12 00	18 47	18 54	22 41 51	1 17 56
2	10 45 30	+ 7 53	+ 0 17	5 14	5 07	12 00	18 44	18 51	22 45 47	1 14 01
3	10 49 07	+ 7 31	+ 0 37	5 15	5 09	11 59	18 42	18 49	22 49 44	1 10 05
4	10 52 44	+ 7 09	+ 0 57	5 17	5 10	11 59	18 40	18 46	22 53 40	1 06 09
5	10 56 21	+ 6 47	+ 1 16	5 19	5 12	11 59	18 37	18 43	22 57 37	1 02 13
6	10 59 57	+ 6 24	+ 1 37	5 20	5 14	11 58	18 35	18 41	23 01 34	0 58 17
7	11 03 33	+ 6 02	+ 1 57	5 22	5 16	11 58	18 33	18 38	23 05 30	0 54 21
8	11 07 09	+ 5 40	+ 2 18	5 23	5 18	11 58	18 31	18 36	23 09 27	0 50 25
9	11 10 45	+ 5 17	+ 2 38	5 25	5 20	11 57	18 28	18 33	23 13 23	0 46 29
10	11 14 21	+ 4 54	+ 2 59	5 27	5 22	11 57	18 26	18 30	23 17 20	0 42 33
11	11 17 56	+ 4 31	+ 3 20	5 28	5 24	11 56	18 24	18 28	23 21 16	0 38 37
12	11 21 31	+ 4 09	+ 3 42	5 30	5 26	11 56	18 21	18 25	23 25 13	0 34 41
13	11 25 07	+ 3 46	+ 4 03	5 32	5 28	11 56	18 19	18 22	23 29 09	0 30 46
14	11 28 42	+ 3 23	+ 4 24	5 33	5 30	11 55	18 17	18 20	23 33 06	0 26 50
15	11 32 17	+ 3 00	+ 4 46	5 35	5 32	11 55	18 14	18 17	23 37 03	0 22 54
16	11 35 52	+ 2 37	+ 5 07	5 36	5 34	11 55	18 12	18 14	23 40 59	0 18 58
17	11 39 27	+ 2 13	+ 5 29	5 38	5 36	11 54	18 10	18 12	23 44 56	0 15 02
18	11 43 02	+ 1 50	+ 5 50	5 40	5 38	11 54	18 07	18 09	23 48 52	0 11 06
19	11 46 37	+ 1 27	+ 6 12	5 41	5 40	11 54	18 05	18 06	23 52 49	0 07 10
20	11 50 12	+ 1 04	+ 6 33	5 43	5 42	11 53	18 03	18 04	23 56 45	{ 0 03 14 / 23 59 18
21	11 53 48	+ 0 40	+ 6 54	5 45	5 44	11 53	18 00	18 01	0 00 42	23 55 22
22	11 57 23	+ 0 17	+ 7 15	5 46	5 46	11 53	17 58	17 58	0 04 38	23 51 26
23	12 00 59	− 0 06	+ 7 36	5 48	5 48	11 52	17 56	17 56	0 08 35	23 47 31
24	12 04 34	− 0 30	+ 7 57	5 50	5 49	11 52	17 53	17 53	0 12 31	23 43 35
25	12 08 10	− 0 53	+ 8 18	5 51	5 51	11 52	17 51	17 50	0 16 28	23 39 39
26	12 11 46	− 1 16	+ 8 39	5 53	5 53	11 51	17 49	17 48	0 20 25	23 35 43
27	12 15 22	− 1 40	+ 8 59	5 55	5 55	11 51	17 46	17 45	0 24 21	23 31 47
28	12 18 59	− 2 03	+ 9 19	5 56	5 57	11 51	17 44	17 43	0 28 18	23 27 51
29	12 22 35	− 2 27	+ 9 39	5 58	5 59	11 50	17 42	17 40	0 32 14	23 23 55
30	12 26 12	− 2 50	+ 9 59	6 00	6 01	11 50	17 39	17 37	0 36 11	23 19 59

DURATION OF TWILIGHT (in minutes)

Latitude	52°	56°	52°	56°	52°	56°	52°	56°
	1 September		11 September		21 September		30 September	
Civil	35	39	34	38	34	37	34	37
Nautical	79	89	76	84	74	82	73	80
Astronomical	127	146	120	135	115	129	113	126

THE NIGHT SKY

Mercury is unsuitably placed for observation throughout the month.

Venus, magnitude −3.9, continues to be visible as a difficult evening object for a short time after sunset, very low above the western horizon. Although it is farther from the Sun at the end of the month compared with the beginning, its rapid southward motion in declination compensates for this increase in elongation so that the time available for observation remains almost exactly the same throughout September.

Mars, magnitude +1.8, is a difficult morning object in the constellation of Leo, passing 1° north of Regulus on the 16th. The planet may be detected after about 0400 hours, low above the eastern horizon.

Jupiter, magnitude −2.5, continues to be visible as a splendid object in the southern half of the sky, from the late evening and through the night. Jupiter commences its retrograde motion after reaching its first stationary point on the 29th, in the constellation of Taurus. The gibbous Moon is near Jupiter and Saturn on the 19th.

Saturn, magnitude 0.0, is still a morning object, some 10° west of Jupiter. Saturn commences its retrograde motion after reaching its first stationary point on the 12th, in the constellation of Taurus.

Zodiacal Light. The morning cone may be seen reaching up from the eastern horizon along the ecliptic, before the beginning of morning twilight, from the beginning of the month to the 11th and again after the 25th.

THE MOON

Day	RA	Dec.	Hor. par.	Semi- diam.	Sun's co- long.	PA of Bright Limb	Phase	Age	Rise 52°	Rise 56°	Transit	Set 52°	Set 56°
	h m	°	'	'	°	°	%	d	h m	h m	h m	h m	h m
1	12 56	− 0.5	58.3	15.9	298	285	9	2.6	8 44	8 46	14 43	20 28	20 24
2	13 47	− 5.5	57.4	15.7	310	286	16	3.6	9 59	10 06	15 30	20 50	20 42
3	14 36	−10.1	56.6	15.4	322	285	24	4.6	11 12	11 23	16 17	21 13	21 01
4	15 26	−14.1	55.8	15.2	335	283	34	5.6	12 22	12 37	17 04	21 40	21 24
5	16 15	−17.3	55.2	15.0	347	280	43	6.6	13 28	13 47	17 52	22 11	21 51
6	17 06	−19.8	54.7	14.9	359	276	53	7.6	14 29	14 51	18 40	22 48	22 26
7	17 56	−21.3	54.4	14.8	11	271	63	8.6	15 25	15 48	19 29	23 32	23 09
8	18 47	−21.9	54.2	14.8	24	266	71	9.6	16 13	16 36	20 17	—	—
9	19 38	−21.5	54.2	14.8	36	261	80	10.6	16 53	17 14	21 06	0 24	0 01
10	20 29	−20.1	54.3	14.8	48	255	87	11.6	17 27	17 45	21 53	1 22	1 02
11	21 19	−17.8	54.6	14.9	60	249	92	12.6	17 55	18 09	22 40	2 26	2 09
12	22 08	−14.7	54.9	15.0	72	242	97	13.6	18 19	18 30	23 26	3 33	3 19
13	22 56	−10.9	55.4	15.1	84	226	99	14.6	18 41	18 47	—	4 42	4 33
14	23 44	− 6.6	55.8	15.2	97	131	100	15.6	19 01	19 03	0 11	5 52	5 47
15	0 31	− 1.9	56.3	15.3	109	86	98	16.6	19 20	19 19	0 56	7 04	7 03
16	1 20	+ 2.9	56.8	15.5	121	78	95	17.6	19 41	19 35	1 42	8 17	8 21
17	2 09	+ 7.7	57.3	15.6	133	77	89	18.6	20 04	19 54	2 29	9 31	9 40
18	3 00	+12.2	57.8	15.7	145	77	82	19.6	20 31	20 17	3 18	10 47	11 00
19	3 54	+16.2	58.2	15.9	157	80	72	20.6	21 04	20 45	4 10	12 03	12 21
20	4 50	+19.3	58.7	16.0	170	84	62	21.6	21 46	21 24	5 05	13 17	13 38
21	5 49	+21.3	59.0	16.1	182	89	51	22.6	22 39	22 16	6 03	14 25	14 48
22	6 50	+22.0	59.4	16.2	194	95	39	23.6	23 44	23 21	7 02	15 24	15 46
23	7 51	+21.3	59.6	16.2	206	101	29	24.6	—	—	8 02	16 11	16 31
24	8 52	+19.2	59.7	16.3	218	107	19	25.6	0 58	0 39	9 01	16 49	17 05
25	9 51	+15.9	59.7	16.3	231	113	11	26.6	2 18	2 03	9 57	17 20	17 31
26	10 48	+11.6	59.5	16.2	243	120	5	27.6	3 39	3 30	10 51	17 46	17 52
27	11 42	+ 6.7	59.1	16.1	255	135	1	28.6	5 00	4 55	11 42	18 08	18 11
28	12 35	+ 1.5	58.6	16.0	267	228	0	0.2	6 19	6 19	12 31	18 30	18 27
29	13 26	− 3.6	57.9	15.8	280	274	2	1.2	7 36	7 41	13 20	18 51	18 44
30	14 16	− 8.5	57.2	15.6	292	280	6	2.2	8 51	9 00	14 08	19 13	19 03

MERCURY

Day	RA	Dec.	Diam.	Phase	Transit	5° high 52°	5° high 56°
	h m	°	"	%	h m	h m	h m
1	11 18	+ 5.9	5	96	12 38	18 33	18 34
3	11 31	+ 4.3	5	94	12 42	18 29	18 29
5	11 43	+ 2.7	5	93	12 47	18 26	18 24
7	11 55	+ 1.2	5	92	12 51	18 22	18 19
9	12 07	− 0.3	5	90	12 55	18 18	18 14
11	12 19	− 1.8	5	89	12 58	18 14	18 08
13	12 30	− 3.3	5	87	13 01	18 09	18 02
15	12 41	− 4.7	5	86	13 04	18 04	17 56
17	12 51	− 6.1	5	84	13 07	17 59	17 50
19	13 02	− 7.5	5	82	13 10	17 54	17 44
21	13 12	− 8.8	6	80	13 12	17 49	17 38
23	13 22	−10.1	6	78	13 14	17 44	17 31
25	13 32	−11.3	6	76	13 16	17 39	17 24
27	13 41	−12.5	6	74	13 17	17 33	17 18
29	13 51	−13.6	6	72	13 19	17 28	17 11
31	14 00	−14.7	6	69	13 20	17 22	17 04

VENUS

Day	RA	Dec.	Diam.	Phase	Transit	5° high 52°	5° high 56°
	h m	°	"	%	h m	h m	h m
1	12 06	+ 0.6	11	93	13 24	18 53	18 49
6	12 28	− 2.0	11	92	13 27	18 42	18 36
11	12 50	− 4.5	11	91	13 29	18 31	18 23
16	13 13	− 7.1	11	90	13 32	18 20	18 10
21	13 35	− 9.6	11	89	13 35	18 09	17 56
26	13 58	−11.9	12	88	13 38	17 58	17 43
31	14 21	−14.2	12	87	13 42	17 48	17 30

MARS

Day	RA	Dec.	Diam.	Phase	Transit	5° high 52°	5° high 56°
1	9 31	+16.0	4	99	10 48	3 58	3 48
6	9 43	+15.0	4	99	10 41	3 56	3 47
11	9 55	+13.9	4	99	10 34	3 55	3 46
16	10 08	+12.8	4	98	10 26	3 53	3 46
21	10 20	+11.7	4	98	10 18	3 51	3 45
26	10 32	+10.6	4	98	10 11	3 49	3 44
31	10 44	+ 9.4	4	98	10 03	3 48	3 43

SUNRISE AND SUNSET

	London		Bristol		Birmingham		Manchester		Newcastle		Glasgow		Belfast	
	0°05′	51°30′	2°35′	51°28′	1°55′	52°28′	2°15′	53°28′	1°37′	54°59′	4°14′	55°52′	5°56′	54°35′
	h m	h m	h m	h m	h m	h m	h m	h m	h m	h m	h m	h m	h m	h m
1	5 13	18 46	5 23	18 56	5 19	18 55	5 19	18 58	5 13	18 58	5 22	19 10	5 31	19 15
2	5 15	18 44	5 25	18 54	5 21	18 53	5 20	18 56	5 15	18 56	5 24	19 08	5 33	19 12
3	5 16	18 42	5 26	18 52	5 22	18 50	5 22	18 53	5 17	18 53	5 26	19 05	5 35	19 10
4	5 18	18 39	5 28	18 49	5 24	18 48	5 24	18 51	5 19	18 51	5 28	19 03	5 37	19 07
5	5 20	18 37	5 30	18 47	5 26	18 46	5 25	18 48	5 21	18 48	5 30	19 00	5 38	19 05
6	5 21	18 35	5 31	18 45	5 27	18 43	5 27	18 46	5 22	18 46	5 32	18 57	5 40	19 02
7	5 23	18 33	5 33	18 43	5 29	18 41	5 29	18 44	5 24	18 43	5 34	18 55	5 42	19 00
8	5 24	18 30	5 34	18 40	5 31	18 39	5 31	18 41	5 26	18 41	5 35	18 52	5 44	18 57
9	5 26	18 28	5 36	18 38	5 32	18 36	5 32	18 39	5 28	18 38	5 37	18 50	5 46	18 55
10	5 28	18 26	5 38	18 36	5 34	18 34	5 34	18 36	5 30	18 36	5 39	18 47	5 48	18 52
11	5 29	18 23	5 39	18 33	5 36	18 32	5 36	18 34	5 32	18 33	5 41	18 44	5 49	18 50
12	5 31	18 21	5 41	18 31	5 37	18 29	5 38	18 32	5 34	18 30	5 43	18 42	5 51	18 47
13	5 32	18 19	5 42	18 29	5 39	18 27	5 39	18 29	5 35	18 28	5 45	18 39	5 53	18 45
14	5 34	18 17	5 44	18 27	5 41	18 25	5 41	18 27	5 37	18 25	5 47	18 36	5 55	18 42
15	5 36	18 14	5 46	18 24	5 42	18 22	5 43	18 24	5 39	18 23	5 49	18 34	5 57	18 40
16	5 37	18 12	5 47	18 22	5 44	18 20	5 45	18 22	5 41	18 20	5 51	18 31	5 59	18 37
17	5 39	18 10	5 49	18 20	5 46	18 17	5 46	18 19	5 43	18 18	5 53	18 28	6 00	18 35
18	5 40	18 07	5 50	18 17	5 47	18 15	5 48	18 17	5 45	18 15	5 55	18 26	6 02	18 32
19	5 42	18 05	5 52	18 15	5 49	18 13	5 50	18 14	5 47	18 12	5 57	18 23	6 04	18 29
20	5 43	18 03	5 53	18 13	5 51	18 10	5 52	18 12	5 48	18 10	5 59	18 21	6 06	18 27
21	5 45	18 00	5 55	18 10	5 52	18 08	5 53	18 09	5 50	18 07	6 01	18 18	6 08	18 24
22	5 47	17 58	5 57	18 08	5 54	18 06	5 55	18 07	5 52	18 05	6 03	18 15	6 10	18 22
23	5 48	17 56	5 58	18 06	5 56	18 03	5 57	18 05	5 54	18 02	6 05	18 13	6 11	18 19
24	5 50	17 54	6 00	18 04	5 57	18 01	5 59	18 02	5 56	18 00	6 06	18 10	6 13	18 17
25	5 51	17 51	6 02	18 01	5 59	17 58	6 00	18 00	5 58	17 57	6 08	18 07	6 15	18 14
26	5 53	17 49	6 03	17 59	6 01	17 56	6 02	17 57	6 00	17 54	6 10	18 05	6 17	18 12
27	5 55	17 47	6 05	17 57	6 02	17 54	6 04	17 55	6 02	17 52	6 12	18 02	6 19	18 09
28	5 56	17 44	6 06	17 54	6 04	17 51	6 06	17 52	6 04	17 49	6 14	17 59	6 21	18 07
29	5 58	17 42	6 08	17 52	6 06	17 49	6 07	17 50	6 05	17 47	6 16	17 57	6 23	18 04
30	6 00	17 40	6 10	17 50	6 07	17 47	6 09	17 48	6 07	17 44	6 18	17 54	6 24	18 02

JUPITER

Day	RA	Dec.	Transit	5° high	
				52°	56°
	h m	° ′	h m	h m	h m
1	4 33.7	+21 03	5 51	22 29	22 13
11	4 36.8	+21 09	5 15	21 52	21 36
21	4 38.7	+21 12	4 37	21 14	20 58
31	4 39.3	+21 12	3 58	20 35	20 19

Diameters – equatorial 42″ polar 39″

SATURN

Day	RA	Dec.	Transit	5° high	
				52°	56°
	h m	° ′	h m	h m	h m
1	3 56.8	+18 12	5 14	22 08	21 56
11	3 57.3	+18 11	4 35	21 29	21 17
21	3 57.0	+18 09	3 56	20 50	20 38
31	3 56.1	+18 04	3 15	20 10	19 58

Diameters – equatorial 19″ polar 17″
Rings – major axis 43″ minor axis 18″

URANUS

Day	RA	Dec.	Transit	10° high	
				52°	56°
	h m	° ′	h m	h m	h m
1	21 22.9	−16 07	22 37	1 54	1 26
11	21 21.5	−16 14	21 57	1 13	0 44
21	21 20.3	−16 19	21 16	0 32	0 03
31	21 19.4	−16 23	20 36	23 47	23 18

Diameter 4″

NEPTUNE

Day	RA	Dec.	Transit	10° high	
				52°	56°
	h m	° ′	h m	h m	h m
1	20 26.3	−18 59	21 41	0 34	23 52
11	20 25.5	−19 02	21 01	23 49	23 12
21	20 24.9	−19 04	20 21	23 09	22 31
31	20 24.5	−19 06	19 41	22 29	21 51

Diameter 2″

 # October 2000

TENTH MONTH, 31 DAYS. *Octo* (eighth), eighth month of Roman pre-Julian calendar

1	*Sunday*	**15th S. after Trinity.** Stanley Holloway b. 1890	275
2	*Monday*	*Michaelmas Law Sittings begin.* Lord Runcie b. 1921	*week* 40 *day* 276
3	*Tuesday*	William Morris d. 1896. A. L. Rowse d. 1997	277
4	*Wednesday*	Ken Wood b. 1916. Janis Joplin d. 1970	278
5	*Thursday*	Jacques Offenbach d. 1880. Oxfam founded 1942	279
6	*Friday*	Lord Tennyson d. 1892. Anwar Sadat d. 1981	280
7	*Saturday*	Battle of Lepanto 1571. Archbishop Laud b. 1573	281
8	*Sunday*	**16th S. after Trinity.** Clement Attlee d. 1967	282
9	*Monday*	YOM KIPPUR. Che Guevara d. 1967	*week* 41 *day* 283
10	*Tuesday*	Verdi b. 1813. Harold Pinter b. 1930	284
11	*Wednesday*	François Mauriac b. 1885. Anton Bruckner d. 1896	285
12	*Thursday*	Edward VI b. 1537. John Denver d. 1997	286
13	*Friday*	Antonio Canova d. 1822. Paul Simon b. 1941	287
14	*Saturday*	FEAST OF TABERNACLES begins. William Penn b. 1644	288
15	*Sunday*	**17th S. after Trinity.** Sarah, Duchess of York b. 1959	289
16	*Monday*	Houses of Parliament destroyed by fire 1834	*week* 42 *day* 290
17	*Tuesday*	John Wilkes b. 1727. Battle of Saratoga 1777	291
18	*Wednesday*	**St Luke.** Charles Babbage d. 1871	292
19	*Thursday*	Ernest Rutherford d. 1937. Jacqueline du Pré d. 1987	293
20	*Friday*	Sir Christopher Wren b. 1632. Sir Richard Burton d. 1890	294
21	*Saturday*	Battle of Trafalgar 1805. Alfred Nobel b. 1833	295
22	*Sunday*	**18th S. after Trinity.** Liszt b. 1811	296
23	*Monday*	First Parliament of Great Britain 1707. John Dunlop d. 1921	*week* 43 *day* 297
24	*Tuesday*	Jane Seymour d. 1537. Tchaikovsky d. 1893	298
25	*Wednesday*	Picasso b. 1881. Vincent Price d. 1993	299
26	*Thursday*	Domenico Scarlatti b. 1685. Igor Sikorsky d. 1972	300
27	*Friday*	Sir John Lennard-Jones b. 1894. Oliver Tambo b. 1917	301
28	*Saturday*	**SS Simon and Jude.** Statue of Liberty unveiled 1886	302
29	*Sunday*	**Last S. after Trinity.** Sir Walter Raleigh d. 1618	303
30	*Monday*	George II b. 1683. Edmund Cartwright d. 1823	*week* 44 *day* 304
31	*Tuesday*	Jan Vermeer b. 1632. Indira Gandhi assassinated 1984	305

ASTRONOMICAL PHENOMENA

d h
6 10 Mercury at greatest elongation E. 26°
15 14 Neptune at stationary point
16 06 Saturn in conjunction with Moon. Saturn 2° N.
17 01 Jupiter in conjunction with Moon. Jupiter 2° N.
18 14 Mercury at stationary point
23 03 Sun's longitude 210° ♏.
24 08 Mars in conjunction with Moon. Mars 3° S.
26 15 Uranus at stationary point
27 18 Mercury in conjunction with Moon. Mercury 6° S.
30 02 Mercury in inferior conjunction
30 10 Venus in conjunction with Moon. Venus 4° S.

MINIMA OF ALGOL

d	h	d	h	d	h
3	02.0	14	13.2	26	00.5
5	22.8	17	10.0	28	21.3
8	19.6	20	06.8	31	18.1
11	16.4	23	03.7		

CONSTELLATIONS

The following constellations are near the meridian at

	d	h		d	h
September	1	24	October	16	21
September	15	23	November	1	20
October	1	22	November	15	19

Ursa Major (below the Pole), Cepheus, Cassiopeia, Cygnus, Lacerta, Andromeda, Pegasus, Capricornus, Aquarius and Piscis Austrinus

THE MOON

Phases, Apsides and Node	d	h	m
☽ First Quarter	5	10	59
○ Full Moon	13	08	53
☾ Last Quarter	20	07	59
● New Moon	27	07	58
Apogee (404,170 km)	6	07	02
Perigee (370,115 km)	19	21	59

Mean longitude of ascending node on October 1, 111°

THE SUN   s.d. 16′.1

Day	Right Ascension	Dec. −	Equation of time	Rise 52°	Rise 56°	Transit	Set 52°	Set 56°	Sidereal time	Transit of First Point of Aries
	h m s	° ′	m s	h m	h m	h m	h m	h m	h m s	h m s
1	12 29 49	3 13	+10 18	6 01	6 03	11 50	17 37	17 35	0 40 07	23 16 03
2	12 33 27	3 36	+10 37	6 03	6 05	11 49	17 35	17 32	0 44 04	23 12 07
3	12 37 04	4 00	+10 56	6 05	6 07	11 49	17 32	17 29	0 48 00	23 08 11
4	12 40 42	4 23	+11 15	6 06	6 09	11 49	17 30	17 27	0 51 57	23 04 16
5	12 44 21	4 46	+11 33	6 08	6 11	11 48	17 28	17 24	0 55 54	23 00 20
6	12 47 59	5 09	+11 51	6 10	6 13	11 48	17 25	17 22	0 59 50	22 56 24
7	12 51 38	5 32	+12 08	6 11	6 15	11 48	17 23	17 19	1 03 47	22 52 28
8	12 55 18	5 55	+12 25	6 13	6 17	11 47	17 21	17 16	1 07 43	22 48 32
9	12 58 58	6 18	+12 42	6 15	6 19	11 47	17 19	17 14	1 11 40	22 44 36
10	13 02 38	6 40	+12 58	6 16	6 21	11 47	17 16	17 11	1 15 36	22 40 40
11	13 06 19	7 03	+13 14	6 18	6 23	11 47	17 14	17 09	1 19 33	22 36 44
12	13 10 00	7 26	+13 29	6 20	6 26	11 46	17 12	17 06	1 23 29	22 32 48
13	13 13 42	7 48	+13 44	6 22	6 28	11 46	17 10	17 04	1 27 26	22 28 52
14	13 17 24	8 10	+13 58	6 23	6 30	11 46	17 08	17 01	1 31 23	22 24 57
15	13 21 07	8 33	+14 12	6 25	6 32	11 46	17 05	16 59	1 35 19	22 21 01
16	13 24 50	8 55	+14 25	6 27	6 34	11 45	17 03	16 56	1 39 16	22 17 05
17	13 28 34	9 17	+14 38	6 29	6 36	11 45	17 01	16 54	1 43 12	22 13 09
18	13 32 19	9 39	+14 50	6 30	6 38	11 45	16 59	16 51	1 47 09	22 09 13
19	13 36 04	10 00	+15 01	6 32	6 40	11 45	16 57	16 49	1 51 05	22 05 17
20	13 39 50	10 22	+15 12	6 34	6 42	11 45	16 55	16 46	1 55 02	22 01 21
21	13 43 37	10 43	+15 22	6 36	6 44	11 45	16 53	16 44	1 58 58	21 57 25
22	13 47 24	11 05	+15 31	6 37	6 46	11 44	16 51	16 42	2 02 55	21 53 29
23	13 51 12	11 26	+15 40	6 39	6 48	11 44	16 49	16 39	2 06 52	21 49 33
24	13 55 00	11 47	+15 48	6 41	6 50	11 44	16 47	16 37	2 10 48	21 45 37
25	13 58 50	12 08	+15 55	6 43	6 53	11 44	16 45	16 35	2 14 45	21 41 42
26	14 02 40	12 28	+16 01	6 44	6 55	11 44	16 43	16 32	2 18 41	21 37 46
27	14 06 31	12 48	+16 07	6 46	6 57	11 44	16 41	16 30	2 22 38	21 33 50
28	14 10 22	13 09	+16 12	6 48	6 59	11 44	16 39	16 28	2 26 34	21 29 54
29	14 14 15	13 29	+16 16	6 50	7 01	11 44	16 37	16 25	2 30 31	21 25 58
30	14 18 08	13 48	+16 20	6 52	7 03	11 44	16 35	16 23	2 34 27	21 22 02
31	14 22 01	14 08	+16 23	6 53	7 05	11 44	16 33	16 21	2 38 24	21 18 06

DURATION OF TWILIGHT (in minutes)

Latitude	52°	56°	52°	56°	52°	56°	52°	56°
	1 October		11 October		21 October		31 October	
Civil	34	37	34	37	34	38	36	40
Nautical	73	80	73	80	74	81	75	83
Astronomical	113	125	112	124	113	124	114	126

THE NIGHT SKY

Mercury is unsuitably placed for observation throughout October, inferior conjunction occurring on the 30th.

Venus is a brilliant object in the early evenings, magnitude −4.0, though still very low in the south-western sky. By the end of the month it is visible for about half-an-hour after sunset, for observers in southern England.

Mars, magnitude +1.8, continues to be visible in the pre-dawn sky, low above the eastern horizon. On the morning of the 24th the old crescent Moon, only three days before New, passes 4° north of Mars.

Jupiter, magnitude −2.7, is in Taurus, about 5° north of Aldebaran. It is becoming visible for the greater part of the night, and by the end of the month is visible low in the east, shortly after 1800 hours. The four Galilean satellites are readily observable with a small telescope, or a good pair of binoculars provided that they are held rigidly. On the morning of the 17th the gibbous Moon passes 3° south of the planet.

Saturn is now visible for the greater part of the night as it approaches opposition next month, magnitude −0.2. The rings of Saturn present a beautiful spectacle to the observer with a small telescope. The Earth passed through the ring plane twice in 1995 and since then the rings have been slowly opening; the diameter of the minor axis is now 19 arcseconds, marginally greater than the polar diameter of the planet itself. The rings will not be at their maximum opening for a couple of years. The gibbous Moon passes 3° below the planet on the morning of the 16th.

THE MOON

Day	RA h m	Dec. °	Hor. par. '	Semi-diam. '	Sun's co-long. °	PA of Bright Limb °	Phase %	Age d	Rise 52° h m	Rise 56° h m	Transit h m	Set 52° h m	Set 56° h m
1	15 07	−12.8	56.5	15.4	304	280	12	3.2	10 04	10 17	14 55	19 38	19 24
2	15 57	−16.5	55.8	15.2	316	279	19	4.2	11 13	11 31	15 44	20 08	19 49
3	16 48	−19.3	55.2	15.0	328	275	27	5.2	12 18	12 39	16 33	20 43	20 21
4	17 39	−21.1	54.7	14.9	341	271	36	6.2	13 17	13 40	17 22	21 24	21 01
5	18 31	−22.0	54.4	14.8	353	267	46	7.2	14 08	14 32	18 10	22 13	21 50
6	19 22	−21.9	54.3	14.8	5	262	55	8.2	14 52	15 14	18 59	23 09	22 47
7	20 12	−20.8	54.3	14.8	17	257	64	9.2	15 28	15 47	19 47	—	23 52
8	21 02	−18.8	54.5	14.8	29	253	73	10.2	15 58	16 14	20 33	0 11	—
9	21 52	−16.0	54.8	14.9	42	248	81	11.2	16 23	16 35	21 19	1 17	1 02
10	22 40	−12.4	55.3	15.1	54	244	88	12.2	16 45	16 53	22 05	2 25	2 14
11	23 28	− 8.1	55.9	15.2	66	239	94	13.2	17 05	17 09	22 50	3 35	3 29
12	0 16	− 3.5	56.5	15.4	78	231	98	14.2	17 25	17 25	23 36	4 47	4 45
13	1 04	+ 1.5	57.1	15.6	90	200	100	15.2	17 45	17 41	—	6 01	6 04
14	1 54	+ 6.4	57.7	15.7	102	101	99	16.2	18 07	17 59	0 24	7 17	7 24
15	2 46	+11.2	58.2	15.8	115	85	97	17.2	18 33	18 20	1 13	8 35	8 46
16	3 40	+15.4	58.6	16.0	127	83	92	18.2	19 04	18 46	2 05	9 53	10 09
17	4 37	+18.8	58.9	16.0	139	85	85	19.2	19 43	19 22	3 00	11 09	11 30
18	5 36	+21.2	59.1	16.1	151	89	75	20.2	20 33	20 09	3 58	12 20	12 44
19	6 36	+22.2	59.2	16.1	163	94	65	21.2	21 34	21 11	4 57	13 22	13 45
20	7 38	+21.8	59.2	16.1	175	99	54	22.2	22 45	22 24	5 57	14 12	14 33
21	8 38	+20.1	59.2	16.1	188	105	43	23.2	—	23 45	6 54	14 52	15 09
22	9 36	+17.1	59.1	16.1	200	110	32	24.2	0 01	—	7 50	15 24	15 37
23	10 32	+13.1	58.9	16.0	212	114	22	25.2	1 21	1 09	8 43	15 50	15 58
24	11 25	+ 8.5	58.6	16.0	224	118	13	26.2	2 40	2 33	9 34	16 12	16 16
25	12 17	+ 3.4	58.2	15.9	236	122	7	27.2	3 58	3 56	10 23	16 33	16 33
26	13 08	− 1.8	57.8	15.7	249	129	2	28.2	5 15	5 17	11 11	16 53	16 49
27	13 58	− 6.8	57.2	15.6	261	161	0	29.2	6 30	6 37	11 58	17 14	17 06
28	14 48	−11.4	56.7	15.4	273	258	1	0.7	7 44	7 56	12 46	17 38	17 25
29	15 38	−15.4	56.1	15.3	285	273	3	1.7	8 56	9 12	13 34	18 05	17 48
30	16 29	−18.6	55.5	15.1	297	274	8	2.7	10 04	10 24	14 23	18 37	18 17
31	17 21	−20.8	55.0	15.0	310	271	14	3.7	11 07	11 30	15 13	19 16	18 53

MERCURY

Day	RA h m	Dec. °	Diam. "	Phase %	Transit h m	5° high 52° h m	5° high 56° h m
1	14 00	−14.7	6	69	13 20	17 22	17 04
3	14 08	−15.7	6	66	13 20	17 17	16 57
5	14 16	−16.6	7	63	13 21	17 11	16 49
7	14 24	−17.4	7	60	13 20	17 05	16 42
9	14 31	−18.1	7	56	13 19	16 59	16 35
11	14 37	−18.7	7	51	13 17	16 53	16 28
13	14 42	−19.2	8	47	13 14	16 47	16 21
15	14 46	−19.5	8	41	13 10	16 40	16 14
17	14 49	−19.6	8	35	13 04	16 34	16 07
19	14 49	−19.6	9	29	12 56	16 27	16 01
21	14 48	−19.3	9	22	12 46	16 20	15 55
23	14 45	−18.7	9	15	12 34	16 13	15 49
25	14 39	−17.8	10	9	12 20	16 06	15 43
27	14 31	−16.6	10	4	12 05	15 58	15 38
29	14 23	−15.3	10	1	11 48	7 47	8 05
31	14 13	−13.8	10	0	11 31	7 21	7 37

VENUS

Day	RA h m	Dec. °	Diam. "	Phase %	Transit h m	5° high 52° h m	5° high 56° h m
1	14 21	−14.2	12	87	13 42	17 48	17 30
6	14 45	−16.4	12	86	13 46	17 38	17 17
11	15 09	−18.3	12	84	13 50	17 29	17 04
16	15 34	−20.1	13	83	13 55	17 21	16 53
21	15 59	−21.7	13	82	14 01	17 14	16 42
26	16 25	−23.0	13	81	14 07	17 09	16 33
31	16 51	−24.1	14	79	14 13	17 06	16 26

MARS

Day	RA h m	Dec. °	Diam. "	Phase %	Transit h m	5° high 52° h m	5° high 56° h m
1	10 44	+ 9.4	4	98	10 03	3 48	3 43
6	10 55	+ 8.3	4	98	9 55	3 46	3 42
11	11 07	+ 7.1	4	97	9 47	3 44	3 41
16	11 18	+ 5.9	4	97	9 39	3 42	3 40
21	11 30	+ 4.6	4	97	9 30	3 40	3 39
26	11 41	+ 3.4	4	96	9 22	3 38	3 38
31	11 53	+ 2.2	4	96	9 14	3 36	3 37

SUNRISE AND SUNSET

	London		Bristol		Birmingham		Manchester		Newcastle		Glasgow		Belfast	
	0°05′	51°30′	2°35′	51°28′	1°55′	52°28′	2°15′	53°28′	1°37′	54°59′	4°14′	55°52′	5°56′	54°35′
	h m	h m	h m	h m	h m	h m	h m	h m	h m	h m	h m	h m	h m	h m
1	6 01	17 38	6 11	17 48	6 09	17 44	6 11	17 45	6 09	17 42	6 20	17 52	6 26	17 59
2	6 03	17 35	6 13	17 45	6 11	17 42	6 13	17 43	6 11	17 39	6 22	17 49	6 28	17 57
3	6 05	17 33	6 15	17 43	6 13	17 40	6 15	17 40	6 13	17 37	6 24	17 46	6 30	17 54
4	6 06	17 31	6 16	17 41	6 14	17 37	6 16	17 38	6 15	17 34	6 26	17 44	6 32	17 52
5	6 08	17 28	6 18	17 38	6 16	17 35	6 18	17 36	6 17	17 32	6 28	17 41	6 34	17 49
6	6 10	17 26	6 19	17 36	6 18	17 33	6 20	17 33	6 19	17 29	6 30	17 39	6 36	17 47
7	6 11	17 24	6 21	17 34	6 19	17 30	6 22	17 31	6 21	17 27	6 32	17 36	6 38	17 44
8	6 13	17 22	6 23	17 32	6 21	17 28	6 24	17 28	6 23	17 24	6 34	17 33	6 39	17 42
9	6 15	17 20	6 24	17 30	6 23	17 26	6 25	17 26	6 25	17 22	6 36	17 31	6 41	17 39
10	6 16	17 17	6 26	17 27	6 25	17 24	6 27	17 24	6 27	17 19	6 38	17 28	6 43	17 37
11	6 18	17 15	6 28	17 25	6 26	17 21	6 29	17 21	6 29	17 17	6 40	17 26	6 45	17 35
12	6 20	17 13	6 30	17 23	6 28	17 19	6 31	17 19	6 30	17 14	6 42	17 23	6 47	17 32
13	6 21	17 11	6 31	17 21	6 30	17 17	6 33	17 17	6 32	17 12	6 44	17 21	6 49	17 30
14	6 23	17 09	6 33	17 19	6 32	17 15	6 34	17 14	6 34	17 09	6 46	17 18	6 51	17 27
15	6 25	17 07	6 35	17 17	6 33	17 12	6 36	17 12	6 36	17 07	6 48	17 16	6 53	17 25
16	6 26	17 04	6 36	17 14	6 35	17 10	6 38	17 10	6 38	17 05	6 50	17 13	6 55	17 23
17	6 28	17 02	6 38	17 12	6 37	17 08	6 40	17 08	6 40	17 02	6 53	17 11	6 57	17 20
18	6 30	17 00	6 40	17 10	6 39	17 06	6 42	17 05	6 42	17 00	6 55	17 08	6 59	17 18
19	6 31	16 58	6 41	17 08	6 41	17 04	6 44	17 03	6 44	16 58	6 57	17 06	7 01	17 16
20	6 33	16 56	6 43	17 06	6 42	17 02	6 46	17 01	6 46	16 55	6 59	17 04	7 03	17 13
21	6 35	16 54	6 45	17 04	6 44	16 59	6 48	16 59	6 48	16 53	7 01	17 01	7 05	17 11
22	6 37	16 52	6 47	17 02	6 46	16 57	6 49	16 57	6 50	16 51	7 03	16 59	7 07	17 09
23	6 38	16 50	6 48	17 00	6 48	16 55	6 51	16 54	6 52	16 48	7 05	16 57	7 09	17 06
24	6 40	16 48	6 50	16 58	6 50	16 53	6 53	16 52	6 54	16 46	7 07	16 54	7 11	17 04
25	6 42	16 46	6 52	16 56	6 51	16 51	6 55	16 50	6 56	16 44	7 09	16 52	7 13	17 02
26	6 44	16 44	6 54	16 54	6 53	16 49	6 57	16 48	6 58	16 42	7 11	16 50	7 15	17 00
27	6 45	16 42	6 55	16 52	6 55	16 47	6 59	16 46	7 00	16 39	7 13	16 47	7 17	16 58
28	6 47	16 40	6 57	16 50	6 57	16 45	7 01	16 44	7 02	16 37	7 16	16 45	7 19	16 56
29	6 49	16 38	6 59	16 48	6 59	16 43	7 03	16 42	7 04	16 35	7 18	16 43	7 21	16 53
30	6 51	16 37	7 01	16 47	7 01	16 41	7 05	16 40	7 07	16 33	7 20	16 41	7 23	16 51
31	6 52	16 35	7 02	16 45	7 02	16 39	7 07	16 38	7 09	16 31	7 22	16 38	7 25	16 49

JUPITER

Day	RA	Dec.	Transit	5° high	
				52°	56°
	h m	° ′	h m	h m	h m
1	4 39.3	+21 12	3 58	20 35	20 19
11	4 38.3	+21 10	3 18	19 55	19 39
21	4 36.0	+21 05	2 37	19 14	18 58
31	4 32.4	+20 57	1 54	18 32	18 16

Diameters – equatorial 46″ polar 43″

SATURN

Day	RA	Dec.	Transit	5° high	
				52°	56°
	h m	° ′	h m	h m	h m
1	3 56.1	+18 04	3 15	20 10	19 58
11	3 54.4	+17 58	2 34	19 30	19 18
21	3 52.1	+17 50	1 53	18 49	18 37
31	3 49.3	+17 41	1 11	18 08	17 56

Diameters – equatorial 20″ polar 18″
Rings – major axis 45″ minor axis 19″

URANUS

Day	RA	Dec.	Transit	10° high	
				52°	56°
	h m	° ′	h m	h m	h m
1	21 19.4	−16 23	20 36	23 47	23 18
11	21 18.7	−16 26	19 56	23 07	22 37
21	21 18.3	−16 27	19 16	22 27	21 57
31	21 18.3	−16 27	18 37	21 48	21 18

Diameter 4″

NEPTUNE

Day	RA	Dec.	Transit	10° high	
				52°	56°
	h m	° ′	h m	h m	h m
1	20 24.5	−19 06	19 41	22 29	21 51
11	20 24.3	−19 07	19 02	21 49	21 12
21	20 24.3	−19 07	18 22	21 10	20 32
31	20 24.5	−19 06	17 43	20 31	19 53

Diameter 2″

November 2000

ELEVENTH MONTH, 30 DAYS. *Novem* (nine), ninth month of Roman pre-Julian calendar

1	*Wednesday*	**All Saints' Day.** L. S. Lowry b. 1887		306
2	*Thursday*	Marie Antoinette b. 1755. Balfour Declaration 1917		307
3	*Friday*	Bellini b. 1801. Conor Cruise O'Brien b. 1917		308
4	*Saturday*	William III b. 1650. Wilfred Owen d. 1918		309
5	*Sunday*	**4th S. before Advent.** Sir John Hackett b. 1910		310
6	*Monday*	Adolphe Sax b. 1814. Jan Paderewski b. 1860	*week 45 day* 311	
7	*Tuesday*	Sir Godfrey Kneller d. 1723. Marie Curie b. 1867		312
8	*Wednesday*	John Milton d. 1674. Prof. Christiaan Barnard b. 1922		313
9	*Thursday*	Edward VII b. 1841. Dylan Thomas d. 1953		314
10	*Friday*	William Hogarth b. 1697. Sir Gordon Richards d. 1986		315
11	*Saturday*	Armistice Day 1918. Dennis Wheatley d. 1977		316
12	*Sunday*	**3rd S. before Advent.** Remembrance Sunday		317
13	*Monday*	R. L. Stevenson b. 1850. Archbishop of Canterbury b. 1935	*week 46 day* 318	
14	*Tuesday*	*Prince of Wales b.* 1948. Sir Frederick Banting b. 1841		319
15	*Wednesday*	Brazil becomes a Republic 1889. J. G. Ballard b. 1930		320
16	*Thursday*	Francis Danby b. 1793. John Walter d. 1812		321
17	*Friday*	Mary I d. 1558. Heitor Villa-Lobos d. 1959		322
18	*Saturday*	Sir William Gilbert b. 1836. Man Ray d. 1976		323
19	*Sunday*	**2nd S. before Advent.** Wolfe Tone d. 1798		324
20	*Monday*	*Queen's Wedding Day* 1947. Admiral Jellicoe d. 1935	*week 47 day* 325	
21	*Tuesday*	Voltaire b. 1694. Natalia Makarova b. 1940		326
22	*Wednesday*	Sir Martin Frobisher d. 1594. J. F. Kennedy assassinated 1963		327
23	*Thursday*	Manuel de Falla b. 1876. Boris Karloff b. 1887		328
24	*Friday*	Ian Botham b. 1955. Freddie Mercury d. 1991		329
25	*Saturday*	Karl Benz b. 1844. Pope John XXIII b. 1881		330
26	*Sunday*	**Christ the King. S. next before Advent**		331
27	*Monday*	Anders Celsius b. 1701. Alexandre Dumas (younger) d. 1895	*week 48 day* 332	
28	*Tuesday*	RAMADAN begins. William Blake b. 1757		333
29	*Wednesday*	Christian Doppler b. 1803. Ada Lovelace d. 1852		334
30	*Thursday*	**St Andrew.** Sir Winston Churchill b. 1874		335

ASTRONOMICAL PHENOMENA

d h
8 02 Mercury at stationary point
12 11 Saturn in conjunction with Moon. Saturn 2° N.
13 04 Jupiter in conjunction with Moon. Jupiter 2° N.
15 06 Mercury at greatest elongation W.19°
19 13 Saturn at opposition
21 21 Mars in conjunction with Moon. Mars 4° S.
22 00 Sun's longitude 240° ♐
24 13 Mercury in conjunction with Moon. Mercury 3° S.
28 02 Jupiter at opposition
29 18 Venus in conjunction with Moon. Venus 2° S.

MINIMA OF ALGOL

d	h	d	h	d	h
3	14.9	15	02.2	26	13.4
6	11.7	17	23.0	29	10.3
9	08.5	20	19.8		
12	05.4	23	16.6		

CONSTELLATIONS

The following constellations are near the meridian at

d	h		d	h
October	1	24	November	15	21
October	16	23	December	1	20
November	1	22	December	16	19

Ursa Major (below the Pole), Cepheus, Cassiopeia, Andromeda, Pegasus, Pisces, Aquarius and Cetus

THE MOON

Phases, Apsides and Node	d	h	m
☽ First Quarter	4	07	27
○ Full Moon	11	21	15
☾ Last Quarter	18	15	24
● New Moon	25	23	11

Apogee (404,377 km)	3	03	30
Perigee (366,047 km)	14	23	01
Apogee (405,273 km)	30	23	39

Mean longitude of ascending node on November 1, 109°

THE SUN   s.d. 16′.2

Day	Right Ascension	Dec. —	Equation of time	Rise 52°	Rise 56°	Transit	Set 52°	Set 56°	Sidereal time	Transit of First Point of Aries
	h m s	° ′	m s	h m	h m	h m	h m	h m	h m s	h m s
1	14 25 56	14 27	+16 24	6 55	7 07	11 44	16 31	16 19	2 42 21	21 14 10
2	14 29 51	14 46	+16 26	6 57	7 10	11 44	16 29	16 17	2 46 17	21 10 14
3	14 33 48	15 05	+16 26	6 59	7 12	11 44	16 28	16 15	2 50 14	21 06 18
4	14 37 45	15 24	+16 26	7 01	7 14	11 44	16 26	16 12	2 54 10	21 02 22
5	14 41 42	15 42	+16 24	7 02	7 16	11 44	16 24	16 10	2 58 07	20 58 27
6	14 45 41	16 00	+16 22	7 04	7 18	11 44	16 22	16 08	3 02 03	20 54 31
7	14 49 40	16 18	+16 19	7 06	7 20	11 44	16 21	16 06	3 06 00	20 50 35
8	14 53 41	16 36	+16 16	7 08	7 22	11 44	16 19	16 04	3 09 56	20 46 39
9	14 57 42	16 53	+16 11	7 10	7 25	11 44	16 17	16 03	3 13 53	20 42 43
10	15 01 44	17 10	+16 06	7 11	7 27	11 44	16 16	16 01	3 17 50	20 38 47
11	15 05 46	17 27	+16 00	7 13	7 29	11 44	16 14	15 59	3 21 46	20 34 51
12	15 09 50	17 43	+15 53	7 15	7 31	11 44	16 13	15 57	3 25 43	20 30 55
13	15 13 55	17 59	+15 45	7 17	7 33	11 44	16 11	15 55	3 29 39	20 26 59
14	15 18 00	18 15	+15 36	7 19	7 35	11 44	16 10	15 53	3 33 36	20 23 03
15	15 22 06	18 30	+15 26	7 20	7 37	11 45	16 08	15 52	3 37 32	20 19 07
16	15 26 13	18 45	+15 16	7 22	7 39	11 45	16 07	15 50	3 41 29	20 15 12
17	15 30 21	19 00	+15 05	7 24	7 41	11 45	16 06	15 48	3 45 25	20 11 16
18	15 34 30	19 14	+14 52	7 25	7 43	11 45	16 04	15 47	3 49 22	20 07 20
19	15 38 39	19 29	+14 39	7 27	7 45	11 45	16 03	15 45	3 53 19	20 03 24
20	15 42 50	19 42	+14 25	7 29	7 47	11 46	16 02	15 44	3 57 15	19 59 28
21	15 47 01	19 56	+14 11	7 30	7 49	11 46	16 01	15 42	4 01 12	19 55 32
22	15 51 13	20 09	+13 55	7 32	7 51	11 46	16 00	15 41	4 05 08	19 51 36
23	15 55 26	20 21	+13 39	7 34	7 53	11 47	15 59	15 40	4 09 05	19 47 40
24	15 59 40	20 34	+13 22	7 35	7 55	11 47	15 58	15 38	4 13 01	19 43 44
25	16 03 54	20 46	+13 04	7 37	7 57	11 47	15 57	15 37	4 16 58	19 39 48
26	16 08 09	20 57	+12 45	7 39	7 59	11 47	15 56	15 36	4 20 54	19 35 52
27	16 12 25	21 08	+12 26	7 40	8 00	11 48	15 55	15 35	4 24 51	19 31 57
28	16 16 42	21 19	+12 06	7 42	8 02	11 48	15 54	15 34	4 28 48	19 28 01
29	16 20 59	21 29	+11 45	7 43	8 04	11 48	15 53	15 33	4 32 44	19 24 05
30	16 25 17	21 39	+11 23	7 45	8 06	11 49	15 53	15 32	4 36 41	19 20 09

DURATION OF TWILIGHT (in minutes)

Latitude	52°	56°	52°	56°	52°	56°	52°	56°
	1 November		11 November		21 November		30 November	
Civil	36	40	37	41	38	43	39	45
Nautical	75	84	78	87	80	90	82	93
Astronomical	115	127	117	130	120	134	123	137

THE NIGHT SKY

Mercury is a morning object, visible low above the south-eastern horizon from after the first week of the month until almost the end of November. During this period its magnitude brightens from +1.1 to −0.7. On the morning of the 24th Mercury may be seen about 3° below the old crescent Moon, only 1.7 days old. This is the most favourable morning apparition of the year for observers in the northern hemisphere.

Venus continues to be visible as a brilliant object for a short time after sunset, low above the west-south-western horizon. By the end of the month it sets about two hours after the Sun. Its magnitude is −4.1. On the evening of the 29th the crescent Moon, four days old, passes about 1° north of the planet.

Mars is still a morning object, magnitude +1.7, moving steadily eastwards in the constellation of Virgo. The Moon is in the vicinity of the planet on the mornings of the 21st and 22nd.

Jupiter reaches opposition on the 28th and is therefore visible throughout the hours of darkness, magnitude −2.9. The Moon, just after Full, is near Jupiter on the nights of the 12th and 13th.

Saturn, magnitude −0.4, reaches opposition on the 19th and thus is visible throughout the hours of darkness. The Full Moon is near the planet on the nights of the 11th and 12th.

Meteors. The Leonid meteor shower, associated with Comet Tempel-Tuttle, does not usually provide a very noticeable display to the casual observer but on rare occasions spectacular displays of short duration have been observed. There is a possibility of such a display in the early morning hours of the 17th, though the Moon, near Last Quarter, will create some interference.

THE MOON

Day	RA	Dec.	Hor. par.	Semi-diam.	Sun's co-long.	PA of Bright Limb	Phase	Age	Rise 52°	Rise 56°	Transit	Set 52°	Set 56°
	h m	°	'	'	°	°	%	d	h m	h m	h m	h m	h m
1	18 13	−22.1	54.6	14.9	322	268	21	4.7	12 02	12 26	16 02	20 03	19 38
2	19 05	−22.3	54.3	14.8	334	264	29	5.7	12 49	13 13	16 51	20 56	20 33
3	19 56	−21.6	54.2	14.8	346	259	38	6.7	13 28	13 49	17 39	21 55	21 35
4	20 46	−19.9	54.3	14.8	358	255	47	7.7	14 00	14 18	18 26	22 59	22 42
5	21 35	−17.3	54.5	14.9	11	251	57	8.7	14 26	14 40	19 12	—	23 53
6	22 23	−14.0	54.9	15.0	23	248	66	9.7	14 49	14 59	19 57	0 06	—
7	23 10	−10.0	55.5	15.1	35	245	75	10.7	15 09	15 15	20 42	1 15	1 06
8	23 58	− 5.4	56.2	15.3	47	242	83	11.7	15 29	15 31	21 27	2 26	2 22
9	0 46	− 0.6	56.9	15.5	59	240	90	12.7	15 48	15 46	22 14	3 39	3 39
10	1 35	+ 4.5	57.7	15.7	71	238	95	13.7	16 09	16 02	23 03	4 54	4 59
11	2 26	+ 9.5	58.4	15.9	83	229	99	14.7	16 33	16 22	23 55	6 12	6 22
12	3 20	+14.1	59.1	16.1	96	145	100	15.7	17 02	16 46	—	7 32	7 47
13	4 18	+17.9	59.5	16.2	108	93	98	16.7	17 38	17 18	0 50	8 53	9 12
14	5 18	+20.8	59.8	16.3	120	90	94	17.7	18 25	18 02	1 49	10 09	10 32
15	6 20	+22.3	59.9	16.3	132	93	87	18.7	19 24	19 00	2 49	11 17	11 41
16	7 23	+22.3	59.8	16.3	144	98	79	19.7	20 33	20 11	3 50	12 12	12 35
17	8 24	+20.8	59.6	16.2	156	103	68	20.7	21 50	21 31	4 50	12 55	13 15
18	9 23	+18.1	59.2	16.1	168	108	57	21.7	23 09	22 55	5 47	13 29	13 44
19	10 20	+14.3	58.8	16.0	181	111	46	22.7	—	—	6 40	13 56	14 06
20	11 13	+ 9.8	58.4	15.9	193	114	35	23.7	0 27	0 19	7 31	14 19	14 25
21	12 04	+ 4.9	57.9	15.8	205	116	25	24.7	1 44	1 41	8 19	14 39	14 41
22	12 54	− 0.2	57.4	15.6	217	118	16	25.7	3 00	3 01	9 06	14 59	14 56
23	13 43	− 5.3	56.9	15.5	229	118	9	26.7	4 14	4 20	9 53	15 19	15 12
24	14 32	−10.0	56.4	15.4	242	119	4	27.7	5 28	5 38	10 39	15 41	15 29
25	15 22	−14.2	55.9	15.2	254	125	1	28.7	6 40	6 54	11 27	16 06	15 50
26	16 12	−17.6	55.5	15.1	266	197	0	0.0	7 50	8 08	12 16	16 35	16 16
27	17 04	−20.3	55.0	15.0	278	264	1	1.0	8 55	9 17	13 05	17 11	16 48
28	17 56	−21.9	54.7	14.9	290	267	4	2.0	9 54	10 18	13 55	17 54	17 30
29	18 48	−22.5	54.4	14.8	302	265	9	3.0	10 45	11 09	14 44	18 45	18 21
30	19 39	−22.1	54.2	14.8	315	261	15	4.0	11 27	11 50	15 33	19 42	19 20

MERCURY

Day	RA	Dec.	Diam.	Phase	Transit	5° high 52°	5° high 56°
	h m	°	"	%	h m	h m	h m
1	14 09	−13.0	10	1	11 23	7 08	7 24
3	14 02	−11.7	10	6	11 11	6 45	7 00
5	13 57	−10.6	9	13	10 56	6 27	6 40
7	13 54	− 9.9	9	22	10 46	6 13	6 25
9	13 55	− 9.6	8	32	10 39	6 04	6 16
11	13 57	− 9.6	8	41	10 35	6 00	6 12
13	14 02	−10.0	7	51	10 32	6 00	6 12
15	14 09	−10.6	7	59	10 32	6 02	6 15
17	14 17	−11.3	6	66	10 32	6 07	6 21
19	14 27	−12.2	6	72	10 34	6 14	6 29
21	14 37	−13.2	6	77	10 36	6 22	6 39
23	14 47	−14.2	6	81	10 39	6 31	6 49
25	14 58	−15.2	6	85	10 42	6 41	7 01
27	15 10	−16.2	5	88	10 46	6 52	7 13
29	15 22	−17.2	5	90	10 50	7 03	7 25
31	15 34	−18.2	5	92	10 55	7 14	7 38

VENUS

Day	RA	Dec.	Diam.	Phase	Transit	5° high 52°	5° high 56°
	h m	°	"	%	h m	h m	h m
1	16 56	−24.3	14	79	14 14	17 05	16 25
6	17 22	−25.0	14	78	14 21	17 05	16 22
11	17 49	−25.4	14	76	14 28	17 08	16 23
16	18 15	−25.5	15	75	14 35	17 14	16 28
21	18 42	−25.3	15	74	14 41	17 23	16 38
26	19 08	−24.9	16	72	14 48	17 35	16 53
31	19 34	−24.1	16	70	14 54	17 49	17 10

MARS

Day	RA	Dec.	Diam.	Phase	Transit	5° high 52°	5° high 56°
1	11 55	+ 1.9	4	96	9 12	3 35	3 37
6	12 06	+ 0.7	4	96	9 04	3 33	3 36
11	12 18	− 0.5	4	95	8 55	3 31	3 35
16	12 29	− 1.7	4	95	8 47	3 29	3 34
21	12 40	− 2.9	4	95	8 38	3 27	3 32
26	12 51	− 4.1	4	94	8 30	3 24	3 31
31	13 03	− 5.3	5	94	8 21	3 22	3 30

SUNRISE AND SUNSET

	London		Bristol		Birmingham		Manchester		Newcastle		Glasgow		Belfast	
	0°05′	51°30′	2°35′	51°28′	1°55′	52°28′	2°15′	53°28′	1°37′	54°59′	4°14′	55°52′	5°56′	54°35′
	h m	h m	h m	h m	h m	h m	h m	h m	h m	h m	h m	h m	h m	h m
1	6 54	16 33	7 04	16 43	7 04	16 37	7 08	16 36	7 11	16 29	7 24	16 36	7 27	16 47
2	6 56	16 31	7 06	16 41	7 06	16 36	7 10	16 34	7 13	16 27	7 26	16 34	7 29	16 45
3	6 58	16 29	7 08	16 39	7 08	16 34	7 12	16 32	7 15	16 25	7 28	16 32	7 31	16 43
4	7 00	16 28	7 09	16 38	7 10	16 32	7 14	16 30	7 17	16 23	7 30	16 30	7 33	16 41
5	7 01	16 26	7 11	16 36	7 12	16 30	7 16	16 28	7 19	16 21	7 32	16 28	7 35	16 39
6	7 03	16 24	7 13	16 34	7 13	16 29	7 18	16 27	7 21	16 19	7 35	16 26	7 37	16 37
7	7 05	16 23	7 15	16 33	7 15	16 27	7 20	16 25	7 23	16 17	7 37	16 24	7 39	16 36
8	7 07	16 21	7 17	16 31	7 17	16 25	7 22	16 23	7 25	16 15	7 39	16 22	7 41	16 34
9	7 08	16 19	7 18	16 30	7 19	16 23	7 24	16 21	7 27	16 13	7 41	16 20	7 43	16 32
10	7 10	16 18	7 20	16 28	7 21	16 22	7 26	16 20	7 29	16 11	7 43	16 18	7 45	16 30
11	7 12	16 16	7 22	16 26	7 23	16 20	7 27	16 18	7 31	16 09	7 45	16 16	7 47	16 28
12	7 14	16 15	7 23	16 25	7 24	16 19	7 29	16 16	7 33	16 08	7 47	16 14	7 49	16 27
13	7 15	16 13	7 25	16 24	7 26	16 17	7 31	16 15	7 35	16 06	7 49	16 13	7 50	16 25
14	7 17	16 12	7 27	16 22	7 28	16 16	7 33	16 13	7 37	16 04	7 51	16 11	7 52	16 23
15	7 19	16 11	7 29	16 21	7 30	16 14	7 35	16 12	7 39	16 03	7 53	16 09	7 54	16 22
16	7 20	16 09	7 30	16 19	7 31	16 13	7 37	16 10	7 41	16 01	7 55	16 08	7 56	16 20
17	7 22	16 08	7 32	16 18	7 33	16 12	7 39	16 09	7 43	16 00	7 57	16 06	7 58	16 19
18	7 24	16 07	7 34	16 17	7 35	16 10	7 40	16 07	7 45	15 58	7 59	16 04	8 00	16 17
19	7 25	16 06	7 35	16 16	7 37	16 09	7 42	16 06	7 47	15 57	8 01	16 03	8 02	16 16
20	7 27	16 04	7 37	16 15	7 38	16 08	7 44	16 05	7 48	15 55	8 03	16 01	8 04	16 14
21	7 29	16 03	7 39	16 13	7 40	16 07	7 46	16 04	7 50	15 54	8 05	16 00	8 06	16 13
22	7 30	16 02	7 40	16 12	7 42	16 05	7 48	16 02	7 52	15 53	8 07	15 58	8 08	16 12
23	7 32	16 01	7 42	16 11	7 43	16 04	7 49	16 01	7 54	15 51	8 09	15 57	8 09	16 11
24	7 34	16 00	7 43	16 10	7 45	16 03	7 51	16 00	7 56	15 50	8 11	15 56	8 11	16 09
25	7 35	15 59	7 45	16 09	7 47	16 02	7 53	15 59	7 58	15 49	8 13	15 55	8 13	16 08
26	7 37	15 58	7 47	16 09	7 48	16 01	7 54	15 58	7 59	15 48	8 15	15 53	8 15	16 07
27	7 38	15 58	7 48	16 08	7 50	16 01	7 56	15 57	8 01	15 47	8 17	15 52	8 16	16 06
28	7 40	15 57	7 50	16 07	7 51	16 00	7 58	15 56	8 03	15 46	8 18	15 51	8 18	16 05
29	7 41	15 56	7 51	16 06	7 53	15 59	7 59	15 55	8 05	15 45	8 20	15 50	8 20	16 04
30	7 43	15 55	7 52	16 05	7 54	15 58	8 01	15 55	8 06	15 44	8 22	15 49	8 21	16 03

JUPITER

Day	RA	Dec.	Transit	5° high	
				52°	56°
	h m	° ′	h m	h m	h m
1	4 32.0	+20 57	1 49	18 27	18 12
11	4 27.3	+20 47	1 05	17 44	17 29
21	4 21.8	+20 35	0 21	17 01	16 46
31	4 16.1	+20 22	23 31	16 17	16 02

Diameters – equatorial 48″ polar 45″

SATURN

Day	RA	Dec.	Transit	5° high	
				52°	56°
	h m	° ′	h m	h m	h m
1	3 49.0	+17 40	1 07	8 05	8 17
11	3 45.9	+17 29	0 24	7 22	7 34
21	3 42.6	+17 19	23 37	6 38	6 50
31	3 39.3	+17 09	22 55	5 55	6 06

Diameters – equatorial 20″ polar 18″
Rings – major axis 46″ minor axis 19″

URANUS

Day	RA	Dec.	Transit	10° high	
				52°	56°
	h m	° ′	h m	h m	h m
1	21 18.3	−16 27	18 33	21 44	21 14
11	21 18.7	−16 25	17 54	21 05	20 36
21	21 19.4	−16 21	17 15	20 27	19 58
31	21 20.4	−16 16	16 37	19 49	19 20

Diameter 4″

NEPTUNE

Day	RA	Dec.	Transit	10° high	
				52°	56°
	h m	° ′	h m	h m	h m
1	20 24.6	−19 06	17 39	20 27	19 50
11	20 25.0	−19 05	17 01	19 49	19 11
21	20 25.8	−19 02	16 22	19 11	18 33
31	20 26.7	−18 59	15 44	18 33	17 55

Diameter 2″

December 2000

TWELFTH MONTH, 31 DAYS. *Decem* (ten), tenth month of Roman pre-Julian calendar

1	*Friday*	Henry I d. 1135. David Ben-Gurion d. 1973	336
2	*Saturday*	Maria Callas b. 1923. Philip Larkin d. 1985	337
3	*Sunday*	**Advent Sunday.** Sir Rowland Hill b. 1795	338
4	*Monday*	Robert Jenkinson d. 1828. Vassily Kandinsky b. 1866	*week 49 day* 339
5	*Tuesday*	Mozart d. 1791. Lord Dainton d. 1997	340
6	*Wednesday*	Henry VI b. 1421. Joseph Gay-Lussac b. 1778	341
7	*Thursday*	Battle of Pearl Harbor 1941. Robert Graves d. 1985	342
8	*Friday*	Mary, Queen of Scots b. 1542. Golda Meir d. 1978	343
9	*Saturday*	Sir Anthony van Dyck d. 1641. Ralph Bunche d. 1951	344
10	*Sunday*	**2nd S. of Advent.** Ada Lovelace b. 1815	345
11	*Monday*	First motor show opened in Paris 1894	*week 50 day* 346
12	*Tuesday*	Sir Marc Brunel d. 1849. Frank Sinatra b. 1915	347
13	*Wednesday*	Abel Tasman discovered New Zealand 1642	348
14	*Thursday*	Nostradamus b. 1503. Sir Stanley Spencer d. 1959	349
15	*Friday*	Alexandre-Gustave Eiffel b. 1832. Sitting Bull d. 1890	350
16	*Saturday*	Beethoven b. 1770. Boston Tea Party 1773	351
17	*Sunday*	**3rd S. of Advent.** Dame Mary Cartwright b. 1900	352
18	*Monday*	Stradivari d. 1737. Steven Spielberg b. 1947	*week 51 day* 353
19	*Tuesday*	Vitus Bering d. 1741. Emily Brontë d. 1848	354
20	*Wednesday*	Artur Rubinstein d. 1982. Carl Sagan d. 1996	355
21	*Thursday*	*Michaelmas Law Sittings end.* Frank Zappa b. 1940	356
22	*Friday*	CHANUCAH begins. Puccini b. 1858	357
23	*Saturday*	Richard Arkwright b. 1732. Thomas Malthus d. 1834	358
24	*Sunday*	**4th S. of Advent.** Christmas Eve	359
25	*Monday*	**Christmas Day.** *Bank Holiday in the UK*	*week 52 day* 360
26	*Tuesday*	**St Stephen.** Boxing Day. *Bank Holiday in the UK*	361
27	*Wednesday*	**St John.** Louis Pasteur b. 1822	362
28	*Thursday*	**Holy Innocents.** Sir Arthur Eddington b. 1882	363
29	*Friday*	William Gladstone b. 1809. Jameson Raid 1895	364
30	*Saturday*	Robert Boyle d. 1691. Josephine Butler d. 1906	365
31	*Sunday*	**1st S. of Christmas.** John Flamsteed d. 1719	366

ASTRONOMICAL PHENOMENA

d	h	
4	14	Pluto in conjunction
9	18	Saturn in conjunction with Moon. Saturn 2° N.
10	08	Jupiter in conjunction with Moon. Jupiter 3° N.
20	10	Mars in conjunction with Moon. Mars 4° S.
21	14	Sun's longitude 270° ♐
25	17	Mercury in conjunction with Moon. Mercury 3° S.
25	17	Partial eclipse of Sun (*see* page 71)
25	19	Mercury in superior conjunction
30	00	Venus in conjunction with Moon. Venus 2° N.

MINIMA OF ALGOL

d	h	d	h	d	h
2	07.1	13	18.3	25	05.6
5	03.9	16	15.2	28	02.4
8	00.7	19	12.0	30	23.3
10	21.5	22	08.8		

CONSTELLATIONS

The following constellations are near the meridian at

d	h		d	h
November	1	24	December	16	21
November	15	23	January	1	20
December	1	22	January	16	19

Ursa Major (below the Pole), Ursa Minor (below the Pole), Cassiopeia, Andromeda, Perseus, Triangulum, Aries, Taurus, Cetus and Eridanus

THE MOON

Phases, Apsides and Node	d	h	m
☽ First Quarter	4	03	55
○ Full Moon	11	09	03
☾ Last Quarter	18	00	41
● New Moon	25	17	22
Perigee (360,602 km)	12	22	21
Apogee (406,192 km)	28	15	05

Mean longitude of ascending node on December 1, 107°

THE SUN

s.d. 16′.3

Day	Right Ascension	Dec. −	Equation of time	Rise 52°	Rise 56°	Transit	Set 52°	Set 56°	Sidereal time	Transit of First Point of Aries
	h m s	° ′	m s	h m	h m	h m	h m	h m	h m s	h m s
1	16 29 36	21 49	+11 01	7 46	8 07	11 49	15 52	15 31	4 40 37	19 16 13
2	16 33 55	21 58	+10 38	7 47	8 09	11 50	15 51	15 30	4 44 34	19 12 17
3	16 38 15	22 07	+10 15	7 49	8 10	11 50	15 51	15 29	4 48 30	19 08 21
4	16 42 36	22 15	+ 9 51	7 50	8 12	11 50	15 50	15 28	4 52 27	19 04 25
5	16 46 57	22 23	+ 9 27	7 51	8 14	11 51	15 50	15 28	4 56 23	19 00 29
6	16 51 18	22 30	+ 9 02	7 53	8 15	11 51	15 49	15 27	5 00 20	18 56 33
7	16 55 40	22 37	+ 8 36	7 54	8 16	11 52	15 49	15 27	5 04 17	18 52 37
8	17 00 03	22 43	+ 8 10	7 55	8 18	11 52	15 49	15 26	5 08 13	18 48 41
9	17 04 26	22 49	+ 7 44	7 56	8 19	11 52	15 49	15 26	5 12 10	18 44 46
10	17 08 50	22 55	+ 7 17	7 57	8 20	11 53	15 48	15 25	5 16 06	18 40 50
11	17 13 13	23 00	+ 6 49	7 58	8 21	11 53	15 48	15 25	5 20 03	18 36 54
12	17 17 38	23 05	+ 6 22	7 59	8 23	11 54	15 48	15 25	5 23 59	18 32 58
13	17 22 02	23 09	+ 5 54	8 00	8 24	11 54	15 48	15 25	5 27 56	18 29 02
14	17 26 27	23 13	+ 5 25	8 01	8 25	11 55	15 48	15 25	5 31 52	18 25 06
15	17 30 52	23 16	+ 4 57	8 02	8 26	11 55	15 49	15 25	5 35 49	18 21 10
16	17 35 18	23 19	+ 4 28	8 03	8 26	11 56	15 49	15 25	5 39 46	18 17 14
17	17 39 44	23 21	+ 3 58	8 03	8 27	11 56	15 49	15 25	5 43 42	18 13 18
18	17 44 10	23 23	+ 3 29	8 04	8 28	11 57	15 49	15 25	5 47 39	18 09 22
19	17 48 36	23 25	+ 2 59	8 05	8 29	11 57	15 50	15 26	5 51 35	18 05 26
20	17 53 02	23 26	+ 2 30	8 05	8 29	11 58	15 50	15 26	5 55 32	18 01 31
21	17 57 29	23 26	+ 2 00	8 06	8 30	11 58	15 51	15 27	5 59 28	17 57 35
22	18 01 55	23 26	+ 1 30	8 06	8 30	11 59	15 51	15 27	6 03 25	17 53 39
23	18 06 22	23 26	+ 1 00	8 07	8 31	11 59	15 52	15 28	6 07 21	17 49 43
24	18 10 48	23 25	+ 0 30	8 07	8 31	12 00	15 52	15 29	6 11 18	17 45 47
25	18 15 14	23 24	0 00	8 08	8 31	12 00	15 53	15 29	6 15 15	17 41 51
26	18 19 41	23 22	− 0 30	8 08	8 32	12 01	15 54	15 30	6 19 11	17 37 55
27	18 24 07	23 19	− 0 59	8 08	8 32	12 01	15 55	15 31	6 23 08	17 33 59
28	18 28 33	23 17	− 1 29	8 08	8 32	12 02	15 55	15 32	6 27 04	17 30 03
29	18 32 59	23 13	− 1 58	8 08	8 32	12 02	15 56	15 33	6 31 01	17 26 07
30	18 37 25	23 10	− 2 27	8 08	8 32	12 03	15 57	15 34	6 34 57	17 22 11
31	18 41 50	23 05	− 2 56	8 08	8 31	12 03	15 58	15 35	6 38 54	17 18 16

DURATION OF TWILIGHT (in minutes)

Latitude	52°	56°	52°	56°	52°	56°	52°	56°
	1 December		11 December		21 December		31 December	
Civil	40	45	41	47	41	47	41	47
Nautical	82	93	84	96	85	97	84	96
Astronomical	123	138	125	141	126	142	125	141

THE NIGHT SKY

Mercury is too close to the Sun for observation throughout the month, superior conjunction occurring on the 25th.

Venus is a magnificent object in the early evening sky, magnitude −4.2, low above the west-south-western horizon. By the end of the month it is visible for over three hours after sunset. The crescent Moon will be seen about 4° below the planet on the evening of the 29th.

Mars, magnitude +1.5, continues to be visible low in the east-south-eastern sky in the early mornings. Mars passes 4° north of Spica on the 11th. On the morning of the 20th the crescent Moon will be seen about 3° above the planet.

Jupiter, magnitude −2.8, is only just past opposition so that it is effectively visible throughout the hours of darkness until morning twilight begins. By the very end of the year it has sunk too low in the west to be visible shortly after 0400 hours. During the night of the 9th to 10th the Full Moon will be seen near Jupiter.

Saturn is an evening object, magnitude −0.2, visible from the end of evening twilight until the early hours of the morning. The Moon passes 2° south of Saturn on the evening of the 9th.

Meteors. The maximum of the well-known Geminid meteor shower occurs on the 13th. Conditions are not favourable since the bright gibbous Moon will be above the horizon.

THE MOON

Day	RA h m	Dec. °	Hor. par. ′	Semi- diam. ′	Sun's co- long. °	PA of Bright Limb °	Phase %	Age d	Rise 52° h m	Rise 56° h m	Transit h m	Set 52° h m	Set 56° h m
1	20 30	−20.7	54.1	14.7	327	257	22	5.0	12 02	12 21	16 20	20 44	20 26
2	21 19	−18.4	54.2	14.8	339	253	30	6.0	12 30	12 46	17 06	21 50	21 35
3	22 07	−15.4	54.4	14.8	351	250	39	7.0	12 53	13 05	17 50	22 57	22 46
4	22 54	−11.6	54.8	14.9	3	248	49	8.0	13 14	13 22	18 34	—	23 59
5	23 40	− 7.4	55.4	15.1	16	246	58	9.0	13 33	13 37	19 18	0 05	—
6	0 27	− 2.7	56.1	15.3	28	245	68	10.0	13 52	13 51	20 03	1 16	1 13
7	1 15	+ 2.3	57.0	15.5	40	244	77	11.0	14 11	14 07	20 50	2 28	2 31
8	2 04	+ 7.2	57.9	15.8	52	245	85	12.0	14 33	14 24	21 40	3 44	3 51
9	2 57	+12.1	58.8	16.0	64	246	92	13.0	14 58	14 45	22 33	5 03	5 15
10	3 53	+16.3	59.6	16.2	76	247	97	14.0	15 31	15 13	23 31	6 24	6 41
11	4 52	+19.8	60.3	16.4	88	235	100	15.0	16 13	15 51	—	7 45	8 06
12	5 55	+21.9	60.7	16.5	100	99	99	16.0	17 08	16 43	0 32	9 00	9 24
13	7 00	+22.6	60.8	16.6	113	96	96	17.0	18 15	17 52	1 36	10 03	10 27
14	8 04	+21.6	60.7	16.5	125	100	90	18.0	19 32	19 12	2 39	10 53	11 14
15	9 06	+19.2	60.3	16.4	137	105	82	19.0	20 53	20 38	3 39	11 32	11 48
16	10 05	+15.5	59.7	16.3	149	109	72	20.0	22 14	22 04	4 36	12 02	12 13
17	11 01	+11.1	59.0	16.1	161	112	62	21.0	23 33	23 28	5 28	12 26	12 33
18	11 53	+ 6.1	58.3	15.9	173	113	50	22.0	—	—	6 18	12 47	12 50
19	12 43	+ 1.0	57.6	15.7	185	114	40	23.0	0 50	0 49	7 05	13 07	13 05
20	13 32	− 4.0	56.9	15.5	198	114	30	24.0	2 04	2 08	7 51	13 26	13 20
21	14 21	− 8.8	56.3	15.3	210	113	21	25.0	3 17	3 25	8 37	13 47	13 37
22	15 09	−13.1	55.8	15.2	222	111	13	26.0	4 28	4 41	9 24	14 10	13 56
23	15 59	−16.7	55.3	15.1	234	108	7	27.0	5 38	5 55	10 11	14 37	14 19
24	16 49	−19.6	54.9	15.0	246	105	3	28.0	6 45	7 06	11 00	15 10	14 48
25	17 41	−21.6	54.6	14.9	259	105	1	29.0	7 46	8 10	11 49	15 50	15 26
26	18 33	−22.5	54.3	14.8	271	253	0	0.3	8 40	9 05	12 39	16 38	16 13
27	19 24	−22.4	54.1	14.7	283	263	1	1.3	9 26	9 49	13 28	17 33	17 10
28	20 15	−21.3	54.0	14.7	295	260	5	2.3	10 03	10 24	14 16	18 33	18 13
29	21 05	−19.3	54.0	14.7	307	257	9	3.3	10 33	10 51	15 02	19 38	19 21
30	21 53	−16.4	54.1	14.7	319	253	16	4.3	10 58	11 12	15 47	20 44	20 31
31	22 40	−12.9	54.3	14.8	332	251	23	5.3	11 19	11 29	16 30	21 51	21 43

MERCURY

Day	RA h m	Dec. °	Diam. ″	Phase %	Transit h m	5° high 52° h m	5° high 56° h m
1	15 34	−18.2	5	92	10 55	7 14	7 38
3	15 47	−19.1	5	93	10 59	7 26	7 51
5	15 59	−20.0	5	95	11 04	7 37	8 05
7	16 12	−20.8	5	96	11 09	7 48	8 18
9	16 25	−21.6	5	97	11 14	7 59	8 31
11	16 38	−22.3	5	98	11 19	8 10	8 44
13	16 51	−22.9	5	98	11 25	8 21	8 57
15	17 05	−23.5	5	99	11 30	8 31	9 09
17	17 18	−23.9	5	99	11 36	8 41	9 20
19	17 32	−24.3	5	100	11 42	8 51	9 31
21	17 46	−24.6	5	100	11 48	8 59	9 41
23	17 59	−24.8	5	100	11 54	9 07	9 50
25	18 13	−25.0	5	100	12 00	14 45	14 02
27	18 27	−25.0	5	100	12 06	14 51	14 08
29	18 42	−24.9	5	100	12 12	14 58	14 16
31	18 56	−24.8	5	100	12 19	15 07	14 25

VENUS

Day	RA h m	Dec. °	Diam. ″	Phase %	Transit h m	5° high 52° h m	5° high 56° h m
1	19 34	−24.1	16	70	14 54	17 49	17 10
6	19 59	−23.0	17	69	14 59	18 04	17 29
11	20 24	−21.7	17	67	15 04	18 20	17 50
16	20 48	−20.2	18	65	15 08	18 37	18 10
21	21 11	−18.4	19	63	15 12	18 53	18 30
26	21 33	−16.5	20	61	15 14	19 10	18 49
31	21 55	−14.4	21	59	15 16	19 25	19 08

MARS

Day	RA h m	Dec. °	Diam. ″	Phase %	Transit h m	5° high 52° h m	5° high 56° h m
1	13 03	− 5.3	5	94	8 21	3 22	3 30
6	13 14	− 6.4	5	94	8 13	3 20	3 29
11	13 25	− 7.5	5	93	8 04	3 18	3 28
16	13 36	− 8.6	5	93	7 56	3 16	3 27
21	13 48	− 9.7	5	93	7 48	3 13	3 25
26	13 59	−10.8	5	92	7 39	3 11	3 24
31	14 10	−11.8	5	92	7 31	3 08	3 23

SUNRISE AND SUNSET

	London		Bristol		Birmingham		Manchester		Newcastle		Glasgow		Belfast	
	0°05′	51°30′	2°35′	51°28′	1°55′	52°28′	2°15′	53°28′	1°37′	54°59′	4°14′	55°52′	5°56′	54°35′
	h m	h m	h m	h m	h m	h m	h m	h m	h m	h m	h m	h m	h m	h m
1	7 44	15 55	7 54	16 05	7 56	15 57	8 02	15 54	8 08	15 43	8 23	15 48	8 23	16 03
2	7 45	15 54	7 55	16 04	7 57	15 57	8 04	15 53	8 09	15 42	8 25	15 48	8 24	16 02
3	7 47	15 54	7 57	16 04	7 59	15 56	8 05	15 52	8 11	15 42	8 27	15 47	8 26	16 01
4	7 48	15 53	7 58	16 03	8 00	15 56	8 06	15 52	8 12	15 41	8 28	15 46	8 27	16 01
5	7 49	15 53	7 59	16 03	8 01	15 55	8 08	15 51	8 14	15 40	8 30	15 45	8 29	16 00
6	7 50	15 52	8 00	16 02	8 03	15 55	8 09	15 51	8 15	15 40	8 31	15 45	8 30	15 59
7	7 52	15 52	8 02	16 02	8 04	15 54	8 10	15 51	8 16	15 39	8 32	15 44	8 31	15 59
8	7 53	15 52	8 03	16 02	8 05	15 54	8 12	15 50	8 18	15 39	8 34	15 44	8 33	15 59
9	7 54	15 51	8 04	16 02	8 06	15 54	8 13	15 50	8 19	15 39	8 35	15 44	8 34	15 58
10	7 55	15 51	8 05	16 01	8 07	15 54	8 14	15 50	8 20	15 38	8 36	15 43	8 35	15 58
11	7 56	15 51	8 06	16 01	8 08	15 54	8 15	15 50	8 21	15 38	8 37	15 43	8 36	15 58
12	7 57	15 51	8 07	16 01	8 09	15 54	8 16	15 50	8 22	15 38	8 39	15 43	8 37	15 58
13	7 58	15 51	8 08	16 01	8 10	15 54	8 17	15 49	8 23	15 38	8 40	15 43	8 38	15 58
14	7 59	15 51	8 09	16 01	8 11	15 54	8 18	15 50	8 24	15 38	8 41	15 43	8 39	15 58
15	8 00	15 51	8 10	16 02	8 12	15 54	8 19	15 50	8 25	15 38	8 42	15 43	8 40	15 58
16	8 00	15 52	8 10	16 02	8 13	15 54	8 20	15 50	8 26	15 38	8 42	15 43	8 41	15 58
17	8 01	15 52	8 11	16 02	8 14	15 54	8 20	15 50	8 27	15 38	8 43	15 43	8 42	15 58
18	8 02	15 52	8 12	16 02	8 14	15 54	8 21	15 50	8 28	15 39	8 44	15 43	8 43	15 58
19	8 03	15 53	8 12	16 03	8 15	15 55	8 22	15 51	8 28	15 39	8 45	15 44	8 43	15 59
20	8 03	15 53	8 13	16 03	8 16	15 55	8 22	15 51	8 29	15 39	8 45	15 44	8 44	15 59
21	8 04	15 53	8 14	16 04	8 16	15 56	8 23	15 52	8 30	15 40	8 46	15 45	8 44	16 00
22	8 04	15 54	8 14	16 04	8 17	15 56	8 23	15 52	8 30	15 40	8 46	15 45	8 45	16 00
23	8 05	15 55	8 14	16 05	8 17	15 57	8 24	15 53	8 30	15 41	8 47	15 46	8 45	16 01
24	8 05	15 55	8 15	16 05	8 17	15 57	8 24	15 53	8 31	15 42	8 47	15 46	8 46	16 01
25	8 05	15 56	8 15	16 06	8 18	15 58	8 25	15 54	8 31	15 42	8 47	15 47	8 46	16 02
26	8 06	15 57	8 15	16 07	8 18	15 59	8 25	15 55	8 31	15 43	8 48	15 48	8 46	16 03
27	8 06	15 57	8 16	16 08	8 18	16 00	8 25	15 56	8 31	15 44	8 48	15 49	8 46	16 04
28	8 06	15 58	8 16	16 08	8 18	16 01	8 25	15 56	8 32	15 45	8 48	15 50	8 46	16 05
29	8 06	15 59	8 16	16 09	8 18	16 02	8 25	15 57	8 32	15 46	8 48	15 51	8 46	16 06
30	8 06	16 00	8 16	16 10	8 18	16 03	8 25	15 58	8 32	15 47	8 48	15 52	8 46	16 07
31	8 06	16 01	8 16	16 11	8 18	16 04	8 25	15 59	8 31	15 48	8 47	15 53	8 46	16 08

JUPITER

Day	RA	Dec.	Transit	5° high	
				52°	56°
	h m	° ′	h m	h m	h m
1	4 16.1	+20 22	23 31	6 50	7 04
11	4 10.5	+20 10	22 46	6 04	6 18
21	4 05.5	+19 58	22 02	5 18	5 33
31	4 01.4	+19 49	21 19	4 34	4 48

Diameters – equatorial 48″ polar 45″

SATURN

Day	RA	Dec.	Transit	5° high	
				52°	56°
	h m	° ′	h m	h m	h m
1	3 39.3	+17 09	22 55	5 55	6 06
11	3 36.2	+17 00	22 12	5 12	5 23
21	3 33.5	+16 53	21 30	4 29	4 40
31	3 31.3	+16 47	20 49	3 47	3 58

Diameters – equatorial 20″ polar 18″
Rings – major axis 46″ minor axis 18″

URANUS

Day	RA	Dec.	Transit	10° high	
				52°	56°
	h m	° ′	h m	h m	h m
1	21 20.4	−16 16	16 37	19 49	19 20
11	21 21.7	−16 10	15 59	19 12	18 43
21	21 23.2	−16 03	15 21	18 35	18 07
31	21 25.0	−15 54	14 44	17 59	17 31

Diameter 4″

NEPTUNE

Day	RA	Dec.	Transit	10° high	
				52°	56°
	h m	° ′	h m	h m	h m
1	20 26.7	−18 59	15 44	18 33	17 55
11	20 27.8	−18 56	15 05	17 55	17 18
21	20 29.0	−18 52	14 27	17 18	16 41
31	20 30.4	−18 47	13 49	16 40	16 04

Diameter 2″

RISING AND SETTING TIMES

TABLE 1. SEMI-DIURNAL ARCS (HOUR ANGLES AT RISING/SETTING)

Dec.	0°	10°	20°	30°	40°	45°	50°	52°	54°	56°	58°	60°	Dec.
	h m	h m	h m	h m	h m	h m	h m	h m	h m	h m	h m	h m	
0°	6 00	6 00	6 00	6 00	6 00	6 00	6 00	6 00	6 00	6 00	6 00	6 00	0°
1°	6 00	6 01	6 01	6 02	6 03	6 04	6 05	6 05	6 06	6 06	6 06	6 07	1°
2°	6 00	6 01	6 03	6 05	6 07	6 08	6 10	6 10	6 11	6 12	6 13	6 14	2°
3°	6 00	6 02	6 04	6 07	6 10	6 12	6 14	6 15	6 17	6 18	6 19	6 21	3°
4°	6 00	6 03	6 06	6 09	6 13	6 16	6 19	6 21	6 22	6 24	6 26	6 28	4°
5°	6 00	6 04	6 07	6 12	6 17	6 20	6 24	6 26	6 28	6 30	6 32	6 35	5°
6°	6 00	6 04	6 09	6 14	6 20	6 24	6 29	6 31	6 33	6 36	6 39	6 42	6°
7°	6 00	6 05	6 10	6 16	6 24	6 28	6 34	6 36	6 39	6 42	6 45	6 49	7°
8°	6 00	6 06	6 12	6 19	6 27	6 32	6 39	6 41	6 45	6 48	6 52	6 56	8°
9°	6 00	6 06	6 13	6 21	6 31	6 36	6 44	6 47	6 50	6 54	6 59	7 04	9°
10°	6 00	6 07	6 15	6 23	6 34	6 41	6 49	6 52	6 56	7 01	7 06	7 11	10°
11°	6 00	6 08	6 16	6 26	6 38	6 45	6 54	6 58	7 02	7 07	7 12	7 19	11°
12°	6 00	6 09	6 18	6 28	6 41	6 49	6 59	7 03	7 08	7 13	7 20	7 26	12°
13°	6 00	6 09	6 19	6 31	6 45	6 53	7 04	7 09	7 14	7 20	7 27	7 34	13°
14°	6 00	6 10	6 21	6 33	6 48	6 58	7 09	7 14	7 20	7 27	7 34	7 42	14°
15°	6 00	6 11	6 22	6 36	6 52	7 02	7 14	7 20	7 27	7 34	7 42	7 51	15°
16°	6 00	6 12	6 24	6 38	6 56	7 07	7 20	7 26	7 33	7 41	7 49	7 59	16°
17°	6 00	6 12	6 26	6 41	6 59	7 11	7 25	7 32	7 40	7 48	7 57	8 08	17°
18°	6 00	6 13	6 27	6 43	7 03	7 16	7 31	7 38	7 46	7 55	8 05	8 17	18°
19°	6 00	6 14	6 29	6 46	7 07	7 21	7 37	7 45	7 53	8 03	8 14	8 26	19°
20°	6 00	6 15	6 30	6 49	7 11	7 25	7 43	7 51	8 00	8 11	8 22	8 36	20°
21°	6 00	6 16	6 32	6 51	7 15	7 30	7 49	7 58	8 08	8 19	8 32	8 47	21°
22°	6 00	6 16	6 34	6 54	7 19	7 35	7 55	8 05	8 15	8 27	8 41	8 58	22°
23°	6 00	6 17	6 36	6 57	7 23	7 40	8 02	8 12	8 23	8 36	8 51	9 09	23°
24°	6 00	6 18	6 37	7 00	7 28	7 46	8 08	8 19	8 31	8 45	9 02	9 22	24°
25°	6 00	6 19	6 39	7 02	7 32	7 51	8 15	8 27	8 40	8 55	9 13	9 35	25°
26°	6 00	6 20	6 41	7 05	7 37	7 57	8 22	8 35	8 49	9 05	9 25	9 51	26°
27°	6 00	6 21	6 43	7 08	7 41	8 03	8 30	8 43	8 58	9 16	9 39	10 08	27°
28°	6 00	6 22	6 45	7 12	7 46	8 08	8 37	8 52	9 08	9 28	9 53	10 28	28°
29°	6 00	6 22	6 47	7 15	7 51	8 15	8 45	9 01	9 19	9 41	10 10	10 55	29°
30°	6 00	6 23	6 49	7 18	7 56	8 21	8 54	9 11	9 30	9 55	10 30	12 00	30°
35°	6 00	6 28	6 59	7 35	8 24	8 58	9 46	10 15	10 58	12 00	12 00	12 00	35°
40°	6 00	6 34	7 11	7 56	8 59	9 48	12 00	12 00	12 00	12 00	12 00	12 00	40°
45°	6 00	6 41	7 25	8 21	9 48	12 00	12 00	12 00	12 00	12 00	12 00	12 00	45°
50°	6 00	6 49	7 43	8 54	12 00	12 00	12 00	12 00	12 00	12 00	12 00	12 00	50°
55°	6 00	6 58	8 05	9 42	12 00	12 00	12 00	12 00	12 00	12 00	12 00	12 00	55°
60°	6 00	7 11	8 36	12 00	12 00	12 00	12 00	12 00	12 00	12 00	12 00	12 00	60°
65°	6 00	7 29	9 25	12 00	12 00	12 00	12 00	12 00	12 00	12 00	12 00	12 00	65°
70°	6 00	7 56	12 00	12 00	12 00	12 00	12 00	12 00	12 00	12 00	12 00	12 00	70°
75°	6 00	8 45	12 00	12 00	12 00	12 00	12 00	12 00	12 00	12 00	12 00	12 00	75°
80°	6 00	12 00	12 00	12 00	12 00	12 00	12 00	12 00	12 00	12 00	12 00	12 00	80°

TABLE 2. CORRECTION FOR REFRACTION AND SEMI-DIAMETER

	m	m	m	m	m	m	m	m	m	m	m	m	
0°	3	3	4	4	4	5	5	5	6	6	6	7	0°
10°	3	3	4	4	4	5	5	6	6	6	7	7	10°
20°	4	4	4	4	5	5	6	7	7	8	8	9	20°
25°	4	4	4	4	5	6	7	8	8	9	11	13	25°
30°	4	4	4	5	6	7	8	9	11	14	21	—	30°

NB: Regarding Table 1. If latitude and declination are of the same sign, take out the respondent directly. If they are of opposite signs, subtract the respondent from 12h.
Example:

Lat.	Dec.	Semi-diurnal arc
+52°	+20°	7h 51m
+52°	−20°	4h 09m

SUNRISE AND SUNSET

The local mean time of sunrise or sunset may be found by obtaining the hour angle from Table 1 and applying it to the time of transit. The hour angle is negative for sunrise and positive for sunset. A small correction to the hour angle, which always has the effect of increasing it numerically, is necessary to allow for the Sun's semi-diameter (16′) and for refraction (34′); it is obtained from Table 2. The resulting local mean time may be converted into the standard time of the country by taking the difference between the longitude of the standard meridian of the country and that of the place, adding it to the local mean time if the place is west of the standard meridian, and subtracting it if the place is east.

Example– Required the New Zealand Mean Time (12h fast on GMT) of sunset on May 23 at Auckland, latitude 36° 50′ S. (or minus), longitude 11h 39m E. Taking the declination as +20°.6 (page 33), we find

	h	m
Tabular entry for Lat. 30° and Dec. 20°, opposite signs	+ 5	11
Proportional part for 6° 50′ of Lat.	−	15
Proportional part for 0°.6 of Dec.	−	2
Correction (Table 2)	+	4
Hour angle	4	58
Sun transits (page 33)	11	57
Longitudinal correction	+	21
New Zealand Mean Time	17	16

MOONRISE AND MOONSET

It is possible to calculate the times of moonrise and moonset using Table 1, though the method is more complicated because the apparent motion of the Moon is much more rapid and also more variable than that of the Sun.

The parallax of the Moon, about 57′, is near to the sum of the semi-diameter and refraction but has the opposite effect on these times. It is thus convenient to neglect all three quantities in the method outlined below.

TABLE 3. LONGITUDE CORRECTION

X A	40m	45m	50m	55m	60m	65m	70m
h	m	m	m	m	m	m	m
1	2	2	2	2	3	3	3
2	3	4	4	5	5	5	6
3	5	6	6	7	8	8	9
4	7	8	8	9	10	11	12
5	8	9	10	11	13	14	15
6	10	11	13	14	15	16	18
7	12	13	15	16	18	19	20
8	13	15	17	18	20	22	23
9	15	17	19	21	23	24	26
10	17	19	21	23	25	27	29
11	18	21	23	25	28	30	32
12	20	23	25	28	30	33	35
13	22	24	27	30	33	35	38
14	23	26	29	32	35	38	41
15	25	28	31	34	38	41	44
16	27	30	33	37	40	43	47
17	28	32	35	39	43	46	50
18	30	34	38	41	45	49	53
19	32	36	40	44	48	51	55
20	33	38	42	46	50	54	58
21	35	39	44	48	53	57	61
22	37	41	46	50	55	60	64
23	38	43	48	53	58	62	67
24	40	45	50	55	60	65	70

Notation

φ = latitude of observer
λ = longitude of observer (measured positively towards the west)
T_{-1} = time of transit of Moon on previous day
T_0 = time of transit of Moon on day in question
T_1 = time of transit of Moon on following day
δ_0 = approximate declination of Moon
δ_R = declination of Moon at moonrise
δ_S = declination of Moon at moonset
h_0 = approximate hour angle of Moon
h_R = hour angle of Moon at moonrise
h_S = hour angle of Moon at moonset
t_R = time of moonrise
t_S = time of moonset

Method

1. With arguments φ, δ_0 enter Table 1 on page 64 to determine h_0 where h_0 is negative for moonrise and positive for moonset.

2. Form approximate times from
$$t_R = T_0 + \lambda + h_0$$
$$t_S = T_0 + \lambda + h_0$$

3. Determine δ_R, δ_S for times t_R, t_S respectively.

4. Re-enter Table 1 on page 64 with
   (a) arguments φ, δ_R to determine h_R
   (b) arguments φ, δ_S to determine h_S

5. Form $t_R = T_0 + \lambda + h_R + AX$
   $$t_S = T_0 + \lambda + h_S + AX$$

where $A = (\lambda + h)$

and $X = (T_0 - T_{-1})$ if $(\lambda + h)$ is negative
$X = (T_1 - T_0)$ if $(\lambda + h)$ is positive

AX is the respondent in Table 3.

Example – To find the times of moonrise and moonset at Vancouver ($\varphi = +49°$, $\lambda = +8h\ 12m$) on 2000 March 4. The starting data (page 26) are

T_{-1} = 10h 07m
T_0 = 10h 55m
T_1 = 11h 43m
δ_0 = −15°

1. h_0 = 4h 48m
2. Approximate values
   t_R = 4d 10h 55m+8h 12m+(−4h 48m)
        = 4d 14h 19m
   t_S = 4d 10h 55m+8h 12m+(+4h 48m)
        = 4d 23h 55m
3. δ_R = −14°.8
   δ_S = −13°.6
4. h_R = −4h 49m
   h_S = +4h 55m
5. t_R = 4d 10h 55m+8h 12m+(−4h 49m)+7m
        = 4d 14h 25m
   t_S = 4d 10h 55m+8h 12m+(+4h 55m)+26m
        = 5d 00h 28m

To get the LMT of the phenomenon the longitude is subtracted from the GMT thus:
Moonrise = 4d 14h 25m−8h 12m = 4d 06h 13m
Moonset = 5d 00h 28m−8h 12m = 4d 16h 16m

ECLIPSES AND OCCULTATIONS 2000

ECLIPSES

There will be six eclipses in 2000, four of the Sun and two of the Moon. (Penumbral eclipses are not mentioned in this section as they are too difficult to observe.)

1. A total eclipse of the Moon on January 21 is visible from northern and western Asia, Asia Minor, Africa, Europe (including the British Isles), Iceland, Greenland, the Atlantic Ocean, the Arctic Ocean, the Americas and the Pacific Ocean (except the western part). The eclipse begins at 03h 01m and ends at 06h 26m. Totality lasts from 04h 04m to 05h 22m.

2. A partial eclipse of the Sun on February 5 is visible from the Southern Ocean and Antarctica. The eclipse begins at 10h 56m and ends at 14h 43m. At maximum eclipse 58 per cent of the Sun is obscured.

3. A partial eclipse of the Sun on July 1 is visible from the South Pacific Ocean and southern South America. The eclipse begins at 18h 07m and ends at 20h 58m. At maximum eclipse 48 per cent of the Sun is obscured.

4. A total eclipse of the Moon on July 16 is visible from southern South America, western North America, the Pacific Ocean, Antarctica, Australasia, Asia, the Indian Ocean, the Middle East, and south and east Africa. The eclipse begins at 11h 57m and ends at 15h 54m. Totality lasts from 13h 02m to 14h 49m.

5. A partial eclipse of the Sun on July 31 is visible from northern Scandinavia, Finland, northern Asia, northern Greenland, the Arctic Ocean, northern and western North America, and the North Pacific Ocean. The eclipse begins at 00h 37m and ends at 03h 49m. At maximum eclipse 60 per cent of the Sun is obscured.

6. A partial eclipse of the Sun on December 25 is visible from the north-eastern part of the Pacific Ocean, North and Central America, southern Greenland, the Caribbean and the North Atlantic Ocean, including the Azores. The eclipse begins at 15h 27m and ends at 19h 43m. At maximum eclipse 72 per cent of the Sun is obscured.

LUNAR OCCULTATIONS

Observations of the times of occultations are made by both amateur and professional astronomers. Such observations are later analysed to yield accurate positions of the Moon; this is one method of determining the difference between ephemeris time and universal time.

Many of the observations made by amateurs are obtained with the use of a stop-watch which is compared with a time-signal immediately after the observation. Thus an accuracy of about one-fifth of a second is obtainable, though the observer's personal equation may amount to one-third or one-half of a second.

The list on page 67 includes most of the occultations visible under favourable conditions in the British Isles. No occultation is included unless the star is at least 10° above the horizon and the Sun sufficiently far below the horizon to permit the star to be seen with the naked eye or with a small telescope. The altitude limit is reduced from 10° to 2° for stars and planets brighter than magnitude 2.0 and such occultations are also predicted in daylight.

The column Phase shows (i) whether a disappearance (D) or reappearance (R) is to be observed; and (ii) whether it is at the dark limb (D) or bright limb (B). The column headed 'El. of Moon' gives the elongation of the Moon from the Sun, in degrees. The elongation increases from 0° at New Moon to 180° at Full Moon and on to 360° (or 0°) at New Moon again. Times and position angles (P), reckoned from the north point in the direction north, east,

south, west, are given for Greenwich (lat. 51° 30′, long. 0°) and Edinburgh (lat. 56° 00′, long. 3° 12′ west).

The coefficients a and b are the variations in the GMT for each degree of longitude (positive to the west) and latitude (positive to the north) respectively; they enable approximate times (to within about 1m generally) to be found for any point in the British Isles. If the point of observation is $\Delta\lambda$ degrees west and $\Delta\phi$ degrees north, the approximate time is found by adding $a.\Delta\lambda + b.\Delta\phi$ to the given GMT.

Example: the disappearance of ZC 364 on February 11 at Coventry, found from both Greenwich and Edinburgh.

	Greenwich	Edinburgh
	°	°
Longitude	0.0	+3.2
Long. of Coventry	+1.5	+1.5
$\Delta\lambda$	+1.5	−1.7
Latitude	+51.5	+56.0
Lat. of Coventry	+52.4	+52.4
$\Delta\phi$	+0.9	−3.6
	h m	h m
GMT	20 09.6	20 01.2
$a.\Delta\lambda$	− 1.5	+ 1.5
$b.\Delta\phi$	− 1.3	+ 3.2
	20 06.8	20 05.9

If the occultation is given for one station but not the other, the reason for the suppression is given by the following code:

N = star not occulted

A = star's altitude less than 10° (2° for bright stars and planets)

S = Sun not sufficiently below the horizon

G = occultation is of very short duration

In some cases the coefficients a and b are not given; this is because the occultation is so short that prediction for other places by means of these coefficients would not be reliable.

LUNAR OCCULTATIONS 2000

Date		ZC No.	Mag.	Phase	El. of Moon	GREENWICH				EDINBURGH			
						UT	a	b	P	UT	a	b	P
					°	h m	m	m	°	h m	m	m	°
January	11	3419	4.5	D.D.	56	18 7.1	0.0	2.0	6	N			
	11	3425	4.6	D.D.	56	18 49.0	−1.1	−1.1	84	18 41.7	−0.9	−0.7	69
	15	405	4.4	D.D.	107	21 51.3	−0.8	1.1	29	21 57.6	G		4
	16	526	6.9	D.D.	120	20 23.3	−1.4	0.3	75	20 21.6	−1.1	0.8	60
	19	888	6.0	D.D.	150	1 34.0	−0.9	−0.6	66	1 29.2	−0.9	−0.2	54
	19	895	5.9	D.D.	151	2 37.3	−0.4	−1.4	93	2 29.7	−0.5	−1.3	84
	19	913	5.2	D.D.	152	S				5 43.9	0.3	−1.3	96
	25	1733	5.2	R.D.	234	S				6 59.9	−1.0	−1.3	260
	27	1950	5.8	R.D.	257	5 21.6	G		218	5 23.7	G		232
	30	2291	5.5	R.D.	292	S				6 57.0	−1.1	−0.2	307
February	11	364	4.3	D.D.	76	20 9.6	−1.0	−1.5	93	20 1.2	−0.9	−0.9	77
	12	491	6.2	D.D.	89	N				21 21.5	G		142
	13	627	6.8	D.D.	101	18 59.1	−1.5	0.3	78	18 57.4	−1.2	0.8	63
	13	636	6.9	D.D.	102	20 49.0	−1.2	0.2	57	20 47.9	−1.1	0.9	40
	13	650	5.7	D.D.	103	22 45.2	−0.9	0.5	37	22 47.1	G		16
	14	800	7.5	D.D.	115	21 50.2	−1.2	−1.9	115	21 39.7	−1.1	−1.1	100
	15	991	6.1	D.D.	130	24 0.2	−1.3	0.3	46	23 59.8	G		29
	16	995	4.1	D.D.	130	0 20.9	−0.6	−1.8	108	0 11.4	−0.7	−1.5	98
	16	1113	5.2	D.D.	141	19 24.2	−0.9	2.8	45	19 39.8	G		16
	16	1127	5.9	D.D.	142	21 46.6	−1.5	0.4	79	21 45.1	−1.3	1.0	65
	26	2223	4.0	R.D.	258	1 36.8	−0.2	−0.2	328	A			
March	10	453	7.3	D.D.	57	18 47.5	−1.1	−1.7	101	S			
	10	462	5.9	D.D.	59	21 8.9	0.0	−3.5	133	20 55.3	−0.3	−2.4	114
	11	618	7.2	D.D.	73	22 59.1	0.0	−1.4	91	22 52.8	−0.1	−1.3	82
	12	764	5.0	D.D.	85	22 16.3	−0.5	−1.4	89	22 8.8	−0.6	−1.2	79
	13	915	4.7	D.D.	97	20 27.4	−1.2	−1.4	106	20 18.6	−1.2	−0.8	93
	14	1077	3.7	D.D.	110	19 47.8	−1.5	−0.1	89	19 44.3	−1.3	0.5	75
	16	1245	7.5	D.D.	127	1 37.9	G		169	1 25.0	0.3	−2.9	159
April	9	888	6.0	D.D.	68	22 7.4	G		158	21 53.4	0.2	−3.0	142
	9	892	6.6	D.D.	69	22 19.4	−0.4	−0.4	49	22 16.3	−0.6	−0.2	38
	9	894	4.6	D.D.	69	22 43.1	−0.3	−0.6	54	22 39.5	−0.4	−0.5	45
	11	1193	5.4	D.D.	95	22 25.9	−0.7	−1.3	88	22 17.8	−0.8	−1.2	81
	12	1205	6.3	D.D.	96	0 51.6	G		34	0 51.9	G		19
	12	1321	6.7	D.D.	107	20 13.4	−1.4	−0.9	107	20 6.0	−1.3	−0.4	97
	13	1345	7.1	D.D.	110	1 47.0	0.3	−1.9	132	1 39.3	0.2	−1.9	129
May	8	1150	6.8	D.D.	64	N				21 15.6	G		168
	9	1310	4.2	D.D.	79	24 3.0	0.3	−1.7	121	23 56.2	0.2	−1.7	118
	22	2747	5.0	R.D.	221	1 15.4	G		203	1 20.0	G		211
	22	2749	5.0	R.D.	222	2 10.5	−1.8	0.9	235	A			
June	6	1387	6.8	D.D.	61	21 59.9	0.0	−1.7	113	S			
	8	1625	5.9	D.D.	88	N				23 36.0	G		191
	9	1741	7.2	D.D.	100	23 17.1	−0.4	−2.0	127	23 7.1	−0.4	−1.9	124
	12	2072	6.7	D.D.	135	23 9.3	−1.9	−0.3	56	23 2.2	G		51
July	10	2148	7.6	D.D.	118	22 32.8	−1.4	−0.5	52	22 26.0	G		46
	11	2271	4.3	D.D.	130	23 52.9	−1.0	−1.6	101	23 42.8	−1.0	−1.5	97
	22	18	6.0	R.D.	241	0 53.8	−0.7	2.2	213	1 1.0	−0.6	2.0	219
	29	Mercury	0.0	D.B.	341	17 42.5	0.3	−1.3	92	17 37.1	0.2	−1.4	88
August	11	2762	6.0	D.D.	144	21 57.0	−1.7	0.1	70	21 52.7	−1.5	0.2	65
	21	364	4.3	R.D.	249	3 35.1	−1.4	1.8	220	3 39.0	−1.0	1.4	232
September	1	1950	5.8	D.D.	45	19 16.7	−0.5	−1.8	108	S			
October	8	3197	6.5	D.D.	128	23 42.2	−1.2	−1.7	100	A			
	14	405	4.4	R.D.	201	23 10.8	−0.3	2.7	197	23 19.9	−0.5	2.1	211
	18	881	5.9	R.D.	243	S				5 49.1	−1.2	0.1	245
	21	1322	6.1	R.D.	282	5 17.9	−1.4	2.1	240	5 21.2	−1.2	1.3	257
November	13	648	3.9	R.D.	197	2 56.2	−1.1	1.6	211	2 57.0	−1.1	0.5	229
	13	658	4.2	R.D.	198	4 30.8	−0.8	−1.2	267	4 21.8	−0.8	−1.7	280
	16	1129	5.3	R.D.	236	1 32.2	G		196	1 48.3	−0.8	2.7	225
	18	1418	5.9	R.D.	265	6 4.9	G		220	6 8.0	−1.7	1.3	240
	30	2961	6.0	D.D.	53	18 42.2	−0.8	−0.9	66	A			
December	1	3078	4.9	D.D.	63	16 38.8	−1.0	1.0	27	16 40.6	−0.7	1.1	17
	4	3458	6.5	D.D.	96	17 19.2	−1.4	1.2	61	17 20.8	−1.1	1.2	54
	7	291	7.1	D.D.	134	21 49.4	−2.0	−1.4	107	21 40.6	−1.5	−0.3	90
	8	306	6.9	D.D.	136	1 29.7	−0.5	0.0	43	1 29.3	−0.4	0.6	26
	8	405	4.4	D.D.	144	17 19.5	−0.5	1.7	76	17 25.9	−0.4	1.8	69
	12	1047	5.2	R.D.	200	20 21.8	−0.1	1.9	241	20 29.6	−0.1	1.7	253
	31	3413	6.4	D.D.	65	18 0.1	−1.7	−0.9	92	17 52.4	−1.3	−0.4	79

MEAN PLACES OF STARS 2000.5

Name	Mag.	RA h m	Dec. ° '	Spectrum
α And Alpheratz	2.1	0 08.4	+29 06	A0p
β Cassiopeiae Caph	2.3	0 09.2	+59 09	F5
γ Pegasi Algenib	2.8	0 13.3	+15 11	B2
β Mensae	2.9	0 25.8	−77 15	G0
α Phoenicis	2.4	0 26.3	−42 18	K0
α Cassiopeiae Schedar	2.2	0 40.5	+56 32	K0
β Ceti Diphda	2.0	0 43.6	−17 59	K0
γ Cassiopeiae*	Var.	0 56.7	+60 43	B0p
β Andromedae Mirach	2.1	1 09.8	+35 37	M0
δ Cassiopeiae	2.7	1 25.8	+60 14	A5
α Eridani Achernar	0.5	1 37.7	−57 14	B5
β Arietis Sheratan	2.6	1 54.7	+20 49	A5
γ Andromedae Almak	2.3	2 03.9	+42 20	K0
α Arietis Hamal	2.0	2 07.2	+23 28	K2
α Ursae Minoris Polaris	2.0	2 32.4	+89 16	F8
β Persei Algol*	Var.	3 08.2	+40 57	B8
α Persei Mirfak	1.8	3 24.4	+49 52	F5
η Tauri Alcyone	2.9	3 47.5	+24 06	B5p
α Tauri Aldebaran	0.9	4 35.9	+16 31	K5
β Orionis Rigel	0.1	5 14.6	− 8 12	B8p
α Aurigae Capella	0.1	5 16.7	+46 00	G0
γ Orionis Bellatrix	1.6	5 25.2	+ 6 21	B2
β Tauri Elnath	1.7	5 26.3	+28 36	B8
δ Orionis	2.2	5 32.0	− 0 18	B0
α Leporis	2.6	5 32.8	−17 49	F0
ε Orionis	1.7	5 36.2	− 1 12	B0
ζ Orionis	1.8	5 40.8	− 1 57	B0
κ Orionis	2.1	5 47.8	− 9 40	B0
α Orionis Betelgeuse*	Var.	5 55.2	+ 7 24	M0
β Aurigae Menkalinan	1.9	5 59.6	+44 57	A0p
β CMa Mirzam	2.0	6 22.7	−17 57	B1
α Carinae Canopus	−0.7	6 24.0	−52 42	F0
γ Geminorum Alhena	1.9	6 37.7	+16 24	A0
α Canis Majoris Sirius	−1.5	6 45.2	−16 43	A0
ε Canis Majoris	1.5	6 58.6	−28 58	B1
δ Canis Majoris	1.9	7 08.4	−26 24	F8p
α Geminorum Castor	1.6	7 34.6	+31 53	A0
α CMi Procyon	0.4	7 39.3	+ 5 13	F5
β Geminorum Pollux	1.1	7 45.3	+28 02	K0
ζ Puppis	2.3	8 03.6	−40 00	Od
γ Velorum	1.8	8 09.5	−47 20	Oap
ε Carinae	1.9	8 22.5	−59 31	K0
δ Velorum	2.0	8 44.7	−54 43	A0
λ Velorum Suhail	2.2	9 08.0	−43 26	K5
β Carinae	1.7	9 13.2	−69 43	A0
ι Carinae	2.2	9 17.1	−59 17	F0
κ Velorum	2.6	9 22.1	−55 01	B3
α Hydrae Alphard	2.0	9 27.6	− 8 40	K2
α Leonis Regulus	1.3	10 08.4	+11 58	B8
γ Leonis Algeiba	1.9	10 20.0	+19 50	K0
β Ursae Majoris Merak	2.4	11 01.9	+56 23	A0
α Ursae Majoris Dubhe	1.8	11 03.8	+61 45	K0
δ Leonis	2.6	11 14.1	+20 31	A3
β Leonis Denebola	2.1	11 49.1	+14 34	A2
γ Ursae Majoris Phecda	2.4	11 53.9	+53 42	A0
γ Corvi	2.6	12 15.8	−17 33	B8
α Crucis	1.0	12 26.6	−63 06	B1
γ Crucis	1.6	12 31.2	−57 07	M3
γ Centauri	2.2	12 41.5	−48 58	A0
γ Virginis	2.7	12 41.7	− 1 27	F0
β Crucis	1.3	12 47.8	−59 41	B1
ε Ursae Majoris Alioth	1.8	12 54.1	+55 57	A0p
α Canum Venaticorum	2.9	12 56.1	+38 19	A0p
ζ Ursae Majoris Mizar	2.1	13 23.9	+54 55	A2p
α Virginis Spica	1.0	13 25.2	−11 10	B2
ε Centauri	2.6	13 39.9	−53 28	B1
η Ursae Majoris Alkaid	1.9	13 47.6	+49 19	B3
β Centauri Hadar	0.6	14 03.9	−60 23	B1
θ Centauri	2.1	14 06.7	−36 22	K0
α Bootis Arcturus	0.0	14 15.7	+19 11	K0
α Centauri Rigil Kent	0.1	14 39.6	−60 50	G0
ε Bootis	2.4	14 45.0	+27 04	K0
β UMi Kochab	2.1	14 50.7	+74 09	K5
γ Ursae Minoris	3.1	15 20.7	+71 50	A2
α CrB Alphecca	2.2	15 34.7	+26 43	A0
β Trianguli Australis	3.0	15 55.2	−63 26	F0
δ Scorpii	2.3	16 00.4	−22 37	B0
β Scorpii	2.6	16 05.5	−19 48	B1
α Scorpii Antares	1.0	16 29.4	−26 26	M0
α Trianguli Australis	1.9	16 48.7	−69 02	K2
ε Scorpii	2.3	16 50.2	−34 18	K0
α Herculis†	Var.	17 14.7	+14 23	M3
λ Scorpii	1.6	17 33.6	−37 06	B2
α Ophiuchi Rasalhague	2.1	17 35.0	+12 34	A5
θ Scorpii	1.9	17 37.4	−43 00	F0
κ Scorpii	2.4	17 42.5	−39 02	B2
γ Draconis	2.2	17 56.6	+51 29	K5
ε Sgr Kaus Australis	1.9	18 24.2	−34 23	A0
α Lyrae Vega	0.0	18 37.0	+38 47	A0
σ Sagittarii	2.0	18 55.3	−26 18	B3
β Cygni Albireo	3.1	19 30.7	+27 58	K0
α Aquilae Altair	0.8	19 50.8	+ 8 52	A5
α Capricorni	3.8	20 18.1	−12 33	G5
γ Cygni	2.2	20 22.2	+40 16	F8p
α Pavonis	1.9	20 25.7	−56 44	B3
α Cygni Deneb	1.3	20 41.4	+45 17	A2p
α Cephei Alderamin	2.4	21 18.6	+62 35	A5
ε Pegasi	2.4	21 44.2	+ 9 53	K0
δ Capricorni	2.9	21 47.1	−16 07	A5
α Gruis	1.7	22 08.3	−46 58	B5
δ Cephei†	3.7	22 29.2	+58 25	†
β Gruis	2.1	22 42.7	−46 53	M3
α PsA Fomalhaut	1.2	22 57.7	−29 37	A3
β Pegasi Scheat	2.4	23 03.8	+28 05	M0
α Pegasi Markab	2.5	23 04.8	+15 12	A0

*γ Cassiopeiae, 1999 mag. 2.5. β Persei, mag. 2.1 to 3.4. α Orionis, mag. 0.1 to 1.2.

†α Herculis, mag. 3.1 to 3.9. δ Cephei, mag. 3.7 to 4.4, spectrum F5 to G0.

The positions of heavenly bodies on the celestial sphere are defined by two co-ordinates, right ascension and declination, which are analogous to longitude and latitude on the surface of the Earth. If we imagine the plane of the terrestrial equator extended indefinitely, it will cut the celestial sphere in a great circle known as the celestial equator. Similarly the plane of the Earth's orbit, when extended, cuts in the great circle called the ecliptic. The two intersections of these circles are known as the First Point of Aries and the First Point of Libra. If from any star a perpendicular be drawn to the celestial equator, the length of this perpendicular is the star's declination. The arc, measured eastwards along the equator from the First Point of Aries to the foot of this perpendicular, is the right ascension. An alternative definition of right ascension is that it is the angle at the celestial pole (where the Earth's axis, if prolonged, would meet the sphere) between the great circles to the First Point of Aries and to the star.

The plane of the Earth's equator has a slow movement, so that our reference system for right ascension and declination is not fixed. The consequent alteration in these quantities from year to year is called precession. In right ascension it is an increase of about 3 seconds a year for equatorial stars, and larger or smaller changes in either direction for stars near the poles, depending on the right ascension of the star. In declination it varies between +20″ and −20″ according to the right ascension of the star.

A star or other body crosses the meridian when the sidereal time is equal to its right ascension. The altitude is then a maximum, and may be deduced by remembering that the altitude of the elevated pole is numerically equal to the latitude, while that of the equator at its intersection with the meridian is equal to the co-latitude, or complement of the latitude.

Thus in London (lat. 51° 30′) the meridian altitude of Sirius is found as follows:

	°	′
Altitude of equator	38	30
Declination south	16	43
Difference	21	47

The altitude of Capella (Dec. +46° 00′) at lower transit is:

	°	′
Altitude of pole	51	30
Polar distance of star	44	00
Difference	7	30

The brightness of a heavenly body is denoted by its magnitude. Omitting the exceptionally bright stars Sirius and Canopus, the twenty brightest stars are of the first magnitude, while the faintest stars visible to the naked eye are of the sixth magnitude. The magnitude scale is a precise one, as a difference of five magnitudes represents a ratio of 100 to 1 in brightness. Typical second magnitude stars are Polaris and the stars in the belt of Orion. The scale is most easily fixed in memory by comparing the stars with Norton's *Star Atlas* (*see* page 71). The stars Sirius and Canopus and the planets Venus and Jupiter are so bright that their magnitudes are expressed by negative numbers. A small telescope will show stars down to the ninth or tenth magnitude, while stars fainter than the twentieth magnitude may be photographed by long exposures with the largest telescopes.

MEAN AND SIDEREAL TIME

Acceleration				Retardation			
h	m s	m s	s	h	m s	m s	s
1	0 10	0 00	0	1	0 10	0 00	0
2	0 20	3 02	1	2	0 20	3 03	1
3	0 30	9 07	2	3	0 29	9 09	2
4	0 39	15 13	3	4	0 39	15 15	3
5	0 49	21 18	4	5	0 49	21 21	4
6	0 59	27 23	5	6	0 59	27 28	5
7	1 09	33 28	6	7	1 09	33 34	6
8	1 19	39 34	7	8	1 19	39 40	7
9	1 29	45 39	8	9	1 28	45 46	8
10	1 39	51 44	9	10	1 38	51 53	9
11	1 48	57 49	10	11	1 48	57 59	10
12	1 58	60 00		12	1 58	60 00	
13	2 08			13	2 08		
14	2 18			14	2 18		
15	2 28			15	2 27		
16	2 38			16	2 37		
17	2 48			17	2 47		
18	2 57			18	2 57		
19	3 07			19	3 07		
20	3 17			20	3 17		
21	3 27			21	3 26		
22	3 37			22	3 36		
23	3 47			23	3 46		
24	3 57			24	3 56		

The length of a sidereal day in mean time is 23h 56m 04s.09. Hence 1h MT = 1h+9s.86 ST and 1h ST = 1h−9s.83 MT.

To convert an interval of mean time to the corresponding interval of sidereal time, enter the acceleration table with the given mean time (taking the hours and the minutes and seconds separately) and add the acceleration obtained to the given mean time. To convert an interval of sidereal time to the corresponding interval of mean time, take out the retardation for the given sidereal time and subtract.

The columns for the minutes and seconds of the argument are in the form known as critical tables. To use these tables, find in the appropriate left-hand column the two entries between which the given number of minutes and seconds lies; the quantity in the right-hand column between these two entries is the required acceleration or retardation. Thus the acceleration for 11m 26s (which lies between the entries 9m 07s and 15m 13s) is 2s. If the given number of minutes and seconds is a tabular entry, the required acceleration or retardation is the entry in the right-hand column above the given tabular entry, e.g. the retardation for 45m 46s is 7s.

Example – Convert 14h 27m 35s from ST to MT

	h	m	s
Given ST	14	27	35
Retardation for 14h		2	18
Retardation for 27m 35s			5
Corresponding MT	14	25	12

For further explanation, *see* pages 73–4.

ECLIPSES AND SHADOW TRANSITS OF JUPITER'S SATELLITES 2000

GMT			Sat.	Phen.
d	h	m		

JANUARY

d	h	m	Sat.	Phen.
6	20	08	II	Ec.D
7	18	21	I	Sh.I
7	20	30	I	Sh.E
8	17	46	I	Ec.R
14	20	18	I	Sh.I
15	17	56	III	Sh.I
15	19	42	I	Ec.R
15	19	57	II	Sh.E
15	19	58	III	Sh.E
22	20	04	II	Sh.I
23	18	52	I	Sh.E
30	18	39	I	Sh.I
31	19	58	II	Ec.R

FEBRUARY

d	h	m	Sat.	Phen.
7	19	57	I	Ec.R
7	20	04	II	Ec.D
9	19	55	III	Ec.D

JUNE

d	h	m	Sat.	Phen.
25	02	21	III	Ec.R

JULY

d	h	m	Sat.	Phen.
1	02	03	I	Sh.E
8	01	48	I	Sh.I
13	00	32	III	Sh.E
14	23	57	II	Sh.I
15	02	30	II	Sh.E
16	00	52	I	Ec.D
17	00	19	I	Sh.E
20	02	37	III	Sh.I
22	02	35	II	Sh.I
23	02	46	I	Ec.D
24	00	04	I	Sh.I
24	02	13	I	Sh.E
30	23	58	II	Ec.D
31	01	58	I	Sh.I
31	23	09	I	Ec.D

AUGUST

d	h	m	Sat.	Phen.
1	22	35	I	Sh.E
7	00	28	III	Ec.D
7	02	24	III	Ec.R
7	02	32	II	Ec.D
8	01	03	I	Ec.D
8	22	20	I	Sh.I
8	23	41	II	Sh.E
9	00	29	I	Sh.E
15	02	57	I	Ec.D
15	23	45	II	Sh.I
16	00	14	I	Sh.I
16	02	18	II	Sh.E
16	02	22	I	Sh.E
23	02	07	I	Sh.I
23	02	22	II	Sh.I
23	23	20	I	Ec.D
24	22	37	III	Sh.I
24	22	44	I	Sh.E
24	23	30	II	Ec.R
25	00	32	III	Sh.E
30	04	01	I	Sh.I
31	01	14	I	Ec.D
31	22	29	I	Sh.I
31	23	31	II	Ec.D

SEPTEMBER

d	h	m	Sat.	Phen.
1	00	38	I	Sh.E
1	02	04	II	Ec.R
1	02	36	III	Sh.I
2	20	51	II	Sh.E
7	03	08	I	Ec.D
8	00	23	I	Sh.I
8	02	05	II	Ec.D
8	02	31	I	Sh.E
8	04	39	II	Ec.R
8	21	37	I	Ec.D
9	20	54	II	Sh.I
9	20	59	I	Sh.I
9	23	28	II	Sh.E
11	20	28	III	Ec.D
11	22	26	III	Ec.R
15	02	16	I	Sh.I
15	04	25	I	Sh.E
15	04	39	II	Ec.D
15	23	31	I	Ec.D
16	20	45	I	Sh.I
16	22	53	I	Sh.E
16	23	31	II	Sh.I
17	02	05	II	Sh.E
18	20	30	II	Ec.R
19	00	28	III	Ec.D
19	02	27	III	Ec.R
22	04	10	I	Sh.I
23	01	25	I	Ec.D
23	22	38	I	Sh.I
24	00	47	I	Sh.E
24	02	08	II	Sh.I
24	04	42	II	Sh.E
24	19	54	I	Sh.E
25	19	15	I	Sh.E
25	20	30	II	Ec.D
26	04	28	III	Ec.D
29	20	32	III	Sh.E
30	03	19	I	Ec.D

OCTOBER

d	h	m	Sat.	Phen.
1	00	31	I	Sh.I
1	02	40	I	Sh.E
1	21	48	I	Ec.D
2	19	00	I	Sh.I
2	21	09	I	Sh.E
2	23	04	II	Sh.E
4	20	38	II	Sh.E
6	22	33	III	Sh.I
7	00	32	III	Sh.E
8	02	25	I	Sh.I
8	23	42	I	Ec.D
9	20	53	I	Sh.I
9	23	02	I	Sh.E
10	01	39	II	Sh.I
11	20	40	II	Sh.I
11	23	14	II	Sh.E
14	02	33	III	Sh.I
16	01	37	I	Ec.D
16	22	47	I	Sh.I
17	00	56	I	Sh.E
17	18	29	III	Ec.R
17	20	05	I	Ec.D
18	19	25	I	Sh.E
18	23	16	II	Sh.I
19	01	51	II	Sh.E
24	00	41	I	Sh.I
24	02	50	I	Sh.E
24	20	28	III	Ec.D
24	21	59	I	Ec.D
24	22	30	III	Ec.R
25	19	09	I	Sh.I
25	21	19	I	Sh.E
26	01	53	II	Sh.I
27	20	05	II	Ec.D
31	02	34	I	Sh.I
31	23	54	I	Ec.D

NOVEMBER

d	h	m	Sat.	Phen.
1	00	28	III	Ec.D
1	21	03	I	Sh.I
1	23	13	I	Sh.E
2	18	22	I	Ec.D
3	22	40	II	Ec.D
5	17	47	II	Sh.I
5	20	23	II	Sh.E
8	01	48	I	Ec.D
8	22	57	I	Sh.I
9	01	07	I	Sh.E
9	20	17	I	Ec.D
10	19	36	I	Sh.E
11	01	16	II	Ec.D
11	18	31	III	Sh.I
11	20	34	III	Sh.E
12	20	24	II	Sh.I
12	23	00	II	Sh.E
16	00	51	I	Sh.I
16	22	11	I	Ec.D
17	19	20	I	Sh.I
17	21	30	I	Sh.E
18	22	31	III	Sh.I
19	00	35	III	Sh.E
19	23	00	II	Sh.I
24	00	06	I	Ec.D
24	21	14	I	Sh.I
24	23	25	I	Sh.E
25	18	35	I	Ec.D
26	17	53	I	Sh.E
28	22	22	II	Ec.R
29	18	35	III	Ec.R
30	17	31	II	Sh.E

DECEMBER

d	h	m	Sat.	Phen.
1	23	09	I	Sh.I
2	22	40	I	Ec.R
3	17	37	I	Sh.I
3	19	48	I	Sh.E
6	22	36	III	Ec.R
7	17	32	II	Sh.I
7	20	08	II	Sh.E
10	19	32	I	Sh.I
10	21	43	I	Sh.E
11	19	04	I	Ec.R
14	20	08	II	Sh.I
14	22	44	II	Sh.E
17	21	27	I	Sh.I
18	20	59	I	Ec.R
19	18	07	I	Sh.E
21	22	45	II	Sh.I
23	19	31	II	Ec.R
24	18	34	III	Sh.I
24	20	41	III	Sh.E
25	22	54	I	Ec.R
26	17	51	I	Sh.I
26	20	02	I	Sh.E
30	22	08	II	Ec.R

Jupiter's satellites transit across the disk from east to west, and pass behind the disk from west to east. The shadows that they cast also transit across the disk. With the exception at times of Satellite IV, the satellites also pass through the shadow of the planet, i.e. they are eclipsed. Just before opposition the satellite disappears in the shadow to the west of the planet and reappears from occultation on the east limb. Immediately after opposition the satellite is occulted at the west limb and reappears from eclipse to the east of the planet. At times approximately two to four months before and after opposition, both phases of eclipses of Satellite III may be seen. When Satellite IV is eclipsed, both phases may be seen.

The times given refer to the centre of the satellite. As the satellite is of considerable size, the immersion and emersion phases are not instantaneous. Even when the satellite enters or leaves the shadow along a radius of the shadow, the phase can last for several minutes. With Satellite IV, grazing phenomena can occur so that the light from the satellite may fade and brighten again without a complete eclipse taking place.

The list of phenomena gives most of the eclipses and shadow transits visible in the British Isles under favourable conditions.

Ec. = Eclipse	R. = Reappearance
Sh. = Shadow transit	I. = Ingress
D. = Disappearance	E. = Egress

EXPLANATION OF ASTRONOMICAL DATA

Positions of the heavenly bodies are given only to the degree of accuracy required by amateur astronomers for setting telescopes, or for plotting on celestial globes or star atlases. Where intermediate positions are required, linear interpolation may be employed.

Definitions of the terms used cannot be given here. They must be sought in astronomical literature and textbooks. Probably the best source for the amateur is Norton's *Star Atlas and Reference Handbook* (Longman, 18th edition, 1989; £26.99), which contains an introduction to observational astronomy, and a series of star maps showing stars visible to the naked eye. Certain more extended ephemerides are available in the British Astronomical Association Handbook, an annual popular among amateur astronomers (Secretary: Burlington House, Piccadilly, London WIV 9AG).

A special feature has been made of the times when the various heavenly bodies are visible in the British Isles. Since two columns, calculated for latitudes 52° and 56°, are devoted to risings and settings, the range 50° to 58° can be covered by interpolation and extrapolation. The times given in these columns are Greenwich Mean Times for the meridian of Greenwich. An observer west of this meridian must add his/her longitude (in time) and vice versa.

In accordance with the usual convention in astronomy, + and − indicate respectively north and south latitudes or declinations.

All data are, unless otherwise stated, for 0h Greenwich Mean Time (GMT), i.e. at the midnight at the beginning of the day named. Allowance must be made for British Summer Time during the period that this is in operation (*see* pages 15 and 75).

PAGE ONE OF EACH MONTH

The calendar for each month is explained on page 15.

Under the heading Astronomical Phenomena will be found particulars of the more important conjunctions of the Sun, Moon and planets with each other, and also the dates of other astronomical phenomena of special interest.

Times of Minima of Algol are approximate times of the middle of the period of diminished light.

The Constellations listed each month are those that are near the meridian at the beginning of the month at 22h local mean time. Allowance must be made for British Summer Time if necessary. The fact that any star crosses the meridian 4m earlier each night or 2h earlier each month may be used, in conjunction with the lists given each month, to find what constellations are favourably placed at any moment. The table preceding the list of constellations may be extended indefinitely at the rate just quoted.

The principal phases of the Moon are the GMTs when the difference between the longitude of the Moon and that of the Sun is 0°, 90°, 180° or 270°. The times of perigee and apogee are those when the Moon is nearest to, and farthest from, the Earth, respectively. The nodes or points of intersection of the Moon's orbit and the ecliptic make a complete retrograde circuit of the ecliptic in about 19 years. From a knowledge of the longitude of the ascending node and the inclination, whose value does not vary much from 5°, the path of the Moon among the stars may be plotted on a celestial globe or star atlas.

PAGE TWO OF EACH MONTH

The Sun's semi-diameter, in arc, is given once a month.

The right ascension and declination (Dec.) is that of the true Sun. The right ascension of the mean Sun is obtained by applying the equation of time, with the sign given, to the right ascension of the true Sun, or, more easily, by applying 12h to the Sidereal Time. The direction in which the equation of time has to be applied in different problems is a frequent source of confusion and error. Apparent Solar Time is equal to the Mean Solar Time plus the Equation of Time. For example, at noon on August 8 the Equation of Time is −5m 34s and thus at 12h Mean Time on that day the Apparent Time is 12h −5m 34s = 11h 54m 26s.

The Greenwich Sidereal Time at 0h and the Transit of the First Point of Aries (which is really the mean time when the sidereal time is 0h) are used for converting mean time to sidereal time and vice versa.

The GMT of transit of the Sun at Greenwich may also be taken as the local mean time (LMT) of transit in any longitude. It is independent of latitude. The GMT of transit in any longitude is obtained by adding the longitude to the time given if west, and vice versa.

LIGHTING-UP TIME

The legal importance of sunrise and sunset is that the Road Vehicles Lighting Regulations 1989 (SI 1989 No. 1796) make the use of front and rear position lamps on vehicles compulsory during the period between sunset and sunrise. Headlamps on vehicles are required to be used during the hours of darkness on unlit roads or whenever visibility is seriously reduced. The hours of darkness are defined in these regulations as the period between half an hour after sunset and half an hour before sunrise.

In all laws and regulations 'sunset' refers to the local sunset, i.e. the time at which the Sun sets at the place in question. This common-sense interpretation has been upheld by legal tribunals. Thus the necessity for providing for different latitudes and longitudes, as already described, is evident.

SUNRISE AND SUNSET

The times of sunrise and sunset are those when the Sun's upper limb, as affected by refraction, is on the true horizon of an observer at sea-level. Assuming the mean refraction to be 34′, and the Sun's semi-diameter to be 16′, the time given is that when the true zenith distance of the Sun's centre is 90° + 34′ + 16′ or 90° 50′, or, in other words, when the depression of the Sun's centre below the true horizon is 50′. The upper limb is then 34′ below the true horizon, but is brought there by refraction. An observer on a ship might see the Sun for a minute or so longer, because of the dip of the horizon, while another viewing the sunset over hills or mountains would record an earlier time. Nevertheless, the moment when the true zenith distance of the Sun's centre is 90° 50′ is a precise time dependent only on the latitude and longitude of the place, and independent of its altitude above sea-level, the contour of its horizon, the vagaries of refraction or the small seasonal change in the Sun's semi-diameter; this moment is suitable in every way as a definition of sunset (or sunrise) for all statutory purposes. (For further information, *see* footnote on page 72.)

TWILIGHT

Light reaches us before sunrise and continues to reach us for some time after sunset. The interval between darkness and sunrise or sunset and darkness is called twilight. Astronomically speaking, twilight is considered to begin or end when the Sun's centre is 18° below the horizon, as no light from the Sun can then reach the observer. As thus defined twilight may last several hours; in high latitudes at the summer solstice the depression of 18° is not reached, and twilight lasts from sunset to sunrise.

The need for some sub-division of twilight is met by dividing the gathering darkness into four stages.

(1) *Sunrise or Sunset*, defined as above
(2) *Civil twilight*, which begins or ends when the Sun's centre is 6° below the horizon. This marks the time when operations requiring daylight may commence or must cease. In England it varies from about 30 to 60 minutes after sunset and the same interval before sunrise
(3) *Nautical twilight*, which begins or ends when the Sun's centre is 12° below the horizon. This marks the time when it is, to all intents and purposes, completely dark
(4) *Astronomical twilight*, which begins or ends when the Sun's centre is 18° below the horizon. This marks theoretical perfect darkness. It is of little practical importance, especially if nautical twilight is tabulated

To assist observers the durations of civil, nautical and astronomical twilights are given at intervals of ten days. The beginning of a particular twilight is found by subtracting the duration from the time of sunrise, while the end is found by adding the duration to the time of sunset. Thus the beginning of astronomical twilight in latitude 52°, on the Greenwich meridian, on March 11 is found as 06h 23m−113m = 04h 30m and similarly the end of civil twilight is 17h 58m+34m = 18h 32m. The letters TAN (twilight all night) are printed when twilight lasts all night.

Under the heading The Night Sky will be found notes describing the position and visibility of the planets and other phenomena.

PAGE THREE OF EACH MONTH

The Moon moves so rapidly among the stars that its position is given only to the degree of accuracy that permits linear interpolation. The right ascension (RA) and declination (Dec.) are geocentric, i.e. for an imaginary observer at the centre of the Earth. To an observer on the surface of the Earth the position is always different, as the altitude is always less on account of parallax, which may reach 1°.

The lunar terminator is the line separating the bright from the dark part of the Moon's disk. Apart from irregularities of the lunar surface, the terminator is elliptical, because it is a circle seen in projection. It becomes the full circle forming the limb, or edge, of the Moon at New and Full Moon. The selenographic longitude of the terminator is measured from the mean centre of the visible disk, which may differ from the visible centre by as much as 8°, because of libration.

Instead of the longitude of the terminator the Sun's selenographic co-longitude (Sun's co-long.) is tabulated. It is numerically equal to the selenographic longitude of the morning terminator, measured eastwards from the mean centre of the disk. Thus its value is approximately 270° at New Moon, 360° at First Quarter, 90° at Full Moon and 180° at Last Quarter.

The Position Angle (PA) of the Bright Limb is the position angle of the midpoint of the illuminated limb, measured eastwards from the north point on the disk. The Phase column shows the percentage of the area of the Moon's disk illuminated; this is also the illuminated percentage of the diameter at right angles to the line of cusps. The terminator is a semi-ellipse whose major axis is the line of cusps, and whose semi-minor axis is determined by the tabulated percentage; from New Moon to Full Moon the east limb is dark, and vice versa.

The times given as moonrise and moonset are those when the upper limb of the Moon is on the horizon for an observer at sea-level. The Sun's horizontal parallax (Hor. par.) is about 9″, and is negligible when considering sunrise and sunset, but that of the Moon averages about 57′. Hence the computed time represents the moment when the true zenith distance of the Moon is 90° 50′ (as for the Sun) minus the horizontal parallax. The time required for the Sun or Moon to rise or set is about four minutes (except in high latitudes). *See also* page 65 and footnote below.

The GMT of transit of the Moon over the meridian of Greenwich is given; these times are independent of latitude but must be corrected for longitude. For places in the British Isles it suffices to add the longitude if west, and vice versa. For other places a further correction is necessary because of the rapid movement of the Moon relative to the stars. The entire correction is conveniently determined by first finding the west longitude λ of the place. If the place is in west longitude, λ is the ordinary west longitude; if the place is in east longitude λ is the complement to 24h (or 360°) of the longitude and will be greater than 12h (or 180°). The correction then consists of two positive portions, namely λ and the fraction $\lambda/24$ (or $\lambda°/360$) multiplied by the difference between consecutive transits. Thus for Christchurch, New Zealand, the longitude is 11h 31m east, so $\lambda = 12$h 29m and the fraction $\lambda/24$ is 0.52. The transit on the local date 2000 June 17 is found as follows:

		d	h	m
GMT of transit at Greenwich	June	17	00	04
λ			12	29
0.52×(24h 04m−23h 16m)				25
GMT of transit at Christchurch		17	12	58
Corr. to NZ Standard Time			12	00
Local standard time of transit		18	00	58

As is evident, for any given place the quantities λ and the correction to local standard time may be combined permanently, being here 24h 29m.

Positions of Mercury are given for every second day, and those of Venus and Mars for every fifth day; they may be interpolated linearly. The diameter (Diam.) is given in seconds of arc. The phase is the illuminated percentage of the disk. In the case of the inner planets this approaches 100 at superior conjunction and 0 at inferior conjunction. When the phase is less than 50 the planet is crescent-shaped or horned; for greater phases it is gibbous. In the case of the exterior planet Mars, the phase approaches 100 at conjunction and opposition, and is a minimum at the quadratures.

Since the planets cannot be seen when on the horizon, the actual times of rising and setting are not given; instead, the time when the planet has an apparent altitude of 5°

has been tabulated. If the time of transit is between 00h and 12h the time refers to an altitude of 5° above the eastern horizon; if between 12h and 24h, to the western horizon. The phenomenon tabulated is the one that occurs between sunset and sunrise. The times given may be interpolated for latitude and corrected for longitude, as in the case of the Sun and Moon.

The GMT at which the planet transits the Greenwich meridian is also given. The times of transit are to be corrected to local meridians in the usual way, as already described.

PAGE FOUR OF EACH MONTH

The GMTs of sunrise and sunset for seven cities, whose adopted positions in longitude (W.) and latitude (N.) are given immediately below the name, may be used not only for these phenomena, but also for lighting-up times (*see* page 71 for a fuller explanation).

The particulars for the four outer planets resemble those for the planets on Page Three of each month, except that, under Uranus and Neptune, times when the planet is 10° high instead of 5° high are given; this is because of the inferior brightness of these planets. The diameters given for the rings of Saturn are those of the major axis (in the plane of the planet's equator) and the minor axis respectively. The former has a small seasonal change due to the slightly varying distance of the Earth from Saturn, but the latter varies from zero when the Earth passes through the ring plane every 15 years to its maximum opening half-way between these periods. The rings were last open at their widest extent (and Saturn at its brightest) in 1988; this will occur again in 2002. The Earth passed through the ring plane in 1995–6 and will do so again in 2009.

TIME

From the earliest ages, the natural division of time into recurring periods of day and night has provided the practical time-scale for the everyday activities of the human race. Indeed, if any alternative means of time measurement is adopted, it must be capable of adjustment so as to remain in general agreement with the natural time-scale defined by the diurnal rotation of the Earth on its axis. Ideally the rotation should be measured against a fixed frame of reference; in practice it must be measured against the background provided by the celestial bodies. If the Sun is chosen as the reference point, we obtain Apparent Solar Time, which is the time indicated by a sundial. It is not a uniform time but is subject to variations which amount to as much as a quarter of an hour in each direction. Such wide variations cannot be tolerated in a practical time-scale, and this has led to the concept of Mean Solar Time in which all the days are exactly the same length and equal to the average length of the Apparent Solar Day.

The positions of the stars in the sky are specified in relation to a fictitious reference point in the sky known as the First Point of Aries (or the Vernal Equinox). It is therefore convenient to adopt this same reference point when considering the rotation of the Earth against the background of the stars. The time-scale so obtained is known as Apparent Sidereal Time.

GREENWICH MEAN TIME

The daily rotation of the Earth on its axis causes the Sun and the other heavenly bodies to appear to cross the sky from east to west. It is convenient to represent this relative motion as if the Sun really performed a daily circuit around a fixed Earth. Noon in Apparent Solar Time may then be defined as the time at which the Sun transits across the observer's meridian. In Mean Solar Time, noon is similarly defined by the meridian transit of a fictitious Mean Sun moving uniformly in the sky with the same average speed as the true Sun. Mean Solar Time observed on the meridian of the transit circle telescope of the Old Royal Observatory at Greenwich is called Greenwich Mean Time (GMT). The mean solar day is divided into 24 hours and, for astronomical and other scientific purposes, these are numbered 0 to 23, commencing at midnight. Civil time is usually reckoned in two periods of 12 hours, designated a.m. (*ante meridiem*, i.e. before noon) and p.m. (*post meridiem*, i.e. after noon).

UNIVERSAL TIME

Before 1925 January 1, GMT was reckoned in 24 hours commencing at noon; since that date it has been reckoned from midnight. To avoid confusion in the use of the designation GMT before and after 1925, since 1928 astronomers have tended to use the term Universal Time (UT) or Weltzeit (WZ) to denote GMT measured from Greenwich Mean Midnight.

In precision work it is necessary to take account of small variations in Universal Time. These arise from small irregularities in the rotation of the Earth. Observed astronomical time is designated UT0. Observed time corrected for the effects of the motion of the poles (giving rise to a 'wandering' in longitude) is designated UT1. There is also a seasonal fluctuation in the rate of rotation of the Earth arising from meteorological causes, often called the annual fluctuation. UT1 corrected for this effect is designated UT2 and provides a time-scale free from short-period fluctuations. It is still subject to small secular and irregular changes.

APPARENT SOLAR TIME

As mentioned above, the time shown by a sundial is called Apparent Solar Time. It differs from Mean Solar Time by an amount known as the Equation of Time, which is the total effect of two causes which make the length of the apparent solar day non-uniform. One cause of variation is that the orbit of the Earth is not a circle but an ellipse, having the Sun at one focus. As a consequence, the angular speed of the Earth in its orbit is not constant; it is greatest at the beginning of January when the Earth is nearest the Sun.

The other cause is due to the obliquity of the ecliptic; the plane of the equator (which is at right angles to the axis of rotation of the Earth) does not coincide with the ecliptic (the plane defined by the apparent annual motion of the Sun around the celestial sphere) but is inclined to it at an angle of 23° 26'. As a result, the apparent solar day is shorter than average at the equinoxes and longer at the solstices. From the combined effects of the components due to obliquity and eccentricity, the equation of time reaches its maximum values in February (−14 minutes) and early November (+16 minutes). It has a zero value on four dates during the year, and it is only on these dates (approximately April 15, June 14, September 1 and December 25) that a sundial shows Mean Solar Time.

SIDEREAL TIME

A sidereal day is the duration of a complete rotation of the Earth with reference to the First Point of Aries. The term sidereal (or 'star') time is a little misleading since the time-scale so defined is not exactly the same as that which would be defined by successive transits of a selected star, as there is a small progressive motion between the stars and the First Point of Aries due to the precession of the Earth's axis. This makes the length of the sidereal day shorter than the true period of rotation by 0.008 seconds. Superimposed on this steady precessional motion are small oscillations (nutation), giving rise to fluctuations in apparent sidereal time amounting to as much as 1.2 seconds. It is therefore customary to employ Mean Sidereal Time, from which these fluctuations have been removed. The conversion of GMT to Greenwich sidereal time (GST) may be performed by adding the value of the GST at 0h on the day in question (Page Two of each month) to the GMT converted to sidereal time using the table on page 69.

Example – To find the GST at August 8d 02h 41m 11s GMT

	h	m	s
GST at 0h	21	07	13
GMT	2	41	11
Acceleration for 2h			20
Acceleration for 41m 11s			7
Sum = GST =	23	48	51

If the observer is not on the Greenwich meridian then his/her longitude, measured positively westwards from Greenwich, must be subtracted from the GST to obtain Local Sidereal Time (LST). Thus, in the above example, an observer 5h east of Greenwich, or 19h west, would find the LST as 4h 48m 51s.

EPHEMERIS TIME

An analysis of observations of the positions of the Sun, Moon and planets taken over an extended period is used in preparing ephemerides. (An ephemeris is a table giving the apparent position of a heavenly body at regular intervals of time, e.g. one day or ten days, and may be used to compare current observations with tabulated positions.) Discrepancies between the positions of heavenly bodies observed over a 300-year period and their predicted positions arose because the time-scale to which the observations were related was based on the assumption that the rate of rotation of the Earth is uniform. It is now known that this rate of rotation is variable. A revised time-scale, Ephemeris Time (ET), was devised to bring the ephemerides into agreement with the observations.

The second of ET is defined in terms of the annual motion of the Earth in its orbit around the Sun (1/31556925.9747 of the tropical year for 1900 January 0d 12h ET). The precise determination of ET from astronomical observations is a lengthy process as the requisite standard of accuracy can only be achieved by averaging over a number of years.

In 1976 the International Astronomical Union adopted a new dynamical time-scale for general use whose scale unit is the SI second (*see* Atomic Time). ET is now of little more than historical interest.

TERRESTRIAL DYNAMICAL TIME

The uniform time system used in computing the ephemerides of the solar system is Terrestrial Dynamical Time (TDT), which has replaced ET for this purpose. Except for the most rigorous astronomical calculations, it may be assumed to be the same as ET. During 2000 the estimated difference TDT–UT is about 65 seconds.

ATOMIC TIME

The fundamental standards of time and frequency must be defined in terms of a periodic motion adequately uniform, enduring and measurable. Progress has made it possible to use natural standards, such as atomic or molecular oscillations. Continuous oscillations are generated in an electrical circuit, the frequency of which is then compared or brought into coincidence with the frequency characteristic of the absorption or emission by the atoms or molecules when they change between two selected energy levels. The National Physical Laboratory (NPL) routinely uses clocks of high stability produced by locking a quartz oscillator to the frequencies defined by caesium or hydrogen atoms.

International Atomic Time (TAI), established through international collaboration, is formed by combining the readings of many caesium clocks and was set close to the astronomically based Universal Time (UT) near the beginning of 1958. It was formally recognized in 1971 and since 1988 January 1 has been maintained by the International Bureau of Weights and Measures (BIPM). The second markers are generated according to the International System (SI) definition adopted in 1967 at the 13th General Conference of Weights and Measures: 'The second is the duration of 9 192 631 770 periods of the radiation corresponding to the transition between the two hyperfine levels of the ground state of the caesium-133 atom.'

Civil time in almost all countries is now based on Co-ordinated Universal Time (UTC), which was adopted for scientific purposes on 1972 January 1. UTC differs from TAI by an integer number of seconds (determined from studies of the rate of rotation of the Earth) and was designed to make both atomic time and UT accessible with accuracies appropriate for most users. The UTC time-scale is adjusted by the insertion (or, in principle, omission) of leap seconds in order to keep it within ±0.9s of UT. These leap seconds are introduced, when necessary, at the same instant throughout the world, either at the end of December or at the end of June. So, for example, the 22nd leap second occurred at 0h UTC on 1999 January 1. All leap seconds so far have been positive, with 61 seconds in the final minute of the UTC month. The time 23h 59m 60s UTC is followed one second later by 0h 0m 00s of the first day of the following month. Notices concerning the insertion of leap seconds are issued by the International Earth Rotation Service (IERS) at the Observatoire de Paris.

RADIO TIME-SIGNALS

UTC is made generally available through time-signals and standard frequency broadcasts such as MSF in the UK, CHU in Canada and WWV and WWVH in the USA. These are based on national time-scales that are maintained in close agreement with UTC and provide traceability to the national time-scale and to UTC. The markers of seconds in the UTC scale coincide with those of TAI.

To disseminate the national time-scale in the UK, special signals are broadcast on behalf of the National Physical Laboratory from the BT (British Telecom) radio station at Rugby (call-sign MSF). The signals are controlled from a caesium beam atomic frequency standard and consist of a precise frequency carrier of 60 kHz which is switched off, after being on for at least half a second, to mark every second. The first second of the minute begins with a period of 500ms with the carrier switched off, to serve as a minute marker. In the other seconds the carrier is always off for at least one tenth of a second at the start and then it carries an on-off code giving the British clock time and date, together with information identifying the start of the next minute. Changes to and from summer time are made following government announcements. Leap seconds are inserted as announced by the IERS and information provided by them on the difference between UTC and UT is also signalled. Other broadcast signals in the UK include the BBC six pips signal, the BT Timeline ('speaking clock'), the NPL Truetime service for computers, and a coded time-signal on the BBC 198 kHz transmitters which is used for timing in the electricity supply industry. From 1972 January 1 the six pips on the BBC have consisted of five short pips from second 55 to second 59 (six pips in the case of a leap second) followed by one lengthened pip, the start of which indicates the exact minute. From 1990 February 5 these signals have been controlled by the BBC with seconds markers referenced to the satellite-based US navigation system GPS (Global Positioning System) and time and day referenced to the MSF transmitter. Formerly they were generated by the Royal Greenwich Observatory. The BT Timeline is compared daily with the National Physical Laboratory caesium beam atomic frequency standard at the Rugby radio station. The NPL Truetime service is directly connected to the national time-scale.

Accurate timing may also be obtained from the signals of international navigation systems such as the ground-based Omega, or the satellite-based American GPS or Russian GLONASS systems.

STANDARD TIME

Since 1880 the standard time in Britain has been Greenwich Mean Time (GMT); a statute that year enacted that the word 'time' when used in any legal document relating to Britain meant, unless otherwise specifically stated, the mean time of the Greenwich meridian. Greenwich was adopted as the universal meridian on 13 October 1884. A system of standard time by zones is used world-wide, standard time in each zone differing from that of the Greenwich meridian by an integral number of hours, either fast or slow. The large territories of the USA and Canada are divided into zones approximately 7.5° on either side of central meridians. (For time zones of countries of the world, *see* Index.)

Variations from the standard time of some countries occur during part of the year; they are decided annually and are usually referred to as Summer Time or Daylight Saving Time.

At the 180th meridian the time can be either 12 hours fast on Greenwich Mean Time or 12 hours slow, and a change of date occurs. The internationally recognized date or calendar line is a modification of the 180th meridian, drawn so as to include islands of any one group on the same side of the line, or for political reasons. The line is indicated by joining up the following co-ordinates:

Lat.	Long.	Lat.	Long.
60° S.	180°	48° N.	180°
51° S.	180°	53° N.	170° E.
45° S.	172.5° W.	65.5° N.	169° W.
15° S.	172.5° W.	75° N.	180°
5° S.	180°		

Changes to the date line would require an international conference.

BRITISH SUMMER TIME

In 1916 an Act ordained that during a defined period of that year the legal time for general purposes in Great Britain should be one hour in advance of Greenwich Mean Time. The Summer Time Acts 1922 and 1925 defined the period during which Summer Time was to be in force, stabilizing practice until the Second World War.

During the war the duration of Summer Time was extended and in the years 1941 to 1945 and in 1947 Double Summer Time (two hours in advance of Greenwich Mean Time) was in force. After the war, Summer Time was extended each year in 1948–52 and 1961–4 by Order in Council.

Between 1968 October 27 and 1971 October 31 clocks were kept one hour ahead of Greenwich Mean Time throughout the year. This was known as British Standard Time.

The most recent legislation is the Summer Time Act 1972, which enacted that 'the period of summer time for the purposes of this Act is the period beginning at two o'clock, Greenwich mean time, in the morning of the day after the third Saturday in March or, if that day is Easter Day, the day after the second Saturday in March, and ending at two o'clock, Greenwich mean time, in the morning of the day after the fourth Saturday in October.'

The duration of Summer Time can be varied by Order in Council and in recent years alterations have been made to bring the operation of Summer Time in Britain closer to similar provisions in other countries of the European Union; for instance, since 1981 the hour of changeover has been 01h Greenwich Mean Time.

The duration of Summer Time in the next two years is:

2000   March 26 01h GMT to October 29 01h GMT
2001   March 25 01h GMT to October 28 01h GMT

MEAN REFRACTION

Alt.	Ref.		Alt.	Ref.		Alt.	Ref.	
° ′	′		° ′	′		° ′	′	
1 20		21	3 12		13	7 54		6
1 30		20	3 34		12	9 27		5
1 41		19	4 00		11	11 39		4
1 52		18	4 30		10	15 00		3
2 05		17	5 06		9	20 42		2
2 19		16	5 50		8	32 20		1
2 35		15	6 44		7	62 17		0
2 52		14	7 54			90 00		
3 12								

The refraction table is in the form of a critical table (*see* page 69)

ASTRONOMICAL CONSTANTS

Solar parallax	8″.794
Astronomical unit	149597870 km
Precession for the year 2000	50″.291
Precession in right ascension	3s.075
Precession in declination	20″.043
Constant of nutation	9″.202
Constant of aberration	20″.496
Mean obliquity of ecliptic (2000)	23° 26′ 22″
Moon's equatorial hor. parallax	57′ 02″.70
Velocity of light in vacuo per second	299792.5 km
Solar motion per second	20.0 km
Equatorial radius of the Earth	6378.140 km
Polar radius of the Earth	6356.755 km
North galactic pole (IAU standard)	
	RA 12h 49m (1950.0). Dec. 27°.4 N.
Solar apex	RA 18h 06m Dec.+30°

Length of year (in mean solar days)

Tropical	365.24219
Sidereal	365.25636
Anomalistic (perihelion to perihelion)	365.25964
Eclipse	346.62000

Length of month (mean values)	d	h	m	s
New Moon to New	29	12	44	02.9
Sidereal	27	07	43	11.5
Anomalistic (perigee to perigee)	27	13	18	33.2

ELEMENTS OF THE SOLAR SYSTEM

Orb	Mean distance from Sun (Earth=1)	Mean distance from Sun km 10⁶	Sidereal period days	Synodic period days	Incl. of orbit to ecliptic ° '	Diameter km	Mass (Earth=1)	Period of rotation on axis days
Sun	—	—	—	—	—	1,392,530	332,946	25–35*
Mercury	0.39	58	88.0	116	7 00	4,879	0.0553	58.646
Venus	0.72	108	224.7	584	3 24	12,104	0.8150	243.019r
Earth	1.00	150	365.3	—	—	12,756e	1.0000	0.997
Mars	1.52	228	687.0	780	1 51	6,794e	0.1074	1.026
Jupiter	5.20	778	4,332.6	399	1 18	{142,984e / 133,708p}	317.89	{0.410e}
Saturn	9.54	1427	10,759.2	378	2 29	{120,536e / 108,728p}	95.18	{0.426e}
Uranus	19.18	2870	30,684.6	370	0 46	51,118e	14.54	0.718r
Neptune	30.06	4497	60,191.0	367	1 46	49,528e	17.15	0.671
Pluto	39.80	5954	91,708.2	367	17 09	2,302	0.002	6.387

e equatorial, p polar, r retrograde, * depending on latitude

THE SATELLITES

Name	Star mag.	Mean distance from primary	Sidereal period of revolution	Name	Star mag.	Mean distance from primary	Sidereal period of revolution
EARTH		km	d	**SATURN**		km	d
I Moon	—	384,400	27.322	VIII Iapetus	11	3,561,300	79.330
MARS				IX Phoebe	16	12,952,000	550.48r
I Phobos	12	9,378	0.319	**URANUS**			
II Deimos	13	23,459	1.262	VI Cordelia	—	49,750	0.335
JUPITER				VII Ophelia	—	53,760	0.376
XVI Metis	17	127,960	0.295	VIII Bianca	—	59,170	0.435
XV Adrastea	19	128,980	0.298	IX Cressida	—	61,780	0.464
V Amalthea	14	181,300	0.498	X Desdemona	—	62,660	0.474
XIV Thebe	16	221,900	0.675	XI Juliet	—	64,360	0.493
I Io	5	421,600	1.769	XII Portia	—	66,100	0.513
II Europa	5	670,900	3.552	XIII Rosalind	—	69,930	0.558
III Ganymede	5	1,070,000	7.155	XIV Belinda	—	75,260	0.624
IV Callisto	6	1,883,000	16.689	S/1986U10	—	77,000	0.638
XIII Leda	20	11,094,000	239	XV Puck	—	86,000	0.762
VI Himalia	15	11,480,000	251	V Miranda	17	129,800	1.413
X Lysithea	18	11,720,000	259	I Ariel	14	191,200	2.520
VII Elara	17	11,737,000	260	II Umbriel	15	266,000	4.144
XII Ananke	19	21,200,000	631r	III Titania	14	435,800	8.706
XI Carme	18	22,600,000	692r	IV Oberon	14	583,600	13.463
VIII Pasiphae	17	23,500,000	735r	S/1997U1	—	7,164,600	579
IX Sinope	18	23,700,000	758r	S/1997U2	—	12,174,700	1,289
SATURN				**NEPTUNE**			
XVIII Pan	—	133,583	0.575	III Naiad	25	48,230	0.294
XV Atlas	18	137,640	0.602	IV Thalassa	24	50,070	0.311
XVI Prometheus	16	139,353	0.613	V Despina	23	52,530	0.335
XVII Pandora	16	141,700	0.629	VI Galatea	22	61,950	0.429
XI Epimetheus	15	151,422	0.695	VII Larissa	22	73,550	0.555
X Janus	14	151,472	0.695	VIII Proteus	20	117,650	1.122
I Mimas	13	185,520	0.942	I Triton	13	354,760	5.877
II Enceladus	12	238,020	1.370	II Nereid	19	5,513,400	360.136
III Tethys	10	294,660	1.888	**PLUTO**			
XIII Telesto	19	294,660	1.888	I Charon	17	19,600	6.387
XIV Calypso	19	294,660	1.888				
IV Dione	10	377,400	2.737				
XII Helene	18	377,400	2.737				
V Rhea	10	527,040	4.518				
VI Titan	8	1,221,850	15.945				
VII Hyperion	14	1,481,100	21.277				

THE EARTH

The shape of the Earth is that of an oblate spheroid or solid of revolution whose meridian sections are ellipses not differing much from circles, whilst the sections at right angles are circles. The length of the equatorial axis is about 12,756 km, and that of the polar axis is 12,714 km. The mean density of the Earth is 5.5 times that of water, although that of the surface layer is less. The Earth and Moon revolve about their common centre of gravity in a lunar month; this centre in turn revolves round the Sun in a plane known as the ecliptic, that passes through the Sun's centre. The Earth's equator is inclined to this plane at an angle of 23.4°. This tilt is the cause of the seasons. In mid-latitudes, and when the Sun is high above the Equator, not only does the high noon altitude make the days longer, but the Sun's rays fall more directly on the Earth's surface; these effects combine to produce summer. In equatorial regions the noon altitude is large throughout the year, and there is little variation in the length of the day. In higher latitudes the noon altitude is lower, and the days in summer are appreciably longer than those in winter.

The average velocity of the Earth in its orbit is 30 km a second. It makes a complete rotation on its axis in about 23h 56m of mean time, which is the sidereal day. Because of its annual revolution round the Sun, the rotation with respect to the Sun, or the solar day, is more than this by about four minutes (*see* page 73). The extremity of the axis of rotation, or the North Pole of the Earth, is not rigidly fixed, but wanders over an area roughly 20 metres in diameter.

TERRESTRIAL MAGNETISM

A magnetic compass points along the horizontal component of a magnetic line of force. These lines of force converge on the 'magnetic dip-poles', the places where a freely suspended magnetized needle would become vertical. Not only do these poles move with time, but their exact locations are ill-defined, particularly so in the case of the north dip-pole where the lines of force on the north side of it, instead of converging radially, tend to bunch into a channel. Although it is therefore unrealistic to attempt to specify the locations of the dip-poles exactly, the present approximate adopted positions are 80°.0 N., 107°.2 W. and 64°.6 S., 138°.4 E. The two magnetic dip-poles are thus not antipodal, the line joining them passing the centre of the Earth at a distance of about 1,250 km. The distances of the magnetic dip-poles from the north and south geographical poles are about 1,200 km and 2,800 km respectively.

There is also a 'magnetic equator', at all points of which the vertical component of the Earth's magnetic field is zero and a magnetized needle remains horizontal. This line runs between 2° and 10° north of the geographical equator in Asia and Africa, turns sharply south off the west African coast, and crosses South America through Brazil, Bolivia and Peru; it recrosses the geographical equator in mid-Pacific.

Reference has already been made to secular changes in the Earth's field. The following table indicates the changes in magnetic declination (or variation of the compass). Declination is the angle in the horizontal plane between the direction of true north and that in which a magnetic compass points. Similar, though much smaller, changes have occurred in 'dip' or magnetic inclination. Secular changes differ throughout the world. Although the London observations suggest a cycle with a period of several hundred years, an exact repetition is unlikely.

London		Greenwich	
1580	11° 15′ E.	1900	16° 29′ W.
1622	5° 56′ E.	1925	13° 10′ W.
1665	1° 22′ W.	1950	9° 07′ W.
1730	13° 00′ W.	1975	6° 39′ W.
1773	21° 09′ W.	1998	3° 32′ W.
1850	22° 24′ W.		

In order that up-to-date information on declination may be available, many governments publish magnetic charts on which there are lines (isogonic lines) passing through all places at which specified values of declination will be found at the date of the chart.

In the British Isles, isogonic lines now run approximately north-east to south-west. Though there are considerable local deviations due to geological causes, a rough value of magnetic declination may be obtained by assuming that at 50° N. on the meridian of Greenwich, the value in 2000 is 2° 37′ west and allowing an increase of 15′ for each degree of latitude northwards and one of 27′ for each degree of longitude westwards. For example, at 53° N., 5° W., declination will be about 2° 37′+45′+135′, i.e. 5° 37′ west. The average annual change at the present time is about 12′ decrease.

The number of magnetic observatories is about 200, irregularly distributed over the globe. There are three in Great Britain, run by the British Geological Survey: at Hartland, north Devon; at Eskdalemuir, Dumfriesshire; and at Lerwick, Shetland Islands. The following are some recent annual mean values of the magnetic elements for Hartland.

Year	Declination West	Dip or inclination	Horizontal force	Vertical force
	° ′	° ′	gauss	gauss
1960	9 59	66 44	0.1871	0.4350
1965	9 30	66 34	0.1887	0.4354
1970	9 06	66 26	0.1903	0.4364
1975	8 32	66 17	0.1921	0.4373
1980	7 44	66 10	0.1933	0.4377
1985	6 56	66 08	0.1938	0.4380
1990	6 15	66 10	0.1939	0.4388
1995	5 33	66 07	0.1946	0.4395
1998	5 03	66 07	0.1949	0.4400

The normal worldwide terrestrial magnetic field corresponds approximately to that of a very strong small bar magnet near the centre of the Earth, but with appreciable smooth spatial departures. The origin and the slow secular change of the normal field are not fully understood but are generally ascribed to electric currents associated with fluid motions in the Earth's core. Superimposed on the normal field are local and regional anomalies whose magnitudes may in places approach that of the normal field; these are due to the influence of mineral deposits in the Earth's crust. A small proportion of the field is of external origin, mostly associated with electric currents in the ionosphere. The configuration of the external field and the ionization of the atmosphere depend on the incident particle and radiation flux from the Sun. There are, therefore, short-term and non-periodic as well as diurnal, 27-day, seasonal and 11-year periodic changes in the magnetic field, dependent upon the position of the Sun and the degree of solar activity.

MAGNETIC STORMS

Occasionally, sometimes with great suddenness, the Earth's magnetic field is subject for several hours to marked disturbance. During a severe storm in 1989 the declination at Lerwick changed by almost 8° in less than an hour. In many instances such disturbances are accompanied by widespread displays of aurorae, marked changes in the incidence of cosmic rays, an increase in the reception of 'noise' from the Sun at radio frequencies, and rapid changes in the ionosphere and induced electric currents within the Earth which adversely affect radio and telegraphic communications. The disturbances are caused by changes in the stream of ionized particles which emanates from the Sun and through which the Earth is continuously passing. Some of these changes are associated with visible eruptions on the Sun, usually in the region of sun-spots. There is a marked tendency for disturbances to recur after intervals of about 27 days, the apparent period of rotation of the Sun on its axis, which is consistent with the sources being located on particular areas of the Sun.

ARTIFICIAL SATELLITES

To consider the orbit of an artificial satellite, it is best to imagine that one is looking at the Earth from a distant point in space. The Earth would then be seen to be rotating about its axis inside the orbit described by the rapidly revolving satellite. The inclination of a satellite orbit to the Earth's equator (which generally remains almost constant throughout the satellite's lifetime) gives at once the maximum range of latitudes over which the satellite passes. Thus a satellite whose orbit has an inclination of 53° will pass overhead all latitudes between 53° S. and 53° N., but would never be seen in the zenith of any place nearer the poles than these latitudes. If we consider a particular place on the earth, whose latitude is less than the inclination of the satellite's orbit, then the Earth's rotation carries this place first under the northbound part of the orbit and then under the southbound portion of the orbit, these two occurrences being always less than 12 hours apart for satellites moving in direct orbits (i.e. to the east). (For satellites in retrograde orbits, the words 'northbound' and 'southbound' should be interchanged in the preceding statement.) As the value of the latitude of the observer increases and approaches the value of the inclination of the orbit, so this interval gets shorter until (when the latitude is equal to the inclination) only one overhead passage occurs each day.

OBSERVATION OF SATELLITES

The regression of the orbit around the Earth causes alternate periods of visibility and invisibility, though this is of little concern to the radio or radar observer. To the visual observer the following cycle of events normally occurs (though the cycle may start in any position): invisibility, morning observations before dawn, invisibility, evening observations after dusk, invisibility, morning observations before dawn, and so on. With reasonably high satellites and for observers in high latitudes around the summer solstice, the evening observations follow the morning observations without interruption as sunlight passing over the polar regions can still illuminate satellites which are passing over temperate latitudes at local midnight. At the moment all satellites rely on sunlight to make them visible, though a satellite with a flashing light has been suggested for a future launching. The observer must be in darkness or twilight in order to make any useful observations. (For durations of twilight; and sunrise and sunset times, *see* Page Two of each month.)

Some of the satellites are visible to the naked eye and much interest has been aroused by the spectacle of a bright satellite disappearing into the Earth's shadow. The event is even more interesting telescopically as the disappearance occurs gradually as the satellite traverses the Earth's penumbral shadow, and during the last few seconds before the eclipse is complete the satellite may change colour (in suitable atmospheric conditions) from yellow to red. This is because the last rays of sunlight are refracted through the denser layers of our atmosphere before striking the satellite.

Some satellites rotate about one or more axes so that a periodic variation in brightness is observed. This was particularly noticeable in several of the Soviet satellites.

Satellite research has provided some interesting results, including a revised value of the Earth's oblateness (1/298.2), and the discovery of the Van Allen radiation belts.

LAUNCHINGS

Apart from their names, e.g. Cosmos 6 Rocket, the satellites are also classified according to their date of launch. Thus 1961 α refers to the first satellite launching of 1961. A number following the Greek letter indicated the relative brightness of the satellites put in orbit. From the beginning of 1963 the Greek letters were replaced by numbers and the numbers by roman letters e.g. 1963−01A. For all satellites successfully injected into orbit the following table gives the designation and names of the main objects, the launch date and some initial orbital data. These are the inclination to the equator (i), the nodal period of revolution (P), and the apogee and perigee heights.

Although most of the satellites launched are injected into orbits less than 1,000 km high, there are an increasing number of satellites in geostationary orbits, i.e. where the orbital inclination is zero, the eccentricity close to zero, and the period of revolution is 1436.1 minutes. Thus the satellite is permanently situated over the equator at one selected longitude at a mean height of 35,786 km. This geostationary band is crowded. In one case there are four television satellites (Astra 1A, Astra 1B, Astra 1C and Astra 1D) orbiting within a few tens of kilometres of each other. In the sky they appear to be separated by only a few arc minutes.

In 1997 a number of *Iridium* satellites were launched into high inclination orbits. These are owned by the mobile telephone company Cellnet. For visual observers, these satellites have the interesting characteristic that the large flat aerials they carry can, when in exactly the right orientation with respect to the Sun and the observer, give off a 'flare' in brightness which can on occasion attain a magnitude of −6, much brighter than Venus. The flare can be visible to the naked eye for nearly a minute.

SPACE STATION MIR

The Russian Space Station, Mir, 1986−17A, which was launched in 1986, is likely to be decommissioned soon. When passing over Britain it has appeared to be almost as bright as Jupiter on favourable transits, though only visible for 4 or 5 minutes on each pass.

The new International Space Station, ISS, 1998−67A, is currently being assembled in an orbit of similar size and inclination. It is already nearly as bright as Mir and will eventually become brighter as more parts are added to it. Predictions for Mir and ISS can be found on the internet at http://www2.gsoc.dlr.de/scripts/satvis.

ARTIFICIAL SATELLITE LAUNCHES 1998–9

Desig-nation	Satellite	Launch date	P	i	Apogee height	Perigee height
1998–			m	°	km	km
015	Progress M, rocket	March 14	90.1	51.6	314	254
016	UHF FO 8	March 16	641.0	24.1	36106	414
017	SPOT 4, rocket	March 24	101.0	98.7	807	802
018	Iridium 51, 61, 55, 57, 58, 59, 60, rocket	March 25	97.3	86.4	636	622
020	TRACE, rocket	April 2	97.2	97.7	642	599
021	Iridium 62-68	April 6	94.9	86.7	522	499
022	STS-90	April 17	89.8	39.0	286	257
023	Globalstar 5-8, rocket	April 24	110.5	52.0	1261	1241
024	Nilesat, BSAT, rocket	April 28	1436.0	0.0	35800	35771
025	Cosmos 2350, rocket, platform, rocket	April 29	1439.6	2.2	35934	35781
026	Iridium XI	May 2	97.4	86.4	644	623
027	Cosmos 2351, platform, platform, platform	May 7	704.9	63.0	39204	514
028	Echostar 4, rocket, platform, rocket	May 7	794.3	15.4	35727	8346
029	USA139, rocket	May 9		(unknown)		
030	NOAA-K	May 13	101.3	98.7	824	809
031	Progress M39	May 14	90.0	51.6	298	254
032	Iridium 70, 72, 73, 74, 75, rocket	May 17	97.4	86.5	644	625
033	Chinastar 1, rocket	May 30	1798.0	24.3	65534	217
034	Shuttle 91	June 2	91.6	51.6	379	369
035	THOR 3, rocket	June 10	1422.3	0.1	36165	34870
036	Cosmos 2352-7, rocket	June 15	118.1	82.5	1875	1310
037	Intelsat 805, rocket	June 18	1045.4	3.2	35694	19798
038	Cosmos 2358, rocket	June 25	89.5	67.0	331	167
039	Cosmos 2359, rocket	June 26	89.9	64.9	302	241
040	Molniya 3-49, platform, rocket	July 1	90.3	62.7	373	208
041	Planet B, rocket	July 3	20896.1	27.3	489366	702
042	Tubsat, rocket	July 7	96.0	78.9	756	396
043	Resurs 01, Fasat-Bravo, TMSAT, Gurwin Techsat 1B, Westpac, SAFIR-2	July 10	101.0	98.8	815	812
044	Sinosat, rocket	July 18	1436.1	0.0	35828	570
045	Cosmos 2360, rocket	July 28	101.7	71.0	852	842
046	Orbcomm FM13-20	August 2	101.0	45.0	822	800
047	Soyuz TM-28	August 13	91.4	51.7	361	347
048	Iridium SV03, SV76	August 19	100.1	86.4	776	773
049	ST-1	August 25	1436.0	0.0	35794	35778
050	Astra 2A	August 30	1436.0	0.0	35847	35724
051	Iridium 82-77	September 8	95.4	86.1	552	544
052	PAS-7, rocket	September 16	1089.9	7.3	57262	169
053	Orbcomm FM21-28, rocket, rocket	September 23	101.3	45.1	834	825
054	Molniya 1-91, rocket, launcher, rocket	September 28	734.4	62.9	40933	2600
055	STEX/ATEX USA 140, rocket	October 3	98.5	85.1	713	681
056	Eutelsat W-2, Sirius 3, rocket, Spelda	October 5	1433.7	0.1	35768	35732
057	Hot Bird 5, rocket	October 9	1407.3	0.4	36649	33814
058	UHF F/O 9, rocket	October 20	1436.2	6.1	36778	34822
059	MAQSAT 3	October 21	641.3	7.1	35515	1018
060	SCD-2 (Brazil), rocket	October 23	100.0	25.0	782	755
061	Deep Space DS-1, SEDSAT-1, rocket, rocket	October 24		(unknown)		
062	Progress M-40, rocket	October 25	91.8	51.7	376	366
063	Afristar, GE-5, rocket	October 28	1430.4	0.1	35754	35616
064	STS-95 Discovery F15, PANSAT, Spartan	October 29	95.8	28.5	572	563
065	Panamsat PAS-8, rocket, launcher, rocket	November 4	768.9	17.3	35952	6916
066	Iridium 2, 86, 85, 84, 83, rocket	November 6	95.2	86.1	546	529
067	Zarya=International Space Station, 1st module, rocket	November 20	89.8	51.6	355	191
068	Bonum 1, rocket	November 22	670.4	19.5	36718	1297
069	STS-88 Endeavour F	December 4	89.7	51.6	336	203
070	Sat Mex 5, rocket	December 6	375.4	6.6	21516	224

ARTIFICIAL SATELLITE LAUNCHES 1998–9

Desig-nation	Satellite	Launch date	P	i	Apogee height	Perigee height
1998–			m	°	km	km
071	SWAS, rocket	December 6	97.6	70.0	662	650
072	Nadezhda 5, Astrid 2, rocket	December 9	105.1	83.0	1025	99
073	Mars Climate Observer, rocket, rocket	December 11	(No elements available)			
074	Iridium 11A, 20A, rocket, Smart Dispenser	December 19	97.6	86.4	668	636
075	Panamsat PAS-6B, rocket	December 22	1197.7	0.7	35789	26195
076	Cosmos 2361, rocket	December 24	105.0	83.0	1026	982
077	Cosmos 2362-2364, rocket, platform, rocket	December 30	675.6	64.9	19147	19128
1999–						
001	Mars payload orbiter	January 3	(Selenocentric orbit)			
002	Rocsat-1	January 27	96.6	35.0	614	601
003	Stardust, rocket	February 7	(Selenocentric orbit)			
004	Globalstar M36, M23, M38 and M40	February 9	103.7	52.0	960	928
005	Telstar 6, rocket, launcher, rocket	February 15	940.5	7.9	35813	15051
006	JCSAT-06, rocket	February 16	2131.1	24.3	65534	267
007	Soyuz TM-29, rocket	February 20	91.7	51.7	377	359
008	Argos, Orsted, Sunsat, rocket	February 23	101.8	98.8	861	844
009	Arabsat 3A, Skynet 4E, rocket, Spelda	February 26	631.9	7.1	35818	234
010	Raduga 1094, rocket, platform, rocket	February 28	1480.3	1.7	36820	36496
011	Wire, rocket	March 5	96.0	97.6	606	552

Time Measurement and Calendars

MEASUREMENTS OF TIME

Measurements of time are based on the time taken by the earth to rotate on its axis (day); by the moon to revolve round the earth (month); and by the earth to revolve round the sun (year). From these, which are not commensurable, certain average or mean intervals have been adopted for ordinary use.

THE DAY

The day begins at midnight and is divided into 24 hours of 60 minutes, each of 60 seconds. The hours are counted from midnight up to 12 noon (when the sun crosses the meridian), and these hours are designated a.m. (*ante meridiem*); and again from noon up to 12 midnight, which hours are designated p.m. (*post meridiem*), except when the 24-hour reckoning is employed. The 24-hour reckoning ignores a.m. and p.m., numbering the hours 0 to 23 from midnight.

Colloquially the 24 hours are divided into day and night, day being the time while the sun is above the horizon (including the four stages of twilight defined on page 72). Day is subdivided into morning, the early part of daytime, ending at noon; afternoon, from noon to about 6 p.m.; and evening, which may be said to extend from 6 p.m. until midnight. Night, the dark period between day and day, begins at the close of astronomical twilight (*see* page 72) and extends beyond midnight to sunrise the next day.

The names of the days are derived from Old English translations or adaptations of the Roman titles.

Sunday	Sun	Sol
Monday	Moon	Luna
Tuesday	Tiw/Tyr (god of war)	Mars
Wednesday	Woden/Odin	Mercury
Thursday	Thor	Jupiter
Friday	Frigga/Freyja (goddess of love)	Venus
Saturday	Saeternes	Saturn

THE MONTH

The month in the ordinary calendar is approximately the twelfth part of a year, but the lengths of the different months vary from 28 (or 29) days to 31.

THE YEAR

The equinoctial or tropical year is the time that the earth takes to revolve round the sun from equinox to equinox, i.e. 365.24219 mean solar days, or 365 days 5 hours 48 minutes and 45 seconds.

The calendar year usually consists of 365 days but a year containing 366 days is called bissextile (*see* Roman calendar, page 89) or leap year, one day being added to the month of February so that a date 'leaps over' a day of the week. In the Roman calendar the day that was repeated was the sixth day before the beginning of March, the equivalent of 24 February.

A year is a leap year if the date of the year is divisible by four without remainder, unless it is the last year of the century. The last year of a century is a leap year only if its number is divisible by 400 without remainder, e.g. the years 1800 and 1900 had only 365 days but the year 2000 has 366 days.

THE SOLSTICE

A solstice is the point in the tropical year at which the sun attains its greatest distance, north or south, from the Equator. In the northern hemisphere the furthest point north of the Equator marks the summer solstice and the furthest point south the winter solstice.

The date of the solstice varies according to locality. For example, if the summer solstice falls on 21 June late in the day by Greenwich time, that day will be the longest of the year at Greenwich though it may be by only a second, but it will fall on 22 June, local date, in Japan, and so 22 June will be the longest day there. The date of the solstice is also affected by the length of the tropical year, which is 365 days 6 hours less about 11 minutes 15 seconds. If a solstice happens late on 21 June in one year, it will be nearly six hours later in the next (unless the next year is a leap year), i.e. early on 22 June, and that will be the longest day.

This delay of the solstice does not continue because the extra day in leap year brings it back a day in the calendar. However, because of the 11 minutes 15 seconds mentioned above, the additional day in leap year brings the solstice back too far by 45 minutes, and the time of the solstice in the calendar is earlier, in a four-year pattern, as the century progresses. The last year of a century is in most cases not a leap year, and the omission of the extra day puts the date of the solstice later by about six hours too much. Compensation for this is made by the fourth centennial year being a leap year. The solstice has become earlier in date throughout this century and, because the year 2000 is a leap year, the solstice will get earlier still throughout the 21st century.

The date of the winter solstice, the shortest day of the year, is affected by the same factors as the longest day.

At Greenwich the sun sets at its earliest by the clock about ten days before the shortest day. The daily change in the time of sunset is due in the first place to the sun's movement southwards at this time of the year, which diminishes the interval between the sun's transit and its setting. However, the daily decrease of the Equation of Time causes the time of apparent noon to be continuously later day by day, which to some extent counteracts the first effect. The rates of the change of these two quantities are not equal or uniform; their combination causes the date of earliest sunset to be 12 or 13 December at Greenwich. In more southerly latitudes the effect of the movement of the sun is less, and the change in the time of sunset depends on that of the Equation of Time to a greater degree, and the date of earliest sunset is earlier than it is at Greenwich, e.g. on the Equator it is about 1 November.

THE EQUINOX

The equinox is the point at which the sun crosses the Equator and day and night are of equal length all over the world. This occurs in March and September.

DOG DAYS

The days about the heliacal rising of the Dog Star, noted from ancient times as the hottest period of the year in the northern hemisphere, are called the Dog Days. Their incidence has been variously calculated as depending on the Greater or Lesser Dog Star (Sirius or Procyon) and their duration has been reckoned as from 30 to 54 days. A generally accepted period is from 3 July to 15 August.

CHRISTIAN CALENDAR

In the Christian chronological system the years are distinguished by cardinal numbers before or after the birth of Christ, the period being denoted by the letters BC (Before Christ) or, more rarely, AC (*Ante Christum*), and AD (*Anno Domini* – In the Year of Our Lord). The correlative dates of the epoch are the fourth year of the 194th Olympiad, the 753rd year from the foundation of Rome, AM 3761 in Jewish chronology, and the 4714th year of the Julian period. The actual date of the birth of Christ is somewhat uncertain.

The system was introduced into Italy in the sixth century. Though first used in France in the seventh century, it was not universally established there until about the eighth century. It has been said that the system was introduced into England by St Augustine (AD 596), but it was probably not generally used until some centuries later. It was ordered to be used by the Bishops at the Council of Chelsea (AD 816).

THE JULIAN CALENDAR

In the Julian calendar (adopted by the Roman Empire in 45 BC, *see* page 89) all the centennial years were leap years, and for this reason towards the close of the 16th century there was a difference of ten days between the tropical and calendar years; the equinox fell on 11 March of the calendar, whereas at the time of the Council of Nicaea (AD 325), it had fallen on 21 March. In 1582 Pope Gregory ordained that 5 October should be called 15 October and that of the end-century years only the fourth should be a leap year (*see* page 81).

THE GREGORIAN CALENDAR

The Gregorian calendar was adopted by Italy, France, Spain and Portugal in 1582, by Prussia, the Roman Catholic German states, Switzerland, Holland and Flanders on 1 January 1583, by Poland in 1586, Hungary in 1587, the Protestant German and Netherland states and Denmark in 1700, and by Great Britain and Dominions (including the North American colonies) in 1752, by the omission of eleven days (3 September being reckoned as 14 September). Sweden omitted the leap day in 1700 but observed leap days in 1704 and 1708, and reverted to the Julian calendar by having two leap days in 1712; the Gregorian calendar was adopted in 1753 by the omission of eleven days (18 February being reckoned as 1 March). Japan adopted the calendar in 1872, China in 1912, Bulgaria in 1915, Turkey and Soviet Russia in 1918, Yugoslavia and Romania in 1919, and Greece in 1923.

In the same year that the change was made in England from the Julian to the Gregorian calendar, the beginning of the new year was also changed from 25 March to 1 January (*see* page 86).

THE ORTHODOX CHURCHES

Some Orthodox Churches still use the Julian reckoning but the majority of Greek Orthodox Churches and the Romanian Orthodox Church have adopted a modified 'New Calendar', observing the Gregorian calendar for fixed feasts and the Julian for movable feasts.

The Orthodox Church year begins on 1 September. There are four fast periods and, in addition to Pascha (Easter), twelve great feasts, as well as numerous commemorations of the saints of the Old and New Testaments throughout the year.

THE DOMINICAL LETTER

The dominical letter is one of the letters A–G which are used to denote the Sundays in successive years. If the first day of the year is a Sunday the letter is A; if the second, B; the third, C; and so on. A leap year requires two letters, the first for 1 January to 29 February, the second for 1 March to 31 December (*see* page 84).

EPIPHANY

The feast of the Epiphany, commemorating the manifestation of Christ, later became associated with the offering of gifts by the Magi. The day was of great importance from the time of the Council of Nicaea (AD 325), as the primate of Alexandria was charged at every Epiphany feast with the announcement in a letter to the churches of the date of the forthcoming Easter. The day was also of importance in Britain as it influenced dates, ecclesiastical and lay, e.g. Plough Monday, when work was resumed in the fields, fell on the Monday in the first full week after Epiphany.

LENT

The Teutonic word *Lent*, which denotes the fast preceding Easter, originally meant no more than the spring season; but from Anglo-Saxon times at least it has been used as the equivalent of the more significant Latin term Quadragesima, meaning the 'forty days' or, more literally, the fortieth day. Ash Wednesday is the first day of Lent, which ends at midnight before Easter Day.

PALM SUNDAY

Palm Sunday, the Sunday before Easter and the beginning of Holy Week, commemorates the triumphal entry of Christ into Jerusalem and is celebrated in Britain (when palm is not available) by branches of willow gathered for use in the decoration of churches on that day.

MAUNDY THURSDAY

Maundy Thursday is the day before Good Friday, the name itself being a corruption of *dies mandati* (day of the mandate) when Christ washed the feet of the disciples and gave them the mandate to love one another.

EASTER DAY

Easter Day is the first Sunday after the full moon which happens on, or next after, the 21st day of March; if the full moon happens on a Sunday, Easter Day is the Sunday after.

This definition is contained in an Act of Parliament (24 Geo. II c. 23) and explanation is given in the preamble to the Act that the day of full moon depends on certain tables that have been prepared. These tables are summarized in the early pages of the Book of Common Prayer. The moon referred to is not the real moon of the heavens, but a hypothetical moon on whose 'full' the date of Easter depends, and the lunations of this 'calendar' moon consist of twenty-nine and thirty days alternately, with certain necessary modifications to make the date of its full agree as nearly as possible with that of the real moon, which is known as the Paschal Full Moon.

A FIXED EASTER

In 1928 the House of Commons agreed to a motion for the third reading of a bill proposing that Easter Day shall, in the calendar year next but one after the commencement of the Act and in all subsequent years, be the first Sunday after the second Saturday in April. Easter would thus fall on the second or third Sunday in April, i.e. between 9 and 15 April (inclusive). A clause in the Bill provided that before it shall come into operation, regard shall be had to any opinion expressed officially by the various Christian churches. Efforts by the World Council of Churches to secure a unanimous choice of date for Easter by its member churches have so far been unsuccessful.

ROGATION DAYS

Rogation Days are the Monday, Tuesday and Wednesday preceding Ascension Day and from the fifth century were observed as public fasts with solemn processions and supplications. The processions were discontinued as religious observances at the Reformation, but survive in the ceremony known as 'beating the parish bounds'. Rogation Sunday is the Sunday before Ascension Day.

EMBER DAYS

The Ember Days at the four seasons are the Wednesday, Friday and Saturday (a) before the third Sunday in Advent, (b) before the second Sunday in Lent, and (c) before the Sundays nearest to the festivals of St Peter and of St Michael and All Angels.

TRINITY SUNDAY

Trinity Sunday is eight weeks after Easter Day, on the Sunday following Pentecost (Whit Sunday). Subsequent Sundays are reckoned in the Book of Common Prayer calendar of the Church of England as 'after Trinity'.

Thomas Becket (1118–70) was consecrated Archbishop of Canterbury on the Sunday after Whit Sunday and his first act was to ordain that the day of his consecration should be held as a new festival in honour of the Holy Trinity. This observance spread from Canterbury throughout the whole of Christendom.

MOVABLE FEASTS TO THE YEAR 2035

Year	Ash Wednesday	Easter	Ascension	Pentecost (Whit Sunday)	Advent Sunday
2000	8 March	23 April	1 June	11 June	3 December
2001	28 February	15 April	24 May	3 June	2 December
2002	13 February	31 March	9 May	19 May	1 December
2003	5 March	20 April	29 May	8 June	30 November
2004	25 February	11 April	20 May	30 May	28 November
2005	9 February	27 March	5 May	15 May	27 November
2006	1 March	16 April	25 May	4 June	3 December
2007	21 February	8 April	17 May	27 May	2 December
2008	6 February	23 March	1 May	11 May	30 November
2009	25 February	12 April	21 May	31 May	29 November
2010	17 February	4 April	13 May	23 May	28 November
2011	9 March	24 April	2 June	12 June	27 November
2012	22 February	8 April	17 May	27 May	2 December
2013	13 February	31 March	9 May	19 May	1 December
2014	5 March	20 April	29 May	8 June	30 November
2015	18 February	5 April	14 May	24 May	29 November
2016	10 February	27 March	5 May	15 May	27 November
2017	1 March	16 April	25 May	4 June	3 December
2018	14 February	1 April	10 May	20 May	2 December
2019	6 March	21 April	30 May	9 June	1 December
2020	26 February	12 April	21 May	31 May	29 November
2021	17 February	4 April	13 May	23 May	28 November
2022	2 March	17 April	26 May	5 June	27 November
2023	22 February	9 April	18 May	28 May	3 December
2024	14 February	31 March	9 May	19 May	1 December
2025	5 March	20 April	29 May	8 June	30 November
2026	18 February	5 April	14 May	24 May	29 November
2027	10 February	28 March	6 May	16 May	28 November
2028	1 March	16 April	25 May	4 June	3 December
2029	14 February	1 April	10 May	20 May	2 December
2030	6 March	21 April	30 May	9 June	1 December
2031	26 February	13 April	22 May	1 June	30 November
2032	11 February	28 March	6 May	16 May	28 November
2033	2 March	17 April	26 May	5 June	27 November
2034	22 February	9 April	18 May	28 May	3 December
2035	7 February	25 March	3 May	13 May	2 December

NOTES

Ash Wednesday (first day in Lent) can fall at earliest on 4 February and at latest on 10 March

Mothering Sunday (fourth Sunday in Lent) can fall at earliest on 1 March and at latest on 4 April

Easter Day can fall at earliest on 22 March and at latest on 25 April

Ascension Day is forty days after Easter Day and can fall at earliest on 30 April and at latest on 3 June

Pentecost (Whit Sunday) is seven weeks after Easter and can fall at earliest on 10 May and at latest on 13 June

Trinity Sunday is the Sunday after Whit Sunday

Corpus Christi falls on the Thursday after Trinity Sunday

Sundays after Pentecost – there are not less than 18 and not more than 23

Advent Sunday is the Sunday nearest to 30 November

EASTER DAYS AND DOMINICAL LETTERS 1500 TO 2035

Dates up to and including 1752 are according to the Julian calendar. For dominical letters in leap years, *see* page 82

		1500–1599	1600–1699	1700–1799	1800–1899	1900–1999	2000–2035
March							
d	22	1573	1668	1761	1818		
e	23	1505/16	1600	1788	1845/56	1913	2008
f	24		1611/95	1706/99		1940	
g	25	1543/54	1627/38/49	1722/33/44	1883/94	1951	2035
A	26	1559/70/81/92	1654/65/76	1749/58/69/80	1815/26/37	1967/78/89	
b	27	1502/13/24/97	1608/87/92	1785/96	1842/53/64	1910/21/32	2005/16
c	28	1529/35/40	1619/24/30	1703/14/25	1869/75/80	1937/48	2027/32
d	29	1551/62	1635/46/57	1719/30/41/52	1807/12/91	1959/64/70	
e	30	1567/78/89	1651/62/73/84	1746/55/66/77	1823/34	1902/75/86/97	
f	31	1510/21/32/83/94	1605/16/78/89	1700/71/82/93	1839/50/61/72	1907/18/29/91	2002/13/24
April							
g	1	1526/37/48	1621/32	1711/16	1804/66/77/88	1923/34/45/56	2018/29
A	2	1553/64	1643/48	1727/38	1809/20/93/99	1961/72	
b	3	1575/80/86	1659/70/81	1743/63/68/74	1825/31/36	1904/83/88/94	
c	4	1507/18/91	1602/13/75/86/97	1708/79/90	1847/58	1915/20/26/99	2010/21
d	5	1523/34/45/56	1607/18/29/40	1702/13/24/95	1801/63/74/85/96	1931/42/53	2015/26
e	6	1539/50/61/72	1634/45/56	1729/35/40/60	1806/17/28/90	1947/58/69/80	
f	7	1504/77/88	1667/72	1751/65/76	1822/33/44	1901/12/85/96	
g	8	1509/15/20/99	1604/10/83/94	1705/87/92/98	1849/55/60	1917/28	2007/12
A	9	1531/42	1615/26/37/99	1710/21/32	1871/82	1939/44/50	2023/34
b	10	1547/58/69	1631/42/53/64	1726/37/48/57	1803/14/87/98	1955/66/77	
c	11	1501/12/63/74/85/96	1658/69/80	1762/73/84	1819/30/41/52	1909/71/82/93	2004
d	12	1506/17/28	1601/12/91/96	1789	1846/57/68	1903/14/25/36/98	2009/20
e	13	1533/44	1623/28	1707/18	1800/73/79/84	1941/52	2031
f	14	1555/60/66	1639/50/61	1723/34/45/54	1805/11/16/95	1963/68/74	
g	15	1571/82/93	1655/66/77/88	1750/59/70/81	1827/38	1900/06/79/90	2001
A	16	1503/14/25/36/87/98	1609/20/82/93	1704/75/86/97	1843/54/65/76	1911/22/33/95	2006/17/28
b	17	1530/41/52	1625/36	1715/20	1808/70/81/92	1927/38/49/60	2022/33
c	18	1557/68	1647/52	1731/42/56	1802/13/24/97	1954/65/76	
d	19	1500/79/84/90	1663/74/85	1747/67/72/78	1829/35/40	1908/81/87/92	
e	20	1511/22/95	1606/17/79/90	1701/12/83/94	1851/62	1919/24/30	2003/14/25
f	21	1527/38/49	1622/33/44	1717/28	1867/78/89	1935/46/57	2019/30
g	22	1565/76	1660	1739/53/64	1810/21/32	1962/73/84	
A	23	1508	1671		1848	1905/16	2000
b	24	1519	1603/14/98	1709/91	1859	1943	2011
c	25	1546	1641	1736	1886		

HINDU CALENDAR

The Hindu calendar is a luni-solar calendar of twelve months, each containing 29 days, 12 hours. Each month is divided into a light fortnight (Shukla or Shuddha) and a dark fortnight (Krishna or Vadya) based on the waxing and waning of the moon. In most parts of India the month starts with the light fortnight, i.e. the day after the new moon, although in some regions it begins with the dark fortnight, i.e. the day after the full moon.

The new year begins in the month of Chaitra (March/April) and ends in the month of Phalgun (March). The twelve months, Chaitra, Vaishakh, Jyeshtha, Ashadh, Shravan, Bhadrapad, Ashvin, Kartik, Margashirsh, Paush, Magh and Phalgun, have Sanskrit names derived from twelve asterisms (constellations). There are regional variations to the names of the months but the Sanskrit names are understood throughout India.

Every lunar month must have a solar transit and is termed pure (shuddha). The lunar month without a solar transit is impure (mala) and called an intercalary month. An intercalary month occurs approximately every 32 lunar months, whenever the difference between the Hindu year of 360 lunar days (354 days 8 hours solar time) and the 365 days 6 hours of the solar year reaches the length of one Hindu lunar month (29 days 12 hours).

The leap month may be added at any point in the Hindu year. The name given to the month varies according to when it occurs but is taken from the month immediately following it. No leap month occurs in 2000.

The days of the week are called Raviwar (Sunday), Somawar (Monday), Mangalwar (Tuesday), Budhawar (Wednesday), Guruwar (Thursday), Shukrawar (Friday) and Shaniwar (Saturday). The names are derived from the Sanskrit names of the Sun, the Moon and five planets, Mars, Mercury, Jupiter, Venus and Saturn.

Most fasts and festivals are based on the lunar calendar but a few are determined by the apparent movement of the Sun, e.g. Sankranti and Pongal (in southern India), which are celebrated on 14/15 January to mark the start of the Sun's apparent journey northwards and a change of season.

Festivals celebrated throughout India are Chaitra (the New Year), Raksha-bandhan (the renewal of the kinship bond between brothers and sisters), Navaratri (a nine-night festival dedicated to the goddess Parvati), Dasara (the victory of Rama over the demon army), Diwali (a festival of lights), Makara Sankranti, Shivaratri (dedicated to Shiva), and Holi (a spring festival).

Regional festivals are Durga-puja (dedicated to the goddess Durga (Parvati)), Sarasvati-puja (dedicated to the goddess Sarasvati), Ganesh Chaturthi (worship of Ganesh on the fourth day (Chaturthi) of the light half of Bhadrapad), Ramanavami (the birth festival of the god Rama) and Janmashtami (the birth festival of the god Krishna).

The main festivals celebrated in Britain are Navaratri, Dasara, Durga-puja, Diwali, Holi, Sarasvati-puja, Ganesh Chaturthi, Raksha-bandhan, Ramanavami and Janmashtami.

For dates of the main festivals in 2000, *see* page 9.

JEWISH CALENDAR

The story of the Flood in the Book of Genesis indicates the use of a calendar of some kind and that the writers recognized thirty days as the length of a lunation. However, after the diaspora, Jewish communities were left in considerable doubt as to the times of fasts and festivals. This led to the formation of the Jewish calendar as used today. It is said that this was done in AD 358 by Rabbi Hillel II, though some assert that it did not happen until much later.

The calendar is luni-solar, and is based on the lengths of the lunation and of the tropical year as found by Hipparchus (*c*.120 BC), which differ little from those adopted at the present day. The year AM 5760 (1999–2000) is the 3rd year of the 304th Metonic (Minor or Lunar) cycle of 19 years and the 20th year of the 206th Solar (or Major) cycle of 28 years since the Era of the Creation. Jews hold that the Creation occurred at the time of the autumnal equinox in the year known in the Christian calendar as 3760 BC (954 of the Julian period). The epoch or starting point of Jewish chronology corresponds to 7 October 3761 BC. At the beginning of each solar cycle, the Tekufah of Nisan (the vernal equinox) returns to the same day and to the same hour.

The hour is divided into 1080 minims, and the month between one new moon and the next is reckoned as 29 days, 12 hours, 793 minims. The normal calendar year, called a Regular Common year, consists of 12 months of 30 days and 29 days alternately. Since 12 months such as these comprise only 354 days, in order that each of them shall not diverge greatly from an average place in the solar year, a 13th month is occasionally added after the fifth month of the civil year (which commences on the first day of the month Tishri), or as the penultimate month of the ecclesiastical year (which commences on the first day of the month Nisan). The years when this happens are called Embolismic or leap years.

Of the 19 years that form a Metonic cycle, seven are leap years; they occur at places in the cycle indicated by the numbers 3, 6, 8, 11, 14, 17 and 19, these places being chosen so that the accumulated excesses of the solar years should be as small as possible.

A Jewish year is of one of the following six types:

Minimal Common	353 days
Regular Common	354 days
Full Common	355 days
Minimal Leap	383 days
Regular Leap	384 days
Full Leap	385 days

The Regular year has alternate months of 30 and 29 days. In a Full year, whether common or leap, Marcheshvan, the second month of the civil year, has 30 days instead of 29;

in Minimal years Kislev, the third month, has 29 instead of 30. The additional month in leap years is called Adar I and precedes the month called Adar in Common years. Adar II is called Adar Sheni in leap years, and the usual Adar festivals are kept in Adar Sheni. Adar I and Adar II always have 30 days, but neither this, nor the other variations mentioned, is allowed to change the number of days in the other months, which still follow the alternation of the normal twelve.

These are the main features of the Jewish calendar, which must be considered permanent because as a Jewish law it cannot be altered except by a great Sanhedrin.

The Jewish day begins between sunset and nightfall. The time used is that of the meridian of Jerusalem, which is 2h 21m in advance of Greenwich Mean Time. Rules for the beginning of sabbaths and festivals were laid down for the latitude of London in the 18th century and hours for nightfall are now fixed annually by the Chief Rabbi.

JEWISH CALENDAR 5760–1

AM 5760 (760) is a Full Leap year of 13 months, 55 sabbaths and 385 days. AM 5761 (761) is a Minimal Common year of 12 months, 50 sabbaths and 353 days.

Month (first day)	AM 5760	AM 5761
Tishri 1	11 September 1999	30 September 2000
Marcheshvan 1	11 October	30 October
Kislev 1	10 November	28 November
Tebet 1	10 December	27 December
Shebat 1	8 January 2000	25 January 2001
*Adar 1	7 February	24 February
†Adar II	8 March	
Nisan 1	6 April	25 March
Iyar 1	6 May	24 April
Sivan 1	4 June	23 May
Tammuz 1	4 July	22 June
Ab 1	2 August	21 July
Elul 1	1 September	20 August

*Known as Adar Rishon in leap years
†Known as Adar Sheni in leap years

JEWISH FASTS AND FESTIVALS

For dates of principal festivals in 2000, *see* page 9.

Tishri 1–2	Rosh Hashanah (New Year)
Tishri 3	*Fast of Gedaliah
Tishri 10	Yom Kippur (Day of Atonement)
Tishri 15–21	Succoth (Feast of Tabernacles)
Tishri 21	Hoshana Rabba
Tishri 22	Shemini Atseret (Solemn Assembly)
Tishri 23	Simchat Torah (Rejoicing of the Law)
Kislev 25	Chanucah (Dedication of the Temple) begins
Tebet 10	Fast of Tebet
†Adar 13	§Fast of Esther
†Adar 14	Purim
†Adar 15	Shushan Purim
Nisan 15–22	Pesach (Passover)
Sivan 6–7	Shavuot (Feast of Weeks)
Tammuz 17	*Fast of Tammuz
Ab 9	*Fast of Ab

*If these dates fall on the sabbath the fast is kept on the following day
†Adar Sheni in leap years
§This fast is observed on Adar 11 (or Adar Sheni 11 in leap years) if Adar 13 falls on a sabbath

THE MUSLIM CALENDAR

The Muslim era is dated from the *Hijrah*, or flight of the Prophet Muhammad from Mecca to Medina, the corresponding date of which in the Julian calendar is 16 July AD 622. The lunar *hijri* calendar is used principally in Iran, Egypt, Malaysia, Pakistan, Mauritania, various Arab states and certain parts of India. Iran uses the solar *hijri* calendar as well as the lunar *hijri* calendar. The dating system was adopted about AD 639, commencing with the first day of the month Muharram.

The lunar calendar consists of twelve months containing an alternate sequence of 30 and 29 days, with the intercalation of one day at the end of the twelfth month at stated intervals in each cycle of 30 years. The object of the intercalation is to reconcile the date of the first day of the month with the date of the actual new moon.

Some adherents still take the date of the evening of the first physical sighting of the crescent of the new moon as that of the first of the month. If cloud obscures the moon the present month may be extended to 30 days, after which the new month will begin automatically regardless of whether the moon has been seen. (Under religious law a month must have less than 31 days.) This means that the beginning of a new month and the date of religious festivals can vary from the published calendars.

In each cycle of 30 years, 19 years are common and contain 354 days, and 11 years are intercalary (leap years) of 355 days, the latter being called *kabisah*. The mean length of the Hijrah years is 354 days 8 hours 48 minutes and the period of mean lunation is 29 days 12 hours 44 minutes.

To ascertain if a year is common or kabisah, divide it by 30: the quotient gives the number of completed cycles and the remainder shows the place of the year in the current cycle. If the remainder is 2, 5, 7, 10, 13, 16, 18, 21, 24, 26 or 29, the year is kabisah and consists of 355 days.

MUSLIM CALENDAR 1420–21

Hijrah year 1420 AH (remainder 10) is a kabisah year; 1421 AH (remainder 11) is a common year.

Month (length)	1420 AH	1421 AH
Muharram (30)	17 April 1999	6 April 2000
Safar (29)	17 May	6 May
Rabi' I (30)	15 June	4 June
Rabi' II (29)	15 July	4 July
Jumada I (30)	13 August	2 August
Jumada II (29)	12 September	1 September
Rajab (30)	11 October	30 September
Sha'ban (29)	10 November	30 October
Ramadân (29)	9 December	28 November
Shawwâl (29)	8 January 2000	28 December
Dhû'l-Qa'da (30)	6 February	26 January 2001
Dhû'l-Hijjah (29 or 30)	7 March	26 February

MUSLIM FESTIVALS

Ramadan is a month of fasting for all Muslims because it is the month in which the revelation of the *Qur'an* (Koran) began. During Ramadan Muslims abstain from food, drink and sexual pleasure from dawn until after sunset throughout the month.

The two major festivals are *Id al-Fitr* and *Id al-Adha*. Id al-Fitr marks the end of the Ramadan fast and is celebrated on the day after the sighting of the new moon of the following month. Id al-Adha, the festival of sacrifice (also known as the great festival), celebrates the submission of the Prophet Ibrahim (Abraham) to God. Id al-Adha falls on the tenth day of Dhul-Hijjah, coinciding with the day when those on *hajj* (pilgrimage to Mecca) sacrifice animals. Other days accorded special recognition are:

Muharram 1	New Year's Day
Muharram 10	Ashura (the day Prophet Noah left the Ark and Prophet Moses was saved from Pharaoh (Sunni), the death of the Prophet's grandson Husain (Shi'ite))
Rabi'u-l-Awwal (Rabi' I) 12	Mawlid al-Nabi (birthday of the Prophet Muhammad)
Rajab 27	Laylat al-Isra' wa'l-Mi'raj (The Night of Journey and Ascension)
Ramadân One of the odd-numbered nights in the last 10 of the month	Laylat al-Qadr (Night of Power)
Dhû'l-Hijjah 10	Id al-Adha (Festival of Sacrifice)

THE SIKH CALENDAR

The Sikh calendar is a lunar calendar of 365 days divided into 12 months. The length of the months varies between 29 and 32 days.

There are no prescribed feast days and no fasting periods. The main celebrations are Baisakhi Mela (the new year and the anniversary of the founding of the Khalsa), Diwali Mela (festival of light), Hola Mohalla Mela (a spring festival held in the Punjab), and the Gurpurbs (anniversaries associated with the ten Gurus).

For dates of the major celebrations in 2000, *see* page 9.

CIVIL AND LEGAL CALENDAR

THE HISTORICAL YEAR

Before 1752, two calendar systems were used in England. The civil or legal year began on 25 March and the historical year on 1 January. Thus the civil or legal date 24 March 1658 was the same day as the historical date 24 March 1659; a date in that portion of the year is written as 24 March 165⅜, the lower figure showing the historical year.

THE NEW YEAR

In England in the seventh century, and as late as the 13th, the year was reckoned from Christmas Day, but in the 12th century the Church in England began the year with the feast of the Annunciation of the Blessed Virgin ('Lady Day') on 25 March and this practice was adopted generally in the 14th century. The civil or legal year in the British Dominions (exclusive of Scotland) began with Lady Day until 1751. But in and since 1752 the civil year has begun with 1 January. New Year's Day in Scotland was changed from 25 March to 1 January in 1600.

Elsewhere in Europe, 1 January was adopted as the first day of the year by Venice in 1522, German states in 1544, Spain, Portugal and the Roman Catholic Netherlands in 1556, Prussia, Denmark and Sweden in 1559, France in 1564, Lorraine in 1579, the Protestant Netherlands in 1583, Russia in 1725, and Tuscany in 1751.

REGNAL YEARS

Regnal years are the years of a sovereign's reign and each begins on the anniversary of his or her accession, e.g. regnal year 49 of the present Queen begins on 6 February 2000.

The system was used for dating Acts of Parliament until 1962. The Summer Time Act 1925, for example, is quoted as 15 and 16 Geo. V c. 64, because it became law in the parliamentary session which extended over part of both of these regnal years. Acts of a parliamentary session during which a sovereign died were usually given two year numbers, the regnal year of the deceased sovereign and the regnal year of his or her successor, e.g. those passed in 1952 were dated 16 Geo. VI and 1 Elizabeth II. Since 1962 Acts of Parliament have been dated by the calendar year.

QUARTER AND TERM DAYS

Holy days and saints days were the usual means in early times for setting the dates of future and recurrent appointments. The quarter days in England and Wales are the feast of the Nativity (25 December), the feast of the Annunciation (25 March), the feast of St John the Baptist (24 June) and the feast of St Michael and All Angels (29 September).

The term days in Scotland are Candlemas (the feast of the Purification), Whitsunday, Lammas (Loaf Mass), and Martinmas (St Martin's Day). These fell on 2 February, 15 May, 1 August and 11 November respectively. However, by the Term and Quarter Days (Scotland) Act 1990, the dates of the term days were changed to 28 February (Candlemas), 28 May (Whitsunday), 28 August (Lammas) and 28 November (Martinmas).

RED-LETTER DAYS

Red-letter days were originally the holy days and saints days indicated in early ecclesiastical calendars by letters printed in red ink. The days to be distinguished in this way were approved at the Council of Nicaea in AD 325.

These days still have a legal significance, as judges of the Queen's Bench Division wear scarlet robes on red-letter days falling during the law sittings. The days designated as red-letter days for this purpose are:

Holy and saints days (for dates, *see* pages 16, 20, etc.)
The Conversion of St Paul, the Purification, Ash Wednesday, the Annunciation, the Ascension, the feasts of St Mark, SS Philip and James, St Matthias, St Barnabas, St John the Baptist, St Peter, St Thomas, St James, St Luke, SS Simon and Jude, All Saints, St Andrew

Civil calendar (for dates, *see* page 9)
The anniversaries of The Queen's accession, The Queen's birthday and The Queen's coronation, The Queen's official birthday, the birthday of the Duke of Edinburgh, the birthday of Queen Elizabeth the Queen Mother, the birthday of the Prince of Wales, St David's Day and Lord Mayor's Day

PUBLIC HOLIDAYS

Public holidays are divided into two categories, common law and statutory. Common law holidays are holidays 'by habit and custom'; in England, Wales and Northern Ireland these are Good Friday and Christmas Day.

Statutory public holidays, known as bank holidays, were first established by the Bank Holidays Act 1871. They were, literally, days on which the banks (and other public institutions) were closed and financial obligations due on that day were payable the following day. The legislation currently governing public holidays in the UK, which is the Banking and Financial Dealings Act 1971, stipulates the days that are to be public holidays in England, Wales, Scotland and Northern Ireland.

Certain holidays (indicated by * below) are granted annually by royal proclamation, either throughout the UK or in any place in the UK. The public holidays are:

England and Wales
*New Year's Day
Easter Monday
*The first Monday in May
The last Monday in May
The last Monday in August
26 December, if it is not a Sunday
27 December when 25 or 26 December is a Sunday

Scotland
New Year's Day, or if it is a Sunday, 2 January
2 January, or if it is a Sunday, 3 January
Good Friday
The first Monday in May
*The last Monday in May
The first Monday in August
Christmas Day, or if it is a Sunday, 26 December
*Boxing Day – if Christmas Day falls on a Sunday, 26 December is given in lieu and an alternative day is given for Boxing Day

Northern Ireland
*New Year's Day
17 March, or if it is a Sunday, 18 March
Easter Monday
*The first Monday in May
The last Monday in May
*12 July, or if it is a Sunday, 13 July
The last Monday in August
26 December, if it is not a Sunday
27 December if 25 or 26 December is a Sunday

For dates of public holidays in 2000 and 2001, *see* pages 10–11.

CHRONOLOGICAL CYCLES AND ERAS

SOLAR (OR MAJOR) CYCLE

The solar cycle is a period of twenty-eight years in any corresponding year of which the days of the week recur on the same day of the month.

METONIC (LUNAR, OR MINOR) CYCLE

In 432 BC, Meton, an Athenian astronomer, found that 235 lunations are very nearly, though not exactly, equal in duration to 19 solar years and so after 19 years the phases of the Moon recur on the same days of the month (nearly). The dates of full moon in a cycle of 19 years were inscribed in figures of gold on public monuments in Athens, and the number showing the position of a year in the cycle is called the golden number of that year.

JULIAN PERIOD

The Julian period was proposed by Joseph Scaliger in 1582. The period is 7980 Julian years, and its first year coincides with the year 4713 BC. The figure of 7980 is the product of the number of years in the solar cycle, the Metonic cycle and the cycle of the Roman indiction (28 × 19 × 15).

ROMAN INDICTION

The Roman indiction is a period of fifteen years, instituted for fiscal purposes about AD 300.

EPACT

The epact is the age of the calendar Moon, diminished by one day, on 1 January, in the ecclesiastical lunar calendar.

CHINESE CALENDAR

A lunar calendar was the sole calendar in use in China until 1911, when the government adopted the new (Gregorian) calendar for official and most business activities. The Chinese tend to follow both calendars, the lunar calendar playing an important part in personal life, e.g. birth celebrations, festivals, marriages; and in rural villages the lunar calendar dictates the cycle of activities, denoting the change of weather and farming activities.

The lunar calendar is used in Hong Kong, Singapore, Malaysia, Tibet and elsewhere in south-east Asia. The calendar has a cycle of 60 years. The new year begins at the first new moon after the sun enters the sign of Aquarius, i.e. the new year falls between 21 January and 19 February in the Gregorian calendar.

Each year in the Chinese calendar is associated with one of 12 animals: the rat, the ox, the tiger, the rabbit, the dragon, the snake, the horse, the goat or sheep, the monkey, the chicken or rooster, the dog, and the pig.

The date of the Chinese new year and the astrological sign for the years 2000–2005 are:

2000	5 February	Dragon
2001	—	Snake
2002	—	Horse
2003	—	Goat or Sheep
2004	—	Monkey
2005	—	Chicken

COPTIC CALENDAR

In the Coptic calendar, which is used in parts of Egypt and Ethiopia, the year is made up of 12 months of 30 days each, followed, in general, by five complementary days. Every fourth year is an intercalary or leap year and in these years there are six complementary days. The intercalary year of the Coptic calendar immediately precedes the leap year of the Julian calendar. The era is that of Diocletian or the Martyrs, the origin of which is fixed at 29 August AD 284 (Julian date).

INDIAN ERAS

In addition to the Muslim reckoning, other eras are used in India. The Saka era of southern India, dating from 3 March AD 78, was declared the national calendar of the Republic of India with effect from 22 March 1957, to be used concurrently with the Gregorian calendar. As revised, the year of the new Saka era begins at the spring equinox, with five successive months of 31 days and seven of 30 days in ordinary years, and six months of each length in leap years. The year AD 2000 is 1922 of the revised Saka era.

The year AD 2000 corresponds to the following years in other eras:

Year 2057 of the Vikram Samvat era
Year 1407 of the Bengali San era
Year 1176 of the Kollam era
Vedanga Jyotisa year 6 of the five-yearly cycle (384th cycle of Paitamah Siddhanta)
Year 6001 of the Kaliyuga era
Year 2544 of the Buddha Nirvana era

JAPANESE CALENDAR

The Japanese calendar is essentially the same as the Gregorian calendar, the years, months and weeks being of the same length and beginning on the same days as those of the Gregorian calendar. The numeration of the years is different, based on a system of epochs or periods each of which begins at the accession of an Emperor or other important occurrence. The method is not unlike the British system of regnal years, except that each year of a period closes on 31 December. The Japanese chronology begins about AD 650 and the three latest epochs are defined by the reigns of Emperors, whose actual names are not necessarily used:

Epoch

Taishō   1 August 1912 to 25 December 1926
Shōwa   26 December 1926 to 7 January 1989
Heisei   8 January 1989

The year Heisei 12 begins on 1 January 2000.

The months are known as First Month, Second Month, etc., First Month being equivalent to January. The days of the week are Nichiyōbi (Sun-day), Getsuyōbi (Moon-day), Kayōbi (Fire-day), Suiyōbi (Water-day), Mokuyōbi (Wood-day), Kinyōbi (Metal-day), Doyōbi (Earth-day).

THE MASONIC YEAR

Two dates are quoted in warrants, dispensations, etc., issued by the United Grand Lodge of England, those for the current year being expressed as *Anno Domini* 2000 – *Anno Lucis* 6000. This *Anno Lucis* (year of light) is based on the Book of Genesis 1:3, the 4000-year difference being derived, in modified form, from *Ussher's Notation*, published in 1654, which places the Creation of the World in 4004 BC.

OLYMPIADS

Ancient Greek chronology was reckoned in Olympiads, cycles of four years corresponding with the periodic Olympic Games held on the plain of Olympia in Elis once every four years. The intervening years were the first, second, etc., of the Olympiad, which received the name of the victor at the Games. The first recorded Olympiad is that of Choroebus, 776 BC.

ZOROASTRIAN CALENDAR

Zoroastrians, followers of the Iranian prophet Zarathushtra (known to the Greeks as Zoroaster) are mostly to be found in Iran and in India, where they are known as Parsees.

The Zoroastrian era dates from the coronation of the last Zoroastrian Sasanian king in AD 631. The Zoroastrian calendar is divided into twelve months, each comprising 30 days, followed by five holy days of the Gathas at the end of each year to make the year consist of 365 days.

In order to synchronize the calendar with the solar year of 365 days, an extra month was intercalated once every 120 years. However, this intercalation ceased in the 12th century and the New Year, which had fallen in the spring, slipped back to August. Because intercalation ceased at different times in Iran and India, there was one month's difference between the calendar followed in Iran (Kadmi calendar) and that followed by the Parsees (Shenshai calendar). In 1906 a group of Zoroastrians decided to bring the calendar back in line with the seasons again and restore the New Year to 21 March each year (Fasli calendar).

The Shenshai calendar (New Year in August) is mainly used by Parsees. The Fasli calendar (New Year, 21 March) is mainly used by Zoroastrians living in Iran, in the Indian subcontinent, or away from Iran.

THE ROMAN CALENDAR

Roman historians adopted as an epoch the foundation of Rome, which is believed to have happened in the year 753 BC. The ordinal number of the years in Roman reckoning is followed by the letters AUC (*ab urbe condita*), so that the year 2000 is 2753 AUC (MMDCCLIII). The calendar that we know has developed from one said to have been established by Romulus using a year of 304 days divided into ten months, beginning with March. To this Numa added January and February, making the year consist of 12 months of 30 and 29 days alternately, with an additional day so that the total was 355. It is also said that Numa ordered an intercalary month of 22 or 23 days in alternate years, making 90 days in eight years, to be inserted after 23 February.

However, there is some doubt as to the origination and the details of the intercalation in the Roman calendar. It is certain that some scheme of this kind was inaugurated and

not fully carried out, for in the year 46 BC Julius Caesar found that the calendar had been allowed to fall into some confusion. He sought the help of the Egyptian astronomer Sosigenes, which led to the construction and adoption (45 BC) of the Julian calendar, and, by a slight alteration, to the Gregorian calendar now in use. The year 46 BC was made to consist of 445 days and is called the Year of Confusion.

In the Roman (Julian) calendar the days of the month were counted backwards from three fixed points, or days, and an intervening day was said to be so many days before the next coming point, the first and last being counted. These three points were the Kalends, the Nones, and the Ides. Their positions in the months and the method of counting from them will be seen in the table below. The year containing 366 days was called *bissextillis annus*, as it had a doubled sixth day (*bissextus dies*) before the March Kalends on 24 February – *ante diem sextum Kalendas Martias*, or a.d. VI Kal. Mart.

Present days of the month	*March, May, July, October have thirty-one days*		*January, August, December have thirty-one days*		*April, June, September, November have thirty days*		*February has twenty-eight days, and in leap year twenty-nine*	
1	Kalendis		Kalendis		Kalendis		Kalendis	
2	VI	ante	IV	ante	IV	ante	IV	ante
3	V	Nonas	III	Nonas	III	Nonas	III	Nonas
4	IV		pridie Nonas		pridie Nonas		pridie Nonas	
5	III		Nonis		Nonis		Nonis	
6	pridie Nonas		VIII		VIII		VIII	
7	Nonis		VII		VII		VII	
8	VIII		VI	ante	VI	ante	VI	ante
9	VII		V	Idus	V	Idus	V	Idus
10	VI	ante	IV		IV		IV	
11	V	Idus	III		III		III	
12	IV		pridie Idus		pridie Idus		pridie Idus	
13	III		Idibus		Idibus		Idibus	
14	pridie Idus		XIX		XVIII		XVI	
15	Idibus		XVIII		XVII		XV	
16	XVII		XVII		XVI		XIV	
17	XVI		XVI		XV		XIII	
18	XV		XV		XIV		XII	
19	XIV		XIV		XIII		XI	
20	XIII		XIII		XII	ante Kalendas	X	ante Kalendas
21	XII		XII	ante Kalendas	XI	(of the month	IX	Martias
22	XI	ante Kalendas	XI	(of the month	X	following)	VIII	
23	X	(of the month	X	following)	IX		VII	
24	IX	following)	IX		VIII		*VI	
25	VIII		VIII		VII		V	
26	VII		VII		VI		IV	
27	VI		VI		V		III	
28	V		V		IV		pridie Kalendas	
29	IV		IV		III			
30	III		III		pridie Kalendas			
31	pridie Kalendas (Aprilis, Iunias, Sextilis, Novembris)		pridie Kalendas (Februarias, Septembris, Iunuarias)		(Maias, Quinctilis, Octobris, Decembris)		*(repeated in leap year)	

Calendar for Any Year 1780–2040

To select the correct calendar for any year between 1780 and 2040, consult the index below
* leap year

1780 N*	1813 K	1846 I	1879 G	1912 D*	1945 C	1978 A	2011 M
1781 C	1814 M	1847 K	1880 J*	1913 G	1946 E	1979 C	2012 B*
1782 E	1815 A	1848 N*	1881 M	1914 I	1947 G	1980 F*	2013 E
1783 G	1816 D*	1849 C	1882 A	1915 K	1948 J*	1981 I	2014 G
1784 J*	1817 G	1850 E	1883 C	1916 N*	1949 M	1982 K	2015 I
1785 M	1818 I	1851 I	1884 F*	1917 C	1950 A	1983 M	2016 L*
1786 A	1819 K	1852 J*	1885 I	1918 E	1951 C	1984 B*	2017 A
1787 C	1820 N*	1853 M	1886 K	1919 G	1952 F*	1985 E	2018 C
1788 F*	1821 C	1854 A	1887 M	1920 J*	1953 I	1986 G	2019 E
1789 I	1822 E	1855 C	1888 B*	1921 M	1954 K	1987 I	2020 H*
1790 K	1823 G	1856 F*	1889 E	1922 A	1955 M	1988 L*	2021 K
1791 M	1824 J*	1857 I	1890 G	1923 C	1956 B*	1989 A	2022 M
1792 B*	1825 M	1858 M	1891 I	1924 F*	1957 E	1990 C	2023 A
1793 E	1826 A	1859 M	1892 L*	1925 I	1958 G	1991 E	2024 D*
1794 G	1827 C	1860 B*	1893 A	1926 K	1959 I	1992 H*	2025 G
1795 I	1828 F*	1861 E	1894 C	1927 M	1960 L*	1993 K	2026 I
1796 L*	1829 I	1862 G	1895 E	1928 B*	1961 A	1994 M	2027 K
1797 A	1830 K	1863 I	1896 H*	1929 E	1962 C	1995 A	2028 N*
1798 C	1831 M	1864 L*	1897 K	1930 G	1963 E	1996 D*	2029 C
1799 E	1832 B*	1865 A	1898 M	1931 I	1964 H*	1997 G	2030 E
1800 G	1833 E	1866 C	1899 A	1932 L*	1965 K	1998 I	2031 G
1801 I	1834 G	1867 E	1900 C	1933 A	1966 M	1999 K	2032 J*
1802 K	1835 I	1868 H*	1901 E	1934 C	1967 A	2000 N*	2033 M
1803 M	1836 L*	1869 K	1902 G	1935 E	1968 D*	2001 C	2034 A
1804 B*	1837 A	1870 M	1903 I	1936 H*	1969 G	2002 E	2035 C
1805 E	1838 C	1871 A	1904 L*	1937 K	1970 I	2003 G	2036 F*
1806 G	1839 E	1872 D*	1905 A	1938 M	1971 K	2004 J*	2037 I
1807 I	1840 H*	1873 G	1906 C	1939 A	1972 N*	2005 M	2038 K
1808 L*	1841 K	1874 I	1907 E	1940 D*	1973 C	2006 A	2039 M
1809 A	1842 M	875 K	1908 H*	1941 G	1974 E	2007 C	2040 B*
1810 C	1843 A	1876 N*	1909 K	1942 I	1975 G	2008 F*	
1811 E	1844 D*	1877 C	1910 M	1943 K	1976 J*	2009 I	
1812 H*	1845 G	1878 E	1911 A	1944 N*	1977 M	2010 K	

A

January
Sun.	1	8	15	22	29
Mon.	2	9	16	23	30
Tue.	3	10	17	24	31
Wed.	4	11	18	25	
Thur.	5	12	19	26	
Fri.	6	13	20	27	
Sat.	7	14	21	28	

February
Sun.	5	12	19	26	
Mon.	6	13	20	27	
Tue.	7	14	21	28	
Wed.	1	8	15	22	
Thur.	2	9	16	23	
Fri.	3	10	17	24	
Sat.	4	11	18	25	

March
Sun.	5	12	19	26	
Mon.	6	13	20	27	
Tue.	7	14	21	28	
Wed.	1	8	15	22	29
Thur.	2	9	16	23	30
Fri.	3	10	17	24	31
Sat.	4	11	18	25	

April
Sun.	2	9	16	23	30
Mon.	3	10	17	24	
Tue.	4	11	18	25	
Wed.	5	12	19	26	
Thur.	6	13	20	27	
Fri.	7	14	21	28	
Sat.	1	8	15	22	29

May
Sun.	7	14	21	28	
Mon.	1	8	15	22	29
Tue.	2	9	16	23	30
Wed.	3	10	17	24	31
Thur.	4	11	18	25	
Fri.	5	12	19	26	
Sat.	6	13	20	27	

June
Sun.	4	11	18	25	
Mon.	5	12	19	26	
Tue.	6	13	20	27	
Wed.	7	14	21	28	
Thur.	1	8	15	22	29
Fri.	2	9	16	23	30
Sat.	3	10	17	24	

July
Sun.	2	9	16	23	30
Mon.	3	10	17	24	31
Tue.	4	11	18	25	
Wed.	5	12	19	26	
Thur.	6	13	20	27	
Fri.	7	14	21	28	
Sat.	1	8	15	22	29

August
Sun.	6	13	20	27	
Mon.	7	14	21	28	
Tue.	1	8	15	22	29
Wed.	2	9	16	23	30
Thur.	3	10	17	24	31
Fri.	4	11	18	25	
Sat.	5	12	19	26	

September
Sun.	3	10	17	24	
Mon.	4	11	18	25	
Tue.	5	12	19	26	
Wed.	6	13	20	27	
Thur.	7	14	21	28	
Fri.	1	8	15	22	29
Sat.	2	9	16	23	30

October
Sun.	1	8	15	22	29
Mon.	2	9	16	23	30
Tue.	3	10	17	24	31
Wed.	4	11	18	25	
Thur.	5	12	19	26	
Fri.	6	13	20	27	
Sat.	7	14	21	28	

November
Sun.	5	12	19	26	
Mon.	6	13	20	27	
Tue.	7	14	21	28	
Wed.	1	8	15	22	29
Thur.	2	9	16	23	30
Fri.	3	10	17	24	
Sat.	4	11	18	25	

December
Sun.	3	10	17	24	31
Mon.	4	11	18	25	
Tue.	5	12	19	26	
Wed.	6	13	20	27	
Thur.	7	14	21	28	
Fri.	1	8	15	22	29
Sat.	2	9	16	23	30

EASTER DAYS
March 26	1815, 1826, 1837, 1967, 1978, 1989
April 2	1809, 1893, 1899, 1961
April 9	1871, 1882, 1939, 1950, 2023, 2034
April 16	1786, 1797, 1843, 1854, 1865, 1911, 1922, 1933, 1995, 2006, 2017
April 23	1905

B (LEAP YEAR)

January
Sun.	1	8	15	22	29
Mon.	2	9	16	23	30
Tue.	3	10	17	24	31
Wed.	4	11	18	25	
Thur.	5	12	19	26	
Fri.	6	13	20	27	
Sat.	7	14	21	28	

February
Sun.	5	12	19	26	
Mon.	6	13	20	27	
Tue.	7	14	21	28	
Wed.	1	8	15	22	29
Thur.	2	9	16	23	
Fri.	3	10	17	24	
Sat.	4	11	18	25	

March
Sun.	4	11	18	25	
Mon.	5	12	19	26	
Tue.	6	13	20	27	
Wed.	7	14	21	28	
Thur.	1	8	15	22	29
Fri.	2	9	16	23	30
Sat.	3	10	17	24	31

April
Sun.	1	8	15	22	29
Mon.	2	9	16	23	30
Tue.	3	10	17	24	
Wed.	4	11	18	25	
Thur.	5	12	19	26	
Fri.	6	13	20	27	
Sat.	7	14	21	28	

May
Sun.	6	13	20	27	
Mon.	7	14	21	28	
Tue.	1	8	15	22	29
Wed.	2	9	16	23	30
Thur.	3	10	17	24	31
Fri.	4	11	18	25	
Sat.	5	12	19	26	

June
Sun.	3	10	17	24	
Mon.	4	11	18	25	
Tue.	5	12	19	26	
Wed.	6	13	20	27	
Thur.	7	14	21	28	
Fri.	1	8	15	22	29
Sat.	2	9	16	23	30

July
Sun.	1	8	15	22	29
Mon.	2	9	16	23	30
Tue.	3	10	17	24	31
Wed.	4	11	18	25	
Thur.	5	12	19	26	
Fri.	6	13	20	27	
Sat.	7	14	21	28	

August
Sun.	5	12	19	26	
Mon.	6	13	20	27	
Tue.	7	14	21	28	
Wed.	1	8	15	22	29
Thur.	2	9	16	23	30
Fri.	3	10	17	24	31
Sat.	4	11	18	25	

September
Sun.	2	9	16	23	30
Mon.	3	10	17	24	
Tue.	4	11	18	25	
Wed.	5	12	19	26	
Thur.	6	13	20	27	
Fri.	7	14	21	28	
Sat.	1	8	15	22	29

October
Sun.	7	14	21	28	
Mon.	1	8	15	22	29
Tue.	2	9	16	23	30
Wed.	3	10	17	24	31
Thur.	4	11	18	25	
Fri.	5	12	19	26	
Sat.	6	13	20	27	

November
Sun.	4	11	18	25	
Mon.	5	12	19	26	
Tue.	6	13	20	27	
Wed.	7	14	21	28	
Thur.	1	8	15	22	29
Fri.	2	9	16	23	30
Sat.	3	10	17	24	

December
Sun.	2	9	16	23	30
Mon.	3	10	17	24	31
Tue.	4	11	18	25	
Wed.	5	12	19	26	
Thur.	6	13	20	27	
Fri.	7	14	21	28	
Sat.	1	8	15	22	29

EASTER DAYS
April 1	1804, 1888, 1956, 2040
April 8	1792, 1860, 1928, 2012
April 22	1832, 1984

C

	January	*February*	*March*
Sun.	7 14 21 28	4 11 18 25	4 11 18 25
Mon.	1 8 15 22 29	5 12 19 26	5 12 19 26
Tue.	2 9 16 23 30	6 13 20 27	6 13 20 27
Wed.	3 10 17 24 31	7 14 21 28	7 14 21 28
Thur.	4 11 18 25	1 8 15 22	1 8 15 22 29
Fri.	5 12 19 26	2 9 16 23	2 9 16 23 30
Sat.	6 13 20 27	3 10 17 24	3 10 17 24 31

	April	*May*	*June*
Sun.	1 8 15 22 29	6 13 20 27	3 10 17 24
Mon.	2 9 16 23 30	7 14 21 28	4 11 18 25
Tue.	3 10 17 24	1 8 15 22 29	5 12 19 26
Wed.	4 11 18 25	2 9 16 23 30	6 13 20 27
Thur.	5 12 19 26	3 10 17 24 31	7 14 21 28
Fri.	6 13 20 27	4 11 18 25	1 8 15 22 29
Sat.	7 14 21 28	5 12 19 26	2 9 16 23 30

	July	*August*	*September*
Sun.	1 8 15 22 29	5 12 19 26	2 9 16 23 30
Mon.	2 9 16 23 30	6 13 20 27	3 10 17 24
Tue.	3 10 17 24 31	7 14 21 28	4 11 18 25
Wed.	4 11 18 25	1 8 15 22 29	5 12 19 26
Thur.	5 12 19 26	2 9 16 23 30	6 13 20 27
Fri.	6 13 20 27	3 10 17 24 31	7 14 21 28
Sat.	7 14 21 28	4 11 18 25	1 8 15 22 29

	October	*November*	*December*
Sun.	7 14 21 28	4 11 18 25	2 9 16 23 30
Mon.	1 8 15 22 29	5 12 19 26	3 10 17 24 31
Tue.	2 9 16 23 30	6 13 20 27	4 11 18 25
Wed.	3 10 17 24 31	7 14 21 28	5 12 19 26
Thur.	4 11 18 25	1 8 15 22 29	6 13 20 27
Fri.	5 12 19 26	2 9 16 23 30	7 14 21 28
Sat.	6 13 20 27	3 10 17 24	1 8 15 22 29

EASTER DAYS

March 25	1883, 1894, 1951, 2035
April 1	1866, 1877, 1923, 1934, 1945, 2018, 2029
April 8	1787, 1798, 1849, 1855, 1917, 2007
April 15	1781, 1827, 1838, 1900, 1906, 1979, 1990, 2001
April 22	1810, 1821, 1962, 1973

E

	January	*February*	*March*
Sun.	6 13 20 27	3 10 17 24	3 10 17 24 31
Mon.	7 14 21 28	4 11 18 25	4 11 18 25
Tue.	1 8 15 22 29	5 12 19 26	5 12 19 26
Wed.	2 9 16 23 30	6 13 20 27	6 13 20 27
Thur.	3 10 17 24 31	7 14 21 28	7 14 21 28
Fri.	4 11 18 25	1 8 15 22	1 8 15 22 29
Sat.	5 12 19 26	2 9 16 23	2 9 16 23 30

	April	*May*	*June*
Sun.	7 14 21 28	5 12 19 26	2 9 16 23 30
Mon.	1 8 15 22 29	6 13 20 27	3 10 17 24
Tue.	2 9 16 23 30	7 14 21 28	4 11 18 25
Wed.	3 10 17 24	1 8 15 22 29	5 12 19 26
Thur.	4 11 18 25	2 9 16 23 30	6 13 20 27
Fri.	5 12 19 26	3 10 17 24 31	7 14 21 28
Sat.	6 13 20 27	4 11 18 25	1 8 15 22 29

	July	*August*	*September*
Sun.	7 14 21 28	4 11 18 25	1 8 15 22 29
Mon.	1 8 15 22 29	5 12 19 26	2 9 16 23 30
Tue.	2 9 16 23 30	6 13 20 27	3 10 17 24
Wed.	3 10 17 24 31	7 14 21 28	4 11 18 25
Thur.	4 11 18 25	1 8 15 22 29	5 12 19 26
Fri.	5 12 19 26	2 9 16 23 30	6 13 20 27
Sat.	6 13 20 27	3 10 17 24 31	7 14 21 28

	October	*November*	*December*
Sun.	6 13 20 27	3 10 17 24	1 8 15 22 29
Mon.	7 14 21 28	4 11 18 25	2 9 16 23 30
Tue.	1 8 15 22 29	5 12 19 26	3 10 17 24 31
Wed.	2 9 16 23 30	6 13 20 27	4 11 18 25
Thur.	3 10 17 24 31	7 14 21 28	5 12 19 26
Fri.	4 11 18 25	1 8 15 22 29	6 13 20 27
Sat.	5 12 19 26	2 9 16 23 30	7 14 21 28

EASTER DAYS

March 24	1799
March 31	1782, 1793, 1839, 1850, 1861, 1907
	1918, 1929, 1991, 2002, 2013
April 7	1822, 1833, 1901, 1985
April 14	1805, 1811, 1895, 1963, 1974
April 21	1867, 1878, 1889, 1935, 1946, 1957, 2019, 2030

D (LEAP YEAR)

	January	*February*	*March*
Sun.	7 14 21 28	4 11 18 25	3 10 17 24 31
Mon.	1 8 15 22 29	5 12 19 26	4 11 18 25
Tue.	2 9 16 23 30	6 13 20 27	5 12 19 26
Wed.	3 10 17 24 31	7 14 21 28	6 13 20 27
Thur.	4 11 18 25	1 8 15 22 29	7 14 21 28
Fri.	5 12 19 26	2 9 16 23	1 8 15 22 29
Sat.	6 13 20 27	3 10 17 24	2 9 16 23 30

	April	*May*	*June*
Sun.	7 14 21 28	5 12 19 26	2 9 16 23 30
Mon.	1 8 15 22 29	6 13 20 27	3 10 17 24
Tue.	2 9 16 23 30	7 14 21 28	4 11 18 25
Wed.	3 10 17 24	1 8 15 22 29	5 12 19 26
Thur.	4 11 18 25	2 9 16 23 30	6 13 20 27
Fri.	5 12 19 26	3 10 17 24 31	7 14 21 28
Sat.	6 13 20 27	4 11 18 25	1 8 15 22 29

	July	*August*	*September*
Sun.	7 14 21 28	4 11 18 25	1 8 15 22 29
Mon.	1 8 15 22 29	5 12 19 26	2 9 16 23 30
Tue.	2 9 16 23 30	6 13 20 27	3 10 17 24
Wed.	3 10 17 24 31	7 14 21 28	4 11 18 25
Thur.	4 11 18 25	1 8 15 22 29	5 12 19 26
Fri.	5 12 19 26	2 9 16 23 30	6 13 20 27
Sat.	6 13 20 27	3 10 17 24 31	7 14 21 28

	October	*November*	*December*
Sun.	6 13 20 27	3 10 17 24	1 8 15 22 29
Mon.	7 14 21 28	4 11 18 25	2 9 16 23 30
Tue.	1 8 15 22 29	5 12 19 26	3 10 17 24 31
Wed.	2 9 16 23 30	6 13 20 27	4 11 18 25
Thur.	3 10 17 24 31	7 14 21 28	5 12 19 26
Fri.	4 11 18 25	1 8 15 22 29	6 13 20 27
Sat.	5 12 19 26	2 9 16 23 30	7 14 21 28

EASTER DAYS

March 24	1940
March 31	1872, 2024
April 7	1844, 1912, 1996
April 14	1816, 1968

F (LEAP YEAR)

	January	*February*	*March*
Sun.	6 13 20 27	3 10 17 24	2 9 16 23 30
Mon.	7 14 21 28	4 11 18 25	3 10 17 24 31
Tue.	1 8 15 22 29	5 12 19 26	4 11 18 25
Wed.	2 9 16 23 30	6 13 20 27	5 12 19 26
Thur.	3 10 17 24 31	7 14 21 28	6 13 20 27
Fri.	4 11 18 25	1 8 15 22 29	7 14 21 28
Sat.	5 12 19 26	2 9 16 23	1 8 15 22 29

	April	*May*	*June*
Sun.	6 13 20 27	4 11 18 25	1 8 15 22 29
Mon.	7 14 21 28	5 12 19 26	2 9 16 23 30
Tue.	1 8 15 22 29	6 13 20 27	3 10 17 24
Wed.	2 9 16 23 30	7 14 21 28	4 11 18 25
Thur.	3 10 17 24	1 8 15 22 29	5 12 19 26
Fri.	4 11 18 25	2 9 16 23 30	6 13 20 27
Sat.	5 12 19 26	3 10 17 24 31	7 14 21 28

	July	*August*	*September*
Sun.	6 13 20 27	3 10 17 24 31	7 14 21 28
Mon.	7 14 21 28	4 11 18 25	1 8 15 22 29
Tue.	1 8 15 22 29	5 12 19 26	2 9 16 23 30
Wed.	2 9 16 23 30	6 13 20 27	3 10 17 24
Thur.	3 10 17 24 31	7 14 21 28	4 11 18 25
Fri.	4 11 18 25	1 8 15 22 29	5 12 19 26
Sat.	5 12 19 26	2 9 16 23 30	6 13 20 27

	October	*November*	*December*
Sun.	5 12 19 26	2 9 16 23 30	7 14 21 28
Mon.	6 13 20 27	3 10 17 24	1 8 15 22 29
Tue.	7 14 21 28	4 11 18 25	2 9 16 23 30
Wed.	1 8 15 22 29	5 12 19 26	3 10 17 24 31
Thur.	2 9 16 23 30	6 13 20 27	4 11 18 25
Fri.	3 10 17 24 31	7 14 21 28	5 12 19 26
Sat.	4 11 18 25	1 8 15 22 29	6 13 20 27

EASTER DAYS

March 23	1788, 1856, 2008
April 6	1828, 1980
April 13	1884, 1952, 2036
April 20	1924

G

January / February / March

	January	*February*	*March*
Sun.	5 12 19 26	2 9 16 23	2 9 16 23 30
Mon.	6 13 20 27	3 10 17 24	3 10 17 24 31
Tue.	7 14 21 28	4 11 18 25	4 11 18 25
Wed.	1 8 15 22 29	5 12 19 26	5 12 19 26
Thur.	2 9 16 23 30	6 13 20 27	6 13 20 27
Fri.	3 10 17 24 31	7 14 21 28	7 14 21 28
Sat.	4 11 18 25	1 8 15 22	1 8 15 22 29

April / May / June

	April	*May*	*June*
Sun.	6 13 20 27	4 11 18 25	1 8 15 22 29
Mon.	7 14 21 28	5 12 19 26	2 9 16 23 30
Tue.	1 8 15 22 29	6 13 20 27	3 10 17 24
Wed.	2 9 16 23 30	7 14 21 28	4 11 18 25
Thur.	3 10 17 24	1 8 15 22 29	5 12 19 26
Fri.	4 11 18 25	2 9 16 23 30	6 13 20 27
Sat.	5 12 19 26	3 10 17 24 31	7 14 21 28

July / August / September

	July	*August*	*September*
Sun.	6 13 20 27	3 10 17 24 31	7 14 21 28
Mon.	7 14 21 28	4 11 18 25	1 8 15 22 29
Tue.	1 8 15 22 29	5 12 19 26	2 9 16 23 30
Wed.	2 9 16 23 30	6 13 20 27	3 10 17 24
Thur.	3 10 17 24	7 14 21 28	4 11 18 25
Fri.	4 11 18 25	1 8 15 22 29	5 12 19 26
Sat.	5 12 19 26	2 9 16 23 30	6 13 20 27

October / November / December

	October	*November*	*December*
Sun.	5 12 19 26	2 9 16 23 30	7 14 21 28
Mon.	6 13 20 27	3 10 17 24	1 8 15 22 29
Tue.	7 14 21 28	4 11 18 25	2 9 16 23 30
Wed.	1 8 15 22 29	5 12 19 26	3 10 17 24 31
Thur.	2 9 16 23 30	6 13 20 27	4 11 18 25
Fri.	3 10 17 24 31	7 14 21 28	5 12 19 26
Sat.	4 11 18 25	1 8 15 22 29	6 13 20 27

EASTER DAYS

March 23	1845, 1913
March 30	1823, 1834, 1902, 1975, 1986, 1997
April 6	1806, 1817, 1890, 1947, 1958, 1969
April 13	1800, 1873, 1879, 1941, 2031
April 20	1783, 1794, 1851, 1862, 1919, 1930, 2003, 2014, 2025

I

January / February / March

	January	*February*	*March*
Sun.	4 11 18 25	1 8 15 22	1 8 15 22 29
Mon.	5 12 19 26	2 9 16 23	2 9 16 23 30
Tue.	6 13 20 27	3 10 17 24	3 10 17 24 31
Wed.	7 14 21 28	4 11 18 25	4 11 18 25
Thur.	1 8 15 22 29	5 12 19 26	5 12 19 26
Fri.	2 9 16 23 30	6 13 20 27	6 13 20 27
Sat.	3 10 17 24 31	7 14 21 28	7 14 21 28

April / May / June

	April	*May*	*June*
Sun.	5 12 19 26	3 10 17 24 31	7 14 21 28
Mon.	6 13 20 27	4 11 18 25	1 8 15 22 29
Tue.	7 14 21 28	5 12 19 26	2 9 16 23 30
Wed.	1 8 15 22 29	6 13 20 27	3 10 17 24
Thur.	2 9 16 23 30	7 14 21 28	4 11 18 25
Fri.	3 10 17 24	1 8 15 22 29	5 12 19 26
Sat.	4 11 18 25	2 9 16 23 30	6 13 20 27

July / August / September

	July	*August*	*September*
Sun.	5 12 19 26	2 9 16 23 30	6 13 20 27
Mon.	6 13 20 27	3 10 17 24 31	7 14 21 28
Tue.	7 14 21 28	4 11 18 25	1 8 15 22 29
Wed.	1 8 15 22 29	5 12 19 26	2 9 16 23 30
Thur.	2 9 16 23 30	6 13 20 27	3 10 17 24
Fri.	3 10 17 24 31	7 14 21 28	4 11 18 25
Sat.	4 11 18 25	1 8 15 22 29	5 12 19 26

October / November / December

	October	*November*	*December*
Sun.	4 11 18 25	1 8 15 22 29	6 13 20 27
Mon.	5 12 19 26	2 9 16 23 30	7 14 21 28
Tue.	6 13 20 27	3 10 17 24	1 8 15 22 29
Wed.	7 14 21 28	4 11 18 25	2 9 16 23 30
Thur.	1 8 15 22 29	5 12 19 26	3 10 17 24 31
Fri.	2 9 16 23 30	6 13 20 27	4 11 18 25
Sat.	3 10 17 24 31	7 14 21 28	5 12 19 26

EASTER DAYS

March 22	1818
March 29	1807, 1891, 1959, 1970
April 5	1795, 1801, 1863, 1874, 1885, 1931, 1942, 1953, 2015, 2026, 2037
April 12	1789, 1846, 1857, 1903, 1914, 1925, 1998, 2009
April 19	1829, 1835, 1981, 1987

H (LEAP YEAR)

January / February / March

	January	*February*	*March*
Sun.	5 12 19 26	2 9 16 23	1 8 15 22 29
Mon.	6 13 20 27	3 10 17 24	2 9 16 23 30
Tue.	7 14 21 28	4 11 18 25	3 10 17 24 31
Wed.	1 8 15 22 29	5 12 19 26	4 11 18 25
Thur.	2 9 16 23 30	6 13 20 27	5 12 19 26
Fri.	3 10 17 24 31	7 14 21 28	6 13 20 27
Sat.	4 11 18 25	1 8 15 22 29	7 14 21 28

April / May / June

	April	*May*	*June*
Sun.	5 12 19 26	3 10 17 24 31	7 14 21 28
Mon.	6 13 20 27	4 11 18 25	1 8 15 22 29
Tue.	7 14 21 28	5 12 19 26	2 9 16 23 30
Wed.	1 8 15 22 29	6 13 20 27	3 10 17 24
Thur.	2 9 16 23 30	7 14 21 28	4 11 18 25
Fri.	3 10 17 24	1 8 15 22 29	5 12 19 26
Sat.	4 11 18 25	2 9 16 23 30	6 13 20 27

July / August / September

	July	*August*	*September*
Sun.	5 12 19 26	2 9 16 23 30	6 13 20 27
Mon.	6 13 20 27	3 10 17 24 31	7 14 21 28
Tue.	7 14 21 28	4 11 18 25	1 8 15 22 29
Wed.	1 8 15 22 29	5 12 19 26	2 9 16 23 30
Thur.	2 9 16 23 30	6 13 20 27	3 10 17 24
Fri.	3 10 17 24 31	7 14 21 28	4 11 18 25
Sat.	4 11 18 25	1 8 15 22 29	5 12 19 26

October / November / December

	October	*November*	*December*
Sun.	4 11 18 25	1 8 15 22 29	6 13 20 27
Mon.	5 12 19 26	2 9 16 23 30	7 14 21 28
Tue.	6 13 20 27	3 10 17 24	1 8 15 22 29
Wed.	7 14 21 28	4 11 18 25	2 9 16 23 30
Thur.	1 8 15 22 29	5 12 19 26	3 10 17 24 31
Fri.	2 9 16 23 30	6 13 20 27	4 11 18 25
Sat.	3 10 17 24 31	7 14 21 28	5 12 19 26

EASTER DAYS

March 29	1812, 1964
April 5	1896
April 12	1868, 1936, 2020
April 19	1840, 1908, 1992

J (LEAP YEAR)

January / February / March

	January	*February*	*March*
Sun.	4 11 18 25	1 8 15 22 29	7 14 21 28
Mon.	5 12 19 26	2 9 16 23	1 8 15 22 29
Tue.	6 13 20 27	3 10 17 24	2 9 16 23 30
Wed.	7 14 21 28	4 11 18 25	3 10 17 24 31
Thur.	1 8 15 22 29	5 12 19 26	4 11 18 25
Fri.	2 9 16 23 30	6 13 20 27	5 12 19 26
Sat.	3 10 17 24 31	7 14 21 28	6 13 20 27

April / May / June

	April	*May*	*June*
Sun.	4 11 18 25	2 9 16 23 30	6 13 20 27
Mon.	5 12 19 26	3 10 17 24 31	7 14 21 28
Tue.	6 13 20 27	4 11 18 25	1 8 15 22 29
Wed.	7 14 21 28	5 12 19 26	2 9 16 23 30
Thur.	1 8 15 22 29	6 13 20 27	3 10 17 24
Fri.	2 9 16 23 30	7 14 21 28	4 11 18 25
Sat.	3 10 17 24	1 8 15 22 29	5 12 19 26

July / August / September

	July	*August*	*September*
Sun.	4 11 18 25	1 8 15 22 29	5 12 19 26
Mon.	5 12 19 26	2 9 16 23 30	6 13 20 27
Tue.	6 13 20 27	3 10 17 24 31	7 14 21 28
Wed.	7 14 21 28	4 11 18 25	1 8 15 22 29
Thur.	1 8 15 22 29	5 12 19 26	2 9 16 23 30
Fri.	2 9 16 23 30	6 13 20 27	3 10 17 24
Sat.	3 10 17 24 31	7 14 21 28	4 11 18 25

October / November / December

	October	*November*	*December*
Sun.	3 10 17 24 31	7 14 21 28	5 12 19 26
Mon.	4 11 18 25	1 8 15 22 29	6 13 20 27
Tue.	5 12 19 26	2 9 16 23 30	7 14 21 28
Wed.	6 13 20 27	3 10 17 24	1 8 15 22 29
Thur.	7 14 21 28	4 11 18 25	2 9 16 23 30
Fri.	1 8 15 22 29	5 12 19 26	3 10 17 24 31
Sat.	2 9 16 23 30	6 13 20 27	4 11 18 25

EASTER DAYS

March 28	1880, 1948, 2032
April 4	1920
April 11	1784, 1852, 2004
April 18	1824, 1976

K

	January	February	March
Sun.	3 10 17 24 31	7 14 21 28	7 14 21 28
Mon.	4 11 18 25	1 8 15 22	1 8 15 22 29
Tue.	5 12 19 26	2 9 16 23	2 9 16 23 30
Wed.	6 13 20 27	3 10 17 24	3 10 17 24 31
Thur.	7 14 21 28	4 11 18 25	4 11 18 25
Fri.	1 8 15 22 29	5 12 19 26	5 12 19 26
Sat.	2 9 16 23 30	6 13 20 27	6 13 20 27

	April	May	June
Sun.	4 11 18 25	2 9 16 23 30	6 13 20 27
Mon.	5 12 19 26	3 10 17 24 31	7 14 21 28
Tue.	6 13 20 27	4 11 18 25	1 8 15 22 29
Wed.	7 14 21 28	5 12 19 26	2 9 16 23 30
Thur.	1 8 15 22 29	6 13 20 27	3 10 17 24
Fri.	2 9 16 23 30	7 14 21 28	4 11 18 25
Sat.	3 10 17 24	1 8 15 22 29	5 12 19 26

	July	August	September
Sun.	4 11 18 25	1 8 15 22 29	5 12 19 26
Mon.	5 12 19 26	2 9 16 23 30	6 13 20 27
Tue.	6 13 20 27	3 10 17 24 31	7 14 21 28
Wed.	7 14 21 28	4 11 18 25	1 8 15 22 29
Thur.	1 8 15 22 29	5 12 19 26	2 9 16 23 30
Fri.	2 9 16 23 30	6 13 20 27	3 10 17 24
Sat.	3 10 17 24 31	7 14 21 28	4 11 18 25

	October	November	December
Sun.	3 10 17 24 31	7 14 21 28	5 12 19 26
Mon.	4 11 18 25	1 8 15 22 29	6 13 20 27
Tue.	5 12 19 26	2 9 16 23 30	7 14 21 28
Wed.	6 13 20 27	3 10 17 24	1 8 15 22 29
Thur.	7 14 21 28	4 11 18 25	2 9 16 23 30
Fri.	1 8 15 22 29	5 12 19 26	3 10 17 24 31
Sat.	2 9 16 23 30	6 13 20 27	4 11 18 25

Easter Days

March 28	1869, 1875, 1937, 2027
April 4	1790, 1847, 1858, 1915, 1926, 1999, 2010, 2021
April 11	1819, 1830, 1841, 1909, 1971, 1982, 1993
April 18	1802, 1813, 1897, 1954, 1965
April 25	1886, 1943, 2038

M

	January	February	March
Sun.	2 9 16 23 30	6 13 20 27	6 13 20 27
Mon.	3 10 17 24 31	7 14 21 28	7 14 21 28
Tue.	4 11 18 25	1 8 15 22	1 8 15 22 29
Wed.	5 12 19 26	2 9 16 23	2 9 16 23 30
Thur.	6 13 20 27	3 10 17 24	3 10 17 24 31
Fri.	7 14 21 28	4 11 18 25	4 11 18 25
Sat.	1 8 15 22 29	5 12 19 26	5 12 19 26

	April	May	June
Sun.	3 10 17 24	1 8 15 22 29	5 12 19 26
Mon.	4 11 18 25	2 9 16 23 30	6 13 20 27
Tue.	5 12 19 26	3 10 17 24 31	7 14 21 28
Wed.	6 13 20 27	4 11 18 25	1 8 15 22 29
Thur.	7 14 21 28	5 12 19 26	2 9 16 23 30
Fri.	1 8 15 22 29	6 13 20 27	3 10 17 24
Sat.	2 9 16 23 30	7 14 21 28	4 11 18 25

	July	August	September
Sun.	3 10 17 24 31	7 14 21 28	4 11 18 25
Mon.	4 11 18 25	1 8 15 22 29	5 12 19 26
Tue.	5 12 19 26	2 9 16 23 30	6 13 20 27
Wed.	6 13 20 27	3 10 17 24 31	7 14 21 28
Thur.	7 14 21 28	4 11 18 25	1 8 15 22 29
Fri.	1 8 15 22 29	5 12 19 26	2 9 16 23 30
Sat.	2 9 16 23 30	6 13 20 27	3 10 17 24

	October	November	December
Sun.	2 9 16 23 30	6 13 20 27	4 11 18 25
Mon.	3 10 17 24 31	7 14 21 28	5 12 19 26
Tue.	4 11 18 25	1 8 15 22 29	6 13 20 27
Wed.	5 12 19 26	2 9 16 23 30	7 14 21 28
Thur.	6 13 20 27	3 10 17 24	1 8 15 22 29
Fri.	7 14 21 28	4 11 18 25	2 9 16 23 30
Sat.	1 8 15 22 29	5 12 19 26	3 10 17 24 31

Easter Days

March 27	1785, 1842, 1853, 1910, 1921, 2005
April 3	1825, 1831, 1983, 1994
April 10	1803, 1814, 1887, 1898, 1955, 1966, 1977, 2039
April 17	1870, 1881, 1927, 1938, 1949, 2022, 2033
April 24	1791, 1859, 2011

L (LEAP YEAR)

	January	February	March
Sun.	3 10 17 24 31	7 14 21 28	6 13 20 27
Mon.	4 11 18 25	1 8 15 22 29	7 14 21 28
Tue.	5 12 19 26	2 9 16 23	1 8 15 22 29
Wed.	6 13 20 27	3 10 17 24	2 9 16 23 30
Thur.	7 14 21 28	4 11 18 25	3 10 17 24 31
Fri.	1 8 15 22 29	5 12 19 26	4 11 18 25
Sat.	2 9 16 23 30	6 13 20 27	5 12 19 26

	April	May	June
Sun.	3 10 17 24	1 8 15 22 29	5 12 19 26
Mon.	4 11 18 25	2 9 16 23 30	6 13 20 27
Tue.	5 12 19 26	3 10 17 24 31	7 14 21 28
Wed.	6 13 20 27	4 11 18 25	1 8 15 22 29
Thur.	7 14 21 28	5 12 19 26	2 9 16 23 30
Fri.	1 8 15 22 29	6 13 20 27	3 10 17 24
Sat.	2 9 16 23 30	7 14 21 28	4 11 18 25

	July	August	September
Sun.	3 10 17 24 31	7 14 21 28	4 11 18 25
Mon.	4 11 18 25	1 8 15 22 29	5 12 19 26
Tue.	5 12 19 26	2 9 16 23 30	6 13 20 27
Wed.	6 13 20 27	3 10 17 24 31	7 14 21 28
Thur.	7 14 21 28	4 11 18 25	1 8 15 22 29
Fri.	1 8 15 22 29	5 12 19 26	2 9 16 23 30
Sat.	2 9 16 23 30	6 13 20 27	3 10 17 24

	October	November	December
Sun.	2 9 16 23 30	6 13 20 27	4 11 18 25
Mon.	3 10 17 24 31	7 14 21 28	5 12 19 26
Tue.	4 11 18 25	1 8 15 22 29	6 13 20 27
Wed.	5 12 19 26	2 9 16 23 30	7 14 21 28
Thur.	6 13 20 27	3 10 17 24	1 8 15 22 29
Fri.	7 14 21 28	4 11 18 25	2 9 16 23 30
Sat.	1 8 15 22 29	5 12 19 26	3 10 17 24 31

Easter Days

March 27	1796, 1864, 1932, 2016
April 3	1836, 1904, 1988
April 17	1808, 1892, 1960

N (LEAP YEAR)

	January	February	March
Sun.	2 9 16 23 30	6 13 20 27	5 12 19 26
Mon.	3 10 17 24 31	7 14 21 28	6 13 20 27
Tue.	4 11 18 25	1 8 15 22 29	7 14 21 28
Wed.	5 12 19 26	2 9 16 23	1 8 15 22 29
Thur.	6 13 20 27	3 10 17 24	2 9 16 23 30
Fri.	7 14 21 28	4 11 18 25	3 10 17 24 31
Sat.	1 8 15 22 29	5 12 19 26	4 11 18 25

	April	May	June
Sun.	2 9 16 23 30	7 14 21 28	4 11 18 25
Mon.	3 10 17 24	1 8 15 22 29	5 12 19 26
Tue.	4 11 18 25	2 9 16 23 30	6 13 20 27
Wed.	5 12 19 26	3 10 17 24 31	7 14 21 28
Thur.	6 13 20 27	4 11 18 25	1 8 15 22 29
Fri.	7 14 21 28	5 12 19 26	2 9 16 23 30
Sat.	1 8 15 22 29	6 13 20 27	3 10 17 24

	July	August	September
Sun.	2 9 16 23 30	6 13 20 27	3 10 17 24
Mon.	3 10 17 24 31	7 14 21 28	4 11 18 25
Tue.	4 11 18 25	1 8 15 22 29	5 12 19 26
Wed.	5 12 19 26	2 9 16 23 30	6 13 20 27
Thur.	6 13 20 27	3 10 17 24 31	7 14 21 28
Fri.	7 14 21 28	4 11 18 25	1 8 15 22 29
Sat.	1 8 15 22 29	5 12 19 26	2 9 16 23 30

	October	November	December
Sun.	1 8 15 22 29	5 12 19 26	3 10 17 24 31
Mon.	2 9 16 23 30	6 13 20 27	4 11 18 25
Tue.	3 10 17 24 31	7 14 21 28	5 12 19 26
Wed.	4 11 18 25	1 8 15 22 29	6 13 20 27
Thur.	5 12 19 26	2 9 16 23 30	7 14 21 28
Fri.	6 13 20 27	3 10 17 24	1 8 15 22 29
Sat.	7 14 21 28	4 11 18 25	2 9 16 23 30

Easter Days

March 26	1780
April 2	1820, 1972
April 9	1944
April 16	2028
April 23	1848, 1916, 2000

GEOLOGICAL TIME

The earth is thought to have come into existence approximately 4,600 million years ago, but for nearly half this time, the Archean era, it was uninhabited. Life is generally believed to have emerged in the succeeding Proterozoic era. The Archean and the Proterozoic eras are often together referred to as the Precambrian.

Although primitive forms of life, e.g. algae and bacteria, existed during the Proterozoic era, it is not until the strata of Palaeozoic rocks is reached that abundant fossilized remains appear.

Since the Precambrian, there have been three great geological eras:

PALAEOZOIC ('ancient life')
*c.*570–*c.*245 million years ago

Cambrian – Mainly sandstones, slate and shales; limestones in Scotland. Shelled fossils and invertebrates, e.g. trilobites and brachiopods, appear

Ordovician – Mainly shales and mudstones, e.g. in north Wales; limestones in Scotland. First fishes

Silurian – Shales, mudstones and some limestones, found mostly in Wales and southern Scotland

Devonian – Old red sandstone, shale, limestone and slate, e.g. in south Wales and the West Country

Carboniferous – Coal-bearing rocks, millstone grit, limestone and shale. First traces of land-living life

Permian – Marls, sandstones and clays. First reptile fossils

There were two great phases of mountain building in the Palaeozoic era: the Caledonian, characterized in Britain by NE–SW lines of hills and valleys; and the later Hercyian, widespread in west Germany and adjacent areas, and in Britain exemplified in E.–W. lines of hills and valleys.

The end of the Palaeozoic era was marked by the extensive glaciations of the Permian period in the southern continents and the decline of amphibians. It was succeeded by an era of warm conditions.

MESOZOIC ('middle forms of life')
*c.*245–*c.*65 million years ago

Triassic – Mostly sandstone, e.g. in the West Midlands

Jurassic – Mainly limestones and clays, typically displayed in the Jura mountains, and in England in a NE–SW belt from Lincolnshire and the Wash to the Severn and the Dorset coast

Cretaceous – Mainly chalk, clay and sands, e.g. in Kent and Sussex

Giant reptiles were dominant during the Mesozoic era, but it was at this time that marsupial mammals first appeared, as well as *Archaeopteryx lithographica*, the earliest known species of bird. Coniferous trees and flowering plants also developed during the era and, with the birds and the mammals, were the main species to survive into the Cenozoic era. The giant reptiles became extinct.

CENOZOIC ('recent life')
from *c.*65 million years ago

Palaeocene ⎫ The emergence of new forms of life,
Eocene   ⎭ including existing species

Oligocene – Fossils of a few still existing species

Miocene – Fossil remains show a balance of existing and extinct species

Pliocene – Fossil remains show a majority of still existing species

Pleistocene – The majority of remains are those of still existing species

Holocene – The present, post-glacial period. Existing species only, except for a few exterminated by man

In the last 25 million years, from the Miocene through the Pliocene periods, the Alpine-Himalayan and the circum-Pacific phases of mountain building reached their climax. During the Pleistocene period ice-sheets repeatedly locked up masses of water as land ice; its weight depressed the land, but the locking-up of the water lowered the sea-level by 100–200 metres. The glaciations and interglacials of the Ice Age are difficult to date and classify, but recent scientific opinion considers the Pleistocene period to have begun approximately 1.64 million years ago. The last glacial retreat, merging into the Holocene period, was 10,000 years ago.

HUMAN DEVELOPMENT

Any consideration of the history of mankind must start with the fact that all members of the human race belong to one species of animal, i.e. *Homo sapiens*, the definition of a species being in biological terms that all its members can interbreed. As a species of mammal it is possible to group man with other similar types, known as the primates. Amongst these is found a sub-group, the apes, which includes, in addition to man, the chimpanzees, gorillas, orang-utans and gibbons. All lack a tail, have shoulder blades at the back, and a Y-shaped chewing pattern on the surface of their molars, as well as showing the more general primate characteristics of four incisors, a thumb which is able to touch the fingers of the same hand, and finger and toe nails instead of claws. The factors available to scientific study suggest that human beings have chimpanzees and gorillas as their nearest relatives in the animal world. However, there remains the possibility that there once lived creatures, now extinct, which were closer to modern man than the chimpanzees and gorillas, and which shared with modern man the characteristics of having flat faces (i.e. the absence of a pronounced muzzle), being bipedal, and possessing large brains.

There are two broad groups of extinct apes recognized by specialists. The ramapithecines, the remains of which, mainly jaw fragments, have been found in east Africa, Asia, and Turkey, lived about 14 to 8 million years ago. From the evidence of their teeth it seems they chewed more in the manner of modern man than the other presently living apes. The second group, the australopithecines, have left more numerous remains amongst which sub-groups may be detected, although the geographic spread is limited to south and east Africa. Living between 5 and 1.5 million years ago, they were closer relatives of modern man to the extent that they walked upright, did not have an extensive muzzle and had similar types of pre-molars. The first australopithecine remains were recognized at Taung in South Africa in 1924 and subsequent discoveries include those at the Olduvai Gorge in Tanzania. The most impressive discovery was made at Hadar, Ethiopia, in 1974 when about half a skeleton, known as 'Lucy', was found.

Also in east Africa, between 2 million and 1.5 million years ago, lived a hominid group which not only walked upright, had a flat face, and a large brain case, but also made simple pebble and flake stone tools. On present evidence these habilines seem to have been the first people to make tools, however crude. This facility is related to the larger brain size and human beings are the only animals to make implements to be used in other processes. These early pebble tool users, because of their distinctive

GEOLOGICAL TIME

Era	Period	Epoch	Date began*	Evolutionary stages
Cenozoic	Quaternary	Holocene	0.01	Man
		Pleistocene	1.64	
	Tertiary	Pliocene	5.2	
		Miocene	23.3	
		Oligocene	35.4	
		Eocene	56.5	
		Palaeocene	65.0	
Mesozoic	Cretaceous		145.6	
	Jurassic		208.0	First birds
	Triassic		245.0	First mammals
Palaeozoic	Permian		290.0	First reptiles
	Carboniferous		362.5	First amphibians and insects
	Devonian		408.5	
	Silurian		439.0	
	Ordovician		510.0	First fishes
	Cambrian		570.0	First invertebrates
Precambrian			4,600.0	First primitive life forms, e.g. algae and bacteria

*millions of years ago

characteristics, have been grouped as a separate sub-species, now extinct, of the genus *Homo* and are known as *Homo habilis*.

The use of fire, again a human characteristic, is associated with another group of extinct hominids whose remains, about a million years old, are found in south and east Africa, China, Indonesia, north Africa and Europe. Mastery of the techniques of making fire probably helped the colonization of the colder northern areas and in this respect the site of Vertesszollos in Hungary is of particular importance. *Homo erectus* is the name given to this group of fossils and it includes a number of famous individual discoveries, e.g. Solo Man, Heidelberg Man, and especially Peking Man who lived at the cave site at Choukoutien which has yielded evidence of fire and burnt bone.

The well-known group Neanderthal Man, or *Homo sapiens neandertalensis*, is an extinct form of modern man who lived between about 100,000 and 40,000 years ago, thus spanning the last Ice Age. Indeed, its ability to adapt to the cold climate on the edge of the ice-sheets is one of its characteristic features, the remains being found only in Europe, Asia and the Middle East. Complete neanderthal skeletons were found during excavations at Tabun in Israel, together with evidence of tool-making and the use of fire. Distinguished by very large brains, it seems that neanderthal man was the first to develop recognizable social customs, especially deliberate burial rites. Why the neanderthalers became extinct is not clear but it may be connected with the climatic changes at the end of the Ice Ages, which would have seriously affected their food supplies; possibly they became too specialized for their own good.

The Swanscombe skull is the only known human fossil remains found in England. Some specialists see Swanscombe Man (or, more probably, woman) as a neanderthaler. Others group these remains together with the Steinheim skull from Germany, seeing both as a separate sub-species. There is too little evidence as yet on which to form a final judgement.

Modern Man, *Homo sapiens sapiens*, the surviving sub-species of *Homo sapiens*, had evolved to our present physical condition and had colonized much of the world by about 30,000 years ago. There are many previously distinguished individual specimens, e.g. Cromagnon Man, which may now be grouped together as *Homo sapiens sapiens*. It was modern man who spread to the American continent by crossing the landbridge between Siberia and Alaska and thence moved south through North America and into South America. Equally it is modern man who over the last 30,000 years has been responsible for the major developments in technology, art and civilization generally.

One of the problems for those studying fossil man is the lack in many cases of sufficient quantities of fossil bone for analysis. It is important that theories should be tested against evidence, rather than the evidence being made to fit the theory. The Piltdown hoax is a well-known example of 'fossils' being forged to fit what was seen in some quarters as the correct theory of man's evolution.

CULTURAL DEVELOPMENT

The Eurocentric bias of early archaeologists meant that the search for a starting point for the development and transmission of cultural ideas, especially by migration, trade and warfare, concentrated unduly on Europe and the Near East. The Three Age system, whereby pre-history was divided into a Stone Age, a Bronze Age and an Iron Age, was devised by Christian Thomsen, curator of the National Museum of Denmark in the early 19th century, to facilitate the classification of the museum's collections. The descriptive adjectives referred to the materials from which the implements and weapons were made and came to be regarded as the dominant features of the societies to which they related. The refinement of the Three Age system once dominated archaeological thought and remains a generally accepted concept in the popular mind. However, it is now seen by archaeologists as an inadequate model for human development.

Common sense suggests that there were no complete breaks between one so-called Age and another, any more than contemporaries would have regarded 1485 as a complete break between medieval and modern English history. Nor can the Three Age system be applied universally. In some areas it is necessary to insert a Copper Age, while in Africa south of the Sahara there would seem to be no Bronze Age at all; in Australia, Old Stone Age societies survived, while in South America, New Stone Age communities existed into modern times. The civilizations in other parts of the world clearly invalidate a Eurocentric theory of human development.

The concept of the 'Neolithic revolution', associated with the domestication of plants and animals, was a development of particular importance in the human cultural pattern. It reflected change from the primitive hunter/gatherer economies to a more settled agricultural way of life and therefore, so the argument goes, made possible the development of urban civilization. However, it can no longer be argued that this 'revolution' took place only in one area from which all development stemmed. Though it appears that the cultivation of wheat and barley was first undertaken, together with the domestication of cattle and goats/sheep in the Fertile Crescent (the area bounded by the rivers Tigris and Euphrates), there is evidence that rice was first deliberately planted and pigs domesticated in south-east Asia, maize first cultivated in Central America and llamas first domesticated in South America. It has been recognized in recent years that cultural changes can take place independently of each other in different parts of the world at different rates and different times. There is no need for a general diffusionist theory.

Although scholars will continue to study the particular societies which interest them, it may be possible to obtain a reliable chronological framework, in absolute terms of years, against which the cultural development of any particular area may be set. The development and refinement of radio-carbon dating and other scientific methods of producing absolute chronologies is enabling the cross-referencing of societies to be undertaken. As the techniques of dating become more rigorous in application and the number of scientifically obtained dates increases, the attainment of an absolute chronology for prehistoric societies throughout the world comes closer to being achieved.

Tidal Tables

CONSTANTS

The constant tidal difference may be used in conjunction with the time of high water at a standard port shown in the predictions data (pages 98–103) to find the time of high water at any of the ports or places listed below.

These tidal differences are very approximate and should be used only as a guide to the time of high water at the places below. More precise local data should be obtained for navigational and other nautical purposes.

All data allow high water time to be found in Greenwich Mean Time; this applies also to data for the months when British Summer Time is in operation and the hour's time difference should be allowed for. Ports marked * are in a different time zone and the standard time zone difference also needs to be added/subtracted to give local time.

EXAMPLE

Required time of high water at Stranraer at 2 January 2000
Appropriate time of high water at Greenock

Afternoon tide 2 January	2026 hrs
Tidal difference	−0020 hrs
High water at Stranraer	2006 hrs

The columns headed 'Springs' and 'Neaps' show the height, in metres, of the tide above datum for mean high water springs and mean high water neaps respectively.

Port		Diff. h m	Springs m	Neaps m
Aberdeen	Leith	−1 19	4.3	3.4
*Antwerp (Prosperpolder)	London	+0 50	5.8	4.8
Ardrossan	Greenock	−0 15	3.2	2.6
Avonmouth	London	−6 45	13.2	9.8
Ayr	Greenock	−0 25	3.0	2.5
Barrow (Docks)	Liverpool	0 00	9.3	7.1
Belfast	London	−2 47	3.5	3.0
Blackpool	Liverpool	−0 10	8.9	7.0
*Boulogne	London	−2 44	8.9	7.2
*Calais	London	−2 04	7.2	5.9
*Cherbourg	London	−6 00	6.4	5.0
Cobh	Liverpool	−5 55	4.2	3.2
Cowes	London	−2 38	4.2	3.5
Dartmouth	London	+4 25	4.9	3.8
*Dieppe	London	−3 03	9.3	7.3
Douglas, IOM	Liverpool	−0 04	6.9	5.4
Dover	London	−2 52	6.7	5.3
Dublin	London	−2 05	4.1	3.4
Dun Laoghaire	London	−2 10	4.1	3.4
*Dunkirk	London	−1 54	6.0	4.9
Fishguard	Liverpool	−4 01	4.8	3.4
Fleetwood	Liverpool	0 00	9.2	7.3
*Flushing	London	−0 15	4.7	3.9
Folkestone	London	−3 04	7.1	5.7
Galway	Liverpool	−6 08	5.1	3.9
Glasgow	Greenock	+0 26	4.7	4.0
Harwich	London	−2 06	4.0	3.4
*Le Havre	London	−3 55	7.9	6.6
Heysham	Liverpool	+0 05	9.4	7.4
Holyhead	Liverpool	−0 50	5.6	4.4
*Hook of Holland	London	−0 01	2.1	1.7
Hull (Albert Dock)	London	−7 40	7.5	5.8
Immingham	London	−8 00	7.3	5.8
Larne	London	−2 40	2.8	2.5
Lerwick	Leith	−3 48	2.2	1.6
Londonderry	London	−5 37	2.7	2.1
Lowestoft	London	−4 25	2.4	2.1
Margate	London	−1 53	4.8	3.9
Milford Haven	Liverpool	−5 08	7.0	5.2
Morecambe	Liverpool	+0 07	9.5	7.4
Newhaven	London	−2 46	6.7	5.1
Oban	Greenock	+5 43	4.0	2.9
*Ostend	London	−1 32	5.1	4.2
Plymouth (Devonport)	London	+4 05	5.5	4.4
Portland	London	+5 09	2.1	1.4
Portsmouth	London	−2 38	4.7	3.8
Ramsgate	London	−2 32	5.2	4.1
Richmond Lock	London	+1 00	4.9	3.7
Rosslare Harbour	Liverpool	−5 24	1.9	1.4
Rosyth	Leith	+0 09	5.8	4.7
*Rotterdam	London	+1 45	2.0	1.7
St Helier	London	+4 48	11.0	8.1
St Malo	London	+4 27	12.2	9.2
St Peter Port	London	+4 54	9.3	7.0
Scrabster	Leith	−6 06	5.0	4.0
Sheerness	London	−1 19	5.8	4.7
Shoreham	London	−2 44	6.3	4.9
Southampton (1st high water)	London	−2 54	4.5	3.7
Spurn Head	London	−8 25	6.9	5.5
Stornoway	Liverpool	−4 16	4.8	3.7
Stranraer	Greenock	−0 20	3.0	2.4
Stromness	Leith	−5 26	3.6	2.7
Swansea	London	−7 35	9.5	7.2
Tees (River Entrance)	Leith	+1 09	5.5	4.3
Tilbury	London	−0 49	6.4	5.4
Tobermory	Liverpool	−5 11	4.4	3.3
Tyne River (North Shields)	London	−1030	5.0	3.9
Ullapool	Leith	−7 40	5.2	3.9
Walton-on-the-Naze	London	−2 10	4.2	3.4
Wick	Leith	−3 26	3.5	2.8
*Zeebrugge	London	−0 55	4.8	3.9

PREDICTIONS

The data on pages 98–103 are daily predictions of the time and height of high water at London Bridge, Liverpool, Greenock and Leith. The time of the data is Greenwich Mean Time; this applies also to data for the months when British Summer Time is in operation and the hour's time difference should be allowed for. The datum of predictions for each port shows the difference of height, in metres from Ordnance data (Newlyn).

The tidal information for London Bridge, Liverpool, Greenock and Leith is reproduced with the permission of the UK Hydrographic Office and the Controller of HMSO. Crown copyright reserved.

JANUARY 2000   *High water*   GMT

		LONDON BRIDGE			LIVERPOOL			GREENOCK			LEITH		
		*Datum of predictions 3.20 m below			*Datum of predictions 4.93 m below			*Datum of predictions 1.62 m below			*Datum of predictions 2.90 m below		
		hr m	ht m	hr	ht m	hr m	ht m	hr	ht m	hr m	ht m	hr	ht m	hr m	ht m	hr	ht m
1	Saturday	09 31	5.9	22 05	6.1	07 11	7.6	19 37	7.8	08 41	3.0	20 26	3.1	10 47	4.5	23 15	4.7
2	Sunday	10 32	6.0	23 01	6.2	08 11	7.9	20 35	8.0	09 46	3.1	21 45	3.1	11 48	4.6	—	—
3	Monday	11 28	6.2	23 53	6.4	09 02	8.2	21 25	8.3	10 37	3.2	22 42	3.1	00 14	4.8	12 42	4.8
4	Tuesday	—	—	12 20	6.4	09 46	8.6	22 07	8.5	11 21	3.3	23 29	3.2	01 05	4.9	13 26	4.9
5	Wednesday	00 39	6.6	13 07	6.6	10 25	8.8	22 45	8.7	—	—	12 01	3.4	01 49	5.0	14 03	5.1
6	Thursday	01 22	6.7	13 48	6.7	11 01	9.0	23 20	8.7	00 09	3.2	12 38	3.5	02 27	5.1	14 37	5.2
7	Friday	01 59	6.7	14 25	6.7	11 36	9.1	23 54	8.8	00 45	3.2	13 10	3.5	03 02	5.1	15 09	5.2
8	Saturday	02 33	6.7	15 00	6.6	—	—	12 11	9.1	01 18	3.2	13 40	3.5	03 36	5.2	15 41	5.3
9	Sunday	03 05	6.7	15 33	6.6	00 28	8.8	12 47	9.1	01 52	3.2	14 11	3.5	04 10	5.2	16 15	5.3
10	Monday	03 38	6.6	16 09	6.7	01 05	8.8	13 23	9.0	02 29	3.2	14 45	3.5	04 46	5.2	16 50	5.2
11	Tuesday	04 12	6.6	16 47	6.7	01 42	8.7	14 01	8.9	03 08	3.2	15 21	3.5	05 23	5.1	17 27	5.2
12	Wednesday	04 50	6.6	17 29	6.6	02 22	8.6	14 42	8.8	03 49	3.2	16 00	3.4	06 04	5.0	18 07	5.1
13	Thursday	05 32	6.5	18 14	6.5	03 05	8.4	15 28	8.6	04 31	3.1	16 42	3.3	06 48	4.9	18 51	5.0
14	Friday	06 19	6.4	19 05	6.4	03 55	8.1	16 22	8.4	05 17	3.0	17 29	3.2	07 38	4.8	19 43	4.9
15	Saturday	07 13	6.3	20 03	6.2	04 54	7.9	17 25	8.2	06 07	3.0	18 26	3.1	08 37	4.7	20 46	4.8
16	Sunday	08 17	6.2	21 09	6.1	06 03	7.8	18 33	8.2	07 06	2.9	19 38	3.0	09 45	4.7	22 00	4.8
17	Monday	09 28	6.2	22 19	6.2	07 14	8.0	19 43	8.4	08 22	3.0	21 07	3.0	10 53	4.8	23 13	5.0
18	Tuesday	10 42	6.3	23 26	6.4	08 23	8.5	20 51	8.8	09 44	3.1	22 21	3.2	11 57	5.0	—	—
19	Wednesday	11 50	6.6	—	—	09 23	9.0	21 50	9.3	10 47	3.3	23 21	3.3	00 19	5.2	12 55	5.3
20	Thursday	00 26	6.7	12 52	7.0	10 17	9.5	22 45	9.6	11 39	3.5	—	—	01 18	5.5	13 46	5.6
21	Friday	01 21	7.0	13 47	7.3	11 08	9.8	23 35	9.8	00 16	3.4	12 28	3.7	02 11	5.7	14 34	5.7
22	Saturday	02 12	7.2	14 38	7.5	11 56	10.0	—	—	01 09	3.5	13 14	3.8	03 00	5.8	15 21	5.8
23	Sunday	02 59	7.2	15 27	7.5	00 23	9.8	12 43	10.0	01 59	3.5	13 58	3.9	03 49	5.8	16 08	5.8
24	Monday	03 44	7.2	16 14	7.5	01 10	9.7	13 28	9.9	02 46	3.5	14 41	3.9	04 37	5.7	16 56	5.7
25	Tuesday	04 27	7.1	16 58	7.3	01 54	9.4	14 12	9.6	03 29	3.4	15 23	3.9	05 24	5.5	17 45	5.5
26	Wednesday	05 07	6.9	17 40	7.0	02 37	9.0	14 55	9.1	04 10	3.4	16 04	3.8	06 13	5.2	18 35	5.3
27	Thursday	05 46	6.7	18 22	6.6	03 19	8.5	15 39	8.6	04 51	3.3	16 46	3.6	07 02	4.9	19 28	5.0
28	Friday	06 26	6.4	19 06	6.2	04 05	8.0	16 27	8.0	05 34	3.1	17 31	3.4	07 54	4.6	20 25	4.7
29	Saturday	07 14	6.1	19 57	5.9	05 00	7.5	17 27	7.5	06 21	3.0	18 19	3.2	08 49	4.4	21 24	4.5
30	Sunday	08 18	5.7	21 02	5.7	06 08	7.3	18 41	7.3	07 15	2.9	19 14	3.0	09 48	4.3	22 28	4.4
31	Monday	09 40	5.6	22 11	5.7	07 24	7.4	19 57	7.4	08 37	2.9	20 27	2.8	10 54	4.3	23 37	4.4

FEBRUARY 2000   *High water*   GMT

		LONDON BRIDGE			LIVERPOOL			GREENOCK			LEITH		
1	Tuesday	10 51	5.8	23 13	5.9	08 29	7.7	20 57	7.7	10 03	3.0	22 13	2.9	—	—	12 03	4.5
2	Wednesday	11 50	6.0	—	—	09 20	8.2	21 45	8.1	10 56	3.1	23 10	2.9	00 40	4.6	13 00	4.7
3	Thursday	00 07	6.2	12 42	6.3	10 04	8.6	22 26	8.4	11 40	3.3	23 53	3.0	01 29	4.8	13 43	4.9
4	Friday	00 56	6.6	13 26	6.6	10 43	8.9	23 03	8.7	—	—	12 18	3.4	02 09	5.0	14 20	5.1
5	Saturday	01 38	6.7	14 07	6.7	11 19	9.1	23 38	8.8	00 30	3.0	12 52	3.4	02 44	5.1	14 53	5.2
6	Sunday	02 17	6.7	14 43	6.7	11 54	9.2	—	—	01 03	3.1	13 21	3.4	03 17	5.2	15 25	5.3
7	Monday	02 52	6.7	15 18	6.8	00 13	8.9	12 30	9.2	01 36	3.1	13 52	3.4	03 50	5.3	15 57	5.4
8	Tuesday	03 25	6.7	15 53	6.8	00 48	9.0	13 06	9.3	02 10	3.1	14 26	3.5	04 24	5.3	16 30	5.4
9	Wednesday	03 57	6.7	16 29	6.8	01 24	9.0	13 43	9.3	02 46	3.2	15 02	3.5	05 00	5.3	17 05	5.4
10	Thursday	04 33	6.8	17 08	6.8	02 01	9.0	14 21	9.2	03 23	3.2	15 39	3.4	05 38	5.2	17 43	5.3
11	Friday	05 12	6.8	17 51	6.7	02 41	8.8	15 04	9.0	04 01	3.2	16 18	3.4	06 20	5.0	18 26	5.2
12	Saturday	05 56	6.7	18 38	6.5	03 26	8.5	15 53	8.6	04 41	3.1	17 00	3.2	07 06	4.9	19 14	5.0
13	Sunday	06 46	6.4	19 31	6.2	04 20	8.1	16 53	8.2	05 26	3.0	17 50	3.1	08 01	4.7	20 14	4.8
14	Monday	07 46	6.2	20 35	5.9	05 28	7.8	18 05	7.9	06 19	2.9	18 55	2.9	09 09	4.6	21 32	4.7
15	Tuesday	08 59	6.0	21 52	5.9	06 46	7.7	19 24	8.0	07 30	2.8	20 42	2.8	10 26	4.6	22 56	4.8
16	Wednesday	10 22	6.0	23 07	6.1	08 06	8.1	20 40	8.4	09 19	2.9	22 14	3.0	11 39	4.8	—	—
17	Thursday	11 38	6.4	—	—	09 13	8.7	21 43	8.9	10 33	3.1	23 17	3.1	00 10	5.0	12 42	5.1
18	Friday	00 11	6.5	12 41	6.8	10 08	9.3	22 36	9.4	11 27	3.4	—	—	01 12	5.3	13 35	5.4
19	Saturday	01 07	6.9	13 36	7.2	10 57	9.7	23 24	9.7	00 11	3.3	12 16	3.6	02 03	5.5	14 22	5.7
20	Sunday	01 57	7.1	14 25	7.4	11 42	9.9	—	—	01 01	3.3	13 01	3.7	02 49	5.7	15 07	5.8
21	Monday	02 43	7.2	15 11	7.5	00 08	9.8	12 26	10.0	01 47	3.4	13 44	3.8	03 33	5.7	15 50	5.8
22	Tuesday	03 26	7.2	15 54	7.4	00 50	9.7	13 07	9.9	02 28	3.4	14 24	3.8	04 16	5.6	16 34	5.8
23	Wednesday	04 04	7.2	16 33	7.2	01 29	9.5	13 46	9.6	03 04	3.4	15 03	3.8	04 58	5.4	17 18	5.6
24	Thursday	04 40	7.0	17 08	7.0	02 06	9.1	14 23	9.2	03 39	3.4	15 40	3.7	05 40	5.2	18 01	5.3
25	Friday	05 14	6.9	17 42	6.7	02 43	8.7	15 01	8.7	04 14	3.3	16 17	3.6	06 22	4.9	18 47	5.0
26	Saturday	05 50	6.6	18 17	6.4	03 21	8.2	15 42	8.1	04 51	3.2	16 56	3.4	07 05	4.6	19 37	4.6
27	Sunday	06 30	6.3	18 58	6.1	04 06	7.7	16 32	7.5	05 32	3.0	17 39	3.1	07 55	4.4	20 34	4.3
28	Monday	07 19	5.9	19 49	5.7	05 05	7.2	17 41	7.0	06 20	2.9	18 29	2.9	08 53	4.2	21 38	4.2
29	Tuesday	08 24	5.5	20 56	5.5	06 27	7.0	19 10	6.9	07 20	2.7	19 30	2.7	09 58	4.1	22 51	4.2

MARCH 2000   *High water*   GMT

		LONDON BRIDGE *Datum of predictions 3.20 m below*				LIVERPOOL *Datum of predictions 4.93 m below*				GREENOCK *Datum of predictions 1.62 m below*				LEITH *Datum of predictions 2.90 m below*			
		hr	ht m	hr	ht m	hr	ht m	hr	ht m	hr	ht m	hr	ht m	hr	ht m	hr	ht m
1	Wednesday	10 00	5.4	22 25	5.6	07 50	7.3	20 27	7.3	09 07	2.7	21 06	2.6	11 13	4.2	——	4.5
2	Thursday	11 18	5.7	23 34	6.0	08 52	7.8	21 20	7.8	10 28	2.9	22 47	2.8	00 08	4.3	12 27	4.5
3	Friday	——	—	12 14	6.2	09 39	8.3	22 03	8.3	11 15	3.1	23 32	2.9	01 04	4.6	13 17	4.7
4	Saturday	00 28	6.3	13 02	6.5	10 20	8.7	22 41	8.6	11 53	3.2	——	—	01 45	4.9	13 55	5.0
5	Sunday	01 15	6.6	13 44	6.7	10 57	9.0	23 17	8.9	00 09	3.0	12 26	3.3	02 20	5.1	14 29	5.2
6	Monday	01 56	6.7	14 22	6.9	11 33	9.2	23 52	9.1	00 43	3.0	12 57	3.3	02 53	5.3	15 01	5.4
7	Tuesday	02 33	6.8	14 58	6.9	——	—	12 08	9.4	01 14	3.1	13 29	3.4	03 26	5.4	15 33	5.5
8	Wednesday	03 07	6.8	15 33	7.0	00 27	9.2	12 45	9.5	01 47	3.1	14 04	3.4	04 00	5.5	16 07	5.6
9	Thursday	03 40	6.9	16 09	7.0	01 03	9.3	13 22	9.5	02 21	3.2	14 41	3.5	04 35	5.5	16 43	5.6
10	Friday	04 16	7.0	16 47	7.0	01 40	9.2	14 01	9.4	02 56	3.3	15 19	3.5	05 14	5.4	17 23	5.5
11	Saturday	04 55	7.0	17 28	6.8	02 19	9.1	14 43	9.1	03 32	3.3	15 57	3.4	05 55	5.2	18 07	5.3
12	Sunday	05 38	6.8	18 12	6.5	03 02	8.7	15 31	8.6	04 11	3.2	16 39	3.2	06 41	5.0	18 57	5.1
13	Monday	06 26	6.5	19 03	6.1	03 55	8.2	16 31	8.0	04 54	3.1	17 28	3.0	07 35	4.7	19 59	4.8
14	Tuesday	07 25	6.1	20 07	5.7	05 04	7.7	17 48	7.6	05 47	2.9	18 33	2.8	08 45	4.5	21 21	4.6
15	Wednesday	08 43	5.8	21 34	5.7	06 29	7.5	19 16	7.7	06 56	2.8	20 42	2.7	10 08	4.5	22 49	4.7
16	Thursday	10 16	5.9	22 54	6.0	07 55	7.9	20 34	8.1	09 02	2.8	22 13	2.9	11 26	4.7	——	—
17	Friday	11 30	6.4	23 57	6.4	09 02	8.5	21 34	8.7	10 19	3.1	23 11	3.1	00 05	4.9	12 31	5.0
18	Saturday	——	—	12 29	6.9	09 56	9.1	22 23	9.2	11 12	3.3	——	—	01 05	5.2	13 23	5.3
19	Sunday	00 51	6.8	13 22	7.2	10 42	9.5	23 07	9.5	00 01	3.2	12 00	3.5	01 52	5.4	14 08	5.6
20	Monday	01 40	7.1	14 09	7.4	11 24	9.8	23 47	9.6	00 46	3.3	12 43	3.6	02 34	5.5	14 49	5.7
21	Tuesday	02 24	7.2	14 52	7.4	——	—	12 04	9.8	01 28	3.3	13 25	3.6	03 13	5.6	15 30	5.7
22	Wednesday	03 04	7.2	15 30	7.3	00 25	9.5	12 42	9.6	02 03	3.3	14 03	3.7	03 52	5.5	16 11	5.7
23	Thursday	03 40	7.1	16 04	7.1	01 01	9.4	13 18	9.4	02 35	3.3	14 39	3.6	04 30	5.3	16 51	5.5
24	Friday	04 13	7.0	16 35	6.9	01 35	9.1	13 52	9.0	03 06	3.3	15 14	3.6	05 07	5.1	17 31	5.2
25	Saturday	04 45	6.8	17 05	6.7	02 09	8.8	14 27	8.6	03 38	3.3	15 49	3.5	05 44	4.9	18 12	4.9
26	Sunday	05 20	6.6	17 40	6.5	02 44	8.4	15 05	8.0	04 13	3.2	16 26	3.3	06 24	4.7	18 58	4.6
27	Monday	05 59	6.3	18 19	6.2	03 24	7.9	15 49	7.5	04 51	3.1	17 08	3.0	07 09	4.5	19 52	4.3
28	Tuesday	06 45	6.0	19 06	5.9	04 15	7.3	16 49	6.9	05 37	2.9	17 58	2.8	08 05	4.2	20 54	4.1
29	Wednesday	07 40	5.6	20 04	5.6	05 29	7.0	18 18	6.7	06 34	2.7	18 58	2.6	09 10	4.1	22 02	4.1
30	Thursday	08 54	5.4	21 25	5.5	07 03	7.0	19 47	7.0	07 47	2.6	20 13	2.6	10 22	4.1	23 18	4.2
31	Friday	10 35	5.6	22 53	5.8	08 15	7.5	20 46	7.6	09 40	2.7	22 04	2.7	11 38	4.3	——	—

APRIL 2000   *High water*   GMT

		LONDON BRIDGE				LIVERPOOL				GREENOCK				LEITH			
1	Saturday	11 39	6.0	23 54	6.1	09 06	8.1	21 32	8.1	10 37	2.9	22 58	2.8	00 24	4.5	12 38	4.6
2	Sunday	——	—	12 29	6.5	09 49	8.6	22 11	8.6	11 16	3.1	23 37	3.0	01 10	4.9	13 21	4.9
3	Monday	00 43	6.5	13 14	6.8	10 27	9.0	22 48	8.9	11 51	3.2	——	—	01 47	5.1	13 57	5.2
4	Tuesday	01 27	6.7	13 54	7.0	11 05	9.3	23 24	9.2	00 12	3.0	12 26	3.3	02 23	5.4	14 32	5.4
5	Wednesday	02 06	6.9	14 33	7.1	11 42	9.5	——	—	00 47	3.1	13 03	3.3	02 57	5.5	15 06	5.6
6	Thursday	02 43	7.0	15 10	7.1	00 02	9.4	12 22	9.6	01 21	3.2	13 42	3.4	03 33	5.6	15 43	5.7
7	Friday	03 21	7.1	15 49	7.1	00 40	9.5	13 02	9.6	01 56	3.3	14 21	3.5	04 11	5.6	16 23	5.7
8	Saturday	04 00	7.2	16 28	7.0	01 20	9.4	13 43	9.5	02 32	3.4	15 01	3.5	04 51	5.5	17 06	5.6
9	Sunday	04 41	7.1	17 09	6.8	02 01	9.2	14 28	9.1	03 09	3.4	15 42	3.4	05 34	5.3	17 53	5.4
10	Monday	05 26	6.9	17 53	6.5	02 47	8.8	15 18	8.5	03 48	3.3	16 26	3.2	06 22	5.0	18 47	5.1
11	Tuesday	06 16	6.5	18 43	6.1	03 41	8.2	16 20	7.9	04 33	3.2	17 20	2.9	07 18	4.8	19 54	4.8
12	Wednesday	07 18	6.1	19 51	5.7	04 52	7.7	17 41	7.5	05 27	3.0	18 38	2.7	08 33	4.6	21 18	4.6
13	Thursday	08 43	5.9	21 23	5.7	06 19	7.6	19 07	7.6	06 41	2.8	20 45	2.7	09 56	4.5	22 41	4.7
14	Friday	10 09	6.1	22 37	6.0	07 49	7.8	20 18	8.1	08 45	2.9	22 01	2.9	11 11	4.7	23 53	4.9
15	Saturday	11 15	6.5	23 37	6.5	08 44	8.4	21 15	8.6	09 59	3.1	22 55	3.1	——	—	12 14	5.0
16	Sunday	——	—	12 11	7.0	09 36	8.9	22 02	9.0	10 52	3.3	23 42	3.2	00 51	5.1	13 06	5.3
17	Monday	00 30	6.8	13 02	7.3	10 21	9.3	22 44	9.3	11 38	3.4	——	—	01 36	5.3	13 49	5.5
18	Tuesday	01 19	7.1	13 48	7.4	11 02	9.4	23 22	9.3	00 24	3.2	12 21	3.4	02 15	5.4	14 30	5.6
19	Wednesday	02 02	7.1	14 28	7.3	11 40	9.4	23 58	9.3	01 02	3.3	13 01	3.4	02 51	5.4	15 09	5.6
20	Thursday	02 41	7.1	15 04	7.1	——	—	12 16	9.3	01 35	3.3	13 38	3.4	03 27	5.4	15 48	5.5
21	Friday	03 17	7.0	15 35	6.9	00 31	9.2	12 50	9.1	02 06	3.3	14 13	3.4	04 02	5.3	16 26	5.3
22	Saturday	03 49	6.8	16 03	6.8	01 05	9.0	13 23	8.8	02 36	3.3	14 48	3.4	04 37	5.1	17 04	5.1
23	Sunday	04 21	6.7	16 34	6.7	01 38	8.8	13 57	8.5	03 07	3.3	15 23	3.3	05 12	5.0	17 44	4.9
24	Monday	04 55	6.6	17 09	6.6	02 13	8.4	14 34	8.1	03 41	3.3	16 01	3.2	05 50	4.8	18 27	4.6
25	Tuesday	05 34	6.4	17 48	6.4	02 52	8.0	15 17	7.6	04 17	3.1	16 43	3.0	06 33	4.6	19 17	4.4
26	Wednesday	06 19	6.1	18 34	6.0	03 38	7.6	16 10	7.1	05 01	2.9	17 33	2.8	07 24	4.4	20 13	4.2
27	Thursday	07 11	5.8	19 28	5.7	04 40	7.2	17 23	6.8	05 56	2.7	18 33	2.7	08 26	4.2	21 17	4.0
28	Friday	08 15	5.6	20 37	5.6	06 04	7.1	18 52	7.0	07 03	2.6	19 40	2.6	09 35	4.2	22 24	4.3
29	Saturday	09 35	5.7	22 00	5.7	07 23	7.4	20 00	7.4	08 22	2.7	20 58	2.7	10 45	4.3	23 30	4.5
30	Sunday	10 51	6.0	23 08	6.0	08 22	7.9	20 51	8.0	09 38	2.8	22 08	2.8	11 47	4.6	——	—

MAY 2000 *High water* GMT

		LONDON BRIDGE			LIVERPOOL				GREENOCK				LEITH			
		Datum of predictions 3.20 m below			*Datum of predictions 4.93 m below*				*Datum of predictions 1.62 m below*				*Datum of predictions 2.90 m below*			
		hr	ht m	hr	ht m	hr	ht m	hr	ht m	hr	ht m	hr	ht m	hr	ht m	hr	ht m

		hr	m	hr	m	hr	m	hr	m	hr	m	hr	m	hr	m	hr	m
1	Monday	11 48	6.4	—	—	09 09	8.4	21 34	8.5	10 29	3.0	22 57	3.0	00 24	4.8	12 38	4.9
2	Tuesday	00 03	6.4	12 38	6.8	09 52	8.9	22 14	9.0	11 12	3.1	23 38	3.1	01 09	5.1	13 20	5.2
3	Wednesday	00 51	6.7	13 22	7.0	10 33	9.3	22 55	9.3	11 53	3.3	—	—	01 49	5.4	14 00	5.5
4	Thursday	01 36	6.9	14 05	7.2	11 15	9.6	23 35	9.5	00 17	3.2	12 37	3.3	02 28	5.6	14 39	5.7
5	Friday	02 19	7.1	14 47	7.2	11 58	9.7	—	—	00 56	3.3	13 20	3.4	03 07	5.7	15 21	5.8
6	Saturday	03 02	7.3	15 29	7.2	00 18	9.6	12 43	9.7	01 34	3.4	14 04	3.4	03 48	5.7	16 05	5.8
7	Sunday	03 46	7.3	16 12	7.1	01 02	9.5	13 29	9.5	02 13	3.5	14 48	3.4	04 31	5.6	16 52	5.7
8	Monday	04 32	7.2	16 55	6.9	01 48	9.3	14 18	9.1	02 52	3.5	15 34	3.3	05 17	5.4	17 44	5.4
9	Tuesday	05 20	7.0	17 41	6.6	02 37	8.9	15 11	8.6	03 34	3.5	16 25	3.1	06 08	5.2	18 41	5.1
10	Wednesday	06 13	6.7	18 34	6.2	03 34	8.4	16 15	8.1	04 21	3.3	17 28	2.9	07 08	4.9	19 50	4.9
11	Thursday	07 17	6.3	19 44	5.9	04 44	8.0	17 30	7.7	05 18	3.1	18 52	2.8	08 23	4.7	21 08	4.7
12	Friday	08 37	6.2	21 05	5.9	06 02	7.8	18 46	7.7	06 34	3.0	20 26	2.8	09 39	4.7	22 22	4.7
13	Saturday	09 49	6.3	22 12	6.2	07 14	8.0	19 52	8.0	08 16	3.0	21 35	2.9	10 49	4.8	23 31	4.8
14	Sunday	10 50	6.6	23 10	6.5	08 17	8.3	20 48	8.4	09 31	3.1	22 29	3.0	11 50	5.0	—	—
15	Monday	11 46	6.9	—	—	09 10	8.7	21 36	8.7	10 26	3.2	23 15	3.1	00 28	5.0	12 43	5.2
16	Tuesday	00 04	6.8	12 37	7.1	09 56	8.9	22 18	9.0	11 13	3.3	23 56	3.2	01 14	5.1	13 29	5.3
17	Wednesday	00 53	6.9	13 22	7.2	10 38	9.0	22 56	9.0	11 56	3.3	—	—	01 53	5.2	14 10	5.3
18	Thursday	01 38	7.0	14 03	7.1	11 16	9.0	23 31	9.0	00 34	3.2	12 36	3.3	02 29	5.2	14 49	5.3
19	Friday	02 19	6.9	14 38	6.9	11 52	8.9	—	—	01 08	3.2	13 13	3.2	03 04	5.3	15 27	5.3
20	Saturday	02 55	6.8	15 08	6.8	00 04	9.0	12 25	8.8	01 40	3.3	13 48	3.2	03 37	5.2	16 04	5.2
21	Sunday	03 28	6.7	15 37	6.7	00 38	8.9	12 58	8.6	02 10	3.3	14 23	3.2	04 10	5.1	16 41	5.0
22	Monday	04 00	6.6	16 08	6.6	01 12	8.7	13 33	8.4	02 42	3.3	15 00	3.1	04 45	5.0	17 20	4.9
23	Tuesday	04 35	6.5	16 44	6.6	01 48	8.5	14 11	8.2	03 15	3.3	15 39	3.0	05 22	4.9	18 01	4.7
24	Wednesday	05 14	6.4	17 23	6.4	02 27	8.2	14 52	7.8	03 50	3.2	16 22	2.9	06 04	4.7	18 46	4.5
25	Thursday	05 58	6.2	18 08	6.2	03 11	7.9	15 40	7.5	04 31	3.0	17 12	2.8	06 50	4.5	19 37	4.4
26	Friday	06 47	6.0	18 59	6.0	04 05	7.6	16 39	7.2	05 21	2.9	18 08	2.7	07 44	4.4	20 34	4.3
27	Saturday	07 45	5.9	20 00	5.8	05 10	7.4	17 50	7.2	06 23	2.7	19 07	2.7	08 47	4.4	21 36	4.4
28	Sunday	08 51	5.9	21 10	5.9	06 21	7.5	19 02	7.5	07 31	2.7	20 10	2.7	09 53	4.4	22 39	4.6
29	Monday	10 00	6.1	22 18	6.1	07 27	7.9	20 02	8.0	08 42	2.8	21 17	2.8	10 56	4.6	23 38	4.8
30	Tuesday	11 03	6.4	23 19	6.4	08 24	8.4	20 54	8.5	09 44	3.0	22 16	2.9	11 53	4.9	—	—
31	Wednesday	—	—	12 00	6.7	09 15	8.9	21 41	9.0	10 37	3.1	23 06	3.1	00 30	5.1	12 43	5.2

JUNE 2000 *High water* GMT

| | | LONDON BRIDGE | | | | LIVERPOOL | | | | GREENOCK | | | | LEITH | | | |
		hr	m	hr	m	hr	m	hr	m	hr	m	hr	m	hr	m	hr	m
1	Thursday	00 15	6.7	12 51	7.0	10 03	9.3	22 26	9.3	11 25	3.2	23 51	3.2	01 17	5.4	13 30	5.5
2	Friday	01 07	7.0	13 40	7.2	10 51	9.5	23 12	9.6	—	—	12 13	3.3	02 00	5.6	14 16	5.7
3	Saturday	01 56	7.2	14 26	7.2	11 39	9.7	23 59	9.7	00 34	3.4	13 03	3.4	02 44	5.7	15 03	5.8
4	Sunday	02 45	7.4	15 12	7.3	—	—	12 28	9.6	01 17	3.5	13 52	3.4	03 28	5.7	15 51	5.8
5	Monday	03 34	7.4	15 58	7.2	00 47	9.6	13 18	9.5	02 00	3.6	14 42	3.3	04 14	5.7	16 41	5.7
6	Tuesday	04 23	7.4	16 44	7.0	01 37	9.4	14 10	9.2	02 42	3.6	15 33	3.3	05 03	5.5	17 35	5.5
7	Wednesday	05 13	7.2	17 32	6.8	02 29	9.2	15 03	8.8	03 27	3.6	16 28	3.1	05 57	5.3	18 33	5.3
8	Thursday	06 07	6.9	18 24	6.5	03 25	8.8	16 01	8.4	04 15	3.4	17 30	3.0	06 58	5.1	19 38	5.0
9	Friday	07 07	6.6	19 27	6.2	04 26	8.4	17 05	8.0	05 11	3.3	18 37	2.9	08 07	4.9	20 46	4.8
10	Saturday	08 14	6.4	20 36	6.1	05 33	8.1	18 13	7.8	06 16	3.1	19 49	2.9	09 15	4.9	21 53	4.7
11	Sunday	09 20	6.4	21 40	6.2	06 41	8.0	19 18	7.9	07 34	3.0	20 57	2.9	10 19	4.8	22 57	4.7
12	Monday	10 19	6.5	22 39	6.4	07 44	8.1	20 16	8.1	08 53	3.0	21 55	3.0	11 21	4.9	23 57	4.8
13	Tuesday	11 15	6.7	23 34	6.6	08 40	8.3	21 07	8.4	09 55	3.1	22 44	3.0	—	—	12 17	5.0
14	Wednesday	—	—	12 07	6.8	09 30	8.5	21 51	8.6	10 47	3.1	23 28	3.1	00 47	4.9	13 07	5.0
15	Thursday	00 26	6.7	12 54	6.9	10 14	8.6	22 31	8.8	11 32	3.1	—	—	01 31	5.0	13 51	5.1
16	Friday	01 14	6.8	13 37	6.9	10 54	8.6	23 07	8.9	00 08	3.2	12 13	3.1	02 09	5.1	14 32	5.1
17	Saturday	01 57	6.8	14 14	6.8	11 30	8.6	23 42	8.9	00 45	3.2	12 51	3.0	02 44	5.1	15 09	5.1
18	Sunday	02 36	6.7	14 46	6.7	—	—	12 04	8.6	01 18	3.3	13 27	3.0	03 17	5.2	15 45	5.1
19	Monday	03 11	6.6	15 17	6.6	00 16	8.8	12 39	8.5	01 50	3.3	14 02	3.0	03 49	5.1	16 21	5.0
20	Tuesday	03 44	6.5	15 49	6.6	00 51	8.8	13 14	8.4	02 20	3.3	14 39	3.0	04 24	5.1	16 57	5.0
21	Wednesday	04 18	6.5	16 24	6.5	01 28	8.6	13 51	8.3	02 53	3.3	15 19	3.0	05 00	5.0	17 36	4.9
22	Thursday	04 56	6.4	17 02	6.4	02 06	8.5	14 30	8.1	03 28	3.2	16 02	2.9	05 39	4.9	18 17	4.7
23	Friday	05 38	6.4	17 44	6.3	02 48	8.3	15 13	7.9	04 07	3.1	16 48	2.9	06 21	4.8	19 03	4.6
24	Saturday	06 24	6.3	18 32	6.2	03 34	8.1	16 03	7.7	04 51	3.0	17 37	2.8	07 07	4.7	19 53	4.5
25	Sunday	07 16	6.2	19 26	6.1	04 29	7.9	17 02	7.6	05 43	2.9	18 30	2.8	08 00	4.6	20 51	4.5
26	Monday	08 15	6.1	20 29	6.1	05 31	7.9	18 08	7.6	06 44	2.8	19 25	2.8	09 01	4.6	21 53	4.6
27	Tuesday	09 19	6.2	21 35	6.2	06 36	8.0	19 14	7.9	07 53	2.8	20 29	2.8	10 07	4.7	22 55	4.8
28	Wednesday	10 24	6.3	22 40	6.3	07 40	8.3	20 16	8.4	09 05	2.9	21 37	2.9	11 11	4.9	23 54	5.0
29	Thursday	11 26	6.6	23 43	6.6	08 41	8.7	21 11	8.9	10 08	3.1	22 37	3.1	—	—	12 11	5.1
30	Friday	—	—	12 24	6.8	09 38	9.1	22 04	9.3	11 04	3.2	23 29	3.2	00 48	5.3	13 07	5.4

JULY 2000 *High water* GMT

		LONDON BRIDGE				LIVERPOOL				GREENOCK				LEITH			
		Datum of predictions 3.20 m below				*Datum of predictions 4.93 m below*				*Datum of predictions 1.62 m below*				*Datum of predictions 2.90 m below*			
		hr	ht m	hr	ht m	hr	ht m	hr	ht m	hr	ht m	hr	ht m	hr	ht m	hr	ht m
1	Saturday	00 42	6.9	13 17	7.0	10 32	9.4	22 54	9.6	11 57	3.3	—	—	01 38	5.5	13 59	5.6
2	Sunday	01 38	7.2	14 08	7.2	11 24	9.6	23 44	9.7	00 18	3.4	12 51	3.3	02 25	5.7	14 49	5.8
3	Monday	02 30	7.4	14 56	7.3	—	—	12 16	9.6	01 04	3.5	13 45	3.3	03 12	5.8	15 39	5.9
4	Tuesday	03 22	7.5	15 44	7.3	00 34	9.8	13 07	9.6	01 50	3.6	14 38	3.3	04 00	5.8	16 30	5.8
5	Wednesday	04 12	7.5	16 31	7.2	01 25	9.7	13 57	9.4	02 34	3.7	15 29	3.3	04 50	5.7	17 22	5.6
6	Thursday	05 01	7.4	17 17	7.0	02 15	9.5	14 46	9.1	03 19	3.7	16 20	3.2	05 42	5.6	18 16	5.4
7	Friday	05 51	7.1	18 04	6.8	03 05	9.1	15 37	8.6	04 05	3.6	17 11	3.1	06 39	5.3	19 13	5.1
8	Saturday	06 43	6.8	18 56	6.5	03 58	8.7	16 31	8.2	04 53	3.5	18 03	3.0	07 40	5.1	20 13	4.8
9	Sunday	07 40	6.5	19 55	6.3	04 55	8.2	17 31	7.8	05 47	3.3	18 57	2.9	08 42	4.9	21 14	4.6
10	Monday	08 42	6.3	21 00	6.1	05 59	7.9	18 37	7.6	06 45	3.1	20 00	2.9	09 43	4.8	22 15	4.5
11	Tuesday	09 42	6.2	22 03	6.1	07 06	7.7	19 41	7.7	07 56	3.0	21 11	2.9	10 45	4.7	23 17	4.5
12	Wednesday	10 40	6.2	23 03	6.2	08 09	7.8	20 37	8.0	09 18	2.9	22 12	2.9	11 48	4.7	—	—
13	Thursday	11 34	6.4	23 59	6.4	09 04	8.0	21 26	8.3	10 23	2.9	23 02	3.1	00 17	4.7	12 45	4.8
14	Friday	—	—	12 25	6.6	09 52	8.2	22 09	8.6	11 13	3.0	23 45	3.2	01 08	4.8	13 34	4.9
15	Saturday	00 50	6.6	13 11	6.7	10 34	8.4	22 48	8.8	11 56	3.0	—	—	01 50	5.0	14 16	5.0
16	Sunday	01 37	6.7	13 52	6.8	11 12	8.5	23 24	8.9	00 25	3.2	12 35	2.9	02 26	5.1	14 53	5.0
17	Monday	02 18	6.7	14 28	6.7	11 48	8.5	23 58	8.9	01 01	3.3	13 11	2.9	03 00	5.1	15 27	5.1
18	Tuesday	02 55	6.6	15 02	6.7	—	—	12 22	8.5	01 32	3.3	13 45	2.9	03 32	5.2	16 00	5.1
19	Wednesday	03 29	6.6	15 34	6.6	00 33	8.9	12 56	8.6	02 01	3.3	14 20	3.0	04 05	5.2	16 35	5.1
20	Thursday	04 02	6.5	16 07	6.5	01 09	8.8	13 31	8.5	02 33	3.3	14 58	3.0	04 39	5.2	17 11	5.0
21	Friday	04 37	6.5	16 42	6.5	01 45	8.8	14 08	8.5	03 07	3.3	15 38	3.0	05 15	5.1	17 49	5.0
22	Saturday	05 16	6.5	17 20	6.5	02 23	8.7	14 46	8.4	03 44	3.2	16 18	3.0	05 53	5.0	18 31	4.9
23	Sunday	05 58	6.5	18 03	6.4	03 05	8.5	15 30	8.2	04 23	3.1	17 01	2.9	06 34	4.9	19 16	4.7
24	Monday	06 45	6.4	18 52	6.3	03 54	8.3	16 22	7.9	05 08	3.0	17 48	2.9	07 20	4.8	20 09	4.7
25	Tuesday	07 39	6.2	19 50	6.2	04 51	8.1	17 25	7.8	06 00	2.9	18 39	2.8	08 16	4.7	21 10	4.6
26	Wednesday	08 41	6.1	20 57	6.1	05 56	8.0	18 34	7.8	07 06	2.8	19 41	2.8	09 24	4.7	22 18	4.7
27	Thursday	09 49	6.1	22 08	6.2	07 06	8.1	19 45	8.1	08 29	2.8	21 00	2.9	10 39	4.8	23 25	4.9
28	Friday	10 58	6.3	23 19	6.4	08 17	8.4	20 50	8.6	09 49	3.0	22 15	3.0	11 49	5.0	—	—
29	Saturday	—	—	12 02	6.6	09 21	8.8	21 48	9.1	10 53	3.1	23 13	3.2	00 26	5.1	12 52	5.3
30	Sunday	00 25	6.8	12 59	6.9	10 19	9.2	22 41	9.6	11 50	3.2	—	—	01 21	5.4	13 47	5.6
31	Monday	01 24	7.1	13 52	7.1	11 13	9.5	23 31	9.8	00 04	3.4	12 45	3.3	02 10	5.7	14 37	5.8

AUGUST 2000 *High water* GMT

		LONDON BRIDGE				LIVERPOOL				GREENOCK				LEITH			
		hr	m	hr	m	hr	m	hr	m	hr	m	hr	m	hr	m	hr	m
1	Tuesday	02 17	7.4	14 41	7.3	—	—	12 03	9.7	00 52	3.6	13 38	3.3	02 57	5.8	15 26	5.9
2	Wednesday	03 08	7.6	15 27	7.3	00 20	9.9	12 52	9.7	01 38	3.7	14 28	3.4	03 44	5.9	16 14	5.8
3	Thursday	03 56	7.5	16 12	7.3	01 07	9.9	13 38	9.5	02 22	3.8	15 14	3.3	04 32	5.9	17 02	5.7
4	Friday	04 42	7.5	16 54	7.2	01 53	9.7	14 22	9.2	03 05	3.8	15 57	3.3	05 21	5.7	17 51	5.4
5	Saturday	05 26	7.2	17 36	7.0	02 37	9.3	15 05	8.8	03 46	3.7	16 38	3.2	06 12	5.5	18 41	5.1
6	Sunday	06 10	6.8	18 17	6.7	03 22	8.8	15 49	8.3	04 28	3.6	17 19	3.1	07 05	5.2	19 33	4.8
7	Monday	06 55	6.4	19 03	6.3	04 10	8.2	16 39	7.8	05 12	3.4	18 03	3.0	08 03	4.9	20 29	4.5
8	Tuesday	07 47	6.1	20 03	6.0	05 07	7.6	17 43	7.4	06 00	3.1	18 53	2.9	09 03	4.6	21 27	4.4
9	Wednesday	08 51	5.8	21 18	5.7	06 18	7.3	18 58	7.3	06 55	2.9	19 58	2.8	10 06	4.5	22 31	4.4
10	Thursday	09 58	5.8	22 30	5.8	07 36	7.3	20 07	7.6	08 08	2.7	21 35	2.9	11 14	4.4	23 40	4.5
11	Friday	11 00	5.9	23 32	6.1	08 40	7.5	21 02	8.0	10 02	2.8	22 37	3.0	—	—	12 22	4.5
12	Saturday	11 55	6.2	—	—	09 31	7.9	21 48	8.4	10 59	2.9	23 24	3.2	00 42	4.7	13 15	4.7
13	Sunday	00 27	6.4	12 45	6.5	10 15	8.2	22 29	8.7	11 43	2.9	—	—	01 29	4.9	13 58	4.9
14	Monday	01 15	6.6	13 30	6.7	10 54	8.5	23 06	8.9	00 05	3.2	12 22	3.0	02 07	5.1	14 33	5.1
15	Tuesday	01 57	6.8	14 09	6.8	11 29	8.6	23 40	9.0	00 41	3.3	12 56	3.0	02 40	5.2	15 05	5.2
16	Wednesday	02 35	6.8	14 45	6.7	—	—	12 03	8.7	01 12	3.3	13 27	3.0	03 12	5.3	15 37	5.3
17	Thursday	03 09	6.7	15 18	6.7	00 14	9.0	12 36	8.7	01 40	3.3	13 59	3.0	03 43	5.4	16 10	5.3
18	Friday	03 42	6.7	15 48	6.6	00 47	9.1	13 09	8.8	02 10	3.3	14 33	3.1	04 15	5.4	16 45	5.3
19	Saturday	04 15	6.7	16 19	6.6	01 22	9.1	13 43	8.8	02 44	3.3	15 09	3.1	04 49	5.4	17 21	5.2
20	Sunday	04 51	6.7	16 55	6.7	01 58	9.0	14 19	8.7	03 20	3.3	15 46	3.1	05 26	5.3	18 01	5.1
21	Monday	05 30	6.6	17 36	6.6	02 37	8.8	15 00	8.5	03 57	3.3	16 24	3.0	06 06	5.2	18 44	4.9
22	Tuesday	06 13	6.4	18 23	6.5	03 23	8.5	15 49	8.1	04 37	3.2	17 06	3.0	06 52	5.0	19 34	4.8
23	Wednesday	07 03	6.2	19 18	6.2	04 19	8.2	16 50	7.8	05 24	3.0	17 55	2.9	07 46	4.8	20 35	4.6
24	Thursday	08 04	5.9	20 25	6.0	05 27	7.8	18 05	7.7	06 26	2.8	18 56	2.8	08 56	4.7	21 49	4.6
25	Friday	09 18	5.8	21 44	6.0	06 45	7.8	19 25	7.9	08 02	2.7	20 27	2.8	10 19	4.7	23 04	4.8
26	Saturday	10 37	6.0	23 05	6.2	08 05	8.1	20 39	8.4	09 43	2.9	22 00	3.0	11 37	4.9	—	—
27	Sunday	11 45	6.4	—	—	09 14	8.6	21 39	9.1	10 51	3.1	23 00	3.3	00 11	5.1	12 44	5.3
28	Monday	00 14	6.7	12 44	6.8	10 10	9.1	22 30	9.6	11 46	3.3	23 51	3.5	01 08	5.4	13 37	5.6
29	Tuesday	01 12	7.1	13 35	7.1	11 00	9.5	23 17	9.9	—	—	12 37	3.3	01 56	5.5	14 25	5.8
30	Wednesday	02 03	7.5	14 23	7.3	11 47	9.7	—	—	00 38	3.6	13 25	3.4	02 41	5.9	15 09	5.9
31	Thursday	02 51	7.6	15 07	7.4	00 02	10.0	12 31	9.7	01 23	3.7	14 10	3.4	03 25	6.0	15 53	5.8

SEPTEMBER 2000   *High water*   GMT

| | | LONDON BRIDGE | | | | LIVERPOOL | | | | GREENOCK | | | | LEITH | | | |
| | | *Datum of predictions 3.20 m below | | | | *Datum of predictions 4.93 m below | | | | *Datum of predictions 1.62 m below | | | | *Datum of predictions 2.90 m below | | | |
		hr	ht m	hr	ht m	hr	ht m	hr	ht m	hr	ht m	hr	ht m	hr	ht m	hr	ht m
1	Friday	03 35	7.6	15 48	7.3	00 45	9.9	13 12	9.5	02 04	3.8	14 49	3.4	04 10	5.9	16 37	5.6
2	Saturday	04 17	7.4	16 27	7.2	01 26	9.7	13 51	9.2	02 44	3.8	15 25	3.4	04 55	5.8	17 20	5.4
3	Sunday	04 55	7.1	17 03	7.0	02 06	9.3	14 29	8.8	03 22	3.8	16 00	3.4	05 41	5.5	18 05	5.1
4	Monday	05 31	6.8	17 39	6.7	02 45	8.7	15 07	8.3	03 59	3.6	16 36	3.3	06 30	5.1	18 51	4.8
5	Tuesday	06 05	6.4	18 17	6.4	03 25	8.1	15 49	7.8	04 38	3.4	17 16	3.2	07 22	4.8	19 41	4.5
6	Wednesday	06 43	6.1	19 04	5.9	04 14	7.5	16 44	7.3	05 21	3.1	18 02	3.0	08 20	4.5	20 39	4.4
7	Thursday	07 32	5.7	20 09	5.5	05 23	7.0	18 06	7.0	06 11	2.9	18 58	2.9	09 24	4.3	21 44	4.3
8	Friday	08 48	5.5	21 51	5.5	06 58	6.9	19 34	7.3	07 15	2.7	20 26	2.8	10 36	4.2	22 56	4.3
9	Saturday	10 20	5.6	23 03	5.8	08 14	7.2	20 36	7.8	09 38	2.7	22 09	3.0	11 53	4.4	——	
10	Sunday	11 24	6.0	——		09 08	7.7	21 24	8.3	10 41	2.9	22 59	3.2	00 09	4.6	12 51	4.7
11	Monday	00 00	6.2	12 17	6.4	09 52	8.2	22 05	8.7	11 23	3.0	23 39	3.3	01 02	4.8	13 33	4.9
12	Tuesday	00 49	6.6	13 04	6.6	10 30	8.5	22 42	9.0	——		12 00	3.1	01 41	5.1	14 07	5.1
13	Wednesday	01 32	6.8	13 45	6.8	11 05	8.7	23 16	9.1	00 15	3.3	12 33	3.1	02 14	5.3	14 39	5.3
14	Thursday	02 10	6.9	14 21	6.8	11 38	8.9	23 49	9.2	00 45	3.3	13 03	3.1	02 46	5.4	15 10	5.4
15	Friday	02 44	6.9	14 54	6.8	——		12 10	9.0	01 14	3.4	13 32	3.2	03 17	5.5	15 43	5.5
16	Saturday	03 17	6.9	15 25	6.8	00 22	9.3	12 43	9.0	01 46	3.4	14 05	3.3	03 49	5.6	16 17	5.5
17	Sunday	03 50	6.9	15 56	6.8	00 57	9.3	13 17	9.0	02 21	3.4	14 39	3.3	04 24	5.6	16 54	5.4
18	Monday	04 25	6.8	16 32	6.8	01 34	9.2	13 54	8.9	02 57	3.4	15 14	3.3	05 01	5.5	17 33	5.3
19	Tuesday	05 03	6.7	17 13	6.8	02 14	9.0	14 35	8.6	03 34	3.4	15 51	3.3	05 44	5.3	18 17	5.1
20	Monday	05 45	6.5	18 00	6.5	02 59	8.6	15 23	8.2	04 13	3.2	16 32	3.2	06 32	5.1	19 07	4.9
21	Thursday	06 32	6.1	18 54	6.2	03 56	8.0	16 25	7.8	04 59	3.0	17 21	3.1	07 29	4.9	20 10	4.7
22	Friday	07 31	5.7	20 04	5.8	05 09	7.6	17 46	7.5	06 02	2.8	18 24	2.9	08 43	4.7	21 30	4.6
23	Saturday	08 54	5.6	21 35	5.8	06 37	7.5	19 16	7.6	07 59	2.7	20 06	2.9	10 11	4.7	22 50	4.8
24	Sunday	10 23	5.8	22 58	6.2	08 02	8.0	20 31	8.4	09 46	2.9	21 46	3.1	11 31	5.0	23 58	5.1
25	Monday	11 31	6.3	——		09 06	8.6	21 27	9.1	10 47	3.2	22 45	3.4	——		12 34	5.3
26	Tuesday	00 02	6.8	12 27	6.8	09 57	9.2	22 15	9.6	11 36	3.3	23 34	3.6	00 53	5.4	13 25	5.6
27	Wednesday	00 57	7.2	13 16	7.1	10 43	9.5	22 59	9.9	——		12 22	3.4	01 39	5.7	14 08	5.7
28	Thursday	01 45	7.5	14 02	7.3	11 25	9.7	23 40	9.9	00 19	3.7	13 05	3.5	02 22	5.9	14 49	5.8
29	Friday	02 30	7.5	14 43	7.3	——		12 05	9.6	01 02	3.8	13 44	3.5	03 04	6.0	15 29	5.7
30	Saturday	03 11	7.4	15 22	7.3	00 20	9.8	12 43	9.5	01 42	3.8	14 18	3.5	03 46	5.9	16 09	5.6

OCTOBER 2000   *High water*   GMT

| | | LONDON BRIDGE | | | | LIVERPOOL | | | | GREENOCK | | | | LEITH | | | |
		hr	ht m	hr	ht m	hr	ht m	hr	ht m	hr	ht m	hr	ht m	hr	ht m	hr	ht m
1	Sunday	03 48	7.2	15 58	7.1	00 57	9.5	13 19	9.2	02 19	3.8	14 50	3.5	04 29	5.7	16 49	5.4
2	Monday	04 21	7.0	16 32	7.0	01 33	9.1	13 53	8.8	02 55	3.7	15 23	3.5	05 12	5.4	17 29	5.1
3	Tuesday	04 51	6.8	17 06	6.7	02 09	8.6	14 28	8.4	03 31	3.6	15 58	3.4	05 57	5.1	18 10	4.9
4	Wednesday	05 22	6.5	17 43	6.4	02 47	8.1	15 08	7.9	04 08	3.4	16 36	3.3	06 45	4.7	18 57	4.6
5	Thursday	05 59	6.2	18 27	6.0	03 31	7.5	15 56	7.4	04 49	3.2	17 21	3.1	07 40	4.4	19 53	4.4
6	Friday	06 41	5.9	19 20	5.6	04 31	6.9	17 07	7.0	05 39	2.9	18 16	3.0	08 42	4.2	20 58	4.3
7	Saturday	07 38	5.5	20 40	5.3	06 08	6.7	18 50	7.1	06 42	2.7	19 25	2.9	09 51	4.2	22 09	4.3
8	Sunday	09 18	5.4	22 24	5.6	07 39	7.0	20 02	7.5	08 07	2.7	21 21	2.9	11 07	4.3	23 23	4.5
9	Monday	10 45	5.7	23 25	6.0	08 36	7.6	20 53	8.1	10 07	2.9	22 23	3.1	——		12 12	4.6
10	Tuesday	11 42	6.1	——		09 21	8.1	21 34	8.6	10 52	3.1	23 05	3.3	00 22	4.8	12 57	4.9
11	Wednesday	00 15	6.4	12 30	6.5	09 59	8.6	22 11	9.0	11 29	3.2	23 39	3.4	01 05	5.0	13 33	5.2
12	Thursday	00 59	6.7	13 13	6.7	10 33	8.9	22 46	9.2	——		12 02	3.3	01 41	5.3	14 07	5.4
13	Friday	01 38	6.9	13 51	6.8	11 07	9.1	23 20	9.4	00 11	3.4	12 33	3.3	02 14	5.5	14 40	5.6
14	Saturday	02 14	7.0	14 26	6.9	11 41	9.2	23 56	9.5	00 45	3.4	13 04	3.4	02 47	5.6	15 14	5.6
15	Sunday	02 50	7.0	15 00	7.0	——		12 16	9.3	01 21	3.5	13 37	3.5	03 22	5.7	15 50	5.7
16	Monday	03 25	7.0	15 36	7.0	00 33	9.5	12 54	9.3	01 59	3.5	14 13	3.5	04 00	5.7	16 28	5.6
17	Tuesday	04 02	6.9	16 16	7.0	01 13	9.3	13 33	9.1	02 37	3.5	14 49	3.6	04 42	5.6	17 09	5.4
18	Wednesday	04 41	6.8	16 59	6.9	01 56	9.0	14 17	8.8	03 16	3.4	15 27	3.5	05 27	5.4	17 55	5.2
19	Thursday	05 23	6.5	17 47	6.6	02 45	8.6	15 08	8.3	03 58	3.3	16 09	3.4	06 19	5.2	18 47	4.9
20	Friday	06 10	6.1	18 44	6.2	03 44	8.0	16 12	7.9	04 48	3.1	16 59	3.3	07 19	4.9	19 54	4.7
21	Saturday	07 09	5.7	19 58	5.9	05 01	7.6	17 36	7.6	06 00	2.8	18 06	3.1	08 38	4.7	21 18	4.7
22	Sunday	08 43	5.6	21 30	5.9	06 32	7.6	19 04	7.9	08 08	2.8	19 53	3.1	10 04	4.8	22 36	4.9
23	Monday	10 07	5.9	22 43	6.4	07 49	8.0	20 14	8.4	09 36	3.0	21 26	3.2	11 19	5.0	23 41	5.2
24	Tuesday	11 10	6.4	23 43	6.9	08 48	8.6	21 09	9.0	10 31	3.3	22 24	3.5	——		12 20	5.3
25	Wednesday	——		12 04	6.8	09 38	9.1	21 56	9.4	11 18	3.4	23 13	3.6	00 35	5.4	13 09	5.5
26	Thursday	00 35	7.2	12 54	7.1	10 22	9.4	22 38	9.6	12 00	3.5	23 57	3.7	01 21	5.7	13 50	5.6
27	Friday	01 23	7.4	13 38	7.3	11 02	9.5	23 18	9.6	——		12 39	3.5	02 03	5.8	14 28	5.6
28	Saturday	02 06	7.4	14 20	7.2	11 39	9.5	23 55	9.5	00 39	3.7	13 15	3.6	02 43	5.8	15 05	5.6
29	Sunday	02 45	7.3	14 58	7.1	——		12 14	9.3	01 18	3.7	13 48	3.6	03 24	5.7	15 43	5.5
30	Monday	03 19	7.0	15 33	7.0	00 30	9.3	12 48	9.1	01 54	3.7	14 20	3.6	04 06	5.5	16 19	5.4
31	Tuesday	03 48	6.8	16 06	6.8	01 04	8.9	13 22	8.9	02 30	3.6	14 53	3.6	04 46	5.3	16 56	5.2

NOVEMBER 2000   *High water*   GMT

		LONDON BRIDGE *Datum of predictions 3.20 m below*				LIVERPOOL *Datum of predictions 4.93 m below*				GREENOCK *Datum of predictions 1.62 m below*				LEITH *Datum of predictions 2.90 m below*			
		hr	ht m	hr	ht m	hr	ht m	hr	ht m	hr	ht m	hr	ht m	hr	ht m	hr	ht m
1	Wednesday	04 16	6.7	16 40	6.6	01 39	8.6	13 57	8.6	03 05	3.5	15 27	3.6	05 28	5.0	17 34	5.0
2	Thursday	04 48	6.6	17 17	6.4	02 16	8.1	14 36	8.2	03 43	3.4	16 04	3.5	06 13	4.7	18 18	4.7
3	Friday	05 25	6.3	17 59	6.1	02 59	7.6	15 21	7.7	04 24	3.2	16 46	3.3	07 03	4.5	19 10	4.5
4	Saturday	06 07	6.0	18 49	5.8	03 52	7.1	16 20	7.3	05 14	3.0	17 38	3.1	08 00	4.3	20 12	4.4
5	Sunday	06 58	5.7	19 50	5.5	05 04	6.8	17 42	7.1	06 15	2.9	18 41	3.0	09 03	4.2	21 20	4.3
6	Monday	08 06	5.5	21 14	5.5	06 42	6.9	19 08	7.4	07 26	2.8	19 58	3.0	10 09	4.3	22 28	4.5
7	Tuesday	09 43	5.6	22 32	5.9	07 51	7.4	20 07	7.9	08 52	2.9	21 22	3.1	11 14	4.6	23 30	4.7
8	Wednesday	10 53	5.9	23 29	6.3	08 40	8.0	20 53	8.4	10 03	3.1	22 16	3.2	—	—	12 08	4.9
9	Thursday	11 46	6.3	—	—	09 20	8.5	21 34	8.9	10 48	3.2	22 58	3.3	00 20	5.0	12 53	5.2
10	Friday	00 17	6.6	12 33	6.6	09 58	8.9	22 12	9.2	11 26	3.3	23 37	3.4	01 03	5.2	13 32	5.4
11	Saturday	01 01	6.9	13 16	6.8	10 35	9.2	22 51	9.5	—	—	12 01	3.4	01 41	5.5	14 10	5.6
12	Sunday	01 43	7.0	13 57	7.0	11 13	9.4	23 32	9.6	00 17	3.5	12 37	3.5	02 19	5.7	14 47	5.7
13	Monday	02 23	7.1	14 38	7.1	11 53	9.5	—	—	00 58	3.5	13 14	3.6	02 59	5.8	15 26	5.7
14	Tuesday	03 03	7.1	15 21	7.2	00 14	9.6	12 35	9.5	01 41	3.6	13 52	3.7	03 41	5.8	16 06	5.7
15	Wednesday	03 44	7.0	16 05	7.2	00 59	9.5	13 20	9.3	02 23	3.5	14 31	3.8	04 27	5.7	16 50	5.5
16	Thursday	04 26	6.8	16 52	7.0	01 46	9.1	14 08	9.0	03 07	3.5	15 11	3.7	05 16	5.6	17 39	5.3
17	Friday	05 10	6.6	17 42	6.7	02 38	8.7	15 01	8.6	03 54	3.3	15 56	3.6	06 10	5.3	18 34	5.1
18	Saturday	05 58	6.2	18 40	6.4	03 39	8.2	16 05	8.2	04 52	3.1	16 49	3.4	07 13	5.0	19 43	4.9
19	Sunday	06 59	5.9	19 53	6.1	04 52	7.8	17 21	8.0	06 11	3.0	17 56	3.3	08 29	4.8	21 03	4.8
20	Monday	08 27	5.8	21 12	6.2	06 11	7.8	18 39	8.1	07 50	3.0	19 26	3.2	09 46	4.8	22 15	5.0
21	Tuesday	09 42	6.0	22 19	6.5	07 23	8.1	19 47	8.4	09 08	3.1	20 55	3.3	10 57	4.9	23 18	5.1
22	Wednesday	10 43	6.4	23 17	6.8	08 23	8.5	20 44	8.8	10 05	3.3	21 57	3.4	11 57	5.1	—	—
23	Thursday	11 38	6.7	—	—	09 14	8.9	21 33	9.1	10 52	3.4	22 49	3.5	00 13	5.3	12 48	5.2
24	Friday	00 09	7.0	12 29	7.0	09 58	9.1	22 17	9.2	11 34	3.5	23 34	3.6	01 02	5.5	13 30	5.4
25	Saturday	00 58	7.2	13 15	7.1	10 38	9.3	22 56	9.3	—	—	12 13	3.5	01 45	5.5	14 08	5.4
26	Sunday	01 41	7.2	13 58	7.1	11 15	9.3	23 32	9.2	00 16	3.5	12 49	3.6	02 27	5.5	14 45	5.4
27	Monday	02 19	7.0	14 37	7.0	11 49	9.2	—	—	00 56	3.5	13 23	3.6	03 07	5.5	15 20	5.4
28	Tuesday	02 52	6.9	15 13	6.8	00 06	9.0	12 23	9.1	01 32	3.5	13 55	3.6	03 47	5.3	15 55	5.3
29	Wednesday	03 20	6.7	15 46	6.7	00 41	8.8	12 57	9.0	02 08	3.4	14 29	3.7	04 25	5.2	16 29	5.2
30	Thursday	03 49	6.6	16 19	6.5	01 16	8.6	13 33	8.7	02 44	3.4	15 03	3.6	05 04	5.0	17 06	5.1

DECEMBER 2000   *High water*   GMT

		LONDON BRIDGE				LIVERPOOL				GREENOCK				LEITH			
1	Friday	04 22	6.5	16 56	6.4	01 53	8.3	14 12	8.4	03 22	3.3	15 38	3.5	05 45	4.8	17 46	4.9
2	Saturday	04 59	6.4	17 37	6.2	02 34	7.9	14 55	8.1	04 04	3.2	16 18	3.4	06 30	4.6	18 33	4.7
3	Sunday	05 40	6.2	18 23	6.0	03 21	7.6	15 45	7.8	04 52	3.1	17 04	3.2	07 19	4.5	19 26	4.5
4	Monday	06 28	6.0	19 16	5.9	04 17	7.2	16 45	7.5	05 46	3.0	17 59	3.1	08 15	4.4	20 28	4.5
5	Tuesday	07 25	5.8	20 18	5.8	05 27	7.1	17 55	7.5	06 46	2.9	19 02	3.0	09 15	4.4	21 33	4.5
6	Wednesday	08 36	5.7	21 27	5.9	06 41	7.3	19 03	7.8	07 51	2.9	20 11	3.0	10 17	4.5	22 35	4.6
7	Thursday	09 50	5.9	22 34	6.2	07 44	7.8	20 02	8.2	08 59	3.0	21 20	3.1	11 16	4.8	23 32	4.9
8	Friday	10 54	6.2	23 32	6.5	08 36	8.3	20 53	8.7	10 00	3.1	22 17	3.2	—	—	12 10	5.0
9	Saturday	11 50	6.5	—	—	09 22	8.8	21 40	9.1	10 49	3.3	23 06	3.4	00 23	5.1	12 58	5.3
10	Sunday	00 25	6.8	12 43	6.8	10 06	9.2	22 26	9.5	11 32	3.4	23 53	3.5	01 11	5.4	13 41	5.5
11	Monday	01 14	7.0	13 32	7.1	10 50	9.5	23 12	9.7	—	—	12 14	3.6	01 56	5.6	14 23	5.7
12	Tuesday	02 00	7.1	14 20	7.2	11 35	9.7	—	—	00 40	3.5	12 56	3.7	02 41	5.8	15 06	5.7
13	Wednesday	02 45	7.1	15 08	7.4	00 00	9.7	12 22	9.7	01 28	3.5	13 38	3.8	03 27	5.9	15 50	5.8
14	Thursday	03 30	7.1	15 56	7.4	00 49	9.6	13 11	9.6	02 16	3.5	14 20	3.9	04 15	5.8	16 36	5.7
15	Friday	04 15	7.0	16 45	7.2	01 39	9.4	14 01	9.4	03 05	3.4	15 04	3.8	05 06	5.7	17 26	5.5
16	Saturday	05 01	6.8	17 36	7.0	02 32	9.0	14 54	9.1	03 56	3.3	15 50	3.8	06 00	5.4	18 22	5.3
17	Sunday	05 50	6.5	18 31	6.7	03 27	8.6	15 50	8.7	04 53	3.2	16 42	3.6	07 00	5.2	19 27	5.1
18	Monday	06 46	6.3	19 34	6.4	04 29	8.2	16 54	8.4	05 58	3.1	17 41	3.5	08 08	4.9	20 38	5.0
19	Tuesday	07 56	6.1	20 43	6.3	05 38	7.9	18 04	8.2	07 10	3.1	18 49	3.3	09 17	4.8	21 45	5.0
20	Wednesday	09 07	6.1	21 47	6.3	06 48	7.9	19 13	8.2	08 25	3.1	20 09	3.3	10 24	4.8	22 49	5.0
21	Thursday	10 10	6.2	22 45	6.5	07 52	8.1	20 15	8.3	09 29	3.2	21 24	3.3	11 27	4.8	23 49	5.0
22	Friday	11 08	6.4	23 40	6.6	08 47	8.4	21 10	8.6	10 22	3.3	22 24	3.3	—	—	12 23	4.9
23	Saturday	—	—	12 02	6.6	09 35	8.7	21 57	8.7	11 08	3.4	23 14	3.3	00 43	5.1	13 11	5.1
24	Sunday	00 30	6.8	12 53	6.8	10 17	8.9	22 38	8.8	11 49	3.5	23 58	3.3	01 31	5.2	13 52	5.2
25	Monday	01 16	6.8	13 38	6.8	10 55	9.1	23 15	8.9	—	—	12 28	3.5	02 14	5.2	14 29	5.3
26	Tuesday	01 56	6.8	14 20	6.8	11 30	9.1	23 50	8.9	00 39	3.3	13 04	3.6	02 54	5.2	15 04	5.3
27	Wednesday	02 31	6.7	14 57	6.7	—	—	12 05	9.1	01 16	3.3	13 38	3.6	03 32	5.2	15 37	5.3
28	Thursday	03 01	6.6	15 30	6.6	00 23	8.8	12 40	9.0	01 51	3.2	14 10	3.6	04 07	5.1	16 10	5.2
29	Friday	03 30	6.6	16 03	6.5	00 58	8.7	13 16	8.9	02 27	3.2	14 43	3.6	04 43	5.0	16 45	5.2
30	Saturday	04 02	6.5	16 38	6.5	01 35	8.5	13 53	8.8	03 04	3.2	15 17	3.5	05 20	4.9	17 22	5.0
31	Sunday	04 38	6.5	17 16	6.4	02 13	8.3	14 32	8.5	03 43	3.2	15 54	3.4	06 00	4.8	18 02	4.9

World Geographical Statistics

THE EARTH

The shape of the Earth is that of an oblate spheroid or solid of revolution whose meridian sections are ellipses, whilst the sections at right angles are circles.

DIMENSIONS

Equatorial diameter = 12,756.27 km (7,926.38 miles)
Polar diameter = 12,713.50 km (7,899.80 miles)
Equatorial circumference = 40,075.01 km (24,901.46 miles)
Polar circumference = 40,007.86 km (24,859.73 miles)

The equatorial circumference is divided into 360 degrees of longitude, which is measured in degrees, minutes and seconds east or west of the Greenwich meridian (0°) to 180°, the meridian 180° E. coinciding with 180° W. This was internationally ratified in 1884.

Distance north and south of the Equator is measured in degrees, minutes and seconds of latitude. The Equator is 0°, the North Pole is 90° N. and the South Pole is 90° S. The Tropics lie at 23° 26′ N. (Tropic of Cancer) and 23° 26′ S. (Tropic of Capricorn). The Arctic Circle lies at 66° 34′ N. and the Antarctic Circle at 66° 34′ S. (NB The Tropics and the Arctic and Antarctic circles are affected by the slow decrease in obliquity of the ecliptic, of about 0.47 arcseconds per year. The effect of this is that the Arctic and Antarctic circles are currently moving towards their respective poles by about 14 metres per century, while the Tropics move towards the Equator by the same amount.

AREA, ETC.

The surface area of the Earth is 510,069,120 km² (196,938,800 miles²), of which the water area is 70.92 per cent and the land area is 29.08 per cent.

The velocity of a given point on the Earth's surface at the Equator is 1,669.79 km per hour (1,037.56 m.p.h.). The Earth's mean velocity in its orbit around the Sun is 107,229 km per hour (66,629 m.p.h.). The Earth's mean distance from the Sun is 149,597,870 km (92,955,807 miles).

OCEANS

AREA

	km²	miles²
Pacific	166,240,000	64,186,300
Atlantic	86,550,000	33,420,000
Indian	73,427,000	28,350,500
Arctic	9,485,000	3,662,000

The division by the Equator of the Pacific into the North and South Pacific and the Atlantic into the North and South Atlantic makes a total of six oceans.

GREATEST DEPTHS

Greatest depth location	metres	feet
Mariana Trench, Pacific	10,920	35,827
Puerto Rico Trench, Atlantic	8,605	28,232
Java (Sunda) Trench, Indian	7,125	23,376
Molloy Deep, Arctic	5,680	18,399

SEAS

AREA

	km²	miles²
South China	2,974,600	1,148,500
Caribbean	2,515,900	971,400
Mediterranean	2,509,900	969,100
Bering	2,261,000	873,000
Gulf of Mexico	1,507,600	582,100
Okhotsk	1,392,000	537,500
Japan	1,012,900	391,100
Hudson Bay	730,100	281,900
East China	664,600	256,600
Andaman	564,880	218,100
Black Sea	507,900	196,100
Red Sea	453,000	174,900
North Sea	427,100	164,900
Baltic Sea	382,000	147,500
Yellow Sea	294,000	113,500
Persian/Arabian Gulf	230,000	88,800

GREATEST DEPTHS

	Maximum depth	
	metres	feet
Caribbean	8,605	28,232
East China (Ryu Kyu Trench)	7,507	24,629
South China	7,258	23,812
Mediterranean (Ionian Basin)	5,150	16,896
Andaman	4,267	14,000
Bering	3,936	12,913
Gulf of Mexico	3,504	11,496
Okhotsk	3,365	11,040
Japan	3,053	10,016
Red Sea	2,266	7,434
Black Sea	2,212	7,257
North Sea	439	1,440
Hudson Bay	111	364
Baltic Sea	90	295
Yellow Sea	73	240
Persian Gulf	73	240

THE CONTINENTS

There are six geographic continents, although America is often divided politically into North and Central America, and South America.

AFRICA is surrounded by sea except for the narrow isthmus of Suez in the north-east, through which is cut the Suez Canal. Its extreme longitudes are 17° 20′ W. at Cape Verde, Senegal, and 51° 24′ E. at Ras Hafun, Somalia. The extreme latitudes are 37° 20′ N. at Cape Blanc, Tunisia, and 34° 50′ S. at Cape Agulhas, South Africa, about 4,400 miles apart. The Equator passes through the middle of the continent.

NORTH AMERICA, including Mexico, is surrounded by ocean except in the south, where the isthmian states of CENTRAL AMERICA link North America with South America. Its extreme longitudes are 168° 5′ W. at Cape Prince of Wales, Alaska, and 55° 40′ W. at Cape Charles,

Newfoundland. The extreme continental latitudes are the tip of the Boothia peninsula, NW Territories, Canada (71° 51′ N.) and 14° 22′ N. at Ocós in the south of Mexico.

SOUTH AMERICA lies mostly in the southern hemisphere; the Equator passes through the north of the continent. It is surrounded by ocean except where it is joined to Central America in the north by the narrow isthmus through which is cut the Panama Canal. Its extreme longitudes are 34° 47′ W. at Cape Branco in Brazil and 81° 20′ W. at Punta Pariña, Peru. The extreme continental latitudes are 12° 25′ N. at Punta Gallinas, Colombia, and 53° 54′ S. at the southernmost tip of the Brunswick peninsula, Chile. Cape Horn, on Cape Island, Chile, lies at 55° 59′ S.

ANTARCTICA lies almost entirely within the Antarctic Circle (66° 34′ S.) and is the largest of the world's glaciated areas. The continent has an area of 5.1 million square miles, 99 per cent of which is permanently ice-covered. The ice amounts to some 7.2 million cubic miles and represents more than 90 per cent of the world's fresh water. The environment is too hostile for unsupported human habitation. *See also* pages 790–1

ASIA is the largest continent and occupies 30 per cent of the world's land surface. The extreme longitudes are 26° 05′ E. at Baba Buran, Turkey and 169° 40′ W. at Mys Dežneva (East Cape), Russia, a distance of about 6,000 miles. Its extreme northern latitude is 77° 45′ N. at Cape Čeljuskin, Russia, and it extends over 5,000 miles south to about 1° 15′ N. of the Equator.

AUSTRALIA is the smallest of the continents and lies in the southern hemisphere. It is entirely surrounded by ocean. Its extreme longitudes are 113° 11′ E. at Steep Point and 153° 11′ E. at Cape Byron. The extreme latitudes are 10° 42′ S. at Cape York and 39° S. at South East Point, Tasmania.

EUROPE, including European Russia, is the smallest continent in the northern hemisphere. Its extreme latitudes are 71° 11′ N. at North Cape in Norway, and 36° 23′ N. at Cape Matapan in southern Greece, a distance of about 2,400 miles. Its breadth from Cabo Carvoeiro in Portugal (9° 34′ W.) in the west to the Kara River, north of the Urals (66° 30′ E.) in the east is about 3,300 miles. The division between Europe and Asia is generally regarded as the watershed of the Ural Mountains; down the Ural river to Gur'yev, Kazakhstan; across the Caspian Sea to Apsheronskiy Poluostrov, near Baku; along the watershed of the Caucasus Mountains to Anapa and thence across the Black Sea to the Bosporus in Turkey; across the Sea of Marmara to Çanakkale Boğazi (Dardanelles).

	Area km²	miles²
Asia	43,998,000	16,988,000
*America	41,918,000	16,185,000
Africa	29,800,000	11,506,000
Antarctica	13,209,000	5,100,000
†Europe	9,699,000	3,745,000
Australia	7,618,493	2,941,526

*North and Central America has an area of 24,255,000 km² (9,365,000 miles²)

†Includes 5,571,000 km² (2,151,000 miles²) of former USSR territory, including the Baltic states, Belarus, Moldova, the Ukraine, that part of Russia west of the Ural Mountains and Kazakhstan west of the Ural river. European Turkey (24,378 km²/9,412 miles²) comprises territory to the west and north of the Bosporus and the Dardanelles

GLACIATED AREAS

It is estimated that 15,915,000 km² (6,145,000 miles²) or 10.73 per cent of the world's land surface is permanently covered with ice.

	Area km²	miles²
South Polar regions	13,830,000	5,340,000
North Polar regions (incl. Greenland or Kalaallit Nunaat)	1,965,000	758,500
Alaska-Canada	58,800	22,700
Asia	37,800	14,600
South America	11,900	4,600
Europe	10,700	4,128
New Zealand	1,015	391
Africa	238	92

The largest glacier is the 515 km/320 mile-long Lambert-Fisher Ice Passage, Antarctica.

PENINSULAS

	Area km²	miles²
Arabian	3,250,000	1,250,000
Southern Indian	2,072,000	800,000
Alaskan	1,500,000	580,000
Labradorian	1,300,000	500,000
Scandinavian	800,300	309,000
Iberian	584,000	225,500

LARGEST ISLANDS

Island, and Ocean	Area km²	miles²
Greenland (Kalaallit Nunaat), Arctic	2,175,500	840,000
New Guinea, Pacific	821,030	317,000
Borneo, Pacific	725,450	280,100
Madagascar, Indian	587,040	226,658
Baffin Island, Arctic	507,451	195,928
Sumatra, Indian	427,350	165,000
Honshu, Pacific	227,413	87,805
*Great Britain, Atlantic	218,077	84,200
Victoria Island, Arctic	217,292	83,897
Ellesmere Island, Arctic	196,236	75,767
Sulawesi (Celebes), Indian	189,036	72,987
South Island, NZ, Pacific	151,213	58,384
Java, Indian	126,650	48,900
North Island, NZ, (Pacific)	115,777	44,702
Cuba, Atlantic	110,862	42,804
Newfoundland, Atlantic	108,855	42,030
Luzon, Pacific	105,880	40,880
Iceland, Atlantic	102,817	39,698
Mindanao, Pacific	95,247	36,775
Ireland, Atlantic	82,462	31,839

*Mainland only

LARGEST DESERTS

	Area (approx.) km²	miles²
The Sahara, N. Africa	8,400,000	3,250,000
Australian Desert	1,550,000	600,000
Arabian Desert	1,200,000	470,000
The Gobi, Mongolia/China	1,040,000	400,000
Kalahari Desert, Botswana/ Namibia/S. Africa	520,000	200,000
Takla Makan, Mongolia/ China	320,000	125,000
*Kara Kum, Turkmenistan	310,000	120,000
Namib Desert, Namibia	285,000	110,000
Thar Desert, India/Pakistan	260,000	100,000
Somali Desert, Somalia	260,000	100,000
Atacama Desert, Chile	180,000	70,000
Sonoran Desert, USA/ Mexico	180,000	70,000
Dasht-e Lut, Iran	52,000	20,000
Mojave Desert, USA	38,850	15,000

*Together with the Kyzyl Kum known as the Turkestan Desert

DEEPEST DEPRESSIONS

	Maximum depth below sea level metres	feet
Dead Sea, Jordan/Israel	408	1,338
Lake Assal, Djibouti	156	511
Turfan Depression, Sinkiang, China	153	505
Qattara Depression, Egypt	132	436
Mangyshlak peninsula, Kazakhstan	131	433
Danakil Depression, Ethiopia	116	383
Death Valley, California, USA	86	282
Salton Sink, California, USA	71	235
W. of Ustyurt plateau, Kazakhstan	70	230
Prikaspiyskaya Nizmennost', Russia/Kazakhstan	67	220
Lake Sarykamysh, Uzbekistan/ Turkmenistan	45	148
El Faiyûm, Egypt	44	147
Valdies peninsula, Lago Enriquillo, Dominican Republic	40	131
Lake Eyre, South Australia	16	52

The world's largest exposed depression is the Prikaspiyskaya Nizmennost' covering the hinterland of the northern third of the Caspian Sea, which is itself 28 m (92 ft) below sea level.

Western Antarctica and Central Greenland largely comprise crypto-depressions under ice burdens. The Antarctic Bentley subglacial trench has a bedrock 2,538 m (8,326 ft) below sea-level. In Greenland (lat. 73° N., long. 39° W.) the bedrock is 365 m (1,197 ft) below sea-level.

More than a quarter of the area of The Netherlands lies marginally below sea-level, an area of more than 10,000 km²/3,860 miles².

LONGEST MOUNTAIN RANGES

Range, and location	Length km	miles
Cordillera de Los Andes, W. South America	7,200	4,500
Rocky Mountains, W. North America	4,800	3,000
Himalaya-Karakoram-Hindu Kush, S. Central Asia	3,800	2,400
Great Dividing Range, E. Australia	3,600	2,250
Trans-Antarctic Mts, Antarctica	3,500	2,200
Atlantic Coast Range, E. Brazil	3,000	1,900
West Sumatran-Javan Range, Indonesia	2,900	1,800
Aleutian Range, Alaska and NW Pacific	2,650	1,650
Tien Shan, S. Central Asia	2,250	1,400
Central New Guinea Range, Irian Jaya/Papua New Guinea	2,000	1,250

HIGHEST MOUNTAINS

The world's 8,000-metre mountains (with six subsidiary peaks) are all in the Himalaya-Karakoram-Hindu Kush ranges.

Mountain	Height metres	feet
Mt Everest*	8,848	29,028
K2 (Chogori)†	8,607	28,238
Kangchenjunga	8,597	28,208
Lhotse	8,511	27,923
Makalu I	8,481	27,824
Lhotse Shar (II)	8,383	27,504
Dhaulagiri I	8,171	26,810
Manaslu I (Kutang I)	8,156	26,760
Cho Oyu	8,153	26,750
Nanga Parbat (Diamir)	8,125	26,660
Annapurna I	8,091	26,546
Gasherbrum I (Hidden Peak)	8,068	26,470
Broad Peak I	8,046	26,400
Shisham Pangma (Gosainthan)	8,046	26,400
Gasherbrum II	8,034	26,360
Makalu South-East	8,010	26,280
Broad Peak Central	8,000	26,246

*Named after Sir George Everest (1790–1866), Surveyor-General of India 1830–43, in 1863. He pronounced his name Eve-rest
†Formerly Godwin-Austin

The culminating summits in the other major mountain ranges are:

Mountain, by range or country	Height metres	feet
Pik Pobedy, Tien Shan	7,439	24,406
Cerro Aconcagua, Cordillera de Los Andes	6,960	22,834
Mt McKinley (S. Peak), Alaska Range	6,194	20,320
Kilimanjaro (Kibo), Tanzania	5,894	19,340
Hkakabo Razi, Myanmar	5,881	19,296
El'brus, (W. Peak), Caucasus	5,642	18,510
Citlaltépetl (Orizaba), Sierra Madre Oriental, Mexico	5,610	18,405
Vinson Massif, E. Antarctica	4,897	16,066
Puncak Jaya, Central New Guinea Range	4,884	16,023

Mountain, by range or country	Height metres	feet
Mt Blanc, Alps	4,807	15,771
Klyuchevskaya Sopka, Kamchatka peninsula, Russia	4,750	15,584
Ras Dashan, Ethiopian Highlands	4,620	15,158
Zard Kūh, Zagros Mts, Iran	4,547	14,921
Mt Kirkpatrick, Trans Antarctic	4,529	14,860
Mt Belukha, Altai Mts, Russia/ Kazakhstan	4,505	14,783
Mt Elbert, Rocky Mountains	4,400	14,433
Mt Rainier, Cascade Range, N. America	4,392	14,410
Nevado de Colima, Sierra Madre Occidental, Mexico	4,268	14,003
Jebel Toubkal, Atlas Mts, N. Africa	4,165	13,665
Kinabalu, Crocker Range, Borneo	4,101	13,455
Kerinci, West Sumatran-Javan Range, Indonesia	3,800	12,467
Jabal an NabīShu'ayb, N. Tihāmat, Yemen	3,760	12,336
Mt Cook (Aorangi), Southern Alps, New Zealand	3,754	12,315
Teotepec, Sierra Madre del Sur, Mexico	3,703	12,149
Thaban Ntlenyana, Drakensberg, South Africa	3,482	11,425
Pico de Bandeira, Atlantic Coast Range	2,890	9,482
Shishaldin, Aleutian Range	2,861	9,387
Kosciusko, Great Dividing Range	2,228	7,310

HIGHEST VOLCANOES

Volcano (last major eruption), and location	Height metres	feet
Ojos del Salado (1981), Andes, Argentina	6,895	22,588
Llullaillaco (1877), Andes, Argentina/Chile	6,723	22,057
San Pedro (1960), Andes, Chile	6,199	20,325
Guallatiri (1960, 1993), Andes, Chile	6,071	19,918
Cotopaxi (1940, 1975), Andes, Ecuador	5,897	19,347
Tupungatito (1986), Andes, Chile	5,640	18,504
Láscar (1995), Andes, Chile	5,591	18,346
Popocatépetl (1998), Mexico	5,426	17,802
Nevado del Ruiz (1985, 1991), Colombia	5,321	17,457
Sangay (1998), Andes, Ecuador	5,188	17,021
Guagua Pichincha (1993), Andes, Ecuador	4,784	15,696
Purace (1977), Colombia	4,756	15,601
Klyuchevskaya Sopka (1997), Kamchatka peninsula, Russia	4,750	15,584
Galeras (1993), Colombia	4,275	14,028
Nevado de Colima (1991, 1994), Mexico	4,268	14,003
Mauna Loa (1984, 1987), Hawaii Is.	4,170	13,680
Cameroon (1982), Cameroon	4,095	13,435

OTHER NOTABLE VOLCANOES

	Height metres	feet
Erebus (1998), Ross Island, Antarctica	3,794	12,450
Fuji (1708), Honshu, Japan	3,775	12,388
Santa Maria (1902, 1998), Guatemala	3,768	12,362
Semeru (1995, 1998), Java, Indonesia	3,675	12,060
Mt Etna (1169, 1669, 1993, 1996, 1997, 1998), Sicily, Italy	3,350	10,990
Raung (1993, 1997), Java, Indonesia	3,322	10,932
Sheveluch (1964, 1997), Kamchatka, Russia	3,283	10,771
Llaima (1995), Chile	3,125	10,253
Mt St Helens (1980, 1986, 1991), Washington State, USA	2,549	8,363
Beerenberg (1985), Jan Mayen Island	2,546	8,347
Pinatubo (1991, 1995), Philippines	1,598	5,249
Hekla (1981, 1991), Iceland	1,491	4,892
Mt Unzen (1792, 1991, 1996), Kyushu, Japan	1,360	4,462
Vesuvius (AD 79, 1631, 1944), Italy	1,281	4,203
Kilauea (1996, 1997–8), Hawaii, USA	1,249	4,009
Soufrière (1979, 1997), St Vincent	1,234	4,048
Soufrière Hills (1997–8), Montserrat	942	3,091
Stromboli (1996, 1997), Lipari Is., Italy	926	3,038
Krakatau (1883, 1995), Sunda Strait, Indonesia	813	2,667
Santorini (Thíra) (1628 BC, 1950), Aegean Sea, Greece	564	1,850
Tristan da Cunha (1961), South Atlantic	243	800
Surtsey (1963–7), off Iceland	173	568

LARGEST LAKES

The areas of some of these lakes are subject to seasonal variation.

	Area km²	miles²	Length km	miles
Caspian Sea, Iran/ Azerbaijan/Russia/ Turkmenistan/ Kazakhstan	371,000	143,000	1,171	728
*Michigan–Huron, USA/Canada	117,610	45,300	1,010	627
Superior, Canada/ USA	82,100	31,700	563	350
Victoria, Uganda/ Tanzania/Kenya	69,500	26,828	362	225
Aral Sea, Kazakhstan/ Uzbekistan	40,000	15,444	134	217
Tanganyika, Dem. Rep. of Congo/ Tanzania/Zambia/ Burundi	32,900	12,665	725	450
Great Bear, Canada	31,328	12,096	309	192
†Baykal (Baikal), Russia	30,500	11,776	620	385
Malawi (Nyasa), Tanzania/Malawi/ Mozambique	29,600	11,150	580	360
Great Slave, Canada	28,570	11,031	480	298
Erie, Canada/USA	25,670	9,910	388	241

	Area km²	miles²	Length km	miles	River, source and outflow	Length km	miles
Winnipeg, Canada	24,390	9,417	428	266	Tigris-Euphrates, R. Murat, E. Turkey		
Ontario, Canada/USA	19,010	7,340	310	193	– Persian Gulf	2,800	1,740
Balkhash, Kazakhstan	18,427	7,115	605	376	Zambezi, NW Zambia – S. Indian		
Ladozhskoye (*Ladoga*),					Ocean	2,735	1,700
Russia	17,700	6,835	193	120	Irrawaddy, R. Mali Hka, Myanmar –		
					Andaman Sea	2,151	1,337

*Lakes Michigan and Huron are regarded as lobes of the same lake.
The Michigan lobe has an area of 57,750 km² (22,300 miles²) and
the Huron lobe an area of 59,570 km² (23,000 miles²)
†World's deepest lake (1,940 m/6,365 ft)

					River, source and outflow	Length km	miles
					Don, SE of Novomoskovsk – Sea of Azov	1,969	1,224

BRITISH ISLES

UNITED KINGDOM, BY COUNTRY

	Area km²	miles²	Length km	miles
Lough Neagh, Northern Ireland	381.73	147.39	28.90	18.00
Loch Lomond, Scotland	71.12	27.46	36.44	22.64
Windermere, England	14.74	5.69	16.90	10.50
Lake Vyrnwy, Wales (artificial)	4.53	1.75	7.56	4.70
Llyn Tegid (*Bala*), Wales (natural)	4.38	1.69	5.80	3.65

River, source and outflow	Length km	miles
Shannon, Co. Cavan, Rep. of Ireland – Atlantic Ocean	386	240
Severn, Powys, Wales – Bristol Channel	354	220
Thames, Gloucestershire, England – North Sea	346	215
Tay, Perthshire, Scotland – North Sea	188	117
Clyde, Lanarkshire, Scotland – Firth of Clyde	158	98½
Tweed, Peeblesshire, Scotland – North Sea	155	96½
Bann (Upper and Lower), Co. Down, N. Ireland – Atlantic Ocean	122	76

LONGEST RIVERS

River, source and outflow	Length km	miles
Nile (*Bahr-el-Nil*), R. Luvironza, Burundi – E. Mediterranean Sea	6,670	4,145
Amazon (*Amazonas*), Lago Villafro, Peru – S. Atlantic Ocean	6,448	4,007
Yangtze-Kiang (*Chang Jiang*), Kunlun Mts, W. China – Yellow Sea	6,380	3,964
Mississippi-Missouri-Red Rock, Montana – Gulf of Mexico	5,970	3,710
Yenisey-Angara, W. Mongolia – Kara Sea	5,540	3,442
Huang He (*Yellow River*), Bayan Har Shan range, central China – Yellow Sea	5,463	3,395
Ob'-Irtysh, W. Mongolia – Kara Sea	5,410	3,362
Zaïre (*Congo*), R. Lualaba, Dem. Rep. of Congo-Zambia – S. Atlantic Ocean	4,700	2,920
Lena-Kirenga, R. Kirenga, W. of Lake Baykal – Laptev Sea, Arctic Ocean	4,400	2,734
Mekong, Lants'ang, Tibet – South China Sea	4,345	2,700
Amur-Argun, R. Argun, Khingan Mts, N. China – Sea of Okhotsk	4,345	2,700
Mackenzie-Peace, Tatlatui Lake, British Columbia – Beaufort Sea	4,240	2,635
Niger, Loma Mts, Guinea – Gulf of Guinea, E. Atlantic Ocean	4,168	2,590
Río de la Plata-Paraná, R. Paranáiba, central Brazil – S. Atlantic Ocean	4,000	2,485
Murray-Darling, SE Queensland – Lake Alexandrina, S. Australia	3,717	2,310
Volga, Valdai plateau – Caspian Sea	3,685	2,290

OTHER NOTABLE RIVERS

	Length km	miles
Rio Grande, USA–Mexian border	3,057	1,900
Ganges-Brahmaputra, R. Matsang, SW Tibet – Bay of Bengal	2,900	1,800
Indus, R. Sengge, SW Tibet – N. Arabian Sea	2,897	1,800
Danube (*Donau*), Black Forest, SW Germany – Black Sea	2,856	1,775

GREATEST WATERFALLS – BY HEIGHT

Waterfall, river and location	Total drop metres	feet	Greatest single leap metres	feet
Saltó Angel, Carrao Auyán Tepuí, Venezuela	979	3,212	807	2,648
Tugela, Tugela, Natal, S. Africa	914	2,014	410	1,350
Utigård, Jostedal Glacier, Norway	800	2,625	600	1,970
Mongefossen, Monge, Norway	774	2,540	—	—
Yosemite, Yosemite Creek, USA	739	2,425	435	1,430
Østre Mardøla Foss, Mardals, Norway	656	2,154	296	974
Tyssestrengane, Tysso, Norway	646	2,120	289	948
Cuquenán, Arabopó, Venezuela	610	2,000	—	—
Sutherland, Arthur, NZ	580	1,904	248	815
*Kjellfossen (Kile), Naeröfjord, Norway	561	1,841	149	490

*Volume often so low the fall atomizes into a 'bridal veil'

BRITISH ISLES, BY COUNTRY

Waterfall, river and location	Total drop metres	feet	Greatest single leap	
Eas a' Chuàl Aluinn, Glas Bheinn, Sutherland, Scotland	200	658		
Powerscourt Falls, Dargle, Co. Wicklow, Rep. of Ireland	106	350		
Pistyll-y-Llyn, Powys/ Dyfed border, Wales	c.72	c.235	(cascades)	
Pistyll Rhyadr, Clwyd/ Powys border, Wales	71.5	235	(single leap)	
Caldron Snout, R. Tees, Cumbria/Durham, England	61	200	(cascades)	

GREATEST WATERFALLS – BY VOLUME

Waterfall, river and location	Mean annual flow m³/sec	galls/sec
Inga (Congo dam site), Dem. Rep. of Congo	43,000	9,460,000
Khône, Mekong, Laos	42,500	9,350,000
Boyoma (Stanley), R. Lualaba, Dem. Rep. of Congo	c.17,000	c.3,750,000
Guayra (Sete Quedas), Brazil	13,000	2,860,000
Rio Paraná, Argentina/ Paraguay	11,900	2,619,000
Niagara (Horseshoe), R. Niagara/Lake Erie–Lake Ontario	6,000	1,320,000
Paulo Afonso, R. São Francisco, Brazil	2,830	622,500
Urubupunga, Alto Paraná, Brazil	2,745	604,000
Cataratas del Iguazú, R. Iguaçu, Brazil/Argentina	1,743	380,000
Patos-Maribando, Rio Grande, Brazil	1,500	330,000
Churchill, R. Churchill, Canada	1,132	215,000
Victoria (Mosi-oa-tunya), R. Zambezi, Zambia/ Zimbabwe	1,087	242,000

TALLEST DAMS

	metres	feet
*Rogun, R. Vakhsh, Tajikistan	335	1,098
Nurek, R. Vakhsh, Tajikistan	300	984
Grande Dixence, Switzerland	285	935
*Longtan, R. Hangshui, China	285	935
Inguri, Georgia	272	892
Manuel M. Torres, Chicoasén, Mexico	261	856
Tehri, R. Bhagivathi, India	261	856

*Under construction

The world's most massive dam is the Syncrude Tailings dam in Alberta, Canada, which will have a volume of 540 million cubic metres/706 million cubic yards.

The Three Gorges Chang Jiang (Yangtze) Dam, China, with a crest length of 1,983 m/6,505 ft, is due for completion in 2009.

The Yacyretá-Apipe dam across the River Paraná, Argentina-Paraguay, is being completed to a length of 69,600 m/43.24 miles.

TALLEST INHABITED BUILDINGS

Building and city	Height metres	feet
Chongqing Tower, China	457	1,499
Petronas Towers I and II, Kuala Lumpur, Malaysia	451.9	1,482
Sears Tower, Chicago[1]	443	1,454
Jin Mao, Shanghai, China (1998)	420	1,378
One World Trade Center Tower, New York[2]	417	1,368
Plaza Rakyat, Kuala Lumpur, Malaysia	382	1,254
Empire State Building, New York[3]	381	1,250
Central Plaza, Hong Kong	373	1,227
Bank of China Tower, Hong Kong	368	1,209
T. & C. Tower, Kaohsiung, Taiwan	347	1,140
Amoco Building, Chicago	346	1,136
John Hancock Center, Chicago	343	1,127
Shun Hing Square, Shenzhen, China	325	1,066
Sky Central Plaza, Guangzhou, China	321	1,056
Chicago Beach Tower, Dubai	321	1,053
Baiyoke Tower, Bangkok, Thailand	320	1,050

1. With TV antennae, 520 m/1,707 ft
2. With TV antennae, 521.2 m/1,710 ft; Two World Trade Center Tower, 415 m/1,362 ft
3. With TV tower (added 1950–1), 430.9 m/1,414 ft

TALLEST STRUCTURES

Structure and location	Height metres	feet
*Warszawa Radio Mast, Konstantynow, Poland	646	2,120
KTHI-TV Mast, Blanchard, North Dakota (guyed)	629	2,063
CN Tower, Metro Centre, Toronto, Canada	555	1,822
Ostankino Tower, Moscow	537	1,762

*Collapsed during renovation, August 1991

LONGEST BRIDGES – BY SPAN

Bridge and location	Length metres	feet
SUSPENSION SPANS		
*Akashi-Kaikyo, Shikoku, Japan (1998)	1,990	6,529
Store Baelt East Bridge, Denmark	1,624	5,328
Humber Estuary, Humberside, England	1,410	4,626
*Jiangyin (Yangtze), China (1999)	1,385	4,544
Tsing Ma, Hong Kong, China	1,377	4,518
Verrazano Narrows, Brooklyn–Staten I, USA	1,298	4,260
Golden Gate, San Francisco Bay, USA	1,280	4,200
Hoga Kustan, Sweden	1,210	3,970
Mackinac Straits, Michigan, USA	1,158	3,800
Minami Bisan-Seto, Japan	1,100	3,609
Bosporus II, Istanbul, Turkey	1,089	3,576
Bosporus I, Istanbul, Turkey	1,074	3,524
George Washington, Hudson River, New York City, USA	1,067	3,500
Kurushima III, Japan	1,030	3,379
Kurushima II, Japan	1,020	3,346
Ponte 25 de Abril (Tagus), Lisbon, Portugal	1,013	3,323
Firth of Forth (road), nr Edinburgh, Scotland	1,006	3,300
Kita Bisan-Seto, Japan	990	3,248
Severn River, Severn Estuary, England	988	3,240

*Under construction

The main span of the 5.15 km/3.2 mile long Second Severn bridging, opened in 1996, is 456 m/1,496 ft.

Bridge and location

	Length	
	metres	feet

CANTILEVER SPANS

	metres	feet
Pont de Québec (rail-road), St Lawrence, Canada	548.6	1,800
Ravenswood, W. Virginia, USA	525.1	1,723
Firth of Forth (rail), nr Edinburgh, Scotland	521.2	1,710
Nanko, Osaka, Japan	510.0	1,673
Commodore Barry, Chester, Pennsylvania, USA	494.3	1,622
Greater New Orleans, Louisiana, USA	480.0	1,575
Howrah (rail-road), Calcutta, India	457.2	1,500

STEEL ARCH SPANS

	metres	feet
New River Gorge, Fayetteville, W. Virginia, USA	518.0	1,700
Bayonne (Kill van Kull), Bayonne, NJ – Staten I., USA	503.5	1,652
Sydney Harbour, Sydney, Australia	502.9	1,650

The 'floating' bridging at Evergreen Point, Seattle, Washington State, USA, is 3,839 m/12,596 ft long, of which 2,310 m/7,578 ft floats.

The longest stretch of bridgings of any kind is that carrying the Interstate 55 and Interstate 10 highways at Manchac, Louisiana, on twin concrete trestles over 55.21 km/34.31 miles.

LONGEST VEHICULAR TUNNELS

Tunnel and location

	Length	
	km	miles

	km	miles
*Seikan (rail), Tsugaru Channel, Japan	53.90	33.49
*Channel Tunnel, Cheriton, Kent – Sangatte, Calais	49.94	31.03
Moscow metro, Belyaevo – Bittsevsky, Moscow, Russia	37.90	23.50
Northern line tube, East Finchley – Morden, London	27.84	17.30
Oshimizu (rail), Honshū, Japan	22.17	13.78
Simplon II (rail), Brigue, Switzerland – Iselle, Italy	19.82	12.31
Simplon I (rail), Brigue, Switzerland – Iselle, Italy	19.80	12.30
*Shin-Kanmon (rail), Kanmon Strait, Japan	18.68	11.61
Great Appennine (rail), Vernio, Italy	18.49	11.49
St Gotthard (road), Göschenen – Airolo, Switzerland	16.32	10.14
Rokko (rail), Ōsaka – Kōbe, Japan	16.09	10.00

*Sub-aqueous

The longest non-vehicular tunnelling in the world is the Delaware Aqueduct in New York State, USA, constructed in 1937–44 to a length of 168.9 km/105 miles.

BRITAIN – RAIL TUNNELS

	miles	yards
Severn, Bristol – Newport	4	484
Totley, Manchester – Sheffield	3	950
Standedge, Manchester – Huddersfield	3	66
Sodbury, Swindon – Bristol	2	924
Disley, Stockport – Sheffield	2	346
Ffestiniog, Llandudno – Blaenau Ffestiniog	2	338

	miles	yards
Bramhope, Leeds – Harrogate	2	241
Cowburn, Manchester – Sheffield	2	182

The longest road tunnel in Britain is the Mersey Road Tunnel, 3.42 km/2 miles 228 yards long. The longest canal tunnel, at Standedge, W. Yorks, is 5.13 km/3 miles 330 yards long; it was closed in 1944 but is currently being restored.

LONGEST SHIP CANALS

Canal (opening date)	Length		Min. depth	
	km	miles	metres	feet
White Sea-Baltic (formerly Stalin) (1933) Canalized river; canal 51.5 km/32 miles	227	141.00	5.0	16.5
*Suez (1869) Links Red and Mediterranean Seas	162	100.60	12.9	42.3
V. I. Lenin Volga-Don (1952) Links Black and Caspian Seas	100	62.20	n/a	n/a
Kiel (or North Sea) (1895) Links North and Baltic Seas	98	60.90	13.7	45.0
*Houston (1940) Links inland city with sea	91	56.70	10.4	34.0
Alphonse XIII (1926) Gives Seville access to sea	85	53.00	7.6	25.0
Panama (1914) Links Pacific Ocean and Caribbean Sea; lake chain, 78.9 km/49 miles dug	82	50.71	12.5	41.0
Manchester Ship (1894) Links city with Irish Channel	64	39.70	8.5	28.0
Welland (1932) Circumvents Niagara Falls and Rapids	43.5	27.00	8.8	29.0
Brussels (Rupel Sea) (1922) Renders Brussels an inland port	32	19.80	6.4	21.0

*Has no locks

The first section of China's Grand Canal, running 1,782 km/1,107 miles from Beijing to Hangzhou, was opened AD 610 and completed in 1283. Today it is limited to 2,000 tonne vessels.

The St Lawrence Seaway comprises Beauharnois, Welland and Welland Bypass and Seaway 54–59 canals, and allows access to Duluth, Minnesota, USA via the Great Lakes from the Atlantic end of Canada's Gulf of St Lawrence, a distance of 3,769 km/2,342 miles. The St Lawrence Canal, completed in 1959, is 293 km/182 miles long.

Distances from London by Air

The list of the distances in statute miles from London, Heathrow, to various cities (airport) abroad was supplied by the publishers of *IATA/Serco Aviation Services Air Distances Manual.*

To	Miles
Abidjan	3,197
Abu Dhabi (International)	3,425
Addis Ababa	3,675
Adelaide (International)	10,111
Aden	3,670
Algiers	1,035
Amman (Queen Alia)	2,287
Amsterdam	230
Ankara (Esenboga)	1,770
Athens	1,500
Atlanta	4,198
Auckland	11,404
Baghdad (Saddam)	2,551
Bahrain	3,163
Baku	2,485
Bangkok	5,928
Barbados	4,193
Barcelona (Muntadas)	712
Basle	447
Beijing (Capital)	5,063
Beirut	2,161
Belfast (Aldergrove)	325
Belgrade	1,056
Berlin (Tegel)	588
Bermuda	3,428
Berne	476
Bogotá	5,262
Bombay (Mumbai)	4,478
Boston	3,255
Brasilia	5,452
Bratislava	817
Brisbane (Eagle Farm)	10,273
Brussels	217
Bucharest (Otopeni)	1,307
Budapest	923
Buenos Aires	6,915
Cairo (International)	2,194
Calcutta	4,958
Calgary	4,357
Canberra	10,563
Cape Town	6,011
Caracas	4,639
Casablanca (Mohamed V)	1,300
Chicago (O'Hare)	3,941
Cologne	331
Colombo (Katunayake)	5,411
Copenhagen	608
Dakar	2,706
Dallas (Fort Worth)	4,736
Dallas (Lovefield)	4,732
Damascus (International)	2,223
Dar-es-Salaam	4,662
Darwin	8,613
Delhi	4,180
Denver	4,655
Detroit (Metropolitan)	3,754
Dhahran	3,143
Dhaka	4,976
Doha	3,253
Dubai	3,414

To	Miles
Dublin	279
Durban	5,937
Düsseldorf	310
Entebbe	4,033
Frankfurt (Main)	406
Freetown	3,046
Geneva	468
Gibraltar	1,084
Gothenburg (Landvetter)	664
Hamburg	463
Harare	5,156
Havana	4,647
Helsinki (Vantaa)	1,148
Ho Chi Minh City	6,345
Hobart	10,826
Hong Kong	5,990
Honolulu	7,220
Houston (Intercontinental)	4,821
Houston (William P. Hobby)	4,837
Islamabad	3,767
Istanbul	1,560
Jakarta (Halim Perdanakusuma)	7,295
Jeddah	2,947
Johannesburg	5,634
Kabul	3,558
Karachi	3,935
Kathmandu	4,570
Khartoum	3,071
Kiev (Borispol)	1,357
Kiev (Julyany)	1,337
Kingston, Jamaica	4,668
Kuala Lumpur (Subang)	6,557
Kuwait	2,903
Lagos	3,107
Larnaca	2,036
Lima	6,303
Lisbon	972
Lomé	3,129
Los Angeles (International)	5,439
Madras	5,113
Madrid	773
Malta	1,305
Manila	6,685
Marseille	614
Mauritius	6,075
Melbourne (Essendon)	10,504
Melbourne (Tullamarine)	10,499
Mexico City	5,529
Miami	4,414
Milan (Linate)	609
Minsk	1,176
Montego Bay	4,687
Montevideo	6,841
Montreal (Mirabel)	3,241
Moscow (Sheremetievo)	1,557
Munich (Franz Josef Strauss)	584
Muscat	3,621
Nairobi (Jomo Kenyatta)	4,248
Naples	1,011
Nassau	4,333
New York (J. F. Kennedy)	3,440
Nice	645
Oporto	806
Oslo (Fornebu)	722
Ottawa	3,321

To	Miles
Palma, Majorca (Son San Juan)	836
Paris (Charles de Gaulle)	215
Paris (Le Bourget)	215
Paris (Orly)	227
Perth, Australia	9,008
Port of Spain	4,404
Prague	649
Pretoria	5,602
Reykjavik (Domestic)	1,167
Reykjavik (Keflavik)	1,177
Rhodes	1,743
Rio de Janeiro	5,745
Riyadh (King Khaled) International	3,067
Rome (Fiumicino)	895
St John's, Newfoundland	2,308
St Petersburg	1,314
Salzburg	651
San Francisco	5,351
São Paulo	5,892
Sarajevo	1,017
Seoul (Kimpo)	5,507
Shanghai	5,725
Shannon	369
Singapore (Changi)	6,756
Sofia	1,266
Stockholm (Arlanda)	908
Suva	10,119
Sydney (Kingsford Smith)	10,568
Tangier	1,120
Tehran	2,741
Tel Aviv	2,227
Tokyo (Narita)	5,956
Toronto	3,544
Tripoli (International)	1,468
Tunis	1,137
Turin (Caselle)	570
Ulan Bator	4,340
Valencia	826
Vancouver	4,707
Venice (Tessera)	715
Vienna (Schwechat)	790
Vladivostok	5,298
Warsaw	912
Washington (Dulles)	3,665
Wellington	11,692
Yangon/Rangoon	5,582
Yokohama (Aomori)	5,647
Zagreb	848
Zürich	490

The United Kingdom

The United Kingdom comprises Great Britain (England, Wales and Scotland) and Northern Ireland. The Isle of Man and the Channel Islands are Crown dependencies with their own legislative systems, and not a part of the United Kingdom.

AREA AS AT 31 MARCH 1981

	Land miles²	km²	*Inland water miles²	km²	Total miles²	km²
United Kingdom	93,006	240,883	1,242	3,218	94,248	244,101
England	50,058	129,652	293	758	50,351	130,410
Wales	7,965	20,628	50	130	8,015	20,758
Scotland	29,767	77,097	653	1,692	30,420	78,789
†Northern Ireland	5,225	13,532	249	628	5,467	14,160
Isle of Man	221	572	—	—	221	572
Channel Islands	75	194	—	—	75	194

*Excluding tidal water
†Excluding certain tidal waters that are parts of statutory areas in Northern Ireland

POPULATION

The first official census of population in England, Wales and Scotland was taken in 1801 and a census has been taken every ten years since, except in 1941 when there was no census because of war. The last official census in the United Kingdom was taken on 21 April 1991 and the next is due in April 2001.

The first official census of population in Ireland was taken in 1841. However, all figures given below refer only to the area which is now Northern Ireland. Figures for Northern Ireland in 1921 and 1931 are estimates based on the censuses taken in 1926 and 1937 respectively.

Estimates of the population of England before 1801, calculated from the number of baptisms, burials and marriages, are:
1570 4,160,221   1670 5,773,646
1600 4,811,718   1700 6,045,008
1630 5,600,517   1750 6,517,035

Thousands	United Kingdom Total	Male	Female	England and Wales Total	Male	Female	Scotland Total	Male	Female	Northern Ireland Total	Male	Female
CENSUS RESULTS ;1801–1991												
1801	—	—	—	8,893	4,255	4,638	1,608	739	869	—	—	—
1811	13,368	6,368	7,000	10,165	4,874	5,291	1,806	826	980	—	—	—
1821	15,472	7,498	7,974	12,000	5,850	6,150	2,092	983	1,109	—	—	—
1831	17,835	8,647	9,188	13,897	6,771	7,126	2,364	1,114	1,250	—	—	—
1841	20,183	9,819	10,364	15,914	7,778	8,137	2,620	1,242	1,378	1,649	800	849
1851	22,259	10,855	11,404	17,928	8,781	9,146	2,889	1,376	1,513	1,443	698	745
1861	24,525	11,894	12,631	20,066	9,776	10,290	3,062	1,450	1,612	1,396	668	728
1871	27,431	13,309	14,122	22,712	11,059	11,653	3,360	1,603	1,757	1,359	647	712
1881	31,015	15,060	15,955	25,974	12,640	13,335	3,736	1,799	1,936	1,305	621	684
1891	34,264	16,593	17,671	29,003	14,060	14,942	4,026	1,943	2,083	1,236	590	646
1901	38,237	18,492	19,745	32,528	15,729	16,799	4,472	2,174	2,298	1,237	590	647
1911	42,082	20,357	21,725	36,070	17,446	18,625	4,761	2,309	2,452	1,251	603	648
1921	44,027	21,033	22,994	37,887	18,075	19,811	4,882	2,348	2,535	1,258	610	648
1931	46,038	22,060	23,978	39,952	19,133	20,819	4,843	2,326	2,517	1,243	601	642
1951	50,225	24,118	26,107	43,758	21,016	22,742	5,096	2,434	2,662	1,371	668	703
1961	52,709	25,481	27,228	46,105	22,304	23,801	5,179	2,483	2,697	1,425	694	731
1971	55,515	26,952	28,562	48,750	23,683	25,067	5,229	2,515	2,714	1,536	755	781
1981	55,848	27,104	28,742	49,155	23,873	25,281	5,131	2,466	2,664	*1,533	750	783
1991	56,467	27,344	29,123	49,890	24,182	25,707	4,999	2,392	2,607	1,578	769	809
†RESIDENT POPULATION: PROJECTIONS (MID-YEAR)												
2001	59,618	29,377	30,241	52,818	26,062	26,756	5,106	2,484	2,622	1,694	830	864
2011	60,929	30,206	30,723	54,151	26,881	27,269	5,059	2,476	2,583	1,720	848	872
2021	62,244	30,916	31,328	55,526	27,614	27,913	4,993	2,449	2,544	1,724	853	871

*Figures include 44,500 non-enumerated persons
† Projections are 1996 based

Source: The Stationery Office – Annual Abstract 1998; ONS – Census reports (Crown copyright)

ISLANDS: Census Results 1901–91

	Isle of Man			Jersey			*Guernsey		
	Total	Male	Female	Total	Male	Female	Total	Male	Female
1901	54,752	25,496	29,256	52,576	23,940	28,636	40,446	19,652	20,794
1911	52,016	23,937	28,079	51,898	24,014	27,884	41,858	20,661	21,197
1921	60,284	27,329	32,955	49,701	22,438	27,263	38,315	18,246	20,069
1931	49,308	22,443	26,865	50,462	23,424	27,038	40,643	19,659	20,984
1951	55,123	25,749	29,464	57,296	27,282	30,014	43,652	21,221	22,431
1961	48,151	22,060	26,091	57,200	27,200	30,000	45,068	21,671	23,397
1971	56,289	26,461	29,828	72,532	35,423	37,109	51,458	24,792	26,666
1981	64,679	30,901	33,778	77,000	37,000	40,000	53,313	25,701	27,612
1991	69,788	33,693	36,095	84,082	40,862	43,220	58,867	28,297	30,570

* Population of Guernsey, Herm, Jethou and Lithou. Figures for 1901–71 record all persons present on census night; census figures for 1981 and 1991 record all persons resident in the islands on census night
Source: 1991 Census

RESIDENT POPULATION

MID-YEAR ESTIMATE

	1987	1997
United Kingdom	57,009,000	59,009,000
England	47,488,000	49,284,000
Wales	2,833,000	2,927,000
Scotland	5,113,000	5,123,000
Northern Ireland	1,575,000	1,675,000

Source: The Stationery Office – *Annual Abstract of Statistics 1999* (Crown copyright)

BY AGE AND SEX 1997

Males	Under 16	65 and over
United Kingdom	6,208,000	3,796,000
England	5,168,000	3,191,000
Wales	307,000	208,000
Scotland	522,000	311,000
Northern Ireland	212,000	86,000

Females	Under 16	60 and over
United Kingdom	5,895,000	6,894,000
England	4,903,000	5,748,000
Wales	293,000	375,000
Scotland	499,000	605,000
Northern Ireland	200,000	166,000

Source: The Stationery Office – *Annual Abstract of Statistics 1999* (Crown copyright)

BY ETHNIC GROUP (1991 Census (Great Britain))

Ethnic group	Estimated population	As % of ethnic minority population
Caribbean	500,000	16.6
African	212,000	7
Other black	178,000	5.9
Indian	840,000	27.9
Pakistani	477,000	15.8
Bangladeshi	163,000	5.4
Chinese	157,000	5.2
Other Asian	198,000	6.6
Other	290,000	9.6
Total ethnic minority groups	3,015,000	100
White	51,874,000	—
All ethnic groups	54,889,000	—

Source: The Stationery Office – *Population Trends* 72 (Crown copyright)

AVERAGE DENSITY *Persons per hectare*

	1981	1991
England	3.55	3.61
Wales	1.34	1.36
Scotland	0.66	0.65
Northern Ireland	1.12	1.11

Sources: ONS – Census reports (Crown copyright)

IMMIGRATION 1997
Acceptances for settlement in the UK by nationality

Region	Number of persons
Europe: total	7,750
European Economic Area	110
Remainder of Europe	7,640
Americas: total	7,790
USA	3,900
Canada	980
Africa: total	13,200
Asia: total	25,610
Indian sub-continent	13,080
Middle East	4,160
Oceania: total	3,100
British Overseas Citizens	540
Stateless	740
Total	58,720

Source: The Stationery Office – *Annual Abstract of Statistics 1999* (Crown copyright)

LIVE BIRTHS AND BIRTH RATES 1997

	Live births	Birth rate*
United Kingdom	726,000	12.3
England and Wales	642,000	12.3
Scotland	59,000	11.6
Northern Ireland	24,000	14.5

*Live births per 1,000 population
Source: The Stationery Office – *Annual Abstract of Statistics 1999* (Crown copyright)

LEGAL ABORTIONS 1997p

Age group	England and Wales	Scotland
Under 16	3,430	289
16–19	29,927	2,428
20–34	113,917	7,929
35–44	22,249	1,410
45 and over	482	24
Total	182,085	

p provisional
Source: The Stationery Office – *Annual Abstract of Statistics 1999*
(Crown copyright)

BIRTHS OUTSIDE MARRIAGE (UK)

Age group	1987	1997
Under 20	48,000	47,000
20–24	68,000	78,000
25–29	37,000	70,000
Over 30	26,000	71,000
Total	179,000	266,000

Source: The Stationery Office – *Annual Abstract of Statistics 1999*
(Crown copyright)

MARRIAGE AND DIVORCE 1996p

	Marriages	Divorces
United Kingdom	317,514p	170,150
England and Wales	278,975p	155,310
Scotland	30,242	12,308
Northern Ireland	8,297	2,532

p provisional
Source: The Stationery Office – *Annual Abstract of Statistics 1999*
(Crown copyright)

DEATHS AND DEATH RATES 1997

Males	Deaths	Death rate[*]
United Kingdom	300,414	10.4
England and Wales	264,865	9.8
Scotland	28,305	11.4
Northern Ireland	7,244	8.8
Females		
United Kingdom	329,332	11.0
England and Wales	290,416	10.5
Scotland	31,189	11.8
Northern Ireland	7,727	9.0

[*] Deaths per 1,000 population
Sources: The Stationery Office – *Annual Abstract of Statistics 1999*
(Crown copyright); ONS; General Register Office for Scotland;
General Register Office (Northern Ireland)

INFANT MORTALITY 1997p
Deaths of infants under 1 year of age per 1,000 live births

	Number
United Kingdom	5.8
England and Wales	5.9
Scotland	5.3
Northern Ireland	5.6

p provisional
Source: The Stationery Office – *Annual Abstract of Statistics 1999*
(Crown copyright)

LIFE EXPECTANCY   LIFE TABLES 1994–96 (INTERIM FIGURES)

	England and Wales		Scotland		Northern Ireland	
Age	Male	Female	Male	Female	Male	Female
0	74.4	79.6	72.1	77.6	73.3	78.7
5	70.0	75.1	67.7	73.2	68.9	74.2
10	65.0	70.1	62.7	68.2	63.9	69.3
15	60.1	65.2	57.8	63.2	59.0	64.3
20	55.2	60.3	53.1	58.3	54.3	59.4
25	50.5	55.3	48.3	53.4	49.6	54.5
30	45.7	50.4	43.6	48.6	44.8	49.6
35	40.9	45.6	38.9	43.7	40.0	44.7
40	36.2	40.7	34.2	38.9	35.3	39.9
45	31.5	36.0	29.6	34.2	30.6	35.1
50	26.9	31.3	25.2	29.6	26.1	30.5
55	22.6	26.8	21.0	25.2	21.7	26.0
60	18.5	22.5	17.2	21.0	17.7	21.7
65	14.8	18.4	13.7	17.2	14.2	17.8
70	11.6	14.7	10.8	13.7	11.0	14.0
75	8.9	11.4	8.3	10.6	8.3	10.8
80	6.6	8.6	6.2	7.9	6.0	7.9
85	4.9	6.3	4.6	5.7	4.2	5.6

Source: The Stationery Office – *Annual Abstract of Statistics 1999* (Crown copyright)

DEATHS ANALYSED BY CAUSE 1997

	England and *Wales*	*Scotland*	*N. Ireland*
TOTAL DEATHS	555,281	59,494	14,967
Deaths from natural causes	536,422	56,932	14,274
Infectious and parasitic diseases	3,496	431	61
Neoplasms	137,618	15,054	3,667
Malignant neoplasm of stomach	6,613	710	171
Malignant neoplasm of trachea, bronchus and lung	29,976	4,106	772
Malignant neoplasm of breast	12,047	1,161	267
Malignant neoplasm of uterus	1,291	106	35
Malignant neoplasm of cervix	1,225	144	26
Benign and unspecified neoplasms	1,624	126	53
Leukaemia	3,587	291	107
Endocrine, nutritional and metabolic diseases and immunity disorders	7,383	727	106
Diabetes mellitus	5,890	510	77
Nutritional deficiencies	65	7	1
Other metabolic and immunity disorders	1,038	167	17
Diseases of blood and blood-forming organs	2,008	200	20
Anaemias	681	71	9
Mental disorders	9,725	1,611	138
Diseases of the nervous system and sense organs	9,772	900	234
Meningitis	224	17	8
Diseases of the circulatory system	228,446	25,911	6,505
Rheumatic heart disease	1,481	183	38
Hypertensive disease	3,084	294	73
Ischaemic heart disease	122,432	14,013	3,764
Diseases of pulmonary circulation and other forms of heart disease	26,609	2,900	635
Cerebrovascular disease	57,747	6,959	1,646
Diseases of the respiratory system	92,517	7,891	2,663
Influenza	347	83	8
Pneumonia	56,719	4,028	1,774
Bronchitis, emphysema	4,116	320	99
Asthma	1,439	113	32
Diseases of the digestive system	20,406	2,428	459
Ulcer of stomach and duodenum	3,959	306	95
Appendicitis	125	14	4
Hernia of the abdominal cavity and other intestinal obstruction	2,106	168	42
Chronic liver disease and cirrhosis	4,107	767	68
Diseases of the genitourinary system	6,757	904	245
Nephritis, nephrotic syndrome and nephrosis	2,930	576	175
Hyperplasia of prostate	247	9	4
Complications of pregnancy, childbirth and the puerperium	35	4	—
Abortion	2	—	—
Diseases of the skin and subcutaneous tissue	1,025	87	25
Diseases of the musculo-skeletal system	3,559	268	44
Congenital anomalies	1,283	182	57
Certain conditions originating in the perinatal period	131	140	69
Birth trauma, hypoxia, birth asphyxia and other respiratory conditions	99	71	26
Signs, symptoms and ill-defined conditions	12,292	383	92
Sudden infant death syndrome	327	52	8
Deaths from injury and poisoning	16,311	2,373	591
All accidents	10,661	1,398	427
Motor vehicle accidents	3,184	384	152
Suicide and self-inflicted injury	3,424	599	120
All other external causes	2,226	376	44

Source: The Stationery Office—*Annual Abstract of Statistics 1999* (Crown copyright)

The National Flag

The national flag of the United Kingdom is the Union Flag, generally known as the Union Jack.

The Union Flag is a combination of the cross of St George, patron saint of England, the cross of St Andrew, patron saint of Scotland, and a cross similar to that of St Patrick, patron saint of Ireland.

Cross of St George: cross Gules in a field Argent (red cross on a white ground)

Cross of St Andrew: saltire Argent in a field Azure (white diagonal cross on a blue ground)

Cross of St Patrick: saltire Gules in a field Argent (red diagonal cross on a white ground)

The Union Flag was first introduced in 1606 after the union of the kingdoms of England and Scotland under one sovereign. The cross of St Patrick was added in 1801 after the union of Great Britain and Ireland.

FLYING THE UNION FLAG

The correct orientation of the Union Flag when flying is with the broader diagonal band of white uppermost in the hoist (i.e. near the pole) and the narrower diagonal band of white uppermost in the fly (i.e. furthest from the pole).

It is the practice to fly the Union Flag daily on some customs houses. In all other cases, flags are flown on government buildings by command of The Queen.

Days for hoisting the Union Flag are notified to the Department for Culture, Media and Sport by The Queen's command and communicated by the department to the other government departments. On the days appointed, the Union Flag is flown on government buildings in the United Kingdom from 8 a.m. to sunset.

DAYS FOR FLYING FLAGS

The Queen's Accession	6 February
Birthday of The Duke of York	19 February
*St David's Day (in Wales only)	1 March
Birthday of The Prince Edward	10 March
Commonwealth Day** (2000)	13 March
Birthday of The Queen	21 April
*St George's Day (in England only)	23 April
†Europe Day	9 May
Coronation Day	2 June
Birthday of The Duke of Edinburgh	10 June
The Queen's Official Birthday (2000)	17 June
Birthday of Queen Elizabeth the Queen Mother	4 August
Birthday of The Princess Royal	15 August
Birthday of The Princess Margaret	21 August
Remembrance Sunday (2000)	12 November
Birthday of The Prince of Wales	14 November
The Queen's Wedding Day	20 November
*St Andrew's Day (in Scotland only)	30 November

‡The opening of Parliament by The Queen
‡The prorogation of Parliament by The Queen

*Where a building has two or more flagstaffs, the appropriate national flag may be flown in addition to the Union Flag, but not in a superior position

**Commonwealth Day is always the second Monday in March

†The Union Flag should fly alongside the European flag. On government buildings that have only one flagpole, the Union Flag should take precedence

‡Flags are flown whether or not The Queen performs the ceremony in person. Flags are flown only in the Greater London area

FLAGS AT HALF-MAST

Flags are flown at half-mast (i.e. two-thirds up between the top and bottom of the flagstaff) on the following occasions:

(a) From the announcement of the death up to the funeral of the Sovereign, except on Proclamation Day, when flags are hoisted right up from 11 a.m. to sunset

(b) The funerals of members of the royal family, subject to special commands from The Queen in each case

(c) The funerals of foreign rulers, subject to special commands from The Queen in each case

(d) The funerals of prime ministers and ex-prime ministers of the UK, subject to special commands from The Queen in each case

(e) Other occasions by special command of The Queen

On occasions when days for flying flags coincide with days for flying flags at half-mast, the following rules are observed. Flags are flown:

(a) although a member of the royal family, or a near relative of the royal family, may be lying dead, unless special commands are received from The Queen to the contrary

(b) although it may be the day of the funeral of a foreign ruler

If the body of a very distinguished subject is lying at a government office, the flag may fly at half-mast on that office until the body has left (provided it is a day on which the flag would fly) and then the flag is to be hoisted right up. On all other government buildings the flag will fly as usual.

THE ROYAL STANDARD

The Royal Standard is hoisted only when The Queen is actually present in the building, and never when Her Majesty is passing in procession.

The Royal Family

THE SOVEREIGN

ELIZABETH II, by the Grace of God, of the United Kingdom of Great Britain and Northern Ireland and of her other Realms and Territories Queen, Head of the Commonwealth, Defender of the Faith

Her Majesty Elizabeth Alexandra Mary of Windsor, elder daughter of King George VI and of HM Queen Elizabeth the Queen Mother
Born 21 April 1926, at 17 Bruton Street, London WI
Ascended the throne 6 February 1952
Crowned 2 June 1953, at Westminster Abbey
Married 20 November 1947, in Westminster Abbey, HRH The Prince Philip, Duke of Edinburgh
Official residences: Buckingham Palace, London SWIA 1AA; Windsor Castle, Berks; Palace of Holyroodhouse, Edinburgh
Private residences: Sandringham, Norfolk; Balmoral Castle, Aberdeenshire

HUSBAND OF THE QUEEN

HRH THE PRINCE PHILIP, DUKE OF EDINBURGH, KG, KT, OM, GBE, AC, QSO, PC, Ranger of Windsor Park
Born 10 June 1921, son of Prince and Princess Andrew of Greece and Denmark (*see* page 129), naturalized a British subject 1947, created Duke of Edinburgh, Earl of Merioneth and Baron Greenwich 1947

CHILDREN OF THE QUEEN

HRH THE PRINCE OF WALES; (Prince Charles Philip Arthur George), KG, KT, GCB and Great Master of the Order of the Bath, AK, QSO, PC, ADC(P)
Born 14 November 1948, created Prince of Wales and Earl of Chester 1958, succeeded as Duke of Cornwall, Duke of Rothesay, Earl of Carrick and Baron Renfrew, Lord of the Isles and Prince and Great Steward of Scotland 1952
Married 29 July 1981 Lady Diana Frances Spencer (Diana, Princess of Wales (1961–97), youngest daughter of the 8th Earl Spencer and the Hon. Mrs Shand Kydd), marriage dissolved 1996
Issue:
(1) HRH Prince William of Wales (Prince William Arthur Philip Louis), *born* 21 June 1982
(2) HRH Prince Henry of Wales (Prince Henry Charles Albert David), *born* 15 September 1984
Residences of the Prince of Wales: St James's Palace, London SWIA 1BS; Highgrove, Doughton, Tetbury, Glos GL8 8TN

HRH THE PRINCESS ROYAL (Princess Anne Elizabeth Alice Louise), KG, GCVO
Born 15 August 1950, declared The Princess Royal 1987
Married (1) 14 November 1973 Captain Mark Anthony Peter Phillips, CVO (*born* 22 September 1948); marriage dissolved 1992; (2) 12 December 1992 Captain Timothy James Hamilton Laurence, MVO, RN (*born* 1 March 1955)
Issue:
(1) Peter Mark Andrew Phillips, *born* 15 November 1977

(2) Zara Anne Elizabeth Phillips, *born* 15 May 1981
Residence: Gatcombe Park, Minchinhampton, Glos

HRH THE DUKE OF YORK (Prince Andrew Albert Christian Edward), CVO, ADC(P)
Born 19 February 1960, created Duke of York, Earl of Inverness and Baron Killyleagh 1986
Married 23 July 1986 Sarah Margaret Ferguson, now Sarah, Duchess of York (*born* 15 October 1959, younger daughter of Major Ronald Ferguson and Mrs Hector Barrantes), marriage dissolved 1996
Issue:
(1) HRH Princess Beatrice of York (Princess Beatrice Elizabeth Mary), *born* 8 August 1988
(2) HRH Princess Eugenie of York (Princess Eugenie Victoria Helena), *born* 23 March 1990
Residences: Buckingham Palace, London SWIA 1AA; Sunninghill Park, Ascot, Berks

HRH THE EARL OF WESSEX (Prince Edward Antony Richard Louis), CVO
Born 10 March 1964, created Earl of Wessex, Viscount Severn 1999
Married 19 June 1999 Sophie Helen Rhys-Jones, now HRH The Countess of Wessex (*born* 20 January 1965, daughter of Mr and Mrs Christopher Rhys-Jones)
Residence: Bagshot Park, Bagshot, Surrey GU19 5PL

SISTER OF THE QUEEN

HRH THE PRINCESS MARGARET, COUNTESS OF SNOWDON, CI, GCVO, Royal Victorian Chain, Dame Grand Cross of the Order of St John of Jerusalem
Born 21 August 1930, younger daughter of King George VI and HM Queen Elizabeth the Queen Mother
Married 6 May 1960 Antony Charles Robert Armstrong-Jones, GCVO (*born* 7 March 1930, created Earl of Snowdon 1961), marriage dissolved 1978
Issue:
(1) David Albert Charles, Viscount Linley, *born* 3 November 1961, *married* 8 October 1993 the Hon. Serena Stanhope, and has issue, *born* 2 July 1999
(2) Lady Sarah Chatto (Sarah Frances Elizabeth), *born* 1 May 1964, *married* 14 July 1994 Daniel Chatto, and has issue, Samuel David Benedict Chatto, *born* 28 July 1996; Arthur Robert Nathaniel Chatto, *born* 5 February 1999
Residence: Kensington Palace, London W8 4PU

MOTHER OF THE QUEEN

HM QUEEN ELIZABETH THE QUEEN MOTHER (Elizabeth Angela Marguerite), Lady of the Garter, Lady of the Thistle, CI, GCVO, GBE, Dame Grand Cross of the Order of St John of Jerusalem, Royal Victorian Chain, Lord Warden and Admiral of the Cinque Ports and Constable of Dover Castle
Born 4 August 1900, youngest daughter of the 14th Earl of Strathmore and Kinghorne
Married 26 April 1923 (as Lady Elizabeth Bowes-Lyon) Prince Albert, Duke of York, afterwards King George VI (*see* page 127)

Residences: Clarence House, St James's Palace, London SW1A 1BA; Royal Lodge, Windsor Great Park, Berks; Castle of Mey, Caithness

---

AUNT OF THE QUEEN

HRH PRINCESS ALICE, DUCHESS OF GLOUCESTER (Alice Christabel), GCB, CI, GCVO, GBE, Grand Cordon of Al Kamal
Born 25 December 1901, third daughter of the 7th Duke of Buccleuch and Queensberry
Married 6 November 1935 (as Lady Alice Montagu-Douglas-Scott) Prince Henry, Duke of Gloucester, third son of King George V (*see* page 127)
Residence: Kensington Palace, London W8 4PU

COUSINS OF THE QUEEN

HRH THE DUKE OF GLOUCESTER (Prince Richard Alexander Walter George), KG, GCVO, Grand Prior of the Order of St John of Jerusalem
Born 26 August 1944
Married 8 July 1972 Birgitte Eva van Deurs, now HRH The Duchess of Gloucester, GCVO (*born* 20 June 1946, daughter of Asger Henriksen and Vivian van Deurs)
Issue:
(1)   Earl of Ulster (Alexander Patrick Gregers Richard), *born* 24 October 1974
(2)   Lady Davina Windsor (Davina Elizabeth Alice Benedikte), *born* 19 November 1977
(3)   Lady Rose Windsor (Rose Victoria Birgitte Louise), *born* 1 March 1980
Residence: Kensington Palace, London W8 4PU

HRH THE DUKE OF KENT (Prince Edward George Nicholas Paul Patrick), KG, GCMG, GCVO, ADC(P)
Born 9 October 1935
Married 8 June 1961 Katharine Lucy Mary Worsley, now HRH The Duchess of Kent, GCVO (*born* 22 February 1933, daughter of Sir William Worsley, Bt.)
Issue:
(1)   Earl of St Andrews (George Philip Nicholas), *born* 26 June 1962, *married* 9 January 1988 Sylvana Tomaselli, and has issue, Edward Edmund Maximilian George, Baron Downpatrick, *born* 2 December 1988; Lady Marina Charlotte Alexandra Katharine Windsor, *born* 30 September 1992; Lady Amelia Sophia Theodora Mary Margaret Windsor, *born* 24 August 1995
(2)   Lady Helen Taylor (Helen Marina Lucy), *born* 28 April 1964, *married* 18 July 1992 Timothy Taylor, and has issue, Columbus George Donald Taylor, *born* 6 August 1994; Cassius Edward Taylor, *born* 26 December 1996
(3)   Lord Nicholas Windsor (Nicholas Charles Edward Jonathan), *born* 25 July 1970
Residence: Wren House, Palace Green, London W8 4PY

HRH PRINCESS ALEXANDRA, THE HON. LADY OGILVY (Princess Alexandra Helen Elizabeth Olga Christabel), GCVO
Born 25 December 1936
Married 24 April 1963 The Rt. Hon. Sir Angus Ogilvy, KCVO (*born* 14 September 1928, second son of 12th Earl of Airlie)
Issue:
(1)   James Robert Bruce Ogilvy, *born* 29 February 1964, *married* 30 July 1988 Julia Rawlinson, and has issue,

Flora Alexandra Ogilvy, *born* 15 December 1994; Alexander Charles Ogilvy, *born* 12 November 1996
(2)   Marina Victoria Alexandra, Mrs Mowatt, *born* 31 July 1966, *married* 2 February 1990 Paul Mowatt (marriage dissolved 1997), and has issue, Zenouska May Mowatt, *born* 26 May 1990; Christian Alexander Mowatt, *born* 4 June 1993
Residence: Thatched House Lodge, Richmond Park, Surrey

HRH PRINCE MICHAEL OF KENT (Prince Michael George Charles Franklin), KCVO
Born 4 July 1942
Married 30 June 1978 Baroness Marie-Christine Agnes Hedwig Ida von Reibnitz, now HRH Princess Michael of Kent (*born* 15 January 1945, daughter of Baron Gunther von Reibnitz)
Issue:
(1)   Lord Frederick Windsor (Frederick Michael George David Louis), *born* 6 April 1979
(2)   Lady Gabriella Windsor (Gabriella Marina Alexandra Ophelia), *born* 23 April 1981
Residences: Kensington Palace, London W8 4PU; Nether Lypiatt Manor, Stroud, Glos.

ORDER OF SUCCESSION

---

1   HRH The Prince of Wales
2   HRH Prince William of Wales
3   HRH Prince Henry of Wales
4   HRH The Duke of York
5   HRH Princess Beatrice of York
6   HRH Princess Eugenie of York
7   HRH The Earl of Wessex
8   HRH The Princess Royal
9   Peter Phillips
10 Zara Phillips
11 HRH The Princess Margaret, Countess of Snowdon
12 Viscount Linley
13 Hon. Charles Patrick Inigo Armstrong-Jones
14 Lady Sarah Chatto
15 Samuel Chatto
16 Arthur Chatto
17 HRH The Duke of Gloucester
18 Earl of Ulster
19 Lady Davina Windsor
20 Lady Rose Windsor
21 HRH The Duke of Kent
22 Baron Downpatrick
23 Lady Marina Charlotte Windsor
24 Lady Amelia Windsor
25 Lord Nicholas Windsor
26 Lady Helen Taylor
27 Columbus Taylor
28 Cassius Taylor
29 Lord Frederick Windsor
30 Lady Gabriella Windsor
31 HRH Princess Alexandra, the Hon. Lady Ogilvy
32 James Ogilvy
33 Alexander Ogilvy
34 Flora Ogilvy
35 Marina, Mrs Paul Mowatt
36 Christian Mowatt
37 Zenouska Mowatt
38 The Earl of Harewood

The Earl of St Andrews and HRH Prince Michael of Kent both lost the right of succession to the throne through marriage to a Roman Catholic. Their children remain in succession provided that they are in communion with the Church of England.

Royal Households

THE QUEEN'S HOUSEHOLD

Office: Buckingham Palace, London SWIA IAA
Tel: 0171-930 4832
Web: http://www.royal.gov.uk

The Lord Chamberlain is the most senior member of The Queen's Household and under him come the heads of the six departments: the Private Secretary, the Keeper of the Privy Purse, the Comptroller of the Lord Chamberlain's Office, the Master of the Household, the Crown Equerry, and the Director of the Royal Collection. Positions in these departments are full-time salaried posts.

There are also a number of honorary or now largely ceremonial appointments which carry no remuneration or a small honorarium. In the following list, most honorary appointments have been placed at the end; however, where this is not the case, such appointments are indicated by an asterisk.

GREAT OFFICERS OF STATE

Lord Chamberlain, The Lord Camoys, GCVO, PC
Lord Steward, The Viscount Ridley, KG, GCVO, TD
Master of the Horse, The Lord Vestey

LADIES-IN-WAITING AND EQUERRIES

Mistress of the Robes, The Duchess of Grafton, GCVO
Ladies of the Bedchamber, The Countess of Airlie, DCVO; The Lady Farnham, CVO
Women of the Bedchamber, Hon. Mary Morrison, DCVO; Lady Susan Hussey, DCVO; Lady Dugdale, DCVO; The Lady Elton, CVO; Mrs Christian Adams (temp.)
Equerry, Sqn. Ldr. S. Brailsford

THE PRIVATE SECRETARY'S OFFICE

Buckingham Palace, London SWIA IAA

Private Secretary to The Queen, Sir Robin Janvrin, KCVO, CB
Deputy Private Secretary, vacant
Communications Secretary, S. Lewis
Assistant Private Secretary, T. Hitchens
Special Assistant to the Private Secretary, A. Dent
Chief Clerk, Mrs G. Middleburgh, MVO
Secretary to the Private Secretary, Miss E. Ash

PRESS OFFICE

Press Secretary, G. Crawford, LVO
Deputy Press Secretary, Miss P. Russell-Smith
Assistant Press Secretaries, R. Arbiter, LVO; D. Tuck

THE QUEEN'S ARCHIVES
Round Tower, Windsor Castle, Berks

Keeper of The Queen's Archives, Sir Robin Janvrin, KCVO, CB
Assistant Keeper, O. Everett, CVO
Registrar, Lady de Bellaigue, MVO

THE PRIVY PURSE AND TREASURER'S OFFICE

Buckingham Palace, London SWIA IAA

Keeper of the Privy Purse and Treasurer to The Queen, Sir Michael Peat, KCVO
Director of Property Services, J. Tiltman, LVO
Director of Royal Travel, Air Cdre the Hon. T. Elworthy
Director of Finance, Property Services and Royal Travel, S. Cawley
Deputy Keeper of the Privy Purse and Deputy Treasurer, J. Parsons, CVO
Chief Accountant and Paymaster, I. McGregor
Personnel Officer, Miss P. Lloyd
Land Agent, Sandringham, M. O'Lone, FRICS
Resident Factor, Balmoral, P. Ord, FRICS

THE LORD CHAMBERLAIN'S OFFICE

Buckingham Palace, London SWIA IAA

Comptroller, Lt.-Col. W. H. M. Ross, CVO, OBE
Assistant Comptroller, Lt.-Col. R. Cartwright
Secretary, J. Spencer, MVO
Assistant Secretary, Miss A. Krysztofiak
State Invitations Assistant, J. O. Hope

Marshal of the Diplomatic Corps, Vice-Adm. Sir James Weatherall, KBE
Vice-Marshal, Mrs K. Colvin

CENTRAL CHANCERY OF THE ORDERS OF KNIGHTHOOD
St James's Palace, London SWIA IBS

Secretary, Lt.-Col. A. Mather, CVO, OBE
Assistant Secretary, Miss R. Wells, MVO

MASTER OF THE HOUSEHOLD'S DEPARTMENT

Buckingham Palace, London SWIA IAA

Master of the Household, Maj.-Gen. Sir Simon Cooper, KCVO
Deputy Master of the Household, Lt.-Col. C. Richards
Assistants to the Master of the Household, M. T. Parker, MVO; A. Jarman; A. Smith
Chief Clerk, M. C. W. N. Jephson, LVO
Chief Housekeeper, Miss H. Colebrook, MVO
Palace Steward, P. S. Croasdale, RVM
Royal Chef, L. Mann, RVM
Superintendent, Windsor Castle, Maj. M. Davidson, MBE, BEM
Superintendent, The Palace of Holyroodhouse, Lt.-Col. D. Anderson, OBE

ROYAL MEWS DEPARTMENT

Buckingham Palace, London SWIW OQH

Crown Equerry, Lt.-Col. S. Gilbert-Denham, CVO
Superintendent, Royal Mews, Buckingham Palace, Maj. I. Kelly

THE ROYAL COLLECTION

St James's Palace, London SWIA IBS

Director of Royal Collection and Surveyor of The Queen's Works of Art, H. Roberts, CVO, FSA
Surveyor of The Queen's Pictures, C. Lloyd, LVO
Librarian, The Royal Library, Windsor Castle, O. Everett, CVO
Deputy Surveyor of The Queen's Works of Art, J. Marsden
Director of Media Affairs, R. Arbiter, LVO
Curator of the Print Room, The Hon. Mrs Roberts, LVO
Financial Director, M. Stevens
Financial Controller, Mrs G. Johnson, MVO
Administrator and Assistant to The Surveyors, D. Rankin-Hunt, MVO, TD
Senior Picture Restorer, Miss V. Pemberton-Pigott, MVO
Chief Restorer, Old Master Drawings, A. Donnithorne

Senior Furniture Restorer, E. Fancourt, LVO, RVM
Armourer, J. Jackson, RVM
Chief Binder, R. Day, MVO, RVM

ROYAL COLLECTION ENTERPRISES LTD
Managing Director, M. E. K. Hewlett, LVO

ECCLESIASTICAL HOUSEHOLD
*Clerk of the Closet, The Bishop of Derby
*Deputy Clerk of the Closet, Revd W. Booth, LVO
*Chaplains and Extra Chaplains to The Queen: approx. 30–40
*Dean of the Chapels Royal, The Bishop of London
Sub-Dean of the Chapels Royal, Revd W. Booth, LVO
*Organist, Choirmaster and Composer, R. J. Popplewell, MVO, FRCO, FRCM
Domestic Chaplain, Buckingham Palace, Revd W. Booth, LVO
Domestic Chaplain, Windsor Castle, The Dean of Windsor
Domestic Chaplain, Sandringham, Revd Canon G. R. Hall, LVO

MEDICAL HOUSEHOLD
*Head of the Medical Household and Physician to The Queen, R. Thompson, DM, FRCP
*Serjeant Surgeon, B. T. Jackson, FRCS
Apothecary to The Queen and to the Household, N. R. Southward, CVO
Apothecary to the Household at Windsor, J. Holliday
Apothecary to the Household at Sandringham, I. K. Campbell, D.Obst., FRCGP
*Coroner of The Queen's Household, J. Burton, CBE

OTHER HONORARY/CEREMONIAL APPOINTMENTS

Lord High Almoner, The Bishop of Wakefield
Master of The Queen's Music, M. Williamson, CBE, AO
Poet Laureate (1999–2009), Prof. Andrew Motion
Keeper of the Royal Philatelic Collection, C. Goodwyn
Bargemaster, R. Crouch
Swan Warden, Prof. C. Perrins, LVO
Swan Marker, D. Barber

POLITICAL (GOVERNMENT WHIPS) (see also page 277)
Captain, Honourable Corps of Gentlemen-at-Arms (Chief Whip in the Lords), The Lord Carter, PC
Captain, Queen's Bodyguard of the Yeomen of the Guard (Deputy Chief Whip in the Lords), The Lord McIntosh of Haringey
Lords-in-Waiting, The Lord Burlison of Rowlands; The Lord Bach
Baronesses-in-Waiting, The Baroness Farrington of Ribbleton; The Baroness Ramsay of Cartvale; The Baroness Amos
Treasurer of the Household (Deputy Chief Whip in the Commons), K. Bradley, MP
Comptroller of the Household, T. McAvoy, MP
Vice-Chamberlain, G. Allen, MP

ARMED FORCES

Gold Sticks, HRH The Princess Royal, KG, GCVO; Gen. Sir Charles Guthrie, GCB, LVO, OBE
Vice-Admiral of the United Kingdom, Adm. Sir Nicholas Hunt, GCB, LVO
Rear-Admiral of the United Kingdom, Adm. Sir Jeremy Black, GBE, KCB, DSO
First and Principal Naval Aide-de-Camp, Adm. Sir Michael Boyce, GCB, OBE
Flag Aide-de-Camp, Adm. Sir John Brigstocke, KCB

Aides-de-Camp-General, Gen. Sir Charles Guthrie, GCB, LVO, OBE; Gen. Sir Roger Wheeler, GCB, CBE; Gen. Sir Michael Walker, KCB, CMG, CBE; Gen. Sir Alex Harley, KBE, CB
Air Aides-de-Camp, Air Chief Marshal Sir Richard Johns, GCB, CBE, LVO; Air Chief Marshal Sir Peter Squire, KCB, DFC, AFC
Gentleman Usher to the Sword of State, Adm. Sir Michael Layard, KCB, CBE
Constable and Governor of Windsor Castle, vacant
Governor of Edinburgh Castle, Maj.-Gen. M. J. Strudwick, CBE

BODYGUARDS

THE HONOURABLE CORPS OF GENTLEMEN-AT-ARMS
Captain, The Lord Carter, PC
Lieutenant, Lt.-Col. R. Mayfield, DSO
Clerk of the Cheque and Adjutant, Col. D. Fanshawe, OBE;
Gentlemen of the Corps: 27
The Queen's Body Guard of the Yeomen of the Guard
Captain, The Lord McIntosh of Haringey
Lieutenant, Col. G. W. Tufnell
Clerk of the Cheque and Adjutant, Col. S. Longsdon
Yeomen of the Guard: 81

THE QUEEN'S HOUSEHOLD IN SCOTLAND

*Hereditary Lord High Constable of Scotland, The Earl of Erroll
*Hereditary Master of the Household in Scotland, The Duke of Argyll
Lord Lyon King of Arms, Sir Malcolm Innes of Edingight, KCVO, WS
*Hereditary Banner-Bearer for Scotland, The Earl of Dundee
*Hereditary Bearer of the National Flag of Scotland, The Earl of Lauderdale
*Hereditary Keeper of the Palace of Holyroodhouse, The Duke of Hamilton and Brandon
*Historiographer, Prof. T. C. Smout, CBE, FBA, FRSE, FSA Scot.
*Botanist, Prof. D. Henderson, CBE, FRSE
*Painter and Limner, vacant
*Sculptor in Ordinary, Prof. Sir Eduardo Paolozzi, CBE, RA
*Astronomer, Prof. J. Brown, ph.D., FRSE
*Heralds and Pursuivants, see Government Departments

ECCLESIASTICAL HOUSEHOLD
*Dean of the Chapel Royal, Very Revd J. Harkness, CB, OBE
*Dean of the Order of the Thistle, Very Revd G. I. Macmillan, CVO
*Chaplains in Ordinary: 10
Domestic Chaplain, Balmoral, Revd R. P. Sloan

MEDICAL HOUSEHOLD
*Physicians in Scotland, P. Brunt, OBE, MD, FRCP; A. Toft, CBE, FRCPE
*Surgeons in Scotland, J. Engeset, FRCS; I. Macintyre
Apothecary to the Household at Balmoral, D. J. A. Glass
Apothecary to the Household at the Palace of Holyroodhouse, Dr J. Cormack, MD, FRCPE, FRCGP

*ROYAL COMPANY OF ARCHERS (QUEEN'S BODYGUARD FOR SCOTLAND)
Captain-General and Gold Stick for Scotland, Maj. Sir Hew Hamilton-Dalrymple, Bt., KCVO
President of the Council and Silver Stick for Scotland, The Duke of Buccleuch and Queensberry, KT, VRD
Adjutant, Maj. the Hon. Sir Lachlan Maclean, Bt.
Secretary, Capt. J. D. B. Younger
Treasurer, J. M. Haldane of Gleneagles
Members on the active list: c.400

HOUSEHOLD OF THE PRINCE PHILIP, DUKE OF EDINBURGH

Office: Buckingham Palace, London SW1A 1AA
Tel: 0171-930 4832

Treasurer, Sir Brian McGrath, KCVO
Private Secretary, Brig. M. G. Hunt-Davis, CVO, CBE
Equerry, Sqn. Ldr. L. Johnson
Temporary Equerries, Capt. P. Wise; Lt.-Col. P. Denning;
Capt. B. Hancock
Chief Clerk and Accountant, G. D. Partington

HOUSEHOLD OF QUEEN ELIZABETH THE QUEEN MOTHER

Office: Clarence House, St James's Palace, London SW1A 1BA
Tel: 0171-930 3141

Lord Chamberlain, The Earl of Crawford and Balcarres, KT,
PC
Private Secretary, Comptroller and Equerry, Capt. Sir Alastair
Aird, GCVO
Assistant Private Secretary and Equerry, Maj. R. Seymour,
CVO
Treasurer and Extra Equerry, Hon. N. Assheton
Treasurer Emeritus and Equerry, Maj. Sir Ralph Anstruther,
Bt., GCVO, MC
Equerry, Capt. W. de Rouet (temp.)
Apothecary to the Household, Dr N. Southward, CVO
Surgeon-Apothecary to the Household (Royal Lodge, Windsor), J.
Holliday
Ladies of the Bedchamber, The Lady Grimthorpe, DCVO; The
Countess of Scarbrough
Women of the Bedchamber, Dame Frances Campbell-Preston,
DCVO; Lady Angela Oswald, LVO; The Hon. Mrs
Rhodes; Mrs Michael Gordon-Lennox
Clerk Comptroller, A. Kirkpatrick-Smith
Information Officer, Mrs R. Murphy, LVO
Clerks, Miss F. Fletcher, LVO; Mrs W. Stevens

HOUSEHOLD OF THE PRINCE OF WALES

Office: St James's Palace, London SW1A 1BS
Tel: 0171-930 4832

Private Secretary and Treasurer, S. M. J. Lamport, CVO
Deputy Private Secretary, M. Bolland
Assistant Private Secretaries, N. S. Archer; Miss E. Buchanan
Press Secretary, Miss S. Henney
Deputy Press Secretary, Mrs C. Harris
Equerry, Lt. Cdr. W. N. Entwisle, RN
Secretary to the Duchy of Cornwall and Keeper of the Records, W.
R. A. Ross

HOUSEHOLD OF THE DUKE OF YORK

Office: Buckingham Palace, London SW1A 1AA
Tel: 0171-930 4832

Private Secretary, Treasurer and Extra Equerry, Capt. R. N.
Blair, LVO, RN
Comptroller and Deputy Private Secretary, Miss C. Manley,
OBE
Equerry, Capt. R. L. Gerrard-Wright

HOUSEHOLD OF THE EARL OF WESSEX

Office: Buckingham Palace, London SW1A 1AA
Tel: 0171-930 4832

Private Secretary, Lt.-Col. S. G. O'Dwyer, LVO
Clerk, Mrs L. Sharp, MVO

HOUSEHOLD OF THE PRINCESS ROYAL

Office: Buckingham Palace, London SW1A 1AA
Tel: 0171-930 4832

Private Secretary, Col. T. Earl
Assistant Private Secretary, Mrs S. Gee
Ladies-in-Waiting, Lady Carew Pole, LVO; Mrs Andrew
Feilden, LVO; The Hon. Mrs Legge-Bourke, LVO; Mrs
William Nunneley, LVO; Mrs Timothy Holderness-
Roddam, LVO; Mrs Charles Ritchie, LVO; Mrs David
Bowes Lyon

HOUSEHOLD OF THE PRINCESS MARGARET, COUNTESS OF SNOWDON

Office: Kensington Palace, London W8 4PU
Tel: 0171-930 3141

Private Secretary, The Viscount Ullswater, PC
Treasurer, Maj. The Lord Napier and Ettrick, KCVO
Lady-in-Waiting, The Hon. Mrs Whitehead, LVO

HOUSEHOLD OF THE DUKE AND DUCHESS OF GLOUCESTER

Office: Kensington Palace, London W8 4PU
Tel: 0171-937 6374

Private Secretary, Comptroller and Equerry, Maj. N. M. L.
Barne, LVO
Assistant Private Secretary to the Duchess of Gloucester, Miss S.
Marland, LVO
Ladies-in-Waiting, Mrs Michael Wigley, CVO; Mrs Euan
McCorquodale, LVO; Mrs Howard Page, LVO

HOUSEHOLD OF PRINCESS ALICE, DUCHESS OF GLOUCESTER

Office: Kensington Palace, London W8 4PU
Tel: 0171-937 6374

Private Secretary, Comptroller and Equerry, Maj. N. M. L.
Barne, LVO
Ladies-in-Waiting, Dame Jean Maxwell-Scott, DCVO; Mrs
Michael Harvey, LVO

HOUSEHOLD OF THE DUKE AND DUCHESS OF KENT

Office: York House, St James's Palace, London SW1 1BQ
Tel: 0171-930 4872

Private Secretary, N. C. Adamson, OBE
Temporary Equerry, Capt. D. Hampshire
Ladies-in-Waiting, Mrs Colin Marsh, LVO; Mrs Julian
Tomkins; Mrs Peter Troughton; Mrs Richard Beckett

HOUSEHOLD OF PRINCE AND PRINCESS
MICHAEL OF KENT

Office: Kensington Palace, London W8 4PU
Tel: 0171-938 3519

Private Secretary, N. Chance
Personal Secretaries, Miss C. Jenkins, Miss K. Garrod
Ladies-in-Waiting, The Hon. Mrs Sanders; Miss A. Frost;
Mrs J. Fellowes

HOUSEHOLD OF PRINCESS ALEXANDRA,
THE HON. LADY OGILVY

Office: Buckingham Palace, London SWIA IAA
Tel: 0171-930 1860

Comptroller and Private Secretary, Capt. N. Blair, LVO, RN
Lady-in-Waiting, Lady Mary Mumford, DCVO

Royal Salutes

ENGLAND

A salute of 62 guns is fired on the wharf at the Tower of
London on the following occasions:
(a) the anniversaries of the birth, accession and
    coronation of the Sovereign
(b) the anniversary of the birth of HM Queen Elizabeth
    the Queen Mother
(c) the anniversary of the birth of HRH Prince Philip,
    Duke of Edinburgh
A salute of 41 guns only is fired on extraordinary and
triumphal occasions, e.g. on the occasion of the Sovereign
opening, proroguing or dissolving Parliament in person,
or when passing through London in procession, except
when otherwise ordered.
A salute of 41 guns is fired from the two saluting
stations in London (the Tower of London and Hyde Park)
on the occasion of the birth of a royal infant.
Constable of the Royal Palace and Fortress of London, Field
Marshal the Lord Inge, GCB
Lieutenant of the Tower of London, Lt.-Gen. Sir Anthony
Denison-Smith, KBE
Resident Governor and Keeper of the Jewel House, Maj.-Gen. G.
Field, CB, OBE

Master Gunner of St James's Park, Field Marshal the Lord
Vincent of Coleshill, GBE, KCB, DSO
Master Gunner within the Tower, Col. S. Lalor

SCOTLAND

Royal salutes are authorized at Edinburgh Castle and
Stirling Castle, although in practice Edinburgh Castle is
the only operating saluting station in Scotland.
A salute of 21 guns is fired on the following occasions:
(a) the anniversaries of the birth, accession and
    coronation of the Sovereign
(b) the anniversary of the birth of HM Queen Elizabeth
    the Queen Mother
(c) the anniversary of the birth of HRH Prince Philip,
    Duke of Edinburgh
A salute of 21 guns is fired in Edinburgh on the
occasion of the opening of the General Assembly of the
Church of Scotland.
A salute of 21 guns may also be fired in Edinburgh on
the arrival of HM The Queen, HM Queen Elizabeth the
Queen Mother, or a member of the royal family who is a
Royal Highness on an official visit.

Royal Finances

FUNDING

THE CIVIL LIST

The Civil List dates back to the late 17th century. It was originally used by the sovereign to supplement hereditary revenues for paying the salaries of judges, ambassadors and other government officers as well as the expenses of the royal household. In 1760 on the accession of George III it was decided that the Civil List would be provided by Parliament to cover all relevant expenditure in return for the King surrendering the hereditary revenues of the Crown. At that time Parliament undertook to pay the salaries of judges, ambassadors, etc. In 1831 Parliament agreed also to meet the costs of the royal palaces in return for a reduction in the Civil List. Each sovereign has agreed to continue this arrangement.

The Civil List paid to The Queen is charged on the Consolidated Fund. Until 1972, the amount of money allocated annually under the Civil List was set for the duration of a reign. The system was then altered to a fixed annual payment for ten years but from 1975 high inflation made an annual review necessary. The system of payments reverted to the practice of a fixed annual payment for ten years from 1 January 1991.

The Civil List Acts provide for other members of the royal family to receive parliamentary annuities from government funds to meet the expenses of carrying out their official duties. Since 1975 The Queen has reimbursed the Treasury for the annuities paid to the Duke of Gloucester, the Duke of Kent and Princess Alexandra. Since 1993 The Queen has reimbursed all the annuities except those paid to herself, Queen Elizabeth the Queen Mother and the Duke of Edinburgh.

The Prince of Wales does not receive a parliamentary annuity. He derives his income from the revenues of the Duchy of Cornwall and these monies meet the official and private expenses of the Prince of Wales and his family.

The annual payments for the years 1991–2000 are:

The Queen	£7,900,000
Queen Elizabeth the Queen Mother	643,000
The Duke of Edinburgh	359,000
*The Duke of York	249,000
*†The Earl of Wessex	141,000
*The Princess Royal	228,000
*The Princess Margaret, Countess of Snowdon	219,000
*Princess Alice, Duchess of Gloucester	87,000
*The Duke of Gloucester	175,000
*The Duke of Kent	236,000
*Princess Alexandra	225,000
	10,462,000
*Refunded to the Treasury	1,560,000
Total	8,947,000

†The Earl of Wessex's annuity was increased from £96,000 upon his marriage in June 1999

GRANTS-IN-AID

The royal household receives grants-in-aid from several government departments to meet various official expenses. The Department for Culture, Media and Sport provides grant-in-aid to pay for the upkeep of English occupied royal palaces, which are used as offices, for official or ceremonial purposes and to which there is public access, and to meet the cost of media and information services.

Royal Travel grant-in-aid is provided by the Department of the Environment, Transport and the Regions to meet the cost of official royal travel by air and rail, using mainly aircraft from 32 (The Royal) Squadron, chartered commercial aircraft for major overseas state visits and the Royal Train.

Grant-in-aid for 1999–2000 is:

Property Services and Communications and Information	£15,000,000
Royal Travel	9,300,000

THE PRIVY PURSE

The funds received by the Privy Purse pay for official expenses incurred by The Queen as head of state and for some of The Queen's private expenditure. The revenues of the Duchy of Lancaster are the principal source of income for the Privy Purse. The revenues of the Duchy were retained by George III in 1760 when the hereditary revenues were surrendered in exchange for the Civil List.

PERSONAL INCOME

The Queen's personal income derives mostly from investments, and is used to meet private expenditure.

DEPARTMENTAL VOTES

Items of expenditure connected with the official duties of the royal family which fall directly on votes of government departments include:

Ministry of Defence – equerries

Foreign and Commonwealth Office – Marshal of the Diplomatic Corps; costs (other than travel costs) associated with overseas visits at the request of government departments

HM Treasury – Central Chancery of the Orders of Knighthood

The Post Office – postal services

TAXATION

The sovereign is not legally liable to pay income tax, capital gains tax or inheritance tax. After income tax was reintroduced in 1842, some income tax was paid voluntarily by the sovereign but over a long period these payments were phased out. In 1992 The Queen offered to pay tax on a voluntary basis from 6 April 1993, and the Prince of Wales to pay tax on a voluntary basis on his income from the Duchy of Cornwall. (He was already taxed in all other respects.)

The main provisions for The Queen and the Prince of Wales to pay tax, set out in a Memorandum of Understanding on Royal Taxation presented to Parliament on 11 February 1993, are that The Queen will pay income tax and capital gains tax in respect of her private income and assets, and on the proportion of the income and capital gains of the Privy Purse used for private purposes. Inheritance tax will be paid on The Queen's assets, except for those which pass to the next sovereign, whether automatically or by gift or bequest. The Prince of Wales will pay income tax on income from the Duchy of Cornwall used for private purposes.

The Prince of Wales has confirmed that he intends to pay tax on the same basis following his accession to the throne.

Other members of the royal family are subject to tax as for any taxpayer.

Military Ranks and Titles

THE QUEEN

Lord High Admiral of the United Kingdom

Colonel-in-Chief
The Life Guards; The Blues and Royals (Royal Horse Guards and 1st Dragoons); The Royal Scots Dragoon Guards (Carabiniers and Greys); The Queen's Royal Lancers; Royal Tank Regiment; Corps of Royal Engineers; Grenadier Guards; Coldstream Guards; Scots Guards; Irish Guards; Welsh Guards; The Royal Welch Fusiliers; The Queen's Lancashire Regiment; The Argyll and Sutherland Highlanders (Princess Louise's); The Royal Green Jackets; Adjutant General's Corps; The Royal Mercian and Lancastrian Yeomanry; The Governor General's Horse Guards (of Canada); The King's Own Calgary Regiment; Canadian Forces Military Engineers Branch; Royal 22e Regiment (of Canada); Governor-General's Foot Guards (of Canada); The Canadian Grenadier Guards; Le Regiment de la Chaudiere (of Canada); 2nd Bn Royal New Brunswick Regiment (North Shore); The 48th Highlanders of Canada; The Argyll and Sutherland Highlanders of Canada (Princess Louise's); The Calgary Highlanders; Royal Australian Engineers; Royal Australian Infantry Corps; Royal Australian Army Ordnance Corps; Royal Australian Army Nursing Corps; The Corps of Royal New Zealand Engineers; Royal New Zealand Infantry Regiment; Royal Malta Artillery; The Malawi Rifles

Affiliated Colonel-in-Chief
The Queen's Gurkha Engineers

Captain-General
Royal Regiment of Artillery; The Honourable Artillery Company; Combined Cadet Force Association; Royal Regiment of Canadian Artillery; Royal Regiment of Australian Artillery; Royal Regiment of New Zealand Artillery; Royal New Zealand Armoured Corps

Patron
Royal Army Chaplains' Department

Air Commodore-in-Chief
Royal Auxiliary Air Force; Royal Air Force Regiment; Air Reserve (of Canada); Royal Australian Air Force Reserve; Territorial Air Force (of New Zealand)

Commandant-in-Chief
Royal Air Force College, Cranwell

Hon. Air Commodore
RAF Marham

HRH THE PRINCE PHILIP, DUKE OF EDINBURGH

Admiral of the Fleet
Field Marshal
Marshal of the Royal Air Force

Admiral of the Fleet, Royal Australian Navy
Field Marshal, Australian Military Forces
Marshal of the Royal Australian Air Force

Admiral of the Fleet, Royal New Zealand Navy
Field Marshal, New Zealand Army
Marshal of the Royal New Zealand Air Force

Captain-General, Royal Marines

Admiral
Royal Canadian Sea Cadets

Colonel-in-Chief
The Royal Gloucestershire, Berkshire and Wiltshire Regiment; The Highlanders (Seaforth, Gordons and Camerons); Corps of Royal Electrical and Mechanical Engineers; Intelligence Corps; Army Cadet Force Association; The Royal Canadian Regiment; The Royal Hamilton Light Infantry (Wentworth Regiment) (of Canada); The Cameron Highlanders of Ottawa; The Queen's Own Cameron Highlanders of Canada; The Seaforth Highlanders of Canada; The Royal Canadian Army Cadets; The Royal Corps of Australian Electrical and Mechanical Engineers; The Australian Cadet Corps

Deputy Colonel-in-Chief
The Queen's Royal Hussars (Queen's Own and Royal Irish)

Colonel
Grenadier Guards

Hon. Colonel
City of Edinburgh Universities Officers' Training Corps; The Trinidad and Tobago Regiment

Air Commodore-in-Chief
Air Training Corps; Royal Canadian Air Cadets

Hon. Air Commodore
RAF Kinloss

HM QUEEN ELIZABETH THE QUEEN MOTHER

Colonel-in-Chief
1st The Queen's Dragoon Guards; The Queen's Royal Hussars (Queen's Own and Royal Irish); 9th/12th Royal Lancers (Prince of Wales's); The King's Regiment; The Royal Anglian Regiment; The Light Infantry; The Black Watch (Royal Highland Regiment); Royal Army Medical Corps; The Black Watch (Royal Highland Regiment) of Canada; The Toronto Scottish Regiment; Canadian Forces Medical Services; Royal Australian Army Medical Corps; Royal New Zealand Army Medical Corps

Hon. Colonel
The Royal Yeomanry; The London Scottish; Inns of Court and City Yeomanry

Commandant-in-Chief
Women in the Royal Navy; Women, Royal Air Force; Royal Air Force Central Flying School

HRH THE PRINCE OF WALES

Rear Admiral, Royal Navy
Major-General, Army
Air Vice-Marshal, Royal Air Force

Colonel-in-Chief
The Royal Dragoon Guards; The 22nd (Cheshire) Regiment; The Royal Regiment of Wales (24th/41st Foot); The Parachute Regiment; The Royal Gurkha Rifles; Army Air Corps; The Royal Canadian Dragoons; Lord Strathcona's Horse (Royal Canadians); Royal Regiment of Canada; Royal Winnipeg Rifles; Air Reserve

Group of Air Command (of Canada); Royal Australian Armoured Corps; The Royal Pacific Islands Regiment

Deputy Colonel-in-Chief
The Highlanders (Seaforth, Gordons and Camerons)

Colonel
Welsh Guards

Air Commodore-in-Chief
Royal New Zealand Air Force

Hon. Air Commodore
RAF Valley

HRH THE DUKE OF YORK

Commander, Royal Navy

Admiral
Sea Cadet Corps

Colonel-in-Chief
The Staffordshire Regiment (The Prince of Wales's); The Royal Irish Regiment (27th (Inniskilling), 83rd, 87th and The Ulster Defence Regiment); Royal New Zealand Army Logistic Regiment; The Queen's York Rangers (First Americans)

Hon. Air Commodore
RAF Lossiemouth

HRH THE PRINCESS ROYAL

Rear Admiral
Chief Commandant for Women in the Royal Navy

Colonel-in-Chief
The King's Royal Hussars; Royal Corps of Signals; The Royal Scots (The Royal Regiment); The Worcestershire and Sherwood Foresters Regiment (29th/45th Foot); The Royal Logistic Corps; 8th Canadian Hussars (Princess Louise's); Canadian Forces Communications and Electronics Branch; The Grey and Simcoe Foresters; The Royal Regina Rifle Regiment; Royal Australian Corps of Signals; Royal New Zealand Corps of Signals; Royal New Zealand Nursing Corps

Colonel
Blues and Royals

Affiliated Colonel-in-Chief
The Queen's Gurkha Signals; The Queen's Own Gurkha Transport Regiment

Hon. Colonel
University of London Officers' Training Corps

Hon. Air Commodore
RAF Lyneham; University of London Air Squadron

HRH THE PRINCESS MARGARET, COUNTESS OF SNOWDON

Colonel-in-Chief
The Light Dragoons; The Royal Highland Fusiliers (Princess Margaret's Own Glasgow and Ayrshire Regiment); Queen Alexandra's Royal Army Nursing Corps; The Highland Fusiliers of Canada; The Princess Louise Fusiliers (of Canada); The Bermuda Regiment

Deputy Colonel-in-Chief
The Royal Anglian Regiment

Hon. Air Commodore
RAF Coningsby

HRH PRINCESS ALICE, DUCHESS OF GLOUCESTER

Air Chief Marshal

Colonel-in-Chief
The King's Own Scottish Borderers; Royal Australian Corps of Transport

Deputy Colonel-in-Chief
The King's Royal Hussars; The Royal Anglian Regiment

Air Chief Commandant
Women, Royal Air Force

HRH THE DUKE OF GLOUCESTER

Hon. Air Marshal

Deputy Colonel-in-Chief
The Royal Gloucestershire, Berkshire and Wiltshire Regiment; The Royal Logistic Corps

Hon. Colonel
Royal Monmouthshire Royal Engineers (Militia)

Hon. Air Commodore
RAF Odiham

HRH THE DUCHESS OF GLOUCESTER

Colonel-in-Chief
Royal Australian Army Educational Corps; Royal New Zealand Army Educational Corps

Deputy Colonel-in-Chief
Adjutant-General's Corps

HRH THE DUKE OF KENT

Field Marshal
Hon. Air Chief Marshal

Colonel-in-Chief
The Royal Regiment of Fusiliers; The Devonshire and Dorset Regiment; The Lorne Scots (Peel, Dufferin and Hamilton Regiment)

Deputy Colonel-in-Chief
The Royal Scots Dragoon Guards (Carabiniers and Greys)

Colonel
Scots Guards

Hon. Air Commodore
RAF Leuchars

HRH THE DUCHESS OF KENT

Hon. Major-General

Colonel-in-Chief
The Prince of Wales's Own Regiment of Yorkshire

Deputy Colonel-in-Chief
The Royal Dragoon Guards; Adjutant-General's Corps; The Royal Logistic Corps

HRH PRINCE MICHAEL OF KENT

Major (retd), The Royal Hussars (Prince of Wales's Own)
Hon. Commodore
  Royal Naval Reserve

HRH PRINCESS ALEXANDRA, THE HON. LADY OGILVY

Patron
  Queen Alexandra's Royal Naval Nursing Service
Colonel-in-Chief
  The King's Own Royal Border Regiment; The Queen's Own Rifles of Canada; The Canadian Scottish Regiment (Princess Mary's)
Deputy Colonel-in-Chief
  The Queen's Royal Lancers; The Light Infantry
Deputy Hon. Colonel
  The Royal Yeomanry
Patron and Air Chief Commandant
  Princess Mary's Royal Air Force Nursing Service

The House of Windsor

King George V assumed by royal proclamation (17 July 1917) for his House and family, as well as for all descendants in the male line of Queen Victoria who are subjects of these realms, the name of Windsor.

KING GEORGE V (George Frederick Ernest Albert), second son of King Edward VII, *born* 3 June 1865; *married* 6 July 1893 HSH Princess Victoria Mary Augusta Louise Olga Pauline Claudine Agnes of Teck (Queen Mary, *born* 26 May 1867; *died* 24 March 1953); *succeeded* to the throne 6 May 1910; *died* 20 January 1936. *Issue:*

1. HRH PRINCE EDWARD Albert Christian George Andrew Patrick David, *born* 23 June 1894, *succeeded* to the throne as King Edward VIII, 20 January 1936; *abdicated* 11 December 1936; created *Duke of Windsor* 1937; *married* 3 June 1937, Mrs Wallis Simpson (Her Grace The Duchess of Windsor, *born* 19 June 1896; *died* 24 April 1986), *died* 28 May 1972

2. HRH PRINCE ALBERT Frederick Arthur George, *born* 14 December 1895, *created* Duke of York 1920; *married* 26 April 1923, Lady Elizabeth Bowes-Lyon, youngest daughter of the 14th Earl of Strathmore and Kinghorne (HM Queen Elizabeth the Queen Mother, *see* page 117), *succeeded* to the throne as King George VI, 11 December 1936; *died* 6 February 1952, having had issue (*see* page 117)

3. HRH PRINCESS (Victoria Alexandra Alice) MARY, *born* 25 April 1897, *created* Princess Royal 1932; *married* 28 February 1922, Viscount Lascelles, later the 6th Earl of Harewood (1882–1947), *died* 28 March 1965. *Issue:*
(1) George Henry Hubert Lascelles, 7th Earl of Harewood, KBE, *born* 7 February 1923; *married* (1) 1949, Maria (Marion) Stein (marriage dissolved 1967); *issue*, (*a*) David Henry George,

Viscount Lascelles, *born* 1950; (*b*) James Edward, *born* 1953; (*c*) (Robert) Jeremy Hugh, *born* 1955; (2) 1967, Mrs Patricia Tuckwell; *issue*, (*d*) Mark Hubert, *born* 1964
(2) Gerald David Lascelles (1924–98), *married* (1) 1952, Miss Angela Dowding (marriage dissolved 1978); *issue*, (*a*) Henry Ulick, *born* 1953; (2) 1978, Mrs Elizabeth Colvin; *issue*, (*b*) Martin David, *born* 1962

4. HRH PRINCE HENRY William Frederick Albert, *born* 31 March 1900, *created* Duke of Gloucester, Earl of Ulster and Baron Culloden 1928, *married* 6 November 1935, Lady Alice Christabel Montagu-Douglas-Scott, daughter of the 7th Duke of Buccleuch (HRH Princess Alice, Duchess of Gloucester, *see* page 118); *died* 10 June 1974. *Issue:*
(1) HRH Prince William Henry Andrew Frederick, *born* 18 December 1941; *accidentally killed* 28 August 1972
(2) HRH Prince Richard Alexander Walter George (HRH The Duke of Gloucester), *see* page 118

5. HRH PRINCE GEORGE Edward Alexander Edmund, *born* 20 December 1902, *created* Duke of Kent, Earl of St Andrews and Baron Downpatrick 1934, *married* 29 November 1934, HRH Princess Marina of Greece and Denmark (*born* 30 November OS, 1906; *died* 27 August 1968); *killed on active service,* 25 August 1942. *Issue:*
(1) HRH Prince Edward George Nicholas Paul Patrick (HRH The Duke of Kent), *see* page 118
(2) HRH Princess Alexandra Helen Elizabeth Olga Christabel (HRH Princess Alexandra, the Hon. Lady Ogilvy), *see* page 118
(3) HRH Prince Michael George Charles Franklin (HRH Prince Michael of Kent), *see* page 118

6. HRH PRINCE JOHN Charles Francis, *born* 12 July 1905; *died* 18 January 1919

Descendants of Queen Victoria

QUEEN VICTORIA (Alexandrina Victoria), *born* 24 May 1819; *succeeded* to the throne 20 June 1837; *married* 10 February 1840 (Francis) Albert Augustus Charles Emmanuel, Duke of Saxony, Prince of Saxe-Coburg and Gotha (HRH Albert, Prince Consort, *born* 26 August 1819, *died* 14 December 1861); *died* 22 January 1901. *Issue:*
1. HRH PRINCESS VICTORIA Adelaide Mary Louisa (Princess Royal) (1840–1901), *m.* 1858, Friedrich III (1831–88), German Emperor March–June 1888. *Issue:*
(1) HIM Wilhelm II (1859–1941), German Emperor 1888–1918, *m.* (1) 1881 Princess Augusta Victoria of Schleswig-Holstein-Sonderburg-Augustenburg (1858–1921); (2) 1922 Princess Hermine of Reuss (1887–1947). *Issue:*
(*a*) Prince Wilhelm (1882–1951), Crown Prince 1888–1918, *m.* 1905 Duchess Cecilie of Mecklenburg-Schwerin; *issue:* Prince Wilhelm (1906–40); Prince Louis Ferdinand (1907–94), *m.* 1938 Grand Duchess Kira (*see* page 128); Prince Hubertus (1909–50); Prince Friedrich Georg (1911–66); Princess Alexandrine Irene (1915–80); Princess Cecilie (1917–75)
(*b*) Prince Eitel-Friedrich (1883–1942), *m.* 1906 Duchess Sophie of Oldenburg (marriage dissolved 1926)
(*c*) Prince Adalbert (1884–1948), *m.* 1914 Duchess Adelheid of Saxe-Meiningen; *issue:* Princess Victoria Marina (1917–81); Prince Wilhelm Victor (1919–89)
(*d*) Prince August Wilhelm (1887–1949), *m.* 1908 Princess Alexandra of Schleswig-Holstein-Sonderburg-Glücksburg (marriage dissolved 1920); *issue:* Prince Alexander (1912–85)
(*e*) Prince Oskar (1888–1958), *m.* 1914 Countess von Ruppin; *issue:* Prince Oskar (1915–39); Prince Wilhelm (1917–88); Princess Herzeleide (1918–89); Prince Wilhelm-Karl (*b.* 1922)
(*f*) Prince Joachim (1890–1920), *m.* 1916 Princess Marie of Anhalt; *issue:* Prince (Karl) Franz Joseph (1916–75), and has issue

(*g*) Princess Viktoria Luise (1892–1980), *m.* 1913 Ernst, Duke of Brunswick 1913–18 (1887–1953); *issue:* Prince Ernst (1914–87); Prince Georg (*b.* 1915), *m.* 1946 Princess Sophie of Greece (*see* page 128) and has issue (two sons, one daughter); Princess Frederika (1917–81), *m.* 1938 Paul I, King of the Hellenes (*see* page 128); Prince Christian (1919–81); Prince Welf Heinrich (*b.* 1923)
(2) Princess Charlotte (1860–1919), *m.* 1878 Bernhard, Duke of Saxe-Meiningen 1914 (1851–1914). *Issue:*
Princess Feodora (1879–1945), *m.* 1898 Prince Heinrich XXX of Reuss
(3) Prince Heinrich (1862–1929), *m.* 1888 Princess Irene of Hesse (*see* page 128). *Issue:*
(*a*) Prince Waldemar (1889–1945), *m.* Princess Calixta Agnes of Lippe
(*b*) Prince Sigismund (1896–1978), *m.* 1919 Princess Charlotte of Saxe-Altenburg; *issue:* Princess Barbara (1920–94); Prince Alfred (*b.* 1924)
(*c*) Prince Heinrich (1900–4)
(4) Prince Sigismund (1864–6)
(5) Princess Victoria (1866–1929), *m.* (1) 1890, Prince Adolf of Schaumburg-Lippe (1859–1916); (2) 1927 Alexander Zubkov
(6) Prince Waldemar (1868–79)
(7) Princess Sophie (1870–1932), *m.* 1889 Constantine I (1868–1923), King of the Hellenes 1913–17, 1920–3. *Issue:*
(*a*) George II (1890–1947), King of the Hellenes 1923–4 and 1935–47, *m.* 1921 Princess Elisabeth of Roumania (marriage dissolved 1935) (*see* page 128)
(*b*) Alexander I (1893–1920), King of the Hellenes 1917–20, *m.*

1919 Aspasia Manos; *issue:* Princess Alexandra (1921–93), *m.*
1944 King Petar II of Yugoslavia (*see* below)
(*c*) Princess Helena (1896–1982), *m.* 1921 King Carol of
Roumania (*see* below), (marriage dissolved 1928)
(*d*) Paul I (1901–64), King of the Hellenes 1947–64, *m.* 1938
Princess Frederika of Brunswick (*see* page 127); *issue:* King
Constantine II (*b.* 1940), *m.* 1964 Princess Anne-Marie of
Denmark (*see* page 129), and has issue (three sons, two
daughters); Princess Sophie (*b.* 1938), *m.* 1962 Juan Carlos I of
Spain (*see* page 129); Princess Irene (*b.* 1942)
(*e*) Princess Irene (1904–74), *m.* 1939 4th Duke of Aosta; *issue:*
Prince Amedeo, 5th Duke of Aosta (*b.* 1943)
(*f*) Princess Katherine (Lady Katherine Brandram) (*b.* 1913), *m.*
1947 Major R. C. A. Brandram, MC, TD; *issue:* R. Paul G. A.
Brandram (*b.* 1948)
(8) Princess Margarethe (1872–1954), *m.* 1893 Prince Friedrich
Karl of Hesse (1868–1940). *Issue:*
(*a*) Prince Friedrich Wilhelm (1893–1916)
(*b*) Prince Maximilian (1894–1914)
(*c*) Prince Philipp (1896–1980), *m.* 1925 Princess Mafalda of
Italy; *issue:* Prince Moritz (*b.* 1926); Prince Heinrich (*b.* 1927);
Prince Otto (*b.* 1937); Princess Elisabeth (*b.* 1940)
(*d*) Prince Wolfgang (1896–1989), *m.* (1) 1924 Princess Marie
Alexandra of Baden; (2) 1948 Ottilie Möller
(*e*) Prince Richard (1901–69)
(*f*) Prince Christoph (1901–43), *m.* 1930 Princess Sophie of
Greece (*see* below) and has issue (two sons, three daughters)

2. HRH PRINCE ALBERT EDWARD (HM KING EDWARD VII), *b.* 9
November 1841, *m.* 1863 HRH Princess Alexandra of Denmark
(1844–1925), *succeeded* to the throne 22 January 1901, *d.* 6 May 1910.
Issue:
(1) Albert Victor, Duke of Clarence and Avondale (1864–92)
(2) George (HM KING GEORGE V) (*see* page 127)
(3) Louise (1867–1931) Princess Royal 1905–31, *m.* 1889 1st
Duke of Fife (1849–1912). *Issue:*
(*a*) Princess Alexandra, Duchess of Fife (1891–1959), *m.* 1913
Prince Arthur of Connaught (*see* page 129)
(*b*) Princess Maud (1893–1945), *m.* 1923 11th Earl of Southesk
(1893–1992); *issue:* The Duke of Fife (*b.* 1929)
(4) Victoria (1868–1935)
(5) Maud (1869–1938), *m.* 1896 Prince Carl of Denmark (1872–
1957), later King Haakon VII of Norway 1905–57. *Issue:*
(*a*) Olav V (1903–91), King of Norway 1957–91, *m.* 1929
Princess Märtha of Sweden (1901–54); *issue:* Princess Ragnhild
(*b.* 1930); Princess Astrid (*b.* 1932); Harald V, King of Norway
(*b.* 1937)
(6) Alexander (6–7 April 1871)

3. HRH PRINCESS ALICE Maud Mary (1843–78), *m.* 1862 Prince
Ludwig (1837–92), Grand Duke of Hesse 1877–92. *Issue:*
(1) Victoria (1863–1950), *m.* 1884 *Admiral of the Fleet* Prince Louis
of Battenberg (1854–1921), *cr.* 1st Marquess of Milford Haven
1917. *Issue:*
(*a*) Alice (1885–1969), *m.* 1903 Prince Andrew of Greece
(1882–1944); *issue:* Princess Margarita (1905–81), *m.* 1931
Prince Gottfried of Hohenlohe-Langenburg (*see* below);
Princess Theodora (1906–69), *m.* Prince Berthold of Baden
(1906–63) and has issue (two sons, one daughter); Princess
Cecilie (1911–37), *m.* George, Grand Duke of Hesse (*see*
below); Princess Sophie (*b.* 1914), *m.* (1) 1930 Prince Christoph
of Hesse (*see* above); (2) 1946 Prince Georg of Hanover (*see*
page 127); Prince Philip, Duke of Edinburgh (*b.* 1921) (*see* page
117)
(*b*) Louise (1889–1965), *m.* 1923 Gustaf VI Adolf (1882–1973),
King of Sweden 1950–73
(*c*) George, 2nd Marquess of Milford Haven (1892–1938), *m.*
1916 Countess Nadejda, daughter of Grand Duke Michael of
Russia; *issue:* Lady Tatiana (1917–88); David Michael, 3rd
Marquess (1919–70)
(*d*) Louis, 1st Earl Mountbatten of Burma (1900–79), *m.* 1922
Edwina Ashley, daughter of Lord Mount Temple; *issue:*
Patricia, Countess Mountbatten of Burma (*b.* 1924), Pamela (*b.*
1929)
(2) Elizabeth (1864–1918), *m.* 1884 Grand Duke Sergius of
Russia (1857–1905)
(3) Irene (1866–1953), *m.* 1888 Prince Heinrich of Prussia (*see*
page 127)
(4) Ernst Ludwig (1868–1937), Grand Duke of Hesse 1892–
1918, *m.* (1) 1894 Princess Victoria Melita of Saxe-Coburg (*see*

below) (marriage dissolved 1901); (2) 1905 Princess Eleonore of
Solms-Hohensolmslich. *Issue:*
(*a*) Princess Elizabeth (1895–1903)
(*b*) George, Hereditary Grand Duke of Hesse (1906–37), *m.*
Princess Cecilie of Greece (*see* above), and had issue, two sons,
accidentally killed with parents 1937
(*c*) Ludwig, Prince of Hesse (1908–68), *m.* 1937 Margaret,
daughter of 1st Lord Geddes
(5) Frederick William (1870–3)
(6) Alix (Tsaritsa of Russia) (1872–1918), *m.* 1894 Nicholas II
(1868–1918) Tsar of All the Russias 1894–1917, assassinated 16
July 1918. *Issue:*
(*a*) Grand Duchess Olga (1895–1918)
(*b*) Grand Duchess Tatiana (1897–1918)
(*c*) Grand Duchess Marie (1899–1918)
(*d*) Grand Duchess Anastasia (1901–18)
(*e*) Alexis, Tsarevich of Russia (1904–18)
(7) Marie (1874–8)

4. HRH PRINCE ALFRED Ernest Albert, Duke of Edinburgh,
Admiral of the Fleet (1844–1900), *m.* 1874 Grand Duchess Marie
Alexandrovna of Russia (1853–1920); succeeded as Duke of Saxe-
Coburg and Gotha 22 August 1893. *Issue:*
(1) Alfred, Prince of Saxe-Coburg (1874–99)
(2) Marie (1875–1938), *m.* 1893 Ferdinand (1865–1927), King of
Roumania 1914–27. *Issue:*
(*a*) Carol II (1893–1953), King of Roumania 1930–40, *m.* (2)
1921 Princess Helena of Greece (*see* above) (marriage
dissolved 1928); *issue:* Michael (*b.* 1921), King of Roumania
1927–30, 1940–7, *m.* 1948 Princess Anne of Bourbon-Parma,
and has issue (five daughters)
(*b*) Elisabeth (1894–1956), *m.* 1921 George II, King of the
Hellenes (*see* page 127)
(*c*) Marie (1900–61), *m.* 1922 Alexander (1888–1934), King of
Yugoslavia 1921–34; *issue:* Petar II (1923–70), King of
Yugoslavia 1934–45, *m.* 1944 Princess Alexandra of Greece (*see*
above) and has issue (Crown Prince Alexander, *b.* 1945);
Prince Tomislav (*b.* 1928), *m.* (1) 1957 Princess Margarita of
Baden (daughter of Princess Theodora of Greece and Prince
Berthold of Baden, *see* above); (2) 1982 Linda Bonney; and has
issue (three sons, one daughter); Prince Andrej (1929–90), *m.*
(1) 1956 Princess Christina of Hesse (daughter of Prince
Christoph of Hesse and Princess Sophie of Greece, *see* above);
(2) 1963 Princess Kira-Melita of Leiningen (*see* below); and has
issue (three sons, two daughters)
(*d*) Prince Nicolas (1903–78)
(*e*) Princess Ileana (1909–91), *m.* (1) 1931 Archduke Anton of
Austria; (2) 1954 Dr Stefan Isarescu; *issue:* Archduke Stefan (*b.*
1932); Archduchess Maria Ileana (1933–59); Archduchess
Alexandra (*b.* 1935); Archduke Dominic (*b.* 1937); Archduchess
Maria Magdalena (*b.* 1939); Archduchess Elisabeth (*b.* 1942)
(*f*) Prince Mircea (1913–16)
(3) Victoria Melita (1876–1936), *m.* (1) 1894 Grand Duke Ernst
Ludwig of Hesse (*see* above) (marriage dissolved 1901); (2) 1905
the Grand Duke Kirill of Russia (1876–1938). *Issue:*
(*a*) Marie Kirillovna (1907–51), *m.* 1925 Prince Friedrich Karl
of Leiningen; *issue:* Prince Emich (1926–91); Prince Karl
(1928–90); Princess Kira-Melita (*b.* 1930), *m.* Prince Andrej of
Yugoslavia (*see* above); Princess Margarita (*b.* 1932); Princess
Mechtilde (*b.* 1936); Prince Friedrich (*b.* 1938)
(*b*) Kira Kirillovna (1909–67), *m.* 1938 Prince Louis Ferdinand
of Prussia (*see* page 127); *issue:* Prince Friedrich Wilhelm (*b.*
1939); Prince Michael (*b.* 1940); Princess Marie (*b.* 1942);
Princess Kira (*b.* 1943); Prince Louis Ferdinand (1944–77);
Prince Christian (*b.* 1946); Princess Xenia (1949–92)
(*c*) Vladimir Kirillovich (1917–92), *m.* 1948 Princess Leonida
Bagration-Mukhransky; *issue:* Grand Duchess Maria (*b.* 1953),
and has issue
(4) Alexandra (1878–1942), *m.* 1896 Ernst, Prince of Hohenlohe
Langenburg. *Issue:*
(*a*) Gottfried (1897–1960), *m.* 1931 Princess Margarita of
Greece (*see* above); *issue:* Prince Kraft (*b.* 1935), Princess
Beatrice (1936–97), Prince Georg Andreas (*b.* 1938), Prince
Ruprecht (1944–76); Prince Albrecht (1944–92)
(*b*) Maria (1899–1967), *m.* 1916 Prince Friedrich of Schleswig-
Holstein-Sonderburg-Glücksburg; *issue:* Prince Peter (1922–
80); Princess Marie (*b.* 1927)
(*c*) Princess Alexandra (1901–63)

(*d*) Princess Irma (1902–86)
(5) Princess Beatrice (1884–1966), *m.* 1909 Alfonso of Orleans, Infante of Spain. *Issue:*
  (*a*) Prince Alvaro (*b.* 1910), *m.* 1937 Carla Parodi-Delfino; *issue:* Doña Gerarda (*b.* 1939); Don Alonso (1941–75); Doña Beatriz (*b.* 1943); Don Alvaro (*b.* 1947)
  (*b*) Prince Alonso (1912–36)
  (*c*) Prince Ataulfo (1913–74)

5. HRH PRINCESS HELENA Augusta Victoria (1846–1923), *m.* 1866 Prince Christian of Schleswig-Holstein-Sonderburg-Augustenburg (1831–1917). *Issue:*
  (1) Prince Christian Victor (1867–1900)
  (2) Prince Albert (1869–1931), Duke of Schleswig-Holstein 1921–31
  (3) Princess Helena (1870–1948)
  (4) Princess Marie Louise (1872–1956), *m.* 1891 Prince Aribert of Anhalt (marriage dissolved 1900)
  (5) Prince Harold (12–20 May 1876)

6. HRH PRINCESS LOUISE Caroline Alberta (1848–1939), *m.* 1871 the Marquess of Lorne, afterwards 9th Duke of Argyll (1845–1914); without issue

7. HRH PRINCE ARTHUR William Patrick Albert, Duke of Connaught, *Field Marshal* (1850–1942), *m.* 1879 Princess Louisa of Prussia (1860–1917). *Issue:*
  (1) Margaret (1882–1920), *m.* 1905 Crown Prince Gustaf Adolf (1882–1973), afterwards King of Sweden 1950–73. *Issue:*
    (*a*) Gustaf Adolf, Duke of Västerbotten (1906–47), *m.* 1932 Princess Sibylla of Saxe-Coburg-Gotha (*see* below); *issue:* Princess Margaretha (*b.* 1934); Princess Birgitta (*b.* 1937); Princess Désirée (*b.* 1938); Princess Christina (*b.* 1943); Carl XVI Gustaf, King of Sweden (*b.* 1946)
    (*b*) Count Sigvard Bernadotte (*b.* 1907), *m.; issue:* Count Michael (*b.* 1944)
    (*c*) Princess Ingrid (Queen Mother of Denmark) (*b.* 1910), *m.* 1935 Frederick IX (1899–1972), King of Denmark 1947–72; *issue:* Margrethe II, Queen of Denmark (*b.* 1940); Princess Benedikte (*b.* 1944); Princess Anne-Marie (*b.* 1946), *m.* 1964 Constantine II of Greece (*see* page 128)
    (*d*) Prince Bertil, Duke of Halland (1912–97), *m.* 1976 Mrs Lilian Craig
    (*e*) Count Carl Bernadotte (*b.* 1916), *m.* (1) 1946 Mrs Kerstin Johnson; (2) 1988 Countess Gunnila Bussler
  (2) Arthur (1883–1938), *m.* 1913 HH the Duchess of Fife (*see* page 128). *Issue:*

Alastair Arthur, 2nd Duke of Connaught (1914–43)
  (3) (Victoria) Patricia (1886–1974), *m.* 1919 Adm. Hon. Sir Alexander Ramsay. *Issue:*
Alexander Ramsay of Mar (*b.* 1919), *m.* 1956 Hon. Flora Fraser (Lady Saltoun)

8. HRH PRINCE LEOPOLD George Duncan Albert, Duke of Albany (1853–84), *m.* 1882 Princess Helena of Waldeck (1861–1922). *Issue:*
  (1) Alice (1883–1981), *m.* 1904 Prince Alexander of Teck (1874–1957), *cr.* 1st Earl of Athlone 1917. *Issue:*
    (*a*) Lady May (1906–94), *m.* 1931 Sir Henry Abel-Smith, KCMG, KCVO, DSO; *issue:* Anne (*b.* 1932); Richard (*b.* 1933); Elizabeth (*b.* 1936)
    (*b*) Rupert, Viscount Trematon (1907–28)
    (*c*) Prince Maurice (March–September 1910)
  (2) Charles Edward (1884–1954), Duke of Albany 1884 until title suspended 1917, Duke of Saxe-Coburg-Gotha 1900–18, *m.* 1905 Princess Victoria Adelheid of Schleswig-Holstein-Sonderburg-Glücksburg. *Issue:*
    (*a*) Prince Johann Leopold (1906–72), and has issue
    (*b*) Princess Sibylla (1908–72), *m.* 1932 Prince Gustav Adolf of Sweden (*see* above)
    (*c*) Prince Dietmar Hubertus (1909–43)
    (*d*) Princess Caroline (1912–83), and has issue
    (*e*) Prince Friedrich Josias (*b.* 1918), and has issue

9. HRH PRINCESS BEATRICE Mary Victoria Feodore (1857–1944), *m.* 1885 Prince Henry of Battenberg (1858–96). *Issue:*
  (1) Alexander, 1st Marquess of Carisbrooke (1886–1960), *m.* 1917 Lady Irene Denison. *Issue:*
Lady Iris Mountbatten (1920–82), *m.; issue:* Robin A. Bryan (*b.* 1957)
  (2) Victoria Eugénie (1887–1969), *m.* 1906 Alfonso XIII (1886–1941) King of Spain 1886–1931. *Issue:*
    (*a*) Prince Alfonso (1907–38)
    (*b*) Prince Jaime (1908–75), and has issue
    (*c*) Princess Beatrice (*b.* 1909), and has issue
    (*d*) Princess Maria (1911–96), and has issue
    (*e*) Prince Juan (1913–93), Count of Barcelona; *issue:* Princess Maria (*b.* 1936); Juan Carlos I, King of Spain (*b.* 1938), *m.* 1962 Princess Sophie of Greece (*see* page 128) and has issue (one son, two daughters); Princess Margarita (*b.* 1939)
    (*f*) Prince Gonzalo (1914–34)
  (3) Major Lord Leopold Mountbatten (1889–1922)
  (4) Maurice (1891–1914), died of wounds received in action

Kings and Queens

HOUSES OF CERDIC AND DENMARK

Reign

927–939 ÆTHELSTAN
Son of Edward the Elder, by Ecgwynn, and grandson of Alfred
Acceded to Wessex and Mercia *c.*924, established direct rule over Northumbria 927, effectively creating the Kingdom of England
Reigned 15 years

939–946 EDMUND I
Born 921, son of Edward the Elder, by Eadgifu
Married (1) Ælfgifu (2) Æthelflæd
Killed aged 25, *reigned* 6 years

946–955 EADRED
Son of Edward the Elder, by Eadgifu
Reigned 9 years

955–959 EADWIG
Born before 943, son of Edmund and Ælfgifu
Married Ælfgifu
Reigned 3 years

959–975 EDGAR I
Born 943, son of Edmund and Ælfgifu
Married (1) Æthelflæd (2) Wulfthryth (3) Ælfthryth
Died aged 32, *reigned* 15 years

975–978 EDWARD I (the Martyr)
Born *c.*962, son of Edgar and Æthelflæd
Assassinated aged *c.*16, *reigned* 2 years

978–1016 ÆTHELRED (the Unready)
Born *c.*968/969, son of Edgar and Ælfthryth
Married (1) Ælfgifu (2) Emma, daughter of Richard I, count of Normandy
1013–14 dispossessed of kingdom by Swegn Forkbeard (king of Denmark 987–1014)
Died aged *c.*47, *reigned* 38 years

1016 EDMUND II (Ironside)
Born before 993, son of Æthelred and Ælfgifu
Married Ealdgyth
Died aged over 23, *reigned* 7 months (April–November)

1016–1035 CNUT (Canute)
Born *c.*995, son of Swegn Forkbeard, king of Denmark, and Gunhild
Married (1) Ælfgifu (2) Emma, widow of Æthelred the Unready
Gained submission of West Saxons 1015, Northumbrians 1016, Mercia 1016, king of all

England after Edmund's death
King of Denmark 1019–35, king of Norway 1028–35
Died aged *c.*40, *reigned* 19 years

1035–1040   HAROLD I (Harefoot)
*Born c.*1016/17, son of Cnut and Ælfgifu
Married Ælfgifu
1035 recognized as regent for himself and his
brother Harthacnut; 1037 recognized as king
Died aged *c.*23, *reigned* 4 years

1040–1042   HARTHACNUT
*Born c.*1018, son of Cnut and Emma
Titular king of Denmark from 1028
Acknowledged king of England 1035–7 with
Harold I as regent; effective king after Harold's
death
Died aged *c.*24, *reigned* 2 years

1042–1066   EDWARD II (the Confessor)
Born between 1002 and 1005, son of Æthelred the
Unready and Emma
Married Eadgyth, daughter of Godwine, earl of
Wessex
Died aged over 60, *reigned* 23 years

1066   HAROLD II (Godwinesson)
*Born c.*1020, son of Godwine, earl of Wessex, and
Gytha
Married (1) Eadgyth (2) Ealdgyth
Killed in battle aged *c.*46, *reigned* 10 months
(January–October)

THE HOUSE OF NORMANDY

1066–1087   WILLIAM I (the Conqueror)
Born 1027/8, son of Robert I, duke of Normandy;
obtained the Crown by conquest
Married Matilda, daughter of Baldwin, count of
Flanders
Died aged *c.*60, *reigned* 20 years

1087–1100   WILLIAM II (Rufus)
Born between 1056 and 1060, third son of William I;
succeeded his father in England only
Killed aged *c.*40, *reigned* 12 years

1100–1135   HENRY I (Beauclerk)
Born 1068, fourth son of William I
Married (1) Edith or Matilda, daughter of
Malcolm III of Scotland (2) Adela, daughter of
Godfrey, count of Louvain
Died aged 67, *reigned* 35 years

1135–1154   STEPHEN
Born not later than 1100, third son of Adela,
daughter of William I, and Stephen, count of Blois
Married Matilda, daughter of Eustace, count of
Boulogne
1141 (February–November) held captive by
adherents of Matilda, daughter of Henry I, who
contested the crown until 1153
Died aged over 53, *reigned* 18 years

THE HOUSE OF ANJOU (PLANTAGENETS)

1154–1189   HENRY II (Curtmantle)
Born 1133, son of Matilda, daughter of Henry I, and
Geoffrey, count of Anjou
Married Eleanor, daughter of William, duke of
Aquitaine, and divorced queen of Louis VII of
France
Died aged 56, *reigned* 34 years

1189–1199   RICHARD I (Coeur de Lion)
Born 1157, third son of Henry II
Married Berengaria, daughter of Sancho VI, king of
Navarre
Died aged 42, *reigned* 9 years

1199–1216   JOHN (Lackland)
Born 1167, fifth son of Henry II
Married (1) Isabella or Avisa, daughter of William,
earl of Gloucester (divorced) (2) Isabella, daughter
of Aymer, count of Angoulême
Died aged 48, *reigned* 17 years

1216–1272   HENRY III
Born 1207, son of John and Isabella of Angoulême

Married Eleanor, daughter of Raymond, count of
Provence
Died aged 65, *reigned* 56 years

1272–1307   EDWARD I (Longshanks)
Born 1239, eldest son of Henry III
Married (1) Eleanor, daughter of Ferdinand III, king
of Castile (2) Margaret, daughter of Philip III of
France
Died aged 68, *reigned* 34 years

1307–1327   EDWARD II
Born 1284, eldest surviving son of Edward I and
Eleanor
Married Isabella, daughter of Philip IV of France
Deposed January 1327, *killed* September 1327 aged
43, *reigned* 19 years

1327–1377   EDWARD III
Born 1312, eldest son of Edward II
Married Philippa, daughter of William, count of
Hainault
Died aged 64, *reigned* 50 years

1377–1399   RICHARD II
Born 1367, son of Edward (the Black Prince), eldest
son of Edward III
Married (1) Anne, daughter of Emperor Charles IV
(2) Isabelle, daughter of Charles VI of France
Deposed September 1399, *killed* February 1400 aged
33, *reigned* 22 years

THE HOUSE OF LANCASTER

1399–1413   HENRY IV
Born 1366, son of John of Gaunt, fourth son of
Edward III, and Blanche, daughter of Henry, duke
of Lancaster
Married (1) Mary, daughter of Humphrey, earl of
Hereford (2) Joan, daughter of Charles, king of
Navarre, and widow of John, duke of Brittany
Died aged *c.*47, *reigned* 13 years

1413–1422   HENRY V
Born 1387, eldest surviving son of Henry IV and
Mary
Married Catherine, daughter of Charles VI of
France
Died aged 34, *reigned* 9 years

1422–1471   HENRY VI
Born 1421, son of Henry V
Married Margaret, daughter of René, duke of Anjou
and count of Provence
Deposed March 1461, *restored* October 1470
Deposed April 1471, *killed* May 1471 aged 49, *reigned*
39 years

THE HOUSE OF YORK

1461–1483   EDWARD IV
Born 1442, eldest son of Richard of York (grandson
of Edmund, fifth son of Edward III, and son of
Anne, great-granddaughter of Lionel, third son of
Edward III)
Married Elizabeth Woodville, daughter of Richard,
Lord Rivers, and widow of Sir John Grey
Acceded March 1461, *deposed* October 1470, *restored*
April 1471
Died aged 40, *reigned* 21 years

1483   EDWARD V
Born 1470, eldest son of Edward IV
Deposed June 1483, *died* probably July–September
1483, aged 12, *reigned* 2 months (April–June)

1483–1485   RICHARD III
Born 1452, fourth son of Richard of York
Married Anne Neville, daughter of Richard, earl of
Warwick, and widow of Edward, Prince of Wales,
son of Henry VI
Killed in battle aged 32, *reigned* 2 years

THE HOUSE OF TUDOR

1485–1509   HENRY VII
Born 1457, son of Margaret Beaufort (great-
granddaughter of John of Gaunt, fourth son of
Edward III) and Edmund Tudor, earl of Richmond

Married Elizabeth, daughter of Edward IV
Died aged 52, *reigned* 23 years

1509–1547   HENRY VIII
Born 1491, second son of Henry VII
Married (1) Catherine, daughter of Ferdinand II,
king of Aragon, and widow of his elder brother
Arthur (divorced) (2) Anne, daughter of Sir
Thomas Boleyn (executed) (3) Jane, daughter of Sir
John Seymour (died in childbirth) (4) Anne,
daughter of John, duke of Cleves (divorced)
(5) Catherine Howard, niece of the Duke of
Norfolk (executed) (6) Catherine, daughter of Sir
Thomas Parr and widow of Lord Latimer
Died aged 55, *reigned* 37 years

1547–1553   EDWARD VI
Born 1537, son of Henry VIII and Jane Seymour
Died aged 15, *reigned* 6 years

1553   JANE
Born 1537, daughter of Frances (daughter of Mary
Tudor, the younger daughter of Henry VII) and
Henry Grey, duke of Suffolk
Married Lord Guildford Dudley, son of the Duke of
Northumberland
Deposed July 1553, *executed* February 1554 aged 16,
reigned 14 days

1553–1558   MARY I
Born 1516, daughter of Henry VIII and Catherine of
Aragon
Married Philip II of Spain
Died aged 42, *reigned* 5 years

1558–1603   ELIZABETH I
Born 1533, daughter of Henry VIII and Anne
Boleyn
Died aged 69, *reigned* 44 years

BRITISH KINGS AND QUEENS SINCE 1603

THE HOUSE OF STUART

Reign
1603–1625   JAMES I (VI OF SCOTLAND)
Born 1566, son of Mary, queen of Scots
(granddaughter of Margaret Tudor, elder daughter
of Henry VII), and Henry Stewart, Lord Darnley
Married Anne, daughter of Frederick II of Denmark
Died aged 58, *reigned* 22 years
(*see also* page 133)

1625–1649   CHARLES I
Born 1600, second son of James I
Married Henrietta Maria, daughter of Henry IV of
France
Executed 1649 aged 48, *reigned* 23 years

COMMONWEALTH DECLARED 19 May 1649
1649–53 Government by a council of state
1653–8 Oliver Cromwell, *Lord Protector*
1658–9 Richard Cromwell, *Lord Protector*

1660–1685   CHARLES II
Born 1630, eldest son of Charles I
Married Catherine, daughter of John IV of Portugal
Died aged 54, *reigned* 25 years

1685–1688   JAMES II (VII of Scotland)
Born 1633, second son of Charles I
Married (1) Lady Anne Hyde, daughter of Edward,
earl of Clarendon (2) Mary, daughter of Alphonso,
duke of Modena
Reign ended with flight from kingdom December
1688
Died 1701 aged 67, *reigned* 3 years
INTERREGNUM 11 December 1688 to 12 February
1689

1689–1702   WILLIAM III
Born 1650, son of William II, prince of Orange, and
Mary Stuart, daughter of Charles I
Married Mary, elder daughter of James II

Died aged 51, *reigned* 13 years
and
1689–1694   MARY II
Born 1662, elder daughter of James II and Anne
Died aged 32, *reigned* 5 years

1702–1714   ANNE
Born 1665, younger daughter of James II and Anne
Married Prince George of Denmark, son of
Frederick III of Denmark
Died aged 49, *reigned* 12 years

THE HOUSE OF HANOVER

1714–1727   GEORGE I (Elector of Hanover)
Born 1660, son of Sophia (daughter of Frederick,
elector palatine, and Elizabeth Stuart, daughter of
James I) and Ernest Augustus, elector of Hanover
Married Sophia Dorothea, daughter of George
William, duke of Lüneburg-Celle
Died aged 67, *reigned* 12 years

1727–1760   GEORGE II
Born 1683, son of George I
Married Caroline, daughter of John Frederick,
margrave of Brandenburg-Anspach
Died aged 76, *reigned* 33 years

1760–1820   GEORGE III
Born 1738, son of Frederick, eldest son of George II
Married Charlotte, daughter of Charles Louis, duke
of Mecklenburg-Strelitz
Died aged 81, *reigned* 59 years

REGENCY 1811–20
Prince of Wales regent owing to the insanity of
George III

1820–1830   GEORGE IV
Born 1762, eldest son of George III
Married Caroline, daughter of Charles, duke of
Brunswick-Wolfenbüttel
Died aged 67, *reigned* 10 years

1830–1837   WILLIAM IV
Born 1765, third son of George III
Married Adelaide, daughter of George, duke of
Saxe-Meiningen
Died aged 71, *reigned* 7 years

1837–1901   VICTORIA
Born 1819, daughter of Edward, fourth son of
George III
Married Prince Albert of Saxe-Coburg and Gotha
Died aged 81, *reigned* 63 years

THE HOUSE OF SAXE-COBURG AND GOTHA

1901–1910   EDWARD VII
Born 1841, eldest son of Victoria and Albert
Married Alexandra, daughter of Christian IX of
Denmark
Died aged 68, *reigned* 9 years

THE HOUSE OF WINDSOR

1910–1936   GEORGE V
Born 1865, second son of Edward VII
Married Victoria Mary, daughter of Francis, duke of
Teck
Died aged 70, *reigned* 25 years

1936   EDWARD VIII
Born 1894, eldest son of George V
Married (1937) Mrs Wallis Simpson
Abdicated 1936, *died* 1972 aged 77, *reigned* 10 months
(20 January to 11 December)

1936–1952   GEORGE VI
Born 1895, second son of George V
Married Lady Elizabeth Bowes-Lyon, daughter of
14th Earl of Strathmore and Kinghorne (*see also*
page 117)
Died aged 56, *reigned* 15 years

1952–   ELIZABETH II
Born 1926, elder daughter of George VI
Married Philip, son of Prince Andrew of Greece (*see
also* page 117)
WHOM GOD PRESERVE

KINGS AND QUEENS OF SCOTS 1016 TO 1603

Reign

1016–1034   MALCOLM II
Born c.954, son of Kenneth II
Acceded to Alba 1005, secured Lothian c.1016,
obtained Strathclyde for his grandson Duncan
c.1016, thus reigning over an area approximately
the same as that governed by later rulers of
Scotland
Died aged c.80, *reigned* 18 years

THE HOUSE OF ATHOLL

1034–1040   DUNCAN I
Son of Bethoc, daughter of Malcolm II, and Crinan,
mormaer of Atholl
Married a cousin of Siward, earl of Northumbria
Reigned 5 years

1040–1057   MACBETH
Born c.1005, son of a daughter of Malcolm II and
Finlaec, mormaer of Moray
Married Gruoch, granddaughter of Kenneth III
Killed aged c.52, *reigned* 17 years

1057–1058   LULACH
Born c.1032, son of Gillacomgan, mormaer of
Moray, and Gruoch (and stepson of Macbeth)
Died aged c.26, *reigned* 7 months (August–March)

1058–1093   MALCOLM III (Canmore)
Born c.1031, elder son of Duncan I
Married (1) Ingiborg (2) Margaret (St Margaret),
granddaughter of Edmund II of England
Killed in battle aged c.62, *reigned* 35 years

1093–1097   DONALD III BÁN
Born c.1033, second son of Duncan I
Deposed May 1094, *restored* November 1094, *deposed*
October 1097, *reigned* 3 years

1094   DUNCAN II
Born c.1060, elder son of Malcolm III and Ingiborg
Married Octreda of Dunbar
Killed aged c.34, *reigned* 6 months (May–November)

1097–1107   EDGAR
Born c.1074, second son of Malcolm III and
Margaret
Died aged c.32, *reigned* 9 years

1107–1124   ALEXANDER I (The Fierce)
Born c.1077, fifth son of Malcolm III and Margaret
Married Sybilla, illegitimate daughter of Henry I of
England
Died aged c.47, *reigned* 17 years

1124–1153   DAVID I (The Saint)
Born c.1085, sixth son of Malcolm III and Margaret
Married Matilda, daughter of Waltheof, earl of
Huntingdon
Died aged c.68, *reigned* 29 years

1153–1165   MALCOLM IV (The Maiden)
Born c.1141, son of Henry, earl of Huntingdon,
second son of David I
Died aged c.24, *reigned* 12 years

1165–1214   WILLIAM I (The Lion)
Born c.1142, brother of Malcolm IV
Married Ermengarde, daughter of Richard, viscount
of Beaumont
Died aged c.72, *reigned* 49 years

1214–1249   ALEXANDER II
Born 1198, son of William I
Married (1) Joan, daughter of John, king of
England (2) Marie, daughter of Ingelram de Coucy
Died aged 50, *reigned* 34 years

1249–1286   ALEXANDER III
Born 1241, son of Alexander II and Marie
Married (1) Margaret, daughter of Henry III of
England (2) Yolande, daughter of the Count of
Dreux
Killed accidentally aged 44, *reigned* 36 years

1286–1290   MARGARET (The Maid of Norway)
Born 1283, daughter of Margaret (daughter of
Alexander III) and Eric II of Norway
Died aged 7, *reigned* 4 years

FIRST INTERREGNUM 1290–2
Throne disputed by 13 competitors. Crown
awarded to John Balliol by adjudication of Edward I
of England

THE HOUSE OF BALLIOL

1292–1296   JOHN (Balliol)
Born c.1250, son of Dervorguilla, great-great-
granddaughter of David I, and John de Balliol
Married Isabella, daughter of John, earl of Surrey
Abdicated 1296, *died* 1313 aged c.63, *reigned* 3 years

SECOND INTERREGNUM 1296–1306
Edward I of England declared John Balliol to have
forfeited the throne for contumacy in 1296 and took
the government of Scotland into his own hands

THE HOUSE OF BRUCE

1306–1329   ROBERT I (Bruce)
Born 1274, son of Robert Bruce and Marjorie,
countess of Carrick, and great-grandson of the
second daughter of David, earl of Huntingdon,
brother of William I
Married (1) Isabella, daughter of Donald, earl of
Mar (2) Elizabeth, daughter of Richard, earl of
Ulster
Died aged 54, *reigned* 23 years

1329–1371   DAVID II
Born 1324, son of Robert I and Elizabeth
Married (1) Joanna, daughter of Edward II of
England (2) Margaret Drummond, widow of Sir
John Logie (divorced)
Died aged 46, *reigned* 41 years

1332 Edward Balliol, son of John Balliol, crowned
King of Scots September, expelled December
1333–6 Edward Balliol restored as King of Scots

THE HOUSE OF STEWART

1371–1390   ROBERT II (Stewart)
Born 1316, son of Marjorie (daughter of Robert I)
and Walter, High Steward of Scotland
Married (1) Elizabeth, daughter of Sir Robert Mure
of Rowallan (2) Euphemia, daughter of Hugh, earl
of Ross
Died aged 74, *reigned* 19 years

1390–1406   ROBERT III
Born c.1337, son of Robert II and Elizabeth
Married Annabella, daughter of Sir John
Drummond of Stobhall
Died aged c.69, *reigned* 16 years

1406–1437   JAMES I
Born 1394, son of Robert III
Married Joan Beaufort, daughter of John, earl of
Somerset
Assassinated aged 42, *reigned* 30 years

1437–1460   JAMES II
Born 1430, son of James I
Married Mary, daughter of Arnold, duke of
Gueldres
Killed accidentally aged 29, *reigned* 23 years

1460–1488   JAMES III
Born 1452, son of James II
Married Margaret, daughter of Christian I of
Denmark
Assassinated aged 36, *reigned* 27 years

1488–1513   JAMES IV
Born 1473, son of James III
Married Margaret Tudor, daughter of Henry VII of
England
Killed in battle aged 40, *reigned* 25 years

1513–1542   JAMES V
Born 1512, son of James IV
Married (1) Madeleine, daughter of Francis I of
France (2) Mary of Lorraine, daughter of the Duc
de Guise
Died aged 30, *reigned* 29 years

1542–1567	MARY
	Born 1542, daughter of James V and Mary
	Married (1) the Dauphin, afterwards Francis II of
	France (2) Henry Stewart, Lord Darnley (3) James
	Hepburn, earl of Bothwell
	Abdicated 1567, prisoner in England from 1568,
	executed 1587, *reigned* 24 years
1567–1625	JAMES VI (and I of England)
	Born 1566, son of Mary, queen of Scots, and Henry,
	Lord Darnley
	Acceded 1567 to the Scottish throne, *reigned* 58
	years
	Succeeded 1603 to the English throne, so joining
	the English and Scottish crowns in one person. The
	two kingdoms remained distinct until 1707 when
	the parliaments of the kingdoms became conjoined
	For British Kings and Queens since 1603, *see* page
	131

WELSH SOVEREIGNS AND PRINCES

Wales was ruled by sovereign princes from the earliest times until the death of Llywelyn in 1282. The first English Prince of Wales was the son of Edward I, who was born in Caernarvon town on 25 April 1284. According to a discredited legend, he was presented to the Welsh chieftains as their prince, in fulfilment of a promise that they should have a prince who 'could not speak a word of English' and should be native born. This son, who afterwards became Edward II, was created 'Prince of Wales and Earl of Chester' at the Lincoln Parliament on 7 February 1301.

The title Prince of Wales is borne after individual conferment and is not inherited at birth, though some Princes have been declared and styled Prince of Wales but never formally so created (*s*). The title was conferred on Prince Charles by The Queen on 26 July 1958. He was invested at Caernarvon on 1 July 1969.

INDEPENDENT PRINCES AD 844 TO 1282

844–878	Rhodri the Great
878–916	Anarawd, son of Rhodri
916–950	Hywel Dda, the Good
950–979	Iago ab Idwal (or Ieuaf)
979–985	Hywel ab Ieuaf, the Bad
985–986	Cadwallon, his brother
986–999	Maredudd ab Owain ap Hywel Dda
999–1008	Cynan ap Hywel ab Ieuaf
1018–1023	Llywelyn ap Seisyll
1023–1039	Iago ab Idwal ap Meurig
1039–1063	Gruffydd ap Llywelyn ap Seisyll
1063–1075	Bleddyn ap Cynfyn
1075–1081	Trahaern ap Caradog
1081–1137	Gruffydd ap Cynan ab Iago
1137–1170	Owain Gwynedd
1170–1194	Dafydd ab Owain Gwynedd
1194–1240	Llywelyn Fawr, the Great
1240–1246	Dafydd ap Llywelyn
1246–1282	Llywelyn ap Gruffydd ap Llywelyn

ENGLISH PRINCES SINCE 1301

1301	Edward (Edward II)
1343	Edward the Black Prince, son of Edward III
1376	Richard (Richard II), son of the Black Prince
1399	Henry of Monmouth (Henry V)
1454	Edward of Westminster, son of Henry VI
1471	Edward of Westminster (Edward V)
1483	Edward, son of Richard III (d. 1484)
1489	Arthur Tudor, son of Henry VII
1504	Henry Tudor (Henry VIII)
1610	Henry Stuart, son of James I (d. 1612)
1616	Charles Stuart (Charles I)

*c.*1638 (*s.*)	Charles Stuart (Charles II)
1688 (*s.*)	James Francis Edward Stuart (The Old Pretender),
	son of James II (d. 1766)
1714	George Augustus (George II)
1729	Frederick Lewis, son of George II (d. 1751)
1751	George William Frederick (George III)
1762	George Augustus Frederick (George IV)
1841	Albert Edward (Edward VII)
1901	George (George V)
1910	Edward (Edward VIII)
1958	Charles, son of Elizabeth II

PRINCESSES ROYAL

The style Princess Royal is conferred at the Sovereign's discretion on his or her eldest daughter. It is an honorary title, held for life, and cannot be inherited or passed on. It was first conferred on Princess Mary, daughter of Charles I, in approximately 1642.

*c.*1642	Princess Mary (1631–60), daughter of Charles I
1727	Princess Anne (1709–59), daughter of George II
1766	Princess Charlotte (1766–1828), daughter of
	George III
1840	Princess Victoria (1840–1901), daughter of Victoria
1905	Princess Louise (1867–1931), daughter of
	Edward VII
1932	Princess Mary (1897–1965), daughter of
	George V
1987	Princess Anne (b. 1950), daughter of Elizabeth II

Precedence

The Sovereign
The Prince Philip, Duke of
  Edinburgh
The Prince of Wales
The Sovereign's younger sons
The Sovereign's grandsons
The Sovereign's cousins
Archbishop of Canterbury
Lord High Chancellor
Archbishop of York
The Prime Minister
Lord President of the Council
Speaker of the House of Commons
Lord Privy Seal
Ambassadors and High
  Commissioners
Lord Great Chamberlain
Earl Marshal
Lord Steward of the Household
Lord Chamberlain of the Household
Master of the Horse
Dukes, according to their patent of
  creation:
  (1) of England
  (2) of Scotland
  (3) of Great Britain
  (4) of Ireland
  (5) those created since the Union
Ministers and Envoys
Eldest sons of Dukes of Blood Royal
Marquesses, according to their patent
  of creation:
  (1) of England
  (2) of Scotland
  (3) of Great Britain
  (4) of Ireland
  (5) those created since the Union
Dukes' eldest sons
Earls, according to their patent of
  creation:
  (1) of England
  (2) of Scotland
  (3) of Great Britain
  (4) of Ireland
  (5) those created since the Union
Younger sons of Dukes of Blood
  Royal
Marquesses' eldest sons
Dukes' younger sons
Viscounts, according to their patent
  of creation:
  (1) of England
  (2) of Scotland
  (3) of Great Britain
  (4) of Ireland
  (5) those created since the Union
Earls' eldest sons
Marquesses' younger sons
Bishops of London, Durham and
  Winchester
Other English Diocesan Bishops,
  according to seniority of
  consecration

Suffragan Bishops, according to
  seniority of consecration
Secretaries of State, if of the degree
  of a Baron
Barons, according to their patent of
  creation:
  (1) of England
  (2) of Scotland
  (3) of Great Britain
  (4) of Ireland
  (5) those created since the Union
Treasurer of the Household
Comptroller of the Household
Vice-Chamberlain of the Household
Secretaries of State under the degree
  of Baron
Viscounts' eldest sons
Earls' younger sons
Barons' eldest sons
Knights of the Garter
Privy Counsellors
Chancellor of the Exchequer
Chancellor of the Duchy of
  Lancaster
Lord Chief Justice of England
Master of the Rolls
President of the Family Division
Vice-Chancellor
Lords Justices of Appeal
Judges of the High Court
Viscounts' younger sons
Barons' younger sons
Sons of Life Peers
Baronets, according to date of patent
Knights of the Thistle
Knights Grand Cross of the Bath
Members of the Order of Merit
Knights Grand Cross of St Michael
  and St George
Knights Grand Commanders of the
  Indian Empire
Knights Grand Cross of the Royal
  Victorian Order
Knights Grand Cross of the British
  Empire
Companions of Honour
Knights Commanders of the Bath
Knights Commanders of St Michael
  and St George
Knights Commanders of the Indian
  Empire
Knights Commanders of the Royal
  Victorian Order
Knights Commanders of the British
  Empire
Knights Bachelor
Vice-Chancellor of the County
  Palatine of Lancaster
Official Referees of the Supreme
  Court
Circuit judges and judges of the
  Mayor's and City of London
  Court
Companions of the Bath
Companions of the Star of India

Companions of St Michael and St
  George
Companions of the Indian Empire
Commanders of the Royal Victorian
  Order
Commanders of the British Empire
Companions of the Distinguished
  Service Order
Lieutenants of the Royal Victorian
  Order
Officers of the British Empire
Companions of the Imperial Service
  Order
Eldest sons of younger sons of Peers
Baronets' eldest sons
Eldest sons of Knights, in the same
  order as their fathers
Members of the Royal Victorian
  Order
Members of the British Empire
Younger sons of the younger sons of
  Peers
Baronets' younger sons
Younger sons of Knights, in the same
  order as their fathers
Naval, Military, Air, and other
  Esquires by office

WOMEN

Women take the same rank as their
husbands or as their brothers; but the
daughter of a peer marrying a commoner retains her title as Lady or
Honourable. Daughters of peers rank
next immediately after the wives of
their elder brothers, and before their
younger brothers' wives. Daughters of
peers marrying peers of lower degree
take the same order of precedence as
that of their husbands; thus the daughter of a Duke marrying a Baron
becomes of the rank of Baroness only,
while her sisters married to common-
ers retain their rank and take precedence of the Baroness. Merely official
rank on the husband's part does not
give any similar precedence to the
wife.

Peeresses in their own right take
the same precedence as peers of the
same rank, i.e. from their date of
creation.

SCOTLAND

For precedence in Scotland, *see* Whitaker's Scottish Almanack.

Forms of address

It is only possible to cover here the forms of address for peers, baronets and knights, their wife and children, and Privy Counsellors. Greater detail should be sought in one of the publications devoted to the subject.

Both formal and social forms of address are given where usage differs; nowadays, the social form is generally preferred to the formal, which increasingly is used only for official documents and on very formal occasions.

F— represents forename
S— represents surname

BARON – *Envelope (formal)*, The Right Hon. Lord —; *(social)*, The Lord —. *Letter (formal)*, My Lord; *(social)*, Dear Lord —. *Spoken*, Lord —.
BARON'S WIFE – *Envelope (formal)*, The Right Hon. Lady —; *(social)*, The Lady —. *Letter (formal)*, My Lady; *(social)*, Dear Lady —. *Spoken*, Lady —.
BARON'S CHILDREN – *Envelope*, The Hon. F— S—. *Letter*, Dear Mr/Miss/Mrs S—. *Spoken*, Mr/Miss/Mrs S—.
BARONESS IN OWN RIGHT – *Envelope*, may be addressed in same way as a Baron's wife or, if she prefers *(formal)*, The Right Hon. the Baroness —; *(social)*, The Baroness —. Otherwise as for a Baron's wife.
BARONET – *Envelope*, Sir F— S—, Bt. *Letter (formal)*, Dear Sir; *(social)*, Dear Sir F—. *Spoken*, Sir F—.
BARONET'S WIFE – *Envelope*, Lady S— *Letter (formal)*, Dear Madam; *(social)*, Dear Lady S— *Spoken*, Lady S—.
COUNTESS IN OWN RIGHT – As for an Earl's wife.
COURTESY TITLES – The heir apparent to a Duke, Marquess or Earl uses the highest of his father's other titles as a courtesy title. (For list, *see* pages 165–6.) The holder of a courtesy title is not styled The Most Hon. or The Right Hon., and in correspondence 'The' is omitted before the title. The heir apparent to a Scottish title may use the title 'Master' (*see* below).
DAME – *Envelope*, Dame F— S—, followed by appropriate post-nominal letters. *Letter (formal)*, Dear Madam; *(social)*, Dear Dame F—. *Spoken*, Dame F—.
DUKE – *Envelope (formal)*, His Grace the Duke of —; *(social)*, The Duke of —. *Letter (formal)*, My Lord Duke; *(social)*, Dear Duke. *Spoken (formal)*, Your Grace; *(social)*, Duke.
DUKE'S WIFE – *Envelope (formal)*, Her Grace the Duchess of —; *(social)*, The Duchess of —. *Letter (formal)*, Dear Madam; *(social)*, Dear Duchess. *Spoken*, Duchess.
DUKE'S ELDEST SON – *see* Courtesy titles.
DUKE'S YOUNGER SONS – *Envelope*, Lord F— S—. *Letter (formal)*, My Lord; *(social)*, Dear Lord F—. *Spoken (formal)*, My Lord; *(social)*, Lord F—.
DUKE'S DAUGHTER – *Envelope*, Lady F— S—. *Letter (formal)*, Dear Madam; *(social)*, Dear Lady F—. *Spoken*, Lady F—.
EARL – *Envelope (formal)*, The Right Hon. the Earl (of) —; *(social)*, The Earl (of) —. *Letter (formal)*, My Lord; *(social)*, Dear Lord —. *Spoken (formal)*, My Lord; *(social)*, Lord —.
EARL'S WIFE – *Envelope (formal)*, The Right Hon. the Countess (of) —; *(social)*, The Countess (of) —. *Letter (formal)*, Madam; *(social)*, Lady —. *Spoken (formal)*, Madam; *(social)*, Lady —.
EARL'S CHILDREN – *Eldest son, see* Courtesy titles. *Younger sons*, The Hon. F— S— (for forms of address, *see* Baron's children). *Daughters*, Lady F— S— (for forms of address, *see* Duke's daughter).
KNIGHT (BACHELOR) – *Envelope*, Sir F— S—. *Letter (formal)*, Dear Sir; *(social)*, Dear Sir F—. *Spoken*, Sir F—.

KNIGHT (ORDERS OF CHIVALRY) – *Envelope*, Sir F— S—, followed by appropriate post-nominal letters. Otherwise as for Knight Bachelor.
KNIGHT'S WIFE – As for Baronet's wife.
LIFE PEER – As for Baron/Baroness in own right.
LIFE PEER'S WIFE – As for Baron's wife.
LIFE PEER'S CHILDREN – As for Baron's children.
MARQUESS – *Envelope (formal)*, The Most Hon. the Marquess of —; *(social)*, The Marquess of —. *Letter (formal)*, My Lord; *(social)*, Dear Lord —. *Spoken (formal)*, My Lord; *(social)*, Lord —.
MARQUESS'S WIFE – *Envelope (formal)*, The Most Hon. the Marchioness of —; *(social)*, The Marchioness of —. *Letter (formal)*, Madam; *(social)*, Dear Lady —. *Spoken*, Lady —.
MARQUESS'S CHILDREN – *Eldest son, see* Courtesy titles. *Younger sons*, Lord F— S— (for forms of address, *see* Duke's younger sons). *Daughters*, Lady F— S— (for forms of address, *see* Duke's daughter).
MASTER – The title is used by the heir apparent to a Scottish peerage, though usually the heir apparent to a Duke, Marquess or Earl uses his courtesy title rather than 'Master'. *Envelope*, The Master of —. *Letter (formal)*, Dear Sir; *(social)*, Dear Master of —. *Spoken (formal)*, Master, or Sir; *(social)*, Master, or Mr S—.
MASTER'S WIFE – Addressed as for the wife of the appropriate peerage style, otherwise as Mrs S—.
PRIVY COUNSELLOR – *Envelope*, The Right (or Rt.) Hon. F— S—. *Letter*, Dear Mr/Miss/Mrs S—. *Spoken*, Mr/Miss/Mrs S—. It is incorrect to use the letters PC after the name in conjunction with the prefix The Right Hon., unless the Privy Counsellor is a peer below the rank of Marquess and so is styled The Right Hon. because of his rank. In this case only, the post-nominal letters may be used in conjunction with the prefix The Right Hon.
VISCOUNT – *Envelope (formal)*, The Right Hon. the Viscount —; *(social)*, The Viscount —. *Letter (formal)*, My Lord; *(social)*, Dear Lord —. *Spoken*, Lord —.
VISCOUNT'S WIFE – *Envelope (formal)*, The Right Hon. the Viscountess —; *(social)*, The Viscountess —. *Letter (formal)*, Madam; *(social)*, Dear Lady —. *Spoken*, Lady —.
VISCOUNT'S CHILDREN – As for Baron's children.

The Peerage

and Members of the House of Lords

The rules which govern the creation and succession of peerages are extremely complicated. There are, technically, five separate peerages, the Peerage of England, of Scotland, of Ireland, of Great Britain, and of the United Kingdom. The Peerage of Great Britain dates from 1707 when an Act of Union combined the two kingdoms of England and Scotland and separate peerages were discontinued. The Peerage of the United Kingdom dates from 1801 when Great Britain and Ireland were combined under an Act of Union. Some Scottish peers have received additional peerages of Great Britain or of the United Kingdom since 1707, and some Irish peers additional peerages of the United Kingdom since 1801.

The Peerage of Ireland was not entirely discontinued from 1801 but holders of Irish peerages, whether pre-dating or created subsequent to the Union of 1801, are not entitled to sit in the House of Lords if they have no additional English, Scottish, Great Britain or United Kingdom peerage. However, they are eligible for election to the House of Commons and to vote in parliamentary elections. An Irish peer holding a peerage of a lower grade which enables him to sit in the House of Lords is introduced there by the title which enables him to sit, though for all other purposes he is known by his higher title.

In the Peerage of Scotland there is no rank of Baron; the equivalent rank is Lord of Parliament, abbreviated to 'Lord' (the female equivalent is 'Lady'). All peers of England, Scotland, Great Britain or the United Kingdom who are 21 years or over, and of British, Irish or Commonwealth nationality are entitled to sit in the House of Lords.

No fees for dignities have been payable since 1937. The House of Lords surrendered the ancient right of peers to be tried for treason or felony by their peers in 1948. In 1999 the Government published a White Paper, *Modernizing Parliament: Reforming the House of Lords*, containing proposals including removing the right of hereditary peers to sit in the House of Lords. For more details, *see* White Papers section.

HEREDITARY WOMEN PEERS

Most hereditary peerages pass on death to the nearest male heir, but there are exceptions, and several are held by women (*see* pages 144 and 156).

A woman peer in her own right retains her title after marriage, and if her husband's rank is the superior she is designated by the two titles jointly, the inferior one second. Her hereditary claim still holds good in spite of any marriage whether higher or lower. No rank held by a woman can confer any title or even precedence upon her husband but the rank of a hereditary woman peer in her own right is inherited by her eldest son (or in some cases daughter).

Since the Peerage Act 1963, hereditary women peers in their own right have been entitled to sit in the House of Lords, subject to the same qualifications as men. The Government's proposals, once enacted, would also remove this right (*see* White Papers section).

LIFE PEERS

Since 1876 non-hereditary or life peerages have been conferred on certain eminent judges to enable the judicial functions of the House of Lords to be carried out. These Lords are known as Lords of Appeal or law lords and, to date, such appointments have all been male.

Since 1958 life peerages have been conferred upon distinguished men and women from all walks of life, giving them seats in the House of Lords in the degree of Baron or Baroness. They are addressed in the same way as hereditary Lords and Barons, and their children have similar courtesy titles.

PEERAGES EXTINCT SINCE THE LAST EDITION

EARLDOM: Lanesborough (*cr.* 1756)
VISCOUNTCY: Whitelaw (*cr.* 1983)
LIFE PEERAGES: Alport (*cr.* 1961); Beloff (*cr.* 1981); Brandon of Oakbrook (*cr.* 1981); Cayzer (*cr.* 1982); Dean of Beswick (*cr.* 1983); Denning (*cr.* 1957); Gillmore of Thamesfield (*cr.* 1996); Grade (*cr.* 1976); Hunt (*cr.* 1966); Lewin (*cr.* 1982); Lowry (*cr.* 1979); Menuhin (*cr.* 1993); Phillips of Ellesmere (*cr.* 1994); Robens of Woldingham (*cr.* 1961); Robson of Kiddington (*cr.* 1974); Sainsbury (*cr.* 1962); Soper (*cr.* 1965)

DISCLAIMER OF PEERAGES

The Peerage Act 1963 enables peers to disclaim their peerages for life. Peers alive in 1963 could disclaim within twelve months after the passing of the Act (31 July 1963); a person subsequently succeeding to a peerage may disclaim within 12 months (one month if an MP) after the date of succession, or of reaching 21, if later. The disclaimer is irrevocable but does not affect the descent of the peerage after the disclaimant's death, and children of a disclaimed peer may, if they wish, retain their precedence and any courtesy titles and styles borne as children of a peer. The disclaimer permits the disclaimant to sit in the House of Commons if elected as an MP. The Government's proposals (*see* White Papers section), once enacted, will permit hereditary peers to sit in the House of Commons without having to disclaim their titles.

The following peerages are currently disclaimed:

EARLDOMS: Durham (1970); Selkirk (1994)
VISCOUNTCIES: Camrose (1995); Hailsham (1963); Stansgate (1963)
BARONIES: Altrincham (1963); Merthyr (1977); Reith (1972); Sanderson of Ayot (1971); Silkin (1972)

PEERS WHO ARE MINORS (i.e. under 21 years of age)
MARQUESSES: Bristol (*b.* 1979)
EARLS: Craven (*b.* 1989)
BARONS: Elphinstone (*b.* 1980)

CONTRACTIONS AND SYMBOLS

S.   Scottish title
I.   Irish title
*   The peer holds also an Imperial title, specified after the name by Engl., Brit. or UK
°   there is no 'of' in the title
b. born
s. succeeded
m. married
w. widower or widow
M. minor
†   heir not ascertained at time of going to press

Hereditary Peers

PEERS OF THE BLOOD ROYAL

Style, His Royal Highness The Duke of __/His Royal Highness the Earl of__
Style of address (formal) May it please your Royal Highness; *(informal)* Sir

Created	Title, order of succession, name, etc.	Heir
	Dukes	
1337	*Cornwall,* Charles, Prince of Wales, *s.* 1952 (*see* page 117)	‡
1398	*Rothesay,* Charles, Prince of Wales, *s.* 1952 (*see* page 117)	‡
1986	*York* (1st), The Prince Andrew, Duke of York (*see* page 117)	None
1928	*Gloucester* (2nd), Prince Richard, Duke of Gloucester, *s.* 1974 (*see* page 118)	Earl of Ulster (*see* page 118)
1934	*Kent* (2nd), Prince Edward, Duke of Kent, *s.* 1942 (*see* page 118)	Earl of St Andrews (*see* page 118)
	Earl	
1999	*Wessex* (1st), The Prince Edward, Earl of Wessex (*see* page 117)	None

‡ The title is not hereditary but is held by the Sovereign's eldest son from the moment of his birth or the Sovereign's accession

DUKES

Coronet, Eight strawberry leaves
Style, His Grace the Duke of __
Wife's style, Her Grace the Duchess of __
Eldest son's style, Takes his father's second title as a courtesy title
Younger sons' style, 'Lord' before forename and family name
Daughters' style, 'Lady' before forename and family name
For forms of address, *see* page 135

Created	Title, order of succession, name, etc.	Heir
1868 I.	*Abercorn* (5th), James Hamilton, KG, (6th *Brit. Marq., Abercorn,* 1790; 14th *Scott. Earl, Abercorn,* 1606) *b.* 1934, *s.* 1979, *m.*	Marquess of Hamilton, *b.* 1969
1701 S.*	*Argyll* (12th), Ian Campbell (5th *UK Duke, Argyll,* 1892), *b.* 1937, *s.* 1973, *m.*	Marquess of Lorne, *b.* 1968
1703 S.	*Atholl* (11th), John Murray, *b.* 1929, *s.* 1996, *m.*	Marquess of Tullibardine, *b.* 1960
1682	*Beaufort* (11th), David Robert Somerset, *b.* 1928, *s.* 1984, *w.*	Marquess of Worcester, *b.* 1952
1694	*Bedford* (13th), John Robert Russell, *b.* 1917, *s.* 1953, *m.*	Marquess of Tavistock, *b.* 1940
1663 S.*	*Buccleuch* (9th) and *Queensberry* (11th) (S. 1684), Walter Francis John Montagu Douglas Scott, KT, VRD (8th *Engl. Earl, Doncaster,* 1662), *b.* 1923, *s.* 1973, *m.*	Earl of Dalkeith, *b.* 1954
1694	*Devonshire* (11th), Andrew Robert Buxton Cavendish, KG, MC, PC, *b.* 1920, *s.* 1950, *m.*	Marquess of Hartington CBE, *b.* 1944
1947	*Edinburgh* (1st), HRH The Prince Philip, Duke of Edinburgh (see page 117).	The Prince of Wales (see page 117)
1900	*Fife* (3rd), James George Alexander Bannerman Carnegie (12th *Scott. Earl, Southesk,* 1633, *s.* 1992), *b.* 1929, *s.* 1959. (*see* page 128)	Earl of Southesk, *b.* 1961
1675	*Grafton* (11th), Hugh Denis Charles FitzRoy, KG, *b.* 1919, *s.* 1970, *m.*	Earl of Euston, *b.* 1947
1643 S.*	*Hamilton* (15th) and *Brandon* (12th) (*Brit.* 1711), Angus Alan Douglas Douglas-Hamilton, *b.* 1938, *s.* 1973. *Premier Peer of Scotland*	Marquess of Douglas and Clydesdale, *b.* 1978
1766 I.*	*Leinster* (8th), Gerald FitzGerald (8th *Brit. Visct., Leinster,* 1747), *b.* 1914, *s.* 1976, *m. Premier Duke and Marquess of Ireland*	Marquess of Kildare, *b.* 1948
1719	*Manchester* (12th), Angus Charles Drogo Montagu, *b.* 1938, *s.* 1985, *m.*	Viscount Mandeville, *b.* 1962
1702	*Marlborough* (11th), John George Vanderbilt Henry Spencer-Churchill, *b.* 1926, *s.* 1972, *m.*	Marquess of Blandford, *b.* 1955
1707 S.*	*Montrose* (8th), James Graham (6th *Brit. Earl, Graham,* 1722), *b.* 1935, *s.* 1992, *m.*	Marquess of Graham, *b.* 1973
1483	*Norfolk* (17th), Miles Francis Stapleton Fitzalan-Howard, KG, GCVO, CB, CBE, MC (12th *Engl. Baron, Beaumont,* 1309, *s.* 1971; 4th *UK Baron Howard of Glossop,* 1869, *s.* 1972), *b.* 1915, *s.* 1975, *m. Premier Duke and Earl Marshal*	Earl of Arundel and Surrey, *b.* 1956
1766	*Northumberland* (12th), Ralph George Algernon Percy, *b.* 1956, *s.* 1995, *m.*	Earl Percy, *b.* 1984

Created	Title, order of succession, name, etc.	Heir
1675	*Richmond* (10th) and *Gordon* (5th) (*UK* 1876), Charles Henry Gordon Lennox (10th *Scott. Duke, Lennox*, 1675), *b.* 1929, *s.* 1989, *m.*	Earl of March and Kinrara, *b.* 1955
1707 s.*	*Roxburghe* (10th), Guy David Innes-Ker (5th *UK Earl, Innes*, 1837), *b.* 1954, *s.* 1974, *m. Premier Baronet of Scotland*	Marquess of Bowmont and Cessford, *b.* 1981
1703	*Rutland* (11th), David Charles Robert Manners, *b.* 1959, *s.* 1999, *m.*	Hon. Edward J. F. *M.*, *b.* 1965
1684	*St Albans* (14th), Murray de Vere Beauclerk, *b.* 1939, *s.* 1988, *m.*	Earl of Burford, *b.* 1965
1547	*Somerset* (19th), John Michael Edward Seymour, *b.* 1952, *s.* 1984, *m.*	Lord Seymour, *b.* 1982
1833	*Sutherland* (6th), John Sutherland Egerton, TD (5th *UK Earl, Ellesmere*, 1846, *s.* 1944), *b.* 1915, *s.* 1963, *m.*	Francis R. *E.*, *b.* 1940
1814	*Wellington* (8th), Arthur Valerian Wellesley, KG, LVO, OBE, MC (9th *Irish Earl, Mornington*, 1760), *b.* 1915, *s.* 1972, *m.*	Marquess of Douro, *b.* 1945
1874	*Westminster* (6th), Gerald Cavendish Grosvenor, OBE, *b.* 1951, *s.* 1979, *m.*	Earl Grosvenor, *b.* 1991

MARQUESSES

Coronet, Four strawberry leaves alternating with four silver balls
Style, The Most Hon. the Marquess (of) __ . In Scotland the spelling 'Marquis' is preferred for pre-Union creations
Wife's style, The Most Hon. the Marchioness (of) __
Eldest son's style, Takes his father's second title as a courtesy title
Younger sons' style, 'Lord' before forename and family name
Daughters' style, 'Lady' before forename and family name
For forms of address, *see* page 135

Created	Title, order of succession, name, etc.	Heir
1916	*Aberdeen and Temair* (6th), Alastair Ninian John Gordon (12th *Scott. Earl, Aberdeen*, 1682), *b.* 1920, *s.* 1984, *m.*	Earl of Haddo, *b.* 1955
1876	*Abergavenny* (5th), John Henry Guy Nevill, KG, OBE, *b.* 1914, *s.* 1954, *m.*	Christopher G. C. *N.*, *b.* 1955
1821	*Ailesbury* (8th), Michael Sidney Cedric Brudenell-Bruce, *b.* 1926, *s.* 1974.	Earl of Cardigan, *b.* 1952
1831	*Ailsa* (8th), Archibald Angus Charles Kennedy (20th *Scott. Earl, Cassillis*, 1509), *b.* 1956, *s.* 1994.	Lord David Kennedy, *b.* 1958
1815	*Anglesey* (7th), George Charles Henry Victor Paget, *b.* 1922, *s.* 1947, *m.*	Earl of Uxbridge, *b.* 1950
1789	*Bath* (7th), Alexander George Thynn, *b.* 1932, *s.* 1992, *m.*	Viscount Weymouth, *b.* 1974
1826	*Bristol* (8th), Frederick William Augustus Hervey, *b.* 1979, *s.* 1999, *M.*	Hon. Ronald F. W. *H.*, *b.* 1919
1796	*Bute* (7th), John Colum Crichton-Stuart (12th *Scott. Earl, Dumfries*, 1633), *b.* 1958, *s.* 1993, *m.*	Earl of Dumfries, *b.* 1989
1812	° *Camden* (6th), David George Edward Henry Pratt, *b.* 1930, *s.* 1983.	Earl of Brecknock, *b.* 1965
1815	*Cholmondeley* (7th), David George Philip Cholmondeley (11th *Irish Visct., Cholmondeley*, 1661), *b.* 1960, *s.* 1990. *Lord Great Chamberlain*	Charles G. *C.*, *b.* 1959
1816 I.*	° *Conyngham* (7th), Frederick William Henry Francis Conyngham (7th *UK Baron, Minster*, 1821), *b.* 1924, *s.* 1974, *m.*	Earl of Mount Charles, *b.* 1951
1791 I.*	*Donegall* (7th), Dermot Richard Claud Chichester, LVO (7th *Brit. Baron, Fisherwick*, 1790; 6th *Brit. Baron, Templemore*, 1831, *s.* 1953), *b.* 1916, *s.* 1975, *m.*	Earl of Belfast, *b.* 1952
1789 I.*	*Downshire* (8th), (Arthur) Robin Ian Hill (8th *Brit. Earl, Hillsborough*, 1772), *b.* 1929, *s.* 1989, *m.*	Earl of Hillsborough, *b.* 1959
1801 I.*	*Ely* (8th), Charles John Tottenham (8th *UK Baron, Loftus*, 1801), *b.* 1913, *s.* 1969, *m.*	Viscount Loftus, *b.* 1943
1801	*Exeter* (8th), (William) Michael Anthony Cecil, *b.* 1935, *s.* 1988, *m.*	Lord Burghley, *b.* 1970
1800 I.*	*Headfort* (6th), Thomas Geoffrey Charles Michael Taylour (4th *UK Baron, Kenlis*, 1831), *b.* 1932, *s.* 1960, *m.*	Earl of Bective, *b.* 1959
1793	*Hertford* (9th), Henry Jocelyn Seymour (10th *Irish Baron, Conway*, 1712), *b.* 1958, *s.* 1997, *m.*	Earl of Yarmouth, *b.* 1993
1599 s.*	*Huntly* (13th), Granville Charles Gomer Gordon (5th *UK Baron, Meldrum*, 1815), *b.* 1944, *s.* 1987, *m. Premier Marquess of Scotland*	Earl of Aboyne, *b.* 1973
1784	*Lansdowne* (9th), Charles Maurice Mercer Nairne Petty-Fitzmaurice (9th *Irish Earl, Kerry*, 1723), *b.* 1941, *s.* 1999, *m.*	Earl of Shelburne, *b.* 1970
1902	*Linlithgow* (4th), Adrian John Charles Hope (10th *Scott. Earl, Hopetoun*, 1703), *b.* 1946, *s.* 1987, *m.*	Earl of Hopetoun, *b.* 1971
1816 I.*	*Londonderry* (9th), Alexander Charles Robert Vane-Tempest-Stewart (6th *UK Earl, Vane*, 1823), *b.* 1937, *s.* 1955, *m.*	Viscount Castlereagh, *b.* 1972
1701 s.*	*Lothian* (12th), Peter Francis Walter Kerr, KCVO (6th *UK Baron, Kerr*, 1821), *b.* 1922, *s.* 1940, *m.*	Earl of Ancram PC, MP, *b.* 1945

Created	Title, order of succession, name, etc.	Heir
1917	*Milford Haven* (4th), George Ivar Louis Mountbatten, *b.* 1961, *s.* 1970, *m.*	Earl of Medina, *b.* 1991
1838	*Normanby* (5th), Constantine Edmund Walter Phipps (9th *Irish Baron, Mulgrave*, 1767), *b.* 1954, *s.* 1994, *m.*	Earl of Mulgrave, *b.* 1994
1812	*Northampton* (7th), Spencer Douglas David Compton, *b.* 1946, *s.* 1978, *m.*	Earl Compton, *b.* 1973
1682 S.	*Queensberry* (12th), David Harrington Angus Douglas, *b.* 1929, *s.* 1954.	Viscount Drumlanrig, *b.* 1967
1926	*Reading* (4th), Simon Charles Henry Rufus Isaacs, *b.* 1942, *s.* 1980, *m.*	Viscount Erleigh, *b.* 1986
1789	*Salisbury* (6th), Robert Edward Peter Cecil, *b.* 1916, *s.* 1972, *m.*	Viscount Cranborne PC, *b.* 1946 (*see also* Baron Cecil, page 139)
1800 I.*	*Sligo* (11th), Jeremy Ulick Browne (11th *UK Baron, Monteagle*, 1806), *b.* 1939, *s.* 1991, *m.*	Sebastian U. B., *b.* 1964
1787	° *Townshend* (7th), George John Patrick Dominic Townshend, *b.* 1916, *s.* 1921, *w.*	Viscount Raynham, *b.* 1945
1694 S.*	° *Tweeddale* (13th), Edward Douglas John Hay (4th *UK Baron Tweeddale*, 1881), *b.* 1947, *s.* 1979.	Lord Charles D. M. H., *b.* 1947
1789 I.*	*Waterford* (8th), John Hubert de la Poer Beresford (8th *Brit. Baron Tyrone*, 1786), *b.* 1933, *s.* 1934, *m.*	Earl of Tyrone, *b.* 1958
1551	*Winchester* (18th), Nigel George Paulet, *b.* 1941, *s.* 1968, *m.* Premier *Marquess of England*	Earl of Wiltshire, *b.* 1969
1892	*Zetland* (4th), Lawrence Mark Dundas (6th *UK Earl, Zetland*, 1838; 7th *Brit. Baron Dundas*, 1794), *b.* 1937, *s.* 1989, *m.*	Earl of Ronaldshay, *b.* 1965

EARLS

Coronet, Eight silver balls on stalks alternating with eight gold strawberry leaves
Style, The Right Hon. the Earl (of) _
Wife's style, The Right Hon. the Countess (of) _
Eldest son's style, Takes his father's second title as a courtesy title
Younger sons' style, 'The Hon.' before forename and family name
Daughters' style, 'Lady' before forename and family name
For forms of address, *see* page 135

Created	Title, order of succession, name, etc.	Heir
1639 S.	*Airlie* (13th), David George Coke Patrick Ogilvy, KT, GCVO, PC, Royal Victorian Chain, *b.* 1926, *s.* 1968, *m.*	Lord Ogilvy, *b.* 1958
1696	*Albemarle* (10th), Rufus Arnold Alexis Keppel, *b.* 1965, *s.* 1979.	Crispian W. J. K., *b.* 1948
1952	° *Alexander of Tunis* (2nd), Shane William Desmond Alexander, *b.* 1935, *s.* 1969, *m.*	Hon. Brian J. A., *b.* 1939
1662 S.	*Annandale and Hartfell.* (11th), Patrick Andrew Wentworth Hope Johnstone, *b.* 1941, claim established 1985, *m.*	Lord Johnstone, *b.* 1971
1789 I.	° *Annesley* (10th), Patrick Annesley, *b.* 1924, *s.* 1979, *m.*	Hon. Philip H. A., *b.* 1927
1785 I.	*Antrim* (9th), Alexander Randal Mark McDonnell, *b.* 1935, *s.* 1977, *m.*	Viscount Dunluce, *b.* 1967
1762 I.*	*Arran* (9th), Arthur Desmond Colquhoun Gore (5th *UK Baron Sudley*, 1884), *b.* 1938, *s.* 1983, *m.*	Paul A. G. CMG, CVO, *b.* 1921
1955	° *Attlee* (3rd), John Richard Attlee, *b.* 1956, *s.* 1991, *m.*	None
1714	*Aylesford* (11th), Charles Ian Finch-Knightley, *b.* 1918, *s.* 1958, *w.*	Lord Guernsey, *b.* 1947
1937	° *Baldwin of Bewdley* (4th), Edward Alfred Alexander Baldwin, *b.* 1938, *s.* 1976, *m.*	Viscount Corvedale, *b.* 1973
1922	*Balfour* (4th), Gerald Arthur James Balfour, *b.* 1925, *s.* 1968, *m.*	Eustace A. G. B., *b.* 1921
1772	° *Bathurst* (8th), Henry Allen John Bathurst, *b.* 1927, *s.* 1943, *m.*	Lord Apsley, *b.* 1961
1919	° *Beatty* (3rd), David Beatty, *b.* 1946, *s.* 1972, *m.*	Viscount Borodale, *b.* 1973
1797 I.	*Belmore* (8th), John Armar Lowry-Corry, *b.* 1951, *s.* 1960, *m.*	Viscount Corry, *b.* 1985
1739 I.*	*Bessborough* (11th), Arthur Mountifort Longfield Ponsonby (8th *UK Baron Duncannon*, 1834), *b.* 1912, *s.* 1993, *m.*	Viscount Duncannon, *b.* 1941
1815	*Bradford* (7th), Richard Thomas Orlando Bridgeman, *b.* 1947, *s.* 1981, *m.*	Viscount Newport, *b.* 1980
1469 S.*	*Buchan* (17th), Malcolm Harry Erskine (8th *UK Baron Erskine*, 1806), *b.* 1930, *s.* 1984, *m.*	Lord Cardross, *b.* 1960
1746	*Buckinghamshire* (10th), (George) Miles Hobart-Hampden, *b.* 1944, *s.* 1983, *m.*	Sir John Hobart, Bt., *b.* 1945
1800	° *Cadogan* (8th), Charles Gerald John Cadogan, *b.* 1937, *s.* 1997, *m.*	Viscount Chelsea, *b.* 1966
1878	° *Cairns* (6th), Simon Dallas Cairns, CBE, *b.* 1939, *s.* 1989, *m.*	Viscount Garmoyle, *b.* 1965
1455 S.	*Caithness* (20th), Malcolm Ian Sinclair, PC, *b.* 1948, *s.* 1965, *w.*	Lord Berriedale, *b.* 1981
1800 I.	*Caledon* (7th), Nicholas James Alexander, *b.* 1955, *s.* 1980, *m.*	Viscount Alexander, *b.* 1990

Created	Title, order of succession, name, etc.	Heir
1661	Carlisle (13th), George William Beaumont Howard (13th Scott. Baron Ruthven of Freeland, 1651), b. 1949, s. 1994.	Hon. Philip C. W. H., b. 1963
1793	Carnarvon (7th), Henry George Reginald Molyneux Herbert, KCVO, KBE, b. 1924, s. 1987, m.	Lord Porchester, b. 1956
1748 I.*	Carrick (10th), David James Theobald Somerset Butler (4th UK Baron Butler, 1912), b. 1953, s. 1992, m.	Viscount Ikerrin, b. 1975
1800 I.	° Castle Stewart (8th), Arthur Patrick Avondale Stuart, b. 1928, s. 1961, m.	Viscount Stuart, b. 1953
1814	° Cathcart (7th), Charles Alan Andrew Cathcart (16th Scott. Baron Cathcart, 1447), b. 1952, s. 1999, m.	Lord Greenock, b. 1986
1647 I.	Cavan. The 12th Earl died in 1988. Heir had not established his claim to the title at the time of going to press	Roger C. Lambart, b. 1944
1827	° Cawdor (7th), Colin Robert Vaughan Campbell, b. 1962, s. 1993, m.	Hon. Frederick W. C., b. 1965
1801	Chichester (9th), John Nicholas Pelham, b. 1944, s. 1944, m.	Richard A. H. P., b. 1952
1803 I.*	Clancarty (9th), Nicholas Power Richard Le Poer Trench (8th UK Visct. Clancarty, 1823), b. 1952, s. 1995.	None
1776 I.*	Clanwilliam (7th), John Herbert Meade (5th UK Baron Clanwilliam, 1828), b. 1919, s. 1989, m.	Lord Gillford, b. 1960
1776	Clarendon (7th), George Frederick Laurence Hyde Villiers, b. 1933, s. 1955, m.	Lord Hyde, b. 1976
1620 I.*	Cork (14th) and Orrery (14th) (I. 1660), John William Boyle, DSC (10th Brit. Baron Boyle of Marston, 1711), b. 1916, s. 1995, m.	Viscount Dungarvan, b. 1945
1850	Cottenham (8th), Kenelm Charles Everard Digby Pepys, b. 1948, s. 1968, m.	Viscount Crowhurst, b. 1983
1762 I.*	Courtown (9th), James Patrick Montagu Burgoyne Winthrop Stopford (8th Brit. Baron Saltersford, 1796), b. 1954, s. 1975, m.	Viscount Stopford, b. 1988
1697	Coventry (11th), George William Coventry, b. 1934, s. 1940, m.	Francis H. C., b. 1912
1857	° Cowley (7th), Garret Graham Wellesley, b. 1934, s. 1975, m.	Viscount Dangan, b. 1965
1892	Cranbrook (5th), Gathorne Gathorne-Hardy, b. 1933, s. 1978, m.	Lord Medway, b. 1968
1801	Craven (9th), Benjamin Robert Joseph Craven, b. 1989, s. 1990, M.	Rupert J. E. C., b. 1926
1398 S.*	Crawford (29th) and Balcarres (12th) (S. 1651), Robert Alexander Lindsay, KT, PC (5th UK Baron, Wigan, 1826; Baron Balniel (life peerage), 1974), b. 1927, s. 1975, m. Premier Earl on Union Roll	Lord Balniel, b. 1958
1861	Cromartie (5th), John Ruaridh Blunt Grant Mackenzie, b. 1948, s. 1989, m.	Viscount Tarbat, b. 1987
1901	Cromer (4th), Evelyn Rowland Esmond Baring, b. 1946, s. 1991, m.	Viscount Errington, b. 1994
1633 S.*	Dalhousie (17th), James Hubert Ramsay (5th UK Baron Ramsay, 1875), b. 1948, s. 1999, m.	Lord Ramsay, b. 1981
1725 I.	Darnley (11th), Adam Ivo Stuart Bligh (20th Engl. Baron Clifton of Leighton Bromswold, 1608), b. 1941, s. 1980, m.	Lord Clifton, b. 1968
1711	Dartmouth (10th), William Legge, b. 1949, s. 1997.	Hon. Rupert L., b. 1951
1761	° De La Warr (11th), William Herbrand Sackville, b. 1948, s. 1988, m.	Lord Buckhurst, b. 1979
1622	Denbigh (12th) and Desmond (11th) (I. 1622), Alexander Stephen Rudolph Feilding, b. 1970, s. 1995, m.	William D. F., b. 1939
1485	Derby (19th), Edward Richard William Stanley, b. 1962, s. 1994, m.	Lord Stanley, b. 1998
1553	Devon (18th), Hugh Rupert Courtenay, b. 1942, s. 1998, m.	Lord Courtenay, b. 1975
1800 I.*	Donoughmore (8th), Richard Michael John Hely-Hutchinson (8th UK Visct. Hutchinson, 1821), b. 1927, s. 1981, m.	Viscount Suirdale, b. 1952
1661 I.*	Drogheda (12th), Henry Dermot Ponsonby Moore (3rd UK Baron Moore, 1954), b. 1937, s. 1989, m.	Viscount Moore, b. 1983
1837	Ducie (7th), David Leslie Moreton, b. 1951, s. 1991, m.	Lord Moreton, b. 1981
1860	Dudley (4th), William Humble David Ward, b. 1920, s. 1969, m.	Viscount Ednam, b. 1947
1660 S.*	Dundee (12th), Alexander Henry Scrymgeour (2nd UK Baron Glassary, 1954), b. 1949, s. 1983, m.	Lord Scrymgeour, b. 1982
1669 S.	Dundonald (15th), Iain Alexander Douglas Blair Cochrane, b. 1961, s. 1986, m.	Lord Cochrane, b. 1991
1686 S.	Dunmore (12th), Malcolm Kenneth Murray, b. 1946, s. 1995, m.	Hon. Geoffrey C. M., b. 1949
1822 I.	Dunraven and Mount-Earl (7th), Thady Windham Thomas Wyndham-Quin, b. 1939, s. 1965, m.	None
1833	Durham. Disclaimed for life 1970. (Antony Claud Frederick Lambton, b.1922, s.1970, m.)	Hon. Edward R. L. (Baron Durham), b. 1961
1837	Effingham (7th), David Mowbray Algernon Howard (17th Engl. Baron Howard of Effingham, 1554), b. 1939, s. 1996, m.	Lord Howard of Effingham, b. 1971
1507 S.*	Eglinton (18th) and Winton (9th) (S. 1600), Archibald George Montgomerie (6th UK Earl Winton, 1859), b. 1939, s. 1966, m.	Lord Montgomerie, b. 1966
1733 I.*	Egmont (11th), Frederick George Moore Perceval (9th Brit. Baron Lovel and Holland, 1762), b. 1914, s. 1932, m.	Viscount Perceval, b. 1934
1821	Eldon (5th), John Joseph Nicholas Scott, b. 1937, s. 1976, m.	Viscount Encombe, b. 1962
1633 S.*	Elgin (11th) and Kincardine (15th) (S. 1647), Andrew Douglas Alexander Thomas Bruce, KT (4th UK Baron, Elgin, 1849), b. 1924, s. 1968, m.	Lord Bruce, b. 1961

Created	Title, order of succession, name, etc.	Heir
1789 I.*	*Enniskillen* (7th), Andrew John Galbraith Cole (5th *UK Baron, Grinstead,* 1815), *b.* 1942, *s.* 1989, *m.*	Arthur G. C., *b.* 1920
1789 I.*	*Erne* (6th), Henry George Victor John Crichton (3rd *UK Baron, Fermanagh,* 1876), *b.* 1937, *s.* 1940, *m.*	Viscount Crichton, *b.* 1971
1452 S.	*Erroll* (24th), Merlin Sereld Victor Gilbert Hay, *b.* 1948, *s.* 1978, *m.* *Hereditary Lord High Constable and Knight Marischal of Scotland*	Lord Hay, *b.* 1984
1661	*Essex* (10th), Robert Edward de Vere Capell, *b.* 1920, *s.* 1981, *m.*	Viscount Malden, *b.* 1944
1711	° *Ferrers* (13th), Robert Washington Shirley, PC, *b.* 1929, *s.* 1954, *m.*	Viscount Tamworth, *b.* 1952
1789	° *Fortescue* (8th), Charles Hugh Richard Fortescue, *b.* 1951, *s.* 1993, *m.*	Hon. Martin D. F., *b.* 1924
1841	*Gainsborough* (5th), Anthony Gerard Edward Noel, *b.* 1923, *s.* 1927, *m.*	Viscount Campden, *b.* 1950
1623 S.*	*Galloway* (13th), Randolph Keith Reginald Stewart (6th *Brit. Baron Stewart of Garlies,* 1796), *b.* 1928, *s.* 1978, *m.*	Andrew C. S., *b.* 1949
1703 S.*	*Glasgow* (10th), Patrick Robin Archibald Boyle (4th *UK Baron, Fairlie,* 1897), *b.* 1939, *s.* 1984, *m.*	Viscount of Kelburn, *b.* 1978
1806 I.*	*Gosford* (7th), Charles David Nicholas Alexander John Sparrow Acheson (5th *UK Baron, Worlingham,* 1835), *b.* 1942, *s.* 1966, *m.*	Hon. Patrick B. V. M. A., *b.* 1915
1945	*Gowrie* (2nd), Alexander Patric Greysteil Hore-Ruthven, PC (3rd *UK Baron Ruthven of Gowrie,* 1919), *b.* 1939, *s.* 1955, *m.*	Viscount Ruthven of Canberra, *b.* 1964
1684 I.*	*Granard* (10th), Peter Arthur Edward Hastings Forbes (5th *UK Baron, Granard,* 1806), *b.* 1957, *s.* 1992, *m.*	Viscount Forbes, *b.* 1981
1833	° *Granville* (6th), Granville George Fergus Leveson-Gower, *b.* 1959, *s.* 1996, *m.*	Hon. Niall J. L.-G., *b.* 1963
1806	° *Grey* (6th), Richard Fleming George Charles Grey, *b.* 1939, *s.* 1963, *m.*	Philip K. G., *b.* 1940
1752	*Guilford* (10th), Piers Edward Brownlow North, *b.* 1971, *s.* 1999, *m.*	Hon. Charles E N., *b.* 1918
1619 S.	*Haddington* (13th), John George Baillie-Hamilton, *b.* 1941, *s.* 1986, *m.*	Lord Binning, *b.* 1985
1919	° *Haig* (2nd), George Alexander Eugene Douglas Haig, OBE, *b.* 1918, *s.* 1928, *m.*	Viscount Dawick, *b.* 1961
1944	*Halifax* (3rd), Charles Edward Peter Neil Wood (5th *UK Visct., Halifax,* 1866), *b.* 1944, *s.* 1980, *m.*	Lord Irwin, *b.* 1977
1898	*Halsbury* (3rd), John Anthony Hardinge Giffard, FRS, FREng., *b.* 1908, *s.* 1943, *w.*	Adam E. G., *b.* 1934
1754	*Hardwicke* (10th), Joseph Philip Sebastian Yorke, *b.* 1971, *s.* 1974.	Charles E. Y., *b.* 1951
1812	*Harewood* (7th), George Henry Hubert Lascelles, KBE, *b.* 1923, *s.* 1947, *m.* (*see also* page 127)	Viscount Lascelles, *b.* 1950 (*see also* page 127)
1742	*Harrington* (11th), William Henry Leicester Stanhope (8th *Brit. Visct. Stanhope of Mahon,* 1717), *b.* 1922, *s.* 1929, *m.*	Viscount Petersham, *b.* 1945
1809	*Harrowby* (7th), Dudley Danvers Granville Coutts Ryder, TD, *b.* 1922, *s.* 1987, *m.*	Viscount Sandon, *b.* 1951
1605 S.	*Home* (15th), David Alexander Cospatrick Douglas-Home, CVO, *b.* 1943, *s.* 1995, *m.*	Lord Dunglass, *b.* 1987
1821	° *Howe* (7th), Frederick Richard Penn Curzon, *b.* 1951, *s.* 1984, *m.*	Viscount Curzon, *b.* 1994
1529	*Huntingdon* (16th), William Edward Robin Hood Hastings Bass, LVO, *b.* 1948, *s.* 1990, *m.*	Hon. Simon A. R. H. H. B., *b.* 1950
1885	*Iddesleigh* (4th), Stafford Henry Northcote, *b.* 1932, *s.* 1970, *m.*	Viscount St Cyres, *b.* 1957
1756	*Ilchester* (9th), Maurice Vivian de Touffreville Fox-Strangways, *b.* 1920, *s.* 1970, *m.*	Hon. Raymond G. F.-S., *b.* 1921
1929	*Inchcape* (4th), (Kenneth) Peter (Lyle) Mackay, *b.* 1943, *s.* 1994, *m.*	Viscount Glenapp, *b.* 1979
1919	*Iveagh* (4th), Arthur Edward Rory Guinness, *b.* 1969, *s.* 1992.	Hon. Rory M. B. G., *b.* 1974
1925	° *Jellicoe* (2nd), George Patrick John Rushworth Jellicoe, KBE, DSO, MC, PC, FRS, *b.* 1918, *s.* 1935, *m.*	Viscount Brocas, *b.* 1950
1697	*Jersey* (10th), (George Francis William Child Villiers (13th *Irish Visct. Grandison,* 1620), *b.* 1976, *s.* 1998.	Hon. Jamie C. V., *b.* 1994
1822 I.	*Kilmorey* (6th), Richard Francis Needham, KT, PC, *b.* 1942, *s.* 1977, *m.*	Viscount Newry and Morne, *b.* 1966
1866	*Kimberley* (4th), John Wodehouse, *b.* 1924, *s.* 1941, *m.*	Lord Wodehouse, *b.* 1951
1768 I.	*Kingston* (11th), Barclay Robert Edwin King-Tenison, *b.* 1943, *s.* 1948, *m.*	Viscount Kingsborough, *b.* 1969
1633 S.*	*Kinnoull* (15th), Arthur William George Patrick Hay (9th *Brit. Baron Hay of Pedwardine,* 1711), *b.* 1935, *s.* 1938, *m.*	Viscount Dupplin, *b.* 1962
1677 S.*	*Kintore* (13th), Michael Canning William John Keith (3rd *UK Visct. Stonehaven,* 1938), *b.* 1939, *s.* 1989, *m.*	Lord Inverurie, *b.* 1976
1914	° *Kitchener of Khartoum* (3rd), Henry Herbert Kitchener, TD, *b.* 1919, *s.* 1937.	None
1624 S.	*Lauderdale* (17th), Patrick Francis Maitland, *b.* 1911, *s.* 1968, *m.*	Viscount Maitland, *b.* 1937
1837	*Leicester* (7th), Edward Douglas Coke, *b.* 1936, *s.* 1994, *m.*	Viscount Coke, *b.* 1965
1641 S.*	*Leven* (14th) and *Melville* (13th) (s. 1690), Alexander Robert Leslie Melville, *b.* 1924, *s.* 1947, *m.*	Lord Balgonie, *b.* 1954
1831	*Lichfield* (5th), Thomas Patrick John Anson, *b.* 1939, *s.* 1960.	Viscount Anson, *b.* 1978
1803 I.*	*Limerick* (6th), Patrick Edmund Pery, KBE (6th *UK Baron Foxford,* 1815), *b.* 1930, *s.* 1967, *m.*	Viscount Glentworth, *b.* 1963

Created	Title, order of succession, name, etc.	Heir
1572	Lincoln (18th), Edward Horace Fiennes-Clinton, b. 1913, s. 1988, m.	Hon. Edward G. F.-C., b. 1943
1633 S.	Lindsay (16th), James Randolph Lindesay-Bethune, b. 1955, s. 1989, m.	Viscount Garnock, b. 1990
1626	Lindsey (14th) and Abingdon (9th) (1682), Richard Henry Rupert Bertie, b. 1931, s. 1963, m.	Lord Norreys, b. 1958
1776 I.	Lisburne (8th), John David Malet Vaughan, b. 1918, s. 1965, m.	Viscount Vaughan, b. 1945
1822 I.*	Listowel (6th), Francis Michael Hare (4th UK Baron Hare, 1869), b. 1964, s. 1997, m.	Hon. Timothy P. H., b. 1966
1905	Liverpool (5th), Edward Peter Bertram Savile Foljambe, b. 1944, s. 1969, m.	Viscount Hawkesbury, b. 1972
1945	° Lloyd George of Dwyfor (3rd), Owen Lloyd George, b. 1924, s. 1968, m.	Viscount Gwynedd, b. 1951
1785 I.*	Longford (7th), Francis Aungier Pakenham, KG, PC (6th UK Baron, Silchester, 1821; 1st UK Baron Pakenham, 1945), b. 1905, s. 1961, m.	Thomas F. D. P., b. 1933
1807	Lonsdale (7th), James Hugh William Lowther, b. 1922, s. 1953, m.	Viscount Lowther, b. 1949
1838	Lovelace (5th), Peter Axel William Locke King (12th Brit. Baron King, 1725), b. 1951, s. 1964, m.	None
1795 I.*	Lucan (7th), Richard John Bingham (3rd UK Baron Bingham, 1934), b. 1934, s. 1964, m.	Lord Bingham, b. 1967
1880	Lytton (5th), John Peter Michael Scawen Lytton (18th Engl. Baron, Wentworth, 1529), b. 1950, s. 1985, m.	Viscount Knebworth, b. 1989
1721	Macclesfield (9th), Richard Timothy George Mansfield Parker, b. 1943, s. 1992, m.	Hon. J. David G. P., b. 1945
1800	Malmesbury (6th), William James Harris, TD, b. 1907, s. 1950, w.	Viscount FitzHarris, b. 1946
1776 & 1792	Mansfield and Mansfield (8th), William David Mungo James Murray (14th Scott. Visct. Stormont, 1621), b. 1930, s. 1971, m.	Viscount Stormont, b. 1956
1565 S.*	Mar (14th) and Kellie (16th) (s. 1616), James Thorne Erskine, b. 1949, s. 1994, m.	Hon. Alexander D. E., b. 1952
1785 I.	Mayo (10th), Terence Patrick Bourke, b. 1929, s. 1962.	Lord Naas, b. 1953
1627 I.*	Meath (15th), John Anthony Brabazon (6th UK Baron, Chaworth, 1831), b. 1941, s. 1998, m.	Lord Ardee, b. 1977
1766 I.	Mexborough (8th), John Christopher George Savile, b. 1931, s. 1980, m.	Viscount Pollington, b. 1959
1813	Minto (6th), Gilbert Edward George Lariston Elliot-Murray-Kynynmound, OBE, b. 1928, s. 1975, m.	Viscount Melgund, b. 1953
1562 S.*	Moray (20th), Douglas John Moray Stuart (12th Brit. Baron Stuart of Castle Stuart, 1796), b. 1928, s. 1974, m.	Lord Doune, b. 1966
1815	Morley (6th), John St Aubyn Parker, KCVO, b. 1923, s. 1962, m.	Viscount Boringdon, b. 1956
1458 S.	Morton (22nd), John Charles Sholto Douglas, b. 1927, s. 1976, m.	Lord Aberdour, b. 1952
1789	Mount Edgcumbe (8th), Robert Charles Edgcumbe, b. 1939, s. 1982.	Piers V. E., b. 1946
1831	Munster (7th), Anthony Charles FitzClarence, b. 1926, s. 1983, m.	None
1805	° Nelson (9th), Peter John Horatio Nelson, b. 1941, s. 1981, m.	Viscount Merton, b. 1971
1660 S.	Newburgh (12th), Don Filippo George Giambattista Camillo Francesco Aldo Ma Rospigliosi, b. 1942, s. 1986, m.	Princess Donna Benedetta F. M. R., b. 1974
1827 I.	Norbury (6th), Noel Terence Graham-Toler, b. 1939, s. 1955, m.	Viscount Glandine, b. 1967
1806 I.*	Normanton (6th), Shaun James Christian Welbore Ellis Agar (9th Brit. Baron, Mendip, 1794; 4th UK Baron, Somerton, 1873), b. 1945, s. 1967, m.	Viscount Somerton, b. 1982
1647 S.	Northesk (14th), David John MacRae Carnegie, b. 1954, s. 1994, m.	Lord Rosehill, b. 1980
1801	Onslow (7th), Michael William Coplestone Dillon Onslow, b. 1938, s. 1971, m.	Viscount Cranley, b. 1967
1696 S.	Orkney (9th), (Oliver) Peter St John, b. 1938, s. 1998, m.	Viscount Kirkwall, b. 1969
1328 I.*	Ormonde and Ossory. The 8th Marquess of Ormonde died in 1997, when the marquessate became extinct. The heir to his earldoms had not established his claim at the time of going to press	Viscount Mountgarret, b. 1936 (see page 146)
1925	Oxford and Asquith (2nd), Julian Edward George Asquith, KCMG, b. 1916, s. 1928, w.	Viscount Asquith OBE, b. 1952
1929	° Peel (3rd), William James Robert Peel (4th UK Visct. Peel, 1895), b. 1947, s. 1969, m.	Viscount Clanfield, b. 1976
1551	Pembroke (17th) and Montgomery (14th) (1605), Henry George Charles Alexander Herbert, b. 1939, s. 1969.	Lord Herbert, b. 1978
1605 S.	Perth (17th), John David Drummond, PC, b. 1907, s. 1951, w.	Viscount Strathallan, b. 1935
1905	Plymouth (3rd), Other Robert Ivor Windsor-Clive (15th Engl. Baron, Windsor, 1529), b. 1923, s. 1943, m.	Viscount Windsor, b. 1951
1785 I.	Portarlington (7th), George Lionel Yuill Seymour Dawson-Damer, b. 1938, s. 1959, m.	Viscount Carlow, b. 1965
1689	Portland (12th), Count Timothy Charles Robert Noel Bentinck, b. 1953, s. 1997, m.	Viscount Woodstock, b. 1984
1743	Portsmouth (10th), Quentin Gerard Carew Wallop, b. 1954, s. 1984, m.	Viscount Lymington, b. 1981
1804	Powis (8th), John George Herbert (9th Irish Baron, Clive, 1762), b. 1952, s. 1993, m.	Viscount Clive, b. 1979
1765	Radnor (8th), Jacob Pleydell-Bouverie, b. 1927, s. 1968, m.	Viscount Folkestone, b. 1955

Created	Title, order of succession, name, etc.	Heir
1831 I.*	*Ranfurly* (7th), Gerald Françoys Needham Knox (8th *UK Baron, Ranfurly*, 1826), *b.* 1929, *s.* 1988, *m.*	Edward J. *K.*, *b.* 1957
1771 I.	*Roden* (10th), Robert John Jocelyn, *b.* 1938, *s.* 1993, *m.*	Viscount Jocelyn, *b.* 1989
1801	*Romney* (7th), Michael Henry Marsham, *b.* 1910, *s.* 1975, *m.*	Julian C. *M.*, *b.* 1948
1703 S.*	*Rosebery* (7th), Neil Archibald Primrose (3rd *UK Earl Midlothian*, 1911), *b.* 1929, *s.* 1974, *m.*	Lord Dalmeny, *b.* 1967
1806 I.	*Rosse* (7th), William Brendan Parsons, *b.* 1936, *s.* 1979, *m.*	Lord Oxmantown, *b.* 1969
1801	*Rosslyn* (7th), Peter St Clair-Erskine, *b.* 1958, *s.* 1977, *m.*	Lord Loughborough, *b.* 1986
1457 S.	*Rothes* (21st), Ian Lionel Malcolm Leslie, *b.* 1932, *s.* 1975, *m.*	Lord Leslie, *b.* 1958
1861	° *Russell* (5th), Conrad Sebastian Robert Russell, FBA, *b.* 1937, *s.* 1987, *m.*	Viscount Amberley, *b.* 1968
1915	° *St Aldwyn* (3rd), Michael Henry Hicks Beach, *b.* 1950, *s.* 1992, *m.*	Hon. David S. *H. B.*, *b.* 1955
1815	*St Germans* (10th), Peregrine Nicholas Eliot, *b.* 1941, *s.* 1988.	Lord Eliot, *b.* 1966
1660	*Sandwich* (11th), John Edward Hollister Montagu, *b.* 1943, *s.* 1995, *m.*	Viscount Hinchingbrooke, *b.* 1969
1690	*Scarbrough* (12th), Richard Aldred Lumley (13th *Irish Visct. Lumley*, 1628), *b.* 1932, *s.* 1969, *m.*	Viscount Lumley, *b.* 1973
1701 S.	*Seafield* (13th), Ian Derek Francis Ogilvie-Grant, *b.* 1939, *s.* 1969, *m.*	Viscount Reidhaven, *b.* 1963
1882	*Selborne* (4th), John Roundell Palmer, KBE, FRS, *b.* 1940, *s.* 1971, *m.*	Viscount Wolmer, *b.* 1971
1646 S.	*Selkirk.* Disclaimed for life 1994. (*see* Lord Selkirk of Douglas, page 161)	Hon. John A. *Douglas-Hamilton*, *b.* 1978
1672	*Shaftesbury* (10th), Anthony Ashley-Cooper, *b.* 1938, *s.* 1961, *m.*	Lord Ashley, *b.* 1977
1756 I.*	*Shannon* (9th), Richard Bentinck Boyle (8th *Brit. Baron Carleton*, 1786), *b.* 1924, *s.* 1963.	Viscount Boyle, *b.* 1960
1442	*Shrewsbury and Waterford* (22nd), (I. 1446), Charles Henry John Benedict Crofton Chetwynd Chetwynd-Talbot (7th *Engl. Earl Talbot*, 1784), *b.* 1952, *s.* 1980, *m. Premier Earl of England and Ireland*	Viscount Ingestre, *b.* 1978
1961	*Snowdon* (1st), Anthony Charles Robert Armstrong-Jones, GCVO, *b.* 1930, *m. Constable of Caernarfon Castle* (*see also* page 117)	Viscount Linley, *b.* 1961 (*see also* page 117)
1765	° *Spencer* (9th), Charles Edward Maurice Spencer, *b.* 1964, *s.* 1992.	Viscount Althorp, *b.* 1994
1703 S.*	*Stair* (14th), John David James Dalrymple (7th *UK Baron, Oxenfoord*, 1841), *b.* 1961, *s.* 1996.	Hon. David H. *D.*, *b.* 1963
1984	*Stockton* (2nd), Alexander Daniel Alan Macmillan, MEP, *b.* 1943, *s.* 1986, *m.*	Viscount Macmillan of Ovenden, *b.* 1974
1821	*Stradbroke* (6th), Robert Keith Rous, *b.* 1937, *s.* 1983, *m.*	Viscount Dunwich, *b.* 1961
1847	*Strafford* (8th), Thomas Edmund Byng, *b.* 1936, *s.* 1984, *m.*	Viscount Enfield, *b.* 1964
1606 S.*	*Strathmore and Kinghorne* (18th), Michael Fergus Bowes Lyon (16th *Scott. Earl, Strathmore*, 1677; 18th *Scott. Earl, Kinghorne*, 1606; 5th *UK Earl, Strathmore and Kinghorne*, 1937), *b.* 1957, *s.* 1987, *m.*	Lord Glamis, *b.* 1986
1603	*Suffolk* (21st) and *Berkshire* (14th) (1626), Michael John James George Robert Howard, *b.* 1935, *s.* 1941, *m.*	Viscount Andover, *b.* 1974
1955	*Swinton* (2nd), David Yarburgh Cunliffe-Lister, *b.* 1937, *s.* 1972, *m.*	Hon. Nicholas J. *C.-L.*, *b.* 1939
1714	*Tankerville* (10th), Peter Grey Bennet, *b.* 1956, *s.* 1980.	Revd the Hon. George A. G. *B.*, *b.* 1925
1822	° *Temple of Stowe* (8th), (Walter) Grenville Algernon Temple-Gore-Langton, *b.* 1924, *s.* 1988, *m.*	Lord Langton, *b.* 1955
1815	*Verulam* (7th), John Duncan Grimston (11th *Irish Visct. Grimston*, 1719; 16th *Scott. Baron Forrester of Corstorphine*, 1633), *b.* 1951, *s.* 1973, *m.*	Viscount Grimston, *b.* 1978
1729	° *Waldegrave* (13th), James Sherbrooke Waldegrave, *b.* 1940, *s.* 1995, *m.*	Viscount Chewton, *b.* 1986
1759	*Warwick* (9th) and *Brooke* (9th) (*Brit.* 1746), Guy David Greville, *b.* 1957, *s.* 1996, *m.*	Lord Brooke, *b.* 1982
1633 S.*	*Wemyss* (12th) and *March* (8th) (S. 1697), Francis David Charteris, KT (5th *UK Baron Wemyss*, 1821), *b.* 1912, *s.* 1937, *m.*	Lord Neidpath, *b.* 1948
1621 I.	*Westmeath* (13th), William Anthony Nugent, *b.* 1928, *s.* 1971, *m.*	Hon. Sean C. W. *N.*, *b.* 1965
1624	*Westmorland* (16th), Anthony David Francis Henry Fane, *b.* 1951, *s.* 1993, *m.*	Hon. Harry St C. *F.*, *b.* 1953
1876	*Wharncliffe* (5th), Richard Alan Montagu Stuart Wortley, *b.* 1953, *s.* 1987, *m.*	Viscount Carlton, *b.* 1980
1801	*Wilton* (7th), Seymour William Arthur John Egerton, *b.* 1921, *s.* 1927, *m.*	Baron Ebury, *b.* 1934 (*see* page 149)
1628	*Winchilsea* (17th) and *Nottingham* (12th) (1681), Daniel James Hatfield Finch Hatton, *b.* 1967, *s.* 1999, *m.*	Robin Heneage *F.-H.*, *b.* 1939
1766 I.	° *Winterton* (8th), (Donald) David Turnour, *b.* 1943, *s.* 1991, *m.*	Robert C. *T.*, *b.* 1950
1956	*Woolton* (3rd), Simon Frederick Marquis, *b.* 1958, *s.* 1969, *m.*	None
1837	*Yarborough* (8th), Charles John Pelham, *b.* 1963, *s.* 1991, *m.*	Lord Worsley, *b.* 1990

COUNTESSES IN THEIR OWN RIGHT

Style, The Right Hon. the Countess (of) —
Husband, Untitled
Children's style, As for children of an Earl
For forms of address, *see* page 135

Created	Title, order of succession, name, etc.	Heir
1643 S.	*Dysart* (11th in line), Rosamund Agnes Greaves, *b.* 1914, *s.* 1975.	Lady Katherine *Grant of Rothiemurchus, b.* 1918
1633 S.	*Loudoun* (13th in line), Barbara Huddleston Abney-Hastings, *b.* 1919, *s.* 1960, *m.*	Lord Mauchline, *b.* 1942
c.1115 S.	*Mar* (31st in line), Margaret of Mar, *b.* 1940, *s.* 1975, *m. Premier Earldom of Scotland*	Mistress of Mar, *b.* 1963
1947	° *Mountbatten of Burma* (2nd in line), Patricia Edwina Victoria Knatchbull, CBE, *b.* 1924, *s.* 1979, *m.*	Lord Romsey, *b.* 1947 (*see also* page 148)
c.1235 S.	*Sutherland* (24th in line), Elizabeth Millicent Sutherland, *b.* 1921, *s.* 1963, *m.*	Lord Strathnaver, *b.* 1947

VISCOUNTS

Coronet, Sixteen silver balls
Style, The Right Hon. the Viscount —
Wife's style, The Right Hon. the Viscountess —
Children's style, 'The Hon.' before forename and family name
In Scotland, the heir apparent to a Viscount may be styled 'The Master of — (title of peer)'
For forms of address, *see* page 135

Created	Title, order of succession, name, etc.	Heir
1945	*Addison* (4th), William Matthew Wand Addison, *b.* 1945, *s.* 1992, *m.*	Hon. Paul W. *A., b.* 1973
1946	*Alanbrooke* (3rd), Alan Victor Harold Brooke, *b.* 1932, *s.* 1972.	None
1919	*Allenby* (3rd), Lt.-Col. Michael Jaffray Hynman Allenby, *b.* 1931, *s.* 1984, *m.*	Hon. Henry J. H. *A., b.* 1968
1911	*Allendale* (3rd), Wentworth Hubert Charles Beaumont, *b.* 1922, *s.* 1956.	Hon. Wentworth P. I. *B., b.* 1948
1642 S.	*of Arbuthnott* (16th), John Campbell Arbuthnott, KT, CBE, DSC, FRSE, *b.* 1924, *s.* 1966, *m.*	Master of Arbuthnott, *b.* 1950
1751 I.	*Ashbrook* (11th), Michael Llowarch Warburton Flower, *b.* 1935, *s.* 1995, *m.*	Hon. Rowland F. W. *F., b.* 1975
1917	*Astor* (4th), William Waldorf Astor, *b.* 1951, *s.* 1966, *m.*	Hon. William W. *A., b.* 1979
1781 I.	*Bangor* (8th), William Maxwell David Ward, *b.* 1948, *s.* 1993, *m.*	Hon. E. Nicholas *W., b.* 1953
1925	*Bearsted* (5th), Nicholas Alan Samuel, *b.* 1950, *s.* 1996, *m.*	Hon. Harry R. *S., b.* 1988
1963	*Blakenham* (2nd), Michael John Hare, *b.* 1938, *s.* 1982, *m.*	Hon. Caspar J. *H., b.* 1972
1935	*Bledisloe* (3rd), Christopher Hiley Ludlow Bathurst, QC, *b.* 1934, *s.* 1979.	Hon. Rupert E. L. *B., b.* 1964
1712	*Bolingbroke* (7th) and *St John* (8th) (1716), Kenneth Oliver Musgrave St John, *b.* 1927, *s.* 1974.	Hon. Henry F. *St J., b.* 1957
1960	*Boyd of Merton* (2nd), Simon Donald Rupert Neville Lennox-Boyd, *b.* 1939, *s.* 1983, *m.*	Hon. Benjamin A. *L.-B., b.* 1964
1717 I.*	*Boyne* (11th), Gustavus Michael Stucley Hamilton-Russell (5th *UK Baron Brancepeth,* 1866), *b.* 1965, *s.* 1995, *m.*	Hon. Brian G. *H.-R., b.* 1940
1929	*Brentford* (4th), Crispin William Joynson-Hicks, *b.* 1933, *s.* 1983, *m.*	Hon. Paul W. *J.-H., b.* 1971
1929	*Bridgeman* (3rd), Robin John Orlando Bridgeman, *b.* 1930, *s.* 1982, *m.*	Hon. William O. C. *B., b.* 1968
1868	*Bridport* (4th), Alexander Nelson Hood (7th *Duke, Brontë in Sicily,* 1799; 6th *Irish Baron Bridport,* 1794), *b.* 1948, *s.* 1969, *m.*	Hon. Peregrine A. N. *H., b.* 1974
1952	*Brookeborough* (3rd), Alan Henry Brooke, *b.* 1952, *s.* 1987, *m.*	Hon. Christopher A. *B., b.* 1954
1933	*Buckmaster* (3rd), Martin Stanley Buckmaster, OBE, *b.* 1921, *s.* 1974.	Hon. Colin J. *B., b.* 1923
1939	*Caldecote* (2nd), Robert Andrew Inskip, KBE, DSC, FREng., *b.* 1917, *s.* 1947, *m.*	Hon. Piers J. H. *I., b.* 1947
1941	*Camrose.* Disclaimed for life 1995. (*see* Baron Hartwell, page 159)	Hon. Adrian M. *Berry, b.* 1937
1954	*Chandos* (3rd), Thomas Orlando Lyttelton, *b.* 1953, *s.* 1980, *m.*	Hon. Oliver A. *L., b.* 1986

Created	Title, order of succession, name, etc.	Heir
1665 I.*	*Charlemont* (14th), John Day Caulfeild (18th *Irish Baron Caulfeild of Charlemont*, 1620), *b.* 1934, *s.* 1985, *m.*	Hon. John D. C., *b.* 1966
1921	*Chelmsford* (3rd), Frederic Jan Thesiger, *b.* 1931, *s.* 1970, *m.*	Hon. Frederic C. P. T., *b.* 1962
1717 I.	*Chetwynd* (10th), Adam Richard John Casson Chetwynd, *b.* 1935, *s.* 1965, *m.*	Hon. Adam D. C., *b.* 1969
1911	*Chilston* (4th), Alastair George Akers-Douglas, *b.* 1946, *s.* 1982, *m.*	Hon. Oliver I. A.-D., *b.* 1973
1902	*Churchill* (3rd), Victor George Spencer (5th *UK Baron Churchill*, 1815), *b.* 1934, *s.* 1973.	None to Viscountcy. To Barony, Richard H. R. S., *b.* 1926
1718	*Cobham* (11th), John William Leonard Lyttelton (8th *Irish Baron Westcote*, 1776), *b.* 1943, *s.* 1977, *m.*	Hon. Christopher C. L., *b.* 1947
1902	*Colville of Culross* (4th), John Mark Alexander Colville, QC (13th *Scott. Baron Colville of Culross*, 1604), *b.* 1933, *s.* 1945, *m.*	Master of Colville, *b.* 1959
1826	*Combermere* (5th), Michael Wellington Stapleton-Cotton, *b.* 1929, *s.* 1969, *m.*	Hon. Thomas R. W. S.-C., *b.* 1969
1917	*Cowdray* (4th), Michael Orlando Weetman Pearson (4th *UK Baron Cowdray*, 1910), *b.* 1944, *s.* 1995, *m.*	Hon. Peregrine J. D. P., *b.* 1994
1927	*Craigavon* (3rd), Janric Fraser Craig, *b.* 1944, *s.* 1974.	None
1886	*Cross* (3rd), Assheton Henry Cross, *b.* 1920, *s.* 1932.	None
1943	*Daventry* (3rd), Francis Humphrey Maurice FitzRoy Newdegate, *b.* 1921, *s.* 1986, *m.*	Hon. James E. F. N., *b.* 1960
1937	*Davidson* (2nd), John Andrew Davidson, *b.* 1928, *s.* 1970, *m.*	Hon. Malcolm W. M. D., *b.* 1934
1956	*De L'Isle* (2nd), Philip John Algernon Sidney, MBE (7th *UK Baron De L'Isle and Dudley*, 1835), *b.* 1945, *s.* 1991, *m.*	Hon. Philip W. E. S., *b.* 1985
1776 I.*	*De Vesci* (7th), Thomas Eustace Vesey (8th *Irish Baron Knapton*, 1750), *b.* 1955, *s.* 1983, *m.*	Hon. Oliver I. V., *b.* 1991
1917	*Devonport* (3rd), Terence Kearley, *b.* 1944, *s.* 1973.	Chester D. H. K., *b.* 1932
1964	*Dilhorne* (2nd), John Mervyn Manningham-Buller, *b.* 1932, *s.* 1980, *m.*	Hon. James E. M.-B., *b.* 1956
1622 I.	*Dillon* (22nd), Henry Benedict Charles Dillon, *b.* 1973, *s.* 1982.	Hon. Richard A. L. D., *b.* 1948
1785 I.	*Doneraile* (10th), Richard Allen St Leger, *b.* 1946, *s.* 1983, *m.*	Hon. Nathaniel W. R. St J. St L., *b.* 1971
1680 I.*	*Downe* (11th), John Christian George Dawnay (4th *UK Baron Dawnay*, 1897), *b.* 1935, *s.* 1965, *m.*	Hon. Richard H. D., *b.* 1967
1959	*Dunrossil* (2nd), John William Morrison, CMG, *b.* 1926, *s.* 1961, *m.*	Hon. Andrew W. R. M., *b.* 1953
1964	*Eccles* (2nd), John Dawson Eccles, CBE, *b.* 1931, *s.* 1999, *m.*	Hon. William David E., *b.* 1960
1897	*Esher* (4th), Lionel Gordon Baliol Brett, CBE, *b.* 1913, *s.* 1963, *m.*	Hon. Christopher L. B. B., *b.* 1936
1816	*Exmouth* (10th), Paul Edward Pellew, *b.* 1940, *s.* 1970, *m.*	Hon. Edward F. P., *b.* 1978
1620 S.	*Falkland* (15th), Lucius Edward William Plantagenet Cary, *b.* 1935, *s.* 1984, *m. Premier Scottish Viscount on the Roll*	Master of Falkland, *b.* 1963
1720	*Falmouth* (9th), George Hugh Boscawen (26th *Engl. Baron Le Despencer*, 1264), *b.* 1919, *s.* 1962, *m.*	Hon. Evelyn A. H. B., *b.* 1955
1720 I.*	*Gage* (8th), (Henry) Nicolas Gage (7th *Brit. Baron Gage*, 1790), *b.* 1934, *s.* 1993, *m.*	Hon. Henry W. G., *b.* 1975
1727 I.	*Galway* (12th), George Rupert Monckton-Arundell, *b.* 1922, *s.* 1980, *m.*	Hon. J. Philip M.-A., *b.* 1952
1478 I.*	*Gormanston* (17th), Jenico Nicholas Dudley Preston (5th *UK Baron Gormanston*, 1868), *b.* 1939, *s.* 1940, *w. Premier Viscount of Ireland*	Hon. Jenico F. T. P., *b.* 1974
1816 I.	*Gort* (9th), Foley Robert Standish Prendergast Vereker, *b.* 1951, *s.* 1995, *m.*	Hon. Robert F. P. V., *b.* 1993
1900	*Goschen* (4th), Giles John Harry Goschen, *b.* 1965, *s.* 1977, *m.*	None
1849	*Gough* (5th), Shane Hugh Maryon Gough, *b.* 1941, *s.* 1951.	None
1937	*Greenwood* (3rd), Michael George Hamar Greenwood, *b.* 1923, *s.* 1998.	†
1929	*Hailsham*. Disclaimed for life 1963. (*see* Lord Hailsham of St Marylebone, page 159)	Rt. Hon. Douglas M. *Hogg* QC, MP, *b.* 1945
1891	*Hambleden* (4th), William Herbert Smith, *b.* 1930, *s.* 1948, *m.*	Hon. William H. B. S., *b.* 1955
1884	*Hampden* (6th), Anthony David Brand, *b.* 1937, *s.* 1975, *m.*	Hon. Francis A. B., *b.* 1970
1936	*Hanworth* (3rd), David Stephen Geoffrey Pollock, *b.* 1946, *s.* 1996, *m.*	Hon. Richard C. S. P., *b.* 1951
1791 I.	*Harberton* (10th), Thomas de Vautort Pomeroy, *b.* 1910, *s.* 1980, *m.*	Henry Robert P., *b.* 1958
1846	*Hardinge* (6th), Charles Henry Nicholas Hardinge, *b.* 1956, *s.* 1984, *m.*	Hon. Andrew H. H., *b.* 1960
1791 I.	*Hawarden* (9th), (Robert) Connan Wyndham Leslie Maude, *b.* 1961, *s.* 1991, *m.*	Hon. Varian J. C. E. M., *b.* 1997
1960	*Head* (2nd), Richard Antony Head, *b.* 1937, *s.* 1983, *m.*	Hon. Henry J. H., *b.* 1980
1550	*Hereford* (18th), Robert Milo Leicester Devereux, *b.* 1932, *s.* 1952. *Premier Viscount of England*	Hon. Charles R. de B. D., *b.* 1975
1842	*Hill* (8th), Antony Rowland Clegg-Hill, *b.* 1931, *s.* 1974, *m.*	Peter D. R. C. C.-H., *b.* 1945
1796	*Hood* (7th), Alexander Lambert Hood (7th *Irish Baron, Hood*, 1782), *b.* 1914, *s.* 1981, *m.*	Hon. Henry L. A. H., *b.* 1958
1956	*Ingleby* (2nd), Martin Raymond Peake, *b.* 1926, *s.* 1966, *w.*	None
1945	*Kemsley* (3rd), Richard Gomer Berry, *b.* 1951, *s.* 1999, *m.*	Hon. Edward A. M., B., *b.* 1960
1911	*Knollys* (3rd), David Francis Dudley Knollys, *b.* 1931, *s.* 1966, *m.*	Hon. Patrick N. M. K., *b.* 1962

Created	*Title, order of succession, name, etc.*	*Heir*
1895	*Knutsford* (6th), Michael Holland-Hibbert, *b.* 1926, *s.* 1986, *m.*	Hon. Henry T. *H.-H., b.* 1959
1945	*Lambert* (3rd), Michael John Lambert, *b.* 1912, *s.* 1989, *m.*	None
1954	*Leathers* (3rd), Christopher Graeme Leathers, *b.* 1941, *s.* 1996, *m.*	Hon. James F. *L., b.* 1969
1922	*Leverhulme* (3rd), Philip William Bryce Lever, KG,TD, *b.* 1915, *s.* 1949, *w.*	None
1781 I.	*Lifford* (9th), (Edward) James Wingfield Hewitt, *b.* 1949, *s.* 1987, *m.*	Hon. James T. W. *H., b.* 1979
1921	*Long* (4th), Richard Gerard Long, CBE, *b.* 1929, *s.* 1967, *m.*	Hon. James R. *L., b.* 1960
1957	*Mackintosh of Halifax* (3rd), (John) Clive Mackintosh, *b.* 1958, *s.* 1980, *m.*	Hon. Thomas H. G. *M., b.* 1985
1955	*Malvern* (3rd), Ashley Kevin Godfrey Huggins, *b.* 1949, *s.* 1978.	Hon. M. James *H., b.* 1928
1945	*Marchwood* (3rd), David George Staveley Penny, *b.* 1936, *s.* 1979, *w.*	Hon. Peter G. W. *P., b.* 1965
1942	*Margesson* (2nd), Francis Vere Hampden Margesson, *b.* 1922, *s.* 1965, *m.*	Maj. Hon. Richard F. D. *M., b.* 1960
1660 I.*	*Massereene* (14th) and *Ferrard* (7th) (1797), John David Clotworthy Whyte-Melville Foster Skeffington (7th *UK Baron, Oriel,* 1821), *b.* 1940, *s.* 1992, *m.*	Hon. Charles J. C. W.-M. F. *S., b.* 1973
1802	*Melville* (9th), Robert David Ross Dundas, *b.* 1937, *s.* 1971, *m.*	Hon. Robert H. K. *D., b.* 1984
1916	*Mersey* (4th), Richard Maurice Clive Bigham (13th *Scott. Lord Nairne,* 1681, *s.* 1995), *b.* 1934, *s.* 1979, *m.*	Hon. Edward J. H. *B.* Master of Nairne, *b.* 1966
1717 I.*	*Midleton* (12th), Alan Henry Brodrick (9th *Brit. Baron Brodrick of Peper Harow,* 1796), *b.* 1949, *s.* 1988, *m.*	Hon. Ashley R. *B., b.* 1980
1962	*Mills* (3rd), Christopher Philip Roger Mills, *b.* 1956, *s.* 1988, *m.*	None
1716 I.	*Molesworth* (12th), Robert Bysse Kelham Molesworth, *b.* 1959, *s.* 1997.	Hon. William J. C. *M., b.* 1960
1801 I.*	*Monck* (7th), Charles Stanley Monck (4th *UK Baron, Monck,* 1866), *b.* 1953, *s.* 1982. (does not use title)	Hon. George S. *M., b.* 1957
1957	*Monckton of Brenchley* (2nd), Maj.-Gen. Gilbert Walter Riversdale Monckton, CB, OBE, MC, *b.* 1915, *s.* 1965, *m.*	Hon. Christopher W. *M., b.* 1952
1946	*Montgomery of Alamein* (2nd), David Bernard Montgomery, CBE, *b.* 1928, *s.* 1976, *m.*	Hon. Henry D. *M., b.* 1954
1550 I.*	*Mountgarret* (17th), Richard Henry Piers Butler (4th *UK Baron Mountgarret,* 1911), *b.* 1936, *s.* 1966, *m.*	Hon. Piers J. R. *B., b.* 1961
1952	*Norwich* (2nd), John Julius Cooper, CVO, *b.* 1929, *s.* 1954, *m.*	Hon. Jason C. D. B. *C., b.* 1959
1651 S.	*of Oxfuird* (13th), George Hubbard Makgill, CBE, *b.* 1934, *s.* 1986, *m.*	Master of Oxfuird, *b.* 1969
1873	*Portman* (10th), Christopher Edward Berkeley Portman, *b.* 1958, *s.* 1999, *m.*	Hon. Luke O. B. *P., b.* 1984
1743 I.*	*Powerscourt* (10th), Mervyn Niall Wingfield (4th *UK Baron Powerscourt,* 1885), *b.* 1935, *s.* 1973, *m.*	Hon. Mervyn A. *W., b.* 1963
1900	*Ridley* (4th), Matthew White Ridley, KG, GCVO, TD, *b.* 1925, *s.* 1964, *m.* Lord Steward	Hon. Matthew W. *R., b.* 1958
1960	*Rochdale* (2nd), St John Durival Kemp, *b.* 1938, *s.* 1993, *m.*	Hon. Jonathan H. D. *K., b.* 1961
1919	*Rothermere* (4th), (Harold) Jonathan Esmond Vere Harmsworth, *b.* 1967, *s.* 1998, *m.*	Hon. Esmond Vyvyan *H., b.* 1967
1937	*Runciman of Doxford* (3rd), Walter Garrison Runciman (Garry), CBE, FBA (4th *UK Baron, Runciman,* 1933), *b.* 1934, *s.* 1989, *m.*	Hon. David W. *R., b.* 1967
1918	*St Davids* (3rd), Colwyn Jestyn John Philipps (20th *Engl. Baron Strange of Knokin,* 1299; 8th *Engl. Baron, Hungerford,* 1426; *Baron De Moleyns,* 1445), *b.* 1939, *s.* 1991, *m.*	Hon. Rhodri C. *P., b.* 1966
1801	*St Vincent* (7th), Ronald George James Jervis, *b.* 1905, *s.* 1940, *m.*	Hon. Edward R. J. *J., b.* 1951
1937	*Samuel* (3rd), David Herbert Samuel, OBE, PH.D., *b.* 1922, *s.* 1978, *m.*	Hon. Dan J. *S., b.* 1925
1911	*Scarsdale* (3rd), Francis John Nathaniel Curzon (7th *Brit. Baron Scarsdale,* 1761), *b.* 1924, *s.* 1977, *m.*	Hon. Peter G. N. *C., b.* 1949
1905	*Selby* (5th), Edward Thomas William Gully, *b.* 1967, *s.* 1997, *m.*	Hon. Christopher R. T. *G., b.* 1993
1805	*Sidmouth* (7th), John Tonge Anthony Pellew Addington, *b.* 1914, *s.* 1976, *m.*	Hon. Jeremy F. *A., b.* 1947
1940	*Simon* (3rd), Jan David Simon, *b.* 1940, *s.* 1993, *m.*	None
1960	*Slim* (2nd), John Douglas Slim, OBE, *b.* 1927, *s.* 1970, *m.*	Hon. Mark W. R. *S., b.* 1960
1954	*Soulbury* (2nd), James Herwald Ramsbotham, *b.* 1915, *s.* 1971, *w.*	Hon. Sir Peter E. *R.* GCMG, GCVO, *b.* 1919
1776 I.	*Southwell* (7th), Pyers Anthony Joseph Southwell, *b.* 1930, *s.* 1960, *m.*	Hon. Richard A. P. *S., b.* 1956
1942	*Stansgate.* Disclaimed for life 1963. (*Rt. Hon. Anthony Neil Wedgwood Benn,* MP, *b.*1925, *s.*1960, *m.*)	Stephen M. W. *B., b.* 1951
1959	*Stuart of Findhorn* (2nd), David Randolph Moray Stuart, *b.* 1924, *s.* 1971, *m.*	Hon. J. Dominic *S., b.* 1948
1957	*Tenby* (3rd), William Lloyd George, *b.* 1927, *s.* 1983, *m.*	Hon. Timothy H. G. L. *G., b.* 1962
1952	*Thurso* (3rd), John Archibald Sinclair, *b.* 1953, *s.* 1995, *m.*	Hon. James A. R. *S., b.* 1984
1721	*Torrington* (11th), Timothy Howard St George Byng, *b.* 1943, *s.* 1961, *m.*	John L. *B.,* MC, *b.* 1919
1936	*Trenchard* (3rd), Hugh Trenchard, *b.* 1951, *s.* 1987, *m.*	Hon. Alexander T. *T., b.* 1978
1921	*Ullswater* (2nd), Nicholas James Christopher Lowther, PC, *b.* 1942, *s.* 1949, *m.*	Hon. Benjamin J. *L., b.* 1975
1621 I.	*Valentia* (15th), Richard John Dighton Annesley, *b.* 1929, *s.* 1983, *m.*	Hon. Francis W. D. *A., b.* 1959

Created	Title, order of succession, name, etc.	Heir
1952	*Waverley* (3rd), John Desmond Forbes Anderson, *b.* 1949, *s.* 1990.	None
1938	*Weir* (3rd), William Kenneth James Weir, *b.* 1933, *s.* 1975, *m.*	Hon. James W. H. *W.*, *b.* 1965
1918	*Wimborne* (4th), Ivor Mervyn Vigors Guest (5th *UK Baron Wimborne*, 1880), *b.* 1968, *s.* 1993.	Hon. Julian J. *G.*, *b.* 1945
1923	*Younger of Leckie* (4th), George Kenneth Hotson Younger, KT, KCVO, TD, PC (*Baron Younger of Prestwick* (life peerage), 1992), *b.* 1931, *s.* 1997, *m.*	Hon. James E. G. *Y.*, *b.* 1955

BARONS/LORDS

Coronet, Six silver balls
Style, The Right Hon. the Lord __. In the Peerage of Scotland there is no rank of Baron; the equivalent rank is Lord of Parliament (*see* page 136) and Scottish peers should always be styled 'Lord', never 'Baron'
Wife's style, The Right Hon. the Lady __
Children's style, 'The Hon.' before forename and family name
In Scotland, the heir apparent to a Lord may be styled 'The Master of __ (title of peer)'
For forms of address, *see* page 135

Created	Title, order of succession, name, etc.	Heir
1911	*Aberconway* (3rd), Charles Melville McLaren, *b.* 1913, *s.* 1953, *m.*	Hon. H. Charles *M.*, *b.* 1948
1873	*Aberdare* (4th), Morys George Lyndhurst Bruce, KBE, PC, *b.* 1919, *s.* 1957, *m.*	Hon. Alastair J. L. *B.*, *b.* 1947
1835	*Abinger* (8th), James Richard Scarlett, *b.* 1914, *s.* 1943, *m.*	Hon. James H. *S.*, *b.* 1959
1869	*Acton* (4th), Richard Gerald Lyon-Dalberg-Acton, *b.* 1941, *s.* 1989, *m.*	Hon. John C. F. H. *L.-D.-A.*, *b.* 1966
1887	*Addington* (6th), Dominic Bryce Hubbard, *b.* 1963, *s.* 1982.	Hon. Michael W. L. *H.*, *b.* 1965
1896	*Aldenham* (6th) and *Hunsdon of Hunsdon* (4th) (1923), Vicary Tyser Gibbs, *b.* 1948, *s.* 1986, *m.*	Hon. Humphrey W. F. *G.*, *b.* 1989
1962	*Aldington* (1st), Toby Austin Richard William Low, KCMG, CBE, DSO, TD, PC, *b.* 1914.	Hon. Charles H. S. *L.*, *b.* 1948
1945	*Altrincham*. Disclaimed for life 1963. (*John Edward Poynder Grigg, b.* 1924, *s.* 1955, *m.*)	Hon. Anthony U. D. D. *G.*, *b.* 1934
1929	*Alvingham* (2nd), Maj.-Gen. Robert Guy Eardley Yerburgh, CBE, *b.* 1926, *s.* 1955, *m.*	Capt. Hon. Robert R. G. *Y.*, *b.* 1956
1892	*Amherst of Hackney* (4th), William Hugh Amherst Cecil, *b.* 1940, *s.* 1980, *m.*	Hon. H. William A. *C.*, *b.* 1968
1881	*Ampthill* (4th), Geoffrey Denis Erskine Russell, CBE, PC, *b.* 1921, *s.* 1973.	Hon. David W. E. *R.*, *b.* 1947
1947	*Amwell* (3rd), Keith Norman Montague, *b.* 1943, *s.* 1990, *m.*	Hon. Ian K. *M.*, *b.* 1973
1863	*Annaly* (6th), Luke Richard White, *b.* 1954, *s.* 1990, *m.*	Hon. Luke H. *W.*, *b.* 1990
1885	*Ashbourne* (4th), Edward Barry Greynville Gibson, *b.* 1933, *s.* 1983, *m.*	Hon. Edward C. d'O. *G.*, *b.* 1967
1835	*Ashburton* (7th), John Francis Harcourt Baring, KG, KCVO, *b.* 1928, *s.* 1991, *m.*	Hon. Mark F. R. *B.*, *b.* 1958
1892	*Ashcombe* (4th), Henry Edward Cubitt, *b.* 1924, *s.* 1962, *m.*	Mark E. *C.*, *b.* 1964
1911	*Ashton of Hyde* (3rd), Thomas John Ashton, TD, *b.* 1926, *s.* 1983, *m.*	Hon. Thomas H. *A.*, *b.* 1958
1800 I.	*Ashtown* (7th), Nigel Clive Crosby Trench, KCMG, *b.* 1916, *s.* 1990, *m.*	Hon. Roderick N. G. *T.*, *b.* 1944
1956	*Astor of Hever* (3rd), John Jacob Astor, *b.* 1946, *s.* 1984, *m.*	Hon. Charles G. J. *A.*, *b.* 1990
1789 I.*	*Auckland* (10th), Robert Ian Burnard Eden (10th *Brit. Baron Auckland*, 1793), *b.* 1962, *s.* 1997, *m.*	Hon. Ronald J. *E.*, *b.* 1931
1313	*Audley.* The 25th Lord Audley died in July 1997, leaving three co-heiresses	
1900	*Avebury* (4th), Eric Reginald Lubbock, *b.* 1928, *s.* 1971, *m.*	Hon. Lyulph A. J. *L.*, *b.* 1954
1718 I.	*Aylmer* (13th), Michael Anthony Aylmer, *b.* 1923, *s.* 1982, *m.*	Hon. A. Julian *A.*, *b.* 1951
1929	*Baden-Powell* (3rd), Robert Crause Baden-Powell, *b.* 1936, *s.* 1962, *m.*	Hon. David M. *B.-P.*, *b.* 1940
1780	*Bagot* (9th), Heneage Charles Bagot, *b.* 1914, *s.* 1979, *m.*	Hon. C. H. Shaun *B.*, *b.* 1944
1953	*Baillieu* (3rd), James William Latham Baillieu, *b.* 1950, *s.* 1973, *m.*	Hon. Robert L. *B.*, *b.* 1979
1607 S.	*Balfour of Burleigh* (8th), Robert Bruce, FRSE, *b.* 1927, *s.* 1967, *m.*	Hon. Victoria B., *b.* 1973
1945	*Balfour of Inchrye* (2nd), Ian Balfour, *b.* 1924, *s.* 1988, *m.*	None
1924	*Banbury of Southam* (3rd), Charles William Banbury, *b.* 1953, *s.* 1981, *m.*	None
1698	*Barnard* (11th), Harry John Neville Vane, TD, *b.* 1923, *s.* 1964.	Hon. Henry F. C. *V.*, *b.* 1959
1887	*Basing* (5th), Neil Lutley Sclater-Booth, *b.* 1939, *s.* 1983, *m.*	Hon. Stuart W. *S.-B.*, *b.* 1969
1917	*Beaverbrook* (3rd), Maxwell William Humphrey Aitken, *b.* 1951, *s.* 1985, *m.*	Hon. Maxwell F. *A.*, *b.* 1977
1647 S.	*Belhaven and Stenton* (13th), Robert Anthony Carmichael Hamilton, *b.* 1927, *s.* 1961, *m.*	Master of Belhaven, *b.* 1953

Created	Title, order of succession, name, etc.	Heir
1848 I.	*Bellew* (7th), James Bryan Bellew, *b.* 1920, *s.* 1981, *m.*	Hon. Bryan E. *B.*, *b.* 1943
1856	*Belper* (4th), (Alexander) Ronald George Strutt, *b.* 1912, *s.* 1956.	Hon. Richard H. *S.*, *b.* 1941
1938	*Belstead* (2nd), John Julian Ganzoni, PC, *b.* 1932, *s.* 1958.	None
1421	*Berkeley* (18th), Anthony Fitzhardinge Gueterbock, OBE, *b.* 1939, *s.* 1992, *m.*	Hon. Thomas F. *G.*, *b.* 1969
1922	*Bethell* (4th), Nicholas William Bethell, MEP, *b.* 1938, *s.* 1967, *m.*	Hon. James N. *B.*, *b.* 1967
1938	*Bicester* (3rd), Angus Edward Vivian Smith, *b.* 1932, *s.* 1968.	Hugh C. V. *S.*, *b.* 1934
1903	*Biddulph* (5th), (Anthony) Nicholas Colin Maitland Biddulph, *b.* 1959, *s.* 1988, *m.*	Hon. Robert J. *M. B.*, *b.* 1994
1938	*Birdwood* (3rd), Mark William Ogilvie Birdwood, *b.* 1938, *s.* 1962, *m.*	None
1958	*Birkett* (2nd), Michael Birkett, *b.* 1929, *s.* 1962, *m.*	Hon. Thomas *B.*, *b.* 1982
1907	*Blyth* (4th), Anthony Audley Rupert Blyth, *b.* 1931, *s.* 1977, *m.*	Hon. Riley A. J. *B.*, *b.* 1955
1797	*Bolton* (7th), Richard William Algar Orde-Powlett, *b.* 1929, *s.* 1963, *m.*	Hon. Harry A. N. *O.-P.*, *b.* 1954
1452 S.	*Borthwick* (24th), John Hugh Borthwick, *b.* 1940, *s.* 1997, *m.*	Hon. James H. A. *B. of Glengelt*, *b.* 1940
1922	*Borwick* (4th), James Hugh Myles Borwick, MC, *b.* 1917, *s.* 1961, *m.*	Hon. Robin S. *B.*, *b.* 1927
1761	*Boston* (10th), Timothy George Frank Boteler Irby, *b.* 1939, *s.* 1978, *m.*	Hon. George W. E. B. *I.*, *b.* 1971
1942	*Brabazon of Tara* (3rd), Ivon Anthony Moore-Brabazon, *b.* 1946, *s.* 1974, *m.*	Hon. Benjamin R. *M.-B.*, *b.* 1983
1880	*Brabourne* (7th), John Ulick Knatchbull, CBE, *b.* 1924, *s.* 1943, *m.*	Lord Romsey, *b.* 1947 (*see* page 144)
1925	*Bradbury* (3rd), John Bradbury, *b.* 1940, *s.* 1994, *m.*	Hon. John *B.*, *b.* 1973
1962	*Brain* (2nd), Christopher Langdon Brain, *b.* 1926, *s.* 1966, *m.*	Hon. Michael C. *B.*, DM, FRCP, *b.* 1928
1938	*Brassey of Apethorpe* (3rd), David Henry Brassey, OBE, *b.* 1932, *s.* 1967, *m.*	Hon. Edward *B.*, *b.* 1964
1788	*Braybrooke* (10th), Robin Henry Charles Neville, *b.* 1932, *s.* 1990, *m.*	George *N.*, *b.* 1943
1957	*Bridges* (2nd), Thomas Edward Bridges, GCMG, *b.* 1927, *s.* 1969, *m.*	Hon. Mark T. *B.*, *b.* 1954
1945	*Broadbridge* (3rd), Peter Hewett Broadbridge, *b.* 1938, *s.* 1972, *m.*	Martin H. *B.*, *b.* 1929
1933	*Brocket* (3rd), Charles Ronald George Nall-Cain, *b.* 1952, *s.* 1967, *m.*	Hon. Alexander C. C. *N.-C.*, *b.* 1984
1860	*Brougham and Vaux* (5th), Michael John Brougham, CBE, *b.* 1938, *s.* 1967.	Hon. Charles W. *B.*, *b.* 1971
1945	*Broughshane* (3rd), (William) Kensington Davison, DSO, DFC, *b.* 1914, *s.* 1995.	None
1776	*Brownlow* (7th), Edward John Peregrine Cust, *b.* 1936, *s.* 1978, *m.*	Hon. Peregrine E. Q. *C.*, *b.* 1974
1942	*Bruntisfield* (2nd), John Robert Warrender, OBE, MC, TD, *b.* 1921, *s.* 1993, *m.*	Hon. Michael J. V. *W.*, *b.* 1949
1950	*Burden* (3rd), Andrew Philip Burden, *b.* 1959, *s.* 1995.	Hon. Fraser W. E. *B.*, *b.* 1964
1529	*Burgh* (7th), Alexander Peter Willoughby Leith, *b.* 1935, *s.* 1959, *m.*	Hon. A. Gregory D. *L.*, *b.* 1958
1903	*Burnham* (6th), Hugh John Frederick Lawson, *b.* 1931, *s.* 1993, *m.*	Hon. Harry F. A. *L.*, *b.* 1968
1897	*Burton* (3rd), Michael Evan Victor Baillie, *b.* 1924, *s.* 1962, *m.*	Hon. Evan M. R. *B.*, *b.* 1949
1643	*Byron* (13th), Robert James Byron, *b.* 1950, *s.* 1989, *m.*	Hon. Charles R. G. *B.*, *b.* 1990
1937	*Cadman* (3rd), John Anthony Cadman, *b.* 1938, *s.* 1966, *m.*	Hon. Nicholas A. J. *C.*, *b.* 1977
1945	*Calverley* (3rd), Charles Rodney Muff, *b.* 1946, *s.* 1971, *m.*	Hon. Jonathan E. *M.*, *b.* 1975
1383	*Camoys* (7th), (Ralph) Thomas Campion George Sherman Stonor, GCVO, PC, *b.* 1940, *s.* 1976, *m. Lord Chamberlain*	Hon. R. William R. T. *S.*, *b.* 1974
1715 I.	*Carbery* (11th), Peter Ralfe Harrington Evans-Freke, *b.* 1920, *s.* 1970, *m.*	Hon. Michael P. *E.-F.*, *b.* 1942
1834 I.*	*Carew* (7th), Patrick Thomas Conolly-Carew (7th *UK Baron, Carew*, 1838), *b.* 1938, *s.* 1994, *m.*	Hon. William P. *C.-C.*, *b.* 1973
1916	*Carnock* (4th), David Henry Arthur Nicolson, *b.* 1920, *s.* 1982.	Nigel *N.*, MBE, *b.* 1917
1796 I.*	*Carrington* (6th), Peter Alexander Rupert Carington, KG, GCMG, CH, MC, PC (6th *Brit. Baron Carrington*, 1797), *b.* 1919, *s.* 1938, *m.*	Hon. Rupert F. J. *C.*, *b.* 1948
1812 I.	*Castlemaine* (8th), Roland Thomas John Handcock, MBE, *b.* 1943, *s.* 1973, *m.*	Hon. Ronan M. E. *H.*, *b.* 1989
1936	*Catto* (2nd), Stephen Gordon Catto, *b.* 1923, *s.* 1959, *m.*	Hon. Innes G. *C.*, *b.* 1950
1918	*Cawley* (3rd), Frederick Lee Cawley, *b.* 1913, *s.* 1954, *m.*	Hon. John F. *C.*, *b.* 1946
1603	*Cecil.* A subsidiary title of the Marquess of Salisbury. His heir Viscount Cranborne, PC, was given a Writ in Acceleration in this title to enable him to sit in the House of Lords whilst his father is still alive (*see also* page 139)	
1937	*Chatfield* (2nd), Ernle David Lewis Chatfield, *b.* 1917, *s.* 1967, *m.*	None
1858	*Chesham* (6th), Nicholas Charles Cavendish, *b.* 1941, *s.* 1989, *m.*	Hon. Charles G. C. *C.*, *b.* 1974
1945	*Chetwode* (2nd), Philip Chetwode, *b.* 1937, *s.* 1950, *m.*	Hon. Roger *C.*, *b.* 1968
1945	*Chorley* (2nd), Roger Richard Edward Chorley, *b.* 1930, *s.* 1978, *m.*	Hon. Nicholas R. D. *C.*, *b.* 1966
1858	*Churston* (5th), John Francis Yarde-Buller, *b.* 1934, *s.* 1991, *m.*	Hon. Benjamin F. A. *Y.-B.*, *b.* 1974
1946	*Citrine* (3rd), Ronald Eric Citrine, *b.* 1919, *s.* 1997, *m.* (does not use title)	None
1800 I.	*Clanmorris* (8th), Simon John Ward Bingham, *b.* 1937, *s.* 1988, *m.*	Robert D. de B. *B.*, *b.* 1942
1672	*Clifford of Chudleigh* (14th), Thomas Hugh Clifford, *b.* 1948, *s.* 1988, *m.*	Hon. Alexander T. H. *C.*, *b.* 1985
1299	*Clinton* (22nd), Gerard Nevile Mark Fane Trefusis, *b.* 1934, *title called out of abeyance* 1965, *m.*	Hon. Charles P. R. F. *T.*, *b.* 1962
1955	*Clitheroe* (2nd), Ralph John Assheton, *b.* 1929, *s.* 1984, *m.*	Hon. Ralph C. *A.*, *b.* 1962
1919	*Clwyd* (3rd), (John) Anthony Roberts, *b.* 1935, *s.* 1987, *m.*	Hon. J. Murray *R.*, *b.* 1971
1948	*Clydesmuir* (3rd), David Ronald Colville, *b.* 1949, *s.* 1996, *m.*	Hon. Richard *C.*, *b.* 1980

Created	Title, order of succession, name, etc.	Heir
1960	*Cobbold* (2nd), David Antony Fromanteel Lytton Cobbold, *b.* 1937, *s.* 1987, *m.*	Hon. Henry F. L. C., *b.* 1962
1919	*Cochrane of Cults* (4th), (Ralph Henry) Vere Cochrane, *b.* 1926, *s.* 1990, *m.*	Hon. Thomas H. V. C., *b.* 1957
1954	*Coleraine* (2nd), (James) Martin (Bonar) Law, *b.* 1931, *s.* 1980, *m.*	Hon. James P. B. L., *b.* 1975
1873	*Coleridge* (5th), William Duke Coleridge, *b.* 1937, *s.* 1984, *m.*	Hon. James D. C., *b.* 1967
1946	*Colgrain* (3rd), David Colin Campbell, *b.* 1920, *s.* 1973, *m.*	Hon. Alastair C. L. C., *b.* 1951
1917	*Colwyn* (3rd), (Ian) Anthony Hamilton-Smith, CBE, *b.* 1942, *s.* 1966, *m.*	Hon. Craig P. H.-S., *b.* 1968
1956	*Colyton* (2nd), Alisdair John Munro Hopkinson, *b.* 1958, *s.* 1996, *m.*	Hon. James P. M. H., *b.* 1983
1841	*Congleton* (8th), Christopher Patrick Parnell, *b.* 1930, *s.* 1967, *m.*	Hon. John P. C. P., *b.* 1959
1927	*Cornwallis* (3rd), Fiennes Neil Wykeham Cornwallis, OBE, *b.* 1921, *s.* 1982, *m.*	Hon. F. W. Jeremy C., *b.* 1946
1874	*Cottesloe* (5th), Cdr. John Tapling Fremantle, *b.* 1927, *s.* 1994, *m.*	Hon. Thomas F. H. F., *b.* 1966
1929	*Craigmyle* (4th), Thomas Columba Shaw, *b.* 1960, *s.* 1998, *m.*	Hon. Alexander F. S., *b.* 1988
1899	*Cranworth* (3rd), Philip Bertram Gurdon, *b.* 1940, *s.* 1964, *m.*	Hon. Sacha W. R. G., *b.* 1970
1959	*Crathorne* (2nd), Charles James Dugdale, *b.* 1939, *s.* 1977, *m.*	Hon. Thomas A. J. D., *b.* 1977
1892	*Crawshaw* (5th), David Gerald Brooks, *b.* 1934, *s.* 1997, *m.*	Hon. John P. B., *b.* 1938
1940	*Croft* (3rd), Bernard William Henry Page Croft, *b.* 1949, *s.* 1997, *m.*	None
1797 I.	*Crofton* (7th), Guy Patrick Gilbert Crofton, *b.* 1951, *s.* 1989, *m.*	Hon. E. Harry P. C., *b.* 1988
1375	*Cromwell* (7th), Godfrey John Bewicke-Copley, *b.* 1960, *s.* 1982, *m.*	Hon. David G. B.-C., *b.* 1997
1947	*Crook* (2nd), Douglas Edwin Crook, *b.* 1926, *s.* 1989, *m.*	Hon. Robert D. E. C., *b.* 1955
1920	*Cullen of Ashbourne* (2nd), Charles Borlase Marsham Cokayne, MBE, *b.* 1912, *s.* 1932, *w.*	Hon. Edmund W. M. C., *b.* 1916
1914	*Cunliffe* (3rd), Roger Cunliffe, *b.* 1932, *s.* 1963, *m.*	Hon. Henry C., *b.* 1962
1927	*Daresbury* (4th), Peter Gilbert Greenall, *b.* 1953, *s.* 1996, *m.*	Hon. Thomas E. G., *b.* 1984
1924	*Darling* (2nd), Robert Charles Henry Darling, *b.* 1919, *s.* 1936, *m.*	Hon. R. Julian H. D., *b.* 1944
1946	*Darwen* (3rd), Roger Michael Davies, *b.* 1938, *s.* 1988, *m.*	Hon. Paul D., *b.* 1962
1932	*Davies* (3rd), David Davies, *b.* 1940, *s.* 1944, *m.*	Hon. David D. D., *b.* 1975
1299	*de Clifford* (27th), John Edward Southwell Russell, *b.* 1928, *s.* 1982, *m.*	Hon. William S. R., *b.* 1930
1851	*De Freyne* (7th), Francis Arthur John French, *b.* 1927, *s.* 1935, *m.*	Hon. Fulke C. A. J. F., *b.* 1957
1838	*de Mauley* (6th), Gerald John Ponsonby, *b.* 1921, *s.* 1962, *m.*	Hon. Col. Thomas M. P., TD, *b.* 1930
1887	*De Ramsey* (4th), John Ailwyn Fellowes, *b.* 1942, *s.* 1993, *m.*	Hon. Freddie J. F., *b.* 1978
1264	*de Ros* (28th), Peter Trevor Maxwell, *b.* 1958, *s.* 1983, *m. Premier Baron of England*	Hon. Finbar J. M., *b.* 1988
1831	*de Saumarez* (7th), Eric Douglas Saumarez, *b.* 1956, *s.* 1991, *m.*	Hon. Victor T. S., *b.* 1956
1910	*de Villiers* (3rd), Arthur Percy de Villiers, *b.* 1911, *s.* 1934.	Hon. Alexander C. de V., *b.* 1940
1812 I.	*Decies* (7th), Marcus Hugh Tristram de la Poer Beresford, *b.* 1948, *s.* 1992, *m.*	Hon. Robert M. D. de la P. B., *b.* 1988
1821	*Delamere* (5th), Hugh George Cholmondeley, *b.* 1934, *s.* 1979, *m.*	Hon. Thomas P. G. C., *b.* 1968
1937	*Denham* (2nd), Bertram Stanley Mitford Bowyer, KBE, PC, *b.* 1927, *s.* 1948, *m.*	Hon. Richard G. G. B., *b.* 1959
1834	*Denman* (5th), Charles Spencer Denman, CBE, MC, TD, *b.* 1916, *s.* 1971, *w.*	Hon. Richard T. S. D., *b.* 1946
1885	*Deramore* (6th), Richard Arthur de Yarburgh-Bateson, *b.* 1911, *s.* 1964, *m.*	None
1881	*Derwent* (5th), Robin Evelyn Leo Vanden-Bempde-Johnstone, LVO, *b.* 1930, *s.* 1986, *m.*	Hon. Francis P. H. V.-B.-J., *b.* 1965
1930	*Dickinson* (2nd), Richard Clavering Hyett Dickinson, *b.* 1926, *s.* 1943, *m.*	Hon. Martin H. D., *b.* 1961
1620 I.*	*Digby* (12th), Edward Henry Kenelm Digby, KCVO (6th *Brit. Baron Digby*, 1765), *b.* 1924, *s.* 1964, *m.*	Hon. Henry N. K. D., *b.* 1954
1615	*Dormer* (17th), Geoffrey Henry Dormer, *b.* 1920, *s.* 1995, *m.*	Hon. William R. D., *b.* 1960
1943	*Dowding* (3rd), Piers Hugh Tremenheere Dowding, *b.* 1948, *s.* 1992.	Hon. Mark D. J. D., *b.* 1949
1800 I.	*Dufferin and Clandeboye.* The 10th Baron died in 1991. Heir had not established his claim to the title at the time of going to press	Sir John *Blackwood*, Bt., *b.* 1944
1929	*Dulverton* (3rd), (Gilbert) Michael Hamilton Wills, *b.* 1944, *s.* 1992.	Hon. Robert A. H. W., *b.* 1983
1800 I.	*Dunalley* (7th), Henry Francis Cornelius Prittie, *b.* 1948, *s.* 1992, *m.*	Hon. Joel H. P., *b.* 1981
1324 I.	*Dunboyne* (28th), Patrick Theobald Tower Butler, VRD, *b.* 1917, *s.* 1945, *m.*	Hon. John F. B., *b.* 1951
1892	*Dunleath* (6th), Brian Henry Mulholland, *b.* 1950, *s.* 1997, *m.*	Hon. Andrew H. M., *b.* 1981
1439 I.	*Dunsany* (20th), Edward John Carlos Plunkett, *b.* 1939, *s.* 1999, *m.*	Hon. Randal P., *b.* 1983
1780	*Dynevor* (9th), Richard Charles Uryan Rhys, *b.* 1935, *s.* 1962.	Hon. Hugo G. U. R., *b.* 1966
1857	*Ebury* (6th), Francis Egerton Grosvenor, *b.* 1934, *s.* 1957, *m.*	Hon. Julian F. M. G., *b.* 1959
1963	*Egremont* (2nd) and *Leconfield* (7th) (1859), John Max Henry Scawen Wyndham, *b.* 1948, *s.* 1972, *m.*	Hon. George R. V. W., *b.* 1983
1643	*Elibank* (14th), Alan D'Ardis Erskine-Murray, *b.* 1923, *s.* 1973, *w.*	Master of Elibank, *b.* 1964
1802	*Ellenborough* (8th), Richard Edward Cecil Law, *b.* 1926, *s.* 1945, *m.*	Maj. Hon. Rupert E. H. L., *b.* 1955
1509 S.*	*Elphinstone* (19th), Alexander Mountstuart Elphinstone (5th *UK Baron, Elphinstone*, 1885), *b.* 1980, *s.* 1994, *M.*	Hon. Angus J. E., *b.* 1982

Created	Title, order of succession, name, etc.	Heir
1934	*Elton* (2nd), Rodney Elton, TD, *b.* 1930, *s.* 1973, *m.*	Hon. Edward P. *E.*, *b.* 1966
1964	*Erroll of Hale* (1st), Frederick James Erroll, TD, PC, *b.* 1914, *m.*	None
1627 S.	*Fairfax of Cameron* (14th), Nicholas John Albert Fairfax, *b.* 1956, *s.* 1964, *m.*	Hon. Edward N. T. *F.*, *b.* 1984
1961	*Fairhaven* (3rd), Ailwyn Henry George Broughton, *b.* 1936, *s.* 1973, *m.*	Maj. Hon. James H. A. *B.*, *b.* 1963
1916	*Faringdon* (3rd), Charles Michael Henderson, *b.* 1937, *s.* 1977, *m.*	Hon. James H. *H.*, *b.* 1961
1756 I.	*Farnham* (12th), Barry Owen Somerset Maxwell, *b.* 1931, *s.* 1957, *m.*	Hon. Simon K. *M.*, *b.* 1933
1856 I.	*Fermoy* (6th), Patrick Maurice Burke Roche, *b.* 1967, *s.* 1984, *m.*	Hon. E. Hugh B. *R.*, *b.* 1972
1826	*Feversham* (6th), Charles Antony Peter Duncombe, *b.* 1945, *s.* 1963, *m.*	Hon. Jasper O. S. *D.*, *b.* 1968
1798 I.	*ffrench* (8th), Robuck John Peter Charles Mario ffrench, *b.* 1956, *s.* 1986, *m.*	Hon. John C. M. J. F. *ff.*, *b.* 1928
1909	*Fisher* (3rd), John Vavasseur Fisher, DSC, *b.* 1921, *s.* 1955, *m.*	Hon. Patrick V. *F.*, *b.* 1953
1295	*Fitzwalter* (21st), (Fitzwalter) Brook Plumptre, *b.* 1914, *title called out of abeyance* 1953, *m.*	Hon. Julian B. *P.*, *b.* 1952
1776	*Foley* (8th), Adrian Gerald Foley, *b.* 1923, *s.* 1927, *m.*	Hon. Thomas H. *F.*, *b.* 1961
1445 S.	*Forbes* (22nd), Nigel Ivan Forbes, KBE, *b.* 1918, *s.* 1953, *m.* Premier Lord of Scotland	Master of Forbes, *b.* 1946
1821	*Forester* (8th), (George Cecil) Brooke Weld-Forester, *b.* 1938, *s.* 1977, *m.*	Hon. C. R. George *W.-F.*, *b.* 1975
1922	*Forres* (4th), Alastair Stephen Grant Williamson, *b.* 1946, *s.* 1978, *m.*	Hon. George A. M. *W.*, *b.* 1972
1917	*Forteviot* (4th), John James Evelyn Dewar, *b.* 1938, *s.* 1993, *m.*	Hon. Alexander J. E. *D.*, *b.* 1971
1951	*Freyberg* (3rd), Valerian Bernard Freyberg, *b.* 1970, *s.* 1993.	None
1917	*Gainford* (3rd), Joseph Edward Pease, *b.* 1921, *s.* 1971, *m.*	Hon. George *P.*, *b.* 1926
1818 I.	*Garvagh* (5th), (Alexander Leopold Ivor) George Canning, *b.* 1920, *s.* 1956, *m.*	Hon. Spencer G. S. de R *C.*, *b.* 1953
1942	*Geddes* (3rd), Euan Michael Ross Geddes, *b.* 1937, *s.* 1975, *m.*	Hon. James G. N. *G.*, *b.* 1969
1876	*Gerard* (5th), Anthony Robert Hugo Gerard, *b.* 1949, *s.* 1992, *m.*	Hon. Rupert B. C. *G.*, *b.* 1981
1824	*Gifford* (6th), Anthony Maurice Gifford, QC, *b.* 1940, *s.* 1961, *m.*	Hon. Thomas A. *G.*, *b.* 1967
1917	*Gisborough* (3rd), Thomas Richard John Long Chaloner, *b.* 1927, *s.* 1951, *m.*	Hon. T. Peregrine L. *C.*, *b.* 1961
1960	*Gladwyn* (2nd), Miles Alvery Gladwyn Jebb, *b.* 1930, *s.* 1996.	None
1899	*Glanusk* (5th), Christopher Russell Bailey, *b.* 1942, *s.* 1997, *m.*	Hon. Charles H. *B.*, *b.* 1976
1918	*Glenarthur* (4th), Simon Mark Arthur, *b.* 1944, *s.* 1976, *m.*	Hon. Edward A. *A.*, *b.* 1973
1911	*Glenconner* (3rd), Colin Christopher Paget Tennant, *b.* 1926, *s.* 1983, *m.*	Hon. Cody *T.*, *b.* 1994
1964	*Glendevon* (2nd), Julian John Somerset Hope, *b.* 1950, *s.* 1996.	Hon. Jonathan C. *H.*, *b.* 1952
1922	*Glendyne* (3rd), Robert Nivison, *b.* 1926, *s.* 1967, *m.*	Hon. John *N.*, *b.* 1960
1939	*Glentoran* (3rd), (Thomas) Robin (Valerian) Dixon, CBE, *b.* 1935, *s.* 1995, *m.*	Hon. Daniel G. *D.*, *b.* 1959
1909	*Gorell* (4th), Timothy John Radcliffe Barnes, *b.* 1927, *s.* 1963, *m.*	Hon. Ronald A. H. *B.*, *b.* 1931
1953	*Grantchester* (3rd), Christopher John Suenson-Taylor, *b.* 1951, *s.* 1995, *m.*	Hon. Jesse D. *S.-T.*, *b.* 1977
1782	*Grantley* (8th), Richard William Brinsley Norton, *b.* 1956, *s.* 1995.	Hon. Francis J. H. *N.*, *b.* 1960
1794 I.	*Graves* (9th), Evelyn Paget Graves, *b.* 1926, *s.* 1994, *m.*	Hon. Timothy E. *G.*, *b.* 1960
1445 S.	*Gray* (22nd), Angus Diarmid Ian Campbell-Gray, *b.* 1931, *s.* 1946, *m.*	Master of Gray, *b.* 1964
1950	*Greenhill* (3rd), Malcolm Greenhill, *b.* 1924, *s.* 1989.	None
1927	*Greenway* (4th), Ambrose Charles Drexel Greenway, *b.* 1941, *s.* 1975, *m.*	Hon. Mervyn S. K. *G.*, *b.* 1942
1902	*Grenfell* (3rd), Julian Pascoe Francis St Leger Grenfell, *b.* 1935, *s.* 1976, *m.*	Francis P. J. *G.*, *b.* 1938
1944	*Gretton* (4th), John Lysander Gretton, *b.* 1975, *s.* 1989.	None
1397	*Grey of Codnor* (6th), Richard Henry Cornwall-Legh, *b.* 1936, *s.* 1996, *m.*	Hon. Richard S. C. *C.-L.*, *b.* 1976
1955	*Gridley* (3rd), Richard David Arnold Gridley, *b.* 1956, *s.* 1996, *m.*	Hon. Carl R. *G.*, *b.* 1981
1964	*Grimston of Westbury* (2nd), Robert Walter Sigismund Grimston, *b.* 1925, *s.* 1979, *m.*	Hon. Robert J. S. *G.*, *b.* 1951
1886	*Grimthorpe* (4th), Christopher John Beckett, OBE, *b.* 1915, *s.* 1963, *m.*	Hon. Edward J. *B.*, *b.* 1954
1945	*Hacking* (3rd), Douglas David Hacking, *b.* 1938, *s.* 1971, *m.*	Hon. Douglas F. *H.*, *b.* 1968
1950	*Haden-Guest* (5th), Christopher Haden-Guest, *b.* 1948, *s.* 1996, *m.*	Hon. Nicholas *H.-G.*, *b.* 1951
1886	*Hamilton of Dalzell* (4th), James Leslie Hamilton, *b.* 1938, *s.* 1990, *m.*	Hon. Gavin G. *H.*, *b.* 1968
1874	*Hampton* (6th), Richard Humphrey Russell Pakington, *b.* 1925, *s.* 1974, *m.*	Hon. John H. A. *P.*, *b.* 1964
1939	*Hankey* (3rd), Donald Robin Alers Hankey, *b.* 1938, *s.* 1996, *m.*	Hon. Alexander M. A. *H.*, *b.* 1947
1958	*Harding of Petherton* (2nd), John Charles Harding, *b.* 1928, *s.* 1989, *m.*	Hon. William A. J. *H.*, *b.* 1969
1910	*Hardinge of Penshurst* (4th), Julian Alexander Hardinge, *b.* 1945, *s.* 1997.	Hon. Hugh F. *H.*, *b.* 1948
1876	*Harlech* (6th), Francis David Ormsby-Gore, *b.* 1954, *s.* 1985, *m.*	Hon. Jasset D. C. *O.-G.*, *b.* 1986
1939	*Harmsworth* (3rd), Thomas Harold Raymond Harmsworth, *b.* 1939, *s.* 1990, *m.*	Hon. Dominic M. E. *H.*, *b.* 1973
1815	*Harris* (8th), Anthony Harris, *b.* 1942, *s.* 1996, *m.*	Ronald G. T. *H.*, *b.* 1911
1954	*Harvey of Tasburgh* (2nd), Peter Charles Oliver Harvey, *b.* 1921, *s.* 1968, *w.*	Charles J. G. *H.*, *b.* 1951
1295	*Hastings* (22nd), Edward Delaval Henry Astley, *b.* 1912, *s.* 1956, *m.*	Hon. Delaval T. H. *A.*, *b.* 1960

Created	Title, order of succession, name, etc.	Heir
1835	*Hatherton* (8th), Edward Charles Littleton, *b.* 1950, *s.* 1985, *m.*	Hon. Thomas E. *L.*, *b.* 1977
1776	*Hawke* (11th), Edward George Hawke, TD, *b.* 1950, *s.* 1992, *m.*	Hon. William M. T. *H.*, *b.* 1995
1927	*Hayter* (3rd), George Charles Hayter Chubb, KCVO, CBE, *b.* 1911, *s.* 1967, *m.*	Hon. G. William M. *C.*, *b.* 1943
1945	*Hazlerigg* (2nd), Arthur Grey Hazlerigg, MC, TD, *b.* 1910, *s.* 1949, *w.*	Hon. Arthur G. *H.*, *b.* 1951
1943	*Hemingford* (3rd), (Dennis) Nicholas Herbert, *b.* 1934, *s.* 1982, *m.*	Hon. Christopher D. C. *H.*, *b.* 1973
1906	*Hemphill* (5th), Peter Patrick Fitzroy Martyn Martyn-Hemphill, *b.* 1928, *s.* 1957, *m.*	Hon. Charles A. M. *M.-H.*, *b.* 1954
1799 I.*	*Henley* (8th), Oliver Michael Robert Eden (6th *UK Baron Northington,* 1885), *b.* 1953, *s.* 1977, *m.*	Hon. John W. O. *E.*, *b.* 1988
1800 I.*	*Henniker* (8th), John Patrick Edward Chandos Henniker-Major, KCMG, CVO, MC (4th *UK Baron Hartismere,* 1866), *b.* 1916, *s.* 1980, *m.*	Hon. Mark I. P. C. *H.-M.*, *b.* 1947
1886	*Herschell* (3rd), Rognvald Richard Farrer Herschell, *b.* 1923, *s.* 1929, *m.*	None
1935	*Hesketh* (3rd), Thomas Alexander Fermor-Hesketh, KBE, PC, *b.* 1950, *s.* 1955, *m.*	Hon. Frederick H. *F.-H.*, *b.* 1988
1828	*Heytesbury* (6th), Francis William Holmes à Court, *b.* 1931, *s.* 1971, *m.*	Hon. James W. *H. à. C.*, *b.* 1967
1886	*Hindlip* (6th), Charles Henry Allsopp, *b.* 1940, *s.* 1993, *m.*	Hon. Henry W. *A.*, *b.* 1973
1950	*Hives* (3rd), Matthew Peter Hives, *b.* 1971, *s.* 1997.	Hon. Michael B. *H.*, *b.* 1926
1912	*Hollenden* (4th), Ian Hampden Hope-Morley, *b.* 1946, *s.* 1999, *m.*	Hon. Edward *H.-M.*, *b.* 1981
1897	*HolmPatrick* (4th), Hans James David Hamilton, *b.* 1955, *s.* 1991, *m.*	Hon. Ion H. J. *H.*, *b.* 1956
1797 I.	*Hotham* (8th), Henry Durand Hotham, *b.* 1940, *s.* 1967, *m.*	Hon. William B. *H.*, *b.* 1972
1881	*Hothfield* (6th), Anthony Charles Sackville Tufton, *b.* 1939, *s.* 1991, *m.*	Hon. William S. *T.*, *b.* 1977
1597	*Howard de Walden.* The 9th Baron Howard de Walden died in 1999, leaving four co-heiresses.	
1930	*Howard of Penrith* (2nd), Francis Philip Howard, *b.* 1905, *s.* 1939, *m.*	Hon. Philip E. *H.*, *b.* 1945
1960	*Howick of Glendale* (2nd), Charles Evelyn Baring, *b.* 1937, *s.* 1973, *m.*	Hon. David E. C. *B.*, *b.* 1975
1796 I.	*Huntingfield* (7th), Joshua Charles Vanneck, *b.* 1954, *s.* 1994, *m.*	Hon. Gerard C. A. *V.*, *b.* 1985
1866	*Hylton* (5th), Raymond Hervey Jolliffe, *b.* 1932, *s.* 1967, *m.*	Hon. William H. M. *J.*, *b.* 1967
1933	*Iliffe* (3rd), Robert Peter Richard Iliffe, *b.* 1944, *s.* 1996, *m.*	Hon. Edward R. *I.*, *b.* 1968
1543 I.	*Inchiquin* (18th), Conor Myles John O'Brien, *b.* 1943, *s.* 1982, *m.*	Murrough R. *O.*, *b.* 1910
1962	*Inchyra* (2nd), Robert Charles Reneke Hoyer Millar, *b.* 1935, *s.* 1989, *m.*	Hon. C. James C. H. *M.*, *b.* 1962
1964	*Inglewood* (2nd), (William) Richard Fletcher-Vane, MEP, *b.* 1951, *s.* 1989, *m.*	Hon. Henry W. F. *F.-V.*, *b.* 1990
1919	*Inverforth* (4th), Andrew Peter Weir, *b.* 1966, *s.* 1982.	Hon. John V. *W.*, *b.* 1935
1941	*Ironside* (2nd), Edmund Oslac Ironside, *b.* 1924, *s.* 1959, *m.*	Hon. Charles E. G. *I.*, *b.* 1956
1952	*Jeffreys* (3rd), Christopher Henry Mark Jeffreys, *b.* 1957, *s.* 1986, *m.*	Hon. Arthur M. H. *J.*, *b.* 1989
1906	*Joicey* (5th), James Michael Joicey, *b.* 1953, *s.* 1993, *m.*	Hon. William J. *J.*, *b.* 1990
1937	*Kenilworth* (4th), (John) Randle Siddeley, *b.* 1954, *s.* 1981, *m.*	Hon. William R. J. *S.*, *b.* 1992
1935	*Kennet* (2nd), Wayland Hilton Young, *b.* 1923, *s.* 1960, *m.*	Hon. W. A. Thoby *Y.*, *b.* 1957
1776 I.*	*Kensington* (8th), Hugh Ivor Edwardes (5th *UK Baron Kensington,* 1886), *b.* 1933, *s.* 1981, *m.*	Hon. W. Owen A. *E.*, *b.* 1964
1951	*Kenswood* (2nd), John Michael Howard Whitfield, *b.* 1930, *s.* 1963, *m.*	Hon. Michael C. *W.*, *b.* 1955
1788	*Kenyon* (6th), Lloyd Tyrell-Kenyon, *b.* 1947, *s.* 1993, *m.*	Hon. Lloyd N. *T.-K.*, *b.* 1972
1947	*Kershaw* (4th), Edward John Kershaw, *b.* 1936, *s.* 1962, *m.*	Hon. John C. E. *K.*, *b.* 1971
1943	*Keyes* (2nd), Roger George Bowlby Keyes, *b.* 1919, *s.* 1945, *m.*	Hon. Charles W. P. *K.*, *b.* 1951
1909	*Kilbracken* (3rd), John Raymond Godley, DSC, *b.* 1920, *s.* 1950.	Hon. Christopher J. *G.*, *b.* 1945
1900	*Killanin* (4th), (George) Redmond Fitzpatrick Morris, *b.* 1947, *s.* 1999, *m.*	Luke M. G. *M.*, *b.* 1975
1943	*Killearn* (3rd), Victor Miles George Aldous Lampson, *b.* 1941, *s.* 1996, *m.*	Hon. Miles H. M. *L.*, *b.* 1977
1789 I.	*Kilmaine* (7th), John David Henry Browne, *b.* 1948, *s.* 1978, *m.*	Hon. John F. S. *B.*, *b.* 1983
1831	*Kilmarnock* (7th), Alastair Ivor Gilbert Boyd, *b.* 1927, *s.* 1975, *m.*	Hon. Robin J. *B.*, *b.* 1941
1941	*Kindersley* (3rd), Robert Hugh Molesworth Kindersley, *b.* 1929, *s.* 1976, *m.*	Hon. Rupert J. M. *K.*, *b.* 1955
1223 I.	*Kingsale* (35th), John de Courcy, *b.* 1941, *s.* 1969. *Premier Baron of Ireland*	Nevinson R. *de C.*, *b.* 1920
1902	*Kinross* (5th), Christopher Patrick Balfour, *b.* 1949, *s.* 1985, *m.*	Hon. Alan I. *B.*, *b.* 1978
1951	*Kirkwood* (3rd), David Harvie Kirkwood, PH.D., *b.* 1931, *s.* 1970, *m.*	Hon. James S. *K.*, *b.* 1937
1800 I.	*Langford* (9th), Col. Geoffrey Alexander Rowley-Conwy, OBE, *b.* 1912, *s.* 1953, *m.*	Hon. Owain G. *R.-C.*, *b.* 1958
1942	*Latham* (2nd), Dominic Charles Latham, *b.* 1954, *s.* 1970.	Anthony M. *L.*, *b.* 1954
1431	*Latymer* (8th), Hugo Nevill Money-Coutts, *b.* 1926, *s.* 1987, *m.*	Hon. Crispin J. A. N. *M.-C.*, *b.* 1955
1869	*Lawrence* (5th), David John Downer Lawrence, *b.* 1937, *s.* 1968.	None
1947	*Layton* (3rd), Geoffrey Michael Layton, *b.* 1947, *s.* 1989, *m.*	Hon. David *L.*, MBE, *b.* 1914
1839	*Leigh* (5th), John Piers Leigh, *b.* 1935, *s.* 1979, *m.*	Hon. Christopher D. P. *L.*, *b.* 1960
1962	*Leighton of St Mellons* (3rd), Robert William Henry Leighton Seager, *b.* 1955, *s.* 1998.	Hon. Simon J. L. *S.*, *b.* 1957
1797	*Lilford* (7th), George Vernon Powys, *b.* 1931, *s.* 1949, *m.*	Hon. Mark V. *P.*, *b.* 1975
1945	*Lindsay of Birker* (3rd), James Francis Lindsay, *b.* 1945, *s.* 1994, *m.*	Alexander S. *L.*, *b.* 1940

Created	Title, order of succession, name, etc.	Heir
1758 I.	*Lisle* (8th), Patrick James Lysaght, *b.* 1931, *s.* 1998.	Hon. John N. G. *L.*, *b.* 1960
1850	*Londesborough* (9th), Richard John Denison, *b.* 1959, *s.* 1968, *m.*	Hon. James F. *D.*, *b.* 1990
1541 I.	*Louth* (16th), Otway Michael James Oliver Plunkett, *b.* 1929, *s.* 1950, *m.*	Hon. Jonathan O. *P.*, *b.* 1952
1458 S.*	*Lovat* (16th), Simon Fraser (5th *UK Baron, Lovat*, 1837), *b.* 1977, *s.* 1995.	Hon. Jack *F.*, *b.* 1984
1663	*Lucas* (11th) and *Dingwall* (14th) (s. 1609), Ralph Matthew Palmer, *b.* 1951, *s.* 1991, *m.*	Hon. Lewis E. *P.*, *b.* 1987
1946	*Lucas of Chilworth* (2nd), Michael William George Lucas, *b.* 1926, *s.* 1967, *m.*	Hon. Simon W. *L.*, *b.* 1957
1929	*Luke* (3rd), Arthur Charles St John Lawson-Johnston, *b.* 1933, *s.* 1996, *m.*	Hon. Ian J. St J. *L.-J.*, *b.* 1963
1914	*Lyell* (3rd), Charles Lyell, *b.* 1939, *s.* 1943.	None
1859	*Lyveden* (6th), Ronald Cecil Vernon, *b.* 1915, *s.* 1973, *m.*	Hon. Jack L. *V.*, *b.* 1938
1959	*MacAndrew* (3rd), Christopher Anthony Colin MacAndrew, *b.* 1945, *s.* 1989, *m.*	Hon. Oliver C. J. *M.*, *b.* 1983
1776 I.	*Macdonald* (8th), Godfrey James Macdonald of Macdonald, *b.* 1947, *s.* 1970, *m.*	Hon. Godfrey E. H. T. *M.*, *b.* 1982
1949	*Macdonald of Gwaenysgor* (2nd), Gordon Ramsay Macdonald, *b.* 1915, *s.* 1966, *m.*	None
1937	*McGowan* (3rd), Harry Duncan Cory McGowan, *b.* 1938, *s.* 1966, *m.*	Hon. Harry J. C. *M.*, *b.* 1971
1922	*Maclay* (3rd), Joseph Paton Maclay, *b.* 1942, *s.* 1969, *m.*	Hon. Joseph P. *M.*, *b.* 1977
1955	*McNair* (3rd), Duncan James McNair, *b.* 1947, *s.* 1989, *m.*	Hon. William S. A. *M.*, *b.* 1958
1951	*Macpherson of Drumochter* (2nd), (James) Gordon Macpherson, *b.* 1924, *s.* 1965, *m.*	Hon. James A. *M.*, *b.* 1979
1937	*Mancroft* (3rd), Benjamin Lloyd Stormont Mancroft, *b.* 1957, *s.* 1987, *m.*	None
1807	*Manners* (5th), John Robert Cecil Manners, *b.* 1923, *s.* 1972, *m.*	Hon. John H. R. *M.*, *b.* 1956
1922	*Manton* (3rd), Joseph Rupert Eric Robert Watson, *b.* 1924, *s.* 1968, *m.*	Maj. Hon. Miles R. M. *W.*, *b.* 1958
1908	*Marchamley* (4th), William Francis Whiteley, *b.* 1968, *s.* 1994.	None
1964	*Margadale* (2nd), James Ian Morrison, TD, *b.* 1930, *s.* 1996, *m.*	Hon. Alastair J. *M.*, *b.* 1958
1961	*Marks of Broughton* (3rd), Simon Richard Marks, *b.* 1950, *s.* 1998, *m.*	Hon. Michael *M.*, *b.* 1989
1964	*Martonmere* (2nd), John Stephen Robinson, *b.* 1963, *s.* 1989.	David A. *R.*, *b.* 1965
1776 I.	*Massy* (9th), Hugh Hamon John Somerset Massy, *b.* 1921, *s.* 1958, *m.*	Hon. David H. S. *M.*, *b.* 1947
1935	*May* (3rd), Michael St John May, *b.* 1931, *s.* 1950, *m.*	Hon. Jasper B. St J. *M.*, *b.* 1965
1928	*Melchett* (4th), Peter Robert Henry Mond, *b.* 1948, *s.* 1973.	None
1925	*Merrivale* (3rd), Jack Henry Edmond Duke, *b.* 1917, *s.* 1951, *m.*	Hon. Derek J. P. *D.*, *b.* 1948
1911	*Merthyr.* Disclaimed for life 1977. (*Trevor Oswin Lewis*, Bt, CBE, *b.* 1935, *s.* 1977, *m.*)	David T. *L.*, *b.* 1977
1919	*Meston* (3rd), James Meston, *b.* 1950, *s.* 1984, *m.*	Hon. Thomas J. D. *M.*, *b.* 1977
1838	*Methuen* (7th), Robert Alexander Holt Methuen, *b.* 1931, *s.* 1994, *m.*	James Paul Archibald *Methuen-Campbell*, *b.* 1952
1711	*Middleton* (12th), (Digby) Michael Godfrey John Willoughby, MC, *b.* 1921, *s.* 1970, *m.*	Hon. Michael C. J. *W.*, *b.* 1948
1939	*Milford* (3rd), Hugo John Laurence Philipps, *b.* 1929, *s.* 1993, *m.*	Hon. Guy W. *P.*, *b.* 1961
1933	*Milne* (2nd), George Douglass Milne, TD, *b.* 1909, *s.* 1948, *m.*	Hon. George A. *M.*, *b.* 1941
1951	*Milner of Leeds* (2nd), Arthur James Michael Milner, AE, *b.* 1923, *s.* 1967, *m.*	Hon. Richard J. *M.*, *b.* 1959
1947	*Milverton* (2nd), Revd Fraser Arthur Richard Richards, *b.* 1930, *s.* 1978, *m.*	Hon. Michael H. *R.*, *b.* 1936
1873	*Moncreiff* (5th), Harry Robert Wellwood Moncreiff, *b.* 1915, *s.* 1942, *w.*	Hon. Rhoderick H. W. *M.*, *b.* 1954
1884	*Monk Bretton* (3rd), John Charles Dodson, *b.* 1924, *s.* 1933, *m.*	Hon. Christopher M. *D.*, *b.* 1958
1885	*Monkswell* (5th), Gerard Collier, *b.* 1947, *s.* 1984, *m.*	Hon. James A. *C.*, *b.* 1977
1728	*Monson* (11th), John Monson, *b.* 1932, *s.* 1958, *m.*	Hon. Nicholas J. *M.*, *b.* 1955
1885	*Montagu of Beaulieu* (3rd), Edward John Barrington Douglas-Scott-Montagu, *b.* 1926, *s.* 1929, *m.*	Hon. Ralph *D.-S.-M.*, *b.* 1961
1839	*Monteagle of Brandon* (6th), Gerald Spring Rice, *b.* 1926, *s.* 1946, *m.*	Hon. Charles J. S. *R.*, *b.* 1953
1943	*Moran* (2nd), (Richard) John (McMoran) Wilson, KCMG, *b.* 1924, *s.* 1977, *m.*	Hon. James M. *W.*, *b.* 1952
1918	*Morris* (3rd), Michael David Morris, *b.* 1937, *s.* 1975, *m.*	Hon. Thomas A. S. *M.*, *b.* 1982
1950	*Morris of Kenwood* (2nd), Philip Geoffrey Morris, *b.* 1928, *s.* 1954, *m.*	Hon. Jonathan D. *M.*, *b.* 1968
1831	*Mostyn* (5th), Roger Edward Lloyd Lloyd-Mostyn, MC, *b.* 1920, *s.* 1965, *m.*	Hon. Llewellyn R. L. *L.-M.*, *b.* 1948
1933	*Mottistone* (4th), David Peter Seely, CBE, *b.* 1920, *s.* 1966, *m.*	Hon. Peter J. P. *S.*, *b.* 1949
1945	*Mountevans* (3rd), Edward Patrick Broke Evans, *b.* 1943, *s.* 1974, *m.*	Hon. Jeffrey de C. R. *E.*, *b.* 1948
1283	*Mowbray* (26th), *Segrave* (27th) (1283) and *Stourton* (23rd) (1448), Charles Edward Stourton, CBE, *b.* 1923, *s.* 1965, *m.*	Hon. Edward W. S. *S.*, *b.* 1953
1932	*Moyne* (3rd), Jonathan Bryan Guinness, *b.* 1930, *s.* 1992, *m.*	Hon. Jasper J. R. *G.*, *b.* 1954
1929	*Moynihan* (4th), Colin Berkeley Moynihan, *b.* 1955, *s.* 1997, *m.*	Hon. Nicholas E. B. *M.*, *b.* 1994
1781 I.	*Muskerry* (9th), Robert Fitzmaurice Deane, *b.* 1948, *s.* 1988, *m.*	Hon. Jonathan F. *D.*, *b.* 1986
1627 S.*	*Napier* (14th) and *Ettrick* (5th) (*UK* 1872), Francis Nigel Napier, KCVO, *b.* 1930, *s.* 1954, *m.*	Master of Napier, *b.* 1962

Created	*Title, order of succession, name, etc.*	*Heir*
1868	*Napier of Magdala* (6th), Robert Alan Napier, *b.* 1940, *s.* 1987, *m.*	Hon. James R. *N.*, *b.* 1966
1940	*Nathan* (2nd), Roger Carol Michael Nathan, *b.* 1922, *s.* 1963, *m.*	Hon. Rupert H. B. *N.*, *b.* 1957
1960	*Nelson of Stafford* (3rd), Henry Roy George Nelson, *b.* 1943, *s.* 1995, *m.*	Hon. Alistair W. H. *N.*, *b.* 1973
1959	*Netherthorpe* (3rd), James Frederick Turner, *b.* 1964, *s.* 1982, *m.*	Hon. Andrew J. E. *T.*, *b.* 1993
1946	*Newall* (2nd), Francis Storer Eaton Newall, *b.* 1930, *s.* 1963, *m.*	Hon. Richard H. E. *N.*, *b.* 1961
1776 I.	*Newborough* (8th), Robert Vaughan Wynn, *b.* 1949, *s.* 1998, *m.*	Hon. Charles H. R. *W.*, *b.* 1923
1892	*Newton* (5th), Richard Thomas Legh, *b.* 1950, *s.* 1992, *m.*	Hon. Piers R. *L.*, *b.* 1979
1930	*Noel-Buxton* (3rd), Martin Connal Noel-Buxton, *b.* 1940, *s.* 1980, *m.*	Hon. Charles C. *N.-B.*, *b.* 1975
1957	*Norrie* (2nd), (George) Willoughby Moke Norrie, *b.* 1936, *s.* 1977, *m.*	Hon. Mark W. J. *N.*, *b.* 1972
1884	*Northbourne* (5th), Christopher George Walter James, *b.* 1926, *s.* 1982, *m.*	Hon. Charles W. H. *J.*, *b.* 1960
1866	*Northbrook* (6th), Francis Thomas Baring, *b.* 1954, *s.* 1990, *m.*	None
1878	*Norton* (8th), James Nigel Arden Adderley, *b.* 1947, *s.* 1993, *m.*	Hon. Edward J. A. *A.*, *b.* 1982
1906	*Nunburnholme* (5th), Charles Thomas Wilson, *b.* 1935, *s.* 1998.	Hon. Stephen C. *W.*, *b.* 1973
	Oaksey. (see Trevethin and Oaksey, page 155)	
1950	*Ogmore* (2nd), Gwilym Rees Rees-Williams, *b.* 1931, *s.* 1976, *m.*	Hon. Morgan *R.-W.*, *b.* 1937
1870	*O'Hagan* (4th), Charles Towneley Strachey, *b.* 1945, *s.* 1961.	Hon. Richard T. *S.*, *b.* 1950
1868	*O'Neill* (4th), Raymond Arthur Clanaboy O'Neill, TD, *b.* 1933, *s.* 1944, *m.*	Hon. Shane S. C. *O'N.*, *b.* 1965
1836 I.*	*Oranmore and Browne* (4th), Dominick Geoffrey Edward Browne (2nd UK Baron, Mereworth, 1926), *b.* 1901, *s.* 1927, *m.*	Hon. Dominick G. T. *B.*, *b.* 1929
1933	*Palmer* (4th), Adrian Bailie Nottage Palmer, *b.* 1951, *s.* 1990, *m.*	Hon. Hugo B. R. *P.*, *b.* 1980
1914	*Parmoor* (4th), (Frederick Alfred) Milo Cripps, *b.* 1929, *s.* 1977.	Michael L. S. *C.*, *b.* 1942
1937	*Pender* (3rd), John Willoughby Denison-Pender, *b.* 1933, *s.* 1965, *m.*	Hon. Henry J. R. *D.-P.*, *b.* 1968
1866	*Penrhyn* (6th), Malcolm Frank Douglas-Pennant, DSO, MBE, *b.* 1908, *s.* 1967, *m.*	Hon. Nigel *D.-P.*, *b.* 1909
1603	*Petre* (18th), John Patrick Lionel Petre, *b.* 1942, *s.* 1989, *m.*	Hon. Dominic W. *P.*, *b.* 1966
1918	*Phillimore* (5th), Francis Stephen Phillimore, *b.* 1944, *s.* 1994, *m.*	Hon. Tristan A. S. *P.*, *b.* 1977
1945	*Piercy* (3rd), James William Piercy, *b.* 1946, *s.* 1981.	Hon. Mark E. P. *P.*, *b.* 1953
1827	*Plunket* (8th), Robin Rathmore Plunket, *b.* 1925, *s.* 1975, *m.*	Hon. Shaun A. F. S. *P.*, *b.* 1931
1831	*Poltimore* (7th), Mark Coplestone Bampfylde, *b.* 1957, *s.* 1978, *m.*	Hon. Henry A. W. *B.*, *b.* 1985
1690 S.	*Polwarth* (10th), Henry Alexander Hepburne-Scott, TD, *b.* 1916, *s.* 1944, *m.*	Master of Polwarth, *b.* 1947
1930	*Ponsonby of Shulbrede* (4th), Frederick Matthew Thomas Ponsonby, *b.* 1958, *s.* 1990.	None
1958	*Poole* (2nd), David Charles Poole, *b.* 1945, *s.* 1993, *m.*	Hon. Oliver J. *P.*, *b.* 1972
1852	*Raglan* (5th), FitzRoy John Somerset, *b.* 1927, *s.* 1964.	Hon. Geoffrey *S.*, *b.* 1932
1932	*Rankeillour* (4th), Peter St Thomas More Henry Hope, *b.* 1935, *s.* 1967.	Michael R. *H.*, *b.* 1940
1953	*Rathcavan* (3rd), Hugh Detmar Torrens O'Neill, *b.* 1939, *s.* 1994, *m.*	Hon. François H. N. *O'N.*, *b.* 1984
1916	*Rathcreedan* (3rd), Christopher John Norton, *b.* 1949, *s.* 1990, *m.*	Hon. Adam G. *N.*, *b.* 1952
1868 I.	*Rathdonnell* (5th), Thomas Benjamin McClintock-Bunbury, *b.* 1938, *s.* 1959, *m.*	Hon. William L. *M.-B.*, *b.* 1966
1911	*Ravensdale* (3rd), Nicholas Mosley, MC, *b.* 1923, *s.* 1966, *m.*	Hon. Shaun N. *M.*, *b.* 1949
1821	*Ravensworth* (8th), Arthur Waller Liddell, *b.* 1924, *s.* 1950, *m.*	Hon. Thomas A. H. *L.*, *b.* 1954
1821	*Rayleigh* (6th), John Gerald Strutt, *b.* 1960, *s.* 1988, *m.*	Hon. John F. *S.*, *b.* 1993
1937	*Rea* (3rd), John Nicolas Rea, MD, *b.* 1928, *s.* 1981, *m.*	Hon. Matthew J. *R.*, *b.* 1956
1628 S.	*Reay* (14th), Hugh William Mackay, *b.* 1937, *s.* 1963, *m.*	Master of Reay, *b.* 1965
1902	*Redesdale* (6th), Rupert Bertram Mitford, *b.* 1967, *s.* 1991, *m.*	None
1940	*Reith.* Disclaimed for life 1972. (*Christopher John Reith, b.* 1928, *s.* 1971, *m.*)	Hon. James H. J. *R.*, *b.* 1971
1928	*Remnant* (3rd), James Wogan Remnant, CVO, *b.* 1930, *s.* 1967, *m.*	Hon. Philip J. *R.*, *b.* 1954
1806 I.	*Rendlesham* (8th), Charles Anthony Hugh Thellusson, *b.* 1915, *s.* 1943, *w.*	Hon. Charles W. B. *T.*, *b.* 1954
1933	*Rennell* (3rd), (John Adrian) Tremayne Rodd, *b.* 1935, *s.* 1978, *m.*	Hon. James R. D. T. *R.*, *b.* 1978
1964	*Renwick* (2nd), Harry Andrew Renwick, *b.* 1935, *s.* 1973, *m.*	Hon. Robert J. *R.*, *b.* 1966
1885	*Revelstoke* (5th), John Baring, *b.* 1934, *s.* 1994.	Hon. James C. *B.*, *b.* 1938
1905	*Ritchie of Dundee* (5th), (Harold) Malcolm Ritchie, *b.* 1919, *s.* 1978, *m.*	Hon. C. Rupert R. *R.*, *b.* 1958
1935	*Riverdale* (3rd), Anthony Robert Balfour, *b.* 1960, *s.* 1998.	Hon. David R. *B.*, *b.* 1938
1961	*Robertson of Oakridge* (2nd), William Ronald Robertson, *b.* 1930, *s.* 1974, *m.*	Hon. William B. E. *R.*, *b.* 1975
1938	*Roborough* (3rd), Henry Massey Lopes, *b.* 1940, *s.* 1992, *m.*	Hon. Massey J. H. *L.*, *b.* 1969
1931	*Rochester* (2nd), Foster Charles Lowry Lamb, *b.* 1916, *s.* 1955, *m.*	Hon. David C. *L.*, *b.* 1944
1934	*Rockley* (3rd), James Hugh Cecil, *b.* 1934, *s.* 1976, *m.*	Hon. Anthony R. *C.*, *b.* 1961
1782	*Rodney* (10th), George Brydges Rodney, *b.* 1953, *s.* 1992, *m.*	Nicholas S. H. *R.*, *b.* 1947
1651 S.*	*Rollo* (14th), David Eric Howard Rollo (5th *UK Baron Dunning*, 1869), *b.* 1943, *s.* 1997, *m.*	Master of Rollo, *b.* 1972
1959	*Rootes* (3rd), Nicholas Geoffrey Rootes, *b.* 1951, *s.* 1992, *m.*	William B. *R.*, *b.* 1944
1796 I.*	*Rossmore* (7th), William Warner Westenra (6th *UK Baron, Rossmore*, 1838), *b.* 1931, *s.* 1958, *m.*	Hon. Benedict W. *W.*, *b.* 1983
1939	*Rotherwick* (3rd), (Herbert) Robin Cayzer, *b.* 1954, *s.* 1996, *m.*	Hon. H. Robin *C.*, *b.* 1989

Created	Title, order of succession, name, etc.	Heir
1885	*Rothschild* (4th), (Nathaniel Charles) Jacob Rothschild, GBE, *b.* 1936, *s.* 1990, *m.*	Hon. Nathaniel P. V. J. *R.*, *b.* 1971
1911	*Rowallan* (4th), John Polson Cameron Corbett, *b.* 1947, *s.* 1993.	Hon. Jason W. P. C. *C.*, *b.* 1972
1947	*Rugby* (3rd), Robert Charles Maffey, *b.* 1951, *s.* 1990, *m.*	Hon. Timothy J. H. *M.*, *b.* 1975
1919	*Russell of Liverpool* (3rd), Simon Gordon Jared Russell, *b.* 1952, *s.* 1981, *m.*	Hon. Edward C. S. *R.*, *b.* 1985
1876	*Sackville* (6th), Lionel Bertrand Sackville-West, *b.* 1913, *s.* 1965, *m.*	Hugh R. I. *S.-W.* MC, *b.* 1919
1964	*St Helens* (2nd), Richard Francis Hughes-Young, *b.* 1945, *s.* 1980, *m.*	Hon. Henry T. *H.-Y.*, *b.* 1986
1559	*St John of Bletso* (21st), Anthony Tudor St John, *b.* 1957, *s.* 1978, *m.*	Hon. Oliver B. *St J.*, *b.* 1995
1887	*St Levan* (4th), John Francis Arthur St Aubyn, DSC, *b.* 1919, *s.* 1978, *m.*	Hon. O. Piers *St. A.*, MC, *b.* 1920
1885	*St Oswald* (6th), Charles Rowland Andrew Winn, *b.* 1959, *s.* 1999, *m.*	Hon. Rowland C. S. H. *W.*, *b.* 1986
1960	*Sanderson of Ayot.* Disclaimed for life 1971. (*Alan Lindsay Sanderson, b.* 1931, *s.* 1971, *m.*)	Hon. Michael *S.*, *b.* 1959
1945	*Sandford* (2nd), Revd John Cyril Edmondson, DSC, *b.* 1920, *s.* 1959, *m.*	Hon. James J. M. *E.*, *b.* 1949
1871	*Sandhurst* (5th), (John Edward) Terence Mansfield, DFC, *b.* 1920, *s.* 1964, *m.*	Hon. Guy R. J. *M.*, *b.* 1949
1802	*Sandys* (7th), Richard Michael Oliver Hill, *b.* 1931, *s.* 1961, *m.*	The Marquess of Downshire (*see* page 138)
1888	*Savile* (3rd), George Halifax Lumley-Savile, *b.* 1919, *s.* 1931.	Hon. Henry L. T. *L.-S.*, *b.* 1923
1447	*Saye and Sele* (21st), Nathaniel Thomas Allen Fiennes, *b.* 1920, *s.* 1968, *m.*	Hon. Richard I. *F.*, *b.* 1959
1826	*Seaford* (6th), Colin Humphrey Felton Ellis, *b.* 1946, *s.* 1999, *m.*	Benjamin F. T. *E.*, *b.* 1976
1932	*Selsdon* (3rd), Malcolm McEacharn Mitchell-Thomson, *b.* 1937, *s.* 1963, *m.*	Hon. Callum M. M. *M.-T.*, *b.* 1969
1489 S.	*Sempill* (21st), James William Stuart Whitemore Sempill, *b.* 1949, *s.* 1995, *m.*	Master of Sempill, *b.* 1979
1916	*Shaughnessy* (3rd), William Graham Shaughnessy, *b.* 1922, *s.* 1938, *w.*	Hon. Michael J. *S.*, *b.* 1946
1946	*Shepherd* (2nd), Malcolm Newton Shepherd, PC, *b.* 1918, *s.* 1954, *w.*	Hon. Graeme G. *S.*, *b.* 1949
1964	*Sherfield* (2nd), Christopher James Makins, *b.* 1942, *s.* 1996, *m.*	Hon. Dwight W. *M.*, *b.* 1951
1902	*Shuttleworth* (5th), Charles Geoffrey Nicholas Kay-Shuttleworth, *b.* 1948, *s.* 1975, *m.*	Hon. Thomas E. *K.-S.*, *b.* 1976
1950	*Silkin.* Disclaimed for life 1972. (*Arthur Silkin, b.* 1916, *s.* 1972, *m.*)	Hon. Christopher L. *S.*, *b.* 1947
1963	*Silsoe* (2nd), David Malcolm Trustram Eve, QC, *b.* 1930, *s.* 1976, *m.*	Hon. Simon R. T. *E.*, *b.* 1966
1947	*Simon of Wythenshawe* (2nd), Roger Simon, *b.* 1913, *s.* 1960, *m.*	Hon. Matthew *S.*, *b.* 1955
1449 S.	*Sinclair* (17th), Charles Murray Kennedy St Clair, CVO, *b.* 1914, *s.* 1957, *m.*	Master of Sinclair, *b.* 1968
1957	*Sinclair of Cleeve* (3rd), John Lawrence Robert Sinclair, *b.* 1953, *s.* 1985.	None
1919	*Sinha* (6th), Arup Kumar Sinha, *b.* 1966, *s.* 1999.	†
1828	*Skelmersdale* (7th), Roger Bootle-Wilbraham, *b.* 1945, *s.* 1973, *m.*	Hon. Andrew *B.-W.*, *b.* 1977
1916	*Somerleyton* (3rd), Savile William Francis Crossley, GCVO, *b.* 1928, *s.* 1959, *m.*	Hon. Hugh F. S. *C.*, *b.* 1971
1784	*Somers* (9th), Philip Sebastian Somers Cocks, *b.* 1948, *s.* 1995.	Alan B. *C.*, *b.* 1930
1780	*Southampton* (6th), Charles James FitzRoy, *b.* 1928, *s.* 1989, *m.*	Hon. Edward C. *F.*, *b.* 1955
1959	*Spens* (3rd), Patrick Michael Rex Spens, *b.* 1942, *s.* 1984, *m.*	Hon. Patrick N. G. *S.*, *b.* 1968
1640	*Stafford* (15th), Francis Melfort William Fitzherbert, *b.* 1954, *s.* 1986, *m.*	Hon. Benjamin J. B. *F.*, *b.* 1983
1938	*Stamp* (4th), Trevor Charles Bosworth Stamp, MD, FRCP, *b.* 1935, *s.* 1987, *m.*	Hon. Nicholas C. T. *S.*, *b.* 1978
1839	*Stanley of Alderley* (8th) and *Sheffield* (8th) (I. 1738), Thomas Henry Oliver Stanley (7th *UK Baron, Eddisbury*, 1848), *b.* 1927, *s.* 1971, *m.*	Hon. Richard O. *S.*, *b.* 1956
1318	*Strabolgi* (11th), David Montague de Burgh Kenworthy, *b.* 1914, *s.* 1953, *m.*	Andrew D. W. *K.*, *b.* 1967
1954	*Strang* (2nd), Colin Strang, *b.* 1922, *s.* 1978, *m.*	None
1955	*Strathalmond* (3rd), William Roberton Fraser, *b.* 1947, *s.* 1976, *m.*	Hon. William G. *F.*, *b.* 1976
1936	*Strathcarron* (2nd), David William Anthony Blyth Macpherson, *b.* 1924, *s.* 1937, *w.*	Hon. Ian D. P. *M.*, *b.* 1949
1955	*Strathclyde* (2nd), Thomas Galloway Dunlop du Roy de Blicquy Galbraith, PC, *b.* 1960, *s.* 1985, *m.*	Hon. Charles W. du R. de B. *G.*, *b.* 1962
1900	*Strathcona and Mount Royal* (4th), Donald Euan Palmer Howard, *b.* 1923, *s.* 1959, *m.*	Hon. D. Alexander S. *H.*, *b.* 1961
1836	*Stratheden* (6th) and *Campbell* (6th) (1841), Donald Campbell, *b.* 1934, *s.* 1987, *m.*	Hon. David A. *C.*, *b.* 1963
1884	*Strathspey* (6th), James Patrick Trevor Grant of Grant, *b.* 1943, *s.* 1992, *m.*	Hon. Michael P. F. *G.*, *b.* 1953
1838	*Sudeley* (7th), Merlin Charles Sainthill Hanbury-Tracy, *b.* 1939, *s.* 1941.	D. Andrew J. *H.-T.*, *b.* 1928
1786	*Suffield* (11th), Anthony Philip Harbord-Hamond, MC, *b.* 1922, *s.* 1951, *w.*	Hon. Charles A. A. *H.-H.*, *b.* 1953
1893	*Swansea* (4th), John Hussey Hamilton Vivian, *b.* 1925, *s.* 1934, *m.*	Hon. Richard A. H. *V.*, *b.* 1957
1907	*Swaythling* (5th), Charles Edgar Samuel Montagu, *b.* 1954, *s.* 1998, *m.*	Hon. Anthony T. S. *M.*, *b.* 1931

Created	Title, order of succession, name, etc.	Heir
1919	*Swinfen* (3rd), Roger Mynors Swinfen Eady, *b.* 1938, *s.* 1977, *m.*	Hon. Charles R. P. S. *E.*, *b.* 1971
1935	*Sysonby* (3rd), John Frederick Ponsonby, *b.* 1945, *s.* 1956.	None
1831 I.	*Talbot of Malahide* (10th), Reginald John Richard Arundell, *b.* 1931, *s.* 1987, *m.*	Hon. Richard J. T. *A.*, *b.* 1957
1946	*Tedder* (3rd), Robin John Tedder, *b.* 1955, *s.* 1994, *m.*	Hon. Benjamin J. *T.*, *b.* 1985
1884	*Tennyson* (5th), Cdr. Mark Aubrey Tennyson, DSC, *b.* 1920, *s.* 1991, *m.*	Lt.-Cdr. James A. *T.* DSC, *b.* 1913
1918	*Terrington* (5th), (Christopher) Montague Woodhouse, DSO, OBE, *b.* 1917, *s.* 1998, *w.*	Hon. Christopher R. J. *W.*, *b.* 1946
1940	*Teviot* (2nd), Charles John Kerr, *b.* 1934, *s.* 1968, *m.*	Hon. Charles R. *K.*, *b.* 1971
1616	*Teynham* (20th), John Christopher Ingham Roper-Curzon, *b.* 1928, *s.* 1972, *m.*	Hon. David J. H. I. *R.-C.*, *b.* 1965
1964	*Thomson of Fleet* (2nd), Kenneth Roy Thomson, *b.* 1923, *s.* 1976, *m.*	Hon. David K. R. *T.*, *b.* 1957
1792	*Thurlow* (8th), Francis Edward Hovell-Thurlow-Cumming-Bruce, KCMG, *b.* 1912, *s.* 1971, *w.*	Hon. Roualeyn R. *H.-T.-C.-B.*, *b.* 1952
1876	*Tollemache* (5th), Timothy John Edward Tollemache, *b.* 1939, *s.* 1975, *m.*	Hon. Edward J. H. *T.*, *b.* 1976
1564 S.	*Torphichen* (15th), James Andrew Douglas Sandilands, *b.* 1946, *s.* 1975, *m.*	Douglas R. A. *S.*, *b.* 1926
1947	*Trefgarne* (2nd), David Garro Trefgarne, PC, *b.* 1941, *s.* 1960, *m.*	Hon. George G. *T.*, *b.* 1970
1921	*Trevethin* (4th) and *Oaksey* (2nd) (1947), John Geoffrey Tristram Lawrence, OBE, *b.* 1929, *s.* 1971, *m.*	Hon. Patrick J. T. *L.*, *b.* 1960
1880	*Trevor* (5th), Marke Charles Hill-Trevor, *b.* 1970, *s.* 1997, *m.*	Hon. Iain R. *H.-T.*, *b.* 1971
1461 I.	*Trimlestown* (21st), Raymond Charles Barnewall, *b.* 1930, *s.* 1997.	None
1940	*Tryon* (3rd), Anthony George Merrik Tryon, *b.* 1940, *s.* 1976.	Hon. Charles G. B. *T.*, *b.* 1976
1935	*Tweedsmuir* (3rd), William de l'Aigle Buchan, *b.* 1915, *s.* 1996, *m.*	Hon. John W. H. de l'A. *B.*, *b.* 1950
1523	*Vaux of Harrowden* (10th), John Hugh Philip Gilbey, *b.* 1915, *s.* 1977, *m.*	Hon. Anthony W. *G.*, *b.* 1940
1800 I.	*Ventry* (8th), Andrew Wesley Daubeny de Moleyns, *b.* 1943, *s.* 1987, *m.*	Hon. Francis W. *D. de M.*, *b.* 1965
1762	*Vernon* (10th), John Lawrance Vernon, *b.* 1923, *s.* 1963, *m.*	Col. William R. D. *Vernon-Harcourt*, OBE, *b.* 1909
1922	*Vestey* (3rd), Samuel George Armstrong Vestey, *b.* 1941, *s.* 1954, *m.*	Hon. William G. *V.*, *b.* 1983
1841	*Vivian* (6th), Nicholas Crespigny Laurence Vivian, *b.* 1935, *s.* 1991, *m.*	Hon. Charles H. C. *V.*, *b.* 1966
1934	*Wakehurst* (3rd), (John) Christopher Loder, *b.* 1925, *s.* 1970, *m.*	Hon. Timothy W. *L.*, *b.* 1958
1723	*Walpole* (10th), Robert Horatio Walpole (8th *Brit. Baron Walpole of Wolterton*, 1756), *b.* 1938, *s.* 1989, *m.*	Hon. Jonathan R. H. *W.*, *b.* 1967
1780	*Walsingham* (9th), John de Grey, MC, *b.* 1925, *s.* 1965, *m.*	Hon. Robert *de. G.*, *b.* 1969
1936	*Wardington* (2nd), Christopher Henry Beaumont Pease, *b.* 1924, *s.* 1950, *m.*	Hon. William S. *P.*, *b.* 1925
1792 I.	*Waterpark* (7th), Frederick Caryll Philip Cavendish, *b.* 1926, *s.* 1948, *m.*	Hon. Roderick A. *C.*, *b.* 1959
1942	*Wedgwood* (4th), Piers Anthony Weymouth Wedgwood, *b.* 1954, *s.* 1970, *m.*	John *W.* CBE, MD, FRCP, *b.* 1919
1861	*Westbury* (5th), David Alan Bethell, CBE, MC, *b.* 1922, *s.* 1961, *m.*	Hon. Richard N. *B.*, MBE, *b.* 1950
1944	*Westwood* (3rd), (William) Gavin Westwood, *b.* 1944, *s.* 1991, *m.*	Hon. W. Fergus *W.*, *b.* 1972
1935	*Wigram* (2nd), (George) Neville (Clive) Wigram, MC, *b.* 1915, *s.* 1960, *w.*	Maj. Hon. Andrew F. C. *W.* MVO, *b.* 1949
1491	*Willoughby de Broke* (21st), Leopold David Verney, *b.* 1938, *s.* 1986, *m.*	Hon. Rupert G. *V.*, *b.* 1966
1946	*Wilson* (2nd), Patrick Maitland Wilson, *b.* 1915, *s.* 1964, *w.*	None
1937	*Windlesham* (3rd), David James George Hennessy, CVO, PC, *b.* 1932, *s.* 1962, *w.*	Hon. James R. *H.*, *b.* 1968
1951	*Wise* (2nd), John Clayton Wise, *b.* 1923, *s.* 1968, *m.*	Hon. Christopher J. C. *W.* PH.D., *b.* 1949
1869	*Wolverton* (7th), Christopher Richard Glyn, *b.* 1938, *s.* 1988.	Hon. Andrew J. *G.*, *b.* 1943
1928	*Wraxall* (2nd), George Richard Lawley Gibbs, *b.* 1928, *s.* 1931.	Hon. Sir Eustace H. B. *G.*, KCVO, CMG, *b.* 1929
1915	*Wrenbury* (3rd), Revd John Burton Buckley, *b.* 1927, *s.* 1940, *m.*	Hon. William E. *B.*, *b.* 1966
1838	*Wrottesley* (6th), Clifton Hugh Lancelot de Verdon Wrottesley, *b.* 1968, *s.* 1977.	Hon. Stephen J. *W.*, *b.* 1955
1919	*Wyfold* (3rd), Hermon Robert Fleming Hermon-Hodge, ERD, *b.* 1915, *s.* 1942.	None
1829	*Wynford* (8th), Robert Samuel Best, MBE, *b.* 1917, *s.* 1943, *m.*	Hon. John P. R. *B.*, *b.* 1950
1308	*Zouche* (18th), James Assheton Frankland, *b.* 1943, *s.* 1965, *m.*	Hon. William T. A. *F.*, *b.* 1984

BARONESSES/LADIES IN THEIR OWN RIGHT

Style, The Right Hon. the Lady __, *or* The Right Hon. the Baroness __, according to her preference. Either style may be used, except in the case of Scottish titles (indicated by s.), which are not baronies (*see* page 136) and whose holders are always addressed as Lady
Husband, Untitled
Children's style, As for children of a Baron
For forms of address, *see* page 135

Created	Title, order of succession, name, etc.	Heir
1664	*Arlington,* Jennifer Jane Forwood, *b.* 1939, *title called out of abeyance* 1999, *m.*	Patrick John Dudley *F., b.* 1967
1455	*Berners* (16th in line), Pamela Vivien Kirkham, *b.* 1929, *title called out of abeyance* 1995, *m.*	Hon. Rupert W. T. *K., b.* 1953
1529	*Braye* (8th in line), Mary Penelope Aubrey-Fletcher, *b.* 1941, *s.* 1985, *m.*	Two co-heiresses
1321	*Dacre* (27th in line), Rachel Leila Douglas-Home, *b.* 1929, *title called out of abeyance* 1970, *w.*	Hon. James T. A. *D.-H., b.* 1952
1332	*Darcy de Knayth* (18th in line), Davina Marcia Ingrams, DBE, *b.* 1938, *s.* 1943, *w.*	Hon. Caspar D. *I., b.* 1962
1439	*Dudley* (14th in line), Barbara Amy Felicity Hamilton, *b.* 1907, *s.* 1972, *m.*	Hon. Jim A. H. *Wallace, b.* 1930
1490 s.	*Herries of Terregles* (14th in line), Anne Elizabeth Fitzalan-Howard, *b.* 1938, *s.* 1975, *m.*	Lady Mary *Mumford,* CVO, *b.* 1940
1602 s.	*Kinloss* (12th in line), Beatrice Mary Grenville Freeman-Grenville, *b.* 1922, *s.* 1944, *m.*	Master of Kinloss, *b.* 1953
1445 s.	*Saltoun* (20th in line), Flora Marjory Fraser, *b.* 1930, *s.* 1979, *m.*	Hon. Katharine I. M. I. *F., b.* 1957
1628	*Strange* (16th in line), (Jean) Cherry Drummond of Megginch, *b.* 1928, *title called out of abeyance* 1986, *m.*	Hon. Adam H. *D. of M., b.* 1953
1544/5	*Wharton* (11th in line), Myrtle Olive Felix Robertson, *b.* 1934, *title called out of abeyance* 1990, *m.*	Hon. Myles C. D. *R., b.* 1964
1313	*Willoughby de Eresby* (27th in line), (Nancy) Jane Marie Heathcote-Drummond-Willoughby, *b.* 1934, *s.* 1983.	Two co-heiresses

Life Peers

NEW LIFE PEERAGES *1 September 1998 to 31 August 1999*
NEW YEAR'S HONOURS (30 December 1998): Sir Peter
Michael Imbert, QPM; Onora Sylvia O'Neill, CBE; Sir
Narendrakumar Babubhai Patel; Sir Alexander
Trotman; Sir David Francis Williamson, GCMG, CB
QUEEN'S BIRTHDAY HONOURS (12 June 1999): Rt. Hon.
Sir Robert Fellowes, GCB, GCVO; Sir Norman Foster,
OM; Sir Ronald Oxburgh, KBE; Usha Prashar, CBE; Sir
Dennis Stevenson, CBE; Viven Stern, CBE
WORKING PEERS (19 June 1999): Catherine Ashton;
Elizabeth Barker; May Blood, MBE; William Bradshaw;
William Brett; Alexander Carlile, QC; Murray Elder;
Richard Faulkner; David Filkin, CBE; Rt. Hon. Sir
Michael Forsyth; Anita Gale; Robert Gavron, CBE;
Peter Goldsmith, QC; Anthony Grabiner, QC; Joan
Hanham, CBE; Angela Harris; Lyndon Harrison;
Rosalind Howells, OBE; Tarsem King; Sir Graham
Kirkham; John Laird; David Lea, OBE; David Lipsey;
Genista McIntosh; Hector MacKenzie; Doreen Massey;
Christopher Rennard, MBE; Dennis Rogan; Colin
Sharman, OBE; Peter Smith; Rt. Hon. William
Waldegrave; Diana Warwick; Alan Watson, CBE; Janet
Whitaker; Rosalie Wilkins; Kenneth Woolmer

CREATED UNDER THE APPELLATE
JURISDICTION ACT 1876 (AS AMENDED)

BARONS
Created
1986   Ackner, Desmond James Conrad Ackner, PC, *b.*
        1920, *m.*
1980   Bridge of Harwich, Nigel Cyprian Bridge, PC, *b.*
        1917, *m.*
1982   Brightman, John Anson Brightman, PC, *b.* 1911, *m.*
1991   Browne-Wilkinson, Nicolas Christopher Henry
        Browne-Wilkinson, PC, *b.* 1930, *m. Lord of Appeal
        in Ordinary*
1996   Clyde, James John Clyde, *b.* 1932, *m. Lord of Appeal
        in Ordinary*
1986   Goff of Chieveley, Robert Lionel Archibald Goff, PC,
        b. 1926, *m.*
1985   Griffiths, (William) Hugh Griffiths, MC, PC, *b.* 1923,
        m.
1998   Hobhouse of Woodborough, John Stewart Hobhouse,
        PC, *b.* 1932. *Lord of Appeal in Ordinary*
1995   Hoffmann, Leonard Hubert Hoffmann, PC, *b.* 1934,
        m. Lord of Appeal in Ordinary
1997   Hutton, (James) Brian (Edward) Hutton, PC, *b.*
        1931, *m. Lord of Appeal in Ordinary*
1988   Jauncey of Tullichettle, Charles Eliot Jauncey, PC, *b.*
        1925, *m.*
1977   Keith of Kinkel, Henry Shanks Keith, GBE, PC, *b.*
        1922, *m.*
1979   Lane, Geoffrey Dawson Lane, AFC, PC, *b.* 1918, *m.*
1993   Lloyd of Berwick, Anthony John Leslie Lloyd, PC, *b.*
        1929, *m. Lord of Appeal in Ordinary*
1998   Millett, Peter Julian Millett, PC, *b.* 1932, *m. Lord of
        Appeal in Ordinary*
1992   Mustill, Michael John Mustill, PC, *b.* 1931, *m.*
1994   Nicholls of Birkenhead, Donald James Nicholls, PC,
        b. 1933, *m. Lord of Appeal in Ordinary*
1994   Nolan, Michael Patrick Nolan, PC, *b.* 1928, *m.*

1986   Oliver of Aylmerton, Peter Raymond Oliver, PC, *b.*
        1921, *m.*
1999   Phillips of Worth Matravers, Nicholas Addison
        Phillips, PC, *b.* 1938, *m. Lord of Appeal in Ordinary*
1997   Saville of Newdigate, Mark Oliver Saville, PC, *b.*
        1936, *m. Lord of Appeal in Ordinary*
1977   Scarman, Leslie George Scarman, OBE, PC, *b.* 1911,
        m.
1992   Slynn of Hadley, Gordon Slynn, PC, *b.* 1930, *m. Lord
        of Appeal in Ordinary*
1995   Steyn, Johan van Zyl Steyn, PC, *b.* 1932, *m. Lord of
        Appeal in Ordinary*
1982   Templeman, Sydney William Templeman, MBE,
        PC, *b.* 1920, *m.*
1964   Wilberforce, Richard Orme Wilberforce, CMG, OBE,
        PC, *b.* 1907, *m.*
1992   Woolf, Harry Kenneth Woolf, PC, *b.* 1933, *m.
        Master of the Rolls*

CREATED UNDER THE LIFE
PEERAGES ACT 1958

BARONS
Created
1998   Ahmed, Nazir Ahmed, *b.* 1957, *m.*
1996   Alderdice, John Thomas Alderdice, *b.* 1955, *m.*
1988   Alexander of Weedon, Robert Scott Alexander, QC, *b.*
        1936, *m.*
1976   Allen of Abbeydale, Philip Allen, GCB, *b.* 1912, *m.*
1998   Alli, Waheed Alli.
1997   Alton of Liverpool, David Patrick Paul Alton, *b.*
        1951, *m.*
1965   Annan, Noël Gilroy Annan, OBE, *b.* 1916, *m.*
1992   Archer of Sandwell, Peter Kingsley Archer, PC, QC,
        b. 1926, *m.*
1992   Archer of Weston-super-Mare, Jeffrey Howard
        Archer, *b.* 1940, *m.*
1988   Armstrong of Ilminster, Robert Temple Armstrong,
        GCB, CVO, *b.* 1927, *m.*
1992   Ashley of Stoke, Jack Ashley, CH, PC, *b.* 1922, *m.*
1993   Attenborough, Richard Samuel Attenborough, CBE,
        b. 1923, *m.*
1998   Bach, William Stephen Goulden Bach, *b.* 1946, *m.*
1997   Bagri, Raj Kumar Bagri, CBE, *b.* 1930, *m.*
1997   Baker of Dorking, Kenneth Wilfred Baker, CH, PC, *b.*
        1934, *m.*
1974   Balniel, The Earl of Crawford and Balcarres. (*see*
        page 140)
1974   Barber, Anthony Perrinott Lysberg Barber, TD, PC,
        b. 1920, *m.*
1992   Barber of Tewkesbury, Derek Coates Barber, *b.* 1918,
        m.
1983   Barnett, Joel Barnett, PC, *b.* 1923, *m.*
1997   Bassam of Brighton, (John) Steven Bassam, *b.* 1953.
1982   Bauer, Prof. Peter Thomas Bauer, D.SC., FBA, *b.*
        1915.
1967   Beaumont of Whitley, Revd Timothy Wentworth
        Beaumont, *b.* 1928, *m.*
1998   Bell, Timothy John Leigh Bell, *b.* 1941, *m.*
1979   Bellwin, Irwin Norman Bellow, *b.* 1923, *m.*
1997   Biffen, (William) John Biffen, PC, *b.* 1930, *m.*
1996   Bingham of Cornhill, Thomas Henry Bingham, PC,
        b. 1933, *m. Lord Chief Justice of England*

1997 *Blackwell*, Norman Roy Blackwell, *b.* 1952, *m.*
1971 *Blake*, Robert Norman William Blake, FBA, *b.* 1916, *w.*
1994 *Blaker*, Peter Allan Renshaw Blaker, KCMG, PC, *b.* 1922, *m.*
1978 *Blease*, William John Blease, *b.* 1914, *m.*
1995 *Blyth of Rowington*, James Blyth, *b.* 1940, *m.*
1980 *Boardman*, Thomas Gray Boardman, MC, TD, *b.* 1919, *m.*
1996 *Borrie*, Gordon Johnson Borrie, QC, *b.* 1931, *m.*
1976 *Boston of Faversham*, Terence George Boston, QC, *b.* 1930, *m.*
1996 *Bowness*, Peter Spencer Bowness, CBE, *b.* 1943, *m.*
1999 *Bradshaw*, William Peter Bradshaw, *b.* 1936, *m.*
1998 *Bragg*, Melvyn Bragg, *b.* 1939, *m.*
1992 *Braine of Wheatley*, Bernard Richard Braine, PC, *b.* 1914, *w.*
1987 *Bramall*, Edwin Noel Westby Bramall, KG, GCB, OBE, MC, *b.* 1923, *m. Field Marshal*
1999 *Brett*, William Henry Brett, *b.* 1942, *m.*
1976 *Briggs*, Asa Briggs, FBA, *b.* 1921, *m.*
1997 *Brooke of Alverthorpe*, Clive Brooke, *b.* 1942, *m.*
1975 *Brookes*, Raymond Percival Brookes, *b.* 1909, *m.*
1998 *Brookman*, David Keith Brookman, *b.* 1937, *m.*
1979 *Brooks of Tremorfa*, John Edward Brooks, *b.* 1927, *m.*
1974 *Bruce of Donington*, Donald William Trevor Bruce, *b.* 1912, *m.*
1976 *Bullock*, Alan Louis Charles Bullock, FBA, *b.* 1914, *m.*
1997 *Burlison*, Thomas Henry Burlison, *b.* 1936, *m.*
1998 *Burns*, Terence Burns, GCB, *b.* 1944, *m.*
1998 *Butler of Brockwell*, (Frederick Edward) Robin Butler, GCB, CVO, *b.* 1938, *m.*
1988 *Butterfield*, (William) John (Hughes) Butterfield, OBE, DM, FRCP, *b.* 1920, *m.*
1985 *Butterworth*, John Blackstock Butterworth, CBE, *b.* 1918, *m.*
1978 *Buxton of Alsa*, Aubrey Leland Oakes Buxton, KCVO, MC, *b.* 1918, *m.*
1987 *Callaghan of Cardiff*, (Leonard) James Callaghan, KG, PC, *b.* 1912, *m.*
1984 *Cameron of Lochbroom*, Kenneth John Cameron, PC, *b.* 1931, *m.*
1981 *Campbell of Alloway*, Alan Robertson Campbell, QC, *b.* 1917, *m.*
1974 *Campbell of Croy*, Gordon Thomas Calthrop Campbell, MC, PC, *b.* 1921, *m.*
1999 *Carlile of Berriew*, Alexander Charles Carlile, QC, *b.* 1948, *m.*
1987 *Carlisle of Bucklow*, Mark Carlisle, QC, PC, *b.* 1929, *m.*
1983 *Carmichael of Kelvingrove*, Neil George Carmichael, *b.* 1921.
1975 *Carr of Hadley*, (Leonard) Robert Carr, PC, *b.* 1916, *m.*
1987 *Carter*, Denis Victor Carter, PC, *b.* 1932, *m.*
1977 *Carver*, (Richard) Michael (Power) Carver, GCB, CBE, DSO, MC, *b.* 1915, *m. Field Marshal*
1990 *Cavendish of Furness*, (Richard) Hugh Cavendish, *b.* 1941, *m.*
1996 *Chadlington*, Peter Selwyn Gummer, *b.* 1942, *m.*
1964 *Chalfont*, (Alun) Arthur Gwynne Jones, OBE, MC, PC, *b.* 1919, *m.*
1985 *Chapple*, Francis (Frank) Joseph Chapple, *b.* 1921, *w.*
1978 *Charteris of Amisfield*, Martin Michael Charles Charteris, GCB, GCVO, OBE, PC, Royal Victorian Chain, *b.* 1913, *m.*
1987 *Chilver*, (Amos) Henry Chilver, FRS, FREng., *b.* 1926, *m.*

1977 *Chitnis*, Pratap Chidamber Chitnis, *b.* 1936, *m.*
1998 *Christopher*, Anthony Martin Grosvenor Christopher, CBE, *b.* 1925, *m.*
1992 *Clark of Kempston*, William Gibson Haig Clark, PC, *b.* 1917, *m.*
1998 *Clarke of Hampstead*, Anthony James Clarke, CBE, *b.* 1932, *m.*
1979 *Cledwyn of Penrhos*, Cledwyn Hughes, CH, PC, *b.* 1916, *m.*
1998 *Clement-Jones*, Timothy Francis Clement-Jones, CBE, *b.* 1949, *m.*
1990 *Clinton-Davis*, Stanley Clinton Clinton-Davis, PC, *b.* 1928, *m.*
1978 *Cockfield*, (Francis) Arthur Cockfield, PC, *b.* 1916, *w.*
1987 *Cocks of Hartcliffe*, Michael Francis Lovell Cocks, PC, *b.* 1929, *m.*
1980 *Coggan*, Rt. Revd (Frederick) Donald Coggan, PC, Royal Victorian Chain, *b.* 1909, *m.*
1981 *Constantine of Stanmore*, Theodore Constantine, CBE, AE, *b.* 1910, *w.*
1992 *Cooke of Islandreagh*, Victor Alexander Cooke, OBE, *b.* 1920, *m.*
1996 *Cooke of Thorndon*, Robin Brunskill Cooke, KBE, PC, Ph.D., *b.* 1926, *m.*
1997 *Cope of Berkeley*, John Ambrose Cope, PC, *b.* 1937, *m.*
1997 *Cowdrey of Tonbridge*, (Michael) Colin Cowdrey, CBE, *b.* 1932, *m.*
1991 *Craig of Radley*, David Brownrigg Craig, GCB, OBE, *b.* 1929, *m. Marshal of the Royal Air Force*
1987 *Crickhowell*, (Roger) Nicholas Edwards, PC, *b.* 1934, *m.*
1978 *Croham*, Douglas Albert Vivian Allen, GCB, *b.* 1917, *w.*
1995 *Cuckney*, John Graham Cuckney, *b.* 1925, *m.*
1996 *Currie of Marylebone*, David Anthony Currie, *b.* 1946, *m.*
1979 *Dacre of Glanton*, Hugh Redwald Trevor-Roper, *b.* 1914, *w.*
1993 *Dahrendorf*, Ralf Dahrendorf, KBE, Ph.D., D.Phil., FBA, *b.* 1929, *m.*
1997 *Davies of Coity*, (David) Garfield Davies, CBE, *b.* 1935, *m.*
1997 *Davies of Oldham*, Bryan Davies, *b.* 1939, *m.*
1993 *Dean of Harptree*, (Arthur) Paul Dean, PC, *b.* 1924, *m.*
1998 *Dearing*, Ronald Ernest Dearing, CB, *b.* 1930, *m.*
1986 *Deedes*, William Francis Deedes, KBE MC, PC, *b.* 1913, *m.*
1991 *Desai*, Prof. Meghnad Jagdishchandra Desai, Ph.D., *b.* 1940, *m.*
1997 *Dholakia*, Navnit Dholakia, OBE, *b.* 1937, *m.*
1970 *Diamond*, John Diamond, *b.* 1907, *m.*
1997 *Dixon*, Donald Dixon, PC, *b.* 1929, *m.*
1993 *Dixon-Smith*, Robert William Dixon-Smith, *b.* 1934, *m.*
1988 *Donaldson of Lymington*, John Francis Donaldson, PC, *b.* 1920, *m.*
1985 *Donoughue*, Bernard Donoughue, D.Phil., *b.* 1934.
1987 *Dormand of Easington*, John Donkin Dormand, *b.* 1919, *m.*
1994 *Dubs*, Alfred Dubs, *b.* 1932, *m.*
1995 *Eames*, Robert Henry Alexander Eames, Ph.D., *b.* 1937, *m.*
1992 *Eatwell*, John Leonard Eatwell, *b.* 1945, *m.*
1983 *Eden of Winton*, John Benedict Eden, PC, *b.* 1925, *m.*
1999 *Elder*, Thomas Murray Elder.
1992 *Elis-Thomas*, Dafydd Elis Elis-Thomas, *b.* 1946, *m.*

1985	*Elliott of Morpeth*, Robert William Elliott, *b.* 1920, *m.*	1994	*Hambro*, Charles Eric Alexander Hambro, *b.* 1930, *m.*
1981	*Elystan-Morgan*, Dafydd Elystan Elystan-Morgan, *b.* 1932, *m.*	1998	*Hamlyn*, Paul Bertrand Hamlyn, CBE, *b.* 1926, *m.*
1980	*Emslie*, George Carlyle Emslie, MBE, PC, FRSE, *b.* 1919, *m.*	1998	*Hanningfield*, Paul Edward Winston White, *b.* 1940
		1983	*Hanson*, James Edward Hanson, *b.* 1922, *m.*
1997	*Evans of Parkside*, John Evans, *b.* 1930, *m.*	1997	*Hardie*, Andrew Rutherford Hardie, QC, PC, *b.* 1946, *m. Lord Advocate*
1998	*Evans of Watford*, David Charles Evans, *b.* 1942, *m.*	1997	*Hardy of Wath*, Peter Hardy, *b.* 1931, *m.*
1992	*Ewing of Kirkford*, Harry Ewing, *b.* 1931, *m.*	1974	*Harmar-Nicholls*, Harmar Harmar-Nicholls, *b.* 1912, *m.*
1983	*Ezra*, Derek Ezra, MBE, *b.* 1919, *m.*		
1997	*Falconer of Thoroton*, Charles Leslie Falconer, QC, *b.* 1951, *m.*	1974	*Harris of Greenwich*, John Henry Harris, PC, *b.* 1930, *m.*
1983	*Fanshawe of Richmond*, Anthony Henry Fanshawe Royle, KCMG, *b.* 1927, *m.*	1998	*Harris of Haringey*, (Jonathan) Toby Harris, *b.* 1953, *m.*
1999	*Faulkner of Worcester*, Richard Oliver Faulkner, *b.* 1946, *m.*	1979	*Harris of High Cross*, Ralph Harris, *b.* 1924, *m.*
1996	*Feldman*, Basil Feldman, *b.* 1926, *m.*	1996	*Harris of Peckham*, Philip Charles Harris, *b.* 1942, *m.*
1999	*Fellowes*, Robert Fellowes, PC, GCB, GCVO, *b.* 1941, *m.*	1999	*Harrison*, Lyndon Henry Arthur Harrison, *b.* 1947, *m.*
1999	*Filkin*, David Geoffrey Nigel Filkin, CBE, *b.* 1944.	1968	*Hartwell*, (William) Michael Berry, MBE, TD, *b.* 1911, *w.*
1983	*Fitt*, Gerard Fitt, *b.* 1926, *w.*		
1979	*Flowers*, Brian Hilton Flowers, FRS, *b.* 1924, *m.*	1993	*Haskel*, Simon Haskel, *b.* 1934, *m.*
1967	*Foot*, John Mackintosh Foot, *b.* 1909, *m.*	1998	*Haskins*, Christopher Robin Haskins, *b.* 1937, *m.*
1999	*Forsyth of Drumlean*, Michael Bruce Forsyth, *b.* 1954, *m.*	1990	*Haslam*, Robert Haslam, *b.* 1923, *m.*
1982	*Forte*, Charles Forte, *b.* 1908, *m.*	1997	*Hattersley*, Roy Sidney George Hattersley, PC, *b.* 1932, *m.*
1999	*Foster of Thames Bank*, Norman Robert Foster, OM, *b.* 1935, *m.*	1992	*Hayhoe*, Bernard John (Barney) Hayhoe, PC, *b.* 1925, *m.*
1989	*Fraser of Carmyllie*, Peter Lovat Fraser, PC, QC, *b.* 1945, *m.*	1992	*Healey*, Denis Winston Healey, CH, MBE, PC, *b.* 1917, *m.*
1997	*Freeman*, Roger Norman Freeman, PC, *b.* 1942, *m.*	1984	*Henderson of Brompton*, Peter Gordon Henderson, KCB, *b.* 1922, *m.*
1982	*Gallacher*, John Gallacher, *b.* 1920, *m.*		
1997	*Garel-Jones*, (William Armand) Thomas Tristan Garel-Jones, PC, *b.* 1941, *m.*	1997	*Higgins*, Terence Langley Higgins, KBE, PC, *b.* 1928, *m.*
1999	*Gavron*, Robert Gavron, CBE, *b.* 1930, *m.*	1979	*Hill-Norton*, Peter John Hill-Norton, GCB, *b.* 1915, *m. Admiral of the Fleet*
1992	*Geraint*, Geraint Wyn Howells, *b.* 1925, *m.*		
1975	*Gibson*, (Richard) Patrick (Tallentyre) Gibson, *b.* 1916, *m.*	1997	*Hogg of Cumbernauld*, Norman Hogg, *b.* 1938, *m.*
1979	*Gibson-Watt*, (James) David Gibson-Watt, MC, PC, *b.* 1918, *m.*	1979	*Holderness*, Richard Frederick Wood, PC, *b.* 1920, *m.*
1997	*Gilbert*, John William Gilbert, PC, PH.D., *b.* 1927, *m.*	1991	*Hollick*, Clive Richard Hollick, *b.* 1945, *m.*
1992	*Gilmour of Craigmillar*, Ian Hedworth John Little Gilmour, PC, *b.* 1926, *m.*	1990	*Holme of Cheltenham*, Richard Gordon Holme, CBE, *b.* 1936, *m.*
1994	*Gladwin of Clee*, Derek Oliver Gladwin, CBE, *b.* 1930, *m.*	1979	*Hooson*, (Hugh) Emlyn Hooson, QC, *b.* 1925, *m.*
1977	*Glenamara*, Edward Watson Short, CH, PC, *b.* 1912, *m.*	1995	*Hope of Craighead*, (James Arthur) David Hope, PC, *b.* 1938, *m. Lord of Appeal in Ordinary*
1999	*Goldsmith*, Peter Henry Goldsmith, QC, *b.* 1950, *m.*	1992	*Howe of Aberavon*, (Richard Edward) Geoffrey Howe, CH, PC, QC, *b.* 1926, *m.*
1997	*Goodhart*, William Howard Goodhart, QC, *b.* 1933, *m.*	1997	*Howell of Guildford*, David Arthur Russell Howell, PC, *b.* 1936, *m.*
1997	*Gordon of Strathblane*, James Stuart Gordon, CBE, *b.* 1936, *m.*	1978	*Howie of Troon*, William Howie, *b.* 1924, *m.*
1999	*Grabiner*, Anthony Stephen Grabiner, QC, *b.* 1945, *m.*	1997	*Hoyle*, (Eric) Douglas Harvey Hoyle, *b.* 1930, *w.*
		1961	*Hughes*, William Hughes, CBE, PC, *b.* 1911, *w.*
1983	*Graham of Edmonton*, (Thomas) Edward Graham, *b.* 1925, *m.*	1997	*Hughes of Woodside*, Robert Hughes, *b.* 1932, *m.*
		1997	*Hunt of Kings Heath*, Philip Alexander Hunt, OBE, *b.* 1949, *m.*
1983	*Gray of Contin*, James (Hamish) Hector Northey Gray, PC, *b.* 1927, *m.*	1980	*Hunt of Tanworth*, John Joseph Benedict Hunt, GCB, *b.* 1919, *m.*
1974	*Greene of Harrow Weald*, Sidney Francis Greene, CBE, *b.* 1910, *m.*	1997	*Hunt of Wirral*, David James Fletcher Hunt, MBE, PC, *b.* 1942, *m.*
1974	*Greenhill of Harrow*, Denis Arthur Greenhill, GCMG, OBE, *b.* 1913, *m.*	1997	*Hurd of Westwell*, Douglas Richard Hurd, CH, CBE, PC, *b.* 1930, *m.*
1975	*Gregson*, John Gregson, *b.* 1924.	1996	*Hussey of North Bradley*, Marmaduke James Hussey, *b.* 1923, *m.*
1968	*Grey of Naunton*, Ralph Francis Alnwick Grey, GCMG, GCVO, OBE, *b.* 1910, *w.*	1978	*Hutchinson of Lullington*, Jeremy Nicolas Hutchinson, QC, *b.* 1915, *m.*
1991	*Griffiths of Fforestfach*, Brian Griffiths, *b.* 1941, *m.*	1999	*Imbert*, Peter Michael Imbert, QPM, *b.* 1933, *m.*
1995	*Habgood*, Rt. Revd John Stapylton Habgood, PC, PH.D., *b.* 1927, *m.*	1997	*Inge*, Peter Anthony Inge, GCB, *b.* 1935, *m. Field Marshal*
1970	*Hailsham of St Marylebone*, Quintin McGarel Hogg, KG, CH, PC, FRS, *b.* 1907, *w.*	1982	*Ingrow*, John Aked Taylor, OBE, TD, *b.* 1917, *m.*

1987 *Irvine of Lairg*, Alexander Andrew Mackay Irvine, PC, QC, *b.* 1940, *m. Lord High Chancellor*
1997 *Islwyn*, Royston John (Roy) Hughes, *b.* 1925, *m.*
1997 *Jacobs*, (David) Anthony Jacobs, *b.* 1931, *m.*
1988 *Jakobovits*, Immanuel Jakobovits, *b.* 1921, *m.*
1997 *Janner of Braunstone*, Greville Ewan Janner, QC, *b.* 1928, *w.*
1987 *Jenkin of Roding*, (Charles) Patrick (Fleeming) Jenkin, PC, *b.* 1926, *m.*
1987 *Jenkins of Hillhead*, Roy Harris Jenkins, OM, PC, *b.* 1920, *m.*
1981 *Jenkins of Putney*, Hugh Gater Jenkins, *b.* 1908, *w.*
1987 *Johnston of Rockport*, Charles Collier Johnston, TD, *b.* 1915, *m.*
1997 *Jopling*, (Thomas) Michael Jopling, PC, *b.* 1930, *m.*
1991 *Judd*, Frank Ashcroft Judd, *b.* 1935, *m.*
1980 *Keith of Castleacre*, Kenneth Alexander Keith, *b.* 1916, *m.*
1997 *Kelvedon*, (Henry) Paul Guinness Channon, PC, *b.* 1935, *m.*
1996 *Kilpatrick of Kincraig*, Robert Kilpatrick, CBE, *b.* 1926, *m.*
1985 *Kimball*, Marcus Richard Kimball, *b.* 1928, *m.*
1983 *King of Wartnaby*, John Leonard King, *b.* 1918, *m.*
1999 *King of West Bromwich*, Tarsem King.
1993 *Kingsdown*, Robert (Robin) Leigh-Pemberton, KG, PC, *b.* 1927, *m.*
1994 *Kingsland*, Christopher James Prout, TD, PC, QC, *b.* 1942.
1999 *Kirkham*, Graham Kirkham, *b.* 1944, *m.*
1975 *Kirkhill*, John Farquharson Smith, *b.* 1930, *m.*
1987 *Knights*, Philip Douglas Knights, CBE, QPM, *b.* 1920, *m.*
1991 *Laing of Dunphail*, Hector Laing, *b.* 1923, *m.*
1999 *Laird*, John Dunn Laird, *b.* 1944, *m.*
1998 *Laming*, (William) Herbert Laming, CBE, *b.* 1936, *m.*
1998 *Lamont of Lerwick*, Norman Stewart Hughson Lamont, PC, *b.* 1942.
1990 *Lane of Horsell*, Peter Stewart Lane, *b.* 1925, *w.*
1997 *Lang of Monkton*, Ian Bruce Lang, PC, *b.* 1940, *m.*
1992 *Lawson of Blaby*, Nigel Lawson, PC, *b.* 1932, *m.*
1999 *Lea of Crondall*, David Edward Lea, OBE, *b.* 1937.
1993 *Lester of Herne Hill*, Anthony Paul Lester, QC, *b.* 1936, *m.*
1997 *Levene of Portsoken*, Peter Keith Levene, KBE, *b.* 1941, *m.*
1997 *Levy*, Michael Abraham Levy, *b.* 1944, *m.*
1989 *Lewis of Newnham*, Jack Lewis, FRS, *b.* 1928, *m.*
1999 *Lipsey*, David Lawrence Lipsey, *b.* 1948, *m.*
1997 *Lloyd-Webber*, Andrew Lloyd Webber, *b.* 1948, *m.*
1997 *Lofthouse of Pontefract*, Geoffrey Lofthouse, *b.* 1925, *w.*
1974 *Lovell-Davis*, Peter Lovell Lovell-Davis, *b.* 1924, *m.*
1984 *McAlpine of West Green*, (Robert) Alistair McAlpine, *b.* 1942, *m.*
1988 *Macaulay of Bragar*, Donald Macaulay, QC, *b.* 1933, *m.*
1975 *McCarthy*, William Edward John McCarthy, D.Phil., *b.* 1925, *m.*
1976 *McCluskey*, John Herbert McCluskey, *b.* 1929, *m.*
1989 *McColl of Dulwich*, Ian McColl, CBE, FRCS, FRCSE, *b.* 1933, *m.*
1995 *McConnell*, Robert William Brian McConnell, PC (NI), *b.* 1922, *m.*
1998 *Macdonald of Tradeston*, Angus John Macdonald, CBE, *b.* 1940, *m.*
1991 *Macfarlane of Bearsden*, Norman Somerville Macfarlane, KT, FRSE, *b.* 1926, *m.*

1982 *McIntosh of Haringey*, Andrew Robert McIntosh, *b.* 1933, *m.*
1991 *Mackay of Ardbrecknish*, John Jackson Mackay, PC, *b.* 1938, *m.*
1979 *Mackay of Clashfern*, James Peter Hymers Mackay, KT, PC, FRSE, *b.* 1927, *m.*
1995 *Mackay of Drumadoon*, Donald Sage Mackay, PC, *b.* 1946, *m.*
1999 *MacKenzie of Culkein*, Hector Uisdean MacKenzie, *b.* 1940.
1998 *Mackenzie of Framwellgate*, Brian Mackenzie, OBE, *b.* 1943, *m.*
1988 *Mackenzie-Stuart*, Alexander John Mackenzie Stuart, *b.* 1924, *m.*
1974 *Mackie of Benshie*, George Yull Mackie, CBE, DSO, DFC, *b.* 1919, *m.*
1996 *MacLaurin*, Ian Charter MacLaurin, *b.* 1937, *w.*
1982 *MacLehose of Beoch*, (Crawford) Murray MacLehose, KT, GBE, KCMG, KCVO, *b.* 1917, *m.*
1995 *McNally*, Tom McNally, *b.* 1943, *m.*
1991 *Marlesford*, Mark Shuldham Schreiber, *b.* 1931, *m.*
1981 *Marsh*, Richard William Marsh, PC, *b.* 1928, *m.*
1998 *Marshall of Knightsbridge*, Colin Marsh Marshall, *b.* 1933, *m.*
1987 *Mason of Barnsley*, Roy Mason, PC, *b.* 1924, *m.*
1997 *Mayhew of Twysden*, Patrick Barnabas Burke Mayhew, QC, PC, *b.* 1929, *m.*
1992 *Merlyn-Rees*, Merlyn Merlyn-Rees, PC, *b.* 1920, *m.*
1978 *Mishcon*, Victor Mishcon, *b.* 1915, *m.*
1981 *Molloy*, William John Molloy, *b.* 1918.
1997 *Molyneaux of Killead*, James Henry Molyneaux, KBE, PC, *b.* 1920.
1997 *Monro of Langholm*, Hector Seymour Peter Monro, AE, PC, *b.* 1922, *m.*
1997 *Montague of Oxford*, Michael Jacob Montague, CBE, *b.* 1932.
1992 *Moore of Lower Marsh*, John Edward Michael Moore, PC, *b.* 1937, *m.*
1986 *Moore of Wolvercote*, Philip Brian Cecil Moore, GCB, GCVO, CMG, PC, *b.* 1921, *m.*
1990 *Morris of Castle Morris*, Brian Robert Morris, D.Phil., *b.* 1930, *m.*
1997 *Morris of Manchester*, Alfred Morris, PC, *b.* 1928, *m.*
1971 *Moyola*, James Dawson Chichester-Clark, PC (NI), *b.* 1923, *m.*
1985 *Murray of Epping Forest*, Lionel Murray, OBE, PC, *b.* 1922, *m.*
1979 *Murton of Lindisfarne*, (Henry) Oscar Murton, OBE, TD, PC, *b.* 1914, *m.*
1997 *Naseby*, Michael Wolfgang Laurence Morris, PC, *b.* 1936, *m.*
1997 *Neill of Bladen*, (Francis) Patrick Neill, QC, *b.* 1926, *m.*
1997 *Newby*, Richard Mark Newby, OBE, *b.* 1953, *m.*
1997 *Newton of Braintree*, Antony Harold Newton, OBE, PC, *b.* 1937, *m.*
1994 *Nickson*, David Wigley Nickson, KBE, FRSE, *b.* 1929, *m.*
1975 *Northfield*, (William) Donald Chapman, *b.* 1923.
1998 *Norton of Louth*, Philip Norton, *b.* 1951.
1997 *Onslow of Woking*, Cranley Gordon Douglas Onslow, KCMG, PC, *b.* 1926, *m.*
1976 *Oram*, Albert Edward Oram, *b.* 1913, *m.*
1997 *Orme*, Stanley Orme, PC, *b.* 1923, *m.*
1992 *Owen*, David Anthony Llewellyn Owen, CH, PC, *b.* 1938, *m.*
1999 *Oxburgh*, Ernest Ronald Oxburgh, KBE, FRS, Ph.D., *b.* 1934, *m.*
1991 *Palumbo*, Peter Garth Palumbo, *b.* 1935, *m.*
1992 *Parkinson*, Cecil Edward Parkinson, PC, *b.* 1931, *m.*

1975 *Parry,* Gordon Samuel David Parry, *b.* 1925, *m.*

1999 *Patel,* Narendrakumar Babubhai Patel, *b.* 1938.

1997 *Patten,* John Haggitt Charles Patten, PC, *b.* 1945, *m.*

1996 *Paul,* Swraj Paul, *b.* 1931, *m.*

1990 *Pearson of Rannoch,* Malcolm Everard MacLaren Pearson, *b.* 1942, *m.*

1979 *Perry of Walton,* Walter Laing Macdonald Perry, OBE, FRS, FRSE, *b.* 1921, *m.*

1987 *Peston,* Maurice Harry Peston, *b.* 1931, *m.*

1983 *Peyton of Yeovil,* John Wynne William Peyton, PC, *b.* 1919, *m.*

1998 *Phillips of Sudbury,* Andrew Wyndham Phillips, OBE, *b.* 1939, *m.*

1996 *Pilkington of Oxenford,* Revd Canon Peter Pilkington, *b.* 1933, *w.*

1992 *Plant of Highfield,* Prof. Raymond Plant, PH.D., *b.* 1945, *m.*

1959 *Plowden,* Edwin Noel Plowden, GBE, KCB, *b.* 1907, *m.*

1987 *Plumb,* (Charles) Henry Plumb, MEP, *b.* 1925, *m.*

1981 *Plummer of St Marylebone,* (Arthur) Desmond (Herne) Plummer, TD, *b.* 1914, *w.*

1990 *Porter of Luddenham,* George Porter, OM, FRS, *b.* 1920, *m.*

1992 *Prentice,* Reginald Ernest Prentice, PC, *b.* 1923, *m.*

1987 *Prior,* James Michael Leathes Prior, PC, *b.* 1927, *m.*

1982 *Prys-Davies,* Gwilym Prys Prys-Davies, *b.* 1923, *m.*

1997 *Puttnam,* David Terence Puttnam, CBE, *b.* 1941, *m.*

1987 *Pym,* Francis Leslie Pym, MC, PC, *b.* 1922, *m.*

1982 *Quinton,* Anthony Meredith Quinton, FBA, *b.* 1925, *m.*

1994 *Quirk,* Prof. (Charles) Randolph Quirk, CBE, FBA, *b.* 1920, *m.*

1997 *Randall of St Budeaux,* Stuart Jeffrey Randall, *b.* 1938, *m.*

1978 *Rawlinson of Ewell,* Peter Anthony Grayson Rawlinson, PC, QC, *b.* 1919, *m.*

1976 *Rayne,* Max Rayne, *b.* 1918, *m.*

1997 *Razzall,* (Edward) Timothy Razzall, CBE, *b.* 1943, *m.*

1987 *Rees,* Peter Wynford Innes Rees, PC, QC, *b.* 1926, *m.*

1988 *Rees-Mogg,* William Rees-Mogg, *b.* 1928, *m.*

1991 *Renfrew of Kaimsthorn,* (Andrew) Colin Renfrew, FBA, *b.* 1937, *m.*

1999 *Rennard,* Christopher John Rennard, MBE, *b.* 1960.

1979 *Renton,* David Lockhart-Mure Renton, KBE, TD, PC, QC, *b.* 1908, *w.*

1997 *Renton of Mount Harry,* (Ronald) Timothy Renton, PC, *b.* 1932, *m.*

1997 *Renwick of Clifton,* Robin William Renwick, KCMG, *b.* 1937, *m.*

1990 *Richard,* Ivor Seward Richard, PC, QC, *b.* 1932, *m.*

1979 *Richardson,* John Samuel Richardson, LVO, MD, FRCP, *b.* 1910, *w.*

1983 *Richardson of Duntisbourne,* Gordon William Humphreys Richardson, KG, MBE, TD, PC, *b.* 1915, *m.*

1992 *Rix,* Brian Norman Roger Rix, CBE, *b.* 1924, *m.*

1997 *Roberts of Conwy,* (Ieuan) Wyn (Pritchard) Roberts, PC, *b.* 1930, *m.*

1999 *Robertson of Port Ellen,* George Islay MacNeill Robertson, PC, *b.* 1946, *m.*

1992 *Rodger of Earlsferry,* Alan Ferguson Rodger, PC, QC, FBA, *b.* 1944.

1992 *Rodgers of Quarry Bank,* William Thomas Rodgers, PC, *b.* 1928, *m.*

1999 *Rogan,* Dennis Robert David Rogan, *b.* 1942, *m.*

1996 *Rogers of Riverside,* Richard George Rogers, RA, RIBA, *b.* 1933, *m.*

1977 *Roll of Ipsden,* Eric Roll, KCMG, CB, *b.* 1907, *w.*

1991 *Runcie,* Rt Revd Robert Alexander Kennedy Runcie, MC, PC, Royal Victorian Chain, *b.* 1921, *m.*

1997 *Russell-Johnston,* (David) Russell Russell-Johnston, *b.* 1932, *m.*

1975 *Ryder of Eaton Hastings,* Sydney Thomas Franklin (Don) Ryder, *b.* 1916, *m.*

1997 *Ryder of Wensum,* Richard Andrew Ryder, OBE, PC, *b.* 1949, *m.*

1996 *Saatchi,* Maurice Saatchi, *b.* 1946, *m.*

1989 *Sainsbury of Preston Candover,* John Davan Sainsbury, KG, *b.* 1927, *m.*

1997 *Sainsbury of Turville,* David John Sainsbury, *b.* 1940, *m.*

1987 *St John of Fawsley,* Norman Antony Francis St John-Stevas, PC, *b.* 1929.

1997 *Sandberg,* Michael Graham Ruddock Sandberg, CBE, *b.* 1927, *m.*

1985 *Sanderson of Bowden,* Charles Russell Sanderson, *b.* 1933, *m.*

1998 *Sawyer,* Lawrence (Tom) Sawyer.

1979 *Scanlon,* Hugh Parr Scanlon, *b.* 1913, *m.*

1978 *Sefton of Garston,* William Henry Sefton, *b.* 1915, *m.*

1997 *Selkirk of Douglas,* James Alexander Douglas-Hamilton, MSP, PC, QC, *b.* 1942, *m.*

1996 *Sewel,* John Buttifant Sewel, CBE, *b.* 1946.

1999 *Sharman,* Colin Morven Sharman, OBE, *b.* 1943, *m.*

1994 *Shaw of Northstead,* Michael Norman Shaw, *b.* 1920, *m.*

1959 *Shawcross,* Hartley William Shawcross, GBE, PC, QC, *b.* 1902, *m.*

1994 *Sheppard of Didgemere,* Allan John George Sheppard, KCVO, *b.* 1932, *m.*

1998 *Sheppard of Liverpool,* David Stuart Sheppard, *b.* 1929, *m.*

1997 *Shore of Stepney,* Peter David Shore, PC, *b.* 1924, *m.*

1980 *Sieff of Brimpton,* Marcus Joseph Sieff, OBE, *b.* 1913, *w.*

1971 *Simon of Glaisdale,* Jocelyn Edward Salis Simon, PC, *b.* 1911, *m.*

1997 *Simon of Highbury,* David Alec Gwyn Simon, CBE, *b.* 1939, *m.*

1997 *Simpson of Dunkeld,* George Simpson, *b.* 1942, *m.*

1991 *Skidelsky,* Robert Jacob Alexander Skidelsky, D.PHIL., *b.* 1939, *m.*

1997 *Smith of Clifton,* Trevor Arthur Smith, *b.* 1937, *m.*

1999 *Smith of Leigh,* Peter Richard Charles Smith.

1990 *Soulsby of Swaffham Prior,* Ernest Jackson Lawson Soulsby, PH.D., *b.* 1926, *m.*

1983 *Stallard,* Albert William Stallard, *b.* 1921, *m.*

1997 *Steel of Aikwood,* David Martin Scott Steel, PC, KBE, MSP, *b.* 1938, *m.*

1991 *Sterling of Plaistow,* Jeffrey Maurice Sterling, CBE, *b.* 1934, *m.*

1987 *Stevens of Ludgate,* David Robert Stevens, *b.* 1936, *m.*

1999 *Stevenson of Coddenham,* Henry Dennistoun Stevenson, CBE, *b.* 1945, *m.*

1992 *Stewartby,* (Bernard Harold) Ian (Halley) Stewart, RD, PC, FBA, FRSE, *b.* 1935, *m.*

1981 *Stodart of Leaston,* James Anthony Stodart, PC, *b.* 1916, *w.*

1983 *Stoddart of Swindon,* David Leonard Stoddart, *b.* 1926, *m.*

1969 *Stokes,* Donald Gresham Stokes, TD, FREng., *b.* 1914, *w.*

1997 *Stone of Blackheath,* Andrew Zelig Stone, *b.* 1942, *m.*

1971 *Tanlaw,* Simon Brooke Mackay, *b.* 1934, *m.*

1996 *Taverne,* Dick Taverne, QC, *b.* 1928, *m.*

1978   *Taylor of Blackburn*, Thomas Taylor, CBE, *b*. 1929, *m*.
1968   *Taylor of Gryfe*, Thomas Johnston Taylor, FRSE, *b*. 1912, *m*.
1996   *Taylor of Warwick*, John David Beckett Taylor, *b*. 1952, *m*.
1992   *Tebbit*, Norman Beresford Tebbit, CH, PC, *b*. 1931, *m*.
1996   *Thomas of Gresford*, Donald Martin Thomas, OBE, QC, *b*. 1937, *m*.
1987   *Thomas of Gwydir*, Peter John Mitchell Thomas, PC, QC, *b*. 1920, *w*.
1997   *Thomas of Macclesfield*, Terence James Thomas, CBE, *b*. 1937, *m*.
1981   *Thomas of Swynnerton*, Hugh Swynnerton Thomas, *b*. 1931, *m*.
1977   *Thomson of Monifieth*, George Morgan Thomson, KT, PC, *b*. 1921, *m*.
1990   *Tombs*, Francis Leonard Tombs, FREng., *b*. 1924, *m*.
1998   *Tomlinson*, John Edward Tomlinson, MEP, *b*. 1939.
1994   *Tope*, Graham Norman Tope, CBE, *b*. 1943, *m*.
1981   *Tordoff*, Geoffrey Johnson Tordoff, *b*. 1928, *m*.
1999   *Trotman*, Alexander Trotman, *b*. 1933.
1993   *Tugendhat*, Christopher Samuel Tugendhat, *b*. 1937, *m*.
1990   *Varley*, Eric Graham Varley, PC, *b*. 1932, *m*.
1996   *Vincent of Coleshill*, Richard Frederick Vincent, GBE, KCB, DSO, *b*. 1931, *m*. (Field Marshal)
1985   *Vinson*, Nigel Vinson, LVO, *b*. 1931, *m*.
1990   *Waddington*, David Charles Waddington, GCVO, PC, QC, *b*. 1929, *m*.
1990   *Wade of Chorlton*, (William) Oulton Wade, *b*. 1932, *m*.
1992   *Wakeham*, John Wakeham, PC, *b*. 1932, *m*.
1999   *Waldegrave of North Hill*, William Arthur Waldegrave, PC, *b*. 1946, *m*.
1997   *Walker of Doncaster*, Harold Walker, PC, *b*. 1927, *m*.
1992   *Walker of Worcester*, Peter Edward Walker, MBE, PC, *b*. 1932, *m*.
1974   *Wallace of Coslany*, George Douglas Wallace, *b*. 1906, *m*.
1995   *Wallace of Saltaire*, William John Lawrence Wallace, PH.D., *b*. 1941, *m*.
1989   *Walton of Detchant*, John Nicholas Walton, TD, FRCP, *b*. 1922, *m*.
1998   *Warner*, Norman Reginald Warner, *b*. 1940, *m*.
1997   *Watson of Invergowrie*, Michael Goodall Watson, MSP, *b*. 1949, *m*.
1999   *Watson of Richmond*, Alan John Watson, CBE, *b*. 1941, *m*.
1992   *Weatherill*, (Bruce) Bernard Weatherill, PC, *b*. 1920, *m*.
1977   *Wedderburn of Charlton*, (Kenneth) William Wedderburn, FBA, QC, *b*. 1927, *m*.
1976   *Weidenfeld*, (Arthur) George Weidenfeld, *b*. 1919, *m*.
1980   *Weinstock*, Arnold Weinstock, *b*. 1924, *m*.
1978   *Whaddon*, (John) Derek Page, *b*. 1927, *m*.
1996   *Whitty*, John Lawrence (Larry) Whitty, *b*. 1943, *m*.
1974   *Wigoder*, Basil Thomas Wigoder, QC, *b*. 1921, *m*.
1985   *Williams of Elvel*, Charles Cuthbert Powell Williams, CBE, *b*. 1933, *m*.
1992   *Williams of Mostyn*, Gareth Wyn Williams, QC, *b*. 1941, *m*.
1999   *Williamson of Horton*, David Francis Williamson, GCMG, CB, *b*. 1934, *m*.
1992   *Wilson of Tillyorn*, David Clive Wilson, GCMG, PH.D., *b*. 1935, *m*.
1995   *Winston*, Robert Maurice Lipson Winston, FRCOG, *b*. 1940, *m*.

1985   *Wolfson*, Leonard Gordon Wolfson, *b*. 1927, *m*.
1991   *Wolfson of Sunningdale*, David Wolfson, *b*. 1935, *m*.
1999   *Woolmer of Leeds*, Kenneth John Woolmer, *b*. 1940, *m*.
1994   *Wright of Richmond*, Patrick Richard Henry Wright, GCMG, *b*. 1931, *m*.
1978   *Young of Dartington*, Michael Young, PH.D., *b*. 1915, *m*.
1984   *Young of Graffham*, David Ivor Young, PC, *b*. 1932, *m*.
1992   *Younger of Prestwick*, The Viscount Younger of Leckie. (*see* page 147)

BARONESSES

Created
1997   *Amos*, Valerie Ann Amos, *b*. 1954.
1996   *Anelay of St Johns*, Joyce Anne Anelay, DBE, *b*. 1947, *m*.
1999   *Ashton of Upholland*, Catherine Margaret Ashton, *m*.
1999   *Barker*, Elizabeth Jean Barker, *b*. 1961.
1987   *Blackstone*, Tessa Ann Vosper Blackstone, PH.D., *b*. 1942.
1987   *Blatch*, Emily May Blatch, CBE, PC, *b*. 1937, *m*.
1999   *Blood*, May Blood, MBE, *b*. 1938.
1990   *Brigstocke*, Heather Renwick Brigstocke, *b*. 1929, *w*.
1964   *Brooke of Ystradfellte*, Barbara Muriel Brooke, DBE, *b*. 1908, *w*.
1998   *Buscombe*, Peta Jane Buscombe, *b*. 1954, *m*.
1996   *Byford*, Hazel Byford, DBE, *b*. 1941, *m*.
1982   *Carnegy of Lour*, Elizabeth Patricia Carnegy of Lour, *b*. 1925.
1990   *Castle of Blackburn*, Barbara Anne Castle, PC, *b*. 1910, *w*.
1992   *Chalker of Wallasey*, Lynda Chalker, PC, *b*. 1942, *m*.
1982   *Cox*, Caroline Anne Cox, *b*. 1937, *m*.
1998   *Crawley*, Christine Mary Crawley, MEP, *b*. 1950, *m*.
1990   *Cumberlege*, Julia Frances Cumberlege, CBE, *b*. 1943, *m*.
1978   *David*, Nora Ratcliff David, *b*. 1913, *w*.
1993   *Dean of Thornton-le-Fylde*, Brenda Dean, PC, *b*. 1943, *m*.
1974   *Delacourt-Smith of Alteryn*, Margaret Rosalind Delacourt-Smith, *b*. 1916, *m*.
1991   *Denton of Wakefield*, Jean Denton, CBE, *b*. 1935.
1990   *Dunn*, Lydia Selina Dunn, DBE, *b*. 1940, *m*.
1990   *Eccles of Moulton*, Diana Catherine Eccles, *b*. 1933, *m*.
1972   *Elles*, Diana Louie Elles, *b*. 1921, *m*.
1997   *Emerton*, Audrey Caroline Emerton, DBE, *b*. 1935.
1974   *Falkender*, Marcia Matilda Falkender, CBE, *b*. 1932.
1994   *Farrington of Ribbleton*, Josephine Farrington, *b*. 1940, *m*.
1974   *Fisher of Rednal*, Doris Mary Gertrude Fisher, *b*. 1919, *w*.
1990   *Flather*, Shreela Flather, *m*.
1997   *Fookes*, Janet Evelyn Fookes, DBE, *b*. 1936.
1999   *Gale*, Anita Gale, *b*. 1940.
1981   *Gardner of Parkes*, (Rachel) Trixie (Anne) Gardner, *b*. 1927, *m*.
1998   *Goudie*, Mary Teresa Goudie, *b*. 1946, *m*.
1993   *Gould of Potternewton*, Joyce Brenda Gould, *b*. 1932, *m*.
1991   *Hamwee*, Sally Rachel Hamwee, *b*. 1947.
1999   *Hanham*, Joan Brownlow Hanham, CBE, *b*. 1939, *m*.
1999   *Harris of Richmond*, Angela Felicity Harris, *b*. 1944.
1996   *Hayman*, Helene Valerie Hayman, *b*. 1949, *m*.
1991   *Hilton of Eggardon*, Jennifer Hilton, QPM, *b*. 1936.

1995   *Hogg,* Sarah Elizabeth Mary Hogg, *b.* 1946, *m.*
1990   *Hollis of Heigham,* Patricia Lesley Hollis, D.Phil., *b.* 1941, *m.*
1985   *Hooper,* Gloria Dorothy Hooper, *b.* 1939.
1999   *Howells of St Davids,* Rosalind Particia-Anne Howells.
1965   *Hylton-Foster,* Audrey Pellew Hylton-Foster, DBE, *b.* 1908, *w.*
1991   *James of Holland Park,* Phyllis Dorothy White (P. D. James), OBE, *b.* 1920, *w.*
1992   *Jay of Paddington,* Margaret Ann Jay, PC, *b.* 1939, *m.* Lord Privy Seal
1979   *Jeger,* Lena May Jeger, *b.* 1915, *w.*
1997   *Kennedy of the Shaws,* Helena Ann Kennedy, QC, *b.* 1950, *m.*
1997   *Knight of Collingtree,* (Joan Christabel) Jill Knight, DBE, *b.* 1923, *w.*
1997   *Linklater of Butterstone,* Veronica Linklater, *b.* 1943, *m.*
1996   *Lloyd of Highbury,* Prof. June Kathleen Lloyd, DBE, FRCP, FRCPE, FRCGP, *b.* 1928.
1978   *Lockwood,* Betty Lockwood, *b.* 1924, *w.*
1997   *Ludford,* Sarah Ann Ludford, MEP, *b.* 1951.
1979   *McFarlane of Llandaff,* Jean Kennedy McFarlane, *b.* 1926.
1999   *McIntosh of Hudnall,* Genista Mary McIntosh, *b.* 1946.
1971   *Macleod of Borve,* Evelyn Hester Macleod, *b.* 1915, *w.*
1997   *Maddock,* Diana Margaret Maddock, *b.* 1945, *m.*
1991   *Mallalieu,* Ann Mallalieu, QC, *b.* 1945, *m.*
1970   *Masham of Ilton,* Susan Lilian Primrose Cunliffe-Lister, *b.* 1935, *m. (Countess of Swinton)*
1999   *Massey of Darwen,* Doreen Elizabeth Massey, *b.* 1938, *m.*
1998   *Miller of Chilthorne Domer,* Susan Elizabeth Miller, *b.* 1954.
1993   *Miller of Hendon,* Doreen Miller, MBE, *b.* 1933, *m.*
1997   *Nicholson of Winterbourne,* Emma Harriet Nicholson, MEP, *b.* 1941, *m.*
1982   *Nicol,* Olive Mary Wendy Nicol, *b.* 1923, *m.*
1991   *O'Cathain,* Detta O'Cathain, OBE, *b.* 1938, *m.*
1999   *O'Neill of Bengarve,* Onora Sylvia O'Neill, CBE, Ph.D., *b.* 1941.
1989   *Oppenheim-Barnes,* Sally Oppenheim-Barnes, PC, *b.* 1930, *m.*
1990   *Park of Monmouth,* Daphne Margaret Sybil Désirée Park, CMG, OBE, *b.* 1921.
1991   *Perry of Southwark,* Pauline Perry, *b.* 1931, *m.*
1974   *Pike,* (Irene) Mervyn (Parnicott) Pike, DBE, *b.* 1918.
1997   *Pitkeathley,* Jill Elizabeth Pitkeathley, OBE, *b.* 1940.
1981   *Platt of Writtle,* Beryl Catherine Platt, CBE, FREng., *b.* 1923, *m.*
1999   *Prashar,* Usha Kumari Prashar, CBE, *b.* 1948, *m.*
1996   *Ramsay of Cartvale,* Margaret Mildred (Meta) Ramsay, *b.* 1936.
1994   *Rawlings,* Patricia Elizabeth Rawlings, *b.* 1939.
1997   *Rendell of Babergh,* Ruth Barbara Rendell, CBE, *b.* 1930, *m.*
1998   *Richardson of Calow,* Kathleen Margaret Richardson, OBE, *b.* 1938, *m.*
1979   *Ryder of Warsaw,* Margaret Susan Cheshire (Sue Ryder), CMG, OBE, *b.* 1923, *w.*
1997   *Scotland of Asthal,* Patricia Janet Scotland, QC, *m.*
1991   *Seccombe,* Joan Anna Dalziel Seccombe, DBE, *b.* 1930, *m.*
1967   *Serota,* Beatrice Serota, DBE, *b.* 1919, *m.*
1998   *Sharp of Guildford,* Margaret Lucy Sharp, *m.*
1973   *Sharples,* Pamela Sharples, *b.* 1923, *m.*

1995   *Smith of Gilmorehill,* Elizabeth Margaret Smith, *b.* 1940, *w.*
1999   *Stern,* Vivien Helen Stern, CBE, *b.* 1941.
1996   *Symons of Vernham Dean,* Elizabeth Conway Symons, *b.* 1951.
1992   *Thatcher,* Margaret Hilda Thatcher, KG, OM, PC, FRS, *b.* 1925, *m.*
1994   *Thomas of Walliswood,* Susan Petronella Thomas, OBE, *b.* 1935, *m.*
1998   *Thornton,* (Dorothea) Glenys Thornton, *b.* 1952, *m.*
1980   *Trumpington,* Jean Alys Barker, PC, *b.* 1922, *w.*
1985   *Turner of Camden,* Muriel Winifred Turner, *b.* 1927, *m.*
1998   *Uddin,* Manzila Pola Uddin, *b.* 1959, *m.*
1985   *Warnock,* Helen Mary Warnock, DBE, *b.* 1924, *w.*
1999   *Warwick of Undercliffe,* Diana Mary Warwick, *b.* 1945, *m.*
1999   *Whitaker,* Janet Alison Whitaker.
1970   *White,* Eirene Lloyd White, *b.* 1909, *w.*
1996   *Wilcox,* Judith Ann Wilcox, *w.*
1999   *Wilkins,* Rosalie Catherine Wilkins, *b.* 1946.
1993   *Williams of Crosby,* Shirley Vivien Teresa Brittain Williams, PC, *b.* 1930, *m.*
1971   *Young,* Janet Mary Young, PC, *b.* 1926, *m.*
1997   *Young of Old Scone,* Barbara Scott Young, *b.* 1948.

Lords Spiritual

The Lords Spiritual are the Archbishops of Canterbury and York and 24 diocesan bishops of the Church of England. The Bishops of London, Durham and Winchester always have seats in the House of Lords; the other 21 seats are filled by the remaining diocesan bishops in order of seniority. The Bishop of Sodor and Man and the Bishop of Gibraltar are not eligible to sit in the House of Lords.

ARCHBISHOPS

Style, The Most Revd and Right Hon. the Lord Archbishop of __
Addressed as Archbishop, *or* Your Grace

Introduced to House of Lords
1991   *Canterbury* (103rd), George Leonard Carey, PC, ph.D., *b.* 1935, *m., cons.* 1987, *trans.* 1991
1990   *York* (96th), David Michael Hope, KCVO, PC, D.phil., *b.* 1940, *cons.* 1985, *elected* 1985, *trans.* 1991, 1995

BISHOPS

Style, The Right Revd the Lord Bishop of __
Addressed as My Lord
elected date of election as diocesan bishop

Introduced to House of Lords (as at mid-1999)
1996   *London* (132nd), Richard John Carew Chartres, *b.* 1947, *m., cons.* 1992
1994   *Durham* (93rd), (Anthony) Michael (Arnold) Turnbull, *b.* 1935, *m., cons.* 1988, *elected* 1988, *trans.* 1994
1996   *Winchester* (96th), Michael Charles Scott-Joynt, *b.* 1943, *m., cons.* 1987
1979   *Chichester* (102nd), Eric Waldram Kemp, DD, *b.* 1915, *m., cons.* 1974, *elected* 1974
1989   *Lichfield* (97th), Keith Norman Sutton, *b.* 1934, *m., cons.* 1978, *elected* 1984
1990   *Bristol* (54th), Barry Rogerson, *b.* 1936, *m., cons.* 1979, *elected* 1985
1993   *Lincoln* (70th), Robert Maynard Hardy, *b.* 1936, *m., cons.* 1980, *elected* 1986
1993   *Oxford* (41st), Richard Douglas Harries, *b.* 1936, *m., cons.* 1987, *elected* 1987
1994   *Birmingham* (7th), Mark Santer, *b.* 1936, *m., cons.* 1981, *elected* 1987
1995   *Blackburn* (7th), Alan David Chesters, *b.* 1937, *m., cons.* 1989, *elected* 1989
1996   *Carlisle* (65th), Ian Harland, *b.* 1932, *m., cons.* 1985, *elected* 1989
1997   *Hereford* (103rd), John Keith Oliver, *b.* 1935, *m., cons.* 1990, *elected* 1990
1997   *Southwark* (9th), Thomas Frederick Butler, *b.* 1940, *m., cons.* 1985, *elected* 1991
1997   *Bath and Wells* (77th), James Lawton Thompson, *b.* 1936, *m., cons.* 1978, *elected* 1991
1997   *Wakefield* (11th), Nigel Simeon McCulloch, *b.* 1942, *m., cons.* 1986, *elected* 1992
1997   *Bradford* (8th), David James Smith, *b.* 1935, *m., cons.* 1987, *elected* 1992
1997   *Manchester* (10th), Christopher John Mayfield, *b.* 1935, *m., cons.* 1985, *elected* 1993

1998   *Salisbury* (77th), David Staffurth Stancliffe, *b.* 1942, *m., cons.* 1993, *elected* 1993
1998   *Gloucester* (39th), David Edward Bentley, *b.* 1935, *m., cons.* 1986, *elected* 1993
1999   *Rochester* (106th), Michael James Nazir-Ali, ph.D., *b.* 1949, *m., cons.* 1984, *elected* 1995
1999   *Guildford* (8th), John Warren Gladwin, *b.* 1942, *m., cons.* 1994, *elected* 1994
1999   *Portsmouth* (8th), Kenneth William Stevenson, *b.* 1949, *m., cons.* 1995, *elected* 1995
1999   *Derby* (6th), Jonathan Sansbury Bailey, *b.* 1940, *m., cons.* 1992, *elected* 1995
1999   *St Albans* (9th), Christopher William Herbert, *b.* 1944, *m., cons.* 1995, *elected* 1995

Bishops awaiting seats, in order of seniority (as at mid-1999)
   Chelmsford (8th), John Freeman Perry, *b.* 1935, *m., cons.* 1989, *elected* 1996
   Peterborough (37th), Ian Cundy, *b.* 1945, *m., cons.* 1992, *elected* 1996
   Chester (40th), Peter Robert Forster, ph.D., *b.* 1950, *cons.* 1996, *elected* 1996
   St Edmundsbury and Ipswich (9th), (John Hubert) Richard Lewis, *b.* 1943, *m., cons.* 1992, *elected* 1997
   Truro (14th), William Ind, *b.* 1942, *m., cons.* 1987, *elected* 1997
   Worcester (112th), Peter Stephen Maurice Selby, *b.* 1941, *cons.* 1984, *elected* 1997
   Newcastle (11th), (John) Martin Wharton, *b.* 1944, *m., cons.* 1992, *elected* 1997
   Sheffield (6th), John Nicholls, *b.* 1943, *m., cons.* 1990, *elected* 1997
   Coventry (8th), Colin J. Bennetts, *b.* 1940, *m., cons.* 1994, *elected* 1997
   Liverpool (7th), James Jones, *b.* 1948, *m., cons.* 1994, *elected* 1998
   Leicester (6th), Timothy John Stevens, *b.* 1946, *m., cons.* 1999, *elected* 1999
   Southwell (10th), George Henry Cassidy, *b.* 1942, *m., cons.* 1999, *elected* 1999

COURTESY TITLES

From this list it will be seen that, for example, the Marquess of Blandford is heir to the Dukedom of Marlborough, and Viscount Amberley to the Earldom of Russell. Titles of second heirs are also given, and the courtesy title of the father of a second heir is indicated by *; e.g. Earl of Burlington, eldest son of *Marquess of Hartington
For forms of address, *see* page 135

MARQUESSES

*Blandford – *Marlborough, D.*
Bowmont and Cessford – *Roxburghe, D.*
Douglas and Clydesdale – *Hamilton, D.*
*Douro – *Wellington, D.*
Graham – *Montrose, D.*
Hamilton – *Abercorn, D.*
*Hartington – *Devonshire, D.*
*Kildare – *Leinster, D.*
Lorne – *Argyll, D.*
*Tavistock – *Bedford, D.*
Tullibardine – *Atholl, D.*
*Worcester – *Beaufort, D.*

EARLS

Aboyne – *Huntly, M.*
Ancram – *Lothian, M.*
Arundel and Surrey – *Norfolk, D.*
*Bective – *Headfort, M.*
*Belfast – *Donegall, M.*
Brecknock – *Camden, M.*
Burford – *St Albans, D.*
Burlington – *Hartington, M.*
*Cardigan – *Ailesbury, M.*
Compton – *Northampton, M.*
*Dalkeith – *Buccleuch, D.*
Dumfries – *Bute, M.*
*Euston – *Grafton, D.*
Glamorgan – *Worcester, M.*
Grosvenor – *Westminster, D.*
*Haddo – *Aberdeen and Temair, M.*
Hillsborough – *Downshire, M.*
Hopetoun – *Linlithgow, M.*
March and Kinrara – *Richmond, D.*
Medina – *Milford Haven, M.*
*Mount Charles – *Conyngham, M.*
Mornington – *Douro, M.*
Mulgrave – *Normanby, M.*
Percy – *Northumberland, D.*
Ronaldshay – *Zetland, M.*
*St Andrews – *Kent, D.*
*Shelburne – *Lansdowne, M.*
*Southesk – *Fife, D.*
Sunderland – *Blandford, M.*
*Tyrone – *Waterford, M.*
Ulster – *Gloucester, D.*
*Uxbridge – *Anglesey, M.*

Wiltshire – *Winchester, M.*
Yarmouth – *Hertford, M.*

VISCOUNTS

Althorp – *Spencer, E.*
Amberley – *Russell, E.*
Andover – *Suffolk and Berkshire, E.*
Anson – *Lichfield, E.*
Asquith – *Oxford and Asquith, E.*
Boringdon – *Morley, E.*
Borodale – *Beatty, E.*
Boyle – *Shannon, E.*
Brocas – *Jellicoe, E.*
Campden – *Gainsborough, E.*
Carlow – *Portarlington, E.*
Carlton – *Wharncliffe, E.*
Castlereagh – *Londonderry, M.*
Chelsea – *Cadogan, E.*
Chewton – *Waldegrave, E.*
Chichester – *Belfast, E.*
Clanfield – *Peel, E.*
Clive – *Powis, E.*
Coke – *Leicester, E.*
Corry – *Belmore, E.*
Corvedale – *Baldwin of Bewdley, E.*
Cranborne – *Salisbury, M.*
Cranley – *Onslow, E.*
Crichton – *Erne, E.*
Crowhurst – *Cottenham, E.*
Curzon – *Howe, E.*
Dangan – *Cowley, E.*
Dawick – *Haig, E.*
Drumlanrig – *Queensberry, M.*
Duncannon – *Bessborough, E.*
Dungarvan – *Cork and Orrery, E.*
Dunluce – *Antrim, E.*
Dunwich – *Stradbroke, E.*
Dupplin – *Kinnoull, E.*
Ebrington – *Fortescue, E.*
Ednam – *Dudley, E.*
Encombe – *Eldon, E.*
Enfield – *Strafford, E.*
Erleigh – *Reading, M.*
Errington – *Cromer, E.*
FitzHarris – *Malmesbury, E.*
Folkestone – *Radnor, E.*
Forbes – *Granard, E.*
Garmoyle – *Cairns, E.*
Garnock – *Lindsay, E.*
Glandine – *Norbury, E.*
Glenapp – *Inchcape, E.*

Glentworth – *Limerick, E.*
Grimstone – *Verulam, E.*
Gwynedd – *Lloyd George of Dwyfor, E.*
Hawkesbury – *Liverpool, E.*
Hinchingbrooke – *Sandwich, E.*
Ikerrin – *Carrick, E.*
Ingestre – *Shrewsbury, E.*
Ipswich – *Euston, E.*
Jocelyn – *Roden, E.*
Kelburn – *Glasgow, E.*
Kilwarlin – *Hillsborough, E.*
Kingsborough – *Kingston, E.*
Kirkwall – *Orkney, E.*
Knebworth – *Lytton, E.*
Lascelles – *Harewood, E.*
Linley – *Snowdon, E.*
Loftus – *Ely, M.*
Lowther – *Lonsdale, E.*
Lumley – *Scarbrough, E.*
Lymington – *Portsmouth, E.*
Macmillan of Ovenden – *Stockton, E.*
Maitland – *Lauderdale, E.*
Malden – *Essex, E.*
Mandeville – *Manchester, D.*
Melgund – *Minto, E.*
Merton – *Nelson, E.*
Moore – *Drogheda, E.*
Newport – *Bradford, E.*
Newry and Mourne – *Kilmorey, E.*
Parker – *Macclesfield, E.*
Perceval – *Egmont, E.*
Petersham – *Harrington, E.*
Pollington – *Mexborough, E.*
Raynham – *Townshend, M.*
Reidhaven – *Seafield, E.*
Ruthven of Canberra – *Gowrie, E.*
St Cyres – *Iddesleigh, E.*
Sandon – *Harrowby, E.*
Savernake – *Cardigan, E.*
Slane – *Mount Charles, E.*
Somerton – *Normanton, E.*
Stopford – *Courtown, E.*
Stormont – *Mansfield, E.*
Strathallan – *Perth, E.*
Stuart – *Castle Stewart, E.*
Suirdale – *Donoughmore, E.*
Tamworth – *Ferrers, E.*
Tarbat – *Cromartie, E.*
Vaughan – *Lisburne, E.*
Weymouth – *Bath, M.*
Windsor – *Plymouth, E.*
Wolmer – *Selborne, E.*
Woodstock – *Portland, E.*

BARONS (LORD)

Aberdour – *Morton, E.*
Apsley – *Bathurst, E.*
Ardee – *Meath, E.*
Ashley – *Shaftesbury, E.*
Balgonie – *Leven and Melville, E.*
Balniel – *Crawford and Balcarres, E.*
Berriedale – *Caithness, E.*
Bingham – *Lucan, E.*
Binning – *Haddington, E.*
Brooke – *Warwick, E.*
Bruce – *Elgin, E.*
Buckhurst – *De La Warr, E.*
Burghley – *Exeter, M.*
Cardross – *Buchan, E.*
Carnegie – *Southesk, E.*
Clifton – *Darnley, E.*
Cochrane – *Dundonald, E.*
Courtenay – *Devon, E.*
Dalmeny – *Rosebery, E.*
Doune – *Moray, E.*
Downpatrick – *St Andrews, E.*
Dunglass – *Home, E.*
Eliot – *St Germans, E.*
Eskdail – *Dalkeith, E.*
Formartine – *Haddo, E.*
Gillford – *Clanwilliam, E.*
Glamis – *Strathmore, E.*
Greenock – *Cathcart, E.*
Guernsey – *Aylesford, E.*
Hay – *Erroll, E.*
Herbert – *Pembroke, E.*
Howard of Effingham – *Effingham, E.*
Howland – *Tavistock, M.*
Hyde – *Clarendon, E.*
Inverurie – *Kintore, E.*
Irwin – *Halifax, E.*
Johnstone – *Annandale and Hartfell, E.*
Kenlis – *Bective, E.*
Langton – *Temple of Stowe, E.*
La Poer – *Tyrone, E.*
Leslie – *Rothes, E.*
Loughborough – *Rosslyn, E.*
Maltravers – *Arundel and Surrey, E.*
Mauchline – *Loudoun, C.*
Medway – *Cranbrook, E.*
Montgomerie – *Eglinton and Winton, E.*
Moreton – *Ducie, E.*
Naas – *Mayo, E.*
Neidpath – *Wemyss and March, E.*
Norreys – *Lindsey and Abingdon, E.*
Ogilvy – *Airlie, E.*

Oxmantown – *Rosse, E.*
Paget de Beaudesert –
  *Uxbridge, E.
Porchester – *Carnarvon, E.*

Ramsay – *Dalhousie, E.*
Romsey – *Mountbatten of
  Burma, C.*
Rosehill – *Northesk, E.*

Scrymgeour – *Dundee, E.*
Seymour – *Somerset, D.*
Stanley – *Derby, E.*
Strathnaver – *Sutherland, C.*

Wodehouse – *Kimberley, E.*
Worsley – *Yarborough, E.*

PEERS' SURNAMES WHICH DIFFER FROM THEIR TITLES

The following symbols
indicate the rank of the
peer holding each title:

B. Baron/Baroness
C. Countess
D. Duke
E. Earl
M. Marquess
V. Viscount
* Life Peer

Abney-Hastings – *Loudoun,
  C.*
Acheson – *Gosford, E.*
Adderley – *Norton, B.*
Addington – *Sidmouth, V.*
Agar – *Normanton, E.*
Aitken – *Beaverbrook, B.*
Akers-Douglas – *Chilston, V.*
Alexander – *A. of Tunis, E.*
Alexander – *A. of Weedon,
  B.**
Alexander – *Caledon, E.*
Allen – *A. of Abbeydale, B.**
Allen – *Croham, B.**
Allsopp – *Hindlip, B.*
Alton – *A. of Liverpool, B.**
Anderson – *Waverley, V.*
Anelay – *A. of St Johns, B.**
Annesley – *Valentia, V.*
Anson – *Lichfield, E.*
Arbuthnott – *of Arbuthnott,
  V.*
Archer – *A. of Sandwell, B.**
Archer – *A. of Weston-super-
  Mare, B.**
Armstrong – *A. of Ilminster,
  B.**
Armstrong-Jones –
  Snowdon, E.
Arthur – *Glenarthur, B.*
Arundell – *T. of Malahide,
  B.*
Ashley – *A. of Stoke, B.**
Ashley-Cooper –
  Shaftesbury, E.
Ashton – *A. of Hyde, B.*
Ashton – *A. of Upholland, B.**
Asquith – *Oxford and
  Asquith, E.*
Assheton – *Clitheroe, B.*
Astley – *Hastings, B.*
Astor – *A. of Hever, B.*
Aubrey-Fletcher – *Braye, B.*
Bailey – *Glanusk, B.*
Baillie – *Burton, B.*
Baillie-Hamilton –
  Haddington, E.
Baker – *B. of Dorking, B.**
Balcarres – *Balniel, B.**
Baldwin – *B. of Bewdley, E.*
Balfour – *B. of Inchrye, B.*

Balfour – *Kinross, B.*
Balfour – *Riverdale, B.*
Bampfylde – *Poltimore, B.*
Banbury – *B. of Southam, B.*
Barber – *B. of Tewkesbury,
  B.**
Baring – *Ashburton, B.*
Baring – *Cromer, E.*
Baring – *H. of Glendale, B.*
Baring – *Northbrook, B.*
Baring – *Revelstoke, B.*
Barker – *Trumpington, B.**
Barnes – *Gorell, B.*
Barnewall – *Trimlestown, B.*
Bassam – *B. of Brighton, B.**
Bathurst – *Bledisloe, V.*
Beauclerk – *St Albans, D.*
Beaumont – *Allendale, V.*
Beaumont – *B. of Whitley,
  B.**
Beckett – *Grimthorpe, B.*
Bellow – *Bellwin, B.**
Benn – *Stansgate, V.*
Bennet – *Tankerville, E.*
Bentinck – *Portland, E.*
Beresford – *Waterford, M.*
Berry – *Hartwell, B.**
Berry – *Kemsley, V.*
Bertie – *Lindsey, E.*
Best – *Wynford, B.*
Bethell – *Westbury, B.*
Bewicke-Copley –
  Cromwell, B.
Bigham – *Mersey, V.*
Bingham – *B. of Cornhill, B.**
Bingham – *Clanmorris, B.*
Bingham – *Lucan, E.*
Bligh – *Darnley, E.*
Blyth – *B. of Rowington, B.**
Bootle-Wilbraham –
  Skelmersdale, B.
Boscawen – *Falmouth, V.*
Boston – *B. of Faversham, B.**
Bourke – *Mayo, E.*
Bowes Lyon – *Strathmore
  and Kinghorne, E.*
Bowyer – *Denham, B.*
Boyd – *Kilmarnock, B.*
Boyle – *Cork, E.*
Boyle – *Glasgow, E.*
Boyle – *Shannon, E.*
Brabazon – *Meath, E.*
Braine – *B. of Wheatley, B.**
Brand – *Hampden, V.*
Brassey – *B. of Apethorpe, B.*
Brett – *Esher, V.*
Bridge – *B. of Harwich, W.**
Bridgeman – *Bradford, E.*
Brodrick – *Midleton, V.*
Brooke – *Alanbrooke, V.*

Brooke – *B. of Alverthorpe,
  B.**
Brooke – *B. of Ystradfellte,
  B.**
Brooke – *Brookeborough, V.*
Brooks – *B. of Tremorfa, B.**
Brooks – *Crawshaw, B.*
Brougham – *Brougham and
  Vaux, B.*
Broughton – *Fairhaven, B.*
Browne – *Kilmaine, B.*
Browne – *Oranmore and
  Browne, B.*
Browne – *Sligo, M.*
Bruce – *Aberdare, B.*
Bruce – *B. of Burleigh, B.*
Bruce – *B. of Donington, B.**
Bruce – *Elgin, E.*
Brudenell-Bruce – *Ailesbury,
  M.*
Buchan – *Tweedsmuir, B.*
Buckley – *Wrenbury, B.*
Butler – *B. of Brockwell, B.**
Butler – *Carrick, E.*
Butler – *Dunboyne, B.*
Butler – *Mountgarret, V.*
Buxton – *B. of Alsa, B.**
Byng – *Strafford, E.*
Byng – *Torrington, V.*
Callaghan – *C. of Cardiff,
  B.**
Cameron – *C. of Lochbroom,
  B.**
Campbell – *Argyll, D.*
Campbell – *C. of Alloway,
  B.**
Campbell – *C. of Croy, B.**
Campbell – *Cawdor, E.*
Campbell – *Colgrain, B.*
Campbell – *Stratheden, B.*
Campbell-Gray – *Gray, B.*
Canning – *Garvagh, B.*
Capell – *Essex, E.*
Carington – *Carrington, B.*
Carlile – *C. of Berriew, B.**
Carlisle – *C. of Bucklow, B.**
Carmichael – *C. of
  Kelvingrove, B.**
Carnegie – *Fife, D.*
Carnegie – *Northesk, E.*
Carr – *C. of Hadley, B.**
Cary – *Falkland, V.*
Castle – *C. of Blackburn, B.**
Caulfeild – *Charlemont, V.*
Cavendish – *C. of Furness,
  B.**
Cavendish – *Chesham, B.*
Cavendish – *Devonshire, D.*
Cavendish – *Waterpark, B.*
Cayzer – *Rotherwick, B.*
Cecil – *A. of Hackney, B.*

Cecil – *Exeter, M.*
Cecil – *Rockley, B.*
Cecil – *Salisbury, M.*
Chalker – *C. of Wallasey, B.**
Chaloner – *Gisborough, B.*
Channon – *Kelvedon, B.**
Chapman – *Northfield, B.*
Charteris – *C. of Amisfield,
  B.**
Charteris – *Wemyss and
  March, E.*
Cheshire – *R. of Warsaw, B**
Chetwynd-Talbot –
  *Shrewsbury and Waterford,
  E.*
Chichester – *Donegall, M.*
Chichester-Clark – *Moyola,
  B.**
Child Villiers – *Jersey, E.*
Cholmondeley – *Delamere,
  B.*
Chubb – *Hayter, B.*
Clark – *C. of Kempston, B.**
Clarke – *C. of Hampstead,
  B.**
Clegg-Hill – *Hill, V.*
Clifford – *C. of Chudleigh, B.*
Cochrane – *C. of Cults, B.*
Cochrane – *Dundonald, E.*
Cocks – *C. of Hartcliffe, B.**
Cocks – *Somers, B.*
Cokayne – *C. of Ashbourne,
  B.*
Coke – *Leicester, E.*
Cole – *Enniskillen, E.*
Collier – *Monkswell, B.*
Colville – *Clydesmuir, B.*
Colville – *C. of Culross, V.*
Compton – *Northampton, M.*
Conolly-Carew – *Carew, B.*
Constantine – *C. of
  Stanmore, B.**
Cooke – *C. of Islandreagh,
  B.**
Cooke – *C. of Thorndon, B.**
Cooper – *Norwich, V.*
Cope – *C. of Berkeley, B.**
Corbett – *Rowallan, B.*
Cornwall-Legh – *G. of
  Codnor, B.*
Courtenay – *Devon, E.*
Cowdrey – *C. of Tonbridge,
  B.**
Craig – *C. of Radley, B.**
Craig – *Craigavon, V.*
Crichton – *Erne, E.*
Crichton-Stuart – *Bute, M.*
Cripps – *Parmoor, B.*
Crossley – *Somerleyton, B.*
Cubitt – *Ashcombe, B.*

Cunliffe-Lister – *M. of Ilton, B.**
Cunliffe-Lister – *Swinton, E.*
Currie – *C. of Marylebone, B.**
Curzon – *Howe, E.*
Curzon – *Scarsdale, V.*
Cust – *Brownlow, B.*
Dalrymple – *Stair, E.*
Daubeny de Moleyns – *Ventry, B.*
Davies – *Darwen, B.*
Davies – *D. of Coity, B.**
Davies – *D. of Oldham, B.**
Davison – *Broughshane, B.*
Dawnay – *Downe, V.*
Dawson-Damer – *Portarlington, E.*
Dean – *D. of Harptree, B.**
Dean – *D. of Thornton-le-Fylde, B.**
Deane – *Muskerry, B.*
de Courcy – *Kingsale, B.*
de Grey – *Walsingham, B.*
Delacourt-Smith – *D. of Alteryn, B.**
de la Poer Beresford – *Decies, B.*
Denison – *Londesborough, B.*
Denison-Pender – *Pender, B.*
Denton – *D. of Wakefield, B.**
Devereux – *Hereford, V.*
Dewar – *Forteviot, B.*
De Yarburgh-Bateson – *Deramore, B.*
Dixon – *Glentoran, B.*
Dodson – *Monk Bretton, B.*
Donaldson – *D. of Lymington, B.**
Dormand – *D. of Easington, B.**
Douglas – *Morton, E.*
Douglas – *Queensberry, M.*
Douglas-Hamilton – *Hamilton, D.*
Douglas-Hamilton – *S. of Douglas, B.**
Douglas-Home – *Dacre, B.*
Douglas-Home – *Home, E.*
Douglas-Pennant – *Penrhyn, B.*
Douglas-Scott-Montagu – *M. of Beaulieu, B.*
Drummond – *Perth, E.*
Drummond of Megginch – *Strange, B.*
Dugdale – *Crathorne, B.*
Duke – *Merrivale, B.*
Duncombe – *Feversham, B.*
Dundas – *Melville, V.*
Dundas – *Zetland, M.*
Eady – *Swinfen, B.*
Eccles – *E. of Moulton, B.**
Eden – *Auckland, B.*
Eden – *E. of Winton, B.**
Eden – *Henley, B.*
Edgcumbe – *Mount Edgcumbe, E.*
Edmondson – *Sandford, B.*

Edwardes – *Kensington, B.*
Edwards – *Crickhowell, B.**
Egerton – *Sutherland, D.*
Egerton – *Wilton, E.*
Eliot – *St Germans, E.*
Elliot-Murray-Kynynmound – *Minto, E.*
Elliott – *E. of Morpeth, B.**
Ellis – *Seaford, B.*
Erroll – *E. of Hale, B.*
Erskine – *Buchan, E.*
Erskine – *Mar and Kellie, E.*
Erskine-Murray – *Elibank, B.*
Evans – *E. of Parkside, B.**
Evans – *E. of Watford, B.**
Evans – *Mountevans, B.*
Evans-Freke – *Carbery, B.*
Eve – *Silsoe, B.*
Ewing – *E. of Kirkford, B.**
Fairfax – *F. of Cameron, B.*
Falconer – *F. of Thoroton, B.**
Fane – *Westmorland, E.*
Farrington – *F. of Ribbleton, B.**
Faulkner – *F. of Worcester, B.**
Feilding – *Denbigh, E.*
Fellowes – *De Ramsey, B.*
Fermor-Hesketh – *Hesketh, B.*
Fiennes – *Saye and Sele, B.*
Fiennes-Clinton – *Lincoln, E.*
Finch Hatton – *Winchilsea, E.*
Finch-Knightley – *Aylesford, E.*
Fisher – *F. of Rednal, B.**
Fitzalan-Howard – *Beaumont, B.*
Fitzalan-Howard – *H. of Terregles, B.*
Fitzalan-Howard – *Norfolk, D.*
FitzClarence – *Munster, E.*
FitzGerald – *Leinster, D.*
Fitzherbert – *Stafford, B.*
FitzRoy – *Grafton, D.*
FitzRoy – *Southampton, B.*
FitzRoy Newdegate – *Daventry, V.*
Fletcher-Vane – *Inglewood, B.*
Flower – *Ashbrook, V.*
Foljambe – *Liverpool, E.*
Forbes – *Granard, E.*
Forbes – *Granard, B.*
Forsyth – *F. of Drumlean, B.**
Forwood – *Arlington, B.*
Foster – *F. of Thames Bank, B.**
Fox-Strangways – *Ilchester, E.*
Frankland – *Zouche, B.*
Fraser – *F. of Carmyllie, B.**
Fraser – *Lovat, B.*
Fraser – *Saltoun, B.*
Fraser – *Strathalmond, B.*

Freeman-Grenville – *Kinloss, B.*
Fremantle – *Cottesloe, B.*
French – *De Freyne, B.*
Galbraith – *Strathclyde, B.*
Ganzoni – *Belstead, B.*
Gardner – *G. of Parkes, B.**
Gathorne-Hardy – *Cranbrook, E.*
Gibbs – *Aldenham, B.*
Gibbs – *Wraxall, B.*
Gibson – *Ashbourne, B.*
Giffard – *Halsbury, E.*
Gilbey – *V. of Harrowden, B.*
Gillmore – *G. of Thamesfield, B.*
Gilmour – *G. of Craigmillar, B.**
Gladwin – *G. of Clee, B.**
Glyn – *Wolverton, B.*
Godley – *Kilbracken, B.*
Goff – *G. of Chieveley, W.**
Gordon – *Aberdeen and Temair, M.*
Gordon – *G. of Strathblane, B.**
Gordon – *Huntly, M.*
Gordon Lennox – *Richmond, D.*
Gore – *Arran, E.*
Gould – *G. of Potternewton, B.**
Graham – *G. of Edmonton, B.**
Graham – *Montrose, D.*
Graham-Toler – *Norbury, E.*
Grant of Grant – *Strathspey, B.*
Gray – *G. of Contin, B.**
Greaves – *Dysart, C.*
Greenall – *Daresbury, B.*
Greene – *G. of Harrow Weald, B.**
Greenhill – *G. of Harrow, B.**
Greville – *Warwick, E.*
Grey – *G. of Naunton, B.**
Griffiths – *G. of Fforestfach, B.**
Grigg – *Altrincham, B.*
Grimston – *G. of Westbury, B.*
Grimston – *Verulam, E.*
Grosvenor – *Ebury, B.*
Grosvenor – *Westminster, D.*
Guest – *Wimborne, V.*
Gueterbock – *Berkeley, B.*
Guinness – *Iveagh, E.*
Guinness – *Moyne, B.*
Gully – *Selby, V.*
Gummer – *Chadlington, B.**
Gurdon – *Cranworth, B.*
Gwynne Jones – *Chalfont, B.**
Hamilton – *Abercorn, D.*
Hamilton – *Belhaven and Stenton, B.*
Hamilton – *Dudley, B.*
Hamilton – *H. of Dalzell, B.*
Hamilton – *HolmPatrick, B.*

Hamilton-Russell – *Boyne, V.*
Hamilton-Smith – *Colwyn, B.*
Hanbury-Tracy – *Sudeley, B.*
Handcock – *Castlemaine, B.*
Harbord-Hamond – *Suffield, B.*
Harding – *H. of Petherton, B.*
Hardinge – *H. of Penshurst, B.*
Hardy – *H. of Wath, B.**
Hare – *Blakenham, V.*
Hare – *Listowel, E.*
Harmsworth – *Rothermere, V.*
Harris – *H. of Greenwich, B.**
Harris – *H. of Haringey, B.**
Harris – *H. of High Cross, B.**
Harris – *H. of Peckham, B.**
Harris – *H. of Richmond, B.**
Harris – *Malmesbury, E.*
Harvey – *H. of Tasburgh, B.**
Hastings Bass – *Huntingdon, E.*
Hay – *Erroll, E.*
Hay – *Kinnoull, E.*
Hay – *Tweeddale, M.*
Heathcote-Drummond-Willoughby – *Willoughby de Eresby, B.*
Hely-Hutchinson – *Donoughmore, E.*
Hely-Hutchinson – *Hutchinson, V.*
Henderson – *Faringdon, B.*
Henderson – *H. of Brompton, B.**
Hennessy – *Windlesham, B.*
Henniker-Major – *Henniker, B.*
Hepburne-Scott – *Polwarth, B.*
Herbert – *Carnarvon, E.*
Herbert – *Hemingford, B.*
Herbert – *Pembroke, E.*
Herbert – *Powis, E.*
Hermon-Hodge – *Wyfold, B.*
Hervey – *Bristol, M.*
Hewitt – *Lifford, V.*
Hicks Beach – *St Aldwyn, E.*
Hill – *Downshire, M.*
Hill – *Sandys, B.*
Hill-Trevor – *Trevor, B.*
Hilton – *H. of Eggardon, B.**
Hobart-Hampden – *Buckinghamshire, E.*
Hobhouse – *H. of Woodborough, W.**
Hogg – *H. of St Marylebone, B.**
Hogg – *H. of Cumbernauld, B.**
Holland-Hibbert – *Knutsford, V.*
Hollis – *H. of Heigham, B.**
Holme – *H. of Cheltenham, B.**

Morris – *Killanin, B.*
Morris – *M. of Castle Morris, B.**
Morris – *M. of Kenwood, B.*
Morris – *M. of Manchester, B.**
Morris – *Naseby, B.**
Morrison – *Dunrossil, V.*
Morrison – *Margadale, B.*
Mosley – *Ravensdale, B.*
Mountbatten – *Milford Haven, M.*
Muff – *Calverley, B.*
Mulholland – *Dunleath, B.*
Murray – *Atholl, D.*
Murray – *Dunmore, E.*
Murray – *Mansfield and Mansfield, E.*
Murray – *M. of Epping Forest, B.**
Murton – *M. of Lindisfarne, B.**
Nall-Cain – *Brocket, B.*
Napier – *Napier and Ettrick, B.*
Napier – *N. of Magdala, B.*
Needham – *Kilmorey, E.*
Neill – *N. of Bladen, B.**
Nelson – *N. of Stafford, B.*
Nevill – *Abergavenny, M.*
Neville – *Braybrooke, B.*
Newton – *N. of Braintree, B.**
Nicholls – *N. of Birkenhead, W.**
Nicholson – *N. of Winterbourne, B.**
Nicolson – *Carnock, B.*
Nivison – *Glendyne, B.*
Noel – *Gainsborough, E.*
North – *Guilford, E.*
Northcote – *Iddesleigh, E.*
Norton – *Grantley, B.*
Norton – *N. of Louth, B.**
Norton – *Rathcreedan, B.*
Nugent – *Westmeath, E.*
O'Brien – *Inchiquin, B.*
Ogilvie-Grant – *Seafield, E.*
Ogilvy – *Airlie, E.*
Oliver – *O. of Aylmerton, W.**
O'Neill – *O. of Bengarve, B.**
O'Neill – *Rathcavan, B.*
Onslow – *O. of Woking, B.**
Orde-Powlett – *Bolton, B.*
Ormsby-Gore – *Harlech, B.*
Page – *Whaddon, B.**
Paget – *Anglesey, M.*
Pakenham – *Longford, E.*
Pakington – *Hampton, B.*
Palmer – *Lucas, B.*
Palmer – *Selborne, E.*
Park – *P. of Monmouth, B.**
Parker – *Macclesfield, E.*
Parker – *Morley, E.*
Parnell – *Congleton, B.*
Parsons – *Rosse, E.*
Paulet – *Winchester, M.*
Peake – *Ingleby, V.*
Pearson – *Cowdray, V.*
Pearson – *P. of Rannoch, B.**

Pease – *Gainford, B.*
Pease – *Wardington, B.*
Pelham – *Chichester, E.*
Pelham – *Yarborough, E.*
Pellew – *Exmouth, V.*
Penny – *Marchwood, V.*
Pepys – *Cottenham, E.*
Perceval – *Egmont, E.*
Percy – *Northumberland, D.*
Perry – *P. of Southwark, B.**
Perry – *P. of Walton, B.**
Pery – *Limerick, E.*
Peyton – *P. of Yeovil, B.**
Philipps – *Milford, B.*
Philipps – *St Davids, V.*
Phillips – *P. of Sudbury, B.**
Phillips – *P. of Worth Matravers, W.**
Phipps – *Normanby, M.*
Pilkington – *P. of Oxenford, B.**
Plant – *P. of Highfield, B.**
Platt – *P. of Writtle, B.**
Pleydell-Bouverie – *Radnor, E.*
Plummer – *P. of St Marylebone, B.**
Plumptre – *Fitzwalter, B.*
Plunkett – *Dunsany, B.*
Plunkett – *Louth, B.*
Pollock – *Hanworth, V.*
Pomeroy – *Harberton, V.*
Ponsonby – *Bessborough, E.*
Ponsonby – *de Mauley, B.*
Ponsonby – *P. of Shulbrede, B.*
Ponsonby – *Sysonby, B.*
Porter – *P. of Luddenham, B.**
Powys – *Lilford, B.*
Pratt – *Camden, M.*
Preston – *Gormanston, V.*
Primrose – *Rosebery, E.*
Prittie – *Dunalley, B.*
Prout – *Kingsland, B.**
Ramsay – *Dalhousie, E.*
Ramsay – *R. of Cartvale, B.**
Ramsbotham – *Soulbury, V.*
Randall – *R. of St Budeaux, B.**
Rawlinson – *R. of Ewell, B.**
Rees-Williams – *Ogmore, B.*
Rendell – *R. of Babergh, B.**
Renfrew – *R. of Kaimsthorn, B.**
Renton – *R. of Mount Harry, B.**
Renwick – *R. of Clifton, B.**
Rhys – *Dynevor, B.*
Richards – *Milverton, B.*
Richardson – *R. of Calow, B.**
Richardson – *R. of Duntisbourne, B.**
Ritchie – *R. of Dundee, B.*
Roberts – *Clwyd, B.*
Roberts – *R. of Conwy, B.**
Robertson – *R. of Oakridge, B.*

Robertson – *R. of Port Ellen, B.**
Robertson – *Wharton, B.*
Robinson – *Martonmere, B.*
Roche – *Fermoy, B.*
Rodd – *Rennell, B.*
Rodger – *R. of Earlsferry, B.**
Rodgers – *R. of Quarry Bank, B.**
Rogers – *R. of Riverside, B.**
Roll – *R. of Ipsden, B.**
Roper-Curzon – *Teynham, B.*
Rospigliosi – *Newburgh, E.*
Rous – *Stradbroke, E.*
Rowley-Conwy – *Langford, B.*
Royle – *F. of Richmond, B.**
Runciman (Garry) – *R. of Doxford, V.*
Russell – *Ampthill, B.*
Russell – *Bedford, D.*
Russell – *de Clifford, B.*
Russell – *R. of Liverpool, B.*
Ryder – *Harrowby, E.*
Ryder – *R. of Eaton Hastings, B.**
Ryder – *R. of Warsaw, B.**
Ryder – *R. of Wensum, B.**
Sackville – *De La Warr, E.*
Sackville-West – *Sackville, B.*
St Aubyn – *St Levan, B.*
St Clair – *Sinclair, B.*
St Clair-Erskine – *Rosslyn, E.*
St John – *Bolingbroke, V.*
St John – *Orkney, V.*
St John – *S. of Bletso, B.*
St John-Stevas – *S. of Fawsley, B.**
St Leger – *Doneraile, V.*
Sainsbury – *S. of Preston Candover, B.**
Sainsbury – *S. of Turville, B.**
Samuel – *Bearsted, V.*
Sanderson – *S. of Ayot, B.*
Sanderson – *S. of Bowden, B.**
Sandilands – *Torphichen, B.*
Saumarez – *de Saumarez, B.*
Savile – *Mexborough, E.*
Saville – *S. of Newdigate, W.**
Scarlett – *Abinger, B.*
Schreiber – *Marlesford, B.**
Sclater-Booth – *Basing, B.*
Scotland – *S. of Asthal, B.**
Scott – *Eldon, E.*
Scrymgeour – *Dundee, E.*
Seager – *L. of St Mellons, B.*
Seely – *Mottistone, B.*
Sefton – *S. of Garston, B.**
Seymour – *Hertford, M.*
Seymour – *Somerset, D.*
Sharp – *S. of Guildford, B.**
Shaw – *Craigmyle, B.*
Shaw – *S. of Northstead, B.**

Sheppard – *S. of Didgemere, B.**
Sheppard – *S. of Liverpool, B.**
Shirley – *Ferrers, E.*
Shore – *S. of Stepney, B.**
Short – *Glenamara, B.**
Siddeley – *Kenilworth, B.*
Sidney – *De L'Isle, V.*
Sieff – *S. of Brimpton, B.**
Simon – *S. of Glaisdale, B.**
Simon – *S. of Highbury, B.**
Simon – *S. of Wythenshawe, B.*
Simpson – *S. of Dunkeld, B.**
Sinclair – *Caithness, E.*
Sinclair – *S. of Cleeve, B.*
Sinclair – *Thurso, V.*
Skeffington – *Massereene, V.*
Slynn – *S. of Hadley, W.**
Smith – *Bicester, B.*
Smith – *Hambleden, V.*
Smith – *Kirkhill, B.*
Smith – *S. of Clifton, B.**
Smith – *S. of Gilmorehill, B.**
Smith – *S. of Leigh, B.**
Somerset – *Beaufort, D.*
Somerset – *Raglan, B.*
Soulsby – *S. of Swaffham Prior, B.**
Spencer – *Churchill, V.*
Spencer-Churchill – *Marlborough, D.*
Spring Rice – *M. of Brandon, B.*
Stanhope – *Harrington, E.*
Stanley – *Derby, E.*
Stanley – *S. of Alderley, B.*
Stapleton-Cotton – *Combermere, V.*
Steel – *S. of Aikwood, B.**
Sterling – *S. of Plaistow, B.**
Stevens – *S. of Ludgate, B.**
Stevenson – *S. of Coddenham, B.**
Stewart – *Galloway, E.*
Stewart – *Stewartby, B.**
Stodart – *S. of Leaston, B.**
Stoddart – *S. of Swindon, B.**
Stone – *S. of Blackheath, B.**
Stonor – *Camoys, B.*
Stopford – *Courtown, E.*
Stourton – *Mowbray, B.*
Strachey – *O'Hagan, B.*
Strutt – *Belper, B.*
Strutt – *Rayleigh, B.*
Stuart – *Castle Stewart, E.*
Stuart – *Mackenzie-Stuart, B.**
Stuart – *Moray, E.*
Stuart – *S. of Findhorn, V.*
Suenson-Taylor – *Grantchester, B.*
Symons – *S. of Vernham Dean, B.**
Taylor – *Ingrow, B.**
Taylor – *T. of Blackburn, B.**
Taylor – *T. of Gryfe, B.**
Taylor – *T. of Warwick, B.**
Taylour – *Headfort, M.*

Temple-Gore-Langton –
  T. of Stowe, E.
Tennant – *Glenconner, B.*
Thellusson – *Rendlesham, B.*
Thesiger – *Chelmsford, V.*
Thomas – *T. of Gresford, B.**
Thomas – *T. of Gwydir, B.**
Thomas – *T. of Macclesfield,*
  B.*
Thomas – *T. of Swynnerton,*
  B.*
Thomas – *T. of Walliswood,*
  B.*
Thomson – *T. of Fleet, B.*
Thomson – *T. of Monifieth,*
  B.*
Thynn – *Bath, M.*
Tottenham – *Ely, M.*
Trefusis – *Clinton, B.*
Trench – *Ashtown, B.*
Trevor-Roper – *D. of*
  Glanton, B.*
Tufton – *Hothfield, B.*
Turner – *Netherthorpe, B.*
Turner – *T. of Camden, B.**
Turnour – *Winterton, E.*
Tyrell-Kenyon – *Kenyon, B.*
Vanden-Bempde-Johnstone
  – *Derwent, B.*
Vane – *Barnard, B.*
Vane-Tempest-Stewart –
  Londonderry, M.
Vanneck – *Huntingfield, B.*
Vaughan – *Lisburne, E.*
Vereker – *Gort, V.*
Verney – *Willoughby de*
  Broke, B.
Vernon – *Lyveden, B.*
Vesey – *De Vesci, V.*
Villiers – *Clarendon, E.*
Vincent – *V. of Coleshill, B.**
Vivian – *Swansea, B.*
Wade – *W. of Chorlton, B.**
Waldegrave – *W. of North*
  Hill, B.*
Walker – *W. of Doncaster,*
  B.*
Walker – *W. of Worcester,*
  B.*
Wallace – *W. of Coslany, B.**
Wallace – *W. of Saltaire, B.**
Wallop – *Portsmouth, E.*
Walton – *W. of Detchant, B.**
Ward – *Bangor, V.*
Ward – *Dudley, E.*
Warrender – *Bruntisfield, B.*
Warwick – *W. of Undercliffe,*
  B.*
Watson – *Manton, B.*
Watson – *W. of Invergowrie,*
  B.*
Watson – *W. of Richmond,*
  B.*
Webber – *Lloyd-Webber, B.**
Wedderburn – *W. of*
  Charlton, B.*
Weir – *Inverforth, B.*
Weld-Forester – *Forester, B.*
Wellesley – *Cowley, E.*
Wellesley – *Wellington, D.*

Westenra – *Rossmore, B.*
White – *Annaly, B.*
White – *Hanningfield, B.**
White – *J. of Holland Park,*
  B.*
Whiteley – *Marchamley, B.*
Whitfield – *Kenswood, B.*
Williams – *W. of Crosby, B.**
Williams – *W. of Elvel, B.**
Williams – *W. of Mostyn, B.**
Williamson – *Forres, B.*
Williamson – *W. of Horton,*
  B.*
Willoughby – *Middleton, B.*
Wills – *Dulverton, B.*
Wilson – *Moran, B.*
Wilson – *Nunburnholme, B.*
Wilson – *W. of Tillyorn, B.**
Windsor – *Gloucester, D.*
Windsor – *Kent, D.*
Windsor-Clive – *Plymouth,*
  E.
Wingfield – *Powerscourt, V.*
Winn – *St Oswald, B.*
Wodehouse – *Kimberley, E.*
Wolfson – *W. of Sunningdale,*
  B.*
Wood – *Halifax, E.*
Wood – *Holderness, B.**
Woodhouse – *Terrington, B.*
Woolmer – *W. of Leeds, B.**
Wright – *W. of Richmond,*
  B.*
Wyndham – *Egremont, B.*
Wyndham-Quin –
  Dunraven and Mount-Earl,
  E.
Wynn – *Newborough, B.*
Yarde-Buller – *Churston, B.*
Yerburgh – *Alvingham, B.*
Yorke – *Hardwicke, E.*
Young – *Kennet, B.*
Young – *Y. of Dartington,*
  B.*
Young – *Y. of Graffham, B.**
Young – *Y. of Old Scone, B.**
Younger – *Y. of Leckie, V.*

Orders of Chivalry

THE MOST NOBLE ORDER
OF THE GARTER (1348)

KG

Ribbon, Blue

Motto, Honi soit qui mal y pense
(*Shame on him who thinks evil of it*)
The number of Knights Companions
is limited to 24

SOVEREIGN OF THE ORDER
The Queen

LADIES OF THE ORDER
HM Queen Elizabeth the Queen
Mother, 1936
HRH The Princess Royal, 1994

ROYAL KNIGHTS
HRH The Prince Philip, Duke of
Edinburgh, 1947
HRH The Prince of Wales, 1958
HRH The Duke of Kent, 1985
HRH The Duke of Gloucester, 1997

EXTRA KNIGHTS COMPANIONS
AND LADIES
HRH Princess Juliana of the
Netherlands, 1958
HRH The Grand Duke of
Luxembourg, 1972
HM The Queen of Denmark, 1979
HM The King of Sweden, 1983
HM The King of Spain, 1988
HM The Queen of the Netherlands,
1989
HIM The Emperor of Japan, 1998

KNIGHTS AND LADY COMPANIONS
The Earl of Longford, 1971
The Marquess of Abergavenny, 1974
The Duke of Grafton, 1976
The Duke of Norfolk, 1983
The Lord Richardson of
Duntisbourne, 1983
The Lord Carrington, 1985
The Lord Callaghan of Cardiff, 1987
The Viscount Leverhulme, 1988
The Lord Hailsham of St
Marylebone, 1988
The Duke of Wellington, 1990
Field Marshal the Lord Bramall,
1990
Sir Edward Heath, 1992
The Viscount Ridley, 1992
The Lord Sainsbury of Preston
Candover, 1992
The Lord Ashburton, 1994
The Lord Kingsdown, 1994

Sir Ninian Stephen, 1994
The Baroness Thatcher, 1995
Sir Edmund Hillary, 1995
The Duke of Devonshire, 1996
Sir Timothy Colman, 1996
The Duke of Abercorn, 1999
Sir William Gladstone, 1999

Prelate, The Bishop of Winchester
Chancellor, The Lord Carrington, KG,
GCMG, CH, MC
Register, The Dean of Windsor
Garter King of Arms, P. Gwynn-Jones,
CVO
Gentleman Usher of the Black Rod, Gen.
Sir Edward Jones, KCB, CBE
Secretary, D. H. B. Chesshyre, LVO

THE MOST ANCIENT AND
MOST NOBLE ORDER OF
THE THISTLE (REVIVED 1687)

KT

Ribbon, Green

Motto, Nemo me impune lacessit (*No
one provokes me with impunity*)
The number of Knights is limited to
16

SOVEREIGN OF THE ORDER
The Queen

LADY OF THE THISTLE
HM Queen Elizabeth the Queen
Mother, 1937

ROYAL KNIGHTS
HRH The Prince Philip, Duke of
Edinburgh, 1952
HRH The Prince of Wales, Duke of
Rothesay, 1977

KNIGHTS AND LADIES
The Earl of Wemyss and March,
1966
Sir Donald Cameron of Lochiel,
1973
The Duke of Buccleuch and
Queensberry, 1978
The Earl of Elgin and Kincardine,
1981
The Lord Thomson of Monifieth,
1981
The Lord MacLehose of Beoch, 1983
The Earl of Airlie, 1985
Capt. Sir Iain Tennant, 1986
The Viscount Younger of Leckie,
1995

The Viscount of Arbuthnott, 1996
The Earl of Crawford and Balcarres,
1996
Lady Marion Fraser, 1996
The Lord Macfarlane of Bearsden,
1996
The Lord Mackay of Clashfern, 1997

Chancellor, The Duke of Buccleuch
and Queensberry, KT, VRD
Dean, The Very Revd G. I.
Macmillan, CVO
Secretary and Lord Lyon King of Arms,
Sir Malcolm Innes of Edingight,
KCVO, WS
Usher of the Green Rod, Rear-Adm.
C. H. Layman, CB, DSO, LVO

THE MOST HONOURABLE
ORDER OF THE BATH
(1725)

GCB *Military*   GCB *Civil*

GCB   Knight (or Dame) Grand Cross
KCB   Knight Commander
DCB   Dame Commander
CB   Companion

Ribbon, Crimson

Motto, Tria juncta in uno (*Three joined
in one*)

Remodelled 1815, and enlarged
many times since. The Order is
divided into civil and military
divisions. Women became eligible for
the Order from 1 January 1971

THE SOVEREIGN

GREAT MASTER AND FIRST OR
PRINCIPAL KNIGHT GRAND CROSS
HRH The Prince of Wales, KG, KT,
GCB

Dean of the Order, The Dean of
Westminster
Bath King of Arms, Gen. Sir Brian
Kenny, GCB, CBE
Registrar and Secretary, Rear-Adm. D.
E. Macey, CB
Genealogist, P. Gwynn-Jones, CVO
Gentleman Usher of the Scarlet Rod, Air
Vice-Marshal Sir Richard Peirse,
KCVO, CB
Deputy Secretary, The Secretary of the
Central Chancery of the Orders of
Knighthood
Chancery, Central Chancery of the
Orders of Knighthood, St James's
Palace, London SWIA IBH

THE ORDER OF MERIT (1902)

OM *Military*   OM *Civil*

OM

Ribbon, Blue and crimson

This Order is designed as a special distinction for eminent men and women without conferring a knighthood upon them. The Order is limited in numbers to 24, with the addition of foreign honorary members. Membership is of two kinds, military and civil, the badge of the former having crossed swords, and the latter oak leaves

THE SOVEREIGN

HRH The Prince Philip, Duke of Edinburgh, 1968
Sir George Edwards, 1971
Revd Prof. Owen Chadwick, KBE, 1983
Sir Andrew Huxley, 1983
Frederick Sanger, 1986
Prof. Sir Ernst Gombrich, 1988
Dr Max Perutz, 1988
Dame Cicely Saunders, 1989
The Lord Porter of Luddenham, 1989
The Baroness Thatcher, 1990
Dame Joan Sutherland, 1991
Prof. Francis Crick, 1991
Dame Ninette de Valois, 1992
Sir Michael Atiyah, 1992
Lucian Freud, 1993
The Lord Jenkins of Hillhead, 1993
Sir Aaron Klug, 1995
Sir John Gielgud, 1996
The Lord Foster of Thames Bank, 1997
Sir Denis Rooke, 1997
HE Cardinal Basil Hume, 1999 (died 1999)
Honorary Member, Nelson Mandela, 1995

Secretary and Registrar, Sir Edward Ford, GCVO, KCB, ERD
Chancery, Central Chancery of the Orders of Knighthood, St James's Palace, London SW1A 1BH

THE MOST DISTINGUISHED ORDER OF ST MICHAEL AND ST GEORGE (1818)

GCMG   KCMG

GCMG   Knight (or Dame) Grand Cross
KCMG   Knight Commander
DCMG   Dame Commander
CMG   Companion

Ribbon, Saxon blue, with scarlet centre
Motto, Auspicium melioris aevi (*Token of a better age*)

THE SOVEREIGN

GRAND MASTER
HRH The Duke of Kent, KG, GCMG, GCVO, ADC

Prelate, The Rt. Revd Simon Barrington-Ward
Chancellor, Sir Antony Acland, GCMG, GCVO
Secretary, The Permanent Under-Secretary of State at the Foreign and Commonwealth Office and Head of the Diplomatic Service
Registrar, Sir John Graham, Bt., GCMG
King of Arms, Sir Ewen Fergusson, GCMG, GCVO
Gentleman Usher of the Blue Rod, Sir John Margetson, KCMG
Dean, The Dean of St Paul's
Deputy Secretary, The Secretary of the Central Chancery of the Orders of Knighthood
Chancery, Central Chancery of the Orders of Knighthood, St James's Palace, London SW1A 1BH

THE MOST EMINENT ORDER OF THE INDIAN EMPIRE (1868)

GCIE   Knight Grand Commander
KCIE   Knight Commander
CIE   Companion

Ribbon, Imperial purple
Motto, Imperatricis auspiciis (*Under the auspices of the Empress*)

THE SOVEREIGN

Registrar, The Secretary of the Central Chancery of the Orders of Knighthood
No conferments have been made since 1947

THE IMPERIAL ORDER OF THE CROWN OF INDIA (1877) FOR LADIES

CI

Badge, the royal cipher in jewels within an oval, surmounted by an heraldic crown and attached to a bow of light blue watered ribbon, edged white
The honour does not confer any rank or title upon the recipient
No conferments have been made since 1947

HM The Queen, 1947
HM Queen Elizabeth the Queen Mother, 1931
HRH The Princess Margaret, Countess of Snowdon, 1947
HRH Princess Alice, Duchess of Gloucester, 1937

THE ROYAL VICTORIAN ORDER (1896)

GCVO   KCVO

GCVO   Knight or Dame Grand Cross
KCVO   Knight Commander
DCVO   Dame Commander
CVO   Commander
LVO   Lieutenant
MVO   Member

Ribbon, Blue, with red and white edges
Motto, Victoria

THE SOVEREIGN

GRAND MASTER
HM Queen Elizabeth the Queen Mother

Chancellor, The Lord Chamberlain
Secretary, The Keeper of the Privy Purse
Registrar, The Secretary of the Central Chancery of the Orders of Knighthood
Chaplain, The Chaplain of the Queen's Chapel of the Savoy
Hon. Genealogist, D. H. B. Chesshyre, LVO

THE MOST EXCELLENT ORDER OF THE BRITISH EMPIRE (1917)

GBE   KBE

The Order was divided into military and civil divisions in December 1918

GBE Knight or Dame Grand Cross
KBE Knight Commander
DBE Dame Commander
CBE Commander
OBE Officer
MBE Member

Ribbon, Rose pink edged with pearl grey with vertical pearl stripe in centre (military division); without vertical pearl stripe (civil division)
Motto, For God and the Empire

THE SOVEREIGN

GRAND MASTER
HRH The Prince Philip, Duke of Edinburgh, KG, KT, OM, GBE, PC

Prelate, The Bishop of London
King of Arms, Air Chief Marshal Sir Patrick Hine, GCB, GBE
Registrar, The Secretary of the Central Chancery of the Orders of Knighthood
Secretary, The Secretary of the Cabinet and Head of the Home Civil Service
Dean, The Dean of St Paul's
Gentleman Usher of the Purple Rod, Sir Robin Gillett, Bt., GBE, RD
Chancery, Central Chancery of the Orders of Knighthood, St James's Palace, London SW1A 1BH

ORDER OF THE COMPANIONS OF HONOUR (1917)

CH

Ribbon, Carmine, with gold edges
This Order consists of one class only and carries with it no title. The number of awards is limited to 65 (excluding honorary members)

Anthony, Rt. Hon. John, 1981
Ashley of Stoke, The Lord, 1975
Astor, Hon. David, 1993
Attenborough, Sir David, 1995
Baker, Dame Janet, 1993
Baker of Dorking, The Lord, 1992

Brenner, Sydney, 1986
Brook, Peter, 1998
Brooke, Rt. Hon. Peter, 1992
Carrington, The Lord, 1983
Cledwyn of Penrhos, The Lord, 1976
de Valois, Dame Ninette, 1981
De Chastelain, Gen. John, 1999
Doll, Prof. Sir Richard, 1995
Fraser, Rt. Hon. Malcolm, 1977
Freud, Lucian, 1983
Gielgud, Sir John, 1977
Glenamara, The Lord, 1976
Gorton, Rt. Hon. Sir John, 1971
Guinness, Sir Alec, 1994
Hailsham of St Marylebone, The Lord, 1974
Hawking, Prof. Stephen, 1989
Healey, The Lord, 1979
Heseltine, Rt. Hon. Michael, 1997
Hobsbawm, Prof. Eric, 1998
Hockney, David, 1997
Howe of Aberavon, The Lord, 1996
Hurd of Westwell, The Lord, 1995
Jones, James, 1977
King, Rt. Hon. Tom, 1992
Lange, Rt. Hon. David, 1989
Lasdun, Sir Denys, 1995
Major, Rt. Hon. John, 1999
Milstein, César, 1994
Owen, The Lord, 1994
Patten, Rt. Hon. Christopher, 1998
Perutz, Dr Max, 1975
Powell, Anthony, 1987
Powell, Sir Philip, 1984
Runciman, Hon. Sir Steven, 1984
Riley, Bridget, 1999
Sanger, Frederick, 1981
Sisson, Charles, 1993
Smith, Sir John, 1993
Somare, Rt. Hon. Sir Michael, 1978
Talboys, Rt. Hon. Sir Brian, 1981
Tebbit, The Lord, 1987
Trudeau, Rt. Hon. Pierre, 1984
Widdowson, Dr Elsie, 1993
Honorary Members, Lee Kuan Yew, 1970; Dr Joseph Luns, 1971

Secretary and Registrar, The Secretary of the Central Chancery of the Orders of Knighthood

THE DISTINGUISHED SERVICE ORDER (1886)

DSO

Ribbon, Red, with blue edges
Bestowed in recognition of especial services in action of commissioned officers in the Navy, Army and Royal Air Force and (since 1942) Mercantile Marine. The members are Companions only. A Bar may be awarded for any additional act of service

THE IMPERIAL SERVICE ORDER (1902)

ISO

Ribbon, Crimson, with blue centre

Appointment as Companion of this Order is open to members of the Civil Services whose eligibility is determined by the grade they hold. The Order consists of The Sovereign and Companions to a number not exceeding 1,900, of whom 1,300 may belong to the Home Civil Services and 600 to Overseas Civil Services. The then Prime Minister announced in March 1993 that he would make no further recommendations for appointments to the Order.

Secretary, The Secretary of the Cabinet and Head of the Home Civil Service
Registrar, The Secretary of the Central Chancery of the Orders of Knighthood, St James's Palace, London SW1A 1BH

THE ROYAL VICTORIAN CHAIN (1902)

It confers no precedence on its holders

HM THE QUEEN
HM Queen Elizabeth the Queen Mother, 1937

HRH Princess Juliana of the Netherlands, 1950
HM The King of Thailand, 1960
HM King Zahir Shah of Afghanistan, 1971
HM The Queen of Denmark, 1974
HM The King of Nepal, 1975
HM The King of Sweden, 1975
The Lord Coggan, 1980
HM The Queen of the Netherlands, 1982
Gen. Antonio Eanes, 1985
HM The King of Spain, 1986
HM The King of Saudi Arabia, 1987
HRH The Princess Margaret, Countess of Snowdon, 1990
The Lord Runcie, 1991
The Lord Charteris of Amisfield, 1992
HE Richard von Weizsäcker, 1992
HM The King of Norway, 1994
The Earl of Airlie, 1997

Baronetage and Knightage

BARONETS

Style, 'Sir' before forename and surname, followed by 'Bt.'
Wife's style, 'Lady' followed by surname
For forms of address, *see* page 135

There are five different creations of baronetcies: Baronets of England (creations dating from 1611); Baronets of Ireland (creations dating from 1619); Baronets of Scotland or Nova Scotia (creations dating from 1625); Baronets of Great Britain (creations after the Act of Union 1707 which combined the kingdoms of England and Scotland); and Baronets of the United Kingdom (creations after the union of Great Britain and Ireland in 1801).

Badge of Baronets of the United Kingdom

Badge of Baronets of Nova Scotia

Badge of Ulster

The patent of creation limits the destination of a baronetcy, usually to male descendants of the first baronet, although special remainders allow the baronetcy to pass, if the male issue of sons fail, to the male issue of daughters of the first baronet. In the case of baronetcies of Scotland or Nova Scotia, a special remainder of 'heirs male and of tailzie' allows the baronetcy to descend to heirs general, including women. There are four existing Scottish baronets with such a remainder.

The Official Roll of Baronets is kept at the Home Office by the Registrar of the Baronetage. Anyone who considers that he is entitled to be entered on the Roll may petition the Crown through the Home Secretary. Every person succeeding to a baronetcy must exhibit proofs of succession to the Home Secretary. A person whose name is not entered on the Official Roll will not be addressed or mentioned by the title of baronet in any official document, nor will he be accorded precedence as a baronet.

BARONETCIES EXTINCT SINCE THE LAST EDITION
Butt (*cr.* 1929); Edwards (*cr.* 1921); Gibson (*cr.* 1926)

Registrar of the Baronetage, Miss C. E. C. Sinclair
Assistant Registrar, Mrs F. G. Bright
Office, Home Office, 50 Queen Anne's Gate, London
SW1H 9AT. Tel: 0171-273 3498

KNIGHTS

Style, 'Sir' before forename and surname, followed by appropriate post-nominal initials if a Knight Grand Cross, Knight Grand Commander or Knight Commander
Wife's style, 'Lady' followed by surname

For forms of address, *see* page 135
The prefix 'Sir' is not used by knights who are clerics of the Church of England, who do not receive the accolade. Their wives are entitled to precedence as the wife of a knight but not to the style of 'Lady'.

ORDERS OF KNIGHTHOOD

Knight Grand Cross, Knight Grand Commander, and Knight Commander are the higher classes of the Orders of Chivalry (*see* pages 171–3). Honorary knighthoods of these Orders may be conferred on men who are citizens of countries of which The Queen is not head of state. As a rule, the prefix 'Sir' is not used by honorary knights.

KNIGHTS BACHELOR

The Knights Bachelor do not constitute a Royal Order, but comprise the surviving representation of the ancient State Orders of Knighthood. The Register of Knights Bachelor, instituted by James I in the 17th century, lapsed, and in 1908 a voluntary association under the title of The Society of Knights (now The Imperial Society of Knights Bachelor by Royal Command) was formed with the primary objects of continuing the various registers dating from 1257 and obtaining the uniform registration of every created Knight Bachelor. In 1926 a design for a badge to be worn by Knights Bachelor was approved and adopted; in 1974 a neck badge and miniature were added.

Knight Principal, Sir Conrad Swan, KCVO
Chairman of Council, Sir Richard Gaskell, Kt.
Prelate, Rt. Revd and Rt. Hon. The Bishop of London
Registrar, Sir Robert Balchin
Hon. Treasurer, Sir Paul Judge, Kt.
Clerk to the Council, R. M. Esden, MBE
Office, 21 Old Buildings, Lincoln's Inn, London WC2A 3UJ

LIST OF BARONETS AND KNIGHTS

Revised to 31 August 1999
Peers are not included in this list

†   Not registered on the Official Roll of the Baronetage at the time of going to press
()   The date of creation of the baronetcy is given in parenthesis
I   Baronet of Ireland
NS   Baronet of Nova Scotia
S   Baronet of Scotland

If a baronet or knight has a double-barrelled or hyphenated surname, he is listed under the final element of the name
A full entry in italic type indicates that the recipient of a knighthood died during the year in which the honour was conferred. The name is included for purposes of record

Abal, Sir Tei, Kt., CBE

Abbott, Sir Albert Francis, Kt., CBE

Abbott, *Adm.* Sir Peter Charles, GBE, KCB

Abdy, Sir Valentine Robert Duff, Bt. (1850)

Abel, Sir Seselo (Cecil) Charles Geoffrey, Kt., OBE

Abercromby, Sir Ian George, Bt. (s. 1636)

Acheson, *Prof.* Sir (Ernest) Donald, KBE

Ackers, Sir James George, Kt.

Ackroyd, Sir Timothy Robert Whyte, Bt. (1956)

Acland, Sir Antony Arthur, GCMG, GCVO

Acland, *Lt.-Col.* Sir (Christopher) Guy (Dyke), Bt., MVO (1890)

Acland, Sir John Dyke, Bt. (1644)

Acland, *Maj.-Gen.* Sir John Hugh Bevil, KCB, CBE

Adam, Sir Christopher Eric Forbes, Bt. (1917)

Adams, Sir Philip George Doyne, KCMG

Adams, Sir William James, KCMG

Adamson, Sir (William Owen) Campbell, Kt.

Adrien, *Hon.* Sir Maurice Latour-, Kt.

Adsetts, Sir William Norman, Kt., OBE

Adye, Sir John Anthony, KCMG

Agnew, Sir Crispin Hamlyn, Bt. (s. 1629)

Agnew, Sir John Keith, Bt. (1895)

Aiken, *Air Chief Marshal* Sir John Alexander Carlisle, KCB

Aikens, Sir Richard John Pearson, Kt., QC

Ainsworth, Sir (Thomas) David, Bt. (1916)

Aird, *Capt.* Sir Alastair Sturgis, GCVO

Aird, Sir (George) John, Bt. (1901)

Airey, Sir Lawrence, KCB

Airy, *Maj.-Gen.* Sir Christopher John, KCVO, CBE

Aitchison, Sir Charles Walter de Lancey, Bt. (1938)

Akehurst, *Gen.* Sir John Bryan, KCB, CBE

Albu, Sir George, Bt. (1912)

Alcock, *Air Chief Marshal* Sir (Robert James) Michael, GCB, KBE

Aldous, *Rt. Hon.* Sir William, Kt.

Alexander, Sir Charles Gundry, Bt. (1945)

Alexander, Sir Claud Hagart-, Bt. (1886)

Alexander, Sir Douglas, Bt. (1921)

Alexander, Sir (John) Lindsay, Kt.

Alexander, *Prof.* Sir Kenneth John Wilson, Kt.

Alexander, Sir Michael O'Donal Bjarne, GCMG

†Alexander, Sir Patrick Desmond William Cable-, Bt. (1809)

Allan, Sir Anthony James Allan Havelock-, Bt. (1858)

Allen, *Prof.* Sir Geoffrey, Kt., PH.D., FRS

Allen, Sir John Derek, Kt., CBE

Allen, *Hon.* Sir Peter Austin Philip Jermyn, Kt.

Allen, Sir Thomas Boaz, Kt., CBE

Allen, Sir William Guilford, Kt.

Allen, Sir (William) Kenneth (Gwynne), Kt.

Alleyne, Sir George Allanmoore Ogarren, Kt.

Alleyne, *Revd* Sir John Olpherts Campbell, Bt. (1769)

Alliance, Sir David, Kt., CBE

Allinson, Sir (Walter) Leonard, KCVO, CMG

Alliott, *Hon.* Sir John Downes, Kt.

Allison, *Air Chief Marshal* Sir John Shakespeare, KCB, CBE

Alment, Sir (Edward) Anthony John, Kt.

Althaus, Sir Nigel Frederick, Kt.

Ambo, *Rt. Revd* George, KBE

Amet, *Hon.* Sir Arnold Karibone, Kt.

Amies, Sir (Edwin) Hardy, KCVO

Amory, Sir Ian Heathcoat, Bt. (1874)

Anderson, Sir John Anthony, KBE

Anderson, *Maj.-Gen.* Sir John Evelyn, KBE

Anderson, Sir John Muir, Kt., CMG

Anderson, *Hon.* Sir Kevin Victor, Kt.

Anderson, Sir Leith Reinsford Steven, Kt., CBE

Anderson, *Vice-Adm.* Sir Neil Dudley, KBE, CB

Anderson, *Prof.* Sir (William) Ferguson, Kt., OBE

Anderton, Sir (Cyril) James, Kt., CBE, QPM

Andrew, Sir Robert John, KCB

Andrews, Sir Derek Henry, KCB, CBE

Andrews, *Hon.* Sir Dormer George, Kt.

Angus, Sir Michael Richardson, Kt.

Annesley, Sir Hugh Norman, Kt., QPM

Anson, *Vice-Adm.* Sir Edward Rosebery, KCB

Anson, Sir John, KCB

Anson, *Rear-Adm.* Sir Peter, Bt., CB (1831)

Anstey, *Brig.* Sir John, Kt., CBE, TD

Anstruther, *Maj.* Sir Ralph Hugo, Bt., GCVO, MC (s. 1694)

Antico, Sir Tristan Venus, Kt.

Antrobus, Sir Charles James, GCMG, OBE

Antrobus, Sir Edward Philip, Bt. (1815)

Appleyard, Sir Leonard Vincent, KCMG

Appleyard, Sir Raymond Kenelm, KBE

Arbuthnot, Sir Keith Robert Charles, Bt. (1823)

Arbuthnot, Sir William Reierson, Bt. (1964)

Arbuthnott, *Prof.* Sir John Peebles, Kt., PH.D., FRSE

Archdale, *Capt.* Sir Edward Folmer, Bt., DSC, RN (1928)

Arculus, Sir Ronald, KCMG, KCVO

Armitage, *Air Chief Marshal* Sir Michael John, KCB, CBE

Armour, *Prof.* Sir James, Kt., CBE

†Armstrong, Sir Christopher John Edmund Stuart, Bt., MBE (1841)

Armytage, Sir John Martin, Bt. (1738)

Arnold, *Rt. Hon.* Sir John Lewis, Kt.

Arnold, Sir Malcolm Henry, Kt., CBE

Arnold, Sir Thomas Richard, Kt.

Arnott, Sir Alexander John Maxwell, Bt. (1896)

Arnott, *Prof.* Sir (William) Melville, Kt., TD, MD

Arrindell, Sir Clement Athelston, GCMG, GCVO, QC

Arthur, *Lt.-Gen.* Sir (John) Norman Stewart, KCB

Arthur, Sir Stephen John, Bt. (1841)

Ash, *Prof.* Sir Eric Albert, Kt., CBE, FRS, FREng.

†Ashburnham, Sir James Fleetwood, Bt. (1661)

Ashe, Sir Derick Rosslyn, KCMG

Ashley, Sir Bernard Albert, Kt.

Ashmore, *Admiral of the Fleet* Sir Edward Beckwith, GCB, DSC

Ashmore, *Vice-Adm.* Sir Peter William Beckwith, KCB, KCVO, DSC

Ashworth, Sir Herbert, Kt.

Aske, *Revd* Sir Conan, Bt. (1922)

Askew, Sir Bryan, Kt.

Asscher, Prof. (Adolf) William, Kt., MD, FRCP

Astill, *Hon.* Sir Michael John, Kt.

Aston, Sir Harold George, Kt., CBE

Astor, *Hon.* Sir John Jacob, Kt., MBE

Astwood, *Hon.* Sir James Rufus, KBE

Atcherley, Sir Harold Winter, Kt.

Atiyah, Sir Michael Francis, Kt., OM, PH.D., FRS

Atkins, *Rt. Hon.* Sir Robert James, Kt.

Atkinson, *Air Marshal* Sir David William, KBE

Atkinson, Sir Frederick John, KCB

Atkinson, Sir John Alexander, KCB, DFC

Atkinson, Sir Robert, Kt., DSC, FREng.

Atopare, Sir Sailas, GCMG

Attenborough, Sir David Frederick, Kt., CH, CVO, CBE, FRS

Atwill, Sir (Milton) John (Napier), Kt.

Audland, Sir Christopher John, KCMG

Audley, Sir George Bernard, Kt.

Augier, *Prof.* Sir Fitz-Roy Richard, Kt.

Auld, *Rt. Hon.* Sir Robin Ernest, Kt.

Austin, Sir Anthony Leonard, Bt. (1894)

Austin, *Vice-Adm.* Sir Peter Murray, KCB

Austin, *Air Marshal* Sir Roger Mark, KCB, AFC

Axford, Sir William Ian, Kt.

Ayckbourn, Sir Alan, Kt., CBE

Aykroyd, Sir James Alexander Frederic, Bt. (1929)

Aykroyd, Sir William Miles, Bt., MC (1920)

Aylmer, Sir Richard John, Bt. (I. 1622)

Bacha, Sir Bhinod, Kt., CMG

Backhouse, Sir Jonathan Roger, Bt. (1901)

Bacon, Sir Nicholas Hickman Ponsonby, Bt. *Premier Baronet of England* (1611 and 1627)

Bacon, Sir Sidney Charles, Kt., CB, FREng.

Baddeley, Sir John Wolsey Beresford, Bt. (1922)

Baddiley, *Prof.* Sir James, Kt., ph.D., D.SC., FRS, FRSE

Badge, Sir Peter Gilmour Noto, Kt.

Badger, Sir Geoffrey Malcolm, Kt.

Baer, Sir Jack Mervyn Frank, Kt.

Bagge, Sir (John) Jeremy Picton, Bt. (1867)

Bagnall, *Air Marshal* Sir Anthony John Crowther, KCB, OBE

Bagnall, *Field Marshal* Sir Nigel Thomas, GCB, CVO, MC

Bailey, Sir Alan Marshall, KCB

Bailey, Sir Brian Harry, Kt., OBE

Bailey, Sir Derrick Thomas Louis, Bt., DFC (1919)

Bailey, Sir John Bilsland, KCB

Bailey, Sir Richard John, Kt., CBE

Bailey, Sir Stanley Ernest, Kt., CBE, QPM

Bailhache, Sir Philip Martin, Kt.

Baillie, Sir Gawaine George Hope, Bt. (1823)

Baines, *Prof.* Sir George Grenfell-, Kt., OBE

Baird, Sir David Charles, Bt. (1809)

†Baird, Sir James Andrew Gardiner, Bt. (s. 1695)

Baird, *Lt.-Gen.* Sir James Parlane, KBE, MD

Baird, *Air Marshal* Sir John Alexander, KBE

Baird, *Vice-Adm.* Sir Thomas Henry Eustace, KCB

Bairsto, *Air Marshal* Sir Peter Edward, KBE, CB

Baker, Sir Bryan William, Kt.

Baker, Sir Robert George Humphrey Sherston-, Bt. (1796)

Baker, *Hon.* Sir (Thomas) Scott (Gillespie), Kt.

Balchin, Sir Robert George Alexander, Kt.

Balcombe, *Rt. Hon.* Sir (Alfred) John, Kt.

Balderstone, Sir James Schofield, Kt.

Baldwin, *Prof.* Sir Jack Edward, Kt., FRS

Baldwin, Sir Peter Robert, KCB

Ball, *Air Marshal* Sir Alfred Henry Wynne, KCB, DSO, DFC

Ball, Sir Charles Irwin, Bt. (1911)

Ball, Sir Christopher John Elinger, Kt.

Ball, *Prof.* Sir Robert James, Kt., ph.D.

Bamford, Sir Anthony Paul, Kt.

Banham, Sir John Michael Middlecott, Kt.

Bannerman, Sir David Gordon, Bt., OBE (s. 1682)

Bannister, Sir Roger Gilbert, Kt., CBE, DM, FRCP

Barber, Sir (Thomas) David, Bt. (1960)

Barbour, *Very Revd* Sir Robert Alexander Stewart, KCVO, MC

Barclay, Sir Colville Herbert Sanford, Bt. (s. 1668)

Barclay, Sir Peter Maurice, Kt., CBE

Barder, Sir Brian Leon, KCMG

Barker, Sir Alwyn Bowman, Kt., CMG

Barker, Sir Colin, Kt.

Barker, *Hon.* Sir (Richard) Ian, Kt.

Barlow, Sir Christopher Hilaro, Bt. (1803)

Barlow, Sir Frank, Kt., CBE

Barlow, Sir (George) William, Kt., FREng.

Barlow, Sir John Kemp, Bt. (1907)

Barlow, Sir Thomas Erasmus, Bt., DSC (1902)

Barnard, Sir Joseph Brian, Kt.

Barnes, Sir (James) David (Francis), Kt., CBE

Barnes, Sir Kenneth, KCB

Barnewall, Sir Reginald Robert, Bt. (I. 1623)

Baron, Sir Thomas, Kt., CBE

Barraclough, *Air Chief Marshal* Sir John, KCB, CBE, DFC, AFC

Barraclough, Sir Kenneth James Priestley, Kt., CBE, TD

Barran, Sir David Haven, Kt.

Barran, Sir John Napoleon Ruthven, Bt. (1895)

Barratt, Sir Lawrence Arthur, Kt.

Barratt, Sir Richard Stanley, Kt., CBE, QPM

Barrett, *Lt.-Gen.* Sir David William Scott-, KBE, MC

Barrett, Sir Stephen Jeremy, KCMG

Barrington, Sir Alexander (Fitzwilliam Croker), Bt. (1831)

Barrington, Sir Nicholas John, KCMG, CVO

Barron, Sir Donald James, Kt.

Barrow, *Capt.* Sir Richard John Uniacke, Bt. (1835)

Barrowclough, Sir Anthony Richard, Kt., QC

Barry, Sir (Lawrence) Edward (Anthony Tress), Bt. (1899)

†Bartlett, Sir Andrew Alan, Bt. (1913)

Barttelot, *Col.* Sir Brian Walter de Stopham, Bt., OBE (1875)

Batchelor, Sir Ivor Ralph Campbell, Kt., CBE

Bate, Sir David Lindsay, KBE

Bate, Sir (Walter) Edwin, Kt., OBE

Bates, Sir Geoffrey Voltelin, Bt., MC (1880)

Bates, Sir Malcolm Rowland, Kt.

Bates, Sir Richard Dawson Hoult, Bt. (1937)

Batho, Sir Peter Ghislain, Bt. (1928)

Bathurst, *Admiral of the Fleet* Sir (David) Benjamin, GCB

Bathurst, Sir Frederick John Charles Gordon Hervey-, Bt. (1818)

Bathurst, Sir Maurice Edward, Kt., CMG, CBE, QC

Batten, Sir John Charles, KCVO

Battersby, *Prof.* Sir Alan Rushton, Kt., FRS

Battishill, Sir Anthony Michael William, GCB

Batty, Sir William Bradshaw, Kt., TD

Baxendell, Sir Peter Brian, Kt., CBE, FREng.

Bayliss, Sir Richard Ian Samuel, KCVO, MD, FRCP

Bayne, Sir Nicholas Peter, KCMG

Baynes, Sir John Christopher Malcolm, Bt. (1801)

Bazley, Sir Thomas John Sebastian, Bt. (1869)

Beach, *Gen.* Sir (William Gerald) Hugh, GBE, KCB, MC

Beale, *Lt.-Gen.* Sir Peter John, KBE, FRCP

Beament, Sir James William Longman, Kt., SC.D., FRS

Beamish, Sir Adrian John, KCMG

Beattie, *Hon.* Sir Alexander Craig, Kt.

Beattie, *Hon.* Sir David Stuart, GCMG, GCVO

Beauchamp, Sir Christopher Radstock Proctor-, Bt. (1745)

Beaumont, *Capt.* the Hon. Sir (Edward) Nicholas (Canning), KCVO

Beaumont, Sir George (Howland Francis), Bt. (1661)

Beaumont, Sir Richard Ashton, KCMG, OBE

Beavis, *Air Chief Marshal* Sir Michael Gordon, KCB, CBE, AFC

Becher, Sir William Fane Wrixon, Bt., MC (1831)

Beck, Sir Edgar Charles, Kt., CBE, FREng.

Beck, Sir Edgar Philip, Kt.

Beckett, *Capt.* Sir (Martyn) Gervase, Bt., MC (1921)

Beckett, Sir Terence Norman, KBE, FREng.

Bedingfeld, *Capt.* Sir Edmund George Felix Paston-, Bt. (1661)

Bedser, Sir Alec Victor, Kt., CBE

Beecham, Sir Jeremy Hugh, Kt.

Beecham, Sir John Stratford Roland, Bt. (1914)

Beeley, Sir Harold, KCMG, CBE

Beetham, *Marshal of the Royal Air Force* Sir Michael James, GCB, CBE, DFC, AFC

Beevor, Sir Thomas Agnew, Bt. (1784)

Beith, Sir John Greville Stanley, KCMG

Beldam, *Rt. Hon.* Sir (Alexander) Roy (Asplan), Kt.

Belich, Sir James, Kt.

Bell, Sir Brian Ernest, KBE

Boolell, Sir Satcam, Kt.
Boord, Sir Nicolas John Charles, Bt. (1896)
Boorman, Lt.-Gen. Sir Derek, KCB
Booth, Sir Christopher Charles, Kt., MD, FRCP
Booth, Hon. Sir David Alwyn Gore-, KCMG, KCVO
Booth, Sir Douglas Allen, Bt. (1916)
Booth, Sir Gordon, KCMG, CVO
Booth, Sir Josslyn Henry Robert Gore-, Bt. (I. 1760)
Booth, Sir Michael Addison John Wheeler-, KCB
Boothby, Sir Brooke Charles, Bt. (1660)
Boreel, Sir Francis David, Bt. (1645)
Boreham, Hon. Sir Leslie Kenneth Edward, Kt.
Bornu, The Waziri of, KCMG, CBE
Borthwick, Sir John Thomas, Bt., MBE (1908)
Bossom, Hon. Sir Clive, Bt. (1953)
Boswall, Sir (Thomas) Alford Houstoun-, Bt. (1836)
Boswell, Lt.-Gen. Sir Alexander Crawford Simpson, KCB, CBE
Bosworth, Sir Neville Bruce Alfred, Kt., CBE
Bottomley, Sir James Reginald Alfred, KCMG
Boughey, Sir John George Fletcher, Bt. (1798)
Boulton, Sir Clifford John, GCB
Boulton, Sir (Harold Hugh) Christian, Bt. (1905)
Boulton, Sir William Whytehead, Bt., CBE, TD (1944)
Bourn, Sir John Bryant, KCB
Bourne, Sir (John) Wilfrid, KCB
Bovell, Hon. Sir (William) Stewart, Kt.
Bowater, Sir Euan David Vansittart, Bt. (1939)
Bowater, Sir (John) Vansittart, Bt. (1914)
Bowden, Sir Andrew, Kt., MBE
Bowden, Sir Frank, Bt. (1915)
Bowen, Sir Geoffrey Fraser, Kt.
Bowen, Sir Mark Edward Mortimer, Bt. (1921)
Bowett, Prof. Sir Derek William, Kt., CBE, QC, FBA
†Bowlby, Sir Richard Peregrine Longstaff, Bt. (1923)
Bowman, Sir Jeffery Haverstock, Kt.
Bowman, Sir Paul Humphrey Armytage, Bt. (1884)
Bowness, Sir Alan, Kt., CBE
Boyce, Adm. Sir Michael Cecil, GCB, OBE
Boyce, Sir Robert Charles Leslie, Bt. (1952)
Boyd, Sir Alexander Walter, Bt. (1916)
Boyd, Sir John Dixon Iklé, KCMG
Boyd, The Hon. Sir Mark Alexander Lennox-, Kt.
Boyd, Prof. Sir Robert Lewis Fullarton, Kt., CBE, D.SC., FRS

Boyes, Sir Brian Gerald Barratt-, KBE
Boyle, Sir Stephen Gurney, Bt. (1904)
Boynton, Sir John Keyworth, Kt., MC
Boys, Rt. Hon. Sir Michael Hardie, GCMG
Boyson, Rt. Hon. Sir Rhodes, Kt.
Brabham, Sir John Arthur, Kt., OBE
Bradbeer, Sir John Derek Richardson, Kt., OBE, TD
Bradbury, Surgeon Vice-Adm. Sir Eric Blackburn, KBE, CB
Bradford, Sir Edward Alexander Slade, Bt. (1902)
Bradman, Sir Donald George, Kt.
Bradshaw, Sir Kenneth Anthony, KCB
Bradshaw, Lt.-Gen. Sir Richard Phillip, KBE
Brain, Sir (Henry) Norman, KBE, CMG
Braithwaite, Sir (Joseph) Franklin Madders, Kt.
Braithwaite, Rt. Hon. Sir Nicholas Alexander, Kt., OBE
Braithwaite, Sir Rodric Quentin, GCMG
Bramley, Prof. Sir Paul Anthony, Kt.
Branigan, Sir Patrick Francis, Kt., QC
Bratza, Sir Nicolas Dušan, Kt., QC
Bray, Sir Theodor Charles, Kt., CBE
Brennan, Hon. Sir (Francis) Gerard, KBE
Brett, Sir Charles Edward Bainbridge, Kt., CBE
Brickwood, Sir Basil Greame, Bt. (1927)
Bridges, Hon. Sir Phillip Rodney, Kt., CMG
Brierley, Sir Ronald Alfred, Kt.
Bright, Sir Graham Frank James, Kt.
Bright, Sir Keith, Kt.
Brigstocke, Adm. Sir John Richard, KCB
Brinckman, Sir Theodore George Roderick, Bt. (1831)
†Brisco, Sir Campbell Howard, Bt. (1782)
Briscoe, Sir John Geoffrey James, Bt. (1910)
Brise, Sir John Archibald Ruggles-, Bt., CB, OBE, TD (1935)
Bristow, Hon. Sir Peter Henry Rowley, Kt.
Brittan, Rt. Hon. Sir Leon, Kt., QC
Brittan, Sir Samuel, Kt.
Britton, Sir Edward Louis, Kt., CBE
Broackes, Sir Nigel, Kt.
†Broadbent, Sir Andrew George, Bt. (1893)
Brocklebank, Sir Aubrey Thomas, Bt. (1885)
Brockman, Vice-Adm. Sir Ronald Vernon, KCB, CSI, CIE, CVO, CBE
Brodie, Sir Benjamin David Ross, Bt. (1834)
Broers, Prof. Sir Alec Nigel, Kt., ph.D., FRS
Bromhead, Sir John Desmond Gonville, Bt. (1806)
Bromley, Sir Michael Roger, KBE

Bromley, Sir Rupert Charles, Bt. (1757)
Bromley, Sir Thomas Eardley, KCMG
†Brooke, Sir Alistair Weston, Bt. (1919)
Brooke, Sir Francis George Windham, Bt. (1903)
Brooke, Rt. Hon. Sir Henry, Kt.
Brooke, Sir (Richard) David Christopher, Bt. (1662)
Brooksbank, Sir (Edward) Nicholas, Bt. (1919)
Broom, Air Marshal Sir Ivor Gordon, KCB, CBE, DSO, DFC, AFC
Broomfield, Sir Nigel Hugh Robert Allen, KCMG
†Broughton, Sir David Delves, Bt. (1661)
Broun, Sir William Windsor, Bt. (S. 1686)
Brown, Sir Allen Stanley, Kt., CBE
Brown, Sir (Austen) Patrick, KCB
Brown, Adm. Sir Brian Thomas, KCB, CBE
Brown, Sir (Cyril) Maxwell Palmer, KCB, CMG
Brown, Vice-Adm. Sir David Worthington, KCB
Brown, Sir Derrick Holden-, Kt.
Brown, Sir Douglas Denison, Kt.
Brown, Hon. Sir Douglas Dunlop, Kt.
Brown, Sir George Francis Richmond, Bt. (1863)
Brown, Sir George Noel, Kt.
Brown, Sir John Douglas Keith, Kt.
Brown, Sir John Gilbert Newton, Kt., CBE
Brown, Sir Mervyn, KCMG, OBE
Brown, Sir Peter Randolph, Kt.
Brown, Hon. Sir Ralph Kilner, Kt., OBE, TD
Brown, Sir Robert Crichton-, KCMG, CBE, TD
Brown, Rt. Hon. Sir Simon Denis, Kt.
Brown, Rt. Hon. Sir Stephen, GBE, Kt.
Brown, Sir Stephen David Reid, KCVO
Brown, Sir Thomas, Kt.
Brown, Sir William Brian Piggott-, Bt. (1903)
Browne, Sir (Edmund) John (Phillip), Kt., FREng.
Brownrigg, Sir Nicholas (Gawen), Bt. (1816)
Browse, Prof. Sir Norman Leslie, Kt., MD, FRCS
Bruce, Sir (Francis) Michael Ian, Bt. (S. 1628)
Bruce, Sir Hervey James Hugh, Bt. (1804)
Bruce, Rt. Hon. Sir (James) Roualeyn Hovell-Thurlow-Cumming-, Kt.
Brunner, Sir John Henry Kilian, Bt. (1895)
Brunton, Sir (Edward Francis) Lauder, Bt. (1908)
Brunton, Sir Gordon Charles, Kt.
Bryan, Sir Arthur, Kt.
Bryan, Sir Paul Elmore Oliver, Kt., DSO, MC

Bryce, *Hon.* Sir (William) Gordon, Kt., CBE

Bryson, *Adm.* Sir Lindsay Sutherland, KCB, FREng.

Buchan, Sir John, Kt., CMG

Buchanan, Sir Andrew George, Bt. (1878)

Buchanan, Sir Charles Alexander James Leith-, Bt. (1775)

Buchanan, *Prof.* Sir Colin Douglas, Kt., CBE

Buchanan, *Vice-Adm.* Sir Peter William, KBE

Buchanan, Sir (Ranald) Dennis, Kt., MBE

Buchanan, Sir Robert Wilson (Robin), Kt.

Buck, Sir (Philip) Antony (Fyson), Kt., QC

Buckland, Sir Ross, Kt.

Buckley, Sir John William, Kt.

Buckley, *Lt.-Cdr.* Sir (Peter) Richard, KCVO

Buckley, *Hon.* Sir Roger John, Kt.

Budd, Sir Alan Peter, Kt.

Bulkeley, Sir Richard Thomas Williams-, Bt. (1661)

Bull, Sir George Jeffrey, Kt.

Bull, Sir Simeon George, Bt. (1922)

Bullard, Sir Julian Leonard, GCMG

Bullus, Sir Eric Edward, Kt.

Bulmer, Sir William Peter, Kt.

Bultin, Sir Bato, Kt., MBE

Bunbury, Sir Michael William, Bt. (1681)

Bunbury, Sir (Richard David) Michael Richardson-, Bt. (I. 1787)

Bunch, Sir Austin Wyeth, Kt., CBE

Bunyard, Sir Robert Sidney, Kt., CBE, QPM

Burbidge, Sir Herbert Dudley, Bt. (1916)

Burdett, Sir Savile Aylmer, Bt. (1665)

Burgen, Sir Arnold Stanley Vincent, Kt., FRS

Burgess, *Gen.* Sir Edward Arthur, KCB, OBE

Burgess, Sir (Joseph) Stuart, Kt., CBE, Ph.D., FRSC

Burgh, Sir John Charles, KCMG, CB

Burke, Sir James Stanley Gilbert, Bt. (I. 1797)

Burke, Sir (Thomas) Kerry, Kt.

Burley, Sir Victor George, Kt., CBE

Burman, Sir (John) Charles, Kt.

Burnet, Sir James William Alexander (Sir Alastair Burnet), Kt.

Burnett, *Air Chief Marshal* Sir Brian Kenyon, GCB, DFC, AFC

Burnett, Sir David Humphery, Bt., MBE, TD (1913)

Burnett, Sir John Harrison, Kt.

Burnett, Sir Walter John, Kt.

Burney, Sir Cecil Denniston, Bt. (1921)

Burns, Sir (Robert) Andrew, KCMG

Burrell, Sir John Raymond, Bt. (1774)

Burrenchobay, Sir Dayendranath, KBE, CMG, CVO

Burrows, Sir Bernard Alexander Brocas, GCMG

Burston, Sir Samuel Gerald Wood, Kt., OBE

Burt, *Hon.* Sir Francis Theodore Page, KCMG

Burton, Sir Carlisle Archibald, Kt., OBE

Burton, Sir George Vernon Kennedy, Kt., CBE

Burton, *Lt.-Gen.* Sir Edmund Fortescue Gerard, KBE

Burton, Sir Graham Stuart, KCMG

Burton, Sir Michael John, Kt., QC

Burton, Sir Michael St Edmund, KCVO, CMG

Bush, *Adm.* Sir John Fitzroy Duyland, GCB, DSC

Butler, *Rt. Hon.* Sir Adam Courtauld, Kt.

Butler, *Hon.* Sir Arlington Griffith, KCMG

Butler, Sir Michael Dacres, GCMG

Butler, Sir (Reginald) Michael (Thomas), Bt. (1922)

Butler, *Hon.* Sir Richard Clive, Kt.

†Butler, Sir Richard Pierce, Bt. (1628)

Butter, *Maj.* Sir David Henry, KCVO, MC

Butterfield, *Hon.* Sir Alexander Neil Logie, Kt.

Buxton, Sir Jocelyn Charles Roden, Bt. (1840)

Buxton, *Rt. Hon.* Sir Richard Joseph, Kt.

Buzzard, Sir Anthony Farquhar, Bt. (1929)

Byatt, Sir Hugh Campbell, KCVO, CMG

Byers, Sir Maurice Hearne, Kt., CBE, QC

Byford, Sir Lawrence, Kt., CBE, QPM

Cable, Sir James Eric, KCVO, CMG

Cadbury, Sir (George) Adrian (Hayhurst), Kt.

Cadbury, Sir (Nicholas) Dominic, Kt.

Cadogan, *Prof.* Sir John Ivan George, Kt., CBE, FRS, FRSE

Cahn, Sir Albert Jonas, Bt. (1934)

Cain, Sir Henry Edney Conrad, Kt.

Caines, Sir John, KCB

Calcutt, Sir David Charles, Kt., QC

Calderwood, Sir Robert, Kt.

Caldwell, *Surgeon Vice-Adm.* Sir (Eric) Dick, KBE, CB

Callan, Sir Ivan Roy, KCVO, CMG

Callaway, *Prof.* Sir Frank Adams, Kt., CMG, OBE

Calman, *Prof.* Sir Kenneth Charles, KCB, MD, FRCP, FRCS, FRSE

Calne, *Prof.* Sir Roy Yorke, Kt., FRS

Calthorpe, Sir Euan Hamilton Anstruther-Gough-, Bt. (1929)

Cameron of Lochiel, Sir Donald Hamish, KT, CVO, TD

Cameron, Sir (Eustace) John, Kt., CBE

Cameron, Sir Hugh Roy Graham, Kt., QPM

Campbell, Sir Alan Hugh, GCMG

Campbell, *Prof.* Sir Colin Murray, Kt.

Campbell, *Prof.* Sir Donald, Kt., CBE, FRCS, FRCPGlas.

Campbell, Sir Ian Tofts, Kt., CBE, VRD

Campbell, Sir Ilay Mark, Bt. (1808)

Campbell, Sir James Alexander Moffat Bain, Bt. (S. 1668)

Campbell, Sir Lachlan Philip Kemeys, Bt. (1815)

Campbell, Sir Niall Alexander Hamilton, Bt. (1831)

Campbell, Sir Robin Auchinbreck, Bt. (S. 1628)

Campbell, Sir Thomas Cockburn-, Bt. (1821)

Campbell, *Hon.* Sir Walter Benjamin, Kt.

Campbell, *Rt. Hon.* Sir William Anthony, Kt.

†Carden, Sir Christopher Robert, Bt. (1887)

Carden, Sir John Craven, Bt. (I. 1787)

Carew, Sir Rivers Verain, Bt. (1661)

Carey, Sir Peter Willoughby, GCB

Carlisle, Sir James Beethoven, GCMG

Carlisle, Sir John Michael, Kt.

Carlisle, Sir Kenneth Melville, Kt.

Carmichael, Sir David Peter William Gibson-Craig-, Bt. (S. 1702 and 1831)

Carnac, *Revd Canon* Sir (Thomas) Nicholas Rivett-, Bt. (1836)

Carnegie, *Lt.-Gen.* Sir Robin Macdonald, KCB, OBE

Carnegie, Sir Roderick Howard, Kt.

Carnwath, Sir Robert John Anderson, Kt., CVO

Caro, Sir Anthony Alfred, Kt., CBE

Carpenter, *Lt.-Gen.* the Hon. Sir Thomas Patrick John Boyd-, KBE

Carr, Sir (Albert) Raymond (Maillard), Kt.

Carrick, *Hon.* Sir John Leslie, KCMG

Carrick, Sir Roger John, KCMG, LVO

Carsberg, *Prof.* Sir Bryan Victor, Kt.

Carswell, *Rt. Hon.* Sir Robert Douglas, Kt.

Carter, Sir Charles Frederick, Kt., FBA

Carter, *Prof.* Sir David Craig, Kt., FRCSE, FRCSGlas., FRCPE

Carter, Sir John, Kt., QC

Carter, Sir John Alexander, Kt.

Carter, Sir John Gordon Thomas, Kt.

Carter, Sir Philip David, Kt., CBE

Carter, Sir Richard Henry Alwyn, Kt.

Carter, Sir William Oscar, Kt.

Cartland, Sir George Barrington, Kt., CMG

Cartledge, Sir Bryan George, KCMG

Cary, Sir Roger Hugh, Bt. (1955)

Casey, *Rt. Hon.* Sir Maurice Eugene, Kt.

Cash, Sir Gerald Christopher, GCMG, GCVO, OBE

Cass, Sir Geoffrey Arthur, Kt.

Cassel, Sir Harold Felix, Bt., TD, QC (1920)

Cassels, Sir John Seton, Kt., CB

Cassels, *Adm.* Sir Simon Alastair
Cassillis, KCB, CBE
Cassidi, *Adm.* Sir (Arthur) Desmond,
GCB
Cater, Sir Jack, KBE
Catford, Sir (John) Robin, KCVO, CBE
Catherwood, Sir (Henry) Frederick
(Ross), Kt.
Catling, Sir Richard Charles, Kt.,
CMG, OBE
Cave, Sir (Charles) Philip Haddon-,
KBE, CMG
†Cave, Sir John Charles, Bt. (1896)
Cave, Sir Robert Cave-Browne-, Bt.
(1641)
Cawley, Sir Charles Mills, Kt., CBE,
ph.D.
Cayley, Sir Digby William David, Bt.
(1661)
Cayzer, Sir James Arthur, Bt. (1904)
Cazalet, *Hon.* Sir Edward Stephen,
Kt.
Cazalet, Sir Peter Grenville, Kt.
Cecil, *Rear-Adm.* Sir (Oswald) Nigel
Amherst, KBE, CB
Chacksfield, *Air Vice-Marshal* Sir
Bernard Albert, KBE, CB
Chadwick, *Revd Prof.* Henry, KBE
Chadwick, *Rt. Hon.* Sir John Murray,
Kt., ED
Chadwick, Sir Joshua Kenneth
Burton, Bt. (1935)
Chadwick, *Revd Prof.* (William)
Owen, OM, KBE, FBA
Chalstrey, Sir (Leonard) John, Kt.,
MD, FRCS
Chan, *Rt. Hon.* Sir Julius, GCMG, KBE
Chance, Sir (George) Jeremy
ffolliott, Bt. (1900)
Chandler, Sir Colin Michael, Kt.
Chandler, Sir Geoffrey, Kt., CBE
Chaney, *Hon.* Sir Frederick Charles,
KBE, AFC
Chantler, *Prof.* Sir Cyril, Kt., MD,
FRCP
Chaplin, Sir Malcolm Hilbery, Kt.,
CBE
Chapman, Sir David Robert
Macgowan, Bt. (1958)
Chapman, Sir George Alan, Kt.
Chapman, Sir Sidney Brookes, Kt.,
MP
Chapple, *Field Marshal* Sir John
Lyon, GCB, GBE
Charles, *Hon.* Sir Arthur William
Hessin, Kt
Charles, Sir George Frederick
Lawrence, KCMG, CBE
Charlton, Sir Robert (Bobby), Kt.,
CBE
Charnley, Sir (William) John, Kt., CB,
FREng.
Chataway, *Rt. Hon.* Sir Christopher,
Kt.
Chatfield, Sir John Freeman, Kt., CBE
Chaytor, Sir George Reginald, Bt.
(1831)
Checketts, *Sqn. Ldr.* Sir David John,
KCVO
Checkland, Sir Michael, Kt.

Cheetham, Sir Nicolas John
Alexander, KCMG
Cheshire, *Air Chief Marshal* Sir John
Anthony, KBE, CB
Chessells, Sir Arthur David (Tim),
Kt.
Chesterman, Sir (Dudley) Ross, Kt.,
ph.D.
Chesterton, Sir Oliver Sidney, Kt.,
MC
Chetwood, Sir Clifford Jack, Kt.
Chetwynd, Sir Arthur Ralph Talbot,
Bt. (1795)
Cheung, Sir Oswald Victor, Kt., CBE
Cheyne, Sir Joseph Lister Watson,
Bt., OBE (1908)
Chichester, Sir (Edward) John, Bt.
(1641)
Chilcot, Sir John Anthony, GCB
Child, Sir (Coles John) Jeremy, Bt.
(1919)
Chilton, *Brig.* Sir Frederick Oliver,
Kt., CBE, DSO
Chilwell, *Hon.* Sir Muir Fitzherbert,
Kt.
Chinn, Sir Trevor Edwin, Kt., CVO
Chipperfield, Sir Geoffrey Howes,
KCB
Chisholm, Sir John Alexander
Raymond, Kt., FREng.
Chitty, Sir Thomas Willes, Bt. (1924)
Cholmeley, Sir Hugh John Frederick
Sebastian, Bt. (1806)
Christie, Sir George William
Langham, Kt.
Christie, Sir William, Kt., MBE
Christopherson, Sir Derman Guy,
Kt., OBE, D.Phil., FRS, FREng.
Chung, Sir Sze-yuen, GBE, FREng.
Clapham, Sir Michael John Sinclair,
KBE
Clark, Sir Francis Drake, Bt. (1886)
Clark, Sir John Allen, Kt.
Clark, Sir John Stewart-, Bt., MEP
(1918)
Clark, Sir Jonathan George, Bt.
(1917)
Clark, Sir Robert Anthony, Kt., DSC
Clark, Sir Robin Chichester-, Kt.
Clark, Sir Terence Joseph, KBE, CMG,
CVO
Clark, Sir Thomas Edwin, Kt.
Clarke, *Hon.* Sir Anthony Peter, Kt.
Clarke, Sir Arthur Charles, Kt., CBE
Clarke, Sir (Charles Mansfield)
Tobias, Bt. (1831)
Clarke, *Prof.* Sir Cyril Astley, KBE,
MD, SC.D., FRS, FRCP
Clarke, Sir Ellis Emmanuel Innocent,
GCMG
Clarke, Sir Jonathan Dennis, Kt.
Clarke, *Maj.* Sir Peter Cecil, KCVO
Clarke, Sir Robert Cyril, Kt.
Clarke, Sir Rupert William John, Bt.,
MBE (1882)
Clay, Sir Richard Henry, Bt. (1841)
Clayton, Sir David Robert, Bt. (1732)
Cleaver, Sir Anthony Brian, Kt.
Cleminson, Sir James Arnold Stacey,
KBE, MC

Clerk, Sir John Dutton, Bt., CBE, VRD
(s. 1679)
Clerke, Sir John Edward
Longueville, Bt. (1660)
Clifford, Sir Roger Joseph, Bt. (1887)
Clothier, Sir Cecil Montacute, KCB,
QC
Clucas, Sir Kenneth Henry, KCB
Clutterbuck, *Vice-Adm.* Sir David
Granville, KBE, CB
Coates, Sir Anthony Robert Milnes,
Bt. (1911)
Coates, Sir David Frederick
Charlton, Bt. (1921)
Coats, Sir Alastair Francis Stuart, Bt.
(1905)
Coats, Sir William David, Kt.
Cobham, Sir Michael John, Kt., CBE
Cochrane, Sir (Henry) Marc
(Sursock), Bt. (1903)
Cockburn, Sir John Elliot, Bt.
(s. 1671)
Cockcroft, Sir Wilfred Halliday, Kt.,
D.Phil.
Cockram, Sir John, Kt.
Cockshaw, Sir Alan, Kt., FREng.
Codrington, Sir Simon Francis
Bethell, Bt. (1876)
Codrington, Sir William Alexander,
Bt. (1721)
Coghill, Sir Egerton James Nevill
Tobias, Bt. (1778)
Coghlin, *Hon.* Sir Patrick, Kt.
Cohen, Sir Edward, Kt.
Cohen, Sir Ivor Harold, Kt., CBE, TD
Cohen, *Prof.* Sir Philip, Kt., ph.D, FRS
Cohen, Sir Stephen Harry Waley-,
Bt. (1961)
Coldstream, Sir George Phillips,
KCB, KCVO, QC
Cole, Sir (Alexander) Colin, KCB,
KCVO, TD
Cole, Sir (Robert) William, Kt.
Coleman, Sir Timothy, KG
Coles, Sir (Arthur) John, GCMG
Colfox, Sir (William) John, Bt. (1939)
Collett, Sir Christopher, GBE
Collett, Sir Ian Seymour, Bt. (1934)
Collins, *Hon.* Sir Andrew David, Kt.
Collins, Sir Arthur James Robert,
KCVO
Collins, Sir Bryan Thomas Alfred,
Kt., OBE, QFSM
Collins, Sir John Alexander, Kt.
Collyear, Sir John Gowen, Kt.,
FREng.
Colman, *Hon.* Sir Anthony David, Kt.
Colman, Sir Michael Jeremiah, Bt.
(1907)
Colquhoun of Luss, Sir Ivar Iain, Bt.
(1786)
Colt, Sir Edward William Dutton, Bt.
(1694)
Colthurst, Sir Richard La Touche,
Bt. (1744)
Coltman, Sir (Arthur) Leycester
Scott, KBE, CMG
Colvin, Sir Howard Montagu, Kt.,
CVO, CBE, FBA

Compston, *Vice-Adm.* Sir Peter Maxwell, KCB

Compton, *Rt. Hon.* Sir John George Melvin, KCMG

Conant, Sir John Ernest Michael, Bt. (1954)

Condon, Sir Paul Leslie, Kt., QPM

Connell, *Hon.* Sir Michael Bryan, Kt.

Conran, Sir Terence Orby, Kt.

Cons, *Hon.* Sir Derek, Kt.

Constable, Sir Frederic Strickland-, Bt. (1641)

Constantinou, Sir Georkios, Kt., OBE

Cook, *Prof.* Sir Alan Hugh, Kt.

Cook, Sir Christopher Wymondham Rayner Herbert, Bt. (1886)

Cooke, Sir Charles Fletcher-, Kt., QC

Cooke, *Col.* Sir David William Perceval, Bt. (1661)

Cooke, Sir Howard Felix Hanlan, GCMG, GCVO

Cooksey, Sir David James Scott, Kt.

Cooper, *Rt. Hon.* Sir Frank, GCB, CMG

Cooper, Sir (Frederick Howard) Michael Craig-, Kt., CBE, TD

Cooper, *Gen.* Sir George Leslie Conroy, GCB, MC

Cooper, Sir Louis Jacques Blom-, Kt., QC

Cooper, Sir Patrick Graham Astley, Bt. (1821)

Cooper, Sir Richard Powell, Bt. (1905)

Cooper, Sir Robert George, Kt., CBE

Cooper, *Maj.-Gen.* Sir Simon Christie, KCVO

Cooper, Sir William Daniel Charles, Bt. (1863)

Coote, Sir Christopher John, Bt., *Premier Baronet of Ireland* (I. 1621)

Copas, *Most Revd* Virgil, KBE, DD

Copisarow, Sir Alcon Charles, Kt.

Corbett, *Maj.-Gen.* Sir Robert John Swan, KCVO, CB

Corby, Sir (Frederick) Brian, Kt.

Corfield, *Rt. Hon.* Sir Frederick Vernon, Kt., QC

Corfield, Sir Kenneth George, Kt., FREng.

Cork, Sir Roger William, Kt.

Corley, Sir Kenneth Sholl Ferrand, Kt.

Cormack, Sir Magnus Cameron, KBE

Cormack, Sir Patrick Thomas, Kt., MP

Corness, Sir Colin Ross, Kt.

Cornforth, Sir John Warcup, Kt., CBE, D.Phil., FRS

Corry, Sir William James, Bt. (1885)

Cortazzi, Sir (Henry Arthur) Hugh, GCMG

Cory, Sir (Clinton Charles) Donald, Bt. (1919)

Cossons, Sir Neil, Kt., OBE

Cotter, *Lt.-Col.* Sir Delaval James Alfred, Bt., DSO (I. 1763)

Cotterell, Sir John Henry Geers, Bt. (1805)

Cotton, Sir John Richard, KCMG, OBE

Cotton, *Hon.* Sir Robert Carrington, KCMG

Cottrell, Sir Alan Howard, Kt., ph.D., FRS, FREng.

†Cotts, Sir Richard Crichton Mitchell, Bt. (1921)

Couper, Sir (Robert) Nicholas (Oliver), Bt. (1841)

Court, *Hon.* Sir Charles Walter Michael, KCMG, OBE

Cousins, *Air Chief Marshal* Sir David, KCB, AFC

Coutts, Sir David Burdett Money-, KCVO

Couzens, Sir Kenneth Edward, KCB

Covacevich, Sir (Anthony) Thomas, Kt., DFC

Cowan, *Gen.* Sir Samuel, KCB, CBE

Coward, *Vice-Adm.* Sir John Francis, KCB, DSO

Cowen, *Rt. Hon. Prof.* Sir Zelman, GCMG, GCVO, QC

Cowie, Sir Thomas (Tom), Kt., OBE

Cowperthwaite, Sir John James, KBE, CMG

Cox, Sir Alan George, Kt., CBE

Cox, *Prof.* Sir David Roxbee, Kt., FRS

Cox, Sir Geoffrey Sandford, Kt., CBE

Cox, *Vice-Adm.* Sir John Michael Holland, KCB

Cradock, *Rt. Hon.* Sir Percy, GCMG

Craig, Sir (Albert) James (Macqueen), GCMG

Craufurd, Sir Robert James, Bt. (1781)

Craven, Sir John Anthony, Kt.

Craven, *Air Marshal* Sir Robert Edward, KBE, CB, DFC

Crawford, *Prof.* Sir Frederick William, Kt., FREng.

Crawford, Sir (Robert) Stewart, GCMG, CVO

Crawford, *Vice-Adm.* Sir William Godfrey, KBE, CB, DSC

Creagh, *Maj.-Gen.* Sir (Kilner) Rupert Brazier-, KBE, CB, DSO

Cresswell, *Hon.* Sir Peter John, Kt.

Crill, Sir Peter Leslie, KBE

Cripps, Sir Cyril Humphrey, Kt.

Crisp, Sir (John) Peter, Bt. (1913)

Critchett, Sir Ian (George Lorraine), Bt. (1908)

Critchley, Sir Julian Michael Gordon, Kt.

Croft, Sir Owen Glendower, Bt. (1671)

Croft, Sir Thomas Stephen Hutton, Bt. (1818)

†Crofton, Sir Hugh Denis, Bt. (1801)

Crofton, *Prof.* Sir John Wenman, Kt.

Crofton, Sir Malby Sturges, Bt. (1838)

Croker, Sir Walter Russell, KBE

Crookenden, *Lt.-Gen.* Sir Napier, KCB, DSO, OBE

Cross, *Air Chief Marshal* Sir Kenneth Brian Boyd, KCB, CBE, DSO, DFC

Crossland, *Prof.* Sir Bernard, Kt., CBE, FREng.

Crossley, Sir Nicholas John, Bt. (1909)

Cruthers, Sir James Winter, Kt.

Cubbon, Sir Brian Crossland, GCB

Cubitt, Sir Hugh Guy, Kt., CBE

Cullen, Sir (Edward) John, Kt., FREng.

Cumming, Sir William Gordon Gordon-, Bt. (1804)

Cuninghame, Sir John Christopher Foggo Montgomery-, Bt. (NS 1672)

Cuninghame, Sir William Henry Fairlie-, Bt. (S. 1630)

Cunliffe, Sir David Ellis, Bt. (1759)

Cunningham, *Lt.-Gen.* Sir Hugh Patrick, KBE

Cunynghame, Sir Andrew David Francis, Bt. (S. 1702)

†Currie, Sir Donald Scott, Bt. (1847)

Currie, Sir Neil Smith, Kt., CBE

Curtis, Sir Barry John, Kt.

Curtis, Sir (Edward) Leo, Kt.

Curtis, *Hon.* Sir Richard Herbert, Kt.

Curtis, Sir William Peter, Bt. (1802)

Curtiss, *Air Marshal* Sir John Bagot, KCB, KBE

Curwen, Sir Christopher Keith, KCMG

Cuschieri, *Prof.* Sir Alfred, Kt.

Cutler, Sir (Arthur) Roden, VC, KCMG, KCVO, CBE

Cutler, Sir Charles Benjamin, KBE, ED

Dacie, *Prof.* Sir John Vivian, Kt., MD, FRS

Dain, Sir David John Michael, KCVO

Dale, Sir William Leonard, KCMG

Dalrymple, *Maj.* Sir Hew Fleetwood Hamilton-, Bt., KCVO (S. 1697)

Dalton, Sir Alan Nugent Goring, Kt., CBE

Dalton, *Vice-Adm.* Sir Geoffrey Thomas James Oliver, KCB

Daly, *Lt.-Gen.* Sir Thomas Joseph, KBE, CB, DSO

Dalyell, Sir Tam (Thomas), Bt., MP (NS 1685)

Daniel, Sir Goronwy Hopkin, KCVO, CB, D.phil.

Daniel, Sir John Sagar, Kt., D.SC.

Daniell, Sir Peter Averell, Kt., TD

Darby, Sir Peter Howard, Kt., CBE, QFSM

Darell, Sir Jeffrey Lionel, Bt., MC (1795)

Dargie, Sir William Alexander, Kt., CBE

Dark, Sir Anthony Michael Beaumont-, Kt.

Darling, Sir Clifford, GCVO

Darvall, Sir (Charles) Roger, Kt., CBE

Dashwood, Sir Francis John Vernon Hereward, Bt., *Premier Baronet of Great Britain* (1707)

Dashwood, Sir Richard James, Bt. (1684)

Daunt, Sir Timothy Lewis Achilles, KCMG

Davey, *Hon.* Sir David Herbert Penry-, Kt.

David, Sir Jean Marc, Kt., CBE, QC

David, *His Hon.* Sir Robin (Robert) Daniel George, Kt., QC

Davidson, Sir Robert James, Kt., FREng.

Davie, Sir John Ferguson-, Bt. (1847)

Davies, *Hon.* Sir (Alfred William) Michael, Kt.

Davies, Sir Alun Talfan, Kt., QC

Davies, Sir (Charles) Noel, Kt.

Davies, *Prof.* Sir David Evan Naughton, Kt., CBE, FRS, FREng.

Davies, Sir David Henry, Kt.

Davies, *Hon.* Sir (David Herbert) Mervyn, Kt., MC, TD

Davies, Sir David John, Kt.

Davies, Sir Frank John, Kt., CBE

Davies, *Prof.* Sir Graeme John, Kt., FREng.

Davies, *Vice-Adm.* Sir Lancelot Richard Bell, KBE

Davies, Sir Peter Maxwell, Kt., CBE

Davies, Sir Victor Caddy, Kt., OBE

Davis, Sir Andrew Frank, Kt., CBE

Davis, Sir Colin Rex, Kt., CBE

Davis, Sir (Ernest) Howard, Kt., CMG, OBE

Davis, Sir John Gilbert, Bt. (1946)

Davis, Sir Peter John, Kt.

Davis, Sir Rupert Charles Hart-, Kt.

Davis, *Hon.* Sir Thomas Robert Alexander Harries, KBE

Davison, *Rt. Hon.* Sir Ronald Keith, GBE, CMG

Davson, Sir Christopher Michael Edward, Bt. (1927)

Dawanincura, Sir John Norbert, Kt., OBE

Dawbarn, Sir Simon Yelverton, KCVO, CMG

Dawson, *Hon.* Sir Daryl Michael, KBE, CB

Dawson, Sir Hugh Michael Trevor, Bt. (1920)

Dawtry, Sir Alan (Graham), Kt., CBE, TD

Day, *Air Marshal* Sir John Romney, KCB, OBE

Day, Sir (Judson) Graham, Kt.

Day, Sir Michael John, Kt., OBE

Day, Sir Robin, Kt.

Day, Sir Simon James, Kt.

Deakin, Sir (Frederick) William (Dampier), Kt., DSO

Deane, *Hon.* Sir William Patrick, KBE

Dear, Sir Geoffrey James, Kt., QPM

de Bellaigue, Sir Geoffrey, GCVO

Debenham, Sir Gilbert Ridley, Bt. (1931)

de Deney, Sir Geoffrey Ivor, KCVO

de Hoghton, Sir (Richard) Bernard (Cuthbert), Bt. (1611)

De la Bère, Sir Cameron, Bt. (1953)

de la Rue, Sir Andrew George Ilay, Bt. (1898)

Dellow, Sir John Albert, Kt., CBE

de Montmorency, Sir Arnold Geoffroy, Bt. (I. 1631)

Denholm, Sir John Ferguson (Ian), Kt., CBE

Denman, Sir (George) Roy, KCB, CMG

Denny, Sir Anthony Coningham de Waltham, Bt. (I. 1782)

Denny, Sir Charles Alistair Maurice, Bt. (1913)

Dent, Sir John, Kt., CBE, FREng.

Denton, *Prof.* Sir Eric James, Kt., CBE, FRS

Derbyshire, Sir Andrew George, Kt.

Derham, Sir Peter John, Kt.

de Trafford, Sir Dermot Humphrey, Bt. (1841)

Deverell, *Lt.-Gen.* Sir John Freegard, KCB, OBE

Devesi, Sir Baddeley, GCMG, GCVO

De Ville, Sir Harold Godfrey Oscar, Kt., CBE

Devitt, Sir James Hugh Thomas, Bt. (1916)

de Waal, Sir (Constant Henrik) Henry, KCB, QC

Dewey, Sir Anthony Hugh, Bt. (1917)

Dewhurst, *Prof.* Sir (Christopher) John, Kt.

d'Eyncourt, Sir Mark Gervais Tennyson-, Bt. (1930)

Dhenin, *Air Marshal* Sir Geoffrey Howard, KBE, AFC, GM, MD

Dhrangadhra, HH the Maharaja Raj Saheb of, KCIE

Dibela, *Hon.* Sir Kingsford, GCMG

Dick, *Maj.-Gen.* Sir Iain Charles Mackay-, KCVO, MBE

Dickenson, Sir Aubrey Fiennes Trotman-, Kt.

Dickinson, Sir Harold Herbert, Kt.

Dickinson, Sir Samuel Benson, Kt.

Dilke, Sir Charles John Wentworth, Bt. (1862)

Dillon, *Rt. Hon.* Sir (George) Brian (Hugh), Kt.

Dixon, Sir Ian Leonard, Kt., CBE

Dixon, Sir Jonathan Mark, Bt. (1919)

Djanogly, Sir Harry Ari Simon, Kt., CBE

Dobbs, *Capt.* Sir Richard Arthur Frederick, KCVO

Dobson, *Vice-Adm.* Sir David Stuart, KBE

Dobson, *Gen.* Sir Patrick John Howard-, GCB

Dodds, Sir Ralph Jordan, Bt. (1964)

Dodson, Sir Derek Sherborne Lindsell, KCMG, MC

Dodsworth, Sir John Christopher Smith-, Bt. (1784)

Doll, *Prof.* Sir (William) Richard (Shaboe), Kt., CH, OBE, FRS, DM, MD, D.SC.

Dollery, Sir Colin Terence, Kt.

Donald, Sir Alan Ewen, KCMG

Donald, *Air Marshal* Sir John George, KBE

Donne, *Hon.* Sir Gaven John, KBE

Donne, Sir John Christopher, Kt.

Dookun, Sir Dewoonarain, Kt.

Dorey, Sir Graham Martyn, Kt.

Dorman, Sir Philip Henry Keppel, Bt. (1923)

Dougherty, *Maj.-Gen.* Sir Ivan Noel, Kt., CBE, DSO, ED

Doughty, Sir William Roland, Kt.

Douglas, Sir (Edward) Sholto, Kt.

Douglas, *Hon.* Sir Roger Owen, Kt.

Douglas, *Rt. Hon.* Sir William Randolph, KCMG

Dover, *Prof.* Sir Kenneth James, Kt., D.Litt., FBA, FRSE

Dowell, Sir Anthony James, Kt., CBE

Down, Sir Alastair Frederick, Kt., OBE, MC, TD

Downes, Sir Edward Thomas, Kt., CBE

Downey, Sir Gordon Stanley, KCB

Downs, Sir Diarmuid, Kt., CBE, FREng.

Downward, *Maj.-Gen.* Peter Aldcroft, KCVO, CB, DSO, DFC

Downward, Sir William Atkinson, Kt.

Dowson, Sir Philip Manning, Kt., CBE, PRA

Doyle, Sir Reginald Derek Henry, Kt., CBE

D'Oyly, Sir Nigel Hadley Miller, Bt. (1663)

Drake, *Hon.* Sir (Frederick) Maurice, Kt., DFC

Dreyer, *Adm.* Sir Desmond Parry, GCB, CBE, DSC

Drinkwater, Sir John Muir, Kt., QC

Driver, Sir Antony Victor, Kt.

Driver, Sir Eric William, Kt.

Drummond, Sir John Richard Gray, Kt., CBE

Drury, Sir (Victor William) Michael, Kt., OBE

Dryden, Sir John Stephen Gyles, Bt. (1733 and 1795)

du Cann, *Rt. Hon.* Sir Edward Dillon Lott, KBE

†Duckworth, Sir Edward Richard Dyce, Bt. (1909)

du Cros, Sir Claude Philip Arthur Mallet, Bt. (1916)

Duff, *Rt. Hon.* Sir (Arthur) Antony, GCMG, CVO, DSO, DSC

Duffell, *Lt.-Gen.* Sir Peter Royson, KCB, CBE, MC

Duffus, *Hon.* Sir William Algernon Holwell, Kt.

Duffy, Sir (Albert) (Edward) Patrick, Kt., PH.D.

Dugdale, Sir William Stratford, Bt., MC (1936)

Dummett, *Prof.* Sir Michael Anthony Eardley, Kt., FBA

Dunbar, Sir Archibald Ranulph, Bt. (S. 1700)

Dunbar, Sir David Hope-, Bt. (S. 1664)

Dunbar, Sir Drummond Cospatrick Ninian, Bt., MC (S. 1698)

Dunbar, Sir James Michael, Bt. (S. 1694)

†Dunbar of Hempriggs, Sir Richard Francis, Bt. (S. 1706)

Duncan, Sir James Blair, Kt.

Duncombe, Sir Philip Digby Pauncefort-, Bt. (1859)

Dunham, Sir Kingsley Charles, Kt., ph.D., FRS, FRSE, FREng.

Dunlop, Sir Thomas, Bt. (1916)

Dunlop, Sir William Norman Gough, Kt.

Dunn, *Air Marshal* Sir Eric Clive, KBE, CB, BEM

Dunn, *Air Marshal* Sir Patrick Hunter, KBE, CB, DFC

Dunn, *Rt. Hon.* Sir Robin Horace Walford, Kt., MC

Dunne, Sir Thomas Raymond, KCVO

Dunning, Sir Simon William Patrick, Bt. (1930)

Dunstan, *Lt.-Gen.* Sir Donald Beaumont, KBE, CB

Dunt, *Vice-Adm.* Sir John Hugh, KCB

†Duntze, Sir Daniel Evans, Bt. (1774)

Dupre, Sir Tumun, Kt., MBE

Dupree, Sir Peter, Bt. (1921)

Durand, Sir Edward Alan Christopher David Percy, Bt. (1892)

Durant, Sir (Robert) Anthony (Bevis), Kt.

Durham, Sir Kenneth, Kt.

Durie, Sir Alexander Charles, Kt., CBE

Durkin, *Air Marshal* Sir Herbert, KBE, CB

Durrant, Sir William Alexander Estridge, Bt. (1784)

Duthie, *Prof.* Sir Herbert Livingston, Kt.

Duthie, Sir Robert Grieve (Robin), Kt., CBE

Dyer, *Prof.* Sir (Henry) Peter (Francis) Swinnerton-, Bt., KBE, FRS (1678)

Dyke, Sir David William Hart, Bt. (1677)

Dyson, *Hon.* Sir John Anthony, Kt.

Eady, *Hon.* Sir David, Kt.

Earle, Sir (Hardman) George (Algernon), Bt. (1869)

Easton, Sir Robert William Simpson, Kt., CBE

Eaton, *Adm.* Sir Kenneth John, GBE, KCB

Eberle, *Adm.* Sir James Henry Fuller, GCB

Ebrahim, Sir (Mahomed) Currimbhoy, Bt. (1910)

Echlin, Sir Norman David Fenton, Bt. (I. 1721)

Eckersley, Sir Donald Payze, Kt., OBE

Edge, *Capt.* Sir (Philip) Malcolm, KCVO

†Edge, Sir William, Bt. (1937)

Edmonstone, Sir Archibald Bruce Charles, Bt. (1774)

Edwardes, Sir Michael Owen, Kt.

Edwards, Sir Christopher John Churchill, Bt. (1866)

Edwards, Sir George Robert, Kt., OM, CBE, FRS, FREng.

Edwards, Sir Llewellyn Roy, Kt.

Edwards, *Prof.* Sir Samuel Frederick, Kt., FRS

Egan, Sir John Leopold, Kt.

Egerton, Sir John Alfred Roy, Kt.

Egerton, Sir (Philip) John (Caledon) Grey-, Bt. (1617)

Egerton, Sir Stephen Loftus, KCMG

Eggleston, *Hon.* Sir Richard Moulton, Kt.

Eichelbaum, *Rt. Hon.* Sir Thomas, GBE

Elias, Sir Patrick, Kt., QC

Eliott of Stobs, Sir Charles Joseph Alexander, Bt. (S. 1666)

Ellerton, Sir Geoffrey James, Kt., CMG, MBE

Elliot, Sir Gerald Henry, Kt.

Elliott, Sir Clive Christopher Hugh, Bt. (1917)

Elliott, Sir David Murray, KCMG, CB

Elliott, *Prof.* Sir John Huxtable, Kt., FBA

Elliott, Sir Randal Forbes, KBE

Elliott, *Prof.* Sir Roger James, Kt., FRS

Elliott, Sir Ronald Stuart, Kt.

Ellis, Sir Ronald, Kt., FREng.

Ellison, *Col.* Sir Ralph Harry Carr-, KCVO, TD

Elphinstone, Sir John, Bt. (S. 1701)

Elphinstone, Sir John Howard Main, Bt. (1816)

Elton, Sir Arnold, Kt., CBE

Elton, Sir Charles Abraham Grierson, Bt. (1717)

Elwes, Sir Jeremy Vernon, Kt., CBE

Elwood, Sir Brian George Conway, Kt., CBE

Elworthy, Sir Peter Herbert, Kt.

Elyan, Sir (Isadore) Victor, Kt.

Emery, *Rt. Hon.* Sir Peter Frank Hannibal, Kt., MP

Empey, Sir Reginald Norman Morgan, Kt., OBE

Engle, Sir George Lawrence Jose, KCB, QC

English, Sir Terence Alexander Hawthorne, KBE, FRCS

Epstein, *Prof.* Sir (Michael) Anthony, Kt., CBE, FRS

Errington, *Col.* Sir Geoffrey Frederick, Bt., OBE (1963)

Errington, Sir Lancelot, KCB

Erskine, Sir (Thomas) David, Bt. (1821)

Esmonde, Sir Thomas Francis Grattan, Bt. (I. 1629)

Espie, Sir Frank Fletcher, Kt., OBE

Esplen, Sir John Graham, Bt. (1921)

Essenhigh, *Adm.* Sir Nigel Richard, Kt.

Eustace, Sir Joseph Lambert, GCMG, GCVO

Evans, Sir Anthony Adney, Bt. (1920)

Evans, *Rt. Hon.* Sir Anthony Howell Meurig, Kt., RD

Evans, *Air Chief Marshal* Sir David George, GCB, CBE

Evans, *Air Chief Marshal* Sir David Parry-, GCB, CBE

Evans, *Hon.* Sir Haydn Tudor, Kt.

Evans, *Prof.* Sir John Grimley, Kt., FRCP

Evans, Sir Richard Harry, Kt., CBE

Evans, Sir Richard Mark, KCMG, KCVO

Evans, Sir Robert, Kt., CBE, FREng.

Evans, Sir (William) Vincent (John), GCMG, MBE, QC

Eveleigh, *Rt. Hon.* Sir Edward Walter, Kt., ERD

Everard, Sir Robin Charles, Bt. (1911)

Everson, Sir Frederick Charles, KCMG

Every, Sir Henry John Michael, Bt. (1641)

Ewans, Sir Martin Kenneth, KCMG

†Ewart, Sir William Michael, Bt. (1887)

Ewbank, *Hon.* Sir Anthony Bruce, Kt.

Ewin, Sir (David) Ernest Thomas Floyd, Kt., OBE, LVO

Ewing, Sir (Alistair) Simon Orr-, Bt. (1963)

Ewing, Sir Ronald Archibald Orr-, Bt. (1886)

Eyre, Sir Graham Newman, Kt., QC

Eyre, *Maj.-Gen.* Sir James Ainsworth Campden Gabriel, KCVO, CBE

Eyre, Sir Reginald Edwin, Kt.

Eyre, Sir Richard Charles Hastings, Kt., CBE

Faber, Sir Richard Stanley, KCVO, CMG

Fadahunsi, Sir Joseph Odeleye, KCMG

Fagge, Sir John William Frederick, Bt. (1660)

Fairbairn, Sir (James) Brooke, Bt. (1869)

Fairclough, Sir John Whitaker, Kt., FREng.

Fairhall, *Hon.* Sir Allen, KBE

Fairweather, Sir Patrick Stanislaus, KCMG

Falconer, *Hon.* Sir Douglas William, Kt., MBE

†Falkiner, Sir Benjamin Simon Patrick, Bt. (I. 1778)

Fall, Sir Brian James Proetel, GCVO, KCMG

Falle, Sir Samuel, KCMG, KCVO, DSC

Fang, *Prof.* Sir Harry, Kt., CBE

Fareed, Sir Djamil Sheik, Kt.

Farmer, Sir Thomas, Kt., CBE

Farndale, *Gen.* Sir Martin Baker, KCB

Farquhar, Sir Michael Fitzroy Henry, Bt. (1796)

Farquharson, *Rt. Hon.* Sir Donald Henry, Kt.

Farquharson, Sir James Robbie, KBE

Farrer, Sir (Charles) Matthew, GCVO

Farrington, Sir Henry Francis Colden, Bt. (1818)

Fat, Sir (Maxime) Edouard (Lim Man) Lim, Kt.

Faulkner, Sir (James) Dennis (Compton), Kt., CBE, VRD

Fawcus, Sir (Robert) Peter, KBE, CMG

Fawkes, Sir Randol Francis, Kt.

Fay, Sir (Humphrey) Michael Gerard, Kt.

Fayrer, Sir John Lang Macpherson, Bt. (1896)

Fearn, Sir (Patrick) Robin, KCMG

Feilden, Sir Bernard Melchior, Kt., CBE

Feilden, Sir Henry Wemyss, Bt., (1846)

Fell, Sir David, KCB

Fellowes, Rt. Hon. Sir Robert, GCB, GCVO

Fender, Sir Brian Edward Frederick, Kt., CMG, ph.D.

Fenn, Sir Nicholas Maxted, GCMG

Fennell, Hon. Sir (John) Desmond Augustine, Kt., OBE

Fennessy, Sir Edward, Kt., CBE

Ferguson, Sir Alexander Chapman, Kt., CBE

Ferguson, Sir Ian Edward Johnson-, Bt. (1906)

Fergusson of Kilkerran, Sir Charles, Bt. (S. 1703)

Fergusson, Sir Ewan Alastair John, GCMG, GCVO

Fergusson, Sir James Herbert Hamilton Colyer-, Bt. (1866)

Feroze, Sir Rustam Moolan, Kt., FRCS

Ferris, Hon. Sir Francis Mursell, Kt., TD

ffolkes, Sir Robert Francis Alexander, Bt, OBE (1774)

Field, Sir Malcolm David, Kt.

Fielding, Sir Colin Cunningham, Kt., CB

Fielding, Sir Leslie, KCMG

Fieldsend, Hon. Sir John Charles Rowell, KBE

Fiennes, Sir Ranulph Twisleton-Wykeham-, Bt., OBE (1916)

Figg, Sir Leonard Clifford William, KCMG

Figgis, Sir Anthony St John Howard, KCVO, CMG

Figures, Sir Colin Frederick, KCMG, OBE

Fingland, Sir Stanley James Gunn, KCMG

Finlay, Sir David Ronald James Bell, Bt. (1964)

Finney, Sir Thomas, Kt., OBE

Firth, Prof. Sir Raymond William, Kt., PH.D., FBA

Fisher, Sir George Read, Kt., CMG

Fisher, Hon. Sir Henry Arthur Pears, Kt.

Fison, Sir (Richard) Guy, Bt., DSC (1905)

†Fitzgerald, Revd (Sir) Daniel Patrick, Bt. (1903)

FitzGerald, Sir George Peter Maurice, Bt., MC (The Knight of Kerry) (1880)

FitzHerbert, Sir Richard Ranulph, Bt. (1784)

Fitzpatrick, Gen. Sir (Geoffrey Richard) Desmond, GCB, GCVO, DSO, MBE, MC

Fitzpatrick, Air Marshal Sir John Bernard, KBE, CB

Flanagan, Sir Ronald, Kt., OBE

Fletcher, Sir Henry Egerton Aubrey-, Bt. (1782)

Fletcher, Sir James Muir Cameron, Kt.

Fletcher, Sir Leslie, Kt., DSC

Floissac, Hon. Sir Vincent Frederick, Kt., CMG, OBE, QC

Floyd, Sir Giles Henry Charles, Bt. (1816)

Foley, Lt.-Gen. Sir John Paul, KCB, OBE, MC

Foley, Sir (Thomas John) Noel, Kt., CBE

Follett, Prof. Sir Brian Keith, Kt., FRS

Foot, Sir Geoffrey James, Kt.

Foots, Sir James William, Kt.

Forbes, Hon. Sir Alastair Granville, Kt.

Forbes, Maj. Sir Hamish Stewart, Bt., MBE, MC (1823)

Forbes of Craigievar, Sir John Alexander Cumnock, Bt. (S. 1630)

Forbes, Vice-Adm. Sir John Morrison, KCB

Forbes, Hon. Sir Thayne John, Kt.

†Forbes of Pitsligo, Sir William Daniel Stuart-, Bt. (S. 1626)

Ford, Sir Andrew Russell, Bt. (1929)

Ford, Sir David Robert, KBE, LVO, OBE

Ford, Maj. Sir Edward William Spencer, GCVO, KCB, ERD

Ford, Air Marshal Sir Geoffrey Harold, KBE, CB, FREng.

Ford, Prof. Sir Hugh, Kt., FRS, FREng.

Ford, Sir James Anson St Clair-, Bt. (1793)

Ford, Sir John Archibald, KCMG, MC

Ford, Gen. Sir Robert Cyril, GCB, CBE

Foreman, Sir Philip Frank, Kt., CBE, FREng.

Forman, Sir John Denis, Kt., OBE

Forrest, Prof. Sir (Andrew) Patrick (McEwen), Kt.

Forrest, Rear-Adm. Sir Ronald Stephen, KCVO

Forster, Sir Archibald William, Kt., FREng.

Forster, Sir Oliver Grantham, KCMG, LVO

Forte, Hon. Sir Rocco John Vincent, Kt.

Forwood, Sir Dudley Richard, Bt. (1895)

Foster, Prof. Sir Christopher David, Kt.

Foster, Sir John Gregory, Bt. (1930)

Foster, Sir Robert Sidney, GCMG, KCVO

Foulis, Sir Ian Primrose Liston-, Bt. (S. 1634)

Foulkes, Sir Nigel Gordon, Kt.

Fountain, Hon. Sir Cyril Stanley Smith, Kt.

Fowden, Sir Leslie, Kt., FRS

Fowke, Sir David Frederick Gustavus, Bt. (1814)

Fowler, Sir (Edward) Michael Coulson, Kt.

Fowler, Rt. Hon. Sir (Peter) Norman, Kt., MP

Fox, Sir (Henry) Murray, GBE

Fox, Rt. Hon. Sir (John) Marcus, Kt., MBE

Fox, Rt. Hon. Sir Michael John, Kt.

Fox, Sir Paul Leonard, Kt., CBE

France, Sir Christopher Walter, GCB

Francis, Sir Horace William Alexander, Kt., CBE, FREng.

Frank, Sir Douglas George Horace, Kt., QC

Frank, Sir Robert Andrew, Bt. (1920)

Franklin, Sir Michael David Milroy, KCB, CMG

Franks, Sir Arthur Temple, KCMG

Fraser, Sir Angus McKay, KCB, TD

Fraser, Sir Charles Annand, KCVO

Fraser, Gen. Sir David William, GCB, OBE

Fraser, Air Marshal Revd Sir (Henry) Paterson, KBE, CB, AFC

Fraser, Sir Iain Michael Duncan, Bt. (1943)

Fraser, Sir Ian James, Kt., CBE, MC

Fraser, Sir (James) Campbell, Kt.

Fraser, Sir William Kerr, GCB

Frederick, Sir Charles Boscawen, Bt. (1723)

Freeland, Sir John Redvers, KCMG

Freeman, Sir James Robin, Bt. (1945)

Freer, Air Chief Marshal Sir Robert William George, GBE, KCB

Freeth, Hon. Sir Gordon, KBE

French, Hon. Sir Christopher James Saunders, Kt.

Frere, Vice-Adm. Sir Richard Tobias, KCB

Fretwell, Sir (Major) John (Emsley), GCMG

Freud, Sir Clement Raphael, Kt.

Froggatt, Sir Leslie Trevor, Kt.

Froggatt, Sir Peter, Kt.

Frossard, Sir Charles Keith, KBE

Frost, Sir David Paradine, Kt., OBE

Frost, Sir Terence Ernest Manitou, Kt., RA

Fry, Sir Peter Derek, Kt.

Fry, Hon. Sir William Gordon, Kt.

Fuchs, Sir Vivian Ernest, Kt., ph.D.

†Fuller, Sir James Henry Fleetwood, Bt. (1910)

Fuller, Hon. Sir John Bryan Munro, Kt.

Fung, Hon. Sir Kenneth Ping-Fan, Kt., CBE

Furness, Sir Stephen Roberts, Bt. (1913)

Gadsden, Sir Peter Drury Haggerston, GBE, FREng.

Gage, Hon. Sir William Marcus, Kt.

Gainsford, Sir Ian Derek, Kt., DDS

Gaius, Rt. Revd Saimon, KBE

Gallwey, Sir Philip Frankland Payne-, Bt. (1812)

Galsworthy, Sir Anthony Charles, KCMG

Gam, Rt. Revd Sir Getake, KBE

Gamble, Sir David Hugh Norman, Bt. (1897)

Gambon, Sir Michael John, Kt., CBE

Garden, *Air Marshal* Sir Timothy, KCB

Gardiner, Sir George Arthur, Kt.

Gardiner, Sir John Eliot, Kt., CBE

Gardner, Sir Edward Lucas, Kt., QC

Gardner, Sir Robert Henry Bruce-, Bt. (1945)

Garland, *Hon.* Sir Patrick Neville, Kt.

Garland, *Hon.* Sir Ransley Victor, KBE

Garlick, Sir John, KCB

Garner, Sir Anthony Stuart, Kt.

Garnett, *Vice-Adm.* Sir Ian David Graham, KCB

Garnier, *Rear-Adm.* Sir John, KCVO, CBE

Garrett, Sir Anthony Peter, Kt., CBE

Garrick, Sir Ronald, Kt., CBE, FREng.

Garrioch, Sir (William) Henry, Kt.

Garrod, *Lt.-Gen.* Sir (John) Martin Carruthers, KCB, OBE

Garthwaite, Sir (William) Mark (Charles), Bt. (1919)

Gaskell, Sir Richard Kennedy Harvey, Kt.

Gatehouse, *Hon.* Sir Robert Alexander, Kt.

Geno, Sir Makena Viora, KBE

George, Sir Arthur Thomas, Kt.

George, *Prof.* Sir Charles Frederick, MD, FRCP

George, Sir Richard William, Kt., CVO

Gerken, *Vice-Adm.* Sir Robert William Frank, KCB, CBE

Gery, Sir Robert Lucian Wade-, KCMG, KCVO

Gethin, Sir Richard Joseph St Lawrence, Bt. (I. 1665)

Getty, Sir (John) Paul, KBE

Ghurburrun, Sir Rabindrah, Kt.

Gibb, Sir Francis Ross (Frank), Kt., CBE, FREng.

Gibbings, Sir Peter Walter, Kt.

Gibbons, Sir (John) David, KBE

Gibbons, Sir William Edward Doran, Bt. (1752)

Gibbs, *Hon.* Sir Eustace Hubert Beilby, KCVO, CMG

Gibbs, *Rt. Hon.* Sir Harry Talbot, GCMG, KBE

Gibbs, *Lt.-Col.* Sir Peter Evan Wyldbore, KCVO

Gibbs, Sir Roger Geoffrey, Kt.

Gibbs, *Field Marshal* Sir Roland Christopher, GCB, CBE, DSO, MC

†Gibson, *Revd* Sir Christopher Herbert, Bt. (1931)

Gibson, *Vice-Adm.* Sir Donald Cameron Ernest Forbes, KCB, DSC

Gibson, Sir Ian, Kt., CBE

Gibson, *Rt. Hon.* Sir Peter Leslie, Kt.

Gibson, *Rt. Hon.* Sir Ralph Brian, Kt.

Giddings, *Air Marshal* Sir (Kenneth Charles) Michael, KCB, OBE, DFC, AFC

Gielgud, Sir (Arthur) John, Kt., OM, CH

Giffard, Sir (Charles) Sydney (Rycroft), KCMG

Gilbert, Sir Arthur, Kt.

Gilbert, *Air Chief Marshal* Sir Joseph Alfred, KCB, CBE

Gilbert, Sir Martin John, Kt., CBE

†Gilbey, Sir Walter Gavin, Bt. (1893)

Giles, *Rear-Adm.* Sir Morgan Charles Morgan-, Kt., DSO, OBE, GM

Gill, Sir Anthony Keith, Kt., FREng.

Gillam, Sir Patrick John, Kt.

Gillen, *Hon.* Sir John de Winter, Kt.

Gillett, Sir Robin Danvers Penrose, Bt., GBE, RD (1959)

Gilmour, *Col.* Sir Allan Macdonald, KCVO, OBE, MC

Gilmour, Sir John Edward, Bt., DSO, TD (1897)

Gina, Sir Lloyd Maepeza, KBE

Gingell, *Air Chief Marshal* Sir John, GBE, KCB, KCVO

Girolami, Sir Paul, Kt.

Girvan, *Hon.* Sir (Frederick) Paul, Kt.

Glasspole, Sir Florizel Augustus, GCMG, GCVO

Glen, Sir Alexander Richard, KBE, DSC

Glenn, Sir (Joseph Robert) Archibald, Kt., OBE

Glidewell, *Rt. Hon.* Sir Iain Derek Laing, Kt.

Glock, Sir William Frederick, Kt., CBE

Glover, *Gen.* Sir James Malcolm, KCB, MBE

Glover, Sir Victor Joseph Patrick, Kt.

Glyn, Sir Richard Lindsay, Bt. (1759 and 1800)

Goavea, Sir Sinaka Vakai, KBE

Godber, Sir George Edward, GCB, DM

Goff, Sir Robert (William) Davis-, Bt. (1905)

Gold, Sir Arthur Abraham, Kt., CBE

Gold, Sir Joseph, Kt.

Goldberg, *Prof.* Sir Abraham, Kt., MD, D.SC., FRCP

Goldberg, *Prof.* Sir David Paul Brandes, Kt.

Goldman, Sir Samuel, KCB

Gombrich, *Prof.* Sir Ernst Hans Josef, Kt., OM, CBE, Ph.D., FBA, FSA

Gooch, Sir Timothy Robert, Bt., MBE (1746)

Gooch, Sir Trevor Sherlock (Sir Peter), Bt. (1866)

Good, Sir John Kennedy-, KBE

Goodall, Sir (Arthur) David Saunders, GCMG

Goodenough, Sir Anthony Michael, KCMG

Goodenough, Sir William McLernon, Bt. (1943)

Goodhart, Sir Philip Carter, Kt.

Goodhart, Sir Robert Anthony Gordon, Bt. (1911)

Goodhew, Sir Victor Henry, Kt.

Goodison, Sir Alan Clowes, KCMG

Goodison, Sir Nicholas Proctor, Kt.

Goodlad, *Rt. Hon.* Sir Alastair Robertson, KCMG

Goodman, Sir Patrick Ledger, Kt., CBE

Goodson, Sir Mark Weston Lassam, Bt. (1922)

Goodwin, Sir Matthew Dean, Kt., CBE

†Goold, Sir George William, Bt. (1801)

Gordon, Sir Andrew Cosmo Lewis Duff-, Bt. (1813)

Gordon, Sir Charles Addison Somerville Snowden, KCB

Gordon, Sir Keith Lyndell, Kt., CMG

Gordon, Sir (Lionel) Eldred (Peter) Smith-, Bt. (1838)

Gordon, Sir Robert James, Bt. (S. 1706)

Gordon, Sir Sidney Samuel, Kt., CBE

Gordon Lennox, Lord Nicholas Charles, KCMG, KCVO

†Gore, Sir Nigel Hugh St George, Bt. (I. 1622)

Gorham, Sir Richard Masters, Kt., CBE, DFC

Goring, Sir William Burton Nigel, Bt. (1627)

Gorman, Sir John Reginald, Kt., CVO, CBE, MC

Gorst, Sir John Michael, Kt.

Gorton, *Rt. Hon.* Sir John Grey, GCMG, CH

Goschen, Sir Edward Christian, Bt., DSO (1916)

Gosling, Sir (Frederick) Donald, Kt.

Goswell, Sir Brian Lawrence, Kt.

Goulden, Sir (Peter) John, KCMG

Goulding, Sir (Ernest) Irvine, Kt.

Goulding, Sir Marrack Irvine, KCMG

Goulding, Sir (William) Lingard Walter, Bt. (1904)

Gourlay, *Gen.* Sir (Basil) Ian (Spencer), KCB, OBE, MC, RM

Gourlay, Sir Simon Alexander, Kt.

Govan, Sir Lawrence Herbert, Kt.

Gow, *Gen.* Sir (James) Michael, GCB

Gowans, Sir James Learmonth, Kt., CBE, FRCP, FRS

Graaff, Sir de Villiers, Bt., MBE (1911)

Grabham, Sir Anthony Henry, Kt.

Graham, Sir Alexander Michael, GBE

Graham, Sir James Bellingham, Bt. (1662)

Graham, Sir James Fergus Surtees, Bt. (1783)

Graham, Sir James Thompson, Kt., CMG

Graham, Sir John Alexander Noble, Bt., GCMG (1906)

Graham, Sir John Moodie, Bt. (1964)

Graham, Sir Norman William, Kt., CB

Graham, Sir Peter, KCB, QC

Graham, Sir Peter Alfred, Kt., OBE

Graham, *Lt.-Gen.* Sir Peter Walter, KCB, CBE

†Graham, Sir Ralph Stuart, Bt. (1629)

Graham, *Hon.* Sir Samuel Horatio, Kt., CMG, OBE

Grandy, *Marshal of the Royal Air Force* Sir John, GCB, GCVO, KBE, DSO

Grant, Sir Archibald, Bt. (s. 1705)

Grant, Sir Clifford, Kt.

Grant, Sir (John) Anthony, Kt.

Grant, Sir (Matthew) Alistair, Kt.

Grant, Sir Patrick Alexander Benedict, Bt. (s. 1688)

Grant, *Lt.-Gen.* Sir Scott Carnegie, KCB

Gray, *Hon.* Sir Charles Anthony St John, Kt., QC

Gray, *Prof.* Sir Denis John Pereira, Kt., OBE, FRCGP

Gray, Sir John Archibald Browne, Kt., SC.D., FRS

Gray, Sir John Walton David, KBE, CMG

Gray, *Lt.-Gen.* Sir Michael Stuart, KCB, OBE

Gray, Sir Robert McDowall (Robin), Kt.

Gray, Sir William Hume, Bt. (1917)

Gray, Sir William Stevenson, Kt.

Graydon, *Air Chief Marshal* Sir Michael James, GCB, CBE

Grayson, Sir Jeremy Brian Vincent Harrington, Bt. (1922)

Green, Sir Allan David, KCB, QC

Green, Sir Andrew Fleming, KCMG

Green, *Hon.* Sir Guy Stephen Montague, KBE

Green, Sir Kenneth, Kt.

Green, Sir Owen Whitley, Kt.

†Green, Sir Stephen Lycett, Bt., TD (1886)

Greenaway, Sir John Michael Burdick, Bt. (1933)

Greenbury, Sir Richard, Kt.

Greene, Sir (John) Brian Massy-, Kt.

Greener, Sir Anthony Armitage, Kt.

Greengross, Sir Alan David, Kt.

Greening, *Rear-Adm.* Sir Paul Woollven, GCVO

Greenstock, Sir Jeremy Quentin, KCMG

Greenwell, Sir Edward Bernard, Bt. (1906)

Gregson, Sir Peter Lewis, GCB

Greig, Sir (Henry Louis) Carron, KCVO, CBE

Grenside, Sir John Peter, Kt., CBE

Grey, Sir Anthony Dysart, Bt. (1814)

Grierson, Sir Michael John Bewes, Bt. (s. 1685)

Grierson, Sir Ronald Hugh, Kt.

Griffin, *Maj.* Sir (Arthur) John (Stewart), KCVO

Griffin, Sir (Charles) David, Kt., CBE

Griffiths, Sir Eldon Wylie, Kt.

Griffiths, Sir John Norton-, Bt. (1922)

Grimwade, Sir Andrew Sheppard, Kt., CBE

Grindrod, *Most Revd* John Basil Rowland, KBE

Grinstead, Sir Stanley Gordon, Kt.

Grose, *Vice-Adm.* Sir Alan, KBE

Grossart, Sir Angus McFarlane McLeod, Kt., CBE

Grotrian, Sir Philip Christian Brent, Bt. (1934)

Grove, Sir Charles Gerald, Bt. (1874)

Grove, Sir Edmund Frank, KCVO

Grugeon, Sir John Drury, Kt.

Grylls, Sir (William) Michael (John), Kt.

Guinness, Sir Alec, Kt., CH, CBE

Guinness, Sir Howard Christian Sheldon, Kt., VRD

Guinness, Sir John Ralph Sidney, Kt., CB

Guinness, Sir Kenelm Ernest Lee, Bt. (1867)

Guise, Sir John Grant, Bt. (1783)

Gull, Sir Rupert William Cameron, Bt. (1872)

Gumbs, Sir Emile Rudolph, Kt.

Gunn, *Prof.* Sir John Currie, Kt., CBE

Gunn, Sir Robert Norman, Kt.

Gunn, Sir William Archer, KBE, CMG

†Gunning, Sir Charles Theodore, Bt. (1778)

Gunston, Sir John Wellesley, Bt. (1938)

Gurdon, *Prof.* Sir John Bertrand, Kt., D.Phil., FRS

Guthrie, *Gen.* Sir Charles Ronald Llewelyn, GCB, LVO, OBE

Guthrie, Sir Malcolm Connop, Bt., (1936)

Guy, *Gen.* Sir Roland Kelvin, GCB, CBE, DSO

Habakkuk, Sir John Hrothgar, Kt., FBA

Hadfield, Sir Ronald, Kt., QPM

Hadlee, Sir Richard John, Kt., MBE

Hadley, Sir Leonard Albert, Kt.

Hague, *Prof.* Sir Douglas Chalmers, Kt., CBE

Halberg, Sir Murray Gordon, Kt., MBE

Hall, Sir Arnold Alexander, Kt., FRS, FREng.

Hall, Sir Basil Brodribb, KCB, MC, TD

Hall, Sir Douglas Basil, Bt., KCMG (s. 1687)

Hall, Sir Ernest, Kt., OBE

Hall, Sir (Frederick) John (Frank), Bt. (1923)

Hall, Sir John, Kt.

Hall, Sir John Bernard, Bt. (1919)

Hall, Sir Peter Edward, KBE, CMG

Hall, *Prof.* Sir Peter Geoffrey, Kt., FBA

Hall, Sir Peter Reginald Frederick, Kt., CBE

Hall, Sir Robert de Zouche, KCMG

Hall, *Brig.* Sir William Henry, KBE, DSO, ED

Halliday, *Vice-Adm.* Sir Roy William, KBE, DSC

Halpern, Sir Ralph Mark, Kt.

Halsey, *Revd* Sir John Walter Brooke, Bt. (1920)

Halstead, Sir Ronald, Kt., CBE

Ham, Sir David Kenneth Rowe-, GBE

Hambling, Sir (Herbert) Hugh, Bt. (1924)

Hamburger, Sir Sidney Cyril, Kt., CBE

Hamer, *Hon.* Sir Rupert James, KCMG, ED

Hamill, Sir Patrick, Kt., QPM

Hamilton, *Rt. Hon.* Sir Archibald Gavin, Kt., MP

Hamilton, Sir Edward Sydney, Bt. (1776 and 1819)

Hamilton, Sir James Arnot, KCB, MBE, FREng.

Hamilton, Sir Malcolm William Bruce Stirling-, Bt. (s. 1673)

Hamilton, Sir Michael Aubrey, Kt.

Hamilton, Sir (Robert Charles) Richard Caradoc, Bt. (s. 1646)

Hammick, Sir Stephen George, Bt. (1834)

Hampel, Sir Ronald Claus, Kt.

Hampshire, Sir Stuart Newton, Kt., FBA

Hampson, Sir Stuart, Kt.

Hampton, Sir (Leslie) Geoffrey, Kt.

Hancock, Sir David John Stowell, KCB

Hancock, *Air Marshal* Sir Valston Eldridge, KBE, CB, DFC

Hand, *Most Revd* Geoffrey David, KBE

Handley, Sir David John Davenport-, Kt., OBE

Hanham, Sir Michael William, Bt., DFC (1667)

Hanley, *Rt. Hon.* Sir Jeremy James, KCMG

Hanley, Sir Michael Bowen, KCB

Hanmer, Sir John Wyndham Edward, Bt. (1774)

Hann, Sir James, Kt., CBE

Hannam, Sir John Gordon, Kt.

Hannay, Sir David Hugh Alexander, GCMG

Hanson, Sir (Charles) Rupert (Patrick), Bt. (1918)

Hanson, Sir John Gilbert, KCMG, CBE

Hardcastle, Sir Alan John, Kt.

Hardie, Sir Douglas Fleming, Kt., CBE

Harding, Sir Christopher George Francis, Kt.

Harding, Sir George William, KCMG, CVO

Harding, *Marshal of the Royal Air Force* Sir Peter Robin, GCB

Harding, Sir Roy Pollard, Kt., CBE

Hardman, Sir Henry, KCB

Hardy, Sir David William, Kt.

Hardy, Sir James Gilbert, Kt., OBE

Hardy, Sir Richard Charles Chandos, Bt. (1876)

Hare, Sir David, Kt., FRSL

Hare, Sir Philip Leigh, Bt. (1818)

Harford, Sir (John) Timothy, Bt. (1934)

Hargroves, *Brig.* Sir Robert Louis, Kt., CBE

Harington, *Gen.* Sir Charles Henry Pepys, GCB, CBE, DSO, MC

Harington, Sir Nicholas John, Bt. (1611)

Harland, *Air Marshal* Sir Reginald Edward Wynyard, KBE, CB

Harley, *Gen.* Sir Alexander George Hamilton, KBE, CB

Harman, *Gen.* Sir Jack Wentworth, GCB, OBE, MC

Harman, *Hon.* Sir Jeremiah LeRoy, Kt.

Harman, Sir John Andrew, Kt.

Harmsworth, Sir Hildebrand Harold, Bt. (1922)

Harris, *Prof.* Sir Alan James, Kt., CBE, FREng.

Harris, *Prof.* Sir Henry, Kt., FRCP, FRCPath., FRS

Harris, Sir Jack Wolfred Ashford, Bt. (1932)

Harris, *Air Marshal* Sir John Hulme, KCB, CBE

Harris, Sir William Gordon, KBE, CB, FREng.

Harrison, Sir David, Kt., CBE, FREng.

Harrison, *Prof.* Sir Donald Frederick Norris, Kt., FRCS

Harrison, Sir Ernest Thomas, Kt., OBE

Harrison, Sir Francis Alexander Lyle, Kt., MBE, QC

Harrison, *Surgeon Vice-Adm.* Sir John Albert Bews, KBE

Harrison, *Hon.* Sir (John) Richard, Kt., ED

Harrison, *Hon.* Sir Michael Guy Vicat, Kt.

Harrison, Sir Michael James Harwood, Bt. (1961)

Harrison, *Prof.* Sir Richard John, Kt., FRS

Harrison, Sir (Robert) Colin, Bt. (1922)

Harrison, Sir Terence, Kt., FREng

Harrop, Sir Peter John, KCB

Hart, Sir Graham Allan, KCB

Hart, *Hon.* Sir Michael Christopher Campbell, Kt.

Hartopp, *Lt. Cdr* Sir Kenneth Alston Cradock-, Bt., MBE, DSC (1796)

Hartwell, Sir (Francis) Anthony Charles Peter, Bt. (1805)

Harvey, Sir Charles Richard Musgrave, Bt. (1933)

Harvie, Sir John Smith, Kt., CBE

Haselhurst, *Rt. Hon.* Sir Alan Gordon Barraclough, Kt., MP

Haskard, Sir Cosmo Dugal Patrick Thomas, KCMG, MBE

Haslam, *Rear-Adm.* Sir David William, KBE, CB

Hassett, *Gen.* Sir Francis George, KBE, CB, DSO, LVO

Hastings, Sir Stephen Lewis Edmonstone, Kt., MC

Hatter, Sir Maurice, Kt.

Hatty, *Hon.* Sir Cyril James, Kt.

Haughton, Sir James, Kt., CBE, QPM

Havelock, Sir Wilfrid Bowen, Kt.

Hawkins, Sir Paul Lancelot, Kt., TD

†Hawkins, Sir Richard Caesar, Bt. (1778)

Hawley, Sir Donald Frederick, KCMG, MBE

†Hawley, Sir Henry Nicholas, Bt. (1795)

Haworth, Sir Philip, Bt. (1911)

Hawthorne, Sir Nigel Barnard, Kt., CBE

Hawthorne, *Prof.* Sir William Rede, Kt., CBE, SC.D., FRS, FREng.

Hay, Sir David Osborne, Kt., CBE, DSO

Hay, Sir David Russell, Kt., CBE, FRCP, MD

Hay, Sir Hamish Grenfell, Kt.

Hay, Sir James Brian Dalrymple-, Bt. (1798)

Hay, Sir John Erroll Audley, Bt. (s. 1663)

†Hay, Sir Ronald Frederick Hamilton, Bt. (s. 1703)

Haydon, Sir Walter Robert, KCMG

Hayes, Sir Brian, Kt., CBE, QPM

Hayes, Sir Brian David, GCB

Hayr, *Air Marshal* Sir Kenneth William, KCB, KBE, AFC

Hayward, Sir Anthony William Byrd, Kt.

Hayward, Sir Jack Arnold, Kt., OBE

Haywood, Sir Harold, KCVO, OBE

Head, Sir Francis David Somerville, Bt. (1838)

Healey, Sir Charles Edward Chadwyck-, Bt. (1919)

Heap, Sir Peter William, KCMG

Hearne, Sir Graham James, Kt., CBE

Heath, *Rt. Hon.* Sir Edward Richard George, KG, MBE, MP

Heath, Sir Mark Evelyn, KCVO, CMG

Heathcote, *Brig.* Sir Gilbert Simon, Bt., CBE (1733)

Heathcote, Sir Michael Perryman, Bt. (1733)

Heatley, Sir Peter, Kt., CBE

Heaton, Sir Yvo Robert Henniker-, Bt. (1912)

Heiser, Sir Terence Michael, GCB

Hellaby, Sir (Frederick Reed) Alan, Kt.

Henderson, Sir Denys Hartley, Kt.

Henderson, Sir (John) Nicholas, GCMG, KCVO

Henderson, Sir William MacGregor, Kt., D.SC., FRS

Henley, Sir Douglas Owen, KCB

Hennessy, Sir James Patrick Ivan, KBE, CMG

†Henniker, Sir Adrian Chandos, Bt. (1813)

Henry, Sir Denis Aynsley, Kt., OBE, QC

Henry, *Rt. Hon.* Sir Denis Robert Maurice, Kt.

Henry, *Hon.* Sir Geoffrey Arama, KBE

†Henry, Sir Patrick Denis, Bt. (1923)

Henry, *Hon.* Sir Trevor Ernest, Kt.

Hepburn, Sir John Alastair Trant Kidd Buchan-, Bt. (1815)

Herbecq, Sir John Edward, KCB

Herbert, *Adm.* Sir Peter Geoffrey Marshall, KCB, OBE

Hermon, Sir John Charles, Kt., OBE, QPM

Heron, Sir Conrad Frederick, KCB, OBE

Heron, Sir Michael Gilbert, Kt.

Hervey, Sir Roger Blaise Ramsay, KCVO, CMG

Heseltine, *Rt. Hon.* Sir William Frederick Payne, GCB, GCVO

Hetherington, Sir Arthur Ford, Kt., DSC, FREng.

Hetherington, Sir Thomas Chalmers, KCB, CBE, TD, QC

Hewetson, Sir Christopher Raynor, Kt., TD

Hewett, Sir Peter John Smithson, Bt., MM (1813)

Hewitt, Sir (Cyrus) Lenox (Simson), Kt., OBE

Hewitt, Sir Nicholas Charles Joseph, Bt. (1921)

Heygate, Sir Richard John Gage, Bt. (1831)

Heywood, Sir Peter, Bt. (1838)

Hezlet, *Vice-Adm.* Sir Arthur Richard, KBE, CB, DSO, DSC

Hibbert, Sir Jack, KCB

Hibbert, Sir Reginald Alfred, GCMG

Hickey, Sir Justin, Kt.

Hickman, Sir (Richard) Glenn, Bt. (1903)

Hicks, Sir Robert, Kt.

Hidden, *Hon.* Sir Anthony Brian, Kt.

Hielscher, Sir Leo Arthur, Kt.

Higgins, *Hon.* Sir Malachy Joseph, Kt.

Higginson, Sir Gordon Robert, Kt., ph.D., FREng.

Hill, Sir Alexander Rodger Erskine-, Bt. (1945)

Hill, Sir Arthur Alfred, Kt., CBE

Hill, Sir Brian John, Kt.

Hill, Sir James Frederick, Bt. (1917)

Hill, Sir John McGregor, Kt., ph.D., FREng.

Hill, Sir John Maxwell, Kt., CBE, DFC

†Hill, Sir John Rowley, Bt. (l. 1779)

Hill, *Vice-Adm.* Sir Robert Charles Finch, KBE, FREng.

Hillary, Sir Edmund, KG, KBE

Hillhouse, Sir (Robert) Russell, KCB

Hills, Sir Graham John, Kt.

Hine, *Air Chief Marshal* Sir Patrick Bardon, GCB, GBE

Hirsch, *Prof.* Sir Peter Bernhard, Kt., ph.D., FRS

Hirst, *Rt. Hon.* Sir David Cozens-Hardy, Kt.

Hirst, Sir Michael William, Kt.

Hoare, Sir Peter Richard David, Bt. (1786)

Hoare, Sir Timothy Edward Charles, Bt., OBE (l. 1784)

Hobart, Sir John Vere, Bt. (1914)

Hobbs, *Maj.-Gen.* Sir Michael Frederick, KCVO, CBE

Hobday, Sir Gordon Ivan, Kt.

Hobhouse, Sir Charles John Spinney, Bt. (1812)

Hockaday, Sir Arthur Patrick, KCB, CMG

Hockley, *Gen.* Sir Anthony Heritage Farrar-, GBE, KCB, DSO, MC

Hoddinott, Sir John Charles, Kt., CBE, QPM

†Hodge, Sir Andrew Rowland, Bt. (1921)

Hodge, Sir James William, KCVO, CMG

Hodge, Sir Julian Stephen Alfred, Kt.

Hodges, *Air Chief Marshal* Sir Lewis MacDonald, KCB, CBE, DSO, DFC

Hodgkin, Sir Gordon Howard Eliot, Kt., CBE

Hodgkinson, *Air Chief Marshal* Sir (William) Derek, KCB, CBE, DFC, AFC

Hodgson, Sir Maurice Arthur Eric, Kt., FREng.

Hodgson, *Hon.* Sir (Walter) Derek (Thornley), Kt.

Hodson, Sir Michael Robin Adderley, Bt. (I. 1789)

Hoffenberg, *Prof.* Sir Raymond, KBE

Hogg, Sir Christopher Anthony, Kt.

Hogg, *Vice-Adm.* Sir Ian Leslie Trower, KCB, DSC

Hogg, Sir Michael David, Bt. (1846)

†Hogg, Sir Michael Edward Lindsay-, Bt. (1905)

Holcroft, Sir Peter George Culcheth, Bt. (1921)

Holden, Sir Edward, Bt. (1893)

Holden, Sir John David, Bt. (1919)

Holder, Sir John Henry, Bt. (1898)

Holder, *Air Marshal* Sir Paul Davie, KBE, CB, DSO, DFC, Ph.D.

Holdgate, Sir Martin Wyatt, Kt., CB, Ph.D.

Holland, *Hon.* Sir Alan Douglas, Kt.

Holland, *Hon.* Sir Christopher John, Kt.

Holland, Sir Clifton Vaughan, Kt.

Holland, Sir Geoffrey, KCB

Holland, Sir Kenneth Lawrence, Kt., CBE, QFSM

Holland, Sir Philip Welsby, Kt.

Holliday, *Prof.* Sir Frederick George Thomas, Kt., CBE, FRSE

Hollings, *Hon.* Sir (Alfred) Kenneth, Kt., MC

Hollis, *Hon.* Sir Anthony Barnard, Kt.

Hollom, Sir Jasper Quintus, Kt.

Holloway, *Hon.* Sir Barry Blyth, KBE

Holm, Sir Carl Henry, Kt., OBE

Holm, Sir Ian (Ian Holm Cuthbert), Kt., CBE

Holman, *Hon.* Sir (Edward) James, Kt.

Holmes, *Prof.* Sir Frank Wakefield, Kt.

Holmes, Sir John Eaton, KBE, CMG, CVO

Holmes, Sir Peter Fenwick, Kt., MC

Holroyd, *Air Marshal* Sir Frank Martyn, KBE, CB, FREng.

Holt, *Prof.* Sir James Clarke, Kt.

Holt, Sir Michael, Kt., CBE

Home, Sir William Dundas, Bt. (S. 1671)

Honeycombe, *Prof.* Sir Robert William Kerr, Kt., FRS, FREng.

Honywood, Sir Filmer Courtenay William, Bt. (1660)

Hood, Sir Harold Joseph, Bt., TD (1922)

Hookway, Sir Harry Thurston, Kt.

Hooper, *Hon.* Sir Anthony, Kt.

Hope, Sir Colin Frederick Newton, Kt.

Hope, *Rt. Revd and Rt. Hon.* David Michael, KCVO

Hope, Sir John Carl Alexander, Bt. (s. 1628)

Hopkin, Sir (William Aylsham) Bryan, Kt., CBE

Hopkins, Sir Anthony Philip, Kt., CBE

Hopkins, Sir Michael John, Kt., CBE, RA, RIBA

Hopwood, *Prof.* Sir David Alan, Kt., FRS

Hordern, *Rt. Hon.* Sir Peter Maudslay, Kt.

Horlick, *Vice-Adm.* Sir Edwin John, KBE, FREng.

Horlick, Sir James Cunliffe William, Bt. (1914)

Horlock, *Prof.* Sir John Harold, Kt., FRS, FREng.

Hornby, Sir Derek Peter, Kt.

Hornby, Sir Simon Michael, Kt.

Horne, Sir Alan Gray Antony, Bt. (1929)

Horsfall, Sir John Musgrave, Bt., MC, TD (1909)

Horsley, *Air Marshal* Sir (Beresford) Peter (Torrington), KCB, CBE, LVO, AFC

†Hort, Sir Andrew Edwin Fenton, Bt. (1767)

Horton, Sir Robert Baynes, Kt.

Hosker, Sir Gerald Albery, KCB, QC

Hoskyns, Sir Benedict Leigh, Bt. (1676)

Hoskyns, Sir John Austin Hungerford Leigh, Kt.

Hotung, Sir Joseph Edward, Kt.

Houghton, Sir John Theodore, Kt., CBE, FRS

†Houldsworth, Sir Richard Thomas Reginald, Bt. (1887)

Hounsfield, Sir Godfrey Newbold, Kt., CBE

Hourston, Sir Gordon Minto, Kt.

House, *Lt.-Gen.* Sir David George, GCB, KCVO, CBE, MC

Houssemayne du Boulay, Sir Roger William, KCVO, CMG

Howard, Sir (Hamilton) Edward de Coucey, Bt., GBE (1955)

Howard, *Prof.* Sir Michael Eliot, Kt., CBE, MC

Howard, *Maj.-Gen.* Lord Michael Fitzalan-, GCVO, CB, CBE, MC

Howell, Sir Ralph Frederic, Kt.

Howells, Sir Eric Waldo Benjamin, Kt., CBE

Howes, Sir Christopher Kingston, KCVO, CB

Howlett, *Gen.* Sir Geoffrey Hugh Whitby, KBE, MC

Hoyle, *Prof.* Sir Fred, Kt., FRS

Hoyos, *Hon.* Sir Fabriciano Alexander, Kt.

Hudson, *Lt.-Gen.* Sir Peter, KCB, CBE

Huggins, *Hon.* Sir Alan Armstrong, Kt.

Hughes, *Hon.* Sir Anthony Philip Gilson, Kt.

Hughes, Sir David Collingwood, Bt. (1773)

Hughes, *Prof.* Sir Edward Stuart Reginald, Kt., CBE

Hughes, Sir Jack William, Kt.

Hughes, Sir Trevor Denby Lloyd-, Kt.

Hughes, Sir Trevor Poulton, KCB

Hugo, *Lt.-Col.* Sir John Mandeville, KCVO, OBE

Hull, *Prof.* Sir David, Kt.

Hulse, Sir Edward Jeremy Westrow, Bt. (1739)

Hume, Sir Alan Blyth, Kt., CB

Humphreys, Sir (Raymond Evelyn) Myles, Kt.

Hunt, Sir John Leonard, Kt.

Hunt, *Adm.* Sir Nicholas John Streynsham, GCB, LVO

Hunt, Sir Rex Masterman, Kt., CMG

Hunt, Sir Robert Frederick, Kt., CBE, FREng.

Hunter, Sir Alistair John, KCMG

Hunter, Sir Ian Bruce Hope, Kt., MBE

Hunter, *Prof.* Sir Laurence Colvin, Kt., CBE, FRSE

Hurn, Sir (Francis) Roger, Kt.

Hurrell, Sir Anthony Gerald, KCVO, CMG

Hurst, Sir Geoffrey Charles, Kt., MBE

Husbands, Sir Clifford Straugh, GCMG

Hutchinson, *Hon.* Sir Ross, Kt., DFC

Hutchison, *Lt.-Cdr.* Sir (George) Ian Clark, Kt., RN

Hutchison, *Rt. Hon.* Sir Michael, Kt.

Hutchison, Sir Peter Craft, Bt. (1956)

Hutchison, Sir Robert, Bt. (1939)

Huxley, *Prof.* Sir Andrew Fielding, Kt., OM, FRS

Huxtable, *Gen.* Sir Charles Richard, KCB, CBE

Hyatali, *Hon.* Sir Isaac Emanuel, Kt.

Hyslop, Sir Robert John (Robin) Maxwell-, Kt.

Ibbs, Sir (John) Robin, KBE

Imray, Sir Colin Henry, KBE, CMG

Ingham, Sir Bernard, Kt.

Ingilby, Sir Thomas Colvin William, Bt. (1866)

Inglis, Sir Brian Scott, Kt.

Inglis of Glencorse, Sir Roderick John, Bt. (s. 1703)

Ingram, Sir James Herbert Charles, Bt. (1893)

Ingram, Sir John Henderson, Kt., CBE

Inkin, Sir Geoffrey David, Kt., OBE

†Innes, Sir David Charles Kenneth Gordon, Bt. (NS 1686)

Innes of Edingight, Sir Malcolm Rognvald, KCVO

Innes, Sir Peter Alexander Berowald, Bt. (s. 1628)

Irvine, Sir Donald Hamilton, Kt., CBE, MD, FRCGP

Irving, *Prof.* Sir Miles Horsfall, Kt., MD, FRCS, FRCSE

Isaacs, Sir Jeremy Israel, Kt.

Isham, Sir Ian Vere Gyles, Bt. (1627)

Jack, *Hon.* Sir Alieu Sulayman, Kt.

Jack, Sir David, Kt., CBE, FRS, FRSE

Jack, Sir David Emmanuel, GCMG, MBE

Jackson, Sir (John) Edward, KCMG

Jackson, Sir Kenneth Joseph, Kt.

Jackson, *Lt.-Gen.* Sir Michael David, KCB, CBE

Jackson, Sir Michael Roland, Bt. (1902)

Jackson, Sir Nicholas Fane St George, Bt. (1913)

Jackson, Sir Robert, Bt. (1815)

Jackson, *Hon.* Sir Rupert Matthew, Kt., QC

Jackson, Sir William Thomas, Bt. (1869)

Jacob, Sir Isaac Hai, Kt., QC

Jacob, *Hon.* Sir Robert Raphael Hayim (Robin), Kt.

Jacobi, Sir Derek George, Kt., CBE

Jacobi, *Dr* Sir James Edward, Kt., OBE

Jacobs, *Hon.* Sir Kenneth Sydney, KBE

Jacobs, Sir Piers, KBE

Jacobs, Sir Wilfred Ebenezer, GCMG, GCVO, OBE, QC

Jacomb, Sir Martin Wakefield, Kt.

Jaffray, Sir William Otho, Bt. (1892)

James, Sir Cynlais Morgan, KCMG

James, Sir Gerard Bowes Kingston, Bt. (1823)

James, Sir John Nigel Courtenay, KCVO, CBE

James, Sir Stanislaus Anthony, GCMG, OBE

Jamieson, *Air Marshal* Sir David Ewan, KBE, CB

Jansen, Sir Ross Malcolm, KBE

Janvrin, Sir Robin Berry, KCVO, CB

Jardine of Applegirth, Sir Alexander Maule, Bt. (s. 1672)

Jardine, Sir Andrew Colin Douglas, Bt. (1916)

Jardine, *Maj.* Sir (Andrew) Rupert (John) Buchanan-, Bt., MC (1885)

Jarman, *Prof.* Sir Brian, Kt., OBE

Jarratt, Sir Alexander Anthony, Kt., CB

Jarvis, Sir Gordon Ronald, Kt.

Jawara, *Hon.* Sir Dawda Kairaba, Kt.

Jay, Sir Antony Rupert, Kt., CVO

Jeewoolall, Sir Ramesh, Kt.

Jefferson, Sir George Rowland, Kt., CBE, FREng.

Jefferson, Sir Mervyn Stewart Dunnington-, Bt. (1958)

Jeffreys, *Prof.* Sir Alec John, Kt., FRS

Jeffries, *Hon.* Sir John Francis, Kt.

Jehangir, Sir Hirji, Bt. (1908)

Jejeebhoy, Sir Rustom, Bt. (1857)

Jenkins, Sir Brian Garton, GBE

Jenkins, Sir Elgar Spencer, Kt., OBE

Jenkins, Sir James Christopher, KCB, QC

Jenkins, Sir Michael Nicholas Howard, Kt., OBE

Jenkins, Sir Michael Romilly Heald, KCMG

Jenkinson, Sir John Banks, Bt. (1661)

†Jenks, Sir Maurice Arthur Brian, Bt. (1932)

Jennings, Sir John Southwood, Kt., CBE, FRSE

Jennings, *Prof.* Sir Robert Yewdall, Kt., QC

Jephcott, Sir (John) Anthony, Bt. (1962)

Jessel, Sir Charles John, Bt. (1883)

Jewkes, Sir Gordon Wesley, KCMG

John, Sir David Glyndwr, KCMG

John, Sir Elton Hercules (Reginald Kenneth Dwight), Kt., CBE

Johns, *Air Chief Marshal* Sir Richard Edward, GCB, CBE, LVO

Johnson, *Rt. Hon.* Sir David Powell Croom-, Kt., DSC, VRD

Johnson, *Gen.* Sir Garry Dene, KCB, OBE, MC

Johnson, Sir John Rodney, KCMG

†Johnson, Sir Patrick Eliot, Bt. (1818)

Johnson, Sir Peter Colpoys Paley, Bt. (1755)

Johnson, *Hon.* Sir Robert Lionel, Kt.

Johnson, Sir Vassel Godfrey, Kt., CBE

Johnston, Sir John Baines, GCMG, KCVO

Johnston, *Lt.-Col.* Sir John Frederick Dame, GCVO, MC

Johnston, *Lt.-Gen.* Sir Maurice Robert, KCB, OBE

Johnston, Sir Thomas Alexander, Bt. (s. 1626)

Johnston, Sir William Robert Patrick Knox- (Sir Robin), Kt., CBE, RD

Johnstone, Sir (George) Richard Douglas, Bt. (s. 1700)

Johnstone, Sir (John) Raymond, Kt., CBE

Jolliffe, Sir Anthony Stuart, GBE

Jones, *Gen.* Sir (Charles) Edward Webb, KCB, CBE

Jones, Sir Christopher Lawrence-, Bt. (1831)

Jones, Sir David Akers-, KBE, CMG

Jones, *Air Marshal* Sir Edward Gordon, KCB, CBE, DSO, DFC

Jones, Sir Ewart Ray Herbert, Kt., D.SC., ph.D., FRS

Jones, Sir (John) Derek Alun-, Kt.

Jones, Sir John Henry Harvey-, Kt., MBE

Jones, Sir John Prichard-, Bt. (1910)

Jones, Sir Keith Stephen, Kt.

Jones, *Hon.* Sir Kenneth George Illtyd, Kt.

Jones, Sir Lyndon, Kt.

Jones, Sir (Owen) Trevor, Kt.

Jones, Sir (Peter) Hugh (Jefferd) Lloyd-, Kt.

Jones, Sir Richard Anthony Lloyd, KCB

Jones, Sir Robert Edward, Kt.

Jones, Sir Simon Warley Frederick Benton, Bt. (1919)

Jones, Sir (Thomas) Philip, Kt., CB

Jones, Sir (William) Emrys, Kt.

Jones, Sir Wynn Normington Hugh-, Kt., LVO

†Joseph, *Hon.* Sir James Samuel, Bt. (1943)

Jowitt, *Hon.* Sir Edwin Frank, Kt.

Joyce, *Lt.-Gen.* Sir Robert John Hayman-, KCB, CBE

Judge, *Rt. Hon.* Sir Igor, Kt.

Judge, Sir Paul Rupert, Kt.

Jugnauth, *Rt. Hon.* Sir Anerood, KCMG, QC

Jungius, *Vice-Adm.* Sir James George, KBE

Jupp, *Hon.* Sir Kenneth Graham, Kt., MC

Kaberry, *Hon.* Sir Christopher Donald, Bt. (1960)

Kalms, Sir (Harold) Stanley, Kt.

Kalo, Sir Kwamala, Kt., MBE

Kan Yuet-Keung, Sir, GBE

Kapi, *Hon.* Sir Mari, Kt., CBE

Kaputin, Sir John Rumet, KBE, CMG

Katsina, The Emir of, KBE, CMG

Katz, Sir Bernard, Kt., FRS

Kausimae, Sir David Nanau, KBE

Kavali, Sir Thomas, Kt., OBE

Kawharu, *Prof.* Sir Ian Hugh, Kt.

Kay, *Prof.* Sir Andrew Watt, Kt.

Kay, *Hon.* Sir John William, Kt.

Kay, *Hon.* Sir Maurice Ralph, Kt.

Kaye, Sir John Phillip Lister Lister-, Bt. (1812)

Kaye, Sir Paul Henry Gordon, Bt. (1923)

Keane, Sir Richard Michael, Bt. (1801)

Keeble, Sir (Herbert Ben) Curtis, GCMG

Keene, *Hon.* Sir David Wolfe, Kt.

Keith, *Prof.* Sir James, KBE

Kellett, Sir Stanley Charles, Bt. (1801)

Kelly, Sir David Robert Corbett, Kt., CBE

Kelly, *Rt. Hon.* Sir (John William) Basil, Kt.

Kelly, Sir William Theodore, Kt., OBE

Kemball, *Air Marshal* Sir (Richard) John, KCB, CBE

Kemp, Sir (Edward) Peter, KCB

Kenilorea, *Rt. Hon.* Sir Peter, KBE

Kennard, *Lt.-Col.* Sir George Arnold Ford, Bt. (1891)

Kennaway, Sir John Lawrence, Bt. (1791)

Kennedy, Sir Francis, KCMG, CBE

Kennedy, *Hon.* Sir Ian Alexander, Kt.

Kennedy, Sir Ludovic Henry Coverley, Kt.

†Kennedy, Sir Michael Edward, Bt., (1836)

Kennedy, *Rt. Hon.* Sir Paul Joseph Morrow, Kt.

Kennedy, *Air Chief Marshal* Sir Thomas Lawrie, GCB, AFC

Kenny, Sir Anthony John Patrick, Kt., D.Phil., D.Litt., FBA

Kenny, *Gen.* Sir Brian Leslie Graham, GCB, CBE

Kentridge, Sir Sydney Woolf, KCMG, QC

Kenyon, Sir George Henry, Kt.

Kermode, Sir (John) Frank, Kt., FBA

Kermode, Sir Ronald Graham Quale, KBE

Kerr, *Hon.* Sir Brian Francis, Kt.

Kerr, *Adm.* Sir John Beverley, GCB

Kerr, Sir John Olav, KCMG

Kerr, *Rt. Hon.* Sir Michael Robert Emanuel, Kt.

Kerruish, Sir (Henry) Charles, Kt., OBE

Kerry, Sir Michael James, KCB, QC

Kershaw, Sir (John) Anthony, Kt., MC

Keswick, Sir John Chippendale Lindley, Kt.

Kidd, Sir Robert Hill, KBE, CB

Kikau, *Ratu* Sir Jone Latianara, KBE

Killen, *Hon.* Denis James, KCMG

Killick, Sir John Edward, GCMG

Kimber, Sir Charles Dixon, Bt. (1904)

King, Sir John Christopher, Bt. (1888)

King, *Vice-Adm.* Sir Norman Ross Dutton, KBE

King, Sir Wayne Alexander, Bt. (1815)

Kingman, *Prof.* Sir John Frank Charles, Kt., FRS

Kingsland, Sir Richard, Kt., CBE, DFC

Kinloch, Sir David, Bt. (s. 1686)

Kinloch, Sir David Oliphant, Bt. (1873)

Kipalan, Sir Albert, Kt.

Kirby, *Hon.* Sir Richard Clarence, Kt.

Kirkpatrick, Sir Ivone Elliott, Bt. (s. 1685)

Kirkwood, *Hon.* Sir Andrew Tristram Hammett, Kt.

Kitcatt, Sir Peter Julian, Kt., CB

Kitson, *Gen.* Sir Frank Edward, GBE, KCB, MC

Kitson, Sir Timothy Peter Geoffrey, Kt.

Kleinwort, Sir Richard Drake, Bt. (1909)

Klevan, *Hon.* Sir Rodney (Conrad), Kt., QC

Klug, Sir Aaron, Kt., OM

Kneller, Sir Alister Arthur, Kt.

Knight, Sir Arthur William, Kt.

Knight, Sir Harold Murray, KBE, DSC

Knight, *Air Chief Marshal* Sir Michael William Patrick, KCB, AFC

Knill, *Prof.* Sir John Lawrence, Kt., FREng.

†Knill, Sir Thomas John Pugin Bartholomew, Bt. (1893)

Knott, Sir John Laurence, Kt., CBE

Knowles, Sir Charles Francis, Bt. (1765)

Knowles, Sir Durward Randolph, Kt., OBE

Knowles, Sir Leonard Joseph, Kt., CBE

Knowles, Sir Richard Marchant, Kt.

Knox, Sir Bryce Muir, KCVO, MC, TD

Knox, Sir David Laidlaw, Kt.

Knox, *Hon.* Sir John Leonard, Kt.

Knox, *Hon.* Sir William Edward, Kt.

Koraea, Sir Thomas, Kt.

Kornberg, *Prof.* Sir Hans Leo, Kt., D.SC., SC.D., Ph.D., FRS

Korowi, Sir Wiwa, GCMG

Krebs, *Prof.* Sir John Richard, Kt., D.Phil., FRS

Kroto, *Prof.* Sir Harold Walter, Kt., FRS

Kulukundis, Sir Elias George (Eddie), Kt., OBE

Kurongku, *Most Revd* Peter, KBE

Lacon, Sir Edmund Vere, Bt. (1818)

Lacy, Sir Hugh Maurice Pierce, Bt. (1921)

Lacy, Sir John Trend, Kt., CBE

Laddie, *Hon.* Sir Hugh Ian Lang, Kt.

Laidlaw, Sir Christophor Charles Fraser, Kt.

Laing, Sir (John) Martin (Kirby), Kt., CBE

Laing, Sir (John) Maurice, Kt.

Laing, Sir (William) Kirby, Kt., FREng.

Laird, Sir Gavin Harry, Kt., CBE

Lake, Sir (Atwell) Graham, Bt. (1711)

Laker, Sir Frederick Alfred, Kt.

Lakin, Sir Michael, Bt. (1909)

Laking, Sir George Robert, KCMG

Lamb, Sir Albert (Larry), Kt.

Lamb, Sir Albert Thomas, KBE, CMG, DFC

Lambert, Sir Anthony Edward, KCMG

Lambert, Sir John Henry, KCVO, CMG

†Lambert, Sir Peter John Biddulph, Bt. (1711)

Lampl, Sir Frank William, Kt.

Landale, Sir David William Neil, KCVO

Landau, Sir Dennis Marcus, Kt.

Lang, *Lt.-Gen.* Sir Derek Boileau, KCB, DSO, MC

Langham, Sir James Michael, Bt. (1660)

Langlands, Sir Robert Alan, Kt.

Langley, *Hon.* Sir Gordon Julian Hugh, Kt.

Langley, *Maj.-Gen.* Sir Henry Desmond Allen, KCVO, MBE

Langrishe, Sir James Hercules, Bt. (I. 1777)

Lankester, Sir Timothy Patrick, KCB

Lapun, *Hon.* Sir Paul, Kt.

Larcom, Sir (Charles) Christopher Royde, Bt. (1868)

Large, Sir Andrew McLeod Brooks, Kt.

Large, Sir Peter, Kt., CBE

Lasdun, Sir Denys Louis, Kt., CH, CBE, FRIBA

Latham, *Hon.* Sir David Nicholas Ramsey, Kt.

Latham, Sir Michael Anthony, Kt.

Latham, Sir Richard Thomas Paul, Bt. (1919)

Latimer, Sir (Courtenay) Robert, Kt., CBE

Latimer, Sir Graham Stanley, KBE

Lauder, Sir Piers Robert Dick-, Bt. (s. 1690)

Laughton, Sir Anthony Seymour, Kt.

Laurantus, Sir Nicholas, Kt., MBE

Laurence, Sir Peter Harold, KCMG, MC

Laurie, Sir Robert Bayley Emilius, Bt. (1834)

Lauterpacht, Sir Elihu, Kt., CBE, QC

Lauti, *Rt. Hon.* Sir Toaripi, GCMG

Lavan, *Hon.* Sir John Martin, Kt.

Law, *Adm.* Sir Horace Rochfort, GCB, OBE, DSC

Lawes, Sir (John) Michael Bennet, Bt. (1882)

Lawler, Sir Peter James, Kt., OBE

Lawrence, Sir David Roland Walter, Bt. (1906)

Lawrence, Sir Guy Kempton, Kt., DSO, OBE, DFC

Lawrence, Sir Ivan John, Kt., QC

Lawrence, Sir John Patrick Grosvenor, Kt., CBE

Lawrence, Sir John Waldemar, Bt., OBE (1858)

Lawrence, Sir William Fettiplace, Bt. (1867)

Laws, *Rt. Hon.* Sir John Grant McKenzie, Kt.

Lawson, Sir Christopher Donald, Kt.

Lawson, *Col.* Sir John Charles Arthur Digby, Bt., DSO, MC (1900)

Lawson, Sir John Philip Howard-, Bt. (1841)

Lawson, *Gen.* Sir Richard George, KCB, DSO, OBE

Lawton, *Prof.* Sir Frank Ewart, Kt.

Lawton, *Rt. Hon.* Sir Frederick Horace, Kt.

Layard, *Adm.* Sir Michael Henry Gordon, KCB, CBE

Layfield, Sir Frank Henry Burland Willoughby, Kt., QC

Lea, *Vice-Adm.* Sir John Stuart Crosbie, KBE

Lea, Sir Thomas William, Bt. (1892)

Leach, *Admiral of the Fleet* Sir Henry Conyers, GCB

Leahy, Sir Daniel Joseph, Kt.

Leahy, Sir John Henry Gladstone, KCMG

Learmont, *Gen.* Sir John Hartley, KCB, CBE

Leask, *Lt.-Gen.* Sir Henry Lowther Ewart Clark, KCB, DSO, OBE

Leather, Sir Edwin Hartley Cameron, KCMG, KCVO

Leaver, Sir Christopher, GBE

Le Bailly, *Vice-Adm.* Sir Louis Edward Stewart Holland, KBE, CB

Le Cheminant, *Air Chief Marshal* Sir Peter de Lacey, GBE, KCB, DFC

Lechmere, Sir Berwick Hungerford, Bt. (1818)

Ledger, Sir Philip Stevens, Kt., CBE, FRSE

Lee, Sir Arthur James, KBE, MC

Lee, *Air Chief Marshal* Sir David John Pryer, GBE, CB

Lee, *Brig.* Sir Leonard Henry, Kt., CBE

Lee, Sir Quo-wei, Kt., CBE

Leeds, Sir Christopher Anthony, Bt. (1812)

Lees, Sir David Bryan, Kt.

Lees, Sir Thomas Edward, Bt. (1897)

Lees, Sir Thomas Harcourt Ivor, Bt. (1804)

Lees, Sir (William) Antony Clare, Bt. (1937)

Leese, Sir John Henry Vernon, Bt. (1908)

Le Fanu, *Maj.* Sir (George) Victor (Sheridan), KCVO

le Fleming, Sir David Kelland, Bt. (1705)

Legard, Sir Charles Thomas, Bt. (1660)

Legg, Sir Thomas Stuart, KCB, QC

Leggatt, *Rt. Hon.* Sir Andrew Peter, Kt.

Leggatt, Sir Hugh Frank John, Kt.

Leggett, Sir Clarence Arthur Campbell, Kt., MBE

Leigh, Sir Geoffrey Norman, Kt.

Leigh, Sir Richard Henry, Bt. (1918)

Leighton, Sir Michael John Bryan, Bt. (1693)

Leitch, Sir George, KCB, OBE

Leith, Sir Andrew George Forbes-, Bt. (1923)

Le Marchant, Sir Francis Arthur, Bt. (1841)

Lemon, Sir (Richard) Dawnay, Kt., CBE

Leng, *Gen.* Sir Peter John Hall, KCB, MBE, MC

Lennard, *Revd* Sir Hugh Dacre Barrett-, Bt. (1801)

Leon, Sir John Ronald, Bt. (1911)

Leonard, *Rt. Revd and Rt. Hon.* Graham Douglas, KCVO

Leonard, *Hon.* Sir (Hamilton) John, Kt.

Lepping, Sir George Geria Dennis, GCMG, MBE

Le Quesne, Sir (Charles) Martin, KCMG

Le Quesne, Sir (John) Godfray, Kt., QC

Leslie, Sir Colin Alan Bettridge, Kt.

Leslie, Sir John Norman Ide, Bt. (1876)

†Leslie, Sir (Percy) Theodore, Bt. (S. 1625)

Leslie, Sir Peter Evelyn, Kt.

Lester, Sir James Theodore, Kt.

Lethbridge, Sir Thomas Periam Hector Noel, Bt. (1804)

Lever, Sir Paul, KCMG

Lever, Sir (Tresham) Christopher Arthur Lindsay, Bt. (1911)

Levey, Sir Michael Vincent, Kt., LVO

Levine, Sir Montague Bernard, Kt.

Levinge, Sir Richard George Robin, Bt. (I. 1704)

Lewando, Sir Jan Alfred, Kt., CBE

Lewinton, Sir Christopher, Kt.

Lewis, Sir David Courtenay Mansel, KCVO

Lewthwaite, *Brig.* Sir Rainald Gilfrid, Bt., CVO, OBE, MC (1927)

Ley, Sir Ian Francis, Bt. (1905)

Leyland, Sir Philip Vyvyan Naylor-, Bt. (1895)

Lickiss, Sir Michael Gillam, Kt.

Liggins, *Prof.* Sir Graham Collingwood, Kt., CBE, FRS

Lightman, *Hon.* Sir Gavin Anthony, Kt.

Lighton, Sir Thomas Hamilton, Bt. (I. 1791)

Limon, Sir Donald William, KCB

Linacre, Sir (John) Gordon (Seymour), Kt., CBE, AFC, DFM

Lindop, Sir Norman, Kt.

Lindsay, Sir James Harvey Kincaid Stewart, Kt.

Lindsay, *Hon.* Sir John Edmund Frederic, Kt.

Lindsay, Sir Ronald Alexander, Bt., (1962)

Lipworth, Sir (Maurice) Sydney, Kt.

Lithgow, Sir William James, Bt. (1925)

Little, *Most Revd* Thomas Francis, KBE

Littler, Sir (James) Geoffrey, KCB

Livesay, *Adm.* Sir Michael Howard, KCB

Llewellyn, Sir Henry Morton, Bt., CBE (1922)

Llewelyn, Sir John Michael Dillwyn-Venables-, Bt. (1890)

Lloyd, *Prof.* Sir Geoffrey Ernest Richard, Kt., FBA

Lloyd, Sir Ian Stewart, Kt.

Lloyd, Sir Nicholas Markley, Kt.

Lloyd, *Rt. Hon.* Sir Peter Robert Cable, Kt., MP

Lloyd, Sir Richard Ernest Butler, Bt. (1960)

Lloyd, *Hon.* Sir Timothy Andrew Wigram, Kt.

Loader, Sir Leslie Thomas, Kt., CBE

Loane, *Most Revd* Marcus Lawrence, KBE

Lobo, Sir Rogerio Hyndman, Kt., CBE

Lockhart, Sir Simon John Edward Francis Sinclair-, Bt. (S. 1636)

†Loder, Sir Edmund Jeune, Bt. (1887)

Logan, Sir Donald Arthur, KCMG

Logan, Sir Raymond Douglas, Kt.

Lokoloko, Sir Tore, GCMG, GCVO, OBE

Lombe, *Hon.* Sir Edward Christopher Evans-, Kt.

Longmore, *Hon.* Sir Andrew Centlivres, Kt.

Loram, *Vice-Adm.* Sir David Anning, KCB, CVO

Lorimer, Sir (Thomas) Desmond, Kt.

Los, *Hon.* Sir Kubulan, Kt., CBE

Lovell, Sir (Alfred Charles) Bernard, Kt., OBE, FRS

Lovelock, Sir Douglas Arthur, KCB

Loveridge, Sir John Warren, Kt.

Lovill, Sir John Roger, Kt., CBE

Low, Sir Alan Roberts, Kt.

Low, Sir James Richard Morrison-, Bt. (1908)

Lowe, *Air Chief Marshal* Sir Douglas Charles, GCB, DFC, AFC

Lowe, Sir Thomas William Gordon, Bt. (1918)

Lowry, Sir John Patrick, Kt., CBE

Lowson, Sir Ian Patrick, Bt. (1951)

Lowther, *Col.* Sir Charles Douglas, Bt. (1824)

Lowther, Sir John Luke, KCVO, CBE

Loyd, Sir Francis Alfred, KCMG, OBE

Loyd, Sir Julian St John, KCVO

Lu, Sir Tseng Chi, Kt.

Lucas, Sir Cyril Edward, Kt., CMG, FRS

Lucas, Sir Thomas Edward, Bt. (1887)

Luce, *Rt. Hon.* Sir Richard Napier, Kt.

Lucy, Sir Edmund John William Hugh Cameron-Ramsay-Fairfax, Bt. (1836)

Luddington, Sir Donald Collin Cumyn, KBE, CMG, CVO

Lumsden, Sir David James, Kt.

Lus, *Hon.* Sir Pita, Kt., OBE

Lush, *Hon.* Sir George Hermann, Kt.

Lushington, Sir John Richard Castleman, Bt. (1791)

Luttrell, *Col.* Sir Geoffrey Walter Fownes, KCVO, MC

Lyell, *Rt. Hon.* Sir Nicholas Walter, Kt., QC, MP

Lygo, *Adm.* Sir Raymond Derek, KCB

Lyle, Sir Gavin Archibald, Bt. (1929)

Lyne, Sir Roderic Michael John, KBE, CMG

Lyons, Sir Edward Houghton, Kt.

Lyons, Sir James Reginald, Kt.

Lyons, Sir John, Kt.

McAlpine, Sir William Hepburn, Bt. (1918)

Macara, Sir Alexander Wiseman, Kt., FRCP, FRCGP

†Macara, Sir Hugh Kenneth, Bt. (1911)

Macartney, Sir John Barrington, Bt. (I. 1799)

McAvoy, Sir (Francis) Joseph, Kt., CBE

McCaffrey, Sir Thomas Daniel, Kt.

McCall, Sir (Charles) Patrick Home, Kt., MBE, TD

McCallum, Sir Donald Murdo, Kt., CBE, FREng.

McCamley, Sir Graham Edward, Kt., MBE

McCarthy, *Rt. Hon.* Sir Thaddeus Pearcey, KBE

McCartney, Sir (James) Paul, Kt., MBE

McClellan, *Col.* Sir Herbert Gerard Thomas, Kt., CBE, TD

McClintock, Sir Eric Paul, Kt.

McColl, Sir Colin Hugh Verel, KCMG

McCollum, *Rt. Hon.* Sir William, Kt.

McConnell, Sir Robert Shean, Bt. (1900)

McCorkell, *Col.* Sir Michael William, KCVO, OBE, TD

McCowan, *Rt. Hon.* Sir Anthony James Denys, Kt.

†McCowan, Sir David William, Bt. (1934)

McCullough, *Hon.* Sir (Iain) Charles (Robert), Kt.

MacDermott, *Rt. Hon.* Sir John Clarke, Kt.

McDermott, Sir (Lawrence) Emmet, KBE

Macdonald of Sleat, Sir Ian Godfrey Bosville, Bt. (s. 1625)

Macdonald, Sir Kenneth Carmichael, KCB

Macdonald, *Vice-Adm.* Sir Roderick Douglas, KBE

McDonald, Sir Tom, Kt., OBE

McDonald, Sir Trevor, Kt., OBE

MacDougall, Sir (George) Donald (Alastair), Kt., CBE, FBA

McDowell, Sir Eric Wallace, Kt., CBE

McDowell, Sir Henry McLorinan, KBE

Mace, *Lt.-Gen.* Sir John Airth, KBE, CB

McEwen, Sir John Roderick Hugh, Bt. (1953)

McFarland, Sir John Talbot, Bt. (1914)

Macfarlane, Sir (David) Neil, Kt.

Macfarlane, Sir George Gray, Kt., CB, FREng.

McFarlane, Sir Ian, Kt.

McGeoch, *Vice-Adm.* Sir Ian Lachlan Mackay, KCB, DSO, DSC

McGrath, Sir Brian Henry, KCVO

Macgregor, Sir Edwin Robert, Bt. (1828)

MacGregor of MacGregor, Sir Gregor, Bt. (1795)

McGregor, Sir Ian Alexander, Kt., CBE, FRS

McGrigor, *Capt.* Sir Charles Edward, Bt. (1831)

McIntosh, *Vice-Adm.* Sir Ian Stewart, KBE, CB, DSO, DSC

McIntosh, Sir Malcolm Kenneth, Kt., ph.D.

McIntosh, Sir Ronald Robert Duncan, KCB

McIntyre, Sir Donald Conroy, Kt., CBE

McIntyre, Sir Meredith Alister, Kt.

MacKay, *Prof.* Sir Donald Iain, Kt., FRSE

McKay, Sir John Andrew, Kt., CBE

Mackechnie, Sir Alistair John, Kt.

McKee, *Maj.* Sir (William) Cecil, Kt., ERD

McKellen, Sir Ian Murray, Kt., CBE

McKenzie, Sir Alexander, KBE

Mackenzie, Sir Alexander Alwyne Henry Charles Brinton Muir-, Bt. (1805)

†Mackenzie, Sir (James William) Guy, Bt. (1890)

Mackenzie, *Gen.* Sir Jeremy John George, GCB, OBE

†Mackenzie, Sir Peter Douglas, Bt. (s. 1673)

†Mackenzie, Sir Roderick McQuhae, Bt. (s. 1703)

McKenzie, Sir Roy Allan, KBE

Mackeson, Sir Rupert Henry, Bt. (1954)

MacKinlay, Sir Bruce, Kt., CBE

McKinnon, Sir James, Kt.

McKinnon, *Hon.* Sir Stuart Neil, Kt.

Mackintosh, Sir Cameron Anthony, Kt.

Macklin, Sir Bruce Roy, Kt., OBE

Mackworth, Sir Digby (John), Bt. (1776)

McLaren, Sir Robin John Taylor, KCMG

†Maclean of Dunconnell, Sir Charles Edward, Bt. (1957)

Maclean, Sir Donald Og Grant, Kt.

MacLean, *Vice-Adm.* Sir Hector Charles Donald, KBE, CB, DSC

Maclean, Sir Lachlan Hector Charles, Bt. (NS 1631)

McLeod, Sir Charles Henry, Bt. (1925)

McLeod, Sir Ian George, Kt.

MacLeod, Sir (John) Maxwell Norman, Bt. (1924)

Macleod, Sir (Nathaniel William) Hamish, KBE

McLintock, Sir (Charles) Alan, Kt.

McLintock, Sir Michael William, Bt. (1934)

Maclure, Sir John Robert Spencer, Bt. (1898)

McMahon, Sir Brian Patrick, Bt. (1817)

McMahon, Sir Christopher William, Kt.

Macmillan, Sir (Alexander McGregor) Graham, Kt.

MacMillan, *Lt.-Gen.* Sir John Richard Alexander, KCB, CBE

McMullin, *Rt. Hon.* Sir Duncan Wallace, Kt.

Macnaghten, Sir Patrick Alexander, Bt. (1836)

McNamara, *Air Chief Marshal* Sir Neville Patrick, KBE

Macnaughton, *Prof.* Sir Malcolm Campbell, Kt.

McNee, Sir David Blackstock, Kt., QPM

McNulty, Sir (Robert William) Roy, Kt., CBE

MacPhail, Sir Bruce Dugald, Kt.

Macpherson, Sir Ronald Thomas Steward (Tommy), CBE, MC, TD

Macpherson of Cluny, *Hon.* Sir William Alan, Kt., TD

McQuarrie, Sir Albert, Kt.

MacRae, Sir (Alastair) Christopher (Donald Summerhayes), KCMG

Macrae, *Col.* Sir Robert Andrew Scarth, KCVO, MBE

Macready, Sir Nevil John Wilfrid, Bt. (1923)

Mactaggart, Sir John Auld, Bt. (1938)

Macwhinnie, Sir Gordon Menzies, Kt., CBE

McWilliam, Sir Michael Douglas, KCMG

McWilliams, Sir Francis, GBE, FREng.

Madden, *Adm.* Sir Charles Edward, Bt., GCB (1919)

Maddocks, Sir Kenneth Phipson, KCMG, KCVO

Maddox, Sir John Royden, Kt.

Madel, Sir (William) David, Kt., MP

Madigan, Sir Russel Tullie, Kt., OBE

Magnus, Sir Laurence Henry Philip, Bt. (1917)

Maguire, *Air Marshal* Sir Harold John, KCB, DSO, OBE

Mahon, Sir (John) Denis, Kt., CBE

Mahon, Sir William Walter, Bt. (1819)

Maiden, Sir Colin James, Kt., D.phil.

Main, Sir Peter Tester, Kt., ERD

Maino, Sir Charles, KBE

†Maitland, Sir Charles Alexander, Bt. (1818)

Maitland, Sir Donald James Dundas, GCMG, OBE

Makins, Sir Paul Vivian, Bt. (1903)

Malcolm, Sir James William Thomas Alexander, Bt. (s. 1665)

Malet, Sir Harry Douglas St Lo, Bt. (1791)

Mallaby, Sir Christopher Leslie George, GCMG, GCVO

Mallick, *Prof.* Sir Netar Prakash, Kt., FRCP, FRCPed.

Mallinson, Sir William James, Bt. (1935)

Malone, *Hon.* Sir Denis Eustace Gilbert, Kt.

Malpas, Sir Robert, Kt., CBE, FREng.

Mamo, Sir Anthony Joseph, Kt., OBE

Mance, *Hon.* Sir Jonathan Hugh, Kt.

Manchester, Sir William Maxwell, KBE

Mander, Sir Charles Marcus, Bt. (1911)

Manduell, Sir John, Kt., CBE

Mann, *Rt. Revd* Michael Ashley, KCVO

Mann, Sir Rupert Edward, Bt. (1905)

Mansel, Sir Philip, Bt. (1622)

Mansfield, *Vice-Adm.* Sir (Edward) Gerard (Napier), KBE, CVO

Mansfield, *Prof.* Sir Peter, Kt., FRS

Mansfield, Sir Philip (Robert Aked), KCMG

Mantell, *Rt. Hon.* Sir Charles Barrie Knight, Kt.

Manton, Sir Edwin Alfred Grenville, Kt.

Manuella, Sir Tulaga, GCMG, MBE

Manzie, Sir (Andrew) Gordon, KCB

Mara, *Rt. Hon. Ratu* Sir Kamisese Kapaiwai Tuimacilai, GCMG, KBE

Margetson, Sir John William Denys, KCMG

Marjoribanks, Sir James Alexander Milne, KCMG

Mark, Sir Robert, GBE
Markham, Sir Charles John, Bt. (1911)
Marking, Sir Henry Ernest, KCVO, CBE, MC
Marling, Sir Charles William Somerset, Bt. (1882)
Marr, Sir Leslie Lynn, Bt. (1919)
Marriner, Sir Neville, Kt., CBE
Marriott, Sir Hugh Cavendish Smith-, Bt. (1774)
Marriott, Sir John Brook, KCVO
†Marsden, Sir Simon Neville Llewelyn, Bt. (1924)
Marsh, *Prof.* Sir John Stanley, Kt., CBE
Marshall, Sir Arthur Gregory George, Kt., OBE
Marshall, Sir Denis Alfred, Kt.
Marshall, *Prof.* Sir (Oshley) Roy, Kt., CBE
Marshall, Sir Peter Harold Reginald, KCMG
Marshall, Sir Robert Braithwaite, KCB, MBE
Marshall, Sir (Robert) Michael, Kt.
Martin, Sir George Henry, Kt., CBE
Martin, *Vice-Adm.* Sir John Edward Ludgate, KCB, DSC
Martin, *Prof.* Sir (John) Leslie, Kt., Ph.D.
Martin, *Prof.* Sir Laurence Woodward, Kt.
Martin, Sir (Robert) Bruce, Kt., QC
Marychurch, Sir Peter Harvey, KCMG
Masefield, Sir Charles Beech Gordon, Kt.
Masefield, Sir Peter Gordon, Kt.
Masire, Sir Ketumile, GCMG
Mason, *Hon.* Sir Anthony Frank, KBE
Mason, Sir (Basil) John, Kt., CB, D.SC., FRS
Mason, *Prof.* Sir David Kean, Kt., CBE
Mason, Sir Frederick Cecil, KCVO, CMG
Mason, Sir Gordon Charles, Kt., OBE
Mason, Sir John Charles Moir, KCMG
Mason, Sir John Peter, Kt., CBE
Mason, *Prof.* Sir Ronald, KCB, FRS
Matane, Sir Paulias Nguna, Kt., CMG, OBE
Mather, Sir (David) Carol (Macdonell), Kt., MC
Mathers, Sir Robert William, Kt.
Matheson of Matheson, Sir Fergus John, Bt. (1882)
Matheson, Sir (James Adam) Louis, KBE, CMG, FREng.
Mathewson, Sir George Ross, Kt., CBE, Ph.D., FRSE
Matthews, Sir Peter Alec, Kt.
Matthews, Sir Peter Jack, Kt., CVO, OBE, QPM
Matthews, Sir Stanley, Kt., CBE
Maud, The Hon. Sir Humphrey John Hamilton, KCMG
Mawhinney, *Rt. Hon.* Sir Brian Stanley, Kt., MP

Maxwell, Sir Michael Eustace George, Bt. (s. 1681)
Maxwell, Sir Nigel Mellor Heron-, Bt. (s. 1683)
May, *Rt. Hon.* Sir Anthony Tristram Kenneth, Kt.
May, Sir Kenneth Spencer, Kt., CBE
May, *Prof.* Sir Robert McCredie, Kt., FRS
Maynard, *Hon.* Sir Clement Travelyan, Kt.
Mayne, *Very Revd* Michael Clement Otway, KCVO
Meadow, *Prof.* Sir (Samuel) Roy, Kt., FRCP, FRCPE
Medlycott, Sir Mervyn Tregonwell, Bt. (1808)
Megarry, *Rt. Hon.* Sir Robert Edgar, Kt., FBA
Meinertzhagen, Sir Peter, Kt., CMG
Melhuish, Sir Michael Ramsay, KBE, CMG
Mellon, Sir James, KCMG
Melville, Sir Harry Work, KCB, Ph.D., D.SC., FRS
Melville, Sir Leslie Galfreid, KBE
Melville, Sir Ronald Henry, KCB
Mensforth, Sir Eric, Kt., CBE, F.Eng.
Menter, Sir James Woodham, Kt., Ph.D., SC.D., FRS
Menteth, Sir James Wallace Stuart-, Bt. (1838)
Meyer, Sir Anthony John Charles, Bt. (1910)
Meyer, Sir Christopher John Rome, KCMG
Meyjes, Sir Richard Anthony, Kt.
Meyrick, Sir David John Charlton, Bt. (1880)
Meyrick, Sir George Christopher Cadafael Tapps-Gervis-, Bt. (1791)
Miakwe, *Hon.* Sir Akepa, KBE
Michael, Sir Peter Colin, Kt., CBE
Middleton, Sir Peter Edward, GCB
Miers, Sir (Henry) David Alastair Capel, KBE, CMG
Milbank, Sir Anthony Frederick, Bt. (1882)
Milburn, Sir Anthony Rupert, Bt. (1905)
Mildmay, Sir Walter John Hugh St John-, Bt. (1772)
Miles, Sir Peter Tremayne, KCVO
Miles, Sir William Napier Maurice, Bt. (1859)
Millais, Sir Geoffrey Richard Everett, Bt. (1885)
Millar, Sir Oliver Nicholas, GCVO, FBA
Millard, Sir Guy Elwin, KCMG, CVO
Miller, Sir Donald John, Kt., FRSE, FREng.
Miller, Sir Harry Holmes, Bt. (1705)
Miller, Sir Hilary Duppa (Hal), Kt.
Miller, *Lt.-Col.* Sir John Mansel, GCVO, DSO, MC
Miller, Sir (Oswald) Bernard, Kt.
Miller, Sir Peter North, Kt.

Miller, Sir Ronald Andrew Baird, Kt., CBE
Miller of Glenlee, Sir Stephen William Macdonald, Bt. (1788)
Millett, *Rt. Hon.* Sir Peter Julian, Kt.
Millichip, Sir Frederick Albert (Bert), Kt.
Mills, *Vice-Adm.* Sir Charles Piercy, KCB, CBE, DSC
Mills, Sir Frank, KCVO, CMG
Mills, Sir John Lewis Ernest Watts, Kt., CBE
Mills, Sir Peter Frederick Leighton, Bt. (1921)
†Milman, Sir David Patrick, Bt. (1800)
Milne, Sir John Drummond, Kt.
Milner, Sir Timothy William Lycett, Bt. (1717)
Mirrlees, *Prof.* Sir James Alexander, Kt., FBA
Mitchell, *Air Cdre* Sir (Arthur) Dennis, KBE, CVO, DFC, AFC
Mitchell, Sir David Bower, Kt.
Mitchell, Sir Derek Jack, KCB, CVO
Mitchell, *Prof.* Sir (Edgar) William John, Kt., CBE, FRS
Mitchell, *Rt. Hon.* Sir James FitzAllen, KCMG
Mitchell, *Very Revd* Patrick Reynolds, KCVO
Mitchell, *Hon.* Sir Stephen George, Kt.
Moate, Sir Roger Denis, Kt.
Mobbs, Sir (Gerald) Nigel, Kt.
Moberly, Sir John Campbell, KBE, CMG
Moberly, Sir Patrick Hamilton, KCMG
Moffat, Sir Brian Scott, Kt., OBE
Moffat, *Lt.-Gen.* Sir (William) Cameron, KBE
Mogg, *Gen.* Sir (Herbert) John, GCB, CBE, DSO
†Moir, Sir Christopher Ernest, Bt. (1916)
Moller, *Hon.* Sir Lester Francis, Kt.
†Molony, Sir Thomas Desmond, Bt. (1925)
Monck, Sir Nicholas Jeremy, KCB
Montgomery, Sir (Basil Henry) David, Bt. (1801)
Montgomery, Sir (William) Fergus, Kt.
Mookerjee, Sir Birendra Nath, Kt.
Moollan, Sir Abdool Hamid Adam, Kt.
Moollan, *Hon.* Sir Cassam (Ismael), Kt.
Moon, Sir Peter Wilfred Giles Graham-, Bt. (1855)
†Moon, Sir Roger, Bt. (1887)
Moore, *Most Revd* Desmond Charles, KBE
Moore, Sir Francis Thomas, Kt.
Moore, Sir Henry Roderick, Kt., CBE
Moore, *Hon.* Sir John Cochrane, Kt.
Moore, *Maj.-Gen.* Sir (John) Jeremy, KCB, OBE, MC
Moore, Sir John Michael, KCVO, CB, DSC

Moore, *Vice Adm.* Sir Michael Antony Claës, KBE, LVO

Moore, *Prof.* Sir Norman Winfrid, Bt. (1919)

Moore, Sir Patrick William Eisdell, Kt., OBE

Moore, Sir William Roger Clotworthy, Bt., TD (1932)

Morauta, Sir Mekere, Kt.

Mordaunt, Sir Richard Nigel Charles, Bt. (1611)

Moreton, Sir John Oscar, KCMG, KCVO, MC

Morgan, *Vice-Adm.* Sir Charles Christopher, KBE

Morgan, *His Hon. Maj.-Gen.* Sir David John Hughes-, Bt., CB, CBE (1925)

Morgan, Sir John Albert Leigh, KCMG

Morison, *Hon.* Sir Thomas Richard Atkin, Kt.

Morland, *Hon.* Sir Michael, Kt.

Morland, Sir Robert Kenelm, Kt.

Morpeth, Sir Douglas Spottiswoode, Kt., TD

Morris, *Air Marshal* Sir Arnold Alec, KBE, CB, FREng.

Morris, Sir (James) Richard (Samuel), Kt., CBE, FREng.

Morris, *Rt. Hon.* Sir John, Kt., QC

Morris, Sir Keith Elliot Hedley, KBE, CMG

Morris, *Prof.* Sir Peter John, Kt., FRS

Morris, Sir Robert Byng, Bt. (1806)

Morris, Sir Trefor Alfred, Kt., CBE, QPM

Morris, *Very Revd* Sir William James, KCVO, Ph.D.

Morrison, Sir (Alexander) Fraser, Kt., CBE

Morrison, *Hon.* Sir Charles Andrew, Kt.

Morrison, Sir Howard Leslie, Kt., OBE

Morritt, *Hon.* Sir (Robert) Andrew, Kt., CVO

Morrow, Sir Ian Thomas, Kt.

Morse, Sir Christopher Jeremy, KCMG

Mortimer, Sir John Clifford, Kt., CBE, QC

Morton, *Adm.* Sir Anthony Storrs, GBE, KCB

Morton, Sir (Robert) Alastair (Newton), Kt.

Moseley, Sir George Walker, KCB

Moser, *Prof.* Sir Claus Adolf, KCB, CBE, FBA

Moses, *Hon.* Sir Alan George, Kt.

†Moss, Sir David John Edwards-, Bt. (1868)

Moss, Sir David Joseph, KCVO, CMG

Mostyn, *Gen.* Sir (Joseph) David Frederick, KCB, CBE

†Mostyn, Sir William Basil John, Bt. (1670)

Mott, Sir John Harmer, Bt. (1930)

Mottram, Sir Richard Clive, KCB

†Mount, Sir (William Robert) Ferdinand, Bt. (1921)

Mountain, Sir Denis Mortimer, Bt. (1922)

Mountfield, Sir Robin, KCB

Mowbray, Sir John, Kt.

Mowbray, Sir John Robert, Bt. (1880)

Muir, Sir Laurence Macdonald, Kt.

†Muir, Sir Richard James Kay, Bt. (1892)

Mulcahy, Sir Geoffrey John, Kt.

Mullens, *Lt.-Gen.* Sir Anthony Richard Guy, KCB, OBE

Mummery, *Hon.* Sir John Frank, Kt.

Munn, Sir James, Kt., OBE

Munro, Sir Alan Gordon, KCMG

†Munro, Sir Kenneth Arnold William, Bt. (s. 1634)

†Munro, Sir Keith Gordon, Bt. (1825)

Munro, Sir Sydney Douglas Gun-, GCMG, MBE

Muria, *Hon.* Sir Gilbert John Baptist, Kt.

Murphy, Sir Leslie Frederick, Kt.

Murray, *Rt. Hon.* Sir Donald Bruce, Kt.

Murray, Sir James, KCMG

Murray, Sir John Antony Jerningham, Kt., CBE

Murray, *Prof.* Sir Kenneth, Kt., FRCPath., FRS, FRSE

Murray, Sir Nigel Andrew Digby, Bt. (s. 1628)

Murray, Sir Patrick Ian Keith, Bt. (s. 1673)

†Murray, Sir Rowland William, Bt. (s. 1630)

Mursell, Sir Peter, Kt., MBE

Musgrave, Sir Christopher Patrick Charles, Bt. (1611)

Musgrave, Sir Richard James, Bt. (I. 1782)

Musson, *Gen.* Sir Geoffrey Randolph Dixon, GCB, CBE, DSO

Myers, Sir Philip Alan, Kt., OBE, QPM

Myers, *Prof.* Sir Rupert Horace, KBE

Mynors, Sir Richard Baskerville, Bt. (1964)

Naipaul, Sir Vidiadhar Surajprasad, Kt.

Nairn, Sir Michael, Bt. (1904)

Nairn, Sir Robert Arnold Spencer-, Bt. (1933)

Nairne, *Rt. Hon.* Sir Patrick Dalmahoy, GCB, MC

Naish, Sir (Charles) David, Kt.

Nall, Sir Michael Joseph, Bt., RN (1954)

Namaliu, *Rt. Hon.* Sir Rabbie Langanai, Kt., CMG

†Napier, Sir Charles Joseph, Bt. (1867)

Napier, Sir John Archibald Lennox, Bt. (s. 1627)

Napier, Sir Oliver John, Kt.

Nasmith, *Prof.* Sir James Duncan Dunbar-, Kt., CBE, RIBA, FRSE

Neal, Sir Eric James, Kt., CVO

Neal, Sir Leonard Francis, Kt., CBE

Neale, Sir Gerrard Anthony, Kt.

Neave, Sir Paul Arundell, Bt. (1795)

Nedd, *Hon.* Sir Robert Archibald, Kt.

Needham, *Rt. Hon.* Sir Richard (The Earl of Kilmorey, *see* page 141)

Neill, *Rt. Hon.* Sir Brian Thomas, Kt.

Neill, *Rt. Hon.* Sir Ivan, Kt., PC (NI)

Neill, Sir (James) Hugh, KCVO, CBE, TD

†Nelson, Sir Jamie Charles Vernon Hope, Bt. (1912)

Nelson, *Hon.* Sir Robert Franklyn, Kt.

Nelson, *Air Marshal* Sir (Sidney) Richard (Carlyle), KCB, OBE, MD

Nepean, *Lt.-Col.* Sir Evan Yorke, Bt. (1802)

Neuberger, *Hon.* Sir David Edmond, Kt.

Neubert, Sir Michael John, Kt.

Neville, Sir Roger Albert Gartside, Kt., VRD

New, *Maj.-Gen.* Sir Laurence Anthony Wallis, Kt., CB, CBE

Newall, Sir Paul Henry, Kt., TD

Newington, Sir Michael John, KCMG

Newman, Sir Francis Hugh Cecil, Bt. (1912)

Newman, Sir Geoffrey Robert, Bt. (1836)

Newman, *Hon.* Sir George Michael, Kt.

Newman, Sir Kenneth Leslie, GBE, QPM

Newman, *Vice-Adm.* Sir Roy Thomas, KCB

Newman, *Col.* Sir Stuart Richard, Kt., CBE, TD

Newsam, Sir Peter Anthony, Kt.

Newton, Sir (Charles) Wilfred, Kt., CBE

Newton, Sir (Harry) Michael (Rex), Bt. (1900)

Newton, Sir Kenneth Garnar, Bt., OBE, TD (1924)

Ngata, Sir Henare Kohere, KBE

Nichol, Sir Duncan Kirkbride, Kt., CBE

Nicholas, Sir David, Kt., CBE

Nicholas, Sir John William, KCVO, CMG

Nicholls, *Air Marshal* Sir John Moreton, KCB, CBE, DFC, AFC

Nicholls, Sir Nigel Hamilton, KCVO, CBE

Nichols, Sir Richard Everard, Kt.

Nicholson, Sir Bryan Hubert, Kt.

†Nicholson, Sir Charles Christian, Bt. (1912)

Nicholson, *Rt. Hon.* Sir Michael, Kt.

Nicholson, Sir Paul Douglas, Kt.

Nicholson, Sir Robin Buchanan, Kt., Ph.D., FRS, FREng.

Nicoll, Sir William, KCMG

Nightingale, Sir Charles Manners Gamaliel, Bt. (1628)

Nightingale, Sir John Cyprian, Kt., CBE, BEM, QPM

Nixon, Sir Simon Michael Christopher, Bt. (1906)

Nixon, Sir Edwin Ronald, Kt., CBE

Noble, Sir David Brunel, Bt. (1902)

Noble, Sir Iain Andrew, Bt., OBE (1923)

Noble, Sir (Thomas Alexander)
Fraser, Kt., MBE
Nombri, Sir Joseph Karl, Kt., ISO,
BEM
Norman, Sir Arthur Gordon, KBE,
DFC
Norman, Sir Mark Annesley, Bt.
(1915)
Norman, Sir Robert Henry, Kt., OBE
Norman, Sir Ronald, Kt., OBE
Norrington, Sir Roger Arthur
Carver, Kt., CBE
Norris, *Air Chief Marshal* Sir
Christopher Neil Foxley-, GCB,
DSO, OBE
Norris, Sir Eric George, KCMG
North, Sir Peter Machin, Kt., CBE,
QC, DCL, FBA
North, Sir Thomas Lindsay, Kt.
North, Sir (William) Jonathan
(Frederick), Bt. (1920)
Norton, *Vice-Adm. Hon.* Sir Nicholas
John Hill-, KCB
Norwood, Sir Walter Neville, Kt.
Nossal, Sir Gustav Joseph Victor, Kt.,
CBE
Nott, *Rt. Hon.* Sir John William
Frederic, KCB
Nourse, *Rt. Hon.* Sir Martin Charles,
Kt.
Nugent, Sir John Edwin Lavallin, Bt.
(I. 1795)
Nugent, *Maj.* Sir Peter Walter James,
Bt. (1831)
Nugent, Sir Robin George Colborne,
Bt. (1806)
Nursaw, Sir James, KCB, QC
Nurse, Sir Paul Maxime, Kt., Ph.D.
Nuttall, Sir Nicholas Keith
Lillington, Bt. (1922)
†Nutting, Sir John Grenfell, Bt., QC
(1903)
Oakeley, Sir John Digby Atholl, Bt.
(1790)
Oakes, Sir Christopher, Bt. (1939)
Oakshott, Hon. Sir Anthony
Hendrie, Bt. (1959)
Oates, Sir Thomas, Kt., CMG, OBE
Obolensky, *Prof.* Sir Dimitri, Kt.
O'Brien, Sir Frederick William
Fitzgerald, Kt.
O'Brien, Sir Richard, Kt., DSO, MC
O'Brien, Sir Timothy John, Bt.
(1849)
O'Brien, *Adm.* Sir William Donough,
KCB, DSC
O'Connell, Sir Maurice James
Donagh MacCarthy, Bt. (1869)
O'Connor, *Rt. Hon.* Sir Patrick
McCarthy, Kt.
O'Dea, Sir Patrick Jerad, KCVO
Odell, Sir Stanley John, Kt.
Odgers, Sir Graeme David William,
Kt.
O'Dowd, Sir David Joseph, Kt., CBE,
QPM
Ogden, Sir (Edward) Michael, Kt.,
QC
Ogilvy, *Rt. Hon.* Sir Angus James
Bruce, KCVO

Ogilvy, Sir Francis Gilbert Arthur,
Bt. (s. 1626)
Ognall, *Hon.* Sir Harry Henry, Kt.
Ohlson, Sir Brian Eric Christopher,
Bt. (1920)
Okeover, *Capt.* Sir Peter Ralph
Leopold Walker-, Bt. (1886)
Olewale, *Hon.* Sir Niwia Ebia, Kt.
Oliphant, Sir Mark (Marcus
Laurence Elwin), KBE, FRS
O'Loghlen, Sir Colman Michael, Bt.
(1838)
Olver, Sir Stephen John Linley, KBE,
CMG
O'Neil, *Hon.* Sir Desmond Henry, Kt.
Ongley, *Hon.* Sir Joseph Augustine,
Kt.
O'Nions, *Prof.* Sir Robert Keith, Kt.,
FRS, Ph.D.
Onslow, Sir John Roger Wilmot, Bt.
(1797)
Oppenheim, Sir Duncan Morris, Kt.
Oppenheimer, Sir Michael Bernard
Grenville, Bt. (1921)
Orde, Sir John Alexander Campbell-,
Bt. (1790)
O'Regan, *Dr* Sir Stephen Gerard
(Tipene), Kt.
Orlebar, Sir Michael Keith Orlebar
Simpson-, KCMG
Orr, Sir David Alexander, Kt., MC
Osborn, Sir John Holbrook, Kt.
Osborn, Sir Richard Henry Danvers,
Bt. (1662)
Osborne, Sir Peter George, Bt.
(I. 1629)
Osifelo, Sir Frederick Aubarua, Kt.,
MBE
Osmond, Sir Douglas, Kt., CBE
Osmond, Sir (Stanley) Paul, Kt., CB
O'Sullevan, Sir Peter John, Kt., CBE
Oswald, *Admiral of the Fleet* Sir (John)
Julian Robertson, GCB
Oswald, Sir (William Richard)
Michael, KCVO
Otton, Sir Geoffrey John, KCB
Otton, *Rt. Hon.* Sir Philip Howard, Kt.
Oulton, Sir Antony Derek Maxwell,
GCB, QC
Ouseley, Sir Herman George, Kt.
Outram, Sir Alan James, Bt. (1858)
Overall, Sir John Wallace, Kt., CBE,
MC
Owen, Sir Geoffrey, Kt.
Owen, Sir Hugh Bernard Pilkington,
Bt. (1813)
Owen, Sir Hugo Dudley Cunliffe-,
Bt. (1920)
Owen, *Hon.* Sir John Arthur Dalziel,
Kt.
Owo, The Olowo of, Kt.
Packard, *Lt.-Gen.* Sir (Charles)
Douglas, KBE, CB, DSO
Page, Sir (Arthur) John, Kt.
Page, Sir Frederick William, Kt., CBE,
FREng.
Page, Sir John Joseph Joffre, Kt., OBE
Paget, Sir Julian Tolver, Bt., CVO
(1871)

Paget, Sir Richard Herbert, Bt.
(1886)
Pain, *Lt.-Gen.* Sir (Horace) Rollo
(Squarey), KCB, MC
Pain, *Hon.* Sir Peter Richard, Kt.
Paine, Sir Christopher Hammon, Kt.,
FRCP, FRCR
Palin, *Air Chief Marshal* Sir Roger
Hewlett, KCB, OBE
Palliser, *Rt. Hon.* Sir (Arthur)
Michael, GCMG
Palmar, Sir Derek James, Kt.
Palmer, Sir (Charles) Mark, Bt.
(1886)
Palmer, *Gen.* Sir (Charles) Patrick
(Ralph), KBE
Palmer, Sir Geoffrey Christopher
John, Bt. (1660)
Palmer, *Rt. Hon.* Sir Geoffrey
Winston Russell, KCMG
Palmer, Sir John Chance, Kt.
Palmer, Sir John Edward Somerset,
Bt. (1791)
Palmer, *Maj.-Gen.* Sir (Joseph)
Michael, KCVO
Palmer, Sir Reginald Oswald, GCMG,
MBE
Pantlin, Sir Dick Hurst, Kt., CBE
Paolozzi, Sir Eduardo Luigi, Kt., CBE,
RA
Parbo, Sir Arvi Hillar, Kt.
Park, *Hon.* Sir Andrew Edward
Wilson, Kt.
Park, *Hon.* Sir Hugh Eames, Kt.
Parker, Sir (Arthur) Douglas Dodds-,
Kt.
Parker, Sir Eric Wilson, Kt.
Parker, *Hon.* Sir Jonathan Frederic,
Kt.
Parker, Sir Peter, KBE, LVO
Parker, Sir Richard (William) Hyde,
Bt. (1681)
Parker, *Rt. Hon.* Sir Roger Jocelyn,
Kt.
Parker, *Vice-Adm.* Sir (Wilfred) John,
KBE, CB, DSC
Parker, Sir William Peter Brian, Bt.
(1844)
Parkes, Sir Edward Walter, Kt., FREng.
Parkinson, Sir Nicholas Fancourt, Kt.
Parsons, Sir (John) Michael, Kt.
Parsons, Sir Richard Edmund
(Clement Fownes), KCMG
Parsons, Sir William Clere Leonard
Brendon Wilmer, Bt. (1677)
Partridge, Sir Michael John Anthony,
KCB
Pascoe, *Gen.* Sir Robert Alan, KCB,
MBE
Pasley, Sir John Malcolm Sabine, Bt.
(1794)
Paterson, Sir Dennis Craig, Kt.
Paterson, Sir John Valentine Jardine,
Kt.
Patnick, Sir (Cyril) Irvine, Kt., OBE
Pattie, *Rt. Hon.* Sir Geoffrey Edwin,
Kt.
Pattinson, Sir (William) Derek, Kt.
Pattison, *Prof.* Sir John Ridley, Kt.,
DM, FRCPath.

Pattullo, Sir (David) Bruce, Kt., CBE
Paul, Sir John Warburton, GCMG, OBE, MC
Paul, *Air Marshal* Sir Ronald Ian Stuart-, KBE
Payne, Sir Norman John, Kt., CBE, FREng.
Peach, Sir Leonard Harry, Kt.
Peacock, *Prof.* Sir Alan Turner, Kt., DSC
Pearce, Sir Austin William, Kt., CBE, Ph.D., FREng.
Pearce, Sir (Daniel Norton) Idris, Kt., CBE, TD
Pearse, Sir Brian Gerald, Kt.
Pearson, Sir Francis Nicholas Fraser, Bt. (1964)
Pearson, *Gen.* Sir Thomas Cecil Hook, KCB, CBE, DSO
Peart, *Prof.* Sir William Stanley, Kt., MD, FRS
Pease, Sir (Alfred) Vincent, Bt. (1882)
Pease, Sir Richard Thorn, Bt. (1920)
Peat, Sir Gerrard Charles, KCVO
Peat, Sir Michael Charles Gerrard, KCVO
Peck, Sir Edward Heywood, GCMG
Peckham, *Prof.* Sir Michael John, Kt., FRCP, FRCPGlas., FRCR, FRCPath.
Pedder, *Air Marshal* Sir Ian Maurice, KCB, OBE, DFC
Peek, *Vice-Adm.* Sir Richard Innes, KBE, CB, DSC
Peek, Sir William Grenville, Bt. (1874)
Peel, Sir John Harold, KCVO
Peel, Sir (William) John, Kt.
Peirse, Sir Henry Grant de la Poer Beresford-, Bt. (1814)
Peirse, *Air Vice-Marshal* Sir Richard Charles Fairfax, KCVO, CB
Pelgen, Sir Harry Friedrich, Kt., MBE
Peliza, Sir Robert John, KBE, ED
Pelly, Sir Richard John, Bt. (1840)
Pemberton, Sir Francis Wingate William, Kt., CBE
Penrose, *Prof.* Sir Roger, Kt., FRS
Pereira, Sir (Herbert) Charles, Kt., D.SC., FRS
Perring, Sir John Raymond, Bt. (1963)
Perris, Sir David (Arthur), Kt., MBE
Perry, Sir David Howard, KCB
Perry, Sir (David) Norman, Kt., MBE
Perry, Sir Michael Sydney, Kt., CBE
Pervez, Sir Mohammed Anwar, Kt., OBE
Pestell, Sir John Richard, KCVO
Peterkin, Sir Neville, Kt.
Peters, *Prof.* Sir David Keith, Kt., FRCP
Petersen, Sir Jeffrey Charles, KCMG
Petersen, Sir Johannes Bjelke-, KCMG
Peterson, Sir Christopher Matthew, Kt., CBE, TD
†Petit, Sir Jehangir, Bt. (1890)
Peto, Sir Henry George Morton, Bt. (1855)

Peto, Sir Michael Henry Basil, Bt. (1927)
Peto, *Prof.* Sir Richard, Kt., FRS
Petrie, Sir Peter Charles, Bt., CMG (1918)
Pettigrew, Sir Russell Hilton, Kt.
Pettit, Sir Daniel Eric Arthur, Kt.
Pettitt, Sir Dennis, Kt.
Philips, *Prof.* Sir Cyril Henry, Kt.
Phillips, Sir Fred Albert, Kt., CVO
Phillips, Sir (Gerald) Hayden, KCB
Phillips, Sir Henry Ellis Isidore, Kt., CMG, MBE
Phillips, Sir Horace, KCMG
Phillips, Sir Peter John, Kt., OBE
Phillips, Sir Robin Francis, Bt. (1912)
Pickard, Sir (John) Michael, Kt.
Pickering, Sir Edward Davies, Kt.
Pickthorn, Sir James Francis Mann, Bt. (1959)
Pidgeon, Sir John Allan Stewart, Kt.
†Piers, Sir James Desmond, Bt. (I. 1661)
Pigot, Sir George Hugh, Bt. (1764)
Pigott, Sir Berkeley Henry Sebastian, Bt. (1808)
Pike, *Lt.-Gen.* Sir Hew William Royston, KCB, DSO, MBE
Pike, Sir Michael Edmund, KCVO, CMG
Pike, Sir Philip Ernest Housden, Kt., QC
Pilditch, Sir Richard Edward, Bt. (1929)
Pile, Sir Frederick Devereux, Bt., MC (1900)
Pilkington, Sir Antony Richard, Kt.
Pilkington, Sir Thomas Henry Milborne-Swinnerton-, Bt. (S. 1635)
Pill, *Rt. Hon.* Sir Malcolm Thomas, Kt.
Pindling, *Rt. Hon.* Sir Lynden Oscar, KCMG
Pinker, Sir George Douglas, KCVO
Pinsent, Sir Christopher Roy, Bt. (1938)
Pippard, *Prof.* Sir (Alfred) Brian, Kt., FRS
Pirie, *Gp Capt* Sir Gordon Hamish, Kt., CVO, CBE
Pitakaka, Sir Moses Puibangara, GCMG
Pitcher, Sir Desmond Henry, Kt.
Pitman, Sir Brian Ivor, Kt.
Pitoi, Sir Sere, Kt., CBE
Pitt, Sir Harry Raymond, Kt., Ph.D., FRS
Pitts, Sir Cyril Alfred, Kt.
Plastow, Sir David Arnold Stuart, Kt.
Platt, Sir Harold Grant, Kt.
Platt, *Prof.* Hon. Sir Peter, Bt. (1959)
Plowman, *Hon.* Sir John Robin, Kt., CBE
Plumb, *Prof.* Sir John Harold, Kt.
Pohai, Sir Timothy, Kt., MBE
Pole, Sir (John) Richard (Walter Reginald) Carew, Bt. (1628)
Pole, Sir Peter Van Notten, Bt. (1791)

Polkinghorne, *Revd Canon* John Charlton, KBE, FRS
Pollen, Sir John Michael Hungerford, Bt. (1795)
Pollock, Sir George Frederick, Bt. (1866)
Pollock, Sir Giles Hampden Montagu-, Bt. (1872)
Pollock, *Admiral of the Fleet* Sir Michael Patrick, GCB, LVO, DSC
Ponsonby, Sir Ashley Charles Gibbs, Bt., KCVO, MC (1956)
Pontin, Sir Frederick William, Kt.
Poole, *Hon.* Sir David Anthony, Kt.
Poore, Sir Herbert Edward, Bt. (1795)
Pope, Sir Joseph Albert, Kt., D.SC., Ph.D.
Popplewell, *Hon.* Sir Oliver Bury, Kt.
†Porritt, Sir Jonathon Espie, Bt. (1963)
Portal, Sir Jonathan Francis, Bt. (1901)
Porter, Sir John Simon Horsbrugh-, Bt. (1902)
Porter, Sir Leslie, Kt.
Porter, *Air Marshal* Sir (Melvin) Kenneth (Drowley), KCB, CBE
Porter, *Rt. Hon.* Sir Robert Wilson, Kt., PC (NI), QC
Posnett, Sir Richard Neil, KBE, CMG
Potter, *Rt. Hon.* Sir Mark Howard, Kt.
Potter, *Maj.-Gen.* Sir (Wilfrid) John, KBE, CB
Potts, *Hon.* Sir Francis Humphrey, Kt.
Pound, Sir John David, Bt. (1905)
Pountain, Sir Eric John, Kt.
Powell, Sir (Arnold Joseph) Philip, Kt., CH, OBE, RA, FRIBA
Powell, Sir Charles David, KCMG
Powell, Sir Nicholas Folliott Douglas, Bt. (1897)
Powell, Sir Raymond, Kt., MP
Powell, Sir Richard Royle, GCB, KBE, CMG
Power, Sir Alastair John Cecil, Bt. (1924)
Power, *Hon.* Sir Noel Plunkett, Kt.
Prance, *Prof.* Sir Ghillean Tolmie, Kt., FRS
Prendergast, Sir (Walter) Kieran, KCVO, CMG
Prentice, *Hon.* Sir William Thomas, Kt., MBE
Prescott, Sir Mark, Bt. (1938)
†Preston, Sir Philip Charles Henry Hulton, Bt. (1815)
Prevost, Sir Christopher Gerald, Bt. (1805)
Price, Sir Charles Keith Napier Rugge-, Bt. (1804)
Price, Sir David Ernest Campbell, Kt.
Price, Sir Francis Caradoc Rose, Bt. (1815)
Price, Sir Frank Leslie, Kt.
Price, Sir (James) Robert, KBE
Price, Sir Norman Charles, KCB
Price, Sir Robert John Green-, Bt. (1874)

Prickett, *Air Chief Marshal* Sir Thomas Other, KCB, DSO, DFC

Prideaux, Sir Humphrey Povah Treverbian, Kt., OBE

†Primrose, Sir John Ure, Bt. (1903)

Pringle, *Air Marshal* Sir Charles Norman Seton, KBE, FREng.

Pringle, *Hon.* Sir John Kenneth, Kt.

Pringle, *Lt.-Gen.* Sir Steuart (Robert), Bt., KCB, RM (S. 1683)

Pritchard, Sir Neil, KCMG

Proby, Sir Peter, Bt. (1952)

Prosser, Sir Ian Maurice Gray, Kt.

Pryke, Sir David Dudley, Bt. (1926)

Puapua, *Rt. Hon.* Sir Tomasi, KBE

Pugh, Sir Idwal Vaughan, KCB

Pullinger, Sir (Francis) Alan, Kt., CBE

Pumfrey, *Hon.* Sir Nicholas Richard, Kt.

Pumphrey, Sir (John) Laurence, KCMG

Purchas, *Rt. Hon.* Sir Francis Brooks, Kt.

Purves, Sir William, Kt., CBE, DSO

Purvis, *Vice-Adm.* Sir Neville, KCB

Quicke, Sir John Godolphin, Kt., CBE

Quigley, Sir (William) George (Henry), Kt., CB, Ph.D.

Quilliam, *Hon.* Sir (James) Peter, Kt.

Quilter, Sir Anthony Raymond Leopold Cuthbert, Bt. (1897)

Quinlan, Sir Michael Edward, GCB

Quinton, Sir James Grand, Kt.

Radcliffe, Sir Sebastian Everard, Bt. (1813)

Radzinowicz, *Prof.* Sir Leon, Kt., LL D

Rae, *Hon.* Sir Wallace Alexander Ramsay, Kt.

Raeburn, Sir Michael Edward Norman, Bt. (1923)

Raeburn, *Maj.-Gen.* Sir (William) Digby (Manifold), KCVO, CB, DSO, MBE

Raikes, *Vice-Adm.* Sir Iwan Geoffrey, KCB, CBE, DSC

Raison, *Rt. Hon.* Sir Timothy Hugh Francis, Kt.

Ralli, Sir Godfrey Victor, Bt., TD (1912)

Ramdanee, Sir Mookteswar Baboolall Kailash, Kt.

Ramphal, Sir Shridath Surendranath, GCMG

Ramphul, Sir Baalkhristna, Kt.

Ramphul, Sir Indurduth, Kt.

Ramsay, Sir Alexander William Burnett, Bt. (1806)

Ramsay, Sir Allan John (Hepple), KBE, CMG

Ramsbotham, *Gen.* Sir David John, GCB, CBE

Ramsbotham, *Hon.* Sir Peter Edward, GCMG, GCVO

Ramsden, Sir John Charles Josslyn, Bt. (1689)

Randle, *Prof.* Sir Philip John, Kt.

Rank, Sir Benjamin Keith, Kt., CMG

Rankin, Sir Ian Niall, Bt. (1898)

Rasch, Sir Simon Anthony Carne, Bt. (1903)

Rashleigh, Sir Richard Harry, Bt. (1831)

Ratford, Sir David John Edward, KCMG, CVO

Rattee, *Hon.* Sir Donald Keith, Kt.

Rattle, Sir Simon Dennis, Kt., CBE

Rault, Sir Louis Joseph Maurice, Kt.

Rawlins, *Surgeon Vice-Adm.* Sir John Stuart Pepys, KBE

Rawlins, *Prof.* Sir Michael David, Kt., FRCP, FRCPED.

Rawlinson, Sir Anthony Henry John, Bt. (1891)

Read, *Air Marshal* Sir Charles Frederick, KBE, CB, DFC, AFC

Read, *Gen.* Sir (John) Antony (Jervis), GCB, CBE, DSO, MC

Read, Sir John Emms, Kt.

†Reade, Sir Kenneth Ray, Bt. (1661)

Reay, *Lt.-Gen.* Sir (Hubert) Alan John, KBE

Redgrave, *Maj.-Gen.* Sir Roy Michael Frederick, KBE, MC

Redmayne, Sir Nicholas, Bt. (1964)

Redmond, Sir James, Kt., FREng.

Redwood, Sir Peter Boverton, Bt. (1911)

Reece, Sir Charles Hugh, Kt.

Reece, Sir James Gordon, Kt.

Rees, Sir (Charles William) Stanley, Kt., TD

Rees, Sir David Allan, Kt., Ph.D., D.SC., FRS

Rees, *Prof.* Sir Martin John, Kt., FRS

Reeve, Sir Anthony, KCMG, KCVO

Reeves, *Most Revd* Paul Alfred, GCMG, GCVO

Reffell, *Adm.* Sir Derek Roy, KCB

Refshauge, *Maj.-Gen.* Sir William Dudley, Kt., CBE

Reid, Sir Alexander James, Bt. (1897)

Reid, Sir (Harold) Martin (Smith), KBE, CMG

Reid, Sir Hugh, Bt. (1922)

Reid, Sir Norman Robert, Kt.

Reid, Sir Robert Paul, Kt.

Reid, Sir William Kennedy, KCB

Reiher, Sir Frederick Bernard Carl, KBE, CMG

Reilly, Sir (D'Arcy) Patrick, GCMG, OBE

Reilly, *Lt.-Gen.* Sir Jeremy Calcott, KCB, DSO

Renals, Sir Stanley, Bt. (1895)

Rennie, Sir John Shaw, GCMG, OBE

Renouf, Sir Clement William Bailey, Kt.

Renshaw, Sir (Charles) Maurice Bine, Bt. (1903)

Renwick, Sir Richard Eustace, Bt. (1921)

Reporter, Sir Shapoor Ardeshirji, KBE

Reynolds, Sir David James, Bt. (1923)

Reynolds, Sir Peter William John, Kt., CBE

Rhodes, Sir Basil Edward, Kt., CBE, TD

Rhodes, Sir John Christopher Douglas, Bt. (1919)

Rhodes, Sir Peregrine Alexander, KCMG

Rice, *Maj.-Gen.* Sir Desmond Hind Garrett, KCVO, CBE

Rice, Sir Timothy Miles Bindon, Kt.

Richard, Sir Cliff, Kt., OBE

Richards, Sir Brian Mansel, Kt., CBE, Ph.D.

Richards, Sir (Francis) Brooks, KCMG, DSC

Richards, *Lt.-Gen.* Sir John Charles Chisholm, KCB, KCVO, RM

Richards, Sir Rex Edward, Kt., D.SC., FRS

Richards, *Hon.* Sir Stephen Price, Kt.

Richardson, Sir Anthony Lewis, Bt. (1924)

Richardson, *Rt. Hon.* Sir Ivor Lloyd Morgan, Kt.

Richardson, Sir (John) Eric, Kt., CBE

Richardson, Sir Michael John de Rougemont, Kt.

Richardson, *Lt.-Gen.* Sir Robert Francis, KCB, CVO, CBE

Richardson, Sir Simon Alaisdair Stewart-, Bt. (S. 1630)

Richmond, Sir John Frederick, Bt. (1929)

Richmond, *Prof.* Sir Mark Henry, Kt., FRS

Ricketts, Sir Robert Cornwallis Gerald St Leger, Bt. (1828)

Riddell, Sir John Charles Buchanan, Bt., CVO (S. 1628)

Ridley, Sir Adam (Nicholas), Kt.

Ridsdale, Sir Julian Errington, Kt., CBE

Rifkind, *Rt. Hon.* Sir Malcolm Leslie, KCMG, QC

Rigby, Sir Anthony John, Bt. (1929)

Rimer, *Hon.* Sir Colin Percy Farquharson, Kt.

Ringadoo, *Hon.* Sir Veerasamy, GCMG

Ripley, Sir Hugh, Bt. (1880)

Risk, Sir Thomas Neilson, Kt.

Ritako, Sir Thomas Baha, Kt., MBE

Rix, *Hon.* Sir Bernard Anthony, Kt.

Rix, Sir John, Kt., MBE, FREng.

Robb, Sir John Weddell, Kt.

Roberts, *Hon.* Sir Denys Tudor Emil, KBE, QC

Roberts, Sir Derek Harry, Kt., CBE, FRS, FREng.

Roberts, Sir (Edward Fergus) Sidney, Kt., CBE

Roberts, *Prof.* Sir Gareth Gwyn, Kt., FRS

Roberts, Sir Gilbert Howland Rookehurst, Bt. (1809)

Roberts, Sir Gordon James, Kt., CBE

Roberts, Sir Samuel, Bt. (1919)

Roberts, Sir Stephen James Leake, Kt.

Roberts, Sir William James Denby, Bt. (1909)

Robertson, Sir John Fraser, KCMG, CBE

Robertson, Sir Lewis, Kt., CBE, FRSE

Robertson, *Prof.* Sir Rutherford Ness, Kt., CMG

Robins, Sir Ralph Harry, Kt., FREng.

Robinson, Sir Albert Edward Phineas, Kt.

†Robinson, Sir Christopher Philipse, Bt. (1854)

Robinson, Sir Dominick Christopher Lynch-, Bt. (1920)

Robinson, Sir John James Michael Laud, Bt. (1660)

Robinson, Sir Wilfred Henry Frederick, Bt. (1908)

Robson, *Prof.* Sir James Gordon, Kt., CBE

Robson, Sir John Adam, KCMG

Roch, *Rt. Hon.* Sir John Ormond, Kt.

Roche, Sir David O'Grady, Bt. (1838)

Roche, Sir Henry John, Kt.

Rodgers, Sir (Andrew) Piers (Wingate Aikin-Sneath), Bt. (1964)

Rodley, *Prof.* Sir Nigel, KBE

Rodrigues, Sir Alberto Maria, Kt., CBE, ED

Roe, *Air Chief Marshal* Sir Rex David, GCB, AFC

Rogers, Sir Frank Jarvis, Kt.

Rogers, *Air Chief Marshal* Sir John Robson, KCB, CBE

Rooke, Sir Denis Eric, Kt., OM, CBE, FRS, FREng.

Ropner, Sir John Bruce Woollacott, Bt. (1952)

Ropner, Sir Robert Douglas, Bt. (1904)

Roscoe, Sir Robert Bell, KBE

Rose, *Rt. Hon.* Sir Christopher Dudley Roger, Kt.

Rose, Sir Clive Martin, GCMG

Rose, Sir David Lancaster, Bt. (1874)

Rose, *Gen.* Sir (Hugh) Michael, KCB, CBE, DSO, QGM

Rose, Sir Julian Day, Bt. (1872 and 1909)

Ross, Sir (James) Keith, Bt., RD, FRCS (1960)

Ross, *Lt.-Col.* Sir Malcolm, KCVO

Ross, *Lt.-Gen.* Sir Robert Jeremy, KCB, OBE

Ross, *Lt.-Col.* Sir Walter Hugh Malcolm, KCVO, OBE

Rosser, Sir Melvyn Wynne, Kt.

Rossi, Sir Hugh Alexis Louis, Kt.

Rotblat, *Prof.* Joseph, KCMG, CBE, FRS

Roth, *Prof.* Sir Martin, Kt., MD, FRCP

Rothschild, Sir Evelyn Robert Adrian de, Kt.

Rougier, *Hon.* Sir Richard George, Kt.

Rowell, Sir John Joseph, Kt., CBE

Rowland, *Air Marshal* Sir James Anthony, KBE, DFC, AFC

Rowland, Sir (John) David, Kt.

Rowlands, *Air Marshal* Sir John Samuel, GC, KBE

Rowley, Sir Charles Robert, Bt. (1836) †(1786)

Roxburgh, *Vice-Adm.* Sir John Charles Young, KCB, CBE, DSO, DSC

Royden, Sir Christopher John, Bt. (1905)

Rudd, Sir (Anthony) Nigel (Russell), Kt.

Rumbold, Sir Henry John Sebastian, Bt. (1779)

Rumbold, Sir Jack Seddon, Kt.

Runchorelal, Sir (Udayan) Chinubhai Madhowlal, Bt. (1913)

Runciman, *Hon.* Sir James Cochran Stevenson (Sir Steven), Kt., CH

Rusby, *Vice-Adm.* Sir Cameron, KCB, LVO

†Russell, Sir (Arthur) Mervyn, Bt. (1812)

Russell, Sir Charles Dominic, Bt. (1916)

Russell, *Hon.* Sir David Sturrock West-, Kt.

Russell, Sir George, Kt., CBE

Russell, *Prof.* Sir Peter Edward Lionel, Kt., D.Litt., FBA

Russell, Sir (Robert) Mark, KCMG

Russell, *Rt. Hon.* Sir (Thomas) Patrick, Kt.

Rutter, Sir Frank William Eden, KBE

Rutter, *Prof.* Sir Michael Llewellyn, Kt., CBE, MD, FRS

Ryan, Sir Derek Gerald, Bt. (1919)

†Rycroft, Sir Richard John, Bt. (1784)

Ryrie, Sir William Sinclair, KCB

Sabola, *Hon.* Sir Joaquim Claudino Gonsalves-, Kt.

Sachs, *Hon.* Sir Michael Alexander Geddes, Kt.

Sainsbury, Sir Robert James, Kt.

Sainsbury, *Rt. Hon.* Sir Timothy Alan Davan, Kt.

†St Aubyn, Sir William Molesworth-, Bt. (1689)

†St George, Sir John Avenel Bligh, Bt. (I. 1766)

St Johnston, Sir Kerry, Kt.

Sainty, Sir John Christopher, KCB

Sakzewski, Sir Albert, Kt.

Salisbury, Sir Robert William, Kt.

Salt, Sir Patrick MacDonnell, Bt. (1869)

Salt, Sir (Thomas) Michael John, Bt. (1899)

Sampson, Sir Colin, Kt., CBE, QPM

Samuel, Sir John Michael Glen, Bt. (1898)

Samuelson, Sir (Bernard) Michael (Francis), Bt. (1884)

Samuelson, Sir Sydney Wylie, Kt., CBE

Sanders, Sir John Reynolds Mayhew-, Kt.

Sanders, Sir Robert Tait, KBE, CMG

Sanderson, Sir Frank Linton, Bt. (1920)

Sarei, Sir Alexis Holyweek, Kt., CBE

Sarell, Sir Roderick Francis Gisbert, KCMG, KCVO

Saunders, *Hon.* Sir John Anthony Holt, Kt., CBE, DSO, MC

Saunders, Sir Peter, Kt.

Savage, Sir Ernest Walter, Kt.

Savile, Sir James Wilson Vincent, Kt., OBE

Say, *Rt. Revd* Richard David, KCVO

Schiemann, *Rt. Hon.* Sir Konrad Hermann Theodor, Kt.

Scholar, Sir Michael Charles, KCB

Scholey, Sir David Gerald, Kt., CBE

Scholey, Sir Robert, Kt., CBE, FREng.

Scholtens, Sir James Henry, KCVO

Schubert, Sir Sydney, Kt.

Scipio, Sir Hudson Rupert, Kt.

Scoon, Sir Paul, GCMG, GCVO, OBE

Scott, Sir Anthony Percy, Bt. (1913)

Scott, Sir (Charles) Peter, KBE, CMG

Scott, Sir David Aubrey, GCMG

Scott, Sir Dominic James Maxwell-, Bt. (1642)

Scott, Sir Ian Dixon, KCMG, KCVO, CIE

Scott, Sir James Jervoise, Bt. (1962)

Scott, Sir Kenneth Bertram Adam, KCVO, CMG

Scott, Sir Michael, KCVO, CMG

Scott, *Rt. Hon.* Sir Nicholas Paul, KBE

Scott, Sir Oliver Christopher Anderson, Bt. (1909)

Scott, *Prof.* Sir Philip John, KBE

Scott, *Rt. Hon.* Sir Richard Rashleigh Folliott, Kt.

Scott, Sir Robert David Hillyer, Kt.

Scott, Sir Walter John, Bt. (1907)

Scott, *Rear-Adm.* Sir (William) David (Stewart), KBE, CB

Scowen, Sir Eric Frank, Kt., MD, D.SC., LL D, FRCP, FRCS

Seale, Sir John Henry, Bt. (1838)

Seaman, Sir Keith Douglas, KCVO, OBE

Sebastian, Sir Cuthbert Montraville, GCMG, OBE

†Sebright, Sir Peter Giles Vivian, Bt. (1626)

Seccombe, Sir (William) Vernon Stephen, Kt.

Secombe, Sir Harry Donald, Kt., CBE

Seconde, Sir Reginald Louis, KCMG, CVO

Sedley, *Rt. Hon.* Sir Stephen John, Kt.

Seely, Sir Nigel Edward, Bt. (1896)

Seeto, Sir Ling James, Kt., MBE

Seeyave, Sir Rene Sow Choung, Kt., CBE

Seligman, Sir Peter Wendel, Kt., CBE

Sellors, Sir Patrick John Holmes-, KCVO, FRCS

Sergeant, Sir Patrick, Kt.

Series, Sir (Joseph Michel) Emile, Kt., CBE

Serota, Sir Nicholas Andrew, Kt.

Serpell, Sir David Radford, KCB, CMG, OBE

†Seton, Sir Charles Wallace, Bt. (S. 1683)

Seton, Sir Iain Bruce, Bt. (S. 1663)

Severne, *Air Vice-Marshal* Sir John de Milt, KCVO, OBE, AFC

Seymour, *Cdr.* Sir Michael Culme-, Bt., RN (1809)

Shackleton, *Prof.* Sir Nicholas John, Kt., PH.D., FRS

Shakerley, Sir Geoffrey Adam, Bt. (1838)

Shakespeare, Sir Thomas William,
Bt. (1942)
Shand, Sir James, Kt., MBE
Sharp, Sir Adrian, Bt. (1922)
Sharp, Sir George, Kt., OBE
Sharp, Sir Kenneth Johnston, Kt., TD
Sharp, Sir Leslie, Kt., QPM
Sharp, Sir Richard Lyall, KCVO, CB
†Sharp, Sir Samuel Christopher
Reginald, Bt. (1920)
Sharpe, Hon. Sir John Henry, Kt., CBE
Sharples, Sir James, Kt., QPM
Shattock, Sir Gordon, Kt.
Shaw, Sir Brian Piers, Kt.
Shaw, Sir (Charles) Barry, Kt., CB, QC
Shaw, Sir (George) Neville Bowan-,
Kt.
Shaw, Prof. Sir John Calman, Kt., CBE,
FRSE
Shaw, Sir (John) Giles (Dunkerley),
Kt.
Shaw, Sir John Michael Robert Best-,
Bt. (1665)
Shaw, Sir Neil McGowan, Kt.
Shaw, Sir Robert, Bt. (1821)
Shaw, Sir Roy, Kt.
Shaw, Sir Run Run, Kt., CBE
Sheehy, Sir Patrick, Kt.
Sheen, Hon. Sir Barry Cross, Kt.
Sheffield, Sir Reginald Adrian
Berkeley, Bt. (1755)
Shehadie, Sir Nicholas Michael, Kt.,
OBE
Sheil, Hon. Sir John, Kt.
Sheldon, Hon. Sir (John) Gervase
(Kensington), Kt.
Shelley, Sir John Richard, Bt. (1611)
Shelton, Sir William Jeremy
Masefield, Kt.
Shepheard, Sir Peter Faulkner, Kt.,
CBE
Shepherd, Sir Colin Ryley, Kt.
Shepperd, Sir Alfred Joseph, Kt.
Sherlock, Sir Philip Manderson, KBE
Sherman, Sir Alfred, Kt.
Sherman, Sir Louis, Kt., OBE
Shields, Sir Neil Stanley, Kt., MC
Shields, Prof. Sir Robert, Kt., MD
Shiffner, Sir Henry David, Bt. (1818)
Shillington, Sir (Robert Edward)
Graham, Kt., CBE
Shinwell, Sir (Maurice) Adrian, Kt.
Shock, Sir Maurice, Kt.
Short, Sir Apenera Pera, KBE
Short, Brig. Sir Noel Edward Vivian,
Kt., MBE, MC
Shuckburgh, Sir Rupert Charles
Gerald, Bt. (1660)
Siaguru, Sir Anthony Michael, KBE
Siddall, Sir Norman, Kt., CBE, FREng.
Sidey, Air Marshal Sir Ernest Shaw,
KBE, CB, MD
Sie, Sir Banja Tejan-, GCMG
Sieff, Hon. Sir David, Kt.
Simeon, Sir John Edmund
Barrington, Bt. (1815)
Simmons, Air Marshal Sir Michael
George, KCB, AFC
Simmons, Sir Stanley Clifford, Kt.,
FRCS, FRCOG

Simms, Sir Neville Ian, Kt., FREng.
Simon, Sir David Alec Gwyn, Kt.,
CBE
Simonet, Sir Louis Marcel Pierre,
Kt., CBE
Simpson, Hon. Sir Alfred Henry, Kt.
Simpson, Lt.-Gen. Sir Roderick
Alexander Cordy-, KBE, CB
Simpson, Sir William James, Kt.
Sims, Sir Roger Edward, Kt.
Sinclair, Sir Clive Marles, Kt.
Sinclair, Sir George Evelyn, Kt.,
CMG, OBE
Sinclair, Sir Ian McTaggart, KCMG,
QC
Sinclair, Air Vice-Marshal Sir
Laurence Frank, GC, KCB, CBE, DSO
Sinclair, Sir Patrick Robert Richard,
Bt. (s. 1704)
Sinden, Sir Donald Alfred, Kt., CBE
Singer, Prof. Sir Hans Wolfgang, Kt.
Singer, Hon. Sir Jan Peter, Kt.
Singh, Hon. Sir Vijay Raghubir, Kt.
Sitwell, Sir (Sacheverell) Reresby, Bt.
(1808)
Skeet, Sir Trevor Herbert Harry, Kt.
Skeggs, Sir Clifford George, Kt.
Skehel, Sir John James, Kt., FRS
Skingsley, Air Chief Marshal Sir
Anthony Gerald, GBE, KCB
Skinner, Sir (Thomas) Keith
(Hewitt), Bt. (1912)
Skipwith, Sir Patrick Alexander
d'Estoteville, Bt. (1622)
Skyrme, Sir (William) Thomas
(Charles), KCVO, CB, CBE, TD
Slack, Sir William Willatt, KCVO,
FRCS
Slade, Sir Benjamin Julian Alfred, Bt.
(1831)
Slade, Rt. Hon. Sir Christopher John,
Kt.
Slaney, Prof. Sir Geoffrey, KBE
Slater, Adm. Sir John (Jock)
Cunningham Kirkwood, GCB, LVO
Sleight, Sir Richard, Bt. (1920)
Sloan, Sir Andrew Kirkpatrick, Kt.,
QPM
Sloman, Sir Albert Edward, Kt., CBE
Smart, Prof. Sir George Algernon,
Kt., MD, FRCP
Smart, Sir Jack, Kt., CBE
Smedley, Hon. Sir (Frank) Brian, Kt.
Smedley, Sir Harold, KCMG, MBE
Smiley, Lt.-Col. Sir John Philip, Bt.
(1903)
Smith, Sir Alan, Kt., CBE, DFC
Smith, Sir Alexander Mair, Kt., ph.D.
Smith, Sir Andrew Colin Hugh-, Kt.
Smith, Lt.-Gen. Sir Anthony Arthur
Denison-, KBE
Smith, Sir Charles Bracewell-, Bt.
(1947)
Smith, Sir Christopher Sydney
Winwood, Bt. (1809)
Smith, Prof. Sir Colin Stansfield, Kt.,
CBE
Smith, Sir Cyril, Kt., MBE
Smith, Prof. Sir David Cecil, Kt., FRS

Smith, Air Chief Marshal Sir David
Harcourt-, GBE, KCB, DFC
Smith, Sir David Iser, KCVO
Smith, Sir Douglas Boucher, KCB
Smith, Sir Dudley (Gordon), Kt.
Smith, Prof. Sir Eric Brian, Kt., ph.D.
Smith, Maj.-Gen. Sir (Francis) Brian
Wyldbore-, Kt., CB, DSO, OBE
Smith, Prof. Sir Francis Graham-, Kt.,
FRS
Smith, Sir Geoffrey Johnson, Kt., MP
Smith, Sir Graham William, Kt., CBE
Smith, Sir John Alfred, Kt., QPM
Smith, Prof. Sir John Cyril, Kt., CBE,
QC, FBA
Smith, Sir John Hamilton-Spencer-,
Bt. (1804)
Smith, Sir John Jonah Walker-, Bt.
(1960)
Smith, Sir John Lindsay Eric, Kt., CH,
CBE
Smith, Sir John Rathbone Vassar-, Bt.
(1917)
Smith, Sir Joseph William Grenville,
Kt., MD, FRCP
Smith, Sir Leslie Edward George, Kt.
Smith, Maj.-Gen. Sir Michael Edward
Carleton-, Kt., CBE
Smith, Sir Michael John Llewellyn,
KCVO, CMG
Smith, Rt. Hon. Sir Murray Stuart-,
Kt.
Smith, Sir (Norman) Brian, Kt., CBE,
ph.D.
†Smith, Sir Peter Frank Graham
Newson-, Bt. (1944)
Smith, Sir Raymond Horace, KBE
Smith, Sir Robert Courtney, Kt., CBE
Smith, Sir Robert Haldane, Kt
Smith, Sir Robert Hill, Bt., MP (1945)
Smith, Prof. Sir Roland, Kt.
Smith, Air Marshal Sir Roy David
Austen-, KBE, CB, CVO, DFC
Smith, Gen. Sir Rupert Anthony, KCB,
DSO, OBE, QGM
Smith, Sir (Thomas) Gilbert, Bt.
(1897)
Smith, Sir (William) Antony (John)
Reardon-, Bt. (1920)
Smith, Sir (William) Richard Prince-,
Bt. (1911)
Smithers, Sir Peter Henry Berry
Otway, Kt., VRD, D.Phil.
Smyth, Sir Thomas Weyland
Bowyer-, Bt. (1661)
Smyth, Sir Timothy John, Bt. (1955)
Soakimori, Sir Frederick Pa-
Nukuanca, KBE, CPM
Soame, Sir Charles John Buckworth-
Herne-, Bt. (1697)
Sobers, Sir Garfield St Auburn, Kt.
Solomon, Sir Harry, Kt.
Somare, Rt. Hon. Sir Michael
Thomas, GCMG, CH
Somers, Rt. Hon. Sir Edward
Jonathan, Kt.
Somerville, Brig. Sir John Nicholas,
Kt., CBE
Somerville, Sir Quentin Charles
Somerville Agnew-, Bt. (1957)

Soulsby, Sir Peter Alfred, Kt.

Soutar, *Air Marshal* Sir Charles John Williamson, KBE

South, Sir Arthur, Kt.

Southby, Sir John Richard Bilbe, Bt. (1937)

Southern, Sir Richard William, Kt., FBA

Southern, Sir Robert, Kt., CBE

Southgate, Sir Colin Grieve, Kt.

Southgate, Sir William David, Kt.

Southward, Sir Leonard Bingley, Kt., OBE

Southwood, *Prof.* Sir (Thomas) Richard (Edmund), Kt., FRS

Souyave, *Hon.* Sir (Louis) Georges, Kt.

Sowrey, *Air Marshal* Sir Frederick Beresford, KCB, CBE, AFC

Sparkes, Sir Robert Lyndley, Kt.

Sparrow, Sir John, Kt.

Spearman, Sir Alexander Young Richard Mainwaring, Bt. (1840)

Spedding, *Prof.* Sir Colin Raymond William, Kt., CBE

Spedding, Sir David Rolland, KCMG, CVO, OBE

Speed, Sir (Herbert) Keith, Kt., RD

Speelman, Sir Cornelis Jacob, Bt. (1686)

Speight, *Hon.* Sir Graham Davies, Kt.

Spencer, Sir Derek Harold, Kt., QC

Spicer, Sir James Wilton, Kt.

Spicer, Sir Nicholas Adrian Albert, Bt., MB (1906)

Spicer, Sir (William) Michael Hardy, Kt., MP

Spiers, Sir Donald Maurice, Kt., CB, TD

Spooner, Sir James Douglas, Kt.

Spotswood, *Marshal of the Royal Air Force* Sir Denis Frank, GCB, CBE, DSO, DFC

Spratt, *Col.* Sir Greville Douglas, GBE, TD

Spring, Sir Dryden Thomas, Kt.

Squire, *Air Chief Marshal* Sir Peter Ted, KCB, DFC, AFC

Stabb, *Hon.* Sir William Walter, Kt., QC

Stainton, Sir (John) Ross, Kt., CBE

Stakis, Sir Reo Argiros, Kt.

Stamer, Sir (Lovelace) Anthony, Bt. (1809)

Stanbridge, *Air Vice-Marshal* Sir Brian Gerald Tivy, KCVO, CBE, AFC

Stanier, Sir Beville Douglas, Bt. (1917)

Stanier, *Field Marshal* Sir John Wilfred, GCB, MBE

Stanley, *Rt. Hon.* Sir John Paul, Kt., MP

†Staples, Sir Gerald James Arland, Bt. (I. 1628)

Stark, Sir Andrew Alexander Steel, KCMG, CVO

Starkey, Sir John Philip, Bt. (1935)

Starrit, Sir James, KCVO

Statham, Sir Norman, KCMG, CVO

Staughton, *Rt. Hon.* Sir Christopher Stephen Thomas Jonathan Thayer, Kt.

Staveley, Sir John Malfroy, KBE, MC

Stear, *Air Chief Marshal* Sir Michael James Douglas, KCB, CBE

Steel, Sir David Edward Charles, Kt., DSO, MC, TD

Steel, *Hon.* Sir David William, Kt.

Steele, Sir (Philip John) Rupert, Kt.

Steere, Sir Ernest Henry Lee-, KBE

Stephen, *Rt. Hon.* Sir Ninian Martin, KG, GCMG, GCVO, KBE

Stephens, Sir (Edwin) Barrie, Kt.

Stephenson, Sir Henry Upton, Bt. (1936)

Sternberg, Sir Sigmund, Kt.

Stevens, Sir Jocelyn Edward Greville, Kt., CVO

Stevens, Sir Laurence Houghton, Kt., CBE

Stevenson, *Vice-Adm.* Sir (Hugh) David, KBE

Stevenson, Sir Simpson, Kt.

Stewart, Sir Alan, KBE

Stewart, Sir Alan d'Arcy, Bt. (I. 1623)

Stewart, Sir David James Henderson-, Bt. (1957)

Stewart, Sir David John Christopher, Bt. (1803)

Stewart, Sir Edward Jackson, Kt.

Stewart, *Prof.* Sir Frederick Henry, Kt., Ph.D., FRS, FRSE

Stewart, Sir Houston Mark Shaw-, Bt., MC, TD (S. 1667)

Stewart, Sir James Douglas, Kt.

Stewart, Sir James Moray, KCB

Stewart, Sir (John) Simon (Watson), Bt. (1920)

Stewart, Sir Robertson Huntly, Kt., CBE

Stewart, Sir Robin Alastair, Bt. (1960)

Stewart, Sir Ronald Compton, Bt. (1937)

Stewart, *Prof.* Sir William Duncan Paterson, Kt., FRS, FRSE

Stibbon, *Gen.* Sir John James, KCB, OBE

Stirling, Sir Alexander John Dickson, KBE, CMG

Stirling, Sir Angus Duncan Aeneas, Kt.

Stockdale, Sir Arthur Noel, Kt.

Stockdale, Sir Thomas Minshull, Bt. (1960)

Stoddart, *Wg Cdr.* Sir Kenneth Maxwell, KCVO, AE

Stoker, *Prof.* Sir Michael George Parke, Kt., CBE, FRCP, FRS, FRSE

Stokes, Sir John Heydon Romaine, Kt.

Stones, Sir William Frederick, Kt., OBE

Stonhouse, *Revd* Sir Michael Philip, Bt. (1628)

Stonor, *Air Marshal* Sir Thomas Henry, KCB

Stoppard, Sir Thomas, Kt., CBE

Storey, *Hon.* Sir Richard, Bt., CBE (1960)

Stormonth Darling, Sir James Carlisle, Kt., CBE, MC, TD

Stott, Sir Adrian George Ellingham, Bt. (1920)

Stoute, Sir Michael Ronald, Kt.

Stow, Sir Christopher Philipson-, Bt., DFC (1907)

Stowe, Sir Kenneth Ronald, GCB, CVO

Stracey, Sir John Simon, Bt. (1818)

Strachan, Sir Curtis Victor, Kt., CVO

Strachey, Sir Charles, Bt. (1801)

Strawson, *Prof.* Sir Peter Frederick, Kt., FBA

Street, *Hon.* Sir Laurence Whistler, KCMG

Streeton, Sir Terence George, KBE, CMG

Stringer, Sir Donald Edgar, Kt., CBE

Strong, Sir Roy Colin, Kt., Ph.D., FSA

Stronge, Sir James Anselan Maxwell, Bt. (1803)

Stroud, *Prof.* Sir (Charles) Eric, Kt., FRCP

Strutt, Sir Nigel Edward, Kt., TD

Stuart, Sir James Keith, Kt.

Stuart, Sir Kenneth Lamonte, Kt.

†Stuart, Sir Phillip Luttrell, Bt. (1660)

Stubblefield, Sir (Cyril) James, Kt., D.SC., FRS

Stubbs, Sir James Wilfrid, KCVO, TD

Stubbs, Sir William Hamilton, Kt., Ph.D.

Stucley, *Lt.* Sir Hugh George Coplestone Bampfylde, Bt. (1859)

Studd, Sir Edward Fairfax, Bt. (1929)

Studd, Sir Peter Malden, GBE, KCVO

Studholme, Sir Henry William, Bt. (1956)

Style, *Lt.-Cdr.* Sir Godfrey William, Kt., CBE, DSC, RN

†Style, Sir William Frederick, Bt. (1627)

Sugden, Sir Arthur, Kt.

Sullivan, *Hon.* Sir Jeremy Mirth, Kt.

Sullivan, Sir Richard Arthur, Bt. (1804)

Sumner, *Hon.* Sir Christopher John, Kt.

Sutherland, Sir John Brewer, Bt. (1921)

Sutherland, Sir Maurice, Kt.

Sutherland, *Prof.* Sir Stewart Ross, Kt., FBA

Sutherland, Sir William George MacKenzie, Kt.

Suttie, Sir James Edward Grant-, Bt. (S. 1702)

Sutton, Sir Frederick Walter, Kt., OBE

Sutton, *Air Marshal* Sir John Matthias Dobson, KCB

Sutton, Sir Richard Lexington, Bt. (1772)

Swaffield, Sir James Chesebrough, Kt., CBE, RD

Swaine, Sir John Joseph, Kt., CBE

Swan, Sir Conrad Marshall John Fisher, KCVO, Ph.D.

Swan, Sir John William David, KBE

Swann, Sir Michael Christopher, Bt., TD (1906)

Swanwick, Sir Graham Russell, Kt., MBE

Swartz, *Hon.* Sir Reginald William Colin, KBE, ED

Sweetnam, Sir (David) Rodney, KCVO, CBE, FRCS

Swinburn, *Lt.-Gen.* Sir Richard Hull, KCB

Swinson, Sir John Henry Alan, Kt., OBE

Swinton, *Maj.-Gen.* Sir John, KCVO, OBE

Swire, Sir Adrian Christopher, Kt.

Swire, Sir John Anthony, Kt., CBE

Swynnerton, Sir Roger John Massy, Kt., CMG, OBE, MC

Sykes, Sir Francis John Badcock, Bt. (1781)

Sykes, Sir Hugh Ridley, Kt.

Sykes, Sir John Charles Anthony le Gallais, Bt. (1921)

Sykes, *Prof.* Sir (Malcolm) Keith, Kt.

Sykes, Sir Richard, Kt.

Sykes, Sir Tatton Christopher Mark, Bt. (1783)

Symington, *Prof.* Sir Thomas, Kt., MD, FRSE

Symons, *Vice-Adm.* Sir Patrick Jeremy, KBE

Synge, Sir Robert Carson, Bt. (1801)

Tait, *Adm.* Sir (Allan) Gordon, KCB, DSC

Talbot, *Hon.* Sir Hilary Gwynne, Kt.

Talboys, *Rt. Hon.* Sir Brian Edward, CH, KCB

Tancred, Sir Henry Lawson-, Bt. (1662)

Tangaroa, *Hon.* Sir Tangoroa, Kt., MBE

Tange, Sir Arthur Harold, Kt., CBE

Tapsell, Sir Peter Hannay Bailey, Kt., MP

Tate, Sir (Henry) Saxon, Bt. (1898)

Tavaiqia, *Ratu* Sir Josaia, KBE

Tavare, Sir John, Kt., CBE

Taylor, *Lt.-Gen.* Sir Allan Macnab, KBE, MC

Taylor, Sir (Arthur) Godfrey, Kt.

Taylor, Sir Cyril Julian Hebden, Kt.

Taylor, Sir Edward Macmillan (Teddy), Kt., MP

Taylor, *Rt. Revd* John Bernard, KCVO

Taylor, Sir John Lang, KCMG

Taylor, Sir Nicholas Richard Stuart, Bt. (1917)

Taylor, *Prof.* Sir William, Kt., CBE

Teagle, *Vice-Adm.* Sir Somerford Francis, KBE

Tebbit, Sir Donald Claude, GCMG

Telford, Sir Robert, Kt., CBE, FREng.

Temple, Sir Rawden John Afamado, Kt., CBE, QC

Temple, *Maj.* Sir Richard Anthony Purbeck, Bt., MC (1876)

Templeton, Sir John Marks, Kt.

Tenison, Sir Richard Hanbury-, KCVO

Tennant, Sir Anthony John, Kt.

Tennant, *Capt.* Sir Iain Mark, KT

Teo, Sir Fiatau Penitala, GCMG, GCVO, ISO, MBE

Terry, *Air Marshal* Sir Colin George, KBE, CB

Terry, Sir Michael Edward Stanley Imbert-, Kt. (1917)

Terry, *Air Chief Marshal* Sir Peter David George, GCB, AFC

Tett, Sir Hugh Charles, Kt.

Thatcher, Sir Denis, Bt., MBE, TD (1990)

Thesiger, Sir Wilfred Patrick, KBE, DSO

Thomas, Sir Derek Morison David, KCMG

Thomas, Sir Frederick William, Kt.

Thomas, Sir (Godfrey) Michael (David), Bt. (1694)

Thomas, Sir Jeremy Cashel, KCMG

Thomas, Sir (John) Alan, Kt.

Thomas, Sir John Maldwyn, Kt.

Thomas, *Prof.* Sir John Meurig, Kt., FRS

Thomas, Sir Keith Vivian, Kt.

Thomas, Sir Quentin Jeremy, Kt., CB

Thomas, Sir Robert Evan, Kt.

Thomas, *Hon.* Sir Roger John Laugharne, Kt.

Thomas, *Hon.* Sir Swinton Barclay, Kt.

Thomas, Sir William James Cooper, Bt., TD (1919)

Thomas, Sir (William) Michael (Marsh), Bt. (1918)

Thompson, Sir Christopher Peile, Bt. (1890)

Thompson, Sir Clive Malcolm, Kt.

Thompson, Sir Donald, Kt.

Thompson, Sir Gilbert Williamson, Kt., OBE

Thompson, *Surgeon Vice-Adm.* Sir Godfrey James Milton-, KBE

Thompson, Sir (Humphrey) Simon Meysey-, Bt. (1874)

Thompson, *Prof.* Sir Michael Warwick, Kt., D.SC

†Thompson, Sir Nicholas Annesley Marler, Bt. (1963)

Thompson, Sir Paul Anthony, Bt. (1963)

Thompson, Sir Peter Anthony, Kt.

Thompson, Sir (Thomas) Lionel Tennyson, Bt. (1806)

Thomson, Sir Adam, Kt., CBE

Thomson, Sir (Frederick Douglas) David, Bt. (1929)

Thomson, Sir John Adam, GCMG

Thomson, Sir John (Ian) Sutherland, KBE, CMG

Thomson, Sir Mark Wilfrid Home, Bt. (1925)

Thomson, Sir Thomas James, Kt., CBE, FRCP

Thorn, Sir John Samuel, Kt., OBE

Thorne, *Maj.-Gen.* Sir David Calthrop, KBE, CVO

Thorne, Sir Neil Gordon, Kt., OBE, TD

Thorne, Sir Peter Francis, KCVO, CBE

Thornton, Sir (George) Malcolm, Kt.

Thornton, *Lt.-Gen.* Sir Leonard Whitmore, KCB, CBE

Thornton, Sir Peter Eustace, KCB

Thornton, Sir Richard Eustace, KCVO, OBE

Thorold, Sir (Anthony) Oliver, Bt. (1642)

Thorpe, *Hon.* Sir Mathew Alexander, Kt.

Thouron, Sir John Rupert Hunt, KBE

Thwaites, Sir Bryan, Kt., ph.D.

Tibbits, *Capt.* Sir David Stanley, Kt., DSC

Tickell, Sir Crispin Charles Cervantes, GCMG, KCVO

Tidbury, Sir Charles Henderson, Kt.

Tikaram, Sir Moti, KBE

Tilt, Sir Robin Richard, Kt.

Tims, Sir Michael David, KCVO

Tindle, Sir Ray Stanley, Kt., CBE

Tippet, *Vice-Adm.* Sir Anthony Sanders, KCB

†Tipping, Sir David Gwynne Evans-, Bt. (1913)

Tirvengadum, Sir Harry Krishnan, Kt.

Titman, Sir John Edward Powis, KCVO

Tod, *Air Marshal* Sir John Hunter Hunter-, KBE, CB

Tod, *Vice-Adm.* Sir Jonathan James Richard, KCB, CBE

Todd, *Prof.* Sir David, Kt., CBE

Todd, Sir Ian Pelham, KBE, FRCS

Todd, *Hon.* Sir (Reginald Stephen) Garfield, Kt.

Tollemache, Sir Lyonel Humphry John, Bt. (1793)

Tololo, Sir Alkan, KBE

Tomkins, Sir Edward Emile, GCMG, CVO

Tomkys, Sir (William) Roger, KCMG

Tomlinson, *Prof.* Sir Bernard Evans, Kt., CBE

Tooley, Sir John, Kt.

Tooth, Sir (Hugh) John Lucas-, Bt. (1920)

ToRobert, Sir Henry Thomas, KBE

Tory, Sir Geofroy William, KCMG

Touche, Sir Anthony George, Bt. (1920)

Touche, Sir Rodney Gordon, Bt. (1962)

Toulson, *Hon.* Sir Roger Grenfell, Kt.

Tovey, Sir Brian John Maynard, KCMG

ToVue, Sir Ronald, Kt., OBE

Towneley, Sir Simon Peter Edmund Cosmo William, KCVO

Townsend, Sir Cyril David, Kt.

Traill, Sir Alan Towers, GBE

Trant, *Gen.* Sir Richard Brooking, KCB

Travers, Sir Thomas à'Beckett, Kt.

Treacher, *Adm.* Sir John Devereux, KCB

Trehane, Sir (Walter) Richard, Kt.

Treitel, *Prof.* Sir Guenter Heinz, Kt., FBA, QC

Warner, *Prof.* Sir Frederick Edward, Kt., FRS, FREng.

Warner, Sir Gerald Chierici, KCMG

Warner, *Hon.* Sir Jean-Pierre Frank Eugene, Kt.

Warren, Sir (Frederick) Miles, KBE

Warren, Sir Kenneth Robin, Kt.

†Warren, Sir Michael Blackley, Bt. (1784)

Wass, Sir Douglas William Gretton, GCB

Waterhouse, *Hon.* Sir Ronald Gough, Kt.

Waterlow, Sir Christopher Rupert, Bt. (1873)

Waterlow, Sir (James) Gerard, Bt. (1930)

Waters, *Gen.* Sir (Charles) John, GCB, CBE

Waters, Sir (Thomas) Neil (Morris), Kt.

Wates, Sir Christopher Stephen, Kt.

Watkins, *Rt. Hon.* Sir Tasker, VC, GBE

†Watson, Sir Andrew Michael Milne-, Bt. (1937)

Watson, Sir Bruce Dunstan, Kt.

Watson, *Prof.* Sir David John, Kt., PH.D.

Watson, Sir (James) Andrew, Bt. (1866)

Watson, Sir John Forbes Inglefield-, Bt. (1895)

Watson, *Vice-Adm.* Sir Philip Alexander, KBE, LVO

Watson, Sir Ronald Matthew, Kt., CBE

Watt, *Surgeon Vice-Adm.* Sir James, KBE, FRCS

Watt, Sir James Harvie-, Bt. (1945)

Watts, Sir Arthur Desmond, KCMG

Watts, *Lt.-Gen.* Sir John Peter Barry Condliffe, KBE, CB, MC

Wauchope, Sir Roger (Hamilton) Don-, Bt. (S. 1667)

Weatherall, *Prof.* Sir David John, Kt., FRS

Weatherall, *Vice-Adm.* Sir James Lamb, KBE

Weatherstone, Sir Dennis, KBE

Weaver, Sir Tobias Rushton, Kt., CB

Webb, Sir Thomas Langley, Kt.

Webster, *Very Revd* Alan Brunskill, KCVO

Webster, *Vice-Adm.* Sir John Morrison, KCB

Webster, *Hon.* Sir Peter Edlin, Kt.

Wedderburn, Sir Andrew John Alexander Ogilvy-, Bt. (1803)

Wedgwood, Sir (Hugo) Martin, Bt. (1942)

Weekes, Sir Everton DeCourcey, KCMG, OBE

Weinberg, Sir Mark Aubrey, Kt.

Weir, Sir Michael Scott, KCMG

Weir, Sir Roderick Bignell, Kt.

Welby, Sir (Richard) Bruno Gregory, Bt. (1801)

Welch, Sir John Kemp-, Kt.

Welch, Sir John Reader, Bt. (1957)

Weldon, Sir Anthony William, Bt. (I. 1723)

Weller, Sir Arthur Burton, Kt., CBE

Wellings, Sir Jack Alfred, Kt., CBE

†Wells, Sir Christopher Charles, Bt. (1944)

Wells, Sir John Julius, Kt.

Wells, Sir William Henry Weston, Kt., FRICS

Westbrook, Sir Neil Gowanloch, Kt., CBE

Westerman, Sir (Wilfred) Alan, Kt., CBE

Weston, Sir Michael Charles Swift, KCMG, CVO

Weston, Sir (Philip) John, KCMG

Whalen, Sir Geoffrey Henry, Kt., CBE

Wheeler, Sir Harry Anthony, Kt., OBE

Wheeler, *Air Chief Marshal* Sir (Henry) Neil (George), GCB, CBE, DSO, DFC, AFC

Wheeler, *Rt. Hon.* Sir John Daniel, Kt.

Wheeler, Sir John Hieron, Bt. (1920)

Wheeler, *Gen.* Sir Roger Neil, GCB, CBE

Wheler, Sir Edward Woodford, Bt. (1660)

Whent, Sir Gerald Arthur, Kt., CBE

Whishaw, Sir Charles Percival Law, Kt.

Whitaker, Sir John James Ingham (Jack), Bt. (1936)

White, Sir Christopher Robert Meadows, Bt. (1937)

White, *Hon.* Sir Christopher Stuart Stuart-, Kt.

White, Sir David Harry, Kt.

White, Sir Frank John, Kt.

White, Sir George Stanley James, Bt. (1904)

White, *Wg Cdr.* Sir Henry Arthur Dalrymple-, Bt., DFC (1926)

White, *Adm.* Sir Hugo Moresby, GCB, CBE

White, *Hon.* Sir John Charles, Kt., MBE

White, Sir John Woolmer, Bt. (1922)

White, Sir Lynton Stuart, Kt., MBE, TD

White, Sir Nicholas Peter Archibald, Bt. (1802)

White, *Adm.* Sir Peter, GBE

Whitehead, Sir John Stainton, GCMG, CVO

Whitehead, Sir Rowland John Rathbone, Bt. (1889)

Whiteley, Sir Hugo Baldwin Huntington-, Bt. (1918)

Whiteley, *Gen.* Sir Peter John Frederick, GCB, OBE, RM

Whitfield, Sir William, Kt., CBE

Whitford, *Hon.* Sir John Norman Keates, Kt.

Whitmore, Sir Clive Anthony, GCB, CVO

Whitmore, Sir John Henry Douglas, Bt. (1954)

Whitney, Sir Raymond William, Kt., OBE, MP

Whittome, Sir (Leslie) Alan, Kt.

Wickerson, Sir John Michael, Kt.

Wicks, Sir Nigel Leonard, GCB, CVO, CBE

†Wigan, Sir Michael Iain, Bt. (1898)

Wiggin, Sir Alfred William (Jerry), Kt., TD

†Wiggin, Sir Charles Rupert John, Bt. (1892)

Wigram, *Revd Canon* Sir Clifford Woolmore, Bt. (1805)

Wilbraham, Sir Richard Baker, Bt. (1776)

Wilford, Sir (Kenneth) Michael, GCMG

Wilkes, *Gen.* Sir Michael John, KCB, CBE

Wilkins, Sir Graham John, Kt.

Wilkinson, Sir (David) Graham (Brook) Bt. (1941)

Wilkinson, *Prof.* Sir Denys Haigh, Kt., FRS

Wilkinson, Sir Peter Allix, KCMG, DSO, OBE

Wilkinson, Sir Philip William, Kt.

Willcocks, Sir David Valentine, Kt., CBE, MC

Williams, Sir Alastair Edgcumbe James Dudley-, Bt. (1964)

Williams, Sir Alwyn, Kt., PH.D., FRS, FRSE

Williams, Sir Arthur Dennis Pitt, Kt.

Williams, Sir (Arthur) Gareth Ludovic Emrys Rhys, Bt. (1918)

Williams, *Prof.* Sir Bernard Arthur Owen, Kt., FBA

Williams, *Prof.* Sir Bruce Rodda, KBE

Williams, Sir Daniel Charles, GCMG, QC

Williams, *Adm.* Sir David, GCB

Williams, *Prof.* Sir David Glyndwr Tudor, Kt.

Williams, Sir David Innes, Kt.

Williams, Sir David Reeve, Kt., CBE

Williams, *Hon.* Sir Denys Ambrose, KCMG

Williams, Sir Donald Mark, Bt. (1866)

Williams, *Prof.* Sir (Edward) Dillwyn, Kt., FRCP

Williams, *Hon.* Sir Edward Stratten, KCMG, KBE

Williams, Sir Francis Owen Garbett, Kt., CBE

Williams, *Prof.* Sir Glanmor, Kt., CBE, FBA

Williams, Sir Henry Sydney, Kt., OBE

Williams, Sir (John) Kyffin, Kt., OBE, DL, RA

Williams, Sir John Robert, KCMG

Williams, Sir (Lawrence) Hugh, Bt. (1798)

Williams, Sir Leonard, KBE, CB

Williams, Sir Osmond, Bt., MC (1909)

Williams, Sir Peter Michael, Kt.

Williams, *Prof.* Sir Robert Evan Owen, Kt., MD, FRCP

Williams, Sir (Robert) Philip Nathaniel, Bt. (1915)

Williams, Sir Robin Philip, Bt. (1953)

Williams, Sir (William) Maxwell (Harries), Kt.

Williamson, *Marshal of the Royal Air Force* Sir Keith Alec, GCB, AFC

Williamson, Sir (Nicholas Frederick) Hedworth, Bt. (1642)

Willink, Sir Charles William, Bt. (1957)

Willis, *Hon.* Sir Eric Archibald, KBE, CMG

Willis, *Vice-Adm.* Sir (Guido) James, KBE

Willis, *Air Chief Marshal* Sir John Frederick, GBE, KCB

Willison, *Lt.-Gen.* Sir David John, KCB, OBE, MC

Willison, Sir John Alexander, Kt., OBE

Wills, Sir David James Vernon, Bt. (1923)

Wills, Sir David Seton, Bt. (1904)

Wills, Sir (Hugh) David Hamilton, Kt., CBE, TD

Wilmot, Sir Henry Robert, Bt. (1759)

Wilmot, Sir Michael John Assheton Eardley-, Bt. (1821)

Wilsey, *Gen.* Sir John Finlay Willasey, GCB, CBE

Wilson, *Lt.-Gen.* Sir (Alexander) James, KBE, MC

Wilson, Sir Anthony, Kt.

Wilson, *Vice-Adm.* Sir Barry Nigel, KCB

Wilson, *Lt.-Col.* Sir Blair Aubyn Stewart-, KCVO

Wilson, Sir Charles Haynes, Kt.

Wilson, *Prof.* Sir Colin Alexander St John, Kt., RA, FRIBA

Wilson, Sir David, Bt. (1920)

Wilson, Sir David Mackenzie, Kt.

Wilson, Sir Geoffrey Masterman, KCB, CMG

Wilson, Sir James William Douglas, Bt. (1906)

Wilson, Sir John Foster, Kt., CBE

Wilson, *Brig.* Sir Mathew John Anthony, Bt., OBE, MC (1874)

Wilson, *Hon.* Sir Nicholas Allan Roy, Kt.

Wilson, Sir Patrick Michael Ernest David McNair-, Kt.

Wilson, Sir Richard Thomas James, KCB

Wilson, Sir Robert, Kt., CBE

Wilson, Sir Robert Donald, KBE

Wilson, *Rt. Revd* Roger Plumpton, KCVO, DD

Wilson, *Air Chief Marshal* Sir (Ronald) Andrew (Fellowes), KCB, AFC

Wilson, *Hon.* Sir Ronald Darling, KBE, CMG

Wilton, Sir (Arthur) John, KCMG, KCVO, MC

Wingate, *Capt.* Sir Miles Buckley, KCVO

Winkley, Sir David Ross, Kt.

Winnington, Sir Francis Salwey William, Bt. (1755)

Winskill, *Air Cdre* Sir Archibald Little, KCVO, CBE, DFC

Winterbottom, Sir Walter, Kt., CBE

Wiseman, Sir John William, Bt. (1628)

Wolfendale, *Prof.* Sir Arnold Whittaker, Kt., FRS

Wolfson, Sir Brian Gordon, Kt.

Wolseley, Sir Charles Garnet Richard Mark, Bt. (1628)

†Wolseley, Sir James Douglas, Bt. (I. 1745)

Wolstenholme, Sir Gordon Ethelbert Ward, Kt., OBE

Wombwell, Sir George Philip Frederick, Bt. (1778)

Womersley, Sir Peter John Walter, Bt. (1945)

Woo, Sir Leo Joseph, Kt.

Woo, Sir Po-Shing, Kt.

Wood, Sir Alan Marshall Muir, Kt., FRS, FREng.

Wood, Sir Andrew Marley, KCMG

Wood, Sir Anthony John Page, Bt. (1837)

Wood, Sir David Basil Hill-, Bt. (1921)

Wood, Sir Frederick Ambrose Stuart, Kt.

Wood, Sir Ian Clark, Kt., CBE

Wood, *Prof.* Sir John Crossley, Kt., CBE

Wood, *Hon.* Sir John Kember, Kt., MC

Wood, Sir Martin Francis, Kt., OBE

Wood, Sir Russell Dillon, KCVO, VRD

Wood, Sir William Alan, KCVO, CB

Woodard, *Rear Adm.* Sir Robert Nathaniel, KCVO

Woodcock, Sir John, Kt., CBE, QPM

Woodfield, Sir Philip John, KCB, CBE

Woodhead, *Vice-Adm.* Sir (Anthony) Peter, KCB

Woodhouse, *Rt. Hon.* Sir (Arthur) Owen, KBE, DSC

Wooding, Sir Norman Samuel, Kt., CBE

Woodroffe, *Most Revd* George Cuthbert Manning, KBE

Woodroofe, Sir Ernest George, Kt., ph.D.

Woodruff, *Prof.* Sir Michael Francis Addison, Kt., D.SC., FRS, FRCS

Woods, Sir Colin Philip Joseph, KCVO, CBE

Woodward, *Hon.* Sir (Albert) Edward, Kt., OBE

Woodward, *Adm.* Sir John Forster, GBE, KCB

Worsley, *Gen.* Sir Richard Edward, GCB, OBE

Worsley, Sir (William) Marcus (John), Bt. (1838)

Worsthorne, Sir Peregrine Gerard, Kt.

Wratten, *Air Chief Marshal* Sir William John, GBE, CB, AFC

Wraxall, Sir Charles Frederick Lascelles, Bt. (1813)

Wrey, Sir George Richard Bourchier, Bt. (1628)

Wrigglesworth, Sir Ian William, Kt.

Wright, Sir Allan Frederick, KBE

Wright, Sir David John, KCMG, LVO

Wright, Sir Denis Arthur Hepworth, GCMG

Wright, Sir Edward Maitland, Kt., D.Phil., LL.D, D.SC., FRSE

Wright, *Hon.* Sir (John) Michael, Kt.

Wright, Sir (John) Oliver, GCMG, GCVO, DSC

Wright, Sir Paul Hervé Giraud, KCMG, OBE

Wright, Sir Peter Robert, Kt., CBE

Wright, Sir Richard Michael Cory-, Bt. (1903)

Wrightson, Sir Charles Mark Garmondsway, Bt. (1900)

Wrigley, *Prof.* Sir Edward Anthony (Sir Tony), Kt., ph.D., PBA

Wu, Sir Gordon Ying Sheung, KCMG

Wynn, Sir David Watkin Williams-, Bt. (1688)

Yacoub, *Prof.* Sir Magdi Habib, Kt., FRCS

Yaki, Sir Roy, KBE

Yang, *Hon.* Sir Ti Liang, Kt.

Yapp, Sir Stanley Graham, Kt.

Yardley, Sir David Charles Miller, Kt., LL D

Yarranton, Sir Peter George, Kt.

Yarrow, Sir Eric Grant, Bt., MBE (1916)

Yellowlees, Sir Henry, KCB

Yocklunn, Sir John (Soong Chung), KCVO

Yoo Foo, Sir (François) Henri, Kt.

Youens, Sir Peter William, Kt., CMG, OBE

Young, Sir Brian Walter Mark, Kt.

Young, Sir Colville Norbert, GCMG, MBE

Young, *Lt.-Gen.* Sir David Tod, KBE, CB, DFC

Young, Sir Dennis Charles, KCMG

Young, *Rt. Hon.* Sir George Samuel Knatchbull, Bt., MP (1813)

Young, *Hon.* Sir Harold William, KCMG

Young, Sir John Kenyon Roe, Bt. (1821)

Young, *Hon.* Sir John McIntosh, KCMG

Young, Sir John Robertson, KCMG

Young, Sir Leslie Clarence, Kt., CBE

Young, Sir Richard Dilworth, Kt.

Young, Sir Robert Christopher Mackworth-, GCVO

Young, Sir Roger William, Kt.

Young, Sir Stephen Stewart Templeton, Bt. (1945)

Young, Sir William Neil, Bt. (1769)

Younger, *Maj.-Gen.* Sir John William, Bt., CBE (1911)

Yuwi, Sir Matiabe, KBE

Zeeman, *Prof.* Sir (Erik) Christopher, Kt., FRS

Zissman, Sir Bernard Philip, Kt.

Zochonis, Sir John Basil, Kt.

Zoleveke, Sir Gideon Pitabose, KBE

Zunz, Sir Gerhard Jacob (Jack), Kt., FREng.

Zurenuoc, Sir Zibang, KBE

Dames Grand Cross and Dames Commanders

Style, 'Dame' before forename and surname, followed by appropriate post-nominal initials. Where such an award is made to a lady already in enjoyment of a higher title, the appropriate initials follow her name
Husband, Untitled
For forms of address, *see* page 135

Dame Grand Cross and Dame Commander are the higher classes for women of the Order of the Bath, the Order of St Michael and St George, the Royal Victorian Order, and the Order of the British Empire. Dames Grand Cross rank after the wives of Baronets and before the wives of Knights Grand Cross. Dames Commanders rank after the wives of Knights Grand Cross and before the wives of Knights Commanders.

Honorary Dames Commanders may be conferred on women who are citizens of countries of which The Queen is not head of state.

LIST OF DAMES
Revised to 31 August 1999

Women peers in their own right and life peers are not included in this list. Female members of the royal family are not included in this list; details of the orders they hold are given on pages 117–8

If a dame has a double barrelled or hyphenated surname, she is listed under the final element of the name
A full entry in italic type indicates that the recipient of an honour died during the year in which the honour was conferred. The name is included for the purposes of record

Abaijah, Dame Josephine, DBE
Abel Smith, Lady, DCVO
Abergavenny, The Marchioness of, DCVO
Airlie, The Countess of, DCVO
Albemarle, The Countess of, DBE
Anderson, *Brig. Hon.* Dame Mary Mackenzie (Mrs Pihl), DBE
Anglesey, The Marchioness of, DBE
Anson, Lady (Elizabeth Audrey), DBE
Anstee, Dame Margaret Joan, DCMG
Arden, *Hon.* Dame Mary Howarth (Mrs Mance), DBE
Baker, Dame Janet Abbott (Mrs Shelley), CH, DBE
Ballin, Dame Reubina Ann, DBE
Barnes, Dame (Alice) Josephine (Mary Taylor), DBE, FRCP, FRCS
Barrow, Dame Jocelyn Anita (Mrs Downer), DBE
Barstow, Dame Josephine Clare (Mrs Anderson), DBE
Basset, Lady Elizabeth, DCVO
Bean, Dame Majorie Louise, DBE
Beaurepaire, Dame Beryl Edith, DBE
Beer, *Prof.* Dame Gillian Patricia Kempster, DBE, FBA
Bergquist, *Prof.* Dame Patricia Rose, DBE
Berry, Dame Alice Miriam, DBE
Blaize, Dame Venetia Ursula, DBE
Blaxland, Dame Helen Frances, DBE
Booth, *Hon.* Dame Margaret Myfanwy Wood, DBE
Bottomley, Dame Bessie Ellen, DBE
Bowman, Dame (Mary) Elaine Kellett-, DBE
Bowtell, Dame Ann Elizabeth, DCB
Boyd, Dame Vivienne Myra, DBE

Bracewell, *Hon.* Dame Joyanne Winifred (Mrs Copeland), DBE
Brain, Dame Margaret Anne (Mrs Wheeler), DBE
Brazill, Dame Josephine (Sister Mary Philippa), DBE
Bridges, Dame Mary Patricia, DBE
Browne, Lady Moyra Blanche Madeleine, DBE
Bryans, Dame Anne Margaret, DBE
Buttfield, Dame Nancy Eileen, DBE
Byatt, Dame Antonia Susan, DBE, FRSL
Bynoe, Dame Hilda Louisa, DBE
Caldicott, Dame Fiona, DBE, FRCP, FRCPsych.
Cartland, Dame Barbara Hamilton, DBE
Cartwright, Dame Silvia Rose, DBE
Casey, Dame Stella Katherine, DBE
Charles, Dame (Mary) Eugenia, DBE
Chesterton, Dame Elizabeth Ursula, DBE
Clark, *Prof.* Dame (Margaret) June, DBE, Ph.D.
Collins, Dame Diana Clavering, DBE
Clay, Dame Marie Mildred, DBE
Clayton, Dame Barbara Evelyn (Mrs Klyne), DBE
Cleland, Dame Rachel, DBE
Coll, Dame Elizabeth Anne Loosemore Esteve-, DBE
Collarbone, Dame Patricia, DBE
Corsar, The Hon. Dame Mary Drummond, DBE
Daws, Dame Joyce Margaretta, DBE
Dell, Dame Miriam Patricia, DBE
Dench, Dame Judith Olivia (Mrs Williams), DBE
de Valois, Dame Ninette, OM, CH, DBE
Devonshire, The Duchess of, DCVO
Digby, Lady, DBE
Donaldson, Dame (Dorothy) Mary (Lady Donaldson of Lymington), GBE
Dugdale, Kathryn, Lady, DCVO
Dumont, Dame Ivy Leona, DCMG
Dyche, Dame Rachael Mary, DBE
Ebsworth, *Hon.* Dame Ann Marian, DBE
Engel, Dame Pauline Frances (Sister Pauline Engel), DBE
Evans, Dame Lois Marie Browne-, DBE

Evison, Dame Helen June Patricia, DBE
Fenner, Dame Peggy Edith, DBE
Fielding, Dame Pauline, DBE
Fitton, Dame Doris Alice (Mrs Mason), DBE
Fort, Dame Maeve Geraldine, DCMG
Fraser, Dame Dorothy Rita, DBE
Friend, Dame Phyllis Muriel, DBE
Fritchie, Dame Irene Tordoff (Dame Rennie Fritchie), DBE
Frost, Dame Phyllis Irene, DBE
Fry, Dame Margaret Louise, DBE
Gallagher, Dame Monica Josephine, DBE
Gardiner, Dame Helen Louisa, DBE, MVO
Giles, *Air Comdt.* Dame Pauline (Mrs Parsons), DBE, RRC
Goodman, Dame Barbara, DBE
Gordon, Dame Minita Elmira, GCMG, GCVO
Gow, Dame Jane Elizabeth (Mrs Whiteley), DBE
Grafton, The Duchess of, GCVO
Grant, Dame Mavis, DBE
Green, Dame Mary Georgina, DBE
Grey, Dame Beryl Elizabeth (Mrs Svenson), DBE
Grimthorpe, The Lady, DCVO
Guilfoyle, Dame Margaret Georgina Constance, DBE
Guthardt, *Revd Dr* Dame Phyllis Myra, DBE
Haig, Dame Mary Alison Glen-, DBE
Hale, *Hon.* Dame Brenda Marjorie (Mrs Farrand), DBE
Hallett, Dame Heather Carol, DBE, QC
Harper, Dame Elizabeth Margaret Way, DBE
Heilbron, *Hon.* Dame Rose, DBE
Henderson, Dame Louise Etiennette Sidonie, DBE
Herbison, Dame Jean Marjory, DBE, CMG
Hercus, *Hon.* Dame (Margaret) Ann, DCMG
Hetet, Dame Rangimarie, DBE
Higgins, *Prof.* Dame Rosalyn, DBE, QC
Hill, *Air Cdre* Dame Felicity Barbara, DBE
Hiller, Dame Wendy (Mrs Gow), DBE
Hine, Dame Deirdre Joan, DBE, FRCP

Decorations and Medals

PRINCIPAL DECORATIONS AND MEDALS
In order of precedence

Victoria Cross (VC), 1856 (*see* page 208)
George Cross (GC), 1940 (*see* pages 208–9)
British Orders of Knighthood, etc.
Baronet's Badge
Knight Bachelor's Badge

Decorations
Conspicuous Gallantry Cross (CGC), 1995
Royal Red Cross Class I (RRC), 1883
Distinguished Service Cross (DSC), 1914. For all ranks for actions at sea
Military Cross (MC), December 1914. For all ranks for actions on land
Distinguished Flying Cross (DFC), 1918. For all ranks for acts of gallantry when flying in active operations against the enemy
Air Force Cross (AFC), 1918. For all ranks for acts of courage when flying, although not in active operations against the enemy
Royal Red Cross Class II (ARRC)
Order of British India
Kaisar-i-Hind Medal
Order of St John

Medals for Gallantry and Distinguished Conduct
Union of South Africa Queen's Medal for Bravery, in Gold
Distinguished Conduct Medal (DCM), 1854
Conspicuous Gallantry Medal (CGM), 1874
Conspicuous Gallantry Medal (Flying)
George Medal (GM), 1940
Queen's Police Medal for Gallantry
Queen's Fire Service Medal for Gallantry
Royal West African Frontier Force Distinguished Conduct Medal
King's African Rifles Distinguished Conduct Medal
Indian Distinguished Service Medal
Union of South Africa Queen's Medal for Bravery, in Silver
Distinguished Service Medal (DSM), 1914
Military Medal (MM), 1916
Distinguished Flying Medal (DFM), 1918
Air Force Medal (AFM)
Constabulary Medal (Ireland)
Medal for Saving Life at Sea
Sea Gallantry Medal
Indian Order of Merit (Civil)
Indian Police Medal for Gallantry
Ceylon Police Medal for Gallantry
Sierra Leone Police Medal for Gallantry
Sierra Leone Fire Brigades Medal for Gallantry
Colonial Police Medal for Gallantry (CPM)
Queen's Gallantry Medal, 1974
Royal Victorian Medal (RVM), Gold, Silver and Bronze
British Empire Medal (BEM), (formerly the Medal of the Order of the British Empire, for Meritorious Service; also includes the Medal of the Order awarded before 29 December 1922)
Canada Medal
Queen's Police (QPM) and Queen's Fire Service Medals (QFSM) for Distinguished Service
Queen's Volunteer Reserves Medal
Queen's Medal for Chiefs

War Medals and Stars (in order of date)
Polar Medals (in order of date)
Police Medals for Valuable Service
Jubilee, Coronation and Durbar Medals
King George V, King George VI and Queen Elizabeth II Long and Faithful Service Medals

Efficiency and Long Service Decorations and Medals
Medal for Meritorious Service
Accumulated Campaign Service Medal
The Medal for Long Service and Good Conduct (Military)
Naval Long Service and Good Conduct Medal
Royal Marines Meritorious Service Medal
Royal Air Force Meritorious Service Medal
Royal Air Force Long Service and Good Conduct Medal
Medal for Long Service and Good Conduct (Ulster Defence Regiment)
Police Long Service and Good Conduct Medal
Fire Brigade Long Service and Good Conduct Medal
Colonial Police and Fire Brigades Long Service Medals
Colonial Prison Service Medal
Hong Kong Disciplined Services Medal
Army Emergency Reserve Decoration (ERD), 1952
Volunteer Officers' Decoration (VD)
Volunteer Long Service Medal
Volunteer Officers' Decoration for India and the Colonies
Volunteer Long Service Medal for India and the Colonies
Colonial Auxiliary Forces Officers' Decoration
Colonial Auxiliary Forces Long Service Medal
Medal for Good Shooting (Naval)
Militia Long Service Medal
Imperial Yeomanry Long Service Medal
Territorial Decoration (TD), 1908
Efficiency Decoration (ED)
Territorial Efficiency Medal
Efficiency Medal
Special Reserve Long Service and Good Conduct Medal
Decoration for Officers, Royal Navy Reserve (RD), 1910
Decoration for Officers, RNVR (VRD)
Royal Naval Reserve Long Service and Good Conduct Medal
RNVR Long Service and Good Conduct Medal
Royal Naval Auxiliary Sick Berth Reserve Long Service and Good Conduct Medal
Royal Fleet Reserve Long Service and Good Conduct Medal
Royal Naval Wireless Auxiliary Reserve Long Service and Good Conduct Medal
Air Efficiency Award (AE), 1942
Volunteer Reserves Service Medal
Ulster Defence Regiment Medal
Northern Ireland Home Service Medal
The Queen's Medal. For champion shots in the RN, RM, RNZN, Army, RAF
Cadet Forces Medal, 1950
Coastguard Auxiliary Service Long Service Medal (formerly Coast Life Saving Corps Long Service Medal)
Special Constabulary Long Service Medal
Royal Observer Corps Medal
Civil Defence Long Service Medal
Ambulance Service (Emergency Duties) Long Service and Good Conduct Medal
Rhodesia Medal
Royal Ulster Constabulary Service Medal
Service Medal of the Order of St John

Badge of the Order of the League of Mercy
Voluntary Medical Service Medal, 1932
Women's Voluntary Service Medal
Colonial Special Constabulary Medal

FOREIGN ORDERS, DECORATIONS AND MEDALS (IN ORDER OF DATE)

THE VICTORIA CROSS (1856)
FOR CONSPICUOUS BRAVERY

VC

Ribbon, Crimson, for all Services (until 1918 it was blue for the Royal Navy)

Instituted on 29 January 1856, the Victoria Cross was awarded retrospectively to 1854, the first being held by Lt. C. D. Lucas, RN, for bravery in the Baltic Sea on 21 June 1854 (gazetted 24 February 1857). The first 62 Crosses were presented by Queen Victoria in Hyde Park, London, on 26 June 1857.

The Victoria Cross is worn before all other decorations, on the left breast, and consists of a cross-pattée of bronze, one and a half inches in diameter, with the Royal Crown surmounted by a lion in the centre, and beneath there is the inscription *For Valour.* Holders of the VC receive a tax-free annuity of £1,300, irrespective of need or other conditions. In 1911, the right to receive the Cross was extended to Indian soldiers, and in 1920 to matrons, sisters and nurses, and the staff of the Nursing Services and other services pertaining to hospitals and nursing, and to civilians of either sex regularly or temporarily under the orders, direction or supervision of the naval, military, or air forces of the Crown.

SURVIVING RECIPIENTS OF THE VICTORIA CROSS
as at 31 August 1999
Agansing Rai, *Capt.,* MM (5th Royal Gurkha Rifles)
1944 *World War*
Annand, *Capt.* R. W. (Durham Light Infantry)
1940 *World War*
Bhan Bhagta Gurung, *Havildar* (2nd Gurkha Rifles)
1945 *World War*
Bhandari Ram, *Capt.* (10th Baluch Regiment)
1944 *World War*
Chapman, *Sgt.* E. T., BEM (Monmouthshire Regiment)
1945 *World War*
Cruickshank, *Flt. Lt.* J. A. (RAFVR)
1944 *World War*
Cutler, *Capt.* Sir Roden, AK, KCMG, KCVO, CBE (Australian Military Forces, 2/5th Field Artillery)
1941 *World War*
Fraser, *Lt.-Cdr.* I. E., DSC (RNR)
1945 *World War*
Gaje Ghale, *Capt.* (5th Royal Gurkha Rifles)
1943 *World War*
Ganju Lama, *Capt.,* MM (7th Gurkha Rifles)
1944 *World War*
Gardner, *Capt.* P. J., MC (Royal Tank Regiment)
1941 *World War*
Gould, *Lt.* T. W. (RN)
1942 *World War*

Jamieson, *Maj.* D. A., CVO (Royal Norfolk Regiment)
1944 *World War*
Kenna, *Pte.* E. (Australian Military Forces, 2/4th (NSW))
1945 *World War*
Kenneally, *Guardsman* J. P. (Irish Guards)
1943 *World War*
Lachhiman Gurung, *Havildar* (8th Gurkha Rifles)
1945 *World War*
Merritt, *Lt.-Col.* C. C. I., CD (South Saskatchewan Regiment)
1942 *World War*
Norton, *Capt.* G. R., MM (South African Forces, Kaffrarian Rifles)
1944 *World War*
Payne, *WO* K., DSC (USA) (Australian Army Training Team)
1969 *Vietnam*
Porteous, *Col.* P. A. (Royal Regiment of Artillery)
1942 *World War*
Rambahadur Limbu, *Capt.,* MVO (10th Princess Mary's Gurkha Rifles)
1965 *Sarawak*
Reid, *Flt. Lt.* W. (RAFVR)
1943 *World War*
Smith, *Sgt.* E. A., CD (Seaforth Highlanders of Canada)
1944 *World War*
Speakman-Pitts, *Sgt.* W. (Black Watch)
1951 *Korea*
Tulbahadur Pun, *Lt.* (6th Gurkha Rifles)
1944 *World War*
Umrao Singh, *Sub Major* (Royal Indian Artillery)
1944 *World War*
Watkins, *Maj. Rt. Hon.* Sir Tasker, GBE (Welch Regiment)
1944 *World War*
Wilson, *Lt.-Col.* E. C. T. (East Surrey Regiment)
1940 *World War*

THE GEORGE CROSS (1940)
FOR GALLANTRY

GC

Ribbon, Dark blue, threaded through a bar adorned with laurel leaves
Instituted 24 September 1940 (with amendments, 3 November 1942)

The George Cross is worn before all other decorations (except the VC) on the left breast (when worn by a woman it may be worn on the left shoulder from a ribbon of the same width and colour fashioned into a bow). It consists of a plain silver cross with four equal limbs, the cross having in the centre a circular medallion bearing a design showing St George and the Dragon. The inscription *For Gallantry* appears round the medallion and in the angle of each limb of the cross is the Royal cypher 'G VI' forming a circle concentric with the medallion. The reverse is plain and bears the name of the recipient and the date of the award. The cross is suspended by a ring from a bar adorned with laurel leaves on dark blue ribbon one and a half inches wide.

The cross is intended primarily for civilians; awards to the fighting services are confined to actions for which purely military honours are not normally granted. It is awarded only for acts of the greatest heroism or of the most conspicuous courage in circumstances of extreme danger. From 1 April 1965, holders of the Cross have received a tax-free annuity, which is now £1,300.

The royal warrant which ordained that the grant of the Empire Gallantry Medal should cease authorized holders of that medal to return it to the Central Chancery of the Orders of Knighthood and to receive in exchange the George Cross. A similar provision applied to posthumous awards of the Empire Gallantry Medal made after the outbreak of war in 1939. In October 1971 all surviving holders of the Albert Medal and the Edward Medal exchanged those decorations for the George Cross.

SURVIVING RECIPIENTS OF THE GEORGE CROSS
as at 31 August 1999

If the recipient originally received the Empire Gallantry Medal (EGM), the Albert Medal (AM) or the Edward Medal (EM), this is indicated by the initials in parenthesis.

Archer, *Col.* B. S. T., GC, OBE, ERD, 1941
Baker, J. T., GC (EM), 1929
Bamford, J., GC, 1952
Beaton, J., GC, CVO, 1974
Bridge, *Lt.-Cdr.* J., GC, GM and bar, 1944
Butson, *Lt.-Col.* A. R. C., GC, CD, MD (AM), 1948
Bywater, R. A. S., GC, GM, 1944
Errington, H., GC, 1941
Farrow, K., GC (AM), 1948
Flintoff, H. H., GC (EM), 1944
Gledhill, A. J., GC, 1967
Gregson, J. S., GC (AM), 1943
Hawkins, E., GC (AM), 1943
Johnson, *WO1* (*SSM*) B., GC, 1990
Kinne, D. G., GC, 1954
Lowe, A. R., GC (AM), 1949
Lynch, J., GC, BEM (AM), 1948
Malta, GC, 1942
Manwaring, T. G., GC (EM), 1949
Moore, R. V., GC, CBE, 1940
Moss, B., GC, 1940
Naughton, F., GC (EGM), 1937
Pearson, Miss J. D. M., GC (EGM), 1940
Pratt, M. K., GC, 1978
Purves, Mrs M., GC (AM), 1949
Raweng, Awang anak, GC, 1951
Riley, G., GC (AM), 1944
Rowlands, *Air Marshal* Sir John, GC, KBE, 1943
Sinclair, *Air Vice-Marshal* Sir Laurence, GC, KCB, CBE, DSO, 1941
Stevens, H. W., GC, 1958
Stronach, *Capt.* G. P., GC, 1943
Styles, *Lt.-Col.* S. G., GC, 1972
Walker, C., GC, 1972
Walker, C. H., GC (AM), 1942
Walton, E. W. K., GC (AM), DSO, 1948
Wilcox, C., GC (EM), 1949
Wiltshire, S. N., GC (EGM), 1930
Wooding, E. A., GC (AM), 1945

Chiefs of Clans and Names in Scotland

Only chiefs of whole Names or Clans are included, except certain special instances (marked *) who, though not chiefs of a whole name, were or are for some reason (e.g. the Macdonald forfeiture) independent. Under decision (*Campbell-Gray*, 1950) that a bearer of a 'double or triple-barrelled' surname cannot be held chief of a part of such, several others cannot be included in the list at present.

THE ROYAL HOUSE: HM The Queen

AGNEW: Sir Crispin Agnew of Lochnaw, Bt., QC, 6 Palmerston Road, Edinburgh EH9 ITN

ANSTRUTHER: Sir Ralph Anstruther of that Ilk, Bt., GCVO, MC, Balcaskie, Pittenweem, Fife KY10 2RD

ARBUTHNOTT: The Viscount of Arbuthnott, KT, CBE, DSC, Arbuthnott House, Laurencekirk, Kincardineshire AB30 IPA

BARCLAY: Peter C. Barclay of Towie Barclay and of that Ilk, 28A Gordon Place, London W8 4JE

BORTHWICK: The Lord Borthwick, Crookston, Heriot, Midlothian EH38 5YS

BOYD: The Lord Kilmarnock, 194 Regent's Park Road, London NW1 8XP

BOYLE: The Earl of Glasgow, Kelburn, Fairlie, Ayrshire KA29 OBE

BRODIE: Ninian Brodie of Brodie, Brodie Castle, Forres, Morayshire IV36 OTE

BRUCE: The Earl of Elgin and Kincardine, KT, Broomhall, Dunfermline, Fife KY11 3DU

BUCHAN: David S. Buchan of Auchmacoy, Auchmacoy House, Ellon, Aberdeenshire

BURNETT: J. C. A. Burnett of Leys, Crathes Castle, Banchory, Kincardineshire

CAMERON: Sir Donald Cameron of Lochiel, KT, CVO, TD, Achnacarry, Spean Bridge, Inverness-shire

CAMPBELL: The Duke of Argyll, Inveraray, Argyll PA32 8XF

CARMICHAEL: Richard J. Carmichael of Carmichael, Carmichael, Thankerton, Biggar, Lanarkshire

CARNEGIE: The Duke of Fife, Elsick House, Stonehaven, Kincardineshire AB3 2NT

CATHCART: vacant

CHARTERIS: The Earl of Wemyss and March, KT, Gosford House, Longniddry, East Lothian EH32 OPX

CLAN CHATTAN: M. K. Mackintosh of Clan Chattan, Maxwell Park, Gwelo, Zimbabwe

CHISHOLM: Hamish Chisholm of Chisholm (*The Chisholm*), Elmpine, Beck Row, Bury St Edmunds, Suffolk

COCHRANE: The Earl of Dundonald, Lochnell Castle, Ledaig, Argyllshire

COLQUHOUN: Sir Ivar Colquhoun of Luss, Bt., Camstraddan, Luss, Dunbartonshire G83 8NX

CRANSTOUN: David A. S. Cranstoun of that Ilk, Corehouse, Lanark

CRICHTON: vacant

CUMMING: Sir William Cumming of Altyre, Bt., Altyre, Forres, Moray

DARROCH: Capt. Duncan Darroch of Gourock, The Red House, Branksome Park Road, Camberley, Surrey

DAVIDSON: Alister G. Davidson of Davidston, 21 Winscombe Street, Takapuna, Auckland, New Zealand

DEWAR: Kenneth Dewar of that Ilk and Vogrie, The Dower House, Grayshott, nr Hindhead, Surrey

DRUMMOND: The Earl of Perth, PC, Stobhall, Perth PH2 6DR

DUNBAR: Sir James Dunbar of Mochrum, Bt., 211 Gardenville Drive, Yorktown, VA 23693, USA

DUNDAS: David D. Dundas of Dundas, 8 Derna Road, Kenwyn 7700, South Africa

DURIE: Andrew Durie of Durie, Finnich Malise, Croftamie, Stirlingshire G63 OHA

ELIOTT: Mrs Margaret Eliott of Redheugh, Redheugh, Newcastleton, Roxburghshire

ERSKINE: The Earl of Mar and Kellie, Erskine House, Kirk Wynd, Alloa, Clackmannan FK10 4JF

FARQUHARSON: Capt. A. Farquharson of Invercauld, MC, Invercauld, Braemar, Aberdeenshire AB35 5TT

FERGUSSON: Sir Charles Fergusson of Kilkerran, Bt., Kilkerran, Maybole, Ayrshire

FORBES: The Lord Forbes, KBE, Balforbes, Alford, Aberdeenshire AB33 8DR

FORSYTH: Alistair Forsyth of that Ilk, Ethie Castle, by Arbroath, Angus DD11 5SP

FRASER: The Lady Saltoun, Inverey House, Aberdeenshire AB35 5YB

*FRASER (OF LOVAT): The Lord Lovat, Beaufort Lodge, Beauly, Inverness-shire IV4 7AZ

GAYRE: R. Gayre of Gayre and Nigg, Minard Castle, Minard, Inverary, Argyll PA32 8YB

GORDON: The Marquess of Huntly, Aboyne Castle, Aberdeenshire AB34 5JP

GRAHAM: The Duke of Montrose, Buchanan Auld House, Drymen, Stirlingshire

GRANT: The Lord Strathspey, The House of Lords, London SW1A OPW

GRIERSON: Sir Michael Grierson of Lag, Bt., 40C Palace Road, London SW2 3NJ

HAIG: The Earl Haig, OBE, Bemersyde, Melrose, Roxburghshire TD6 9DP

HALDANE: Martin Haldane of Gleneagles, Gleneagles, Auchterarder, Perthshire

HANNAY: Ramsey Hannay of Kirkdale and of that Ilk, Cardoness House, Gatehouse-of-Fleet, Kirkcudbrightshire

HAY: The Earl of Erroll, Woodbury Hall, Sandy, Beds

HENDERSON: John Henderson of Fordell, 7 Owen Street, Toowoomba, Queensland, Australia

HUNTER: Pauline Hunter of Hunterston, Plovers Ridge, Lon Cecrist, Treaddur Bay, Holyhead, Gwynedd

IRVINE OF DRUM: David C. Irvine of Drum, Holly Leaf Cottage, Inchmarlo, Banchory, Aberdeenshire AB31 4BR

JARDINE: Sir Alexander Jardine of Applegirth, Bt., Ash House, Thwaites, Millom, Cumbria LA18 5HY

JOHNSTONE: The Earl of Annandale and Hartfell, Raehills, Lockerbie, Dumfriesshire

KEITH: The Earl of Kintore, The Stables, Keith Hall, Inverurie, Aberdeenshire AB51 OLD

KENNEDY: The Marquess of Ailsa, Cassillis House, Maybole, Ayrshire

KERR: The Marquess of Lothian, KCVO, Ferniehurst Castle, Jedburgh, Roxburghshire TN8 6NX

LAMONT: Peter N. Lamont of that Ilk, St Patrick's College, Manly, NSW 2095, Australia

LEASK: Madam Leask of Leask, 1 Vincent Road, Sheringham, Norfolk

LENNOX: Edward J. H. Lennox of that Ilk, Pools Farm, Downton on the Rock, Ludlow, Shropshire

LESLIE: The Earl of Rothes, Tanglewood, West Tytherley, Salisbury, Wilts SP5 ILX

LINDSAY: The Earl of Crawford and Balcarres, KT, PC, Balcarres, Colinsburgh, Fife

LOCKHART: Angus H. Lockhart of the Lee, Newholme, Dunsyre, Lanark

LUMSDEN: Gillem Lumsden of that Ilk and Blanerne, Stapely Howe, Hoe Benham, Newbury, Berks

MACALESTER: William St J. S. McAlester of Loup and Kennox, 2 Avon Road East, Christchurch, Dorset

McBAIN: J. H. McBain of McBain, 7025 North Finger Rock Place, Tucson, Arizona, USA

MACDONALD: The Lord Macdonald (*The Macdonald of Macdonald*), Kinloch Lodge, Sleat, Isle of Skye

*MACDONALD OF CLANRANALD: Ranald A. Macdonald of Clanranald, Mornish House, Killin, Perthshire FK21 8TX

*MACDONALD OF SLEAT (CLAN HUSTEAIN): Sir Ian Macdonald of Sleat, Bt., Thorpe Hall, Rudston, Driffield, N. Humberside YO25 OJE

*MACDONELL OF GLENGARRY: Ranald MacDonell of Glengarry, Elonbank, Castle Street, Fortrose, Ross-shire IV10 8TH

MACDOUGALL: vacant

MACDOWALL: Fergus D. H. Macdowall of Garthland, 9170 Ardmore Drive, North Saanich, British Columbia, Canada

MACGREGOR: Brig. Sir Gregor MacGregor of MacGregor, Bt., Bannatyne, Newtyle, Blairgowrie, Perthshire PH12 8TR

MACINTYRE: James W. MacIntyre of Glenoe, 15301 Pine Orchard Drive, Apartment 3H, Silver Spring, Maryland, USA

MACKAY: The Lord Reay, House of Lords, London SW1

MACKENZIE: The Earl of Cromartie, Castle Leod, Strathpeffer, Ross-shire IV14 9AA

MACKINNON: Madam Anne Mackinnon of Mackinnon, 16 Purleigh Road, Bridgwater, Somerset

MACKINTOSH: *The Mackintosh of Mackintosh*, Moy Hall, Inverness IV13 7YQ

MACLACHLAN: vacant

MACLAREN: Donald MacLaren of MacLaren and Achleskine, Achleskine, Kirkton, Balquhidder, Lochearnhead

MACLEAN: The Hon. Sir Lachlan Maclean of Duart, Bt., Arngask House, Glenfarg, Perthshire PH2 9QA

MACLENNAN: vacant

MACLEOD: John MacLeod of MacLeod, Dunvegan Castle, Isle of Skye

MACMILLAN: George MacMillan of MacMillan, Finlaystone, Langbank, Renfrewshire

MACNAB: J. C. Macnab of Macnab (*The Macnab*), Leuchars Castle Farmhouse, Leuchars, Fife KY16 0EY

MACNAGHTEN: Sir Patrick Macnaghten of Macnaghten and Dundarave, Bt., Dundarave, Bushmills, Co. Antrim

MACNEACAIL: Iain Macneacail of Macneacail and Scorrybreac, 12 Fox Street, Ballina, NSW, Australia

MACNEIL OF BARRA: Ian R. Macneil of Barra (*The Macneil of Barra*), 95/6 Grange Loan, Edinburgh

MACPHERSON: The Hon. Sir William Macpherson of Cluny, TD, Newtown Castle, Blairgowrie, Perthshire

MACTAVISH: E. S. Dugald MacTavish of Dunardry, c/o 2519 Vivaldi Lane, Four Seasons Estates, Gambrills, MD 21054, USA

MACTHOMAS: Andrew P. C. MacThomas of Finegand, c/o Roslin Cottage, Pitmedden, Aberdeenshire AB41 7NY

MAITLAND: The Earl of Lauderdale, 12 St Vincent Street, Edinburgh

MAKGILL: The Viscount of Oxfuird, Hill House, St Mary Bourne, Andover, Hants SP11 6BG

MALCOLM (MACCALLUM): Robin N. L. Malcolm of Poltalloch, Duntrune Castle, Lochgilphead, Argyll

MAR: The Countess of Mar, St Michael's Farm, Great Witley, Worcs WR6 6JB

MARJORIBANKS: Andrew Marjoribanks of that Ilk, 10 Newark Street, Greenock

MATHESON: Maj. Sir Fergus Matheson of Matheson, Bt., Old Rectory, Hedenham, Bungay, Suffolk NR35 2LD

MENZIES: David R. Menzies of Menzies, Wester Auchnagallin Farmhouse, Braes of Castle Grant, Grantown on Spey PH26 3PL

MOFFAT: Madam Moffat of that Ilk, St Jasual, Bullocks Farm Lane, Wheeler End Common, High Wycombe

MONCREIFFE: vacant

MONTGOMERIE: The Earl of Eglinton and Winton, Balhomie, Cargill, Perth PH2 6DS

MORRISON: Dr Iain M. Morrison of Ruchdi, Magnolia Cottage, The Street, Walberton, Sussex

MUNRO: Hector W. Munro of Foulis, Foulis Castle, Evanton, Ross-shire IV16 9UX

MURRAY: The Duke of Atholl, Blair Castle, Blair Atholl, Perthshire

NESBITT (or NISBET): Robert Nesbitt of that Ilk, Upper Roundhurst Farm, Roundhurst, Haslemere, Surrey

NICOLSON: The Lord Carnock, 90 Whitehall Court, London SW1A 2EL

OGILVY: The Earl of Airlie, KT, GCVO, PC, Cortachy Castle, Kirriemuir, Angus

RAMSAY: The Earl of Dalhousie, KT, GCVO, GBE, MC, Brechin Castle, Brechin, Angus DD7 6SH

RATTRAY: James S. Rattray of Rattray, Craighall, Rattray, Perthshire

ROBERTSON: Alexander G. H. Robertson of Struan (*Struan-Robertson*), The Breach Farm, Goudhurst Road, Cranbrook, Kent

ROLLO: The Lord Rollo, Pitcairns, Dunning, Perthshire

ROSE: Miss Elizabeth Rose of Kilravock, Kilravock Castle, Croy, Inverness

ROSS: David C. Ross of that Ilk, Shandwick, Perth Road, Stanley, Perthshire

RUTHVEN: The Earl of Gowrie, PC, 34 King Street, Covent Garden, London WC2

SCOTT: The Duke of Buccleuch and Queensberry, KT, VRD, Bowhill, Selkirk

SCRYMGEOUR: The Earl of Dundee, Birkhill, Cupar, Fife

SEMPILL: The Lord Sempill, 3 Vanburgh Place, Edinburgh, EH6 8AE

SHAW: John Shaw of Tordarroch, Newhall, Balblair, by Conon Bridge, Ross-shire

SINCLAIR: The Earl of Caithness, 137 Claxton Grove, London W6 8HB

SKENE: Danus Skene of Skene, Nether Pitlour, Strathmiglo, Fife

STIRLING: Fraser J. Stirling of Cader, 44A Oakley Street, London SW3 5HA

STRANGE: Maj. Timothy Strange of Balcaskie, Little Holme, Porton Road, Amesbury, Wilts

SUTHERLAND: The Countess of Sutherland, House of Tongue, Brora, Sutherland

SWINTON: John Swinton of that Ilk, 123 Superior Avenue SW, Calgary, Alberta, Canada

TROTTER: Alexander Trotter of Mortonhall, Charterhall, Duns, Berwickshire

URQUHART: Kenneth T. Urquhart of Urquhart, 507 Jefferson Park Avenue, Jefferson, New Orleans, Louisiana 70121, USA

WALLACE: Ian F. Wallace of that Ilk, 5 Lennox Street, Edinburgh EH4 1QB

WEDDERBURN OF THAT ILK: The Master of Dundee, Birkhill, Cupar, Fife

WEMYSS: David Wemyss of that Ilk, Invermay, Forteviot, Perthshire

The Privy Council

The Sovereign in Council, or Privy Council, was the chief source of executive power until the system of Cabinet government developed in the 18th century. Now the Privy Council's main functions are to advise the Sovereign and to exercise its own statutory responsibilities independent of the Sovereign in Council (*see also* page 215).

Membership of the Privy Council is automatic upon appointment to certain government and judicial positions in the United Kingdom, e.g. Cabinet ministers must be Privy Counsellors and are sworn in on first assuming office. Membership is also accorded by The Queen to eminent people in the UK and independent countries of the Commonwealth of which Her Majesty is Queen, on the recommendation of the British Prime Minister. Membership of the Council is retained for life, except for very occasional removals.

The administrative functions of the Privy Council are carried out by the Privy Council Office (*see* page 331) under the direction of the President of the Council, who is always a member of the Cabinet.

President of the Council, The Rt. Hon. Margaret Beckett, MP
Clerk of the Council, A. Galloway

MEMBERS *as at 31 August 1999*

HRH The Duke of Edinburgh, 1951
HRH The Prince of Wales, 1977

Aberdare, Lord, 1974
Ackner, Lord, 1980
Airlie, Earl of, 1984
Aldington, Lord, 1954
Aldous, Sir William, 1995
Alebua, Ezekiel, 1988
Alison, Michael, 1981
Alport, Lord, 1960
Ampthill, Lord, 1995
Ancram, Michael, 1996
Anthony, Douglas, 1971
Arbuthnot, James, 1998
Archer of Sandwell, Lord, 1977
Armstrong, Hilary, 1999
Arnold, Sir John, 1979
Arthur, Hon. Owen, 1995
Ashdown, Paddy, 1989
Ashley of Stoke, Lord, 1979
Atkins, Sir Robert, 1995
Auld, Sir Robin, 1999
Baker of Dorking, Lord, 1984
Balcombe, Sir John, 1985

Barber, Lord, 1963
Barnett, Lord, 1975
Beckett, Margaret, 1993
Beith, Alan, 1992
Beldam, Sir Roy, 1989
Belstead, Lord, 1983
Benn, Anthony, 1964
Bennett, Sir Frederic, 1985
Biffen, Lord, 1979
Bingham of Cornhill, Lord, 1986
Birch, William, 1992
Bisson, Sir Gordon, 1987
Blair, Anthony, 1994
Blaker, Lord, 1983
Blanchard, Peter, 1998
Blatch, Baroness, 1993
Blunkett, David, 1997
Boateng, Paul, 1999
Bolger, James, 1991
Booth, Albert, 1976
Boothroyd, Betty, 1992
Boscawen, Hon. Robert, 1992
Bottomley, Virginia, 1992
Boyson, Sir Rhodes, 1987
Braine of Wheatley, Lord, 1985
Brathwaite, Sir Nicholas, 1991
Bridge of Harwich, Lord, 1975
Brightman, Lord, 1979
Brittan, Sir Leon, 1981
Brook, Sir Henry, 1996
Brooke, Peter, 1988
Brown, Gordon, 1996
Brown, Nicholas, 1997
Brown, Sir Simon, 1992
Brown, Sir Stephen, 1983
Browne-Wilkinson, Lord, 1983
Butler, Sir Adam, 1984
Butler-Sloss, Dame Elizabeth, 1988
Buxton, Sir Richard, 1997
Byers, Stephen, 1998
Caborn, Richard, 1999
Caithness, Earl of, 1990
Callaghan of Cardiff, Lord, 1964
Cameron of Lochbroom, Lord, 1984
Camoys, Lord, 1997
Campbell of Croy, Lord, 1970
Campbell, Walter Menzies, 1998
Campbell, Sir William, 1999
Canterbury, The Archbishop of, 1991
Carlisle of Bucklow, Lord, 1979
Carr of Hadley, Lord, 1963
Carrington, Lord, 1959
Carswell, Sir Robert, 1993
Carter, Lord, 1997
Casey, Sir Maurice, 1986
Castle of Blackburn, Baroness, 1964
Chadwick, Sir John, 1997
Chalfont, Lord, 1964
Chalker of Wallasey, Baroness, 1987
Chan, Sir Julius, 1981
Charteris of Amisfield, Lord, 1972
Chataway, Sir Christopher, 1970

Clark, Alan, 1991
Clark, David, 1997
Clark, Helen, 1990
Clark of Kempston, Lord, 1990
Clarke, Sir Anthony, 1998
Clarke, Kenneth, 1984
Clarke, Thomas, 1997
Cledwyn of Penrhos, Lord, 1966
Clinton-Davis, Lord, 1998
Clyde, Lord, 1996
Cockfield, Lord, 1982
Cocks of Hartcliffe, Lord, 1976
Coggan, Lord, 1961
Colman, Fraser, 1986
Compton, Sir John, 1983
Concannon, John, 1978
Cook, Robin, 1996
Cooke of Thorndon, Lord, 1977
Cooper, Sir Frank, 1983
Cope of Berkeley, Lord, 1988
Corfield, Sir Frederick, 1970
Cowen, Sir Zelman, 1981
Cradock, Sir Percy, 1993
Cranborne, Viscount, 1994
Crawford and Balcarres, Earl of, 1972
Crickhowell, Lord, 1979
Croom-Johnson, Sir David, 1984
Cullen, *Hon.* Lord, 1997
Cumming-Bruce, Sir Roualeyn, 1977
Cunningham, Jack, 1993
Curry, David, 1996
Darling, Alistair, 1997
Davies, Denzil, 1978
Davies, Ronald, 1997
Davis, David, 1997
Davison, Sir Ronald, 1978
Dean of Harptree, Lord, 1991
Dean of Thornton-le-Fylde, Baroness, 1998
Deedes, Lord, 1962
Dell, Edmund, 1970
Denham, Lord, 1981
Devonshire, Duke of, 1964
Dewar, Donald, 1996
Diamond, Lord, 1965
Dillon, Sir Brian, 1982
Dixon, Lord, 1996
Dobson, Frank, 1997
Donaldson of Lymington, Lord, 1979
Dorrell, Stephen, 1994
Douglas, Sir William, 1977
du Cann, Sir Edward, 1964
Duff, Sir Antony, 1980
Dunn, Sir Robin, 1980
East, Paul, 1998
Eden of Winton, Lord, 1972
Eggar, Timothy, 1995
Eichelbaum, Sir Thomas, 1989
Emery, Sir Peter, 1993
Emslie, Lord, 1972
Erroll of Hale, Lord, 1960
Esquivel, Manuel, 1986
Evans, Sir Anthony, 1992

Eveleigh, Sir Edward, 1977
Farquharson, Sir Donald, 1989
Fellowes, Lord, 1990
Ferrers, Earl, 1982
Field, Frank, 1997
Floissac, Sir Vincent, 1992
Foot, Michael, 1974
Forsyth of Drumlean, The Lord, 1995
Forth, Eric, 1997
Foster, Derek, 1993
Fowler, Sir Norman, 1979
Fox, Sir Marcus, 1995
Fox, Sir Michael, 1981
Fraser, Malcolm, 1976
Fraser of Carmyllie, Lord, 1989
Freeman, John, 1966
Freeman, Lord, 1993
Freeson, Reginald, 1976
Garel-Jones, Lord, 1992
Gault, Thomas, 1992
George, Edward, 1999
Georges, Telford, 1986
Gibbs, Sir Harry, 1972
Gibson, Sir Peter, 1993
Gibson, Sir Ralph, 1985
Gibson-Watt, Lord, 1974
Gilbert, Lord, 1978
Gilmour of Craigmillar, Lord, 1973
Glenamara, Lord, 1964
Glidewell, Sir Iain, 1985
Goff of Chieveley, Lord, 1982
Goodlad, Sir Alastair, 1992
Gorton, Sir John, 1968
Gowrie, Earl of, 1984
Graham, Douglas, 1998
Graham of Edmonton, Lord, 1998
Gray of Contin, Lord, 1982
Griffiths, Lord, 1980
Gummer, John, 1985
Habgood, Rt. Revd Lord, 1983
Hague, William, 1995
Hailsham of St Marylebone, Lord, 1956
Hamilton, Sir Archie, 1991
Hanley, Sir Jeremy, 1994
Hardie, Lord, 1997
Hardie Boys, Sir Michael, 1989
Harman, Harriet, 1997
Harris of Greenwich, Lord, 1998
Harrison, Walter, 1977
Haselhurst, Sir Alan, 1999
Hattersley, Lord, 1975
Hayhoe, Lord, 1985
Healey, Lord, 1964
Heath, Sir Edward, 1955
Heathcoat-Amory, David, 1996
Henry, Sir Denis, 1993
Henry, John, 1996
Heseltine, Michael, 1979
Heseltine, Sir William, 1986
Hesketh, Lord, 1991
Higgins, Lord, 1979
Hirst, Sir David, 1992
Hobhouse, Sir John, 1993
Hoffmann, Lord, 1992
Hogg, Hon. Douglas, 1992
Holderness, Lord, 1959
Hollis of Heigham, Baroness, 1999
Hope of Craighead, Lord, 1989

Hordern, Sir Peter, 1993
Howard, Michael, 1990
Howe of Aberavon, Lord, 1972
Howell of Guildford, Lord, 1979
Hughes, Lord, 1970
Hunt, Jonathan, 1989
Hunt of Wirral, Lord, 1990
Hurd of Westwell, Lord, 1982
Hutchison, Sir Michael, 1995
Hutton, Lord, 1988
Ingraham, Hubert, 1993
Ingram, Adam, 1998
Irvine of Lairg, Lord, 1997
Jack, Michael, 1997
Janvrin, Sir Robin, 1998
Jauncey of Tullichettle, Lord, 1988
Jay of Paddington, Baroness, 1998
Jellicoe, Earl, 1963
Jenkin of Roding, Lord, 1973
Jenkins of Hillhead, Lord, 1964
Jones, Aubrey, 1955
Jones, Barry, 1999
Jopling, Lord, 1979
Jowell, Tessa, 1998
Judge, Sir Igor, 1996
Jugnauth, Sir Anerood, 1987
Kaufman, Gerald, 1978
Keith, Sir Kenneth, 1998
Keith of Kinkel, Lord, 1976
Kelly, Sir Basil, 1984
Kelvedon, Lord, 1980
Kenilorea, Sir Peter, 1979
Kennedy, Sir Paul, 1992
Kerr, Sir Michael, 1981
King, Thomas, 1979
Kingsdown, Lord, 1987
Kingsland, Lord, 1994
Kinnock, Neil, 1983
Knight, Gregory, 1995
Lamont, Norman, 1986
Lane, Lord, 1975
Lang of Monkton, Lord, 1990
Lange, David, 1984
Lansdowne, Marquess of, 1964
Latasi, Kamuta, 1996
Lauti, Sir Toaripi, 1979
Laws, Sir John, 1999
Lawson of Blaby, Lord, 1981
Lawton, Sir Frederick, 1972
Leggatt, Sir Andrew, 1990
Leonard, Rt. Revd Graham, 1981
Liddell, Helen, 1998
Lilley, Peter, 1990
Lloyd of Berwick, Lord, 1984
Lloyd, Sir Peter, 1994
London, The Bishop of, 1995
Longford, Earl of, 1948
Louisy, Allan, 1981
Luce, Sir Richard, 1986
Lyell, Sir Nicholas, 1990
Mabon, Dickson, 1977
McCarthy, Sir Thaddeus, 1968
McCartney, Ian, 1999
McCollum, Sir Liam, 1997
McCowan, Sir Anthony, 1989
MacDermott, Sir John, 1987
Macdonald of Tradeston, Lord, 1999
MacGregor, John, 1985
MacIntyre, Duncan, 1980
Mackay, Andrew, 1998

McKay, Ian, 1992
Mackay of Ardbrecknish, Lord, 1996
Mackay of Clashfern, Lord, 1979
Mackay of Drumadoon, Lord, 1996
McKinnon, Donald, 1992
Maclean, David, 1995
Maclennan, Robert, 1997
McMullin, Sir Duncan, 1980
Major, John, 1987
Mance, Sir Jonathan, 1999
Mandelson, Peter, 1998
Mantell, Sir Charles, 1997
Mara, Ratu Sir Kamisese, 1973
Marsh, Lord, 1966
Mason of Barnsley, Lord, 1968
Maude, Hon. Francis, 1992
Mawhinney, Sir Brian, 1994
May, Sir Anthony, 1998
Mayhew of Twysden, Lord, 1986
Meacher, Michael, 1997
Megarry, Sir Robert, 1978
Mellor, David, 1990
Merlyn-Rees, Lord, 1974
Michael, Alun, 1998
Milburn, Alan, 1998
Millan, Bruce, 1975
Millett, Sir Peter, 1994
Mitchell, Sir James, 1985
Molyneaux of Killead, Lord, 1983
Monro of Langholm, Lord, 1995
Moore, Michael, 1990
Moore of Lower Marsh, Lord, 1986
Moore of Wolvercote, Lord, 1977
Morris, Charles, 1978
Morris, Sir John, 1970
Morris of Manchester, Lord, 1979
Morritt, Sir Robert, 1994
Mowlam, Marjorie, 1997
Moyle, Roland, 1978
Mummery, Sir John, 1996
Murphy, Paul, 1998
Murray, Hon. Lord, 1974
Murray, Sir Donald, 1989
Murray of Epping Forest, Lord, 1976
Murton of Lindisfarne, Lord, 1976
Mustill, Lord, 1985
Nairne, Sir Patrick, 1982
Namaliu, Sir Rabbie, 1989
Naseby, Lord, 1994
Needham, Sir Richard, 1994
Neill, Sir Brian, 1985
Newton of Braintree, Lord, 1988
Nicholls of Birkenhead, Lord, 1995
Nicholson, Sir Michael, 1995
Nolan, Lord, 1991
Nott, Sir John, 1979
Nourse, Sir Martin, 1985
Oakes, Gordon, 1979
O'Connor, Sir Patrick, 1980
O'Donnell, Turlough, 1979
O'Flynn, Francis, 1987
Ogilvy, Sir Angus, 1997
Oliver of Aylmerton, Lord, 1980
Onslow of Woking, Lord, 1988
Oppenheim-Barnes, Baroness, 1979
Orme, Lord, 1974
Otton, Sir Philip, 1995
Owen, Lord, 1976
Paeniu, Bikenibeu, 1991
Palliser, Sir Michael, 1983

Palmer, Sir Geoffrey, 1986
Parker, Sir Roger, 1983
Parkinson, Lord, 1981
Patten, Christopher, 1989
Patten, Lord, 1990
Patterson, Percival, 1993
Pattie, Sir Geoffrey, 1987
Perth, Earl of, 1957
Peters, Winston, 1998
Peyton of Yeovil, Lord, 1970
Phillips, Sir Nicholas, 1995
Pill, Sir Malcolm, 1995
Pindling, Sir Lynden, 1976
Portillo, Michael, 1992
Potter, Sir Mark, 1996
Prentice, Lord, 1966
Prescott, John, 1994
Price, George, 1982
Prior, Lord, 1970
Puapua, Sir Tomasi, 1982
Purchas, Sir Francis, 1982
Pym, Lord, 1970
Quin, Joyce, 1998
Radice, Giles, 1999
Raison, Sir Timothy, 1982
Ramsden, James, 1963
Rawlinson of Ewell, Lord, 1964
Redwood, John, 1993
Rees, Lord, 1983
Reid, John, 1998
Renton, Lord, 1962
Renton of Mount Harry, Lord, 1989
Richard, Lord, 1993
Richardson, Sir Ivor, 1978
Richardson of Duntisbourne, Lord,
    1976
Rifkind, Sir Malcolm, 1986
Roberts of Conwy, Lord, 1991
Robertson of Port Ellen, Lord, 1997
Roch, Sir John, 1993
Rodger of Earlsferry, Lord, 1992
Rodgers of Quarry Bank, Lord, 1975
Rose, Sir Christopher, 1992
Ross, *Hon.* Lord, 1985
Rumbold, Dame Angela, 1991
Runcie, Lord, 1980
Russell, Sir Patrick, 1987

Ryder of Wensum, Lord, 1990
Sainsbury, Sir Timothy, 1992
St John of Fawsley, Lord, 1979
Sandiford, Erskine, 1989
Saville of Newdigate, Lord, 1994
Scarman, Lord, 1973
Schiemann, Sir Konrad, 1995
Scott, Sir Nicholas, 1989
Scott, Sir Richard, 1991
Seaga, Edward, 1981
Sedley, Sir Stephen, 1999
Selkirk of Douglas, Lord, 1996
Shawcross, Lord, 1946
Shearer, Hugh, 1969
Sheldon, Robert, 1977
Shephard, Gillian, 1992
Shepherd, Lord, 1965
Shipley, Jennifer, 1998
Shore of Stepney, Lord, 1967
Short, Clare, 1997
Simmonds, Kennedy, 1984
Simon of Glaisdale, Lord, 1961
Sinclair, Ian, 1977
Slade, Sir Christopher, 1982
Slynn of Hadley, Lord, 1992
Smith, Andrew, 1997
Smith, Christopher, 1997
Smith, Sir Geoffrey Johnson, 1996
Somare, Sir Michael, 1977
Somers, Sir Edward, 1981
Stanley, Sir John, 1984
Staughton, Sir Christopher, 1988
Steel of Aikwood, Lord, 1977
Stephen, Sir Ninian, 1979
Stephenson, Sir John, 1971
Stewartby, Lord, 1989
Steyn, Lord, 1992
Stodart of Leaston, Lord, 1974
Strang, Gavin, 1997
Strathclyde, Lord, 1995
Straw, Jack, 1997
Stuart-Smith, Sir Murray, 1988
Talboys, Sir Brian, 1977
Taylor, Ann, 1997
Tebbit, Lord, 1981
Templeman, Lord, 1978
Thatcher, Baroness, 1970

Thomas, Edmund, 1996
Thomas, Sir Swinton, 1994
Thomas of Gwydir, Lord, 1964
Thomson, David, 1981
Thomson of Monifieth, Lord, 1966
Thorpe, Jeremy, 1967
Thorpe, Sir Matthew, 1995
Tipping, Andrew, 1998
Tizard, Robert, 1986
Trefgarne, Lord, 1989
Trimble, David, 1997
Trumpington, Baroness, 1992
Tuckey, Sir Simon, 1998
Ullswater, Viscount, 1994
Varley, Lord, 1974
Waddington, Lord, 1987
Waite, Sir John, 1993
Wakeham, Lord, 1983
Waldegrave, William, 1990
Walker of Doncaster, Lord, 1979
Walker of Worcester, Lord, 1970
Walker, Sir Robert, 1997
Waller, Sir Mark, 1996
Ward, Sir Alan, 1995
Watkins, Sir Tasker, 1980
Weatherill, Lord, 1980
Wheeler, Sir John, 1993
Widdecombe, Ann, 1997
Wigley, Dafydd, 1997
Wilberforce, Lord, 1964
Williams, Alan, 1977
Williams of Crosby, Baroness, 1974
Williams of Mostyn, Lord
Windlesham, Lord, 1973
Wingti, Paias, 1987
Withers, Reginald, 1977
Woodhouse, Sir Owen, 1974
Woolf, Lord, 1986
Wylie, *Hon.* Lord, 1970
York, The Archbishop of, 1991
Young, Baroness, 1981
Young, Sir George, 1993
Young of Graffham, Lord, 1984
Younger of Leckie, Viscount, 1979
Zacca, Edward, 1992

The Privy Council of Northern Ireland

The Privy Council of Northern Ireland had responsibilities in Northern Ireland similar to those of the Privy Council in Great Britain until the Northern Ireland Act 1974 instituted direct rule and a UK Cabinet minister became responsible for the functions previously exercised by the Northern Ireland government.

Membership of the Privy Council of Northern Ireland is retained for life. The postnominal initials PC (NI) are used to differentiate its members from those of the Privy Council.

MEMBERS *as at 31 August 1999*

Bailie, Robin, 1971
Bleakley, David, 1971
Craig, William, 1963
Dobson, John, 1969
Kelly, Sir Basil, 1969
Kirk, Herbert, 1962
Long, William, 1966
Lowry, The Lord, 1971
McConnell, The Lord, 1964
McIvor, Basil, 1971
Moyola, The Lord, 1966

Neill, Sir Ivan, 1950
Porter, Sir Robert, 1969
Taylor, John, MP, 1970
West, Henry, 1960

Parliament

The United Kingdom constitution is not contained in any single document but has evolved in the course of time, formed partly by statute, partly by common law and partly by convention. A constitutional monarchy, the United Kingdom is governed by Ministers of the Crown in the name of the Sovereign, who is head both of the state and of the government.

The organs of government are the legislature (Parliament), the executive and the judiciary. The executive consists of HM Government (Cabinet and other Ministers) (*see* pages 272–3), government departments (*see* pages 276–350), local authorities (*see* Local Government), and public corporations operating nationalized industries or social or cultural services (*see* pages 276–350). The judiciary (*see* Law Courts and Offices) pronounces on the law, both written and unwritten, interprets statutes and is responsible for the enforcement of the law; the judiciary is independent of both the legislature and the executive.

THE MONARCHY

The Sovereign personifies the state and is, in law, an integral part of the legislature, head of the executive, head of the judiciary, commander-in-chief of all armed forces of the Crown and 'Supreme Governor' of the Church of England. The seat of the monarchy is in the United Kingdom. In the Channel Islands and the Isle of Man, which are Crown dependencies, the Sovereign is represented by a Lieutenant-Governor. In the member states of the Commonwealth of which the Sovereign is head of state, her representative is a Governor-General; in UK dependencies the Sovereign is usually represented by a Governor, who is responsible to the British Government.

Although in practice the powers of the monarchy are now very limited, restricted mainly to the advisory and ceremonial, there are important acts of government which require the participation of the Sovereign. These include summoning, proroguing and dissolving Parliament, giving royal assent to bills passed by Parliament, appointing important office-holders, e.g. government ministers, judges, bishops and governors, conferring peerages, knighthoods and other honours, and granting pardon to a person wrongly convicted of a crime. The Sovereign appoints the Prime Minister; by convention this office is held by the leader of the political party which enjoys, or can secure, a majority of votes in the House of Commons. In international affairs the Sovereign as head of state has the power to declare war and make peace, to recognize foreign states and governments, to conclude treaties and to annex or cede territory. However, as the Sovereign entrusts executive power to Ministers of the Crown and acts on the advice of her Ministers, which she cannot ignore, royal prerogative powers are in practice exercised by Ministers, who are responsible to Parliament.

Ministerial responsibility does not diminish the Sovereign's importance to the smooth working of government. She holds meetings of the Privy Council (*see* below), gives audiences to her Ministers and other officials at home and overseas, receives accounts of Cabinet decisions, reads dispatches and signs state papers; she must be informed and consulted on every aspect of national life; and she must show complete impartiality.

COUNSELLORS OF STATE

In the event of the Sovereign's absence abroad, it is necessary to appoint Counsellors of State under letters patent to carry out the chief functions of the Monarch, including the holding of Privy Councils and giving royal assent to acts passed by Parliament. The normal procedure is to appoint as Counsellors three or four members of the royal family among those remaining in the UK.

In the event of the Sovereign on accession being under the age of 18 years, or at any time unavailable or incapacitated by infirmity of mind or body for the performance of the royal functions, provision is made for a regency.

THE PRIVY COUNCIL

The Sovereign in Council, or Privy Council, was the chief source of executive power until the system of Cabinet government developed. Nowadays its main function is to advise the Sovereign to approve Orders in Council and to advise on the issue of royal proclamations. The Council's own statutory responsibilities (independent of the powers of the Sovereign in Council) include powers of supervision over the registering bodies for the medical and allied professions. A full Council is summoned only on the death of the Sovereign or when the Sovereign announces his or her intention to marry. (For full list of Counsellors, *see* pages 212–4.)

There are a number of advisory Privy Council committees, whose meetings the Sovereign does not attend. Some are prerogative committees, such as those dealing with legislative matters submitted by the legislatures of the Channel Islands and the Isle of Man or with applications for charters of incorporation; and some are provided for by statute, e.g. those for the universities of Oxford and Cambridge and the Scottish universities.

The Judicial Committee of the Privy Council is the final court of appeal from courts of the UK dependencies, courts of independent Commonwealth countries which have retained the right of appeal, courts of the Channel Islands and the Isle of Man, some professional and disciplinary committees, and church sources. The Committee is composed of Privy Counsellors who hold, or have held, high judicial office, although usually only three or five hear each case.

Administrative work is carried out by the Privy Council Office under the direction of the President of the Council, a Cabinet Minister.

PARLIAMENT

Parliament is the supreme law-making authority and can legislate for the UK as a whole or for any parts of it separately (the Channel Islands and the Isle of Man are Crown dependencies and not part of the UK). The main functions of Parliament are to pass laws, to provide (by voting taxation) the means of carrying on the work of government and to scrutinize government policy and administration, particularly proposals for expenditure.

International treaties and agreements are by custom presented to Parliament before ratification.

Parliament emerged during the late 13th and early 14th centuries. The officers of the King's household and the King's judges were the nucleus of early Parliaments, joined by such ecclesiastical and lay magnates as the King might summon to form a prototype 'House of Lords', and occasionally by the knights of the shires, burgesses and proctors of the lower clergy. By the end of Edward III's reign a 'House of Commons' was beginning to appear; the first known Speaker was elected in 1377.

Parliamentary procedure is based on custom and precedent, partly formulated in the Standing Orders of both Houses of Parliament, and each House has the right to control its own internal proceedings and to commit for contempt. The system of debate in the two Houses is similar; when a motion has been moved, the Speaker proposes the question as the subject of a debate. Members speak from wherever they have been sitting. Questions are decided by a vote on a simple majority. Draft legislation is introduced, in either House, as a bill. Bills can be introduced by a Government Minister or a private Member, but in practice the majority of bills which become law are introduced by the Government. To become law, a bill must be passed by each House (for parliamentary stages, *see* Bill, page 220) and then sent to the Sovereign for the royal assent, after which it becomes an Act of Parliament.

Proceedings of both Houses are public, except on extremely rare occasions. The minutes (called Votes and Proceedings in the Commons, and Minutes of Proceedings in the Lords) and the speeches (The Official Report of Parliamentary Debates, *Hansard*) are published daily. Proceedings are also recorded for transmission on radio and television and stored in the Parliamentary Recording Unit before transfer to the National Sound Archive. Television cameras have been allowed into the House of Lords since 1985 and into the House of Commons since 1989; committee meetings may also be televised.

By the Parliament Act of 1911, the maximum duration of a Parliament is five years (if not previously dissolved), the term being reckoned from the date given on the writs for the new Parliament. The maximum life has been prolonged by legislation in such rare circumstances as the two world wars (31 January 1911 to 25 November 1918; 26 November 1935 to 15 June 1945). Dissolution and writs for a general election are ordered by the Sovereign on the advice of the Prime Minister. The life of a Parliament is divided into sessions, usually of one year in length, beginning and ending most often in October or November.

DEVOLUTION

The Scottish Parliament elected in 1999 has legislative power over all devolved matters, i.e. matters not reserved to Westminster or otherwise outside its powers. The National Assembly for Wales elected in May 1999 has power to make secondary legislation in the areas where executive functions have been transferred to it. The New Northern Ireland Assembly elected in June 1998 was due to be formally established by legislation in 1999; this had not yet happened at time of going to press. It will have legislative authority in the fields currently administered by the Northern Ireland departments. For further details, *see* Regional Assemblies supplement and Local Government section.

THE HOUSE OF LORDS

London SW1A 0PW
Tel 0171-219 3000
Information Office: 0171–219 3107
E-mail: hlinfo@parliament.uk
Web site: http://www.parliament.uk

The House of Lords consists of the Lords Spiritual and Temporal. The Lords Spiritual are the Archbishops of Canterbury and York, the Bishops of London, Durham and Winchester, and the 21 senior diocesan bishops of the Church of England. The Lords Temporal currently consist of all hereditary peers of England, Scotland, Great Britain and the UK who have not disclaimed their peerages, life peers created under the Life Peerages Act 1958, and those Lords of Appeal in Ordinary created life peers under the Appellate Jurisdiction Act 1876, as amended (i.e. law lords). In January 1999 the Government introduced legislation removing the right of hereditary peers to sit in the House of Lords. An amendment to the legislation was later agreed that would allow 92 hereditary peers (42 Conservative, 28 cross-bench, three Liberal Democrat, two Labour, the Earl Marshal, the Lord Great Chamberlain and 15 others) to remain in the House of Lords until longer-term reform of the House had been carried out; elections to select those who would remain would be held in October and November 1999. At the time of going to press the legislation had passed through all its Commons stages and was awaiting its third reading in the House of Lords. The Government has also announced its intention of establishing an independent Appointments Commission to oversee the future nomination of life peers. A Royal Commission on the longer-term reform of the House of Lords was set up in February 1999 and is due to report by the end of 1999.

Disclaimants of a hereditary peerage lose their right to sit in the House of Lords but gain the right to vote at parliamentary elections and to offer themselves for election to the House of Commons. Those peers disqualified from sitting in the House include:

– aliens, i.e. any peer who is not a British citizen, a Commonwealth citizen (under the British Nationality Act 1981) or a citizen of the Republic of Ireland
– peers under the age of 21
– undischarged bankrupts or, in Scotland, those whose estate is sequestered
– peers convicted of treason

Peers who do not wish to attend sittings of the House of Lords may apply for leave of absence for the duration of a Parliament.

Until the beginning of this century the House of Lords had considerable power, being able to veto any bill submitted to it by the House of Commons, but those powers were greatly reduced by the Parliament Acts of 1911 and 1949 (*see* page 221).

Combined with its legislative role, the House of Lords has judicial powers as the ultimate Court of Appeal for courts in Great Britain and Northern Ireland, except for criminal cases in Scotland. These powers are exercised by the Lord Chancellor and the Lords of Appeal in Ordinary (the law lords) (*see* page 354).

Members of the House of Lords are unpaid. However, they are entitled to reimbursement of travelling expenses on parliamentary business within the UK and certain other expenses incurred for the purpose of attendance at sittings of the House, within a maximum for each day of £80.50 for overnight subsistence, £35.50 for day subsistence and incidental travel, and £34.50 for secretarial costs, postage and certain additional expenses.

COMPOSITION *as at 1 July 1999*
Archbishops and Bishops, 26
Peers by succession, 751 (17 women)
Hereditary peers of first creation (including the Prince of Wales), 8
Life peers under the Appellate Jurisdiction Act 1876, 27
Life peers under the Life Peerages Act 1958, 477 (87 women)
Total 1,289
Of whom:
  Peers without writs of summons, 67 (3 minors)
  Peers on leave of absence from the House, 57

STATE OF PARTIES *as at 1 July 1999**
More than half of the members of the House of Lords take the whip of one of the three main political parties. The other members have no political affiliations and more than 300 sit on the cross-benches as independents.

Conservative, 471
Labour, 176
Liberal Democrats, 66
Cross-bench, 339
Other (including Lords Spiritual), 113
* Excluding peers without writs of summons and peers on leave of absence from the House

OFFICERS

The House is presided over by the Lord Chancellor, who is *ex officio* Speaker of the House. A panel of deputy Speakers is appointed by Royal Commission. The first deputy Speaker is the Chairman of Committees, appointed at the beginning of each session, a salaried officer of the House who takes the chair in committee of the whole House and in some select committees. He is assisted by a panel of deputy chairmen, headed by the salaried Principal Deputy Chairman of Committees, who is also chairman of the European Communities Committee of the House.

The permanent officers include the Clerk of the Parliaments, who is in charge of the administrative and procedural staff collectively known as the Parliament Office; the Gentleman Usher of the Black Rod, who is also Serjeant-at-Arms in attendance upon the Lord Chancellor and is responsible for security and for accommodation and services in the House of Lords; and the Yeoman Usher who is Deputy Serjeant-at-Arms and assists Black Rod in his duties.

Speaker (£160,011), The Lord Irvine of Lairg, PC, QC
  Private Secretary, Ms E. Hutchinson
Chairman of Committees (£64,426), The Lord Boston of Faversham, QC
Principal Deputy Chairman of Committees (£60,032), The Lord Tordoff

DEPARTMENT OF THE CLERK OF THE PARLIAMENTS
Clerk of the Parliaments (£123,787), J. M. Davies
Clerk Assistant and Clerk of Legislation (£73,250–£110,300), P. D. G. Hayter, LVO
Reading Clerk and Principal Finance Officer (£61,110–£98,400), M. G. Pownall
Counsel to Chairman of Committees (£61,110–£98,400), Sir James Nursaw, KCB, QC: Dr C. S. Kerse; D. W. Saunders
Principal Clerks (£55,750–£92,930), J. A. Vallance White, CB (*Judicial Office and Fourth Clerk at the Table*); B. P. Keith (*Journals*); D. R. Beamish (*Committees and Overseas Office*); R. H. Walters, D.Phil. (*Establishment Officer*); Dr F. P. Tudor (*Private Bills*); E. C. Ollard (*Public Bills*); A. Makower; T. V. Mohan (*Select Committees*)

Senior Clerks (£31,283–£47,399), S. P. Burton; Miss M. B. Robertson (*seconded as Secretary to the Leader of the House and Chief Whip*); T. E. Radice; D. J. Batt; E. R. Morgan; Dr E. A. Hopkins; Miss L. J. Mouland; J. A. Vaughan
Clerks (£16,306–£28,336), A. J. Mackersie; Miss K. S. Ball
Clerk of the Records (£45,810–£73,470), S. K. Ellison
Assistant Clerks of the Records (£30,431–£46,108), D. L. Prior; Dr C. Shenton
Librarian (£50,510–£82,650), D. L. Jones
Deputy Librarian (£35,427–£57,481), P. G. Davis, PH.D.
Senior Library Clerks (£31,283–£47,399), Miss I. L. Victory, PH.D.; S. Kennedy; H. C. Deadman
Library Clerk (£19,103–£25,022), I. S. Cruse
Examiners of Petitions for Private Bills, Dr F. P. Tudor; W. A. Proctor
Editor, Official Report (*Hansard*), (£45,810–£73,470), Mrs M. E. E. C. Villiers
Deputy Editor, Official Report (£34,462–£55,915), Mrs C. J. Boden

DEPARTMENT OF THE GENTLEMAN USHER OF THE BLACK ROD
Gentleman Usher of the Black Rod and Serjeant-at-Arms (£61,110–£98,400), Gen. Sir Edward Jones, KCB, CBE
Yeoman Usher of the Black Rod and Deputy Serjeant-at-Arms (£30,431–£46,108), Brig. H. D. C. Duncan, MBE

SELECT COMMITTEES

The main House of Lords select committees, as at 7 June 1999, are as follows:

European Communities – Sub-committees:
  A (*Economic and Financial Affairs, Trade and External Relations*) – *Chair*, The Lord Grenfell; *Clerk*, Dr E. A. Hopkins
  B (*Energy, Industry and Transport*) – *Chair*, The Lord Geddes; *Clerk*, R. Morgan
  C (*Environment, Transport and Consumer Protection*) – *Chair*, The Earl of Cranbrook; *Clerk*, T. Radice
  D (*Agriculture, Fisheries and Food*) – *Chair*, The Lord Reay; *Clerk*, J. A. Vaughan
  E (*Law and Institutions*) – *Chair*, The Lord Hope of Craighead, PC; *Clerk*, T. Radice
  F (*Social Affairs, Education and Home Affairs*) – *Chair*, The Lord Wallace of Saltaire, PH.D.; *Clerk*, T. V. Mohar
Science and Technology – *Chair*, The Lord Winston, FRCOG; *Clerk*, A. Makower
Delegated Powers and Deregulation – *Chair*, The Lord Alexander of Weedon, QC; *Clerk*, Dr F. P. Tudor
Monetary Policy Committee of the Bank of England – *Chair*, The Lord Peston; *Clerk*, D. J. Batt

THE HOUSE OF COMMONS
London SW1A 0AA
Tel 0171-219 3000
Information Office: 0171-219 4272
Forthcoming business: 0171-219 5532
E-mail: hcinfo@parliament.uk
Web site: http://www.parliament.uk

The members of the House of Commons are elected by universal adult suffrage. For electoral purposes, the United Kingdom is divided into constituencies, each of which returns one member to the House of Commons, the member being the candidate who obtains the largest number of votes cast in the constituency. To ensure equitable representation, the four Boundary Commissions (*see* page 283) keep constituency boundaries under review and recommend any redistribution of seats which may seem necessary because of population movements, etc. The number of seats was raised to 640 in 1945, reduced to 625 in 1948, and subsequently rose to 630 in 1955, 635 in 1970, 650 in 1983, 651 in 1992 and 659 in 1997. Of the present 659 seats, there are 529 for England, 40 for Wales, 72 for Scotland and 18 for Northern Ireland. The number of Scottish MPs at Westminster is to be cut by about 12 by 2007.

An electoral reform commission headed by Lord Jenkins of Hillhead proposed in October 1998 that the 'first-past-the-post' system of electing members of the House of Commons should be replaced by an alternative vote top-up system, under which 80–85 per cent of MPs would be elected by an alternative vote method and the remaining 15–20 per cent by an open-list system of proportional representation. A referendum will be held on the proposals at an unspecified future date.

ELECTIONS

Elections are by secret ballot, each elector casting one vote; voting is not compulsory. For entitlement to vote in parliamentary elections, *see* Legal Notes section. When a seat becomes vacant between general elections, a by-election is held.

British subjects and citizens of the Irish Republic can stand for election as Members of Parliament (MPs) provided they are 21 or over and not subject to disqualification. Those disqualified from sitting in the House include:
– undischarged bankrupts
– people sentenced to more than one year's imprisonment
– clergy of the Church of England, Church of Scotland, Church of Ireland and Roman Catholic Church
– members of the House of Lords
– holders of certain offices listed in the House of Commons Disqualification Act 1975, e.g. members of the judiciary, Civil Service, regular armed forces, police forces, some local government officers and some members of public corporations and government commissions

A candidate does not require any party backing but his or her nomination for election must be supported by the signatures of ten people registered in the constituency. A candidate must also deposit with the returning officer £500, which is forfeit if the candidate does not receive more than 5 per cent of the votes cast. All election expenses at a general election, except the candidate's personal expenses, are subject to a statutory limit of £4,965, plus 4.2 pence for each elector in a borough constituency or 5.6 pence for each elector in a county constituency.

See pages 226–33 for an alphabetical list of MPs, pages 236–68 for the results of the last general election, and page 233 for the results of by-elections since the general election.

STATE OF PARTIES *as at 26 July 1999*

Conservative, 162 (14 women)
Labour, 416 (101 women)
Liberal Democrats, 46 (3 women)
Plaid Cymru, 4
Scottish Labour, 1
Scottish Nationalist, 6 (2 women)
Sinn Fein, 2
Social Democratic and Labour, 3
Ulster Democratic Unionist, 2
Ulster Unionist, 10
United Kingdom Unionist, 1
Independent, 1
Member for Falkirk West (Dennis Canavan), 1
The Speaker and three Deputy Speakers, 4 (1 woman)
Total, 659 (121 women)
Government majority, 178

BUSINESS

The week's business of the House is outlined each Thursday by the Leader of the House, after consultation between the Chief Government Whip and the Chief Opposition Whip. A quarter to a third of the time will be taken up by the Government's legislative programme and the rest by other business. As a rule, bills likely to raise political controversy are introduced in the Commons before going on to the Lords, and the Commons claims exclusive control in respect of national taxation and expenditure. Bills such as the Finance Bill, which imposes taxation, and the Consolidated Fund Bills, which authorize expenditure, must begin in the Commons. A bill of which the financial provisions are subsidiary may begin in the Lords; and the Commons may waive its rights in regard to Lords' amendments affecting finance.

The Commons has a public register of MPs' financial and certain other interests; this is published annually as a House of Commons paper. Members must also disclose any relevant financial interest or benefit in a matter before the House when taking part in a debate, in certain other proceedings of the House, or in consultations with other MPs, with Ministers or with civil servants.

MEMBERS' PAY AND ALLOWANCES

Since 1911 members of the House of Commons have received salary payments; facilities for free travel were introduced in 1924. Salary rates since 1911 are as follows:

1911	£400 p.a.	1983 June	£15,308 p.a.
1931	360	1984 Jan	16,106
1934	380	1985 Jan	16,904
1935	400	1986 Jan	17,702
1937	600	1987 Jan	18,500
1946	1,000	1988 Jan	22,548
1954	1,250	1989 Jan	24,107
1957	1,750	1990 Jan	26,701
1964	3,250	1991 Jan	28,970
1972 Jan	4,500	1992 Jan	30,854
1975 June	5,750	1994 Jan	31,687
1976 June	6,062	1995 Jan	33,189
1977 July	6,270	1996 Jan	34,085
1978 June	6,897	1996 July	43,000
1979 June	9,450	1997 April	43,860
1980 June	11,750	1998 April	45,066
1981 June	13,950	1999 April	47,008
1982 June	14,510		

In 1969 MPs were granted an allowance for secretarial and research expenses, now known as the Office Costs Allowance. From April 1999 the allowance is £50,264 a year.

Since 1972 MPs have been able to claim reimbursement for the additional cost of staying overnight away from their main residence while on parliamentary business; this is known as the Additional Costs Allowance and from April 1999 is £12,984 a year.

Since 1980 each MP in receipt of the Office Costs Allowance has been able to contribute sums to an approved pension scheme for the provision of a pension, or other benefits, for or in respect of persons whose salary is met by him/her from the Office Costs Allowance.

MEMBERS' PENSIONS

Pension arrangements for MPs were first introduced in 1964. The arrangements currently provide a pension of one-fiftieth of salary for each year of pensionable service with a maximum of two-thirds of salary at age 65. Pension is payable normally at age 65, for men and women, or on later retirement. Pensions may be paid earlier, e.g. on retirement due to ill health or at age 60 after 20 years' service. The widow/widower of a former MP receives a pension of five-eighths of the late MP's pension. Pensions are index-linked. Members currently contribute 6 per cent of salary to the pension fund; there is an Exchequer contribution, currently slightly more than the amount contributed by MPs.

The House of Commons Members' Fund provides for annual or lump sum grants to ex-MPs, their widows or widowers, and children whose incomes are below certain limits or who are experiencing severe hardship. Members contribute £24 a year and the Exchequer £215,000 a year to the fund.

OFFICERS AND OFFICIALS

The House of Commons is presided over by the Speaker, who has considerable powers to maintain order in the House. A deputy Speaker, called the Chairman of Ways and Means, and two Deputy Chairmen may preside over sittings of the House of Commons; they are elected by the House, and, like the Speaker, neither speak nor vote other than in their official capacity.

The staff of the House are employed by a Commission chaired by the Speaker. The heads of the six House of Commons departments are permanent officers of the House, not MPs. The Clerk of the House is the principal adviser to the Speaker on the privileges and procedures of the House, the conduct of the business of the House, and committees. The Serjeant-at-Arms is responsible for security, ceremonial, and for accommodation in the Commons part of the Palace of Westminster.

Speaker (£111,315), The Rt. Hon. Betty Boothroyd, MP (West Bromwich West)
Chairman of Ways and Means (£80,367), The Rt. Hon. Sir Alan Haselhurst, MP (Saffron Walden)
First Deputy Chairman of Ways and Means (£76,326), Michael Martin, MP (Glasgow Springburn)
Second Deputy Chairman of Ways and Means (£76,326), Michael Lord, MP (Suffolk Central and Ipswich North)

OFFICES OF THE SPEAKER AND CHAIRMAN OF WAYS AND MEANS

Speaker's Secretary (£45,810–£73,470), N. Bevan, CB
Chaplain to the Speaker, Revd Canon R. Wright
Secretary to the Chairman of Ways and Means (£30,271 – £45,795), C. Stanton

DEPARTMENT OF THE CLERK OF THE HOUSE

Clerk of the House of Commons (£123,787), W. R. McKay, CB
Clerk Assistant (£66,900–£104,190), G. Cubie
Clerk of Committees (£66,900–£104,190), C. B. Winnifrith, CB
Clerk of Legislation (£66,900–£104,190), R. B. Sands
Principal Clerks (£61,110–£98,400)
    Journals, A. J. Hastings, CB
    Table Office, D. G. Millar
    Domestic Committees, M. R. Jack, PH.D.
Principal Clerks (£50,510–£82,650)
    Overseas Office, R. W. G. Wilson
    Bills, Ms H. E. Irwin
    Select Committees, Mrs J. Sharpe; F. A. Cranmer; R. J. Rogers
    Delegated Legislation, W. A. Proctor
Deputy Principal Clerks (£45,810–£73,470), Ms A. Barry; C. R. M. Ward, PH.D.; D. W. N. Doig; A. Sandall; D. L. Natzler; E. P. Silk; A. R. Kennon; L. C. Laurence Smyth; S. J. Patrick; D. J. Gerhold; C. J. Poyser; D. F. Harrison; S. J. Priestley; A. H. Doherty; P. A. Evans; R. I. S. Phillips; R. G. James, PH.D.; Ms P. A. Helme; D. R. Lloyd; B. M. Hutton; J. S. Benger, D.PHIL.; Ms E. C. Samson; N. P. Walker; M. D. Hamlyn; Mrs E. J. Flood; P. C. Seaward, D.PHIL.; A. Y. A. Azad

Senior Clerks (£30,271–£45,795), C. G. Lee; C. D. Stanton; C. A. Shaw; Ms L. M. Gardner; K. J. Brown; F. J. Reid; M. Hennessy; G. R. Devine; P. G. Moon; M. Clark; Mrs J. N. St J. Mulley; T. W. P. Healey; Mrs S. A. R. Davies; J. D. Whatley; K. C. Fox; J. D. W. Rhys; Ms J. A. Long; Miss E. S. Payne; Ms S. McGlashan; Ms J. Eldred *(acting)*; S. T. Fiander *(acting)*; D. H. Griffiths *(acting)*; Ms R. Melling, CBE *(acting)*; C. Wilson *(acting)*
Examiners of Petitions for Private Bills, Ms H. E. Irwin; Dr F. P. Tudor
Registrar of Members' Interests (£50,510–£82,650), R. J. Willoughby *(seconded to Speaker's Office)*
Taxing Officer, W. A. Proctor

Vote Office

Deliverer of the Vote (£45,810–£73,470), J. F. Collins
Deputy Deliverers of the Vote (£30,271–£45,795), vacant *(Distribution)*; O. B. T. Sweeney *(Parliamentary)*; F. W. Hallett *(Production)*

Speaker's Counsel

Speaker's Counsel (£61,110–£98,400), J. Mason, CB
Speaker's Counsel (European legislation) (£61,110–£98,400), J. E. G. Vaux
Speaker's Assistant Counsel (£45,810–£73,470), A. Akbar; J. R. Mallinson

DEPARTMENT OF THE SERJEANT-AT-ARMS

Serjeant-at-Arms (£61,110–£98,400), P. N. W. Jennings, CVO (until Dec. 1999); M. J. A. Cummins (from Jan. 2000)
Deputy Serjeant-at-Arms (£45,810–£73,470), M. J. A. Cummins (until Dec. 1999)
Assistant Serjeants-at-Arms (£34,283–£55,524), P. A. J. Wright; J. M. Robertson; M. Harvey

DEPARTMENT OF THE LIBRARY

Librarian (£61,110–£98,400), Miss J. B. Tanfield (until Dec. 1999); Miss P. Baines (from Jan. 2000)
Directors (£45,810–£73,470), Miss P. Baines (until Dec. 1999); K. G. Cuninghame; Mrs J. Wainwright; R. Clements; R. Ware, D.PHIL.
Heads of Sections (£34,283–£55,524), C. Pond, PH.D.; Mrs C. Andrews; Mrs J. Lourie; C. Barclay; Mrs J. Fiddick; Mrs C. Gillie; R. Twigger; Mrs G. Allen; R. Cracknell
Senior Library Clerks (£30,271–£45,795), Ms F. Poole; T. Edmonds; Ms O. Gay; Miss E. McInnes; Dr D. Gore; B. Winetrobe; Miss M. Baber; Ms A. Walker; Mrs H. Holden; Mrs P. Carling; Miss J. Seaton; Mrs K. Greener; Ms P. Strickland; Miss V. Miller; M. P. Hillyard; Ms J. Roll; Ms W. Wilson; S. Wise; E. Wood; P. Bowers, PH.D.; T. Dodd; A. Seely; Mrs J. Hough; G. Danby, PH.D.; Dr P. M. Richards; B. C. Morgan; Ms K. Wright; Miss L. Conway; C. Blair, PH.D.; G. Vidler; C. Sear; M. Oakes *(period)*; D. Maddison *(period)*; A. Presland *(period)*; Ms F. Whittle *(acting)*

DEPARTMENT OF FINANCE AND ADMINISTRATION

Director of Finance and Administration (£61,110–£98,400), A. Walker
Head of the Establishments Office (£50,510–£82,650), B. Wilson
Head of the Fees Office (£45,810–£73,470), A. Cameron
Head of the Finance Office (£45,810–£73,470), M. Barram

DEPARTMENT OF THE OFFICIAL REPORT

Editor (£50,510–£82,650), I. Church
Deputy Editors (£41,550–£65,270), W. G. Garland; Miss L. Sutherland; Ms C. Fogarty

REFRESHMENT DEPARTMENT

Director of Catering Services (£50,510–£82,650), Mrs S. Harrison

Operations Manager (£30,271–£45,795), vacant

Executive Chef (£30,271–£45,795), D. Dorricott

Financial Controller (£30,271–£45,795), Mrs J. Rissen

SELECT COMMITTEES

The more important committees, as at August 1999, are:

DEPARTMENTAL COMMITTEES

Agriculture – Chair, Peter Luff, MP; *Clerk*, Ms L. M. Gardner

Culture, Media and Sport – Chair, Rt. Hon. Gerald Kaufman, MP; *Clerks*, C. G. Lee; Ms T. H. L. Brufal

Defence – Chair, Bruce George, MP; *Clerks*, P. A. Evans; Ms S. McGlashan

Education and Employment – Clerks, B. M. Hutton; K. C. Fox
    Sub-committees: Education – Chair, Malcolm Wicks, MP; *Clerk*, B. M. Hutton; *Employment* – Chair, Rt. Hon. Derek Foster, MP; *Clerk*, T. W. P. Healey

Environment, Transport and the Regions – Chairs, Andrew Bennett, MP; Gwyneth Dunwoody, MP; *Clerk*, D. F. Harrison
    Sub-committees: Environment – Chair, Andrew Bennett, MP; *Clerk*, H. A. Yardley; *Transport* – Chair, Gwyneth Dunwoody, MP; *Clerk*, G. R. Devine

Foreign Affairs – Chair, Donald Anderson, MP; *Clerks*, E. P. Silk; one vacancy

Health – Chair, David Hinchliffe, MP; *Clerks*, J. S. Benger, D.Phil.; J. D. Whatley

Home Affairs – Chair, Chris Mullin, MP; *Clerks*, A. R. Kennon; M. P. Atkins

International Development – Chair, Bowen Wells, MP; *Clerks*, A. Y. A. Azad; Ms J. Hughes

Northern Ireland – Chair, Rt. Hon. Peter Brooke, CH, MP; *Clerk*, C. R. M. Ward

Science and Technology – Chair, Dr Michael Clark, MP; *Clerk*, Mrs J. N. St J. Mulley

Scottish Affairs – Chair, David Marshall, MP; *Clerk*, Ms A. Barry

Social Security – Chair, Archy Kirkwood, MP; *Clerk*, L. C. Laurence Smyth

Trade and Industry – Chair, Martin O'Neill, MP; *Clerks*, D. L. Natzler; M. Egan

Treasury – Chair, Rt. Hon. Giles Radice, MP; *Clerks*, S. J. Patrick; one vacancy
    Treasury sub-committee: Chair, Sir Michael Spicer, MP; *Clerk*, vacant

Welsh Affairs – Chair, Martyn Jones, MP; *Clerk*, Ms P. A. Helme

NON-DEPARTMENTAL COMMITTEES

Deregulation – Chair, Peter Pike, MP; *Clerk*, J. D. W. Rhys

Environmental Audit – Chair, John Horam, MP; *Clerk*, F. J. Reid

European Legislation – Chair, James Hood, MP; *Clerks*, Mrs E. J. Flood; Mrs S. Craig

Modernization – Chair, Rt. Hon. Margaret Beckett, MP; *Clerks*, C. B. Winnifrith, CB; A. Sandall

Procedure – Chair, Nicholas Winterton, MP; *Clerks*, Ms E. C. Samson; S. Mark

Public Accounts – Chair, Rt. Hon. David Davis, MP; *Clerk*, K. J. Brown, OBE

Public Administration – Chair, Tony Wright, MP; *Clerk*, Dr P. C. Seaward

Standards and Privileges – Chair, Rt. Hon. Robert Sheldon, MP; *Clerks*, A. Sandall; Mrs S. A. R. Davies

PARLIAMENTARY INFORMATION

The following is a short glossary of aspects of the work of Parliament. Unless otherwise stated, references are to House of Commons procedures.

BILL – Proposed legislation is termed a bill. The stages of a public bill (for private bills, *see* page 221) in the House of Commons are as follows:

First Reading: This stage nowadays merely constitutes an order to have the bill printed

Second Reading: The debate on the principles of the bill

Committee Stage: The detailed examination of a bill, clause by clause. In most cases this takes place in a standing committee, or the whole House may act as a committee. A special standing committee may take evidence before embarking on detailed scrutiny of the bill. Very rarely, a bill may be examined by a select committee (*see* page 221)

Report Stage: Detailed review of a bill as amended in committee

Third Reading: Final debate on a bill

Public bills go through the same stages in the House of Lords, except that in almost all cases the committee stage is taken in committee of the whole House.

A bill may start in either House, and has to pass through both Houses to become law. Both Houses have to agree the same text of a bill, so that the amendments made by the second House are then considered in the originating House, and if not agreed, sent back or themselves amended, until agreement is reached.

CHILTERN HUNDREDS – A nominal office of profit under the Crown, the acceptance of which requires an MP to vacate his/her seat. The Manor of Northstead is similar. These are the only means by which an MP may resign.

CONSOLIDATED FUND BILL – A bill to authorize issue of money to maintain Government services. The bill is dealt with without debate.

EARLY DAY MOTION – A motion put on the notice paper by an MP without in general the real prospect of its being debated. Such motions are expressions of back-bench opinion.

FATHER OF THE HOUSE – The Member whose continuous service in the House of Commons is the longest. The present Father of the House is the Rt. Hon. Sir Edward Heath, KG, MBE, MP, elected first in 1950.

HOURS OF MEETING – The House of Commons normally meets Monday, Tuesday and Thursday at 2.30 p.m., and on Wednesday and Friday at 9.30 a.m.; there are ten Fridays without sittings in each session. From January 1999 until the end of the 1999–2000 session the Commons is experimenting with sitting from 11.30 a.m. on Thursdays. (*See also* Westminster Hall Sittings, below). The House of Lords normally meets at 2.30 p.m. Monday to Wednesday and at 3 p.m. on Thursday. In the latter part of the session, the House of Lords sometimes sits on Fridays at 11 a.m.

LEADER OF THE OPPOSITION – In 1937 the office of Leader of the Opposition was recognized and a salary was assigned to the post. Since April 1999 the salary has been £105,957 (including parliamentary salary of £47,008). The present Leader of the Opposition is the Rt. Hon. William Hague, MP.

THE LORD CHANCELLOR – The Lord High Chancellor of Great Britain is (*ex officio*) the Speaker of the House of Lords. Unlike the Speaker of the House of Commons, he is a member of the Government, takes part in debates and votes in divisions. He has none of the powers to maintain order that the Speaker in the Commons has, these powers being exercised in the Lords by the House as a whole. The Lord Chancellor sits in the Lords on one of the Woolsacks, couches covered with red cloth and stuffed with wool. If he wishes to address the House in any way except formally as Speaker, he leaves the Woolsack.

NORTHERN IRELAND GRAND COMMITTEE – The Northern Ireland Grand Committee consists of all MPs representing constituencies in Northern Ireland, together with not more than 25 other MPs nominated by the Committee of Selection. The business of the committee includes questions, short debates, ministerial statements, bills, legislative proposals and other matters relating exclusively to Northern Ireland, and delegated legislation. In autumn 1999 the House will debate a proposal to suspend the work of the Committee during the experiment with sittings in Westminster Hall (*see* page 222).

The Northern Ireland Affairs Committee is one of the departmental select committees, empowered to examine the expenditure, administration and policy of the Northern Ireland Office and the administration and expenditure of the Crown Solicitor's Office.

OPPOSITION DAY – A day on which the topic for debate is chosen by the Opposition. There are 20 such days in a normal session. On 17 days, subjects are chosen by the Leader of the Opposition; on the remaining three days by the leader of the next largest opposition party.

PARLIAMENT ACTS 1911 AND 1949 – Under these Acts, bills may become law without the consent of the Lords, though the House of Lords has the power to delay a public bill for 13 months from its first second reading in the House of Commons.

PRIME MINISTER'S QUESTIONS – The Prime Minister answers questions from 3.00 to 3.30 p.m. on Wednesdays.

PRIVATE BILL – A bill promoted by a body or an individual to give powers additional to, or in conflict with, the general law, and to which a special procedure applies to enable people affected to object.

PRIVATE MEMBER'S BILL – A public bill promoted by a Member who is not a member of the Government.

PRIVATE NOTICE QUESTION – A question adjudged of urgent importance on submission to the Speaker (in the Lords, the Leader of the House), answered at the end of oral questions, usually at 3.30 p.m.

PRIVILEGE – The following are covered by the privilege of Parliament:
(i) freedom from interference in going to, attending at, and going from, Parliament
(ii) freedom of speech in parliamentary proceedings
(iii) the printing and publishing of anything relating to the proceedings of the two Houses is subject to privilege
(iv) each House is the guardian of its dignity and may punish any insult to the House as a whole

QUESTION TIME – Oral questions are answered by Ministers in the Commons from 2.30 to 3.30 p.m. every day except Friday. From January 1999 until the end of the 1999–2000 session the Commons is experimenting with taking questions on Thursdays from 11.30 a.m. to 12.30 p.m. Questions are also taken at the start of the Lords sittings, with a daily limit of four oral questions.

ROYAL ASSENT – The royal assent is signified by letters patent to such bills and measures as have passed both Houses of Parliament (or bills which have been passed under the Parliament Acts 1911 and 1949). The Sovereign has not given royal assent in person since 1854. On occasion, for instance in the prorogation of Parliament, royal assent may be pronounced to the two Houses by Lords Commissioners. More usually royal assent is notified to each House sitting separately in accordance with the Royal Assent Act 1967. The old French formulae for royal assent are then endorsed on the acts by the Clerk of the Parliaments.

The power to withhold assent resides with the Sovereign but has not been exercised in the UK since 1707.

SCOTTISH GRAND COMMITTEE – Established in its present form in 1957, the committee consists of all 72 MPs representing Scottish constituencies, with a quorum of ten. The functions of the committee are to consider the principle of all public bills relating exclusively to Scotland (constituting in effect the bill's second reading); to consider the Scottish estimates on not less than six days a session; and to consider matters relating exclusively to Scotland on not more than six days a session. From the beginning of the 1994–5 session, the committee's powers were enhanced to allow oral questions, short debates, ministerial statements, and consideration of appropriate statutory instruments. The committee can meet on appointed days at specified places in Scotland. In autumn 1999 the House will debate a proposal to suspend the work of the Committee during the experiment with sittings in Westminster Hall (*see* page 222).

The Scottish Affairs Committee, one of the departmental select committees, was empowered to examine the expenditure, administration and policy of the Scottish Office, and the expenditure and administration of the Lord Advocate's Office. Following devolution, the role of the select committee has been questioned. If it continues, it will be concerned with the role and responsibilities of the relevant Secretary of State and on occasion the policy of the UK departments as it affects Scotland.

SELECT COMMITTEES – Consisting usually of ten to 15 members of all parties, select committees are a means used by both Houses in order to investigate certain matters.

Most select committees in the House of Commons are tied to departments: each committee investigates subjects within a government department's remit. There are other select committees dealing with public accounts (i.e. the spending by the Government of money voted by Parliament) and European legislation, and also domestic committees dealing, for example, with privilege and procedure. Major select committees usually take evidence in public; their evidence and reports are published by The Stationery Office. House of Commons select committees are reconstituted after a general election. For main committees, *see* page 220.

The principal select committee in the House of Lords is that on the European Communities, which has, at present, six sub-committees dealing with all areas of Community policy. The House of Lords also has a select committee on science and technology, which appoints sub-committees to deal with specific subjects, and a select committee on delegated powers and deregulation. For committees, *see* page 217. In addition, *ad hoc* select committees have been set up from time to time to investigate specific subjects. There are also some joint committees of the two Houses, e.g. the committees on statutory instruments and on parliamentary privilege.

THE SPEAKER – The Speaker of the House of Commons is the spokesman and president of the Chamber. He or she is elected by the House at the beginning of each Parliament or when the previous Speaker retires or dies. The Speaker neither speaks in debates nor votes in divisions except when the voting is equal.

VACANT SEATS – When a vacancy occurs in the House of Commons during a session of Parliament, the writ for the by-election is moved by a Whip of the party to which the member whose seat has been vacated belonged. If the House is in recess, the Speaker can issue a warrant for a writ, should two members certify to him that a seat is vacant.

WELSH GRAND COMMITTEE – First appointed in the 1959–60 session, the committee consists of all 40 MPs representing Welsh constituencies plus not more than five other members nominated by the Committee of Selection. The functions of the committee are to consider the principle of all public bills referred to it (constituting in effect the second reading of such a bill); and to consider matters relating exclusively to Wales. Since 1996 the business of the committee may also include questions, ministerial statements and short debates. Since June 1996 members of the committee have been permitted to speak in Welsh. In autumn 1999 the House will debate a proposal to suspend the work of the Committee during the experiment with sittings in Westminster Hall (*see* below).

The Welsh Affairs Committee, one of the departmental select committees, was empowered to examine the expenditure, administration and policy of the Welsh Office. Following devolution, the role of the select committee has been questioned. If it continues, it will be concerned with the role and responsibilities of the relevant Secretary of State and on occasion the policy of the UK departments as it affects Wales.

WESTMINSTER HALL SITTINGS – Following a report by the Modernization of the House of Commons Select Committee, the Commons decided in May 1999 to set up a second debating forum for an experimental period from the start of the 1999–2000 session. It will be known as 'Westminster Hall' and sittings will be in the Grand Committee Room on Tuesdays from 10 a.m. to 1 p.m., Wednesdays from 9.30 a.m. to 2 p.m. and Thursdays from 2.30 p.m. for up to three hours. Sittings will be open to the public at the times indicated.

WHIPS – In order to secure the attendance of Members of a particular party in Parliament, particularly on the occasion of an important vote, Whips (originally known as 'Whippers-in') are appointed. The written appeal or circular letter issued by them is also known as a 'whip', its urgency being denoted by the number of times it is underlined. Failure to respond to a three-line whip is tantamount in the Commons to secession (at any rate temporarily) from the party. Whips are provided with office accommodation in both Houses, and Government and some Opposition Whips receive salaries from public funds.

PARLIAMENTARY EDUCATION UNIT – Norman Shaw Building (North), London SW1A 2TT. Tel: 0171-219 2105 E-mail: edunit@parliament.uk

GOVERNMENT OFFICE

The Government is the body of Ministers responsible for the administration of national affairs, determining policy and introducing into Parliament any legislation necessary to give effect to government policy. The majority of Ministers are members of the House of Commons but members of the House of Lords or of neither House may

also hold ministerial responsibility. The Lord Chancellor is always a member of the House of Lords. The Prime Minister is, by current convention, always a member of the House of Commons.

THE PRIME MINISTER

The office of Prime Minister, which had been in existence for nearly 200 years, was officially recognized in 1905 and its holder was granted a place in the table of precedence. The Prime Minister, by tradition also First Lord of the Treasury and Minister for the Civil Service, is appointed by the Sovereign and is usually the leader of the party which enjoys, or can secure, a majority in the House of Commons. Other Ministers are appointed by the Sovereign on the recommendation of the Prime Minister, who also allocates functions amongst Ministers and has the power to obtain their resignation or dismissal individually.

The Prime Minister informs the Sovereign of state and political matters, advises on the dissolution of Parliament, and makes recommendations for important Crown appointments, the award of honours, etc.

As the chairman of Cabinet meetings and leader of a political party, the Prime Minister is responsible for translating party policy into government activity. As leader of the Government, the Prime Minister is responsible to Parliament and to the electorate for the policies and their implementation.

The Prime Minister also represents the nation in international affairs, e.g. summit conferences.

THE CABINET

The Cabinet developed during the 18th century as an inner committee of the Privy Council, which was the chief source of executive power until that time. The Cabinet is composed of about 20 Ministers chosen by the Prime Minister, usually the heads of government departments (generally known as Secretaries of State unless they have a special title, e.g. Chancellor of the Exchequer), the leaders of the two Houses of Parliament, and the holders of various traditional offices.

The Cabinet's functions are the final determination of policy, control of government and co-ordination of government departments. The exercise of its functions is dependent upon enjoying majority support in the House of Commons. Cabinet meetings are held in private, taking place once or twice a week during parliamentary sittings and less often during a recess. Proceedings are confidential, the members being bound by their oath as Privy Counsellors not to disclose information about the proceedings.

The convention of collective responsibility means that the Cabinet acts unanimously even when Cabinet Ministers do not all agree on a subject. The policies of departmental Ministers must be consistent with the policies of the Government as a whole, and once the Government's policy has been decided, each Minister is expected to support it or resign.

The convention of ministerial responsibility holds a Minister, as the political head of his or her department, accountable to Parliament for the department's work. Departmental Ministers usually decide all matters within their responsibility, although on matters of political importance they normally consult their colleagues collectively. A decision by a departmental Minister is binding on the Government as a whole.

POLITICAL PARTIES

Before the reign of William and Mary the principal officers of state were chosen by and were responsible to the Sovereign alone and not to Parliament or the nation at large. Such officers acted sometimes in concert with one another but more often independently, and the fall of one did not, of necessity, involve that of others, although all were liable to be dismissed at any time.

In 1693 the Earl of Sunderland recommended to William III the advisability of selecting a ministry from the political party which enjoyed a majority in the House of Commons and the first united ministry was drawn in 1696 from the Whigs, to which party the King owed his throne. This group became known as the Junto and was regarded with suspicion as a novelty in the political life of the nation, being a small section meeting in secret apart from the main body of Ministers. It may be regarded as the forerunner of the Cabinet and in course of time it led to the establishment of the principle of joint responsibility of Ministers, so that internal disagreement caused a change of personnel or resignation of the whole body of Ministers.

The accession of George I, who was unfamiliar with the English language, led to a disinclination on the part of the Sovereign to preside at meetings of his Ministers and caused the appearance of a Prime Minister, a position first acquired by Robert Walpole in 1721 and retained by him without interruption for 20 years and 326 days.

DEVELOPMENT OF PARTIES

In 1828 the Whigs became known as Liberals, a name originally given to it by its opponents to imply laxity of principles, but gradually accepted by the party to indicate its claim to be pioneers and champions of political reform and progressive legislation. In 1861 a Liberal Registration Association was founded and Liberal Associations became widespread. In 1877 a National Liberal Federation was formed, with headquarters in London. The Liberal Party was in power for long periods during the second half of the 19th century and for several years during the first quarter of the 20th century, but after a split in the party the numbers elected were small from 1931. In 1988, a majority of the Liberals agreed on a merger with the Social Democratic Party under the title Social and Liberal Democrats; since 1989 they have been known as the Liberal Democrats. A minority continue separately as the Liberal Party.

Soon after the change from Whig to Liberal the Tory Party became known as Conservative, a name believed to have been invented by John Wilson Croker in 1830 and to have been generally adopted about the time of the passing of the Reform Act of 1832 to indicate that the preservation of national institutions was the leading principle of the party. After the Home Rule crisis of 1886 the dissentient Liberals entered into a compact with the Conservatives, under which the latter undertook not to contest their seats, but a separate Liberal Unionist organization was maintained until 1912, when it was united with the Conservatives.

Labour candidates for Parliament made their first appearance at the general election of 1892, when there were 27 standing as Labour or Liberal-Labour. In 1900 the Labour Representation Committee was set up in order to establish a distinct Labour group in Parliament, with its own whips, its own policy, and a readiness to co-operate with any party which might be engaged in promoting legislation in the direct interest of labour. In 1906 the LRC became known as the Labour Party.

The Council for Social Democracy was announced by four former Labour Cabinet Ministers in January 1981 and in March 1981 the Social Democratic Party was launched. Later that year the SDP and the Liberal Party formed an electoral alliance. In 1988 a majority of the SDP agreed on a merger with the Liberal Party but a minority continued as a separate party under the SDP title. In 1990 it was decided to wind up the party organization and its three sitting MPs were known as independent social democrats. None were returned at the 1992 general election.

Plaid Cymru was founded in 1926 to provide an independent political voice for Wales and to campaign for self-government in Wales.

The Scottish National Party was founded in 1934 to campaign for independence for Scotland.

The Social Democratic and Labour Party was founded in 1970, emerging from the civil rights movement of the 1960s, with the aim of promoting reform, reconciliation and partnership across the sectarian divide in Northern Ireland and of opposing violence from any quarter.

The Ulster Democratic Unionist Party was founded in 1971 to resist moves by the Ulster Unionist Party which were considered a threat to the Union. Its aim is to maintain Northern Ireland as an integral part of the UK.

The Ulster Unionist Council first met formally in 1905. Its objectives are to maintain Northern Ireland as an integral part of the UK and to promote the aims of the Ulster Unionist Party.

GOVERNMENT AND OPPOSITION

The government of the day is formed by the party which wins the largest number of seats in the House of Commons at a general election, or which has the support of a majority of members in the House of Commons. By tradition, the leader of the majority party is asked by the Sovereign to form a government, while the largest minority party becomes the official Opposition with its own leader and a 'Shadow Cabinet'. Leaders of the Government and Opposition sit on the front benches of the Commons with their supporters (the back-benchers) sitting behind them.

FINANCIAL SUPPORT

Financial support to Opposition parties in the House of Commons was introduced in 1975 and is commonly known as Short Money, after Edward Short, the Leader of the House at that time, who introduced the scheme. For 1999–2000 financial support is:

Conservative	£3,377,973
Liberal Democrats	1,085,010
Plaid Cymru	61,859
SNP	134,643
SDLP	54,112
Democratic Unionists	33,871
Ulster Unionsts	138,750

A specific allocation for the Leader of the Opposition's office was introduced in April 1999 and has been set at £500,000 a year.

Financial support to the Opposition parties in the House of Lords was introduced in 1996 and is commonly known as Cranborne Money.

The parties included here are those with MPs sitting in the House of Commons in the present Parliament. Addresses of other political parties may be found in the Societies and Institutions section.

CONSERVATIVE AND UNIONIST PARTY

Central Office, 32 Smith Square, London
SW1P 3HH
Tel 0171-222 9000; fax 0171-222 1135
E-mail: ccoffice@conservative-party.org.uk
Web: http://www.conservative-party.org.uk

Chairman, Rt. Hon. Michael Ancram, QC, MP
Deputy Chairman and Chief Executive, The Hon. David Prior, MP
Senior Vice-Chairman, Tim Collins, CBE, MP
Vice-Chairmen, N. Evans, MP (*Wales*); John Hayes, MP
Treasurer, M. Ashcroft
SHADOW CABINET *as at August 1999*
Leader of the Opposition, Rt. Hon. William Hague, MP
Agriculture, Fisheries and Food, Tim Yeo, MP
Cabinet Office, Duchy of Lancaster and Policy Renewal, Andrew Lansley, CBE, MP
Culture, Media and Sport, Peter Ainsworth, MP
Defence, Iain Duncan Smith, MP
Education and Employment, Theresa May, MP
Environment, Transport and the Regions, Rt. Hon. John Redwood, MP
Foreign and Commonwealth Affairs, John Maples, MP
Health, Dr Liam Fox, MP
Home Affairs, Rt. Hon. Ann Widdecombe, MP
International Development, Gary Streeter, MP
Leader of the House of Commons and Constitutional Affairs, Rt. Hon. Sir George Young, Bt., MP
Leader of the House of Lords and Constitutional Affairs, The Lord Strathclyde, PC
Northern Ireland, Rt. Hon. Andrew Mackay, MP
Social Security, David Willetts, MP
Trade and Industry, Angela Browning, MP
Transport, Bernard Jenkin, MP
Treasury, Rt. Hon. Francis Maude, MP
Chief Secretary to the Treasury, Rt. Hon. David Heathcoat-Amory, MP
Conservative Party Chairman, Rt. Hon. Michael Ancram, QC, MP

CHIEF WHIPS
House of Lords, The Lord Henley
House of Commons, Rt. Hon. James Arbuthnot, MP (*Chief Whip*); Patrick McLoughlin, MP (*Deputy Chief Whip*)

SCOTTISH CONSERVATIVE AND UNIONIST CENTRAL OFFICE

Suite 1/1, 14 Links Place, Leith, Edinburgh
EH6 7EZ
Tel 0131-555 2900
E-mail: scuco@scottish.tory.org.uk

Chairman, R. Robertson
Deputy Chairman, Mrs K. Donald
Hon. Treasurer, D. Mitchell, CBE
Head of Campaigns and Operations, D. Canzini

LABOUR PARTY

Millbank Tower, Millbank, London SW1P 4GT
Tel 0171-802 1000; fax 0171-802 1234
E-mail: labour-party@geo2.poptel.org.uk
Web: http://www.labour.org.uk

Parliamentary Party Leader, Rt. Hon. Anthony Blair, MP
Deputy Party Leader, Rt. Hon. John Prescott, MP
Leader in the Lords, The Baroness Jay of Paddington
Chair, R. Rosser
Vice-Chair, Rt. Hon. Clare Short, MP
Treasurer, Ms M. Prosser
General Secretary, Ms M. McDonagh
General Secretary, Scottish Labour Party, A. Rowley

LIBERAL DEMOCRATS

4 Cowley Street, London SW1P 3NB
Tel 0171-222 7999; fax 0171-799 2170
E-mail: libedems@cix.co.uk
Web: http://www.libdems.org.uk

President, The Baroness Maddock
Hon. Treasurer, The Lord Razzall, CBE
Chief Executive, Ms E. Pamplin
Parliamentary Party Leader, Charles Kennedy, MP
Leader in the Lords, The Lord Rodgers of Quarry Bank, PC
LIBERAL DEMOCRAT SPOKESMEN *as at August 1999*
Deputy Leader, Home and Legal Affairs, Alan Beith, MP
Agriculture and Rural Affairs, Paul Tyler, MP
Culture, Media and Sport, Constitution, Rt. Hon. Robert Maclennan, MP
Education and Employment, Don Foster, MP
Environment and Transport, Matthew Taylor, MP
Foreign Affairs, Defence and Europe, Menzies Campbell, MP
Health, Simon Hughes, MP
Local Government and Housing, Paul Burstow, MP
Social Security and Welfare, David Rendel, MP
Trade and Industry, David Chidgey, MP
Treasury, Malcolm Bruce, MP
Women, Jackie Ballard, MP
Young People, Lembit Opik, MP
Northern Ireland, Lembit Opik, MP
Scotland, Jim Wallace, MP
Wales, Richard Livsey, MP

LIBERAL DEMOCRAT WHIPS
House of Lords, The Lord Harris of Greenwich, PC
House of Commons, Paul Tyler, MP (*Chief Whip*); Andrew Stunell, MP (*Deputy Whip*)

LIBERAL DEMOCRATS WALES

Bay View House, 102 Bute Street, Cardiff
CF1 6AD
Tel 01222-313400; fax 01222-313401
E-mail: ldwales@cix.co.uk

Party President, A. Carlile, QC
Party Leader, Richard Livsey, CBE, MP
Chairman, P. Lloyd
Treasurer, A. Joyce
Secretary, Ms K. Lloyd
Administrative Officer, Ms H. Northmore-Thomas

SCOTTISH LIBERAL DEMOCRATS

4 Clifton Terrace, Edinburgh EH12 5DR
Tel 0131-337 2314; fax 0131-337 3566
E-mail: scotlibdem@cix.co.uk
Web: http://www.scotlibdems.org.uk

Party President, R. Thomson
Party Leader, Jim Wallace, MP, MSP
Convener, Cllr I. Yuill
Treasurer, D. R. Sullivan
Chief Executive, W. Rennie

PLAID CYMRU – THE PARTY OF WALES
18 Park Grove, Cardiff CF10 3BN
Tel 01222-646000; fax 01222-646001
E-mail: post@plaidcymru.org
Web: http://www.plaidcymru.org
Party President, Dafydd Wigley, MP
Chairman, M. Phillips
Hon. Treasurer, vacant
Chief Executive/General Secretary, K. Davies

SCOTTISH NATIONAL PARTY
6 North Charlotte Street, Edinburgh EH2 4JH
Tel 0131-226 3661; fax 0131-225 9597
Web: http://www.snp.org.uk

Parliamentary Party Leader, Alasdair Morgan, MP, MSP
Chief Whip, Alasdair Morgan, MP, MSP
National Convener, Alex Salmond, MP
Senior Vice-Convener, John Swinney, MP
National Treasurer, I. Blackford
National Secretary, Colin Campbell, MSP

NORTHERN IRELAND

SOCIAL DEMOCRATIC AND LABOUR
PARTY
121 Ormeau Road, Belfast BT7 1SH
Tel 01232-247700; fax 01232-236699
E-mail: sdlp@indigo.ie
Web: http://www.indigo.ie/sdlp

Parliamentary Party Leader, John Hume, MP, MEP
Deputy Leader, Seamus Mallon, MP
Chief Whip, Eddie McGrady, MP
Chairman, J. Lennon
Hon. Treasurer, H. Doherty
General Secretary, Mrs G. Cosgrove

ULSTER DEMOCRATIC UNIONIST PARTY
91 Dundela Avenue, Belfast BT4 3BU
Tel 01232-471155; fax 01232-471797
E-mail: info@dup.org.uk
Web: http://www.dup.org.uk

Parliamentary Party Leader, Ian Paisley, MP, MEP
Deputy Leader, Peter Robinson, MP
Chairman, W. J. McClure
Chief Executive, A. Ewart
Hon. Treasurer, G. Campbell
Party Secretary, N. Dodds

ULSTER UNIONIST PARTY
3 Glengall Street, Belfast BT12 5AE
Tel 01232-324601; fax 01232-246738
E-mail: uup@uup.org.uk
Web: http://www.uup.org

Party Leader, Rt. Hon. David Trimble, MP
Chief Whip, Revd Martin Smyth, MP

ULSTER UNIONIST COUNCIL
President, J. Cunningham
Chairman, The Lord Rogan
Hon. Treasurer, J. Allen, OBE
General Secretary, D. Boyd

MEMBERS OF PARLIAMENT as at 27 July 1999

For abbreviations, *see* page 235
* Member of last Parliament
† Elected at a by-election since the general election
For late amendments *see* Stop-press

*Abbott, Ms Diane J. (*b.* 1953) *Lab., Hackney North and Stoke Newington*, maj. 15,627

Adams, Gerard (Gerry) (*b.* 1948) *SF, Belfast West*, maj. 7,909

*Adams, Mrs K. Irene (*b.* 1948) *Lab., Paisley North*, maj. 12,814

*Ainger, Nicholas R. (*b.* 1949) *Lab., Carmarthen West and Pembrokeshire South*, maj. 9,621

*Ainsworth, Peter M. (*b.* 1956) *C., Surrey East*, maj. 15,093

*Ainsworth, Robert W. (*b.* 1952) *Lab., Coventry North East*, maj. 22,569

†Alexander, Douglas G. (*b.* 1967) *Lab., Paisley South*, maj. 2,731

Allan, Richard B. (*b.* 1966) *LD, Sheffield Hallam*, maj. 8,271

*Allen, Graham W. (*b.* 1953) *Lab., Nottingham North*, maj. 18,801

*Amess, David A. A. (*b.* 1952) *C., Southend West*, maj. 2,615

*Ancram, Rt. Hon. Michael A. F. J. K. (Earl of Ancram) (*b.* 1945) *C., Devizes*, maj. 9,782

*Anderson, Donald (*b.* 1939) *Lab., Swansea East*, maj. 25,569

*Anderson, Mrs Janet (*b.* 1949) *Lab., Rossendale and Darwen*, maj. 10,949

*Arbuthnot, Rt. Hon. James N. (*b.* 1952) *C., Hampshire North East*, maj. 14,398

*Armstrong, Miss Hilary J. (*b.* 1945) *Lab., Durham North West*, maj. 24,754

*Ashdown, Rt. Hon. J. J. D. (Paddy) (*b.* 1941) *LD, Yeovil*, maj. 11,403

*Ashton, Joseph W. (*b.* 1933) *Lab., Bassetlaw*, maj. 17,460

Atherton, Ms Candice K. (*b.* 1955) *Lab., Falmouth and Camborne*, maj. 2,688

Atkins, Ms Charlotte (*b.* 1950) *Lab., Staffordshire Moorlands*, maj. 10,049

*Atkinson, David A. (*b.* 1940) *C., Bournemouth East*, maj. 4,346

*Atkinson, Peter L. (*b.* 1943) *C., Hexham*, maj. 222

*Austin-Walker, John E. (*b.* 1944) *Lab., Erith and Thamesmead*, maj. 17,424

Baker, Norman J. (*b.* 1957) *LD, Lewes*, maj. 1,300

*Baldry, Antony B. (*b.* 1950) *C., Banbury*, maj. 4,737

Ballard, Mrs Jacqueline M. (*b.* 1953) *LD, Taunton*, maj. 2,443

*Banks, Anthony L. (*b.* 1943) *Lab., West Ham*, maj. 19,494

*Barnes, Harold (*b.* 1936) *Lab., Derbyshire North East*, maj. 18,321

*Barron, Kevin J. (*b.* 1946) *Lab., Rother Valley*, maj. 23,485

*Battle, John D. (*b.* 1951) *Lab., Leeds West*, maj. 19,771

*Bayley, Hugh (*b.* 1952) *Lab., City of York*, maj. 20,523

Beard, C. Nigel (*b.* 1936) *Lab., Bexleyheath and Crayford*, maj. 3,415

*Beckett, Rt. Hon. Margaret M. (*b.* 1943) *Lab., Derby South*, maj. 16,106

Begg, Ms Anne (*b.* 1955) *Lab., Aberdeen South*, maj. 3,365

*Beggs, Roy (*b.* 1936) *UUP, Antrim East*, maj. 6,389

*Beith, Rt. Hon. Alan J. (*b.* 1943) *LD, Berwick upon Tweed*, maj. 8,042

Bell, Martin, OBE (*b.* 1938) *Ind., Tatton*, maj. 11,077

*Bell, Stuart (*b.* 1938) *Lab., Middlesbrough*, maj. 25,018

*Benn, Rt. Hon. Anthony N. W. (*b.* 1925) *Lab., Chesterfield*, maj. 5,775

†Benn, Hilary J. (*b.* 1953) *Lab., Leeds Central*, maj. 2,293

*Bennett, Andrew F. (*b.* 1939) *Lab., Denton and Reddish*, maj. 20,311

*Benton, Joseph E. (*b.* 1933) *Lab., Bootle*, maj. 28,421

Bercow, John S. (*b.* 1963) *C., Buckingham*, maj. 12,386

*Beresford, Sir Paul (*b.* 1946) *C., Mole Valley*, maj. 10,221

*Bermingham, Gerald E. (*b.* 1940) *Lab., St Helens South*, maj. 23,739

*Berry, Roger L., D.PHIL. (*b.* 1948) *Lab., Kingswood*, maj. 14,253

Best, Harold (*b.* 1939) *Lab., Leeds North West*, maj. 3,844

*Betts, Clive J. C. (*b.* 1950) *Lab., Sheffield Attercliffe*, maj. 21,818

Blackman, Ms Elizabeth M. (*b.* 1949) *Lab., Erewash*, maj. 9,135

*Blair, Rt. Hon. Anthony C. L. (*b.* 1953) *Lab., Sedgefield*, maj. 25,143

Blears, Hazel A. (*b.* 1956) *Lab., Salford*, maj. 17,069

Blizzard, Robert J. (*b.* 1950) *Lab., Waveney*, maj. 12,453

*Blunkett, Rt. Hon. David (*b.* 1947) *Lab., Sheffield Brightside*, maj. 19,954

Blunt, Crispin J. R. (*b.* 1960) *C., Reigate*, maj. 7,741

*Boateng, Paul Y. (*b.* 1951) *Lab., Brent South*, maj. 19,691

*Body, Sir Richard (*b.* 1927) *C., Boston and Skegness*, maj. 647

*Boothroyd, Rt. Hon. Betty (*b.* 1929) *The Speaker, West Bromwich West*, maj. 15,423

Borrow, David S. (*b.* 1952) *Lab., Ribble South*, maj. 5,084

*Boswell, Timothy E. (*b.* 1942) *C., Daventry*, maj. 7,378

*Bottomley, Peter J. (*b.* 1944) *C., Worthing West*, maj. 7,713

*Bottomley, Rt. Hon. Virginia H. B. M. (*b.* 1948) *C., Surrey South West*, maj. 2,694

*Bradley, Keith J. C. (*b.* 1950) *Lab., Manchester Withington*, maj. 18,581

Bradley, Peter C. S. (*b.* 1953) *Lab., Wrekin, The*, maj. 3,025

Bradshaw, Benjamin P. J. (*b.* 1960) *Lab., Exeter*, maj. 11,705

Brady, Graham (*b.* 1967) *C., Altrincham and Sale West*, maj. 1,505

Brake, Thomas A. (*b.* 1962) *LD, Carshalton and Wallington*, maj. 2,267

Brand, Dr Peter (*b.* 1947) *LD, Isle of Wight*, maj. 6,406

*Brazier, Julian W. H., TD (*b.* 1953) *C., Canterbury*, maj. 3,964

Breed, Colin E. (*b.* 1947) *LD, Cornwall South East*, maj. 6,480

Brinton, Ms Helen R. (*b.* 1954) *Lab., Peterborough*, maj. 7,323

*Brooke, Rt. Hon. Peter L., CH (*b.* 1934) *C., Cities of London and Westminster*, maj. 4,881

*Brown, Rt. Hon. J. Gordon, PH.D. (*b.* 1951) *Lab., Dunfermline East*, maj. 18,751

*Brown, Nicholas H. (*b.* 1950) *Lab., Newcastle upon Tyne East and Wallsend*, maj. 23,811

Brown, Russell L. (*b.* 1951) *Lab., Dumfries*, maj. 9,643

Browne, Desmond (*b.* 1952) *Lab., Kilmarnock and Loudoun*, maj. 7,256

*Browning, Mrs Angela F. (*b.* 1946) *C., Tiverton and Honiton*, maj. 1,653

*Bruce, Ian C. (*b.* 1947) *C., Dorset South*, maj. 77

*Bruce, Malcolm G. (*b.* 1944) *LD, Gordon*, maj. 6,997

Buck, Ms Karen P. (*b.* 1958) *Lab., Regent's Park and Kensington North*, maj. 14,657

*Burden, Richard H. (*b.* 1954) *Lab., Birmingham Northfield*, maj. 11,443

Burgon, Colin (*b.* 1948) *Lab., Elmet*, maj. 8,779

Burnett, John P. A. (*b.* 1945) *LD, Devon West and Torridge*, maj. 1,957

*Burns, Simon H. M. (*b.* 1952) *C., Chelmsford West*, maj. 6,691

Burstow, Paul K. (*b.* 1962) *LD, Sutton and Cheam*, maj. 2,097

Butler, Ms Christine M. (*b.* 1943) *Lab., Castle Point,* maj. 1,116

*Butterfill, John V. (*b.* 1941) *C., Bournemouth West,* maj. 5,710

*Byers, Rt. Hon. Stephen J. (*b.* 1953) *Lab., Tyneside North,* maj. 26,643

Cable, Dr J. Vincent (*b.* 1943) *LD, Twickenham,* maj. 4,281

*Caborn, Richard G. (*b.* 1943) *Lab., Sheffield Central,* maj. 16,906

Campbell, Alan (*b.* 1957) *Lab., Tynemouth,* maj. 11,273

*Campbell, Mrs Anne (*b.* 1940) *Lab., Cambridge,* maj. 14,137

*Campbell, Ronald (*b.* 1943) *Lab., Blyth Valley,* maj. 17,736

*Campbell, Rt. Hon. W. Menzies, CBE, QC (*b.* 1941) *LD, Fife North East,* maj. 10,356

*Campbell-Savours, Dale N. (*b.* 1943) *Lab., Workington,* maj. 19,656

*Canavan, Dennis A. (*b.* 1942) *Lab., Falkirk West,* maj. 13,783

*Cann, James C. (*b.* 1946) *Lab., Ipswich,* maj. 10,439

Caplin, Ivor K. (*b.* 1958) *Lab., Hove,* maj. 3,959

Casale, Roger M. (*b.* 1960) *Lab., Wimbledon,* maj. 2,980

*Cash, William N. P. (*b.* 1940) *C., Stone,* maj. 3,818

Caton, Martin P. (*b.* 1951) *Lab., Gower,* maj. 13,007

Cawsey, Ian A. (*b.* 1960) *Lab., Brigg and Goole,* maj. 6,389

*Chapman, J. K. (Ben) (*b.* 1940) *Lab., Wirral South,* maj. 7,004

*Chapman, Sir Sydney (*b.* 1935) *C., Chipping Barnet,* maj. 1,035

Chaytor, David M. (*b.* 1949) *Lab., Bury North,* maj. 7,866

*Chidgey, David W. G. (*b.* 1942) *LD, Eastleigh,* maj. 754

*Chisholm, Malcolm G. R. (*b.* 1949) *Lab., Edinburgh North and Leith,* maj. 10,978

Chope, Christopher R., OBE (*b.* 1947) *C., Christchurch,* maj. 2,165

*Church, Mrs Judith A. (*b.* 1953) *Lab., Dagenham,* maj. 17,054

*Clapham, Michael (*b.* 1943) *Lab., Barnsley West and Penistone,* maj. 17,267

*Clappison, W. James (*b.* 1956) *C., Hertsmere,* maj. 3,075

Clark, Rt. Hon. Alan K. M. (*b.* 1928) *C., Kensington and Chelsea,* maj. 9,519

*Clark, Rt. Hon. David G., PH.D. (*b.* 1939) *Lab., South Shields,* maj. 22,153

Clark, Ms Lynda M. (*b.* 1949) *Lab., Edinburgh Pentlands,* maj. 4,862

*Clark, Dr Michael, PH.D. (*b.* 1935) *C., Rayleigh,* maj. 10,684

Clark, Paul G. (*b.* 1957) *Lab., Gillingham,* maj. 1,980

Clarke, Anthony R. (*b.* 1963) *Lab., Northampton South,* maj. 744

Clarke, Charles R. (*b.* 1950) *Lab., Norwich South,* maj. 14,239

*Clarke, Eric L. (*b.* 1933) *Lab., Midlothian,* maj. 9,870

*Clarke, Rt. Hon. Kenneth H., QC (*b.* 1940) *C., Rushcliffe,* maj. 5,055

*Clarke, Rt. Hon. Thomas, CBE (*b.* 1941) *Lab., Coatbridge and Chryston,* maj. 19,295

*Clelland, David G. (*b.* 1943) *Lab., Tyne Bridge,* maj. 22,906

*Clifton-Brown, Geoffrey R. (*b.* 1953) *C., Cotswold,* maj. 11,965

*Clwyd, Mrs Ann (*b.* 1937) *Lab., Cynon Valley,* maj. 19,755

Coaker, Vernon R. (*b.* 1953) *Lab., Gedling,* maj. 3,802

*Coffey, Ms M. Ann (*b.* 1946) *Lab., Stockport,* maj. 18,912

*Cohen, Harry M. (*b.* 1949) *Lab., Leyton and Wanstead,* maj. 15,186

Coleman, Iain (*b.* 1958) *Lab., Hammersmith and Fulham,* maj. 3,842

Collins, Timothy W. G. (*b.* 1964) *C., Westmorland and Lonsdale,* maj. 4,521

Colman, Anthony (*b.* 1943) *Lab., Putney,* maj. 2,976

*Colvin, Michael K. B. (*b.* 1932) *C., Romsey,* maj. 8,585

*Connarty, Michael (*b.* 1947) *Lab., Falkirk East,* maj. 13,385

*Cook, Francis (*b.* 1935) *Lab., Stockton North,* maj. 21,357

*Cook, Rt. Hon. R. F. (Robin) (*b.* 1946) *Lab., Livingston,* maj. 11,747

Cooper, Ms Yvette (*b.* 1969) *Lab., Pontefract and Castleford,* maj. 25,725

*Corbett, Robin (*b.* 1933) *Lab., Birmingham Erdington,* maj. 12,657

*Corbyn, Jeremy B. (*b.* 1949) *Lab., Islington North,* maj. 19,955

*Cormack, Sir Patrick (*b.* 1939) *C., Staffordshire South,* maj. 7,821

*Corston, Ms Jean A. (*b.* 1942) *Lab., Bristol East,* maj. 16,159

Cotter, Brian J. (*b.* 1938) *LD, Weston-Super-Mare,* maj. 1,274

*Cousins, James M. (*b.* 1944) *Lab., Newcastle upon Tyne Central,* maj. 16,480

*Cox, Thomas M. (*b.* 1930) *Lab., Tooting,* maj. 15,011

*Cran, James D. (*b.* 1944) *C., Beverley and Holderness,* maj. 811

Cranston, Ross F. (*b.* 1948) *Lab., Dudley North,* maj. 9,457

Crausby, David A. (*b.* 1946) *Lab., Bolton North East,* maj. 12,669

Cryer, Mrs C. Ann (*b.* 1939) *Lab., Keighley,* maj. 7,132

Cryer, John R. (*b.* 1964) *Lab., Hornchurch,* maj. 5,680

*Cummings, John S. (*b.* 1943) *Lab., Easington,* maj. 30,012

*Cunliffe, Lawrence F. (*b.* 1929) *Lab., Leigh,* maj. 24,496

*Cunningham, Rt. Hon. Dr. J. A. (Jack), PH.D. (*b.* 1939) *Lab., Copeland,* maj. 11,944

*Cunningham, James D. (*b.* 1941) *Lab., Coventry South,* maj. 10,953

*Cunningham, Ms Roseanna (*b.* 1951) *SNP, Perth,* maj. 3,141

*Curry, Rt. Hon. David M. (*b.* 1944) *C., Skipton and Ripon,* maj. 11,620

Curtis-Tansley, Ms Claire (*b.* 1958) *Lab., Crosby,* maj. 7,182

*Dafis, Cynog G. (*b.* 1938) *PC, Ceredigion,* maj. 6,961

*Dalyell, Tam (Sir Thomas Dalyell of the Binns, Bt.) (*b.* 1932) *Lab., Linlithgow,* maj. 10,838

*Darling, Rt. Hon. Alistair M. (*b.* 1953) *Lab., Edinburgh Central,* maj. 11,070

Darvill, Keith E. (*b.* 1948) *Lab., Upminster,* maj. 2,770

Davey, Edward J. (*b.* 1965) *LD, Kingston and Surbiton,* maj. 56

Davey, Ms Valerie (*b.* 1940) *Lab., Bristol West,* maj. 1,493

*Davidson, Ian G. (*b.* 1950) *Lab. Co-op., Glasgow Pollok,* maj. 13,791

*Davies, Rt. Hon. D. J. Denzil (*b.* 1938) *Lab., Llanelli,* maj. 16,039

Davies, Geraint R. (*b.* 1960) *Lab., Croydon Central,* maj. 3,897

*Davies, J. Quentin (*b.* 1944) *C., Grantham and Stamford,* maj. 2,692

*Davies, Rt. Hon. Ronald (*b.* 1946) *Lab., Caerphilly,* maj. 25,839

*Davis, Rt. Hon. David M. (*b.* 1948) *C., Haltemprice and Howden,* maj. 7,514

*Davis, Terence A. G. (*b.* 1938) *Lab., Birmingham Hodge Hill,* maj. 14,200

Dawson, T. Hilton (*b.* 1953) *Lab., Lancaster and Wyre,* maj. 1,295

*Day, Stephen R. (*b.* 1948) *C., Cheadle,* maj. 3,189

Dean, Ms Janet E. A. (*b.* 1949) *Lab., Burton,* maj. 6,330

*Denham, John Y. (*b.* 1953) *Lab., Southampton Itchen,* maj. 14,209

*Dewar, Rt. Hon. Donald C. (*b.* 1937) *Lab., Glasgow Anniesland,* maj. 15,154

Dismore, Andrew H. (*b.* 1954) *Lab., Hendon,* maj. 6,155

Dobbin, James (*b.* 1941) *Lab. Co-op., Heywood and Middleton,* maj. 17,542

*Dobson, Rt. Hon. Frank G. (*b.* 1940) *Lab., Holborn and St Pancras,* maj. 17,903

Donaldson, Jeffrey M. (*b.* 1962) *UUP, Lagan Valley,* maj. 16,925

*Donohoe, Brian H. (*b.* 1948) *Lab., Cunninghame South,* maj. 14,869

Doran, Frank (*b.* 1949) *Lab., Aberdeen Central,* maj. 10,801

*Dorrell, Rt. Hon. Stephen J. (*b.* 1952) *C., Charnwood,* maj. 5,900

*Dowd, James P. (*b.* 1951) *Lab., Lewisham West,* maj. 14,337

Drew, David E. (*b.* 1952) *Lab. Co-op., Stroud,* maj. 2,910

Drown, Ms Julia K. (*b.* 1962) *Lab., Swindon South,* maj. 5,645

*Duncan, Alan J. C. (*b.* 1957) *C., Rutland and Melton,* maj. 8,836

*Duncan Smith, G. Iain (*b.* 1954) *C., Chingford and Woodford Green,* maj. 5,714

*Dunwoody, Hon. Mrs Gwyneth P. (*b.* 1930) *Lab., Crewe and Nantwich,* maj. 15,798

*Eagle, Ms Angela (*b.* 1961) *Lab., Wallasey,* maj. 19,074

Eagle, Ms Maria (*b.* 1961) *Lab., Liverpool Garston,* maj. 18,417

Edwards, Huw W. E. (*b.* 1953) *Lab., Monmouth,* maj. 4,178

Efford, Clive S. (*b.* 1958) *Lab., Eltham,* maj. 10,182

Ellman, Ms Louise J. (*b.* 1945) *Lab. Co-op., Liverpool Riverside,* maj. 21,799

*Emery, Rt. Hon. Sir Peter (*b.* 1926) *C., Devon East,* maj. 7,489

*Ennis, Jeffrey (*b.* 1952) *Lab., Barnsley East and Mexborough,* maj. 26,763

*Etherington, William (*b.* 1941) *Lab., Sunderland North,* maj. 19,697

*Evans, Nigel M. (*b.* 1957) *C., Ribble Valley,* maj. 6,640

*Ewing, Mrs Margaret A. (*b.* 1945) *SNP, Moray,* maj. 5,566

*Faber, David J. C. (*b.* 1961) *C., Westbury,* maj. 6,068

*Fabricant, Michael L. D. (*b.* 1950) *C., Lichfield,* maj. 238

Fallon, Michael C (*b.* 1952) *C., Sevenoaks,* maj. 10,461

Fearn, Ronald C., OBE (*b.* 1931) *LD, Southport,* maj. 6,160

*Field, Rt. Hon. Frank (*b.* 1942) *Lab., Birkenhead,* maj. 21,843

*Fisher, Mark (*b.* 1944) *Lab., Stoke-on-Trent Central,* maj. 19,924

Fitzpatrick, James (*b.* 1952) *Lab., Poplar and Canning Town,* maj. 18,915

Fitzsimons, Ms Lorna (*b.* 1967) *Lab., Rochdale,* maj. 4,545

Flight, Howard E. (*b.* 1948) *C., Arundel and South Downs,* maj. 14,035

Flint, Ms Caroline L. (*b.* 1961) *Lab., Don Valley,* maj. 14,659

*Flynn, Paul P. (*b.* 1935) *Lab., Newport West,* maj. 14,537

Follett, Ms D. Barbara (*b.* 1942) *Lab., Stevenage,* maj. 11,582

*Forsythe, Clifford (*b.* 1929) *UUP, Antrim South,* maj. 16,611

*Forth, Rt. Hon. Eric (*b.* 1944) *C., Bromley and Chislehurst,* maj. 11,118

*Foster, Rt. Hon. Derek (*b.* 1937) *Lab., Bishop Auckland,* maj. 21,064

*Foster, Donald M. E. (*b.* 1947) *LD, Bath,* maj. 9,319

Foster, Michael J. (*b.* 1946) *Lab., Hastings and Rye,* maj. 2,560

Foster, Michael J. (*b.* 1963) *Lab., Worcester,* maj. 7,425

*Foulkes, George (*b.* 1942) *Lab. Co-op., Carrick, Cumnock and Doon Valley,* maj. 21,062

*Fowler, Rt. Hon. Sir Norman (*b.* 1938) *C., Sutton Coldfield,* maj. 14,885

*Fox, Dr Liam (*b.* 1961) *C., Woodspring,* maj. 7,734

Fraser, Christopher J. (*b.* 1962) *C., Dorset Mid and Poole North,* maj. 681

*Fyfe, Ms Maria (*b.* 1938) *Lab., Glasgow Maryhill,* maj. 14,264

*Galbraith, Samuel L. (*b.* 1945) *Lab., Strathkelvin and Bearsden,* maj. 16,292

*Gale, Roger J. (*b.* 1943) *C., Thanet North,* maj. 2,766

*Galloway, George (*b.* 1954) *Lab., Glasgow Kelvin,* maj. 9,665

*Gapes, Michael J. (*b.* 1952) *Lab. Co-op., Ilford South,* maj. 14,200

Gardiner, Barry S. (*b.* 1957) *Lab., Brent North,* maj. 4,019

*Garnier, Edward H., QC (*b.* 1952) *C., Harborough,* maj. 6,524

George, Andrew H. (*b.* 1958) *LD, St Ives,* maj. 7,170

*George, Bruce T. (*b.* 1942) *Lab., Walsall South,* maj. 11,312

*Gerrard, Neil F. (*b.* 1942) *Lab., Walthamstow,* maj. 17,149

Gibb, Nicholas J. (*b.* 1960) *C., Bognor Regis and Littlehampton,* maj. 7,321

Gibson, Dr Ian (*b.* 1938) *Lab., Norwich North,* maj. 9,470

*Gillan, Mrs Cheryl E. K. (*b.* 1952) *C., Chesham and Amersham,* maj. 13,859

*Gill, Christopher J. F., RD (*b.* 1936) *C., Ludlow,* maj. 5,909

Gilroy, Mrs Linda (*b.* 1949) *Lab. Co-op., Plymouth Sutton,* maj. 9,440

*Godman, Norman A., PH.D. (*b.* 1938) *Lab., Greenock and Inverclyde,* maj. 13,040

*Godsiff, Roger D. (*b.* 1946) *Lab., Birmingham Sparkbrook and Small Heath,* maj. 19,526

Goggins, Paul G. (*b.* 1953) *Lab., Wythenshawe and Sale East,* maj. 15,019

*Golding, Ms Llinos (*b.* 1933) *Lab., Newcastle under Lyme,* maj. 17,206

Gordon, Mrs Eileen (*b.* 1946) *Lab., Romford,* maj. 649

*Gorman, Mrs Teresa E. (*b.* 1931) *C., Billericay,* maj. 1,356

Gorrie, Donald C. E. (*b.* 1933) *LD, Edinburgh West,* maj. 7,253

*Graham, Thomas (*b.* 1944) *SLI, Renfrewshire West,* maj. 7,979

*Grant, Bernard A. M. (*b.* 1944) *Lab., Tottenham,* maj. 20,200

Gray, James W. (*b.* 1954) *C., Wiltshire North,* maj. 3,475

Green, Damian H. (*b.* 1956) *C., Ashford,* maj. 5,355

*Greenway, John R. (*b.* 1946) *C., Ryedale,* maj. 5,058

Grieve, Dominic C. R. (*b.* 1956) *C., Beaconsfield,* maj. 13,987

Griffiths, Ms Jane P. (*b.* 1954) *Lab., Reading East,* maj. 3,795

*Griffiths, Nigel (*b.* 1955) *Lab., Edinburgh South,* maj. 11,452

*Griffiths, Winston J. (*b.* 1943) *Lab., Bridgend,* maj. 15,248

*Grocott, Bruce J. (*b.* 1940) *Lab., Telford,* maj. 11,290

Grogan, John T. (*b.* 1961) *Lab., Selby,* maj. 3,836

*Gummer, Rt. Hon. John S. (*b.* 1939) *C., Suffolk Coastal,* maj. 3,254

*Gunnell, W. John (*b.* 1933) *Lab., Morley and Rothwell,* maj. 14,750

*Hague, Rt. Hon. William J. (*b.* 1961) *C., Richmond,* maj. 10,051

*Hain, Peter G. (*b.* 1950) *Lab., Neath,* maj. 26,741

*Hall, Michael T. (*b.* 1952) *Lab., Weaver Vale,* maj. 13,448

Hall, Patrick (*b.* 1951) *Lab., Bedford,* maj. 8,300

*Hamilton, Rt. Hon. Sir Archibald (*b.* 1941) *C., Epsom and Ewell,* maj. 11,525

Hamilton, Fabian (*b.* 1955) *Lab., Leeds North East,* maj. 6,959

Hammond, Philip (*b.* 1955) *C., Runnymede and Weybridge,* maj. 9,875

Hancock, Michael T., CBE (*b.* 1946) *LD, Portsmouth South,* maj. 4,327

*Hanson, David G. (*b.* 1957) *Lab., Delyn,* maj. 11,693

*Harman, Rt. Hon. Harriet (*b.* 1950) *Lab., Camberwell and Peckham,* maj. 16,351

Harris, Dr Evan (*b.* 1965) *LD, Oxford West and Abingdon,* maj. 6,285

*Harvey, Nicholas B. (*b.* 1961) *LD, Devon North,* maj. 6,181

*Haselhurst, Rt. Hon. Sir Alan (*b.* 1937) *C., Saffron Walden,* maj. 10,573

*Hawkins, Nicholas J. (*b.* 1957) *C., Surrey Heath,* maj. 16,287

Hayes, John H. (*b.* 1958) *C., South Holland and the Deepings,* maj. 7,991

Heal, Mrs Sylvia L. (*b.* 1942) *Lab. Co-op., Halesowen and Rowley Regis,* maj. 10,337

*Heald, Oliver (*b.* 1954) *C., Hertfordshire North East,* maj. 3,088

Healey, John (*b.* 1960) *Lab., Wentworth,* maj. 23,959

*Heath, Rt. Hon. Sir Edward, KG, MBE (*b.* 1916) *C., Old Bexley and Sidcup,* maj. 3,569

Heath, David W. St J. (*b.* 1954) *LD, Somerton and Frome,* maj. 130

*Heathcoat-Amory, Rt. Hon. David P. (*b.* 1949) *C., Wells,* maj. 528

*Henderson, Douglas J. (*b.* 1949) *Lab., Newcastle upon Tyne North,* maj. 19,332

Henderson, Ivan J. (*b.* 1958) *Lab., Harwich,* maj. 1,216

Hepburn, Stephen (*b.* 1959) *Lab., Jarrow,* maj. 21,933

*Heppell, John B. (*b.* 1948) *Lab., Nottingham East,* maj. 15,419

*Heseltine, Rt. Hon. Michael R. D., CH (*b.* 1933) *C., Henley,* maj. 11,167

Hesford, Stephen (*b.* 1957) *Lab., Wirral West,* maj. 2,738

Hewitt, Ms Patricia H. (*b.* 1948) *Lab., Leicester West,* maj. 12,864

*Hill, T. Keith (*b.* 1943) *Lab., Streatham,* maj. 18,423

*Hinchliffe, David M. (*b.* 1948) *Lab., Wakefield,* maj. 14,604

*Hodge, Mrs Margaret E., MBE (*b.* 1944) *Lab., Barking,* maj. 15,896

*Hoey, Ms Catharine (Kate) L. (*b.* 1946) *Lab., Vauxhall,* maj. 18,660

*Hogg, Rt. Hon. Douglas M., QC (*b.* 1945) *C., Sleaford and North Hykeham,* maj. 5,123

*Home Robertson, John D. (*b.* 1948) *Lab., East Lothian,* maj. 14,221

*Hood, James (*b.* 1948) *Lab., Clydesdale,* maj. 13,809

*Hoon, Geoffrey W. (*b.* 1953) *Lab., Ashfield,* maj. 22,728

Hope, Philip I. (*b.* 1955) *Lab. Co-op., Corby,* maj. 11,860

Hopkins, Kelvin P. (*b.* 1941) *Lab., Luton North,* maj. 9,626

*Horam, John R. (*b.* 1939) *C., Orpington,* maj. 2,952

*Howard, Rt. Hon. Michael, QC (*b.* 1941) *C., Folkestone and Hythe,* maj. 6,332

*Howarth, Alan T., CBE (*b.* 1944) *Lab., Newport East,* maj. 13,523

*Howarth, George E. (*b.* 1949) *Lab., Knowsley North and Sefton East,* maj. 26,147

Howarth, J. Gerald D. (*b.* 1947) *C., Aldershot,* maj. 6,621

*Howells, Kim S., PH.D. (*b.* 1946) *Lab., Pontypridd,* maj. 23,129

Hoyle, Lindsay H. (*b.* 1957) *Lab., Chorley,* maj. 9,870

*Hughes, Ms Beverley J. (*b.* 1950) *Lab., Stretford and Urmston,* maj. 13,640

*Hughes, Kevin M. (*b.* 1952) *Lab., Doncaster North,* maj. 21,937

*Hughes, Simon H. W. (*b.* 1951) *LD, Southwark North and Bermondsey,* maj. 3,387

Humble, Mrs Jovanka (Joan) (*b.* 1951) *Lab., Blackpool North and Fleetwood,* maj. 8,946

Hume, John, MEP (*b.* 1937) *SDLP, Foyle,* maj. 13,664

*Hunter, Andrew R. F. (*b.* 1943) *C., Basingstoke,* maj. 2,397

Hurst, Alan A. (*b.* 1945) *Lab., Braintree,* maj. 1,451

*Hutton, John M. P. (*b.* 1955) *Lab., Barrow and Furness,* maj. 14,497

Iddon, Brian (*b.* 1940) *Lab., Bolton South East,* maj. 21,311

*Illsley, Eric E. (*b.* 1955) *Lab., Barnsley Central,* maj. 24,501

*Ingram, Rt. Hon. Adam P. (*b.* 1947) *Lab., East Kilbride,* maj. 17,384

*Jack, Rt. Hon. J. Michael (*b.* 1946) *C., Fylde,* maj. 8,963

*Jackson, Ms Glenda M., CBE (*b.* 1936) *Lab., Hampstead and Highgate,* maj. 13,284

*Jackson, Mrs Helen M. (*b.* 1939) *Lab., Sheffield Hillsborough,* maj. 16,451

*Jackson, Robert V. (*b.* 1946) *C., Wantage,* maj. 6,039

*Jamieson, David C. (*b.* 1947) *Lab., Plymouth Devonport,* maj. 19,067

*Jenkin, Hon. Bernard C. (*b.* 1959) *C., Essex North,* maj. 5,476

*Jenkins, Brian D. (*b.* 1942) *Lab., Tamworth,* maj. 7,496

Johnson, Alan A. (*b.* 1950) *Lab., Hull West and Hessle,* maj. 15,525

Johnson, Ms Melanie J. (*b.* 1955) *Lab., Welwyn Hatfield,* maj. 5,595

*Johnson Smith, Rt. Hon. Sir Geoffrey (*b.* 1924) *C., Wealden,* maj. 14,204

*Jones, Rt. Hon. S. Barry (*b.* 1938) *Lab., Alyn and Deeside,* maj. 16,403

Jones, Ms Fiona E. A. (*b.* 1957) *Lab., Newark,* maj. 3,016

Jones, Ms Helen M. (*b.* 1954) *Lab., Warrington North,* maj. 19,527

*Jones, Ieuan W. (*b.* 1949) *PC, Ynys Môn,* maj. 2,481

Jones, Ms Jennifer G. (*b.* 1948) *Lab., Wolverhampton South West,* maj. 5,118

*Jones, Jonathan O. (*b.* 1954) *Lab. Co-op., Cardiff Central,* maj. 7,923

*Jones, Ms Lynne M., PH.D. (*b.* 1951) *Lab., Birmingham Selly Oak,* maj. 14,088

*Jones, Martyn D. (*b.* 1947) *Lab., Clwyd South,* maj. 13,810

*Jones, Nigel D. (*b.* 1948) *LD, Cheltenham,* maj. 6,645

*Jowell, Rt. Hon. Tessa J. H. D. (*b.* 1947) *Lab., Dulwich and West Norwood,* maj. 16,769

*Kaufman, Rt. Hon. Gerald B. (*b.* 1930) *Lab., Manchester Gorton,* maj. 17,342

Keeble, Ms Sally C. (*b.* 1951) *Lab., Northampton North,* maj. 10,000

Keen, Mrs Ann L. (*b.* 1948) *Lab., Brentford and Isleworth,* maj. 14,424

*Keen, D. Alan (*b.* 1937) *Lab. Co-op., Feltham and Heston,* maj. 15,273

Keetch, Paul S. (*b.* 1961) *LD, Hereford,* maj. 6,648

Kelly, Ms Ruth M. (*b.* 1968) *Lab., Bolton West,* maj. 7,072

Kemp, Fraser (*b.* 1958) *Lab., Houghton and Washington East,* maj. 26,555

*Kennedy, Charles P. (*b.* 1959) *LD, Ross, Skye and Inverness West,* maj. 4,019

*Kennedy, Mrs Jane E. (*b.* 1958) *Lab., Liverpool Wavertree,* maj. 19,701

*Key, S. Robert (*b.* 1945) *C., Salisbury,* maj. 6,276

*Khabra, Piara S. (*b.* 1924) *Lab., Ealing Southall,* maj. 21,423

Kidney, David N. (*b.* 1955) *Lab., Stafford,* maj. 4,314

*Kilfoyle, Peter (*b.* 1946) *Lab., Liverpool Walton,* maj. 27,038

King, Andrew (*b.* 1948) *Lab., Rugby and Kenilworth,* maj. 495

King, Ms Oona T. (*b.* 1967) *Lab., Bethnal Green and Bow,* maj. 11,285

*King, Rt. Hon. Thomas J., CH (*b.* 1933) *C., Bridgwater,* maj. 1,796

Kingham, Ms Teresa J. (*b.* 1963) *Lab., Gloucester,* maj. 8,259

Kirkbride, Miss Julie (*b.* 1960) *C., Bromsgrove,* maj. 4,895

*Kirkwood, Archibald J. (*b.* 1946) *LD, Roxburgh and Berwickshire,* maj. 7,906

Kumar, Dr Ashok (*b.* 1956) *Lab., Middlesbrough South and Cleveland East,* maj. 10,607

Ladyman, Dr Stephen J. (*b.* 1952) *Lab., Thanet South,* maj. 2,878

Laing, Mrs Eleanor F. (*b.* 1958) *C., Epping Forest,* maj. 5,252

Lait, Ms Jacqueline A. H. (*b.* 1947) *C., Beckenham,* maj. 1,227

Lansley, Andrew D. (*b.* 1956) *C., Cambridgeshire South,* maj. 8,712

Lawrence, Mrs Jacqueline R. (*b.* 1948) *Lab., Preseli Pembrokeshire,* maj. 8,736

Laxton, Robert (*b.* 1944) *Lab., Derby North,* maj. 10,615

*Leigh, Edward J. E. (*b.* 1950) *C., Gainsborough,* maj. 6,826

Lepper, David (*b.* 1945) *Lab. Co-op., Brighton Pavilion,* maj. 13,181

Leslie, Christopher M. (*b.* 1972) *Lab., Shipley,* maj. 2,996

Letwin, Oliver (*b.* 1956) *C., Dorset West,* maj. 1,840

Levitt, Tom (*b.* 1954) *Lab., High Peak,* maj. 8,791

Lewis, Ivan (*b.* 1967) *Lab., Bury South,* maj. 12,433

Lewis, Dr Julian M. (*b.* 1951) *C., New Forest East,* maj. 5,215

*Lewis, Terence (*b.* 1935) *Lab., Worsley,* maj. 17,741

*Liddell, Rt. Hon. Helen (*b.* 1950) *Lab., Airdrie and Shotts,* maj. 15,412

*Lidington, David R., PH.D. (*b.* 1956) *C., Aylesbury,* maj. 8,419

*Lilley, Rt. Hon. Peter B. (*b.* 1943) *C., Hitchin and Harpenden,* maj. 6,671

Linton, J. Martin (*b.* 1944) *Lab., Battersea,* maj. 5,360

*Livingstone, Kenneth R. (*b.* 1945) *Lab., Brent East,* maj. 15,882

Livsey, Richard A. L., CBE (*b.* 1935) *LD, Brecon and Radnorshire,* maj. 5,097

*Lloyd, Anthony J. (*b.* 1950) *Lab., Manchester Central,* maj. 19,682

*Lloyd, Rt. Hon. Sir Peter (*b.* 1937) *C., Fareham,* maj. 10,358

*Llwyd, Elfyn (*b.* 1951) *PC, Meirionnydd nant Conwy,* maj. 6,805

Lock, David A. (*b.* 1960) *Lab., Wyre Forest,* maj. 6,946

*Lord, Michael N. (*b.* 1938) *C., Suffolk Central and Ipswich North,* maj. 3,538

Loughton, Timothy P. (*b.* 1962) *C., Worthing East and Shoreham,* maj. 5,098

Love, Andrew (*b.* 1949) *Lab. Co-op., Edmonton,* maj. 13,472

*Luff, Peter J. (*b.* 1955) *C., Worcestershire Mid,* maj. 9,412

*Lyell, Rt. Hon. Sir Nicholas, QC (*b.* 1938) *C., Bedfordshire North East,* maj. 5,883

*McAllion, John (*b.* 1948) *Lab., Dundee East,* maj. 9,961

*McAvoy, Thomas M. (*b.* 1943) *Lab. Co-op., Glasgow Rutherglen,* maj. 15,007

McCabe, Stephen J. (*b.* 1955) *Lab., Birmingham Hall Green,* maj. 8,420

McCafferty, Ms Christine (*b.* 1945) *Lab., Calder Valley,* maj. 6,255

*McCartney, Ian (*b.* 1951) *Lab., Makerfield,* maj. 26,177

*McCartney, Robert L., QC (NI) (*b.* 1936) *UKU, Down North,* maj. 1,449

McDonagh, Ms Siobhain A. (*b.* 1960) *Lab., Mitcham and Morden,* maj. 13,741

*Macdonald, Calum A., PH.D. (*b.* 1956) *Lab., Western Isles,* maj. 3,576

McDonnell, John M. (*b.* 1951) *Lab., Hayes and Harlington,* maj. 14,291

*McFall, John (*b.* 1944) *Lab. Co-op., Dumbarton,* maj. 10,883

*McGrady, Edward K. (*b.* 1935) *SDLP, Down South,* maj. 9,933

*MacGregor, Rt. Hon. John R. R., OBE (*b.* 1937) *C., Norfolk South,* maj. 7,378

McGuinness, Martin (*b.* 1950) *SF, Ulster Mid,* maj. 1,883

McGuire, Mrs Anne (*b.* 1949) *Lab., Stirling,* maj. 6,411

McIntosh, Miss Anne C. B. (*b.* 1954) *C., Vale of York,* maj. 9,721

McIsaac, Ms Shona (*b.* 1960) *Lab., Cleethorpes,* maj. 9,176

*Mackay, Rt. Hon. Andrew J. (*b.* 1949) *C., Bracknell,* maj. 10,387

McKenna, Ms Rosemary (*b.* 1941) *Lab., Cumbernauld and Kilsyth,* maj. 11,128

*MacKinlay, Andrew S. (*b.* 1949) *Lab., Thurrock,* maj. 17,256

*Maclean, Rt. Hon. David J. (*b.* 1953) *C., Penrith and the Border,* maj. 10,233

*McLeish, Henry B. (*b.* 1948) *Lab., Fife Central,* maj. 13,713

*Maclennan, Rt. Hon. Robert A. R. (*b.* 1936) *LD, Caithness, Sutherland and Easter Ross,* maj. 2,259

*McLoughlin, Patrick A. (*b.* 1957) *C., Derbyshire West,* maj. 4,885

*McNamara, J. Kevin (*b.* 1934) *Lab., Hull North,* maj. 19,705

McNulty, Anthony J. (*b.* 1958) *Lab., Harrow East,* maj. 9,738

*MacShane, Denis, PH.D. (*b.* 1948) *Lab., Rotherham,* maj. 21,469

MacTaggart, Ms Fiona M. (*b.* 1953) *Lab., Slough,* maj. 13,071

McWalter, Tony (*b.* 1945) *Lab. Co-op., Hemel Hempstead,* maj. 3,636

*McWilliam, John D. (*b.* 1941) *Lab., Blaydon,* maj. 16,605

*Madel, Sir David (*b.* 1938) *C., Bedfordshire South West,* maj. 132

*Maginnis, Kenneth (*b.* 1938) *UUP, Fermanagh and South Tyrone,* maj. 13,688

*Mahon, Mrs Alice (*b.* 1937) *Lab., Halifax,* maj. 11,212

*Major, Rt. Hon. John, CH (*b.* 1943) *C., Huntingdon,* maj. 18,140

Malins, Humfrey J., CBE (*b.* 1945) *C., Woking,* maj. 5,678

Mallaber, Ms C. Judith (*b.* 1951) *Lab., Amber Valley,* maj. 11,613

*Mallon, Seamus (*b.* 1936) *SDLP, Newry and Armagh,* maj. 4,889

*Mandelson, Rt. Hon. Peter B. (*b.* 1953) *Lab., Hartlepool,* maj. 17,508

Maples, John C. (*b.* 1943) *C., Stratford-upon-Avon,* maj. 14,106

*Marek, John, PH.D. (*b.* 1940) *Lab., Wrexham,* maj. 11,762

*Marsden, Gordon (*b.* 1953) *Lab., Blackpool South,* maj. 11,616

Marsden, Paul W. B. (*b.* 1968) *Lab., Shrewsbury and Atcham,* maj. 1,670

*Marshall, David, PH.D (*b.* 1941) *Lab., Glasgow Shettleston,* maj. 15,868

*Marshall, James, PH.D. (*b.* 1941) *Lab., Leicester South,* maj. 16,493

Marshall-Andrews, Robert G., QC (*b.* 1944) *Lab., Medway,* maj. 5,354

*Martin, Michael J. (*b.* 1945) *Lab., Glasgow Springburn,* maj. 17,326

*Martlew, Eric A. (*b.* 1949) *Lab., Carlisle,* maj. 12,390

*Mates, Michael J. (*b.* 1934) *C., Hampshire East,* maj. 11,590

Maude, Rt. Hon. Francis A. A. (*b.* 1953) *C., Horsham,* maj. 14,862

*Mawhinney, Rt. Hon. Sir Brian, PH.D. (*b.* 1940) *C., Cambridgeshire North West,* maj. 7,754

*Maxton, John A. (*b.* 1936) *Lab., Glasgow Cathcart,* maj. 12,245

May, Mrs Theresa M. (*b.* 1956) *C., Maidenhead,* maj. 11,981

*Meacher, Rt. Hon. Michael H. (*b.* 1939) *Lab., Oldham West and Royton,* maj. 16,201

*Meale, J. Alan (*b.* 1949) *Lab., Mansfield,* maj. 20,518

Merron, Ms Gillian J. (*b.* 1959) *Lab., Lincoln,* maj. 11,130

*Michael, Rt. Hon. Alun E. (*b.* 1943) *Lab. Co-op., Cardiff South and Penarth,* maj. 13,881

*Michie, Mrs J. Ray (*b.* 1934) *LD, Argyll and Bute,* maj. 6,081

*Michie, William (*b.* 1935) *Lab., Sheffield Heeley,* maj. 17,078

*Milburn, Rt. Hon. Alan (*b.* 1958) *Lab., Darlington,* maj. 16,025

*Miller, Andrew P. (*b.* 1949) *Lab., Ellesmere Port and Neston,* maj. 16,036

*Mitchell, Austin V., D.PHIL. (*b.* 1934) *Lab., Great Grimsby,* maj. 16,244

Moffatt, Mrs Laura J. (*b.* 1954) *Lab., Crawley,* maj. 11,707

*Moonie, Dr Lewis G. (*b.* 1947) *Lab. Co-op., Kirkcaldy,* maj. 10,710

Moore, Michael K. (*b.* 1965) *LD, Tweeddale, Ettrick and Lauderdale,* maj. 1,489

Moran, Ms Margaret (*b.* 1955) *Lab., Luton South,* maj. 11,319

Morgan, Alasdair N. (*b.* 1945) *SNP, Galloway and Upper Nithsdale,* maj. 5,624

*Morgan, H. Rhodri (*b.* 1939) *Lab., Cardiff West,* maj. 15,628

Morgan, Ms Julie (*b.* 1944) *Lab., Cardiff North,* maj. 8,126

*Morley, Elliot A. (*b.* 1952) *Lab., Scunthorpe,* maj. 14,173

*Morris, Ms Estelle (*b.* 1952) *Lab., Birmingham Yardley,* maj. 5,315

*Morris, Rt. Hon. John, QC (*b.* 1931) *Lab., Aberavon,* maj. 21,571

*Moss, Malcolm D. (*b.* 1943) *C., Cambridgeshire North East,* maj. 5,101

Mountford, Ms Kali C. J. (*b.* 1954) *Lab., Colne Valley,* maj. 4,840

*Mowlam, Rt. Hon. Marjorie, Ph.D. (b. 1949) Lab., Redcar, maj. 21,664
*Mudie, George E. (b. 1945) Lab., Leeds East, maj. 17,466
*Mullin, Christopher J. (b. 1947) Lab., Sunderland South, maj. 19,638
Murphy, Denis (b. 1948) Lab., Wansbeck, maj. 22,367
Murphy, James (b. 1967) Lab., Eastwood, maj. 3,236
*Murphy, Paul P. (b. 1948) Lab., Torfaen, maj. 24,536
Naysmith, J. Douglas (b. 1941) Lab. Co-op., Bristol North West, maj. 11,382
*Nicholls, Patrick C. M. (b. 1948) C., Teignbridge, maj. 281
Norman, Archibald J. (b. 1954) C., Tunbridge Wells, maj. 7,506
Norris, Dan (b. 1960) Lab., Wansdyke, maj. 4,799
Oaten, Mark (b. 1964) LD, Winchester, maj. 21,556
*O'Brien, Michael (b. 1954) Lab., Warwickshire North, maj. 14,767
†O'Brien, Stephen (b. 1957) C., Eddisbury, maj. 1,606
*O'Brien, William (b. 1929) Lab., Normanton, maj. 15,893
*O'Hara, Edward (b. 1937) Lab., Knowsley South, maj. 30,708
*Olner, William J. (b. 1942) Lab., Nuneaton, maj. 13,540
*O'Neill, Martin J. (b. 1945) Lab., Ochil, maj. 4,652
Opik, Lembit (b. 1965) LD, Montgomeryshire, maj. 6,303
Organ, Ms Diana M. (b. 1952) Lab., Forest of Dean, maj. 6,343
Osborne, Mrs Sandra C. (b. 1956) Lab., Ayr, maj. 6,543
*Ottaway, Richard G. J. (b. 1945) C., Croydon South, maj. 11,930
*Page, Richard L. (b. 1941) C., Hertfordshire South West, maj. 10,021
*Paice, James E. T. (b. 1949) C., Cambridgeshire South East, maj. 9,349
*Paisley, Revd Ian R. K., MEP (b. 1926) DUP, Antrim North, maj. 10,574
Palmer, Nicholas D. (b. 1950) Lab., Broxtowe, maj. 5,575
Paterson, Owen W. (b. 1956) C., Shropshire North, maj. 2,195
*Pearson, Ian P., Ph.D. (b. 1959) Lab., Dudley South, maj. 13,027
*Pendry, Thomas (b. 1934) Lab., Stalybridge and Hyde, maj. 14,806
Perham, Ms Linda (b. 1947) Lab., Ilford North, maj. 3,224
*Pickles, Eric J. (b. 1952) C., Brentwood and Ongar, maj. 9,690
*Pickthall, Colin (b. 1944) Lab., Lancashire West, maj. 17,119
*Pike, Peter L. (b. 1937) Lab., Burnley, maj. 17,062
Plaskitt, James A. (b. 1954) Lab., Warwick and Leamington, maj. 3,398
Pollard, Kerry P. (b. 1944) Lab., St Albans, maj. 4,459
Pond, Christopher R. (b. 1952) Lab., Gravesham, maj. 5,779
*Pope, Gregory J. (b. 1960) Lab., Hyndburn, maj. 11,448
Pound, Stephen P. (b. 1948) Lab., Ealing North, maj. 9,160
*Powell, Sir Raymond (b. 1928) Lab., Ogmore, maj. 24,447
*Prentice, Ms Bridget T. (b. 1952) Lab., Lewisham East, maj. 12,127
*Prentice, Gordon (b. 1951) Lab., Pendle, maj. 10,824
*Prescott, Rt. Hon. John L. (b. 1938) Lab., Hull East, maj. 23,318
*Primarolo, Ms Dawn (b. 1954) Lab., Bristol South, maj. 19,328
Prior, Hon. David G. L. (b. 1954) C., Norfolk North, maj. 1,293
Prosser, Gwynfor M. (b. 1943) Lab., Dover, maj. 11,739
*Purchase, Kenneth (b. 1939) Lab. Co-op., Wolverhampton North East, maj. 12,987
*Quin, Rt. Hon. Joyce G. (b. 1944) Lab., Gateshead East and Washington West, maj. 24,950
Quinn, Lawrence W. (b. 1956) Lab., Scarborough and Whitby, maj. 5,124
*Radice, Rt. Hon. Giles H. (b. 1936) Lab., Durham North, maj. 26,299
Rammell, William E. (b. 1959) Lab., Harlow, maj. 10,514

Randall, A. John (b. 1955) C., Uxbridge, maj. 3,766
Rapson, Sydney N. J. (b. 1942) Lab., Portsmouth North, maj. 4,323
*Raynsford, W. R. N. (Nick) (b. 1945) Lab., Greenwich and Woolwich, maj. 18,128
*Redwood, Rt. Hon. John A., D.Phil. (b. 1951) C., Wokingham, maj. 9,365
Reed, Andrew J. (b. 1964) Lab., Loughborough, maj. 5,712
*Reid, Rt. Hon. John, Ph.D. (b. 1947) Lab., Hamilton North and Bellshill, maj. 17,067
*Rendel, David D. (b. 1949) LD, Newbury, maj. 8,517
*Robathan, Andrew R. G. (b. 1951) C., Blaby, maj. 6,474
*Robertson, Rt. Hon. George I. M. (b. 1946) Lab., Hamilton South, maj. 15,878
Robertson, Laurence A. (b. 1958) C., Tewkesbury, maj. 9,234
*Robinson, Geoffrey (b. 1938) Lab., Coventry North West, maj. 16,601
*Robinson, Peter D. (b. 1948) DUP, Belfast East, maj. 6,754
*Roche, Mrs Barbara M. R. (b. 1954) Lab., Hornsey and Wood Green, maj. 20,499
*Roe, Mrs Marion A. (b. 1936) C., Broxbourne, maj. 6,653
*Rogers, Allan R. (b. 1932) Lab., Rhondda, maj. 24,931
*Rooker, Jeffrey W. (b. 1941) Lab., Birmingham Perry Barr, maj. 18,957
*Rooney, Terence H. (b. 1950) Lab., Bradford North, maj. 12,770
*Ross, Ernest (b. 1942) Lab., Dundee West, maj. 11,859
*Ross, William (b. 1936) UUP, Londonderry East, maj. 3,794
*Rowe, Andrew J. B. (b. 1935) C., Faversham and Kent Mid, maj. 4,173
*Rowlands, Edward (b. 1940) Lab., Merthyr Tydfil and Rhymney, maj. 27,086
Roy, Frank (b. 1958) Lab., Motherwell and Wishaw, maj. 12,791
Ruane, Christopher S. (b. 1958) Lab., Vale of Clwyd, maj. 8,955
*Ruddock, Mrs Joan M. (b. 1943) Lab., Lewisham Deptford, maj. 18,878
Ruffley, David L. (b. 1962) C., Bury St Edmunds, maj. 368
Russell, Ms Christine M. (b. 1945) Lab., City of Chester, maj. 10,553
Russell, Robert E. (b. 1946) LD, Colchester, maj. 1,581
Ryan, Ms Joan M. (b. 1955) Lab., Enfield North, maj. 6,822
St Aubyn, Nicholas F. (b. 1955) C., Guildford, maj. 4,791
*Salmond, Alexander E. A. (b. 1954) SNP, Banff and Buchan, maj. 12,845
Salter, Martin J. (b. 1954) Lab., Reading West, maj. 2,997
Sanders, Adrian M. (b. 1959) LD, Torbay, maj. 12
Sarwar, Mohammad (b. 1952) Lab., Glasgow Govan, maj. 2,914
Savidge, Malcolm K. (b. 1946) Lab., Aberdeen North, maj. 10,010
Sawford, Philip A. (b. 1950) Lab., Kettering, maj. 189
Sayeed, Jonathan (b. 1948) C., Bedfordshire Mid, maj. 7,090
*Sedgemore, Brian C. J. (b. 1937) Lab., Hackney South and Shoreditch, maj. 14,980
Shaw, Jonathan R. (b. 1966) Lab., Chatham and Aylesford, maj. 2,790
*Sheerman, Barry J. (b. 1940) Lab. Co-op., Huddersfield, maj. 15,848
*Sheldon, Rt. Hon. Robert E. (b. 1923) Lab., Ashton under Lyne, maj. 22,965
*Shephard, Rt. Hon. Gillian P. (b. 1940) C., Norfolk South West, maj. 2,464
*Shepherd, Richard C. S. (b. 1942) C., Aldridge-Brownhills, maj. 2,526
Shipley, Ms Debra A. (b. 1957) Lab., Stourbridge, maj. 5,645
*Short, Rt. Hon. Clare (b. 1946) Lab., Birmingham Ladywood, maj. 23,082

*Simpson, Alan J. (*b.* 1948) *Lab., Nottingham South,* maj. 13,364

Simpson, Keith (*b.* 1949) *C., Norfolk Mid,* maj. 1,336

Singh, Marsha (*b.* 1954) *Lab., Bradford West,* maj. 3,877

*Skinner, Dennis E. (*b.* 1932) *Lab., Bolsover,* maj. 27,149

*Smith, Rt. Hon. Andrew D. (*b.* 1951) *Lab., Oxford East,* maj. 16,665

Smith, Ms Angela E. (*b.* 1959) *Lab. Co-op., Basildon,* maj. 13,280

*Smith, Rt. Hon. Christopher R., Ph.D. (*b.* 1951) *Lab., Islington South and Finsbury,* maj. 14,563

Smith, Ms Geraldine (*b.* 1961) *Lab., Morecambe and Lunesdale,* maj. 5,965

Smith, Ms Jacqueline J. (*b.* 1962) *Lab., Redditch,* maj. 6,125

Smith, John W. P. (*b.* 1951) *Lab., Vale of Glamorgan,* maj. 10,532

*Smith, Llewellyn T. (*b.* 1944) *Lab., Blaenau Gwent,* maj. 28,035

Smith, Sir Robert, Bt. (*b.* 1958) *LD, Aberdeenshire West and Kincardine,* maj. 2,662

*Smyth, Revd W. Martin (*b.* 1931) *UUP, Belfast South,* maj. 4,600

*Snape, Peter C. (*b.* 1942) *Lab., West Bromwich East,* maj. 13,584

*Soames, Hon. A. Nicholas W. (*b.* 1948) *C., Sussex Mid,* maj. 6,854

*Soley, Clive S. (*b.* 1939) *Lab., Ealing Acton and Shepherd's Bush,* maj. 15,647

Southworth, Ms Helen M. (*b.* 1956) *Lab., Warrington South,* maj. 10,807

*Spellar, John F. (*b.* 1947) *Lab., Warley,* maj. 15,451

Spelman, Mrs Caroline A. (*b.* 1958) *C., Meriden,* maj. 582

*Spicer, Sir Michael (*b.* 1943) *C., Worcestershire West,* maj. 3,846

*Spring, Richard J. G. (*b.* 1946) *C., Suffolk West,* maj. 1,867

*Squire, Ms Rachel A. (*b.* 1954) *Lab., Dunfermline West,* maj. 12,354

*Stanley, Rt. Hon. Sir John (*b.* 1942) *C., Tonbridge and Malling,* maj. 10,230

Starkey, Mrs Phyllis M. (*b.* 1947) *Lab., Milton Keynes South West,* maj. 10,292

*Steen, Sir Anthony (*b.* 1939) *C., Totnes,* maj. 877

*Steinberg, Gerald N. (*b.* 1945) *Lab., City of Durham,* maj. 22,504

*Stevenson, George W. (*b.* 1938) *Lab., Stoke-on-Trent South,* maj. 18,303

Stewart, David J. (*b.* 1956) *Lab., Inverness East, Nairn and Lochaber,* maj. 2,339

Stewart, Ian (*b.* 1950) *Lab., Eccles,* maj. 21,916

Stinchcombe, Paul D. (*b.* 1962) *Lab., Wellingborough,* maj. 187

Stoate, Howard G. A. (*b.* 1954) *Lab., Dartford,* maj. 4,328

*Stott, Roger, CBE (*b.* 1943) *Lab., Wigan,* maj. 22,643

*Strang, Rt. Hon. Gavin S., Ph.D. (*b.* 1943) *Lab., Edinburgh East and Musselburgh,* maj. 14,530

*Straw, Rt. Hon. J. W. (Jack) (*b.* 1946) *Lab., Blackburn,* maj. 14,451

*Streeter, Gary N. (*b.* 1955) *C., Devon South West,* maj. 7,433

Stringer, Graham E. (*b.* 1950) *Lab., Manchester Blackley,* maj. 19,588

Stuart, Mrs Gisela G. (*b.* 1955) *Lab., Birmingham Edgbaston,* maj. 4,842

Stunell, Andrew (*b.* 1942) *LD, Hazel Grove,* maj. 11,814

*Sutcliffe, Gerard (*b.* 1953) *Lab., Bradford South,* maj. 12,936

Swayne, Desmond A. (*b.* 1956) *C., New Forest West,* maj. 11,332

Swinney, John R. (*b.* 1964) *SNP, Tayside North,* maj. 4,160

Syms, Robert A. R. (*b.* 1956) *C., Poole,* maj. 5,298

*Tapsell, Sir Peter (*b.* 1930) *C., Louth and Horncastle,* maj. 6,900

Taylor, Ms Dari J. (*b.* 1944) *Lab., Stockton South,* maj. 11,585

Taylor, David L. (*b.* 1946) *Lab., Leicestershire North West,* maj. 13,219

*Taylor, Sir Edward (Teddy) (*b.* 1937) *C., Rochford and Southend East,* maj. 4,225

*Taylor, Ian C., MBE (*b.* 1945) *C., Esher and Walton,* maj. 14,528

*Taylor, Rt. Hon. John D. (*b.* 1937) *UUP, Strangford,* maj. 5,852

*Taylor, John M. (*b.* 1941) *C., Solihull,* maj. 11,397

*Taylor, Matthew O. J. (*b.* 1963) *LD, Truro and St Austell,* maj. 12,501

*Taylor, Rt. Hon. W. Ann (*b.* 1947) *Lab., Dewsbury,* maj. 8,323

*Temple-Morris, Peter (*b.* 1938) *Lab., Leominster,* maj. 8,835

Thomas, Gareth (*b.* 1954) *Lab., Clwyd West,* maj. 1,848

Thomas, Gareth R. (*b.* 1967) *Lab., Harrow West,* maj. 1,240

Thompson, William J. (*b.* 1939) *UUP, Tyrone West,* maj. 1,161

*Timms, Stephen C. (*b.* 1955) *Lab., East Ham,* maj. 19,358

*Tipping, S. P. (Paddy) (*b.* 1949) *Lab., Sherwood,* maj. 16,812

Todd, Mark W. (*b.* 1954) *Lab., Derbyshire South,* maj. 13,967

Tonge, Dr Jennifer L. (*b.* 1941) *LD, Richmond Park,* maj. 2,951

*Touhig, J. Donnelly (Don) (*b.* 1947) *Lab. Co-op., Islwyn,* maj. 23,931

*Townend, John E. (*b.* 1934) *C., Yorkshire East,* maj. 3,337

*Tredinnick, David A. S. (*b.* 1950) *C., Bosworth,* maj. 1,027

*Trend, Hon. Michael St J., CBE (*b.* 1952) *C., Windsor,* maj. 9,917

*Trickett, Jon H. (*b.* 1950) *Lab., Hemsworth,* maj. 23,992

*Trimble, Rt. Hon. W. David (*b.* 1944) *UUP, Upper Bann,* maj. 9,252

Truswell, Paul A. (*b.* 1955) *Lab., Pudsey,* maj. 6,207

*Turner, Dennis (*b.* 1942) *Lab. Co-op., Wolverhampton South East,* maj. 15,182

Turner, Desmond S. (*b.* 1939) *Lab., Brighton Kemptown,* maj. 3,534

Turner, Dr George (*b.* 1940) *Lab., Norfolk North West,* maj. 1,339

Twigg, J. Derek (*b.* 1959) *Lab., Halton,* maj. 23,650

Twigg, Stephen (*b.* 1966) *Lab., Enfield Southgate,* maj. 1,433

*Tyler, Paul A., CBE (*b.* 1941) *LD, Cornwall North,* maj. 13,933

*Tyrie, Andrew G. (*b.* 1957) *C., Chichester,* maj. 9,734

*Vaz, N. Keith A. S. (*b.* 1956) *Lab., Leicester East,* maj. 18,422

*Viggers, Peter J. (*b.* 1938) *C., Gosport,* maj. 6,258

Vis, R. J. (Rudi) (*b.* 1941) *Lab., Finchley and Golders Green,* maj. 3,189

*Walker, A. Cecil (*b.* 1924) *UUP, Belfast North,* maj. 13,024

*Wallace, James R. (*b.* 1954) *LD, Orkney and Shetland,* maj. 6,968

*Walley, Ms Joan L. (*b.* 1949) *Lab., Stoke-on-Trent North,* maj. 17,392

Walter, Robert J. (*b.* 1948) *C., Dorset North,* maj. 2,746

Ward, Ms Claire M. (*b.* 1972) *Lab., Watford,* maj. 5,792

*Wardle, Charles F. (*b.* 1939) *C., Bexhill and Battle,* maj. 11,100

*Wareing, Robert N. (*b.* 1930) *Lab., Liverpool West Derby,* maj. 25,965

*Waterson, Nigel C. (*b.* 1950) *C., Eastbourne,* maj. 1,994

Watts, David L. (*b.* 1951) *Lab., St Helens North,* maj. 23,417

Webb, Prof. Steven J. (*b.* 1965) *LD, Northavon,* maj. 2,137

*Wells, Bowen (*b.* 1935) *C., Hertford and Stortford,* maj. 6,885

*Welsh, Andrew P. (*b.* 1944) *SNP, Angus,* maj. 10,189

White, Brian A. R. (*b.* 1957) *Lab., Milton Keynes North East,* maj. 240

Whitehead, Alan P. V. (*b.* 1950) *Lab., Southampton Test,* maj. 13,684

*Whitney, Sir Raymond, OBE (*b.* 1930) *C., Wycombe,* maj. 2,370

*Whittingdale, John F. L., OBE (*b.* 1959) *C., Maldon and Chelmsford East,* maj. 10,039

*Wicks, Malcolm H. (*b.* 1947) *Lab., Croydon North,* maj. 18,398

*Widdecombe, Rt. Hon. Ann N. (*b.* 1947) *C., Maidstone and the Weald,* maj. 9,603

*Wigley, Rt. Hon. Dafydd (*b.* 1943) *PC, Caernarfon,* maj. 7,949

*Wilkinson, John A. D. (*b.* 1940) *C., Ruislip-Northwood,* maj. 7,794

*Willetts, David L. (*b.* 1956) *C., Havant,* maj. 3,729

*Williams, Rt. Hon. Alan J. (*b.* 1930) *Lab., Swansea West,* maj. 14,459

*Williams, Dr Alan W. (*b.* 1945) *Lab., Carmarthen East and Dinefwr,* maj. 3,450

Williams, Mrs Betty H. (*b.* 1944) *Lab., Conwy,* maj. 1,596

Willis, G. Philip (*b.* 1941) *LD, Harrogate and Knaresborough,* maj. 6,236

Wills, Michael D. (*b.* 1952) *Lab., Swindon North,* maj. 7,688

*Wilshire, David (*b.* 1943) *C., Spelthorne,* maj. 3,473

*Wilson, Brian D. H. (*b.* 1948) *Lab., Cunninghame North,* maj. 11,039

*Winnick, David J. (*b.* 1933) *Lab., Walsall North,* maj. 12,588

*Winterton, Mrs J. Ann (*b.* 1941) *C., Congleton,* maj. 6,130

*Winterton, Nicholas R. (*b.* 1938) *C., Macclesfield,* maj. 8,654

Winterton, Ms Rosalie (*b.* 1958) *Lab., Doncaster Central,* maj. 17,856

*Wise, Mrs Audrey (*b.* 1935) *Lab., Preston,* maj. 18,680

Wood, Michael R. (*b.* 1946) *Lab., Batley and Spen,* maj. 6,141

Woodward, Shaun A. (*b.* 1958) *C., Witney,* maj. 7,028

Woolas, Philip J. (*b.* 1959) *Lab., Oldham East and Saddleworth,* maj. 3,389

*Worthington, Anthony (*b.* 1941) *Lab., Clydebank and Milngavie,* maj. 13,320

*Wray, James (*b.* 1938) *Lab., Glasgow Baillieston,* maj. 14,840

Wright, Anthony D. (*b.* 1954) *Lab., Great Yarmouth,* maj. 8,668

*Wright, Anthony W., D.PHIL. (*b.* 1948) *Lab., Cannock Chase,* maj. 14,478

Wyatt, Derek M. (*b.* 1949) *Lab., Sittingbourne and Sheppey,* maj. 1,929

*Yeo, Timothy S. K. (*b.* 1945) *C., Suffolk South,* maj. 4,175

*Young, Rt. Hon. Sir George, BT. (*b.* 1941) *C., Hampshire North West,* maj. 11,551

BY-ELECTIONS SINCE THE GENERAL ELECTION (*see also* Stop-press)

UXBRIDGE
(31 July 1997)
*E.*57,733 *T.*55.2%

J. Randall, *C.*	16,288
A. Slaughter, *Lab.*	12,522
K. Kerr, *LD*	1,792
'Lord Sutch', *Loony*	396
Ms J. Leonard, *Soc.*	259
Ms F. Taylor, *BNP*	205
I. Anderson, *Nat. Dem.*	157
J. McCauley, *NF*	110
H. Middleton, *Original Lib. Party*	69
J. Feisenberger, *UK Ind.*	39
R. Carroll, *Emerald Rainbow Islands Dream Ticket*	30
C. majority	3,766

PAISLEY SOUTH
(6 November 1997)
*E.*54,040 *T.*42%

D. Alexander, *Lab.*	10,346
I. Blackford, *SNP*	7,615
Ms E. McCartin, *LD*	2,582
Ms S. Laidlaw, *C.*	1,643
J. Deighan, *ProLife*	578
F. Curran, *Soc. All. Fighting Corruption*	306
C. McLauchlan, *Scottish Ind. Lab.*	155
C. Herriot, *Soc. Lab.*	153
K. Blair, *NLP*	57
Lab. majority	2,731

BECKENHAM
(20 November 1997)
*E.*72,807 *T.*43.7%

Ms J. Lait, *C.*	13,162
R. Hughes, *Lab.*	11,935
Ms R. Vetterlein, *LD*	5,864
P. Rimmer, *Lib.*	330
J. McAuley, *NF*	267
L. Mead, *New Britain Ref.*	237
T. Campion, *Social Foundation*	69
J. Small, *NLP*	44
C. majority	1,227

WINCHESTER
(20 November 1997)
*E.*78,884 *T.*68.7%

M. Oaten, *LD*	37,006
G. Malone, *C.*	15,450
P. Davies, *Lab.*	944
R. Page, *Ref./UK Ind. Alliance*	521
'Lord' Sutch, *Loony*	316
R. Huggett, *Literal Dem.*	59
Ms R. Barry, *NLP*	48
R. Everest, *European C.*	40
LD majority	21,556

LEEDS CENTRAL
(10 June 1999)
*E.*66,983 *T.*19.6%

H. Benn, *Lab.*	6,361
P. Wild, *LD*	4,068
E. Wild, *C.*	1,618
Lab. majority	2,293

EDDISBURY
(22 July 1999)
*E.*67,086 *T.*51.4 %

S. O'Brien, *C.*	15,465
Ms M. Hanson, *Lab.*	13,859
P. Roberts, *LD*	4,757
A. Hope, *Loony*	238
R. Everest, *Ind. Euro C.*	98
Ms D. Grice, *NLP*	80
C. majority	1,606

General Election statistics

PRINCIPAL PARTIES IN PARLIAMENT SINCE 1970

	1970	1974 Feb.	1974 Oct.	1979	1983	1987	1992	1997
Conservative	330*	296	276	339	397	375	336	165
Labour	287	301	319	268	209	229	270	418
Liberal/LD	6	14	13	11	17	17	20	46
Social Democrat	—	1	—	—	6	5	—	—
Independent	5†	1	1	2	—	—	—	1
Plaid Cymru	—	2	3	2	2	3	4	4
Scottish Nationalist	1	7	11	2	2	3	3	6
Democratic Unionist	—	—	—	3	3	3	3	2
SDLP	—	1	1	1	1	3	4	3
Sinn Fein	—	—	—	—	1	1	—	2
Ulster Popular Unionist	—	—	—	—	1	1	1	—
Ulster Unionist‡	*	11	10	6	10	9	9	10
UK Unionist	—	—	—	—	—	—	—	1
The Speaker	1	1	1	1	1	1	1	1
Total	630	635	635	635	650	650	651	659

* Including 8 Ulster Unionists
† Comprising: Independent Labour 1, Independent Unity 1, Protestant Unity 1, Republican Labour 1, Unity 1
‡ Comprises:
  1974 (February) United Ulster Unionist Council 11
  1974 (October) United Ulster Unionist 10
  1979 Ulster Unionist 5, United Ulster Unionist 1
  1983 Official Unionist 10

PARLIAMENTS SINCE 1970

		Duration		
Assembled	*Dissolved*	*yr*	*m.*	*d.*
29 June 1970	8 February 1974	3	7	10
6 March 1974	20 September 1974	0	6	14
22 October 1974	7 April 1979	4	5	16
9 May 1979	13 May 1983	4	0	4
15 June 1983	18 May 1987	3	11	3
17 June 1987	16 March 1992	4	8	28
27 April 1992	8 April 1997	4	11	12
7 May 1997				

MAJORITIES IN THE COMMONS SINCE 1970

Year	*Party*	*Maj.*
1970	Conservative	31
1974 *Feb.*	No majority	
1974 *Oct.*	Labour	5
1979	Conservative	43
1983	Conservative	144
1987	Conservative	102
1992	Conservative	21
1997	Labour	178

VOTES CAST 1992 AND 1997

	1992	1997
Conservative	14,089,722	9,600,940
Labour	11,567,764	13,517,911
Liberal Democrats	6,027,552	5,243,440
Scottish Nationalist	629,564	622,260
Plaid Cymru	154,390	161,030
N. Ireland parties	740,859	780,920
Others	401,239	1,361,701
Total	33,619,090	31,287,702

DISTRIBUTION OF SEATS BY COUNTRY 1997

	England	Wales	Scotland	N. Ireland
Conservative	165	—	—	—
Labour	328	34	56	—
Lib. Dem.	34	2	10	—
SNP	—	—	6	—
Plaid Cymru	—	4	—	—
Other	2*	—	—	18

* Includes the Speaker

SIZE OF ELECTORATE 1997

England	36,806,557
Wales	2,222,533
Scotland	3,984,406
Northern Ireland	1,190,198
Total	44,203,694

PARLIAMENTARY CONSTITUENCIES AS AT 1 MAY 1997 (*see also* Stop-press)

The results of voting in each parliamentary division at the general election of 1 May 1997 are given below. The majority in the 1992 general election, and any by-election between 1987 and 1992, is given below the 1992 result where the constituency covers the same area as in 1992. Where the boundaries of a constituency have changed since 1992, a notional result for 1992 is given.

Symbols
E. Total number of electors in the constituency at the 1997 general election
T. Turnout of electors at the 1997 general election
* Member of the last Parliament in unchanged constituency
† Member of the last Parliament in different constituency or one affected by boundary changes

Abbreviations
All.	Alliance Party (NI)
C.	Conservative
DUP	Democratic Unionist Party
Green	Green Party
Ind.	Independent
Lab.	Labour
Lab. Co-op.	Labour Co-operative
LD	Liberal Democrat
PC	Plaid Cymru
SDLP	Social Democratic and Labour Party
SF	Sinn Fein
SNP	Scottish National Party
UKU	United Kingdom Unionist
UUP	Ulster Unionist Party
ACA	Anti-Child Abuse
ACC	Anti-Corruption Candidate
Albion	Albion Party
Alt.	Alternative
ANP	All Night Party
Anti-maj.	Independent Anti-majority Democracy
AS	Anti-sleaze
Barts	Independent Save Barts Candidate
BDP	British Democratic Party
Beanus	Space Age Superhero from Planet Beanus
Beaut.	Independently Beautiful Party
Bert.	Berties Party
BFAIR	British Freedom and Individual Rights
BHMBCM	Black Haired Medium Build Caucasian Male
BHR	British Home Rule
B. Ind.	Beaconsfield Independent: Unity Through Electoral Reform
BIPF	British Isles People First Party
BNP	British National Party
Bypass	Newbury Bypass Stop Construction Now
Byro	Lord Byro versus the Scallywag Tories
Care	Care in the Community
CASC	Conservatives Against the Single Currency
CFSS	Country Field and Shooting Sports
Ch. D.	Christian Democrat
Ch. Nat.	Christian Nationalist

Choice	People's Choice
Ch. P.	Christian Party
Ch. U.	Christian Unity
Comm. L.	Communist League
Comm. P.	Communist Party of Britain
Constit.	Constitutionalist
Consult.	Independent Democracy Means Consulting the People
CRP	Community Representative Party
CSSPP	Common Sense Sick of Politicians Party
Cvty	Conservatory
D. Nat.	Democratic Nationalist
Dream	Rainbow Dream Ticket Party
Dynamic	First Dynamic Party
EDP	English Democratic Party
Embryo	Anti-Abortion Euthanasia Embryo Experiments
EUP	European Unity Party
Fair	Building a Fair Society
FDP	Fancy Dress Party
Fellowship	Fellowship Party for Peace and Justice
FEP	Full Employment Party
FP	Freedom Party
Glow	Glow Bowling Party
GRLNSP	Green Referendum Lawless Naturally Street Party
Heart	Heart 106.2 Alien Party
Hemp	Hemp Coalition
HR	Human Rights '97
Hum.	Humanist Party
IAC	Independent Anti-Corruption in Government/ TGWU
Ind. AFE	Independent Against a Federal Europe
Ind. BB	Independent Back to Basics
Ind. CRP	Independent Conservative Referendum Party
Ind. Dean	Independent Royal Forest of Dean
Ind. Dem.	Independent Democrat
Ind. ECR	Independent English Conservative and Referendum
Ind. Euro C.	Independent Euro Conservative
Ind. F.	Independent Forester
Ind. Green	Independent Green: Your Children's Future
Ind. Hum.	English Independent Humanist Party
Ind. Is.	Island Independent
Ind. JRP	Justice and Renewal Independent Party
Ind. No	Independent No to Europe
IZB	Islam Zinda Baad Platform
JP	Justice Party
Juice	Juice Party
KBF	Keep Britain Free and Independent Party
Lab. Change	Labour Time for Change Candidate
LC	Loyal Conservative
LCP	Legalize Cannabis Party
LGR	Local Government Reform
Lib.	Liberal
Loc.	Local
Logic	Logic Party Truth Only Allowed
Loony	Monster Raving Loony Party
Mal	Mal Voice of the People Party
Miss M.	Miss Moneypenny's Glamorous One Party
MK	Mebyon Kernow

Mongolian	Mongolian Barbeque Great Place to Party
MRAC	Multi-racial Anti-Corruption Alliance
Nat. Dem.	National Democrat
New Way	New Millennium New Way Hemp Candidate
NF	National Front
NIFT	Former Captain NI Football Team
NIP	Northern Ireland Party
NI Women	Northern Ireland Women's Coalition
NLP	Natural Law Party
NLPC	New Labour Party Candidate
None	None of the Above Parties
NPC	Non-party Conservative
Pacifist	Pacifist for Peace, Justice, Co-operation, Environment
PAYR	Protecting All Your Rights Locally Effectively
PF	Pathfinders
PLP	People's Labour Party
Plymouth	Plymouth First Group
PP	People's Party
PPP	People's Party Party
ProLife	ProLife Alliance
PUP	Progressive Unionist Party
RA	Residents Association
Rain. Is.	Rainbow Connection Your Island Candidate
Rain. Ref.	Rainbow Referendum
R. Alt.	Radical Alternative
Ref.	Referendum Party
Ren. Dem.	Renaissance Democrat
Rep. GB	Republican Party of Great Britain
Rights	Charter for Basic Rights
Ronnie	Ronnie the Rhino Party
Route 66	Route 66 Party Posse Party
Scrapit	Scrapit Stop Avon Ring Road Now
SCU	Scottish Conservative Unofficial
SEP	Socialist Equality Party
SFDC	Stratford First Democratic Conservative
SG	Sub-genus Party
Shields	Pro Interests of South Shields People
SIP	Sheffield Independent Party
SLI	Scottish Labour Independent
Slough	People in Slough Shunning Useless Politicians
SLU	Scottish Labour Unofficial
Soc.	Socialist Party
Soc. Dem.	Social Democrat
Soc. Lab.	Socialist Labour Party
SPGB	Socialist Party of Great Britain
Spts All.	Sportsman's Alliance: Anything but Mellor
SSA	Scottish Socialist Alliance
Stan	Happiness Stan's Freedom to Party Party
Teddy	Teddy Bear Alliance Party
Top	Top Choice Liberal Democrat
21st Cent.	21st Century Independent Foresters
UA	Universal Alliance
UK Ind.	UK Independence Party
UKPP	UK Pensioners Party
WCCC	West Cheshire College in Crisis Party
Wessex	Wessex Regionalist
WP	Workers' Party
WRP	Workers' Revolutionary Party

ENGLAND

ALDERSHOT
E.76,189   T.71.07%
G. Howarth, C.   23,119
A. Collett, LD   16,498
T. Bridgeman, Lab.   13,057
J. Howe, UK Ind.   794
A. Pendragon, Ind.   361
Dr D. Stevens, BNP   322
C. majority 6,621
(Boundary change: notional C.)

ALDRIDGE-BROWNHILLS
E.62,441   T.74.26%
*R. Shepherd, C.   21,856
J. Toth, Lab.   19,330
Ms C. Downie, LD   5,184
C. majority 2,526
(April 1992, C. maj. 11,024)

ALTRINCHAM AND SALE WEST
E.70,625   T.73.32%
G. Brady, C.   22,348
Ms J. Baugh, Lab.   20,843
M. Ramsbottom, LD   6,535
A. Landes, Ref.   1,348
J. Stephens, ProLife   313
Dr R. Mrozinski, UK Ind.   270
J. Renwick, NLP   125
C. majority 1,505
(Boundary change: notional C.)

AMBER VALLEY
E.72,005   T.76.07%
Ms J. Mallaber, Lab.   29,943
†P. Oppenheim, C.   18,330
R. Shelley, LD   4,219
Mrs I. McGibbon, Ref.   2,283
Lab. majority 11,613
(Boundary change: notional C.)

ARUNDEL AND SOUTH DOWNS
E.67,641   T.75.90%
H. Flight, C.   27,251
J. Goss, LD   13,216
R. Black, Lab.   9,376
J. Herbert, UK Ind.   1,494
C. majority 14,035
(Boundary change: notional C.)

ASHFIELD
E.72,269   T.70.02%
†G. Hoon, Lab.   32,979
M. Simmonds, C.   10,251
W. Smith, LD   4,882
M. Betts, Ref.   1,896
S. Belshaw, BNP   595
Lab. majority 22,728
(Boundary change: notional Lab.)

ASHFORD
E.74,149   T.74.57%
D. Green, C.   22,899
J. Ennals, Lab.   17,544
J. Williams, LD   10,901
C. Cruden, Ref.   3,201
R. Boden, Green   660
S. Tyrell, NLP   89
C. majority 5,355
(April 1992, C. maj. 17,359)

ASHTON UNDER LYNE
E.72,206   T.65.48%
†Rt. Hon. R. Sheldon, Lab.   31,919

R. Mayson, C.   8,954
T. Pickstone, LD   4,603
Mrs L. Clapham, Ref.   1,346
Prince Cymbal, Loony   458
Lab. majority 22,965
(Boundary change: notional Lab.)

AYLESBURY
E.79,047   T.72.81%
†D. Lidington, C.   25,426
Ms S. Bowles, LD   17,007
R. Langridge, Lab.   12,759
M. John, Ref.   2,196
L. Sheaff, NLP   166
C. majority 8,419
(Boundary change: notional C.)

BANBURY
E.77,456   T.75.46%
†A. Baldry, C.   25,076
Ms H. Peperell, Lab.   20,339
Mrs C. Bearder, LD   9,761
J. Ager, Ref.   2,245
Ms B. Cotton, Green   530
Mrs L. King, UK Ind.   364
I. Pearson, NLP   131
C. majority 4,737
(Boundary change: notional C.)

BARKING
E.53,682   T.61.41%
†Mrs M. Hodge, Lab.   21,698
K. Langford, C.   5,802
M. Marsh, LD   3,128
C. Taylor, Ref.   1,283
M. Tolman, BNP   894
D. Mearns, ProLife   159
Lab. majority 15,896
(Boundary change: notional Lab.)

BARNSLEY CENTRAL
E.61,133   T.59.68%
†E. Illsley, Lab.   28,090
S. Gutteridge, C.   3,589
D. Finlay, LD   3,481
J. Walsh, Ref.   1,325
Lab. majority 24,501
(Boundary change: notional Lab.)

**BARNSLEY EAST AND
MEXBOROUGH**
E.67,840   T.63.88%
†J. Ennis, Lab.   31,699
Miss J. Ellison, C.   4,936
D. Willis, LD   4,489
K. Capstick, Soc. Lab.   1,213
A. Miles, Ref.   797
Ms J. Hyland, SEP   201
Lab. majority 26,763
(Boundary change: notional Lab.)

**BARNSLEY WEST AND
PENISTONE**
E.64,894   T.65.04%
*M. Clapham, Lab.   25,017
P. Watkins, C.   7,750
Mrs W. Knight, LD   7,613
Mrs J. Miles, Ref.   1,828
Lab. majority 17,267
(April 1992, Lab. maj. 14,504)

BARROW AND FURNESS
E.66,960   T.72.03%
*J. Hutton, Lab.   27,630
R. Hunt, C.   13,133
Mrs A. Metcalfe, LD   4,264
J. Hamzeian, PLP   1,995
D. Mitchell, Ref.   1,208
Lab. majority 14,497
(April 1992, Lab. maj. 3,578)

BASILDON
E.73,989   T.71.74%
Ms A. Smith, Lab. Co-op.   29,646
J. Baron, C.   16,366
Ms L. Granshaw, LD   4,608
C. Robinson, Ref.   2,462
Lab. Co-op. majority 13,280
(Boundary change: notional C.)

BASINGSTOKE
E.77,035   T.74.16%
†A. Hunter, C.   24,751
N. Lickley, Lab.   22,354
M. Rimmer, LD   9,714
E. Selim, Ind.   310
C. majority 2,397
(Boundary change: notional C.)

BASSETLAW
E.68,101   T.70.37%
†J. Ashton, Lab.   29,298
M. Cleasby, C.   11,838
M. Kerrigan, LD   4,950
R. Graham, Ref.   1,838
Lab. majority 17,460
(Boundary change: notional Lab.)

BATH
E.70,815   T.76.24%
†D. Foster, LD   26,169
Ms A. McNair, C.   16,850
T. Bush, Lab.   8,828
A. Cook, Ref.   1,192
R. Scrase, Green   580
P. Sandell, UK Ind.   315
N. Pullen, NLP   55
LD majority 9,319
(Boundary change: notional LD)

BATLEY AND SPEN
E.64,209   T.73.14%
M. Wood, Lab.   23,213
†Mrs E. Peacock, C.   17,072
Mrs K. Pinnock, LD   4,133
E. Wood, Ref.   1,691
R. Smith, BNP   472
C. Lord, Green   384
Lab. majority 6,141
(Boundary change: notional C.)

BATTERSEA
E.66,928   T.70.82%
M. Linton, Lab.   24,047
†J. Bowis, C.   18,687
Ms P. Keaveney, LD   3,482
M. Slater, Ref.   804
R. Banks, UK Ind.   250
J. Marshall, Dream   127
Lab. majority 5,360
(Boundary change: notional C.)

BEACONSFIELD
E.68,959   *T*.72.80%
D. Grieve, *C.*   24,709
P. Mapp, *LD*   10,722
A. Hudson, *Lab.*   10,063
H. Lloyd, *Ref.*   2,197
C. Story, *CASC*   1,434
C. Cooke, *UK Ind.*   451
Ms G. Duval, *ProLife*   286
T. Dyball, *NLP*   193
R. Matthews, *B. Ind.*   146
C. majority 13,987
(Boundary change: notional C.)

BECKENHAM
E.72,807   *T*.74.65%
†P. Merchant, *C.*   23,084
R. Hughes, *Lab.*   18,131
Ms R. Vetterlein, *LD*   9,858
L. Mead, *Ref.*   1,663
P. Rimmer, *Lib.*   720
C. Pratt, *UK Ind.*   506
J. Mcauley, *NF*   388
C. majority 4,953
(Boundary change: notional C.)
See also page 233

BEDFORD
E.66,560   *T*.73.53%
P. Hall, *Lab.*   24,774
R. Blackman, *C.*   16,474
C. Noyce, *LD*   6,044
P. Conquest, *Ref.*   1,503
Ms P. Saunders, *NLP*   149
Lab. majority 8,300
(Boundary change: notional C.)

BEDFORDSHIRE MID
E.66,979   *T*.78.41%
J. Sayeed, *C.*   24,176
N. Mallett, *Lab.*   17,086
T. Hill, *LD*   8,823
Mrs S. Marler, *Ref.*   2,257
M. Lorys, *NLP*   174
C. majority 7,090
(Boundary change: notional C.)

BEDFORDSHIRE NORTH EAST
E.64,743   *T*.77.83%
†Rt. Hon. Sir N. Lyell, *C.*   22,311
J. Lehal, *Lab.*   16,428
P. Bristow, *LD*   7,119
J. Taylor, *Ref.*   2,490
L. Foley, *Ind. C.*   1,842
B. Bence, *NLP*   138
C. majority 5,883
(Boundary change: notional C.)

BEDFORDSHIRE SOUTH WEST
E.69,781   *T*.75.76%
†Sir D. Madel, *C.*   21,534
A. Date, *Lab.*   21,402
S. Owen, *LD*   7,559
Ms R. Hill, *Ref.*   1,761
T. Wise, *UK Ind.*   446
A. Le Carpentier, *NLP*   162
C. majority 132
(Boundary change: notional C.)

BERWICK-UPON-TWEED
E.56,428   *T*.74.08%
*A. Beith, *LD*   19,007
P. Brannen, *Lab.*   10,965

N. Herbert, *C.*   10,056
N. Lambton, *Ref.*   1,423
I. Dodds, *UK Ind.*   352
LD majority 8,042
(April 1992, LD maj. 5,043)

BETHNAL GREEN AND BOW
E.73,008   *T*.61.20%
Ms O. King, *Lab.*   20,697
K. Choudhury, *C.*   9,412
S. N. Islam, *LD*   5,361
D. King, *BNP*   3,350
T. Milson, *Lib.*   2,963
S. Osman, *Real Lab.*   1,117
S. Petter, *Green*   812
M. Abdullah, *Ref.*   557
A. Hamid, *Soc. Lab.*   413
Lab. majority 11,285
(Boundary change: notional Lab.)

BEVERLEY AND HOLDERNESS
E.71,916   *T*.73.62%
†J. Cran, *C.*   21,629
N. O'Neill, *Lab.*   20,818
J. Melling, *LD*   9,689
D. Barley, *UK Ind.*   695
S. Withers, *NLP*   111
C. majority 811
(Boundary change: notional C.)

BEXHILL AND BATTLE
E.65,584   *T*.74.70%
†C. Wardle, *C.*   23,570
Mrs K. Field, *LD*   12,470
R. Beckwith, *Lab.*   8,866
Mrs V. Thompson, *Ref.*   3,302
J. Pankhurst, *UK Ind.*   786
C. majority 11,100
(Boundary change: notional C.)

BEXLEYHEATH AND CRAYFORD
E.63,334   *T*.76.14%
N. Beard, *Lab.*   21,942
†D. Evennett, *C.*   18,527
Mrs F. Montford, *LD*   5,391
B. Thomas, *Ref.*   1,551
Ms P. Smith, *BNP*   429
W. Jenner, *UK Ind.*   383
Lab. majority 3,415
(Boundary change: notional C.)

BILLERICAY
E.76,550   *T*.72.40%
†Mrs T. Gorman, *C.*   22,033
P. Richards, *Lab.*   20,677
G. Williams, *LD*   8,763
B. Hughes, *LC*   3,377
J. Buchanan, *ProLife*   570
C. majority 1,356
(Boundary change: notional C.)

BIRKENHEAD
E.59,782   *T*.65.78%
*F. Field, *Lab.*   27,825
J. Crosby, *C.*   5,982
R. Wood, *LD*   3,548
M. Cullen, *Soc. Lab.*   1,168
R. Evans, *Ref.*   800
Lab. majority 21,843
(April 1992, Lab. maj. 17,613)

BIRMINGHAM EDGBASTON
E.70,204   *T*.69.03%
Mrs G. Stuart, *Lab.*   23,554

A. Marshall, *C.*   18,712
J. Gallagher, *LD*   4,691
J. Oakton, *Ref.*   1,065
D. Campbell, *BDP*   443
Lab. majority 4,842
(Boundary change: notional C.)

BIRMINGHAM ERDINGTON
E.66,380   *T*.60.87%
†R. Corbett, *Lab.*   23,764
A. Tompkins, *C.*   11,107
I. Garrett, *LD*   4,112
G. Cable, *Ref.*   1,424
Lab. majority 12,657
(Boundary change: notional Lab.)

BIRMINGHAM HALL GREEN
E.58,767   *T*.71.16%
S. McCabe, *Lab.*   22,372
*A. Hargreaves, *C.*   13,952
A. Dow, *LD*   4,034
P. Bennett, *Ref.*   1,461
Lab. majority 8,420
(April 1992, C. maj. 3,665)

BIRMINGHAM HODGE HILL
E.56,066   *T*.60.91%
*T. Davis, *Lab.*   22,398
E. Grant, *C.*   8,198
H. Thomas, *LD*   2,891
P. Johnson, *UK Ind.*   660
Lab. majority 14,200
(April 1992, Lab. maj. 7,068)

BIRMINGHAM LADYWOOD
E.70,013   *T*.54.24%
†Ms C. Short, *Lab.*   28,134
S. Vara, *C.*   5,052
S. S. Marwa, *LD*   3,020
Mrs R. Gurney, *Ref.*   1,086
A. Carmichael, *Nat. Dem.*   685
Lab. majority 23,082
(Boundary change: notional Lab.)

BIRMINGHAM NORTHFIELD
E.56,842   *T*.68.34%
†R. Burden, *Lab.*   22,316
A. Blumenthal, *C.*   10,873
M. Ashall, *LD*   4,078
D. Gent, *Ref.*   1,243
K. Axon, *BNP*   337
Lab. majority 11,443
(Boundary change: notional Lab.)

BIRMINGHAM PERRY BARR
E.71,031   *T*.64.60%
†J. Rooker, *Lab.*   28,921
A. Dunnett, *C.*   9,964
R. Hassall, *LD*   4,523
S. Mahmood, *Ref.*   843
A. Baxter, *Lib.*   718
L. Windridge, *BNP*   544
A. S. Panesar, *Fourth Party*   374
Lab. majority 18,957
(Boundary change: notional Lab.)

BIRMINGHAM SELLY OAK
E.72,049   *T*.70.16%
*Dr L. Jones, *Lab.*   28,121
G. Greene, *C.*   14,033
D. Osborne, *LD*   6,121
L. Marshall, *Ref.*   1,520
Dr G. Gardner, *ProLife*   417

P. Sherriff-Knowles, *Loony*   253
H. Meads, *NLP*   85
Lab. majority 14,088
(April 1992, Lab. maj. 2,060)

BIRMINGHAM SPARKBROOK AND
SMALL HEATH
E.73,130   T. 57.11%
†R. Godsiff, *Lab.*   26,841
K. Hardeman, *C.*   7,315
R. Harmer, *LD*   3,889
A. Clawley, *Green*   959
R. Dooley, *Ref.*   737
P. Patel, *Fourth Party*   538
R. M. Syed, *PAYR*   513
Ms S. Bi, *Ind.*   490
C. Wren, *Soc. Lab.*   483
Lab. majority 19,526
(Boundary change: notional Lab.)

BIRMINGHAM YARDLEY
E.53,058   T. 71.22%
*Ms E. Morris, *Lab.*   17,778
J. Hemming, *LD*   12,463
Mrs A. Jobson, *C.*   6,736
D. Livingston, *Ref.*   646
A. Ware, *UK Ind.*   164
Lab. majority 5,315
(April 1992, Lab. maj. 162)

BISHOP AUCKLAND
E.66,754   T. 68.88%
†Rt. Hon. D. Foster, *Lab.*   30,359
Mrs J. Fergus, *C.*   9,295
L. Ashworth, *LD*   4,223
D. Blacker, *Ref.*   2,104
Lab. majority 21,064
(Boundary change: notional Lab.)

BLABY
E.70,471   T. 76.05%
†A. Robathan, *C.*   24,564
R. Willmott, *Lab.*   18,090
G. Welsh, *LD*   8,001
R. Harrison, *Ref.*   2,018
J. Peacock, *BNP*   523
T. Stokes, *Ind.*   397
C. majority 6,474
(Boundary change: notional C.)

BLACKBURN
E.73,058   T. 65.01%
*J. Straw, *Lab.*   26,141
Ms S. Sidhu, *C.*   11,690
S. Fenn, *LD*   4,990
D. Bradshaw, *Ref.*   1,892
Mrs T. Wingfield, *Nat. Dem.*   671
Mrs H. Drummond, *Soc. Lab.*   637
R. Field, *Green*   608
Mrs M. Carmichael-Grimshaw,
    KBF   506
W. Batchelor, *CSSPP*   362
Lab. majority 14,451
(April 1992, Lab. maj. 6,027)

BLACKPOOL NORTH AND
FLEETWOOD
E.74,989   T. 71.67%
Mrs J. Humble, *Lab.*   28,051
†H. Elletson, *C.*   19,105
Mrs B. Hill, *LD*   4,600
Ms K. Stacey, *Ref.*   1,704
J. Ellis, *BNP*   288

Lab. majority 8,946
(Boundary change: notional C.)

BLACKPOOL SOUTH
E.75,720   T. 67.80%
G. Marsden, *Lab.*   29,282
R. Booth, *C.*   17,666
Mrs D. Holt, *LD*   4,392
Lab. majority 11,616
(Boundary change: notional C.)

BLAYDON
E.64,699   T. 70.98%
*J. McWilliam, *Lab.*   27,535
P. Maughan, *LD*   10,930
M. Watson, *C.*   6,048
R. Rook, *Ind. Lab.*   1,412
Lab. majority 16,605
(April 1992, Lab. maj. 13,343)

BLYTH VALLEY
E.61,761   T. 68.78%
*R. Campbell, *Lab.*   27,276
A. Lamb, *LD*   9,540
Mrs B. Musgrave, *C.*   5,666
Lab. majority 17,736
(April 1992, Lab. maj. 8,044)

BOGNOR REGIS AND
LITTLEHAMPTON
E.66,480   T. 69.86%
N. Gibb, *C.*   20,537
R. Nash, *Lab.*   13,216
Dr J. Walsh, *LD*   11,153
G. Stride, *UK Ind.*   1,537
C. majority 7,321
(Boundary change: notional C.)

BOLSOVER
E.66,476   T. 71.32%
†D. Skinner, *Lab.*   35,073
R. Harwood, *C.*   7,924
I. Cox, *LD*   4,417
Lab. majority 27,149
(Boundary change: notional Lab.)

BOLTON NORTH EAST
E.67,930   T. 72.44%
D. Crausby, *Lab.*   27,621
R. Wilson, *C.*   14,952
Dr E. Critchley, *LD*   4,862
D. Staniforth, *Ref.*   1,096
W. Kelly, *Soc. Lab.*   676
Lab. majority 12,669
(Boundary change: notional Lab.)

BOLTON SOUTH EAST
E.66,459   T. 65.23%
B. Iddon, *Lab.*   29,856
P. Carter, *C.*   8,545
F. Harasiwka, *LD*   3,805
W. Pickering, *Ref.*   973
L. Walch, *NLP*   170
Lab. majority 21,311
(Boundary change: notional Lab.)

BOLTON WEST
E.63,535   T. 77.37%
Ms R. Kelly, *Lab.*   24,342
†T. Sackville, *C.*   17,270
Mrs B. Ronson, *LD*   5,309
Mrs D. Kelly, *Soc. Lab.*   1,374
Mrs G. Frankl-Slater, *Ref.*   865

Lab. majority 7,072
(Boundary change: notional C.)

BOOTLE
E.57,284   T. 66.73%
†J. Benton, *Lab.*   31,668
R. Mathews, *C.*   3,247
K. Reid, *LD*   2,191
J. Elliott, *Ref.*   571
P. Glover, *Soc.*   420
S. Cohen, *NLP*   126
Lab. majority 28,421
(Boundary change: notional Lab.)

BOSTON AND SKEGNESS
E.67,623   T. 68.87%
†Sir R. Body, *C.*   19,750
P. McCauley, *Lab.*   19,103
J. Dodsworth, *LD*   7,721
C. majority 647
(Boundary change: notional C.)

BOSWORTH
E.68,113   T. 76.57%
†D. Tredinnick, *C.*   21,189
A. Furlong, *Lab.*   20,162
J. Ellis, *LD*   9,281
S. Halborg, *Ref.*   1,521
C. majority 1,027
(Boundary change: notional C.)

BOURNEMOUTH EAST
E.61,862   T. 70.20%
†D. Atkinson, *C.*   17,997
D. Eyre, *LD*   13,651
Mrs J. Stevens, *Lab.*   9,181
A. Musgrave-Scott, *Ref.*   1,808
K. Benney, *UK Ind.*   791
C. majority 4,346
(Boundary change: notional C.)

BOURNEMOUTH WEST
E.62,028   T. 66.22%
†J. Butterfill, *C.*   17,115
Ms J. Dover, *LD*   11,405
D. Gritt, *Lab.*   10,093
R. Mills, *Ref.*   1,910
Mrs L. Tooley, *UK Ind.*   281
J. Morse, *BNP*   165
A. Springham, *NLP*   103
C. majority 5,710
(Boundary change: notional C.)

BRACKNELL
E.79,292   T. 74.52%
†A. Mackay, *C.*   27,983
Ms A. Snelgrove, *Lab.*   17,596
A. Hilliar, *LD*   9,122
J. Tompkins, *New Lab.*   1,909
W. Cairns, *Ref.*   1,636
L. Boxall, *UK Ind.*   569
Ms D. Roberts, *ProLife*   276
C. majority 10,387
(Boundary change: notional C.)

BRADFORD NORTH
E.66,228   T. 63.26%
*T. Rooney, *Lab.*   23,493
R. Skinner, *C.*   10,723
T. Browne, *LD*   6,083
H. Wheatley, *Ref.*   1,227
W. Beckett, *Loony*   369
Lab. majority 12,770
(April 1992, Lab. maj. 7,664)

BRADFORD SOUTH
*E.*68,391   *T.* 65.88%
*G. Sutcliffe, *Lab.*   25,558
Mrs A. Hawkesworth, *C.*   12,622
A. Wilson-Fletcher, *LD*   5,093
Mrs M. Kershaw, *Ref.*   1,785
Lab. majority 12,936
(April 1992, Lab. maj. 4,902)
(June 1994, Lab. maj. 9,664)

BRADFORD WEST
*E.*71,961   *T.* 63.32%
M. Singh, *Lab.*   18,932
M. Riaz, *C.*   15,055
Mrs H. Wright, *LD*   6,737
A. Khan, *Soc. Lab.*   1,551
C. Royston, *Ref.*   1,348
J. Robinson, *Green*   861
G. Osborn, *BNP*   839
S. Shah, *Soc.*   245
Lab. majority 3,877
(April 1992, Lab. maj. 9,502)

BRAINTREE
*E.*72,772   *T.* 76.37%
A. Hurst, *Lab.*   23,729
†Rt. Hon. A. Newton, *C.*   22,278
T. Ellis, *LD*   6,418
N. Westcott, *Ref.*   2,165
J. Abbott, *Green*   712
M. Nolan, *New Way*   274
Lab. majority 1,451
(Boundary change: notional C.)

BRENT EAST
*E.*53,548   *T.* 65.87%
†K. Livingstone, *Lab.*   23,748
M. Francois, *C.*   7,866
I. Hunter, *LD*   2,751
S. Keable, *Soc. Lab.*   466
A. Shanks, *ProLife*   218
Ms C. Warrilo, *Dream*   120
D. Jenkins, *NLP*   103
Lab. majority 15,882
(Boundary change: notional Lab.)

BRENT NORTH
*E.*54,149   *T.* 70.50%
B. Gardiner, *Lab.*   19,343
†Rt. Hon. Sir R. Boyson, *C.*   15,324
P. Lorber, *LD*   3,104
A. Davids, *NLP*   204
G. Clark, *Dream*   199
Lab. majority 4,019
(Boundary change: notional C.)

BRENT SOUTH
*E.*53,505   *T.* 64.48%
†P. Boateng, *Lab.*   25,180
S. Jackson, *C.*   5,489
J. Brazil, *LD*   2,670
Ms J. Phythian, *Ref.*   497
D. Edler, *Green*   389
C. Howard, *Dream*   175
Ms A. Mahaldar, *NLP*   98
Lab. majority 19,691
(Boundary change: notional Lab.)

BRENTFORD AND ISLEWORTH
*E.*79,058   *T.* 71.00%
Mrs A. Keen, *Lab.*   32,249
†N. Deva, *C.*   17,825
Dr G. Hartwell, *LD*   4,613

J. Bradley, *Green*   687
Mrs B. Simmerson, *UK Ind.*   614
M. Ahmed, *NLP*   147
Lab. majority 14,424
(Boundary change: notional C.)

BRENTWOOD AND ONGAR
*E.*66,005   *T.* 76.85%
†E. Pickles, *C.*   23,031
Mrs E. Bottomley, *LD*   13,341
M. Young, *Lab.*   11,231
Mrs A. Kilmartin, *Ref.*   2,658
Capt. D. Mills, *UK Ind.*   465
C. majority 9,690
(Boundary change: notional C.)

BRIDGWATER
*E.*73,038   *T.* 74.79%
*Rt. Hon. T. King, *C.*   20,174
M. Hoban, *LD*   18,378
R. Lavers, *Lab.*   13,519
Ms F. Evens, *Ref.*   2,551
C. majority 1,796
(April 1992, C. maj. 9,716)

BRIGG AND GOOLE
*E.*63,648   *T.* 73.53%
I. Cawsey, *Lab.*   23,493
D. Stewart, *C.*   17,104
Mrs M.-R. Hardy, *LD*   4,692
D. Rigby, *Ref.*   1,513
Lab. majority 6,389
(Boundary change: notional C.)

BRIGHTON KEMPTOWN
*E.*65,147   *T.* 70.81%
D. Turner, *Lab.*   21,479
†Sir A. Bowden, *C.*   17,945
C. Gray, *LD*   4,478
D. Inman, *Ref.*   1,526
Ms H. Williams, *Soc. Lab.*   316
J. Bowler, *NLP*   172
Ms L. Newman, *Loony*   123
R. Darlow, *Dream*   93
Lab. majority 3,534
(Boundary change: notional C.)

BRIGHTON PAVILION
*E.*66,431   *T.* 73.69%
D. Lepper, *Lab. Co-op.*   26,737
†Sir D. Spencer, *C.*   13,556
K. Blanshard, *LD*   4,644
P. Stocken, *Ref.*   1,304
P. West, *Green*   1,249
R. Huggett, *Ind. C.*   1,098
F. Stevens, *UK Ind.*   179
R. Dobbs, *SG*   125
A. Card, *Dream*   59
Lab. Co-op. majority 13,181
(Boundary change: notional C.)

BRISTOL EAST
*E.*68,990   *T.* 69.87%
†Ms J. Corston, *Lab.*   27,418
E. Vaizey, *C.*   11,259
P. Tyzack, *LD*   7,121
G. Philp, *Ref.*   1,479
P. Williams, *Soc. Lab.*   766
J. McLaggan, *NLP*   158
Lab. majority 16,159
(Boundary change: notional Lab.)

BRISTOL NORTH WEST
*E.*75,009   *T.* 73.65%
D. Naysmith, *Lab. Co-op.*   27,575
†M. Stern, *C.*   16,193
I. Parry, *LD*   7,263
C. Horton, *Ind. Lab.*   1,718
J. Quintanilla, *Ref.*   1,609
G. Shorter, *Soc. Lab.*   482
S. Parnell, *BNP*   265
T. Leighton, *NLP*   140
Lab. Co-op. majority 11,382
(Boundary change: notional Lab.
Co-op.)

BRISTOL SOUTH
*E.*72,393   *T.* 68.87%
†Ms D. Primarolo, *Lab.*   29,890
M. Roe, *C.*   10,562
S. Williams, *LD*   6,691
D. Guy, *Ref.*   1,486
J. Boxall, *Green*   722
I. Marshall, *Soc.*   355
Louis Taylor, *Glow*   153
Lab. majority 19,328
(Boundary change: notional Lab.)

BRISTOL WEST
*E.*84,870   *T.* 73.81%
Ms V. Davey, *Lab.*   22,068
†Rt. Hon. W. Waldegrave, *C.*   20,575
C. Boney, *LD*   17,551
Lady M. Beauchamp, *Ref.*   1,304
J. Quinnell, *Green*   852
R. Nurse, *Soc. Lab.*   244
J. Brierley, *NLP*   47
Lab. majority 1,493
(Boundary change: notional C.)

BROMLEY AND CHISLEHURST
*E.*71,104   *T.* 74.17%
†Rt. Hon. E. Forth, *C.*   24,428
R. Yeldham, *Lab.*   13,310
Dr P. Booth, *LD*   12,530
R. Bryant, *UK Ind.*   1,176
Ms F. Speed, *Green*   640
M. Stoneman, *NF*   369
G. Aitman, *Lib.*   285
C. majority 11,118
(Boundary change: notional C.)

BROMSGROVE
*E.*67,744   *T.* 77.07%
Miss J. Kirkbride, *C.*   24,620
P. McDonald, *Lab.*   19,725
Mrs J. Davy, *LD*   6,200
Mrs D. Winsor, *Ref.*   1,411
Mrs G. Wetton, *UK Ind.*   251
C. majority 4,895
(Boundary change: notional C.)

BROXBOURNE
*E.*66,024   *T.* 70.41%
†Mrs M. Roe, *C.*   22,952
B. Coleman, *Lab.*   16,299
Mrs J. Davies, *LD*   5,310
D. Millward, *Ref.*   1,633
D. Bruce, *BNP*   610
B. Cheetham, *Third Way*   172
C. majority 6,653
(Boundary change: notional C.)

BROXTOWE
*E.*74,144   *T.* 78.41%
N. Palmer, *Lab.*   27,343

†Sir J. Lester, *C.* 21,768
T. Miller, *LD* 6,934
R. Tucker, *Ref.* 2,092
Lab. majority 5,575
(Boundary change: notional C.)

BUCKINGHAM
*E.*62,945   *T.* 78.48%
J. Bercow, *C.* 24,594
R. Lehmann, *Lab.* 12,208
N. Stuart, *LD* 12,175
Dr G. Clements, *NLP* 421
C. majority 12,386
(Boundary change: notional C.)

BURNLEY
*E.*67,582   *T.* 66.95%
*P. Pike, *Lab.* 26,210
W. Wiggin, *C.* 9,148
G. Birtwistle, *LD* 7,877
R. Oakley, *Ref.* 2,010
Lab. majority 17,062
(April 1992, Lab. maj. 11,491)

BURTON
*E.*72,601   *T.* 75.08%
Ms J. Dean, *Lab.* 27,810
†Sir I. Lawrence, *C.* 21,480
D. Fletcher, *LD* 4,617
K. Sharp, *Nat. Dem.* 604
Lab. majority 6,330
(Boundary change: notional C.)

BURY NORTH
*E.*70,515   *T.* 78.07%
D. Chaytor, *Lab.* 28,523
*A. Burt, *C.* 20,657
N. Kenyon, *LD* 4,536
R. Hallewell, *Ref.* 1,337
Lab. majority 7,866
(April 1992, C. maj. 4,764)

BURY SOUTH
*E.*66,568   *T.* 75.60%
I. Lewis, *Lab.* 28,658
†D. Sumberg, *C.* 16,225
V. D'Albert, *LD* 4,227
B. Slater, *Ref.* 1,216
Lab. majority 12,433
(Boundary change: notional C.)

BURY ST EDMUNDS
*E.*74,017   *T.* 75.02%
D. Ruffley, *C.* 21,290
M. Ereira-Guyer, *Lab.* 20,922
D. Cooper, *LD* 10,102
I. McWhirter, *Ref.* 2,939
Mrs J. Lillis, *NLP* 272
C. majority 368
(Boundary change: notional C.)

CALDER VALLEY
*E.*74,901   *T.* 75.39%
Ms C. McCafferty, *Lab.* 26,050
*Sir D. Thompson, *C.* 19,795
S. Pearson, *LD* 8,322
A. Mellor, *Ref.* 1,380
Ms V. Smith, *Green* 488
C. Jackson, *BNP* 431
Lab. majority 6,255
(April 1992, C. maj. 4,878)

CAMBERWELL AND PECKHAM
*E.*50,214   *T.* 56.71%
†Ms H. Harman, *Lab.* 19,734

K. Humphreys, *C.* 3,383
N. Williams, *LD* 3,198
N. China, *Ref.* 692
Ms A. Ruddock, *Soc. Lab.* 685
G. Williams, *Lib.* 443
Ms J. Barker, *Soc.* 233
C. Eames, *WRP* 106
Lab. majority 16,351
(Boundary change: notional Lab.)

CAMBRIDGE
*E.*71,669   *T.* 71.63%
*Mrs A. Campbell, *Lab.* 27,436
D. Platt, *C.* 13,299
G. Heathcock, *LD* 8,287
W. Burrows, *Ref.* 1,262
Ms M. Wright, *Green* 654
Ms A. Johnstone, *ProLife* 191
R. Athow, *WRP* 107
Ms P. Gladwin, *NLP* 103
Lab. majority 14,137
(April 1992, Lab. maj. 580)

CAMBRIDGESHIRE NORTH EAST
*E.*76,056   *T.* 72.87%
†M. Moss, *C.* 23,855
Mrs V. Bucknor, *Lab.* 18,754
A. Nash, *LD* 9,070
M. Bacon, *Ref.* 2,636
C. Bennett, *Soc. Lab.* 851
L. Leighton, *NLP* 259
C. majority 5,101
(Boundary change: notional C.)

CAMBRIDGESHIRE NORTH WEST
*E.*65,791   *T.* 74.20%
†Rt. Hon. Dr B. Mawhinney, *C.* 23,488
L. Steptoe, *Lab.* 15,734
Mrs B. McCoy, *LD* 7,388
A. Watt, *Ref.* 1,939
W. Wyatt, *UK Ind.* 269
C. majority 7,754
(Boundary change: notional C.)

CAMBRIDGESHIRE SOUTH
*E.*69,850   *T.* 76.85%
A. Lansley, *C.* 22,572
J. Quinlan, *LD* 13,860
A. Gray, *Lab.* 13,485
R. Page, *Ref.* 3,300
D. Norman, *UK Ind.* 298
F. Chalmers, *NLP* 168
C. majority 8,712
(Boundary change: notional C.)

CAMBRIDGESHIRE SOUTH EAST
*E.*75,666   *T.* 75.08%
†J. Paice, *C.* 24,397
R. Collinson, *Lab.* 15,048
Ms S. Brinton, *LD* 14,246
J. Howlett, *Ref.* 2,838
K. Lam, *Fair* 167
P. While, *NLP* 111
C. majority 9,349
(Boundary change: notional C.)

CANNOCK CHASE
*E.*72,362   *T.* 72.37%
†Dr A. Wright, *Lab.* 28,705
J. Backhouse, *C.* 14,227
R. Kirby, *LD* 4,537
P. Froggatt, *Ref.* 1,663

W. Hurley, *New Lab.* 1,615
M. Conroy, *Soc. Lab.* 1,120
M. Hartshorn, *Loony* 499
Lab. majority 14,478
(Boundary change: notional Lab.)

CANTERBURY
*E.*74,548   *T.* 72.58%
†J. Brazier, *C.* 20,913
Ms C. Hall, *Lab.* 16,949
M. Vye, *LD* 12,854
J. Osborne, *Ref.* 2,460
G. Meaden, *Green* 588
J. Moore, *UK Ind.* 281
A. Pringle, *NLP* 64
C. majority 3,964
(Boundary change: notional C.)

CARLISLE
*E.*59,917   *T.* 72.78%
†E. Martlew, *Lab.* 25,031
R. Lawrence, *C.* 12,641
C. Mayho, *LD* 4,576
A. Fraser, *Ref.* 1,233
W. Stevens, *NLP* 126
Lab. majority 12,390
(Boundary change: notional Lab.)

CARSHALTON AND
WALLINGTON
*E.*66,038   *T.* 73.33%
T. Brake, *LD* 18,490
*N. Forman, *C.* 16,223
A. Theobald, *Lab.* 11,565
J. Storey, *Ref.* 1,289
P. Hickson, *Green* 377
G. Ritchie, *BNP* 261
L. Povey, *UK Ind.* 218
LD majority 2,267
(April 1992, C. maj. 9,943)

CASTLE POINT
*E.*67,146   *T.* 72.34%
Ms C. Butler, *Lab.* 20,605
*Dr R. Spink, *C.* 19,489
D. Baker, *LD* 4,477
H. Maulkin, *Ref.* 2,700
Miss L. Kendall, *Consult.* 1,301
Lab. majority 1,116
(April 1992, C. maj. 16,830)

CHARNWOOD
*E.*72,692   *T.* 77.28%
†Rt. Hon. S. Dorrell, *C.* 26,110
D. Knaggs, *Lab.* 20,210
R. Wilson, *LD* 7,224
H. Meechan, *Ref.* 2,104
M. Palmer, *BNP* 525
C. majority 5,900
(Boundary change: notional C.)

CHATHAM AND AYLESFORD
*E.*69,172   *T.* 71.07%
J. Shaw, *Lab.* 21,191
R. Knox-Johnston, *C.* 18,401
R. Murray, *LD* 7,389
K. Riddle, *Ref.* 1,538
A. Harding, *UK Ind.* 493
T. Martel, *NLP* 149
Lab. majority 2,790
(Boundary change: notional C.)

CHEADLE
E.67,627　T.77.58%
†S. Day, C. 22,944
Mrs P. Calton, LD 19,755
P. Diggett, Lab. 8,253
P. Brook, Ref. 1,511
C. majority 3,189
(Boundary change: notional C.)

CHELMSFORD WEST
E.76,086　T.76.99%
†S. Burns, C. 23,781
M. Bracken, LD 17,090
Dr R. Chad, Lab. 15,436
T. Smith, Ref. 1,536
G. Rumens, Green 411
M. Levin, UK Ind. 323
C. majority 6,691
(Boundary change: notional C.)

CHELTENHAM
E.67,950　T.74.03%
†N. Jones, LD 24,877
J. Todman, C. 18,232
B. Leach, Lab. 5,100
Mrs A. Powell, Ref. 1,065
K. Hanks, Loony 375
G. Cook, UK Ind. 302
Ms A. Harriss, ProLife 245
Ms S. Brighouse, NLP 107
LD majority 6,645
(Boundary change: notional LD)

CHESHAM AND AMERSHAM
E.69,244　T.75.38%
†Mrs C. Gillan, C. 26,298
M. Brand, LD 12,439
P. Farrelly, Lab. 10,240
P. Andrews, Ref. 2,528
C. Shilson, UK Ind. 618
H. Godfrey, NLP 74
C. majority 13,859
(Boundary change: notional C.)

CHESTER, CITY OF
E.71,730　T.78.43%
Ms C. Russell, Lab. 29,806
†G. Brandreth, C. 19,253
D. Simpson, LD 5,353
R. Mullen, Ref. 1,487
I. Sanderson, Loony 204
J. Gerrard, WCCC 154
Lab. majority 10,553
(Boundary change: notional C.)

CHESTERFIELD
E.72,472　T.70.91%
*Rt. Hon. A. Benn, Lab. 26,105
A. Rogers, LD 20,330
M. Potter, C. 4,752
N. Scarth, Ind. OAP 202
Lab. majority 5,775
(April 1992, Lab. maj. 6,414)

CHICHESTER
E.74,489　T.74.88%
A. Tyrie, C. 25,895
Prof. P. Gardiner, LD 16,161
C. Smith, Lab. 9,605
D. Denny, Ref. 3,318
J. Rix, UK Ind. 800
C. majority 9,734
(Boundary change: notional C.)

CHINGFORD AND WOODFORD
GREEN
E.62,904　T.70.66%
†I. Duncan Smith, C. 21,109
T. Hutchinson, Lab. 15,395
G. Seeff, LD 6,885
A. Gould, BNP 1,059
C. majority 5,714
(Boundary change: notional C.)

CHIPPING BARNET
E.69,049　T.71.78%
†Sir S. Chapman, C. 21,317
G. Cooke, Lab. 20,282
S. Hooker, LD 6,121
V. Ribekow, Ref. 1,190
B. Miskin, Loony 253
B. Scallan, ProLife 243
Ms D. Dirksen, NLP 159
C. majority 1,035
(Boundary change: notional C.)

CHORLEY
E.74,387　T.77.58%
L. Hoyle, Lab. 30,607
†D. Dover, C. 20,737
S. Jones, LD 4,900
A. Heaton, Ref. 1,319
P. Leadbetter, NLP 143
Lab. majority 9,870
(Boundary change: notional C.)

CHRISTCHURCH
E.71,488　T.78.61%
C. Chope, C. 26,095
†Mrs D. Maddock, LD 23,930
C. Mannan, Lab. 3,884
R. Spencer, Ref. 1,684
R. Dickinson, UK Ind. 606
C. majority 2,165
(Boundary change: notional C.)

CITIES OF LONDON AND
WESTMINSTER
E.69,047　T.58.16%
†Rt. Hon. P. Brooke, C. 18,981
Ms K. Green, Lab. 14,100
M. Dumigan, LD 4,933
Sir A. Walters, Ref. 1,161
Ms P. Wharton, Barts 266
C. Merton, UK Ind. 215
R. Johnson, NLP 176
N. Walsh, Loony 138
G. Webster, Hemp 112
J. Sadowitz, Dream 73
C. majority 4,881
(Boundary change: notional C.)

CLEETHORPES
E.68,763　T.73.40%
Ms S. McIsaac, Lab. 26,058
†M. Brown, C. 16,882
K. Melton, LD 5,746
J. Berry, Ref. 1,787
Lab. majority 9,176
(Boundary change: notional C.)

COLCHESTER
E.74,743　T.69.58%
R. Russell, LD 17,886
S. Shakespeare, C. 16,305
R. Green, Lab. 15,891
J. Hazell, Ref. 1,776

Ms L. Basker, NLP 148
LD majority 1,581
(Boundary change: notional C.)

COLNE VALLEY
E.73,338　T.76.92%
Ms K. Mountford, Lab. 23,285
*G. Riddick, C. 18,445
N. Priestley, LD 12,755
A. Brooke, Soc. Lab. 759
A. Cooper, Green 493
J. Nunn, UK Ind. 478
Ms M. Staniforth, Loony 196
Lab. majority 4,840
(April 1992, C. maj. 7,225)

CONGLETON
E.68,873　T.77.56%
†Mrs A. Winterton, C. 22,012
Mrs J. Walmsley, LD 15,882
Ms H. Scholey, Lab. 14,714
J. Lockett, UK Ind. 811
C. majority 6,130
(Boundary change: notional C.)

COPELAND
E.54,263　T.76.19%
*Rt. Hon. Dr J. Cunningham,
　Lab. 24,025
A. Cumpsty, C. 12,081
R. Putnam, LD 3,814
C. Johnston, Ref. 1,036
G. Hanratty, ProLife 389
Lab. majority 11,944
(April 1992, Lab. maj. 2,439)

CORBY
E.69,252　T.77.91%
P. Hope, Lab. Co-op. 29,888
*W. Powell, C. 18,028
I. Hankinson, LD 4,045
S. Riley-Smith, Ref. 1,356
I. Gillman, UK Ind. 507
Ms J. Bence, NLP 133
Lab. Co-op. majority 11,860
(April 1992, C. maj. 342)

CORNWALL NORTH
E.80,076　T.73.16%
*P. Tyler, LD 31,186
N. Linacre, C. 17,253
Ms A. Lindo, Lab. 5,523
Ms F. Odam, Ref. 3,636
J. Bolitho, MK 645
R. Winfield, Lib. 186
N. Cresswell, NLP 152
LD majority 13,933
(April 1992, LD maj. 1,921)

CORNWALL SOUTH EAST
E.75,825　T.75.74%
C. Breed, LD 27,044
W. Lightfoot, C. 20,564
Mrs D. Kirk, Lab. 7,358
J. Wonnacott, UK Ind. 1,428
P. Dunbar, MK 573
W. Weights, Lib 268
Ms M. Hartley, NLP 197
LD majority 6,480
(April 1992, C. maj. 7,704)

COTSWOLD
E.67,333　T.75.92%
†G. Clifton-Brown, C. 23,698

D. Gayler, *LD* — 11,733
D. Elwell, *Lab.* — 11,608
R. Lowe, *Ref.* — 3,393
Ms V. Michael, *Green* — 560
H. Brighouse, *NLP* — 129
C. majority 11,965
(Boundary change: notional C.)

COVENTRY NORTH EAST
*E.*74,274   *T.*64.74%
†R. Ainsworth, *Lab.* — 31,856
M. Burnett, *C.* — 9,287
G. Sewards, *LD* — 3,866
N. Brown, *Lib.* — 1,181
R. Hurrell, *Ref.* — 1,125
H. Khamis, *Soc. Lab.* — 597
C. Sidwell, *Dream* — 173
Lab. majority 22,569
(Boundary change: notional Lab.)

COVENTRY NORTH WEST
*E.*76,439   *T.*71.07%
†G. Robinson, *Lab.* — 30,901
P. Bartlett, *C.* — 14,300
Dr N. Penlington, *LD* — 5,690
D. Butler, *Ref.* — 1,269
D. Spencer, *Soc. Lab.* — 940
R. Wheway, *Lib.* — 687
P. Mills, *ProLife* — 359
L. Francis, *Dream* — 176
Lab. majority 16,601
(Boundary change: notional Lab.)

COVENTRY SOUTH
*E.*71,826   *T.*69.79%
†J. Cunningham, *Lab.* — 25,511
P. Ivey, *C.* — 14,558
G. MacDonald, *LD* — 4,617
D. Nellist, *Soc.* — 3,262
P. Garratt, *Ref.* — 943
R. Jenking, *Lib.* — 725
J. Astbury, *BNP* — 328
Ms A.-M. Bradshaw, *Dream* — 180
Lab. majority 10,953
(Boundary change: notional C.)

CRAWLEY
*E.*69,040   *T.*73.03%
Mrs L. Moffatt, *Lab.* — 27,750
Miss J. Crabb, *C.* — 16,043
H. de Souza, *LD* — 4,141
R. Walters, *Ref.* — 1,931
E. Saunders, *UK Ind.* — 322
A. Kahn, *JP* — 230
Lab. majority 11,707
(Boundary change: notional C.)

CREWE AND NANTWICH
*E.*68,694   *T.*73.67%
†Mrs G. Dunwoody, *Lab.* — 29,460
M. Loveridge, *C.* — 13,662
D. Cannon, *LD* — 5,940
P. Astbury, *Ref.* — 1,543
Lab. majority 15,798
(Boundary change: notional Lab.)

CROSBY
*E.*57,190   *T.*77.18%
Ms C. Curtis-Tansley, *Lab.* — 22,549
†Sir M. Thornton, *C.* — 15,367
P. McVey, *LD* — 5,080
J. Gauld, *Ref.* — 813
J. Marks, *Lib.* — 233

W. Hite, *NLP* — 99
Lab. majority 7,182
(Boundary change: notional C.)

CROYDON CENTRAL
*E.*80,152   *T.*69.62%
G. Davies, *Lab.* — 25,432
†D. Congdon, *C.* — 21,535
G. Schlich, *LD* — 6,061
C. Cook, *Ref.* — 1,886
M.-S. Barnsley, *Green* — 595
J. Woollcott, *UK Ind.* — 290
Lab. majority 3,897
(Boundary change: notional C.)

CROYDON NORTH
*E.*77,063   *T.*68.21%
†M. Wicks, *Lab.* — 32,672
I. Martin, *C.* — 14,274
M. Morris, *LD* — 4,066
R. Billis, *Ref.* — 1,155
J. Feisenberger, *UK Ind.* — 396
Lab. majority 18,398
(Boundary change: notional C.)

CROYDON SOUTH
*E.*73,787   *T.*73.45%
†R. Ottaway, *C.* — 25,649
C. Burling, *Lab.* — 13,719
S. Gauge, *LD* — 11,441
A. Barber, *Ref.* — 2,631
P. Ferguson, *BNP* — 354
A. Harker, *UK Ind.* — 309
M. Samuel, *Choice* — 96
C. majority 11,930
(Boundary change: notional C.)

DAGENHAM
*E.*58,573   *T.*61.74%
†Mrs J. Church, *Lab.* — 23,759
J. Fairrie, *C.* — 6,705
T. Dobrashian, *LD* — 2,704
S. Kraft, *Ref.* — 1,411
W. Binding, *BNP* — 900
R. Dawson, *Ind.* — 349
M. Hipperson, *Nat. Dem.* — 183
Ms K. Goble, *ProLife* — 152
Lab. majority 17,054
(Boundary change: notional Lab.)

DARLINGTON
*E.*65,140   *T.*73.95%
*A. Milburn, *Lab.* — 29,658
P. Scrope, *C.* — 13,633
L. Boxell, *LD* — 3,483
M. Blakey, *Ref.* — 1,399
Lab. majority 16,025
(April 1992, Lab. maj. 2,798)

DARTFORD
*E.*69,726   *T.*74.57%
H. Stoate, *Lab.* — 25,278
†R. Dunn, *C.* — 20,950
Mrs D. Webb, *LD* — 4,827
P. McHale, *BNP* — 428
P. Homden, *FDP* — 287
J. Pollitt, *Ch. D.* — 228
Lab. majority 4,328
(Boundary change: notional C.)

DAVENTRY
*E.*80,151   *T.*77.04%
†T. Boswell, *C.* — 28,615

K. Ritchie, *Lab.* — 21,237
J. Gordon, *LD* — 9,233
Mrs B. Russocki, *Ref.* — 2,018
B. Mahoney, *UK Ind.* — 443
R. France, *NLP* — 204
C. majority 7,378
(Boundary change: notional C.)

DENTON AND REDDISH
*E.*68,866   *T.*66.92%
†A. Bennett, *Lab.* — 30,137
Ms B. Nutt, *C.* — 9,826
I. Donaldson, *LD* — 6,121
Lab. majority 20,311
(Boundary change: notional Lab.)

DERBY NORTH
*E.*76,116   *T.*73.76%
R. Laxton, *Lab.* — 29,844
*Rt. Hon. G. Knight, *C.* — 19,229
R. Charlesworth, *LD* — 5,059
P. Reynolds, *Ref.* — 1,816
J. Waters, *ProLife* — 195
Lab. majority 10,615
(April 1992, C. maj. 4,453)

DERBY SOUTH
*E.*76,386   *T.*67.84%
†Rt. Hon. Mrs M. Beckett, *Lab.* — 29,154
J. Arain, *C.* — 13,048
J. Beckett, *LD* — 7,438
J. Browne, *Ref.* — 1,862
R. Evans, *Nat. Dem.* — 317
Lab. majority 16,106
(Boundary change: notional Lab.)

DERBYSHIRE NORTH EAST
*E.*71,653   *T.*72.54%
*H. Barnes, *Lab.* — 31,425
S. Elliott, *C.* — 13,104
S. Hardy, *LD* — 7,450
Lab. majority 18,321
(April 1992, Lab. maj. 6,270)

DERBYSHIRE SOUTH
*E.*76,672   *T.*78.21%
M. Todd, *Lab.* — 32,709
†Mrs E. Currie, *C.* — 18,742
R. Renold, *LD* — 5,408
R. North, *Ref.* — 2,491
Dr I. Crompton, *UK Ind.* — 617
Lab. majority 13,967
(Boundary change: notional C.)

DERBYSHIRE WEST
*E.*72,716   *T.*78.23%
†P. McLoughlin, *C.* — 23,945
S. Clamp, *Lab.* — 19,060
C. Seeley, *LD* — 9,940
J. Gouriet, *Ref.* — 2,499
G. Meynell, *Ind. Green* — 593
H. Price, *UK Ind.* — 484
N. Delves, *Loony* — 281
M. Kyslun, *Ind. BB* — 81
C. majority 4,885
(Boundary change: notional C.)

DEVIZES
*E.*80,383   *T.*74.69%
†Rt. Hon. M. Ancram, *C.* — 25,710
A. Vickers, *LD* — 15,928
F. Jeffrey, *Lab.* — 14,551
J. Goldsmith, *Ref.* — 3,021

S. Oram, *UK Ind.* 622
S. Haysom, *NLP* 204
C. majority 9,782
(Boundary change: notional C.)

DEVON EAST
*E.*69,094   *T.*76.06%
†Rt. Hon. Sir P. Emery, *C.* 22,797
Miss R. Trethewey, *LD* 15,308
A. Siantonas, *Lab.* 9,292
W. Dixon, *Ref.* 3,200
G. Halliwell, *Lib.* 1,363
C. Giffard, *UK Ind.* 459
G. Needs, *Nat. Dem.* 131
C. majority 7,489
(Boundary change: notional C.)

DEVON NORTH
*E.*70,350   *T.*77.94%
†N. Harvey, *LD* 27,824
R. Ashworth, *C.* 21,643
Mrs E. Brenton, *Lab.* 5,367
LD majority 6,181
(Boundary change: notional LD)

DEVON SOUTH WEST
*E.*69,293   *T.*76.22%
†G. Streeter, *C.* 22,695
C. Mavin, *Lab.* 15,262
K. Baldry, *LD* 12,542
R. Sadler, *Ref.* 1,668
Mrs H. King, *UK Ind.* 491
J. Hyde, *NLP* 159
C. majority 7,433
(Boundary change: notional C.)

DEVON WEST AND TORRIDGE
*E.*75,919   *T.*77.91%
J. Burnett, *LD* 24,744
I. Liddell-Grainger, *C.* 22,787
D. Brenton, *Lab.* 7,319
R. Lea, *Ref.* 1,946
M. Jackson, *UK Ind.* 1,841
M. Pithouse, *Lib.* 508
LD majority 1,957
(Boundary change: notional C.)

DEWSBURY
*E.*61,523   *T.*70.01%
†Mrs A. Taylor, *Lab.* 21,286
Dr P. McCormick, *C.* 12,963
K. Hill, *LD* 4,422
Ms F. Taylor, *BNP* 2,232
Ms W. Goff, *Ref.* 1,019
D. Daniel, *Ind. Lab.* 770
I. McCourtie, *Green* 383
Lab. majority 8,323
(Boundary change: notional Lab.)

DONCASTER CENTRAL
*E.*67,965   *T.*63.92%
Ms R. Winterton, *Lab.* 26,961
D. Turtle, *C.* 9,105
S. Tarry, *LD* 4,091
M. Cliff, *Ref.* 1,273
M. Kenny, *Soc. Lab.* 854
J. Redden, *ProLife* 697
P. Davies, *UK Ind.* 462
Lab. majority 17,856
(April 1992, Lab. maj. 10,682)

DONCASTER NORTH
*E.*63,019   *T.*63.30%
†K. Hughes, *Lab.* 27,843

P. Kennerley, *C.* 5,906
M. Cook, *LD* 3,369
R. Thornton, *Ref.* 1,589
M. Swan, *AS Lab.* 1,181
Lab. majority 21,937
(Boundary change: notional Lab.)

DON VALLEY
*E.*65,643   *T.*66.35%
Ms C. Flint, *Lab.* 25,376
Mrs C. Gledhill, *C.* 10,717
P. Johnston, *LD* 4,238
P. Davis, *Ref.* 1,379
N. Ball, *Soc. Lab.* 1,024
S. Platt, *Green* 493
Ms C. Johnson, *ProLife* 330
Lab. majority 14,659
(Boundary change: notional Lab.)

DORSET MID AND POOLE NORTH
*E.*67,049   *T.*75.67%
C. Fraser, *C.* 20,632
A. Leaman, *LD* 19,951
D. Collis, *Lab.* 8,014
D. Nabarro, *Ref.* 2,136
C. majority 681
(Boundary change: notional C.)

DORSET NORTH
*E.*68,923   *T.*76.30%
R. Walter, *C.* 23,294
Mrs P. Yates, *LD* 20,548
J. Fitzmaurice, *Lab.* 5,380
Mrs M. Evans, *Ref.* 2,564
Revd D. Wheeler, *UK Ind.* 801
C. majority 2,746
(Boundary change: notional C.)

DORSET SOUTH
*E.*66,318   *T.*74.16%
†I. Bruce, *C.* 17,755
J. Knight, *Lab.* 17,678
M. Plummer, *LD* 9,936
P. McAndrew, *Ref.* 2,791
Capt. M. Shakesby, *UK Ind.* 861
G. Napper, *NLP* 161
C. majority 77
(Boundary change: notional C.)

DORSET WEST
*E.*70,369   *T.*76.10%
O. Letwin, *C.* 22,036
R. Legg, *LD* 20,196
R. Bygraves, *Lab.* 9,491
P. Jenkins, *UK Ind.* 1,590
M. Griffiths, *NLP* 239
C. majority 1,840
(Boundary change: notional C.)

DOVER
*E.*68,669   *T.*78.93%
G. Prosser, *Lab.* 29,535
†D. Shaw, *C.* 17,796
M. Corney, *LD* 4,302
Mrs S. Anderson, *Ref.* 2,124
C. Hyde, *UK Ind.* 443
Lab. majority 11,739
(Boundary change: notional C.)

DUDLEY NORTH
*E.*68,835   *T.*69.45%
R. Cranston, *Lab.* 24,471
C. MacNamara, *C.* 15,014

G. Lewis, *LD* 3,939
M. Atherton, *Soc. Lab.* 2,155
S. Bavester, *Ref.* 1,201
G. Cartwright, *NF* 559
S. Darby, *Nat. Dem.* 469
Lab. majority 9,457
(Boundary change: notional Lab.)

DUDLEY SOUTH
*E.*66,731   *T.*71.78%
†I. Pearson, *Lab.* 27,124
M. Simpson, *C.* 14,097
R. Burt, *LD* 5,214
C. Birch, *Ref.* 1,467
Lab. majority 13,027
(Boundary change: notional Lab.)

DULWICH AND WEST NORWOOD
*E.*69,655   *T.*65.49%
†Ms T. Jowell, *Lab.* 27,807
R. Gough, *C.* 11,038
Mrs S. Kramer, *LD* 4,916
B. Coles, *Ref.* 897
Dr A. Goldie, *Lib.* 587
D. Goodman, *Dream* 173
E. Pike, *UK Ind.* 159
Capt. Rizz, *Rizz Party* 38
Lab. majority 16,769
(Boundary change: notional Lab.)

DURHAM NORTH
*E.*67,891   *T.*69.48%
†G. Radice, *Lab.* 33,142
M. Hardy, *C.* 6,843
B. Moore, *LD* 5,225
I. Parkin, *Ref.* 1,958
Lab. majority 26,299
(Boundary change: notional Lab.)

DURHAM NORTH WEST
*E.*67,156   *T.*68.97%
†Miss H. Armstrong, *Lab.* 31,855
Mrs L. St J. Howe, *C.* 7,101
A. Gillings, *LD* 4,991
R. Atkinson, *Ref.* 2,372
Lab. majority 24,754
(Boundary change: notional Lab.)

DURHAM, CITY OF
*E.*69,340   *T.*70.86%
*G. Steinberg, *Lab.* 31,102
R. Chalk, *C.* 8,598
Dr N. Martin, *LD* 7,499
Ms M. Robson, *Ref.* 1,723
P. Kember, *NLP* 213
Lab. majority 22,504
(April 1992, Lab. maj. 15,058)

EALING ACTON AND SHEPHERD'S BUSH
*E.*72,078   *T.*66.68%
†C. Soley, *Lab.* 28,052
Mrs B. Yerolemou, *C.* 12,405
A. Mitchell, *LD* 5,163
C. Winn, *Ref.* 637
J. Gilbert, *Soc. Lab.* 635
J. Gomm, *UK Ind.* 385
P. Danon, *ProLife* 265
C. Beasley, *Glow* 209
W. Edwards, *Ch. P.* 163
K. Turner, *NLP* 150
Lab. majority 15,647
(Boundary change: notional Lab.)

EALING NORTH
E.78,144   T.71.31%
S. Pound, *Lab.*	29,904
†H. Greenway, *C.*	20,744
A. Gupta, *LD*	3,887
G. Slysz, *UK Ind.*	689
Ms A. Siebe, *Green*	502

Lab. majority 9,160
(Boundary change: notional C.)

EALING SOUTHALL
E.81,704   T.66.88%
†P. Khabra, *Lab.*	32,791
J. Penrose, *C.*	11,368
Ms N. Thomson, *LD*	5,687
H. Brar, *Soc. Lab.*	2,107
N. Goodwin, *Green*	934
B. Cherry, *Ref.*	854
Ms K. Klepacka, *ProLife*	473
Dr R. Mead, *UK Ind.*	428

Lab. majority 21,423
(Boundary change: notional Lab.)

EASINGTON
E.62,518   T.67.01%
*J. Cummings, *Lab.*	33,600
J. Hollands, *C.*	3,588
J. Heppell, *LD*	3,025
R. Pulfrey, *Ref.*	1,179
S. Colborn, *SPGB*	503

Lab. majority 30,012
(April 1992, Lab. maj. 26,390)

EASTBOURNE
E.72,347   T.72.80%
†N. Waterson, *C.*	22,183
C. Berry, *LD*	20,189
D. Lines, *Lab.*	6,576
T. Lowe, *Ref.*	2,724
Mrs T. Williamson, *Lib.*	741
J. Dawkins, *UK Ind.*	254

C. majority 1,994
(Boundary change: notional C.)

EAST HAM
E.65,591   T.60.81%
†S. Timms, *Lab.*	25,779
Miss A. Bray, *C.*	6,421
I. Khan, *Soc. Lab.*	2,697
M. Sole, *LD*	2,599
C. Smith, *BNP*	1,258
Mrs J. McCann, *Ref.*	845
G. Hardy, *Nat. Dem.*	290

Lab. majority 19,358
(Boundary change: notional Lab.)

EASTLEIGH
E.72,155   T.76.91%
†D. Chidgey, *LD*	19,453
S. Reid, *C.*	18,699
A. Lloyd, *Lab.*	14,883
V. Eldridge, *Ref.*	2,013
P. Robinson, *UK Ind.*	446

LD majority 754
(Boundary change: notional C.)

ECCLES
E.69,645   T.65.60%
I. Stewart, *Lab.*	30,468
G. Barker, *C.*	8,552
R. Boyd, *LD*	4,905
J. De Roeck, *Ref.*	1,765

Lab. majority 21,916
(Boundary change: notional Lab.)

EDDISBURY
E.65,256   T.75.78%
†Rt. Hon. A. Goodlad, *C.*	21,027
Ms M. Hanson, *Lab.*	19,842
D. Reaper, *LD*	6,540
Ms N. Napier, *Ref.*	2,041

C. majority 1,185
(Boundary change: notional C.)
See also page 233

EDMONTON
E.63,718   T.70.37%
A. Love, *Lab. Co-op.*	27,029
*Dr I. Twinn, *C.*	13,557
A. Wiseman, *LD*	2,847
J. Wright, *Ref.*	708
B. Cowd, *BNP*	437
Mrs P. Weald, *UK Ind.*	260

Lab. Co-op. majority 13,472
(April 1992, C. maj. 593)

ELLESMERE PORT AND NESTON
E.67,573   T.77.79%
†A. Miller, *Lab.*	31,310
Mrs L. Turnbull, *C.*	15,274
Ms J. Pemberton, *LD*	4,673
C. Rodden, *Ref.*	1,305

Lab. majority 16,036
(Boundary change: notional Lab.)

ELMET
E.70,423   T.76.81%
C. Burgon, *Lab.*	28,348
*S. Batiste, *C.*	19,569
B. Jennings, *LD*	4,691
C. Zawadski, *Ref.*	1,487

Lab. majority 8,779
(April 1992, C. maj. 3,261)

ELTHAM
E.57,358   T.75.71%
C. Efford, *Lab.*	23,710
C. Blackwood, *C.*	13,528
Ms A. Taylor, *LD*	3,701
M. Clark, *Ref.*	1,414
H. Middleton, *Lib.*	584
W. Hitches, *BNP*	491

Lab. majority 10,182
(Boundary change: notional C.)

ENFIELD NORTH
E.67,680   T.70.43%
Ms J. Ryan, *Lab.*	24,148
M. Field, *C.*	17,326
M. Hopkins, *LD*	4,264
R. Ellingham, *Ref.*	857
Ms J. Griffin, *BNP*	590
Mrs J. O'Ware, *UK Ind.*	484

Lab. majority 6,822
(April 1992, C. maj. 9,430)

ENFIELD SOUTHGATE
E.65,796   T.70.72%
S. Twigg, *Lab.*	20,570
†Rt. Hon. M. Portillo, *C.*	19,137
J. Browne, *LD*	4,966
N. Luard, *Ref.*	1,342
A. Storkey, *Ch. D.*	289
A. Malakouna, *Mal*	229

Lab. majority 1,433
(Boundary change: notional C.)

EPPING FOREST
E.72,795   T.72.82%
Mrs E. Laing, *C.*	24,117
S. Murray, *Lab.*	18,865
S. Robinson, *LD*	7,074
J. Berry, *Ref.*	2,208
P. Henderson, *BNP*	743

C. majority 5,252
(Boundary change: notional C.)

EPSOM AND EWELL
E.73,222   T.74.00%
†Rt. Hon. Sir A. Hamilton, *C.*	24,717
P. Woodford, *Lab.*	13,192
J. Vincent, *LD*	12,380
C. Macdonald, *Ref.*	2,355
H. Green, *UK Ind.*	544
H. Charlton, *Green*	527
Ms K. Weeks, *ProLife*	466

C. majority 11,525
(Boundary change: notional C.)

EREWASH
E.77,402   T.77.95%
Ms E. Blackman, *Lab.*	31,196
†Mrs A. Knight, *C.*	22,061
Dr M. Garnett, *LD*	5,181
S. Stagg, *Ref.*	1,404
M. Simmons, *Soc. Lab.*	496

Lab. majority 9,135
(Boundary change: notional C.)

ERITH AND THAMESMEAD
E.62,887   T.66.13%
†J. Austin-Walker, *Lab.*	25,812
N. Zahawi, *C.*	8,388
A. Grigg, *LD*	5,001
J. Flunder, *Ref.*	1,394
V. Dooley, *BNP*	718
M. Jackson, *UK Ind.*	274

Lab. majority 17,424
(Boundary change: notional Lab.)

ESHER AND WALTON
E.72,382   T.74.14%
†I. Taylor, *C.*	26,747
Ms J. Reay, *Lab.*	12,219
G. Miles, *LD*	10,937
A. Cruickshank, *Ref.*	2,904
B. Collignon, *UK Ind.*	558
Ms S. Kay, *Dream*	302

C. majority 14,528
(Boundary change: notional C.)

ESSEX NORTH
E.68,008   T.75.30%
†B. Jenkin, *C.*	22,480
T. Young, *Lab.*	17,004
A. Phillips, *LD*	10,028
R. Lord, *UK Ind.*	1,202
Ms S. Ransome, *Green*	495

C. majority 5,476
(Boundary change: notional C.)

EXETER
E.79,154   T.78.16%
B. Bradshaw, *Lab.*	29,398
Dr A. Rogers, *C.*	17,693
D. Brewer, *LD*	11,148
D. Morrish, *Lib.*	2,062
P. Edwards, *Green*	643
Mrs C. Haynes, *UK Ind.*	638
J. Meakin, *UKPP*	282

Lab. majority 11,705
(Boundary change: notional C.)

FALMOUTH AND CAMBORNE
*E.*71,383   *T.*75.13%
Ms C. Atherton, *Lab.* | 18,151
*S. Coe, *C.* | 15,463
Mrs T. Jones, *LD* | 13,512
P. de Savary, *Ref.* | 3,534
J. Geach, *Ind. Lab.* | 1,691
P. Holmes, *Lib.* | 527
R. Smith, *UK Ind.* | 355
Ms R. Lewarne, *MK* | 238
G. Glitter, *Loony* | 161
Lab. majority 2,688
(April 1992, C. maj. 3,267)

FAREHAM
*E.*68,787   *T.*75.85%
†Rt. Hon. Sir P. Lloyd, *C.* | 24,436
M. Pryor, *Lab.* | 14,078
Mrs G. Hill, *LD* | 10,234
D. Markham, *Ref.* | 2,914
W. O'Brien, *Ind. No* | 515
C. majority 10,358
(Boundary change: notional C.)

FAVERSHAM AND KENT MID
*E.*67,490   *T.*73.50%
†A. Rowe, *C.* | 22,016
A. Stewart, *Lab.* | 17,843
B. Parmenter, *LD* | 6,138
R. Birley, *Ref.* | 2,073
N. Davidson, *Loony* | 511
M. Cunningham, *UK Ind.* | 431
D. Currer, *Green* | 380
Ms C. Morgan, *GRLNSP* | 115
N. Pollard, *NLP* | 99
C. majority 4,173
(Boundary change: notional C.)

FELTHAM AND HESTON
*E.*71,093   *T.*65.58%
†A. Keen, *Lab. Co-op.* | 27,836
P. Ground, *C.* | 12,563
C. Penning, *LD* | 4,264
R. Stubbs, *Ref.* | 1,099
R. Church, *BNP* | 682
D. Fawcett, *NLP* | 177
Lab. Co-op. majority 15,273
(Boundary change: notional Lab. Co-op.)

FINCHLEY AND GOLDERS GREEN
*E.*72,225   *T.*69.65%
R. Vis, *Lab.* | 23,180
†J. Marshall, *C.* | 19,991
J. Davies, *LD* | 5,670
G. Shaw, *Ref.* | 684
A. Gunstock, *Green* | 576
D. Barraclough, *UK Ind.* | 205
Lab. majority 3,189
(Boundary change: notional C.)

FOLKESTONE AND HYTHE
*E.*71,153   *T.*73.15%
†Rt. Hon. M. Howard, *C.* | 20,313
D. Laws, *LD* | 13,981
P. Doherty, *Lab.* | 12,939
J. Aspinall, *Ref.* | 4,188
J. Baker, *UK Ind.* | 378
E. Segal, *Soc.* | 182
R. Saint, *CFSS* | 69

C. majority 6,332
(Boundary change: notional C.)

FOREST OF DEAN
*E.*63,465   *T.*79.07%
Ms D. Organ, *Lab.* | 24,203
†P. Marland, *C.* | 17,860
Dr A. Lynch, *LD* | 6,165
J. Hopkins, *Ref.* | 1,624
G. Morgan, *Ind. Dean* | 218
C. Palmer, *21st Cent.* | 80
S. Porter, *Ind. F.* | 34
Lab. majority 6,343
(Boundary change: notional Lab.)

FYLDE
*E.*71,385   *T.*72.94%
†Rt. Hon. M. Jack, *C.* | 25,443
J. Garrett, *Lab.* | 16,480
W. Greene, *LD* | 7,609
D. Britton, *Ref.* | 2,372
T. Kerwin, *NLP* | 163
C. majority 8,963
(Boundary change: notional C.)

GAINSBOROUGH
*E.*64,106   *T.*74.56%
†E. Leigh, *C.* | 20,593
P. Taylor, *Lab.* | 13,767
N. Taylor, *LD* | 13,436
C. majority 6,826
(Boundary change: notional C.)

GATESHEAD EAST AND WASHINGTON WEST
*E.*64,114   *T.*67.19%
†Miss J. Quin, *Lab.* | 31,047
Miss J. Burns, *C.* | 6,097
A. Ord, *LD* | 4,622
M. Daley, *Ref.* | 1,315
Lab. majority 24,950
(Boundary change: notional Lab.)

GEDLING
*E.*68,820   *T.*75.80%
V. Coaker, *Lab.* | 24,390
*A. Mitchell, *C.* | 20,588
R. Poynter, *LD* | 5,180
J. Connor, *Ref.* | 2,006
Lab. majority 3,802
(April 1992, C. maj. 10,637)

GILLINGHAM
*E.*70,389   *T.*72.00%
P. Clark, *Lab.* | 20,187
†J. Couchman, *C.* | 18,207
R. Sayer, *LD* | 9,649
G. Cann, *Ref.* | 1,492
C. MacKinlay, *UK Ind.* | 590
D. Robinson, *Loony* | 305
C. Jury, *BNP* | 195
Ms G. Duguay, *NLP* | 58
Lab. majority 1,980
(Boundary change: notional C.)

GLOUCESTER
*E.*78,682   *T.*73.61%
Ms T. Kingham, *Lab.* | 28,943
†D. French, *C.* | 20,684
P. Munisamy, *LD* | 6,069
A. Reid, *Ref.* | 1,482
A. Harris, *UK Ind.* | 455
Ms M. Hamilton, *NLP* | 281

Lab. majority 8,259
(Boundary change: notional C.)

GOSPORT
*E.*68,830   *T.*70.25%
*P. Viggers, *C.* | 21,085
I. Gray, *Lab.* | 14,827
S. Hogg, *LD* | 9,479
A. Blowers, *Ref.* | 2,538
P. Ettie, *Ind.* | 426
C. majority 6,258
(April 1992, C. maj. 16,318)

GRANTHAM AND STAMFORD
*E.*72,310   *T.*73.25%
†Q. Davies, *C.* | 22,672
P. Denning, *Lab.* | 19,980
J. Sellick, *LD* | 6,612
Ms M. Swain, *Ref.* | 2,721
M. Charlesworth, *UK Ind.* | 556
Ms R. Clark, *ProLife* | 314
I. Harper, *NLP* | 115
C. majority 2,692
(Boundary change: notional C.)

GRAVESHAM
*E.*69,234   *T.*76.92%
C. Pond, *Lab.* | 26,460
†J. Arnold, *C.* | 20,681
Dr M. Canet, *LD* | 4,128
Mrs P. Curtis, *Ref.* | 1,441
A. Leyshon, *Ind.* | 414
D. Palmer, *NLP* | 129
Lab. majority 5,779
(Boundary change: notional C.)

GREAT GRIMSBY
*E.*65,043   *T.*66.26%
*A. Mitchell, *Lab.* | 25,765
D. Godson, *C.* | 9,521
A. De Freitas, *LD* | 7,810
Lab. majority 16,244
(April 1992, Lab. maj. 7,504)

GREAT YARMOUTH
*E.*68,625   *T.*71.23%
A. Wright, *Lab.* | 26,084
*M. Carttiss, *C.* | 17,416
D. Wood, *LD* | 5,381
Lab. majority 8,668
(April 1992, C. maj. 5,309)

GREENWICH AND WOOLWICH
*E.*61,352   *T.*65.85%
†N. Raynsford, *Lab.* | 25,630
M. Mitchell, *C.* | 7,502
Mrs C. Luxton, *LD* | 5,049
D. Ellison, *Ref.* | 1,670
R. Mallone, *Fellowship* | 428
D. Martin-Eagle, *Constit.* | 124
Lab. majority 18,128
(Boundary change: notional Lab.)

GUILDFORD
*E.*75,541   *T.*75.40%
N. St Aubyn, *C.* | 24,230
Mrs M. Sharp, *LD* | 19,439
J. Burns, *Lab.* | 9,945
J. Gore, *Ref.* | 2,650
R. McWhirter, *UK Ind.* | 400
J. Morris, *Pacifist* | 294
C. majority 4,791
(Boundary change: notional C.)

HACKNEY NORTH AND STOKE
NEWINGTON
E.62,045 *T*.52.95%
*Ms D. Abbott, *Lab.* 21,110
M. Lavender, *C.* 5,483
D. Taylor, *LD* 3,806
Yen Chit Chong, *Green* 1,395
B. Maxwell, *Ref.* 544
D. Tolson, *None* 368
Miss L. Lovebucket, *Rain. Ref.* 146
Lab. majority 15,627
(April 1992, Lab. maj. 10,727)

HACKNEY SOUTH AND
SHOREDITCH
E.61,728 *T*.54.67%
†B. Sedgemore, *Lab.* 20,048
M. Pantling, *LD* 5,068
C. O'Leary, *C.* 4,494
T. Betts, *New Lab.* 2,436
R. Franklin, *Ref.* 613
G. Callow, *BNP* 531
M. Goldman, *Comm. P.* 298
Ms M. Goldberg, *NLP* 145
W. Rogers, *WRP* 113
Lab. majority 14,980
(Boundary change: notional Lab.)

HALESOWEN AND ROWLEY REGIS
E.66,245 *T*.73.61%
Mrs S. Heal, *Lab.* 26,366
J. Kennedy, *C.* 16,029
Ms E. Todd, *LD* 4,169
P. White, *Ref.* 1,244
Ms K. Meeds, *Nat. Dem.* 592
T. Weller, *Green* 361
Lab. majority 10,337
(Boundary change: notional C.)

HALIFAX
E.71,701 *T*.70.51%
*Mrs A. Mahon, *Lab.* 27,465
R. Light, *C.* 16,253
E. Waller, *LD* 6,059
Mrs C. Whitaker, *UK Ind.* 779
Lab. majority 11,212
(April 1992, Lab. maj. 478)

HALTEMPRICE AND HOWDEN
E.65,602 *T*.75.53%
†Rt. Hon. D. Davis, *C.* 21,809
Ms D. Wallis, *LD* 14,295
G. McManus, *Lab.* 11,701
T. Pearson, *Ref.* 1,370
G. Bloom, *UK Ind.* 301
B. Stevens, *NLP* 74
C. majority 7,514
(Boundary change: notional C.)

HALTON
E.64,987 *T*.68.38%
D. Twigg, *Lab.* 31,497
P. Balmer, *C.* 7,847
Ms J. Jones, *LD* 3,263
R. Atkins, *Ref.* 1,036
D. Proffitt, *Lib.* 600
J. Alley, *Rep. GB* 196
Lab. majority 23,650
(Boundary change: notional Lab.)

HAMMERSMITH AND FULHAM
E.78,637 *T*.68.70%
I. Coleman, *Lab.* 25,262

†M. Carrington, *C.* 21,420
Ms A. Sugden, *LD* 4,728
Mrs M. Bremner, *Ref.* 1,023
W. Johnson-Smith, *New Lab.* 695
Ms E. Streeter, *Green* 562
G. Roberts, *UK Ind.* 183
A. Phillips, *NLP* 79
A. Elston, *Care* 74
Lab. majority 3,842
(Boundary change: notional C.)

HAMPSHIRE EAST
E.76,604 *T*.75.88%
†M. Mates, *C.* 27,927
R. Booker, *LD* 16,337
R. Hoyle, *Lab.* 9,945
J. Hayter, *Ref.* 2,757
I. Foster, *Green* 649
S. Coles, *UK Ind.* 513
C. majority 11,590
(Boundary change: notional C.)

HAMPSHIRE NORTH EAST
E.69,111 *T*.73.95%
†J. Arbuthnot, *C.* 26,017
I. Mann, *LD* 11,619
P. Dare, *Lab.* 8,203
D. Rees, *Ref.* 2,420
K. Jessavala, *Ind.* 2,400
C. Berry, *UK Ind.* 452
C. majority 14,398
(Boundary change: notional C.)

HAMPSHIRE NORTH WEST
E.73,222 *T*.74.66%
†Rt. Hon. Sir G. Young, Bt., *C.*
  24,730
C. Fleming, *LD* 13,179
M. Mumford, *Lab.* 12,900
Mrs P. Callaghan, *Ref.* 1,533
T. Rolt, *UK Ind.* 1,383
W. Baxter, *Green* 486
H. Anscomb, *Bypass* 231
R. Dodd, *Ind.* 225
C. majority 11,551
(Boundary change: notional C.)

HAMPSTEAD AND HIGHGATE
E.64,889 *T*.67.86%
†Ms G. Jackson, *Lab.* 25,275
Miss E. Gibson, *C.* 11,991
Mrs B. Fox, *LD* 5,481
Ms M. Siddique, *Ref.* 667
J. Leslie, *NLP* 147
R. Carroll, *Dream* 141
Miss P. Prince, *UK Ind.* 123
R. J. Harris, *Hum.* 105
Capt. Rizz, *Rizz Party* 101
Lab. majority 13,284
(Boundary change: notional Lab.)

HARBOROUGH
E.70,424 *T*.75.27%
†E. Garnier, *C.* 22,170
M. Cox, *LD* 15,646
N. Holden, *Lab.* 13,332
N. Wright, *Ref.* 1,859
C. majority 6,524
(Boundary change: notional C.)

HARLOW
E.64,072 *T*.74.62%
W. Rammell, *Lab.* 25,861

†J. Hayes, *C.* 15,347
Ms L. Spenceley, *LD* 4,523
M. Wells, *Ref.* 1,422
G. Batten, *UK Ind.* 340
J. Bowles, *BNP* 319
Lab. majority 10,514
(Boundary change: notional C.)

HARROGATE AND
KNARESBOROUGH
E.65,155 *T*.73.14%
P. Willis, *LD* 24,558
†Rt. Hon. N. Lamont, *C.* 18,322
Ms B. Boyce, *Lab.* 4,159
J. Blackburn, *LC* 614
LD majority 6,236
(Boundary change: notional C.)

HARROW EAST
E.79,846 *T*.71.37%
A. McNulty, *Lab.* 29,927
†H. Dykes, *C.* 20,189
B. Sharma, *LD* 4,697
B. Casey, *Ref.* 1,537
A. Scholefield, *UK Ind.* 464
A. Planton, *NLP* 171
Lab. majority 9,738
(Boundary change: notional C.)

HARROW WEST
E.72,005 *T*.72.92%
G. Thomas, *Lab.* 21,811
*R. Hughes, *C.* 20,571
Mrs P. Nandhra, *LD* 8,127
H. Crossman, *Ref.* 1,997
Lab. majority 1,240
(Boundary change: notional C.)

HARTLEPOOL
E.67,712 *T*.65.65%
*P. Mandelson, *Lab.* 26,997
M. Horsley, *C.* 9,489
R. Clark, *LD* 6,248
Miss M. Henderson, *Ref.* 1,718
Lab. majority 17,508
(April 1992, Lab. maj. 8,782)

HARWICH
E.75,775 *T*.70.62%
I. Henderson, *Lab.* 20,740
†I. Sproat, *C.* 19,524
Mrs A. Elvin, *LD* 7,037
J. Titford, *Ref.* 4,923
R. Knight, *CRP* 1,290
Lab. majority 1,216
(Boundary change: notional C.)

HASTINGS AND RYE
E.70,388 *T*.69.71%
M. Foster, *Lab.* 16,867
*Mrs J. Lait, *C.* 14,307
M. Palmer, *LD* 13,717
C. McGovern, *Ref.* 2,511
Ms J. Amstad, *Lib.* 1,046
W. Andrews, *UK Ind.* 472
D. Howell, *Loony* 149
Lab. majority 2,560
(April 1992, C. maj. 6,634)

HAVANT
E.68,420 *T*.70.63%
†D. Willetts, *C.* 19,204
Ms L. Armstrong, *Lab.* 15,475

M. Kooner, *LD* 10,806
A. Green, *Ref.* 2,395
M. Atwal, *BIPF* 442
C. majority 3,729
(Boundary change: notional C.)

HAYES AND HARLINGTON
*E.*56,829   *T.*72.31%
J. McDonnell, *Lab.* 25,458
A. Retter, *C.* 11,167
A. Little, *LD* 3,049
F. Page, *Ref.* 778
J. Hutchins, *NF* 504
D. Farrow, *ANP* 135
Lab. majority 14,291
(Boundary change: notional C.)

HAZEL GROVE
*E.*63,694   *T.*77.46%
A. Stunell, *LD* 26,883
B. Murphy, *C.* 15,069
J. Lewis, *Lab.* 5,882
J. Stanyer, *Ref.* 1,055
G. Black, *UK Ind.* 268
D. Firkin-Flood, *Ind. Hum.* 183
LD majority 11,814
(April 1992, C. maj. 929)

HEMEL HEMPSTEAD
*E.*71,468   *T.*77.09%
A. McWalter, *Lab. Co-op.* 25,175
†R. Jones, *C.* 21,539
Mrs P. Lindsley, *LD* 6,789
P. Such, *Ref.* 1,327
Ms D. Harding, *NLP* 262
Lab. Co-op. majority 3,636
(Boundary change: notional C.)

HEMSWORTH
*E.*66,964   *T.*67.91%
†J. Trickett, *Lab.* 32,088
N. Hazell, *C.* 8,096
Ms J. Kirby, *LD* 4,033
D. Irvine, *Ref.* 1,260
Lab. majority 23,992
(Boundary change: notional Lab.)

HENDON
*E.*76,195   *T.*65.67%
A. Dismore, *Lab.* 24,683
†Sir J. Gorst, *C.* 18,528
W. Casey, *LD* 5,427
S. Rabbow, *Ref.* 978
B. Wright, *UK Ind.* 267
Ms S. Taylor, *WRP* 153
Lab. majority 6,155
(Boundary change: notional C.)

HENLEY
*E.*66,424   *T.*77.60%
†Rt. Hon. M. Heseltine, *C.* 23,908
T. Horton, *LD* 12,741
D. Enright, *Lab.* 11,700
S. Sainsbury, *Ref.* 2,299
Mrs S. Miles, *Green* 514
N. Barlow, *NLP* 221
T. Hibbert, *Whig Party* 160
C. majority 11,167
(Boundary change: notional C.)

HEREFORD
*E.*69,864   *T.*75.22%
P. Keetch, *LD* 25,198

†Sir C. Shepherd, *C.* 18,550
C. Chappell, *Lab.* 6,596
C. Easton, *Ref.* 2,209
LD majority 6,648
(Boundary change: notional C.)

HERTFORD AND STORTFORD
*E.*71,759   *T.*76.03%
†B. Wells, *C.* 24,027
S. Speller, *Lab.* 17,142
M. Wood, *LD* 9,679
H. Page Croft, *Ref.* 2,105
B. Smalley, *UK Ind.* 1,223
M. Franey, *ProLife* 259
D. Molloy, *Logic* 126
C. majority 6,885
(Boundary change: notional C.)

HERTFORDSHIRE NORTH EAST
*E.*67,161   *T.*77.42%
†O. Heald, *C.* 21,712
I. Gibbons, *Lab.* 18,624
S. Jarvis, *LD* 9,493
J. Grose, *Ref.* 2,166
C. majority 3,088
(Boundary change: notional C.)

HERTFORDSHIRE SOUTH WEST
*E.*71,671   *T.*77.31%
†R. Page, *C.* 25,462
M. Wilson, *Lab.* 15,441
Mrs A. Shaw, *LD* 12,381
T. Millward, *Ref.* 1,853
C. Adamson, *NLP* 274
C. majority 10,021
(Boundary change: notional C.)

HERTSMERE
*E.*68,011   *T.*74.03%
†J. Clappison, *C.* 22,305
Ms E. Kelly, *Lab.* 19,230
Mrs A. Gray, *LD* 6,466
J. Marlow, *Ref.* 1,703
R. Saunders, *UK Ind.* 453
N. Kahn, *NLP* 191
C. majority 3,075
(Boundary change: notional C.)

HEXHAM
*E.*58,914   *T.*77.52%
*P. Atkinson, *C.* 17,701
I. McMinn, *Lab.* 17,479
Dr P. Carr, *LD* 7,959
R. Waddell, *Ref.* 1,362
D. Lott, *UK Ind.* 1,170
C. majority 222
(April 1992, C. maj. 13,438)

HEYWOOD AND MIDDLETON
*E.*73,898   *T.*68.41%
J. Dobbin, *Lab. Co-op.* 29,179
S. Grigg, *C.* 11,637
D. Clayton, *LD* 7,908
Mrs C. West, *Ref.* 1,076
P. Burke, *Lib.* 750
Lab. Co-op. majority 17,542
(Boundary change: notional Lab. Co-op.)

HIGH PEAK
*E.*72,315   *T.*79.03%
T. Levitt, *Lab.* 29,052
†C. Hendry, *C.* 20,261

Mrs S. Barber, *LD* 6,420
C. Hanson-Orr, *Ref.* 1,420
Lab. majority 8,791
(Boundary change: notional C.)

HITCHIN AND HARPENDEN
*E.*67,219   *T.*77.99%
†Rt. Hon. P. Lilley, *C.* 24,038
Ms R. Sanderson, *Lab.* 17,367
C. White, *LD* 10,515
D. Cooke, *NLP* 290
J. Horton, *Soc.* 217
C. majority 6,671
(Boundary change: notional C.)

HOLBORN AND ST PANCRAS
*E.*63,037   *T.*60.28%
†F. Dobson, *Lab.* 24,707
J. Smith, *C.* 6,804
Ms J. McGuinness, *LD* 4,750
Mrs J. Carr, *Ref.* 790
T. Beddington, *NLP* 191
S. Smith, *JP* 173
Ms B. Conway, *WRP* 171
M. Rosenthal, *Dream* 157
P. Rice-Evans, *EUP* 140
B. Quintavalle, *ProLife* 114
Lab. majority 17,903
(Boundary change: notional Lab.)

HORNCHURCH
*E.*60,775   *T.*72.30%
J. Cryer, *Lab.* 22,066
*R. Squire, *C.* 16,386
R. Martins, *LD* 3,446
R. Khilkoff-Boulding, *Ref.* 1,595
Miss J. Trueman, *Third Way* 259
J. Sowerby, *ProLife* 189
Lab. majority 5,680
(April 1992, C. maj. 9,165)

HORNSEY AND WOOD GREEN
*E.*74,537   *T.*69.08%
*Mrs B. Roche, *Lab.* 31,792
Mrs H. Hart, *C.* 11,293
Ms L. Featherstone, *LD* 5,794
Ms H. Jago, *Green* 1,214
Ms R. Miller, *Ref.* 808
P. Sikorski, *Soc. Lab.* 586
Lab. majority 20,499
(April 1992, Lab. maj. 5,177)

HORSHAM
*E.*75,432   *T.*75.78%
Rt. Hon. F. Maude, *C.* 29,015
Mrs M. Millson, *LD* 14,153
Ms M. Walsh, *Lab.* 10,691
R. Grant, *Ref.* 2,281
H. Miller, *UK Ind.* 819
M. Corbould, *FEP* 206
C. majority 14,862
(Boundary change: notional C.)

HOUGHTON AND WASHINGTON EAST
*E.*67,343   *T.*62.10%
F. Kemp, *Lab.* 31,946
P. Booth, *C.* 5,391
K. Miller, *LD* 3,209
J. Joseph, *Ref.* 1,277
Lab. majority 26,555
(Boundary change: notional Lab.)

HOVE
E.69,016   T.69.72%
I. Caplin, *Lab.* | 21,458
R. Guy, *C.* | 17,499
T. Pearce, *LD* | 4,645
S. Field, *Ref.* | 1,931
J. Furness, *Ind. C.* | 1,735
P. Mulligan, *Green* | 644
J. Vause, *UK Ind.* | 209
Lab. majority 3,959
(April 1992, C. maj. 12,268)

HUDDERSFIELD
E.65,824   T.67.69%
*B. Sheerman, *Lab. Co-op.* | 25,171
W. Forrow, *C.* | 9,323
G. Beever, *LD* | 7,642
P. McNulty, *Ref.* | 1,480
J. Phillips, *Green* | 938
Lab. Co-op. majority 15,848
(April 1992, *Lab. majority* 7,258)

HULL EAST
E.68,733   T.58.90%
*Rt. Hon. J. Prescott, *Lab.* | 28,870
A. West, *C.* | 5,552
J. Wastling, *LD* | 3,965
G. Rogers, *Ref.* | 1,788
Ms M. Nolan, *ProLife* | 190
D. Whitley, *NLP* | 121
Lab. majority 23,318
(April 1992, Lab. maj. 18,719)

HULL NORTH
E.68,106   T.56.96%
*K. McNamara, *Lab.* | 25,542
D. Lee, *C.* | 5,837
D. Nolan, *LD* | 5,667
A. Scott, *Ref.* | 1,533
T. Brotheridge, *NLP* | 215
Lab. majority 19,705
(April 1992, Lab. maj. 15,384)

HULL WEST AND HESSLE
E.65,840   T.58.25%
A. Johnson, *Lab.* | 22,520
R. Tress, *LD* | 6,995
C. Moore, *C.* | 6,933
R. Bate, *Ref.* | 1,596
B. Franklin, *NLP* | 310
Lab. majority 15,525
(Boundary change: notional Lab.)

HUNTINGDON
E.76,094   T.74.86%
†Rt. Hon. J. Major, *C.* | 31,501
J. Reece, *Lab.* | 13,361
M. Owen, *LD* | 8,390
D. Bellamy, *Ref.* | 3,114
C. Coyne, *UK Ind.* | 331
Ms V. Hufford, *Ch. D.* | 177
D. Robertson, *Ind.* | 89
C. majority 18,140
(Boundary change: notional C.)

HYNDBURN
E.66,806   T.72.26%
†G. Pope, *Lab.* | 26,831
P. Britcliffe, *C.* | 15,383
L. Jones, *LD* | 4,141
P. Congdon, *Ref.* | 1,627
J. Brown, *IAC* | 290

Lab. majority 11,448
(Boundary change: notional Lab.)

ILFORD NORTH
E.68,218   T.71.60%
Ms L. Perham, *Lab.* | 23,135
†V. Bendall, *C.* | 19,911
A. Dean, *LD* | 5,049
P. Wilson, *BNP* | 750
Lab. majority 3,224
(Boundary change: notional C.)

ILFORD SOUTH
E.72,104   T.69.37%
†M. Gapes, *Lab. Co-op.* | 29,273
Sir N. Thorne, *C.* | 15,073
Ms A. Khan, *LD* | 3,152
D. Hodges, *Ref.* | 1,073
B. Ramsey, *Soc. Lab.* | 868
A. Owens, *BNP* | 580
Lab. Co-op. majority 14,200
(Boundary change: notional C.)

IPSWICH
E.66,947   T.72.24%
†J. Cann, *Lab.* | 25,484
S. Castle, *C.* | 15,045
N. Roberts, *LD* | 5,881
T. Agnew, *Ref.* | 1,637
W. Vinyard, *UK Ind.* | 208
E. Kaplan, *NLP* | 107
Lab. majority 10,439
(Boundary change: notional Lab.)

ISLE OF WIGHT
E.101,680   T.71.95%
Dr P. Brand, *LD* | 31,274
A. Turner, *C.* | 24,868
Ms D. Gardiner, *Lab.* | 9,646
T. Bristow, *Ref.* | 4,734
M. Turner, *UK Ind.* | 1,072
H. Rees, *Ind. Is.* | 848
P. Scivier, *Green* | 544
C. Daly, *NLP* | 87
J. Eveleigh, *Rain. Is.* | 86
LD majority 6,406
(April 1992, C. maj. 1,827)

ISLINGTON NORTH
E.57,385   T.62.49%
*J. Corbyn, *Lab.* | 24,834
J. Kempton, *LD* | 4,879
S. Fawthrop, *C.* | 4,631
C. Ashby, *Green* | 1,516
Lab. majority 19,955
(April 1992, Lab. maj. 12,784)

ISLINGTON SOUTH AND FINSBURY
E.55,468   T.63.67%
†C. Smith, *Lab.* | 22,079
Ms S. Ludford, *LD* | 7,516
D. Berens, *C.* | 4,587
Miss J. Bryett, *Ref.* | 741
A. Laws, *ACA* | 171
M. Creese, *NLP* | 121
E. Basarik, *Ind.* | 101
Lab. majority 14,563
(Boundary change: notional Lab.)

JARROW
E.63,828   T.68.84%
S. Hepburn, *Lab.* | 28,497

M. Allatt, *C.* | 6,564
T. Stone, *LD* | 4,865
A. LeBlond, *Ind. Lab.* | 2,538
P. Mailer, *Ref.* | 1,034
J. Bissett, *SPGB* | 444
Lab. majority 21,933
(Boundary change: notional Lab.)

KEIGHLEY
E.67,231   T.76.57%
Mrs A. Cryer, *Lab.* | 26,039
*G. Waller, *C.* | 18,907
M. Doyle, *LD* | 5,064
C. Carpenter, *Ref.* | 1,470
Lab. majority 7,132
(April 1992, C. maj. 3,596)

KENSINGTON AND CHELSEA
E.67,786   T.54.71%
Rt. Hon. A. Clark, *C.* | 19,887
R. Atkinson, *Lab.* | 10,368
R. Woodthorpe Browne, *LD* | 5,668
Ms A. Ellis-Jones, *UK Ind.* | 540
E. Bear, *Teddy* | 218
G. Oliver, *UKPP* | 176
Ms S. Hamza, *NLP* | 122
P. Sullivan, *Dream* | 65
P. Parliament, *Heart* | 44
C. majority 9,519
(Boundary change: notional C.)
See also Stop-press

KETTERING
E.75,153   T.75.79%
P. Sawford, *Lab.* | 24,650
†Rt. Hon. R. Freeman, *C.* | 24,461
R. Aron, *LD* | 6,098
A. Smith, *Ref.* | 1,551
Mrs R. le Carpentier, *NLP* | 197
Lab. majority 189
(Boundary change: notional C.)

KINGSTON AND SURBITON
E.73,879   T.75.35%
E. Davey, *LD* | 20,411
†R. Tracey, *C.* | 20,355
Ms S. Griffin, *Lab.* | 12,811
Mrs G. Tchiprout, *Ref.* | 1,470
Ms P. Burns, *UK Ind.* | 418
C. Port, *Dream* | 100
M. Leighton, *NLP* | 100
LD majority 56
(Boundary change: notional C.)

KINGSWOOD
E.77,026   T.77.75%
†Dr R. Berry, *Lab.* | 32,181
J. Howard, *C.* | 17,928
Mrs J. Pinkerton, *LD* | 7,672
Ms A. Reather, *Ref.* | 1,463
P. Hart, *BNP* | 290
A. Harding, *NLP* | 238
A. Nicolson, *Scrapit* | 115
Lab. majority 14,253
(Boundary change: notional C.)

KNOWSLEY NORTH AND SEFTON EAST
E.70,918   T.70.09%
†G. Howarth, *Lab.* | 34,747
C. Doran, *C.* | 8,600
D. Bamber, *LD* | 5,499
C. Jones, *Soc. Lab.* | 857

Lab. majority 26,147
(Boundary change: notional Lab.)

KNOWSLEY SOUTH
*E.*70,532   *T.*67.47%
†E. O'Hara, *Lab.*   36,695
G. Robertson, *C.*   5,987
C. Mainey, *LD*   3,954
A. Wright, *Ref.*   954
Lab. majority 30,708
(Boundary change: notional Lab.)

LANCASHIRE WEST
*E.*73,175   *T.*74.79%
†C. Pickthall, *Lab.*   33,022
C. Varley, *C.*   15,903
A. Wood, *LD*   3,938
M. Carter, *Ref.*   1,025
J. Collins, *NLP*   449
D. Hill, *Home Rule*   392
Lab. majority 17,119
(Boundary change: notional Lab.)

LANCASTER AND WYRE
*E.*78,168   *T.*75.30%
H. Dawson, *Lab.*   25,173
†K. Mans, *C.*   23,878
J. Humberstone, *LD*   6,802
Mrs V. Ivell, *Ref.*   1,516
J. Barry, *Green*   795
Dr J. Whittaker, *UK Ind.*   698
Lab. majority 1,295
(Boundary change: notional C.)

LEEDS CENTRAL
*E.*67,664   *T.*54.70%
†D. Fatchett, *Lab.*   25,766
E. Wild, *C.*   5,077
D. Freeman, *LD*   4,164
P. Myers, *Ref.*   1,042
D. Rix, *Soc. Lab.*   656
C. Hill, *Soc.*   304
Lab. majority 20,689
(Boundary change: notional Lab.)
See also page 233

LEEDS EAST
*E.*56,963   *T.*62.83%
*G. Mudie, *Lab.*   24,151
J. Emsley, *C.*   6,685
Mrs M. Kirk, *LD*   3,689
L. Parish, *Ref.*   1,267
Lab. majority 17,466
(April 1992, Lab. maj. 12,697)

LEEDS NORTH EAST
*E.*63,185   *T.*72.03%
F. Hamilton, *Lab.*   22,368
*T. Kirkhope, *C.*   15,409
Dr W. Winlow, *LD*   6,318
I. Rose, *Ref.*   946
Ms J. Egan, *Soc. Lab.*   468
Lab. majority 6,959
(April 1992, C. maj. 4,244)

LEEDS NORTH WEST
*E.*69,972   *T.*70.57%
H. Best, *Lab.*   19,694
*Dr K. Hampson, *C.*   15,850
Mrs B. Pearce, *LD*   11,689
S. Emmett, *Ref.*   1,325
R. Lamb, *Soc. Lab.*   335
R. Toone, *ProLife*   251

D. Duffy, *Ronnie*   232
Lab. majority 3,844
(April 1992, C. maj. 7,671)

LEEDS WEST
*E.*63,965   *T.*62.88%
*J. Battle, *Lab.*   26,819
J. Whelan, *C.*   7,048
N. Amor, *LD*   3,622
W. Finley, *Ref.*   1,210
D. Blackburn, *Green*   896
N. Nowosielski, *Lib.*   625
Lab. majority 19,771
(April 1992, Lab. maj. 13,828)

LEICESTER EAST
*E.*64,012   *T.*69.37%
*K. Vaz, *Lab.*   29,083
S. Milton, *C.*   10,661
J. Matabudul, *LD*   3,105
P. Iwaniw, *Ref.*   1,015
S. Sidhu, *Soc. Lab.*   436
N. Slack, *Glow*   102
Lab. majority 18,422
(April 1992, Lab. maj. 11,316)

LEICESTER SOUTH
*E.*71,750   *T.*67.06%
*J. Marshall, *Lab.*   27,914
C. Heaton-Harris, *C.*   11,421
B. Coles, *LD*   6,654
J. Hancock, *Ref.*   1,184
J. Dooher, *Soc. Lab.*   634
K. Sills, *Nat. Dem.*   307
Lab. majority 16,493
(April 1992, Lab. maj. 9,440)

LEICESTER WEST
*E.*64,570   *T.*63.36%
Ms P. Hewitt, *Lab.*   22,580
R. Thomas, *C.*   9,716
M. Jones, *LD*   5,795
W. Shooter, *Ref.*   970
G. Forse, *Green*   586
D. Roberts, *Soc. Lab.*   452
Ms J. Nicholls, *Soc.*   327
A. Belshaw, *BNP*   302
C. Potter, *Nat. Dem.*   186
Lab. majority 12,864
(April 1992, Lab. maj. 3,978)

LEICESTERSHIRE NORTH WEST
*E.*65,069   *T.*79.95%
D. Taylor, *Lab.*   29,332
R. Goodwill, *C.*   16,113
S. Heptinstall, *LD*   4,492
M. Abney-Hastings, *Ref.*   2,088
Lab. majority 13,219
(Boundary change: notional C.)

LEIGH
*E.*69,908   *T.*65.69%
†L. Cunliffe, *Lab.*   31,652
E. Young, *C.*   7,156
P. Hough, *LD*   5,163
R. Constable, *Ref.*   1,949
Lab. majority 24,496
(Boundary change: notional Lab.)

LEOMINSTER
*E.*65,993   *T.*76.60%
†P. Temple-Morris, *C.*   22,888
T. James, *LD*   14,053

R. Westwood, *Lab.*   8,831
A. Parkin, *Ref.*   2,815
Ms F. Norman, *Green*   1,086
R. Chamings, *UK Ind.*   588
J. Haycock, *BNP*   292
C. majority 8,835
(Boundary change: notional C.)

LEWES
*E.*64,340   *T.*76.42%
N. Baker, *LD*   21,250
†T. Rathbone, *C.*   19,950
Dr M. Patton, *Lab.*   5,232
Mrs L. Butler, *Ref.*   2,481
J. Harvey, *UK Ind.*   256
LD majority 1,300
(Boundary change: notional C.)

LEWISHAM DEPTFORD
*E.*58,141   *T.*57.87%
†Mrs J. Ruddock, *Lab.*   23,827
Mrs I. Kimm, *C.*   4,949
K. Appiah, *LD*   3,004
J. Mulrenan, *Soc. Lab.*   996
Ms S. Shepherd, *Ref.*   868
Lab. majority 18,878
(Boundary change: notional Lab.)

LEWISHAM EAST
*E.*56,333   *T.*66.41%
†Ms B. Prentice, *Lab.*   21,821
P. Hollobone, *C.*   9,694
D. Buxton, *LD*   4,178
S. Drury, *Ref.*   910
R. Croucher, *NF*   431
P. White, *Lib.*   277
Capt. Rizz, *Dream*   97
Lab. majority 12,127
(Boundary change: notional Lab.)

LEWISHAM WEST
*E.*58,659   *T.*64.00%
*J. Dowd, *Lab.*   23,273
Mrs C. Whelan, *C.*   8,936
Miss K. McGrath, *LD*   3,672
A. Leese, *Ref.*   1,098
N. Long, *Soc. Lab.*   398
Ms E. Oram, *Lib.*   167
Lab. majority 14,337
(April 1992, Lab. maj. 1,809)

LEYTON AND WANSTEAD
*E.*62,176   *T.*63.24%
†H. Cohen, *Lab.*   23,922
R. Vaudry, *C.*   8,736
C. Anglin, *LD*   5,920
S. Duffy, *ProLife*   488
A. Mian, *Ind.*   256
Lab. majority 15,186
(Boundary change: notional Lab.)

LICHFIELD
*E.*62,720   *T.*77.48%
†M. Fabricant, *C.*   20,853
Ms S. Woodward, *Lab.*   20,615
Dr P. Bennion, *LD*   5,473
G. Seward, *Ref.*   1,652
C. majority 238
(Boundary change: notional C.)

LINCOLN
*E.*65,485   *T.*71.08%
Ms G. Merron, *Lab.*   25,563

A. Brown, *C.*	14,433
Ms L. Gabriel, *LD*	5,048
J. Ivory, *Ref.*	1,329
A. Myers, *NLP*	175
Lab. majority 11,130	
(Boundary change: notional Lab.)	

LIVERPOOL GARSTON
*E.*66,755   *T.*65.14%

Ms M. Eagle, *Lab.*	26,667
Ms F. Clucas, *LD*	8,250
N. Gordon-Johnson, *C.*	6,819
F. Dunne, *Ref.*	833
G. Copeland, *Lib.*	666
J. Parsons, *NLP*	127
S. Nolan, *SEP*	120
Lab. majority 18,417	
(Boundary change: notional Lab.)	

LIVERPOOL RIVERSIDE
*E.*73,429   *T.*51.93%

Ms L. Ellman, *Lab. Co-op.*	26,858
Ms B. Fraenkel, *LD*	5,059
D. Sparrow, *C.*	3,635
Ms C. Wilson, *Soc.*	776
D. Green, *Lib.*	594
G. Skelly, *Ref.*	586
Ms H. Neilson, *ProLife*	277
D. Braid, *MRAC*	179
G. Gay, *NLP*	171
Lab. Co-op. majority 21,799	
(Boundary change: notional Lab. Co-op.)	

LIVERPOOL WALTON
*E.*67,527   *T.*59.54%

*P. Kilfoyle, *Lab.*	31,516
R. Roberts, *LD*	4,478
M. Kotecha, *C.*	2,551
C. Grundy, *Ref.*	620
Ms L. Mahmood, *Soc.*	444
Ms H. Williams, *Lib.*	352
Ms V. Mearns, *ProLife*	246
Lab. majority 27,038	
(April 1992, Lab. maj. 28,299)	

LIVERPOOL WAVERTREE
*E.*73,063   *T.*62.85%

†Ms J. Kennedy, *Lab.*	29,592
R. Kemp, *LD*	9,891
C. Malthouse, *C.*	4,944
P. Worthington, *Ref.*	576
K. McCullough, *Lib.*	391
Ms R. Kingsley, *ProLife*	346
Ms C. Corkhill, *WRP*	178
Lab. majority 19,701	
(Boundary change: notional Lab.)	

LIVERPOOL WEST DERBY
*E.*68,682   *T.*61.38%

†R. Wareing, *Lab.*	30,002
S. Radford, *Lib.*	4,037
Ms A. Hines, *LD*	3,805
N. Morgan, *C.*	3,656
P. Forrest, *Ref.*	657
Lab. majority 25,965	
(Boundary change: notional Lab.)	

LOUGHBOROUGH
*E.*68,945   *T.*75.95%

A. Reed, *Lab.*	25,448
K. Andrew, *C.*	19,736
Ms D. Brass, *LD*	6,190

R. Gupta, *Ref.*	991
Lab. majority 5,712	
(Boundary change: notional C.)	

LOUTH AND HORNCASTLE
*E.*68,824   *T.*72.58%

†Sir P. Tapsell, *C.*	21,699
J. Hough, *Lab.*	14,799
Mrs F. Martin, *LD*	12,207
Ms R. Robinson, *Green*	1,248
C. majority 6,900	
(Boundary change: notional C.)	

LUDLOW
*E.*61,267   *T.*75.55%

†C. Gill, *C.*	19,633
I. Huffer, *LD*	13,724
Ms N. O'Kane, *Lab.*	11,745
T. Andrewes, *Green*	798
E. Freeman-Keel, *UK Ind.*	385
C. majority 5,909	
(Boundary change: notional C.)	

LUTON NORTH
*E.*64,618   *T.*73.25%

K. Hopkins, *Lab.*	25,860
D. Senior, *C.*	16,234
Mrs K. Newbound, *LD*	4,299
C. Brown, *UK Ind.*	689
A. Custance, *NLP*	250
Lab. majority 9,626	
(Boundary change: notional C.)	

LUTON SOUTH
*E.*68,395   *T.*70.45%

Ms M. Moran, *Lab.*	26,428
†Sir G. Bright, *C.*	15,109
K. Fitchett, *LD*	4,610
C. Jacobs, *Ref.*	1,205
C. Lawman, *UK Ind.*	390
M. Scheimann, *Green*	356
Ms C. Perrin, *NLP*	86
Lab. majority 11,319	
(Boundary change: notional C.)	

MACCLESFIELD
*E.*72,049   *T.*75.22%

†N. Winterton, *C.*	26,888
Ms J. Jackson, *Lab.*	18,234
M. Flynn, *LD*	9,075
C. majority 8,654	
(Boundary change: notional C.)	

MAIDENHEAD
*E.*67,302   *T.*75.61%

Mrs T. May, *C.*	25,344
A. Ketteringham, *LD*	13,363
Ms D. Robson, *Lab.*	9,205
C. Taverner, *Ref.*	1,638
D. Munkley, *Lib.*	896
N. Spiers, *UK Ind.*	277
K. Ardley, *Glow*	166
C. majority 11,981	
(Boundary change: notional C.)	

MAIDSTONE AND THE WEALD
*E.*72,466   *T.*73.98%

†Rt. Hon. Miss A. Widdecombe, *C.*	23,657
J. Morgan, *Lab.*	14,054
Mrs J. Nelson, *LD*	11,986
Ms S. Hopkins, *Ref.*	1,998
Ms M. Cleator, *Soc. Lab.*	979

Ms P. Kemp, *Green*	480
Mrs R. Owen, *UK Ind.*	339
J. Oldbury, *NLP*	115
C. majority 9,603	
(Boundary change: notional C.)	

MAKERFIELD
*E.*67,358   *T.*66.83%

†I. McCartney, *Lab.*	33,119
M. Winstanley, *C.*	6,942
B. Hubbard, *LD*	3,743
A. Seed, *Ref.*	1,210
Lab. majority 26,177	
(Boundary change: notional Lab.)	

MALDON AND CHELMSFORD EAST
*E.*66,184   *T.*76.13%

†J. Whittingdale, *C.*	24,524
K. Freeman, *Lab.*	14,485
G. Pooley, *LD*	9,758
L. Overy-Owen, *UK Ind.*	935
Ms E. Burgess, *Green*	685
C. majority 10,039	
(Boundary change: notional C.)	

MANCHESTER BLACKLEY
*E.*62,227   *T.*57.46%

G. Stringer, *Lab.*	25,042
S. Barclay, *C.*	5,454
S. Wheale, *LD*	3,937
P. Stanyer, *Ref.*	1,323
Lab. majority 19,588	
(Boundary change: notional Lab.)	

MANCHESTER CENTRAL
*E.*63,815   *T.*52.55%

†A. Lloyd, *Lab.*	23,803
Ms A. Firth, *LD*	4,121
S. McIlwaine, *C.*	3,964
F. Rafferty, *Soc. Lab.*	810
J. Maxwell, *Ref.*	742
T. Rigby, *Comm L.*	97
Lab. majority 19,682	
(Boundary change: notional Lab.)	

MANCHESTER GORTON
*E.*64,349   *T.*56.43%

†Rt. Hon. G. Kaufman, *Lab.*	23,704
Dr J. Pearcey, *LD*	6,362
G. Senior, *C.*	4,249
K. Hartley, *Ref.*	812
Dr S. Fitz-Gibbon, *Green*	683
T. Wongsam, *Soc. Lab.*	501
Lab. majority 17,342	
(Boundary change: notional Lab.)	

MANCHESTER WITHINGTON
*E.*66,116   *T.*66.59%

†K. Bradley, *Lab.*	27,103
J. Smith, *C.*	8,522
Dr Y. Zalzala, *LD*	6,000
M. Sheppard, *Ref.*	1,079
S. Caldwell, *ProLife*	614
Ms J. White, *Soc.*	376
S. Kingston, *Dream*	181
M. Gaskell, *NLP*	152
Lab. majority 18,581	
(Boundary change: notional Lab.)	

MANSFIELD
*E.*67,057   *T.*70.72%

*A. Meale, *Lab.*	30,556

T. Frost, *C.*   10,038
P. Smith, *LD*   5,244
W. Bogusz, *Ref.*   1,588
Lab. majority 20,518
(April 1992, Lab. maj. 11,724)

MEDWAY
*E.*61,736   *T.*72.47%
R. Marshall-Andrews, *Lab.*   21,858
*Dame P. Fenner, *C.*   16,504
R. Roberts, *LD*   4,555
J. Main, *Ref.*   1,420
Mrs S. Radlett, *UK Ind.*   405
Lab. majority 5,354
(April 1992, C. maj. 8,786)

MERIDEN
*E.*76,287   *T.*71.73%
Mrs C. Spelman, *C.*   22,997
B. Seymour-Smith, *Lab.*   22,415
A. Dupont, *LD*   7,098
P. Gilbert, *Ref.*   2,208
C. majority 582
(April 1992, C. maj. 14,699)

MIDDLESBROUGH
*E.*70,931   *T.*64.99%
†S. Bell, *Lab.*   32,925
L. Benham, *C.*   7,907
Miss A. Charlesworth, *LD*   3,934
R. Edwards, *Ref.*   1,331
Lab. majority 25,018
(Boundary change: notional Lab.)

MIDDLESBROUGH SOUTH AND
CLEVELAND EAST
*E.*70,481   *T.*76.03%
Dr A. Kumar, *Lab.*   29,319
†M. Bates, *C.*   18,712
H. Garrett, *LD*   4,004
R. Batchelor, *Ref.*   1,552
Lab. majority 10,607
(Boundary change: notional C.)

MILTON KEYNES NORTH EAST
*E.*70,395   *T.*72.78%
B. White, *Lab.*   20,201
†P. Butler, *C.*   19,961
G. Mabbutt, *LD*   8,907
M. Phillips, *Ref.*   1,492
A. Francis, *Green*   576
M. Simson, *NLP*   99
Lab. majority 240
(Boundary change: notional C.)

MILTON KEYNES SOUTH WEST
*E.*71,070   *T.*71.42%
Mrs P. Starkey, *Lab.*   27,298
*B. Legg, *C.*   17,006
P. Jones, *LD*   6,065
H. Kelly, *NLP*   389
Lab. majority 10,292
(April 1992, C. maj. 4,687)

MITCHAM AND MORDEN
*E.*65,385   *T.*73.33%
Ms S. McDonagh, *Lab.*   27,984
*Rt. Hon. Dame A. Rumbold, *C.*

                                            14,243
N. Harris, *LD*   3,632
P. Isaacs, *Ref.*   810
Ms L. Miller, *BNP*   521
T. Walsh, *Green*   415

K. Vasan, *Ind.*   144
J. Barrett, *UK Ind.*   117
N. Dixon, *ACC*   80
Lab. majority 13,741
(April 1992, C. maj. 1,734)

MOLE VALLEY
*E.*69,140   *T.*78.86%
†Sir P. Beresford, *C.*   26,178
S. Cooksey, *LD*   15,957
C. Payne, *Lab.*   8,057
N. Taber, *Ref.*   2,424
R. Burley, *Ind. CRP*   1,276
Capt. I. Cameron, *UK Ind.*   435
Ms J. Thomas, *NLP*   197
C. majority 10,221
(Boundary change: notional C.)

MORECAMBE AND LUNESDALE
*E.*68,013   *T.*72.41%
Ms G. Smith, *Lab.*   24,061
†Sir M. Lennox-Boyd, *C.*   18,096
Mrs J. Greenwell, *LD*   5,614
I. Ogilvie, *Ref.*   1,313
D. Walne, *NLP*   165
Lab. majority 5,965
(Boundary change: notional C.)

MORLEY AND ROTHWELL
*E.*68,385   *T.*67.12%
†J. Gunnell, *Lab.*   26,836
A. Barraclough, *C.*   12,086
M. Galdas, *LD*   5,087
D. Mitchell-Innes, *Ref.*   1,359
R. Wood, *BNP*   381
Ms P. Sammon, *ProLife*   148
Lab. majority 14,750
(Boundary change: notional Lab.)

NEW FOREST EAST
*E.*65,717   *T.*74.64%
Dr J. Lewis, *C.*   21,053
G. Dawson, *LD*   15,838
A. Goodfellow, *Lab.*   12,161
C. majority 5,215
(Boundary change: notional C.)

NEW FOREST WEST
*E.*66,522   *T.*74.79%
D. Swayne, *C.*   25,149
R. Hale, *LD*   13,817
D. Griffiths, *Lab.*   7,092
Mrs M. Elliott, *Ref.*   2,150
M. Holmes, *UK Ind.*   1,542
C. majority 11,332
(Boundary change: notional C.)

NEWARK
*E.*69,763   *T.*74.50%
Ms F. Jones, *Lab.*   23,496
*R. Alexander, *C.*   20,480
P. Harris, *LD*   5,960
G. Creedy, *Ref.*   2,035
Lab. majority 3,016
(April 1992, C. maj. 8,229)

NEWBURY
*E.*73,680   *T.*76.65%
†D. Rendel, *LD*   29,887
R. Benyon, *C.*   21,370
P. Hannon, *Lab.*   3,107
E. Snook, *Ref.*   992
Ms R. Stark, *Green*   644

R. Tubb, *UK Ind.*   302
Ms K. Howse, *Soc. Lab.*   174
LD majority 8,517
(Boundary change: notional C.)

NEWCASTLE-UNDER-LYME
*E.*66,686   *T.*73.67%
*Mrs L. Golding, *Lab.*   27,743
M. Hayes, *C.*   10,537
Dr R. Studd, *LD*   6,858
Ms K. Suttle, *Ref.*   1,510
S. Mountford, *Lib.*   1,399
Ms B. Bell, *Soc. Lab.*   1,082
Lab. majority 17,206
(April 1992, Lab. maj. 9,839)

NEWCASTLE UPON TYNE
CENTRAL
*E.*69,781   *T.*66.05%
†J. Cousins, *Lab.*   27,272
B. Newmark, *C.*   10,792
Ms R. Berry, *LD*   6,911
C. Coxon, *Ref.*   1,113
Lab. majority 16,480
(Boundary change: notional Lab.)

NEWCASTLE UPON TYNE EAST
AND WALLSEND
*E.*63,272   *T.*65.73%
†N. Brown, *Lab.*   29,607
J. Middleton, *C.*   5,796
G. Morgan, *LD*   4,415
P. Cossins, *Ref.*   966
Ms B. Carpenter, *Soc. Lab.*   642
M. Levy, *Comm. P.*   163
Lab. majority 23,811
(Boundary change: notional Lab.)

NEWCASTLE UPON TYNE
NORTH
*E.*65,357   *T.*69.20%
*D. Henderson, *Lab.*   28,125
G. White, *C.*   8,793
P. Allen, *LD*   6,578
Mrs D. Chipchase, *Ref.*   1,733
Lab. majority 19,332
(April 1992, Lab. maj. 8,946)

NORFOLK MID
*E.*75,311   *T.*76.29%
K. Simpson, *C.*   22,739
D. Zeichner, *Lab.*   21,403
Mrs S. Frary, *LD*   8,617
N. Holder, *Ref.*   3,229
A. Park, *Green*   1,254
B. Parker, *NLP*   215
C. majority 1,336
(Boundary change: notional C.)

NORFOLK NORTH
*E.*77,113   *T.*76.27%
D. Prior, *C.*   21,456
N. Lamb, *LD*   20,163
M. Cullingham, *Lab.*   14,736
J. Allen, *Ref.*   2,458
C. majority 1,293
(April 1992, C. maj. 12,545)

NORFOLK NORTH WEST
*E.*77,083   *T.*74.72%
Dr G. Turner, *Lab.*   25,250
*H. Bellingham, *C.*   23,911
Ms E. Knowles, *LD*   5,513

R. Percival, *Ref.*   2,923
Lab. majority 1,339
(April 1992, C. maj. 11,564)

NORFOLK SOUTH
E.79,239   T.78.37%
†Rt. Hon. J. MacGregor, *C.*   24,935
Mrs B. Hacker, *LD*   17,557
Ms J. Ross, *Lab.*   16,188
Mrs P. Bateson, *Ref.*   2,533
Mrs S. Ross-Wagenknecht, *Green*   484
A. Boddy, *UK Ind.*   400
C. majority 7,378
(Boundary change: notional C.)

NORFOLK SOUTH WEST
E.80,236   T.73.28%
†Rt. Hon. Mrs G. Shephard, *C.*   24,694
A. Heffernan, *Lab.*   22,230
D. Buckton, *LD*   8,178
R. Hoare, *Ref.*   3,694
C. majority 2,464
(Boundary change: notional C.)

NORMANTON
E.62,980   T.68.28%
†W. O'Brien, *Lab.*   26,046
Miss F. Bulmer, *C.*   10,153
D. Ridgway, *LD*   5,347
K. Shuttleworth, *Ref.*   1,458
Lab. majority 15,893
(Boundary change: notional Lab.)

NORTHAMPTON NORTH
E.73,664   T.70.18%
Ms S. Keeble, *Lab.*   27,247
†A. Marlow, *C.*   17,247
Ms L. Dunbar, *LD*   6,579
D. Torbica, *UK Ind.*   464
B. Spivack, *NLP*   161
Lab. majority 10,000
(Boundary change: notional C.)

NORTHAMPTON SOUTH
E.79,384   T.71.94%
A. Clarke, *Lab.*   24,214
†Rt. Hon. M. Morris, *C.*   23,470
A. Worgan, *LD*   6,316
C. Petrie, *Ref.*   1,405
D. Clark, *UK Ind.*   1,159
G. Woollcombe, *NLP*   541
Lab. majority 744
(Boundary change: notional C.)

NORTHAVON
E.78,943   T.79.21%
Prof. S. Webb, *LD*   26,500
†Rt. Hon. Sir J. Cope, *C.*   24,363
R. Stone, *Lab.*   9,767
J. Parfitt, *Ref.*   1,900
LD majority 2,137
(Boundary change: notional C.)

NORWICH NORTH
E.72,521   T.75.92%
Dr I. Gibson, *Lab.*   27,346
Dr R. Kinghorn, *C.*   17,876
P. Young, *LD*   6,951
A. Bailey-Smith, *Ref.*   1,777
H. Marks, *LCP*   512
J. Hood, *Soc. Lab.*   495
Mrs D. Mills, *NLP*   100
Lab. majority 9,470
(Boundary change: notional C.)

NORWICH SOUTH
E.70,009   T.72.56%
C. Clarke, *Lab.*   26,267
B. Khanbhai, *C.*   12,028
A. Aalders-Dunthorne, *LD*   9,457
Dr D. Holdsworth, *Ref.*   1,464
H. Marks, *LCP*   765
A. Holmes, *Green*   736
B. Parsons, *NLP*   84
Lab. majority 14,239
(Boundary change: notional Lab.)

NOTTINGHAM EAST
E.65,581   T.60.60%
*J. Heppell, *Lab.*   24,755
A. Raca, *C.*   9,336
K. Mulloy, *LD*   4,008
B. Brown, *Ref.*   1,645
Lab. majority 15,419
(April 1992, Lab. maj. 7,680)

NOTTINGHAM NORTH
E.65,698   T.63.02%
*G. Allen, *Lab.*   27,203
Ms G. Shaw, *C.*   8,402
Ms R. Oliver, *LD*   3,301
J. Neal, *Ref.*   1,858
A. Belfield, *Soc.*   637
Lab. majority 18,801
(April 1992, Lab. maj. 10,743)

NOTTINGHAM SOUTH
E.72,418   T.67.00%
*A. Simpson, *Lab.*   26,825
B. Kirsch, *C.*   13,461
G. Long, *LD*   6,265
K. Thompson, *Ref.*   1,523
Ms S. Edwards, *Nat. Dem.*   446
Lab. majority 13,364
(April 1992, Lab. maj. 3,181)

NUNEATON
E.72,032   T.74.29%
*W. Olner, *Lab.*   30,080
R. Blunt, *C.*   16,540
R. Cockings, *LD*   4,732
R. English, *Ref.*   1,533
D. Bray, *Loc. Ind.*   390
P. Everitt, *UK Ind.*   238
Lab. majority 13,540
(April 1992, Lab. maj. 1,631)

OLD BEXLEY AND SIDCUP
E.68,044   T.75.53%
†Rt. Hon. Sir E. Heath, *C.*   21,608
R. Justham, *Lab.*   18,039
I. King, *LD*   8,284
B. Reading, *Ref.*   2,457
C. Bullen, *UK Ind.*   489
Ms V. Tyndall, *BNP*   415
R. Stephens, *NLP*   99
C. majority 3,569
(Boundary change: notional C.)

OLDHAM EAST AND
SADDLEWORTH
E.73,189   T.73.92%
P. Woolas, *Lab.*   22,546
†C. Davies, *LD*   19,157
J. Hudson, *C.*   10,666
D. Findlay, *Ref.*   1,116
J. Smith, *Soc. Lab.*   470
I. Dalling, *NLP*   146

Lab. majority 3,389
(Boundary change: notional C.)

OLDHAM WEST AND ROYTON
E.69,203   T.66.09%
†M. Meacher, *Lab.*   26,894
J. Lord, *C.*   10,693
H. Cohen, *LD*   5,434
G. Choudhury, *Soc. Lab.*   1,311
P. Etherden, *Ref.*   1,157
Mrs S. Dalling, *NLP*   249
Lab. majority 16,201
(Boundary change: notional Lab.)

ORPINGTON
E.78,749   T.76.40%
†J. Horam, *C.*   24,417
C. Maines, *LD*   21,465
Ms S. Polydorou, *Lab.*   10,753
D. Clark, *Ref.*   2,316
J. Carver, *UK Ind.*   526
R. Almond, *Lib.*   494
N. Wilton, *ProLife*   191
C. majority 2,952
(Boundary change: notional C.)

OXFORD EAST
E.69,339   T.69.05%
†A. Smith, *Lab.*   27,205
J. Djanogly, *C.*   10,540
G. Kershaw, *LD*   7,038
M. Young, *Ref.*   1,391
C. Simmons, *Green*   975
W. Harper-Jones, *Embryo*   318
Dr P. Gardner, *UK Ind.*   234
J. Thompson, *NLP*   108
P. Mylvaganam, *Anti-maj.*   68
Lab. majority 16,665
(Boundary change: notional Lab.)

OXFORD WEST AND ABINGDON
E.79,329   T.77.14%
Dr E. Harris, *LD*   26,268
L. Harris, *C.*   19,983
Ms S. Brown, *Lab.*   12,361
Mrs G. Eustace, *Ref.*   1,258
Dr M. Woodin, *Green*   691
R. Buckton, *UK Ind.*   258
Mrs L. Hodge, *ProLife*   238
Ms A.-M. Wilson, *NLP*   91
J. Rose, *LGR*   48
LD majority 6,285
(Boundary change: notional C.)

PENDLE
E.63,049   T.74.60%
*G. Prentice, *Lab.*   25,059
J. Midgeley, *C.*   14,235
A. Greaves, *LD*   5,460
D. Hockney, *Ref.*   2,281
Lab. majority 10,824
(April 1992, Lab. maj. 2,113)

PENRITH AND THE BORDER
E.66,496   T.73.63%
†Rt. Hon. D. Maclean, *C.*   23,300
G. Walker, *LD*   13,067
Mrs M. Meling, *Lab.*   10,576
C. Pope, *Ref.*   2,018
C. majority 10,233
(Boundary change: notional C.)

PETERBOROUGH
E.65,926   T.73.46%

Ms H. Brinton, *Lab.*	24,365
Mrs J. Foster, *C.*	17,042
D. Howarth, *LD*	5,170
P. Slater, *Ref.*	924
C. Brettell, *NLP*	334
J. Linskey, *UK Ind.*	317
S. Goldspink, *ProLife*	275

Lab. majority 7,323
(Boundary change: notional C.)

PLYMOUTH DEVONPORT
E.74,483   T.69.76%

†D. Jamieson, *Lab.*	31,629
A. Johnson, *C.*	12,562
R. Copus, *LD*	5,570
C. Norsworthy, *Ref.*	1,486
Mrs C. Farrand, *UK Ind.*	478
S. Ebbs, *Nat. Dem.*	238

Lab. majority 19,067
(Boundary change: notional Lab.)

PLYMOUTH SUTTON
E.70,666   T.67.43%

Mrs L. Gilroy, *Lab. Co-op.*	23,881
A. Crisp, *C.*	14,441
S. Melia, *LD*	6,613
T. Hanbury, *Ref.*	1,654
R. Bullock, *UK Ind.*	499
K. Kelway, *Plymouth*	396
F. Lyons, *NLP*	168

Lab. Co-op. majority 9,440
(Boundary change: notional C.)

PONTEFRACT AND CASTLEFORD
E.62,350   T.66.39%

Ms Y. Cooper, *Lab.*	31,339
A. Flook, *C.*	5,614
W. Paxton, *LD*	3,042
R. Wood, *Ref.*	1,401

Lab. majority 25,725
(April 1992, Lab. maj. 23,495)

POOLE
E.66,078   T.70.84%

R. Syms, *C.*	19,726
A. Tetlow, *LD*	14,428
H. White, *Lab.*	10,100
J. Riddington, *Ref.*	1,932
P. Tyler, *UK Ind.*	487
Mrs J. Rosta, *NLP*	137

C. majority 5,298
(Boundary change: notional C.)

POPLAR AND CANNING TOWN
E.67,172   T.58.46%

J. Fitzpatrick, *Lab.*	24,807
B. Steinberg, *C.*	5,892
Ms J. Ludlow, *LD*	4,072
J. Tyndall, *BNP*	2,849
I. Hare, *Ref.*	1,091
Ms J. Joseph, *Soc. Lab.*	557

Lab. majority 18,915
(Boundary change: notional Lab.)

PORTSMOUTH NORTH
E.64,539   T.70.14%

S. Rapson, *Lab.*	21,339
†P. Griffiths, *C.*	17,016
S. Sollitt, *LD*	4,788
S. Evelegh, *Ref.*	1,757
P. Coe, *UK Ind.*	298

C. Bex, *Wessex*	72

Lab. majority 4,323
(Boundary change: notional C.)

PORTSMOUTH SOUTH
E.80,514   T.64.21%

M. Hancock, *LD*	20,421
*D. Martin, *C.*	16,094
A. Burnett, *Lab.*	13,086
C. Trim, *Ref.*	1,629
J. Thompson, *Lib.*	184
Mrs J. Evans, *UK Ind.*	141
W. Treend, *NLP*	140

LD majority 4,327
(April 1992, C. maj. 242)

PRESTON
E.72,933   T.65.92%

†Mrs A. Wise, *Lab.*	29,220
P. Gray, *C.*	10,540
W. Chadwick, *LD*	7,045
J. C. Porter, *Ref.*	924
J. Ashforth, *NLP*	345

Lab. majority 18,680
(Boundary change: notional Lab.)

PUDSEY
E.70,922   T.74.35%

P. Truswell, *Lab.*	25,370
P. Bone, *C.*	19,163
Dr J. Brown, *LD*	7,375
D. Crabtree, *Ref.*	823

Lab. majority 6,207
(April 1992, C. maj. 8,972)

PUTNEY
E.60,176   T.73.11%

A. Colman, *Lab.*	20,084
*Rt. Hon. D. Mellor, *C.*	17,108
R. Pyne, *LD*	4,739
Sir J. Goldsmith, *Ref.*	1,518
W. Jamieson, *UK Ind.*	233
L. Beige, *Stan*	101
M. Yardley, *Spts All.*	90
J. Small, *NLP*	66
Ms A. Poole, *Beaut.*	49
D. Vanbraam, *Ren. Dem.*	7

Lab. majority 2,976
(April 1992, C. maj. 7,526)

RAYLEIGH
E.68,737   T.74.65%

†Dr M. Clark, *C.*	25,516
R. Ellis, *Lab.*	14,832
S. Cumberland, *LD*	10,137
A. Farmer, *Lib.*	829

C. majority 10,684
(Boundary change: notional C.)

READING EAST
E.71,586   T.70.15%

Ms J. Griffiths, *Lab.*	21,461
†J. Watts, *C.*	17,666
R. Samuel, *LD*	9,307
D. Harmer, *Ref.*	1,042
J. Buckley, *NLP*	254
Miss A. Thornton, *UK Ind.*	252
Ms B. Packer, *BNP*	238

Lab. majority 3,795
(Boundary change: notional C.)

READING WEST
E.69,073   T.70.05%

M. Salter, *Lab.*	21,841

N. Bennett, *C.*	18,844
Mrs D. Tomlin, *LD*	6,153
S. Brown, *Ref.*	976
I. Dell, *BNP*	320
D. Black, *UK Ind.*	255

Lab. majority 2,997
(Boundary change: notional C.)

REDCAR
E.68,965   T.70.99%

†Dr M. Mowlam, *Lab.*	32,972
A. Isaacs, *C.*	11,308
Ms J. Benbow, *LD*	4,679

Lab. majority 21,664
(Boundary change: notional Lab.)

REDDITCH
E.60,841   T.73.55%

Ms J. Smith, *Lab.*	22,280
Miss A. McIntyre, *C.*	16,155
M. Hall, *LD*	4,935
R. Cox, *Ref.*	1,151
P. Davis, *NLP*	227

Lab. majority 6,125
(Boundary change: notional C.)

REGENT'S PARK AND
KENSINGTON NORTH
E.73,752   T.64.19%

Ms K. Buck, *Lab.*	28,367
P. McGuinness, *C.*	13,710
Miss E. Gasson, *LD*	4,041
Ms S. Dangoor, *Ref.*	867
J. Hinde, *NLP*	192
Ms D. Sadowitz, *Dream*	167

Lab. majority 14,657
(Boundary change: notional Lab.)

REIGATE
E.64,750   T.74.40%

C. Blunt, *C.*	21,123
A. Howard, *Lab.*	13,382
P. Samuel, *LD*	9,615
†Sir G. Gardiner, *Ref.*	3,352
R. Higgs, *Ind.*	412
S. Smith, *UK Ind.*	290

C. majority 7,741
(Boundary change: notional C.)

RIBBLE SOUTH
E.71,670   T.77.06%

D. Borrow, *Lab.*	25,856
†Rt. Hon. R. Atkins, *C.*	20,772
T. Farron, *LD*	5,879
G. Adams, *Ref.*	1,475
N. Ashton, *C.*	1,127
Ms B. Leadbetter, *NLP*	122

Lab. majority 5,084
(Boundary change: notional C.)

RIBBLE VALLEY
E.72,664   T.78.75%

†N. Evans, *C.*	26,702
M. Carr, *LD*	20,062
M. Johnstone, *Lab.*	9,013
J. Parkinson, *Ref.*	1,297
Miss N. Holmes, *NLP*	147

C. majority 6,640
(Boundary change: notional C.)

RICHMOND (Yorks)
E.65,058   T.73.38%

†Rt. Hon. W. Hague, *C.*	23,326

S. Merritt, *Lab.* 13,275
Mrs J. Harvey, *LD* 8,773
A. Bentley, *Ref.* 2,367
C. majority 10,051
(Boundary change: notional C.)

RICHMOND PARK
E.71,572   T.79.43%
Dr J. Tonge, *LD* 25,393
†Rt. Hon. J. Hanley, *C.* 22,442
Ms S. Jenkins, *Lab.* 7,172
J. Pugh, *Ref.* 1,467
D. Beaupre, *Loony* 204
B. D'Arcy, *NLP* 102
P. Davies, *Dream* 73
LD majority 2,951
(Boundary change: notional C.)

ROCHDALE
E.68,529   T.70.16%
Ms L. Fitzsimons, *Lab.* 23,758
†Miss E. Lynne, *LD* 19,213
M. Turnberg, *C.* 4,237
G. Bergin, *BNP* 653
S. Mohammed, *IZB* 221
Lab. majority 4,545
(Boundary change: notional LD)

ROCHFORD AND SOUTHEND
EAST
E.72,848   T.63.97%
†Sir E. Taylor, *C.* 22,683
N. Smith, *Lab.* 18,458
Ms P. Smith, *LD* 4,387
B. Lynch, *Lib.* 1,070
C. majority 4,225
(Boundary change: notional C.)

ROMFORD
E.59,611   T.70.66%
Mrs E. Gordon, *Lab.* 18,187
†Sir M. Neubert, *C.* 17,538
N. Meyer, *LD* 3,341
S. Ward, *Ref.* 1,431
T. Hurlstone, *Lib.* 1,100
M. Carey, *BNP* 522
Lab. majority 649
(Boundary change: notional C.)

ROMSEY
E.67,306   T.76.99%
†M. Colvin, *C.* 23,834
M. Cooper, *LD* 15,249
Ms J. Ford, *Lab.* 9,623
Dr A. Sked, *UK Ind.* 1,824
M. Wigley, *Ref.* 1,291
C. majority 8,585
(Boundary change: notional C.)

ROSSENDALE AND DARWEN
E.69,749   T.73.42%
†Mrs J. Anderson, *Lab.* 27,470
Mrs P. Buzzard, *C.* 16,521
B. Dunning, *LD* 5,435
R. Newstead, *Ref.* 1,108
A. Wearden, *BNP* 674
Lab. majority 10,949
(Boundary change: notional Lab.)

ROTHER VALLEY
E.68,622   T.67.26%
*K. Barron, *Lab.* 31,184
S. Stanbury, *C.* 7,699

S. Burgess, *LD* 5,342
S. Cook, *Ref.* 1,932
Lab. majority 23,485
(April 1992, Lab. maj. 17,222)

ROTHERHAM
E.59,895   T.62.86%
*D. MacShane, *Lab.* 26,852
S. Gordon, *C.* 5,383
D. Wildgoose, *LD* 3,919
R. Hollibone, *Ref.* 1,132
A. Neal, *ProLife* 364
Lab. majority 21,469
(April 1992, Lab. maj. 17,561)

RUGBY AND KENILWORTH
E.79,384   T.77.10%
A. King, *Lab.* 26,356
†J. Pawsey, *C.* 25,861
J. Roodhouse, *LD* 8,737
M. Twite, *NLP* 251
Lab. majority 495
(Boundary change: notional C.)

RUISLIP-NORTHWOOD
E.60,393   T.74.24%
†J. Wilkinson, *C.* 22,526
P. Barker, *Lab.* 14,732
C. Edwards, *LD* 7,279
Ms C. Griffin, *NLP* 296
C. majority 7,794
(Boundary change: notional C.)

RUNNYMEDE AND WEYBRIDGE
E.72,177   T.71.44%
P. Hammond, *C.* 25,051
I. Peacock, *Lab.* 15,176
G. Taylor, *LD* 8,397
P. Rolt, *Ref.* 2,150
S. Slater, *UK Ind.* 625
J. Sleeman, *NLP* 162
C. majority 9,875
(Boundary change: notional C.)

RUSHCLIFFE
E.78,735   T.78.89%
*Rt. Hon. K. Clarke, *C.* 27,558
Ms J. Pettit, *Lab.* 22,503
S. Boote, *LD* 8,851
Miss S. Chadd, *Ref.* 2,682
J. Moore, *NLP* 403
Ms A. Maszwska, *NLP* 115
C. majority 5,055
(April 1992, C. maj. 19,766)

RUTLAND AND MELTON
E.70,150   T.75.02%
†A. Duncan, *C.* 24,107
J. Meads, *Lab.* 15,271
K. Lee, *LD* 10,112
R. King, *Ref.* 2,317
J. Abbott, *UK Ind.* 823
C. majority 8,836
(Boundary change: notional C.)

RYEDALE
E.65,215   T.74.80%
†J. Greenway, *C.* 21,351
J. Orrell, *LD* 16,293
Ms A. Hiles, *Lab.* 8,762
J. Mackfall, *Ref.* 1,460
S. Feaster, *UK Ind.* 917
C. majority 5,058
(Boundary change: notional C.)

SAFFRON WALDEN
E.74,097   T.76.99%
†Sir A. Haselhurst, *C.* 25,871
M. Caton, *LD* 15,298
M. Fincken, *Lab.* 12,275
R. Glover, *Ref.* 2,308
I. Evans, *UK Ind.* 658
B. Tyler, *Ind.* 486
C. Edwards, *NLP* 154
C. majority 10,573
(Boundary change: notional C.)

ST ALBANS
E.65,560   T.77.49%
K. Pollard, *Lab.* 21,338
D. Rutley, *C.* 16,879
A. Rowlands, *LD* 10,692
J. Warrilow, *Ref.* 1,619
Ms S. Craigen, *Dream* 166
I. Docker, *NLP* 111
Lab. majority 4,459
(Boundary change: notional C.)

ST HELENS NORTH
E.71,380   T.68.97%
D. Watts, *Lab.* 31,953
P. Walker, *C.* 8,536
J. Beirne, *LD* 6,270
D. Johnson, *Ref.* 1,276
R. Waugh, *Soc. Lab.* 832
R. Rudin, *UK Ind.* 363
Lab. majority 23,417
(April 1992, Lab. maj. 16,244)

ST HELENS SOUTH
E.66,526   T.66.53%
†G. Bermingham, *Lab.* 30,367
Ms M. Russell, *C.* 6,628
B. Spencer, *LD* 5,919
W. Holdaway, *Ref.* 1,165
Ms H. Jump, *NLP* 179
Lab. majority 23,739
(Boundary change: notional Lab.)

ST IVES
E.71,680   T.75.20%
A. George, *LD* 23,966
W. Rogers, *C.* 16,796
C. Fegan, *Lab.* 8,184
M. Faulkner, *Ref.* 3,714
Mrs P. Garnier, *UK Ind.* 567
G. Stephens, *Lib.* 425
K. Lippiatt, *R. Alt.* 178
W. Hitchins, *BHMBCM* 71
LD majority 7,170
(April 1992, C. maj. 1,645)

SALFORD
E.58,610   T.56.51%
Ms H. Blears, *Lab.* 22,848
E. Bishop, *C.* 5,779
N. Owen, *LD* 3,407
R. Cumpsty, *Ref.* 926
Ms S. Herman, *NLP* 162
Lab. majority 17,069
(Boundary change: notional Lab.)

SALISBURY
E.78,973   T.73.75%
*R. Key, *C.* 25,012
Ms Y. Emmerson-Peirce, *LD* 18,736
R. Rogers, *Lab.* 10,242
N. Farage, *UK Ind.* 3,332

H. Soutar, *Green* 623
W. Holmes, *Ind.* 184
Mrs S. Haysom, *NLP* 110
C. majority 6,276
(April 1992, C. maj. 8,973)

SCARBOROUGH AND WHITBY
*E.*75,862   *T.*71.61%
L. Quinn, *Lab.* 24,791
*J. Sykes, *C.* 19,667
M. Allinson, *LD* 7,672
Ms S. Murray, *Ref.* 2,191
Lab. majority 5,124
(April 1992, C. maj. 11,734)

SCUNTHORPE
*E.*60,393   *T.*68.84%
†E. Morley, *Lab.* 25,107
M. Fisher, *C.* 10,934
G. Smith, *LD* 3,497
P. Smith, *Ref.* 1,637
B. Hopper, *Soc. Lab.* 399
Lab. majority 14,173
(Boundary change: notional Lab.)

SEDGEFIELD
*E.*64,923   *T.*72.57%
†Rt. Hon. A. Blair, *Lab.* 33,526
Mrs E. Pitman, *C.* 8,383
R. Beadle, *LD* 3,050
Miss M. Hall, *Ref.* 1,683
B. Gibson, *Soc. Lab.* 474
Lab. majority 25,143
(Boundary change: notional Lab.)

SELBY
*E.*75,141   *T.*74.95%
J. Grogan, *Lab.* 25,838
K. Hind, *C.* 22,002
E. Batty, *LD* 6,778
D. Walker, *Ref.* 1,162
P. Spence, *UK Ind.* 536
Lab. majority 3,836
(Boundary change: notional C.)

SEVENOAKS
*E.*66,474   *T.*75.44%
M. Fallon, *C.* 22,776
J. Hayes, *Lab.* 12,315
R. Walshe, *LD* 12,086
N. Large, *Ref.* 2,138
Ms M. Lawrence, *Green* 443
M. Ellis, *PF* 244
A. Hankey, *NLP* 147
C. majority 10,461
(Boundary change: notional C.)

SHEFFIELD ATTERCLIFFE
*E.*68,548   *T.*64.65%
*C. Betts, *Lab.* 28,937
B. Doyle, *C.* 7,119
Mrs G. Smith, *LD* 6,973
J. Brown, *Ref.* 1,289
Lab. majority 21,818
(April 1992, Lab. maj. 15,480)

SHEFFIELD BRIGHTSIDE
*E.*58,930   *T.*57.47%
*D. Blunkett, *Lab.* 24,901
F. Butler, *LD* 4,947
C. Buckwell, *C.* 2,850
B. Farnsworth, *Ref.* 624
P. Davidson, *Soc. Lab.* 482

R. Scott, *NLP* 61
Lab. majority 19,954
(April 1992, Lab. maj. 22,681)

SHEFFIELD CENTRAL
*E.*68,667   *T.*53.04%
†R. Caborn, *Lab.* 23,179
A. Qadar, *LD* 6,273
M. Hess, *C.* 4,341
A. D'Agorne, *Green* 954
A. Brownlow, *Ref.* 863
K. Douglas, *Soc.* 466
Ms M. Aitken, *ProLife* 280
M. Driver, *WRP* 63
Lab. majority 16,906
(Boundary change: notional Lab.)

SHEFFIELD HALLAM
*E.*62,834   *T.*72.38%
R. Allan, *LD* 23,345
†Sir I. Patnick, *C.* 15,074
S. Conquest, *Lab.* 6,147
I. Davidson, *Ref.* 788
P. Booler, *SIP* 125
LD majority 8,271
(Boundary change: notional C.)

SHEFFIELD HEELEY
*E.*66,599   *T.*64.96%
*W. Michie, *Lab.* 26,274
R. Davison, *LD* 9,196
J. Harthman, *C.* 6,767
D. Mawson, *Ref.* 1,029
Lab. majority 17,078
(April 1992, Lab. maj. 14,954)

SHEFFIELD HILLSBOROUGH
*E.*74,642   *T.*71.04%
*Mrs H. Jackson, *Lab.* 30,150
A. Dunworth, *LD* 13,699
D. Nuttall, *C.* 7,707
J. Rusling, *Ref.* 1,468
Lab. majority 16,451
(April 1992, Lab. maj. 7,068)

SHERWOOD
*E.*74,788   *T.*75.59%
*P. Tipping, *Lab.* 33,071
R. Spencer, *C.* 16,259
B. Moult, *LD* 4,889
L. Slack, *Ref.* 1,882
P. Ballard, *BNP* 432
Lab. majority 16,812
(April 1992, Lab. maj. 2,910)

SHIPLEY
*E.*69,281   *T.*76.32%
C. Leslie, *Lab.* 22,962
*Rt. Hon. Sir M. Fox, *C.* 19,966
J. Cole, *LD* 7,984
Dr S. Ellams, *Ref.* 1,960
Lab. majority 2,996
(April 1992, C. maj. 12,382)

SHREWSBURY AND ATCHAM
*E.*73,542   *T.*75.25%
P. Marsden, *Lab.* 20,484
*D. Conway, *C.* 18,814
Mrs A. Woolland, *LD* 13,838
D. Barker, *Ref.* 1,346
D. Rowlands, *UK Ind.* 477
A. Dignan, *CFSS* 257
A. Williams, *PPP* 128

Lab. majority 1,670
(April 1992, C. maj. 10,965)

SHROPSHIRE NORTH
*E.*70,852   *T.*72.71%
O. Paterson, *C.* 20,730
I. Lucas, *Lab.* 18,535
J. Stevens, *LD* 10,489
D. Allen, *Ref.* 1,764
C. majority 2,195
(Boundary change: notional C.)

SITTINGBOURNE AND SHEPPEY
*E.*63,850   *T.*72.30%
D. Wyatt, *Lab.* 18,723
†Sir R. Moate, *C.* 16,794
R. Truelove, *LD* 8,447
P. Moull, *Ref.* 1,082
C. Driver, *Loony* 644
N. Risi, *UK Ind.* 472
Lab. majority 1,929
(Boundary change: notional C.)

SKIPTON AND RIPON
*E.*72,042   *T.*75.44%
†Rt. Hon. D. Curry, *C.* 25,294
T. Mould, *LD* 13,674
R. Marchant, *Lab.* 12,171
Mrs N. Holdsworth, *Ref.* 3,212
C. majority 11,620
(Boundary change: notional C.)

SLEAFORD AND NORTH
HYKEHAM
*E.*71,486   *T.*74.39%
†Rt. Hon. D. Hogg, *C.* 23,358
S. Harriss, *Lab.* 18,235
J. Marriott, *LD* 8,063
P. Clery, *Ref.* 2,942
R. Overton, *Ind.* 578
C. majority 5,123
(Boundary change: notional C.)

SLOUGH
*E.*70,283   *T.*67.91%
Ms F. MacTaggart, *Lab.* 27,029
Mrs P. Buscombe, *C.* 13,958
C. Bushill, *LD* 3,509
Ms A. Bradshaw, *Lib.* 1,835
T. Sharkey, *Ref.* 1,124
P. Whitmore, *Slough* 277
Lab. majority 13,071
(Boundary change: notional Lab.)

SOLIHULL
*E.*78,898   *T.*74.66%
†J. Taylor, *C.* 26,299
M. Southcombe, *LD* 14,902
Ms R. Harris, *Lab.* 14,334
M. Nattrass, *Ref.* 2,748
J. Caffery, *ProLife* 623
C. majority 11,397
(Boundary change: notional C.)

SOMERTON AND FROME
*E.*73,988   *T.*77.58%
D. Heath, *LD* 22,684
†M. Robinson, *C.* 22,554
R. Ashford, *Lab.* 9,385
R. Rodwell, *Ref.* 2,449
R. Gadd, *UK Ind.* 331
LD majority 130
(Boundary change: notional C.)

SOUTHAMPTON ITCHEN
E.76,869 T.70.06%
†J. Denham, Lab.	29,498
P. Fleet, C.	15,289
D. Harrison, LD	6,289
J. Clegg, Ref.	1,660
K. Rose, Soc. Lab.	628
C. Hoar, UK Ind.	172
G. Marsh, Soc.	113
Ms R. Barry, NLP	110
F. McDermott, ProLife	99

Lab. majority 14,209
(Boundary change: notional Lab.)

SOUTHAMPTON TEST
E.72,983 T.71.85%
A. Whitehead, Lab.	28,396
†Sir J. Hill, C.	14,712
A. Dowden, LD	7,171
P. Day, Ref.	1,397
H. Marks, LCP	388
A. McCabe, UK Ind.	219
P. Taylor, Glow	81
J. Sinel, NLP	77

Lab. majority 13,684
(Boundary change: notional Lab.)

SOUTHEND WEST
E.66,493 T.69.95%
†D. Amess, C.	18,029
Mrs N. Stimson, LD	15,414
A. Harley, Lab.	10,600
C. Webster, Ref.	1,734
B. Lee, UK Ind.	636
P. Warburton, NLP	101

C. majority 2,615
(April 1992, C. maj. 11,902)

SOUTH HOLLAND AND THE DEEPINGS
E.69,642 T.71.98%
J. Hayes, C.	24,691
J. Lewis, Lab.	16,700
P. Millen, LD	7,836
G. Erwood, NPC	902

C. majority 7,991
(Boundary change: notional C.)

SOUTHPORT
E.70,194 T.72.08%
R. Fearn, LD	24,346
*M. Banks, C.	18,186
Ms S. Norman, Lab.	6,125
F. Buckle, Ref.	1,368
Ms S. Ashton, Lib.	386
E. Lines, NLP	93
M. Middleton, Nat. Dem.	92

LD majority 6,160
(April 1992, C. maj. 3,063)

SOUTH SHIELDS
E.62,261 T.62.60%
†Dr D. Clark, Lab.	27,834
M. Hoban, C.	5,681
D. Ord, LD	3,429
A. Loraine, Ref.	1,660
I. Wilburn, Shields	374

Lab. majority 22,153
(Boundary change: notional Lab.)

SOUTHWARK NORTH AND BERMONDSEY
E.65,598 T.62.19%
†S. Hughes, LD	19,831
J. Fraser, Lab.	16,444
G. Shapps, C.	2,835
M. Davidson, BNP	713
W. Newton, Ref.	545
I. Grant, Comm L.	175
J. Munday, Lib.	157
Ms I. Yngvison, Nat. Dem.	95

LD majority 3,387
(Boundary change: notional LD)

SPELTHORNE
E.70,562 T.73.58%
*D. Wilshire, C.	23,306
K. Dibble, Lab.	19,833
E. Glynn, LD	6,821
B. Coleman, Ref.	1,495
J. Fowler, UK Ind.	462

C. majority 3,473
(April 1992, C. maj. 19,843)

STAFFORD
E.67,555 T.76.64%
D. Kidney, Lab.	24,606
D. Cameron, C.	20,292
Mrs P. Hornby, LD	5,480
S. Culley, Ref.	1,146
A. May, Loony	248

Lab. majority 4,314
(Boundary change: notional C.)

STAFFORDSHIRE MOORLANDS
E.66,095 T.77.34%
Ms C. Atkins, Lab.	26,686
Dr A. Ashworth, C.	16,637
Mrs C. Jebb, LD	6,191
D. Stanworth, Ref.	1,603

Lab. majority 10,049
(Boundary change: notional Lab.)

STAFFORDSHIRE SOUTH
E.68,896 T.74.19%
†Sir P. Cormack, C.	25,568
Ms J. LeMaistre, Lab.	17,747
Mrs J. Calder, LD	5,797
P. Carnell, Ref.	2,002

C. majority 7,821
(Boundary change: notional C.)

STALYBRIDGE AND HYDE
E.65,468 T.65.80%
†T. Pendry, Lab.	25,363
N. de Bois, C.	10,557
M. Cross, LD	5,169
R. Clapham, Ref.	1,992

Lab. majority 14,806
(Boundary change: notional Lab.)

STEVENAGE
E.66,889 T.76.82%
Ms B. Follett, Lab.	28,440
†T. Wood, C.	16,858
A. Wilcock, LD	4,588
J. Coburn, Ref.	1,194
D. Bundy, ProLife	196
A. Calcraft, NLP	110

Lab. majority 11,582
(Boundary change: notional C.)

STOCKPORT
E.65,232 T.71.54%
†Ms A. Coffey, Lab.	29,338
S. Fitzsimmons, C.	10,426
Mrs S. Roberts, LD	4,951
W. Morley-Scott, Ref.	1,280
G. Southern, Soc. Lab.	255
C. Newitt, Loony	213
C. Dronfield, Ind.	206

Lab. majority 18,912
(Boundary change: notional Lab.)

STOCKTON NORTH
E.64,380 T.69.08%
†F. Cook, Lab.	29,726
B. Johnston, C.	8,369
Mrs S. Fletcher, LD	4,816
K. McConnell, Ref.	1,563

Lab. majority 21,357
(Boundary change: notional Lab.)

STOCKTON SOUTH
E.68,470 T.76.12%
Ms D. Taylor, Lab.	28,790
†T. Devlin, C.	17,205
P. Monck, LD	4,721
J. Horner, Ref.	1,400

Lab. majority 11,585
(Boundary change: notional C.)

STOKE-ON-TRENT CENTRAL
E.64,113 T.62.77%
*M. Fisher, Lab.	26,662
N. Jones, C.	6,738
E. Fordham, LD	4,809
P. Stanyer, Ref.	1,071
M. Coleman, BNP	606
Ms F. Oborski, Lib.	359

Lab. majority 19,924
(April 1992, Lab. maj. 13,420)

STOKE-ON-TRENT NORTH
E.59,030 T.65.50%
†Ms J. Walley, Lab.	25,190
C. Day, C.	7,798
H. Jebb, LD	4,141
Ms J. Tobin, Ref.	1,537

Lab. majority 17,392
(Boundary change: notional Lab.)

STOKE-ON-TRENT SOUTH
E.69,968 T.66.08%
*G. Stevenson, Lab.	28,645
Mrs S. Scott, C.	10,342
P. Barnett, LD	4,710
R. Adams, Ref.	1,103
Mrs A. Micklem, Lib.	580
S. Batkin, BNP	568
B. Lawrence, Nat. Dem.	288

Lab. majority 18,303
(April 1992, Lab. maj. 6,909)

STONE
E.68,242 T.77.77%
†W. Cash, C.	24,859
J. Wakefield, Lab.	21,041
B. Stamp, LD	6,392
Ms A. Winfield, Lib.	545
Ms D. Grice, NLP	237

C. majority 3,818
(Boundary change: notional C.)

STOURBRIDGE
E.64,966 T.76.50%
Ms D. Shipley, Lab.	23,452
†W. Hawksley, C.	17,807
C. Bramall, LD	7,123
P. Quick, Ref.	1,319

Lab. majority 5,645
(Boundary change: notional C.)

STRATFORD-ON-AVON
*E.*81,434   *T.*76.26%

J. Maples, *C.*	29,967
Dr S. Juned, *LD*	15,861
S. Stacey, *Lab.*	12,754
A. Hilton, *Ref.*	2,064
J. Spilsbury, *UK Ind.*	556
J. Brewster, *NLP*	307
S. Marcus, *SFDC*	306
Ms S. Miller, *ProLife*	284

C. majority 14,106
(Boundary change: notional C.)

STREATHAM
*E.*74,509   *T.*60.24%

†K. Hill, *Lab.*	28,181
E. Noad, *C.*	9,758
R. O'Brien, *LD*	6,082
J. Wall, *Ref.*	864

Lab. majority 18,423
(Boundary change: notional Lab.)

STRETFORD AND URMSTON
*E.*69,913   *T.*69.65%

Ms B. Hughes, *Lab.*	28,480
J. Gregory, *C.*	14,840
J. Bridges, *LD*	3,978
Ms C. Dore, *Ref.*	1,397

Lab. majority 13,640
(Boundary change: notional Lab.)

STROUD
*E.*77,494   *T.*80.45%

D. Drew, *Lab. Co-op.*	26,170
†R. Knapman, *C.*	23,260
P. Hodgkinson, *LD*	9,502
J. Marjoram, *Green*	3,415

Lab. Co-op. majority 2,910
(Boundary change: notional C.)

SUFFOLK CENTRAL AND IPSWICH NORTH
*E.*70,222   *T.*75.22%

†M. Lord, *C.*	22,493
Ms C. Jones, *Lab.*	18,955
Dr M. Goldspink, *LD*	10,886
Ms S. Bennell, *Ind.*	489

C. majority 3,538
(Boundary change: notional C.)

SUFFOLK COASTAL
*E.*74,219   *T.*75.80%

†Rt. Hon. J. Gummer, *C.*	21,696
M. Campbell, *Lab.*	18,442
Ms A. Jones, *LD*	12,036
S. Caulfield, *Ref.*	3,416
A. Slade, *Green*	514
Ms F. Kaplan, *NLP*	152

C. majority 3,254
(Boundary change: notional C.)

SUFFOLK SOUTH
*E.*67,323   *T.*77.20%

†T. Yeo, *C.*	19,402
P. Bishop, *Lab.*	15,227
Mrs K. Pollard, *LD*	14,395
C. de Chair, *Ref.*	2,740
Mrs A. Holland, *NLP*	211

C. majority 4,175
(Boundary change: notional C.)

SUFFOLK WEST
*E.*68,638   *T.*71.51%

†R. Spring, *C.*	20,081
M. Jefferys, *Lab.*	18,214
A. Graves, *LD*	6,892
J. Carver, *Ref.*	3,724
A. Shearer, *NLP*	171

C. majority 1,867
(Boundary change: notional C.)

SUNDERLAND NORTH
*E.*64,711   *T.*59.05%

†W. Etherington, *Lab.*	26,067
A. Selous, *C.*	6,370
G. Pryke, *LD*	3,973
M. Nicholson, *Ref.*	1,394
K. Newby, *Loony*	409

Lab. majority 19,697
(Boundary change: notional Lab.)

SUNDERLAND SOUTH
*E.*67,937   *T.*58.77%

†C. Mullin, *Lab.*	27,174
T. Schofield, *C.*	7,536
J. Lennox, *LD*	4,606
M. Wilkinson, *UK Ind.*	609

Lab. majority 19,638
(Boundary change: notional Lab.)

SURREY EAST
*E.*72,852   *T.*75.02%

†P. Ainsworth, *C.*	27,389
Ms B. Ford, *LD*	12,296
D. Ross, *Lab.*	11,573
M. Sydney, *Ref.*	2,656
A. Stone, *UK Ind.*	569
Ms S. Bartrum, *NLP*	173

C. majority 15,093
(Boundary change: notional C.)

SURREY HEATH
*E.*73,813   *T.*74.14%

†N. Hawkins, *C.*	28,231
D. Newman, *LD*	11,944
Ms S. Jones, *Lab.*	11,511
J. Gale, *Ref.*	2,385
R. Squire, *UK Ind.*	653

C. majority 16,287
(Boundary change: notional C.)

SURREY SOUTH WEST
*E.*72,350   *T.*78.03%

*Rt. Hon. Mrs V. Bottomley, *C.*

	25,165
N. Sherlock, *LD*	22,471
Ms M. Leicester, *Lab.*	5,333
Mrs J. Clementson, *Ref.*	2,830
J. Kirby, *UK Ind.*	401
Ms J. Quintavalle, *ProLife*	258

C. majority 2,694
(April 1992, C. maj. 14,975)

SUSSEX MID
*E.*68,784   *T.*77.73%

†N. Soames, *C.*	23,231
Mrs M. Collins, *LD*	16,377
M. Hamilton, *Lab.*	9,969
T. Large, *Ref.*	3,146
J. Barnett, *UK Ind.*	606
E. Tudway, *Ind. JRP*	134

C. majority 6,854
(Boundary change: notional C.)

SUTTON AND CHEAM
*E.*62,785   *T.*75.01%

P. Burstow, *LD*	19,919
*Lady O. Maitland, *C.*	17,822
M. Allison, *Lab.*	7,280
P. Atkinson, *Ref.*	1,784
S. McKie, *UK Ind.*	191
Ms D. Wright, *NLP*	96

LD majority 2,097
(April 1992, C. maj. 10,756)

SUTTON COLDFIELD
*E.*71,864   *T.*72.92%

*Rt. Hon. Sir N. Fowler, *C.*	27,373
A. York, *Lab.*	12,488
J. Whorwood, *LD*	10,139
D. Hope, *Ref.*	2,401

C. majority 14,885
(April 1992, C. maj. 26,036)

SWINDON NORTH
*E.*65,535   *T.*73.66%

M. Wills, *Lab.*	24,029
G. Opperman, *C.*	16,341
M. Evemy, *LD*	6,237
Ms G. Goldsmith, *Ref.*	1,533
A. Fiskin, *NLP*	130

Lab. majority 7,688
(Boundary change: notional Lab.)

SWINDON SOUTH
*E.*70,207   *T.*72.87%

Ms J. Drown, *Lab.*	23,943
†S. Coombs, *C.*	18,298
S. Pajak, *LD*	7,371
D. Mackintosh, *Ref.*	1,273
R. Charman, *Route 66*	181
K. Buscombe, *NLP*	96

Lab. majority 5,645
(Boundary change: notional C.)

TAMWORTH
*E.*67,205   *T.*74.18%

†B. Jenkins, *Lab.*	25,808
Lady A. Lightbown, *C.*	18,312
Mrs J. Pinkett, *LD*	4,025
Mrs D. Livesey, *Ref.*	1,163
C. Lamb, *UK Ind.*	369
Ms C. Twelvetrees, *Lib.*	177

Lab. majority 7,496
(Boundary change: notional C.)

TATTON
*E.*63,822   *T.*76.45%

M. Bell, *Ind.*	29,354
†N. Hamilton, *C.*	18,277
S. Hill, *Ind.*	295
S. Kinsey, *Ind.*	187
B. Penhaul, *Miss M.*	128
J. Muir, *Albion*	126
M. Kennedy, *NLP*	123
D. Bishop, *Byro*	116
R. Nicholas, *Ind.*	113
J. Price, *Juice*	73

Ind. majority 11,077
(Boundary change: notional C.)

TAUNTON
*E.*79,783   *T.*76.47%

Mrs J. Ballard, *LD*	26,064
*D. Nicholson, *C.*	23,621
Ms E. Lisgo, *Lab.*	8,248
B. Ahern, *Ref.*	2,760

L. Andrews, *BNP* — 318
LD majority 2,443
(April 1992, C. maj. 3,336)

TEIGNBRIDGE
*E.*81,667   *T.*77.08%
†P. Nicholls, *C.* — 24,679
R. Younger-Ross, *LD* — 24,398
Ms S. Dann, *Lab.* — 11,311
S. Stokes, *UK Ind.* — 1,601
N. Banwell, *Green* — 817
Mrs L. Golding, *Dream* — 139
C. majority 281
(Boundary change: notional C.)

TELFORD
*E.*56,558   *T.*65.62%
†B. Grocott, *Lab.* — 21,456
B. Gentry, *C.* — 10,166
N. Green, *LD* — 4,371
C. Morris, *Ref.* — 1,119
Lab. majority 11,290
(Boundary change: notional Lab.)

TEWKESBURY
*E.*68,208   *T.*76.46%
L. Robertson, *C.* — 23,859
J. Sewell, *LD* — 14,625
K. Tustin, *Lab.* — 13,665
C. majority 9,234
(Boundary change: notional C.)

THANET NORTH
*E.*71,112   *T.*68.84%
*R. Gale, *C.* — 21,586
Ms I. Johnston, *Lab.* — 18,820
P. Kendrick, *LD* — 5,576
M. Chambers, *Ref.* — 2,535
Ms J. Haines, *UK Ind.* — 438
C. majority 2,766
(April 1992, C. maj. 18,210)

THANET SOUTH
*E.*62,792   *T.*71.65%
Dr S. Ladyman, *Lab.* — 20,777
†Rt. Hon. J. Aitken, *C.* — 17,899
Ms B. Hewett-Silk, *LD* — 5,263
C. Crook, *UK Ind.* — 631
D. Wheatley, *Green* — 418
Lab. majority 2,878
(Boundary change: notional C.)

THURROCK
*E.*71,600   *T.*65.94%
*A. MacKinlay, *Lab.* — 29,896
A. Rosindell, *C.* — 12,640
J. White, *LD* — 3,843
P. Compobassi, *UK Ind.* — 833
Lab. majority 17,256
(April 1992, Lab. maj. 1,172)

TIVERTON AND HONITON
*E.*75,744   *T.*78.06%
†Mrs A. Browning, *C.* — 24,438
Dr J. Barnard, *LD* — 22,785
J. King, *Lab.* — 7,598
S. Lowings, *Ref.* — 2,952
Mrs J. Roach, *Lib.* — 635
Ms E. McIvor, *Green* — 485
D. Charles, *Nat. Dem.* — 236
C. majority 1,653
(Boundary change: notional C.)

TONBRIDGE AND MALLING
*E.*64,798   *T.*75.97%
†Rt. Hon. Sir J. Stanley, *C.* — 23,640
Mrs B. Withstandley, *Lab.* — 13,410
K. Brown, *LD* — 9,467
J. Scrivenor, *Ref.* — 2,005
Mrs B. Bullen, *UK Ind.* — 502
G. Valente, *NLP* — 205
C. majority 10,230
(Boundary change: notional C.)

TOOTING
*E.*66,653   *T.*69.17%
*T. Cox, *Lab.* — 27,516
J. Hutchings, *C.* — 12,505
S. James, *LD* — 4,320
Mrs A. Husband, *Ref.* — 829
J. Rattray, *Green* — 527
P. Boddington, *BFAIR* — 161
J. Koene, *Rights* — 94
D. Bailey-Bond, *Dream* — 83
P. Miller, *NLP* — 70
Lab. majority 15,011
(April 1992, Lab. maj. 4,107)

TORBAY
*E.*72,258   *T.*73.79%
A. Sanders, *LD* — 21,094
*R. Allason, *C.* — 21,082
M. Morey, *Lab.* — 7,923
G. Booth, *UK Ind.* — 1,962
B. Cowling, *Lib.* — 1,161
P. Wild, *Dream* — 100
LD majority 12
(April 1992, C. maj. 5,787)

TOTNES
*E.*70,473   *T.*76.30%
†Sir A. Steen, *C.* — 19,637
R. Chave, *LD* — 18,760
V. Ellery, *Lab.* — 8,796
Ms P. Cook, *Ref.* — 2,552
C. Venmore, *Loc. C.* — 2,369
H. Thomas, *UK Ind.* — 999
A. Pratt, *Green* — 548
J. Golding, *Dream* — 108
C. majority 877
(Boundary change: notional C.)

TOTTENHAM
*E.*66,173   *T.*56.98%
*B. Grant, *Lab.* — 26,121
A. Scantlebury, *C.* — 5,921
N. Hughes, *LD* — 4,064
P. Budge, *Green* — 1,059
Ms E. Tay, *ProLife* — 210
C. Anglin, *WRP* — 181
Ms T. Kent, *SEP* — 148
Lab. majority 20,200
(April 1992, Lab. maj. 11,968)

TRURO AND ST AUSTELL
*E.*76,824   *T.*73.87%
*M. Taylor, *LD* — 27,502
N. Badcock, *C.* — 15,001
M. Dooley, *Lab.* — 8,697
C. Hearn, *Ref.* — 3,682
A. Haithwaite, *UK Ind.* — 576
Mrs D. Robinson, *Green* — 482
D. Hicks, *MK* — 450
Mrs L. Yelland, *PP* — 240
P. Boland, *NLP* — 117

LD majority 12,501
(April 1992, LD maj. 7,570)

TUNBRIDGE WELLS
*E.*65,259   *T.*74.10%
A. Norman, *C.* — 21,853
A. Clayton, *LD* — 14,347
P. Warner, *Lab.* — 9,879
T. Macpherson, *Ref.* — 1,858
M. Anderson Smart, *UK Ind.* — 264
P. Levy, *NLP* — 153
C. majority 7,506
(Boundary change: notional C.)

TWICKENHAM
*E.*73,281   *T.*79.34%
Dr V. Cable, *LD* — 26,237
†T. Jessel, *C.* — 21,956
Ms E. Tutchell, *Lab.* — 9,065
Miss J. Harrison, *Ind. ECR* — 589
T. Haggar, *Dream* — 155
A. Hardy, *NLP* — 142
LD majority 4,281
(Boundary change: notional C.)

TYNE BRIDGE
*E.*61,058   *T.*57.08%
†D. Clelland, *Lab.* — 26,767
A. Lee, *C.* — 3,861
Mrs M. Wallace, *LD* — 2,785
G. Oswald, *Ref.* — 919
Ms E. Brunskill, *Soc.* — 518
Lab. majority 22,906
(Boundary change: notional Lab.)

TYNEMOUTH
*E.*66,341   *T.*77.11%
A. Campbell, *Lab.* — 28,318
M. Callanan, *C.* — 17,045
A. Duffield, *LD* — 4,509
C. Rook, *Ref.* — 819
Dr F. Rogers, *UK Ind.* — 462
Lab. majority 11,273
(Boundary change: notional C.)

TYNESIDE NORTH
*E.*66,449   *T.*67.90%
†S. Byers, *Lab.* — 32,810
M. McIntyre, *C.* — 6,167
T. Mulvenna, *LD* — 4,762
M. Rollings, *Ref.* — 1,382
Lab. majority 26,643
(Boundary change: notional Lab.)

UPMINSTER
*E.*57,149   *T.*72.30%
K. Darvill, *Lab.* — 19,085
†Sir N. Bonsor, *C.* — 16,315
Mrs P. Peskett, *LD* — 3,919
T. Murray, *Ref.* — 2,000
Lab. majority 2,770
(Boundary change: notional C.)

UXBRIDGE
*E.*57,497   *T.*72.26%
†Sir M. Shersby, *C.* — 18,095
D. Williams, *Lab.* — 17,371
Dr A. Malyan, *LD* — 4,528
G. Aird, *Ref.* — 1,153
Ms J. Leonard, *Soc.* — 398
C. majority 724
(Boundary change: notional C.)
See also page 233

VALE OF YORK
E.70,077   T.76.01%
Miss A. McIntosh, *C.* 23,815
M. Carter, *Lab.* 14,094
C. Hall, *LD* 12,656
C. Fairclough, *Ref.* 2,503
A. Pelton, *Soc. Dem.* 197
C. majority 9,721
(Boundary change: notional C.)

VAUXHALL
E.70,402   T.55.49%
†Ms K. Hoey, *Lab.* 24,920
K. Kerr, *LD* 6,260
R. Bacon, *C.* 5,942
I. Driver, *Soc. Lab.* 983
S. Collins, *Green* 864
R. Headicar, *SPGB* 97
Lab. majority 18,660
(Boundary change: notional Lab.)

WAKEFIELD
E.73,210   T.68.96%
†D. Hinchliffe, *Lab.* 28,977
J. Peacock, *C.* 14,373
D. Dale, *LD* 5,656
S. Shires, *Ref.* 1,480
Lab. majority 14,604
(Boundary change: notional Lab.)

WALLASEY
E.63,714   T.73.52%
*Ms A. Eagle, *Lab.* 30,264
Mrs P. Wilcock, *C.* 11,190
P. Reisdorf, *LD* 3,899
R. Hayes, *Ref.* 1,490
Lab. majority 19,074
(April 1992, Lab. maj. 3,809)

WALSALL NORTH
E.67,587   T.64.07%
*D. Winnick, *Lab.* 24,517
M. Bird, *C.* 11,929
Ms T. O'Brien, *LD* 4,050
D. Bennett, *Ref.* 1,430
M. Pitt, *Ind.* 911
A. Humphries, *NF* 465
Lab. majority 12,588
(April 1992, Lab. maj. 3,824)

WALSALL SOUTH
E.64,221   T.67.33%
*B. George, *Lab.* 25,024
L. Leek, *C.* 13,712
H. Harris, *LD* 2,698
Dr T. Dent, *Ref.* 1,662
Mrs L. Meads, *NLP* 144
Lab. majority 11,312
(April 1992, Lab. maj. 3,178)

WALTHAMSTOW
E.63,818   T.62.76%
†N. Gerrard, *Lab.* 25,287
Mrs J. Andrew, *C.* 8,138
Dr J. Jackson, *LD* 5,491
Revd G. Hargreaves, *Ref.* 1,139
Lab. majority 17,149
(Boundary change: notional Lab.)

WANSBECK
E.62,998   T.71.70%
D. Murphy, *Lab.* 29,569
A. Thompson, *LD* 7,202

P. Green, *C.* 6,299
P. Gompertz, *Ref.* 1,146
Dr N. Best, *Green* 956
Lab. majority 22,367
(April 1992, Lab. maj. 18,174)

WANSDYKE
E.69,032   T.79.27%
D. Norris, *Lab.* 24,117
M. Prisk, *C.* 19,318
J. Manning, *LD* 9,205
K. Clinton, *Ref.* 1,327
T. Hunt, *UK Ind.* 438
P. House, *Loony* 225
Ms S. Lincoln, *NLP* 92
Lab. majority 4,799
(Boundary change: notional C.)

WANTAGE
E.71,657   T.78.23%
*R. Jackson, *C.* 22,311
Ms C. Wilson, *Lab.* 16,272
Ms J. Riley, *LD* 14,822
S. Rising, *Ref.* 1,549
Ms M. Kennet, *Green* 640
Count N. Tolstoy-Miloslausky,
   UK Ind. 465
C. majority 6,039
(April 1992, C. maj. 16,473)

WARLEY
E.59,758   T.65.08%
†J. Spellar, *Lab.* 24,813
C. Pincher, *C.* 9,362
J. Pursehouse, *LD* 3,777
K. Gamre, *Ref.* 941
Lab. majority 15,451
(Boundary change: notional Lab.)

WARRINGTON NORTH
E.72,694   T.70.50%
Ms H. Jones, *Lab.* 31,827
Ms R. Lacey, *C.* 12,300
I. Greenhalgh, *LD* 5,308
Dr A. Smith, *Ref.* 1,816
Lab. majority 19,527
(Boundary change: notional Lab.)

WARRINGTON SOUTH
E.72,262   T.76.23%
Ms H. Southworth, *Lab.* 28,721
C. Grayling, *C.* 17,914
P. Walker, *LD* 7,199
G. Kelly, *Ref.* 1,082
S. Ross, *NLP* 166
Lab. majority 10,807
(Boundary change: notional C.)

WARWICK AND LEAMINGTON
E.79,374   T.75.71%
J. Plaskitt, *Lab.* 26,747
†Sir D. Smith, *C.* 23,349
N. Hicks, *LD* 7,133
Mrs V. Davis, *Ref.* 1,484
P. Baptie, *Green* 764
G. Warwick, *UK Ind.* 306
M. Gibbs, *EDP* 183
R. McCarthy, *NLP* 125
Lab. majority 3,398
(Boundary change: notional C.)

WARWICKSHIRE NORTH
E.72,602   T.74.71%
†M. O'Brien, *Lab.* 31,669

S. Hammond, *C.* 16,902
W. Powell, *LD* 4,040
R. Mole, *Ref.* 917
C. Cooke, *UK Ind.* 533
I. Moorecroft, *Bert.* 178
Lab. majority 14,767
(Boundary change: notional Lab.)

WATFORD
E.74,015   T.74.63%
Ms C. Ward, *Lab.* 25,019
R. Gordon, *C.* 19,227
A. Canning, *LD* 9,272
Dr P. Roe, *Ref.* 1,484
L. Davis, *NLP* 234
Lab. majority 5,792
(Boundary change: notional C.)

WAVENEY
E.75,266   T.75.21%
R. Blizzard, *Lab.* 31,846
†D. Porter, *C.* 19,393
C. Thomas, *LD* 5,054
N. Clark, *Ind.* 318
Lab. majority 12,453
(Boundary change: notional C.)

WEALDEN
E.79,519   T.74.32%
†Rt. Hon. Sir G. Johnson Smith,
   C. 29,417
M. Skinner, *LD* 15,213
N. Levine, *Lab.* 10,185
B. Taplin, *Ref.* 3,527
Mrs M. English, *UK Ind.* 569
P. Cragg, *NLP* 188
C. majority 14,204
(Boundary change: notional C.)

WEAVER VALE
E.66,011   T.73.17%
†M. Hall, *Lab.* 27,244
J. Byrne, *C.* 13,796
T. Griffiths, *LD* 5,949
R. Cockfield, *Ref.* 1,312
Lab. majority 13,448
(Boundary change: notional Lab.)

WELLINGBOROUGH
E.74,955   T.75.10%
P. Stinchcombe, *Lab.* 24,854
*Sir P. Fry, *C.* 24,667
P. Smith, *LD* 5,279
A. Ellwood, *UK Ind.* 1,192
Ms A. Lowrys, *NLP* 297
Lab. majority 187
(April 1992, C. maj. 11,816)

WELLS
E.72,178   T.78.11%
*Rt. Hon. D. Heathcoat-Amory,
   C. 22,208
Dr P. Gold, *LD* 21,680
M. Eavis, *Lab.* 10,204
Mrs P. Phelps, *Ref.* 2,196
Ms L. Royse, *NLP* 92
C. majority 528
(April 1992, C. maj. 6,649)

WELWYN HATFIELD
E.67,395   T.78.59%
Ms M. Johnson, *Lab.* 24,936
†D. Evans, *C.* 19,341

R. Schwartz, *LD* 7,161
E. Cox, *RA* 1,263
Ms H. Harold, *ProLife* 267
Lab. majority 5,595
(Boundary change: notional C.)

WENTWORTH
*E.*63,951   *T.*65.33%
J. Healey, *Lab.* 30,225
K. Hamer, *C.* 6,266
J. Charters, *LD* 3,867
A. Battley, *Ref.* 1,423
Lab. majority 23,959
(April 1992, Lab. maj. 22,449)

WEST BROMWICH EAST
*E.*63,401   *T.*65.44%
†P. Snape, *Lab.* 23,710
B. Matsell, *C.* 10,126
M. Smith, *LD* 6,179
G. Mulley, *Ref.* 1,472
Lab. majority 13,584
(Boundary change: notional Lab.)

WEST BROMWICH WEST
*E.*67,496   *T.*54.37%
†Rt. Hon. Miss B. Boothroyd, *Speaker*
23,969
R. Silvester, *Lab. Change* 8,546
S. Edwards, *Nat. Dem.* 4,181
Speaker majority 15,423
(Boundary change: notional Lab.)

WESTBURY
*E.*74,301   *T.*76.38%
†D. Faber, *C.* 23,037
J. Miller, *LD* 16,969
K. Small, *Lab.* 11,969
G. Hawkins, *Lib.* 1,956
N. Hawkings-Byass, *Ref.* 1,909
R. Westbury, *UK Ind.* 771
C. Haysom, *NLP* 140
C. majority 6,068
(Boundary change: notional C.)

WEST HAM
*E.*57,058   *T.*58.99%
†A. Banks, *Lab.* 24,531
M. MacGregor, *C.* 5,037
Ms S. McDonough, *LD* 2,479
K. Francis, *BNP* 1,198
T. Jug, *Loony* 300
J. Rainbow, *Dream* 116
Lab. majority 19,494
(Boundary change: notional Lab.)

WESTMORLAND AND LONSDALE
*E.*68,389   *T.*74.29%
T. Collins, *C.* 21,470
S. Collins, *LD* 16,949
J. Harding, *Lab.* 10,459
M. Smith, *Ref.* 1,931
C. majority 4,521
(Boundary change: notional C.)

WESTON-SUPER-MARE
*E.*72,445   *T.*73.68%
B. Cotter, *LD* 21,407
Mrs M. Daly, *C.* 20,133
D. Kraft, *Lab.* 9,557
T. Sewell, *Ref.* 2,280
LD majority 1,274
(Boundary change: notional C.)

WIGAN
*E.*64,689   *T.*67.74%
†R. Stott, *Lab.* 30,043
M. Loveday, *C.* 7,400
T. Beswick, *LD* 4,390
A. Bradborne, *Ref.* 1,450
C. Maile, *Green* 442
W. Ayliffe, *NLP* 94
Lab. majority 22,643
(Boundary change: notional Lab.)
See also Stop-press

WILTSHIRE NORTH
*E.*77,237   *T.*75.11%
J. Gray, *C.* 25,390
S. Cordon, *LD* 21,915
N. Knowles, *Lab.* 8,261
Ms M. Purves, *Ref.* 1,774
A. Wood, *UK Ind.* 410
Ms J. Forsyth, *NLP* 263
C. majority 3,475
(Boundary change: notional C.)

WIMBLEDON
*E.*64,070   *T.*75.47%
R. Casale, *Lab.* 20,674
*Dr C. Goodson-Wickes, *C.* 17,694
Ms A. Willott, *LD* 8,014
H. Abid, *Ref.* 993
R. Thacker, *Green* 474
Ms S. Davies, *ProLife* 346
M. Kirby, *Mongolian* 112
G. Stacey, *Dream* 47
Lab. majority 2,980
(April 1992, C. maj. 14,761)

WINCHESTER
*E.*78,884   *T.*78.66%
M. Oaten, *LD* 26,100
†G. Malone, *C.* 26,098
P. Davies, *Lab.* 6,528
P. Strand, *Ref.* 1,598
R. Huggett, *Top* 640
D. Rumsey, *UK Ind.* 476
J. Browne, *Ind. AFE* 307
P. Stockton, *Loony* 307
LD majority 2
(Boundary change: notional C.)
See also page 233

WINDSOR
*E.*69,132   *T.*73.46%
†M. Trend, *C.* 24,476
C. Fox, *LD* 14,559
Mrs A. Williams, *Lab.* 9,287
J. McDermott, *Ref.* 1,676
P. Bradshaw, *Lib.* 388
Mrs E. Bigg, *UK Ind.* 302
Mr R. Parr, *Dynamic* 93
C. majority 9,917
(Boundary change: notional C.)

WIRRAL SOUTH
*E.*59,372   *T.*81.01%
†B. Chapman, *Lab.* 24,499
L. Byrom, *C.* 17,495
P. Gilchrist, *LD* 5,018
D. Wilcox, *Ref.* 768
Ms J. Nielsen, *ProLife* 264
G. Mead, *NLP* 51
Lab. majority 7,004
(Boundary change: notional C.)

WIRRAL WEST
*E.*60,908   *T.*76.98%
S. Hesford, *Lab.* 21,035
*Rt. Hon. D. Hunt, *C.* 18,297
J. Thornton, *LD* 5,945
D. Wharton, *Ref.* 1,613
Lab. majority 2,738
(April 1992, C. maj. 11,064)

WITNEY
*E.*73,520   *T.*76.72%
S. Woodward, *C.* 24,282
A. Hollingsworth, *Lab.* 17,254
Mrs A. Lawrence, *LD* 11,202
G. Brown, *Ref.* 2,262
M. Montgomery, *UK Ind.* 765
Ms S. Chapple-Perrie, *Green* 636
C. majority 7,028
(Boundary change: notional C.)

WOKING
*E.*70,053   *T.*72.68%
H. Malins, *C.* 19,553
P. Goldenberg, *LD* 13,875
Ms K. Hanson, *Lab.* 10,695
H. Bell, *Ind. C.* 3,933
C. Skeate, *Ref.* 2,209
M. Harvey, *UK Ind.* 512
Miss D. Sleeman, *NLP* 137
C. majority 5,678
(Boundary change: notional C.)

WOKINGHAM
*E.*66,161   *T.*75.74%
†Rt. Hon. J. Redwood, *C.* 25,086
Dr R. Longton, *LD* 15,721
Ms P. Colling, *Lab.* 8,424
P. Owen, *Loony* 877
C. majority 9,365
(Boundary change: notional C.)

WOLVERHAMPTON NORTH EAST
*E.*61,642   *T.*67.17%
K. Purchase, *Lab. Co-op.* 24,534
D. Harvey, *C.* 11,547
B. Niblett, *LD* 2,214
C. Hallmark, *Lib.* 1,560
A. Muchall, *Ref.* 1,192
M. Wingfield, *Nat. Dem.* 356
Lab. Co-op. majority 12,987
(Boundary change: notional Lab. Co-op.)

WOLVERHAMPTON SOUTH EAST
*E.*54,291   *T.*64.15%
*D. Turner, *Lab. Co-op.* 22,202
W. Hanbury, *C.* 7,020
R. Whitehouse, *LD* 3,292
T. Stevenson-Platt, *Ref.* 980
N. Worth, *Soc. Lab.* 689
K. Bullman, *Lib.* 647
Lab. Co-op. majority 15,182
(April 1992, Lab. maj. 10,240)

WOLVERHAMPTON SOUTH WEST
*E.*67,482   *T.*72.49%
Ms J. Jones, *Lab.* 24,657
*N. Budgen, *C.* 19,539
M. Green, *LD* 4,012
M. Hyde, *Lib.* 713
Lab. majority 5,118
(April 1992, C. maj. 4,966)

WOODSPRING
E.69,964   T.78.51%
†Dr L. Fox, C.	24,425
Mrs N. Kirsen, LD	16,691
Ms D. Sander, Lab.	11,377
R. Hughes, Ref.	1,614
Dr R. Lawson, Green	667
A. Glover, Ind.	101
M. Mears, NLP	52

C. majority 7,734
(Boundary change: notional C.)

WORCESTER
E.69,234   T.74.56%
M. Foster, Lab.	25,848
N. Bourne, C.	18,423
P. Chandler, LD	6,462
Mrs P. Wood, UK Ind.	886

Lab. majority 7,425
(Boundary change: notional C.)

WORCESTERSHIRE MID
E.68,381   T.74.32%
†P. Luff, C.	24,092
Mrs D. Smith, Lab.	14,680
D. Barwick, LD	9,458
T. Watson, Ref.	1,780
D. Ingles, UK Ind.	646
A. Dyer, NLP	163

C. majority 9,412
(Boundary change: notional C.)

WORCESTERSHIRE WEST
E.64,712   T.76.25%
†Sir M. Spicer, C.	22,223
M. Hadley, LD	18,377
N. Stone, Lab.	7,738
Ms S. Cameron, Green	1,006

C. majority 3,846
(Boundary change: notional C.)

WORKINGTON
E.65,766   T.75.08%
†D. Campbell-Savours, Lab.	31,717
R. Blunden, C.	12,061
P. Roberts, LD	3,967
G. Donnan, Ref.	1,412
C. Austin, UA	217

Lab. majority 19,656
(Boundary change: notional Lab.)

WORSLEY
E.68,978   T.67.82%
†T. Lewis, Lab.	29,083
D. Garrido, C.	11,342
R. Bleakley, LD	6,356

Lab. majority 17,741
(Boundary change: notional Lab.)

WORTHING EAST AND SHOREHAM
E.70,771   T.72.87%
T. Loughton, C.	20,864
M. King, LD	15,766
M. Williams, Lab.	12,335
J. McCulloch, Ref.	1,683
Mrs R. Jarvis, UK Ind.	921

C. majority 5,098
(Boundary change: notional C.)

WORTHING WEST
E.71,329   T.72.12%
†P. Bottomley, C.	23,733
C. Hare, LD	16,020
J. Adams, Lab.	8,347
N. John, Ref.	2,313
T. Cross, UK Ind.	1,029

C. majority 7,713
(Boundary change: notional C.)

WREKIN, THE
E.59,126   T.76.56%
P. Bradley, Lab.	21,243
P. Bruinvels, C.	18,218
I. Jenkins, LD	5,807

Lab. majority 3,025
(Boundary change: notional C.)

WYCOMBE
E.73,589   T.71.10%
†Sir R. Whitney, C.	20,890
C. Bryant, Lab.	18,520
P. Bensilum, LD	9,678
A. Fulford, Ref.	2,394
J. Laker, Green	716
M. Heath, NLP	121

C. majority 2,370
(Boundary change: notional C.)

WYRE FOREST
E.73,063   T.75.35%
D. Lock, Lab.	26,843
†A. Coombs, C.	19,897
D. Cropp, LD	4,377
W. Till, Ref.	1,956
C. Harvey, Lib.	1,670
J. Millington, UK Ind.	312

Lab. majority 6,946
(Boundary change: notional C.)

WYTHENSHAWE AND SALE EAST
E.71,986   T.63.25%
P. Goggins, Lab.	26,448
P. Fleming, C.	11,429
Ms V. Tucker, LD	5,639
B. Stanyer, Ref.	1,060
J. Flannery, Soc. Lab.	957

Lab. majority 15,019
(Boundary change: notional Lab.)

YEOVIL
E.74,165   T.72.88%
†Rt. Hon. J. D. D. Ashdown, LD	26,349
N. Cambrook, C.	14,946
P. Conway, Lab.	8,053
J. Beveridge, Ref.	3,574
D. Taylor, Green	728
J. Archer, Musician	306
C. Hudson, Dream	97

LD majority 11,403
(Boundary change: notional LD)

YORK, CITY OF
E.79,383   T.73.50%
*H. Bayley, Lab.	34,956
S. Mallett, C.	14,433
A. Waller, LD	6,537
J. Sheppard, Ref.	1,083
M. Hill, Green	880
E. Wegener, UK Ind.	319
A. Lightfoot, Ch. Nat.	137

Lab. majority 20,523
(April 1992, Lab. maj. 6,342)

YORKSHIRE EAST
E.69,409   T.70.55%
†J. Townend, C.	20,904
I. Male, Lab.	17,567
D. Leadley, LD	9,070
R. Allerston, Soc. Dem.	1,049
M. Cooper, Nat. Dem.	381

C. majority 3,337
(Boundary change: notional C.)

WALES

ABERAVON
E.50,025   T.71.89%
*Rt. Hon. J. Morris, Lab.	25,650
R. McConville, LD	4,079
P. Harper, C.	2,835
P. Cockwell, PC	2,088
P. David, Ref.	970
Capt. Beany, Beanus	341

Lab. majority 21,571
(April 1992, Lab. maj. 21,310)

ALYN AND DEESIDE
E.58,091   T.72.21%
†B. Jones, Lab.	25,955
T. Roberts, C.	9,552
Mrs E. Burnham, LD	4,076
M. Jones, Ref.	1,627
Mrs S. Hills, PC	738

Lab. majority 16,403
(Boundary change: notional Lab.)

BLAENAU GWENT
E.54,800   T.72.32%
*L. Smith, Lab.	31,493
Mrs G. Layton, LD	3,458
Mrs M. Williams, C.	2,607
J. Criddle, PC	2,072

Lab. majority 28,035
(April 1992, Lab. maj. 30,067)

BRECON AND RADNORSHIRE
E.52,142   T.82.24%
R. Livsey, LD	17,516
*J. Evans, C.	12,419
C. Mann, Lab.	11,424
Ms E. Phillips, Ref.	900
S. Cornelius, PC	622

LD majority 5,097
(April 1992, C. maj. 130)

BRIDGEND
E.59,721   T.72.44%
*W. Griffiths, Lab.	25,115
D. Davies, C.	9,867
A. McKinlay, LD	4,968

T. Greaves, *Ref.* 1,662
D. Watkins, *PC* 1,649
Lab. majority 15,248
(April 1992, Lab. maj. 7,326)

CAERNARFON
E.46,815   T.72.65%
*D. Wigley, *PC* 17,616
E. Williams, *Lab.* 9,667
E. Williams, *C.* 4,230
Ms M. McQueen, *LD* 1,686
C. Collins, *Ref.* 811
PC majority 7,949
(April 1992, PC maj. 14,476)

CAERPHILLY
E.64,621   T.70.05%
*R. Davies, *Lab.* 30,697
R. Harris, *C.* 4,858
L. Whittle, *PC* 4,383
A. Ferguson, *LD* 3,724
M. Morgan, *Ref.* 1,337
Mrs C. Williams, *ProLife* 270
Lab. majority 25,839
(April 1992, Lab. maj. 22,672)

CARDIFF CENTRAL
E.60,354   T.70.01%
*J. Owen Jones, *Lab. Co-op.* 18,464
Mrs J. Randerson, *LD* 10,541
D. Melding, *C.* 8,470
T. Burns, *Soc. Lab.* 2,230
W. Vernon, *PC* 1,504
N. Lloyd, *Ref.* 760
C. James, *Loony* 204
A. Hobbs, *NLP* 80
Lab. Co-op. majority 7,923
(April 1992, Lab. maj. 3,465)

CARDIFF NORTH
E.60,430   T.80.24%
Ms J. Morgan, *Lab.* 24,460
*G. Jones, *C.* 16,334
R. Rowland, *LD* 5,294
Dr C. Palfrey, *PC* 1,201
E. Litchfield, *Ref.* 1,199
Lab. majority 8,126
(April 1992, C. maj. 2,969)

CARDIFF SOUTH AND PENARTH
E.61,838   T.68.57%
*A. Michael, *Lab. Co-op.* 22,647
Mrs C. Roberts, *C.* 8,766
Dr S. Wakefield, *LD* 3,964
J. Foreman, *New Lab.* 3,942
D. Haswell, *PC* 1,356
P. Morgan, *Ref.* 1,211
M. Shepherd, *Soc.* 344
Ms B. Caves, *NLP* 170
Lab. Co-op. majority 13,881
(April 1992, Lab. maj. 10,425)

CARDIFF WEST
E.58,198   T.69.21%
†R. Morgan, *Lab.* 24,297
S. Hoare, *C.* 8,669
Ms J. Gasson, *LD* 4,366
Ms G. Carr, *PC* 1,949
T. Johns, *Ref.* 996
Lab. majority 15,628
(Boundary change: notional Lab.)

CARMARTHEN EAST AND DINEFWR
E.53,079   T.78.62%
†Dr A. Wynne Williams, *Lab.* 17,907
R. Thomas, *PC* 14,457
E. Hayward, *C.* 5,022
Mrs J. Hughes, *LD* 3,150
I. Humphreys-Evans, *Ref.* 1,196
Lab. majority 3,450
(Boundary change: notional Lab.)

CARMARTHEN WEST AND PEMBROKESHIRE SOUTH
E.55,724   T.76.52%
†N. Ainger, *Lab.* 20,956
O. J. Williams, *C.* 11,335
R. Llewellyn, *PC* 5,402
K. Evans, *LD* 3,516
Mrs J. Poirrier, *Ref.* 1,432
Lab. majority 9,621
(Boundary change: notional Lab.)

CEREDIGION
E.54,378   T.73.90%
†C. Dafis, *PC* 16,728
R. Harris, *Lab.* 9,767
D. Davies, *LD* 6,616
Dr F. Aubel, *C.* 5,983
J. Leaney, *Ref.* 1,092
PC majority 6,961
(Boundary change: notional PC)

CLWYD SOUTH
E.53,495   T.73.62%
†M. Jones, *Lab.* 22,901
B. Johnson, *C.* 9,091
A. Chadwick, *LD* 3,684
G. Williams, *PC* 2,500
A. Lewis, *Ref.* 1,207
Lab. majority 13,810
(Boundary change: notional Lab.)

CLWYD WEST
E.53,467   T.75.29%
G. Thomas, *Lab.* 14,918
†R. Richards, *C.* 13,070
E. Williams, *PC* 5,421
G. Williams, *LD* 5,151
Ms H. Collins, *Ref.* 1,114
D. Neal, *Cvty* 583
Lab. majority 1,848
(Boundary change: notional C.)

CONWY
E.55,092   T.75.44%
Mrs B. Williams, *Lab.* 14,561
R. Roberts, *LD* 12,965
D. Jones, *C.* 10,085
R. Davies, *PC* 2,844
A. Barham, *Ref.* 760
R. Bradley, *Alt. LD* 250
D. Hughes, *NLP* 95
Lab. majority 1,596
(April 1992, C. maj. 995)

CYNON VALLEY
E.48,286   T.69.22%
*Mrs A. Clwyd, *Lab.* 23,307
A. Davies, *PC* 3,552
H. Price, *LD* 3,459
A. Smith, *C.* 2,262
G. John, *Ref.* 844

Lab. majority 19,755
(April 1992, Lab. maj. 21,364)

DELYN
E.53,693   T.74.02%
†D. Hanson, *Lab.* 22,300
Mrs K. Lumley, *C.* 10,607
P. Lloyd, *LD* 4,160
A. Drake, *PC* 1,558
Ms E. Soutter, *Ref.* 1,117
Lab. majority 11,693
(Boundary change: notional Lab.)

GOWER
E.57,691   T.75.12%
M. Caton, *Lab.* 23,313
A. Cairns, *C.* 10,306
H. Evans, *LD* 5,624
E. Williams, *PC* 2,226
R. Lewis, *Ref.* 1,745
A. Popham, *FP* 122
Lab. majority 13,007
(April 1992, Lab. maj. 7,018)

ISLWYN
E.50,540   T.72.03%
*D. Touhig, *Lab. Co-op.* 26,995
C. Worker, *LD* 3,064
R. Walters, *C.* 2,864
D. Jones, *PC* 2,272
Mrs S. Monaghan, *Ref.* 1,209
Lab. Co-op. majority 23,931
(April 1992, Lab. maj. 24,728)
(Feb. 1995, Lab. maj. 13,097)

LLANELLI
E.58,323   T.70.66%
†Rt. Hon. D. Davies, *Lab.* 23,851
M. Phillips, *PC* 7,812
A. Hayes, *C.* 5,003
N. Burree, *LD* 3,788
J. Willock, *Soc. Lab.* 757
Lab. majority 16,039
(Boundary change: notional Lab.)

MEIRIONNYDD NANT CONWY
E.32,345   T.75.98%
*E. Llwyd, *PC* 12,465
H. Rees, *Lab.* 5,660
J. Quin, *C.* 3,922
Mrs B. Feeley, *LD* 1,719
P. Hodge, *Ref.* 809
PC majority 6,805
(April 1992, PC maj. 4,613)

MERTHYR TYDFIL AND RHYMNEY
E.56,507   T.69.27%
*T. Rowlands, *Lab.* 30,012
D. Anstey, *LD* 2,926
J. Morgan, *C.* 2,508
A. Cox, *PC* 2,344
A. Cowdell, *Old Lab.* 691
R. Hutchings, *Ref.* 660
Lab. majority 27,086
(April 1992, Lab. maj. 26,713)

MONMOUTH
E.60,703   T.80.76%
H. Edwards, *Lab.* 23,404
*R. Evans, *C.* 19,226
M. Williams, *LD* 4,689
N. Warry, *Ref.* 1,190

A. Cotton, *PC* — 516
Lab. majority 4,178
(April 1992, C. maj. 3,204)

MONTGOMERYSHIRE
*E.*42,618   *T.*74.91%
L. Opik, *LD* — 14,647
G. Davies, *C.* — 8,344
Ms A. Davies, *Lab.* — 6,109
Ms H. M. Jones, *PC* — 1,608
J. Bufton, *Ref.* — 879
Ms S. Walker, *Green* — 338
LD majority 6,303
(April 1992, LD maj. 5,209)

NEATH
*E.*55,525   *T.*74.28%
*P. Hain, *Lab.* — 30,324
D. Evans, *C.* — 3,583
T. Jones, *PC* — 3,344
F. Little, *LD* — 2,597
P. Morris, *Ref.* — 975
H. Marks, *LCP* — 420
Lab. majority 26,741
(April 1992, Lab. maj. 23,975)

NEWPORT EAST
*E.*50,997   *T.*73.06%
†A. Howarth, *Lab.* — 21,481
D. Evans, *C.* — 7,958
A. Cameron, *LD* — 3,880
A. Scargill, *Soc. Lab.* — 1,951
G. Davis, *Ref.* — 1,267
C. Holland, *PC* — 721
Lab. majority 13,523
(April 1992, Lab. maj. 9,899)

NEWPORT WEST
*E.*53,914   *T.*74.57%
*P. Flynn, *Lab.* — 24,331
P. Clarke, *C.* — 9,794
S. Wilson, *LD* — 3,907
C. Thompsett, *Ref.* — 1,199
H. Jackson, *PC* — 648
H. Moelwyn Hughes, *UK Ind.* — 323
Lab. majority 14,537
(April 1992, Lab. maj. 7,779)

OGMORE
*E.*52,078   *T.*73.10%
*Sir R. Powell, *Lab.* — 28,163
D. Unwin, *C.* — 3,716
Ms K. Williams, *LD* — 3,510
J. Rogers, *PC* — 2,679
Lab. majority 24,447
(April 1992, Lab. maj. 23,827)

PONTYPRIDD
*E.*64,185   *T.*71.44%
*Dr K. Howells, *Lab.* — 29,290
N. Howells, *LD* — 6,161
J. Cowen, *C.* — 5,910
O. Llewelyn, *PC* — 2,977
J. Wood, *Ref.* — 874
P. Skelly, *Soc. Lab.* — 380
R. Griffiths, *Comm. P.* — 178
A. Moore, *NLP* — 85
Lab. majority 23,129
(April 1992, Lab. maj. 19,797)

PRESELI PEMBROKESHIRE
*E.*54,088   *T.*78.40%
Mrs J. Lawrence, *Lab.* — 20,477
R. Buckland, *C.* — 11,741
J. Clarke, *LD* — 5,527
A. Lloyd Jones, *PC* — 2,683
D. Berry, *Ref.* — 1,574
Ms M. Scott Cato, *Green* — 401
Lab. majority 8,736
(Boundary change: notional C.)

RHONDDA
*E.*57,105   *T.*71.46%
*A. Rogers, *Lab.* — 30,381
Ms L. Wood, *PC* — 5,450
Dr R. Berman, *LD* — 2,307
S. Whiting, *C.* — 1,551
S. Gardiner, *Ref.* — 658
K. Jakeway, *Green* — 460
Lab. majority 24,931
(April 1992, Lab. maj. 28,816)

SWANSEA EAST
*E.*57,373   *T.*67.41%
*D. Anderson, *Lab.* — 29,151
Ms C. Dibble, *C.* — 3,582
E. Jones, *LD* — 3,440
Ms M. Pooley, *PC* — 1,308
Ms C. Maggs, *Ref.* — 904
R. Job, *Soc.* — 289
Lab. majority 25,569
(April 1992, Lab. maj. 23,482)

SWANSEA WEST
*E.*58,703   *T.*68.94%
*Rt. Hon. A. Williams, *Lab.* — 22,748
A. Baker, *C.* — 8,289
J. Newbury, *LD* — 5,872
D. Lloyd, *PC* — 2,675
D. Proctor, *Soc. Lab.* — 885
Lab. majority 14,459
(April 1992, Lab. maj. 9,478)

TORFAEN
*E.*60,343   *T.*71.67%
*P. Murphy, *Lab.* — 29,863
N. Parish, *C.* — 5,327
Ms J. Gray, *LD* — 5,249
Ms D. Holler, *Ref.* — 1,245
R. Gough, *PC* — 1,042
R. Coghill, *Green* — 519
Lab. majority 24,536
(April 1992, Lab. maj. 20,754)

VALE OF CLWYD
*E.*52,418   *T.*74.65%
C. Ruane, *Lab.* — 20,617
D. Edwards, *C.* — 11,662
D. Munford, *LD* — 3,425
Ms G. Kensler, *PC* — 2,301
S. Vickers, *Ref.* — 834
S. Cooke, *UK Ind.* — 293
Lab. majority 8,955
(Boundary change: notional C.)

VALE OF GLAMORGAN
*E.*67,213   *T.*80.21%
J. Smith, *Lab.* — 29,054
†W. Sweeney, *C.* — 18,522
Mrs S. Campbell, *LD* — 4,945
Ms M. Corp, *PC* — 1,393
Lab. majority 10,532
(Boundary change: notional C.)

WREXHAM
*E.*50,741   *T.*71.78%
Dr J. Marek, *Lab.* — 20,450
S. Andrew, *C.* — 8,688
A. Thomas, *LD* — 4,833
J. Cronk, *Ref.* — 1,195
K. Plant, *PC* — 1,170
N. Low, *NLP* — 86
Lab. majority 11,762
(Boundary change: notional Lab.)

YNYS MÔN
*E.*52,952   *T.*75.41%
*I. W. Jones, *PC* — 15,756
O. Edwards, *Lab.* — 13,275
G. Owen, *C.* — 8,569
D. Burnham, *LD* — 1,537
H. Gray Morris, *Ref.* — 793
PC majority 2,481

SCOTLAND

ABERDEEN CENTRAL
*E.*54,257   *T.*65.64%
F. Doran, *Lab.* — 17,745
Mrs J. Wisely, *C.* — 6,944
B. Topping, *SNP* — 5,767
J. Brown, *LD* — 4,714
J. Farquharson, *Ref.* — 446
Lab. majority 10,801
(Boundary change: notional Lab.)

ABERDEEN NORTH
*E.*54,302   *T.*70.74%
M. Savidge, *Lab.* — 18,389

B. Adam, *SNP* — 8,379
J. Gifford, *C.* — 5,763
M. Rumbles, *LD* — 5,421
A. Mackenzie, *Ref.* — 463
Lab. majority 10,010
(Boundary change: notional Lab.)

ABERDEEN SOUTH
*E.*60,490   *T.*72.84%
Ms A. Begg, *Lab.* — 15,541
N. Stephen, *LD* — 12,176
†R. Robertson, *C.* — 11,621

J. Towers, *SNP* — 4,299
R. Wharton, *Ref.* — 425
Lab. majority 3,365
(Boundary change: notional C.)

ABERDEENSHIRE WEST AND KINCARDINE
*E.*59,123   *T.*73.05%
Sir R. Smith, *LD* — 17,742
†G. Kynoch, *C.* — 15,080
Ms J. Mowatt, *SNP* — 5,639
Ms Q. Khan, *Lab.* — 3,923

S. Ball, *Ref.* 805
LD majority 2,662
(Boundary change: notional C.)

AIRDRIE AND SHOTTS
*E.*57,673   *T.*71.40%
†Mrs H. Liddell, *Lab.* 25,460
K. Robertson, *SNP* 10,048
Dr N. Brook, *C.* 3,660
R. Wolseley, *LD* 1,719
C. Semple, *Ref.* 294
Lab. majority 15,412
(Boundary change: notional Lab.)

ANGUS
*E.*59,708   *T.*72.14%
†A. Welsh, *SNP* 20,792
S. Leslie, *C.* 10,603
Ms C. Taylor, *Lab.* 6,733
Dr R. Speirs, *LD* 4,065
B. Taylor, *Ref.* 883
SNP majority 10,189
(Boundary change: notional SNP)

ARGYLL AND BUTE
*E.*49,451   *T.*72.23%
*Mrs R. Michie, *LD* 14,359
Prof. N. MacCormick, *SNP* 8,278
R. Leishman, *C.* 6,774
A. Syed, *Lab.* 5,596
M. Stewart, *Ref.* 713
LD majority 6,081
(April 1992, LD maj. 2,622)

AYR
*E.*55,829   *T.*80.17%
Mrs S. Osborne, *Lab.* 21,679
†P. Gallie, *C.* 15,136
I. Blackford, *SNP* 5,625
Miss C. Hamblen, *LD* 2,116
J. Enos, *Ref.* 200
Lab. majority 6,543
(Boundary change: notional Lab.)

BANFF AND BUCHAN
*E.*58,493   *T.*68.69%
†A. Salmond, *SNP* 22,409
W. Frain-Bell, *C.* 9,564
Ms M. Harris, *Lab.* 4,747
N. Fletcher, *LD* 2,398
A. Buchan, *Ref.* 1,060
SNP majority 12,845
(Boundary change: notional SNP)

CAITHNESS, SUTHERLAND AND EASTER ROSS
*E.*41,566   *T.*70.18%
†R. Maclennan, *LD* 10,381
J. Hendry, *Lab.* 8,122
E. Harper, *SNP* 6,710
T. Miers, *C.* 3,148
Ms C. Ryder, *Ref.* 369
J. Martin, *Green* 230
M. Carr, *UK Ind.* 212
LD majority 2,259
(Boundary change: notional LD)

CARRICK, CUMNOCK AND DOON VALLEY
*E.*65,593   *T.*74.96%
†G. Foulkes, *Lab. Co-op.* 29,398
A. Marshall, *C.* 8,336
Mrs C. Hutchison, *SNP* 8,190

D. Young, *LD* 2,613
J. Higgins, *Ref.* 634
Lab. Co-op. majority 21,062
(Boundary change: notional Lab. Co-op.)

CLYDEBANK AND MILNGAVIE
*E.*52,092   *T.*75.03%
†A. Worthington, *Lab.* 21,583
J. Yuill, *SNP* 8,263
Ms N. Morgan, *C.* 4,885
K. Moody, *LD* 4,086
I. Sanderson, *Ref.* 269
Lab. majority 13,320
(Boundary change: notional Lab.)

CLYDESDALE
*E.*63,428   *T.*71.60%
*J. Hood, *Lab.* 23,859
A. Doig, *SNP* 10,050
M. Izatt, *C.* 7,396
Mrs S. Grieve, *LD* 3,796
K. Smith, *BNP* 311
Lab. majority 13,809
(April 1992, Lab. maj. 10,187)

COATBRIDGE AND CHRYSTON
*E.*52,024   *T.*72.30%
†T. Clarke, *Lab.* 25,697
B. Nugent, *SNP* 6,402
A. Wauchope, *C.* 3,216
Mrs M. Daly, *LD* 2,048
B. Bowsley, *Ref.* 249
Lab. majority 19,295
(Boundary change: notional Lab.)

CUMBERNAULD AND KILSYTH
*E.*48,032   *T.*75.00%
Ms R. McKenna, *Lab.* 21,141
C. Barrie, *SNP* 10,013
I. Sewell, *C.* 2,441
J. Biggam, *LD* 1,368
Ms J Kara, *ProLife* 609
K. McEwan, *SSA* 345
Ms P. Cook, *Ref.* 107
Lab. majority 11,128
(April 1992, Lab. maj. 9,215)

CUNNINGHAME NORTH
*E.*55,526   *T.*74.07%
*B. Wilson, *Lab.* 20,686
Mrs M. Mitchell, *C.* 9,647
Ms K. Nicoll, *SNP* 7,584
Ms K. Freel, *LD* 2,271
Ms L. McDaid, *Soc. Lab.* 501
I. Winton, *Ref.* 440
Lab. majority 11,039
(April 1992, Lab. maj. 2,939)

CUNNINGHAME SOUTH
*E.*49,543   *T.*71.54%
*B. Donohoe, *Lab.* 22,233
Mrs M. Burgess, *SNP* 7,364
Mrs P. Paterson, *C.* 3,571
E. Watson, *LD* 1,604
K. Edwin, *Soc. Lab.* 494
A. Martlew, *Ref.* 178
Lab. majority 14,869
(April 1992, Lab. maj. 10,680)

DUMBARTON
*E.*56,229   *T.*73.39%
*J. McFall, *Lab. Co-op.* 20,470

W. Mackechnie, *SNP* 9,587
P. Ramsay, *C.* 7,283
A. Reid, *LD* 3,144
L. Robertson, *SSA* 283
G. Dempster, *Ref.* 255
D. Lancaster, *UK Ind.* 242
Lab. Co-op. majority 10,883
(April 1992, Lab. maj. 6,129)

DUMFRIES
*E.*62,759   *T.*78.92%
R. Brown, *Lab.* 23,528
S. Stevenson, *C.* 13,885
R. Higgins, *SNP* 5,977
N. Wallace, *LD* 5,487
D. Parker, *Ref.* 533
Ms E. Hunter, *NLP* 117
Lab. majority 9,643
(Boundary change: notional C.)

DUNDEE EAST
*E.*58,388   *T.*69.41%
†J. McAllion, *Lab.* 20,718
Ms S. Robison, *SNP* 10,757
B. Mackie, *C.* 6,397
Dr G. Saluja, *LD* 1,677
E. Galloway, *Ref.* 601
H. Duke, *SSA* 232
Ms E. MacKenzie, *NLP* 146
Lab. majority 9,961
(Boundary change: notional Lab.)

DUNDEE WEST
*E.*57,346   *T.*67.67%
†E. Ross, *Lab.* 20,875
J. Dorward, *SNP* 9,016
N. Powrie, *C.* 5,105
Dr E. Dick, *LD* 2,972
Ms M. Ward, *SSA* 428
J. MacMillan, *Ref.* 411
Lab. majority 11,859
(Boundary change: notional Lab.)

DUNFERMLINE EAST
*E.*52,072   *T.*70.25%
†Rt. Hon. G. Brown, *Lab.* 24,441
J. Ramage, *SNP* 5,690
I. Mitchell, *C.* 3,656
J. Tolson, *LD* 2,164
T. Dunsmore, *Ref.* 632
Lab. majority 18,751
(Boundary change: notional Lab.)

DUNFERMLINE WEST
*E.*52,467   *T.*69.44%
†Ms R. Squire, *Lab.* 19,338
J. Lloyd, *SNP* 6,984
Mrs E. Harris, *LD* 4,963
K. Newton, *C.* 4,606
J. Bain, *Ref.* 543
Lab. majority 12,354
(Boundary change: notional Lab.)

EAST KILBRIDE
*E.*65,229   *T.*74.81%
†A. Ingram, *Lab.* 27,584
G. Gebbie, *SNP* 10,200
C. Herbertson, *C.* 5,863
Mrs K. Philbrick, *LD* 3,527
J. Deighan, *ProLife* 1,170
Ms J. Gray, *Ref.* 306
E. Gilmour, *NLP* 146

Lab. majority 17,384
(Boundary change: notional Lab.)

EAST LOTHIAN
E.57,441   T.75.61%
†J. Home Robertson, Lab.	22,881
M. Fraser, C.	8,660
D. McCarthy, SNP	6,825
Ms A. MacAskill, LD	4,575
N. Nash, Ref.	491

Lab. majority 14,221
(Boundary change: notional Lab.)

EASTWOOD
E.66,697   T.78.32%
J. Murphy, Lab.	20,766
P. Cullen, C.	17,530
D. Yates, SNP	6,826
Dr C. Mason, LD	6,110
D. Miller, Ref.	497
Dr M. Tayan, ProLife	393
D. McPherson, UK Ind.	113

Lab. majority 3,236
(Boundary change: notional C.)

EDINBURGH CENTRAL
E.63,695   T.67.09%
†A. Darling, Lab.	20,125
M. Scott-Hayward, C.	9,055
Ms F. Hyslop, SNP	6,750
Ms K. Utting, LD	5,605
Ms L. Hendry, Green	607
A. Skinner, Ref.	495
M. Benson, Ind. Dem.	98

Lab. majority 11,070
(Boundary change: notional Lab.)

EDINBURGH EAST AND MUSSELBURGH
E.59,648   T.70.61%
†Dr G. Strang, Lab.	22,564
D. White, SNP	8,034
K. Ward, C.	6,483
Dr C. MacKellar, LD	4,511
J. Sibbet, Ref.	526

Lab. majority 14,530
(Boundary change: notional Lab.)

EDINBURGH NORTH AND LEITH
E.61,617   T.66.45%
†M. Chisholm, Lab.	19,209
Ms A. Dana, SNP	8,231
E. Stewart, C.	7,312
Ms H. Campbell, LD	5,335
A. Graham, Ref.	441
G. Brown, SSA	320
P. Douglas-Reid, NLP	97

Lab. majority 10,978
(Boundary change: notional Lab.)

EDINBURGH PENTLANDS
E.59,635   T.76.70%
Ms L. Clark, Lab.	19,675
†Rt. Hon. M. Rifkind, C.	14,813
S. Gibb, SNP	5,952
Dr J. Dawe, LD	4,575
M. McDonald, Ref.	422
R. Harper, Green	224
A. McConnachie, UK Ind.	81

Lab. majority 4,862
(Boundary change: notional C.)

EDINBURGH SOUTH
E.62,467   T.71.78%
†N. Griffiths, Lab.	20,993
Miss E. Smith, C.	9,541
M. Pringle, LD	7,911
Dr J. Hargreaves, SNP	5,791
I. McLean, Ref.	504
B. Dunn, NLP	98

Lab. majority 11,452
(Boundary change: notional Lab.)

EDINBURGH WEST
E.61,133   T.77.91%
D. Gorrie, LD	20,578
†Rt. Hon. Lord J. Douglas-Hamilton, C.	13,325
Ms L. Hinds, Lab.	8,948
G. Sutherland, SNP	4,210
Dr S. Elphick, Ref.	277
P. Coombes, Lib.	263
A. Jack, AS	30

LD majority 7,253
(Boundary change: notional C.)

FALKIRK EAST
E.56,792   T.73.24%
†M. Connarty, Lab.	23,344
K. Brown, SNP	9,959
M. Nicol, C.	5,813
R. Spillane, LD	2,153
S. Mowbray, Ref.	326

Lab. majority 13,385
(Boundary change: notional Lab.)

FALKIRK WEST
E.52,850   T.72.60%
†D. Canavan, Lab.	22,772
D. Alexander, SNP	8,989
Mrs C. Buchanan, C.	4,639
D. Houston, LD	1,970

Lab. majority 13,783
(Boundary change: notional Lab.)

FIFE CENTRAL
E.58,315   T.69.90%
†H. McLeish, Lab.	23,912
Mrs P. Marwick, SNP	10,199
J. Rees-Mogg, C.	3,669
R. Laird, LD	2,610
J. Scrymgeour-Wedderburn, Ref.	375

Lab. majority 13,713
(Boundary change: notional Lab.)

FIFE NORTH EAST
E.58,794   T.71.16%
*M. Campbell, LD	21,432
A. Bruce, C.	11,076
C. Welsh, SNP	4,545
C. Milne, Lab.	4,301
W. Stewart, Ref.	485

LD majority 10,356
(Boundary change: notional LD)

GALLOWAY AND UPPER NITHSDALE
E.52,751   T.79.65%
A. Morgan, SNP	18,449
†Rt. Hon. I. Lang, C.	12,825
Ms K. Clark, Lab.	6,861
J. McKerchar, LD	2,700
R. Wood, Ind.	566
A. Kennedy, Ref.	428
J. Smith, UK Ind.	189

SNP majority 5,624
(Boundary change: notional C.)

GLASGOW ANNIESLAND
E.52,955   T.63.98%
†Rt. Hon. D. Dewar, Lab.	20,951
Dr W. Wilson, SNP	5,797
A. Brocklehurst, C.	3,881
C. McGinty, LD	2,453
A. Majid, ProLife	374
W. Bonnar, SSA	229
A. Milligan, UK Ind.	86
Ms G. McKay, Ref.	84
T. Pringle, NLP	24

Lab. majority 15,154
(Boundary change: notional Lab.)

GLASGOW BAILLIESTON
E.51,152   T.62.27%
†J. Wray, Lab.	20,925
Mrs P. Thomson, SNP	6,085
M. Kelly, C.	2,468
Ms S. Rainger, LD	1,217
J. McVicar, SSA	970
J. McClafferty, Ref.	188

Lab. majority 14,840
(Boundary change: notional Lab.)

GLASGOW CATHCART
E.49,312   T.69.17%
†J. Maxton, Lab.	19,158
Ms M. Whitehead, SNP	6,913
A. Muir, C.	4,248
C. Dick, LD	2,302
Ms Z. Indyk, ProLife	687
R. Stevenson, SSA	458
S. Haldane, Ref.	344

Lab. majority 12,245
(Boundary change: notional Lab.)

GLASGOW GOVAN
E.49,836   T.64.70%
M. Sarwar, Lab.	14,216
Ms N. Sturgeon, SNP	11,302
W. Thomas, C.	2,839
R. Stewart, LD	1,915
A. McCombes, SSA	755
P. Paton, SLU	325
I. Badar, SLI	319
Z. J. Abbasi, SCU	221
K. MacDonald, Ref.	201
J. White, BNP	149

Lab. majority 2,914
(Boundary change: notional Lab.)

GLASGOW KELVIN
E.57,438   T.56.85%
†G. Galloway, Lab.	16,643
Ms S. White, SNP	6,978
Ms E. Buchanan, LD	4,629
D. McPhie, C.	3,539
A. Green, SSA	386
R. Grigor, Ref.	282
V. Vanni, SPGB	102
G. Stidolph, NLP	95

Lab. majority 9,665
(Boundary change: notional Lab.)

GLASGOW MARYHILL
E.52,523   T.56.59%
†Ms M. Fyfe, Lab.	19,301
J. Wailes, SNP	5,037
Ms E. Attwooll, LD	2,119

S. Baldwin, *C.* 1,747
Ms L. Blair, *NLP* 651
Ms A. Baker, *SSA* 409
J. Hanif, *ProLife* 344
R. Paterson, *Ref.* 77
S. Johnstone, *SEP* 36
Lab. majority 14,264
(Boundary change: notional Lab.)

GLASGOW POLLOK
*E.*49,284   *T.*66.56%
†I. Davidson, *Lab. Co-op.* 19,653
D. Logan, *SNP* 5,862
T. Sheridan, *SSA* 3,639
E. Hamilton, *C.* 1,979
D. Jago, *LD* 1,137
Ms M. Gott, *ProLife* 380
D. Haldane, *Ref.* 152
Lab. Co-op. majority 13,791
(Boundary change: notional Lab. Co-op.)

GLASGOW RUTHERGLEN
*E.*50,646   *T.*70.14%
†T. McAvoy, *Lab. Co-op.* 20,430
I. Gray, *SNP* 5,423
R. Brown, *LD* 5,167
D. Campbell Bannerman, *C.* 3,288
G. Easton, *Ind. Lab.* 812
Ms R. Kane, *SSA* 251
Ms J. Kerr, *Ref.* 150
Lab. Co-op. majority 15,007
(Boundary change: notional Lab. Co-op.)

GLASGOW SHETTLESTON
*E.*47,990   *T.*55.87%
†D. Marshall, *Lab.* 19,616
H. Hanif, *SNP* 3,748
C. Simpson, *C.* 1,484
Ms K. Hiles, *LD* 1,061
Ms C. McVicar, *SSA* 482
R. Currie, *BNP* 191
T. Montguire, *Ref.* 151
J. Graham, *WRP* 80
Lab. majority 15,868
(Boundary change: notional Lab.)

GLASGOW SPRINGBURN
*E.*53,473   *T.*59.05%
†M. Martin, *Lab.* 22,534
J. Brady, *SNP* 5,208
M.Holdsworth, *C.* 1,893
J. Alexander, *LD* 1,349
J. Lawson, *SSA* 407
A. Keating, *Ref.* 186
Lab. majority 17,326
(Boundary change: notional Lab.)

GORDON
*E.*58,767   *T.*71.89%
†M. Bruce, *LD* 17,999
J. Porter, *C.* 11,002
R. Lochhead, *SNP* 8,435
Ms L. Kirkhill, *Lab.* 4,350
F. Pidcock, *Ref.* 459
LD majority 6,997
(Boundary change: notional C.)

GREENOCK AND INVERCLYDE
*E.*48,818   *T.*71.05%
†Dr N. Godman, *Lab.* 19,480
B. Goodall, *SNP* 6,440

R. Ackland, *LD* 4,791
H. Swire, *C.* 3,976
Lab. majority 13,040
(Boundary change: notional Lab.)

HAMILTON NORTH AND
BELLSHILL
*E.*53,607   *T.*70.88%
†Dr J. Reid, *Lab.* 24,322
M. Matheson, *SNP* 7,255
G. McIntosh, *C.* 3,944
K. Legg, *LD* 1,924
R. Conn, *Ref.* 554
Lab. majority 17,067
(Boundary change: notional Lab.)

HAMILTON SOUTH
*E.*46,562   *T.*71.07%
†G. Robertson, *Lab.* 21,709
I. Black, *SNP* 5,831
R. Kilgour, *C.* 2,858
R. Pitts, *LD* 1,693
C. Gunn, *ProLife* 684
S. Brown, *Ref.* 316
Lab. majority 15,878
(Boundary change: notional Lab.)
See also Stop-press

INVERNESS EAST, NAIRN AND
LOCHABER
*E.*65,701   *T.*72.71%
D. Stewart, *Lab.* 16,187
F. Ewing, *SNP* 13,848
S. Gallagher, *LD* 8,364
Mrs M. Scanlon, *C.* 8,355
Ms W. Wall, *Ref.* 436
M. Falconer, *Green* 354
D. Hart, *Ch. U.* 224
Lab. majority 2,339
(Boundary change: notional LD)

KILMARNOCK AND LOUDOUN
*E.*61,376   *T.*77.24%
D. Browne, *Lab.* 23,621
A. Neil, *SNP* 16,365
D. Taylor, *C.* 5,125
J. Stewart, *LD* 1,891
W. Sneddon, *Ref.* 284
W. Gilmour, *NLP* 123
Lab. majority 7,256
(April 1992, Lab. maj. 6,979)

KIRKCALDY
*E.*52,186   *T.*67.02%
†L. Moonie, *Lab. Co-op.* 18,730
S. Hosie, *SNP* 8,020
Miss C. Black, *C.* 4,779
J. Mainland, *LD* 3,031
V. Baxter, *Ref.* 413
Lab. Co-op. majority 10,710
(Boundary change: notional Lab. Co-op.)

LINLITHGOW
*E.*53,706   *T.*73.84%
†T. Dalyell, *Lab.* 21,469
K. MacAskill, *SNP* 10,631
T. Kerr, *C.* 4,964
A. Duncan, *LD* 2,331
K. Plomer, *Ref.* 259
Lab. majority 10,838
(Boundary change: notional Lab.)

LIVINGSTON
*E.*60,296   *T.*71.04%
†Rt. Hon. R. Cook, *Lab.* 23,510
P. Johnston, *SNP* 11,763
H. Craigie Halkett, *C.* 4,028
E. Hawthorn, *LD* 2,876
Ms H. Campbell, *Ref.* 444
M. Culbert, *SPGB* 213
Lab. majority 11,747
(Boundary change: notional Lab.)

MIDLOTHIAN
*E.*47,552   *T.*74.13%
†E. Clarke, *Lab.* 18,861
L. Millar, *SNP* 8,991
Miss A. Harper, *C.* 3,842
R. Pinnock, *LD* 3,235
K. Docking, *Ref.* 320
Lab. majority 9,870
(Boundary change: notional Lab.)

MORAY
*E.*58,302   *T.*68.21%
†Mrs M. Ewing, *SNP* 16,529
A. Findlay, *C.* 10,963
L. Macdonald, *Lab.* 7,886
Ms D. Storr, *LD* 3,548
P. Mieklejohn, *Ref.* 840
SNP majority 5,566
(Boundary change: notional SNP)

MOTHERWELL AND WISHAW
*E.*52,252   *T.*70.08%
F. Roy, *Lab.* 21,020
J. McGuigan, *SNP* 8,229
S. Dickson, *C.* 4,024
A. Mackie, *LD* 2,331
C. Herriot, *Soc. Lab.* 797
T. Russell, *Ref.* 218
Lab. majority 12,791
(Boundary change: notional Lab.)

OCHIL
*E.*56,572   *T.*77.40%
†M. O'Neill, *Lab.* 19,707
G. Reid, *SNP* 15,055
A. Hogarth, *C.* 6,383
Mrs A. Watters, *LD* 2,262
D. White, *Ref.* 210
I. McDonald, *D. Nat.* 104
M. Sullivan, *NLP* 65
Lab. majority 4,652
(Boundary change: notional Lab.)

ORKNEY AND SHETLAND
*E.*32,291   *T.*64.00%
*J. Wallace, *LD* 10,743
J. Paton, *Lab.* 3,775
W. Ross, *SNP* 2,624
H. Vere Anderson, *C.* 2,527
F. Adamson, *Ref.* 820
Ms C. Wharton, *NLP* 116
A. Robertson, *Ind.* 60
LD majority 6,968
(April 1992, LD maj. 5,033)

PAISLEY NORTH
*E.*49,725   *T.*68.65%
†Mrs I. Adams, *Lab.* 20,295
I. Mackay, *SNP* 7,481
K. Brookes, *C.* 3,267
A. Jelfs, *LD* 2,365
R. Graham, *ProLife* 531

E. Mathew, *Ref.*   196
Lab. majority 12,814
(Boundary change: notional Lab.)

PAISLEY SOUTH
*E.*54,040   *T.*69.12%
†G. McMaster, *Lab. Co-op.*   21,482
W. Martin, *SNP*   8,732
Ms E. McCartin, *LD*   3,500
R. Reid, *C.*   3,237
J. Lardner, *Ref.*   254
S. Clerkin, *SSA*   146
Lab. Co-op. majority 12,750
(Boundary change: notional Lab.
Co-op.)
See also page 233

PERTH
*E.*60,313   *T.*73.87%
†Ms R. Cunningham, *SNP*   16,209
J. Godfrey, *C.*   13,068
D. Alexander, *Lab.*   11,036
C. Brodie, *LD*   3,583
R. MacAuley, *Ref.*   366
M. Henderson, *UK Ind.*   289
SNP majority 3,141
(Boundary change: notional C.)

RENFREWSHIRE WEST
*E.*52,348   *T.*76.00%
†T. Graham, *Lab.*   18,525
C. Campbell, *SNP*   10,546
C. Cormack, *C.*   7,387
B. MacPherson, *LD*   3,045
S. Lindsay, *Ref.*   283
Lab. majority 7,979
(Boundary change: notional Lab.)

ROSS, SKYE AND INVERNESS
WEST
*E.*55,639   *T.*71.81%
†C. Kennedy, *LD*   15,472
D. Munro, *Lab.*   11,453
Mrs M. Paterson, *SNP*   7,821
Miss M. Macleod, *C.*   4,368
L. Durance, *Ref.*   535
A. Hopkins, *Green*   306
LD majority 4,019
(Boundary change: notional LD)

ROXBURGH AND BERWICKSHIRE
*E.*47,259   *T.*73.91%
†A. Kirkwood, *LD*   16,243
D. Younger, *C.*   8,337
Ms H. Eadie, *Lab.*   5,226
M. Balfour, *SNP*   3,959
J. Curtis, *Ref.*   922
P. Neilson, *UK Ind.*   202
D. Lucas, *NLP*   42
LD majority 7,906
(Boundary change: notional LD)

STIRLING
*E.*52,491   *T.*81.84%
Mrs A. McGuire, *Lab.*   20,382
†Rt. Hon. M. Forsyth, *C.*   13,971
E. Dow, *SNP*   5,752
A. Tough, *LD*   2,675
W. McMurdo, *UK Ind.*   154
Ms E. Olsen, *Value Party*   24
Lab. majority 6,411
(Boundary change: notional C.)

STRATHKELVIN AND BEARSDEN
*E.*62,974   *T.*78.94%
†S. Galbraith, *Lab.*   26,278

D. Sharpe, *C.*   9,986
G. McCormick, *SNP*   8,111
J. Morrison, *LD*   4,843
D. Wilson, *Ref.*   339
Ms J. Fisher, *NLP*   155
Lab. majority 16,292
(Boundary change: notional Lab.)

TAYSIDE NORTH
*E.*61,398   *T.*74.25%
J. Swinney, *SNP*   20,447
†W. Walker, *C.*   16,287
I. McFatridge, *Lab.*   5,141
P. Regent, *LD*   3,716
SNP majority 4,160
(Boundary change: notional C.)

TWEEDDALE, ETTRICK AND
LAUDERDALE
*E.*50,891   *T.*76.64%
M. Moore, *LD*   12,178
K. Geddes, *Lab.*   10,689
A. Jack, *C.*   8,623
I. Goldie, *SNP*   6,671
C. Mowbray, *Ref.*   406
J. Hein, *Lib.*   387
D. Paterson, *NLP*   47
LD majority 1,489
(Boundary change: notional LD)

WESTERN ISLES
*E.*22,983   *T.*70.08%
*C. Macdonald, *Lab.*   8,955
Dr A. Lorne Gillies, *SNP*   5,379
J. McGrigor, *C.*   1,071
N. Mitchison, *LD*   495
R. Lionel, *Ref.*   206
Lab. majority 3,576

NORTHERN IRELAND

ANTRIM EAST
*E.*58,963   *T.*58.26%
†R. Beggs, *UUP*   13,318
S. Neeson, *All.*   6,929
J. McKee, *DUP*   6,682
T. Dick, *C.*   2,334
W. Donaldson, *PUP*   1,757
D. O'Connor, *SDLP*   1,576
R. Mason, *Ind.*   1,145
Ms C. McAuley, *SF*   543
Ms M. McCann, *NLP*   69
UUP majority 6,389
(Boundary change: notional UUP)

ANTRIM NORTH
*E.*72,411   *T.*63.78%
*Revd I. Paisley, *DUP*   21,495
J. Leslie, *UUP*   10,921
S. Farren, *SDLP*   7,333
J. McCarry, *SF*   2,896
Dr D. Alderdice, *All.*   2,845
Ms B. Hinds, *NI Women*   580
J. Wright, *NLP*   116
DUP majority 10,574
(April 1992, DUP maj. 14,936)

ANTRIM SOUTH
*E.*69,414   *T.*57.91%
†C. Forsythe, *UUP*   23,108

D. McClelland, *SDLP*   6,497
D. Ford, *All.*   4,668
H. Smyth, *PUP*   3,490
H. Cushinan, *SF*   2,229
Ms B. Briggs, *NLP*   203
UUP majority 16,611
(Boundary change: notional UUP)

BELFAST EAST
*E.*61,744   *T.*63.21%
†P. Robinson, *DUP*   16,640
R. Empey, *UUP*   9,886
J. Hendron, *All.*   9,288
Miss S. Dines, *C.*   928
D. Corr, *SF*   810
Mrs P. Lewsley, *SDLP*   629
D. Dougan, *NIFT*   541
J. Bell, *WP*   237
D. Collins, *NLP*   70
DUP majority 6,754
(Boundary change: notional DUP)

BELFAST NORTH
*E.*64,577   *T.*64.19%
†C. Walker, *UUP*   21,478
A. Maginness, *SDLP*   8,454
G. Kelly, *SF*   8,375
T. Campbell, *All.*   2,221
P. Emerson, *Green*   539

P. Treanor, *WP*   297
Ms A. Gribben, *NLP*   88
UUP majority 13,024
(Boundary change: notional UUP)

BELFAST SOUTH
*E.*63,439   *T.*62.24%
†Revd M. Smyth, *UUP*   14,201
Dr A. McDonnell, *SDLP*   9,601
D. Ervine, *PUP*   5,687
S. McBride, *All.*   5,112
S. Hayes, *SF*   2,019
Ms A. Campbell, *NI Women*   1,204
Miss M. Boal, *C.*   962
N. Cusack, *Ind. Lab.*   292
P. Lynn, *WP*   286
J. Anderson, *NLP*   120
UUP majority 4,600
(Boundary change: notional UUP)

BELFAST WEST
*E.*61,785   *T.*74.27%
G. Adams, *SF*   25,662
†Dr J. Hendron, *SDLP*   17,753
F. Parkinson, *UUP*   1,556
J. Lowry, *WP*   721
L. Kennedy, *HR*   102
Ms M. Daly, *NLP*   91
SF majority 7,909
(Boundary change: notional SDLP)

DOWN NORTH
E.63,010   T.58.03%
†R. McCartney, *UKU*   12,817
A. McFarland, *UUP*   11,368
Sir O. Napier, *All.*   7,554
L. Fee, *C.*   1,810
Miss M. Farrell, *SDLP*   1,602
Ms J. Morrice, *NI Women*   1,240
T. Mullins, *NLP*   108
R. Mooney, *NIP*   67
UKU majority 1,449
(Boundary change: notional Popular
Unionist)

DOWN SOUTH
E.69,855   T.70.84%
†E. McGrady, *SDLP*   26,181
D. Nesbitt, *UUP*   16,248
M. Murphy, *SF*   5,127
J. Crozier, *All.*   1,711
Ms R. McKeon, *NLP*   219
SDLP majority 9,933
(Boundary change: notional SDLP)

FERMANAGH AND SOUTH
TYRONE
E.64,600   T.74.75%
†K. Maginnis, *UUP*   24,862
G. McHugh, *SF*   11,174
T. Gallagher, *SDLP*   11,060
S. Farry, *All.*   977
S. Gillan, *NLP*   217
UUP majority 13,688
(Boundary change: notional UUP)

FOYLE
E.67,620   T.70.71%
†J. Hume, *SDLP*   25,109
M. McLaughlin, *SF*   11,445
W. Hay, *DUP*   10,290
Mrs H.-M. Bell, *All.*   817
D. Brennan, *NLP*   154

SDLP majority 13,664
(Boundary change: notional SDLP)

LAGAN VALLEY
E.71,225   T.62.21%
J. Donaldson, *UUP*   24,560
S. Close, *All.*   7,635
E. Poots, *DUP*   6,005
Ms D. Kelly, *SDLP*   3,436
S. Sexton, *C.*   1,212
Ms S. Ramsey, *SF*   1,110
Ms F. McCarthy, *WP*   203
H. Finlay, *NLP*   149
UUP majority 16,925
(Boundary change: notional UUP)

LONDONDERRY EAST
E.58,831   T.64.77%
†W. Ross, *UUP*   13,558
G. Campbell, *DUP*   9,764
A. Doherty, *SDLP*   8,273
M. O'Kane, *SF*   3,463
Ms Y. Boyle, *All.*   2,427
J. Holmes, *C.*   436
Ms C. Gallen, *NLP*   100
I. Anderson, *Nat. Dem.*   81
UUP majority 3,794
(Boundary change: notional UUP)

NEWRY AND ARMAGH
E.70,652   T.75.40%
†S. Mallon, *SDLP*   22,904
D. Kennedy, *UUP*   18,015
P. McNamee, *SF*   11,218
P. Whitcroft, *All.*   1,015
D. Evans, *NLP*   123
SDLP majority 4,889
(Boundary change: notional SDLP)

STRANGFORD
E.69,980   T.59.47%
†Rt. Hon. J. Taylor, *UUP*   18,431

Mrs I. Robinson, *DUP*   12,579
K. McCarthy, *All.*   5,467
P. O'Reilly, *SDLP*   2,775
G. Chalk, *C.*   1,743
G. O Fachtna, *SF*   503
Mrs S. Mullins, *NLP*   121
UUP majority 5,852
(Boundary change: notional UUP)

TYRONE WEST
E.58,168   T.79.55%
W. Thompson, *UUP*   16,003
J. Byrne, *SDLP*   14,842
P. Doherty, *SF*   14,280
Ms A. Gormley, *All.*   829
T. Owens, *WP*   230
R. Johnstone, *NLP*   91
UUP majority 1,161
(Boundary change: notional DUP)

ULSTER MID
E.58,836   T.86.12%
M. McGuinness, *SF*   20,294
†Revd W. McCrea, *DUP*   18,411
D. Haughey, *SDLP*   11,205
E. Bogues, *All.*   460
Mrs M. Donnelly, *WP*   238
Ms M. Murray, *NLP*   61
SF majority 1,883
(Boundary change: notional DUP)

UPPER BANN
E.70,398   T.67.88%
*D. Trimble, *UUP*   20,836
Ms B. Rodgers, *SDLP*   11,584
Ms B. O'Hagan, *SF*   5,773
M. Carrick, *DUP*   5,482
Dr W. Ramsay, *All.*   3,017
T. French, *WP*   554
B. Price, *C.*   433
J. Lyons, *NLP*   108
UUP majority 9,252

COMMONWEALTH PARLIAMENTARY ASSOCIATION (1911)

The Commonwealth Parliamentary Association consists of 143 branches in the national, state, provincial or territorial parliaments in the countries of the Commonwealth. Conferences and general assemblies are held every year in different countries of the Commonwealth.

President (1999–2000), Rt. Hon. Betty Boothroyd, MP, Speaker of the House of Commons, United Kingdom
Chairman of the Executive Committee (1996–9), Hon. Billie Miller, MP (Barbados)
Secretary-General, A. R. Donahoe, QC, Suite 700, Westminster House, 7 Millbank, London SW1P 3JA

UNITED KINGDOM BRANCH

Hon. Presidents, The Lord Chancellor; Madam Speaker
Chairman of Branch, Rt. Hon. Tony Blair, MP
Chairman of Executive Committee, Donald Anderson, MP

Secretary, A. Pearson, Westminster Hall, Houses of Parliament, London, SW1A 0AA

THE INTER-PARLIAMENTARY UNION (1889)

The Union exists to facilitate personal contact between members of all parliaments in the promotion of representative institutions, peace and international co-operation.

Secretary-General, A. Johnsson, Place du Petit-Saconnex, CP 438, 1211 Geneva 19, Switzerland

BRITISH GROUP

Palace of Westminster, London SW1A 0AA

Hon. Presidents, The Lord Chancellor; Madam Speaker
President, Rt. Hon. Tony Blair, MP
Chairman, David Marshall, MP
Secretary, D. Ramsay

European Parliament

European Parliament elections take place at five-yearly intervals; the first direct elections to the Parliament were held in 1979. In mainland Britain MEPs were elected in all constituencies on a first-past-the-post basis until the elections of June 1999; in Northern Ireland three MEPs have been elected by the single transferable vote system of proportional representation since 1979. From 1979 to 1994 the number of seats held by the UK in the European Parliament was 81. At the June 1994 election the number of seats increased to 87 (England 71, Wales 5, Scotland, 8, Northern Ireland 3).

At the European Parliament elections held on 10 June 1999, all British MEPs were elected under a 'closed-list' regional system of proportional representation, with England being divided into nine regions and Scotland and Wales each constituting a region. Parties submitted a list of candidates for each region in their own order of preference. Voters voted for a party or an independent candidate, and the first seat in each region was allocated to the party or candidate with the highest number of votes. The rest of the seats in each region were then allocated broadly in proportion to each party's share of the vote. Each region returned the following number of members: East Midlands, 6; Eastern, 8; London, 10; North East, 4; North West, 10; South East, 11; South West, 7; West Midlands, 8; Yorkshire and the Humber, 7; Wales, 5; Scotland, 8.

British subjects and citizens of the Irish Republic are eligible for election to the European Parliament provided they are 21 or over and not subject to disqualification. Since 1994, nationals of member states of the European Union have had the right to vote in elections to the European Parliament in the UK as long as they are entered on the electoral register.

MEPs currently receive a salary from the parliaments or governments of their respective member states, set at the level of the national parliamentary salary and subject to national taxation rules (for salary of British MPs, *see* page 218). A proposal that all MEPs should be paid the same rate of salary out of the EU budget, and subject to the EC tax rate, was under negotiation between the European Parliament and the Council of Ministers at the time of going to press.

UK MEMBERS AS AT 10 JUNE 1999

*Denotes membership of the last European Parliament

Atkins, Rt. Hon. Sir Robert (*b.* 1946), *C., North West*
Attwooll, Ms Elspeth M.-A. (*b.* 1943), *LD, Scotland*
*Balfe, Richard A. (*b.* 1944), *Lab., London*
Beazley, Christopher J. P. (*b.* 1952), *C., Eastern*
Bethell, The Lord (*b.* 1938), *C., London*
*Bowe, David R. (*b.* 1955), *Lab., Yorkshire and the Humber*
Bowis, John C., OBE (*b.* 1945), *C., London*
Bradbourn, Philip, OBE (*b.* 1951), *C., West Midlands*
Bushill-Matthews, Philip (*b.* 1943), *C., West Midlands*
Callanan, Martin (*b.* 1961), *C., North East*
Cashman, Michael (*b.* 1950), *Lab., West Midlands*
*Chichester, Giles B. (*b.* 1946), *C., South West*
Clegg, Nicholas W. P. (*b.* 1967), *LD, East Midlands*
*Corbett, Richard (*b.* 1955), *Lab., Yorkshire and the Humber*
*Corrie, John A. (*b.* 1935), *C., West Midlands*

Davies, Christopher G. (*b.* 1954), *LD, North West*
Deva, Niranjan J. A. (Nirj), FRSA (*b.* 1948), *C., South East*
*Donnelly, Alan J. (*b.* 1957), *Lab., North East*
Dover, Den (*b.* 1938), *C., North West*
Duff, Andrew N. (*b.* 1950), *LD, Eastern*
*Elles, James E. M. (*b.* 1949), *C., South East*
Evans, Ms Jillian R. (*b.* 1959), *PC, Wales*
Evans, Jonathan P., FRSA (*b.* 1950), *C., Wales*
*Evans, Robert J. E. (*b.* 1956), *Lab., London*
Farage, Nigel (*b.* 1964), *UK Ind., South East*
*Ford, J. Glyn (*b.* 1950), *Lab., South West*
Foster, Mrs Jacqui (*b.* 1947), *C., North West*
Gill, Ms Neena (*b.* 1956), *Lab., West Midlands*
Goodwill, Robert (*b.* 1956), *C., Yorkshire and the Humber*
*Green, Mrs Pauline (*b.* 1948), *Lab., London*
Hannan, Daniel (*b.* 1971), *C., South East*
Harbour, Malcolm (*b.* 1947), *C., West Midlands*
Heaton-Harris, Christopher (*b.* 1967), *C., East Midlands*
Helmer, Roger (*b.* 1944), *C., East Midlands*
Holmes, Michael (*b.* 1938), *UK Ind., South West*
*Howitt, Richard (*b.* 1961), *Lab., Eastern*
Hudghton, Ian (*b.* 1951), *SNP, Scotland*
*Hughes, Stephen S. (*b.* 1952), *Lab., North East*
Huhne, Christopher M. P., OBE (*b.* 1954), *LD, South East*
*Hume, John, MP (*b.* 1937), *SDLP, Northern Ireland*
Inglewood, The Lord (*b.* 1951), *C., North West*
*Jackson, Mrs Caroline F., D.PHIL. (*b.* 1946), *C., South West*
Khanbhai, Bashir (*b.* 1945), *C., Eastern*
*Kinnock, Mrs Glenys E. (*b.* 1944), *Lab., Wales*
Kirkhope, Timothy J. R. (*b.* 1945), *C., Yorkshire and the Humber*
Lambert, Ms Jean D. (*b.* 1950), *Green, London*
Lucas, Ms Caroline, PH.D. (*b.* 1960), *Green, South East*
Ludford, The Baroness (*b.* 1951), *LD, London*
Lynne, Ms Elizabeth (*b.* 1948), *LD, West Midlands*
*McAvan, Ms Linda (*b.* 1962), *Lab., Yorkshire and the Humber*
*McCarthy, Ms Arlene (*b.* 1960), *Lab., North West*
MacCormick, Prof. D. Neil, FBA (*b.* 1941), *SNP, Scotland*
*McMillan-Scott, Edward H. C. (*b.* 1949), *C., Yorkshire and the Humber*
*McNally, Mrs Eryl M. (*b.* 1942), *Lab., Eastern*
*Martin, David W. (*b.* 1954), *Lab., Scotland*
*Miller, William (*b.* 1954), *Lab., Scotland*
Moraes, Claude (*b.* 1965), *Lab., London*
*Morgan, Ms Eluned (*b.* 1967), *Lab., Wales*
*Murphy, Simon F., PH.D. (*b.* 1962), *Lab., West Midlands*
Newton Dunn, William F. (Bill) (*b.* 1941), *C., East Midlands*
Nicholson of Winterbourne, The Baroness (*b.* 1941), *LD, South East*
*Nicholson, James F. (*b.* 1945), *UUP, Northern Ireland*
O'Toole, Ms Barbara M. (Mo) (*b.* 1960), *Lab., North East*
*Paisley, Revd Ian R. K., MP (*b.* 1926), *DUP, Northern Ireland*
Parish, Neil (*b.* 1956), *C., South West*
*Perry, Roy J. (*b.* 1943), *C., South East*
*Provan, James L. C. (*b.* 1936), *C., South East*
Purvis, John R., CBE (*b.* 1938), *C., Scotland*
*Read, Ms I. M. (Mel) (*b.* 1939), *Lab., East Midlands*
*Simpson, Brian (*b.* 1953), *Lab., North West*
*Skinner, Peter W. (*b.* 1959), *Lab., South East*
Stevenson, Struan (*b.* 1948), *C., Scotland*
Stockton, The Earl of (*b.* 1943), *C., South West*
*Sturdy, Robert W. (*b.* 1944), *C., Eastern*
Sumberg, David A. G. (*b.* 1941), *C., North West*
Tannock, Dr Charles (*b.* 1957), *C., London*

Taylor, Ms Catherine D. (*b.* 1973), *Lab., Scotland*
Titford, Jeffrey (*b.* 1933), *UK Ind., Eastern*
*Titley, Gary (*b.* 1950), *Lab., North West*
Van Orden, Geoffrey (*b.* 1945), *C., Eastern*
Villiers, Ms Theresa (*b.* 1968), *C., London*
Wallis, Ms Diana P. (*b.* 1954), *LD, Yorkshire and the Humber*

*Watson, Graham R. (*b.* 1956), *LD, South West*
*Watts, Mark F. (*b.* 1964), *Lab., South East*
*Whitehead, Philip (*b.* 1937), *Lab., East Midlands*
Wyn, Eurig (*b.* 1944), *PC, Wales*
*Wynn, Terence (*b.* 1946), *Lab., North West*

UK REGIONS AS AT 10 JUNE 1999

Abbreviations

ACPFCA	Anti-Corruption Pro Family Christian Alliance
AHRPE	Architect Human Rights Peace in Europe
Anti VAT	Independent Anti Value Added Tax
EFP	English Freedom Party
Ind. Profit	Independent Making a Profit in Europe
Ind. Stable	Independent Open Democracy for Stability
Lower Tax	Account for Lower Scottish Taxes
MEP Ind.	MEP Independent Labour
Soc. All.	Socialist Alliance
SSP	Scottish Socialist Party
WW	Weekly Worker

For other abbreviations, *see* page 235

EASTERN
(Bedfordshire; Cambridgeshire; Essex; Hertfordshire; Luton; Norfolk; Peterborough; Southend-on-Sea; Suffolk; Thurrock)
E.4,019,916　T.24.74%

C.	425,091 (42.75%)
Lab.	250,132 (25.15%)
LD	118,822 (11.95%)
UK Ind.	88,452 (8.89%)
Green	61,334 (6.17%)
Lib.	16,861 (1.70%)
Pro Euro C.	16,340 (1.64%)
BNP	9,356 (0.94%)
Soc. Lab.	6,143 (0.62%)
NLP	1,907 (0.19%)
C. majority	174,959

(June 1994, Lab. maj. 90,087)

MEMBERS ELECTED
*R. Sturdy, *C.*
C. Beazley, *C.*
B. Khanbhai, *C.*
G. Van Orden, *C.*
*Ms E. McNally, *Lab.*
*R. Howitt, *Lab.*
A. Duff, *LD*
J. Titford, *UK Ind.*

EAST MIDLANDS
(Derby; Derbyshire; Leicester; Leicestershire; Lincolnshire; Northamptonshire; Nottingham; Nottinghamshire; Rutland)
E.3,170,517　T.22.83%

C.	285,662 (39.47%)
Lab.	206,756 (28.57%)
LD	92,398 (12.77%)
UK Ind.	54,800 (7.57%)
Green	38,954 (5.38%)

Alt. Lab.	17,409 (2.41%)
Pro Euro C.	11,359 (1.57%)
BNP	9,342 (1.29%)
Soc. Lab.	5,528 (0.76%)
NLP	1,525 (0.21%)
C. majority	78,906

(June 1994, Lab. maj. 229,680)

MEMBERS ELECTED
R. Helmer, *C.*
W. Newton Dunn, *C.*
C. Heaton-Harris, *C.*
*Ms M. Read, *Lab.*
*P. Whitehead, *Lab.*
N. Clegg, *LD*

LONDON
E.4,940,493　T.23.10%

Lab.	399,466 (35.00%)
C.	372,989 (32.68%)
LD	133,058 (11.66%)
Green	87,545 (7.67%)
UK Ind.	61,741 (5.41%)
Soc. Lab.	19,632 (1.72%)
BNP	17,960 (1.57%)
Lib.	16,951 (1.49%)
Pro Euro C.	16,383 (1.44%)
AHRPE	4,851 (0.43%)
Anti VAT	2,596 (0.23%)
Hum.	2,586 (0.23%)
Hemp	2,358 (0.21%)
NLP	2,263 (0.20%)
WW	846 (0.07%)
Lab. majority	26,477

(June 1994, Lab. maj. 346,850)

MEMBERS ELECTED
Miss T. Villiers, *C.*
Dr C. Tannock, *C.*
The Lord Bethell, *C.*
J. Bowis, *C.*
*Ms P. Green, *Lab.*
C. Moraes, *Lab.*
*R. Evans, *Lab.*
*R. Balfe, *Lab.*
Ms S. Ludford, *LD*
Ms J. Lambert, *Green*

NORTH EAST
(Co. Durham; Darlington; Hartlepool; Middlesbrough; Northumberland; Redcar and Cleveland; Stockton-on-Tees; Tyne and Wear)
E.1,954,076　T.19.74%

Lab.	162,573 (42.15%)
C.	105,573 (27.37%)
LD	52,070 (13.50%)

UK Ind.	34,063 (8.83%)
Green	18,184 (4.71%)
Soc. Lab.	4,511 (1.17%)
BNP	3,505 (0.91%)
Pro Euro C.	2,926 (0.76%)
SPGB	1,510 (0.39%)
NLP	826 (0.21%)
Lab. majority	57,000

(June 1994, Lab. maj. 330,689)

MEMBERS ELECTED
M. Callanan, *C.*
*A. Donnelly, *Lab.*
*S. Hughes, *Lab.*
Ms M. O'Toole, *Lab.*

NORTHERN IRELAND
Northern Ireland forms a three-member seat with a single transferable vote system
E.1,190,160　T.57.77%
First Count

*Revd I. Paisley, *DUP*	192,762
*J. Hume, *SDLP*	190,731
*J. Nicholson, *UUP*	119,507
M. McLaughlin, *SF*	117,643
D. Ervine, *PUP*	22,494
R. McCartney, *UKU*	20,283
S. Neeson, *All.*	14,391
J. Anderson, *NLP*	998

MEMBERS ELECTED
*Revd I. Paisley, *DUP*
*J. Hume, *SDLP*
*J. Nicholson, *UUP* (elected on third count)

NORTH WEST
(Blackburn-with-Darwen; Blackpool; Cheshire; Cumbria; Greater Manchester; Halton; Lancashire; Merseyside; Warrington)
E.5,170,524　T.19.67%

C.	360,027 (35.39%)
Lab.	350,511 (34.46%)
LD	119,376 (11.74%)
UK Ind.	66,779 (6.57%)
Green	56,828 (5.59%)
Lib.	22,640 (2.23%)
BNP	13,587 (1.34%)
Soc. Lab.	11,338 (1.11%)
Pro Euro C.	9,816 (0.97%)
ACPFCA	2,251 (0.22%)
NLP	2,114 (0.21%)
Ind. Hum.	1,049 (0.10%)
WW	878 (0.09%)
C. majority	9,516

(June 1994, Lab. maj. 444,569)

MEMBERS ELECTED
The Lord Inglewood, *C.*
Sir Robert Atkins, *C.*
D. Sumberg, *C.*
D. Dover, *C.*
Mrs J. Foster, *C.*
*Ms A. McCarthy, *Lab.*
*G. Titley, *Lab.*
*T. Wynn, *Lab.*
*B. Simpson, *Lab.*
C. Davies, *LD*

SCOTLAND

*E.*3,979,845   *T.*24.83%

Lab.	283,490 (28.68%)
SNP	268,528 (27.17%)
C.	195,296 (19.76%)
LD	96,971 (9.81%)
Green	57,142 (5.78%)
SSP	39,720 (4.02%)
Pro Euro C.	17,781 (1.80%)
UK Ind.	12,549 (1.27%)
Soc. Lab.	9,385 (0.95%)
BNP	3,729 (0.38%)
NLP	2,087 (0.21%)
Lower Tax	1,632 (0.17%)
Lab. majority	14,962

(June 1994, Lab. maj. 148,718)

MEMBERS ELECTED
S. Stevenson, *C.*
J. Purvis, *C.*
*D. Martin, *Lab.*
*W. Miller, *Lab.*
Ms C. Taylor, *Lab.*
Ms E. Attwooll, *LD*
*I. Hughdton, *SNP*
Prof. N. MacCormick, *SNP*

SOUTH EAST

(Bracknell Forest; Brighton and
Hove; Buckinghamshire; East Sussex;
Hampshire; Isle of Wight; Kent;
Medway; Milton Keynes;
Oxfordshire; Portsmouth; Reading;
Slough; Southampton; Surrey; West
Berkshire; West Sussex; Windsor and
Maidenhead; Wokingham)

*E.*5,972,945   *T.*24.95%

C.	661,931 (44.42%)
Lab.	292,146 (19.61%)
LD	228,136 (15.31%)
UK Ind.	144,514 (9.70%)
Green	110,571 (7.42%)
Pro Euro C.	27,305 (1.83%)
BNP	12,161 (0.82%)
Soc. Lab.	7,281 (0.49%)
NLP	2,767 (0.19%)
Ind. Stable	1,857 (0.12%)
Ind. Profit	1,400 (0.09%)
C. majority	369,785

(June 1994, C. maj. 230,122)

MEMBERS ELECTED
*J. Provan, *C.*
*R. Perry, *C.*
D. Hannan, *C.*
*J. Elles, *C.*
N. Deva, *C.*
*P. Skinner, *Lab.*
*M. Watts, *Lab.*

The Baroness Nicholson of
Winterbourne, *LD*
C. Huhne, *LD*
Dr Caroline Lucas, *Green*
N. Farage, *UK Ind.*

SOUTH WEST

(Bath and North-East Somerset;
Bournemouth; Bristol; Cornwall;
Devon; Dorset; Gloucestershire;
North Somerset; Plymouth; Poole;
Scilly Isles; Somerset; South
Gloucestershire; Swindon; Torbay;
Wiltshire)

*E.*3,747,620   *T.*27.81%

C.	434,645 (41.70%)
Lab.	188,362 (18.07%)
LD	171,498 (16.45%)
UK Ind.	111,012 (10.65%)
Green	86,630 (8.31%)
Lib.	21,645 (2.08%)
Pro Euro C.	11,134 (1.07%)
BNP	9,752 (0.94%)
Soc. Lab.	5,741 (0.55%)
NLP	1,968 (0.19%)
C. majority	246,283

(June 1994, LD maj. 3,796)

MEMBERS ELECTED
*Dr Caroline Jackson, *C.*
*G. Chichester, *C.*
The Earl of Stockton, *C.*
N. Parish, *C.*
*G. Ford, *Lab.*
*G. Watson, *LD*
M. Holmes, *UK Ind.*

WALES

*E.*2,211,162   *T.*28.33%

Lab.	199,690 (31.88%)
PC	185,235 (29.57%)
C.	142,631 (22.77%)
LD	51,283 (8.19%)
UK Ind.	19,702 (3.15%)
Green	16,146 (2.58%)
Pro Euro C.	5,834 (0.93%)
Soc. Lab.	4,283 (0.68%)
NLP	1,621 (0.26%)
Lab. majority	14,455

(June 1994, Lab. maj. 368,271)

MEMBERS ELECTED
J. Evans, *C.*
*Ms G. Kinnock, *Lab.*
*Ms E. Morgan, *Lab.*
Ms J. Evans, *PC*
E. Wyn, *PC*

WEST MIDLANDS

(Herefordshire; Shropshire;
Staffordshire; Stoke-on-Trent;
Telford and Wrekin; Warwickshire;
West Midlands Metropolitan
County; Worcestershire)

*E.*4,001,942   *T.*21.21%

C.	321,719 (37.91%)
Lab.	237,671 (28.00%)
LD	95,769 (11.28%)
UK Ind.	49,621 (5.85%)
Green	49,440 (5.83%)
MEP Ind.	36,849 (4.34%)

Lib.	14,954 (1.76%)
BNP	14,344 (1.69%)
Pro Euro C.	11,144 (1.31%)
Soc. All.	7,203 (0.85%)
Soc. Lab.	5,257 (0.62%)
EFP	3,066 (0.36%)
NLP	1,647 (0.19%)
C. majority	84,048

(June 1994, Lab. maj. 268,888)

MEMBERS ELECTED
*J. Corrie, *C.*
P. Bushill-Matthews, *C.*
M. Harbour, *C.*
P. Bradbourn, *C.*
*S. Murphy, *Lab.*
M. Cashman, *Lab.*
Ms N. Gill, *Lab.*
Ms E. Lynne, *LD*

YORKSHIRE AND THE HUMBER

(East Riding of Yorkshire; Kingston-
upon-Hull; North East Lincolnshire;
North Lincolnshire; North
Yorkshire; South Yorkshire; West
Yorkshire; York)

*E.*3,767,227   *T.*19.75%

C.	272,653 (36.64%)
Lab.	233,024 (31.32%)
LD	107,168 (14.40%)
UK Ind.	52,824 (7.10%)
Green	42,604 (5.73%)
Alt. Lab.	9,554 (1.28%)
BNP	8,911 (1.20%)
Pro Euro C.	8,075 (1.09%)
Soc. Lab.	7,650 (1.03%)
NLP	1,604 (0.22%)
C. majority	39,629

(June 1994, Lab. maj. 344,310)

MEMBERS ELECTED
*E. McMillan-Scott, *C.*
T. Kirkhope, *C.*
R. Goodwill, *C.*
*Ms L. McAvan, *Lab.*
*D. Bowe, *Lab.*
*R. Corbett, *Lab.*
Ms D. Wallis, *LD*

BY-ELECTIONS SINCE THE LAST EDITION

SCOTLAND NORTH EAST
(26 November 1998)

E. 584,061   *T.* 20.53%

I. Hughdton, *SNP*	57,445
S. Stevenson, *C.*	23,744
Mrs K. Walker Shaw, *Lab.*	22,086
K. Raffar, *LD*	11,753
H. Duke, *SSP*	2,510
R. Harper, *Green*	2,067
SNP majority	33,701

The Government

THE CABINET AS AT 4 AUGUST 1999

Prime Minister, First Lord of the Treasury and Minister for the Civil Service
The Rt. Hon. Anthony (Tony) Blair, MP, since May 1997
Deputy Prime Minister and Secretary of State for the Environment, Transport and the Regions
The Rt. Hon. John Prescott, MP, since May 1997
Chancellor of the Exchequer
The Rt. Hon. Gordon Brown, MP, since May 1997
Secretary of State for Foreign and Commonwealth Affairs
The Rt. Hon. Robin Cook, MP, since May 1997
Lord Chancellor
The Lord Irvine of Lairg, PC, QC, since May 1997
Secretary of State for the Home Department
The Rt. Hon. Jack Straw, MP, since May 1997
Secretary of State for Education and Employment
The Rt. Hon. David Blunkett, MP, since May 1997
President of the Council and Leader of the House of Commons
The Rt. Hon. Margaret Beckett, MP, since July 1998
Minister for the Cabinet Office and Chancellor of the Duchy of Lancaster
The Rt. Hon. Dr Jack Cunningham, MP, since July 1998
Secretary of State for Scotland
The Rt. Hon. Dr John Reid, MP, since May 1999
Secretary of State for Defence
The Lord Robertson of Port Ellen, PC (until October 1999), since May 1997
Secretary of State for Health
The Rt. Hon. Frank Dobson, MP, since May 1997
Parliamentary Secretary to the Treasury (Chief Whip)
The Rt. Hon. Ann Taylor, MP
Secretary of State for Culture, Media and Sport
The Rt. Hon. Chris Smith, MP, since May 1997
Secretary of State for Northern Ireland
The Rt. Hon. Dr Marjorie (Mo) Mowlam, MP, since May 1997
Secretary of State for Wales
The Rt. Hon. Paul Murphy, MP, since July 1999
Secretary of State for International Development
The Rt. Hon. Clare Short, MP, since May 1997
Secretary of State for Social Security
The Rt. Hon. Alistair Darling, MP, since July 1998
Minister of Agriculture, Fisheries and Food
The Rt. Hon. Nick Brown, MP, since July 1998
Leader of the House of Lords and Minister for Women
The Baroness Jay of Paddington*, since July 1998
Secretary of State for Trade and Industry
The Rt. Hon. Stephen Byers, MP, since January 1999
Chief Secretary to the Treasury
The Rt. Hon. Alan Milburn, MP, since January 1999

The Minister of State at the Department of the Environment, Transport and the Regions with responsibility for Transport, and the Government Chief Whip in the House of Lords will attend Cabinet meetings although they are not members of the Cabinet.
* Appointed as Lord Privy Seal

LAW OFFICERS

Attorney-General
The Lord Williams of Mostyn, QC, since July 1999
Lord Advocate
The Lord Hardie, PC, QC, since May 1997
Solicitor-General
Ross Cranston, MP, since July 1998
Solicitor-General for Scotland
Colin Boyd, QC
Advocate-General for Scotland
Lynda Clark, MP

MINISTERS OF STATE

Agriculture, Fisheries and Food
The Rt. Hon. Joyce Quin, MP
The Baroness Hayman
Cabinet Office
The Lord Falconer of Thoroton, QC
Ian McCartney, MP
Defence
John Spellar, MP (*Armed Forces*)
The Baroness Symons of Vernham Dean (*Defence Procurement*)
Education and Employment
The Rt. Hon. Andrew Smith, MP (*Employment*)
Estelle Morris, MP (*School Standards*)
The Baroness Blackstone, PH.D. (*Lifelong Learning*)
Environment, Transport and the Regions
The Lord Macdonald of Tradeston (*Transport*)
The Rt. Hon. Michael Meacher, MP (*Environment*)
The Rt. Hon. Hilary Armstrong, MP (*Local Government, Regions*)
The Rt. Hon. Nick Raynsford, MP (*Housing, Planning, London*)
Foreign and Commonwealth Office
Geoffrey Hoon, MP (*Minister for Europe*)
Peter Hain, MP
John Battle, MP
Health
John Denham, MP (*NHS Structure and Resources*)
The Rt. Hon. Tessa Jowell, MP (*Public Health, Women's Issues*)
Home Office
The Rt. Hon. Paul Boateng, MP
Charles Clarke, MP
Barbara Roche, MP
Northern Ireland Office
The Rt. Hon. Adam Ingram, MP (*Security, Victims, Europe, Constitution*)
Scotland Office
Brian Wilson, MP
Social Security
Jeff Rooker, MP
Trade and Industry
The Rt. Hon. Helen Liddell, MP (*Energy, Competitiveness in Europe*)
The Rt. Hon. Richard Caborn, MP (*Trade*)
Patricia Hewitt, MP

Treasury
Dawn Primarolo, MP (*Paymaster-General*)
Stephen Timms, MP (*Financial Secretary*)
Melanie Johnson, MP (*Economic Secretary*)

UNDER-SECRETARIES OF STATE

Agriculture, Fisheries and Food
Elliot Morley, MP
Culture, Media and Sport
Alan Howarth, MP (*Arts*)
Kate Hoey, MP (*Sport*)
Janet Anderson, MP (*Tourism, Film, Broadcasting*)
Defence
Peter Kilfoyle, MP
Education and Employment
Margaret Hodge, MP (*Employment, Under 5s*)
Malcolm Wicks, MP (*Lifelong Learning*)
Jacqui Smith, MP (*School Standards*)
Michael Wills, MP (*Information and Communications Technology*)
Environment, Transport and the Regions
The Lord Whitty
Keith Hill, MP
Chris Mullin, MP
Beverley Hughes, MP
Foreign and Commonwealth Office
The Baroness Scotland of Asthal
Health
John Hutton, MP
The Lord Hunt of Kings Heath
Gisela Stuart, MP
Home Office
Michael O'Brien, MP
The Lord Bassam of Brighton
International Development
George Foulkes, MP
Lord Chancellor's Department
Keith Vaz, MP
David Lock, MP
Northern Ireland Office
John McFall, MP (*Education, Economic Development*)
The Lord Dubs (*Environment, Agriculture*)
George Howarth, MP (*Political Development, Equality, Human Rights*)
Privy Council Office
Paddy Tipping, MP
Social Security
The Baroness Hollis of Heigham, D.Phil. (*Child Benefit, Child Support, War Pensions*)
Angela Eagle, MP (*Income-related Benefits, International and Green Issues*)
Hugh Bayley, MP (*Disability and Sickness Benefits, Deregulation, Independent Living Fund*)
Trade and Industry
Dr Kim Howells, MP (*Competition, Consumer Affairs*)
Alan Johnson, MP (*Employment Relations, the Post Office, Industry*)
The Lord Sainsbury of Turville§ (*Science*)
Welsh Office
David Hanson, MP
§ Unpaid

GOVERNMENT WHIPS

HOUSE OF LORDS

Captain of the Honourable Corps of Gentlemen-at-Arms (Chief Whip)
The Lord Carter, PC
Captain of The Queen's Bodyguard of the Yeoman of the Guard (Deputy Chief Whip)
The Lord McIntosh of Haringey
Lords-in-Waiting
The Lord Burlison; The Lord Bach
Baronesses-in-Waiting
The Baroness Farrington of Ribbleton; The Baroness Ramsay of Cartvale; The Baroness Amos

HOUSE OF COMMONS

Parliamentary Secretary to the Treasury (Chief Whip)
The Rt. Hon. Ann Taylor, MP
Treasurer of HM Household (Deputy Chief Whip)
Keith Bradley, MP
Comptroller of HM Household
Thomas McAvoy, MP
Vice-Chamberlain of HM Household
Graham Allen, MP
Lords Commissioners
Robert Ainsworth, MP; James Dowd, MP; Clive Betts, MP; David Jamieson, MP; Jane Kennedy, MP
Assistant Whips
David Clelland, MP; Kevin Hughes, MP; Anne McGuire, MP; Michael Hall, MP; Gregory Pope, MP; Gerry Sutcliffe, MP

Government Legislative Programme 1998–9 and Budget Summary

The Queen's Speech

The Queen's Speech was delivered in the House of Lords on 24 November 1998. It included the following main legislative proposals:
– a Bill to end the internal market, require hospitals to meet minimum standards of clinical care, abolish GP fundholding and create Primary Care Trusts
– a Bill to make it easier for hospitals to recover some of the costs of treating road accident victims from insurance companies
– a Bill to reform disability benefits and benefits for new widows and widowers, introduce stakeholder pensions and enable pensions to be split on divorce
– a Bill to guarantee a minimum income for working families, introduce a contribution to child care costs and replace the disability working allowance with a disabled person's tax credit
– a Bill to introduce a Disability Rights Commission
– a Bill to transfer the functions of the Contributions Agency to the Inland Revenue
– a Bill to modernize youth courts, introduce a 'contract of behaviour' for first-time offenders under 17 who plead guilty and are not discharged or jailed, and give greater protection to vulnerable witnesses
– a Bill to modernize the legal aid system
– a Bill to lower the age of consent for homosexuals to 16 in England, Wales and Scotland and 17 in Northern Ireland, and protect vulnerable teenagers from sexual advances by those in a position of trust or authority
– a Bill to remove the right of hereditary peers to sit and vote in the House of Lords as the first stage of reform of the Upper House
– a Bill to reform the treatment of asylum seekers with the aim of reducing the incentive to economic migration, and to restructure the appeals system and regulate immigration advisers
– a Bill to abolish compulsory competitive tendering in local authorities and require authorities to deliver 'best value' and review their services every five years
– a Bill to require local councils to adopt a code of conduct and set up a standards committee, and to enable them to have an elected mayor or a cabinet with a leader
– a Bill to establish a Greater London Authority headed by an elected mayor, transfer responsibility for policing in London from the Home Office to the Authority, and establish a transport executive and a development agency
– a Bill to give employees new rights, including greater protection against unfair dismissal, improved parental leave and the right to union recognition
– a Bill to close a loophole relating to the rating valuation of non-domestic properties
– a Bill to provide a fair basis for water charges and to remove from water companies the power to disconnect householders for non-payment
– a Bill to bring intensive pig farms, poultry batteries and other parts of the food industry under the control of pollution inspectors and establish a single pollution regime called Integrated Pollution Prevention and Control

– a Bill to increase the borrowing limit of Scottish Enterprise
– a Bill to establish the remit of the Financial Services Authority, a new single statutory regulatory body for the financial services industry, and set up a single ombudsman, compensation and appeals scheme
– a Bill to regulate electronic commerce
– a Bill to convert the Commonwealth Development Corporation into a public-private partnership
– a Bill to establish regional development agencies
The Queen's Speech also included the following pledges made on behalf of the Government:
– to continue with economic policies designed to build long-term stability
– to aim for high and stable levels of economic growth and employment
– to raise achievement in schools and improve standards of teaching, including the introduction of a consultation paper on the reform of the teaching profession
– to take forward proposals to establish a Food Standards Agency
– to increase expenditure on health and education
– to work for the successful establishment of the Scottish Parliament and the Welsh Assembly and the full implementation of all aspects of the Belfast Agreement
– to publish a White Paper setting out arrangements for a new system of appointing life peers and to establish a Royal Commission on the Reform of the House of Lords
– to publish a draft Freedom of Information Bill, to be subject to pre-legislative scrutiny in both Houses of Parliament
– to publish draft legislation on the reform of political party funding, the conduct of local councils' business and the establishment of a Strategic Rail Authority
– to tackle global poverty and promote sustainable development
– to play a leading role in preparing the EU for the challenge of enlargement, encouraging the reform of the CAP, making the EU's foreign and security policy more effective and ensuring that the EU meets the concerns of the UK's citizens
– to encourage preparations in the UK for the introduction of the Euro in other member states of the EU
– to ensure strong defence arrangements based on NATO and promote international peace and security
– to pursue reform of the UN and an early resolution of its financial crisis
– to promote human rights, fight against terrorism and serious crime and take a leading role in protecting the environment

The Budget

The Chancellor of the Exchequer (Gordon Brown) presented his Budget to the House of Commons on 9 March 1999. It included the following main points:
– a new 10p rate of income tax to be introduced on the first £1,500 of earnings from April 1999; the 20p tax rate to

be abolished; the basic rate of income tax to be cut from 23p to 22p from April 2000

– personal tax allowances for pensioners to be raised by more than the rate of inflation

– no national insurance to be paid on the first £87 per week of earnings from April 2001; the upper limit for NI contributions to be raised to £575 per week

– the married couple's tax allowance to be abolished from April 2001, except for pensioners, and replaced by a child tax credit worth £416 a year

– child benefit to be raised to £15 a week for the first child and £10 a week for subsequent children, from April 2000

– mortgage interest relief (MIRAS) to be abolished from April 2000

– stamp duty to be raised by 0.5 per cent for houses worth more than £250,000 from 16 March 1999

– pensioners' winter allowance to be raised from £20 to £100

– a guaranteed minimum income of £78 for a single pensioner and £121 for a couple

– petrol up 3.79p a litre for unleaded petrol and 4.25p a litre for leaded

– excise duty cut by £55 from June 1999 for cars with engines below 1,100 cc

– excise duty from autumn 2000 to be based on carbon dioxide emission rate

– cigarettes up 17.5p a packet from midnight on 9 March

– the capital gains tax threshold to be raised to £7,100 from April 1999

– the inheritance tax threshold to be raised to £231,000 from April 1999

– corporation tax to be cut by 1p from April 1999; a new 10p rate to be introduced for new small businesses from April 2000

– a new research and development tax credit for small businesses

– a new energy levy on industry from April 2001

– a new share ownership scheme for employees

– a 'computers for all' programme to be launched, including a national network of 1,000 computer learning centres

– a £60-a-week credit for over-50s moving off welfare into work

Government Departments and Public Offices

For changes notified after 31 August, *see* Stop-press

This section covers central government departments, executive agencies, regulatory bodies, other statutory independent organizations, and bodies which are government-financed or whose head is appointed by a government minister.

THE CIVIL SERVICE

Under the Next Steps programme, launched in 1988, many semi-autonomous executive agencies have been established to carry out much of the work of the Civil Service. Executive agencies operate within a framework set by the responsible minister which specifies policies, objectives and available resources. All executive agencies are set annual performance targets by their minister. Each agency has a chief executive, who is responsible for the day-to-day operations of the agency and who is accountable to the minister for the use of resources and for meeting the agency's targets. The minister accounts to Parliament for the work of the agency. Nearly 60 per cent of civil servants now work in executive agencies. Customs and Excise, the Inland Revenue, the Crown Prosecution Service and the Serious Fraud Office, which employ a further 17 per cent of civil servants, also operate on 'Next Steps' lines. In January 1999 there were about 463,700 permanent civil servants.

The Senior Civil Service was created in 1996 and comprises about 3,000 staff from Permanent Secretary to the former Grade 5 level, including all agency chief executives. All government departments and executive agencies are now responsible for their own pay and grading systems for civil servants outside the Senior Civil Service. In practice the grades of the former Open structure are still in use in some organizations. The Open structure represented the following:

Grade	Title
1	Permanent Secretary
1A	Second Permanent Secretary
2	Deputy Secretary
3	Under-Secretary
4	Chief Scientific Officer B, Professional and Technology Directing A
5	Assistant Secretary, Deputy Chief Scientific Officer, Professional and Technology Directing B
6	Senior Principal, Senior Principal Scientific Officer, Professional and Technology Superintending Grade
7	Principal, Principal Scientific Officer, Principal Professional and Technology Officer

SALARIES 1999–2000

MINISTERIAL SALARIES from 1 April 1999

Ministers who are Members of the House of Commons receive a parliamentary salary (£47,008) in addition to their ministerial salary.

*Prime Minister	£107,179
*Cabinet minister (Commons)	£64,307
*†Cabinet minister (Lords)	£83,560
Minister of State (Commons)	£33,359
Minister of State (Lords)	£64,426
Parliamentary Under-Secretary (Commons)	£25,319
Parliamentary Under-Secretary (Lords)	£55,631

* These ministers have yet to decide whether to take the full salaries provided for them for the financial year 1999–2000. For the time being they will draw the following ministerial salaries: Prime Minister, £62,760; Cabinet minister (Commons), £47,149; Cabinet minister (Lords), £70,608

† Except the Lord Chancellor, who receives a salary of £160,011

SPECIAL ADVISERS' SALARIES from 1 April 1999

Special advisers to government ministers are paid out of public funds; their salaries are negotiated individually, but are usually in the range £26,728 to £78,186. At March 1999 there were 66 special advisers.

CIVIL SERVICE SALARIES from 1 April 1999

Senior Civil Service (SCS)

Secretary of the Cabinet and Head of the Home Civil Service	£98,400–£168,910
Permanent Secretary	£98,400–£168,910
Band 9	£87,460–£123,860
Band 8	£80,020–£116,860
Band 7	£73,250–£110,300
Band 6	£66,900–£104,190
Band 5	£61,110–£98,400
Band 4	£55,750–£92,930
Band 3	£50,510–£82,650
Band 2	£45,810–£73,470
Band 1	£41,550–£65,270

Staff are placed in pay bands according to their level of responsibility and taking account of other factors such as experience and marketability. Movement within and between bands is based on performance. A recruitment and retention allowance of up to £3,000 may be paid in certain circumstances in addition to the salary ranges shown for bands 1 to 9.

Other Civil Servants

Following the delegation of responsibility for pay and grading to government departments and agencies from 1 April 1996, it is no longer possible to show service-wide pay rates for staff outside the Senior Civil Service. The following table will however give an indication of the percentage of civil servants at a given salary level.

Non-Industrial Staff by Gross Salary Band as at 1 April 1998

Salary Band	Per Cent
£5,001–£10,000	8.9
£10,001–£15,000	38.8
£15,001–£20,000	23.4
£20,001–£25,000	16.1
£25,001–£30,000	5.5
£30,001–£35,000	2.7
£35,001–£40,000	1.9
£40,001–£45,000	1.0
£45,001–£50,000	0.6
£50,001–£55,000	0.4
£55,001–£60,000	0.2
£60,001–£65,000	0.1
£65,001–£70,000	0.1
£70,001–£75,000	0.0
£75,001 +	0.1

Source: Government Statistical Service – *Civil Service Statistics 1998*

ADJUDICATOR'S OFFICE
Haymarket House, 28 Haymarket, London SW1Y 4SP
Tel 0171-930 2292; fax 0171-930 2298

The Adjudicator's Office opened in 1993 and investigates complaints about the way the Inland Revenue (including the Valuation Office Agency) and Customs and Excise have handled an individual's affairs.
The Adjudicator, Dame Barbara Mills, DBE, QC
Head of Office, M. Savage

ADVISORY, CONCILIATION AND ARBITRATION SERVICE
Brandon House, 180 Borough High Street, London
SE1 1LW
Tel 0171-210 3613; fax 0171-210 3708

The Advisory, Conciliation and Arbitration Service (ACAS) was set up under the Employment Protection Act 1975 (the provisions now being found in the Trade Union and Labour Relations (Consolidation) Act 1992). ACAS is directed by a Council consisting of a full-time chairman and part-time employer, trade union and independent members, all appointed by the Secretary of State for Trade and Industry. The functions of the Service are to promote the improvement of industrial relations in general, to provide facilities for conciliation, mediation and arbitration as means of avoiding and resolving industrial disputes, and to provide advisory and information services on industrial relations matters to employers, employees and their representatives.

ACAS has regional offices in Birmingham, Bristol, Cardiff, Fleet, Glasgow, Leeds, Liverpool, London, Manchester, Newcastle upon Tyne and Nottingham.
Chairman, J. Hougham, CBE
Chief Conciliator (*G4*), D. Evans

MINISTRY OF AGRICULTURE, FISHERIES AND FOOD
Nobel House, 17 Smith Square, London SW1P 3JR
Tel 0171-238 6000; fax 0171-238 6591
E-mail: helpline@inf.maff.gov.uk
Web: http://www.maff.gov.uk/maffhome.htm

The Ministry of Agriculture, Fisheries and Food is responsible for government policies on agriculture, horticulture and fisheries in England and for policies relating to the safety and quality of food in the UK as a whole, including composition, labelling, additives, contaminants and new production processes. In association with the agriculture departments of the Scottish Executive, the National Assembly for Wales and the Northern Ireland Office and with the Intervention Board (*see* page 314), the Ministry is responsible for negotiations in the EU on the common agricultural and fisheries policies, and for single European market questions relating to its responsibilities. Its remit also includes international agricultural and food trade policy.

The Ministry exercises responsibilities for the protection and enhancement of the countryside and the marine environment, for flood defence and for other rural issues. It is the licensing authority for veterinary medicines and the registration authority for pesticides. It administers policies relating to the control of animal, plant and fish diseases. It provides scientific, technical and professional services and advice to farmers, growers and ancillary industries, and it commissions research to assist in the formulation and assessment of policy and to underpin applied research and development work done by industry. Responsibility for food safety and standards will be transferred to the new Food Standards Agency, expected to be in operation by mid 2000.
Minister of Agriculture, Fisheries and Food, The Rt. Hon. Nick Brown, MP
    Principal Private Secretary (*G7*), Ms S. Hendry
    Private Secretary (*SEO*), C. Porro
    Parliamentary Private Secretary, Ms R. Kelly, MP
Minister of State, The Rt. Hon. Joyce Quin, MP
    Private Secretary, Ms T. Hart
Minister of State, The Baroness Hayman
    Private Secretary, Mrs K. Lepper
Parliamentary Secretary, Elliot Morley, MP
    Private Secretary, M. Livesey
Parliamentary Clerk, M. Stickings
Permanent Secretary (*SCS*), R. J. Packer
    Private Secretary, A. Lawrence

ESTABLISHMENTS GROUP
Director of Establishments (*SCS*), R. A. Saunderson

ESTABLISHMENTS (GENERAL) AND OFFICE SERVICES DIVISION
Head of Division (*SCS*), Dr Mandy Bailey

PERSONNEL MANAGEMENT AND DEVELOPMENT DIVISION
Head of Division (*SCS*), vacant

BUILDING AND ESTATE MANAGEMENT
Eastbury House, 30–34 Albert Embankment,
London SE1 7TL
Tel 0171-238 6000
Head of Division (*SCS*), J. A. S. Nickson

INFORMATION TECHNOLOGY DIRECTORATE
Room 755, St Christopher House, Southwark Street,
London SE1 0UD
Tel 0171-921 1886
Director (*SCS*), A. G. Matthews

Government Buildings, Epsom Road, Guildford, Surrey
GU1 2LD
Tel 01483-403757
Head of Strategies (*G6*), P. Barber
Head of Applications (*G6*), D. D. Brown
Head of Infrastructure (*G6*), S. Soper

COMMUNICATIONS DIRECTORATE
Tel 0171-238 6000; helpline 0645-335577
Director of Communications (*SCS*), R. Lowson
Chief Press Officer (*G7*), M. Smith
Chief Publicity Officer (*G7*), N. Wagstaffe
Principal Librarian (*G7*), P. McShane

AGENCY OWNERSHIP UNIT
Head of Unit (*SCS*), Dr M. Tas

FINANCE DEPARTMENT
3–8 Whitehall Place (West Block), London SW1A 2HH
Tel 0171-238 6000
Principal Finance Officer (*SCS*), P. Elliott

FINANCIAL POLICY DIVISION
Head of Division (*SCS*), B. J. Harding

PROCUREMENT AND CONTRACTS DIVISION
19–29 Woburn Place, London WC1H 0LU
Tel 0171-273 3000

Head of Division (*SCS*), D. Rabey

AUDIT, CONSULTANCY AND MANAGEMENT SERVICES
19–29 Woburn Place, London WC1H 0LU
Tel 0171-273 3000

Director of Audit (*SCS*), D. V. Fisher

RESOURCE MANAGEMENT STRATEGY UNIT
19–29 Woburn Place, London WC1H 0LU
Tel 0171-273 3000

Head of Unit (*SCS*), D. V. Fisher

RESOURCE MANAGEMENT DIVISION
Foss House, Kings Pool, 1–2 Peasholme Green, York
YO1 7PX
Tel 01904-455328

Head of Division (*G6*), Mrs J. Flint

BUSINESS PLANNING UNIT
Head of Unit (*G7*), G. Holt

LEGAL DEPARTMENT
55 Whitehall, London SW1A 2EY
Tel 0171-238 6000

Legal Adviser and Solicitor (*SCS*), Miss K. M. S. Morton
Principal Assistant Solicitors (*SCS*), D. J. Pearson; Ms C. A.
Crisham

LEGAL DIVISIONS

Assistant Solicitor, Division A1 (*SCS*), P. Davis
Assistant Solicitor, Division A2 (*SCS*), P. Kent
Assistant Solicitor, Division A3 (*SCS*), C. Gregory
Assistant Solicitor, Division A4 (*SCS*), C. Allen
Assistant Solicitor, Division A5 (*SCS*), vacant
Assistant Solicitor, Division B1 (*SCS*), Dr Gisela Davis
Assistant Solicitor, Division B2 (*SCS*), Ms S. B. Spence
Assistant Solicitor, Division B3 (*SCS*), A. I. Corbett
Assistant Solicitor, Division B4 (*SCS*), N. Lambert

INVESTIGATION UNIT
Chief Investigation Officer, Miss J. Panting

ECONOMICS AND STATISTICS
3–8 Whitehall Place (West Block), London SW1A 2HH
Tel 0171-238 6000

Under-Secretary (*SCS*), D. Thompson

DIVISIONS

Senior Economic Adviser, Economics and Statistics (*Farm Business*) (*G6*), H. Fearn
Senior Economic Adviser, Economics (*International*) (*SCS*), N. Atkinson
Senior Economic Adviser, Economics (*Resource Use*) (*SCS*), J. P. Muriel

STATISTICS DIVISION
Foss House, Kings Pool, 1–2 Peasholme Green, York
YO1 7PX
Tel 01904-455332

Chief Statistician (*Commodities and Food*) (*SCS*), S. Platt
Chief Statistician (*Census and Surveys*) (*SCS*), P. F. Helm

CHIEF SCIENTIST'S GROUP
*St Christopher House, 80–112 Southwark Street, London
SE1 0UD
Tel 0171-928 3666

Chief Scientist (*SCS*), Dr D. W. F. Shannon

DIVISIONS

Head, Agriculture, Environment and Food Technology (*SCS*),
Dr J. C. Sherlock
Head, Veterinary, Food and Aquatic Science (*SCS*),
Dr K. J. MacOwan
Head, Research Policy and International (*SCS*), A. R. Burne

FISHERIES DEPARTMENT
Fisheries Secretary (*SCS*), S. Wentworth

DIVISIONS

Head, Fisheries I (*SCS*), P. M. Boyling
Head, Fisheries II (*SCS*), C. I. Llewellyn
Head, Fisheries III (*SCS*), Miss S. Brown
Head, Fisheries IV (*SCS*), B. S. Edwards
Chief Inspector, Sea Fisheries Inspectorate (*G6*), S. G. Ellson

AGRICULTURAL CROPS AND
COMMODITIES DIRECTORATE
3–8 Whitehall Place (West Block), London SW1A 2HH
Tel 0171-238 6000

Deputy Secretary (*SCS*), Ms V. K. Timms, CB

EUROPEAN UNION AND INTERNATIONAL
POLICY
Under-Secretary (*SCS*), A. J. Lebrecht

DIVISIONS

Head, European Union (*SCS*), Miss V. Smith
Head, Trade Policy and Tropical Foods (*SCS*), J. Robbs

AGRICULTURE GROUP
Head of Group (*SCS*), D. Hunter

DIVISIONS

Head, Horticulture, Potatoes and HMI (*SCS*), G. W. Noble
Head, New Crops and Sugar (*SCS*), H. B. Brown
Head, Arable Crops (*SCS*), A. Kuyk
Head, Beef and Sheep (*SCS*), R. Cowan
Head, Livestock Schemes (*SCS*), A. Taylor
Head, Milk, Pigs, Eggs and Poultry (*SCS*), P. Nash

FOOD INDUSTRY, COMPETITIVENESS AND
CONSUMERS
Under-Secretary (*SCS*), N. Thornton

DIVISIONS

Head, Food and Drinks Industry (*SCS*), Miss C. J. Rabagliati
Head, International Relations and Export Promotion (*SCS*),
D. V. Orchard
Head, Agricultural Resources and Better Regulation (*SCS*), Mrs
A. Blackburn
Head, Marketing, Competition and Consumers (*SCS*), Ms J.
Allfrey
Heads, Inquiry Liaison Unit (*SCS*), D. Dawson; (*G6*), Mrs A.
Waters

REGIONAL SERVICES AND DEFENCE GROUP
3–8 Whitehall Place (West Block), London SW1A 2HH
Tel 0171-238 6000

Under-Secretary (*SCS*), Mrs K. J. A. Brown

DIVISIONS

Head, Plant Health, and Plant Health and Seeds Inspectorate
(*SCS*), A. J. Perrins
Head, Flood and Coastal Protection (*SCS*), Dr J. Park
Head of CAP Schemes Management Division (*SCS*), Mrs J.
Purnell

PLANT VARIETY RIGHTS OFFICE AND SEEDS DIVISION
White House Lane, Huntingdon Road, Cambridge
CB3 0LF
Tel 01223-277151
Head of Office (SCS), D. A. Boreham

REGIONAL ORGANIZATION
Head, Regional Support Unit (G7), D. Putley
Regional Service Centres
ANGLIA REGION, Block B, Government Buildings,
Brooklands Avenue, Cambridge CB2 2DR. Tel: 01223-
462727. *Regional Director*, M. Edwards
EAST MIDLANDS REGION, Block 7, Government
Buildings, Chalfont Drive, Nottingham NG8 3SN. Tel:
0115-929 0634. *Regional Director*, G. Norbury
NORTH-EAST REGION, Government Buildings, Crosby
Road, Northallerton, N. Yorks DL6 1AD. Tel: 01609-
773751. *Regional Director*, P. Watson
NORTHERN REGION, Eden Bridge House, Lowther
Street, Carlisle, Cumbria CA3 8DX. Tel: 01228-523400.
Regional Director, I. G. Pearson
NORTH MERCIA REGION, Electra Way, Crewe Business
Park, Crewe, Cheshire CW1 6GL. Tel: 01270-
754000. *Regional Director*, F. Whitehouse
SOUTH-EAST REGION, Block A, Government Buildings,
Coley Park, Reading, Berks RG1 6DT. Tel: 01889-
581222. *Regional Director*, Mrs V. Silvester
SOUTH MERCIA REGION, Block C, Government
Buildings, Whittington Road, Worcester WR5 2LQ. Tel:
01905-763355. *Regional Director*, B. Davies
SOUTH-WEST REGION, Clyst House, Winslade Park,
Clyst St Mary, Exeter EX5 1DY. Tel: 01392-447400.
Regional Director, M. R. W. Highman
WESSEX REGION, Block 3, Government Buildings,
Burghill Road, Westbury-on-Trym, Bristol
BS10 6NJ. Tel: 0117-959 1000. *Regional Director*, Mrs
A. J. L. Ould

FOOD SAFETY AND ENVIRONMENT GROUP
Deputy Secretary (SCS), R. J. D. Carden, CB

ENVIRONMENT GROUP
Under-Secretary (SCS), D. J. Coates
Head, Rural Division (SCS), Ms L. Cornish
Head, Conservation Management Division (SCS), T. J.
Osmond
Head, Rural and Marine Environment (SCS), D. E. Jones

FOOD SAFETY AND STANDARDS GROUP
Under-Secretary (SCS), G. Podger

DIVISIONS
Head, Additives and Novel Foods (SCS), Dr J. R. Bell
Head, Food Contaminants (SCS), Dr R. Burt
Head, Food Labelling and Standards (SCS), G. F. Meekings
Head, Radiological Safety and Nutrition (SCS), Dr M. G. Segal
Head, Food Hygiene (SCS), R. J. Harding
Head, Meat Hygiene I (SCS), R. C. McIvor
Head, Meat Hygiene II (SCS), C. J. Lawson
Head, Food Standards Agency Division (SCS), Miss
E. J. Wordley

VETERINARY PUBLIC HEALTH UNIT
Assistant Chief Veterinary Officer (SCS), D. Taylor, CBE
Head of Unit (SCS), P. Hewson

ANIMAL HEALTH GROUP
*Government Buildings, Hook Rise South, Tolworth,
Surbiton, Surrey KT6 7NF
Tel 0181-330 4411
Under-Secretary (SCS), B. H. B. Dickinson

DIVISIONS
Head, Animal Health (BSE and International Trade) (SCS), T.
E. D. Eddy
Head, Animal Health (Disease Control) (SCS), T. D.
Rossington
Head, Services (G6), R. Gurd
Head, Animal Welfare (SCS), C. J. Ryder
Head, Bovine Tuberculosis (SCS), R. Hathaway

CHIEF VETERINARY OFFICER'S GROUP
*Government Buildings, Hook Rise South, Tolworth,
Surbiton, Surrey KT6 7NF
Tel 0181-330 8057
Chief Veterinary Officer (SCS), J. M. Scudamore
Assistant Chief Veterinary Officer (SCS), R. J. G. Cawthorne

DIVISIONS
Head, Veterinary International Trade Team (SCS), R. A. Bell
*Head, Veterinary Notifiable Disease Team (Exotic Diseases and
TSE) (SCS)*, Dr D. Matthews
*Head, Veterinary Notifiable Disease Team (Endemic Animal
Diseases and Zoonoses) (SCS)*, Dr Debby Reynolds
Head, Welfare Team (SCS), A. T. Turnbull

VETERINARY FIELD SERVICE
*Government Buildings, Hook Rise South, Tolworth,
Surbiton, Surrey KT15 3NB
Tel 0181-330 4411
Director of Veterinary Field Services (SCS), M. J. Atkinson
* During the autumn of 1999 staff at the Tolworth and St Christopher
House sites will begin to be relocated to: 1A Page Street, London
SW1P 4PQ. Tel: 0171-904 3000

EXECUTIVE AGENCIES

CENTRAL SCIENCE LABORATORY
Sand Hutton, York YO41 1LZ
Tel 01904-462000; fax 01904-462111
The agency provides MAFF with technical support and
policy advice on the protection and quality of the food
supply and on related environmental issues.
Chief Executive (G3), Prof. P. I. Stanley
Research Directors (G5), Prof. A. R. Hardy (*Agriculture and
Environment*); Prof. J. Gilbert (*Food*)

CENTRE FOR ENVIRONMENT, FISHERIES AND
AQUACULTURE SCIENCE
Pakefield Road, Lowestoft, Suffolk NR33 0HT
Tel 01502-562244; fax: 01502-513865
The Agency, established in April 1997, provides research
and consultancy services in fisheries science and manage-
ment, aquaculture, fish health and hygiene, environmental
impact assessment, and environmental quality assessment.
Chief Executive, Dr P. Greig-Smith

FARMING AND RURAL CONSERVATION AGENCY
Nobel House, 17 Smith Square, London SW1P 3JR
Tel 0171-238 5432; fax 0171-238 5588
The Agency, established in April 1997, is responsible
jointly to MAFF and the National Assembly for Wales. It
assists the Government in the design, development and
implementation of policies on the integration of farming
and conservation, environmental protection and the rural
economy. This includes agri-environment schemes such as

Environmentally Sensitive Areas, Countryside Stewardship and access schemes, rural development, milk hygiene
inspections and wildlife management.
Chief Executive (SCS), Miss S. Nason

INTERVENTION BOARD
— *see* page 314

MEAT HYGIENE SERVICE
Foss House, Kings Pool, 1–2 Peasholme Green, York
YOI 7PX
Tel 01904-455655; fax 01904-455502
The Agency was launched in April 1995. It protects public
health and promotes animal welfare through veterinary
supervision and meat inspection in licensed fresh meat
establishments.
Chief Executive (G4), J. McNeill

PESTICIDES SAFETY DIRECTORATE
Mallard House, Kings Pool, 3 Peasholme Green, York
YOI 7PX
Tel 01904-640500; fax 01904-455733
The Pesticides Safety Directorate is responsible for the
evaluation and approval of pesticides and the development
of policies relating to them, in order to protect consumers,
users and the environment.
Chief Executive (G4), G. K. Bruce
Director (Policy) (G5), J. A. Bainton
Director (Approvals) (G5), Dr A. D. Martin

VETERINARY LABORATORIES AGENCY
Woodham Lane, New Haw, Addlestone, Surrey KTI5 3NB
Tel 01932-341111; fax 01932-347046
The Veterinary Laboratories Agency provides scientific
and technical expertise in animal and public health.
Chief Executive (G3), Dr T. W. A. Little
Director of Research (G5), Dr J. A. Morris
Director of Laboratory Services (G5), Dr S. Edwards
Director of Surveillance (G5), J. W. Harkness
Director of Finance (G6), I. Grattage
Laboratory Secretary (G6), C. Edwards

VETERINARY MEDICINES DIRECTORATE
Woodham Lane, New Haw, Addlestone, Surrey KTI5 3LS
Tel 01932-336911; fax 01932-336618
The Veterinary Medicines Directorate is responsible for
all aspects of the authorization and control of veterinary
medicines, including post-authorization surveillance of
residues in meat and animal products, and the provision of
policy advice to ministers.
Chief Executive and Director of Veterinary Medicines (G4),
Dr J. M. Rutter
Director (Policy) (G5), R. Anderson
Director (Licensing) (G5), S. Dean
Secretary and Head of Business Unit (G6), J. FitzGerald
Licensing Manager, Pharmaceuticals and Feed Additives (G6),
J. P. O'Brien
Licensing Manager, Immunologicals (G6), Dr D. J. K. Mackay

COLLEGE OF ARMS (OR HERALDS
COLLEGE)
Queen Victoria Street, London EC4V 4BT
Tel 0171-248 2762; fax 0171-248 6448

The Sovereign's Officers of Arms (Kings, Heralds and
Pursuivants of Arms) were first incorporated by Richard
III. The powers vested by the Crown in the Earl Marshal
(the Duke of Norfolk) with regard to state ceremonial are
largely exercised through the College. The College is also
the official repository of the arms and pedigrees of English,
Welsh, Northern Irish and Commonwealth (except Canadian) families and their descendants, and its records include
official copies of the records of Ulster King of Arms, the
originals of which remain in Dublin. The 13 officers of the
College specialize in genealogical and heraldic work for
their respective clients.
Arms have been and still are granted by letters patent
from the Kings of Arms. A right to arms can only be
established by the registration in the official records of the
College of Arms of a pedigree showing direct male line
descent from an ancestor already appearing therein as
being entitled to arms, or by making application through
the College of Arms for a grant of arms. Grants are made
to corporations as well as to individuals.
The College of Arms is open Monday–Friday 10–4.
Earl Marshal, The Duke of Norfolk, KG, GCVO, CB, CBE, MC

KINGS OF ARMS
Garter, P. L. Gwynn-Jones, CVO, FSA
Clarenceux (and Registrar), D. H. B. Chesshyre, LVO, FSA
Norroy and Ulster, T. Woodcock, LVO, FSA

HERALDS
Richmond (and Earl Marshal's Secretary), P. L. Dickinson
York, H. E. Paston-Bedingfeld
Chester, T. H. S. Duke
Lancaster, R. J. B. Noel
Windsor, W. G. Hunt, TD

PURSUIVANTS
Rouge Croix, D. V. White
Rouge Dragon, C. E. A. Cheesman, PH.D.

COURT OF THE LORD LYON
HM New Register House, Edinburgh EHI 3YT
Tel 0131-556 7255; fax 0131-557 2148

The Court of the Lord Lyon is the Scottish Court of
Chivalry (including the genealogical jurisdiction of the *Ri-
Sennachie* of Scotland's Celtic Kings). The Lord Lyon King
of Arms has jurisdiction, subject to appeal to the Court of
Session and the House of Lords, in questions of heraldry
and the right to bear arms. The Court also administers the
Scottish Public Register of All Arms and Bearings and the
Public Register of All Genealogies. Pedigrees are established by decrees of Lyon Court and by letters patent. As
Royal Commissioner in Armory, the Lord Lyon grants
patents of arms (which constitute the grantee and heirs
noble in the Noblesse of Scotland) to 'virtuous and well-
deserving' Scotsmen and to petitioners (personal or
corporate) in The Queen's overseas realms of Scottish
connection, and issues birthbrieves.
Lord Lyon King of Arms, Sir Malcolm Innes of Edingight,
KCVO, WS

HERALDS
Albany, J. A. Spens, MVO, RD, WS
Rothesay, Sir Crispin Agnew of Lochnaw, Bt., QC
Ross, C. J. Burnett, FSA Scot.

PURSUIVANTS
Kintyre, J. C. G. George, FSA Scot.
Unicorn, Alastair Campbell of Airds, FSA Scot.
Carrick, Mrs C. G. W. Roads, MVO, FSA Scot.

Lyon Clerk and Keeper of Records, Mrs C. G. W. Roads, MVO,
FSA Scot.
Procurator-Fiscal, D. F. Murby, WS
Herald Painter, Mrs J. Phillips
Macer, A. M. Clark

ARTS COUNCILS

The Arts Council of Great Britain was established as an independent body in 1946 to be the principal channel for the Government's support of the arts. In 1994 the Scottish and Welsh Arts Councils became autonomous and the Arts Council of Great Britain became the Arts Council of England.

The Arts Councils are responsible for the distribution of the proceeds of the National Lottery allocated to the arts (*see* Lotteries and Gaming section).

ARTS COUNCIL OF ENGLAND
14 Great Peter Street, London SW1P 3NQ
Tel 0171-333 0100; fax 0171-973 6590

The Arts Council of England's objectives are to develop and improve the understanding and practice of the arts and to increase their accessibility to the public. The Council funds the major arts organizations in England and the ten Regional Arts Boards. It is funded by the Department for Culture, Media and Sport but operates at 'arm's length' from Government as regards artistic decision-making, although it is expected to account for such decisions to the Government and the public. The Council also provides advice, information and help to artists and arts organizations. Its members are unpaid.

The Council distributes an annual grant from the Department for Culture, Media and Sport; the grant for 1999–2000 is £218.8 million.
Chairman, G. Robinson
Members, D. Anderson; D. Brierley, CBE; Ms D. Bull, CBE; Prof. C. Frayling; A. Gormley; A. Kapoor; Prof. J. MacGregor; Prof. A. Motion; Ms P. Skene; Ms H. Strong
Chief Executive, P. Hewitt

REGIONAL ARTS BOARDS

EASTERN ARTS BOARD, Cherry Hinton Hall, Cherry Hinton Road, Cambridge CB1 8DW. Tel: 01223-215355. *Chair*, Prof. S. Timperley
EAST MIDLANDS ARTS BOARD, Mountfields House, Epinal Way, Loughborough, Leics LE11 0QE. Tel: 01509-218292. *Chair*, Prof. R. Cowell
LONDON ARTS BOARD, Elme House, 133 Long Acre, London WC2E 9AF. Tel: 0171-240 1313. *Chair*, T. Phillips, OBE
NORTHERN ARTS BOARD, 9–10 Osborne Terrace, Newcastle upon Tyne NE2 1NZ. Tel: 0191-281 6334. *Chair*, G. Loggie
NORTH-WEST ARTS BOARD, Manchester House, 22 Bridge Street, Manchester M3 3AB. Tel: 0161-834 6644. *Chair*, Prof. B. Cox, CBE, FRSL
SOUTH-EAST ARTS BOARD, Union House, Eridge Road, Tunbridge Wells, Kent TN4 8HF. Tel: 01892-507205. *Chair*, R. Reed
SOUTHERN ARTS BOARD, 13 St Clement Street, Winchester SO23 9DQ. Tel: 01962-855099. *Chair*, D. Astor
SOUTH-WEST ARTS BOARD, Bradninch Place, Gandy Street, Exeter EX4 3LS. Tel: 01392-218188. *Chair*, vacant
WEST MIDLANDS ARTS BOARD, 82 Granville Street, Birmingham B1 2LH. Tel: 0121-631 3121. *Chair*, R. Natkiel
YORKSHIRE ARTS BOARD, 21 Bond Street, Dewsbury, W. Yorks WF13 1AX. Tel: 01924-455555. *Chair*, C. Price

SCOTTISH ARTS COUNCIL
12 Manor Place, Edinburgh EH3 7DD
Tel 0131-226 6051; fax 0131-225 9833

The Scottish Arts Council funds arts organizations in Scotland and is funded directly by the Scottish Executive. The grant for 1999–2000 is £28.097 million.
Chairman, M. Linklater
Members, Ms S. Ainsley; H. Buchanan; Cllr Elizabeth Cameron; R. Chester; W. English; J. Faulds; Ms D. Idiens; Ms M. Marshall; Dr Ann Matheson, OBE; J. Scott Moncrieff; W. Speirs; Ms J. Urquart
Director, Ms T. Jackson

ARTS COUNCIL OF WALES
9 Museum Place, Cardiff CF1 3NX
Tel 01222-376500; fax 01222-221447

The Arts Council of Wales funds arts organizations in Wales and is funded by the National Assembly for Wales. The grant for 1999–2000 is about £14.7 million.
Chairman, Ms E. Bennet; Ms A. Davies; R. Davies; K. Evans; Ms K. Gass; D. Johnston; G. S. Jones; L. Jones; G. Lewis; A. Lloyd; A. Roberts; Ms C. Thomas; Ms M. Vincentelli
Chief Executive, Ms J. Weston

ARTS COUNCIL OF NORTHERN IRELAND
MacNeice House, 77 Malone Road, Belfast BT9 6AQ
Tel 01232-385200; fax 01232-661715

The Arts Council of Northern Ireland is the prime distributor of government funds in support of the arts in Northern Ireland. It is funded by the Department of Education for Northern Ireland, and the grant for 1999–2000 is £6.89 million.
Chairman, Prof. B. Walker
Vice-Chairman, Ms M. O'Neill
Members, Cllr M. Bradley; W. Burns; S. Burnside; P. Donnelly; Dr Tess Hurson; Mrs R. McMullan; G. Patterson; Ms C. Poulter; Ms I. Sandford; A. Shortt
Chief Executive, B. Ferran

ART GALLERIES, ETC.

ROYAL FINE ART COMMISSION (former)
— *see* Commission for Architecture and the Built Environment

ROYAL FINE ART COMMISSION FOR SCOTLAND
Bakehouse Close, 146 Canongate, Edinburgh EH8 8DD
Tel 0131-556 6699; fax 0131-556 6633

The Commission was established in 1927 and advises ministers and local authorities on the visual impact and quality of design of construction projects. It is an independent body and gives its opinions impartially.
Chairman, The Lord Cameron of Lochbroom, PC, FRSE
Commissioners, Prof. G. Benson; W. A. Cadell; Mrs K. Dalyell; Ms J. Malvenan; R. G. Maund; M. Murray; D. Page; B. Rae; R. Russell; M. Turnbull; A. Wright
Secretary, C. Prosser

NATIONAL GALLERY
Trafalgar Square, London WC2N 5DN
Tel 0171-839 3321; fax 0171-747 2403

The National Gallery, which houses a permanent collection of western painting from the 13th to the 20th century, was founded in 1824, following a parliamentary grant of £60,000 for the purchase and exhibition of the Angerstein collection of pictures. The present site was first occupied in 1838; an extension to the north of the building with a public entrance in Orange Street was opened in 1975, and the Sainsbury wing was opened in 1991. Total government grant-in-aid for 1999–2000 is £19.478 million.

BOARD OF TRUSTEES
Chairman, P. Hughes, CBE
Trustees, Lady Bingham; Sir Mark Richmond, SC.D., FRS; Lady Monck; Sir Ewen Fergusson, GCMG, GCVO; R. Gavron, CBE; C. Le Brun; The Hon. R. G. H. Seitz; Dr D. Landau; Sir Colin Southgate; J. Snow; Prof. Dawn Ades; Lady Hopkins

OFFICERS
Director, R. N. MacGregor
Keeper, Dr N. Penny
Senior Curator, D. Jaffé
Chief Restorer, M. H. Wyld, CBE
Head of Exhibitions, M. J. Wilson
Scientific Adviser, Dr A. Roy
Director of Administration, J. MacAuslan
Head of Press and Public Relations, Miss J. Liddiard

NATIONAL PORTRAIT GALLERY
St Martin's Place, London WC2H OHE
Tel 0171-306 0055; fax 0171-306 0058
A grant was made in 1856 to form a gallery of the portraits of the most eminent persons in British history. The present building was opened in 1896 and an extension in 1933. There are four regional partnerships displaying portraits in appropriate settings: Montacute House, Gawthorpe Hall, Beningbrough Hall and Bodelwyddan Castle. Total government grant-in-aid for 1999–2000 is £4.997 million.

BOARD OF TRUSTEES
Chairman, H. Keswick
Trustees, The Lord President of the Council (*ex officio*); The President of the Royal Academy of Arts (*ex officio*); The Lord Morris of Castle Morris, D.Phil.; Prof. N. Lynton; J. Tusa; Mrs J. E. Benson, LVO, OBE; Lady Tumim, OBE; Sir David Scholey, CBE; Mrs C. Tomalin; Baroness Willoughby de Eresby; M. Hastings; Prof. The Earl Russell, FBA; T. Phillips, RA; Prof. C. Matthew
Director (*G3*), C. Saumarez Smith, PH.D.

TATE GALLERY
Millbank, London SW1P 4RG
Tel 0171-887 8000; fax 0171-887 8007
The Tate Gallery comprises the national collections of British painting and 20th-century painting and sculpture. The Gallery was opened in 1897, the cost of erection (£80,000) being defrayed by Sir Henry Tate, who also contributed the nucleus of the present collection. The Turner wing was opened in 1910, galleries to contain the collection of modern foreign painting in 1926, and a new sculpture hall in 1937. In 1979 a further extension was built, and the Clore Gallery, for the Turner collection, was opened in 1987. The Tate Gallery Liverpool opened in 1988 and the Tate Gallery St Ives in 1993. The new Tate Gallery of Modern Art at Bankside is due to open in May 2000, with the Millbank gallery then being devoted to British art. Total government grant-in-aid for 1999–2000 is £19.727 million.

BOARD OF TRUSTEES
Chairman, D. Verey
Trustees, Prof. Dawn Ades; The Hon. Mrs J. de Botton; Sir Richard Carew Pole; Prof. M. Craig-Martin; P. Doig; Sir Christopher Mallaby, GCMG, GCVO; Sir Mark Richmond; Mrs P. Ridley, OBE; W. Woodrow

OFFICERS
Director, Sir Nicholas Serota
Director of National Programmes, S. Nairne

Director of Collections, J. Lewison
Director, Tate Gallery of Modern Art, L. Nittve
Director, Tate Gallery of British Art, S. Deuchar
Curator, Tate Gallery Liverpool, L. Biggs
Curator, Tate Gallery St Ives, M. Tooby

WALLACE COLLECTION
Hertford House, Manchester Square, London WIM 6BN
Tel 0171-935 0687; fax 0171-224 2155
The Wallace Collection was bequeathed to the nation by the widow of Sir Richard Wallace, Bt. in 1897, and Hertford House was subsequently acquired by the Government. Total government grant-in-aid for 1999–2000 is £2.453 million.
Director, Miss R. J. Savill
Head of Administration, A. W. Houldershaw

NATIONAL GALLERIES OF SCOTLAND
The Mound, Edinburgh EH2 2EL
Tel 0131-624 6200; fax 0131-343 3250
The National Galleries of Scotland comprise the National Gallery of Scotland, the Scottish National Portrait Gallery, the Scottish National Gallery of Modern Art and the Dean Gallery. There are also outstations at Paxton House, Berwickshire, and Duff House, Banffshire. Total government grant-in-aid for 1999–2000 is £10.197 million.

TRUSTEES
Chairman of the Trustees, The Countess of Airlie, CVO
Trustees, Ms V. Atkinson; J. H. Blair; G. J. N. Gemmell, CBE; Lord Gordon of Strathblane, CBE; A. P. Leitch; Prof. Christina Lodder; Dr I. McKenzie Smith, OBE; Dr M. Shea; G. Weaver; Prof. I. Whyte

OFFICERS
Director (*G4*), T. Clifford
Keeper of Conservation (*G6*), M. Gallagher
Head of Press and Information (*G7*), Mrs A. M. Wagener
Keeper of Education (*G7*), M. Cassin
Registrar (*G7*), Miss A. Buddle
Secretary (*G6*), Ms S. Edwards
Buildings (*G7*), R. Galbraith
Keeper, National Gallery of Scotland (*G6*), M. Clarke
Keeper, Scottish National Portrait Gallery (*G6*), J. Holloway
Curator of Photography, Miss S. F. Stevenson
Keeper, Scottish National Gallery of Modern Art and Dean Gallery (*G6*), R. Calvocoressi

ASSEMBLY OMBUDSMAN FOR NORTHERN IRELAND AND NORTHERN IRELAND COMMISSIONER FOR COMPLAINTS
Progressive House, 33 Wellington Place, Belfast BT1 6HN
Tel 01232-233821; fax 01232-234912

The Ombudsman is appointed under legislation with powers to investigate complaints by people claiming to have sustained injustice in consequence of maladministration arising from action taken by a Northern Ireland government department, or any other public body within his remit. Staff are presently seconded from the Northern Ireland Civil Service.
Ombudsman, G. Burns, MBE
Deputy Ombudsman, J. MacQuarrie
Directors, C. O'Hare; R. Doherty; H. Mallon

UK ATOMIC ENERGY AUTHORITY

Harwell, Didcot, Oxon OX11 ORA
Tel 01235-820220; fax 01235-436401

The UKAEA was established by the Atomic Energy Authority Act 1954 and took over responsibility for the research and development of the civil nuclear power programme. The Authority's commercial arm, AEA Technology PLC, was privatized in 1996. UKAEA is responsible for the safe management and decommissioning of its radioactive plant and for maximizing the income from the buildings and land on its sites. UKAEA also undertakes special nuclear tasks for the Government, including the UK's contribution to the international fusion programme.

Chairman, Adm. Sir Kenneth Eaton
Chief Executive, Dr J. McKeown

AUDIT COMMISSIONS

AUDIT COMMISSION FOR LOCAL AUTHORITIES AND THE NATIONAL HEALTH SERVICE IN ENGLAND AND WALES

1 Vincent Square, London SW1P 2PN
Tel 0171-828 1212; fax 0171-976 6187

The Audit Commission was set up in 1983 and is responsible for appointing external auditors to local authorities and local National Health Service bodies in England and Wales. It is also responsible for promoting the proper stewardship of public finances and value for money in the services provided by local authorities and health bodies.

The Commission has a chairman, a deputy chairman and up to 18 members who, though appointed by the Secretary of State for the Environment, Transport and the Regions in consultation with the Health Secretaries in England and Wales, are responsible to Parliament.

Chairman, Dame Helena Shovelton, DBE
Deputy Chairman, J. Orme
Controller of Audit, A. Foster
Commission Secretary, Ms C. Baldwinson
Chief Executive of District Audit Service, D. Prince

ACCOUNTS COMMISSION FOR SCOTLAND

18 George Street, Edinburgh EH2 2QU
Tel 0131-477 1234; fax 0131-477 4567

The Commission was set up in 1975. It is responsible for securing the audit of the accounts of Scottish local authorities and certain joint boards and joint committees, and for value-for-money audits of authorities. In 1995 it assumed responsibility for securing the audit of National Health Service bodies in Scotland. The Commission is required to deal with reports made by the Controller of Audit on items of account contrary to law; on incorrect accounting; and on losses due to misconduct, negligence and failure to carry out statutory duties.

Members are appointed by the First Minister.

Chairman, Prof. J. P. Percy, CBE
Controller of Audit, R. W. Black
Secretary, W. F. Magee

THE BANK OF ENGLAND

Threadneedle Street, London EC2R 8AH
Tel 0171-601 4444; fax 0171-601 4771

The Bank of England was incorporated in 1694 under royal charter. It is the banker of the Government and manages the note issue. Since May 1997 it has been operationally independent and its Monetary Policy Committee has had responsibility for setting short-term interest rates to meet the Government's inflation target. As the central reserve bank of the country, the Bank keeps the accounts of British banks, who maintain with it a proportion of their cash resources, and of most overseas central banks. The Bank is divided into two divisions, Monetary Stability and Financial Stability. Its responsibility for banking supervision has been transferred to the Financial Services Authority. (*See also* page 635).

Governor, The Rt. Hon. E. A. J. George
Deputy Governors, D. Clementi; M. A. King
Non-Executive Directors, C. J. Allsopp; R. Bailie, OBE; A. R. F. Buxton; Sir David Cooksey; H. J. Davies; Sir Ian Gibson; G. Hawker; Mrs F. A. Heaton; Sir John Keswick; Dame Sheila Masters, DBE; Ms S. McKechnie, OBE; W. Morris; J. Neill, CBE, PH.D.; Ms K. O'Donovan; N. I. Simms; J. Stretton
Monetary Policy Committee, The Governor; the Deputy Governors; I. Plenderleith; Prof. C. Goodhart; Dr D. Julius; Prof. W. Buiter; J. Vickers; Dr S. Wadhwani
Advisers to the Governor, Sir Peter Petrie; L. Berkowitz; D. Brealey
Chief Cashier and Deputy Director, Banking and Market Services, Ms M. V. Lowther
Chief Registrar, G. P. Sparkes
General Manager, Printing Works, A. W. Jarvis
Secretary, P. D. Rodgers
The Auditor, K. Butler

BOUNDARY COMMISSIONS

The Commissions are constituted under the Parliamentary Constituencies Act 1986. The Speaker of the House of Commons is *ex officio* chairman of all four commissions in the UK. Each of the four commissions is required by law to keep the parliamentary constituencies in their part of the UK under review. The latest review was completed in 1995 and its proposals took effect at the 1997 general election. The next review is due to be completed between 2002 and 2006.

ENGLAND
1 Drummond Gate, London SW1V 2QQ
Tel 0171-533 5177; fax 0171-533 5176

Deputy Chairman, The Hon. Mr Justice Harrison
Joint Secretaries, R. Farrance; S. Limpkin

WALES
1 Drummond Gate, London SW1V 2QQ
Tel 0171-533 5172; fax 0171-533 5176

Deputy Chairman, The Hon. Mr Justice Kay
Joint Secretaries, R. Farrance; S. Limpkin

SCOTLAND
3 Drumsheugh Gardens, Edinburgh EH3 7QJ
Tel 0131-538 7200; fax 0131-538 7240

Deputy Chairman, The Hon. Lady Cosgrove
Secretary, R. Smith

NORTHERN IRELAND
REL Division, 11 Millbank, London SW1P 4PN
Tel 0171-210 6569

Deputy Chairman, The Hon. Mr Justice Coghlin
Secretary, Mrs L. Rogers

BRITISH BROADCASTING CORPORATION

Broadcasting House, Portland Place, London WIA IAA
Tel 0171-580 4468; fax 0171-637 1630
Television Centre, Wood Lane, London W12 7RJ
Tel 0181-743 8000; fax 0181-749 7520

The BBC was incorporated under royal charter in 1926 as successor to the British Broadcasting Company Ltd. The BBC's current charter came into force on 1 May 1996 and extends to 31 December 2006. The chairman, vice-chairman and other governors are appointed by The Queen-in-Council. The BBC is financed by revenue from receiving licences for the home services and by grant-in-aid from Parliament for the World Service (radio). For services, *see* Broadcasting section.

BOARD OF GOVERNORS

Chairman (£67,420), Sir Christopher Bland
Vice-Chairman (£17,300), The Baroness Young of Old Scone
National Governors (*each* £17,300), Prof. F. Monds
  (*N. Ireland*); R. S. Jones, OBE (*Wales*); Sir Robert Smith
  (*Scotland*)
Chairman, English National Forum (£13,000), R. Sondhi
Governors (*each* £8,660), Sir David Scholey, CBE; Sir
  Richard Eyre, CBE; A. White, CBE; Dame Pauline
  Neville-Jones, DCMG; A. Young; Ms H. Rabbatts

BOARD OF MANAGEMENT

EXECUTIVE COMMITTEE
Director-General and Editor-in-Chief (£387,000), Sir John
  Birt (until April 2000); G. Dyke (from April 2000)
Chief Executives, M. Bannister (*BBC Production*); W. Wyatt
  (*BBC Broadcast*); T. Hall (*BBC News*); R. Lynch (*BBC
  Resources Ltd*); R. Gavin (*BBC Worldwide*); M. Byford
  (*World Service*)
Directors, Ms M. Salmon (*Personnel*); Ms P. Hodgson (*Policy
  and Planning*); J. Smith (*Finance*); C. Browne (*Corporate
  Affairs*)

OTHER BOARD OF MANAGEMENT MEMBERS
Directors, A. Yentob (*Television*); Ms J. Abramsky (*Radio*);
  Ms J. Drabble (*Education*); M. Thompson (*Regional
  Broadcasting*)

OTHER SENIOR STAFF

The Secretary, C. Graham
Director, Continuous News, R. Mosey
Controller, BBC1, P. Salmon
Controller, BBC2, Ms J. Root
Controller, Radio 1, A. Parfitt
Controller, Radio 2, J. Moir
Controller, Radio 3, R. Wright
Controller, Radio 4, J. Boyle
Controller, Radio 5 Live, R. Mosey
Controller, BBC Proms and Millennium Programmes,
  N. Kenyon
Controller, BBC Scotland, J. McCormick
Controller, BBC Wales, G. Talfan Davies
Controller, BBC N. Ireland, P. Loughrey
Controller, English Regions, A. Griffee

THE BRITISH COUNCIL

10 Spring Gardens, London SW1A 2BN
Tel 0171-930 8466; fax 0171-839 6347
Bridgewater House, 58 Whitworth Street, Manchester
M15 4AA
Tel 0161-957 7755; fax 0161-957 7762
Arts Division: 11 Portland Place, London W1N 4EJ
Tel 0171-389 3001; fax 0171-389 3199

The British Council was established in 1934, incorporated by royal charter in 1940 and granted a supplemental charter in 1993. It is an independent, non-political organization which promotes Britain abroad. It is the UK's international network for education, culture and development services. The Council is represented in 230 towns and cities in 109 countries and runs 209 libraries, 95 teaching centres and 29 resource centres around the world.

Total income in 1998–9, including Foreign and Commonwealth Office grants and contracted money, was £424.639 million.
Chairman, The Baroness Kennedy of The Shaws, QC
Deputy Chairman, Sir Tim Lankester, KCB
Director-General, D. Green

BRITISH FILM COMMISSION

70 Baker Street, London W1M 1DJ
Tel 0171-224 5000; fax 0171-224 1013

The British Film Commission was set up in 1991 and is funded by the Department for Culture, Media and Sport. The Commission promotes the UK as an international production centre, encourages the use of locations, facilities, services and personnel, and provides, at no charge to the film makers, comprehensive advice and information relating to the practical aspects of filming in the UK.

The Government has announced plans to establish a new film body by April 2000 which would incorporate the work currently undertaken by the Commision.
Commissioner and Chief Executive, S. Norris

BRITISH FILM INSTITUTE

21 Stephen Street, London W1P 2LN
Tel 0171-255 1444; fax 0171-436 7950

The British Film Institute was founded in 1933 and is now established by royal charter. It is the UK national agency with responsibility for encouraging the arts of film and television and conserving them in the national interest. The BFI has three main operating departments: bfi Collections, which runs the National Film and Television Archive; bfi Exhibition, which runs the National Film Theatre and the London Film Festival; and bfi Education, which comprises the National Library, publishing and education projects. Total government funding for 1999–2000 is £16.8 million.

The Government has announced plans to establish a new film body by April 2000 which would incorporate the work currently undertaken by the Institute.
Chairman, A. Parker, CBE
Deputy Chairman, Ms J. Bakewell, CBE
Director, J. Woodward
Deputy Director, J. Teckman

BRITISH PHARMACOPOEIA COMMISSION

Market Towers, 1 Nine Elms Lane, London sw8 5NQ
Tel 0171-273 0561; fax 0171-273 0566

The British Pharmacopoeia Commission sets standards for medicinal products used in human and veterinary medicines and is responsible for publication of the British Pharmacopoeia (a publicly available statement of the standard that a product must meet throughout its shelf-life), the British Pharmacopoeia (Veterinary) and the selection of British Approved Names. It has 13 members who are appointed by the Secretary of State for Health, the Minister for Agriculture, Fisheries and Food, the Scottish ministers, the National Assembly for Wales, and the relevant Northern Ireland departments.

Chairman, Prof. D. Calam, OBE, D.Phil.
Vice-Chairman, Prof. J. A. Goldsmith
Secretary and Scientific Director, Dr R. C. Hutton

BRITISH RAILWAYS BOARD and SHADOW STRATEGIC RAIL AUTHORITY

26 Old Queen Street, London SW1H 9HP
Tel 0171-960 1500; fax 0171-960 1501

The British Railways Board came into being in 1963 under the terms of the Transport Act 1962. Under the Railways Act 1993, the activities of the Board were restructured and largely transferred to the private sector. Its residual responsibilities include disposing of surplus land and advising the Government on rail policy issues.

The Government announced in July 1998 that British Rail's residual functions would be taken over by a Strategic Rail Authority, which has been operating in shadow form since 1 April 1999 and will do so until the required legislation in enacted, probably in 2000. When the authority is set up it will also incorporate the functions of the Passenger Franchising Director and some functions currently exercised by the Rail Regulator and the Department of the Environment, Transport and the Regions. Its main responsibilities will be strategic planning, co-ordinating and supervising the activities of the rail industry, and the disbursement of public funds.

Chairman, British Railways Board and Shadow Strategic Rail Authority (£130,000), Sir Alastair Morton
Vice-Chairman, J. J. Jerram, CBE
Non-executive Members (part-time), M. J. Grant (The Franchising Director, *ex officio*); D. A. Begg; Miss K. T. Kantor
Secretary, P. Trewin

BRITISH STANDARDS INSTITUTION (BSI)

389 Chiswick High Road, London w4 4AL
Tel 0181-996 9000; fax 0181-996 7344

The British Standards Institution is the recognized authority in the UK for the preparation and publication of national standards for industrial and consumer products. About 90 per cent of its standards work is now internationally linked. British Standards are issued for voluntary adoption, though in a number of cases compliance with a British Standard is required by legislation. Industrial and consumer products certified as complying with the relevant British Standard may carry the Institution's certification trade mark, known as the 'Kitemark'.

Chairman, V. E. Thomas, CBE
Chief Executive, K. Tozzi

BRITISH TOURIST AUTHORITY

Thames Tower, Black's Road, London w6 9EL
Tel 0181-846 9000; fax 0181-563 0302

Established under the Development of Tourism Act 1969, the British Tourist Authority is responsible for promoting tourism to Great Britain from overseas. It also has a general responsibility for the promotion and development of tourism and tourist facilities within Great Britain as a whole, and for advising the Secretary of State for Culture, Media and Sport on tourism matters.

Chairman (part-time), D. Quarmby
Chief Executive, J. Hamblin

BRITISH WATERWAYS

Willow Grange, Church Road, Watford, Herts wd1 3QA
Tel 01923-226422; fax 01923-201400

British Waterways conserves and manages over 2,000 miles of canals and rivers in England, Scotland and Wales. It is responsible to the Secretary of State for the Environment, Transport and the Regions. Its responsibilities include maintaining the waterways and structures on and around them; looking after wildlife and the waterway environment; and ensuring that canals and rivers are safe and enjoyable places to visit.

Chairman (part-time), Dr G. Greener
Members (part-time), D. H. R. Yorke; Sir Neil Cossons; Ms J. Elvey; Ms J. Lewis-Jones; Ms C. Dobson; P. King; P. Soulsby; C. Christie
Chief Executive, D. Fletcher
Director of Corporate Services, R. J. Duffy

BROADCASTING STANDARDS COMMISSION

7 The Sanctuary, London SW1P 3JS
Tel 0171-233 0544; fax 0171-233 0397

The Commission was established in April 1997 under the Broadcasting Act 1996. It is an independent organization representing the interests of the consumer, and its remit covers all television and radio broadcasting. The Commission considers the portrayal of violence and sexual conduct and matters of taste and decency. It also provides redress for people who believe they have been unfairly treated or subjected to unwarranted infringement of privacy. The Commission conducts research into standards and fairness in broadcasting and produces codes of practice, and it considers and adjudicates on complaints. Members of the Commission are appointed by the Secretary of State for Culture, Media and Sport. The appointments are part-time.

Chair (£45,210), vacant
Deputy Chairmen (£34,000–£36,000), Ms J. Leighton; Mrs S. Warner
Commissioners (each £14,960), Ms D. Barr; D. Boulton; Dame Fiona Caldicott, DBE; U. Dholakia; S. Heppel, CB; Revd Rose Hudson Wilkin; J. Mitchell; Ms S. O'Sullivan; M. Unger; Ms S. Wyn Thomas
Director, S. Whittle

BUILDING SOCIETIES COMMISSION
12th Floor, 25 The North Colonnade, Canary Wharf,
London E14 5HS
Tel 0171-676 1000

The Building Societies Commission was established by the Building Societies Act 1986. The Commission is responsible for the supervision of building societies and administers the system of prudential regulation. It also advises the Treasury and other government departments on matters relating to building societies.

The Government has proposed to Parliament that the functions of the Commission should pass to the Financial Services Authority (*see* page 635) on implementation of the Financial Services and Markets Bill.

BUILDING SOCIETIES COMMISSION
Chairman, G. E. Fitchew
Deputy Chairman, Ms C. Sergeant
Commissioners, S. Mundy; J. M. Palmer; *F. G. Sunderland; *Sir James Birrell; *N. Fox Bassett; *F. E. Worsley
* part-time

COMMISSION STAFF
Assistant Commissioners, W. Champion; E. Engstrom
Secretary, G. Johnson

THE BROADS AUTHORITY
Thomas Harvey House, 18 Colegate, Norwich NR3 1BQ
Tel 01603-610734; fax 01603-765710

The Broads Authority is a special statutory authority set up under the Norfolk and Suffolk Broads Act 1988. The functions of the Authority are to conserve and enhance the natural beauty of the Broads; to provide integrated management of the land and water space of the area; to promote the enjoyment of the Broads by the public; and to protect the interests of navigation. The Authority comprises 35 members, appointed by the local authorities in the area covered, environmental conservation bodies, the Environment Agency, and the Great Yarmouth Port Authority.
Chairman, The Viscountess Knollys
Chief Executive, Prof. M. A. Clark, OBE

THE CABINET OFFICE
70 Whitehall, London SW1A 2AS
Tel 0171-270 3000
*Horse Guards Road, London SW1P 3AL
Tel 0171-270 1234
Web: http://www.open.gov.uk/co/

The Cabinet Office comprises the Secretariat, who support Ministers collectively in the conduct of Cabinet business; and units responsible for modernizing government and helping to improve the quality, coherence and responsiveness of public services. It is also responsible for Senior Civil Service and public appointments, market testing and efficiency in the Civil Service, and Civil Service recruitment. The Cabinet Office supports the Prime Minister in his capacity as Minister for the Civil Service, with responsibility for day-to-day supervision delegated to the Minister for the Cabinet Office, who is also responsible for the Central Office of Information (*see* page 288).

Prime Minister and Minister for the Civil Service,
    The Rt. Hon. Tony Blair, MP
Minister for the Cabinet Office and Chancellor of the Duchy of Lancaster, The Rt. Hon. Dr Jack Cunningham, MP

Principal Private Secretary (SCS), Dr J. Fuller
Private Secretary, Ms B. Feeny
Special Advisers, T. Walker; Ms A. Healy
Minister of State, The Lord Falconer of Thoroton, QC
Private Secretary, M. Langdale
Parliamentary Private Secretary, C. Leslie, MP
Minister of State, Ian McCartney, MP
Private Secretary, Ms N. Pitts
Secretary of the Cabinet and Head of the Home Civil Service, Sir Richard Wilson, KCB
Private Secretary (SCS), S. Wood
Second Permanent Secretary, B. Bender, CB
Private Secretary, M. Sweeney
Parliamentary Clerk, S. Brown
Chief Scientific Adviser, Sir Robert May, FRS

PRIME MINISTER'S OFFICE
10 Downing Street, London SW1A 2AA
Tel 0171-270 3000; fax 0171-925 0918
Web: http://www.number-10.gov.uk

Principal Private Secretary, J. J. Heywood
Chief of Staff (£91,014), J. Powell
Private Secretaries, J. Sawers (*Foreign Affairs*); R. Read
    (*Parliamentary Affairs*); D. North (*Home Affairs*); O.
    Barder (*Economic Affairs*); P. Barton (*Assistant on Foreign
    Affairs*)
Diary Secretary, Ms K. Garvey
Special Assistant for Presentation and Planning, Ms A. Hunter
Assistant to Mrs Blair, Ms F. Millar
Political Secretary, Ms S. Morgan
Head of Policy Unit, D. Miliband
Policy Unit, G. Mulgan; R. Liddle; D. Scott; Ms E. Lloyd;
    P. Hyman; J. Purnell; P. McFadden; R. Hill; G. Norris;
    Ms S. White; A. Adonis
Parliamentary Private Secretary, B. Grocott, MP
Chief Press Secretary (£91,014), A. Campbell
Deputy Press Secretary, G. Smith
Special Advisers, Press Office, Ms H. Coffman; L. Price
Press Officers, P. Willinson; Ms L. McNeil; D. Peel; J.
    Braithwaite; Mrs M. Cleaver
Strategic Communications Unit, A. Evans; P. Bassett; D.
    Bradshaw; J. Humphreys; Ms S. Kenny; A. Silverman
*Secretary for Appointments, and Ecclesiastical Secretary to the
    Lord Chancellor,* J. Holroyd, CB, CVO
Parliamentary Clerk, Mrs H. Murray

SECRETARIAT

ECONOMIC AND DOMESTIC SECRETARIAT
Head (SCS), W. Rickett
Deputy Heads (SCS), J. Gallagher; P. Britton
Adviser on Parliamentary Procedures (SCS), A. Kennon

DEFENCE AND OVERSEAS AFFAIRS SECRETARIAT
Head of Secretariat and Chairman of Joint Intelligence Committee
    (SCS), The Hon. M. Pakenham, CMG
Deputy Head (SCS), D. Fisher
Head of Division (SCS), N. Sanderson
Chief of the Assessments Staff (SCS), R. Gozney

INTELLIGENCE CO-ORDINATION GROUP
Head (SCS), J. Alpass
Head of Security Division (SCS), Ms E.Chivers

EUROPEAN SECRETARIAT
Head (SCS), D. Bostock
Deputy Head (SCS), M. Donnelly
Head of Division (SCS), M. Kirk

CONSTITUTION SECRETARIAT
Head (SCS), Sir Quentin Thomas, CB
Head of Devolution Team (SCS), D. Brew
Head of Other Constitutional Reform Team (SCS), Ms J. Simpson
Head of Legal Advisers, Ms R. Jefferys

*CENTRAL SECRETARIAT
Head (SCS), D. A. Wilkinson, CB
Deputy Head (SCS), Ms S. Phippard

CEREMONIAL BRANCH
Ashley House, 2 Monck Street, London SW1P 2BQ
Tel 0171-270 1234
Honours Nomination Unit: Tel 0171-276 2775
Ceremonial Officer (SCS), A. J. Merifield, CB

PUBLIC SERVICE DELIVERY

*MODERNIZING PUBLIC SERVICES GROUP
Tel 0171-270 1838
Director (SCS), J. Rees
Deputy Directors (SCS), Mrs G. Craig; S. O'Leary, OBE; B. Avery

CENTRAL IT UNIT
53 Parliament Street, London SW1A 2NG
Tel 0171-238 2000
Director (SCS), D. Cooke
Deputy Directors (SCS), Ms M. Mayer; J. Crump; M. Gladwyn; Ms A. Steward; I. White; P. Waller

*REGULATORY IMPACT UNIT
Director (SCS), M. Stanley
Deputy Directors (SCS), M. Herron; P. Hayes; Ms A. French
Legal Adviser, P. Bovey

*MODERNIZING GOVERNMENT
Director, A. Wells
Head of Secretariat (SCS), J. Cowper

CIVIL SERVICE MANAGEMENT

*CIVIL SERVICE CORPORATE MANAGEMENT COMMAND
Senior Director (SCS), B. M. Fox, CB
Directors (SCS), J. Barker; Ms S. Hinkley, CBE
Deputy Directors (SCS), Ms A. Schofield; Ms J. Lemprière; C. J. Parry; Ms E. Goodison; D. G. Pain; S. Mitha

CENTRE FOR MANAGEMENT AND POLICY STUDIES
Director-General, Prof. R. Amman
Directors (SCS), R. Green; B. Behrens

GOVERNMENT INFORMATION AND COMMUNICATION SERVICES
Head of Government Information and Communication Services (SCS), M. Granatt
Director, Development Centre (SCS), C. Skinner
Deputy Director, Ms S. Jenkins

*OFFICE OF THE COMMISSIONER FOR PUBLIC APPOINTMENTS (OCPA)
Tel 0171-270 6472

The role of the Commissioner for Public Appointments (CPA) is to monitor, regulate and approve departmental procedures for ministerial appointments to advisory and executive non-departmental public bodies, public corporations, nationalized industries, regulators and NHS bodies. The Commissioner is appointed by Order-in-Council.
Commissioner, Dame Rennie Fritchie
Head of Office (SCS), J. Barron

*OFFICE OF THE CIVIL SERVICE COMMISSIONERS (OCSC)
Tel 0171-270 5081; fax 0171-270 5967

First Commissioner, Sir Michael Bett, CBE
Commissioners (part-time), D. J. Burr; Ms S. Forbes; H. J. F. McLean, CBE; Sir Leonard Peach; J. Shrigley; K. Singh; C. Stevens, CB; Dame Rennie Fritchie
Secretary to the Commissioners and Head of the Office (SCS), J. Barron

CROSS-CUTTING ISSUES

*SOCIAL EXCLUSION UNIT
Tel 0171-270 5211
Director of Unit (SCS), Ms M. Wallace, OBE
Deputy Directors, J. Bright; Ms Z. Peatfield; M. Wheatley

*CENTRAL DRUGS CO-ORDINATION UNIT
Tel 0171-270 5399
UK Anti-Drugs Co-ordinator (£106,057), K. Hellawell
Deputy Co-ordinator, M. Trace
Head of Unit, J. Critchley

WOMEN'S UNIT
10 Great George Street, London SW1P 3AE
Tel 0171-273 8808
Head of Unit (SCS), Ms F. Reynolds, CBE
Deputy Director, K. Palmer

*PERFORMANCE AND INNOVATION UNIT
Tel 0171-270 1512
Director (SCS), S. Chakrabarti
Deputy Director (SCS), J. Rentoul
Chief Economist, S. Aldridge
Directors, J. Norton; D. Instone; A. Lean; G. Wilkinson; Ms J. Hutcheon

INFORMATION, ESTABLISHMENT AND ORGANIZATION
Queen Anne's Chambers, 28 Broadway, London SW1H 9JS
Director of Information (SCS), B. Sutlieff
Principal Establishment and Finance Officer (SCS), Mrs N. A. Oppenheimer
Deputy Directors (SCS), Miss E. Chennells; D. Brennan; R. Harris; K. Tolladay
Ministers' Adviser on Agencies, C. Brendish, CBE

HER MAJESTY'S STATIONERY OFFICE
St Clements House, 2–16 Colegate, Norwich NR3 1BQ
Tel 01603-621000
Controller (SCS), Mrs C. Tullo

EXECUTIVE AGENCIES

THE BUYING AGENCY
Royal Liver Building, Pier Head, Liverpool L3 1PE
Tel 0151-227 4262; fax 0151-227 3315

The Agency provides a professional purchasing service to government departments and other public bodies. From April 2000 it will be part of the new Office of Government Commerce reporting to the Chief Secretary to the Treasury.
Chief Executive (SCS), S. P. Sage

CCTA (CENTRAL COMPUTER AND TELECOMMUNICATIONS AGENCY)
Rosebery Court, St Andrew's Business Park, Norwich NR7 0HS
Tel 01603-704567; fax 01603-704817
Steel House, 11 Tothill Street, London SW1H 9NF
Tel 0171-273 6565; fax 0171-273 6555

---

* Unless otherwise stated, this is the address and telephone number of directorates of the Board

CCTA's objective is to develop, maintain and make available expertise about information technology which public sector organizations can draw on in order to operate more effectively and efficiently. From April 2000 it will be part of the new Office of Government Commerce reporting to the Chief Secretary to the Treasury.
Chief Executive, R. Assirati

CIVIL SERVICE COLLEGE
Sunningdale Park, Ascot, Berks SL5 0QE
Tel 01344-634000; fax 01344-634781
11 Belgrave Road, London SW1V 1RB
Tel 0171-834 6644; fax 01344-634451
199 Cathedral Street, Glasgow G4 0QU
Tel 0141-553 6021; fax 0141-553 6171
Suite 19, 1 St Colme Street, Edinburgh EH3 6AA
Tel 0131-220 8267; fax 0131-220 8367

The College provides training in management and professional skills for the public and private sectors.
Director (G3), E. Wooldridge
Business Executives (G5/G6), M. N. Barnes; R. Behrens;
    G. W. Llewellyn; Ms L. Oliver (*Non-Executive Director*);
    P. Tebby; M. Timmis; Dr A. Wyatt

GOVERNMENT CAR AND DESPATCH AGENCY
46 Ponton Road, London SW8 5AX
Tel 0171-217 3839; fax 0171-217 3840

The Agency provides secure transport and document transfers between government departments.
Chief Executive, N. Matheson

PROPERTY ADVISERS TO THE CIVIL ESTATE
6th Floor, Trevelyan House, Great Peter Street, London SW1P 2BY
Tel 0171-271 2626; fax 0171-271 2622

The Agency promotes co-operation between government departments to enable them to obtain best value for money in the management of their property assets. It also provides them with property guidance and other property-related services. From April 2000 it will be part of the new Office of Government Commerce reporting to the Chief Secretary to the Treasury.
Chief Executive, J. C. Locke, FRICS

CENTRAL ADJUDICATION SERVICES
Quarry House, Quarry Hill, Leeds LS2 7UB
Tel 0113-232 4000; fax 0113-232 4841
New Court, 48 Carey Street, London WC2A 2LS
Tel 0171-412 1504; fax 0171-412 1220

The Chief Adjudication Officer is appointed by the Secretary of State for Social Security to give advice to adjudication officers on making decisions for social security claims and to keep under review the standards of adjudication of the Benefits Agency and the Employment Service. He reports annually to the Secretary of State.
    From 28 November 1999 under the Social Security Act 1998 all responsibility for standards of decision making will pass to the chief executives of the Benefits Agency and the Employment Service.
Chief Adjudication Officer, D. Petch (until 28 November 1999)

CENTRAL OFFICE OF INFORMATION
Hercules Road, London SE1 7DU
Tel 0171-928 2345; fax 0171-928 5037

The Central Office of Information (COI) is a government department which offers consultancy, procurement and project management services to central government for publicity. Though the majority of the COI's work is for government departments in the UK, it also procures a range of publicity materials for overseas consumption. Administrative responsibility for the COI rests with the Minister for the Cabinet Office.
Chief Executive (G3), Ms C. Fisher
    Senior Personal Secretary, Ms I. MacMull

MANAGEMENT BOARD
Members, K. Williamson; P. Buchanan; I. Hamilton; R. Haslam; Ms S. Whetton; M. Reid
Secretary, Ms I. MacMull

DIRECTORS
Director, Client Services (G6), I. Hamilton
Director, Marketing Communications (G6), P. Buchanan
Director, Films, Radio and Events (G6), S. Whetton
Director, Publications (G6), M. Reid
Director, Central Services (G5), K. Williamson
Director, Regional Network (G6), R. Haslam

NETWORK OFFICES

EASTERN, 2nd Floor, Block A1, Westbrook Centre, Milton Road, Cambridge CB4 1YG. *Network Director (G7),* P. Powell
MIDLANDS EAST, 1st Floor, Severns House, 20 Middle Pavement, Nottingham NG1 7DW. *Network Director (G7),* P. Smith
MIDLANDS WEST, Five Ways House, Islington Row, Middleway, Edgbaston, Birmingham B15 1SH. *Network Director (G6),* B. Garner
NORTH-EAST, Wellbar House, Gallowgate, Newcastle upon Tyne NE1 4TB. *Network Director (G7),* Ms L. Taylor
NORTH-WEST, Sunley Tower, Piccadilly Plaza, Manchester M1 4BD. *Network Director (G7),* Mrs E. Jones
SOUTH-EAST, Hercules Road, London SE1 7DU. *Network Director (G6),* Ms V. Burdon
SOUTH-WEST, The Pithay, Bristol BS1 2NF. *Network Director (G7),* P. Whitbread
YORKSHIRE AND HUMBERSIDE, City House, New Station Street, Leeds LS1 4JG. *Network Director (G7),* Ms W. Miller

CERTIFICATION OFFICE FOR TRADE UNIONS AND EMPLOYERS' ASSOCIATIONS
180 Borough High Street, London SE1 1LW
Tel 0171-210 3734/5; fax 0171-210 3612

The Certification Office is an independent statutory authority. The Certification Officer is appointed by the Secretary of State for Trade and Industry and is responsible for receiving and scrutinizing annual returns from trade unions and employers' associations; for investigating allegations of financial irregularities in the affairs of a trade union or employers' association; for dealing with complaints concerning trade union elections; for ensuring observance of statutory requirements governing political funds and trade union mergers; and for certifying the independence of trade unions.
Certification Officer, E. G. Whybrew
Assistant Certification Officer, G. S. Osborne

SCOTLAND
58 Frederick Street, Edinburgh EH2 1LN
Tel 0131-226 3224; fax 0131-200 1300
Assistant Certification Officer for Scotland, J. L. J. Craig

CHARITY COMMISSION

Harmsworth House, 13–15 Bouverie Street, London EC4Y
8DP
Tel 0870-333 0123; fax 0171-674 2310
2nd Floor, 20 King's Parade, Queen's Dock, Liverpool
L3 4DQ
Tel 0151-703 1500; fax 0151-703 1557
Woodfield House, Tangier, Taunton, Somerset TA1 4BL
Tel 01823-345000; fax 01823-345008

The Charity Commission is established under the Charities
Act 1993 with the general function of promoting the
effective use of charitable resources in England and Wales.
The Commission gives information and advice to charity
trustees to make the administration of their charity more
effective; investigates misconduct and the abuse of charitable assets, and takes or recommends remedial action; and
maintains a public register of charities. The Commission
does not have at its disposal any funds with which to make
grants to organizations or individuals.

At the end of 1998 there were 186,248 registered
charities.

Chief Commissioner (G3), J. Stoker
Legal Commissioner (G3), M. Carpenter
Commissioners (part-time) (G4), J. Bonds; Ms J. Warburton;
Ms J. Unwin
Heads of Legal Sections (G5), J. A. Dutton; G. S. Goodchild;
K. M. Dibble; S. Slack
Executive Director (G4), Ms L. Berry
Head of Policy Division (G5), R. Carter
Establishment Officer (G5), Ms C. Stewart
Information Systems Controller (G5), Ms G. Cruickshank

The offices responsible for charities in Scotland and
Northern Ireland are:
SCOTLAND – Scottish Charities Office, Crown Office, 25
Chambers Street, Edinburgh EH1 1LA. Tel: 0131-226
2626
NORTHERN IRELAND – Department of Health and
Social Services, Charities Branch, Annexe 3, Castle
Buildings, Stormont Estate, Belfast BT4 3RA. Tel: 01232-
522780

CHIEF ADJUDICATION OFFICER
— *see* Central Adjudication Services

CHILD SUPPORT AGENCY
— *see* page 342

CHURCH COMMISSIONERS
1 Millbank, London SW1P 3JZ
Tel 0171-222 7010; fax 0171-233 0171

The Church Commissioners were established in 1948 by
the amalgamation of Queen Anne's Bounty (established
1704) and the Ecclesiastical Commissioners (established
1836). They are responsible for the management of most
of the Church of England's assets, the income from which
is predominantly used to pay, house and pension the clergy.
The Commissioners own 51,000 acres of agricultural land,
a number of residential estates in central London, and
commercial property in Great Britain. They also carry out
administrative duties in connection with pastoral reorganization and redundant churches.

The Commissioners are: the Archbishops of Canterbury
and of York; four bishops, three clergy and four lay persons
elected by the respective houses of the General Synod;

two deans or provosts elected by all the deans and provosts;
three persons nominated by The Queen; three persons
nominated by the Archbishops of Canterbury and York;
three persons nominated by the Archbishops after consultation with others including the lord mayors of London
and York and the vice-chancellors of the universities of
Oxford and Cambridge; the First Lord of the Treasury;
the Lord President of the Council; the Home Secretary;
the Lord Chancellor; the Secretary of State for Culture,
Media and Sport; and the Speaker of the House of
Commons.

INCOME AND EXPENDITURE
for year ended 31 December 1998

	£ million
Total income	139.9
Net income	128.6
Investments	76.2
Property	45.9
Interest from loans, etc.	17.8
	158.9
Total expenditure	
Parochial ministry support	20.0
Bishop and cathedral clergy stipends	6.3
Bishops' housing	3.0
Grants to cathedrals	2.4
Financial provision for resigning clergy	1.8
Clergy pensions	108.2
Church buildings	1.1
Bishops' working cost	8.8
Commissioners' administration and administration	5.3
of central church functions	
Administration costs of other church bodies	2.0
Deficit for year	19.0

CHURCH ESTATES COMMISSIONERS
First, J. Sclater, CVO
Second, S. Bell, MP
Third, The Viscountess Brentford

OFFICERS
Secretary, H. H. Hughes
Deputy Secretary (Finance and Investment), C. W. Daws
Official Solicitor, N. I. Johnson
Assistant Secretaries:
    The Accountant, G. C. Baines
    Management Accountant, B. J. Hardy
    Chief Surveyor, A. C. Brown
    Computer Manager, J. W. Ferguson
    Bishoprics Secretary, E. G. Peacock
    Investments Manager, A. S. Hardy
    Pastoral, Houses and Redundant Churches, M. D. Elengorn
    Senior Architect, J. A. Taylor

CIVIL AVIATION AUTHORITY
CAA House, 45–59 Kingsway, London WC2B 6TE
Tel 0171-379 7311; fax: 0171-240 1153

The CAA is responsible for the economic regulation of
UK airlines and for the safety regulation of UK civil
aviation by the certification of airlines and aircraft and by
licensing aerodromes, flight crew and aircraft engineers.
Through its subsidiary company, National Air Traffic
Services Ltd (NATS), it is also responsible for the provision
of air traffic control and telecommunications services. The
Government announced in July 1999 that it planned to
separate safety regulation from service provision and sell
51 per cent of NATS to the private sector.

The CAA advises the Government on aviation issues,

represents consumer interests, conducts economic and scientific research, produces statistical data, and provides specialist services and other training and consultancy services to clients world-wide.
Chairman, Sir Malcolm Field
Secretary, R. J. Britton

THE COAL AUTHORITY
200 Lichfield Lane, Mansfield, Notts NG18 4RG
Tel 01623-427162; fax: 01623-622072

The Coal Authority was established under the Coal Industry Act 1994 to manage certain functions previously undertaken by British Coal, including ownership of unworked coal. It is responsible for licensing coal mining operations and for providing information on coal reserves and past and future coal mining. It settles subsidence claims not falling on coal mining operators. It deals with the management and disposal of property, and with surface hazards such as abandoned coal mine shafts.
Chairman, J. Harris
Chief Executive, K. J. Fergusson

COMMISSION FOR ARCHITECTURE AND THE BUILT ENVIRONMENT
7 St James's Square, London SW1Y 4JU
Tel 0171-839 6537; fax 0171-839 8475

The Commission for Architecture and the Built Environment (CABE) replaced the Royal Fine Art Commission (RFAC) in August 1999. It has taken over the RFAC's design review function, and is also responsible for promoting the importance of high quality architecture and urban design and encouraging the understanding of architecture through educational initiatives and grant programmes.
Chairman, S. A. Lipton
Secretary, F. Golding

COMMISSION FOR INTEGRATED TRANSPORT
Great Minster House, 76 Marsham Street, London SW1P 4DR
Tel 0171-890 4918/4453/4813; fax 0171-676 2167

The Commission for Integrated Transport was proposed in the 1998 Transport White Paper and was set up in June 1999. Its role is to provide independent expert advice to the Government in order to achieve a transport system that supports sustainable development. Members of the Commission are appointed by the Secretary of State for the Environment, Transport and the Regions.
Chairman (£25,000), Prof. D. Begg
Vice-Chairman (£17,500), Sir Trevor Chinn
Members (£5,000 each), Prof. B. Bradshaw; L. Christensen, CBE; N. Gavron; S. Joseph; D. Leeder; Ms L. Matson; W. Morris; J. O'Brien; Ms V. Palmer; M. Parker; N. Reilly
Ex-Officio Members, Sir Malcolm Field (*Chairman, Civil Aviation Authority*); L. Haynes (*Chief Executive, Highways Agency*); Sir Alastair Morton (*Chairman, British Railways Board and Head, Shadow Strategic Rail Authority*); Ms J. Wilmot (*Chair, Disabled Persons Transport Advisory Committee*)
Secretary (G7), P. Carey

COMMONWEALTH DEVELOPMENT CORPORATION
1 Bessborough Gardens, London SW1V 2JQ
Tel 0171-828 4488; fax 0171-828 6505

The Commonwealth Development Corporation (CDC) assists overseas countries in the development of their economies. Its sponsoring department is the Department for International Development. Its main activity is providing long-term finance, as loans and risk capital, for financially viable and developmentally sound business enterprises. CDC's area of operations includes UK overseas territories and, with ministerial approval, Commonwealth or other developing countries. At present, CDC is authorized to operate in more than 60 countries and territories. Its investments at the end of 1998 were US$2.4 billion.

Legislation was introduced in Parliament in November 1998 under which the CDC would become a public limited company and operate as a public/private partnership.
Chairman (*part-time*), The Earl Cairns, CBE
Deputy Chair (*part-time*), Ms J. Almond
Chief Executive, Dr R. Reynolds

COMMONWEALTH SECRETARIAT
— *see* Index

COMMONWEALTH WAR GRAVES COMMISSION
2 Marlow Road, Maidenhead, Berks SL6 7DX
Tel 01628-634221; fax 01628-771208

The Commonwealth War Graves Commission (formerly Imperial War Graves Commission) was founded by royal charter in 1917. It is responsible for the commemoration of 1,695,098 members of the forces of the Commonwealth who fell in the two world wars. More than one million graves are maintained in 23,216 burial grounds throughout the world. Over three-quarters of a million men and women who have no known grave or who were cremated are commemorated by name on memorials built by the Commission.

The funds of the Commission are derived from the six participating governments, i.e. the UK, Canada, Australia, India, New Zealand and South Africa.
President, HRH The Duke of Kent, KG, GCMG, GCVO, ADC
Chairman, The Secretary of State for Defence in the UK
Vice-Chairman, Adm. Sir John Kerr, GCB
Members, The High Commissioners in London for Canada, New Zealand, India, South Africa and Australia; The Viscount Ridley, KG, GCVO, TD; Prof. R. J. O'Neill, AO; Mrs L. Golding, MP; J. Wilkinson, MP; Sir John Gray, KBE, CMG; P. D. Orchard-Lisle, CBE, TD; Air Chief Marshal Sir Michael Stear, KCB, CBE; Gen. Sir John Wilsey, GCB, CBE
Director-General and Secretary to the Commission, D. Kennedy, CMG
Deputy Director-General, R. J. Dalley
Legal Adviser and Solicitor, G. C. Reddie
Directors, D. R. Parker (*Personnel*); A. Coombe (*Works*); R. D. Wilson (*Finance*); D. C. Parker (*Horticulture*); L. J. Hanna (*Information and Secretariat*)

IMPERIAL WAR GRAVES ENDOWMENT FUND
Trustees, The Lord Remnant, CVO, FCA (*Chairman*); A. C. Barker; Adm. Sir John Kerr, GCB
Secretary to the Trustees, R. D. Wilson

COMPETITION COMMISSION
New Court, 48 Carey Street, London WC2A 2JT
Tel 0171-271 0100; fax 0171-271 0367

The Commission was established in 1948 as the Monopolies and Restrictive Practices Commission (later the Monopolies and Mergers Commission); it became the Competition Commission in April 1999 under the Competition Act 1998. Its role is to investigate and report on matters which are referred to it by the Secretary of State for Trade and Industry or the Director-General of Fair Trading or, in the case of regulated utilities, by the appropriate regulator. It has no power to initiate its own investigations.

The Appeal Tribunals of the Competition Commission will hear appeals against decisions by the Director-General of Fair Trading and the utility regulators in respect of the prohibitions on anti-competitive agreements and abuse of a dominant position to be introduced in March 2000 under the Competition Act 1998.

The Commission has a full-time chairman, two part-time deputy chairmen and about 35 reporting panel members to carry out investigations. All are appointed by the Secretary of State for Trade and Industry.
Chairman (£123,600), D. Morris, PH.D.
Deputy Chairmen (£54,106–£72,141), P. G. Corbett, CBE; Ms D. Kingsmill
President-designate, Appeal Tribunals, His Hon. Judge Bellamy, QC
Members (£15,628 each), H. Aldous; Prof. J. Beatson, QC; R. Bertram; Mrs S. Brown; Prof. M. Cave; A. T. Clothier; R. H. F. Croft, CB; C. Darke; N. H. Finney, OBE; Prof. P. Geroski; Prof. C. Graham; D. B. Hammond; Ms J. C. Hanratty; C. Henderson, CB; D. J. Jenkins, MBE; R. Lyons; P. MacKay, CB; Dr Elizabeth Monck; Ms K. M. H. Mortimer; R. J. Munson; Prof. D. M. G. Newbery, FBA; Dr Gill Owen; M. R. Prosser; A. Pryor, CB; R. Rawlinson; Prof. Judith Rees; T. S. Richmond, MBE; J. Rickford; Dame Helena Shovelton, DBE; G. H. Stacy, CBE; D. Start; Prof. A. Steele
Secretary, Miss P. Boys

COUNTRYSIDE AGENCY
John Dower House, Crescent Place, Cheltenham, Glos GL50 3RA
Tel 01242-521381; fax 01242-584270

The Countryside Agency was set up in April 1999 by the merger of the Countryside Commission with parts of the Rural Development Commission. It is an independent agency which promotes the conservation and enhancement of the countryside in England and undertakes activities aimed at stimulating job creation and the provision of essential services in the countryside. The Agency is funded by an annual grant from the Department of the Environment, Transport and the Regions, and board members are appointed by the Secretary of State.
Chairman, E. Cameron
Deputy Chair, Ms P. Warhurst
Members, Ms K. Ashbrook; Ms J. Bradbury; the Rt. Revd Bishop of Blackburn; M. Doughty; Dr Victoria Edwards, FRICS; Prof. P. Lowe; Ms C. Mack; M. Middleton, CBE, FCA; Ms F. Rowe; D. Woodhall, CBE
Chief Executive, R. G. Wakeford
Directors, Miss M. A. Clark, OBE; R. Clarke; D. Coleman

COUNTRYSIDE COUNCIL FOR WALES/CYNGOR CEFN GWLAD CYMRU
Plas Penrhos, Ffordd Penrhos, Bangor LL57 2LQ
Tel 01248-385500; fax 01248-385505

The Countryside Council for Wales is the Government's statutory adviser on sustaining natural beauty, wildlife and the opportunity for outdoor enjoyment in Wales and its inshore waters. It is funded by the National Assembly for Wales and accountable to the First Secretary, who appoints its members.
Chairman, E. M. W. Griffith, CBE
Chief Executive, P. E. Loveluck, CBE
Senior Director and Chief Scientist, Dr M. E. Smith
Director, Countryside Policy, Dr J. Taylor
Director, Conservation, Dr D. Parker

COVENT GARDEN MARKET AUTHORITY
Covent House, New Covent Garden Market, London SW8 5NX
Tel 0171-720 2211; fax 0171-622 5307

The Covent Garden Market Authority is constituted under the Covent Garden Market Acts 1961 to 1977, the members being appointed by the Minister of Agriculture, Fisheries and Food. The Authority owns and operates the 56-acre New Covent Garden Markets (fruit, vegetables, flowers) which have been trading since 1974.
Chairman (part-time), L. Mills, CBE
General Manager, Dr P. M. Liggins
Secretary, C. Farey

CRIMINAL CASES REVIEW COMMISSION
Alpha Tower, Suffolk Street Queensway, Birmingham B1 1TT
Tel 0121-633 1800; fax 0121-633 1823/1804

The Criminal Cases Review Commission is an independent body set up under the Criminal Appeal Act 1995. It is a non-departmental public body reporting to Parliament via the Home Secretary. It is responsible for investigating suspected miscarriages of justice in England, Wales and Northern Ireland, and deciding whether or not to refer cases back to an appeal court. Membership of the Commission is by royal appointment; the senior executive staff are appointed by the Commission.
Chairman, Sir Frederick Crawford, FREng.
Members, B. Capon; L. Elks; A. Foster; Ms J. Gort; Ms F. King; J. Knox; D. Kyle; J. Leckey; Prof. L. Leigh; J. MacKeith; K. Singh; B. Skitt; E. Weiss
Chief Executive, Ms G. Stacey
Director of Finance and Personnel, D. Robson
Legal Advisers, J. Wagstaff; M. Aspinall
Police Adviser, R. Barrington

For Scotland, *see* Scottish Criminal Cases Review Commission

CRIMINAL INJURIES COMPENSATION AUTHORITY AND BOARD
Morley House, Holborn Viaduct, London EC1A 2JQ
Tel 0171-842 6800; fax 0171-436 0804
Tay House, 300 Bath Street, Glasgow G2 4JR
Tel 0141-331 2726; fax 0141-331 2287

All applications for compensation for personal injury arising from crimes of violence in England, Scotland and

Wales are dealt with at the above locations. (Separate arrangements apply in Northern Ireland.) Applications received up to 31 March 1996 are assessed on the basis of common law damages under the 1990 compensation scheme by the Criminal Injuries Compensation Board (CICB), which was founded in 1964 under the prerogative powers of the Crown. The CICB also hears appeals. Applications received on or after 1 April 1996 are assessed under a tariff-based scheme, made under the Criminal Injuries Compensation Act 1995, by the Criminal Injuries Compensation Authority (CICA); there is a separate avenue of appeal to the Criminal Injuries Compensation Appeals Panel (CICAP). In 1998–9 total compensation paid was £194.5 million.

Chairman of the Criminal Injuries Compensation Board (part-time) (£36,951), The Lord Carlisle of Bucklow, PC, QC
Director of the Board and Chief Executive of the Criminal Injuries Compensation Authority, H. Webber
Head of Legal Services, Mrs A. M. Johnstone
Operations Manager, E. McKeown
Chairman of the Criminal Injuries Compensation Appeals Panel, M. Lewer, QC
Secretary to the Panel, Miss V. Jenson

CROFTERS COMMISSION
4–6 Castle Wynd, Inverness IV2 3EQ
Tel 01463-663450; fax 01463-711820

The Crofters Commission was established in 1955 under the Crofters (Scotland) Act. It advises the Scottish ministers on all matters relating to crofting. It seeks to develop and promote thriving crofting communities and to simplify relevant legislation. It administers the Crofting Counties Agricultural Grants Scheme, Livestock Improvement Schemes and the Croft Entrant Scheme. It also provides a free enquiry service.
Chairman, I. MacAskill
Secretary (G6), M. Grantham

CROWN ESTATE
16 Carlton House Terrace, London SW1Y 5AH
Tel 0171-210 4377; fax 0171-930 8187

The Crown Estate includes substantial blocks of urban property, primarily in London, almost 120,000 hectares of agricultural land and extensive marine holdings throughout the United Kingdom. Its origins go back to the reign of King Edward the Confessor and, until the accession of King George III, the Sovereign received its rents and profits. However, since 1760 the annual surplus, after deducting management expenses, has been surrendered by the Sovereign to Parliament to help meet the cost of civil government. In return, the Sovereign receives the Civil List and the Government meets other official expenditure incurred in support of the Sovereign.

In the year ended 31 March 1999, the gross revenue from the Crown Estate totalled £173.6 million and £125.8 million was paid to the Exchequer as surplus revenue.
First Commissioner and Chairman (part-time), Sir Denys Henderson
Second Commissioner and Chief Executive, Sir Christopher Howes, KCVO, CB
Commissioners (part-time), Mrs H. M. R. Chapman, CBE, FRICS; The Lord De Ramsey; I. D. Grant, CBE; D. E. G. Griffiths, CBE; J. H. M. Norris, CBE; R. R. Spinney, FRICS
Director of Finance and Administration, R. Bright

Director of Urban Estates, N. Borrett
Urban Estates Managers, D. A. Bickmore; M. W. Dillon; R. Wyatt
Development and Investment Manager, L. Colgan
Agricultural Estates Manager, C. Bourchier
Marine Estates Manager, F. G. Parrish
Finance Manager, J. G. Lelliott
Information Systems Manager, D. Kingston-Smith
Internal Audit Manager, J. E. Ford
Corporate Policy and Personnel Manager, M. J. Gravestock
Communications Manager, Miss I. Belcher

SCOTLAND
10 Charlotte Square, Edinburgh EH2 4BR
Tel 0131-226 7241; fax 0131-220 1366
Head of Scottish Estates, M. Cunliffe

WINDSOR ESTATE
The Great Park, Windsor, Berks SL4 2HT
Tel 01753-860222; fax 01753-859617
Deputy Ranger, P. Everrett

CROWN PROSECUTION SERVICE
— *see* pages 362–3

DEPARTMENT FOR CULTURE, MEDIA AND SPORT
2–4 Cockspur Street, London SW1Y 5DH
Tel 0171-211 6200; fax 0171-211 6032
E-mail: enquiries@culture.gov.uk
Web: http://www.culture.gov.uk

The Department for Culture, Media and Sport was established in July 1997 and is responsible for government policy relating to the arts, broadcasting, the press, museums and galleries, libraries, sport and recreation, historic buildings and ancient monuments, tourism, and the music industry. It is responsible for policy on the National Lottery and the Millennium, and sponsors the Millennium Commission.
Secretary of State for Culture, Media and Sport, The Rt. Hon. Chris Smith, MP
  Private Secretary, F. Muir
  Special Advisers, J. Newbigin; A. Burnham; B. Jefferson; R. Cotton; D. McGonigal
  Parliamentary Private Secretary, Ms F. Mactaggart, MP
Parliamentary Under-Secretaries, Alan Howarth, MP (*Arts*); Kate Hoey, MP (*Sport*); Janet Anderson, MP (*Tourism, Film and Broadcasting*)
  Private Secretaries, D. Fitzgerald; N. Hughes; D. Tambling
Parliamentary Clerk, T. English
Permanent Secretary (SCS), R. Young
  Private Secretary, K. Gibbins

MUSEUMS, GALLERIES, LIBRARIES AND HERITAGE GROUP
Head of Group (SCS), Ms A. Stewart
Head, Libraries and Information Division (SCS), N. MacKay
Head, Buildings, Monuments and Sites (SCS), N. Pittman
Head, Museums, Galleries and Cultural Property (SCS), H. Corner
Director, Government Art Collection (SCS), Ms P. Johnson

STRATEGY AND COMMUNICATION GROUP
Head of Group (SCS), P. Bolt
Head of News, I. Hepplewhite
Head of Information, G. Newsom
Head of Strategy, Ms Z. McNeill-Ritchie

CORPORATE SERVICES GROUP
Head of Group (SCS), A. Ramsay
Head, Finance Division (SCS), A. McLellan
Head, National Lottery Division (SCS), vacant
Head, Personnel and Central Services Division (SCS), Ms R. Siemaszko
Head, Central Appointments Unit, Ms R. Griggs
Head, Internal Audit, D. Rix

CREATIVE INDUSTRIES, MEDIA AND BROADCASTING GROUP
Head of Group (SCS), N. J. Kroll
Head, Broadcasting Division (SCS), Ms M. Leech
Head, Media Division (SCS), Ms J. Evans
Head, Creative Industries, A. Ferries

REGIONS, TOURISM, MILLENNIUM AND INTERNATIONAL GROUP
Head of Group, B. Leonard
Head, Tourism Division (SCS), S. Broadley
Head, Millennium Unit, Miss C. Pillman
Head, Local, Regional and International Division (SCS), P. Douglas

EDUCATION, TRAINING, ARTS AND SPORT
Head of Group, Ms P. Drew
Head, Arts Division (SCS), W. Nye
Head, Sports Division (SCS), vacant
Head, Education (SCS), A. Dyer

EXECUTIVE AGENCY

ROYAL PARKS AGENCY
The Old Police House, Hyde Park, London W2 2UH
Tel 0171-298 2000; fax 0171-298 2005

The Agency is responsible for maintaining and developing the royal parks.
Chief Executive (G5), D. Welch, CBE

BOARD OF CUSTOMS AND EXCISE
*New King's Beam House, 22 Upper Ground, London
SE1 9PJ
Tel 0171-620 1313
Web: http://www.open.gov.uk/customs/c&ehome.htm

Commissioners of Customs were first appointed in 1671 and housed by the King in London. The Excise Department was formerly under the Inland Revenue Department and was amalgamated with the Customs Department in 1909.

HM Customs and Excise is responsible for collecting and administering customs and excise duties and VAT, and advises the Chancellor of the Exchequer on any matters connected with them. The Department is also responsible for preventing and detecting the evasion of revenue laws and for enforcing a range of prohibitions and restrictions on the importation of certain classes of goods. In addition, the Department undertakes certain agency work on behalf of other departments, including the compilation of UK overseas trade statistics from customs import and export documents.

THE BOARD
Chairman (G1), Dame Valerie Strachan, DCB
    Private Secretaries, Ms J. Mellon; P. Gerrard
Deputy Chairman, T. Walker

---

* Unless otherwise stated, this is the address and telephone number of directorates of the Board

Commissioners (G3), P. R. H. Allen; A. R. Rawsthorne; D. J. Howard; A. Paynter; M. R. Brown; R. N. McAfee; M. W. Norgrove; T. Byrne
Head of Board's Secretariat, J. Bone
Solicitor, D. Pickup

PUBLIC RELATIONS OFFICE
Tel 0171-865 5581
Head of Public Relations, P. Rose

CORPORATE SERVICES DIRECTORATE
Director, A. Paynter

INFORMATION SYSTEMS DIRECTORATE
Alexander House, 21 Victoria Avenue, Southend-on-Sea
SS99 IAA
Tel 01702-348944
Director, vacant

CUSTOMS POLICY DIRECTORATE
Director, A. R. Rawsthorne

EXCISE AND CENTRAL POLICY DIRECTORATE
Director, D. J. Howard

VAT POLICY DIRECTORATE
Director, M. R. Brown

PERSONNEL AND FINANCE DIRECTORATE
Director, P. R. H. Allen

OUTFIELD
Director, R. N. McAfee
Tariff and Statistical Office
Portcullis House, 27 Victoria Avenue, Southend-on-Sea
SS2 6AL
Tel 01702-348944
Controller, M. McDowall
Accounting Services Division
Alexander House, 21 Victoria Avenue, Southend-on-Sea
SS99 IAA
Tel 01702-348944
Accountant and Comptroller-General, D. Robinson

OPERATIONS (COMPLIANCE) DIRECTORATE
Director, M. W. Norgrove

OPERATIONS (PREVENTION) DIRECTORATE
Director, T. Byrne
National Investigation Service
Custom House, Lower Thames Street, London EC3R 6EE
Tel 0171-283 5353
Chief Investigation Officer, P. Evans

SOLICITOR'S OFFICE
Solicitor, D. Pickup
Deputy Solicitor, G. Fotherby

COLLECTORS OF HM CUSTOMS AND EXCISE
(G5)
Anglia, M. Hill
Central England, D. Garlick
Eastern England, A. Durrant
London Airports, M. Peach
London Central, J. Maclean
Northern England, H. Peden
Northern Ireland, T. W. Logan
North-west England, A. Allen
Scotland, I. Mackay
South-east England, J. Tullberg
South London and Thames, J. Hendry
Southern England, H. Burnard
Thames Valley, J. Barnard
Wales, the West and Borders, B. Flavill

OFFICE OF THE DATA PROTECTION
REGISTRAR
Wycliffe House, Water Lane, Wilmslow, Cheshire
SK9 5AF
Tel 01625-545745; fax 01625-524510

The Office of the Data Protection Registrar was created
by the Data Protection Act 1984; the Registrar will be
renamed the Data Protection Commissioner on 1 March
2000 under the Data Protection Act 1998, which will
implement the EU Data Protection Directive (95/46/EC)
in the UK. It is the Registrar's duty to compile and maintain
the register of data users and computer bureaux and to
provide facilities for members of the public to examine the
register; to promote observance of data protection principles; to consider complaints made by data subjects; to
disseminate information about the Data Protection Act; to
encourage the production of codes of practice by trade
associations and other bodies; to guide data users in
complying with data protection principles; and to co-
operate with other parties to the Council of Europe
Convention and act as UK authority for the purposes of
Article 13 of the Convention.
Registrar, Mrs E. France

DEER COMMISSION FOR SCOTLAND
Knowsley, 82 Fairfield Road, Inverness IV3 5LH
Tel 01463-231751; fax 01463-712931

The Deer Commission for Scotland has the general
functions of furthering the conservation and control of deer
in Scotland. It has the statutory duty, with powers, to
prevent damage to agriculture, forestry and the habitat by
deer. It is funded by the Scottish Executive.
Chairman (part-time), A. Raven
Director, A. Rinning
Technical Director, R. W. Youngson

MINISTRY OF DEFENCE
— *see* pages 384–96

DESIGN COUNCIL
34 Bow Street, London WC2E 7DL
Tel 0171-420 5200; fax 0171-420 5300

The Design Council is incorporated by royal charter and
is a registered charity. It works with government, industry
and academia to generate information and practical tools
for uptake in industry and education which demonstrate
the contribution, value and effectiveness of design. Its
sponsoring department is the Department of Trade and
Industry.
Chairman, J. Sorrell, CBE
Chief Executive, A. Summers

THE DUCHY OF CORNWALL
10 Buckingham Gate, London SW1E 6LA
Tel 0171-834 7346; fax 0171-931 9541

The Duchy of Cornwall was created by Edward III in 1337
for the support of his eldest son Edward, later known as
the Black Prince. It is the oldest of the English duchies.
The duchy is acquired by inheritance by the sovereign's
eldest son either at birth or on the accession of his parent
to the throne, whichever is the later. The primary purpose
of the estate remains to provide an income for the Prince
of Wales. The estate is mainly agricultural, consisting of
129,000 acres in 24 counties mainly in the south-west of
England. The duchy also has some residential property, a
number of shops and offices, and a Stock Exchange
portfolio. Prince Charles is the 24th Duke of Cornwall.

THE PRINCE'S COUNCIL
Chairman, HRH The Prince of Wales, KG, KT, GCB
Lord Warden of the Stannaries, The Earl Peel
Receiver-General, The Earl Cairns, CBE
Attorney-General to the Prince of Wales, N. Underhill, QC
Secretary and Keeper of the Records, W. R. A. Ross
Other members, Earl of Shelburne; J. E. Pugsley;
  A. M. J. Galsworthy; C. Howes, CB; W. N. Hood, CBE; S.
  Lamport; R. Broadhurst

OTHER OFFICERS
Auditors, I. Brindle; R. Hughes
Sheriff (1999–2000), Lt.-Cdr. N. J. Trefusis

THE DUCHY OF LANCASTER
Lancaster Place, Strand, London WC2E 7ED
Tel 0171-836 8277; fax 0171-836 3098

The estates and jurisdiction known as the Duchy of
Lancaster have belonged to the reigning monarch since
1399 when John of Gaunt's son came to the throne as
Henry IV. As the Lancaster Inheritance it goes back as far
as 1265 when Henry III granted his youngest son Edmund
lands and possessions following the Baron's war. In 1267
Henry gave Edmund the County, Honor and Castle of
Lancaster and created him the first Earl of Lancaster. In
1351 Edward III created Lancaster a County Palatine.
  The Chancellor of the Duchy of Lancaster is responsible
for the administration of the Duchy, the appointment of
justices of the peace in Lancashire, Greater Manchester
and Merseyside and ecclesiastical patronage in the Duchy
gift.
*Chancellor of the Duchy of Lancaster (and Minister for the
  Cabinet Office)*, The Rt. Hon. Dr Jack Cunningham, MP
  (*see also* page 286)
Attorney-General, R. G. B. McCombe, QC
Receiver-General, Sir Michael Peat, KCVO
Clerk of the Council, M. K. Ridley, CVO
Chief Clerk and Secretary for Appointments, Col. F. N. J. Davies

ECGD (EXPORT CREDITS GUARANTEE
DEPARTMENT)
PO Box 2200, 2 Exchange Tower, Harbour Exchange
Square, London E14 9GS
Tel 0171-512 7000; fax 0171-512 7649

ECGD (Export Credits Guarantee Department), the UK's
official export credit insurer, is a government department
responsible to the Secretary of State for Trade and Industry
and functions under the Export and Investment Guarantees
Act 1991. This enables ECGD to facilitate UK exports by
making available export credit insurance to firms engaged
in selling overseas and to guarantee repayment to banks
providing finance for capital goods. The Act also empowers
ECGD to insure UK companies investing overseas against
political risks such as war, expropriation and restrictions
on remittances.
Chief Executive, H. V. B. Brown

Group Directors *(G3)*, V. P. Lunn-Rockliffe *(Asset Management)*; J. R. Weiss *(Underwriting)*; T. M. Jaffray *(Resource Management)*

DIVISIONS

Director, Finance *(G5)*, R. J. Healey
Director, Central Services *(G5)*, P. J. Callaghan
Directors, Underwriting Divisions *(G5)*, G. G. W. Welsh *(Division 1)*; J. C. W. Croall *(Division 2)*; M. D. Pentecost *(Division 3)*; R. Gotts *(Division 4)*; S. R. Dodgson *(Division 5)*; C. J. Leeds *(Division 6)*
Director, Office of the General Counsel *(G5)*, N. Ridley
Director, International Debt *(G5)*, Ms L. Woods
Director, Claims *(G5)*, R. F. Lethbridge
Director, Treasury and Export Finance *(G5)*, J. S. Snowdon
Director, Risk Management *(G5)*, P. J. Radford
Director, External Relations *(G5)*, Mrs M. E. Maddox
Director, IT Services *(G6)*, E. J. Walsby
Director, Internal Audit *(G6)*, G. Cassell
Director, Operational Research *(G6)*, Ms R. Kaufman

EXPORT GUARANTEES ADVISORY COUNCIL
Chairman, D. H. A. Harrison
Other Members, Ms E. Airey; Dr A. K. Banerji; R. F. T. Binyon; A. Brown; S. J. Doughty; Ms L. Knox; G. W. Lynch, OBE; D. McLachlan; P. J. Mason; R. H. Maudslay; Sir David Wright, KCMG, LVO

DEPARTMENT FOR EDUCATION AND EMPLOYMENT

Sanctuary Buildings, Great Smith Street, London SW1P 3BT
Tel 0870-001 2345; fax 0171-925 6000
E-mail: info@dfee.gov.uk
Web: http://www.dfee.gov.uk
Caxton House, Tothill Street, London SW1H 9NF
Tel 0171-273 3000; fax 0171-273 5124
Moorfoot, Sheffield S1 4PQ
Tel 0114-275 3275; fax 0114-259 4724
Mowden Hall, Staindrop Road, Darlington DL3 9BG
Tel 01325-460155

The Department for Education and Employment was formed in July 1995, bringing together the functions of the former Department for Education with the training and labour market functions of the former Employment Department Group. It includes an executive agency, the Employment Service. The Department aims to support economic growth and improve the nation's competitiveness and quality of life by raising standards of educational achievement and skill and by promoting an efficient and flexible labour market.

Secretary of State for Education and Employment, The Rt. Hon. David Blunkett, MP
Principal Private Secretary, M. Wardle
Special Advisers, C. Ryan; Ms S. Linden; N. Pearce; T. Engel
Parliamentary Private Secretary, Ms J. Corston, MP
Minister of State, The Rt. Hon. Andrew Smith, MP *(Employment)*
Private Secretary, D. Nickerson
Parliamentary Private Secretary, Ms J. Ryan, MP
Minister of State, Estelle Morris, MP *(School Standards)*
Private Secretary, J. Whitfield
Minister in the Lords, The Baroness Blackstone, PH.D. *(Lifelong Learning)*
Private Secretary, E. Wilkinson
Parliamentary Private Secretary, T. McNulty, MP

Parliamentary Under-Secretaries of State, Margaret Hodge, MP *(Employment, Under 5s)*; Malcolm Wicks, MP *(Lifelong Learning)*; Jacqui Smith, MP *(School Standards)*; Michael Wills, MP *(Information and Communications Technology)*
Private Secretaries, G. Walker; Ms J. Loosley; D. McGrath
Permanent Secretary, Sir Michael Bichard, KCB
Private Secretary, M. Doherty

EMPLOYMENT, LIFELONG LEARNING AND INTERNATIONAL DIRECTORATE
Director-General, N. Stuart

INTERNATIONAL
Director, C. Tucker, CB
Heads of Divisions, Ms W. Harris *(European Union)*; Ms E. Trewartha *(European Social Fund)*; B. Shaw *(International Relations)*

SKILLS AND LIFELONG LEARNING
Director, D. Grover, CB
Heads of Divisions, J. Temple *(Skills Unit)*; vacant *(Individual Learning)*; Mrs L. Ammon, CBE *(Learning at Work)*; Dr J. Pugh *(University for Industry)*

EMPLOYMENT POLICY
Director, M. J. Richardson
Heads of Divisions, M. Neale *(Structural Unemployment Policy)*; E. Galvin *(Employment and Benefits Policy)*; C. Barnham *(Welfare to Work)*; B. Wells *(Economy and Labour Market)*

EQUAL OPPORTUNITIES, TECHNOLOGY AND OVERSEAS LABOUR
Director, B. Niven
Heads of Divisions, Ms S. Trundle, OBE *(Childcare Unit)*; Ms J. Eastabrook *(Sex and Race Equality)*; Miss D. Fordham *(Disability Policy)*; P. Chorley *(Family Friendly Employment)*; N. Atkinson *(Overseas Labour Service)*

FINANCE AND ANALYTICAL SERVICES DIRECTORATE
Director-General, P. Shaw

FINANCE
Heads of Divisions, Mrs S. Todd *(Expenditure)*; S. Burt *(Private Finance)*; Mrs C. Hunter *(Programmes)*; R. Wye *(Efficiency)*; P. Connor *(Financial Accounting)*; N. Thirtle *(Internal Audit)*

ANALYTICAL SERVICES
Director, D. Allnutt
Heads of Divisions, M. Britton *(Qualifications, Pupil Assessment and International)*; J. Elliott *(Youth and Further Education)*; S. Field *(Higher Education)*; B. Butcher *(Employability and Adult Learning)*; R. Bartholomew *(Equal Opportunities and Research Programmes)*; Ms A. Brown *(Schools, Teachers and Resources)*

FURTHER AND HIGHER EDUCATION AND YOUTH TRAINING DIRECTORATE
Director-General, R. Dawe

QUALIFICATIONS
Director, R. Hull
Heads of Divisions, C. Johnson *(School and College Qualifications)*; J. West *(Qualifications for Work)*; A. Clarke *(Standards, Quality and Access)*

FURTHER EDUCATION AND YOUTH TRAINING
Director, D. Forrester

Heads of Divisions, Ms C. Tyler (*Investing in Young People*); S. Geary (*Careers and Information*); S. Hillier (*Funding and Organization*); A. Davies (*Partnership Skills and Young People*)

HIGHER EDUCATION
Director, A. C. Clark
Heads of Divisions, M. Hipkins (*Higher Education Funding*); N. Flint (*Student Support 1*); B. Evans (*Student Support 2*); T. Fellowes (*Higher Education and Employment*)

LEGAL ADVISER'S OFFICE
Legal Adviser, D. Macrae
Heads of Divisions, F. Clarke; S. Harker; Miss D. Collins

OPERATIONS DIRECTORATE
Director, J. Hedger, CB
Heads of Divisions, P. Houten (*TECs Operational Policy, Planning, Communications and Transition*); P. Lauener (*Post-16 Review Group*); Ms S. Orr (*Quality and Finance Assurance*); G. McKinsie (*Regional Development and Government Offices*); J. Fuller (*National Training Organizations*); P. Mucklow (*Structures and Learning Skills Councils*); A. McCully (*Legislation*)

PERSONNEL AND SUPPORT SERVICES DIRECTORATE
Director, Mrs H. Douglas
Heads of Divisions, R. Hinchcliffe (*Information Systems*); M. Shipp (*Personnel*); P. Neill (*Procurement and Contracting*); J. Gordon (*Training and Development*); L. Webb (*Facilities Management*); G. Archer (*Corporate Change and Senior Staff*); B. Hillon (*Senior Equal Opportunities Adviser*)

SCHOOLS DIRECTORATE
Director-General, D. Normington

SCHOOLS ORGANIZATION AND FUNDING
Director, Ms H. Williams
Heads of Divisions, Ms E. Wylie (*LEA Support*); A. Sevier (*School Framework and Governance*); K. Beeton (*School Capital and Buildings*); A. Wye (*Schools and LEA Funding*); Ms C. Macready (*School Admissions and Organization*)

TEACHERS
Director, P. Makeham
Heads of Divisions, Ms A. Jackson (*Teachers' Pay and Policy*); G. Holley (*Teacher Supply and Training*); Ms P. Jones (*Teachers' Standards and Pensions*); Ms C. Bienkowska (*Teacher Development and Leadership*)

PUPIL SUPPORT AND INCLUSION
Director, R. Smith
Heads of Divisions, P. Cohen (*School Inclusion*); C. Wells (*Study Support, Business and Community Links and Youth*); M. Phipps (*Pupil Support and Independent Schools*); S. Crowne (*Special Educational Needs*); A. Cranston (*Early Years*)
Head of Sure Start Unit, Ms N. Eisenstadt
Deputy Head of Sure Start Unit, Ms S. Thomson

CURRICULUM, COMMUNICATIONS, TECHNOLOGY AND PARENTS
Director, Ms I. Wilde
Heads of Divisions, I. Berry (*Curriculum*); S. Edwards (*School Communications*); R. Tabberer (*Education and Training Technology*); N. Baxter (*Parents and Performance Tables*)

STANDARDS AND EFFECTIVENESS UNIT
Head of Unit, Prof. M. Barber
Heads of Divisions, S. Adamson (*Standards*); Ms S. Scales (*LEA Effectiveness*); D. Sandeman (*School Effectiveness*)

STRATEGY AND COMMUNICATIONS DIRECTORATE
Director, P. Wanless
Heads of Divisions, Ms J. Simpson (*Head of News*); T. Cook (*Media Relations*); J. Ross (*Publicity*); R. Harrison (*Strategy and Board Secretariat*); G. McKenzie (*Briefing*)

EXECUTIVE AGENCY

THE EMPLOYMENT SERVICE
Caxton House, Tothill Street, London SW1H 9NA
Tel 0171-273 6060; fax 0171-273 6099

The aims of the Employment Service are to contribute to high levels of employment and growth by helping all people without a job to find work and by helping employers to fill their vacancies, and to help individuals lead rewarding working lives.
Chief Executive, L. Lewis
Director of Jobcentre Services, J. Turner, CB
Director of Human Resources, K. White
Director of Welfare to Work Delivery, R. Foster
Director of Finance and Commercial Policy, P. Collis
Non-Executive Directors, R. Dykes; Ms L. de Groot; C. Cox
Regional Directors, M. Groves (*East Midlands and Eastern*); S. Holt, OBE (*London and South-East*); P. Robson (*Northern*); Ms M. John (*North-West*); K. Pascoe (*South-West*); Ms R. Thew (*West Midlands*); R. Lasko (*Yorkshire and Humberside*)
Director for Scotland, A. R. Brown
Director for Wales, Mrs S. Keyse

ELECTRICITY REGULATION, OFFICE OF
(former)
— *see* Gas and Electricity Markets, Office of

OFFICE FOR THE REGULATION OF ELECTRICITY AND GAS
Brookmount Buildings, 42 Fountain Street, Belfast BT1 5EE
Tel 01232-311575 (*Electricity*); 01232-314212 (*Gas*); fax 01232-311740

The Office for the Regulation of Electricity and Gas (OFREG) is the combined regulatory body for the electricity and gas supply industries in Northern Ireland.
Director-General of Electricity Supply and Director-General of Gas for Northern Ireland, D. B. McIldoon
Deputy Director-General of Electricity and Gas, C. H. Coulthard

ENGLISH HERITAGE
— *see* Historic Buildings and Monuments Commission for England

---

ENGLISH NATURE
Northminster House, Peterborough PE1 1UA
Tel 01733-455000; fax 01733-568834

English Nature (the Nature Conservancy Council for England) was established in 1991 and is responsible for advising the Secretary of State for the Environment, Transport and the Regions on nature conservation in England. It promotes, directly and through others, the conservation of England's wildlife and natural features. It selects, establishes and manages National Nature Reserves and identifies and notifies Sites of Special Scientific Interest. It provides advice and information about nature conservation, and supports and conducts research relevant to these functions. Through the Joint Nature Conservation Committee (*see* page 326), it works with its sister organizations in Scotland and Wales on UK and international nature conservation issues.

Chairman, The Baroness Young of Old Scone
Chief Executive, Dr D. R. Langslow
Directors, Dr K. L. Duff; Miss C. E. M. Wood; Ms S. Collins

DEPARTMENT OF THE ENVIRONMENT, TRANSPORT AND THE REGIONS

Eland House, Bressenden Place, London SWIE 5DU
Great Minster House, 76 Marsham Street, London SWIP 4DR
Ashdown House, 123 Victoria Street, London SWIE 6DE
Tel 0171-890 3000
Web: http://www.detr.gov.uk

The Department of the Environment, Transport and the Regions (DETR) was formed in June 1997 by the merger of the Department of the Environment and the Department of Transport. It is responsible for policies relating to the environment, housing, transport services, rural affairs, planning, local government, regional development, regeneration, the construction industry and health and safety.

The Department's ministers are based at Eland House.

Deputy Prime Minister and Secretary of State for the Environment, Transport and the Regions, The Rt. Hon. John Prescott, MP
Private Secretary, P. Unwin
Special Advisers, J. Irvin; Ms J. Hammell
Minister for Transport, The Lord Macdonald of Tradeston
Private Secretary, S. Davies
Minister of State, The Rt. Hon. Michael Meacher, MP (*Environment*)
Private Secretary, C. Bird
Parliamentary Private Secretary, T. Rooney, MP
Minister of State, The Rt. Hon. Hilary Armstrong, MP (*Local Government, Regions*)
Private Secretary, N. Carter
Special Adviser, D. Murphy
Parliamentary Private Secretary, K. Hill, MP
Minister of State, Nick Raynsford, MP (*Housing, Planning, London*)
Private Secretary, E. West
Special Adviser, P. Hackett
Parliamentary Private Secretary, B. Chapman, MP
Parliamentary Under-Secretaries of State, The Lord Whitty; Keith Hill, MP; Chris Mullin, MP; Beverley Hughes, MP
Private Secretaries, Ms J. Borg; Ms K. Braddick; Ms J. Matthew; R. O'Donnell
Parliamentary Clerk, Ms P. Gaunt
Permanent Secretary (*SCS*), Sir Richard Mottram, KCB
Private Secretary, Mrs S. Bishop

*DIRECTORATE OF COMMUNICATION

Director (*SCS*), vacant
Deputy Directors (*SCS*), C. Skinner (*Publicity*); D. Plews (*Press*)

†ENVIRONMENT PROTECTION GROUP

Director-General (*SCS*), Miss D. A. Nichols

ENERGY, ENVIRONMENT AND WASTE DIRECTORATE
Director (*SCS*), P. Ward
Heads of Divisions (*SCS*), L. Packer (*Sustainable Energy Policy*); D. Vincent (*Energy Environment and Best Practice*); H. Cleary (*Environment and Business 1–5*); B. Ryder (*Environment and Business 6–7*); Ms L. Simcock (*Waste Policy*); D. Prior (*Joint Environmental Markets Unit*)

ENVIRONMENT: RISK AND ATMOSPHERE DIRECTORATE
Director (*SCS*), H. Derwent
Heads of Divisions (*SCS*), Dr P. Hinchcliffe (*Chemicals and Biotechnology*); Dr S. Brown (*Radioactive Substances*); P. Betts (*Global Atmosphere*); M. Hurst (*Air and Environment Quality 1–5*); M. Williams (*Air and Environment Quality 6–10*)

ENVIRONMENT PROTECTION STRATEGY DIRECTORATE
Director (*SCS*), A. Burchell
Heads of Divisions (*SCS*), Mrs H. C. Hillier (*EP Statistics and Information Management*); B. Glicksman (*Environment Agency Sponsorship and Navigation*); Ms S. McCabe (*Environment Protection International*); R. Wilson (*Environment Protection Economics*); J. Adams (*Sustainable Development Unit*)

WATER AND LAND DIRECTORATE
Director (*SCS*), A. H. Davis
Heads of Divisions (*SCS*), M. Rouse (*Drinking Water Inspectorate*); A. Simcock (*Marine, Land and Liabilities*); S. Hoggan (*Water Quality*); B. Dinwiddy (*Water Supply and Regulation*)

†FINANCE GROUP

Director and Principal Finance Officer (*SCS*), J. Ballard
Heads of Divisions (*SCS*), R. Bennett (*Finance Programmes*); I. McBrayne (*Finance Sponsorship and Programme*); R. Anderson (*Finance Departmental Administration*); A. Beard (*Finance Accounting Services, Resource Accounting and Budgeting*); C. Arnott (*Internal Audit*)

*HOUSING, CONSTRUCTION, REGENERATION AND COUNTRYSIDE GROUP

Director-General (*SCS*), Mrs M. McDonald, CB

HOUSING
Director (*SCS*), M. Gahagan
Heads of Divisons (*SCS*), Mrs J. Littlewood (*Research, Analysis and Evaluation*); B. Oelman (*Housing Data and Statistics*); P. Cox (*Housing and Urban Economics*); Ms R. Sharpe (*Housing Policy, Renewal and Ownership*); M. Faulkner (*Housing Private Rented Sector*); Mrs H. Chipping (*Local Authority Housing Finance*); R. Horsman (*Housing Associations and Private Finance*); A. Allberry (*Homelessness and Housing Management*)

CONSTRUCTION DIRECTORATE
Director (*SCS*), J. Hobson
Heads of Divisions (*SCS*), N. Dorling (*Construction Industry Sponsorship*); J. Stambollouian (*Construction Innovation and Research Management*); R. Wood (*Export Promotion and Construction Materials*); P. Everall (*Building Regulations*); B. Davies (*Construction Market Intelligence*)

WILDLIFE AND COUNTRYSIDE DIRECTORATE
Director (*SCS*), Ms S. Lambert
Heads of Divisions (*SCS*), R. M. Pritchard (*European Wildlife*); R. Hepworth (*Global Wildlife*); Ms D. Kahn (*Rural Development*); Ms S. Carter (*Countryside*); C. Braun (*Countryside Legislation*)

REGENERATION DIRECTORATE
Director (*SCS*), P. Evans
Heads of Divisions (*SCS*), J. Roberts; W. Chapman; Ms L. Derrick; Ms H. Ghosh

---

* Based at Eland House
† Based at Ashdown House
‡ Based at Great Minster House

LONDON ROUGH SLEEPERS UNIT
Director (SCS), Ms L. Casey
Head of Division (SCS), Ms J. Bailey

*LEGAL GROUP
Director-General (SCS), D. Hogg

COUNTRYSIDE, PLANNING AND TRANSPORT
Director (SCS), Ms S. Unerman
Heads of Divisions (SCS), N. Lefton (*Countryside and Environmental Liability*); Ms G. Hedley-Dent (*Planning*); R. Lines (*Highways*); N. Thomas (*Road Traffic*); A. Jones (*Aviation*); C. Ingram (*Marine*); Ms J.-A. McKenzie (*Railways*)

COMMERCIAL, ENVIRONMENT, HOUSING AND LOCAL GOVERNMENT
Director (SCS), C. Muttukamaru
Heads of Divisions (SCS), J. Comber (*Environment (National)*); D. Jordan (*Local Government (Finance)*); Ms P. Conlon (*Local Government (General)*); K. Baublys (*Housing and Land*); Ms S. Headley (*Special Projects*); D. Aries (*Commercial and Establishments*); Ms D. Phillips (*Devolution and Regional Government*)

ENVIRONMENT (INTERNATIONAL AND EC)
Director (SCS), P. Szell
Head of Division (SCS), A. McGlone

LEGISLATIVE UNIT
Director (SCS), A. Roberts

*LOCAL AND REGIONAL GOVERNMENT GROUP
Director-General (SCS), P. Wood

LOCAL GOVERNMENT DIRECTORATE
Director (SCS), A. Whetnall
Heads of Divisions (SCS), P. Rowsell (*Local Government Sponsorship*); J. R. Footitt (*Local Government Competition and Quality*); T. Redpath (*Local Government Legislation*); T. Crossley (*Local Government Pensions*)

LOCAL GOVERNMENT FINANCE POLICY DIRECTORATE
Director (SCS), M. Lambirth
Heads of Divisions (SCS), R. J. Gibson (*Local Government Grant Distribution*); Mrs P. Penneck (*Local Government Finance Statistics*); Ms P. Williams (*Local Government Capital Finance*); S. Hughes (*Local Government Taxation*); I. Scotter (*Local Government Revenue Expenditure*)

GOVERNMENT OFFICES AND REGIONAL POLICY DIRECTORATE
Director (SCS), Miss L. Bell
Heads of Divisions (SCS), M. Coulshed; M. Ross; A. Murray; Mrs J. Scoones (*Government Offices Central Unit*)

REGIONAL OFFICES
— *see* pages 303–4

‡PLANNING, ROADS AND LOCAL TRANSPORT
Director-General (SCS), C. J. S. Brearley, CB

MOBILITY UNIT
Head of Unit (SCS), Miss E. A. Frye, OBE

PLANNING DIRECTORATE
Director (SCS), J. Jacobs
Heads of Divisions (SCS), J. Channing (*Planning and Policies*); C. Bowden (*Development Control Policy*); M. R. Ash (*Plans and Compensation*); J. Zetter (*Environmental Assessment, International and Research*); A. M. Oliver (*Planning and Land Use Statistics*); L. Hicks (*Minerals and Waste Planning*); J. M. Leigh-Pollitt (*Land and Property*)

NATIONAL ROADS POLICY DIRECTORATE
Director (SCS), Ms D. Phillips
Heads of Divisions (SCS), T. Worsley (*Highways, Economics and Traffic Appraisal*); N. McDonald (*Roads Policy*); M. Talbot (*Traffic Management and Tolls*); R. Donachie (*Transport Statistics: Roads*)

INTEGRATED AND LOCAL TRANSPORT
Director (SCS), R. Bird
Heads of Divisions (SCS), E. C. Neve (*Buses and Taxis*); P. McCarthy (*Local Transport Policy*); A. S. D. Whybrow (*Charging and Local Transport*); M. Walsh (*Economics, Local Transport and General*); P. Capell (*Transport Statistics: Personal Travel*)

ROAD AND VEHICLE SAFETY
Director (SCS), J. Plowman
Heads of Divisions (SCS), M. Fendick (*Vehicle Standards and Engineering*); R. Peal (*Road Safety*); R. Jones (*Licensing and Enforcement*); Dr T. Carter (*Chief Medical Adviser*); M. Brasher (*Driver, Vehicle Operator Task Force*); I. Todd (*Vehicle, Environment and Taxation*)

‡RAILWAYS, AVIATION LOGISTICS AND MARITIME
Director-General (SCS), D. Rowlands

RAILWAYS
Director (SCS), vacant
Heads of Divisions (SCS), M. Fuhr, OBE (*Channel Tunnel Rail Link*); S. Connolly (*Railways Economics and Finance*); P. Thomas (*Railways International and General*); B. Linnard (*Railways Sponsorship*)

AVIATION
Director (SCS), R. Griffins
Heads of Divisions (SCS), M. Fawcett (*Airports Policy*); M. C. Mann (*Economics, Aviation, Maritime and International*); Ms E. Duthie (*Aviation Environmental*); M. Smethers (*Multilateral*); A. T. Baker (*International Aviation*); D. McMillan (*Civil Aviation*)

AIR ACCIDENTS INVESTIGATION BRANCH
Defence Evaluation and Research Agency, Farnborough, Hants GU14 6TD
Tel 01252-510300
Chief Inspector of Air Accidents, K. P. R. Smart, CBE
Deputy Chief Inspector, R. McKinlay

LOGISTICS AND MARITIME TRANSPORT
Director (SCS), B. Wadsworth
Heads of Divisions (SCS), Ms A. Moss (*Road Haulage*); M. Hughes (*Transport Statistics Freight*); D. Liston-Jones (*Traffic Area Network Unit*); D. Cooke (*Shipping Policy 1*); G. D. Rowe (*Shipping Policy 2*); J. F. Wall, CMG (*Shipping Policy 3*); C. Young (*Radioactive Materials Transport*); S. Reeves (*Ports*)

MARINE ACCIDENTS INVESTIGATION BRANCH
5–7 Brunswick Place, Southampton SO1 2AN
Tel 01703-395500
Chief Inspector of Marine Accidents, Rear-Adm. J. Lang
Deputy Chief Inspector, S. Harwood

TRANSPORT SECURITY
Director (SCS), D. Lord
Head of Division and Deputy Director (SCS), W. Gillan

---

* Based at Eland House
† Based at Ashdown House
‡ Based at Great Minster House

*STRATEGY AND CORPORATE SERVICES
GROUP
Director-General (SCS), R. S. Dudding
Heads of Divisions (SCS), I. Heawood (*Information Management*); I. Harris (*Working Environment*); P. Walton (*Corporate, Business and Agencies*); G. Jones (*Procurement, Policy and Advice*); J. O'Callaghan (*IT Services*)

PERSONNEL AND CHANGE MANAGEMENT
Director (SCS), Ms J. Cotton
Heads of Divisions (SCS), M. Bailey (*Personnel Support*); E. Gibbons (*Group Facing Teams*); K. Arnold (*Pay and Industrial Relations*); B. Meakins (*Change Management, Development and Training*)

CHIEF ECONOMIST
Director and Chief Economist (SCS), C. Riley
Head of Division (SCS), vacant (*Central Economics and Policy*)

CENTRAL STRATEGY (AND CHIEF SCIENTIST)
Director (and Chief Scientist) (SCS), D. Fisk
Heads of Divisions (SCS), J. Stevens (*Europe, Transport and General*); M. Devine (*Health and Safety Sponsorship*); A. Apling (*Science and Technology Policy*); Ms B. Hill (*Transport Strategy and Awareness*)

EXECUTIVE AGENCIES

DRIVER AND VEHICLE LICENSING AGENCY
Longview Road, Morriston, Swansea SA6 7JL
Tel 01792-772151 (*drivers*); 01792-772134 (*vehicles*)
The Agency issues driving licences, registers and licenses vehicles, and collects excise duty.
Chief Executive, Dr S. J. Ford, CBE

DRIVING STANDARDS AGENCY
Stanley House, Talbot Street, Nottingham NG1 5GU
Tel 0115-947 4222; fax 0115-955 7334
The Agency's role is to carry out driving tests and approve driving instructors.
Chief Executive, vacant

HIGHWAYS AGENCY
St Christopher House, Southwark Street, London SE1 0TE
Tel 0645-556575
The Agency is responsible for the operation, management and maintenance of the motorway and trunk road network and for road construction and improvement.
Chief Executive, L. J. Haynes

MARITIME AND COASTGUARD AGENCY
Spring Place, 105 Commercial Road, Southampton
SO15 1EG
Tel 01703-329100
The Agency was formed in April 1998 by the merger of the Coastguard Agency and the Marine Safety Agency. Its role is to develop, promote and enforce high standards of marine safety; to minimize loss of life amongst seafarers and coastal users; and to minimize pollution from ships of the sea and coastline.
Chief Executive, M. Storey
Chief Coastguard, J. Astbury

PLANNING INSPECTORATE
Tollgate House, Houlton Street, Bristol BS2 9DJ
Tel 0117-987 8000
The Inspectorate is responsible for casework involving planning, housing, roads, environmental and related legislation. It is a joint executive agency of the Department of the Environment, Transport and the Regions and the National Assembly for Wales.
Chief Executive and Chief Planning Inspector, C. Shepley

QUEEN ELIZABETH II CONFERENCE CENTRE
Broad Sanctuary, London SW1P 3EE
Tel 0171-222 5000; fax 0171-798 4200
The Centre provides conference and banqueting facilities for both private sector and government use.
Chief Executive, M. C. Buck

VEHICLE CERTIFICATION AGENCY
1 Eastgate Office Centre, Eastgate Road, Bristol BS5 6XX
Tel 0117-951 5151; fax 0117-952 4103
The Agency tests and certificates vehicles to UK and international standards.
Chief Executive, D. W. Harvey

VEHICLE INSPECTORATE
Berkeley House, Croydon Street, Bristol BS5 0DA
Tel 0117-954 3200; fax 0117-954 3212
The Agency carries out annual testing and inspection of heavy goods and other vehicles and administers the MOT testing scheme.
Chief Executive, R. J. Oliver

TRAFFIC AREA OFFICES AND
COMMISSIONERS
Senior Traffic Commissioner, M. W. Betts, CBE
Eastern, G. Simms
North-Eastern and North-Western, K. R. Waterworth
Scottish, M. W. Betts, CBE
South-Eastern and Metropolitan, Brig. M. H. Turner
Wales, D. Dixon
Western, C. Heaps
West Midlands, D. Dixon

TRAFFIC DIRECTOR FOR LONDON
College House, Great Peter Street, London SW1P 3LN
Tel 0171-222 4545; fax 0171-976 8640
The Traffic Director for London is a non-departmental public body which is independent from the Department of the Environment, Transport and the Regions but is responsible to the Secretary of State and to Parliament. Its role is to co-ordinate the Priority (Red) Route Network in London and monitor its operation.
Traffic Director for London, D. Turner

THE ENVIRONMENT AGENCY
25th Floor, Millbank Tower, 21–24 Millbank, London
SW1P 4XL
Tel 0171-863 8600; fax 0171-863 8650
Rio House, Waterside Drive, Aztec West, Almondsbury, Bristol BS32 4UD
Tel 01454-624400; fax 01454-624409

The Environment Agency was established in 1996 under the Environment Act 1995 and is a non-departmental public body sponsored by the Department of the Environment, Transport and the Regions, MAFF and the National Assembly for Wales. The Agency is responsible for pollution prevention and control in England and Wales, and for the management and use of water resources, including flood defences, fisheries and navigation. It has head offices in London and Bristol and eight regional offices.

THE BOARD
Chairman, The Lord De Ramsey (until Dec. 1999)

Deputy Chairman, Sir John Harman
Members, C. Beardwood; A. J. P. Dalton; A. Dare, CBE;
E. Gallagher; N. Haigh, OBE; C. Hampson, CBE; Prof. R.
Macrory; Prof. Jacqueline McGlade; G. Manning, OBE;
Dr A. Powell; Prof. D. Ritchie; A. Rogers; G. Wardell

THE EXECUTIVE
Chief Executive, E. Gallagher
Director of Finance, N. Reader
Director of Personnel, G. Duncan
Director of Environmental Protection, Dr P. Leinster
Director of Water Management, G. Mance
Director of Operations, A. Robertson
Director of Corporate Affairs, M. Wilson
Director of Legal Services, R. Navarro
Chief Scientist, J. Pentreath

ROYAL COMMISSION ON
ENVIRONMENTAL POLLUTION
1st Floor, Steel House, 11 Tothill Street, London
SW1H 9RE
Tel 0171-273 6635

The Commission was set up in 1970 to advise on national
and international matters concerning the pollution of the
environment.
Chairman, Prof. Sir Thomas Blundell
Members, Sir Geoffrey Allen, FRS; Revd Prof. M. C.
Banner; Prof. G. S. Boulton, FRS, FRSE; Prof. R. Clift,
OBE, FREng.; J. Flemming; Sir Martin Holdgate, CB; Prof.
B. Hoskins, CBE, FRS; Prof. R. Macrory; Prof.
M. G. Marmot, PH.D.; Prof. J. G. Morris, CBE, FRS; Dr
Susan Owens, OBE; J. Roberts; Dr Penelope A. Rowlatt
Secretary, D. R. Lewis

EQUAL OPPORTUNITIES COMMISSION
Overseas House, Quay Street, Manchester M3 3HN
Tel 0161-833 9244; fax 0161-835 1657

Press Office, 36 Broadway, London SW1H 0XH. Tel: 0171-
222 1110
Other Offices, Stock Exchange House, 7 Nelson Mandela
Place, Glasgow G2 1QW. Tel: 0141-248 5833; Windsor
House, Windsor Place, Cardiff. Tel: 01222-343552

The Commission was set up in 1975 as a result of the
passing of the Sex Discrimination Act. It works towards
the elimination of discrimination on the grounds of sex or
marital status and to promote equality of opportunity
between men and women generally. It is responsible to the
Department for Education and Employment.
Chair, Ms J. Mellor
Deputy Chairs, Mrs E. Hodder; Ms G. James
Members, P. Smith; Ms M. Berg; R. Grayson; Dr J. Stringer;
Prof. T. Rees; R. Penn; Ms J. Rubin; Prof. M. Schofield;
Ms K. Carberry; Ms J. Watson; Ms T. Woodcraft
Chief Executive (*acting*), F. Spencer

EQUAL OPPORTUNITIES COMMISSION FOR NORTHERN
IRELAND
Chamber of Commerce House, 22 Great Victoria Street,
Belfast BT2 7BA
Tel 01232-242752; fax 01232-331047
Chair, Mrs J. Smyth, CBE
Chief Executive, Ms E. Collins

OFFICE OF FAIR TRADING
Field House, Bream's Buildings, London EC4A 1PR
(from the end of 1999) Fleetbank House, 2–6 Salisbury
Square, London EC4Y 8JX
Tel 0171-211 8000; fax 0171-211 8800

The Office of Fair Trading is a non-ministerial government
department headed by the Director-General of Fair
Trading. It keeps commercial activities in the UK under
review and seeks to protect consumers against unfair
trading practices. The Director-General's consumer protection duties under the Fair Trading Act 1973, together
with his responsibilities under the Consumer Credit Act
1974, the Estate Agents Act 1979, the Control of Misleading
Advertisements Regulations 1988, and the Unfair Terms
in Consumer Contracts Regulations 1994, are administered
by the Office's Consumer Affairs Division. The Competition Policy Division is concerned with monopolies and
mergers (under the Fair Trading Act 1973) and the
Director-General's other responsibilities for competition
matters, including those under the Restrictive Trade
Practices Acts 1976 and 1977, the Resale Prices Act 1976,
the Competition Act 1980, the Financial Services Act 1986
and the Broadcasting Act 1990. In March 2000 the new
provisions in the Competition Act 1998 will replace the
Restrictive Trade Practices Acts 1976 and 1977, the Resale
Prices Act 1976 and most of the Competition Act 1980.
The Office is the UK competent authority on the
application of the European Commission's competition
rules, and also liaises with the Commission on consumer
protection initiatives.
Director-General, J. Bridgeman

CONSUMER AFFAIRS DIVISION
Director (*G3*), Miss C. Banks
Assistant Directors (*G5*), R. Watson; M. Graham; D. Wray

COMPETITION POLICY DIVISION
Director (*G3*), Mrs M. J. Bloom
Assistant Directors (*G5*), A. J. White; H. L. Emden;
E. L. Whitehorn; S. Wood; P. G. A. Bamford

LEGAL DIVISION
Director (*G3*), Miss P. Edwards
Assistant Directors (*G5*), M. A. Khan; S. Brindley
Establishment and Finance Officer (*G5*), Mrs R. Heyhoe
Chief Information Officer (*G6*), D. Hill

FOREIGN AND COMMONWEALTH
OFFICE
Downing Street, London SW1A 2AL
Tel 0171-270 3000
Web: http://www.fco.gov.uk

The Foreign and Commonwealth Office provides, mainly
through diplomatic missions, the means of communication
between the British Government and other governments
and international governmental organizations for the
discussion and negotiation of all matters falling within the
field of international relations. It is responsible for alerting
the Government to the implications of developments
overseas; for protecting British interests overseas; for
protecting British citizens abroad; for explaining British
policies to, and cultivating friendly relations with, governments overseas; and for the discharge of British responsibilities to the UK overseas territories.
Secretary of State for Foreign and Commonwealth Affairs, The
Rt. Hon. Robin Cook, MP

Principal Private Secretary, S. L. Cowper-Coles, CMG, LVO
Private Secretaries, T. Barrow, LVO; A. Patrick
Special Advisers, A. Hood; D. Clark
Parliamentary Private Secretary, K. Purchase, MP
Minister for Europe, Geoffrey Hoon, MP
  Private Secretary, N. Hopton
Minister of State, Peter Hain, MP
Minister of State, John Battle, MP
  Private Secretaries to the Ministers of State, F. Baker; Ms P. Phillips
Parliamentary Under-Secretary of State, The Baroness Scotland of Asthal
  Private Secretary, C. Newns
Permanent Under-Secretary of State and Head of HM Diplomatic Service, Sir John Kerr, KCMG
  Private Secretary, D. Frost
Chief Executive, †*British Trade International,* Sir David Wright, KCMG, LVO
Deputy Under-Secretaries, C. Hum, CMG (*Chief Clerk*); C. Budd, CMG (*EU/Economic Director*); E. Jones Parry, CMG (*Political Director*); D. Manning, CMG; J. Shepherd, CMG; Sir Franklin Berman, KCMG, QC (*Legal Adviser*)
Directors, Ms A. Grant, CMG (*Africa and Commonwealth*); P. J. Westmacott, CMG (*Americas/Overseas Territories*); P. Ricketts, CMG, CVO (*International Security*); S. J. L. Wright, CMG (*Wider Europe*); N. E. Sheinwald, CMG (*European Union*); R. E. Dibble (*Chief Executive, FCO Services*); A. R. Brenton (*Global Issues*); C. Crawford (*Deputy Political Director*); D. Plumbly, CMG (*Middle East/ North Africa*); R. F. Cooper (*Asia, Pacific*); D. Hall, CMG (*Export Promotion*); R. Dalton (*Personnel*); D. N. Reddaway, CMG, MBE (*Public Services*); P. S. Collecott (*Resources*); C. Butler (*Chief Economic Adviser*)

HEADS OF DEPARTMENTS

African Department (Equatorial), J. Bevan
African Department (Southern), N. R. Chrimes
Aviation and Maritime Department, N. A. Ling
Central and North-West European Department, Sir John Ramsden, Bt.
Change Management Unit, Ms S. Matthews
China/Hong Kong Department, D. A. Warren
Common Foreign and Security Policy Department, C. Roberts
Commonwealth Co-ordination Department, C. C. Bright
Consular Division, D. J. R. Taylor
Counter-Terrorism Policy Department, V. Fean
Cultural Relations Department, Ms A. W. Lewis
Devolved Administration Department, Dr J. Milligan
Drugs and International Crime Department, M. Ryder
Eastern Department, A. F. Pringle
Eastern Adriatic Department, T. R. V. Phillips
Economic Relations Department, C. Butler
Environment, Science and Energy Department, J. Ashton
European Union Department (Bi-lateral), J. Cresswell, CVO
European Union Department (External), S. Featherstone
European Union Department (Internal), M. J. Lyall-Grant
FCO Services, N. Hook (*Head, Conference and Visits Group*); Ms V. Life (*Head, Consultancy Group*); J. Elgie (*Head, Estates Group*); J. Thompson, MBE (*Head, Information Management Group*); Ms J. Link (*Head, Resource Management Group*); M. Carr (*Head, Support Group*); N. Stickells (*Head, Technical Group*)
Financial Compliance Unit, M. Purves
Financial Policy Department, M. J. Brown
Honours Department, R. M. Sands
Human Rights Policy Department, R. A. E. Gordon, OBE
Information Department, P. J. Dun
*Internal Audit Department, R. A. Elias
†*Invest in Britain Bureau,* A. Fraser (*Chief Executive*)

†*Joint Export Promotion Directorate,* D. Hall, CMG
Latin America and Caribbean Department, H. G. Hogger
Middle East Department, E. G. M. Chaplin
Migration and Visa Department, R. M. White, MBE
Near East and North Africa Department, C. N. R. Prentice
News Department, N. K. Darroch, CMG
Non-Proliferation Department, P. W. Hare, LVO
North America Department, P. J. Priestley, CBE
North-East Asia and Pacific Department, P. Carter
OSCE and Council of Europe Department, A. E. Huckle
Parliamentary Relations Department, A. Henderson (*Head*); P. R. O. Bromley (*Deputy Head and Parliamentary Clerk*)
Personnel Command, P. Jones (*Asst. Director, Personnel Management*); T. Simmons (*Asst. Director, Performance Issues*); Ms E. Kennedy (*Asst. Director, *Medical and Welfare*); S. Wightman (*Asst. Director, Personnel Policy*); R. T. Fell, CVO (*Asst. Director, Personnel Services*); C. Edgerton, OBE, T. Malcomson (*Asst. Directors, Prosper*); Ms A. Cookson-Hall (*Head, Recruitment*); Dr Vanessa Davies (*Head, Diplomatic Service Language Centre*); Mrs C. Dharwarker (*Head, Training*); Ms J. Bennet, Ms A. Kirk (*Heads, Grading Review Team*)
Policy Planning Staff, Mrs A. M. Leslie
Protocol Department, M. B. L. Dalton, LVO, OBE (*Head of Department and First Assistant Marshal of the Diplomatic Corps*)
Purchasing Directorate, M. J. H. Gower
Republic of Ireland Department, G. Fergusson
Research Analysts, R. D. Lavers
Royal Matters Department, B. England
Security Strategy Unit, T. J. Duggin
Security Policy Department, A. M. Thompson
South Asian Department, S. N. Evans, OBE
South-East Asian Department, N. J. Cox
Southern European Department, J. Hill
United Nations Department, Ms R. M. Marsden
Whitehall Liaison Department, L. Parker

EXECUTIVE AGENCY

WILTON PARK CONFERENCE CENTRE
Wiston House, Steyning, W. Sussex BN44 3DZ
Tel 01903-815020; fax 01903-816373

The Centre organizes international affairs conferences and is hired out to government departments and commercial users.
Chief Executive and Director, C. B. Jennings

CORPS OF QUEEN'S MESSENGERS
Support Group, Foreign and Commonwealth Office, London SW1
Tel 0171-270 2779

Superintendent of the Corps of Queen's Messengers, A. C. Brown
Queen's Messengers, P. Allen; R. Allen; Maj. A. N. D. Bols; Lt.-Cdr. K. E. Brown; Lt.-Col. W. P. A. Bush; Lt.-Col. M. B. de S. Clayton; Maj. P. C. H. Dening-Smitherman; Sqn. Ldr. J. S. Frizzell; Capt. N. C. E. Gardner; Maj. D. A. Griffiths; A. Hill; R. Long; A. Rix; Maj. K. J. Rowbottom; Maj. M. R. Senior; Cdr. K. M. C. Simmons, AFC; Maj. P. M. O. Springfield; Maj. J. S. Steele

---

* Joint Foreign and Commonwealth Office/Department for International Development department
† Joint Foreign and Commonwealth Office/Department of Trade and Industry directorate

FOREIGN COMPENSATION COMMISSION
Room 3.G.9, 1 Palace Street, London SW1E 5HE
Tel 0171-238 4419; fax 0171-238 4594

The Commission was set up by the Foreign Compensation Act 1950 primarily to distribute, under Orders in Council, funds received from other governments in accordance with agreements to pay compensation for expropriated British property and other losses sustained by British nationals.
Chairman, A. W. E. Wheeler, CBE
Secretary, A. N. Grant

FORESTRY COMMISSION
231 Corstorphine Road, Edinburgh EH12 7AT
Tel 0131-334 0303; fax 0131-334 3047

The Forestry Commission is the government department responsible for forestry policy in Great Britain. It reports directly to forestry ministers (i.e. the Minister of Agriculture, Fisheries and Food, the Scottish ministers and the National Assembly for Wales), to whom it is responsible for advice on forestry policy and for the implementation of that policy.

The Commission's principal objectives are to protect Britain's forests and woodlands; expand Britain's forest area; enhance the economic value of the forest resources; conserve and improve the biodiversity, landscape and cultural heritage of forests and woodlands; develop opportunities for woodland recreation; and increase public understanding of and community participation in forestry. Forest Enterprise, a trading body operating as an executive agency of the Commission, manages its forestry estate on a multi-use basis.
Chairman (part-time), Sir Peter Hutchison, Bt., CBE
Director-General and Deputy Chairman (G2), D. J. Bills
Secretary to the Commissioners (G5), F. Strang

FOREST ENTERPRISE HEADQUARTERS, 231
Corstorphine Road, Edinburgh EH12 7AT. Tel: 0131-334
0303. *Chief Executive*, Dr B. McIntosh
FOREST RESEARCH, Alice Holt Lodge, Wrecclesham,
Farnham, Surrey GU10 4LU. Tel: 01420-222555;
Northern Research Station, Roslin, Midlothian
EH25 9SY. Tel: 0131-445 2176. *Chief Executive*, J. Dewar

FRANCHISING, OFFICE OF PASSENGER RAIL
— *see* Transport section

REGISTRY OF FRIENDLY SOCIETIES
Victory House, 30–34 Kingsway, London WC2B 6ES
Tel 0171-663 5282/5124/5269/5299

The Registry of Friendly Societies is a non-ministerial government department now comprising the Registry of Friendly Societies and the Assistant Registrar of Friendly Societies for Scotland.

The Central Office of the Registry of Friendly Societies provides a public registry for mutual organizations registered under the Building Societies Act 1986, the Friendly Societies Acts 1974 and 1992, and the Industrial and Provident Societies Act 1965. The Chief Registrar is responsible for the supervision of credit unions, and advises the Government on issues affecting them.

The Registry of Friendly Societies will be subsumed into the Financial Services Authority (*see* page 635) at a date to be fixed following the enactment of the Financial Services and Markets Bill.

CENTRAL OFFICE OF THE REGISTRY
Chief Registrar, G. E. Fitchew
Assistant Registrars, A. J. Perrett; Ms S. Eden; S. Mundy; E. Engstrom; N. Fawcett
Legal Adviser, A. J. Perrett
Establishment and Finance Officer, R. E. Merrick

REGISTRY OF FRIENDLY SOCIETIES, SCOTLAND
58 Frederick Street, Edinburgh EH2 1NB
Tel 0131-226 3224
Assistant Registrar (G5), J. L. J. Craig, WS

FRIENDLY SOCIETIES COMMISSION
15th Floor, 25 The North Colonnade, Canary Wharf,
London E14 5HS
Tel 0171-676 1000; fax 0171-676 0059

The Friendly Societies Commission was established by the Friendly Societies Act 1992. It is responsible for the supervision of friendly societies and administers the system of prudential regulation. It also advises the Treasury and other government departments on matters relating to friendly societies.

The Government has proposed to Parliament that the functions of the Commission should pass to the Financial Services Authority (*see* page 635) on implementation of the Financial Services and Markets Bill.

FRIENDLY SOCIETIES COMMISSION
Chairman, *M. Roberts
Commissioners, F. da Rocha; *B. Richardson; *J. A. Geddes;
*Ms S. Brown; *Ms P. Triggs
* part-time

SECRETARIAT
Secretary, Ms J. Erskine

GAMING BOARD FOR GREAT BRITAIN
Berkshire House, 168–173 High Holborn, London
WC1V 7AA
Tel 0171-306 6200; fax 0171-306 6266

The Board was established in 1968 and is responsible to the Home Secretary. It is the regulatory body for casinos, bingo clubs, gaming machines and the larger society and all local authority lotteries in Great Britain. Its functions are to ensure that those involved in organizing gaming and lotteries are fit and proper to do so and to keep gaming free from criminal infiltration; to ensure that gaming and lotteries are run fairly and in accordance with the law; and to advise the Home Secretary on developments in gaming and lotteries.
Chairman (part-time) (£37,650), P. Dean, CBE
Secretary, T. Kavanagh

OFFICE OF GAS AND ELECTRICITY MARKETS
Stockley House, 130 Wilton Road, London SW1V 1LQ
Tel 0171-828 0898; fax 0171-932 1600
SCOTLAND: Regent Court, 70 West Regent Street,
Glasgow G2 2QZ
Tel 0141-331 2678; fax 0141-331 2777

The Office of Gas and Electricity Markets (Ofgem) was formed in 1999 by the merger of the separate regulators for electricity and gas set up under the Electricity Act 1989 and the Gas Act 1986 respectively. It is headed by the Director-General for Electricity and Gas Supply and is the independent regulatory body for the electricity and gas supply industries in England, Scotland and Wales. Its functions are to promote competition and to protect customers' interests in relation to prices, security of supply and quality of services.

Director-General for Electricity and Gas Supply, C. McCarthy
Deputy Directors-General, A. J. Boorman (*Customers*); Dr Eileen Marshall, CBE (*Supply Chain*); R. Morse (*Electricity and Gas Transportation Regulation*)
Chief Operating Officer, Ms G. Whittington
Director, Public Affairs, Ms S. Harrison
Legal Adviser, W. Sprigge

GOVERNMENT ACTUARY'S DEPARTMENT

New King's Beam House, 22 Upper Ground, London SE1 9RJ
Tel 0171-211 2600; fax 0171-211 2640

The Government Actuary provides a consulting service to government departments, the public sector, and overseas governments. The actuaries advise on social security schemes and superannuation arrangements in the public sector at home and abroad, on population and other statistical studies, and on government supervision of insurance companies, friendly societies and pension funds.

Government Actuary, C. D. Daykin, CB
Directing Actuaries, D. G. Ballantine; T. W. Hewitson; A. G. Young
Chief Actuaries, E. I. Battersby; A. J. M. Chamberlain; Ms C. Cresswell; Mrs B. J. Hall; A. I. Johnston; D. Lewis; J. C. A. Rathbone; G. T. Russell

---

GOVERNMENT HOSPITALITY FUND

8 Cleveland Row, London SW1A 1DH
Tel 0171-210 4282; fax 0171-930 1148

The Government Hospitality Fund was instituted in 1908 for the purpose of organizing official hospitality on a regular basis with a view to the promotion of international goodwill. It is responsible to the Foreign and Commonwealth Office.

Minister in Charge, The Baroness Symons of Vernham Dean
Secretary, Col. T. Earl

GOVERNMENT OFFICES FOR THE REGIONS

The Government Offices for the Regions were established in 1994. The regional directors are accountable to the Secretary of State for the Environment, Transport and the Regions, the Secretary of State for Trade and Industry, and the Secretary of State for Education and Employment. The offices' role is to promote a coherent approach to competitiveness, sustainable economic development and regeneration using public and private resources.

CENTRAL UNIT, 1st Floor, Eland House, Bressenden Place, London SW1E 5DU
Tel 0171-890 5157; fax 0171-890 5019

Director (*G3*), Miss L. Bell
Head of Unit (*G5*), Mrs J. Scoones

EAST MIDLANDS
Secretariat: The Belgrave Centre, Stanley Place, Talbot Street, Nottingham NG1 5GG
Tel 0115-971 9971; fax 0115-971 2769

Regional Director (G3), D. Morrison
Directors (*G5*), Dr S. Kennett (*Environment and Community Development*); R. Poole (*Competitiveness and European Policy*); P. Mucklow (*Skills and Enterprise*); (*G6*), K. Lussey (*Corporate Affairs*)

EAST OF ENGLAND
Secretariat: Building A, Westbrook Centre, Milton Road, Cambridge CB4 1YG
Tel 01223-346700; fax 01223-346701

Regional Director (*G3*), A. Riddell
Directors (*G5*), C. Dunabin (*Housing, Environment and Regeneration*); Ms C. Bowdler (*Planning and Transport*); M. Oldham (*Economic Development*); J. Street (*Skills and Enterprise*); (*G6*), vacant (*Strategy and Resources*)

LONDON
Secretariat: Riverwalk House, 157–161 Millbank, London SW1P 4RR
Tel 0171-217 3456; fax 0171-217 3450

Director of Office (*G2*), Miss E. C. Turton, CB
Directors (*G3*), J. A. Owen (*Skills, Education and Regeneration*); S. Lord (*Transport and Corporate*); R. Allan (*New London Governance*); (*G5*), A. Sargent (*Skills and Education*); Mrs J. Bridges (*Planning*); Ms A. Munro (*Transport Division*); K. Timmins (*Enterprise and North-West*); Ms M. Winckler (*London East and European Programmes*); S. Gooding (*London Transport Division*); P. Sanders (*Transport for London Bill Division*); A. Melville (*Greater London Authority Implementation*); Ms E. Meek (*GLA Division*); A. Weedon (*Transport Task Force*); Ms C. Lyons (*Corporate*); J. Sienkiewicz (*London Development Unit*); R. Wragg (*Operations and Business Management*); N. Robinson (*Exports and Trade, and Business Development*); P. Fiddeman (*Regeneration London South*); B. Mann (*Home Office Liaison*); Z. Kowalczyk (*London Readiness 2000/Millennium Access*); I. Jordan (*Transport for London Project Division*)

NORTH-EAST
Secretariat: Wellbar House, Gallowgate, Newcastle upon Tyne NE1 4TD
Tel 0191-201 3300; fax 0191-202 3744

Regional Director (*G3*), Dr R. Dobbie
Directors (*G5*), J. Darlington (*Planning, Environment and Transport*); Miss D. Caudle (*Education, Skills, Enterprise and Regeneration*); A. Dell (*Europe, Industry, Trade and Technology*); (*G6*), Mrs D. Pearce (*Strategy and Resources*)

NORTH-WEST
Secretariat: 12th Floor, Sunley Tower, Piccadilly Plaza, Manchester M1 4BE
Tel 0161-952 4000; fax 0161-952 4099

Regional Director (*G3*), Ms M. Neville-Rolfe
Directors, (*G5*), Dr B. Isherwood (*Strategy and Regional Issues*); P. Styche (*Environment and Transport*); Dr D. Higham (*Business and Europe*); D. Duff (*Skills and Enterprise*); (*G6*), Ms E. Hughes (*Planning*); I. Jamieson (*Europe, Manchester*); Ms S. Yates (*Europe, Liverpool*); D. Hopewell (*Corporate Services*); N. Burke (*Operations, Skills and Enterprise*) (*acting*)

SOUTH-EAST
Secretariat: 2nd Floor, Bridge House, 1 Walnut Tree Close, Guildford, Surrey GU1 4GA
Tel 01483-882481; fax 01483-882259

Regional Director (*G3*), D. Saunders

Directors (*G5*), Ms L. Robinson (*Hants/IOW*); N. Wilson (*Berks/Oxon/Bucks*); A. Campbell (*Kent*); D. Andrews (*Surrey/E. and W. Sussex*); Mrs C. Dixon (*Regional Strategy Team*)

SOUTH-WEST
Secretariat: 4th Floor, The Pithay, Bristol BS1 2PB
Tel 0117-900 1792; fax 0117-900 1900
Regional Director (*G3*), Ms J. Henderson
Directors (*G5*), R. Bayly (*Devon and Cornwall*); Ms B. Houlden (*Environment and Regeneration*); T. Shearer (*Competitiveness and Skills*); Ms C. Carrington (*Corporate Services*)

WEST MIDLANDS
Secretariat: 6th Floor, 77 Paradise Circus, Queensway, Birmingham B1 2DT
Tel 0121-212 5000; fax 0121-212 5456
Regional Director (*G3*), D. Ritchie
Directors (*G5*), C. Marsh (*Policy Co-ordination and Europe Division*); Mrs P. Holland (*Local Government Division*); D. Way (*Business and Learning*); (*G6*), K. Griffiths (*Resource Management Division*)

YORKSHIRE AND THE HUMBER
Secretariat: PO Box 213, City House, New Station Street, Leeds LS1 4US
Tel 0113-280 0600; fax 0113-283 6394
Regional Director (*G3*), Mrs F. Everiss
Directors (*G5*), G. Dyche (*Strategy and Europe*); S. Perryman (*Business, Enterprise and Skills*); (*G6*), J. Jarvis (*Planning and Transport*); M. Doxey (*Personnel and Resources*); Ms M. Jackson (*Regeneration*) (*acting*)

DEPARTMENT OF HEALTH
Richmond House, 79 Whitehall, London SW1A 2NL
Tel 0171-210 2000
Web: http://www.open.gov.uk/doh/dhhome.htm

The Department of Health is responsible for the provision of the National Health Service in England and for social care, including oversight of personal social services run by local authorities in England for children (except day care, which is now the responsibility of the DfEE), the elderly, the infirm, the handicapped and other persons in need. It is responsible for health promotion and has functions relating to public and environmental health, food safety and nutrition. The Department is also responsible for the ambulance and emergency first aid services, under the Civil Defence Act 1948. The Department represents the UK at the European Union and other international organizations including the World Health Organization. It also supports UK-based healthcare and pharmaceutical industries.

Responsibility for food safety will be transferred to the new Food Standards Agency, expected to be in operation by mid 2000.

Secretary of State for Health, The Rt. Hon. Frank Dobson, MP
  Principal Private Secretary, J. Grauberg
  Private Secretaries, H. Rogers; M. Ferrero
  Special Advisers, J. McCrea; S. Stevens
  Parliamentary Private Secretary, Mrs A. Keen, MP
Minister of State, John Denham, MP (*NHS Structure and Resources*)
  Private Secretary, J. Adedji
  Parliamentary Private Secretary, P. Goggins, MP
Minister of State, The Rt. Hon. Tessa Jowell, MP (*Public Health, Women's Issues*)
  Private Secretary, R. Carter

Parliamentary Private Secretary, J. Ennis, MP
Parliamentary Under-Secretaries of State, John Hutton, MP; The Lord Hunt of Kings Heath; Gisela Stuart, MP
  Private Secretaries, N. Paterson; Ms H. McLain; vacant
Parliamentary Clerk, J. Fowles
Permanent Secretary (*SCS*), C. Kelly
  Private Secretary, Miss S. Foster
Chief Medical Officer (*SCS*), Prof. L. Donaldson, QHP, FRCSEd., FRCP
Chief Executive, NHS Executive (*SCS*), Sir Alan Langlands
Deputy Chief Medical Officers (*SCS*), Dr Patricia Troop; Dr Sheila Adam

REGIONAL CHAIRMEN'S MEETING
Chairman, The Secretary of State for Health
Members, John Denham, MP (*Minister of State*); The Rt. Hon. Tessa Jowell, MP (*Minister of State*); John Hutton, MP (*Parliamentary Under-Secretary*); The Lord Hunt of Kings Heath (*Parliamentary Under-Secretary*); Gisela Stuart, MP (*Parliamentary Under-Secretary*); Prof. L. Donaldson, QHP, FRCSEd., FRCP (*Chief Medical Officer*); Sir Alan Langlands (*Chief Executive, NHS Executive*); C. Kelly (*Permanent Secretary*); vacant (*Chief Nursing Officer*); C. Wilkinson; Mrs Z. Manzoor, CBE; P. Hammersley; Mrs R. Varley; Miss J. Trotter, OBE; I. Mills; W. Wells; Prof. A. Breckenridge, CBE; A. D. M. Liddell, CBE

CORPORATE MANAGEMENT DIRECTORATE GROUP
Head of Group (*SCS*), Ms A. Perkins

STATISTICS DIVISION
Director of Statistics (*SCS*), J. Fox
Chief Statisticians (*SCS*), R. K. Willmer; A. Roberts (*acting*)

PERSONNEL SERVICES
Director of Personnel (*SCS*), F. Goldhill
Heads of Branches (*SCS*), C. Muir; I. Forsyth; S. Redmond

INFORMATION SERVICES DIVISION
Head of Division (*SCS*), Dr A. A. Holt
Heads of Branches, Mrs L. Wishart; C. Horsey; M. Rainsford; Mrs J. Dainty; R. Long; P. G. Cobb; P. Charman

RESOURCE MANAGEMENT AND FINANCE
Head of Division (*SCS*), D. Clark
Heads of Branches, P. Kendall; B. Burleigh; J. Stopes-Roe; A. McNeil

ECONOMICS AND OPERATIONAL RESEARCH DIVISION (HEALTH)
Chief Economic Adviser (*SCS*), C. H. Smee, CB
Heads of Branches, Dr S. Harding; Dr G. Royston; A. Hare; N. York

COMMUNICATIONS DIRECTORATE
Director of Communications (*SCS*), Mrs H. McCallum
Deputy Directors, vacant (*Media Centre*); W. Roberts (*Publicity*); P. Addison-Child (*NHS Communications*) (*acting*)

POLICY MANAGEMENT UNIT
Head of Branch (*acting*), R. Walsh

SOLICITOR'S OFFICE
Solicitor (*SCS*), M. Morgan
Director of Legal Services (*SCS*), Mrs G. S. Kerrigan

PUBLIC HEALTH POLICY GROUP

PROTECTION OF HEALTH DIVISION
Head of Division (*SCS*), Dr Eileen Rubery, CB
Head of Branches, Dr E. Smales; A. Smith; J. Walden

JOINT FOOD SAFETY AND STANDARDS DIVISION
Head of Division (SCS), G. Podger
Heads of Branches, Dr R. Skinner; Ms P. Stewart; Miss J.
Wordley; S. Catling

HEALTH PROMOTION DIVISION
Head of Division (SCS), D. P. Walden
Heads of Branches (SCS), Miss A. Mithani; M. Fry; Miss A.
Edwards; E. Waterhouse

SOCIAL CARE GROUP
Chief Social Services Inspector, Ms D. Platt
Head of Social Care Policy, D. Walden
Deputy Chief Inspectors, D. Gilroy; Ms A. Nottage
Heads of Branches (SCS), S. Mitchell; N. Boyd; J. Kennedy;
T. Jeffery; Miss A. Stephenson; R Wilson (*Section Head*)
Assistant Chief Inspector (HQ), J. Cleary
Assistant Chief Inspectors (Regions), S. Allard; J. Cypher;
B. Riddell; A. Jones; Mrs P. K. Hall; C. P. Brearley; J.
Fraser; Mrs L. Hoare; Ms J. Owen; Miss F. McCabe

NURSING GROUP
Chief Nursing Officer/Director of Nursing (SCS), vacant
Assistant Chief Nursing Officers (SCS), Mrs G. Stephens; D.
Moore; Mrs E. Fradd

RESEARCH AND DEVELOPMENT DIVISION
Director of Research and Development, Prof. Sir John Pattison
Deputy Director of Research and Development (SCS), Dr C.
Henshall
Heads of Branches (SCS), Dr P. Greenaway; Mrs J. Griffin;
Ms A. Kauder; M. Taylor

NHS EXECUTIVE
Quarry House, Quarry Hill, Leeds LS2 7UE
Tel 0113-254 5000
Chief Executive, Sir Alan Langlands
Director of Human Resources, H. Taylor
Director of Finance and Performance, C. Reeves, CBE
Medical Director, Dr Sheila Adam
Chief Nursing Officer, vacant
Director of Research and Development, Prof. Sir John Pattison
Director of Planning and Performance Management,
A. D. M. Liddell, CBE
Director of NHS Clinical Governance Support Team, Prof. A.
Halligan

CORPORATE AFFAIRS
Head of Corporate Affairs (SCS), M. Staniforth

HUMAN RESOURCES
Deputy Director of Human Resources (SCS), S. Barnett

INFORMATION POLICY UNIT
Head of Unit (SCS), Dr P. Drury

PLANNING DIRECTORATE
Director (SCS), A. D. M. Liddell, CBE
Chief Economic Adviser, C. Smee, CB
Head of Planning, L. Bradley
Head of Communications, vacant
Director of Statistics, J. Fox

HEALTH SERVICES DIRECTORATE
Director (SCS), Dr Sheila Adam
Heads of Branches, M. Brown; Mrs L. Wolstenholme; Ms J.
McKessack; L. Percival; Dr G. Radford; D. Hewlett; Ms
K. Tyson

PRIMARY CARE DIVISION
Head of Division, A. McKeon
Fraud Supremo, J. Gee
Chief Dental Officer, J. R. Wild

Chief Pharmaceutical Officer (acting), Mrs J. Howe
Heads of Branches, Miss H. Robinson (*Dental and Optical
Services*); K. Guinness (*Pharmacy and Prescribing*); Miss
H. Gwynn (*White Paper Implementation Team*); M. Farrar
(*General Medical Services*)

FINANCE AND PERFORMANCE DIRECTORATE
Director (SCS), C. L. Reeves
Deputy Directors, R. Douglas; B. McCarthy
Heads of Branches, J. Lawler; Dr S. Peck; M. Sturges; A.
Angilley; M. A. Harris, CBE; J. Thomlinson; P. Coates; J.
Copeland

REGIONAL OFFICES
– see Social Welfare section

ADVISORY COMMITTEES

ADVISORY COMMITTEE ON THE MICROBIOLOGICAL
SAFETY OF FOOD, Room 502A, Skipton House, 80
London Road, London SE1 6LH. Tel: 0171-972 5050.
Chairman, Prof. D. Georgarla, CBE, Ph.D.
COMMITTEE ON THE SAFETY OF MEDICINES, Market
Towers, 1 Nine Elms Lane, London SW8 5NQ. Tel:
0171-273 0451. *Chairman*, Prof. A. M. Breckenridge, CBE,
FRCP, FRCPEd., FRSE
MEDICINES COMMISSION, Market Towers, 1 Nine Elms
Lane, London SW8 5NQ. Tel: 0171-273 0652. *Chairman*,
Prof. D. H. Lawson, CBE, FRCPEd., FRCP(Glas.)

SPECIAL HEALTH AUTHORITIES

DENTAL VOCATIONAL TRAINING AUTHORITY,
Master's House, Temple Grove, Compton Place Road,
Eastbourne, E. Sussex BN20 8AD. Tel: 01323-431189.
Chairman, R. Davies; *Secretary*, Ms J. Verity
FAMILY HEALTH SERVICES APPEAL AUTHORITY, 30
Victoria Avenue, Harrogate HG1 5PR. Tel: 01423-
535415. *Chief Executive*, D. J. Laverick
HEALTH EDUCATION AUTHORITY, Trevelyan House,
30 Great Peter Street, London SW1P 2HW. Tel: 0171-222
5300. *Chair*, Ms Y. Buckland; *Chief Executive*, S.
Fortescue
MENTAL HEALTH ACT COMMISSION – *see* page 320
MICROBIOLOGICAL RESEARCH AUTHORITY, Porton
Down, Salisbury, Wilts SP4 0JG. Tel: 01980-612100.
Chairman, Sir William Stewart, FRS; *Director*, Dr R. H.
Gilmour
NATIONAL BLOOD AUTHORITY, Oak House, Reeds
Crescent, Watford, Herts WD1 1QH. Tel: 01923-486800.
Chairman, M. Fogden; *Chief Executive*, M. Gorham
NATIONAL INSTITUTE OF CLINICAL EXCELLENCE, 90
Long Acre, London WC2E 9RZ. Tel: 0171-849 3444.
Chairman, Sir Michael Rawlins; *Chief Executive*, A.
Dillon
NHS INFORMATION AUTHORITY, 15 Frederick Road,
Edgbaston, Birmingham B15 1JD. Tel: 0121-625 1992.
Chairman, Prof. A. Bellingham, CBE; *Chief Executive*, N.
Bell
NHS LITIGATION AUTHORITY, 5 Pemberton Row,
London EC4A 3BA. Tel: 0171-936 4400. *Chairman*, Sir
Bruce Martin, QC; *Chief Executive*, S. Walker
NHS SUPPLIES, Premier House, 60 Caversham Road,
Reading, Berks RG1 7EB. Tel 0118-980 8600. *Chairman*,
D. Hall, CBE, TD; *Chief Executive*, T. Hunt, CBE
PRESCRIPTION PRICING AUTHORITY, Bridge House,
152 Pilgrim Street, Newcastle upon Tyne NE1 6SN. Tel:
0191-232 5371. *Chairman*, Prof. D. J. Johns; *Chief
Executive*, N. Scholte

UK Transplant Support Service Authority, Fox Den Road, Stoke Gifford, Bristol BS34 8RR. Tel: 0117-975 7575. *Chairman,* J. F. Shaw; *Chief Executive,* Mrs R. Balderson

SPECIAL HOSPITALS

Ashworth Hospital, Parkbourn, Maghull, Merseyside L31 1HW. Tel: 0151-473 0303. *Chief Executive (acting),* P. Clarke

Broadmoor Hospital, Crowthorne, Berks RG45 7EG. Tel: 01344-773111. *Chief Executive,* Dr J. Hollyman

Rampton Hospital, Retford, Notts DN22 0PD. Tel: 01777-248321. *Chief Executive,* Mrs S. Foley

EXECUTIVE AGENCIES

Medicines Control Agency
Market Towers, 1 Nine Elms Lane, London SW8 5NQ
Tel 0171-273 0000; fax 0171-273 0353

The Agency controls medicines through licensing, monitoring and inspection, and enforces safety standards.
Chief Executive, Dr K. H. Jones, CB

Medical Devices Agency
Hannibal House, Elephant and Castle, London SE1 6TQ
Tel 0171-972 8000; fax 0171-972 8108

The Agency safeguards the performance, quality and safety of medical devices and ensures that they comply with relevant EU directives.
Chief Executive, A. Kent

NHS Estates
1 Trevelyan Square, Boar Lane, Leeds LS1 6AE
Tel 0113-254 7000; fax 0113-254 7299

NHS Estates provides advice and support in the area of healthcare estate functions to the NHS and the healthcare industry.
Chief Executive, Mrs K. Priestley

NHS Pensions
Hesketh House, 200–220 Broadway, Fleetwood, Lancs FY7 8LG
Tel 01253-774774; fax 01253-774860

NHS Pensions administers the NHS occupational pension scheme.
Chief Executive, A. F. Cowan

HEALTH AND SAFETY COMMISSION
Rose Court, 2 Southwark Bridge, London SE1 9HS
Tel 0171-717 6000; fax 0171-717 6717

The Health and Safety Commission was created under the Health and Safety at Work etc. Act 1974, with duties to reform health and safety law, to propose new regulations, and generally to promote the protection of people at work and of the public from hazards arising from industrial and commercial activity, including major industrial accidents and the transportation of hazardous materials. The members of the Commission are appointed by the Secretary of State for the Environment, Transport and the Regions. The Commission is made up of representatives of employers, trades unions and local authorities, and has a full-time chairman.
Chairman, W. Callaghan
Members, Ms A. Gibson; Dr M. McKiernan; Ms J. Edmond-Smith; G. Brumwell; Ms M. Burns; S. Hamid; A. Chowdry; O. Tudor; R. Symons, CBE
Secretary, T. A. Gates

HEALTH AND SAFETY EXECUTIVE
Rose Court, 2 Southwark Bridge, London SE1 9HS
Tel 0171-717 6000; fax 0171-717 6717

The Health and Safety Executive is the Health and Safety Commission's major instrument. Through its inspectorates it enforces health and safety law in the majority of industrial premises. The Executive advises the Commission in its major task of laying down safety standards through regulations and practical guidance for many industrial processes. The Executive is also the licensing authority for nuclear installations and the reporting officer on the severity of nuclear incidents in Britain, and it is responsible for the Channel Tunnel Safety Authority.
Director-General, Miss J. H. Bacon, CB
Deputy Director-General, D. C. T. Eves, CB (*HM Chief Inspector of Factories*)
Director, Field Operations Directorate, Dr A. Ellis
Director, Science and Technology, Dr J. McQuaid, CB
Director, Safety Policy, C. Norris
Director, Health Directorate, Dr P. J. Graham
Director, Resources and Planning, R. Hillier
HM Chief Inspector of Nuclear Installations, Dr L. G. Williams
HM Chief Inspector of Mines, B. Langdon, CBE
HM Chief Inspecting Officer of Railways, V. Coleman

HIGHLANDS AND ISLANDS ENTERPRISE
Bridge House, 20 Bridge Street, Inverness IV1 1QR
Tel 01463-234171; fax 01463-244241

Highlands and Islands Enterprise (HIE) was set up under the Enterprise and New Towns (Scotland) Act 1991. Its role is to design, direct and deliver enterprise development, training, environmental and social projects and services. HIE is made up of a strategic core body and ten Local Enterprise Companies (LECs) to which many of its individual functions are delegated.
Chairman, Dr J. Hunter
Chief Executive, I. A. Robertson, CBE

HISTORIC BUILDINGS AND MONUMENTS COMMISSION FOR ENGLAND (ENGLISH HERITAGE)
23 Savile Row, London W1X 1AB
Tel 0171-973 3000; fax 0171-973 3001

English Heritage was established under the National Heritage Act 1983, and its duties are to offer expert advice and skills and give grants to secure the preservation of listed buildings, cathedrals, churches, archaeological sites, ancient monuments and historic houses in England; to encourage the imaginative re-use of historic buildings to aid regeneration of the centres of cities, towns and villages; to manage the historic houses and monuments in its care; and to promote access to and enjoyment of ancient monuments and historic buildings in England. It is funded by the Department for Culture, Media and Sport.
On 1 April 1999 English Heritage merged with the Royal Commission on the Historical Monuments of England (RCHME). It is therefore now responsible for the National Monuments Record, which includes all the material gathered since the formation of the RCHME in 1908 and now contains over 12 million photographs, maps and drawings.
Chairman, Sir Jocelyn Stevens, CVO (until March 2000)

Commissioners, Miss A. Arrowsmith; Ms B. Cherry; Cllr P. Davis; A. Fane; The Lord Faringdon; Prof. E. Fernie, CBE; Lady Gass; HRH The Duke of Gloucester, KG, GCVO; L. Grossman; Mrs C. Lycett-Green; Ms K. McLeod; Prof. R. Morris, FSA; Miss S. Underwood
Chief Executive, Ms P. Alexander

NATIONAL MONUMENTS RECORD, National Monuments Record Centre, Kemble Drive, Swindon SN2 2GZ. Tel: 01793-414600; fax: 01793-414606. *London Search Room:* 55 Blandford Street, London W1H 3AF. Tel: 0171-208 8200; fax: 0171-224 5333

HISTORIC BUILDINGS COUNCIL FOR SCOTLAND
Longmore House, Salisbury Place, Edinburgh EH9 1SH
Tel 0131-668 8600; fax 0131-668 8788

The Historic Buildings Council for Scotland is the advisory body to the Scottish ministers on matters related to buildings of special architectural or historical interest and in particular to proposals for awards by them of grants for the repair of buildings of outstanding architectural or historical interest or lying within outstanding conservation areas.
Chairman, Sir Raymond Johnstone, CBE
Members, R. Cairns; Mrs P. Chalmers; Mrs A. Dundas-Bekker; Dr J. Frew; D. Gauci; J. Hunter Blair; E. Jamieson; K. Martin; Revd C. Robertson; Mrs P. Robertson; Ms F. Sinclair
Secretary, Ms S. Adams

HISTORIC BUILDINGS COUNCIL FOR WALES
Cathays Park, Cardiff CF1 3NQ
Tel 01222-500200; fax 01222-826375

The Council's function is to advise the National Assembly for Wales on the built heritage through Cadw: Welsh Historic Monuments (*see* page 350), which is an executive agency of the Assembly.
Chairman, T. Lloyd, FSA
Members, Dr P. Morgan; Mrs S. Furse; Dr S. Unwin; Dr E. Wiliam; Miss E. Evans; Dr R. Wools
Secretary, Mrs J. Booker

HISTORIC ROYAL PALACES
Hampton Court Palace, East Molesey, Surrey KT8 9AU
Tel 0181-781 9500; fax 0181-781 9754

Historic Royal Palaces was formerly an executive agency of the Department for Culture, Media and Sport; it now has charitable trust status. The Secretary of State for Culture, Media and Sport is still accountable to Parliament for the care and presentation of the palaces, which are owned by the Sovereign in right of the Crown. The chairman of the trustees is appointed by The Queen on the advice of the Secretary of State.
Historic Royal Palaces is responsible for the Tower of London, Hampton Court Palace, Kensington Palace State Apartments and the Royal Ceremonial Dress Collection, Kew Palace with Queen Charlotte's Cottage, and the Banqueting House, Whitehall.

TRUSTEES
Chairman, The Earl of Airlie, KT, GCVO, PC

Appointed by The Queen, The Lord Camoys, GCVO, PC; Sir Michael Peat, KCVO; H. Roberts, CVO, FSA
Appointed by the Secretary of State, M. Herbert; Ms A. Heylin; S. Jones; Ms J. Sharman
Ex officio, Field Marshal the Lord Inge, GCB (*Constable of the Tower of London*)

OFFICERS
Chief Executive, A. Coppin
Director of Finance, Ms A. McLeish
Director of Human Resources, M. Bridger
Surveyor of the Fabric, R. Davidson
Curator, Historic Royal Palaces, Dr E. Impey
Director, Palaces Group, D. McGuinness
Resident Governor, HM Tower of London, Maj.-Gen. G. Field, CB, OBE

Royal Commission on the Historical Monuments of England (former)
— *see* Historic Buildings and Monuments Commission for England (English Heritage)

ROYAL COMMISSION ON THE ANCIENT AND HISTORICAL MONUMENTS OF SCOTLAND
John Sinclair House, 16 Bernard Terrace, Edinburgh EH8 9NX
Tel 0131-662 1456; fax 0131-662 1477

The Royal Commission was established in 1908 and is appointed to provide for the survey and recording of ancient and historical monuments connected with the culture, civilization and conditions of life of the people in Scotland from the earliest times. It is funded by the Scottish Executive. The Commission compiles and maintains the National Monuments Record of Scotland as the national record of the archaeological and historical environment. The National Monuments Record is open for reference Monday–Thursday 9.30–4.30, Friday 9.30–4.
Chairman, Sir William Fraser, GCB, FRSE
Commissioners, Prof. J. M. Coles, Ph.D., FBA; Prof. Rosemary Cramp, CBE, FSA; Prof. T. C. Smout, CBE, FRSE, FBA; Dr Deborah Howard, FSA; Prof. R. A. Paxton, FRSE; Dr Barbara Crawford, FSA, FSA Scot.; Miss A. Riches; J. Simpson, FSA Scot.; Ms M. Mackay, Ph.D.
Secretary, R. J. Mercer, FSA, FRSE

ROYAL COMMISSION ON THE ANCIENT AND HISTORICAL MONUMENTS OF WALES
Crown Building, Plas Crug, Aberystwyth SY23 1NJ
Tel 01970-621200; fax 01970-627701

The Royal Commission was established in 1908 and is currently empowered by a royal warrant of 1992 to survey, record, publish and maintain a database of ancient and historical and maritime sites and structures, and landscapes in Wales. The Commission is funded by the National Assembly for Wales and is also responsible for the National Monuments Record of Wales, which is open daily for public reference, for the supply of archaeological information to the Ordnance Survey, for the co-ordination of archaeological aerial photography in Wales, and for sponsorship of the regional Sites and Monuments Records.

Chairman, Prof. R. A. Griffiths, PH.D., D.Litt.
Commissioners, D. Gruffyd Jones; Prof. G. B. D. Jones,
  D.Phil., FSA; Mrs A. Nicol; Prof. P. Sims-Williams, FBA;
  Prof. G. J. Wainwright, MBE, PH.D., FSA; E. Wiliam, PH.D.,
  FSA
Secretary, P. R. White, FSA

ANCIENT MONUMENTS BOARD FOR SCOTLAND
Longmore House, Salisbury Place, Edinburgh EH9 1SH
Tel 0131-668 8764; fax 0131-668 8765

The Ancient Monuments Board for Scotland advises the
Scottish ministers on the exercise of their functions, under
the Ancient Monuments and Archaeological Areas Act
1979, of providing protection for monuments of national
importance.
Chairman, Prof. M. Lynch, PH.D., FRSE, PSA Scot.
Members, A. Wright, FRSA; Mrs K. Dalyell, FSA Scot.; P.
  Clarke, FSA; Ms A. Ritchie, OBE, PH.D., FSA, FSA Scot.;
  Prof. C. D. Morris, FRSE, FSA, FSA Scot.; R. J. Mercer,
  FRSE, FSA, FSA Scot.; Miss L. M. Thoms, FSA Scot.; J.
  Higgitt, FSA; Ms C. Swanson, PH.D., FSA Scot.; M.
  Baughan; Ms J. Cannizzo, PH.D.; S. Peake , PH.D.; M.
  Taylor; Ms J. Harden, FSA Scot.
Secretary, R. A. J. Dalziel
Assessor, D. J. Breeze, PH.D., FRSE, FSA, FSA Scot.

ANCIENT MONUMENTS BOARD FOR WALES
Cathays Park, Cardiff CFI 3NQ
Tel 01222-500200; fax 01222-826375

The Ancient Monuments Board for Wales advises the
National Assembly for Wales on its statutory functions in
respect of ancient monuments.
Chairman, Prof. R. R. Davies, CBE, D.Phil., FBA
Members, R. G. Keen; Mrs F. M. Lynch Llewellyn, FSA;
  Prof. W. H. Manning, PH.D., FSA; Prof. Wendy Davies,
  PH.D., FBA; M. J. Garner; Prof. R. A. Griffiths, PH.D., D.Litt.
Secretary, Mrs J. Booker

HOME-GROWN CEREALS AUTHORITY
Caledonia House, 223 Pentonville Road, London N1 9NG
Tel 0171-520 3926; fax 0171-520 3954

Set up under the Cereals Marketing Act 1965, the Authority
consists of seven members representing UK cereal growers,
seven representing dealers in, or processors of, grain and
two independent members. The Authority's functions are
to improve the production and marketing of UK-grown
cereals and oilseeds through a research and development
programme, to provide a market information service, and
to promote UK cereals in export markets.
Chairman (part-time) (£21,324), A. Pike
Chief Executive, P. V. Biscoe

HOME OFFICE
50 Queen Anne's Gate, London SW1H 9AT
Tel 0171-273 4000; fax 0171-273 2190
E-mail: gen.ho@gtnet.gov.uk
Web: http://www.homeoffice.gov.uk

The Home Office deals with those internal affairs in
England and Wales which have not been assigned to other
government departments. The Home Secretary is particularly concerned with the administration of justice; criminal
law; the treatment of offenders, including probation and
the prison service; the police; immigration and nationality;
passport policy matters; community relations; certain
public safety matters; and fire and civil emergencies
services. The Home Secretary personally is the link
between The Queen and the public, and exercises certain
powers on her behalf, including that of the royal pardon.
  Other subjects dealt with include electoral arrangements;
ceremonial and formal business connected with honours;
scrutiny of local authority by-laws; granting of licences for
scientific procedures involving animals; cremations, burials
and exhumations; firearms; dangerous drugs and poisons;
general policy on laws relating to shops, liquor licensing,
gaming and marriage; theatre and cinema licensing; and
race relations policy.
  The Home Secretary is also the link between the UK
government and the governments of the Channel Islands
and the Isle of Man.
Secretary of State for the Home Department, The Rt. Hon. Jack
  Straw, MP
  Principal Private Secretary (SCS), Ms H. Jackson
  Private Secretaries, Ms C. Sumner; S. Harrison; Ms M.
    Goldstein
  Special Advisers, E. Owen; J. Russell
Minister of State, The Rt. Hon. Paul Boateng, MP
  Private Secretary, S. Hayes
Minister of State, Charles Clarke, MP
  Private Secretary, Ms C. French
Minister of State, Barbara Roche, MP
  Private Secretary, J. Payne
Parliamentary Under-Secretaries of State, Michael O'Brien,
  MP; The Lord Bassam of Brighton
  Private Secretaries, T. Wright; P. Morrison
Parliamentary Clerk, Mrs J. Thorne
Permanent Under-Secretary of State (SCS), D. B. Omand
  Private Secretary, Miss A. Rutherford
Chief Medical Officer (at Department of Health), Prof. L.
  Donaldson, QHP, FRCSEd., FRCP

COMMUNICATION DIRECTORATE
Director (SCS), B. Butler
Deputy Head of Communication (Head of News) (SCS), Ms P.
  Teare
Head of Publicity and Corporate Services (SCS), Miss A. Nash
Assistant Director, News (G6), vacant
Assistant Director and Head of Information Services Group (G6),
  P. Griffiths

CONSTITUTIONAL AND COMMUNITY POLICY DIRECTORATE
Director (SCS), Miss C. Sinclair
Heads of Units (SCS), Mrs G. Catto; R. Evans; M. de
  Pulford; E. Grant; L. Hughes; Ms S. Marshall; N.
  Varney

ANIMALS (SCIENTIFIC PROCEDURES) INSPECTORATE
Chief Inspector (SCS), Dr J. Richmond
Superintendent Inspector (SCS), Dr J. Anderson
Inspectors (G6), Dr R. Curtis; Dr V. Navaratnam; Dr C.
  Wilkins

GAMING BOARD FOR GREAT BRITAIN
— *see* page 302

CORPORATE DEVELOPMENT DIRECTORATE
Director (SCS), Dr D. Pepper
Heads of Units (SCS), T. Edwards; Ms S. Rae; Ms E.
  Sparrow; C. Welsh; S. Wharton

Senior Principals (G6), Mrs C. Burrows; S. Thornton; T. Williams

CORPORATE RESOURCES DIRECTORATE
Grenadier House, 99–105 Horseferry Road, London
SW1P 2DD
Tel 0171-273 4000
Queen Anne's Gate, London SW1H 9AT
Tel 0171-273 4000

Director (SCS), Ms L. Lockyer
Heads of Units (SCS), T. Cobley; Ms E. Moody
Senior Principals (G6), R. Creedon; A. Ford; J. G. Jones; D. Rigby

CRIMINAL POLICY group
Directors (SCS), J. Halliday, CB; W. Fittall; Mrs S. Street
Heads of Units (SCS), S. Atkins; M. Boyle; Ms K. Bramwell; Ms C. Byrne; I. Chisholm; J. Duke-Evans; S. Hickson; H. Marriage; A. Norbury; J. Powls; Miss C. Stewart; J. Thompson; H. Webber
Senior Principals (G6), J. Furniss; Mrs A. Johnstone; A. Macfarlane; J. Nicholson; Ms L. Rogerson; S. Thornton

HOME OFFICE CRIME PREVENTION COLLEGE
The Hawkhills, Easingwold, York YO6 3EG
Tel 01347-825060
Director, S. Trimmins

HM INSPECTORATE OF PROBATION
Chief Inspector (SCS), Sir Graham Smith, CBE
Assistant Chief Inspector (G6), G. Childs

FIRE AND EMERGENCY PLANNING DIRECTORATE
Horseferry House, Dean Ryle Street, London SW1P 2AW
Tel 0171-273 4000
50 Queen Anne's Gate, London SW1H 9AT
Tel 0171-273 4000

Director (SCS), C. Everett
Heads of Units (SCS), P. Davies; E. Guy; Mrs V. Harris; Miss S. Hart; Dr D. Peace

HM FIRE SERVICE INSPECTORATE
HM Chief Inspector, G. Meldrum, CBE, QFSM
HM Territorial Inspectors, A. R. Currie, OBE, QFSM; P. Morphew, QFSM; A. Rule, QFSM; J. G. Russel, QFSM
Lay Inspector, vacant
HM Inspectors, R. A. M. Baillie, QFSM; D. Berry; G. P. Bowles; S. D. Christian; D. Kent; C. Moseley; R. Pearce; E. G. Pearn, OBE, QFSM; K. Phillips; M. Robinson; B. J. Unger; A. C. Wells, QFSM
Principal (G7), Miss G. Kirton

EMERGENCY PLANNING COLLEGE
The Hawkhills, Easingwold, Yorks YO6 3EG
Tel 01347-821406

IMMIGRATION AND NATIONALITY DIRECTORATE, AND EU AND INTERNATIONAL UNIT
Whitgift Centre, Block A, 15 Wellesley Road, Croydon, Surrey CR9 3LY
Tel 0181-686 7766
Apollo House, 36 Wellesley Road, Croydon, Surrey CR9 3RR
Tel 0181-686 0333
50 Queen Anne's Gate, London SW1H 9AT
Tel 0171-273 4000
India Buildings, 3rd Floor, Water Street, Liverpool L2 0QN
Tel 0151-237 5200

Director-General (SCS), S. Boys Smith
Deputy Directors-General (SCS), M. J. Eland (*Policy*); Miss K. Collins (*Operations*); Dr C. Mace (*Projects*)
Heads of Directorates (SCS), J. Acton; Miss V. M. Dews; B. Eagle; Mrs E. C. L. Pallett; J. Potts; R. M. Whalley; R. G. Yates
Senior Principals (G6), P. Dawson; B. Downie; P. Wheelhouse

IMMIGRATION SERVICE
Director (Ports) (SCS), T. Farrage, CBE
Deputy Director (G6), V. Hogg
Director (Enforcement) (SCS), I. Boon
Deputy Director (G6), C. Harbin

EU AND INTERNATIONAL UNIT
Head of Unit (SCS), P. Edwards

LEGAL ADVISERS' BRANCH
Legal Adviser (SCS), Miss J. Wheldon, CB
Deputy Legal Advisers (SCS), Mrs S. A. Evans; T. Middleton
Assistant Legal Advisers (SCS), R. J. Clayton; J. R. O'Meara; R. Green; S. A. Parker

ORGANIZED AND INTERNATIONAL CRIME DIRECTORATE
Director (SCS), J. Warne

PLANNING AND FINANCE DIRECTORATE
50 Queen Anne's Gate, London SW1H 9AT
Tel 0171-273 4000
Horseferry House, Dean Ryle Street, London SW1P 2AW
Tel 0171-273 4000

Director (SCS), R. Fulton
Heads of Units (SCS), C. Harnett; A. Mortimer
Senior Principal (G6), P. Dare

POLICE POLICY DIRECTORATE
Director (SCS), J. Lyon
Heads of Units (SCS), N. Benger; Miss D. Loudon
Senior Principal (G6), R. Ginman

NATIONAL DIRECTORATE OF POLICE TRAINING
National Director of Police Training, P. Hermitage, QPM

Corporate Services
Senior Principal (G6), S. Wells

NATIONAL POLICE TRAINING
Bramshill House, Bramshill, Hook, Hants RG27 0JW
Tel 01256-602100
Head of Higher Training, I. McDonald

HENDON DATA CENTRE
Aerodrome Road, Colindale, London NW9 5LN
Tel 0181-200 2424
Head of Unit (G6), J. Ladley

POLICE SCIENTIFIC DEVELOPMENT BRANCH
Sandridge, St Albans, Herts AL4 9HQ
Tel 01727-865051

Director (SCS), B. R. Coleman, OBE
Chief Scientist/Deputy Director (G6), Dr P. Young

Langhurst House, Langhurstwood Road, Nr Horsham, W. Sussex RH12 4WX
Tel 01403-255451
Head of Langhurst Facility (G6), Dr G. Thomas

HM INSPECTORATE OF CONSTABULARY
HM Chief Inspector of Constabulary (SCS), Sir David O'Dowd, CBE, QPM

HM Inspectors (SCS), D. Crompton, CBE, QPM; K. Povey, QPM; C. Smith, CBE, CVO, QPM; P. J. Winship, CBE, QPM; D. Blakey, CBE, QPM

Senior Principal (G6), L. Davidoff

METROPOLITAN POLICE COMMITTEE AND SECRETARIAT
Clive House, Petty France, London SW1H 9HD
Tel 0171-273 4000

Head of Secretariat (SCS), P. Honour

RESEARCH, DEVELOPMENT AND STATISTICS DIRECTORATE
Director (SCS), Dr P. Wiles
Heads of Units (SCS), Dr G. Laycock; C. Lewis; D. Moxon; R. Price; P. Ward; Dr J. Youell
Senior Principals (G6), G. Barclay; Ms M. Colledge; P. Collier; Mrs P. Dowdeswell; Ms M. FitzGerald; P. Goldblatt; Mrs C. Lehman; Mrs P. Mayhew, OBE; R. Walmsley; B. Webb

STRATEGY UNIT
Head of Unit (SCS), R. Weatherill

HM INSPECTORATE OF PRISONS
HM Chief Inspector, Gen. Sir David Ramsbotham, GCB, CBE
HM Deputy Chief Inspector, C. Allen
HM Inspectors (Governor 1), R. Jacques; G. Hughes

PRISONS OMBUDSMAN
— see page 331

PAROLE BOARD FOR ENGLAND AND WALES
— see page 329

HM PRISON SERVICE
— see pages 380–2

FIRE SERVICE COLLEGE
Moreton-in-Marsh, Glos GL56 0RH
Tel 01608-650831
An executive agency of the Home Office.
Chief Executive and Commandant, T. Glossop, QFSM
College Secretary, P. Taylor

UK PASSPORT AGENCY
Clive House, Petty France, London SW1H 9HD
Tel 0171-799 2728
An executive agency of the Home Office.
Chief Executive (SCS), B. L. Herdan
Deputy Chief Executive and Director of Operations (G6), K. J. Sheehan
Director of Systems (G6), J. Davies
CRIMINAL RECORDS BUREAU, Room 466/68, India Buildings, Water Street, Liverpool L2 0UZ. Tel: 0151-224 8068. *Programme Manager (G6)*, G. Ryan

HORSERACE TOTALISATOR BOARD
74 Upper Richmond Road, London SW15 2SU
Tel 0181-874 6411; fax 0181-874 6107

The Horserace Totalisator Board (the Tote) was established by the Betting, Gaming and Lotteries Act 1963. Its function is to operate totalisators on approved racecourses in Great Britain, and it also provides on- and off-course cash and credit offices. Under the Horserace Totalisator and Betting Levy Board Act 1972, it is further empowered to offer bets at starting price (or other bets at fixed odds) on any sporting event, and under the Horserace Totalisator Board Act 1997 to take bets on any event, except the National Lottery. The chairman and members of the Board are appointed by the Home Secretary.

The Government announced in May 1999 that the Tote would be made available for sale, subject to the necessary legislation going through Parliament.
Chairman (£78,225), P. I. Jones
Chief Executive, W. J. Heaton

HOUSE OF LORDS, ROYAL COMMISSION ON THE REFORM OF
— *see* Royal Commission on the Reform of the House of Lords

HOUSING CORPORATION
149 Tottenham Court Road, London W1P 0BN
Tel 0171-393 2000; fax 0171-393 2111

Established by Parliament in 1964, the Housing Corporation regulates, funds and promotes the proper performance of registered social landlords, which are non-profit making bodies run by voluntary committees. There are over 2,200 registered social landlords, most of which are housing associations, and they now provide homes for more than 1.5 million people. Under the Housing Act 1996, the Corporation's regulatory role was widened to embrace new types of landlords, in particular local housing companies. The Corporation is funded by the Department of the Environment, Transport and the Regions.
Chairman, The Baroness Dean of Thornton-le-Fylde, PC
Deputy Chairman, E. Armitage
Chief Executive, A. Mayer

HUMAN FERTILIZATION AND EMBRYOLOGY AUTHORITY
Paxton House, 30 Artillery Lane, London E1 7LS
Tel 0171-377 5077; fax 0171-377 1871

The Human Fertilization and Embryology Authority (HFEA) was established under the Human Fertilization and Embryology Act 1990. Its function is to license persons carrying out any of the following activities: the creation or use of embryos outside the body in the provision of infertility treatment services; the use of donated gametes in infertility treatment; the storage of gametes or embryos; and research on human embryos. It maintains a confidential database of all such treatments and of egg and sperm donors, and provides information to patients, clinics and the public. The HFEA also keeps under review information about embryos and, when requested to do so, gives advice to the Secretary of State for Health.
Chairman, Mrs R. Deech
Deputy Chairman, Mrs J. Denton
Members, Prof. Brenda Almond; Dr G. Bahadur; Prof. D. Barlow; Mrs M. E. Coath; Prof. Christine Gosden; Prof. A. Grubb; Prof. H. Leese; Prof. S. Lewis; Dr B. Lieberman; Dr Anne McLaren; Dr S. Muhammed; Ms S. Nathan; Ms S. Nebhrajani; The Rt. Revd Bishop of Rochester; Dr Joan Stringer; Prof. A. Templeton; Julia, Lady Tugendhat; Prof. J. Williams
Chief Executive, Mrs S. McCarthy

HUMAN GENETICS ADVISORY COMMISSION
Room 1/5, Albany House, 94–98 Petty France, London
SW1H 9ST
Tel 0171-271 2131; fax 0171-271 2028

The Human Genetics Advisory Commission was established in 1996. It is an advisory body with the remit of taking a broad view of developments in human genetics and advising ministers on ways to build public confidence in the application of the new science. Members of the Commission are appointed by the Secretary of State for Trade and Industry and the Secretary of State for Health.
Chairman, The Baroness O'Neill, CBE, FBA
Members, Prof. C. Aitken, CBE; Dr Michaela Aldred; Prof. M. Bobrow; Mrs D. Littlejohn, CBE; Prof. N. Nevin; Dr G. Poste, FRS; Revd Dr J. Polkinghorne, KBE, FRS; Ms M. Stuart
Head of Secretariat, Dr Amanda Goldin

INDEPENDENT COMMISSION FOR POLICE COMPLAINTS FOR NORTHERN IRELAND
Chamber of Commerce House, 22 Great Victoria Street, Belfast BT2 7LP
Tel 01232-244821; fax 01232-248563

The Independent Commission for Police Complaints was established under the Police (Northern Ireland) Order 1987. It has powers to supervise the investigation of certain categories of serious complaints, can direct that disciplinary charges be brought, and has oversight of the informal resolution procedure for less serious complaints.
Under the Police (Northern Ireland) Act 1998 the Commission will be replaced by a Police Ombudsman. This is expected to happen in early 2000.
Chairman, P. A. Donnelly
Chief Executive, B. McClelland

INDEPENDENT HOUSING OMBUDSMAN
Norman House, 105–109 Strand, London WC2R 0AA
Tel 0171-836 3630; 0345-125973; fax 0171-836 3900

The Independent Housing Ombudsman was established in 1997 under the Housing Act 1996. The Ombudsman deals with complaints against registered social landlords (not including local authorities).
Ombudsman, R. Jefferies
Chair of Board, Ms P. Brown
General Manager, L. Greenberg

INDEPENDENT INTERNATIONAL COMMISSION ON DECOMMISSIONING
Dublin Castle, Block M, Ship Street, Dublin 2
Tel 00 353 1-478 0111; fax 00 353 1-478 0600
Rosepark House, Upper Newtownards Road, Belfast BT4 3NX
Tel 01232-488600; fax 01232-488601

The Commission was established by agreement between the British and Irish governments in August 1997. Its objective is to facilitate the decommissioning of illegally-held firearms and explosives in accordance with the relevant legislation in both jurisdictions. Its members are appointed jointly by the two governments; staff are appointed by the Commission. All are drawn from countries other than the UK and the Republic of Ireland.
Chairman, Gen. J. de Chastelain (Canada)
Commissioners, Brig. T. Nieminen (Finland); Ambassador D. C. Johnson (USA)
Chief of Staff, C. E. Garrard (Canada)

INDEPENDENT REVIEW SERVICE FOR THE SOCIAL FUND
4th Floor, Centre City Podium, 5 Hill Street, Birmingham B5 4UB
Tel 0121-606 2100; fax 0121-606 2180

The Social Fund Commissioner is appointed by the Secretary of State for Social Security. The Commissioner appoints Social Fund Inspectors, who provide an independent review of decisions made by Social Fund Officers in the Benefits Agency of the Department of Social Security.
Social Fund Commissioner, J. Scampion

INDEPENDENT TELEVISION COMMISSION
33 Foley Street, London W1P 7LB
Tel 0171-255 3000; fax 0171-306 7800

The Independent Television Commission replaced the Independent Broadcasting Authority in 1991. The Commission is responsible for licensing and regulating all commercially funded television services broadcast from the UK. Members are appointed by the Secretary of State for Culture, Media and Sport.
Chairman (£67,420), Sir Robin Biggam
Deputy Chairman (£17,300), The Lord Holme of Cheltenham, CBE
Members (*part-time*) (£12,980), A. Balls, CB; Dr J. Beynon, FREng.; Sir Michael Checkland; Ms J. Goffe; Dr Maria Moloney; Prof. D. L. Morgan, D.Phil. (*Member for Wales*); J. Ranelagh; Dr M. Shea, CVO (*Member for Scotland*)
Chief Executive (£175,000), P. Rogers
Secretary and Director of Administration, M. Redley

INDUSTRIAL INJURIES ADVISORY COUNCIL
6th Floor, The Adelphi, 1–11 John Adam Street, London WC2N 6HT
Tel 0171-962 8066; fax 0171-712 2255

The Industrial Injuries Advisory Council is a statutory body under the Social Security Administration Act 1992 which considers and advises the Secretary of State for Social Security on regulations and other questions relating to industrial injuries benefits or their administration.
Chairman, Prof. A. J. Newman Taylor, OBE, FRCP
Secretary, A. Packer

BOARD OF INLAND REVENUE
Somerset House, Strand, London WC2R 1LB
Tel 0171-438 6622

The Board of Inland Revenue was constituted under the Inland Revenue Board Act 1849. The Board administers and collects direct taxes – income tax, corporation tax, capital gains tax, inheritance tax, stamp duty, and petroleum revenue tax – and advises the Chancellor of the Exchequer on policy questions involving them. The Department's Valuation Office is an executive agency responsible for valuing property for tax purposes. The Contributions Agency of the Department of Social Security, which is responsible for the collection of contributions under the National Insurance scheme, became part of the Inland Revenue in April 1999 and is now an executive office called the National Insurance Contributions Office. The Contributions Unit of the Social Security Agency in Northern Ireland also transferred to the Inland Revenue in April 1999.

THE BOARD

Chairman (G1), N. Montagu, CB
   Private Secretary, Ms C. Lunney
Deputy Chairmen (G2), S. C. T. Matheson, CB; G. H. Bush, CB
Director-General (G2), T. J. Flesher

DIVISIONS

Director, Human Resources Division (G3), J. Gant
Director, Business and Management Services Division (G3), J. Yard
Head, Strategy and Planning Division, P. Wardle
Principal Finance Officer (G3), R. R. Martin
Director, Business Operations Division (G3), D. A. Smith
Director, Statistics and Economics Division (G3), R. G. Ward
Director, Business Tax Division (G3), Ms J. Williams
Director, Management Services Unit (G3), K. Hodgson
Director, International Division (G3), G. Makhlouf
Director, Compliance Division (G3), E. J. Gribbon
Director, Personal Tax Division (G3), B. A. Mace
Director, Capital and Savings Division (G3), D. Hartnett

EXECUTIVE OFFICES

ACCOUNTS OFFICE (CUMBERNAULD), St Mungo's Road, Cumbernauld, Glasgow G70 5TR. *Director*, A. Geddes, OBE
ACCOUNTS OFFICE (SHIPLEY), Shipley, Bradford, W. Yorks BD98 8AA. *Director*, R. J. Warner
CAPITAL TAXES OFFICE, Ferrers House, PO Box 38, Castle Meadow Road, Nottingham NG2 1BB. *Director*, E. McKeegan
CAPITAL TAXES OFFICE (SCOTLAND), Mulberry House, 16 Picardy Place, Edinburgh EH1 3NB. *Registrar*, Mrs J. Templeton
COMMUNICATIONS UNITS, North-West Wing, Bush House, London WC2B 4PP. *Head of External Communications Unit*, P. Whyatt; *Head of Internal Communications Unit*, Ms N. Walters
ENFORCEMENT OFFICE, Durrington Bridge House, Barrington Road, Worthing, W. Sussex BN12 4SE. *Director*, Mrs C. A. Mellor
FINANCIAL ACCOUNTING OFFICE, South Block, Barrington Road, Worthing, W. Sussex BN12 4XH. *Director*, J. D. Easey
FINANCIAL INTERMEDIARIES AND CLAIMS OFFICE, St John's House, Merton Road, Bootle L26 9BB; Fitz Roy House, PO Box 46, Castle Meadow, Nottingham NG2 1BD. *Director*, J. Johnson
INTERNAL AUDIT OFFICE, North-West Wing, Bush House, London WC2B 4PP. *Director*, N. R. Buckley
NATIONAL INSURANCE CONTRIBUTIONS OFFICE, DSS Longbenton, Benton Park Road, Newcastle upon Tyne NE98 1YX. *Chief Executive (G3)*, G. Bertram, CB
OIL TAXATION OFFICE, Melbourne House, Aldwych, London WC2B 4LL. *Director*, G. Nield

PENSION SCHEME OFFICE, Yorke House, PO Box 62, Castle Meadow Road, Nottingham NG2 1BG. *Director*, S. J. McManus
SOLICITOR'S OFFICE, East Wing, Somerset House, London WC2R 1LB. *Solicitor (G2)*, P. Ridd
SOLICITOR'S OFFICE (SCOTLAND), Clarendon House, 114–116 George Street, Edinburgh EH2 4LH. *Solicitor*, I. K. Laing
SPECIAL COMPLIANCE OFFICE, Angel Court, 199 Borough High Street, London SE1 1HZ. *Director*, F. J. Brannigan
STAMP OFFICE, South-West Wing, Bush House, Strand, London WC2B 4QN. *Director*, K. S. Hodgson, OBE
TRAINING OFFICE, Lawress Hall, Riseholme Park, Lincoln LN2 2BJ. *Director*, T. Kuczys

REGIONAL EXECUTIVE OFFICES

INLAND REVENUE EAST, Churchgate, New Road, Peterborough PE1 1TD. *Director*, M. J. Hodgson
INLAND REVENUE LARGE BUSINESS OFFICE, 6th Floor, North-West Wing, Bush House, Strand, London WC2B 4BB. *Director*, Mrs M. E. Williams
INLAND REVENUE LONDON, New Court, Carey Street, London WC2A 2JE. *Director*, J. F. Carling
INLAND REVENUE NORTH, Ground Floor, Regent House, 10 Commercial Street, Darlington DL3 6JF. *Director*, R. Cooke
INLAND REVENUE NORTH-WEST, The Triad, Stanley Road, Bootle, Merseyside L75 2DD. *Director*, G. W. Lunn
INLAND REVENUE SOUTH-EAST, Dukes Court, Dukes Street, Woking GU21 5XR. *Director*, T. Sleeman
INLAND REVENUE SOUTH-WEST, 3rd Floor, Longbrook House, New North Road, Exeter EX4 4UA. *Director*, R. S. Hurcombe
INLAND REVENUE SOUTH YORKSHIRE, Concept House, 5 Young Street, Sheffield S1 4LF. *Director*, Ms M. Hay
INLAND REVENUE WALES AND MIDLANDS, 1st Floor, Phase II Building, Ty Glas Avenue, Llanishen, Cardiff CF4 5TS; 550 Streetsbrook Road, Solihull, West Midlands B91 1QU. *Director*, M. W. Kirk
INLAND REVENUE SCOTLAND, Clarendon House, 114–116 George Street, Edinburgh EH2 4LH. *Director*, I. S. Gerrie
INLAND REVENUE NORTHERN IRELAND, Dorchester House, 52–58 Great Victoria Street, Belfast BT2 7QE. *Director*, D. Hinstridge

VALUATION OFFICE AGENCY
New Court, 48 Carey Street, London WC2A 2JE
Tel 0171-506 1700; fax 0171-506 1998
50 Frederick Street, Edinburgh EH2 1NG
Tel 0131-465 0700; fax 0131-465 0799

Chief Executive, M. A. Johns
Chief Valuer, Scotland, A. Ainslie

ADJUDICATOR'S OFFICE
— see page 277

INTELLIGENCE SERVICES TRIBUNAL
PO Box 4823, London SW1A 9XD
Tel 0171-273 4383

The Intelligence Services Act 1994 established a tribunal of three senior members of the legal profession, independent of the Government and appointed by The Queen, to investigate complaints from any person about anything which they believe the Secret Intelligence Service or the

Government Communications Headquarters has done to them or to their property.
President, The Rt. Hon. Lord Justice Simon Brown
Vice-President, Sheriff J. McInnes, QC
Member, Sir Richard Gaskell
Secretary, N. Brooks

INTERCEPTION COMMISSIONER
c/o PO Box 12376, London SW1P 1XU
Tel 0171-273 4096

The Commissioner is appointed by the Prime Minister. He keeps under review the issue by Secretaries of State of warrants under the Interception of Communications Act 1985 and safeguards made in respect of intercepted material obtained through the use of such warrants. He is also required to give all such assistance as the Interception of Communications Tribunal may require to enable it to carry out its functions, and to submit an annual report to the Prime Minister with respect to the carrying out of his functions.
Commissioner, The Lord Nolan, PC
  Private Secretary, N. Brooks

INTERCEPTION OF COMMUNICATIONS TRIBUNAL
PO Box 12376, London SW1P 1XU
Tel 0171-273 4096

Under the Interception of Communications Act 1985, the Tribunal is required to investigate complaints from any person who believes that communications sent to or by them have been intercepted in the course of their transmission by post or by means of a public telecommunications system. The Tribunal comprises senior members of the legal profession, who are appointed by The Queen.
President, Sir William Macpherson of Cluny
Vice-President, Sir David Calcutt, QC
Members, P. Scott, QC; R. Seabrook, QC; W. Carmichael
Secretary, N. Brooks

DEPARTMENT FOR INTERNATIONAL DEVELOPMENT
94 Victoria Street, London SW1E 5JL
Tel 0171-917 7000; fax 0171-917 0016
Web: http://www.dfid.gov.uk
Abercrombie House, Eaglesham Road, East Kilbride, Glasgow G75 8EA
Tel 01355-844000; fax 01355-844099

The Department for International Development (DFID) was established in May 1997 from the former Overseas Development Administration of the Foreign and Commonwealth Office. It takes the lead on British policy towards developing countries. It also manages the development assistance budget, including financial aid and technical assistance (specialist staff abroad and training facilities in the UK), whether provided directly to developing countries or through the various multilateral aid organizations, including the EU, the World Bank and the UN agencies.
Secretary of State for International Development, The Rt. Hon. Clare Short, MP
  Private Secretary, A. Smith
  Special Advisers, D. Harris; D. Mepham
  Parliamentary Private Secretary, D. Turner, MP

Parliamentary Under-Secretary, George Foulkes, MP
Permanent Secretary (*SCS*), Sir John Vereker, KCB
  Private Secretary, M. James

PROGRAMMES
Director-General (*SCS*), B. R. Ireton
Head, Conflict and Humanitarian Affairs Department (*SCS*), Dr M. Kapila

AFRICA
Director (*SCS*), P. D. M. Freeman
Heads of Departments (*SCS*), Mrs B. M. Kelly, CBE (*Africa, Greater Horn and Co-ordination*); B. Thomson (*West and North Africa*); D. Fish (*Nairobi*); J. R. Drummond (*Harare*); J. H. S. Chard (*Pretoria*)

ASIA
Director (*SCS*), S. Unsworth
Heads of Departments (*SCS*), C. Myhill (*East Asia and Pacific*); R. Graham-Harrison (*India*); Ms M. H. Vowles (*Western Asia*); A. K. C. Wood (*South-East Asia*); K. L. Sparkhall (*Bangladesh*); Ms S. Wardell (*Nepal*); Ms J. Creighton (*Pacific*)

EASTERN EUROPE AND WESTERN HEMISPHERE
Director (*SCS*), J. Kerby
Heads of Departments (*SCS*), A. Coverdale (*Eastern Europe and Central Asia*); J. S. Laing (*Central and South-Eastern Europe*); B. P. Thomson (*Caribbean*)
Heads of Departments, D. R. Curran (*Latin America, Caribbean and Atlantic*); J. D. Moye (*EBRD Unit*)

ECONOMICS, STATISTICS AND ENTERPRISE
Director, and Chief Economic Adviser (*SCS*), A. Coverdale
Chief Statistician (*SCS*), A. B. Williams
Head, Asia Regional and Economic Policy, P. J. Ackroyd
Head, Africa Policy and Economics, P. J. Landymore
Head, Development Economics Research (*SCS*), P. D. Grant
Head, Enterprise Development, D. L. Wright
Head, Governance Department (*SCS*), R. J. Wilson

HUMAN RESOURCE DEVELOPMENT
Chief Health and Population Adviser (*acting*), Ms J. Cleves
Chief Social Development Adviser (*SCS*), Dr R. Eyben
Chief Education Adviser (*SCS*), Ms M. A. Harrison

RURAL LIVELIHOODS AND ENVIRONMENT
Director, and Chief Natural Resources Adviser (*SCS*), A. J. Bennett, CMG
Head, Environment Policy Department (*SCS*), D. P. Turner
Head, Natural Resources Policy and Advisory Department, and Deputy Chief Natural Resources Adviser (*SCS*), J. M. Scott
Head, Natural Resources Research Department (*SCS*), Dr J. Tarbit, OBE
Senior Environment and Research Adviser, Ms L. C. Brown
Senior Fisheries Adviser, R. W. Beales
Senior Forestry Advisers, J. M. Hudson; I. A. Napier
Senior Animal Health Advisers, G. G. Freeland; Ms L. M. Bell
Chief Engineering Adviser and Head, Infrastructure and Urban Development Department (*SCS*), J. W. Hodges

RESOURCES
Director-General (*SCS*), R. G. Manning
Heads of Departments (*SCS*), M. J. Dinham (*Head of Personnel and Principal Establishment Officer*); D. Sands-Smith (*Procurement, Appointments and NGO*); R. Calvert (*Information*); G. M. Stegmann (*Head, Aid Policy and Resources and Principal Finance Officer*); A. D. Davis (*Information Systems and Services*); R. A. Elias (*Internal Audit Unit*); C. P. Raleigh (*Evaluation*)
Head of Department, R. Plumb (*Overseas Pensions*)

INTERNATIONAL DEVELOPMENT AFFAIRS
Director (SCS), J. A. L. Faint
Heads of Departments (SCS), M. Lowcock *(European Union)*;
D. J. Batt *(International Economic Policy)*; G. Toulmin
(United Nations and Commonwealth); M. E. Cund
(International Financial Institutions)

INTERVENTION BOARD
PO Box 69, Reading RGI 3YD
Tel 0118-958 3626; fax 0118-953 1370

The Intervention Board was established as a government
department in 1972 and became an executive agency in
1990. The Board is responsible for the implementation of
European Union regulations covering the market support
arrangements of the Common Agricultural Policy. Mem-
bers are appointed by and are responsible to the four
agriculture ministers in the UK.
Chairman, I. Kent
Chief Executive (G3), G. Trevelyan
Directors (G5), H. MacKinnon *(Operations)*; J. P. Bradbury
(Operations, Newcastle); Mrs A. Parker *(Corporate
Services)*; P. Kent *(Legal)*; G. Trantham *(Finance)*

LAND REGISTRIES

HM LAND REGISTRY
Lincoln's Inn Fields, London WC2A 3PH
Tel 0171-917 8888; fax 0171-955 0110
The registration of title to land was first introduced in
England and Wales by the Land Registry Act 1862; HM
Land Registry operates today under the Land Registration
Acts 1925 to 1988. The object of registering title to land is
to create and maintain a register of landowners whose title
is guaranteed by the state and so to simplify the transfer,
mortgage and other dealings with real property. Registra-
tion on sale is now compulsory throughout England and
Wales. The register has been open to inspection by the
public since 1990.
  HM Land Registry is an executive agency administered
under the Lord Chancellor by the Chief Land Registrar.

HEADQUARTERS OFFICE
Chief Land Registrar and Chief Executive, P. Collis
Solicitor to Land Registry, C. J. West
Director of Corporate Services, E. G. Beardsall
Senior Land Registrar, J. V. Timothy
Director of Operations, A. Howarth
Director of Information Technology, P. J. Smith, OBE
Director of Management Services, P. R. Laker
Land Registrar, M. L. Wood
Deputy Establishment Officer, J. Hodder
Controller of Operations Development, P. Norman
Head of Legal Practice, P. Morris
Head of Survey and Plans Practice, M. K. Brown

COMPUTER SERVICES DIVISION
Burrington Way, Plymouth PL5 3LP
Tel 01752-635600
Head of IT Services Division, P. A. Maycock
Head of IT Development Division, J. Formby
Head of National Land Information Service (NLIS), P. Sizer
Head of IT Management Services, K. Deards

LAND CHARGES AND AGRICULTURAL CREDITS
DEPARTMENT
Burrington Way, Plymouth PL5 3LP
Tel 01752-635600

Superintendent of Land Charges, J. Hughes

DISTRICT LAND REGISTRIES
BIRKENHEAD (OLD MARKET HOUSE) – Old Market
House, Hamilton Street, Birkenhead L41 5FL. Tel: 0151-
473 1110. *District Land Registrar*, P. J. Brough
BIRKENHEAD (ROSEBRAE COURT) – Rosebrae Court,
Woodside Ferry Approach, Birkenhead L41 6DU. Tel:
0151-472 6666. *District Land Registrar*, M. G. Garwood
COVENTRY – Leigh Court, Torrington Avenue,
Coventry CV4 9XZ. Tel: 01203-860860. *District Land
Registrar*, T. H. O. Lewis
CROYDON – Sunley House, Bedford Park, Croydon
CR9 3LE. Tel: 0181-781 9100. *District Land Registrar*, F.
M. Twambley
DURHAM (BOLDON HOUSE) – Boldon House,
Wheatlands Way, Pity Me, Durham DHI 5GJ. Tel: 0191-
301 2345. *District Land Registrar*, R. B. Fearnley
DURHAM (SOUTHFIELD HOUSE) – Southfield House,
Southfield Way, Durham DHI 5TR. Tel: 0191-301 3500.
District Land Registrar, P. J. Timothy
GLOUCESTER – Twyver House, Bruton Way, Gloucester
GLI IDQ. Tel: 01452-511111. *District Land Registrar*,
W. W. Budden
HARROW – Lyon House, Lyon Road, Harrow, Middx
HAI 2EU. Tel: 0181-235 1181. *District Land Registrar*, C.
Tate
KINGSTON UPON HULL – Earle House, Portland Street,
Hull HU2 8JN. Tel: 01482-223244. *District Land Registrar*,
S. R. Coveney
LANCASHIRE – Birkenhead House, East Beach, Lytham,
Lancs FY8 5AB. Tel: 01253-849849. *District Land
Registrar*, Mrs L. Wallwork
LEICESTER – Westbridge Place, Leicester LE3 5DR. Tel:
0116-265 4000. *District Land Registrar*, Mrs
J. A. Goodfellow
LYTHAM – Birkenhead House, East Beach, Lytham,
Lancs FY8 5AB. Tel: 01253-849849. *District Land
Registrar*, J. G. Cooper
NOTTINGHAM (EAST) – Robins Wood Road,
Nottingham NG8 3RQ. Tel: 0115-906 5353. *District Land
Registrar*, P. A. Brown
NOTTINGHAM (WEST) – Chalfont Drive, Nottingham
NG8 3RN. Tel: 0115-935 1166. *District Land Registrar*, Ms
A. M. Goss
PETERBOROUGH – Touthill Close, City Road,
Peterborough PEI IXN. Tel: 01733-288288. *District Land
Registrar*, C. W. Martin
PLYMOUTH – Plumer House, Tailyour Road, Crownhill,
Plymouth PL6 5HY. Tel: 01752-636000. *District Land
Registrar*, A. J. Pain
PORTSMOUTH – St Andrews Court, St Michael's Road,
Portsmouth POI 2JH. Tel: 01705-768888. *District Land
Registrar*, S. R. Sehrawat
STEVENAGE – Brickdale House, Swingate, Stevenage,
Herts SGI IXG. Tel: 01438-788888. *District Land Registrar*,
M. Croker
SWANSEA – Ty Bryn Glas, High Street, Swansea SAI IPW.
Tel: 01792-458877. *District Land Registrar*, T. M. Lewis
TELFORD – Parkside Court, Hall Park Way, Telford
TF3 4LR. Tel: 01952-290355. *District Land Registrar*, A. M.
Lewis
TUNBRIDGE WELLS – Forest Court, Forest Road,
Tunbridge Wells, Kent TN2 5AQ. Tel: 01892-510015.
District Land Registrar, G. R. Tooke
WALES – Ty Cwm Tave, Phoenix Way, Llansamlet,
Swansea SA7 9FQ. Tel: 01792-355000. *District Land
Registrar*, G. A. Hughes
WEYMOUTH – Melcombe Court, 1 Cumberland Drive,
Weymouth, Dorset DT4 9TT. Tel: 01305-363636.
District Land Registrar, Mrs P. M. Reeson

YORK – James House, James Street, York YO1 3YZ. Tel: 01904-450000. *District Land Registrar,* Mrs R. F. Lovel

REGISTERS OF SCOTLAND
Meadowbank House, 153 London Road, Edinburgh EH8 7AU
Tel 0131-659 6111; fax 0131-479 3688

Registers of Scotland is an executive agency of the Scottish Executive. It is responsible for framing and maintaining records relating to property and other legal documents. The agency holds 15 registers: two property registers (General Register of Sasines and Land Register of Scotland) and 13 chancery and judicial registers (Register of Deeds in the Books of Council and Session; Register of Protests; Register of Judgments; Register of Service of Heirs; Register of the Great Seal; Register of the Quarter Seal; Register of the Prince's Seal; Register of Crown Grants; Register of Sheriffs' Commissions; Register of the Cachet Seal; Register of Inhibitions and Adjudications; Register of Entails; and Register of Hornings).

Chief Executive and Keeper of the Registers of Scotland, A. W. Ramage
Deputy Keeper, A. G. Rennie
Managing Director, F. Manson

LAW COMMISSION
Conquest House, 37–38 John Street, London WC1N 2BQ
Tel 0171-453 1220; fax 0171-453 1297

The Law Commission was set up in 1965, under the Law Commissions Act 1965, to make proposals to the Government for the examination of the law in England and Wales and for its revision where it is unsuited for modern requirements, obscure, or otherwise unsatisfactory. It recommends to the Lord Chancellor programmes for the examination of different branches of the law and suggests whether the examination should be carried out by the Commission itself or by some other body. The Commission is also responsible for the preparation of Consolidation and Statute Law (Repeals) Bills.

Chairman, The Hon. Mr Justice Carnwath, CVO
Commissioners, C. Harpum; A. S. Burrows; Miss D. Faber; S. Silber, QC
Secretary, M. W. Sayers

SCOTTISH LAW COMMISSION
140 Causewayside, Edinburgh EH9 1PR
Tel 0131-668 2131; fax 0131-662 4900

The Commission keeps the law in Scotland under review and makes proposals for its development and reform. It is responsible to the Scottish Courts Administration (*see* pages 364–5).

Chairman (part-time), The Hon. Lord Gill
Commissioners (full-time), Dr E. M. Clive; N. R. Whitty; *(part-time)* Prof. K. G. C. Reid; P. S. Hodge, QC
Secretary, N. Raven

LAW OFFICERS' DEPARTMENTS
Legal Secretariat to the Law Officers, Attorney-General's Chambers, 9 Buckingham Gate, London SW1E 6JP
Tel 0171-271 2400; fax 0171-271 2434
Attorney-General's Chambers, Royal Courts of Justice, Belfast BT1 3JY
Tel 01232-235111; fax 01232-546049

The Law Officers of the Crown for England and Wales are the Attorney-General and the Solicitor-General. The

Attorney-General, assisted by the Solicitor-General, is the chief legal adviser to the Government and is also ultimately responsible for all Crown litigation. He has overall responsibility for the work of the Law Officers' Departments (the Treasury Solicitor's Department, the Crown Prosecution Service, the Serious Fraud Office and the Legal Secretariat to the Law Officers). He has a specific statutory duty to superintend the discharge of their duties by the Director of Public Prosecutions (who heads the Crown Prosecution Service) and the Director of the Serious Fraud Office. The Director of Public Prosecutions for Northern Ireland is also responsible to the Attorney-General for the performance of his functions. The Attorney-General has additional responsibilities in relation to aspects of the civil and criminal law.

Attorney-General (*£68,332), The Lord Williams of Mostyn, QC
  Private Secretary, R. Cazalet
  Parliamentary Private Secretary, M. Foster, MP
Solicitor-General (*£56,031), Ross Cranston, MP
  Private Secretary, R. Cazalet
Legal Secretary (G2), D. Seymour
Deputy Legal Secretary (G3), S. Parkinson
* In addition to a parliamentary salary of £47,008

LEGAL AID BOARD
85 Gray's Inn Road, London WC1X 8AA
Tel 0171-813 1000

The Legal Aid Board has the general function of ensuring that advice, assistance, mediation and representation are available to those who need them within the framework of the Legal Aid Act 1988. In 1989 the Board took over from the Law Society responsibility for administering legal aid. The Board is a non-departmental government body whose members are appointed by the Lord Chancellor.

Chairman, Sir Tim Chessells
Deputy Chairman, H. Hodge, OBE
Members, S. Orchard, CBE (*Chief Executive*); M. Barnes, CBE; Ms D. Charnock; Ms J. Dunkley; P. Ely; B. Harvey; Mrs S. Hewitt; P. Hollingworth; J. Shearer

SCOTTISH LEGAL AID BOARD
44 Drumsheugh Gardens, Edinburgh EH3 7SW
Tel 0131-226 7061; fax 0131-220 4878

The Scottish Legal Aid Board was set up under the Legal Aid (Scotland) Act 1986. It is responsible for ensuring that advice, assistance and representation are available in accordance with the Act. Members are appointed by the First Minister.

Chairman, Mrs J. Couper
Members, B. C. Adair; Mrs K. Blair; Prof. P. H. Grinyer; Sheriff A. Jessop; N. Kuenssberg; D. O'Carroll; Mrs Y. Osman; Ms M. Scanlan; M. C. Thomson, QC; A. F. Wylie, QC
Chief Executive, L. Montgomery

OFFICE OF THE LEGAL SERVICES OMBUDSMAN
22 Oxford Court, Oxford Street, Manchester M2 3WQ
Tel 0161-236 9532; fax 0161-236 2651

The Legal Services Ombudsman is appointed by the Lord Chancellor under the Courts and Legal Services Act 1990

to oversee the handling of complaints against solicitors, barristers, licensed conveyancers and legal executives by their professional bodies. A complainant must first complain to the relevant professional body before raising the matter with the Ombudsman. The Ombudsman is independent of the legal profession and her services are free of charge.
Legal Services Ombudsman, Ms A. Abraham
Secretary, S. D. Entwisle

OFFICE OF THE SCOTTISH LEGAL SERVICES OMBUDSMAN
Mulberry House, 16–22 Picardy Place, Edinburgh EH1 3JT
Tel 0131-556 5574; fax 0131-556 1519
Scottish Legal Services Ombudsman, G. S. Watson

LIBRARIES

LIBRARY AND INFORMATION COMMISSION
19–29 Woburn Place, London WC1H 0LU
Tel 0171-273 8700; fax 0171-273 8701

The Commission is an independent body set up in 1995 to advise the Government and others on library and information matters, notably in the areas of research strategy and international links. It also aims to promote co-operation and co-ordination between different types of information services.

The Commission will merge with the Museums and Galleries Commission in 2000 to form the Museums, Libraries and Archives Council.
Chairman, M. Evans, CBE
Commissioners, Cllr E. Arram; Mrs L. Brindley; Sir Charles Chadwyck-Healey; Prof. M. Collier; Prof. Judith Elkin; Prof. W. Ewart, OBE; Ms G. Kempster, OBE; Dr B. Lang (*ex officio*); D. Law; Dr R. McKee; Ms C. Rayner, OBE; Dr Sandra Ward; M. Wood
Chief Executive, Ms M. Haines

THE BRITISH LIBRARY
96 Euston Road, London NW1 2DB
Tel 0171-412 7000

The British Library was established in 1973. It is the UK's national library and occupies a key position in the library and information network. The Library aims to serve scholarship, research, industry, commerce and all other major users of information. Its services are based on collections which include over 18 million volumes, 1 million discs, and 55,000 hours of tape recordings. The Library is now based at two sites: London (St Pancras and Colindale) and Boston Spa, W. Yorks. Government grant-in-aid to the British Library in 1999–2000 is £83.2 million. The Library's sponsoring department is the Department for Culture, Media and Sport.

Access to the reading rooms at St Pancras is limited to holders of a British Library Reader's Pass; information about eligibility is available from the Reader Admissions Office. The exhibition galleries and public areas are open to all, free of charge.

Opening hours of services vary; some services may close for one week each year. Specific information should be checked by telephone.

In April 1999 the British Library's research function was transferred to the Library and Information Commission.

BRITISH LIBRARY BOARD
Chairman, Dr J. M. Ashworth
Chief Executive and Deputy Chairman, Dr B. Lang
Deputy Chief Executive, D. Russon
Director-General, Collections and Services, D. Bradbury

Part-time Members, The Hon. E. Adeane, CVO; Prof. M. Anderson, FBA, FRSE; Sir Matthew Farrer, GCVO; C. G. R. Leach, Ph.D.; Mrs P. M. Lively, OBE; B. Naylor; Dr Jessica Rawson, CBE, FBA; J. Ritblat; The Viscount Runciman of Doxford, CBE, FBA; P. Scherer

BRITISH LIBRARY, BOSTON SPA
Boston Spa, Wetherby, W. Yorks LS23 7BQ
Tel 01937-546000

BIBLIOGRAPHIC SERVICES AND DOCUMENT SUPPLY, *Director,* M. Smith
NATIONAL BIBLIOGRAPHIC SERVICE. Tel: 01937-546585. *Director,* R. Smith
London Unit, 96 Euston Road, London NW1 2DB. Tel: 0171-412 7077
COLLECTION MANAGEMENT, *Director,* S. Ede
INFORMATION SYSTEMS. Tel: 01937-546879. *Director,* J. R. Mahoney

BRITISH LIBRARY, ST PANCRAS
96 Euston Road, London NW1 2DB
Tel 0171-412 7000

PLANNING AND RESOURCES. Tel: 0171-412 7132
PRESS AND PUBLIC RELATIONS. Tel: 0171-412 7111
EXHIBITIONS SERVICE, EDUCATION SERVICE AND VISITOR SERVICES. Tel: 0171-412 7332

READER SERVICES AND COLLECTION DEVELOPMENT. *Director,* M. J. Crump
Reader Admissions. Tel: 0171-412 7677
Reader Services. Tel: 0171-412 7676
West European Collections, Slavonic and East European Collections, English Language Collections. Tel: 0171-412 7676
Newspaper Library, Colindale Avenue, London NW9 5HE. Tel: 0171-412 7353

PRESERVATION SERVICE (NATIONAL PRESERVATION OFFICE). Tel: 0171-412 7612

SPECIAL COLLECTIONS. Tel: 0171-412 7513. *Director,* Dr A. Prochaska
Oriental and India Office Collections. Tel: 0171-412 7873
Western Manuscripts. Tel: 0171-412 7513
Map Library. Tel: 0171-412 7700
Music Library. Tel: 0171-412 7635
Philatelic Collections. Tel: 0171-412 7729
National Sound Archive. Tel: 0171-412 7440

SCIENCE, TECHNOLOGY AND BUSINESS
Science and Technology. Tel: 0171-412 7494/7496
British and EPO Patents. Tel: 0171-412 7919
Foreign Patents. Tel: 0171-412 7902
Business. Tel: 0171-412 7454
Social Policy Information Service. Tel: 0171-412 7536

NATIONAL LIBRARY OF SCOTLAND
George IV Bridge, Edinburgh EH1 1EW
Tel 0131-226 4531; fax 0131-622 4803

The Library, which was founded as the Advocates' Library in 1682, became the National Library of Scotland in 1925. It is funded by the Scottish Executive. It contains about six million books and pamphlets, 18,000 current periodicals, 230 newspaper titles and 100,000 manuscripts. It has an unrivalled Scottish collection.

The Reading Room is for reference and research which cannot conveniently be pursued elsewhere. Admission is by ticket issued to an approved applicant. Opening hours: Reading Room, weekdays, 9.30–8.30 (Wednesday, 10–8.30); Saturday 9.30–1. Map Library, weekdays, 9.30–5 (Wednesday, 10–5); Saturday 9.30–1. Exhibition, weekdays,

10–5; Saturday 10–5; Sunday 2–5. Scottish Science Library, weekdays, 9.30–5 (Wednesday, 10–8.30).
Chairman of the Trustees, The Earl of Crawford and Balcarres, PC
Librarian and Secretary to the Trustees (*G4*), I. D. McGowan
Secretary of the Library (*G6*), M. C. Graham
Keeper of Printed Books (*G6*), Ms A. Matheson, OBE, Ph.D.
Keeper of Manuscripts (*G6*), I. C. Cunningham
Director of Public Services (*G6*), A. M. Marchbank, Ph.D.

NATIONAL LIBRARY OF WALES/LLYFRGELL GENEDLAETHOL CYMRU
Aberystwyth SY23 3BU
Tel 01970-632800; fax 01970-615709

The National Library of Wales was founded by royal charter in 1907, and is funded by the National Assembly for Wales. It contains about four million printed books, 40,000 manuscripts, four million deeds and documents, numerous maps, prints and drawings, and a sound and moving image collection. It specializes in manuscripts and books relating to Wales and the Celtic peoples. It is the repository for pre-1858 Welsh probate records, manorial records and tithe documents, and certain legal records. Readers' room open weekdays, 9.30–6 (Saturday 9.30–5); closed first week of October. Admission by reader's ticket.
President, Dr R. Brinley Jones
Librarian (*G4*), A. M. W. Green
Heads of Departments (*G6*), M. W. Mainwaring (*Administration and Technical Services*); G. Jenkins (*Manuscripts and Records*); Dr W. R. M. Griffiths (*Printed Books*); Dr D. H. Owen (*Pictures and Maps*)

LIGHTHOUSE AUTHORITIES

CORPORATION OF TRINITY HOUSE
Trinity House, Tower Hill, London EC3N 4DH
Tel 0171-481 6900; fax 0171-480 7662

Trinity House, the first general lighthouse and pilotage authority in the kingdom, was granted its first charter by Henry VIII in 1514. The Corporation is the general lighthouse authority for England, Wales and the Channel Islands and maintains 72 lighthouses, 13 major floating aids to navigation (e.g. light vessels) and more than 420 buoys. The Corporation also has certain statutory jurisdiction over aids to navigation maintained by local harbour authorities and is responsible for dealing with wrecks dangerous to navigation, except those occurring within port limits or wrecks of HM ships.

The Trinity House Lighthouse Service is maintained out of the General Lighthouse Fund which is provided from light dues levied on ships calling at ports of the UK and the Republic of Ireland. The Corporation is also a deep-sea pilotage authority and a charitable organization.

The affairs of the Corporation are controlled by a board of Elder Brethren and the Secretary. A separate board, which comprises Elder Brethren, senior staff and outside representatives, currently controls the Lighthouse Service. The Elder Brethren also act as nautical assessors in marine cases in the Admiralty Division of the High Court of Justice.

ELDER BRETHREN
Master, HRH The Prince Philip, Duke of Edinburgh, KG, KT
Deputy Master, Rear-Adm. P. B. Rowe, CBE, LVO
Wardens, Capt. C. M. C. Stewart; Sir Brian Shaw

Elder Brethren, HRH The Prince of Wales, KG, KT; HRH The Duke of York, CVO, ADC; Capt. Sir David Tibbits, DSC, RN; Capt. D. A. G. Dickins; Capt. J. E. Bury; Capt. J. A. N. Bezant, DSC, RD, RNR (retd.); Capt. D. J. Cloke; Capt. Sir Miles Wingate, KCVO; The Rt. Hon. Sir Edward Heath, KG, MBE, MP; Capt. I. R. C. Saunders; Capt. P. F. Mason, CBE; Capt. T. Woodfield, OBE; The Lord Simon of Glaisdale, PC; Capt. D. T. Smith, RN; Cdr. Sir Robin Gillett, Bt., GBE, RD, RNR; Capt. Sir Malcolm Edge, KCVO; The Lord Cuckney; Capt. D. J. Orr; The Lord Carrington, KG, GCMG, CH, MC, PC; The Lord Mackay of Clashfern, KT, PC; Sir Adrian Swire; Capt. P. H. King; The Lord Sterling of Plaistow, CBE, RNR; Cdr. M. J. Rivett-Carnac, RN; Adm. Sir Jock Slater, GCB, LVO, ADC; Capt. J. R. Burton-Hall, RD; Capt. I. Gibb, FRSA; Cdre P. J. Melson, CBE, RN; Capt. D. C. Glass

OFFICERS
Secretary, R. F. Dobb
Director of Finance, K. W. Clark
Director of Engineering, M. G. B. Wannell
Director of Administration, D. I. Brewer
Human Resources Manager, C. A. Jameson
Legal and Insurance Manager, J. D. Price
Navigation Manager, Mrs K. Hossain
Head of Management Services, S. J. W. Dunning
Deputy Director of Engineering, P. N. Hyde
Senior Inspector of Shipping, J. R. Dunnett
Media and Communication Officer, H. L. Cooper

NORTHERN LIGHTHOUSE BOARD
84 George Street, Edinburgh EH2 3DA
Tel 0131-473 3100; fax 0131-220 2093

The Lighthouse Board is the general lighthouse authority for Scotland and the Isle of Man. The board owes its origin to an Act of Parliament passed in 1786. At present the Commissioners operate under the Merchant Shipping Act 1894 and are 19 in number.

The Commissioners control 84 major automatic lighthouses, 116 minor lights and many lighted and unlighted buoys. They have a fleet of two motor vessels.

COMMISSIONERS
The Lord Advocate; the Solicitor-General for Scotland; the Lord Provosts of Edinburgh, Glasgow and Aberdeen; the Provost of Inverness; the Convener of Argyll and Bute Council; the Sheriffs-Principal of North Strathclyde, Tayside, Central and Fife, Grampian, Highlands and Islands, South Strathclyde, Dumfries and Galloway, Lothians and Borders, and Glasgow and Strathkelvin; A. J. Struthers; W. F. Hay, CBE; Capt. D. M. Cowell; Adm. Sir Michael Livesay, KCB; The Lord Maclay

OFFICERS
Chief Executive, Capt. J. B. Taylor, RN
Director of Finance, D. Gorman
Director of Engineering, W. Paterson
Director of Operations and Navigational Requirements, P. J. Christmas

LOCAL COMMISSIONERS

COMMISSION FOR LOCAL ADMINISTRATION IN ENGLAND
21 Queen Anne's Gate, London SW1H 9BU
Tel 0171-915 3210; fax 0171-233 0396

Local Commissioners (local government ombudsmen) are responsible for investigating complaints from members of the public against local authorities (but not town and parish councils); police authorities; the Commission for New Towns (housing functions); education appeal committees and certain other authorities. The Commissioners are appointed by the Crown on the recommendation of the Secretary of State for the Environment, Transport and the Regions.

Certain types of action are excluded from investigation, including personnel matters and commercial transactions unless they relate to the purchase or sale of land. Complaints can be sent direct to the Local Government Ombudsman or through a councillor, although the Local Government Ombudsman will not consider a complaint unless the council has had an opportunity to investigate and reply to a complainant.

A free leaflet *Complaint about the council? How to complain to the Local Government Ombudsman* is available from the Commission's office.

Chairman and Chief Executive of the Commission and Local
  Commissioner (£123,787), E. B. C. Osmotherly, CB
Vice-Chairman and Local Commissioner (£93,810), Mrs
  P. A. Thomas
Local Commissioner (£92,810), J. R. White
Member (*ex officio*), The Parliamentary Commissioner for
  Administration
Deputy Chief Executive and Secretary (£59,059), N. J. Karney

COMMISSION FOR LOCAL ADMINISTRATION IN WALES

Derwen House, Court Road, Bridgend CF31 1BN
Tel 01656-661325; fax 01656-658317

The Local Commissioner for Wales has similar powers to the Local Commissioners in England. The Commissioner is appointed by the Crown on the recommendation of the First Secretary. A free leaflet *Your Local Ombudsman in Wales* is available from the Commission's office.

Local Commissioner, E. R. Moseley
Secretary, D. Bowen
Member (*ex officio*), The Parliamentary Commissioner for
  Administration

COMMISSIONER FOR LOCAL ADMINISTRATION IN SCOTLAND

23 Walker Street, Edinburgh EH3 7HX
Tel 0131-225 5300; fax 0131-225 9495

The Local Commissioner for Scotland has similar powers to the Local Commissioners in England, and is appointed by the Crown on the recommendation of the First Minister.

Local Commissioner, F. C. Marks, OBE
Deputy Commissioner and Secretary, Ms J. H. Renton

LONDON REGIONAL TRANSPORT

55 Broadway, London SW1H 0BD
Tel 0171-222 5600

Subject to the financial objectives and principles approved by the Secretary of State for the Environment, Transport and the Regions, London Regional Transport has a general duty to provide or secure the provision of public transport services for Greater London.

Chairman (*non-executive*), Sir Malcolm Bates
Chief Executive, D. Tunnicliffe, CBE
Member, and Managing Director of London Transport Buses, C.
  Hodson, CBE
Member, and Managing Director of London Underground Ltd,
  D. Smith

OFFICE OF THE LORD ADVOCATE

Crown Office, 25 Chambers Street, Edinburgh EH1 1LA
Tel 0131-226 2626; fax 0131-226 6910

The Law Officers for Scotland are the Lord Advocate and the Solicitor-General for Scotland.

Lord Advocate, The Lord Hardie, PC, QC
Solicitor-General for Scotland, Colin Boyd, QC
  Private Secretary to the Law Officers, J. Gibbons

LORD CHANCELLOR'S DEPARTMENT

Selborne House, 54–60 Victoria Street, London SW1E 6QW
Tel 0171-210 8500
E-mail: enquiries.lcdhq@gtnet.gov.uk
Web: http://www.open.gov.uk/lcd

The Lord Chancellor appoints Justices of the Peace (except in the Duchy of Lancaster) and advises the Crown on the appointment of most members of the higher judiciary. He is responsible for promoting general reforms in the civil law, for the procedure of the civil courts and for legal aid. He is a member of the Cabinet. He also has ministerial responsibility for magistrates' courts, which are administered locally. Administration of the Supreme Court and county courts in England and Wales was taken over by the Court Service, an executive agency of the department, in 1995.

The Lord Chancellor is also responsible for ensuring that letters patent and other formal documents are passed in the proper form under the Great Seal of the Realm, of which he is the custodian. The work in connection with this is carried out under his direction in the Office of the Clerk of the Crown in Chancery.

The Lord Chancellor is also the senior Lord of Appeal in Ordinary and speaker of the House of Lords.

Lord Chancellor (£160,011), The Lord Irvine of Lairg, PC,
  QC
  Principal Private Secretary, Ms J. Rowe
  Special Adviser, G. Hart
Parliamentary Secretaries, Keith Vaz, MP; David Lock, MP
  Private Secretaries, R. Moore; Ms D. Hulin
Permanent Secretary (SCS), Sir Hayden Phillips, KCB
  Private Secretary, M. Camley

CROWN OFFICE
House of Lords, London SW1A 0PW
Tel 0171-219 4713

Clerk of the Crown in Chancery (SCS), Sir Hayden Phillips,
  KCB
Deputy Clerk of the Crown in Chancery (SCS), M. Huebner, CB
Clerk of the Chamber, C. I. P. Denyer

JUDICIAL GROUP
Tel 0171-210 8500

Head of Group (SCS), M. Huebner, CB
Heads of Divisions (SCS), D. E. Staff (*Policy and Conditions of
  Service*); Mrs M. Pigott (*Senior Appointment and Silk*);
  Miss J. Killick (*Senior Appointment and Silk*); J. Tanner
  (*District Bench and Tribunals*); S. Humphries (*Magistrates'
  Appointments*); P. L. Jacob (*Judicial Policy*)

Judicial Studies Board
9th Floor, Millbank Tower, London SW1P 4QW
Tel 0171-925 4762

Secretary (SCS), E. S. Adams

POLICY GROUP
Tel 0171-210 8719

Director-General (SCS), Ms J. MacNaughton
Heads of Divisions (SCS), A. Cogbill (*Civil Justice and Legal Services Directorate*); D. Gladwell (*Civil Justice*); R. Sams (*Civil Law Development*); D. A. Hill (*Access to Justice Bill Team*); C. Myerscough (*Community Legal Services*); Ms A. Finlay (*Public and Private Rights Directorate*); W. Arnold (*Family Policy*); A. Shaw (*Administrative Justice*); M. Ormerod (*Magistrates' Courts and Criminal Policy Directorate*); P. White (*Magistrates' Courts IT*); vacant (*Human Rights Act Implementation Team*); vacant (*Criminal Policy*); Mrs K. Allen (*Policy Group Secretariat and Agency Monitoring Unit*); Mrs J. Brown (*Social Policy Unit*)

LEGAL ADVISER'S GROUP
Tel 0171-210 0711

Legal Adviser (SCS), P. Jenkins
Heads of Divisions (SCS), M. H. Collon (*Legal Advice and Litigation*); A. Wallace (*International and Common Law Services*); M. Kron (*Drafting Services*)

COMMUNICATIONS GROUP
Tel 0171-210 8672

Director of Communications (SCS), A. Percival, LVO

CORPORATE SERVICES GROUP
Tel 0171-210 8503

Director of Corporate Services and Principal Establishment and Finance Officer (SCS), Mrs E. Grimsey
Heads of Divisions (SCS), Mrs S. Anderson (*Personnel Management*); Mrs S. Webber (*Personnel Management*); S. Smith (*Finance*); K. Cregeen, OBE (*Facilities and Support Services*); A. Rummins (*Internal Assurance*); K. Garrett (*Statutory Publications Office*)

ECCLESIASTICAL PATRONAGE
10 Downing Street, London SW1A 2AA
Tel 0171-930 4433

Secretary for Ecclesiastical Patronage, J. H. Holroyd, CB
Assistant Secretary for Ecclesiastical Patronage, N. C. Wheeler

HM MAGISTRATES' COURTS' SERVICE INSPECTORATE
Southside, 105 Victoria Street, London SW1E 6QJ
Tel 0171-210 1655

Chief Inspector (SCS), C. J. A. Chivers
Senior Inspectors (SCS), D. Gear; C. Monson; Ms S. Steel

LORD CHANCELLOR'S ADVISORY COMMITTEE ON STATUTE LAW
67 Tufton Street, London SW1P 3QS
Tel 0171-210 2615

The Advisory Committee advises the Lord Chancellor on all matters relating to the revision, modernization and publication of the statute book.
Chairman, The Lord Chancellor
Deputy Chairman, Sir Hayden Phillips, KCB
Members, The Hon. Mr Justice Carnwath, CVO; The Hon. Lord Gill; Sir James Jenkins, KCB, QC; Mrs E. Grimsey; J. M. Davies; J. C. McCluskie, CB, QC; A. H. Hammond, CB, QC; R. Henderson; P. Jenkins; Mrs C. Tullo; W. R. McKay, CB; K. Garrett; C. Carey; First Legislative Counsel of Northern Ireland
Secretary (acting), M. Heseltine

EXECUTIVE AGENCIES

THE COURT SERVICE
Southside, 105 Victoria Street, London SW1E 6QT
Tel 0171-210 1672; fax 0171-210 1797

The Court Service provides administrative support to the Supreme Court of England and Wales, county courts and a number of tribunals.

Chief Executive (SCS), I. Magee
Director of Operational Policy (SCS), Miss B. Kenny
Director of Finance (SCS), vacant
Change Director (SCS), K. Pogson
Director of Purchasing and Contract Management (SCS), vacant
Head of Information Services Division (SCS), Ms A. Vernon
Head of Personnel and Training (SCS), Ms H. Dudley
Director of Civil and Family Operations (SCS), S. Smith
Director of Criminal Operations (SCS), N. J. Smedley
Director of Tribunals (SCS), P. Stockton

Supreme Court Group
Strand, London WC2A 2LL
Tel 0171-936 6000
Director (SCS), I. Hyams

For Supreme Court departments and offices and circuit administrators, *see* Law Courts and Offices section

HM LAND REGISTRY
— *see* page 314

PUBLIC RECORD OFFICE
— *see* page 333

PUBLIC TRUST OFFICE
— *see* page 332

LORD GREAT CHAMBERLAIN'S OFFICE
House of Lords, London SW1A 0PW
Tel 0171-219 3100; fax 0171-219 2500

The Lord Great Chamberlain is a Great Officer of State, the office being hereditary since the grant of Henry I to the family of De Vere, Earls of Oxford. It is now a joint hereditary office between the Cholmondeley and Carington families. The Lord Great Chamberlain is responsible for the royal apartments of the Palace of Westminster, i.e. The Queen's Robing Room, the Royal Gallery and, in conjunction with the Lord Chancellor and the Speaker, Westminster Hall. The Lord Great Chamberlain has particular responsibility for the internal administrative arrangements within the House of Lords for State Openings of Parliament.
Lord Great Chamberlain, The Marquess of Cholmondeley
Secretary to the Lord Great Chamberlain, Gen. Sir Edward Jones, KCB, CBE
Clerks to the Lord Great Chamberlain, Miss C. J. Bostock; Miss R. M. Wilkinson

---

LORD PRIVY SEAL'S OFFICE
Privy Council Office, 68 Whitehall, London SW1A 2AT
Tel 0171-270 3000

The Lord Privy Seal is a member of the Cabinet and Leader of the House of Lords. She has no departmental portfolio, but is a member of a number of domestic and economic Cabinet committees. She is responsible to the Prime Minister for the organization of government business in the House and has a responsibility to the House itself to advise it on procedural matters and other difficulties which arise.
Lord Privy Seal, Leader of the House of Lords and Minister for Women, The Baroness Jay of Paddington, PC
Principal Private Secretary, W. Connon
Private Secretary (House of Lords), Miss M. Robertson
Special Adviser, Ms J. Gibbons

LOTTERY COMMISSION, NATIONAL
— *see* page 325

OFFICE OF MANPOWER ECONOMICS
Oxford House, 76 Oxford Street, London WIN 9FD
Tel 0171-467 7244; fax 0171-467 7248

The Office of Manpower Economics was set up in 1971. It is an independent non-statutory organization which is responsible for servicing independent review bodies which advise on the pay of various public service groups (see Review Bodies, pages 334–5), the Pharmacists Review Panel and the Police Negotiating Board. The Office is also responsible for servicing *ad hoc* bodies of inquiry and for undertaking research into pay and associated matters as requested by the Government.
OME Director, M. J. Horsman
Director, Health Secretariat, and OME Deputy Director, G. S. Charles
Director, Armed Forces' and Teachers' Secretariats, G. McGregor
Director, Senior Salaries Secretariat, Mrs C. Haworth
Press Liaison Officer, M. C. Cahill

MENTAL HEALTH ACT COMMISSION
Maid Marian House, 56 Hounds Gate, Nottingham
NG1 6BG
Tel 0115-943 7100; fax 0115-943 7101

The Mental Health Act Commission was established in 1983. Its functions are to keep under review the operation of the Mental Health Act 1983; to visit and meet patients detained under the Act; to investigate complaints falling within the Commission's remit; to operate the consent to treatment safeguards in the Mental Health Act; to publish a biennial report on its activities; to monitor the implementation of the Code of Practice; and to advise ministers. Commissioners are appointed by the Secretary of State for Health.
Chairman (acting), G. Lakes
Vice-Chairman, Prof. R. Williams
Chief Executive (G6), W. Bingley

MILLENNIUM COMMISSION
Portland House, Stag Place, London SW1E 5EZ
Tel 0171-880 2001; fax 0171-880 2000

The Millennium Commission was established in February 1994 and is accountable to the Department for Culture, Media and Sport. It is an independent body which distributes money from National Lottery proceeds to projects to mark the millennium.
Chairman, The Rt. Hon. Chris Smith, MP
Members, The Rt. Hon. Dr Jack Cunningham, MP; Prof. Heather Couper, FRAS; Earl of Dalkeith; The Lord Glentoran, CBE; Sir John Hall; The Rt. Hon. M. Heseltine, MP; S. Jenkins; The Baroness Scotland of Asthal, QC
Director, M. O'Connor

MONOPOLIES AND MERGERS COMMISSION (FORMER)
— *see* Competition Commission

MUSEUMS

MUSEUMS AND GALLERIES COMMISSION
16 Queen Anne's Gate, London SW1H 9AA
Tel 0171-233 4200; fax 0171-233 3686

Established in 1931 as the Standing Commission on Museums and Galleries, the Commission was renamed in 1981. Its sponsor department is the Department for Culture, Media and Sport. The Commission advises the Government, and the relevant ministers in Scotland, Wales and Northern Ireland, on museum affairs. Commissioners are appointed by the Prime Minister.

The Commission's executive functions include providing the services of the Museums Security Adviser; allocating grants to the seven Area Museum Councils in England; funding and monitoring the work of the Museum Documentation Association; and administering grant schemes for non-national museums. The Commission administers the arrangements for government indemnities and the acceptance of works of art in lieu of inheritance tax, and its Conservation Unit advises on conservation and environmental standards. A registration scheme for museums in the UK is operated by the Commission.

The Commission will merge with the Library and Information Commission in 2000 to form the Museums, Libraries and Archives Council.
Chairman, J. Joll
Members, Prof. P. Bateson, FRS (*Vice-Chairman*); The Baroness Brigstocke; Prof. R. Buchanan; Ms R. Butler; Penelope, Viscountess Cobham; R. Foster; L. Grossman; R. Hiscox; Adm. Sir John Kerr, GCB; Dr I. McKenzie Smith, RSA; A. Warhurst, CBE; Mrs C. Wilson
Director and Secretary, T. Mason

THE BRITISH MUSEUM
Great Russell Street, London WC1B 3DG
Tel 0171-636 1555; fax 0171-323 8614

The British Museum houses the national collection of antiquities, ethnography, coins and paper money, medals, and prints and drawings. The British Museum may be said to date from 1753, when Parliament approved the holding of a public lottery to raise funds for the purchase of the collections of Sir Hans Sloane and the Harleian manuscripts, and for their proper housing and maintenance. The building (Montagu House) was opened in 1759. The present buildings were erected between 1823 and the present day, and the original collection has increased to its present dimensions by gifts and purchases. Total government grant-in-aid for 1999–2000 is £34.7 million.

BOARD OF TRUSTEES
Appointed by the Sovereign, HRH The Duke of Gloucester, KG, GCVO
Appointed by the Prime Minister, N. Barber; Prof. Gillian Beer, FBA; Sir John Boyd; E. J. P. Browne, FREng.; Sir Matthew Farrer, GCVO; Sir Michael Hopkins, CBE, RA, RIBA; Sir Joseph Hotung; Prof. M. Kemp, FBA; S. Keswick; Hon. Mrs M. Marten, OBE; Sir John Morgan, KCMG; The Rt. Hon. Sir Timothy Raison; Sir Martin Rees, FRS; Prof. Sir Gunter Treitel, DCL, FBA, QC
Nominated by the Learned Societies, Prof. Jean Thomas, CBE (*Royal Society*); A. Jones, RA (*Royal Academy*); Sir Claus Moser, KCB, CBE, FBA (*British Academy*); The Lord Renfrew of Kaimsthorn, FBA, FSA (*Society of Antiquaries*)
Appointed by the Trustees of the British Museum, G. C. Greene, CBE (*Chairman*); Sir David Attenborough, CH, CVO, CBE, FRS; Prof. Rosemary Cramp, CBE, FSA; The Lord Egremont; Dr Jennifer Montagu, FBA

OFFICERS
Director, Dr R. G. W. Anderson, FRSC, FSA
Managing Director, Ms S. Taverne
Director of Marketing and Public Affairs, Dr C. Homden
Director of Finance and Resources, A. B. Blackstock
Secretary, Mrs C. Nihoul Parker
Head of Public Services, G. A. L. House
Head of Press and Public Relations, A. E. Hamilton
Head of Design, Miss M. Hall, OBE
Head of Education, J. F. Reeve
Head of Administration, C. E. I. Jones
Head of Building Development and Planning, K. T. Stannard
Head of Building Management, T. R. A. Giles
Head of Finance, Miss S. E. Davies
Head of Personnel and Office Services, Miss B. A. Hughes

KEEPERS
Keeper of Prints and Drawings, A. V. Griffiths
Keeper of Coins and Medals, Dr A. M. Burnett
Keeper of Egyptian Antiquities, W. V. Davies
Keeper of Western Asiatic Antiquities, Dr J. E. Curtis
Keeper of Greek and Roman Antiquities, Dr D. J. R. Williams
Keeper of Medieval and Later Antiquities, J. Cherry
Keeper of Prehistoric and Romano-British Antiquities, Dr T. M. Potter
Keeper of Japanese Antiquities, V. T. Harris
Keeper of Oriental Antiquities, R. J. Knox
Keeper of Ethnography, B. J. Mack
Keeper of Scientific Research, Dr S. G. E. Bowman
Keeper of Conservation, W. A. Oddy

NATURAL HISTORY MUSEUM
Cromwell Road, London SW7 5BD
Tel 0171-942 5000
The Natural History Museum originates from the natural history departments of the British Museum, which grew extensively during the 19th century; in 1860 the natural history collection was moved from Bloomsbury to a new location. Part of the site of the 1862 International Exhibition in South Kensington was acquired for the new museum, and the Museum opened to the public in 1881. In 1963 the Natural History Museum became completely independent with its own board of trustees. The Walter Rothschild Zoological Museum, Tring, bequeathed by the second Lord Rothschild, has formed part of the Museum since 1938. The Geological Museum merged with the Natural History Museum in 1985. Total government grant-in-aid for 1999–2000 is £29.583 million.

BOARD OF TRUSTEES
Appointed by the Prime Minister, The Lord Oxburgh, KBE, Ph.D., FRS (*Chairman*); Sir Crispin Tickell, GCMG, KCVO; Dame Anne McLaren, DBE, FRS, FRCOG; Sir Richard Sykes, FRS; Miss J. Mayhew; Ms J. Bennett; Prof. M. Hassell, FRS; O. Stocken
Appointed by the Secretary of State for Culture, Media and Sport, Prof. C. Leaver, FRS, FRSE
Appointed by the Trustees of the Natural History Museum, The Lord Palumbo; Prof. K. O'Nions, FRS; Prof. Linda Partridge, FRS, FRSE

SENIOR STAFF
Director, N. R. Chalmers, Ph.D.
Director of Science, Prof. P. Henderson, D.Phil.
Head of Audit and Review, D. Thorpe
Keeper of Botany, S. Blackmore, Ph.D.
Head of Development and Marketing, Ms T. Burman
Keeper of Entomology, Dr R. Vane-Wright
Head of Estates, G. Pellow
Head of Education and Exhibitions, Dr G. Clarke
Head of Finance, N. Greenwood

Head of Library and Information Services, Dr R. G. Lester
Keeper of Mineralogy, Prof. A. Fleet
Keeper of Palaeontology, Prof. S. K. Donovan
Head of Human Resources, Mrs J. Rowe
Head of Visitor Services, M. Baron
Keeper of Zoology, Prof. P. Rainbow
Policy and Planning Co-ordinator, P. Kirkman
Director, Tring Zoological Museum, Mrs T. Wild

THE SCIENCE MUSEUM
Exhibition Road, London SW7 2DD
Tel 0171-938 8000; fax 0171-938 8112

The Science Museum, part of the National Museum of Science and Industry, houses the national collections of science, technology, industry and medicine. The Museum began as the science collection of the South Kensington Museum and first opened in 1857. In 1883 it acquired the collections of the Patent Museum and in 1909 the science collections were transferred to the new Science Museum, leaving the art collections with the Victoria and Albert Museum.

Some of the Museum's commercial aircraft, agricultural machinery, and road and rail transport collections are at Wroughton, Wilts. The National Museum of Science and Industry also incorporates the National Railway Museum, York and the National Museum of Photography, Film and Television, Bradford.

Total government grant-in-aid for 1999–2000 is £20.759 million.

BOARD OF TRUSTEES
Chairman, Sir Peter Williams, CBE, Ph.D., FREng.
Members, HRH The Duke of Kent, KG, GCMG, GCVO, ADC; Dr M. Archer; G. Dyke; Dr A. Grocock; Mrs A. Higham, OBE; Mrs J. Kennedy, OBE; Dame Bridget Ogilvie, DBE; The Lord Puttnam, CBE; Sir Michael Quinlan, GCB; D. E. Rayner, CBE; Sir Christopher Wates

OFFICERS
Director, Sir Neil Cossons, OBE, FSA
Assistant Director and Head of Resource Management Division, J. Tucker
Head of Personnel and Legal Services, vacant
Head of Finance, Ms A. Caine
Head of Information Systems, S. Gordon
Head of Estates, J. Bevin
Assistant Director and Head of Collections Division, D. Swade
Head of Physical Sciences and Engineering Group (acting), Dr A. Q. Morton
Head of Life and Communications Technologies Group, Dr R. F. Bud
Head of Collections Management Group, Dr S. Keene
Assistant Director and Head of Public Affairs Division, C. M. Pemberton
Head of Corporate Relations, F. Kirk
Head of Commercial Development, M. Sullivan
Head of Marketing and Communications, H. Roderick
Head of Wellcome Wing Commercial and Access, B. Jones
Assistant Director, Wellcome Wing Project Director and Head of Science Communication Division, Prof. J. R. Durant
Head of Education and Programmes, Dr R. Jackson
Head of Exhibition and Wellcome Wing Content, Dr G. Farmelo
Head of Design, T. Molloy
Head of National Railway Museum, A. Scott
Head of National Museum of Photography, Film and Television, Ms A. Nevill

VICTORIA AND ALBERT MUSEUM
Cromwell Road, London SW7 2RL
Tel 0171-942 2000

The Victoria and Albert Museum is the national museum of fine and applied art and design. It descends directly from the Museum of Manufactures, which opened in Marlborough House in 1852 after the Great Exhibition of 1851. The Museum was moved in 1857 to become part of the South Kensington Museum. It was renamed the Victoria and Albert Museum in 1899. It also houses the National Art Library and Print Room.

The Museum administers three branch museums: the National Museum of Childhood in Bethnal Green, the Theatre Museum in Covent Garden, and the Wellington Museum at Apsley House. The museum in Bethnal Green was opened in 1872 and the building is the most important surviving example of the type of glass and iron construction used by Paxton for the Great Exhibition. Total government grant-in-aid for 1999–2000 is £30.084 million.

BOARD OF TRUSTEES
Chairman, Mrs P. Ridley
Deputy Chairman, J. Scott, CBE, FSA
Members, Miss N. Campbell; Penelope, Viscountess Cobham; Lady Copisarow; R. Fitch, CBE; Prof. C. Frayling, PH.D.; Sir Terence Heiser, GCB; Mrs A. Heseltine; A. Irby III; A. Snow; Prof. J. Steer, FSA, DLitt.; A. Wheatley; Prof. C. White, CVO, FBA
Secretary to the Board of Trustees, P. A. Wilson

OFFICERS
Director, Dr A. C. N. Borg, CBE, FSA
Assistant Directors, T. J. Stevens (*Collections*); J. W. Close (*Administration*)
Head of Buildings and Estate, R. P. Whitehouse
Chief Curator, Ceramics and Glass, Dr O. Watson
Head of Conservation, Dr J. Ashley-Smith
Head of Education, D. Anderson, OBE
Chief Curator, Far Eastern, Miss R. Kerr
Head of Finance and Central Services, Miss R. M. Sykes
Chief Curator, Furniture and Woodwork, C. Wilk
Chief Curator, Indian and South-East Asian, Dr D. Swallow
Head of Information Systems Services, A. Cooper
Head of Major Projects, Mrs G. F. Miles
Chief Curator, Metalwork, Silver and Jewellery, vacant
Chief Librarian, National Art Library, J. F. van den Wateren
Head of Personnel, Mrs G. Henchley
Chief Curator, Prints, Drawings and Paintings, Miss S. B. Lambert
Head of Public Services, R. Cole-Hamilton
Head of Records and Collections Services, A. Seal
Head of Research, P. Greenhalgh
Head of Safety and Security, R. Bland
Chief Curator, Sculpture, Dr P. E. D. Williamson
Chief Curator, Textiles and Dress, Mrs V. D. Mendes
Managing Director, V. and A. Enterprises Ltd, M. Cass
Director of Development, vacant
Head of National Museum of Childhood (acting), Dr S. Laurence
Head of Theatre Museum, Miss M. Benton
Head of Wellington Museum, Miss A. Robinson

MUSEUM OF LONDON
London Wall, London EC2Y 5HN
Tel 0171-600 3699; fax 0171-600 1058

The Museum of London illustrates the history of London from prehistoric times to the present day. It opened in 1976 and is based on the amalgamation of the former Guildhall Museum and London Museum. The Museum is controlled by a Board of Governors, appointed (nine each) by the Government and the Corporation of London. The Museum is currently funded jointly by the Department for Culture, Media and Sport and the Corporation of London, each contributing £4.360 million in 1999–2000.
Chairman of Board of Governors, R. Hambro
Director, Dr S. Thurley

COMMONWEALTH INSTITUTE
Kensington High Street, London W8 6NQ
Tel 0171-603 4535; fax 0171-602 7374

The Commonwealth Institute is responsible for promoting the Commonwealth in the UK and other member countries through exhibitions, educational programmes, publications, resources and information. The Institute houses the Commonwealth Resource Centre (CRC) and Literature Library and a Conference and Events Centre.

The Institute was established in 1958 and is an independent statutory body funded by the British government with contributions from other Commonwealth governments. It is controlled by a board of governors which includes the high commissioners of all Commonwealth countries represented in London.
Chairman, D. A. Thompson
Director-General, D. French
Administrative and Commercial Director, P. Kennedy
Director of Education, S. Brace
Director of Public Affairs, G. Carter

IMPERIAL WAR MUSEUM
Lambeth Road, London SE1 6HZ
Tel 0171-416 5000; fax 0171-416 5374

The Museum, founded in 1917, illustrates and records all aspects of the two world wars and other military operations involving Britain and the Commonwealth since 1914. It was opened in its present home, formerly Bethlem Hospital or Bedlam, in 1936. The Museum also administers HMS *Belfast* in the Pool of London, Duxford Airfield near Cambridge and the Cabinet War Rooms in Westminster.

Total government grant-in-aid for 1999–2000 is £11.662 million.

OFFICERS
Director-General, R. W. K. Crawford
Secretary, J. J. Chadwick, OBE
Assistant Directors, D. A. Needham (*Administration*); Miss K. J. Carmichael (*Collections*); G. Marsh (*Planning and Development*)
Director of Duxford Airfield, E. O. Inman, OBE
Director of HMS Belfast, E. J. Wenzel

KEEPERS
Department of Museum Services, C. Dowling, D.Phil.
Department of Documents, R. W. A. Suddaby
Department of Exhibits and Firearms, D. J. Penn
Department of Printed Books, R. Golland
Department of Art, Miss A. H. Weight
Department of Film, R. B. N. Smither
Department of Photographs, Ms B. Kinally
Department of Sound Records, Mrs M. A. Brooks
Department of Marketing and Trading, Miss A. Godwin
Curator of the Cabinet War Rooms, P. Reed

NATIONAL MARITIME MUSEUM
Greenwich, London SE10 9NF
Tel 0181-858 4422; fax 0181-312 6632

Established by Act of Parliament in 1934, the National Maritime Museum illustrates the maritime history of Great Britain in the widest sense, underlining the importance of the sea and its influence on the nation's power, wealth, culture, technology and institutions. The Museum is in

three groups of buildings in Greenwich Park – the main building, the Queen's House (built by Inigo Jones, 1616–35) and the Royal Observatory (including Wren's Flamsteed House). Total government grant-in-aid for 1999–2000 is £10.425 million.
Director, R. L. Ormond

NATIONAL ARMY MUSEUM
Royal Hospital Road, London SW3 4HT
Tel 0171-730 0717; fax 0171-823 6573

The National Army Museum covers the history of five centuries of the British Army. It was established by royal charter in 1960. Total government grant-in-aid for 1999–2000 is £3.2 million.
Director, I. G. Robertson
Assistant Directors, D. K. Smurthwaite; A. J. Guy; Maj. P. R. Bateman

ROYAL AIR FORCE MUSEUM
Grahame Park Way, London NW9 5LL
Tel 0181-205 2266; fax 0181-200 1751

Situated on the former airfield at RAF Hendon, the Museum illustrates the development of aviation from before the Wright brothers to the present-day RAF. Total government grant-in-aid for 1999–2000, including funding for the aerospace museum at Cosford, is £3.5 million.
Director, Dr M. A. Fopp
Assistant Directors, H. Hall; A. Wright
Senior Keeper, P. Elliott

NATIONAL MUSEUMS AND GALLERIES ON MERSEYSIDE
PO Box 33, 127 Dale Street, Liverpool L69 3LA
Tel 0151-207 0001; fax 0151-478 4190

The Board of Trustees of the National Museums and Galleries on Merseyside is responsible for the Liverpool Museum, the Merseyside Maritime Museum (incorporating HM Customs and Excise National Museum), the Museum of Liverpool Life, the Lady Lever Art Gallery, the Walker Art Gallery and Sudley House, and the Conservation Centre. Total government grant-in-aid for 1999–2000 is £13.6 million.
Chairman of the Board of Trustees, D. McDonnell
Director, R. Foster
Keeper of Art Galleries, J. Treuherz
Keeper of Conservation, A. Durham
Keeper, Liverpool Museum, Ms L. Knowles
Keeper, Merseyside Maritime Museum and Museum of Liverpool Life, M. Stammers

NATIONAL MUSEUMS AND GALLERIES OF WALES/AMGUEDDFEYDD AC ORIELAU CENEDLAETHOL CYMRU
Cathays Park, Cardiff CF1 3NP
Tel 01222-573500; fax 01222-577010

The National Museums and Galleries of Wales comprise the National Museum and Gallery, the Museum of Welsh Life, the Roman Legionary Museum, Turner House Gallery, the Welsh Slate Museum, the Segontium Roman Museum and the Museum of the Welsh Woollen Industry. Total funding from the National Assembly for Wales for 1999–2000 is £13.516 million.
President, M. C. T. Prichard, CBE
Vice-President, A. Thomas

OFFICERS
Director, A. Southall

Assistant Directors, C. Thomas (*Public Affairs*); I. Fell (*Exhibitions and Interpretation*); Dr E. William (*Collections and Education and Deputy Director*); J. Williams-Davies (*Social and Industrial History, and Keeper, Museum of Welsh Life*); M. Tooby (*Arts and Sciences, and Keeper, National Museum and Gallery*)
Keeper of Geology, M. G. Bassett, PH.D.
Keeper of Bio-diversity and Systematic Biology, Dr P. G. Oliver
Keeper of Art, O. Fairclough
Keeper of Archaeology, R. Brewer
Manager, Roman Legionary Museum, vacant
Keeper in Charge, Turner House Gallery, O. Fairclough
Keeper, Welsh Slate Museum and Segontium Roman Museum, D. Roberts, PH.D.
Manager, Museum of the Welsh Woollen Industry, S. Moss

NATIONAL MUSEUMS OF SCOTLAND
Chambers Street, Edinburgh EH1 1JF
Tel 0131-225 7534; fax 0131-220 4819

The National Museums of Scotland comprise the Royal Museum of Scotland, the Scottish United Services Museum, the Scottish Agricultural Museum, the Museum of Flight, Shambellie House Museum of Costume and the Museum of Scotland. Total funding from the Scottish Executive for 1999–2000 is £19.9 million.

BOARD OF TRUSTEES
Chairman, Sir Robert Smith, FSA SCOT.
Members, Prof. T. Devine; Dr L. Glasser, MBE, FRSE; S. G. Gordon, CBE; Dr V. van Heyingen, FRSE; G. Johnston, OBE, TD; Ms C. Macaulay; N. McIntosh, CBE; Prof. A. Manning, OBE; Prof. J. Murray; Sir William Purves, CBE, DSO; Dr A. Ritchie, OBE; The Countess of Rosebery; I. Smith; The Lord Wilson of Tillyorn, GCMG

OFFICERS
Director, M. Jones, FSA, FSA SCOT., FRSA
Depute Director (Resources) and Project Director, Museum of Scotland, I. Hooper, FSA SCOT.
Depute Director (Collections) and Keeper of History and Applied Art, Miss D. Idiens, FRSA, FSA SCOT.
Development Director, C. McCallum
Keeper of Archaeology, D. V. Clarke, PH.D., FSA, FSA SCOT.
Keeper of Geology and Zoology, M. Shaw, D.PHIL.
Keeper of Social and Technological History, G. Sprott
Head of Public Affairs, Ms M. Bryden
Head of Museum Services, S. R. Elson, FSA SCOT.
Head of Administration, A. G. Young
Keeper, Scottish United Services Museum, S. C. Wood
Curator, Scottish Agricultural Museum, G. Sprott
Curator, Museum of Flight, A. Smith
Keeper, Shambellie House Museum of Costume, Miss N. Tarrant

NATIONAL ASSEMBLY FOR WALES
— *see* Wales, National Assembly for

NATIONAL AUDIT OFFICE
157–197 Buckingham Palace Road, London SW1W 9SP
Tel 0171-798 7000; fax 0171-828 3774
22 Melville Street, Edinburgh EH3 7NS
Tel 0131-244 2736; fax 0131-244 2721
Audit House, 23–24 Park Place, Cardiff CF1 3BA
Tel 01222-378661; fax 01222-388415

The National Audit Office came into existence under the National Audit Act 1983 to replace and continue the work of the former Exchequer and Audit Department. The Act reinforced the Office's total financial and operational independence from the Government and brought its head, the Comptroller and Auditor-General, into a closer relationship with Parliament as an officer of the House of Commons.

The National Audit Office provides independent information, advice and assurance to Parliament and the public about all aspects of the financial operations of government departments and many other bodies receiving public funds. It does this by examining and certifying the accounts of these organizations and by regularly publishing reports to Parliament on the results of its value for money investigations of the economy, efficiency and effectiveness with which public resources have been used. The National Audit Office is also the auditor by agreement of the accounts of certain international and other organizations. In addition, the Office authorizes the issue of public funds to government departments.

Comptroller and Auditor-General, Sir John Bourn, KCB
Private Secretary, M. Davies
Deputy Comptroller and Auditor-General, R. N. Le Marechal, CB
Assistant Auditors-General, T. Burr; J. Colman; L. H. Hughes, CB; J. Marshall; Miss C. Mawhood; M. C. Pfleger; M. Sinclair
Directors, Mrs C. Allen; Miss J. Angus; J. Ashcroft; T. Banfield; Ms G. Body; A. Burchell; P. Cannon; J. Cavanagh; D. Clarke; M. Daynes; S. Doughty; R. Eales; A. Fiander; R. Frith; N. Gale; F. Grogan; Mrs A. Hands; K. Hawkeswell; J. Jones; J. Jones; Mrs P. Leahy; J. McEwen; R. Maggs; G. Miller; R. Parker; J. Pearce; Ms M. Radford; J. Rickleton; A. Roberts; J. Robertson; N. Sloan; Mrs P. Smith; I. Summers; R. Swan; J. Thorpe; Miss J. Wheeler; M. Whitehouse; D. Woodward; P. Woodward

NATIONAL CONSUMER COUNCIL
20 Grosvenor Gardens, London SW1W 0DH
Tel 0171-730 3469; fax 0171-730 0191

The National Consumer Council was set up by the Government in 1975 to give an independent voice to consumers in the UK. Its role is to advocate the consumer interest to decision-makers in national and local government, industry and regulatory bodies, business and the professions. It does this through a combination of research and campaigning. It is largely funded by grant-in-aid from the Department of Trade and Industry.
Chairman, D. Hatch, CBE
Vice-Chairman, Mrs D. Hutton, CBE
Director, Ms A. Bradley

NATIONAL DEBT OFFICE
— *see* National Investment and Loans Office

NATIONAL ENDOWMENT FOR SCIENCE, TECHNOLOGY AND THE ARTS
1st Floor, Gainsborough House, 33 Throgmorton Street, London EC2N 2BR
Tel 0171-861 9670; fax 0171-861 9675

The National Endowment for Science, Technology and the Arts (NESTA) was established under the National Lottery Act 1998 with a £200 million endowment from the proceeds of the National Lottery. Its aims are to help talented individuals; to enable innovative ideas to be successfully commercially exploited; and to promote public knowledge of science, technology and the arts.
Chairman, The Lord Puttnam, CBE
Trustees, Dame Bridget Ogilvie, DBE; Prof. Sir Martin Rees, FRS; Dr C. Evans, OBE; Ms C. Vorderman; D. Wardell; F. Matarasso; C. Gillinson; The Baroness McIntosh of Hudnall; Ms C. McKeever; Ms J. Kirkpatrick; Ms S. Hunter; D. Alexander
Chief Executive, J. Newton

NATIONAL HERITAGE MEMORIAL FUND
7 Holbein Place, London SW1W 8NR
Tel 0171-591 6000; fax 0171-591 6001

The National Heritage Memorial Fund is an independent body established in 1980 as a memorial to those who have died for the UK. The Fund is empowered by the National Heritage Act 1980 to give financial assistance towards the cost of acquiring, maintaining or preserving land, buildings, works of art and other objects of outstanding interest which are also of importance to the national heritage. The Fund is administered by 15 trustees who are appointed by the Prime Minister.

The National Lottery Act 1993 designated the Fund as distributor of the heritage share of proceeds from the National Lottery. As a result, the Fund now operates two funds: the Heritage Memorial Fund and the Heritage Lottery Fund. The Heritage Memorial Fund receives an annual grant from the Department for Culture, Media and Sport; the grant for 1999–2000 is £2.5 million.
Chairman, Dr E. Anderson
Trustees, Prof. C. Baines; R. Boas; Sir Richard Carew Pole, Bt.; Sir Angus Grossart; Sir Ernest Hall; Mrs C. Hubbard; J. Keegan; Mrs P. Lankester; Prof. P. J. Newbould; Miss S. Palmer; Mrs C. Porteous; Prof. T. Pritchard; Ms M. A. Sieghart; Dame Sue Tinson, DBE
Director, Ms A. Case

NATIONAL INSURANCE JOINT AUTHORITY
The Adelphi, 1–11 John Adam Street, London WC2N 6HT
Tel 0171-962 8529; fax 0171-962 8647

The Authority's function is to co-ordinate the operation of social security legislation in Great Britain and Northern Ireland, including the necessary financial adjustments between the two National Insurance Funds.
Members, The Secretary of State for Social Security; the Head of the Department of Health and Social Services for Northern Ireland
Secretary, vacant

NATIONAL INVESTMENT AND LOANS OFFICE
1 King Charles Street, London SW1A 2AP
Tel 0171-270 3861; fax 0171-270 6075

The National Investment and Loans Office is a non-ministerial government department which was set up in 1980 by the merger of the National Debt Office and the Public Works Loan Board. The Office provides the staff and administrative support for the National Debt Commissioners, the Public Works Loan Commissioners and the Office of HM Paymaster-General. The National Debt

Office is responsible for managing the investment portfolios of certain public funds and the management of some residual operations relating to the national debt. The function of the Public Works Loan Board is to make loans from the National Loans Fund to local authorities and certain other statutory bodies, primarily for capital purposes.

The Office of HM Paymaster-General has continuously existed in its present form since 1836; the Paymaster-General has responsibilities assigned from time to time by the Prime Minister and is currently a Treasury minister. The Assistant Paymaster-General is responsible for the banking and financial information services provided to the Government and public sector bodies by the Office of HM Paymaster-General.

Director, I. H. Peattie
Establishment Officer, A. Lawrie

NATIONAL DEBT OFFICE
0171-270 3868

Comptroller-General, I. H. Peattie

PUBLIC WORKS LOAN BOARD
0171-270 3874

Chairman, A. D. Loehnis, CMG
Deputy Chairman, Miss V. J. Di Palma, OBE
Other Commissioners, Dame Sheila Masters, DBE; Mrs R. V. Hale; R. Burton; J. A. Parkes, CBE; J. Andrews; B. Tanner, CBE; T. Fellowes; Mrs R. Terry; D. W. Midgley; L. M. Nippers
Secretary, I. H. Peattie
Assistant Secretary, D. Hockey

OFFICE OF HM PAYMASTER-GENERAL
0171-270 6074

Paymaster-General, Dawn Primarolo, MP
Assistant Paymaster-General, I. H. Peattie
Head of Banking, L. Palmer

BANKING OPERATIONS, National Investment and Loans Office, Sutherland House, Russell Way, Crawley, W. Sussex RH10 1UH. Tel: 01293-604410. *Banking Manager,* P. Harris

NATIONAL LOTTERY CHARITIES BOARD
St Vincent House, 16 Suffolk Street, London SW1Y 4NL
Tel 0171-747 5299; fax 0171-747 5347

The Board was set up under the National Lottery Act 1993 to distribute funds from the Lottery to support charitable, benevolent and philanthropic organizations. The chairman and members are appointed by the Secretary of State for Culture, Media and Sport. The Board's main aim is to help meet the needs of those at greatest disadvantage in society and to improve the quality of life in the community through grants programmes in the UK and an international grants programme for UK-based agencies working abroad.
Chair, Lady Brittan, CBE
Deputy Chairman, Sir Adam Ridley
Members, Mrs T. Baring, CBE; A. Bhatia, OBE; S. Burkeman; J. Carroll; Mrs A. Clark; Ms K. Hampton; T. Jones, OBE; Ms A. Jordan; Mrs B. Lowndes, MBE; R. Martineau; W. Osborne; R. Partington; J. Simpson, OBE; N. Stewart, OBE; Mrs E. Watkins
Chief Executive, T. Hornsby

NATIONAL LOTTERY COMMISSION
2 Monck Street, London SW1P 2BQ
Tel 0171-227 2000; fax 0171-227 2005

The National Lottery Commission replaced the Office of the National Lottery (OFLOT) in April 1999 under the National Lottery Act 1998. The Commission is responsible for the granting, varying and enforcing of licences to run the National Lottery. Its duties are to ensure that the National Lottery is run with all due propriety, that the interests of players are protected, and, subject to these two objectives, that returns to the 'good causes' are maximized.
Chairman, B. Pomeroy
Commissioners, Ms H. Blume; Dame Helena Shovelton, DBE; Ms H. Spicer; R. Squire
Chief Executive, M. Harris
Director of Operations, K. Jones

For details of National Lottery operations, *see* National Lottery section

NATIONAL PHYSICAL LABORATORY
Queens Road, Teddington, Middx TW11 0LW
Tel 0181-977 3222; fax 0181-943 6458

The Laboratory is the UK's national standards laboratory. It develops, maintains and disseminates national measurement standards for physical quantities such as mass, length, time, temperature, voltage, force and pressure. It also conducts underpinning research on engineering materials and information technology and disseminates good measurement practice. It is government-owned but contractor-operated.
Managing Director, Dr J. Rae
Director of Marketing and Communications, D. C. Richardson

NATIONAL RADIOLOGICAL
PROTECTION BOARD
Chilton, Didcot, Oxon OX11 0RQ
Tel 01235-831600; fax 01235-833891

The National Radiological Protection Board is an independent statutory body created by the Radiological Protection Act 1970. It is the national point of authoritative reference on radiological protection for both ionizing and non-ionizing radiations, and has issued recommendations on limiting human exposure to electromagnetic fields and radiation from a range of sources, including X-rays, the Sun and power generators. Its sponsoring department is the Department of Health.
Chairman, Sir Walter Bodmer, PH.D., FRCPath., FRS
Director, Prof. R. H. Clarke

NATIONAL SAVINGS
Charles House, 375 Kensington High Street, London
W14 8SD
Tel 0171-605 9300; fax 0171-605 9438

National Savings was established as a government department in 1969. It became an executive agency of the Treasury in 1996 and is responsible for the design, marketing and administration of savings and investment products for personal savers and investors. In April 1999 the German electronics group Siemens took over all the back office functions at National Savings.

Chief Executive, P. Bareau
Personnel Director, D. S. Speedie
Finance Director, R. Douglas
Commercial Director, C. Moxey
Funding Director, M. Corcoran
Sourcing Director, Ms J. Bevan

For details of schemes, *see* National Savings section

OFFICE FOR NATIONAL STATISTICS
1 Drummond Gate, London SW1V 2QQ
Tel 0171-533 6363; fax 0171-533 5719

The Office for National Statistics was created in 1996 by the merger of the Central Statistical Office and the Office of Population, Censuses and Surveys. It is an executive agency of the Treasury and is responsible for preparing and interpreting key economic statistics for government policy; collecting and publishing business statistics; publishing annual and monthly statistical digests; providing researchers, analysts and other customers with a statistical service; administration of the marriage laws and local registration of births, marriages and deaths in England and Wales; provision of population estimates and projections and statistics on health and other demographic matters in England and Wales; population censuses in England and Wales; surveys for government departments and public bodies; and promoting these functions within the UK, the European Union and internationally to provide a statistical service to meet European Union and international requirements.

The Office for National Statistics is also responsible for establishing and maintaining a central database of key economic and social statistics produced to common classifications, definitions and standards.

Chief Executive, Registrar-General for England and Wales and Head of the Government Statistical Service, Prof. T. Holt (until the end of 1999)
Directors (G3), J. Calder (*Methods and Quality*); vacant (*Census, Population and Health*); J. Kidgell (*Economic Statistics*); D. Roberts (*Administration and Registration*); M. Pepper (*Business Statistics*); J. Pullinger (*Social Statistics*)
Principal Establishment Officer (G5), E. Williams
Principal Finance Officer (G5), P. Murphy
Head of Information (G6), I. Scott
Parliamentary Clerk, L. Land

FAMILY RECORDS CENTRE, 1 Myddelton Street, London EC1R 1UW. Tel: 0181-392 5300. Open Mon., Wed., Fri. 9 a.m.–5 p.m.; Tues. 10 a.m.–7 p.m.; Thurs. 9 a.m.–7 p.m.; Sat. 9.30 a.m.–5 p.m.

JOINT NATURE CONSERVATION COMMITTEE
Monkstone House, City Road, Peterborough PE1 1JY
Tel 01733-562626; fax 01733-555948

The Committee was established under the Environmental Protection Act 1990. It advises the Government and others on UK and international nature conservation issues and disseminates knowledge on these subjects. It establishes common standards for the monitoring of nature conservation and research, and provides guidance to English Nature, Scottish Natural Heritage, the Countryside Council for Wales and the Department of the Environment for Northern Ireland.

Chairman, Sir Angus Stirling
Managing Director, D. Steer
Director, Dr M. A. Vincent

NEW OPPORTUNITIES FUND
Dacre House, Dacre Street, London SW1H 0DH
Tel 0171-222 3084; fax 0171-222 3085

The New Opportunities Fund was established under the National Lottery Act 1998 and is responsible for distributing funds allocated from the proceeds of the National Lottery to health, education and environment projects within initiatives determined by the Government.
Chair of the Board, The Baroness Pitkeathley
Members of the Board, Ms J. Barrow; Prof. E. Bolton, CB; Ms N. Clarke; Prof. A. Patmore, CBE; D. Mackie; D. Campbell; Ms J. Hutt; Dr S. Griffiths; Ms R. McDonough
Chief Executive, S. Dunmore

NORTHERN IRELAND AUDIT OFFICE
106 University Street, Belfast BT7 1EU
Tel 01232-251000; fax 01232-251106

The primary aim of the Northern Ireland Audit Office is to provide independent assurance, information and advice to Parliament on the proper accounting for Northern Ireland departmental and certain other public expenditure; revenue, assets and liabilities; on regularity and propriety; and on the economy, efficiency and effectiveness of the use of resources.
Comptroller and Auditor-General for Northern Ireland, J. M. Dowdall

NORTHERN IRELAND HUMAN RIGHTS COMMISSION
Temple Court, 39–41 North Street, Belfast BT1 1NA
Tel 01232-243987; fax 01232-247844

The Northern Ireland Human Rights Commission was set up in March 1999. Its main functions are to keep under review the law and practice relating to human rights in Northern Ireland, to advise the Government and to promote an awareness of human rights in Northern Ireland. The Commission consists of one full-time commissioner and nine part-time commissioners, all appointed by the Secretary of State for Northern Ireland.
Chief Commissioner (£55,000), Prof. B. Dickson
Commissioners (£8,000 each), Ms C. Bell; Ms M-A. Dinsmore, QC; T. Donnelly, MBE; The Revd H. Good, OBE; Prof. T. Hadden; Ms A. Hegarty; Ms P. Kelly; Ms I. McCormack; F. McGuinness

NORTHERN IRELAND OFFICE
11 Millbank, London SW1P 4PN
Tel 0171-210 3000
Castle Buildings, Stormont, Belfast BT4 3SG
Tel 01232-520700; fax 01232-528195
Web: http://www.nics.gov.uk/centgov/nio/nio.htm

The Northern Ireland Office was established in 1972, when the Northern Ireland (Temporary Provisions) Act transferred the legislative and executive powers of the Northern

Ireland Parliament and Government to the UK Parliament and a Secretary of State.

The Northern Ireland Office is responsible primarily for security issues, law and order and prisons, and for matters relating to the political and constitutional future of the province. It also deals with international issues as they affect Northern Ireland. The Northern Ireland departments are responsible for the administration of social, industrial and economic policies.

Under the terms of the 1998 Belfast Agreement, power was due to be devolved to the New Northern Ireland Assembly in 1999; the Assembly would then take on responsibility for the relevant areas of work currently undertaken by the departments of the Northern Ireland Office. In December 1998 the creation of ten new departments was agreed: agriculture and rural development; the environment; regional development; social development; education; higher education, training and employment; enterprise, trade and investment, culture, arts and leisure; health, social services and public safety; and finance and personnel. Each department would be headed by a member of the power-sharing executive (three each by the UUP and the SDLP and two each by the DUP and Sinn Fein), which would be headed by the First Minister and Deputy First Minister. Six cross-border implementation bodies would also be established, dealing with inland waterways, food safety, trade and business development, EU programmes, language, and aquaculture.

It is anticipated that the number of ministers at the Northern Ireland Office would be reduced in the event of devolution.

The names of most civil servants are not listed for security reasons.

Secretary of State for Northern Ireland, The Rt. Hon. Dr Marjorie (Mo) Mowlam, MP
Special Advisers, N. Warner; A. Lappin
Parliamentary Private Secretary, H. Jackson, MP
Minister of State, The Rt. Hon. Adam Ingram, MP (*Security, Victims, Europe, Constitution*)
Parliamentary Private Secretary, T. Colman, MP
Parliamentary Under-Secretaries of State, The Lord Dubs (*Environment, Agriculture*); John McFall, MP (*Education, Economic Development*); George Howarth, MP (*Political Development, Equality, Human Rights*)
Permanent Under-Secretary of State (*SCS*), J. Pilling, CB
Second Permanent Under-Secretary of State, Head of the Northern Ireland Civil Service, J. Semple, CB

LONDON
SCS, (Political Director)
SCS, (Associate Political Director); (International and Planning); (Constitutional and Political); (Rights and European); (Personnel and Office Services)
SCS, (Director of Information Services)

BELFAST
SCS, (Political Director)
SCS, (Associate Political Director); (Security); (Criminal Justice); (Political); (Personnel and Finance)

NORTHERN IRELAND INFORMATION SERVICE
Castle Buildings, Stormont, Belfast BT4 3SG
Tel 01232-520700

Director of Communications

EXECUTIVE AGENCIES
COMPENSATION AGENCY, Royston House, Upper Queen Street, Belfast BT1 6FD. Tel: 01232-2499444
FORENSIC SCIENCE AGENCY, Seapark, 151 Belfast Road, Carrickfergus, Co. Antrim BT38 8PL. Tel: 01232-365744
NORTHERN IRELAND PRISON SERVICE, *see* page 383

DEPARTMENT OF AGRICULTURE FOR NORTHERN IRELAND
Dundonald House, Upper Newtownards Road, Belfast BT4 3SB
Tel 01232-520100; fax 01232-525015

Parliamentary Under-Secretary of State, The Lord Dubs
Permanent Secretary (*SCS*)
Under-Secretaries (*SCS*), (Central Services and Rural Development); (Food, Farm and Environmental Policy); (Veterinary); (Science); (Agri-Food Development)

EXECUTIVE AGENCIES
INTERVENTION BOARD
— *see* page 314
RIVERS AGENCY, 4 Hospital Road, Belfast BT8 8JP. Tel: 01232-253355
FOREST SERVICE, Dundonald House, Upper Newtownards Road, Belfast BT4 3SB. Tel: 01232-524480

DEPARTMENT OF ECONOMIC DEVELOPMENT NORTHERN IRELAND
Netherleigh, Massey Avenue, Belfast BT4 2JP
Tel 01232-529900; fax 01232-529550

Parliamentary Under-Secretary of State, John McFall, MP
Permanent Secretary (*SCS*)
Under-Secretaries (*SCS*), (Resources Group); (Regulatory Services Group)
INDUSTRIAL DEVELOPMENT BOARD, IDB House, 64 Chichester Street, Belfast BT1 4JX. Tel: 01232-233233

EXECUTIVE AGENCIES
INDUSTRIAL RESEARCH AND TECHNOLOGY UNIT, 17 Antrim Road, Lisburn BT28 3AL. Tel: 01846-623000
TRAINING AND EMPLOYMENT AGENCY (NORTHERN IRELAND), Adelaide House, Adelaide Street, Belfast BT2 8FD. Tel: 01232-257777

DEPARTMENT OF EDUCATION FOR NORTHERN IRELAND
Rathgael House, Balloo Road, Bangor, Co. Down BT19 7PR
Tel 01247-279279; fax 01247-279100

Parliamentary Under-Secretary of State, John McFall, MP
Permanent Secretary (*SCS*)
Deputy Secretaries (*SCS*), (Schools); (Finance and Corporate Services)
Chief Inspector (*SCS*), (Education and Training Inspectorate)

DEPARTMENT OF THE ENVIRONMENT FOR NORTHERN IRELAND
Clarence Court, 10–18 Adelaide Street, Belfast BT2 8GB
Tel 01232-540540

Parliamentary Under-Secretary of State, The Lord Dubs
Permanent Secretary (*SCS*)
Under-Secretaries (*SCS*), (Personnel, Finance, Housing and Local Government); (Rural and Urban Affairs); (Roads, Water and Transport); (Planning, Works and Environment)

EXECUTIVE AGENCIES
CONSTRUCTION SERVICE, Churchill House, Victoria Square, Belfast BT1 4QW. Tel: 01232-250284
DRIVER AND VEHICLE LICENSING AGENCY (NORTHERN IRELAND), County Hall, Castlerock Road, Coleraine, Co. Londonderry BT51 3HS. Tel: 01265-41200

DRIVER AND VEHICLE TESTING AGENCY (NORTHERN IRELAND), Balmoral Road, Belfast BT12 6QL. Tel: 01232-681831

ENVIRONMENT AND HERITAGE SERVICE, Commonwealth House, Castle Street, Belfast BT1 1GU. Tel: 01232-251477

LAND REGISTERS OF NORTHERN IRELAND, Lincoln Building, 27–45 Great Victoria Street, Belfast BT2 7SL. Tel: 01232-251515

ORDNANCE SURVEY OF NORTHERN IRELAND, Colby House, Stranmillis Court, Belfast BT9 5BJ. Tel: 01232-255755

PLANNING SERVICE, Clarence Court, 10–18 Adelaide Street, Belfast BT2 8GB. Tel: 01232-540540

PUBLIC RECORD OFFICE (NORTHERN IRELAND) – see page 334

RATE COLLECTION AGENCY (NORTHERN IRELAND), Oxford House, 49–55 Chichester Street, Belfast BT1 4HH. Tel: 01232-252252

ROADS SERVICE, Clarence Court, 10–18 Adelaide Street, Belfast BT2 8GB. Tel: 01232-540540

WATER SERVICE, Northland House, 3 Frederick Street, Belfast BT1 2NR. Tel: 01232-244711

ADVISORY BODIES

HISTORIC BUILDINGS COUNCIL FOR NORTHERN IRELAND, c/o Environment and Heritage Service, Historic Monuments and Buildings, Commonwealth House, Castle Street, Belfast BT1 1GU. Tel: 01232-251477

COUNCIL FOR NATURE CONSERVATION AND THE COUNTRYSIDE, c/o Environment and Heritage Service, Commonwealth House, Castle Street, Belfast BT1 1GU. Tel: 01232-251477

DEPARTMENT OF FINANCE AND PERSONNEL
Parliament Buildings, Stormont, Belfast BT4 3SG
Tel 01232-520400

Minister of State, The Rt. Hon. Adam Ingram, MP
Permanent Secretary (SCS)
Under-Secretaries (SCS), (Supply Group); (Resources Control and Professional Services Group); (Central Personnel Group); (Government Purchasing Service)

NORTHERN IRELAND CIVIL SERVICE (NICS)
Parliament Buildings, Stormont, Belfast BT4 3TT
Tel 01232-520700

Head of Civil Service (SCS), J. Semple, CB
Under-Secretaries (SCS), (Central Secretariat); (Legal Services); (Office of the Legislative Council)

GENERAL REGISTER OFFICE (NORTHERN IRELAND), Oxford House, 49–65 Chichester Street, Belfast BT1 4HL. Tel: 01232-252000. *Registrar-General* (G6)

EXECUTIVE AGENCIES

BUSINESS DEVELOPMENT SERVICE, Craigantlet Buildings, Stoney Road, Belfast BT4 3SX. Tel: 01232-520400

GOVERNMENT PURCHASING AGENCY, Rosepark House, Upper Newtownards Road, Belfast BT4 3NR. Tel: 01232-520400

NORTHERN IRELAND STATISTICS AND RESEARCH AGENCY, The Arches Centre, 11–13 Bloomfield Avenue, Belfast BT5 5HD. Tel: 01232-526093

VALUATION AND LANDS AGENCY, Queen's Court, 56–66 Upper Queen Street, Belfast BT4 6FD. Tel: 01232-250700

DEPARTMENT OF HEALTH AND SOCIAL SERVICES NORTHERN IRELAND
Castle Buildings, Stormont, Belfast BT4 3PP
Tel 01232-520000; fax 01232-520572

Parliamentary Under-Secretary of State, George Howarth, MP
Permanent Secretary (SCS)
Chief Medical Officer (SCS)
Under-Secretaries (SCS), (Health and Social Services Executive); (Health and Social Policy); (Medical and Allied Services); (Central Management and Social Security Policy Group)

HEALTH AND SOCIAL SERVICES BOARDS
— see Social Welfare section

EXECUTIVE AGENCIES

NORTHERN IRELAND CHILD SUPPORT AGENCY, Great Northern Tower, 17 Great Victoria Street, Belfast BT2 7AD. Tel: 01232-339000

NORTHERN IRELAND HEALTH AND SOCIAL SERVICES ESTATES AGENCY, Stoney Road, Dundonald, Belfast BT16 1US. Tel: 01232-520025

NORTHERN IRELAND SOCIAL SECURITY AGENCY, Castle Buildings, Stormont, Belfast BT4 3SJ. Tel: 01232-520520

OCCUPATIONAL PENSIONS REGULATORY AUTHORITY
Invicta House, Trafalgar Place, Brighton BN1 4DW
Tel 01273-627600; fax 01273-627688

The Occupational Pensions Regulatory Authority (OPRA) was set up under the Pensions Act 1995 and became fully operational on 6 April 1997. It is the independent, statutory regulator of occupational pension schemes in the UK.
Chairman, J. Hayes, CBE
Chief Executive, Mrs C. Instance

OMBUDSMEN
— see Local Commissioners *and* Parliamentary Commissioner. For non-statutory Ombudsmen, *see* Index

---

ORDNANCE SURVEY
Romsey Road, Maybush, Southampton SO16 4GU
Tel 01703-792000; fax 01703-792452

Ordnance Survey is the national mapping agency for Britain. It is a government department funded by parliamentary vote, and reports to the Secretary of State for the Environment, Transport and the Regions.
Director-General and Chief Executive, Prof. D. Rhind

PARADES COMMISSION
12th Floor, Windsor House, 6–12 Bedford Street, Belfast BT2 7EL
Tel 01232-895900; fax 01232-322988

The Parades Commission was set up under the Public Processions (Northern Ireland) Act 1998. Its function is to encourage and facilitate local accommodation on contentious parades; where this is not possible, the Commission is empowered to make legal determinations about such parades, which may include imposing conditions on aspects of the notified parade.

The chairman and members are appointed by the

Secretary of State for Northern Ireland; the membership must, as far as is practicable, be representative of the community in Northern Ireland.

Chairman, A. Graham

Members, D. Hewitt, CBE; Mrs R. A. McCormick; A. Canavan; F. Guckian, CBE; W. Martin; Dr Barbara Erwin

Secretary (G5), Mrs H. Robinson

OFFICE OF THE PARLIAMENTARY COMMISSIONER FOR ADMINISTRATION AND HEALTH SERVICE COMMISSIONER
Millbank Tower, Millbank, London SW1P 4QP
Tel 0845-015 4033; fax 0171-217 4000

The Parliamentary Commissioner for Administration (the Parliamentary Ombudsman) is independent of Government and is an officer of Parliament. He is responsible for investigating complaints referred to him by MPs from members of the public who claim to have sustained injustice in consequence of maladministration by or on behalf of government departments and certain non-departmental public bodies. In March 1999 an additional 158 public bodies were brought within the jurisdiction of the Parliamentary Commissioner. Certain types of action by government departments or bodies are excluded from investigation. The Parliamentary Commissioner is also responsible for investigating complaints, referred by MPs, alleging that access to official information has been wrongly refused under the Code of Practice on Access to Government Information 1994.

The Health Service Commissioners (the Health Service Ombudsman) for England, for Scotland and for Wales are responsible for investigating complaints against National Health Service authorities and trusts that are not dealt with by those authorities to the satisfaction of the complainant. Complaints can be referred direct by the member of the public who claims to have sustained injustice or hardship in consequence of the failure in a service provided by a relevant body, failure of that body to provide a service or in consequence of any other action by that body. The Ombudsmens' jurisdiction now covers complaints about family doctors, dentists, pharmacists and opticians, and complaints about actions resulting from clinical judgment. The Health Service Ombudsmen are also responsible for investigating complaints that information has been wrongly refused under the Code of Practice on Openness in the National Health Service 1995. The three offices are presently held by the Parliamentary Commissioner.

Parliamentary Commissioner and Health Service Commissioner (G1), M. S. Buckley

Deputy Parliamentary Commissioner (G3), J. E. Avery, CB

Deputy Health Service Commissioner (G3), Ms H. Scott

Directors, Parliamentary Commissioner (G5), Ms J. Binstead; N. Cleary; Mrs S. P. Maunsell; G. Monk; A. Watson

Directors, Health Service Commissioners (G5), Ms H. Bainbridge; N. J. Jordan; D. R. G. Pinchin; R. Tyrrell

Finance and Establishment Officer (G5), J. Stevens

For Scotland, *see* Scottish Parliamentary Commissioner for Administration

For Wales, *see* Welsh Administration Ombudsman

PARLIAMENTARY COMMISSIONER FOR STANDARDS
House of Commons, London SW1A 0AA
Tel 0171-219 0320

Following recommendations of the Committee on Standards in Public Life, the House of Commons agreed to the appointment of an independent Parliamentary Commissioner for Standards with effect from November 1995. The Commissioner has responsibility for maintaining and monitoring the operation of the Register of Members' Interests; advising Members of Parliament and the select committee on standards and privileges, on the interpretation of the rules on disclosure and advocacy, and on other questions of propriety; and receiving and, if she thinks fit, investigating complaints about the conduct of MPs.

Parliamentary Commissioner for Standards, Miss E. Filkin

PARLIAMENTARY COUNSEL
36 Whitehall, London SW1A 2AY
Tel 0171-210 6637; fax 0171-210 6632

Parliamentary Counsel draft all government bills (i.e. primary legislation) except those relating exclusively to Scotland, the latter being drafted by the Lord Advocate's Department. They also advise on all aspects of parliamentary procedure in connection with such bills and draft government amendments to them as well as any motions (including financial resolutions) necessary to secure their introduction into, and passage through, Parliament.

First Counsel (SCS), E. G. Caldwell, CB

Counsel (SCS), E. G. Bowman, CB; G. B. Sellers, CB; E. R. Sutherland, CB; P. F. A. Knowles, CB; S. C. Laws, CB; R. S. Parker, CB; Miss C. E. Johnston; P. J. Davies; J. M. Sellers

PAROLE BOARD FOR ENGLAND AND WALES
Abell House, John Islip Street, London SW1P 4LH
Tel 0171-217 5314; 0171-217 5793

The Board was constituted under the Criminal Justice Act 1967 and continued under the Criminal Justice Act 1991. It is an executive non-departmental public body and its duty is to advise the Home Secretary with respect to matters referred to it by him which are connected with the early release or recall of prisoners. Its functions include giving directions concerning the release on licence of prisoners serving discretionary life sentences and of certain prisoners serving long-term determinate sentences.

Chairman, The Baroness Prashar, CBE

Vice-Chairman, The Hon. Mr Justice Tucker

Chief Executive, J. Casey

PAROLE BOARD FOR SCOTLAND
Saughton House, Broomhouse Drive, Edinburgh EH11 3XD
Tel 0131-244 8755; fax 0131-244 6974

The Board directs and advises the First Minister on the release of prisoners on licence, and related matters.

Chairman, I. McNee

Vice-Chairmen, Sheriff G. Shiach; Ms J. Freeman

Secretary, H. P. Boyle

PATENT OFFICE
Concept House, Cardiff Road, Newport NP9 1RH
Tel 0645-500505; fax 01633-814444

The Patent Office is an executive agency of the Department of Trade and Industry. The duties of the Patent Office are to administer the Patent Acts, the Registered Designs Act and the Trade Marks Act, and to deal with questions relating to the Copyright, Designs and Patents Act 1988. The Search and Advisory Service carries out commercial searches through patent information. In 1997 the Office granted 2,792 patents and registered 9,592 designs and 27,897 trade marks.

Comptroller-General, Ms A. Brimelow
Director, Intellectual Property Policy Directorate, G. Jenkins
Director, Patents and Designs, R. J. Marchant
Director and Assistant Registrar of Trade Marks, P. Lawrence
Director, Administration and Resources and Secretary to the Patent Office, C. Octon
Director, Copyright, J. Startup
Director, Finance, J. Thompson

HM PAYMASTER-GENERAL, OFFICE OF
— *see* National Investment and Loans Office

PENSIONS COMPENSATION BOARD
11 Belgrave Road, London SW1V 1RB
Tel 0171-828 9794; fax 0171-931 7239

The Pensions Compensation Board was established under the Pensions Act 1995 and is funded by a levy paid by all eligible occupational pension schemes. Its function is to compensate occupational pension schemes for losses due to dishonesty where the employer is solvent.

Chairman, Dr J. T. Farrand, QC
Secretary, M. Lydon

OFFICE OF THE PENSIONS OMBUDSMAN
6th Floor, 11 Belgrave Road, London SW1V 1RB
Tel 0171-834 9144; fax 0171-821 0065

The Pensions Ombudsman is appointed under the Pension Schemes Act 1993 as amended by the Pensions Act 1995. He investigates and decides complaints and disputes concerning occupational pension schemes. Complaints concerning personal pensions would normally be dealt with only if outside the jurisdiction of the Personal Investment Authority. The Ombudsman is completely independent and there is no charge for bringing a complaint or dispute to him.

Pensions Ombudsman, Dr J. T. Farrand, QC

POLICE COMPLAINTS AUTHORITY
10 Great George Street, London SW1P 3AE
Tel 0171-273 6450; fax 0171-273 6401

The Police Complaints Authority was established under the Police and Criminal Evidence Act 1984 to provide an independent system for dealing with complaints by members of the public against police officers in England and Wales. It is funded by the Home Office. The authority has powers to supervise the investigation of certain categories of serious complaints and certain statutory

functions in relation to the disciplinary aspects of complaints. It does not deal with police operational matters; these are usually dealt with by the Chief Constable of the relevant force.

Chairman, P. Moorhouse
Deputy Chairman, Ms M. Meacher
Members, Mrs L. Allan; I. Bynoe; Ms J. Dobry; J. Elliott; Miss M. Mian; Mrs C. Mitchell; A. Potts; Mrs M. Scorer; Ms L. Whyte; A. Williams, MBE

INDEPENDENT COMMISSION FOR POLICE COMPLAINTS FOR NORTHERN IRELAND
— *see* page 311

POLITICAL HONOURS SCRUTINY COMMITTEE
Ashley House, 2 Monck Street, London SW1P 2BQ
Tel 0171-276 2770; fax 0171-276 2766

The function of the Political Honours Scrutiny Committee (a committee of Privy Councillors) was last set out in full in an Order in Council in May 1997. Subsequent Orders in Council have been made announcing changes in the committee's membership. The Prime Minister submits certain particulars to the Committee about persons proposed to be recommended for honour for their political services. The Committee, after such enquiry as it thinks fit, reports to the Prime Minister whether, so far as it believes, the persons whose names are submitted are fit and proper persons to be recommended.

Chairman, The Lord Thomson of Monifieth, KT, PC
Members, The Baroness Dean of Thornton-le-Fylde, PC; The Lord Hurd of Westwell, CH, CBE
Secretary, A. J. Merifield, CB

PORT OF LONDON AUTHORITY
Devon House, 58–60 St Katharine's Way, London E1 9LB
Tel 0171-265 2656; fax 0171-265 2699

The Port of London Authority is a public trust constituted under the Port of London Act 1908 and subsequent legislation. It is the governing body for the Port of London, covering the tidal portion of the River Thames from Teddington to the seaward limit. The Board comprises a chairman and up to seven but not less than four non-executive members appointed by the Secretary of State for the Environment, Transport and the Regions, and up to four but not less than one executive members appointed by the Board.

Chairman, Sir Brian Shaw
Vice-Chairman, J. H. Kelly, CBE
Chief Executive, S. Cuthbert
Secretary, G. E. Ennals

THE POST OFFICE
148 Old Street, London EC1V 9HQ
Tel 0171-490 2888

Crown services for the carriage of government dispatches were set up in about 1516. The conveyance of public correspondence began in 1635 and the mail service was made a parliamentary responsibility with the setting up of a Post Office in 1657. Telegraphs came under Post Office control in 1870 and the Post Office Telephone Service began in 1880. The National Girobank service of the Post

Office began in 1968. The Post Office ceased to be a government department in 1969 when responsibility for the running of the postal, telecommunications, giro and remittance services was transferred to a public authority called The Post Office. The 1981 British Telecommunications Act separated the functions of the Post Office, making it solely responsible for postal services and Girobank. Girobank was privatized in 1990. In July 1999 the Government announced plans to turn the Post Office into a public limited company, give it greater commercial freedom and set up an independent regulator to protect consumer interests.

The chairman, chief executive and members of the Post Office Board are appointed by the Secretary of State for Trade and Industry but responsibility for the running of the Post Office as a whole rests with the Board in its corporate capacity.

FINANCIAL RESULTS £m	1997–8	1998–9
Post Office Group		
Turnover	6,759	7,010
Profit before tax	664	608
Royal Mail		
Turnover	5,411	5,570
Profit before tax	560	485
Parcelforce		
Turnover	465	474
Profit (loss) before tax	(14)	(25)
Post Office Counters		
Turnover	1,130	1,148
Profit before tax	33	22

POST OFFICE BOARD
Chairman, Dr N. Bain
Chief Executive, J. Roberts, CBE
Members, R. Close (*Managing Director, Finance*); J. Cope (*Managing Director, Strategy and Personnel*)
Secretary, R. Adams

For postal services, *see* Communications section

PRIME MINISTER'S OFFICE
— *see* page 286

PRISONS OMBUDSMAN FOR ENGLAND AND WALES
Ashley House, 2 Monck Street, London SW1P 2BQ
Tel 0171-276 2876; fax 0171-276 2860

The post of Prisons Ombudsman was instituted in 1994. The Ombudsman is appointed by the Home Secretary and is an independent point of appeal for prisoners' grievances about their lives in prison, including disciplinary issues. The Ombudsman cannot investigate grievances relating to issues which are the subject of litigation or criminal proceedings, the merits of decisions taken by ministers (although from May 1999 he may investigate the advice upon which ministers' decisions were made), or actions of bodies outside the prison service.
Prisons Ombudsman, S. Shaw

For Scotland, *see* Scottish Prisons Complaints Commission

PRIVY COUNCIL OFFICE
2 Carlton Gardens, London SW1Y 5AA
Tel 0171-270 0474; fax 0171-270 0109

The Office is responsible for the arrangements leading to the making of all royal proclamations and Orders in Council; for certain formalities connected with ministerial changes; for considering applications for the granting (or amendment) of royal charters; for the scrutiny and approval of by-laws and statutes of chartered bodies; and for the appointment of high sheriffs and many Crown and Privy Council appointments to governing bodies.
President of the Council (and Leader of the House of Commons),
   The Rt. Hon. Margaret Beckett, MP
   Private Secretary, Ms V. A. Scarborough
Parliamentary Secretary, Paddy Tipping, MP
Clerk of the Council, A. K. Galloway
Deputy Clerk of the Council, G. C. Donald
Senior Clerk, Miss M. A. McCullagh
Registrar, J. A. C. Watherston

PROCURATOR FISCAL SERVICE
— *see* page 366

PUBLIC HEALTH LABORATORY SERVICE
61 Colindale Avenue, London NW9 5DF
Tel 0181-200 1295; fax 0181-200 8130

The Public Health Laboratory Service comprises nine groups of laboratories, the Central Public Health Laboratory, the Communicable Disease Surveillance Centre and the Headquarters. The PHLS seeks to protect the population from infection through detection, diagnosis, surveillance, prevention and control of infections and communicable diseases. It keeps track of what infections are appearing where, advises on remedial or preventive action and provides clinical diagnostic services.
Chairman (£15,125), Prof. Sir Leslie Turnberg, MD
Deputy Chairman, R. Tabor
Director, Dr Diana Walford, FRCP, FRCPath.
Deputy Directors, Prof. B. I. Duerden, MD, FRCPath.
   (*Programmes*); K. M. Saunders (*Corporate Planning and Resources*)
Board Secretary, K. M. Saunders

CENTRAL PUBLIC HEALTH LABORATORY
Colindale Avenue, London NW9 5HT
Director, Prof. S. P. Borriello

COMMUNICABLE DISEASES SURVEILLANCE CENTRE
Colindale Avenue, NW9 5EQ
Director, Dr C. L. R. Bartlett

PHLS GROUPS OF LABORATORIES AND GROUP DIRECTORS
East, Dr P. M. B. White
Midlands, Dr R. E. Warren
North, Dr N. F. Lightfoot
North-West, Prof. P. Morgan-Capner
South-West, Prof. K. A. V. Cartwright
Thames, Dr R. Gross
Trent, Dr P. J. Wilkinson
Wessex, Dr S. A. Rousseau
Wales, Dr A. J. Howard

OTHER SPECIAL LABORATORIES AND UNITS
ANAEROBE REFERENCE UNIT, Public Health Laboratory, Cardiff. *Head,* Prof. B. I. Duerden

ANTIVIRAL SUSCEPTIBILITY REFERENCE UNIT, Public Health Laboratory, Birmingham. *Head,* Dr D. P. Pillay
CRYPTOSPRORIDIUM REFERENCE UNIT, Public Health Laboratory, Rhyl. *Head,* Dr D. Casemore
FOOD MICROBIOLOGY RESEARCH UNIT, Public Health Laboratory, Exeter. *Head,* Prof. T. J. Humphrey
GENITO-URINARY INFECTIONS REFERENCE LABORATORY, Public Health Laboratory, Bristol. *Head,* Dr A. J. Herring
LEPTOSPIRA REFERENCE LABORATORY, Public Health Laboratory, Hereford. *Director,* Dr T. J. Coleman
LYME DISEASE REFERENCE UNIT, Public Health Laboratory, Southampton. *Head,* Dr S. O'Connell
MALARIA REFERENCE LABORATORY, London School of Hygiene and Tropical Medicine, London WC1E 7HT. *Directors,* Prof. D. J. Bradley; Dr D. C. Warhurst
MENINGOCOCCAL REFERENCE LABORATORY, Public Health Laboratory, Manchester. *Director,* Dr B. A. Oppenheim
MYCOBACTERIUM REFERENCE UNIT, Public Health Laboratory, Dulwich, London. *Director,* Dr F. Drobniewski
MYCOLOGY REFERENCE LABORATORY, Public Health Laboratory, Bristol. *Head,* Dr D. Warnock; University of Leeds. *Head,* Prof. E. G. V. Evans
PARASITOLOGY REFERENCE LABORATORY, Hospital for Tropical Diseases, London. *Director,* Dr P. L. Chiodini
TOXOPLASMA REFERENCE LABORATORY, Public Health Laboratory, Swansea. *Head,* D. H. M. Joynson
WATER AND ENVIRONMENTAL MICROBIOLOGY RESEARCH UNIT, Public Health Laboratory, Nottingham. *Head,* Dr J. V. Lee

---

REGISTRAR OF PUBLIC LENDING RIGHT
Bayheath House, Prince Regent Street,
Stockton-on-Tees TS18 1DF
Tel 01642-604699; fax 01642-615641

Under the Public Lending Right system, in operation since 1983, payment is made from public funds to authors whose books are lent out from public libraries. Payment is made once a year and the amount each author receives is proportionate to the number of times (established from a sample) that each registered book has been lent out during the previous year. The Registrar of PLR, who is appointed by the Secretary of State for Culture, Media and Sport, compiles the register of authors and books. Only living authors resident in the UK or Germany are eligible to apply. (The term 'author' covers writers, illustrators, translators, and some editors/compilers.)

A payment of 2.07 pence was made in 1998–9 for each estimated loan of a registered book, up to a top limit of £6,000 for the books of any one registered author; the money for loans above this level is used to augment the remaining PLR payments. In February 1999, the sum of £4.159 million was made available for distribution to 17,192 registered authors and assignees as the annual payment of PLR.
Registrar, Dr J. G. Parker
Chairman of Advisory Committee, M. Holroyd

PUBLIC RECORD OFFICE
— *see* page 333

PUBLIC TRUST OFFICE
Stewart House, 24 Kingsway, London WC2B 6JX
Tel 0171-664 7000; fax 0171-664 7702
COURT FUNDS OFFICE, 22 Kingsway, London WC2B 6LE
Tel 0171-936 6000

The Public Trust Office became an executive agency of the Lord Chancellor's Department in 1994. The chief executive of the agency holds the statutory titles of Public Trustee and Accountant-General of the Supreme Court.

The Public Trustee is a trust corporation created to undertake the business of executorship and trusteeship; she can act as executor or administrator of the estate of a deceased person, or as trustee of a will or settlement. The Public Trustee is also responsible for the performance of all the administrative, but not the judicial, tasks required of the Court of Protection under Part VII of the Mental Health Act 1983, relating to the management and administration of the property and affairs of persons suffering from mental disorder. The Public Trustee also acts as Receiver when so directed by the Court, usually where there is no other person willing or able so to act. It also deals with the registration of Enduring Powers of Attorney.

The Accountant-General of the Supreme Court, through the Court Funds Office, is responsible for the investment and accounting of funds in court for persons under a disability, monies in court subject to litigation and statutory deposits.
Chief Executive (Public Trustee and Accountant-General), Ms J. C. Lomas
Assistant Public Trustee, vacant
Investment Manager, H. Stevenson
Chief Property Adviser, A. Nightingale

MENTAL HEALTH SECTOR
Director of Mental Health, Mrs H. M. Bratton
Principal of Receivership Division, W. K. Middleton
Principal of Protection Division, P. L. Hales

TRUSTS AND FUNDS SECTOR
Director of Trusts and Funds, F. J. Eddy
Divisional Manager, Court Funds Office, P. MacDermott
Divisional Manager, Trust Division, M. Munt
Finance Officer, M. Guntrip

PLANNING AND PAY POLICY
Head of Human Resources and Planning, D. Adams

PUBLIC WORKS LOAN BOARD
— *see* National Investment and Loans Office

QUEST (THE QUALITY, EFFICIENCY AND STANDARDS TEAM)
c/o Department for Culture, Media and Sport, 2-4 Cockspur Street, London SW1Y 5DH
Tel 0171-211 6200; fax 0171-211 6032

Quest was established in 1999. Its role is to monitor efficiency and financial management in organizations sponsored by the Department for Culture, Media and Sport and to provide independent advice to the Secretary of State.
Chairman, K. Oates
Chief Executive, T. Suter

COMMISSION FOR RACIAL EQUALITY
Elliot House, 10–12 Allington Street, London SW1E 5EH
Tel 0171-828 7022; fax 0171-630 7605

The Commission was established in 1977 under the Race Relations Act 1976. Its duties are to work towards the elimination of discrimination and promote equality of opportunity, to encourage good relations between different racial groups and to monitor the working of the Race Relations Act. It is funded by the Home Office.
Chairman, Sir Herman Ouseley (until Jan. 2000)
Deputy Chairmen, H. Harris; Dr M. Jogee
Commissioners, M. Amran; Dr R. Chandran; M. Hastings; S. Malik; Ms J. Mellor; P. Passley; Ms S. Patel; R. Purkiss; Ms C. Short; Dr J. Singh; R. Singh
Chief Executive, Ms S. Parsons

THE RADIO AUTHORITY
Holbrook House, 14 Great Queen Street, London WC2B 5DG
Tel 0171-430 2724; fax 0171-405 7062

The Radio Authority was established in 1991 under the Broadcasting Act 1990. It is the regulator and licensing authority for all independent radio services. Members of the Authority are appointed by the Secretary of State for Culture, Media and Sport; senior executive staff are appointed by the Authority.
Chairman, Sir Peter Gibbings
Deputy Chairman, M. Moriarty, CB
Members, Lady Sheil; A. Reid; Mrs H. Tennant; F. Sharkey; Ms S. Hewitt; D.Witherow; Ms S. Nathan
Chief Executive, A. Stoller
Deputy Chief Executive, D. Vick
Secretary to the Authority and Head of Legal Affairs, Ms E. Salomon

OFFICE OF THE RAIL REGULATOR
1 Waterhouse Square, 138–142 Holborn, London EC1N 2TQ
Tel 0171-282 2000; fax 0171-282 2040

The Office of the Rail Regulator was set up under the Railways Act 1993. The Regulator's main functions are the licensing of operators of railway assets; the approval of agreements for access by those operators to track, stations and light maintenance depots; the enforcement of domestic competition law; and consumer protection. The Regulator also sponsors a network of Rail Users' Consultative Committees, which represent the interests of passengers.

Subject to parliamentary approval of the necessary legislation, the consumer protection function of the Rail Regulator will be taken over by the new Strategic Rail Authority when it is set up, and the Rail Regulator will become subject to strategic guidance from the Secretary of State.
Rail Regulator, T. Winsor
Director, Economic Regulation Group, vacant
Director, Railway Network Group, M. Beswick
Director, Passenger Services Group, vacant
Chief Legal Adviser, M. R. Brocklehurst
Chief Economic Adviser, vacant
Director, Resources and RUCC Sponsorship, vacant
Director, Communications, K. R. Webb

RECORD OFFICES

ADVISORY COUNCIL ON PUBLIC RECORDS
Secretariat: Public Record Office, Kew, Richmond, Surrey TW9 4DU
Tel 0181-876 3444 ext. 2351; fax 0181-392 5295

Council members are appointed by the Lord Chancellor, under the Public Records Act 1958, to advise him on matters concerning public records in general and, in particular, on those aspects of the work of the Public Record Office which affect members of the public who make use of it.
Chairman, The Master of the Rolls
Secretary, T. R. Padfield

THE PUBLIC RECORD OFFICE
Kew, Richmond, Surrey TW9 4DU
Tel 0181-876 3444; fax 0181-878 8905

The Public Record Office, originally established in 1838 under the Master of the Rolls, was placed under the direction of the Lord Chancellor in 1958; it became an executive agency in 1992. The Lord Chancellor appoints a Keeper of Public Records, whose duties are to co-ordinate and supervise the selection of records of government departments and the law courts for permanent preservation, to safeguard the records and to make them available to the public. There is a separate record office for Scotland, now called the National Archives of Scotland (*see* page 334).

The Office holds records of central government dating from the Domesday Book (1086) to the present. Under the Public Records Act 1967 they are normally open to inspection when 30 years old, and are then available, without charge, in the reading rooms (Monday, Wednesday, Friday, Saturday, 9.30–5; Tuesday 10–7; Thursday 9.30–7).
Keeper of Public Records (G3), Mrs S. Tyacke, CB
Director, Public Services Division (G5), Dr E. Hallam Smith
Director, Government, Corporate and Information Services Division (G5), Dr D. Simpson

HOUSE OF LORDS RECORD OFFICE (THE PARLIAMENTARY ARCHIVES)
House of Lords, London SW1A 0PW
Tel 0171-219 3074; fax 0171-219 2570

Since 1497, the records of Parliament have been kept within the Palace of Westminster. They are in the custody of the Clerk of the Parliaments. In 1946 a record department was established to supervise their preservation and their availability to the public. The search room of the office is open to the public Monday–Friday, 9.30–5 (Tuesday to 8, by appointment).

Some three million documents are preserved, including Acts of Parliament from 1497, journals of the House of Lords from 1510, minutes and committee proceedings from 1610, and papers laid before Parliament from 1531. Amongst the records are the Petition of Right, the Death Warrant of Charles I, the Declaration of Breda, and the Bill of Rights. The House of Lords Record Office also has charge of the journals of the House of Commons (from 1547), and other surviving records of the Commons (from 1572), including documents relating to private bill legislation from 1818. Among other documents are the records of the Lord Great Chamberlain, the political papers of certain members of the two Houses, and documents relating to Parliament acquired on behalf of the nation. A permanent exhibition was established in the Royal Gallery in 1979.
Clerk of the Records, S. K. Ellison
Assistant Clerks of the Records, D. L. Prior; Dr C. Shenton

ROYAL COMMISSION ON HISTORICAL
MANUSCRIPTS
Quality House, Quality Court, Chancery Lane, London
WC2A 1HP
Tel 0171-242 1198; fax 0171-831 3550

The Commission was set up by royal warrant in 1869 to
enquire and report on collections of papers of value for the
study of history which were in private hands. In 1959 a
new warrant enlarged these terms of reference to include
all historical records, wherever situated, outside the Public
Records and gave it added responsibilities as a central co-
ordinating body to promote, assist and advise on their
proper preservation and storage. The Commission is
sponsored by the Department for Culture, Media and
Sport.

The Commission also maintains the National Register
of Archives (NRA), which contains over 41,000 unpublished
lists and catalogues of manuscript collections describing
the holdings of local record offices, national and university
libraries, specialist repositories and others in the UK and
overseas. The NRA can be searched using computerized
indices which are available in the Commission's search
room.

The Commission also administers the Manorial and
Tithe Documents Rules on behalf of the Master of the
Rolls.

Chairman, The Lord Bingham of Cornhill, PC
Commissioners, Sir Patrick Cormack, FSA, MP; The Lord
   Egremont and Leconfield; Sir Matthew Farrer, GCVO;
   Sir John Sainty, KCB, FSA; Very Revd
   H. E. C. Stapleton, FSA; Sir Keith Thomas, FBA; Mrs
   C. M. Short; The Earl of Scarbrough; Mrs A. Dundas-
   Bekker; G. E. Aylmer, D.Phil, FBA; Mrs S. J. Davies, Ph.D.;
   Mrs A. Prochaska, Ph.D.; Prof. H. C. G. Matthew, D.Phil,
   FBA; Miss R. Dunhill, FSA; Dr Caroline Barron, FSA;
   Prof. T. C. Smout, CBE, Ph.D., FBA, FRSE, FSAScot.
Secretary, C. J. Kitching, Ph.D., FSA

SCOTTISH RECORDS ADVISORY COUNCIL
HM General Register House, Edinburgh EH1 3YY
Tel 0131-535 1314; fax 0131-535 1360

The Council was established under the Public Records
(Scotland) Act 1937. Its members are appointed by the
First Minister and it may submit proposals or make
representations to the First Minister, the Lord Justice
General or the Lord President of the Court of Session on
questions relating to the public records of Scotland.
Chairman, Prof. Anne Crowther
Secretary, Ms A. Rosie

NATIONAL ARCHIVES OF SCOTLAND
HM General Register House, Edinburgh EH1 3YY
Tel 0131-535 1314; fax 0131-535 1360

The history of the national archives of Scotland can be
traced back to the 13th century. The National Archives of
Scotland (formerly the Scottish Record Office) is an
executive agency of the Scottish Executive and keeps the
administrative records of pre-Union Scotland, the registers
of central and local courts of law, the public registers of
property rights and legal documents, and many collections
of local and church records and private archives. Certain
groups of records, mainly the modern records of government departments in Scotland, the Scottish railway records,
the plans collection, and private archives of an industrial
or commercial nature, are preserved in the branch
repository at the West Register House in Charlotte Square.
The search rooms in both buildings are open Monday–
Friday, 9–4.45. A permanent exhibition at the West Register

House and changing exhibitions at the General Register
House are open to the public on weekdays, 10–4. The
National Register of Archives (Scotland) is based in the
West Register House.
Keeper of the Records of Scotland, P. M. Cadell
Deputy Keeper, Dr P. D. Anderson

PUBLIC RECORD OFFICE (NORTHERN
IRELAND)
66 Balmoral Avenue, Belfast BT9 6NY
Tel 01232-251318; fax 01232-255999

The Public Record Office (Northern Ireland) is responsible
for identifying and preserving Northern Ireland's archival
heritage and making it available to the public. It is an
executive agency of the Department of the Environment
for Northern Ireland. The search room is open on weekdays,
9.15–4.15 (Thursday, 9.15–8.45).
Chief Executive, vacant

CORPORATION OF LONDON RECORDS
OFFICE
Guildhall, London EC2P 2EJ
Tel 0171-332 1251; fax 0171-710 8682

The Corporation of London Records Office contains the
municipal archives of the City of London which are
regarded as the most complete collection of ancient
municipal records in existence. The collection includes
charters of William the Conqueror, Henry II, and later
kings and queens to 1957; ancient custumals: Liber Horn,
Dunthorne, Custumarum, Ordinacionum, Memorandorum
and Albus, Liber de Antiquis Legibus, and collections of
statutes; continuous series of judicial rolls and books from
1252 and Council minutes from 1275; records of the Old
Bailey and Guildhall sessions from 1603; financial records
from the 16th century; the records of London Bridge from
the 12th century; and numerous subsidiary series and
miscellanea of historical interest. The Readers' Room is
open Monday–Friday, 9.30–4.45.
Keeper of the City Records, The Town Clerk
City Archivist, J. R. Sewell
Deputy City Archivist, Mrs J. M. Bankes

RESEARCH COUNCILS
— *see* Organizations section

REVIEW BODIES

The secretariat for these bodies is provided by the Office
of Manpower Economics (*see* page 320)

ARMED FORCES PAY
The Review Body on Armed Forces Pay was appointed in
1971 to advise the Prime Minister on the pay and
allowances of members of naval, military and air forces of
the Crown and of any women's service administered by
the Defence Council.
Chairman, The Baroness Dean of Thornton-le-Fylde, PC
Members, Mrs K. Coleman, OBE; J. Davies; Vice-Adm. Sir
   Toby Frere, KCB; The Lord Gladwin of Clee, CBE; Prof.
   D. Greenaway; Ms G. Haskins; M. Ward

DOCTORS' AND DENTISTS' REMUNERATION
The Review Body on Doctors' and Dentists' Remuneration
was set up in 1971 to advise the Government on the
remuneration of doctors and dentists taking any part in the
National Health Service.
Chairman, C. B. Gough

Members, Mrs M. Alderson; Prof. N. Bourne;
A. Hawksworth; Miss C. Hui; Dr G. Jones; C. King, CBE;
Prof. Sheila McLean; D. Penton

NURSING STAFF, MIDWIVES, HEALTH VISITORS AND PROFESSIONS ALLIED TO MEDICINE

The Review Body for nursing staff, midwives, health visitors and professions allied to medicine was set up in 1983 to advise the Government on the remuneration of nursing staff, midwives and health visitors employed in the National Health Service; and also of physiotherapists, radiographers, occupational therapists, orthoptists, chiropodists, dietitians and related grades employed in the National Health Service.
Chairman, Prof. C. Booth
Members, Ms U. Bannerjee; J. Bartlett; Mrs M. Davies; Mrs
S. Gleig; M. Malone-Lee, CB; K. Miles; C. Monks, OBE;
Prof. G. Raab; Prof. P. Weetman

SCHOOL TEACHERS

The School Teachers' Review Body (STRB) was set up under the School Teachers' Pay and Conditions Act 1991. It is required to examine and report on such matters relating to the statutory conditions of employment of school teachers in England and Wales as may be referred to it by the Secretary of State for Education and Employment.
Chairman, A. R. Vineall
Members, P. Gedling; M. Harding; V. Harris; Miss J.
Langdon; R. Pearson; J. Singh; Mrs P. Sloane

SENIOR SALARIES

The Senior Salaries Review Body (formerly the Top Salaries Review Body) was set up in 1971 to advise the Prime Minister on the remuneration of the judiciary, senior civil servants and senior officers of the armed forces. In 1993 its remit was extended to cover the pay, pensions and allowances of MPs, ministers and others whose pay is determined by a Ministerial and Other Salaries Order, and the allowances of peers.
Chairman, Sir Michael Perry, CBE
Members, The Hon. M. Beloff, QC; D. Clayman; Prof. S.
Dawson; Mrs R. Day; The Baroness Dean of Thornton-le-Fylde, PC; Sir Terry Heiser, GCB; Sir Sydney
Lipworth, QC; Miss P. Mann, OBE; Prof. Sir David
Williams, QC

ROYAL BOTANIC GARDEN EDINBURGH

20A Inverleith Row, Edinburgh EH3 5LR
Tel 0131-552 7171; fax 0131-248 2901

The Royal Botanic Garden Edinburgh (RBGE) originated as the Physic Garden, established in 1670 beside the Palace of Holyroodhouse. The Garden moved to its present 28-hectare site at Inverleith, Edinburgh, in 1821. There are also three specialist gardens: Younger Botanic Garden Benmore, near Dunoon, Argyllshire; Logan Botanic Garden, near Stranraer, Wigtownshire; and Dawyck Botanic Garden, near Stobo, Peeblesshire. Since 1986 RBGE has been administered by a board of trustees established under the National Heritage (Scotland) Act 1985. It receives an annual grant from the Rural Affairs Department of the Scottish Executive.

RBGE is an international centre for scientific research on plant diversity and for horticulture education and conservation. It has an extensive library and a herbarium with over two million dried plant specimens. Public

opening hours: Edinburgh site, daily (except Christmas Day and New Year's Day) November–January 9.30–4; February and October 9.30–5; March and September 9.30–6; April–August 9.30–7; specialist gardens, 1 March–31 October 9.30–6. Admission free to Edinburgh site; admission charge to specialist gardens.
Chairman of the Board of Trustees, Dr P. Nicholson
Regius Keeper, Prof. S. Blackmore

ROYAL BOTANIC GARDENS KEW

Richmond, Surrey TW9 3AB
Tel 0181-332 5000; fax 0181-332 5197
Wakehurst Place, Ardingly, nr Haywards Heath,
W. Sussex RH17 6TN
Tel 01444-894066; fax 01444-894069

The Royal Botanic Gardens (RBG) Kew were originally laid out as a private garden for Kew House for George III's mother, Princess Augusta, in 1759. They were much enlarged in the 19th century, notably by the inclusion of the grounds of the former Richmond Lodge. In 1965 the garden at Wakehurst Place was acquired; it is owned by the National Trust and managed by RBG Kew. Under the National Heritage Act 1983 a board of trustees was set up to administer the gardens, which in 1984 became an independent body supported by grant-in-aid from the Ministry of Agriculture, Fisheries and Food.

The functions of RBG Kew are to carry out research into plant sciences, to disseminate knowledge about plants and to provide the public with the opportunity to gain knowledge and enjoyment from the gardens' collections. There are extensive national reference collections of living and preserved plants and a comprehensive library and archive. The main emphasis is on plant conservation and bio-diversity.

The gardens are open daily (except Christmas Day and New Year's Day) from 9.30 a.m. (Wakehurst, 10 a.m.). The closing hour varies from 4 p.m. in mid-winter to 6 p.m. on weekdays and 7.30 p.m. on Sundays and Bank Holidays in mid-summer. Admission, 1999, £5.00; concessionary schemes available. Glasshouses (Kew only), 9.30–4.30 (winter); 9.30–5.30 (summer). No dogs except guide-dogs for the blind.

BOARD OF TRUSTEES
Chairman, The Viscount Blakenham
Members, Sir Jeffery Bowman (*Queen's Trustee*);
R. P. Bauman; Miss M. Black, CBE; Prof. M. Crawley;
Prof. H. Dickinson; Miss A. Ford; Ms R. Franklin; S. de
Grey, CBE; R. Lapthorne; Lady Lennox-Boyd; I. Oag;
Prof. J. S. Parker; Prof. C. Payne, OBE
Director, Prof. P. Crane

ROYAL COMMISSION FOR THE EXHIBITION OF 1851

Sherfield Building, Imperial College of Science, Technology and Medicine, London SW7 2AZ
Tel 0171-594 8790; fax 0171-594 8794

The Royal Commission was incorporated by supplemental charter as a permanent commission after winding up the affairs of the Great Exhibition of 1851. Its object is to promote scientific and artistic education by means of funds derived from its Kensington estate, purchased with the surplus left over from the Great Exhibition. Annual charitable expenditure on educational grants is about £1 million.

President, HRH The Prince Philip, Duke of Edinburgh,
  KG, KT, PC
Chairman, Board of Management, Sir Denis Rooke, OM,
  CBE, FRS, FREng.
Secretary to Commissioners, J. P. W. Middleton, CB

ROYAL COMMISSION ON THE REFORM OF
THE HOUSE OF LORDS
4 Central Buildings, Matthew Parker Street, London SW1H
9NL
Tel 0171-210 0450; fax 0171-210 0451

The Royal Commission was established by Royal Warrant
dated 18 February 1999. Its terms of reference are to
consider and make recommendations on the role and
functions of a second chamber; to make recommendations
on the method or combination of methods of composition
required to constitute a second chamber fit for that role
and those functions; and to report by 31 December 1999.
Chairman, The Lord Wakeham, PC
Members, Ms A. Beynon; The Lord Butler of Brockwell,
  GCB, CVO; The Baroness Dean of Thornton-le-Fylde,
  PC; The Rt. Revd R. Harries; The Lord Hurd of
  Westwell, CH, CBE, PC; G. Kaufman, PC, MP; Prof. A.
  King; W. Morris; K. Munro; Prof. Dawn Oliver; Sir
  Michael Wheeler-Booth, CB
Secretary, D. J. R. Hill

THE ROYAL MINT
Llantrisant, Pontyclun CF72 8YT
Tel 01443-623000; fax 01443-623190

The prime responsibility of the Royal Mint is the provision
of United Kingdom coinage, but it actively competes in
world markets for a share of the available circulating coin
business and about two-thirds of the 18,000 tonnes of coins
it produces annually are exported. The Mint also manufactures special proof and uncirculated quality coins in gold,
silver and other metals; military and civil decorations and
medals; commemorative and prize medals; and royal and
official seals.
  The Royal Mint became an executive agency of the
Treasury in 1990. The Government announced in July
1999 that the Royal Mint would be given greater
commercial freedom to expand its business into new areas
and develop partnerships with the private sector.
Master of the Mint, The Chancellor of the Exchequer (*ex
officio*)
Deputy Master and Comptroller, R. de L. Holmes

ROYAL NATIONAL THEATRE BOARD
South Bank, London, SE1 9PX
Tel 0171-452 3333; fax 0171-452 3344

The chairman and members of the Board of the Royal
National Theatre are appointed by the Secretary of State
for Culture, Media and Sport.
Chairman, Sir Christopher Hogg
Members, Ms J. Bakewell, CBE; The Hon. P. Benson;
  Gabrielle Lady Greenbury; Sir David Hancock, KCB; G.
  Hutchings; Ms K. Jones; Ms S. MacGregor, OBE; Sir Ian
  McKellen; M. Oliver; Sir Tom Stoppard, CBE;
  P. Wiegand
Company Secretary, Mrs M. McGregor
Director, T. Nunn, CBE
Executive Director, The Baroness McIntosh of Hudnall

SCOTLAND OFFICE
Dover House, Whitehall, London SW1A 2AU
Tel 0171-270 3000; fax 0171-270 6730

The Scotland Office is the Office of the Secretary of State
for Scotland, who represents Scottish interests in the
Cabinet on matters reserved to the UK Parliament, i.e.
national financial and economic matters, social security,
defence and international relations, and employment. *See
also* Scottish Executive.
Secretary of State for Scotland, The Rt. Hon. Dr John Reid,
  MP
  Private Secretary (SCS), Ms J. Coulquhoun
Minister of State, Brian Wilson, MP
  Private Secretary, D. Ferguson
Advocate-General for Scotland, Lynda Clark, MP
Head of Office (SCS), I. Gordon

SCOTTISH COURTS ADMINISTRATION
— see page 364–5

SCOTTISH CRIMINAL CASES REVIEW
COMMISSION
5th Floor, Portland House, 17 Renfield Street, Glasgow
G2 5AH
Tel 0141-730 7030; fax 0141-730 7040

The Commission is a non-departmental public body which
started operating on 1 April 1999. It took over from the
Secretary of State for Scotland powers to consider alleged
miscarriages of justice in Scotland and refer cases meeting
the relevant criteria to the Appeal Court for review.
Members are appointed by the First Minister; senior
executive staff are appointed by the Commission.
Chairperson (£360 per day), Prof. Sheila McLean
Members (£210 per day), A. Bonnington; Prof. P. Duff; The
  Very Revd G. Forbes; A. Gallen; Sheriff G. Gordon,
  CBE, QC; W. Taylor, QC
Chief Executive, R. Eadie

SCOTTISH ENTERPRISE
120 Bothwell Street, Glasgow G2 7JP
Tel 0141-248 2700; fax 0141-221 3217

Scottish Enterprise was established in 1991 and its purpose
is to create jobs and prosperity for the people of Scotland.
It is funded largely by the Scottish Executive and is
responsible to the Scottish ministers. Working in partnership with the private and public sectors, Scottish Enterprise
aims to further the development of Scotland's economy, to
enhance the skills of the Scottish workforce and to promote
Scotland's international competitiveness. Through Locate
in Scotland (*see* page 338), Scottish Enterprise is concerned
with attracting firms to Scotland, and through Scottish
Trade International (*see* page 338) it helps Scottish
companies to compete in world export markets. Scottish
Enterprise has a network of 13 Local Enterprise Companies
that deliver economic development services at local level.
Chairman (£31,567), Sir Ian Wood, CBE
Chief Executive, C. Beveridge, CBE

SCOTTISH ENVIRONMENT PROTECTION AGENCY
Erskine Court, The Castle Business Park, Stirling FK9 4TR
Tel 01786-457700; fax 01786-446885

The Scottish Environment Protection Agency came into being on 1 April 1996 under the Environment Act 1995. It is responsible for controlling pollution to land, air and water in Scotland. It receives funding from the Scottish Executive.
Chairman, K. Collins
Chief Executive, A. Paton
Director of Finance, J. Ford
Director of Environmental Strategy, Ms P. Henton
Director, North Region, Prof. D. Mackay
Director, East Region, W. Halcrow
Director, West Region, J. Beveridge

SCOTTISH EXECUTIVE
St Andrew's House, Edinburgh EH1 3DG
Tel 0131-556 8400; fax 0131-244 8240
E-mail: ceu@scotland.gov.uk
Web: http://www.scotland.gov.uk

The Scottish Executive is responsible in Scotland for all matters not reserved to Westminster under devolution, including education, health, social work, law and order, agriculture and the environment.   In addition there are a number of Scottish departments for which the Executive has some degree of responsibility; these include the Scottish Courts Administration, the General Register Office, the National Archives of Scotland (formerly the Scottish Record Office) and the Department of the Registers of Scotland. *See also* Scotland Office and National Assemblies supplement.
First Minister, The Rt. Hon. Donald Dewar, MP, MSP
Deputy First Minister and Minister for Justice, Jim Wallace, QC, MP, MSP
Finance Minister, Jack McConnell, MSP
Minister for Health and Community Care, Susan Deacon, MSP
Minister for Communities, Wendy Alexander, MSP
Minister for Transport and the Environment, Sarah Boyack, MSP
Minister for Enterprise and Lifelong Learning, Henry McLeish, MP, MSP
Minister for Rural Affairs, Ross Finnie, MSP
Minister for Education and Children, Sam Galbraith, MP, MSP
Minister for Parliament and Chief Whip, Tom McCabe, MSP
Lord Advocate, The Lord Hardie, PC, QC

SCOTTISH EXECUTIVE CORPORATE SERVICES
16 Waterloo Place, Edinburgh EH1 3DN
Tel 0131-556 8400
Principal Establishment Officer (SCS), C. C. MacDonald, CB
Head of Personnel (SCS), D. F. Middleton

DIRECTORATE OF ADMINISTRATIVE SERVICES
Saughton House, Broomhouse Drive, Edinburgh EH11 3DX
Tel 0131-556 8400
Director of Administrative Services (SCS), A. M. Brown
Chief Estates Officer, J. A. Andrew
Head of Information Technology (SCS), Ms M. McGinn
Director of Telecommunications, K. Henderson, OBE
Chief Quantity Surveyor (SCS), A. J. Wyllie
James Craig Walk, Edinburgh EH1 3BA
Head of Purchasing and Supplies (SCS), N. Bowd

SCOTTISH EXECUTIVE FINANCE
Victoria Quay, Edinburgh EH6 6QQ
Tel 0131-556 8400
Principal Finance Officer (SCS), Dr P. S. Collings
Assistant Secretaries (SCS), M. T. S. Batho; J. G. Henderson; D. G. N. Reid; W. T. Tait
Head of Accountancy Services Unit, I. M. Smith
Assistant Director of Finance Strategy, I. A. McLeod

SCOTTISH EXECUTIVE SECRETARIAT
St Andrew's House, Regent Road, Edinburgh EH1 3DG
Tel 0131-556 8400
Head of Secretariat, R. S. B. Gordon
Constitutional Policy, J. A. Ewing
Scotland Act Implementation (SCS), W. G. Burgess
Functions and Whitehall Negotiations (SCS), I. N. Walford
Legal Adviser, J. L. Jamieson, CBE

MANAGEMENT GROUP SUPPORT STAFF UNIT
Head of Unit (SCS), P. J. Rycroft

SCOTTISH EXECUTIVE INFORMATION DIRECTORATE
For the Scottish Executive and certain UK services in Scotland
Head of Information Directorate (SCS), R. Williams

SOLICITOR'S OFFICE
For the Scottish Executive
Solicitor (SCS), R. M. Henderson
Deputy Solicitor (SCS), J. S. G. Maclean
Divisional Solicitors (SCS), R. Bland (*seconded to Scottish Law Commission*); G. C. Duke; I. H. Harvie; H. F. Macdiarmid; J. G. S. Maclean; N. Raven; Mrs L. A. Towers

SCOTTISH EXECUTIVE RURAL AFFAIRS DEPARTMENT
Pentland House, 47 Robb's Loan, Edinburgh EH14 1TY
Tel 0131-556 8400
Secretary (SCS), J. S. Graham
Under-Secretaries (SCS), T. A. Cameron (*Agriculture*); S. F. Hampson (*Environment*)
Fisheries Secretary (SCS), Dr P. Brady
Assistant Secretaries (SCS), I. R. Anderson; D. R. Dickson; D. Feeley; Ms I. M. Low; Ms J. Polley; A. J. Rushworth; Dr P. Rycroft; G. M. D. Thomson; J. R. Wildgoose
Chief Agricultural Officer (SCS), A. J. Robertson
Assistant Chief Agricultural Officers, W. A. Aitken; J. Henderson; A. Robb
Chief Agricultural Economist, D. J. Greig
Chief Food and Dairy Officer, S. D. Rooke
Senior Principal Scientific Officers, Mrs L. A. D. Turl; Dr R. Waterhouse

ENVIRONMENTAL AFFAIRS GROUP
Head of Group (SCS), S. F. Hampson
Heads of Divisions (SCS), A. G. Dickson; Ms B. Campbell
Chief Water Engineer, P. Wright
Ecological Adviser, Dr J. Miles

STRATEGY AND CO-ORDINATION UNIT
Head of Unit, A. J. Cameron

EXECUTIVE AGENCIES

FISHERIES RESEARCH SERVICES
Marine Laboratory, PO Box 101, Victoria Road, Aberdeen AB11 9DB
Tel 01224-876544; fax 01224-295511
The Agency provides scientific information and advice on

marine and freshwater fisheries, aquaculture and the protection of the aquatic environment and its wildlife.
Director, Dr A. D. Hawkins
Deputy Director, Dr J. M. Davies

FRESHWATER FISHERIES LABORATORY
Faskally, Pitlochry, Perthshire PH6 5LB
Tel 01796-472060

Senior Principal Scientific Officers, Dr R. M. Cook; Dr J. M. Davies; Dr A. E. Ellis; R. G. J. Shelton; Dr R. Stagg; Dr P. A. Stewart; Dr C. S. Wardle
Inspector of Salmon and Freshwater Fisheries for Scotland, D. A. Dunkley

INTERVENTION BOARD
— *see* page 314

SCOTTISH AGRICULTURAL SCIENCE AGENCY
East Craig, Edinburgh EH12 8NJ
Tel 0131-244 8890; fax 0131-244 8988

The Agency provides scientific information and advice on agricultural and horticultural crops and the environment, and has various statutory and regulatory functions.
Director, Dr R. K. M. Hay
Deputy Director, S. R. Cooper
Senior Principal Scientific Officer, W. J. Rennie

SCOTTISH FISHERIES PROTECTION AGENCY
Pentland House, 47 Robb's Loan, Edinburgh EH14 1TY
Tel 0131-556 8400; fax 0131-244 6086

The Agency enforces fisheries law and regulations in Scottish waters and ports.
Chief Executive, Capt. P. Du Vivier, RN
Director of Corporate Strategy and Resources, J. B. Roddin
Director of Operational Enforcement, R. J. Walker
Marine Superintendent, Capt. W. A. Brown

SCOTTISH EXECUTIVE DEVELOPMENT DEPARTMENT
Victoria Quay, Edinburgh EH6 6QQ
Tel 0131-556 8400

Head of Department (*SCS*), K. MacKenzie
Heads of Groups (*SCS*), D. J. Belfall; J. S. B. Martin
Heads of Divisions (*SCS*), M. T. Affolter; A. M. Burnside; E. C. Davidson; J. D. Gallacher; R. A. Grant; D. S. Henderson; Mrs D. Mellon; W. J. R. McQueen; R. Tait
Senior Economic Adviser (*SCS*), C. L. Wood

PROFESSIONAL STAFF
Chief Planner (*SCS*), A. Mackenzie, CBE
Deputy Chief Architect (*SCS*), Dr J. P. Cornish
Chief Statistician (*SCS*), C. R. MacLean

INQUIRY REPORTERS
Robert Stevenson House, 2 Greenside Lane, Edinburgh EH1 3AG
Tel 0131-244 5680
Chief Reporter (*SCS*), R. M. Hickman
Deputy Chief Reporter (*SCS*), J. M. McCulloch

NATIONAL ROADS DIRECTORATE
Victoria Quay, Edinburgh EH6 6QQ
Tel 0131-556 8400

Deputy Chief Engineers (*SCS*), J. A. Howison (*Roads*); N. B. MacKenzie (*Bridges*)

SCOTTISH EXECUTIVE EDUCATION DEPARTMENT
Victoria Quay, Edinburgh EH6 6QQ
Tel 0131-556 8400

Secretary (*SCS*), J. Elvidge

Under-Secretaries (*SCS*), D. J. Crawley; Mrs G. Stewart
Assistant Secretaries (*SCS*), R. N. Irvine; J. W. L. Lonie; S. Y. MacDonald; A. K. MacLeod; G. McHugh; Mrs R. Menlowe; Ms J. Morgan
Chief Statistician (*SCS*), C. R. MacLean
Chief Architect (*SCS*), J. E. Gibbons, PH.D., FSA Scot.
Chief Inspector of Social Work Services, A. Skinner
Assistant Chief Inspectors, Mrs G. Ottley; D. Pia; I. C. Robertson

HM INSPECTORS OF SCHOOLS
Senior Chief Inspector (*SCS*), D. A. Osler
Depute Senior Chief Inspectors (*SCS*), F. Crawford; G. H. C. Donaldson
Chief Inspectors (*SCS*), P. Banks; J. Boyes; Miss K. M. Fairweather; D. E. Kelso; J. J. McDonald; A. S. McGlynn; H. M. Stalker
There are 79 Grade 6 Inspectors

EXECUTIVE AGENCIES

HISTORIC SCOTLAND
Longmore House, Salisbury Place, Edinburgh EH9 1SH
Tel 0131-668 8600; fax 0131-668 8699

The agency's role is to protect Scotland's historic monuments, buildings and lands, and to promote public understanding and enjoyment of them.
Chief Executive (*G3*), G. N. Munro
Directors (*G5*), F. J. Lawrie; I. Maxwell; B. Naylor; B. O'Neil; L. Wilson
Chief Inspector of Ancient Monuments, Dr D. J. Breeze
Chief Inspector, Historic Buildings, R. Emerson, FSA, FSAScot.

SCOTTISH PUBLIC PENSIONS AGENCY
St Margaret's House, 151 London Road, Edinburgh EH8 7TG
Tel 0131-556 8400; fax 0131-244 3334

The Agency is responsible for the pension arrangements of some 300,000 people, mainly NHS and teaching services employees and pensioners.
Chief Executive, R. Garden
Directors, G. Mowat (*Policy*); A. M. Small (*Operations*); M. J. McDermott (*Resources and Customer Services*)

SCOTTISH EXECUTIVE ENTERPRISE AND LIFELONG LEARNING DEPARTMENT
Victoria Quay, Edinburgh EH6 6QQ
Tel 0131-556 8400

Secretary (*SCS*), E. Frizzell
Under-Secretaries (*SCS*), E. J. Weeple; M. B. Foulis
Assistant Secretaries (*SCS*), C. Smith; J. A. Brown; I. McGhee; D. A. Stewart; G. F. Dickson; C. M. Reeves

INDUSTRIAL EXPANSION
Meridian Court, 5 Cadogan Street, Glasgow G2 6AT
Tel 0141-248 2855

Under-Secretary (*SCS*), G. Robson
Industrial Adviser, D. Blair
Scientific Adviser, Prof. D. J. Tedford
Assistant Secretaries (*SCS*), W. Malone; J. K. Mason; Dr J. Rigg

LOCATE IN SCOTLAND
120 Bothwell Street, Glasgow G2 7JP
Tel 0141-248 2700

Director (*SCS*), M. Togneri

SCOTTISH TRADE INTERNATIONAL
120 Bothwell Street, Glasgow G2 7JP
Tel 0141-248 2700

Director, D. Taylor

EXECUTIVE AGENCY

STUDENT AWARDS AGENCY FOR SCOTLAND
Gyleview House, 3 Redheughs Rigg, Edinburgh EH12 9HH
Tel 0131-476 8212; fax 0131-244 5887
Chief Executive, K. MacRae

SCOTTISH EXECUTIVE HEALTH DEPARTMENT
St Andrew's House, Edinburgh EH1 3DG
Tel 0131-556 8400

NATIONAL HEALTH SERVICE IN SCOTLAND
MANAGEMENT EXECUTIVE
Chief Executive (SCS), G. R. Scaife, CB
Director of Purchasing (SCS), Dr K. J. Woods
Director of Primary Care (SCS), Mrs A. Robson
Director of Finance (SCS), J. Aldridge
Director of Human Resources (SCS), G. Marr
Director of Nursing, Miss A. Jarvie
Director of Community Care, Ms E. Lewis
Medical Director (SCS), Dr A. Fraser
Director of Trusts (SCS), P. Wilson
Director of Information Services, NHS, C. B. Knox
Director of Estates, H. R. McCallum
Chief Pharmacist (SCS), W. Scott
Chief Scientist, Prof. G. R. D. Catto
Chief Dental Officer, T. R. Watkins

PUBLIC HEALTH POLICY UNIT
Head of Unit and Chief Medical Officer (SCS), Prof. Sir David Carter, FRCSE, FRCSGlas., FRCPE
Deputy Chief Medical Officer (SCS), Dr A. Fraser
Head of Group (SCS), Mrs N. Munro
Assistant Secretary (SCS), J. T. Brown
Principal Medical Officers, Dr J. B. Louden *(part-time)*; Dr A. MacDonald *(part-time)*; Dr R. Skinner; Dr E. Sowler
Senior Medical Officers, Dr Angela Anderson; Dr E. Bashford; Dr K. G. Brotherston; Dr D. Campbell; Dr J. Cumming; Dr B. Davis; Dr D. J. Ewing; Dr D. Findlay; Dr G. R. Foster; Dr A. Keel; Dr Patricia Madden; Dr H. Whyte; Dr D. Will

STATE HOSPITAL
Carstairs Junction, Lanark ML11 8RP
Tel 01555-840293
Chairman, D. N. James
General Manager, R. Manson

COMMON SERVICES AGENCY
Trinity Park House, South Trinity Road, Edinburgh EH5 3SE
Tel 0131-552 6255
Chairman, G. R. Scaife, CB
General Manager, Dr F. Gibb

HEALTH BOARDS
— *see* Social Welfare section

SCOTTISH EXECUTIVE JUSTICE DEPARTMENT
Saughton House, Broomhouse Drive, Edinburgh EH11 3XD
Tel 0131-556 8400
Secretary (SCS), J. Hamill, CB
Under-Secretaries (SCS), C. Baxter; N. G. Campbell
Assistant Secretaries (SCS), Mrs M. H. Brannan; Mrs M. B. Gunn; R. S. T. MacEwen
Chief Research Officer, Dr C. P. A. Levein
Senior Principal Research Officer, Mrs A. Millar

SCOTTISH COURTS ADMINISTRATION
— *see* pages 364–5

SOCIAL WORK SERVICES GROUP
James Craig Walk, Edinburgh EH1 3BA
Tel 0131-556 8400
Under-Secretary (SCS), N. G. Campbell
Assistant Secretaries (SCS), G. A. Anderson; Dr J. M. Francis; Mrs V. M. Macniven

OTHER APPOINTMENTS
HM Chief Inspector of Constabulary, W. Taylor, QPM
HM Chief Inspector of Prisons, C. Fairweather, OBE
Commandant, Scottish Police College, H. I. Watson, OBE, QPM
HM Chief Inspector of Fire Services, D. Davis, CBE, QFSM
Commandant, Scottish Fire Service Training School, D. Grant, QFSM

OFFICE OF THE SCOTTISH PARLIAMENTARY COUNSEL
Victoria Quay, Edinburgh EH6 6QQ
Tel 0131-556 8400

First Scottish Parliamentary Counsel, J. C. McCluskie, CB, QC
Scottish Parliamentary Counsel, G. M. Clark; C. A. M. Wilson
Depute Scottish Parliamentary Counsel, J. D. Harkness; Miss M. Mackenzie
Assistant Scottish Parliamentary Counsel, A. C. Gordon

PRIVATE LEGISLATION OFFICE UNDER THE PRIVATE LEGISLATION PROCEDURE (SCOTLAND) ACT 1936
50 Frederick Street, Edinburgh EH2 1EN
Tel 0131-226 6499

Senior Counsel, G. S. Douglas, QC
Junior Counsel, N. M. P. Morrison

EXECUTIVE AGENCIES

NATIONAL ARCHIVES OF SCOTLAND
— *see* page 334

REGISTERS OF SCOTLAND
— *see* page 315

SCOTTISH PRISON SERVICE
— *see* pages 382–3

GENERAL REGISTER OFFICE FOR SCOTLAND
New Register House, Edinburgh EH1 3YT
Tel 0131-334 0380; fax 0131-314 4400

The General Register Office for Scotland is a department forming part of the Scottish Executive. It is the office of the Registrar-General for Scotland, who has responsibility for civil registration and the taking of censuses in Scotland and has in his custody the following records: the statutory registers of births, deaths, still births, adoptions, marriages and divorces; the old parish registers (recording births, deaths and marriages, etc., before civil registration began in 1855); and records of censuses of the population in Scotland. Hours of public access: Monday–Friday 9–4.30.
Registrar-General (SCS), J. N. Randall
Deputy Registrar-General, B. V. Philp
Census Manager, D. A. Orr
Heads of Branches, D. B. L. Brownlee; R. C. Lawson; F. D. Garvie; G. Compton; G. W. L. Jackson; F. G. Thomas

MENTAL WELFARE COMMISSION FOR SCOTLAND
K Floor, Argyle House, 3 Lady Lawson Street, Edinburgh EH3 9SH
Tel 0131-222 6111

Chairman, Sir William Reid, KCB
Vice-Chairman, Mrs N. Bennie
Commissioners (part-time), C. Campbell, QC; Mrs F. Cotter;
W. Gent; Dr P. Jauhar; Dr Shainool Jiwa; Dr
Elizabeth McCall-Smith; D. J. Macdonald; Dr J.
Morrow; M. D. Murray; Dr Linda Pollock; A. Robb;
Mrs M. Ross; Dr Margaret Thomas; Dr M. Whoriskey
Director, Dr J. A. T. Dyer

SCOTTISH HOMES
Thistle House, 91 Haymarket Terrace, Edinburgh
EH12 5HE
Tel 0131-313 0044; fax 0131-313 2680

Scottish Homes, the national housing agency for Scotland,
aims to improve the quality and variety of housing available
in Scotland by working in partnership with the public and
private sectors. The agency is a major funder of new and
improved housing provided by housing associations and
private developers. It is currently transferring its own
rented houses to alternative landlords. It is also involved in
housing research. Board members are appointed by the
First Minister.
Chairman, J. Ward, CBE
Chief Executive, P. McKinlay, CBE

SCOTTISH NATURAL HERITAGE
12 Hope Terrace, Edinburgh EH9 2AS
Tel 0131-447 4784; fax 0131-446 2277

Scottish Natural Heritage was established in 1992 under
the Natural Heritage (Scotland) Act 1991. It provides
advice on nature conservation to all those whose activities
affect wildlife, landforms and features of geological interest
in Scotland, and seeks to develop and improve facilities for
the enjoyment and understanding of the Scottish countryside. It is funded by the Scottish Executive.
Chairman, Dr J. Markland, CBE
Chief Executive, R. Crofts
Chief Scientific Adviser, M. B. Usher
Directors of Operations, J. Thomson (*West*); I. Jardine (*East*); J.
Watson (*North*)
Director of Corporate Services, vacant

SCOTTISH OFFICE (former)
— *see* Scotland Office

SCOTTISH PARLIAMENTARY
COMMISSIONER FOR ADMINISTRATION
28 Thistle Street, Edinburgh EH2 1EN
Tel 0845-601 0456; fax 0131-226 4447

The Scottish Parliamentary Commissioner for Administration was appointed in July 1999 to investigate complaints
made to him by Members of the Scottish Parliament on
behalf of members of the public who have suffered an
injustice through maladministration by the Scottish Executive and a wide range of public bodies involved in
devolved Scottish affairs.
Scottish Parliamentary Commissioner for Administration, M. S.
Buckley

SCOTTISH PRISONS COMPLAINTS
COMMISSION
Government Buildings, Broomhouse Drive, Edinburgh
EH11 3XD
Tel 0131-244 8423; fax 0131-244 8430

The Commission was established in 1994. It is an
independent body to which prisoners in Scottish prisons
can make application in relation to any matter where they
have failed to obtain satisfaction from the Prison Service's
internal grievance procedures. Clinical judgments made by
medical officers, matters which are the subject of legal
proceedings and matters relating to sentence, conviction
and parole decision-making are excluded from the Commission's jurisdiction. The Commissioner is appointed by
the First Minister.
Commissioner, Dr J. McManus

SEA FISH INDUSTRY AUTHORITY
18 Logie Mill, Logie Green Road, Edinburgh EH7 4HG
Tel 0131-558 3331; fax 0131-558 1442

Established under the Fisheries Act 1981, the Authority is
required to promote the efficiency of the sea fish industry.
It carries out research relating to the industry and gives
advice on related matters. It provides training, promotes
the marketing, consumption and export of sea fish and sea
fish products, and may provide financial assistance for the
improvement of fishing vessels in respect of essential safety
equipment. It is responsible to the Ministry of Agriculture,
Fisheries and Food.
Chairman, E. Davey
Chief Executive, A. C. Fairbairn

THE SECURITY AND INTELLIGENCE
SERVICES

Under the Intelligence Services Act 1994, the Intelligence
and Security Committee of Parliamentarians was established to oversee the work of GCHQ, MI5 and MI6; in
1999 an Investigator was appointed to the committee in
order to reinforce the authority of its findings and establish
public confidence in the oversight system. The Act also
established the Intelligence Services Tribunal (*see* pages
312–3), which hears complaints made against GCHQ and
MI6. The Security Service Tribunal and Commissioner
(*see* below) investigate complaints about MI5.

DEFENCE INTELLIGENCE STAFF
— *see* Defence section

GOVERNMENT COMMUNICATIONS
HEADQUARTERS (GCHQ)
Priors Road, Cheltenham, Glos GL52 5AJ
Tel 01242-221491; fax 01242-226816

GCHQ produces signals intelligence in support of national
security and the UK's economic wellbeing, and in the
prevention or detection of serious crime. It also provides
advice and assistance to government departments, the
armed forces and other national infrastructure bodies on
the security of their communications and information
systems. It was placed on a statutory footing by the
Intelligence Services Act 1994 and is headed by a director
who is directly accountable to the Foreign Secretary.
Director, F. N. Richards, CVO, CMG

NATIONAL CRIMINAL INTELLIGENCE SERVICE
PO Box 8000, London SEII 5EN
Tel: 0171-238 8000

The National Criminal Intelligence Service (NCIS) provides intelligence about serious and organized crime to law enforcement, government and other relevant national and international agencies. On 1 April 1998 NCIS was placed on a statutory footing. It is accountable to the NCIS Service Authority.

Director-General, J. Abbott, QPM
Deputy Director-General (Director (Intelligence)),
R. Gaspar, QPM
Director, International Division, N. Bailey
Director, UK Division, V. Harvey
Director, Resources Division, J. Bamfield

SERVICE AUTHORITY
PO Box 2600, London SWIV 2WG
Tel: 0171-238 2600

The Service Authority for NCIS is responsible for ensuring its effective operation. It operates with the Service Authority for the National Crime Squad (*see* page 374). There are 26 members of the authorities, of whom the chairman and nine others serve as 'core members' on both authorities.

Chairman, Rt. Hon. Sir John Wheeler
Clerk, T. Simmons
Treasurer, P. Derrick

THE SECRET INTELLIGENCE SERVICE (MI6)
PO Box 1300, London SEI IBD

The Secret Intelligence Service produces secret intelligence in support of the Government's security, defence, foreign and economic policies. It was placed on a statutory footing by the Intelligence Services Act 1994 and is headed by a chief, known as 'C', who is directly accountable to the Foreign Secretary.

Chief, R. B. Dearlove, OBE

THE SECURITY SERVICE (MI5)
Thames House, PO Box 3255, London SWIP IAE
Tel 0171-930 9000

The function of the Security Service is the protection of national security, in particular against threats from espionage, terrorism, sabotage and the proliferation of weapons of mass destruction, from the activities of agents of foreign powers, and from actions intended to overthrow or undermine parliamentary democracy by political, industrial or violent means. It is also the Service's function to safeguard the economic well-being of the UK against threats posed by the actions or intentions of persons outside the British Islands. Under the Security Service Act 1996, the Service's role was extended to support the police and customs in the prevention and detection of serious crime.

The Security Service was placed on a statutory footing by the Security Service Act 1989 and is headed by a director-general who is directly accountable to the Home Secretary.

Director-General, S. Lander

SECURITY SERVICE COMMISSIONER
c/o PO Box 18, London SEI OTZ
Tel 0171-273 4095

The Commissioner is appointed by the Prime Minister. He keeps under review the issue of warrants by the Home Secretary under the Intelligence Services Act 1994, and is required to help the Security Service Tribunal by investigating complaints which allege interference with property and by offering all such assistance in discharging its functions as it may require. He is also required to submit an annual report on the discharge of his functions to the Prime Minister.

Commissioner, The Rt. Hon. Lord Justice Stuart-Smith
Private Secretary, N. R. Brooks

SECURITY SERVICE TRIBUNAL
PO Box 18, London SEI OTZ
Tel 0171-273 4095

The Security Service Act 1989 established a tribunal of three to five senior members of the legal profession, independent of the Government and appointed by The Queen, to investigate complaints from any person about anything which they believe the Security Service has done to them or to their property.

President, The Rt. Hon. Lord Justice Simon Brown
Vice-President, Sheriff J. McInnes, QC
Member, Sir Richard Gaskell
Secretary, N. R. Brooks

SENTENCE REVIEW COMMISSIONERS
PO Box 1011, Belfast BT2 7SR
Tel 01232-549412; fax 01232-549427

The Sentence Review Commissioners are appointed by the Secretary of State for Northern Ireland to consider applications from prisoners serving sentences in Northern Ireland for declarations that they are entitled to early release in accordance with the provisions of the Northern Ireland (Sentences) Act 1998. The commissioners have been appointed until 31 July 2000 and are served by staff seconded from the Northern Ireland Office.

Joint Chairmen, Sir John Belloch, KCB; B. Currin
Commissioners, Dr Silvia Casale; Dr P. Curran; I. Dunbar, CB; Mrs M. Gilpin; Dr A. Grounds; Ms C. McGrory; Dr D. Morrow; D. Wall
Secretary (SCS)

SERIOUS FRAUD OFFICE
Elm House, 10–16 Elm Street, London WCIX OBJ
Tel 0171-239 7272; fax 0171-837 1689

The Serious Fraud Office works under the superintendence of the Attorney-General. Its remit is to investigate and prosecute serious and complex fraud. (Other fraud cases are handled by the fraud divisions of the Crown Prosecution Service.) The scope of its powers covers England, Wales and Northern Ireland. The staff includes lawyers, accountants and other support staff; investigating teams work closely with the police.

Director, Mrs R. Wright

DEPARTMENT OF SOCIAL SECURITY
Richmond House, 79 Whitehall, London SWIA 2NS
Tel 0171-238 0800

The Department of Social Security (DSS) is responsible for the payment of benefits including child benefit, one-parent benefit, income support and family credit. It administers the Social Fund, and is responsible for assessing the means of applicants for legal aid. It is also responsible for the payment of war pensions and the operation of the child maintenance system. Responsibility for the operation of the national insurance contributions scheme was transferred from the DSS to the Inland Revenue in April 1999.

Secretary of State for Social Security, The Rt. Hon. Alistair Darling, MP
    Principal Private Secretary, R. Clark
    Special Advisers, J. McTernan; A. Maugham
    Parliamentary Private Secretary, Ms A. Coffey, MP
Minister of State, Jeff Rooker, MP
    Private Secretary, D. Higlett
Parliamentary Under-Secretaries of State, The Baroness Hollis of Heigham, D.Phil. (*Family Policy, Child Benefit, Child Support, War Pensions*); Angela Eagle, MP (*Income-related Benefits, International and Green Issues*); Hugh Bayley, MP (*Disability and Sickness Benefits, Deregulation, Independent Living Fund*)
    Private Secretaries, B. Stayte; D. Topping; Ms V. Hutchinson; Ms H. McCarthy; R. Sanguinaza; Ms L. Wright
Permanent Secretary (*SCS*), Ms R. Lomax
    Private Secretary, C. Jackson

CORPORATE MANAGEMENT GROUP
Director (*SCS*), J. Tross

PERSONNEL AND HQ SUPPORT SERVICES DIRECTORATE
Director, S. Hewitt
Section Heads (*SCS*), T. Perl; (*G7*), R. Yeats; B. Glew; J. Elliott

ANALYTICAL SERVICES DIVISION
The Adelphi, 1–11 John Adam Street, London WC2N 6HT
Tel 0171-962 8000

Director (*SCS*), D. Stanton
Chief Statistician (*SCS*), N. Dyson
Senior Economic Advisers (*SCS*), J. Ball; G. Harris; R. D'Souza
Deputy Chief Scientific Officer (*SCS*), D. Barnbrook
Chief Research Officers (*SCS*), Ms S. Duncan; S. Rice

FINANCE DIVISION
Grade 3, S. Lord

INFORMATION DIRECTORATE
Director of Information (*SCS*), S. MacDowall
Deputy Head of Information (*G6*), J. Bretherton
Chief Press Officer (*G7*), Ms S. Lewis
Chief Publicity Officer (*G7*), Mrs A. Hall

SOCIAL SECURITY POLICY GROUP
Head of Policy Group (*SCS*), P. R. C. Gray
Policy Directors (*SCS*), M. Cayley; Miss M. Peirson, CB; D. Brereton; U. Brennan
Policy Managers (*SCS*), L. Richards; C. Ramsden; B. O'Gorman; M. Street; J. Groombridge; Mrs C. Rookes; B. Calderwood; D. Allsop, CBE; C. Evans; J. Hughes; P. Cleasby; P. Morgan; Mrs L. Richards; Ms J. Shersby; (*G6*), B. Layton; I. Williams; P. Barrett; J. Griffiths-Chayes; K. Sadler; N. Ward

SOLICITOR'S OFFICE
Solicitor (*SCS*), Mrs M. A. Morgan, CB

SOLICITOR'S DIVISION A
New Court, 48 Carey Street, London WC2A 2LS
Tel 0171-412 1466
Principal Assistant Solicitor (*SCS*), J. A. Catlin

Assistant Solicitors (*SCS*), J. M. Swainson; Mrs G. Massiah; Mrs F. A. Logan; C. Cooper; H. Connell; P. Milledge

SOLICITOR'S DIVISION B
New Court, 48 Carey Street, London WC2A 2LS
Tel 0171-412 1528
Solicitor (*SCS*), Mrs M. A. Morgan, CB
Assistant Solicitors (*SCS*), R. G. S. Aitken; Ms S. Edwards; S. Cooper

SOLICITOR'S DIVISION C
New Court, 48 Carey Street, London WC2A 2LS
Tel 0171-412 1342
Principal Assistant Solicitor (*SCS*), Mrs G. S. Kerrigan
Assistant Solicitors (*SCS*), R. J. Dormer; Miss M. E. Trefgarne; Mrs S. Walker; G. Aitkin

BENEFITS FRAUD INSPECTORATE
Berkeley House, 12A North Park Road, Harrogate HG1 5QA
Tel 01423-832922
Director-General (*SCS*), C. Bull

EXECUTIVE AGENCIES
APPEALS SERVICE AGENCY
— *see* Tribunals

BENEFITS AGENCY
Quarry House, Quarry Hill, Leeds LS2 7UA
Tel 0113-232 4000

The Agency administers claims for and payments of social security benefits.
Chief Executive, P. Mathison
    Private Secretary, R. Baldwin
Directors, J. Codling (*Finance*); M. Fisher (*Personnel and Communications*); S. Heminsley (*Strategic and Planning*); A. Cleveland (*Operations Support*); N. Haighton (*Projects*)
Medical Policy
Principal Medical Officers, Dr M. Aylward; Dr P. Dewis; Dr P. Sawney; Dr A. Braidwood; Dr P. Stidolph

CHILD SUPPORT AGENCY
DSS Long Benton, Benton Park Road, Newcastle upon Tyne NE98 1YX
Tel 0191-213 5000

The Agency was set up in April 1993. It is responsible for the administration of the Child Support Act and for the assessment, collection and enforcement of maintenance payments for all new cases.
Chief Executive, Ms F. Boardman
Directors, M. Davison; C. Peters; M. Isaacs; T. Read

INFORMATION TECHNOLOGY SERVICES AGENCY
4th Floor, Verulam Point, Station Way, St Albans, Herts AL1 5HE
Tel 01727-815835; fax 01727-833740

The Agency maintains and oversees policies on information technology strategy, procurement, technical standards and security.
Chief Executive, G. McCorkell
Directors, J. Thomas; J. Brewood; G. Brown; B. Barnes; B. Gormley; J. Delamere; C. Nicholls
Non-Executive Directors, K. Pfotzer; K. Bogg

WAR PENSIONS AGENCY
Norcross, Blackpool, Lancs FY5 3WP
Tel 01253-856123

The Agency administers the payment of war disablement and war widows' pensions and provides welfare services

and support to war disablement pensioners, war widows and their dependants and carers.
Chief Executive, G. Hextall

Central Advisory Committee on War Pensions
6th Floor, The Adelphi, 1–11 John Adam Street, London WC2N 6HT
Tel 0171-962 8062
Secretary, C. Pike

ADVISORY BODIES

NATIONAL DISABILITY COUNCIL, Level 4, Caxton House, Tothill Street, London SW1H 9NA. Tel: 0171-273 5636. *Chairman,* D. Grayson, OBE; *Secretary,* R. Timm
SOCIAL SECURITY ADVISORY COMMITTEE, New Court, Carey Street, London WC2A 2LS. Tel 0171-412 1508. *Chairman,* Lt.-Gen. Sir Thomas Boyd-Carpenter, KBE; *Secretary,* Ms G. Saunders

SPORTS COUNCIL
— *see* United Kingdom Sports Council

OFFICE FOR STANDARDS IN EDUCATION (OFSTED)
Alexandra House, 33 Kingsway, London WC2B 6SE
Tel 0171-421 6800; fax 0171-421 6707

The Office is a non-ministerial government department established in 1992 to keep the Secretary of State and the public informed about the standards and management of schools in England, and to establish and monitor an independent inspection system for maintained schools in England. *See also* Education section.
HM Chief Inspector, C. Woodhead
Directors of Inspection, M.J. Tomlinson, CBE; D. Taylor
Director of Policy, Planning and Resources, Miss J. M. Phillips, CBE

DIVISION MANAGERS

Personnel Management, C. Payne
Contracts, C. Bramley
Communications, Media and Public Relations, J. Lawson
Information Systems, M. Worthy
Administrative Support and Estate Management, K. Francis
Inspection Quality, P. Matthews
LEA Reviews, Reorganization Proposals, D. Singleton
School Improvement, Ms E. Passmore, OBE
Nursery and Primary, K. Lloyd
Secondary and Independent, vacant
Post-Compulsory, D. West
Special Educational Needs, C. Marshall
Research, Analysis and International, Ms C. Agambar
Teacher Education and Training, C. Gould
Nursery Education Scheme, D. Bradley
Subject Specialist Advisers, N. Bufton; B. Ponchaud; A. Dobson; M. Ive; P. Smith; Ms J. Mills; G. Clay; P. Jones; J. Hertrich; Ms B. Wintersgill; S. Harrison
There are about 200 HM Inspectors

COMMITTEE ON STANDARDS IN PUBLIC LIFE
Horse Guards Road, London SW1P 3AL
Tel 0171-270 5875; fax 0171-270 5874

The Committee on Standards in Public Life was set up in October 1994. It is a standing body whose chairman and members are appointed by the Prime Minister; three members are nominated by the leaders of the three main political parties. The committee's remit is to examine concerns about standards of conduct of all holders of public office, including arrangements relating to financial and commercial activities, and to make recommendations as to any changes in present arrangements which might be required to ensure the highest standards of propriety in public life. It is also charged with reviewing issues in relation to the funding of political parties. The committee does not investigate individual allegations of misconduct.
Chairman, The Lord Neill of Bladen, QC
Members, Sir Clifford Boulton, GCB; Prof. Alice Brown; Sir Anthony Cleaver; The Lord Goodhart, QC; Ms F. Heaton; Prof. A. King; The Rt. Hon. J. MacGregor, OBE, MP; The Lord Shore of Stepney, PC; Sir William Utting, CB; Ms D. Warwick
Secretary (SCS), Mrs S. Tyerman

STRATEGIC RAIL AUTHORITY (SHADOW)
— *see* British Railways Board

OFFICE OF TELECOMMUNICATIONS
50 Ludgate Hill, London EC4M 7JJ
Tel 0171-634 8700; fax 0171- 634 8943

The Office of Telecommunications (Oftel) is a non-ministerial government department responsible for supervising telecommunications activities and broadcast transmission in the UK. Its goal is to achieve the best deal for UK telecommunications customers in terms of quality, choice and value for money. It is responsible for ensuring that holders of telecommunications licences comply with their licence conditions and for maintaining and promoting effective competition in telecommunications.
The Director-General has powers to deal with anti-competitive practices and monopolies. He also has a duty to consider all reasonable complaints and representations about telecommunication apparatus and services.
Director-General, D. Edmonds
Director of Operations, Miss A. Lambert
Director of Regulatory Policy, Mrs A. Taylor
Director of Compliance, Mrs J. Whittles
Director of Technology, P. Walker
Director of Strategy and Forecasting, A. Bell
Director of Business Support, D. Smith
Director of Communications, D. Stroud

TOURIST BOARDS
(For British Tourist Authority, *see* page 285)

The English Tourism Council, the Scottish Tourist Board, the Wales Tourist Board and the Northern Ireland Tourist Board are responsible for developing and marketing the tourist industry in their respective countries.
ENGLISH TOURISM COUNCIL, Thames Tower, Black's Road, London W6 9EL. Tel: 0181-846 9000. *Chief Executive* (*acting*), Ms E. Noble
SCOTTISH TOURIST BOARD, 23 Ravelston Terrace, Edinburgh EH4 3EU. Tel: 0131-332 2433; Thistle House, Beechwood Park North, Inverness IV2 3ED. Tel: 01463-716996. *Chief Executive,* T. Buncle
WALES TOURIST BOARD, Brunel House, 2 Fitzalan Road, Cardiff CF2 1UY. Tel: 01222-475272. *Chief Executive,* J. Jones

NORTHERN IRELAND TOURIST BOARD, St Anne's Court, 59 North Street, Belfast BT1 INB. Tel: 01232-231221. *Chief Executive*, I. Henderson

---

DEPARTMENT OF TRADE AND INDUSTRY

1 Victoria Street, London SW1H 0ET
Tel 0171-215 5000; fax 0171-222 2629
Web: http://www.dti.gov.uk

The Department is responsible for international trade policy, including the promotion of UK trade interests in the European Union, GATT, OECD, UNCTAD and other international organizations; the promotion of UK exports and assistance to exporters; policy in relation to industry and commerce, including industrial relations policy; policy towards small firms; regional industrial assistance; legislation and policy in relation to the Post Office; competition policy and consumer protection; the development of national policies in relation to all forms of energy and the development of new sources of energy, including international aspects of energy policy; policy on science and technology research and development; space policy; standards, quality and design; and company legislation.

Secretary of State for Trade and Industry, The
Rt. Hon. Stephen Byers, MP
Principal Private Secretary, A. Phillipson
Private Secretaries, C. Woolard; E. Barker
Minister of State, The Rt. Hon. Helen Liddell, MP (*Energy, Competitiveness in Europe*)
Minister of State, The Rt. Hon. Richard Caborn, MP (*Trade*)
Minister of State, Patricia Hewitt, MP
Parliamentary Under-Secretaries of State, Dr Kim Howells, MP (*Competition, Consumer Affairs*); Alan Johnson, MP (*Employment Relations, the Post Office, Industry*); The Lord Sainsbury of Turville (*Science*)
Private Secretaries, Ms D. Parr; Ms P. Ciniewicz; S. Evans
Parliamentary Clerk, T. Williams
Permanent Secretary, Sir Michael Scholar, KCB
Private Secretary, Ms J. Dav
Chief Scientific Adviser and Head of Office of Science and Technology, Sir Robert May, FRS
Private Secretary, R. Clay
British Trade International Chief Executive, Sir David Wright, KCMG, LVO
Directors-General, Dr J. Taylor, OBE, FREng., FRS (*Director-General of the Research Councils*); A. Hutton, CB (*Trade Policy*); D. Durie, CMG (*Enterprise and Regions*); Dr C. Bell (*Corporate and Consumer Affairs*); D. Nissen, CB (*The Solicitor*); Ms A. Walker (*Energy*); J. Spencer (*Resources and Services*); A. Macdonald, CB (*Industry*)

DIVISIONAL ORGANIZATION

†BRITISH NATIONAL SPACE CENTRE
Director-General (*SCS*), D. R. Davis
Deputy Director-General (*SCS*), D. Leadbeater
Directors (*SCS*), A. Cooper; Dr P. Murdin; Dr D. Lumley

BUSINESS LINK DIRECTORATE
Director of Business Link (*SCS*), P. Waller
Directors (*SCS*), P. Bentley; Mrs P. Jackson; T. Evans; Ms H. Merrifield

CENTRAL DIRECTORATE
Director of Competitiveness Unit (*SCS*), D. Evans
Directors (*SCS*), Ms S. Chambers; J. Reynolds

†CHEMICALS AND BIOTECHNOLOGY DIRECTORATE

Director of Chemicals and Biotechnology (*SCS*), M. Baker
Directors (*SCS*), Ms G. Alliston; Ms M. Darnbrough

COMMUNICATIONS DIRECTORATE
Director of News (*SCS*), M. Tee
Director of Publicity and Internal Communications (*SCS*), P. Burke

†COMMUNICATIONS AND INFORMATION INDUSTRIES DIRECTORATE
Director of Communications and Information Industries (*SCS*), W. MacIntyre
Directors (*SCS*), N. Worman; D. Lumley; D. Love; C. Holmes; P. Williams; S. Price

COMPANY LAW AND INVESTIGATIONS DIRECTORATE
Director of Company Law and Investigations (*SCS*), R. Rogers
Directors (*SCS*), J. Grewe; G. Harp; J. Gardner; J. Sibley; R. Burns; Ms B. Chase; A. Robertshaw

COMPETITION POLICY AND UTILITIES REVIEW TEAM
Director of Team (*SCS*), Ms R. Anderson
Directors (*SCS*), Dr A. Eggington; D. Miner; J. May; R. Bent

CONSUMER AFFAIRS DIRECTORATE
Director of Consumer Affairs (*SCS*), S. Haddrill
Directors (*SCS*), P. Mason; Ms J. Munday; H. Ewing; A. Willcocks

CONSUMER GOODS, BUSINESS AND POSTAL SERVICES DIRECTORATE
Director of Consumer Goods, Business and Postal Services (*SCS*), M. Baker
Directors (*SCS*), B. Hopson; Ms J. Britton

ECONOMICS AND STATISTICS DIRECTORATE
Chief Economic Adviser (*SCS*), D. R. Coates
Directors (*SCS*), K. Warwick; Ms J. Dougharty; M. Bradbury

EMPLOYMENT RELATIONS DIRECTORATE
Director of Industrial Relations (*SCS*), P. Salvidge
Directors (*SCS*), Dr E. Baker; R. Niblett; Ms N. Carter; K. Masson; M. Beatson

ENERGY POLICY, ANALYSIS, TECHNOLOGY AND COAL DIRECTORATE
Director of Energy Policy, Analysis, Technology and Coal (*SCS*), N. Hirst
Directors (*SCS*), G. C. White; N. Peace; G. Bevan; M. Atkinson; A. Wright

†ENGINEERING INDUSTRIES DIRECTORATE
Director of Engineering Industries (*SCS*), M. O'Shea
Directors (*SCS*), J. Neilson; M. Ralph; R. Kingcombe; H. Brown; R. Poole; A. Vinall; Ms A. Wilks

ENGINEERING INSPECTORATE
Director of Engineering Inspectorate (*SCS*), Dr P. Fenwick

†ENVIRONMENT DIRECTORATE
Director of Environment (*SCS*), Dr C. Hicks
Director (*SCS*), D. Prior

†ESTATES AND FACILITIES MANAGEMENT DIRECTORATE
Director (*SCS*), M. Coolican

EUROPEAN POLICY DIRECTORATE
Kingsgate House, 66–74 Victoria Street, London SW1E 6SW
Director (*SCS*), N. McMillan, CMG

EXPORT CONTROL AND NON-PROLIFERATION DIRECTORATE
Kingsgate House, 66–74 Victoria Street, London SW1E 6SW

Director of Export Control and Non-Proliferation (*SCS*), Dr R. Heathcote
Directors (*SCS*), J. Neve; S. Haird

EXPORT PROMOTION DIRECTORATES
Kingsgate House, 66–74 Victoria Street, London SW1E 6SW

Director, Markets and Sectors (*SCS*), M. Gibson
Directors (*SCS*), M. Mowlam (*The Americas*); M. Cohen (*Asia Pacific*); K. Levinson (*Central and Eastern Europe*); S. Lyle Smythe (*Business in Europe*); M. Khan (*Middle East, Near East and North Africa*); V. Fean (*Sub-Saharan Africa and South Asia*); R. Lamb (*Sectors, Services and Outward Investment*)

EXPORT SERVICES DIRECTORATE
Kingsgate House, 66–74 Victoria Street, London SW1E 6SW

Director (*SCS*), A. Reynolds

FINANCE AND RESOURCE MANAGEMENT DIRECTORATE
Director of Finance and Resource Management (*SCS*), J. Phillips
Directors (*SCS*), E. Hosker; K. Hills; N. Nandra; H. Savill

†INDUSTRY ECONOMICS AND STATISTICS DIRECTORATE
Director (*SCS*), Dr N. Owen

†INFORMATION MANAGEMENT AND PROCESS ENGINEERING DIRECTORATE
Director (*SCS*), R. Wheeler

INFRASTRUCTURE AND ENERGY PROJECTS DIRECTORATE
Director of Infrastructure and Energy Projects (*SCS*), J. Rhodes
Directors (*SCS*), G. Atkinson; Dr K. Forrest; B. Gallagher; J. Campbell

†INNOVATION POLICY AND STANDARDS DIRECTORATE
Director of Innovation Policy and Standards (*SCS*), R. Foster
Directors (*SCS*), J. M. Barber; J. Hobday; D. Reed; P. Bunn

†INNOVATION UNIT
Director (*SCS*), Dr A. Keddie

†INTERNAL AUDIT DIRECTORATE
Director of Internal Audit (*SCS*), R. Louth

INTERNATIONAL ECONOMICS DIRECTORATE
Kingsgate House, 66–74 Victoria Street, London SW1E 6SW

Director (*SCS*), C. Moir

INVEST IN BRITAIN BUREAU (FCO/DTI)
Chief Executive (*SCS*), A. Fraser

JOINT EXPORT PROMOTION DIRECTORATE (FCO/DTI)
Kingsgate House, 66–74 Victoria Street, London SW1E 6SW

Director (*SCS*), D. Hall, CMG

LEGAL RESOURCE MANAGEMENT AND BUSINESS LAW UNIT
10 Victoria Street, London SW1H 0NN

The Solicitor and Director-General (*SCS*), D. Nissen, CB
Director (*SCS*), P. Burke

LEGAL SERVICES DIRECTORATE A
10 Victoria Street, London SW1H 0NN

Director of Legal A (*SCS*), J. Stanley
Legal Directors (*SCS*), J. Roberts; Miss N. O'Flynn; S. Hyett; Miss G. Richmond

LEGAL SERVICES DIRECTORATE B
10 Victoria Street, London SW1H 0NN

Director of Legal B (*SCS*), P. Bovey
Legal Directors (*SCS*), R. Baker; B. Welch; R. Perkins; Ms S. Hardy; C. Raikes; Ms N. Arora

LEGAL SERVICES DIRECTORATE C
10 Victoria Street, London SW1H 0NN

Director of Legal C (*SCS*), Ms A. Brett-Holt
Legal Directors (*SCS*), M. Bucknill; A. Woods; C. Osborne; T. Susman

LEGAL SERVICES DIRECTORATE D
10 Victoria Street, London SW1H 0NN

Director of Legal D (*SCS*), Mrs T. Dunstan
Directors (*SCS*), S. Milligan; L. Nawbatt

MANAGEMENT BEST PRACTICE
Director of Management Best Practice, Dr K. Poulter
Deputy Director (*SCS*), Dr I. Harrison

NEW ISSUES AND DEVELOPING COUNTRIES
Kingsgate House, 66–74 Victoria Street, London SW1E 6SW

Director (*SCS*), C. Bridge

NUCLEAR INDUSTRIES DIRECTORATE
Director of Nuclear Industries (*SCS*), H. Leiser
Directors (*SCS*), Dr M. Draper; Dr E. Drage; I. Downing; S. Bowen; D. Walker

OFFICE OF SCIENCE AND TECHNOLOGY: SCIENCE AND ENGINEERING BASE DIRECTORATE
Albany House, 84–86 Petty France, London SW1H 9ST

Director, Science and Engineering Base (*SCS*), A. Quigley
Directors (*SCS*), Ms F. Price; Dr K. Root

OFFICE OF SCIENCE AND TECHNOLOGY: TRANSDEPARTMENTAL SCIENCE AND TECHNOLOGY DIRECTORATE
Albany House, 84–86 Petty France, London SW1H 9ST

Director, Transdepartmental Science and Technology (*SCS*), Ms J. Durning
Directors (*SCS*), S. Spivey; Mrs P. Sellers; M. Parker; Ms J. Darrell

OIL AND GAS DIRECTORATE
1 Victoria Street, London SW1H 0ET

Director of Oil and Gas (*SCS*), G. Dart
Directors (*SCS*), J. R. V. Brooks, CBE; G. Riggs; S. Toole; M. Graham

Atholl House, 86–88 Guild Street, Aberdeen AB11 6AR
Tel 01224-254059

Director of Oil and Gas (*SCS*), S. Toole

REGIONAL ASSISTANCE DIRECTORATE
Director of Regional Assistance (*SCS*), A. Steele
Director (*SCS*), S. Robins

REGIONAL EUROPEAN FUNDS DIRECTORATE
Director (*SCS*), vacant

REGIONAL POLICY DIRECTORATE
Director (*SCS*), D. Smith

SENIOR STAFF MANAGEMENT DIRECTORATE
Director (*SCS*), Ms K. Elliott

SMALL AND MEDIUM-SIZED ENTERPRISES (SME) POLICY DIRECTORATE
Director (*SCS*), C. Johnston

SMALL AND MEDIUM-SIZED ENTERPRISES (SME) TECHNOLOGY DIRECTORATE
Director (*SCS*), R. Allpress

STAFF PERSONNEL OPERATIONS DIRECTORATE
Director (*SCS*), R. Wright

---

† At 151 Buckingham Palace Road, London SW1W 9SS

STAFF POLICY AND PAY DIRECTORATE
Director (SCS), Ms B. Habberjam

TRADE FACILITATION AND IMPORT POLICY
DIRECTORATE
Kingsgate House, 66–74 Victoria Street, London SW1E 6SW
Director (SCS), A. Berry

TRADE POLICY DIRECTORATE
Kingsgate House, 66–74 Victoria Street, London SW1E 6SW
Director (SCS), J. Hunt

BRITISH TRADE INTERNATIONAL
Kingsgate House, 66–74 Victoria Street, London SW1E 6SW
Tel 0171-215 5000

British Trade International replaced the British Overseas Trade Board in June 1999. It is responsible for international trade promotion and development.
Chairmen, Brian Wilson, MP (*Minister for Trade, DTI*);
  Geoffrey Hoon, MP (*Minister of State, FCO*)
Vice-Chairmen, HRH The Duke of Kent, KG, GCMG, GCVO;
  Sir Martin Laing, CBE
Chief Executive, Sir David Wright, KCMG, LVO
Members, R. Turner, OBE; V. Brown; J. Shepherd, CMG; A.
  Summers; Ms G. Goucher, MBE; Sir David John; R.
  Orgill; K. Pathak; W. Thomson; G. Robson; D. Jones;
  M. Bohill; D. Durie, CMG

REGIONAL OFFICES
— *see* pages 303–4

EXECUTIVE AGENCIES

COMPANIES HOUSE
Companies House, Crown Way, Cardiff CF4 3UZ
Tel 01222-380801; fax 01222-380900
London Information Centre, 21 Bloomsbury Street, London
WC1B 3XD
37 Castle Terrace, Edinburgh EH1 2EB
Tel 0131-535 5800; fax 0131-535 5820

Companies House incorporates companies, registers company documents and provides company information.
Registrar of Companies for England and Wales, J. Holden
Registrar for Scotland, J. Henderson

EMPLOYMENT TRIBUNALS SERVICE
19–29 Woburn Place, London WC1H 0LU
Tel 0171-273 8666; fax 0171-273 8670

The Service became an executive agency in 1997 and brought together the administrative support for the employment tribunals and the Employment Appeal Tribunal.
Chief Executive, I. Jones

THE INSOLVENCY SERVICE
PO Box 203, 21 Bloomsbury Street, London WC1B 3QW
Tel 0171-637 1110; fax 0171-636 4709

The Service administers and investigates the affairs of bankrupts and companies in compulsory liquidation; deals with the disqualification of directors in all corporate failures; regulates insolvency practitioners and their professional bodies; provides banking and investment services for bankruptcy and liquidation estates; and advises ministers on insolvency policy issues.
Inspector-General and Chief Executive, P. R. Joyce
Deputy Inspectors-General, D. J. Flynn; L. T. Cramp

NATIONAL WEIGHTS AND MEASURES LABORATORY
Stanton Avenue, Teddington, Middx TW11 0JZ
Tel 0181-943 7272; fax 0181-943 7270

---

† At 151 Buckingham Palace Road, London SW1W 9SS

The Laboratory administers weights and measures legislation, carries out type examination, calibration and testing, and runs courses on metrological topics.
Chief Executive, Dr S. Bennett

PATENT OFFICE
— *see* page 330

RADIOCOMMUNICATIONS AGENCY
Wyndham House, 189 Marsh Wall, London E14 9SX
Tel 0171-211 0211; fax 0171-211 0507

The Agency is responsible for the management of the radio spectrum used for civilian purposes within the UK. It also represents UK radio interests internationally.
Chief Executive, D. Hendon

HM TREASURY
Parliament Street, London SW1P 3AG
Tel 0171-270 5000
Web: http://www.hm-treasury.gov.uk

The Office of the Lord High Treasurer has been continuously in commission for well over 200 years. The Lord High Commissioners of HM Treasury are the First Lord of the Treasury (who is also the Prime Minister), the Chancellor of the Exchequer and five junior Lords (who are government whips in the House of Commons). This Board of Commissioners is assisted at present by the Chief Secretary, the Parliamentary Secretary who is also the government Chief Whip, the Paymaster-General, the Financial Secretary, the Economic Secretary, the Minister of State and the Permanent Secretary.

The Prime Minister is not primarily concerned in the day-to-day aspects of Treasury business; the management of the Treasury devolves upon the Chancellor of the Exchequer and the other Treasury ministers.

The Chief Secretary is responsible for public expenditure planning and control; public sector pay; value for money in the public services; public/private partnerships and procurement policy; strategic oversight of banking, financial services and insurance; departmental investment strategies; welfare reform; devolution; and resource accounting and budgeting. From April 2000 he will be responsible for a new Office of Government Commerce which will centralize government procurement activities.

The Paymaster-General is responsible for the Inland Revenue, Customs and Excise and the Treasury, with overall responsibility for the Finance Bill. She leads on personal and business taxation, VAT and European/international tax issues. The Paymaster-General's Office is part of the National Investment and Loans Office (*see* pages 324–5).

The Financial Secretary is responsible for growth and productivity; small firms and venture capital; science, research and development; competition and deregulation policy; environmental issues; export credit; most Customs and Excise taxes; vehicle excise duty; and parliamentary financial business.

The Economic Secretary is responsible for National Savings, the Debt Management Office, the National Investment and Loans Office, the Office for National Statistics, the Royal Mint, and the Government Actuary's Department; banking, financial services and insurance; foreign exchange reserves; debt management policy; women's issues; and charity taxation.
Prime Minister and First Lord of the Treasury, The Rt. Hon.
  Tony Blair, MP
Chancellor of the Exchequer, The Rt. Hon. Gordon Brown, MP

Principal Private Secretary, T. Scholar
Private Secretaries, J. Papps; Ms T. Finkelstein
Special Advisers, E. Balls; E. Miliband; S. Livermore; I. Austin
Council of Economic Advisers, C. Wales; P. Gregg; Ms S. Vadera
Parliamentary Private Secretary, vacant
Chief Secretary to the Treasury, The Rt. Hon. Alan Milburn, MP
Private Secretary, P. Schofield
Paymaster-General, Dawn Primarolo, MP
Private Secretary, Ms S. Knight
Parliamentary Private Secretary, A. Johnson, MP
Financial Secretary to the Treasury, Stephen Timms, MP
Private Secretary, S. Field
Economic Secretary, Melanie Johnson, MP
Private Secretary, Ms A. King
Parliamentary Secretary to the Treasury and Government Chief Whip (*£64,307), The Rt. Hon. Ann Taylor, MP
Private Secretary, M. Maclean
Treasurer of HM Household and Deputy Chief Whip (*£33,359), Keith Bradley, MP
Comptroller of HM Household (*£21,467), Thomas McAvoy, MP
Vice-Chamberlain of HM Household (*21,467), Graham Allen, MP
Lord Commissioners of the Treasury (*£21,467), Robert Ainsworth, MP; James Dowd, MP; Clive Betts, MP; David Jamieson, MP; Jane Kennedy, MP
Assistant Whips (*£21,467), David Clelland, MP; Kevin Hughes, MP; Greg Pope, MP; Anne McGuire, MP; Michael Hall, MP; Gerry Sutcliffe, MP
Parliamentary Clerk, D. S. Martin
Permanent Secretary to the Treasury, Sir Andrew Turnbull, KCB, CVO
Private Secretary, Ms S. Riach
Head of Government Accountancy Service and Chief Accountancy Adviser to the Treasury, A. Likierman

DIRECTORATES

Leader, Ministerial Support Team (SCS), T. Scholar
Leader, Communications Team (SCS), J. Kingman
Leader, Strategy Team (SCS), Dr R. Kosmin

MACROECONOMIC POLICY AND PROSPECTS
Director, and Head of the Government Economic Service (SCS), A. O'Donnell
Deputy Directors (SCS), J. Grice; J. Taylor
Team Leaders (SCS), M. Bradbury; D. Deaton; C. M. Kelly; Ms S. Killen; A. Kilpatrick; D. Ramsden

INTERNATIONAL FINANCE
Director (SCS), Sir Nigel Wicks, GCB, CVO, CBE
Deputy Directors (SCS), J. Cunliffe; P. McIntyre
Team Leaders (SCS), S. Brooks; A. Gibbs; D. Lawton; M. Richardson; R. Todd

BUDGET AND PUBLIC FINANCES
Director (SCS), R. Culpin
Deputy Directors (SCS), N. Macpherson; C. J. Mowl
Team Leaders (SCS), P. Curwen; Ms M. Dawes; S. N. Matthews; D. Savage; M. Swan; I. Taylor; M. Williams; P. Wynn Owen

PUBLIC SERVICES
Director (SCS), E. J. W. Gieve, CB
Deputy Directors (SCS), †N. Glass; Miss G. M. Noble, CB; P. N. Sedgwick; A. Sharples

is entitled to the ministerial salary shown but in common with other Cabinet ministers takes only £47,149
Team Leaders (SCS), Ms A. Charlesworth; T. Dowse; E. Evans; D. Franklin; N. Holgate; A. Hudson; P. Kane; Ms B. Kelly; J. Moore; M. Parkinson; A. Ritchie; P. Sedgwick; A. Sharples; Ms C. Slocock; Ms A. Tuffs

FINANCIAL MANAGEMENT, REPORTING AND AUDIT
Director (Chief Accountancy Adviser) (SCS), A. Likierman
Deputy Director (SCS), †J. E. Mortimer
Team Leaders (SCS), J. Breckenbridge; C. Butler; Mrs R. M. Dunn; Dr R. Kosmin; Ms A. M. Jones; D. Loweth; K. Ross

FINANCE, REGULATION AND INDUSTRY
Director (SCS), S. Robson, CB
Deputy Directors (SCS), H. J. Bush; R. Fellgett; B. Rigby; M. Roberts
Team Leaders (SCS), R. Allen; Ms S. Beckett; M. Burt; P. Casey; J. Colling; Mrs P. C. Diggle; C. Farthing; C. Ford; D. Griffiths; J. Halligan; Mrs S. Lewis; J. May; C. R. Pickering; D. Roe; P. Rutman; P. Schofield; Ms C. Speck; J. Whitlock; T. Wilson

PERSONNEL, ACCOMMODATION AND INFORMATION SERVICES
Director (SCS), Ms M. O'Mara
Team Leaders (SCS), I. Cooper; J. Dodds; J. Hibberd
† Combined deputy director and head of team

EXECUTIVE AGENCIES

NATIONAL SAVINGS
— see page 325–6

OFFICE FOR NATIONAL STATISTICS
— see pages 326

ROYAL MINT
— see page 336

UNITED KINGDOM DEBT MANAGEMENT OFFICE
Cheapside House, 138 Cheapside, London EC2V 6BB
Tel 0171-862 6500; fax 0171 862 6509

The UK Debt Management Office was launched as an executive agency of the Treasury in April 1998 after the transfer from the Bank of England to the Treasury of responsibility for debt management, the sale of gilts and oversight of the gilts market. It will in due course take over responsibility for the management of the Exchequer's daily cash flow.
Chief Executive, M. L. Williams

THE TREASURY SOLICITOR
DEPARTMENT OF HM PROCURATOR-GENERAL AND TREASURY SOLICITOR
Queen Anne's Chambers, 28 Broadway, London SW1H 9JS
Tel 0171-210 3000; fax 0171-210 3004

The Treasury Solicitor's Department provides legal services for many government departments. Those without their own lawyers are provided with legal advice, and both they and other departments are provided with litigation services. The Treasury Solicitor is also the Queen's Proctor, and is responsible for collecting Bona Vacantia on behalf of the Crown. The Department became an executive agency in 1996.
HM Procurator-General and Treasury Solicitor (SCS), A. H. Hammond, CB
Deputy Treasury Solicitor (SCS), A. M. Inglese

---

* In addition to a parliamentary salary of £47,008; the Chief Whip

LITIGATION DIVISION
SCS, R. Aitken; Mrs D. Babar; D. Brummell; A. D. Lawton; A. Leithead; B. McKay; P. R. Messer; Ms L. Nicoll; Mrs J. B. C. Oliver; D. Palmer; S. Parkinson; R. J. Phillips; A. J. Sandal

QUEEN'S PROCTOR DIVISION
Queen's Proctor (SCS), A. H. Hammond, CB
Assistant Queen's Proctor (SCS), Mrs D. Babar

RESOURCES AND SERVICES DIVISION
Principal Establishment and Finance Officer and Security Officer (SCS), J. P. Burnett
Deputy Establishment Officer (G7), Ms H. Donnelly
Finance Officer (G7), C. A. Woolley
Information Systems Manager (G7), M. Gabbidon
Business Support Manager (SEO), E. Blishen

BONA VACANTIA DIVISION
SCS, Ms L. Addison

EUROPEAN DIVISION
SCS, J. E. Collins; A. Ridout; M. C. P. Thomas

CULTURE, MEDIA AND SPORT DIVISION
SCS, Ms I. Letwin

CABINET OFFICE AND CENTRAL ADVISORY DIVISION
SCS, M. C. L. Carpenter; P. Kilgarriff

MINISTRY OF DEFENCE ADVISORY DIVISION
Metropole Building, Northumberland Avenue, London WC2N 5BL
Tel 0171-218 4691
SCS, N. Beach; Mrs V. Collett; M. Hemming; Ms F. Nash

DEPARTMENT FOR EDUCATION AND EMPLOYMENT ADVISORY DIVISION
Caxton House, Tothill Street, London SW1H 9NF
Tel 0171-273 3000
SCS, F. D. W. Clarke; Ms D. Collins; S. T. Harker; C. House; N. A. D. Lambert; D. Macrae

HM TREASURY ADVISORY DIVISION
Treasury Chambers, Parliament Street, London SW1P 3AG
Tel 0171-270 3000
SCS, M. A. Blythe; J. R. J. Braggins; Ms R. Ford; J. Jones; R. Ricks; Miss J. V. Stokes

CONSTITUTIONAL REFORM DIVISION
70 Whitehall, London SW1A 2AS
Tel 0171-270 6093
SCS, Miss R. A. Jeffreys

COUNCIL ON TRIBUNALS
7th Floor, 22 Kingsway, London WC2B 6LE
Tel 0171-936 7045; fax 0171-936 7044

The Council on Tribunals is an independent body that operates under the Tribunals and Inquiries Act 1992. It consists of 16 members appointed by the Lord Chancellor and the Lord Advocate; one member is appointed to represent the interests of people in Wales. The Scottish Committee of the Council generally considers Scottish tribunals and matters relating only to Scotland.

The Council advises on and keeps under review the constitution and working of administrative tribunals, and considers and reports on administrative procedures relating to statutory inquiries. Some 70 tribunals are currently under the Council's supervision. It is consulted by and advises government departments on a wide range of subjects relating to adjudicative procedures.

Chairman, vacant
Members, The Parliamentary Commissioner for Administration *(ex officio)*; R. J. Elliot, WS *(Chairman of the Scottish Committee)*; Mrs C. Berkeley; S. M. D. Brown; S. R. Davie, CB; J. H. Eames; Mrs A. Galbraith; ; Mrs S. R. Howdle; I. J. Irvine; S. Jones, CBE; Prof. T. M. Partington; I. D. Penman, CB; D. G. Readings; E. P. Roberts; P. A. A. Waring
Secretary, Mrs P. J. Fairbairn

SCOTTISH COMMITTEE OF THE COUNCIL ON TRIBUNALS
44 Palmerston Place, Edinburgh EH12 5BJ
Tel 0131-220 1236; fax 0131-225 4271
Chairman, R. J. Elliot, WS
Members, The Parliamentary Commissioner for Administration *(ex officio)*; Mrs P. Y. Berry, MBE; Mrs B. Bruce; I. J. Irvine; Mrs A. Middleton; I. D. Penman, CB; Mrs H. Sheerin, OBE
Secretary, Mrs E. M. MacRae

TRIBUNALS
— *see* pages 370–3

UNITED KINGDOM SPORTS COUNCIL (UK SPORT)
Walkden House, 10 Melton Street, London NW1 2EB
Tel 0171-380 8000; fax 0171-380 8010

The UK Sports Council (UK Sport) was established by Royal Charter in January 1997. Its role is to focus on high performance sport at UK level, with the aim of achieving sporting excellence in world competition. It promotes the development of sport and fosters the provision of sporting facilities. It works to combat drug misuse, deals with international relations and organizes major events. It also distributes the funds allocated to sport from the proceeds of the National Lottery.
Chairman, Sir Rodney Walker
Chief Executive, R. Callicott

UNRELATED LIVE TRANSPLANT REGULATORY AUTHORITY
Department of Health, c/o Room 311, Wellington House, 133–155 Waterloo Road, London SE1 8UG
Tel 0171-972 4812; fax 0171-972 4852

The Unrelated Live Transplant Regulatory Authority (ULTRA) is a statutory body established in 1990. In every case where the transplant of an organ within the definition of the Human Organ Transplants Act 1989 is proposed between a living donor and a recipient who are not genetically related, the proposal must be referred to ULTRA. Applications must be made by registered medical practitioners.

The Authority comprises a chairman and ten members appointed by the Secretary of State for Health. The secretariat is provided by Department of Health officials.
Chairman, Prof. R. N. M. MacSween
Members, Mrs J. H. Callman; Dr J. F. Douglas; Dr H. Draper; Miss P. M. Franklin; Dr S. Fuggle; A. J. Hooker; S. G. Macpherson; Prof. Sir Netar Mallick; Prof. A. Rees; Mrs S. J. Sullivan
Administrative Secretary, E. Scarlett
Medical Secretary, Dr P. Doyle

NATIONAL ASSEMBLY FOR WALES
Cathays Park, Cardiff CF1 3NQ
Tel 01222-825111
National Assembly Information Line: 01222-898200
E-mail: webmaster@wales.gov.uk
Web: http://www.wales.gov.uk

The National Assembly for Wales has responsibility in Wales for ministerial functions relating to health and personal social services; education, except for terms and conditions of service and student awards; training; the Welsh language, arts and culture; the implementation of the Citizen's Charter in Wales; local government; housing; water and sewerage; environmental protection; sport; agriculture and fisheries; forestry; land use, including town and country planning and countryside and nature conservation; new towns; non-departmental public bodies and appointments in Wales; ancient monuments and historic buildings and the Welsh Arts Council; roads; tourism; financial assistance to industry; the Strategic Development Scheme in Wales and the Programme for the Valleys; and the operation of the European Regional Development Fund in Wales and other European Union matters. *See also* Welsh Office, and National Assemblies supplement.

First Secretary of the Assembly, The Rt. Hon. Alun Michael, MP, AM
  Private Secretary, Ms A. Coleman
  Special Advisers, Ms J. Crowley; A. Bold
Secretary for Economic Development, Rhodri Morgan, MP, AM
Secretary for Education Up to Age 16, Rosemary Butler, AM
Secretary for Health and Social Services, Jane Hutt, AM
Secretary for Post-16 Education and Training, Tom Middlehurst, AM
Secretary for Agriculture and the Rural Economy, Christine Gwyther, AM
Secretary for the Environment, Peter Law, AM
Trefnydd Manager, Andrew Davies, AM
Finance Secretary, Edwina Hart, AM

Permanent Secretary (G1), J. D. Shortridge
Clerk to the Assembly, J. W. Lloyd, CB

OFFICE OF THE PRESIDING OFFICER
Deputy Clerk (G3), B. J. Mitchell

COMMITTEE SECRETARIAT
Grade 5, Ms M. Knox

CABINET SECRETARIAT
Grade 5, L. Conway

OFFICE OF THE COUNSEL GENERAL
Counsel General, W. Roddick, QC

COMMUNICATIONS DIRECTORATE
Head of Publicity (G7), W. J. Edwards
Chief Press Officer (G7), D. Clifford

ESTABLISHMENT GROUP
Principal Establishment Officer (G3), Mrs B. Wilson
Heads of Divisions (G5), Dr A. G. Thornton; Ms K. Cassidy; Mrs M. Evans; N. Finlayson
Chief Statistician (G5), W. R. L. Alldritt
Head of Health Statistics and Analysis Unit (G6), P. Demery

FINANCE GROUP
Principal Finance Officer (G3), D. T. Richards
Head of Division (G5), L. A. Pavelin
Senior Economic Adviser (G5), M. G. Phelps
Head of Internal Audit (G6), D. A. McNeill

ECONOMIC AFFAIRS
Deputy Secretary (G2), D. W. Jones

AGRICULTURE DEPARTMENT
Head of Department (G3), H. D. Brodie

ECONOMIC DEVELOPMENT GROUP
Head of Group (G3), M. J. Cochlin
Heads of Divisions (G5), A. D. Lansdown; L. Conway; P. Fullerton

INDUSTRY AND TRAINING DEPARTMENT
Director (G3), D. W. Jones
Industrial Director (G4), vacant
Heads of Divisions (G5), R. Keveren; N. E. Thomas; W. G. Davies; *(G6),* Dr R. J. Loveland

SOCIAL POLICY
Deputy Secretary (G2), G. C. G. Craid

EDUCATION DEPARTMENT
Head of Department (G3), R. J. Davies
†*Heads of Divisions (G5),* R. Thomas; D. R. Adams; J. Howells; Mrs E. A. Taylor

OFFICE OF HM CHIEF INSPECTOR FOR SCHOOLS IN WALES
†*Chief Inspector (G4),* Miss S. Lewis
†*Staff Inspectors (G5),* M. G. Haines; C. Abbott
There are 45 Grade 6 Inspectors.
Head of Administration (G7), Mrs S. Howells

LOCAL GOVERNMENT GROUP
Head of Group (G3), Mrs H. F. O. Thomas
Heads of Divisions (G5), M. J. Shanahan; J. Atkins
Chief Inspector, Social Services Inspectorate (Wales) (G5), G. Williams
Deputy Chief Inspectors, R. Tebboth; R. C. Woodward; Mrs P. E. White

NHS DIRECTORATE
Director (G3), P. R. Gregory
Heads of Divisions (G5), B. Wilcox; R. C. Williams; Ms S. Beaver; J. Morgan

HEALTH PROTECTION AND IMPROVEMENT DIRECTORATE
Chief Medical Officer (G3), Dr R. Hall
Principal Medical Officers (G4), Dr B. Fuge; Dr M. Pontin
Senior Medical Officers (G5), Dr J. Ludlow; Dr H. N. Williams; Dr D. Salter
Chief Dental Officer (G5), P. Langmaid
Chief Scientific Adviser (G5), Dr J. A. V. Pritchard
Deputy Scientific Adviser (G6), Dr E. O. Crawley
Chief Pharmaceutical Adviser (G5), Miss C. W. Howells
Chief Environmental Health Adviser (G5), R. Alexander
Deputy Environmental Health Adviser (G6), D. Worthington

NURSING DIVISION
Chief Nursing Officer, Miss R. Kennedy
Nursing Officers, P. Johnson; M. F. Tonkin; Mrs H. Wood; Mrs R. Johnson

TRANSPORT, PLANNING AND ENVIRONMENT GROUP
Head of Group (G3), M. L. Evans
Director of Highways (G4), K. J. Thomas, CBE
Heads of Divisions (G5), J. R. Rees (*Roads Construction*); G. A. Thomas (*Transport Policy*); *(G6),* R. J. Shaw (*Network Management*); B. H. Hawker, OBE (*Roads Major Projects*)
Grade 7, R. H. Powell; I. P. Davies; R. K. Cones; K. J. A. Tengy; T. J. Collins; S. C. Shouler; M. J. Gilbert; T. C. Dorken; M. J. A. Parker; I. A. Grindulis; A. D. Perry; Dr M. C. Dunn

---

† Based at Ty Glas Road, Llanishen, Cardiff CF4 5LE. Tel: 01222-761456

HEALTH AUTHORITIES
— *see* Social Welfare section

EXECUTIVE AGENCIES

CADW: WELSH HISTORIC MONUMENTS
Crown Building, Cathays Park, Cardiff CF1 3NQ
Tel 01222-500200; fax 01222-826375

Cadw supports the preservation, conservation, appreciation and enjoyment of the built heritage in Wales.
Chief Executive, T. Cassidy
Director of Policy and Administration, R. W. Hughes
Conservation Architect, J. D. Hogg
Principal Inspector of Ancient Monuments and Historic Buildings, J. R. Avent
Head of Presentation, A. J. Hood
Head of Corporate Services, J. Jenkins
Head of Administration, Mrs J. Booker
National Manager, Cadwraeth Cymru, M. B. R. Watkins

FARMING AND RURAL CONSERVATION AGENCY
— *see* page 279–80

INTERVENTION BOARD
— *see* pages 314

PLANNING INSPECTORATE
Crown Buildings, Cathays Park, Cardiff CF1 3NQ
Tel 01222-823892; fax 01222-825150

The Inspectorate is a joint executive agency of the Department of the Environment, Transport and the Regions and the National Assembly for Wales.
Chief Executive and Chief Planning Inspector (*G3*), C. Shepley
Director (*G5*), R. Davies

WALES YOUTH AGENCY
Leslie Court, Lon-y-Llyn, Caerphilly CF83 1BQ
Tel 01222-855700; fax 01222-855701

The Wales Youth Agency is an independent organization funded by the National Assembly for Wales. Its functions include the encouragement and development of the partnership between statutory and voluntary agencies relating to young people; the promotion of staff development and training; and the extension of marketing and information services in the relevant fields. The board of directors do not receive a salary.
Chairman of the Board of Directors, R. Noble
Vice-Chairman of the Board of Directors, Dr H. Williamson
Chief Executive, B. Williams

OFFICE OF WATER SERVICES
Centre City Tower, 7 Hill Street, Birmingham B5 4UA
Tel 0121-625 1300; fax 0121-625 1400

The Office of Water Services (Ofwat) was set up under the Water Act 1989 and is a non-ministerial government department headed by the Director-General of Water Services. It is the independent economic regulator of the water and sewerage companies in England and Wales. Ofwat's main duties are to ensure that the companies can finance and carry out the functions specified in the Water Industry Act 1991 and to protect the interests of water customers. There are ten regional customer service committees which are concerned solely with the interests of water customers. Representation of customer interests at national level is the responsibility of the Ofwat National Customer Council (ONCC).
Director-General of Water Services, I. C. R. Byatt
Chairman, Ofwat National Customer Council, Ms S. Reiter

WELSH ADMINISTRATION OMBUDSMAN
5th Floor, Capital Tower, Greyfriars Road, Cardiff CF10 3AG
Tel 0845-601 0987; fax 01222-226909

The Welsh Administration Ombudsman was appointed in July 1999 to investigate complaints by members of the public who have suffered an injustice through maladministration by the National Assembly for Wales and certain public bodies involved in devolved Welsh affairs.
Welsh Administration Ombudsman, M. S. Buckley

WELSH DEVELOPMENT AGENCY
Principality House, The Friary, Cardiff CF10 3FE
Tel 01443-845500; fax 01443-845589

The Agency was established under the Welsh Development Agency Act 1975. Its remit is to help further the regeneration of the economy and improve the environment in Wales. Under the Government of Wales Act 1998, the Land Authority for Wales and the Development Board for Rural Wales merged with the Welsh Development Agency. The Agency is sponsored by the National Assembly for Wales.

The Agency's priorities are to create new businesses and to encourage existing small firms to grow. Its main activities include promoting Wales as a location for inward investment, helping to boost the growth, profitability and competitiveness of indigenous Welsh companies, providing investment capital for industry, encouraging investment by the private sector in property development, grant-aiding land reclamation, and stimulating quality urban and rural development.
Chairman, D. Rowe-Beddoe
Deputy Chairman, G. Hawker
Chief Executive, W. B. Willott, CB

WELSH OFFICE
Gwydyr House, Whitehall, London SW1A 2ER
Tel 0171-270 3000

The Welsh Office is the Office of the Secretary of State for Wales, who represents Welsh interests in the Cabinet. *See also* National Assembly for Wales.
Secretary of State for Wales, The Rt. Hon. Paul Murphy, MP
Parliamentary Under-Secretary, David Hanson, MP
Head of Department, Ms A. Jackson

WOMEN'S NATIONAL COMMISSION
Room 56/4, Cabinet Office, Horse Guards Road, London SW1P 3AL
Tel 0171-238 0386; fax 0171-238 0387

The Women's National Commission is an independent advisory committee to the Government. Its remit is to ensure that the informed opinions of women are given their due weight in the deliberations of the Government and in public debate on matters of public interest including those of special interest to women. The Commission's sponsoring department is the Cabinet Office.
Chair, Miss V. Evans, CBE
Secretary, Ms J. Veitch

Prime Ministers since 1782

Over the centuries there has been some variation in the determination of the dates of appointment of Prime Ministers. Where possible, the date given is that on which a new Prime Minister kissed the Sovereign's hands and accepted the commission to form a ministry. However, until the middle of the 19th century the dating of a commission or transfer of seals could be the date of taking office. Where the composition of the Government changed, e.g. became a coalition, but the Prime Minister remained the same, the date of the change of government is given.

The Marquess of Rockingham, *Whig*, 27 March 1782
The Earl of Shelburne, *Whig*, 4 July 1782
The Duke of Portland ,*Coalition*, 2 April 1783
William Pitt, *Tory*, 19 December 1783
Henry Addington, *Tory*, 17 March 1801
William Pitt, *Tory*, 10 May 1804
The Lord Grenville, *Whig*, 11 February 1806
The Duke of Portland ,*Tory*, 31 March 1807
Spencer Perceval, *Tory*, 4 October 1809
The Earl of Liverpool, *Tory*, 8 June 1812
George Canning ,*Tory*, 10 April 1827
Viscount Goderich, *Tory*, 31 August 1827
The Duke of Wellington, *Tory*, 22 January 1828
The Earl Grey, *Whig*, 22 November 1830
The Viscount Melbourne, *Whig*, 16 July 1834
The Duke of Wellington, *Tory*, 17 November 1834
Sir Robert Peel, *Tory*, 10 December 1834
The Viscount of Melbourne, *Whig*, 18 April 1835
Sir Robert Peel, *Tory*, 30 August 1841
Lord John Russell (subsequently the Earl Russell), *Whig*, 30 June 1846
The Earl of Derby, *Tory*, 23 February 1852
The Earl of Aberdeen, *Peelite*, 19 December 1852
The Viscount Palmerston, *Liberal*, 6 February 1855
The Earl of Derby, *Conservative*, 20 February 1858
The Viscount Palmerston, *Liberal*, 12 June 1859
The Earl Russell, *Liberal*, 29 October 1865

The Earl of Derby, *Conservative*, 28 June 1866
Benjamin Disraeli, *Conservative*, 27 February 1868
William Gladstone, *Liberal*, 3 December 1868
Benjamin Disraeli, *Conservative*, 20 February 1874
William Gladstone, *Liberal*, 23 April 1880
The Marquess of Salisbury, *Conservative*, 23 June 1885
William Gladstone, *Liberal*, 1 February 1886
The Marquess of Salisbury, *Conservative*, 25 July 1886
William Gladstone, *Liberal*, 15 August 1892
The Earl of Rosebery, *Liberal*, 5 March 1894
The Marquess of Salisbury, *Conservative*, 25 June 1895
Arthur Balfour, *Conservative*, 12 July 1902
Sir Henry Campbell-Bannerman, *Liberal*, 5 December 1905
Herbert Asquith, *Liberal*, 7 April 1908
Herbert Asquith, *Coalition*, 25 May 1915
David Lloyd-George, *Coalition*, 7 December 1916
Andrew Bonar Law, *Conservative*, 23 October 1922
Stanley Baldwin, *Conservative*, 22 May 1923
Ramsay MacDonald, *Labour*, 22 January 1924
Stanley Baldwin, *Conservative*, 4 November 1924
Ramsay MacDonald, *Labour*, 5 June 1929
Ramsay MacDonald, *Coalition*, 24 August 1931
Stanley Baldwin, *Coalition*, 7 June 1935
Neville Chamberlain, *Coalition*, 28 May 1937
Winston Churchill, *Coalition*, 10 May 1940
Winston Churchill, *Conservative*, 23 May 1945
Clement Attlee, *Labour*, 26 July 1945
Sir Winston Churchill, *Conservative*, 26 October 1951
Sir Anthony Eden, *Conservative*, 6 April 1955
Harold Macmillan, *Conservative*, 10 January 1957
Sir Alec Douglas-Home, *Conservative*, 19 October 1963
Harold Wilson, *Labour*, 16 October 1964
Edward Heath, *Conservative*, 19 June 1970
Harold Wilson, *Labour*, 4 March 1974
James Callaghan, *Labour*, 5 April 1976
Margaret Thatcher, *Conservative*, 4 May 1979
John Major, *Conservative*, 28 November 1990
Anthony Blair, *Labour*, 2 May 1997

Speakers of the Commons since 1708

The date of appointment given is the day on which the Speaker was first elected by the House of Commons. The appointment requires royal approbation before it is confirmed and this is usually given within a few days. The present Speaker is the 155th.

PARLIAMENT OF GREAT BRITAIN

Sir Richard Onslow (*Lord Onslow*), 16 November 1708
William Bromley, 25 November 1710
Sir Thomas Hanmer, 16 February 1714
Spencer Compton (*Earl of Wilmington*), 17 March 1715
Arthur Onslow, 23 January 1728
Sir John Cust, 3 November 1761
Sir Fletcher Norton (*Lord Grantley*), 22 January 1770
Charles Cornwall, 31 October 1780
Hon. William Grenville (*Lord Grenville*), 5 January 1789
Henry Addington (*Viscount Sidmouth*), 8 June 1789

PARLIAMENT OF THE UNITED KINGDOM

Sir John Mitford (*Lord Redesdale*), 11 February 1801
Charles Abbot (*Lord Colchester*), 10 February 1802
Charles Manners-Sutton (*Viscount Canterbury*), 2 June 1817

James Abercromby (*Lord Dunfermline*), 19 February 1835
Charles Shaw-Lefevre (*Viscount Eversley*), 27 May 1839
J. Evelyn Denison (*Viscount Ossington*), 30 April 1857
Sir Henry Brand (*Viscount Hampden*), 9 February 1872
Arthur Wellesley Peel (*Viscount Peel*), 26 February 1884
William Gully (*Viscount Selby*), 10 April 1895
James Lowther (*Viscount Ullswater*), 8 June 1905
John Whitley, 27 April 1921
Hon. Edward Fitzroy, 20 June 1928
Douglas Clifton-Brown (*Viscount Ruffside*), 9 March 1943
William Morrison (*Viscount Dunrossil*), 31 October 1951
Sir Harry Hylton-Foster, 20 October 1959
Horace King (*Lord Maybray-King*), 26 October 1965
Selwyn Lloyd (*Lord Selwyn-Lloyd*), 12 January 1971
George Thomas (*Viscount Tonypandy*), 2 February 1976
Bernard Weatherill (*Lord Weatherill*), 15 June 1983
Betty Boothroyd, 27 April 1992

CIVIL SERVICE STAFF

By Main Departments *as at 1 April 1998*

	Total	Of whom in agencies
Agriculture, Fisheries and Food	9,657	3,844
Cabinet Office (including Office of Public Service)	2,477	1,413
Culture, Media and Sport	612	231
Customs and Excise	23,400	—
Defence	104,163	59,526
Education and Employment	33,117	28,612
Environment, Transport and the Regions	15,215	10,457
Foreign Office	5,449	37
Health	4,596	1,104
HM Prison Service	39,363	39,363
Home Office	10,840	2,767
Inland Revenue	53,412	4,029
International Development	1,055	—
Lord Chancellor's Department	10,048	9,213
Northern Ireland Office	205	—
Scottish Departments	13,098	8,200
Social Security	87,218	84,448
Trade and Industry	8,493	4,059
Treasury	893	—
Welsh Office	2,110	170
Other departments	37,845	20,008
TOTAL	463,266	*277,481

*Excluding Inland Revenue (other than Valuation Office), Customs and Excise, Crown Prosecution Service and the Serious Fraud Office, which operate on Next Steps lines.

Source: Government Statistical Service – *Civil Service Statistics 1998* (Crown copyright)

Law Courts and Offices

THE JUDICIAL COMMITTEE OF THE PRIVY COUNCIL

The Judicial Committee of the Privy Council is primarily the final court of appeal for the United Kingdom overseas and those independent Commonwealth countries which have retained the avenue of appeal upon achieving independence (Antigua and Barbuda, The Bahamas, Barbados, Belize, Brunei, Dominica, Jamaica, Kiribati, Mauritius, New Zealand, St Christopher and Nevis, St Lucia, St Vincent and the Grenadines, Trinidad and Tobago, and Tuvalu). The Committee also hears appeals from the Channel Islands and the Isle of Man and the disciplinary and health committees of the medical and allied professions. It has a limited jurisdiction to hear appeals under the Pastoral Measure 1983. In 1998 the Judicial Committee heard 58 appeals and 85 petitions for special leave to appeal.

Following devolution, the Judicial Committee assumes a new role as Scotland's principal constitutional court and will be the final arbiter in disputes between the UK and Scottish Parliaments regarding legislative competence.

The members of the Judicial Committee include the Lord Chancellor, the Lords of Appeal in Ordinary (*see* page 354), other Privy Counsellors who hold or have held high judicial office and certain judges from the Commonwealth.

PRIVY COUNCIL OFFICE (JUDICIAL COMMITTEE), Downing Street, London SWIA 2AJ. Tel: 0171-270 0483. *Registrar of the Privy Council,* J. A. C. Watherston; *Chief Clerk,* F. G. Hart

The Judicature of England and Wales

The legal system of England and Wales is separate from those of Scotland and Northern Ireland and differs from them in law, judicial procedure and court structure, although there is a common distinction between civil law (disputes between individuals) and criminal law (acts harmful to the community).

The supreme judicial authority for England and Wales is the House of Lords, which is the ultimate Court of Appeal from all courts in Great Britain and Northern Ireland (except criminal courts in Scotland) for all cases except those concerning the interpretation and application of European Community law, including preliminary rulings requested by British courts and tribunals, which are decided by the European Court of Justice (*see* pages 773–81). Under the Human Rights Act 1998, which is due to come into force on 2 October 2000, the European Convention on Human Rights will be incorporated into British law; unresolved cases will still be referred to the European Court of Human Rights. As a Court of Appeal the House of Lords consists of the Lord Chancellor and the Lords of Appeal in Ordinary (law lords).

SUPREME COURT OF JUDICATURE

The Supreme Court of Judicature comprises the Court of Appeal, the High Court of Justice and the Crown Court. The High Court of Justice is the superior civil court and is divided into three divisions. The Chancery Division is concerned mainly with equity, bankruptcy and contentious probate business. The Queen's Bench Division deals with commercial and maritime law, serious personal injury and medical negligence cases, cases involving a breach of contract and professional negligence actions. The Family Division deals with matters relating to family law. Sittings are held at the Royal Courts of Justice in London or at 126 district registries outside the capital. High Court judges sit alone to hear cases at first instance. Appeals from lower courts are heard by two or three judges, or by single judges of the appropriate division. The Restrictive Practices Court, set up under the Restrictive Trade Practices Act 1956, and the Technology and Construction Court, which deals with cases which require expert evidence on technical and other issues concerning mainly the construction industry, defective products, property valuations, and landlord and tenant disputes, are also currently part of the High Court, although the Restrictive Practices Court is due to be abolished following the establishment of the Competition Commission (*see* page 291). Appeals from the High Court are heard in the Court of Appeal (Civil Division), presided over by the Master of the Rolls, and may go on to the House of Lords.

CRIMINAL CASES

In criminal matters the decision to prosecute in the majority of cases rests with the Crown Prosecution Service, the independent prosecuting body in England and Wales (*see* pages 362–3). The Service is headed by the Director of Public Prosecutions, who works under the superintendence of the Attorney-General. Certain categories of offence continue to require the Attorney-General's consent for prosecution.

The Crown Court sits in about 90 centres, divided into six circuits, and is presided over by High Court judges, full-time circuit judges, and part-time recorders and assistant recorders, sitting with a jury in all trials which are contested. There were 266 assistant recorders at 30 June 1999. The Crown Court deals with trials of the more serious criminal offences, the sentencing of offenders committed for sentence by magistrates' courts (when the magistrates consider their own power of sentence inadequate), and appeals from magistrates' courts. Magistrates usually sit with a circuit judge or recorder to deal with appeals and committals for sentence. Appeals from the Crown Court, either against sentence or conviction, are made to the Court of Appeal (Criminal Division), presided over by the Lord Chief Justice. A further appeal from the Court of Appeal to the House of Lords can be brought if a point of law of general public importance is considered to be involved.

Minor criminal offences (summary offences) are dealt with in magistrates' courts, which usually consist of three unpaid lay magistrates (justices of the peace) sitting without a jury, who are advised on points of law and procedure by a legally-qualified clerk to the justices. There were 30,260 justices of the peace at 1 January 1999. In busier courts a full-time, salaried and legally-qualified stipendiary magistrate presides alone. Cases involving people under 18 are heard in youth courts, specially constituted magistrates' courts which sit apart from other courts. Preliminary proceedings in a serious case to decide whether there is evidence to justify committal for trial in the Crown Court are also dealt with in the magistrates' courts. Appeals from magistrates' courts against sentence or conviction are made to the Crown Court. Appeals upon a point of law are made to the High Court, and may go on to the House of Lords.

CIVIL CASES

Most minor civil cases are dealt with by the county courts, of which there are about 270 (details may be found in the local telephone directory). Cases are heard by circuit judges or district judges. There were 356 district judges at 31 May 1999. For cases involving small claims there are special simplified procedures. Where there are financial limits on county court jurisdiction, claims which exceed those limits may be tried in the county courts with the consent of the parties, or in certain circumstances on transfer from the High Court. Outside London, bankruptcy proceedings can be heard in designated county courts. Magistrates' courts can deal with certain classes of civil case and committees of magistrates license public houses, clubs and betting shops. For the implementation of the Children Act 1989, a new structure of hearing centres was set up in 1991 for family proceedings cases, involving magistrates' courts (family proceedings courts), divorce county courts, family hearing centres and care centres. Appeals in family matters heard in the family proceedings courts go to the Family Division of the High Court; affiliation appeals and appeals from decisions of the licensing committees of magistrates go to the Crown Court. Appeals from county courts are heard in the Court of Appeal (Civil Division), and may go on to the House of Lords.

CORONERS' COURTS

Coroners' courts investigate violent and unnatural deaths or sudden deaths where the cause is unknown. Cases may be brought before a local coroner (a senior lawyer or doctor) by doctors, the police, various public authorities or members of the public. Where a death is sudden and the cause is unknown, the coroner may order a post-mortem examination to determine the cause of death rather than hold an inquest in court.

Judicial appointments are made by The Queen; the most senior appointments are made on the advice of the Prime Minister and other appointments on the advice of the Lord Chancellor.

Under the provisions of the Criminal Appeal Act 1995, a Commission was set up to direct and supervise investigations into possible miscarriages of justice and to refer cases to the courts on the grounds of conviction and sentence (*see* page 291); these functions were formerly the responsibility of the Home Secretary.

THE HOUSE OF LORDS
AS FINAL COURT OF APPEAL

The Lord High Chancellor (£160,011)
The Rt. Hon. the Lord Irvine of Lairg, *born* 1940, *apptd* 1997

LORDS OF APPEAL IN ORDINARY (each £147,214)
Style, The Rt. Hon. Lord —

Rt. Hon. Lord Browne-Wilkinson, *born* 1930, *apptd* 1991

Rt. Hon. Lord Slynn of Hadley, *born* 1930, *apptd* 1992
Rt. Hon. Lord Nicholls of Birkenhead, *born* 1933, *apptd* 1994
Rt. Hon. Lord Steyn, *born* 1932, *apptd* 1995
Rt. Hon. Lord Hoffman, *born* 1934, *apptd* 1995
Rt. Hon. Lord Hope of Craighead, *born* 1938, *apptd* 1996
Rt. Hon. Lord Clyde, *born* 1932, *apptd* 1996
Rt. Hon. Lord Hutton, *born* 1931, *apptd* 1997
Rt. Hon. Lord Saville of Newdigate, *born* 1936, *apptd* 1997
Rt. Hon. Lord Hobhouse of Woodborough, *born* 1932, *apptd* 1998
Rt. Hon. Lord Millett, *born* 1932, *apptd* 1998
Rt. Hon. Lord Phillips of Worth Matravers, *born* 1938, *apptd* 1999

Judicial Office of the House of Lords, House of Lords, London SWIA OPW. Tel: 0171-219 3111
Registrar, The Clerk of the Parliaments (*see* page 217)

SUPREME COURT OF JUDICATURE

COURT OF APPEAL

The Master of the Rolls (£147,214), The Rt. Hon. Lord Woolf, *born* 1933, *apptd* 1996
Secretary, Mrs L. Grace
Clerk, Ms J. Jones

LORDS JUSTICES OF APPEAL (each £139,931)
Style, The Rt. Hon. Lord/Lady Justice [surname]

Rt. Hon. Sir Martin Nourse, *born* 1932, *apptd* 1985
Rt. Hon. Sir Murray Stuart-Smith, *born* 1927, *apptd* 1988
Rt. Hon. Sir Roy Beldam, *born* 1925, *apptd* 1989
Rt. Hon. Sir Paul Kennedy, *born* 1935, *apptd* 1992
Rt. Hon. Sir Simon Brown, *born* 1937, *apptd* 1992
Rt. Hon. Sir Anthony Evans, *born* 1934, *apptd* 1992
Rt. Hon. Sir Christopher Rose, *born* 1937, *apptd* 1992
Rt. Hon. Sir John Roch, *born* 1934, *apptd* 1993
Rt. Hon. Sir Peter Gibson, *born* 1934, *apptd* 1993
Rt. Hon. Sir Denis Henry, *born* 1931, *apptd* 1993
Rt. Hon. Sir Swinton Thomas, *born* 1931, *apptd* 1994
Rt. Hon. Sir Andrew Morritt, CVO, *born* 1938, *apptd* 1994
Rt. Hon. Sir Philip Otton, *born* 1933, *apptd* 1995
Rt. Hon. Sir Robin Auld, *born* 1937, *apptd* 1995
Rt. Hon. Sir Malcolm Pill, *born* 1938, *apptd* 1995
Rt. Hon. Sir William Aldous, *born* 1936, *apptd* 1995
Rt. Hon. Sir Alan Ward, *born* 1938, *apptd* 1995
Rt. Hon. Sir Konrad Schiemann, *born* 1937, *apptd* 1995
Rt. Hon. Sir Mathew Thorpe, *born* 1938, *apptd* 1995
Rt. Hon. Sir Mark Potter, *born* 1937, *apptd* 1996
Rt. Hon. Sir Henry Brooke, *born* 1936, *apptd* 1996
Rt. Hon. Sir Igor Judge, *born* 1941, *apptd* 1996
Rt. Hon. Sir Mark Waller, *born* 1940, *apptd* 1996
Rt. Hon. Sir John Mummery, *born* 1938, *apptd* 1996
Rt. Hon. Sir Charles Mantell, *born* 1937, *apptd* 1997
Rt. Hon. Sir John Chadwick, ED, *born* 1941, *apptd* 1997
Rt. Hon. Sir Robert Walker, *born* 1938, *apptd* 1997
Rt. Hon. Sir Richard Buxton, *born* 1938, *apptd* 1997
Rt. Hon. Sir Anthony May, *born* 1940, *apptd* 1997
Rt. Hon. Sir Simon Tuckey, *born* 1941, *apptd* 1998
Rt. Hon. Sir Anthony Clarke, *born* 1943, *apptd* 1998
Rt. Hon. Sir John Laws, *born* 1945, *apptd* 1999
Rt. Hon. Sir Stephen Sedley, *born* 1939, *apptd* 1999
Rt. Hon. Sir Jonathan Mance, *born* 1943, *apptd* 1999
Rt. Hon. Dame Brenda Hale, *born* 1945, *apptd* 1999

Ex officio Judges, The Lord High Chancellor; the Lord Chief Justice of England; the Master of the Rolls; the President of the Family Division; and the Vice-Chancellor

COURT OF APPEAL (CRIMINAL DIVISION)

Vice-President, The Rt. Hon. Lord Justice Rose
Judges, The Lord Chief Justice of England; the Master of the Rolls; Lords Justices of Appeal; and Judges of the High Court of Justice

COURTS-MARTIAL APPEAL COURT

Judges, The Lord Chief Justice of England; the Master of the Rolls; Lords Justices of Appeal; and Judges of the High Court of Justice

HIGH COURT OF JUSTICE

CHANCERY DIVISION

President, The Lord High Chancellor
The Vice-Chancellor (£139,931), The Rt. Hon. Sir Richard Scott, *born* 1934, *apptd* 1994
Clerk, W. Northfield, BEM

JUDGES (each £123,787)
Style, The Hon. Mr/Mrs Justice [surname]

Hon. Sir Donald Rattee, *born* 1937, *apptd* 1989
Hon. Sir Francis Ferris, TD, *born* 1932, *apptd* 1990
Hon. Sir Jonathan Parker, *born* 1937, *apptd* 1991
Hon. Sir John Lindsay, *born* 1935, *apptd* 1992
Hon. Dame Mary Arden, DBE, *born* 1947, *apptd* 1993
Hon. Sir Edward Evans-Lombe, *born* 1937, *apptd* 1993
Hon. Sir Robin Jacob, *born* 1941, *apptd* 1993
Hon. Sir William Blackburne, *born* 1944, *apptd* 1993
Hon. Sir Gavin Lightman, *born* 1939, *apptd* 1994
Hon. Sir Robert Carnwath, *born* 1945, *apptd* 1994
Hon. Sir Colin Rimer, *born* 1944, *apptd* 1994
Hon. Sir Hugh Laddie, *born* 1946, *apptd* 1995
Hon. Sir Timothy Lloyd, *born* 1946, *apptd* 1996
Hon. Sir David Neuberger, *born* 1948, *apptd* 1996
Hon. Sir Andrew Park, *born* 1939, *apptd* 1997
Hon. Sir Nicholas Pumfrey, *born* 1951, *apptd* 1997
Hon. Sir Michael Hart, *born* 1948, *apptd* 1998

HIGH COURT OF JUSTICE IN BANKRUPTCY

Judges, The Vice-Chancellor and judges of the Chancery Division of the High Court

COMPANIES COURT

Judges, The Vice Chancellor and judges of the Chancery Division of the High Court

PATENT COURT (APPELLATE SECTION)

Judge, The Hon. Mr Justice Jacob

QUEEN'S BENCH DIVISION

The Lord Chief Justice of England (£157,511) The Rt. Hon. the Lord Bingham of Cornhill, *born* 1933, *apptd* 1996
Private Secretary, E. Adams
Clerk, J. Bond
Vice-President, The Rt. Hon. Lord Justice Kennedy

JUDGES (each £123,787)
Style, The Hon. Mr/Mrs Justice [surname]

Hon. Sir Oliver Popplewell, *born* 1927, *apptd* 1983
Hon. Sir Richard Tucker, *born* 1930, *apptd* 1985
Hon. Sir Patrick Garland, *born* 1929, *apptd* 1985
Hon. Sir Michael Turner, *born* 1931, *apptd* 1985
Hon. Sir John Alliott, *born* 1932, *apptd* 1986
Hon. Sir Harry Ognall, *born* 1934, *apptd* 1986
Hon. Sir John Owen, *born* 1925, *apptd* 1986
Hon. Sir Humphrey Potts, *born* 1931, *apptd* 1986
Hon. Sir Richard Rougier, *born* 1932, *apptd* 1986
Hon. Sir Ian Kennedy, *born* 1930, *apptd* 1986

Hon. Sir Stuart McKinnon, *born* 1938, *apptd* 1988
Hon. Sir Scott Baker, *born* 1937, *apptd* 1988
Hon. Sir Edwin Jowitt, *born* 1929, *apptd* 1988
Hon. Sir Douglas Brown, *born* 1931, *apptd* 1996
Hon. Sir Michael Morland, *born* 1929, *apptd* 1989
Hon. Sir Roger Buckley, *born* 1939, *apptd* 1989
Hon. Sir Anthony Hidden, *born* 1936, *apptd* 1989
Hon. Sir Michael Wright, *born* 1932, *apptd* 1990
Hon. Sir John Blofeld, *born* 1932, *apptd* 1990
Hon. Sir Peter Cresswell, *born* 1944, *apptd* 1991
Hon. Dame Ann Ebsworth, DBE, *born* 1937, *apptd* 1992
Hon. Sir David Latham, *born* 1942, *apptd* 1992
Hon. Sir Christopher Holland, *born* 1937, *apptd* 1992
Hon. Sir John Kay, *born* 1943, *apptd* 1992
Hon. Sir Richard Curtis, *born* 1933, *apptd* 1992
Hon. Dame Janet Smith, DBE, *born* 1940, *apptd* 1992
Hon. Sir Anthony Colman, *born* 1938, *apptd* 1992
Hon. Sir John Dyson, *born* 1943, *apptd* 1993
Hon. Sir Thayne Forbes, *born* 1938, *apptd* 1993
Hon. Sir Michael Sachs, *born* 1932, *apptd* 1993
Hon. Sir Stephen Mitchell, *born* 1941, *apptd* 1993
Hon. Sir Rodger Bell, *born* 1939, *apptd* 1993
Hon. Sir Michael Harrison, *born* 1939, *apptd* 1993
Hon. Sir Bernard Rix, *born* 1944, *apptd* 1993
Hon. Dame Heather Steel, DBE, *born* 1940, *apptd* 1993
Hon. Sir William Gage, *born* 1938, *apptd* 1993
Hon. Sir Andrew Longmore, *born* 1944, *apptd* 1993
Hon. Sir Thomas Morison, *born* 1939, *apptd* 1993
Hon. Sir David Keene, *born* 1941, *apptd* 1994
Hon. Sir Andrew Collins, *born* 1942, *apptd* 1994
Hon. Sir Maurice Kay, *born* 1942, *apptd* 1995
Hon. Sir Brian Smedley, *born* 1934, *apptd* 1995
Hon. Sir Anthony Hooper, *born* 1937, *apptd* 1995
Hon. Sir Alexander Butterfield, *born* 1942, *apptd* 1995
Hon. Sir George Newman, *born* 1941, *apptd* 1995
Hon. Sir David Poole, *born* 1938, *apptd* 1995
Hon. Sir Martin Moore-Bick, *born* 1946, *apptd* 1995
Hon. Sir Gordon Langley, *born* 1943, *apptd* 1995
Hon. Sir Roger Thomas, *born* 1947, *apptd* 1996
Hon. Sir Robert Nelson, *born* 1942, *apptd* 1996
Hon. Sir Roger Toulson, *born* 1946, *apptd* 1996
Hon. Sir Michael Astill, *born* 1938, *apptd* 1996
Hon. Sir Alan Moses, *born* 1945, *apptd* 1996
Hon. Sir Timothy Walker, *born* 1946, *apptd* 1996
Hon. Sir David Eady, *born* 1943, *apptd* 1997
Hon. Sir Jeremy Sullivan, *born* 1945, *apptd* 1997
Hon. Sir David Penry-Davey, *born* 1942, *apptd* 1997
Hon. Sir Stephen Richards, *born* 1950, *apptd* 1997
Hon. Sir David Steel, *born* 1943, *apptd* 1998
Hon. Sir Rodney Klevan, *born* 1940, *apptd* 1998
Hon. Sir Charles Gray, *born* 1942, *apptd* 1998
Hon. Sir Nicolas Bratza, *born* 1945, *apptd* 1998
Hon. Sir Michael Burton, *born* 1946, *apptd* 1998
Hon. Sir Rupert Jackson, *born* 1948, *apptd* 1998
Hon. Dame Heather Hallett, *born* 1949, *apptd* 1999
Hon. Sir Patrick Elias, *born* 1947, *apptd* 1999
Hon. Sir Richard Aikens, *born* 1948, *apptd* 1999

FAMILY DIVISION

President (£139,931), The Rt. Hon. Dame Elizabeth Butler-Sloss, DBE, *born* 1933, *apptd* 1999
Secretary, Mrs S. Leung
Clerk, Mrs S. Bell

JUDGES (each £123,787)
Style, The Hon. Mr/Mrs Justice [surname]

Hon. Sir Edward Cazalet, *born* 1936, *apptd* 1988
Hon. Sir Robert Johnson, *born* 1933, *apptd* 1989
Hon. Dame Joyanne Bracewell, DBE., *born* 1934, *apptd* 1990

Hon. Sir Michael Connell, *born* 1939, *apptd* 1991
Hon. Sir Peter Singer, *born* 1944, *apptd* 1993
Hon. Sir Nicholas Wilson, *born* 1945, *apptd* 1993
Hon. Sir Nicholas Wall, *born* 1945, *apptd* 1993
Hon. Sir Andrew Kirkwood, *born* 1944, *apptd* 1993
Hon. Dame Brenda Hale, DBE, *born* 1945, *apptd* 1994
Hon. Sir Hugh Bennett, *born* 1943, *apptd* 1995
Hon. Sir Edward Holman, *born* 1947, *apptd* 1995
Hon. Dame Mary Hogg, DBE, *born* 1947, *apptd* 1995
Hon. Sir Christopher Sumner, *born* 1939, *apptd* 1996
Hon. Sir Anthony Hughes, *born* 1948, *apptd* 1997
Hon. Sir Arthur Charles, *born* 1948, *apptd* 1998
Hon. Sir David Bodey, *born* 1947, *apptd* 1998

RESTRICTIVE PRACTICES COURT
Room 410, Thomas More Building, Royal Courts of
Justice, Strand, London WC2A 2LL
Tel 0171-936 6727

President, The Hon. Mr Justice Buckley
Judges, The Hon. Mr Justice Ferris; The Hon. Mr Justice
  Lightman
Lay Members, B. M. Currie; Sir Lewis Robertson, CBE; R.
  Garrick, CBE; S. J. Ahearne; J. A. Graham; Mrs D. H.
  Hatfield; J. A. Scott; B. D. Colgate; J. A. C. King
Clerk of the Court, M. Buckley

TECHNOLOGY AND CONSTRUCTION
COURT
St Dunstan's House, 133–137 Fetter Lane, London
EC4A 1HD
Tel 0171-936 7427

JUDGES (each £100,209)
  The Hon. Mr Justice Dyson (*Presiding Judge*)
  His Hon. Judge Bowsher, QC
  His Hon. Judge Hicks, QC
  His Hon. Judge Havery, QC
  His Hon. Judge Lloyd, QC
  His Hon. Judge Newman, QC
  His Hon. Judge Thornton, QC
  His Hon. Judge Wilcox
  His Hon. Judge Toulmin, CMG, QC

Court Manager, Miss B. Joy

LORD CHANCELLOR'S DEPARTMENT
— *see* Government Departments and Public Offices

SUPREME COURT DEPARTMENTS AND
OFFICES
Royal Courts of Justice, London WC2A 2LL
Tel 0171-936 6000

DIRECTOR'S OFFICE

Director, I. Hyams
Group Manager and Deputy Director, J. Selch
Group Manager, Family Proceedings and Probate Service, R. P.
  Knight
Finance and Performance Officer, K. T. Fairweather

ADMIRALTY AND COMMERCIAL REGISTRY AND
MARSHAL'S OFFICE
Registrar (£74,464), P. Miller
Admiralty Marshal and Court Manager, K. Houghton

BANKRUPTCY DEPARTMENT
Chief Registrar (£92,810), M. C. B. Buckley

Bankruptcy Registrars (£74,464), W. S. James; J. A.
  Simmonds; P. J. S. Rawson; S. Baister; G. W. Jaques
Court Manager, M. A. Brown

CENTRAL OFFICE OF THE SUPREME COURT
Senior Master of the Supreme Court (*QBD*)*, and Queen's*
  Remembrancer (£92,810), R. L. Turner
Masters of the Supreme Court (*QBD*) (£74,464), D. L. Prebble;
  G. H. Hodgson; J. Trench; M. Tennant; P. Miller; N. O.
  Murray; I. H. Foster; G. H. Rose; P. G. A. Eyre; H. J.
  Leslie; J. G. G. Ungley
Senior Court Manager, P. Emery

CHANCERY DIVISION
Senior Court Manager, P. Emery

CHANCERY CHAMBERS
Chief Master of the Supreme Court (£92,810), J. I. Winegarten
Masters of the Supreme Court (£74,464), J. A. Moncaster; R.
  A. Bowman; N. W. Bragge; T. J. Bowles
Court Manager, G. Robinson
Conveyancing Counsel of the Supreme Court, W. D. Ainger; H.
  M. Harrod; A. C. Taussig

COMPANIES COURT
Registrar (£74,464), M. Buckley
Court Manager, M. A. Brown

COURT OF APPEAL CIVIL DIVISION
Head of the Civil Appeals Office (£92,810), R. Venne
Court Manager, Miss H. M. Goddard

COURT OF APPEAL CRIMINAL DIVISION
Registrar (£92,810), M. McKenzie, CB, QC
Deputy Registrar, Mrs L. G. Knapman
Chief Clerk, M. Bishop

COURTS-MARTIAL APPEALS OFFICE
Registrar (£92,810), M. McKenzie, CB, QC
Chief Clerk, M. Bishop

CROWN OFFICE OF THE SUPREME COURT
Master of the Crown Office, and Queen's Coroner and Attorney
  (£92,810), M. McKenzie, CB, QC
Head of Crown Office, Mrs L. G. Knapman
Chief Clerk, M. Bishop

EXAMINERS OF THE COURT
Empowered to take examination of witnesses in all
Divisions of the High Court
  A. G. Dyer; A. W. Hughes; Mrs G. M. Kenne; R. M.
  Planterose; Miss V. E. I. Selvaratnam

RESTRICTIVE PRACTICES COURT
Clerk of the Court, M. Buckley
Court Manager, M. A. Brown

SUPREME COURT COSTS OFFICE
Senior Cost Judge (£92,810), P. T. Hurst
Masters of the Supreme Court (£74,464), M. Ellis; T. H.
  Seager Berry; C. C. Wright; P. R. Rogers; G. N. Pollard;
  J. E. O'Hare; C. D. N. Campbell
Court Manager, Mrs H. Oakey

COURT OF PROTECTION
Stewart House, 24 Kingsway, London WC2B 6HD
Tel 0171-664 7000
Master (£92,810), D. A. Lush

ELECTION PETITIONS OFFICE
Room E113, Royal Courts of Justice, Strand, London
WC2A 2LL

Tel 0171-936 6131

The office accepts petitions and deals with all matters relating to the questioning of parliamentary, European Parliament and local government elections, and with applications for relief under the Representation of the People legislation.

Prescribed Officer, R. L. Turner

Chief Clerk, Miss J. L. Waine

OFFICE OF THE LORD CHANCELLOR'S VISITORS
Stewart House, 24 Kingsway, London WC2B 6HD
Tel 0171-664 7317

Legal Visitor, A. R. Tyrrell

Medical Visitors, K. Khan; W. B. Sprey; E. Mateu; S. E. Mahapatra; A. Bailey; A. Kaeser

OFFICIAL RECEIVERS' DEPARTMENT
21 Bloomsbury Street, London WC1B 3SS
Tel 0171-323 3090

Senior Official Receiver, M. C. A. Osborne

Official Receivers, M. J. Pugh; L. T. Cramp; J. Norris

OFFICIAL SOLICITOR'S DEPARTMENT
81 Chancery Lane, London WC2B 6HD
Tel 0171-911 7105

Official Solicitor to the Supreme Court, P. M. Harris

Deputy Official Solicitor, H. J. Baker

Chief Clerk, R. Lancaster

PRINCIPAL REGISTRY (FAMILY DIVISION)
First Avenue House, 42–49 High Holborn, London
WC1V 6NP
Tel 0171-936 6000

Senior District Judge (£92,810), G. B. N. A. Angel

District Judges (£74,464), B. P. F. Kenworthy-Browne; Mrs K. T. Moorhouse; M. J. Segal; R. Conn; Miss I. M. Plumstead; G. J. Maple; Miss H. C. Bradley; K. J. White; A. R. S. Bassett-Cross; N. A. Grove; M. C. Berry; Miss S. M. Bowman; C. Million; P. Waller; Miss P. Cushing; R. Harper; G. C. Brasse; Miss D. C. Redgrave

Family and Probate Service Group Manager, R. P. Knight

District Probate Registrars

Birmingham and Stoke-on-Trent, C. Marsh

Brighton and Maidstone, P. Ellwood

Bristol, Exeter and Bodmin, R. H. P. Joyce

Cardiff, Bangor and Carmarthen, R. F. Yeldam

Ipswich, Norwich and Peterborough, D. N. Mee

Leeds, Lincoln and Sheffield, A. P. Dawson

Liverpool, Lancaster and Chester, C. Fox

Manchester and Nottingham, M. A. Moran

Newcastle, Carlisle, York and Middlesbrough, P. Sanderson

Oxford, Gloucester and Leicester, R. R. Da Costa

Winchester, A. K. Biggs

JUDGE ADVOCATES

OFFICE OF THE JUDGE ADVOCATE OF THE FLEET
c/o Group Manager's Office, The Court Service, Concorde House, 10–12 London Road, Maidstone ME16 8QA
Tel 01622-200120

Judge Advocate of the Fleet (£92,810), His Hon. Judge Sessions

OFFICE OF THE JUDGE ADVOCATE-GENERAL OF THE FORCES
(*Joint Service for the Army and the Royal Air Force*)
22 Kingsway, London WC2B 6LE

Tel 0171-218 8079

Judge Advocate-General (£100,209), His Hon. Judge J. W. Rant, CB, QC

Vice-Judge Advocate-General (£89,306), E. G. Moelwyn-Hughes

Judge Advocates (£74,464), D. M. Berkson; M. A. Hunter; J. P. Camp; Miss S. E. Woollam; R. C. C. Seymour; I. H. Pearson; R. G. Chapple; J. F. T. Bayliss

Style for Judge Advocates, Judge Advocate [surname]

HIGH COURT AND CROWN COURT CENTRES

First-tier centres deal with both civil and criminal cases and are served by High Court and circuit judges. Second-tier centres deal with criminal cases only and are served by High Court and circuit judges. Third-tier centres deal with criminal cases only and are served only by circuit judges.

MIDLAND AND OXFORD CIRCUIT

First-tier – Birmingham, Lincoln, Nottingham, Oxford, Stafford, Warwick

Second-tier – Leicester, Northampton, Shrewsbury, Worcester

Third-tier – Coventry, Derby, Grimsby, Hereford, Peterborough, Stoke-on-Trent, Wolverhampton

Circuit Administrator, P. Handcock, The Priory Courts, 6th Floor, 33 Bull Street, Birmingham B4 6DS. Tel: 0121-681 3000

Group Managers: Birmingham Group, Mrs K. Hoyte; *Coventry Group*, Mrs D. Ponsonby; *Lincoln Group*, A. Phillips; *Northampton Group*, K. Dickerson; *Nottingham Group*, Mrs E. A. Folman; *Stafford Group*, D. Bennett

NORTH-EASTERN CIRCUIT

First-tier – Leeds, Newcastle upon Tyne, Sheffield, Teesside

Second-tier – Bradford, York

Third-tier – Doncaster, Durham, Kingston-upon-Hull

Circuit Administrator, P. J. Farmer, 18th Floor, West Riding House, Albion Street, Leeds LS1 5AA. Tel: 0113-251 1200

Group Managers: Bradford Group, F. Taylor; *Leeds Group*, P. M. Norris; *Newcastle upon Tyne Group*, Miss S. Proudlock; *Sheffield Group*, G. Bingham, OBE; *Teesside Group*, Miss E. Yates

NORTHERN CIRCUIT

First-tier – Carlisle, Liverpool, Manchester (Crown Square), Preston

Third-tier – Barrow-in-Furness, Bolton, Burnley, Lancaster; Manchester (Minshull Street)

Circuit Administrator, R. A. Vincent, 15 Quay Street, Manchester M60 9FD. Tel: 0161-833 1005

Group Managers: Liverpool Group, Mrs J. Roche; *Manchester Central Group*, Mrs C. A. Mayer; *Outer Manchester Group*, S. Townley; *Preston Group*, B. Wilson

SOUTH-EASTERN CIRCUIT

First-tier – Chelmsford, Croydon, Lewes, Norwich

Second-tier – Chichester, Ipswich, London (Central Criminal Court), Luton, Maidstone, Reading, St Albans

Third-tier – Aylesbury, Basildon, Bury St Edmunds, Cambridge, Canterbury, Guildford, Hove, King's Lynn, London (Blackfriars, Harrow, Inner London Sessions House, Isleworth, Kingston, Knightsbridge, Middlesex Guildhall, Snaresbrook, Southend, Southwark, Wood Green, Woolwich)

Circuit Administrator, R. J. Clarke, New Cavendish House, 18 Maltravers Street, London WC2R 3EU. Tel: 0171-936 7235

Provincial Administrator, J. Powell, 1st Floor, Steeple House, Church Lane, Chelmsford CM1 1NH. Tel: 01245-257425

Group Managers: Chelmsford Group, M. Littlewood; *Kingston Group*, D. Thompson; *Lewes Group*, B. Macbeth; *London Group (Civil)*, D. Marsh; *London Group (Crime)*, K. Budgen; *Luton Group*, M. McIver; *Maidstone Group*, Mrs L. Lennon

The High Court in Greater London sits at the Royal Courts of Justice.

WALES AND CHESTER CIRCUIT

First-tier – Caernarfon, Cardiff, Chester, Mold, Swansea
Second-tier – Carmarthen, Merthyr Tydfil, Newport, Welshpool
Third-tier – Dolgellau, Haverfordwest, Knutsford, Warrington
Circuit Administrator, P. Risk, Churchill House, Churchill Way, Cardiff CF10 4HH. Tel: 01222-415501
Group Managers: Cardiff Group, G. Pickett; *Chester Group*, G. Kenney; *Swansea Group*, Mrs D. Thomas

WESTERN CIRCUIT

First-tier – Bristol, Exeter, Truro, Winchester
Second-tier – Dorchester, Gloucester, Plymouth, Weymouth
Third-tier – Barnstaple, Bournemouth, Newport (IOW), Portsmouth, Salisbury, Southampton, Swindon, Taunton
Circuit Administrator, D. Ryan, Bridge House, Sion Place, Clifton, Bristol BS8 4BN. Tel: 0117-974 3763
Group Managers: Bristol Group, N. Jeffery; *Exeter Group*, D. Gentry; *Winchester Group*, A. Bean

CIRCUIT JUDGES

Senior Circuit Judges, each £100,209
Circuit Judges at the Central Criminal Court, London (Old Bailey Judges), each £100,209
Circuit Judges, each £92,810
Style, His/Her Hon. Judge [surname]
Senior Presiding Judge, The Rt. Hon. Lord Justice Judge
MIDLAND AND OXFORD CIRCUIT
Presiding Judges, The Hon. Mr Justice Jowitt; The Hon. Mr Justice Astill

F. A. Allan; Miss C. Alton; B. J. Appleby, QC; D. P. Bennett; R. S. A. Benson; J. G. Boggis, QC; R. W. A. Bray; D. W. Brunning; N. B. Cameron Coles, QC; J. J. Cavell; F. A. Chapman; P. N. R. Clark; M. F. Coates; R. R. B. Cole; T. G. E. Corrie; P. F. Crane; *P. J. Crawford, QC (*Recorder of Birmingham*); Mrs P. A. Deeley; P. N. de Mille; T. M. Dillon, QC; C. H. Durman; B. A. Farrer, QC; Miss E. N. Fisher; J. E. Fletcher; A. C. Geddes; R. J. H. Gibbs, QC; J. Hall; V. E. Hall; D. R. D. Hamilton; S. T. Hammond; G. C. W. Harris, QC; M. J. Heath; Miss E. J. Hindley, QC; C. R. Hodson; J. R. Hopkin; Mrs H. M. Hughes; R. H. Hutchinson; R. A. G. Inglis; A. A. Jenkins; R. P. V. Jenkins; A. W. P. King; M. K. Lee, QC; D. L. McCarthy; A. W. McCreath; A. G. MacDuff, QC; D. D. McEvoy, QC; J. V. Machin; M. H. Mander; L. Marshall; K. Matthewman, QC; W. D. Matthews; H. R. Mayor, QC; N. J. Mitchell; P. R. Morrell; J. I. Morris; M. D. Mott; A. J. D. Nicholl; R. T. N. Orme; R. C. C. O'Rorke; J. F. F. Orrell; D. S. Perrett, QC; C. J. Pitchers; R. F. D. Pollard; D. P. Pugsley; J. R. Pyke; R. J. Rubery; J. A. O. Shand; D. P. Stanley; P. J. Stretton; G.

C. Styler; A. B. Taylor; J. J. Teare; R. S. W. F. Tonking; J. J. Wait; J. C. Warner; H. Wilson; J. W. Wilson

NORTH-EASTERN CIRCUIT

Presiding Judges, The Hon. Mr Justice Hooper; The Hon. Mr Justice Bennett

J. R. S. Adams; J. Altman; P. M. Baker, QC; T. W. Barber; J. E. Barry; G. N. Barr Young; R. Bartfield; C. O. J. Behrens; D. R. Bentley, QC; P. H. Bowers; A. N. J. Briggs; D. M. A. Bryant; J. W. M. Bullimore; B. Bush; M. C. Carr; M. L. Cartlidge; P. J. Charlesworth; P. J. Cockroft; G. J. K. Coles, QC; J. Crabtree; M. T. Cracknell; W. H. R. Crawford, QC; Mrs J. Davies; I. J. Dobkin; E. J. Faulks; P. J. Fox, QC; A. N. Fricker, QC; M. S. Garner; A. R. Goldsack, QC; R. A. Grant; S. P. Grenfell; S. J. Gullick; G. F. R. Harkins; T. S. A. Hawkesworth, QC; P. J. M. Heppel, QC; *T. D. T. Hodson (*Recorder of Newcastle upon Tyne*); P. M. L. Hoffman; D. P. Hunt; A. E. Hutchinson, QC; N. H. Jones, QC; R. A. Jordan; G. H. Kamil; T. D. Kent-Jones, TD; G. M. Lightfoot; R. P. Lowden; A. G. McCallum; C. I. McGonigal; M. K. Mettyear; R. J. Moore; A. L. Myerson, QC; D. A. Orde; Miss H. E. Paling; J. Prophet; P. E. Robertshaw; R. M. Scott; A. Simpson; L. Spittle; Mrs L. Sutcliffe; J. A. Swanson; M. J. Taylor; R. C. Taylor; J. D. G. Walford; M. Walker; P. H. C. Walker; *B. Walsh, QC; C. T. Walton; G. Whitburn, QC; J. S. Wolstenholme; D. R. Wood

NORTHERN CIRCUIT

Presiding Judges, The Hon. Mr Justice Forbes; The Hon. Mr Justice Douglas Brown

M. P. Allweis; J. F. Appleton; S. W. Baker; A. W. Bell; R. C. W. Bennett; Miss I. Bernstein; M. S. Blackburn; A. N. H. Blake; C. Bloom, QC; R. Brown; J. K. Burke, QC; I. B. Campbell; F. B. Carter, QC; B. I. Caulfield; D. Clark; *D. C. Clarke, QC (*Recorder of Liverpool*); G. M. Clifton; I. W. Crompton; *R. E. Davies, QC (*Recorder of Manchester*); Miss A. E. Downey; B. R. Duckworth; S. B. Duncan; Miss D. B. Eaglestone; T. K. Earnshaw; G. A. Ensor; D. M. Evans, QC; S. J. D. Fawcus; P. S. Fish; J. R. B. Geake; D. S. Gee; W. George; J. A. D. Gilliland, QC; J. A. Hammond; M. Hedley; T. B. Hegarty, QC; M. J. Henshell; F. R. B. Holloway; R. C. Holman; N. J. G. Howarth; G. W. Humphries; C. E. F. James; P. M. Kershaw, QC (*Commercial Circuit Judge*); H. L. Lachs; P. M. Lakin; B. W. Lewis; R. J. D. Livesey, QC; D. Lynch; D. I. Mackay; J. B. Macmillan; D. G. Maddison; B. C. Maddocks; C. J. Mahon; J. A. Morgan; W. P. Morris; T. J. Mort; *C. P. L. Openshaw; QC; F. D. Owen, TD; J. A. Phillips; J. C. Phipps; D. A. Pirie; A. J. Proctor; J. H. Roberts; Miss G. D. Ruaux; H. S. Singer; E. Slinger; A. C. Smith; W. P. Smith; Miss E. M. Steel; D. R. Swift; C. B. Tetlow; J. P. Townend; I. J. C. Trigger; P. W. G. Urquhart; K. H. P. Wilkinson; B. Woodward

SOUTH-EASTERN CIRCUIT

Presiding Judges, The Hon. Mr Justice Gage; The Hon. Mr Justice Moses

J. D. R. Adams; M. F. Addison; P. C. Ader; Mrs S. C. Andrew; A. R. L. Ansell; M. G. Anthony; S. A. Anwyl, QC; M. F. Baker, QC; A. F. Balston; G. S. Barham; C. J. A. Barnett, QC; W. E. Barnett, QC; R. A. Barratt, QC; K. Bassingthwaighte; *G. A. Bathurst Norman; P. J. L. Beaumont, QC; N. E. Beddard; Mrs C. V. Bevington; M. G. Binning; J. E. Bishop; B. M. B. Black; H. O. Blacksell, QC; J. G. Boal, QC; A. V. Bradbury; P. N. Brandt; R. G. Brown; J. M. Bull, QC; *N. M. Butter, QC; The Hon. C. W. Byers; H. J. Byrt, QC; C. V. Callman; J. Q. Campbell; M. J. Carroll; B. E. F. Catlin; *B. L. Charles, QC; P. C. L. Clark; P. C. Clegg; Miss S. Coates; N. J. Coleman; S. H. Colgan; P. H. Collins;

C. C. Colston, QC; S. S. Coltart; Viscount Colville of Culross, QC; J. S. Colyer, QC; C. D. Compston; T. A. C. Coningsby, QC; J. G. Connor; R. D. Connor; M. J. Cook; R. A. Cooke; M. R. Coombe; P. E. Copley; Dr E. Cotran; P. R. Cowell; R. C. Cox; M. L. S. Cripps; J. F. Crocker; D. L. Croft, QC; H. M. Crush; D. M. Cryan; P. Curl; G. L. Davies; I. H. Davies, TD; W. L. M. Davies, QC; M. Dean, QC; W. N. Denison, QC (*Common Serjeant*); J. E. Devaux; M. N. Devonshire, TD; P. H. Downes; W. H. Dunn, QC; C. M. Edwards; D. F. Elfer; QC; D. R. Ellis; R. C. Elly; C. Elwen; F. P. L. Evans; J. D. Farnworth; P. Fingret; P. E. J. Focke, QC; P. Ford; G. C. F. Forrester; Ms D. A. Freedman; R. Gee; L. Gerber; C. A. H. Gibson; Miss A. F. Goddard, QC; S. A. Goldstein; C. G. M. Gordon; J. B. Gosschalk; M. Graham, QC; B. S. Green, QC; D. J. Griffiths; G. D. Grigson; R. B. Groves, TD, VRD; N. T. Hague, QC; D. F. Hallett; A. B. R. Hallgarten, QC; Miss G. Hallon; J. Hamilton; Miss S. Hamilton, QC; C. R. H. Hardy; B. Hargrove, OBE, QC; M. F. Harris; A. M. Harvey; R. G. Hawkins, QC; J. M. Haworth; R. J. Haworth; R. M. Hayward; A. N. Hitching; D. Holden; J. F. Holt; A. C. W. Hordern, QC; K. A. D. Hornby; M. Hucker; Sir David Hughes-Morgan, Bt., CB, CBE; J. G. Hull, QC; M. J. Hyam (*Recorder of London*); D. A. Inman; A. B. Issard-Davies; Dr P. J. E. Jackson; T. J. C. Joseph; I. G. F. Karsten, QC; S. S. Katkhuda; C. J. B. Kemp; M. Kennedy, QC; A. M. Kenny; T. R. King; B. J. Knight, QC; L. G. Krikler; L. H. C. Lait; P. St J. H. Langan, QC; Capt. J. B. R. Langdon, RN; P. H. Latham; R. Laurie; T. Lawrence; D. M. Levy, QC; C. C. D. Lindsay, QC; S. H. Lloyd; F. R. Lockhart; Mrs C. M. Ludlow; Capt. S. Lyons; A. G. McDowall; R. J. McGregor-Johnson; K. M. McHale; K. A. Machin, QC; R. G. McKinnon; W. N. McKinnon; K. C. Macrae; T. Maher; F. J. M. Marr-Johnson; D. N. N. Martineau; N. A. Medawar, QC; D. B. Meier; D. J. Mellor; G. D. Mercer; D. Q. Miller; Miss A. E. Mitchell; F. I. Mitchell; H. M. Morgan; D. Morton Jack; R. T. Moss; Miss M. J. S. Mowat; T. M. E. Nash; M. H. D. Neligan; Mrs M. F. Norrie; Brig. A. P. Norris, OBE; P. W. O'Brien; M. A. Oppenheimer; D. C. J. Paget, QC; D. J. Parry; Mrs N. Pearce; Prof. D. S. Pearl; Miss V. A. Pearlman; B. P. Pearson; J. R. Peppitt, QC; N. A. J. Philpot; T. D. Pillay; D. C. Pitman; J. R. Platt; J. R. Playford, QC; P. B. Pollock; T. G. Pontius; W. D. C. Poulton; H. C. Pownall, QC; S. Pratt; R. J. C. V. Prendergast; J. E. Previté, QC; B. H. Pryor, QC; J. E. Pullinger; D. W. Radford; J. W. Rant, CB, QC; E. V. P. Reece; J. R. Reid, QC; M. P. Reynolds; G. K. Rice; M. S. Rich, QC; N. P. Riddell; G. Rivlin, QC; S. D. Robbins; D. A. H. Rodwell, QC; G. H. Rooke, TD, QC; W. M. Rose; P. C. R. Rountree; J. H. Rucker; T. R. G. Ryland; J. E. A. Samuels, QC; R. B. Sanders; A. R. G. Scott-Gall; J. S. Sennitt; D. Serota, QC; J. L. Sessions; D. R. A. Sich; A. G. Simmons; K. T. Simpson; P. R. Simpson; M. Singh, QC; S. P. Sleeman; C. M. Smith, QC; S. A. R. Smith; R. J. Southan; S. B. Spence; S. M. Stephens, QC; N. A. Stewart; W. F. C. Thomas; P. J. Thompson; A. G. Y. Thorpe; C. H. Tilling; C. J. M. Tyrer; Mrs A. P. Uziell-Hamilton; J. E. van der Werff; A. O. R. Vick, QC; T. L. Viljoen; Miss A. P. Wakefield; R. Wakefield; R. Walker; S. P. Waller; D. B. Watling, QC; A. R. Webb; C. S. Welchman; A. F. Wilkie, QC; S. R. Wilkinson; R. J. Winstanley; D. Worsley; E. G. Wrintmore; M. P. Yelton; K. H. Zucker, QC

WALES AND CHESTER CIRCUIT

Presiding Judges, The Hon. Mr Justice Maurice Kay; The Hon. Mr Justice Connell; The Hon. Mr Justice Thomas

K. E. Barnett; M. R. Burr; G. H. F. Carson; S. P. Clarke; T. R. Crowther, QC; J. T. Curran; Miss J. M. P. Daley; G. H. M. Daniel; D. T. A. Davies; J. B. S. Diehl, QC; R. T.

Dutton; D. E. H. Edwards; G. O. Edwards, QC; The Lord Elystan-Morgan; *D. R. Evans, QC; M. R. Furness; J. W. Gaskell; D. R. Halbert; D. J. Hale; Miss J. E. Hayward; R. P. Hughes; P. J. Jacobs; G. J. Jones; H. D. H. Jones; G. E. Kilfoil; C. G. Masterman; D. G. Morgan; D. G. Morris; D. C. Morton; T. H. Moseley, QC; P. J. Price, QC; E. J. Prosser, QC; D. W. Richards; J. M. T. Rogers, QC; A. A. Wallace

WESTERN CIRCUIT

Presiding Judges, The Hon. Mr Justice Butterfield; The Hon. Mr Justice Toulson

P. R. Barclay; J. F. Beashel; R. H. Bond; Miss J. A. M. Bonvin; C. L. Boothman; M. J. L. Brodrick; J. M. J. Burford, QC; R. D. H. Bursell, QC; A. V. Chubb; M. G. Cotterill; G. W. A. Cottle; K. C. Cutler; P. M. Darlow; S. C. Darwall Smith; Mrs S. P. Darwall Smith; Mrs L. H. Davies; *M. Dyer; Ms J. A. Exton; J. D. Foley; D. L. Griffiths; J. D. Griggs; Mrs C. M. A. Hagen; P. J. C. R. Hooton; G. B. Hutton; R. E. Jack, QC; A. G. H. Jones; T. Longbotham; T. N. Mackean; Miss S. M. D. McKinney; I. S. McKintosh; J. G. McNaught; The Lord Meston, QC; T. J. Milligan; J. Neligan; S. K. O'Malley; S. K. Overend; R. Price; R. C. Pryor, QC; M. W. Roach; J. N. P. Rudd; A. Rutherford; Miss A. O. H. Sander; D. H. D. Selwood; R. M. Shawcross; D. A. Smith, QC; W. E. M. Taylor; P. M. Thomas; A. A. R. Thompson, QC; D. K. Ticehurst, QC; D. M. Webster, QC; J. H. Weeks, QC; J. S. Wiggs; J. A. J. Wigmore; J. C. Willis

RECORDERS
(each £422 per day)

F. A. Abbott; R. D. I. Adam; J. F. Akast; D. J. Ake; R. Akenhead, QC; I. D. G. Alexander, QC; C. D. Allan, QC; C. J. Alldis; J. H. Allen, QC; D. M. Altaras; A. J. Anderson, QC; W. P. Andreae-Jones, QC; Mrs E. H. Andrew; P. J. Andrews, QC; R. A. Anelay, QC; J. M. Appleby; Miss L. E. Appleby, QC; B. J. Argyle; E. K. Armitage, QC; P. J. B. Armstrong; G. K. Arran; S. J. Ashurst; E. G. Aspley; P. Atherton; R. K. Atherton; N. J. Atkinson, QC; D. J. M. Aubrey, QC; D. S. Aubrey; M. G. Austin-Smith; M. J. S. Axtell; W. S. Aylen, QC; P. D. Babb; J. F. Badenoch, QC; P. G. N. Badge; Miss P. H. Badley; E. H. Bailey; A. B. Baillie; N. R. J. Baker, QC; Miss A. Ball, QC; C. G. Ball, QC; A. Barker, QC; B. J. Barker, QC; G. E. Barling, QC; D. N. Barnard; H. J. Barnes; T. P. Barnes, QC; A. J. Barnett; Miss F. J. Baron, QC; D. A. Bartlett; G. R. Bartlett, QC; J. C. T. Barton, QC; D. C. Bate, QC; S. D. Batten, QC; P. D. Batty, QC; J. J. Baughan, QC; J. F. T. Bayliss; R. A. Bayliss; D. M. Bean; J. Beatson; S. J. Bedford; R. V. M. E. Behar; R. W. Belben; J. K. Benson; P. C. Benson; R. A. Benson, QC; H. L. Bentham, QC; D. M. Berkson; C. R. Berry; M. Bethel, QC; P. V. Bevan; Mrs M. O. Bickford-Smith; N. Bidder; I. G. Bing; P. V. Birkett, QC; M. I. Birnbaum; W. J. Birtles; P. W. Birts, QC; Mrs J. M. Black, QC; M. J. Black, QC; B. G. D. Blair, QC; W. J. L. Blair, QC; P. E. Bleasdale; R. H. L. Blomfield, TD; D. J. Blunt, QC; O. S. P. Blunt, QC; Miss B. M. Bolton; G. T. K. Boney, QC; Ms C. Booth, QC; J. J. Boothby; D. J. Boulton; S. N. Bourne-Arton, QC; M. J. Bowerman; Ms M. R. Bowron; W. Boyce; S. C. Boyd, QC; J. J. Boyle; D. L. Bradshaw; W. T. S. Braithwaite, QC; G. B. Breen; D. J. Brennan, QC; M. L. Brent, QC; G. J. B. G. Brice, QC; A. J. Brigden; D. R. Bright; R. P. Brittain; R. A. Britton; J. Bromley-Davenport; L. F. M. Brown; S. C. Brown, QC; D. J. M. Browne, QC; J. N. Browne; A. J. N. Brunner, QC; R. V. Bryan; Miss B. M. Bucknall, QC; J. E. Bullen; J. P. Burke, QC; L. S. Burn; H. W. Burnett, QC; R. H. Burns; S. J. Burnton, QC; F. G. Burrell, QC; K. Bush; A. J. Butcher, QC; C. M. Butler; Miss J. Butler; M. D. Byrne; D. W. Caddick;

D. Calvert-Smith, QC; R. Camden Pratt, QC; Miss S. M. C.
Cameron, QC; A. N. Campbell, QC; J. M. Caplan, QC; G. M.
C. Carey, QC; A. C. Carlile, QC, MP; H. B. H. Carlisle, QC; J.
J. Carter-Manning, QC; R. Carus, QC; Mrs J. R. Case; P. D.
Cattan; Miss M. T. Catterson; R. M. Challinor; N. M.
Chambers, QC; Miss D. C. Champion; C. B. Chandler; V.
R. Chapman; J. M. Cherry, QC; A. C. Chippindall; C. F.
Chruszcz, QC; C. H. Clark, QC; C. S. S. Clarke, QC; P.
W. Clarke; P. R. J. Clarkson, QC; T. Clayson; A. S. L.
Cleary; W. Clegg, QC; P. Clements; G. Cliffe; T. A.
Clover; W. P. Coates; D. J. Cocks, QC; J. J. Coffey, QC; T.
A. Coghlan, QC; J. L. Cohen; L. F. R. Cohen, QC; W. J.
Coker, QC; A. J. S. Coleman; P. J. D. Coleridge, QC; A. R.
Collender, QC; P. N. Collier, QC; M. G. Collins, QC; I.
Collis; Mrs J. R. Comyns; D. G. Conlin; A. D. Conrad; C.
S. Cook; J. L. Cooke, QC; N. O. Cooke; K. B. Coonan, QC;
A. E. M. Cooper; P. J. Cooper, QC; C. J. Cornwall; P. J.
Cosgrove, QC; Miss D. R. Cotton, QC; J. S. Coward, QC; T.
G. Cowling; Mrs L. M. Cox, QC; P. Crampin, QC; L. S.
Crawford; N. Crichton; D. I. Crigman, QC; C. A.
Critchlow; D. R. Crome; S. R. Crookenden, QC; Mrs J. E.
Crowley; J. D. Crowley, QC; T. S. Culver; Miss E. A. M.
Curnow, QC; P. D. Curran; J. W. O. Curtis, QC; M. J.
Curwen; A. J. G. Dalziel; Mrs P. M. T. Dangor; A. M.
Darroch; C. P. M. Davidson; A. M. Davies; A. R. M.
Davies; H. Davies; J. T. L. Davies; Miss N. V. Davies, QC;
R. L. Davies, QC; N. A. L. Davis, QC; W. E. Davis; A. W.
Dawson; D. H. Day, QC; P. G. Dedman; Ms M. R. de Haas,
QC; P. A. de la Piquerie; M. A. de Navarro, QC; R. L.
Denyer, QC; H. A. D. de Silva; P. N. Digney; C. E. Dines;
A. D. Dinkin, QC; D. R. Dobbin; R. S. Dodds; P. Dodgson;
R. A. M. Doggett; Ms B. Dohmann, QC; D. T. Donaldson,
QC; A. M. Donne, QC; A. F. S. Donovan; A. K. Dooley; Ms
J. M. R. Dowell; J. Dowse; M. J. Dudley; J. R. Duggan; P.
R. Dunkels, QC; J. D. Durham Hall, QC; R. M. Eades; H.
W. P. Eccles, QC; C. N. Edelman, QC; A. J. C. Edis, QC; A.
H. Edwards; Miss S. M. Edwards, QC; A. J. C. Edwards-
Stuart, QC; A. J. Elleray, QC; G. Elias, QC; E. A. Elliott; J. A.
Elvidge; R. M. Englehart, QC; D. A. Evans, QC; D. H.
Evans, QC; F. W. H. Evans; G. J. Evans; G. W. R.
Evans, QC; I. Evans; M. Evans; M. J. Evans; M. A.
Everall, QC; Miss D. Faber; T. M. Faber; R. B. Farley, QC;
P. M. Farmer, QC; D. J. Farrer, QC; P. E. Feinberg, QC; J. F.
Q. Fenwick, QC; R. Fernyhough, QC; M. C. Field; R. A.
Field, QC; J. E. Finestein; Miss A. C. Finnerty; D. T. Fish;
D. P. Fisher, QC; G. D. Flather, CBE, QC; R. A. Flowerdew;
N. M. Ford, QC; R. A. Fordham, QC; B. C. Forster; M. D. P.
Fortune; D. R. Foskett, QC; I. H. Foster; J. R. Foster, QC; D.
P. Friedman, QC; S. A. Furst, QC; C. J. E. Gardner, QC; P.
R. Garlick, QC; C. R. Garside, QC; R. C. Gaskell; J. B.
Gateshill; S. A. G. L. Gault; A. H. Gee, QC; I. W. Geering,
QC; D. S. Geey; C. R. George, QC; S. M. Gerlis; D. C.
Gerrey; J. S. Gibbons, QC; A. J. Gilbart, QC; F. H. S.
Gilbert, QC; N. J. Gilchrist; K. Gillance; N. B. D. Gilmour,
QC; L. Giovenne; R. P. Glancy, QC; A. T. Glass, QC; M. G.
J. Gledhill; H. B. Globe, QC; Miss E. Gloster, QC; H. K.
Goddard, QC; H. A. Godfrey, QC; Ms L. S. Godfrey, QC; J.
J. Goldberg, QC; I. S. Goldrein, QC; J. B. Goldring, QC; P.
H. Goldsmith, QC; A. J. Goldstaub, QC; L. C. Goldstone,
QC; A. J. J. Gompertz, QC; Miss R. M. Goode; J. R. W.
Goss; T. J. C. Goudie, QC; A. A. Goymer; G. Gozem; The
Lord Grabiner, QC; M. H. Green, QC; Miss J. E. G.
Greenberg, QC; A. E. Greenwood; J. Greenwood; J. G.
Grenfell, QC; D. E. Griffith-Jones; R. H. Griffith-Jones; J.
P. G. Griffiths, QC; M. G. Grills; M. S. E. Grime, QC; P.
Grobel; P. H. Gross, QC; B. P. Gulbenkian; J. D. Guthrie,
QC; A. S. Hacking, QC; J. W. Haines; N. J. Hall; S. J. Hall; J.
P. N. Hallam; A. N. R. Hamilton; G. M. Hamilton, TD, QC;
I. M. Hamilton; P. L. Hamlin; J. L. Hand, QC; G. T.
Harrap; M. K. Harington; P. J. Harrington, QC; D. M.

Harris, QC; R. D. Harrison; R. M. Harrison, QC; H. M.
Harrod; J. M. Harrow; C. A. Hart-Leverton, QC; B.
Harvey; J. G. Harvey; M. L. T. Harvey, QC; D. W. Hatton,
QC; A. M. D. Havelock-Allan, QC; The Hon. P. N. Havers,
QC; W. G. Hawkesworth; R. W. P. H. Hay; Prof. D. J.
Hayton; R. Hayward-Smith, QC; R. Hedgeland; A. T.
Hedworth, QC; R. A. Henderson, QC; R. H. Q. Henriques,
QC; R. C. Herman; M. S. Heslop QC; T. Hewitt; G. R.
Hickinbottom; J. W. Hillyer; A. J. H. Hilton, QC; J. W.
Hirst, QC; W. T. J. Hirst; J. D. Hitchen; S. A. Hockman,
QC; H. E. G. Hodge, OBE; A. J. C. Hoggett, QC; T. V.
Holroyde, QC; R. M. Hone; G. A. J. Hooper; A. D. Hope; S.
J. Hopkins; M. A. P. Hopmeier; M. Horowitz, QC; Miss R.
Horwood-Smart; C. P. Hotten, QC; B. F. Houlder, QC; M.
N. Howard, QC; C. I. Howells; M. J. Hubbard, QC; D. L.
Hughes; Miss J. C. A. Hughes, QC; Miss K. L. Hughes; P.
T. Hughes, QC; T. M. Hughes, QC; L. D. Hull; Capt. D. R.
Humphrey, RN; W. G. B. Hungerford; D. R. N. Hunt, QC;
P. J. Hunt, QC; I. G. A. Hunter, QC; M. A. Hunter; G. N. N.
Huskinson; M. Hussain, QC; J. G. K. Hyland; R. Ibbotson;
M. D. Inman, QC; P. R. Isaacs; S. L. Isaacs, QC; S. M. Jack;
D. G. A. Jackson; M. R. Jackson; I. E. Jacob; N. F. B.
Jarman, QC; J. M. Jarvis, QC; J. R. Jarvis; A. H. Jeffreys; D.
A. Jeffreys, QC; J. D. Jenkins, QC; Miss A. M. A. Jolles; D. A. F.
Jones; D. L. Jones; N. G. Jones; P. H. F. Jones; S. E. Jones,
QC; W. J. Jones; R. C. Jose; Ms W. R. Joseph, QC; H. M.
Joy; P. S. L. Joyce, QC; R. W. S. Juckes; M. L. Kallipetis,
QC; Miss L. N. R. Kamill; R. G. Kaye, QC; C. B. Kealy; K.
R. Keen, QC; Mrs S. M. Keen; B. R. Keith, QC; W. A.
Kennedy; D. Kennett Brown; D. M. Kerr; L. D. Kershen,
QC; M. I. Khan; G. M. P. F. Khayat, QC; C. A. Kinch; T. R.
A. King, QC; Mrs F. M. Kirkham; M. S. Knott; Miss P. E.
Knowles; C. J. Knox; Miss J. C. M. Korner, QC; S. E.
Kramer, QC; Miss L. J. Kushner, QC; P. E. Kyte, QC; N. R.
W. Lambert; D. C. Lamdin; A. T. Lancaster; D. A. Landau;
D. G. Lane, QC; B. F. J. Langstaff, QC; R. B. Latham, QC; S.
W. Lawler, QC; Sir Ivan Lawrence, QC; Miss E. A. Lawson,
QC; M. H. Lawson, QC; G. S. Lawson-Rogers, QC; P. L. O.
Leaver, QC; D. Lederman, QC; B. W. T. Leech; I. Leeming,
QC; C. H. de V. Leigh, QC; H. B. G. Lett; B. L. Lever; B. H.
Leveson, QC; A. E. Levy, QC; M. E. Lewer, QC; J. A. Lewis;
K. M. J. Lewison, QC; S. J. Linehan, QC; R. A. Lissack, QC;
G. W. Little; B. J. E. Livesey, QC; C. G. Llewellyn-Jones,
QC; L. J. R. Lobo; C. J. Lockhart-Mummery, QC; A. J. C.
Lodge, QC; D. C. Lovell-Pank, QC; A. C. Lowcock; G. W.
Lowe; J. A. M. Lowen; Rt. Hon. Sir Nicholas Lyell, QC,
MP; A. P. Lyon; P. G. McCahill, QC; R. G. B. McCombe,
QC; G. F. McDermott; A. E. McFarlane, QC; K. M. P.
Macgill; R. D. Machell, QC; B. M. McIntyre; C. C.
Mackay, QC; D. L. Mackie; N. A. McKittrick; I. A. B.
McLaren, QC; I. McLeod; N. R. B. Macleod; QC; A. G.
Mainds; A. H. R. Maitland; A. R. Malcolm; H. J. Malins;
M. E. Mann, QC; The Hon. G. R. J. Mansfield; R. L. Marks;
J. W. Marrin, QC; A. L. Marriott, QC; M. A. Marriott; A. S.
Marron, QC; P. Marsh; R. G. Marshall-Andrews, QC; G. C.
Marson; H. R. A. Martineau; S. A. Maskrey, QC; C. P.
Mather; D. Matheson, QC; P. R. Matthews; Mrs S. P.
Matthews, QC; P. B. Mauleverer, QC; R. B. Mawrey, QC; J.
F. M. Maxwell; R. Maxwell, QC; Mrs P. R. May; R. M. J.
Meeke; G. M. Mercer; N. F. Merriman, QC; C. S. J.
Metcalf; J. T. Milford, QC; K. S. H. Miller; P. W. Miller; R.
A. Miller; S. M. Miller, QC; C. J. Millington; C. E. Million;
J. B. M. Milmo, QC; D. C. Milne, QC; C. J. M. Miskin, QC;
Miss C. M. Miskin; A. P. Mitchell; A. R. Mitchell, QC; C.
R. Mitchell; D. C. Mitchell; J. R. Mitchell; J. E. Mitting,
QC; F. R. Moat; E. G. Moelwyn-Hughes; C. R. D. Moger,
QC; Mrs J. P. Moir; D. P. R. Mole, QC; M. G. C.
Moorhouse; A. G. Moran, QC; D. W. Morgan; P. B.
Morgan; A. P. Morris, QC; C. Morris-Coole; H. A. C.
Morrison, OBE; R. F. Morrison; G. E. Morrow, QC; M. G.

M. Morse; C. J. Moss, QC; P. C. Mott, QC; R. W. Moxon-Brown, QC; J. H. Muir; F. J. Muller, QC; A. H. Munday, QC; G. S. Murdoch, QC; I. P. Murphy, QC; M. J. A. Murphy, QC; A. C. Murray; C. M. Murray; N. O. G. Murray; N. J. Mylne, QC; H. G. Narayan; A. R. H. Newman, QC; Miss L. A. Newton; A. I. Niblett; G. Nice, QC; A. E. R. Noble; B. Nolan, QC; M. C. Norman; J. M. Norris; P. H. Norris; G. Nuttall; J. G. Nutting, QC; D. P. O'Brien, QC; Mrs F. M. T. Oldham, QC; M. D. Oldham; S. Oliver-Jones, QC; R. W. Onions; M. N. O'Sullivan; D. B. W. Ouseley, QC; N. D. Padfield, QC; Miss A. M. Page, QC; S. R. Page; A. O. Palmer, QC; A. W. Palmer, QC; D. P. Pannick, QC; A. D. W. Pardoe, QC; S. A. B. Parish; P. L. Parker; G. C. Parkins, QC; G. E. Parkinson; M. P. Parroy, QC; D. J. T. Parry; E. O. Parry; N. S. K. Pascoe, QC; A. Patience, QC; Miss A. E. H. Pauffley, QC; J. G. Paulusz; W. E. Pawlak; F. M. Pearce; D. J. Pearce-Higgins, QC; R. J. Pearse Wheatley; The Hon. I. J. C. Peddie, QC; J. V. Pegden; J. Perry, QC; M. Pert, QC; N. M. Peters; J. R. D. Philips; D. J. Phillips, QC; W. B. Phillips; M. A. Pickering, QC; J. K. Pickup; C. J. Pitchford, QC; The Hon. B. M. D. Pitt; Miss E. F. Platt, QC; R. Platts; R. O. Plender, QC; Miss J. C. Plumptre; Miss I. M. Plumstead; S. D. Popat; A. R. Porten, QC; L. R. Portnoy; J. R. L. Posnansky, QC; Mrs R. M. Poulet, QC; S. R. Powles, QC; D. Price; G. A. L. Price, QC; J. A. Price, QC; J. C. Price; N. P. L. Price, QC; R. Price Lewis; R. B. L. Prior; F. S. K. Privett; H. W. Prosser; A. C. Pugh, QC; G. V. Pugh, QC; G. F. Pulman, QC; C. P. B. Purchas, QC; R. M. Purchas, QC; N. R. Purnell, QC; P. O. Purnell, QC; Q. C. W. Querelle; N. P. Quinn; D. A. Radcliffe; Mrs N. P. Radford, QC; Ms A. J. Rafferty, QC; T. W. H. Raggatt, QC; Miss E. A. Ralphs; J. Y. Randall, QC; A. D. Rawley, QC; J. E. Rayner James, QC; P. R. Raynor, QC; J. H. Reddihough; M. H. Redfern, QC; A. R. F. Redgrave, QC; D. W. Rees; G. W. Rees; P. Rees; C. E. Reese, QC; P. C. Reid; D. J. Rennie; R. E. Rhodes, QC; D. J. Richardson; T. Rigby; S. V. Riordan, QC; G. Risius; Miss J. H. Ritchie, QC; J. M. Roberts; J. M. G. Roberts, QC; T. D. Roberts; A. J. Robertson; G. R. Robertson, QC; V. Robinson, QC; D. E. H. Robson, QC; G. W. Roddick, QC; Miss M. B. Roddy; Miss D. J. Rodgers; P. F. G. Rook, QC; J. G. Ross; J. G. Ross Martyn; P. C. Rouch; J. J. Rowe, QC; R. J. Royce; M. W. Rudland; P. E. B. M. Rueff; A. A. Rumbelow, QC; N. J. Rumfitt, QC; R. J. Rundell; J. R. T. Rylance; C. R. A. Sallon, QC; C. N. Salmon; D. A. Salter; G. R. Sankey, QC; N. L. Sarony; J. H. B. Saunders, QC; M. P. Sayers, QC; R. J. Scholes; T. J. W. Scott; Miss P. Scriven, QC; R. J. Seabrook, QC; C. Seagroatt, QC; W. P. L. Sellick; O. M. Sells, QC; R. W. Seymour, QC; A. J. Seys-Llewellyn; A. R. F. Sharp; P. P. Shears; S. J. Sher, QC; Miss D. A. Sherwin; Miss J. Shipley; S. R. Silber, QC; P. C. H. Simon, QC; Miss E. A. Slade, QC; A. C. Smith, QC; A. T. Smith, QC; D. Smith; P. W. Smith, QC; R. D. H. Smith, QC; Ms Z. P. Smith; C. J. Smyth; R. C. Southwell, QC; R. C. E. Southwell; M. H. Spence, QC; Sir Derek Spencer, QC; J. Spencer, QC; M. G. Spencer, QC; R. G. Spencer; S. M. Spencer, QC; R. V. Spencer Bernard; D. P. Spens, QC; R. W. Spon-Smith; D. Steer, QC; M. T. Steiger, QC; Mrs L. J. Stern, QC; A. W. Stevenson, TD; J. S. H. Stewart, QC; S. P. Stewart, QC; W. R. Stewart Smith; A. C. Steynor; G. J. C. Still; D. A. Stockdale, QC; Mrs D. M. Stocken; D. M. A. Stokes, QC; M. G. T. Stokes, QC; J. B. Storey, QC; T. M. F. Stow, QC; D. M. A. Strachan, QC; M. Stuart-Moore, QC; J. H. Stuart-Smith, QC; F. R. C. Such; A. B. Suckling, QC; Ms L. E. Sullivan, QC; D. M. Sumner; J. P. C. Sumption, QC; M. A. Supperstone, QC; P. J. Susman; R. P. Sutton, QC; N. H. Sweeney; Miss C. J. Swift, QC; M. R. Swift, QC; Miss H. H. Swindells; P. Sycamore; C. J. M. Symons, QC; J. P. Tabor, QC; J. A. Tackaberry, QC; P. J. Talbot, QC; R. K. K. Talbot; R. B. Tansey, QC; J. B. C. Tanzer; Miss S. A. M. Tapping; G. F. Tattersall, QC; E. T. H. Teague; N. J. M.

Teare, QC; R. H. Tedd, QC; A. D. Temple, QC; V. B. A. Temple, QC; M. H. Tennant; The Lord Thomas of Gresford, OBE, QC; P. A. Thomas; R. L. Thomas, QC; R. M. Thomas; R. U. Thomas, QC; Miss S. M. Thomas; C. F. J. Thompson; R. E. T. Thorn, QC; A. R. Thornhill, QC; P. R. Thornton, QC; A. C. Tickle; M. B. Tillett, QC; J. W. Tinnion; R. N. Titheridge, QC; S. M. Tomlinson, QC; P. J. H. Towler; J. B. S. Townend, QC; C. M. Treacy, QC; H. B. Trethowan; A. D. H. Trollope, QC; M. G. Tugendhat, QC; H. W. Turcan; D. A. Turner, QC; J. Turner; P. A. Twigg, QC; J. F. Uff, QC; R. P. A. Ullstein, QC; N. E. Underhill, QC; J. G. G. Ungley; H. V. C. Vagg; N. P. Valios, QC; N. C. van der Bijl; D. A. J. Vaughan, QC; M. J. D. Vere-Hodge, QC; C. J. Vosper; J. P. Wadsworth, QC; S. P. Waine; R. M. Wakerley, QC; Mrs E. A. Walker; R. A. Walker, QC; R. J. Walker, QC; Sir Jonah Walker-Smith, Bt.; T. M. Walsh; J. J. Wardlow; B. B. Warner; J. Warren, QC; N. J. Warren; N. R. Warren, QC; D. E. B. Waters; Miss B. J. Watson; Sir James Watson, Bt.; B. J. Waylen; A. S. Webster, QC; M. R. West; L. J. West-Knights; G. B. N. White; W. J. M. White; D. R. B. Whitehouse; R. P. Whitehurst; P. G. Whiteman, QC; P. J. M. Whiteman, TD; A. Whitfield, QC; S. J. P. Widdup; C. T. Wide, QC; R. Wigglesworth; Mrs M. Wilby; N. V. M. Wilkinson; Miss E. Willers; G. H. G. Williams, QC; Miss J. A. Williams; J. G. Williams, QC; J. L. Williams, QC; M. J. Williams; W. L. Williams, QC; Miss H. E. Williamson, QC; S. W. Williamson, QC; A. J. D. Wilson, QC; A. M. Wilson, QC; I. K. R. Wilson; C. Wilson-Smith, QC; G. W. Wingate-Saul, QC; Miss S. E. Wollam; H. Wolton, QC; M. M. Wood, QC; N. A. Wood; R. L. J. Wood, QC; W. R. Wood; Miss S. Woodley, QC; J. T. Woods; W. C. Woodward, QC; Miss S. E. Woollam; A. P. L. Woolman; T. H. Workman; Miss A. M. Worrall, QC; P. F. Worsley, QC; J. J. Wright; N. A. Wright; D. E. M. Young, QC; M. K. Zeidman, QC

STIPENDIARY MAGISTRATES

PROVINCIAL
(each £74,464)

Cheshire, P. K. Dodd, OBE, *apptd* 1991
Derbyshire, M. J. Friel, *apptd* 1997; Mrs J. H. Alderson, *apptd* 1997
Devon, P. H. Wassall, *apptd* 1994
Dorset, P. R. Farmer, *apptd* 1998
East and West Sussex, P. C. Tain, *apptd* 1992
Essex, K. A. Gray, *apptd* 1995
Greater Manchester, A. Berg, *apptd* 1994; C. R. Darnton, *apptd* 1994; M. A. Abelson, *apptd* 1998
Hampshire, T. G. Cowling, *apptd* 1989; J. I. Woollard, *apptd* 1998
Humberside, N. H. White, *apptd* 1985
Lancashire/Merseyside, J. Finestein, *apptd* 1992
Leicestershire, D. M. Meredith, *apptd* 1995; R. Holland, *apptd* 1999
Merseyside, D. R. G. Tapp, *apptd* 1992; P. S. Ward, *apptd* 1994; P. J. Firth, *apptd* 1994
Middlesex, N. A. McKittrick, *apptd* 1989; S. N. Day, *apptd* 1991; C. S. Wiles, *apptd* 1996
Mid Glamorgan, Miss P. J. Watkins, *apptd* 1995
Norfolk, N. P. Heley, *apptd* 1994
North-East London, G. E. Cawdron, *apptd* 1993
Nottinghamshire, P. F. Nuttall, *apptd* 1991; M. L. R. Harris, *apptd* 1991
Shropshire, P. H. R. Browning, *apptd* 1994
South Glamorgan, G. R. Watkins, *apptd* 1993
South Wales and Gwent, D. V. Manning-Davies, *apptd* 1996; Miss P. J. Watkins, *apptd* 1995

South Yorkshire, J. A. Browne, *apptd* 1992; W. D. Thomas, *apptd* 1989; M. A. Rosenberg, *apptd* 1993; P. H. F. Jones, *apptd* 1995; Mrs S. E. Driver, *apptd* 1995
Staffordshire, P. G. G. Richards, *apptd* 1991
West Midlands, W. M. Probert, *apptd* 1983; B. Morgan, *apptd* 1989; I. Gillespie, *apptd* 1991; M. F. James, *apptd* 1991; C. M. McColl, *apptd* 1994; J. A. Jellema, *apptd* 1998; D. J. Chinery, *apptd* 1998
West Yorkshire, Mrs P. A. Hewitt, *apptd* 1990; G. A. K. Hodgson, *apptd* 1993; N. R. Cadbury, *apptd* 1997

METROPOLITAN

Chief Metropolitan Stipendiary Magistrate and Chairman of Magistrates' Courts Committee for Inner London Area
(£92,810), G. E. Parkinson, *apptd* 1997 (*Bow Street*)
Magistrates (each £74,464)
Bow Street, The Chief Magistrate; R. D. Bartle, *apptd* 1972; C. L. Pratt, *apptd* 1990; H. N. Evans, *apptd* 1994
Camberwell Green, C. P. M. Davidson, *apptd* 1984; B. Loosley, *apptd* 1989; H. Gott, *apptd* 1992; Miss E. Roscoe, *apptd* 1994; R. House, *apptd* 1995; Miss C. S. R. Tubbs, *apptd* 1996
Greenwich, D. A. Cooper, *apptd* 1991; M. Kelly, *apptd* 1992; P. S. Wallis, *apptd* 1993; H. C. F. Riddle, *apptd* 1995
Highbury Corner, M. A. Johnstone, *apptd* 1980; Miss D. Quick, *apptd* 1986; J. M. Baker, *apptd* 1990; A. T. Evans, *apptd* 1990; Mrs L. Morgan, *apptd* 1995; P. A. M. Clark, *apptd* 1996
Horseferry Road, A. R. Davies, *apptd* 1985; G. Breen, *apptd* 1986; T. Workman, *apptd* 1986; Mrs K. R. Keating, *apptd* 1987; Mrs E. Rees, *apptd* 1994
Inner London and City Family Proceedings Court, N. Crichton, *apptd* 1987
Marylebone, D. Kennett Brown, *apptd* 1982; K. Maitland-Davies, *apptd* 1984; A. C. Baldwin, *apptd* 1990; Ms G. Babington-Browne, *apptd* 1991
South-Western, C. D. Voelcker, *apptd* 1982; A. W. Ormerod, *apptd* 1988; Miss D. Wickham, *apptd* 1989
Thames, Mrs J. Comyns, *apptd* 1982; S. E. Dawson, *apptd* 1984; G. Wicks, *apptd* 1987; I. G. Bing, *apptd* 1989; W. A. Kennedy, *apptd* 1991
Tower Bridge, C. S. F. Black, *apptd* 1993; M. Read, *apptd* 1993; S. Somjee, *apptd* 1995
West London Magistrates' Court, Miss A. Jennings, *apptd* 1972; T. English, *apptd* 1986; J. Philips, *apptd* 1989; D. L. Thomas, *apptd* 1990; D. Simpson, *apptd* 1993; J. Coleman, *apptd* 1995
'Floaters', Miss D. Lachhar, *apptd* 1996; J. V. Perkins, *apptd* 1999; K. Grant, *apptd* 1999

MAGISTRATES' COURTS COMMITTEE FOR THE INNER LONDON AREA
65 Romney Street, London SW1P 3RD
Tel 0171-799 3332

Justices' Chief Executive and Clerk to the Committee (£84,015), Miss C. Glenn
Justices' Clerk (*Training*) (£26,305–£35,546), vacant

CROWN PROSECUTION SERVICE
50 Ludgate Hill, London EC4M 7EX
Tel 0171-273 8000

The Crown Prosecution Service (CPS) is responsible for the independent review and conduct of criminal proceedings instituted by police forces in England and Wales, with the exception of cases conducted by the Serious Fraud Office (*see* page 341) and certain minor offences.
The Service is headed by the Director of Public Prosecutions (DPP), who works under the superintendence of the Attorney- General, and a chief executive. The Service was reorganized in April 1999 and now comprises a headquarters office and 42 Areas, each Area corresponding to a police area in England and Wales. Each Area is headed by a Chief Crown Prosecutor, supported by an Area Business Manager.

Director of Public Prosecutions (SCS), D. Calvert-Smith, QC
Chief Executive (SCS), M. E. Addison
Directors (SCS), C. Newell (*Casework*); G. Patten (*Policy*); J. Graham (*Finance*); L. Carey (*Business Information Systems*); Ms T. Newell (*acting*) (*Personnel Strategy*); Ms T. Fisher (*acting*) (*Personnel Operations*)
Head of Communications (SCS), Ms L. Salisbury

CPS AREAS

ENGLAND

CPS AVON AND SOMERSET, 1st Floor, Froomsgate House, Rupert Street, Bristol BS1 2QJ. Tel: 0117-930 2800. *Chief Crown Prosecutor* (SCS), D. Archer; *Area Business Manager*, Ms L. Burton
CPS BEDFORDSHIRE, Sceptre House, 7–9 Castle Street, Luton LU1 3AJ. Tel: 01582-816600. *Chief Crown Prosecutor* (SCS), Ms M. Townsend; *Area Business Manager*, Ms J. Altham
CPS CAMBRIDGESHIRE, Justinian House, Spitfire Close, Ermine Business Park, Huntingdon, Cambs PE18 6XY. Tel: 01480-825200. *Chief Crown Prosecutor* (SCS), R. Crowley; *Area Business Manager*, I. Farrell
CPS CHESHIRE, 2nd Floor, Windsor House, Pepper Street, Chester CH1 1TD. Tel: 01244-408600. *Chief Crown Prosecutor* (SCS), B. Hughes; *Area Business Manager*, Ms E. Sherwood
CPS CLEVELAND, Linthorpe Road, Middlesbrough, Cleveland TS1 1TX. Tel: 01642-204500. *Chief Crown Prosecutor* (SCS), D. Magson; *Area Business Manager*, Ms M. Phillips
CPS CUMBRIA, 1st Floor, Stocklund House, Castle Street, Carlisle CA3 8SY. Tel: 01228-882900. *Chief Crown Prosecutor* (SCS), D. Farmer; *Area Business Manager*, J. Pears
CPS DERBYSHIRE, 5th Floor, St Peter's House, Gower Street, Derby DE1 1SB. Tel: 01332-614000. *Chief Crown Prosecutor* (SCS), D. Adams; *Area Business Manager*, Ms A. Clarke
CPS DEVON AND CORNWALL, Hawkins House, Pynes Hill, Rydon Lane, Exeter EX2 5SS. Tel: 01392-288000. *Chief Crown Prosecutor* (SCS), A. Cresswell; *Area Business Manager*, J. Nettleton
CPS DORSET, 1st Floor, Oxford House, Oxford Road, Bournemouth BH8 8HA. Tel: 01202-498700. *Chief Crown Prosecutor* (SCS), J. Revell; *Area Business Manager*, J. Putman
CPS DURHAM, Elvet House, Hallgarth Street, Durham DH1 3AT. Tel: 0191-383 5800. *Chief Crown Prosecutor* (SCS), J. Corringhan; *Area Business Manager*, B. Feetham
CPS ESSEX, County House, 100 New London Road, Chelmsford CM2 0RG. Tel: 01245-455800. *Chief Crown Prosecutor* (SCS), J. Bell; *Area Business Manager*, P. Overett
CPS GLOUCESTERSHIRE, 2 Kimbrose Way, Gloucester GL1 2DB. Tel: 01452-872400. *Chief Crown Prosecutor* (SCS), W. Cole; *Area Business Manager*, W. Hollins
CPS GREATER MANCHESTER, PO Box 237, 8th Floor, Sunlight House, Quay Street, Manchester M60 3PS. Tel: 0161-827 4700. *Chief Crown Prosecutor* (SCS), T. Taylor; *Area Business Manager*, K. Fox

CPS HAMPSHIRE, 3rd Floor, Black Horse House, 8–10 Leigh Road, Eastleigh, Hants so50 9FH. Tel: 01703-673800. *Chief Crown Prosecutor (SCS)*, R. Daw; *Area Business Manager*, M. Sunderland

CPS HERTFORDSHIRE, Queen's House, 58 Victoria Street, St Albans, Herts ALI 3HZ. Tel: 01727-798700. *Chief Crown Prosecutor (SCS)*, C. Ingham; *Area Business Manager*, L. Carroll

CPS HUMBERSIDE, 2nd Floor, King William House, Lowgate, Hull HUI IRS. Tel: 01482-621000. *Chief Crown Prosecutor (SCS)*, B. Marshall; *Area Business Manager*, Ms C. Skidmore

CPS KENT, Priory Gate, 29 Union Street, Maidstone, Kent ME14 IPT. Tel: 01622-356600. *Chief Crown Prosecutor (SCS)*, Ms E. Howe; *Area Business Manager*, K. Mitchell

CPS LANCASHIRE, 3rd Floor, Unicentre, Lord's Walk, Preston PRI IDH. Tel: 01772-208100. *Chief Crown Prosecutor (SCS)*, D. Dickenson; *Area Business Manager*, G. Rankin

CPS LEICESTERSHIRE, Princes Court, 34 York Road, Leicester LEI 5TU. Tel: 0116-204 6700. *Chief Crown Prosecutor (SCS)*, M. Howard; *Area Business Manager*, Ms L. Jones

CPS LINCOLNSHIRE, Crosstrent House, 10A Newport, Lincoln LNI 3DF. Tel: 01633-261100. *Chief Crown Prosecutor (SCS)*, Ms A. Kerr; *Area Business Manager*, Ms A. Garbett

CPS LONDON (METROPOLITAN), 4th Floor, 50 Ludgate Hill, London EC4M 7EX. Tel: 0171-796 8000. *Chief Crown Prosecutor (SCS)*, P. Boeuf; *Assistant Chief Crown Prosecutors (SCS)*, Ms A. Saunders; Ms M. Werrett; H. Cohen; *Area Business Manager*, A. Machray

CPS MERSEYSIDE, 7th Floor (South), Royal Liver Building, Pier Head, Liverpool L3 IHN. Tel: 0151-239 6400. *Chief Crown Prosecutor (SCS)*, J. Holt; *Area Business Manager*, Ms D. King

CPS NORFOLK, Haldin House, Old Bank of England Court, Queen Street, Norwich NR2 4SX. Tel: 01603-693000. *Chief Crown Prosecutor (SCS)*, P. Tidey; *Area Business Manager*, A. Mardell

CPS NORTH YORKSHIRE, 6th Floor, Ryedale Building, 60 Piccadilly, York YOI INS. Tel: 01904-731700. *Chief Crown Prosecutor (SCS)*, B. Turnbull; *Area Business Manager*, R. Cragg

CPS NORTHAMPTONSHIRE, Beaumont House, Cliftonville, Northampton NNI 5BE. Tel: 01604-823600. *Chief Crown Prosecutor (SCS)*, C. Chapman; *Area Business Manager*, J. Stephenson

CPS NORTHUMBRIA, 1st Floor, Benton House, 136 Sandyford Road, Newcastle upon Tyne NE2 IQE. Tel: 0191-260 4200. *Chief Crown Prosecutor (SCS)*, Ms N. Reasbeck; *Area Business Manager*, S. Guy

CPS NOTTINGHAMSHIRE, 2 King Edward Court, King Edward Street, Nottingham NGI IEL. Tel: 0115-852 3300. *Chief Crown Prosecutor (SCS)*, P. Lewis; *Area Business Manager*, Ms G. Pessol

CPS SOUTH YORKSHIRE, Greenfield House, 32 Scotland Street, Sheffield s3 7DQ. Tel: 0114-229 8600. *Chief Crown Prosecutor (SCS)*, Ms J. Bermingham; *Area Business Manager*, C. Day

CPS STAFFORDSHIRE, 11A Princes Street, Stafford STI6 2EU. Tel: 01785-272200. *Chief Crown Prosecutor (SCS)*, H. Ireland; *Area Business Manager*, B. Laybourne

CPS SUFFOLK, Saxon House, 1 Cromwell Square, Ipswich IPI ITS. Tel: 01473-282100. *Chief Crown Prosecutor (SCS)*, C. Yule; *Area Business Manager*, Ms D. Waddington

CPS SURREY, One Onslow Street, Guildford, Surrey GUI 4YA. Tel: 01483-468200. *Chief Crown Prosecutor (SCS)*, Ms S. Hebblethwaite; *Area Business Manager*, M. Wray

CPS SUSSEX, Unit 3, Clifton Mews, Clifton Hill, Brighton BNI 3HR. Tel: 01273-765600. *Chief Crown Prosecutor (SCS)*, M. Kennedy; *Area Business Manager*, B. Shepherd

CPS THAMES VALLEY, The Courtyard, Lombard Street, Abingdon, Oxon OXI4 5SE. Tel: 01235-551900. *Chief Crown Prosecutor (SCS)*, S. Clements; *Area Business Manager*, G. Choldcroft

CPS WARWICKSHIRE, Rossmore House, 10 Newbold Terrace, Leamington Spa, Warks CV32 4EA. Tel: 01926-450088. *Chief Crown Prosecutor (SCS)*, M. Lynn; *Area Business Manager*, Ms S. Petyt

CPS WEST MERCIA, Artillery House, Heritage Way, Droitwich, Worcester WR9 8YB. Tel: 01905-825000. *Chief Crown Prosecutor (SCS)*, J. England; *Area Business Manager*, L. Sutton

CPS WEST MIDLANDS, 14th Floor, Colmore Gate, 2 Colmore Row, Birmingham B3 2QA. Tel: 0121-262 1300. *Chief Crown Prosecutor (SCS)*, D. Blundell; *Area Business Manager*, M. Grist

CPS WEST YORKSHIRE, 4–5 South Parade, Wakefield, W. Yorks WFI ILR. Tel: 01924-205200. *Chief Crown Prosecutor (SCS)*, N. Franklin; *Area Business Manager*, R. Stevenson

CPS WILTSHIRE, 2nd Floor, Fox Talbot House, Bellinger Close, Malmesbury Road, Chippenham, Wilts SNI5 IBN. Tel: 01249-766100. *Chief Crown Prosecutor (SCS)*, N. Hawkins; *Area Business Manager*, N. Nabi

WALES

CPS DYFED-POWYS, Heol Penlanffos, Tanerdy, Carmarthen, Dyfed SA3I 2EZ. Tel: 01267-242100. *Chief Crown Prosecutor (SCS)*, S. Rowlands; *Area Business Manager*, Ms C. Jones

CPS GWENT, 7th Floor, Chartist Tower, Dock Street, Newport, Gwent NP9 IDW. Tel: 01633-241100. *Chief Crown Prosecutor (SCS)*, C. Woolley; *Area Business Manager*, B. Fullerton

CPS NORTH WALES, Llys Eirias, Heritage Gate, Abergele Road, Colwyn Bay, Conwy LL29 8BW. Tel: 01492-806800. *Chief Crown Prosecutor (SCS)*, P. Whittaker; *Area Business Manager*, Ms A. Walsh

CPS SOUTH WALES, 21st Floor, Capital Tower, Greyfriars Road, Cardiff CFI 3PL. Tel: 01222-803800. *Chief Crown Prosecutor (SCS)*, H. Heycock; *Area Business Manager*, I. Edmondson

The Scottish Judicature

Scotland has a legal system separate from and differing greatly from the English legal system in enacted law, judicial procedure and the structure of courts.

In Scotland the system of public prosecution is headed by the Lord Advocate and is independent of the police, who have no say in the decision to prosecute. The Lord Advocate, discharging his functions through the Crown Office in Edinburgh, is responsible for prosecutions in the High Court, sheriff courts and district courts. Prosecutions in the High Court are prepared by the Crown Office and conducted in court by one of the law officers, by an advocate-depute, or by a solicitor advocate. In the inferior courts the decision to prosecute is made and prosecution is preferred by procurators fiscal, who are lawyers and full-time civil servants subject to the directions of the Crown Office. A permanent legally-qualified civil servant known as the Crown Agent is responsible for the running of the Crown Office and the organization of the Procurator Fiscal Service, of which he is the head.

Scotland is divided into six sheriffdoms, each with a full-time sheriff principal. The sheriffdoms are further divided into sheriff court districts, each of which has a legally-qualified resident sheriff or sheriffs, who are the judges of the court.

In criminal cases sheriffs principal and sheriffs have the same powers; sitting with a jury of 15 members, they may try more serious cases on indictment, or, sitting alone, may try lesser cases under summary procedure. Minor summary offences are dealt with in district courts which are administered by the district and the islands local government authorities and presided over by lay justices of the peace (of whom there are about 4,000) and, in Glasgow only, by stipendiary magistrates. Juvenile offenders (children under 16) may be brought before an informal children's hearing comprising three local lay people. The superior criminal court is the High Court of Justiciary which is both a trial and an appeal court. Cases on indictment are tried by a High Court judge, sitting with a jury of 15, in Edinburgh and on circuit in other towns. Appeals from the lower courts against conviction or sentence are heard also by the High Court, which sits as an appeal court only in Edinburgh. There is no further appeal to the House of Lords in criminal cases.

In civil cases the jurisdiction of the sheriff court extends to most kinds of action. Appeal against decisions of the sheriff may be made to the sheriff principal and thence to the Court of Session, or direct to the Court of Session, which sits only in Edinburgh. The Court of Session is divided into the Inner and the Outer House. The Outer House is a court of first instance in which cases are heard by judges sitting singly, sometimes with a jury of 12. The Inner House, itself subdivided into two divisions of equal status, is mainly an appeal court. Appeals may be made to the Inner House from the Outer House as well as from the sheriff court. An appeal may be made from the Inner House to the House of Lords.

The judges of the Court of Session are the same as those of the High Court of Justiciary, the Lord President of the Court of Session also holding the office of Lord Justice General in the High Court. Senators of the College of Justice are Lords Commissioners of Justiciary as well as judges of the Court of Session. On appointment, a Senator takes a judicial title, which is retained for life. Although styled 'The Hon./Rt. Hon. Lord —', the Senator is not a peer.

The office of coroner does not exist in Scotland. The local procurator fiscal inquires privately into sudden or suspicious deaths and may report findings to the Crown Agent. In some cases a fatal accident inquiry may be held before the sheriff.

COURT OF SESSION AND HIGH COURT OF JUSTICIARY

The Lord President and Lord Justice General (£147,214)
The Rt. Hon. the Lord Rodger of Earlsferry, *born* 1944, *apptd* 1996
Secretary, A. Maxwell

INNER HOUSE

Lords of Session (each £139,931)
FIRST DIVISION
The Lord President
Hon. Lord Sutherland (Ranald Sutherland), *born* 1932, *apptd* 1985
Hon. Lord Prosser (William Prosser), *born* 1934, *apptd* 1986
Hon. Lord Caplan (Philip Caplan), *born* 1929, *apptd* 1989

SECOND DIVISION
Lord Justice Clerk (£139,931), The Rt. Hon. Lord Cullen (William Cullen), *born* 1935, *apptd* 1997
Rt. Hon. The Lord McCluskey, *born* 1929, *apptd* 1984
Hon. Lord Kirkwood (Ian Kirkwood), *born* 1932, *apptd* 1987
Hon. Lord Coulsfield (John Cameron), *born* 1934, *apptd* 1987

OUTER HOUSE

Lords of Session (each £123,787)

Hon. Lord Milligan (James Milligan), *born* 1934, *apptd* 1988
Rt. Hon. The Lord Cameron of Lochbroom, *born* 1931, *apptd* 1989
Hon. Lord Marnoch (Michael Bruce), *born* 1938, *apptd* 1990
Hon. Lord MacLean (Ranald MacLean), *born* 1938, *apptd* 1990
Hon. Lord Penrose (George Penrose), *born* 1938, *apptd* 1990
Hon. Lord Osborne (Kenneth Osborne), *born* 1937, *apptd* 1990
Hon. Lord Abernethy (Alistair Cameron), *born* 1938, *apptd* 1992
Hon. Lord Johnston (Alan Johnston), *born* 1942, *apptd* 1994
Hon. Lord Gill (Brian Gill), *born* 1942, *apptd* 1994
Hon. Lord Hamilton (Arthur Hamilton), *born* 1942, *apptd* 1995
Hon. Lord Dawson (Thomas Dawson), *born* 1948, *apptd* 1995
Hon. Lord Macfadyen (Donald Macfadyen), *born* 1945, *apptd* 1995
Hon. Lady Cosgrove (Hazel Aronson), *born* 1946, *apptd* 1996
Hon. Lord Nimmo Smith (William Nimmo Smith), *born* 1942, *apptd* 1996
Hon. Lord Philip (Alexander Philip), *born* 1942, *apptd* 1996
Hon. Lord Kingarth (Derek Emslie), *born* 1949, *apptd* 1997
Hon. Lord Bonomy (Iain Bonomy), *born* 1946, *apptd* 1997
Hon. Lord Eassie (Ronald Mackay), *born* 1945, *apptd* 1997
Hon. Lord Reed (Robert Reed), *born* 1956, *apptd* 1998

COURT OF SESSION AND HIGH COURT OF JUSTICIARY
Parliament House, Parliament Square, Edinburgh EH1 1HQ
Tel 0131-225 2595

Principal Clerk of Session and Justiciary (£32,293–£53,879), J. L. Anderson
Deputy Principal Clerk of Justiciary and Administration (£28,314–£43,873), T. Fyffe
Deputy Principal Clerk of Session and Principal Extractor (£28,314–£43,873), G. McKeand
Deputy Principal Clerk (Keeper of the Rolls) (£28,314–£43,873), T. Thomson
Depute Clerks of Session and Justiciary (£21,613–£28,414), N. J. Dowie; I. F. Smith; T. Higgins; T. B. Cruickshank; Q. A. Oliver; F. Shannly; A. S. Moffat; G. G. Ellis; W. Dunn; A. M. Finlayson; C. C. Armstrong; R. Jenkins; J. O. McLean; M. Weir; R. M. Sinclair; E. G. Appelbe; B. Watson; D. W. Cullen; D. J. Cullum; I. D. Martin; N. McGinley; J. Lynn; E. Dickson; K. D. Carter; F. Petrie

SCOTTISH COURTS ADMINISTRATION
Hayweight House, 23 Lauriston Street, Edinburgh
EH3 9DQ
Tel 0131-229 9200

The Scottish Courts Administration is responsible to the Scottish Ministers for the performance of the Scottish Court Service and central administration pertaining to the judiciary in the Supreme and Sheriff Courts. It is also responsible for policy in relation to civil court procedures and jurisdiction, the law of diligence, evidence, arbitration and dispute resolution, private international law, law reform and other matters.
Director, J. Hamill, CB
Deputy Director (Legal Policy) (Assistant Solicitor) (G5), P. M. Beaton
Deputy Director (Resources and Liaison), D. Stewart

SCOTTISH COURT SERVICE
Hayweight House, 23 Lauriston Street, Edinburgh
EH3 9DQ
Tel 0131-229 9200

The Scottish Court Service became an executive agency within the Scottish Courts Administration in 1995. It is responsible to the Scottish Ministers for the provision of staff, court houses and associated services for the Supreme and Sheriff Courts.
Chief Executive, M. Ewart

SHERIFF COURT OF CHANCERY
27 Chambers Street, Edinburgh EH1 1LB
Tel 0131-225 2525

The Court deals with service of heirs and completion of title in relation to heritable property.
Sheriff of Chancery, C. G. B. Nicholson, QC

HM COMMISSARY OFFICE
27 Chambers Street, Edinburgh EH1 1LB
Tel 0131-225 2525

The Office is responsible for issuing confirmation, a legal document entitling a person to execute a deceased person's will, and other related matters.
Commissary Clerk, J. M. Ross

SCOTTISH LAND COURT
1 Grosvenor Crescent, Edinburgh EH12 5ER
Tel 0131-225 3595

The court deals with disputes relating to agricultural and crofting land in Scotland.
Chairman (£100,209), The Hon. Lord McGhie (James McGhie), QC
Members, D. J. Houston; D. M. Macdonald; J. Kinloch (*part-time*)
Principal Clerk, K. H. R. Graham, WS

SHERIFFDOMS

SALARIES

Sheriff Principal	£100,209
Sheriff	£92,810
Area Director	£32,293–£63,490
Sheriff Clerk	£12,719–£43,873

*Floating Sheriff

GRAMPIAN, HIGHLANDS AND ISLANDS
Sheriff Principal, D. J. Risk, QC
Area Director North, J. Robertson

SHERIFFS AND SHERIFF CLERKS
Aberdeen and Stonehaven, D. Kelbie; L. A. S. Jessop; A. Pollock; Mrs A. M. Cowan; C. J. Harris, QC; I. H. L. Miller; *G. K. Buchanan; *Sheriff Clerks*, Mrs E. Laing (*Aberdeen*); B. McBride (*Stonehaven*)
Peterhead and Banff, K. A. McLernan; *Sheriff Clerk*, A. Hempseed (*Peterhead*); *Sheriff Clerk Depute*, Mrs F. L. MacPherson (*Banff*)
Elgin, N. McPartlin; *Sheriff Clerk*, M. McBey
Inverness, Lochmaddy, Portree, Stornoway, Dingwall, Tain, Wick and Dornoch, W. J. Fulton; D. Booker-Milburn; J. O. A. Fraser; I. A. Cameron; *Sheriff Clerks*, J. Robertson (*Inverness*); W. Cochrane (*Dingwall*); *Sheriff Clerks Depute*, Miss M. Campbell (*Lochmaddy and Portree*); Miss A. B. Armstrong (*Stornoway*); L. MacLachlan (*Tain*); Mrs J. McEwan (*Wick*); K. Kerr (*Dornoch*)
Kirkwall and Lerwick, C. S. Mackenzie; *Sheriff Clerks Depute*, vacant (*Kirkwall*); M. Flanagan (*Lerwick*)
Fort William, C. G. McKay (also *Oban*); *Sheriff Clerk Depute*, D. Hood

TAYSIDE, CENTRAL AND FIFE
Sheriff Principal, J. F. Wheatley, QC
Area Director East, M. Bonar

SHERIFFS AND SHERIFF CLERKS
Arbroath and Forfar, K. A. Veal; *C. N. R. Stein; *Sheriff Clerks*, M. Herbertson (*Arbroath*); S. Munro (*Forfar*)
Dundee, R. A. Davidson; A. L. Stewart, QC; *J. P. Scott; G. J. Evans (also *Cupar*); *Sheriff Clerk*, D. Nicoll
Perth, J. C. McInnes, QC; Mrs F. L. Reith, QC; *Sheriff Clerk*, J. Murphy
Falkirk, A. V. Sheehan; A. J. Murphy; *Sheriff Clerk*, R. McMillan
Stirling, The Hon. R. E. G. Younger; *Sheriff Clerk*, J. Clark
Alloa, W. M. Reid; *Sheriff Clerk*, R. G. McKeand
Cupar, G. J. Evans (also *Dundee*); *Sheriff Clerk*, R. Hughes
Dunfermline, J. S. Forbes; C. W. Palmer; *Sheriff Clerk*, W. McCulloch
Kirkcaldy, F. J. Keane; Mrs L. G. Patrick; *I. D. Dunbar; *B. G. Donald; *Sheriff Clerk*, W. Jones

LOTHIAN AND BORDERS
Sheriff Principal, C. G. B. Nicholson, QC
Area Director East, M. Bonar

SHERIFFS AND SHERIFF CLERKS
Edinburgh, R. G. Craik, QC (also *Peebles*); R. J. D. Scott (also *Peebles*); Miss I. A. Poole; A. M. Bell; J. M. S. Horsburgh, QC; G. W. S. Presslie (also *Haddington*); J. A. Farrell; *A. Lothian; I. D. Macphail, QC; C. N. Stoddart; A. B. Wilkinson, QC; Mrs D. J. B. Robertson; N. M. P. Morrison, QC; *Miss M. M. Stephen; Mrs M. L. E. Jarvie, QC; *Sheriff Clerk*, J. Ross
Peebles, R. G. Craik, QC (also *Edinburgh*); R. J. D. Scott (also *Edinburgh*); *Sheriff Clerk Depute*, M. L. Kubeczka
Linlithgow, H. R. MacLean; G. R. Fleming; *K. A. Ross; *Sheriff Clerk*, R. D. Sinclair
Haddington, G. W. S. Presslie (also *Edinburgh*); *Sheriff Clerk*, J. O'Donnell
Jedburgh and Duns, J. V. Paterson; *Sheriff Clerk*, I. W. Williamson
Selkirk, J. V. Paterson; *Sheriff Clerk Depute*, L. McFarlane

NORTH STRATHCLYDE
Sheriff Principal, B. A. Kerr, QC
Area Director West, I. Scott

SHERIFFS AND SHERIFF CLERKS

Oban, C. G. McKay (also *Fort William*); *Sheriff Clerk Depute*, J. G. Whitelaw
Dumbarton, J. T. Fitzsimons; T. Scott; S. W. H. Fraser; *Sheriff Clerk*, P. Corcoran
Paisley, J. Spy; C. K. Higgins; N. Douglas; D. J. Pender; *W. Dunlop; G. C. Kavanagh (also *Campbeltown*); *Sheriff Clerk*, Miss S. Hindes
Greenock, J. Herald (also *Rothesay*); Sir Stephen Young; *Sheriff Clerk*, J. Tannahill
Kilmarnock, T. M. Croan; D. B. Smith; T. F. Russell; *Sheriff Clerk*, G. Waddell
Dunoon, Mrs C. M. A. F. Gimblett; *Sheriff Clerk Depute*, Mrs C. Carson
Campbeltown, *W. Dunlop (also *Paisley*); *Sheriff Clerk Depute*, P. G. Hay
Rothesay, J. Herald (also *Greenock*); *Sheriff Clerk Depute*, Mrs C. K. McCormick

GLASGOW AND STRATHKELVIN

Sheriff Principal, E. F. Bowen, QC
Area Director West, I. Scott

SHERIFFS AND SHERIFF CLERKS

Glasgow, B. Kearney; G. H. Gordon, CBE, Ph.D., QC; B. A. Lockhart; Mrs A. L. A. Duncan; A. C. Henry; J. K. Mitchell; A. G. Johnston; J. P. Murphy; Miss S. A. O. Raeburn, QC; D. Convery; J. McGowan; I. A. S. Peebles, QC; C. W. McFarlane, QC; K. M. Maciver; H. Matthews, QC; J. A. Baird; Miss R. E. A. Rae, QC; T. A. K. Drummond, QC; Mrs P. M. M. Bowman; A. W. Noble; *J. D. Friel; *Mrs D. M. MacNeill, QC; J. A. Taylor; C. A. L. Scott; *Sheriff Clerk*, R. Cockburn

SOUTH STRATHCLYDE, DUMFRIES AND GALLOWAY

Sheriff Principal, G. L. Cox, QC
Area Director West, I. Scott

SHERIFFS AND SHERIFF CLERKS

Hamilton, L. Cameron; D. C. Russell; V. J. Canavan (also *Airdrie*); W. E. Gibson; J. H. Stewart; H. S. Neilson; S. C. Pender; *Sheriff Clerk*, P. Feeney
Lanark, J. D. Allan; *Sheriff Clerk*, A. Whyte
Ayr, N. Gow, QC; R. G. McEwan, QC; *C. B. Miller; *Sheriff Clerk*, Miss C. D. Cockburn
Stranraer and Kirkcudbright, J. R. Smith (also *Dumfries*); *Sheriff Clerks*, W. McIntosh (*Stranraer*); B. Lindsay (*Kirkcudbright*)
Dumfries, K. G. Barr; M. J. Fletcher; J. R. Smith (also *Stranraer and Kirkcudbright*); *Sheriff Clerk*, P. McGonigle
Airdrie, V. J. Canavan (also *Hamilton*); R. H. Dickson; I. C. Simpson; J. C. Morris, QC; *Sheriff Clerk*, D. Forrester

STIPENDIARY MAGISTRATES

GLASGOW

R. Hamilton, *apptd* 1984; J. B. C. Nisbet, *apptd* 1984; R. B. Christie, *apptd* 1985; Mrs J. A. M. MacLean, *apptd* 1990

PROCURATOR FISCAL SERVICE

CROWN OFFICE
25 Chambers Street, Edinburgh EH1 1LA
Tel 0131-226 2626

Crown Agent (£80,020–£116,860), A. C. Normand
Deputy Crown Agent (£55,750–£92,930), F. R. Crowe

PROCURATORS FISCAL

SALARIES

Regional Procurator Fiscal – grade 3	£61,110–£98,400
Regional Procurator Fiscal – grade 4	£55,750–£92,930
Procurator Fiscal – upper level	£41,550–£65,270
Procurator Fiscal – lower level	£36,000–£43,822

GRAMPIAN, HIGHLANDS AND ISLANDS REGION

Regional Procurator Fiscal, L. A. Higson (*Aberdeen*)
Procurators Fiscal, E. K. Barbour (*Stonehaven*); A. J. M. Colley (*Banff*); A. N. Perry (*Peterhead*); D. J. Dickson (*Elgin*); A. N. Perry (*Wick*); J. Bamber (*Portree, Lochmaddy*); F. Redman (*Stornoway*); G. Napier (*Inverness*); R. W. Urquhart (*Kirkwall, Lerwick*); D. J. Buchanan (*Fort William*); A. N. MacDonald (*Dingwall, Tain*)

TAYSIDE, CENTRAL AND FIFE REGION

Regional Procurator Fiscal, B. K. Heywood (*Dundee*)
Procurators Fiscal, J. I. Craigen (*Forfar*); I. A. McLeod (*Perth*); W. J. Gallacher (*Falkirk*); C. Ritchie (*Stirling and Alloa*); E. B. Russell (*Cupar*); R. G. Stott (*Dunfermline*); Miss H. M. Clark (*Kirkcaldy*)

LOTHIAN AND BORDERS REGION

Regional Procurator Fiscal, N. McFadyen (*Edinburgh*)
Procurators Fiscal, Miss L. M. Ruxton (*Linlithgow*); A. J. P. Reith (*Haddington*); A. R. G. Fraser (*Duns, Jedburgh*); D. MacNeill (*Selkirk*)

NORTH STRATHCLYDE REGION

Regional Procurator Fiscal, W. A. Gilchrist (*Paisley*)
Procurators Fiscal, I. Henderson (*Campbeltown*); C. C. Donnelly (*Dumbarton*); W. S. Carnegie (*Greenock*); D. L. Webster (*Dunoon*); J. G. MacGlennan (*Kilmarnock*); B. R. Maguire (*Oban*)

GLASGOW AND STRATHKELVIN REGION

Regional Procurator Fiscal, A. D. Vannet (*Glasgow*)

SOUTH STRATHCLYDE, DUMFRIES AND GALLOWAY REGION

Regional Procurator Fiscal, D. A. Brown (*Hamilton*)
Procurators Fiscal, S. R. Houston (*Lanark*); J. T. O'Donnell (*Ayr*); F. R. Crowe (*Stranraer*); A. S. Kennedy (*Stranraer, Kirkcudbright*); D. J. Howdle (*Dumfries*); D. Spiers (*Airdrie*)

Northern Ireland Judicature

In Northern Ireland the legal system and the structure of courts closely resemble those of England and Wales; there are, however, often differences in enacted law.

The Supreme Court of Judicature of Northern Ireland comprises the Court of Appeal, the High Court of Justice and the Crown Court. The practice and procedure of these courts is similar to that in England. The superior civil court is the High Court of Justice, from which an appeal lies to the Northern Ireland Court of Appeal; the House of Lords is the final civil appeal court.

The Crown Court, served by High Court and county court judges, deals with criminal trials on indictment. Cases are heard before a judge and, except those involving offences specified under emergency legislation, a jury. Appeals from the Crown Court against conviction or sentence are heard by the Northern Ireland Court of Appeal; the House of Lords is the final court of appeal.

The decision to prosecute in cases tried on indictment and in summary cases of a serious nature rests in Northern Ireland with the Director of Public Prosecutions, who is responsible to the Attorney-General. Minor summary offences are prosecuted by the police.

Minor criminal offences are dealt with in magistrates' courts by a legally qualified resident magistrate and, where an offender is under 17, by juvenile courts each consisting of a resident magistrate and two lay members specially qualified to deal with juveniles (at least one of whom must be a woman). On 6 August 1999 there were 937 justices of the peace in Northern Ireland. Appeals from magistrates' courts are heard by the county court, or by the Court of Appeal on a point of law or an issue as to jurisdiction.

Magistrates' courts in Northern Ireland can deal with certain classes of civil case but most minor civil cases are dealt with in county courts. Judgments of all civil courts are enforceable through a centralized procedure administered by the Enforcement of Judgments Office.

SUPREME COURT OF JUDICATURE

The Royal Courts of Justice, Belfast BT1 3JF
Tel 01232-235111
Lord Chief Justice of Northern Ireland (£147,214)
The Rt. Hon. Sir Robert Carswell, *born* 1934, *apptd* 1997
  Principal Secretary, G. W. Johnston

LORDS JUSTICES OF APPEAL (each £139,931)
Style, The Rt. Hon. Lord Justice [surname]

Rt. Hon. Sir Michael Nicholson, *born* 1933, *apptd* 1995
Rt. Hon. Sir William McCollum, *born* 1933, *apptd* 1997
Rt. Hon. Sir Anthony Campbell, *born* 1936, *apptd* 1998

PUISNE JUDGES (each £123,787)
Style, The Hon. Mr Justice [surname]

Hon. Sir John Sheil, *born* 1938, *apptd* 1989
Hon. Sir Brian Kerr, *born* 1948, *apptd* 1993
Hon. Sir John Pringle, *born* 1929, *apptd* 1993
Hon. Sir Malachy Higgins, *born* 1944, *apptd* 1993
Hon. Sir Paul Girvan, *born* 1948, *apptd* 1995
Hon. Sir Patrick Coghlin, *born* 1945, *apptd* 1997
Hon. Sir John Gillen, *born* 1947, *apptd* 1998

MASTERS OF THE SUPREME COURT (each £74,464)
Master, Queen's Bench and Appeals and Clerk of the Crown, J.
  W. Wilson, QC
Master, High Court, Mrs D. M. Kennedy
Master, Office of Care and Protection, F. B. Hall
Master, Chancery Office, R. A. Ellison
Master, Bankruptcy and Companies Office, C. W. G. Redpath
Master, Probate and Matrimonial Office, Miss M.
  McReynolds
Master, Taxing Office, J. C. Napier

OFFICIAL SOLICITOR
Official Solicitor to the Supreme Court of Northern Ireland, Miss
  B. M. Donnelly

COUNTY COURTS

JUDGES (each £100,209)
Style, His/Her Hon. Judge [surname]

Judge Curran, QC; Judge Gibson, QC; Judge Petrie, QC; Judge Smyth, QC; Judge Markey, QC; Judge McKay, QC; Judge Martin, QC (*Chief Social Security and Child Support Commissioner*); Judge Brady, QC; Judge Rodgers; Judge Foote, QC; Her Hon. Judge Philpott, QC; Judge McFarland; Judge Lockie

RECORDERS (each £100,209)
Belfast, Judge Hart, QC
Londonderry, Judge Burgess

MAGISTRATES' COURTS

RESIDENT MAGISTRATES (each £74,464)
There are 17 resident magistrates in Northern Ireland.

CROWN SOLICITOR'S OFFICE

PO Box 410, Royal Courts of Justice, Belfast BT1 3JY
Tel 01232-542555

Crown Solicitor, N. P. Roberts

DEPARTMENT OF THE DIRECTOR OF PUBLIC PROSECUTIONS

Royal Courts of Justice, Belfast BT1 3NX
Tel 01232-542444

Director of Public Prosecutions, A. Fraser, CB, QC
Deputy Director of Public Prosecutions, W. R. Junkin

NORTHERN IRELAND COURT SERVICE

Windsor House, Bedford Street, Belfast BT2 7LT
Tel 01232-328594

Director (*G3*)

Ecclesiastical Courts

Original jurisdiction is exercised by the consistory court of each diocese in England, presided over by the Chancellor of that diocese. Appellate jurisdiction is exercised by the provincial courts detailed below, by the Court for Ecclesiastical Causes Reserved, and by commissions of review (the membership of these being newly constituted for each case).

COURT OF ARCHES (PROVINCE OF CANTERBURY)
Registry, 16 Beaumont Street, Oxford OX1 2LZ
Tel 01865-241974

Dean of the Arches, The Rt. Worshipful Sir John Owen

COURT OF THE VICAR-GENERAL OF THE PROVINCE OF CANTERBURY
Registry, 16 Beaumont Street, Oxford OX1 2LZ
Tel 01865-241974

Vicar-General, The Rt. Worshipful Miss S. Cameron, QC

CHANCERY COURT OF YORK
Registry, Stamford House, Piccadilly, York YO1 9PP
Tel 01904-623487

Auditor, The Rt. Worshipful Sir John Owen

THE VICAR-GENERAL OF THE PROVINCE OF YORK
Registry, Stamford House, Piccadilly, York YO1 9PP
Tel 01904-623487

Vicar-General, His Honour the Worshipful Judge
   T. A. C. Coningsby, QC

COURT OF FACULTIES
Registry, 1 The Sanctuary, London SW1P 3JT
Tel 0171-222 5381

Office for the issue of special and common marriage licences, appointment of notaries public, etc. Office hours, Monday–Friday, 10–4.

Master of the Faculties, The Rt. Worshipful Sir John Owen

The Probation Service

ENGLAND AND WALES

The Probation Service is currently organized into 54 areas. It is employed in each area by an independent committee and it provides a professional service to the courts, with responsibility for a wide range of duties which include:

(a) a pre-sentence report service for the criminal courts
(b) provision of a range of non-custodial measures involving the supervision of offenders in the community
(c) supervision of offenders released from custody, together with work in penal establishments and help for the families of those serving sentences
(d) an enquiry, conciliation and supervision service in the divorce and domestic courts
(e) support for and promotion of preventive and containment measures in the community designed to reduce the level of crime and domestic breakdown

It is a direct grant service funded 80 per cent from the Home Office and 20 per cent from the relevant local authority. In April 1999 the Government announced plans to reform the Probation Service for England and Wales. A new, unified Probation Service will be led by a Director, responsible to the Home Secretary. There will be 42 local service areas, matching existing police force boundaries. Local Probation Boards are to take a more strategic role, and the Service will be entirely funded by central government.

Its national representative bodies are:

THE CENTRAL PROBATION COUNCIL, 4th Floor, 8–9 Grosvenor Place, London SW1X 7SH. Tel: 0171-245 9364. *Director*, M. Wargent

THE ASSOCIATION OF CHIEF OFFICERS OF PROBATION, 4th Floor, 8–9 Grosvenor Place, London SW1X 7SH. Tel: 0171-823 2551. *Chair*, G. Dobson

THE NATIONAL ASSOCIATION OF PROBATION OFFICERS, 4 Chivalry Road, London SW11 1HT. Tel: 0171-223 4887. *General Secretary*, Ms J. McKnight

SCOTLAND

The probation service in Scotland is a statutory duty of local authorities under section 27 of the Social Work (Scotland) Act 1968. Social workers supervise and provide advice, guidance and assistance to those persons living in their area who are subject to a court's supervision order. This is done by social workers as part of their normal duties and not by a separate probation staff.

NORTHERN IRELAND

The Probation Board for Northern Ireland provides a probation service throughout Northern Ireland. Its function and range of duties is similar to that of the Probation Service in England and Wales (*see* above), except that in Northern Ireland work in divorce and domestic courts is the responsibility of the social services and not the Probation Board. The Probation Board is a statutory body whose 14 members are appointed by the Secretary of State for Northern Ireland and it receives its funding from the Northern Ireland Office.

Tribunals

AGRICULTURAL LAND TRIBUNALS

c/o Rural and Marine Environment Division, Ministry of Agriculture, Fisheries and Food, Nobel House, 17 Smith Square, London SW1P 3JR
Tel 0171-238 6991

Agricultural Land Tribunals settle disputes and other issues between agricultural landlords and tenants, and drainage disputes between neighbours.

There are seven tribunals covering England and one covering Wales. For each tribunal the Lord Chancellor appoints a chairman and one or more deputies (barristers or solicitors of at least seven years standing). The Lord Chancellor also appoints lay members to three statutory panels: the 'landowners' panel, the 'farmers' panel and the 'drainage' panel.

Each tribunal is an independent statutory body with jurisdiction only within its own area. A separate tribunal is constituted for each case, and consists of a chairman (who may be the chairman or one of the deputy chairmen) and two lay members nominated by the chairman.

Chairmen (England) (£271 a day), W. D. Greenwood; K. J. Fisher; P. A. de la Piquerie; A. G. Donn; His Hon. Judge Lee; G. L. Newsom; His Hon. Judge Robert Taylor
Chairman (Wales) (£271 a day), W. J. Owen

THE APPEALS SERVICE

Whittington House, 19–30 Alfred Place, London WC1E 7LW
Tel 0171-814 6520

The Service (formerly the Independent Tribunal Service) is responsible for the functioning of tribunals hearing appeals concerning child support assessments, social security benefits and vaccine damage payments. Judicial authority for the Service rests with the President, while administrative responsibility is exercised by the Appeals Service Agency, which is an executive agency of the Department of Social Security.
President, His Hon. Judge Michael Harris
Chief Executive, Appeals Service Agency, N. Ward

COMMONS COMMISSIONERS

Room 818, Tollgate House, Houlton Street, Bristol BS2 9DJ
Tel 0117-987 8928

The Commons Commissioners are responsible for deciding disputes arising under the Commons Registration Act 1965 and the Common Land (Rectification of Registers) Act 1989. They also enquire into the ownership of unclaimed common land. Commissioners are appointed by the Lord Chancellor.
Chief Commons Commissioner (part-time) (£37,164), D. M. Burton
Commissioner, I. L. R. Romer
Clerk, H. Thomas

COPYRIGHT TRIBUNAL

Harmsworth House, 13–15 Bouverie Street, London EC4Y 8DP
Tel 0171-596 6510; fax 0171-596-6526

The Copyright Tribunal resolves disputes over copyright licences, principally where there is collective licensing.

The chairman and two deputy chairmen are appointed by the Lord Chancellor. Up to eight ordinary members are appointed by the Secretary of State for Trade and Industry.
Chairman (£316 a day), C. P. Tootal
Secretary, Miss J. E. M. Durdin

DATA PROTECTION TRIBUNAL

c/o The Home Office, Queen Anne's Gate, London SW1H 9AT
Tel 0171-273 3755

The Data Protection Tribunal determines appeals against decisions of the Data Protection Registrar (Commissioner from March 2000) (*see* page 294). The chairman and deputy chairman are appointed by the Lord Chancellor and must be legally qualified. Lay members are appointed by the Home Secretary to represent the interests of data users or data subjects. A tribunal consists of a legally-qualified chairman sitting with equal numbers of the lay members appointed to represent the interests of data users and data subjects.
Chairman (£394 a day), J. A. C. Spokes, QC
Secretary, R. Hartley

EMPLOYMENT TRIBUNALS

CENTRAL OFFICE (ENGLAND AND WALES)

19–29 Woburn Place, London WC1H 0LU
Tel 0171-273 8666

Employment Tribunals for England and Wales sit in 11 regions. The tribunals deal with matters of employment law, redundancy, dismissal, contract disputes, sexual, racial and disability discrimination, and related areas of dispute which may arise in the workplace. A central registration unit records all applications and maintains a public register at Southgate Street, Bury St Edmunds, Suffolk IP33 2AQ. The tribunals are funded by the Department of Trade and Industry; administrative support is provided by the Employment Tribunals Service (*see* page 346).

Chairmen, who may be full-time or part-time, are legally qualified. They are appointed by the Lord Chancellor. Tribunal members are appointed by the Secretary of State for Trade and Industry.
President, His Hon. Judge Prophet

CENTRAL OFFICE (SCOTLAND)

Eagle Building, 215 Bothwell Street, Glasgow G2 7TS
Tel 0141-204 0730

Tribunals in Scotland have the same remit as those in England and Wales. Chairmen are appointed by the Lord President of the Court of Session and lay members by the Secretary of State for Trade and Industry.
President (£100,209), Mrs D. Littlejohn, CBE

EMPLOYMENT APPEAL TRIBUNAL
Central Office: Audit House, 58 Victoria Embankment,
London EC4Y 0DS
Tel 0171-273 1041
Divisional Office: 52 Melville Street, Edinburgh EH3 7HF
Tel 0131-225 3963

The Employment Appeal Tribunal hears appeals on a
question of law arising from any decision of an employment
tribunal. A tribunal consists of a high court judge and two
lay members, one from each side of industry. They are
appointed by The Queen on the recommendation of the
Lord Chancellor and the Secretary of State for Trade and
Industry. Administrative support is provided by the
Employment Tribunals Service (*see* page 346).
President, The Hon. Mr Justice Lindsay
Scottish Chairman, The Hon. Lord Johnston
Registrar, Miss V. J. Selio

IMMIGRATION APPELLATE AUTHORITIES
Taylor House, 88 Rosebery Avenue, London
ECIR 4QU
Tel 0171-862 4200

The Immigration Appeal Adjudicators hear appeals from
immigration decisions concerning the need for, and refusal
of, leave to enter or remain in the UK, refusals to grant
asylum, decisions to make deportation orders and directions
to remove persons subject to immigration control from the
UK. The Immigration Appeal Tribunal hears appeals
direct from decisions to make deportation orders in matters
concerning conduct contrary to the public good, and from
refusals to grant asylum. Its principal jurisdiction is,
however, the hearing of appeals from adjudicators by the
party (Home Office or individual) who is aggrieved by the
decision. Appeals are subject to leave being granted by the
tribunal.
An adjudicator sits alone. The tribunal sits in divisions
of three, normally a legally qualified member and two lay
members. Members of the tribunal and adjudicators are
appointed by the Lord Chancellor.

IMMIGRATION APPEAL TRIBUNAL
President, The Hon. Mr Justice Collins
Vice-Presidents, Mrs J. Chatwani; A. F. Hatt; M. Rapinet; A.
O'Brien-Quinn

IMMIGRATION APPEAL ADJUDICATORS
Chief Adjudicator, His Hon. Judge Dunn, QC
Deputy Chief Adjudicator, J. Latter

INDUSTRIAL TRIBUNALS AND THE FAIR EMPLOYMENT TRIBUNAL (NORTHERN IRELAND)
Long Bridge House, 20–24 Waring Street, Belfast
BT1 2EB
Tel 01232-327666

The industrial tribunal system in Northern Ireland was set
up in 1965 and has a similar remit to the employment
tribunals in the rest of the UK. There is also in Northern
Ireland a Fair Employment Tribunal, which hears and
determines individual cases of alleged religious or political
discrimination in employment. Employers can appeal to
the Fair Employment Tribunal if they consider the
directions of the Fair Employment Commission to be

unreasonable, inappropriate or unnecessary, and the Fair
Employment Commission can make application to the
Tribunal for the enforcement of undertakings or directions
with which an employer has not complied.
The president, vice-president and part-time chairmen
of the Fair Employment Tribunal are appointed by the
Lord Chancellor. The full-time chairman and the part-
time chairmen of the industrial tribunals and the panel
members to both the industrial tribunals and the Fair
Employment Tribunal are appointed by the Department
of Economic Development Northern Ireland.
*President of the Industrial Tribunals and the Fair Employment
Tribunal* (£100,209), J. Maguire, CBE
*Vice-President of the Industrial Tribunals and the Fair
Employment Tribunal,* Mrs M. P. Price
Secretary, Mrs P. McVeigh

LANDS TRIBUNAL
48–49 Chancery Lane, London WC2A IJR
Tel 0171-936 7200

The Lands Tribunal is an independent judicial body which
determines questions relating to the valuation of land,
rating appeals from valuation tribunals, the discharge or
modification of restrictive covenants, and compulsory
purchase compensation. The tribunal may also arbitrate
under references by consent. The president and members
are appointed by the Lord Chancellor.
President, G. R. Bartlett, QC
Members (£92,810), P. H. Clarke, FRICS; N. J. Rose, FRICS; P.
R. Francis
Member (part-time), His Hon. Judge Rich, QC
Member (part-time) (£400 a day), A. P. Musto, FRICS
Registrar, C. A. McMullan

LANDS TRIBUNAL FOR SCOTLAND
1 Grosvenor Crescent, Edinburgh EH12 5ER
Tel 0131-225 7996

The Lands Tribunal for Scotland has the same remit as
the tribunal for England and Wales but also covers
questions relating to tenants' rights. The president is
appointed by the Lord President of the Court of Session.
President, The Hon. Lord McGhie, QC
Members (£92,810), J. Devine, FRICS; A. R. MacLeary,
FRICS
Members (part-time) (£33,409), Sheriff A. C. Henry; R. A.
Edwards, CBE, WS
Clerk, N. M. Tainsh

MENTAL HEALTH REVIEW TRIBUNALS
Secretariat: Health Service Directorate, Room 302A
Wellington House, 133–155 Waterloo Road, London
SEI 8UG
Tel 0171-972 4503

The Mental Health Review Tribunals are independent
judicial bodies which review the cases of patients compulsorily detained under the provisions of the Mental Health
Act 1983. They have the power to discharge the patient, to
recommend leave of absence, delayed discharge, transfer
to another hospital or that a guardianship order be made,
to reclassify both restricted and unrestricted patients, and
to recommend consideration of a supervision application.
There are four tribunals in England, each headed by a

regional chairman who is appointed by the Lord Chancellor on a part-time basis. Each tribunal is made up of at least three members, and must include a lawyer, who acts as president (£239 a day), a medical member (£226 a day) and a lay member (£97 a day).

There are five regional offices:

LIVERPOOL, 3rd Floor, Cressington House, 249 St Mary's Road, Garston, Liverpool L19 0NF. Tel: 0151-494 0095

LONDON (NORTH), Spur 3, Block 1, Government Buildings, Honeypot Lane, Stanmore, Middx HA7 1AY. Tel: 0171-972 3734

LONDON (SOUTH), Block 3, Crown Offices, Kingston Bypass Road, Surbiton, Surrey KT6 5QN. Tel: 0181-268 4520

NOTTINGHAM, Spur A, Block 5, Government Buildings, Chalfont Drive, Western Boulevard, Nottingham NG8 3RZ. Tel: 0115-929 4222

WALES, 4th Floor, Crown Buildings, Cathays Park, Cardiff CF1 3NQ. Tel: 01222-825328

NATIONAL HEALTH SERVICE TRIBUNAL

The NHS Tribunal considers representations that the continued inclusion of a doctor, dentist, optician or pharmacist on a health authority's list would be prejudicial to the efficiency of the service concerned. The tribunal sits when required, about eight times a year, and usually in London. The chairman is appointed by the Lord Chancellor and members by the Secretary of State for Health.
Chairman, A. Whitfield, QC
Deputy Chairmen, Miss E. Platt, QC; Dr R. N. Ough
Clerk, I. D. Keith, East Hookers, Twineham, nr Haywards Heath, W. Sussex RH17 5NN. Tel: 01444-881345

NATIONAL HEALTH SERVICE TRIBUNAL (SCOTLAND)
Clerk: 66 Queen Street, Edinburgh EH2 4NE
Tel 0131-226 4771

The tribunal considers representations that the continued inclusion of a doctor, dentist, optometrist or pharmacist on a health board's list would be prejudicial to the efficiency of the service concerned. The tribunal sits when required and is composed of a chairman, one lay member, and one practitioner member drawn from a representative professional panel. The chairman is appointed by the Lord President of the Court of Session, and the lay member and the members of the professional panel are appointed by the First Minister.
Chairman, M. G. Thomson, QC
Lay member, J. D. M. Robertson
Clerk to the Tribunal, D. G. Brash, WS

PENSIONS APPEAL TRIBUNALS

CENTRAL OFFICE (ENGLAND AND WALES)
48–49 Chancery Lane, London WC2A 1JR
Tel 0171-936 7032/3/4

The Pensions Appeal Tribunals are responsible for hearing appeals from ex-servicemen or women and widows who have had their claims for a war pension rejected by the Secretary of State for Social Security. The Entitlement Appeal Tribunals hear appeals in cases where the Secretary of State has refused to grant a war pension. The Assessment Appeal Tribunals hear appeals against the Secretary of State's assessment of the degree of disablement caused by an accepted condition. The tribunal members are appointed by the Lord Chancellor.
President (£74,464), Dr H. M. G. Concannon
Secretary, Miss N. Collins

PENSIONS APPEAL TRIBUNALS FOR SCOTLAND
20 Walker Street, Edinburgh EH3 7HS
Tel 0131-220 1404
President (£298 a day), C. N. McEachran, QC

OFFICE OF THE SOCIAL SECURITY AND CHILD SUPPORT COMMISSIONERS
5th Floor, Newspaper House, 8–16 Great New Street, London EC4A 3BN
Tel 0171-353 5145
23 Melville Street, Edinburgh EH3 7PW
Tel 0131-225 2201

The Social Security Commissioners are the final statutory authority to decide appeals relating to entitlement to social security benefits. The Child Support Commissioners are the final statutory authority to decide appeals relating to child support. Appeals may be made in relation to both matters only on a point of law. The Commissioners' jurisdiction covers England, Wales and Scotland. There are 17 commissioners; they are all qualified lawyers.
Chief Social Security Commissioner and Chief Child Support Commissioner, His Hon. Judge Machin, QC
Secretary, S. Hill (*London*); Mrs M. Watts (*Edinburgh*)

OFFICE OF THE SOCIAL SECURITY COMMISSIONERS AND CHILD SUPPORT COMMISSIONERS FOR NORTHERN IRELAND
Lancashire House, 5 Linenhall Street, Belfast BT2 8AA
Tel 01232-332344

The role of Northern Ireland Social Security Commissioners and Child Support Commissioners is similar to that of the Commissioners in Great Britain. There are two commissioners for Northern Ireland.
Chief Commissioner, His Hon. Judge Martin, QC
Registrar of Appeals, W. D. Pollock

THE SOLICITORS' DISCIPLINARY TRIBUNAL
113 Chancery Lane, London WC2A 1PL
Tel 0171-242 0219

The Solicitors' Disciplinary Tribunal is an independent statutory body whose members are appointed by the Master of the Rolls. The tribunal considers applications made to it alleging either professional misconduct and/or a breach of the statutory rules by which solicitors are bound against an individually named solicitor, former solicitor, registered foreign lawyer, or solicitor's clerk. The president and solicitor members do not receive remuneration.
President, G. B. Marsh
Clerk, Mrs S. C. Elson

THE SCOTTISH SOLICITORS' DISCIPLINE TRIBUNAL
22 Rutland Square, Edinburgh EH1 2BB
Tel 0131-229 5860

The Scottish Solicitors' Discipline Tribunal is an independent statutory body with a panel of 18 members, ten of whom are solicitors; members are appointed by the Lord President of the Court of Session. Its principal function is to consider complaints of misconduct against solicitors in Scotland.
Chairman, J. W. Laughland
Clerk, J. M. Barton, WS

SPECIAL COMMISSIONERS OF INCOME TAX
15–19 Bedford Avenue, London WC1B 3AS
Tel 0171-631 4242

The Special Commissioners are an independent body appointed by the Lord Chancellor to hear complex appeals against decisions of the Board of Inland Revenue and its officials. In addition to the Presiding Special Commissioner there are two full-time and 13 deputy special commissioners; all are legally qualified.
Presiding Special Commissioner, His Hon. Stephen Oliver, QC
Special Commissioners (£92,810), T. H. K. Everett; one vacancy
Clerk, R. P. Lester

SPECIAL IMMIGRATION APPEALS COMMISSION
Taylor House, 88 Rosebery Avenue, London EC1R 4QU
Tel 0171-862 4200

The Commission was set up under the Special Immigration Appeals Commission Act 1998. Its main function is to consider appeals against orders for deportations in cases which involve, in the main, considerations of national security. Members are appointed by the Lord Chancellor.
Chairman, The Hon. Mr Justice Potts
Secretary, Ms P. Dews

TRAFFIC COMMISSIONERS
c/o Scottish Traffic Area, Argyle House, 3 Lady Lawson Street, Edinburgh EH3 9SE
Tel 0131-529 8500

The Traffic Commissioners are responsible for licensing operators of heavy goods and public service vehicles. They also have responsibility for appeals relating to the licensing of operators and for disciplinary cases involving the conduct of drivers of these vehicles. There are six Commissioners in the seven traffic areas covering Britain. Each Traffic Commissioner constitutes a tribunal for the purposes of the Tribunals and Inquiries Act 1971. For Traffic Area Offices and Commissioners, *see* page 299.
Senior Traffic Commissioner (£59,431), M. W. Betts, CBE

TRANSPORT TRIBUNAL
48–49 Chancery Lane, London WC2A 1JR
Tel 0171-936 7493

The Transport Tribunal hears appeals against decisions made by Traffic Commissioners at public inquiries. The tribunal consists of a legally-qualified president, two legal members who may sit as chairmen, and five lay members. The president and legal members are appointed by the Lord Chancellor and the lay members by the Secretary of State for the Environment, Transport and the Regions.
President (part-time), H. B. H. Carlisle, QC
Legal member (part-time) (£290 a day), His Hon. Judge Brodrick
Lay members (£232 a day), D. Yeomans; J. W. Whitworth; Ms P. Steel; P. Rogers; L. Milliken
Secretary, P. J. Fisher

VALUATION TRIBUNALS
c/o Warwickshire Valuation Tribunal, 2nd Floor, Walton House, 11 Parade, Leamington Spa, Warks CV32 4DG
Tel 01926-421875

The Valuation Tribunals hear appeals concerning the council tax, non-domestic rating and land drainage rates in England and Wales, and have residual jurisdiction to hear appeals concerning the community charge, the pre-1990 rating list, disabled rating and mixed hereditaments. There are 56 tribunals in England and eight in Wales; those in England are funded by the Department of the Environment, Transport and the Regions and those in Wales by the National Assembly for Wales. A separate tribunal is constituted for each hearing, and normally consists of a chairman and two other members. Members are appointed by the local authorities and serve on a voluntary basis. A National Association of Valuation Tribunals considers all matters affecting valuations tribunals in England, and the Council of Wales Valuation Tribunals performs the same function in Wales.
President, National Association of Valuation Tribunals, P. Wood
Valuation Tribunals National Officer, B. P. Massen
President, Council of Wales Valuation Tribunals, J. H. Owens

VAT AND DUTIES TRIBUNALS
15–19 Bedford Avenue, London WC1B 3AS
Tel 0171-631 4242

VAT and Duties Tribunals are administered by the Lord Chancellor in England and Wales, and by the First Minister in Scotland. They are independent, and decide disputes between taxpayers and Customs and Excise. In England and Wales, the president and chairmen are appointed by the Lord Chancellor and members by the Treasury. Chairmen in Scotland are appointed by the Lord President of the Court of Session.
President, His Hon. Stephen Oliver, QC
Vice-President, England and Wales (£92,810), A. W. Simpson
Vice-President, Scotland (£92,810), T. G. Coutts, QC
Vice-President, Northern Ireland (£92,810), His Hon. J. McKee, QC
Registrar, R. P. Lester

The Police Service

There are 52 police forces in the United Kingdom, each responsible for policing in its area. Most forces' area is coterminous with one or more local authority areas. Policing in London is carried out by the Metropolitan Police and the City of London Police; in Northern Ireland by the Royal Ulster Constabulary; and by the Isle of Man, States of Jersey, and Guernsey forces in their respective islands and bailiwicks. National services include the National Missing Persons Bureau and the National Crime Squad.

The police authorities of English and Welsh forces comprise local councillors, magistrates and independent members. In Scotland, there are six joint police boards made up of local councillors; the other two police authorities are councils. In London the authority for the Metropolitan Police is the Home Secretary, advised by the Metropolitan Police Committee; for the City of London Police the authority is a committee of the Corporation of London and includes councillors and magistrates. In Northern Ireland the Secretary of State appoints the police authority.

Police authorities are financed by central and local government grants and a precept on the council tax. Subject to the approval of the Home Secretary (in England and Wales) and to regulations, they appoint the chief constable. In England and Wales they are responsible for publishing annual policing plans and annual reports, setting local objectives and a budget, and levying the precept. The police authorities in Scotland are responsible for setting a budget, providing the resources necessary to police the area adequately, appointing officers of the rank of Assistant Chief Constable and above, and determining the number of officers and civilian staff in the force. The structure and responsibilities of the police authority in Northern Ireland are under review.

The Home Secretary, the Secretary of State for Northern Ireland and the Scottish Executive are responsible for the organization, administration and operation of the police service. They make regulations covering matters such as police ranks, discipline, hours of duty, and pay and allowances. All police forces are subject to inspection by HM Inspectors of Constabulary, who report to the Home Secretary, Scottish Executive or Secretary of State for Northern Ireland. In Scotland, a review of the structure of police forces began in April 1998. In Northern Ireland a commission on policing was established by the Belfast Agreement in April 1998. It made recommendations to the Secretary of State in September 1999.

In April 1999 the Home Secretary set targets for recruitment of officers from ethnic minorities for each force in England and Wales to achieve within ten years. From 2000 targets for promotion and retention of these officers will also be set.

COMPLAINTS

The investigation and resolution of a serious complaint against a police officer in England and Wales is subject to the scrutiny of the Police Complaints Authority. An officer who is dismissed, required to resign or reduced in rank, whether as a result of a complaint or not, may appeal to a police appeals tribunal established by the relevant police authority. In Scotland, chief constables are obliged to investigate a complaint against one of their officers; if there is a suggestion of criminal activity, the complaint is investigated by an independent public prosecutor. In Northern Ireland complaints are investigated by the Independent Commission for Police Complaints, which will be replaced by the Police Ombudsman in by April 2000.

BASIC RATES OF PAY
since 1 September 1998

Chief Constable	
No fixed term	£71,058–£101,613
Fixed term appointment	£74,616–£106,569
Assistant Chief Constable – designated Deputy	
No fixed term	80% of their Chief Constable's pay or £68,064, whichever is higher
Fixed term appointment	80% of their Chief Constable's pay or £71,466, whichever is higher
Assistant Chief Constable	
No fixed term	£59,292–£68,064
Fixed term appointment	£62,259–£71,466
Superintendent	£43,143–£53,556
Chief Inspector	£35,454–£38,307
Inspector	£31,719–£36,918
Sergeant	£24,525–£28,605
Constable	£16,056–£25,410

Metropolitan Police

Metropolitan Commissioner	£121,300–£137,000
Deputy Commissioner	£99,570–£112,509
Assistant Commissioner	£90,036–£99,129
Commander	£59,292–£71,466

The rank of Chief Superintendent was abolished in April 1995. Existing appointments continue and receive the higher ranges of the pay scale for Superintendents
1999 pay negotiations still in progress at time of going to press

THE SPECIAL CONSTABULARY

Each police force has its own special constabulary, made up of volunteers who work in their spare time. Special Constables have full police powers within their force and adjoining force areas, and assist regular officers.

NATIONAL CRIME SQUAD

The National Crime Squad (NCS) was established on 1 April 1998, replacing the six regional crime squads in England and Wales. It investigates national and international organized and serious crime. It also supports police forces investigating serious crime. The squad is accountable to the National Crime Squad Service Authority.
Headquarters: PO Box 2500, London
SW1V 2WF. Tel: 0171-238 2500
Director General, Roy Penrose, OBE, QPM

NCS SERVICE AUTHORITY

The Service Authority is responsible for ensuring the effective operation of the National Crime Squad. It fulfills a similar role to a police authority. It works alongside the National Criminal Intelligence Service Service Authority. There are 26 members, of whom the chairman and nine others serve as 'core members' on both authorities.

Headquarters: PO Box 2600, London SW1V 2WG. Tel: 0171-238 2600
Chairman, Rt. Hon. Sir John Wheeler
Clerk, T. Simmons
Treasurer, P. Derrick

NATIONAL MISSING PERSONS BUREAU

The Police National Missing Persons Bureau (PNMPB) acts as a central clearing house of information, receiving reports about vulnerable missing persons that are still outstanding after 28 days and details of unidentified persons or remains within 48 hours of being found from all forces in England and Wales. Reports are also received from Scottish police forces, the RUC, and foreign police forces via Interpol.
Headquarters: New Scotland Yard, Broadway, London SW1H 0BG. Tel: 0171-230 1212
Director, C. J. Coombes

POLICE INFORMATION TECHNOLOGY ORGANIZATION

The Police Information Technology Organization (PITO) became a non-departmental public body on 1 April 1998. It develops and manages the delivery of national police information technology services, such as the Police National Computer, co-ordinates the development of local information technology systems where common standards and systems are needed, and provides a procurement service.
Headquarters: Horseferry House, Dean Ryle Street, London SW1P 2AW. Tel: 0181-358 5497
Chairman, Sir Trefor Morris
Chief Executive, vacant

FORENSIC SCIENCE SERVICE

The Forensic Science Service (FSS) provides forensic science support to the police forces in England and Wales for the investigation of scenes of crime, scientific analysis of material, and interpretation of scientific results. The FSS is organized into serious crime, volume crime, drugs and specialist services, supported by intelligence and consultancy services. Laboratories are located at Birmingham., Chepstow, Chorley, Huntingdon, London and Wetherby.
Headquarters: Priory House, Gooch Street North, Birmingham B5 6QQ. Tel: 0121-607 6800
Chief Executive, Dr J. Thompson

POLICE FORCES AND AUTHORITIES

Strength: actual strength of force as at mid 1999
Chair: chairman/convener of the police authority/police committee/joint police board

ENGLAND

AVON AND SOMERSET CONSTABULARY, *HQ,* PO Box 37, Valley Road, Portishead, Bristol BS20 8QJ. Tel: 01275-818181. *Strength,* 3,016; *Chief Constable,* S. Pilkington, QPM; *Chair,* J. Cristenson

BEDFORDSHIRE POLICE, *HQ,* Woburn Road, Kempston, Bedford MK43 9AX. Tel: 01234-841212. *Strength,* 1,054; *Chief Constable,* M. O'Byrne, QPM; *Chair,* A. Heffernan

CAMBRIDGESHIRE CONSTABULARY, *HQ,* Hinchingbrooke Park, Huntingdon, Cambs PE18 8NP. Tel: 01480-456111. *Strength,* 1,295; *Chief Constable,* D. G. Gunn, QPM; *Chair,* J. Reynolds

CHESHIRE CONSTABULARY, *HQ,* Nuns Road, Chester CH1 2PP. Tel: 01244-350000. *Strength,* 2,053; *Chief Constable,* N. Burgess, QPM; *Chair,* Mrs M. Chapman

CLEVELAND POLICE, *HQ,* PO Box 70, Ladgate Lane, Middlesbrough TS8 9EH. Tel: 01642-326326. *Strength,* 1,400 *Chief Constable,* B. D. D. Shaw, QPM; *Chair,* K. Walker

CUMBRIA CONSTABULARY, *HQ,* Carleton Hall, Penrith, Cumbria CA10 2AU. Tel: 01768-891999. *Strength,* 1,118; *Chief Constable,* C. Phillips, QPM; *Chair,* R. Watson

DERBYSHIRE CONSTABULARY, *HQ,* Butterley Hall, Ripley, Derbyshire DE5 3RS. Tel: 01773-570100. *Strength,* 1,770; *Chief Constable,* J. F. Newing, CBE, QPM; *Chair,* K. Wilkinson

DEVON AND CORNWALL CONSTABULARY, *HQ,* Middlemoor, Exeter EX2 7HQ. Tel: 0990-777444. *Strength,* 2,871; *Chief Constable,* J. S. Evans, QPM; *Chair,* O. May

DORSET POLICE FORCE, *HQ,* Winfrith, Dorchester, Dorset DT2 8DZ. Tel: 01929-462727. *Strength,* 1,284; *Chief Constable,* Mrs J. Stichbury; *Chair,* P. I. Jones

DURHAM CONSTABULARY, *HQ,* Aykley Heads, Durham DH1 5TT. Tel: 0191-386 4929. *Strength,* 1,570; *Chief Constable,* G. Hedges, QPM; *Chair,* J. Knox

ESSEX POLICE, *HQ,* PO Box 2, Springfield, Chelmsford CM2 6DA. Tel: 01245-491491. *Strength,* 2,928; *Chief Constable,* D. F. Stevens, QPM; *Chair,* E. A. Peel

GLOUCESTERSHIRE CONSTABULARY, *HQ,* Holland House, Lansdown Road, Cheltenham, Glos GL51 6QH. Tel: 01242-521321. *Strength,* 1,122; *Chief Constable,* A. J. P. Butler, QPM; *Chair,* Brig. M. A. Browne, CBE

GREATER MANCHESTER POLICE, *HQ,* PO Box 22 (S. West PDO), Chester House, Boyer Street, Manchester M16 0RE. Tel: 0161-872 5050. *Strength,* 6,840; *Chief Constable,* D. Wilmot, QPM; *Chair,* S. Murphy

HAMPSHIRE CONSTABULARY, *HQ,* West Hill, Winchester, Hants SO22 5DB. Tel: 01962-841500. *Strength,* 3,468; *Chief Constable,* Sir John Hoddinott, CBE, QPM; *Chair,* W. H. Wheeler

HERTFORDSHIRE CONSTABULARY, *HQ,* Stanborough Road, Welwyn Garden City, Herts AL8 6XF. Tel: 01707-354200. *Strength,* 1,767; *Chief Constable,* P. Sharpe, QPM; *Chair,* P. Holland

HUMBERSIDE POLICE, *HQ,* Queens Gardens, Kingston upon Hull HU1 3DJ. Tel: 01482-326111. *Strength,* 1,975; *Chief Constable,* D. Westwood; *Chair,* K. Townsend

KENT CONSTABULARY, *HQ,* Sutton Road, Maidstone, Kent ME15 9BZ. Tel: 01622-690690. *Strength,* 3,300; *Chief Constable,* J. D. Phillips, QPM; *Chair,* Mrs P. F. Stubbs

LANCASHIRE CONSTABULARY, *HQ,* PO Box 77, Hutton, Preston, Lancs PR4 5SB. Tel: 01772-614444. *Strength,* 3,299; *Chief Constable,* Mrs P. A. Clare, QPM; *Chair,* Dr R. B. Henig

LEICESTERSHIRE CONSTABULARY, *HQ,* St Johns, Narborough, Leicester LE9 5BX. Tel: 0116-222 2222. *Strength,* 1,896; *Chief Constable,* D. J. Wyrko, QPM; *Chair,* D. J. Saville

LINCOLNSHIRE POLICE, *HQ,* PO Box 999, Lincoln LN5 7PH. Tel: 01522-532222. *Strength,* 1,139; *Chief Constable,* R. J. N. Childs, QPM; *Chair,* M. D. Kennedy

MERSEYSIDE POLICE, *HQ,* PO Box 59, Canning Place, Liverpool L69 1JD. Tel: 0151-709 6010. *Strength,* 4,211; *Chief Constable,* N. Bettison; *Chair,* Ms C. Gustafson

NORFOLK CONSTABULARY, *HQ,* Martineau Lane, Norwich NR1 2DJ. Tel: 01603-768769. *Strength,* 1,394; *Chief Constable,* K. R. Williams, QPM; *Chair,* B. J. Landale

NORTHAMPTONSHIRE POLICE, *HQ,* Wootton Hall, Northampton NN4 0JQ. Tel: 01604-700700. *Strength,* 1,150; *Chief Constable,* C. Fox, QPM; *Chair,* Dr M. Dickie

NORTHUMBRIA POLICE, *HQ,* Ponteland, Newcastle upon Tyne NE20 0BL. Tel: 01661-872555. *Strength,* 3,800; *Chief Constable,* C. Strachan, QPM; *Chair,* G. Gill

NORTH YORKSHIRE POLICE, *HQ,* Newby Wiske Hall, Newby Wiske, Northallerton, N. Yorks DL7 9HA. Tel: 01609-783131. *Strength,* 1,353; *Chief Constable,* D. R. Kenworthy, QPM; *Chair,* Mrs A. F. Harris

NOTTINGHAMSHIRE POLICE, *HQ,* Sherwood Lodge, Arnold, Nottingham NG5 8PP. Tel: 0115-967 0999. *Strength,* 2,234; *Chief Constable,* C. F. Bailey, QPM; *Chair,* R. A. Hassett

SOUTH YORKSHIRE POLICE, *HQ,* Snig Hill, Sheffield S3 8LY. Tel: 0114-220 2020. *Strength,* 3,195; *Chief Constable,* M. Hedges; *Chair,* C. Swindell

STAFFORDSHIRE POLICE, *HQ,* Cannock Road, Stafford ST17 0QG. Tel: 01785-257717. *Strength,* 2,255; *Chief Constable,* J. W. Giffard, QPM; *Chair,* J. T. Meir

SUFFOLK CONSTABULARY, *HQ,* Martlesham Heath, Ipswich IP5 3QS. Tel: 01473-613500. *Strength,* 1,185; *Chief Constable,* P. J. Scott-Lee, QPM; *Chair,* M. N. Smith

SURREY POLICE, *HQ,* Mount Browne, Sandy Lane, Guildford, Surrey GU3 1HG. Tel: 01483-571212. *Strength,* 1,690; *Chief Constable,* I. Blair, QPM; *Chair,* A. Peirce

SUSSEX POLICE, *HQ,* Malling House, Church Lane, Lewes, E. Sussex BN7 2DZ. Tel: 0845-6070999. *Strength,* 3,038; *Chief Constable,* P. Whitehouse, QPM; *Chair,* K. C. Bodfish

THAMES VALLEY POLICE, *HQ,* Oxford Road, Kidlington, Oxon OX5 2NX. Tel: 01865-846000. *Strength,* 3,800; *Chief Constable,* C. Pollard, QPM; *Chair,* G. Maybury

WARWICKSHIRE CONSTABULARY, *HQ,* PO Box 4, Leek Wootton, Warwick CV35 7QB. Tel: 01926-415000. *Strength,* 923; *Chief Constable,* A. C. Timpson; *Chair,* J. Rennie

WEST MERCIA CONSTABULARY, *HQ,* Hindlip Hall, PO Box 55, Hindlip, Worcester WR3 8SP. Tel: 01905-723000. *Strength,* 2,007; *Chief Constable,* P. Hampson, QPM; *Chair,* D. B. Watkins

WEST MIDLANDS POLICE, *HQ,* PO Box 52, Lloyd House, Colmore Circus, Queensway, Birmingham B4 6NQ. Tel: 0121-626 5000. *Strength,* 7,322; *Chief Constable,* E. Crew, QPM; *Chair,* R. Jones

WEST YORKSHIRE POLICE, *HQ,* PO Box 9, Laburnum Road, Wakefield, W. Yorks WF1 3QP. Tel: 01924-375222. *Strength,* 4,982; *Chief Constable,* G. Moore, QPM; *Chair,* N. Taggart

WILTSHIRE CONSTABULARY, *HQ,* London Road, Devizes, Wilts SN10 2DN. Tel: 01380-722341. *Strength,* 1,085; *Chief Constable,* Miss E. Neville, QPM; PH.D.; *Chair,* H. A. Woolnough

WALES

DYFED-POWYS POLICE, *HQ,* PO Box 99, Llangunnor, Carmarthen SA31 2PF. Tel: 01267-222020. *Strength,* 1,021; *Chief Constable,* R. White, CBE, QPM; *Chair,* Ms M. Roberts

GWENT POLICE, *HQ,* Croesyceiliog, Cwmbran NP44 2XJ. Tel: 01633-838111. *Strength,* 1,200; *Chief Constable (acting),* K. Turner; *Chair,* D. Turnbull

NORTH WALES POLICE, *HQ,* Glan-y-don, Colwyn Bay, Conwy LL29 8AW. Tel: 01492-517171. *Strength,* 1,414; *Chief Constable,* M. J. Argent, QPM; *Chair,* J. Anderson, OBE

SOUTH WALES POLICE, *HQ,* Cowbridge Road, Bridgend CF31 3SU. Tel: 01656-655555. *Strength,* 2,999; *Chief Constable,* A. T. Burden, QPM; *Chair,* R. Thomas

SCOTLAND

CENTRAL SCOTLAND POLICE, *HQ,* Randolphfield, Stirling FK8 2HD. Tel: 01786-456000. *Strength,* 713; *Chief Constable,* W. J. M. Wilson, QPM; *Convener,* I. Miller

DUMFRIES AND GALLOWAY CONSTABULARY, *HQ,* Cornwall Mount, Dumfries DG1 1PZ. Tel: 01387-252112. *Strength,* 439; *Chief Constable,* W. Rae, QPM; *Chair,* B. Conchie

FIFE CONSTABULARY, *HQ,* Detroit Road, Glenrothes, Fife KY6 2RJ. Tel: 01592-418888. *Strength,* 840; *Chief Constable,* J. P. Hamilton, QPM; *Chair,* A. Keddie

GRAMPIAN POLICE, *HQ,* Queen Street, Aberdeen AB10 1ZA. Tel: 01224-386000. *Strength,* 1,220; *Chief Constable,* A. G. Brown, QPM; *Chair,* Ms M. Stewart

LOTHIAN AND BORDERS POLICE, *HQ,* Fettes Avenue, Edinburgh EH4 1RB. Tel: 0131-311 3131. *Strength,* 2,615; *Chief Constable,* Sir R. Cameron, QPM; *Convenor,* Ms L. Hinds

NORTHERN CONSTABULARY, *HQ,* Old Perth Road, Inverness IV2 3SY. Tel: 01463-715555. *Strength,* 659; *Chief Constable,* W. A. Robertson, QPM; *Chair,* Mrs J. Home

STRATHCLYDE POLICE, *HQ,* 173 Pitt Street, Glasgow G2 4JS. Tel: 0141-532 2000. *Strength,* 7,008; *Chief Constable,* J. Orr, OBE, QPM; *Chair,* W. Timoney

TAYSIDE POLICE, *HQ,* PO Box 59, West Bell Street, Dundee DD1 9JU. Tel: 01382-223200. *Strength,* 1,150; *Chief Constable,* W. A. Spence, QPM; *Chair,* J. Corrigan

NORTHERN IRELAND

ROYAL ULSTER CONSTABULARY, *HQ,* Brooklyn, Knock Road, Belfast BT5 6LD. Tel: 01232-650222. *Strength,* 8,450; *Chief Constable,* Sir Ronald Flanagan, OBE; *Chair,* P. Armstrong

ISLANDS

ISLAND POLICE FORCE, *HQ,* Hospital Lane, St Peter Port, Guernsey GY1 2QN. Tel: 01481-725111. *Strength,* 147; *Chief Officer,* M. H. Wyeth; *President, States Committee for Home Affairs,* M. W. Torode

STATES OF JERSEY POLICE, *HQ,* Rouge Bouillon, PO Box 789, St Helier, Jersey JE4 8ZD. Tel: 01534-612612. *Strength,* 241; *Chief Officer,* R. H. Le Breton; *President, Defence Committee,* M. Wavell

ISLE OF MAN CONSTABULARY, *HQ,* Glencrutchery Road, Douglas, Isle of Man IM2 4RG. Tel: 01624-631212. *Strength,* 226; *Chief Constable,* R. E. N. Oake, QPM; *Chairman, Police Committee,* Hon. A. R. Bell

---

METROPOLITAN POLICE SERVICE
New Scotland Yard, Broadway, London SW1H 0BG
Tel 0171-230 1212

Establishment, 26,425

Commissioner, (until January 2000) Sir Paul Condon, QPM; (from January 2000) J. Stevens, QPM
Deputy Commissioner (until January 2000), J. Stevens, QPM
Receiver, P. Fletcher
Chair, Sir John Quinton

OPERATIONAL AREAS
Assistant Commissioners, A. Dunn, QPM (*North London*); P. A. Manning, QPM (*Realignment Programme*); W. I. R. Johnston, QPM (*Central London*); D. F. O'Connor, QPM (*South London*)
Deputy Assistant Commissioner, R. Clark, QPM; D. Flanders, QPM; J. G. D. Grieve, QPM; W. I. Griffiths, BEM, QPM; J. Townsend, QPM; A. S. Trotter; B. Wilding; M. Todd

Commanders, M. Briggs, QPM; M. R. Campbell; P. J. Clarke; M. Craik; D. N. Croll, QPM; R. Culzen; R. Currie, QPM; R. Gaspar; P. C. Hagen; A. C. Hayman; C. A. Howlett; G. P. James; D. M. T. Kendrick, OBE, QPM; T. D. Laidlaw, LVO, QPM; M. Messinger; S. C. Pilkington; D. A. Ray, QPM; S. Roberts; A. L. Rowe, QPM; A. G. Shave; D. L. Smith;

SPECIALIST OPERATIONS DEPARTMENT
Assistant Commissioner, D. C. Veness, QPM
Deputy Assistant Commissioner, A. G. Fry, QPM
Commanders, B. G. Moss, QPM; N. G. Mulvihill, QPM; R. C. Pearce

COMPLAINTS INVESTIGATION BUREAU
Commander, I. G. Quinn, QPM

INSPECTORATE
Commander, B. J. Luckhurst, QPM

OTHER DEPARTMENTS
Director, Strategic Co-ordination, Commander T. C. Lloyd, QPM
Director, Personnel, Mrs P. Woods
Director, Consultancy and Information Services, Mrs S. Merchant
Director, Public Affairs, R. Fedorcio
Solicitor, D. Hamilton
Director, Technology, N. Boothman
Director, Property Services, T. G. Lawrence

CITY OF LONDON POLICE
26 Old Jewry, London EC2R 8DJ
Tel 0171-601 2222

Strength, 778
The City of London Police is responsible for policing the City of London. Though small, the area includes one of the most important financial centres in the world and the force has particular expertise in areas such as fraud investigation as well as the areas required of any police force.
    The force has a wholly elected police authority, the police committee of the Corporation of London, which appoints the Commissioner.
Commissioner (£99,129), P. Nove, QPM
Assistant Commissioner (acting) (£79,302), J. Hart, QPM
Commander (acting) (£71,466), J. Davison
Chairman of Police Committee, L. St J. T. Jackson

BRITISH TRANSPORT POLICE
15 Tavistock Place, London WC1H 9SJ
Tel 0171-388 7541

Strength (March 1999), 2,106
British Transport Police is the national police force for the railways in England, Wales and Scotland, including the London Underground system, the Docklands Light Railway and the Midland Metro Tram system. The Chief Constable reports to the British Transport Police Committee. The members of the Committee are appointed by the British Railways Board and include representatives of Railtrack and London Underground Ltd as well as independent members. Officers are paid the same as other police forces.
Chief Constable, D. J. Williams, QPM
Deputy Chief Constable, A. Parker, QPM

MINISTRY OF DEFENCE POLICE
MDP Wethersfield, Braintree, Essex CM7 4AZ
Tel 01371-854000

Strength (March 1999), 3,577
The Ministry of Defence Police is an agency of the Ministry of Defence. It is a national civilian police force whose officers are appointed by the Secretary of State for Defence. It is responsible for the policing of all military land, stations and establishments in the United Kingdom. The agency also has certain responsibilities for the civilian Ministry of Defence Guard Service.
Chief Constable, W. E. E. Boreham, OBE
Deputy Chief Constable, A. V. Comben
Head of Secretariat, P. A. Crowther

ROYAL PARKS CONSTABULARY
The Old Police House, Hyde Park, London W2 2UH
Tel 0171-298 2000

Strength (July 1999), 155
The Royal Parks Constabulary is maintained by the Royal Parks Agency, an executive agency of the Department for Culture, Media and Sport, and is responsible for the policing of eight royal parks in and around London. These comprise an area in excess of 6,300 acres. Officers of the force are appointed under the Parks Regulations Act 1872 as amended and are paid around 85 per cent of the Metropolitan Police rate.
Chief Officer, W. Ross, OBE
Deputy Chief Officer, A. McLean

UK ATOMIC ENERGY AUTHORITY CONSTABULARY
Building E6, Culham Science Centre, Abingdon, Oxon OX14 3DB
Tel 01235-463760

Strength (June 1999), 498
The Constabulary is responsible for policing UK Atomic Energy Authority and British Nuclear Fuels PLC establishments and for escorting nuclear material between establishments. The Chief Constable is responsible, through the Atomic Energy Authority Police Authority, to the President of the Board of Trade. Officers are paid around 95 per cent of the rate paid to other police forces.
Chief Constable, W. F. Pryke
Assistant Chief Constable, P. P. Crossan

STAFF ASSOCIATIONS

Police officers are not permitted to join a trade union or to take strike action. All ranks have their own staff associations.
ASSOCIATION OF CHIEF POLICE OFFICERS OF ENGLAND, WALES AND NORTHERN IRELAND, 7th Floor, 25 Victoria Street, London SW1H 0EX. Tel: 0171-227 3434. Represents Chief Constables, Deputy and Assistant Chief Constables in England, Wales and Northern Ireland; officers of the rank of Commander and above in the Metropolitan and City of London Police and senior civilian members of these forces.
General Secretary, Miss M. C. E. Barton, OBE

THE POLICE SUPERINTENDENTS' ASSOCIATION OF
ENGLAND AND WALES, 67A Reading Road,
Pangbourne, Reading RG8 7JD. Tel: 0118-984 4005.
Represents officers of the rank of Superintendent.
Secretary, Supt. P. Williams

THE POLICE FEDERATION OF ENGLAND AND WALES,
15–17 Langley Road, Surbiton, Surrey KT6 6LP. Tel:
0181-399 2224. Represents officers up to and including
the rank of Chief Inspector. *General Secretary,* J. Moseley

ASSOCIATION OF CHIEF POLICE OFFICERS IN
SCOTLAND, Police Headquarters, Fettes Avenue,
Edinburgh EH4 1RB. Tel: 0131-311 3051. Represents the
Chief Constables, Deputy and Assistant Chief
Constables of the Scottish police forces. *Hon. Secretary,*
H. R. Cameron, QPM

THE ASSOCIATION OF SCOTTISH POLICE
SUPERINTENDENTS, Secretariat, 173 Pitt Street,
Glasgow G2 4JS. Tel: 0141-221 5796. Represents officers
of the rank of Superintendent. *President,* Chief Supt. S.
Davidson

THE SCOTTISH POLICE FEDERATION, 5 Woodside
Place, Glasgow G3 7QF. Tel: 0141-332 5234. Represents
officers up to and including the rank of Chief Inspector.
General Secretary, D. J. Keil, QPM

THE SUPERINTENDENTS' ASSOCIATION OF
NORTHERN IRELAND, RUC Training Centre,
Garnerville Road, Belfast BT4 2NX. Tel: 01232-700660.
Represents Superintendents and Chief Superintendents
in the RUC. *Hon. Secretary,* Supt. W. T. Brown

THE POLICE FEDERATION FOR NORTHERN IRELAND,
Royal Ulster Constabulary, Garnerville, Garnerville
Road, Belfast BT4 2NX. Tel: 01232-760831. Represents
officers up to and including the rank of Chief Inspector.
Secretary, D. A. McClurg

POLICE STRENGTHS 1999

	Male	Female	Total
ENGLAND AND WALES p			
Total officers	105,973	20,123	126,096
Ethnic minority officers	2,016	529	2,545
Special constables	10,860	5,624	16,484
Civilians	20,441	32,590	53,031
SCOTLAND*			
Officers	12,762	2,226	14,988
Special constables	–	–	1,723
Support staff	–	–	4,670
NORTHERN IRELAND			
Officers	7,512	957	8,469
Special constables	785	424	1,209
Civilians	1,192	2,314	3,506

p provisonal
* Figures for Scotland as at 31 March 1998
Sources: Home Office; Scottish Office; RUC

The Prison Service

The prison services in the United Kingdom are the responsibility of the Home Secretary, the Scottish Executive Justice Department and the Secretary of State for Northern Ireland. The chief executive officers of the Prison Service, the Scottish Prison Service and the Northern Ireland Prison Service are responsible for the day-to-day running of the system.

There are 135 prison establishments (136 from December 1999) in England and Wales, 23 in Scotland and four in Northern Ireland. Convicted prisoners are classified according to their assessed security risk and are housed in establishments appropriate to that level of security. There are no open prisons in Northern Ireland. Female prisoners are housed in women's establishments or in separate wings of mixed prisons. Remand prisoners are, where possible, housed separately from convicted prisoners. Offenders under the age of 21 are usually detained in a young offenders' institution, which may be a separate establishment or part of a prison.

Seven prisons are now run by the private sector, and in England and Wales all escort services have been contracted out to private companies. Four prisons are being built and financed under the Private Finance Initiative and will also be run by private contractors. In Scotland, one prison (Kilmarnock) was built and financed by the private sector and is being operated by private contractors.

There are independent prison inspectorates in England and Wales (see page 310) and Scotland (see page 339) which report annually on conditions and the treatment of prisoners. HM Chief Inspector of Prisons for England and Wales also performs an inspectorate role for prisons in Northern Ireland. Every prison establishment also has an independent board of visitors or visiting committee made up of local volunteers. Any prisoner whose complaint is not satisfied by the internal complaints procedures may complain to the Prisons Ombudsman for England and Wales (see page 331) or the Scottish Prisons Complaints Commission (see page 340). There is no Prisons Ombudsman for Northern Ireland, but complaints by prisoners regarding maladministration may be made to the Parliamentary Commissioner for Administration (see page 329).

AVERAGE PRISON POPULATION 1998–9 (UK)

	Remand	Sentenced	Other
ENGLAND AND WALES*			
Male	11,900	49,700	—
Female	700	2,400	—
Total	12,600	52,100	600
SCOTLAND			
Male	n/a	n/a	—
Female	n/a	n/a	—
Total	971	5,057	—
N. IRELAND			
Male	340	1,028	9
Female	9	15	1
Total	349	1,043	10
UK TOTAL	13,920	58,200	610
* 1998 figures			

The projected prison population for 2006 in England and Wales is 66,700 if custody rates and sentence lengths remain at 1998 levels

Sources: Home Office – Statistical Bulletin 1/99; Scottish Prison Service – Annual Report and Accounts 1998–9; Northern Ireland Prison Service – Annual Report 1998–9

SENTENCED PRISON POPULATION BY SEX AND OFFENCE (ENGLAND AND WALES) as at June 1997

	Male	Female
Violence against the person	9,836	387
Sexual offences	3,973	9
Burglary	7,642	96
Robbery	6,069	154
Theft, handling, fraud and forgery	5,068	453
Drugs offences	6,309	675
Other offences	5,242	193
Offence not known	2,599	100
Total	46,739	2,066

Source: Home Office – Statistical Bulletin 5/98

AVERAGE SENTENCED POPULATION BY LENGTH OF SENTENCE 1997 (ENGLAND AND WALES)

	Adults	Young Offenders
Up to 18 months	9,724	3,267
18 months–4 years	10,777	3,019
Over 4 years	19,950	1,534
Total	40,451	7,820

Source: HMSO – Annual Abstract of Statistics 1999

AVERAGE DAILY SENTENCED POPULATION BY LENGTH OF SENTENCE 1998–9 (SCOTLAND)

	Adults	Young Offenders
Less than 4 years	2,036	518
4 years or over (including life)	2,312	191
Total	4,348	710

Source: Scottish Prison Service – Annual Report and Accounts 1998–9

PRISON SUICIDES 1998–9 (ENGLAND AND WALES)

Adults	71
Young offenders	11
Total	82

Source: HM Prison Service – Annual Report and Accounts 1998–9

AVERAGE NUMBER OF PRISON SERVICE STAFF 1998–9 (GREAT BRITAIN)

	England and Wales	Scotland
No. of prison service staff	41,196	4,974

Sources: HM Prison Service – Annual Report and Accounts 1998–9; Scottish Prison Service – Annual Report and Accounts 1998–9

OPERATING COSTS OF PRISON SERVICE IN ENGLAND AND WALES 1998–9

	£ million
Staff costs	995.2
Other operating costs	859.0
Operating income	(16.8)
Net operating costs before notional charge on capital employed	1,837.4
Charge on capital employed	251.7
Net operating costs	2,089.1
Average cost per prisoner place (reflecting establishment costs only)	£22,649

Source: HM Prison Service – Annual Report and Accounts 1998–9

OPERATING COSTS OF SCOTTISH PRISON SERVICE
1998–9

	£
Total income	1,996,000
Total expenditure	183,137,000
Staff costs	119,760,000
Running costs	45,284,000
Other current expenditure	18,093,000
Operating deficit	(181,141,000)
Cost of capital charges	(22,925,000)
Interest payable and similar charges	(14,000)
Interest receivable	105,000
Deficit for financial year	(203,975,000)
Average annual cost per prisoner per place	£26,912

Source: Scottish Prison Service – *Annual Report and Accounts 1998–9*

OPERATING COSTS OF NORTHERN IRELAND PRISON
SERVICE 1998–9

	£
Custodial	117,975,548
Non-custodial	5,489,720
Headquarters	7,269,975
Total	130,735,243
Average annual cost per prisoner place	73,612

Source: Northern Ireland Prison Service

THE PRISON SERVICES

HM PRISON SERVICE

Cleland House, Page Street, London SW1P 4LN
Tel 0171-217 6000; Fax 0171-217 6403
SALARIES 1998–9

Governor 1	£52,349–£54,156
Governor 2	£47,270–£48,721
Governor 3	£40,823–£41,977
Governor 4	£34,233–£36,055
Governor 5	£29,596–£32,295

For civil service salaries, *see* page 276

THE PRISON SERVICE STRATEGY BOARD

Chairman, The Rt. Hon. Paul Boateng, MP (*Home Office minister for prisons and probation*)
Director-General (SCS), M. Narey
 Private Secretary, Ms R. Goodwin
 Staff Officer, J. Heavens
Deputy Director-General (SCS), P. Wheatley
Director of High Security Prisons (SCS), B. Clark
Director of Security (SCS), Ms E. Bailey
Director of Personnel (SCS), G. Hadley
Director of Finance (SCS), J. Le Vay
Director of Corporate Affairs (SCS), Ms C. Pelham
Director of Regimes (SCS), K. D. Sutton
Director of Health Care (SCS), Dr M. Longfield (until end 1999)
Non-Executive Members, Sir Duncan Nichol, CBE; Mrs R. Thomson, CBE; Mrs P. A. Clare, QPM; P. Carter
Board Secretary and Head of Secretariat, Ms C. Checksfield
Chaplain-General and Archdeacon of the Prison Service, Ven. D. Fleming
Senior Roman Catholic Chaplain, Mgr J. Branson

AREA MANAGERS (*SCS*)

Central, J. Dring; *East Midlands*, M. Egan; *Kent*, T. Murtagh, OBE; *London North and East Anglia*, I. Ward; *London South*, P. Atherton; *Mercia*, D. Curtis; *Mersey and Manchester*, A. Fitzpatrick; *North-East*, R. Mitchell; *North-West*, D. I. Lockwood; *South Coast*, A. Smith; *Wales and the West*, J. May; *Yorkshire*, P. Earnshaw

PRISON ESTABLISHMENTS
CNA Average number of in use certified normal accommodation places without overcrowding 1998–9
Prisoners/Young Offenders Average number of prisoners/young offenders 1998–9
ACKLINGTON, Morpeth, Northumberland NE65 9XH. *CNA*, 662. *Prisoners*, 631. *Governor*, Ms H. Banks
ALBANY, Newport, Isle of Wight PO30 5RS. *CNA*, 436. *Prisoners*, 429. *Governor*, K. Munns
ALTCOURSE (private prison), Higher Lane, Fazakerley, Liverpool L9 7AG. *CNA*, 600. *Prisoners*, 669. *Director*, W. MacGowan
††ASHFIELD (from December 1999), Shortwood Road, Pucklechurch, Bristol BS16 9QT. *CNA*, 400. *Director*, N. Pascoe
ASHWELL, Oakham, Leics LE15 7LF. *CNA*, 484. *Prisoners*, 491. *Governor*, C. Bushell
*‡ASKHAM GRANGE, Askham Richard, York YO2 3PT. *CNA*, 130. *Prisoners and Young Offenders*, 121. *Governor*, H. E. Crew
‡AYLESBURY, Bierton Road, Aylesbury, Bucks HP20 1EH. *CNA*, 433. *Young Offenders*, 443. *Governor*, S. Bryans
BEDFORD, St Loyes Street, Bedford MK40 1HG. *CNA*, 352. *Prisoners*, 400. *Governor*, T. Ireson
†BELMARSH, Western Way, Thamesmead, London SE28 0EB. *CNA*, 843. *Prisoners*, 788. *Governor*, W. S. Duff
BIRMINGHAM, Winson Green Road, Birmingham B18 4AS. *CNA*, 734. *Prisoners*, 1,100. *Governor*, C. Scott, OBE
BLAKENHURST (private prison), Hewell Lane, Redditch, Worcs B97 6QS. *CNA*, 647. *Prisoners*, 850. *Director*, P. Siddons
BLANTYRE HOUSE, Goudhurst, Cranbrook, Kent TN17 2NH. *CNA*, 120. *Prisoners*, 120. *Governor*, E. McLennan-Murray
BLUNDESTON, Lowestoft, Suffolk NR32 5BG. *CNA*, 352. *Prisoners*, 385. *Governor*, S. Robinson
††BRINSFORD, New Road, Featherstone, Wolverhampton WV10 7PY. *CNA*, 477. *Young Offenders*, 509. *Governor*, C. Davidson
BRISTOL, Cambridge Road, Bristol BS7 8PS. *CNA*, 487. *Prisoners*, 602. *Governor*, N. Hall
BRIXTON, PO Box 369, Jebb Avenue, London SW2 5XF. *CNA*, 693. *Prisoners*, 659. *Governor*, R. Chapman
*††BROCKHILL, Redditch, Worcs B97 6RD. *CNA*, 159. *Prisoners and Young Offenders*, 159. *Governor*, V. Bird
BUCKLEY HALL (private prison), Buckley Farm Lane, Rochdale, Lancs OL12 9DP. *CNA*, 350. *Prisoners*, 382. *Director*, S. Mitson
BULLINGDON, PO Box 50, Bicester, Oxon OX6 0PR. *CNA*, 773. *Prisoners*, 897. *Governor*, J. Cann
*†BULLWOOD HALL, High Road, Hockley, Essex SS5 4TE. *CNA*, 140. *Prisoners and Young Offenders*, 140. *Governor*, Mrs V. Hart
CAMP HILL, Newport, Isle of Wight PO30 5PB. *CNA*, 460. *Prisoners*, 472. *Governor*, W. Preston
CANTERBURY, 46 Longport, Canterbury CT1 1PJ. *CNA*, 196. *Prisoners*, 283. *Governor*, Ms J. Galbally
††CARDIFF, Knox Road, Cardiff CF2 1UG. *CNA*, 525. *Prisoners and Young Offenders*, 722. *Governor*, J. Thomas-Ferrand
‡CASTINGTON, Morpeth, Northumberland NE65 9XG. *CNA*, 450. *Young Offenders*, 398. *Governor*, M. Lees
CHANNINGS WOOD, Denbury, Newton Abbot, Devon TQ12 6DW. *CNA*, 594. *Prisoners*, 615. *Governor*, R. Mullen
††CHELMSFORD, 200 Springfield Road, Chelmsford, Essex CM2 6LQ. *CNA*, 388. *Prisoners and Young Offenders*, 409. *Governor*, Ms A. Gomme
COLDINGLEY, Bisley, Woking, Surrey GU24 9EX. *CNA*, 286. *Prisoners*, 290. *Governor*, E. R. Butt

*COOKHAM WOOD, Rochester, Kent ME1 3LU. *CNA*, 120. *Prisoners*, 149. *Governor*, Miss C. Kershaw

DARTMOOR, Princetown, Yelverton, Devon PL20 6RR. *CNA*, 671. *Prisoners*, 692. *Governor*, J. Lawrence

‡DEERBOLT, Bowes Road, Barnard Castle, Co. Durham DL12 9BG. *CNA*, 450. *Young Offenders*, 405. *Governor*, P. Atkinson

††DONCASTER (private prison), Off North Bridge, Marshgate, Doncaster DN5 8UX. *CNA*, 771. *Prisoners and Young Offenders*, 1,052. *Director*, H. Jones

††DORCHESTER, North Square, Dorchester DT1 1JD. *CNA*, 213. *Prisoners and Young Offenders*, 230. *Governor*, Mrs D. Calvert

‡DOVER, The Citadel, Western Heights, Dover CT17 9DR. *CNA*, 264. *Young Offenders*, 247. *Governor*, B. Pollett

DOWNVIEW, Sutton Lane, Sutton, Surrey SM2 5PD. *CNA*, 327. *Prisoners*, 340. *Governor*, C. Lambert

*‡DRAKE HALL, Eccleshall, Staffs ST21 6LQ. *CNA*, 295. *Prisoners and Young Offenders*, 295. *Governor*, P. Tidball

*†DURHAM, Old Elvet, Durham DH1 3HU. *CNA*, 686. *Prisoners*, 902. *Governor*, M. Newell

*‡EAST SUTTON PARK, Sutton Valence, Maidstone, Kent ME17 3DF. *CNA*, 94. *Prisoners and Young Offenders*, 79. *Governor*, Revd R. Carter

*†‡EASTWOOD PARK, Falfield, Wotton-under-Edge, Glos GL12 8DB. *CNA*, 255. *Prisoners and Young Offenders*, 288. *Governor*, P. Winkley.

ELMLEY, Church Road, Eastchurch, Sheerness, Kent ME12 4AY. *CNA*, 763. *Prisoners*, 886. *Governor*, A. Smith

ERLESTOKE HOUSE, Devizes, Wilts SN10 5TU. *CNA*, 310. *Prisoners*, 300. *Governor (acting)*, I. Acheson

EVERTHORPE, Brough, E. Yorks HU15 1RB. *CNA*, 438. *Prisoners*, 464. *Governor*, P. Midgley

††EXETER, New North Road, Exeter EX4 4EX. *CNA*, 321. *Prisoners and Young Offenders*, 527. *Governor*, N. Evans

FEATHERSTONE, New Road, Wolverhampton WV10 7PU. *CNA*, 599. *Prisoners*, 599. *Governor*, M. Pascoe

††FELTHAM, Bedfont Road, Feltham, Middx TW13 4ND. *CNA*, 802. *Prisoners and Young Offenders*, 878. *Governor*, C. Welsh

FORD, Arundel, W. Sussex BN18 0BX. *CNA*, 501. *Prisoners*, 355. *Governor*, K. Kan

FOREST BANK (from December 1999), Agecroft Road, Pendlebury, Manchester M27 8UE. *CNA*, 800. *Director*, M. Goodwin

*‡FOSTON HALL, Foston, Derbys DE65 5DN. *CNA*, 174. *Prisoners and Young Offenders*, 174. *Governor*, Ms P. Scriven

FRANKLAND, Brasside, Durham DH1 5YD. *CNA*, 655. *Prisoners*, 530. *Governor*, I. Woods

FULL SUTTON, Full Sutton, York YO41 1PS. *CNA*, 602. *Prisoners*, 530. *Governor*, D. Roberts

GARTH, Ulnes Walton Lane, Leyland, Preston PR5 3NE. *CNA*, 633. *Prisoners*, 646. *Governor*, W. Rose-Quirie, OBE

GARTREE, Gallow Field Road, Market Harborough, Leics LE16 7RP. *CNA*, 366. *Prisoners*, 366. *Governor*, S. Rimmer

††GLEN PARVA, Tigers Road, Wigston, Leicester LE8 4TN. *CNA*, 720. *Young Offenders*, 845. *Governor*, B. Payling

††GLOUCESTER, Barrack Square, Gloucester GL1 2JN. *CNA*, 235. *Prisoners and Young Offenders*, 327. *Governor*, R. Booty

GRENDON/SPRING HILL, HMP Grendon, Grendon Underwood, Aylesbury, Bucks HP18 0TL. *CNA*, 497. *Prisoners*, 489. *Governor*, T. C. Newell

‡GUYS MARSH, Shaftesbury, Dorset SP7 0AH. *CNA*, 487. *Prisoners and Young Offenders*, 507. *Governor*, D. Godfrey

§HASLAR, 2 Dolphin Way, Gosport, Hants PO12 2AW. *CNA*, 160. *Prisoners*, 142. *Governor*, R. Oliver

‡HATFIELD, Thorne Road, Hatfield, Doncaster DN7 6EL. *CNA*, 180. *Young Offenders*, 155. *Governor*, Ms C. Davies

HAVERIGG, Millom, Cumbria LA18 4NA. *CNA*, 530. *Prisoners*, 530. *Governor*, G. Brunskill

HEWELL GRANGE, Redditch, Worcs B97 6QQ. *CNA*, 203. *Prisoners*, 203. *Governor*, N. Croft

HIGH DOWN, Sutton Lane, Sutton, Surrey SM2 5PJ. *CNA*, 649. *Prisoners*, 779. *Governor*, D. Wilson

*HIGHPOINT, Stradishall, Newmarket, Suffolk CB8 9YG. *CNA*, 649. *Prisoners*, 836. *Governor*, R. Woolford

††HINDLEY, Gibson Street, Bickershaw, Wigan, Lancs WN2 5TH. *CNA*, 531. *Prisoners and Young Offenders*, 493. *Governor*, C. Sheffield

‡HOLLESLEY BAY COLONY, Woodbridge, Suffolk IP12 3JW. *CNA*, 365. *Prisoners and Young Offenders*, 353. *Governor*, J. Forster

*†‡HOLLOWAY, Parkhurst Road, London N7 0NU. *CNA*, 477. *Prisoners and Young Offenders*, 492. *Governor*, D. Lancaster

HOLME HOUSE, Holme House Road, Stockton-on-Tees TS18 2QU. *CNA*, 971. *Prisoners*, 944. *Governor*, D. Crouch

††HULL, Hedon Road, Hull HU9 5LS. *CNA*, 572. *Prisoners and Young Offenders*, 494. *Governor*, S. Wagstaffe

‡HUNTERCOMBE, Huntercombe Place, Nuffield, Henley-on-Thames RG9 5SB. *CNA*, 368. *Young Offenders*, 376. *Governor*, P. Manwaring

KINGSTON, 122 Milton Road, Portsmouth PO3 6AS. *CNA*, 193. *Prisoners*, 175. *Governor*, S. McLean

KIRKHAM, Freckleton Road, Preston PR4 2RA. *CNA*, 702. *Prisoners*, 658. *Governor*, A. F. Jennings, OBE

KIRKLEVINGTON GRANGE, Yarm, Cleveland TS15 9PA. *CNA*, 183. *Prisoners*, 178. *Governor*, Ms S. Anthony

LANCASTER, The Castle, Lancaster LA1 1YL. *CNA*, 218. *Prisoners*, 216. *Governor*, J. Illingsworth

††LANCASTER FARMS, Far Moor Lane, Stone Row Head, off Quernmore Road, Lancaster LA1 3QZ. *CNA*, 496. *Prisoners and Young Offenders*, 456. *Governor*, D. Thomas

LATCHMERE HOUSE, Church Road, Ham Common, Richmond, Surrey TW10 5HH. *CNA*, 193. *Prisoners*, 171. *Governor*, T. Hinchliffe

LEEDS, Armley, Leeds LS12 2TJ. *CNA*, 1,056. *Prisoners*, 1,233. *Governor*, R. Daly

LEICESTER, Welford Road, Leicester LE2 7AJ. *CNA*, 219. *Prisoners*, 331. *Governor*, D. Bamber

††LEWES, Brighton Road, Lewes, E. Sussex BN7 1EA. *CNA*, 485. *Prisoners and Young Offenders*, 483. *Governor*, J. F. Dixon

LEYHILL, Wotton-under-Edge, Glos GL12 8BT. *CNA*, 410. *Prisoners*, 422. *Governor*, D. T. Williams

LINCOLN, Greetwell Road, Lincoln LN2 4BD. *CNA*, 360. *Prisoners*, 430. *Governor*, B. McCourt

LINDHOLME, Bawtry Road, Hatfield Woodhouse, Doncaster DN7 6EE. *CNA*, 686. *Prisoners*, 666. *Governor*, A. Holman

LITTLEHEY, Perry, Huntingdon, Cambs PE18 0SR. *CNA*, 624. *Prisoners*, 648. *Governor*, C. Morris

LIVERPOOL, 68 Hornby Road, Liverpool L9 3DF. *CNA*, 1,216. *Prisoners*, 1,510. *Governor*, W. Abbott

LONG LARTIN, South Littleton, Evesham, Worcs WR11 5TZ. *CNA*, 456. *Prisoners*, 344. *Governor*, J. Mullen

LOWDHAM GRANGE (private prison), Lowdham, Notts NG14 7TA. *CNA*, 504. *Prisoners*, 498. *Director*, R. Tasker

---

* Women's establishment or establishment with units for women
† Remand Centre or establishment with units for remand prisoners
‡ Young Offender Institution or establishment with units for young offenders
§ Immigration Holding Centre

*†‡LOW NEWTON, Brasside, Durham DH1 5SD. *CNA, 215. Prisoners and Young Offenders, 295. Governor,* M. Kirby
MAIDSTONE, 36 County Road, Maidstone ME14 1UZ. *CNA,* 551. *Prisoners, 541. Governor,* M. Conway
MANCHESTER, Southall Street, Manchester M60 9AH. *CNA, 953. Prisoners, 1,074. Governor,* J. Smith
‡MOORLAND, Bawtry Road, Hatfield Woodhouse, Doncaster DN7 6BW. *CNA, 740. Prisoners and Young Offenders, 760. Governor,* D. J. Waplington, OBE
MORTON HALL, Swinderby, Lincoln LN6 9PS. *CNA, 208. Prisoners, 158. Governor,* M. Murphy
THE MOUNT, Molyneaux Avenue, Bovingdon, Hemel Hempstead HP3 0NZ. *CNA, 705. Prisoners, 745. Governor,* P. Wailen
*†‡NEW HALL, Dial Wood, Flockton, Wakefield WF4 4AX. *CNA, 327. Prisoners and Young Offenders, 366. Governor,* M. Shepherd
†‡NORTHALLERTON, 15A East Road, Northallerton, N. Yorks DL6 1NW. *CNA, 152. Prisoners and Young Offenders, 271. Governor,* D. P. G. Appleton
NORTH SEA CAMP, Freiston, Boston, Lincs PE22 0QX. *CNA, 177. Prisoners, 197. Governor,* M. A. Lewis
†‡NORWICH, Mousehold, Norwich NR1 4LU. *CNA, 564. Prisoners and Young Offenders, 744. Governor,* M. Spurr
NOTTINGHAM, Perry Road, Sherwood, Nottingham NG5 3AG. *CNA, 466. Prisoners, 431. Governor,* K. Beaumont
‡ONLEY, Willoughby, Rugby, Warks CV23 8AP. *CNA, 400. Young Offenders, 400. Governor,* J. N. Brooke
†‡PARC (private prison), Heol Hopcyn John, Bridgend CF35 6AR. *CNA, 800. Prisoners and Young Offenders, 411. Director,* R. Dixon
PARKHURST, Newport, Isle of Wight PO30 5NX. *CNA, 482. Prisoners, 443. Governor,* D. M. Morrison
PENTONVILLE, Caledonian Road, London N7 8TT. *CNA, 897. Prisoners, 1,175. Governor,* R. Duncan
‡PORTLAND, Easton, Portland, Dorset DT5 1DL. *CNA, 516. Young Offenders, 534. Governor,* K. Lockyer
‡PRESCOED, 47 Maryport Street, Usk, Gwent NP5 1XP. *CNA, see* Usk. *Prisoners and Young Offenders, see* Usk. *Governor,* R. J. Comber
PRESTON, 2 Ribbleton Lane, Preston PR1 5AB. *CNA, 445. Prisoners, 679. Governor,* A. Scott
RANBY, Ranby, Retford, Notts DN22 8EV. *CNA, 710. Prisoners, 720. Governor,* J. Slater
†‡READING, Forbury Road, Reading RG1 3HY. *CNA, 203. Prisoners and Young Offenders, 245. Governor,* C. Norman
*RISLEY, Risley, Warrington WA3 6BP. *CNA, 851. Prisoners, 868. Governor,* C. Sheffield
†‡ROCHESTER, 1 Fort Road, Rochester, Kent ME1 3QS. *CNA, 433. Prisoners and Young Offenders, 366. Governor,* T. Robson
*SEND, Ripley Road, Send, Woking, Surrey GU23 7LJ. *CNA, 80. Prisoners, 80. Governor,* T. Beeston
SHEPTON MALLET, Cornhill, Shepton Mallet, Somerset BA4 5LU. *CNA, 162. Prisoners, 224. Governor,* R. Bennett
SHREWSBURY, The Dana, Shrewsbury SY1 2HR. *CNA, 323. Prisoners, 323. Governor,* A. Bramley
STAFFORD, 54 Gaol Road, Stafford ST16 3AW. *CNA, 627. Prisoners, 627. Governor,* P. Wright
STANDFORD HILL, Church Road, Eastchurch, Isle of Sheppey, Kent ME12 4AA. *CNA, 384. Prisoners, 217. Governor,* K. Naisbitt
STOCKEN, Stocken Hall Road, Stretton, nr Oakham, Leics LE15 7RD. *CNA, 556. Prisoners, 576. Governor,* R. Curtis
‡STOKE HEATH, Stoke Heath, Market Drayton, Shropshire TF9 2JL. *CNA, 646. Young Offenders, 633. Governor,* J. Alldridge
*‡STYAL, Wilmslow, Cheshire SK9 4HR. *CNA, 284. Prisoners and Young Offenders, 280. Governor,* Ms M. Moulden

SUDBURY, Ashbourne, Derbys DE6 5HW. *CNA, 511. Prisoners, 492. Governor,* P. E. Salter
SWALESIDE, Brabazon Road, Eastchurch, Isle of Sheppey, Kent ME12 4AX. *CNA, 632. Prisoners, 616. Governor,* J. Podmore
†SWANSEA, 200 Oystermouth Road, Swansea SA1 3SR. *CNA, 251. Prisoners, 336. Governor,* G. Deighton
‡SWINFEN HALL, Lichfield, Staffs WS14 9QS. *CNA, 255. Young Offenders, 295. Governor,* Ms J. P. Francis
‡THORN CROSS, Arley Road, Appleton Thorn, Warrington WA4 4RL. *CNA, 316. Young Offenders, 224. Governor,* I. Windebank
USK, 47 Maryport Street, Usk, Gwent NP5 1XP. *CNA (Usk and Prescoed), 206. Prisoners (Usk and Prescoed), 281. Governor,* R. J. Comber
THE VERNE, Portland, Dorset DT5 1EQ. *CNA, 552. Prisoners, 570. Governor,* M. Cook
WAKEFIELD, 5 Love Lane, Wakefield WF2 9AG. *CNA, 747. Prisoners, 555. Governor,* D. Shaw
WANDSWORTH, Heathfield Road, London SW18 3HS. *CNA, 1,102. Prisoners, 1,094. Governor,* M. Knight
WAYLAND, Griston, Thetford, Norfolk IP25 6RL. *CNA, 618. Prisoners, 648. Governor,* Mrs K. Crawley
WEALSTUN, Wetherby, W. Yorks LS23 7AZ. *CNA, 632. Prisoners, 603. Governor,* S. Tasker
WEARE, Portland Dock, Castletown, Portland, Dorset DT5 1PZ. *CNA, 400. Prisoners, 312. Governor,* Ms S. F. McCormick
WELLINGBOROUGH, Millers Park, Doddington Road, Wellingborough, Northants NN8 2NH. *CNA, 368. Prisoners, 338. Governor,* E. Willetts
‡WERRINGTON, Werrington, Stoke-on-Trent ST9 0DX. *CNA, 188. Young Offenders, 106. Governor,* S. Habgood
‡WETHERBY, York Road, Wetherby, W. Yorks LS22 5ED. *CNA, 360. Young Offenders, 347. Governor,* D. Hall
WHATTON, 14 Cromwell Road, Nottingham NG13 9FQ. *CNA, 275. Prisoners, 272. Governor,* D. Walmesley
WHITEMOOR, Longhill Road, March, Cambs PE15 0PR. *CNA, 522. Prisoners, 454. Governor,* T. Williams
*WINCHESTER, Romsey Road, Winchester SO22 5DF. *CNA, 463. Prisoners, 576. Governor,* R. J. Gaines
THE WOLDS (private prison), Everthorpe, Brough, E. Yorks HU15 2JZ. *CNA, 360. Prisoners, 399. Director,* D. McDonnell
†‡§WOODHILL, Tattenhoe Street, Milton Keynes MK4 4DA. *CNA, 672. Prisoners and Young Offenders, 693. Governor,* Mrs M. Boon
WORMWOOD SCRUBS, PO Box 757, Du Cane Road, London W12 0AE. *CNA, 746. Prisoners, 1,122. Governor,* S. Moore
WYMOTT, Ulnes Walton Lane, Leyland, Preston PR5 3LW. *CNA, 809. Prisoners, 797. Governor,* R. Doughty

SCOTTISH PRISON SERVICE

Calton House, 5 Redheughs Rigg, Edinburgh EH12 9HW
Tel 0131-556 8400

SALARIES 1998–9

Senior managers in the Scottish Prison Service, including governors and deputy governors of prisons, are paid across three pay bands:

Band I	£36,000–£55,600
Band H	£30,000 –£46,350
Band G	£25,100–£38,150

Chief Executive of Scottish Prison Service (SCS), E. W. Frizzell
Director of Custody, J. Durno, OBE
Director, Human Resources, P. Russell

Director, Finance and Information Systems, W. Pretswell
Director, Strategy and Corporate Affairs, Ms J. Hutchison
Deputy Director, Regime Services and Supplies, J. McNeill
Deputy Director, Estates and Buildings, B. Paterson
Area Director, South and West, M. Duffy
Area Director, North and East, P. Withers
Head of Training, Scottish Prison Service College, J. Matthews
Head of Communications, M. Mulford

PRISON ESTABLISHMENTS

Prisoners/Young Offenders Average number of
prisoners/young offenders 1998–9

*ABERDEEN, Craiginches, Aberdeen AB9 2HN. *Prisoners*, 181.
Governor, I. Gunn

BARLINNIE, Barlinnie, Glasgow G33 2QX. *Prisoners*, 1,124.
Governor, R. L. Houchin

CASTLE HUNTLY, Castle Huntly, Longforgan, nr
Dundee DD2 5HL. *Prisoners*, 106. *Governor*, K. Rennie

*‡CORNTON VALE, Cornton Road, Stirling FK9 5NY.
Prisoners and Young Offenders, 180. *Governor*, Mrs K.
Donegan

*‡DUMFRIES, Terregles Street, Dumfries DG2 9AX. *Young
Offenders*, 137. *Governor*, G. Taylor

DUNGAVEL, Dungavel House, Strathaven, Lanarkshire
ML10 6RF. *Prisoners*, 113. *Governor*, T. Pitt

EDINBURGH, 33 Stenhouse Road, Edinburgh EH1 3LN.
Prisoners, 731. *Governor*, A. Spencer

FRIARTON, Friarton, Perth PH2 8DW. *Prisoners*, 77.
Governor, Mrs A. Mooney

‡GLENOCHIL, King O'Muir Road, Tullibody,
Clackmannanshire FK10 3AD. *Prisoners and Young
Offenders*, 573. *Governor*, L. McBain, OBE

GREENOCK, Gateside, Greenock PA16 9AH. *Prisoners*, 236.
Governor, R. MacCowan

*INVERNESS, Porterfield, Inverness IV2 3HH. *Prisoners*, 122.
Governor, H. Ross

KILMARNOCK (private prison), Bowhouse, Mauchline
Road, Kilmarnock KA1 5JH. *Prisoners*, 500. *Director*, J.
Bywalec

LONGRIGGEND, Longriggend, nr Airdrie, Lanarkshire
ML6 7TL. *Prisoners*, 158. *Governor*, Ms R. Kite

LOW MOSS, Low Moss, Bishopbriggs, Glasgow G64 2QB.
Prisoners, 362. *Governor*, E. Murch

NATIONAL INDUCTION UNIT, Shotts ML7 4LE. *Prisoners*,
48. *Governor*, J. Gerrie

NORANSIDE, Noranside, Fern, by Forfar, Angus DD8 3QY.
Prisoners, 102. *Governor*, A. MacDonald

PENNINGHAME, Penninghame, Newton Stewart DG8 6RG.
Prisoners, 89. *Governor*, S. Swan

PERTH, 3 Edinburgh Road, Perth PH2 8AT. *Prisoners*, 477.
Governor, W. Millar

PETERHEAD, Salthouse Head, Peterhead, Aberdeenshire
AB4 6YY. *Prisoners*, 297. *Governor*, W. Rattray; *Governor,
Peterhead Unit*, B. McConnell

‡POLMONT, Brightons, Falkirk, Stirlingshire FK2 0AB.
Young Offenders, 443. *Governor*, D. Gunn

SHOTTS, Shotts ML7 4LF. *Prisoners*, 467. *Governor*, W.
McKinlay; *Governor, Shotts Unit*, G. Storer

NORTHERN IRELAND PRISON SERVICE

Dundonald House, Upper Newtownards Road, Belfast
BT4 3SU
Tel 01232-520700; fax 01232-525160

SALARIES 1998–9

Governor 1	£52,349
Governor 2	£47,270
Governor 3	£40,923
Governor 4	£34,233–£35,107
Governor 5	£29,596–£31,810

A Northern Ireland allowance is also payable

PRISON ESTABLISHMENTS

Prisoners/Young Offenders Average number of
prisoners/young offenders 1998–9

‡HYDEBANK WOOD, Hospital Road, Belfast BT8 8NA.
Young Offenders, 173

*‡MAGHABERRY, Old Road, Ballinderry Upper, Lisburn,
Co. Antrim BT28 2PT. *Prisoners and Young Offenders*, 502

MAGILLIGAN, Point Road, Magilligan, Co. Londonderry
BT49 0LR. *Prisoners*, 340

MAZE, Halftown Road, Maze, Lisburn, Co. Antrim
BT27 5RF (due to close by late 2000). *Prisoners*, 387

---

* Women's establishment or establishment with units for women
† Remand Centre or establishment with units for remand prisoners
‡ Young Offender Institution or establishment with units for young
offenders
§ Immigration Holding Centre

Defence

The armed forces of the United Kingdom comprise the Royal Navy, the Army and the Royal Air Force. The Queen is commander-in-chief of all the armed forces. The Ministry of Defence, headed by a Secretary of State, provides the support structure for the armed forces. Within the Ministry of Defence, the Defence Council has overall responsibility for running the armed forces. The Chief of Staff of each service reports through the Chief of the Defence Staff to the Secretary of State on matters relating to the running of his service. The Chief of Staff also chairs the executive committee of the appropriate service board, which manages the service in accordance with centrally determined objectives and budgets. The military-civilian Central Staffs, headed by the Vice-Chief of the Defence Staff and the Second Permanent Under-Secretary of State, are responsible for policy, operational requirements, commitments, financial management, resource planning and civilian personnel management. The Defence Procurement Agency is responsible for purchasing equipment. The Defence Scientific Staff and the Defence Intelligence Staff also form part of the Ministry of Defence.

A permanent Joint Headquarters for the conduct of joint operations was set up at Northwood in 1996. The Joint Headquarters connects the policy and strategic functions of the MoD Head Office with the conduct of operations and is intended to strengthen the policy/executive division. A Joint Rapid Deployment Force was established in August 1996 and a Joint Rapid Reaction Force was set up in April 1999 and will be fully in place by October 2001.

Britain pursues its defence and security policies through its membership of NATO (to which most of its armed forces are committed), the Western European Union, the European Union, the Organization for Security and Co-operation in Europe and the UN (*see* International Organizations section).

ARMED FORCES STRENGTHS *as at 1 April 1999*

All Services	208,600
Men	192,500
Women	16,100
Royal Naval Services	43,700
Army	109,700
Royal Air Force	55,200

Source: The Stationery Office: *UK Defence Statistics 1999*

SERVICE PERSONNEL

1 April

	Royal Navy	Army	RAF	All Services
1975 strength	76,200	167,100	95,000	338,300
1990 strength	63,200	152,800	89,700	305,700
1999 strength	43,700	109,700	55,200	208,600

Source: The Stationery Office: *UK Defence Statistics 1999*

CIVILIAN PERSONNEL

1 April

1975 level	316,700
1990 level	172,300
1999 level	117,700

Source: The Stationery Office: *UK Defence Statistics 1999*

DEPLOYMENT OF UK PERSONNEL

Service personnel in UK *as at 1 July 1998*	173,400
England	144,600
Wales	3,200
Scotland	14,200
N. Ireland	11,000
Service personnel overseas *as at 1 April 1999*	49,924
Royal Naval Services	5,454
Army	31,412
Royal Air Force	8,650

Forces overseas were deployed in Continental Europe, Gibraltar, Cyprus and elsewhere in the Mediterranean, the Near East, the Gulf, the Far East and other locations.

There were also 3,977 locally entered army personnel as at 1 April 1999, of whom 2,087 were deployed in the UK, 352 in Gibraltar, 853 in Brunei and 685 in Nepal.

At 1 August 1998 there were 11,646 US forces personnel based in the UK (including 9,000 Air Force, 1,540 Navy and 376 Army personnel).

Sources: Ministry of Defence; *The Military Balance 1998–9* (OUP)

NUCLEAR FORCES

Britain's nuclear forces comprise four ballistic missile submarines carrying Trident missiles and equipped with nuclear warheads. All nuclear free-fall bombs have been taken out of service.

ARMS CONTROL

The 1990 Conventional Armed Forces in Europe Treaty (the CFE Treaty), which is currently being revised, commits all NATO and former Warsaw Pact members to limiting five major classes of conventional weapons. In 1968 Britain signed the Nuclear Non-Proliferation Treaty, which was indefinitely and unconditionally extended in 1995. In 1996 it signed a Comprehensive Nuclear Test Ban Treaty. Britain was a party to the 1972 Biological and Toxin Weapons Convention, which provides for a world-wide ban on biological weapons, and the 1993 Chemical Weapons Convention, which came into force in 1997 and provides for a world-wide ban on chemical weapons. In 1997 Britain signed the Ottawa Convention, which provides for an immediate ban on the use, production and transfer of anti-personnel land-mines; Britain ratified the Convention on 31 July 1998 and it came into force on 1 March 1999.

DEFENCE BUDGET

	£ million
1998–9 estimated outturn	22,549
1999–2000 estimated outturn	22,280

The Government estimated in July 1998 that defence expenditure as a percentage of GDP would fall from 2.7 per cent in 1998–9 to 2.4 per cent by 2001–2.

Sources: The Stationery Office: *UK Defence Statistics 1999*; Ministry of Defence: *The Strategic Defence Review*

MINISTRY OF DEFENCE
Main Building, Whitehall, London SW1A 2HB
Tel 0171-218 9000
Public Enquiry Office: Tel 0171-218 6645
Web http://www.mod.uk

For ministerial and civil service salaries, *see* page 276
For Services salaries, *see* pages 394–6
Officers promoted in an acting capacity to a more senior

rank are listed under the more senior rank. Promotion to five-star rank is no longer usual in peacetime.
For changes after 31 August 1999, *see* Stop-press

Secretary of State for Defence, The Lord Robertson of Port Ellen, PC (until Oct. 1999)
  Private Secretary (SCS), T. C. McKane
  Special Advisers, A. McGowan; B. Gray
  Parliamentary Private Secretary, Ms S. Heal, MP
Minister of State for the Armed Forces, John Spellar, MP
  Private Secretary (SCS), D. Applegate
Minister of State for Defence Procurement, The Baroness Symons of Vernham Dean
  Private Secretary (SCS), D. Hatcher
Parliamentary Under-Secretary of State, Peter Kilfoyle, MP
  Private Secretary (SCS), A. Dwyer
Permanent Under-Secretary of State (SCS), K. R. Tebbit, CMG
Chief of the Defence Staff, Gen. Sir Charles Guthrie, GCB, LVO, OBE, ADC (*Gen.*)

THE DEFENCE COUNCIL

The Defence Council is responsible for running the Armed Forces. It is chaired by the Secretary of State for Defence and consists of: the Ministers of State; the Parliamentary Under-Secretary of State; the Chief of the Defence Staff; the Permanent Under-Secretary of State; the Chief of the Naval Staff; the Chief of the General Staff; the Chief of the Air Staff; the Vice-Chief of the Defence Staff; the Chief Scientific Adviser; the Chief of Defence Procurement; and the Second Permanent Under-Secretary of State.

CHIEFS OF STAFF

CHIEF OF THE NAVAL STAFF

Chief of the Naval Staff and First Sea Lord, Adm. Sir Michael Boyce, GCB, OBE, ADC
Asst Chief of the Naval Staff, Rear-Adm. J. M. Burnell-Nugent (from 6 Dec. 1999)
Secretariat (*Naval Staff*) (SCS), C. Verey

CHIEF OF THE GENERAL STAFF

Chief of the General Staff, Gen. Sir Roger Wheeler, GCB, CBE, ADC (*Gen.*) (until April 2000); Gen. Sir Michael Walker, KCB, CMG, CBE, ADC (*Gen.*) (from April 2000)
Asst Chief of the General Staff, Maj.-Gen. K. O'Donoghue, CBE
Director-General, Development and Doctrine, Maj.-Gen. A. D. Pigott, CBE (until Feb. 2000); Maj.-Gen. C. L. Elliott, CB, MBE (from Feb. 2000)

CHIEF OF THE AIR STAFF

Chief of the Air Staff, Air Chief Marshal Sir Richard Johns, GCB, CBE, LVO, ADC
Asst Chief of the Air Staff, Air Vice-Marshal G. E. Stirrup, AFC
Secretariat (*Air Staff*) (SCS), M. J. D. Fuller
British-American Community Relations Co-ordinator, Air Marshal Sir John Kemball, KCB, CBE, RAF (retd)
Chief Executive, National Air Traffic Services (SCS), D. J. McLauchlan
Director, Airspace Policy, Air Vice-Marshal J. R. D. Arscott

CENTRAL STAFFS

Vice-Chief of the Defence Staff, Adm. Sir Peter Abbott, GBE, KCB
Second Permanent Under-Secretary of State (SCS), R. T. Jackling, CB, CBE
Deputy CDS (*Equipment Capability*), Vice-Adm. Sir Jeremy Blackham, KCB
Asst CDS, Operational Requirements (*Sea Systems*), Rear-Adm. R. J. G. Ward

Asst CDS, Operational Requirements (*Land Systems*), Maj.-Gen. P. J. Russell-Jones, OBE
Asst CDS, Operational Requirements (*Air Systems*), Air Vice-Marshal S. M. Nicholl, CBE, AFC
Deputy CDS (*Personnel*), Air Marshal M. D. Pledger, OBE, AFC
Asst CDS (*Programmes*), Maj.-Gen. J. P. Kiszely, MC
Asst Under-Secretary of State (*Service Personnel Policy*) (SCS), D. Bowen
Defence Housing Executive (SCS), C. J. I. James
Surgeon-General, Air Marshal Sir John Baird, KBE, QHP (until Feb. 2000); Lt.-Gen. R. C. Menzies, OBE, QHS (from Feb. 2000)
Chief of Staff to the Surgeon-General, Rear-Adm. C. D. Stanford
Chief Executive, Defence Medical Training Organization, and Chief Executive, Defence Secondary Care Agency, Maj.-Gen. C. G. Callow, OBE, QHP
Deputy Under-Secretary of State (*Resources, Programmes and Finance*) (SCS), C. V. Balmer
Asst Under-Secretary of State (*Programmes*) (SCS), T. A. Woolley
Asst Under-Secretary of State (*Systems*) (SCS), N. K. J. Witney
Asst Under-Secretary of State (*Financial Management*) (SCS), D. G. Jones
Asst Under-Secretary of State (*General Finance*) (SCS), C. Sanders
Defence Services Secretary, Rear-Adm. R. B. Lees
Deputy CDS (*Commitments*), Air Marshal Sir John Day, KCB, OBE
Asst CDS (*Operations*), Rear-Adm. S. Moore
Asst Under-Secretary of State (*Home and Overseas*) (SCS), E. V. Buckley, CB
Chief of Defence Logistics, Gen. Sir Samuel Cowan, KCB, CBE
Chief of Staff to the Chief of Defence Logistics, Air Vice-Marshal I. Brackenbury, OBE
Deputy to the Chief of Defence Logistics, J. R. C. Oughton
Asst CDS (*Logistics*), Air Vice-Marshal D. C. Couzens
Director of Policy (SCS), R. P. Hatfield, CBE
Asst CDS (*Policy*), Maj.-Gen. C. F. Drewry, CBE
Deputy Under-Secretary of State (*Civilian Management*) (SCS), J. Howe
Asst Under-Secretary of State, Civilian Management (*Personnel*) (SCS), B. A. E. Taylor
Chief Constable, MOD Police, W. E. E. Boreham, OBE
Asst Under-Secretary of State (*Security and Support*) (SCS), A. G. Rucker
Legal Adviser (SCS), M. J. Hemming
Director-General, Information and Communications Services (SCS), A. C. Sleigh
Defence Estate Organization (SCS), B. L. Hirst
Commandant, Joint Services Command and Staff College, Maj.-Gen. T. J. Granville-Chapman, CBE

DEFENCE INFORMATION STAFF

Director-General of Corporate Communications (SCS), J. Pitt-Brooke
Director, Information Strategy and News (SCS), Ms O. Muirhead
Director, Internal Communications and Media Training (SCS), A. Boardman
Director, Public Relations (*Navy*), Cdre H. Edelston
Director, Public Relations (*Army*), Brig. S. Roberts
Director, Public Relations (*RAF*), Air Cdre D. Walker

DEFENCE INTELLIGENCE STAFF

Old War Office Building, Whitehall, London SW1A 2EU
Tel 0171-218 6645; fax 0171-218 1562
Chief of Defence Intelligence, Vice-Adm. A. W. J. West, DSC

*Deputy Chief of Defence Intelligence and Head of Defence
Intelligence Analysis Staff (SCS)*, J. N. L. Morrison
Director, Intelligence Programmes and Resources (SCS), P. I.
Bailey
*Director, Defence Intelligence Secretariat and Communications
Information Systems (SCS)*, R. C. Hack
Director, Regional Assessments, Brig. N. J. Cottam, OBE
Director, Intelligence Global Issues (SCS), J. M. Cunningham
Director-General, Intelligence and Geographic Resources, Air
Vice-Marshal J. C. French, CBE

DEFENCE SCIENTIFIC STAFF

Chief Scientific Adviser (SCS), Prof. Sir David Davies, KBE
(until Jan. 2000); Prof. Sir Keith O'Nions, FRS (from Jan.
2000)
Chief Scientist (SCS), G. H. B. Jordan
Deputy Chief Scientists (Scrutiny and Analysis) (SCS), M. J.
Earwicker; P. M. Sutcliffe
Asst Chief Scientific Adviser (Nuclear) (SCS), P. W. Roper
Nuclear Weapon Safety Adviser (SCS), Dr A. Ferguson

SECOND SEA LORD/COMMANDER-IN-CHIEF NAVAL HOME COMMAND

Second Sea Lord and C.-in-C. Naval Home Command, Adm. Sir
John Brigstocke, KCB, ADC
*Director-General, Naval Personnel (Strategy and Plans) and
Chief of Staff to Second Sea Lord and C.-in-C. Naval Home
Command*, Rear-Adm. P. A. Dunt
Asst Under-Secretary of State (Naval Personnel) (SCS), B.
Miller
*Flag Officer Training and Recruiting and Chief Executive, Naval
Recruiting and Training Agency*, Rear-Adm. J. Chadwick
Naval Secretary and Chief Executive, Naval Manning Agency,
Rear-Adm. J. M. de Halpert
Director-General, Naval Medical Services, vacant
Director-General, Naval Chaplaincy Services, Revd Dr C.
Stewart

NAVAL SUPPORT COMMAND

Chief of Fleet Support, Vice-Adm. Sir John Dunt, KCB
Director-General, Fleet Support (Operations and Plans), Rear-
Adm. M. G. Wood, CBE
Asst Under-Secretary of State (Fleet Support) (SCS), D. J.
Gould
Chief Executive, Ships Support Agency (SCS), J. Coles
Chief Executive, Naval Bases and Supply Agency,, Rear-Adm.
B. B. Perowne
Chief Naval Engineering Officer, Rear-Adm. J. A. Burch, CBE
Director-General, Aircraft (Navy), vacant
*Flag Officer Scotland, N. England and N. Ireland, and Naval
Base Commander Clyde*, Rear-Adm. A. M. Gregory, OBE

COMMANDER-IN-CHIEF FLEET

C.-in-C. Fleet, Adm. Sir Nigel Essenhigh, KCB
Deputy Commander Fleet, Vice-Adm. F. M. Malbon
Chief of Staff (Operations) and Flag Officer Submarines, Rear-
Adm. R. P. Stevens, OBE
Flag Officer Surface Flotilla, Rear-Adm. P. M. Franklyn, CB,
MVO (until Feb. 2000); Rear-Adm. I. A. Forbes, CBE
(from Feb. 2000)
Flag Officer Sea Training, Rear-Adm. A. K. Backus, OBE
*Commander, UK Task Group/Commander, Anti-Submarine
Warfare Strike Force*, Rear-Adm. I. A. Forbes, CBE (until
Feb. 2000); Rear-Adm. S. R. Meyer (from Feb. 2000)
Flag Officer Naval Aviation, Rear-Adm. I. R. Henderson, CBE
Commandant-General, Royal Marines, Maj.-Gen. R. H. G.
Fulton

QUARTERMASTER-GENERAL'S DEPARTMENT

Quartermaster-General, Lt.-Gen. Sir Scott Grant, KCB
Chief of Staff, Maj.-Gen. C. L. Elliott, CB, MBE (until Feb.
2000)
Asst Under-Secretary (Quartermaster) (SCS), N. H. R. Evans
Director of Contracts (Army) (SCS), P. D. Batt
Director-General, Logistic Support (Army), Maj.-Gen. A. W.
Lyons, CBE
Director-General, Equipment Support (Army), Maj.-Gen. D. L.
Judd

ADJUTANT-GENERAL'S DEPARTMENT

Adjutant-General, Gen. Sir Alexander Harley, KBE, CB, ADC
Chief of Staff, Maj.-Gen. A. P. N. Currie
Head, Command Secretariat (SCS), M. E. McLoughlin
*Director-General, Army Training and Recruiting and Chief
Executive, Army Training and Recruiting Agency*, Maj.-Gen.
A. M. D. Palmer, CBE
Chaplain-General, Revd Dr V. Dobbin, MBE, QHC
Director-General, Army Medical Services, Maj.-Gen. R. C.
Menzies, OBE, QHS (until Feb. 2000)
Director, Army Legal Services, Maj.-Gen. G. Risius
Military Secretary and Chief Executive, Army Personnel Centre,
Maj.-Gen. A. S. H. Irwin, CBE
Commandant, Royal Military Academy, Sandhurst, Maj.-Gen.
A. G. Denaro, CBE
Commandant, Royal Military College of Science, Maj.-Gen. J. C.
B. Sutherell

COMMANDER-IN-CHIEF LAND COMMAND

C.-in-C., Land Command, Gen. Sir Michael Walker, KCB,
CMG, CBE, ADC (Gen.) (until April 2000); Gen. Sir
Michael Jackson, KCB, CBE (from April 2000)
*Deputy C.-in-C., Land Command, and Inspector-General,
Territorial Army*, Lt.-Gen. Sir John Deverell, KCB, OBE
Chief of Staff, HQ Land Command, Maj.-Gen. P. C. C.
Trousdell
Deputy Chief of Staff, HQ Land Command, Maj.-Gen. P. A.
Chambers, MBE

HQ STRIKE COMMAND

Air Officer Commanding-in-Chief, Air Chief Marshal Sir
Peter Squire, KCB, DFC, AFC, ADC
Chief of Staff and Deputy C.-in-C., Air Marshal T. I. Jenner,
CB
*Senior Air Staff Officer and Air Officer Commanding, No. 38
Group*, Air Vice-Marshal P. O. Sturley, MBE
Air Officer Logistics and Communications Information Systems,
Air Vice-Marshal P. J. Scott
Air Officer Administration, Air Vice-Marshal A. J. Burton
Head, Command Secretariat (SCS), C. J. Wright
Air Officer Commanding, No. 1 Group, Air Vice-Marshal J. H.
Thompson
Air Officer Commanding, No. 11/18 Group, Air Vice-Marshal
B. K. Burridge, CBE

HQ LOGISTICS COMMAND

Air Officer Commanding-in-Chief, Air Vice-Marshal G.
Skinner, CBE
*Chief of Staff (Air Officer Commanding Directly Administered
Units)*, vacant
Command Secretary (SCS), H. Griffiths
*Air Officer Communications Information Systems and Support
Services*, Air Vice-Marshal P. Liddell
Director-General, Support Management (RAF), Air Vice-
Marshal P. W. Henderson, MBE

HQ PERSONNEL AND TRAINING COMMAND

Air Member for Personnel and Air Officer Commanding-in-Chief, Air Marshal Sir Anthony Bagnall, KCB, OBE
Chief of Staff, Air Vice-Marshal R. A. Wright, AFC
Chief Executive, Training Group Defence Agency, Air Vice-Marshal A. J. Stables, CBE
Commandant, RAF College, Cranwell, Air Vice-Marshal T. W. Rimmer, OBE
Air Secretary and Chief Executive, RAF Personnel Management Agency, Air Vice-Marshal I. M. Stewart, AFC
Director-General, Medical Services (RAF), Air Vice-Marshal C. J. Sharples, QHP
Director, Legal Services (RAF), Air Vice-Marshal J. Weeden
Chaplain-in-Chief (RAF), Revd A. P. Bishop, QHC
Command Secretary (SCS), L. D. Kyle

DEFENCE PROCUREMENT AGENCY

MOD Abbey Wood, Bristol BS34 8JH
Tel 0117-913 0000

Chief of Defence Procurement and Chief Executive, Defence Procurement Agency, Vice-Adm. Sir Robert Walmsley, KCB
Deputy Chief of Defence Procurement (Operations) and Controller of the Navy, Air Marshal P. C. Norriss, CB, AFC
Deputy Chief Executive (SCS), J. F. Howe, CB, OBE
Executive Director 1 (SCS), I. Fauset
Executive Director 2, Maj.-Gen. D. J. M. Jenkins, CBE
Executive Director 3 (SCS), G. N. Beaven
Executive Director 4, Rear-Adm. P. Spencer (until Jan. 2000); Rear-Adm. N. C. F. Guild (from Jan. 2000)
Executive Director 5 (SCS), S. Porter
Executive Director 6 (SCS), S. Webb
Change Adviser (SCS), J. Allen
Integration and Aerospace Adviser, Air Vice-Marshal A. A. Nicholson, CBE, LVO
Engineering Adviser, Maj.-Gen. L. D. Curran
Head of Defence Export Services (SCS), L. A. Edwards

OTHER DEFENCE AGENCIES

ARMED FORCES PERSONNEL ADMINSTRATION AGENCY, Building 182, RAF Innsworth, Gloucester GL3 1HW. Tel: 01452-712612 ext. 7347. *Chief Executive,* T. S. Lord
ARMY BASE REPAIR ORGANIZATION, Building 200, Monxton Road, Andover, Hants SP11 8HT. Tel: 01264-383295. *Chief Executive,* J. R. Drew, CBE
ARMY PERSONNEL CENTRE, Kentigern House, 65 Brown Street, Glasgow G2 8EX. Tel: 0141-248 7890. *Chief Executive,* Maj.-Gen. A. S. H. Irwin, CBE
ARMY TECHNICAL SUPPORT AGENCY, Room 60/1, HQ QMG, Monxton Road, Andover, Hants SP11 8HT. Tel: 01264-383161. *Chief Executive,* Brig. A. D. Ball, CBE
ARMY TRAINING AND RECRUITING AGENCY, Trenchard Lines, Upavon, Pewsey, Wilts SN9 6BE. Tel: 01980-615024. *Chief Executive,* Maj.-Gen. A. M. D. Palmer, CBE
BRITISH FORCES POST OFFICE, Inglis Barracks, Mill Hill, London NW7 1PX. Tel: 0181-818 6313. *Director and Chief Executive,* Brig. B. J. Cash
DEFENCE ANALYTICAL SERVICES AGENCY, Northumberland House, Northumberland Avenue, London WC2N 5BP. Tel: 0171-218 0729. *Chief Executive,* C. Youngson
DEFENCE AVIATION REPAIR AGENCY, DARA Head Office, Building 145, St Athan, Barry, Vale of Glamorgan CF62 4WA. Tel: 01446-798893. *Chief Executive,* S. R. Hill, OBE

DEFENCE BILLS AGENCY, Room 410, Mersey House, Drury Lane, Liverpool L2 7PX. Tel: 0151-242 2234. *Chief Executive,* I. S. Elrick
DEFENCE CLOTHING AND TEXTILES AGENCY, Skimmingdish Lane, Caversfield, Oxon OX6 9TS. Tel: 01869-875501. *Chief Executive,* Brig. M. J. Roycroft
DEFENCE CODIFICATION AIR LOGISTICS DOCUMENTATION, Defence Codification, Room 2.4.23, Kentigern House, 65 Brown Street, Glasgow G2 8EX. Tel: 0141-224 2066. *Chief Executive,* K. A. Bradshaw
DEFENCE COMMUNICATION SERVICES AGENCY, Building 111, Basil Hill Barracks, Park Lane, Corsham, Wilts SN13 9NR. Tel: 01225-814886. *Chief Executive,* Maj-Gen. A. J. Raper, CBE
DEFENCE DENTAL AGENCY, RAF Halton, Aylesbury, Bucks HP22 5PG. Tel: 01296-623535, ext. 6851. *Chief Executive,* Air Vice-Marshal I. G. McIntyre, QHDS
DEFENCE ESTATES, St George's House, Blakemore Drive, Sutton Coldfield, W. Midlands B95 7RL. Tel: 0121-311 2140. *Chief Executive,* I. Andrews, CBE
DEFENCE EVALUATION AND RESEARCH AGENCY, Ively Road, Farnborough, Hants GU14 0LX. Tel: 01252-394500. *Chief Executive,* Sir John Chisholm
DEFENCE HOUSING EXECUTIVE, 8th Floor, St Christopher House, Southwark Street, London SE1 0TE. Tel: 0171-921 1033. *Chief Executive,* J. Wilson
DEFENCE INTELLIGENCE AND SECURITY CENTRE, Chicksands, Shefford, Beds SG17 5PR. Tel: 01462-752125. *Chief Executive,* Brig. C. G. Holtom
DEFENCE MEDICAL TRAINING ORGANIZATION, Building 87, Fort Blockhouse, Gosport, Hants PO12 2AB. Tel: 01705-765284/765438. *Chief Executive,* Maj.-Gen. C. G. Callow, OBE, QHP
DEFENCE SECONDARY CARE AGENCY, Room 564, St Giles Court, 1–13 St Giles High Street, London WC2H 8LD. Tel: 0171-305 6190. *Chief Executive,* Maj.-Gen. C. G. Callow, OBE, QHP
DEFENCE STORAGE AND DISTRIBUTION AGENCY, Ploughley Road, Lower Arncott, Bicester, Oxon OX6 0LD. Tel: 01869-256840. *Chief Executive,* Brig. P. D. Foxton
DEFENCE TRANSPORT AND MOVEMENTS AGENCY, Monxton Road, Andover, Hants SP11 8HT. Tel: 01264-382537. *Chief Executive,* Air Cdre P. T. W. Leaning
DEFENCE VETTING AGENCY, Room 4/54, Metropole Building, Northumberland Avenue, London WC2N 5BL. Tel: 0171-807 0435. *Chief Executive,* M. P. B. G. Wilson
DISPOSAL SALES AGENCY, 7th Floor, 6 Hercules Road, London SE1 7DJ. Tel: 0171-261 8853. *Chief Executive,* S. Taylor
JOINT AIR RECONNAISSANCE INTELLIGENCE CENTRE, RAF Brampton, Huntingdon, Cambs PE18 8QL. Tel: 01480-52151, ext. 7837. *Chief Executive,* Gp Capt S. J. Lloyd
LOGISTIC INFORMATION SYSTEMS AGENCY, Monxton Road, Andover, Hants SP11 8HT. Tel: 01264-382025. *Chief Executive,* Brig. P. A. Flanagan
MEDICAL SUPPLIES AGENCY, Drummond Barracks, Ludgershall, Andover, Hants SP11 9RU. Tel: 01980-608606. *Chief Executive,* B. E. Nimick
METEOROLOGICAL OFFICE, London Road, Bracknell, Berks RG12 2SZ. Tel: 01344-420242. *Chief Executive,* P. D. Ewins, CB, FEng.
MILITARY SURVEY, Elmwood Avenue, Feltham, Middx TW13 7AH. Tel: 0181-818 2181. *Chief Executive,* Brig. P. R. Wildman, OBE
MINISTRY OF DEFENCE POLICE, Wethersfield, Braintree, Essex CM7 4AZ. Tel: 01371-854000. *Chief Executive,* Chief Constable W. E. E. Boreham, OBE

NAVAL BASES AND SUPPLY AGENCY, Room 8, C Block, Ensleigh, Bath BA1 5AB. Tel: 01225-467400. *Chief Executive*, Rear-Adm. B. B. Perowne

NAVAL MANNING AGENCY, Victory Building, HM Naval Base, Portsmouth PO1 3LS. Tel: 01705-727402. *Chief Executive*, Rear-Adm. J. M. de Halpert

NAVAL RECRUITING AND TRAINING AGENCY, Victory Building, HM Naval Base, Portsmouth PO1 3LS. Tel: 01705-727602. *Chief Executive*, Rear-Adm. J. Chadwick

PAY AND PERSONNEL AGENCY, Warminster Road, Bath BA1 5AA. Tel: 01225-828533. *Chief Executive*, M. A. Rowe

RAF LOGISTICS SUPPORT SERVICES, H014, RAF Wyton, PO Box 70, Huntingdon, Cambs PE17 2PY. Tel: 01480-52451, ext. 6604. *Chief Executive*, Air Cdre I. Sloss

RAF PERSONNEL MANAGEMENT AGENCY, RAF Innsworth, Gloucester GL3 1EZ. Tel: 01452-712612, ext. 7010. *Chief Executive*, Air Vice-Marshal I. M. Stewart, AFC

RAF SIGNALS ENGINEERING ESTABLISHMENT, RAF Henlow, Beds SG16 6DN. Tel: 01462-851515, ext. 7625. *Chief Executive*, Air Cdre C. M. Davison

SERVICE CHILDREN'S EDUCATION, HQ SCE, Building 5, Wegberg Military Complex, BFPO 40. Tel: 00-49 2161-908 2372. *Chief Executive*, D. G. Wadsworth

SHIPS SUPPORT AGENCY, B Block, Room 102, Foxhill, Bath BA1 5AB. Tel: 01225-882348. *Chief Executive*, J. D. Coles

TRAINING GROUP DEFENCE AGENCY, RAF Innsworth, Gloucester GL3 1EZ. Tel: 01452-712612, ext. 5344. *Chief Executive*, Air Vice-Marshal A. J. Stables, CBE

UNITED KINGDOM HYDROGRAPHIC OFFICE, Admiralty Way, Taunton, Somerset TA1 2DN. Tel: 01823-337900. *Chief Executive, and Hydrographer of the Royal Navy*, Rear-Adm. J. P. Clarke, CB, LVO, MBE

The Royal Navy

LORD HIGH ADMIRAL OF THE UNITED KINGDOM
HM The Queen

ADMIRALS OF THE FLEET
HRH The Prince Philip, Duke of Edinburgh, KG, KT, OM, GBE, AC, QSO, PC, *apptd* 1953
The Lord Hill-Norton, GCB, *apptd* 1971
Sir Michael Pollock, GCB, LVO, DSC, *apptd* 1974
Sir Edward Ashmore, GCB, DSC, *apptd* 1977
Sir Henry Leach, GCB, *apptd* 1982
Sir Julian Oswald, GCB, *apptd* 1993
Sir Benjamin Bathurst, GCB, *apptd* 1995

ADMIRALS
Boyce, Sir Michael, GCB, OBE, ADC (*Chief of the Naval Staff and First Sea Lord*)
Abbott, Sir Peter, GBE, KCB (*Vice-Chief of the Defence Staff*)
Brigstocke, Sir John, KCB, ADC (*C.-in-C. Naval Home Command and Second Sea Lord*)
Essenhigh, Sir Nigel, KCB (*C.-in-C. Fleet, C.-in-C. Eastern Atlantic Area and Commander Allied Forces North-Western Europe*)

VICE-ADMIRALS
Dunt, Sir John, KCB (*Chief of Fleet Support*)
Garnett, Sir Ian, KCB (*Chief of Joint Operations*)
Haddacks, P. K. (*UK Military Rep. at NATO HQ*)
Blackham, Sir Jeremy, KCB (*Deputy CDS (Equipment Capability)*)
Blackburn, D. A. J., CB, LVO (*Chief of Staff, Commander Naval Forces South Atlantic*)

West, A. W. J., DSC (*Chief of Defence Intelligence*)
McAnally, J. H. S., LVO (*Commandant, Royal College of Defence Studies*)
Malbon, F. M. (*Deputy Commander Fleet*)
Band, J. (*Team Leader, Defence Training and Education Study*) (from 11 Jan. 2000)

REAR-ADMIRALS
Clarke, J. P., CB, LVO, MBE (*Hydrographer of the Navy and Chief Executive, UK Hydrographic Office*)
Franklyn, P. M., CB, MVO (*Flag Officer Surface Flotilla*) (until Feb. 2000)
Perowne, J. F., OBE (*Dep. SACLANT*)
Lees, R. B. (*Defence Services Secretary*)
Spencer, P. (*Executive Director 4, Defence Procurement Agency*) (until Jan. 2000)
Ross, A. B., CB, CBE (*Asst Director Operations Divn International Military Staff*)
Perowne, B. B. (*Chief Executive, Naval Bases and Supply Agency*)
Forbes, I. A., CBE (*Commander, UK Task Group/Commander, Anti-Submarine Warfare Strike Force*) (until Feb. 2000); (*Flag Officer Surface Flotilla*) (from Feb. 2000)
Gough, A. B. (*Asst CDS (Policy and Requirements) to Supreme Allied Commander Europe*)
Lippiett, R. J., MBE (*Chief of Staff to Commander, Allied Naval Forces Southern Europe, and Senior British Officer Southern Region*)
Gregory, A. M., OBE (*Flag Officer Scotland, N. England and N. Ireland, and Naval Base Commander Clyde*)
Moore, S. (*Asst CDS (Operations)*)
Dunt, P. A. (*Director-General, Naval Personnel (Strategy and Plans) and Chief of Staff to Second Sea Lord and C.-in-C. Naval Home Command*)
Burch, J. A., CBE (*Chief Naval Engineering Officer*)
Rickard, H. W. (*Senior Directing Staff (Naval), Royal College of Defence Studies*)
Stevens, R. P., OBE (*Chief of Staff (Operations), Flag Officer Submarines, COMSUBEASTLANT and COMSUBNORTHWEST*)
Henderson, I. R., CBE (*Flag Officer Naval Aviation*)
Chadwick, J. (*Flag Officer Training and Recruiting and Chief Executive, Naval Recruiting and Training Agency*)
de Halpert, J. M. (*Naval Secretary/Chief Executive, Naval Manning Agency*)
HRH The Prince of Wales, KG, KT, GCB and Great Master of the Order of the Bath, AK, QSO, PC, ADC(P)
Wood, M. G., CBE (*Director-General, Fleet Support (Operations and Plans)*)
Stanford, C. D. (*Chief of Staff to the Surgeon-General*)
Burnell-Nugent, J. M. (*Asst Chief of the Naval Staff*) (from 6 Dec. 1999)
Meyer, S. R. (*Military Adviser to the High Representative in Sarajevo*) (until Feb. 2000); (*Commander, UK Task Group/Commander, Anti-Submarine Warfare Strike Force*) (from Feb. 2000)
Backus, A. K., OBE (*Flag Officer Sea Training*)
Clare, R. A. G. (*Director of Operational Management, NATO Regional Command North*)
Guild, N. C. F. (*Executive Director 4, Defence Procurement Agency*) (from Jan. 2000)
Ward, R. J. G. (*Asst CDS Operational Requirements (Sea Systems)*)

Enquiries regarding records of serving officers should be directed to The Naval Secretary, Room 161, Victory Building, HM Naval Base, Portsmouth, Hants PO1 3LS. Tel: 01705-727431.

HM FLEET *as at autumn 1999*

SUBMARINES

Trident	Vanguard, Vengeance, Victorious, Vigilant
Fleet	Sceptre, Sovereign, Spartan, Splendid, Superb, Talent, Tireless, Torbay, Trafalgar, Trenchant, Triumph, Turbulent
ANTI-SUBMARINE WARFARE CARRIERS	Ark Royal, Illustrious, Invincible
ASSAULT SHIPS	Fearless, Intrepid
LANDING PLATFORM HELICOPTER	Ocean

DESTROYERS

Type 42	Birmingham, Cardiff, Edinburgh, Exeter, Glasgow, Gloucester, Liverpool, Manchester, Newcastle, Nottingham, Southampton, York

FRIGATES

Type 23	Argyll, Grafton, Iron Duke, Lancaster, Marlborough, Monmouth, Montrose, Norfolk, Northumberland, Richmond, Somerset, Sutherland, Westminster
Type 22	Brave, Campbeltown, Chatham, Cornwall, Coventry, Cumberland, Sheffield

OFFSHORE PATROL

Castle Class	Dumbarton Castle, Leeds Castle
Island Class	Alderney, Anglesey, Guernsey, Lindisfarne, Shetland

MINEHUNTERS

Hunt Class	Atherstone, Berkeley, Bicester, Brecon, Brocklesby, Cattistock, Chiddingfold, Cottesmore, Dulverton, Hurworth, Ledbury, Middleton, Quorn
Sandown Class	Bridport, Cromer, Grimsby, Inverness, Pembroke, Penzance, Sandown, Walney

PATROL CRAFT

River Class	Orwell
Coastal Training Craft*	Archer, Biter, Blazer, Charger, Dasher, Example, Exploit, Explorer, Express, Puncher, Pursuer, Raider, Smiter, Tracker
Gibraltar Search and Rescue Craft	Ranger, Trumpeter
ICE PATROL SHIP	Endurance
SURVEY SHIPS	Beagle, Bulldog, Gleaner, Herald, Roebuck, Scott
SOLD/DECOMMISSIONED 1998–9	Arun, Beaver, Blackwater, Boxer, London, Orkney, Spey

* Operated by the University Royal Naval Units

OTHER PARTS OF THE NAVAL SERVICE

ROYAL MARINES

The Royal Marines were formed in 1664 and are part of the Naval Service. Their primary purpose is to conduct amphibious and land warfare. The principal operational units are 3 Commando Brigade Royal Marines, an amphibious all-arms brigade trained to operate in arduous environments, which is a core element of the UK's Joint Rapid Reaction Force; Comacchio Group Royal Marines, which is responsible for the security of nuclear weapon facilities; and Special Boat Service Royal Marines, the maritime special forces. The Royal Marines also provide detachments for warships and land-based naval parties as required. The Royal Marines Band Service provides military musical support for the Naval Service. The headquarters of the Royal Marines is at Portsmouth, along with the Royal Marines School of Music, and principal bases at Plymouth, Arbroath, Poole, Taunton and Chivenor. The Corps of Royal Marines is about 6,500 strong.

Commandant-General, Royal Marines, Maj.-Gen. R. H. G. Fulton

Chief of Staff, NATO Joint Headquarters North, Maj.-Gen. D. Wilson, OBE (from Dec. 1999)

Director-General, Joint Doctrine and Concepts Centre, Maj.-Gen. A. A. Milton, OBE, ADC

ROYAL MARINES RESERVE (RMR)

The Royal Marines Reserve is a commando-trained volunteer force with the principal role, when mobilized, of supporting the Royal Marines. There are RMR centres in London, Glasgow, Bristol, Liverpool and Newcastle. The current strength of the RMR is about 1,000.

Director, RMR, Lt.-Col. A. W. MacCormick

ROYAL FLEET AUXILIARY SERVICE (RFA)

The Royal Fleet Auxiliary Service is a civilian-manned flotilla of 22 ships. Its primary role is to supply the Royal Navy at sea with food, fuel, ammunition and spares, enabling it to maintain operations away from its home ports. In addition the RFA provides the Royal Navy with sea-borne aviation training facilities as well as secure logistic support and amphibious operations capability for the Army and Royal Marines.

FLEET AIR ARM

The Fleet Air Arm was founded in 1914 as the Royal Naval Air Service and operates some 240 fixed wing aircraft and helicopters for the Royal Navy. Sea Harrier fighters provide air defence/strike capability for the fleet, and Sea King and Lynx helicopters provide commando support, anti-submarine, anti-surface, airborne early warning and search and rescue capability. In 1999 the strength of the FAA was 5,600.

ROYAL NAVAL RESERVE (RNR)

The Royal Naval Reserve is an integral part of the Naval Service. It comprises up to 3,850 men and women nationwide who volunteer to train in their spare time to enable the Royal Navy to meet its operational commitments, at sea and ashore, in crisis or war.

The standard annual training commitment is 24 days, including 12 days' continuous training. Daily pay scales range from £35 to £110 for officers and from £22 to £56

for ratings. A single bounty is also payable, the amount depending on the length of service.
Director, Naval Reserves, Capt J. A. Rimington, RN

QUEEN ALEXANDRA'S ROYAL NAVAL NURSING SERVICE

The first nursing sisters were appointed to naval hospitals in 1884 and the Queen Alexandra's Royal Naval Nursing Service (QARNNS) gained its current title in 1902. Nursing ratings were introduced in 1960 and men were integrated into the Service in 1982; both men and women serve as officers and ratings. Female medical assistants were introduced in 1987.
Patron, HRH Princess Alexandra, the Hon. Lady Ogilvy, GCVO
Matron-in-Chief, Capt. P. M. Hambling, QHNS

The Army

THE QUEEN

FIELD MARSHALS

HRH The Prince Philip, Duke of Edinburgh, KG, KT, OM, GBE, AC, QSO, PC, *apptd* 1953
The Lord Carver, GCB, CBE, DSO, MC, *apptd* 1973
Sir Roland Gibbs, GCB, CBE, DSO, MC, *apptd* 1979
The Lord Bramall, KG, GCB, OBE, MC, *apptd* 1982
Sir John Stanier, GCB, MBE, *apptd* 1985
Sir Nigel Bagnall, GCB, CVO, MC, *apptd* 1988
The Lord Vincent of Coleshill, GBE, KCB, DSO (Col. Cmdt. RA), *apptd* 1991
Sir John Chapple, GCB, CBE, *apptd* 1992
HRH The Duke of Kent, KG, GCMG, GCVO, ADC, *apptd* 1993
The Lord Inge, GCB (Col. Green Howards, Col. Cmdt. APTC), *apptd* 1994

GENERALS

Guthrie, Sir Charles, GCB, LVO, OBE, ADC (*Gen.*), Col. LG (*Chief of the Defence Staff*)
Wheeler, Sir Roger, GCB, CBE, ADC (*Gen.*), Col. Cmdt. Int. Corps, Col. R. Irish (*Chief of the General Staff*) (until April 2000)
Walker, Sir Michael, KCB, CMG, CBE, ADC (*Gen.*), Col. Cmdt. The Queen's Division, Col. Cmdt. AAC (*C.-in-C., Land*) (until April 2000); (*Chief of the General Staff*) (from April 2000)
Harley, Sir Alexander, KBE, CB, ADC (*Gen.*), Col. Cmdt. RHA (*Adjutant-General*)
Cowan, Sir Samuel, KCB, CBE, Col. Cmdt. Bde of Gurkhas (*Chief of Defence Logistics*)
Smith, Sir Rupert, KCB, DSO, OBE, QGM, Col. Cmdt. REME (*D. SACEUR*)

LIEUTENANT-GENERALS

Pike, Sir Hew, KCB, DSO, MBE (*GOC Northern Ireland*)
Grant, Sir Scott, KCB, Col. Cmdt. King's Division, Col. Cmdt. RE, Chief Royal Engineer (*Quartermaster-General*)
Jackson, Sir Michael, KCB, CBE, Col. Cmdt. Parachute Regiment, Col. Cmdt. AG Corps (*Commander ACE Rapid Reaction Corps*) (until April 2000); (*C.-in-C., Land*) (in the rank of General, from April 2000)
Burton, Sir Edmund, KBE, Col. Cmdt. RA (until early 2000)
Deverell, Sir John, KCB, OBE, Col. LI, Col. Cmdt. SASC (*Deputy C.-in-C., Land Command, and Inspector-General, Territorial Army*)
Willcocks, M. A., CB (*Deputy Commander (Operations) SFOR Bosnia-Hercegovina*)

MAJOR-GENERALS

Cordingley, P. A. J., DSO (*Senior British Loan Service Officer, Oman*)
Pigott, A. D., CBE, Col. The Queen's Gurkha Engineers, Col. Cmdt. RE (*Director-General, Development and Doctrine*) (until Feb. 2000)
McAfee, R. W. M., CB, Col. Cmdt. RTR (*Commander Multinational Divn Central (Airmobile)*)
Vyvyan, C. G. C., CBE, Col. Cmdt. RGJ (*Head of British Defence Staff, Washington*)
Jenkins, D. J. M., CBE, Col. Cmdt. REME, Col. Cmdt. RAC, Col. QRH (*Executive Director 2, Defence Procurement Agency*)
Granville-Chapman, T. J., CBE (*Commandant, Joint Services Command and Staff College*)
Drewienkiewicz, K. J., CB, Col. Cmdt. RE (*Head of British Contingent to Kosovo Monitoring Mission*)
Sulivan, T. J., CBE (*GOC HQ 4 Divn*)
Drewry, C. F., CBE (*Asst CDS (Policy)*)
Elliott, C. L., CB, MBE (*Chief of Staff, HQ Quartermaster-General*) (until Feb. 2000); (*Director-General, Development and Doctrine*) (from Feb. 2000)
Kiszely, J. P., MC (*Asst CDS (Programmes)*)
O'Donoghue, K., CBE (*Asst Chief of the General Staff*)
Webb-Carter, E. J., OBE, Col. DWR (*GOC London District*)
Callow, C. G., OBE, QHP (*Chief Executive, Defence Medical Training Organization, and Chief Executive, Defence Secondary Care Agency*)
Denaro, A. G., CBE (*Commandant, RMAS*)
Irwin, A. S. H., CBE (*Military Secretary and Chief Executive, Army Personnel Centre*)
Trousdell, P. C. C., Col. The Queen's Own Gurkha Transport Regiment (*Chief of Staff, HQ Land Command*)
Besgrove, P. V. R., CBE, Col. Cmdt. REME
Searby, R. V. (*GOC HQ 5 Divn*)
Russell-Jones, P. J., OBE (*Asst CDS, Operational Requirements (Land Systems)*)
Risius, G. (*Director, Army Legal Services*)
Chambers, P. A., MBE (*Deputy Chief of Staff, HQ Land Command*)
Reith, J. G., CBE (*Commander Allied Command Europe Mobile Force*)
Milne, J. (*Director Support, HQ Allied Land Forces Central Europe*)
Pringle, A. R. D., CBE, Col. Cmdt. RGJ (*Chief of Staff to Chief of Joint Operations*)
Raper, A. J., CBE (*Chief Executive, Defence Communications Services Agency*)
Truluck, A. E. G., CBE (*Executive Assistant to the Chief of Staff Supreme HQ Allied Powers Europe*)
Ridgway, A. P., CBE (*Chief of Staff HQ ACE Rapid Reaction Corps*)
Watt, C. R., CBE (*GOC 1 (UK) Armd Divn*)
Ramsay, A. I., CBE, DSO, Col. Cmdt. RHF (*Commander British Forces Cyprus*)
Strudwick, M. J., CBE, Col. Cmdt. The Scottish Division (*GOC Scotland*)
Currie, A. P. N. (*Chief of Staff to Adjutant-General*)
Lyons, A. W., CBE (*Director-General, Logistic Support (Army)*)
HRH The Prince of Wales, KG, KT, GCB and Great Master of the Order of the Bath, AK, QSO, PC, ADC(P)
Curran, L. D. (*Engineering Adviser, Defence Procurement Agency*)
Dannatt, F. R., CBE, MC (*GOC 3 (UK) Divn*)
Grant Peterkin, A. P., OBE (*Senior Army Member, Royal College of Defence Studies*)
Palmer, A. M. D., CBE (*Director-General, Army Training and Recruiting and Chief Executive, Army Training and Recruiting Agency*)
Delves, C. N. G. (*Chief of Joint Forces Operational Readiness and Training*)

Sutherell, J. C. B. (*Commandant, RMCS*)

Viggers, F. R., MBE (*Comd. Multinational Divn (SW) SFOR Bosnia-Hercegovina*)

Menzies, R. C., OBE, QHS (*Director-General, Army Medical Services*) (until Feb. 2000); (*Surgeon-General*) (in the rank of Lieutenant-General, from Feb. 2000)

Gordon, R. D. S., CBE (*GOC HQ 2 Divn*)

Moore-Bick, J. D., CBE (*Leader, Study into the Future of Shrivenham/Watchfield*)

Judd, D. L. (*Director-General, Equipment Support (Army)*)

CONSTITUTION OF THE ARMY

The regular forces include the following arms, branches and corps. They are listed in accordance with the order of precedence within the British Army. All enquiries with regard to records of serving personnel (Regular and Territorial Army) should be directed to Relations with the Public, Army Personnel Office, Kentigern House, 65 Brown Street, Glasgow G2 8EX. Tel: 0141-224 8883/8880/8881/8884.

THE ARMS

HOUSEHOLD CAVALRY – The Household Cavalry Regiment (The Life Guards and The Blues and Royals)

ROYAL ARMOURED CORPS – Cavalry Regiments: 1st The Queen's Dragoon Guards; The Royal Scots Dragoon Guards (Carabiniers and Greys); The Royal Dragoon Guards; The Queen's Royal Hussars (The Queen's Own and Royal Irish); 9th/12th Royal Lancers (Prince of Wales's); The King's Royal Hussars; The Light Dragoons; The Queen's Royal Lancers; Royal Tank Regiment, comprising two regular regiments

ARTILLERY – Royal Regiment of Artillery

ENGINEERS – Corps of Royal Engineers

SIGNALS – Royal Corps of Signals

THE INFANTRY

The Foot Guards and regiments of Infantry of the Line are grouped in divisions as follows:

GUARDS DIVISION – Grenadier, Coldstream, Scots, Irish and Welsh Guards. *Divisional Office*, HQ Infantry, Imber Road, Warminster, Wilts. *Training Centre*, Infantry Training Centre, Vimy Barracks, Catterick, N. Yorks

SCOTTISH DIVISION – The Royal Scots (The Royal Regiment); The Royal Highland Fusiliers (Princess Margaret's Own Glasgow and Ayrshire Regiment); The King's Own Scottish Borderers; The Black Watch (Royal Highland Regiment); The Highlanders (Seaforth, Gordons and Camerons); The Argyll and Sutherland Highlanders (Princess Louise's). *Divisional Office*, HQ Infantry, Imber Road, Warminster, Wilts. *Training Centre*, Infantry Training Centre, Vimy Barracks, Catterick, N. Yorks

QUEEN'S DIVISION – The Princess of Wales's Royal Regiment (Queen's and Royal Hampshire's); The Royal Regiment of Fusiliers; The Royal Anglian Regiment. *Divisional Office*, HQ Infantry, Imber Road, Warminster, Wilts. *Training Centre*, Infantry Training Centre, Vimy Barracks, Catterick, N. Yorks

KING'S DIVISION – The King's Own Royal Border Regiment; The King's Regiment; The Prince of Wales's Own Regiment of Yorkshire; The Green Howards (Alexandra, Princess of Wales's Own Yorkshire Regiment); The Queen's Lancashire Regiment; The Duke of Wellington's Regiment (West Riding). *Divisional Office*, HQ Infantry, Imber Road, Warminster, Wilts. *Training Centre*, Infantry Training Centre, Vimy Barracks, Catterick, N. Yorks

THE ROYAL IRISH REGIMENT (one general service and six home service battalions) – 27th (Inniskilling), 83rd, 87th and the Ulster Defence Regiment. *Regimental HQ* and *Training Centre*, St Patrick's Barracks, BFPO 808

PRINCE OF WALES'S DIVISION – The Devonshire and Dorset Regiment; The Cheshire Regiment; The Royal Welch Fusiliers; The Royal Regiment of Wales (24th/41st Foot); The Royal Gloucestershire, Berkshire and Wiltshire Regiment; The Worcestershire and Sherwood Foresters Regiment (29th/45th Foot); The Staffordshire Regiment (The Prince of Wales's). *Divisional Office*, HQ Infantry, Imber Road, Warminster, Wilts. *Training Centre*, Infantry Training Centre, Vimy Barracks, Catterick, N. Yorks

LIGHT DIVISION – The Light Infantry; The Royal Green Jackets. *Divisional Office*, HQ Infantry, Imber Road, Warminster, Wilts. *Training Centre*, Infantry Training Centre, Vimy Barracks, Catterick, N. Yorks

BRIGADE OF GURKHAS – The Royal Gurkha Rifles; The Queen's Gurkha Engineers; Queen's Gurkha Signals; The Queen's Own Gurkha Transport Regiment. *Regimental HQ*, Queen Elizabeth Barracks, Church Crookham, Fleet, Aldershot, Hants. *Gurkha Training Wing*, Infantry Training Centre, Vimy Barracks, Catterick, N. Yorks

THE PARACHUTE REGIMENT (three regular battalions) – *Regimental HQ*, Browning Barracks, Aldershot, Hants. *Training Centre*, Infantry Training Centre, Vimy Barracks, Catterick, N. Yorks

SPECIAL AIR SERVICE REGIMENT – *Regimental HQ* and *Training Centre*, Stirling Lines, Hereford

ARMY AIR CORPS – *Regimental HQ* and *Training Centre*, Middle Wallop, Stockbridge, Hants

SERVICES/ARMS*

Royal Army Chaplains' Department – *Regimental HQ*, HQ AG, Upavon, Pewsey, Wilts. *Training Centre*, Armed Forces Chaplaincy Centre, Amport House, Amport, Andover, Hants

The Royal Logistic Corps – *Regimental HQ*, Blackdown Barracks, Deepcut, Camberley, Surrey. *Training Centre*, Princess Royal Barracks, Deepcut, Camberley, Surrey

Royal Army Medical Corps – *Regimental HQ*, Keogh Barracks, Ash Vale, Aldershot, Hants. *Training Centre*, Defence Medical Services Training Centre, Keogh Barracks, Ash Vale, Aldershot, Hants

Corps of Royal Electrical and Mechanical Engineers – *Regimental HQ* and *Training Centre*, Hazebrouck Barracks, Isaac Newton Road, Arborfield, Reading, Berks

Adjutant-General's Corps – *Corps HQ* and *Training Centre*, Worthy Down, Winchester, Hants

Royal Army Veterinary Corps – *Regimental HQ*, Keogh Barracks, Ash Vale, Aldershot, Hants. *Training Centre*, Defence Animal Centre, Welby Lane, Melton Mowbray, Leics

Small Arms School Corps – *Corps HQ* and *Training Centre*, School of Infantry, Imber Road, Warminster, Wilts

Royal Army Dental Corps – *Regimental HQ*, Keogh Barracks, Ash Vale, Aldershot, Hants. *Training Centre*, Defence Dental Agency Training Establishment, Evelyn Woods Road, Aldershot, Hants

*Intelligence Corps – *Corps HQ* and *Training Centre*, Chicksands, Shefford, Beds

Army Physical Training Corps – *Regimental HQ* and *Depot*, Queen's Avenue, Aldershot, Hants

General Service Corps

Queen Alexandra's Royal Army Nursing Corps – *Regimental HQ*, Keogh Barracks, Ash Vale, Aldershot, Hants. *Training Centre*, Health Studies Division, Royal Defence Medical College, Vulcan Block, Fort Blockhouse, Gosport, Hants

Corps of Army Music – *Corps HQ* and *Training Centre*, Army School of Music, Kneller Hall, Kneller Road, Twickenham, Middx

ARMY EQUIPMENT HOLDINGS *as at August 1999*

Tanks	373
Armoured combat vehicles	2,920
Artillery pieces	406
Large landing craft	2
Helicopters	232

THE TERRITORIAL ARMY (TA)

The Territorial Army provides formed units and individuals as an essential part of the Army's order of battle for operations across all military tasks in order to ensure that the Army is capable of mounting and sustaining operations at nominated states of readiness. It also provides a basis for regeneration, while at the same time maintaining links with the local community and society at large. From 1 July 1999 its established strength is 41,204.

Members of the TA receive pay at the rate appropriate to their rank. From 1 April 1999, the minimum daily rates of pay for officers range between £28.26 and £86.27, and for soldiers between £25.34 and £60.38. Members who complete their annual training requirements (27 and 19 days respectively for members of the Independent and Specialist TA) and are certified as efficient receive a single bounty ranging from £100 to £1,050.

Inspector-General, Lt.-Gen. Sir John Deverell, KCB, OBE

QUEEN ALEXANDRA'S ROYAL ARMY NURSING CORPS

The Queen Alexandra's Royal Army Nursing Corps (QARANC) was founded in 1902 as Queen Alexandra's Imperial Military Nursing Service (QAIMNS) and gained its present title in 1949. The QARANC has trained nurses for the register since 1950 and also trains and employs health care assistants. Qualified Registered General Nurses are also recruited. Since 1992 men have been eligible to join the QARANC. Members of the Corps serve in military hospitals in the UK and abroad and in MOD hospital units in the UK.

Colonel-in-Chief, HRH The Princess Margaret, Countess of Snowdon, GCVO, CI

Matron-in-Chief (Army) and Director, Army Nursing Services, Col. B. C. McEvilly, QHNS

The Royal Air Force

THE QUEEN

MARSHALS OF THE ROYAL AIR FORCE

HRH The Prince Philip, Duke of Edinburgh, KG, KT, OM, GBE, AC, QSO, PC, *apptd* 1953
Sir John Grandy, GCB, GCVO, KBE, DSO, *apptd* 1971
Sir Denis Spotswood, GCB, CBE, DSO, DFC, *apptd* 1974
Sir Michael Beetham, GCB, CBE, DFC, AFC, *apptd* 1982
Sir Keith Williamson, GCB, AFC, *apptd* 1985
The Lord Craig of Radley, GCB, OBE, *apptd* 1988

AIR CHIEF MARSHALS

Johns, Sir Richard, GCB, CBE, LVO, ADC (*Chief of the Air Staff*)
Cheshire, Sir John, KBE, CB (*C.-in-C. Allied Forces NW Europe*)
Squire, Sir Peter, KCB, DFC, AFC, ADC (*Air Officer Commanding-in-Chief, HQ Strike Command, and Commander Allied Air Forces NW Europe*)

AIR MARSHALS

Bagnall, Sir Anthony, KCB, OBE (*Air Member for Personnel and Air Officer C.-in-C., HQ Personnel and Training Command*)
Baird, Sir John, KBE, QHP (*Surgeon-General*) (until Feb. 2000)
Day, Sir John, KCB, OBE (*Deputy CDS (Commitments)*)
Coville, C. C. C., CB (*Deputy C.-in-C. Allied Forces Central Europe*)
Jenner, T. I., CB (*Chief of Staff and Deputy C.-in-C., HQ Strike Command*)
Norriss, P. C., CB, AFC (*Deputy Chief of Defence Procurement (Operations) and Controller of the Navy*)
Pledger, M. D., OBE, AFC (*Deputy CDS (Personnel)*)
Goodall, R. H., CB, CBE, AFC (*Chief of Staff, Component Command Air North*)

AIR VICE-MARSHALS

Stables, A. J., CBE (*Chief Executive, Training Group Defence Agency*)
French, J. C., CBE (*Director-General, Intelligence and Geographic Resources*)
Spink, C. R., CBE (*Director-General, Saudi Arabia Armed Forces Project*)
Thompson, J. H. (*AOC No. 1 Group*)
Stewart, I. M., AFC (*Air Secretary and Chief Executive, RAF Personnel Management Agency*)
Weeden, J. (*Director, Legal Services (RAF)*)
Stirrup, G. E., AFC (*Asst Chief of the Air Staff*)
Wright, R. A., AFC (*Chief of Staff, HQ Personnel and Training Command*)
McIntyre, I. G., QHDS (*Chief Executive, Defence Dental Agency*)
Sharples, C. J., QHP (*Director-General, Medical Services (RAF)*)
Burridge, B. K., CBE (*AOC No. 11/18 Group*)
Filbey, K. D., CBE (*Senior Directing Staff (Air), Royal College of Defence Studies*)
Sturley, P. O., MBE (*Senior Air Staff Officer, HQ Strike Command, and AOC No. 38 Group*)
Brackenbury, I., OBE (*Chief of Staff to Chief of Defence Logistics*)
Henderson, P. W., MBE (*Director-General, Support Management, HQ Logistics Command*)
Nicholl, S. M., CBE, AFC (*Asst CDS Operational Requirements (Air Systems)*)
Niven, D. M., CBE (*Commander, Joint Helicopter Command*)
Scott, P. J. (*Air Officer Logistics and Communications Information Systems, HQ Strike Command*)
Burton, A. J., OBE (*Air Officer Administration, HQ Strike Command*)
Rimmer, T. W., OBE (*Commandant, RAF College, Cranwell*)
Nicholson, A. A., CBE, LVO (*Integration and Aerospace Adviser, Defence Procurement Agency*)
HRH The Prince of Wales, KG, KT, GCB and Great Master of the Order of the Bath, AK, QSO, PC, ADC(P)
Gardiner, M. J., OBE (*Deputy Commander, Interim Combined Air Operations Centre No. 4*)
Couzens, D. C. (*Asst CDS (Logistics)*)
Liddell, P. (*Air Officer Communications Information Systems and Support Services*)
Harris, P. V., AFC
Arscott, J. R. D. (*Director, Airspace Policy*)
Skinner, G., CBE (*Air Officer C.-in-C., HQ Logistics Command*)

CONSTITUTION OF THE ROYAL AIR FORCE

The RAF consists of three commands: Strike Command, Personnel and Training Command and Logistics Command. Strike Command is responsible for all the RAF's front-line forces. Its roles include strike/attack, air defence, reconnaissance, maritime patrol, strategic air transport, air-to-air refuelling, search and rescue, and aero-medical facilities. Personnel and Training Command is responsible for personnel administration and training in the RAF. Logistics Command is responsible for all logistics, engineering and materiel support.

Enquiries regarding records of serving officers should be directed to the RAF Personnel Management Agency (*see* Defence Agencies, above).

RAF EQUIPMENT *as at 1 July 1999*

AIRCRAFT

Tornado ADV	93
Tornado IDS	127
Harrier	64
Jaguar	53
Canberra	7
Nimrod	27
VC10	24
Tristar	9
Hercules	55
BAe 125	6
BAe 146	3
Sentry	7
Hawk	107
Bulldog	105
Domenie	10
Islander	2
Jetstream	11
Tucano	86

HELICOPTERS

Chinook	38
Puma	41
Sea King	25
Wessex	15
Gazelle	1

ROYAL AUXILIARY AIR FORCE (RAuxAF)

Formed in 1924, the Auxiliary Air Force received the prefix 'Royal' in 1947 in recognition of its war record. The RAuxAF amalgamated with the Royal Air Force Volunteer Reserve in 1997. The RAuxAF supports the RAF in many roles, including maritime air operations, air and ground defence of airfields, air movements, aero-medical evacuation, intelligence and public relations. In May 1999 there were 1,715 reservists in the RAuxAF; under the Strategic Defence Review, the Reserve Air Forces' establishment is expected to increase to 2,920 (these figures include elements of the Royal Air Force Reserve).

The minimum annual commitment for reservists is 27 days, including 15 days' continuous training. Pay scales are equivalent to regular rates less a percentage, made on a pro-rata daily basis. A single bounty is also payable, the amount depending on the length of service.

Air Commodore-in-Chief, HM The Queen
Controller of Reserve Forces (RAF), Air Cdre C. Davison, MBE

PRINCESS MARY'S ROYAL AIR FORCE
NURSING SERVICE

The Princess Mary's Royal Air Force Nursing Service (PMRAFNS) offers commissions to Registered General Nurses (RGN) with a minimum of two years experience after obtaining RGN and normally with a second qualification. RGNs with no additional experience or qualification are recruited as non-commissioned officers in the grade of Staff Nurse.

Air Chief Commandant, HRH Princess Alexandra, the Hon. Lady Ogilvy, GCVO
Matron-in-Chief, Air Cdre R. H. Williams, QHNS

SERVICE SALARIES

The following rates of pay apply from 1 April 1999. Annual salaries are derived from daily rates in whole pence and rounded to the nearest £.

The pay rates shown are for Army personnel. The rates apply also to personnel of equivalent rank and pay band in the other services (*see* page 395 for table of relative ranks).

OFFICERS' SALARIES

MAIN SCALE

Rank	Daily	Annual
Second Lieutenant	£43.12	£15,782
Lieutenant		
On appointment	57.00	20,862
After 1 year in the rank	58.50	21,411
After 2 years in the rank	60.00	21,960
After 3 years in the rank	61.50	22,509
After 4 years in the rank	63.00	23,058
Captain		
On appointment	72.71	26,612
After 1 year in the rank	74.67	27,329
After 2 years in the rank	76.63	28,047
After 3 years in the rank	78.59	28,764
After 4 years in the rank	80.55	29,481
After 5 years in the rank	82.51	30,199
After 6 years in the rank	84.47	30,916
Major		
On appointment	92.02	33,679
After 1 year in the rank	94.29	34,510
After 2 years in the rank	96.56	35,341
After 3 years in the rank	98.83	36,172
After 4 years in the rank	101.10	37,003
After 5 years in the rank	103.37	37,833
After 6 years in the rank	105.64	38,664
After 7 years in the rank	107.91	39,495
After 8 years in the rank	110.18	40,326
Special List Lieutenant-Colonel	127.23	46,566
Lieutenant-Colonel		
On appointment with less than 19 years' service	129.77	47,496
After 2 years in the rank or with 19 years' service	133.19	48,746

Rank	Daily	Annual
Lieutenant-Colonel *contd*		
After 4 years in the rank or with 21 years' service	£136.61	£49,999
After 6 years in the rank or with 23 years' service	140.03	51,251
After 8 years in the rank or with 25 years' service	143.45	52,503
Colonel		
On appointment	150.85	55,211
After 2 years in the rank	154.82	56,664
After 4 years in the rank	158.79	58,117
After 6 years in the rank	162.76	59,570
After 8 years in the rank	166.73	61,023
Brigadier	184.79	67,633
Major-General		
Range 1	195.68	71,423
Range 2	200.98	73,358
Range 3	207.85	75,865
Lieutenant-General		
Range 4	223.00	81,396
Range 5	240.12	87,642
General		
Range 6	298.82	109,069
Range 7	314.32	114,727
Range 8	384.49	140,339

Field Marshal – appointments to this rank will not usually be made in peacetime. The salary for existing holders of the rank is equivalent to the salary of a range 8 General

---

SALARIES OF OFFICERS COMMISSIONED FROM THE RANKS (LIEUTENANTS AND CAPTAINS ONLY)

YEARS OF COMMISSIONED SERVICE	YEARS OF NON-COMMISSIONED SERVICE FROM AGE 18					
	Less than 12 years		12 years but less than 15 years		15 years or more	
	Daily	Annual	Daily	Annual	Daily	Annual
On commissioning	£80.07	£29,306	£84.16	£30,803	£88.25	£32,300
After 1 year's service	82.11	30,052	86.20	31,549	89.72	32,838
After 2 years' service	84.16	30,803	88.25	32,300	91.04	33,321
After 3 years' service	86.20	31,549	89.72	32,838	92.36	33,804
After 4 years' service	88.25	32,300	91.04	33,321	93.68	34,287
After 5 years' service	89.72	32,838	92.36	33,804	95.00	34,770
After 6 years' service	91.04	33,321	93.68	34,287	96.32	35,253
After 8 years' service	92.36	33,804	95.00	34,770	97.64	35,736
After 10 years' service	93.68	34,287	96.32	35,253	97.64	35,736
After 12 years' service	95.00	34,770	97.64	35,736	97.64	35,736
After 14 years' service	96.32	35,253	97.64	35,736	97.64	35,736
After 16 years' service	97.64	35,736	97.64	35,736	97.64	35,736

SOLDIERS' SALARIES

The pay structure below officer level is divided into pay bands. Jobs at each rank are allocated to bands according to their score in the job evaluation system. Length of service is from age 18.

Scale A: committed to serve for less than 6 years, or those with less than 9 years' service who are serving on Open Engagement

Scale B: committed to serve for 6 years but less than 9 years

Scale C: committed to serve for 9 years or more, or those with more than 9 years' service who are serving on Open Engagement

Daily rates of pay effective from 1 April 1999 are:

RANK	SCALE A		
	Band 1	Band 2	Band 3
Private			
Class 4	£27.05	£ —	£ —
Class 3	30.44	35.33	40.76
Class 2	34.02	38.95	44.38
Class 1	37.00	41.92	47.34
Lance Corporal			
Class 3	37.00	41.92	47.34
Class 2	39.38	44.30	50.15
Class 1	42.36	47.28	53.13
Corporal			
Class 2	45.26	50.16	56.00
Class 1	48.59	53.47	59.31

	Band 4	Band 5	Band 6	Band 7
Sergeant	£53.44	£58.75	£64.54	£ —
Staff Sergeant	56.50	61.80	67.63	74.63
Warrant Officer				
Class 2	60.41	65.73	72.88	80.05
Class 1	64.42	69.73	76.98	84.12

	SCALE B		
	Band 1	Band 2	Band 3
Private			
Class 4	£27.35	£ —	£ —
Class 3	30.74	35.63	41.06
Class 2	34.32	39.25	44.68
Class 1	37.30	42.22	47.64

SCALE B			
	Band 1	Band 2	Band 3
Lance Corporal			
Class 3	37.30	42.22	47.64
Class 2	39.68	44.60	50.45
Class 1	42.66	47.58	53.43
Corporal			
Class 2	45.56	50.46	56.30
Class 1	48.89	53.77	59.61

	Band 4	Band 5	Band 6	Band 7
Sergeant	£53.74	£59.05	£64.84	£ —
Staff Sergeant	56.80	62.10	67.93	74.93
Warrant Officer				
Class 2	60.71	66.03	73.18	80.35
Class 1	64.72	70.03	77.28	84.42

SCALE C			
	Band 1	Band 2	Band 3
Private			
Class 4	£27.80	£ —	£ —
Class 3	31.19	36.08	41.51
Class 2	34.77	39.70	45.13
Class 1	37.75	42.67	48.09
Lance Corporal			
Class 3	37.75	42.67	48.09
Class 2	40.13	45.05	50.90
Class 1	43.11	48.03	53.88
Corporal			
Class 2	46.01	50.91	56.75
Class 1	49.34	54.22	60.06

	Band 4	Band 5	Band 6	Band 7
Sergeant	£54.19	£59.50	£65.29	£ —
Staff Sergeant	57.25	62.55	68.38	75.38
Warrant Officer				
Class 2	61.16	66.48	73.63	80.80
Class 1	65.17	70.48	77.73	84.87

RELATIVE RANK – ARMED FORCES

	Royal Navy		*Army*		*Royal Air Force*
1	Admiral of the Fleet	1	Field Marshal	1	Marshal of the RAF
2	Admiral (Adm.)	2	General (Gen.)	2	Air Chief Marshal
3	Vice-Admiral (Vice-Adm.)	3	Lieutenant-General (Lt.-Gen.)	3	Air Marshal
4	Rear-Admiral (Rear-Adm.)	4	Major-General (Maj.-Gen.)	4	Air Vice-Marshal
5	Commodore (Cdre)	5	Brigadier (Brig.)	5	Air Commodore (Air Cdre)
6	Captain (Capt.)	6	Colonel (Col.)	6	Group Captain (Gp Capt)
7	Commander (Cdr.)	7	Lieutenant-Colonel (Lt.-Col.)	7	Wing Commander (Wg Cdr.)
8	Lieutenant-Commander (Lt.-Cdr.)	8	Major (Maj.)	8	Squadron Leader (Sqn Ldr)
9	Lieutenant (Lt.)	9	Captain (Capt.)	9	Flight Lieutenant (Flt. Lt.)
10	Sub-Lieutenant (Sub-Lt.)	10	Lieutenant (Lt.)	10	Flying Officer (FO)
11	Acting Sub-Lieutenant (Acting Sub-Lt.)	11	Second Lieutenant (2nd Lt.)	11	Pilot Officer (PO)

SERVICE RETIRED PAY ON COMPULSORY RETIREMENT

Those who leave the services having served at least five years, but not long enough to qualify for the appropriate immediate pension, now qualify for a preserved pension and terminal grant, both of which are payable at age 60. The tax-free resettlement grants shown below are payable on release to those who qualify for a preserved pension and who have completed nine years service from age 21 (officers) or 12 years from age 18 (other ranks).

The annual rates for army personnel are given. The rates apply also to personnel of equivalent rank in the other services, including the nursing services.

OFFICERS

Applicable to officers who give full pay service on the active list on or after 31 March 1999. Senior officers (*) can elect to receive a pension calculated as a percentage of their pensionable earnings.

No. of years reckonable service over age 21	Capt. and below	Major	Lt.-Col.	Colonel	Brigadier	Major-General*	Lieutenant-General*	General*
16	£ 8,811	£10,546	£13,893	£ —	£ —	£ —	£ —	£ —
17	9,219	11,047	14,536	—	—	—	—	—
18	9,628	11,547	15,179	17,643	—	—	—	—
19	10,036	12,048	15,821	18,390	—	—	—	—
20	10,445	12,549	16,464	19,137	—	—	—	—
21	10,853	13,049	17,107	19,884	—	—	—	—
22	11,262	13,550	17,750	20,631	23,784	—	—	—
23	11,670	14,051	18,393	21,378	24,536	—	—	—
24	12,079	14,551	19,036	22,125	25,287	27,535	—	—
25	12,487	15,052	19,678	22,873	26,039	28,353	—	—
26	12,895	15,553	20,321	23,620	26,790	29,171	—	—
27	13,304	16,053	20,964	24,367	27,542	29,990	34,418	—
28	13,712	16,554	21,607	25,114	28,293	30,808	35,357	—
29	14,121	17,055	22,250	25,861	29,045	31,626	36,296	—
30	14,529	17,555	22,893	26,608	29,796	32,444	37,235	49,298
31	14,938	18,056	23,535	27,355	30,548	33,263	38,174	50,541
32	15,346	18,557	24,178	28,102	31,299	34,081	39,114	51,784
33	15,755	19,057	24,821	28,849	32,051	34,899	40,053	53,027
34	16,163	19,558	25,464	29,596	32,802	35,717	40,992	54,271

*Field Marshal** – active list half pay at the rate of £70,170 a year

WARRANT OFFICERS, NCOs AND PRIVATES

Applicable to soldiers who give full pay service on or after 31 March 1999.

No. of years reckonable service	Below Corporal	Corporal	Sergeant	Staff Sergeant	Warrant Officer Class II	Warrant Officer Class I
22	£5,121	£6,499	£ 7,198	£ 8,194	£ 8,470	£ 9,364
23	5,300	6,726	7,449	8,480	8,770	9,701
24	5,478	6,953	7,701	8,766	9,070	10,037
25	5,657	7,180	7,952	9,052	9,370	10,374
26	5,836	7,406	8,203	9,338	9,670	10,710
27	6,015	7,633	8,454	9,624	9,970	11,047
28	6,193	7,860	8,706	9,910	10,270	11,383
29	6,372	8,087	8,957	10,196	10,570	11,720
30	6,551	8,314	9,208	10,482	10,871	12,056
31	6,730	8,541	9,459	10,768	11,171	12,393
32	6,908	8,768	9,711	11,054	11,471	12,729
33	7,087	8,995	9,962	11,340	11,771	13,066
34	7,266	9,221	10,213	11,626	12,071	13,402
35	7,445	9,448	10,464	11,912	12,371	13,739
36	7,623	9,675	10,716	12,198	12,671	14,075
37	7,802	9,902	10,967	12,484	12,971	14,412

RESETTLEMENT GRANTS

Terminal grants are in each case three times the rate of retired pay or pension. There are special rates of retired pay for certain other ranks not shown above. Lower rates are payable in cases of voluntary retirement.

A gratuity of £2,995 is payable for officers with short service commissions for each year completed. Resettlement grants are: officers £10,305; non-commissioned ranks £6,771.

Religion in the UK

There are two established, i.e. state, churches in the United Kingdom: the Church of England and the Church of Scotland. There are no established churches in Wales or Northern Ireland, though the Church in Wales, the Scottish Episcopal Church and the Church of Ireland are members of the Anglican Communion.

About 65 per cent of the population of the UK (38.1 million people) would call itself broadly Christian (in the Trinitarian sense), with 45 per cent (26.1 million) identifying with Anglican churches, 10 per cent (5.7 million) with the Roman Catholic Church, 4 per cent (2.6 million) with Presbyterian Churches, 2 per cent (1.3 million) with the Methodist Churches and 4 per cent (2.6 million) with other Christian churches; but only about 8.7 per cent of the population of Great Britain (3.98 million people) regularly attends a Christian church. Church attendance in Northern Ireland is estimated at 30–35 per cent of the population.

About 2 per cent of the population (1.3 million people) is affiliated to non-Trinitarian churches, e.g. Jehovah's Witnesses, the Church of Jesus Christ of Latter-Day Saints (Mormons), the Church of Christ, Scientist and the Unitarian churches.

A further 5 per cent of the population (3.25 million people) are adherents of other faiths, including Hinduism, Islam, Judaism and Sikhism.

About 28 per cent of the population is non-religious.

ADHERENTS TO RELIGIONS IN UK *(millions)*

	1975	1985	1995
Christian (Trinitarian)	40.2	39.1	38.1
Non-Trinitarian	0.7	1.0	1.3
Hindu	0.3	0.4	0.4
Jew	0.4	0.3	0.3
Muslim	0.4	0.9	1.2
Sikh	0.2	0.3	0.6
Other	0.1	0.3	0.3
Total	42.3	42.3	42.2

PERCENTAGE OF UK POPULATION ADHERING TO RELIGIONS

	1975	1985	1995
Christian (Trinitarian)	72	69	65
Non-Trinitarian	1	2	2
Non-Christian religions	3	3	5
All religions	76	74	72

Source: Christian Research/Paternoster Publishing – *UK Christian Handbook Religious Trends No. 1 1998–9*; figures in text are for 1995

INTER-CHURCH AND INTER-FAITH CO-OPERATION

The main umbrella body for the Christian churches in the UK is the Churches Together in Britain and Ireland (formerly the Council of Churches for Britain and Ireland). There are also ecumenical bodies in each of the constituent countries of the UK: Churches Together in England, Action of Churches Together in Scotland, CYTUN (Churches Together in Wales), and the Irish Council of Churches. The Free Churches' Council comprises most of the Free Churches in England and Wales, and the Evangelical Alliance represents evangelical Christians.

The Inter Faith Network for the United Kingdom promotes co-operation between faiths, and the Council of Christians and Jews works to improve relations between the two religions. Churches Together in Britain and Ireland also has a Commission on Inter Faith Relations.

ACTION OF CHURCHES TOGETHER IN SCOTLAND, Scottish Churches House, Kirk Street, Dunblane, Perthshire FK15 0AJ. Tel: 01786-823588. *General Secretary,* Revd Dr K. Franz

CHURCHES TOGETHER IN BRITAIN AND IRELAND, Inter-Church House, 35–41 Lower Marsh, London SE1 7RL. Tel: 0171-620 4444. *General Secretary,* Dr D. Goodbourn

CHURCHES TOGETHER IN ENGLAND, 101 Queen Victoria Street, London EC4V 4EN. Tel: 0171-332 8230. *Administration Officer,* Ms J. Lampard

COUNCIL OF CHRISTIANS AND JEWS, Drayton House, 30 Gordon Street, London WC1H 0AN. Tel: 0171-388 3322. *Director,* Sr M. Shepherd, NDS

CYTUN (CHURCHES TOGETHER IN WALES) - Ty John Penri, 11 St Helen's Road, Swansea SA1 4AL. Tel: 01792-460876. *General Secretary,* Revd G. Abraham-Williams

EVANGELICAL ALLIANCE, Whitefield House, 186 Kennington Park Road, London SE11 4BT. Tel: 0171-207 2100. *General Director,* Revd J. Edwards

FREE CHURCHES' COUNCIL, 27 Tavistock Square, London WC1H 9HH. Tel: 0171-387 8413. *General Secretary,* Revd G. H. Roper

INTER FAITH NETWORK FOR THE UNITED KINGDOM, 5–7 Tavistock Place, London WC1H 9SN. Tel: 0171-388 0008. *Director,* B. Pearce

IRISH COUNCIL OF CHURCHES, Inter-Church Centre, 48 Elmwood Avenue, Belfast BT9 6AZ. Tel: 01232-663145. *General Secretary,* Dr R. D. Stevens

Christianity

The faith was slowly formulated in the first millennium of the Christian era. Between AD 325 and 787 there were seven Oecumenical Councils at which bishops from the entire Christian world assembled to resolve various doctrinal disputes. The estrangement between East and West began after Constantine moved the centre of the Roman Empire from Rome to Constantinople, and it gained momentum after the temporal administration was divided. Linguistic and cultural differences between Greek East and Latin West served to encourage separate ecclesiastical developments which became pronounced in the tenth and early 11th centuries.

Administration of the church was divided between five ancient patriarchates: Rome and all the West, Constantinople (the imperial city – the 'New Rome'), Jerusalem and all Palestine, Antioch and all the East, and Alexandria and all Africa. Of these, only Rome was in the Latin West and after the schism in 1054, Rome developed a structure of authority centralized on the Papacy, while the Orthodox East maintained the style of localized administration.

Papal authority over the doctrine and jurisdiction of the Church in western Europe was unrivalled after the split with the Eastern Orthodox Church until the Protestant Reformation in the 16th century.

CHRISTIANITY IN BRITAIN

A Church of England already existed when Pope Gregory sent Augustine to evangelize the English in AD 596. Conflicts between Church and State during the Middle Ages culminated in the Act of Supremacy in 1534, which repudiated papal supremacy and declared King Henry VIII to be the supreme head of the Church in England. Since 1559 the English monarch has been termed the Supreme Governor of the Church of England.

In 1560 the jurisdiction of the Roman Catholic Church in Scotland was abolished and the first assembly of the

Church of Scotland ratified the Confession of Faith, drawn up by a committee including John Knox. In 1592 Parliament passed an Act guaranteeing the liberties of the Church and its presbyterian government. King James VI (James I of England) and later Stuart monarchs attempted to reintroduce episcopacy, but a presbyterian church was finally restored in 1690 and secured by the Act of Settlement (1690) and the Act of Union (1707).

PORVOO DECLARATION

The Porvoo Declaration was drawn up by representatives of the British and Irish Anglican churches and the Nordic and Baltic Lutheran churches and was approved by the General Synod of the Church of England in July 1995. Churches that approve the Declaration regard baptized members of each other's churches as members of their own, and allow free interchange of episcopally ordained ministers within the rules of each church.

For Christian churches in the UK, *see* pages 401–423

Non-Christian Religions

BUDDHISM

Buddhism originated in northern India, in the teachings of Siddharta Gautama, who was born near Kapilavastu about 560 BC.

Fundamental to Buddhism is the concept that there is no such thing as a permanent soul or self; when someone dies, consciousness is the only one of the elements of which they were composed which is lost. All the other elements regroup in a new body and carry with them the consequences of the conduct of the earlier life (known as the law of *karma*). This cycle of death and rebirth is broken only when the state of *nirvana* has been reached. Buddhism steers a middle path between belief in personal immortality and belief in death as the final end.

The Four Noble Truths of Buddhism (*dukkha*, suffering; *tanha*, a thirst or desire for continued existence which causes dukkha; *nirvana*, the final liberation from desire and ignorance; and *ariya*, the path to nirvana) are all held to be universal and to sum up the *dhamma* or true nature of life. Necessary qualities to promote spiritual development are *sila* (morality), *samadhi* (meditation) and *panna* (wisdom).

There are two main schools of Buddhism: *Theravada* Buddhism, the earliest extant school, which is more traditional, and *Mahayana* Buddhism, which began to develop about 100 years after the Buddha's death and is more liberal; it teaches that all people may attain Buddhahood. Important schools which have developed within Mahayana Buddhism are *Zen* Buddhism, *Nichiren* Buddhism and Pure Land Buddhism or *Amidism*. There are also distinctive Tibetan forms of Buddhism. Buddhism began to establish itself in the West in the early 20th century.

The scripture of Theravada Buddhism is the *Pali Canon*, which dates from the first century BC. Mahayana Buddhism uses a Sanskrit version of the Pali Canon but also has many other works of scripture.

There is no set time for Buddhist worship, which may take place in a temple or in the home. Worship centres around *paritta* (chanting), acts of devotion centering on an image of the Buddha, and, where possible, offerings to a relic of the Buddha. Buddhist festivals vary according to local traditions and within Theravada and Mahayana Buddhism. For religious purposes Buddhists use solar and lunar calendars, the New Year being celebrated in April. Other festivals mark events in the life of the Buddha.

There is no supreme governing authority in Buddhism.

In the United Kingdom communities representing all schools of Buddhism have developed and operate independently. The Buddhist Society was established in 1924; it runs courses and lectures, and publishes books about Buddhism. It represents no one school of Buddhism.

There are estimated to be at least 300 million Buddhists world-wide, and more than 500 groups and centres, an estimated 25,000 adherents and up to 20 temples or monasteries in the UK.

THE BUDDHIST SOCIETY, 58 Eccleston Square, London SW1V 1PH. Tel: 0171-834 5858. *General Secretary*, R. C. Maddox

HINDUISM

Hinduism has no historical founder but had become highly developed in India by about 1200 BC. Its adherents originally called themselves Aryans; Muslim invaders first called the Aryans 'Hindus' (derived from 'Sindhu', the name of the river Indus) in the eighth century.

Most Hindus hold that *satya* (truthfulness), *ahimsa* (non-violence), honesty, physical labour and tolerance of other faiths are essential for good living. They believe in one supreme spirit (*Brahman*), and in the transmigration of *atman* (the soul). Most Hindus accept the doctrine of *karma* (consequences of actions), the concept of *samsara* (successive lives) and the possibility of all atmans achieving *moksha* (liberation from samsara) through *jnana* (knowledge), *yoga* (meditation), *karma* (work or action) and *bhakti* (devotion).

Most Hindus offer worship to *murtis* (images or statues) representing different aspects of Brahman, and follow their *dharma* (religious and social duty) according to the traditions of their *varna* (social class), *ashrama* (stage in life), *jati* (caste) and *kula* (family).

Hinduism's sacred texts are divided into *shruti* ('heard' or divinely inspired), including the *Vedas*, or *smriti* ('remembered' tradition), including the *Ramayana*, the *Mahabharata*, the *Puranas* (ancient myths), and the sacred law books. Most Hindus recognize the authority of the *Vedas*, the oldest holy books, and accept the philosophical teachings of the *Upanishads*, the *Vedanta Sutras* and the *Bhagavad-Gita*.

Brahman is formless, limitless and all-pervading, and is represented in worship by murtis which may be male or female and in the form of a human, animal or bird. Brahma, Vishnu and Shiva are the most important gods worshipped by Hindus; their respective consorts are Saraswati, Lakshmi and Durga or Parvati, also known as Shakti. There are believed to have been ten *avatars* (incarnations) of Vishnu, of whom the most important are Rama and Krishna. Other popular gods are Ganesha, Hanuman and Subrahmanyam. All gods are seen as aspects of the supreme God, not as competing deities.

Orthodox Hindus revere all gods and goddesses equally, but there are many sects, including the Hare-Krishna movement (ISKCon), the Arya Samaj, the Swami Narayan Hindu mission and the Satya Sai-Baba movement, in which worship is concentrated on one deity to the exclusion of others. In some sects a human *guru* (spiritual teacher) is revered more than the deity, while in other sects the guru is seen as the source of spiritual guidance.

Hinduism does not have a centrally-trained and ordained priesthood. The pronouncements of the *shankaracharyas* (heads of monasteries) of Shringeri, Puri, Dwarka and Badrinath are heeded by the orthodox but may be ignored by the various sects.

The commonest form of worship is a *puja*, in which offerings of red and yellow powders, rice grains, water, flowers, food, fruit, incense and light are made to the *murti* (image) of a deity. Puja may be done either in a home shrine or a *mandir* (temple). Many British Hindus celebrate life-cycle rituals with Sanskrit mantras for naming a baby, the sacred thread (an initiation ceremony), marriage and cremation. For details of the Hindu calendar, main festivals etc, *see* pages 84–5.

The largest communities of Hindus in Britain are in Leicester, London, Birmingham and Bradford, and developed as a result of immigration from India, eastern Africa and Sri Lanka.

There are an estimated 800 million Hindus world-wide; there are about 360,000 adherents and over 150 temples in the UK.

ARYA PRATINIDHI SABHA (UK) AND ARYA SAMAJ LONDON, 69A Argyle Road, London W13 OLY. Tel: 0181-991 1732. *President*, Prof. S. N. Bharadwaj

BHARATIYA VIDYA BHAVAN, Institute of Indian Art and Culture, 4A Castletown Road, London W14 9HQ. Tel: 0171-381 4608. *Executive Director*, Dr M. N. Nandakumara

INTERNATIONAL SOCIETY FOR KRISHNA CONSCIOUSNESS (ISKCon), Bhaktivedanta Manor, Dharam Marg, Hilfield Lane, Aldenham, Watford, Herts WD2 8EZ. Tel: 01923-857244. *Governing Body Commissioner*, P. Latai

NATIONAL COUNCIL OF HINDU TEMPLES (UK), Bhakrivedanta Manor, Dharam Marg, Hilfield Lane, Aldenham, Watford WD2 8EZ. Tel: 01923-856269. *Secretary*, V. P. Aery

SWAMINARAYAN HINDU MISSION, 105–119 Brentfield Road, London NW10 8JP. Tel: 0181-965 2651. *Chairman*, Sadhu Atmaswarup Das

VISHWA HINDU PARISHAD (UK), 48 Wharfedale Gardens, Thornton Heath, Surrey CR7 6LB. Tel: 0181-684 9716. *General Secretary*, K. Ruparelia

ISLAM

Islam (which means 'peace arising from submission to the will of Allah' in Arabic) is a monotheistic religion which was taught in Arabia by the Prophet Muhammad, who was born in Mecca (Makkah) in AD 570. Islam spread to Egypt, North Africa, Spain and the borders of China in the century following the prophet's death, and is now the predominant religion in Indonesia, the Near and Middle East, northern and parts of western Africa, Pakistan, Bangladesh, Malaysia and some of the former Soviet republics. There are also large Muslim communities in other countries.

For Muslims (adherents of Islam), there is one God (*Allah*), who holds absolute power. His commands were revealed to mankind through the prophets, who include Abraham, Moses and Jesus, but his message was gradually corrupted until revealed finally and in perfect form to Muhammad through the angel *Jibril* (Gabriel) over a period of 23 years. This last, incorruptible message has been recorded in the *Qur'an* (Koran), which contains 114 divisions called *surahs*, each made up of *ayahs*, and is held to be the essence of all previous scriptures. The *Ahadith* are the records of the Prophet Muhammad's deeds and sayings (the *Sunnah*) as recounted by his immediate followers. A culture and a system of law and theology gradually developed to form a distinctive Islamic civilization. Islam makes no distinction between sacred and worldly affairs and provides rules for every aspect of human life. The *Shari'ah* is the sacred law of Islam based upon prescriptions derived from the Qur'an and the Sunnah of the Prophet.

The 'five pillars of Islam' are *shahadah* (a declaration of faith in the oneness and supremacy of Allah and the messengership of Muhammad); *salat* (formal prayer, to be performed five times a day facing the *Ka'bah* (sacred house)

in the holy city of Mecca); *zakat* (welfare due); *sawm* (fasting during the month of Ramadan); and *hajj* (pilgrimage to Mecca); some Muslims would add *jihad* (striving for the cause of good and resistance to evil).

Two main groups developed among Muslims. *Sunni* Muslims accept the legitimacy of Muhammad's first four *caliphs* (successors as head of the Muslim community) and of the authority of the Muslim community as a whole. About 90 per cent of Muslims are Sunni Muslims. *Shi'ites* recognize only Muhammad's son-in-law Ali as his rightful successor and the *Imams* (descendants of Ali, not to be confused with *imams* (prayer leaders or religious teachers)) as the principal legitimate religious authority. The largest group within Shi'ism is *Twelver Shi'ism*, which has been the official school of law and theology in Iran since the 16th century; other subsects include the *Ismailis* and the *Druze*, the latter being an offshoot of the Ismailis and differing considerably from the main body of Muslims.

There is no organized priesthood, but learned men such as *ulama*, *imams* and *ayatollahs* are accorded great respect. The *Sufis* are the mystics of Islam. Mosques are centres for worship and teaching and also for social and welfare activities. For details of the Muslim calendar and festivals, *see* page 86.

Islam was first known in western Europe in the eighth century AD when 800 years of Muslim rule began in Spain. Later, Islam spread to eastern Europe. More recently, Muslims came to Europe from Africa, the Middle East and Asia in the late 19th century. Both the Sunni and Shi'ah traditions are represented in Britain, but the majority of Muslims in Britain adhere to Sunni Islam.

There is no central organization, but the Islamic Cultural Centre, which is the London Central Mosque, and the Imams and Mosques Council are influential bodies; there are many other Muslim organizations in Britain.

There are about 1,000 million Muslims world-wide, with more than one million adherents and about 900 mosques in Britain.

IMAMS AND MOSQUES COUNCIL, 20–22 Creffield Road, London W5 3RP. Tel: 0181-992 6636. *Director of the Council and Principal of the Muslim College*, Dr M. A. Z. Badawi

ISLAMIC CULTURAL CENTRE, 146 Park Road, London NW8 7RG. Tel: 0171-724 3363. *Director*, H. Al-Majed

MUSLIM COUNCIL OF BRITAIN, P.O. Box 52, Wembley, Middx HA9 7AL. Tel: 0181-903 9024. *Secretary-General*, Iqbal Sacranie

MUSLIM WORLD LEAGUE, 46 Goodge Street, London W1P 1FJ. Tel: 0171-636 7568. *Deputy Director*, G. Rahman

UNION OF MUSLIM ORGANIZATIONS OF THE UK AND EIRE, 109 Campden Hill Road, London W8 7TL. Tel: 0171-229 0538. *General Secretary*, Dr S. A. Pasha

JUDAISM

Judaism is the oldest monotheistic faith. The primary authority of Judaism is the Hebrew Bible or *Tanakh*, which records how the descendants of Abraham were led by Moses out of their slavery in Egypt to Mount Sinai where God's law (*Torah*) was revealed to them as the chosen people. The *Talmud*, which consists of commentaries on the *Mishnah* (the first text of rabbinical Judaism), is also held to be authoritative, and may be divided into two main categories: the *halakah* (dealing with legal and ritual matters) and the *Aggadah* (dealing with theological and ethical matters not directly concerned with the regulation of conduct). The *Midrash* comprises rabbinic writings containing biblical interpretations in the spirit of the Aggadah. The *halakah* has become a source of division; Orthodox Jews regard Jewish law as derived from God and therefore unalterable; Reform and Liberal Jews seek to interpret it in the light of contemporary considerations; and Conservative Jews aim to maintain most of the traditional rituals but to allow changes in accordance with tradition. Reconstructionist Judaism, a 20th-century movement, regards Judaism as a culture rather than a theological system and accepts all forms of Jewish practice.

The family is the basic unit of Jewish ritual, with the synagogue playing an important role as the centre for public worship and religious study. A synagogue is led by a group of laymen who are elected to office. The Rabbi is primarily a teacher and spiritual guide. The Sabbath is the central religious observance. For details of the Jewish calendar, fasts and festivals, *see* page 85. Most British Jews are descendants of either the *Ashkenazim* of central and eastern Europe or the *Sephardim* of Spain and Portugal.

The Chief Rabbi of the United Hebrew Congregations of the Commonwealth is appointed by a Chief Rabbinate Conference, and is the rabbinical authority of the Orthodox sector of the Ashkenazi Jewish community. His authority is not recognized by the Reform Synagogues of Great Britain (the largest progressive group), the Union of Liberal and Progressive Synagogues, the Union of Orthodox Hebrew Congregations, the Federation of Synagogues, the Sephardi community, or the Assembly of Masorti Synagogues. He is, however, generally recognized both outside the Jewish community and within it as the public religious representative of the totality of British Jewry. The Chief Rabbi is President of the *Beth Din* of the United Synagogue.

A *Beth Din* (Court of Judgment) is a rabbinic court. The *Dayanim* (Assessors) adjudicate in disputes or on matters of Jewish law and tradition; they also oversee dietary law administration.

The Board of Deputies of British Jews, established in 1760, is the representative body of British Jewry. The basis of representation is mainly synagogal, but communal organizations are also represented. It watches over the interests of British Jewry, acts as the central voice of the community and seeks to counter anti-Jewish discrimination and antisemitic activities.

In November 1998 a Consultative Committee was established comprising representatives of the Assembly of Masorti Synagogues, Reform Synagogues of Great Britain, Union of Liberal and Progressive Synagogues and the United Synagogue. The Committee holds discussions to further communal harmony and development.

There are over 12.5 million Jews world-wide; in Great Britain and Ireland there are an estimated 285,000 adherents and about 365 synagogues. Of these, 191 congregations and about 150 rabbis and ministers are under the jurisdiction of the Chief Rabbi; 99 orthodox congregations have a more independent status; and 75 congregations do not recognize the authority of the Chief Rabbi.

CHIEF RABBINATE, 735 High Road, London NI2 OUS. Tel: 0181-343 6301. *Chief Rabbi*, Prof. Jonathan Sacks; *Executive Director*, Mrs S. Weinberg

BETH DIN (COURT OF THE CHIEF RABBI), 735 High Road, London NI2 OUS. Tel: 0181-343 6280. *Registrar*, vacant; *Dayanim*, Rabbi C. Ehrentreu; Rabbi I. Binstock; Rabbi C. D. Kaplin; Rabbi M. Gelley

BOARD OF DEPUTIES OF BRITISH JEWS, Commonwealth House, 1–19 New Oxford Street, London WCIA INF. Tel: 0171-543 5400. *President*, E. Tabachnik, QC; *Director-General*, N. A. Nagler

ASSEMBLY OF MASORTI SYNAGOGUES, 1097 Finchley Road, London NWII OPU. Tel: 0181-201 8772. *Director*, H. Freedman

FEDERATION OF SYNAGOGUES, 65 Watford Way, London NW4 3AQ. Tel: 0181-202 2263. *Head of Administration*, G. D. Coleman

BETH DIN OF THE FEDERATION OF SYNAGOGUES, 65 Watford Way, London NW4 3AQ. Tel: 0181-202 2263. *Registrar*, Rabbi S. Zaiden; *Dayanim*, Dayan Y. Y. Lichtenstein, Dayan B. Berkovits, Dayan M. D. Elzas

REFORM SYNAGOGUES OF GREAT BRITAIN, The Sternberg Centre for Judaism, 80 East End Road, London N3 2SY. Tel: 0181-349 4731. *Chief Executive*, Rabbi T. Bayfield

SPANISH AND PORTUGUESE JEWS' CONGREGATION, 2 Ashworth Road, London W9 IJY. Tel: 0171-289 2573. *Chief Administrator and Secretary*, H. Miller

UNION OF LIBERAL AND PROGRESSIVE SYNAGOGUES, The Montagu Centre, 21 Maple Street, London WIP 6DS. Tel: 0171-580 1663. *Executive Director*, Rabbi Dr C. H. Middleburgh

UNION OF ORTHODOX HEBREW CONGREGATIONS, 140 Stamford Hill, London NI6 6QT. Tel: 0181-802 6226.

UNITED SYNAGOGUE HEAD OFFICE, 735 High Road, London NI2 OUS. Tel: 0181-343 8989. *Chief Executive*, George Willman

SIKHISM

The Sikh religion dates from the birth of Guru Nanak in the Punjab in 1469. 'Guru' means teacher but in Sikh tradition has come to represent the divine presence of God giving inner spiritual guidance. Nanak's role as the human vessel of the divine guru was passed on to nine successors, the last of whom (Guru Gobind Singh) died in 1708. The immortal guru is now held to reside in the sacred scripture, *Guru Granth Sahib*, and so to be present in all Sikh gatherings.

Guru Nanak taught that there is one God and that different religions are like different roads leading to the same destination. He condemned religious conflict, ritualism and caste prejudices. The fifth Guru, Guru Arjan Dev, largely compiled the Sikh Holy Book, a collection of hymns (*gurbani*) known as the *Adi Granth*. It includes the writings of the first five Gurus and the ninth Guru, and selected writings of Hindu and Muslim saints whose views are in accord with the Gurus' teachings. Guru Arjan Dev also built the Golden Temple at Amritsar, the centre of Sikhism. The tenth Guru, Guru Gobind Singh, passed on the guruship to the sacred scripture, Guru Granth Sahib. He also founded the *Khalsa*, an order intended to fight against tyranny and injustice. Male initiates to the order added 'Singh' to their given names and women added 'Kaur'. Guru Gobind Singh also made five symbols obligatory: *kaccha* (a special undergarment), *kara* (a steel bangle), *kirpan* (a small sword), *kesh* (long unshorn hair, and consequently the wearing of a turban), and *kangha* (a comb). These practices are still compulsory for those Sikhs who are initiated into the Khalsa (the *Amritdharis*). Those who do not seek initiation are known as *Sehajdharis*.

There are no professional priests in Sikhism; anyone with a reasonable proficiency in the Punjabi language can conduct a service. Worship can be offered individually or communally, and in a private house or a *gurdwara* (temple). Sikhs are forbidden to eat meat prepared by ritual slaughter; they are also asked to abstain from smoking, alcohol and other intoxicants. Such abstention is compulsory for the *Amritdharis*. For details of the Sikh calendar and main celebrations, *see* page 86.

There are about 20 million Sikhs world-wide and about 400,000 adherents and 250 gurdwaras in Great Britain. Every gurdwara manages its own affairs and there is no central body in the UK. The Sikh Missionary Society provides an information service.

The Churches

For changes notified after 31 August, *see* Stop-press

The Church of England

The Church of England is the established (i.e. state) church in England and the mother church of the Anglican Communion. The Thirty-Nine Articles, a set of doctrinal statements which, together with the Book of Common Prayer of 1662 and the Ordinal, define the position of the Church of England, were adopted in their final form in 1571 and include the emphasis on personal faith and the authority of the scriptures common to the Protestant Reformation throughout Europe.

THE ANGLICAN COMMUNION

The Anglican Communion consists of 38 independent provincial or national Christian churches throughout the world, many of which are in Commonwealth countries and originated from missionary activity by the Church of England. Every ten years all the bishops in the Communion meet at the Lambeth Conference, convened by the Archbishop of Canterbury. The Conference has no policy-making authority but is an important forum for the discussion of issues of common concern. The Anglican Consultative Council was set up in 1968 to liaise between the member churches and provinces of the Anglican Communion. It meets every two to three years. Meetings of the Anglican primates have taken place every two years since 1979.

There are about 70 million Anglicans and 800 archbishops and bishops world-wide.

STRUCTURE

The Church of England is divided into the two provinces of Canterbury and York, each under an archbishop. The two provinces are subdivided into 44 dioceses.

Decisions on matters concerning the Church of England are made by the General Synod, established in 1970. It also discusses and expresses opinion on any other matter of religious or public interest. The General Synod has 574 members in total, divided between three houses: the House of Bishops, the House of Clergy and the House of Laity. It is presided over jointly by the Archbishops of Canterbury and York and normally meets twice a year. The Synod has the power, delegated by Parliament, to frame statute law (known as a Measure) on any matter concerning the Church of England. A Measure must be laid before both Houses of Parliament, who may accept or reject it but cannot amend it. Once accepted the Measure is submitted for royal assent and then has the full force of law. There are a number of committees, boards and councils answerable to the Synod, which deal with, or advise on, a wide range of matters. In addition to the General Synod, there are synods of clergy and laity at diocesan level.

The Archbishops' Council was established in January 1999. Its creation was the result of changes to the Church of England's national structure proposed in 1995 and subsequently approved by the Synod and Parliament. The Council undertakes strategic planning, co-ordinates the work of all the central institutions and oversees the internal and external affairs of the Church of England. It reports frequently to the General Synod and seeks Synodical approval of its decisions. The Archbishops' Council comprises seven *ex-officio* members: the Archbishops of

Canterbury and York (joint Presidents), the prolocutors of the Convocations of Canterbury and York, the chairman and vice-chairman of the House of Laity and a Church Estates Commissioner; six elected members: two bishops, two clergy and two lay members each elected by their respective Houses of the General Synod and up to six members appointed by the two archbishops.

GENERAL SYNOD OF THE CHURCH OF ENGLAND, Church House, Great Smith Street, London SW1P 3NZ. Tel: 0171-222 9011. *Secretary-General*, P. Mawer
HOUSE OF BISHOPS: *Chairman*, The Archbishop of Canterbury; *Vice-Chairman*, The Archbishop of York
HOUSE OF CLERGY: *Chairmen (alternating)*, Canon J. Stanley; Canon H. Wilcox
HOUSE OF LAITY: *Chairman*, Dr Christina Baxter; *Vice-Chairman*, Dr P. Giddings
ARCHBISHOPS' COUNCIL, Church House, Great Smith Street, London SW1P 3NZ. Tel: 0171-222 9011. *Secretary-General*, P. Mawer

THE ORDINATION OF WOMEN

The canon making it possible for women to be ordained to the priesthood was promulged in the General Synod in February 1994 and the first 32 women priests were ordained on 12 March 1994.

MEMBERSHIP

In 1997 the Church of England had an electoral roll membership of 1.3 million, and each week about 1 million people attended Sunday services. At mid-1999 there were two archbishops and 106 diocesan, suffragan and (stipendiary) assistant bishops. In 1998 there were 8,984 other male and 919 female full-time stipendiary clergy, and over 16,000 churches and places of worship. (The Diocese in Europe is not included in these figures.)

FULL-TIME DIOCESAN CLERGY 1998 AND CHURCH ELECTORAL ROLLS 1997

	Clergy		Membership
	Male	Female	
Bath and Wells	223	25	42,500
Birmingham	189	31	19,600
Blackburn	233	12	37,700
Bradford	112	9	13,200
Bristol	133	24	19,800
Canterbury	171	13	21,600
Carlisle	140	12	25,100
Chelmsford	375	39	52,500
Chester	266	19	49,400
Chichester	336	7	60,000
Coventry	132	16	17,900
Derby	170	13	21,300
Durham	206	30	27,700
Ely	141	20	20,900
Europe	–	–	8,800
Exeter	245	13	34,100
Gloucester	147	14	26,500
Guildford	169	26	31,000
Hereford	103	15	19,400
Leicester	140	18	16,600

	Clergy		Membership
	Male	*Female*	
Lichfield	332	42	53,500
Lincoln	197	40	32,100
Liverpool	220	34	32,900
London	500	48	55,600
Manchester	267	28	39,000
Newcastle	141	11	17,800
Norwich	180	15	26,400
Oxford	393	67	62,200
Peterborough	147	15	19,900
Portsmouth	103	9	18,400
Ripon	136	24	19,600
Rochester	208	25	31,900
St Albans	248	42	44,900
St Edmundsbury			
and Ipswich	151	15	25,600
Salisbury	214	19	45,800
Sheffield	174	23	21,000
Sodor and Man	22	0	2,900
Southwark	316	63	45,500
Southwell	159	29	18,500
Truro	125	3	18,000
Wakefield	159	16	23,700
Winchester	230	15	43,000
Worcester	144	18	22,600
York	256	26	38,300
TOTAL	8,653	983	1,324,700

STIPENDS 1999–2000

Archbishop of Canterbury	£53,370
Archbishop of York	£46,760
Bishop of London	£43,580
Other diocesan bishops	£28,930
Suffragan bishops	£23,790
Deans and provosts	£23,790
Residentiary canons	£19,460
Incumbents and clergy of similar status	£15,910*

*national average, provisional estimate

CANTERBURY

103RD ARCHBISHOP AND PRIMATE OF ALL ENGLAND
Most Revd and Rt. Hon. George L. Carey, PH.D., *cons.* 1987, *trans.* 1991, *apptd* 1991; Lambeth Palace, London SE1 7JU. *Signs* George Cantuar:

BISHOPS SUFFRAGAN
Dover, Rt. Revd Stephen S. Venner, *cons* 1994, *apptd* 1999; Upway, St Martin's Hill, Canterbury, Kent CT1 1PR
Maidstone, Rt. Revd Gavin H. Reid, *cons.* 1992, *apptd* 1992; Bishop's House, Pett Lane, Charing, Ashford, Kent TN27 0DL
Ebbsfleet, Rt. Revd Michael A. Houghton, *cons.* 1998, *apptd* 1998 (provincial episcopal visitor); 8 Goldney Avenue, Bristol BS8 4RA
Richborough, Rt. Revd Edwin Barnes, *cons.* 1995, *apptd* 1995 (provincial episcopal visitor); 14 Hall Place Gardens, St Albans, Herts AL1 3SP

DEAN
Very Revd John Arthur Simpson, *apptd* 1986

CANONS RESIDENTIARY
P. Brett, *apptd* 1983; R. H. C. Symon, *apptd* 1994; Dr M. Chandler, *apptd* 1995; Ven. J. Pritchard, *apptd* 1996

Organist, D. Flood, FRCO, *apptd* 1988

ARCHDEACONS
Canterbury, Ven. J. Pritchard, *apptd* 1996
Maidstone, Ven. P. Evans, *apptd* 1989
Vicar-General of Province and Diocese, Chancellor S. Cameron, QC
Commissary-General, His Hon. Judge Richard Walker
Joint Registrars of the Province, F. E. Robson, OBE; B. J. T. Hanson, CBE
Diocesan Registrar and Legal Adviser, R. H. B. Sturt
Diocesan Secretary, D. Kemp, Diocesan House, Lady Wootton's Green, Canterbury CT1 1NQ. Tel: 01227-459401

YORK

96TH ARCHBISHOP AND PRIMATE OF ENGLAND
Most Revd and Rt. Hon. David M. Hope, KCVO, D.Phil., LL D, *cons.* 1985, *trans.* 1995, *apptd* 1995; Bishopthorpe, York YO23 2GE. *Signs* David Ebor:

BISHOPS SUFFRAGAN
Hull, Rt. Revd Richard M. C. Frith, *cons.* 1998, *apptd* 1998; Hullen House, Woodfield Lane, Hessle, Hull HU13 0ES
Selby, Rt. Revd Humphrey V. Taylor, *cons.* 1991, *apptd* 1991; 10 Precentor's Court, York YO1 2ES
Whitby, Rt. Revd Robert S. Ladds, *cons.* 1999, *apptd* 1999; 60 West Green, Stokesley, Middlesbrough TS9 5BD
Beverley, Rt. Revd John Gaisford, *cons.* 1994, *apptd* 1994 (provincial episcopal visitor); 3 North Lane, Roundhay, Leeds LS8 2QJ

DEAN
Very Revd Raymond Furnell, *apptd* 1994

CANONS RESIDENTIARY
G. Webster., *apptd* 1999; R. Metcalfe, *apptd* 1988; P. J. Ferguson, *apptd* 1995; E. R. Norman, PH.D., DD, *apptd* 1999

Organist, P. Moore, FRCO, *apptd* 1983

ARCHDEACONS
Cleveland, Ven. C. J. Hawthorn, *apptd* 1991
East Riding, Ven. P. R. W. Harrison, *apptd* 1998
York, Ven. R. Seed, *apptd* 1999

Official Principal and Auditor of the Chancery Court, Sir John Owen, QC
Chancellor of the Diocese, His Hon. Judge Coningsby, QC, *apptd* 1977
Vicar-General of the Province and Official Principal of the Consistory Court, His Hon. Judge Coningsby, QC
Registrar and Legal Secretary, L. P. M. Lennox
Diocesan Secretary, C. Sheppard, Church House, Ogleforth, York YO1 7JE. Tel: 01904-611696

LONDON (Province of Canterbury)

132ND BISHOP
Rt. Revd and Rt. Hon Richard J. C. Chartres, *cons.* 1992, *apptd. 1995*; The Old Deanery, Dean's Court, London EC4V 5AA. *Signs* Richard Londin:

AREA BISHOPS
Edmonton, Rt. Revd Peter W. Wheatley, *cons.* 1999, *apptd* 1999; 27 Thurlow Road, London NW3 5PP
Kensington, Rt. Revd Michael Colclough, *cons.* 1996, *apptd* 1996; 19 Campden Hill Square, London W8 7JY
Stepney, Rt. Revd Dr John M. Sentamu, *cons.* 1996, *apptd* 1996; 63 Coborn Road, London E3 2DB

Willesden, Rt. Revd Graham G. Dow, *cons.* 1992, *apptd* 1992; 173 Willesden Lane, London NW6 7YN

BISHOP SUFFRAGAN
Fulham, Rt. Revd John Broadhurst, *cons.* 1996, *apptd* 1996; 26 Canonbury Park South, London N1 2FN

DEAN OF ST PAUL'S
Very Revd John H. Moses, PH.D., *apptd* 1996

CANONS RESIDENTIARY
R. J. Halliburton, *apptd* 1990; M. J. Saward, *apptd* 1991; S. J. Oliver, *apptd* 1997

Registrar and Receiver of St Paul's, Brig. R. W. Acworth, CBE

Organist, J. Scott, FRCO, *apptd* 1990

ARCHDEACONS
Charing Cross, Ven. Dr W. Jacob, *apptd* 1996
Hackney, Ven. L. Dennen, *apptd* 1999
Hampstead, Ven. M. Lawson, *apptd* 1999
London, Middlesex, Ven. M. Colmer, *apptd* 1996
Northolt, Ven. P. Broadbent, *apptd* 1995

Chancellor, Miss S. Cameron, QC, *apptd* 1992
Registrar and Legal Secretary, P. C. E. Morris
Diocesan Secretary, vacant

DURHAM (Province of York)

70TH BISHOP
Rt. Revd A. Michael A. Turnbull, *cons.* 1988, *apptd* 1994; Auckland Castle, Bishop Auckland DL14 7NR. *Signs* Michael Dunelm:

BISHOP SUFFRAGAN
Jarrow, Rt. Revd Alan Smithson, *cons.* 1990, *apptd* 1990; The Old Vicarage, Hallgarth, Pittington, Durham DH6 1AB

DEAN
Very Revd John R. Arnold, *apptd* 1989

CANONS RESIDENTIARY
D. W. Brown, *apptd* 1990; T. Willmott, *apptd* 1997; M. Kitchen, *apptd* 1997; D. J. Whittington, *apptd* 1998; N. Stock, *apptd* 1998

Organist, J. B. Lancelot, FRCO, *apptd* 1985

ARCHDEACONS
Auckland, Ven. G. G. Gibson, *apptd* 1993
Durham, Ven. T. Willmott, *apptd* 1997
Sunderland, Ven. F. White, *apptd* 1997

Chancellor, His Hon. Judge Bursell, QC, *apptd* 1989
Registrar and Legal Secretary, A. N. Fairclough
Diocesan Secretary, J. P. Cryer, Auckland Castle, Bishop Auckland, Co. Durham DL14 7QJ. Tel: 01388-604515

WINCHESTER (Canterbury)

96TH BISHOP
Rt. Revd Michael C. Scott-Joynt, *cons.* 1987, *trans.* 1995, *apptd* 1995; Wolvesey, Winchester SO23 9ND. *Signs* Michael Winton:

BISHOPS SUFFRAGAN
Basingstoke, Rt. Revd Dr. Geoffrey Rowell, *cons.* 1994, *apptd* 1994; Bishopswood End, Kingswood Rise, Four Marks, Alton, Hants GU34 5BD
Southampton, Rt. Revd Jonathan M. Gledhill, *cons.* 1996, *apptd* 1996; Ham House, The Crescent, Romsey SO51 7NG

DEAN
Very Revd Michael Till, *apptd* 1996

Dean of Jersey (*A Peculiar*), Very Revd John Seaford, *apptd* 1993
Dean of Guernsey (*A Peculiar*), Very Revd Marc Trickey, *apptd* 1995

CANONS RESIDENTIARY
A. K. Walker, *apptd* 1987; P. B. Morgan, *apptd* 1994; C. Stewart, *apptd* 1997; Ven. J. A. Guille, *apptd* 1998

Organist, D. Hill, FRCO, *apptd* 1988

ARCHDEACONS
Basingstoke, Ven. J. A. Guille, *apptd* 1998
Winchester, Ven. A. G. Harbidge, *apptd* 1998

Chancellor, C. Clark, *apptd* 1993
Registrar and Legal Secretary, P. M. White
Diocesan Secretary, R. Anderton, Church House, 9 The Close, Winchester, Hants SO23 9LS. Tel: 01962-844644

BATH AND WELLS (Canterbury)

76TH BISHOP
Rt. Revd James L. Thompson, *cons.* 1978, *apptd* 1991; The Palace, Wells BA5 2PD. *Signs* James Bath & Wells

BISHOP SUFFRAGAN
Taunton, Rt. Revd Andrew John Radford, *cons.* Dec. 1998, *apptd* 1998; The Bishop's Lodge, Monkton Heights, West Monkton, Taunton, Somerset TA2 8LU

DEAN
Very Revd Richard Lewis, *apptd* 1990

CANONS RESIDENTIARY
R. Acworth, *apptd* 1993;
P. G. Walker, *apptd* 1994; M. W. Matthews, *apptd* 1997

Organist, M. Archer, *apptd* 1996

ARCHDEACONS
Bath, Ven. R. J. S. Evens, *apptd* 1996
Taunton, Ven. J. P. C. Reed, *apptd* 1999
Wells, Ven. R. Acworth, *apptd* 1993

Chancellor, T. Briden, *apptd* 1993
Registrar and Legal Secretary, T. Berry
Diocesan Secretary, N. Denison, The Old Deanery, Wells, Somerset BA5 2UG. Tel: 01749-670777

BIRMINGHAM (Canterbury)

7TH BISHOP
Rt. Revd Mark Santer, *cons.* 1981, *apptd* 1987; Bishop's Croft, Harborne, Birmingham B17 0BG. *Signs* Mark Birmingham

BISHOP SUFFRAGAN
Aston, Rt. Revd John Austin, *cons.* 1992, *apptd* 1992; Strensham House, 8 Strensham Hill, Moseley, Birmingham B13 8AG

PROVOST
vacant

CANONS RESIDENTIARY
Ven. C. J. G. Barton, *apptd* 1990; Revd D. Lee, *apptd* 1996; Revd G. O'Neill, *apptd* 1997

Organist, M. Huxley, FRCO, *apptd* 1986

ARCHDEACONS
Aston, Ven. C. J. G. Barton, *apptd* 1990
Birmingham, Ven. J. F. Duncan, *apptd* 1985

Chancellor, His Hon. Judge Aglionby, *apptd* 1970
Registrar and Legal Secretary, H. Carslake
Diocesan Secretary, J. Drennan, 175 Harborne Park Road,
  Harborne, Birmingham B17 0BH. Tel: 0121-427 5141

BLACKBURN (York)

7TH BISHOP
Rt. Revd Alan D. Chesters, *cons.* 1989, *apptd* 1989; Bishop's
  House, Ribchester Road, Blackburn BB1 9EF. *Signs* Alan
  Blackburn

BISHOPS SUFFRAGAN
Burnley, Rt. Revd Martyn W. Jarrett, *cons.* 1994, *apptd* 1994;
  Dean House, 449 Padiham Road, Burnley BB12 6TE
Lancaster, Rt. Revd Stephen Pedley, *cons.* 1998, *apptd* 1997;
  The Vicarage, Shireshead, Forton, Preston PR3 0AE

PROVOST
Very Revd David Frayne, *apptd* 1992

CANONS RESIDENTIARY
D. M. Galilee, *apptd* 1995; A. D. Hindley, *apptd* 1996; P. J.
  Ballard, *apptd* 1998

Organist, R. Tanner, *apptd* 1998

ARCHDEACONS
Blackburn, Ven. F. J. Marsh, *apptd* 1996
Lancaster, vacant

Chancellor, J. W. M. Bullimore, *apptd* 1990
Registrar and Legal Secretary, T. A. Hoyle
Diocesan Secretary, Revd M. J. Wedgeworth, Diocesan
  Office, Cathedral Close, Blackburn BB1 5AA. Tel: 01254-
  54421

BRADFORD (York)

8TH BISHOP
Rt. Revd David J. Smith, *cons.* 1987, *apptd* 1992;
  Bishopscroft, Ashwell Road, Heaton, Bradford BD9 4AU.
  Signs David Bradford

PROVOST
Very Revd John S. Richardson, *apptd* 1990

CANONS RESIDENTIARY
C. G. Lewis, *apptd* 1993; G. Smith, *apptd* 1996

Organist, A. Horsey, FRCO, *apptd* 1986

ARCHDEACONS
Bradford, Ven. G. A. Wilkinson, *apptd* 1999
Craven, Ven. M. L. Grundy, *apptd* 1994

Chancellor, J. de G. Walford, *apptd* 1999
Registrar and Legal Secretary, J. G. H. Mackrell
Diocesan Secretary, M. Halliday, Cathedral Hall, Stott Hill,
  Bradford BD1 4ET. Tel: 01274-725958

BRISTOL (Canterbury)

54TH BISHOP
Rt. Revd Barry Rogerson, *cons.* 1979, *apptd* 1985;
  Bishop's House, Clifton Hill, Bristol BS8 1BW. *Signs*
  Barry Bristol

BISHOP SUFFRAGAN
Swindon, Rt. Revd Michael Doe, *cons.* 1994, *apptd* 1994;
  Mark House, Field Rise, Old Town, Swindon SN1 4HP

DEAN
Very Revd Robert W. Grimley, *apptd* 1997

CANONS RESIDENTIARY
P. F. Johnson, *apptd* 1990; D. R. Holt, *apptd* 1998; B. D.
  Clover, *apptd* 1999

Organist, M. Lee, *apptd* 1998

ARCHDEACONS
Bristol, Ven. T. E. McClure, apptd 1999
Swindon, Ven. A. F. Hawker, *apptd* 1998

Chancellor, Sir David Calcutt, QC, *apptd* 1971
Registrar and Legal Secretary, T. Berry
Diocesan Secretary, Mrs L. Farrall, Diocesan Church House,
  23 Great George Street, Bristol, Avon BS1 5QZ. Tel:
  0117-921 4411

CARLISLE (York)

65TH BISHOP
Rt. Revd Ian Harland, *cons.* 1985, *apptd* 1989; Rose Castle,
  Dalston, Carlisle CA5 7BZ. *Signs* Ian Carliol:

BISHOP SUFFRAGAN
Penrith, Rt. Revd Richard Garrard, *cons.* 1994, *apptd* 1994;
  Holm Croft, Castle Road, Kendal, Cumbria LA9 7AU

DEAN
Very Revd Graeme P. Knowles, *apptd* 1998

CANONS RESIDENTIARY
R. A. Chapman, *apptd* 1978; Ven. D. C. Turnbull, *apptd*
  1993; D. W. V. Weston, *apptd* 1994; C. Hill, *apptd* 1996

Organist, J. Suter, FRCO, *apptd* 1991

ARCHDEACONS
Carlisle, Ven. D. C. Turnbull, *apptd* 1993
West Cumberland, Ven. A. N. Davis, *apptd* 1996
Westmorland and Furness, vacant

Chancellor, His Hon. Judge Aglionby, *apptd* 1991
Registrar and Legal Secretary, Mrs S. Holmes
Diocesan Secretary, Canon C. Hill, Church House, West
  Walls, Carlisle CA3 8UE. Tel: 01228-522573

CHELMSFORD (Canterbury)

8TH BISHOP
Rt. Revd John F. Perry, *cons.* 1989, *apptd* 1996;
  Bishopscourt, Margaretting, Ingatestone CM4 0HD. *Signs*
  John Chelmsford

BISHOPS SUFFRAGAN
Barking, Rt. Revd Roger F. Sainsbury, *cons.* 1991, *apptd*
  1991; 110 Capel Road, Forest Gate, London E7 0JS
Bradwell, Rt. Revd Laurence Green, *cons.* 1993, *apptd* 1993;
  The Vicarage, Orsett Road, Horndon-on-the-Hill,
  Stanford-le-Hope, Essex SS17 8NS
Colchester, Rt. Revd Edward Holland, *cons.* 1986, *apptd*
  1995; 1 Fitzwalter Road, Lexden, Colchester CO3 3SS

PROVOST
Very Revd Peter S. M. Judd, *apptd* 1997

CANONS RESIDENTIARY
T. Thompson, *apptd* 1988; B. P. Thompson, *apptd* 1988; D.
  Knight, *apptd* 1991; A. Knowles, *apptd* 1998

Master of Music, Dr G. Elliott, ph.d., frco, *apptd* 1981

ARCHDEACONS
Colchester, Ven. M. W. Wallace, *apptd* 1997
Harlow, Ven. P. F. Taylor, *apptd* 1996
Southend, Ven. D. Jennings, *apptd* 1992
West Ham, Ven. M. J. Fox, *apptd* 1996

Chancellor, Miss S. M. Cameron, qc, *apptd* 1970
Registrar and Legal Secretary, B. Hood
Diocesan Secretary, D.Phillips, 53 New Street, Chelmsford, Essex cmi iat. Tel: 01245-266731

CHESTER (York)

40TH BISHOP
Rt. Revd Peter R. Forster, ph.d., *cons.* 1996, *apptd* 1996; Bishop's House, Chester chi 2jd. *Signs* Peter Cestr:

BISHOPS SUFFRAGAN
Birkenhead, (until March 2000) Rt. Revd Michael L. Langrish, *cons.* 1993, *apptd* 1993; Bishop's Lodge, 67 Bidston Road, Oxton, Birkenhead ch43 6tr
Stockport, Rt. Revd Geoffrey M. Turner, *cons.* 1994, *apptd* 1994; Bishop's Lodge, Back Lane, Dunham Town, Altrincham, Cheshire wa14 4sg

DEAN
Very Revd Dr Stephen S. Smalley, *apptd* 1986

CANONS RESIDENTIARY
R. M. Rees, *apptd* 1990; O. A. Conway, *apptd* 1991; Dr T. J. Dennis, *apptd* 1994; J. W. S. Newcome, *apptd* 1994

Organist and Director of Music, D. G. Poulter, frco, *apptd* 1997

ARCHDEACONS
Chester, Ven. C. Hewetson, *apptd* 1994
Macclesfield, Ven. R. J. Gillings, *apptd* 1994

Chancellor, D. G. P. Turner, *apptd* 1998
Registrar and Legal Secretary, A. K. McAllester
Diocesan Secretary, S. P. A. Marriott, Church House, Lower Lane, Aldford, Chester ch3 6hp. Tel: 01244-620444

CHICHESTER (Canterbury)

102ND BISHOP
Rt. Revd Eric W. Kemp, dd, *cons.* 1974, *apptd* 1974; The Palace, Chichester po19 1py. *Signs* Eric Cicestr:

BISHOPS SUFFRAGAN
Horsham, Rt. Revd Lindsay G. Urwin, *cons.* 1993, *apptd* 1993; Bishop's House, 21 Guildford Road, Horsham, W. Sussex rh12 1lu
Lewes, Rt. Revd Wallace P. Benn, *cons.* 1997, *apptd* 1997; 16a Prideaux Road, Eastbourne, E. Sussex bn21 2nb

DEAN
Very Revd John D. Treadgold, lvo, *apptd* 1989

CANONS RESIDENTIARY
R. T. Greenacre, *apptd* 1975; F. J. Hawkins, *apptd* 1981; P. G. Atkinson, *apptd* 1997; C. Lansdale, *apptd* 1999; D. McKittrick, *apptd* 1999

Organist, A. J. Thurlow, frco, *apptd* 1980

ARCHDEACONS
Chichester, Ven. M. Brotherton, *apptd* 1991
Horsham, Ven. W. C. L. Filby, *apptd* 1983
Lewes and Hastings, Ven. N. S. Reade, *apptd* 1997

Chancellor, vacant
Registrar and Legal Secretary, C. Butcher
Diocesan Secretary, J. Prichard, Diocesan Church House, 211 New Church Road, Hove, E. Sussex bn3 4ed. Tel: 01273-421021

COVENTRY (Canterbury)

8TH BISHOP
Rt. Revd Colin J. Bennetts; *cons.* 1994, *apptd* 1997; The Bishop's House, 23 Davenport Road, Coventry cv5 6pw. *Signs* Colin Coventry

BISHOP SUFFRAGAN
Warwick, Rt. Revd Anthony M. Priddis, *cons.* 1996, *apptd* 1996; 139 Kenilworth Road, Coventry cv4 7af

PROVOST
Very Revd John F. Petty, *apptd* 1987

CANONS RESIDENTIARY
V. Faull, *apptd* 1994; J. C. Burch, *apptd* 1995; A. White, *apptd* 1998

Director of Music, R. Jeffcoat, *apptd* 1997

ARCHDEACONS
Coventry, Ven. H. I. L. Russell, *apptd* 1989
Warwick, Ven. M. J. J. Paget-Wilkes, *apptd* 1990

Chancellor, Sir William Gage, *apptd* 1980
Registrar and Legal Secretary, D. J. Dumbleton
Diocesan Secretary, Mrs I. Chapman, Church House, Palmerston Road, Coventry cv5 6fj. Tel: 01203-674328

DERBY (Canterbury)

6TH BISHOP
Rt. Revd Jonathan S. Bailey, *cons.* 1992, *apptd* 1995; Derby Church House, Full Street, Derby de1 3dr. *Signs* Jonathan Derby

BISHOP SUFFRAGAN
Repton, Rt. Revd David C. Hawtin, *cons.*1999, *apptd* 1999; Repton House, Lea, Matlock, Derbys de4 5jp

PROVOST
Very Revd Michael F. Perham, *apptd* 1998

CANONS RESIDENTIARY
G. A. Chesterman, *apptd* 1989; Ven. I. Gatford, *apptd* 1992; G. O. Marshall, *apptd* 1992; D. C. Truby, *apptd* 1998

Organist, P. Gould, *apptd* 1982

ARCHDEACONS
Chesterfield, Ven. D. C. Garnett, *apptd* 1996
Derby, Ven. I. Gatford, *apptd* 1992

Chancellor, J. W. M. Bullimore, *apptd* 1981
Registrar and Legal Secretary, J. S. Battie
Diocesan Secretary, R. J. Carey, Derby Church House, Full Street, Derby de1 3dr. Tel: 01332-382233

ELY (Canterbury)

BISHOP
vacant

BISHOP SUFFRAGAN
Huntingdon, Rt. Revd John R. Flack, *cons.* 1997, *apptd* 1996; 14 Lynn Road, Ely, Cambs cb6 1da

DEAN
Very Revd Michael Higgins, *apptd* 1991

CANONS RESIDENTIARY
J. Inge, *apptd* 1996

Organist, P. Trepte, FRCO, *apptd* 1991

ARCHDEACONS
Ely, Ven. J. Watson, *apptd* 1993
Huntingdon, Ven. J. Beer, *apptd* 1997
Wisbech, Ven. J. Rone, *apptd* 1995

Chancellor, W. Gage, QC
Joint Registrars, W. H. Godfrey; P. F. B. Beesley (*Legal Secretary*)
Diocesan Secretary, Dr M. Lavis, Bishop Woodford House, Barton Road, Ely, Cambs CB7 4DX. Tel: 01353-652701

EXETER (Canterbury)

70TH BISHOP
(from March 2000) Rt. Revd Michael L. Langrish, *cons.* 1993, *apptd* 2000; The Palace, Exeter, EX1 1HY. *Signs* Michael Exon

BISHOPS SUFFRAGAN
Crediton, Rt. Revd Richard S. Hawkins, *cons.* 1988, *apptd* 1996;,10 The Close, Exeter EX1 1EZ
Plymouth, Rt. Revd John H. Garton, *cons.* 1996, *apptd* 1996; 31 Riverside Walk, Tamerton Foliot, Plymouth PL5 4AQ

DEAN
Very Revd Keith B. Jones, *apptd* 1996

CANONS RESIDENTIARY
K. C. Parry, *apptd* 1991; N. Collings, *apptd* 1999

Organist, L. A. Nethsingha, FRCO, *apptd* 1973

ARCHDEACONS
Barnstaple, Ven. T. Lloyd, *apptd* 1989
Exeter, Ven. A. F. Tremlett, *apptd* 1994
Plymouth, Ven. R. G. Ellis, *apptd* 1982
Totnes, Preb. R. T. Gilpin, *apptd* 1996

Chancellor, Sir David Calcutt, QC, *apptd* 1971
Registrar and Legal Secretary, R. K. Wheeler
Diocesan Secretary, M. Beedell, Diocesan House, Palace Gate, Exeter, Devon EX1 1HX. Tel: 01392-72686

GIBRALTAR IN EUROPE (Canterbury)

BISHOP
Rt. Revd John Hind, *cons.* 1991, *apptd* 1993; 14 Tufton Street, London SW1P 3QZ

BISHOP SUFFRAGAN
In Europe Rt. Revd Henry Scriven, *cons.* 1995, *apptd* 1994; 14 Tufton Street, London SW1P 3QZ

Dean, Cathedral Church of the Holy Trinity, Gibraltar, Very Revd W. G. Reid
Chancellor, Pro-Cathedral of St Paul, Valletta, Malta, Canon A. Woods
Chancellor, Pro-Cathedral of the Holy Trinity, Brussels, Belgium, Canon N. Walker

ARCHDEACONS
Eastern, Ven. S. J. B. Peake
North-West Europe, Ven. G. G. Allen

France, Ven. M. Draper, OBE
Gibraltar, Ven. K. Robinson
Italy, Ven. W. E. Edebohls
Scandinavia and Germany, Ven. D. Ratcliff
Switzerland, Ven. P. J. Hawker, OBE

Chancellor, Sir David Calcutt, QC
Registrar and Legal Secretary, J. G. Underwood
Diocesan Secretary, A. C. Mumford, 14 Tufton Street, London SW1P 3QZ. Tel: 0171-976 8001

GLOUCESTER (Canterbury)

39TH BISHOP
Rt. Revd David Bentley, *cons.* 1986, *apptd* 1993; Bishopscourt, Gloucester GL1 2BQ. *Signs* David Gloucestr

BISHOP SUFFRAGAN
Tewkesbury, Rt. Revd John S. Went, *cons.* 1995, *apptd* 1995; Green Acre, Hempsted, Gloucester GL2 6LG

DEAN
Very Revd Nicholas A. S. Bury, *apptd* 1997

CANONS RESIDENTIARY
R. D. M. Grey, *apptd* 1982; N. Chatfield, *apptd* 1992; N. Heavisides, *apptd* 1993; C. H. Morgan, *apptd* 1996

Organist, D. Briggs, FRCO, *apptd* 1994

ARCHDEACONS
Cheltenham, Ven. H. S. Ringrose, *apptd* 1998
Gloucester, Ven. C. J. H. Wagstaff, *apptd* 1982

Chancellor and Vicar-General, Ms D. J. Rodgers, *apptd* 1990
Registrar and Legal Secretary, C. G. Peak
Diocesan Secretary, M. Williams, Church House, College Green, Gloucester GL1 2LY. Tel: 01452-410022

GUILDFORD (Canterbury)

8TH BISHOP
Rt. Revd John W. Gladwin, *cons.* 1994, *apptd* 1994; Willow Grange, Woking Road, Guildford GU4 7QS. *Signs* John Guildford

BISHOP SUFFRAGAN
Dorking, Rt. Revd Ian Brackley, *cons.* 1996, *apptd* 1995; Dayspring, 13 Pilgrims Way, Guildford GU4 8AD

DEAN
Very Revd Alexander G. Wedderspoon, *apptd* 1987

CANONS RESIDENTIARY
Dr Maureen Palmer, *apptd* 1996

Organist, A. Millington, FRCO, *apptd* 1982

ARCHDEACONS
Dorking, Ven. M. Wilson, *apptd* 1995
Surrey, Ven. R. Reiss, *apptd* 1995

Chancellor, His Hon. Judge Goodman
Registrar and Legal Secretary, P. F. B. Beesley
Diocesan Secretary, vacant

HEREFORD (Canterbury)

103RD BISHOP
Rt. Revd John Oliver, *cons.* 1990, *apptd* 1990; The Palace, Hereford HR4 9BN. *Signs* John Hereford

BISHOP SUFFRAGAN
Ludlow, Rt. Revd Dr John Saxbee, *cons.* 1994, *apptd* 1994; Bishop's House, Halford, Craven Arms, Shropshire SY7 9BT

DEAN
Very Revd Robert A. Willis, *apptd* 1992

CANONS RESIDENTIARY
P. Iles, *apptd* 1983; J. Tiller, *apptd* 1984; M. W. Hooper, *apptd* 1997

Organist, Dr R. Massey, FRCO, *apptd* 1974

ARCHDEACONS
Hereford, Ven. M. W. Hooper, *apptd* 1997
Ludlow, Rt. Revd J. C. Saxbee, *apptd* 1992

Chancellor, J. M. Henty
Joint Registrars and Legal Secretaries, V. T. Jordan; P. F. B. Beesley
Diocesan Secretary, Miss S. Green, The Palace, Hereford HR4 9BL. Tel: 01432-353863

LEICESTER (Canterbury)

6TH BISHOP
Rt. Revd Timothy J. Stevens, *cons.* 1995, *apptd* 1999; Bishop's Lodge, 10 Springfield Road, Leicester LE2 3BD. *Signs* Timothy Leicester

STIPENDIARY ASSISTANT BISHOP
Rt. Revd William Down, *cons.* 1990, *apptd* 1995

PROVOST
Vacant

CANONS RESIDENTIARY
M. T. H. Banks, *apptd* 1988; M. Wilson, *apptd* 1988

Organist, J. T. Gregory, *apptd* 1994

ARCHDEACONS
Leicester, Ven. M. Edson, *apptd* 1994
Loughborough, Ven. I. Stanes, *apptd* 1992

Chancellor, N. Seed, *apptd* 1989
Registrars and Legal Secretaries, P. C. E. Morris; R. H. Bloor
Diocesan Secretary, A. Howard; Church House, 3–5 St Martin's East, Leicester LEI 5FX. Tel: 0116-262 7445

LICHFIELD (Canterbury)

97TH BISHOP
Rt. Revd Keith N. Sutton, *cons.* 1978, *apptd* 1984; Bishop's House, The Close, Lichfield WS13 7LG. *Signs* Keith Lichfield

BISHOPS SUFFRAGAN
Shrewsbury, Rt. Revd David M. Hallatt, *cons.* 1994, *apptd* 1994; 68 London Road, Shrewsbury SY2 6PG
Stafford, Rt. Revd Christopher J. Hill, *cons.* 1996, *apptd* 1996; Ash Garth, Broughton Crescent, Barlaston, Staffs ST12 9DD
Wolverhampton, Rt. Revd Michael G. Bourke, *cons.* 1993, *apptd* 1993; 61 Richmond Road, Wolverhampton WV3 9JH

DEAN
Very Revd Michael Yorke, *apptd* 1999

CANONS RESIDENTIARY
A. N. Barnard, *apptd* 1977; C. W. Taylor, *apptd* 1995; Ven. G. Frost, *apptd* 1998

Organist, A. Lumsden, *apptd* 1992

ARCHDEACONS
Lichfield, Ven. G. Frost, *apptd* 1998
Salop, Ven . J. B. Hall, *apptd* 1998
Stoke-on-Trent, Ven. A. G. C. Smith, *apptd* 1997
Walsall, Ven. A. G. Sadler, *apptd* 1997

Chancellor, His Hon. Judge Shand
Registrar and Legal Secretary, J. P. Thorneycroft
Diocesan Secretary, D. R. Taylor, St Mary's House, The Close, Lichfield, Staffs WS13 7LD. Tel: 01543-306030

LINCOLN (Canterbury)

70TH BISHOP
Rt. Revd Robert M. Hardy, *cons.* 1980, *apptd* 1987; Bishop's House, Eastgate, Lincoln LN2 1QQ. *Signs* Robert Lincoln

BISHOPS SUFFRAGAN
Grantham, Rt. Revd Alastair L. J. Redfern, *cons.* 1997, *apptd* 1997; Fairacre, 234 Barrowby Road, Grantham, Lincs NG31 8NP
Grimsby, Rt. Revd David Tustin, *cons.* 1979, *apptd* 1979; Bishop's House, Church Lane, Irby-upon-Humber, Grimsby DN37 7JR

DEAN
Very Revd Alexander F. Knight, *apptd* 1998

CANONS RESIDENTIARY
B. R. Davis, *apptd* 1977; A. J. Stokes, *apptd* 1992; V. White, *apptd* 1994

Organist, C. S. Walsh, FRCO, *apptd* 1988

ARCHDEACONS
Lincoln, Ven. A. Hawes, *apptd* 1995
Lindsey, vacant
Stow, Ven. R. J. Wells, *apptd* 1989

Chancellor, Peter N. Collier, QC, *apptd* 1999
Registrar and Legal Secretary, D. M. Wellman
Diocesan Secretary, P. Hamlyn Williams, The Old Palace, Lincoln LN2 1PU. Tel: 01522-529241

LIVERPOOL (York)

7TH BISHOP
Rt. Revd James Jones, *cons.* 1994, *apptd* 1998; Bishop's Lodge, Woolton Park, Liverpool L25 6DT. *Signs* James Liverpool

BISHOP SUFFRAGAN
Warrington, Rt. Revd John Packer, *cons.* 1996, *apptd* 1996; 34 Central Avenue, Eccleston Park, Prescot, Merseyside L34 2QP

DEAN
(from February 2000) Rt. Revd Dean Dr Rupert W. N. Hoare

CANONS RESIDENTIARY
D. J. Hutton, *apptd* 1983; M. C. Boyling, *apptd* 1994; N. T. Vincent, *apptd* 1995; C. Byworth, *apptd* 1999

Organist, Prof. I. Tracey, *apptd* 1980

ARCHDEACONS
Liverpool, Ven. R. L. Metcalf, *apptd* 1994
Warrington, Ven. C. D. S. Woodhouse, *apptd* 1981

Chancellor, R. G. Hamilton
Registrar and Legal Secretary, R. H. Arden

Diocesan Secretary, K. Cawdron, Church House, 1 Hanover Street, Liverpool LI 3DW. Tel: 0151-709 9722

MANCHESTER (York)

10TH BISHOP
Rt. Revd Christopher J. Mayfield, *cons.* 1985, *apptd* 1993; Bishopscourt, Bury New Road, Manchester M7 4LE. *Signs* Christopher Manchester

BISHOPS SUFFRAGAN
Bolton, Rt. Revd David K. Gillett, *cons.* 1999, *apptd* 1999; 4 Bishop's Lodge, Bolton Road, Hawkshaw, Bury BL8 4JN
Hulme, Rt. Revd Stephen R. Lowe, *cons.* 1999, *apptd.* 1999; 14 Moorgate Avenue, Withington, Manchester M20 IHE
Middleton, vacant

DEAN
Very Revd Kenneth Riley, *apptd* 1993

CANONS RESIDENTIARY
J. R. Atherton, PH.D., *apptd* 1984; A. E. Radcliffe, *apptd* 1991; P. Denby, *apptd* 1995

Organist, C. Stokes, *apptd* 1992

ARCHDEACONS
Bolton, Ven. L. M. Davies, *apptd* 1992
Manchester, Ven A. Wolstencroft, *apptd* 1998
Rochdale, Ven. J. M. M. Dalby, *apptd* 1991

Chancellor, J. Holden, *apptd* 1997
Registrar and Legal Secretary, M. Darlington
Diocesan Secretary, Mrs J. Park, Diocesan Church House, 90 Deansgate, Manchester M3 2GH. Tel: 0161-833 9521

NEWCASTLE (York)

11TH BISHOP
Rt. Revd J. Martin Wharton, *cons.* 1992, *apptd* 1997; Bishop's House, 29 Moor Road South, Gosforth, Newcastle upon Tyne NE3 IPA. *Signs* Martin Newcastle

STIPENDIARY ASSISTANT BISHOP
Rt. Revd Paul Richardson, *cons.* 1987, *apptd* 1999

PROVOST
Very Revd Nicholas G. Coulton, *apptd* 1990

CANONS RESIDENTIARY
R. Langley, *apptd* 1985; P. R. Strange, *apptd* 1986; Ven. P. Elliott, *apptd* 1993; G. V. Miller, *apptd* 1999

Organist, T. G. Hone, FRCO, *apptd* 1987

ARCHDEACONS
Lindisfarne, Ven. M. E. Bowering, *apptd* 1987
Northumberland, Ven. P. Elliott, *apptd* 1993

Chancellor, Prof. D. McClean, *apptd* 1998
Registrar and Legal Secretary, Mrs B. J. Lowdon
Diocesan Secretary, P. Davies, Church House, Grainger Park Road, Newcastle upon Tyne NE4 8SX. Tel: 0191-273 0120

NORWICH (Canterbury)

71ST BISHOP
vacant; (from January 2000) Rt Revd Graham R. James, *cons.* 1993, *apptd* 2000; Bishop's House, Norwich NR3 ISB. *Signs* Graham Norvic

BISHOPS SUFFRAGAN
Lynn, Rt. Revd A. C. Foottit, *cons.* 1999, *apptd* 1999
Thetford, Rt. Revd Hugo F. de Waal, *cons.* 1992, *apptd* 1992; Rectory Meadow, Bramerton, Norwich NR14 7DW

DEAN
Very Revd Stephen Platten, *apptd* 1995

CANONS RESIDENTIARY
J. M. Haselock, *apptd* 1998; Ven. C. J. Offer, *apptd* 1994; R. J. Hanmer, *apptd* 1994; M. Kitchener, *apptd* 1999

Organist, D. Dunnett, *apptd* 1996

ARCHDEACONS
Lynn, Ven. M. C. Gray, *apptd* 1999
Norfolk, Ven. A. M. Handley, *apptd* 1993
Norwich, Ven. C. J. Offer, *apptd* 1994

Chancellor, The Hon. Mr Justice Blofeld, *apptd* 1998
Registrar and Legal Secretary, J. W. F. Herring
Diocesan Secretary, D. Adeney, Diocesan House, 109 Dereham Road, Easton, Norwich, Norfolk NR9 5ES. Tel: 01603-880853

OXFORD (Canterbury)

41ST BISHOP
Rt. Revd Richard D. Harries, *cons.* 1987, *apptd* 1987; Diocesan Church House, North Hinksey, Oxford OX2 ONB. *Signs* Richard Oxon:

AREA BISHOPS
Buckingham, Rt. Revd Michael A. Hill *cons.* 1998, *apptd* 1998; 28 Church Street, Great Missenden, Bucks HP16 OAZ
Dorchester, Rt. Revd Anthony J. Russell, *cons.* 1988, *apptd* 1988; Holmby House, Sibford Ferris, Banbury, Oxon OX15 5RG
Reading, Rt. Revd Dominic Walker, *cons.* 1997, *apptd* 1997; Bishop's House, Tidmarsh Lane, Tidmarsh, Reading RG8 8HA

DEAN OF CHRIST CHURCH
Very Revd John H. Drury, *apptd* 1991

CANONS RESIDENTIARY
O. M. T. O'Donovan, D.Phil., *apptd* 1982; J. M. Pierce, *apptd* 1987; J. S. K. Ward, *apptd* 1991; R. Jeffery, *apptd* 1996; Prof. J. Webster, *apptd* 1996; Prof. H. M. R. E. Mayr-Harting, *apptd* 1997; Ven. J. A. Morrison, *apptd* 1998

Organist, S. Darlington, FRCO, *apptd* 1985

ARCHDEACONS
Berkshire, Ven. N. A. Russell, *apptd* 1998
Buckingham, Ven. D. Goldie, *apptd* 1998
Oxford, Ven. J. A. Morrison, *apptd* 1998

Chancellor, P. T. S. Boydell, QC, *apptd* 1958
Registrar and Legal Secretary, Dr F. E. Robson
Diocesan Secretary, R. Pearce, Diocesan Church House, North Hinksey, Oxford OX2 ONB. Tel: 01865-208202

PETERBOROUGH (Canterbury)

37TH BISHOP
Rt. Revd Ian P. M. Cundy, *cons.* 1992, *apptd* 1996; The Palace, Peterborough PEI IYA. *Signs* Ian Petriburg:

BISHOP SUFFRAGAN
Brixworth, Rt. Revd Paul E. Barber, *cons.* 1989, *apptd* 1989; 4 The Avenue, Dallington, Northampton NNI 4RZ

DEAN
Very Revd Michael Bunker, *apptd* 1992

CANONS RESIDENTIARY
T. R. Christie, *apptd* 1980; J. Higham, *apptd* 1983; P. A. Spence, *apptd* 1998
Organist, C. S. Gower, FRCO, *apptd* 1977

ARCHDEACONS
Northampton, Ven. M. R. Chapman, *apptd* 1991
Oakham, vacant

Chancellor, T. A. C. Coningsby, QC, *apptd* 1989
Registrar and Legal Secretary, R. Hemingray
Diocesan Secretary, Revd Canon R. J. Cattle, The Palace, Peterborough, Cambs PE1 1YB. Tel: 01733-64448

PORTSMOUTH (Canterbury)

8TH BISHOP
Rt. Revd Dr Kenneth W. Stevenson, *cons.* 1995, *apptd* 1995; Bishopsgrove, 26 Osborn Road, Fareham, Hants PO16 7DQ. *Signs* Kenneth Portsmouth

PROVOST
vacant

CANONS RESIDENTIARY
D. T. Isaac, *apptd* 1990; Jane B. Hedges, *apptd* 1993; G. Kirk, *apptd* 1998; I. Jagger, *apptd* 1998
Organist, D. J. C. Price, *apptd* 1996

ARCHDEACONS
Isle of Wight, Ven. K. M. L. H. Banting, *apptd* 1996
Portsmouth, Ven. C. Lowson, *apptd* 1999

Chancellor, His Hon. Judge Aglionby, *apptd* 1978
Registrar and Legal Secretary, Miss H. A. G. Tyler
Diocesan Secretary, M. F. Jordan, Cathedral House, St Thomas's Street, Portsmouth, Hants PO1 2HA. Tel: 01705-825731

RIPON (York)

BISHOP
vacant

BISHOP SUFFRAGAN
Knaresborough, Rt. Revd Frank V. Weston, *cons.* 1997, *apptd* 1997; 16 Shaftesbury Avenue, Roundhay, Leeds LS8 1DT

DEAN
Very Revd John Methuen, *apptd* 1995

CANONS RESIDENTIARY
M. R. Glanville-Smith, *apptd* 1990; K. Punshon, *apptd* 1996; J. Bell, *apptd* 1997
Organist, K. Beaumont, FRCO, *apptd* 1994

ARCHDEACONS
Leeds, Ven. J. M. Oliver, *apptd* 1992
Richmond, Ven. K. Good, *apptd* 1993

Chancellor, His Hon. Judge Grenfell, *apptd* 1992
Registrars and Legal Secretaries, C. T. Tunnard, Mrs N. Harding
Diocesan Secretary, P. M. Arundel, Diocesan Office, St Mary's Street, Leeds LS9 7DP. Tel: 0113-248 7487

ROCHESTER (Canterbury)

106TH BISHOP
Rt. Revd Dr Michael Nazir-Ali, *cons.* 1984, *apptd* 1994; Bishopscourt, Rochester ME1 1TS. *Signs* Michael Roffen:

BISHOP SUFFRAGAN
Tonbridge, Rt. Revd Brian A. Smith, *cons.* 1993, *apptd* 1993; Bishop's Lodge, 48 St Botolph's Road, Sevenoaks TN13 3AG

DEAN
Very Revd Edward F. Shotter, *apptd* 1990

CANONS RESIDENTIARY
E. R. Turner, *apptd* 1981; J. M. Armson, *apptd* 1989; N. L. Warren, *apptd* 1989; C. J. Meyrick, *apptd* 1998
Organist, R. Sayer, FRCO, *apptd* 1995

ARCHDEACONS
Bromley, Ven. G. Norman, *apptd* 1994
Rochester, Ven. N. L. Warren, *apptd* 1989
Tonbridge, Ven. Judith Rose, *apptd* 1996

Chancellor, His Hon. Judge Goodman, *apptd* 1971
Registrar and Legal Secretary, M. Thatcher
Diocesan Secretary, P. Law, St Nicholas Church, Boley Hill, Rochester ME1 1SL. Tel: 01634-830333

ST ALBANS (Canterbury)

9TH BISHOP
Rt. Revd Christopher W. Herbert, *cons.* 1995, *apptd* 1995; Abbey Gate House, St Albans AL3 4HD. *Signs* Christopher St Albans

BISHOPS SUFFRAGAN
Bedford, Rt. Revd John H. Richardson, *cons.* 1994, *apptd* 1994; 168 Kimbolton Road, Bedford MK41 8DN
Hertford, Rt. Revd Robin J. N. Smith, *cons.* 1990, *apptd* 1990; Hertford House, Abbey Mill Lane, St Albans AL3 4HE

DEAN
Very Revd Christopher Lewis, *apptd* 1993

CANONS RESIDENTIARY
G. R. S. Ritson, *apptd* 1987; M. Sansom, *apptd* 1988; C. R. J. Foster, *apptd* 1994
Organist, A. Lucas, *apptd* 1998

ARCHDEACONS
Bedford, Ven. M. L. Lesiter, *apptd* 1993
Hertford, Ven. T. P. Jones, *apptd* 1997
St Albans, Ven. R. I. Cheetham, *apptd* 1999

Chancellor, His Hon. Judge Bursell, QC, *apptd* 1992
Registrar and Legal Secretary, D. N. Cheetham
Diocesan Secretary, L. Nicholls, Holywell Lodge, 41 Holywell Hill, St Albans AL1 1HE. Tel: 01727-854532

ST EDMUNDSBURY AND IPSWICH (Canterbury)

9TH BISHOP
Rt. Revd J. H. Richard Lewis, *cons.* 1992, *apptd* 1997; Bishop's House, 4 Park Road, Ipswich IP1 3ST. *Signs* Richard St Edmundsbury and Ipswich

BISHOP SUFFRAGAN
Dunwich, Rt. Revd Clive Young, *cons.* 1999, *apptd* 1999; 28 Westerfield Road, Ipswich IP4 2UJ

PROVOST
Very Revd J. Atwell, *apptd* 1995

CANONS RESIDENTIARY
A. M. Shaw, *apptd* 1989; M. E. Mingins, *apptd* 1993; J. Parr, *apptd* 1999
Organist, J. Thomas, *apptd* 1997

ARCHDEACONS
Ipswich, Ven. T. A. Gibson, *apptd* 1987
Sudbury, Ven. J. Cox, *apptd* 1995
Suffolk, Ven. G. Arrand, *apptd* 1994

Chancellor, The Hon. Mr Justice Blofeld, *apptd* 1974
Registrar and Legal Secretary, J. Hall
Diocesan Secretary, N. Edgell, 13–15 Tower Street, Ipswich IP1 3BG. Tel: 01473-211028

SALISBURY (Canterbury)

77TH BISHOP
Rt. Revd David S. Stancliffe, *cons.* 1993, *apptd* 1993; South Canonry, The Close, Salisbury SP1 2ER. *Signs* David Sarum

BISHOPS SUFFRAGAN
Ramsbury, Rt. Revd Peter F. Hullah, *cons.* 1999, *apptd* 1999
Sherborne, Rt. Revd John D. G. Kirkham, *cons.* 1976, *apptd* 1976; Little Bailie, Sturminster Marshall, Wimborne BH21 4AD

DEAN
Very Revd Derek Watson, *apptd* 1996

CANONS RESIDENTIARY
D. J. C. Davies, *apptd* 1985; D. M. K. Durston, *apptd* 1992; June Osborne, *apptd* 1995
Organist, S. R. A. Lole, *apptd* 1997

ARCHDEACONS
Dorset, Ven. G. E. Walton, *apptd* 1982
Sherborne, Ven. P. C. Wheatley, *apptd* 1991
Wilts, Ven. B. J. Hopkinson, *apptd* 1986 (Sarum), 1998 (Wilts)

Chancellor, His Hon. Judge Wiggs, *apptd* 1997
Registrar and Legal Secretary, A. Johnson
Diocesan Secretary, Revd Karen Curnock, Church House, Crane Street, Salisbury SP1 2QB. Tel: 01722-411922

SHEFFIELD (York)

6TH BISHOP
Rt. Revd John (Jack) Nicholls, *cons.* 1990, *apptd* 1997; Bishopscroft, Snaithing Lane, Sheffield S10 3LG. *Signs* Jack Sheffield

BISHOP SUFFRAGAN
Doncaster, Rt. Revd Michael F. Gear, *cons.* 1993, *apptd* 1993; Bishops Lodge, Hooton Roberts, Rotherham S65 4PF

PROVOST
Very Revd Michael Sadgrove, *apptd* 1995

CANONS RESIDENTIARY
T. M. Page, *apptd* 1982; C. M. Smith, *apptd* 1991; Jane E. M. Sinclair, *apptd* 1993; Ven. R. F. Blackburn, *apptd* 1999

Organist, N. Taylor, *apptd* 1997

ARCHDEACONS
Doncaster, Ven. B. L. Holdridge, *apptd* 1994
Sheffield, Ven. R. F. Blackburn, *apptd* 1999

Chancellor, Prof. J. D. McClean, *apptd* 1992
Registrar and Legal Secretary, Mrs M. Myers
Diocesan Secretary, C. A. Beck, FCIS, Diocesan Church House, 95–99 Effingham Street, Rotherham S65 1BL. Tel: 01709-511116

SODOR AND MAN (York)

79TH BISHOP
Rt. Revd Noel D. Jones, CB, *cons.* 1989, *apptd* 1989; The Bishop's House, Quarterbridge Road, Douglas, Isle of Man IM2 3RF. *Signs* Noel Sodor and Man

CANONS
B. H. Kelly, *apptd* 1980; F. H. Bird, *apptd* 1993; D. Whitworth, *apptd* 1996; M. Convery, *apptd* 1999

ARCHDEACON
Isle of Man, Ven. B. H. Partington, *apptd* 1996

Vicar-General and Chancellor, Ms C. Faulds
Registrar and Legal Secretary, C. J. Callow
Diocesan Secretary, The Hon. C. Murphy, c/o 26 The Fountains, Ramsey, Isle of Man IM8 1NN. Tel: 01624-816545

SOUTHWARK (Canterbury)

9TH BISHOP
Rt. Revd Thomas F. Butler, PH.D, LL D, *cons.* 1985, *apptd* 1998; Bishop's House, 38 Tooting Bec Gardens, London SW16 1QZ. *Signs* Thomas Southwark

AREA BISHOPS
Croydon, Rt. Revd Dr Wilfred D. Wood, DD, *cons.* 1985, *apptd* 1985; St Matthew's House, George Street, Croydon CR0 1PE
Kingston upon Thames, Rt Revd Peter B. Price, *cons.* 1997, *apptd* 1998; *Kingston Episcopal Area Office*, Whitelands College, West Hill, London SW15 3SN
Woolwich, Rt. Revd Colin O. Buchanan, *cons.* 1985, *apptd* 1996; 37 South Road, Forest Hill, London SE23 2UJ

PROVOST
Very Revd Colin B. Slee, *apptd* 1994

CANONS RESIDENTIARY
D. Painter, *apptd* 1991; Helen Cunliffe, *apptd* 1995; J. John, *apptd* 1997; B. Saunders, *apptd* 1997; A. P. Nunn, *apptd* 1999
Organist, P. Wright, FRCO, *apptd* 1989

ARCHDEACONS
Croydon, Ven. V. A. Davies, *apptd* 1994
Lambeth, Ven. C. R. B. Bird, *apptd* 1988
Lewisham, Ven. D. J. Atkinson, *apptd* 1996
Reigate, Ven. M. Baddeley, *apptd* 1996
Southwark, Ven. D. L. Bartles-Smith, *apptd* 1985
Wandsworth, Ven. D. Gerrard, *apptd* 1989

Chancellor, C. George, QC
Registrar and Legal Secretary, P. Morris
Diocesan Secretary, S. Parton, Trinity House, 4 Chapel Court, Borough High Street, London SE1 1HW. Tel: 0171-403 8686

SOUTHWELL (York)

10TH BISHOP
Rt. Revd George H. Cassidy, *cons.* 1999, *apptd* 1999;
Bishop's Manor, Southwell NG25 0JR. *Signs* George
Southwell

BISHOP SUFFRAGAN
Sherwood, Rt. Revd Alan W. Morgan, *cons.* 1989, *apptd* 1989;
Sherwood House, High Oakham Road, Mansfield
NG18 5AJ

PROVOST
Very Revd David Leaning, *apptd* 1991

CANONS RESIDENTIARY
I. G. Collins, *apptd* 1985; G. A. Hendy *apptd* 1997

Organist, P. Hale, *apptd* 1989

ARCHDEACONS
Newark, Ven. N. Peyton, *apptd* 1999
Nottingham, Ven. G. Ogilvie, *apptd* 1996

Chancellor, J. Shand, *apptd* 1981
Registrar and Legal Secretary, C. C. Hodson
Diocesan Secretary, P. Prentis, Dunham House, Westgate,
Southwell, Notts NG25 0JL. Tel: 01636-814331

TRURO (Canterbury)

14TH BISHOP
Rt. Revd William Ind, *cons.* 1987, *apptd* 1997; Lis Escop,
Truro TR3 6QQ. *Signs* William Truro

BISHOP SUFFRAGAN
St Germans, vacant

DEAN
Very Revd Michael A. Moxon, LVO, *apptd* 1998

CANONS RESIDENTIARY
P. R. Gay, *apptd* 1994; K. P. Mellor, *apptd* 1994; P. D.
Goodridge, *apptd* 1996; P. Robson, *apptd* 1999

Organist, A. Nethsingha, FRCO, *apptd* 1994

ARCHDEACONS
Cornwall, (until 31 December 1999)Ven. J. T. McCabe,
apptd 1996; (from 1 January 2000) Ven. R. D. C.
Whiteman
Bodmin, vacant

Chancellor, T. Briden, *apptd* 1998
Registrar and Legal Secretary, M. J. Follett
Diocesan Secretary, B. C. Laite, Diocesan House, Kenwyn,
Truro TR1 3DU. Tel: 01872-274351

WAKEFIELD (York)

11TH BISHOP
Rt. Revd Nigel S. McCulloch, *cons.* 1986, *apptd* 1992;
Bishop's Lodge, Woodthorpe Lane, Wakefield WF2 6JL.
Signs Nigel Wakefield

BISHOP SUFFRAGAN
Pontefract, Rt. Revd David C. James, *cons.* 1998, *apptd* 1998;
Pontefract House, 181A Manygates Lane, Wakefield
WF2 7DR

PROVOST
Very Revd George P. Nairn-Briggs, *apptd* 1997

CANONS RESIDENTIARY
R. Capper, *apptd* 1997; R. Gage, *apptd* 1997; I. Gaskell,
apptd 1998; J. Holmes, *apptd* 1998

Organist, J. Bielby, FRCO, *apptd* 1972

ARCHDEACONS
Halifax, Ven. R. Inwood, *apptd* 1995
Pontefract, Ven. A. Robinson, *apptd* 1997

Chancellor, P. Collier, QC, *apptd* 1992
Registrar and Legal Secretary, L. Box
Diocesan Secretary, A. W. Ellis, Church House, 1 South
Parade, Wakefield WF1 1LP. Tel: 01924-371802

WORCESTER (Canterbury)

112TH BISHOP
Rt. Revd Dr Peter S. M. Selby, *cons.* 1984, *apptd* 1997; The
Bishop's House, Hartlebury Castle, Kidderminster
DY11 7XX. *Signs* Peter Wigorn:

BISHOP SUFFRAGAN
Dudley, (until February 2000) Rt. Revd Dr Rupert Hoare,
cons. 1993, *apptd* 1993; The Bishop's House, Brooklands,
Halesowen Road, Cradley Heath B64 7JF

DEAN
Very Revd Peter J. Marshall, *apptd* 1997

CANONS RESIDENTIARY
I. M. MacKenzie, *apptd* 1989; B. Ruddock, *apptd.* 1999; J. D.
Tetley, *apptd* 1999

Organist, A. Lucas, *apptd* 1996

ARCHDEACONS
Dudley, Ven. J. Gathercole, *apptd* 1987
Worcester, Ven. Dr J. Tetley

Chancellor, C. Mynors, *apptd* 1999
Registrar and Legal Secretary, M. Huskinson
Diocesan Secretary, R. Higham, The Old Palace, Deansway,
Worcester WR1 2JE. Tel: 01905-20537

ROYAL PECULIARS

WESTMINSTER
The Collegiate Church of St Peter
Dean, Very Revd Dr A. W. Carr, *apptd* 1997
Sub Dean and Archdeacon, A. E. Harvey, *apptd* 1987
Canons of Westminster, D. H. Hutt, *apptd* 1995; M. J.
Middleton, *apptd* 1997; R. Wright, *apptd* 1998
Chapter Clerk and Receiver-General, Maj.-Gen. D. Burden,
CB, CBE
Organist, J. O'Donnell
Registrar, S. J. Holmes, MVO, 20 Dean's Yard, London
SW1P 3PA
Legal Secretary, C. L. Hodgetts

WINDSOR
*The Queen's Free Chapel of St George within Her Castle of
Windsor*
Dean, Rt. Revd D. J. Conner, *apptd* 1998
Canons Residentiary, J. A. White, *apptd* 1982; L. F. P.
Gunner, *apptd* 1996; B. P. Thompson, PH.D., *apptd* 1998;
J. A. Ovenden, *apptd* 1998
Chapter Clerk, Lt.-Col. N. J. Newman, *apptd* 1990, Chapter
Office, The Cloisters, Windsor Castle, Windsor, Berks
SL4 1NJ
Organist, J. Rees-Williams, FRCO, *apptd* 1991

Other Anglican Churches

THE CHURCH IN WALES

The Anglican Church was the established church in Wales from the 16th century until 1920, when the estrangement of the majority of Welsh people from Anglicanism resulted in disestablishment. Since then the Church in Wales has been an autonomous province consisting of six sees. The bishops are elected by an electoral college comprising elected lay and clerical members, who also elect one of the diocesan bishops as Archbishop of Wales.

The legislative body of the Church in Wales is the Governing Body, which has 365 members divided between the three orders of bishops, clergy and laity. Its President is the Archbishop of Wales and it meets twice annually. Its decisions are binding upon all members of the Church. The Church's property and finances are the responsibility of the Representative Body. There are about 96,000 members of the Church in Wales, with about 700 stipendiary clergy and 1,142 parishes.

THE GOVERNING BODY OF THE CHURCH IN WALES, 39 Cathedral Road, Cardiff CF1 9XF. Tel: 01222-231638. *Secretary-General*, J. W. D. McIntyre

10TH ARCHBISHOP OF WALES, vacant

BISHOPS
Bangor (79th), vacant
Llandaff (102nd), Rt. Revd Dr Barry C. Morgan, b. 1947, *cons.* 1993, *elected* 1999; Llys Esgob, The Cathedral Green, Llandaff, Cardiff CF5 2YE. *Signs* Barry Landav. *Stipendiary clergy*, 164
Monmouth (8th), Rt. Revd Rowan D. Williams, *b* 1950, *cons.* 1992, *elected* 1992; Bishopstow, Stow Hill, Newport NP2 4EA. *Signs* Rowan Monmouth. *Stipendiary clergy*, 115
St Asaph (74th), Rt. Revd John S. Davies, b. 1943, *cons.* 1999, *elected* 1999; Esgobty, St Asaph, Clwyd LL17 0TW. *Signs* Cambrensis. *Stipendiary clergy*, 112
St David's (126th), Rt. Revd D. Huw Jones, b. 1934, *cons.* 1993, *elected* 1995; Llys Esgob, Abergwili, Carmarthen SA31 2JG. *Signs* Huw St Davids. *Stipendiary clergy*, 135
Swansea and Brecon (8th), Rt. Revd Anthony E. Pierce, b. 1941, *cons.* 1999, *elected* 1999; Ely Tower, Brecon, Powys LD3 9DE. *Signs* Anthony Swansea & Brecon. *Stipendiary clergy*, 100

The stipend of a diocesan bishop of the Church in Wales is £26,674 a year from 1998

THE SCOTTISH EPISCOPAL CHURCH

The Scottish Episcopal Church was founded after the Act of Settlement (1690) established the presbyterian nature of the Church of Scotland. The Scottish Episcopal Church is in full communion with the Church of England but is autonomous. The governing authority is the General Synod, an elected body of 180 members which meets once a year. The diocesan bishop who convenes and presides at meetings of the General Synod is called the Primus and is elected by his fellow bishops.

There are 51,353 members of the Scottish Episcopal Church, of whom 32,047 are communicants. There are seven bishops, 175 stipendiary clergy, and 320 churches and places of worship.

THE GENERAL SYNOD OF THE SCOTTISH EPISCOPAL CHURCH, 21 Grosvenor Crescent, Edinburgh EH12 5EE. Tel: 0131-225 6357. *Secretary-General*, J. F. Stuart

PRIMUS OF THE SCOTTISH EPISCOPAL CHURCH, Most Revd Richard F. Holloway (Bishop of Edinburgh), *elected* 1992

BISHOPS
Aberdeen and Orkney, A. Bruce Cameron, b. 1941, *cons.* 1992, *elected* 1992. *Clergy*, 23
Argyll and the Isles, Douglas M. Cameron, b. 1935, *cons.* 1993, *elected* 1992. *Clergy*, 8
Brechin, Neville Chamberlain, b. 1939, *cons.* 1997, *elected* 1997. *Clergy*, 16
Edinburgh, Richard F. Holloway, b. 1933, *cons.* 1986, *elected* 1986. *Clergy*, 52
Glasgow and Galloway, Idris Jones, b. 1943, *cons.* 1998, *elected* 1998. *Clergy*, 41
Moray, Ross and Caithness, John Crook, b. 1940, Bishop Elect. *Clergy*, 10
St Andrews, Dunkeld and Dunblane, Michael H. G. Henley, b. 1938, *cons.* 1995, *elected* 1995. *Clergy*, 25

The minimum stipend of a diocesan bishop of the Scottish Episcopal Church was £22,410 in 1998 (i.e. 1.5 × the minimum clergy stipend of £14,940)

THE CHURCH OF IRELAND

The Anglican Church was the established church in Ireland from the 16th century but never secured the allegiance of a majority of the Irish and was disestablished in 1871. The Church in Ireland is divided into the provinces of Armagh and Dublin, each under an archbishop. The provinces are subdivided into 12 dioceses.

The legislative body is the General Synod, which has 660 members in total, divided between the House of Bishops and the House of Representatives. The Archbishop of Armagh is elected by the House of Bishops; other episcopal elections are made by an electoral college.

There are about 375,000 members of the Church of Ireland, with two archbishops, ten bishops, about 600 clergy and about 1,000 churches and places of worship.

CENTRAL OFFICE, Church of Ireland House, Church Avenue, Rathmines, Dublin 6. Tel: 00-353-1-4978422. *Chief Officer and Secretary of the Representative Church Body*, R. H. Sherwood; *Assistant Secretary of the General Synod*, V. F. Beatty

PROVINCE OF ARMAGH

ARCHBISHOP OF ARMAGH AND PRIMATE OF ALL IRELAND, Most Revd Robert H. A. Eames, PH.D., b. 1937, *cons.* 1975, *trans.* 1986. *Clergy*, 51
BISHOPS
Clogher, Brian D. A. Hannon, b. 1936, *cons.* 1986, *apptd* 1986. *Clergy*, 32
Connor, James E. Moore, b. 1933, *cons.* 1995, *apptd* 1995. *Clergy*, 106
Derry and Raphoe, James Mehaffey, PH.D., b. 1931, *cons.* 1980, *apptd* 1980. *Clergy*, 50
Down and Dromore, Harold C. Miller, b. 1950, *cons.* 1997, *apptd* 1997. *Clergy*, 109
Kilmore, Elphin and Ardagh, Michael H. G. Mayes, b. 1941, *cons.* 1993, *apptd* 1993. *Clergy*, 24
Tuam, Killala and Achonry, Richard C. A. Henderson, b. 1957, *cons.* 1998, *apptd* 1998. *Clergy*, 12

PROVINCE OF DUBLIN

ARCHBISHOP OF DUBLIN, BISHOP OF GLENDALOUGH, AND PRIMATE OF IRELAND, Most Revd Walton N. F. Empey, *b.* 1934, *cons.* 1981, *trans.* 1985, 1996. *Clergy,* 90
BISHOPS
Cashel and Ossory, John R. W. Neill, *b.* 1945, *cons.* 1986, *trans.* 1997. *Clergy,* 37
Cork, Cloyne and Ross, W. Paul Colton, *b.* 1960, *cons.* 1999, *apptd* 1999. *Clergy,* 28
Limerick and Killaloe, Edward F. Darling, *b.* 1933, *cons.* 1985, *apptd* 1985. *Clergy,* 23
Meath and Kildare, (Most Revd) Robert L. Clarke, PH.D., *b.* 1949, *cons.* 1996, *apptd* 1996. *Clergy,* 23

OVERSEAS

PRIMATES

PRIMATE AND PRESIDING BISHOP OF AOTEAROA, NEW ZEALAND AND POLYNESIA, Rt. Revd John Paterson (Bishop of Auckland), *cons.* 1995, *apptd* 1998
PRIMATE OF AUSTRALIA, (until November 1999; election due February 2000) Most Revd Keith Rayner (Archbishop of Melbourne), *cons.* 1969, *apptd* 1991
PRIMATE OF BRAZIL, Most Revd Glauco Soares de Lima (Bishop of São Paulo), *cons.* 1989, *apptd* 1994
ARCHBISHOP OF THE PROVINCE OF BURUNDI, Most Revd Samuel Ndayisenga (Bishop of Buye), *apptd* 1998
ARCHBISHOP AND PRIMATE OF CANADA, Most Revd Michael G. Peers, *cons.* 1977, *elected* 1986
ARCHBISHOP OF THE PROVINCE OF CENTRAL AFRICA, Most Revd Walter P. K. Makhulu (Bishop of Botswana), *cons.* 1979, *apptd* 1980
PRIMATE OF THE CENTRAL REGION OF AMERICA, Most Revd Cornelius J. Wilson (Bishop of Costa Rica), *cons.* 1978, *apptd* 1998
ARCHBISHOP OF THE PROVINCE OF CONGO, Most Revd Byankya Njojo (Bishop of Boga), *cons.* 1980, *apptd* 1992
PRIMATE OF THE PROVINCE OF HONG KONG SHENG KUNG HUI, Most Revd Peter Kwong (Bishop of Hong Kong Island), *cons.*1981, *apptd* 1998
ARCHBISHOP OF THE PROVINCE OF THE INDIAN OCEAN, Most Revd Remi Rabenirina (Bishop of Antananarivo), *cons.* 1984, *apptd* 1995
PRIMATE OF JAPAN, Rt. Revd John M. Takeda (Bishop of Tokyo), *cons.* 1988, *apptd* 1998
PRESIDENT-BISHOP OF JERUSALEM AND THE MIDDLE EAST, (until May 2000) Rt. Revd Ghais A. Malik (Bishop of Egypt), *cons.* 1984, *apptd* 1996
ARCHBISHOP OF THE PROVINCE OF KENYA, Most Revd Dr David M. Gitari (Bishop of Nairobi), *cons.* 1975, *apptd* 1996
ARCHBISHOP OF THE PROVINCE OF KOREA, Most Revd Matthew Chul Bum Chung (Bishop of Seoul), *cons.* 1995, *apptd* 1998
ARCHBISHOP OF THE PROVINCE OF MELANESIA, Most Revd Ellison L. Pogo (Bishop of Central Melanesia), *cons.* 1981, *apptd* 1994
ARCHBISHOP OF MEXICO, Most Revd Samuel Espinoza (Bishop of Western Mexico), *cons.* 1981, *elected* 1995
ARCHBISHOP OF THE PROVINCE OF MYANMAR, Most Revd Andrew Mya Han (Bishop of Yangon), *cons.* 1988, *apptd* 1988
ARCHBISHOP OF THE PROVINCE OF NIGERIA, (until December 1999) Most Revd Joseph Adetiloye (Bishop of Lagos), *cons.* 1970, *apptd* 1991

ARCHBISHOP OF PAPUA NEW GUINEA, Most Revd James Ayong (Bishop of Aipo Rongo), *cons.* 1995, *elected* 1996
PRIME BISHOP OF THE PHILIPPINES, Most Revd Ignacio C. Soliba, *cons.* 1991, *apptd* 1997
ARCHBISHOP OF THE PROVINCE OF RWANDA, Most Revd Kolini Mboni (Bishop of Kigali), *cons.* 1980, *apptd* 1997
PRIMATE OF THE PROVINCE OF SOUTH EAST ASIA, Most Revd Moses Tay (Bishop of Singapore), *cons.* 1982 *apptd* 1996
METROPOLITAN OF THE PROVINCE OF SOUTHERN AFRICA, Most Revd Winston H. N. Ndungane (Archbishop of Cape Town), *cons.* 1991, *trans.* 1996
PRESIDING BISHOP OF THE SOUTHERN CONE OF AMERICA, Rt. Revd Maurice Sinclair (Bishop of Northern Argentina), *cons.* 1990
ARCHBISHOP OF THE PROVINCE OF THE SUDAN,vacant; election due February 2000
ARCHBISHOP OF THE PROVINCE OF TANZANIA, Most Revd Donald L. Mtetemela (Bishop of Ruaha), *cons.* 1982, *apptd* 1998
ARCHBISHOP OF THE PROVINCE OF UGANDA, Most Revd Mpalanyi-Nkoyoyo. *cons.* 1980
PRESIDING BISHOP AND PRIMATE OF THE USA, Most Revd Frank T. Griswold III, *cons.* 1985, *apptd* 1997
ARCHBISHOP OF THE PROVINCE OF WEST AFRICA, Most Revd Robert Okine (Bishop of Koforidua), *cons.* 1981, *apptd* 1993
ARCHBISHOP OF THE PROVINCE OF THE WEST INDIES, Most Revd Drexel Wellington Gomez (Bishop of Nassau and the Bahamas), *cons.* 1972, *apptd* 1998

OTHER CHURCHES AND EXTRA-PROVINCIAL DIOCESES

ANGLICAN CHURCH OF BERMUDA, Rt. Revd Ewen Ratteray, *apptd* 1996
CHURCH OF CEYLON: This Church comes under the Metropolitical authority of the Archbishop of Canterbury.
Bishop of Colombo, Rt. Revd. Kenneth Michael James Fernando, *cons.* 1992
Bishop of Kurunagala, Rt. Revd Andrew O. Kumarage, *cons.* 1984
EPISCOPAL CHURCH OF CUBA, Rt. Revd Jorge Perera Hurtado, *apptd* 1995
LUSITANIAN CHURCH (*Portuguese Episcopal Church*), Rt. Revd Fernando da Luz Soares, *apptd* 1971
SPANISH REFORMED EPISCOPAL CHURCH, Rt. Revd Carlos Lozano Lopez, *apptd* 1995
EXTRA-PROVINCIAL TO PROVINCE IX OF THE EPISCOPAL CHURCH IN THE USA:
PUERTO RICO, Rt. Revd David Andres Alvarez-Velazquez, *cons.* 1987
VENEZUELA, Rt. Revd Orlando Guerrero, *cons.* 1995

MODERATORS OF CHURCHES IN FULL COMMUNION WITH THE ANGLICAN COMMUNION

CHURCH OF NORTH INDIA, Rt. Revd Vinod Anandrao R. Peter (Bishop of Nagpur), *apptd* 1998
CHURCH OF SOUTH INDIA, Most Revd William Moses (Bishop of Coimbatore), *cons.* 1987, *apptd* 1998
CHURCH OF PAKISTAN, Rt. Revd Samuel Azariah, Bishop of Raiwind
CHURCH OF BANGLADESH, Rt. Revd Barnabas Mondal, *cons.* 1975, *apptd* 1975

The Church of Scotland

The Church of Scotland is the established (i.e. national) church of Scotland. The Church is Reformed and evangelical in doctrine, and presbyterian in constitution, i.e. based on a hierarchy of councils of ministers and elders and, since 1990, of members of a diaconate. At local level the kirk session consists of the parish minister and ruling elders. At district level the presbyteries, of which there are 47, consist of all the ministers in the district, one ruling elder from each congregation, and those members of the diaconate who qualify for membership. The General Assembly is the supreme authority, and is presided over by a Moderator chosen annually by the Assembly. The Sovereign, if not present in person, is represented by a Lord High Commissioner who is appointed each year by the Crown.

The Church of Scotland has about 700,000 members, 1,200 ministers and 1,600 churches. There are about 100 ministers and other personnel working overseas.

Lord High Commissioner (1999), The Lord Hogg of
    Cumbernauld
Moderator of the General Assembly (1999), The Rt. Revd John
    B. Cairns
Principal Clerk, Revd F. A. J. Macdonald
Depute Clerk, Revd M. A. MacLean
Procurator, R. A. Dunlop, QC
Law Agent and Solicitor of the Church, Mrs J. S. Wilson
Parliamentary Agent, I. McCulloch (*London*)
General Treasurer, D. F. Ross
Secretary, Church and Nation Committee, Revd Dr D. Sinclair
CHURCH OFFICE, 121 George Street, Edinburgh
EH2 4YN. Tel: 0131-225 5722

PRESBYTERIES AND CLERKS
Edinburgh, Revd W. P. Graham
West Lothian, Revd D. Shaw
Lothian, J. D. McCulloch

Melrose and Peebles, Revd J. H. Brown
Duns, Revd A. C. D. Cartwright
Jedburgh, Revd A. D. Reid

Annandale and Eskdale, Revd C. B. Haston
Dumfries and Kirkcudbright, Revd G. M. A. Savage
Wigtown and Stranraer, Revd D. Dutton

Ayr, Revd J. Crichton
Irvine and Kilmarnock, Revd C. G. F. Brockie
Ardrossan, Revd D. Broster

Lanark, Revd I. D. Cunningham
Paisley, Revd D. Kay
Greenock, Revd D. Mill
Glasgow, Revd A. Cunningham
Hamilton, Revd J. H. Wilson
Dumbarton, Revd D. P. Munro

South Argyll, M. A. J. Gossip
Dunoon, Revd R. Samuel
Lorn and Mull, Revd W. Hogg

Falkirk, Revd D. E. McClements
Stirling, Revd B. W. Dunsmore

Dunfermline, Revd W. E. Farquhar
Kirkcaldy, Revd B. L. Tomlinson
St Andrews, Revd P. Meager

Dunkeld and Meigle, Revd A. B. Reid
Perth, Revd A. M. Millar
Dundee, Revd J. A. Roy
Angus, Revd M. I. G. Rooney

Aberdeen, Revd A. Douglas
Kincardine and Deeside, Revd J. W. S. Brown
Gordon, Revd I. U. Thomson
Buchan, Revd R. Neilson
Moray, Revd D. J. Ferguson

Abernethy, Revd J. A. I. MacEwan
Inverness, Revd A. S. Younger
Lochaber, Revd A. Ramsay

Ross, Revd R. M. MacKinnon
Sutherland, Revd J. L. Goskirk
Caithness, Revd M. G. Mappin
Lochcarron/Skye, Revd A. I. Macarthur
Uist, Revd M. Smith
Lewis, Revd T. S. Sinclair

Orkney (*Finstown*), Revd T. Hunt
Shetland (*Lerwick*), Revd N. R. Whyte
England (*London*), Revd W. A. Cairns

Europe (*Geneva*), Revd J. W. McLeod

The minimum stipend of a minister in the Church of Scotland in 1998 was £16,737

The Roman Catholic Church

The Roman Catholic Church is one world-wide Christian Church acknowledging as its head the Bishop of Rome, known as the Pope (Father). The Pope is held to be the successor of St Peter and thus invested with the power which was entrusted to St Peter by Jesus Christ. A direct line of succession is therefore claimed from the earliest Christian communities. With the fall of the Roman Empire the Pope also became an important political leader. His temporal power is now limited to the 107 acres of the Vatican City State.

The Pope exercises spiritual authority over the Church with the advice and assistance of the Sacred College of Cardinals, the supreme council of the Church. He is also advised about the concerns of the Church locally by his ambassadors, who liaise with the Bishops' Conference in each country.

In addition to advising the Pope, those members of the Sacred College of Cardinals who are under the age of 80 also elect a successor following the death of a Pope. The assembly of the Cardinals at the Vatican for the election of a new Pope is known as the Conclave in which, in complete seclusion, the Cardinals elect by a secret ballot; a two-thirds majority is necessary before the vote can be accepted as final. When a Cardinal receives the necessary votes, the Dean of the Sacred College formally asks him if he will accept election and the name by which he wishes to be known. On his acceptance of the office the Conclave is dissolved and the First Cardinal Deacon announces the election to the assembled crowd in St Peter's Square. On the first Sunday or Holyday following the election, the new Pope assumes the pontificate at High Mass in St Peter's Square. A new pontificate is dated from the assumption of the pontificate.

The number of cardinals was fixed at 70 by Pope Sixtus V in 1586, but has been steadily increased since the pontificate of John XXIII and at the end of June 1999 stood at 157, plus two cardinals created 'in pectore' (their names being kept secret by the Pope for fear of persecution; they are thought to be Chinese).

The Roman Catholic Church universally and the Vatican City State are run by the Curia, which is made up of the Secretariat of State, the Sacred Council for the Public Affairs of the Church, and various congregations, secretariats and tribunals assisted by commissions and offices. The congregations are permanent commissions for conducting the affairs of the Church and are made up of cardinals, one of whom occupies the office of prefect. Below the Secretariat of State and the congregations are the secretariats and tribunals, all of which are headed by cardinals. (The Curial cardinals are analagous to ministers in charge of government departments.)

The Vatican State has its own diplomatic service, with representatives known as nuncios. Papal nuncios with full diplomatic recognition are given precedence over all other ambassadors to the country to which they are appointed; where precedence is not recognized the Papal representative is known as a pro-nuncio. Where the representation is only to the local churches and not to the government of a country, the Papal representative is known as an apostolic delegate. The Roman Catholic Church has an estimated 890.9 million adherents world-wide.

SOVEREIGN PONTIFF

His Holiness Pope John Paul II (Karol Wojtyla), *born* Wadowice, Poland, 18 May 1920; *ordained priest* 1946; *appointed Archbishop* of Krakow 1964; *created Cardinal* 1967; *assumed pontificate* 16 October 1978

SECRETARIAT OF STATE

Secretary of State, HE Cardinal Angelo Sodano
First Section (General Affairs), Mgr G. Re (Archbishop of Vescovio)
Second Section (Relations with other states), Mgr J. L. Tauran (Archbishop of Telepte)

BISHOPS' CONFERENCE

The Roman Catholic Church in England and Wales is governed by the Bishops' Conference, membership of which includes the Diocesan Bishops, the Apostolic Exarch of the Ukrainians, the Bishop of the Forces and the Auxiliary Bishops. The Conference is headed by the President and Vice-President. There are five departments, each with an episcopal chairman: the Department for Christian Life and Worship (the Archbishop of Southwark), the Department for Mission and Unity (the Bishop of Arundel and Brighton), the Department for Catholic Education and Formation (the Bishop of Leeds), the Department for Christian Responsibility and Citizenship (the Bishop of Plymouth), and the Department for International Affairs.

The Bishops' Standing Committee, made up of all the Archbishops and the chairman of each of the above departments, has general responsibility for continuity and policy between the plenary sessions of the Conference. It prepares the Conference agenda and implements its decisions. It is serviced by a General Secretariat. There are also agencies and consultative bodies affiliated to the Conference.

The Bishops' Conference of Scotland has as its president Archbishop Winning of Glasgow and is the permanently constituted assembly of the Bishops of Scotland. To promote its work, the Conference establishes various agencies which have an advisory function in relation to the Conference. The more important of these agencies are called Commissions and each one has a Bishop President who, with the other members of the Commissions, are appointed by the Conference.

The Irish Episcopal Conference has as its acting president Archbishop Connell of Dublin. Its membership comprises all the Archbishops and Bishops of Ireland and it appoints various Commissions to assist it in its work.

There are three types of Commissions: (a) those made up of lay and clerical members chosen for their skills and experience, and staffed by full-time expert secretariats; (b) Commissions whose members are selected from existing institutions and whose services are supplied on a part-time basis; and (c) Commissions of Bishops only.

The Roman Catholic Church in Britain and Ireland has an estimated 8,992,000 members, 11 archbishops, 67 bishops, 11,260 priests, and 8,588 churches and chapels open to the public.

Bishops' Conferences secretariats:

ENGLAND AND WALES, 39 Eccleston Square, London SW1V 1PD. Tel: 0171-630 8220. *General Secretary*, The Rt. Revd Arthur Roche

SCOTLAND, Candida Casa, 8 Corsehill Road, Ayr, Scotland KA7 2ST. Tel: 01292-256750. *General Secretary*, The Rt. Revd Maurice Taylor (Bishop of Galloway)

IRELAND, Iona, 65 Newry Road, Dundalk, Co. Louth. *Executive Secretary*, Revd Hugh G. Connelly

GREAT BRITAIN

APOSTOLIC NUNCIO TO GREAT BRITAIN

The Most Revd Pablo Puente, 54 Parkside, London SW19 5NE. Tel: 0181-946 1410

ENGLAND AND WALES

THE MOST REVD ARCHBISHOPS

Westminster, vacant
Auxiliaries, Vincent Nichols, *cons.* 1992; James J. O'Brien, *cons.* 1977; Patrick O'Donoghue, *cons.* 1993
Clergy, 789
Archbishop's Residence, Archbishop's House, Ambrosden Avenue, London SW1P 1QJ. Tel: 0171-798 9033
Birmingham, vacant
Auxiliaries, Philip Pargeter, *cons.* 1990
Clergy, 490
Diocesan Curia, Cathedral House, St Chad's Queensway, Birmingham B4 6EX. Tel: 0121-236 5535
Cardiff, John A. Ward, *cons.* 1980, *apptd* 1983
Clergy, 137
Diocesan Curia, Archbishop's House, 41–43 Cathedral Road, Cardiff CF1 9HD. Tel: 01222-220411
Liverpool, Patrick Kelly, *cons.* 1984, *apptd* 1996
Auxiliary, Vincent Malone, *cons.* 1989
Clergy, 533
Diocesan Curia, 152 Brownlow Hill, Liverpool L3 5RQ. Tel: 0151-709 4801
Southwark, Michael Bowen, *cons.* 1970, *apptd* 1977
Auxiliaries, Charles Henderson, *cons.* 1972; Howard Tripp, *cons.* 1980; John Jukes, *cons.* 1980
Clergy, 516
Diocesan Curia, Archbishop's House, 150 St George's Road, London SE1 6HX. Tel: 0171-928 5592

THE RT. REVD BISHOPS

Arundel and Brighton, Cormac Murphy-O'Connor, *cons.* 1977. *Clergy*, 313. *Diocesan Curia*, Bishop's House, The Upper Drive, Hove, E. Sussex BN3 6NE. Tel: 01273-506387
Brentwood, Thomas McMahon, *cons.* 1980, *apptd* 1980. *Clergy*, 174. *Bishop's Office*, Cathedral House, Ingrave Road, Brentwood, Essex CM15 8AT. Tel: 01277-232266
Clifton, Mervyn Alexander, *cons.* 1972, *apptd* 1974. *Clergy*, 251. *Diocesan Curia*, Egerton Road, Bishopston, Bristol BS7 8HU. Tel: 0117-983 3907

East Anglia, Peter Smith, *cons.* 1995, *apptd* 1995. *Clergy*, 173. *Diocesan Curia*, The White House, 21 Upgate, Poringland, Norwich NR14 7SH. Tel: 01508-492202

Hallam, John Rawsthorne, *cons.* 1981, *apptd* 1997. *Clergy*, 89. *Bishop's Residence*, 'Quarters', Carsick Hill Way, Sheffield S10 3LY. Tel: 0114-230 9101

Hexham and Newcastle, Michael Ambrose Griffiths, *cons.* 1992. *Clergy*, 259. *Diocesan Curia*, Bishop's House, East Denton Hall, 800 West Road, Newcastle upon Tyne NE5 2BJ. Tel: 0191-228 0003

Lancaster, John Brewer, *cons.* 1971, *apptd* 1985. *Clergy*, 256. *Bishop's Residence*, Bishop's House, Cannon Hill, Lancaster LA1 5NG. Tel: 01524-32231

Leeds, David Konstant, *cons.* 1977, *apptd* 1985. *Clergy*, 253. *Diocesan Curia*, 7 St Marks Avenue, Leeds LS2 9BN. Tel: 0113-244 4788

Menevia (Wales), Daniel Mullins, *cons.* 1970, *apptd* 1987. *Clergy*, 61. *Diocesan Curia*, 27 Convent Street, Swansea SA1 2BX. Tel: 01792-644017

Middlesbrough, John Crowley, *cons.* 1986, *apptd* 1992. *Clergy*, 187. *Diocesan Curia*, 50A The Avenue, Linthorpe, Middlesbrough, Cleveland TS5 6QT. Tel: 01642-850505

Northampton, Patrick Leo McCartie, *cons.* 1977, *apptd* 1990. *Clergy*, 154. *Diocesan Curia*, Bishop's House, Marriott Street, Northampton NN2 6AW. Tel: 01604-715635

Nottingham, James McGuinness, *cons.* 1972, *apptd* 1974. *Clergy*, 217. *Diocesan Curia*, Willson House, Derby Road, Nottingham NG1 5AW. Tel: 0115-953 9800

Plymouth, Christopher Budd, *cons.* 1986. *Clergy*, 143. *Diocesan Curia*, Bishop's House, 31 Wyndham Street West, Plymouth PL1 5RZ. Tel: 01752-224414

Portsmouth, F. Crispian Hollis, *cons.* 1987, *apptd* 1989. *Clergy*, 268. *Bishop's Residence*, Bishop's House, Edinburgh Road, Portsmouth, Hants PO1 3HG. Tel: 01705-820894

Salford, Terence J. Brain, *cons.* 1991, *apptd* 1997. *Clergy*, 394. *Diocesan Curia*, Cathedral House, 250 Chapel Street, Salford M3 5LL. Tel: 0161-834 9052

Shrewsbury, Brian Noble, *cons.* 1995, *apptd* 1995. *Clergy* 196. *Diocesan Curia*, 2 Park Road South, Birkenhead, Merseyside L43 4UX. Tel: 0151-652 9855

Wrexham (Wales), Edwin Regan, *apptd* 1994. *Clergy*, 86. *Diocesan Curia*, Bishop's House, Sontley Road, Wrexham, Clwyd LL13 7EW. Tel: 01978-262726

SCOTLAND

THE MOST REVD ARCHBISHOPS
St Andrews and Edinburgh, Keith Patrick O'Brien, *cons.* 1985 *Clergy*, 192
Diocesan Curia, 113 Whitehouse Loan, Edinburgh EH9 1BD. Tel: 0131-452 8244
Glasgow, HE Cardinal Thomas Winning, *cons.* 1971, *apptd* 1974
Clergy, 253
Diocesan Curia, 196 Clyde Street, Glasgow G1 4JY. Tel: 0141-226 5898

THE RT. REVD BISHOPS
Aberdeen, Mario Conti, *cons.* 1977. *Clergy*, 58. *Bishop's Residence*, 3 Queen's Cross, Aberdeen AB2 6BR. Tel: 01224-319154
Argyll and the Isles, vacant. *Clergy*, 33. *Diocesan Curia*, St Columba's Cathedral, Esplanade, Oban, Argyll PA34 5AB. Tel: 01631-571003
Dunkeld, Vincent Logan, *cons.* 1981. *Clergy*, 51. *Diocesan Curia*, 29 Roseangle, Dundee DD1 4LR. Tel: 01382-25453
Galloway, Maurice Taylor, *cons.* 1981. *Clergy*, 66. *Diocesan Curia*, 8 Corsehill Road, Ayr KA7 2ST. Tel: 01292-266750
Motherwell, Joseph Devine, *cons.* 1977, *apptd* 1983. *Clergy*, 168. *Diocesan Curia*, Coursington Road, Motherwell ML1 1PW. Tel: 01698-269114

Paisley, John A. Mone, *cons.* 1984, *apptd* 1988. *Clergy*, 86. *Diocesan Curia*, Cathedral House, 8 East Buchanan Street, Paisley, Renfrewshire PA1 1HS. Tel: 0141-889 3601

BISHOPRIC OF THE FORCES

Francis Walmsley, *cons.* 1979. Administration: AGPDO, Middle Hill, Aldershot, Hants GU11 1PP. Tel: 01252-349004

IRELAND

There is one hierarchy for the whole of Ireland. Several of the dioceses have territory partly in the Republic of Ireland and partly in Northern Ireland.

APOSTOLIC NUNCIO TO IRELAND
Most Revd Giovanni Ceirano (titular Archbishop of Tigimma), 183 Navan Road, Dublin 7. Tel: 00 353 1-380577

THE MOST REVD ARCHBISHOPS
Armagh, Sean Brady, *cons.* 1995, *apptd* 1996
Auxiliary, Gerard Clifford, *cons.* 1991
Clergy, 183
Diocesan Curia, Ara Coeli, Armagh BT61 7QY. Tel: 01861-522045
Cashel, Dermot Clifford, *cons.* 1986, *apptd* 1988
Clergy, 136
Archbishop's Residence, Archbishop's House, Thurles, Co. Tipperary. Tel: 00 353 504-21512
Dublin, Desmond Connell, *cons.* 1988, *apptd* 1988
Auxiliaries, James Moriarty, *cons.* 1991; Eamonn Walsh, *cons.* 1990; Fiachra O'Ceallaigh, *cons* 1994; Martin Drennan, *cons.* 1997; Raymond Field, *cons.* 1997
Clergy, 994
Archbishop's Residence, Archbishop's House, Drumcondra, Dublin 9. Tel: 00 353 1-8373732
Tuam, Michael Neary, *cons.* 1992, *apptd* 1995
Clergy, 180
Archbishop's Residence, Archbishop's House, Tuam, Co. Galway. Tel: 00 353 93-24166

THE MOST REVD BISHOPS
Achonry, Thomas Flynn, *cons.* 1975. *Clergy*, 62. *Bishop's Residence*, Bishop's House, Ballaghadaderreen, Co. Roscommon. Tel: 00 353 907-60021
Ardagh and Clonmacnois, Colm O'Reilly, *cons.* 1983. *Clergy*, 100. *Diocesan Office*, Bishop's House, St Michael's, Longford, Co. Longford. Tel: 00 353 43-46432
Clogher, Joseph Duffy, *cons.* 1979. *Clergy*, 108. *Bishop's Residence*, Bishop's House, Monaghan. Tel: 00 353 47-81019
Clonfert, Joseph Kirby, *cons.* 1988. *Clergy*, 71. *Bishop's Residence*, St Brendan's, Coorheen, Loughrea, Co. Galway. Tel: 00 353 91-41560
Cloyne, John Magee, *cons.* 1987. *Clergy*, 158. *Diocesan Centre*, Cobh, Co. Cork. Tel: 00 353 21-811430
Cork and Ross, John Buckley, *cons.* 1984, *apptd* 1998. *Clergy*, 338. *Diocesan Office*, Bishop's House, Redemption Road, Cork. Tel: 00 353 21-301717
Derry, Seamus Hegarty, *cons.* 1984, *apptd* 1994. *Clergy*, 157. *Bishop's Residence*, Bishop's House, St Eugene's Cathedral, Derry BT48 9AP. Tel: 01504-262302
Auxiliary, Francis Lagan, *cons.* 1988
Down and Connor, Patrick J. Walsh, *cons.* 1983, *apptd* 1991. *Clergy*, 248. *Bishop's Residence*, Lisbreen, 73 Somerton Road, Belfast, Co. Antrim BT15 4DE. Tel: 01232-776185
Auxiliaries, Anthony Farquhar, *cons.* 1983; Michael Dallat, *cons.* 1994

Dromore, Francis Brooks, *cons.* 1976. *Clergy*, 78. *Bishop's Residence*, Bishop's House, Violet Hill, Newry, Co. Down BT35 6PN. Tel: 01693-62444

Elphin, Christopher Jones, *cons.* 1994. *Clergy*, 101. *Bishop's Residence*, St Mary's, Sligo. Tel: 00 353 71-62670

Ferns, Brendon Comiskey, *cons.* 1980. *Clergy*, 161. *Bishop's Office*, Bishop's House, Summerhill, Wexford. Tel: 00 353 53-22177

Galway and Kilmacduagh, James McLoughlin, *cons.* 1993. *Clergy*, 90. *Diocesan Office*, The Cathedral, Galway. Tel: 00 353 91-63566

Kerry, William Murphy, *cons.* 1995. *Clergy*, 149. *Bishop's Residence*, Bishop's House, Killarney, Co. Kerry. Tel: 00 353 64-31168

Kildare and Leighlin, Laurence Ryan, *cons.* 1984. *Clergy*, 136. *Bishop's Residence*, Bishop's House, Carlow. Tel: 00 353 503-31102

Killala, Thomas Finnegan, *cons.* 1970. *Clergy*, 62. *Bishop's Residence*, Bishop's House, Ballina, Co. Mayo. Tel: 00 353 96-21518

Killaloe, William Walsh, *cons.* 1994. *Clergy*, 149. *Bishop's Residence*, Westbourne, Ennis, Co. Clare. Tel: 00 353 65-28638

Kilmore, Francis McKiernan, *cons.* 1972. *Coadjutor*, Leo O'Reilly. *Clergy*, 115. *Bishop's Residence*, Bishop's House, Cullies, Co. Cavan. Tel: 00 353 49-31496

Limerick, Donal Murray, *cons.* 1996. *Clergy*, 152. *Diocesan Offices*, 66 O'Connell Street, Limerick. Tel: 00 353 61-315856

Meath, Michael Smith, *cons.* 1984, *apptd* 1990. *Clergy*, 141. *Bishop's Residence*, Bishop's House, Dublin Road, Mullingar, Co. Westmeath. Tel: 00 353 44-48841

Ossory, Laurence Forristal, *cons.* 1980. *Clergy*, 111. *Bishop's Residence*, Sion House, Kilkenny. Tel: 00 353 56-62448

Raphoe, Philip Boyce, *cons.* 1994. *Clergy*, 96. *Bishop's Residence*, Ard Adhamhnáin, Letterkenny, Co. Donegal. Tel: 00 353 74-21208

Waterford and Lismore, William Lee, *cons.* 1993. *Clergy*, 130. *Bishop's Residence*, Woodleigh, Summerville Avenue, Waterford. Tel: 00 353 51-71432

PATRIARCHS IN COMMUNION WITH THE ROMAN CATHOLIC CHURCH

Alexandria, HB Stephanos II Ghattas (Patriarch for Catholic Copts)

Antioch, HB Ignace Antoine II Hayek (Patriarch for Syrian rite Catholics); HB Maximos V. Hakim (Patriarch for Greek Melkite rite Catholics); HE Cardinal Nasrallah Pierre Sfeir (Patriarch for Maronite rite Catholics)

Jerusalem, HB Michel Sabbah (Patriarch for Latin rite Catholics); HB Maximos V. Hakim (Patriarch for Greek Melekite rite Catholics)

Babilonia of the Chaldeans, HB Raphael I Bidawid

Cilicia of the Armenians, HB Jean Pierre XVIII Kasparian (Patriarch for Armenian rite Catholics)

Oriental India, Archbishop Raul Nicolau Gonsalves

Lisbon, vacant

Venice, HE Cardinal Marco Ce

Other Churches in the UK

AFRICAN AND AFRO-CARIBBEAN CHURCHES

There are more than 160 Christian churches or groups of African or Afro-Caribbean origin in the UK. These include the Apostolic Faith Church, the Cherubim and Seraphim Church, the New Testament Church Assembly, the New Testament Church of God, the Wesleyan Holiness Church and the Aladura Churches.

The Afro-West Indian United Council of Churches and the Council of African and Afro-Caribbean Churches UK (which was initiated as the Council of African and Allied Churches in 1979 to give one voice to the various Christian churches of African origin in the UK) are the media through which the member churches can work jointly to provide services they cannot easily provide individually.

There are about 70,000 adherents of African and Afro-Caribbean churches in the UK, and about 1,000 congregations. The Afro-West Indian United Council of Churches has about 30,000 individual members, 135 ministers and 65 places of worship. The Council of African and Afro-Caribbean Churches UK has about 17,000 members, 250 ministers and 75 congregations.

AFRO-WEST INDIAN UNITED COUNCIL OF CHURCHES, c/o New Testament Church of God, Arcadian Gardens, High Road, London N22 5AA. Tel: 0181-888 9427. *Secretary*, Bishop E. Brown

COUNCIL OF AFRICAN AND AFRO-CARIBBEAN CHURCHES UK, 31 Norton House, Sidney Road, London SW9 0UJ. Tel: 0171-274 5589. *Chairman*, His Grace The Most Revd Father Olu A. Abiola

ASSOCIATED PRESBYTERIAN CHURCHES OF SCOTLAND

The Associated Presbyterian Churches came into being in 1989 as a result of a division within the Free Presbyterian Church of Scotland. Following two controversial disciplinary cases, the culmination of deepening differences within the Church, a presbytery was formed calling itself the Associated Presbyterian Churches (APC). The Associated Presbyterian Churches has about 1,000 members, 15 ministers and 20 churches.

Clerk of the Scottish Presbytery, Revd Dr M. MacInnes, Drumalin, 16 Drummond Road, Inverness IV2 4NB. Tel: 01463-223983

THE BAPTIST CHURCH

Baptists trace their origins to John Smyth, who in 1609 in Amsterdam reinstituted the baptism of conscious believers as the basis of the fellowship of a gathered church. Members of Smyth's church established the first Baptist church in England in 1612. They came to be known as 'General' Baptists and their theology was Arminian, whereas a later group of Calvinists who adopted the baptism of believers came to be known as 'Particular' Baptists. The two sections of the Baptists were united into one body, the Baptist Union of Great Britain and Ireland, in 1891. In 1988 the title was changed to the Baptist Union of Great Britain.

Baptists emphasize the complete autonomy of the local church, although individual churches are linked in various kinds of associations. There are international bodies (such as the Baptist World Alliance) and national bodies, but some Baptist churches belong to neither. However, in Great Britain the majority of churches and associations belong to the Baptist Union of Great Britain. There are also Baptist Unions in Wales, Scotland and Ireland which are much smaller than the Baptist Union of Great Britain, and there is some overlap of membership.

There are over 40 million Baptist church members world-wide; in the Baptist Union of Great Britain there are 147,089 members, 1,780 pastors and 2,114 churches. In the Baptist Union of Scotland there are 13,587 members, 140 pastors and 171 churches. In the Baptist Union of Wales there are 21,800 members, 110 pastors and 527 churches. In the Association of Baptist Churches (formerly the Baptist Union of Ireland) there are 8,378 members, 90 pastors and 110 churches.

President of the Baptist Union of Great Britain (1999–2000), Revd M. I. Bochenski

General Secretary, Revd D. R. Coffey, Baptist House, PO Box 44, 129 Broadway, Didcot, Oxon OX11 8RT. Tel: 01235-517700

THE CONGREGATIONAL FEDERATION

The Congregational Federation was founded by members of Congregational churches in England and Wales who did not join the United Reformed Church (see p. 422) in 1972. There are also churches in Scotland and Australia affiliated to the Federation. The Federation exists to encourage congregations of believers to worship in free assembly, but it has no authority over them and emphasizes their right to independence and self-government.

The Federation has 11,923 members, 71 recognized ministers and 313 churches in England, Wales and Scotland.

President of the Federation (1999–2000), Revd. R. Waddington

General Secretary, G. M. Adams, The Congregational Centre, 4 Castle Gate, Nottingham NG1 7AS. Tel: 0115-911 1460

THE FREE CHURCH OF ENGLAND

The Free Church of England is a union of two bodies in the Anglican tradition, the Free Church of England, founded in 1844 as a protest against the Oxford Movement in the established Church, and the Reformed Episcopal Church, founded in America in 1873 but which also had congregations in England. As both Churches sought to maintain the historic faith, tradition and practice of the Anglican Church since the Reformation, they decided to unite as one body in England in 1927. The historic episcopate was conferred on the English Church in 1876 through the line of the American bishops, who had pioneered an open table Communion policy towards members of other denominations.

The Free Church of England has 1,500 members, 42 ministers and 25 churches in England. It also has three house churches and three ministers in New Zealand, two churches and one minister in Queensland, Australia, and one church and one minister in St Petersburg, Russia.

General Secretary, Revd W. J. Lawler, 45 Broughton Road, Wallasey, Merseyside CH44 4DT. Tel: 0151-638 2564

THE FREE CHURCH OF SCOTLAND

The Free Church of Scotland was formed in 1843 when over 400 ministers withdrew from the Church of Scotland as a result of interference in the internal affairs of the church by the civil authorities. In 1900, all but 26 ministers joined with others to form the United Free Church (most of which rejoined the Church of Scotland in 1929). In 1904 the remaining 26 ministers were recognized by the House of Lords as continuing the Free Church of Scotland.

The Church maintains strict adherence to the Westminster Confession of Faith (1648) and accepts the Bible as the sole rule of faith and conduct. Its General Assembly meets annually. It also has links with Reformed Churches overseas. The Free Church of Scotland has 6,000 members, 110 ministers and 140 churches.

General Treasurer, I. D. Gill, The Mound, Edinburgh EH1 2LS. Tel: 0131-226 5286

THE FREE PRESBYTERIAN CHURCH OF SCOTLAND

The Free Presbyterian Church of Scotland was formed in 1893 by two ministers of the Free Church of Scotland who refused to accept a Declaratory Act passed by the Free Church General Assembly in 1892. The Free Presbyterian Church of Scotland is Calvinistic in doctrine and emphasizes observance of the Sabbath. It adheres strictly to the Westminster Confession of Faith of 1648.

The Church has about 3,000 members in Scotland and about 4,000 in overseas congregations. It has 20 ministers and 50 churches.

Moderator, Revd G. G. Hutton, Free Presbyterian Manse, Broadford, Isle of Skye IV49 4AQ

Clerk of Synod, Revd J. MacLeod, 16 Matheson Road, Stornoway, Isle of Lewis HS1 2LA. Tel: 01851-702755

THE INDEPENDENT METHODIST CHURCHES

The Independent Methodist Churches seceded from the Wesleyan Methodist Church in 1805 and remained independent when the Methodist Church in Great Britain was formed in 1932. They are mainly concentrated in the industrial areas of the north of England.

The churches are Methodist in doctrine but their organization is congregational. All the churches are members of the Independent Methodist Connexion of Churches. The controlling body of the Connexion is the Annual Meeting, to which churches send delegates. The Connexional President is elected annually. Between annual meetings the affairs of the Connexion are handled by departmental committees. Ministers are appointed by the churches and trained through the Connexion. The ministry is open to both men and women and is unpaid.

There are 3,050 members, 106 ministers and 98 churches in Great Britain.

Connexional President (1999–2000), J. Dolan

General Secretary, J. M. Day, The Old Police House, Croxton, Stafford ST21 6PE. Tel: 0163-062 0671

THE LUTHERAN CHURCH

Lutheranism is based on the teachings of Martin Luther, the German leader of the Protestant Reformation. The authority of the scriptures is held to be supreme over Church tradition and creeds, and the key doctrine is that of justification by faith alone.

Lutheranism is one of the largest Protestant denominations and it is particularly strong in northern Europe and the USA. Some Lutheran churches are episcopal, while others have a synodal form of organization; unity is based on doctrine rather than structure. Most Lutheran churches are members of the Lutheran World Federation, based in Geneva.

Lutheran services in Great Britain are held in seventeen languages to serve members of different nationalities. English-language congregations are members either of the Lutheran Church in Great Britain, or of the Evangelical Lutheran Church of England. The Lutheran Church in Great Britain and other Lutheran churches in Britain are members of the Lutheran Council of Great Britain.

There are over 70 million Lutherans world-wide; in Great Britain there are about 50,000 members, 50 clergy and 100 congregations.

General Secretary of the Lutheran Council of Great Britain, Revd T. Bruch, 30 Thanet Street, London WC1H 9QH. Tel: 0171-383 3081

THE METHODIST CHURCH

The Methodist movement started in England in 1729 when the Revd John Wesley, an Anglican priest, and his brother Charles met with others in Oxford and resolved to conduct their lives and study by 'rule and method'. In 1739 the Wesleys began evangelistic preaching and the first Methodist chapel was founded in Bristol in the same year. In 1744 the first annual conference was held, at which the Articles of Religion were drawn up. Doctrinal emphases included repentance, faith, the assurance of salvation, social concern and the priesthood of all believers. After John Wesley's death in 1791 the Methodists withdrew from the established Church to form the Methodist Church. Methodists gradually drifted into many groups, but in 1932 the Wesleyan Methodist Church, the United Methodist Church and the Primitive Methodist Church united to form the Methodist Church in Great Britain as it now exists.

The governing body and supreme authority of the Methodist Church is the Conference, but there are also 33 district synods, consisting of all the ministers and selected lay people in each district, and circuit meetings of the ministers and lay people of each circuit.

There are over 60 million Methodists world-wide; in Great Britain (1998 figures) there are 353,330 members, 3,727 ministers, 10,746 lay preachers and 6,452 churches.

President of the Conference in Great Britain (1999–2000), Revd S. Burgess
Vice-President of the Conference (1999–2000), B. Thornton
Secretary of the Conference, Revd Dr N. T. Collinson,
Methodist Church, Conference Office, 25 Marylebone Road, London NW1 5JR. Tel: 0171-486 5502

THE METHODIST CHURCH IN IRELAND

The Methodist Church in Ireland is closely linked to British Methodism but is autonomous. It has 16,956 members, 201 ministers, 290 lay preachers and 228 churches.

President of the Methodist Church in Ireland (1999–2000), Revd Dr K. A. Wilson, 137 Wheatfield, Bray, Co. Wicklow, Republic of Ireland. Tel: 1-286 9647

Secretary of the Methodist Church in Ireland, Revd E. T. I. Mawhinney, 1 Fountainville Avenue, Belfast BT9 6AN. Tel: 01232-324554

THE (EASTERN) ORTHODOX CHURCH

The Eastern (or Byzantine) Orthodox Church is a communion of self-governing Christian churches recognizing the honorary primacy of the Oecumenical Patriarch of Constantinople.

The position of Orthodox Christians is that the faith was fully defined during the period of the Oecumenical Councils. In doctrine it is strongly trinitarian, and stresses the mystery and importance of the sacraments. It is episcopal in government. The structure of the Orthodox Christian year differs from that of western Churches (*see* page 82).

Orthodox Christians throughout the world are estimated to number about 300 million.

PATRIARCHS OF THE EASTERN ORTHODOX CHURCH
Archbishop of Constantinople, New Rome and Oecumenical Patriarch, Bartholomew, *elected* 1991
Pope and Patriarch of Alexandria and All Africa, Petros VII, *elected* 1997
Patriarch of Antioch and All the East, Ignatios IV, *elected* 1979
Patriarch of Jerusalem and All Palestine, Diodoros, *elected* 1981
Patriarch of Moscow and All Russia, Alexei II, *elected* 1990
Archbishop of Pec, Metropolitan of Belgrade and Karlovci, Patriarch of Serbia, Pavle, *elected* 1990
Archbishop of Bucharest and Patriarch of Romania, Teoctist, *elected* 1986
Metropolitan of Sofia and Patriarch of Bulgaria, Maxim, *elected* 1971
Archbishop of Tbilisi and Mtskheta, Catholicos-Patriarch of All Georgia, Ilia II, *elected* 1977

HEADS OF AUTOCEPHALOUS ORTHODOX CHURCHES
Archbishop of Cyprus, Chrysostomos, *elected* 1977
Archbishop of Athens and All Greece, Christodoulos, *elected* 1998
Metropolitan of Warsaw and All Poland, Sawa, *elected* 1998
Archbishop of Tirana and All Albania, Anastas, *elected* 1992
Archbishop of Prague and All the Czech Lands and Slovakia, Dorotej, *elected* 1964

EASTERN ORTHODOX CHURCHES IN THE UK

THE PATRIARCHATE OF ANTIOCH

There are ten parishes served by 13 clergy. In Great Britain the Patriarchate is represented by the Revd Fr Samir Gholam, 1A Redhill Street, London NW1 4BG. Tel: 0171-383 0403.

THE GREEK ORTHODOX CHURCH (PATRIARCHATE OF CONSTANTINOPLE)

The presence of Greek Orthodox Christians in Britain dates back at least to 1677 when Archbishop Joseph Geogirenes of Samos fled from Turkish persecution and came to London. The present Greek cathedral in Moscow Road, Bayswater, was opened for public worship in 1879 and the Diocese of Thyateira and Great Britain was established in 1922. There are now 110 parishes and other communities (including monasteries) in Great Britain, served by six bishops, 95 clergy and about 100 churches.

In Great Britain the Patriarchate of Constantinople is

represented by Archbishop Gregorios of Thyateira and Great Britain, 5 Craven Hill, London W2 3EN. Tel: 0171-723 4787.

THE RUSSIAN ORTHODOX CHURCH (PATRIARCHATE OF MOSCOW) AND THE RUSSIAN ORTHODOX CHURCH OUTSIDE RUSSIA
The records of Russian Orthodox Church activities in Britain date from the visit to England of Tsar Peter I in the early 18th century. Clergy were sent from Russia to serve the chapel established to minister to the staff of the Imperial Russian Embassy in London.

In Great Britain the Patriarchate of Moscow is represented by Metropolitan Anthony of Sourozh, 67 Ennismore Gardens, London SW7 1NH. Fax only: 0171-584 9864. He is assisted by one archbishop, one vicar bishop and 26 clergy. There are 27 parishes and smaller communities.

The Russian Orthodox Church Outside Russia is represented by Archbishop Mark of Berlin, Germany and Great Britain, c/o 57 Harvard Road, London W4 4ED. Tel: 0181-742 3493. There are eight communities, including two monasteries, served by eight clergy.

THE SERBIAN ORTHODOX CHURCH (PATRIARCHATE OF SERBIA)
There are 33 parishes and smaller communities in Great Britain served by 12 clergy. The Patriarchate of Serbia is represented by the Episcopal Vicar, the Very Revd Milenko Zebic, 131 Cob Lane, Bournville, Birmingham B30 1QE. Tel: 0121-458 5273.

OTHER NATIONALITIES
Most of the Ukrainian parishes in Britain have joined the Patriarchate of Constantinople, leaving a small number of Ukrainian parishes in Britain under the care of other patriarchates (not all of which are recognized by the other Orthodox churches). The Latvian, Polish and some Belorussian parishes are also under the care of the Patriarchate of Constantinople. The Patriarchate of Romania has one parish served by two clergy. The Patriarchate of Bulgaria has one parish served by one priest. The Belorussian Autocephalous Orthodox Church has five parishes served by two priests.

THE ORIENTAL ORTHODOX CHURCHES

The term 'Oriental Orthodox Churches' is now generally used to describe a group of six ancient eastern churches which reject the Christological definition of the Council of Chalcedon (AD 451) and use Christological terms in different ways from the Eastern Orthodox Church. There are about 34 million members of the Oriental Orthodox Churches.

PATRIARCHS OF THE ORIENTAL ORTHODOX CHURCHES
ARMENIAN ORTHODOX CHURCH – Supreme Patriarch Catholicos of All Armenians (Etchmiadzin), vacant; Catholicos of Cilicia, Aram I, elected 1995; Patriarch of Jerusalem, Torkom II, elected 1994; Patriarch of Constantinople, Mesrob II, elected 1998
COPTIC ORTHODOX CHURCH – Pope of Alexandria and Patriarch of the See of St Mark, Shenouda III, elected 1971
ERITREAN ORTHODOX CHURCH – Patriarch of Eritrea, Philipos I, elected 1998
ETHIOPIAN ORTHODOX CHURCH – Patriarch of Ethiopia, Paulos, elected 1992
MALANKARA ORTHODOX SYRIAN CHURCH – Catholicos of the East, Basilios Mar Thoma Mathews II, elected 1991

SYRIAN ORTHODOX CHURCH – Patriarch of Antioch and All the East, Ignatius Zakka I, elected 1980

ORIENTAL ORTHODOX CHURCHES IN THE UK

THE ARMENIAN ORTHODOX CHURCH
(PATRIARCHATE OF ETCHMIADZIN)
The Armenian Orthodox Church is the longest-established Oriental Orthodox community in Great Britain. It is represented by Archbishop Yeghishe Gizirian, Armenian Primate of Great Britain, Armenian Vicarage, Iverna Gardens, London W8 6TP. Tel: 0171-937 0152.

THE COPTIC ORTHODOX CHURCH
The Coptic Orthodox Church is the largest Oriental Orthodox community in Great Britain. It has four dioceses (Birmingham; Scotland, Ireland and North-East England; the British Orthodox Church; and churches directly under Pope Shenouda III). The senior bishop in Great Britain is Metropolitan Seraphim, 10 Heathwood Gardens, London SE7 8EP. Tel: 0181-854 3090.

THE ERITREAN ORTHODOX CHURCH
In Great Britain the Eritrean Orthodox Church is represented by Bishop Markos, 11 Anfield Close, Weir Road, London SW12 0NT. Tel: 0181-675 5115.

THE ETHIOPIAN ORTHODOX CHURCH
The acting head of the Ethiopian Orthodox Church in Europe is Revd Berhanu Beserat, 33 Jupiter Crescent, London NW1 8HA. Tel: 0956-513700.

THE MALANKARA ORTHODOX SYRIAN CHURCH
The Malankara Orthodox Syrian Church is part of the Diocese of Europe under Metropolitan Thomas Mar Makarios. His representative in Great Britain is Fr M. S. Skariah, Paramula House, 44 Newbury Road, Newbury Park, Ilford, Essex IG2 7HD. Tel: 0181-599 3836.

THE SYRIAN ORTHODOX CHURCH
The Syrian Orthodox Church in Great Britain comes under the Patriarchal Vicar, whose representative is Fr Touma Hazim Dakkama, Antiochian, 5 Canning Road, Croydon CR0 6QA. Tel: 0181-654 7531. The Indian congregation under the Syrian Patriarch of Antioch is represented by Fr Eldhose Koungampillil, 1 Roslyn Court, Roslyn Avenue, East Barnet, Herts EN4 8DJ. Tel: 0181-368 2794.

THE COUNCIL OF ORIENTAL ORTHODOX CHURCHES, 34 Chertsey Road, Church Square, Shepperton, Middx TW17 9LF. Tel: 0181-368 8447. Secretary, Deacon Aziz M. A. Nour

PENTECOSTAL CHURCHES

Pentecostalism is inspired by the descent of the Holy Spirit upon the apostles at Pentecost. The movement began in Los Angeles, USA, in 1906 and is characterized by baptism with the Holy Spirit, divine healing, speaking in tongues (glossolalia), and a literal interpretation of the scriptures. The Pentecostal movement in Britain dates from 1907. Initially, groups of Pentecostalists were led by laymen and did not organize formally. However, in 1915 the Elim Foursquare Gospel Alliance (more usually called the Elim Pentecostal Church) was founded in Ireland by George Jeffreys and in 1924 about 70 independent assemblies formed a fellowship, the Assemblies of God in Great Britain and Ireland. The Apostolic Church grew out of the

1904–5 revivals in South Wales and was established in 1916, and the New Testament Church of God was established in England in 1953. In recent years many aspects of Pentecostalism have been adopted by the growing charismatic movement within the Roman Catholic, Protestant and Eastern Orthodox churches.

There are about 105 million Pentecostalists world-wide, with about 200,000 adult adherents in Great Britain and Ireland.

THE APOSTOLIC CHURCH, International Administration Offices, PO Box 389, 24–27 St Helens Road, Swansea SA1 1ZH. Tel: 01792-473992. *President*, Pastor R. W. Jones; *Administrator*, Pastor A. Saunders. The Apostolic Church has about 130 churches, 5,500 adherents and 83 ministers

THE ASSEMBLIES OF GOD IN GREAT BRITAIN AND IRELAND, General Offices, 16 Bridgford Road, West Bridgford, Nottingham NG2 6AF. Tel: 0115-981 1188. *General Superintendent*, P.C. Weaver; *General Administrator*, D. H. Gill. The Assemblies of God has 640 churches, about 75,000 adherents (including children) and 860 accredited ministers

THE ELIM PENTECOSTAL CHURCH, PO Box 38, Cheltenham, Glos GL50 3HN. Tel: 01242-519904. *General Superintendent*, Pastor I. W. Lewis; *Administrator*, Pastor B. Hunter. The Elim Pentecostal Church has 600 churches, 68,500 adherents and 650 accredited ministers

THE NEW TESTAMENT CHURCH OF GOD, Main House, Overstone Park, Overstone, Northampton NN6 0AD. Tel: 01604-643311. *National Overseer*, Revd Dr R. O. Brown. The New Testament Church of God has 110 organized congregations, 7,971 baptized members, about 20,000 adherents and 242 accredited ministers

THE PRESBYTERIAN CHURCH IN IRELAND

The Presbyterian Church in Ireland is Calvinistic in doctrine and presbyterian in constitution. Presbyterianism was established in Ireland as a result of the Ulster plantation in the early 17th century, when English and Scottish Protestants settled in the north of Ireland.

There are 21 presbyteries and five regional synods under the chief court known as the General Assembly. The General Assembly meets annually and is presided over by a Moderator who is elected for one year. The ongoing work of the Church is undertaken by 18 boards under which there are a number of specialist committees.

There are about 290,000 Presbyterians in Ireland, mainly in the north, in 562 congregations and with 400 ministers. *Moderator* (1999–2000), Rt. Revd J. Lockington

Clerk of Assembly and General Secretary, Very Revd Dr S. Hutchinson, Church House, Belfast BT1 6DW. Tel: 01232-322284

THE PRESBYTERIAN CHURCH OF WALES

The Presbyterian Church of Wales or Calvinistic Methodist Church of Wales is Calvinistic in doctrine and presbyterian in constitution. It was formed in 1811 when Welsh Calvinists severed the relationship with the established church by ordaining their own ministers. It secured its own confession of faith in 1823 and a Constitutional Deed in 1826, and since 1864 the General Assembly has met annually, presided over by a Moderator elected for a year. The doctrine and constitutional structure of the

Presbyterian Church of Wales was confirmed by Act of Parliament in 1931–2.

The Church has 47,535 members, 127 ministers and 894 churches.

Moderator (1999–2000), Revd G. Tudwal Jones

General Secretary, Revd W. G. Edwards, 53 Richmond Road, Cardiff CF24 3WJ. Tel: 01222-494913

THE RELIGIOUS SOCIETY OF FRIENDS (QUAKERS)

Quakerism is a movement, not a church, which was founded in the 17th century by George Fox and others in an attempt to revive what they saw as 'primitive Christianity'. The movement was based originally in the Midlands, Yorkshire and north-west England, but there are now Quakers in 36 countries around the world. The colony of Pennsylvania, founded by William Penn, was originally Quaker.

Emphasis is placed on the experience of God in daily life rather than on sacraments or religious occasions. There is no church calendar. Worship is largely silent and there are no appointed ministers; the responsibility for conducting a meeting is shared equally among those present. Social reform and religious tolerance have always been important to Quakers, together with a commitment to non-violence in resolving disputes.

There are 213,800 Quakers world-wide, with over 19,000 in Great Britain and Ireland. There are about 490 meeting houses in Great Britain.

CENTRAL OFFICES: (GREAT BRITAIN) Friends House, Euston Road, London NW1 2BJ. Tel: 0171-663 1000; (IRELAND) Swanbrook House, Morehampton Road, Dublin 4. Tel: 00 353 1-683684

THE SALVATION ARMY

The Salvation Army was founded by a Methodist minister, William Booth, in the east end of London in 1865, and has since become established in 104 countries world-wide. It was first known as the Christian Mission, and took its present name in 1878 when it adopted a quasi-military command structure intended to inspire and regulate its endeavours and to reflect its view that the Church was engaged in spiritual warfare. Salvationists emphasize evangelism, social work and the relief of poverty.

The world leader, known as the General, is elected by a High Council composed of the Chief of the Staff and senior ranking officers known as commissioners.

There are about 1.5 million members, 17,201 active officers (full-time ordained ministers) and 15,670 worship centres and outposts world-wide. In Great Britain and Ireland there are 62,836 members, 1,638 active officers and 810 worship centres.

General, J. Gowans

UK Territorial Commander, A. Hughes

TERRITORIAL HEADQUARTERS, 101 Newington Causeway, London SE1 6BN. Tel: 0171-367 4500

THE SEVENTH-DAY ADVENTIST CHURCH

The Seventh-day Adventist Church was founded in 1863 in the USA. Its members look forward to the second coming of Christ and observe the Sabbath (the seventh day) as a day of rest, worship and ministry. The Church bases its faith and practice wholly on the Bible and has developed 27 fundamental beliefs.

The World Church is divided into 12 divisions, each made up of unions of churches. The Seventh-day Adventist Church in the British Isles is known as the British Union of Seventh-day Adventists and is a member of the Trans-European Division. In the British Isles the administrative organization of the church is arranged in three tiers: the local churches; the regional conferences for south England, north England, Wales, Scotland and Ireland; and the national 'union' conference.

There are about 9 million Adventists and 42,321 churches in 204 countries world-wide. In the UK and Ireland there are 19,702 members, 152 ministers and 238 churches.
President of the British Union Conference, Pastor C. R. Perry
BRITISH ISLES HEADQUARTERS, Stanborough Park, Watford WD2 6JP. Tel: 01923-672251

UNDEB YR ANNIBYNWYR CYMRAEG
The Union of Welsh Independents

The Union of Welsh Independents was formed in 1872 and is a voluntary association of Welsh Congregational Churches and personal members. It is entirely Welsh-speaking. Congregationalism in Wales dates back to 1639 when the first Welsh Congregational Church was opened in Gwent. Member churches are Calvinistic in doctrine and congregationalist in organization. Each church has complete independence in the government and administration of its affairs.

The Union has 39,174 members, 231 ministers and 535 member churches.
President of the Union (1999–2000), C. Evans
General Secretary, Revd D. Myrddin Hughes, Tŷ John Penry, 11 Heol Sant Helen, Swansea SA1 4AL. Tel: 01792-652542

THE UNITED REFORMED CHURCH

The United Reformed Church was formed by the union of most of the Congregational churches in England and Wales with the Presbyterian Church of England in 1972.

Congregationalism dates from the mid 16th century. It is Calvinistic in doctrine, and its followers form independent self-governing congregations bound under God by covenant, a principle laid down in the writings of Robert Browne (1550–1633). From the late 16th century the movement was driven underground by persecution, but the cause was defended at the Westminster Assembly in 1643 and the Savoy Declaration of 1658 laid down its principles. Congregational churches formed county associations for mutual support and in 1832 these associations merged to form the Congregational Union of England and Wales.

The Presbyterian Church in England also dates from the mid 16th century, and was Calvinistic and evangelical in its doctrine. It was governed by a hierarchy of courts.

In the 1960s there was close co-operation locally and nationally between Congregational and Presbyterian Churches. This led to union negotiations and a Scheme of Union, supported by Act of Parliament in 1972. In 1981 a further unification took place, with the Reformed Association of Churches of Christ becoming part of the URC. In its basis the United Reformed Church reflects local church initiative and responsibility with a conciliar pattern of oversight. The General Assembly is the central body, and is made up of equal numbers of ministers and lay members.

The United Reformed Church is divided into 12 Synods,

each with a Synod Moderator, and 75 Districts. There are 96,917 members, 650 full-time stipendiary ministers, 190 non-stipendiary ministers and 1,739 local churches.
General Secretary, Revd A. G. Burnham, 86 Tavistock Place, London WC1H 9RT. Tel: 0171-916 2020

THE WESLEYAN REFORM UNION

The Wesleyan Reform Union was founded by Methodists who left or were expelled from Wesleyan Methodism in 1849 following a period of internal conflict. Its doctrine is conservative evangelical and its organization is congregational, each church having complete independence in the government and administration of its affairs. The main concentration of churches is in Yorkshire.

The Union has 2,187 members, 22 ministers, 125 lay preachers and 113 churches.
President (1999–2000), J. B. Kay
General Secretary, Revd A. J. Williams, Wesleyan Reform Church House, 123 Queen Street, Sheffield S1 2DU. Tel: 0114-272 1938

Non-Trinitarian Churches

THE CHURCH OF CHRIST, SCIENTIST

The Church of Christ, Scientist was founded by Mary Baker Eddy in the USA in 1879 to 'reinstate primitive Christianity and its lost element of healing'. Christian Science teaches the need for spiritual regeneration and salvation from sin, but is best known for its reliance on prayer alone in the healing of sickness. Adherents believe that such healing is a law, or Science, and is in direct line with that practised by Jesus Christ (revered, not as God, but as the Son of God) and by the early Christian Church.

The denomination consists of The First Church of Christ, Scientist, in Boston, Massachusetts, USA (the Mother Church) and its branch churches in over 60 countries world-wide. Branch churches are democratically governed by their members, while a five-member Board of Directors, based in Boston, is authorized to transact the business of the Mother Church. The Bible and Mary Baker Eddy's book, *Science and Health with Key to the Scriptures*, are used at services; there are no clergy. Those engaged in full-time healing are called practitioners, of whom there are 3,500 world-wide.

No membership figures are available, since Mary Baker Eddy felt that numbers are no measure of spiritual vitality and ruled that such statistics should not be published. There are over 2,400 branch churches world-wide, including nearly 200 in the UK.
CHRISTIAN SCIENCE COMMITTEE ON PUBLICATION, 2 Elysium Gate, 126 New Kings Road, London SW6 4LZ. Tel: 0171-371 0600. *District Manager for Great Britain and Ireland*, H. Joynes

THE CHURCH OF JESUS CHRIST OF LATTER-DAY SAINTS

The Church (often referred to as 'the Mormons') was founded in New York State, USA, in 1830, and came to Britain in 1837. The oldest continuous branch in the world is to be found in Preston, Lancs. Mormons are Christians who claim to belong to the 'Restored Church' of Jesus Christ. They believe that true Christianity died when the last original apostle died, but that it was given back to the world by God and Christ through Joseph Smith, the Church's founder and first president. They accept and use the Bible as scripture, but believe in continuing revelation from God and use additional scriptures, including *The Book of Mormon: Another Testament of Jesus Christ.* The importance of the family is central to the Church's beliefs and practices. Church members set aside Monday evenings as Family Home Evenings when Christian family values are taught. Polygamy was formally discontinued in 1890.

The Church has no paid ministry; local congregations are headed by a leader chosen from amongst their number. The world governing body, based in Utah, USA, is the three-man First Presidency, assisted by the Quorum of the Twelve Apostles.

There are more than 10 million members world-wide, with about 180,000 adherents in Britain in over 350 congregations.

President of the Europe North Area (including Britain), Elder S. J. Condie

BRITISH HEADQUARTERS, Church Offices, 751 Warwick Road, Solihull, W. Midlands B91 3DQ. Tel: 0121-712 1202

JEHOVAH'S WITNESSES

The movement now known as Jehovah's Witnesses grew from a Bible study group formed by Charles Taze Russell in 1872 in Pennsylvania, USA. In 1896 it adopted the name of the Watch Tower Bible and Tract Society, and in 1931 its members became known as Jehovah's Witnesses. Jehovah's (God's) Witnesses believe in the Bible as the word of God, and consider it to be inspired and historically accurate. They take the scriptures literally, except where there are obvious indications that they are figurative or symbolic, and reject the doctrine of the Trinity. Witnesses also believe that the earth will remain for ever and that all those approved of by Jehovah will have eternal life on a cleansed and beautified earth; only 144,000 will go to heaven to rule with Christ. They believe that the second coming of Christ began in 1914 and his thousand-year reign on earth is imminent, and that Armageddon (a final battle in which evil will be defeated) will precede Christ's rule of peace. They refuse to take part in military service, and do not accept blood transfusions. They publish two magazines, *The Watchtower* and *Awake!*

The 12-member world governing body is based in New York, USA. Witnesses world-wide are divided into branches, countries or areas, districts, circuits and congregations. There are overseers at each level, and two assemblies are held annually for each circuit. There is no paid ministry, but each congregation has elders assigned to look after various duties and every Witness is assigned homes to visit in their congregation.

There are over 5 million Jehovah's Witnesses world-wide, with 130,000 Witnesses in the UK organized into over 1,400 congregations.

BRITISH ISLES HEADQUARTERS, Watch Tower House, The Ridgeway, London NW7 1RN. Tel: 0181-906 2211

UNITARIAN AND FREE CHRISTIAN CHURCHES

Unitarianism has its historical roots in the Judaeo-Christian tradition but rejects the deity of Christ and the doctrine of the trinity. It allows the individual to embrace insights from all the world's faiths and philosophies, as there is no fixed creed. It is accepted that beliefs may evolve in the light of personal experience.

Unitarian communities first became established in Poland and Transylvania in the 16th century. The first avowedly Unitarian place of worship in the British Isles opened in London in 1774. The General Assembly of Unitarian and Free Christian Churches came into existence in 1928 as the result of the amalgamation of two earlier organizations. There are about 7,000 Unitarians in Great Britain and Ireland, and 150 Unitarian ministers. About 200 self-governing congregations and fellowship groups, including a small number overseas, are members of the General Assembly.

GENERAL ASSEMBLY OF UNITARIAN AND FREE CHRISTIAN CHURCHES, Essex Hall, 1–6 Essex Street, Strand, London WC2R 3HY. Tel: 0171-240 2384. *General Secretary,* J. J. Teagle

Education

For addresses of national education departments, *see* Government Departments and Public Offices. For other addresses, *see* Education Directory

Responsibility for education in England lies with the Secretary of State for Education and Employment; in Wales, with the First Secretary of the National Assembly for Wales; in Scotland, with the Scottish Ministers ; and in Northern Ireland, with the Secretary of State for Northern Ireland.

The main concerns of the education departments (the Department for Education and Employment (DfEE), the National Assembly for Wales Education Department, the Scottish Executive Education Department and Enterprise and Lifelong Learning Department and the Department of Education for Northern Ireland (DENI)) are the formulation of national policies for education and the maintenance of consistency in educational standards. They are responsible for the broad allocation of resources for education, for the rate and distribution of educational building and for the supply, training and superannuation of teachers.

Expenditure

In the UK in 1996–7, expenditure on education was (£ million):

Schools	21,650.2
Further and higher education	9,543.5
Other education and related expenditure	1,445.8

Most of this expenditure is incurred by local authorities, which make their own expenditure decisions according to their local situations and needs. Expenditure on education by central government departments, in real terms, was (£ million):

	1998–9 estimated outturn	1999–2000 planned
DfEE	14,451	15,606
Welsh Office (now National Assembly for Wales)	451.5	523.1
SOEID (now Scottish Executive Education Dept.)	1,309	1,450
DENI	1,336	1,429

The bulk of direct expenditure by the DfEE, the National Assembly for Wales and the Scottish Executive is directed towards supporting higher education in universities and colleges through the Higher Education Funding Councils (HEFCs) and further education and sixth form colleges through the Further Education Funding Councils (FEFCs). In addition, the DfEE funds student support in England and Wales, the City Technology Colleges (CTCs), the City College for the Technology of the Arts, and pays grants under the specialist schools programme. In Wales the National Assembly also funds curriculum development, educational services and research and supports bilingual education. In Scotland the main elements of central government expenditure, in addition to those outlined above, are grant-aided special schools, student awards and bursaries (through the Student Awards Agency for Scotland), teachers, curriculum development, special educational needs, community education and further and higher education through the Funding Councils. The Department of Education for Northern Ireland directly funds higher education, teacher education, teacher salaries and superannuation, student awards, further education, grant-maintained integrated schools, and voluntary grammar schools.

Current net expenditure on education by local education authorities in England, Wales, and Scotland, and education and library boards in Northern Ireland is (£ million):

	1998–9 estimated outturn	1999–2000 planned
England	20,032	20,400
Wales	1,355	1,427
Scotland	2,475	2,605
Northern Ireland	913	938

Local Education Administration

In England and Wales the education service is administered by local education authorities (LEAs), which carry the day-to-day responsibility for providing most state primary and secondary education in their areas. They share with the FEFCs the duty to provide adult education to meet local needs.

The LEAs own and maintain most schools and some colleges, build new ones and provide equipment. LEAs are financed largely from the council tax and aggregate external finance (AEF) from the Department for the Environment, Transport and the Regions in England and the National Assembly for Wales.

All LEA-maintained schools manage their own budgets. The LEA allocates funds to the school, largely on the basis of pupil numbers, and the school governing body is responsible for overseeing spending and for most aspects of staffing, including appointments and dismissals. LEAs have powers to monitor, maintain and improve standards. An Education Association can be set up to take over the management of failing schools where both the LEA and the governing body have not brought about improvements identified as necessary by inspection.

The duty of providing education locally in Scotland rests with the education authorities. They are responsible for the construction of buildings, the employment of teachers and other staff and the provision of equipment and materials. Devolved School Management is in place for all primary, secondary and special schools.

Education authorities are required to establish school boards consisting of parents and teachers as well as co-opted members, responsible among other things for the appointment of staff.

Education is administered locally in Northern Ireland by five education and library boards, whose costs are met in full by DENI. All grant-aided schools include elected parents and teachers on their boards of governors. Provision has been made for schools wishing to provide integrated education to have grant-maintained integrated status from the outset. All schools and colleges of further education have full responsibility for their own budgets, including staffing costs. The Council for Catholic Maintained Schools forms an upper tier of management for Catholic schools and provides advice on matters relating to management and administration.

THE INSPECTORATE

The Office for Standards in Education (OFSTED) is a non-ministerial government department in England headed by HM Chief Inspector of Schools (HMCI). OFSTED's remit is regularly to inspect and report on all maintained and independent schools; local education authorities (on a five-year cycle from 2000, supported by the Audit Commission); initial teacher training; adult and youth education and nursery education providers using independent registered nursery education inspectors. All state schools are inspected by teams of OFSTED-trained accredited inspectors, including educationalists and lay people and headed by registered inspectors. The inspection is carried out according to the *Framework for Inspection of Schools* to ensure consistency in the process of inspection and the criteria used. HM Inspectors (HMI) within OFSTED report on good practice in schools and on other educational issues based on inspection evidence. From 1997 for secondary and from 1998 for primary, schools are inspected once every six years or more frequently if there is cause. A summary of the inspection report must be sent to the parents of each pupil by the school, followed by a copy of the governors' action plan thereon. The inspection of further and higher education in England is the responsibility of inspectors appointed to the respective Funding Councils.

There are 200 HMIs on OFSTED's permanent staff, 2,000 trained registered inspectors and 9,500 team inspectors.

Estyn: Arolygiaeth Ei Mawrhydi Dros Addysg A Hyfforddiant yng Nghymru (Her Majesty's Inspectorate for Education and Training in Wales) has a similar remit to OFSTED and carries out the inspection of funded nursery provision, maintained and independent schools on a five-year cycle. Estyn also inspects establishments of further education at the request of the Further Education Funding Council for Wales. Its remit also includes advice to government on education and training matters.

There are 38 HMIs, about 350 registered inspectors and 820 team members in Wales.

HM Inspectors of Schools in Scotland inspect schools and publish reports on further education institutions and community education, and are involved in assessing the quality of teacher education. HMIs work in teams alongside lay people and associate assessors, who are practising teachers seconded for the inspection. The inspection of higher education is the responsibility of inspectors appointed to the Higher Education Funding Council for Scotland.

There are 83 HMIs and eight Chief Inspectors in Scotland.

Inspection is carried out in Northern Ireland by the Department of Education's Education and Training Inspectorate, using teams which, on occasion, include lay people. The Inspectorate also performs an advisory function to the Secretary of State for Northern Ireland. From September 1999 a seven-year cycle of inspection was introduced.

There is one Chief Inspector and 62 members of the Inspectorate in Northern Ireland.

SCHOOLS AND PUPILS

Schooling is compulsory in Great Britain for all children between five and 16 years and between four and 16 years in Northern Ireland. Provision is being increased for preschool children and many pupils remain at school after the minimum leaving age. No fees are charged in any publicly maintained school in England, Wales and Scotland. In Northern Ireland, fees may be charged in voluntary schools and are paid by pupils in preparatory departments of grammar schools, but pupils admitted to the secondary departments of grammar schools, unless they come from outside the province, do not pay fees.

The 'Parents' Charter', available free from education departments, is a booklet telling parents about the education system. Schools are now required to make available information about themselves, their truancy rates, destinations of leavers, their public examination and (in England, Wales and Northern Ireland) national test results. Parents in England and Wales must receive a written yearly progress report on all aspects of their child's achievements. There is a similar commitment for Northern Ireland. In Scotland the school report card gives parents information on their child's progress.

FALL AND RISE IN NUMBERS

In nursery and primary education, and increasingly in secondary education, pupil numbers in the UK declined through the 1980s. In maintained nursery and primary schools they reached their lowest figure of 4.6 million in 1986, had risen to 5.2 million by 1998 and are expected to decline to 5.1 million by 2002. In secondary schools pupil numbers peaked at 4.6 million in 1981, had fallen to 3.7 million by 1998 but are projected to rise to about 4 million by 2006.

ENGLAND AND WALES

There are two main types of school in England and Wales: publicly maintained schools, which charge no fees; and independent schools, which charge fees (*see* page 428). Publicly maintained schools, with the exception of City Technology Colleges, are maintained by local education authorities.

From September 1999, all existing publicly funded schools were incorporated into a new school framework comprising community, voluntary (subdivided into voluntary controlled and voluntary aided) and foundation schools. They are non-denominational and provide primary and secondary education. The voluntary category is retained as before but now comprises two categories, voluntary controlled and voluntary aided, which latter now includes the former special agreement schools. Voluntary schools provide primary and secondary education. Although the buildings are in many cases provided by the voluntary bodies (mainly religious denominations), they are financially maintained by an LEA. In the case of voluntary controlled schools the LEA bears all costs. In voluntary aided schools, although the managers or governors are responsible for the building, repairs, improvements and alterations to the building, central government may reimburse up to 85 per cent of approved capital expenditure, while the LEA pays for internal maintenance and other running costs. In the case of former special agreement schools, the LEA may, by special agreement, pay between one-half and three-quarters of the cost of building a new, or extending an existing, school, usually a secondary school. Most grant-maintained schools (*see* below) have been categorised as foundation schools. It is proposed that schools have the opportunity to change category.

The number of schools by category in 1998 was:

	England	Wales
Maintained schools	27,487	2,210
County	13,917	1,628
Voluntary	6,785	291
controlled	2,805	121
aided	3,942	170
special agreement*	38	–
Grant-maintained	1,177	18
CTCs and CCTAs*	15	–
Independent schools	2,227	59
TOTAL	30,906	2,287

* In England only

Under the Local Management of Schools (LMS) initiative, LEAs are required, from April 2000, to delegate the entire school budget, including staffing costs, directly to those schools that wish it. LEAs continue to retain responsibility for various common services, including transport and special educational needs units. The LEA acts as admission authority for most community and some voluntary schools.

Governing bodies – All publicly maintained schools have a governing body, usually made up of a number of parent and local community representatives, governors appointed by the LEA if the school is LEA maintained, the headteacher (unless he or she chooses otherwise), and serving teachers. Schools can appoint up to four sponsor governors from business who will be expected to provide financial and managerial assistance. Governing bodies are responsible for the overall policies of schools and their academic aims and objectives. They also control matters of school discipline, the appointment and dismissal of staff and act as the admission authority for voluntary aided and all foundation schools. Governing bodies select inspectors for their schools, are responsible for action as a result of inspection reports and are required to make those reports and their action plans thereon available to parents.

The Specialist Schools Programme is open to all state secondary schools in England which teach the national curriculum and wish to specialise in the teaching of technology, mathematics and science (technology colleges), modern foreign languages (language colleges), sports colleges and arts colleges. In addition to the normal funding arrangements, the schools receive business sponsorship (up to four sponsor governors may sit on governing bodies) and complementary capital grants up to £100,000 from central government, together with extra annual funding of £100 a pupil to assist the delivery of an enhanced curriculum. By September 1999, there were 242 technology colleges, 61 language colleges, 33 sports colleges and 29 arts colleges.

Grant-maintained (GM) schools – Under the previous administration all secondary and primary schools, whether maintained or independent, were eligible to apply for grant-maintained status subject to a ballot of parents. GM schools were initially maintained directly by the Secretary of State (through the Funding Agency for Schools) and the former Welsh Office, not the LEA; those arrangements no longer apply and they are now included in LEA funding arrangements. They are wholly run by their own governing body. About 60 per cent of GM schools were secondary schools. From 1 September 1999, the name and status of GM schools changed. Those schools originally in the county and voluntary controlled categories and those established by the Funding Agency for Schools became foundation schools, while former voluntary aided and special agreement schools and those founded by promoters entered the voluntary aided subdivision of the voluntary category, with an option to express a preference as to category.

City Technology Colleges (CTCs) and *City Colleges for the Technology of the Arts (CCTAs)* are state-aided but independent of LEAs. Their aim is to widen the choice of secondary education in disadvantaged urban areas and to teach a broad curriculum with an emphasis on science, technology, business understanding and arts technologies. Capital costs are shared by government and business sponsors, and running costs are covered by a per capita grant from the DfEE in line with comparable costs in an LEA maintained school. The first city technology college opened in 1988 in Solihull. The first CCTA, known as Britschool, opened in Croydon in 1991.

SCOTLAND

Education authority schools (known as public schools) are financed by local government, partly through revenue support grants from central government, and partly from local taxation. Devolved management from the local authority to the school is in place for more than 88 per cent of all school level expenditure. A small number of grant-aided schools, mainly in the special sector, are conducted by boards of managers and receive grants direct from the Scottish Executive Education Department. There are, in addition, two self-governing schools in the public sector which are managed entirely by a board of management. At present they are funded by direct government grant but it is proposed to return them to the education authority framework. Independent schools receive no direct grant and charge fees, but are subject to inspection and registration.

Education authorities are required to establish school boards to participate in the administration and management of schools. These boards consist of elected parents and staff members as well as co-opted members.

The number of schools by category in 1998 was:

Publicly maintained schools:	
Education authority	3,711
Self-governing	2
Independent schools	114
TOTAL	3,827

NORTHERN IRELAND

Controlled schools are maintained by the education and library boards with all costs paid from public funds. Voluntary maintained schools, mainly under Roman Catholic management, receive grants towards capital costs and running costs in whole or in part. Voluntary grammar schools may be under denominational or non-denominational management and receive grants from DENI. Voluntary maintained and voluntary grammar schools can apply for designation as a new category of voluntary school, which is eligible for a 100 per cent as opposed to 85 per cent grant. Such schools are managed by a board of governors on which no single interest group has a majority of nominees. All grant-aided schools include elected parents and teachers on their boards of governors, whose responsibilities also include financial management under the Local Management of Schools (LMS) initiative. All schools now have fully delegated budgets. The majority of children in Northern Ireland are educated in schools which in practice are segregated on religious lines. Integrated schools exist to educate Protestant and Roman Catholic children together. There are two types: grant-maintained integrated schools which are funded by DENI; and controlled integrated schools funded by the education and library boards. Procedures are in place for balloting parents in existing segregated schools to determine whether they want instead to have integrated schools, subject to the satisfaction of certain criteria. By September 1999, 43 integrated schools had been established, 16 of them secondary.

The number of schools by category in 1998–9 was:

Grant-aided schools:
Controlled	653
Voluntary maintained	547
Voluntary grammar	54
Integrated schools	40
Independent schools	22
TOTAL	1,316

THE STATE SYSTEM

NURSERY EDUCATION – Nursery education is for children from two to five years and is not compulsory, although a free place is available for each four-year-old who requires it and free provision for three-year-olds is being increased. Northern Ireland has a compulsory school starting age of four as of September each year but there too pre-school provision is being increased. Nursery education takes place in nursery schools (1,685 in the public sector in 1998) or, in England, nursery classes in primary schools. The number of children receiving nursery education in the UK in 1997—8 was (thousands):

In maintained nursery schools	78.4
In primary schools	994.3
In non-maintained nursery schools	69.3
In special schools	8.0
TOTAL	1,150.0

Education authorities are responsible for planning, co-ordinating and delivering nursery education in their areas using a range of providers on the basis of an Early Years Development Plan, in partnership with parents and the private and voluntary sectors. All providers of pre-school education are subject to inspection.

PRIMARY EDUCATION – Primary education begins at five years in Great Britain and four years in Northern Ireland, and is almost always co-educational. In England, Wales and Northern Ireland the transfer to secondary school is generally made at 11 years. In Scotland, the primary school course lasts for seven years and pupils transfer to secondary courses at about the age of 12.

Primary schools consist mainly of infant schools for children aged five to seven, junior schools for those aged seven to 11, and combined junior and infant schools for both age groups. First schools in some parts of England cater for ages five to ten as the first stage of a three-tier system: first, middle and secondary. Many primary schools provide nursery classes for children under five (*see* above).

Primary schools (UK) 1997	8
No. of primary schools	23,213
No. of pupils (thousands)	5,413.8
Pupils under five years	379.0

Pupil-teacher ratios in maintained primary schools were:

	1996–7	1997–8
England	23.4	23.7
Wales	22.6	n/a
Scotland	19.6	19.9
Northern Ireland	19.8	19.9
UK	21.3	21.2

The average size of classes 'as taught' was 25.6 in 1997 .

MIDDLE SCHOOLS – Middle schools (which take children from first schools), mostly in England, cover varying age ranges between eight and 14 and usually lead on to comprehensive upper schools.

SECONDARY EDUCATION – Secondary schools are for children aged 11 to 16 and for those who choose to stay on to 18. At 16, many students prefer to move on to tertiary or sixth form colleges (*see* page 432–3). Most secondary schools in England, Wales and Scotland are co-educational. The largest secondary schools have over 1,500 pupils but only 31.3 per cent of the schools take over 1,000 pupils.

Secondary schools 1998
	England and Wales	Scotland	N. Ireland
No. of pupils (000s)	30,273.1	314.9	153.1
% 16 and 17 years old	74.1%	53.6%	45.5%
Average class size	42.5	19.2	n/a
Pupil-teacher ratio	32.6	13.2	14.5

In England and Wales the main types of maintained secondary schools are: comprehensive schools (86.7 per cent of pupils in England, 100 per cent in Wales), whose admission arrangements are without reference to ability or aptitude; deemed middle schools for children aged variously between eight and 14 who then move on to senior comprehensive schools at 12, 13 or 14 (5.1 per cent of pupils in England); secondary modern schools (2.7 per cent of pupils in England) providing a general education with a practical bias; secondary grammar schools (4.2 per cent of pupils in England) with selective intake providing an academic course from 11 to 16–18 years; and technical schools (0.2 per cent of pupils in England), providing an integrated academic and technical education.

In Scotland all pupils in education authority secondary schools attend schools with a comprehensive intake. Most of these schools provide a full range of courses appropriate to all levels of ability from first to sixth year.

In most areas of Northern Ireland there is a selective system of secondary education with pupils transferring either to grammar schools (40.4 per cent of pupils in 1999) or secondary schools (59.6 per cent of pupils in 1999) at 11–12 years of age. Parents can choose the school they would like their children to attend and all those who apply must be admitted if they meet the criteria. If a school is over-subscribed beyond its standard admissions number, selection is on the basis of published criteria, which, for most grammar schools, place emphasis on performance in the transfer procedure tests which are set and administered by the Northern Ireland Council for the Curriculum, Examinations and Assessment. When parents consider that a school has not applied its criteria fairly they have access to independent appeals tribunals. Grammar schools provide an academic type of secondary education with A-levels at the end of the seventh year, while secondary non-grammar schools follow a curriculum suited to a wider range of aptitudes and abilities.

SPECIAL EDUCATION – Special education is provided for children with special educational needs. Wherever possible, such children are educated in ordinary schools, taking the parents' wishes into account, and schools are required to publish their policy for pupils with special educational needs. LEAs in England and Wales and Education and Library Boards in Northern Ireland are required to identify and secure provision for the needs of children with learning difficulties, to involve the parents in any decision and draw up a formal statement of the child's special educational needs and how they intend to meet them, all within statutory time limits. Parents have a right to appeal to a Special Educational Needs (SEN) Tribunal if they disagree with the statement. In Scotland, school placing is a matter of agreement between education authorities and parents. Parents have the right to say which school they want their child to attend, and a right of appeal where their wishes are not being met. Whenever possible, children with special needs are integrated into ordinary schools.

Maintained special schools are run by education authorities which pay all the costs of maintenance, but under the terms of Local Management of Schools (LMS), those able and wishing to manage their own budgets may choose to do so. Non-maintained special schools are run by voluntary bodies; they may receive some grant from central government for capital expenditure and for equipment but their current expenditure is met primarily from the fees charged to education authorities for pupils placed in the schools. Some independent schools provide education wholly or mainly for children with special educational needs and are required to meet similar standards to those for maintained and non-maintained special schools. It is intended that pupils with special educational needs should have access to as much of the national curriculum as possible, but there is provision for them to be exempt from it or for it to be modified to suit their capabilities.

The number of pupils with statements of special needs in January 1998 was (thousands):

In special schools: total	101.7
England	87.9
Wales	3.5
Scotland	6.4
N. Ireland	3.8
In public sector primary and secondary schools: total	166.0
England	141.0
Wales	12.7
Scotland	8.2
N. Ireland	4.1

ALTERNATIVE PROVISION

There is no legal obligation on parents in the UK to educate their children at school provided that the local education authority is satisfied that the child is receiving full-time education suited to its age, abilities and aptitudes. The education authority need not be informed that a child is being educated at home unless the child is already registered at a state school. In this case the parents must arrange for the child's name to be removed from the school's register (by writing to the headteacher) before education at home can begin. Failure to do so leaves the parents liable to prosecution for condoning non-attendance.

INDEPENDENT SCHOOLS

Independent schools charge fees and are owned and managed under special trusts, with profits being used for the benefit of the schools concerned. There is a wide variety of provision, from kindergartens to large day and boarding schools, and from experimental schools to traditional institutions. A number of independent schools have been instituted by religious and ethnic minorities.

All independent schools in the UK are open to inspection by approved inspectors (*see* page 425) and must register with the appropriate government education department. The education departments lay down certain minimum standards and can make schools remedy any unacceptable features of their building or instruction and exclude any unsuitable teacher or proprietor. Most independent schools offer a similar range of courses to state schools and enter pupils for the same public examinations. Introduction of the national curriculum and the associated education targets and assessment procedures is not obligatory in the independent sector.

The term public schools is often applied to those independent schools in membership of the Headmasters'

and Headmistresses' Conference, the Governing Bodies Association or the Governing Bodies of Girls' Schools Association. Most public schools are single-sex but there are some mixed schools and an increasing number of schools have mixed sixth forms.

Preparatory schools are so-called because they prepare pupils for the common entrance examination to senior independent schools. Most cater for pupils from about seven to 13 years. The common entrance examination is set by the Common Entrance Examination Board, but marked by the independent school to which the pupil intends to go. It is taken at 13 by boys, and between 11 and 13 by girls.

The number of schools and pupils in 1997–8 was:

	No. of schools	No. of pupils (000s)	% of school population	Pupil-teacher ratio
England	2,231	572.2	6.9	10.2
Wales	59	9.9	1.9	10.0
Scotland	176	31.7	3.7	10.7
N. Ireland	22	1.2	0.3	9.3

Most independent schools in Scotland follow the same examination system as England, Wales and Northern Ireland, i.e. GCSE followed by A-levels, although some take the Scottish Certificate of Education examinations.

ASSISTED PLACES SCHEME

The Assisted Places Scheme ceased to operate after September 1997 and is being phased out. Pupils in secondary education holding their places at the beginning of the 1997–8 school year will keep them until they have completed their education at their current school. Those at the primary stage will hold them until they have completed that phase of their education, although some may exceptionally be allowed to so for a further period to complete their secondary education. The scheme enables children to attend independent secondary schools which their parents could not otherwise afford. It provides help with tuition fees and other expenses, except boarding costs, on a sliding scale depending on the family's income. The proportion of pupils receiving full fee remission is about 42.5 per cent. In the 1998–9 academic year, about 30,600 places were offered at the 466 participating schools in England and Wales. In Scotland about 2,800 pupils participated in the scheme in 50 schools in 1998–9.

The scheme is administered and funded in England by the DfEE and in Wales and Scotland by the respective education departments. The scheme does not operate in Northern Ireland as the independent sector admits non-fee-paying pupils. There is, however, a similar scheme known as the Talented Children's Scheme to help pupils gifted in music and dance.

Further information can be obtained from the Independent Schools Information Service (*see* Education Directory).

THE CURRICULUM

ENGLAND AND WALES

The national curriculum was introduced in primary and secondary schools between autumn 1989 and autumn 1996, for the period of compulsory schooling from five to 16. It is mandatory in all maintained schools. As originally proposed, it was widely criticised for being too prescriptive and time-consuming. Following revision in 1994 its requirements were substantially reduced; the revisions were implemented in August 1995 for key stages one to three and from August 1996 for key stage four. A review of the curriculum is under way and the new courses/structures will be introduced in schools from September 2000 including, for the first time, Citizenship. As a first step, primary schools have been allowed greater flexibility in teaching the non-core curriculum subjects (which remain compulsory) in order to allow priority to be given to literacy and numeracy.

The statutory subjects at key stages one and two (five–11-year olds) are:

Core subjects	Foundation subjects
English	Design and technology
Welsh (Welsh-speaking	Information technology
schools in Wales)	
Mathematics	History
Science	Geography
	Welsh (generally a second language in non-Welsh-speaking schools in Wales)
	Art
	Music
	PE

At key stage three (11- to 14-year-olds) all pupils must study a modern foreign language. At key stage four (14- to 16-year-olds) pupils are required to continue to study the core subjects, PE, and, in England only, a modern foreign language, design and technology and information technology. Other foundation subjects are optional. Religious education must be taught across all key stages, following a locally agreed syllabus; parents have the right to remove their children if they wish. In Wales the national curriculum has separate and distinctive characteristics which are reflected, where appropriate, in the programmes of study.

Statutory assessment takes place on entry to primary school and national tests and tasks in English, Welsh (in Welsh-speaking schools in Wales) and mathematics at key stage one, with the addition of science at key stages two and three, are in place. Teachers make their own assessments of their pupils' progress to set alongside the test results. At key stage four the GCSE and vocational equivalents are the main form of assessment.

The DfEE and the National Assembly for Wales publish tables showing pupils' performance in A-level, AS-level, GCSE and GNVQ examinations school by school. In England only, local education authorities are required to publish similar information in November each year showing the results of national curriculum tests and teacher assessments for seven-, 11- and 14-year-olds. Approximately 600,000 pupils in each of the age groups take the tests each year in England and Wales (38,000).

NATIONAL TESTING AND TEACHERS' ASSESSMENT RESULTS IN CORE SUBJECTS 1998

Percentage of pupils reaching the expected level of performance at that age:

	Key stage 1 7-year olds (level 2)	Key stage 2 11-year olds (level 4)	Key stage 3 14-year olds (level 5)
ENGLAND			
English	81.0	65.0	58.5
Mathematics	84.5	62.0	62.0
Science	86.0	70.0	60.5
WALES			
English	80.0	65.0	62.0
Welsh (first language)	86.0	63.0	71.0
Mathematics	84.0	65.0	64.0
Science	85.0	71.0	60.0

National targets have been set for 11-year-olds in England: 80 per cent to reach level four in the English test and 75

per cent to reach level four in the mathematics test by 2002. In Wales the targets are: 70–80 per cent to reach the expected level of performance for that age at key stages two and three in English, Welsh, mathematics and science by 2002.

In Wales, Welsh is a compulsory subject for all pupils at key stages one, two and three where it is taught either as a first or second language. It is now compulsory also at key stage four in both Welsh-speaking and non Welsh-speaking schools. In 1997 some 27 per cent of primary schools used Welsh as the sole or main medium of instruction and a further 6 per cent used it for part of the curriculum. Nearly 22 per cent of secondary schools taught Welsh both as a first and second language.

In October 1997 in England the Qualifications and Curriculum Authority (QCA) was formed by the amalgamation of the School Curriculum and Assessment Authority and the National Council for Vocational Qualifications. An independent government agency funded by the DfEE, its remit ranges from the under-fives to higher level vocational qualifications. It is responsible for ensuring that the curriculum and qualifications available to young people and adults are of high quality, coherent and flexible. In Wales, Awdurdod Cymwysterau, Cwricwlwm ac Asesu Cymru (ACCAC)/the Qualifications, Curriculum and Assessment Authority for Wales exercises similar functions. ACCAC is funded by the National Assembly for Wales.

SCOTLAND

The content and management of the curriculum in Scotland are not prescribed by statute but are the responsibility of education authorities and individual headteachers. Advice and guidance are provided by the Scottish Executive Education Department and the Scottish Consultative Council on the Curriculum, which also has a developmental role. Guidance for the pre-school sector describes the nature of the pre-school experience, sets out features of learning in key aspects of the child's early development and identifies appropriate learning experiences for children and opportunities for collaboration with other agencies. For the five–14 age group there are guidelines on the structure and balance of the curriculum as well as for each of the curriculum areas, although they are currently under review. There are also guidelines on assessment across the whole curriculum, on reporting to parents, and on standardised national tests for English language and mathematics at five levels. The curriculum for 14- to 16-year-olds includes study within each of eight modes: language and communication, mathematical studies, science, technology, social studies, creative activities, physical education, and religious and moral education. There are recommendations for the percentage of time to be devoted to each area over the two years. Provision is made for teaching in Gaelic in Gaelic-speaking areas. Testing is carried out on a voluntary basis when the teacher deems it appropriate; most pupils are expected to move from one level to the next at roughly two-year intervals. National testing is largely in place in most primary schools but secondary school participation rates are lower.

For 16- to 18-year-olds, there is available a modular system of vocational courses, certificated by the Scottish Qualifications Authority (SQA), in addition to academic courses. A new unified framework of courses and awards, known as 'Higher Still', which will bring together both academic and vocational courses was introduced in 1999 (*see* page 431). The SQA will award the new certificates.

NORTHERN IRELAND

A curriculum common to all grant-aided schools exists. Pupils are required to study religious education and, depending on which key stage they have reached, certain subjects from six broad areas of study: English, mathematics, science and technology; the environment and society; creative and expressive studies and, in key stages three and four, language studies. The statutory curriculum requirements at key stages one to three have been revised and new programmes of study were introduced in September 1996. Six cross-curricular educational themes, which include information technology and education for mutual understanding, are woven through the main subjects of the curriculum. Irish is a foundation subject in schools that use it as a medium of instruction.

The assessment of pupils is broadly in line with practice in England and Wales and takes place at the ages of eight, 11 and 14. The GCSE is used to assess 16-year-olds.

NATIONAL TESTING AND TEACHERS' ASSESSMENT RESULTS IN CORE SUBJECTS 1999 (1998 KEY STAGE 3)
Percentage of pupils reaching the expected level of performance at that age (at key stage 3, teacher assessed level (test level in brackets)):

	Key stage 1 8-year olds (level 2)	Key stage 2 11-year olds (level 4)	Key stage 3 14-year olds (level 5)
English	93	68	73(69)
Mathematics	93	73	70(66)
Science	—	—	70(66)

National targets have been set for 11-year-olds: 80 per cent to reach level four in English and mathematics by 2002.

The Northern Ireland Council for the Curriculum, Examinations and Assessment (NICCEA) monitors and advises DENI and teachers on all matters relating to the curriculum, assessment arrangements and examinations in grant-aided schools. It conducts GCSE, A- and AS-level examinations, pupil assessment at key stages one, two and three and administers the transfer procedure tests.

THE PUBLIC EXAMINATION SYSTEM

ENGLAND, WALES AND NORTHERN IRELAND
Until the end of 1987, secondary school pupils at the end of compulsory schooling around the age of 16, and others, took the General Certificate of Education (GCE) Ordinary-level or the Certificate of Secondary Education (CSE). From 1988 these were replaced by a single system of examinations, the General Certificate of Secondary Education (GCSE), which is usually taken after five years of secondary education. The GCSE is the main method of assessing the performance of pupils at age 16 in all national curriculum subjects required to be assessed at the end of compulsory schooling. The structure of the examination is being adapted in accordance with national curriculum requirements; new subject criteria were published in 1995 to govern GCSE syllabuses introduced in 1996 for first examination in 1998. GCSE short-course qualifications are available in some subjects. As a rule the syllabus takes half the time of a full GCSE course.

The GCSE differs from its predecessors in that there are syllabuses based on national criteria covering course objectives, content and assessment methods; differentiated assessment (i.e. different papers or questions for different ranges of ability) and grade-related criteria (i.e. grades awarded on absolute rather than relative performance). The GCSE certificates are awarded on a seven-point scale, A to G. From 1994 there has been an additional 'starred' A grade (A*), to recognise the achievement of the highest attainers at GCSE. Grades A to C are the equivalent of the corresponding O-level grades A to C or CSE grade 1. Grades D, E, F and G record achievement at least as high

as that represented by CSE grades 2 to 5. All GCSE syllabuses, assessments and grading procedures are monitored by the Qualifications and Curriculum Authority (*see* page 429) to ensure that they conform to the national criteria

In the UK in 1997–8, 94.5 per cent of all 16-year-olds achieved one or more graded GCSE, SCE Standard Grade, or equivalent result, while 48.4 per cent achieved five or more GCSEs at grade C or better (England, Wales and Northern Ireland).

In Wales the Certificate of Education is intended for 16-year-olds for whom no suitable examination exists. In 1997, 27,520 candidates took the examination, of whom 94.4 per cent obtained pass or better.

Many maintained schools offer BTEC Firsts (*see* page 433) and an increasing number offer BTEC Nationals. National Vocational Qualifications in the form of General NVQs are also available to students in schools (*see* page 434). The Part 1 GNVQ is a shortened version of the full GNVQ. Designed for 14- to 16-year-olds, it is a two-year course at foundation and intermediate levels, the former broadly equivalent to two GCSEs at grades D to G, and the latter at grades A* to C. It has been piloted from 1995 and has been available in schools since September 1999.

Advanced (A-level) examinations are taken by those who choose to continue their education after GCSE. A-level courses last two years and have traditionally provided the foundation for entry to higher education. Revised A-level syllabuses from September 2000 will offer candidates the choice between end-of-course or staged assessment, with limits on coursework. A-levels are marked on a seven-point scale: pass, from A to E; N (narrow failure) which will be phased out; and U (unclassified), which is not certificated.

Advanced Supplementary level (AS-level) examinations were introduced in 1987 as an alternative to, and to complement, A-level examinations. AS-levels are for full-time A-level students but are also open to other students. An AS-level syllabus has heretofore covered not less than half the amount of ground covered by the corresponding A-level syllabus and, where possible, has been related to it. An AS-level course lasts two years and requires not less than half the teaching time of the corresponding A-level course, and two AS-levels are equivalent to one A-level. From September 2000 a new AS (Advanced Subsidiary) qualification will represent the first half of a full A-level. AS-level passes are graded A to E, with grade standards related to the A-level grades.

In the UK in 1996–7, 296,000 students (45.3 per cent boys, 54.7 per cent girls) achieved one or more passes at A-level or SCE H-grade (an increase of 4.3 per cent on the previous year). Of those in Great Britain who entered for at least one A-level, or at least two SCE H-grades, 32 per cent studied sciences (59 per cent boys, 41 per cent girls) and 68 per cent studied arts/social studies (43.5 per cent of boys, 56.5 per cent of girls).

Most examining boards allow the option of an additional paper of greater difficulty to be taken by A-level candidates to obtain what is known as a Special-level or Scholarship-level qualification. S-level papers are available in most of the traditional academic subjects and are marked on a three-point scale. From September 2000 they will be replaced by 'world class test' special papers.

The City & Guilds Diploma of Vocational Education is intended for a wide ability range. The Diploma provides recognition of achievement at two levels: foundation at pre-16 and intermediate at post-16. The intermediate level is being phased out in favour of the corresponding GNVQs. Within guidelines and to meet specified criteria, schools and colleges design their own courses, which stress activity-based learning, core skills which include application of number, communication and information technology, and work experience. The Diploma is of value to those who want to find out what aptitudes they may have and to prepare themselves for work, but who may not yet be committed to a particular occupation. At foundation level, it can be taken alongside GCSEs and can provide a context for the introduction of GNVQ units into the key stage four curriculum.

The various examining boards in England have combined into three unitary awarding bodies, which offer both academic and vocational qualifications: GNVQs, GCSEs and A-levels. The new bodies are Edexcel, the Assessment and Qualifications Alliance (AQA), and Oxford, Cambridge and RSA Examinations (OCR). At present the existing examination boards are still separate bodies, working in alliance to develop single courses.

SCOTLAND

Scotland has its own system of public examinations. At the end of the fourth year of secondary education, at about the age of 16, or earlier if appropriate, pupils take the Standard Grade of the Scottish Certificate of Education. Standard Grade courses and examinations have been designed to suit every level of ability, with assessment against nationally determined standards of performance.

For most courses there are three separate examination papers at the end of the two-year Standard Grade course. They are set at Credit (leading to awards at grade 1 or 2), General (leading to awards at grade 3 or 4) and Foundation (leading to awards at grade 5 or 6) levels. Grade 7 is available to those who, although they have completed the course, have not attained any of these levels. Normally pupils will take examinations covering two pairs of grades, either grades 1–4 or grades 3–6. Most candidates take seven or eight Standard Grade examinations.

Above Standard Grade, Higher Grade will be available after a one-year course in the fifth or sixth year of secondary school until 2000/1. The one-year Certificate of Sixth Year Studies (CSYS) will be available until 2001–2.

A new system of courses and qualifications is being phased in under the "Higher Still" reforms, bringing together academic and vocational qualifications. It will replace Highers, CSYS and National Certificate modules, for everyone studying beyond Standard Grade in Scottish schools, and for non-advanced students in further education colleges. Qualifications will be available at five levels: Access, Intermediate 1, Intermediate 2, Higher, and Advanced Higher, the latter not available until 2000–1. Courses will be made up of internally assessed units with external assessment of the full course determining the grade (A to C). Students possessing a number of units and courses may be able to build them into a Scottish Group Award. The core skills of communication, numeracy, problem-solving, information technology and working with others are embedded in the Higher Still qualifications, although the skills and levels covered vary between subjects; there will also be separate core skills units.

All of these qualifications are awarded by the Scottish Qualifications Authority (SQA), which on 1 April 1997 assumed the functions of the Scottish Examinations Board and the Scottish Vocational Education Council.

THE INTERNATIONAL BACCALAUREATE

The International Baccalaureate is an internationally recognised two-year pre-university course and examination designed to facilitate the mobility of students and to promote international understanding. Candidates must offer one subject from each of six subject groups, at least three at higher level and the remainder at subsidiary level. Single subjects can be offered, for which a certificate is received. There are 33 schools and colleges in the UK which offer the International Baccalaureate diploma.

RECORDS OF ACHIEVEMENT

The National Record of Achievement (NRA) is under review. Subject to evaluation, it will be replaced in England, Wales and Northern Ireland by the 'Progress file' after a three year trial period starting in July 1999. It is not compulsory in Scotland where, from 1999–2000, the Scottish Qualifications Authority will issue a Scottish Qualifications Certificate recording all qualifications achieved at all levels which it has either awarded or accredited.

TEACHERS

ENGLAND AND WALES

To obtain Qualified Teacher Status (QTS) it is necessary to have successfully completed a course of initial teacher training, traditionally either a Bachelor of Education (B Ed) degree or the Postgraduate Certificate of Education (PGCE) at an accredited institution. New entrants to the profession are statutorily required to serve a one-year induction period during which they will have a structured programme of support. In recent years various employment-based routes to teaching have been developed. The Graduate Teacher Programme allows graduates with teaching experience to undergo between one term's and one year's school-based training. The Registered Teacher Scheme is designed to attract into the teaching profession entrants over 24 years of age without formal teaching qualifications but with relevant training and experience; entrants are paid a salary and undertake one to two years higher education depending on whether they possess relevant teaching experience. Teachers in further education are not required to have Qualified Teacher Status, though roughly half have a teaching qualification and most have industrial, commercial or professional experience. A mandatory qualification for aspiring head-teachers, the National Professional Qualification for Headship (NPQH), was introduced in September 1997.

The national curriculum for initial teacher training is in place in both England and Wales in all core subjects of the national curriculum.

Teacher training is now largely school-based, with student teachers on secondary PGCE courses spending two-thirds of their training in the classroom. Changes have also been made to primary phase teacher training to make it more school-based and to give schools a role in course design and delivery. Individual schools or consortia of schools and CTCs can bid for funds from the DfEE to carry out their own teacher training, including recruitment of students, subject to approval of their proposed training programme by the Teacher Training Agency (TTA) and monitoring and evaluation by OFSTED and Estyn. Funds are given to schools to meet the costs of designing and delivering the courses.

The TTA funds all types of teacher training in England, whether run by universities, colleges or schools, and some educational research. In Wales funding is undertaken by the Higher Education Funding Council for Wales. On an integrated England and Wales basis the TTA also acts as a central source of information and advice about entry to teaching, and has responsibilities relating to the continuing professional development of teachers. An independent professional council, the General Teaching Council, is to be established to advise the Secretary of State and the TTA, with a separate council for Wales.

The Specialist Teacher Assistant (STA) scheme was introduced in September 1994 to provide trained support to qualified teachers in the teaching of reading, writing and arithmetic to young pupils.

SHORTAGE SUBJECTS

Because of a shortage of teachers in certain secondary subjects, from September 1999 a £5,000 incentive was introduced for graduates training for a PGCE who then take up a post as teachers of mathematics or science. Furthermore, providers of initial teacher training in England and Wales may receive funds from the TTA to help promote courses in certain subjects and to offer students on courses in those subjects financial support. The subjects are: science; mathematics; modern languages (including Welsh in Wales); design and technology; information technology; religious education; music, and geography.

SCOTLAND

The General Teaching Council (GTC) for Scotland advises central government on matters relating to teachers and teacher education. All teachers in maintained schools must be registered with the GTC, initially for a two-year probationary period which can be extended if necessary. Only graduates are accepted as entrants to the profession; primary school teachers undertake either a four-year vocational degree course or a one-year postgraduate course, while teachers of academic subjects in secondary schools undertake the latter. Most initial teacher training is classroom-based. The Scottish Qualification for Headship has been introduced for aspiring head teachers. The colleges of education provide both in-service and pre-service training for teachers which is subject to inspection by HM Inspectors. All pre-service courses must be approved by the Scottish Executive Education Department and, if appropriate, validated by a higher education institution and accredited by the GTC. The colleges are funded by the Scottish Higher Education Funding Council.

NORTHERN IRELAND

All new entrants to teaching in grant-aided schools are graduates and hold an approved teaching qualification. Teacher training is provided by the two universities and two colleges of education. The colleges are concerned with teacher education mainly for the primary school sector. They also provide B Ed courses for intending secondary school teachers of religious education, commercial studies, and craft, design and technology. With these exceptions, the professional training of teachers for secondary schools is provided in the education departments of the universities. A review of primary and secondary teacher training has taken place as a result of which all student teachers spend more time in the classroom. All newly qualified teachers undertake a two-year induction period. The General Teaching Council for Northern Ireland is in the process of being established to advise government on professional issues, to maintain a register of teachers and to act as a disciplinary body.

ACCREDITATION OF TRAINING INSTITUTIONS

Advice to central government on the accreditation, content and quality of initial teacher training courses is given in England by the TTA, in Wales by the HEFCW and in Northern Ireland by validating bodies (by the General Teaching Council for Northern Ireland when established). These bodies also monitor and disseminate good practice, assisted in Northern Ireland by the Teacher Education Committee. In Scotland the General Teaching Council advises the Scottish Executive Education Department on the professional suitability of all training courses in colleges of education.

SERVING TEACHERS 1996–7 *(full-time and part-time)* (thousands)

	All	% graduate
Public sector schools	450.0	56.6
Nursery and primary	211.0	52.0
Secondary	222.0	74.0
Special	17.0	44.0
FE and HE establishments	133.0	82.0
TOTAL	583.0	69.3

SALARIES

Qualified teachers in England, Wales and Northern Ireland, other than heads and deputy heads, are paid on an 18-point scale. Entry points and placement depend on qualifications, experience, responsibilities, excellence and recruitment and retention factors as calculated by the relevant body, i.e. the governing body or the LEA. A new career grade of 'Advanced Skills Teacher' has been introduced to enhance prospects in the classroom for the most able teachers. There is a statutory superannuation scheme in maintained schools.

Teachers in Scotland are paid on a ten-point scale. The entry point depends on type of qualification, and additional allowances are payable under certain circumstances.

*Salaries from 1 September 1999**

	England, Wales and N. Ireland	Scotland
Head	£31,155–£70,002	£27,846–£51,582
Deputy head	£27,258–£44,841	£27,846–£38,589
Advanced skills teacher	£26,082–£41,607	
Teacher	£13,830–£37,041	£13,206–£28,893

* From 1 April 1998 for Scotland: award pending

FURTHER EDUCATION

Further education is defined as all provision outside schools to people aged over 16 of education up to and including A-level and its equivalent.

ENGLAND AND WALES

Further education and sixth form colleges are funded directly by central government through the Further Education Funding Council for England (FEFCE) and the Further Education Funding Council for Wales (FEFCW). The Councils have a duty to secure provision of adequate facilities in their areas and are also responsible for the assessment of quality, in which their inspectorates play a key role. The colleges are controlled by autonomous further education corporations, which include substantial representation from industry and commerce, and which own their own assets and employ their own staff. Their funding is determined in part by the number of students enrolled and their level of achievement.

In England and Wales further education courses are taught at a variety of institutions. These include universities which were formerly polytechnics, colleges of higher education, colleges of further education (some of which also offer higher education courses) and tertiary colleges and sixth form colleges, which concentrate on the provision of normal sixth form school courses as well as a range of vocational courses. A number of institutions specific to a particular form of training, e.g. the Royal College of Music, are also involved.

Teaching staff in further education establishments are not necessarily required to have teaching qualifications although many do so, but they are subject to regular appraisal of teaching performance. It is planned to introduce a mandatory professional qualification for college principals.

Further education tends to be broadly vocational in purpose and employers are often involved in designing courses. It ranges from lower-level technical and commercial courses and government-sponsored training, through courses for those aiming at higher-level posts in industry, commerce and administration, to professional courses. Facilities exist for GCE A- and AS-levels, GCSEs, GNVQs and a full range of vocational qualifications (see pages 430–1). These courses can form the foundation for progress to higher education qualifications. Many students attend part-time, either through day or block release from employment, or in the evenings.

The main courses and examinations in the vocational field, all of which link in with the National Vocational Qualification (NVQ) framework (see page 434), are offered by the following bodies, but there are also many others.

The Edexcel Foundation was formed by the merger of the Business and Technology Education Council (BTEC) and London Examinations. It provides programmes of study across a wide range of subject areas. The main qualifications offered are GCSEs, A-levels, GNVQs, NVQs, BTEC First, National and Higher National diplomas and certificates, key skills and entry certificates.

City & Guilds specialize in developing qualifications and assessments for work-related and leisure qualifications. They offer nationally and internationally recognized certificates in over 500 vocational qualifications. The progressive structure of awards spans seven levels, from foundation to the highest level of professional competence.

RSA Examinations Board schemes cover a wide range of vocational qualifications, including accounting, business administration, customer service, management, language schemes, information technology and teaching qualifications. A wide range of NVQs and GNVQs are offered and a policy operates of credit accumulation, so that candidates can take a single unit or complete qualifications.

There are 453 further education establishments (of which 110 are sixth form colleges) in England and 26 in Wales. In England (1998–9) there were 746.9 thousand full-time and sandwich-course students and 1,618.5 thousand part-time students. In Wales (1996–7) there were 39.9 thousand full-time and sandwich students and 103.8 thousand part-time students.

SCOTLAND

Further education comprises non-advanced courses up to SCE Higher Grade, occasionally GCE A-level and GSVQ work-based awards. Courses are taught mainly at colleges of further education, but may also be provided in schools, in higher education institutions and in the workplace.

Responsibility for further education lies with the Scottish Executive under the Minister for Enterprise and Lifelong Learning through the Scottish Further Education Funding Council. There are 47 further education colleges of which 43 are self-governing incorporated colleges run by their own boards of management. The boards include the principal, staff and student representatives among their ten to 16 members; at least half the members must have experience of commerce, industry or the practice of a profession. Two colleges, on Orkney and Shetland, are under Islands Council control and two further colleges, Sabhal Mor Ostaig (the Gaelic college on Skye) and Newbattle Abbey are run by trustees.

The Scottish Qualifications Authority (SQA) awards qualifications for most occupations. It awards at non-advanced level the National Certificate, which is available in over 4,000 individual modules and covers the whole range of non-advanced further education provision. Students may study for the National Certificate on a full-time, part-time, open learning or work-based learning basis. National Certificate modules can be taken in further education colleges, secondary schools and other centres, normally from the age of 16 onwards. New unified qualifications for non-advanced post-16 education began to be phased in from August 1999 under the Higher Still reforms, which bring together academic and vocational qualifications. Higher Still courses will be available at five levels, (Access, Intermediate 1, Intermediate 2, Higher and Advanced Higher) and will replace Higher Grades, CSYS, General Scottish Vocational Qualifications (GSVQ) and National Certificate modules, but not Standard Grade or Scottish Vocational Qualifications (SVQ).

The SQA also offers modular advanced-level HNC/HND qualifications, which are available in further education colleges and higher education institutions. SQA accredits and awards SVQs which have mutual recognition with the NVQs available in the rest of the UK. SVQs are work-place assessed, but can also be taken in further education colleges and other centres where work-place conditions can be simulated. The SQA will issue the Scottish Qualifications Certificate from 1999–2000, which replaces the National Record of Achievement in Scotland (see above).

In the academic year 1997–8 there were 35,750 full-time and sandwich-course students and 249,215 part-time students on non-advanced vocational courses of further education in further education colleges (excluding Newbattle Abbey College).

NORTHERN IRELAND

All further education colleges are free-standing corporate bodies like their counterparts in the rest of the UK. Planning is the responsibility of the Department of Education for Northern Ireland, which funds the colleges directly. The colleges own their own property, are responsible for their own services and employ their own staff.

The governing bodies of the colleges must include at least 50 per cent membership from the professions, local business or industry, or other fields of employment relevant to the activities of the college.

In 1998–9 Northern Ireland had 17 institutions of further education, and there were 20,594 full-time students and 55,827 part-time students on non-advanced vocational courses of further education.

STUDENT SUPPORT

At present 16 to 19-year-olds may receive means-tested discretionary payments from LEAs, while adults may apply for access funds allocated by central government through the FEFCs. New arrangements are being piloted comprising the means-tested Education Maintenance Allowance (EMA) for 16 to 18-year-old students in both schools and colleges and extension of the access fund scheme.

COURSE INFORMATION

Applications for further education courses are generally made directly to the colleges concerned.

NATIONAL VOCATIONAL QUALIFICATIONS

National Vocational Qualifications (NVQs) are work-place based occupational qualifications. In September 1992 General National Vocational Qualifications (GNVQs) were introduced into colleges and schools as a vocational alternative to academic qualifications. They cover six broad categories in the NVQ framework and are aimed at those wishing to familiarize themselves with a range of opportunities. Advanced GNVQ, sometimes known as the "vocational A-level" is equivalent to two A-levels; from September 2000 a revised version equivalent to a single A-level is to be introduced. Intermediate GNVQ is equivalent to four GCSEs at A* to C grade. Foundation GNVQ is equivalent to four GCSEs at D to G grade.

Bodies responsible for the regulation of GNVQs and NVQs in the UK are: in England, the Qualifications and Curriculum Authority (QCA); in Wales, Awdurdod Cymwysterau, Cwricwlwm ac Asesu Cymru (ACCAC)/ the Curriculum and Assessment Authority; in Northern Ireland, the Council for the Curriculum, Examinations and Assessment (NICCEA); and in Scotland, the Scottish Qualifications Authority (SQA). With the exception of the SQA those bodies do not award qualifications but accredit NVQs, GNVQs and core skills. Assessment is carried out through awarding bodies who bestow the qualifications where candidates reach the required standards.

HIGHER EDUCATION

The term higher education is used to describe education above A-level, Higher and Advanced Higher Grade and their equivalent, which is provided in universities, colleges of higher education and in some further education colleges.

The Further and Higher Education Act 1992 and parallel legislation in Scotland removed the distinction between higher education provided by the universities and that provided in England and Wales by the former polytechnics and colleges of higher education and in Scotland by the former central institutions and others, allowing all polytechnics, and other higher education institutions which satisfy the necessary criteria, to award their own taught course and research degrees and to adopt the title of university. All the polytechnics, art colleges and some colleges of higher education have since adopted the title of university. The change of name does not affect the legal constitution of the institutions. Funding is by the Higher Education Funding Councils for England, Wales and Scotland and directly by the Department of Education in Northern Ireland.

The number of students in higher education in the UK in 1997–8 was (thousands):

Full-time, sandwich	1,230.4
% female	51.7%
Part-time	708.0
% female	54.2%
TOTAL	1,938.4
of which overseas	10.8%

The proportion of 18- to 21-year-olds undertaking full-time and part-time courses in higher education in the UK was 34 per cent in 1997–8. The number of mature entrants (those aged 21 and over when starting an undergraduate course and 25 and over when starting a postgraduate course) to higher education in Great Britain in 1997–8 (including those at the Open University) was 1,070.9 thousand. The number of full-time and part-time students on science courses (excluding medicine and related courses) in 1997–8 was 421.5 thousand, of whom 31.4 per cent were female.

UNIVERSITIES AND COLLEGES

The universities are self-governing institutions established in most cases by royal charter or Act of Parliament. They have academic freedom and are responsible for their own academic appointments, curricula and student admissions and award their own degrees.

Responsibility for universities rests in England with the Secretary of State for Education and Employment, in their territories with the Secretaries of State for Wales and Northern Ireland and with the Scottish Executive. Advice to government on matters relating to the universities is provided by the Higher Education Funding Councils for England, Wales and Scotland, and by the Higher Education Council in Northern Ireland. The HEFCs receive a block grant from central government which they allocate to the universities and colleges. The grant is allocated directly to institutions by central government in Northern Ireland on the advice of the Northern Ireland Higher Education Council.

There are now 88 universities in the UK, where only 47 existed prior to the Further and Higher Education Acts 1992. Of the 88, 71 are in England (including one federal university), two (one a federal institution) in Wales, 13 in Scotland and two in Northern Ireland.

The pre-1992 universities each have their own system of internal government but broad similarities exist. Most are run by two main bodies: the senate, which deals primarily with academic issues and consists of members elected from within the university; and the council, which is the supreme body and is responsible for all appointments and promotions, and bidding for and allocation of financial resources. At least half the members of the council are drawn from outside the university. Joint committees of senate and council are becoming increasingly common.

Those universities which were formerly polytechnics (38) or other higher education institutions (three) and the colleges of higher education (60) are run by higher education corporations (HECs), which are controlled by boards of governors. At least half the members of each board must be drawn from industry, business, commerce and the professions.

ENGLAND AND WALES

In 1997–8 full-time and part-time student enrolments were (thousands):

England

Undergraduates	1,173.2
% overseas	9.3%
Postgraduates	323.6
% overseas	21%

Wales

Undergraduates	76.2
% overseas	8.5%
Postgraduates	16.9
% overseas	22.7%

Higher education courses funded by the respective HEFCs are also taught in some further education colleges. In England in 1997–8 there were about 35.6 thousand students (2.3 per cent of total higher education student numbers) on such courses and about 500 (0.5 per cent of higher education student numbers) in Wales.

SCOTLAND

The Scottish Higher Education Funding Council (SHEFC) funds 21 institutions of higher education, including 13 universities. The universities are broadly managed as described above and the remaining colleges are managed by independent governing bodies which include representatives of industrial, commercial, professional and educational interests. Most of the courses outside the universities have a vocational orientation and a substantial number are sandwich courses.

Student enrolments in 1997–8 in universities and other higher education institutions were (thousands):

Undergraduates	130.9
% overseas	8.9%
Postgraduates	37.9
% overseas	23.8%

There were 38.4 thousand students on higher education courses in further education colleges, 22.9 per cent of total higher education students.

NORTHERN IRELAND

In Northern Ireland advanced courses are provided by 17 colleges of further education, the two universities and the two colleges of education. As well as offering first and postgraduate degrees, the University of Ulster offers courses leading to the BTEC Higher National Diploma and professional qualifications. Applications to undertake courses of higher education other than degree courses are made to the institutions direct. Higher education student enrolments in 1997–8 were (thousands):

Undergraduates	32.8
% overseas	13.4%
Postgraduates	9.6
% overseas	15.5%

There were 9,879 students enrolled on advanced courses of higher education in the institutions of further education, 23.3 per cent of higher education student numbers.

The non-residential Open University provides courses nationally leading to degrees. Teaching is through a combination of television and radio programmes, correspondence, tutorials, short residential courses and local audio-visual centres. No qualifications are needed for entry. The Open University offers a modular programme of undergraduate courses by credit accumulation and post-experience and postgraduate courses, including a programme of higher degrees which comprises BPhil, MPhil and PhD through research, and MA, MBA and MSc through taught courses. The Open University throughout the UK is funded by the Higher Education Funding Council for England, although Scottish students, from 2000–1, will be funded by the Scottish Higher Education Funding Council. Its recurrent grant for 1997–8 was £116.9 million from the Higher Education Funding Council for England and £6.6 million from the Teacher Training Agency. In 1999, about 113,000 undergraduates were registered of whom about 53 per cent were women. Estimated cost (1999) of a six-credit degree was around £4,200 including course fees of about £3,000.

The independent University of Buckingham provides a two-year course leading to a bachelor's degree and its tuition fees were £9,996 for 1999. It receives no capital or recurrent income from the Government. Its academic year consists of four terms of ten weeks each.

ACADEMIC STAFF

Each university and college appoints its own academic staff on its own conditions. However, there is a common salary structure and, except for Oxford and Cambridge, a common career structure in those universities formerly funded by the UFC and a common salary structure for the former PCFC sector. The Universities and Colleges Employers Association (UCEA) acts as a pay agency for universities and colleges.

Teaching staff in higher education require no formal teaching qualification, but the Institute of Teaching and Learning in Higher Education, funded by the Higher Education Funding Councils, has been established to set up an accreditation scheme for higher education teachers and to encourage innovation in teaching and learning. Teacher trainers are required to spend a certain amount of time in schools to ensure that they have sufficient recent practical experience.

In 1997–8, there were 102,517 full-time and part-time teaching and research staff (UK nationals) in institutions of higher education in the UK.

Salary scales for staff in the pre-1992 universities sector differ from those in the former polytechnics and colleges; it is planned eventually to amalgamate them. The salary scales for non-clinical academic staff in universities formerly funded by the UFC are:

Professor	from £35,120
Senior lecturer	£30,498–£34,464
Lecturer grade B	£22,726–£29,048
Lecturer grade A	£15,735 –£21,815

The salaries of clinical academic staff are kept broadly comparable to those of doctors and dentists in the National Health Service.

Salary scales for lecturers in the former polytechnics, now universities, and colleges of higher education in England, Wales and Northern Ireland are:

	March 1999
Head of Department	from £26,304
Principal lecturer	£27,746–£35,204
Senior lecturer	£22,400–£29,600
Lecturer	£14,398–£24,002

The salary scales for such staff in Scotland are determined at individual college level.

FINANCE

Although universities and colleges are expected to look to a wider range of funding sources than before, and to generate additional revenue in collaboration with industry, they are still largely financed, directly or indirectly, from government resources.

In 1997–8 the total income of institutions of higher education in the UK was £11,616.7 million (£11,049.9 million in 1996–7). Grants from the funding councils amounted to £4,507.6 million (£4,371.8 million in 1996–7), forming 38.8 per cent of total income (39.5 per cent in 1996–7). Income from research grants and contracts was £1,733.3 million, 14.9 per cent of total income (14.7 per cent in 1996–7).

In the academic year 1997–8 the HEFCs' recurrent grant to institutions outside their sector for the provision of higher education courses was £62.8 million.

COURSES

In the UK all universities, including the Open University, and some colleges award their own degrees and other qualifications and may act as awarding and validating bodies for neighbouring colleges which are not yet accredited. The Quality Assurance Agency for Higher Education, funded by institutional contributions, advises government on applications for degree-awarding powers.

Higher education courses last full-time for at least four weeks or, if part-time, involve more than 60 hours of instruction. Facilities exist for full-time and part-time study, day release, sandwich or block release. Credit accumulation and transfer (CATS) is a system of study which is becoming widely available. It allows a student to achieve a final qualification by accumulating credits for courses of study successfully achieved, or even professional experience, over a period. Credit transfer information and values are carried on an electronic database called ECCTIS 2000, which is available in most careers offices and many schools and colleges.

Higher education courses comprise: first degree and postgraduate (including research); Diploma in Higher Education (DipHE); Higher National Diploma (HND) and Higher National Certificate (HNC); and preparation for professional examinations. The in-service training of teachers is also included, but from September 1994 has been funded in England by the TTA (*see* page 431), not the HEFCE.

The Diploma of Higher Education (DipHE) is a two-year diploma usually intended to serve as a stepping-stone to a degree course or other further study. The DipHE is awarded by the institution itself if it is accredited; by an accredited institution of its choice if not. The BTEC Higher National Certificate (HNC) is awarded after two years part-time study. The BTEC Higher National Diploma (HND) is awarded after two years full-time, or three years sandwich-course or part-time study.

With the exception of certain Scottish universities where master is sometimes used for a first degree in arts subjects, undergraduate courses lead to the title of Bachelor, Bachelor of Arts (BA) and Bachelor of Science (BSc) being the most common. For a higher degree the titles are: Master of Arts (MA), Master of Science (MSc) (usually taught courses) and the research degrees of Master of Philosophy (MPhil) and Doctor of Philosophy (PhD or, at a few universities, DPhil).

Most undergraduate courses at universities and colleges of higher education run for three years, but some take four years or more.

Postgraduate studies vary in length. Taught courses such as certificates, diplomas or masters degrees usually take one year full-time or two years part-time. Research degrees take from two to three years full-time. Details of taught courses and research degree opportunities can be found in the *Directory of Graduate Studies*, published annually for the Careers Research and Advisory Centre (CRAC).

Post-experience short courses are forming an increasing part of higher education provision, reflecting the need to update professional and technical training. Most of these courses fund themselves.

ADMISSIONS

The target number of students entering full-time higher education is 31 to 33 per cent of the 18- to 19-year-old age group in 1999–2000. Institutions suffer financial penalties if the number of students laid down for them by the Funding Councils is exceeded, but the individual university or college decides which students to accept. The formal entry requirements to most degree courses are two A-levels at grade E or above (or equivalent), and to HND courses one A-level (or equivalent). In practice, most offers of places require qualifications in excess of this, higher requirements usually reflecting the popularity of a course. These requirements do not, however, exclude applications from students with a variety of non-GCSE qualifications or unquantified experience and skills.

For admission to a degree, DipHE or HND, potential students apply through a central clearing house, Universities and Colleges Admission Service (UCAS). Applicants are supplied with an application form and a *UCAS Handbook*, available from schools, colleges and careers offices or directly from UCAS, and may apply to a maximum of six institutions/courses. The only exception among universities is the Open University, which conducts its own admissions.

Applications for undergraduate teacher training courses are made through UCAS. Details of initial teacher training courses in Scotland can be obtained from colleges of education and those universities offering such courses, and from the Committee of Scottish Higher Education Principals (COSHEP).

For admission as a postgraduate student, universities and colleges normally require a good first degree in a subject related to the proposed course of study or research, but other experience and qualifications will be considered on merit. Most applications are made to individual institutions but there are two clearing houses of relevance. Postgraduate teacher training courses in England and Wales utilize the Graduate Teacher Training Registry. Applications to postgraduate teacher training courses in Scotland are made through the Teacher Education Admissions Clearing House (TEACH). Applications for PGCE courses at institutions in Northern Ireland are made to the Department of Education for Northern Ireland. For social work the Social Work Admissions System operates.

FEES

From September 1998 new entrants to undergraduate courses have paid, directly to the institution, an annual contribution to their fees (up to £1,025 in 1999–2000) depending on their own level of income and that of their spouse or parents. Among the classes of students exempt from payment are: existing students with mandatory awards (*see below*), for whom the grant-awarding body pays; postgraduate certificate of education students; Scottish and EU students in the fourth year of a four-year degree course at a Scottish institution; and medical students in the fifth year of their course. Students from EU member countries pay fees at home student rates and will also be liable to make an annual contribution to fees assessed against family income.

Universities and colleges are free to set their own charges for students from non-EU countries, whose fees are meant to cover the cost of their education. Financial help is available under a number of schemes. Information about them is available from British Council offices worldwide.

For postgraduate students, the maximum tuition fee that will be reimbursed through the awards system is £2,675 in 1999–2000.

STUDENT SUPPORT

STUDENT GRANTS

Students in the UK who started a full-time or sandwich undergraduate course of higher education since the academic year commencing in September 1998 are no longer eligible for a grant. Grants for such students have been replaced by loans which are partly income-contingent, although some students, such as single parents and those with dependants are entitled to a means-tested grant for help in meeting certain living costs. Disabled students are eligible for non means-tested disabled students allowances. Students who started their courses before September 1998 continue to be eligible for means-tested maintenance grants, from which a parental contribution is deductible on a sliding scale dependent on income or, for married students, from their spouse's income. However, a parental contribution is not deducted from the grant to students over 25 years of age who have been self-supporting for at least three years. The main rates of mandatory grant have been frozen since 1991–2, while the amount available as a loan has increased in compensation.

Grants are paid by the local education authority for the area in which the student lives in England, Wales and Northern Ireland. The cost is reimbursed by central government. For students resident in Scotland grants are made by central government through the Student Awards Agency.

The means-tested maintenance grant, usually paid once a term, covers periods of attendance during term as well as the Christmas and Easter vacations, but not the summer vacation. The basic grant rates for 1999–2000 (rates for Scottish students in parentheses) are:

Living in

College/lodgings in London area	£2,280 (£2,200)
College/lodgings outside London area	£1,855 (£1,780)
Parental home	£1,515 (£1,360)

Additional allowances are available if, for example, the course requires a period of study abroad.

Expenditure on student fees and maintenance in 1997–8 was £2,378.7 million; about 943 thousand mandatory awards were made.

STUDENT LOANS

In the academic year 1999–2000 students are eligible to apply for interest-free but indexed loans of up to £4,480 through LEAs in England and Wales, education and library boards in Northern Ireland and the Student Awards Agency in Scotland.

Loans are available to students on designated courses, which are those full-time or sandwich courses leading to: a degree; the Diploma of Higher Education; the Higher National Diploma; initial teacher-training courses, including those for the postgraduate certificate of education and the art teachers' certificate or diploma; a university certificate or diploma course lasting at least three years and other qualifications which are specifically designated as being comparable to first degree courses. Certain residency conditions also apply. From autumn 2000 loans of up to £500 will be available to part-time students on low incomes. In 1997–8, 615.1 thousand loans were taken up, to the value of £941.0 million. Repayment arrangements differ for students who embarked upon higher education courses before the 1998–99 academic year and those starting thereafter. The former normally repay over five to seven years, although repayment can be deferred if annual income is at or below 85 per cent of national average earnings (£17,784 at 31 August 1999). The latter will not be required to make repayments if their annual income is below £10,000; otherwise a percentage of the income above that amount is taken to repay the loan.

ACCESS FUNDS

Access funds are allocated by central government to the appropriate Funding Councils in England, Wales and Scotland and administered by further and higher education institutions. In Northern Ireland they are allocated by central government directly to the institution. They are available to students whose access to education might otherwise be inhibited by financial considerations or where real financial difficulties are faced. For the academic year 1999–2000, provision in the UK is £72 million.

POSTGRADUATE AWARDS

Grants for postgraduate study are of two types, both discretionary: 30-week bursaries, which are means-tested and are available for certain vocational and diploma courses; and studentship awards, which cover students undertaking research degrees or taught masters degrees, are dependent on the class of first degree (especially for research degrees) and are not means-tested. Postgraduate students, with the exception of students on loan-bearing diploma courses such as teacher training, are not eligible to apply for student loans. For students resident in England and Wales funding is provided by the DfEE, research councils, the Ministry of Agriculture, Fisheries and Food and the British Academy.

In Scotland postgraduate funding is provided by central government through the Student Awards Agency for Scotland, the Scottish Executive Rural Affairs Department and the research councils as in England and Wales.

Awards in Northern Ireland are made by DENI, the Department of Agriculture for Northern Ireland and the Medical Research Council.

The rates for 30-week bursaries for non loan-bearing courses of professional and vocational training in 1999–2000 (Scottish rates in parenthesis) are:

Living in

College/lodgings in London area	£4,010* (£3,749)
College/lodgings outside London area	£3,085 (£2,958)
Parental home	£2,585 (£2,235)

*1998–9 rate

Studentship awards are payable at between £5,455 and £7,060 a year (1999–2000).

ADULT AND CONTINUING EDUCATION

The term adult education covers a broad spectrum of educational activities. In the UK, the responsibility for securing adult and continuing education leading to academic or vocational qualifications is statutory. In England, Wales and Scotland it is shared between various bodies: the Further Education Funding Councils are responsible for and fund those courses which take place in their sector and lead to academic and vocational qualifications, prepare students to undertake further or higher education courses, or confer basic skills; the Higher Education Funding Councils fund advanced courses of continuing education. The LEAs have the power, although not the duty, to provide those courses which do not fall within the remit of the Funding Councils. Funding in Northern Ireland is through the education and library boards.

Adult education takes place in 'area' adult education centres (England and Wales), vocational further education colleges (47 in 1998) and evening centres (Scotland), community schools (Northern Ireland), the adult studies departments of colleges of further and higher education and universities.

The involvement of universities in adult education and continuing education has diversified considerably. Birkbeck College in the University of London caters solely for part-time students. Those institutions and colleges formerly in the PCFC sector in England and Wales, because of their range of courses and flexible patterns of student attendance, provide opportunities in the field of adult and continuing education. The Forum for the Advancement of Continuing Education (FACE) promotes collaboration between institutions of higher education active in this area. The Open University, in partnership with the BBC, provides distance teaching leading to first degrees, and also offers post-experience and higher degree courses.

Of the voluntary bodies, the biggest is the Workers' Educational Association (WEA) which operates throughout the UK, reaching about 150,000 adult students annually. The FEFCs and LEAs make grants towards provision.

NIACE, the national organisation for adult learning has a broad remit to promote lifelong learning opportunities for adults. NIACE works to develop increased participation in education and training. It does this through research and project work, conferences, publications and the provision of an information service to educational providers. NIACE Cymru, the Welsh committee, receives financial support from the National Assembly for Wales, support in kind from local authorities, and advises government, voluntary bodies and education providers on adult continuing education and training matters in Wales. In Scotland advice on adult and community education, and promotion thereof, is provided by the Scottish Community Education Council. Following the demise of the Northern Ireland Council for Adult Education, its functions have been taken over by DENI until a successor body can be set up.

The Universities' Association for Continuing Education (UACE) represents the continuing education community within higher education and is open to universities and higher education institutions in the UK with additional provision for international, associate and individual members.

COURSES

Although lengths vary, most courses are part-time. Long-term residential colleges in England and Wales are grant-aided by the FEFCs and provide full-time courses lasting one or two years. Some colleges and centres offer short-term residential courses in a wide range of subjects. Local education authorities directly sponsor many of the colleges, while others are sponsored by universities or voluntary organizations. A directory of learning holidays, *Time to Learn*, is published by NIACE.

GRANTS

Adult education bursaries for students at the long-term residential colleges of adult education are the responsibility of the colleges themselves. The awards are administered for the colleges by the Awards Officer of the Residential Colleges Committee for students resident in England and are funded by the FEFC for England in English colleges; for colleges in Wales they are funded and administered by the FEFC for Wales; for colleges in Scotland they are funded by central government and administered by the Scottish FEFCs; and for colleges in Northern Ireland they are funded by central government and administered by the education and library boards.

Education Directory

LOCAL EDUCATION AUTHORITY

ENGLAND

COUNTY COUNCILS

BEDFORDSHIRE, County Hall, Cauldwell Street, Bedford MK42 9AP. Tel: 01234-363222. *Director,* P. Brett

BUCKINGHAMSHIRE, County Hall, Walton Street, Aylesbury HP20 1UA. Tel: 01296-382602. *Director,* D. McGahey

CAMBRIDGESHIRE, Education Information Office, Box ELH 1500, Shire Hall, Cambridge CB3 0AP. Tel: 01223-717667. *Director,* A. Baxter

CHESHIRE, County Hall, Chester CH1 1SQ. Tel: 01244-602201. *Director,* D. Cracknell

CORNWALL, County Hall, Truro TR1 3AY. Tel: 01872-322000. *Director,* J. Harris

CUMBRIA, 5 Portland Square, Carlisle CA1 1PU. Tel: 01228-606868. *Director,* J. Nellist

DERBYSHIRE, County Hall, Matlock DE4 3AG. Tel: 01629-585641. *Director (acting),* R. V. Taylor

DEVON, County Hall, Topsham Road, Exeter EX2 4QD. Tel: 01392-382059. *Director of Education, Arts and Libraries,* A Smith

DORSET, County Hall, Colliton Park, Dorchester DT1 1XJ. Tel: 01305-224171. *Director,* R. Ely

DURHAM, County Hall, Durham DH1 5UL. Tel: 0191-383 3319. *Director,* K. Mitchell

EAST SUSSEX, County Hall, St Anne's Crescent, Lewes BN7 1SG. Tel: 01273-481316. *County Education Officer,* D. Mallen, CBE

ESSEX, PO Box 47, Victoria Road South, Chelmsford CM1 1LD. Tel: 01245-492211. *Director of Learning Services,* P. A. Lincoln

GLOUCESTERSHIRE, Shire Hall, Westgate Street, Gloucester GL1 2TG. Tel: 01452-425300. *Director,* R. Crouch

HAMPSHIRE, The Castle, Winchester SO23 8UG. Tel: 01962-841841. *County Education Officer,* A. J. Seber

HERTFORDSHIRE, County Hall, Pegs Lane, Hertford SG13 8DE. Tel: 01992-555827. *Director,* R. Shostak

ISLE OF WIGHT, County Hall, High Street, Newport PO30 1UD. Tel: 01983-823400. *Director,* A. Kaye

KENT, Sessions House, County Hall, Maidstone ME14 1XQ. Tel: 01622-671411. *Director,* N. Henwood

LANCASHIRE, PO Box 61, County Hall, Preston PR1 8RJ. Tel: 01772-254868. *Director of Education and Cultural Services,* C. J. Trinick

LEICESTERSHIRE, County Hall, Glenfield, Leicester LE3 8RF. Tel: 0116-265 6634. *Director,* Mrs J. A. M. Strong

LINCOLNSHIRE, County Offices, Newland, Lincoln LN1 1YL. Tel: 01522-552222. *Director of Education and Cultural Services,* N. J. Riches

NORFOLK, County Hall, Martineau Lane, Norwich NR1 2DH. Tel: 01603-222146. *Director,* Dr B. C. Slater

NORTHAMPTONSHIRE, Education and Community Learning Directorate, PO Box 149, County Hall, Northampton NN1 1AU. Tel: 01604-236252. *Director,* Mrs B. Bignold

NORTHUMBERLAND, County Hall, Morpeth NE61 2EF. Tel: 01670-533601. *Director,* Dr L. Davis

NORTH YORKSHIRE, County Hall, Northallerton, N. Yorks DL7 8AE. Tel: 01609-780780. *Director,* Miss C. Welbourn

NOTTINGHAMSHIRE, County Hall, West Bridgford, Nottingham NG2 7QP. Tel: 0115-982 3823. *Director,* R. Valentine

OXFORDSHIRE, Macclesfield House, New Road, Oxford OX1 1NA. Tel: 01865-815449. *Chief Education Officer,* G. Badman

SHROPSHIRE, The Shirehall, Abbey Foregate, Shrewsbury SY2 6ND. Tel: 01743-254307. *Director,* Mrs C. Adams

SOMERSET, County Hall, Taunton TA1 4DY. Tel: 01823-355790. *Director,* M. Jennings

STAFFORDSHIRE, Tipping Street, Stafford ST16 2DH. Tel: 01785-223121. *Director,* Dr P. J. Hunter

SUFFOLK, St Andrew House, County Hall, Ipswich IP14 1LJ. Tel: 01473-584627. *Director,* D. J. Peachey

SURREY, County Hall, Penrhyn Road, Kingston upon Thames KT1 2DN. Tel: 0181-541 9500. *Director,* Dr P. Gray

WARWICKSHIRE, PO Box 24, 22 Northgate Street, Warwick CV34 4SR. Tel: 01926-410410. *Director,* E. Wood

WEST SUSSEX, County Hall, Chichester PO19 1RF. Tel: 01243-777129. *Director,* R. D. C. Bunker

WILTSHIRE, County Hall, By The Sea Road, Trowbridge BA14 8JB. Tel: 01225-713750. *Director,* vacant

WORCESTERSHIRE, County Hall, Spetchley Road, Worcester WR5 2NP. Tel: 01905-763763. *Director of Educational Services,* J. Kramer

UNITARY COUNCILS

BARNSLEY, Berneslai Close, Barnsley S70 2HS. Tel: 01226-773500. *Director,* D. Dalton

BATH AND NORTH-EAST SOMERSET, PO Box 25, Riverside, Temple Street, Keynsham, Bristol BS31 1DN. Tel: 01225-477000. *Strategic Director (Education and Culture),* R. Jones

BIRMINGHAM, Margaret Street, Birmingham B3 3BU. Tel: 0121-303 2500. *Director,* Prof. T. Brighouse

BLACKBURN WITH DARWEN, Town Hall, Blackburn BB1 7DY. Tel: 01254-585541. *Director,* Dr M. Pattison

BLACKPOOL, Progress House, Clifton Road, Blackpool FY4 4US. Tel: 01253-476555. *Director,* Dr D. Sanders

BOLTON, Paderborn House, Civic Centre, Bolton BL1 1RU. Tel: 01204-522311. *Director,* Mrs M. Blenkinsop

BOURNEMOUTH, Dorset House, 20–22 Christchurch Road, Bournemouth BH1 3NL. Tel: 01202-451451. *Director,* K. Shaikh

BRACKNELL FOREST, Edward Elgar House, Skimped Hill Lane, Bracknell, Berks RG12 1LY. Tel: 01344-424642. *Director,* A. Eccleston

BRADFORD, Flockton House, Flockton Road, Bradford BD7 7RY. Tel: 01274-751840. *Director,* Mrs D. Cavanagh

BRIGHTON AND HOVE, PO Box 2503, Kings House, Grand Avenue, Hove BN3 2SU. Tel: 01273-290000. *Director,* D. Hawker

BRISTOL, The Council House, College Green, Bristol BS1 5TR. Tel: 0117-903 7961. *Director,* R. Riddell

BURY, Athenaeum House, Market Street, Bury BL9 0SW. Tel: 0161-253 5652. *Director,* H. Williams

CALDERDALE, Northgate House, Northgate, Halifax HX1 1UN. Tel: 01422-357257. *Director,* Ms C. White

COVENTRY, Council Offices, Earl Street, Coventry CV1 5RS. Tel: 01203-831500. *Director,* Ms C. Goodwin

DARLINGTON, Town Hall, Darlington DL1 5QT. Tel: 01325-380651. *Director,* G. Pennington

DERBY, Middleton House, 27 St Mary's Gate, Derby DEI 3NN. Tel: 01332-716924. *Director*, vacant

DONCASTER, 7th Floor, The Council House, College Road, Doncaster DNI 3AD. Tel: 01302-737103. *Executive Director*, M. Simpson

DUDLEY, Westox House, 1 Trinity Road, Dudley DYI IDQ. Tel: 01384-814225. *Chief Education Officer*, R. P. Colligan

EAST RIDING OF YORKSHIRE, County Hall, Beverley HUI7 9BA. Tel: 01482-887700. *Director*, J. Ginnever

GATESHEAD, Civic Centre, Regent Street, Gateshead NE8 IHH. Tel: 0191-477 1011. *Director*, B. H. Edwards

HALTON, Grosvenor House, Halton Lea, Runcorn WA7 2ED. Tel: 0151-424 2061. *Director*, G. Talbot

HARTLEPOOL, Civic Centre, Victoria Road, Hartlepool TS24 8AY. Tel: 01429-266522. *Director*, J. J. Fitt

HEREFORDSHIRE, PO Box 185, Blackfriars Street, Hereford HR4 9ZR. Tel: 01432-260908. *Director*, Dr E. Oram

KINGSTON UPON HULL, Essex House, Manor Street, Hull HUI IYD. Tel: 01482-613161. *Director*, Miss J. E. Taylor

KIRKLEES, Oldgate House, 2 Oldgate, Huddersfield HDI 6QW. Tel: 01484-225242. *Chief Education Officer*, G. Tonkin

KNOWSLEY, Huyton Hey Road, Huyton, Knowsley L36 9YH. Tel: 0151-443 3220. *Director*, P. Wylie

LEEDS, Merrion House, Merrion Way, Leeds LS2 8DT. Tel: 0113-247 5876. *Director*, K. Burton

LEICESTER, Marlborough House, 38 Welford Road, Leicester LE2 7AA. Tel: 0116-252 7807. *Director*, T. Warren

LIVERPOOL, 14 Sir Thomas Street, Liverpool LI 6BJ. Tel: 0151-233 3000. *Director*, M. F. Cogley

LUTON, Unity House, 111 Stuart Street, Luton LUI 5NP. Tel: 01582-546000. *Director*, T. Dessent

MANCHESTER, Cumberland House, Crown Square, Manchester M60 3BB. Tel: 0161-234 7125. *Director*, D. Johnston

MEDWAY, Compass Centre, Chatham Maritime, Chatham, Kent ME7 4OD. Tel: 01634-881638. *Director*, R Bolsin

MIDDLESBROUGH, PO Box 69, Vancouver House, Gurney Street, Middlesborough TSI IQP. Tel: 01642-262001. *Corporate Director of Education and Leisure*, Ms C. Berry

MILTON KEYNES, Saxon Court, 502 Avebury Boulevard, Milton Keynes MK9 3HS. Tel: 01908-253325. *Director*, A. Flack

NEWCASTLE UPON TYNE, Civic Centre, Newcastle upon Tyne NEI 8PU. Tel: 0191-232 8520 ext. 5301. *Director*, D. Bell

NORTH EAST LINCOLNSHIRE, 7 Eleanor Street, Grimsby DN32 9DU. Tel: 01472-324021. *Director*, G. Hill

NORTH LINCOLNSHIRE, PO Box 35, Hewson House, Station Road, Brigg DN20 8XJ. Tel: 01724-297011. *Director*, T. Thomas

NORTH SOMERSET, Town Hall, Weston-super-Mare BS23 IAE. Tel: 01934-888822. *Director*, J. Simpson

NORTH TYNESIDE, Town Hall, High Street East, Wallsend, Tyne & Wear NE28 7RR. Tel: 0191-200 6565. *Executive Director*, L. Watson

NOTTINGHAM CITY, Sandfield Centre, Sandfield Road, Nottingham NG7 IQH. Tel: 0115-915 5555. *Director*, P. Roberts

OLDHAM, PO Box 40, Civic Centre, West Street, Oldham OLI IXJ. Tel: 0161-911 4200. *Director*, M. Willis

PETERBOROUGH, Bayard Place, Broadway, Peterborough PEI IFB. Tel: 01733-748000. *Director*, W. Goodwin

PLYMOUTH, Civic Centre, Armada Way, Plymouth PLI 2EW. Tel: 01752-307461. *Director*, S. Faruqi

POOLE, Civic Centre, Poole, Dorset BHI5 2RU. Tel: 01202-633203. *Director*, F. Davies

PORTSMOUTH, Civic Offices, Guildhall Square, Portsmouth POI 2AL. Tel: 01705-822251. *Director*, J. Gaskin

READING, Civic Centre, Reading RGI 7TD. Tel: 0118-939 0900. *Director*, A. Daykin

REDCAR AND CLEVELAND, Council Offices, Kirkleatham Street, Redcar TSIO IYA. Tel: 01642-444342. *Director*, P. Scott

ROCHDALE, PO Box 70, Municipal Offices, Smith Street, Rochdale OLI6 IYD. Tel: 01706-647474. *Director*, B. Atkinson

ROTHERHAM, Norfolk House, Walker Place, Rotherham S60 IQT. Tel: 01709-822500. *Director*, H. C. Bower

RUTLAND, Catmose, Oakham, Rutland LEI5 6HP. Tel: 01572-772700. *Head of Education Service*, Ms C. Chambers

ST HELENS, Rivington Centre, Rivington Road, St Helens WAIO 4ND. Tel: 01744-456000. *Director*, C. Hilton

SALFORD, Chapel Street, Salford M3 5TL. Tel: 0161-832 9751. *Director of Education and Leisure*, M. Carriline

SANDWELL, PO Box 41, Shaftesbury House, 402 High Street, West Bromwich B70 9LT. Tel: 0121-525 7366. *Director*, S. Gallacher

*SEFTON, Town Hall, Trinity Road, Bootle, Merseyside L20 7AE. Tel: 0151-922 4040. *Director*, B. Marsh

SHEFFIELD, Leopold Street, Sheffield SI IRJ. Tel: 0114-273 5722. *Director*, J. Crossley-Holland

SLOUGH, Town Hall, Bath Road, Slough SLI 3UQ. Tel: 01753-875712. *Chief Officer*, J. Christie

SOLIHULL, PO Box 19, Council House, Solihull B9I 3QT. Tel: 0121-704 6656. *Director*, D. Nixon

SOUTHAMPTON, Civic Centre, Southampton SOI4 7LY. Tel: 01703-832771. *Director*, R. Hogg

SOUTH GLOUCESTERSHIRE, Bowling Hill, Chipping Sodbury, S. Glos BS37 6JX. Tel: 01454-863253. *Director*, Ms T. Gillespie

SOUTHEND, Civic Centre, Victoria Avenue, Southend-on-Sea SS2 6ER. Tel: 01702-215890. *Director*, S. Hay

SOUTH TYNESIDE, Town Hall and Civic Offices, Westoe Road, South Shields NE33 2RL. Tel: 0191-427 1717. *Director*, I. Reid

STOCKPORT, Town Hall, Stockport SKI 3XE. Tel: 0161-474 3808. *Director*, M. K. J. Hunt

STOCKTON-ON-TEES, Municipal Buildings, Church Road, Stockton-on-Tees TSI8 ILD. Tel: 01642-393441. *Director*, S. T. Bradford

STOKE-ON-TRENT, PO Box 758, Swann House, Boothen Road, Stoke-on-Trent ST4 IRU. Tel: 01782-234567. *Director*, N. Rigby

SUNDERLAND, PO Box 100, Civic Centre, Sunderland SR2 7DN. Tel: 0191-553 1355. *Director*, Dr J. W. Williams, ph.D

SWINDON, Civic Offices, Euclid Street, Swindon SNI 2JH. Tel: 01793-463069. *Director*, M. Lusty

TAMESIDE, Council Offices, Wellington Road, Ashton under Lyne, Lancs OL6 6DL. Tel: 0161-342 2201. *Director of Education and Leisure Services*, P. Lawday

TELFORD AND WREKIN, Civic Offices, Telford, Shropshire TF3 4LD. Tel: 01952-202402. *Director*, Ms C. Davies

THURROCK, PO Box 118, Grays, Essex RMI7 6GF. Tel: 01375-652283. *Director*, R. Wilkins

TORBAY, Oldway Mansion, Paignton, Devon TQ3 2TE. Tel: 01803-208208. *Director*, G. Cane

TRAFFORD, PO Box 40, Trafford Town Hall, Talbot Road, Stretford, Trafford, Greater Manchester M32 OEL. Tel: 0161-912 1212. *Director Education, Arts and Leisure*, C. Pratt

WAKEFIELD, County Hall, Wakefield WF1 2QW. Tel: 01924-305500. *Director*, J. McLeod

WALSALL, Civic Centre, Darwall Street, Walsall WS1 1TP. Tel: 01922-652301. *Director*, T. Howard

WARRINGTON, New Town House, Buttermarket Street, Warrington, Cheshire WA1 2NH. Tel: 01925-442901. *Director*, M. Roxborgh

WEST BERKSHIRE, Avon Bank House, West Street, Newbury, Berks RG14 1BZ. Tel: 01635-519722. *Director*, J. Mercer

WIGAN, Gateway House, Standishgate, Wigan, Lancs WN1 1AE. Tel: 01942-828891. *Director*, R. J. Clark

WINDSOR AND MAIDENHEAD, Town Hall, St Ives Road, Maidenhead, Berks SL6 1RF. Tel: 01628-796367. *Director*, M. Peckham

WIRRAL, Hamilton Building, Conway Street, Birkenhead CH41 4FD. Tel: 0151-666 2121. *Director*, C. Rice

WOKINGHAM, PO Box 156, Shute End, Wokingham, Berks RG40 1WN. Tel: 0118-974 6100. *Director*, Mrs J. Griffin

WOLVERHAMPTON, Civic Centre, St Peter's Square, Wolverhampton WV1 1RR. Tel: 01902-554100. *Director*, R. Lockwood

YORK, 10–12 George Hudson Street, York YO1 1ZG. Tel: 01904-613161. *Director*, M. Peters

LONDON

*Inner London borough

BARKING AND DAGENHAM, Town Hall, Barking, Essex IG11 7LU. Tel: 0181-592 4500. *Director*, A. Larbalestier

BARNET, The Old Town Hall, Friern Barnet Lane, London N11 3DL. Tel: 0181-359 3004. *Head of Education*, Ms L. Stone

BEXLEY, Hill View, Hill View Drive, Welling, Kent DA16 3RY. Tel: 0181-303 7777. *Director*, P. McGee

BRENT, Chesterfield House, 9 Park Lane, Wembley, Middx HA9 7RW. Tel: 0181-937 3190. *Director*, vacant

BROMLEY, Civic Centre, Stockwell Close, Bromley BR1 3UH. Tel: 0181-313 4066. *Director*, K. Davis

*CAMDEN, Crowndale Centre, 218–220 Eversholt Street, London NW1 1BD. Tel: 0171-911 1505. *Director*, R. Litchfield

*CITY OF LONDON, Education Department, Corporation of London, PO Box 270, Guildhall, London EC2P 2EJ. Tel: 0171-332 1750. *City Education Officer*, D. Smith

*CITY OF WESTMINSTER, City Hall, 64 Victoria Street, London SW1E 6QP. Tel: 0171-641 1947. *Director*, J. Harris

CROYDON, Taberner House, Park Lane, Croydon CR9 3JS. Tel: 0181-760 5555. *Director*, D. Sands

EALING, Perceval House, 14–16 Uxbridge Road, London W5 2HL. Tel: 0181-758 5410. *Director*, A. Parker

ENFIELD, PO Box 56, Civic Centre, Silver Street, Enfield, Middx EN1 3XQ. Tel: 0181-379 3200. *Director*, Ms E. Graham

*GREENWICH, Riverside House, Woolwich High Street, London SE18 6DN. Tel: 0181-312 5638. *Director*, G. Gyte

*HACKNEY, Edith Cavell Building, Enfield Road, London N1 5BA. Tel: 0181-356 5000. *Director*, Ms E. Reid

*HAMMERSMITH AND FULHAM, Cambridge House, Cambridge Grove, London W6 0LE. Tel: 0181-748 3020. *Director*, Ms C. Whatford

HARINGEY, 48 Station Road, Wood Green, London N22 4TY. Tel: 0181-489 0000. *Director*, Ms F. Magee

HARROW, PO Box 22, Civic Centre, Station Road, Harrow HA1 2UW. Tel: 0181-424 1304. *Director*, P. Osburn

HAVERING, The Broxhill Centre, Broxhill Road, Harold Hill, Romford RM14 1XN. Tel: 01708-773839. *Executive Director Children and Lifelong Learning*, S. Evans

HILLINGDON, Civic Centre, High Street, Uxbridge UB8 1UW. Tel: 01895-250528. *Director*, P. O'Hear

HOUNSLOW, Civic Centre, Lampton Road, Hounslow, Middx TW3 4DN. Tel: 0181-862 5352. *Director*, J. D. Tricket

*ISLINGTON, Laycock Street, Islington, London N1 1TH. Tel: 0171-527 5753. *Director*, A. Roberts

*KENSINGTON AND CHELSEA, Town Hall, Hornton Street, London W8 7NX. Tel: 0171-361 3303. *Director*, R. Wood

KINGSTON UPON THAMES, Guildhall 2, Kingston upon Thames KT1 1EU. Tel: 0181-547 5220. *Director*, J. Braithwaite

*LAMBETH, International House, Canterbury Crescent, London SW9 7QE. Tel: 0171-926 1000. *Director*, Ms H. Du Quesnay

*LEWISHAM, 3rd Floor, Laurence House, 1 Catford Road, London SE6 4RU. Tel: 0181-314 8527. *Director*, Ms A. Efunshile

MERTON, Civic Centre, London Road, Morden, Surrey SM4 5DX. Tel: 0181-545 3251. *Director*, Ms J. Cairns

NEWHAM, Broadway House, 322 High Street, Stratford, London E15 1AJ. Tel: 0181-555 5552. *Director*, I. Harrison

REDBRIDGE, Lynton House, 255–259 High Road, Ilford, Essex IG1 1NY. Tel: 0181-478 3020. *Chief Education Officer*, D. Capper

RICHMOND UPON THAMES, 1st Floor, Regal House, London Road, Twickenham TW1 3QS. Tel: 0181-891 7500. *Chief Executive (acting)*, R. Hancock

*SOUTHWARK, 1 Bradenham Close, London SE17 2QA. Tel: 0171-525 5050. *Director Education and Leisure Services*, G. Mott

SUTTON, The Grove, Carshalton, Surrey SM5 3AL. Tel: 0181-770 5000. *Strategic Director*, Dr I. Birnbaum

*TOWER HAMLETS, Mulberry Place, 5 Clove Crescent, London E14 2BG. Tel: 0171-364 5000. *Director of Education and Community Services*, Ms C. Gilbert

WALTHAM FOREST, Leyton Municipal Offices, High Road, Leyton, London E10 5QJ. Tel: 0181-527 5544 ext. 5001. *Chief Education Officer*, A. Lockhart

*WANDSWORTH, Town Hall, Wandsworth High Street, London SW18 2PU. Tel: 0181-871 8013. *Director*, P. Robinson

WALES

ANGLESEY, Swyddfa'r Sir, Llangefni, Anglesey LL77 7EY. Tel: 01248-752921. *Director*, R. P. Jones

BLAENAU GWENT, Festival House, Victoria Business Park, Ebbw Vale NP23 6ER. Tel: 01495-355434. *Director*, B. Mawby

BRIDGEND, Sunnyside, Sunnyside Road, Bridgend CF31 4AR. Tel: 01656-642600. *Director*, D. Matthews

CAERPHILLY, Council Offices, Caerphilly Road, Ystrad Mynach, Hengoed CF82 7EP. Tel: 01443-815588. *Director*, N. Harries

CARDIFF, County Hall, Atlantic Wharf, Cardiff CF1 5UW. Tel: 01222-872700. *Director*, T. Davies

CARMARTHENSHIRE, Pibwrlwyd, Carmarthen SA31 2NH. Tel: 01267-224501. *Director*, K. Davies

CEREDIGION, Swyddfa'r Sir, Marine Terrace, Aberystwyth SY23 2DE. Tel: 01970-633600. *Director*, R. Williams

CONWY, Government Buildings, Dinerth Road, Rhos-on-Sea LL28 4UL. Tel: 01492-575031. *Director*, R. E. Williams

DENBIGHSHIRE, Phase 4, County Hall, Mold, Flintshire CH7 6GR. Tel: 01824-706777. *Director*, E. Lewis

FLINTSHIRE, County Hall, Mold CH7 6NW. Tel: 01352-704010. *Director of Education, Libraries and Information*, K. McDonogh

GWYNEDD, Shirehall Street, Caernarfon LL55 1SH. Tel: 01286-677162. *Director*, D. Whittall

MERTHYR TYDFIL, Ty Keir Hardie, Riverside Court, Avenue De Clichy, Merthyr Tydfil CF47 8XD. Tel: 01685-724614. *Director,* D. Jones

MONMOUTHSHIRE, County Hall, Cwmbran NP44 2XH. Tel: 01633-644487. *Director,* D. Young

NEATH PORT TALBOT, Civic Centre, Port Talbot SA13 1PJ. Tel: 01639-763298. *Director,* V. Thomas

NEWPORT, Civic Centre, Newport NP20 4UR. Tel: 01633-232204. *Director,* G. Bingham

PEMBROKESHIRE, County Hall, Haverfordwest SA61 1TP. Tel: 01437-764551. *Director,* G. Davies

POWYS, County Hall, Llandrindod Wells LD1 5LG. Tel: 01597-826000. *Director,* M. Barker

RHONDDA, CYNON, TAFF, Education Centre, Grawen Street, Porth CF39 0BU. Tel: 01443-687666. *Director,* vacant

SWANSEA, County Hall, Oystermouth Road, Swansea SA1 3SN. Tel: 01792-636351. *Director,* R. Parry

TORFAEN, County Hall, Croesyceiliog, Cwmbran, Torfaen NP44 2WR. Tel: 01633-648069. *Director,* M. de Val

VALE OF GLAMORGAN, Civic Offices, Holton Road, Barry CF63 4RU. Tel: 01446-709138. *Director,* A. Davies

WREXHAM, Roxburgh House, Hill Street, Wrexham LL11 1SN. Tel: 01978-297420. *Director,* T. Garner

SCOTLAND

ABERDEEN CITY, Summerhill Education Centre, Stronsay Drive, Aberdeen AB15 6JA. Tel: 01224-346060. *Director,* J. Stodter

ABERDEENSHIRE, Woodhill House, Westburn Road, Aberdeen AB16 5GB. Tel: 01224-665420. *Director,* M. White

ANGUS, County Buildings, Market Street, Forfar DD8 3WE. Tel: 01307-461460. *Director,* J. Anderson

ARGYLL AND BUTE, Argyll House, Alexandra Parade, Dunoon PA23 8AG. Tel: 01369-704000. *Director,* A. Morton

CITY OF EDINBURGH, Wellington Court, 10 Waterloo Place, Edinburgh EH1 3EG. Tel: 0131-469 3000. *Director,* R. Jobson

CLACKMANNANSHIRE, Lime Tree House, Alloa FK10 1EX. Tel: 01259-452431. *Director,* K. Bloomer

DUMFRIES AND GALLOWAY, Education Department, 30 Edinburgh Road, Dumfries DG1 1JG. Tel: 01387-260000. *Director (acting),* F. Sanderson

DUNDEE CITY, 8th Floor, Tayside House, Crichton Street, Dundee DD1 3RJ. Tel: 01382-434000. *Director,* Ms A. Wilson

EAST AYRSHIRE, Council Headquarters, London Road, Kilmarnock KA3 7BU. Tel: 01563-576017. *Director,* J. Mulgrew

EAST DUNBARTONSHIRE, Boclair House, 100 Milngavie Road, Bearsden, Glasgow G61 2TQ. Tel: 0141-578 8000. *Director,* I. Mills

EAST LOTHIAN, John Muir House, Haddington EH41 3HA. Tel: 01620-827562. *Director,* A. Blackie

EAST RENFREWSHIRE, Council Offices, Eastwood Park, Rouken Glen Road, Giffnock G46 6UG. Tel: 0141-577 3431. *Director,* Mrs E. J. Currie

EILEAN SIAR/WESTERN ISLES, Council Offices, Sandwick Road, Stornoway, Isle of Lewis HS1 2BW. Tel: 01851-703773. *Director (acting),* M. Macleod

FALKIRK, McLaren House, Marchmont Avenue, Polmont, Falkirk FK2 0NZ. Tel: 01324-506600. *Director,* Dr G. Young

FIFE, Rothesay House, North Street, Glenrothes KY7 5PN. Tel: 01592-413656. *Director,* A. McKay

GLASGOW CITY, Nye Bevan House, 20 India Street, Glasgow G2 4PF. Tel: 0141-287 6898. *Director,* K. Corsar

HIGHLAND, Council Buildings, Glenurquhart Road, Inverness IV3 5NX. Tel: 01463-702802. *Director,* B. Robertson

INVERCLYDE, 105 Dalrymple Street, Greenock PA15 1HT. Tel: 01475-712824. *Director,* B. McLeary

MIDLOTHIAN, Fairfield House, 8 Lothian Road, Dalkeith EH22 3ZJ. Tel: 0131-270 7500. *Director,* D. MacKay

MORAY, Council Offices, High Street, Elgin IV30 1BX. Tel: 01343-563170. *Director,* K. Gavin

NORTH AYRSHIRE, Cunninghame House, Irvine KA12 8EE. Tel: 01294-324400. *Director,* J. Travers

NORTH LANARKSHIRE, Municipal Buildings, Kildonan Street, Coatbridge ML5 3BT. Tel: 01236-812222. *Director,* M. O'Neill

ORKNEY ISLANDS, Council Offices, School Place, Kirkwall, Orkney KW15 1NY. Tel: 01856-873535. *Director,* L. Manson

PERTH AND KINROSS, Blackfriars, Perth PH1 5LU. Tel: 01738-476200. *Director,* R. McKay

RENFREWSHIRE, Council Headquarters, South Building, Cotton Street, Paisley PA1 1LE. Tel: 0141-842 5601. *Director,* Ms S. Rae

SCOTTISH BORDERS, Council Headquarters, Newtown St Boswells, Melrose, Roxburghshire TD6 0SA. Tel: 01835-824000. *Director,* J. Christie

SHETLAND ISLANDS, Hayfield House, Hayfield Lane, Lerwick, Shetland ZE1 0QD. Tel: 01595-744000. *Director,* J. Halcrow

SOUTH AYRSHIRE, County Buildings, Wellington Square, Ayr KA7 1DR. Tel: 01292-612000. *Director,* M. McCabe

SOUTH LANARKSHIRE, Council Headquarters, Almada Street, Hamilton ML3 0AA. Tel: 01698-454545. *Executive Director,* Ms M. Allan

STIRLING, Viewforth, Stirling FK8 2ET. Tel: 01786-442678. *Director,* G. Jeyes

WEST DUNBARTONSHIRE, Garshake Road, Dumbarton G82 3PU. Tel: 01389-737301. *Director,* I. McMurdo

WEST LOTHIAN, Lindsay House, South Bridge Street, Bathgate EH48 1TS. Tel: 01506-776000. *Corporate Manager,* R. Stewart

NORTHERN IRELAND

EDUCATION AND LIBRARY BOARDS

BELFAST, 40 Academy Street, Belfast BT1 2NQ. Tel: 01232-564122. *Chief Executive,* D. Cargo

NORTH, County Hall, 182 Galgorm Road, Ballymena, Co. Antrim BT42 1HN. Tel: 01266-653333. *Chief Executive,* G. Topping

SOUTH EASTERN, Grahamsbridge Road, Dundonald BT16 2HS. Tel: 01232-381188. *Chief Executive,* J. B. Fitzsimons

SOUTHERN, 3 Charlemont Place, The Mall, Armagh BT61 9AX. Tel: 01861-512200. *Chief Executive,* Mrs H. McClenaghan

WESTERN, 1 Hospital Road, Omagh, Co. Tyrone BT79 0AW. Tel: 01662-411411. *Chief Executive,* P. J. Martin

ISLANDS

GUERNSEY, Grange Road, St Peter Port, Guernsey GY1 1RQ. Tel: 01481-710821. *Director,* D. T. Neale

JERSEY, PO Box 142, Jersey JE4 8QJ. Tel: 01534-509500. *Director,* T. W. McKeon

ISLE OF MAN, Murray House, 5–11 Mount Havelock, Douglas, Isle of Man IM1 2SG. Tel: 01624-685820. *Director,* R. B. Cowin

ISLES OF SCILLY, Town Hall, St Mary's, Isles of Scilly TR21 0LW. Tel: 01720-422537 ext. 145. *Secretary for Education,* P. S. Hygate

ADVISORY BODIES

SCHOOLS

EDUCATION OTHERWISE, PO Box 7420, London N9 9SG.
Tel: Helpline: 0870-730 0074

BRITISH EDUCATIONAL COMMUNICATIONS AND
TECHNOLOGY AGENCY (formerly National Council
for Educational Technology), Milburn Hill Road,
Science Park, Coventry CV4 7JJ. Tel: 01203-416994.
Chief Executive, O. Lynch

INTERNATIONAL BACCALAUREATE ORGANIZATION,
Peterson House, Fortran Road, St Mellons, Cardiff
CF3 0WB. Tel: 01222-774000. *Director of Academic Affairs*,
Dr H. Drennen

NATIONAL ADVISORY COUNCIL FOR EDUCATION AND
TRAINING TARGETS, Dunford Lodge, Storth Lane,
Ranmoor, Sheffield S10 3HN. Tel: 0114-259 7887.
Director, J. Dewsbury

SCOTTISH COUNCIL FOR EDUCATIONAL
TECHNOLOGY, 74 Victoria Crescent Road, Glasgow
G12 9JN. Tel: 0141-337 5000. *Chief Executive*, R. Pietrasik

SPECIAL EDUCATIONAL NEEDS TRIBUNAL, 7th Floor,
Windsor House, 50 Victoria Street, London SW1H 0NW.
Tel: 0171-925 6925. *President*, T. Aldridge; *Secretary*,
P. Craggs

INDEPENDENT SCHOOLS

GOVERNING BODIES ASSOCIATION, The Ancient
Foresters, Bush End, Takeley, Bishop's Stortford, Herts
CM22 6NN. Tel: 01279-871865. *Chief Executive*,
F. V. Morgan

GOVERNING BODIES OF GIRLS' SCHOOLS
ASSOCIATION, The Ancient Foresters, Bush End,
Takeley, Bishop's Stortford, Herts CM22 6NN. Tel:
01279-871865. *Chief Executive*, F. V. Morgan

INDEPENDENT SCHOOLS COUNCIL, Grosvenor Gardens
House, 35–37 Grosvenor Gardens, London SW1W 0BS.
Tel: 0171-798 1590. *General Secretary*, Dr A. B. Cooke

INDEPENDENT SCHOOLS EXAMINATIONS BOARD,
Jordan House, Christchurch Road, New Milton, Hants
BH25 6QJ. Tel: 01425-621111. *Secretary-General*,
Mrs J. Williams

INDEPENDENT SCHOOLS INFORMATION SERVICE, 21
Melville Street, Edinburgh EH3 7PE. Tel: 0131-220 2106.
Administrator, Mrs F. Valpy

INDEPENDENT SCHOOLS INFORMATION SERVICE, 35-
37 Grosvenor Gardens, London SW1W 0BS. Tel: 0171-
798 1500. *Secretary*, Mrs C. Parrish

SCOTTISH COUNCIL OF INDEPENDENT SCHOOLS, 21
Melville Street, Edinburgh EH3 7PE. Tel: 0131-220 2106.
Director, Mrs J. Sischy

FURTHER EDUCATION

FURTHER EDUCATION DEVELOPMENT AGENCY
(FEDA), Citadel Place, Tinworth Street, London
SE11 5EH. Tel: 0171-840 5400. *Chief Executive*, C. Hughes

Regional Advisory Councils

ASSOCIATION OF COLLEGES IN THE EASTERN REGION,
Merlin Place, Milton Road, Cambridge CB4 0DP. Tel:
01223-424022. *Chief Executive*, J. Graystone

CENTRA (EDUCATION AND TRAINING SERVICES) LTD,
Duxbury Park, Duxbury Hall Road, Chorley, Lancs
PR7 4AT. Tel: 01257-241428. *Chief Executive*, P. Wren;
Chairman, R. Chapman

EMFEC (East Midland Further Education Council),
Robins Wood House, Robins Wood Road, Aspley,
Nottingham NG8 3NH. Tel: 0115-929 3291. *Chief
Executive*, Ms J. Gardiner

NCFE (formerly Northern Council for Further
Education), Portland House, 2nd Floor, Block D, New
Bridge Street, Newcastle upon Tyne NE1 8AN. Tel:
0191-201 3100. *Chief Executive*, J. F. Pearce

SOUTHERN REGIONAL COUNCIL FOR EDUCATION AND
TRAINING, Building 33, The University of Reading,
London Road, Reading RG1 5AQ. Tel: 0118-931 6320.
Chief Executive, B. J. Knowles

SOUTH WEST ASSOCIATION FOR EDUCATION AND
TRAINING, Bishops Hull House, Bishops Hull,
Taunton, Somerset TA1 5RA. Tel: 01823-335491. *Chief
Executive*, Ms L. McGrath

WELSH JOINT EDUCATION COMMITTEE, 245 Western
Avenue, Cardiff CF5 2YX. Tel: 01222-265000.
Examinations Secretary, B. Evans

YORKSHIRE AND HUMBERSIDE ASSOCIATION FOR
FURTHER AND HIGHER EDUCATION, 13 Wellington
Road East, Dewsbury, W. Yorks WF13 1XG. Tel: 01924-
450900. *Director (acting)*, C. Daniel

HIGHER EDUCATION

ASSOCIATION OF COMMONWEALTH UNIVERSITIES,
John Foster House, 36 Gordon Square, London
WC1H 0PF. Tel: 0171-387 8572. *Secretary-General*,
Prof. M. G. Gibbons

COMMITTEE OF SCOTTISH HIGHER EDUCATION
PRINCIPALS (COSHEP), 53 Hanover Street,
Edinburgh EH2 2PJ. Tel: 0131-226 1111. *Secretary*,
Dr R. L. Crawford

COMMITTEE OF VICE-CHANCELLORS AND PRINCIPALS
OF THE UNIVERSITIES OF THE UNITED KINGDOM,
Woburn House, 20 Tavistock Square, London
WC1H 9HQ. Tel: 0171-419 4111. *Chairman*, H. Newby;
Chief Executive, Ms D. Warwick

NORTHERN IRELAND HIGHER EDUCATION COUNCIL,
Rathgael House, Balloo Road, Bangor BT19 7PR. Tel:
01247-279333. *Chairman*, Sir Kenneth Bloomfield, KCB

QUALITY ASSURANCE AGENCY FOR HIGHER
EDUCATION, Southgate House, Southgate Street,
Gloucester GL1 1UB. Tel: 01452-557000. *Chief Executive*,
J. Randall

SCOTTISH STUDENTSHIP ADVISORY GROUP, c/o
Student Awards Agency for Scotland, Gyleview House,
3 Redheughs Rigg, Edinburgh EH12 9HH. Tel: 0131-244
5846. *Chairman*, Prof. D. Harding; *Secretary*,
Mrs A. Hampson

CURRICULUM COUNCILS

AWDURDOD CYMWYSTERAU CWRICWLWM AC ASESU
CYMRU/QUALIFICATIONS, CURRICULUM AND
ASSESSMENT AUTHORITY FOR WALES, Castle
Buildings, Womanby Street, Cardiff CF1 9SX. Tel:
01222-375400. *Chief Executive*, J. V. Williams

NORTHERN IRELAND COUNCIL FOR THE
CURRICULUM, EXAMINATIONS AND ASSESSMENT,
Clarendon Dock, 29 Clarendon Road, Belfast BT1 3BG.
Tel: 01232-261200. *Acting Chief Executive*, Dr A. Hamill

QUALIFICATIONS AND CURRICULUM AUTHORITY, 29
Bolton Street, London W1Y 7PD. Tel: 0171-509 5555.
Chairman, Sir William Stubbs, PH.D.

SCOTTISH CONSULTATIVE COUNCIL ON THE
CURRICULUM, Gardyne Road, Broughty Ferry,
Dundee DD5 1NY. Tel: 01382-455053. *Chief Executive*,
M. Baughan

EXAMINING BODIES

UNITARY AWARDING BODIES
ASSESSMENT AND QUALIFICATIONS ALLIANCE (AQA).
Tel: 0161-953 1180. *Publicity Officer,* Ms H. Hallett
THE EDEXCEL FOUNDATION, Stewart House, 32 Russell
Square, London WC1B 5DN. Tel: 0171-393 4444. *Chief
Executive,* Ms C. Townsend, PH.D.
OXFORD, CAMBRIDGE AND RSA EXAMINATIONS
(OCR), 1 Regent Street, Cambridge CB2 1GG. Tel:
01223-552552. *Chief Executive,* B. Swift; *Chairman,*
Dr K. Pretty

GCSE
THE EDEXCEL FOUNDATION, *see above*
NORTHERN EXAMINATIONS AND ASSESSMENT BOARD,
Devas Street, Manchester M15 6EX. Tel: 0161-953 1180.
Chief Executive, Miss H. M. James
NORTHERN IRELAND COUNCIL FOR THE
CURRICULUM, EXAMINATIONS AND ASSESSMENT.
Tel: 01232-261200. *Chief Executive,* Dr A. Hamill
OXFORD, CAMBRIDGE AND RSA EXAMINATIONS
SEG (SOUTHERN EXAMINING GROUP), Stag Hill
House, Guildford, Surrey GU2 5XJ. Tel: 01483-506506.
Secretary-General, Dr C. P. Hughes
WELSH JOINT EDUCATION COMMITTEE, 245 Western
Avenue, Cardiff CF5 2YX. Tel: 01222-265000. *Chief
Executive,* I. Hume

A-LEVEL
THE ASSOCIATED EXAMINING BOARD, Stag Hill House,
Guildford, Surrey GU2 5XJ. Tel: 01483-506506.
Secretary-General, Dr C. P. Hughes
THE EDEXCEL FOUNDATION, *see above*
NORTHERN EXAMINATIONS AND ASSESSMENT BOARD,
Devas Street, Manchester M15 6EX. Tel: 0161-953 1180.
Chief Executive, Ms H. M. James; *Secretary,* J. Coote
NORTHERN IRELAND COUNCIL FOR THE
CURRICULUM, EXAMINATIONS AND ASSESSMENT,
Clarendon Dock, 29 Clarendon Road, Belfast BT1 3BG.
Tel: 01232-261200. *Chief Executive,* Mrs C. Coxhead
OXFORD, CAMBRIDGE AND RSA EXAMINATIONS
WELSH JOINT EDUCATION COMMITTEE, 245 Western
Avenue, Cardiff CF5 2YX. Tel: 01222-265000. *Chief
Executive,* I. Hume

SCOTLAND
SCOTTISH QUALIFICATIONS AUTHORITY, Hanover
House, 24 Douglas Street, Glasgow G2 7NQ. Tel: 0141-
248 7900. *Chief Executive,* R. Tuck; *Chairman,* D. Miller

FURTHER EDUCATION
CITY & GUILDS, 1 Giltspur Street, London EC1A 9DD.
Tel: 0171-294 2468. *Director-General,* N. Carey, PH.D.
THE EDEXCEL FOUNDATION, *see above*
OXFORD, CAMBRIDGE AND RSA EXAMINATIONS

FUNDING COUNCILS

SCHOOLS
FUNDING AGENCY FOR SCHOOLS, Albion Wharf, 25
Skeldergate, York YO1 2XL. Tel: 01904-661661.
Chairman, Vice-Adm. Sir Antony Tippett, KCB

FURTHER EDUCATION
FURTHER EDUCATION FUNDING COUNCIL FOR
ENGLAND, Cheylesmore House, Quinton Road,
Coventry CV1 2WT. Tel: 01203-863000. *Chief Executive,*
Prof. D. Melville
FURTHER EDUCATION FUNDING COUNCIL FOR
WALES, Linden Court, The Orchards, Ty Glas
Avenue, Cardiff CF14 5DZ. Tel: 01222-761861. *Chief
Executive,* Prof. J. Andrews
SCOTTISH FURTHER EDUCATION FUNDING COUNCIL,
Donaldson House, 97 Haymarket Terrace, Edinburgh
EH12 5HD. Tel: 0131-313 6590. *Chief Executive,*
Prof. J. Sizer, CBE

HIGHER EDUCATION
HIGHER EDUCATION FUNDING COUNCIL FOR
ENGLAND, Northavon House, Coldharbour Lane,
Bristol BS16 1QD. Tel: 0117-931 7317. *Chief Executive,*
Sir Brian Fender, Kt.
HIGHER EDUCATION FUNDING COUNCIL FOR WALES,
Linden Court, The Orchards, Ty Glas Avenue, Cardiff
CF14 5DZ. Tel: 01222-761861. *Chief Executive,*
Prof. J. A. Andrews
SCOTTISH HIGHER EDUCATION FUNDING COUNCIL,
Donaldson House, 97 Haymarket Terrace, Edinburgh
EH12 5HD. Tel: 0131-313 6500. *Chief Executive,*
Prof. J. Sizer, CBE; *Secretary,* L. Howells
STUDENT AWARDS AGENCY FOR SCOTLAND, Gyleview
House, 3 Redheughs Rigg, Edinburgh EH12 9HH. Tel:
0131-244 5868. *Chief Executive,* K. MacRae
STUDENT LOANS COMPANY LTD, 100 Bothwell Street,
Glasgow G2 7JD. Tel: 0141-306 2000. *Chief Executive,*
C. Ward
TEACHER TRAINING AGENCY, Portland House, Stag
Place, London SW1E 5TT. Tel: 0171-925 3700. *Chairman,*
Prof. C. Booth

ADMISSIONS AND COURSE INFORMATION

CAREERS RESEARCH AND ADVISORY CENTRE, Sheraton
House, Castle Park, Cambridge CB3 0AX. Tel: 01223-
460277. *Chief Executive,* D. McGregor
COMMITTEE OF SCOTTISH HIGHER EDUCATION
PRINCIPALS (COSHEP), St Andrew House, 141 West
Nile Street, Glasgow G1 2RN. Tel: 0141-353 1880.
Secretary, Dr R. L. Crawford
GRADUATE TEACHER TRAINING REGISTRY, Rosehill,
New Barn Lane, Cheltenham, Glos GL52 3LZ. Tel:
01242-544600. *Registrar,* Mrs M. Griffiths; *Chief
Executive,* Ms A. Millett
SOCIAL WORK ADMISSIONS SYSTEM, Rosehill, New
Barn Lane, Cheltenham, Glos GL52 3LZ. Tel: 01242-
544600. *Admissions Officer,* Mrs M. Griffiths
UNIVERSITIES AND COLLEGES ADMISSIONS SERVICE,
Rosehill, New Barn Lane, Cheltenham, Glos GL52 3LZ.
Tel: 01242-222444. *Chief Executive,* M. A. Higgins, PH.D.

UNIVERSITIES

THE UNIVERSITY OF ABERDEEN (1495)
Regent Walk, Aberdeen AB24 3FX
Tel 01224-272000
Full-time students (1998–9), 11,061
Chancellor, The Lord Wilson of Tillyorn, GCMG (1997)
Vice-Chancellor and Principal, Prof. C. D. Rice
Secretary, S. Cannon
Rector, Miss C. Dickson Wright

THE UNIVERSITY OF ABERTAY DUNDEE (1994)
Bell Street, Dundee DD1 1HG
Tel 01382-308000
Full-time students (1998–9), 3,957
Chancellor, The Earl of Airlie, KT, GCVO, PC (1994)
Vice-Chancellor and Principal, Prof. B. King
Registrar, Dr D. Button
Secretary, D. Hogarth

ANGLIA POLYTECHNIC UNIVERSITY (1992)
Bishop Hall Lane, Chelmsford CM1 1SQ
Tel 01245-493131
Full-time students (1998–9), 16,800
Chancellor, The Lord Prior, PC (1992)
Vice-Chancellor, M. Malone-Lee, CB
Secretary, S. G. Bennett

ASTON UNIVERSITY (1966)
Aston Triangle, Birmingham B4 7ET
Tel 0121-359 3611
Full-time students (1998–9), 4,710
Chancellor, Sir Adrian Cadbury (1979)
Vice-Chancellor, Prof. M. Wright
Registrar and Secretary, R. D. A. Packham

THE UNIVERSITY OF BATH (1966)
Claverton Down, Bath BA2 7AY
Tel 01225-826826
Full-time students (1998–9), 7,475
Chancellor, The Lord Tugendhat (1998)
Vice-Chancellor, Prof. V. D. Vandelinde
Registrar, J. A. Bursey

THE UNIVERSITY OF BIRMINGHAM (1900)
Edgbaston, Birmingham B15 2TT
Tel 0121-414 3344
Full-time students (1998–9), 20,000
Chancellor, Sir Alexander Jarratt, CB (1983)
Vice-Chancellor, Prof. M. Irvine, Ph.D., FRSE
Registrar and Secretary, D. J. Allen

BOURNEMOUTH UNIVERSITY (1992)
Talbot Campus, Fern Barrow, Poole BH12 5BB
Tel 01202-524111
Full-time students (1998–9), 7,714
Chancellor, The Baroness Cox (1992)
Vice-Chancellor, Prof. G. Slater
Registrar, N. O. G. Richardson

THE UNIVERSITY OF BRADFORD (1966)
Bradford BD7 1DP
Tel 01274-232323
Full-time students (1998–9), 7,517
Chancellor, The Baroness Lockwood (1997)
Vice-Chancellor, Prof. C. Bell
Registrar and Secretary, N. J. Andrew

THE UNIVERSITY OF BRIGHTON (1992)
Mithras House, Lewes Road, Brighton BN2 4AT
Tel 01273-600900
Full-time students (1998–9), 9,750
Academic Registrar, P. Reynolds
Deputy Director, D. E. House
Director, Prof. Sir David Watson
Rector, C. Lawlor

THE UNIVERSITY OF BRISTOL (1909)
Senate House, Tyndall Avenue, Bristol BS8 1TH
Tel 0117-928 9000
Full-time students (1998–9), 12,224
Chancellor, Sir Jeremy Morse, KCMG (1989)
Vice-Chancellor, Sir John Kingman, FRS

Registrar, D. Pretty
Secretary, Ms K. E. McKenzie, D.Phil.

BRUNEL UNIVERSITY (1966)
Uxbridge, Middx UB8 3PH
Tel 01895-274000
Full-time students (1998–9), 12,320
Chancellor, The Lord Wakeham, PC (1998)
Vice-Chancellor and Principal, Prof. M. J. H. Sterling, Ph.D.,
  FREng.
Academic Registrar, J. B. Alexander

THE UNIVERSITY OF BUCKINGHAM (1983)
Buckingham MK18 1EG
Tel 01280-814080
Full-time students (1998–9), 584
Chancellor, Sir Martin Jacomb (1998)
Vice-Chancellor, Prof. R. H. Taylor
Registrar and Secretary, S. Cooksey

THE UNIVERSITY OF CAMBRIDGE
University Offices, The Old Schools, Cambridge CB2 1TN
Tel 01223-337733
Undergraduates (1998–9) 17,350

UNIVERSITY OFFICERS, ETC.
Chancellor, HRH The Prince Philip, Duke of Edinburgh,
  KG, KT, OM, GBE, PC (1977)
Vice-Chancellor, Prof. Sir Alec Broers, FRS (1996)
High Steward, The Lord Runcie, PC, DD (1991)
Deputy High Steward,
  The Lord Richardson of Duntisbourne, MBE, TD, PC
  (1983)
Commissary, The Lord Oliver of Aylmerton (*Trinity Hall*),
  PC (1989)
Orator, A. J. Bowen (*Jesus*), (1993)
Librarian, P. K. Fox (*Selwyn*), (1994)
Director of the Fitzwilliam Museum, D. D. Robinson (*Clare*),
  (1995)
Registrary, T. J. Mead (*Wolfson*), Ph.D. (1997)
Secretary-General of the Faculties, D. A. Livesey (*Emmanuel*),
  Ph.D. (1992)
Treasurer, Mrs J. Womack (*Trinity Hall*), (1993)

COLLEGES AND HALLS, ETC.
with dates of foundation
CHRIST'S (1505), *Master,* A. J. Munro, Ph.D. (1995)
CHURCHILL (1960), *Master,* Sir John Boyd, KCMG (1996)
CLARE (1326), *Master,* Prof. B. A. Hepple, LLD (1993)
CLARE HALL (1966), *President,*
  Prof. Dame Gillian Beer, DBE, Litt.D., FBA (1994)
CORPUS CHRISTI (1352), *Master,*
  Prof. Sir Tony Wrigley, Ph.D. (1994)
DARWIN (1964), *Master,*
  Prof. Sir Geoffrey Lloyd, Ph.D., FBA (1989)
DOWNING (1800), *Master,* Prof. D. A. King, FRS (1995)
EMMANUEL (1584), *Master,* Prof. J. E. Ffowcs-
  Williams, SC.D. (1996)
FITZWILLIAM (1966), *Master,* Prof. B. F. G. Johnston
GIRTON (1869), *Mistress,* Prof. A. M. Strathern, Ph.D.
  (1998)
GONVILLE AND CAIUS (1348), *Master,* N. McKendrick
  (1996)
HOMERTON (1824) (for B.Ed. Students), *Principal,*
  Mrs K. B. Pretty, Ph.D. (1991)
HUGHES HALL (1885) (for post-graduate students),
  President, Prof. P. Richards (1998)
JESUS (1496), *Master,* Prof. D. G. Crighton, SC.D., FRS (1997)
KING'S (1441), *Provost,* Prof. P. P. G. B. Bateson, SC.D., FRS
  (1987)

*Lucy Cavendish College (1965) (for women research students and mature and affiliated undergraduates), *President,*
The Baroness Perry of Southwark (1994)
Magdalene (1542), *Master,*
Prof. Sir John Gurdon, D.phil., FRS (1995)
*New Hall (1954), *President,* Mrs A. Lonsdale (1996)
*Newnham (1871), *Principal,* Baroness O'Neill, CBE (1992)
Pembroke (1347), *Master,* Sir Roger Tomkys, KCMG (1992)
Peterhouse (1284), *Master,*
Prof. Sir John Meurig Thomas, FRS (1993)
Queens' (1448), *President,* The Lord Eatwell
Robinson (1977), *Warden,*
Prof. the Lord Lewis of Newnham, SC.D., FRS (1977)
Selwyn (1882), *Master,*
Sir David Harrison, CBE, SC.D., FREng. (1993)
Sidney Sussex (1596), *Master,* Prof. S. N. Dawson (1999)
St Catharine's (1473), *Master,*
Prof. Sir Terence English (1993)
St Edmund's (1896), *Master,* Prof. R. B. Heap, SC.D. (1996)
St John's (1511), *Master,* Prof. P. Goddard, ph.D., FRS (1994)
Trinity (1546), *Master,* Prof. A. K. Sen (1998)
Trinity Hall (1350), *Master,* Sir John Lyons, ph.D. (1984)
Wolfson (1965), *President,* G. Johnson ph.D. (1994)
*College for women only

UNIVERSITY OF CENTRAL ENGLAND IN
  BIRMINGHAM (1992)
Perry Barr, Birmingham B42 2SU
Tel 0121-331 5000
Full-time students (1998–9), 10,750
Chancellor, I. McArdle
Vice-Chancellor, Dr P. C. Knight, CBE
Registrar and Secretary, Ms M. Penlington

UNIVERSITY OF CENTRAL LANCASHIRE (1992)
Preston PRI 2HE
Tel 01772-201201
Full-time students (1998–9), 15,450
Chancellor, Sir Francis Kennedy, KCMG, CBE (1995)
Vice-Chancellor, Dr M. McVicar
Registrar, Ms L. Munro
Secretary, Mrs P. M. Ackroyd

CITY UNIVERSITY (1966)
Northampton Square, London ECIV OHB
Tel 0171-477 8000
Full-time students (1998–9), 7,729
Chancellor, The Rt. Hon. the Lord Mayor of London
Vice-Chancellor, Prof. D. W. Rhind
Academic Registrar, A. H. Seville, ph.D.
Secretary, M. M. O'Hara

COVENTRY UNIVERSITY (1992)
Priory Street, Coventry CVI 5FB
Tel 01203-887688
Full-time students (1998–9), 16,000
Chancellor, The Lord Plumb, MEP (1995)
Vice-Chancellor, Dr M. Goldstein, CBE, ph.D., D.SC.
Academic Registrar, Dr J. Gledhill, ph.D.
Secretary, Mrs L. Arlidge

CRANFIELD UNIVERSITY (1969)
Cranfield, Beds MK43 OAL
Tel 01234-750111
Full-time students (1998–9), 2,248

Chancellor, The Lord Vincent of Coleshill, GBE, KCB, DSO (1998)
Vice-Chancellor, Prof. F. R. Hartley, D.SC.
Academic Registrar and Secretary, D. J. Buck

DE MONTFORT UNIVERSITY (1992)
The Gateway, Leicester LEI 9BH
Tel 0116-255 1551
Full-time students (1998–9), 17,350
Chancellor, Dr J. White (1998)
Vice-Chancellor, Prof. P. Tasker
Academic Registrar, V. E. Critchlow

UNIVERSITY OF DERBY (1993)
Kedleston Road, Derby DE22 1GB
Tel 01332-622222
Full-time students (1998–9), 14,000
Chancellor, Sir Christopher Ball, FRSA
Vice-Chancellor, Prof. R. Waterhouse
Registrar, Mrs J. Fry
Secretary, R. Gillis, FRSA

THE UNIVERSITY OF DUNDEE (1967)
Dundee DDI 4HN
Tel 01382-344000
Full-time students (1998–9), 8,355
Chancellor, Sir James Black, FRCP, FRS (1992)
Vice-Chancellor and Principal, Dr I. J. Graham-Bryce
Secretary, R. Seaton
Rector, T. Slattery, 1998–2001

THE UNIVERSITY OF DURHAM
Old Shire Hall, Durham DHI 3HP
Tel 0191-374 2000
Full-time students (1998–9), 9,902
Chancellor, Sir Peter Ustinov, CBE, FRSL
Vice-Chancellor, Prof. Sir Kenneth Calman, KCB, MD, FRCP, FRCGP, FRCR, FRSE, ph.D.
Registrar and Secretary, J. V. Hogan, ph.D.

Colleges
Collingwood *Principal,* Prof. G. H. Blake, ph.D.
Graduate Society *Principal,* M. Richardson, ph.D.
Grey *Master,* V. E. Watts
Hatfield *Master,* Prof. T. P. Burt, ph.D.
St Aidan's *Principal,* J. S. Ashworth
St Chad's *Principal,* Revd J. P. M. Cassidy, ph.D.
St Cuthbert's Society *Principal,* vacant
St Hild and St Bede *Principal,*
  Revd Prof. D. J. Davies, ph.D.
St John's *Principal,* Rt. Revd S. W. Sykes
St Mary's *Principal,* Miss J. L. Hobbs
Trevelyan *Principal,* Prof. M. Todd, D.Litt
University *Master,* Prof. M. E. Tucker, ph.D.
Ushaw *President,* Revd J. O'Keefe
Van Mildert *Principal,* Prof. I. R. Taylor, ph.D.

THE UNIVERSITY OF EAST ANGLIA (1963)
Norwich NR4 7TJ
Tel 01603-456161
Full-time students (1998–9), 11,730
Chancellor, Sir Geoffrey Allen, FRS, FREng. (1994)
Vice-Chancellor, V. Watts
Registrar and Secretary, B. Summers

UNIVERSITY OF EAST LONDON (1992)
Longbridge Road, Dagenham, Essex RM8 2AS
Tel 0181-223 3000
Full-time students (1998–9), 12,500
Chancellor, The Lord Rix, CBE (1997)
Vice-Chancellor, Prof. F. W. Gould
Registrar and Secretary, A. Ingle

THE UNIVERSITY OF EDINBURGH (1583)
Old College, South Bridge, Edinburgh EH8 9YL
Tel 0131-650 1000
Full-time students (1998–9), 18,300
Chancellor, HRH The Prince Philip, Duke of Edinburgh,
   KG, KT, OM, GBE, PC, FRS (1952)
Vice-Chancellor and Principal, Prof. Sir Stewart Sutherland,
   FBA, FRSE
Secretary, M. J. B. Lowe, PH.D.
Rector, J. Colquhoun (1997–2000)

THE UNIVERSITY OF ESSEX (1964)
Wivenhoe Park, Colchester CO4 3SQ
Tel 01206-873333
Full-time students (1998–9), 5,710
Chancellor, The Lord Nolan, PC (1997)
Vice-Chancellor, Prof. I. Crewe
Registrar and Secretary, T. Rich, PH.D.

THE UNIVERSITY OF EXETER (1955)
Northcote House, The Queen's Drive, Exeter EX4 4QJ
Tel 01392-263263
Full-time students (1998–9), 9,140
Chancellor, The Lord Alexander of Weedon, QC (1998)
Vice-Chancellor, Sir Geoffrey Holland, KCB
Registrar and Secretary, I. H. C. Powell

UNIVERSITY OF GLAMORGAN (1992)
Treforest, Pontypridd CF37 1DL
Tel 01443-480480
Full-time students (1998–9), 10,657
Chancellor, The Lord Merlyn-Rees, PC, QC (1994)
Vice-Chancellor, Prof. A. L. Webb
Registrar, J. O'Shea
Secretary, J. L. Bracegirdle

THE UNIVERSITY OF GLASGOW (1451)
University Avenue, Glasgow G12 8QQ
Tel 0141-339 8855
Full-time students (1998–9), 19,900
Chancellor, Sir William Fraser, GCB, FRSE
Vice-Chancellor, Prof. Sir Graeme Davies, FREng, FRSE
Secretary, D. Mackie, FRSA
Rector, R. Kemp, 1999–2002

GLASGOW CALEDONIAN UNIVERSITY (1993)
Cowcaddens Road, Glasgow G4 0BA
Tel 0141-331 3000
Full-time students (1998–9), 8,500
Chancellor, The Lord Nickson, KBE (1993)
Vice-Chancellor and Principal, Dr I. A. Johnston, PH.D., CB
Head of Academic Registration, E. B. Ferguson

UNIVERSITY OF GREENWICH (1992)
Bexley Road, Eltham, London SE9 2PQ
Tel 0181-331 8000
Full-time students (1998–9), 14,007
Chancellor, Lord Holme of Cheltenham, CBE
Vice-Chancellor, Dr D. E. Fussey
Secretary, J. M. Charles

HERIOT-WATT UNIVERSITY (1966)
Riccarton, Edinburgh EH14 4AS
Tel 0131-449 5111
Full-time students (1998–9), 5,800, plus 9,000 full-time
   distance learning students
Chancellor, The Lord Mackay of Clashfern, PC, QC, FRSE
   (1979)
Vice-Chancellor and Principal, Prof. J. S. Archer, FREng.
Secretary, P. L. Wilson

UNIVERSITY OF HERTFORDSHIRE (1992)
College Lane, Hatfield, Herts AL10 9AB
Tel 01707-284000
Full-time students (1998–9), 18,015
Chancellor, The Lord MacLaurin of Knebworth (1996)
Vice-Chancellor, Prof. N. K. Buxton
Registrar and Secretary, P. G. Jeffreys

UNIVERSITY OF HUDDERSFIELD (1992)
Queensgate, Huddersfield HD1 3DH
Tel 01484-422288
Full-time students (1998–9), 17,000
Chancellor, Sir Ernest Hall, OBE (1996)
Vice-Chancellor, Prof. J. R. Tarrant
Registrar and Secretary, Mrs M. H. Andrew

THE UNIVERSITY OF HULL (1954)
Cottingham Road, Hull HU6 7RX
Tel 01482-346311
Full-time students (1998–9), 10,800
Chancellor, The Lord Armstrong of Ilminster, GCB, CVO
   (1994)
Vice-Chancellor, Prof. D. N. Dilks, FRSL
Registrar and Secretary, D. J. Lock

KEELE UNIVERSITY (1962)
Newcastle under Lyme, Staffs ST5 5BG
Tel 01782-621111
Full-time students (1998–9), 6,400
Chancellor, Sir Claus Moser, KCB, CBE, FBA (1986)
Vice-Chancellor, Prof. J. V. Finch, CBE
Registrar and Secretary, S. J. Morris

THE UNIVERSITY OF KENT AT CANTERBURY
   (1965)
Canterbury CT2 7NZ
Tel 01227-764000
Full-time students (1998–9), 7,185
Chancellor, Sir Crispin Tickell, GCMG, KCVO
Vice-Chancellor, Prof. R. Sibson, PH.D.
Registrar and Secretary, N. A. McHard

KINGSTON UNIVERSITY (1992)
Kingston upon Thames, Surrey KT1 1LQ
Tel 0181-547 2000
Full-time students (1998–9), 14,000
Chancellor, Sir Frank Lampl
Vice-Chancellor, Prof. P. Scott
Registrar, Ms A. M. Stokes
Secretary, R. S. Abdulla, MBE

THE UNIVERSITY OF LANCASTER (1964)
Bailrigg, Lancaster LA1 4YW
Tel 01524-65201
Full-time students (1998–9), 8,684
Chancellor, HRH Princess Alexandra, the Hon. Lady Ogilvy,
   GCVO (1964)
Vice-Chancellor, Prof. W. Ritchie, OBE
Academic Registrar, Mrs M. McClintock
Secretary, Ms F. Aiken

THE UNIVERSITY OF LEEDS (1904)
Leeds LS2 9JT
Tel 0113-243 1751
Full-time students (1998–9), 23,244
Chancellor, Lord Bragg
Vice-Chancellor, Prof. A. G. Wilson
Registrar and Secretary, D. S. Robinson, PH.D.

LEEDS METROPOLITAN UNIVERSITY (1992)
Calverley Street, Leeds LS1 3HE
Tel 0113-283 2600
Full-time students (1998–9), 14,000
Chancellor, L. Silver (1989)
Vice-Chancellor, Prof. L. Wagner
Registrar, Ms C. Orange
Secretary, M. Wilkinson

THE UNIVERSITY OF LEICESTER (1957)
University Road, Leicester LE1 7RH
Tel 0116-252 2522
Full-time students (1998–9), 8,476
Chancellor, Sir Michael Atiyah, OM, FRS, Ph.D., D.SC (1995)
Vice-Chancellor, Prof. R. Burgess, Ph.D.
Registrar and Secretary, K. J. Julian

UNIVERSITY OF LINCOLNSHIRE AND
   HUMBERSIDE
Humberside campus: Hull HU6 7RT
Tel 01482-440550
Lincoln campus: Lincoln LN2 4VF
Tel 01522-882000
Full-time students (1998–9), 7,000
Chancellor, Dr J. H. Hooper, CBE
Vice-Chancellor, Prof. R. P. King
Registrar, F. Marks
Secretary, R. Graham

THE UNIVERSITY OF LIVERPOOL (1903)
Senate House, Abercromby Square, Liverpool L69 3BX
Tel 0151-794 2000
Full-time students (1998–9), 13,200
Chancellor, The Lord Owen, CH, PC (1996)
Vice-Chancellor, Prof. P. N. Love, CBE
Registrar and Secretary, M. D. Carr

LIVERPOOL JOHN MOORES UNIVERSITY (1992)
Rodney House, 70 Mount Pleasant, Liverpool L3 5UX
Tel 0151-231 2121
Full-time students (1998–9), 20,000
Chancellor, Ms C. Booth, QC
Vice-Chancellor, Prof. P. Toyne
Registrar and Secretary, Ms A. Wild

THE UNIVERSITY OF LONDON (1836)
Senate House, Malet Street, London WC1E 7HU
Tel 0171-862 8000
Internal students (1998–9), 102,000; External students,
   26,000
Chancellor, HRH The Princess Royal, KG, GCVO, FRS (1981)
Vice-Chancellor, Prof. G. Zellick, Ph.D.
Academic Registrar, Mrs G. F. Roberts
Director of Administration, J. R. Davidson
Chairman of the Council, The Lord Woolf, PC
Chairman of Convocation, D. D. A. Leslie
Visitor, HM The Queen in Council

COLLEGES

BIRKBECK COLLEGE, Malet Street, London WC1E 7HX.
   Master, Prof. T. O'Shea
CHARING CROSS AND WESTMINSTER MEDICAL
   SCHOOL, *see* Imperial College of Science, Technology
   and Medicine
GOLDSMITHS COLLEGE, Lewisham Way, New Cross,
   London SE14 6NW. *Warden*, Prof. B. Pimlott, FBA
HEYTHROP COLLEGE, Kensington Square, London
   W8 5HQ. *Principal*, Revd Dr J. McBade, SJ

IMPERIAL COLLEGE OF SCIENCE, TECHNOLOGY AND
   MEDICINE (includes Imperial College Schools of
   Medicine at Charing Cross, Hammersmith and St
   Mary's hospitals and at the National Heart and Lung
   Institute), South Kensington, London SW7 2AZ. *Rector*,
   Prof. Sir Ronald Oxburgh, KBE, FRS
KING'S COLLEGE LONDON, (includes King's College
   School of Medicine and Dentistry, United Medical and
   Dental Schools of Guy's and St Thomas' Hospitals),
   Strand, London WC2R 2LS. *Principal*, Prof. A. Lucas, PH.D.
LONDON BUSINESS SCHOOL, Sussex Place, Regent's
   Park, London NW1 4SA. *Principal*, Prof. J. Quelch
THE LONDON HOSPITAL MEDICAL COLLEGE, *see*
   Queen Mary and Westfield College
LONDON SCHOOL OF ECONOMICS AND POLITICAL
   SCIENCE, Houghton Street, London WC2A 2AE. *Director*,
   Prof. A. Giddens
LONDON SCHOOL OF HYGIENE AND TROPICAL
   MEDICINE, Keppel Street, London WC1E 7HT. *Dean*,
   Prof. H. Spencer
LONDON SCHOOL OF JEWISH STUDIES, 44A Albert
   Road, London NW4 2SJ. *Principal*, Prof. D. H. Ruben
QUEEN MARY AND WESTFIELD COLLEGE,
   (incorporating St Bartholomew's and the Royal London
   School of Medicine and Dentistry and the London
   Hospital Medical College), Mile End Road, London
   E1 4NS. *Principal*, Prof. A. Smith
ROYAL FREE HOSPITAL SCHOOL OF MEDICINE, *see*
   University College London
ROYAL HOLLOWAY, Egham Hill, Egham, Surrey TW20
   0EX. *Principal*, Prof. N. Gower (until Feb 2000);
   Prof. D. Bone (from Feb 2000)
ROYAL POSTGRADUATE MEDICAL SCHOOL, *see* Imperial
   College of Science, Technology and Medicine
ROYAL VETERINARY COLLEGE, Royal College Street,
   London NW1 0TU. *Principal and Dean*,
   Prof. L. E. Lanyon, PH.D.
SCHOOL OF ORIENTAL AND AFRICAN STUDIES,
   Thornhaugh Street, Russell Square, London WC1H 0XG.
   Director, Sir Tim Lankester, KCB
SCHOOL OF PHARMACY, 29–39 Brunswick Square,
   London WC1N 1AX. *Dean*,
   Prof. A. T. Florence, CBE, PH.D., FRSE
ST BARTHOLOMEW'S AND THE ROYAL LONDON
   SCHOOL OF MEDICINE AND DENTISTRY, *see* Queen
   Mary and Westfield College
ST GEORGE'S HOSPITAL MEDICAL SCHOOL, Cranmer
   Terrace, London SW17 0RE. *Dean*, Prof. R. Boyd, FRCP
UNITED MEDICAL AND DENTAL SCHOOLS OF GUY'S
   AND ST THOMAS' HOSPITALS, *see* King's College
   London
UNIVERSITY COLLEGE LONDON, (including UCL
   Medical School), Gower Street, London WC1E 6BT.
   Provost, Prof. C. Llewellyn-Smith, FRS
WYE COLLEGE, Wye, near Ashford, Kent TN25 5AH.
   Principal, Prof. J. H. D. Prescott, PH.D.

INSTITUTES

BRITISH INSTITUTE IN PARIS, 9–11 rue de Constantine,
   75340 Paris Cedex 07, France. *Director*,
   Prof. C. L. Campos, CBE, PH.D. *London office:* Senate House,
   Malet Street, London WC1E 7HU
CENTRE FOR DEFENCE STUDIES, King's College
   London, Strand, London WC2R 2LS. *Director*,
   Prof. L. Freedman, CBE, FBA
COURTAULD INSTITUTE OF ART, North Block,
   Somerset House, Strand, London WC2R 0RN. *Director*,
   Prof. E. C. Fernie, CBE, FSA, FRSE
UNIVERSITY MARINE BIOLOGICAL STATION
   MILLPORT, Isle of Cumbrae, Scotland KA28 0EG.
   Director, Dr R. Ormond

SCHOOL OF ADVANCED STUDY, Senate House, Malet Street, London WC1E 7HU. *Dean*, Prof. T. C. Daintith
Comprises:
INSTITUTE OF ADVANCED LEGAL STUDIES, Charles Clore House, 17 Russell Square, London WC1B 5DR. *Director*, Prof. B. A. K. Rider
INSTITUTE OF CANCER RESEARCH, Royal Cancer Hospital, Chester Beatty Laboratories, 17A Onslow Gardens, London SW7 3AL. *Chief Executive*, Dr P. Rigby
INSTITUTE OF CLASSICAL STUDIES, Senate House, Malet Street, London WC1E 7HU. *Director*, Prof. G. B. Waywell, FSA
INSTITUTE OF COMMONWEALTH STUDIES, 27–28 Russell Square, London WC1B 5DS. *Director*, Prof. P. Caplan
INSTITUTE OF EDUCATION, 20 Bedford Way, London WC1H 0AL. *Director*, Prof. P. Mortimore, OBE
INSTITUTE OF ENGLISH STUDIES, Senate House, Malet Street, London WC1E 7HU. *Director*, Prof. W. Gould
INSTITUTE OF GERMANIC STUDIES, 29 Russell Square, London WC1B 5DP. *Director*, Prof. R. Görner
INSTITUTE OF HISTORICAL RESEARCH, Senate House, Malet Street, London WC1E 7HU. *Director*, Prof. D. Cannadine
INSTITUTE OF LATIN AMERICAN STUDIES, 31 Tavistock Square, London WC1H 9HA. *Director*, Prof. J. Dunkerley
INSTITUTE OF PSYCHIATRY, De Crespigny Park, Denmark Hill, London SE5 8AF. *Dean*, Prof. S. Checkley
INSTITUTE OF ROMANCE STUDIES, Senate House, Malet Street, London WC1E 7HU. *Director*, Prof. J. Labanyi
INSTITUTE OF UNITED STATES STUDIES, Senate House, Malet Street, London WC1E 7HU. *Director*, Prof. G. L. McDowell, PH.D.
WARBURG INSTITUTE, Woburn Square, London WC1H 0AB. *Director*, Prof. C. N. J. Mann, PH.D., CBE

ASSOCIATE INSTITUTIONS

INSTITUTE OF ZOOLOGY, Royal Zoological Society, Regent's Park, London NW1 4RY. *Director*, Prof. M. Gosling
ROYAL ACADEMY OF MUSIC, Marylebone Road, London NW1 2BS. *Director*, Dr C. Price
TRINITY COLLEGE OF MUSIC, 11–13 Mandeville Place, London W1M 6AQ. *Principal*, G. Henderson

LONDON GUILDHALL UNIVERSITY (1993)
31 Jewry Street, London EC3N 2EY
Tel 0171-320 1000
Full-time students (1998–9), 14,387
Academic Registrar, Ms J. Grinstead
Deputy Provost, M. Weaver
Patron, HRH The Prince Philip, Duke of Edinburgh, KG, KT, OM, GBE, PC (1952)
Provost, Prof. R. Floud, D.Phil.

LOUGHBOROUGH UNIVERSITY (1966)
Loughborough, Leics LE11 3TU
Tel 01509-263171
Full-time students (1998–9), 9,757
Chancellor, Sir Denis Rooke, CBE, FRS, FREng. (1989)
Vice-Chancellor, Prof. D. Wallace, FRS, FRSE
Registrar, vacant

UNIVERSITY OF LUTON (1993)
Park Square, Luton LU1 3JU
Tel 01582-734111
Full-time students (1998–9), 10,000
Chancellor, Sir David Plastow
Vice-Chancellor, Dr D. John
Registrar, R. Harris
Secretary, vacant

THE UNIVERSITY OF MANCHESTER
Manchester M13 9PL
Tel 0161-275 2000
Full-time students (1998–9), 18,968
Chancellor, The Lord Flowers, FRS (1994)
Vice-Chancellor, Prof. M. B. Harris, CBE, PH.D.
Registrar and Secretary, E. Newcomb

UNIVERSITY OF MANCHESTER INSTITUTE OF SCIENCE AND TECHNOLOGY (UMIST) (1824)
PO Box 88, Manchester M60 1QD
Tel 0161-236 3311
Full-time students (1998–9), 6,747
Chancellor, Prof. Sir Roland Smith, PH.D. (1995)
Vice-Chancellor, Prof. R. F. Boucher, FREng., PH.D.
Registrar and Secretary, P. C. C. Stephenson

MANCHESTER METROPOLITAN UNIVERSITY (1992)
All Saints, Manchester M15 6BH
Tel 0161-247 2000
Full-time students (1998–9), 20,000
Chancellor, The Duke of Westminster, OBE, TD (1993)
Vice-Chancellor, Mrs A. V. Burslem, OBE
Academic Registrar, J. D. M. Karczewski-Slowikowski
Secretary, T. A. Hendley

MIDDLESEX UNIVERSITY (1992)
White Hart Lane, London N17 8HR
Tel 0181-362 5000
Full-time students (1998–9), 19,365
Chancellor, The Baroness Platt of Writtle (1993)
Vice-Chancellor, Prof. M. Driscoll
Registrar, G. Jones

NAPIER UNIVERSITY (1992)
219 Colinton Road, Edinburgh EH14 1DJ
Tel 0131-444 2266
Full-time students (1998–9), 10,387
Chancellor, The Viscount Younger of Leckie, KT, KCVO, TD, PC, FRSE (1993)
Vice-Chancellor and Principal, Prof. J. Mavor
Secretary, Dr G. Webber

THE UNIVERSITY OF NEWCASTLE UPON TYNE
6 Kensington Terrace, Newcastle upon Tyne NE1 7RU
Tel 0191-222 6000
Full-time students (1998–9), 12,321
Chancellor, Rt. Hon. C. Patten, CH
Vice-Chancellor, J. R. G. Wright
Registrar, D. E. T. Nicholson

UNIVERSITY OF NORTH LONDON (1992)
166–220 Holloway Road, London N7 8DB
Tel 0171-607 2789
Full-time students (1998–9), 13,189
Vice-Chancellor, B. A. Roper
Registrar, Ms M. Storey
Secretary, J. McParland

UNIVERSITY OF NORTHUMBRIA AT NEWCASTLE (1992)
Ellison Place, Newcastle upon Tyne NE1 8ST
Tel 0191-232 6002
Full-time students (1998–9), 13,500
Chancellor, The Lord Glenamara, CH, PC (1984)
Vice-Chancellor, Prof. G. Smith
Registrar, Ms C. Penna
Secretary, R. A. Bott
Rector, Revd. A. Shipton

THE UNIVERSITY OF NOTTINGHAM (1948)
University Park, Nottingham NG7 2RD
Tel 0115-951 5151
Full-time students (1998–9), 15,000
Chancellor, The Lord Dearing, CB (1993)
Vice-Chancellor, Prof. Sir Colin Campbell
Registrar, K. H. Jones

NOTTINGHAM TRENT UNIVERSITY (1992)
Burton Street, Nottingham NG1 4BU
Tel 0115-948 8418
Full-time students (1998–9), 20,838
Vice-Chancellor, Prof. R. Cowell, PH.D.
Academic Registrar, D. W. Samson
Secretary, D. Skellett

THE UNIVERSITY OF OXFORD
University Offices, Wellington Square, Oxford OX1 2JD
Tel 01865-270000
Students in residence 1998–9, 16,185
Chancellor, The Lord Jenkins of Hillhead (*Balliol*), *elected* 1987, OM, PC
Vice-Chancellor, Dr C. R. Lucas (*Balliol*), *elected* 1997
High Steward, The Lord Goff of Chieveley (*Lincoln* and *New College*), *elected* 1990, PC
Proctors, Dr R. H. A. Jenkyns (*Lady Margaret Hall*); P. W. Smith (*Pembroke*), *elected* 1999
Assessor, Prof. R. A. Mayou (*Nuffield*), *elected* 1999
Public Orator, Prof. J. Griffin (*Balliol*), *elected* 1992
Bodley's Librarian, R. P. Carr (*Balliol*), *elected* 1997
Keeper of Archives, D. G. Vaisey (*Exeter*), *elected* 1995
Director of the Ashmolean Museum, Dr C. Brown (*Worcester*), *elected* 1998
Registrar of the University, D. R. Holmes (*St John's*), *elected* 1998
Surveyor to the University, P. M. R. Hill (*St Cross*), *elected* 1993
Secretary of Faculties, A. P. Weale (*Worcester*), *elected* 1984
Secretary of the Chest, J. R. Clements (*Merton*), *elected* 1995

OXFORD COLLEGES AND HALLS
with dates of foundation
ALL SOULS (1438), *Warden,* Prof. J. Davis, FBA, PH.D. (1995)
BALLIOL (1263), *Acting Master,* A. Graham (1998)
BLACKFRIARS (1221), *Regent,* Revd F. G. Kerr (1998)
BRASENOSE (1509), *Principal,* The Lord Windlesham, BT, CVO, PC, D.Litt (1989)
CAMPION HALL (1896), *Master,* Revd G. J. Hughes, D.phil. (1998)
CHRIST CHURCH (1546), *Dean,* Very Revd J. H. Drury (1991)
CORPUS CHRISTI (1517), *President,* Prof. Sir Keith Thomas, FBA (1986)
EXETER (1314), *Rector,* Dr M. Butler (1993)
GREEN (1979), *Warden,* Sir John Hanson, KCMG, CBE (1997)
GREYFRIARS (1910), *Warden,* Revd T. G. Weinandy, PH.D. (1996)

HARRIS MANCHESTER (1786), *Principal,* Revd R. Waller, ph.D. (1990)
HERTFORD (1874), *Principal,* Sir Walter Bodmer, FRS, FRCPath. (1996)
JESUS (1571), *Principal,* Sir Peter North, CBE, QC, FBA (1984)
KEBLE (1868), *Warden,* Dr A. Cameron, FBA, FSA (1994)
KELLOGG (1990), *President,* Dr G. P. Thomas (1990)
LADY MARGARET HALL (1878), *Principal,* Sir Brian Fall, GVCO, KCMG (1995)
LINACRE (1962), *Principal,* Dr P. A. Slack, FBA (1996)
LINCOLN (1427), *Rector,* Dr W. E. K. Anderson, FRSE (1994)
MAGDALEN (1458), *President,* A. D. Smith, CBE (1988)
MANSFIELD (1886), *Principal,* Prof. D. I. Marquand (1996)
MERTON (1264), *Warden,* Dr. J Rawson, CBE, FBA (1994)
NEW COLLEGE (1379), *Warden,* Dr. A. J. Ryan, FBA (1996)
NUFFIELD (1958), *Warden,* A. Atkinson, FBA (1994)
ORIEL (1326), *Provost,* Dr E. W. Nicholson, DD, FBA (1990)
PEMBROKE (1624), *Master,* Dr R. Stevens, DCL (1993)
QUEEN'S (1340), *Provost,* Sir Alan Budd (1999)
REGENT'S PARK (1810), *Principal,* Revd P. S. Fiddes, D.phil. (1989)
SOMERVILLE (1879), *Principal,* Dame Fiona Caldicott, DBE, FRCP, FRCPsych., FRCPI (1996)
ST ANNE'S (1952 (Society of Oxford Home-Students (1879)), *Principal,* Mrs R. L. Deech (1991)
ST ANTONY'S (1953), *Warden,* Sir Marrack Goulding, KCMG (1997)
ST BENET'S HALL (1897), *Master,* Revd H. Wansbrough, OSB (1991)
ST CATHERINE'S (1963), *Master,* The Lord Plant of Highfield (1994)
ST CROSS (1965), *Master,* Dr R. C. Repp (1987)
ST EDMUND HALL (c.1278), *Principal,* Prof. D. M. P. Mingos (1999)
*ST HILDA'S (1893), *Principal,* Miss E. Llewellyn-Smith, CB (1990)
ST HUGH'S (1886), *Principal,* D. Wood, CBE, QC (1991)
ST JOHN'S (1555), *President,* Dr W. Hayes (1987)
ST PETER'S (1929), *Master,* Dr J. P. Barron, FSA (1991)
TEMPLETON (1965), *President,* Sir David Rowland (1998)
TRINITY (1554), *President,* The Hon. Michael J. Beloff, QC (1996)
UNIVERSITY (1249), *Master,* Baron Butler of Brockwell, GCB, CVO (1998)
WADHAM (1610), *Warden,* J. S. Flemming, FBA (1993)
WOLFSON (1966), *President,* Sir David Smith, D.phil., FRS, FRSE (1994)
WORCESTER (1714), *Provost,* R. G. Smethurst (1991)
WYCLIFFE HALL (1877), *Principal,* Revd A. E. McGrath, D.phil. (1995)

*College for women only

OXFORD BROOKES UNIVERSITY (1993)
Headington, Oxford OX3 0BP
Tel 01865-484851
Full-time students (1998–9), 10,200
Chancellor, Baroness Kennedy of the Shaws, QC
Vice-Chancellor, Prof. G. Upton
Academic Registrar, Ms E. N. Winders

UNIVERSITY OF PAISLEY (1992)
Paisley PA1 2BE
Tel 0141-848 3000
Full-time students (1998–9), 8,500
Chancellor, Sir Robert Easton, CBE (1993)
Vice-Chancellor, Prof. R. W. Shaw, CBE
Registrar, D. Rigg
Secretary, J. Fraser

UNIVERSITY OF PLYMOUTH (1992)
Drake Circus, Plymouth PL4 8AA
Tel 01752-600600
Full-time students (1998–9), 15,424
Vice-Chancellor, Prof. J. Bull
Academic Registrar and Secretary, Miss J. Hopkinson

UNIVERSITY OF PORTSMOUTH (1992)
University House, Winston Churchill Avenue,
    Portsmouth PO1 2UP
Tel 01705-848484
Full-time students (1998–9), 14,500
Chancellor, The Lord Palumbo (1992)
Vice-Chancellor, Prof. J. Craven
Academic Registrar, A. Rees
Secretary, Dr M. Bateman

THE QUEEN'S UNIVERSITY OF BELFAST (1908)
Belfast BT7 1NN
Tel 01232-245133
Full-time students (1995–6), 14,500
Chancellor, Sen. G. Mitchell
Vice-Chancellor, Prof. G. Bain
Registrar, J. Town

THE UNIVERSITY OF READING (1926)
Whiteknights, PO Box 217, Reading RG6 6AH
Tel 0118-987 5123
Full-time students (1998–9), 12,000
Chancellor, The Lord Carrington, KG, GCMG, CH, MC, PC
    (1992)
Vice-Chancellor, Prof. R. Williams
Registrar, D. C. R. Frampton

THE ROBERT GORDON UNIVERSITY (1992)
Schoolhill, Aberdeen AB10 1FR
Tel 01224-262000
Full-time students (1998–9), 7,582
Chancellor, Sir Bob Reid (1993)
Vice-Chancellor and Principal, Prof. W. Stevely
Secretary, D. Caldwell

ROYAL COLLEGE OF MUSIC
London SW7 2BS
Tel 0171-589 3643
Full-time students (1998–9), 610
Registrar and Secretary, K. A. Porter
Dean and Deputy Director, Dr J. Cox
Director, Dr J. Ritterman

THE UNIVERSITY OF ST ANDREWS (1411)
College Gate, St Andrews KY16 9AJ
Tel 01334-476161
Full-time students (1998–9), 5,843
Chancellor, Sir Kenneth Dover, DLitt., FRSE, FBA (1981)
Vice-Chancellor and Principal, Prof. S. Arnott, CBE, FRS, FRSE
Secretary and Registrar, D. J. Corner
Rector, D. R. Findlay, QC, FRSA (1996–1999)

THE UNIVERSITY OF SALFORD (1967)
Salford M5 4WT
Tel 0161-295 5000
Full-time students (1998–9), 20,000
Chancellor, Sir Walter Bodmer, Ph.D., FRS
Vice-Chancellor, Prof. M. Harloe
Registrar, Dr M. D. Winton, Ph.D.

THE UNIVERSITY OF SHEFFIELD (1905)
Western Bank, Sheffield S10 2TN
Tel 0114-222 2000
Full-time students (1998–9), 15,639
Chancellor, Sir Peter Middleton, GCB
Vice-Chancellor, Prof. Sir Gareth Roberts, Kt, FRS, Ph.D.
Registrar and Secretary, D. Fletcher, Ph.D.

SHEFFIELD HALLAM UNIVERSITY (1992)
Howard Street, Sheffield S1 1WB
Tel 0114-225 5555
Full-time students (1998–9), 17,147
Chancellor, Sir Bryan Nicholson (1992)
Vice-Chancellor, Ms D. Green
Registrar, Ms J. Tory
Secretary, Ms S. Neocosmos

THE UNIVERSITY OF SOUTHAMPTON (1952)
Highfield, Southampton SO17 1BJ
Tel 01703-595000
Full-time students (1998–9), 15,777
Chancellor, The Earl of Selbourne, KBE, FRS (1996)
Vice-Chancellor, Prof. H. Newby, CBE, Ph.D.
Registrar and Secretary, J. F. D. Lauwerys
Academic Registrar, R. Knight

SOUTH BANK UNIVERSITY (1992)
103 Borough Road, London SE1 0AA
Tel 0171-928 8989
Full-time students (1998–9), 10,594
Chancellor, Sir Trevor McDonald
Vice-Chancellor, Prof. G. Bernbaum
Registrar, R. Phillips
Secretary, Mrs L. Gander

STAFFORDSHIRE UNIVERSITY (1992)
College Road, Stoke-on-Trent ST4 2DE
Tel 01782-294000
Full-time students (1998–9), 11,734
Chancellor, The Lord Ashley of Stoke, CH, PC (1993)
Vice-Chancellor, Prof. C. E. King, Ph.D.
Academic Registrar, Ms F. Francis
Secretary, K. Sproston

THE UNIVERSITY OF STIRLING (1967)
Stirling FK9 4LA
Tel 01786-473171
Full-time students (1998–9), 5,887
Chancellor, Dame Diana Rigg, DBE
Vice-Chancellor, Prof. A. Miller, CBE, FRSE
Academic Registrar, D. G. Wood
Secretary, K. J. Clarke

THE UNIVERSITY OF STRATHCLYDE (1964)
McCance Building, John Anderson Campus, Glasgow
    G1 1XQ
Tel 0141-552 4400
Full-time students (1998–9), 16,528
Chancellor, The Lord Hope of Craighead, PC (1998)
Vice-Chancellor and Principal, Prof. Sir John Arbuthnott,
    FRSE, FRCPath
Secretary, P. W. A. West

UNIVERSITY OF SUNDERLAND (1992)
Langham Tower, Ryhope Road, Sunderland SR2 7EE
Tel 0191-515 2000
Full-time students (1998–9), 11,587
Chancellor, The Lord Puttnam, CBE (1998)
Vice-Chancellor, Prof. P. Fidler, MBE
Academic Registrar, S. Porteous
Secretary, J. D. Pacey

THE UNIVERSITY OF SURREY (1966)
Guildford, Surrey GU2 5XH
Tel 01483-300800
Full-time students (1998–9), 9,100
Chancellor, HRH The Duke of Kent, KG, GCMG, GCVO (1977)
Vice-Chancellor, Prof. P. J. Dowling, FRS, FREng.
Registrar, P. J. Beardsley
Secretary, H. W. B. Davies

THE UNIVERSITY OF SUSSEX (1961)
Falmer, Brighton BN1 9RH
Tel 01273-606755
Full-time students (1998–9), 9,176
Chancellor, The Lord Attenborough (1998)
Vice-Chancellor, Prof. M. A. M. Smith
Registrar (acting), G. Ivey

UNIVERSITY OF TEESSIDE (1992)
Middlesbrough TS1 3BA
Tel 01642-218121
Full-time students (1997–8), 8,216
Chancellor, The Rt. Hon. Sir Leon Brittan, QC (1993)
Vice-Chancellor, Prof. D. Fraser
Registrar, Ms J. Walters
Secretary, J. M. McClintock

THAMES VALLEY UNIVERSITY (1992)
St Mary's Road, Ealing, London W5 5RF
Tel 0181-579 5000
Full-time students (1997–8), 5,793
Chancellor, The Lord Hamlyn, CBE
Secretary, S. Denton
Vice-Chancellor (acting), Sir William Taylor

THE UNIVERSITY OF ULSTER (1984)
Cromore Road, Coleraine BT52 1SA
Tel 01265-44141
Full-time students (1998–9), 20,042
Chancellor, Rabbi J. Neuberger (1993)
Vice-Chancellor, Prof. P. G. McKenna, Ph.D.
Academic Registrar, Dr K. I. Miller, Ph.D.

THE UNIVERSITY OF WALES (1893)
King Edward VII Avenue, Cathays Park, Cardiff CF10 3NS
Tel 01222-382656
Students (1998–9), 48,017
Chancellor, HRH The Prince of Wales, KG, KT, GCB, PC (1976)
Senior Vice-Chancellor, Prof. K. G. Robbins, FRSE, D.Litt
Secretary-General, J. D. Pritchard

MEMBER INSTITUTIONS

UNIVERSITY OF WALES BANGOR, Bangor LL57 2DG. Tel: 01248-351151. *Vice-Chancellor,* Prof. H. R. Evans, Ph.D., FREng. (1995)
UNIVERSITY OF WALES COLLEGE OF MEDICINE, Heath Park, Cardiff CF14 4XN. Tel: 01222-747747. *Vice-Chancellor,* Prof. I. R. Cameron, DM, FRCP (1994)
UNIVERSITY OF WALES COLLEGE, NEWPORT, Caerleon Campus, PO Box 179, Newport NP6 1YG. Tel: 01633-430088. *Principal,* Prof. K. J. Overshott, Ph.D. (1990)
UNIVERSITY OF WALES INSTITUTE, CARDIFF, Llandaff Centre, Western Avenue, Cardiff CF5 2SG. Tel: 01222-506070. *Principal,* A. J. Chapman, Ph.D. (1998)
UNIVERSITY OF WALES SWANSEA, Singleton Park, Swansea SA2 8PP. Tel: 01792-205678. *Vice-Chancellor,* Prof. R. H. Williams, Ph.D., D.SC, FRS (1994)
UNIVERSITY OF WALES, ABERYSTWYTH, Old College, King Street, Aberystwyth SY23 2AX. Tel: 01970-623111. *Vice-Chancellor,* Prof. D. Llwyd Morgan, D.Phil, D.Litt

UNIVERSITY OF WALES, CARDIFF, PO Box 920, Cardiff CF10 3XP. Tel: 01222-874000. *Vice-Chancellor,* Prof. Sir Brian Smith, Ph.D., D.SC. (1993)
UNIVERSITY OF WALES, LAMPETER, Lampeter SA48 7ED. Tel: 01570-422351. *Vice-Chancellor,* Prof. K. G. Robbins, D.Litt., D.Phil., FRSE (1992)

THE UNIVERSITY OF WARWICK (1965)
Coventry CV4 7AL
Tel 01203-523523
Full-time students (1998–9), 15,900
Chancellor, Sir Shridath Surendranath Ramphal, GCMG, QC (1989)
Vice-Chancellor, Prof. Sir Brian Follett, FRS
Registrar, Dr J. W. Nicholls

UNIVERSITY OF WESTMINSTER (1992)
309 Regent Street, London W1R 8AL
Tel 0171-911 5000
Full-time students (1998–9), 10,947
Vice-Chancellor and Rector, Dr G. M. Copland (1996)
Academic Registrar, Ms E. Green
Secretary, A. Strang

UNIVERSITY OF THE WEST OF ENGLAND (1992)
Coldharbour Lane, Bristol BS16 1QY
Tel 0117-965 6261
Full-time students (1998–9), 16,630
Chancellor, The Rt. Hon. Dame Elizabeth Butler-Sloss, DBE (1993)
Vice-Chancellor, A. C. Morris
Assistant Academic Registrar, Ms M. J. Carter
Academic Secretary, Ms C. Webb

THE UNIVERSITY OF WOLVERHAMPTON (1992)
Wulfruna Street, Wolverhampton WV1 1SB
Tel 01902-321000
Full-time students (1998–9), 14,170
Chancellor, vacant
Vice-Chancellor, Prof. J. S. Brooks, Ph.D.
Registrar, J. F. Baldwin
Secretary, A. W. Lee

THE UNIVERSITY OF YORK (1963)
Heslington, York YO10 5DD
Tel 01904-430000
Full-time students (1998–9), 7,000
Chancellor, Dame Janet Baker, CH, DBE (1991)
Vice-Chancellor, Prof. R. U. Cooke, Ph.D., D.SC.
Registrar and Secretary, D. J. Foster

THE OPEN UNIVERSITY (1969)
Walton Hall, Milton Keynes MK7 6AA
Tel 01908-274066
Students and clients (1999), c.165,000
Chancellor, The Rt. Hon. Betty Boothroyd, MP
Vice-Chancellor, Sir John Daniel
Secretary, F. Woodburn
Registry, H. Niven

ROYAL COLLEGE OF ART (1837)
Kensington Gore, London SW7 2EU
Tel 0171-590 4444
Students (1998–9), 780 (all postgraduate)
Registrar, A. Selby
Director of Administration, G. Philpott
Provost, The Earl of Snowdon, GCVO (1995)
Rector and Vice-Provost, Prof. C. Frayling

COLLEGES

It is not possible to name here all the colleges offering courses of higher or further education. The list does not include colleges forming part of a polytechnic or a university. The English colleges that follow are confined to those in the Higher Education Funding Council for England sector; there are many more colleges in England providing higher education courses, some with HEFCFE funding.

The list of colleges in Wales, Scotland and Northern Ireland includes institutions providing at least one full-time course leading to a first degree granted by an accredited validating body.

ENGLAND

BATH SPA UNIVERSITY COLLEGE, Newton Park, Newton St Loe, Bath BA2 9BN. Tel 01225-875875. *Director*, F. Morgan

BISHOP GROSSETESTE COLLEGE, Lincoln LN1 3DY. Tel 01522-527347. *Principal*, Prof. E. Baker

BOLTON INSTITUTE OF HIGHER EDUCATION, Deane Road, Bolton BL3 5AB. Tel 01204-528851. *Principal*, Ms M. Temple

BRETTON HALL, West Bretton, Wakefield, W. Yorks WF4 4LG. Tel 01924-830261. *Principal*, Prof. G. H. Bell

BUCKINGHAMSHIRE CHILTERNS UNIVERSITY COLLEGE, Queen Alexandra Road, High Wycombe, Bucks HP11 2JZ. Tel 01494-522141. *Director*, Prof. P. B. Mogford

CANTERBURY CHRIST CHURCH UNIVERSITY COLLEGE, North Holmes Road, Canterbury, Kent CT1 1QU. Tel 01227-767700. *Principal*, Prof. M. Wright

THE CENTRAL SCHOOL OF SPEECH AND DRAMA, Embassy Theatre, 64 Eton Avenue, London NW3 3HY. Tel 0171-722 8183. *Principal*, Prof. R. S. Fowler

CHELTENHAM AND GLOUCESTER COLLEGE OF HIGHER EDUCATION, PO Box 220, The Park, Cheltenham, Glos GL50 2QF. Tel 01242-532700. *Director*, Miss J. O. Trotter, OBE

THE COLLEGE OF RIPON AND YORK ST JOHN, Lord Mayor's Walk, York YO31 7EX. Tel 01904-656771. *Principal*, Prof. D. Willcocks

DARTINGTON COLLEGE OF ARTS, Totnes, Devon TQ9 6EJ. Tel 01803-862224. *Principal*, Prof. K. Thompson

EDGE HILL COLLEGE OF HIGHER EDUCATION, St Helens Road, Ormskirk, Lancs L39 4QP. Tel 01695-575171. *Chief Executive*, Dr J. Cater

FALMOUTH COLLEGE OF ARTS, Woodlane, Falmouth, Cornwall TR11 4RH. Tel 01326-211077. *Principal*, Prof. A. G. Livingston

HARPER ADAMS UNIVERSITY COLLEGE, Newport, Shropshire TF10 8NB. Tel 01952-820280. *Principal*, Prof. E. W. Jones

HOMERTON COLLEGE, Cambridge CB2 2PH. Tel 01223-507111. *Principal*, Dr K. Pretty, PH.D.

KENT INSTITUTE OF ART AND DESIGN, Oakwood Park, Maidstone, Kent ME16 8AG. Tel 01622-757286. *Director*, Prof. V. Grylls

KING ALFRED'S COLLEGE, Sparkford Road, Winchester, Hants SO22 4NR. Tel 01962-841515. *Principal*, Prof. J. P. Dickinson

LIVERPOOL HOPE UNIVERSITY COLLEGE, Hope Park, Liverpool L16 9JD. Tel 0151-291 3000. *Rector and Chief Executive*, Prof. S. Lee

THE LONDON INSTITUTE, 65 Davies Street, London W1Y 2AA. Tel 0171-514 6000. *Rector*, Sir William Stubbs

NEWMAN COLLEGE OF HIGHER EDUCATION, Genners Lane, Bartley Green, Birmingham B32 3NT. Tel 0121-476 1181. *Principal*, Prof. B. Ray

RCN INSTITUTE, The Royal College of Nursing, 20 Cavendish Square, London W1M 0AB. Tel 0171-647 3700. *Director*, Prof. A. L. Kitson

ROEHAMPTON INSTITUTE LONDON, Whitelands College, West Hill, London SW15 3SN. Tel 0181-392 3232. *Rector*, Dr B. Porter

ROSE BRUFORD COLLEGE, Lamorbey Park, Sidcup, Kent DA15 9DF. Tel 0181-300 3024. *Principal*, Prof. R. Ely

ROYAL AGRICULTURAL COLLEGE, Cirencester, Glos GL7 6JS. Tel 01285-652531. *Principal*, Prof. J. B. Dent

ROYAL NORTHERN COLLEGE OF MUSIC, 124 Oxford Road, Manchester M13 9RD. Tel 0161-907 5200. *Principal*, Prof. E. Gregson

SOUTHAMPTON INSTITUTE, East Park Terrace, Southampton SO14 0YN. Tel 01703-319000. *Principal*, Dr R. Brown

SURREY INSTITUTE OF ART AND DESIGN, UNIVERSITY COLLEGE, Falkner Road, Farnham, Surrey GU9 7DS. Tel 01252-722441. *Director*, Prof. N. J. Taylor

TRINITY AND ALL SAINTS' COLLEGE, Brownberrie Lane, Horsforth, Leeds LS18 5HD. Tel 0113-283 7100. *Principal*, Dr M. J. Coughlan

THE UNIVERSITY OF BIRMINGHAM, WESTHILL, Weoley Park Road, Selly Oak, Birmingham B29 6LL. Tel 0121-472 7245. *Principal and Vice-Chancellor*, Prof. J. H. Y. Briggs

UNIVERSITY COLLEGE CHESTER, Parkgate Road, Chester CH1 4BJ. Tel 01244-375444. *Principal*, Prof. T. J. Wheeler

UNIVERSITY COLLEGE CHICHESTER, College Lane, Chichester, W. Sussex PO19 4PE. Tel 01243-816000. *Director*, P. E. D. Robinson

UNIVERSITY COLLEGE NORTHAMPTON, Park Campus, Boughton Green Road, Northampton NN2 7AL. Tel 01604-733500. *Rector*, Dr S. M. Gaskell

UNIVERSITY COLLEGE OF ST MARK AND ST JOHN, Derriford Road, Plymouth PL6 8BH. Tel 01752-636700. *Principal*, Dr W. J. Rea

UNIVERSITY COLLEGE OF ST MARTIN, Lancaster LA1 3JD. Tel 01524-384384. *Principal*, Prof. C. J. Carr

UNIVERSITY COLLEGE SCARBOROUGH, Filey Road, Scarborough YO11 3AZ. Tel 01723-362392. *Principal*, Dr. R. A. Withers

UNIVERSITY COLLEGE WORCESTER, Henwick Grove, Worcester WR2 6AJ. Tel 01905-855000. *Principal*, Ms D. Urwin

WESTMINSTER COLLEGE, Oxford OX2 9AT. Tel 01865-247644. *Principal*, Revd Dr R. Ralph

WINCHESTER SCHOOL OF ART, Park Avenue, Winchester, Hants SO23 8DL. Tel 01703-596900. *Principal*, P. Pilgrim

WALES

CARMARTHENSHIRE COLLEGE, Graig Campus, Sandy Road, Llanelli SA15 4DN. Tel 01554-748000. *Principal*, B. Robinson

LLANDRILLO COLLEGE, Llandudno Road, Rhos-on-Sea, Colwyn Bay, Conwy LL28 4HZ. Tel 01492-546666. *Principal*, W. S. H. Evans

NORTH EAST WALES INSTITUTE OF HIGHER EDUCATION, Plas Coch, Mold Road, Wrexham LL11 2AW. Tel 01978-290666. *Principal*, Prof. J. O. Williams

SWANSEA INSTITUTE OF HIGHER EDUCATION, Mount Pleasant, Swansea SA1 6ED. Tel 01792-481000. *Principal*, Prof. D. Warner

TRINITY COLLEGE, Carmarthen SA31 3EP. Tel 01267-676767. *Principal,* D. C. Jones-Davies, OBE

UNIVERSITY OF WALES INSTITUTE CARDIFF, Llandaff Campus, Western Avenue, Cardiff CF5 2YB. Tel 01222-416070. *Principal,* Prof A. J. Chapman, ph.D.

WELSH COLLEGE OF MUSIC AND DRAMA, Castle Grounds, Cathays Park, Cardiff CF10 3ER. Tel 01222-342854. *Principal,* E. Fivet

SCOTLAND

BELL COLLEGE OF TECHNOLOGY, Almada Street, Hamilton, Lanarkshire ML3 0JB. Tel 01698-283100. *Principal,* Dr K. J. MacCallum

DUMFRIES AND GALLOWAY COLLEGE, Heathhall, Dumfries DG1 3QZ. Tel 01387-261261. *Principal,* J. Neil

FIFE COLLEGE OF FURTHER AND HIGHER EDUCATION, St Brycedale Avenue, Kirkcaldy, Fife KY1 1EX. Tel 01592-268591. *Principal,* Mrs J. S. R. Johnston

GLASGOW SCHOOL OF ART, 167 Renfrew Street, Glasgow G3 6RQ. Tel 0141-353 4500. *Director,* Ms S. Reid

INVERNESS COLLEGE, Longman Road, Inverness IV1 1SA. Tel 01463-236681. *Principal,* Dr G. Clark

LEWS CASTLE COLLEGE, Stornoway, Isle of Lewis HS2 0XR. Tel 01851-703311. *Principal,* Dr D. Green

MORAY COLLEGE, Moray Street, Elgin, Moray IV30 1JJ. Tel 01343-554321. *Principal,* Dr R. J. Chalmers

NORTHERN COLLEGE, Hilton Place, Aberdeen AB24 4FA. Tel 01224-283500. *Principal,* D. Adams

ORKNEY COLLEGE, Kirkwall, Orkney KW15 1LX. Tel 01856-872839. *Principal,* P. Scott

QUEEN MARGARET UNIVERSITY COLLEGE, Duke Street, Edinburgh EH6 8HF. Tel 0131-317 3000. *Principal,* Dr J. Stringer

ROYAL SCOTTISH ACADEMY OF MUSIC AND DRAMA, 100 Renfrew Street, Glasgow G2 3DB. Tel 0141-332 4101. *Principal,* Sir Philip Ledger, Kt., CBE, FRSE

SÀBHAL MOR OSTAIG, Sleat, Isle of Skye IV44 8RQ. Tel 01471-844373. *Director,* N. N. Gillies

SAC (SCOTTISH AGRICULTURAL COLLEGE), Central Office, West Mains Road, Edinburgh EH9 3JG. Tel 0131-535 4000. *Principal,* K. A. Linklater

THURSO COLLEGE, Ormlie Road, Thurso, Caithness KW14 7EE. Tel 01847-896161. *Principal,* R. Murray

NORTHERN IRELAND

EAST DOWN INSTITUTE OF FURTHER AND HIGHER EDUCATION, Market Street, Downpatrick, Co. Down BT30 6ND. Tel 01396-615815.

ST MARY'S UNIVERSITY COLLEGE, 191 Falls Road, Belfast BT12 6FE. Tel 01232-327678. *Principal,* Very Revd Prof. M. O'Callaghan

STRANMILLIS COLLEGE, Stranmillis Road, Belfast BT9 5DY. Tel 01232-381271.

ADULT CONTINUING EDUCATION

FORUM FOR THE ADVANCEMENT OF CONTINUING EDUCATION (FACE), Centre for Access, Advice and Continuing Education, University of East London, Romford Road, London E15 4LZ. Tel 0181-849 3696. *Joint Chairs,* J. Storan; Ms L. Chiswick

NATIONAL INSTITUTE OF ADULT CONTINUING EDUCATION, 21 De Montfort Street, Leicester LE1 7GE. Tel 0116-204 4200

NIACE CYMRU, 245 Western Avenue, Cardiff CF5 2YX. Tel 01222-265002. *Director for Wales,* Ms A. Poole

THE RESIDENTIAL COLLEGES COMMITTEE, c/o Ruskin College, Oxford OX1 2HE. Tel 01865-556360. *Awards Officer,* Mrs F. A. Bagchi

COMMUNITY LEARNING SCOTLAND, Rosebery House, 9 Haymarket Terrace, Edinburgh EH12 5EZ. Tel 0131-313 2488. *Chief Executive,* C. McConnell

THE UNIVERSITIES ASSOCIATION FOR CONTINUING EDUCATION, University of Cambridge Board of Continuing Education, Madingley Hall, Madingley, Cambridge CB3 8AQ. Tel 01954-280279. *Administrator,* Ms S. Irwin

WORKERS' EDUCATIONAL ASSOCIATION, Temple House, 17 Victoria Park Square, London E2 9PB. Tel 0181-983 1515. *General Secretary,* R. Lochrie

LONG-TERM RESIDENTIAL COLLEGES FOR ADULT EDUCATION

COLEG HARLECH, Harlech, Gwynedd LL46 2PU. Tel 01766-780363. *Warden (Acting),* Dr D. Wiltshire

CO-OPERATIVE COLLEGE, Stanford Hall, Loughborough, Leics LE12 5QP. Tel 01509-857218. *Chief Executive,* R. Wildgust

FIRCROFT COLLEGE, 1018 Bristol Road, Selly Oak, Birmingham B29 6LH. Tel 0121-472 0116. *Principal,* Ms F. Larden

HILLCROFT COLLEGE, South Bank, Surbiton, Surrey KT6 6DF. Tel 0181-399 2688. *Principal,* Ms J. Ireton

NEWBATTLE ABBEY COLLEGE, Dalkeith, Midlothian EH22 3LL. Tel 0131-663 1921. *Principal,* W. M. Conboy

NORTHERN COLLEGE, Wentworth Castle, Stainborough, Barnsley, S. Yorks S75 3ET. Tel 01226-776000. *Principal,* Dr J. A. Jowitt

PLATER COLLEGE, Pullens Lane, Oxford OX3 0DT. Tel 01865-740500. *Principal,* M. Blades

RUSKIN COLLEGE, Walton Street, Oxford OX1 2HE. Tel 01865-554331. *Principal,* J. Durcan

PROFESSIONAL EDUCATION
Excluding postgraduate study

The organizations listed below are those which, by providing specialist training or conducting examinations, control entry into a profession, or are responsible for maintaining a register of those with professional qualifications in their sector.

Many professions now have a largely graduate entry, and possession of a first degree can exempt entrants from certain of the professional examinations. Enquiries about obtaining professional qualifications should be made to the relevant professional organization(s). Details of higher education providers of first degrees may be found in *University and College Entrance: Official Guide* (available from UCAS, *see* page 444).

EC RECOGNITION

It is now possible for those with professional qualifications obtained in the UK to have these recognized in other European Union countries. A booklet, *Europe Open for Professions,* and further information can be obtained from:

DEPARTMENT OF TRADE AND INDUSTRY, Bay 212, Kingsgate House, 66–74 Victoria Street, London SW1E 6SW. Tel: 0171-215 4648. *Contact,* Ms A. Wilson

ACCOUNTANCY

The main bodies granting membership on examination after a period of practical work are:

ASSOCIATION OF CHARTERED CERTIFIED ACCOUNTANTS (ACCA), 29 Lincoln's Inn Fields, London WC2A 3EE. Tel: 0171-242 6855. *Chief Executive,* Mrs A. L. Rose

CHARTERED INSTITUTE OF MANAGEMENT ACCOUNTANTS, 63 Portland Place, London WIN 4AB. Tel: 0171-637 2311. *Secretary,* J. S. Chester, OBE

CHARTERED INSTITUTE OF PUBLIC FINANCE AND ACCOUNTANCY (CIPFA), 3 Robert Street, London WC2N 6BH. Tel: 0171-543 5600. *Chief Executive,* D. Adams

INSTITUTE OF CHARTERED ACCOUNTANTS IN ENGLAND AND WALES, Chartered Accountants' Hall, PO Box 433, Moorgate Place, London EC2P 2BJ. Tel: 0171-920 8100. *Chief Executive,* J. Collier

INSTITUTE OF CHARTERED ACCOUNTANTS OF SCOTLAND, 27 Queen Street, Edinburgh EH2 ILA. Tel: 0131-225 5673. *Chief Executive,* P. W. Johnston

ACTUARIAL SCIENCE

Two professional organizations grant qualifications after examination:

FACULTY OF ACTUARIES IN SCOTLAND, 18 Dublin Street, Edinburgh EH1 3PP. Tel: 0131-240 1300. *Secretary,* W. W. Mair

INSTITUTE OF ACTUARIES, Staple Inn Hall, High Holborn, London WC1V 7QJ. Tel: 0171-632 2100. *Secretary-General,* G. B. L. Campbell. Education enquiries to Napier House, 4 Worcester Street, Oxford OXI 2AW. Tel: 01865-268200

ARCHITECTURE

The Education Committee of the Royal Institute of British Architects sets standards and guides the whole system of architectural education throughout the UK. RIBA recognizes courses at 35 schools of architecture in the UK for exemption from their own examinations as well as 65 courses overseas.

ARCHITECTS REGISTRATION BOARD, 73 Hallam Street, London WIN 6EE. Tel: 0171-580 5861. *Chief Officer and Registrar,* A. Finch

THE ROYAL INSTITUTE OF BRITISH ARCHITECTS, 66 Portland Place, London WIN 4AD. Tel: 0171-580 5533. Information Unit: 0891-234400. *President,* M. Goldschmied; *Director-General,* A. Reid, PH.D.

Schools of architecture outside the universities include:

THE ARCHITECTURAL ASSOCIATION, 34–36 Bedford Square, London WC1B 3ES. Tel: 0171-887 4000. *Secretary,* E. A. Le Maistre

THE SCHOOL OF ARCHITECTURE AND THE BUILDING ARTS, 14–15 Gloucester Gate, London NWI 4HG. Tel: 0171-916 7380. *Director,* Prof. A. Gale

BANKING

Professional organizations granting qualifications after examination are:

CHARTERED INSTITUTE OF BANKERS, 90 Bishopsgate, London EC2N 4AS. Tel: 0171-444 7111. *Chief Executive,* G. Shreeve

CHARTERED INSTITUTE OF BANKERS IN SCOTLAND, Drumsheugh House, 38B Drumsheugh Gardens, Edinburgh EH3 7SW. Tel: 0131-473 7777. *Chief Executive,* C. W. Munn

BUILDING

Examinations are conducted by:

CHARTERED INSTITUTE OF BUILDING, Englemere, King's Ride, Ascot, Berks SL5 7TB. Tel: 01344-630700. *Chief Executive,* K. Banbury

INSTITUTE OF BUILDING CONTROL, 92–104 East Street, Epsom, Surrey KT17 IEB. Tel: 01372-745577. *Chief Executive,* G. Parrott

INSTITUTE OF CLERKS OF WORKS OF GREAT BRITAIN, 41 The Mall, London W5 3TJ. Tel: 0181-579 2917/8. *Secretary,* vacant

BUSINESS, MANAGEMENT AND ADMINISTRATION

Professional bodies conducting training and/or examinations in business, administration, management or commerce include:

AMETS (ASSOCIATION FOR MANAGEMENT EDUCATION AND TRAINING IN SCOTLAND), c/o Cottrell Building, University of Stirling, Stirling FK9 4LA. Tel: 01786-450906. *Chairman,* Prof. F. Pignatelli

THE ASSOCIATION OF MBAS, 15 Duncan Terrace, London NI 8BZ. Tel: 0171-837 3375. Publishes a directory giving details of MBA programmes worldwide. *Director,* M. Jones

CAM FOUNDATION (COMMUNICATIONS, ADVERTISING AND MARKETING EDUCATION FOUNDATION), Abford House, 15 Wilton Road, London SW1V INJ. Tel: 0171-828 7506. *Chief Executive,* D. Royston-Lee

CHARTERED INSTITUTE OF HOUSING, Octavia House, Westwood Business Park, Westwood Way, Coventry CV4 8JP. Tel: 01203-851700. *Chief Executive,* D. Butler

CHARTERED INSTITUTE OF MARKETING, Moor Hall, Cookham, Maidenhead, Berks SL6 9QH. Tel: 01628-427500. *Chief Executive,* J. Stubbs

CHARTERED INSTITUTE OF PURCHASING AND SUPPLY, Easton House, Easton on the Hill, Stamford, Lincs PE9 3NZ. Tel: 01780-756777. *Chief Executive,* C. Holden

CHARTERED INSTITUTE OF TRANSPORT, 80 Portland Place, London WIN 4DP. Tel: 0171-467 9400. *Director,* Mrs D. de Carvalho

HENLEY MANAGEMENT COLLEGE, Greenlands, Henley-on-Thames, Oxon RG9 3AU. Tel: 01491-571454. *Principal,* Prof. R. Wild, PH.D., D.SC.

INSTITUTE OF ADMINISTRATIVE MANAGEMENT, 40 Chatsworth Parade, Petts Wood, Orpington, Kent BR5 IRW. Tel: 01689-875555. *Chief Executive,* Prof. G. Robinson

INSTITUTE OF CHARTERED SECRETARIES AND ADMINISTRATORS, 16 Park Crescent, London WIN 4AH. Tel: 0171-580 4741. *Chief Executive,* M. J. Ainsworth

INSTITUTE OF CHARTERED SHIPBROKERS, 3 St Helen's Place, London EC3A 6EJ. Tel: 0171-628 5559. *Director,* Ms B. Fletcher

INSTITUTE OF EXPORT, Export House, 64 Clifton Street, London EC2A 4HB. Tel: 0171-247 9812. *Director-General,* I. J. Campbell

INSTITUTE OF HEALTHCARE MANAGEMENT, 7–10 Chandos Street, London WIM 9DE. Tel: 0171-460 7654. *Director,* S. Marples

INSTITUTE OF MANAGEMENT, Management House, Cottingham Road, Corby, Northants NN17 ITT. Tel: 01536-204222. *Director-General,* Mrs M. Chapman

INSTITUTE OF PERSONNEL AND DEVELOPMENT, IPD House, Camp Road, London SW19 4UX. Tel: 0181-971 9000. *Director-General,* G. Armstrong

INSTITUTE OF PRACTITIONERS IN ADVERTISING, 44 Belgrave Square, London SW1X 8QS. Tel: 0171-235 7020. *Secretary*, J. Raad

INSTITUTE OF QUALITY ASSURANCE, 12 Grosvenor Crescent, London SW1X 7EE. Tel: 0171-245 6722. *Chief Executive*, Frank Steer, MBE

CHIROPRACTIC

Chiropractic is accorded statutory regulation by the Chiropractic Act 1994. There were previously four professional associations operating voluntary registration schemes. These registers were replaced by the General Chiropractic Council, which opened a new register in June 1999, although the Associations still exist. It is illegal for anyone to call themselves a chiropractor unless they have undertaken a recognized course of training and are registered with the General Chiropractic Council.

There are currently five training centres for chiropractic. Two of these provide four-year part-time training programmes leading to internal academic awards; the other three provide full-time training leading to a B.Sc. and M.Sc. in chiropractic. In future, the General Chiropractic Council will determine the training requirements to qualify for registration and accredit courses.

BRITISH CHIROPRACTIC ASSOCIATION, Blagrave House, 17 Blagrave Street, Reading RG1 1QB. Tel: 0118-950 5950. *Executive Director*, Ms S. A. Wakefield

GENERAL CHIROPRACTIC COUNCIL, 3rd Floor, North Wing, 344–354 Gray's Inn Road, London WC1X 8BP. Tel: 0171-713 5155. *Chief Executive and Registrar*, Mrs M. Coats

SCOTTISH CHIROPRACTIC ASSOCIATION, St Boswells Chiropractic Clinic, 16 Jenny Moores Road, St Boswells, Melrose TD6 0AL. Tel: 01835-823645. *Secretary*, Dr C. I. How

DANCE

The Council for Dance Education and Training (CDET) has accredited courses at the following: Arts Education Schools, Tring Park and London; Central School of Ballet; Doreen Bird College of Performing Arts; Elmhurst–The School for Dance and Performing Arts; English National Ballet School; The Hammond School; The Italia Conti Academy of Theatre Arts Ltd; Laban Centre, London; Laine Theatre Arts Ltd; London Contemporary Dance School; London Studio Centre; Midlands Academy of Dance and Drama; Merseyside Dance and Drama Centre; Northern Ballet School; Performers College; Stella Mann College; Studios La Pointe; Royal Academy of Dancing; The Urdang Academy.

The accreditation of a course in a school does not necessarily imply that other courses of a different type or duration in the same school are also accredited.

CDET has approved the teacher registration systems of the following: Association of American Dancing; British Ballet Organization; British Theatre Dance Association; Cecchetti Society; Imperial Society of Teachers of Dancing; Royal Academy of Dancing.

COUNCIL FOR DANCE EDUCATION AND TRAINING (UK), Studio 8, The Glasshouse, 49A Goldhawk Road, London W12 8QP. Tel: 0181-746 0076. *Chairman*, Clive Priestley, CB

IMPERIAL SOCIETY OF TEACHERS OF DANCING, Imperial House, 22–26 Paul Street, London EC2A 4QE. Tel: 0171-377 1577. *Chief Executive*, M. J. Browne

INTERNATIONAL DANCE TEACHERS' ASSOCIATION, International House, 76 Bennett Road, Brighton BN2 5JL. Tel: 01273-685652. *Chief Executive*, J. Dearling

ROYAL ACADEMY OF DANCING, 36 Battersea Square, London SW11 3RA. Tel: 0171-223 0091. *Chief Executive*, L. Rittner; *Artistic Director*, Miss L. Wallis

ROYAL BALLET SCHOOL, 155 Talgarth Road, London W14 9DE. Tel: 0181-748 6335. Also at White Lodge, Richmond Park, Surrey TW10 5HR. Tel: 0181-876 5547. *Director*, Ms G. Stock

DEFENCE

ROYAL COLLEGE OF DEFENCE STUDIES, Seaford House, 37 Belgrave Square, London SW1X 8NS. Tel: 0171-915 4800. Prepares selected senior officers and officials for responsibilities in the direction and management of defence, security and related areas. *Commandant*, Vice-Adm. J. H. S. McAnally, LVO

JOINT SERVICES COMMAND AND STAFF COLLEGE, Bracknell, Berks RG12 9DD. Tel: 01344-454593. *Commandant*, Maj.-Gen. T. J. Granville-Chapman, CBE; *Dean of Academic Studies*, Prof. G. Till, PH.D.

ROYAL NAVAL COLLEGE

BRITANNIA ROYAL NAVAL COLLEGE, Dartmouth, Devon TQ6 0HJ. Tel: 01803-832141. Provides professional training and education for all new entry RN officers and officers from foreign and Commonwealth navies. *Commodore*, Cdre M. W. G. Kerr

MILITARY COLLEGES

DIRECTORATE OF EDUCATIONAL AND TRAINING SERVICES, Trenchard Lines, Upavon, Pewsey, Wilts SN9 6BE. Tel: 01980-618719. *Director*, Brig. P. S. Purves, DSC

ROYAL MILITARY ACADEMY SANDHURST, Camberley, Surrey GU15 4PQ. Tel: 01276-63344. *Commandant*, Maj.-Gen. A. G. Denaro, CBE

ROYAL MILITARY COLLEGE OF SCIENCE, Shrivenham, Swindon, Wilts SN6 8LA. Tel: 01793-785435. Students from UK and overseas study from degree to postgraduate levels in engineering, management, science and technology. The College is a faculty of Cranfield University. *Commandant*, Maj.-Gen. J. C. B. Sutherall, CBE; *Principal*, Prof. P. Hutchinson

ROYAL AIR FORCE COLLEGES

ROYAL AIR FORCE COLLEGE, Cranwell, Sleaford, Lincs. NG34 8HB. Provides initial training for all officer entrants to the RAF. Also provides initial specialist and postgraduate training for engineering and supply officers. The RAF College is the site of the Joint Elementary Flying School for pilots of all three services, Number 3 Flying Training School and the RAF Central Flying School. It is also the headquarters for the RAF University Air Squadrons, and is responsible for supervision of the Air Cadet Organization. *Air Officer Commanding and Commandant*, Air Vice-Marshal T. W. Rimmer, OBE

ROYAL AIR FORCE TRAINING, DEVELOPMENT AND SUPPORT UNIT, RAF Halton, Aylesbury, Bucks HP22 5PG. Tel: 01296-623535. *Commanding Officer*, Gp Capt. A. Harris

DENTISTRY

In order to practise in the UK, a dentist must be entered in the Dentists Register. To be registered, a person must hold the degree or diploma in dental surgery of a university in the UK or the diploma of any of the licensing authorities (the Royal Colleges of Surgeons of England and of Edinburgh, and the Royal College of Physicians and Surgeons of Glasgow). Nationals of EU or European

Economic Area member states holding an appropriate European diploma, and holders of certain overseas diplomas, may also be registered. Temporary registration may be available for those dentists who do not hold a diploma described above. The Dentists Register is maintained by:
THE GENERAL DENTAL COUNCIL, 37 Wimpole Street, London WIM 8DQ. Tel: 0171-887 3800. *Chief Executive and Registrar*, Mrs R. M. J. Hepplewhite

DIETETICS
See also FOOD AND NUTRITION SCIENCE

The professional association is the British Dietetic Association. Full membership is open to dietitians holding a recognized qualification, who may also become State Registered Dietitians through the Council for Professions Supplementary to Medicine (*see* Medicine).
THE BRITISH DIETETIC ASSOCIATION, 5th Floor, Elizabeth House, 22 Suffolk Street, Queensway, Birmingham BI ILS. Tel: 0121-616 4900. *Secretary*, J. Grigg

DRAMA

The national validating body for courses providing training in drama for the professional theatre is the National Council for Drama Training. It currently has accredited courses at the following: Academy of Live and Recorded Arts; Arts Educational Schools; Birmingham School of Speech Training and Dramatic Art; Bristol Old Vic Theatre School; Central School of Speech and Drama; Drama Centre, London; Drama Studio, London; Guildford School of Acting; Guildhall School of Music and Drama, London; London Academy of Music and Dramatic Art; Manchester Metropolitan University School of Theatre; Mountview Theatre School; Oxford School of Drama, Woodstock; Queen Margaret University College, Edinburgh; Rose Bruford College, Sidcup; Royal Academy of Dramatic Art, London; Royal Scottish Academy of Music and Drama; Webber Douglas Academy of Dramatic Art, London; Welsh College of Music and Drama.
The accreditation of a course in a school does not necessarily imply that other courses of different type or duration in the same school are also accredited.
THE NATIONAL COUNCIL FOR DRAMA TRAINING, 5 Tavistock Place, London WCIH 9SS. *Executive Secretary*, Mrs A. Bailey

ENGINEERING

The Engineering Council supervises the engineering profession through the 39 nominated engineering institutions who are represented on its Board for Engineers' Regulation. Working with and through the institutions, the Council sets the standards for the registration of individuals, and also the accreditation for academic courses in universities and colleges and the practical training in industry.
THE ENGINEERING COUNCIL, 10 Maltravers Street, London WC2R 3ER. Tel: 0171-240 7891. *Director-General*, M. Shirley

The principal qualifying bodies are:
BRITISH COMPUTER SOCIETY, 1 Sanford Street, Swindon SNI IHJ. Tel: 01793-417417. *Chief Executive*, Mrs J. M. Scott
BRITISH INSTITUTE OF NON-DESTRUCTIVE TESTING, 1 Spencer Parade, Northampton NNI 5AA. Tel: 01604-630124. *Secretary*, M. E. Gallagher
CHARTERED INSTITUTION OF BUILDING SERVICES ENGINEERS, 222 Balham High Road, London SWI2 9BS. Tel: 0181-675 5211. *Secretary*, R. John

INSTITUTION OF AGRICULTURAL ENGINEERS, West End Road, Silsoe, Bedford MK45 4DU. Tel: 01525-861096. *Chief Executive*, J. H. Neville
INSTITUTE OF BRITISH FOUNDRYMEN, Bordesley Hall, The Holloway, Alvechurch, Birmingham B48 7QA. Tel: 01527-596100. *Secretary*, G. A. Schofield
INSTITUTION OF CHEMICAL ENGINEERS, Davis Building, 165–189 Railway Terrace, Rugby, Warks CV21 3HQ. Tel: 01788-578214. *Chief Executive*, Dr T. J. Evans
INSTITUTION OF CIVIL ENGINEERS, 1 Great George Street, London SWIP 3AA. Tel: 0171-222 7722. *Director-General*, M. Casebourne
INSTITUTION OF ELECTRICAL ENGINEERS, Savoy Place, London WC2R OBL. Tel: 0171-240 1871. *Chief Executive*, Dr A. Roberts
INSTITUTE OF ENERGY, 18 Devonshire Street, London WIN 2AU. Tel: 0171-580 7124. *Secretary and Chief Executive*, Ms L. Evans
INSTITUTION OF ENGINEERING DESIGNERS, Courtleigh, Westbury Leigh, Westbury, Wilts BA13 3TA. Tel: 01373-822801. *Secretary*, M. Osborne
INSTITUTION OF FIRE ENGINEERS, 148 New Walk, Leicester LEI 7QB. Tel: 0116-255 3654. *General Secretary*, D. W. Evans
INSTITUTION OF GAS ENGINEERS, 21 Portland Place, London WIN 3AF. Tel: 0171-636 6603. *Secretary*, Ms J. Sedgwick
INSTITUTE OF HEALTHCARE ENGINEERING AND ESTATE MANAGEMENT, 2 Abingdon House, Cumberland Business Centre, Northumberland Road, Portsmouth PO5 IDS. Tel: 01705-823186. *Secretary*, W. R. Pym
INSTITUTION OF INCORPORATED ENGINEERS, Savoy Hill House, Savoy Hill, London WC2R OBS. Tel: 0171-836 3357. *Chief Executive*, P. F. Wason
INSTITUTION OF INCORPORATED EXECUTIVE ENGINEERS, Wix Hill House, West Horsley, Surrey KT24 6DZ. Tel: 01483-222383. *Secretary*, D. Dacam, OBE
INSTITUTE OF LIGHTING ENGINEERS, Lennox House, 9 Lawford Road, Rugby CV21 2DZ. Tel: 01788-576492. *Chief Executive*, R. G. Frost
INSTITUTE OF MARINE ENGINEERS, 80 Coleman Street, London EC2R 5BJ. Tel: 0171-382 2600. *Director-General*, K. F. Read
INSTITUTE OF MATERIALS, 1 Carlton House Terrace, London SWIY 5DB. Tel: 0171-451 7300. *Chief Executive*, Dr B. A. Rickinson
INSTITUTE OF MEASUREMENT AND CONTROL, 87 Gower Street, London WCIE 6AA. Tel: 0171-387 4949. *Secretary*, M. J. Yates
INSTITUTION OF MECHANICAL ENGINEERS, 1 Birdcage Walk, London SWIH 9JJ. Tel: 0171-222 7899. *Director-General*, Sir Michael Moore, KBE, LVO
INSTITUTION OF MINING AND METALLURGY, Danum House, 6A South Parade, Doncaster DNI 2DY. Tel: 01302-320486. *Secretary*, Dr G. J. M. Woodrow
INSTITUTION OF NUCLEAR ENGINEERS, 1 Penerley Road, London SE6 2LQ. Tel: 0181-698 1500. *Secretary*, W. J. Hurst
INSTITUTE OF PHYSICS, 76 Portland Place, London WIN 3DH. Tel: 0171-470 4800. *Chief Executive*, Dr A. D. W. Jones
INSTITUTION OF PLANT ENGINEERS, 77 Great Peter Street, London SWIP 2EZ. Tel: 0171-233 2855. *Secretary*, P. F. Tye
INSTITUTE OF PLUMBING, 64 Station Lane, Hornchurch, Essex RMI2 6NB. Tel: 01708-472791. *Chief Executive*, W. A. Watts, MBE

INSTITUTE OF QUALITY ASSURANCE, 12 Grosvenor Crescent, London SW1X 7EE. Tel: 0171-245 6722. *Secretary-General*, D. Campbell
INSTITUTION OF STRUCTURAL ENGINEERS, 11 Upper Belgrave Street, London SW1X 8BH. Tel: 0171-235 4535. *Chief Executive*, Dr K. J. Eaton.
INSTITUTION OF WATER OFFICERS, Heriot House, 12 Summerhill Terrace, Newcastle upon Tyne NE4 6EB. Tel: 0191-230 5150. *Company Secretary (acting)*, Ms L. Harding
ROYAL AERONAUTICAL SOCIETY, 4 Hamilton Place, London W1V 0BQ. Tel: 0171-499 3515. *Director*, K. Mans
ROYAL INSTITUTION OF NAVAL ARCHITECTS, 10 Upper Belgrave Street, London SW1X 8BQ. Tel: 0171-235 4622. *Chief Executive*, T. Blakeley
THE WELDING INSTITUTE, Abington Hall, Abington, Cambridge CB1 6AL. Tel: 01223-891162. *Chief Executive*, B. Braithwaite, OBE

FILM AND TELEVISION

Postgraduate training for those intending to make a career in film and television production is provided by the National Film and Television School, which provides courses in television producing and direction, animation direction, documentary direction, fiction direction, screenwriting, screen design, editing, cinematography, screen sound, art direction and screen music. Short courses to enable professionals to update or expand their skills are also provided.
NATIONAL FILM AND TELEVISION SCHOOL, Beaconsfield Studios, Station Road, Beaconsfield, Bucks HP9 1LG. Tel: 01494-671234. Web: http://www.nftsfilm-tv.ac.uk. *Director*, S. Bayly

FOOD AND NUTRITION SCIENCE
See also DIETETICS

Scientific and professional bodies include:
INSTITUTE OF FOOD SCIENCE & TECHNOLOGY, 5 Cambridge Court, 210 Shepherd's Bush Road, London W6 7NJ. Tel: 0171-603 6316. *Chief Executive*, Ms H. G. Wild

FORESTRY AND TIMBER STUDIES

Professional organizations include:
COMMONWEALTH FORESTRY ASSOCIATION, c/o Oxford Forestry Institute, South Parks Road, Oxford OX1 3RB. Tel: 01865-271037. *Chairman*, Dr J. S. Maini
INSTITUTE OF CHARTERED FORESTERS, 7A St Colme Street, Edinburgh EH3 6AA. Tel: 0131-225 2705. *Secretary*, Ms L. Kennedy
ROYAL FORESTRY SOCIETY OF ENGLAND, WALES AND NORTHERN IRELAND, 102 High Street, Tring, Herts HP23 4AF. Tel: 01442-822028. *Director*, J. E. Jackson, PH.D.
ROYAL SCOTTISH FORESTRY SOCIETY, The Stables, Dalkeith Country Park, Dalkeith, Midlothian EH22 2NA. Tel: 0131-660 9480. *Director*, M. Osborne

FUEL AND ENERGY SCIENCE

The principal professional bodies are:
INSTITUTE OF ENERGY, 18 Devonshire Street, London W1N 2AU. Tel: 0171-580 7124. *Secretary*, Mrs D. Davy
INSTITUTION OF GAS ENGINEERS, 21 Portland Place, London W1N 3AF. Tel: 0171-636 6603. *Secretary*, Mrs S. M. Raine
INSTITUTE OF PETROLEUM, 61 New Cavendish Street, London W1M 8AR. Tel: 0171-467 7100. *Director-General*, J. G. Pym

HOTELKEEPING, CATERING AND INSTITUTIONAL MANAGEMENT
See also DIETETICS, AND FOOD AND NUTRITION SCIENCE

The qualifying professional body in these areas is:
HOTEL AND CATERING INTERNATIONAL MANAGEMENT ASSOCIATION, 191 Trinity Road, London SW17 7HN. Tel: 0181-672 4251. *Chief Executive*, D. Wood

INDUSTRIAL AND VOCATIONAL TRAINING

The NTO National Council represents the network of employer-led national training organizations (NTOs). NTOs represent the education and training interests of their respective sectors to government and ensure the development and adoption of occupational standards, particularly through National and Scottish Vocational Qualifications and learning initiatives including Modern Apprenticeship and National Traineeship.
NTO NATIONAL COUNCIL, 10 Meadowcourt, Amos Road, Sheffield S9 1BX. Tel: 0114-261 9926. *Chief Executive*, Dr. A. Powell

INSURANCE

Organizations conducting examinations and awarding diplomas are:
ASSOCIATION OF AVERAGE ADJUSTERS, 200 Aldersgate Street, London EC1A 4JJ. Tel: 0171-956 0099. *Secretary*, D. W. Taylor
CHARTERED INSTITUTE OF LOSS ADJUSTERS, Manfield House, 1 Southampton Street, London WC2R 0LR. Tel: 0171-240 1496. *Director*, G. L. Cave
CHARTERED INSURANCE INSTITUTE, 20 Aldermanbury, London EC2V 7HY. Tel: 0171-417 4425. *Director-General*, Prof. D. E. Bland

JOURNALISM

Courses for trainee newspaper journalists are available at 30 centres. One-year full-time courses are available for selected students and 18-week courses for graduates. Particulars of all these courses are available from the National Council for the Training of Journalists. Short courses for mid-career development can be arranged, as can various distance learning courses. The NCTJ also offers Assessor, Internal Verifier (IV) and Accreditation of Prior Achievement (APA) training, and NVQs.
For periodical journalists, there are nine centres running courses approved by the Periodicals Training Council (PTC). The PTC also offers NVQs and information on best practice training.
THE NATIONAL COUNCIL FOR TRAINING OF JOURNALISTS, Latton Bush Centre, Southern Way, Harlow, Essex CM18 7BL. Tel: 01279-430009. *Chief Executive*, R. Selwood
THE PERIODICALS TRAINING COUNCIL, Queen's House, 55–56 Lincoln's Inn Fields, London WC2A 3LJ. Tel: 0171-404 4168. *Director*, Ms J. Butcher

LAW

THE BAR

Admission to the Bar of England and Wales is controlled by the Inns of Court, admission to the Bar of Northern Ireland by the Honorable Society of the Inn of Court of Northern Ireland and admission as an Advocate of the Scottish Bar is controlled by the Faculty of Advocates. The governing body of the barristers' branch of the legal profession in England and Wales is the General Council of the Bar (the Bar Council). The governing body in Northern Ireland is the Honorable Society of the Inn of Court of Northern Ireland, and the Faculty of Advocates is the governing body of the Scottish Bar. The education and examination of students training for the Bar of England and Wales is regulated by the General Council of the Bar. Those who intend to practise at the Bar of England and Wales must pass the Bar's vocational course. The Inns of Court School of Law is the largest provider of initial training for those wishing to practise at the Bar, but seven other institutions have been validated to provide the course. Applications are handled by the Bar Council's Centralised Applications Clearing House (CACH).

FACULTY OF ADVOCATES, Advocates Library, Parliament House, Edinburgh EH1 1RF. Tel: 0131-226 5071. *Dean*, G. N. H. Emslie, QC; *Clerk*, I. G. Armstrong

THE GENERAL COUNCIL OF THE BAR, 3 Bedford Row, London WC1R 4DB. Tel: 0171-242 0082. *Chairman*, D. Brennan, QC; *Chief Executive*, N. Morison

CACH, Education and Training Department, 2–3 Cursitor Street, London EC4A 1NE. Tel: 0171-440 4000

THE HONORABLE SOCIETY OF THE INN OF COURT OF NORTHERN IRELAND, Royal Courts of Justice, Belfast BT1 3JF. Tel: 01232-235111. *Treasurer* (1999), Hon. Mr Justice Kerr; *Under-Treasurer*, J. W. Wilson, QC

INNS OF COURT SCHOOL OF LAW, 4 Gray's Inn Place, Gray's Inn, London WC1R 5DX. Tel: 0171-404 5787. *Chairman*, The Hon. Mr Justice Hooper; *Principal*, Prof. R. Stone

The Inns of Court

GRAY'S INN, 8 South Square, London WC1R 5EU. Tel: 0171-458 7900. *Treasurer*, Rt. Hon. Sir Anthony Evans, Kt., QC; *Under-Treasurer*, D. Machin

THE INNER TEMPLE, London EC4Y 7HL. Tel: 0171-797 8250. *Treasurer*, The Rt. Hon. The Lord Lloyd of Berwick; *Sub-Treasurer*, Brig. P. A. Little, CBE

LINCOLN'S INN, London WC2A 3TL. Tel: 0171-405 1393. *Treasurer*, The Rt. Hon. Sir John Balcombe, Kt., QC; *Under-Treasurer*, Col. D. H. Hills, MBE

THE MIDDLE TEMPLE, London EC4Y 9AT. Tel: 0171-427 4800. *Treasurer*, Hon. Sir Charles McCullough, Kt., QC; *Under-Treasurer*, Brig. C. T. J. Wright

SOLICITORS

Qualifications for solicitors are obtainable only from one of the Law Societies, which control the education and examination of trainee solicitors and the admission of solicitors.

THE COLLEGE OF LAW provides courses for the Common Professional Examination and Legal Practice Course at Braboeuf Manor, St Catherine's, Guildford, Surrey GU3 1HA; 14 Store Street, London WC1E 7DE; Christleton Hall, Chester CH3 7AB; Bishopthorpe Road, York YO23 2GA. The college also provides the Bar Vocational Course at its London branch

LAW SOCIETY OF ENGLAND AND WALES, 113 Chancery Lane, London WC2A 1PL. Tel: 0171-242 1222. *President* (1999–2000), R. Sayer; *Secretary-General*, Mrs J. M. Betts

LAW SOCIETY OF NORTHERN IRELAND, Law Society House, 98 Victoria Street, Belfast BT1 3JZ. Tel: 01232-231614. *Chief Executive*, J. W. Bailie

LAW SOCIETY OF SCOTLAND, 26 Drumsheugh Gardens, Edinburgh EH3 7YR. Tel: 0131-226 7411. *President* (1999–2000), M. Scanlan; *Secretary*, D. R. Mill

OFFICE FOR THE SUPERVISION OF SOLICITORS, Victoria Court, 8 Dormer Place, Leamington Spa, Warks CV32 5AE. Tel: 01926-820082. The Office is an establishment of the Law Society set up to handle complaints about solicitors and regulate solicitors' practices

LIBRARIANSHIP AND INFORMATION SCIENCE/MANAGEMENT

The Library Association accredits degree and postgraduate courses in library and information science which are offered by 17 universities in the UK. A full list of accredited degree and postgraduate courses is available from its Information Services and on its web site (*see* below). The Association also maintains a professional register of Chartered Members open to graduate ordinary members of the Association.

THE LIBRARY ASSOCIATION, 7 Ridgmount Street, London WC1E 7AE. Tel: 0171-636 7543. Web: http://www.la-hq.org.uk. *Chief Executive*, Dr R. McKee

MATERIALS STUDIES

The qualifying body is:
INSTITUTE OF MATERIALS, 1 Carlton House Terrace, London SW1Y 5DB. Tel: 0171-451 7300. *Chief Executive*, Dr B. A. Rickinson

MEDICINE

All doctors must be registered with the General Medical Council. In order to register, medical students must complete an undergraduate medical degree at one of the 19 universities with medical schools, followed by a year of general clinical training. Once registered, doctors undertake general professional and basic specialist training as senior house officers. Further specialist training is provided by the royal colleges, faculties and societies listed below. The General Medical Council keeps a register of those doctors who have been awarded Certificates of Completion of Specialist Training.

The United Examining Board holds qualifying examinations for candidates who have trained overseas. These candidates must also have spent a period at a UK medical school.

GENERAL MEDICAL COUNCIL, 178 Great Portland Street, London W1N 6JE. Tel: 0171-580 7642. *President*, Sir Donald Irvine, CBE, MD, FRGCP; *Chief Executive*, F. Scott

UNITED EXAMINING BOARD, Apothecaries Hall, Black Friars Lane, London EC4V 6EJ. Tel: 0171-236 1180. *Chairman*, Prof. J. S. P. Lumley, FRCS; *Registrar*, A. M. Wallington-Smith

COLLEGES/SOCIETIES HOLDING POSTGRADUATE MEMBERSHIP AND DIPLOMA EXAMINATIONS

FACULTY OF ACCIDENT AND EMERGENCY MEDICINE, Royal College of Surgeons of England, 35–43 Lincoln's Inn Fields, London WC2A 3PN. Tel: 0171-405 7071. *President (from 2 December 1999)*, I. W. R. Anderson

FACULTY OF OCCUPATIONAL MEDICINE, 6 St Andrew's Place, London NW1 4LB. Tel: 0171-317 5890. *Secretary*, Ms F. M. Quinn

FACULTY OF PHARMACEUTICAL MEDICINE, 1 St Andrew's Place, London NW1 4LB. Tel: 0171-224 0343. *Administrator*, Ms K. Wright

FACULTY OF PUBLIC HEALTH MEDICINE, 4 St Andrew's Place, London NW1 4LB. Tel: 0171-935 0243. *Secretary*, P. Scourfield

ROYAL COLLEGE OF ANAESTHETISTS, 48–49 Russell Square, London WC1B 4JY. Tel: 0171-813 1900. *President*, Prof. L. Strunin; *Chief Executive*, Ms W. Cogger

ROYAL COLLEGE OF GENERAL PRACTITIONERS, 14 Princes Gate, London SW7 1PU. Tel: 0171-581 3232. *President*, Prof. Sir Denis Gray, Kt., OBE, FRCGP; *Secretary* (from Nov. 1999), Dr M. Baker, FRCGP

ROYAL COLLEGE OF OBSTETRICIANS AND GYNAECOLOGISTS, 27 Sussex Place, London NW1 4RG. Tel: 0171-772 6200. *President*, Prof. R. W. Shaw; *Secretary*, P. A. Barnett

ROYAL COLLEGE OF PAEDIATRICS AND CHILD
HEALTH, 50 Hallam Street, London WIN 6DE. Tel:
0171-307 5600. *President*, Prof. J. D. Baum; *Secretary*, L.
Tyler

ROYAL COLLEGE OF PATHOLOGISTS, 2 Carlton House
Terrace, London SWIY 5AF. Tel: 0171-930 5861.
President (from November 1999), Prof. J. Lilleyman; *Deputy
Secretary*, Ms E. Evans

ROYAL COLLEGE OF PHYSICIANS, 11 St Andrew's Place,
London NWI 4LE. Tel: 0171-935 1174. *President*, Prof. K.
G. M. M. Alberti, FRCP; *Secretary*, P. Masterton-Smith

ROYAL COLLEGE OF PHYSICIANS AND SURGEONS OF
GLASGOW, 232–242 St Vincent Street, Glasgow G2 5RJ.
Tel: 0141-221 6072. *President*, C. Mackay; *Hon. Secretary*,
Dr C. Semple

ROYAL COLLEGE OF PHYSICIANS OF EDINBURGH,
9 Queen Street, Edinburgh EH2 1JQ. Tel: 0131-225 7324.
President, Prof. J. C. Petrie; *Secretary*, Dr A. C. Parker

ROYAL COLLEGE OF PSYCHIATRISTS, 17 Belgrave
Square, London SWIX 8PG. Tel: 0171-235 2351. *President*,
Prof. J. Cox; *Secretary*, Mrs V. Cameron

ROYAL COLLEGE OF RADIOLOGISTS, 38 Portland Place,
London WIN 4QJ. Tel: 0171-636 4432. *President*, Prof. P.
Armstrong; *General Secretary*, A. J. Cowles

ROYAL COLLEGE OF SURGEONS OF EDINBURGH,
Nicolson Street, Edinburgh EH8 9DW. Tel: 0131-527
1600. *President*, Prof. A. G. D. Maran; *Executive Secretary*,
Ms A. S. Campbell

ROYAL COLLEGE OF SURGEONS OF ENGLAND, 35–43
Lincoln's Inn Fields, London WC2A 3PN. Tel: 0171-405
3474. *President*, B. T. Jackson, FRCS; *Secretary*, C. Duncan

SOCIETY OF APOTHECARIES OF LONDON, 14 Black
Friars Lane, London EC4V 6EJ. Tel: 0171-236 1189.
Clerk, Lt.-Col. R. J. Stringer

PROFESSIONS SUPPLEMENTARY TO MEDICINE

The standard of professional education in art, drama and
music therapies, biomedical sciences, chiropody, dietetics,
occupational therapy, orthoptics, prosthetics and orthotics,
physiotherapy and radiography is the responsibility of nine
professional boards, which also publish an annual register
of qualified practitioners. The work of the boards is co-
ordinated by the Council for Professions Supplementary
to Medicine.

In June 1999 the Government announced that three new
boards would be established, covering speech and language
therapists, clinical scientists and paramedics.

THE COUNCIL FOR PROFESSIONS SUPPLEMENTARY TO
MEDICINE, Park House, 184 Kennington Park Road,
London SEII 4BU. Tel: 0171-582 0866. *Registrar*, M. D.
Hall

ART, DRAMA AND MUSIC THERAPIES

A postgraduate qualification in the relevant therapy is
required. There are five institutions in the UK offering
courses in art therapy and six offering courses in music
therapy.

BRITISH ASSOCIATION OF ART THERAPISTS, Mary
Ward House, 5 Tavistock Place, London WCIH 9SN.
Tel: 0171-383 3774. *Administrator*, Ms. D. Haworth

ASSOCIATION OF PROFESSIONAL MUSIC THERAPISTS,
26 Hamlyn Road, Glastonbury, Somerset BA6 8HT
(enquirers should enclose a stamped addressed
envelope). Tel: 01458-834919

BRITISH ASSOCIATION OF DRAMATHERAPISTS, 41
Broomhouse Lane, London SW6 3DP (enquirers should
enclose a stamped addressed envelope). Tel: 0171-731
0160

BIOMEDICAL SCIENCES

Qualifications from higher education establishments and
training in medical laboratories are required for membership of the Institute of Biomedical Science.

INSTITUTE OF BIOMEDICAL SCIENCE, 12 Coldbath
Square, London ECIR 5HL. Tel: 0171-713 0214. *Chief
Executive*, A. Potter

CHIROPODY

Professional recognition is granted by the Society of
Chiropodists and Podiatrists to students who are awarded
B.Sc. degrees in Podiatry or Podiatric Medicine after
attending a course of full-time training for three or four
years at one of the 14 recognized schools in the UK (11 in
England and Wales, two in Scotland and one in Northern
Ireland). Qualifications granted and degrees recognized by
the Society are approved by the Chiropodists Board for
the purpose of State Registration, which is a condition of
employment within the National Health Service.

THE SOCIETY OF CHIROPODISTS AND PODIATRISTS,
53 Welbeck Street, London WIM 7HE. Tel: 0171-486
3381. *Chief Executive*, Ms H. de Lyon

See also DIETETICS

OCCUPATIONAL THERAPY

The professional qualification may be obtained upon
successful completion of a validated course in any of the
28 institutions approved by the College of Occupational
Therapists. The courses are normally degree-level courses
based in higher education institutions.

COLLEGE OF OCCUPATIONAL THERAPISTS, 106–114
Borough High Street, London SEI ILB. Tel: 0171-357
6480. *Secretary*, J. Thompson

ORTHOPTICS

Orthoptists undertake the diagnosis and treatment of all
types of squint and other anomalies of binocular vision,
working in close collaboration with ophthalmologists. The
training and maintenance of professional standards are the
responsibility of the Orthoptists Board of the Council for
the Professions Supplementary to Medicine. The professional body is the British Orthoptic Society. Training is at
degree level.

THE BRITISH ORTHOPTIC SOCIETY, Tavistock House
North, Tavistock Square, London WCIH 9HX. Tel: 0171-
387 7992. *Hon. Secretary*, Ms R. Auld

PHYSIOTHERAPY

Full-time three- or four-year degree courses are available
at 29 recognized schools in the UK. Information about
courses leading to eligibility for Membership of the
Chartered Society of Physiotherapy and to State Registration is available from the Chartered Society of Physiotherapy.

THE CHARTERED SOCIETY OF PHYSIOTHERAPY, 14
Bedford Row, London WCIR 4ED. Tel: 0171-306 6666.
Chief Executive, P. Gray

PROSTHETICS AND ORTHOTICS

Prosthetists provide artificial limbs, while orthotists provide
devices to support or control a part of the body. It is
necessary to obtain an honours degree to become a
prosthetist or orthotist. Courses are available at two
institutions in the UK.

BRITISH ASSOCIATION OF PROSTHETISTS AND
ORTHOTISTS, Sir James Clark Building, Abbey Mill
Business Centre, Paisley PAI ITJ. Tel: 0141-561 7217

RADIOGRAPHY AND RADIOTHERAPY

In order to practise both diagnostic and therapeutic radiography in the UK, it is necessary to have successfully completed a course of education and training approved by the Privy Council. Such courses are offered by universities throughout the UK and lead to the award of a degree in radiography. Further information is available from the college.

THE COLLEGE OF RADIOGRAPHERS, 2 Carriage Row, 183 Eversholt Street, London NW1 1BU. Tel: 0171-391 4500. *Chief Executive*, S. Evans

COMPLEMENTARY MEDICINE

Professional courses are validated by:
INSTITUTE FOR COMPLEMENTARY MEDICINE, PO Box 194, London SE16 1QZ. Tel: 0171-237 5165. *Director*, A. Baird

MERCHANT NAVY TRAINING SCHOOLS

OFFICERS

WARSASH MARITIME CENTRE, Southampton Institute, Newtown Road, Warsash, Southampton SO31 9ZL. Tel: 01489-576161. *Dean*, Capt. G. B. Angas

SEAFARERS

NATIONAL SEA TRAINING CENTRE, North West Kent College, Dering Way, Gravesend, Kent DA12 2JJ. Tel: 01322-629600. *Director of Faculty*, R. MacDonald

MUSIC

ASSOCIATED BOARD OF THE ROYAL SCHOOLS OF MUSIC, 14 Bedford Square, London WC1B 3JG. Tel: 0171-636 5400. The Board conducts graded music examinations in over 80 countries and provides other services to music education through its professional development department and publishing company. *Chief Executive*, R. Morris

GUILDHALL SCHOOL OF MUSIC AND DRAMA, Silk Street, London EC2Y 8DT. Tel: 0171-628 2571. *Principal*, I. Horsbrugh

LONDON COLLEGE OF MUSIC AND MEDIA, Thames Valley University, St Mary's Road, London W5 5RF. Tel: 0181-231 2304. *Dean*, Mrs P. Thompson

ROYAL ACADEMY OF MUSIC, Marylebone Road, London NW1 5HT. Tel: 0171-873 7373. *Principal*, Prof. C. Price

ROYAL COLLEGE OF ORGANISTS, 7 St Andrew Street, London EC4A 3LQ. Tel: 0171-936 3606. *Senior Executive*, A. Dear

ROYAL NORTHERN COLLEGE OF MUSIC, 124 Oxford Road, Manchester M13 9RD. Tel: 0161-907 5200. *Principal*, Prof. E. Gregson

ROYAL SCOTTISH ACADEMY OF MUSIC AND DRAMA, 100 Renfrew Street, Glasgow G2 3DB. Tel: 0141-332 4101. *Principal*, Dr P. Ledger, CBE, FRSE

TRINITY COLLEGE OF MUSIC, 11–13 Mandeville Place, London W1M 6AQ. Tel: 0171-935 5773. *Principal*, G. Henderson

NURSING

All nurses must be registered with the UK Central Council for Nursing, Midwifery and Health Visiting. Courses leading to registration as a nurse are at least three years in length. There are also some programmes which are combined with degrees. Students study in colleges of nursing or in institutions of higher education. Courses offer a combination of theoretical and practical experience in a variety of settings. Different courses lead to different types of registration, including: Registered Nurse (RN), Registered Mental Nurse (RMN), Registered Mental Handicap Nurse (RMHN), Registered Sick Children's Nurse (RSCN), Registered Midwife (RM) and Registered Health Visitor (RHV). The various national boards, listed below, are responsible for validating courses in nursing. In February 1999 the Government announced plans to replace these boards and the UK Central Council with a single UK-wide body. Health visitors will continue to have separate registration and representation on the new body.

The Royal College of Nursing is the largest professional union representing nurses and provides higher education through its Institute.

ENGLISH NATIONAL BOARD FOR NURSING, MIDWIFERY AND HEALTH VISITING, Victory House, 170 Tottenham Court Road, London W1P 0HA. Tel: 0171-388 3131. *Chief Executive*, A. P. Smith, CBE

NATIONAL BOARD FOR NURSING, MIDWIFERY AND HEALTH VISITING FOR NORTHERN IRELAND, Centre House, 79 Chichester Street, Belfast BT1 4JE. Tel: 01232-238152. *Chief Executive*, Prof. O. D'A. Slevin, Ph.D.

NATIONAL BOARD FOR NURSING, MIDWIFERY AND HEALTH VISITING FOR SCOTLAND, 22 Queen Street, Edinburgh EH2 1NT. Tel: 0131-226 7371. *Chief Executive*, D. C. Benton

THE ROYAL COLLEGE OF NURSING OF THE UNITED KINGDOM, 20 Cavendish Square, London W1M 0AB. Tel: 0171-409 3333. *General Secretary*, Miss C. Hancock; *Director of the RCN Institute*, Prof. A. Kitson

WELSH NATIONAL BOARD FOR NURSING, MIDWIFERY AND HEALTH VISITING, 2nd Floor, Golate House, 101 St Mary Street, Cardiff CF10 1DX. Tel: 01222-261400. *Chief Executive*, D. A. Ravey

UK CENTRAL COUNCIL FOR NURSING, MIDWIFERY AND HEALTH VISITING, 23 Portland Place, London W1N 4JT. Tel: 0171-637 7181. *Chief Executive and Registrar*, Ms S. Norman

OPHTHALMIC AND DISPENSING OPTICS

Professional bodies are:
THE ASSOCIATION OF BRITISH DISPENSING OPTICIANS, 6 Hurlingham Business Park, Sulivan Road, London SW6 3DU. Tel: 0171-736 0088. Grants qualifications as a dispensing optician. *Registrar*, D. G. Baker

THE COLLEGE OF OPTOMETRISTS, 42 Craven Street, London WC2N 5NG. Tel: 0171-839 6000. Grants qualifications as an optometrist. *General Secretary*, P. D. Leigh

OSTEOPATHY

Osteopathy is accorded statutory regulation by the Osteopaths Act 1993. The existing voluntary registration schemes were taken over by the General Osteopathic Council, which opened a new statutory register on 9 May 1998. From 2000 it will be an offence for anyone who is not on the statutory register to call themselves an osteopath.

The General Osteopathic Council is now responsible for regulating, developing and promoting the profession. Osteopathic education is currently undergoing considerable change. Courses vary in length from four to six years, granting various qualifications from diploma to honours degree. Shorter courses are available for qualified doctors. Details of accrediting institutions and courses can be obtained from the General Osteopathic Council.

GENERAL OSTEOPATHIC COUNCIL, Osteopathy House, 176 Tower Bridge Road, London SE1 3LU. Tel: 0171-357 6655. *Chief Executive and Registrar*, Miss M. Craggs

PHARMACY

Information may be obtained from the Secretary and Registrar of the Royal Pharmaceutical Society of Great Britain.

ROYAL PHARMACEUTICAL SOCIETY OF GREAT BRITAIN, 1 Lambeth High Street, London SE1 7JN. Tel: 0171-735 9141. *Secretary and Registrar*, A. Lewis, OBE

PHOTOGRAPHY

The professional body is:

BRITISH INSTITUTE OF PROFESSIONAL PHOTOGRAPHY, Fox Talbot House, Amwell End, Ware, Herts SG12 9HN. Tel: 01920-464011. *Chief Executive*, A. Mair

PRINTING

Details of training courses in printing can be obtained from the Institute of Printing and the British Printing Industries Federation. In addition to these examining and organizing bodies, examinations are held by various independent regional examining boards in further education.

BRITISH PRINTING INDUSTRIES FEDERATION, 11 Bedford Row, London WC1R 4DX. Tel: 0171-242 6904. *Chief Executive*, T. P. E. Machin

INSTITUTE OF PRINTING, The Mews, Hill House, Clanricarde Road, Tunbridge Wells, Kent TN1 1PJ. Tel: 01892-538118. *Secretary-General*, D. Freeland

SCIENCE

Professional qualifications are awarded by:

GEOLOGICAL SOCIETY, Burlington House, Piccadilly, London W1V 0JU. Tel: 0171-434 9944. *Chief Executive*, E. Nickless

INSTITUTE OF BIOLOGY, 20–22 Queensberry Place, London SW7 2DZ. Tel: 0171-581 8333. *President*, Dr J. Norris; *Chief Executive*, Prof. A. Malcolm

INSTITUTE OF PHYSICS, 76 Portland Place, London W1N 3DH. Tel: 0171-470 4800. *Chief Executive*, Dr A. D. W. Jones

ROYAL SOCIETY OF CHEMISTRY, Burlington House, Piccadilly, London W1V 0BN. Tel: 0171-437 8656. *President*, Prof. A. Ledwith, CBE, FRS; *Secretary-General*, T. D. Inch, PH.D., D.SC.

SOCIAL WORK

The Central Council for Education and Training in Social Work promotes education and training for social work and social care in the UK. It approves education and training programmes, including those leading to its qualifying award, the Diploma in Social Work.

THE CENTRAL COUNCIL FOR EDUCATION AND TRAINING IN SOCIAL WORK, Derbyshire House, St Chad's Street, London WC1H 8AD. Tel: 0171-278 2455. *Chairperson*, Ms Z. Alexander; *Chief Executive*, J. Bernard

SPEECH AND LANGUAGE THERAPY

The Royal College of Speech and Language Therapists provides details of courses leading to qualification as a speech and language therapist. Other professionals may become Affiliates of the College. A directory of registered members is published annually.

THE ROYAL COLLEGE OF SPEECH AND LANGUAGE THERAPISTS, 7 Bath Place, Rivington Street, London EC2A 3SU. Tel: 0171-613 3855. *Director*, Mrs P. Evans

SURVEYING

The qualifying professional bodies include:

ARCHITECTURE AND SURVEYING INSTITUTE, St Mary House, 15 St Mary Street, Chippenham, Wilts SN15 3WD. Tel: 01249-444505. *Chief Executive*, I. N. Norris

ASSOCIATION OF BUILDING ENGINEERS, Jubilee House, Billing Brook Road, Weston Favell, Northampton NN3 8NW. Tel: 01604-404121. *Chief Executive*, D. R. Gibson

INCORPORATED SOCIETY OF VALUERS AND AUCTIONEERS (1968), 3 Cadogan Gate, London SW1X 0AS. Tel: 0171-235 2282. *Chief Executive*, C. Evans

INSTITUTE OF REVENUES, RATING AND VALUATION, 41 Doughty Street, London WC1N 2LF. Tel: 0171-831 3505. *Director*, Ms K. Aldred

ROYAL INSTITUTION OF CHARTERED SURVEYORS (incorporating The Institute of Quantity Surveyors), 12 Great George Street, London SW1P 3AD. Tel: 0171-222 7000. *Chief Executive*, J. H. A. J. Armstrong

TEACHING

Teachers in maintained schools must acquire Qualified Teacher Status (QTS) by completing a programme of Initial Teacher Training. Those without a first degree may take a Bachelor of Education (B.Ed) or a Bachelor of Arts/Science (BA/B.Sc) with QTS, full-time for three or four years, depending on the programme followed. These degrees combine subject and professional studies with teaching practice. Shortened courses of these degrees are available for those who have successfully completed one or two years of higher education. Flexible routes into teaching are increasing, including part-time, distance learning and modular courses. Alternatively, teachers can gain QTS through employment-based training, following individual training plans while in post.

For those who already have a first degree, the most common route is through a one-year Postgraduate Certificate of Education (PGCE). This may be taken full-time or part-time, or as a distance-learning programme. Postgraduates may also gain QTS through training in a school (School-Centred Initial Teacher Training). Since January 1998, graduates have been able to join the Graduate Teacher Programme which provides teaching and training for one year.

Details of courses in England and Wales are contained in the *NATFHE Handbook of Initial Teacher Training in England and Wales 1999*, in *University and College Entrance: 1999 (The Big Book)* published by UCAS and on the UCAS website. Further information about teaching in England and Wales is available from the Teaching Information Line, 01245-454454. Details of courses in Scotland can be obtained from universities and the Graduate Teacher Training Registry (GTTR). Each university chooses whether to receive applications direct or through the GTTR. Details of courses in Northern Ireland can be obtained from the Department of Education for Northern Ireland. Applications for teacher training courses in Northern Ireland are made to the institutions direct.

TEACHER TRAINING AGENCY COMMUNICATION CENTRE, PO Box 3210, Chelmsford, Essex CM1 3WA

UCAS WEB: http://www.ucas.ac.uk

TEXTILES

THE TEXTILE INSTITUTE, 4th Floor, St James's Buildings, Oxford Street, Manchester M1 6FQ. Tel: 0161-237 1188. *Director-General*, T. Hennessey

THEOLOGICAL COLLEGES

The number of students training for the ministry in the academic year 1998–9 is shown in parenthesis. Those marked * show figures for 1997–8.

ANGLICAN

COLLEGE OF THE RESURRECTION, Mirfield, W. Yorks wf14 0bw. Tel: 01924-481910. (40). *Principal*, Revd C. Irvine

CRANMER HALL, St John's College, Durham dh1 3rj. Tel: 0191-374 3579. (69). *Principal*, Rt. Revd S. W. Sykes

OAK HILL COLLEGE, Chase Side, London n14 4ps. Tel: 0181-449 0467. (90). *Principal*, Revd Dr D. Peterson

RIDLEY HALL, Cambridge cb3 9hg. Tel: 01223-741080. (60). *Principal*, Revd G. A. Cray

RIPON COLLEGE, Cuddesdon, Oxford ox44 9ex. Tel: 01865-874427. (75). *Principal*, Revd J. Clarke

ST JOHN' S COLLEGE, Chilwell Lane, Bramcote, Nottingham ng9 3ds. Tel: 0115-925 1114. (70). *Principal*, Revd Canon Dr C. Baxter

ST MICHAEL' S THEOLOGICAL COLLEGE, Llandaff, Cardiff cf5 2yj. Tel: 01222-563379. (40). *Principal*, Revd Dr J. I. Holdsworth

ST STEPHEN' S HOUSE, 16 Marston Street, Oxford ox4 1jx. Tel: 01865-247874. (c.60). *Principal*, Revd Dr J. P. Sheehy

THEOLOGICAL INSTITUTE OF THE SCOTTISH EPISCOPAL CHURCH, Old Coates House, 32 Manor Place, Edinburgh eh3 7eb. Tel: 0131-220 2272. (28).

TRINITY COLLEGE, Stoke Hill, Bristol bs9 1jp. Tel: 0117-968 2803. (200). *Principal*, Revd Dr F. Bridges (from Nov. 1999)

WESTCOTT HOUSE, Jesus Lane, Cambridge cb5 8bp. Tel: 01223-741000. (65). *Principal*, Revd M. G. V. Roberts

WYCLIFFE HALL, 54 Banbury Road, Oxford ox2 6pw. Tel: 01865-274200. (70). *Principal*, Revd Dr A. E. McGrath

BAPTIST

BRISTOL BAPTIST COLLEGE, The Promenade, Clifton, Bristol bs8 3nf. Tel: 0117-946 7050. (26). *Principal*, Revd Dr B. Haymes

NORTHERN BAPTIST COLLEGE, Luther King House, Brighton Grove, Rusholme, Manchester m14 5jp. Tel: 0161-224 2214. (30). *Principal*, Revd Dr R. L. Kidd

NORTH WALES BAPTIST COLLEGE, Ffordd Ffriddoedd, Bangor ll57 2eh. Tel: 01248-362608. (5*). *Warden*, Revd Dr D. D. Morgan

REGENT' S PARK COLLEGE, Oxford ox1 2lb. Tel: 01865-288120. (25). *Principal*, Revd Dr P. S. Fiddes

THE SCOTTISH BAPTIST COLLEGE, 12 Aytoun Road, Glasgow g41 5rn. Tel: 0141-424 0747. (14). *Principal*, Revd Dr K. B. E. Roxburgh

SOUTH WALES BAPTIST COLLEGE, 54 Richmond Road, Cardiff cf24 3ur. Tel: 01222-256066. (26). *Principal*, Revd D. H. Matthews

CHURCH OF SCOTLAND

TRINITY COLLEGE, Faculty of Divinity, University of Glasgow, Glasgow g12 8qq. Tel: 0141-330 6840. (20). *Principal*, Revd Dr D. M. Murray

CONGREGATIONAL

SCOTTISH CONGREGATIONAL COLLEGE, 340 Catherdral Street, Glasgow g1 2bq. Tel: 0141-332 7667. (4) *Principal*, Revd Dr J. W. Dyce

METHODIST

EDGHILL THEOLOGICAL COLLEGE, 9 Lennoxvale, Belfast bt9 5by. Tel: 01232-665870. (25). *Principal*, Revd Dr W. D. D. Cooke

HARTLEY VICTORIA COLLEGE, Luther King House, Brighton Grove, Manchester m14 5jp. Tel: 0161-224 2215. (30). *Principal*, Revd Dr J. A. Harrod

WESLEY COLLEGE, College Park Drive, Henbury Road, Bristol bs10 7qd. Tel: 0117-959 1200. (49*). *Principal*, Revd Dr N. Richardson

WESLEY HOUSE, Jesus Lane, Cambridge cb5 8bj. Tel: 01223-741033. (30). *Principal*, Revd Dr P. Luscombe

WESLEY STUDY CENTRE, 55 The Avenue, Durham dh1 4eb. Tel: 0191-374 3580. (20). *Director*, Revd R. Walton

NON-DENOMINATIONAL

CHRIST' S COLLEGE, 25 High Street, Old Aberdeen ab24 3ee. Tel: 01224-272380. (30). *Master*, Very Revd Prof. A. Main

NEW COLLEGE, Mound Place, Edinburgh eh1 2lx. Tel: 0131-650 8916. (15). *Principal*, Revd Dr D. Lyall

QUEENS ' COLLEGE, Somerset Road, Edgbaston, Birmingham b15 2qh. Tel: 0121-454 1527. (56). *Principal*, Revd P. Fisher

ST MARY'S COLLEGE, The University, St Andrews, Fife ky16 9ju. Tel: 01334-462850. (7*). *Principal*, Dr R. A. Piper

SPURGEON' S COLLEGE, South Norwood Hill, London se25 6dj. Tel: 0181-653 0850. (100). *Principal*, Revd Dr M. J. Quicke

PRESBYTERIAN

UNION THEOLOGICAL COLLEGE, 108 Botanic Avenue, Belfast bt7 1jt. Tel: 01232-205080. (200). *Principal*, Revd Prof. J. C. McCullough

PRESBYTERIAN CHURCH OF WALES

UNITED THEOLOGICAL COLLEGE, Aberystwyth sy23 2lt. Tel: 01970-624574. (3). *Principal*, Revd Dr J. T. Williams

ROMAN CATHOLIC

ALLEN HALL, 28 Beaufort Street, London sw3 5aa. Tel: 0171-351 1296. (35). *Principal*, Revd J. Overton, stl

CAMPION HOUSE COLLEGE, 112 Thornbury Road, Isleworth, Middx tw7 4nn. Tel: 0181-560 1924. (c.12). *Principal*, Revd M. Barrow, sj

OSCOTT COLLEGE, Chester Road, Sutton Coldfield, W. Midlands b73 5aa. Tel: 0121-354 7117. (40). *Rector*, Very Revd Mgr K. McDonald

ST JOHN' S SEMINARY, Wonersh, Guildford, Surrey gu5 0qx. Tel: 01483-892217. (45). *Rector*, Revd K. Haggerty, stl

SCOTUS COLLEGE, 2 Chesters Road, Bearsden, Glasgow g61 4ag. Tel: 0141-942 8384. (25). *Rector*, Revd N. Donnachie

USHAW COLLEGE, Durham dh7 9rh. Tel: 0191-373 1366. (32). *President*, Revd J. P. O'Keefe

UNITARIAN

UNITARIAN COLLEGE, Luther King House, Brighton Grove, Rusholme, Manchester m14 5jp. Tel: 0161-224 2849. (5). *Principal*, Revd Dr L. Smith

UNITED REFORMED

MANSFIELD COLLEGE, Mansfield Road, Oxford ox1 3tf. Tel: 01865-270999. (20). *Principal*, Prof. D. Marquand

NORTHERN COLLEGE, Luther King House, Brighton Grove, Rusholme, Manchester M14 5JP. Tel: 0161-224 4381. (44). *Principal*, Revd Dr D. R. Peel

WESTMINSTER COLLEGE, Madingley Road, Cambridge CB3 0AA. Tel: 01223-741084. (45). *Principal*, Revd Dr D. G. Cornick

JEWISH

JEWS' COLLEGE, Schaller House, Albert Road, London NW4 2SJ. Tel: 0181-203 6427. (6). *Director*, Prof. D. H. Ruben

LEO BAECK COLLEGE, Sternberg Centre for Judaism, 80 East End Road, London N3 2SY. Tel: 0181-349 4525. (27). *Principal*, Rabbi Prof. J. Magonet

TOWN AND COUNTRY PLANNING

Degree and diploma courses in town planning are accredited by the Royal Town Planning Institute.

THE ROYAL TOWN PLANNING INSTITUTE, 26 Portland Place, London WIN 4BE. Tel: 0171-636 9107. *Secretary-General*, R. Upton

TRANSPORT

Qualifying examinations in transport management and logistics leading to professional status are conducted by the Institute of Logistics and Transport.

THE INSTITUTE OF LOGISTICS AND TRANSPORT, 80 Portland Place, London WIN 4DP. Tel: 0171-467 9400. *Director*, Mrs D. de Carvalho

VETERINARY MEDICINE

The regulatory body for veterinary medicine is the Royal College of Veterinary Surgeons, which keeps the register of those entitled to practise veterinary medicine. In order to be registered, a person must complete a five-year undergraduate degree (BVetMed, BVSc., BVMS, BVM and S) at one of the six authorized institutions in the UK.

The British Veterinary Association is the professional body representing veterinary surgeons. The British Veterinary Nursing Association is the professional body representing veterinary nurses who are also registered with the Royal College of Veterinary Surgeons.

BRITISH VETERINARY ASSOCIATION, 7 Mansfield Street, London WIM 0AT. Tel: 0171-636 6541. *Chief Executive*, J. Baird

BRITISH VETERINARY NURSING ASSOCIATION, Level 15, Terminus House, Terminus Street, Harlow, Essex CM20 1XA. Tel: 01279-450567. *Chairman*, Ms J. More

ROYAL COLLEGE OF VETERINARY SURGEONS, Belgravia House, 62–64 Horseferry Road, London SWIP 2AF. Tel: 0171-222 2001. *President*, Prof A. R. Michell; *Registrar*, Miss J. C. Hern

Independent Schools

The following pages list those independent schools whose
Head is a member of the Headmasters' and Headmistress'
Conference, the Society of Headmasters and
Headmistresses of Independent Schools or the Girls'
Schools Association

THE HEADMASTERS' AND HEADMISTRESSES' CONFERENCE

Chairman (1990), J. Sabben-Clare (Winchester College)
T. D. Wheare (Bryanston) (from Jan. 2000)
Secretary, V. S. Anthony, 130 Regent Road, Leicester LEI 7PG.
Tel: 0116-285 4810
Membership Secretary, D. E. Prince. Tel: 0116-255 1567
The annual meeting is held early in October

* Woodard Corporation School, 1 The Sanctuary, London
SWIP 3JT. Tel: 0171-222 5381
† Girls in VI form
‡ Co-educational

Name of School	Foun-ded	No. of pupils	Annual fees £		Head (with date of appointment)
			Boarding	Day	
ENGLAND AND WALES					
Abbotsholme School, Rocester	1889	134‡	13,860	9,270	Dr S. Tommis (1999)
Abingdon School, Oxon	1256	790	12,294	6,669	M. St J. Parker (1975)
Ackworth School, W. Yorks	1779	340‡	11,406	6,486	M. J. Dickinson (1995)
Aldenham School, Elstree, Herts	1597	405†	13,890	9,615	S. R. Borthwick (1994)
Alleyn's School, London SE22	1619	917‡	—	7,005	Dr C. H. R. Niven (1992)
Ampleforth College (*RC*), N. Yorks	1802	483†	14,805	7,644	Revd G. F. L. Chamberlain, OSB (1993)
*Ardingly College, Haywards Heath	1858	420‡	13,455	10,185	J. Franklin (1998)
Arnold School, Blackpool	1896	800‡	—	4,635	W. T. Gillen (1993)
Ashville College, Harrogate	1877	586‡	11,010	5,916	M. H. Crosby (1987)
Bablake School, Coventry	1560	850‡	—	4,497	Dr S. Nuttall (1991)
Bancroft's School, Woodford Green, Essex	1727	780‡	—	6,915	Dr P. R. Scott (1996)
Barnard Castle School, Co. Durham	1883	470‡	10,548	6,243	M. D. Featherstone (1997)
Batley Grammar School, W. Yorks	1612	503‡	—	4,887	B. Battye (1998)
Bedales School, Petersfield	1893	400‡	15,798	12,078	Mrs A. A. Willcocks (1995)
Bedford Modern School	1566	1,100	11,325	6,114	S. Smith (1997)
Bedford School	1552	688	13,440	8,460	Dr I. P. Evans (1990)
Berkhamsted Collegiate School, Herts	1541	1,000†	12,834	8,067	Dr P. Chadwick (*Principal*) (1996)
Birkdale School, Sheffield	1904	520†	—	5,364	R. J. Court (1998)
Birkenhead School, Merseyside	1860	620	—	4,776	S. J. Haggett (1988)
Bishop's Stortford College, Herts	1868	350‡	12,075	8,706	J. G. Trotman (1997)
*Bloxham School, Banbury	1860	345‡	15,150	11,460	D. K. Exham (1991)
Blundell's School, Tiverton	1604	370‡	14,070	8,580	J. Leigh (1992)
Bolton School	1641	850	—	5,298	A. W. Wright (1983)
Bootham School, York	1823	373‡	12,150	7,950	I. M. Small (1988)
Bradfield College, Reading	1850	580‡	15,105	11,328	P. B. Smith (1985)
Bradford Grammar School	1662	1,068‡	—	5,300	S. R. Davidson (1996)
Brentwood School, Essex	1557	1,080‡	11,991	6,891	J. A. B. Kelsall (1993)
Brighton College, E. Sussex	1845	540‡	14,724	9,498	Dr A. F. Seldon (1997)
Bristol Cathedral School	1140	470†	—	4,362	K. J. Riley (1993)
Bristol Grammar School	1532	1,030‡	—	4,776	Dr D. J. Mascord (1999)
Bromsgrove School, Worcs	1553	650‡	12,075	7,470	T. M. Taylor (1986)
Bryanston School, Blandford Forum	1928	640‡	15,807	11,382	T. D. Wheare (1983)
Bury Grammar School, Lancs	1634	650	—	4,470	K. Richards (1990)
Canford School, Wimbourne	1923	570‡	15,270	11,460	J. D. Lever (1992)
Caterham School, Surrey	1811	690‡	13,914	7,458	R. A. E. Davey (1995)
Charterhouse, Godalming	1611	675†	15,588	12,882	Revd J. S. Witheridge (1996)
Cheadle Hulme School, Cheshire	1855	1,083‡	—	5,085	D. J. Wilkinson (1990)
Cheltenham College, Glos	1841	520‡	14,700	11,055	P. A. Chamberlain (1997)
Chetham's School of Music, Manchester	1653	270‡	17,595	13,620	Mrs C. Moreland (1999)
Chigwell School, Essex	1629	400‡	11,571	7,611	D. F. Gibbs (1996)
Christ College, Brecon	1541	300‡	12,102	9,378	D. P. Jones (1996)

Name of School	Founded	No. of pupils	Annual fees £ Boarding	Day	Head (with date of appointment)
Christ's Hospital, Horsham	1552	800‡	13,067	—	Dr P. C. D. Southern (1996)
Churcher's College, Petersfield	1722	560‡	—	6,180	G. W. Buttle (1988)
City of London Freemen's School, Ashtead	1854	400‡	11,997	7,497	D. C. Haywood (1986)
City of London, London EC4	1442	875	—	7,137	D. Levin (1999)
Clifton College, Bristol	1862	667‡	14,790	10,140	A. H. Monro (1990)
Colfe's School, London SE12	1652	669‡	—	6,345	Dr D. J. Richardson (1990)
Colston's Collegiate School, Bristol	1710	500‡	10,800	4,700	D. G. Crawford (1995)
Cranleigh School, Surrey	1865	480†	14,535	10,755	G. Waller (1997)
Culford School, Bury St Edmunds	1881	365‡	13,038	8,484	J. S. Richardson (1992)
Dame Allan's Boys' School, Newcastle upon Tyne	1705	810†	—	4,692	D. W. Welsh (*Principal*) (1996)
Dauntsey's School, Devizes	1542	660‡	13,119	8,001	S. B. Roberts (1997)
Dean Close School, Cheltenham	1886	440‡	14,865	10,380	Revd T. M. Hastie-Smith (1998)
*Denstone College, Uttoxeter	1868	350‡	10,650	7,050	D. M. Derbyshire (1997)
Downside School (*RC*), Somerset	1606	280	13,368	6,786	Revd Dom. A. Sutch (1995)
Dulwich College, London SE21	1619	1,200	14,805	7,575	G. G. Able (*Master*) (1997)
*Durham School	1414	272‡	12,966	8,487	N. G. Kern (1997)
Eastbourne College	1867	500‡	14,460	9,690	C. M. P. Bush (1993)
*Ellesmere College, Shropshire	1884	435‡	12,900	8,541	B. J. Wignall (1996)
Eltham College, London SE9	1842	590†	14,150	6,850	D. M. Green (1990)
Emanuel School, London SW11	1594	760‡	—	6,384	Mrs A-M. Sutcliffe (1998)
Epsom College, Surrey	1853	655‡	14,415	10,710	A. H. Beadles (1992)
Eton College, Windsor	1440	1,288	15,660	—	J. E. Lewis (1994)
Exeter School	1633	670‡	9,900	5,220	N. W. Gamble (1992)
Felsted School, Dunmow, Essex	1564	390‡	14,970	11,790	S. C. Roberts (1993)
Forest School, London E17	1834	1,000‡	11,001	7,008	A. G. Boggis (*Warden*) (1992)
Framlingham College, Woodbridge, Suffolk	1864	420‡	12,111	7,773	Mrs. G. M. Randall (1994)
Frensham Heights, Farnham	1925	300‡	13,800	9,000	P. M. de Voil (1993)
Giggleswick School, Settle	1499	325‡	14,394	9,552	A. P. Millard (1993)
The Grange School, Northwich, Cheshire	1933	650‡	—	4,215	Mrs J. E. Stephen (1997)
Gresham's School, Holt, Norfolk	1555	520‡	14,670	10,455	J. H. Arkell (1991)
Haberdashers' Aske's School, Elstree, Herts	1690	1,100	—	7,164	J. W. R. Goulding (1996)
Haileybury, Hertford	1862	620‡	15,510	11,220	S. A. Westley (*Master*) (1996)
Hampton School, Middx	1556	950	—	6,555	B. R. Martin (1997)
Harrow School, Middx	1572	790	15,900	—	B. J. Lenon (1999)
Hereford Cathedral School	1384	620‡	—	5,535	Dr H. C. Tomlinson (1987)
Highgate School, London N6	1565	575	—	8,640	R. P. Kennedy (1989)
Hulme Grammar School, Oldham	1611	648	—	4,455	T. J. Turvey (1995)
*Hurstpierpoint College, Hassocks, W. Sussex	1849	350‡	13,830	10,710	S. D. A. Meek (1995)
Hymers College, Hull	1889	740‡	—	4,518	J. C. Morris (1990)
Ipswich School	1390	585‡	10,599	6,144	I. G. Galbraith (1993)
John Lyon School, Harrow	1876	524	—	6,870	Revd T. J. Wright (1986)
Kelly College, Tavistock	1877	350‡	13,815	8,685	M. Turner (1995)
Kent College, Canterbury	1885	480‡	13,005	7,242	E. B. Halse (1995)
Kimbolton School, Huntingdon	1600	560‡	11,205	6,615	R. V. Peel (1987)
King Edward VI School, Southampton	1553	950‡	—	5,925	P. B. Hamilton (1996)
King Edward VII and Queen Mary School, Lytham St Annes	1908	795‡	—	4,500	P. J. Wilde, *Principal* (1999)
King Edward's School, Bath	1552	685‡	—	5,631	P. J. Winter (1993)
King Edward's School, Birmingham	1552	883	—	5,523	R. M. Dancey (*Chief Master*) (1998)
King Edward's School, Witley, Surrey	1553	480‡	11,385	7,785	R. J. Fox (1988)
King Henry VIII School, Coventry	1545	799‡	—	4,497	D. N. Ireland (*Acting Head*) (1999)
*King's College, Taunton	1879	430‡	13,950	9,180	R. S. Funnell (1988)
King's College School, London SW19	1829	700	—	8,400	A. C. V. Evans (1997)
King's School, Bruton, Somerset	1519	360‡	13,050	9,435	R. I. Smyth (1993)
King's School, Canterbury	600	754‡	15,780	11,010	Revd Canon K. H. Wilkinson (1996)
King's School, Chester	1541	540†	—	5,112	A. R. D. Wickson (1981)
King's School, Ely	973	395‡	13,325	9,150	R. H. Youdale (1992)
King's School, Gloucester	1541	300‡	11,000	7,500	P. Lacey (1992)
King's School, Macclesfield	1502	1,050‡	—	5,010	A. G. Silcock (1987)
King's School, Rochester, Kent	604	327‡	14,808	8,538	Dr I. R. Walker (1987)

Name of School	Founded	No. of pupils	Annual fees £ Boarding	Day	Head (with date of appointment)
*King's School, Tynemouth	1860	628‡	—	4,851	Dr D. Younger (1993)
King's School, Worcester	1541	788‡	—	6,273	T. H. Keyes (1998)
Kingston Grammar School, Surrey	1561	605‡	—	6,897	C. D. Baxter (1991)
Kingswood School, Bath	1748	486‡	13,999	7,954	G. M. Best (1987)
*Lancing College, W. Sussex	1848	463‡	14,850	11,100	P. M. Tinniswood (1998)
Latymer Upper School, London W6	1624	950†	—	7,560	C. Diggory (1991)
Leeds Grammar School	1552	1,010	—	6,204	Dr M. Bailey (1999)
Leicester Grammar School	1981	650‡	—	5,250	J. B. Sugden (1989)
Leighton Park School, Reading	1890	340‡	13,455	9,414	J. Dunston (1996)
The Leys School, Cambridge	1875	500‡	13,680	10,080	Revd Dr J. C. A. Barrett (1990)
Liverpool College	1840	700‡	—	5,685	J. P. Siviter (*Principal*) (1997)
Llandovery College, Carmarthenshire	1848	210‡	11,652	7,737	Dr C. E. Evans (*Warden*) (1988)
Lord Wandsworth College, Long Sutton, Hants	1912	485‡	14,445	9,675	I. G. Power (1997)
Loughborough Grammar School	1495	970	9,504	5,238	P. B. Fisher (1998)
Magdalen College School, Oxford	1480	540	—	6,033	A. D. Halls (*Master*) (1998)
Malvern College, Worcs	1862	551‡	15,030	10,920	H. C. K. Carson (1997)
Manchester Grammar School	1515	1,425	—	5,040	Dr G. M. Stephen (*High Master*) (1994)
Marlborough College, Wilts	1843	800‡	15,555	11,670	E. J. H. Gould (*Master*) (1993)
Merchant Taylors' School, Liverpool	1620	728	—	4,599	S. J. R. Dawkins (1986)
Merchant Taylors' School, Northwood, Middx	1561	775	13,500	8,000	J. R. Gabitass (1991)
Millfield, Street, Somerset	1935	1,215‡	15,855	10,455	P. M. Johnson (1998)
Mill Hill School, London NW7	1807	565‡	14,085	9,225	W. R. Winfield (1995)
Monkton Combe School, Bath	1868	330‡	14,460	9,870	M. J. Cuthbertson (1990)
Monmouth School	1614	570	10,368	6,222	T. H. P. Haynes (1995)
Mount St Mary's College (*RC*), Sheffield	1842	280‡	10,920	6,270	P. MacDonald (1998)
Newcastle-under-Lyme School	1872	1,100‡	—	4,488	Dr R. M. Reynolds (*Principal*) (1990)
Norwich School	1156	615†	—	5,610	C. D. Brown, MA (1984)
Nottingham High School	1513	832	—	5,688	C. S. Parker (1995)
Oakham School, Rutland	1584	778‡	14,190	8,490	A. R. M. Little (1996)
The Oratory School (*RC*), Woodcote, Berks	1859	382	14,460	10,125	S. W. Barrow (1991)
Oundle School, Northants	1556	830‡	15,273	—	Dr R. Townsend (1999)
Pangbourne College, Berks	1917	320‡	13,920	9,750	A. B. E. Hudson (1988)
Perse School, Cambridge	1615	570†	—	6,078	N. P. V. Richardson (1994)
Plymouth College	1877	598‡	11,316	5,745	A. J. Morsley (1992)
Pocklington School, York	1514	585‡	10,000	6,200	J. N. D. Gray (1992)
Portsmouth Grammar School	1732	800‡	—	5,595	Dr T. R. Hands, D.Phil. (1997)
Prior Park College (*RC*), Bath	1830	500‡	12,765	7,062	Dr R. G. G. Mercer, D.Phil. (1996)
Queen Elizabeth GS, Wakefield	1591	680†	—	5,307	R. P. Mardling (1985)
Queen Elizabeth's GS, Blackburn	1567	908†	—	4,977	Dr D. S. Hempsall (1995)
Queen Elizabeth's Hospital, Bristol	1590	540	9,015	4,815	Dr R. Gliddon (1985)
Queen's College, Taunton	1843	473‡	11,340	7,434	C. T. Bradnock (1991)
Radley College, Abingdon	1847	620	15,375	—	R. M. Morgan (*Warden*) (1991)
Ratcliffe College (*RC*), Leicester	1844	495‡	10,899	7,269	P. Farrar (1999)
Reading Blue Coat School	1646	607†	11,760	6,450	S. J. W. McArthur (1997)
Reed's School, Cobham, Surrey	1813	320†	12,690	9,591	D. W. Jarrett (1997)
Reigate Grammar School, Surrey	1675	802‡	—	6,324	P. V. Dixon (1996)
Rendcomb College, Cirencester	1920	250‡	12,420	9,840	G. Holden (1999)
Repton School, Derby	1557	542‡	14,250	10,620	G. E. Jones (1987)
Rossall School, Fleetwood, Lancs	1844	390‡	13,500	5,025	R. D. W. Rhodes (1987)
Royal Grammar School, Guildford	1509	840	—	7,311	T. M. S. Young (1992)
Royal Grammar School, Newcastle upon Tyne	1545	925	—	4,842	J. F. X. Miller (1994)
Royal Grammar School, Worcester	1291	731	—	5,436	W. A. Jones (1993)
Royal Hospital School, Ipswich	1712	690‡	10,452	6,774	N. K. D. Ward (1995)
Rugby School	1567	719‡	15,375	9,225	M. B. Mavor, CVO (1990)
Rydal Penrhos School, Colwyn Bay	1885	452‡	11,577	7,674	M. S. James (1998)
Ryde School with Upper Chine, Isle of Wight	1921	420‡	10,290	5,040	Dr N. J. England (1997)
St Albans School	948	680†	—	6,900	A. R. Grant (1993)
St Bede's College (*RC*), Manchester	1876	1,002‡	—	4,170	J. Byrne (1983)
St Bees School, Cumbria	1583	300‡	13,425	9,075	Mrs J. D. Pickering (1998)

Name of School	Foun-ded	No. of pupils	Annual fees £ Boarding	Annual fees £ Day	Head (with date of appointment)
St Benedict's School (RC), London w5	1902	548†	—	6,135	Dr A. J. Dachs (1986)
St Dunstan's College, London se6	1888	930‡	—	6,480	D. I. Davies (1998)
St Edmund's College (RC), Ware, Herts	1568	373‡	11,985	7,575	D. J. J. McEwen (1984)
St Edmund's School, Canterbury	1749	270‡	14,688	9,480	A. N. Ridley (1994)
St Edward's School, Oxford	1863	569‡	15,150	10,995	D. Christie (Warden) (1988)
St George's College (RC), Addlestone, Surrey	1869	986‡	—	7,650	J. A. Peake (1994)
St John's School, Leatherhead, Surrey	1851	420†	13,200	9,300	C. H. Tongue (1993)
St Lawrence College in Thanet, Ramsgate	1879	370‡	14,595	9,360	M. Slater (1996)
St Mary's College (RC), Liverpool	1919	620‡	—	4,500	W. Hammond (1991)
St Paul's School, London sw13	1509	778	14,910	9,810	R. S. Baldock (High Master) (1992)
St Peter's School, York	627	500‡	12,228	7,119	A. F. Trotman (1995)
Sedbergh School, Cumbria	1525	288	14,760	10,920	C. H. Hirst (1995)
Sevenoaks School, Kent	1432	960‡	15,213	9,651	T. R. Cookson (1996)
Sherborne School, Dorset	1550	500	15,525	11,640	P. H. Lapping (1988)
Shrewsbury School	1552	700	15,150	10,665	F. E. Maidment (1988)
Silcoates School, Wakefield	1820	450‡	—	6,354	A. P. Spillane (1992)
Solihull School	1560	799†	—	5,277	P. S. J. Derham (1996)
Stamford School, Lincs	1532	511	10,500	5,400	Dr P. R. Mason (Principal) (1997)
Stockport Grammar School	1487	1,005‡	—	4,833	I. Mellor (1996)
Stonyhurst College (RC), Clitheroe	1593	400‡	14,028	8,466	A. J. F. Aylward (1996)
Stowe School, Bucks	1923	575†	15,690	11,760	J. G. L. Nichols (1989)
Sutton Valence School, Kent	1576	400‡	13,830	8,850	N. A. Sampson (1994)
Taunton School	1846	465‡	13,185	8,460	J. P. Whiteley (1997)
Tettenhall College, Wolverhampton	1863	300‡	10,800	6,594	Dr P. C. Bodkin (1994)
Tonbridge School, Kent	1553	710	15,846	11,196	J. M. Hammond (1990)
Trent College, Nottingham	1868	640‡	12,382	7,628	J. S. Lee (1988)
Trinity School, Croydon	1596	860	—	6,828	C. J. Tarrant (1999)
Truro School	1880	752‡	10,668	5,571	G. A. G. Dodd (1993)
University College School, London nw3	1830	700	—	8,475	K. J. Durham (1996)
Uppingham School, Oakham, Rutland	1584	660†	15,420	10,800	Dr S. C. Winkley, d.phil. (1991)
Warwick School	914	800	11,667	5,466	Dr P. J. Cheshire (1988)
Wellingborough School, Northants	1595	348‡	—	6,570	F. R. Ullmann (1993)
Wellington College, Crowthorne, Berks	1859	805†	15,525	11,400	C. J. Driver (Master) (1989)
Wellington School, Somerset	1837	556‡	9,828	5,388	A. J. Rogers (1990)
Wells Cathedral School, Somerset	909	568‡	12,306	7,308	J. S. Baxter (1985)
West Buckland School, Barnstaple, Devon	1858	489‡	10,350	6,210	J. F. Vick (1997)
Westminster School, London sw1	1560	652‡	16,068	11,130	T. Jones-Parry (1998)
Whitgift School, South Croydon	1596	1,100	—	7,269	C. A. Barnett, d.phil. (1991)
William Hulme's GS, Manchester	1887	660‡	—	4,785	B. J. Purvis (1997)
Winchester College	1382	680	16,110	12,474	J. P. Sabben-Clare (1985)
Wisbech Grammar School, Cambs	1379	702‡	—	5,685	R. S. Repper (1988)
Wolverhampton Grammar School	1512	760‡	—	6,000	Dr B. Trafford (1990)
Woodbridge School, Suffolk	1662	547‡	11,640	6,846	S. H. Cole (1994)
Woodhouse Grove School, Bradford	1812	600‡	10,995	6,420	D. C. Humphreys (1996)
*Worksop College, Notts	1895	380‡	12,930	8,865	R. A. Collard (1994)
Worth School (RC), Crawley	1959	405	13,971	9,861	Fr C. Jamison (1994)
Wrekin College, Telford	1880	310‡	13,740	8,310	S. G. Drew (1998)
Wycliffe College, Stonehouse, Glos	1882	400‡	15,750	10,035	Dr R. A. Collins (1998)
Yarm School, Stockton-on-Tees	1978	560†	—	6,141	D. M. Dunn (1999)

SCOTLAND

Name of School	Foun-ded	No. of pupils	Annual fees £ Boarding	Annual fees £ Day	Head (with date of appointment)
Daniel Stewart's and Melville College, Edinburgh	1855	760†	10,650	5,436	P. J. F. Tobin (Principal) (1989)
Dollar Academy, Clackmannanshire	1818	749‡	11,340	5,121	J. S. Robertson (Rector) (1994)
The High School of Dundee	1239	720‡	—	4,950	A. M. Duncan (1997)
The Edinburgh Academy	1824	463†	12,645	5,931	J. V. Light (Rector) (1995)
Fettes College, Edinburgh	1870	392‡	14,886	10,044	M. C. B. Spens (1998)
George Heriot's School, Edinburgh	1628	885‡	—	4,815	A. G. Hector (1998)
George Watson's College, Edinburgh	1741	1,273‡	10,662	5,133	F. E. Gerstenberg (Principal) (1985)
Glasgow Academy	1845	600‡	—	5,142	D. Comins (Rector) (1994)
Glenalmond College, Perth	1841	366‡	14,370	9,585	I. G. Templeton (Warden) (1992)

Name of School	Foun- ded	No. of pupils	Annual fees £		Head (with date of appointment)
			Boarding	Day	
Gordonstoun School, Elgin	1935	430‡	14,241	9,192	M. C. Pyper (1990)
High School of Glasgow	1124	668‡	—	5,175	R. G. Easton (Rector) (1983)
Hutcheson's Grammar School, Glasgow	1641	1,250‡	—	4,617	J. Knowles (Rector) (1999)
Kelvinside Academy, Glasgow	1878	320‡	—	5,400	J. L. Broadfoot (Rector) (1998)
Loretto School, Musselburgh	1827	290‡	14,385	9,600	K. J. Budge (1995)
Merchiston Castle School, Edinburgh	1833	350	14,280	9,675	A. R. Hunter (1998)
Morrison's Academy, Crieff	1860	362‡	12,825	4,950	G. H. Edwards (Rector) (1996)
Robert Gordon's College, Aberdeen	1729	960‡	—	5,060	B. R. W. Lockhart (1996)
St Aloysius' College, Glasgow	1859	847‡	—	3,975	Fr. A. Porter, SJ (1995)
St Colomba's School, Kilmacolm	1897	360‡	—	4,713	A. H. Livingstone (1987)
Strathallan School, Perth	1912	400‡	14,040	9,672	A. W. McPhail (1993)
NORTHERN IRELAND					
Bangor Grammar School	1856	494	—	245	N. D. Argent (1998)
Belfast Royal Academy	1785	1,387‡	—	80	W. M. Sillery (1980)
Campbell College, Belfast	1894	690	6,759	1,389	Dr R. J. I. Pollock (1987)
Coleraine Academical Institution	1860	406	—	75	R. S. Forsythe (1984)
Methodist College, Belfast	1865	570‡	6,940	3,390	T. W. Mulryne (Principal) (1988)
Portora Royal School, Enniskillen	1608	110	—	42	R. L. Bennett (1983)
Royal Belfast Academical Institution	1810	1,050	—	510	R. M. Ridley (Principal) (1990)
CHANNEL ISLANDS AND ISLE OF MAN					
Elizabeth College, Guernsey	1563	500†	7,815	3,090	D. E. Toze (1998)
King William's College, Isle of Man	1668	280‡	13,545	9,630	P. K. Fulton-Peebles (Principal) (1996)
Victoria College, Jersey	1852	617†	—	2,268	vacant
EUROPE					
Aiglon College, Switzerland	1949	230‡	Fr.60,460	Fr.39,560	R. McDonald (1994)
British School in The Netherlands	1935	590‡	—	Gld.21,950	J. Hollis (1997)
British School of Brussels	1969	560‡	—	Euro.17,798	Ms J. M. Bray (Principal) (1990)
British School of Paris	1954	360‡	Fr.119,000	Fr.86,000	M. W. Honour (Principal) (1992)
The International School of Geneva	1924	1,140‡	—	Fr.19,615	G. Walker, OBE (Director-General) (1991)
King's College, Madrid	1969	600‡	Pesetas2.07m	Pesetas1.3m	C. T. Gill Leech (1996)
St Columba's College, Dublin	1843	305‡	Ir£7,140	Ir£4,125	T. E. Macey (1988)
St Edward's College, Malta	1929	330†	—	LM.858	W. Dimech (1997)
St George's English School, Rome	1958	280‡	—	L.21.2m	Mrs B. Gardner (Principal) (1994)

OTHER OVERSEAS MEMBERS

AFRICA

DIOCESAN COLLEGE, Rondebosch, SA. Head, C. N. Watson

FALCON COLLEGE, Esigodini, Zimbabwe. Head, P. N. Todd

HILTON COLLEGE, Kwazulu-Natal, SA. Head, M. J. Nicholson

MICHAELHOUSE, Balgowan, SA. Head, R. D. Forde

PETERHOUSE, Marondera, Zimbabwe. Head, M. W. Bawden

ST ANDREW'S COLLEGE, Grahamstown, SA. Head, A. R. Clark

ST GEORGE'S COLLEGE, Harare, Zimbabwe. Head, acting head

ST STITHIAN'S COLLEGE, Transvaal, SA. Head, D. B. Wylde

AUSTRALIA

BALLARAT AND CLARENDON COLLEGE, Ballarat, Victoria. Head, D. S. Shepherd

BRIGHTON GRAMMAR SCHOOL, Brighton, Victoria. Head, M. S. Urwin

BRISBANE BOYS' COLLEGE, Toowong, Queensland. Head, M. Norris

CAMBERWELL GRAMMAR SCHOOL, Deepdene DC, Victoria. Head, C. F. Black

CANBERRA GRAMMAR SCHOOL, Red Hill, ACT. Head, T. C. Murray

CAULFIELD GRAMMAR SCHOOL, Elsternwick, Victoria. Head, S. H. Newton

CHRIST CHURCH GRAMMAR SCHOOL, Claremont, W. Australia. Head, J. J. S. Madin

CRANBROOK SCHOOL, Bellevue Hill, NSW. Head, Dr B. N. Carter

THE GEELONG COLLEGE, Newtown, Victoria. Head, Dr P. Turner

GEELONG GRAMMAR SCHOOL, Corio, Victoria. Head, L. Hannah

GUILDFORD GRAMMAR SCHOOL, Guildford, W. Australia. Head, K. Walton

HAILEYBURY COLLEGE, Keysborough, Victoria. Head, A. H. M. Aikman

THE HALE SCHOOL, Wembley Downs, W. Australia. *Head,* R. J. Inverarity, MBE

IVANHOE GRAMMAR SCHOOL, Ivanhoe, Victoria. *Head,* R. D. Fraser

KINROSS WOLAROI SCHOOL, Orange, NSW. *Head,* A. E. S. Anderson

KNOX GRAMMAR SCHOOL, Wahroonga, NSW. *Head,* Dr I. Paterson

MELBOURNE GRAMMAR SCHOOL, South Yarra, Victoria. *Head,* A. P. Sheahan

MENTONE GRAMMAR SCHOOL, Mentone, Victoria. *Head,* N. Clark

NEWINGTON COLLEGE, Sydney, NSW. *Head,* M. H. Smee

ST PETER'S COLLEGE, St Peter's, S. Australia. *Head,* R. L. Burchnall

SCOTCH COLLEGE, Torrens Park, S. Australia. *Head,* K. Webb

SCOTCH COLLEGE, Hawthorn, Victoria. *Head,* Dr F. G. Donaldson

THE SCOTS COLLEGE, Bellevue Hill, NSW. *Head,* Dr R. L. Iles

THE SOUTHPORT SCHOOL, Southport, Queensland. *Head,* B. A. Cook

SYDNEY CHURCH OF ENGLAND GRAMMAR SCHOOL, North Sydney, NSW. *Head,* R. A. I. Grant

SYDNEY GRAMMAR SCHOOL, Darlinghurst, NSW. *Head,* Dr R. D. Townsend

TRINITY GRAMMAR SCHOOL, Summer Hill, NSW. *Head,* G. M. Cujes

WESLEY COLLEGE, Prahran, Victoria. *Head,* D. Loader

WESTBOURNE GRAMMAR SCHOOL, Werribee, Victoria. *Head,* G. G. Ryan

BERMUDA

SALTUS GRAMMAR SCHOOL, Hamilton. *Head,* R. T. Rowell

CANADA

BRENTWOOD COLLEGE SCHOOL, Mill Bay, BC. *Head,* W. T. Ross

GLENLYON-NORFOLK SCHOOL, Victoria, BC. *Head,* C. E. G. Peacock

HILLFIELD STRATHALLAN COLLEGE, Hamilton, Ontario. *Head,* W. S. Boyer

RIDLEY COLLEGE, St Catharines, Ontario. *Head,* R. D. Lane

ST ANDREW'S COLLEGE, Aurora, Ontario. *Head,* E. Staunton

UPPER CANADA COLLEGE, Toronto, Ontario. *Head,* J. D. Blakey

HONG KONG

ISLAND SCHOOL, Borrett Road. *Head,* D. J. James

KING GEORGE V SCHOOL, Kowloon. *Head,* M. J. Behennah

INDIA

BISHOP COTTON SCHOOL, Shimla. *Head,* K. K. Mustafi

THE CATHEDRAL AND JOHN CONNON SCHOOL, Bombay. *Head,* Mrs M. Isaacs

THE LAWRENCE SCHOOL, Sanawar. *Head,* Dr H. S. Dhillon

THE SCINDIA SCHOOL, Gwalior. *Head,* A. N. Dar

INDONESIA

THE BRITISH INTERNATIONAL SCHOOL, Jakarta. *Head,* J. Birchall

MALAYSIA

KOLEJ TUANKU JA'AFAR, Negeri Sembilan. *Head,* P. D. Briggs

MIDDLE EAST

THE INDIAN SCHOOL, Sultanate of Oman. *Head,* B. S. Bhatnagar

NEW ZEALAND

CHRIST'S COLLEGE, Christchurch. *Head,* R. A. Zordan

KING'S COLLEGE, Auckland. *Head,* J. S. Taylor

ST ANDREW'S COLLEGE, Christchurch. *Head,* B. J. Maister

WANGANUI COLLEGIATE SCHOOL, Wanganui. *Head,* J. R. Hensman

PAKISTAN

AITCHISON COLLEGE, Lahore. *Head,* S. Khan

KARACHI GRAMMAR SCHOOL, Karachi. *Head,* H. H. A. Pullan

SOUTH AND CENTRAL AMERICA

ACADEMIA BRITANICA CUSCATLECA, Santa Tecla, El Salvador. *Head,* R. Braund

THE BRITISH SCHOOLS, Montevideo, Uruguay. *Head,* C. D. T. Smith

MARKHAM COLLEGE, Lima, Peru. *Head,* W. J. Baker

ST ANDREW'S SCOTS SCHOOL, Buenos Aires, Argentina. *Head,* A. G. F. Fisher

ST GEORGE'S COLLEGE, Buenos Aires, Argentina. *Head,* N. P. O. Green

ST PAUL'S SCHOOL, São Paulo, Brazil. *Head,* M. T. M. C. McCann

USA

ST MARK'S COLLEGE, Southborough, Massachusetts. *Head,* A. J de V. Hill

SOCIETY OF HEADMASTERS AND HEADMISTRESSES OF INDEPENDENT SCHOOLS

The Society was founded in 1961 and, in general, represents smaller boarding schools.

General Secretary, I. D. Cleland, Celedston, Rhosesmor Road, Halkyn, Holywell CH8 8DL. Tel: 01352-781102

Headmasters/mistresses of the following schools are members of both HMC and SHMIS; details of these schools appear in the HMC list: Abbotsholme School, Ackworth School, Bedales School, Churcher's College, Colston's Collegiate School, King's School, Gloucester, King's School, Tynemouth, Leighton Park School, Lord Wandsworth College, Pangbourne College, Reading Blue Coat School, Reed's School, Rendcomb College, Royal Hospital School, Rydal Penrhos School, Ryde School, St George's College, Shiplake College, Silcoates School, Tettenhall College, Wisbech Grammar School, Yarm School

The Headmistress of King Edward VI High School for Girls is a member of both SHMIS and GSA; details of the school are given in the GSA list

CSC   Church Schools Company, Church Schools House, Chapel Street, Titchmarsh, Kettering, Northants NN14 3DA. Tel: 01832-735105

* Woodard Corporation School
† Girls in VI form
‡ Co-educational

Name of School	Foun-ded	No. of pupils	Annual fees £		Head (with date of appointment)
			Boarding	Day	
ENGLAND AND WALES					
Abbey Gate College, Saighton, Chester	1977	248‡	—	5,085	E. W. Mitchell (1991)
Austin Friars School (*RC*), Carlisle	1951	295‡	—	5,565	Revd D. Middleton (1996)
Battle Abbey School, E. Sussex	1912	130‡	11,100	6,900	R. Clark (1998)
Bearwood College, Wokingham	1827	250‡	12,225	7,170	S. G. G. Aiano (1998)
Bedstone College, Bucknell, Shropshire	1948	165‡	11,994	6,450	M. S. Symonds (1990)
Bentham Grammar School, N. Yorks	1726	183‡	10,950	5,550	Miss R. E. Colman (1999)
Bethany School, Cranbrook, Kent	1866	290‡	11,136	7,125	N. Dorey (1998)
Box Hill School, Dorking	1959	290‡	12,219	7,110	Dr R. A. S. Atwood (1987)
Claremont Fan Court School, Esher	1932	300‡	11,415	7,425	Mrs. P. B. Farrar (*Principal*) (1994)
Claysmore School, Blandford Forum	1896	299‡	13,335	9,450	D. J. Beeby (1986)
Cokethorpe School, Witney, Oxon	1957	280‡	13,850	4,620	P. J. S. Cantwell (1995)
Duke of York's Royal Military School, Dover	1803	500‡	900	—	J. Cummings (1999)
Elmhurst - The School for Dance and Performing Arts, Camberley	1922	61‡	11,490	8,427	J. McNamara (*Principal*) (1995)
Embley Park School, Romsey, Hants	1946	285‡	11,395	6,870	D. F. Chapman (1987)
Ewell Castle School, Epsom	1926	300	—	5,205	R. A. Fewtrell (*Principal*) (1983)
Friends' School, Saffron Walden	1702	200‡	12,285	7,371	Ms J. E. Laing (1996)
Fulneck School, Pudsey, W. Yorks	1753	260‡	10,485	5,685	Mrs H. Gordon, (*Principal*) (1996)
*Grenville College, Bideford	1954	270‡	11,631	5,760	Dr M. C. V. Cane (1992)
Halliford School, Shepperton, Middx	1921	320†	—	5,550	J. R. Crook (1984)
Hipperholme Grammar School, Halifax	1648	320†	—	4,620	C. C. Robinson (1988)
Keil School, Dumbarton	1915	180‡	11,805	6,618	T. S. Smith (1999)
Kingham Hill School, Chipping Norton	1886	230‡	11,874	7,128	M. H. Payne (1990)
Kirkham Grammar School, Preston	1549	620‡	8,895	4,590	B. Stacey (1991)
Langley School, Norwich	1910	270‡	12,630	6,555	J. G. Malcolm (1997)
Lincoln Minster School (*CSC*)	1996	285‡	10,512	5,556	C. Rickart (1999)
Lomond School, Helensburgh, Argyll and Bute	1977	385‡	11,865	5,535	A. D. Macdonald (1986)
Milton Abbey School, Blandford Forum	1954	80	14,175	10,275	W. J. Hughes-D'Aeth (1995)
Oswestry School, Shropshire	1407	310‡	12,120	7,230	P. K. Smith (1995)
The Purcell School (music), Harrow	1962	119‡	16,677	9,993	J. Tolputt (1999)
Rannoch School, Rannoch, By Pitlochry	1959	220‡	13,230	6,930	Dr J. D. Halliday (1997)
Rishworth School, W. Yorks	1724	350‡	11,250	5,340	R. A. Baker (1999)
Rougemont School, Newport	1974	330‡	—	5,163	I. Brown (1995)
Royal Russell School, Croydon	1853	485‡	12,480	6,540	Dr J. R. Jennings (1996)
Royal School, Dungannon, N. Ireland	1608	630‡	4,069	110	P. D. Hewitt (1984)
Royal Wolverhampton School	1850	303‡	12,675	6,210	Mrs B. A. Evans (1995)
Ruthin School, Denbighshire	1574	170‡	11,685	7,485	J. S. Rowlands (1993)
St Bede's School, Hailsham	1978	530‡	13,650	8,265	R. A. Perrin (1978)
St Christopher School, Letchworth	1915	360‡	13,317	7,548	C. Reid (1980)
St David's College, Llandudno	1965	220‡	11,658	7,581	W. Seymour (1991)
St Edward's School, Cheltenham	1987	450‡	—	6,390	A. J. Martin (1991)
Scarborough College, N. Yorks	1898	355‡	10,959	5,943	T. L. Kirkup (1996)
Seaford College, Petworth, W. Sussex	1884	302‡	12,600	8,400	T. J. Mullins (1997)

Name of School	Foun-ded	No. of pupils	Annual fees £		Head (with date of appointment)
			Boarding	Day	
Shebbear College, North Devon	1841	200‡	11,478	6,174	L. D. Clark (1997)
Shiplake College, Henley-on-Thames	1959	290†	13,590	9,165	N. V. Bevan (1988)
Sibford School, Banbury	1842	250‡	12,120	6,015	Ms S. Freestone (1997)
Sidcot School, North Somerset	1808	342‡	11,850	6,840	A. Slesser (1997)
Stafford Grammar School	1982	300‡	—	4,710	M. Darley (1998)
Stanbridge Earls School, Romsey, Hants	1952	190‡	14,175	10,560	H. Moxon (1984)
Sunderland High School (*CSC*)	1884	300‡	—	4,170	Dr A. Slater (1998)
Thetford Grammar School, Norfolk	1119	200‡	—	5,112	J. R. Weeks (1990)
Warminster School, Wilts	1707	300‡	11,160	6,300	D. Dowdles (1998)
Yehudi Menuhin School (music), Surrey	1963	51‡	varies	—	P. N. Chisholm (1988)

GIRLS' SCHOOLS ASSOCIATION

THE GIRL'S SCHOOLS ASSOCIATION, 130 Regent Road, Leicester LE1 7PG. Tel: 0116-254 1619
President, Mrs L. Warrington (from 1.1.2000)
Secretary, Ms S. Cooper

Headmasters/mistresses of the following schools are members of both HMC and GSA; details of these schools appear in the HMC list: Berkhamsted Collegiate School, Rydal Penrhos School, Stamford Endowed Schools

CSC Church Schools Company
§ Girls Day School Trust, 100 Rochester Row, London SW1P 1JP. Tel: 0171-393 6666
* Woodard Corporation School
† Boys in VI form
‡ Co-educational

Name of School	Foun-ded	No. of pupils	Annual fees £		Head (with date of appointment)
			Boarding	Day	
ENGLAND AND WALES					
Abbey School, Reading	1887	673	—	5,385	Miss B. C. L. Sheldon (1991)
Abbot's Hill, Hemel Hempstead	1912	164	12,525	7,500	Mrs K. Lewis (1997)
Adcote School for Girls, Shrewsbury	1907	80	11,460	6,585	Mrs A. E. Read (1997)
Alderley Edge School for Girls	1880	100	—	4,635	Ms P. A. Bristow (1997)
Alice Ottley School, Worcester	1883	500	—	6,678	Ms M. Chapman (1999)
Amberfield School, Ipswich	1952	151	—	4,410	Mrs L. A. Lewis (1992)
Ashford School, Kent	1910	340	13,671	7,869	Mrs J. Burnett (1997)
§Atherley School, Southampton (*CSC*)	1926	200	—	4,992	Mrs M. Bradley (1999)
Badminton School, Bristol	1858	380	13,425	7,425	Mrs J. A. Scarrow (1997)
Bedford High School	1882	668	10,890	5,832	Mrs B. E. Stanley (1995)
Bedgebury School, Goudhurst, Kent	1860	259	13,230	8,220	Mrs L. J. Griffin (until Dec 1999); vacant (from Jan 2000)
Beechwood Sacred Heart (*RC*), Tunbridge Wells	1915	130	12,540	7,680	N. R. Beesley (1999)
Benenden School, Cranbrook, Kent	1923	450	15,870	—	Mrs G. D. du Charme (1985)
Bolton School	1877	794	—	5,298	Miss E. J. Panton (1994)
Bradford Girls' Grammar School	1875	641	—	5,130	Mrs L. J. Warrington (1987)
Brigidine School, Windsor	1948	150	—	5,820	Mrs M. B. Cairns (1986)
Bruton School, Somerset	1900	457	10,035	5,445	Mrs B. Bates (1999)
Burgess Hill School, W. Sussex	1906	370	11,265	6,660	Mrs R. F. Lewis (1992)
Bury Grammar School, Lancs	1884	761	—	4,470	Miss C. H. Thompson (1998)
Casterton School, Carnforth, Lancs	1823	354	11,403	7,254	A. F. Thomas (1990)
Channing School, London N6	1885	350	—	6,735	Mrs E. Radice (1999)
Cheltenham Ladies' College, Glos	1853	840	14,340	9,105	Mrs A. V. Tuck (*Principal*) (1996)
City of London School for Girls, London EC2	1894	546	—	6,795	Mrs Y. A. Burne, PH.D. (1995)
Clifton High School, Bristol	1877	345	9,060	5,250	Mrs M. C. Culligan (1998)
Cobham Hall, Kent	1962	200	13,500	7,500	Mrs R. J. McCarthy (1989)
Colston's Girls' School, Bristol	1891	456	—	4,545	Mrs J. P. Franklin (1989)
Combe Bank School, Sevenoaks	1868	218	—	7,380	Miss N. Spurr (1993)
Cranford House School, Moulsford, Oxon	1931	87	—	5,850	Mrs A. B. Gray (1992)
Croham Hurst School, South Croydon	1899	350	—	5,850	Miss S. C. Budgen (1994)
Dame Alice Harpur School, Bedford	1882	721	—	5,769	Mrs R. Randle (1990)
Dame Allan's Girls' School, Newcastle upon Tyne	1705	430†	—	4,692	D. W. Welsh (*Principal*) (1996)

Name of School	Founded	No. of pupils	Annual fees £ Boarding	Day	Head (with date of appointment)
*Derby High School for Girls	1892	300	—	5,070	Dr G. H. Goddard, Ph.D. (1983)
Downe House, Newbury	1907	551	14,955	10,842	Mrs E. McKendrick (1997)
Dunottar School, Reigate	1926	255	—	6,090	Miss M. J. Skinner (1997)
Durham High School for Girls	1884	256	—	5,592	Mrs A. J. Templeman (1998)
Edgbaston Church of England College, Birmingham	1886	149	—	5,100	Mrs A. Varley-Tipton (1992)
Edgbaston High School for Girls, Birmingham	1876	500	—	5,085	Miss E. M. Mullenger (1998)
*Elmslie Girls' School, Blackpool	1918	130	—	5,100	Miss S. J. Woodward (1997)
Farlington School, Horsham	1896	250	11,745	7,275	Mrs P. M. Mawer (1992)
Farnborough Hill, Hants	1889	500	—	5,802	Miss J. Thomas (1997)
Farringtons and Stratford House, Chislehurst	1911	280	12,480	6,330	Mrs C. E. James (1999)
Francis Holland School, London NW1	1878	375	—	2,265	Mrs G. Low (1998)
Francis Holland School, London SW1	1881	250	—	7,605	Miss S. J. Pattenden (1997)
Gateways School, Harewood, W. Yorks	1941	190	—	5,094	Mrs D. Davidson (1997)
Godolphin and Latymer School, London W6	1905	700	—	6,996	Miss M. Rudland (1986)
Godolphin School, Salisbury	1726	395	13,164	7,887	Miss M. J. Horsburgh (1996)
Greenacre School, Banstead	1933	225	—	6,000	Mrs P. M. Wood (1990)
§Guildford High School (CSC)	1888	570	—	6,390	Mrs S. H. Singer (1991)
Haberdashers' Aske's School for Girls, Elstree, Herts	1873	834	—	5,400	Mrs P. Penney (1991)
Haberdashers' Monmouth School	1891	575	10,422	5,937	Dr B. Despontin, Ph.D. (1997)
Harrogate Ladies' College	1893	360	11,700	7,170	Dr M. J. Hustler (1996)
Headington School, Oxford	1915	543	11,925	6,525	Mrs H. A. Fender (1996)
Heathfield School, Ascot, Berks	1899	235	15,450	—	Mrs J. M. Benammar (1992)
Hethersett Old Hall School, Norwich	1928	183	11,295	5,670	Mrs B. M. Garrard (acting) (until Dec 1999); Mrs J. Mark (from Jan 2000)
Highclare School, Birmingham	1932	205†	—	4,875	Mrs C. A. Hanson (1974)
Hollygirt School, Nottingham	1877	231	—	4,305	Mrs M. I. Connolly (1997)
Holy Child School, Birmingham	1936	152	—	5,367	Mrs J. M. C. Hill (1993)
Holy Trinity College, Bromley	1886	222	—	5,274	Mrs D. A. Bradshaw (1994)
Holy Trinity School, Kidderminster	1903	170	—	4,650	Mrs E. L. Thomas (1998)
Howell's School, Denbigh	1859	220	11,085	7,485	Mrs S. Gordon (1998)
§Hull High School (CSC)	1890	164	—	4,824	Mrs M. A. Benson (1994)
Hulme Grammar School, Oldham	1895	511	—	4,455	Miss M. S. Smolenski (1992)
James Allen's Girls' School, London SE22	1741	740	—	7,059	Mrs M. O. Gibbs (1994)
Kent College, Tunbridge Wells	1886	240	13,740	8,100	Miss B. J. Crompton (1990)
King Edward VI High School for Girls, Birmingham	1883	543	—	5,385	Ms S. H. Evans (1996)
King's High School for Girls, Warwick	1879	547	—	5,355	Mrs J. M. Anderson (1987)
Kingsley School, Leamington Spa	1884	460	—	4,725	Mrs Mannion Watson (1997)
Lady Eleanor Holles School, Hampton, Middx	1710	719	—	7,062	Miss E. M. Candy (1981)
La Retraite School, Salisbury	1953	92‡	—	5,625	Mrs R. A. Simmons (1994)
La Sagesse High School, Newcastle upon Tyne	1906	320	—	5,058	Miss L. Clark (1994)
Lavant House and Rosemead, Chichester	1952	95	12,060	6,780	Mrs S. E. Watkins (1996)
Leeds Girls' High School	1876	615	—	5,511	Mrs S. Fishburn (1997)
Leicester High School	1906	297	—	5,235	Mrs P. A. Watson (1992)
Lodge School, Purley, Surrey	1916	120	—	5,430	Miss P. Maynard (1998)
Loughborough High School	1850	558	—	4,995	Miss J. E. L. Harvatt (1978)
Luckley-Oakfield School, Wokingham	1895	283	11,103	6,507	R. C. Blake (1994)
Malvern Girls' College, Worcs	1893	430	13,800	9,210	Mrs P. M. C. Leggate (1997)
Manchester High School	1874	729	—	4,830	Mrs C. Lee-Jones (1998)
Manor House School, Little Bookham, Surrey	1927	170	8,848	6,543	Mrs L. A. Mendes (1989)
Marymount International School, Kingston upon Thames	1955	242	16,335	9,510	Sr R. Sheridan (1990)
Maynard School, Exeter	1877	429	—	5,310	Miss F. Murdin (1980)
Merchant Taylors' School, Liverpool	1888	660	—	4,356	Mrs J. I. Mills (1994)
Moira House School, Eastbourne	1875	210	13,500	8,400	Mrs A. Harris (Principal) (1997)
More House School, London SW1	1953	220	—	6,660	Mrs L. Falconer (1999)
Moreton Hall, Oswestry	1913	260	14,085	9,660	J. Forster (1992)
Mount School, York	1785	265	12,075	7,575	Miss B. J. Windle (1986)
Newcastle upon Tyne Church High School	1885	372	—	4,845	Mrs L. G. Smith (1995)

Name of School	Foun- ded	No. of pupils	Annual fees £		Head (with date of appointment)
			Boarding	Day	
New Hall School, Chelmsford	1642	395	12,720	8,280	Sr Anne-Marie (1996)
Northampton High School	1878	570	—	5,040	Mrs L. A. Mayne (1988)
North Foreland Lodge, Hook	1909	180	14,550	8,700	Miss S. Cameron (1996)
North London Collegiate School, Edgware	1850	760	—	6,360	Mrs B. McCabe (1997)
Northwood College, Middx	1878	448	—	6,108	Mrs A. Mayou (1991)
Notre Dame Senior School, Cobham, Surrey	1937	330	—	5,625	Mrs M. McSwiggan (1999)
Ockbrook School, Derby	1799	430	8,505	4,635	Miss D. P. Bolland (1995)
Old Palace School, Croydon	1889	547	—	5,298	Miss K. L. Hilton (1974)
Palmers Green High School, London N21	1905	140	—	5,625	Mrs S. Grant (1989)
Parsons Mead, Ashtead, Surrey	1897	160	11,688	6,600	Miss E. B. Plant (1990)
Perse School for Girls, Cambridge	1881	530	—	5,862	Miss H. S. Smith (1989)
*Peterborough High School	1895	160	10,623	5,289	Mrs S. A. Dixon (1999)
Pipers Corner School, High Wycombe	1930	270	11,670	6,990	Mrs V. M. Stattersfield (1996)
Polam Hall School, Darlington	1848	289	11,595	5,391	Mrs H. C. Hamilton (1987)
Princess Helena College, Hitchin, Herts	1820	150	12,285	8,385	Mrs A. M. Hodgkiss (1997)
Prior's Field, Godalming	1902	235	11,670	7,800	Mrs J. Dwyer (1999)
Queen Anne's School, Reading	1894	320	14,010	9,180	Mrs D. Forbes (1993)
*Queen Ethelburga's College, York	1912	200	13,497	8,325	Mrs E. I. E. Taylor (1997)
*Queen Margaret's School, York	1901	365	12,594	7,980	Dr G. A. H. Chapman (1993)
Queen's College, London W1	1848	80	—	7,410	Miss M. M. Connell (1999)
Queen's Gate School, London SW7	1891	250	—	6,750	Mrs A. M. Holyoak (*Principal*) (1989)
Queen's School, Chester	1878	468	—	5,145	Miss D. M. Skilbeck (1989)
Queenswood, Hatfield, Herts	1894	371	14,430	8,940	Ms C. Farr (*Principal*) (1996)
Redland High School for Girls, Bristol	1882	490	—	4,944	Mrs C. Lear (1971)
Red Maids' School, Bristol	1634	495	8,940	4,470	Miss S. Hampton (1987)
Roedean School, Brighton	1885	410	15,750	9,750	Mrs P. Metham (1997)
Royal Masonic School, Herts	1788	520	9,876	6,009	Mrs I. M. Andrews (1992)
Rye St Antony School (*RC*), Oxford	1930	330	10,455	5,985	Miss A. M. Jones (1990)
St Albans High School	1889	556	—	5,940	Mrs C. Y. Daly (1994)
St Andrew's School, Bedford	1897	154	—	5,007	Mrs J. M. Mark (1995)
St Anne's School, Windermere	1863	150‡	11,385	6,845	R. D. Hunter (1996)
St Antony's-Leweston School (*RC*), Sherborne	1891	240	13,023	8,580	H. J. MacDonald (*Acting Head*) (1999)
St Catherine's School, Guildford	1885	490	11,865	7,230	Mrs C. M. Oulton (1994)
St David's School, Ashford, Middx	1716	234†	11,550	6,390	Ms P. A. Bristow (1999)
St Dunstan's Abbey School, Plymouth	1850	160†	10,365	5,580	Mrs B. K. Brown (1998)
*St Elphin's School, Matlock	1844	160	11,670	6,798	Mrs V. E. Fisher (1995)
St Felix School, Southwold, Suffolk	1897	150	12,015	7,950	R. Williams (1998)
St Francis' College (*RC*), Letchworth	1933	182	12,210	6,270	Miss M. Hegarty (1993)
St Gabriel's School, Newbury	1929	187	—	6,108	D. J. Cobb (1990)
St George's School, Ascot, Berks	1923	280	14,070	8,970	Mrs J. Grant Peterkin (1999)
School of St Helen and St Katharine, Abingdon	1903	590	—	5,574	Mrs C. L. Hall (1993)
St Helen's School, Northwood, Middx	1899	634	11,610	6,108	Mrs D. M. Jefkins (1994)
St James' School, West Malvern	1896	150	13,890	8,070	Mrs S. Kershaw (1998)
St Joseph's Convent School (*RC*), Reading	1894	330	—	5,220	Mrs V. Brookes (1990)
St Leonards-Mayfield School, Mayfield	1872	460	12,900	8,600	Sr J. Sinclair (1980)
St Margaret's School, Bushey, Herts	1749	320	11,775	7,056	Miss M. de Villiers (1992)
*St Margaret's School, Exeter	1904	356	—	5,085	Mrs M. D'Albertanson (1993)
St Martin's School, Solihull	1941	240	—	5,250	Mrs S. J. Williams (1988)
*School of S. Mary and S. Anne, Abbots Bromley, Staffs	1874	186	12,675	8,136	Mrs M. Steel (1998)
St Mary's Convent School, Worcester	1934	200	—	4,230	C. Garner (1997)
St Mary's Hall, Brighton	1836	240	10,833	6,975	Mrs S. M. Meek (1997)
St Mary's School (*RC*), Ascot, Berks	1885	353	14,310	9,390	Mrs M. Breen (1999)
St Mary's School, Calne, Wilts	1872	300	14,490	9,150	Mrs C. J. Shaw (1996)
St Mary's School, Cambridge	1898	460	9,985	5,520	Mrs G. Piotrowska (1998)
St Mary's School, Colchester	1908	225	—	4,665	Mrs G. M. G. Mouser (1981)
St Mary's School, Gerrards Cross	1872	148	—	5,900	Mrs F. Balcombe (1995)
St Mary's School (*RC*), Shaftesbury	1945	316	12,150	7,875	Mrs S. Pennington (1998)
St Mary's School, Wantage, Oxon	1873	200	13,950	9,300	Mrs S. Bodinham (1994)
St Nicholas' School, Fleet, Hants	1935	156	—	5,340	Mrs A. V. Whatmough (1995)
St Paul's Girls' School, London W6	1904	657	—	7,782	Miss E. Diggory (*High Mistress*) (1998)

Name of School	Foun-ded	No. of pupils	Annual fees £		Head (with date of appointment)
			Boarding	Day	
St Swithun's School, Winchester	1884	462	13,620	8,250	Dr H. L. Harvey (1995)
St Teresa's School, Dorking	1928	360	11,700	6,450	Mrs M. E. Prescott (1997)
Sherborne School for Girls, Dorset	1899	390	14,970	11,250	Mrs G. Kerton-Johnson (1999)
Sir William Perkins's School, Chertsey, Surrey	1725	583	—	5,430	Miss S. Ross (1994)
Stonar School, Melksham, Wilts	1921	325	11,205	6,225	Mrs C. Homan (1997)
Stover School, Newton Abbot	1932	210	10,485	5,235	P. E. Bujak (1994)
§Surbiton High School, Kingston-upon-Thames (CSC)	1884	612	—	6,060	Miss M. G. Perry (1993)
Talbot Heath, Bournemouth	1886	398	10,650	6,150	Mrs C. Dipple (1991)
Teesside High School, Stockton-on-Tees	1970	350	—	4,965	Miss J. F. Hamilton (1995)
Tormead School, Guildford	1905	522	—	6,330	Mrs H. E. M. Alleyne (1992)
Truro High School	1880	380	9,795	5,355	J. Graham-Brown (1992)
Tudor Hall School, Banbury	1850	262	12,780	7,980	Miss N. Godfrey (1984)
Wakefield Girls' High School	1878	717†	—	5,300	Mrs P. A. Langham (1988)
Walthamstow Hall, Sevenoaks	1838	250	14,220	8,010	Mrs J. S. Lang (1984)
Wentworth College, Bournemouth	1871	235	10,545	6,615	Miss S. D. Coe (1991)
Westfield School, Newcastle upon Tyne	1962	235	—	5,085	Mrs M. Farndale (1991)
Westholme School, Blackburn	1923	685	—	4,305	Mrs L. Croston (Principal) (1988)
Westonbirt School, Tetbury, Glos	1928	200	13,728	9,180	Mrs M. Henderson (1999)
Wispers School, Haslemere, Surrey	1946	115	11,460	7,374	L. H. Beltran (1980)
Withington Girls' School, Manchester	1890	530	—	4,710	Mrs M. Kenyon (1986)
Woldingham School, Surrey	1842	550	14,085	8,523	Mrs M. M. Ribbins (1997)
Wychwood School, Oxford	1897	138	8,820	5,550	Mrs S. Wingfield Digby (1997)
Wycombe Abbey School, High Wycombe	1896	513	15,000	11,250	Mrs P. E. Davies (1998)
Wykeham House School, Fareham, Hants	1913	150	—	4,824	Mrs R. M. Kamaryc (1995)
SCOTLAND					
Kilgraston School, Bridge of Earn, Perth	1920	200	12,720	7,500	Mrs J. L. Austin (1993)
Laurel Park School, Glasgow	1996	465	—	4,653	Mrs E. Surber (1995)
Mary Erskine School, Edinburgh	1694	691‡	10,650	5,130	P. F. J. Tobin (Principal) (1989)
St George's School, Edinburgh	1888	550	10,905	5,580	Dr J. McClure (1994)
St Leonards School, St Andrews	1877	251†	14,430	7,950	Mrs M. James (1988)
St Margaret's School, Aberdeen	1846	200	—	4,536	Miss A. C. Ritchie (1998)
St Margaret's School and St Denis and Cranley, Edinburgh	1890	370	10,050	4,950	Miss A. Mitchell (1994)
CHANNEL ISLANDS					
The Ladies' College, Guernsey	1872	350	—	2,340	Miss M. E. Macdonald (Principal) (1992)

Health

SELECTED CAUSES OF DEATH, BY GENDER AND AGE
1997 (UNITED KINGDOM)
Percentages and number*

	Under 1†	1–15	16–24	25–34	35–54	55–64	65–74	75 and over	All ages
Males									
Circulatory diseases	4	6	4	9	33	42	44	44	41
Cancer	1	15	7	11	27	36	34	22	27
Respiratory diseases	10	8	3	4	5	8	12	21	15
Injury and poisoning	5	31	66	53	15	3	1	1	4
Infectious diseases	9	5	2	3	2	1	1	—	1
Other causes	71	36	19	21	18	10	8	11	11
All males (number)	2,400	1,200	2,700	4,600	22,400	33,700	77,900	155,600	300,400
Females									
Circulatory diseases	3	5	7	10	17	28	38	46	41
Cancer	2	19	14	30	51	49	36	15	23
Respiratory diseases	14	8	6	5	6	9	13	20	17
Injury and poisoning	5	22	41	28	8	2	1	1	2
Infectious diseases	10	7	6	4	1	1	1	—	1
Other causes	67	40	26	24	17	12	11	17	16
All females (number)	1,900	900	1,000	2,000	14,700	21,000	55,700	232,200	329,300

* Percentages may not total 100 per cent because of rounding
† Excluding deaths at ages under 28 days
Source: The Stationery Office – *Social Trends 29* (Crown copyright)

NOTIFICATIONS OF INFECTIOUS DISEASES (UK) 1997

Measles	4,844
Mumps	2,264
Rubella	4,205
Whooping cough	3,669
Scarlet fever	4,639
Dysentery	2,427
Food poisoning	105,579
Typhoid and paratyphoid fevers	249
Hepatitis	3,601
Tuberculosis	6,367
Malaria	1,549

Source: The Stationery Office – *Annual Abstract of Statistics 1999* (Crown copyright)

HIV/AIDS AND SEXUALLY TRANSMITTED DISEASES
(ENGLAND)

	1986	1996
HIV cases diagnosed	2,114	2,230
Exposure category		
Homosexual intercourse	76%	59%
Heterosexual intercourse	6%	29%
Injecting drug use	11%	6%
Blood products	4%	1%
Aids cases diagnosed	450	1,257
Sexually transmitted diseases (new cases)		
All, except HIV/Aids	—	424,300
Syphilis	2,400	1,200
Gonorrhoea	46,300	14,400
Chlamydia	—	44,700
Herpes	18,900	27,600
Wart virus	52,200	97,800

Source: The Stationery Office – *Health and Personal Social Services Statistics for England 1998* (Crown copyright)

PREVALENCE OF SMOKING CIGARETTES (ENGLAND)
Percentages among adults aged 16 and over, by sex

	1986	1997
Males		
Current smoker	34	30
Ex-regular smoker	33	27
Never smoked	33	42
Females		
Current smoker	31	29
Ex-regular smoker	18	19
Never smoked	51	52

Source: The Stationery Office – *All Change? The Health Education Monitoring Survey One Year On* (Crown copyright)

ALCOHOL CONSUMPTION - UNITS PER WEEK
(ENGLAND) 1997
Percentage

Men	
Non-drinker	6
Under one	6
1–10	35
11–21	23
22–35	17
36–50	7
51 and over	6
Women	
Non-drinker	9
Under one	16
1–7	41
8–14	17
15–25	12
26–35	2
36 and over	3

Source: The Stationery Office – *All Change? The Health Education Monitoring Survey One Year On* (Crown copyright)

People Who Have Used Drugs in the Past Year
(England and Wales) 1997
by sex, age and type of drug
Percentage

Age	16–29	30–54	All aged 16–54
Men			
Cannabis	28	7	14
Hallucinants	18	2	7
Opiates	6	1	3
Other	3	1	1
Any drug	31	7	15
Women			
Cannabis	22	4	10
Hallucinants	10	1	4
Opiates	1	0	0
Other	1	0	0
Any drug	24	4	11

Source: The Stationery Office – *All Change? The Health Education Monitoring Survey One Year On* (Crown copyright)

HEALTH IN ENGLAND

A report, *Health in England 1996*, was published by the Health Education Authority and the Office for National Statistics in May 1997. In 1998 a follow-up survey, *All Change? The Health Education Monitoring Survey One Year On*, was published. It included the following main findings:
– 30 per cent of men and 29 per cent of women were cigarette smokers
– the mean alcohol consumption was 17.0 units a week for men and 7.3 units a week for women
– 26 per cent of respondents were sedentary
– 15 per cent of men and 11 per cent of women had taken drugs in the past year
– 16 per cent of men and 10 per cent of women aged 16–54 had had two or more sexual partners in the previous year

HEALTH TARGETS

In February 1997 the Government published a Green Paper, *Our Healthier Nation*, which identified four main areas of illness in England (heart disease and stroke, accidents, cancer and mental health) to be improved, and replaced the targets in *The Health of the Nation* (a White Paper published in 1992) with four main targets:
– a reduction in the number of deaths from coronary heart disease and strokes by two-fifths by 2010
– a reduction in the number of deaths from cancer by one fifth by 2010
– a reduction in the number of deaths by suicide by one sixth by 2010
– a reduction in the number of deaths from accidents by one fifth by 2010
Similar reviews are being undertaken in Wales and Northern Ireland. In Scotland a White Paper, *Towards a Healthier Scotland*, was presented in February 1999.

Consumption of Foods Containing Fibre and Starchy Carbohydrates (England) 1996 *by age and sex*
Percentage consuming each food

Age	16–24	25–34	35–44	45–54	55–64	65–74	Total
Men							
Eats wholemeal bread	7	14	16	21	23	22	17
Eats bread daily	83	77	87	84	89	92	84
Eats fruit, vegetables and salad daily	43	51	56	69	72	73	59
Eats potatoes, pasta or rice daily	35	51	55	56	63	66	53
Eats bread; fruit, vegetables and salad; and potatoes, pasta or rice daily	19	31	34	41	45	51	36
Women							
Eats wholemeal bread	16	23	24	30	29	34	25
Eats bread daily	76	75	79	83	83	93	81
Eats fruit, vegetables and salad daily	57	60	74	81	86	83	72
Eats potatoes, pasta or rice daily	44	51	55	62	67	64	56
Eats bread; fruit, vegetables and salad; and potatoes, pasta or rice daily	24	32	38	45	53	53	40

Source: The Stationery Office – *Health in England 1996* (Crown copyright)

Frequency of at Least Moderate-Intensity Exercise for 30 Minutes or More *by age and sex*
Percentages

Age	16–24	25–34	35–44	45–54	55–64	65–74	Total
Men							
Less than one day a week	9	19	20	26	38	42	24
1–2 days a week	21	20	25	25	23	29	23
3–4 days a week	14	12	12	11	7	14	12
5 or more days a week	56	48	43	39	32	14	41
Women							
Less than one day a week	20	18	19	22	37	46	26
1–2 days a week	29	27	33	28	33	28	30
3–4 days a week	18	15	14	14	9	11	14
5 or more days a week	32	39	34	35	21	14	31

Source: The Stationery Office – *Health in England 1996* (Crown copyright)

Social Welfare

National Health Service

The National Health Service (NHS) came into being on 5 July 1948 under the National Health Service Act 1946, covering England and Wales, and under separate legislation for Scotland and Northern Ireland. The NHS is now administered by the Secretary of State for Health (in England), the National Assembly for Wales, the Scottish Executive and the Secretary of State for Northern Ireland.

The function of the NHS is to provide a comprehensive health service designed to secure improvement in the physical and mental health of the people and to prevent, diagnose and treat illness. It was founded on the principle that treatment should be provided according to clinical need rather than ability to pay, and should be free at the point of delivery. However, prescription charges were provided for by legislation in 1949 and implemented in 1952, and charges for some dental and ophthalmic treatment have also been introduced.

The NHS covers a comprehensive range of hospital, specialist, family practitioner (medical, dental, ophthalmic and pharmaceutical), artificial limb and appliance, ambulance, and community health services. Everyone normally resident in the UK is entitled to use any of these services.

STRUCTURE

The structure of the NHS remained relatively stable for the first 30 years of its existence. In 1974, a three-tier management structure comprising Regional Health Authorities, Area Health Authorities and District Management Teams was introduced in England, and the NHS became responsible for community health services. In 1979 Area Health Authorities were abolished and District Management Teams were replaced by District Health Authorities.

The National Health Service and Community Care Act 1990 provided for more streamlined Regional Health Authorities and District Health Authorities, and for the establishment of Family Health Services Authorities (FHSAs) and NHS Trusts. The concept of the 'internal market' was introduced into health care, whereby care was provided through NHS contracts where health authorities or boards and GP fundholders (the purchasers) were responsible for buying health care from hospitals, non-fundholding GPs, community services and ambulance services (the providers).

NHS Trusts operate as self-governing health care providers independent of health authority control and responsible to the Secretary of State. Until 1999 they derived their income principally from contracts to provide services to health authorities and fund-holding GPs. In Northern Ireland, 20 health and social services trusts are responsible for providing health and social services in an organizational model unique to Northern Ireland.

The Act also paved the way for the Community Care reforms, which were introduced in April 1993 and changed the way care is administered for elderly people, the mentally ill, the physically handicapped and people with learning disabilities.

The eight Regional Health Authorities in England were abolished in April 1996 and replaced by eight regional offices which, together with the headquarters in Leeds, form the NHS Executive. The regional offices are part of the Department of Health, and their functions include financial and performance monitoring of local purchasers and providers, public health, regional research and development, and education programmes.

In April 1996 the District Health Authorities and Family Health Service Authorities were merged to form 100 unified Health Authorities (HAs) in England. The HAs are responsible for health and health services in their areas. They are also responsible for assessing the health care needs of the local population and developing integrated strategies for meeting these needs in partnership with GPs and in consultation with the public, hospitals and others. HAs' resources are allocated by the NHS Executive headquarters, to which they are also accountable for their performance. HA chairmen are appointed by the Health Secretary and non-executive members by the regional offices of the NHS Executive.

In Wales the chairman and non-executive members of the five HAs which replaced the former 17 HAs and FHSAs in April 1996 are appointed by the First Secretary. Health Solutions Wales provides a range of specialist services to the NHS in Wales. In Scotland there are 15 Health Boards with similar responsibilities to those of HAs. In Northern Ireland there are four Health and Social Services Boards.

There are also Community Health Councils (called Local Health Councils in Scotland and Health and Social Services Councils in Northern Ireland) throughout the UK; their role is to represent the interests of the public to health authorities and boards. The Government announced in March 1998 that public consultation and patient representation in the NHS would be increased.

Under the Health Act 1999 the NHS internal market in England was replaced by teams of GPs and community nurses working together in primary care groups (*see* page 481) from 1 April 1999. Long-term service agreements are beginning to replace annual contracts between primary care groups, health authorities, and NHS Trusts. A National Institute for Clinical Excellence has been established to produce new national guidelines and National Service Frameworks are being prepared to guarantee consistency in access to services. The first of these, to be published in late 1999, will address mental health and coronary heart disease services. A Commission for Health Improvement is being established in autumn 1999 to promote best practice. In Scotland, the Act replaced the internal market with Local Health Care Co-operatives (see page 481) from 1 April 1999. The NHS Trusts were reorganized into 13 primary care trusts and 15 acute care trusts, responsible to the Health Boards. In Wales the internal market was replaced by a system of Local Health Groups (see page 481). In Scotland the Scottish Health Technology Assessment Centre will provide guidelines to promote best practice.

FINANCE

UNITED KINGDOM

The NHS is still funded mainly (75.3 per cent in England for 1998–9) through general taxation, although in recent years more reliance has been placed on the NHS element of National Insurance contributions (13 per cent in England for 1998–9), patient charges and other sources of income.

Total UK expenditure on the NHS in 1998–9 was £49,125 million, of which £45,315 million was from public monies and £3,810 million from patient charges and other receipts. NHS expenditure represented 5.8 per cent of GDP. The total cost per head was £830. The planned expenditure for 1999–2000 is £52,376 million. The Government announced in July 1998 that an additional £21,000 million would be spent on the NHS between 1999 and 2002.

NATIONAL HEALTH CURRENT EXPENDITURE 1997–8

	£ million
National Health Service:	
Hospitals, Community Health Services and Family Health Services	40,993
Departmental administration	245
Other central services	3,242
Less payments by patients	−919
TOTAL	43,561

PERSONAL SOCIAL SERVICES CURRENT EXPENDITURE 1997–8

	£ million
Central government	73
Local authorities running expenses	10,484
Capital expenditure	213
TOTAL	10,770

Source: The Stationery Office – *Annual Abstract of Statistics 1999* (Crown copyright)

WALES

CENTRAL GOVERNMENT HEALTH FUNDING 1997–8

	£ thousand
Central administration	6,904
Hospital, community and cash limited family health services	1,851,757
NHS Trusts	159,266
Demand-led (non-cash limited) family health services	425,705
Other health services	61,951
Welfare foods	12,773
TOTAL	2,518,356

Source: Welsh Office

SCOTLAND

NET COSTS OF THE NATIONAL HEALTH SERVICE 1996–7

	£ thousand
Central administration	8,378
Total NHS cost	4,377,923
NHS contributions	468,770
Net costs to Exchequer	3,909,153
Health Board administration	89,282
Hospital and community health services	3,108,575
Family practitioner services	986,616
Central health services	120,586
State hospital	22,400
Training	3,326
Research	10,517
Disabled services	2,331
Welfare foods	13,835
Miscellaneous health services	20,455
TOTAL	4,386,301

Source: Scottish Office – *Annual Abstract of Statistics 1998* (Crown copyright)

ORGANIZATIONS

HEALTH AUTHORITIES (ENGLAND)

There are 100 health authorities in England. For details, contact the relevant NHS Executive regional office (*see* below).

NHS EXECUTIVE REGIONAL OFFICES
EASTERN, 6–12 Capital Drive, Linford Wood, Milton Keynes MK14 6QP. Tel: 01908-844400. *Chairman*, Mrs R. Varley; *Regional Director*, P. Houghton
LONDON, 40 Eastbourne Terrace, London W2 3QR. Tel: 0171-725 5300. *Chairman*, I. Mills; *Regional Director*, N. Crisp
NORTHERN AND YORKSHIRE, John Snow House, Durham University Science Park, Durham DH1 3YG. Tel: 0191-301 1325. *Chairman*, Mrs Z. Manzoor; *Regional Director*, P. Garland
NORTH WEST, 930–932 Birchwood Boulevard, Millennium Park, Birchwood, Warrington WA3 7QN. Tel: 01925-704000. *Chairman*, Prof. A. Breckenridge; *Regional Director*, Prof. R. Tinston
SOUTH EAST, 40 Eastbourne Terrace, London W2 3QR. Tel: 0171-725 2500. *Chairman*, Sir William Wells; *Regional Director*, B. Stocking
SOUTH WEST, Westward House, Lime Kiln Close, Stoke Gifford, Bristol BS34 8SR. Tel: 0117-984 1750. *Chairman*, Miss J. Trotter, OBE; *Regional Director*, A. Laurance
TRENT, Fulwood House, Old Fulwood Road, Sheffield S10 3TH. Tel: 0114-263 0300. *Chairman*, P. Hammersley; *Regional Director*, N. McKay
WEST MIDLANDS, Bartholomew House, 142 Hagley Road, Birmingham B16 9PA. Tel: 0121-224 4600. *Chairman*, C. Wilkinson; *Regional Director*, S. Day

HEALTH BOARDS (SCOTLAND)

ARGYLL AND CLYDE, Ross House, Hawkhead Road, Paisley PA2 7BN. Tel: 0141-842 7200. *Chairman*, M. D. Jones; *General Manager*, N. McConachie
AYRSHIRE AND ARRAN, PO Box 13, Boswell House, 10 Arthur Street, Ayr KA7 1QJ. Tel: 01292-611040. *Chairman*, Dr J. Morrow; *General Manager*, Mrs W.-Y. Hatton
BORDERS, Newstead, Melrose, Roxburghshire TD9 0SE. Tel: 01896-825500. *Chairman*, D. A. C. Kilshaw, OBE; *General Manager*, Dr L. Burley
DUMFRIES AND GALLOWAY, Grierson House, The Crichton, Bankend Road, Dumfries DG1 4ZG. Tel: 01387-272700. *Chairman*, J. Ross, CBE; *General Manager*, N. Campbell
FIFE, Springfield House, Cupar KY15 9UP. Tel: 01334-656200. *Chairman*, Mrs C. Stenhouse; *General Manager*, M. Murray
FORTH VALLEY, 33 Spittal Street, Stirling FK8 1DX. Tel: 01786-457248. *Chairman*, E. Bell-Scott; *General Manager*, D. Hird
GRAMPIAN, Summerfield House, 2 Eday Road, Aberdeen AB15 6RE. Tel: 01224-663456. *Chairman*, Dr C. E. MacLeod, CBE; *General Manager*, F. E. L. Hartnett, OBE
GREATER GLASGOW, Dalian House, PO Box 15329, 350 St Vincent Street, Glasgow G3 8YZ. Tel: 0141-201 4444. *Chairman*, Prof. D. Hamblen; *Chief Executive*, C. J. Spry
HIGHLAND, Beechwood Park, Inverness IV2 3HG. Tel: 01463-717123. *Chairman*, Mrs C. Thomson; *General Manager (acting)*, E. Baigal
LANARKSHIRE, 14 Beckford Street, Hamilton, Lanarkshire ML3 0TA. Tel: 01698-281313. *Chairman*, I. Livingstone, CBE; *General Manager*, Prof. T. A. Divers

LOTHIAN, Deaconess House, 148 Pleasance, Edinburgh EH8 9RS. Tel: 0131-536 9000. *Chairman,* Mrs M. Ford; *General Manager,* T. Jones

ORKNEY, Garden House, New Scapa Road, Kirkwall, Orkney KW15 1BQ. Tel: 01856-885400. *Chairman,* I. Leslie; *General Manager,* J. Wellden

SHETLAND, Brevik House, South Road, Lerwick ZE1 OTG. Tel: 01595-696767. *Chairman,* J. Telford; *General Manager,* B. J. Atherton

TAYSIDE, Gateway House, Luna Place, Dundee Technology Park, Dundee DD2 1TP. Tel: 01382-561818. *Chairman,* Mrs F. Havenga; *General Manager,* T. Brett

WESTERN ISLES, 37 South Beach Street, Stornoway, Isle of Lewis HS1 2BN. Tel: 01851-702997. *Chairman,* A. Matheson; *General Manager,* M. Maclennan

HEALTH AUTHORITIES (WALES)

BRO TAF, 17 Churchill House, Churchill Way, Cardiff CF10 4TW. Tel: 01222-402402. *Chairman,* Mrs K. Thomas; *Chief Executive,* D. Hands

DYFED POWYS, St David's Hospital, Carmarthen SA31 3HB. Tel: 01267-225077. *Chairman,* Ms M. Price; *Chief Executive,* P. Stansbie

GWENT, Mamhilad House, Mamhilad Park Estate, Pontypool NP4 0YP. Tel: 01495-765065. *Chairman,* Mrs F. Peel; *Chief Executive,* G. Coomber

MORGANNWG, 41 High Street, Swansea SA1 1LT. Tel: 01792-458066. *Chairman,* D. H. Thomas; *Chief Executive,* Mrs J. V. Williams

NORTH WALES, Preswylfa, Hendy Road, Mold CH7 1PZ. Tel: 01352-700227. *Chairman,* Mrs E. Rowlands; *Chief Executive,* B. Jones

HEALTH SOLUTIONS WALES, National Assembly for Wales, Pierhead Street, Capital Waterside, Cardiff CF1 5XT. Tel: 01222-500500.

NORTHERN IRELAND HEALTH AND SOCIAL SERVICES BOARDS

EASTERN, Champion House, 12–22 Linenhall Street, Belfast BT2 8BS. Tel: 01232-321313. *Chairman,* J. D. Thompson, CBE; *Chief Executive,* Dr M. P. J. Kilbane, FRCP

NORTHERN, County Hall, 182 Galgorm Road, Ballymena BT42 1QB. Tel: 01266-653333. *Chairman,* R. J. Hanna; *Chief Executive,* J. S. MacDonell

SOUTHERN, Tower Hill, Armagh BT61 9DR. Tel: 01861-410041. *Chairman,* W. Gillespie; *Chief Executive,* B. P. Cunningham

WESTERN, 15 Gransha Park, Clooney Road, Londonderry BT47 6TG. Tel: 01504-860086. *Chairman,* R. G. Toland; *Chief Executive,* T. J. Frawley

HEALTH PROMOTION AUTHORITIES

HEALTH EDUCATION AUTHORITY, Trevelyan House, 30 Great Peter Street, London SW1P 2HW. Tel: 0171-222 5300. *Chair,* Ms Y. Buckland; *Chief Executive,* vacant. The Health Education Authority will be replaced by a new Health Development Agency in early 2000

NATIONAL ASSEMBLY FOR WALES HEALTH PROMOTION DIVISION, *see* page 349

HEALTH EDUCATION BOARD FOR SCOTLAND, Woodburn House, Canaan Lane, Edinburgh EH10 4SG. Tel 0131-536 5500. *Chairman,* D. R. Campbell; *Chief Executive,* Prof. A. Tannahill

HEALTH PROMOTION AGENCY FOR NORTHERN IRELAND, 18 Ormeau Avenue, Belfast BT2 8HS. Tel: 01232-311611

EMPLOYEES AND SALARIES

EMPLOYEES

HEALTH AND PERSONAL SOCIAL SERVICES WORKFORCE (*Great Britain*) as at 30 September 1997

General medical practitioners	35,206
General dental practitioners	19,598
Ophthalmic medical practitioners	*830
Ophthalmic opticians	*7,847
Medical staff	64,316
Dental staff	3,078
Nursing and midwifery staff	353,933
Professional and technical staff	107,158
Administrative and clerical staff	177,957
Health care assistants and support staff	91,774
Ambulance staff	16,424
Other Health Service staff	3,337
†Personal social services staff	229,439

* Figures for England and Wales relate to 31 December 1997. Figures for Scotland relate to 31 March 1997. Those with contracts with more than one authority/board will be counted more than once.
† England only
Source: The Stationery Office – *Annual Abstract of Statistics 1999* (Crown copyright)

SALARIES *as at 1 April 1999*

General Practitioners (GPs), dentists, optometrists and pharmacists are self-employed, and are employed by the NHS under contract. GPs are paid for their NHS work in accordance with a scheme of remuneration which includes a basic practice allowance, capitation fees, reimbursement of certain practice expenses and payments for out-of-hours work. Dentists receive payment for items of treatment for individual adult patients and, in addition, a continuing care payment for those registered with them. Optometrists receive approved fees for each sight test they carry out. Pharmacists receive professional fees from the NHS and are refunded the cost of prescriptions supplied.

Consultant	£47,345–£61,605
Specialist Registrar	£23,300–£33,965
Registrar	£23,300–£28,625
Senior House Officer	£20,845–£27,845
House Officer	£16,710–£18,860
GP	*£52,600
Nursing Grades G–I (Senior Ward Sister)	£20,145–£28,240
Nursing Grade F (Ward Sister)	£17,075–£20,925
Nursing Grade E (Senior Staff Nurse)	£15,395–£17,830
Nursing Grade D (Staff Nurse)	£14,400–£15,905
Nursing Grade C (Enrolled Nurse)	£11,735–£13,915
Nursing Grades A–B (Nursing Auxiliary)	£8,705–£11,735

* average intended net remuneration

HEALTH SERVICES

PRIMARY AND COMMUNITY HEALTH CARE

Primary and community health care services comprise the family health services (i.e. the general medical, personal medical, pharmaceutical, dental, and ophthalmic services) and community services (including preventive activities such as vaccination, immunization and fluoridation) commissioned by HAs and provided by NHS Trusts, health centres and clinics. Nursing services including practice nurses, district nurses and health visitors, community psychiatric nurses, school nurse and ante- and post-natal care are also an integral part of primary and community health care.

FAMILY DOCTOR SERVICE

In England and Wales the Family Doctor Service (or General Medical Service) is now the responsibility of the HAs. In late 1999 a pilot scheme of 19 walk-in centres, where people may consult a doctor without an appointment between the hours of 7 a.m. and 10 p.m., will begin operation. They are responsible to HAs and will work closely with primary care groups.

Any doctor may take part in the Family Doctor Service (provided the area in which he/she wishes to practise has not already an adequate number of doctors) and about 29,000 GPs in England and Wales do so. The distribution of GPs is controlled by the Medical Practices Committee, a statutory body. The average number of patients on a doctor's list in 1997 was:

England	1,878
Wales	1,706
Scotland	1,478

GPs may also have private fee-paying patients.

The Government has replaced the fundholding system by allowing the new primary care groups and trusts to assume one of four levels of responsibility. In April 1999 481 primary care groups became operational in England, covering populations of between 46,000 and 257,000. They operate as a committee of a Health Authority and are responsible for health improvement, primary and community health service development and commissioning secondary care services where appropriate. Primary care groups operate at one of two levels of responsibility. At level one, the group advises the Health Authority and is responsible for less than 40 per cent of the group's unified budget. Level two primary care groups are responsible for 40 per cent of the group's unified budget, rising to 60 per cent in their second year of operation. A board consisting of GPs, nurses, a social services officer, a health authority representative and a local member of the public administers each group.

From 1 April 2000, Primary Care Trusts will become operational in England. They will be free-standing statutory bodies undertaking many of the functions presently exercised by Health Authorities. They will operate at one of two levels. Level three Trusts will be able to commission services with greater scope than a level two primary care group, but not directly provide them. Those at level four will be able to commission and directly provide services and run community hospitals and health services.

In Scotland, fundholding was replaced by over 70 Local Health Care Co-operatives on 1 April 1999. These, consisting of GPs and others involved in primary care, are responsible for developing health care in their area.

In Wales 22 Local Health Groups were set up by the Health Authorities and began work in April 1999. They are coterminous with local authority areas. Initially they will advise Health Authorities but in the future they will assume responsibility for commissioning services and devising strategies for improved health. They will also integrate the delivery of primary and community care. A governing body including GPs and other health professionals, social services and community representatives administers each group.

Everyone aged 16 or over can choose their doctor (parents or guardians choose for children under 16); the doctor is free to accept a person or not. Should a patient have difficulty in registering with a doctor, HAs have powers to assign the patient to a GP. A person may change

their doctor if they wish, by going to the surgery of a GP of their choice who is willing to accept them, and either handing in their medical card to register or filling in a form. When people are away from home they can still use the Family Doctor Service if they ask to be treated as temporary residents, and in an emergency, any doctor in the service will give treatment and advice. A number of drop-in medical centres are being set up where anyone can consult a doctor.

PHARMACEUTICAL SERVICE

Patients may obtain medicines, appliances and oral contraceptives prescribed under the NHS from any pharmacy whose owner has entered into arrangements with the HA to provide this service; the number of these pharmacies in England and Wales in March 1998 was about 10,500. There are also some appliance suppliers who only provide special appliances. In rural areas, where access to a pharmacy may be difficult, patients may be able to obtain medicines, etc., from their doctor.

Except for contraceptives (for which there is no charge), a charge of £5.90 is payable for each item supplied unless the patient is exempt and the declaration on the back of the prescription form is completed. Prepayment certificates (£30.80 valid for four months, £84.60 valid for a year) may be purchased by those patients not entitled to exemption who require frequent prescriptions.

The following people are exempt from prescription charges:
- children under 16
- full-time students under 19
- men and women aged 60 and over
- pregnant women who hold an exemption certificate
- women who have had a baby in the last 12 months and who hold an exemption certificate
- people suffering from certain medical conditions who hold an exemption certificate
- people who receive income support, full working families' tax credit or credit reduced by up to £70, full disabled person's tax credit or credit reduced by up to £70 or income-based jobseeker's allowance, and their partners
- people who are named on an HC2 certificate issued by the Health Benefits Division
- war pensioners (for their accepted disablements)

Booklet HC11, available from main post offices and local social security offices, gives further details.

The number of prescriptions dispensed in the community in 1998 was:

England	513,200,000
Wales	46,659,000
Scotland	35,670,000
Northern Ireland	22,171,000

DENTAL SERVICE

Dentists, like doctors, may take part in the NHS and also have private patients. About 17,000 dentists in England provide NHS general dental services. They are responsible to the HAs in whose areas they provide services.

Patients may go to any dentist who is taking part in the NHS and is willing to accept them. Patients are required to pay 80 per cent of the cost of NHS dental treatment. Since 1 April 1999 the maximum charge for a course of treatment has been £348. There is no charge for arrest of bleeding or repairs to dentures; home visits by the dentist or re-opening a surgery in an emergency are charged for as treatment given in the normal way. The following people are exempt from dental charges or have charges remitted:
- people under 18
- full-time students under 19
- women who were pregnant when accepted for treatment
- women who have had a child in the previous 12 months

– people who receive income support, full working families' tax credit or credit reduced by up to £70, full disabled person's tax credit or credit reduced by up to £70, or income-based jobseeker's allowance, and their partners
– people who are named on an HC2 certificate issued by the Health Benefits Division
Booklet HC11, available from main post offices and local social security offices, gives further details.

General Dental Service 1998–9 (England)

Number of dentists	17,319
Number of patients registered	
Adults	16,800,000
Children	6,900,000
Number of courses of treatment	
Adults	26,200,000
Expenditure (£ million)	
Gross expenditure	1,400
Paid by patients	400
Paid out of public funds	1,000

Source: NHS Executive

General Ophthalmic Services

General Ophthalmic Services are administered by HAs. Testing of sight may be carried out by any ophthalmic medical practitioner or ophthalmic optician (optometrist). The optician must give the prescription to the patient, who can take this to any supplier of glasses to have them dispensed. Only registered opticians can supply glasses to children and to people registered as blind or partially sighted.

The NHS sight test costs £14.57. Those on a low income may qualify for help with the cost. The test is available free to:
– people aged 60 or over
– children under 16*
– full-time students under 19*
– people who receive income support, income-based jobseeker's allowance, full working families' tax credit or credit reduced by up to £70, full disabled person's tax credit or credit reduced by up to £70, and their partners*
– people who are named on an HC2 certificate issued by the Health Benefits Division*
– people prescribed complex lenses*
– people registered as blind or partially sighted
– diagnosed diabetic and glaucoma patients
– people advised by an ophthalmologist that they are at risk of glaucoma

The categories indicated by * above are automatically entitled to help with the purchase of glasses under an NHS voucher scheme, as are people whose spectacles are lost or damaged as a result of illness. Booklet HC11, available from main post offices and local social security offices, gives further details.

Diagnosis and specialist treatment of eye conditions, and the provision of special glasses, are available through the Hospital Eye Service.

Community Child Health Services

Pre-school services at GP surgeries or child health clinics provide regular monitoring of children's physical, mental and emotional health and development, and advice to parents on their children's health and welfare.

The School Health Service provides for the medical and dental examination of schoolchildren, and advises the local education authority, the school, the parents and the pupil of any health factors which may require special consideration during the pupil's school life. GPs are increasingly undertaking child health monitoring in order to improve the preventive health care of children.

Health Action Zones

Health Action Zones aim to improve health services and tackle health inequalities in certain areas, working with the primary care groups in their area. The first 11 zones were set up in April 1998 and by April 1999 a total of 26 were in existence. Each zone receives funding for seven years.

Hospitals and Other Services

Hospital, medical, dental, nursing, ophthalmic and ambulance services are provided by the NHS to meet all reasonable requirements. Facilities for the care of expectant and nursing mothers and young children, and other services required for the diagnosis and treatment of illness, are also provided. Rehabilitation services (occupational therapy, physiotherapy and speech therapy) may also be provided, and surgical and medical appliances are supplied where appropriate. Specialists and consultants who work in NHS hospitals can also engage in private practice, including the treatment of their private patients in NHS hospitals.

Private Finance Initiative

The Private Finance Initiative (PFI) was launched in 1992, and involves the private sector in designing, building, financing and operating new hospitals, which are then leased to the NHS. In July 1997 a new programme of hospital building under the PFI was announced by the Government.

Charges

Certain hospitals have accommodation in single rooms or small wards which, if not required for patients who need privacy for medical reasons, may be made available to patients who desire it as an amenity for a small charge. These patients are still NHS patients and are treated as such.

In a number of hospitals, accommodation is available for the treatment of private in-patients who undertake to pay the full costs of hospital accommodation and services and (usually) separate medical fees to a specialist as well. The amount of the medical fees is a matter for agreement between doctor and patient. Hospital charges for private in-patients are set locally at a commercial rate.

There is no charge for drugs supplied to NHS hospital in-patients, but out-patients pay £5.90 an item unless they are exempt. With certain exceptions, hospital out-patients have to pay fixed charges for dentures, contact lenses and certain appliances. Glasses may be obtained either from the hospital or an optician, and the charge will be related to the type of lens prescribed and the choice of frame.

Ambulance Service

The NHS provides emergency ambulance services free of charge via the 999 emergency telephone service. There are 37 ambulance services in the UK. Helicopter ambulances are used in some areas where access may be difficult or heavy traffic could hinder road progress, and an air ambulance service is available throughout Scotland. Non-emergency ambulance services are provided free of charge to patients who are deemed to require them on medical grounds.

In 1998–9 in England about 3,800,000 emergency calls were made to the ambulance service, an increase of 7.6 per cent on the previous year. There were about 2,700,000 emergency patient journeys. The Patients' Charter requires emergency ambulances to respond to 95 per cent of calls within 14 minutes in urban areas and 19 minutes in rural areas, and to reach 50 per cent of cases within eight minutes. In 1998–9 10 ambulance services met the Charter standard for responding to life-threatening emergencies and seven met the standard for non-life threatening emegencies. Of the 21 ambulance services whose calls are not prioritized, 10 achieved the Charter Standard.

NHS DIRECT

NHS Direct is a telephone service staffed by nurses which gives patients advice on how to look after themselves as well as directing them to the appropriate part of the NHS for treatment if necessary. The Government intends that the service will cover all parts of England by the end of 2000.

BLOOD SERVICES

There are four national bodies which co-ordinate the blood donor programme in each constituent country of the UK. About two million donations of blood are given each year; donors give blood at local centres on a voluntary basis.
NATIONAL BLOOD AUTHORITY, Oak House, Reeds Crescent, Watford, Herts WD1 1QH. Tel: 01923-486800. *Chairman*, M. Fogden, CB; *Chief Executive*, M. Gorham
SCOTTISH NATIONAL BLOOD TRANSFUSION SERVICE, 21 Ellens Glen Road, Edinburgh EH17 7QT. Tel: 0131-536 5701. *National Director*, A. McMillan-Douglas
WELSH BLOOD SERVICE, Ely Valley Road, Talbot Green, Pontyclun CF72 9WB. Tel: 01443-622000. *Director*, Dr F. G. Williams
NORTHERN IRELAND BLOOD TRANSFUSION SERVICE, Belfast City Hospital Complex, Lisburn Road, Belfast BT9 7TS. Tel: 01232-321414

HOSPICES

Hospice or palliative care may be available for patients with life-threatening illnesses. It may be provided at the patient's home or in a voluntary or NHS hospice or in hospital, and is intended to ensure the best possible quality of life for the patient during their illness, and to provide help and support to both the patient and the patient's family. The National Council for Hospices and Specialist Palliative Care Services co-ordinates NHS and voluntary services in England, Wales and Northern Ireland; the Scottish Partnership Agency for Palliative and Cancer Care performs the same function in Scotland.
NATIONAL COUNCIL FOR HOSPICE AND SPECIALIST PALLIATIVE CARE SERVICES, 7th Floor, 1 Great Cumberland Place, London W1H 7AL. Tel: 0171-723 1639. *Executive Director*, Ms E. S. Richardson
SCOTTISH PARTNERSHIP AGENCY FOR PALLIATIVE AND CANCER CARE, 1A Cambridge Street, Edinburgh EH1 2DY. Tel: 0131-229 0538. *Director*, Mrs M. Stevenson

NUMBER OF BEDS AND PATIENT ACTIVITY 1997

	England*	Wales
In-patients:		
Average daily available beds	199,000	15,200
Average daily occupation of beds	162,000	12,000
Persons waiting for admission at 31 March	†1,158,000	69,900
Day-case admissions	2,958,000	309,700
Ordinary admissions	8,381,000	521,100
Out-patient attendances:		
New patients	11,298,000	693,300
Total attendances	40,864,000	2,643,300
Accident and emergency:		
New patients	12,439,000	826,600
Total attendances	14,080,000	997,900
Ward attendances	1,027,000	n/a

* 1996 figures
† 1997 figure
n/a not available

SCOTLAND

In-patients:	
Average available staffed beds	38,400
Average occupied beds	30,900
Out-patient attendances:	
New patients	2,675,000
Total attendances	6,272,000

Source: The Stationery Office – *Annual Abstract of Statistics 1999* (Crown copyright)

WAITING LISTS

At the end of June 1999 the total number of patients waiting to be admitted to NHS hospitals in England was 1,094,300, a decrease of 15 per cent on the previous year. The number of patients who had been waiting more than one year was 48,700, a decrease of 32 per cent on the previous year. Some 70 per cent of elective patients are treated within three months of being placed on a waiting list. Under the Patient's Charter, patients are guaranteed admission within 18 months of being placed on a waiting list.

NHS CHARTERS

The original Patient's Charter was published in 1991 and came into force in 1992; an expanded version was published in 1995. The Charter sets out the rights of patients in relation to the NHS (i.e. the standards of service which all patients will receive at all times); and patients' reasonable expectations (i.e. the standards of service that the NHS aims to provide, even if they cannot in exceptional circumstances be met). The Charter covers areas such as access to services, personal treatment of patients, the provision of information, registering with a doctor, hospital waiting times, care in hospitals, community services, ambulance waiting times, dental, optical and pharmaceutical services, and maternity services. In England there are separate Patient's Charter leaflets setting out standards in relation to services for children and young people, maternity services, mental health services and blood donation.

The Government is developing a new NHS Charter and a consultation document is expected to be published in autumn 1999. The Charter is due to be issued in April 2000, with local charters in place by 2001. Further information is available free of charge from the national Health Information Service (Tel 0800-665544).

Health authorities and boards, NHS Trusts and GP practices may also have their own local charters setting out the standard of service they aim to provide.

COMPLAINTS

The Patient's Charter includes the right to have any complaint about the service provided by the NHS dealt with quickly, with a full written reply being provided by a relevant chief executive. There are two levels to the NHS complaints procedure: the first level involves resolution of a complaint locally, following a direct approach to the relevant service provider; the second level involves an independent review procedure if the complaint is not resolved locally. As a final resort, patients may approach the Health Service Commissioner or Ombudsman (*see* page 329) (in Northern Ireland, the Commissioner for Complaints if they are dissatisfied with the response of the NHS to a complaint.

In 1997–8 there were 88,757 written complaints about hospital and community health services, of which 65 per cent were resolved locally within the target period of four weeks; two per cent of complainants requested an independent review. There were 38,093 written complaints about family health services and in 1,390 cases the complainant requested an independent review.

NHS TRIBUNALS

The National Health Service Tribunal and the National Health Service Tribunal (Scotland) (*see* page 372) consider representations that the continued inclusion of a doctor, dentist, optician or pharmacist on the list of a health authority or health board would be prejudicial to the efficiency of the service concerned. The Mental Health Review Tribunals (*see* page 371) are responsible for reviewing the cases of patients compulsorily detained under the Mental Health Act 1983.

RECIPROCAL ARRANGEMENTS

Citizens of countries in the European Economic Area (EEA - *see* page 778) are entitled to receive emergency health care either free of charge or for a reduced charge when they are temporarily visiting other member states of the EEA. Form E111, available at post offices, should be obtained before travelling. Non-EEA nationals, or visitors receiving routine, non-emergency care, are normally required to pay for treatment in Britain. There are bilateral agreements with several other countries, including Australia and New Zealand, for the provision of urgent medical treatment either free of charge or for a reduced charge.

Personal Social Services

The Secretary of State for Health is responsible, under the Local Authority Social Services Act 1970, for the provision of social services for elderly people, disabled people, families and children, and those with mental disorders. Personal Social Services are administered by local authorities according to policies and standards set by central government. Each authority has a Director of Social Services and a Social Services Committee responsible for the social services functions placed upon them. Local authorities provide, enable and commission care after assessing the needs of their population. The private and voluntary sectors also play an important role in the delivery of social services, and an estimated six million people in Great Britain provide substantial regular care for a member of their family.

The Community Care reforms introduced in 1993 were intended to enable vulnerable groups to live in the community rather than in residential homes wherever possible, and to offer them as independent a lifestyle as possible.

At 31 March 1997, there were 519,115 places in residential and nursing care homes in England. About 240,000 residents were supported by local authorities (an increase of 12 per cent on the previous year). Of the local authority-supported residents, 24 per cent were in local authority-run homes (down from 29 per cent), 46 per cent were in independent residential care homes (up from 42 per cent) and 27 per cent were in independent nursing homes (the same percentage as in the previous year).

FINANCE

The Personal Social Services programme is financed partly by central government, with decisions on expenditure allocations being made at local authority level.

STAFF

STAFF OF LOCAL AUTHORITY SOCIAL SERVICES DEPARTMENTS 1997 (ENGLAND)
Full-time equivalents

Area office/field work staff	114,900
Residential care staff	65,400
Day care staff	30,800
Central/strategic HQ staff	16,400
Other staff	1,900
Total staff	229,400

Source: Department of Health

ELDERLY PEOPLE

Services for elderly people are designed to enable them to remain living in their own homes for as long as possible. Local authority services include advice, domestic help, meals in the home, alterations to the home to aid mobility, emergency alarm systems, day and/or night attendants, laundry services and the provision of day centres and recreational facilities. Charges may be made for these services. Respite care may also be provided in order to allow carers temporary relief from their responsibilities.

Local authorities and the private sector also provide 'sheltered housing' for elderly people, sometimes with resident wardens.

If an elderly person is admitted to a residential home, charges are made according to a means test; if the person cannot afford to pay, the costs are met by the local authority.

The Royal Commission on Long-Term Care reported in March 1999. Its proposals are being considered by the Government.

DISABLED PEOPLE

Services for disabled people are designed to enable them to remain living in their own homes wherever possible. Local authority services include advice, adaptations to the home, meals in the home, help with personal care, occupational therapy, educational facilities and recreational facilities. Respite care may also be provided in order to allow carers temporary relief from their responsibilities.

Special housing may be available for disabled people who can live independently, and residential accommodation for those who cannot.

FAMILIES AND CHILDREN

Local authorities are required to provide services aimed at safeguarding the welfare of children in need and, wherever possible, allowing them to be brought up by their families. Services include advice, counselling, help in the home and the provision of family centres. Many authorities also provide short-term refuge accommodation for women and children.

DAY CARE

In allocating day-care places to children, local authorities give priority to children with special needs, whether in terms of their health, learning abilities or social needs. They also provide a registration and inspection service in relation to childminders, play groups and private day nurseries in the local authority area. In England in 1997 there were 6,100 day nurseries providing 194,000 places, 98,500 registered child-minders providing 365,000 places, and 15,800 play groups providing 384,000 places.

A national child care strategy is being developed by the Government, under which day care and out-of-school child care facilities will be extended to match more closely the needs of working parents.

CHILD PROTECTION

Children considered to be at risk of physical injury, neglect or sexual abuse are placed on the local authority's child protection register. Local authority social services staff, school nurses, health visitors and other agencies work together to prevent and detect cases of abuse. In England at 31 March 1997 there were 16,400 boys and 15,700 girls on child protection registers. Of these, 38 per cent were at risk of neglect, 34 per cent of physical abuse, 23 per cent of sexual abuse and 16 per cent of emotional abuse.

LOCAL AUTHORITY CARE

Local authorities are required to provide accommodation for children who have no parent or guardian or whose parents or guardians are unable or unwilling to care for them. A family proceedings court may also issue a care order in cases where a child is being neglected or abused, or is not attending school; the court must be satisfied that this would positively contribute to the well-being of the child.

The welfare of children in local authority care must be properly safeguarded. Children may be placed with foster families, who receive payments to cover the expenses of caring for the child or children, or in residential care. Children's homes may be run by the local authority or by the private or voluntary sectors; all homes are subject to inspection procedures. In England at 31 March 1997, 51,600 children were in the care of local authorities. Of these, 65 per cent were placed with foster parents and 5 per cent were placed for adoption.

ADOPTION

Local authorities are required to provide an adoption service, either directly or via approved voluntary societies. In England and Wales in 1996, 6,000 children (3,000 boys and 3,000 girls) were adopted.

PEOPLE WITH LEARNING DISABILITIES

Services for people with learning disabilities (i.e. mental handicap) are designed to enable them to remain living in the community wherever possible. Local authority services include short-term care, support in the home, the provision of day care centres, and help with other activities outside the home. Residential care is provided for the severely or profoundly disabled.

MENTALLY ILL PEOPLE

Under the Care Programme Approach, mentally ill people should be assessed by specialist services and receive a care plan, and a key worker should be appointed for each patient. Regular reviews of the patient's progress should be conducted. Local authorities provide help and advice to mentally ill people and their families, and places in day centres and social centres. Social workers can apply for a mentally disturbed person to be compulsorily detained in hospital. Where appropriate, mentally ill people are provided with accommodation in special hospitals, local authority accommodation, or homes run by private or voluntary organizations. Patients who have been discharged from hospitals may be placed on a supervision register. In July 1998 the Government announced that the system of care for mentally ill people would be replaced. The Mental Health Act 1983 is under review. A Mental Health National Service Framework is due to be published in autumn 1999 and enter into force in spring 2000, introducing national standards of care throughout England. In Scotland a committee has been established to review mental health legislation and will report to the Scottish Parliament in mid-2000.

TOTAL PLACES IN RESIDENTIAL AND NURSING HOMES (ENGLAND) *as at 31 March 1997*

By client group

Elderly people	374,302
Physically/sensorily disabled adults	11,494
Elderly mentally infirm people	39,373
People with mental illness	22,646
People with learning disabilities	50,872
Other people	20,428
All client groups	519,115

Source: Department of Health

LOCAL AUTHORITY-SUPPORTED RESIDENTS IN STAFFED RESIDENTIAL AND NURSING CARE (ENGLAND) *as at 31 March 1997*

All staffed homes	236,335
Local authority	58,747
Independent residential care	111,530
Independent nursing care	66,058
Elderly people	180,471
Physically/sensorily disabled adults	8,628
People with mental health problems	17,271
People with learning disabilities	26,872
Other people	3,093

Source: The Stationery Office – *Health and Personal Social Services Statistics for England 1998* (Crown copyright)

LOCAL AUTHORITY PERSONAL SOCIAL SERVICES GROSS EXPENDITURE BY CLIENT GROUP 1996–7 (ENGLAND)
£ million

	Elderly	Children	Learning disability	Adults	Mental health	HQ costs	Total
HQ costs	—	—	—	—	—	123	123
Area officers/seniormanagers	95	143	21	23	25	—	308
Care management/care assessment	284	321	58	74	86	—	823
Residential care	2,685	657	665	181	185	—	4,373
Non-residential care	1,466	907	451	357	153	—	3,333
Field social work	44	113	14	16	19	—	207
Other	—	—	—	96	—	—	96
TOTAL	4,575	2,142	1,208	748	468	123	9,263

Source: The Stationery Office – *Health and Personal Social Services Statistics for England 1998* (Crown copyright)

National Insurance and Related Cash Benefits

NB All leaflets referred to in this section can be obtained from local social security offices unless an alternative source is given

The state insurance and assistance schemes, comprising schemes of national insurance and industrial injuries insurance, national assistance, and non-contributory old age pensions, came into force from 5 July 1948. The Ministry of Social Security Act 1966 replaced national assistance and non-contributory old age pensions with a scheme of non-contributory benefits. These and subsequent measures relating to social security provision in Great Britain were consolidated by the Social Security Act 1975, the Social Security (Consequential Provisions) Act 1975, and the Industrial Injuries and Diseases (Old Cases) Act 1975. Corresponding measures were passed for Northern Ireland. The Social Security Pensions Act 1975 introduced a new state pensions scheme in 1978, and the graduated pension scheme 1961 to 1975 has been wound up, existing rights being preserved. Under the Pensions Act 1995 the age of retirement is to be 65 for both men and women, this being phased in between 2010 and 6 April 2020. The Pensioners' Payments and Social Security Act 1979 provided for a Christmas bonus for pensioners in 1979 and in succeeding years. The Child Benefit Act 1975 replaced family allowances (introduced 1946) with child benefit and one-parent benefit. Some of this legislation has been superseded by the provisions of the Social Security Acts 1969 to 1992. The Government is reforming the social security system. The Welfare Reform and Pensions Bill was published in February 1999 and is expected to become law in autumn 1999. If it is enacted, changes in benefits will come into effect from April 2001. Details of proposed changes, where known, are included.

NATIONAL INSURANCE SCHEME

The National Insurance (NI) scheme operates under the Social Security Contributions and Benefits Act 1992 and the Social Security Administration Act 1992, and orders and regulations made thereunder. The scheme is financed by contributions payable by earners, employers and others (*see* below) and by a Treasury grant. Money collected under the scheme is used to finance the National Insurance Fund (from which contributory benefits are paid) and to contribute to the cost of the National Health Service.

NATIONAL INSURANCE FUND

Approximate receipts and payments of the National Insurance Fund for the year ended 31 March 1999 were:

Receipts	£'000
Balance, 1 April 1998 (provisional)	9,608,000
Contributions under the Social Security Acts (net of SSP and SMP)	48,934,000
Treasury grant	0
Compensation from Consolidated Fund for SSP and SMP recoveries	558,000
Compensation from Consolidated Fund for contribution holidays for employers taking on formerly long-term unemployed	3,000
Income from investments	675,000
State scheme premiums	88,000
Other receipts	115,000
	50,373,000

Payments	£'000
Benefits	44,337,000
Personal pensions contracted-out rebates	1,937,000
Age-related rebates for contracted-out money purchase schemes	80,000
Transfers to Northern Ireland	315,000
Administration	993,000
Redundancy payments (net)	106,000
Other payments	20,000
Balance, 31 March 1999	12,253,000
	60,041,000

CONTRIBUTIONS

There are six classes of NI contributions:

Class 1   paid by employees and their employers

Class 1A   paid by employers who provide employees with cars/fuel for private use

Class 1B   paid by employers in value of any items included on a PAYE settlement with the Inland Revenue

Class 2   paid by self-employed people

Class 3   voluntary contributions paid to protect entitlement to certain benefits

Class 4   paid by the self-employed on their taxable profits over a set limit

The lower and upper earnings limits and the percentage rates referred to below apply from 6 April 1999 to 5 April 2000.

CLASS 1

Class 1 contributions are paid where a person:
– is an employed earner (employee) or office holder (e.g. company director)
– is 16 or over and under state pension age
– earns at or above the lower earning limit of £66.00 per week (including overtime pay, bonus, commission, etc.), without deduction of superannuation contributions)

Class 1 contributions are made up of primary and secondary contributions. Primary contributions are those paid by the employee and these are deducted from earnings by the employer. Primary contributions are not paid on earnings below the lower earnings limit. They are payable at the rate of 10 per cent on earnings between the lower earnings limit and the upper earnings limit of £500.00 per week (8.4 per cent for contracted-out employment, *see* page 488).

Some married women or widows pay a reduced rate of 3.85 per cent on earnings between the lower and upper earnings limits. It is no longer possible to elect to pay the reduced rate but those who had reduced liability before 12 May 1977 may retain it so long as certain conditions are met. *See* leaflet CA09 (widows) or leaflet CA13 (married women).

Secondary contributions are paid by employers of employed earners at the rate of 12.2 per cent on all earnings at or above the secondary earnings threshold of £83.00 per week. Employers operating contracted-out salary related schemes (*see* page 488) pay reduced contributions of 9.2 per cent; those with contracted-out money-purchase schemes (*see* page 488) pay 11.6 per cent. There is no upper earnings limit for employers' contributions. The contracted-out rate applies only to that portion of earnings between the lower and upper earnings limits. Employers' contributions below and above those respective limits are assessed at the appropriate not contracted-out rate.

CLASS 2

Class 2 contributions are paid where a person is self-employed and is 16 or over and under state pension age. Contributions are paid at a flat rate of £6.55 per week regardless of the amount earned. However, those with earnings of less than £3,770 a year can apply for Small Earnings Exception, i.e. exemption from liability to pay Class 2 contributions. Those granted exemption from Class 2 contributions may pay Class 2 or Class 3 contributions voluntarily. Self-employed earners (whether or not they pay Class 2 contributions) may also be liable to pay Class 4 contributions based on profits. There are special rules for those who are concurrently employed and self-employed.

Married women and widows can no longer choose not to pay Class 2 contributions but those who elected not to pay Class 2 contributions before 12 May 1977 may retain the right so long as certain conditions are met.

Class 2 contributions are collected by the National Insurance Contributions Office (NICO), an executive agency of the Inland Revenue, by direct debit or quarterly bills. *See* leaflets CA03 and CA02.

Class 3

Class 3 contributions are voluntary flat-rate contributions of £6.45 per week payable by persons over the age of 16 who would otherwise be unable to qualify for retirement pension and certain other benefits because they have an insufficient record of Class 1 or Class 2 contributions. This may include those who are not working, those not liable for Class 1 or Class 2 contributions or those excepted from Class 2 contributions. Married women and widows who on or before 11 May 1977 elected not to pay Class 1 (full rate) or Class 2 contributions cannot pay Class 3 contributions while they retain this right.

Class 3 contributions are collected by the NICO by quarterly bills or direct debit. *See* leaflet CA08.

Class 4

Self-employed people whose profits and gains are over £7,530 a year pay Class 4 contributions in addition to Class 2 contributions. This applies to self-employed earners over 16 and under the state pension age. Class 4 contributions are calculated at 6 per cent of annual profits or gains between £7,530 and £26,000. The maximum Class 4 contribution payable on £26,000 or more is £1,108.20.

Class 4 contributions are assessed and collected by the Inland Revenue together with Schedule D tax. It is possible, in some circumstances, to apply for exceptions from liability to pay Class 4 contributions or to have the amount of contribution reduced (where Class 1 contributions are payable on earnings assessed for Class 4 contributions). *See* leaflet CA03.

PENSIONS

The Social Security Pensions Act came into force in 1978. It aimed to:
- reduce reliance on means-tested benefit in old age, widowhood and chronic ill-health
- ensure that occupational pension schemes which are contracted out of the state scheme fulfil the conditions of a good scheme
- ensure that pensions are adequately protected against inflation
- ensure that men and women are treated equally in state and occupational schemes

Legislation and regulations introduced since 1978 go further towards fulfilling these aims and more changes came into effect in April 1997 (*see* below). One of the changes is to equalize the state pension age for men (currently 65 years) and women (currently 60 years) from 6 April 2020. The change will be phased in over the ten

years leading up to 6 April 2020. As a result the state pension age is as follows:
- the pension age for men remains at 65
- the pension age for women born on or before 5 April 1950 remains at 60
- the pension age for women born on or after 6 April 1955 is now 65
- for women born after 5 April 1950 and before 6 April 1955, the pension age is 60 plus one month for every month, or part of a month, that their date of birth fell after 5 April 1950.

The Welfare Reform and Pensions Bill provides for the sharing of pensions between divorcing couples.

State Pension Scheme

The state pension scheme consists of the basic flat-rate pension and the state earnings-related pension scheme (SERPS), also known as additional pension.

The amount of basic pension paid is dependent on the number of 'qualifying years' a person has in their 'working life'. A 'qualifying year' is a tax year in which a person pays Class 1 (at the standard rate), 2 or 3 NI contributions for the whole year (*see* above). Those in receipt of invalid care allowance, disabled person's tax credit, jobseeker's allowance, incapacity benefit, severe disablement allowance or approved training have contributions credited to them for each week they receive benefit or fulfil certain other conditions. For those reaching pensionable age on or after 6 April 1999, a Class 3 credit of earnings will be awarded for each week from 6 April 1995 that family credit or, subsequently, working families tax credit, has been received. 'Working life' is counted from the start of the tax year in which a person reaches 16 to the end of the tax year before the one in which they reach pensionable age: for men this is normally 49 years and for women this varies between 44 and 49 years because the pension ages vary (*see* above). To get the full rate (100 per cent) basic pension a person must have qualifying years for about 90 per cent of their working life. To get the minimum basic pension (25 per cent) a person will need ten or eleven qualifying years. Married women who are not entitled to a pension on their own contributions may get a pension on their husband's contributions. It is possible for people who are unable to work because they care for children or a sick or disabled person at home to reduce the number of qualifying years required. This is called home responsibilities protection (HRP) and can be given for any tax year since April 1978; the number of years for which HRP is given is deducted from the number of qualifying years needed.

The amount of SERPS or additional pension paid depends on the amount of earnings a person has between the lower and upper earnings limits (*see* page 486) for each complete tax year between 6 April 1978 (when the scheme started) and the tax year before they reach state pension age. The right to additional pension does not depend on the person's right to basic pension. The amount of additional pension paid also depends on when a person reaches retirement; changes being phased in from 6 April 1999 mean that pensions will be calculated differently from that date. Women widowed before 6 April 2000 will inherit all their late husband's additional pension and women widowed on or after this date will inherit half of the husband's additional pension.

There are four categories of state pension provided under the Social Security Contributions and Benefits Act 1992:
- Category A, a contributory pension made up of basic and additional elements, payable to those of pensionable age who satisfy the entitlement conditions described above (*see* pages 490–1)

– Category B, a contributory pension made up of basic and additional elements, payable to married women and widows and based on their husband's contributions. This category of pension is to be extended to men whose wives were born after 5 April 1950 from 6 April 2010 (*see* pages 490–1)
– Category C, a non-contributory pension payable to those who reached pensionable age before 5 July 1948 (*see* page 492)
– Category D, a non-contributory pension for those over 80 (*see* page 492)

Graduated retirement benefit is also available to those who paid graduated NI contributions into the scheme when it existed between April 1961 and April 1975.

It is possible to find out how much basic and additional pension a person might receive by filling in form BR19, available from local social security offices or by telephoning 0191-225 5240.

The Welfare Reform and Pensions Bill proposes changes to pensions. SERPS will be replaced by a second state pension from 2002, subject to the legislation being passed. This will initially be earnings-related, but will subsequently be paid at a flat rate, targeted towards low earners. It will provide a guaranteed minimum income. Under certain circumstances, people not working (such as disabled people and those caring for children or sick relatives) will receive credits into the scheme as though they had earned £9,000 per year. As with SERPS, a person will be entitled to contract out into an occupational, personal or new stakeholder pension scheme. Subject to the passage of the Welfare Reform Bill, stakeholder pensions will be available from 2001. They will be targeted at those earning between £9,000 and £18,500 who have no occupational or appropriate personal scheme to join. Higher earners will also be able to join a stakeholder scheme if they wish.

CONTRACTED-OUT OCCUPATIONAL AND PERSONAL PENSION SCHEMES

Under the Pensions Schemes Act 1993, an employer can contract out of SERPS those employees who are members of an occupational scheme, so long as the occupational scheme satisfies certain conditions. The occupational pension took the place of the additional pension from April 1997 (previously it took the place of part of the additional pension); the state remains responsible for the flat rate state basic pension. Until April 1997 members of contracted-out occupational and personal pension schemes accrued additional pension in the same way as someone who is not contracted-out but the rate payable was reduced by contracted-out deductions. Since 5 April 1997, it has not been possible to accrue any SERPS while being a member of a contracted-out occupational or personal pension scheme. Members are still entitled to those rights earned before April 1997. Since April 1997 there have been age-related NI contribution rebates for people who leave SERPS and become members of either a COMP (*see* below) or an appropriate personal pension scheme; these will be lower for younger people and higher for older people.

There are three types of contracted-out occupational schemes.

Contracted-Out Salary-Related Scheme (COSR)

– this scheme must provide a pension related to earnings
– the pension provided must not be less than a person's guaranteed minimum pension (GMP), i.e. worth about the same as the additional pension provided by the state scheme had the member remained in the State scheme

– any notional additional pension earned from 6 April 1978 to 5 April 1997 will be reduced by the amount of GMP earned during that period (the contracted-out deduction)
– from 6 April 1997 these schemes no longer provide a GMP but do have to satisfy a new scheme-based test, certified by an actuary, before a contracting-out certificate can be issued

Contracted-Out Money Purchase Scheme (COMP)

– this scheme must provide a pension based on the value of the fund built up, i.e. the money paid in, along with returns from investment
– part of the pension, known as protected rights, takes the place of the additional pension. A contracted-out deduction, which may be more or less than the pension provided by the scheme, will be made from any additional pension earned from 6 April 1987 to 5 April 1997

In contracted-out occupational pension schemes, both the employee and employer pay lower NI contribution rates in recognition that SERPS will not be paid.

Contracted-Out Mixed Benefit Scheme (COMBS)

A mixed benefit scheme has two active sections, one salary-related and the other money purchase. Scheme rules set out which section individual employees may join and the circumstances (if any) in which members may move between sections. Each section must satisfy the respective contracting-out conditions for COSRs and COMPs.

Appropriate Personal Pension Schemes

The option of a personal pension scheme is open to all employees, even if their employer has an occupational pension scheme. A personal pension scheme must provide a pension based on the value of the fund built up, i.e. the money paid in, along with returns from investment. Part of the pension, known as protected rights, takes the place of the additional pension. A contracted-out deduction, which may be more or less than the pension provided by the scheme, will be made from any additional pension earned from 6 April 1987 to 5 April 1997.

Employees who are members of a personal pension plan and their employers pay NI contributions at the full rate and the Inland Revenue pays the difference between the full rate and the contracted-out rate into the personal pension scheme.

A Pensions Ombudsman deals with complaints about maladministration of pensions schemes. The Occupational Pensions Board, which supervised contracting-out and approved personal pension schemes, was abolished in April 1997 and replaced by the Occupational Pensions Regulatory Authority. *See* leaflet NP46.

BENEFITS

Leaflets relating to the various benefits and contribution conditions for different benefits are available from local social security offices; leaflets NI196 *Social Security Benefit Rates*, FB2 *Which Benefit?* and MG1 *A Guide to Benefits* are general guides to benefits, benefit rates and contributions.

The benefits payable under the Social Security Acts are:

CONTRIBUTORY BENEFITS
Jobseeker's allowance (contribution-based)
Incapacity benefit
Maternity allowance
Widow's benefit (comprising widow's payment, widowed mother's allowance and widow's pension)
Retirement pensions, categories A and B

NON-CONTRIBUTORY BENEFITS AND TAX CREDITS
Child benefit
Guardian's allowance
Jobseeker's allowance (income-based)
Invalid care allowance
Severe disablement allowance
Attendance allowance
Disability living allowance
Disabled person's tax credit
Retirement pensions, categories C and D
Income support
Working families tax credit
Housing benefit
Council tax benefit
Social fund

BENEFITS FOR INDUSTRIAL INJURIES AND
DISABLEMENT

OTHER
Statutory sick pay
Statutory maternity pay

TAX CREDITS

Under the Tax Credits Act 1999, Family Credit and Disability Working Allowance (both non-contributory benefits) were replaced by Working Families Tax Credit and Disabled Person's Tax Credit from 5 October 1999. . Both of these are administered by the Inland Revenue. The first payments will be made from April 2000. People receiving Family Credit or Disability Working Allowance on 5 October 1999 will continue to receive their benefits until the award expires, when they will be able to change to the new tax credits. Until March 2000 the tax credits will be paid directly to the applicant by the Inland Revenue. From April 2000 employees will receive the credits from their employer along with their wages or salary. Self-employed applicants will be paid direct by the Inland Revenue. Further information and application forms are available from Inland Revenue Tax Enquiry Centres, Benefits Agency offices, Jobcentres, post offices and Citizens' Advice Bureaux.

WORKING FAMILIES TAX CREDIT

Working Families Tax Credit is a system of tax credits paid to couples (married or unmarried) or lone parents who have at least one child living with them and where at least one partner works at least 16 hours per week. The credit is not payable if any savings exceed £8,000.

Working Families Tax Credit will usually be paid at the same rate for 26 weeks. There are four elements:
- a basic credit of £52.30 per family per week
- a credit of £11.05 per week where one earner works at least 30 hours per week
- a credit for each child at the rate of £19.85 per week from birth (rising by £1.10 plus inflation from April 2000), £20.90 from the September following their 11th birthday and £25.95 from the September following their 16th birthday up to the day before their 19th birthday
- a childcare credit (in certain circumstances) of up to 70 per cent of eligible childcare costs up to a maximum of £100 per week for one child and £150 per week for two or more children

If net income is below £90 per week, the maximum tax credit is payable. If net income exceeds £90 per week, the total tax credit is reduced by 55p for each £1.00 above £90.

DISABLED PERSON'S TAX CREDIT

Disabled Person's Tax Credit is a system of tax credits for people who are working at least 16 hours per week but

have an illness or disability which puts them at a disadvantage in getting a job. To qualify, a person must have one of the 'qualifying benefits' or have had them up to 182 days before applying. The credit is not payable if any savings exceed £16,000.

Disabled Person's Tax Credit will usually be paid at the same rate for 26 weeks. There are five elements:
- a basic credit of £54.30 per week for a single person or £83.55 for a couple
- a credit of £11.05 per week where one applicant works at least 30 hours per week
- a credit for each child at the rate of £19.85 from birth (rising by £1.10 plus inflation from April 2000), £20.90 from the September following their 11th birthday and £25.95 from the September following their 16th birthday up to the day before their 19th birthday
- a disabled child's tax credit of £21.90 per week
- a childcare credit (in certain circumstances) of up to 70 per cent of eligible childcare costs up to a maximum of £100 per week for one child and £150 per week for two or more children

If net income is below £70 per week for a single person or £90 per week for a couple or lone parent, the maximum tax credit is payable. If net income exceeds these thresholds, the total tax credit is reduced by 55p for each £1.00 above the threshold.

CONTRIBUTORY BENEFITS

Entitlement to contributory benefits depends on contribution conditions being satisfied either by the claimant or by some other person (depending on the kind of benefit). The class or classes of contribution which for this purpose are relevant to each benefit are:

Jobseeker's allowance (contribution-based)	Class 1
Incapacity benefit	Class 1 or 2
Maternity allowance	Class 1 or 2
Widow's benefits	Class 1, 2 or 3
Retirement pensions, categories A and B	Class 1, 2 or 3

The system of contribution conditions relates to yearly levels of earnings on which contributions have been paid.

JOBSEEKER'S ALLOWANCE

Jobseeker's allowance (JSA) replaced unemployment benefit and income support for unemployed people under pension age from 7 October 1996. There are two routes of entitlement. Contribution-based JSA is paid as a personal rate (i.e. additional benefit for dependants is not paid) to those who have made sufficient NI contributions in two particular tax years. Savings and partner's earnings are not taken into account and payment can be made for up to six months. Those who do not qualify for contribution-based JSA, those who have exhausted their entitlement to contribution-based JSA or those for whom contribution-based JSA provides insufficient income may qualify for income-based JSA. The amount paid depends on age and number of dependants and income and savings are taken into account. Income-based JSA may comprise three parts: a personal allowance for the jobseeker and his/her partner and one for each child or young person for whom they are responsible; premiums for groups of people with special needs; and housing costs. This is payable for the claimant and their dependants for as long as they satisfy the rules. Rates of jobseeker's allowance correspond to income support rates.

Claims for this benefit are made through Employment Service Jobcentres. A person wishing to claim jobseeker's allowance must be unemployed, capable of work and available for any work which they can reasonably be expected to do, usually for at least 40 hours per week.

They must agree and sign a 'jobseeker's agreement', which will set out each claimant's plans to find work, and must actively seek work. If they refuse work or training their benefit may be suspended for between two and six weeks.

A person will be disqualified from jobseeker's allowance if they have left a job voluntarily or through misconduct, if they refuse to take up an offer of employment or if they fail to attend a training scheme or employment programme. In these circumstances, it may be possible to receive hardship payments, particularly where the claimant or their family is vulnerable, e.g. if sick or pregnant, or for those with children or caring responsibilities. *See* leaflet JSAL5.

INCAPACITY BENEFIT

Incapacity benefit is available to those who are incapable of work but cannot get statutory sick pay from their employer. It is not payable to those over state pension age. However, people who are already in receipt of short-term incapacity benefit when they reach state pension age may continue to receive this benefit for up to 52 weeks. The Welfare Reform and Pensions Bill proposes restricting eligibility for incapacity benefit to people who have paid National Insurance contributions in the previous two years. The Bill also provides for the reduction of the amount of incapacity benefit payable where a claimant receives more than a specified amount of occupational or personal pension. Severely disabled people aged between 16 and 19 should receive incapacity benefit without meeting the national insurance contribution conditions under the Government's proposals. There are three rates of incapacity benefit:
- short-term lower rate for the first 28 weeks of sickness
- short-term higher rate from weeks 29 to 52
- long-term rate after week 52

The terminally ill and those entitled to the highest rate care component of disability living allowance are paid the long-term rate after 28 weeks. Incapacity benefit is taxable after 28 weeks.

Two rates of age addition are paid with long-term benefit based on the claimant's age when incapacity started. The higher rate is payable where incapacity for work commenced before the age of 35; and the lower rate where incapacity commenced before the age of 45. Increases for dependants are also payable with short and long-term incapacity benefit.

There are two medical tests of incapacity: the 'own occupation' test and the 'all work' test. Those who worked before becoming incapable of working will be assessed, for the first 28 weeks of incapacity, on their ability to do their own job. After 28 weeks (or from the start of incapacity for those who were not working) claimants are assessed on their ability to carry out a range of work-related activities. The 'all work' test applies to most former sickness and invalidity benefit claimants. The Government plans to replace the 'all work' test with a new 'personal capability assessment.' *See* leaflets IB202 and SD1.

MATERNITY ALLOWANCE

The maternity allowance (MA) scheme covers women who are self-employed or otherwise do not qualify for statutory maternity pay (*see* page 495). In order to qualify, the woman must have been working and paying standard rate NI contributions for at least 26 weeks in the 66-week period which ends with the week before the week in which the baby is due. A woman can choose to start receiving MA between the beginning of the 11th week before the week in which the baby is due and the Sunday after the baby is born, depending on when she stops working. MA is paid

for a period of up to 18 weeks. MA is only paid while the woman is not working. *See* leaflet NI17A.

WIDOW'S BENEFITS

Only the late husband's contributions of any class count for widow's benefit in any of its three forms:

Widow's payment – may be received by a woman who at her husband's death is under 60, or whose husband was not entitled to a Category A retirement pension when he died. It is a single tax-free lump sum payable immediately the woman becomes a widow

Widowed mother's allowance – a taxable benefit payable to a widow if she is entitled or treated as entitled to child benefit, or if she is expecting her husband's baby

Widow's pension – a widow may receive this pension if aged 45 or over at the time of her husband's death (40 or over if widowed before 11 April 1988) or when her widowed mother's allowance ends. If aged 55 or over (50 or over if widowed before 11 April 1988) she will receive the full widow's pension rate

It is not possible to receive widowed mother's allowance and widow's pension at the same time, and widow's benefit in any form ceases upon remarriage or during a period in which a widow lives with a man as his wife. Different rules and conditions (other than those mentioned) apply to women widowed before 11 April 1988. The Welfare Reform and Pensions Bill proposes the replacement of widow's payment with a £2,000 bereavement payment and the introduction of widowed parent's allowance and bereavement allowance. All of the new benefits will be payable to both widowers and widows who are eligible. See leaflet NP45.

RETIREMENT PENSION: CATEGORIES A AND B

A Category A pension is payable for life to men and women who reach state pension age and who satisfy the contributions conditions (*see* page 486). A Category B pension is payable for life to a woman and is based on her husband's contributions. It becomes payable only when the husband has claimed his pension and the woman has reached state pension age. It is also payable on widowhood after 60 regardless of whether the late husband had qualified for his pension. There are special rules for those who are widowed before reaching pensionable age.

A person may defer claiming their pension for five years after state pension age. In doing so they may earn increments which will increase the weekly amount paid when they claim their pension. If a married man defers his Category A pension, his wife cannot claim a Category B pension on his contributions but she may earn increments on her pension during this time. A woman can defer her Category B pension, and earn increments, even if her husband is claiming his Category A pension.

The basic state pension is £66.75 per week plus any additional (earnings-related) pension the person may be entitled to (*see* page 486). An increase of £39.95 is paid for an adult dependant, providing the dependant's earnings do not exceed the rate of jobseeker's allowance for a single person (*see* below). It is also possible to get an increase of Category A and B pensions for a child or children. An age addition of 25p per week is payable if a retirement pensioner is aged 80 or over.

Since 1989 pensioners have been allowed to have unlimited earnings without affecting their retirement pension. Income support is payable on top of a pension where a pension does not give the person enough to live on and to those who are entitled to retirement pension but who have not claimed it. Pensioners may also be entitled to housing and council tax benefits.

GRADUATED RETIREMENT BENEFIT

Graduated NI contributions were first payable from 1961 and were calculated as a percentage of earnings between certain bands. They were discontinued in 1975. Any graduated pension which an employed person over 18 and under 70 (65 for a woman) had earned by paying graduated contributions will be paid when the contributor claims retirement pension or at 70 (65 for a woman), in addition to any retirement pension for which he or she qualifies. A wife can get a graduated pension in return for her own graduated contributions, but not for her husband's.

Graduated retirement benefit is at a weekly rate for each 'unit' of graduated contributions paid by the employee (half a unit or more counts as a whole unit); the rate varies from person to person. A unit of graduated pension can be calculated by adding together all graduated contributions and dividing by 7.5 (men) or 9.0 (women). If a person defers making a claim beyond 65 (60 for a woman), entitlement may be increased by one seventh of a penny per £1 of its weekly rate for each complete week of deferred retirement, as long as the retirement is deferred for a minimum of seven weeks.

WEEKLY RATES OF BENEFIT
from April 1999

Jobseeker's allowance (contribution-based)

Person under 18	£30.30
Person aged 18–24	39.85
Person over 25	50.35

Short-term incapacity benefit

Person under pension age – lower rate	48.80
*Person under pension age – higher rate	57.70
Increase for adult dependant	31.15
*Person over pension age	62.05
Increase for adult dependant	38.40

*Long-term incapacity benefit

Person (under or over pension age)	64.70
Increase for adult dependant	39.95
Age addition – lower rate	6.80
Age addition – higher rate	13.60

Invalidity allowance: maximum amount payable

Higher rate	13.60
Middle rate	8.60
Lower rate	4.30

Maternity allowance

Employed	57.70
Self-employed or unemployed	50.10

Widow's benefits

Widow's payment (lump sum)	1,000.00*
†Widowed mother's allowance	66.75
†Widow's pension	66.75

*Retirement pension: categories A and B

Single person	66.75
Increase for wife/other adult dependant	39.95

*These benefits attract an increase for each dependent child (in addition to child benefit) of £9.90 for the first or only child and £11.35 for each subsequent child

†To rise to £2,000 and be extended to widowers once Welfare Reform and Pensions Bill becomes law

NON-CONTRIBUTORY BENEFITS

These benefits are paid from general taxation and are not dependent on NI contributions. Unless otherwise stated, a benefit is tax-free and is not means tested.

CHILD BENEFIT

Child benefit is payable for virtually all children aged under 16, and for those aged 16 to 18 who are studying full-time up to and including A-level or equivalent standard. It is also payable for a short period if the child has left school recently and is registered for work or work-based training for young people at a careers office.

A higher rate of benefit (child benefit (lone parent)) may be paid to a person who is responsible for bringing up one or more children on his/her own. It is a flat rate benefit payable for the eldest child only. Since 6 July 1998 child benefit (lone parent) has not been available to new lone parents but it may still be payable in certain circumstances. *See* leaflets CH1 and CH11.

GUARDIAN'S ALLOWANCE

Where the parents of a child are dead, the person who has the child in his/her family may claim a guardian's allowance in addition to child benefit. In exceptional circumstances the allowance is payable on the death of only one parent. *See* leaflet NI14.

INVALID CARE ALLOWANCE

Invalid care allowance (ICA) is a taxable benefit payable to people of working age who give up the opportunity of full-time paid employment because they are regularly and substantially engaged (spending at least 35 hours per week as a carer) in caring for a severely disabled person. To qualify for ICA a person must be caring for someone in receipt of one of the following benefits:

- the middle or highest rate of disability living allowance care component
- either rate of attendance allowance
- constant attendance allowance, paid at not less than the normal maximum rate, under the industrial injuries or war pension schemes

See leaflets FB31 and SD1.

SEVERE DISABLEMENT ALLOWANCE

Persons who have been incapable of work for a continuous period of at least 28 weeks but who do not qualify for contributory incapacity benefit may be entitled to severe disablement allowance (SDA). This benefit is available to people over 16 and under 65. Those who are over 65 can only get SDA if they were entitled to it on the day before their 65th birthday. People who became incapable of work on or before their 20th birthday do not have to have their disability assessed but those who became incapable after their 20th birthday must be assessed as at least 80 per cent disabled. If the Welfare Reform and Pensions Bill is enacted, Severe Disablement Allowance will not be available to new claimants from April 2001. *See* leaflet NI252.

ATTENDANCE ALLOWANCE

This is payable to disabled people who claim after the age of 65 and who need a lot of care or supervision because of physical or mental disability for a period of at least six months. People not expected to live for six months because of an illness do not have to wait six months. The allowance has two rates: the lower rate is for day or night care, and the higher rate is for day and night care. *See* leaflets DS702 and SD1.

DISABILITY LIVING ALLOWANCE

This is payable to disabled people who claim before the age of 65 who have personal care and mobility needs because of an illness or disability for a period of at least three months and are likely to have those needs for a further six months or more. People not expected to live for six months because of an illness do not have to wait three months. The allowance has two components: the care component, which has three rates, and the mobility component, which has two rates. The rates depend on the care and mobility needs of the claimant. The mobility component is currently payable only to those aged five or over, but the Government plans to extend it to those aged over three. A Disability Income Guarantee will also be introduced. *See* leaflets DS704 and SD1.

RETIREMENT PENSION: CATEGORIES C AND D

A Category C pension is provided, subject to a residence test, for persons who were over pensionable age on 5 July 1948, and for the wives and widows of men who qualified if they are over pension age. A Category D pension is provided for people aged 80 and over if they are not entitled to another category of pension or are entitled to less than the Category D rate.

WEEKLY RATES OF BENEFIT
from April 1998

Child benefit	
Eldest child	£14.40
Eldest child of certain lone parents	17.10
Each subsequent child	9.60
Guardian's allowance	
Eldest child	7.30
Each subsequent child	11.35
*Invalid care allowance	
	39.95
Increase for wife/other adult dependant	23.90
*Severe disablement allowance	
†Basic rate	40.35
Under 40	14.05
40–49	8.90
50–59	4.45
Increase for wife/other adult dependant	23.95
Attendance allowance	
Higher rate	52.95
Lower rate	35.40
Disability living allowance	
Care component	
Higher rate	52.95
Middle rate	35.40
Lowest rate	14.05
Mobility component	
Higher rate	37.00
Lower rate	14.05
Retirement pension: categories *C and D	
Single person	39.95
Increase for wife/other adult dependant	23.95
(not payable with Category D pension)	

*These benefits attract an increase for each dependent child (in addition to child benefit) of £9.90 for the first or only child and £11.35 for each subsequent child
†The age addition applies to the age when incapacity began

INCOME SUPPORT

Income support is a benefit for those aged 16 and over whose income is below a certain level. It can be paid to people who are not expected to sign on as unemployed (income support for unemployed people was replaced by jobseeker's allowance in October 1996) and who are:
– incapable of work due to sickness or disability
– bringing up children alone
– 60 or over
– looking after a person who has a disability
– registered blind

Some people who are not in these categories may also be able to claim income support.

Income support is also payable to people who work for less than 16 hours a week on average (or 24 hours for a partner). Some people can claim income support if they work longer hours.

Income support is not payable if the claimant, or claimant and partner, have capital or savings in excess of £8,000. For capital and savings in excess of £3,000, a deduction of £1 is made for every £250 or part of £250 held. Different limits apply to people permanently in residential care and nursing homes: the upper limit is £16,000 and deductions apply for capital in excess of £10,000.

Sums payable depend on fixed allowances laid down by law for people in different circumstances. If both partners are entitled to income support, either may claim it for the couple. People receiving income support may be able to receive housing benefit, help with mortgage or home loan interest and help with health care. They may also be eligible for help with exceptional expenses from the Social Fund. Special rates may apply to some people living in residential care or nursing homes. Leaflet IS20 gives a detailed explanation of income support.

In October 1998 the Government's voluntary New Deal for Lone Parents programme became available throughout the UK. All lone parents receiving income support are assigned a personal adviser at a jobcentre who will provide guidance and support with a view to enabling the claimant to find work.

INCOME SUPPORT PREMIUMS

Income support premiums are additional weekly payments for those with special needs. People qualifying for more than one premium will normally only receive the highest single premium for which they qualify. However, family premium, disabled child premium, severe disability premium and carer premium are payable in addition to other premiums.

People with children may qualify for:
– the family premium if they have at least one child (a higher rate is paid to lone parents, although from 6 April 1998 it has not generally been available to new claimants)
– the disabled child premium if they have a child who receives disability living allowance or is registered blind
Carers may qualify for:
– the carer premium if they or their partner are in receipt of invalid care allowance
Long-term sick or disabled people may qualify for:
– the disability premium if they or their partner are receiving certain benefits because they are disabled or cannot work; are registered blind; or if the claimant has been incapable of work or receiving statutory sick pay for at least 364 days (196 days if the person is terminally ill), including periods of incapacity separated by eight weeks or less
– the severe disability premium if the person lives alone and receives attendance allowance or the middle or higher rate of disability living allowance care component and no one receives invalid care allowance for caring for that person. This premium is also available to couples where both partners meet the above conditions
People aged 60 and over may qualify for:
– the pensioner premium if they or their partner are aged 60 to 74
– the enhanced pensioner premium if they or their partner are aged 75 to 79
– the higher pensioner premium if they or their partner are aged 80 or over. This is also available to people over 60 who receive attendance allowance, disability living allowance, long-term incapacity benefit or severe disablement allowance, or who are registered blind

WEEKLY RATES OF BENEFIT
from April 1999

Income support

Single person

under 18	£30.95
under 18 (higher)	40.70
aged 18–24	40.70
aged 25 and over	51.40
aged 18 and over and a single parent	51.40

Couples*

one or both aged 18 or over	80.65

For each child in a family

until September following 11th birthday	20.20
from September following 11th birthday to September following 16th birthday	25.90
†from September following 16th birthday to day before 19th birthday	30.95

Premiums

Family premium	13.90
Family (lone parent) premium	15.75
Disabled child premium	21.90
Carer premium	13.95
Disability premium	
Single	21.90
Couple	31.25
Severe disability premium	
Single	39.75
Couple (one person qualified)	39.75
Couple (both qualified)	79.50
Pensioner premium	
Single	23.60
Couple	35.95
Higher pensioner premium	
Single	30.85
Couple	39.20
Enhanced pensioner premium	
Single	25.90
Couple	39.20

*Where one or both partners are aged under 18, their personal allowance will depend on their situation
†If in full-time education up to A-level or equivalent standard

HOUSING BENEFIT

Housing benefit is designed to help people with rent (including rent for accommodation in guest houses, lodgings or hostels). It does not cover mortgage payments. The amount of benefit paid depends on:

- the income of the claimant, and partner if there is one, including earned income, unearned income (any other income including some other benefits) and savings
- number of dependants
- certain extra needs of the claimant, partner or any dependants
- number and gross income of people sharing the home who are not dependent on the claimant
- how much rent is paid

Housing benefit is not payable if the claimant, or claimant and partner, have savings of over £16,000. The amount of benefit is affected if savings held exceed £3,000. Housing benefit is not paid for meals, fuel or certain service charges that may be included in the rent. Deductions are also made for most non-dependants who live in the same accommodation as the claimant (and their partner).

The maximum amount of benefit (which is not necessarily the same as the amount of rent paid) may be paid where the claimant is in receipt of income support or income-based jobseeker's allowance or where the claimant's income is less than the amount allowed for their needs. Any income over that allowed for their needs will mean that their benefit is reduced.

Claims for housing benefit are made to the local council. Those who are also claiming income support or income-based jobseeker's allowance may claim housing benefit at the local benefits or employment services office. *See* leaflets RR1 and RR2.

COUNCIL TAX BENEFIT

Nearly all the rules which apply to housing benefit apply to council tax benefit, which helps people on low incomes to pay council tax bills. The amount payable depends on how much council tax is paid and who lives with the claimant. The benefit may be available to those receiving income support or income-based jobseeker's allowance or to those whose income is less than that allowed for their needs. Any income over that allowed for their needs will mean that their council tax benefit is reduced. Deductions are made for non-dependants.

The maximum amount that is payable for those living in properties in council tax bands A to E is 100 per cent of the claimant's council tax liability. This also applies to those living in properties in bands F to H who were in receipt of the benefit at 31 March 1998 if they have remained in the same property. From 1 April 1998 council tax benefit for new claimants living in property bands F to H (or existing claimants moving into these bands) was restricted to the level payable for band E.

If a person shares a home with one or more adults (not their partner) who are on a low income, it may be possible to claim a second adult rebate. Those who are entitled to both council tax benefit and second adult rebate will be awarded whichever is the greater. Second adult rebate may be claimed by those not in receipt of council tax benefit.

THE SOCIAL FUND

The Social Fund helps people with expenses which are difficult to meet from regular income. Regulated maternity and funeral payments are decided by Decision Makers; cold weather payments and winter fuel payments are made automatically. These payments are not limited by the district's Social Fund budget. Discretionary community care grants, and budgeting and crisis loans are decided by Social Fund Officers and come out of a yearly budget which is allocated to each district (1999–2000, grants £98 million; loans £436.7 million; £0.5 million set aside as a contingency reserve). *See* leaflet SB16.

REGULATED PAYMENTS

Maternity Payments

A payment of up to £100 for each baby expected, born, adopted, or the subject of a parental order (in the case of surrogacy). From April 2000 the Maternity Payment Scheme will be replaced by the State Maternity Grant Scheme. The payment will double to £200 and will be linked to the claimant seeking advice on the welfare of the baby. It is payable to people on income support, income-based jobseeker's allowance, disabled person's tax credit and working families tax credit and does not have to be repaid.

Funeral Payments

Payable for the necessary cost of burial or cremation, plus other funeral expenses reasonably incurred up to £600, to people receiving income support, income-based jobseeker's allowance, disabled person's tax credit, working families' tax credit, council tax benefit or housing benefit who have good reason for taking responsibility for the funeral expenses. These payments are recoverable from any estate of the deceased.

Cold Weather Payments

A payment of £8.50 when the average temperature over seven consecutive days is recorded as or forecast to be 0°C or below in their area. Payments are made to people on income support or income-based jobseeker's allowance and who have a child under five or whose benefit includes a pensioner or disability premium. They do not have to be repaid.

Winter Fuel Payments

An annual payment of £100 per household paid automatically to eligible pensioners. Payments are made before Christmas and do not have to be repaid.

DISCRETIONARY PAYMENTS

Community Care Grants

These are intended to help people on income support or income-based jobseeker's allowance (or those likely to receive these benefits on leaving residential or institutional accommodation) to live as independently as possible in the community; ease exceptional pressures on families; care for a prisoner or young offender released on temporary licence; help people set up home as part of a resettlement programme and/or assist with certain travelling expenses. They do not have to be repaid.

Budgeting Loans

These are interest-free loans to people who have been receiving income support or income-based jobseeker's allowance for at least 26 weeks, for intermittent expenses that may be difficult to budget for.

Crisis Loans

These are interest-free loans to anyone, whether receiving benefit or not, who is without resources in an emergency, where there is no other means of preventing serious damage or serious risk to their health or safety.

SAVINGS

Savings over £500 (£1,000 for people aged 60 or over) are taken into account for maternity and funeral payments, community care grants and budgeting loans. All savings are taken into account for crisis loans. Savings are not taken into account for cold weather or winter fuel payments.

INDUSTRIAL INJURIES AND DISABLEMENT BENEFITS

The industrial injuries scheme, administered under the Social Security Contributions and Benefits Act 1992, provides a range of benefits designed to compensate for disablement resulting from an industrial accident (i.e. an accident arising out of and in the course of an employed earner's employment) or from a prescribed disease due to the nature of a person's employment. Those who are self-employed are not covered by this scheme.

INDUSTRIAL INJURIES DISABLEMENT BENEFIT

A person must be at least 14 per cent disabled (except for certain respiratory diseases) in order to qualify for this benefit. The amount paid depends on the degree of disablement:
– those assessed as 14–19 per cent disabled are paid at the 20 per cent rate
– those with disablement of over 20 per cent will have the percentage rounded up or down to the nearest 10 per cent, e.g. a disablement of 44 per cent will be paid at the 40 per cent rate while a disablement of 45 per cent will be paid at the 50 per cent rate

Benefit is payable 15 weeks (90 days) after the date of the accident or onset of the disease and may be payable for a limited period or for life. The benefit is payable whether the person works or not and those who are incapable of work are entitled to draw statutory sick pay or incapacity benefit in addition to industrial injuries disablement benefit. It may also be possible to claim the following allowances:
– reduced earnings allowance for those who are unable to return to their regular work or work of the same standard and who had their accident (or whose disease started) before 1 October 1990
– retirement allowance for those who were entitled to reduced earnings allowance who have reached state pension age
– constant attendance allowance for those with a disablement of 100 per cent who need constant care. There are four rates of allowance depending on how much care the person needs
– exceptionally severe disablement allowance for those who are entitled to constant care attendance allowance at one of the higher rates and who need constant care permanently

See leaflets NI6 and N12.

OTHER BENEFITS

People who are disabled because of an accident or disease that was the result of work that they did before 5 July 1948 are not entitled to industrial injuries disablement benefit. They may, however, be entitled to payment under the workmen's compensation scheme or the pneumoconiosis, byssinosis and miscellaneous diseases benefit scheme. *See* leaflets WS1 and PN1.

WEEKLY RATES OF BENEFIT
from April 1999

*Disablement benefit/pension	
Degree of disablement	
100 per cent	£108.10
90	97.29
80	86.48
70	75.67
60	64.86
50	54.05
40	43.24
30	32.43
20	21.62
†Unemployability supplement	66.75
Addition for adult dependant (subject to earnings rule)	39.95
Reduced earnings allowance (maximum)	43.24
Retirement allowance (maximum)	10.81
Constant attendance allowance (normal maximum rate)	43.30
Exceptionally severe disablement allowance	43.30

*There is a weekly benefit for those under 18 with no dependants which is set at a lower rate
†This benefit attracts an increase for each dependent child (in addition to child benefit) of £9.90 for the first child and £11.35 for each subsequent child

---

CLAIMS AND QUESTIONS

With a few exceptions, claims and questions relating to social security benefits are decided in agencies. The decision makers act impartially. *See* leaflets GL24 and NI260(DMA).

Entitlement to benefit (including disablement questions) and regulated Social Fund payments is determined by decision makers. A claimant who is dissatisfied with that decision can ask for an explanation and review of the decision. If they are still dissatisfied they can go to the Appeals Service, an independent tribunal. There is a further right of appeal to a Social Security Commissioner against the tribunal's decision but leave to appeal must first be obtained. Appeals to the Commissioner must be on a point of law. Provision is also made for the determination of certain questions by the Secretary of State for Social Security.

Decisions on applications to the discretionary Social Fund are made by Social Fund Officers. Applicants can ask for a review within 28 days of the date on the decision letter. The Social Fund Review Officer will review the case and there is a further right of review to an independent Social Fund Inspector.

Reviews of housing and council tax benefit decisions are dealt with initially by the council. The claimant must ask for a review within six weeks of being told how much benefit they will receive. Further reviews are dealt with by an independent review board.

OTHER BENEFITS

Statutory Sick Pay

Employers usually pay statutory sick pay (SSP) to their employees for up to 28 weeks of sickness in any period of incapacity for work that lasts longer than four days. SSP is paid at £59.55 per week and is subject to PAYE tax and NI deductions. Employees who cannot obtain SSP may be able to claim incapacity benefit. Employers may be able to recover some SSP costs. See leaflets NI244 and NI245.

Statutory Maternity Pay

In general, employers pay statutory maternity pay (SMP) to pregnant women who have been employed by them full or part-time for at least 26 weeks before the end of the 'qualifying week', which is 15 weeks before the week the baby is due, and whose earnings on average at least equal the lower earnings limit applied to NI contributions. All women who meet these conditions receive payment of 90 per cent of their average earnings for six weeks, followed by a maximum of 12 weeks at £59.55. SMP can be paid from the beginning of the 11th week before the week in which the baby is due but women can decide to begin maternity leave later than this. SMP is not payable for any week in which the woman works. Employers are reimbursed for 92 per cent of the SMP they pay (105 per cent for those whose annual NI liability (excluding Class 1A) is £20,000 or less). *See* Leaflet NI17A.

War Pensions

The War Pensions Agency, an executive agency of the Department of Social Security (DSS), awards war pensions under The Naval, Military and Air Forces, Etc. (Disablement and Death) Service Pensions Order 1983 to members of the armed forces in respect of service after 4 August 1914. There is also a scheme for civilians and civil defence workers in respect of the 1939–45 war, and other schemes for groups such as merchant seamen and Polish armed forces who served under British command.

Pensions

War disablement pension is awarded for the disabling effects of any injury, wound or disease which is the result of, or has been aggravated by, conditions of service in the armed forces. It can only be paid once the person has left the armed forces. The amount of pension paid depends on the severity of disablement, which is assessed by comparing the health of the claimant with that of a healthy person of the same age and sex. The person's earning capacity or occupation are not taken into account in this assessment. A pension is awarded if the person has a disablement of 20 per cent or more and a lump sum is usually payable to those with a disablement of less than 20 per cent. No award is made for noise-induced sensorineural hearing loss where the assessment of disablement is less than 20 per cent.

War widow's pension is payable where the husband's death was due to, or hastened by, his service in the armed forces or where the husband was in receipt of a war disablement pension constant attendance allowance (or would have been had he not been in hospital). A war widow's pension is also payable if the husband was getting unemployability supplement at the time of his death and his pensionable disablement was at least 80 per cent. Most war widows receive a standard rank-related rate but a lower weekly rate is payable to war widows of men below the rank of Lieutenant-Colonel who are under the age of 40, without children and capable of maintaining themselves. This is increased to the standard rate at age 40. Allowances are paid for children (in addition to child benefit) and adult dependents. An age allowance may also be given when the woman reaches 65 and increased at age 70 and age 80.

A war widower's pension may be payable to a man whose wife died because of service in the armed forces, if he was dependent on his wife before her death and cannot support himself.

All war pensions and war widow's pensions are tax-free and pensioners living overseas receive the same amount as those resident in the UK.

Supplementary Allowances

A number of supplementary allowances may be awarded to a war pensioner which are intended to meet various needs which may result from disablement or death and take account of its particular effect on the pensioner or spouse. The principal supplementary allowances are unemployability supplement, allowance for lowered standard of occupation and constant attendance allowance. Others include exceptionally severe disablement allowance, severe disablement occupational allowance, treatment allowance, mobility supplement, comforts allowance, clothing allowance, age allowance and widow's age allowance. There is a rent allowance available on a war widow's pension.

Social Security Benefits

Most social security benefits are paid in addition to the basic war disablement pension or war widow's pension. Any retirement pension for which a war widow qualifies on her own NI contribution record can be paid in addition to her war widow's pension.

A war pensioner or war widow who claims income support, working families tax credit or disabled person's tax credit has the first £10 a week of pension disregarded. A similar provision operates for housing benefit and council tax benefit; but the local authority may, at its discretion, disregard any or all of the balance.

Claims and Questions

To claim a war pension it is necessary to contact the nearest war pensioners' welfare service office, the address of which is available from local social security offices, or to write to the War Pensions Agency, Norcross, Blackpool FY5 3WP.

Regional Development

ENGLISH PARTNERSHIPS
16–18 Old Queen Street
London SW1H 9HP
Tel 0171-976 7070; fax 0171-976 7740
English Partnerships was established in April 1999 by the merger of the Commission for the New Towns (CNT) and the Urban Regeneration Agency (URA, formally known as English Partnerships). Its role is to work with central and local government, the regional development agencies (RDAs, see below), the private sector and other partners to bring about sustainable economic regeneration and development in the English regions. It has taken on the URA's responsibility for regenerating derelict, vacant and under-used land and buildings, and the CNT's responsibility for dealing with the residual assets and liabilities of the former new towns and urban development corporations in England. The regional assets and operations of the URA, with the exception of its London operation, were transferred to the RDAs on 1 April 1999.
Chairman, Sir Alan Cockshaw, FREng.
Non-Executive Board Members, Sir Idris Pearce, CBE, FRICS; M. Mallinson, CBE, FRICS; A. Fraser; Sir Brian Jenkins, GBE; W. Jordan, CBE; D. Mapp; Sir Dennis Stevenson, CBE; The Lord Thomas of Macclesfield, CBE
Chief Executive, Mrs P. Hay-Plumb
Corporate Strategy and Communications Director, T. Beattie
Commercial Director, J. Gill
Finance and Administration Directors, D. Hone (*CNT*); J. Walker (*EP*)
Development Director, D. Shelton

REGIONAL DEVELOPMENT AGENCIES

The creation of business-led regional development agencies in England was announced in a White Paper *Building Partnerships for Prosperity* in December 1997. The agencies were established in December 1998 and took on their responsibilities in April 1999. Their role is to improve regional economic performance and enhance regional competitiveness. They are the lead bodies at regional level for co-ordinating inward investment, raising people's skills, improving the competitiveness of business and bringing about social and physical regeneration. They will produce regional strategies and give advice to the Government. There are eight agencies in England outside London; a London agency will be set up at a later date. The regional operations (except those relating to London) of the former URA and the rural regeneration work of the former Rural Development Commission have been transferred to the agencies. Regional chambers are being established to provide a mechanism through which the RDAs can take account of regional views and account for their activities.

EASTERN
EAST OF ENGLAND DEVELOPMENT AGENCY, Compass House, Chivers Way, Histon, Cambridge CB4 9ZR. Tel: 01223-713900; fax: 01223-713910. *Chairman*, V. Watts; *Chief Executive*, W. Samuel

EAST MIDLANDS
EAST MIDLANDS DEVELOPMENT AGENCY, c/o East Midlands Development Company, 2–4 Weekday Cross, Nottingham NG1 2GB. Tel: 0115-952 7870; fax: 0115-958 5292. *Chairman*, D. Mapp; *Chief Executive*, M. Briggs

NORTH-EAST
ONE NORTH EAST, Great North House, Sandyford Road, Newcastle upon Tyne NE1 8ND. Tel: 0191-261 0026; fax 0191-232 9069. *Chairman*, J. Bridge; *Chief Executive*, M. Collier

NORTH-WEST
NORTH WEST DEVELOPMENT AGENCY, New Town House, Buttermarket Street, Warrington WA1 2LF. Tel: 01925-644683; fax: 01925-644671. *Chairman*, The Lord Thomas of Macclesfield, CBE; *Chief Executive*, M. Shields

SOUTH-EAST
SOUTH EAST ENGLAND DEVELOPMENT AGENCY (SEEDA), SEEDA Headquarters, Cross Lanes, Guildford GU1 1YA. Tel: 01483-484226; fax: 01483-484247. *Chairman*, A. Willett; *Chief Executive*, A. Dunnett

SOUTH-WEST
SOUTH WEST OF ENGLAND REGIONAL DEVELOPMENT AGENCY, The Gaunts' House, Denmark Street, Bristol BS1 5DR. Tel: 0117-922 0353; fax: 0117-922 0354. *Chairman*, Sir Michael Lickiss; *Chief Executive*, Ms J. Barrow

WEST MIDLANDS
ADVANTAGE WEST MIDLANDS, 2 Priestley Wharf, Holt Street, Aston Science Park, Birmingham B7 4BZ. Tel: 0121-380 3500; fax: 0121-380 3501. *Chairman*, A. Stephenson; *Chief Executive*, A. Cassidy

YORKSHIRE AND THE HUMBER
YORKSHIRE FORWARD, Westgate House, 100 Wellington Street, Leeds LS1 4LT. Tel: 0113-242 6268; fax: 0113-243 1088. *Chairman*, G. Hall; *Chief Executive*, M. Havenhand

---

DEVELOPMENT CORPORATIONS

URBAN DEVELOPMENT CORPORATIONS
Urban development corporations were established under the Local Government, Planning and Land Act 1980, as short-life public bodies. Their objectives were to bring land and buildings back into effective use; to develop existing and new industry and commerce; to improve the environment; and to ensure that housing and social facilities are available in the area. All the corporations in England have now been wound up.

CARDIFF BAY (1987), Baltic House, Mount Stuart Square, Cardiff CF1 6DH. Tel: 01222-585858. *Chairman*, Sir Geoffrey Inkin, OBE; *Chief Executive*, M. Boyce. Area, 1,094 hectares
LAGANSIDE (1989), Clarendon Building, 15 Clarendon Road, Belfast BT1 3BG. Tel: 01232-328507. *Chairman*, A. Hopkins; *Chief Executive*, M. Smith. Area, 200 hectares

OTHER DEVELOPMENT CORPORATIONS
Wales
DEVELOPMENT BOARD FOR RURAL WALES (1977), merged with Welsh Development Agency in October 1998 (*see* page 350)

The Water Industry

ENGLAND AND WALES

In England and Wales the Secretary of State for the Environment, Transport and the Regions and the National Assembly for Wales have overall responsibility for water policy and set the environmental and health and safety standards for the water industry. The Director-General of Water Services, as the independent economic regulator, is responsible for ensuring that the private water companies are able to fulfil their statutory obligation to provide water supply and sewerage services, and for protecting the interests of consumers.

The Minister of Agriculture, Fisheries and Food and the National Assembly for Wales are responsible for policy relating to land drainage, flood protection, sea defences and the protection and development of fisheries.

The Environment Agency is responsible for water quality and the control of pollution, the management of water resources and nature conservation. The Drinking Water Inspectorate and local authorities are responsible for the quality of drinking water.

THE WATER COMPANIES

Until 1989 nine regional water authorities in England and the Welsh Water Authority in Wales were responsible for water supply and the development of water resources, sewerage and sewage disposal, pollution control, freshwater fisheries, flood protection, water recreation, and environmental conservation. The Water Act 1989 provided for the creation of a privatized water industry under public regulation, and the functions of the regional water authorities were taken over by ten holding companies and the regulatory bodies.

Of the 99 per cent of the population of England and Wales who are connected to a public water supply, 78 per cent are supplied by the water companies (through their principal operating subsidiaries, the water service companies). The remaining 22 per cent are supplied by statutory water companies which were already in the private sector. Most of these have public limited company (PLC) status and many are now in foreign ownership or are part of larger multi-utility companies. They are represented by Water UK, which also represents the ten water service companies responsible for sewerage and sewage disposal in England and Wales, and the state-owned water authorities of Scotland and Northern Ireland. Water UK is the trade association for all the water service companies except Mid Kent Water.

Limited competition exists in the water industry, with large industrial customers being able to negotiate separate supply arrangements. Discussions are underway to determine the feasibility and future extent of competition.

WATER UK, 1 Queen Anne's Gate, London, SW1H 9BT. Tel: 0171-344 1844. *Chief Executive*, Ms P. Taylor

Water Service Companies

ANGLIAN WATER SERVICES LTD, Anglian House, Ambury Road, Huntingdon, Cambs PE18 6NZ

DWR CYMRU (WELSH WATER), Cambrian Way, Brecon, Powys LD3 7HP

NORTHUMBRIAN WATER LTD, Abbey Road, Pity Me, Durham DH1 5FJ

NORTH WEST WATER LTD, Dawson House, Liverpool Road, Great Sankey, Warrington WA5 3LW

SEVERN TRENT WATER LTD, 2297 Coventry Road, Sheldon, Birmingham B26 3PU

SOUTHERN WATER SERVICES LTD, Southern House, Yeoman Road, Worthing, W. Sussex BN13 3NX

SOUTH WEST WATER SERVICES LTD, Peninsula House, Rydon Lane, Exeter EX2 7HR

THAMES WATER UTILITIES LTD, Gainsborough House, Manor Farm Road, Reading RG2 0JN

WESSEX WATER SERVICES LTD, Wessex House, Passage Street, Bristol BS2 0JQ

YORKSHIRE WATER SERVICES LTD, Western House, Western Way, Halifax Road, Bradford BD6 2LZ

WATER SUPPLY AND CONSUMPTION 1997–8

	Supply		Consumption			
	Supply from treatment works (*Ml/day*)	Total leakage (*Ml/day*)	Household (*l/head/day*) Unmetered	Metered	Non-household (*l/prop/day*) Unmetered	Metered
WATER SERVICE COMPANIES						
Anglian	1,164.3	235.0	171.0	155.1	617.1	3,329.2
Dwr Cymru (Welsh)	990.0	336.7	168.2	169.6	776.9	2,832.1
North West	2,083.4	578.8	157.0	140.8	703.9	2,817.9
Northumbrian	788.8	184.5	164.7	130.0	922.8	5,037.8
Severn Trent	1,918.0	399.0	153.1	139.5	600.0	2,722.2
South West	445.1	101.1	177.1	127.2	1,113.4	1,757.3
Southern	603.4	98.8	173.8	148.0	837.7	2,769.8
Thames	2,664.7	905.5	191.8	166.3	767.9	3,602.6
Wessex	402.0	109.8	164.0	132.1	1,894.2	2,742.9
Yorkshire	1,292.1	368.1	155.3	135.7	127.4	2,864.3
Total	12,351.8	3,317.2	—	—	—	—
Average	—	—	167.0	146.7	745.6	3,000.6
WATER COMPANIES						
Total	3,331.0	664.3	—	—	—	—
Average	—	—	177.6	153.8	952.9	3,258.0

Source: Office of Water Services

REGULATORY BODIES

The Office of Water Services (Ofwat) (*see* page 350) was set up under the Water Act 1989 and is the independent economic regulator of the water and sewerage companies in England and Wales. Ofwat's main duty is to ensure that the companies can finance and carry out their statutory functions and to protect the interests of water customers. Ofwat is a non-ministerial government department headed by the Director-General of Water Services, who is appointed by the Secretary of State for the Environment, Transport and the Regions and the Secretary of State for Wales. Under the Competition Act 1998, from 1 March 2000 the Competition Commission (*see* page 291) will hear appeals against the regulator's decisions regarding anti-competitive agreements and abuse of a dominant position in the marketplace.

The Environment Agency (*see* page 299) has statutory duties and powers in relation to water resources, pollution control, flood defence, fisheries, recreation, conservation and navigation in England and Wales.

The Drinking Water Inspectorate is responsible for assessing the quality of the drinking water supplied by the water companies, inspecting the companies themselves and investigating any accidents affecting drinking water quality. The Chief Inspector presents an annual report to the Secretary of State for the Environment, Transport and the Regions and to the National Assembly for Wales.

METHODS OF CHARGING

In England and Wales, most domestic customers still pay for domestic water supply and sewerage services through charges based on the old rateable value of their property, although about 18 per cent of householders are now charged according to consumption, which is recorded by meter. Industrial and most commercial customers are charged according to consumption.

Under the Water Industry Act 1999, water companies can continue basing their charges on the old rateable value of property. Domestic customers can continue paying on an unmeasured basis unless they choose to pay according to consumption. After having a meter installed (which is free of charge), a customer can revert to unmeasured charging within 12 months. Domestic, school and hospital customers cannot be disconnected for non-payment.

In November 1999 Ofwat will decide the new pricing structure for 2000–2005. Both the Regulator and the Government have indicated that they expect charges to customers to be reduced.

SCOTLAND

Overall responsibility for national water policy in Scotland rested with the Secretary of State for Scotland until July 1999 when it was devolved to the Scottish Executive.

Until The Local Government etc. (Scotland) Act 1994, water supply and sewerage services were local authority responsibilities. The Central Scotland Water Development Board had the function of developing new sources of water supply for the purpose of providing water in bulk to water authorities whose limits of supply were within the board's area. Under the Act, three new public water authorities, covering the north, east and west of Scotland respectively, took over the provision of water and sewerage services from April 1996. The Central Scotland Water Development Board was then abolished. The new authorities were responsible to the Secretary of State for Scotland, and since July 1999 have been responsible to the Scottish Executive. The Act also established the Scottish Water and Sewerage Customers Council representing consumer interests. It monitored the performance of the authorities; approved

charges schemes; investigated complaints; and advised the Secretary of State. The Water Industries Act 1999, whose Scottish provisions were accepted by the Scottish Executive, abolished the Scottish Water and Sewerage Customers Council. It will be replaced in late 1999 by a Water Industry Commissioner who will promote the interests of customers. The Commissioner will make long-term recommendations about charging and efficiency to the Scottish Executive and will be advised by three water industry consultative committees (one for each water authority).

The Scottish Environment Protection Agency (SEPA) (*see* page 337) is responsible for promoting the cleanliness of Scotland's rivers, lochs and coastal waters. SEPA is also responsible for controlling pollution.

WATER RESOURCES 1997

	No.	Yield (Ml/day)
Reservoirs and lochs	287	3,018
Feeder intakes	27	—
River intakes	223	422
Bore-holes	35	77
Underground springs	103	46
Total	*676	3,562

* Including compensation reservoirs

WATER CONSUMPTION 1997

TOTAL (Ml/day)	2,336.3
Potable	2,320.3
Unmetered	1,781.7
Metered	538.5
Non-potable†	16.0
TOTAL (l/head/day)	468.6
Unmetered	357.4
Metered and non-potable†	109.9

† 'Non-potable' supplied for industrial purposes. Metered supplies in general relate to commercial and industrial use and unmetered to domestic use
Source: The Scottish Office

EAST OF SCOTLAND WATER AUTHORITY, Pentland Gait, 597 Calder Road, Edinburgh EH11 4HJ. Tel: 0131-453 7500. *Chief Executive,* R. Rennet

NORTH OF SCOTLAND WATER AUTHORITY, Cairngorm House, Beechwood Business Park, Inverness IV2 3ED. Tel: 01463-245400. *Chief Executive,* A. Findlay

SCOTTISH WATER AND SEWERAGE CUSTOMERS COUNCIL, Ochil House, Springkerse Business Park, Stirling FK7 7XE. Tel: 01786-430200. (The Council will be replaced by the Water Industry Commissioner at the same address)

WEST OF SCOTLAND WATER AUTHORITY, 419 Balmore Road, Glasgow G22 6NU. Tel: 0141-355 5333. *Chief Executive,* E. Chambers

METHODS OF CHARGING

The water authorities set charges for domestic and non-domestic water and sewerage provision through charges schemes which have to be approved by the Scottish Water and Sewerage Customers Council. The authorities must publish a summary of their charges schemes.

NORTHERN IRELAND

In Northern Ireland ministerial responsibility for water services lies with the Secretary of State for Northern Ireland. The Water Service, which is an executive agency of the Department of the Environment for Northern Ireland, is responsible for policy and co-ordination with regard to supply, distribution and cleanliness of water, and the provision and maintenance of sewerage services.

The Water Service (*see* page 328) is divided into four regions, the Eastern, Northern, Western and Southern Divisions. These are based in Belfast, Ballymena, Londonderry and Craigavon respectively.

On major issues the Department of the Environment for Northern Ireland seeks the views of the Northern Ireland Water Council, a body appointed to advise the Department on the exercise of its water and sewerage functions. The Council includes representatives from agriculture, angling, industry, commerce, tourism, trade unions and local government.

METHODS OF CHARGING

Usually householders do not pay separately for water and sewerage services; the costs of these services are allowed for in the Northern Ireland regional rate. Water consumed by industry, commerce and agriculture in excess of 100 cubic metres (22,000 gallons) per half year is charged through meters. Traders operating from industrially derated premises are required to pay for the treatment and disposal of the trade effluent which they discharge into the public sewerage system.

Energy

The main primary sources of energy in Britain are oil, natural gas, coal, nuclear power and water power. The main secondary sources (i.e. sources derived from the primary sources) are electricity, coke and smokeless fuels, and petroleum products. The Department of the Environment, Transport and the Regions is responsible for promoting energy efficiency.

INDIGENOUS PRODUCTION OF PRIMARY FUELS
Million tonnes of oil equivalent

	1997	1998p
Coal	31.5	27.0
Petroleum	140.4	145.2
Natural gas	86.2	90.3
Primary electricity		
Nuclear	22.99	23.28
Natural flow hydro	0.41	0.50
Total	281.9	286.2

p provisional

INLAND ENERGY CONSUMPTION BY PRIMARY FUEL
Million tonnes of oil equivalent, seasonally adjusted

	1997	1998p
Coal	42.9	43.1
Petroleum	77.0	76.7
Natural gas	88.7	92.2
Primary electricity	24.83	25.19
Nuclear	22.99	23.28
Natural flow hydro	0.42	0.50
Net imports	1.42	1.41
Total	233.5	237.2

p provisional

TRADE IN FUELS AND RELATED MATERIALS 1998

	Quantity*	Value†
IMPORTS		
Coal and other solid fuel	15.1	687
Crude petroleum	40.0	2,170
Petroleum products	17.8	1,414
Natural gas	0.4	43
Electricity	1.1	335
Total	74.5	4,648
Total (fob)‡	—	4,105
EXPORTS		
Coal and other solid fuel	0.9	69
Crude petroleum	79.6	4,441
Petroleum products	37.1	2,886
Natural gas	1.5	76
Electricity	—	3
Total	119.0	7,475
Total (fob)‡	—	7,475

* Million tonnes of oil equivalent
† £ million
‡ Adjusted to exclude estimated costs of insurance, freight, etc.
Source: Department of Trade and Industry – *Energy Trends May 1999*
(Crown copyright)

OIL

Until the 1960s Britain imported almost all its oil supplies. In 1969 oil was discovered in the Arbroath field of the UK Continental Shelf (UKCS). The first oilfield to be brought into production was the Argyll field in 1975, and since the mid-1970s Britain has been a major producer of crude oil.

Licences for exploration and production are granted to companies by the Department of Trade and Industry; the leading British oil companies are British Petroleum (BP) and Shell Transport and Trading. At the end of 1998, 1,021 offshore licences and 150 onshore licences had been awarded, and there were 121 offshore oilfields in production. In 1998 there were 10 oil refineries and four smaller refining units processing crude and process oils. There are estimated to be reserves of 1,800 million tonnes of oil in the UKCS. Royalties are payable on fields approved before April 1982 and petroleum revenue tax is levied on fields approved between 1975 and March 1993.

DRILLING ACTIVITY 1998

Number of wells started	Offshore	Onshore
Exploration and appraisal	80	14
Exploration	47	—
Appraisal	33	—
Development	281	21

VALUE OF UKCS OIL AND GAS PRODUCTION AND INVESTMENT
£ million

	1997	1998p
Total income	18,955	16,950
Operating costs	4,150	4,190
Exploration expenditure	1,194	762
Gross trading profits*	13,832	11,289
Percentage contribution to GDP	1.9	1.5
Capital investment	4,333	5,086
Percentage contribution to industrial investment	18	18

* Net of stock appreciation
p provisional

INDIGENOUS PRODUCTION AND REFINERY RECEIPTS

	1997	1998p
Indigenous production (thousand tonnes)	128,234	132,633
Crude oil	120,321	124,222
NGLs*	7,913	8,411
Refinery receipts (thousand tonnes)		
Indigenous	47,589	46,382
Other†	794	1,255
Net foreign imports	48,649	46,434

p provisional
* Natural gas liquids: condensates and petroleum gases derived at onshore treatment plants
† Mainly recycled products

DELIVERIES OF PETROLEUM PRODUCTS FOR INLAND CONSUMPTION BY ENERGY USE
Thousand tonnes

	1997	1998
Electricity generators	1,393	924
Gas works	46	47
Iron and steel industry	730	499
Other industries	5,751	5,678
Transport	47,317	47,831
Domestic	3,057	3,190
Other	3,253	3,042
Total	61,547	61,210

Source: Department of Trade and Industry – *Energy Trends May 1999*
(Crown copyright)

GAS

From the late 18th century gas in Britain was produced from coal. In the 1960s town gas began to be produced from oil-based feedstocks using imported oil. In 1965 gas was discovered in the North Sea in the West Sole field, which became the first gasfield in production in 1967, and from the late 1960s natural gas began to replace town gas. Britain is now the world's fourth largest producer of gas and in 1998 only 1.5 per cent of gas available for consumption in the UK was imported. From October 1998 Britain was connected to the continental European gas system via a pipeline from Bacton, Norfolk to Zeebrugge, Belgium.

By the end of 1998 there were 80 offshore gasfields producing natural gas and associated gas (mainly methane). There is estimated to be 1,795,000 million cubic metres of recoverable gas reserves. There are about 9,419 km of major submarine pipelines for transporting hydrocarbons, and onshore pipelines for carrying refined products and chemicals. Natural gas is transported around Britain by about 273,000 km of pipelines supplied by seven coastal terminals. This pipeline system is owned by Transco but BG's competitors are allowed access under a network code. New arrangements for trading within the pipeline system were introduced on 1 October 1999. Greater efficiency in balancing supply and demand is expected to achieve savings which will be reflected in lower prices.

The Office of Gas and Electricity Markets (see page 302) is the regulator for the gas industry. It was formed in 1999 by the merger of the Office of Gas Supply and the Office of Electricity Regulation. Under the Competition Act 1998, from 1 March 2000 the Competition Commission (see page 291) will hear appeals against the regulator's decisions regarding anti-competitive agreements and abuse of a dominant position in the marketplace.

The gas industry in Britain was nationalized in 1949 and operated as the Gas Council. The Gas Council was replaced by the British Gas Corporation in 1972 and the industry became more centralized. The British Gas Corporation was privatized in 1986 as British Gas PLC.

In 1993 the Monopolies and Mergers Commission found that British Gas's integrated business in Great Britain as a gas trader and the owner of the gas transportation system could be expected to operate against the public interest. In February 1997 British Gas demerged its trading arm and now operates as two separate companies: BG PLC, which runs the Transco pipeline business in Britain and oil and gas exploration and production in the UK and abroad; and Centrica PLC, which runs the trading, service and retail operations under the British Gas brand name in Great Britain.

Competition was gradually introduced into the industrial gas market from 1986. Supply of gas to the domestic market was opened to companies other than British Gas, starting in April 1996 with a pilot project in the West Country and Wales. From spring 1997 competition was progressively introduced throughout the rest of Britain in stages which were completed in May 1998. With the electricity market also open, many suppliers now offer their customers both gas and electricity. Some gas companies have become part of larger multi-utility companies, often operating internationally.

BG PLC, 100 Thames Valley Park Drive, Reading RG6 1PT. Tel: 0118-935 3222. *Chairman,* R. V. Giordano; *Chief Executive,* D. Varney

CENTRICA PLC, Charter Court, 50 Windsor Road, Slough, Berks SL1 2HA. Tel: 01753-758000. *Chief Executive,* R. Gardner

NATURAL GAS PRODUCTION AND SUPPLY
GWh

	1997	1998p
Gross gas production	998,343	1,048,353
Exports	21,666	31,604
Imports	14,062	10,582
Gas available	927,790	956,076
Gas transmitted‡	911,798	948,401

p provisional
‡ Figures differ from gas available mainly because of stock changes

NATURAL GAS CONSUMPTION
GWh

	1997	1998p
Electricity generators	243,361	253,348
Iron and steel industry	20,725	22,754
Other industries	174,763	175,747
Domestic	341,347	360,266
Public administration, commerce and agriculture	112,347	118,860
Total	892,544	930,975

p provisional
Source: Department of Trade and Industry – *Energy Trends May 1999* (Crown copyright)

COAL

Coal has been mined in Britain for centuries and the availability of coal was crucial to the industrial revolution of the 18th and 19th centuries. Mines were in private ownership until 1947 when they were nationalized and came under the management of the National Coal Board, later the British Coal Corporation. In addition to producing coal at its own deep-mine and opencast sites, of which there were 850 in 1955, British Coal was responsible for licensing private operators.

Under the Coal Industry Act 1994, the Coal Authority (see page 290) was established to take over ownership of coal reserves and to issue licences to private mining companies as part of the privatization of British Coal. The Coal Authority also deals with the physical legacy of mining, e.g. subsidence damage claims, and is responsible for holding and making available all existing records. The mines were sold as five separate businesses in 1994 and coal production in the UK is now undertaken entirely in the private sector. At the end of 1997 there were 20 large deep mines in operation.

The main UK customer for coal is the electricity supply industry, but the latter's demand for coal declined and National Power (see page 503) announced that it expected to close ten of its 18 coal-fired power stations by 2000. However, following a review of energy policy, the Government announced measures in its October 1998 Energy White Paper which included a freeze on new applications to build gas-fired power stations in order to increase opportunities for coal-fired power stations; there is a possibility that the EU might challenge the Government's plans. The Government also hopes that reform of the electricity wholesale market (the Pool, see below) will allow coal to compete better with other fuels.

COAL PRODUCTION AND FOREIGN TRADE
Thousand tonnes

	1997	1998p
Total production	48,495	41,428
Deep-mined	30,281	25,014
Opencast	16,700	15,033
Imports	19,756	21,233
Exports	1,147	944

p provisional

INLAND COAL USE
Thousand tonnes

Fuel producers	1997	1998p
Collieries	8	5
Electricity generators	47,058	48,521
Coke ovens	8,751	8,695
Other conversion industries	846	643
Total	63,075	63,039
Final users		
Industry	3,174	2,714
Domestic	2,587	2,182
Public administration, commerce and agriculture	651	279

p provisional
Source: Department of Trade and Industry

ELECTRICITY

The first power station in Britain generating electricity for public supply began operating in 1882. In the 1930s a national transmission grid was developed, and it was reconstructed and extended in the 1950s and 1960s. Power stations were operated by the Central Electricity Generating Board.

Under the Electricity Act 1989, 12 regional electricity companies (RECs), which are responsible for the distribution of electricity from the national grid to consumers, were formed from the former area electricity boards in England and Wales. Four companies were formed from the Central Electricity Generating Board: three generating companies (National Power PLC, Nuclear Electric PLC and PowerGen PLC) and the National Grid Company PLC, which owns and operates the transmission system. National Power and PowerGen were floated on the stock market in 1991. Nuclear Electric was split into two parts in 1995; the part comprising the more modern nuclear stations was incorporated into a new company, British Energy, which was floated on the stock market in 1996. Magnox Electric, which owns the magnox nuclear reactors, remained in the public sector and was integrated into British Nuclear Fuels (BNFL) in 1999. Ownership of the National Grid Company was transferred to the RECs and it was subsequently floated in 1995.

Generators sell the electricity they produce into an open commodity market (the Pool) from which buyers purchase. The Regulator and Government have announced their intention to replace the Pool. The introduction of competition into the domestic electricity market was completed in May 1999. With the gas market also open, many suppliers now offer their customers both gas and electricity.

Electricity companies can now also sell gas to their customers. Similarly, gas companies can also offer electricity. Some electricity companies have bought others, and there is a trend towards larger multi-utility companies, often operating internationally.

In Scotland, three new companies were formed under the Electricity Act 1989: Scottish Power PLC and Scottish Hydro-Electric PLC, which are responsible for generation, transmission, distribution and supply; and Scottish Nuclear Ltd. Scottish Power and Scottish Hydro-Electric were floated on the stock market in 1991 (the latter merged with Southern Electric in 1998 to become Scottish and Southern Energy PLC); Scottish Nuclear was incorporated into British Energy in 1995.

In Northern Ireland, Northern Ireland Electricity PLC was set up in 1993 under a 1991 Order in Council. It is responsible for transmission, distribution and supply and has been floated on the stock market. There is no Pool in Northern Ireland; three private companies are responsible for electricity generation and the electricity is sold to Northern Ireland Electricity under a series of power purchase agreements.

The Office of Gas and Electricity Markets (*see* page 302) is the regulator for the electricity industry. It was formed in 1999 by the merger of the Office of Electricity Regulation and the Office of Gas Supply. Under the Competition Act 1998, from 1 March 2000 the Competition Commission (*see* page 291) will hear appeals against the regulator's decisions regarding anti-competitive agreements and abuse of a dominant position in the marketplace.

The Electricity Association is the electricity industry's main trade association, providing representational and professional services for the electricity companies. EA Technology Ltd provides distribution and utilization research, development and technology transfer.

NUCLEAR POWER

Nuclear reactors began to supply electricity to the national grid in 1956. It is generated at six magnox reactors, seven advanced gas-cooled reactors (AGRs) and one pressurized water reactor (PWR), Sizewell 'B' in Suffolk. Nuclear stations now generate about 29 per cent of the UK's electricity.

In preparation for privatization, the nuclear industry was restructured in December 1995. A holding company, British Energy PLC, was formed with two operational subsidiaries, Nuclear Electric Ltd and Scottish Nuclear Ltd. Nuclear Electric operates the five AGRs and the PWR in England and Wales; Scottish Nuclear operates the two AGRs in Scotland. British Energy was floated on the stock market in 1996. The Magnox reactors were transferred to Magnox Electric PLC, and later to British Nuclear Fuels Ltd (BNFL, *see* above). BNFL is in public ownership, providing reprocessing, waste management and effluent treatment services. The UK Atomic Energy Authority (*see* page 283) is responsible for the decommissioning of nuclear reactors and other nuclear facilities used in research and development. UK Nirex, which is owned by the nuclear generating companies and the Government, is responsible for the disposal of intermediate and some low-level nuclear waste. The Nuclear Installations Inspectorate of the Health and Safety Executive (*see* page 306) is the nuclear industry's regulator.

ELECTRICITY UTILITIES

BRITISH ENERGY PLC, 10 Lochside Place, Edinburgh EH12 9DF. Tel: 0131-527 2000

BNFL MAGNOX GENERATION PLC, Berkeley Centre, Berkeley, Glos GL13 9PB. Tel: 01453-810451

EAST MIDLANDS ELECTRICITY PLC, PO Box 44, Wollaton, Nottingham NG8 1EZ. Tel: 0115-901 0101

EASTERN ELECTRICITY PLC, PO Box 40, Wherstead Park, Wherstead, Ipswich IP9 2AQ. Tel: 01473-688688

FIRST HYDRO COMPANY, Bala House, Lakeside Business Village, St David's Park, Ewloe CH5 3XJ. Tel: 01244-520234

GUERNSEY ELECTRICITY, PO Box 4, Electricity House, North Side, Vale, Guernsey GY1 3AD. Tel: 01481-46931

HYDER PLC, Newport Road, St Mellons, Cardiff CF3 9XW. Tel: 01222-792111

JERSEY ELECTRICITY, PO Box 45, Queens Road, St Helier, Jersey JE4 8NY. Tel: 01534-505000

LONDON ELECTRICITY PLC, Templar House, 81–87 High Holborn, London WC1V 6NU. Tel: 0171-242 9050

MANWEB PLC, Manweb House, Kingsfield Court, Chester Business Park, Chester CH4 9RF. Tel: 0845-272 3636

MANX ELECTRICITY AUTHORITY, PO Box 177,
Douglas, Isle of Man IM99 IPS. Tel: 01624-687687

MIDLANDS ELECTRICITY PLC, Mucklow Hill,
Halesowen, W. Midlands B62 8BP Tel: 0121-423 2345

NATIONAL GRID COMPANY PLC, National Grid House,
Kirby Corner Road, Coventry CV4 8JY. Tel: 01203-
423000

NATIONAL POWER PLC, Windmill Hill Business Park,
Whitehill Way, Swindon, Wilts SN5 6PB. Tel: 01793-
877777

NIGEN LTD., Kilroot Power Station, Larne Road,
Carrickfergus, Co. Antrim BT38 7LX. Tel: 01960-351644

NORTHERN ELECTRIC PLC, Carliol House, Market
Street, Newcastle upon Tyne NE1 6NE. Tel: 0191-210
2000

NORTHERN IRELAND ELECTRICITY PLC, 120 Malone
Road, Belfast BT9 5HT. Tel: 01232-661100

NORWEB PLC, Talbot Road, Manchester M16 0HQ. Tel:
0161-873 8000

POWERGEN PLC, Westwood Way, Westwood Business
Park, Coventry CV4 8LG. Tel: 01203-424000

PREMIER POWER LTD, Ballylumford, Islandmagee,
Larne, Co. Antrim BT40 3RS. Tel: 01960-381100

SCOTTISH AND SOUTHERN ENERGY PLC, 10 Dunkeld
Road, Perth PH1 5WA. Tel: 01738-455040

SCOTTISHPOWER PLC, 1 Atlantic Quay, Glasgow G2 8SP.
Tel: 0141-248 8200

SEEBOARD PLC, Forest Gate, Brighton Road, Crawley, W.
Sussex RHII 9BH. Tel: 01293-565888

SWEB PLC, 800 Park Avenue, Aztec West, Almondsbury,
Bristol BS32 4SE. Tel: 01454-201101

YORKSHIRE ELECTRICITY GROUP PLC, Wetherby Road,
Scarcroft, Leeds LS14 3HS. Tel: 0113-289 2123

ELECTRICITY ASSOCIATION LTD, 30 Millbank, London
SW1P 4RD. Tel: 0171-963 5700

EA TECHNOLOGY LTD, Capenhurst, Chester CH1 6ES.
Tel: 0151-339 4181

ELECTRICITY GENERATION, SUPPLY AND
CONSUMPTION
GWh

	1996	1997
Electricity generated: total	347,386	345,342
Major power producers: total	326,287	324,143
Conventional steam stations	160,565	133,132
Nuclear stations	94,671	98,146
Gas turbines and oil engines	226	459
Combined cycle gas turbine stations	65,880	86,974
Hydro-electric stations:		
Natural flow	2,801	3,337
Pumped storage	1,556	1,486
Renewables other than hydro	588	609
Other generators	21,099	21,199
Electricity used on works: total	17,728	16,369
Major generating companies	16,064	15,404
Other generators	1,664	956
Electricity supplied (gross): total	329,641	328,973
Major power producers: total	309,612	308,739
Conventional steam stations	153,170	127,075
Nuclear stations	85,820	89,341
Gas turbines and oil engines	216	436
Combined cycle gas turbine stations	65,604	86,609
Hydro-electric stations:		
Natural flow	2,763	3,299
Pumped storage	1,507	1,439
Renewables other than hydro	533	540
Other generators	20,028	20,234

Electricity used in pumping		
Major power producers	2,430	2,477
Electricity supplied (net): total	327,209	326,496
Major power producers	307,181	306,262
Other generators	20,028	20,234
Net imports	16,677	16,575
Electricity available	343,886	343,071
Losses in transmission, etc.	29,601	25,585
Electricity consumption: total	314,285	317,486
Fuel industries	8,629	8,235
Final users: total	305,656	309,251
Industrial sector	103,129	104,743
Domestic sector	107,513	104,455
Other sectors	95,014	100,053

Source: The Stationery Office – Annual Abstract of Statistics 1999

RENEWABLE SOURCES

Renewable sources of energy principally include biofuels,
hydro, wind and solar. Renewable sources accounted for
2.7 million tonnes of oil equivalent of primary energy use
in 1998; of this, about 1.7 million tonnes was used to
generate electricity and about 0.9 million tonnes to generate
heat.

The Non-Fossil Fuel Obligation (NFFO) Renewables
Orders are the Government's principal mechanism for
developing renewable energy sources. NFFO Renewables
Orders require the regional electricity companies to buy
specified amounts of electricity from specified non-fossil
fuel sources. The technologies covered by NFFO Orders
have been landfill gas, municipal and industrial waste,
small-scale hydro, onshore wind and energy crops. The
fifth NFFO Renewables Order was made in September
1998. In Scotland a similar system of Scottish Renewables
Orders exists. The third Order was made in February 1999
and covers wave energy, the first time that this technology
has been supported by a Renewables Order. Energy policy
was devolved to the Scottish Parliament in July 1999.

The Government intends to achieve 10 per cent of the
UK's electricity needs from renewables by 2010. Plans are
also being made to determine how renewables can
contribute to meeting commitments to future reductions
in greenhouse gases.

RENEWABLE ENERGY SOURCES 1998

	Percentages
Biofuels	79.8
Landfill gas	15.1
Sewage gas	6.9
Wood combustion	26.8
Straw combustion	2.7
Refuse combustion	21.4
Other biofuels	6.9
Hydro	16.9
Large-scale	16.3
Small-scale	0.6
Wind	2.9
Active solar heating	0.4
Total	100

Source: Department of Trade and Industry

Transport

CIVIL AVIATION

Since the privatization of British Airways in 1987, UK airlines have been operated entirely by the private sector. In 1998, total capacity on British airlines amounted to 40,017,000 tonne-km, of which 29,756,000 tonne-km was on scheduled services. British airlines carried 93.1 million passengers, 61.7 million on scheduled services and 31.4 million on charter flights.

Leading British airlines include British Airways, Britannia Airways, British Midland, Monarch Airlines and Virgin Atlantic.

There are 142 licensed civil aerodromes in Britain, with Heathrow and Gatwick handling the highest volume of passengers. BAA PLC owns and operates the seven major airports: Heathrow, Gatwick, Stansted, Southampton, Glasgow, Edinburgh and Aberdeen, which between them handle about 70 per cent of air passengers and 81 per cent of air cargo traffic in Britain. Many other airports, including Manchester, are controlled by local authorities or private companies. In the 1999 Budget, the Government announced it was setting up a review of competition in the airports sector.

The Civil Aviation Authority, an independent statutory body, is responsible for the economic regulation of UK airlines and for the safety regulation of the UK civil aviation industry. Through its wholly-owned subsidiary company National Air Traffic Services Ltd the CAA is also responsible for the provision of air traffic control services over Britain and its surrounding seas and at most major British airports. The Government has announced plans to privatize a majority holding in National Air Traffic Services.

The CAA is responsible for ensuring that UK airlines provide services at the lowest charges possible, given the requirement to meet stringent safety standards. It is also responsible for the economic regulation of the larger airports.

All commercial airline companies must be granted an Air Operator's Certificate, which is issued by the CAA to operators meeting the required safety standards. The CAA also issues airport safety licences, which must be obtained by any airport used for public transport and training flights. All British-registered aircraft must be granted an airworthiness certificate, and the CAA also issues professional licences to pilots, flight crew, ground engineers and air traffic controllers.

AIR PASSENGERS 1998*

ALL UK AIRPORTS: TOTAL	160,248,019
LONDON AREA AIRPORTS: TOTAL	102,216,797
Battersea Heliport	4,709
Gatwick (BAA)	29,173,130
Heathrow (BAA)	60,683,988
London City	1,360,187
Luton	4,132,818
Southend	4,063
Stansted (BAA)	6,862,611
OTHER UK AIRPORTS: TOTAL	58,026,513
Aberdeen (BAA)	2,662,960
Barra	9,045
Barrow-in-Furness	105
Belfast City	1,316,792
Belfast International	2,671,848
Benbecula (HIAL)	36,519
Biggin Hill	6,987
Birmingham	6,709,086
Blackpool	94,312
Bournemouth	315,537
Bristol	1,838,219
Cambridge	16,689
Campbeltown (HIAL)	9,595
Cardiff	1,263,225
Carlisle	966
Coventry	2,639
Dundee	10,583
East Midlands	2,142,005
Edinburgh (BAA)	4,588,507
Exeter	250,806
Glasgow (BAA)	6,566,927
Gloucestershire	2,246
Hawarden	6,394
Humberside	345,661
Inverness (HIAL)	340,742
Islay (HIAL)	21,282
Isle of Man	727,611
Kent International	2,269
Kirkwall (HIAL)	90,610
Leeds/Bradford	1,406,948
Lerwick (Tingwall)	4,029
Liverpool	873,172
Londonderry	49,146
Lydd	2,370
Manchester	17,351,162
Newcastle upon Tyne	2,984,724
Norwich	318,549
Penzance Heliport	119,800
Plymouth	139,930
Prestwick	564,043
St Mary's, Isles of Scilly	131,617
Scatsta	104,356
Sheffield City	46,527
Shoreham	2,156
Southampton (BAA)	737,463
Stornoway (HIAL)	96,070
Sumburgh (HIAL)	305,740
Teesside	655,218
Tiree (HIAL)	4,988
Tresco, Isles of Scilly (H)	35,475
Unst	1,806
Wick (HIAL)	41,057
CHANNEL IS. AIRPORTS: TOTAL	2,789,624
Alderney	77,198
Guernsey	963,674
Jersey	1,748,752

*Total terminal, transit, scheduled and charter passengers
Source: Civil Aviation Authority

RAILWAYS

Britain pioneered railways and a railway network was developed across Britain by private companies in the course of the 19th century. In 1948 the main railway companies were nationalized and were run by a public authority, the British Transport Commission. The Commission was replaced by the British Railways Board in 1963, operating as British Rail. On 1 April 1994, responsibility for managing the railway infrastructure passed to a newly-formed company, Railtrack; the British Railways Board continued as operator of all train services until they were sold or franchised to the private sector. All passenger activities have now been franchised and all British Rail's freight, technical support and specialist function businesses have been sold. The Board still has certain functions, including overall responsibility for the British Transport Police (*see* page 377).

PRIVATIZATION

Since 1 April 1994, ownership of operational track and land has been vested in Railtrack, which was floated on the Stock Exchange in 1996. Railtrack manages the track and charges for access to it and is responsible for signalling and timetabling. It does not operate train services. It owns the stations, and leases most of them out to the train operating companies. Infrastructure support functions are now provided by private sector companies. Railtrack invests in infrastructure principally using finance raised by track charges, and takes investment decisions in consultation with rail operators. Railtrack is also responsible for overall safety on the railways.

Proposals to privatize part of London Underground were announced in July 1997 with more details being given in June 1999. The Government intends the infrastructure to be run by private companies, with the operating company remaining in public ownership. In June 1999 the Government announced that the lines would be leased in three groups. The first group, lines close to the surface, would be leased to Railtrack with a view to integrating them into the national railway network. The remaining lines will be leased in two groups. In 1997–8 there were 832 million passenger journeys, including 384 million using season tickets.

RAIL REGULATOR

The independent Rail Regulator is responsible for the licensing of new railway operators, approving access agreements, promoting the use and development of the network, preventing anti-competitive practices (in conjunction with the Director General of Fair Trading) and protecting the interests of rail users. The Regulator will publish the conclusions of his review of Railtrack's funding arrangements in July 2000, for implementation in April 2001. He has indicated that he will seek to promote improvements in the infrastructure. The White Paper *New Deal for Transport* contains proposals to strengthen the Regulator's power to impose sanctions and broaden the scope of his duties.

Separate regulations, which took effect on 28 June 1998, established licensing and access arrangements for certain international train services in Great Britain. These are overseen by the International Rail Regulator, a position held by the Rail Regulator.

The White Paper *New Deal for Transport*, published in July 1998, announced plans to establish a Strategic Rail Authority (SRA) to manage passenger railway franchising, take responsibility for increasing the use of the railways for freight transport, and lead strategic planning of passenger and freight rail services. In July 1999 the Government published its Railways Bill which will give the SRA its full powers.

The SRA began work in shadow form in April 1999, using the existing powers of the Franchising Director and British Rail.

SERVICES

For privatization, domestic passenger services were divided into 25 train-operating units, which have been franchised to private sector operators via a competitive tendering process overseen by the Director of the Office of Passenger Rail Franchising (OPRAF). The franchise agreements are for between five and 15 years. The Government continues to subsidize loss-making but socially necessary rail services. The Franchising Director is responsible for monitoring the performance of the franchisees, allocating and administering government subsidy payments, proposing closures to the Rail Regulator and designating experimental services.

There are currently 25 train operating companies: Anglia Railways; Cardiff Railway; Central Trains; Chiltern Railways; Connex South Central; Connex South Eastern; Eurostar (which is not subject to a franchise agreement); Gatwick Express; Great Eastern Railway; Great North Eastern Railway; Great Western Trains; Island Line (Isle of Wight); LTS Rail (London to Southend and Shoeburyness); Merseyrail Electrics; Midland Mainline; North Western Trains; Northern Spirit; Scotrail Railways; Silverlink Train Services (North London); South West Trains; Thameslink Rail; Thames Trains; Virgin Trains (which operates two franchises); Wales and West Passenger Trains; and West Anglia Great Northern Railway.

Railtrack publishes a national timetable which contains details of rail services operated over the Railtrack network, coastal shipping information and connections with Ireland, the Isle of Man, the Isle of Wight, the Channel Islands and some European destinations.

The national rail enquiries service offers information about train times and fares for any part of the country:

National Rail Enquiries   0345-484950
London Transport   0171-222 1234
Eurostar   0345-303030

Rail Users' Consultative Committees monitor the policies and performance of train and station operators in their area (there are nine, covering Great Britain). They are statutory bodies and have a legal right to make recommendations for changes. The London Regional Passengers Committee represents users of buses, the Underground and the Docklands Light Railway as well as users of rail services in the London area.

British Rail's passenger rolling stock was divided between three subsidiary companies, which were privatized in 1996. The companies lease rolling stock to passenger service operators. On privatization, British Rail's bulk freight haulage companies and Rail Express Systems, which carries Royal Mail traffic, were sold to English, Welsh and Scottish Railways, which also purchased Railfreight Distribution (international freight) in 1997. In 1997–8 an average 1,159,000 tonnes of freight was transported by an average of 1,900 trains a day.

BRITISH RAILWAYS BOARD, *see* page 285

RAILTRACK, Railtrack House, Euston Square, London NW1 2EE. Tel: 0171-557 8000. *Chairman*, Sir Robert Horton. *Chief Executive*, G. Corbett

ASSOCIATION OF TRAIN OPERATING COMPANIES, 40 Bernard Street, London WC1N 1BY. Tel: 0171-904 3010. *Chairman*, I. W. Warburton

OFFICE OF PASSENGER RAIL FRANCHISING (OPRAF), Golding's House, 2 Hay's Lane, London SE1 2HB. Tel: 0171-940 4200. *Franchising Director*, M. Grant

OFFICE OF THE RAIL REGULATOR (ORR) 1
Waterhouse Square, 138–142 Holborn, London
ECIN 2ST. Tel: 0171-282 2000. *Rail Regulator*, T. Winsor
SHADOW STRATEGIC RAIL AUTHORITY, 26 Old Queen
Street, London SWIH 9HP. Tel: 0171-960 1500. *Chairman*,
Sir Alastair Morton

RAILTRACK

At 31 March 1998, Railtrack had about 20,000 miles of
standard gauge lines and sidings in use, representing 10,343
miles of route of which 3,208 miles were electrified.
Standard rail on main line has a weight of 110 lb per yard.
Railtrack owns 2,495 stations, 90 light maintenance depots,
about 40,000 bridges, viaducts and tunnels, and over 9,000
level crossings.

Passenger journeys made in 1998–9 totalled 892.3
million, including 390 million made by holders of season
tickets. The average distance of each passenger journey on
ordinary fare was 28.97 miles; and on season ticket, 16
miles. Passenger stations in use numbered 2,500. The
number of ticket transactions in the year was 329.3 million,
earning a total ticket revenue of £3,100 million.

In 1998–9 Railtrack showed an operating profit of £471
million and a pre-tax profit of £428 million. On 31 March
1998 Railtrack employed 10,622 staff.

	£ million
Income	
Passenger	2,169
Freight	169
Property rental	131
Other	63
Total	2,573
Costs	
Production and management	547
Infrastructure maintenance	694
Joint industry costs	227
Depreciation	634
Total	2,102

RAIL SAFETY

The Railways (Safety Case) Regulations 1994 require
infrastructure controllers (e.g. Railtrack, London Underground) to have systems in place to manage safety on the
railway networks for which they are responsible.

The infrastructure controllers are required to present a
safety case to the Railway Inspectorate (part of the Health
and Safety Executive). The safety case must be accepted
by the Inspectorate, and is subsequently subject to regular
compliance audits.

The infrastructure controllers require companies bidding to operate services to present a safety case. The safety
case must be accepted by the infrastructure controller
before a service operator can receive a licence and begin
to provide services. If any variation is required, the safety
case must be re-presented. Safety cases must be reviewed
at least every three years. The Inspectorate may examine
the safety case of service operators as part of its compliance
audit of infrastructure operators.

ACCIDENTS ON RAILWAYS

	1996–7	1997–8
Train accidents: total	1,753	1,864
Persons killed: total	1	10
Passengers	1	7
Railway staff	0	0
Others	0	3
Persons injured: total	257	244
Passengers	182	190
Railway staff	61	39
Others	14	15

	1996–7	1997–8
Other accidents through movement of railway vehicles		
Persons killed	20	33
Persons injured	828	883
Other accidents on railway premises		
Persons killed	4	5
Passengers	3	3
Railway staff	0	0
Others	1	2
Persons injured	3,668	4,186
Trespassers and suicides		
Persons killed	251	264
Persons injured	106	136

THE CHANNEL TUNNEL

The earliest recorded scheme for a submarine transport
connection between Britain and France was in 1802.
Tunnelling has begun simultaneously on both sides of the
Channel three times: in 1881, in the early 1970s, and on 1
December 1987, when construction workers began to bore
the first of the three tunnels which form the Channel
Tunnel. They 'holed through' the first tunnel (the service
tunnel) on 1 December 1990 and tunnelling was completed
in June 1991. The tunnel was officially inaugurated by The
Queen and President Mitterrand of France on 6 May 1994.

The submarine link comprises three tunnels. There are
two rail tunnels, each carrying trains in one direction,
which measure 24.93 ft (7.6 m) in diameter. Between them
lies a smaller service tunnel, measuring 15.75 ft (4.8 m) in
diameter. The service tunnel is linked to the rail tunnels
by 130 cross-passages for maintenance and safety purposes.
The tunnels are 31 miles (50 km) long, 24 miles (38 km) of
which is under the sea-bed at an average depth of 132 ft
(40 m). The rail terminals are situated at Folkestone and
Calais, and the tunnels go underground at Shakespeare
Cliff, Dover, and Sangatte, west of Calais.

Passenger services (Eurostar) run from Waterloo station
in London and Ashford, Kent, to Paris, Brussels and Lille.
Connecting services from Edinburgh and Manchester via
London began in 1997. The introduction of through
services from these cities, not stopping in London, is the
subject of a government review, due to report in late 1999.
Vehicle shuttle services operate between Folkestone and
Calais.

RAIL LINKS

The route for the British Channel Tunnel Rail Link will
run from Folkestone to a new terminal at St Pancras
station, London, with new intermediate stations at Ebbsfleet, Kent, and Stratford, east London; at present services
run into a terminal at Waterloo station, London.

Construction of the rail link is financed by the private
sector with a substantial government contribution. A
private sector consortium, London and Continental Railways Ltd (LCR), is responsible for the design, construction
and ownership of the rail link, and comprises Union
Railways and the UK operator of Eurostar. Construction
was expected to be completed in 2003, but on 28 January
1998 LCR informed the Government that it was unable to
fulfil its obligations. On 3 June 1998 the Government
announced a new funding agreement with LCR. The rail
link will be constructed in two phases: phase one, from the
Channel Tunnel to Fawkham Junction (where an existing
connection allows trains to continue to Waterloo), began
in October 1998 and will be completed in 2003; phase two,
from Fawkham Junction to St Pancras, will be built between
2001 and 2007. Railtrack will buy phase one when it is
completed and has an option to buy phase two by 2003.

Infrastructure developments in France have been completed and high-speed trains run from Calais to Paris, linking the Channel Tunnel with the high-speed European network.

ROADS

HIGHWAY AUTHORITIES

The powers and responsibilities of highway authorities in England and Wales are set out in the Highways Acts 1980; for Scotland there is separate legislation.

Responsibility for trunk road motorways and other trunk roads in Great Britain rests in England with the Secretary of State for the Environment, Transport and the Regions, in Scotland with the Scottish Executive, and in Wales with the National Assembly for Wales. The costs of construction, improvement and maintenance are paid for by central government. The White Paper *New Deal for Transport*, published in July 1998, restated and revised the Highways Agency's responsibility for operating, maintaining and improving the trunk road network.

The highway authority for non-trunk roads in England, Wales and Scotland is, in general, the unitary authority, county council or London borough council in whose area the roads lie.

In Northern Ireland the Department of the Environment for Northern Ireland is the statutory road authority responsible for public roads and their maintenance and construction; the Roads Service executive agency (*see* page 328) carries out these functions on behalf of the Department.

FINANCE

The Government contributes towards capital expenditure through grants and credit approvals in England and Transport Grant (TG) in Wales. Grant rates are determined by the Secretary of State for the Environment, Transport and the Regions in England, the Scottish Executive and the National Assembly for Wales in each country respectively. Grant is paid at 50 per cent of expenditure accepted for grant in England and Wales.

In England Transport Supplementary Grant (TSG) is paid towards capital spending on highways, principal carriageways and the regulation of traffic; other capital spending is financed by credit approvals and specific grants. Current expenditure is funded by revenue support grant (i.e. central government grants to local authorities for non-specific services). TSG is also paid towards capital spending on bridge assessment and strengthening; towards structural maintenance on the primary route network; and towards all principal 'A' roads. In Wales TG is paid towards capital expenditure only; current expenditure is funded by revenue support grant.

For the financial year 1999–2000 local authorities in England will receive £158 million in TSG and £465 million in credit approvals. Total estimated expenditure on building and maintaining motorways and trunk roads in England in 1998–9 was £1,429 million; estimated outturn for 1999–2000 is £1,487 million.

For the financial year 1999–2000 local authorities in Wales will receive up to £18.8 million in TG. Total expenditure on motorways and trunk roads in Wales in 1998–9 was £114 million and estimated expenditure in 1999–2000 is £112.5 million.

Until 1999, the Scottish Office received a block vote from Parliament, and the Secretary of State for Scotland determined how much was spent on roads. Since 1 July 1999 all decisions on transport expenditure have been devolved to the Scottish Executive. Total expenditure on building and maintaining trunk roads in Scotland was estimated at £170 million in 1997–8.

In Northern Ireland estimated expenditure on roads for 1998–9 was £147.7 million and £155.6 million has been allocated for expenditure in 1999–2000.

The Government is currently considering the possibility of introducing tolls on certain roads. The White Paper *New Deal for Transport* contains proposals to enable local authorities to levy charges for driving cars in congested areas and for workplace parking; the income would be used to improve local transport.

PRIVATE FINANCE

Contracts have been let which allow greater involvement by the private sector in the design, finance, construction and operation of roads.

ROADS REVIEW

The Roads Review was published in July 1998 and the Government announced a reduction of over two-thirds in the road building programme in England. Greater emphasis is to be given to making better use of existing roads, including traffic management, network control and driver information. Thirty-seven schemes will go ahead and will be built by 2005 at a cost of £1,400 million (known as the Targeted Programme of Improvements (TPI)). The Government has begun studies to address trunk road problems not covered by the TPI. In Wales, a review resulted in four schemes going ahead, six being cancelled, eight being referred for further study and three deferred. A separate review of roads policy in Scotland is to be published in November 1998.

ROAD LENGTHS

(in miles) *as at April 1998*

	Total roads	Trunk roads (including motorways)	Motorways[*]
England	176,587	6,535	1,730
Wales	21,344	1,068	83
Scotland	32,999	2,019	212
N. Ireland	15,211	153†	82

[*]There were in addition 43.9 miles of local authority motorway in England
†1997 figure

MOTORWAYS

England and Wales:

M1	London to Yorkshire
M2	London to Faversham
M3	London to Southampton
M4	London to South Wales
M5	Birmingham to Exeter
M6	Catthorpe to Carlisle
M10	St Albans spur
M11	London to Cambridge
M18	Rotherham to Goole
M20	London to Folkestone
M23	London to Gatwick
M25	London orbital
M26	M20 to M25 spur
M27	Southampton bypass
M32	M4 to Bristol spur
M40	London to Birmingham
M41	London to West Cross
M42	South-west of Birmingham to Measham
M45	Dunchurch spur
M50	Ross spur
M53	Chester to Birkenhead
M54	M6 to Telford
M55	Preston to Blackpool
M56	Manchester to Chester
M57	Liverpool outer ring

M58	Liverpool to Wigan
M61	Manchester to Preston
M62	Liverpool to Hull
M63	Manchester southern ring road
M65	Calder Valley
M66	Manchester eastern ring road to Rochdale
M67	Manchester Hyde to Denton
M69	Coventry to Leicester
M180	South Humberside

Scotland:

M8	Edinburgh-Newhouse, Baillieston-West Ferry Interchange
M9	Edinburgh to Dunblane
M73	Maryville to Mollinsburn
M74	Glasgow-Paddy's Rickle Bridge, Cleuchbrae-Gretna
M77	Ayr Road Route
M80	Stirling to Haggs/Glasgow (M8) to Stepps
M90	Inverkeithing to Perth
M876	Dennyloanhead (M80) to Kincardine Bridge

Northern Ireland:

M1	Belfast to Dungannon
M2	Belfast to Antrim
M2	Ballymena bypass
M3	Belfast Cross Harbour Bridge
M5	M2 to Greencastle
M12	M1 to Craigavon
M22	Antrim to Randalstown

ROAD USE

ESTIMATED TRAFFIC ON ALL ROADS (GREAT BRITAIN) 1998

Million vehicle kilometres

All motor vehicles	459,400
Cars and taxis	375,900
Two-wheeled motor vehicles	4,000
Buses and coaches	5,000
Light vans	42,000
Other goods vehicles	32,100
Total goods vehicles	74,600
Pedal cycles	4,000

ROAD GOODS TRANSPORT (GREAT BRITAIN) 1998
Analysis by mode of working and by gross weight of vehicle

Estimated tonne kilometres (thousand million)	151.9
Own account	37.6
Public haulage	114.3
By gross weight of vehicle (billion tonne kilometres)	
Not over 25 tonnes	22.5
Over 25 tonnes	129.4
Estimated tonnes carried (millions)	1,630.0
Own account	589.0
Public haulage	1,041.0
By gross weight of vehicle (million tonnes)	
Not over 25 tonnes	382.0
Over 25 tonnes	1,248.0

ROAD PASSENGER SERVICES

Until 1988 most road passenger transport services in Great Britain were provided by the public sector; the National Bus Company was the largest bus and coach operator in England and Wales and the Scottish Bus Group the largest operator in Scotland. The privatization of the National Bus Company was completed in 1988 and that of the Scottish Bus Group in 1991. London Transport's bus operating subsidiaries were privatized by the end of 1994. Almost all bus and coach services in Great Britain are now provided by private sector companies.

Bus services outside London were deregulated in 1986,

although local authorities can subsidise the provision of socially necessary services after competitive tendering. In London, London Transport retains overall responsibility for the provision of services.

The largest bus operators in Great Britain are Stagecoach Holdings, FirstGroup (formerly FirstBus) and Arriva (formerly Cowie British Bus), which between them account for over 50 per cent of all bus services (by turnover). There are also 17 municipal bus companies in England and Wales, and thousands of smaller private sector operators. National Express runs a national network of coach routes, mainly operating through franchises.

In Northern Ireland, almost all passenger transport services are provided by subsidiaries of Translink (formerly the Northern Ireland Transport Holding Company), which is publicly owned. The two main operators are Citybus Ltd (in Belfast) and Ulsterbus Ltd (outside Belfast). There are also about 75 small private sector operators.

The transport White Paper announced plans to promote bus use, primarily through agreements between local authorities and bus operators to improve the standard and efficiency of services in an area.

There are about 64,000 licensed taxis in Great Britain, of which about 19,000 are in London. There are also about 74,000 licensed private hire vehicles in Great Britain outside London, and an estimated 60,000 in London; an exact figure is not known because a new licensing system is to take effect in 1999.

BUSES AND COACHES (GREAT BRITAIN) 1997–8

Number of vehicles (31 March 1998)	76,200
Vehicle kilometres (millions)	4,191
Local bus passenger journeys (millions)	4,337
Passenger receipts (£ million)	3,778

ROAD SAFETY

The Government in 1987 set a target of reducing road traffic casualties by a third by the year 2000 compared to the average for 1981–5. Measures to achieve this were successful in reducing the number of deaths on the road by 36 per cent by 1997, and the number of serious casualties by 42 per cent. Over the same period the number of slight casualties increased by 16 per cent, but as road traffic increased by 52 per cent, the number of casualties per 100 km travelled has increased by only 1 per cent. In 1998, fatalities were reduced by 5 per cent from 1997, and all casualties decreased by 1 per cent.

Government consultations with local authorities, the police and road safety organizations in 1996 produced strong support for setting new road safety targets.

Proposals for discussion were produced in autumn 1997, and in autumn 1999 the Government will set new road safety targets for Britain for the period to 2010; similar targets are being set in Northern Ireland.

ROAD ACCIDENTS 1998

Road accidents	238,923
Vehicles involved:	
Pedal cycles	23,423
Motor vehicles	413,172
Total casualties	325,212
Pedestrians	44,886
Vehicle users	280,326
Killed*	3,421
Pedestrians	906
Pedal cycles	158
All two-wheeled motor vehicles	498
Cars and taxis	1,696
Others	163

*Died within 30 days of accident

	Killed	Injured
1965	7,952	389,985
1970	7,499	355,869
1975	6,366	318,584
1980	6,010	323,000
1985	5,165	312,359
1990	5,217	335,924
1995	3,621	306,885
1996	3,598	316,704
1997	3,599	323,945
1998	3,421	321,791

Source: Department of the Environment, Transport and the Regions

DRIVING LICENCES

It is necessary to hold a valid full licence in order to drive on public roads in the UK. Learner drivers must obtain a provisional driving licence before starting to learn to drive and must then pass theory and practical tests to obtain a full driving licence. Application forms for a driving licence (form D1) are available from post offices. A phased introduction of driving licences including the driver's photograph began in July 1998; all licences for newly qualified drivers will include a photograph, and qualified drivers will be issued with the new licence when their licence details need updating.

There are separate tests for driving motor cycles, cars, passenger-carrying vehicles (PCVs) and large goods vehicles (LGVs). Drivers must hold full car entitlement before they can apply for PCV or LGV entitlements. At 3 April 1999, 38 million people in the UK (20.9 male, 17.1 female) held a valid driving licence (full or provisional). The minimum age for driving motor cars, light goods vehicles up to 3.5 tonnes and motor cycles is 17 (moped, 16). Since June 1997, drivers who collect six or more penalty points within two years of qualifying lose their licence and are required to take another test. A leaflet, *What You Need to Know About Driving Licences* (form D100), is available from post offices.

The Driver and Vehicle Licensing Agency is responsible for issuing driving licences, registering and licensing vehicles, and collecting excise duty in Great Britain. In Northern Ireland the Driver and Vehicle Licensing Agency (Northern Ireland) has similar responsibilities.

Driving Licence Fees *as at 1 April 1999*

First provisional licence	£23.50
Changing a provisional to a full licence after passing a driving test	£8.50
Renewal of licence	£8.50
Renewal of licence including PCV or LGV entitlements	£28.50
Renewal after disqualification	£24.50
Renewal after drinking and driving disqualification	£33.50
Medical renewal	free
Medical renewal (over 70)	free
Duplicate Licence	£13.50
Exchange licence	£13.50
Removing endorsements	£13.50
Replacement (change of name or address)	free

Driving Tests

The Driving Standards Agency is responsible for carrying out driving tests and approving driving instructors in Great Britain. In Northern Ireland the Driver and Vehicle Testing Agency (Northern Ireland) is responsible for testing drivers and vehicles.

In 1998–9, almost 1.2 million car driving tests were conducted in Great Britain, of which 45.9 per cent resulted in a pass. In addition over 49,000 lorry tests were undertaken, of which 51.9 per cent were successful. Over 83,000 motorcycle tests were undertaken, of which 67.9 per cent were successful. There were more than 7,600 bus tests, with a pass rate of 47.8 per cent. In the same period, 1.2 million theory tests were conducted. A new, longer driving test was introduced on 4 May 1999.

Since 1 March 1997 driving test candidates have been required to produce photographic confirmation of their identity.

*Driving Test Fees (weekday rate/evening and Saturday rate) *as at 1 April 1999*

For cars	£36.75/£46
†For motor cycles	£45/£55
For lorries, buses	£73.50/£92

*Since 1 July 1996 most candidates for car and motor cycle tests have also been required to take a written driving theory test, for which there is a separate fee of £15.50. Theory tests for lorry and bus drivers were introduced on 1 January 1997
†Before riding on public roads, learner motor cyclists and learner moped riders are required to have completed Compulsory Basic Training, provided by DSA-approved training bodies. The Compulsory Basic Training certificate costs £8.00. All exemptions from CBT were removed on 1 January 1997

An extended driving test was introduced in 1992 for those convicted of dangerous driving. The fee is £73.50/£92 (car) or £90/£110 (motorcycle).

MOTOR VEHICLES

Vehicles must be licensed by the DVLA or the DVLNI before they can be driven on public roads. They must also be approved as roadworthy by the Vehicle Certification Agency. The Vehicle Inspectorate carries out annual testing and inspection of goods vehicles, buses and coaches.

There were 27.9 million vehicles registered at the DVLA at December 1998:

Private and light goods	24,840,942
Motor cycles, scooters, mopeds	701,692
Coaches and buses	80,862
Large goods vehicles	419,526
Electric vehicles	11,020
Others	1,926,884
Total	27,980,926

Vehicle Licences

Registration and first licensing of vehicles is through local offices (known as Vehicle Registration Offices) of the Driver and Vehicle Licensing Agency in Swansea (*see* page 299). Local facilities for relicensing are available at any post office which deals with vehicle licensing. Applicants will need to take their vehicle registration document; if this is not available the applicant must complete form V62 which is held at post offices. Postal applications can be made to the post offices shown on form V100, available at any post office. This form also provides guidance on registering and licensing vehicles.

Details of the present duties chargeable on motor vehicles are available at post offices and Vehicle Registration Offices. The Vehicle Excise and Registration Act 1994 provides *inter alia* that any vehicle kept on a public road but not used on roads is chargeable to excise duty as if it were in use. All non-commercial vehicles constructed before 1 January 1973 are exempt from vehicle excise duty.

Vehicle Excise Duty Rates
from 10 March 1999

	Twelve months £	Six months £
Motor Cars		
Light vans, cars, taxis, etc.	155.00	85.25
Under 1100cc†	100.00	55.00
Over 1100cc†	155.00	85.25
Motor Cycles		
With or without sidecar, not over 150 cc	15.00	—
With or without sidecar, 150–250 cc	40.00	—
Others	60.00	33.00
Electric motorcycles (including tricycles)	15.00	—
Tricycles (not over 450 kg)		
Not over 150 cc	15.00	—
Others	60.00	33.00
*Buses**		
Seating 9–16 persons	160.00	88.00
	(155.00)	(85.25)
Seating 17–35 persons	210.00	115.50
	(155.00)	(85.25)
Seating 36–60 persons	320.00	176.00
	(155.00)	(85.25)
Seating over 60 persons	480.00	264.00
	(155.00)	(85.25)

*Figures in parentheses refer to reduced pollution vehicles.
†Rate from 1 June 1999

MoT Testing

Cars, motor cycles, motor caravans, light goods and dual-purpose vehicles more than three years old must be covered by a current MoT test certificate. The certificate must be renewed annually. The MoT testing scheme is administered by the Vehicle Inspectorate.

A fee is payable to MoT testing stations, which must be authorized to carry out tests. The maximum fees, which are prescribed by regulations, are:

For cars and light vans	£30.87
For solo motor cycles	£12.74
For motor cycle combinations	£21.28
For three-wheeled vehicles	£25.02
For non-public service vehicle buses	£38.08
For light goods vehicles between 3,000 and 3,500 kg	£32.77

Method of Travel to Work, *Great Britain (percentage*)*

	1993	1997
Car, van, minibus, works van	68	71
Bus, coach, private bus	9	8
Train (incl. Underground and light rail)	5	6
Walk	12	11
Other	5	5
All	100	100

*All figures are rounded
Source: DETR/The Stationery Office – *Focus on Personal Travel 1998* (Crown copyright)

SHIPPING AND PORTS

Since earliest times sea trade has played a central role in Britain's economy. By the 17th century Britain had built up a substantial merchant fleet and by the early 20th century it dominated the world shipping industry. In recent years the size and tonnage of the UK-registered trading fleet have declined; the UK-flagged merchant fleet now constitutes about 1 per cent of the world fleet. In December 1998 the Government published a document, *British Shipping: Charting a New Course*, which outlined strategies to promote the long-term interests of British shipping.

Freight is carried by liner and bulk services, almost all scheduled liner services being containerized. About 95 per cent by weight of Britain's overseas trade is carried by sea; this amounts to 75 per cent of its total value. Passengers and vehicles are carried by roll-on, roll-off ferries, hovercraft, hydrofoils and high-speed catamarans. There are about 57 million ferry passengers a year, of whom 36 million travel internationally. The leading British operators of passenger services are P. & O. Stena, Stena Line (which has a Swedish parent company) and P. & O. European Ferries.

Lloyd's of London provides the most comprehensive shipping intelligence service in the world. *Lloyd's Shipping Index*, published daily, lists some 25,000 ocean-going vessels and gives the latest known report of each.

Ports

There are about 70 commercially significant ports in Great Britain, including such ports as London, Dover, Forth, Tees and Hartlepool, Grimsby and Immingham, Sullom Voe, Milford Haven, Southampton, Felixstowe and Liverpool. Belfast is the principal freight port in Northern Ireland.

Broadly speaking, ports are owned and operated by private companies, local authorities or trusts. The largest operator is Associated British Ports (formerly the British Transport Docks Board, privatized in 1981), which owns 23 ports. Total traffic through British ports in 1998 amounted to 568 million tonnes, an increase of 2 per cent on the previous year.

Marine Safety

By 1 October 2002 all roll-on, roll-off ferries operating to and from the UK will be required to meet the new international safety standards on stability established by the Stockholm Agreement.

The Maritime and Coastguard Agency (MCA) was established on 1 April 1998 by the merger of the Coastguard Agency and the Marine Safety Agency. It is an executive agency of the Department of the Environment, Transport and the Regions. The Agency's aims are to develop, promote and enforce high standards of marine safety, to minimize loss of life amongst seafarers and coastal users, and to minimize pollution of the sea and coastline from ships. In 1998 HM Coastguard co-ordinated 11,553 incidents requiring search and rescue facilities. Assistance was rendered on 6,328 occasions and 249 lives were lost.

Locations hazardous to shipping in coastal waters are marked by lighthouses and other lights and buoys. The lighthouse authorities are the Corporation of Trinity House (for England, Wales and the Channel Islands), the Northern Lighthouse Board (for Scotland and the Isle of Man), and the Commissioners of Irish Lights (for Northern Ireland and the Republic of Ireland). Trinity House maintains 72 lighthouses, 13 major floating aids to navigation and more than 429 buoys; and the Northern Lighthouse Board 84 lighthouses, 116 minor lights and many buoys.

Harbour authorities are responsible for pilotage within their harbour areas; and the Ports Act 1991 provides for the transfer of lights and buoys to harbour authorities where these are used for mainly local navigation.

PRINCIPAL MERCHANT FLEETS 1998

Flag	No	Gross tonnage
Panama	6,143	98,222,372
Liberia	1,717	60,492,104
Bahamas	1,286	27,715,783
Greece	1,545	25,224,543
Malta	1,416	24,074,712
Cyprus	1,602	23,301,517
Singapore	1,677	20,370,399
Norway (NIS)	750	19,918,331
Japan	8,922	17,780,396
China (Taiwan)	3,214	16,503,355
*United States of America	5,626	11,851,660
Russia	4,723	11,089,922
Philippines	1,726	8,508,313
Germany	1,158	8,083,620
St Vincent	1,317	7,875,497
Italy	1,329	6,818,632
India	947	6,777,102
Marshall Islands	207	6,441,843
Turkey	1,135	6,251,395
Hong Kong, China	391	6,170,705
Korea (South)	2,381	5,694,216
China (Taiwan)	686	5,491,718
Malaysia	828	5,209,049
Denmark (DIS)	473	5,091,330
Bermuda	127	4,810,939
Netherlands	1,214	4,263,326
Isle of Man	207	4,202,970
Brazil	504	4,170,577
United Kingdom	1,421	4,084,970
Iran	382	3,347,429
Indonesia	2,359	3,252,093
Norway	1,575	3,218,007
Antigua and Barbuda	575	2,787,829
French Antarctic Territory	91	2,683,295
Sweden	562	2,552,365
Canada	835	2,501,274
Kuwait	202	2,459,004
Belize	1,308	2,382,478
Australia	617	2,188,146
Romania	389	2,088,166
Other countries	22,261	45,941,914
WORLD TOTAL	85,828	531,893,296

DIS Danish International Register of Shipping – offshore registry
NIS Norwegian International Ship Register – offshore registry
*Excluding ships of United States Reserve Fleet

Source: Lloyd's Register of Shipping

MERCHANT SHIPS COMPLETED 1998

Country of Build	No	Gross tonnage
Japan	561	10,206,334
Korea (South)	160	7,243,180
China (People's Republic)	130	1,440,184
Germany	77	1,049,545
Italy	37	811,571
Poland	48	696,929
Denmark	21	455,399
China (Taiwan)	22	447,046
Spain	107	435,903
Netherlands	96	291,267
Croatia	12	280,685
Finland	9	219,924
*United States of America	86	213,680
Norway	57	180,689
Singapore	39	170,355
France	15	148,345
United Kingdom	23	134,231
Romania	21	105,868
Bulgaria	8	93,774
Turkey	21	89,646
Brazil	4	86,077
Ukraine	4	75,135
Indonesia	22	69,485
Philippines	6	62,146
Russia	8	60,794
Other countries	132	229,305

For Registration in		
Panama	338	7,910,235
Liberia	93	2,921,791
Germany	127	1,699,035
Greece	23	1,307,404
Singapore	98	1,050,703
Hong Kong, China	29	917,874
Cyprus	37	699,300
Malaysia	35	695,162
Bahamas	26	637,977
Japan	163	636,824
Denmark (DIS)	16	597,782
Norway (NIS)	21	518,665
Netherlands	59	478,545
United Kingdom	39	459,961
Italy	33	429,056
China (People's Republic)	26	421,993
Kuwait	4	413,314
Malta	21	349,258
Philippines	21	288,746
Marshall Islands	7	246,327
Norway	43	206,239
China (Taiwan)	8	197,147
*United States of America	71	184,627
Sweden	10	151,916
Antigua and Barbuda	16	142,609
Other countries	362	1,735,007
WORLD TOTAL	1,726	25,297,497

DIS Danish International Register of Shipping – offshore registry
NIS Norwegian International Ship Register – offshore registry
*Excluding ships of United States reserve fleet

Source: Lloyd's Register of Shipping

UK-REGISTERED TRADING VESSELS of 500 Gross Tons and Over *as at end 1997*

Type of vessel	No	Gross tonnage
Tankers[1]	123	2,704,000
Bulk carriers[2]	35	1,408,000
Specialized carriers[3]	11	43,000
Container (fully cellular)	60	1,626,000
Ro-Ro[4]	85	827,000
Other general cargo	156	654,000
Passenger[5]	16	548,000
Total	486	7,809,000

1 Includes oil, gas, chemical and other specialized tankers
2 Includes combination bulk carriers: ore/oil and ore/bulk/oil carriers
3 Includes livestock, car and chemical carriers
4 Roll-on, roll-off passenger and cargo vessels
5 Cruise liner and other passenger vessels

Source: The Stationery Office – *Annual Abstract of Statistics 1999*

SEABORNE TRADE OF THE UK 1996
Exports (Including Re-exports) Plus Imports by Sea

	Million tonnes
By weight	
All cargo	354.3
Dry cargo	203.4
Tanker cargo	150.9

	£ million
By value	
All cargo	260,900
Dry cargo	244,700
Tanker cargo	16,300

Source: The Stationery Office – *Annual Abstract of Statistics 1999*

PASSENGER MOVEMENT BY SEA 1997p

Arrivals plus departures at UK seaports by place of embarkation or landing*

All passenger movements	33,975,000
Irish Republic	4,055,000
Belgium	1,883,000
France†	26,960,000
Netherlands	1,934,000
Other EU countries	970,000
Other European and Mediterranean countries‡	172,000

p provisional
* Passengers are included at both departure and arrival if their journeys begin and end at a UK seaport
† Includes hovercraft passengers
‡ Includes North Africa and Middle East Mediterranean countries

Source: The Stationery Office – *Annual Abstract of Statistics 1999*

Communications

Postal Services

Responsibility for running postal services rests in the UK with the Post Office (*see* pages 330–1), which the Government plans to change from a public authority into a public limited company. All shares will be owned by the Government. An independent postal services regulator will be appointed. The Secretary of State for Trade and Industry has powers to suspend the letter monopoly of the Post Office in certain areas and to issue licences to other bodies to provide an alternative service. Non-Post Office bodies are permitted to transfer mail between document exchanges and to deliver letters, provided that a minimum fee of £1 per letter is charged. From 1 April 2000 this minimum fee will be reduced to 50 pence. Charitable organizations are allowed to carry and deliver Christmas and New Year cards.

INLAND POSTAL SERVICES AND REGULATIONS

INLAND LETTER POST RATES*

Not over	1st class†	2nd class†
60 g	26p	19p
100 g	39p	31p
150 g	52p	40p
200 g	66p	50p
250 g	77p	61p
300 g	88p	70p
350 g	£1.00	80p
400 g	£1.14	92p
450 g	£1.30	£1.05
500 g	£1.45	£1.20
600 g	£1.75	£1.40
700 g	£2.20	£1.60
750 g	£2.35	£1.70 (not
800 g	£2.55	admissible
900 g	£2.80	over 750 g)
1,000 g	£3.05	
Each extra 250 g or part thereof	75p	

UK PARCEL RATES

Not over	
1 kg	£2.85
2 kg	£3.90
4 kg	£5.95
6 kg	£6.45
8 kg	£7.40
10 kg	£7.95

*Postcards travel at the same rates as letter post
†There is a two-tier postal delivery system in the UK with first class letters normally being delivered the following day and second class post within three days

OVERSEAS POSTAL SERVICES AND REGULATIONS

Details of overseas parcel rates are available from Parcelforce Worldwide by telephoning 0800 884422.

OVERSEAS SURFACE MAIL RATES

Letters

Not over		Not over	
20 g	34p	450 g	£3.04
60 g	56p	500 g	£3.36
100 g	80p	750 g	£4.96
150 g	£1.12	1,000 g	£6.59
200 g	£1.44	1,250 g	£7.84
250 g	£1.76	1,500 g	£9.76
300 g	£2.08	1,750 g	£11.36
350 g	£2.40	2,000 g	£12.96
400 g	£2.72		

Postcards travel at 20 g letter rate

AIRMAIL LETTER RATES

Europe: Letters

Not over		Not over	
20 g	30p	280 g	£1.95
40 g	44p	300 g	£2.07
60 g	56p	320 g	£2.20
80 g	69p	340 g	£2.32
100 g	82p	360 g	£2.45
120 g	94p	380 g	£2.57
140 g	£1.07	400 g	£2.70
160 g	£1.19	420 g	£2.82
180 g	£1.32	440 g	£2.95
200 g	£1.44	460 g	£3.08
220 g	£1.57	480 g	£3.20
240 g	£1.69	500 g	£3.33
260 g	£1.82	1,000 g	£6.50
		*2,000 g	£13.08

* Max. 2 kg
Postcards to Europe travel at 20 g letter rate

Outside Europe: Letters

	Not over 10 g	Not over 20 g	Over 20 g	Post- cards
Zone 1	44p	64p	varies	44p
Zone 2	44p	64p	varies	44p

For airmail letter zones outside Europe, *see* pages 518–19

STAMPS

Postage stamps are sold in values of 1p, 2p, 4p, 5p, 6p, 10p, 19p, 20p, 25p, 26p, 29p, 30p, 31p, 35p, 36p, 37p, 38p, 39p, 41p, 43p, 50p, 63p, £1, £1.50, £2.00, £5.00, and £10.00. Books or rolls of first and second class stamps are also available. Stamps are sold at Post Offices and some other outlets, including stationers and newsagents.

PREPAID STATIONERY

Aerogrammes to all destinations are 37p, with a packet of six costing £2.05. Pictorial aerogrammes are 45p; a packet of six, £2.50. Forces aerogrammes are free to certain destinations.

Special Delivery prepaid envelopes:
Not over

500 g (C4 and C5 size)	£3.65

For items over 500g add additional payment

up to 1 kg	£1.10
2 kg	£2.35
10 kg	£11.35

Guaranteed services	Special Delivery	Registered	Registered Plus
C4, 500g	£3.65	£3.80	£4.85
C5, 250g	£3.20	£3.60	£4.55

Printed postage stamps cut from envelopes, postcards, newspaper wrappers, etc., may be used as stamps in payment of postage, provided that they are not imperfect or defaced.

POSTAL ORDERS

Postal orders (British pattern) are issued and paid at nearly all post offices in the UK and in many other countries.

Postal orders are printed with a counterfoil for denominations of 50p and £1, followed by £1 steps to £10, £15 and £20. Postage stamps may be affixed in the space provided to increase the value of the postal order by up to 49p. Charges (in addition to the value of the postal order): up to £1, 25p; £2–£4, 45p; £5–£7, 65p; £8–£10, 80p; £15, 90p; £20, 95p.

The name of the payee must be inserted on the postal order. If not presented within six months of the last day of the month of issue, orders must be sent to the local customer services manager of Post Office Counters Ltd (listed in the telephone directory) to ascertain whether the order may still be paid. If the counterfoil has been retained postal orders not more than four years out of date may be paid when presented with the counterfoil at a post office.

RESTRICTIONS

Articles which may not be sent in the post include offensive or dangerous articles (such as explosives, articles containing batteries, or aerosol products), packets likely to impede Post Office sorters, and certain kinds of advertisement. Certain other articles (such as biological specimens, liquids, or perishable foodstuffs) may be posted only if packed correctly. Advice is available from Royal Mail (tel: 0345-740740) for letters and small packets; Parcelforce (tel: 0800-224466) for parcels; or local post office counter staff.

The exportation of some goods by post is prohibited except under Department of Trade licence. Enquiries should be addressed to the Export Data Branch, Overseas Trade Divisions, Department of Trade and Industry, 1 Victoria Street, London SW1H 0ET. Tel: 0171-215 5000.

SPECIAL DELIVERY SERVICES

DATAPOST

A guaranteed service for the delivery of documents and packages: (i) Datapost Sameday offers same working day collection and delivery in many areas; (ii) Datapost 10 (for delivery before 10 a.m.) and Datapost 12 (for delivery before noon) offer next working day delivery nationwide and are available only to certain destinations. Items may be collected or handed in at post offices. There are also Datapost links with a number of overseas countries. Parcelforce 24 (next working day delivery) and 48 (delivery in two working days) offer a similar guaranteed service.

ROYAL MAIL SPECIAL DELIVERY

A guaranteed next working day delivery service by 12.30 p.m. to most UK destinations for first class letters and packets. The fee is £3.35. Compensation of up to £250 can

be awarded for a 100 g item if next working day delivery is not achieved, provided that items are posted before latest recommended posting times. Details of other compensation levels can be obtained by telephoning 0345-740740.

SWIFTAIR

An express airmail service. Items are placed on the first available flight to the destination country. Although Swiftair mail receives priority treatment, delivery times are not guaranteed. Charge (in addition to postage): £2.85.

OTHER SERVICES

ADVICE OF DELIVERY

Written confirmation of delivery from the post office at the stated destination. Charge: 33p (inland); 40p (international); plus postage.

CERTIFICATE OF POSTING

Issued free on request at time of posting.

COMPENSATION (INLAND AND INTERNATIONAL)

Inland: compensation up to a maximum of £26 may be paid where it can be shown that a letter was damaged or lost in the post due to the fault of the Post Office, its employees or agents. The Post Office does not accept responsibility for loss or damage arising from faulty packing.

International: if a certificate of posting is produced, compensation up to a maximum of £26 may be given for loss or damage in the UK to uninsured parcels to or from most overseas countries. No compensation will be paid for any loss or damage due to the action of the Queen's Enemies.

INTERNATIONAL REPLY COUPONS

Coupons used to prepay replies to letters, exchangeable abroad for stamps representing the lowest airmail letter rate from the country concerned to the UK. Charge: 60p each.

NEWSPAPER POST

Copies of newspapers registered at the Post Office may be posted only by the publisher or their agents in open-ended wrappers or unsealed envelopes approved by the Post Office, or tied with string removable without cutting. Wrappers and envelopes must be prominently marked 'newspaper post' in the top left-hand corner. The only additional writing or printing permitted is 'with compliments', the name and address of sender, request for return if undeliverable, and a page reference. Items receive first class letter service.

POSTE RESTANTE

Poste Restante is solely for travellers and is for three months in any one town. A packet may be addressed to any post office, except town sub-offices, and should state 'Poste Restante' or 'to be called for' in the address. Redirection from a Poste Restante is undertaken for up to three months. Letters for an expected ship at a port are kept for two months, otherwise letters are kept for two weeks, or one month if from abroad. At the end of this period mail is treated as undeliverable or is returned.

PRIVATE BOX

Provides an alternative address (e.g. PO Box 123) and mail is held at the local delivery office for collection. Charges: £42 (six months); £52 (12 months).

RECORDED MAIL

Provides a record of posting and delivery of letters and ensures a signature on delivery. This service is recommended for items of little or no monetary value. All packets must be handed to the post office and a certificate of posting issued. Charges: 60p plus postage (inland); £2.60 plus postage (international).

REDIRECTION

By agent of addressee: mail other than parcels, business reply and freepost items may be reposted free not later than the day after delivery (not counting Sundays and public holidays) if unopened and if original addressee's name is unobscured. Parcels may be redirected free within the same time limits only if the original and substituted address are in the same local parcel delivery area (or the London postal area). Registered packets must be taken to a post office and are re-registered free up to the day after delivery.

By the Post Office: a printed form obtainable from the Post Office must be signed by the person to whom the letters are to be addressed. A fee is payable for each different surname on the application form. Charges: up to 1 calendar month, £6.00 (abroad, £12.00); up to 3 calendar months, £13.00 (£26.00); up to 12 calendar months, £30.00 (£60.00).

REGISTERED MAIL (INTERNATIONAL)

All packets must be handed to the post office and a certificate of posting obtained. Charges (plus postage):

Compensation up to	Registered fee plus postage
£500	£3.15
£2,200	£4.20

Compensation in respect of currency or other forms of monetary worth is given only if money is sent by registered letter post. Compensation cannot be paid in the case of any packet containing prohibited articles (*see* Restrictions). Compensation is only paid for well-packed fragile articles and not for exceptionally fragile or perishable articles.

SMALL PACKETS POST AND PRINTED PAPERS (INTERNATIONAL)

Permits the transmission of goods up to 2 kg to all countries, in the same mails as printed papers. Packets can be sealed and can contain personal correspondence relating to the contents. Registration is allowed as insurance as long as the item is packed in a way complying with any insurance regulations. A customs declaration is required and the packet must be marked with 'small packet' and a return address. Instructions for the disposal of undelivered packets must be given at the time of posting. An undeliverable packet will be returned to the sender at his/her expense.

Surface mail: worldwide

Not over		Not over	
100 g	54p	450 g	£1.80
150 g	72p	500 g	£1.98
200 g	90p	750 g	£2.70
250 g	£1.08	1,000 g	£3.78
300 g	£1.26	1,500 g	£5.58
350 g	£1.44	2,000 g	£7.38
400 g	£1.62		

Printed papers only, per extra 50 g, 17p

UNDELIVERED AND UNPAID MAIL

Undelivered mail is returned to the sender provided the return address is indicated either on the outside of the envelope or inside. If the sender's address is not available items not containing property are destroyed. If the packet contains something of value it is retained for up to three months. Undeliverable second class mail containing newspapers, magazines or commercial advertising is destroyed.

All unpaid or underpaid letters are treated as second class mail. The recipient is charged the amount of underpayment plus 15p per item. Parcels over 750 g are charged at first class rates plus 15p.

Public Telecommunications Services

Under the British Telecommunications Act 1981 British Telecom (now BT) was created to provide a national public telecommunications service. The Telecommunications Act 1984 removed BT's monopoly on running the public telecommunications system and BT was privatized in 1984.

The Telecommunications Act 1984 also established the Office of Telecommunications (Oftel) as the independent regulatory body for the telecommunications industry (*see also* Government Departments and Public Offices).

PUBLIC TELECOMMUNICATIONS OPERATORS

Until 1991 the three licensed fixed-link public telecommunications operators (PTOs) in the UK were BT, Mercury Communications Ltd, and Kingston Communications (Hull) PLC. In 1991 the Government announced that it was opening up the existing duopoly of the two major fixed-link operators, BT and Mercury, and would be encouraging applications for telecommunications licences. The Department of Trade and Industry has granted over 280 PTO licences.

BT's obligations under its operating licence continue to include the provision of a universal telecommunications service, including a service in rural areas; and essential services, such as public call boxes and emergency services.

Cable and Wireless Communications PLC (which was formed from the merger of Mercury Communications with other communications companies in 1997) is licensed to provide national and international public telecommunications services for residential and business customers. These services utilize the digital network created by Mercury. Cable and Wireless can also provide the following services: public and private telephone services; national and international switched voice and data services; electronic messaging (private circuits and networks (national and international), integrated voice and data); data network services; customer equipment cable television, Internet service provision and mobile communications services.

In December 1996 the Government liberalized international facilities licensing in the UK. The end of the BT/Mercury duopoly means that other operators are now able to apply for licences to own and operate their own international telecommunications networks. By July 1999, over 100 operators had been granted international facilities licences. In January 1998 the telecommunications market throughout the European Union was liberalized.

PREMIUM RATE TELEPHONE SERVICES

There are over 1,000 premium rate telephone companies which offer information on a variety of subjects such as the weather, stock market analysis, horoscopes, etc., on the various networks.

The lines and equipment are provided by telecommunications operators under condition that services adhere to the codes of practice of the Independent Committee for the Supervision of Standards of Telephone Information Services. Services are charged at different rates from 5p to £1.50 per minute.

MOBILE TELEPHONE SYSTEMS

Cellular telephone network systems allow calls to be made to and from mobile telephones. The four companies licensed by the Department of Trade and Industry to provide competing cellular telephone systems are BT Cellnet, jointly owned by BT and Securicor; One-2-One, jointly owned by Cable and Wireless and MediaOne; Orange; and Vodafone AirTouch.

INLAND TELEPHONES

An individual customer can install an extension telephone socket or apparatus in their own home without the need to buy the items from any of the licensed public telecommunications operators. Although an individual need not buy or rent an apparatus from a PTO, a telephone bought from a retail outlet must be of an approved standard compatible with the public network (indicated by a green disc on the label).

BT EXCHANGE LINE RENTALS
(*including VAT*)

	Per quarter
Residential, exclusive	£26.77
Light user scheme	from £9.24
Business, exclusive	£43.88

BT TELEPHONE APPARATUS RENTAL
Per quarter

Residential	from £4.47
Business	from £5.53
Private payphone	from £50.53

EXCHANGE LINE CONNECTION AND TAKE-OVER
CHARGES
(*including VAT*)
BT

New line	£99.00
Removing customer	£0.00
Take-over of existing lines:	
Simultaneous (same day)	£0.00
Non-simultaneous	£0.00

Cable and Wireless

Monthly line rental	£7.98

RATES

BT and Cable and Wireless local and dialled national calls are charged by the second. Calls made from payphones are charged in 10p units. There is a 5p minimum charge on all BT calls and a minimum charge of at least 3.5p on Cable and Wireless calls depending on the charging package. All charges are subject to VAT, except those from payphones which are VAT inclusive. VAT charges on ordinary lines are calculated as a percentage of the total quarterly (BT)/monthly (Cable and Wireless) bill.

The charge per second depends on the time of day and the distance of the call:

BT	Cable and Wireless	
Daytime	Daytime	Monday to Friday 8 a.m. to 6 p.m.
Evening and night-time	Evening	Monday to Friday 6 p.m. to 8 a.m.
Weekend	Weekend	Midnight Friday to midnight Sunday

Local rate
Regional rate – up to 35 miles (56 km)
National rate – over 35 miles (56 km) (including Channel Islands and Isle of Man)
Calls to mobile phones

DIALLED CALL TIME
pence per minute charges (*including VAT*)*

BT	Local rate
Daytime	3.95
Evening and night-time	1.49
Weekend	1.00
Regional rate	
Daytime	7.91
Evening and night-time	3.95
Weekend	2.95
National rate	
Daytime	7.91
Evening and night-time	4.18
Weekend	2.95

Calls to mobile phones

	Daytime	Evening and night-time	Weekend
BT Cellnet	19.8	19.2	2.0
Vodafone AirTouch	20.6	15.0	7.4
One-2-One	25.3	17.9	8.0
Orange	24.8	17.8	7.9

*Cable and Wireless customers choose from a range of packages depending on the time of day they use the telephone most and the distance of their calls. Charges vary with each package.

OPERATOR-CONNECTED CALLS

Operator-connected calls from ordinary lines are generally subject to a one-minute minimum charge (and thereafter by the minute) which varies with distance and time of day. Operator-connected calls from payphones are charged in three-minute periods at the payphone tariff. There is also a £1.80 handling charge for operator-connected calls. For calls that have to be placed through the operator because a dialled call has failed, the charge is equivalent to the dialled rate, subject normally to the one-minute minimum.

Higher charges apply to other operator-connected calls, including special services calls and those to mobile phones, the Irish Republic and the Channel Islands.

PHONECARDS

BT phonecards to the value of £2, £5, £10 and £20 are available from post offices and other outlets for use in specially designated public telephone boxes. Each phonecard unit is equivalent to a 10p coin in a payphone. Special public payphones at major railway stations and airports also accept commercial credit cards.

INTERNATIONAL TELEPHONES

All UK customers have access to International Direct Dialling (IDD) and can dial direct to numbers on most exchanges in over 230 countries worldwide. Details about how to make calls are given in dialling code information and in the International Telephone Guide.

For countries without IDD, calls have to be made through the International Operator. All operator-connected calls are subject to a £1.80 handling charge. Thereafter the call is charged by the minute.

Countries which can be called on IDD fall into one of 18 international charge bands depending on location. Charges in each band also vary according to the time of day; cheap rate dialled calls are available to all countries at certain times, but there is no reduced rate for operator-connected calls. Details of current international telephone charges can be obtained from the International Operator.

For International Dialling Codes, *see* pages 518–19.

OTHER TELECOMMUNICATIONS SERVICES

TELEX SERVICE

There are now more than 240 countries that can be reached by the BT telex network from the UK. Calls can be sent to mobile terminals, including ships via the Inmarsat satellite service. Call charges start at 4.8p per minute for inland calls. International calls are charged by the second.

TELEMESSAGE

Telemessages can be sent by telephone or telex within the UK for 'hard copy' delivery the next working day, including Saturdays. To achieve this, a telemessage must be telephoned/telexed before 10 p.m. Monday to Saturday (7 p.m. Sundays and Bank Holidays). Dial 0800-190190 and ask for the Telemessage Service.

A telemessage costs £8.99 for the first 50 words and £5.00 for each subsequent group of 50 words – the name and address are free. A sender's copy costs £1.20. A selection of cards is available for special occasions at £1.00 per card. (All prices are include VAT.)

BT SERVICES

OPERATOR SERVICES – 100
  For difficulties
  For the following call services: alarm calls (booking charge £2.70); advice of duration and charge (charge £1.80); charge card calls (charge £1.50); freephone calls; international personal calls (charge £2.15–£4.30); transferred charge calls (charge £1.80); subscriber controlled transfer (All charges exclude VAT)
INTERNATIONAL OPERATOR – 155
DIRECTORY ENQUIRIES – 192 (35p charge per call)
INTERNATIONAL DIRECTORY ENQUIRIES – 153 (£1.10 charge per minute)
EMERGENCY SERVICES – 999
  Services include fire service; police service; ambulance service; coastguard; lifeboat; cave rescue; mountain rescue
FAULTS – 151 (residential), 154 (business)
TELEMESSAGE – 0800-190190
INTERNATIONAL TELEGRAMS – 100
MARITIME SERVICES – 100
  Includes Ship's Telegram Service and Ship's Telephone Service
BT INMARSAT SATELLITE SERVICE – 155
ALL OTHER CALL ENQUIRIES – 100

Airmail and IDD Codes

AIRMAIL ZONES (AZ)
The table includes airmail letter zones for countries outside Europe, and destinations to which European and European Union airmail letter rates apply (*see also* page 513).
(*Source:* Post Office)
1 airmail zone 1
2 airmail zone 2
e Europe

INTERNATIONAL DIRECT DIALLING (IDD)
International dialling codes are composed of four elements which are dialled in sequence:

(i) the international code
(ii) the country code (*see* below)
(iii) the area code
(iv) the customer's telephone number

Calls to some countries must be made via the international operator. (*Source:* BT)

† Connection is currently unavailable
‡ Calls must be made via the international operator
p A pause in dialling is necessary whilst waiting for a second tone
* Varies in some areas
** Varies depending on carrier

Country	AZ	IDD from UK	IDD to UK
Afghanistan	1	†	†
Albania	e	00 355	00 44
Algeria	1	00 213	00*p*44
Andorra	e	00 376	00 44
Angola	1	00 244	00 44
Anguilla	1	00 1 264	011 44
Antigua and Barbuda	1	00 1 268	011 44
Argentina	1	00 54	00 44
Armenia	e	00 374	810 44
Aruba	1	00 297	00 44
Ascension Island	1	00 247	00 44
Australia	2	00 61	00 11 44
Austria	e	00 43	00 44
Azerbaijan	e	00 994	810 44
Azores	e	00 351	00 44
Bahamas	1	00 1 242	011 44
Bahrain	1	00 973	0 44
Bangladesh	1	00 880	00 44
Barbados	1	00 1 246	011 44
Belarus	e	00 375	810 44
Belgium	e	00 32	00 44
Belize	1	00 501	00 44
Benin	1	00 229	00*p*44
Bermuda	1	00 1 441	011 44
Bhutan	1	00 975	00 44
Bolivia	1	00 591	00 44
Bosnia-Hercegovina	e	00 387	00 44
Botswana	1	00 267	00 44
Brazil	1	00 55	00 44
British Virgin Islands	1	00 1 284	011 44
Brunei	1	00 673	00 44
Bulgaria	e	00 359	00 44
Burkina Faso	1	00 226	00 44
Burundi	1	00 257	90 44
Cambodia	1	00 855	00 44
Cameroon	1	00 237	00 44
Canada	1	00 1	011 44
Canary Islands	e	00 34	00 44
Cape Verde	1	00 238	0 44
Cayman Islands	1	00 1 345	011 44
Central African Republic	1	00 236	19 44
Chad	1	00 235	15 44
Chile	1	00 56	00 44
China	2	00 86	00 44
Hong Kong	1	00 852	001 44
Colombia	1	00 57	009 44
Comoros	1	00 269	00 44
Congo, Dem. Rep. of	1	00 243	00 44
Congo, Republic of	1	00 242	00 44
Cook Islands	2	00 682	00 44
Costa Rica	1	00 506	00 44
Côte d'Ivoire	1	00 225	00 44
Croatia	e	00 385	00 44
Cuba	1	00 53	119 44
Cyprus	e	00 357	00 44
Czech Republic	e	00 420	00 44
Denmark	e	00 45	00 44
Djibouti	1	00 253	00 44
Dominica	1	00 1 767	011 44
Dominican Republic	1	00 1 809	011 44
Ecuador	1	00 593	00 44
Egypt	1	00 20	00 44
Equatorial Guinea	1	00 240	00 44
Eritrea	1	00 291	00 44
Estonia	e	00 372	800 44
Ethiopia	1	00 251	00 44
Falkland Islands	1	00 500	0 44
Faroe Islands	e	00 298	009 44
Fiji	2	00 679	05 44
Finland	e	00 358	00 44**
France	e	00 33	00 44
French Guiana	1	00 594	00 44
French Polynesia	2	00 689	00 44
Gabon	1	00 241	00 44
The Gambia	1	00 220	00 44
Georgia	e	00 995	810 44
Germany	e	00 49	00 44
Ghana	1	00 233	00 44
Gibraltar	1	00 350	00 44
Greece	e	00 30	00 44
Greenland	e	00 299	009 44
Grenada	1	00 1 473	011 44
Guadeloupe	1	00 590	00 44
Guam	2	00 1 671	001 44
Guatemala	1	00 502	00 44
Guinea	1	00 224	00 44
Guinea-Bissau	1	00 245	099 44
Guyana	1	00 592	001 44
Haiti	1	00 509	00 44
Honduras	1	00 504	00 44
Hungary	e	00 36	00 44
Iceland	e	00 354	00 44
India	1	00 91	00 44
Indonesia			001 44**
	1	00 62	00844**
Iran	1	00 98	00 44
Iraq	1	00 964	00 44
Ireland, Republic of	e	00 353	00 44
Israel	1	00 972	00 44**
Italy	e	00 39	00 44
Jamaica	1	00 1 876	011 44
Japan			001 44**
			004144**
	2	00 81	006144**
Jordan	1	00 962	00 44*
Kazakhstan	e	00 7	810 44
Kenya	1	00 254	00 44

Country	AZ	IDD from UK	IDD to UK	Country	AZ	IDD from UK	IDD to UK
Kiribati	2	00 686	00 44	Russia	e	00 7	810 44
Korea, North	2	00 850	00 44	Rwanda	1	00 250	00 44
Korea, South			001 44**	St Christopher and			
	2	00 82	00244**	Nevis	1	00 1 869	011 44
Kuwait	1	00 965	00 44	St Helena	1	00 290	0 44
Kyrgystan	e	00 996	00 44	St Lucia	1	00 1 758	011 44
Laos	1	00 856	00 44	St Pierre and			
Latvia	e	00 371	00 44	Miquelon	1	00 508	00 44
Lebanon	1	00 961	00 44	St Vincent and the			
Lesotho	1	00 266	00 44	Grenadines	1	00 1 784	001 44
Liberia	1	00 231	00 44	El Salvador	1	00 503	0 44
Libya	1	00 218	00 44	Samoa	2	00 685	0 44
Liechtenstein	e	00 423	00 44	Samoa, American	2	00 684	00 44
Lithuania	e	00 370	810 44	San Marino	e	00 378	00 44
Luxembourg	e	00 352	00 44	São Tomé and			
Macao	1	00 853	00 44	Príncipe	1	00 239	00 44
Macedonia	e	00 389	99 44	Saudi Arabia	1	00 966	00 44
Madagascar	1	00 261	00 44	Senegal	1	00 221	00p44
Madeira	e	00 351 91	00 44*	Serbia	e	00 381	99 44
Malawi	1	00 265	101 44	Seychelles	1	00 248	00 44
Malaysia	1	00 60	00 44	Sierra Leone	1	00 232	00 44
Maldives	1	00 960	00 44	Singapore	1	00 65	001 44
Mali	1	00 223	00 44	Slovak Republic	e	00 421	00 44
Malta	e	00 356	00 44	Slovenia	e	00 386	00 44
Mariana Islands,				Solomon Islands	2	00 677	00 44
Northern	2	00 1 670	011 44	Somalia	1	00 252	16 44
Marshall Islands	2	00 692	011 44	South Africa	1	00 27	09 44
Martinique	1	00 596	00 44	Spain	e	00 34	00 44
Mauritania	1	00 222	00 44	Sri Lanka	1	00 94	00 44
Mauritius	1	00 230	00 44	Sudan	1	00 249	00 44
Mayotte	1	00 269	10 44	Suriname	1	00 597	00 44
Mexico	1	00 52	98 44	Swaziland	1	00 268	00 44
Micronesia, Federated				Sweden			007 44**
States of	2	00 691	011 44				00944**
Moldova	e	00 373	810 44		e	00 46	008744**
Monaco	e	00 377	00 44	Switzerland	e	00 41	00 44
Mongolia	2	00 976	00 44	Syria	1	00 963	00 44
Montenegro	e	00 381	99 44	Taiwan	2	00 886	002 44
Montserrat	1	00 1 664	011 44	Tajikistan	e	00 7	810 44
Morocco	1	00 212	00p44	Tanzania	1	00 255	00 44
Mozambique	1	00 258	00 44	Thailand	1	00 66	001 44
Myanmar	1	00 95	00 44	Tibet	1	00 86	00 44
Namibia	1	00 264	00 44	Togo	1	00 228	00 44
Nauru	2	00 674	00 44	Tonga	2	00 676	00 44
Nepal	1	00 977	00 44	Trinidad and Tobago	1	00 1 868	011 44
Netherlands	e	00 31	00 44	Tristan da Cunha	1	00 2 897	‡
Netherlands Antilles	1	00 599	00 44	Tunisia	1	00 216	00 44
New Caledonia	2	00 687	00 44	Turkey	e	00 90	00 44
New Zealand	2	00 64	00 44	Turkmenistan	e	00 993	810 44
Nicaragua	1	00 505	00 44	Turks and Caicos Is-			
Niger	1	00 227	00 44	lands	1	00 1 649	0 44
Nigeria	1	00 234	009 44	Tuvalu	2	00 688	00 44
Niue	2	00 683	00 44	Uganda	1	00 256	00 44
Norfolk Island	2	00 672	0101 44	Ukraine	e	00 380	810 44
Norway	e	00 47	00 44	United Arab Emirates	1	00 971	00 44
Oman	1	00 968	00 44	Uruguay	1	00 598	00 44
Pakistan	1	00 92	00 44	USA	1	00 1	011 44
Palau	2	00 680	011 44	Alaska		00 1 907	011 44
Panama	1	00 507	00 44	Hawaii		00 1 808	011 44
Papua New Guinea	2	00 675	05 44	Uzbekistan	e	00 998	810 44
Paraguay	1	00 595	00 44**	Vanuatu	2	00 678	00 44
			003 44**	Vatican City State	e	00 390 66982	00 44
Peru	1	00 51	00 44	Venezuela	1	00 58	00 44
Philippines	2	00 63	00 44	Vietnam	1	00 84	00 44
Poland	e	00 48	00 44	Virgin Islands (US)	1	00 1 340	011 44
Portugal	e	00 351	00 44	Yemen	1	00 967	00 44
Puerto Rico	1	00 1 787	011 44	Yugoslav Fed. Rep.	e	00 381	99 44
Qatar	1	00 974	00 44	Zambia	1	00 260	00 44
Réunion	1	00 262	00 44	Zimbabwe	1	00 263	00 44
Romania	e	00 40	00 44				

The Internet

The Internet is a rapidly-growing worldwide network of computer networks which use the same protocols (agreed methods of communication). It has its origins in the Advanced Research Projects Agency Network (ARPANET), a government-funded defence network in the USA, and other research and academic networks, such as the UK Joint Academic Network (JANET), a network linking universities and higher education institutions in the UK. JANET has extensive links to international and other national academic networks, and also to commercial and public network services. It is funded by the higher education funding agencies in the UK.

The main protocol used by the networks is Transmission Control Protocol/Internet Protocol (TCP/IP). Other protocols include:
- file transfer protocol (ftp), which allows files to be transferred between computers
- simple mail transfer protocol (smtp), which allows electronic mail (e-mail) to be sent
- hypertext transfer protocol (http), which allows hypertext facilities to be provided
- telnet, a facility which allows users to log on to other computers on the Internet

The most common uses of the Internet include:
- sending and receiving e-mail; text can be sent directly to another computer linked to the Internet
- playing computer games
- commercial transactions
- mailing lists, which enable users to send and receive information on specialist interests
- 'newsgroups' or bulletin boards, where messages on specialist interests can be left for users to read
- the publication of information

The World Wide Web (WWW or the Web) is a vast collection of computers able to support multi-media formats and accessible via Web 'browsers' (search and navigation tools). Data stored on these computers (servers) is organized into pages with hypertext links; each page has a unique address. It is estimated that 800 million pages of the Web are searchable, but the extent of the Internet which is indexed by search engines is diminishing rapidly and no engine is currently indexing more than about 16 per cent of the Web. For practical purposes the WWW and the Internet are now almost synonymous. The main Web browsers are Netscape Navigator and Internet Explorer. The Internet is increasingly used by commercial organizations for the conduct of electronic business. Policies and standards are being developed to ensure an appropriate level of privacy; tools include access control mechanisms, data labelling and cryptography standards.

The speed of access to Internet sources and of downloading information depends on the number of users on the system (which varies according to the time of day), the location of the information, and the amount of information being downloaded.

CONNECTIONS

Connection to the Internet usually requires access to a computer, a modem and a telephone line, although it is now possible to receive television-based Internet services. Internet service providers (ISPs) supply an Internet address and password, an electronic mailbox and some or all of the necessary software. Most providers provide only a connection to the Internet, but a few also offer more sophisticated on-line services which are usually easier to use but more expensive than direct Internet access. Leading service providers include AOL, CompuServe, Demon, UU net and Microsoft Network. Details of providers are available in computer magazines and specialist Internet publications.

The main methods of connecting to the Internet are by a dial-up connection or a leased-line connection. A dial-up connection may be made over standard telephone lines or over ISDN lines. There are two types of dial-up connection: an online account, which allows the user to log on to an account on a remote computer which is connected to the Internet; and a dial-up IP connection, where a full Internet connection is made from the user's computer. The latter requires more complicated software. A permanent leased-line connection (a data line requiring no modem) is likely to be used where there are a large number of potential users, e.g. where all the users on a local area network (LAN) are to be connected.

The total number of Internet users in the UK is estimated to exceed 12.5 million adults by the end of 1999. Some 15 per cent of the UK population have home access and 14 per cent work access. The number of people on-line worldwide is estimated to be about 179 million as at June 1999.

TERMS

Home page – the introductory section of a site on the Web

Hypertext mark-up language (HTML) – a standard document mark-up language used on the Web

Java – a programming language for writing client/server and networked applications; its uses include creating interactive Web sites

Search engine – a means of finding Web pages or other material on the Internet containing specific words or phrases

Server – a computer storing data and software which can be used by other computers on a network

Uniform/Universal resource locators (URLs) – the address system for the Web

Users' network (USENET) – a large bulletin board system on the Internet

Local Government

Major changes in local government were introduced in England and Wales in 1974 and in Scotland in 1975 by the Local Government Act 1972 and the Local Government (Scotland) Act 1973. Further significant alterations were made in England by the Local Government Acts of 1985 and 1992.

The structure in England was based on two tiers of local authorities (county councils and district councils) in the non-metropolitan areas; and a single tier of metropolitan councils in the six metropolitan areas of England and London borough councils in London.

Following reviews of the structure of local government in England by the Local Government Commission, 46 unitary (all-purpose) authorities were created between April 1995 and April 1998 to cover certain areas in the non-metropolitan counties. The remaining county areas continue to have two tiers of local authorities. The county and district councils in the Isle of Wight were replaced by a single unitary authority on 1 April 1995; the former counties of Avon, Cleveland, Humberside and Berkshire have been replaced by unitary authorities; and Hereford and Worcester was replaced by a new county council for Worcestershire (with district councils) and a unitary authority for Herefordshire.

The Local Government (Wales) Act 1994 and the Local Government etc. (Scotland) Act 1994 abolished the two-tier structure in Wales and Scotland with effect from 1 April 1996, replacing it with a single tier of unitary authorities.

Local authorities are empowered or required by various Acts of Parliament to carry out functions in their areas. The legislation concerned comprises public general Acts and 'local' Acts which local authorities have promoted as private bills.

ELECTIONS

Local elections are normally held on the first Thursday in May. Generally, all British subjects, citizens of the Republic of Ireland, Commonwealth and other European Union citizens who are 18 years or over and resident on the qualifying date in the area for which the election is being held, are entitled to vote at local government elections. A register of electors is prepared and published annually by local electoral registration officers.

A returning officer has the overall responsibility for an election. Voting takes place at polling stations, arranged by the local authority and under the supervision of a presiding officer specially appointed for the purpose. Candidates, who are subject to various statutory qualifications and disqualifications designed to ensure that they are suitable persons to hold office, must be nominated by electors for the electoral area concerned.

In England, the Local Government Commission is responsible for carrying out periodic reviews of electoral arrangements and making recommendations to the Secretary of State for changes found necessary. In Wales and Scotland these matters are the responsibility of the Local Government Boundary Commission for Wales and the Local Boundary Commission for Scotland respectively.

LOCAL GOVERNMENT COMMISSION FOR ENGLAND, Dolphyn Court, 10–11 Great Turnstile, Lincoln's Inn Fields, London WC1V 7JU. Tel: 0171-430 8400

LOCAL GOVERNMENT BOUNDARY COMMISSION FOR WALES, 1–6 St Andrew's Place, Cardiff CF1 3BE. Tel: 01222-395031
LOCAL GOVERNMENT BOUNDARY COMMISSION FOR SCOTLAND, 3 Drumsheugh Gardens, Edinburgh EH3 7QJ. Tel: 0131-538 7510

INTERNAL ORGANIZATION

The council as a whole is the final decision-making body within any authority. Councils are free to a great extent to make their own internal organizational arrangements. The Government has published a draft Local Government (Organization and Standards) Bill, proposing new management arrangements with a separate executive arm of the council.

Normally, questions of policy are settled by the full council, while the administration of the various services is the responsibility of committees of councillors. Day-to-day decisions are delegated to the council's officers, who act within the policies laid down by the councillors.

FINANCE

Local government in England, Wales and Scotland is financed from four sources: the council tax, non-domestic rates, government grants, and income from fees and charges for services. (For arrangements in Northern Ireland, see page 526.)

COUNCIL TAX

Under the Local Government Finance Act 1992, from 1 April 1993 the council tax replaced the community charge (which had been introduced in April 1989 in Scotland and April 1990 in England and Wales in place of domestic rates).

The council tax is a local tax levied by each local council. Liability for the council tax bill usually falls on the owner-occupier or tenant of a dwelling which is their sole or main residence. Council tax bills may be reduced because of the personal circumstances of people resident in a property, and there are discounts in the case of dwellings occupied by fewer than two adults.

In England, each county council, each district council and each police authority sets its own council tax rate. The district councils collect the combined council tax, and the county councils and police authorities claim their share from the district councils' collection funds. In Wales, each unitary authority and each police authority sets its own council tax rate. The unitary authorities collect the combined council tax and the police authorities claim their share from the funds. In Scotland, each island council and unitary authority sets its own rate of council tax.

The tax relates to the value of the dwelling. Each dwelling is placed in one of eight valuation bands, ranging from A to H, based on the property's estimated market value as at 1 April 1991.

The valuation bands and ranges of values in England, Wales and Scotland are:

England

A	Up to £40,000	E	£88,001–£120,000
B	£40,001–£52,000	F	£120,001–£160,000
C	£52,001–£68,000	G	£160,001–£320,000
D	£68,001–£88,000	H	Over £320,000

Wales

A	Up to £30,000	E	£66,001–£90,000
B	£30,001–£39,000	F	£90,001–£120,000
C	£39,001–£51,000	G	£120,001–£240,000
D	£51,001–£66,000	H	Over £240,000

Scotland

A	Up to £27,000	E	£58,001–£80,000
B	£27,001–£35,000	F	£80,001–£106,000
C	£35,001–£45,000	G	£106,001–£212,000
D	£45,001–£58,000	H	Over £212,000

The council tax within a local area varies between the different bands according to proportions laid down by law. The charge attributable to each band as a proportion of the Band D charge set by the council is approximately:

A	67%	E	122%
B	78%	F	144%
C	89%	G	167%
D	100%	H	200%

The band D rate is given in the tables on pages 543–8 (England), 555 (London), 558 (Wales), and 564 (Scotland). There may be variations from the given figure within each district council area because of different parish or community precepts being levied.

Non-Domestic Rates

Non-domestic (business) rates are collected by billing authorities; these are the district councils in those areas of England with two tiers of local government and unitary authorities in other parts of England, in Wales and in Scotland. In respect of England and Wales, the Local Government Finance Act 1988 provides for liability for rates to be assessed on the basis of a poundage (multiplier) tax on the rateable value of property (hereditaments). Separate multipliers are set by the Secretary of State for the Environment, Transport and the Regions in England, the National Assembly for Wales and the Scottish Executive, and rates are collected by the billing authority for the area where a property is located. Rate income collected by billing authorities is paid into a national non-domestic rating (NNDR) pool and redistributed to individual authorities on the basis of the adult population figure as prescribed by the Secretary of State for the Environment, Transport and the Regions, the National Assembly for Wales or the Scottish Executive. The rates pools are maintained separately in England, Wales and Scotland. For the years 1995–6 to 1999–2000 actual payment of rates in certain cases is subject to transitional arrangements, to phase in the larger increases and reductions in rates resulting from the effects of the 1995 revaluation.

Rates are levied in Scotland in accordance with the Local Government (Scotland) Act 1975. For 1995–6, the Secretary of State for Scotland prescribed a single non-domestic rates poundage to apply throughout the country at the same level as the uniform business rate (UBR) in England. Rate income is pooled and redistributed to local authorities on a per capita basis. For the year 1995–6 payment of rates was subject to transitional arrangements to phase in the effect of the 1995 revaluation.

Rateable values for the 1995 rating lists came into force on 1 April 1995. They are derived from the rental value of property as at 1 April 1993 and determined on certain statutory assumptions by the Valuation Office Agency in England and Wales, and by Regional Assessors in Scotland. New property which is added to the list, and significant changes to existing property, necessitate amendments to the rateable value on the same basis. Rating lists (valuation rolls in Scotland) remain in force until the next general revaluation. Such revaluations take place every five years,

the next being in 2005. New rating lists come into force on 1 April 2000 based on rental levels as at 1 April 1998.

Certain types of property are exempt from rates, e.g. agricultural land and buildings, certain businesses and places of public religious worship. Charities and other non-profit-making organizations may receive full or partial relief. Empty property is liable to pay rates at 50 per cent, except for certain specified classes which are exempt entirely.

Government Grants

In addition to specific grants in support of revenue expenditure on particular services, central government pays revenue support grant to local authorities. This grant is paid to each local authority so that if each authority spends at the level of its standard spending assessment, all authorities in the same class can set broadly the same council tax.

COMPLAINTS

Commissioners for Local Administration in England, Wales and Scotland (*see* page 317) are responsible for investigating complaints from members of the public who claim to have suffered injustice as a consequence of maladministration in local government or in certain local bodies.

The Northern Ireland Commissioner for Complaints fulfils a similar function in Northern Ireland, investigating complaints about local authorities and certain public bodies.

Complaints are made to the relevant local authority in the first instance and complainants may approach the Commissioners if not satisfied. Complaints may also be made directly to the Commissioners.

THE QUEEN'S REPRESENTATIVES

The Lord-Lieutenant of a county is the permanent local representative of the Crown in that county. The appointment of Lord-Lieutenants is now regulated by the Lieutenancies Act 1997. They are appointed by the Sovereign on the recommendation of the Prime Minister. The retirement age is 75. The office of Lord-Lieutenant dates from 1557, and its holder was originally responsible for the maintenance of order and for local defence in the county. The duties of the post include attending on royalty during official visits to the county, performing certain duties in connection with armed forces of the Crown (and in particular the reserve forces), and making presentations of honours and awards on behalf of the Crown. In England, Wales and Northern Ireland, the Lord-Lieutenant usually also holds the office of *Custos Rotulorum*. As such, he or she acts as head of the county's commission of the peace (which recommends the appointment of magistrates).

The office of Sheriff (from the Old English shire-reeve) of a county was created in the tenth century. The Sheriff was the special nominee of the Sovereign, and the office reached the peak of its influence under the Norman kings. The Provisions of Oxford (1258) laid down a yearly tenure of office. Since the mid-16th century the office has been purely civil, with military duties taken over by the Lord-Lieutenant of the county. The Sheriff (commonly known as 'High Sheriff') attends on royalty during official visits to the county, acts as the returning officer during parliamentary elections in county constituencies, attends the opening ceremony when a High Court judge goes on circuit, executes High Court writs, and appoints under-sheriffs to act as deputies. The appointments and duties of the High Sheriffs in England and Wales are laid down by the Sheriffs Act 1887.

The serving High Sheriff submits a list of names of

possible future sheriffs to a tribunal which chooses three names to put to the Sovereign. The tribunal nominates the High Sheriff annually on 12 November and the Sovereign picks the name of the Sheriff to succeed in the following year. The term of office runs from 25 March to the following 24 March (the civil and legal year before 1752). No person may be chosen twice in three years if there is any other suitable person in the county.

CIVIC DIGNITIES

District councils in England may petition for a royal charter granting borough or 'city' status to the district. Local councils in Wales may petition for a royal charter granting county borough or 'city' status to the council.

In England and Wales the chairman of a borough or county borough council may be called a mayor, and the chairman of a city council a Lord Mayor. Parish councils in England and community councils in Wales may call themselves 'town councils', in which case their chairman is the town mayor.

In Scotland the chairman of a local council may be known as a convenor; a provost is the equivalent of a mayor. The chairmen of the councils for the cities of Aberdeen, Dundee, Edinburgh and Glasgow are Lord Provosts.

ENGLAND

There are currently 34 non-metropolitan counties; all are divided into non-metropolitan districts. In addition, there are 45 unitary authorities (13 created in April 1996, 13 in April 1997 and 19 in April 1998). At present there are 238 non-metropolitan districts. The populations of most of the new unitary authorities are in the range of 100,000 to 300,000. The non-metropolitan districts have populations broadly in the range of 60,000 to 100,000; some, however, have larger populations, because of the need to avoid dividing large towns, and some in mainly rural areas have smaller populations.

The main conurbations outside Greater London – Tyne and Wear, West Midlands, Merseyside, Greater Manchester, West Yorkshire and South Yorkshire – are divided into 36 metropolitan districts, most of which have a population of over 200,000.

There are also about 10,000 parishes, in 219 of the non-metropolitan and 18 of the metropolitan districts.

ELECTIONS

For districts, non-metropolitan counties and for about 8,000 parishes, there are elected councils, consisting of directly elected councillors. The councillors elect annually one of their number as chairman.

Generally, councillors serve four years and there are no elections of district and parish councillors in county election years. In metropolitan districts, one-third of the councillors for each ward are elected each year except in the year when county elections take place elsewhere. Non-metropolitan districts can choose whether to have elections by thirds or whole council elections. In the former case, one-third of the council, as nearly as may be, is elected in each year of metropolitan district elections. If whole council elections are chosen, these are held in the year midway between county elections.

FUNCTIONS

In non-metropolitan areas, functions are divided between the districts and counties, those requiring the larger area

or population for their efficient performance going to the county. The metropolitan district councils, with the larger population in their areas, already had wider functions than non-metropolitan councils, and following abolition of the metropolitan county councils were given most of their functions also. A few functions continue to be exercised over the larger area by joint bodies, made up of councillors from each district.

The allocation of functions is as follows:

County councils: education; strategic planning; traffic, transport and highways; fire service; consumer protection; refuse disposal; smallholdings; social services; libraries

Non-metropolitan district councils: local planning; housing; highways (maintenance of certain urban roads and off-street car parks); building regulations; environmental health; refuse collection; cemeteries and crematoria

Unitary councils: their functions are all those listed above, except that the fire service is exercised by a joint body

Concurrently by county and district councils: recreation (parks, playing fields, swimming pools); museums; encouragement of the arts, tourism and industry

The Police and Magistrates Court Act 1994 set up police authorities in England and Wales separate from the local authorities.

PARISH COUNCILS

Parishes with 200 or more electors must generally have parish councils, which means that over three-quarters of the parishes have councils. A parish council comprises at least five members, the number being fixed by the district council. Elections are held every four years, at the time of the election of the district councillor for the ward including the parish. All parishes have parish meetings, comprising the electors of the parish. Where there is no council, the meeting must be held at least twice a year.

Parish council functions include: allotments; encouragement of arts and crafts; community halls, recreational facilities (e.g. open spaces, swimming pools), cemeteries and crematoria; and many minor functions. They must also be given an opportunity to comment on planning applications. They may, like county and district councils, spend limited sums for the general benefit of the parish. They levy a precept on the district councils for their funds.

The Local Government and Rating Act 1997 gave additional powers to parish councils to spend money on community transport initiatives and crime prevention equipment.

FINANCE

Aggregate external finance for 1999–2000 was originally determined at £39,545 million. Of this, specific and special grants were estimated at £5,905 million; £19,902 million was in respect of revenue support grant and £13,612 million was support from the national non-domestic rate pool. Total standard spending by local authorities considered for grant purposes was £50,639 million.

The average council taxes, expressed in terms of Band D, two-adult properties for 1999–2000, were: inner London boroughs and the City of London £679; outer London boroughs £760; metropolitan districts £878; shire areas £792. The average for England was £664.

National non-domestic rate (or uniform business rate) for 1999–2000 is 48.9p. The provisional amount estimated to be raised from central, local and Crown lists is £12,700 million. Total rateable value held on draft local authority lists at 31 December 1998 was £29,300 million. The amount to be redistributed to authorities from the pool in 1999–2000 is £13,600 million.

Under the Local Government and Housing Act 1989, local authorities have four main ways of paying for capital expenditure: borrowing and other forms of extended credit; capital grants from central government towards some types of capital expenditure; 'usable' capital receipts from the sale of land, houses and other assets; and revenue.

The amount of capital expenditure which a local authority can finance by borrowing (or other forms of credit) is effectively limited by the credit approvals issued to it by central government. Most credit approvals can be used for any local authority service; these are known as basic credit approvals. Others (supplementary credit approvals) are for particular projects or services.

Generally, the 'usable' part of a local authority's capital receipts consists of 25 per cent of receipts from the sale of council houses. The balance has to be set aside as provision for repaying debt and meeting other credit liabilities. Since 1 September 1998, local authorities have been free to use all receipts from the sale of other property and assets.

EXPENDITURE

Local authority budgeted net revenue expenditure for 1999–2000 was (1999–2000 cash prices):

Service	£m
Education	22,564
Personal social services	9,673
Police	7,078
Highway maintenance	1,741
Fire	1,497
Civil defence and other Home Office services	577
Magistrates courts	316
Public transport and parking	685
Housing benefit administration	5,693
Non-housing revenue account housing	424
Libraries, culture and heritage	934
Sport	536
Local environmental services	5,933
Other services	415
Net current expenditure	58,066
Capital charges	2,137
Capital charged to revenue	762
Other non-current expenditure	2,303
Interest receipts	−767
Gross revenue expenditure	62,502
Specific and special grants outside AEF	−8,744
Revenue expenditure	53,758
Specific and special grants inside AEF	−2,340
Net revenue expenditure	51,418

AEF = aggregate external finance

LONDON

Since the abolition of the Greater London Council in 1986, the Greater London area has not had a single local government body. The area is divided into 32 borough councils, which have a status similar to the metropolitan district councils in the rest of England, and the Corporation of the City of London.

In March 1998 the Government announced proposals for a Greater London Authority (GLA) covering the area of the 32 London boroughs and the City of London, which would comprise a directly elected mayor and a 25-member assembly. A referendum was held in London on 7 May 1998; the turnout was approximately 34 per cent, of whom 72 per cent voted in favour of the GLA. The GLA will be responsible for transport, economic development, strategic planning, culture, health, the environment, the police and fire and emergency planning. The separately elected assembly will scrutinize the mayor's activities and approve plans and budgets. Fourteen of the assembly's members will be directly elected from constituencies made up of two or three London boroughs. The 11 additional members will be elected on a London-wide basis, either as independents or from party political lists on the basis of proportional representation. Parties or independent candidates must secure at least five per cent of the vote to be entitled to additional seats. Legislation to establish the GLA was introduced in Parliament in December 1998 and the Government plans to hold the first elections for the Mayor and Assembly on 4 May 2000, with the Authority assuming its responsibilities on 3 July 2000.

LONDON BOROUGH COUNCILS

The London boroughs have whole council elections every four years, in the year immediately following the county council election year. The next elections will be in 2002.

The borough councils have responsibility for the following functions: building regulations; cemeteries and crematoria; consumer protection; education; youth employment; environmental health; electoral registration; food; drugs; housing; leisure services; libraries; local planning; local roads; museums; parking; recreation (parks, playing fields, swimming pools); refuse collection and street cleansing; social services; town planning; and traffic management.

THE CORPORATION OF LONDON
(*see also* pages 550–2)

The Corporation of London is the local authority for the City of London. Its legal definition is 'The Mayor and Commonalty and Citizens of the City of London'. It is governed by the Court of Common Council, which consists of the Lord Mayor, 24 other aldermen, and 130 common councilmen. The Lord Mayor and two sheriffs are nominated annually by the City guilds (the livery companies) and elected by the Court of Aldermen. Aldermen and councilmen are elected from the 25 wards into which the City is divided; councilmen must stand for re-election annually. The Council is a legislative assembly, and there are no political parties.

The Corporation has the same functions as the London borough councils. In addition, it runs the City of London Police; is the health authority for the Port of London; has health control of animal imports throughout Greater London, including at Heathrow airport; owns and manages public open spaces throughout Greater London; runs the Central Criminal Court; and runs Billingsgate, Smithfield and Spitalfields markets.

THE CITY GUILDS (LIVERY COMPANIES)

The livery companies of the City of London grew out of early medieval religious fraternities and began to emerge as trade and craft guilds, retaining their religious aspect, in the 12th century. From the early 14th century, only members of the trade and craft guilds could call themselves citizens of the City of London. The guilds began to be called livery companies, because of the distinctive livery worn by the most prosperous guild members on ceremonial occasions, in the late 15th century.

By the early 19th century the power of the companies within their trades had begun to wane, but those wearing the livery of a company continued to play an important role in the government of the City of London. Liverymen still have the right to nominate the Lord Mayor and sheriffs, and most members of the Court of Common Council are liverymen (*see also* page 552).

GREATER LONDON SERVICES

After the abolition of the Greater London Council (GLC) in 1986, the London boroughs took over most of its functions. Successor bodies have also been set up for certain functions. The London Residuary Body (LRB) was set up in 1986 to deal with residual matters of the GLC. It completed its work and was wound up in 1995.

WALES

The Local Government (Wales) Act 1994 abolished the two-tier structure of eight county and 37 district councils which had existed since 1974, and replaced it, from 1 April 1996, with 22 unitary authorities. The new authorities were elected in May 1995. Each unitary authority has inherited all the functions of the previous county and district councils, except fire services (which are provided by three combined fire authorities, composed of representatives of the unitary authorities) and National Parks (which are the responsibility of three independent National Park authorities).

The Police and Magistrates Courts Act 1994 set up four police authorities with effect from 1 April 1995: Dyfed-Powys, Gwent, North Wales, and South Wales.

COMMUNITY COUNCILS

In Wales community councils are the equivalent of parishes in England. Unlike England, where many areas are not in any parish, communities have been established for the whole of Wales, approximately 865 communities in all. Community meetings may be convened as and when desired.

Community councils exist in 735 communities and further councils may be established at the request of a community meeting. Community councils have broadly the same range of powers as English parish councils. Community councillors are elected at the same time as a unitary authority election and for a term of four years.

FINANCE

Aggregate external finance for 1998–9 is £2,701.9 million. This comprises revenue support grant of £1,799.9 million, specific grants of £258.9 million, support from the national non-domestic rate pool of £612 million, and £31.2 million in council tax reduction grants. Total standard spending by local authorities considered for grant purposes is £3,090.5 million.

The average Band D council tax levied in Wales for 1998–9 is £555, comprising unitary authorities £513, police authorities £57, community councils £16 and an average grant reduction of £31.

National non-domestic rates (or uniform business rate) in Wales for 1998–9 is 42.9p. The amount estimated to be raised is £612 million. Total rateable value held on local authority lists at 31 December 1997 was £1,342 million.

EXPENDITURE

Local authority budgeted net revenue expenditure for 1999–2000 was (1999–2000 cash prices):

Service	£m
Education	1,427
Personal social services	616
Police	372
Highway maintenance	145

Fire	95
Probation and other Home Office services	35
Magistrates courts	19
Public transport and parking	18
Housing and council tax benefit	360
Non-housing revenue account housing	17
Libraries, museums and art galleries	50
Swimming pools and recreation	55
Local environmental services	314
Other services	97
Net current expenditure	3,620
Capital charges	259
Capital charged to revenue	19
Other non-current expenditure	11
Interest receipts	−20
Gross revenue expenditure	3,890
Specific grants outside AEF	−459
Revenue expenditure	3,431
Specific grants inside AEF	−68
Net revenue expenditure	3,362

AEF = aggregate external finance

SCOTLAND

The Local Government etc. (Scotland) Act 1994 abolished the two-tier structure of nine regional and 53 district councils which had existed since 1975 and replaced it, from 1 April 1996, with 29 unitary authorities on the mainland; the three islands councils remained. The new authorities were elected in April 1995. Each unitary authority has inherited all the functions of the regional and district councils, except water and sewerage (now provided by three public bodies whose members were appointed by the Secretary of State for Scotland; this power has now been devolved to the Scottish Executive) and reporters panels (now a national agency).

In July 1999 the Scottish Parliament assumed responsibility for legislation on local government. The Government had established a Commission on Local Government and the Scottish Parliament (the McIntosh Commission) to make recommendations on the relationship between local authorities and the new Parliament and on increasing local authorities' accountability. The Commission reported to the First Minister of the Scottish Parliament in June 1999. Among its recommendations were that joint working agreements and arrangements be set up between the Scottish Parliament, Scottish ministers and local councils; that councils should review their management and working practices with a view to becoming more accountable; and that councils should be elected for four years by proportional representation.

ELECTIONS

The unitary authorities consist of directly elected councillors. Elections take place every three years; the next elections are in 2002. In 1999 the register showed 4,027,433 electors in Scotland.

FUNCTIONS

The functions of the councils and islands councils are: education; social work; strategic planning; the provision of infrastructure such as roads; consumer protection; flood prevention; coast protection; valuation and rating; the police and fire services; civil defence; electoral registration; public transport; registration of births, deaths and marriages;

housing; leisure and recreation; development control and building control; environmental health; licensing; allotments; public conveniences; and the administration of district courts.

COMMUNITY COUNCILS

Unlike the parish councils and community councils in England and Wales, Scottish community councils are not local authorities. Their purpose as defined in statute is to ascertain and express the views of the communities they represent, and to take in the interests of their communities such action as appears to be expedient or practicable. Over 1,000 community councils have been established under schemes drawn up by district and islands councils in Scotland.

Since April 1996 community councils have had an enhanced role, becoming statutory consultees on local planning issues and on the decentralization schemes which the new councils have to draw up for delivery of services.

FINANCE

Figures for 1998–9 show total receipts from non-domestic rates of £441,126,663 (provisional) and £1,046 million from the council tax. The unified business rate for 1998–9 was 48p for property with a rateable value of less than £10,000 and 48.9p otherwise. The average Band D council tax payable was £827.

EXPENDITURE

Local authority current expenditure supported by aggregate external finance for 1999–2000 was (1999–2000 cash prices):

Service	£m
Tourism	8
Roads and transport	355
Housing	4
Other environmental services	749
Law, order and protective services	914
Education	2,875
Arts and libraries	115
Social work services	1,172
Housing benefit administration	30
Sheltered employment	10
Consumer protection	19
Total	6,251
Total excluding housing benefits, sheltered employment and consumer protection	6,192

NORTHERN IRELAND

For the purpose of local government Northern Ireland has a system of 26 single-tier district councils.

ELECTIONS

There are 582 members of the councils, elected for periods of four years at a time on the principle of proportional representation.

FUNCTIONS

The district councils have three main roles. These are:
Executive: responsibility for a wide range of local services including building regulations; community services; consumer protection; cultural facilities; environmental health; miscellaneous licensing and registration provisions, including dog control; litter prevention; recreational and social facilities; refuse collection and disposal; street cleansing; and tourist development

Representative: nominating representatives to sit as members of the various statutory bodies responsible for the administration of regional services such as drainage, education, fire, health and personal social services, housing, and libraries
Consultative: acting as the medium through which the views of local people are expressed on the operation in their area of other regional services, notably conservation (including water supply and sewerage services), planning and roads, provided by those departments of central government which have an obligation, statutory or otherwise, to consult the district councils about proposals affecting their areas

FINANCE

Local government in Northern Ireland is funded by a system of rates (a local property tax calculated by using the rateable value of a property multiplied by an amount per pound of rateable value). Rates are collected by the Rate Collection Agency, an executive agency within the Department of the Environment for Northern Ireland. A general revaluation of non-domestic properties became effective on 1 April 1997. As a result of this, separate regional rates are now made at standard uniform amounts by the Department of Finance and Personnel for both domestic and non-domestic sectors. District councils now make their individual district rates on the same basis.

In 1997–8 approximately £495 million was raised in rates. The average domestic poundage levied was 189.59p and the average non-domestic rate poundage was 41.37p.

Political Composition of Local Councils

AS AT END MAY 1999

Abbreviations:

C.	Conservative
Com.	Communist
Dem.	Democrat
Green	Green
Ind.	Independent
Lab.	Labour
Lib.	Liberal
LD	Liberal Democrat
MK	Mebyon Kernow
NP	Non-policital/Non-party
PC	Plaid Cymru
RA	Ratepayers'/Resident's Associations
SD	Social Democrat
SNP	Scottish National Party

ENGLAND

COUNTY COUNCILS

Bedfordshire	*C.* 25, *Lab.* 14, *LD* 10
Buckinghamshire	*C.* 38, *LD* 10, *Lab.* 5, *Ind.* 1
Cambridgeshire	*C.* 33, *Lab.* 10, *LD* 16
Cheshire	*Lab.* 19, *C.* 19, *LD* 10
Cornwall	*LD* 35, *Ind.* 27 *C.* 8, *Lab.* 8, *MK* 1
Cumbria	*Lab.* 43, *C.* 24, *LD* 12, *Ind.* 4
Derbyshire	*Lab.* 44, *C.* 12, *LD* 6, *Ind.* 2
Devon	*LD* 30, *C.* 14, *Lab.* 4, *Ind.* 3, *Lib.* 2, *Ind. LD* 1
Dorset	*LD* 21, *C.* 15, *Lab.* 5, *Ind.* 1
Durham	*Lab.* 52, *Ind.* 4, *C.* 2, *LD* 2, *vacant* 1
East Sussex	*C.* 20, *LD* 17, *Lab.* 7
Essex	*C.* 38, *Lab.* 24, *LD* 15, *Ind.* 2
Gloucestershire	*LD* 21, *C.* 22, *Lab.* 17, *Ind.* 3
Hampshire	*C.* 42, *LD* 22, *Lab.* 8, *Ind.* 2
Hertfordshire	*C.* 39, *Lab.* 29, *LD* 9
Kent	*C.* 45, *Lab.* 23, *LD* 16
Lancashire	*Lab.* 45, *C.* 23, *LD* 7, *Other* 2, *vacant* 1
Leicestershire	*C.* 25, *Lab.* 17, *LD* 11, *others* 1
Lincolnshire	*C.* 43, *Lab.* 19, *LD* 11, *Ind.* 3
Norfolk	*C.* 37, *Lab.* 33, *LD* 13, *Ind.* 1
Northamptonshire	*Lab.* 38, *C.* 27, *LD* 3
Northumberland	*Lab.* 42, *Ind.C.* 14, *LD* 8, *Ind.* 1, *Green* 1
North Yorkshire	*C.* 36, *Lab.* 11, *Ind.* 8, *Ind. Lab.* 19
Nottinghamshire	*Lab.* 42, *C.* 17, *LD* 4
Oxfordshire	*C.* 27, *Lab.* 22, *LD* 19, *Green* 2
Shropshire	*C.* 19, *LD* 13, *Lab.* 6, *others* 6
Somerset	*LD* 37, *C.* 17, *Lab.* 3
Staffordshire	*Lab.* 40, *C.* 20, *LD* 2
Suffolk	*Lab.* 31, *C.* 31, *LD* 15, *Ind.* 2, *vacant* 1
Surrey	*C.* 47, *LD* 17, *Lab.* 6, *Ind.* 3, *RA* 3
Warwickshire	*Lab.* 31, *C.* 21, *LD* 7, *Ind.* 2, *other* 1
West Sussex	*C.* 38, *LD* 23, *Lab.* 9, *Ind.* 1
Wiltshire	*C.* 23, *LD* 19, *Lab.* 4, *Ind.* 1
Worcestershire	*C.* 25, *Lab* 21, *LD* 8, *Ind.* 1, *Lib.* 1, *Ind. Lab.* 1

UNITARY COUNCILS

Barnsley	*Lab.* 57, *Ind.* 3, *C.* 2, *LD* 2 *vacant* 2
Bath and North-East Somerset	*LD* 30, *Lab.* 17, *C.* 16, *Ind.Lab.* 2
Birmingham	*Lab.* 77, *C.* 20, *LD* 16, *Ind.* 3, *vacant* 1
Blackburn with Darwen	*Lab.* 43, *C.* 16, *LD* 3
Blackpool	*Lab.* 33, *C.* 8, *LD* 3
Bolton	*Lab.* 41, *C.* 10, *LD* 9
Bournemouth	*LD* 19, *C.* 26, *Ind.* 6, *Lab.* 6
Bracknell Forest	*C.* 22, *Lab.* 18
Bradford	*Lab.* 54, *C.* 26, *LD* 10
Brighton and Hove	*Lab.* 45, *C.* 27, *Green* 3, *LD* 3
Bristol	*Lab.* 37, *LD* 23, *C.* 10
Bury	*Lab.* 37, *C.* 8, *LD* 3
Calderdale	*Lab.* 20, *C.* 19, *LD* 14, *Ind.* 1
Coventry	*Lab.* 44, *C.* 8, *others* 2
Darlington	*Lab.* 35, *C.* 15, *LD* 2
Derby	*Lab.* 34, *C.* 6, *LD* 4
Doncaster	*Lab.* 42, *LD* 9, *Ind.* 5, *C.* 5, *Ind. Lab.* 1, *other* 1
Dudley	*Lab.* 54, *C.* 8, *LD* 10
East Riding of Yorkshire	*C.* 27, *LD* 22, *Lab.* 12, *Ind.* 4, *SDP* 2
Gateshead	*Lab.* 49, *LD* 16, *Lib.* 1
Halton	*Lab.* 46, *LD* 8, *C.* 1, *vacant* 1
Hartlepool	*Lab.* 30, *LD* 10, *C.* 6, *Ind.* 1
Herefordshire	*LD* 31, *Ind.* 16, *C.* 8, *Lab.* 2, *others* 2, *vacant* 1
Isle of Wight	*LD* 16, *C.* 15, *Ind.* 9, *Ind. Lab.* 4, *Lib.* 2, *others* 2
Kingston upon Hull	*Lab.* 50, *Ind. Lab.* 4, *LD* 5, *C.* 1
Kirklees	*Lab.* 35, *LD* 23, *C.* 10, *Green* 3, *Ind.* 1
Knowsley Metropolitan Borough	*Lab.* 64, *LD* 2
Leeds	*Lab.* 70, *C.* 12, *LD* 14, *Green* 1, *others* 2
Leicester	*Lab.* 30, *LD* 16, *C.* 10
Liverpool	*LD* 59, *Lab.* 29, *Lib.* 5, *Ind.* 1, *others* 5
Luton	*Lab.* 36, *LD* 9, *C.* 3
Manchester	*Lab.* 79, *LD* 19, *vacant* 1
Medway	*Lab.* 39, *LD* 20, *C.* 21, *other* 1
Middlesbrough	*Lab.* 41, *LD* 7, *C.* 4, *Ind.* 1
Milton Keynes	*Lab.* 27, *LD* 19, *C.* 4, *Ind.* 1
Newcastle upon Tyne	*Lab.* 62, *LD* 15, *vacant* 1
North-East Lincolnshire	*Lab.* 22, *LD* 5, *C.* 11, *Ind.* 4
North Lincolnshire	*Lab.* 23, *C.* 19
North Somerset	*C.* 32, *Lab.* 13, *LD* 11, *Ind.* 4, *others* 1
North Tyneside	*Lab.* 39, *C.* 13, *LD* 8
Nottingham	*Lab.* 48, *C.* 4, *LD* 3
Oldham	*Lab.* 33, *LD* 26, *C.* 1
Peterborough	*Lab.* 26, *C.* 24, *Ind. Lab.* 1, *Lib.* 3, *LD* 2, *other* 1
Plymouth	*Lab.* 47, *C.* 13
Poole	*LD* 19, *C.* 17, *Lab.* 3
Portsmouth	*Lab.* 20, *C.* 10, *LD* 9
Reading	*Lab.* 36, *LD* 6, *C.* 3
Redcar and Cleveland	*Lab.* 32, *LD* 11, *Ind.* 2
Rochdale	*Lab.* 35, *LD* 18, *C.* 6, *vacant* 1
Rotherham	*Lab.* 63, *C.* 2, *LD* 1

Rutland — *Ind.* 8, *LD* 4, *C.* 1, *Lab.* 2, *Green* 1, *Ind. C.* 1, *others* 3

St Helens — *Lab.* 37, *LD* 14, *C.* 3

Salford — *Lab.* 56, *LD* 4

Sandwell — *Lab.* 61, *Lib.* 9, *C.* 2

Sefton — *Lab.* 30, *LD* 24, *C.* 15

Sheffield — *LD* 47, *Lab.* 39, *C.* 1

Slough — *Lab.* 32, *C.* 6, *Lib.* 3

Solihull — *C.* 24, *Lab.* 15, *LD* 11, *Ind.* 1

Southampton — *Lab.* 27, *LD* 14, *C.* 4

South Gloucestershire — *LD* 37, *Lab.* 25, *C.* 7, *vacant* 1

Southend — *C.* 19, *LD* 12, *Lab.* 8

South Tyneside — *Lab.* 51, *LD* 6, *others* 3

Stockport — *LD* 32, *Lab.* 25, *Ind.* 4, *C.* 2

Stockton-on-Tees — *Lab.* 38, *C.* 12, *LD* 5

Stoke-on-Trent — *Lab.* 48, *LD* 4, *C.* 2, *Ind.* 6

Sunderland — *Lab.* 64, *C.* 8, *LD* 2, *Lib.* 1

Swindon — *Lab.* 39, *LD* 10, *C.* 5

Tameside — *Lab.* 48, *C.* 4, *LD* 2

Telford and Wrekin — *Lab.* 38, *C.* 8, *LD* 4, *Ind. C.* 1, *Ind.* 2, *RA* 1

Thurrock — *Lab.* 45, *C.* 4

Torbay — *LD* 20, *C.* 13, *Lab.* 2, *others* 1

Trafford — *Lab.* 33, *C.* 27, *LD* 3

Wakefield — *Lab.* 58, *C.* 3, *Ind.* 2

Walsall — *Lab.* 31, *C.* 22, *Lib.* 6, *Ind.* 1

Warrington — *Lab.* 45, *LD* 11, *C.* 4

West Berkshire — *LD* 38, *C.* 14, *Ind.* 1, *vacant* 1

Wigan — *Lab.* 70, *LD* 2

Windsor and Maidenhead — *LD* 30, *C.* 20, *Ind.* 7, *Lab.* 1

Wirral — *Lab.* 39, *C.* 17, *LD* 10

Wokingham — *C.* 30, *LD* 24

Wolverhampton — *Lab.* 39, *C.* 17, *LD* 3

York — *Lab.* 27, *LD* 22, *C.* 3, *Ind.* 1

DISTRICT COUNCILS

*Denotes councils where one-third of councillors retire each year except in the year of county council elections

*Adur — *Lab.* 15, *LD* 13, *C.* 9, *RA* 2

Allerdale — *Lab.* 33, *Ind.* 3, *others* 10, *LD* 7, *vacant* 3

Alnwick — *LD* 13, *Lab.* 2, *others* 1, *C.* 2, *Ind.* 12

Amber Valley — *Lab.* 32, *C.* 11

Arun — *C.* 35, *LD* 10, *Lab.* 8, *Ind.* 2, *vacant* 1

Ashfield — *Lab.* 29, *C.* 1, *Ind.* 2, *LD* 1

Ashford — *C.* 24, *LD* 9, *Lab.* 12, *Ind. C.* 1, *Ind.* 2, *others* 1

Aylesbury Vale — *LD* 26, *C.* 24, *Ind.* 7, *Lab.* 1

Babergh — *Ind.* 13, *C.* 10, *Lab.* 5, *LD* 13, *others* 1

*Barrow-in-Furness — *Lab.* 18, *C.* 17, *others* 3

*Basildon — *Lab.* 23, *LD* 8, *C.* 11

*Basingstoke and Deane — *C.* 24, *Lab.* 15, *LD* 14, *Ind.* 3, *others* 1

*Bassetlaw — *Lab.* 32, *C.* 12, *LD* 3, *Ind.* 2, *vacant* 1

*Bedford — *Lab.* 19, *LD* 18, *C.* 9, *Ind.* 7

Berwick-upon-Tweed — *LD* 18, *Ind.* 9, *C.* 1, *Lab.* 1

Blaby — *C.* 25, *LD* 8, *Lab.* 6

Blyth Valley — *Lab.* 36, *LD* 9, *Ind.* 3, *C.* 2

Bolsover — *Lab.* 32, *Ind.* 4, *RA* 1

Boston — *Lab.* 11, *Ind.* 6, *C.* 12, *LD* 3

Braintree — *Lab.* 31, *C.* 17, *Ind.* 7, *LD* 3, *Green* 2

Breckland — *C.* 34, *Lab.* 14, *Ind.* 3, *LD* 2

*Brentwood — *LD* 25, *C.* 10, *Lab.* 2, *Lib.* 1, *Ind. C.* 1

Bridgnorth — *Ind.* 9, *Lab.* 4, *LD* 4, *Ind. C.* 4, *C.* 4, *others* 8

Broadland — *C.* 25, *Lab.* 12, *LD* 9, *Ind.* 3

Bromsgrove — *C.* 30, *Lab.* 7, *RA* 2

*Broxbourne — *C.* 33, *Lab.* 5

Broxtowe — *Lab.* 27, *C.* 10, *LD* 11, *Ind.* 1

*Burnley — *Lab.* 31, *LD* 9, *Ind.* 5, *C.* 3

*Cambridge — *Lab.* 21, *LD* 3, *C.* 18

*Cannock Chase — *Lab.* 33, *LD* 5, *C.* 3, *vacant* 1

Canterbury — *LD* 17, *Lab.* 14, *C.* 18

Caradon — *Ind.* 20, *LD* 18, *Lab.* 2, *C.* 1

*Carlisle — *C.* 28, *Lab.* 16, *Ind.* 2, *LD* 6

Carrick — *LD* 27, *Ind.* 7, *C.* 9, *Lab.* 2

Castle Morpeth — *Ind.* 12, *Lab.* 9, *C.* 4, *LD* 7, *Green* 1

Castle Point — *Lab.* 24, *C.* 15

Charnwood — *Lab.* 24, *C.* 21, *LD* 6, *Ind.* 1

Chelmsford — *LD* 28, *C.* 21, *Lab.* 5, *Ind.* 2

*Cheltenham — *C.* 18, *LD* 17, *Lab.* 1, *others* 5

*Cherwell — *C.* 26, *Lab.* 19, *LD* 5, *Ind.* 2

Chesterfield — *Lab.* 28, *LD* 19

Chester-le-Street — *Lab.* 30, *C.* 1, *Ind.* 1, *Lib.* 1

*Chester — *Lab.* 22, *LD* 18, *C.* 18, *Ind.* 2

Chichester — *C.* 29, *LD* 19, *Ind.* 2

Chiltern — *C.* 29, *LD* 19, *RA* 2

*Chorley — *Lab.* 31, *C.* 9, *LD* 6, *Ind.* 2

Christchurch — *C.* 17, *Ind.* 3, *LD* 5

*Colchester — *LD* 26, *Lab.* 15, *C.* 18, *Ind.* 1

*Congleton — *LD* 38, *Lab.* 2, *C.* 8

Copeland — *Lab.* 31, *C.* 17, *Ind.* 2, *LD* 1

Corby — *Lab.* 27, *C.* 1, *LD* 1

Cotswold — *Ind.* 15, *LD* 7, *Ind. C.* 2, *Lab.* 2, *C.* 14, *others* 5

*Craven — *C.* 19, *LD* 5, *Ind.* 10

*Crawley — *Lab.* 25, *C.* 5, *LD* 2

*Crewe and Nantwich — *Lab.* 29, *C.* 20, *LD* 5, *Ind.* 2

Dacorum — *C.* 26, *Lab.* 20, *LD* 6

Dartford — *Lab.* 28, *C.* 14, *Ind. Lab.* 1, *others* 4

*Daventry — *C.* 20, *Lab.* 13, *LD* 3, *Ind.* 2

Derbyshire Dales — *C.* 21, *LD* 9, *Lab.* 6, *Ind.* 3

Derwentside — *Lab.* 47, *Ind.* 7, *others* 1

Dover — *Lab.* 28, *C.* 26, *LD* 1, *Ind.* 1

Durham — *Lab.* 33, *LD* 13, *Ind.* 3

Easington — *Lab.* 45, *Lib.* 1, *Ind.* 4, *Ind. Lab.* 1

*Eastbourne — *LD* 15, *C.* 15

East Cambridgeshire — *LD* 20, *Ind.* 8, *NP* 4, *Lab.* 4, *C.* 1

East Devon — *C.* 39, *LD* 14, *Ind.* 5, *Lab.* 1, *Lib.* 1

East Dorset — *C.* 26, *LD* 9, *Ind.* 1

East Hampshire — *C.* 22, *LD* 17, *Ind.* 3

East Hertfordshire — *C.* 31, *LD* 9, *Lab.* 8, *Ind.* 2

*Eastleigh — *LD* 29, *Lab.* 8, *C.* 7

East Lindsey — *Ind.* 28, *Lab.* 9, *LD* 7, *C.* 6, *Green* 1, *others* 8, *vacant* 1

East Northamptonshire — *C.* 20, *Lab.* 15, *Ind.* 1

East Staffordshire — *Lab.* 28, *C.* 15, *LD* 3

Eden — *Ind.* 30, *LD* 3, *C.* 3, *Lab.* 2

*Ellesmere Port and Neston — *Lab.* 37, *C.* 5, *LD* 1

*Elmbridge — *C.* 24, *RA* 21, *LD* 8, *Lab.* 6, *Ind.* 1

*Epping Forest — *C.* 19, *LD* 15, *Lab.* 14, *others* 8, *Ind.* 3

Epsom and Ewell — *RA* 27, *LD* 9, *Lab.* 3

Erewash — *Lab.* 29, *C.* 16, *LD* 4, *Ind.* 3

*Exeter — *Lab.* 22, *LD* 8, *C.* 3, *Lib.* 3

*Fareham — C. 23, LD 14, Lab. 5
Fenland — C. 28, Lab. 7, Ind. 3, LD 1, vacant 1
Forest Heath — C. 21, Ind. 1, LD 2, Lab. 1
Forest of Dean — Lab. 30, Ind. 12, LD 6, C. 1, NP 2
Fylde — C. 21, Lab. 2, LD 3, Ind. 12, others 11
Gedling — C. 28, Lab. 18, LD 7, others 3
*Gloucester — Lab. 23, LD 8, C. 8
*Gosport — Lab. 11, C. 10, others 2, LD 7
Gravesham — Lab. 29, C. 15
*Great Yarmouth — Lab. 29, C. 19
Guildford — LD 20, C. 17, Ind. 2, Lab. 6
Hambleton — C. 35, Ind. 6, Lab. 2, LD 4
Harborough — C. 16, LD 14, Lab. 3, Ind. 4
*Harlow — Lab. 34, LD 4, C. 4
*Harrogate — LD 41, C. 15, Lab. 3
*Hart — C. 16, LD 13, Ind. 4, Ind. C. 2
*Hastings — Lab. 19, LD 11, C. 2
*Havant — C. 16, LD 11, Lab. 9, Ind. 3, Ind. Lab. 2, Lib. 1
*Hertsmere — C. 20, Lab. 13, LD 6
High Peak — Lab. 27, LD 5, C. 10, Ind. 2
Hinckley and Bosworth — LD 14, Lab. 9, C. 11
Horsham — C. 24, LD 16, Ind. 3
*Huntingdonshire — C. 36, LD 14, vacant 1, Ind. 2
*Hyndburn — Lab. 23, C. 23, Ind. C. 1
*Ipswich — Lab. 36, C. 10, Ind. 1, LD 1
Kennet — C. 20, Ind. 11, Lab. 4, LD 4, Ind. C. 1
Kerrier — Ind. 18, Lab. 11, LD 11, C. 4
Kettering — Lab. 22, C. 18, Ind. 4, LD 1
King's Lynn and West Norfolk — Lab. 27, C. 26, LD 5, Ind. 2
Lancaster — Ind. 22, Lab. 17, C. 8, LD 6, Ind. C. 1, Green 5, NP 1
Lewes — LD 30, C. 16, Ind. 1, RA 1
Lichfield — C. 29, Lab. 24, LD 2, Ind. 1
*Lincoln — Lab. 31, C. 2
*Macclesfield — C. 37, Lab. 7, LD 13, others 3
*Maidstone — LD 22, Lab. 13, C. 15, Ind. 5
Maldon — C. 17, Ind. 6, Lab. 6, Ind. C. 1
Malvern Hills — LD 21, C. 10, Ind. 8, Lab. 1, Ind. C. 2
Mansfield — Lab. 39, C. 5, LD 2
Melton — Lab. 13, C. 7, Ind. 6
Mendip — LD 16, Lab. 10, C. 18, Ind. 2
Mid Bedfordshire — C. 34, Lab. 7, Ind. 6, LD 6
Mid Devon — Ind. 18, LD 18, Lab. 1, Lib. 1, C. 2
Mid Suffolk — LD 14, C. 14, Lab. 6, Ind. 3, Ind. Lab. 2, vacant 1
*Mid Sussex — C. 29, LD 21, Ind. 2, Lab. 2
*Mole Valley — C. 17, LD 16, Ind. 7, Lab. 1
Newark and Sherwood — Lab. 26, C. 20, LD 5, Ind. 3
*Newcastle under Lyme — Lab. 36, Lib. 12, C. 7, Ind. 1
New Forest — C. 30, LD 25, Ind. 3
Northampton — Lab. 28, LD 11, C. 8
North Cornwall — Ind. 24, LD 10, C. 3, MK 1
North Devon — LD 26, Ind. 12, NP 1, C. 5
North Dorset — C. 17, LD 10, Ind. 6
North East Derbyshire — Lab. 38, C. 9, LD 3, Ind. Lab. 1, Ind. 2
*North Hertfordshire — C. 28, Lab. 18, LD 3
North Kesteven — C. 14, LD 10, Ind. 9, Lab. 7
North Norfolk — Lab. 10, LD 12, others 17, Ind. 7
North Shropshire — Ind. 9, Lab. 5, LD 1, C. 9, others 16
North Warwickshire — Ind. Lab. 22, C. 9, Lib. 2, Lab. 1

North West Leicestershire — Lab. 31, C. 8, Ind. 1
North Wiltshire — LD 26, C. 20, Lab. 4, Ind. 2
*Norwich — Lab. 33, LD 15
*Nuneaton and Bedworth — Lab. 40, C. 5
*Oadby and Wigston — LD 22, C. 4
Oswestry — Ind. 11, Lab. 6, C. 4, LD 5, Ind. Lab. 3
*Oxford — Lab. 28, LD 16, Green 7
*Pendle — LD 23, Lab. 20, C. 7, Ind. 1
*Penwith — LD 9, C. 9, Ind. 8, Lab. 5, MK 2, vacant 1
*Preston — Lab. 28, C. 13, LD 13, Ind. Lab. 2, Ind. 1
*Purbeck — C. 13, LD 5, Ind. 5, Lab. 1
*Redditch — Lab. 20, C. 6, LD 3
*Reigate and Banstead — C. 22, Lab. 13, LD 8, RA 6
Restormel — LD 17, Ind. 12, Lab. 1, C. 13, MK 1
Ribble Valley — C. 19, LD 18, Ind. 2
Richmondshire — Ind. 18, LD 9, C. 6, SDP 1
*Rochford — LD 13, Lab. 12, C. 11, RA 3, Ind. 1
*Rossendale — Lab. 21, C. 15
Rother — C. 28, LD 8, Ind. 4, Lab. 5
*Rugby — Lab. 22, C. 11, LD 7, Ind. 6, others 2
*Runnymede — C. 25, Lab. 9, Ind. 6, LD 2
Rushcliffe — C. 31, Lab. 11, LD 11, Ind. 1
*Rushmoor — C. 20, Lab. 13, LD 12
Ryedale — Ind. 6, LD 5, C. 11, Lab. 1
*St Albans — LD 21, Lab. 16, C. 21
St Edmundsbury — C. 23, Lab. 16, LD 2, Ind. 3
Salisbury — LD 16, Lab. 11, C. 27, Ind. 4
Scarborough — C. 17, Lab. 13, Ind. 14, LD 5
Sedgefield — Lab. 43, Ind. 4, LD 2
Sedgemoor — C. 31, Lab. 16, LD 2, Ind. 1
Selby — Lab. 19, C. 15, Ind. 6, vacant 1
Sevenoaks — C. 33, LD 9, Lab. 9, Ind. 2
Shepway — C. 30, LD 13, Lab. 13
*Shrewsbury and Atcham — Lab. 20, LD 11, C. 13, Ind. 4
*South Bedfordshire — LD 18, Lab. 16, C. 16, Ind. 3
South Bucks — C. 27, Ind. 10, LD 3
*South Cambridgeshire — C. 18, LD 14, Lab. 8, Ind. 14, vacant 1
South Derbyshire — Lab. 24, C. 9, Ind. C. 1
South Hams — C. 29, Ind. 4, LD 4, Lab. 3
South Holland — C. 20, Ind. 10, Lab. 3, Ind. Lab. 1, LD 1, NP 3
South Kesteven — C. 29, Ind. 14, Lab. 12, LD 3
*South Lakeland — LD 22, C. 17, Lab. 9, Ind. 4
South Norfolk — LD 27, C. 16, Lab. 2, Ind. 2
South Northamptonshire — C. 28, Lab. 7, Ind. 4, LD 3
South Oxfordshire — LD 20, Lab. 7, C. 20, Ind. 3
South Ribble — Lab. 21, C. 18, LD 12, others 3
South Shropshire — Ind. 16, LD 14, Green 2, others 8
South Somerset — LD 41, C. 13, Ind. 6
South Staffordshire — C. 37, Lab. 10, LD 1, Ind. 2
Spelthorne — C. 27, Lab. 9, LD 4
*Staffordshire Moorlands — Ind. C. 17, Lab. 15, RA 11, LD 9, Ind. 3, others 12
Stafford — Lab. 28, C. 23, LD 8, Ind. C. 1
*Stevenage — Lab. 33, LD 3, C. 3
*Stratford — C. 24, LD 20, Ind. 7, Lab. 4
*Stroud — Lab. 24, C. 17, LD 5, Ind. 4, Green 4, others 1
Suffolk Coastal — Lab. 36, Lab. 8, LD 10, Ind. 1
Surrey Heath — C. 22 LD 7, Lab. 7
*Swale — LD 23, Lab. 17, C. 9
*Tamworth — Lab. 27, C. 2, Ind. 1

*Tandridge	C. 18, LD 17, Lab. 7
Taunton Deane	LD 23, C. 21, Lab. 5, Ind. 4, Green 1
Teesdale	Ind. 12, Lab. 10, NP 8, C. 1
Teignbridge	Ind. 19, LD 16, C. 19, Lab. 2, others 2
Tendring	Lab. 23, Ind. 11, C. 17, LD 9
Test Valley	C. 28, LD 15, others 1
Tewkesbury	C. 13, Ind. 11, LD 4, Lab. 8
Thanet	Lab. 35, C. 16, Ind. 3
*Three Rivers	LD 26, C. 15, Lab. 7
*Tonbridge and Malling	C. 27, LD 21, Lab. 7
Torridge	Ind. 20, LD 12, Lab. 2, C. 1, Green 1
*Tunbridge Wells	C. 28, LD 12, Lab. 7, Ind. 1
Tynedale	Lab. 14, LD 10, C. 22, Ind. 6
Uttlesford	LD 18, C. 16, Ind. 6, Lab. 2
Vale of White Horse	LD 33, C. 15, Lab. 2, Ind. 1
Vale Royal	Lab. 33, C. 16, LD 8
Wansbeck	Lab. 25, LD 20
Warwick	Lab. 16, C. 10, LD 13, Ind. 6
*Watford	Lab. 19, LD 10, C. 7
*Waveney	Lab. 38, C. 5, LD 3, Ind. 2
Waverley	C. 31, LD 24, Lab. 2
Wealden	C. 34, LD 22, Ind. 2
Wear Valley	Lab. 30, Ind. 5, LD 5
Wellingborough	Lab. 20, C. 16
*Welwyn Hatfield	Lab. 24, C. 24
West Devon	LD 8, Ind. 13, C. 9
West Dorset	C. 22, LD 15, others 14, Lab. 4
*West Lancashire	Lab. 32, C. 21, Ind. 2
*West Lindsey	LD 16, Ind. 8, Lab. 3, C. 10
*West Oxfordshire	C. 19, Ind. 10, LD 13, Lab. 7
West Somerset	C. 17, Ind. 8, Lab. 5, LD 1
West Wiltshire	LD 27, C. 10, Lab. 2, Ind. 2, others 2
*Weymouth and Portland	Lab. 15, LD 12, Ind. 6, C. 2
*Winchester	LD 34, C. 12, Ind. 5, Lab. 4
*Woking	LD 14, C. 13, Lab. 7, Ind. 1
*Worcester	Lab. 20, C. 11, Ind. 3, LD 2
*Worthing	C. 20, LD 16
Wychavon	C. 31, LD 11, Lab. 5, Ind. 2
Wycombe	C. 42, LD 7, Lab. 9, Ind. 2
Wyre	C. 35, Lab. 19, LD 2
*Wyre Forest	Lab. 18, LD 4, C. 5, Lib. 3, Ind. 5, others 7

GREATER LONDON COUNCILS

Barking and Dagenham	Lab. 46, RA 3, LD 2
Barnet	C. 28, Lab. 26, LD 6
Bexley	C. 32, Lab. 24, LD 6
Brent	Lab. 43, C. 19, LD 4
Bromley	C. 29, LD 24, Lab. 7
Camden	Lab. 42, C. 11, LD 6
City of Westminster	C. 47, Lab. 13
Croydon	Lab. 38, C. 31, LD 1
Ealing	Lab. 53, C. 15, LD 3
Enfield	Lab. 43, C. 23
Greenwich	Lab. 52, C. 8, LD 2
Hackney	Lab. 29, LD 16, C. 13, Green 1, Ind. 1
Hammersmith and Fulham	Lab. 35, C. 14, Ind. 1
Haringey	Lab. 54, LD 3, C. 2
Harrow	Lab. 32, C. 20, Lib. 9, Ind. 2
Havering	Lab. 30, RA 16, C. 14, LD 3
Hillingdon	C. 33, Lab. 32, LD 4
Hounslow	Lab. 44, C. 11, LD 4, Ind. Lab. 1
Islington	Lab. 26, LD 26

Kensington and Chelsea	C. 39, Lab. 15
Kingston upon Thames	C. 21, LD 19, Lab. 10
Lambeth	Lab. 41, LD 18, C. 5
Lewisham	Lab. 59, LD 4, C. 2, others 1, vacant 1
Merton	Lab. 39, C. 12, Ind. 3, LD 3
Newham	Lab. 59, Ind. Lab. 1
Redbridge	Lab. 29, C. 24, LD 9
Richmond upon Thames	LD 34, C. 14, Lab. 4
Southwark	Lab. 32, LD 27, C. 4, Ind. 1
Sutton	LD 46, C. 5, Lab. 5
Tower Hamlets	Lab. 41, LD 9
Waltham Forest	Lab. 30, C. 14, LD 12, Ind. C. 1
Wandsworth	C. 50, Lab. 11

WALES

Anglesey	Ind. 27, PC 9, Lab. 4
Blaenau Gwent	Lab. 34, RA 4, Ind. 2, Lib. 1, Ind. Lab. 1
Bridgend	Lab. 42, Ind. 3, C. 1, LD 5, Ind. Lab. 1, PC 2
Caerphilly	PC 39, Lab. 28, Ind. 3, LD 3
Cardiff	Lab. 50, LD 18, C. 5, PC 1, Ind. Lab. 1
Carmarthenshire	Lab. 28, Ind. 25, PC 14, Ind. Lab 4, RA 2, LD 1
Ceredigion	Ind. 20, LD 7, PC 14, Lab. 1, others 2
Conwy	Lab. 19, C. 5, Ind. 14, LD 14, PC 7
Denbighshire	Ind. 17, Lab. 13, PC 8, C. 2, LD 1, others 5, vacant 1
Flintshire	Lab. 42, LD 7, PC 2, others 19
Gwynedd	PC 44, Ind. 19, Lab. 12, LD 6, others 2
Merthyr Tydfil	Lab. 16, Ind. 13, PC 4
Monmouthshire	C. 19, Lab. 18, Ind. 4, LD 1
Neath Port Talbot	Lab. 40, PC 10, RA 5, Ind. 3, LD 2, SDP 3, Ind.Lab. 1
Newport	Lab. 40, C. 5, others 2
Pembrokeshire	Ind. 38, Lab. 13, LD 3, PC 2, vacant 1, C. 3
Powys	Ind. 57, Lab. 7, LD 8, C. 1
Rhondda, Cynon, Taff	PC 42, Lab. 26, Ind. 5, LD 2
Swansea	Lab. 47, Ind. 8, LD 10, C. 4, PC 2, others 1
Torfaen	Lab. 39, C. 1, Ind. 3, LD 1
Vale of Glamorgan	C. 22, Lab. 19, PC 6
Wrexham	Lab. 26, C. 4, Ind. 8, others 2, Ind. Lab. 5, LD 7

SCOTLAND

Aberdeen City	Lab. 22, LD 12, C. 6, SNP 3
Aberdeenshire	LD 28, SNP 23, Ind. 10, C. 7
Angus	SNP 21, Ind. 3, C. 2, LD 2, Lab.1
Argyll and Bute	Ind. 19, LD 6, SNP 5, C. 4, Lab. 1, NP 1
City of Edinburgh	Lab. 31, C. 13, LD 13, SNP 1
Clackmannanshire	SNP 9, Lab. 8, Com.1
Dumfries and Galloway	Ind. 15, Lab. 13, C. 8, LD 6, SNP 5
Dundee City	Lab. 14, SNP 10, C. 4, Ind. Lab. 1

East Ayrshire	*Lab.* 17, *SNP* 14, *C.* 1
East Dunbartonshire	*Lab.* 11, *LD* 10, *C.* 3
East Lothian	*Lab.* 17, *C.* 5, *SNP* 1
East Renfrewshire	*Lab.* 9, *C.* 8, *LD* 2, *RA* 1
Eilean Siar/Western Isles	*NP* 22, *Lab.* 6, *SNP* 3
Falkirk	*Lab.* 15, *SNP* 9, *Ind.* 5, *C.* 2, *Ind. Lab.* 1
Fife	*Lab.* 43, *LD* 21, *SNP* 9, *Ind.* 2, *C.* 1, *Comm.* 1, *Dem. Left* 1
Glasgow City	*Lab.* 74, *SNP* 2, *C.* 1, *LD* 1, *other* 1
Highland	*Ind.* 50, *LD* 12, *Lab.* 10, *SNP* 8
Inverclyde	*Lab.* 11, *LD* 8, *C.* 1
Midlothian	*Lab.* 17, *LD* 1
Moray	*Ind.* 13, *Lab.* 6, *LD* 2, *SNP* 2, *Scottish Ind.* 2, *C.* 1
North Ayrshire	*Lab.* 25, *C.* 2, *SNP* 2, *Ind.* 1
North Lanarkshire	*Lab.* 56, *SNP* 12, *Ind.* 2
Orkney Islands	*Ind.* 20, *vacant* 1
Perth and Kinross	*SNP* 16, *C.* 11, *Lab.* 6, *LD* 6, *Ind.* 2
Renfrewshire	*Lab.* 21, *SNP* 15, *LD* 3, *C.* 1
Scottish Borders	*Ind.* 14, *LD* 14, *SNP* 4, *Lab.* 1, *C.* 1
Shetland Islands	*Ind.* 13, *LD* 8, *Ind. LD* 1
South Ayrshire	*Lab.* 17, *C.* 13
South Lanarkshire	*Lab.* 54, *SNP* 10, *C.* 2, *LD* 1
Stirling	*Lab.* 11, *C.* 9, *SNP* 2
West Dunbartonshire	*Lab.* 14, *SNP* 7, *Ind.* 1
West Lothian	*Lab.* 20, *SNP* 11, *C.* 1

England

The Kingdom of England lies between 55° 46' and 49° 57' 30" N. latitude (from a few miles north of the mouth of the Tweed to the Lizard), and between 1° 46' E. and 5° 43' W. (from Lowestoft to Land's End). England is bounded on the north by the Cheviot Hills; on the south by the English Channel; on the east by the Straits of Dover (Pas de Calais) and the North Sea; and on the west by the Atlantic Ocean, Wales and the Irish Sea. It has a total area of 50,351 sq. miles (130,410 sq. km): land 50,058 sq. miles (129,652 sq. km); inland water 293 sq. miles (758 sq. km).

POPULATION

The population at the 1991 census was 47,055,204 (males 22,812,889; females 24,242,315). The average density of the population in 1991 was 3.6 persons per hectare.

FLAG

The flag of England is the cross of St George, a red cross on a white field (cross gules in a field argent). The cross of St George, the patron saint of England, has been used since the 13th century.

RELIEF

There is a marked division between the upland and lowland areas of England. In the extreme north the Cheviot Hills (highest point, The Cheviot, 2,674 ft) form a natural boundary with Scotland. Running south from the Cheviots, though divided from them by the Tyne Gap, is the Pennine range (highest point, Cross Fell, 2,930 ft), the main orological feature of the country. The Pennines culminate in the Peak District of Derbyshire (Kinder Scout, 2,088 ft). West of the Pennines are the Cumbrian mountains, which include Scafell Pike (3,210 ft), the highest peak in England, and to the east are the Yorkshire Moors, their highest point being Urra Moor (1,490 ft).

In the west, the foothills of the Welsh mountains extend into the bordering English counties of Shropshire (the Wrekin, 1,334 ft; Long Mynd, 1,694 ft) and Hereford and Worcester (the Malvern Hills – Worcestershire Beacon, 1,394 ft). Extensive areas of highland and moorland are also to be found in the south-western peninsula formed by Somerset, Devon and Cornwall: principally Exmoor (Dunkery Beacon, 1,704 ft), Dartmoor (High Willhays, 2,038 ft) and Bodmin Moor (Brown Willy, 1,377 ft). Ranges of low, undulating hills run across the south of the country, including the Cotswolds in the Midlands and south-west, the Chilterns to the north of London, and the North (Kent) and South (Sussex) Downs of the south-east coastal areas.

The lowlands of England lie in the Vale of York, East Anglia and the area around the Wash. The lowest-lying are the Cambridgeshire Fens in the valleys of the Great Ouse and the River Nene, which are below sea-level in places. Since the 17th century extensive drainage has brought much of the Fens under cultivation. The North Sea coast between the Thames and the Humber, low-lying and formed of sand and shingle for the most part, is subject to erosion and defences against further incursion have been built along many stretches.

HYDROGRAPHY

The Severn is the longest river in Great Britain, rising in the north-eastern slopes of Plynlimon (Wales) and entering England in Shropshire with a total length of 220 miles (354 km) from its source into its outflow into the Bristol Channel, where it receives on the east the Bristol Avon, and on the

west the Wye, its other tributaries being the Vyrnwy, Tern, Stour, Teme and Upper (or Warwickshire) Avon. The Severn is tidal below Gloucester, and a high bore or tidal wave sometimes reverses the flow as high as Tewkesbury (13½ miles above Gloucester). The scenery of the greater part of the river is very picturesque and beautiful, and the Severn is a noted salmon river, some of its tributaries being famous for trout. Navigation is assisted by the Gloucester and Berkeley Ship Canal (16¾ miles), which admits vessels of 350 tons to Gloucester. The Severn Tunnel was begun in 1873 and completed in 1886 at a cost of £2 million and after many difficulties from flooding. It is 4 miles 628 yards in length (of which 2¼ miles are under the river). The Severn road bridge between Haysgate, Gwent, and Almondsbury, Glos, with a centre span of 3,240 ft, was opened in 1966.

The longest river wholly in England is the Thames, with a total length of 215 miles (346 km) from its source in the Cotswold hills to the Nore, and is navigable by ocean-going ships to London Bridge. The Thames is tidal to Teddington (69 miles from its mouth) and forms county boundaries almost throughout its course; on its banks are situated London, Windsor Castle, the oldest royal residence still in regular use, Eton College and Oxford, the oldest university in the kingdom.

Of the remaining English rivers, those flowing into the North Sea are the Tyne, Wear, Tees, Ouse and Trent from the Pennine Range, the Great Ouse (160 miles), which rises in Northamptonshire, and the Orwell and Stour from the hills of East Anglia. Flowing into the English Channel are the Sussex Ouse from the Weald, the Itchen from the Hampshire Hills, and the Axe, Teign, Dart, Tamar and Exe from the Devonian hills. Flowing into the Irish Sea are the Mersey, Ribble and Eden from the western slopes of the Pennines and the Derwent from the Cumbrian mountains.

The English Lakes, noteworthy for their picturesque scenery and poetic associations, lie in Cumbria, the largest being Windermere (10 miles long), Ullswater and Derwent Water.

ISLANDS

The Isle of Wight is separated from Hampshire by the Solent. The capital, Newport, stands at the head of the estuary of the Medina, Cowes (at the mouth) being the chief port. Other centres are Ryde, Sandown, Shanklin, Ventnor, Freshwater, Yarmouth, Totland Bay, Seaview and Bembridge.

Lundy (the name means Puffin Island), 11 miles north-west of Hartland Point, Devon, is about two miles long and about half a mile wide on average, with a total area of about 1,116 acres, and a population of about 20. It became the property of the National Trust in 1969 and is now principally a bird sanctuary.

The Isles of Scilly consist of about 140 islands and skerries (total area, 6 sq. miles/10 sq. km) situated 28 miles south-west of Land's End. Only five are inhabited: St Mary's, St Agnes, Bryher, Tresco and St Martin's. The population is 1,978. The entire group has been designated a Conservation Area, a Heritage Coast, and an Area of Outstanding Natural Beauty, and has been given National Nature Reserve status by the Nature Conservancy Council because of its unique flora and fauna. Tourism and the winter/spring flower trade for the home market form the basis of the economy of the Isles. The island group is a recognized rural development area.

EARLY HISTORY

Archaeological evidence suggests that England has been inhabited since at least the Palaeolithic period, though the extent of the various Palaeolithic cultures was dependent upon the degree of glaciation. The succeeding Neolithic and Bronze Age cultures have left abundant remains throughout the country, the best-known of these being the henges and stone circles of Stonehenge (ten miles north of Salisbury, Wilts) and Avebury (Wilts), both of which are believed to have been of religious significance. In the latter part of the Bronze Age the Goidels, a people of Celtic race, and in the Iron Age other Celtic races of Brythons and Belgae, invaded the country and brought with them Celtic civilization and dialects, place names in England bearing witness to the spread of the invasion over the whole kingdom.

THE ROMAN CONQUEST

The Roman conquest of Gaul (57–50 BC) brought Britain into close contact with Roman civilization, but although Julius Caesar raided the south of Britain in 55 BC and 54 BC, conquest was not undertaken until nearly 100 years later. In AD 43 the Emperor Claudius dispatched Aulus Plautius, with a well-equipped force of 40,000, and himself followed with reinforcements in the same year. Success was delayed by the resistance of Caratacus (Caractacus), the British leader from AD 48–51, who was finally captured and sent to Rome, and by a great revolt in AD 61 led by Boudicca (Boadicea), Queen of the Iceni; but the south of Britain was secured by AD 70, and Wales and the area north to the Tyne by about AD 80.

In AD 122, the Emperor Hadrian visited Britain and built a continuous rampart, since known as Hadrian's Wall, from Wallsend to Bowness (Tyne to Solway). The work was entrusted by the Emperor Hadrian to Aulus Platorius Nepos, legate of Britain from AD 122 to 126, and it was intended to form the northern frontier of the Roman Empire.

The Romans administered Britain as a province under a Governor, with a well-defined system of local government, each Roman municipality ruling itself and its surrounding territory, while London was the centre of the road system and the seat of the financial officials of the Province of Britain. Colchester, Lincoln, York, Gloucester and St Albans stand on the sites of five Roman municipalities, and Wroxeter, Caerleon, Chester, Lincoln and York were at various times the sites of legionary fortresses. Well-preserved Roman towns have been uncovered at or near Silchester (*Calleva Atrebatum*), ten miles south of Reading, Wroxeter (*Viroconium Cornoviorum*), near Shrewsbury, and St Albans (*Verulamium*) in Hertfordshire.

Four main groups of roads radiated from London, and a fifth (the Fosse) ran obliquely from Lincoln through Leicester, Cirencester and Bath to Exeter. Of the four groups radiating from London, one ran south-east to Canterbury and the coast of Kent, a second to Silchester and thence to parts of western Britain and south Wales, a third (later known as Watling Street) ran through Verulamium to Chester, with various branches, and the fourth reached Colchester, Lincoln, York and the eastern counties.

In the fourth century Britain was subject to raids along the east coast by Saxon pirates, which led to the establishment of a system of coastal defences from the Wash to Southampton Water, with forts at Brancaster, Burgh Castle (Yarmouth), Walton (Felixstowe), Bradwell, Reculver, Richborough, Dover, Lympne, Pevensey and Porchester (Portsmouth). The Irish (Scoti) and Picts in the north were also becoming more aggressive; from about AD 350 incursions became more frequent and more formidable. As the Roman Empire came under attack increasingly towards the end of the fourth century, many troops were removed from Britain for service in other parts of the empire. The island was eventually cut off from Rome by the Teutonic conquest of Gaul, and with the withdrawal of the last Roman garrison early in the fifth century, the Romano-British were left to themselves.

SAXON SETTLEMENT

According to legend, the British King Vortigern called in the Saxons to defend him against the Picts, the Saxon chieftains being Hengist and Horsa, who landed at Ebbsfleet, Kent, and established themselves in the Isle of Thanet; but the events during the one and a half centuries between the final break with Rome and the re-establishment of Christianity are unclear. However, it would appear that in the course of this period the raids turned into large-scale settlement by invaders traditionally known as Angles (England north of the Wash and East Anglia), Saxons (Essex and southern England) and Jutes (Kent and the Weald), which pushed the Romano-British into the mountainous areas of the north and west, Celtic culture outside Wales and Cornwall surviving only in topographical names. Various kingdoms were established at this time which attempted to claim overlordship of the whole country, hegemony finally being achieved by Wessex (capital, Winchester) in the ninth century. This century also saw the beginning of raids by the Vikings (Danes), which were resisted by Alfred the Great (871–899), who fixed a limit to the advance of Danish settlement by the Treaty of Wedmore (878), giving them the area north and east of Watling Street, on condition that they adopt Christianity.

In the tenth century the kings of Wessex recovered the whole of England from the Danes, but subsequent rulers were unable to resist a second wave of invaders. England paid tribute (*Danegeld*) for many years, and was invaded in 1013 by the Danes and ruled by Danish kings from 1016 until 1042, when Edward the Confessor was recalled from exile in Normandy. On Edward's death in 1066 Harold Godwinson (brother-in-law of Edward and son of Earl Godwin of Wessex) was chosen King of England. After defeating (at Stamford Bridge, Yorkshire, 25 September) an invading army under Harald Hadraada, King of Norway (aided by the outlawed Earl Tostig of Northumbria, Harold's brother), Harold was himself defeated at the Battle of Hastings on 14 October 1066, and the Norman conquest secured the throne of England for Duke William of Normandy, a cousin of Edward the Confessor.

CHRISTIANITY

Christianity reached the Roman province of Britain from Gaul in the third century (or possibly earlier); Alban, traditionally Britain's first martyr, was put to death as a Christian during the persecution of Diocletian (22 June 303), at his native town Verulamium; and the Bishops of Londinium, Eboracum (York), and Lindum (Lincoln) attended the Council of Arles in 314. However, the Anglo-Saxon invasions submerged the Christian religion in England until the sixth century when conversion was undertaken in the north from 563 by Celtic missionaries from Ireland led by St Columba, and in the south by a mission sent from Rome in 597 which was led by St Augustine, who became the first archbishop of Canterbury. England appears to have been converted again by the end of the seventh century and followed, after the Council of Whitby in 663, the practices of the Roman Church, which brought the kingdom into the mainstream of European thought and culture.

PRINCIPAL CITIES

BIRMINGHAM

Birmingham is Britain's second city. It is a focal point in national communications networks with a rapidly expanding international airport. The generally accepted derivation of 'Birmingham' is the *ham* (dwelling-place) of the *ing* (family) of *Beorma*, presumed to have been Saxon. During the Industrial Revolution the town grew into a major manufacturing centre and in 1889 was granted city status.

Despite the decline in manufacturing, Birmingham is still a major hardware trade and motor component industry centre. As well as the National Exhibition Centre and the Aston Science Park, recent developments include the International Convention Centre, the National Indoor Arena and Brindleyplace.

The principal buildings are the Town Hall (1834–50); the Council House (1879); Victoria Law Courts (1891); Birmingham University (1906–9); the 13th-century Church of St Martin-in-the-Bull-Ring (rebuilt 1873); Our Lady, Help of Christians Church; the Cathedral (formerly St Philip's Church) (1711) and the Roman Catholic Cathedral of St Chad (1839–41).

BRADFORD

Bradford lies on the southern edge of the Yorkshire Dales National Park, including within its boundaries the village of Haworth, home of the Brontë sisters, and Ilkley Moor.

Originally a Saxon township, Bradford received a market charter in 1251 but developed only slowly until the industrialization of the textile industry brought rapid growth during the 19th century; it was granted its city charter in 1897. The prosperity of that period is reflected in much of the city's architecture, particularly the public buildings: City Hall (1873), Wool Exchange (1867), St George's Hall (Concert Hall, 1853), Cartwright Hall (Art Gallery, 1904) and the Technical College (1882). Other chief buildings are the Cathedral (15th century) and Bolling Hall (14th century).

Textiles still play an important part in the city's economy but industry is now more broadly based, including engineering, micro-electronics, printing and chemicals. The city has a strong financial services sector, and a growing tourism industry.

BRISTOL

Bristol was a Royal Borough before the Norman Conquest. The earliest form of the name is *Bricgstow*. In 1373 Edward III granted Bristol county status.

The chief buildings include the 12th-century Cathedral (with later additions), with Norman chapter house and gateway, the 14th-century Church of St Mary Redcliffe, Wesley's Chapel, Broadmead, the Merchant Venturers' Almshouses, the Council House (1956), Guildhall, Exchange (erected from the designs of John Wood in 1743), Cabot Tower, the University and Clifton College. The Roman Catholic Cathedral at Clifton was opened in 1973.

The Clifton Suspension Bridge, with a span of 702 feet over the Avon, was projected by Brunel in 1836 but was not completed until 1864. Brunel's SS *Great Britain*, the first ocean-going propeller-driven ship, is now being restored in the City Docks from where she was launched in 1843. The docks themselves have been extensively restored and

redeveloped and are becoming a focus for the arts and recreation.

CAMBRIDGE

Cambridge, a settlement far older than its ancient University, lies on the River Cam or Granta. The city is a county town and regional headquarters. Its industries include electronics, high technology research and development, and biotechnology. Among its open spaces are Jesus Green, Sheep's Green, Coe Fen, Parker's Piece, Christ's Pieces, the University Botanic Garden, and the Backs, or lawns and gardens through which the Cam winds behind the principal line of college buildings. East of the Cam, King's Parade, upon which stand Great St Mary's Church, Gibbs' Senate House and King's College Chapel with Wilkins' screen, joins Trumpington Street to form one of the most beautiful throughfares in Europe.

University and college buildings provide the outstanding features of Cambridge architecture but several churches (especially St Benet's, the oldest building in the city, and St Sepulchre's, the Round Church) are also notable. The Guildhall (1939) stands on a site of which at least part has held municipal buildings since 1224.

CANTERBURY

Canterbury, the Metropolitan City of the Anglican Communion, dates back to prehistoric times. It was the Roman *Durovernum Cantiacorum* and the Saxon *Cant-wara-byrig* (stronghold of the men of Kent). Here in 597 St Augustine began the conversion of the English to Christianity, when Ethelbert, King of Kent, was baptized.

Of the Benedictine St Augustine's Abbey, burial place of the Jutish Kings of Kent (whose capital Canterbury was), only ruins remain. St Martin's Church, on the eastern outskirts of the city, is stated by Bede to have been the place of worship of Queen Bertha, the Christian wife of King Ethelbert, before the advent of St Augustine.

In 1170 the rivalry of Church and State culminated in the murder in Canterbury Cathedral, by Henry II's knights, of Archbishop Thomas Becket. His shrine became a great centre of pilgrimage, as described in Chaucer's *Canterbury Tales*. After the Reformation pilgrimages ceased, but the prosperity of the city was strengthened by an influx of Huguenot refugees, who introduced weaving. The poet and playwright Christopher Marlowe was born and reared in Canterbury, and there are also literary associations with Defoe, Dickens, Joseph Conrad and Somerset Maugham.

The Cathedral, with architecture ranging from the 11th to the 15th centuries, is world famous. Modern pilgrims are attracted particularly to the Martyrdom, the Black Prince's Tomb, the Warriors' Chapel and the many examples of medieval stained glass.

The medieval city walls are built on Roman foundations and the 14th-century West Gate is one of the finest buildings of its kind in the country.

The 1,000-seat Marlowe Theatre is a centre for the Canterbury Arts Festival each autumn.

CARLISLE

Carlisle is situated at the confluence of the River Eden and River Caldew, 309 miles north-west of London and about ten miles from the Scottish border. It was granted a charter in 1158.

The city stands at the western end of Hadrian's Wall and dates from the original Roman settlement of *Luguvalium*. Granted to Scotland in the tenth century, Carlisle is not included in the Domesday Book. William Rufus reclaimed the area in 1092 and the castle and city walls were built to guard Carlisle and the western border; the citadel is a Tudor addition to protect the south of the city. Border disputes were common until the problem of the Debateable Lands was settled in 1552. During the Civil War the city remained Royalist; in 1745 Carlisle was besieged for the last time by the Young Pretender.

The Cathedral, originally a 12th-century Augustinian priory, was enlarged in the 13th and 14th centuries after the diocese was created in 1133. To the south is a restored Tithe Barn and nearby the 18th-century church of St Cuthbert, the third to stand on a site dating from the seventh century.

Carlisle is the major shopping, commercial and agricultural centre for the area, and industries include the manufacture of metal goods, biscuits and textiles. However, the largest employer is the services sector, notably in central and local government, retailing and transport. The city has an important communications position at the centre of a network of major roads, as a stage on the main west coast rail services, and with its own airport at Crosby-on-Eden.

CHESTER

Chester is situated on the River Dee, and was granted borough and city status in 1974. Its recorded history dates from the first century when the Romans founded the fortress of *Deva*. The city's name is derived from the Latin *castra* (a camp or encampment). During the Middle Ages, Chester was the principal port of north-west England but declined with the silting of the Dee estuary and competition from Liverpool. The city was also an important military centre, notably during Edward I's Welsh campaigns and the Elizabethan Irish campaigns. During the Civil War, Chester supported the King and was besieged from 1643 to 1646. Chester's first charter was granted *c.* 1175 and the city was incorporated in 1506. The office of Sheriff is the earliest created in the country (*c.* 1120s), and in 1992 the Mayor was granted the title of Lord Mayor. He/she also enjoys the title 'Admiral of the Dee'.

The city's architectural features include the city walls (an almost complete two-mile circuit), the unique 13th-century Rows (covered galleries above the street-level shops), the Victorian Gothic Town Hall (1869), the Castle (rebuilt 1788 and 1822) and numerous half-timbered buildings. The Cathedral was a Benedictine abbey until the Dissolution. Remaining monastic buildings include the chapter house, refectory and cloisters and there is a modern free-standing bell tower. The Norman church of St John the Baptist was a cathedral church in the early Middle Ages.

Chester is a thriving retail, business and tourist centre.

COVENTRY

Coventry is an important industrial centre, producing vehicles, machine tools, agricultural machinery, man-made fibres, aerospace components and telecommunications equipment. New investment has come from financial services, power transmission, professional services, leisure and education.

The city owes its beginning to Leofric, Earl of Mercia, and his wife Godiva who, in 1043, founded a Benedictine monastery. The guildhall of St Mary dates from the 14th century, three of the city's churches date from the 14th and 15th centuries, and 16th-century almshouses may still be seen. Coventry's first cathedral was destroyed at the Reformation, its second in the 1940 blitz (the walls and spire remain) and the new cathedral designed by Sir Basil Spence, consecrated in 1962, now draws numerous visitors.

Coventry is the home of the University of Warwick and its Science Park, Coventry University, the Westwood Business Park, the Cable and Wireless College, the Museum of British Road Transport and the Coventry Arena.

DERBY

Derby stands on the banks of the River Derwent, and its name dates back to 880 when the Danes settled in the locality and changed the original Saxon name of *Northworthy* to *Deoraby*.

Derby has a wide range of industries including aero engines, cars, pipework, specialized mechanical engineering equipment, textiles, chemicals, plastics and the Royal Crown Derby porcelain. The city is an established railway centre with rail research, engineering, safety testing, infrastructure and train-operating companies.

Buildings of interest include St Peter's Church and the Old Abbey Building (14th century), the Cathedral (1525), St Mary's Roman Catholic Church (1839) and the Industrial Museum, formerly the Old Silk Mill (1721). The traditional city centre is complemented by the Eagle Centre and 'out-of-centre' retail developments. In addition to the Derby Playhouse, the Assembly Rooms are a multi-purpose venue.

The first charter granting a Mayor and Aldermen was that of Charles I in 1637. Previous charters date back to 1154. It was granted city status in 1977.

DURHAM

The city of Durham is a district in the county of Durham and a major tourist attraction because of its prominent Norman Cathedral and Castle set high on a wooded peninsula overlooking the River Wear. The Cathedral was founded as a shrine for the body of St Cuthbert in 995. The present building dates from 1093 and among its many treasures is the tomb of the Venerable Bede (673–735). Durham's Prince Bishops had unique powers up to 1836, being lay rulers as well as religious leaders. As a palatinate Durham could have its own army, nobility, coinage and courts. The Castle was the main seat of the Prince Bishops for nearly 800 years; it is now used as a college by the University. The University, founded on the initiative of Bishop William Van Mildert, is England's third oldest.

Among other buildings of interest is the Guildhall in the Market Place which dates originally from the 14th century. Work has been carried out to conserve this area as part of the city's contribution to the Council of Europe's Urban Renaissance Campaign. Annual events include Durham's Regatta in June (claimed to be the oldest rowing event in Britain) and the Annual Gala (formerly Durham Miners' Gala) in July.

The economy has undergone a significant change with the replacement of mining as the dominant industry by 'white collar' employment. Although still a predominantly rural area, the industrial and commercial sector is growing and a wide range of manufacturing and service industries are based on industrial estates in and around the city. A research and development centre, linked to the University, also plays an important role in the local economy.

EXETER

Exeter lies on the River Exe ten miles from the sea. It was granted a charter by Henry II. The Romans founded *Isca Dumnoniorum* in the first century AD, and in the third century a stone wall (much of which remains) was built, providing protection against Saxon, and then Danish invasions. After the Conquest, the city led resistance to William in the west until reduced by siege. The Normans built the ringwork castle of Rougemont, the gatehouse and one tower of which remain, although the rest was pulled down in 1784. The first bridge across the Exe was built in the early 13th century. The city's main port was situated downstream at Topsham until the construction in the 1560s of the first true canal in England, the redevelopment of which in 1700 brought seaborne trade direct to the city. Exeter was the Royalist headquarters in the west during the Civil War.

The diocese of Exeter was established by Edward the Confessor in 1050, although a minster existed near the Cathedral site from the late seventh century. A new cathedral was built in the 12th century but the present building, which incorporates the Norman Towers, was begun *c.* 1275 and completed about a century later. The Guildhall dates from the 12th century and there are many other medieval buildings in the city, as well as architecture in the Georgian and Regency styles, and the Custom House (1680). Damage suffered by bombing in 1942 led to the redevelopment of the city centre.

Exeter's prosperity from medieval times was based on trade in wool and woollen cloth (commemorated by Tuckers Hall), which flourished until the late 18th century when export trade was hit by the French wars. Subsequently Exeter has developed as an administrative and commercial centre, notably in the distributive trades, light manufacturing industries and tourism.

KINGSTON UPON HULL

Hull (officially Kingston upon Hull) lies at the junction of the River Hull with the Humber, 22 miles from the North Sea. It is one of the major seaports of the United Kingdom, comprising 2,000 acres in four main dock installations. The port provides a wide range of cargo services, including ro-ro and container traffic, and handles a million passengers annually on daily sailings to Rotterdam and Zeebrugge. There is a variety of manufacturing and service industries, as well as increasing tourism and conference business.

The city, restored after heavy air raid damage during the Second World War, has good office and administrative buildings, its municipal centre being the Guildhall, its educational centres the University of Hull and the University of Lincolnshire and Humberside and its religious centre the Parish Church of the Holy Trinity. The old town area has been renovated and includes a marina and shopping complex. Just west of the city is the Humber Bridge, the world's longest single-span suspension bridge.

Kingston upon Hull was so named by Edward I. City status was accorded in 1897 and the office of Mayor raised to the dignity of Lord Mayor in 1914.

LEEDS

Leeds, situated in the lower Aire Valley, is a junction for road, rail, canal and air services and an important manufacturing and commercial centre. Seventy-three per cent of employment is in services, notably the distributive trades, public administration, medical services and business services. The main manufacturing industries are mechanical engineering, printing and publishing, metal goods and furniture.

The principal buildings are the Civic Hall (1933), the Town Hall (1858), the Municipal Buildings and Art Gallery (1884) with the Henry Moore Gallery (1982), the Corn Exchange (1863) and the University. The Parish Church (St Peter's) was rebuilt in 1841; the 17th-century St John's Church has a fine interior with a famous English Renaissance screen; the last remaining 18th-century church in the city is Holy Trinity in Boar Lane (1727). Kirkstall Abbey (about three miles from the centre of the city),

founded by Henry de Lacy in 1152, is one of the most complete examples of Cistercian houses now remaining. Temple Newsam, birthplace of Lord Darnley, was acquired by the Council in 1922. The present house was largely rebuilt by Sir Arthur Ingram in about 1620. Adel Church, about five miles from the centre of the city, is a fine Norman structure. The new Royal Armouries Museum houses the collection of antique arms and armour formerly held at the Tower of London.

Leeds was first incorporated by Charles I in 1626. The earliest forms of the name are *Loidis* or *Ledes*, the origins of which are obscure.

LEICESTER

Leicester is situated geographically in the centre of England. It dates back to pre-Roman times and was one of the Five Boroughs of the Danelaw. In 1589 Queen Elizabeth I granted a charter to the city and the ancient title was confirmed by letters patent in 1919.

The principal industries are hosiery, knitwear, footwear manufacturing and engineering. The growth of Leicester as a hosiery centre increased rapidly from the introduction there of the first stocking frame in 1670 and today it has some of the largest hosiery factories in the world.

The principal buildings are the Town Hall, the New Walk Centre, the University of Leicester, De Montfort University, De Montfort Hall, one of the finest concert halls in the provinces seating over 2,750 people, and the Granby Halls, an indoor sports facility. The ancient churches of St Martin (now Leicester Cathedral), St Nicholas, St Margaret, All Saints, St Mary de Castro, and buildings such as the Guildhall, the 14th-century Newarke Gate, the Castle and the Jewry Wall Roman site still exist. The Haymarket Theatre was opened in 1973 and The Shires shopping centre in 1992.

LINCOLN

Situated 40 miles inland on the River Witham, Lincoln derives its name from a contraction of *Lindum Colonia*, the settlement founded in AD 48 by the Romans to command the crossing of Ermine Street and Fosse Way. Sections of the third-century Roman city wall can be seen, including an extant gateway (Newport Arch), and excavations have discovered traces of a sewerage system unique in Britain. The Romans also drained the surrounding fenland and created a canal system, laying the foundations of Lincoln's agricultural prosperity and also of the city's importance in the medieval wool trade as a port and Staple town.

As one of the Five Boroughs of the Danelaw, Lincoln was an important trading centre in the ninth and tenth centuries and medieval prosperity from the wool trade lasted until the 14th century, enabling local merchants to build parish churches (of which three survive), and attracting in the 12th century a Jewish community (Jew's House and Court, Aaron's House). However, the removal of the Staple to Boston in 1369 heralded a decline from which the city only recovered fully in the 19th century when improved fen drainage made Lincoln agriculturally important and improved canal and rail links led to industrial development, mainly in the manufacture of machinery, components and engineering products.

The castle was built shortly after the Conquest and is unusual in having two mounds; on one motte stands a Keep (Lucy's Tower) added in the 12th century. It currently houses one of the four surviving copies of the Magna Carta. The Cathedral was begun *c.* 1073 when the first Norman bishop moved the see of Lindsey to Lincoln, but was mostly destroyed by fire and earthquake in the 12th century. Rebuilding was begun by St Hugh and completed over a century later. Other notable architectural features are the 12th-century High Bridge, the oldest in Britain still to carry buildings, and the Guildhall situated above the 15th–16th-century Stonebow gateway.

LIVERPOOL

Liverpool, on the right bank of the River Mersey, three miles from the Irish Sea, is the United Kingdom's foremost port for the Atlantic trade. Tunnels link Liverpool with Birkenhead and Wallasey.

There are 2,100 acres of dockland on both sides of the river and the Gladstone and Royal Seaforth Docks can accommodate Panamax-sized vessels. Approximately 31 million tonnes of cargo is handled annually. The main cargoes are crude oil, grain, fossil fuels, edible oils, timber, scrap metal, containers and break-bulk cargo. Liverpool Free Port, Britain's largest, was opened in 1984.

Liverpool was created a free borough in 1207 and a city in 1880. From the early 18th century it expanded rapidly with the growth of industrialization and the Atlantic trade. Surviving buildings from this period include the Bluecoat Chambers (1717, formerly the Bluecoat School), the Town Hall (1754, rebuilt to the original design 1795), and buildings in Rodney Street, Canning Street and the suburbs. Notable from the 19th and 20th centuries are the Anglican Cathedral, built from the designs of Sir Giles Gilbert Scott (the foundation stone was laid in 1904, and the building was completed only in 1980), the Catholic Metropolitan Cathedral (designed by Sir Frederick Gibberd, consecrated 1967) and St George's Hall (1838–54), regarded as one of the finest modern examples of classical architecture. The refurbished Albert Dock (designed by Jesse Hartley) contains the Merseyside Maritime Museum and Tate Gallery, Liverpool.

In 1852 an Act was obtained for establishing a public library, museum and art gallery; as a result Liverpool had one of the first public libraries in the country. The Brown, Picton and Hornby libraries now form one of the country's major libraries. The Victoria Building of Liverpool University, the Royal Liver, Cunard and Mersey Docks & Harbour Company buildings at the Pier Head, the Municipal Buildings and the Philharmonic Hall are other examples of the city's fine buildings.

MANCHESTER

Manchester (the *Mamucium* of the Romans, who occupied it in AD 79) is a commercial and industrial centre with a population engaged in the engineering, chemical, clothing, food processing and textile industries and in education. Banking, insurance and a growing leisure industry are among the prime commercial activities. The city is connected with the sea by the Manchester Ship Canal, opened in 1894, 35½ miles long, and accommodating ships up to 15,000 tons. Manchester Airport handles 15 million passengers yearly.

The principal buildings are the Town Hall, erected in 1877 from the designs of Alfred Waterhouse, with a large extension of 1938; the Royal Exchange (1869, enlarged 1921); the Central Library (1934); Heaton Hall; the 17th-century Chetham Library; the Rylands Library (1900), which includes the Althorp collection; the University precinct; the 15th-century Cathedral (formerly the parish church) and G-MEX exhibition centre. Recent developments include the Manchester Arena, the largest indoor arena in Europe, and the Bridgewater Hall. Manchester is the home of the Hallé Orchestra, the Royal Northern College of Music, the Royal Exchange Theatre and seven public art galleries. Metrolink, the light rail system, opened in 1992.

The Commonwealth Games are to be held in Manchester in 2002 and new sports facilities include a stadium, a swimming pool complex and the National Cycling Centre.

The town received its first charter of incorporation in 1838 and was created a city in 1853.

NEWCASTLE UPON TYNE

Newcastle upon Tyne, on the north bank of the River Tyne, is eight miles from the North Sea. A cathedral and university city, it is the administrative, commercial and cultural centre for north-east England and the principal port. It is an important manufacturing centre with a wide variety of industries.

The principal buildings include the Castle Keep (12th century), Black Gate (13th century), Blackfriars (13th century), West Walls (13th century), St Nicholas's Cathedral (15th century, fine lantern tower), St Andrew's Church (12th–14th century), St John's (14th–15th century), All Saints (1786 by Stephenson), St Mary's Roman Catholic Cathedral (1844), Trinity House (17th century), Sandhill (16th-century houses), Guildhall (Georgian), Grey Street (1834–9), Central Station (1846–50), Laing Art Gallery (1904), University of Newcastle Physics Building (1962) and Medical Building (1985), Civic Centre (1963), Central Library (1969) and Eldon Square Shopping Development (1976). Open spaces include the Town Moor (927 acres) and Jesmond Dene. Nine bridges span the Tyne at Newcastle.

The city's name is derived from the 'new castle' (1080) erected as a defence against the Scots. In 1400 it was made a county, and in 1882 a city.

NORWICH

Norwich grew from an early Anglo-Saxon settlement near the confluence of the Rivers Yare and Wensum, and now serves as provincial capital for the predominantly agricultural region of East Anglia. The name is thought to relate to the most northerly of a group of Anglo-Saxon villages or *wics*. The city's first known charter was granted in 1158 by Henry II.

Norwich serves its surrounding area as a market town and commercial centre, banking and insurance being prominent among the city's businesses. From the 14th century until the Industrial Revolution, Norwich was the regional centre of the woollen industry, but now the biggest single industry is financial services and principal trades are engineering, printing, shoemaking, double glazing, the production of chemicals and clothing, food processing and technology. Norwich is accessible to seagoing vessels by means of the River Yare, entered at Great Yarmouth, 20 miles to the east.

Among many historic buildings are the Cathedral (completed in the 12th century and surmounted by a 15th-century spire 315 feet in height), the keep of the Norman castle (now a museum and art gallery), the 15th-century flint-walled Guildhall (now a tourist information centre), some thirty medieval parish churches, St Andrew's and Blackfriars' Halls, the Tudor houses preserved in Elm Hill and the Georgian Assembly House. The University of East Anglia is on the city's western boundary.

NOTTINGHAM

Nottingham stands on the River Trent and is connected by canal with the Atlantic Ocean and the North Sea. *Snotingaham* or *Notingeham*, literally the homestead of the people of Snot, is the Anglo-Saxon name for the Celtic settlement of *Tigguocobauc*, or the house of caves. In 878,

Nottingham became one of the Five Boroughs of the Danelaw. William the Conqueror ordered the construction of Nottingham Castle, while the town itself developed rapidly under Norman rule. Its laws and rights were later formally recognized by Henry II's charter in 1155. The Castle became a favoured residence of King John. In 1642 King Charles I raised his personal standard at Nottingham Castle at the start of the Civil War.

Nottingham is home to Notts County FC (the world's oldest football league side), Nottingham Racecourse and the National Watersports Centre. The principal industries include textiles, pharmaceuticals, food manufacturing, engineering and telecommunications. There are two universities within the city boundaries.

Architecturally, Nottingham has a wealth of notable buildings, particularly those designed in the Victorian era by T. C. Hine and Watson Fothergill. The City Council owns the Castle, of Norman origin but restored in 1878, Wollaton Hall (1580–8), Newstead Abbey (home of Lord Byron), the Guildhall (1888) and Council House (1929). St Mary's, St Peter's and St Nicholas's Churches are of interest, as is the Roman Catholic Cathedral (Pugin, 1842–4).

Nottingham was granted city status in 1897.

OXFORD

Oxford is a university city, an important industrial centre, and a market town. Industry played a minor part in Oxford until the motor industry was established in 1912.

It is for its architecture that Oxford is of most interest to the visitor, its oldest specimens being the reputedly Saxon tower of St Michael's church, the remains of the Norman castle and city walls, and the Norman church at Iffley. It is chiefly famous, however, for its Gothic buildings, such as the Divinity Schools, the Old Library at Merton College, William of Wykeham's New College, Magdalen College and Christ Church and many other college buildings. Later centuries are represented by the Laudian quadrangle at St John's College, the Renaissance Sheldonian Theatre by Wren, Trinity College Chapel, and All Saints Church; Hawksmoor's mock-Gothic at All Souls College, and the 18th-century Queen's College. In addition to individual buildings, High Street and Radcliffe Square, just off it, both form architectural compositions of great beauty. Most of the Colleges have gardens, those of Magdalen, New College, St John's and Worcester being the largest.

PLYMOUTH

Plymouth is situated on the borders of Devon and Cornwall at the confluence of the Rivers Tamar and Plym. The city has a long maritime history; it was the home port of Sir Francis Drake and the starting point for his circumnavigation of the world, as well as the last port of call for the *Mayflower* when the Pilgrim Fathers sailed for the New World in 1620. Today Plymouth is host to many international yacht races. The Barbican harbour area has many Elizabethan buildings and on Plymouth Hoe stands Smeaton's lighthouse, the third to be built on the Eddystone Rocks 13 miles offshore.

The city centre was rebuilt following extensive war damage, and comprises a large shopping centre, municipal offices, law courts and public buildings. The main employment is provided at the naval base, though many industrial firms and service industries have become established in the post-war period and the city is a growing tourism centre. In 1982 the Theatre Royal was opened. In conjunction with the Cornwall County Council, the Tamar Bridge was constructed linking the city by road with Cornwall.

PORTSMOUTH

Portsmouth occupies Portsea Island, Hampshire, with boundaries extending to the mainland. It is a centre of industry and commerce, including many high technology and manufacturing industries. It is the British headquarters of several major international companies. The Royal Navy base still has a substantial work-force, although this has decreased in recent years. The commercial port and continental ferry port is owned and run by the City Council, and carries passengers and vehicles to France and northern Spain.

A major port since the 16th century, Portsmouth is also a thriving seaside resort catering for thousands of visitors annually. Among many historic attractions are Lord Nelson's flagship, HMS *Victory*, the Tudor warship *Mary Rose*, Britain's first 'ironclad' warship, HMS *Warrior*, the D-Day Museum, Charles Dickens' birthplace at 393 Old Commercial Road, the Royal Naval and Royal Marine museums, Southsea Castle (built by Henry VIII), Fort Nelson on Portsdown Hill, the Sealife Centre and the Round Tower and Point Battery, which for hundreds of years have guarded the entrance to Portsmouth Harbour.

ST ALBANS

The origins of St Albans, situated on the River Ver, stem from the Roman town of *Verulamium*. Named after the first Christian martyr in Britain, who was executed here, St Albans has developed around the Norman Abbey and Cathedral Church (consecrated 1115), built partly of materials from the old Roman city. The museums house Iron Age and Roman artefacts and the Roman Theatre, unique in Britain, has a stage as opposed to an amphitheatre. Archaeological excavations in the city centre have revealed evidence of pre-Roman, Saxon and medieval occupation.

The town's significance grew to the extent that it was a signatory and venue for the drafting of the Magna Carta. It was also the scene of riots during the Peasants' Revolt, where French King John was imprisoned there after the Battle of Poitiers, and heavy fighting took place there during the Wars of the Roses.

Previously controlled by the Abbot, the town achieved a charter in 1553 and city status in 1877. The street market, first established in 1553, is still an important feature of the city, as are many hotels and inns which survive from the days when St Albans was an important coach stop. Tourist attractions include historic churches and houses, and a 15th-century clock tower.

The city now contains a wide range of firms, with special emphasis on information and legal services. In addition, it is the home of the Royal National Rose Society, and of Rothamsted Park, the agricultural research centre.

SHEFFIELD

Sheffield, the centre of the special steel and cutlery trades, is situated at the junction of the Sheaf, Porter, Rivelin and Loxley valleys with the River Don. Though its cutlery, silverware and plate have long been famous, Sheffield has other and now more important industries: special and alloy steels, engineering, tool-making, medical equipment and media-related industries (in its new Cultural Industries Quarter). Sheffield has two universities and is an important research centre.

The parish church of St Peter and St Paul, founded in the 12th century, became the Cathedral Church of the Diocese of Sheffield in 1914. The Roman Catholic Cathedral Church of St Marie (founded 1847) was created Cathedral for the new diocese of Hallam in 1980. Parts of the present building date from c.1435. The principal buildings are the Town Hall (1897), the Cutlers' Hall (1832), City Hall (1932), Graves Art Gallery (1934), Mappin Art Gallery, the Crucible Theatre and the restored 19th-century Lyceum theatre, which dates from 1897 and was reopened in 1990. Three major sports venues were opened in 1990 to 1991. The National Centre for Popular Music was opened in 1999.

Sheffield was created a city in 1893.

Master Cutler of the Company of Cutlers in Hallamshire 1998–9, D. B. Liversidge

SOUTHAMPTON

Southampton is the leading British deep-sea port on the Channel and is situated on one of the finest natural harbours in the world. The first charter was granted by Henry II and Southampton was created a county of itself in 1447. In 1964 it was granted city status.

There were Roman and Saxon settlements on the site of the city, which has been an important port since Anglo-Saxon times due to its natural deep-water harbour. The oldest church is St Michael's (1070) which has an unusually tall spire built in the 18th century as a landmark for navigators of Southampton Water. Other buildings and monuments within the city walls are the Bargate, the Tudor House Museum, God's House Tower, the Tudor Merchants Hall, the Weigh-house, West Gate, King John's House, Long House, Wool House, the ruins of Holy Rood Church, St Julien's Church and the Mayflower Memorial. The medieval town walls, built for artillery, are among the most complete in the UK. Public open spaces total over 1,000 acres and comprise 9 per cent of the city's area. The Common covers an area of 328 acres in the central district of the city and is mostly natural parkland. A recent addition to work in marine technology in Southampton is Europe's leading oceanography research centre, which is part of the University.

STOKE-ON-TRENT

Stoke-on-Trent, standing on the River Trent and familiarly known as The Potteries, is the main centre of employment for the population of North Staffordshire. The city is the largest clayware producer in the world (china, earthenware, sanitary goods, refractories, bricks and tiles) and also has a wide range of other manufacturing industry, including steel, chemicals, engineering and tyres. Extensive reconstruction has been carried out in recent years.

The city was formed by the federation of the separate municipal authorities of Tunstall, Burslem, Hanley, Stoke, Fenton, and Longton in 1910 and received its city status in 1925.

WINCHESTER

Winchester, the ancient capital of England, is situated on the River Itchen. The city is rich in architecture of all types but the Cathedral takes pride of place. The longest Gothic cathedral in the world, it was built in 1079–93 and exhibits examples of Norman, Early English and Perpendicular styles. The author Jane Austen is buried in the Cathedral. Winchester College, founded in 1382, is one of the most famous public schools, the original building (1393) remaining largely unaltered. St Cross Hospital, another great medieval foundation, lies one mile south of the city. The almshouses were founded in 1136 by Bishop Henry de Blois, and Cardinal Henry Beaufort added a new almshouse of 'Noble Poverty' in 1446. The chapel and dwellings are of great architectural interest, and visitors may still receive the 'Wayfarer's Dole' of bread and ale.

Excavations have done much to clarify the origins and development of Winchester. Part of the forum and several of the streets of the Roman town have been discovered; excavations in the Cathedral Close have uncovered the entire site of the Anglo-Saxon cathedral (known as the Old Minster) and parts of the New Minster which was built by Alfred's son Edward the Elder and is the burial place of the Alfredian dynasty. The original burial place of St Swithun, before his remains were translated to a site in the present cathedral, was also uncovered.

Excavations in other parts of the city have thrown much light on Norman Winchester, notably on the site of the Royal Castle (adjacent to which the new Law Courts have been built) and in the grounds of Wolvesey Castle, where the great house built by Bishops Giffard and Henry de Blois in the 12th century has been uncovered. The Great Hall, built by Henry III between 1222 and 1236 survives and houses the Arthurian Round Table.

YORK

The city of York is an archiepiscopal seat. Its recorded history dates from AD 71, when the Roman Ninth Legion established a base under Petilius Cerealis which later became the fortress of *Eburacum.* In Anglo-Saxon times the city was the royal and ecclesiastical centre of Northumbria, and after capture by a Viking army in AD 866 it became the capital of the Viking kingdom of Jorvik. By the 14th century the city had become a great mercantile centre, mainly because of its control of the wool trade, and was used as the chief base against the Scots. Under the Tudors its fortunes declined, though Henry VIII made it the headquarters of the Council of the North. Excavations on many sites, including Coppergate, have greatly expanded knowledge of Roman, Viking and medieval urban life.

With its development as a railway centre in the 19th century the commercial life of York expanded. The principal industries are the manufacture of chocolate, scientific instruments and sugar. It is the location of several government departments.

The city is rich in examples of architecture of all periods. The earliest church was built in AD 627 and, in the 12th to 15th centuries, the present Minster was built in a succession of styles. Other examples within the city are the medieval city walls and gateways, churches and guildhalls. Domestic architecture includes the Georgian mansions of The Mount, Micklegate and Bootham.

English Counties and Shires

LORD-LIEUTENANTS AND HIGH SHERIFFS

County/Shire	Lord-Lieutenant	High Sheriff, 1999–2000
Bedfordshire	S. C. Whitbread	C. R. Kilroy
Berkshire	P. L. Wroughton	M. J. B. Todhunter
Bristol	J. Tidmarsh, MBE	J. R. Pool
Buckinghamshire	Sir Nigel Mobbs	The Hon. Sir William McAlpine, Bt.
Cambridgeshire	J. G. P. Crowden	J. E. Heading
Cheshire	W. A. Bromley-Davenport	M. D. A. Clarke
Cornwall	Lady Holborow	Lt.-Cdr. N. J. Trefusis
Cumbria	J. A. Cropper	A. I. Bullough
Derbyshire	J. K. Bather	D. R. Penrose, MBE
Devon	E. Dancer, CBE	Sir Simon Day
Dorset	Capt. M. Fulford-Dobson, RN	A. G. Yeatman
Durham	Sir Paul Nicholson	F. Nicholson
East Riding of Yorkshire	R. Marriott, TD	A. L. Marr
East Sussex	Admiral Sir Lindsay Bryson, KCB, FRSE, FREng.	K. M. H. Millar
Essex	The Lord Braybrooke	G. R. Capel Cure
Gloucestershire	H. W. G. Elwes	The Hon. M. W. Vestey
Greater London	The Lord Imbert, QPM	R. J. L. Bramble
Greater Manchester	Col. J. B. Timmins, OBE, TD	N. K. Stoller
Hampshire	Mrs F. M. Fagan	V. A. L. Powell
Herefordshire	Sir Thomas Dunne, KCVO	Mrs R. J. Dawes
Hertfordshire	S. A. Bowes Lyon	H. M. Neal, CBE
Isle of Wight	C. D. J. Bland	S. H. G. Twining, LVO, OBE
Kent	The Lord Kingsdown, KG, PC	J. B. Sunley
Lancashire	The Lord Shuttleworth	Lady Shuttleworth
Leicestershire	T. G. M. Brooks	Mrs A. Grahame Wilson, CBE
Lincolnshire	Mrs B. K. Cracroft-Eley	F. J. F. M. Dymoke
Merseyside	A. W. Waterworth	D. H. Morris
Norfolk	Sir Timothy Colman, KG	N. W. D. Foster
Northamptonshire	Lady Juliet Townsend, LVO	D. Reynolds
Northumberland	The Viscount Ridley, KG, GCVO, TD	Mrs E. M. Fairbairn
North Yorkshire	The Lord Crathorne	A. V. Hudson
Nottinghamshire	Sir Andrew Buchanan, Bt.	A. M. Nall
Oxfordshire	H. L. J. Brunner	A. J. Feilden
Rutland	Air Chief Marshal Sir Thomas Kennedy, GCB, AFC	Mrs W. M. L. Goldring
Shropshire	A. E. H. Heber-Percy	J. R. B. Lovegrove-Fielden
Somerset	Lady Gass	T. A. H. Yandle
South Yorkshire	The Earl of Scarbrough	D. B. Shaw
Staffordshire	J. A. Hawley, TD	D. E. D. Johnson
Suffolk	The Lord Belstead, PC	Col. D. H. C. Gordon Lennox
Surrey	Mrs S. J. F. Goad	P. R. Nutting
Tyne and Wear	Sir Ralph Carr-Ellison, KCVO, TD	M. Bird
Warwickshire	M. Dunne	M. C. Fetherston-Dilke
West Midlands	R. R. Taylor, OBE	R. S. Burman, CBE
West Sussex	H. Wyatt	Mrs J. Buckland, MBE
West Yorkshire	J. Lyles, CBE	P. A. H. Hartley, CBE
Wiltshire	Lt.-Gen. Sir Maurice Johnston, KCB, OBE	P. J. Miles
Worcestershire	Sir Thomas Dunne, KCVO	Mrs R. J. Dawes

COUNTY COUNCILS: Area, Population, Finance

Council	Administrative headquarters	Area (hectares)	Population	Total demand upon collection fund 1999– 2000
Bedfordshire	County Hall, Bedford	119,220	524,105	£92,756,000
Buckinghamshire	County Hall, Aylesbury	156,538	632,487	118,700,000
Cambridgeshire	Shire Hall, Cambridge	305,399	645,125	107,300,000
Cheshire	County Hall, Chester	208,344	956,616	171,543,844
Cornwall	County Hall, Truro	354,810	468,425	95,665,000
Cumbria	The Courts, Carlisle	681,000	483,163	106,644,000
Derbyshire	County Hall, Matlock	262,858	928,636	161,471,440
Devon	County Hall, Exeter	670,343	1,009,950	616,240,000
Dorset	County Hall, Dorchester	254,375	645,166	101,144,947
Durham	County Hall, Durham	223,180	593,430	94,113,602
East Sussex	Pelham House, St Andrew's Lane, Lewes	172,500	690,447	117,085,000
Essex	County Hall, Chelmsford	344,781	1,528,577	292,692,000
Gloucestershire	Shire Hall, Gloucester	265,535	528,370	369,000,000
Hampshire	The Castle, Winchester	367,915	1,541,547	280,805,000
Hertfordshire	County Hall, Hertford	164,306	975,829	238,025,212
Kent	County Hall, Maidstone	354,296	1,508,873	293,876,314
Lancashire	County Hall, Preston	289,780	1,383,998	260,156,000
Leicestershire	County Hall, Glenfield, Leicester	208,380	867,521	126,035,000
Lincolnshire	County Offices, Newland, Lincoln	588,000	584,534	433,411,000
Norfolk	County Hall, Norwich	537,234	745,613	161,910,340
Northamptonshire	County Hall, Northampton	236,737	578,807	118,053,000
Northumberland	County Hall, Morpeth	502,594	307,709	71,500,000
North Yorkshire	County Hall, Northallerton	830,399	556,200	122,900,000
Nottinghamshire	County Hall, Nottingham	208,510	993,872	174,592,555
Oxfordshire	County Hall, Oxford	260,595	547,584	131,000,000
Shropshire	The Shirehall, Shrewsbury	319,736	406,387	59,673,000
Somerset	County Hall, Taunton	345,233	460,368	103,551,885
Staffordshire	County Buildings, Stafford	262,355	1,031,135	150,640,000
Suffolk	County Hall, Ipswich	380,207	636,266	131,600,000
Surrey	County Hall, Kingston upon Thames	167,011	1,018,003	271,100,000
Warwickshire	Shire Hall, Warwick	198,054	484,247	115,333,810
West Sussex	County Hall, Chichester	199,025	702,290	175,870,000
Wiltshire	County Hall, Trowbridge	348,070	564,471	94,231,000
Worcestershire	County Hall, Worcester	173,529	531,909	107,497,073

COUNTY COUNCILS: Officers and Chairmen

Council	Chief Executive	County Treasurer	Chairman of County Council
Bedfordshire	D. Cleggett	W. Dodds	J. Saunders
Buckinghamshire	I. Crookall	§S. Nolan	K. I. Ross
Cambridgeshire	A. Barnish	D. T. Earle	J. Eddy
Cheshire	C. Cheesman	A. Cope	D. Newton
Cornwall	J. F. Mills	F. P. Twyning	J. M. Philp
Cumbria	W. A. Swarbrick	°R. F. Mather	R. Watson
Derbyshire	A. R. N. Hodgson	P. Swaby	G. Bratt
Devon	P. Jenkinson	‡J. Glasby	K. J. Turner
Dorset	D. Jenkins	A. P. Peel	Mrs P. Hymers
Durham	K. W. Smith	J. Kirkby	J. Richardson
East Sussex	Mrs C. Miller	J. Howes	M. Skilton
Essex	K. W. S. Ashurst	K. D. Neale	Mrs J. E. Beard
Gloucestershire	R. Cockcroft	R. Cockcroft	Ms M. Rutter
Hampshire	P. C. B. Robertson	J. C. Pittam	F. A. J. Emery-Wallis
Hertfordshire	W. D. Ogley	*C. Sweeney	R. Smith
Kent	M. Pitt	*D. Lewis	F. Fox
Lancashire	G. A. Johnson	B. G. Aldred	Dr R. Henig
Leicestershire	J. B. Sinnott	A. Youd	G. Perkins
Lincolnshire	D. Bowles	†M. Spink	J. Fisher
Norfolk	T. J. Byles	*R. D. Summers	Mrs T. I. Paines
Northamptonshire	J. V. Picking	Mrs L. Charker *(acting)*	C. Kalyan
Northumberland	J. M. McCall *(acting)*	*C. Burns	L. B. Smith
North Yorkshire	J. Walker	J. S. Moore	Lt. Col. J. H. Jacob MC
Nottinghamshire	P. J. Housden	R. Latham	J. K. Stobbart
Oxfordshire	J. Harwood	C. Gray	H. Wyatt
Shropshire	N. T. Pursey	N. T. Pursey	Mrs P. Larney
Somerset	Dr D. Radford	C. N. Bilsland	R. B. Clark
Staffordshire	B. A. Price, CBE	R. G. Tettenborn, OBE	T. R. Wright
Suffolk	Mrs L. Homer	R. Whiteman	Dr A. D. Lower
Surrey	P. Coen	§M. Taylor	Mrs H. Hawker
Warwickshire	I. G. Caulfield	S. R. Freer	Mrs J. Tandy
West Sussex	D. P. Rigg	Mrs H. Kilpatrick	I. R. W. Elliott
Wiltshire	Dr K. Robinson	D. Chalker	Brig. R. J. Baddeley
Worcestershire	R. Sykes	M. Weaver	N. Knowles

* Director of Finance
° Director of Corporate Finance
† Director of Finance and Resources
‡ Director of Resources
§ Head of Finance

Unitary Councils

SMALL CAPITALS denote CITY status
§ Denotes Borough council

Council	Population	Band D charge 1999*	Chief Executive	Mayor (a)Lord Mayor (b)Chairman 1999–2000
§Barnsley	220,937	£818.93	J. Edwards, OBE	A. Whittaker
Bath and North-East Somerset	164,700	778.92	J. Everitt	J. Bailey
BIRMINGHAM	961,041	892.53	M. Lyons	(a) I. McArdle
§Blackburn with Darwen	136,612	914.84	P. S. Watson	S. R. Kiani
§Blackpool	151,200	683.07	G. E. Essex-Crosby	W. Burgess
§Bolton	258,584	885.49	B. Knight	J. Monaghan
§Bournemouth	160,700	737.56	D. Newell	J. Courtney
§Bracknell Forest	110,000	711.46	G. Mitchell	J. C. Finnie FRICS
BRADFORD	457,344	808.17	I. Stewart	(a) H. Mason
§Brighton and Hove	245,000	697.00	G. Jones	Ms J. Langston
BRISTOL	399,600	992.15	Ms L. de Groot	(a) G. Robertson
§Bury	176,760	811.20	D. Taylor	J. P. Costello
§Calderdale	191,585	876.19	P. Sheehan	P. Coles
COVENTRY	294,387	968.00	I. Roxburgh	(a) Mrs J. Wright
§Darlington	101,000	687.49	B. Keel	W. Dixon
DERBY	235,238	786.75	R. H. Cowlishaw	Ms S. F. Bolton
§Doncaster	288,854	760.86	A. M. Taylor	Mrs M. J. Robinson
§Dudley	304,615	779.19	A. Sparke	F. S. Hunt
East Riding of Yorkshire	310,800	857.37	D. Stephenson	(b) Ms D. Clark
§Gateshead	199,588	868.94	L. N. Elton	B. Coates
§Halton	123,038	678.81	M. Cuff	R. Gilligan
Hartlepool	92,000	976.82	B. J. Dinsdale	R. Watts
Herefordshire	167,000	729.11	N. Pringle	(b) G. Hyde
Isle of Wight	125,466	784.47	B. Quoroll	(b) Mrs B. Foster
KINGSTON UPON HULL	266,900	793.33	I. Crookham	(a) B. Wilkinson
§Kirklees	373,127	868.00	T. Elson	H. Fox
§Knowsley	152,091	948.87	D. G. Henshaw	J. King
LEEDS	680,722	687.00	P. Rogerson	(a) K. Parker
LEICESTER	270,493	791.80	R. Green	(a) P. Swift
LIVERPOOL	452,450	1,171.54	P. Bounds	(a) J. Devaney
§Luton	181,500	706.81	Mrs K. Jones	R. Saleem
§MANCHESTER	404,861	987.28	H. Bernstein	(a) A. Burns
Medway	239,978	670.47	Ms J. Armitt	D. Liyanage
Middlesbrough	144,500	805.81	¶J. E. Foster	M. J. Carr
§Milton Keynes	204,415	742.00	H. Miller	K. Beeley
NEWCASTLE UPON TYNE	259,541	977.30	K. G. Lavery	(a) J. Cunningham
North-East Lincolnshire	168,000	864.53	R. Bentham	G. Mitchell
North Lincolnshire	152,423	983.97	Dr M. Garnett	Ms B. Martin
North Somerset	177,000	739.92	P. May	R. Moon
§North Tyneside	192,286	904.74	Executive Directorate	Ms M. Mulgrove
NOTTINGHAM	284,000	886.08	E. F. Cantle	(a) D. A. Jones
§Oldham	216,531	933.76	A. W. Kilburn	J. B. Battye
PETERBOROUGH	159,900	752.24	P. Martin	J. Bartlett
PLYMOUTH	255,800	701.89	Mrs A. Stone	(a) T. Savery
§Poole	139,200	702.99	J. Brookes	F. J. Wretham
PORTSMOUTH	190,400	680.31	N. Gurney	(a) D. Horne
§Reading	142,851	868.13	Ms J. Markham	S. Waite
Redcar and Cleveland	140,200	1,042.60	A. W. Kilburn	M. Stephen
§Rochdale	202,164	870.88	Mrs F. W. Done	D. Murphy
§Rotherham	251,637	808.96	A. G. Carruthers	M. G. Judge
Rutland	34,600	944.89	Dr J. R. Morphet	(b) Wg Cdr. R. D. Toy
§St Helens	178,764	962.88	Mrs C. Hudson	P. Jackson
SALFORD	220,463	1,198.02	J. C. Willis	W. B. Pennington
§Sandwell	290,091	856.01	F. N. Summers	J. Edwards
§Sefton	289,542	913.85	G. J. Haywood	R. J. Brennan
SHEFFIELD	501,202	883.50	R. W. Kerslake	(a) T. Bagshaw
§Slough	108,000	725.44	Ms C. Coppell	Mrs O. E. Mansell
§Solihull	199,859	894.63	Dr N. H. Perry	A. Harper

Council	Population	Band D charge 1999*	Chief Executive	Mayor (a)Lord Mayor (b)Chairman 1999–2000
SOUTHAMPTON	214,859	708.96	J. Cairns	D. Burke
South Gloucestershire	239,000	781.57	M. Robinson	(b) A. Adams
§Southend	172,300	675.75	J. K. M. Krawiec	A. S. North
§South Tyneside	154,697	884.25	‡P. J. Haigh	Ms M. Chenery
§Stockport	284,395	916.65	J. R. Schultz	Ms I. Shaw
§Stockton-on-Tees	179,000	852.87	G. Garlick	Mrs J. Kitchen
STOKE-ON-TRENT	254,300	750.97	B. Smith	(a) R. G. Booth
§SUNDERLAND	289,040	814.61	C. W. Sinclair, PH.D.	D. R.Wares
§Swindon	177,118	672.00	P. Doherty	Ms J. Brunt
§Tameside	216,431	898.20	M. J. Greenwood	F. Robinson
Telford and Wrekin	151,500	756.99	C. Barber (acting)	vacant
§Thurrock	132,283	672.48	K. Barnes	C. Morris
§Torbay	119,674	751.96	A. J. Hodgkiss	J. Turner
§Trafford	212,731	689.22	W. A. Lewis	R. Bowker
WAKEFIELD	310,915	742.52	†M. Pullan	B. Bullock
§Walsall	259,488	802.92	D. C. Winchurch	Mrs D. Farrell
§Warrington	187,000	738.48	S. Broomhead	T. Swift
West Berkshire	144,000	810.58	Ms S. Manzie	(b) J. Cottam
§Wigan	306,521	834.52	S. M. Jones	W. Smith
§Windsor and Maidenhead	132,465	743.73	D. C. Lunn	Mrs S. Hopkins
§Wirral	330,795	977.00	S. Maddox	H. Lloyd
Wokingham	142,767	820.61	Ms J. Earl	(b) Mrs P. Hellier-Symons
§Wolverhampton	242,190	954.72	D. Anderson	P. A. Bilson
YORK	175,925	691.43	D. Clark	(a) P. Vaughan

* For explanation of council tax, see pages 521–2
† The Chief Officer
‡ Head of Paid Service
¶ Managing Director

District Councils

SMALL CAPITALS denote CITY status
§ Denotes Borough status
For explanation of council tax, see pages 521–2
* Executive Director
** 1996 figure
† General Manager
‡ Head of Paid Service
¶ Managing Director

Council	Population	Band D charge 1999*	Chief Executive	Chairman (a)Mayor (b)Lord Mayor 1999–2000
Adur, W. Sussex	58,019	£797.44	I. Lowrie	G. Howitt
§Allerdale, Cumbria	95,702	856.45	C. J. Hart	(a) Mrs M. Snaith
Alnwick, Northumberland	30,081	901.27	L. A. B. St Ruth	G. R. Arckless
Amber Valley, Derbys	111,897	869.30	P. M. Carney	(a) M. B. Gent
Arun, W. Sussex	129,357	765.94	I. Sumnall	H. Parris
Ashfield, Notts	108,364	925.50	E. N. Bernasconi	Mrs C. Young
§Ashford, Kent	92,331	736.37	A. Baker	(a) Mrs B. A. Simmons
Aylesbury Vale, Bucks	145,931	762.05	B. Hurley	C. R. James
Babergh, Suffolk	79,632	765.34	P. Barnes	P. Jones
§Barrow-in-Furness, Cumbria	73,125	891.66	T. O. Campbell	(a) Mrs J. Waiting
Basildon, Essex	161,124	806.06	J. Robb	Mrs L. Gordon
§Basingstoke and Deane, Hants	144,790	749.08	Mrs K. E. P. Sporle	(a) L. Jones
Bassetlaw, Notts	103,979	930.00	J. Molloy	J. Napier
§Bedford, Beds	133,692	859.93	L. W. Gould	(a) Ms C. Ellis
§Berwick-upon-Tweed, Northumberland	26,731	890.31	E. O. Cawthorn, TD	(a) N. N. Ferguson

Council	Population	Band D charge 1999*	Chief Executive	Chairman (a)Mayor (b)Lord Mayor 1999–2000
Blaby, Leics	82,700	814.36	E. Hemsley	B. Garner
§Blyth Valley, Northumberland	79,584	883.06	G. Paul	(a) Mrs M. A. Parker
Bolsover, Derbys	70,437	904.50	J. R. Fotherby	R. Brooks
§Boston, Lincs	53,226	962.33	M. James	(a) P. Goodale
Braintree, Essex	118,883	761.04	Ms A. F. Ralph	F. Card
Breckland, Norfolk	107,167	735.31	R. N. Garnett	K. Martin
§Brentwood, Essex	70,597	760.77	C. P. Sivell	(a) H. Bailey
Bridgnorth, Salop	50,511	782.61	Mrs T. M. Elliott	Mrs M. Winckler
Broadland, Norfolk	106,292	777.15	J. Bryant	G. E. Debbage
Bromsgrove, Worcs	91,544	712.43	D. A. H. Bryant	R. J. Deeming
§Broxbourne, Herts	81,449	721.02	M. J. Walker	(a) R. L. Groucott
§Broxtowe, Notts	107,137	918.14	M. Brown	(a) F. Prince
§Burnley, Lancs	91,130	948.24	R. Ellis	(a) E. Fisk
CAMBRIDGE	91,933	737.49	R. Hammond	(a) R. Smith
Cannock Chase, Staffs	88,833	966.58	M. G. Kemp	A. B. Hill
CANTERBURY, Kent	123,947	752.00	C. Carmichael	(b) Miss J. Samper
Caradon, Cornwall	76,516	744.89	Dr J. Neal	T. G. Smale
CARLISLE, Cumbria	100,562	883.39	R. S. Brackley	(a) J. R. Collier
Carrick, Cornwall	82,725	755.78	J. P. Winskill	Mrs S. C. Shaw
§Castle Morpeth, Northumberland	50,299	908.15	P. Wilson	(a) E. M. Coe
§Castle Point, Essex	86,560	797.13	B. Rollinson	(a) A. Hurd
§Charnwood, Leics	141,806	785.97	S. M. Peatfield	(a) J. B. Powell
§Chelmsford, Essex	152,418	774.35	M. Easteal	(a) M. J. Mackrory
§Cheltenham, Glos	103,115	703.71	L. Davison	(a) D. J. Banyard
Cherwell, Oxon	117,832	759.24	G. J. Handley	R. Laynes
§Chesterfield, Derbys	99,403	849.13	D. R. Shaw	(a) T. Gilby
Chester-le-Street, Co. Durham	52,641	830.27	J. A. Greensmith	Mrs I. Howey
CHESTER, Cheshire	115,971	860.08	P. F. Durham	(b) E. Plenderleath
Chichester, W. Sussex	101,358	749.12	J. S. Marsland	C. W. Spawton
Chiltern, Bucks	89,838	711.43	A. Goodrum	D. W. Phillips
§Chorley, Lancs	96,504	888.04	J. W. Davies	(a) Ms F. Molyneaux
§Christchurch, Dorset	40,865	816.02	M. A. Turvey	(a) R. J. R. McArthur
§Colchester, Essex	142,515	760.21	J. Cobley	(a) M. Hunt
§Congleton, Cheshire	84,525	857.17	P. Cooper	(a) R. Parry
§Copeland, Cumbria	71,296	852.00	†Dr J. Stanforth	(a) G. Blackwell
§Corby, Northants	53,044	765.59	N. Rudd	(a) E. Gordon
Cotswold, Glos	73,965	759.58	N. C. Abbott	B. I. Evans
Craven, N. Yorks	49,891	740.99	*Ms R. Mann (acting)	A. Dixon
§Crawley, W. Sussex	87,644	754.83	M. D. Sander	(a) R. Calcott
§Crewe and Nantwich, Cheshire	103,164	858.82	A. Wenham	(a) C. G. Thorley
§Dacorum, Herts	134,733	736.23	K. Hunt	(a) R. Jameson
§Dartford, Kent	79,439	750.10	C. R. Shepherd	(a) I. Jones
Daventry, Northants	62,886	719.63	P. Cook	Mrs I. Taylor
Derbyshire Dales, Derbys	67,562	877.56	D. Wheatcroft	Mrs J. N. Bevan
Derwentside, Co. Durham	86,046	897.58	vacant	Ms E. Wilson
Dover, Kent	103,216	744.38	J. P. Moir, TD	F. E. Woodbridge MBE
DURHAM	80,669	836.90	C. Shearsmith	(a) Mrs M. A. Adair
Easington, Co. Durham	97,824	921.83	vacant	G. Martin
§Eastbourne, E. Sussex	81,395	789.34	Mrs S. E. Conway	(a) Mrs B. Healy
East Cambridgeshire	60,416	703.25	R. C. Carr	Ms S. Friend-Smith
East Devon	115,873	761.07	F. J. Vallender	B. C. J. Hughes
East Dorset	78,698	837.15	A. Breakwell	G. W. Russell
East Hampshire	103,460	800.06	Miss J. Hunter	Dr J. Happel
East Hertfordshire	115,818	717.12	R. J. Bailey	R. Parker
§Eastleigh, Hants	105,999	784.00	C. Tapp	(a) Ms J. Welsh
East Lindsey, Lincs	116,957	755.45	P. Haigh	Mrs F. M. Martin
East Northamptonshire	67,686	681.29	R. K. Heath	M. L. Peacock
§East Staffordshire	97,105	790.14	F. W. Saunders	(a) D. Tilling
Eden, Cumbria	45,581	822.17	I. W. Bruce	Ms N. Walker
§Ellesmere Port and Neston, Cheshire	80,873	875.55	S. Ewbank	(a) S. M. Earley

Council	Population	Band D charge 1999*	Chief Executive	Chairman (a)Mayor (b)Lord Mayor 1999–2000
§Elmbridge, Surrey	114,479	779.56	M. Lockwood	(a) T. Stewart
Epping Forest, Essex	116,027	766.98	J. Burgess	S. Goodwin
§Epsom and Ewell, Surrey	67,007	748.95	D. J. Smith	(a) E. Kington
§Erewash, Derbys	106,101	854.71	G. A. Pook	(a) E. A. Bishop
EXETER, Devon	98,125	749.17	P. Bostock	(a) R. Hill
Fareham, Hants	99,262	762.84	A. A. Davies	(a) R. H. Price
Fenland, Cambs	74,426	728.00	N. R. Topliss	J. L. Baker
Forest Heath, Suffolk	54,843	719.21	‡D. W. Burnip	W. J. Bishop
Forest of Dean, Glos	75,351	759.25	Ms M. Holborow	W. Hobman
§Fylde, Lancs	70,999	885.46	J. R. Wilkinson	(a) Miss M. Procopides
§Gedling, Notts	110,133	903.27	D. Kennedy	(a) J. F. Glass
GLOUCESTER	101,608	758.65	G. Garbutt	(a) A. Meredith
§Gosport, Hants	75,061	786.22	M. Crocker	(a) K. P. J. Searle
§Gravesham, Kent	92,454	728.24	E. C. Anderson	(a) J. Jaggon
§Great Yarmouth, Norfolk	87,724	775.07	R. W. Packham	J. Barnes
§Guildford, Surrey	127,500	751.44	D. T. Watts	(a) R. E. Blundell
Hambleton, N. Yorks	79,425	695.29	P. Simpson	G. W. Ellis
Harborough, Leics	67,607	808.59	M. C. Wilson	P. R. Fewkes
Harlow, Essex	74,629	872.49	D. F. Byrne	J. McCree
§Harrogate, N. Yorks	143,526	760.22	P. M. Walsh	(a) G. Crowther OBE
Hart, Hants	80,921	779.32	G. R. Jelbart	J. Stocks
§Hastings, E. Sussex	80,820	813.35	R. Mawford	(a) R. Stevens
§Havant, Hants	119,697	775.08	R. D. Smith	(a) D. M. Farrow
§Hertsmere, Herts	87,590	747.85	P. H. Copland	(a) J. M. Donne
§High Peak, Derbys	87,900	865.61	R. P. H. Brady	(a) D. Bond
§Hinckley and Bosworth, Leics	96,201	763.43	J. Corry (acting)	(a) D. R. Bown
Horsham, W. Sussex	108,562	724.60	M. J. Pearson	E. D. Jenkins
Huntingdonshire, Cambs	144,075	695.15	D. Monks	Mrs P. Newbon
§Hyndburn, Lancs	78,390	939.87	M. J. Chambers	(a) B. Dawson
§Ipswich, Suffolk	116,956	828.63	J. D. Hehir	(a) J. C. Mowles
Kennet, Wilts	68,526	769.06	M. J. Boden	Mrs S. M. Findlay
Kerrier, Cornwall	87,566	757.00	G. G. Cox	M. Jeffery
§Kettering, Northants	78,200	773.94	P. Walker	(a) J. West
§King's Lynn and West Norfolk	131,000	775.19	Dr G. Taylor	(a) Dr P. Richards
LANCASTER, LANCS	123,856	883.88	D. Corker	(a) Mrs S. Rostron
Lewes, E. Sussex	87,389	811.45	J. N. Crawford	J. E. Lewry
Lichfield, Staffs	92,679	766.23	J. T. Thompson	J. A. Nichols
LINCOLN	81,987	800.67	A. Taylor	(a) Ms L. Woolley
§Macclesfield, Cheshire	151,590	852.40	B. W. Longden	(a) Miss C. M. Andrew
§Maidstone, Kent	137,000	797.20	J. D. Makepeace	(a) Ms F. Brown
Maldon, Essex	52,843	739.57	E. A. P. Plumridge	R. Pipe
Malvern Hills, Worcs	86,902	688.17	C. J. Bocock	R. J. Farmer
Mansfield, Notts	100,386	934.40	R. P. Goad	G. Harper
§Melton, Leics	45,112	799.21	P. M. Murphy	(a) R. Holt
Mendip, Somerset	95,603	779.02	G. Jeffs	C. Lockey
Mid Bedfordshire, Beds	109,801	858.81	C. A. Tucker	Ms F. Chapman
Mid Devon, Devon	64,258	794.16	M. I. R. Bull	D. F. Pugsley
Mid Suffolk, Suffolk	78,383	759.59	G. R. Chilton	Mrs W. Marchant
Mid Sussex, W. Sussex	126,000	762.72	W. J. H. Hatton	Mrs C. Field
Mole Valley, Surrey	79,220	748.58	Mrs H. Kerswell	Mrs B. Douglass
Newark and Sherwood, Notts	102,784	940.32	R. G. Dix	E. Jackson
§Newcastle under Lyme, Staffs	119,091	768.15	F. Harley	(a) Mrs B. Blaise
New Forest, Hants	160,456	799.25	¶I. B. Mackintosh	Mrs P. A. Wyeth
§Northampton	180,567	787.97	R. J. B. Morris	(a) A. McCutcheon
North Cornwall	73,800	720.01	D. Brown	R. W. Flower
North Devon	84,800	772.99	D. T. Cunliffe	A. E. Cook
North Dorset	52,110	808.67	vacant	Mrs D. Jones MBE
North East Derbyshire	97,570	905.13	‡Ms C. A. Gilby	J. A. Dargue
North Hertfordshire	111,994	758.89	S. Philp	D. Ashley
North Kesteven, Lincs	79,942	797.60	Mrs R. Marlow	Mrs B. Wells
North Norfolk	90,461	779.04	B. A. Barrell	C. Durrant

Council	Population	Band D charge 1999*	Chief Executive	Chairman (a)Mayor (b)Lord Mayor 1999–2000
North Shropshire	52,873	810.95	R. J. Hughes	Mrs P. A. Dee
§North Warwickshire	60,747	874.00	J. Hutchinson	(a) R. Spencer
North West Leicestershire	80,566	827.51	M. J. Diaper	S. D. Sheahan
North Wiltshire	111,974	789.64	R. Marshall	B. E. Atfield
NORWICH, Norfolk	120,895	817.70	J. R. Packer, OBE	(b) D. Underwood
§Nuneaton and Bedworth, Warks	117,052	850.93	Ms C. Kerr	(a) Ms M. Beaumont
§Oadby and Wigston, Leics	51,547	801.58	Mrs R. E. Hyde	(a) P. Swift
§Oswestry, Salop	33,508	800.71	B. D. Catton (acting)	(a) W. O. Jones
OXFORD	134,800	825.90	R. S. Block	(b) Ms V. Smith
§Pendle, Lancs	85,111	947.00	S. Barnes	(a) Mrs E. D. Sargeant
Penwith, Cornwall	59,251	738.46	‡D. H. Hosken	Mrs S. M. Menadue
§Preston, Lancs	126,082	958.52	J. E. Carr	(a) G. Threlfell Swabrick
Purbeck, Dorset	42,445	823.87	P. B. Croft	R. Anderson
§Redditch, Worcs	78,106	758.92	Ms K. Kerswell	(a) J. Witherspoon
§Reigate and Banstead, Surrey	117,777	707.00	M. Bacon	(a) B. Cowle
§Restormel, Cornwall	86,519	740.45	Mrs P. Crowson	J. Weller
§Ribble Valley, Lancs	51,767	897.99	D. G. Morris	(a) B. Collis
Richmondshire, N. Yorks	44,179	771.60	H. Tabiner	Ms H. Grant
Rochford, Essex	75,395	796.09	P. Warren	D. Helson
§Rossendale, Lancs	65,681	944.36	J. S. Hartley	(a) A. Neal
Rother, E. Sussex	81,683	777.95	D. F. Powell, FRICS	Mrs P. Bullock
§Rugby, Warks	81,683	839.39	Mrs D. M. Colley	(a) J. M. Roodhouse
§Runnymede, Surrey	71,789	688.59	T. N. Williams	(a) P. Poole
§Rushcliffe, Notts	97,567	882.52	K. Beaumont	(a) B. Nicholls
§Rushmoor, Hants	82,526	779.42	J. A. Lloyd	(a) D. E. Clifford
Ryedale, N. Yorks	47,981	778.97	H. W. Mosley	A. A. Aslett
ST ALBANS, Herts	128,700	763.78	E. A. Hackford	(a) M. Morrell
§St Edmundsbury, Suffolk	91,731	744.53	G. R. N. Toft	(a) Mrs M. M. L. Horbury
Salisbury, Wilts	105,318	778.68	R. Sheard	D. Parker
§Scarborough, N. Yorks	106,221	751.00	J. M. Trebble	(a) H. Dixon
§Sedgefield, Co. Durham	90,530	967.18	N. Vaulks	(a) Mrs A. Mumford
Sedgemoor, Somerset	97,763	760.68	A. G. Lovell	D. S. Alder
Selby, N. Yorks	89,428	744.65	M. Connor	D. N. Bain Mackay
Sevenoaks, Kent	109,742	765.27	N. Howells	Mrs S. Dunckley
Shepway, Kent	96,020	771.94	R. J. Thompson	Mrs S. Newlands
§Shrewsbury and Atcham, Salop	94,600	775.66	D. Bradbury	(a) R. Jones
South Bedfordshire	108,941	922.00	J. Ruddick	K. Sharer
South Bucks	62,482	757.17	C. R. Furness	R. Worrall
South Cambridgeshire	124,500	703.40	J. S. Ballantyne	A. W. Wyatt
South Derbyshire	71,772	848.97	D. J. Dugdale	K. Richards
South Hams, Devon	77,565	777.30	P. G. West (acting)	Mrs R. Rowe
South Holland, Lincs	70,386	795.28	C. J. Simpkins	J. Clark
South Kesteven, Lincs	108,945	767.84	C. Farmer	P. Taylor
South Lakeland, Cumbria	96,897	n/a	P. J. Cunliffe	Mrs J. S. Borer
South Norfolk	102,612	787.56	G. Rivers	W. Dinneen
South Northamptonshire	70,685	797.19	R. Tinlin	J. Byrom
South Oxfordshire	119,476	786.43	R. Watson	D. Turner
§South Ribble, Lancs	102,001	887.36	P. Halsall	(a) Mrs M. R. Smith
South Shropshire	38,230	820.17	G. C. Biggs, MBE	M. R. Williams
South Somerset	145,000	781.40	Ms E. Peters	N. Speakman, MBE, TD
South Staffordshire	105,487	655.40	L. T. Barnfield	Mrs C. Young
§Spelthorne, Surrey	89,748	761.39	M. B. Taylor	(a) E. O'Hara
Staffordshire Moorlands	95,072	965.00	B. J. Preedy	Ms S. Ralphs
§Staffordshire	117,788	754.70	D. Rawlings	(a) C. Baron
§Stevenage, Herts	75,147	625.18	I. Paske	(a) E. Webb
Stratford, Warks	109,400	771.26	I. B. Prosser	K. Lambert
Stroud, Glos	106,300	817.68	R. M. Ollin	Mrs L. Williams
Suffolk Coastal	107,970	752.85	T. K. Griffin	I. K. Jowers
§Surrey Heath	80,800	766.00	B. R. Catchpole	(a) K. Pedder
§Swale, Kent	115,769	744.40	C. Edwards	(a) Ms A. McLean
§Tamworth, Staffs	70,065	736.01	C. Moore	(a) Mrs P. Dix
Tandridge, Surrey	76,316	765.70	P. Thomas	Mrs W. Weston

Council	Population	Band D charge 1999*	Chief Executive	Chairman (a)Mayor (b)Lord Mayor 1999–2000
§Taunton Deane, Somerset	93,696	760.00	Mrs S. Douglas	(a) R. Parrish
Teesdale, Co. Durham	24,068	831.83	C. M. Anderson	J. L. Armstrong
Teignbridge, Devon	108,258	782.79	B. T. Jones	Mrs J. Collis
Tendring, Essex	130,900	769.40	J. Hawkins	Mrs R. Smith
§Test Valley, Hants	103,261	755.56	A. Jones	(a) Ms M. Kerley
§Tewkesbury, Glos	70,709	725.93	H. Davis	(a) Mrs B. A. Cromwell
Thanet, Kent	123,665	776.13	D. Ralls, CBE, DFC	R. Dickinson
Three Rivers, Herts	78,457	766.64	A. Robertson	I. Ambrose
§Tonbridge and Malling, Kent	101,763	748.13	T. Thompson	(a) Ms A. Oakley
Torridge, Devon	52,129	783.55	R. K. Brasington	J. Rawlinson
§Tunbridge Wells, Kent	99,538	769.41	R. J. Stone	(a) J. Ealden
Tynedale, Northumberland	57,275	878.93	A. Baty	W. Garrett
Uttlesford, Essex	67,500	795.72	K. Ivory	R. C. Dean
Vale of White Horse, Oxon	109,922	748.52	T. A. Stock	Mrs J. Hutchinson
§Vale Royal, Cheshire	114,700	850.94	J. W. Page	(a) Ms M. Bowhay-Merritt
Wansbeck, Northumberland	63,171	901.98	R. A. Stephenson	J. Young
Warwick	116,299	806.00	Miss J. M. Barrett	Mrs J. Compton
§Watford, Herts	74,566	831.51	Ms C. Hassan	(a) Ms R. Bell
Waveney, Suffolk	106,751	675.08	M. Berridge	J. Taylor
§Waverley, Surrey	113,212	776.51	Ms C. L. Pointer	(a) P. Betlem
Wealden, E. Sussex	130,214	821.90	D. R. Holness	Mrs S. M. Tidy
Wear Valley, Co. Durham	62,746	867.70	*Mrs C. Hughes	D. Kingston
§Wellingborough, Northants	**67,900	682.46	T. McArdle	(a) R. Cotter
Welwyn Hatfield, Herts	92,366	764.57	M. Saminaden	J. Mansfield
§West Devon	45,895	778.00	D. J. Incoll	(a) Mrs M. Gaston
West Dorset	85,463	831.46	R. C. Rennison	Mrs N. M. Penfold
West Lancashire	107,978	915.20	W. J. Taylor	S. J. Jones
West Lindsey, Lincs	76,218	799.39	R. W. Nelsey	A. D. Caine
West Oxfordshire	90,251	623.31	G. Bonner	A. Walker
West Somerset	31,651	776.54	C. W. Rockall	Mrs J. M. David
West Wiltshire	107,803	772.61	J. Ligo	R. J. Brice
§Weymouth and Portland, Dorset	61,233	679.96	T. Grainger	(a) Ms T. Roebuck
WINCHESTER, Hants	96,386	779.27	D. H. Cowan	(a) A. Mitchell
§Woking, Surrey	86,765	789.57	P. Russell	(a) I. D. F. Fidler
WORCESTER	89,481	730.86	D. Wareing	(a) Ms J. Hodges
§Worthing, W. Sussex	96,157	756.81	M. J. Ball	(a) B. McLuskie
Wychavon, Worcs	101,716	728.30	W. S. Nott	Mrs E. Hope
Wycombe, Bucks	162,000	768.77	R. J. Cummins	R. C. Pushman
§Wyre, Lancs	101,818	895.43	M. Brown	(a) H. Taylor
Wyre Forest, Worcs	94,814	748.79	W. S. Baldwin	J. Gordon

1	Stockton-on-Tees	22	Walsall
2	Middlesbrough	23	Sandwell
3	Blackpool	24	Dudley
4	Blackburn	25	Birmingham
	with Darwen	26	Solihull
5	Bolton	27	Coventry
6	Bury	28	Peterborough
7	Rochdale	29	South Glos
8	Salford	30	Bristol
9	Oldham	31	Bath and
10	Liverpool		NE Somerset
11	Knowsley	32	Windsor and
12	St Helens		Maidenhead
13	Halton	33	Slough
14	Warrington	34	Reading
15	Trafford	35	Wokingham
16	Manchester	36	Bracknell Forest
17	Tameside	37	Thurrock
18	Stockport	38	Southend
19	Nottingham	39	Medway
20	Telford and	40	Plymouth
	Wrekin	41	Torbay
21	Wolverhampton		

LONDON

1	Hillingdon	18	Kensington and Chelsea
2	Harrow	19	City of Westminster
3	Barnet	20	City of London
4	Enfield	21	Tower Hamlets
5	Waltham Forest	22	Richmond upon Thames
6	Redbridge	23	Wandsworth
7	Barking and Dagenham	24	Lambeth
8	Havering	25	Southwark
9	Ealing	26	Lewisham
10	Brent	27	Greenwich
11	Camden	28	Bexley
12	Haringey	29	Kingston upon Thames
13	Islington	30	Merton
14	Hackney	31	Sutton
15	Newham	32	Croydon
16	Hounslow	33	Bromley
17	Hammersmith and Fulham		

London

THE CORPORATION OF LONDON
(see also page 524)

The City of London is the historic centre at the heart of London known as 'the square mile' around which the vast metropolis has grown over the centuries. The City's residential population is 5,500. The civic government is carried on by the Corporation of London through the Court of Common Council.

The City is an international financial centre, generating over £20 billion a year for the British economy. It includes the head offices of the principal banks, insurance companies and mercantile houses, in addition to buildings ranging from the historic Roman Wall and the 15th-century Guildhall, to the massive splendour of St Paul's Cathedral and the architectural beauty of Wren's spires.

The City of London was described by Tacitus in AD 62 as 'a busy emporium for trade and traders'. Under the Romans it became an important administration centre and hub of the road system. Little is known of London in Saxon times, when it formed part of the kingdom of the East Saxons. In 886 Alfred recovered London from the Danes and reconstituted it a burgh under his son-in-law. In 1066 the citizens submitted to William the Conqueror who in 1067 granted them a charter, which is still preserved, establishing them in the rights and privileges they had hitherto enjoyed.

THE MAYORALTY

The Mayoralty was probably established about 1189, the first Mayor being Henry Fitz Ailwyn who filled the office for 23 years and was succeeded by Fitz Alan (1212–14). A new charter was granted by King John in 1215, directing the Mayor to be chosen annually, which has ever since been done, though in early times the same individual often held the office more than once. A familiar instance is that of 'Whittington, thrice Lord Mayor of London' (in reality four times, 1397, 1398, 1406, 1419); and many modern cases have occurred. The earliest instance of the phrase 'Lord Mayor' in English is in 1414. It was used more generally in the latter part of the 15th century and became invariable from 1535 onwards. At Michaelmas the liverymen in Common Hall choose two Aldermen who have served the office of Sheriff for presentation to the Court of Aldermen, and one is chosen to be Lord Mayor for the following mayoral year.

LORD MAYOR'S DAY

The Lord Mayor of London was previously elected on the feast of St Simon and St Jude (28 October), and from the time of Edward I, at least, was presented to the King or to the Barons of the Exchequer on the following day, unless that day was a Sunday. The day of election was altered to 16 October in 1346, and after some further changes was fixed for Michaelmas Day in 1546, but the ceremonies of admittance and swearing-in of the Lord Mayor continued to take place on 28 and 29 October respectively until 1751. In 1752, at the reform of the calendar, the Lord Mayor was continued in office until 8 November, the 'New Style' equivalent of 28 October. The Lord Mayor is now presented to the Lord Chief Justice at the Royal Courts of Justice on the second Saturday in November to make the final declaration of office, having been sworn in at Guildhall on the preceding day. The procession to the Royal Courts of Justice is popularly known as the Lord Mayor's Show.

REPRESENTATIVES

Aldermen are mentioned in the 11th century and their office is of Saxon origin. They were elected annually between 1377 and 1394, when an Act of Parliament of Richard II directed them to be chosen for life.

The Common Council, elected annually on the first Friday in December, was, at an early date, substituted for a popular assembly called the *Folkmote*. At first only two representatives were sent from each ward, but the number has since been greatly increased. The Corporation is reducing the number of Common Councilmen from 130 to 100 through natural wastage. The Government has introduced legislation to remove anomalies from the election system and to extend the non-resident franchise.

OFFICERS

Sheriffs were Saxon officers; their predecessors were the *wic-reeves* and *portreeves* of London and Middlesex. At first they were officers of the Crown, and were named by the Barons of the Exchequer; but Henry I (in 1132) gave the citizens permission to choose their own Sheriffs, and the annual election of Sheriffs became fully operative under King John's charter of 1199. The citizens lost this privilege, as far as the election of the Sheriff of Middlesex was concerned, by the Local Government Act 1888; but the liverymen continue to choose two Sheriffs of the City of London, who are appointed on Midsummer Day and take office at Michaelmas.

The office of Chamberlain is an ancient one, the first contemporary record of which is 1237. The Town Clerk (or Common Clerk) is mentioned in 1274.

ACTIVITIES

The work of the Corporation is assigned to a number of committees which present reports to the Court of Common Council. These Committees are: City Lands and Bridge House Grants Estates, Policy and Resources, Finance, Planning and Transportation, Central Markets, Billingsgate and Leadenhall Markets, Spitalfields Market, Police, Port and City of London Health and Social Services, Libraries, Art Galleries and Records, Board of Governors of City of London Freemen's School, Music and Drama (Guildhall School of Music and Drama), Establishment, Housing and Sports Development, Gresham (City side), Hampstead Heath Management, Epping Forest and Open Spaces, West Ham Park, Privileges, Barbican Residential and Barbican Centre (Barbican Arts and Conference Centre).

The City's estate, in the possession of which the Corporation of London differs from other municipalities, is managed by the City Lands and Bridge House Grants Estates Committee, the chairmanship of which carries with it the title of Chief Commoner.

The Honourable the Irish Society, which manages the Corporation's estates in Ulster, consists of a Governor and five other Aldermen, the Recorder, and 19 Common Councilmen, of whom one is elected Deputy Governor.

THE LORD MAYOR 1998–9*

The Rt. Hon. the Lord Mayor, Lord Levene of Portsoken, KBE
  Secretary, Air Vice-Marshal M. Dicken, CB

THE SHERIFFS 1999–2000

R. G. Finch (*Alderman, Coleman Street*) and Mrs P. A. Halliday (*Councilman, Walbrook*); *elected*, 8 July 1999; *assumed office*, 29 September 1999

---

* The Lord Mayor for 1999–2000 was elected on Michaelmas Day. *See* Stop-press

OFFICERS, ETC

Town Clerk and Chamberlain, B. P. Harty
Chief Commoner (1999), Mrs P. B. Newman
Clerk, The Honourable the Irish Society, S. Waley, The Irish Chamber, 1st Floor, 75 Watling Street, London EC4M 9BJ

THE ALDERMEN

Name and Ward	CC	Ald.	Shff.	Lord Mayor
Sir Peter Gadsden, GBE, *Farringdon Wt.*	1969	1971	1970	1979
Sir Christopher Leaver, GBE, *Dowgate*	1973	1974	1979	1981
Sir Alan Traill, GBE, *Langbourn*	1970	1975	1982	1984
Sir David Rowe-Ham, GBE, *Bridge* and *Bridge Wt.*	—	1976	1984	1986
Sir Christopher Collett, GBE, *Broad Street*	1973	1979	1985	1988
Sir Alexander Graham, GBE, *Queenhithe*	1978	1979	1986	1990
Sir Brian Jenkins, GBE, *Cordwainer*	—	1980	1987	1991
Sir Paul Newall, TD, *Walbrook*	1980	1981	1989	1993
Sir Christopher Walford, *Farringdon Wn.*	—	1982	1990	1994
Sir John Chalstrey, *Vintry*	1981	1984	1993	1995
Sir Roger Cork, *Tower*	1978	1983	1992	1996
Richard Nichols, *Candlewick*	1983	1984	1994	1997
Lord Levene of Portsoken, KBE, *Portsoken*	1983	1984	1995	1998

All the above have passed the Civic Chair

	CC	Ald.	Shff.
Clive Martin, OBE, TD, *Aldgate*	—	1985	1996
David Howard, *Cornhill*	1972	1986	1997
James Oliver, *Bishopsgate*	1980	1987	1997
Peter Bull, *Cheap*	1968	1984	
Gavyn Arthur, *Cripplegate*	1988	1991	1998
Robert Finch, *Coleman Street*	—	1992	
Richard Agutter, *Castle Baynard*	—	1995	
Michael Savory, *Bread Street*	1980	1996	
David Brewer, *Bassishaw*	1992	1996	
Nicholas Anstee, *Aldersgate*	1987	1996	
Michael Everard, CBE, *Lime Street*	—	1996	
John Hughesdon, *Billingsgate*	1991	1997	

THE COMMON COUNCIL

Deputy: Each Common Councilman so described serves as deputy to the Alderman of her/his ward.

Absalom, J. D. (1994)	*Farringdon Wt.*
Altman, L. P., CBE (1996)	*Cripplegate Wn.*
Angell, E. H. (1991)	*Cripplegate Wt.*
Archibald, *Deputy* W. W. (1986)	*Cornhill*
Ayers, K. E. (1996)	*Bassishaw*
Balls, H. D. (1970)	*Castle Baynard*
Barker, *Deputy* J. A. (1981)	*Cripplegate Wn.*
Barnes-Yallowley, H. M. F. (1986)	*Coleman Street*
Beale, *Deputy* M. J. (1979)	*Lime Street*
Bird, J. L., OBE (1977)	*Bridge*
Biroum-Smith, P. L. (1988)	*Dowgate*
Bowman, J. C. R. (1995)	*Aldgate*
Bradshaw, D. J. (1991)	*Cripplegate Wn.*
Bramwell, F. M. (1983)	*Langbourn*
Branson, N. A. C. (1996)	*Bassishaw*
Brewster, J. W., OBE (1994)	*Bassishaw*

Brighton, R. L. (1984)	*Portsoken*
Brooks, W. I. B. (1988)	*Billingsgate*
Byllam-Barnes, J. C. F. B. (1997)	*Cheap*
Caspi, D. R. (1994)	*Bridge*
Cassidy, *Deputy* M. J. (1989)	*Coleman Street*
Catt, B. F. (1982)	*Farringdon Wn.*
Chadwick, R. A. H. (1994)	*Tower*
Challis, G. H., CBE (1978)	*Langbourn*
Charkham, J. P. (1996)	*Farringdon Wt.*
Cohen, Mrs C. M. (1986)	*Lime Street*
Cole, Lt.-Col. Sir Colin, KCB, KCVO, TD (1964)	*Castle Baynard*
Cotgrove, D. (1991)	*Lime Street*
Currie, *Deputy* Miss S. E. M. (1985)	*Cripplegate Wt.*
Daily-Hunt, R. B. (1989)	*Cripplegate Wt.*
Darwin, G. E. (1995)	*Farringdon Wt.*
Davis, C. B. (1991)	*Bread Street*
Dove, W. H., MBE (1993)	*Bishopsgate*
Dunitz, A. A. (1984)	*Portsoken*
Eskenzi, *Deputy* A. N. (1970)	*Farringdon Wn.*
Eve, R. A. (1980)	*Cheap*
Everett, K. M. (1984)	*Candlewick*
Falk, F. A., TD (1997)	*Broad Street*
Farr, M. C. (1998)	*Walbrook*
Farrow, M. W. W. (1996)	*Farringdon Wt.*
Farthing, R. B. C. (1981)	*Aldgate*
Fell, J. A. (1982)	*Queenhithe*
FitzGerald, *Deputy* R. C. A. (1981)	*Bread Street*
Forbes, G. B. (1993)	*Bishopsgate*
Fraser, S. J. (1993)	*Coleman Street*
Fraser, W. B. (1981)	*Vintry*
Galloway, A. D. (1981)	*Broad Street*
Gillon, G. M. F. (1995)	*Cordwainer*
Ginsburg, S. (1990)	*Bishopsgate*
Gowman, Miss A. J. (1991)	*Dowgate*
Graves, A. C. (1985)	*Bishopsgate*
Green, C. (1994)	*Aldersgate*
Griffiths, Mrs R. M. (1996)	*Cripplegate Wt.*
Hall, B. R. H. (1995)	*Farringdon Wn.*
Halliday, Mrs P. (1992)	*Walbrook*
Hardwick, Dr P. B. (1987)	*Aldgate*
Harris, B. N. (1996)	*Broad Street*
Hart, *Deputy* M. G. (1970)	*Bridge*
Haynes, J. E. H. (1986)	*Cornhill*
Henderson, J. S., OBE (1975)	*Langbourn*
Henderson-Begg, M. (1977)	*Coleman Street*
Holland, *Deputy* J., CBE (1972)	*Aldgate*
Holliday, Mrs E. H. L. (1987)	*Vintry*
Horlock, *Deputy* H. W. S. (1969)	*Farringdon Wn.*
Jackson, L. St J. T. (1978)	*Bread Street*
Kellett, Mrs M. W. F. (1986)	*Tower*
Kemp, D. L. (1984)	*Coleman Street*
Knowles, S. K. (1984)	*Candlewick*
Lawrence, G. A. (1994)	*Farringdon Wt.*
Lawson, G. C. H. (1971)	*Portsoken*
Leck, P. (1998)	*Aldersgate*
Littlechild, Mrs V. (1998)	*Cripplegate Wt.*
Littlestone, N. (1993)	*Aldersgate*
Luder, I. D. (1998)	*Farringdon Wt.*
McGuinness, C. (1997)	*Castle Baynard*
MacLellan, *Deputy* A. P. W. (1989)	*Walbrook*
McNeil, I. D. (1977)	*Lime Street*
Malins, *Deputy* J. H., QC (1981)	*Farringdon Wt.*
Martinelli, *Deputy* P. J. (1994)	*Bassishaw*
Mayhew, Miss J. (1986)	*Queenhithe*
Mayhew, J. P. (1996)	*Aldersgate*
Mead, Mrs W. (1997)	*Farringdon Wt.*
Mitchell, *Deputy* C. R. (1971)	*Castle Baynard*
Mizen, *Deputy* D. H. (1979)	*Broad Street*
Mobsby, *Deputy* D. J. L. (1985)	*Billingsgate*

Mooney, B. D. F. (1998)   *Queenhithe*
Morgan, *Deputy* B. L., CBE (1963)   *Bishopsgate*
Moss, A. D. (1989)   *Tower*
Nash, *Deputy* Mrs J. C. (1983)   *Aldersgate*
Newman, Mrs P. B. (1989)   *Aldersgate*
O'Ferrall, P. C. K., OBE (1996)   *Aldgate*
Owen, Mrs J. (1975)   *Langbourn*
Owen-Ward, J. R. (1983)   *Bridge*
Parmley, A. C., PH.D. (1992)   *Vintry*
Pembroke, *Deputy* Mrs A. M. F. (1978)   *Cheap*
Platts-Mills, J. F. F., QC   *Farringdon Wt.*
Ponsonby of Shulbrede, *Deputy* Lady
  (1981)   *Farringdon Wt.*
Price, E. E. (1996)   *Farringdon Wt.*
Pulman, *Deputy* G. A. G. (1983)   *Tower*
Punter, C. (1993)   *Cripplegate Wn.*
Quilter, S. D. (1998)   *Cripplegate Wt.*
Regan, R. D. (1998)   *Farringdon Wn.*
Revell-Smith, *Deputy* P. A., CBE (1959)   *Vintry*
Rigby, P. P., CBE (1972)   *Farringdon Wn.*
Robinson, Mrs D. C. (1989)   *Bishopsgate*
Roney, *Deputy* E. P. T., CBE (1974)   *Bishopsgate*
Samuel, *Deputy* Mrs I., MBE (1971)   *Portsoken*
Sargant, K. A. (1991)   *Cornhill*
Saunders, *Deputy* R. (1975)   *Candlewick*
Scriven, R. G., CBE (1984)   *Candlewick*
Sellon, S. A., OBE, TD (1990)   *Cordwainer*
Shalit, D. M. (1972)   *Farringdon Wn.*
Sharp, *Deputy* Mrs I. M. (1974)   *Queenhithe*
Sherlock, M. R. C. (1992)   *Dowgate*
Snyder, *Deputy* M. J. (1986)   *Cordwainer*
Spanner, J. H., TD (1984)   *Broad Street*
Stevenson, F. P. (1994)   *Cripplegate Wn.*
Taylor, J. A. F., TD (1991)   *Bread Street*
Thorp, C. R. (1996)   *Billingsgate*
Thorp, D. A. R. (1998)   *Dowgate*
Trotter, J. (1993)   *Billingsgate*
Walsh, S. (1989)   *Farringdon Wt.*
Warner, D. W. (1994)   *Cripplegate Wn.*
White, Dr J. W. (1986)   *Cornhill*
Willoughby, P. J. (1985)   *Bishopsgate*
Wilmot, R. T. D. (1973)   *Cordwainer*
Wixley, G. R. A., CBE, TD (1964)   *Coleman Street*

The City Guilds
(Livery Companies)

The constitution of the livery companies has been unchanged for centuries. There are three ranks of membership: freemen, liverymen and assistants. A person can become a freeman by patrimony (through a parent having been a freeman); by servitude (through having served an apprenticeship to a freeman); or by redemption (by purchase).

Election to the livery is the prerogative of the company, who can elect any of its freemen as liverymen. Assistants are usually elected from the livery and form a Court of Assistants which is the governing body of the company. The Master (in some companies called the Prime Warden) is elected annually from the assistants.

As at June 1998, 22,923 liverymen of the guilds were entitled to vote at elections at Common Hall.

The order of precedence, omitting extinct companies, is given in parenthesis after the name of each company in the list below. In certain companies the election of Master or Prime Warden for the year does not take place until the

autumn. In such cases the Master or Prime Warden for 1998–9 is given.

THE TWELVE GREAT COMPANIES
In order of civic precedence

MERCERS (*1*). *Hall*, Ironmonger Lane, London EC2V 8HE. *Livery*, 253. *Clerk*, C. H. Parker. *Master*, P. R. Withers Green

GROCERS (*2*). *Hall*, Princes Street, London EC2R 8AD. *Livery*, 325. *Clerk*, P. P. Rawlins, MBE. *Master*, His Honour Judge S. Coltart

DRAPERS (*3*). *Hall*, Throgmorton Avenue, London EC2N 2DQ. *Livery*, 252. *Clerk*, A. L. Lang, MBE. *Master*, J. M. F. Padovan

FISHMONGERS (*4*). *Hall*, London Bridge, London EC4R 9EL. *Livery*, 363. *Clerk*, K. S. Waters. *Prime Warden*, The Earl of Clarendon

GOLDSMITHS (*5*). *Hall*, Foster Lane, London EC2V 6BN. *Livery*, 280. *Clerk*, R. D. Buchanan-Dunlop, CBE. *Prime Warden*, Sir Nigel Broackes

MERCHANT TAYLORS (*6/7*). *Hall*, 30 Threadneedle Street, London EC2R 8JB. *Livery*, 300. *Clerk*, D. A. Peck. *Master*, Alderman Sir Brian Jenkins, GBE

SKINNERS (*6/7*). *Hall*, 8 Dowgate Hill, London EC4R 2SP. *Livery*, 400. *Clerk*, Capt. D. Hart Dyke, CBE, LVO, RN. *Master*, Sir Andrew Wilson, KCB, AFC

HABERDASHERS (*8*). *Clerk*, Capt. R. J. Fisher, RN, *Hall*, *Livery*, 320. 39-40 Bartholomew Close, London EC1A 7JN. *Master*, M. D. G. Wheldon, FRICS

SALTERS (*9*). *Hall*, 4 Fore Street, London EC2Y 5DE. *Livery*, 165. *Clerk*, Col. M. P. Barneby. *Master*, The Hon. A. H. Todd

IRONMONGERS (*10*). *Hall*, Shaftesbury Place, Barbican, London EC2Y 8AA. *Livery*, 130. *Clerk*, J. A. Oliver. *Master*, Sir Richard Evans, KCMG, KCVO

VINTNERS (*11*). *Hall*, Upper Thames Street, London EC4V 3BG. *Livery*, 300. *Clerk*, Brig. M. Smythe, OBE. *Master*, A. J. Buchanan

CLOTHWORKERS (*12*). *Hall*, Dunster Court, Mincing Lane, London EC3R 7AH. *Livery*, 200. *Clerk*, M. G. T. Harris. *Master*, Sir John B. Hall, Bt.

OTHER CITY GUILDS
In alphabetical order

ACTUARIES (*91*). *Livery*, 187. *Clerk*, Mrs J. V. Evans, 81 Worrin Road, Shenfield, Brentwood, Essex CM15 8JN. *Master*, S. J. Green

AIR PILOTS AND AIR NAVIGATORS, GUILD OF (*81*). *Livery*, 500. *Grand Master*, HRH The Prince Philip, Duke of Edinburgh, KG, KT, OM, GBE, PC. *Clerk*, Air Vice-Marshal R. G. Peters, CB, Cobham House, 291 Grays Inn Road, London WC1X 8QF. *Master*, Capt J. C. Hutchinson

APOTHECARIES, SOCIETY OF (*58*). *Hall*, 14 Black Friars Lane, London EC4V 6EJ. *Livery*, 1700. *Clerk*, Lt.-Col. R. J. Stringer. *Master*, R. J. Parker

ARBITRATORS (*93*). *Livery*, 160. *Clerk*, Mrs G. Duffy, 13 Hall Gardens, Colney Heath, St Albans, Herts AL4 0QF. *Master*, J. Mackie

ARMOURERS AND BRASIERS (*22*). *Hall*, 81 Coleman Street, London EC2R 5BJ. *Livery*, 120. *Clerk*, Cdr. T. J. K. Sloane, OBE, RN. *Master*, G. Archer Garnett

BAKERS (*19*). *Hall*, Harp Lane, London EC3R 6DP. *Livery*, 390. *Clerk*, J. W. Tompkins. *Master*, C. Gilford

BARBERS (*17*). *Hall*, Monkwell Square, Wood Street, London EC2Y 5BL. *Livery*, 312. *Clerk*, Brig. A. F. Eastburn. *Master*, The Rt. Hon. The Lord McColl of Dulwich, CBE, FRCS

BASKETMAKERS (*52*). *Livery*, 317. *Clerk*, Maj. G. J. Flint-Shipman, TD, 48 Seymour Walk, London SW10 9NF. *Prime Warden*, Deputy G. A. G. Pulman

BLACKSMITHS (*40*). *Livery*, 237. *Clerk*, C. Jerl, 48 Upwood Road, London SE12 8AN. *Prime Warden*, H. A. E. Adams

BOWYERS (*38*). *Livery*, 108. *Clerk*, J. R. Owen-Ward, 11 Aldermans Hill, London N13 4YD. *Master*, W. P. Forrester

BREWERS (*14*). *Hall*, Aldermanbury Square, London EC2V 7HR. *Livery*, 140. *Clerk*, C. W. Dallmeyer. *Master*, R. H. B. Neame

BRODERERS (*48*). *Livery*, 168. *Clerk*, P. J. C. Crouch, 11 Bridge Road, East Molesey, Surrey KT8 9EU. *Master*, A. T. Peck

BUILDERS MERCHANTS (*88*). *Livery*, 185. *Clerk*, Miss S. M. Robinson, TD, 4 College Hill, London EC4R 2RB. *Master*, S. B. Tusting

BUTCHERS (*24*). *Hall*, 87 Bartholomew Close, London EC1A 7EB. *Livery*, 648. *Clerk*, G. J. Sharp. *Master*, G. A. Jackman

CARMEN (*77*). *Livery*, 430. *Clerk*, Cdr. R. M. H. Bawtree, OBE, RN, 35/37 Ludgate Hill, London EC4M 7JN. *Master*, J. M. Silbermann, OBE, FRSA

CARPENTERS (*26*). *Hall*, 1 Throgmorton Avenue, London EC2N 2JJ. *Livery*, 174. *Clerk*, Maj.-Gen. P. T. Stevenson, OBE. *Master*, N. B. C. Evelegh, MBE

CHARTERED ACCOUNTANTS (*86*). *Livery*, 340. *Clerk*, C. Bygrave, The Rustlings, Valley Close, Studham, Dunstable LU6 2QN. *Master*, D. T. Young

CHARTERED ARCHITECTS (*98*). *Livery*, 112. *Clerk*, J. Griffiths, 28 Palace Road, East Molesey, Surrey KT8 9DL. *Master*, Prof. P. Dale

CHARTERED SECRETARIES AND ADMINISTRATORS (*87*). *Livery*, 240. *Clerk*, Maj. I. F. Stewart, Sadler's Hall, 3rd Floor, 40 Gutter Lane, London EC2V 6BR. *Master*, W. C. Hammond, MBE

CHARTERED SURVEYORS (*85*). *Livery*, 350. *Clerk*, Mrs A. L. Jackson, 16 St Mary-at-Hill, London EC3R 8EE. *Master*, Miss D. F. Patman

CLOCKMAKERS (*61*). *Livery*, 230. *Clerk*, Gp Capt. P. H. Gibson, MBE, Room 66-67 Albert Buildings, 49 Queen Victoria Street, London EC4N 4SE. *Master*, Prof. A. Boksenberg, CBE, FRS

COACHMAKERS AND COACH-HARNESS MAKERS (*72*). *Livery*, 420. *Clerk*, Gp Capt. G. Bunn, CBE, Charlcote House, Burfield Road, Chorleywood, Herts WD3 5NS. *Master*, P. Ashfield

CONSTRUCTORS (*99*). *Livery*, 130. *Clerk*, L. L. Brace, 181 Fentiman Road, London SW8 1JY. *Master*, D. A. Hutchison, MBE

COOKS (*35*). *Livery*, 75. *Clerk*, M. C. Thatcher, Registry Chambers, The Old Deanery, Deans Court, London EC4V 5AA. *Master*, P. D. Herbage

COOPERS (*36*). *Hall*, 13 Devonshire Square, London EC2M 4TH. *Livery*, 265. *Clerk*, J. A. Newton. *Master*, M. J. Howell

CORDWAINERS (*27*). *Livery*, 163. *Clerk*, Lt.-Col. J. R. Blundell, RM, Eldon Chambers, 30 Fleet Street, London EC4Y 1AA. *Master*, Dr R. K. H. Parker

CURRIERS (*29*). *Livery*, 96. *Clerk*, Gp Capt. F. J. Hamilton, Kestrel Cottage, East Knoyle, Salisbury SP3 6AD. *Master*, C. W. Rome

CUTLERS (*18*). *Hall*, Warwick Lane, London EC4M 7BR. *Livery*, 100. *Clerk*, K. S. G. Hinde, OBE, TD. *Master*, C. M. Li Evans

DISTILLERS (*69*). *Livery*, 270. *Clerk*, C. V. Hughes, 71 Lincoln's Inn Fields, London WC2A 3JF. *Master*, R. H. Nicholson

DYERS (*13*). *Hall*, 10 Dowgate Hill, London EC4R 2ST. *Livery*, 123. *Clerk*, J. R. Chambers. *Prime Warden*, Lt. Col. M. A. Marshall

ENGINEERS (*94*). *Livery*, 282. *Clerk*, Cdr. B. D. Gibson, Kiln Bank, Bodle Street Green, Hailsham, E. Sussex BN27 4UA. *Master*, R. H. Rooley, FREng.

ENVIRONMENTAL CLEANERS (*97*). *Livery*, 235. *Clerk*, J. C. M. Chapman, Woodside Cottage, 44 New Road, Bengeo, Herts SG14 3JL. *Master*, D. A. S. Grant

FAN MAKERS (*76*). *Livery*, 202. *Clerk*, Lt.-Col. I. R. P. Green, 2 Bolts Hill, Castle Camps, Cambridge CB1 6TL. *Master*, M. H. Davis

FARMERS (*80*). *Hall*, 3 Cloth Street, London EC1A 7LD. *Livery*, 300. *Clerk*, Miss M. L. Winter. *Master*, J. H. Cossins, CBE

FARRIERS (*55*). *Livery*, 375. *Clerk*, Mrs C. C. Clifford, 19 Queen Street, Chipperfield, Kings Langley, Herts WD4 9BT. *Master*, R. J. Crocker

FELTMAKERS (*63*). *Livery*, 170. *Clerk*, Lt.-Col. C. J. Holroyd, Providence Cottage, Chute Cadley, Andover, Hants SP11 9EB. *Master*, Cdre I. R. Welsey-Harding

FLETCHERS (*39*). *Hall*, 3 Cloth Street, London EC1A 7LD. *Livery*, 108. *Clerk*, J. R. Owen-Ward. *Master*, R. H. Upton

FOUNDERS (*33*). *Hall*, Number One, Cloth Fair, London EC1A 7HT. *Livery*, 175. *Clerk*, A. J. Gillett. *Master*, L. W. Kemp

FRAMEWORK KNITTERS (*64*). *Livery*, 211. *Clerk*, H. W. H. Ellis, Whitegarth Chambers, 37 The Uplands, Loughton, Essex IG10 1NQ. *Master*, T. D. P. Turnbull

FRUITERERS (*45*). *Livery*, 262. *Clerk*, Lt.-Col. L. G. French, Chapelstones, 84 High Street, Codford St Mary, Warminster BA12 0ND. *Master*, L. S. Olins

FUELLERS (*95*). *Livery*, 66. *Clerk*, R. A. Riley, 22 Broadfields, Headstone Lane, Hatch End, Middx HA2 6NH. *Master*, V. M. F. Williams

FURNITURE MAKERS (*83*). *Livery*, 292. *Clerk*, Mrs J. A. Wright, Painters' Hall, 9 Little Trinity Lane, London EC4V 2AD. *Master*, J. A. Jacobs

GARDENERS (*66*). *Livery*, 247. *Clerk*, Col. N. G. S. Gray, 25 Luke Street, London EC2A 4AR. *Master*, The Revd Canon P. Delaney

GIRDLERS (*21*). *Hall*, Basinghall Avenue, London EC2V 5DD. *Livery*, 80. *Clerk*, Lt.-Col. R. Sullivan. *Master*, A. R. Westall

GLASS-SELLERS (*71*). *Livery*, 167. *Hon. Clerk*, B. J. Rawles, 43 Aragon Avenue, Thames Ditton, Surrey KT7 0PY. *Master*, The Rt. Revd J. Waine, KCVO

GLAZIERS AND PAINTERS OF GLASS (*53*). *Hall*, 9 Montague Close, London SE1 9DD. *Livery*, 240. *Clerk*, Col. D. W. Eking. *Master*, P. R. Batchelor

GLOVERS (*62*). *Livery*, 270. *Clerk*, Mrs M. Hood, 71 Ifield Road, London SW10 9AU. *Master*, Mrs M. Linton

GOLD AND SILVER WYRE DRAWERS (*74*). *Livery*, 310. *Clerk*, R. P. Williams, 50 Cheyne Avenue, London E18 2DR. *Master*, K. P. Kirby

GUNMAKERS (*73*). *Livery*, 268. *Clerk*, J. M. Riches, The Proof House, 48-50 Commercial Road, London E1 1LP. *Master*, Col. D. C. Munn

HORNERS (*54*). *Livery*, 244. *Clerk*, A. R. Layard. Whitethorns, Rannoch Road, Crowborough, E. Sussex TN6 1RA. *Master*, L. P. Smith

INFORMATION TECHNOLOGISTS (*100*). *Livery*, 300. *Clerk*, Mrs G. Davies, 30 Aylesbury Street, London EC1R 0ER. *Master*, P. Cropper

INNHOLDERS (*32*). *Hall*, 30 College Street, London EC4R 2RH. *Livery*, 129. *Clerk*, J. R. Edwardes Jones. *Master*, Dr R. Glover

INSURERS (*92*). *Hall*, 20 Aldermanbury, London EC2V 7HY. *Livery*, 380. *Clerk*, L. J. Walters. *Master*, M. J. Pickard

JOINERS AND CEILERS (*41*). *Livery*, 125. *Clerk*, Mrs A. L. Jackson, 75 Meadway Drive, Horsell, Woking, Surrey GU21 4TF. *Master*, R. W. E. Rogan

LAUNDERERS (*89*). *Hall*, 9 Montague Close, London Bridge, London SE1 9DD. *Livery*, 250. *Clerk*, Mrs J. Polek. *Master*, T. A. Elliott

LEATHERSELLERS (*15*). *Hall*, 15 St Helen's Place, London EC3A 6DQ, *Livery*, 150. *Clerk*, Capt. J. G. F. Cooke, OBE, RN. *Master*, R. S. Whitmore

LIGHTMONGERS (*96*). *Livery*, 145. *Clerk*, D. B. Wheatley, Crown Wharf, 11a Coldharbour, Blackwall Reach, London E14 9NS. *Master*, E. H. Ring

LORINERS (*57*). *Livery*, 353. *Clerk*, G. B. Forbes, 50 Cheyne Avenue, London E18 2DR. *Master*, E. I. Walker-Arnott

MAKERS OF PLAYING CARDS (*75*). *Livery*, 148. *Clerk*, M. J. Smyth, 6 The Priory, Godstone, Surrey RH9 8NL. *Master*, G. H. E. Robson

MARKETORS (*90*). *Livery*, 220. *Clerk*, Mrs G. Duffy, 13 Hall Gardens, Colney Heath, St Albans, Herts AL4 0PF. *Master*, Prof. J. A. P. Treasure

MASONS (*30*). *Livery*, 125. *Clerk*, P. F. Clark, 22 Cannon Hill, Southgate, London N14 6LG. *Master*, B. J. Rushton

MASTER MARINERS, HONOURABLE COMPANY OF (*78*). HQS Wellington, Temple Stairs, Victoria Embankment, London WC2R 2PN. *Livery*, 220. *Admiral*, HRH The Prince Philip, Duke of Edinburgh, KG, KT, OM, GBE, PC. *Clerk*, J. A. V. Maddock. *Master*, Capt G. M. Pepper

MUSICIANS (*50*). *Livery*, 359. *Clerk*, S. F. N. Waley, 75 Watling Street, London EC4M 9BJ. *Master*, Sir Alan Traill, CBE, QSD

NEEDLEMAKERS (*65*). *Livery*, 230. *Clerk*, M. G. Cook, 5 Staple Inn, London WC1V 7QH. *Master*, Sir Anthony Wilson

PAINTER-STAINERS (*28*). *Hall*, 9 Little Trinity Lane, London EC4V 2AD. *Livery*, 320. *Clerk*, Col. W. J. Chesshyre. *Master*, The Hon. M. Robson

PATTENMAKERS (*70*). *Livery*, 200. *Clerk*, Lt. Col. R. W. Murfin, TD, Vanguard House, Sutton Valence, Kent ME17 3JA. *Master*, R. P. Ziff

PAVIORS (*56*). *Livery*, 230. *Clerk*, J. L. White, 3 Ridgemount Gardens, Enfield, Middx EN2 8QL. *Master*, P. D. Marriott Gell

PEWTERERS (*16*). *Hall*, Oat Lane, London EC2V 7DE. *Livery*, 119. *Clerk*, Cdr. A. St J. Steiner, OBE, RN. *Master*, W. Grant

PLAISTERERS (*46*). *Hall*, 1 London Wall, London EC2Y 5JU. *Livery*, 205. *Clerk*, R. Vickers. *Master*, C. Towlson

PLUMBERS (*31*). *Livery*, 347. *Clerk*, Lt.-Col. R. J. A. Paterson-Fox, Room 28, 49 Queen Victoria Street, London EC4N 4SA. *Master*, J. H. Mayfield

POULTERS (*34*). *Livery*, 180. *Clerk*, A. W. Scott, 23 Orchard Drive, Chorleywood, Herts WD3 5QN. *Master*, C. R. S. Link

SADDLERS (*25*). *Hall*, 40 Gutter Lane, London EC2V 6BR. *Livery*, 75. *Clerk*, Gp Capt. W. S. Brereton Martin, CBE. *Master*, M. R. Quirk, OBE

SCIENTIFIC INSTRUMENT MAKERS (*84*). *Hall*, 9 Montague Close, London SE1 9DD. *Livery*, 235. *Clerk*, F. G. Everard. *Master*, M. T. Dixon

SCRIVENERS (*44*). *Livery*, 245. *Clerk*, G. A. Hill, HQS Wellington, Temple Stairs, Victoria Embankment, London WC2R 2PN. *Master*, N. Grimston

SHIPWRIGHTS (*59*). *Livery*, 400. *Permanent Master*, HRH The Prince Philip, Duke of Edinburgh, KG, KT, OM, GBE, PC. *Clerk*, Capt. R. F. Channon, RN, Ironmongers Hall, Barbican, London EC2Y 8AA. *Prime Warden*, P. Tudball, CBE

SOLICITORS (*79*). *Livery*, 260. *Clerk*, Miss S. M. Robinson, TD, 4 College Hill, London EC2R 2RB. *Master*, M. R. Mathews

SPECTACLE MAKERS (*60*). *Livery*, 230. *Clerk*, Lt.-Col. J. A. B. Salmon, OBE, LLB, Apothecaries' Hall, Black Friars Lane, London EC4V 6EL. *Master*, A. H. Chignell, FRCS

STATIONERS AND NEWSPAPER MAKERS (*47*). *Hall*, Ave Maria Lane, London EC4M 7DD. *Livery*, 446. *Clerk*, Brig. D. G. Sharp, AFC. *Master*, R. T. H. Harrison

TALLOW CHANDLERS (*21*). *Hall*, 4 Dowgate Hill, London EC4R 2SH. *Livery*, 180. *Clerk*, Brig. W. K. L. Prosser, CBE, MC. *Master*, Brig. N. H. Thompson, CBE

TIN PLATE WORKERS (ALIAS WIRE WORKERS) (*67*). *Livery*, 200. *Clerk*, M. Henderson-Begg, Bartholomew House, 66 Westbury Road, New Malden, Surrey KT3 5AS. *Master*, Dr B. T. K. Barry

TOBACCO PIPE MAKERS AND TOBACCO BLENDERS (*82*). *Livery*, 161. *Clerk*, N. J. Hallings-Pott, Hackhurst Farm, Lower Dicker, Hailsham, E. Sussex BN27 4BP. *Master*, The Hon. M. H. Richards

TURNERS (*51*). *Livery*, 190. *Clerk*, E. A. Windsor Clive, c/o Apothecaries' Hall, Black Friars Lane, London EC4V 6EL. *Master*, Dr J. M. Slater, BScM, PhD

TYLERS AND BRICKLAYERS (*37*). *Livery*, 126. *Clerk*, J. A. Norris, Hawthorns, Claygate Lane, Thames Ditton, Surrey KT7 0DT. *Master*, Sir Idris Pearce, CBE, TD

UPHOLDERS (*49*). *Livery*, 225. *Clerk*, J. P. Cody, Hall in the Wood, 46 Quail Gardens, Selsdon Vale, Croydon CR2 8TF. *Master*, C. B. Roffe

WAX CHANDLERS (*20*). *Hall*, Gresham Street, London EC2V 7AD. *Livery*, 119. *Clerk*, Cdr J. Stevens. *Master*, B. E. A. Reynolds

WEAVERS (*42*). *Livery*, 125. *Clerk*, Mrs F. Newcombe, Saddlers' House, Gutter Lane, London EC2V 6BR. *Upper Bailiff*, R. H. W. Graham-Palmer

WHEELWRIGHTS (*68*). *Livery*, 212. *Clerk*, P. J. C. Crouch, 11 Bridge Road, East Molesey, Surrey KT8 9EU. *Master*, T. W. P. Bridges

WOOLMEN (*43*). *Livery*, 135. *Clerk*, F. Allen, Hollands, Hedsor Road, Bourne End, Bucks SL8 5EE. *Master*, P. F. Valpy

FIREFIGHTERS (*No livery*). *Freemen*, 127. *Clerk*, G. P. Ellis, The Insurance Hall, 20 Aldermanbury, London EC2V 7GF. *Master*, Prof. D. E. Bland, OBE

PARISH CLERKS (*No livery*). *Members*, 95. *Clerk*, Lt. Col. B. J. N. Coombes, c/o 1 Dean Trench Street, London SW1P 3HB. *Master*, W. H. Dove, MBE

WATER CONSERVATORS (*No livery*). *Hall*, 16 St Mary-at-Hill, London EC2R 8EE. *Freemen*. *Hon. Clerk*, H. B. Berridge, MBE. *Master*, Dr E. W. Jackson

WATERMEN AND LIGHTERMEN (*No livery*). *Hall*, 16 St Mary-at-Hill, London EC3R 8EF. *Craft Owning Freemen*, 360. *Clerk*, C. Middlemiss. *Master*, J. Johnson

WORLD TRADERS (*No livery*). *Freemen*, 146. *Clerk*, N. R. Pullman, 36 Ladbroke Grove, London W11 2PA. *Master*, Sir Roger Cork

LONDON BOROUGH COUNCILS

Council	Municipal offices	Population	Band D charge 1999	Chief Executive (*Managing Director)	Mayor (a) Lord Mayor 1999–2000
Barking and Dagenham;	°Dagenham, RM10 7BN	143,681	£738.00	W. C. Smith	W. Dale
Barnet	†The Burroughs, Hendon, NW4 4BG	293,564	760.85	M. Caller	J. Cohen
Bexley	‡Bexleyheath, Kent DA6 7LB	215,615	750.18	C. Duffield	Mrs L. Bailey
Brent	†Forty Lane, Wembley, HA9 9EZ	243,025	678.46	G. Daniel	J. Lebor
Bromley	°Bromley, BR1 3UH	290,609	669.96	Dr M. Blanch	Ms S. Polydoru
§Camden	†Judd Street, WC1H 9JE	170,444	896.57	S. Bundred	R. Shaw
§CITY OF WESTMINSTER	City Hall, Victoria Street, SW1E 6QP	174,814	350.00	W. Roots	(a) A. Segal
Croydon	Taberner House, Park Lane, Croydon, CR9 3JS	313,510	758.39	D. Wechsler	S. Khan
Ealing	†Uxbridge Road, W5 2HL	275,257	643.00	Ms G. Guy	P. Portwood
Enfield	°Silver Street, Enfield, EN1 3XA	257,417	732.61	D. Plank	E. Smythe
§Greenwich	†Wellington Street, SE18 6PW	207,650	883.35	D. Brooks	J. Fahy
§Hackney	†Mare Street, E8 1EA	181,248	789.60	*S. Ebanja (acting)	J. Lobenstein, MBE
§Hammersmith and Fulham	†King Street, W6 9JU	148,502	827.02	*R. Harbord	A. Slaughter
Haringey	°High Road, N22 4LE	202,204	898.00	G. Singh	Ms M. Dewar
Harrow	°Harrow, HA1 2UJ	200,100	787.53	A. Redmond	Ms A. Groves
Havering	†Romford, RM1 3BD	229,492	724.00	H. W. Tinworth	Mrs M. Whitelock
Hillingdon	°High Street, Uxbridge, UB8 1UW	231,602	763.66	D. Leatham	M. Lancaster
Hounslow	°Lampton Road, Hounslow, TW3 4DN	204,397	795.43	D. Myers	G. Dhillon
§Islington	†Upper Street, N1 2UD	164,686	912.00	Ms L. Fullick	Ms J. Sands
§Kensington and Chelsea (RB)	†Hornton Street, W8 7NX	138,394	572.79	A. Taylor	Mrs P. Frazer
Kingston upon Thames (RB)	Guildhall, Kingston upon Thames, KT1 1EU	132,996	793.58	vacant	Ms J. Smith
§Lambeth	†Brixton Hill, SW2 1RW	244,834	642.00	Ms H. Rabbatts	S. Bourne
§Lewisham	†Catford, SE6 4RU	230,983	727.87	Dr B. Quirk	D. Sullivan
Merton	°London Road, Morden, SM4 5DX	168,470	784.24	R. Paine	Ms J. Paton
§Newham	†East Ham, E6 2RP	212,170	704.43	Dr W. Thomson	R. A. Mirza
Redbridge	†Ilford, IG1 1DD	226,218	750.00	M. Frater	F. Maravala
Richmond upon Thames	°Richmond Road, Twickenham, TW1 3BZ	160,732	834.44	Mrs G. Norton	M. Jones
§Southwark	†Peckham Road, SE5 8UB	218,541	808.60	R. Coomber	C. Cherrill
Sutton	‡St Nicholas Way, Sutton, SM1 1EA	168,880	748.62	Mrs P. Hughes	Ms S. Stears
§Tower Hamlets	107A Commercial Street, E1 6BG	160,064	674.02	Ms S. Pierce	Ms D. Jones
Waltham Forest	†Forest Road, Walthamstow, E17 4JF	212,033	840.29	A. Tobias	P. J. Dawe
§Wandsworth	†Wandsworth High Street, SW18 2PU	252,425	369.87	G. K. Jones	Mrs. L. Ayonrinde

§ Inner London Borough
RB Royal Borough
° Civic Centre
† Town Hall
‡ Civic Offices
For explanation of council tax, see pages 521–2

Wales

The Principality of Wales (Cymru) occupies the extreme west of the central southern portion of the island of Great Britain, with a total area of 8,015 sq. miles (20,758 sq. km): land 7,965 sq. miles (20,628 sq. km); inland water 50 sq. miles (130 sq. km). It is bounded on the north by the Irish Sea, on the south by the Bristol Channel, on the east by the English counties of Cheshire, Shropshire, Worcestershire and Gloucestershire, and on the west by St George's Channel.

Across the Menai Straits is the island of Anglesey (Ynys Môn) (276 sq. miles), communication with which is facilitated by the Menai Suspension Bridge (1,000 ft long) built by Telford in 1826, and by the tubular railway bridge (1,100 ft long) built by Stephenson in 1850. Holyhead harbour, on Holy Isle (north-west of Anglesey), provides accommodation for ferry services to Dublin (70 miles).

POPULATION

The population at the 1991 census was 2,835,073 (males 1,370,104; females 1,464,969). The average density of population in 1991 was 1.36 persons per hectare.

RELIEF

Wales is a country of extensive tracts of high plateau and shorter stretches of mountain ranges deeply dissected by river valleys. Lower-lying ground is largely confined to the coastal belt and the lower parts of the valleys. The highest mountains are those of Snowdonia in the north-west (Snowdon, 3,559 ft), Berwyn (Aran Fawddwy, 2,971 ft), Cader Idris (Pen y Gadair, 2,928 ft), Dyfed (Plynlimon, 2,467 ft), and the Black Mountain, Brecon Beacons and Black Forest ranges in the south-east (Carmarthen Van, 2,630 ft, Pen y Fan, 2,906 ft, Waun Fâch, 2,660 ft).

HYDROGRAPHY

The principal river rising in Wales is the Severn (*see also* page 532), which flows from the slopes of Plynlimon to the English border. The Wye (130 miles) also rises in the slopes of Plynlimon. The Usk (56 miles) flows into the Bristol Channel, through Gwent. The Dee (70 miles) rises in Bala Lake and flows through the Vale of Llangollen, where an aqueduct (built by Telford in 1805) carries the Pontcysyllte branch of the Shropshire Union Canal across the valley. The estuary of the Dee is the navigable portion, 14 miles in length and about five miles in breadth, and the tide rushes in with dangerous speed over the 'Sands of Dee'. The Towy (68 miles), Teifi (50 miles), Taff (40 miles), Dovey (30 miles), Taf (25 miles) and Conway (24 miles), the last named broad and navigable, are wholly Welsh rivers.

The largest natural lake is Bala (Llyn Tegid) in Gwynedd, nearly four miles long and about one mile wide. Lake Vyrnwy is an artificial reservoir, about the size of Bala, and forms the water supply of Liverpool; Birmingham is supplied from reservoirs in the Elan and Claerwen valleys.

WELSH LANGUAGE

According to the 1991 census results, the percentage of persons of three years and over able to speak Welsh was:

Clwyd	18.2	Powys	20.2
Dyfed	43.7	S. Glamorgan	6.5
Gwent	2.4	W. Glamorgan	15.0
Gwynedd	61.0		
Mid Glamorgan	8.5	Wales	18.7

The 1991 figure represents a slight decline from 18.9 per cent in 1981 (1971, 20.8 per cent; 1961, 26 per cent).

FLAG

The flag of Wales, the Red Dragon (Y Ddraig Goch), is a red dragon on a field divided white over green (per fess argent and vert a dragon passant gules). The flag was augmented in 1953 by a royal badge on a shield encircled with a riband bearing the words *Ddraig Goch Ddyry Cychwyn* and imperially crowned, but this augmented flag is rarely used.

EARLY HISTORY

The earliest inhabitants of whom there is any record appear to have been subdued or exterminated by the Goidels (a people of Celtic race) in the Bronze Age. A further invasion of Celtic Brythons and Belgae followed in the ensuing Iron Age. The Roman conquest of southern Britain and Wales was for some time successfully opposed by Caratacus (Caractacus or Caradog), chieftain of the Catuvellauni and son of Cunobelinus (Cymbeline). South-east Wales was subjugated and the legionary fortress at Caerleon-on-Usk established by about AD 75–77; the conquest of Wales was completed by Agricola about AD 78. Communications were opened up by the construction of military roads from Chester to Caerleon-on-Usk and Caerwent, and from Chester to Conwy (and thence to Carmarthen and Neath). Christianity was introduced during the Roman occupation, in the fourth century.

ANGLO-SAXON ATTACKS

The Anglo-Saxon invaders of southern Britain drove the Celts into the mountain stronghold of Wales, and into Strathclyde (Cumberland and south-west Scotland) and Cornwall, giving them the name of *Waelisc* (Welsh), meaning 'foreign'. The West Saxons' victory at Deorham (AD 577) isolated Wales from Cornwall and the battle of Chester (AD 613) cut off communication with Strathclyde and northern Britain. In the eighth century the boundaries of the Welsh were further restricted by the annexations of Offa, King of Mercia, and counter-attacks were largely prevented by the construction of an artificial boundary from the Dee to the Wye (Offa's Dyke).

In the ninth century Rhodri Mawr (844–878) united the country and successfully resisted further incursions of the Saxons by land and raids of Norse and Danish pirates by sea, but at his death his three provinces of Gwynedd (north), Powys (mid) and Deheubarth (south) were divided among his three sons, Anarawd, Mervyn and Cadell. Cadell's son Hywel Dda ruled a large part of Wales and codified its laws but the provinces were not united again until the rule of Llewelyn ap Seisyllt (husband of the heiress of Gwynedd) from 1018 to 1023.

THE NORMAN CONQUEST

After the Norman conquest of England, William I created palatine counties along the Welsh frontier, and the Norman barons began to make encroachments into Welsh territory. The Welsh princes recovered many of their losses during the civil wars of Stephen's reign and in the early 13th century Owen Gruffydd, prince of Gwynedd, was the dominant figure in Wales. Under Llywelyn ap Iorwerth (1194–1240) the Welsh united in powerful resistance to English incursions and Llywelyn's privileges and *de facto* independence were recognized in Magna Carta. His grandson, Llywelyn ap Gruffydd, was the last native prince; he was killed in 1282 during hostilities between the Welsh and English, allowing Edward I of England to establish his authority over the country. On 7 February 1301, Edward of Caernarvon, son of Edward I, was created Prince of Wales, a title which has subsequently been borne by the eldest son of the sovereign.

Strong Welsh national feeling continued, expressed in the early 15th century in the rising led by Owain Glyndŵr, but the situation was altered by the accession to the English throne in 1485 of Henry VII of the Welsh House of Tudor. Wales was politically assimilated to England under the Act of Union of 1535, which extended English laws to the Principality and gave it parliamentary representation for the first time.

EISTEDDFOD

The Welsh are a distinct nation, with a language and literature of their own, and the national bardic festival (Eisteddfod), instituted by Prince Rhys ap Griffith in 1176, is still held annually. These *Eisteddfodau* (sessions) form part of the *Gorsedd* (assembly), which is believed to date from the time of Prydian, a ruling prince in an age many centuries before the Christian era.

PRINCIPAL CITIES

CARDIFF

Cardiff, at the mouth of the Rivers Taff, Rhymney and Ely, is the capital city of Wales and a major administrative, commercial and business centre. The National Assembly for Wales was opened in Cardiff in 1999. It has many industries, including steel, and its flourishing port is within the Cardiff Bay area, subject of a major redevelopment continuing until the year 2000.

The many fine buildings include the City Hall, the National Museum of Wales, University Buildings, Law Courts, Welsh Office, County Hall, Police Headquarters, the Temple of Peace and Health, Llandaff Cathedral, the Welsh National Folk Museum at St Fagans, Cardiff Castle, the New Theatre, the Sherman Theatre and the Welsh College of Music and Drama. More recent buildings include St David's Hall, Cardiff International Arena and World Trade Centre, and the Welsh National Ice Rink. The Millennium Stadium is under construction for the 1999 rugby World Cup and the Centre for Visual Arts opened in 1999.

SWANSEA

Swansea (*Abertawe*) is a city and a seaport. The Gower peninsula was brought within the city boundary under local government reform in 1974. The trade of the port includes coal, steel products, containerized goods, petroleum products and petrochemicals.

The principal buildings are the Norman Castle (rebuilt *c*.1330), the Royal Institution of South Wales, founded in 1835 (including Library), the University of Wales Swansea at Singleton, and the Guildhall, containing Frank Brangwyn's British Empire panels. The Dylan Thomas Centre,

formerly the old Guildhall, was restored in 1995. More recent buildings include the County Hall, the new Maritime Quarter and Marina and the leisure centre.

Swansea was chartered by the Earl of Warwick, *c*. 1158–84, and further charters were granted by King John, Henry III, Edward II, Edward III and James II, Cromwell (two) and the Marcher Lord William de Breos.

LOCAL COUNCILS

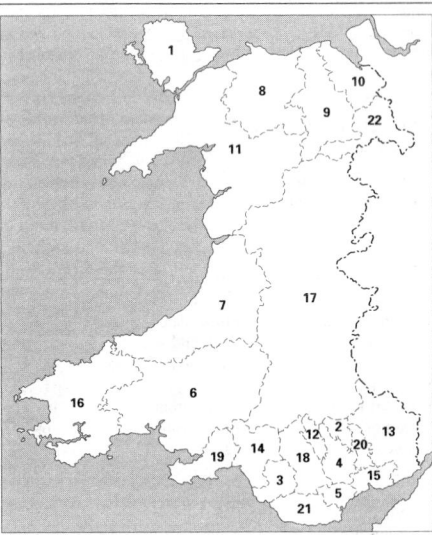

Key	Council
1	Anglesey
2	Blaenau Gwent
3	Bridgend
4	Gwynedd
5	Caerphilly
6	Cardiff
7	Carmarthenshire
8	Ceredigion
9	Conwy
10	Denbighshire
11	Flintshire
12	Merthyr Tydfil
13	Monmouthshire
14	Neath Port Talbot
15	Newport
16	Pembrokeshire
17	Powys
18	Rhondda, Cynon, Taff
19	Swansea
20	Torfaen
21	The Vale of Glamorgan
22	Wrexham

LORD-LIEUTENANTS AND HIGH SHERIFFS

County/Shire	Lord-Lieutenant	High Sheriff, 1999–2000
Clwyd	Sir William Gladstone, Bt., KG	D. E. Williams
Dyfed	Sir David Mansel Lewis, KCVO	J. M. G. Andrews
Gwent	Sir Richard Hanbury Tenison, KCVO	Mrs J. C. Johnson
Gwynedd	vacant	W. D. I. Edwards
Mid Glamorgan	M. A. McLaggan	D. H. Thomas, CBE
Powys	The Hon. Mrs E. S. Legge-Bourke, LVO	J. G. Coltman-Rogers
S. Glamorgan	Capt. N. Lloyd-Edwards	Mrs M. Watkins
W. Glamorgan	R. C. Hastie, CBE	H. A. Steane

LOCAL COUNCILS

SMALL CAPITALS denote CITY status
§ Denotes Borough status

Council	Administrative headquarters	Population	Band D charge 1999	Chief Executive	Chairman 1999–2000 (a) Mayor (b) Lord Mayor
Anglesey	Llangefni	67,055	£534.26¶	G. F. Edwards	R. J. Jones
Blaenau Gwent	Ebbw Vale	73,200	566.54	R. Leadbeter, OBE	(a) Mrs K. M. Williams
Bridgend	Bridgend	128,340	607.56	I. K. Lewis	(a) L. Jenkins
Caerphilly	Hengoed	69,100	637.00	M. Davies	D. Potter
CARDIFF	Cardiff	315,040	572.66	B. Davies	(b) R. Goodway
Carmarthenshire	Carmarthen	169,108	665.85	B. Roynon	K. Maynard
Ceredigion	Aberaeron	69,545	670.00	O. Watkin	W. T. K. Raw-Rees MBE
§Conwy	Conwy	110,600	487.52	C. D. Barker	G. Rees
Denbighshire	Ruthin	90,400	647.00	H. V. Thomas	E. Edwards
Flintshire	Mold	144,900	591.60	P. McGreevy	I. Roberts MBE
Gwynedd	Caernarfon	116,000	614.74	G. R. Jones	W. A. Evans
§Merthyr Tydfil	Merthyr Tydfil	58,100	711.43	G. Meredith	(a) L. C. Elliott
Monmouthshire	Cwmbran	86,248	490.24	Ms J. Redfearn	R. J. B. Wilcox
§Neath Port Talbot	Port Talbot	139,459	749.66	K. R. Sawyers	(a) M. Harris
§Newport	Newport	136,800	656.44	R. D. Blair	(a) F. J. Sweeting
Pembrokeshire	Haverfordwest	114,400	451.71	B. Parry-Jones	B. Phillips
Powys	Llandrindod Wells	124,400	551.98	Miss J. Tonge	G. Morgan
§Rhondda, Cynon, Taff	Tonypandy	240,117	671.92	K. Ryley	G. Beard
SWANSEA	Swansea	230,200	604.18	Ms V. Sugar	(b) R. Lloyd
§Torfaen	Pontypool	90,527	563.87	Dr C. Grace	(a) Ms B. Ryan
Vale of Glamorgan	Barry	119,500	522.00	D. Foster	T. H. Jarvie
§Wrexham	Wrexham	125,200	537.15	D. Griffin	(a) R. Davies

¶ Managing Director

THE NATIONAL ASSEMBLY FOR WALES
(see also pages 1280–91)

In July 1997 the Government announced plans to establish a National Assembly for Wales. In a referendum on 18 September 1997 about 50 per cent of the electorate voted, of whom 50.3 per cent voted in favour of the Assembly. Elections are to be held every four years. The first elections were held on 6 May 1999 when about 46 per cent of the electorate voted. The first session was held on 10 May 1999 and the Assembly was officially opened on 26 May at Crickhowell House, Cardiff; a new building to house the Assembly is under construction in Cardiff.

The Assembly has 60 members (including the Presiding Officer), comprising 40 constituency members and 29 additional regional members from party lists. It can introduce only secondary legislation and has no power to raise or lower income tax.

The National Assembly for Wales is responsible for education, health, training, environment, economic development, local government, housing, planning, financial assistance to industry, tourism, some transport, heritage and the arts, agriculture, forestry and food standards.

SALARIES FROM 1 APRIL 1999:

First Secretary	£64,308 (plus AM salary)
Ministers	£33,360 (plus AM salary)
AMs	£34,438*

* Reduced by two-thirds if the member is already an MP or an MEP

THE WELSH CABINET

First Secretary, The Rt. Hon. Alun Michael, MP, AM (*Lab.*)
Secretary for Economic Development, Rhodri Morgan, MP, AM (*Lab.*)
Secretary for Education Up to Age 16, Rosemary Butler, AM (*Lab.*)
Secretary for Post-16 Education and Training, Tom Middlehurst, AM (*Lab.*)
Secretary for Health and Social Services, Jane Hutt, AM (*Lab.*)
Secretary for Agriculture and the Rural Economy, Christine Gwyther, AM (*Lab.*)
Secretary for the Environment, Peter Law, AM (*Lab.*)
Trefnydd Manager, Andrew Davies, AM (*Lab.*)
Finance Secretary, Edwina Hart, AM (*Lab.*)

STATE OF THE PARTIES *as at May 1999*

	Constituency AMs	Regional AMs	Total
Labour	27	1	28
Plaid Cymru	8†	8	16†
Conservative	1	8	9
Liberal Democrats	3	3	6
Presiding Officer (The Lord Elis-Thomas, AM)	1	0	1

† Excludes the Presiding Officer, who has no party allegiance while in post

Scotland

The Kingdom of Scotland occupies the northern portion of the main island of Great Britain and includes the Inner and Outer Hebrides, and the Orkney, Shetland, and many other islands. It lies between 60° 51′ 30″ and 54° 38′ N. latitude and between 1° 45′ 32″ and 6° 14′ W. longitude, with England to the south, the Atlantic Ocean on the north and west, and the North Sea on the east.

The greatest length of the mainland (Cape Wrath to the Mull of Galloway) is 274 miles, and the greatest breadth (Buchan Ness to Applecross) is 154 miles. The customary measurement of the island of Great Britain is from the site of John o' Groats house, near Duncansby Head, Caithness, to Land's End, Cornwall, a total distance of 603 miles in a straight line and approximately 900 miles by road.

The total area of Scotland is 30,420 sq. miles (78,789 sq. km); land 29,767 sq. miles (77,097 sq. km), inland water 653 sq. miles (1,692 sq. km).

POPULATION

The population at the 1991 census was 4,998,567 (males 2,391,961; females 2,606,606). The average density of the population in 1991 was 0.65 persons per hectare.

RELIEF

There are three natural orographic divisions of Scotland. The southern uplands have their highest points in Merrick (2,766 ft), Rhinns of Kells (2,669 ft), and Cairnsmuir of Carsphairn (2,614 ft), in the west; and the Tweedsmuir Hills in the east (Hartfell 2,651 ft, Dollar Law 2,682 ft, Broad Law 2,756 ft).

The central lowlands, formed by the valleys of the Clyde, Forth and Tay, divide the southern uplands from the northern Highlands, which extend almost from the extreme north of the mainland to the central lowlands, and are divided into a northern and a southern system by the Great Glen.

The Grampian Mountains, which entirely cover the southern Highland area, include in the west Ben Nevis (4,406 ft), the highest point in the British Isles, and in the east the Cairngorm Mountains (Cairn Gorm 4,084 ft, Braeriach 4,248 ft, Ben Macdui 4,296 ft). The north-western Highland area contains the mountains of Wester and Easter Ross (Carn Eige 3,880 ft, Sgurr na Lapaich 3,775 ft).

Created, like the central lowlands, by a major geological fault, the Great Glen (60 miles long) runs between Inverness and Fort William, and contains Loch Ness, Loch Oich and Loch Lochy. These are linked to each other and to the north-east and south-west coasts of Scotland by the Caledonian Canal, providing a navigable passage between the Moray Firth and the Inner Hebrides.

HYDROGRAPHY

The western coast is fragmented by peninsulas and islands, and indented by fjords (sea-lochs), the longest of which is Loch Fyne (42 miles long) in Argyll. Although the east coast tends to be less fractured and lower, there are several great drowned inlets (firths), e.g. Firth of Forth, Firth of Tay, Moray Firth, as well as the Firth of Clyde in the west.

The lochs are the principal hydrographic feature. The largest in Scotland and in Britain is Loch Lomond (27 sq. miles), in the Grampian valleys; the longest and deepest is Loch Ness (24 miles long and 800 feet deep), in the Great Glen; and Loch Shin (20 miles long) and Loch Maree in the Highlands.

The longest river is the Tay (117 miles), noted for its salmon. It flows into the North Sea, with Dundee on the estuary, which is spanned by the Tay Bridge (10,289 ft)

opened in 1887 and the Tay Road Bridge (7,365 ft) opened in 1966. Other noted salmon rivers are the Dee (90 miles) which flows into the North Sea at Aberdeen, and the Spey (110 miles), the swiftest flowing river in the British Isles, which flows into Moray Firth. The Tweed, which gave its name to the woollen cloth produced along its banks, marks in the lower stretches of its 96-mile course the border between Scotland and England.

The most important river commercially is the Clyde (106 miles), formed by the junction of the Daer and Portrail water, which flows through the city of Glasgow to the Firth of Clyde. During its course it passes over the picturesque Falls of Clyde, Bonnington Linn (30 ft), Corra Linn (84 ft), Dundaff Linn (10 ft) and Stonebyres Linn (80 ft), above and below Lanark. The Forth (66 miles), upon which stands Edinburgh, the capital, is spanned by the Forth (Railway) Bridge (1890), which is 5,330 feet long, and the Forth (Road) Bridge (1964), which has a total length of 6,156 feet (over water) and a single span of 3,000 feet.

The highest waterfall in Scotland, and the British Isles, is Eas a'Chùal Aluinn with a total height of 658 feet (200 m), which falls from Glas Bheinn in Sutherland. The Falls of Glomach, on a head-stream of the Elchaig in Wester Ross, have a drop of 370 feet.

GAELIC LANGUAGE

According to the 1991 census, 1.4 per cent of the population of Scotland, mainly in the Highlands and western coastal regions, were able to speak the Scottish form of Gaelic.

LOWLAND SCOTTISH LANGUAGE

Several regional Lowland Scottish dialects, known variously as Scots, Scotch, Lallans or Doric, are widely spoken. The General Register Office (Scotland) has estimated that 1.5 million people, or 30 per cent of the population, are Scots speakers.

FLAG

The flag of Scotland is known as the Saltire. It is a white diagonal cross on a blue field (saltire argent in a field azure) and represents St Andrew, the patron saint of Scotland.

THE SCOTTISH ISLANDS

ORKNEY

The Orkney Islands (total area 375½ sq. miles) lie about six miles north of the mainland, separated from it by the Pentland Firth. Of the 90 islands and islets (holms and skerries) in the group, about one-third are inhabited.

The total population at the 1991 census was 19,612; the 1991 populations of the islands shown here include those of smaller islands forming part of the same civil parish.

Mainland, 15,128	Rousay, 291
Burray, 363	Sanday, 533
Eday, 166	Shapinsay, 322
Flotta and Fara, 126	South Ronaldsay, 943
Graemsay and Hoy, 477	Stronsay, 382
North Ronaldsay, 92	Westray, 704
Papa Westray, 85	

The islands are rich in prehistoric and Scandinavian remains, the most notable being the Stone Age village of Skara Brae, the burial chamber of Maeshowe, the many brochs (towers) and the 12th-century St Magnus Cathedral. Scapa Flow, between the Mainland and Hoy, was the war station of the British Grand Fleet from 1914 to 1919 and the scene of the scuttling of the surrendered German High Seas Fleet (21 June 1919).

Most of the islands are low-lying and fertile, and farming (principally beef cattle) is the main industry. Flotta, to the south of Scapa Flow, is the site of the oil terminal for the Piper, Claymore and Tartan fields in the North Sea. The capital is Kirkwall (population 6,881) on Mainland.

SHETLAND

The Shetland Islands have a total area of 551 sq. miles and a population at the 1991 census of 22,522. They lie about 50 miles north of the Orkneys, with Fair Isle about half-way between the two groups. Out Stack, off Muckle Flugga, one mile north of Unst, is the most northerly part of the British Isles (60° 51′ 30″ N. lat.).

There are over 100 islands, of which 16 are inhabited. Populations at the 1991 census were:

Mainland, 17,596	Muckle Roe, 115
Bressay, 352	Trondra, 117
East Burra, 72	Unst, 1,055
Fair Isle, 67	West Burra, 857
Fetlar, 90	Whalsay, 1,041
Housay, 85	Yell, 1,075

Shetland's many archaeological sites include Jarlshof, Mousa and Clickhimin, and its long connection with Scandinavia has resulted in a strong Norse influence on its place-names and dialect.

Industries include fishing, knitwear and farming. In addition to the fishing fleet there are fish processing factories, while the traditional handknitting of Fair Isle and Unst is supplemented now with machine-knitted garments. Farming is mainly crofting, with sheep being raised on the moorland and hills of the islands. Latterly the islands have become a centre of the North Sea oil industry, with pipelines from the Brent and Ninian fields running to the terminal at Sullom Voe, the largest of its kind in Europe. Lerwick is the main centre for supply services for offshore oil exploration and development.

The capital is Lerwick (population 7,901) on Mainland.

THE HEBRIDES

Until the late 13th century the Hebrides included other Scottish islands in the Firth of Clyde, the peninsula of Kintyre (Argyll), the Isle of Man, and the (Irish) Isle of Rathlin. The origin of the name is stated to be the Greek *Eboudai*, latinized as *Hebudes* by Pliny, and corrupted to its present form. The Norwegian name *Sudreyjar* (Southern Islands) was latinized as *Sodorenses*, a name that survives in the Anglican bishopric of Sodor and Man.

There are over 500 islands and islets, of which about 100 are inhabited, though mountainous terrain and extensive peat bogs mean that only a fraction of the total area is under cultivation. Stone, Bronze and Iron Age settlement has left many remains, including those at Callanish on Lewis, and Norse colonization influenced language, customs and place-names. Occupations include farming (mostly crofting and stock-raising), fishing and the manufacture of tweeds and other woollens. Tourism is also an important factor in the economy.

The Inner Hebrides lie off the west coast of Scotland and relatively close to the mainland. The largest and best-known is Skye (area 643 sq. miles; pop. 8,868; chief town, Portree), which contains the Cuillin Hills (Sgurr Alasdair 3,257 ft), the Red Hills (Beinn na Caillich 2,403 ft) and Bla Bheinn (3,046 ft) and The Storr (2,358 ft). Skye is also famous as the refuge of the Young Pretender in 1746. Other islands in the Highland council area include Raasay (pop. 163), Rum, Eigg and Muck.

Further south the Inner Hebridean islands include Arran (pop. 4,474) containing Goat Fell (2,868 ft); Coll and Tiree (pop. 940); Colonsay and Oronsay (pop. 106); Islay (area 235 sq. miles; pop. 3,538); Jura (area 160 sq. miles; pop. 196) with a range of hills culminating in the Paps of Jura (Beinn-

an-Oir, 2,576 ft, and Beinn Chaolais, 2,477 ft); and Mull (area 367 sq. miles; pop. 2,708; chief town Tobermory) containing Ben More (3,171 ft).

The Outer Hebrides, separated from the mainland by the Minch, now form the Eilean Siar Western Isles Islands Council area (area 1,119 sq. miles; population at the 1991 census 29,600). The main islands are Lewis with Harris (area 770 sq. miles, pop. 21,737), whose chief town, Stornoway, is the administrative headquarters; North Uist (pop. 1,404); South Uist (pop. 2,106); Baleshare (55); Benbecula (pop. 1,803) and Barra (pop. 1,244). Other inhabited islands include Bernera (262), Berneray (141), Eriskay (179), Grimsay (215), Scalpay (382) and Vatersay (72).

EARLY HISTORY

There is evidence of human settlement in Scotland dating from the third millennium BC, the earliest settlers being Middle Stone Age hunters and fishermen. Early in the second millennium BC, New Stone Age farmers began to cultivate crops and rear livestock; their settlements were on the west coast and in the north, and included Skara Brae and Maeshowe (Orkney). Settlement by the Early Bronze Age 'Beaker folk', so-called from the shape of their drinking vessels, in eastern Scotland dates from about 1800 BC. Further settlement is believed to have occurred from 700 BC onwards, as tribes were displaced from further south by new incursions from the Continent and the Roman invasions from AD 43.

Julius Agricola, the Roman governor of Britain AD 77–84, extended the Roman conquests in Britain by advancing into Caledonia, culminating with a victory at Mons Graupius, probably in AD 84; he was recalled to Rome shortly afterwards and his forward policy was not pursued. Hadrian's Wall, mostly completed by AD 30, marked the northern frontier of the Roman empire except for the period between about AD 144 and 190 when the frontier moved north to the Forth–Clyde isthmus and a turf wall, the Antonine Wall, was manned.

After the Roman withdrawal from Britain, there were centuries of warfare between the Picts, Scots, Britons, Angles and Vikings. The Picts, believed to be a non-Indo-European race, occupied the area north of the Forth. The Scots, a Gaelic-speaking people of northern Ireland, colonized the area of Argyll and Bute (the kingdom of Dalriada) in the fifth century AD and then expanded eastwards and northwards. The Britons, speaking a Brythonic Celtic language, colonized Scotland from the south from the first century BC; they lost control of south-eastern Scotland (incorporated into the kingdom of Northumbria) to the Angles in the early seventh century but retained Strathclyde (south-western Scotland and Cumbria). Viking raids from the late eighth century were followed by Norse settlement in the western and northern isles, Argyll, Caithness and Sutherland from the mid-ninth century onwards.

UNIFICATION

The union of the areas which now comprise Scotland began in AD 843 when Kenneth mac Alpin, king of the Scots from c.834, became also king of the Picts, joining the two lands to form the kingdom of Alba (comprising Scotland north of a line between the Forth and Clyde rivers). Lothian, the eastern part of the area between the Forth and the Tweed, seems to have been leased to Kenneth II of Alba (reigned 971–995) by Edgar of England c.973/4, and Scottish possession was confirmed by Malcolm II's victory over a Northumbrian army at Carham c.1016. At about this time Malcolm II (reigned 1005–34) placed his grandson Duncan on the throne of the British kingdom of Strathclyde, bringing under Scots rule virtually all of what is now Scotland.

The Norse possessions were incorporated into the kingdom of Scotland from the 12th century onwards. An uprising in the mid-12th century drove the Norse from most of mainland Argyll. The Hebrides were ceded to Scotland by the Treaty of Perth in 1266 after a Norwegian expedition in 1263 failed to maintain Norse authority over the islands. Orkney and Shetland fell to Scotland in 1468–9 as a pledge for the unpaid dowry of Margaret of Denmark, wife of James III, though Danish claims of suzerainty were relinquished only with the marriage of Anne of Denmark to James VI in 1590.

From the 11th century, there were frequent wars between Scotland and England over territory and the extent of England's political influence. The failure of the Scottish royal line with the death of Margaret of Norway in 1290 led to disputes over the throne which were resolved by the adjudication of Edward I of England. He awarded the throne to John Balliol in 1292 but Balliol's refusal to be a puppet king led to war. Balliol surrendered to Edward I in 1296 and Edward attempted to rule Scotland himself. Resistance to Scotland's loss of independence was led by William Wallace, who defeated the English at Stirling Bridge (1297), and Robert Bruce, crowned in 1306, who held most of Scotland by 1311 and routed Edward II's army at Bannockburn (1314). England recognized the independence of Scotland in the Treaty of Northampton in 1328. Subsequent clashes include the disastrous battle of Flodden (1513) in which James IV and many of his nobles fell.

THE UNION

In 1603 James VI of Scotland succeeded Elizabeth I on the throne of England (his mother, Mary Queen of Scots, was the great-granddaughter of Henry VII), his successors reigning as sovereigns of Great Britain. Political union of the two countries did not occur until 1707.

THE JACOBITE REVOLTS

After the abdication (by flight) in 1688 of James VII and II, the crown devolved upon William III (grandson of Charles I) and Mary II (elder daughter of James VII and II). In 1689 Graham of Claverhouse roused the Highlands on behalf of James VII and II, but died after a military success at Killiecrankie.

After the death of Anne (younger daughter of James VII and II), the throne devolved upon George I (great-grandson of James VI and I). In 1715, armed risings on behalf of James Stuart (the Old Pretender, son of James VII and II) led to the indecisive battle of Sheriffmuir, and the Jacobite movement died down until 1745, when Charles Stuart (the Young Pretender) defeated the Royalist troops at Prestonpans and advanced to Derby (1746). From Derby, the adherents of 'James VIII and III' (the title claimed for his father by Charles Stuart) fell back on the defensive and were finally crushed at Culloden (16 April 1746).

PRINCIPAL CITIES

ABERDEEN

Aberdeen, 130 miles north-east of Edinburgh, received its charter as a Royal Burgh in 1179. Scotland's third largest city, Aberdeen is the second largest Scottish fishing port and the main centre for offshore oil exploration and production. It is also an ancient university town and distinguished research centre. Other industries include engineering, food processing, textiles, paper manufacturing and chemicals.

Places of interest include King's College, St Machar's

Cathedral, Brig o' Balgownie, Duthie Park and Winter Gardens, Hazlehead Park, the Kirk of St Nicholas, Mercat Cross, Marischal College and Marischal Museum, Provost Skene's House, Art Gallery, Gordon Highlanders Museum, Satrosphere Hands-On Discovery Centre, and Aberdeen Maritime Museum in Provost Ross's House.

DUNDEE

Dundee, a Royal Burgh, is situated on the north bank of the Tay estuary. The city's port and dock installations are important to the offshore oil industry and the airport also provides servicing facilities. Principal industries include textiles, computers and other electronic industries, lasers, printing, tyre manufacture, food processing, carpets, engineering, clothing manufacture and tourism.

The unique City Churches – three churches under one roof, together with the 15th-century St Mary's Tower – are the most prominent architectural feature. Dundee has two historic ships: the Dundee-built RRS *Discovery* which took Capt. Scott to the Antarctic lies alongside Discovery Quay, and the frigate *Unicorn*, the only British-built wooden warship still afloat, is moored in Victoria Dock. Places of interest include Mills Public Observatory, the Tay road and rail bridges, McManus Galleries, Barrack Street Museum, Claypotts Castle, Broughty Castle and Verdant Works (Textile Heritage Centre).

EDINBURGH

Edinburgh is the capital of and seat of government in Scotland. The city is built on a group of hills and contains in Princes Street one of the most beautiful thoroughfares in the world.

The principal buildings are the Castle, which now houses the Stone of Scone and also includes St Margaret's Chapel, the oldest building in Edinburgh, and near it, the Scottish National War Memorial; the Palace of Holyroodhouse; Parliament House, the present seat of the judicature; three universities (Edinburgh, Heriot-Watt, Napier); St Giles' Cathedral; St Mary's (Scottish Episcopal) Cathedral (Sir George Gilbert Scott); the General Register House (Robert Adam); the National and the Signet Libraries; the National Gallery; the Royal Scottish Academy; National Portrait Gallery; and the Edinburgh International Conference Centre, opened in 1995. A new Scottish Parliament building is under construction at Holyrood.

GLASGOW

Glasgow, a Royal Burgh, is the principal commercial and industrial centre in Scotland. The city occupies the north and south banks of the Clyde, formerly one of the chief commercial estuaries in the world. The principal industries include engineering, electronics, finance, chemicals and printing. The city has also developed recently as a tourism and conference centre.

The chief buildings are the 13th-century Gothic Cathedral, the University (Sir George Gilbert Scott), the City Chambers, the Royal Concert Hall, St Mungo Museum of Religious Life and Art, Pollok House, the School of Art (Mackintosh), Kelvingrove Art Galleries, the Gallery of Modern Art, the Burrell Collection museum and the Mitchell Library. The city is home to the Scottish National Orchestra, Scottish Opera and Scottish Ballet.

LORD-LIEUTENANTS

Title	Name
Aberdeenshire	A. D. M. Farquharson
Angus	The Earl of Airlie, KT, GCVO, PC
Argyll and Bute	The Duke of Argyll
Ayrshire and Arran	Maj. R. Y. Henderson, TD
Banffshire	J. A. S. McPherson, CBE
Berwickshire	Maj.-Gen. Sir John Swinton, KCVO, OBE
Caithness	Maj. G. T. Dunnett, TD
Clackmannan	Lt.-Col. R. C. Stewart, CBE, TD
Dumfries	Capt. R. C. Cunningham-Jardine
Dunbartonshire	Brig. D. D. G. Hardie, TD
East Lothian	Sir Hew Hamilton-Dalrymple, Bt., KCVO
Eilean Siar/Western Isles	The Viscount Dunrossil, CMG
Fife	Mrs C. M. Dean
Inverness	The Lord Gray of Contin, PC
Kincardineshire	The Viscount of Arbuthnott, KT, CBE, DSC, FRSE
Lanarkshire	H. B. Sneddon, CBE
Midlothian	Capt. G. W. Burnet, LVO
Moray	Air Vice-Marshal G. A. Chesworth, CB, OBE, DFC
Nairn	E. Brodie
Orkney	G. R. Marwick
Perth and Kinross	Sir David Montgomery, Bt.
Renfrewshire	C. H. Parker, OBE
Ross and Cromarty	Capt. R. W. K. Stirling of Fairburn, TD
Roxburgh, Ettrick and Lauderdale	Dr June Paterson-Brown
Shetland	J. H. Scott
Stirling and Falkirk	Lt.-Col. J. Stirling of Garden, CBE, TD, FRICS
Sutherland	Maj.-Gen. D. Houston, CBE
The Stewartry of Kirkcudbright	Lt.-Gen. Sir Norman Arthur, KCB
Tweeddale	Capt. J. D. B. Younger
West Lothian	The Earl of Morton
Wigtown	Maj. E. S. Orr-Ewing

The Lord Provosts of the four city districts of Aberdeen, Dundee, Edinburgh and Glasgow are Lord-Lieutenants for those districts *ex officio*.

LOCAL COUNCILS

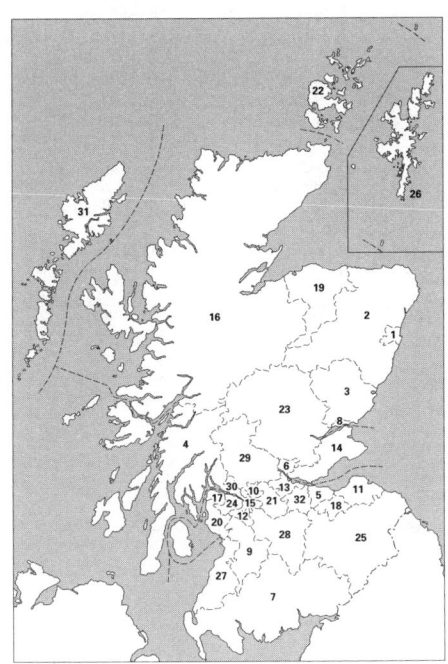

Key	Council
1	Aberdeen City
2	Aberdeenshire
3	Angus
4	Argyll and Bute
5	City of Edinburgh
6	Clackmannanshire
7	Dumfries and Galloway
8	Dundee City
9	East Ayrshire
10	East Dunbartonshire
11	East Lothian
12	East Renfrewshire
13	Eilean Siar/Western Isles
14	Falkirk
15	Fife
16	Glasgow City
17	Highland
18	Inverclyde
19	Midlothian
20	Moray
21	North Ayrshire
22	North Lanarkshire
23	Orkney
24	Perth and Kinross
25	Renfrewshire
26	Scottish Borders
27	Shetland
28	South Ayrshire
29	South Lanarkshire
30	Stirling
31	West Dunbartonshire
32	West Lothian

LOCAL COUNCILS

Council	Administrative headquarters	Population (latest estimate)	Band D charge 1999	Chief Executive	Chairman (a) Convener (b) Provost (c) Lord Provost
Aberdeen City	Aberdeen	213,070	£1,033.25	D. Paterson	(c) Ms M. Smith
Aberdeenshire	Aberdeen	226,260	719.00	A. G. Campbell	(a) R. Bisset
Angus	Forfar	110,070	938.60	A. B. Watson	(b) Mrs F. E. Duncan
Argyll and Bute	Lochgilphead	89,980	1,070.10	J. A. McLellan	(a) D. C. Currie
City of Edinburgh	Edinburgh	450,180	889.00	T. N. Aitchison	(c) Rt. Hon. E. Milligan
Clackmannanshire	Alloa	48,560	753.00	R. Allan	(b) W. McAdam
Dumfries and Galloway	Dumfries	147,300	766.00	P. N. Jones	(a) A. Campbell
Dundee City	Dundee	146,690	1,238.60	A. Stephen	(c) Rt. Hon. Ms H. W. Wright
East Ayrshire	Kilmarnock	121,300	1,037.80	D. Montgomery	(b) J. Boyd
East Dunbartonshire	Glasgow	109,570	830.00	Dr V. Nash	(b) R. McSkimming
East Lothian	Haddington	89,570	789.00	J. Lindsay	(a) P. O'Brien
East Renfrewshire	Giffnock	87,980	765.00	P. Daniels	(b) A. Steele
Eilean Siar/Western Isles	Stornoway	27,940	898.95	N. Galbraith (acting)	(a) A. A. Macdonald
Falkirk	Falkirk	144,110	892.00	Ms M. Pitcaithly	(b) D. Goldie
Fife	Glenrothes	348,900	986.50	D. Sinclair	(a) J. MacDougall
Glasgow City	Glasgow	619,680	1,263.10	J. Andrews	(c) A. Mosson
Highland	Inverness	208,300	799.00	A. D. McCourt	(a) D. Green
Inverclyde	Greenock	85,400	863.00	R. Cleary	(b) D. Roach
Midlothian	Dalkeith	80,860	936.00	T. Muir	(b) S. Campbell
Moray	Elgin	85,870	724.00	B. Stewart	(a) E. Aldridge
North Ayrshire	Irvine	139,660	977.10	B. Devine	(a) S. Taylor
North Lanarkshire	Motherwell	326,720	844.00	A. Cowe	(b) B. McCulloch
Orkney Islands	Kirkwall	19,550	624.00	A. Buchan	(a) H. Halcro-Johnston
Perth and Kinross	Perth	133,040	758.00	H. Robertson	(b) M. O'Malley
Renfrewshire	Paisley	177,830	972.10	T. Scholes	(b) J. McDowell
Scottish Borders	Newtown St Boswells	106,300	639.00	A. M. Croall	(a) A. L. Tulley
Shetland Islands	Lerwick	22,910	830.75	B. Bennett	(a) T. Stove
South Ayrshire	Ayr	114,440	792.00	G. W. F. Thorley	(b) Ms E. Foulkes
South Lanarkshire	Hamilton	306,860	880.00	vacant	(b) A. Dick
Stirling	Stirling	83,130	819.00	K. Yates	(b) T. Brookes
West Dunbartonshire	Dumbarton	94,880	1,170.10	T. Huntingford (acting)	(b) A. Macdonald
West Lothian	Livingston	153,090	1,044.00	A. M. Linkston	(b) J. Thomas

THE SCOTTISH PARLIAMENT (see also pages 1280–91)

In July 1997 the Government announced plans to establish a Scottish Parliament. In a referendum on 11 September 1997 about 62 per cent of the electorate voted of whom 74.3 per cent voted in favour of the Parliament and 63.5 per cent in favour of its having tax-raising powers. Elections are to be held every four years. The first elections were held on 6 May 1999 when about 59 per cent of the electorate voted. The first session was held on 12 May 1999 and the Scottish Parliament was officially opened on 1 July 1999 at the Edinburgh Assembly Hall; a new building to house the Parliament is under construction in Edinburgh.

The Scottish Parliament has 129 members (including the Presiding Officer), comprising 73 constituency members and 65 additional regional members from party lists. It can introduce primary legislation and has the power to raise or lower the basic rate of income tax by up to three pence in the pound.

The Scottish Parliament is responsible for education, health, law, environment, economic development, local government, housing, police, fire services, planning, financial assistance to industry, tourism, some transport, heritage and the arts, agriculture, forestry, food standards

SALARIES FROM 1 APRIL 1999:

First Minister	£64,308 (plus MSP salary)
Ministers	£33,360 (plus MSP salary)
Lord Advocate	£43,585
Solicitor-General for Scotland	£31,515
Junior Ministers	£17,305 (plus MSP salary)
MSPs	£40,092*
Presiding Officer	£33,360 (plus MSP salary)
Deputy Presiding Officers	£17,305 (plus MSP salary)

* Reduced by two-thirds (to £13,364) if the member is already an MP or an MEP
MSPs and officers are paid by the Scottish Parliamentary Corporate Body; ministers are paid out of the Scottish Consolidated Fund.

THE SCOTTISH EXECUTIVE

First Minister, The Rt. Hon. Donald Dewar, MP, MSP (*Lab.*)
Deputy First Minister and Minister for Justice, Jim Wallace, QC, MP, MSP (*LD*)
Finance Minister, Jack McConnell, MSP (*Lab.*)
Minister for Health and Community Care, Susan Deacon, MSP (*Lab.*)
Minister for Communities, Wendy Alexander, MSP (*Lab.*)
Minister for Transport and the Environment, Sarah Boyack, MSP (*Lab.*)
Minister for Enterprise and Lifelong Learning, Henry McLeish, MP, MSP (*Lab.*)
Minister for Rural Affairs, Ross Finnie, MSP (*LD*)
Minister for Education and Children, Sam Galbraith, MP, MSP (*Lab.*)
Minister for Parliament and Chief Whip, Tom McCabe, MSP (*Lab.*)
Lord Advocate, The Lord Hardie, QC (*Lab.*)

JUNIOR MINISTERS (NOT MEMBERS OF THE SCOTTISH EXECUTIVE)

Deputy Minister for Justice, Angus Mackay, MSP (*Lab.*)
Deputy Minister for Community Care, Iain Gray, MSP (*Lab.*)
Deputy Minister for Local Government, Frank McAveety, MSP (*Lab. Co-op.*)
Deputy Minister for Social Inclusion, Equality and the Voluntary Sector, Jackie Baillie, MSP (*Lab.*)
Deputy Minister for Enterprise and Lifelong Learning, Nicol Stephen, MSP (*LD*)
Deputy Minister for Highlands and Islands and Gaelic, Alasdair Morrison, MSP (*Lab.*)
Deputy Minister for Fisheries, John Home Robertson, MSP (*Lab.*)
Deputy Minister for Culture and Sport, Rhona Brankin, MSP (*Lab. Co-op.*)
Deputy Minister for Children and Education, Peter Peacock, MSP (*Lab.*)
Deputy Minister for Parliament and Whip, Iain Smith, MSP (*LD*)
Solicitor-General for Scotland, Colin Boyd, QC

STATE OF THE PARTIES *as at May 1999*

	Constituency MSPs	Regional MSPs	Total
Scottish Labour Party	53	3	56
Scottish National Party	7	28	35
Scottish Conservative and Unionist Party	0	18	18
Scottish Liberal Democrats	12	4†	16†
Scottish Green Party	0	1	1
Scottish Socialist Party	0	1	1
Independent (Dennis Canavan)	1	0	1
Presiding Officer (Rt. Hon. Sir David Steel, PC, KBE, MSP)	0	1	1

† Excludes the Presiding Officer, who has no party allegiance while in post
Deputy Presiding Officers, George Reid, MSP (*SNP*); Patricia Ferguson, MSP (*Lab.*)

Northern Ireland

Northern Ireland has a total area of 5,467 sq. miles (14,144 sq. km): land, 5,225 sq. miles (13,532 sq. km); inland water and tideways, 249 sq. miles (628 sq. km).

The population of Northern Ireland at the 1991 census was 1,577,836 (males, 769,071; females, 808,765). The average density of population in 1991 was 1.11 persons per hectare.

In 1991 the number of persons in the various religious denominations (expressed as percentages of the total population) were: Roman Catholic, 38.4; Presbyterian, 21.4; Church of Ireland, 17.7; Methodist, 3.8; others 7.7; none, 3.7; not stated, 7.3.

FLAG

The official national flag of Northern Ireland is now the Union Flag. The flag formerly in use (a white, six-pointed star in the centre of a red cross on a white field, enclosing a red hand and surmounted by a crown) has not been used since the imposition of direct rule.

PRINCIPAL CITIES

BELFAST

Belfast, the administrative centre of Northern Ireland, is situated at the mouth of the River Lagan at its entrance to Belfast Lough. The city grew, owing to its easy access by sea to Scottish coal and iron, to be a great industrial centre.

The principal buildings are of a relatively recent date and include the Parliament Buildings at Stormont, the City Hall, Waterfront Hall, the Law Courts, the Public Library and the Museum and Art Gallery.

Belfast received its first charter of incorporation in 1613 and was created a city in 1888; the title of Lord Mayor was conferred in 1892.

LONDONDERRY

Londonderry (originally Derry) is situated on the River Foyle, and has important associations with the City of London. The Irish Society was created by the City of London in 1610, and under its royal charter of 1613 it fortified the city and was for long closely associated with its administration. Because of this connection the city was incorporated in 1613 under the new name of Londonderry.

The city is famous for the great siege of 1688–9, when for 105 days the town held out against the forces of James II until relieved by sea. The city walls are still intact and form a circuit of almost a mile around the old city.

Interesting buildings are the Protestant Cathedral of St Columb's (1633) and the Guildhall, reconstructed in 1912 and containing a number of beautiful stained glass windows, many of which were presented by the livery companies of London.

CONSTITUTIONAL DEVELOPMENTS

Northern Ireland is subject to the same fundamental constitutional provisions which apply to the rest of the United Kingdom. It had its own parliament and government from 1921 to 1972, but after increasing civil unrest the Northern Ireland (Temporary Provisions) Act 1972 transferred the legislative and executive powers of the Northern Ireland parliament and government to the UK Parliament and a Secretary of State. The Northern Ireland Constitution Act 1973 provided for devolution in Northern Ireland

through an assembly and executive, but a power-sharing executive formed by the Northern Ireland political parties in January 1974 collapsed in May 1974; since then Northern Ireland has been governed by direct rule under the provisions of the Northern Ireland Act 1974. This allows Parliament to approve all laws for Northern Ireland and places the Northern Ireland department under the direction and control of the Secretary of State for Northern Ireland.

Attempts were made by successive governments to find a means of restoring a widely acceptable form of devolved government to Northern Ireland. In 1985 the governments of the United Kingdom and the Republic of Ireland signed the Anglo-Irish Agreement, establishing an intergovernmental conference in which the Irish government may put forward views and proposals on certain aspects of Northern Ireland affairs.

Discussions between the British and Irish governments and the main Northern Ireland parties began in 1991. It was agreed that any political settlement would need to address relationships within Northern Ireland, within the island of Ireland (north/south) and between the British and Irish governments (east/west). Although round table talks ended in 1992 the process continued from September 1993 as separate bilateral discussions with three of the Northern Ireland parties (the DUP declined to participate).

In December 1993 the British and Irish governments published the Joint Declaration complementing the political talks, and making clear that any settlement would need to be founded on principles of democracy and consent. The declaration also stated that all democratically mandated parties could be involved in political talks as long as they permanently renounced paramilitary violence.

The provisional IRA and loyalist paramilitary groups announced cease-fires on 31 August and 13 October 1994 respectively. The Government initiated exploratory meetings with Sinn Fein and loyalist representatives in December 1994.

In February 1995 the then Prime Minister (John Major) launched *A Framework for Accountable Government in Northern Ireland* and, with the Irish Prime Minister, *A New Framework for Agreement*. These outlined what a comprehensive political settlement might look like. The ideas were intended to facilitate multilateral dialogue involving the Northern Ireland parties and the British government.

In autumn 1995 the Prime Minister said that Sinn Fein would not be invited to all-party talks until the IRA had decommissioned its arms; the IRA ruled out any decommissioning of weapons in advance of a political settlement. An international body chaired by a former US senator, George Mitchell, reported in January 1996 that no weapons would be decommissioned before the start of all-party talks and that a compromise agreement was necessary under which weapons would be decommissioned during negotiations. The Prime Minister accepted the report and proposed the election of representatives to conduct all-party talks. On 9 February 1996 the IRA called off its cease-fire.

PEACE TALKS

Following elections on 30 May 1996, all-party talks opened at Stormont Castle on 10 June 1996 which included nine of the ten parties returned at the election; Sinn Fein representatives were turned away because the IRA had failed to reinstate its cease-fire. On 29 July 1996 the all-party talks were suspended after disagreements over the issue of decommissioning arms. An opening agenda for the talks was agreed in October 1996.

On 25 June 1997 the newly-elected Labour Government

said that substantive negotiations should begin in September 1997 with a view to reaching conclusions by May 1998. The British and Irish governments issued a joint paper outlining their proposals for resolving the decommissioning issue. The Government also indicated that if the IRA were to call a cease-fire, it would assess whether it was genuine over a period of six weeks, and if satisfied that it was so, would then invite Sinn Fein to the talks. An IRA cease-fire was declared on 20 July 1997.

When the UK Government announced in August 1997 that Sinn Fein would be present when the substantive talks opened on 15 September, the Unionist and loyalist parties, unhappy at the terms on which Sinn Fein had been admitted, boycotted the opening session. The Ulster Unionist Party, the Progressive Unionist Party and the Ulster Democratic Party re-entered the negotiations on 17 September. Full-scale peace talks began on 7 October. The parties had agreed to concentrate on constitutional issues, with the issue of decommissioning terrorist weapons to be handled by a new independent commission.

On 12 January 1998 the British and Irish governments issued a joint document, *Propositions on Heads of Agreement*, proposing the establishment of various new cross-border bodies; further proposals were presented on 27 January. A draft peace settlement was issued by the talks' chairman, Sen. George Mitchell, on 6 April 1998 but was rejected by the Unionists the following day. On 10 April agreement was reached between the British and Irish governments and the eight Northern Ireland political parties still involved in the talks (the Good Friday/Belfast Agreement). The agreement provided for an elected New Northern Ireland Assembly; a North/South Ministerial Council, and a British-Irish Council comprising representatives of the British, Irish, Channel Islands and Isle of Man governments and members of the new assemblies for Scotland, Wales and Northern Ireland. Further points included the abandonment of the Republic of Ireland's constitutional claim to Northern Ireland; the decommissioning of weapons; the release of paramilitary prisoners; and changes in policing.

Referendums on the agreement were held in Northern Ireland and the Republic of Ireland on 22 May 1998. In Northern Ireland the turnout was 81 per cent, of which 71.12 per cent voted in favour of the agreement. In the Republic of Ireland, the turnout was about 55 per cent, of which 94.4 per cent voted in favour of both the agreement and the necessary constitutional change. In the UK, the Northern Ireland Act 1998, enshrining the provisions of the Agreement, received Royal Assent in November 1998.

NORTHERN IRELAND ASSEMBLY

The Assembly has 108 members elected by single transferable vote (six from each of the 18 Westminster constituencies). The first elections took place on 25 June 1998 and members met for the first time on 1 July. Safeguards ensure that key decisions have cross-community support. The executive powers of the Assembly will be discharged by an executive committee comprising a First Minister and Deputy First Minister (jointly elected by the Assembly on a cross-community basis) and up to ten ministers with departmental responsibilities. Ministerial posts will be allocated on the basis of the number of seats each party holds.

The Assembly met in shadow form several times, pending the establishment of an Executive and the transfer of powers from Parliament. After devolution it will have executive and legislative authority over those areas formerly the responsibility of the Northern Ireland government departments (*see* page 326). Its powers might be extended further in future.

Power was initially due to be transferred to the new Executive on 10 March 1999, but disagreements emerged over whether Sinn Fein should be allowed to enter the Executive before IRA weapons had been decommissioned. Further deadlines of 2 April and 30 June were also missed. On 15 July the Assembly met to nominate ministers, with the transfer of power to follow on 18 July. However, as the decommissioning issue had still not been resolved, Unionists failed to nominate ministers (the UUP boycotting the meeting itself) and the process collapsed. On 20 July the British and Irish Governments initiated a review of the implementation of the Agreement and asked former Senator George Mitchell to act as facilitator. The review will resume in September 1999 with the aim of resolving the disagreements over decommissioning and formation of the Executive. (*See also* Events of the Year and Stop-press.)

Composition

Party	Seats
UUP	28
SDLP	24
DUP	20
Sinn Fein	18
Alliance Party	6
UK Unionist Party	5
Progressive Unionist Party	2
Northern Ireland Women's Coalition	2
Others	3

OTHER BODIES

Consultations between the First Minister and Deputy First Minister, the British and Irish Governments and the political parties concluded in early 1999 with an agreement to establish six areas for cross-border bodies and a further six areas for co-operation. Treaties between the British and Irish governments establishing the bodies and parallel domestic legislation to underpin them are now in place.

The intergovernmental conference established by the 1985 Anglo-Irish Agreement (*see* page 566) was replaced by a new British-Irish Intergovernmental Conference which will discuss all areas of mutual bilateral interest.

The British-Irish Council will operate on the basis of consensus and may reach agreements and pursue common policies in areas of mutual interest.

ECONOMY

FINANCE

Taxation in Northern Ireland is largely imposed and collected by the UK government. After deducting the cost of collection and of Northern Ireland's contributions to the European Union, the balance, known as the Attributed Share of Taxation, is paid over to the Northern Ireland Consolidated Fund. Northern Ireland's revenue is insufficient to meet its expenditure and is supplemented by a grant-in-aid.

	1998-9*	1999-2000**
Public income	£6,639,768,864	£7,541,000,000
Public expenditure	6,949,890,984	7,541,000,000

* Outturn
** Estimate

PRODUCTION

The products of the engineering and allied industries, which employed 29,500 persons in 1996, were valued at £4,403 million. The textiles industry (manufacture of textiles and textile products), employing about 25,200 persons, produced goods valued at approximately £1,266 million. The food products, beverages and tobacco industry, employing about 20,900 persons, produced goods valued at £3,512 million.

In 1998, 1,523 persons were employed in mining and quarrying operations in Northern Ireland and the minerals raised (22,356,000 tonnes) were valued at £58,989,000.

COMMUNICATIONS

The total tonnage handled by Northern Ireland ports in 1998 was 12.23 million. Regular ferry, freight and container services operate to ports in Great Britain and Europe from a number of ports, with most trade passing through Belfast (60 per cent of the total), Larne and Warrenpoint.

The Northern Ireland Transport Holding Company is largely responsible for the supervision of the subsidiary companies, Ulsterbus and Citybus (which operate the public road passenger services) and Northern Ireland Railways (collectively known as Translink). Road freight

services are also provided by a large number of hauliers operating competitively under licence.

Belfast International Airport, owned by TBI International, provides scheduled and chartered services on domestic and international routes. In 1997–8 the airport handled approximately 2.5 million passengers and 41,000 tonnes of freight. Scheduled services also operate from Belfast City Airport (BCA, owned by Shorts Bombardier Aerospace) to 20 UK destinations. In 1997–8 the airport handled approximately 1.3 million passengers. City of Derry Airport (Londonderry, owned and operated by Derry City Council) provides services to 15 UK and European destinations and to Belfast, providing links to many of the locations serviced by BCA. In 1997–8 City of Derry Airport served approximately 68,000 passengers.

NORTHERN IRELAND COUNTIES

County	Area* (sq. miles)	Lord-Lieutenant	High Sheriff, 1999
Antrim	1,093	The Lord O'Neill, TD	Mrs P. Traill
Armagh	484	The Earl of Caledon	Mrs E. Cullen
‡Belfast City	25	Col. J. E. Wilson, OBE	R. Newton
Down	945	W. J. Hall	Mrs M. E. Crawford
Fermanagh	647	The Earl of Erne	Mrs P. G. Moore
†Londonderry	798	Sir Michael McCorkell, KCVO, OBE, TD	Mrs D. Hutchinson
‡Londonderry City	3.4	J. T. Eaton, CBE, TD	Mrs M. Hasson
Tyrone	1,211	The Duke of Abercorn, KG	Miss A. F. Colhoun

* Excluding inland waters and tideways
‡ Denotes County Borough
† Excluding the City of Londonderry

DISTRICT COUNCILS

SMALL CAPITALS denotes CITY status
§ Denotes Borough Council

Council	Population (September 1998)	Net Annual Value	Council Clerk	Chairman †Mayor 1999
§Antrim, Co. Antrim	47,500	£31,487,895	S. J. Magee	†P. Marks
§Ards, Co. Down	67,800	28,984,295	D. J. Fallows	†G. Ennis
§ARMAGH, Co. Armagh	53,200	20,155,297	D. R. D. Mitchell	†R. Turner
§Ballymena, Co. Antrim	58,200	34,032,137	M. G. Rankin	†J. Currie
§Ballymoney, Co. Antrim	24,900	8,786,335	J. Dempsey	†F. Campbell
Banbridge, Co. Down	37,700	14,406,488	R. Gilmore	S. Doyle
BELFAST, Co. Antrim and Co. Down	297,200	287,458,969	B. Hanna	D. Alderdice
§Carrickfergus, Co. Antrim	35,700	15,786,964	R. Boyd	†J. Cramsey
§Castlereagh, Co. Down	64,500	33,301,018	A. Donaldson	†J. Beattie
§Coleraine, Co. Londonderry	54,700	29,126,980	W. Moore	†J. McClure
Cookstown, Co. Tyrone	31,800	14,758,461	M. J. McGuckin	P. McAleer
§Craigavon, Co. Armagh	79,100	44,658,976	T. Reaney	†M. Carrick
DERRY, Co. Londonderry	104,700	59,358,072	T. J. Keanie	†J. Miller
Down, Co. Down	61,200	23,064,131	O. O'Connor	J. McIlhernon
Dungannon, Co. Tyrone	47,100	23,700,171	W. J. Beattie	J. Canning
Fermanagh, Co. Fermanagh	55,500	27,797,576	Mrs A. McGinley	P. McCaffrey
§Larne, Co. Antrim	30,300	17,373,878	C. McGarry	†Mrs J. Drummond
§Limavady, Co. Londonderry	30,800	11,886,598	J. K. Stevenson	†S. Gault
§Lisburn, Co. Antrim and Co. Down	106,600	58,153,699	N. Davidson	†P. O'Hagan
Magherafelt, Co. Londonderry	37,900	15,078,309	J. A. McLaughlin	R. A. Montgomery
Moyle, Co. Antrim	15,000	4,792,815	R. G. Lewis	H. Harding
Newry and Mourne, Co. Down and Co. Armagh	84,900	35,404,701	K. O'Neill	B. Curran
§Newtownabbey, Co. Antrim	79,600	43,371,929	N. Dunn	†N. Crilly
§North Down, Co. Down	73,500	38,920,296	T. Polley (acting)	†M. Fitzsimons
Omagh, Co. Tyrone	47,000	22,308,485	J. P. McKinney	S. Clarke
Strabane, Co. Tyrone	36,800	13,265,922	D. McSorley	I. Barr

The Isle of Man
Ellan Vannin

The Isle of Man is an island situated in the Irish Sea, in latitude 54° 3'–54° 25' N. and longitude 4° 18'–4° 47' W., nearly equidistant from England, Scotland and Ireland. Although the early inhabitants were of Celtic origin, the Isle of Man was part of the Norwegian Kingdom of the Hebrides until 1266, when this was ceded to Scotland. Subsequently granted to the Stanleys (Earls of Derby) in the 15th century and later to the Dukes of Atholl, it was brought under the administration of the Crown in 1765. The island forms the bishopric of Sodor and Man.

The total land area is 221 sq. miles (572 sq. km). The report on the 1991 census showed a resident population of 69,788 (males, 33,693; females, 36,095). The main language in use is English. There are no remaining native speakers of Manx Gaelic but 643 people are able to speak the language.

CAPITAL – ΨDouglas; population (1991), 22,214. ΨCastletown (3,152) is the ancient capital; the other towns are ΨPeel (3,829) and ΨRamsey (6,496)

FLAG – A red flag charged with three conjoined armoured legs in white and gold

TYNWALD DAY – 5 July

GOVERNMENT

The Isle of Man is a self-governing Crown dependency, having its own parliamentary, legal and administrative system. The British Government is responsible for international relations and defence. Under the UK Act of Accession, Protocol 3, the island's relationship with the European Union is limited to trade alone and does not extend to financial aid. The Lieutenant-Governor is The Queen's personal representative in the island.

The legislature, Tynwald, is the oldest parliament in the world in continuous existence. It has two branches: the Legislative Council and the House of Keys. The Council consists of the President of Tynwald, the Bishop of Sodor and Man, the Attorney-General (who does not have a vote) and eight members elected by the House of Keys. The House of Keys has 24 members, elected by universal adult suffrage. The branches sit separately to consider legislation and sit together, as Tynwald Court, for most other parliamentary purposes.

The presiding officer in Tynwald Court is the President of Tynwald, elected by the members, who also presides over sittings of the Legislative Council. The presiding officer of the House of Keys is Mr Speaker, who is elected by members of the House.

The principal members of the Manx Government are the Chief Minister and nine departmental ministers, who comprise the Council of Ministers.

Lieutenant-Governor, HE Sir Timothy Daunt, KCMG
  ADC to the Lieutenant-Governor, C. J. Tummon
President of Tynwald, The Hon. Sir Charles Kerruish, OBE
Speaker, House of Keys, The Hon. N. Q. Cringle
The First Deemster and Clerk of the Rolls, His Honour T. W. Cain
Clerk of Tynwald, Secretary to the House of Keys and Counsel to the Speaker, Prof. T. St J. N. Bates
Clerk of Legislative Council and Clerk Assistant of Tynwald, T. A. Bawden
Attorney-General, W. J. H. Corlett, QC
Chief Minister, The Hon. D. J. Gelling
Chief Secretary, J. F. Kissack
Chief Financial Officer, J. A. Cashen

ECONOMY

Most of the income generated in the island is earned in the services sector with financial and professional services accounting for just over half of the national income. Tourism and manufacturing are also major generators of income whilst the island's other traditional industries of agriculture and fishing now play a smaller role in the economy.

Under the terms of Protocol 3, the island has tariff-free access to EU markets for its goods.

The island's unemployment rate is approximately 1.5 per cent and price inflation is around 2 per cent per annum.

FINANCE

The budget for 1999–2000 provided for net revenue expenditure of £287 million. The principal sources of government revenue are taxes on income and expenditure. Income tax is payable at a rate of 15 per cent on the first £9,900 of taxable income for single resident individuals and 20 per cent on the balance, after personal allowances of £7,350. These bands are doubled for married couples. The rate of income tax is 15 per cent on the first £100,000 of taxable income of companies, rising to 20 per cent on the balance. Non-residents are charged tax at the rate of 20 per cent. By agreement with the British Government, the island keeps most of its rates of indirect taxation (VAT and duties) the same as those in the United Kingdom, but this agreement may be terminated by either party. However, VAT on tourist accommodation is charged at 5 per cent. A reciprocal agreement on national insurance benefits and pensions exists between the governments of the Isle of Man and the United Kingdom. Taxes are also charged on property (rates), but these are comparatively low.

The major government expenditure items are health, social security and education, which account for 60 per cent of the government budget. The island makes a voluntary annual contribution to the United Kingdom for defence and other external services.

The island has a special relationship with the European Union and neither contributes money to nor receives funds from the EU budget.

The Channel Islands

The Channel Islands, situated off the north-west coast of France (at distances of from ten to 30 miles), are the only portions of the Dukedom of Normandy still belonging to the Crown, to which they have been attached since the Conquest. They were the only British territory to come under German occupation during the Second World War, following invasion on 30 June to 1 July 1940. The islands were relieved by British forces on 9 May 1945, and 9 May (Liberation Day) is now observed as a bank and public holiday.

The islands consist of Jersey (28,717 acres/11,630 ha), Guernsey (15,654 acres/6,340 ha), and the dependencies of Guernsey: Alderney (1,962 acres/795 ha), Brechou (74/30), Great Sark (1,035/419), Little Sark (239/97), Herm (320/130), Jethou (44/18) and Lihou (38/15) – a total of 48,083 acres/19,474 ha, or 75 sq. miles/194 sq. km. In 1991 the population of Jersey was 84,082; and of Guernsey, 58,867; Alderney, 2,297 and Sark, 575. The official languages are English and French but French is being supplanted by English, which is the language in daily use. In country districts of Jersey and Guernsey and throughout Sark a Norman-French *patois* is also in use, though to a declining extent.

GOVERNMENT

The islands are Crown dependencies with their own legislative assemblies (the States in Jersey, Guernsey and Alderney, and the Court of Chief Pleas in Sark), and systems of local administration and of law, and their own courts. Acts passed by the States require the sanction of The Queen-in-Council. The British Government is responsible for defence and international relations. The Channel Islands have trading rights alone within the European Union; these rights do not include financial aid.

In both Bailiwicks the Lieutenant-Governor and Commander-in-Chief, who is appointed by the Crown, is the personal representative of The Queen and the channel of communication between the Crown (via the Privy Council) and the island's government.

The government of each Bailiwick is conducted by committees appointed by the States. Justice is administered by the Royal Courts of Jersey and Guernsey, each consisting of the Bailiff and 12 elected Jurats. The Bailiffs of Jersey and Guernsey, appointed by the Crown, are President of the States and of the Royal Courts of their respective islands.

Each Bailiwick constitutes a deanery under the jurisdiction of the Bishop of Winchester (*see* Index).

ECONOMY

A mild climate and good soil have led to the development of intensive systems of agriculture and horticulture, which form a significant part of the economy. Equally important are invisible earnings, principally from tourism and banking and finance, the low rate of income tax (20p in the £ in Jersey and Guernsey; no tax of any kind in Sark) and the absence of super-tax and death duties making the islands a popular tax-haven.

Principal exports are agricultural produce and flowers; imports are chiefly machinery, manufactured goods, food, fuel and chemicals. Trade with the UK is regarded as internal.

British currency is legal tender in the Channel Islands but each Bailiwick issues its own coins and notes (*see* page 613). They also issue their own postage stamps; UK stamps are not valid.

JERSEY

Lieutenant-Governor and Commander-in-Chief of Jersey, HE Gen. Sir Michael Wilkes, KCB, CBE, *apptd* 1995
  Secretary and ADC, Lt.-Col. A. J. C. Woodrow, OBE, MC
Bailiff of Jersey, Sir Philip Bailhache, Kt.
Deputy Bailiff, F. C. Hamon
Attorney-General, M. C. St J. Burt, QC
Receiver-General, Gp Capt. R. Green, OBE
Solicitor-General, Miss S. C. Nicolle, QC
Greffier of the States, G. H. C. Coppock
States Treasurer, G. M. Baird

FINANCE

Year to 31 Dec.	1997	1998
Revenue income	£423,764,968	£442,434,776
Revenue expenditure	395,662,095	357,773,867
Capital expenditure	93,476,388	82,380,488
Public debt	0	0

CHIEF TOWN – ΨSt Helier, on the south coast of Jersey
FLAG – A white field charged with a red saltire cross, and the arms of Jersey in the upper centre

GUERNSEY AND DEPENDENCIES

Lieutenant-Governor and Commander-in-Chief of the Bailiwick of Guernsey and its Dependencies, HE Vice-Adm. Sir John Coward, KCB, DSO, *apptd* 1994
  Secretary and ADC, Capt. D. P. L. Hodgetts
Bailiff of Guernsey, de V. G. Carey
Deputy Bailiff, A. C. K. Day, QC
HM Procureur and Receiver-General, G. R. Rowland, QC
HM Comptroller, H. E. Roberts
States Supervisor, M. J. Brown

FINANCE

Year to 31 Dec.	1996	1997
Revenue	£182,016,695	£183,273,000
Expenditure	166,817,571	168,712,000

CHIEF TOWNS – ΨSt Peter Port, on the east coast of Guernsey; St Anne on Alderney
FLAG – White, bearing a red cross of St George, with a gold cross overall in the centre

ALDERNEY

President of the States, J. Kay-Mouat, OBE
Clerk of the States, D. V. Jenkins
Clerk of the Court, A. Johnson

SARK

Seigneur of Sark, J. M. Beaumont
The Seneschal, L. P. de Carteret
The Greffier, J. P. Hamon

OTHER DEPENDENCIES

Brechou, Lihou and Jethou are leased by the Crown. Herm is leased by the States of Guernsey.

The Environment

THE RIO EARTH SUMMIT

At the UN Conference on Environment and Development (UNCED) in Rio, Brazil, in 1992, 103 heads of state or government adopted the Rio Declaration, 27 principles intended to guide governments in pursuing economic development in ways that would benefit all and protect the environment. In particular the declaration stressed that the environment should be protected as part of development and that poorer developing countries should be helped to develop in ways that would minimize damage to the environment. The measures needed to ensure such sustainable development were outlined in the document *Agenda 21*. Neither the Rio Declaration nor Agenda 21 were binding agreements. The UN Commission on Sustainable Development was set up to monitor the progress of Agenda 21.

The second UNCED took place in New York in June 1997. It was found that progress towards the goals set at Rio had been slow. The UK agreed to reverse the decline in the amount of aid it was giving to developing countries and to reduce greenhouse gas emissions to 20 per cent below their 1990 levels by 2010.

CONVENTION ON BIOLOGICAL DIVERSITY

This binding agreement was adopted by 153 states at Rio, came into force in December 1993 and was ratified by the UK in June 1994. Its aim is to lessen the destruction of biological species and habitats, and parties to the convention are required to take inventories of their plants and animals, to protect endangered species and to ensure the diversity of species and habitats in the world. The convention is being implemented through a series of scientific advisory meetings and meetings of parties to the convention.

FRAMEWORK CONVENTION ON CLIMATE CHANGE

This convention, also a binding agreement, was adopted by 153 states at Rio, ratified by the UK in December 1993 and came into force in March 1994. It is intended to reduce the risks of global warming by limiting 'greenhouse' gas emissions. It recommended that industrialized countries reduce 'greenhouse' gas emissions to 1990 levels by 2000.

Progress towards the convention's targets is reviewed at regular conferences. The most recent of these was held in Kyoto, Japan, in December 1997 and the 159 countries represented agreed the Kyoto Protocol, which covers the six main 'greenhouse' gases (carbon dioxide, methane, nitrous oxide, hydrofluorocarbons (HFCs), perfluorocarbons (PFCs), sulphur hexafluoride (SF_6)). Under the protocol:

– 38 industrial countries agreed to legally binding targets for cutting their emissions of greenhouse gases to at least 5.2 per cent below 1990 levels between 2008 and 2012. EU members agreed to an 8 per cent reduction in emissions. The UK has agreed to a 12.5 per cent reduction
– nations are permitted to trade carbon permits, i.e. those close to their ceiling of allowed emissions could buy the right to pollute from those who had not used up their capacity
– nations can also offset emissions by using features such as forests that absorb carbon gases

Sanctions for those not meeting their targets are to be agreed at a later date. A timetable for implementing the protocol was agreed at Buenos Aires in November 1998. Trading in carbon permits will begin in 2000, when the Clean Development Mechanism will also be established. Developed countries will provide less polluting technology to developing countries, in return for carbon credits to offset their own emissions.

STATEMENT OF PRINCIPLES ON FORESTS

This non-binding agreement was intended to preserve tropical rain forests. It was recognized that forests must meet human needs (as a national resource providing timber and fuel) and that forests are important for absorbing carbon dioxide. The statement recommends the development of sustainable forest management policies and financial aid to developing countries so that they can preserve their forests.

EUROPEAN UNION PROGRAMMES

The first environmental action plan was adopted in 1972. These programmes are underpinned by the following principles: preventative action; the rectification of environmental damage at source where possible; and the 'polluter pays' principle (i.e. the polluter meets the full cost of the control of pollution). EU directives must be transposed into national law and policy to be effective.

The EC (now EU) Fifth Environmental Action Programme, called 'Towards Sustainability', was endorsed in December 1992 setting out a programme for sustainable development to 2000. It involves joint action by national and local government, private companies and individuals. A review of the programme, setting out priorities for further action, including further integration of environmental considerations into other policy areas, was completed in 1998.

The European Environment Agency was established in 1993 to monitor the state of the environment in the EU and to provide comparable environmental information.

UK MEASURES

The UK's international commitments on the environment have been incorporated into annual white papers called *This Common Inheritance*, summarizing the Government's commitments, achievements and future action and targets. Among the issues covered by the reports are climate change, wildlife and habitats, rural and urban development, air and water quality, pollution and waste, forestry and soil, and transport.

UK governments have increasingly seen environmental policy as part of the broader concept of sustainable development. This involves achieving environmental, economic and social objectives simultaneously, with environmental impact taken into account in all areas of policy rather than being considered in isolation. Government policy and operations are subject to scrutiny by the parliamentary environmental audit committee.

The UK produced its first national sustainable development strategy in 1994 and its first set of sustainable development indicators in 1996. A new strategy, 'A Better Quality of Life' was published in May 1999 which included revised indicators and targets. The Ministry of Agriculture, Fisheries and Food is working on a set of indicators of some of the pressures that agriculture exerts on the environment.

BIOLOGICAL DIVERSITY

The UK Biodiversity Group was set up after the Rio Earth Summit to identify and draw up costed action plans to protect the most threatened and declining species in the UK. The group's report, published in December 1995, identified 1,250 species and 38 key habitats which require action to protect them.

CLIMATE CHANGE AND POLLUTION

The Climate Change Impact Review Group was set up after Rio and in July 1996 published the *Review of the Potential Effects of Climate Change in the UK*, a sector by sector analysis of the impacts of climate change on sea level, the natural environment, energy and transport for the 2020s and 2050s in the UK. The Government intends to introduce legislation in the Finance Bill 2000 to provide for a climate change levy on businesses from April 2001.

The National Air Quality Strategy was adopted in March 1997. It is a framework for improving air quality. It sets quality standards for the main air pollutants and specific air quality objectives to be met by 2005, and outlines how industry, central and local government, transport and other sectors can contribute to improving air quality. A revised strategy was published in January 1999.

The draft UK Climate Change Consultation Paper was published in October 1998. It was followed by a period of consultation and a draft UK Climate Change Programme will be published in late 1999. The new programme is expected to be in place by 2001.

LOCAL AGENDA 21

Local authorities (and local communities) are being encouraged to play their part in meeting the UK's commitments under Agenda 21 and to a lesser degree the Biological Diversity and Climate Change Conventions. Under Local Agenda 21, local authorities draw up a sustainable development strategy for their areas. The main aims of the strategy are to protect and enhance the local environment, ensure prudent use of natural resources, meet social needs and promote economic success.

Each strategy should identify the local sustainability issues, set explicit objectives and priorities, state which organizations or sectors will take which actions, show how the objectives will be achieved and progress assessed, and outline the procedures for updating the strategy over time. Issues that might be covered by a local sustainability strategy include health, housing, home energy conservation, development plans, transport, air quality, biodiversity and recycling.

Local Agenda 21 is overseen in the UK by the Local Agenda 21 Steering Group, made up of representatives from the Local Government Association, the Convention of Scottish Local Authorities, the Association of Local Authorities of Northern Ireland, the TUC, the Advisory Committee on Business and the Environment, the World-Wide Fund for Nature, and other organizations. The International Council for Local Environmental Initiatives (ICLEI) is co-ordinating the international Local Agenda 21 initiative and the results of these efforts are reported via local government associations to the United Nations Commission on Sustainable Development.

Local authorities are under no statutory obligation to take part in Local Agenda 21 but a survey in 1998 found that 84 per cent of local authorities are engaged in or committed to Local Agenda 21. The Government wants all local authorities to adopt a Local Agenda 21 strategy by December 2000.

BUSINESSES

The Environmental Technology Best Practice Programme was set up in 1994 to help businesses to improve their environmental performance. The programme publishes free guides to good practice and case studies on low-cost waste minimization measures, cleaner technologies and on specific sectors and pollutants. The specific sectors covered so far are foundries, metal finishing, volatile organic compounds (solvents), textiles, paper and board, glass, printing, food and drink, chemicals, engineering, ceramics, plastics and packaging.

The Environment and Energy Helpline offers advice to business on any environmental issue.

UK TARGETS AND RECENT ACHIEVEMENTS
as at July 1999

Global Atmosphere

- reduce greenhouse gas emissions to 12.5 per cent below 1990 levels by 2010 (9 per cent reduction was achieved by 1997)
- reduce carbon dioxide emissions to 20 per cent below 1990 levels by 2010 (8 per cent reduction was achieved by 1997)
- phase out production and supply of CFCs by end of 1994 (achieved)
- return atmospheric chlorine and bromide to 1994 levels by 2012
- phase out HCFCs by 2015
- cut consumption of methyl bromide by 25 per cent by 1998 (*achieved*) and phase it out by 2005

Air Quality and Noise

- reduce sulphur dioxide emissions by 80 per cent on 1980 levels by 2010
- maintain emissions of oxides of nitrogen at 1987 levels from 1994 (*being achieved*)
- cut emissions from large combustion plants by 60 per cent between 1980 and 2003 (sulphur dioxide) and by 30 per cent between 1980 and 1988 (oxides of nitrogen)

Fresh Water and the Sea

- bring drinking water standards up to EC Directive standards by the mid-1990s (*largely achieved: in 1995, 99.5 per cent of tests in England and Wales met standards*)
- bring bathing waters fully up to EC Directive standards by the mid-1990s (*90 per cent of UK bathing waters met the standards in 1996*)
- phase out dumping of waste from collieries at sea by 1997 (*achieved in 1995*) and dumping of sewage sludge at sea by end of 1998
- halve atmospheric inputs of 17 harmful substances by 1999

Forestry

- double England's forest in the next 50 years (currently 7.5 per cent of total land area), subject to the necessary Common Agricultural Policy reform
- increase woodland cover in Wales by 50 per cent in next 50 years (currently 12 per cent of total land area)

Energy

- achieve energy savings of 250 petajoules per year by 2000
- achieve 15 per cent improvement in energy efficiency of government estate over five years to March 1996 (*achieved 14.5 per cent improvement*). New target set of 20 per cent improvement by 2000
- create 1500 MW of new electricity generating capacity from renewable resources by 2000

Waste

- reduce industrial and commercial waste going to landfill to 85 per cent of 1998 levels by 2005:

- recover 40 per cent of municipal waste by 2005, 45 per cent by 2010 and two-thirds by 2015
- recycle or compost 25 per cent of household waste by 2000
- 1 million tonnes of organic household waste a year to be composted by 2000, and 40 per cent of domestic properties with a garden to carry out composting by 2000
- 40 per cent of soil improvers and growing media in UK to be supplied by non-peat materials by 2005
- maintain at least 90 per cent recycling rate for waste lead-acid batteries
- increase use of waste/recycled materials as aggregates in England from about 30 to 55 million tonnes a year by 2006
- recover 50–65 per cent of packaging waste by 2001 and recycle 25–45 per cent by 2001 (minimum of 15 per cent for each material)
- ensure 40 per cent of UK newspaper feedstock to be waste paper by 2000
- recover 65 per cent of scrap tyres
- achieve easily accessible recycling facilities for 80 per cent of households by 2000

Housing
- reduce the proportion of homes lying empty to 3 per cent by 2005
- ensure that half of all new housing is built on re-used sites by 2005
- reduce number of government-owned empty homes.

ADDRESSES

ADVISORY COMMITTEE ON BUSINESS AND THE ENVIRONMENT, Floor 6/D9, Ashdown House, 123 Victoria Street, London SW1E 6DE. Tel: 0171-890 6624

ENVIRONMENT AGENCY, *see* page 299

ENVIRONMENTAL TECHNOLOGY BEST PRACTICE PROGRAMME, The Environment and Energy Helpline: 0800-585794. Web: http://www.environment.detr.gov.uk/bpp/helpline.htm

EUROPEAN ENVIRONMENT AGENCY, Kongens Nytorv 6, DK-1050 Copenhagen K, Denmark. Tel: Copenhagen 3336 7100. Web: http://www.eea.eu.int

GOVERNMENT PANEL ON SUSTAINABLE DEVELOPMENT, Zone 4/D9 Ashdown House, 123 Victoria Street, London SW1E 6DE. Tel: 0171-890 4962. Web: http://www.detr.gov.uk/environment

INTERNATIONAL COUNCIL FOR LOCAL ENVIRONMENTAL INITIATIVES (ICLEI), Sixteenth Floor, West Tower, City Hall, 100 Queen Street West, Toronto, Ontario M5H 2N2, Canada. Tel: Toronto 392 1462. Web: http://www.iclei.org

LOCAL AGENDA 21, Improvement and Development Agency, Layden House, 76-78 Turnmill Street, London EC1M 5QU. Tel: 0171-296 6599. Web: http://www.la21-uk.org.uk

ROYAL COMMISSION ON ENVIRONMENTAL POLLUTION, *see* page 300

SCOTTISH ENVIRONMENT PROTECTION AGENCY, *see* page 337

UK BIODIVERSITY GROUP, c/o Biodiversity Action Plan Secretariat, European Wildlife Division, Department of the Environment, Transport and the Regions, Room 902D Tollgate House, Houlton Street, Bristol BS2 9DJ. Tel: 0117-987 8974. Web: http://www.jncc.gov.uk/ukbg

UK ROUND TABLE ON SUSTAINABLE DEVELOPMENT, Zone 4/F4 Ashdown House, 123 Victoria Street, London SW1E 6DE. Tel: 0171-890 4962

UN COMMISSION ON SUSTAINABLE DEVELOPMENT, Division for Sustainable Development, Room DC2, 2220 United Nations, New York, NY 10017, USA. Tel: New York 963 3170

Conservation and Heritage

Conservation of the Countryside

NATIONAL PARKS

ENGLAND AND WALES

The ten National Parks of England and Wales were set up under the provisions of the National Parks and Access to the Countryside Act 1949 to conserve and protect scenic landscapes from inappropriate development and to provide access to the land for public enjoyment.

The Countryside Agency (established on 1 April 1999 from the merger of the Countryside Commission and the Rural Development Commission) is the statutory body which has the power to designate National Parks in England, and the Countryside Council for Wales is responsible for National Parks in Wales. Designations in England are confirmed by the Secretary of State for the Environment, Transport and the Regions and those in Wales by the National Assembly for Wales. The designation of a National Park does not affect the ownership of the land or remove the rights of the local community. The majority of the land in the National Parks is owned by private landowners (74 per cent) or by bodies such as the National Trust (7 per cent) and the Forestry Commission (7 per cent). The National Park Authorities own only 2.3 per cent of the land.

The Environment Act 1995 replaced the existing National Park boards and committees with free-standing National Park Authorities (NPAs). NPAs are the sole local planning authorities for their areas and as such influence land use and development, and deal with planning applications. Their duties include conserving and enhancing the natural beauty, wildlife and cultural heritage of the National Parks; promoting opportunities for public understanding and enjoyment of the National Parks; and fostering the economic and social well-being of the communities within National Parks. The NPAs publish management plans as statements of their policies and appoint their own officers and staff.

Membership of the NPAs differs slightly between England and Wales. In England membership is split between representatives of the constituent local authorities and members appointed by the Secretary of State (of whom one half minus one are nominated by the parish councils in the park), with the local authority representatives in a majority of one. The Countryside Agency advises the Secretary of State on appointments not nominated by the parish councils. In Wales two-thirds of NPA members are appointed by the constituent local authorities and one-third by the National Assembly for Wales, advised by the Countryside Council for Wales.

Central government provides 75 per cent of the funding for the parks through the National Park Grant. The remaining 25 per cent is supplied by the local authorities concerned. Approved net expenditure for all National Parks in 1999–2000 was £25,036,000 for England and £6,694,000 for Wales.

Two areas considered as having equivalent status are the Broads and the New Forest (*see* page 575).

The National Parks (with date designation confirmed) are:

BRECON BEACONS (1957), Powys (66 per cent)/Carmarthenshire/Rhondda, Cynon and Taff/Merthyr Tydfil/Blaenau Gwent/Monmouthshire, 1,351 sq. km/522 sq. miles – The park is centred on the Beacons, Pen y Fan, Corn Du and Cribyn, but also includes the valley of the Usk, the Black Mountains to the east and the Black Mountain to the west. There are information centres at Brecon, Craig-y-nos Country Park, Abergavenny and Llandovery, a study centre at Danywenallt and a day visitor centre near Libanus. *Information Office*, 7 Glamorgan Street, Brecon, Powys LD3 7DP. Tel: 01874-624437. *National Park Officer*, M. Fitton

DARTMOOR (1951 and 1994), Devon, 954 sq. km/368 sq. miles – The park consists of moorland and rocky granite tors, and is rich in prehistoric remains. There are information centres at Newbridge, Tavistock, Bovey Tracey, Steps Bridge, Princetown and Postbridge. *Information Office*, Parke, Haytor Road, Bovey Tracey, Devon TQ13 9JQ. Tel: 01626-832093. *National Park Officer*, N. Atkinson

EXMOOR (1954), Somerset (71 per cent)/Devon, 693 sq. km/268 sq. miles – Exmoor is a moorland plateau inhabited by wild ponies and red deer. There are many ancient remains and burial mounds. There are information centres at Lynmouth, County Gate, Dulverton and Combe Martin. *Information Office*, Exmoor House, Dulverton, Somerset TA22 9HL. Tel: 01398-23665. *National Park Officer*, K. Bungay

LAKE DISTRICT (1951), Cumbria, 2,292 sq. km/885 sq. miles – The Lake District includes England's highest mountains (Scafell Pike, Helvellyn and Skiddaw) but it is most famous for its glaciated lakes. There are information centres at Keswick, Waterhead, Hawkshead, Seatoller, Bowness, Grasmere, Coniston, Glenridding and Pooley Bridge, an information van at Gosforth and a park centre at Brockhole, Windermere. *Information Office*, Brockhole, Windermere, Cumbria LA23 1LJ. Tel: 01539-446601. *National Park Officer*, P. Tiplady

NORTHUMBERLAND (1956), Northumberland, 1,049 sq. km/405 sq. miles – The park is an area of hill country stretching from Hadrian's Wall to the Scottish Border. There are information centres at Ingram, Once Brewed, Rothbury, Housesteads, Harbottle and Kielder, and an information caravan at Cawfields. *Information Office*, Eastburn, South Park, Hexham, Northumberland NE46 1BS. Tel: 01434-605555. *National Park Officer*, G. Taylor

NORTH YORK MOORS (1952), North Yorkshire (96 per cent)/Redcar and Cleveland, 1,436 sq. km/554 sq. miles – The park consists of woodland and moorland, and includes the Hambleton Hills and the Cleveland Way. There are information centres at Danby, Pickering, Sutton Bank, Ravenscar, Helmsley and Hutton-le-Hole, and a day study centre at Danby. *Information Office*, The Old Vicarage, Bondgate, Helmsley, York YO6 5BP. Tel: 01439-70657. *National Park Officer*, D. Arnold-Forster

PEAK DISTRICT (1951), Derbyshire (64 per cent)/Staffordshire/South Yorkshire/Cheshire/West Yorkshire/Greater Manchester, 1,438 sq. km/555 sq. miles – The Peak District includes the gritstone moors

of the 'Dark Peak' and the limestone dales of the 'White Peak'. There are information centres at Bakewell, Edale, Fairholmes and Castleton, and information points at Torside (in the Longdendale Valley) and at Hartington (former station).
Information Office, Aldern House, Baslow Road, Bakewell, Derbyshire DE45 1AE. Tel: 01629-814321. *National Park Officer*, C. Harrison

PEMBROKESHIRE COAST (1952 and 1995), Pembrokeshire, 584 sq. km/225 sq. miles – The park includes cliffs, moorland and a number of islands, including Skomer. There are information centres at Tenby, St David's, Pembroke, Newport, Kilgetty, Haverfordwest and Broad Haven.
Information Office, Winch Lane, Haverfordwest, Pembrokeshire SA61 1PY. Tel: 01437-764636. *National Park Officer*, N. Wheeler

SNOWDONIA (1951), Gwynedd/Conwy, 2,142 sq. km/827 sq. miles – Snowdonia is an area of deep valleys and rugged mountains. There are information centres at Aberdyfi, Bala, Betws y Coed, Blaenau Ffestiniog, Conwy, Harlech, Dolgellau and Llanberis.
Information Office, Penrhyndeudraeth, Gwynedd LL48 6LF. Tel: 01766-770274. *National Park Officer*, I. Huws

YORKSHIRE DALES (1954), North Yorkshire (88 per cent)/Cumbria, 1,769 sq. km/683 sq. miles – The Yorkshire Dales are composed primarily of limestone overlaid in places by millstone grit. The three peaks of Ingleborough, Whernside and Pen-y-Ghent are within the park. There are information centres at Clapham, Grassington, Hawes, Aysgarth Falls, Malham and Sedbergh.
Information Office, Yorebridge House, Bainbridge, Leyburn, N. Yorks DL8 3BP. Tel: 01969-50456. *National Park Officer*, H. Hancock

Two other areas considered to have equivalent status to national parks are the Broads and the New Forest. The Broads Authority, a special statutory authority, was established in 1989 to develop, conserve and manage the Norfolk and Suffolk Broads (*see also* page 286). The Government declared in 1992 its intention of giving the New Forest a status equivalent to that of a National Park by declaring it an 'area of national significance'.

THE BROADS (1989), Norfolk, 303 sq. km/117 sq. miles – The Broads are located between Norwich and Great Yarmouth on the flood plains of the five rivers flowing through the area to the sea. The area is one of fens, winding waterways, woodland and marsh. The 40 or so broads are man-made, and are connected to the rivers by dykes, providing over 200 km of navigable waterways. There are information centres at Beccles, Hoveton, North-west Tower (Yarmouth), Ranworth and Toad Hole.
Broads Authority, Thomas Harvey House, 18 Colegate, Norwich NR3 1BQ. Tel: 01603-610734. *Chief Executive*, A. Clark

THE NEW FOREST, Hampshire, 376 sq. km/145 sq. miles – The forest has been protected since 1079 when it was declared a royal hunting forest. The area consists of forest, ancient woodland and heathland. Much of the Forest is managed by the Forestry Commission, which provides several camp-sites. The main villages are Brockenhurst, Burley and Lyndhurst, which has a visitor centre.
The Forestry Commission, Office of the Deputy Surveyor of the New Forest and the New Forest Committee, The Queen's House, Lyndhurst, Hants SO43 7NH. Tel: 01703-284149

SCOTLAND AND NORTHERN IRELAND

The National Parks and Access to the Countryside Act 1949 dealt only with England and Wales and made no provision for Scotland or Northern Ireland. Although there are no national parks in these two countries, there is power to designate them in Northern Ireland under the Amenity Lands Act 1965 and the Nature Conservation and Amenity Lands Order (Northern Ireland) 1985. In 1998 Scottish Natural Heritage submitted proposals to the Government for the designation of National Parks in Scotland. It will be for the Scottish Parliament to legislate in this area.

AREAS OF OUTSTANDING NATURAL BEAUTY

ENGLAND AND WALES

Under the National Parks and Access to the Countryside Act 1949, provision was made for the designation of Areas of Outstanding Natural Beauty (AONBs) by the Countryside Commission. The Countryside Agency is now responsible for AONBs in England and since April 1991 the Countryside Council for Wales has been responsible for the Welsh AONBs. Designations in England are confirmed by the Secretary of State for the Environment, Transport and the Regions and those in Wales by the National Assembly for Wales.

Although less emphasis is placed upon the provision of open-air enjoyment for the public than in the national parks, AONBs are areas which are no less beautiful and require the same degree of protection to conserve and enhance the natural beauty of the countryside. This includes protecting flora and fauna, geological and other landscape features. In AONBs planning and management responsibilities are split between county and district councils; where unitary authorities exist they have sole responsibility for planning and management. Several AONBs cross local authority boundaries. Finance for the AONBs is provided by grant-aid.

The 41 Areas of Outstanding Natural Beauty (with date designation confirmed) are:

ANGLESEY (1967), Anglesey, 221 sq. km/85 sq. miles
ARNSIDE AND SILVERDALE (1972), Cumbria/Lancashire, 75 sq. km/29 sq. miles
BLACKDOWN HILLS (1991), Devon/Somerset, 370 sq. km/143 sq. miles
CANNOCK CHASE (1958), Staffordshire, 68 sq. km/26 sq. miles
CHICHESTER HARBOUR (1964), Hampshire/West Sussex, 74 sq. km/29 sq. miles
CHILTERNS (1965; extended 1990), Bedfordshire/Hertfordshire/Buckinghamshire/Oxfordshire, 833 sq. km/322 sq. miles
CLWYDIAN RANGE (1985), Denbighshire/Flintshire, 157 sq. km/60 sq. miles
CORNWALL (1959; Camel estuary 1983), 958 sq. km/370 sq. miles
COTSWOLDS (1966; extended 1990), Gloucestershire/Wiltshire/Warwickshire/Worcestershire/Somerset, 2,038 sq. km/787 sq. miles
CRANBORNE CHASE AND WEST WILTSHIRE DOWNS (1983), Dorset/Hampshire/Somerset/Wiltshire, 983 sq. km/379 sq. miles
DEDHAM VALE (1970; extended 1978, 1991), Essex/Suffolk, 90 sq. km/35 sq. miles
DORSET (1959), 1,129 sq. km/436 sq. miles
EAST DEVON (1963), 268 sq. km/103 sq. miles
EAST HAMPSHIRE (1962), 383 sq. km/148 sq. miles
FOREST OF BOWLAND (1964), Lancashire/North Yorkshire, 802 sq. km/310 sq. miles

GOWER (1956), Swansea, 189 sq. km/73 sq. miles

HIGH WEALD (1983), Kent/Surrey/East Sussex/West Sussex, 1,460 sq. km/564 sq. miles

HOWARDIAN HILLS (1987), North Yorkshire, 204 sq. km/79 sq. miles

ISLE OF WIGHT (1963), 189 sq. km/73 sq. miles

ISLES OF SCILLY (1976), 16 sq. km/6 sq. miles

KENT DOWNS (1968), 878 sq. km/339 sq. miles

LINCOLNSHIRE WOLDS (1973), 558 sq. km/215 sq. miles

LLŶN (1957), Gwynedd, 161 sq. km/62 sq. miles

MALVERN HILLS (1959), Herefordshire/Worcestershire/Gloucestershire, 105 sq. km/40 sq. miles

MENDIP HILLS (1972; extended 1989), Somerset, 198 sq. km/76 sq. miles

NIDDERDALE (1994), North Yorkshire, 603 sq. km/233 sq. miles

NORFOLK COAST (1968), 451 sq. km/174 sq. miles

NORTH DEVON (1960), 171 sq. km/66 sq. miles

NORTH PENNINES (1988), Cumbria/Durham/Northumberland, 1,983 sq. km/766 sq. miles

NORTHUMBERLAND COAST (1958), 135 sq. km/52 sq. miles

QUANTOCK HILLS (1957), Somerset, 99 sq. km/38 sq. miles

SHROPSHIRE HILLS (1959), 804 sq. km/310 sq. miles

SOLWAY COAST (1964), Cumbria, 115 sq. km/44 sq. miles

SOUTH DEVON (1960), 337 sq. km/130 sq. miles

SOUTH HAMPSHIRE COAST (1967), 77 sq. km/30 sq. miles

SUFFOLK COAST AND HEATHS (1970), 403 sq. km/156 sq. miles

SURREY HILLS (1958), 419 sq. km/162 sq. miles

SUSSEX DOWNS (1966), 983 sq. km/379 sq. miles

TAMAR VALLEY (1995), Cornwall/Devon, 195 sq. km/115 sq. miles

NORTH WESSEX DOWNS (1972), Berkshire/Hampshire/Oxfordshire/Wiltshire, 1,730 sq. km/668 sq. miles

WYE VALLEY (1971), Monmouthshire/Gloucestershire/Herefordshire, 326 sq. km/126 sq. miles

NORTHERN IRELAND

The Department of the Environment for Northern Ireland, with advice from the Council for Nature Conservation and the Countryside, designates Areas of Outstanding Natural Beauty in Northern Ireland. At present there are nine and these cover a total area of approximately 284,948 hectares (704,121 acres).

ANTRIM COAST AND GLENS, Co. Antrim, 70,600 ha/174,452 acres

CAUSEWAY COAST, Co. Antrim, 4,200 ha/10,378 acres

LAGAN VALLEY, Co. Down, 2,072 ha/5,119 acres

LECALE COAST, Co. Down, 3,108 ha/7,679 acres

MOURNE, Co. Down, 57,012 ha/140,876 acres

NORTH DERRY, Co. Londonderry, 12,950 ha/31,999 acres

RING OF GULLION, Co. Armagh, 15,353 ha/37,938 acres

SPERRIN, Co. Tyrone/Co. Londonderry, 101,006 ha/249,585 acres

STRANGFORD LOUGH, Co. Down, 18,647 ha/46,077 acres

NATIONAL SCENIC AREAS

In Scotland, National Scenic Areas have a broadly equivalent status to AONBs. Scottish Natural Heritage recognizes areas of national scenic significance. At mid 1999 there were 40, covering a total area of 1,001,800 hectares (2,475,448 acres).

Development within National Scenic Areas is dealt with by local authorities, who are required to consult Scottish Natural Heritage concerning certain categories of development. Disagreements between Scottish Natural Heritage and local authorities are referred to the Scottish Executive. Land management uses can also be modified in the interest of scenic conservation.

ASSYNT-COIGACH, Highland, 90,200 ha/222,884 acres

BEN NEVIS AND GLEN COE, Highland/Argyll and Bute/Perth and Kinross, 101,600 ha/251,053 acres

CAIRNGORM MOUNTAINS, Highland/Aberdeenshire/Moray, 67,200 ha/166,051 acres

CUILLIN HILLS, Highland, 21,900 ha/54,115 acres

DEESIDE AND LOCHNAGAR, Aberdeenshire/Angus, 40,000 ha/98,840 acres

DORNOCH FIRTH, Highland, 7,500 ha/18,532 acres

EAST STEWARTRY COAST, Dumfries and Galloway, 4,500 ha/11,119 acres

EILDON AND LEADERFOOT, Scottish Borders, 3,600 ha/8,896 acres

FLEET VALLEY, Dumfries and Galloway, 5,300 ha/13,096 acres

GLEN AFFRIC, Highland, 19,300 ha/47,690 acres

GLEN STRATHFARRAR, Highland, 3,800 ha/9,390 acres

HOY AND WEST MAINLAND, Orkney Islands, 14,800 ha/36,571 acres

JURA, Argyll and Bute, 21,800 ha/53,868 acres

KINTAIL, Highland, 15,500 ha/38,300 acres

KNAPDALE, Argyll and Bute, 19,800 ha/48,926 acres

KNOYDART, Highland, 39,500 ha/97,604 acres

KYLE OF TONGUE, Highland, 18,500 ha/45,713 acres

KYLES OF BUTE, Argyll and Bute, 4,400 ha/10,872 acres

LOCH NA KEAL, MULL, Argyll and Bute, 12,700 ha/31,382 acres

LOCH LOMOND, Argyll and Bute/Stirling/West Dunbartonshire, 27,400 ha/67,705 acres

LOCH RANNOCH AND GLEN LYON, Perth and Kinross/Stirling, 48,400 ha/119,596 acres

LOCH SHIEL, Highland, 13,400 ha/33,111 acres

LOCH TUMMEL, Perth and Kinross, 9,200 ha/22,733 acres

LYNN OF LORN, Argyll and Bute, 4,800 ha/11,861 acres

MORAR, MOIDART AND ARDNAMURCHAN, Highland, 13,500 ha/33,358 acres

NORTH-WEST SUTHERLAND, Highland, 20,500 ha/50,655 acres

NITH ESTUARY, Dumfries and Galloway, 9,300 ha/22,980 acres

NORTH ARRAN, North Ayrshire, 23,800 ha/58,810 acres

RIVER EARN, Perth and Kinross, 3,000 ha/7,413 acres

RIVER TAY, Perth and Kinross, 5,600 ha/13,838 acres

ST KILDA, Western Isles, 900 ha/2,224 acres

SCARBA, LUNGA AND THE GARVELLACHS, Argyll and Bute, 1,900 ha/4,695 acres

SHETLAND, Shetland Islands, 11,600 ha/28,664 acres

SMALL ISLES, Highland, 15,500 ha/38,300 acres

SOUTH LEWIS, HARRIS AND NORTH UIST, Western Isles, 109,600 ha/270,822 acres

SOUTH UIST MACHAIR, Western Isles, 6,100 ha/15,073 acres

THE TROSSACHS, Stirling, 4,600 ha/11,367 acres

TROTTERNISH, Highland, 5,000 ha/12,355 acres

UPPER TWEEDDALE, Scottish Borders, 10,500 ha/25,945 acres

WESTER ROSS, Highland, 145,300 ha/359,036 acres

THE NATIONAL FOREST

The National Forest is being planted in about 200 square miles of Derbyshire, Leicestershire and Staffordshire. About 30 million trees, of mixed species but mainly broadleaved, will be planted over the next 20 years and beyond, and will eventually cover about one-third of the designated area. The project is funded by the Department of the Environment, Transport and the Regions. It was developed in 1992–5 by the Countryside Commission and is now run by the National Forest Company, which was established in April 1995. Since then almost 3 million trees have been planted on 1,518 hectares of land across 384 sites. Under the National Forest tender scheme, anybody wishing to undertake a project can submit a competitive bid to the National Forest Company.

NATIONAL FOREST COMPANY, Enterprise Glade, Bath Lane, Moira, Swadlincote, Derbys DE12 6BD. Tel: 01283-551211. *Chief Executive*, Miss S. Bell

Nature Conservation Areas

SITES OF SPECIAL SCIENTIFIC INTEREST

Site of Special Scientific Interest (SSSI) is a legal notification applied to land in England, Scotland or Wales which English Nature (EN), Scottish Natural Heritage (SNH), or the Countryside Council for Wales (CCW) identifies as being of special interest because of its flora, fauna, geological or physiographical features. In some cases, SSSIs are managed as nature reserves.

EN, SNH and CCW must notify the designation of a SSSI to the local planning authority, every owner/occupier of the land, and the Secretary of State for the Environment, Transport and the Regions, the Scottish Executive or the National Assembly for Wales. Forestry and agricultural departments and a number of other bodies are also informed of this notification.

Objections to the notification of a SSSI can be made and ultimately considered at a full meeting of the Council of EN or CCW. In Scotland an objection will be dealt with by the appropriate regional board or the main board of SNH, depending on the nature of the objection. Unresolved objections on scientific grounds must be referred to the Advisory Committee for SSSI.

The protection of these sites depends on the co-operation of individual landowners and occupiers. Owner-/occupiers must consult EN, SNH or CCW and gain written consent before they can undertake certain listed activities on the site. Funds are available through management agreements and grants to assist owners and occupiers in conserving sites' interests. As a last resort a site can be purchased.

The number and area of SSSIs in Britain as at 31 March 1999 was:

	no.	hectares	acres
England*	4,012	980,539	2,422,912
Scotland	1,448	919,597	2,272,324
Wales	963	223,332	551,853

*Figures as at 30 September 1998

NORTHERN IRELAND
In Northern Ireland 161 Areas of Special Scientific Interest (ASSIs) have been established by the Department of the Environment for Northern Ireland. These cover a total area of 83,465.476 hectares (206,243.19 acres).

NATIONAL NATURE RESERVES

National Nature Reserves are defined in the National Parks and Access to the Countryside Act 1949 as land designated for the study and preservation of flora and fauna, or of geological or physiographical features.

English Nature (EN), Scottish Natural Heritage (SNH) or the Countryside Council for Wales (CCW) can designate as a National Nature Reserve land which is being managed as a nature reserve under an agreement with one of the statutory nature conservation agencies; land held and managed by EN, SNH or CCW; or land held and managed as a nature reserve by another approved body. EN, SNH or CCW can make by-laws to protect reserves from undesirable activities; these are subject to confirmation by the Secretary of State for the Environment, Transport and the Regions, the National Assembly for Wales or the Scottish Executive.

The number and area of National Nature Reserves in Britain as at 31 March 1999 was:

	no.	hectares	acres
England*	194	79,666	196,855
Scotland	71	114,277	282,378
Wales	62	23,308	57,594

*Figures as at 30 September 1998

NORTHERN IRELAND
National Nature Reserves are established and managed by the Department of the Environment for Northern Ireland, with advice from the Council for Nature Conservation and the Countryside. There are 45 National Nature Reserves covering 4,322.1 hectares (10,676 acres).

LOCAL NATURE RESERVES

Local Nature Reserves are defined in the National Parks and Access to the Countryside Act 1949 as land designated for the study and preservation of flora and fauna, or of geological or physiographical features. The Act gives local authorities in England, Scotland and Wales the power to acquire, declare and manage local nature reserves in consultation with English Nature, Scottish Natural Heritage and the Countryside Council for Wales. Conservation trusts can also own and manage non-statutory local nature reserves.

The number and area of designated Local Nature Reserves in Britain as at 31 March 1999 was:

	no.	hectares	acres
England	598	29,032	71,738
Scotland	29	9,297	22,973
Wales	41	4,283	10,583

An additional 38 km of linear trails are designated as Local Nature Reserves.

FOREST NATURE RESERVES

Forest Enterprise (an executive agency of the Forestry Commission) is responsible for the management of the

Commission's forests. It has created 46 Forest Nature Reserves with the aim of protecting and conserving special forms of natural habitat, flora and fauna. There are about 300 SSSIs on the estates, some of which are also Nature Reserves.

Forest Nature Reserves extend in size from under 50 hectares (124 acres) to over 500 hectares (1,236 acres). The largest include the Black Wood of Rannoch, by Loch Rannoch; Cannop Valley Oakwoods, Forest of Dean; Culbin Forest, near Forres; Glen Affric, near Fort Augustus; Kylerhea, Skye; Pembrey, Carmarthen Bay; Starr Forest, in Galloway Forest Park; and Wyre Forest, near Kidderminster.

Forest Enterprise also manages 18 Caledonian Forest Reserves in Scotland. These reserves are intended to protect and expand 16,000 hectares of native oak and pine woods in the Scottish highlands.

NORTHERN IRELAND

There are 36 Forest Nature Reserves in Northern Ireland, covering 1,759 hectares (4,346 acres). They are designated and administered by the Forest Service, an agency of the Department of Agriculture for Northern Ireland. There are also 15 National Nature Reserves on Forest Service-owned property.

MARINE NATURE RESERVES

The Secretary of State for the Environment, Transport and the Regions, the National Assembly for Wales and the Scottish Executive have the power to designate Marine Nature Reserves. English Nature, Scottish Natural Heritage and the Countryside Council for Wales select and manage these reserves. Marine Nature Reserves may be established in Northern Ireland under a 1985 Order.

Marine Nature Reserves provide protection for marine flora and fauna, and geological and physiographical features on land covered by tidal waters or parts of the sea in or adjacent to the UK. Reserves also provide opportunities for study and research.

The three statutory Marine Nature Reserves are:

LUNDY
(1986), Bristol Channel
SKOMER
(1990), Dyfed
STRANGFORD LOUGH
(1995), Northern Ireland

Two other areas proposed for designation as reserves are: the Menai Strait, and Bardsey Island and part of the Llŷn peninsula, both in Wales.

A number of non-statutory marine reserves have been set up by conservation groups.

EUROPEAN MARINE SITES

The 1992 EC Habitats Directive and the 1979 Birds Directive allow the UK government to establish Special Areas of Conservation (SACs) on land and at sea. Where the designated area includes sea or seashore it is described as a European marine site. The UK marine SACs project is a demonstration initiative, funded by the EU, to establish management schemes for twelve of the marine SACs in the UK.

Conservation of Wildlife and Habitats

The United Kingdom is party to a number of international conservation conventions.

RAMSAR CONVENTION

The Convention on Wetlands of International Importance especially as Waterfowl Habitat was adopted at Ramsar, Iran, in 1971 and ratified by the UK in 1976. By July 1999, 116 countries were party to promote the convention. The aim of the convention is to the conservation and wise use of wetlands (e.g. areas of marsh, fen) and their flora and fauna, especially waterfowl. Governments who are party to the convention are obliged to designate wetlands in their territory for inclusion in the List of Wetlands of International Importance and to include wetland conservation considerations in their national land-use planning. As at 10 May 1999, there were 148 sites in the UK.

RAMSAR CONVENTION BUREAU, Rue Mauverney 28, CH-1196 Gland, Switzerland. Tel: Gland 999 0170. Web: http://www.ramsar.org

BONN CONVENTION

The Bonn Convention on the Conservation of Migratory Species of Wild Animals was adopted in 1979 and came into force in the UK on 1 October 1979. The convention requires the protection of listed endangered migratory species and encourages international agreements covering these and other threatened species.

The United Kingdom has signed and ratified three regional agreements under the convention: the Agreement on the Conservation of Small Cetaceans of the Baltic and North Seas (ASCOBANS), protecting dolphins and porpoises, etc; the Agreement on the Conservation of Bats in Europe and the African-Eurasian Migratory Waterbird Agreement (AEWA), which is aimed at protecting migrant waterbirds, and is working towards becoming a signatory (on behalf of Gibraltar) to the Agreement on the Conservation of Cetaceans in the Mediterranean and Black Seas (ACCOBAMS).

UNEP/CMS SECRETARIAT, United Nations Premises in Bonn, Martin-Luther-King Strasse 8, D-53175 Bonn, Germany. Tel: Bonn 815 2401. Web: http://www.wcmc.org.uk/cms

BERN CONVENTION

The Convention on the Conservation of European Wildlife and Natural Habitats was adopted in 1979 and ratified by the UK in 1982. The aim of the convention is to conserve flora and fauna and their natural habitats in Europe. Particular emphasis is placed on the protection of endangered and vulnerable species (both endemic and migratory) and on those species and habitats whose conservation requires the co-operation of several states.

Parties to the convention undertake to maintain populations (or take steps to increase populations where necessary) of species covered by the convention while taking account of local cultural, economic and recreational requirements and the requirements of sub-species. They must also ensure that national and local planning and development policies take account of wildlife and fauna.

SECRETARIAT OF THE BERN CONVENTION STANDING COMMITTEE, Council of Europe, F-67075 Strasbourg Cedex, France. Tel: Strasbourg 8841 2253. Web: http://www.nature.coe.int

HABITATS DIRECTIVE

The Council (EC) Directive on the Conservation of Natural Habitats of Wild Fauna and Flora was adopted by the Council in 1992 and became law in the UK in 1994 as the Conservation (Natural Habitats) Regulations. Under this directive EU members are required to maintain or restore natural habitats and wild species (other than birds) and to designate Special Areas of Conservation (SACs). SACs are those areas that are considered to be of European-wide importance because they are rare, threatened or important for the maintenance of biological diversity in Europe. The directive specifies the habitat types and species which require site designation: 75 habitat types and 47 species are proposed for site designation in the UK.

Member states compile a national list from which a final list of European importance will be drawn by 2004. By June 1999 the UK had submitted a total of 340 candidate sites to the Commission.

BIRDS DIRECTIVE

The Council (EC) Directive on the Conservation of Wild Birds was adopted by the Council in 1979 and came into force in April 1981. Under this directive EU members are required to maintain populations of wild birds and to preserve the diversity and area of their habitats. The species that are to be protected are listed in Annex 1 to the directive and are those species that are in danger of extinction, rare, or vulnerable to changes in their habitat.

Members are also obliged, under the directive, to notify the Commission of sites which are of particular importance to the conservation of wild birds. These sites are designated as Special Protection Areas (SPAs). Any site that is to be designated as a SPA in the UK must first have been notified as a Site of Special Scientific Interest or Area of Special Scientific Interest (see page 577). Sites may be designated as SPAs if they are of national or international importance. New guidelines for the selection of SPAs were agreed in June 1999 and a definitive list of SPAs is expected to be published in spring 2000.

By June 1999, a total of 2,436 SPAs had been designated, of which 200 are in the UK. The UK designations cover over 930,000 hectares.

CITES

The Convention on Trade in Endangered Species of Wild Fauna and Flora (CITES) was agreed in 1973 and came into force in 1975. It aims to prevent international trade in wildlife and their products, e.g. skins, from species threatened with extinction. Plant and animal species subject to regulation are listed according to the degree of protection they need:

- appendix I is a list of species threatened with extinction that are, or may be, affected by trade. International trade in these species is prohibited
- appendix II is a list of species which might become threatened if trade in them is not controlled. A permit is required to trade in these species
- appendix III is a list of species, protected within individual countries, where the country has asked other parties to the convention to assist in controlling international trade. A permit is required to trade in these species

Approximately 30,000 species are covered by the regulations.

The Wildlife Licensing and Registration Service (Wildlife and Countryside Directorate) of the Department of Environment, Transport and the Regions (see page 297) is responsible for issuing permits and compiling annual trade reports. The Joint Nature Conservation Committee (*see* page 326) and the Royal Botanic Gardens (*see* page 335) are the officially designated scientific authorities (on animals and plants respectively) who provide the expertise on which import and export approvals are based. CITES is financed by contributions from the member countries. CITES Secretariat, 15 Chemin des Anémones, CH-1219 Châtelaine, Geneva, Switzerland. Tel: Geneva 2979 9139

European Wildlife Trade Regulation

The Council (EC) Regulation on the Protection of Species of Wild Fauna and Flora by Regulating Trade Therein came into force in the UK on 1 June 1997. It is intended to standardize wildlife trade regulations across Europe and to improve the application of CITES. Approximately 30,000 plant and animal species are protected under the regulation.

UK Legislation

The Wildlife and Countryside Act 1981 gives legal protection to a wide range of wild animals and plants. Subject to parliamentary approval, the Secretary of State for the Environment, Transport and the Regions may vary the animals and plants given legal protection. The most recent variation of Schedules 5 and 8 came into effect in March and April 1998.

Under Section 9 and Schedule 5 of the Act it is illegal without a licence to kill, injure, take, possess or sell any of the listed animals (whether alive or dead) and to disturb its place of shelter and protection or to destroy that place.

Under Section 13 and Schedule 8 of the Act it is illegal without a licence to pick, uproot, sell or destroy any of the listed plants and, unless authorized, to uproot any wild plant.

The Act lays down a close season for wild birds (other than game birds) from 1 February to 31 August inclusive, each year. Exceptions to these dates are made for:

Capercaillie and (except Scotland) *Woodcock* – 1 February to 30 September

Snipe – 1 February to 11 August

Wild Duck and *Wild Goose* (below high water mark) – 21 February to 31 August

Birds which may be killed or taken outside the close season (except on Sundays and on Christmas Day in Scotland, and on Sundays in prescribed areas of England and Wales) are the above-named, plus coot, certain wild duck (gadwall, goldeneye, mallard, pintail, pochard, shoveler, teal, tufted duck, wigeon), certain wild geese (Canada, greylag, pink-footed, white-fronted (in England and Wales only)), moorhen, golden plover and woodcock.

Certain wild birds may be killed or taken subject to the conditions of a general licence at any time by authorized persons: crow, collared dove, gull (great and lesser black-backed or herring), jackdaw, jay, magpie, pigeon (feral or wood), rook, sparrow (house), and starling. Conditions usually apply where the birds pose a threat to agriculture, public health, air safety, other bird species, and to prevent the spread of disease.

All other British birds are fully protected by law throughout the year.

Animals

‡Adder (*Vipera berus*)
Anemone, Ivell's Sea (*Edwardsia ivelli*)
Anemone, Starlet Sea (*Nematostella vectensis*)
Apus, Tadpole shrimp (*Triops cancriformis*)
Bat, Horseshoe (*Rhinolophidae*, all species)
Bat, Typical (*Vespertilonidae*, all species)
Beetle (*Graphoderus zonatus*)

Beetle (*Hypebaeus flavipes*)
Beetle, Lesser Silver Water (*Hydrochara caraboides*)
§§Beetle, Mire Pill (*Curimopsis nigrita*)
Beetle, Rainbow Leaf (*Chrysolina cerealis*)
*Beetle, Stag (*Lucanus cervus*)
Beetle, Violet Click (*Limoniscus violaceus*)
Beetle, Water (*Graphoderus zonatus*)
Beetle, Water (*Paracymus aeneus*)
Burbot (*Lota lota*)
*Butterfly, Adonis Blue (*Lysandra bellargus*)
*Butterfly, Black Hairstreak (*Strymonidia pruni*)
*Butterfly, Brown Hairstreak (*Thecla betulae*)
*Butterfly, Chalkhill Blue (*Lysandra coridon*)
*Butterfly, Chequered Skipper (*Carterocephalus palaemon*)
*Butterfly, Duke of Burgundy Fritillary (*Hamearis lucina*)
*Butterfly, Glanville Fritillary (*Melitaea cinxia*)
Butterfly, Heath Fritillary (*Mellicta athalia* (or *Melitaea athalia*))
Butterfly, High Brown Fritillary (*Argynnis adippe*)
Butterfly, Large Blue (*Maculinea arion*)
Butterfly, Large Copper (*Lycaena dispar*)
*Butterfly, Large Heath (*Coenonympha tullia*)
*Butterfly, Large Tortoiseshell (*Nymphalis polychloros*)
*Butterfly, Lulworth Skipper (*Thymelicus acteon*)
Butterfly, Marsh Fritillary (*Eurodryas aurinia*)
*Butterfly, Mountain Ringlet (*Erebia epiphron*)
*Butterfly, Northern Brown Argus (*Aricia artaxerxes*)
*Butterfly, Pearl-bordered Fritillary (*Boloria euphrosyne*)
*Butterfly, Purple Emperor (*Apatura iris*)
*Butterfly, Silver Spotted Skipper (*Hesperia comma*)
*Butterfly, Silver-studded Blue (*Plebejus argus*)
*Butterfly, Small Blue (*Cupido minimus*)
Butterfly, Swallowtail (*Papilio machaon*)
*Butterfly, White Letter Hairstreak (*Stymonida w-album*)
*Butterfly, Wood White (*Leptidea sinapis*)
Cat, Wild (*Felis silvestris*)
Cicada, New Forest (*Cicadetta montana*)
**Crayfish, Atlantic stream (*Austropotamobius pallipes*)
Cricket, Field (*Gryllus campestris*)
Cricket, Mole (*Gryllotalpa gryllotalpa*)
Damselfly, Southern (*Coenagrion mercuriale*)
Dolphin (*Cetacea*)
Dormouse (*Muscardinus avellanarius*)
Dragonfly, Norfolk Aeshna (*Aeshna isosceles*)
*Frog, Common (*Rana temporaria*)
Goby, Couch's (*Gobius couchii*)
Goby, Giant (*Gobius cobitis*)
Grasshopper, Wart-biter (*Decticus verrucivorus*)
Hatchet Shell, Northern (*Thyasira gouldi*)
Hydroid, Marine (*Clavopsella navis*)
Lagoon Snail (*Paludinella littorina*)
Lagoon Snail, De Folin's (*Caecum armoricum*)
Lagoon Worm, Tentacled (*Alkmaria romijni*)
Leech, Medicinal (*Hirudo medicinalis*)
Lizard, Sand (*Lacerta agilis*)
‡Lizard, Viviparous (*Lacerta vivipara*)
Marten, Pine (*Martes martes*)
Moth, Barberry Carpet (*Pareulype berberata*)
Moth, Black-veined (*Siona lineata* (or *Idaea lineata*))
Moth, Essex Emerald (*Thetidia smaragdaria*)
Moth, Fiery clearwing (*Bembecia chrysidiformis*)
Moth, Fisher's estuarine (*Gortyna borelii*)
Moth, New Forest Burnet (*Zygaena viciae*)
Moth, Reddish Buff (*Acosmetia caliginosa*)
Moth, Sussex Emerald (*Thalera fimbrialis*)
††Mussel, Fan (*Atrina fragilis*)
†Mussel, Freshwater Pearl (*Margaritifera margaritifera*)
Newt, Great Crested (or Warty) (*Triturus cristatus*)
*Newt, Palmate (*Triturus helveticus*)
*Newt, Smooth (*Triturus vulgaris*)

Otter, Common (*Lutra lutra*)
Porpoise (*Cetacea*)
Sandworm, Lagoon (*Armandia cirrhosa*)
††Sea Fan, Pink (*Eunicella verrucosa*)
Sea-Mat, Trembling (*Victorella pavida*)
Sea Slug, Lagoon (*Tenellia adspersa*)
‡‡Shad, Allis (*alosa alosa*)
§§Shad, Twaite (*alosa fallax*)
Shark, Basking (*Cetorhinus maximus*)
Shrimp, Fairy (*Chirocephalus diaphanus*)
Shrimp, Lagoon Sand (*Gammarus insensibilis*)
‡Slow-worm (*Anguis fragilis*)
Snail, Glutinous (*Myxas glutinosa*)
Snail, Sandbowl (*Catinella arenaria*)
‡Snake, Grass (*Natrix natrix* (*Natrix helvetica*))
Snake, Smooth (*Coronella austriaca*)
Spider, Fen Raft (*Dolomedes plantarius*)
Spider, Ladybird (*Eresus niger*)
Squirrel, Red (*Sciurus vulgaris*)
Sturgeon (*Acipenser sturio*)
*Toad, Common (*Bufo bufo*)
Toad, Natterjack (*Bufo calamita*)
Turtle, Marine (*Dermochelyidae* and *Cheloniidae*, all species)
Vendace (*Coregonus albula*)
§§Vole, Water (*Arvicola terrestris*)
Walrus (*Odobenus rosmarus*)
Whale (*Cetacea*)
Whitefish (*Coregonus lavaretus*)
*   The offence relates to 'sale' only
** The offence relates to 'taking' and 'sale' only
†   The offence relates to 'killing and injuring' only
‡   The offence relates to 'killing, injuring and sale'
§   The offence relates to 'killing, injuring and taking'
§§ The offence relates only to damaging, destroying or obstructing access to a shelter or protection
†† The offence relates to killing, injuring, taking, possession and sale
‡‡ The offence relates to killing, injuring, taking and damaging, etc., a shelter

Plants

Adder's tongue, Least (*Ophioglossum lusitanicum*)
Alison, Small (*Alyssum alyssoides*)
Blackwort (*Southbya nigrella*)
°Bluebell (*Hyacinthoides non-scripta*)
Broomrape, Bedstraw (*Orobanche caryophyllacea*)
Broomrape, Oxtongue (*Orobanche loricata*)
Broomrape, Thistle (*Orobanche reticulata*)
Cabbage, Lundy (*Rhynchosinapis wrightii*)
Calamint, Wood (*Calamintha sylvatica*)
Caloplaca, Snow (*Caloplaca nivalis*)
Catapyrenium, Tree (*Catapyrenium psoromoides*)
Catchfly, Alpine (*Lychnis alpina*)
Catillaria, Laurer's (*Catellaria laureri*)
Centaury, Slender (*Centaurium tenuiflorum*)
Cinquefoil, Rock (*Potentilla rupestris*)
Cladonia, Upright Mountain (*Cladonia stricta*)
Clary, Meadow (*Salvia pratensis*)
Club-rush, Triangular (*Scirpus triquetrus*)
Colt's-foot, Purple (*Homogyne alpina*)
Cotoneaster, Wild (*Cotoneaster integerrimus*)
Cottongrass, Slender (*Eriophorum gracile*)
Cow-wheat, Field (*Melampyrum arvense*)
Crocus, Sand (*Romulea columnae*)
Crystalwort, Lizard (*Riccia bifurca*)
Cudweed, Broad-leaved (*Filago pyramidata*)
Cudweed, Jersey (*Gnaphalium luteoalbum*)
Cudweed, Red-tipped (*Filago lutescens*)
Cut-grass (*Leersia oryzoides*)
Diapensia (*Diapensia lapponica*)
Dock, Shore (*Rumex rupestris*)
Earwort, Marsh (*Jamesoniella undulifolia*)

Eryngo, Field (*Eryngium campestre*)
Fern, Dickie's bladder (*Cystopteris dickieana*)
Fern, Killarney (*Trichomanes speciosum*)
Flapwort, Norfolk (*Leiocolea rutheana*)
Fleabane, Alpine (*Erigeron borealis*)
Fleabane, Small (*Pulicaria vulgaris*)
Fleawort, South stack (*Tephroseris integrifolia* (*ssp maritima*))
Frostwort, Pointed (*Gymnomitrion apiculatum*)
Fungus, Hedgehog (*Hericium erinaceum*)
Fungus, Oak polypore (*Buglossoporus pulvinus*)
Fungus, Royal bolete (*Boletus regius*)
Fungus, Sandy stilt puffball (*Battarraea phalloides*)
Galingale, Brown (*Cyperus fuscus*)
Gentian, Alpine (*Gentiana nivalis*)
Gentian, Dune (*Gentianella uliginosa*)
Gentian, Early (*Gentianella anglica*)
Gentian, Fringed (*Gentianella ciliata*)
Gentian, Spring (*Gentiana verna*)
Germander, Cut-leaved (*Teucrium botrys*)
Germander, Water (*Teucrium scordium*)
Gladiolus, Wild (*Gladiolus illyricus*)
Goosefoot, Stinking (*Chenopodium vulvaria*)
Grass-poly (*Lythrum hyssopifolia*)
Grimmia, Blunt-leaved (*Grimmia unicolor*)
Gyalecta, Elm (*Gyalecta ulmi*)
Hare's-ear, Sickle-leaved (*Bupleurum falcatum*)
Hare's-ear, Small (*Bupleurum baldense*)
Hawk's-beard, Stinking (*Crepis foetida*)
Hawkweed, Northroe (*Hieracium northroense*)
Hawkweed, Shetland (*Hieracium zetlandicum*)
Hawkweed, Weak-leaved (*Hieracium attenuatifolium*)
Heath, Blue (*Phyllodoce caerulea*)
Helleborine, Red (*Cephalanthera rubra*)
Helleborine, Young's (*Epipactis youngiana*)
Horsetail, Branched (*Equisetum ramosissimum*)
Hound's-tongue, Green (*Cynoglossum germanicum*)
Knawel, Perennial (*Scleranthus perennis*)
Knotgrass, Sea (*Polygonum maritimum*)
Lady's-slipper (*Cypripedium calceolus*)
Lecanactis, Churchyard (*Lecanactis hemisphaerica*)
Lecanora, Tarn (*Lecanora achariana*)
Lecidea, Copper (*Lecidea inops*)
Leek, Round-headed (*Allium sphaerocephalon*)
Lettuce, Least (*Lactuca saligna*)
Lichen, Alpine sulphur-tresses (*Alectoria ochroleuca*)
Lichen, Arctic kidney (*Nephroma arcticum*)
Lichen, Ciliate strap (*Heterodermia leucomelos*)
Lichen, Convoluted cladonia (*Cladonia convoluta*)
Lichen, Coralloid rosette (*Heterodermia propagulifera*)
Lichen, Ear-lobed dog (*Peltigera lepidophora*)
Lichen, Forked hair (*Bryoria furcellata*)
Lichen, Goblin lights (*Catolechia wahlenbergii*)
Lichen, Golden hair (*Teloschistes flavicans*)
Lichen, New Forest beech-lichen (*Enterographa elaborata*)
Lichen, Orange fruited Elm (*Caloplaca luteoalba*)
Lichen, River jelly (*Collema dichotomum*)
Lichen, Scaly breck (*Squamarina lentigera*)
Lichen, Stary breck (*Buellia asterella*)
Lichen, Upright mountain cladonia (*Cladonia stricta*)
Lily, Snowdon (*Lloydia serotina*)
Liverwort, Leafy (*Petallophyllum ralfsi*)
Liverwort, Lindenberg's (*Adelanthus lindenbergianus*)
Marsh-mallow, Rough (*Althaea hirsuta*)
Marshwort, Creeping (*Apium repens*)
Milk-parsley, Cambridge (*Selinum carvifolia*)
Moss (*Drepanocladius vernicosus*)
Moss, Alpine copper (*Mielichoferia mielichoferi*)
Moss, Anomodon, long-leaved (*Anomodon longifolius*)
Moss, Baltic bog (*Sphagnum balticum*)
Moss, Blue dew (*Saelania glaucescens*)

Moss, Blunt-leaved bristle (*Orthotrichum obtusifolium*)
Moss, Bright green cave (*Cyclodictyon laetevirens*)
Moss, Cordate beard (*Barbula cordata*)
Moss, Cornish path (*Ditrichum cornubicum*)
Moss, Derbyshire feather (*Thamnobryum angustifolium*)
Moss, Dune thread (*Bryum mamillatum*)
Moss, Flamingo (*Desmatodon cernuus*)
Moss, Glaucous beard (*Barbula glauca*)
Moss, Green shield (*Buxbaumia viridis*)
Moss, Hair silk (*Plagiothecium piliferum*)
Moss, Knothole (*Zygodon forsteri*)
Moss, Large yellow feather (*Scorpidium turgescens*)
Moss, Millimetre (*Micromitrium tenerum*)
Moss, Multifruited river (*Cryphaea lamyana*)
Moss, Nowell's limestone (*Zygodon gracilis*)
Moss, Polar feather-moss (*Hygrohypnum polare*)
Moss, Rigid apple (*Bartramia stricta*)
Moss, Round-leaved feather (*Rhyncostegium rotundifolium*)
Moss, Schleicher's thread (*Bryum schleicheri*)
Moss, Threadmoss, long-leaved (*Bryum neodamense*)
Moss, Triangular pygmy (*Acaulon triquetrum*)
Moss, Vaucher's feather (*Hypnum vaucheri*)
Mudwort, Welsh (*Limosella australis*)
Naiad, Holly-leaved (*Najas marina*)
Naiad, Slender (*Najas flexilis*)
Orache, Stalked (*Halimione pedunculata*)
Orchid, Early spider (*Ophrys sphegodes*)
Orchid, Fen (*Liparis loeselii*)
Orchid, Ghost (*Epipogium aphyllum*)
Orchid, Lapland marsh (*Dactylorhiza lapponica*)
Orchid, Late spider (*Ophrys fuciflora*)
Orchid, Lizard (*Himantoglossum hircinum*)
Orchid, Military (*Orchis militaris*)
Orchid, Monkey (*Orchis simia*)
Panneria, Caledonia (*Panneria ignobilis*)
Parmelia, New Forest (*Parmelia minarum*)
Parmentaria, Oil stain (*Parmentaria chilensis*)
Pear, Plymouth (*Pyrus cordata*)
Penny-cress, Perfoliate (*Thlaspi perfoliatum*)
Pennyroyal (*Mentha pulegium*)
Pertusaria, Alpine moss (*Pertusaria bryontha*)
Physcia, Southern grey (*Physcia tribacioides*)
Pigmyweed (*Crassula aquatica*)
Pine, Ground (*Ajuga chamaepitys*)
Pink, Cheddar (*Dianthus gratianopolitanus*)
Pink, Childing (*Petroraghia nanteuilii*)
Pink, Deptford (*Dianthus armeria*) (England and Wales
   only)
Plantain, Floating water (*Luronium natans*)
Pseudocyphellaria, Ragged (*Pseudocyphellaria lacerata*)
Psora, Rusty Alpine (*Psora rubiformis*)
Ragwort, Fen (*Senecio paludosus*)
Ramping-fumitory, Martin's (*Fumaria martinii*)
Rampion, Spiked (*Phyteuma spicatum*)
Restharrow, Small (*Ononis reclinata*)
Rock-cress, Alpine (*Arabis alpina*)
Rock-cress, Bristol (*Arabis stricta*)
Rustwort, Western (*Marsupella profunda*)
Sandwort, Norwegian (*Arenaria norvegica*)
Sandwort, Teesdale (*Minuartia stricta*)
Saxifrage, Drooping (*Saxifraga cernua*)
Saxifrage, Marsh (*Saxifrage hirulus*)
Saxifrage, Tufted (*Saxifraga cespitosa*)
Solenopsora, Serpentine (*Solenopsora liparina*)
Solomon's-seal, Whorled (*Polygonatum verticillatum*)
Sow-thistle, Alpine (*Cicerbita alpina*)
Spearwort, Adder's-tongue (*Ranunculus ophioglossifolius*)
Speedwell, Fingered (*Veronica triphyllos*)
Speedwell, Spiked (*Veronica spicata*)
Spike rush, Dwarf (*Eleocharis parvula*)

Star-of-Bethlehem, Early (*Gagea bohemica*)
Starfruit (*Damasonium alisma*)
Stonewort, Bearded (*Chara canescens*)
Stonewort, Foxtail (*Lamprothamnium papulosum*)
Strapwort (*Corrigiola litoralis*)
Turpswort (*Geocalyx graveolens*)
Violet, Fen (*Viola persicifolia*)
Viper's-grass (*Scorzonera humilis*)
Water-plantain, Ribbon-leaved (*Alisma gramineum*)
Wood-sedge, Starved (*Carex depauperata*)
Woodsia, Alpine (*Woodsia alpina*)
Woodsia, Oblong (*Woodsia ilvensis*)
Wormwood, Field (*Artemisia campestris*)
Woundwort, Downy (*Stachys germanica*)
Woundwort, Limestone (*Stachys alpina*)
Yellow-rattle, Greater (*Rhinanthus serotinus*)
° The sale of plants taken from the wild is prohibited; the sale of
cultivated plants is still permitted

MOST UNDER THREAT

The animals and birds considered to be most under threat
in Great Britain by the Joint Nature Conservation
Committee are the high brown fritillary butterfly; violet
click beetle; new forest burnet moth; corncrake; aquatic
warbler; tree sparrow; wryneck; water vole; red squirrel;
allis shad; and twaite shad.

Close Seasons and Times

GAME BIRDS

In each case the dates are inclusive:

Black game – 11 December to 19 August (31 August in Somerset, Devon and New Forest)
*Grouse – 11 December to 11 August
*Partridge – 2 February to 31 August
*Pheasant – 2 February to 30 September
*Ptarmigan – (Scotland only) 11 December to 11 August
*It is also unlawful in England and Wales to kill this game on a Sunday or Christmas Day

HUNTING AND GROUND GAME

There is no statutory close time for fox-hunting or rabbit-shooting, nor for hares. However, by an Act passed in 1892 the sale of hares or leverets in Great Britain is prohibited from 1 March to 31 July inclusive. The recognized date for the opening of the fox-hunting season is 1 November, and it continues till the following April.

DEER

The statutory close seasons for deer (all dates inclusive) are:

	England and Wales	Scotland
Fallow deer		
Male	1 May–31 July	1 May–31 July
Female	1 Mar.–31 Oct.	16 Feb.–20 Oct.
Red deer		
Male	1 May–31 July	21 Oct.–30 June
Female	1 Mar.–31 Oct.	16 Feb.–20 Oct.
Roe deer		
Male	1 Nov.–31 Mar.	21 Oct.–31 Mar.
Female	1 Mar.–31 Oct.	1 April–20 Oct.
Sika deer		
Male	1 May–31 July	21 Oct.–30 June
Female	1 Mar.–31 Oct.	16 Feb.–20 Oct.
Red/Sika hybrids		
Male	—	21 Oct.–30 June
Female	—	16 Feb.–20 Oct

ANGLING

GAME FISHING

Where local by-laws neither specify nor dispense with an annual close season, the statutory close times for game fishing are: Trout, 1 October to end February; Salmon, 1 November to 31 January. New national by-laws concerning salmon came into force from 15 April 1999. The main provisions are that angling for salmon before 16 June is only permitted with artificial fly or artificial lure and any salmon caught before 16 June must be returned to the water with minimum injury.

COARSE FISHING

Responsibility for the fisheries function of the National Rivers Authority, including licensing and regulation, passed to the Environment Agency on 1 April 1996. The statutory close season for coarse fish in England and Wales runs from 15 March to 15 June on all rivers, streams and drains. Close season arrangements for canals vary from region to region. The close season on all lakes, ponds and reservoirs is at the discretion of the fishery owner, except on the Norfolk Broads and certain Sites of Special Scientific Interest where the statutory close season still applies. It is necessary in all cases to check with the local Environment Agency office (telephone 0645-333111).

LICENCES

Purchase of a national rod fishing licence is legally required of anglers aged 12 or over wishing to fish with rod and line in all waters within the area of the Environment Agency.

	Salmon and sea trout	Non-migratory trout and coarse fish
Full	£57.00	£18.00
Concessionary	28.50	9.00
Eight-day	16.50	6.50
One-day	5.50	2.50

Concessionary licences are available for juniors (12–16 years), for senior citizens (65 years and over), and disabled who are in receipt of long-term incapacity benefit, short-term incapacity benefit (at the higher rate) or severe disablement allowance. Those in receipt of a war pension which includes unemployability supplements are also eligible. Licences can be purchased by telephone on 0870-166 2662.

Historic Buildings and Monuments

LISTING

Under the Planning (Listed Buildings and Conservation Areas) Act 1990, the Secretary of State for Culture, Media and Sport has a statutory duty to compile lists of buildings or groups of buildings in England which are of special architectural or historic interest. Under the Ancient Monuments and Archaeological Areas Act 1979 as amended by the National Heritage Act 1983, the Secretary of State is also responsible for compiling a schedule of ancient monuments. Decisions are taken on the advice of English Heritage (see page 296).

Listed buildings are classified into Grade I, Grade II* and Grade II. There are currently about 500,000 individual listed buildings in England, of which about 95 per cent are Grade II listed. Almost all pre-1700 buildings are listed, and most buildings of 1700 to 1840. English Heritage is carrying out thematic surveys of particular types of buildings with a view to making recommendations for listing, and members of the public may propose a building for consideration. The main purpose of listing is to ensure that care is taken in deciding the future of a building. No changes which affect the architectural or historic character of a listed building can be made without listed building consent (in addition to planning permission where relevant). Applications for listed building consent are normally dealt with by the local planning authority, although English Heritage is always consulted about proposals affecting Grade I and Grade II* properties. It is a criminal offence to demolish a listed building, or alter it in such a way as to affect its character, without consent.

There are currently about 22,500 scheduled monuments in England. English Heritage is carrying out a Monuments Protection Programme assessing archaeological sites with a view to making recommendations for scheduling, and members of the public may propose a monument for consideration. All monuments proposed for scheduling are considered to be of national importance. Where buildings are both scheduled and listed, ancient monuments legislation takes precedence. The main purpose of scheduling a monument is to preserve it for the future and to protect it from damage, destruction or any unnecessary interference. Once a monument has been scheduled, scheduled monument consent is required before any works are carried out. The scope of the control is more extensive and more detailed than that applied to listed buildings, but certain minor works, as detailed in the Ancient Monuments (Class Consents) Order 1994, may be carried out without consent. It is a criminal offence to carry out unauthorized work to scheduled monuments.

Under the Planning (Listed Buildings and Conservation Areas) Act 1990 and the Ancient Monuments and Archaeological Areas Act 1979, the Secretary of State for Wales is responsible for listing buildings and scheduling monuments in Wales on the advice of Cadw (see page 350), the Historic Buildings Council for Wales (see page 307) and the Ancient Monuments Board for Wales (see page 307). The criteria for evaluating buildings are similar to those in England and the same listing system is used. In April 1997 there were 19,161 listed buildings and 2,999 scheduled monuments in Wales.

Under the Planning (Listed Buildings and Conservation Areas) (Scotland) Act 1997 and the Ancient Monuments and Archaeological Areas Act 1979, the Secretary of State for Scotland is responsible for listing buildings and scheduling monuments in Scotland on the advice of Historic Scotland (see page 338), the Historic Buildings Council for Scotland (see page 307) and the Ancient Monuments Board for Scotland (see page 308). The criteria for evaluating buildings are similar to those in England but an A, B, C grading system is used. There are about 44,462 listed buildings and about 7,035 scheduled monuments in Scotland.

Under the Planning (Northern Ireland) Order 1991 and the Historic Monuments and Archaeological Objects (Northern Ireland) Order 1995, the Department of the Environment for Northern Ireland (see page 327) is responsible for listing buildings and scheduling monuments in Northern Ireland on the advice of the Historic Buildings Council for Northern Ireland and the Historic Monuments Council for Northern Ireland. The criteria for evaluating buildings are similar to those in England but no statutory grading system is used. In March 1999 there were 8,563 listed buildings and 1,365 scheduled monuments in Northern Ireland.

OPENING TO THE PUBLIC

The following is a selection of the many historic buildings and monuments open to the public. The admission charges given are the standard charges for 1999–2000; many properties have concessionary rates for children, etc. Opening hours vary. Many properties are closed in winter and some are also closed in the mornings. Most properties are closed on Christmas Eve, Christmas Day, Boxing Day and New Year's Day, and many are closed on Good Friday. During the winter season, most English Heritage monuments are closed on Mondays and Tuesdays and monuments in the care of Cadw are closed on Sunday mornings. In Northern Ireland most monuments are closed on Mondays except on bank holidays. Information about a specific property should be checked by telephone.

*Closed in winter (usually November–March)
†Closed in winter, and in mornings in summer

ENGLAND

EH English Heritage property
NT National Trust property

*A LA RONDE (NT), Exmouth, Devon. Tel: 01395-265514. Closed Fri. and Sat. Adm. £3.20. Unique 16-sided house completed c.1796

†ALNWICK CASTLE, Northumberland. Tel: 01665-510777. Adm. £5.95. Seat of the Dukes of Northumberland since 1309; Italian Renaissance-style interior

ALTHORP, Northants. Tel: 01604-770107, ticket reservations 01604-592020. Open 1 July to 30 August. Adm £9.50. Spencer family seat. Diana, Princess of Wales memorabilia

†ANGLESEY ABBEY (NT), Cambs. Tel: 01223-811200. Closed Mon. (except Bank Holidays), Tues. and Good Friday. Gardens open daily July to Sept. Adm. £6.00 (£7.00 Sun. and Bank Holiday Mon.); gardens only, £3.50. House built c.1600. Outstanding grounds with unique statuary

APSLEY HOUSE, London W1. Tel: 0171-499 5676. Closed Mon. Adm. £4.50. Built by Robert Adam 1771–8, home of the Dukes of Wellington since 1817 and known as 'No. 1 London'. Collection of fine and decorative arts

†ARUNDEL CASTLE, W. Sussex. Tel: 01903-883136. Closed Sat. and Good Friday. Adm. £6.70. Castle dating from the Norman Conquest. Seat of the Dukes of Norfolk

AVEBURY (NT), Wilts. Tel: 01672-539250. Adm. free. Remains of stone circles constructed 4,000 years ago surrounding the later village of Avebury. Also *Alexander Keiller Museum*. Adm. £1.70

BANQUETING HOUSE, Whitehall, London SW1. Tel: 0171-930 4179. Closed Sun. and Bank Holidays. Adm. £3.60. Designed by Inigo Jones; ceiling paintings by Rubens. Site of the execution of Charles I

†BASILDON PARK (NT), Berks. Tel: 0118-984 3040. Closed Mon. (except Bank Holidays), Tues. and Good Friday. Adm. £4.10; grounds only, £1.80. Palladian house built in 1776–83

BATTLE ABBEY (EH), E. Sussex. Tel: 01424-773792. Adm. £4.00. Remains of the abbey founded by William the Conqueror on the site of the Battle of Hastings

BEAULIEU, Hants. Tel: 01590-612345. Adm. £9.00. House and gardens, Beaulieu Abbey and exhibition of monastic life, National Motor Museum (*see also* page 591)

BEESTON CASTLE (EH), Cheshire. Tel: 01829-260464. Adm. £2.80. Thirteenth-century inner ward with gatehouse and towers, and remains of outer ward

†BELTON HOUSE (NT), Grantham, Lincs. Tel: 01476-566116. Closed Mon. (except Bank Holidays), Tues. and Good Friday. Adm. £5.20. Fine 17th-century house in landscaped park

*BELVOIR CASTLE, nr Grantham, Lincs. Tel: 01476-870262. Closed Mon. (except Bank Holidays) and Fri.; also closed Mon.-Sat. in Oct. Adm. £5.00. Seat of the Dukes of Rutland; 19th-century Gothic-style castle

*BERKELEY CASTLE, Glos. Tel: 01453-810332. Opening times vary. Adm. £4.95. Completed 1153; site of the murder of Edward II (1327)

*BLENHEIM PALACE, Woodstock, Oxon. Tel: 01993-811325. Adm. £8.50. Seat of the Dukes of Marlborough and Winston Churchill's birthplace; designed by Vanbrugh

†BLICKLING HALL (NT), Norfolk. Tel: 01263-738030. Closed Mon. (except Bank Holidays) and Tues. Adm. £6.20; garden only, £3.50. Jacobean house with state rooms, temple and 18th-century orangery

BODIAM CASTLE (NT), E. Sussex. Tel: 01580-830436. Closed Mon. in winter. Adm. £3.50. Well-preserved medieval moated castle

BOLSOVER CASTLE (EH), Derbys. Tel: 01246-823349. Closed Mon. and Tues. in winter. Adm. £3.10. Notable 17th-century buildings

BOSCOBEL HOUSE (EH), Shropshire. Tel: 01902-850244. Closed Mon. and Tues. in winter; also closed in Jan. Adm. £4.00. Timber-framed 17th-century hunting lodge, refuge of fugitive Charles II

†BOUGHTON HOUSE, Northants. Tel: 01536-515731. House open Aug. only; grounds May to Sept. except Fri.; state rooms by prior booking. Adm. £6.00; grounds, £1.50. A 17th-century house with French-style additions

*BOWOOD HOUSE, Wilts. Tel: 01249-812102. Adm. £5.50. An 18th-century house in Capability Brown park, with lake, temple and arboretum

†BROADLANDS, Hants. Tel: 01794-505010. Open June-Sept. Adm. £5.50. Palladian mansion in Capability Brown parkland. Mountbatten exhibition

BRONTË PARSONAGE, Haworth, W. Yorks. Tel: 01535-642323. Closed 10 Jan.-4 Feb. 2000. Adm. £3.80. Home of the Brontë sisters; museum and memorabilia

BUCKFAST ABBEY, Devon. Tel: 01364-642519. Adm. free. Benedictine monastery on medieval foundations

*BUCKINGHAM PALACE, London SW1. Tel: 0171-839 1377. Open daily for eight weeks from early Aug. each year. Adm. £10.00. Purchased by George III in 1762, and the Sovereign's official London residence since 1837. Eighteen state rooms, including the Throne Room, and Picture Gallery

BUCKLAND ABBEY (NT), Devon. Tel: 01822-853607. Closed Thurs.; in winter open only weekend afternoons, closed 3 Jan.–18 Feb. 2000. Adm. £4.40; grounds only, £2.30. A 13th-century Cistercian monastery. Home of Sir Francis Drake

BURGHLEY HOUSE, Stamford, Lincs. Tel: 01780-752451. Adm. £6.10. Late Elizabethan house; vast state apartments

†CALKE ABBEY (NT), Derbys. Tel: 01332-863822. Closed Thurs. and Fri. Adm. £5.00, by timed ticket; garden only, £2.30. Baroque 18th-century mansion

CARISBROOKE CASTLE (EH), Isle of Wight. Tel: 01983-522107. Adm. £4.50. Norman castle; prison of Charles I 1647-8

CARLISLE CASTLE (EH), Cumbria. Tel: 01228-606000. Adm. £3.00. Medieval castle, prison of Mary Queen of Scots

*CARLYLE'S HOUSE (NT), Cheyne Row, London SW3. Tel: 0171-352 7087. Closed Mon. (except Bank Holidays), Tues. and Good Friday. Adm. £3.30. Home of Thomas Carlyle

CASTLE ACRE PRIORY (EH), Norfolk. Tel: 01760-755394. Closed Mon. and Tues. in winter. Adm. £3.10. Remains include 12th-century church and prior's lodgings

*CASTLE DROGO (NT), Devon. Tel: 01647-433306. Castle closed Fri. (except Good Friday). Adm. £5.30; grounds only, £2.50. Granite castle designed by Lutyens

*CASTLE HOWARD, N. Yorks. Tel: 01653-648444. Adm. £7.00; grounds only, £4.50. Designed by Vanbrugh 1699–1726; mausoleum designed by Hawksmoor

CASTLE RISING CASTLE (EH), Norfolk. Tel: 01553-631330. Closed Mon. and Tues. in winter. Adm. £2.75. A 12th-century keep in a massive earthwork with gatehouse and bridge

*CHARTWELL (NT), Kent. Tel: 01732-866368. Closed Mon. (except Bank Holidays) and Tues. (except July and Aug.). Adm. £5.50 by timed ticket; grounds only, £2.75. Home of Sir Winston Churchill

*CHATSWORTH, Derbys. Tel: 01246-582204. Adm. £6.50; garden only, £3.75. Tudor mansion in magnificent parkland

CHESTERS ROMAN FORT (EH), Northumberland. Tel: 01434-681379. Adm. £2.80. Roman cavalry fort

*CHYSAUSTER ANCIENT VILLAGE (EH), Cornwall. Tel: 0831-757934. Adm. £1.60. Romano-Cornish village, 2nd and 3rd century AD, on a probably late Iron Age site

CLIFFORD'S TOWER (EH), York. Tel: 01904-646940. Adm. £1.80. A 13th-century tower built on a mound

†CLIVEDEN (NT), Berks. Tel: 01628-605069. House open Thurs. and Sun. only, gardens daily. Adm. £5.00; £1.00 extra for house. Former home of the Astors, now an hotel set in garden and woodland

CORBRIDGE ROMAN SITE (EH), Northumberland. Tel: 01434-632349. Closed Mon. and Tues. in winter. Adm. £2.80. Excavated central area of a Roman town and successive military bases

CORFE CASTLE (NT), Dorset. Tel: 01929-481294. Adm. £4.00. Ruined former royal castle dating from 11th century

†CROFT CASTLE (NT), Herefordshire. Tel: 01568-780246. Closed Mon. (except Bank Holidays), Tues. and Good Friday; April and Oct. open weekends and Bank Holiday Mon. only; grounds open all year. Adm. £3.40; grounds only, £2.00 per car. Pre-Conquest border castle with Georgian-Gothic interior

DEAL CASTLE (EH), Kent. Tel: 01304-372762. Closed Mon. and Tues. in winter. Adm. £3.00. Largest of the coastal defence forts built by Henry VIII

DICKENS HOUSE, Doughty Street, London WC1. Tel: 0171-405 2127. Closed Sun. Adm. £3.50. House occupied by Dickens 1837–9; manuscripts, furniture and portraits

DR JOHNSON'S HOUSE, 17 Gough Square, London EC4. Tel: 0171-353 3745. Closed Sun. and Bank Holidays. Adm. £3.00. Home of Samuel Johnson

DOVE COTTAGE, Grasmere, Cumbria. Tel: 01539-435544. Closed Jan. and early Feb. Adm. £4.40; museum only, £2.20. Wordsworth's home 1799-1808; museum

DOVER CASTLE (EH), Kent. Tel: 01304-201628. Adm. £6.90. Castle with Roman, Saxon and Norman features; wartime operations rooms

DUNSTANBURGH CASTLE (EH), Northumberland. Tel: 01665-576231. Closed Mon. and Tues. in winter. Adm. £1.80. A 14th-century castle on a cliff, with a substantial gatehouse-keep

ELTHAM PALACE (EH), London SE9. Tel: 0181-294 2548. Closed Mon. (except Bank Holidays), Tues. and Sat. Adm. £5.50; grounds only, £3.30. 1930s house and remains of medieval palace

FARLEIGH HUNGERFORD CASTLE (EH), Somerset. Tel: 01225-754026. Closed Mon. and Tues. in winter. Adm. £2.30. Late 14th-century castle with two courts; chapel with tomb of Sir Thomas Hungerford

*FARNHAM CASTLE KEEP (EH), Surrey. Tel: 01252-713393. Adm. £2.00. Large 12th-century shell-keep

FOUNTAINS ABBEY (NT), nr Ripon, N. Yorks. Tel: 01765-608888. Closed Fri. Nov.-Jan.; deer park open daily all year. Adm. £4.30; visitor centre, deer park and St Mary's Church free. Ruined Cistercian monastery; 18th-century landscaped gardens of Studley Royal estate

FRAMLINGHAM CASTLE (EH), Suffolk. Tel: 01728-724189. Closed Mon. and Tues. in winter. Adm. £3.10. Castle (*c.*1200) with high curtain walls enclosing an almshouse (1639)

FURNESS ABBEY (EH), Cumbria. Tel: 01229-823420. Closed Mon. and Tues. in winter. Adm. £2.60. Remains of church and conventual buildings founded in 1123

GLASTONBURY ABBEY, Somerset. Tel: 01458-832267. Adm. £3.00. Ruins of a 12th-century abbey rebuilt after fire. Site of an early Christian settlement

GOODRICH CASTLE (EH), Herefordshire. Tel: 01600-890538. Adm. £3.10. Remains of 13th- and 14th-century castle with 12th-century keep

GREENWICH, London SE10. *Royal Observatory.* Tel: 0181-858 4422. Adm. £9.50 (joint ticket for Royal Observatory and National Maritime Museum). Former Royal Observatory (founded 1675) housing the time ball and zero meridian of longitude. *The Queen's House.* Tel: 0181-858 4422. Closed until Dec. 1999. Adm. charge. Designed for Queen Anne, wife of James I, by Inigo Jones. *Painted Hall and Chapel* (Royal Naval College). Visitors admitted to Sunday service (11 a.m.) in the chapel during college term

GRIME'S GRAVES (EH), Norfolk. Tel: 01842-810656. Closed Mon. and Tues. in winter. Adm. £1.85. Neolithic flint mines. One shaft can be descended

GUILDHALL, London EC2. Tel: 0171-332 1460. Closed Sun. in winter. Adm. free. Centre of civic government of the City. Built *c.*1440; facade built 1788-9

*HADDON HALL, Derbys. Tel: 01629-812855. Adm. £5.50. Well-preserved 12th-century manor house

HAILES ABBEY (EH), Glos. Tel: 01242-602398. Closed Mon. to Fri. in winter. Adm. £2.60. Ruins of a 13th-century Cistercian monastery

†HAM HOUSE (NT), Richmond, Surrey. Tel: 0181-940 1950. Closed Thurs. and Fri. Adm. £5.00. Garden open all year except Thurs. and Fri. Adm. £1.50. Stuart house with fine interiors

HAMPTON COURT PALACE, East Molesey, Surrey. Tel: 0181-781 9500. Adm. £10.00. A 16th-century palace with additions by Wren. Gardens with maze; Tudor tennis court (summer only)

†HARDWICK HALL (NT), Derbys. Tel: 01246-850430. Closed Mon. (except Bank Holidays), Tues. and Fri.; grounds open daily, all year. Adm. £6.00; grounds only, £3.00. Built 1591–7 for Bess of Hardwick; notable furnishings

*HARDY'S COTTAGE (NT), Higher Bockhampton, Dorset. Tel: 01305-262366. Closed Fri. (except Good Friday) and Sat. Adm. £2.60. Birthplace of Thomas Hardy

*HAREWOOD HOUSE, W. Yorks. Tel: 0113-288 6331. Adm. £6.95. An 18th-century house designed by John Carr and Robert Adam; park by Capability Brown

†HATFIELD HOUSE, Herts. Tel: 01707-262823. Closed Mon. (except Bank Holidays) and Good Friday. Adm. £6.00; grounds, £1.50. Jacobean house built by Robert Cecil; surviving wing of Royal Palace of Hatfield (1497)

HELMSLEY CASTLE (EH), N. Yorks. Tel: 01439-770442. Closed Mon. and Tues. in winter. Adm. £2.30. A 12th-century keep and curtain wall with 16th-century buildings. Spectacular earthwork defences

†HEVER CASTLE, Kent. Tel: 01732-865224. Adm. £7.30; gardens only, £5.80. A 13th-century double-moated castle, childhood home of Anne Boleyn

*HOLKER HALL, Cumbria. Tel: 015395-58328. Closed Sat. Adm. £6.00; grounds only, £3.35. Former home of the Dukes of Devonshire; award-winning gardens

†HOLKHAM HALL, Norfolk. Tel: 01328-710227. Closed Fri. and Sat. Adm. £4.00. Fine Palladian mansion

HOUSESTEADS ROMAN FORT (EH), Northumberland. Tel: 01434-344363. Adm. £2.80. Excavated infantry fort on Hadrian's Wall with extra-mural civilian settlement

†HUGHENDEN MANOR (NT), High Wycombe. Tel: 01494-532580. Closed Mon. (except Bank Holidays) and Tues.; open weekends only in March. Adm. £4.10. Home of Disraeli; small formal garden

JANE AUSTEN'S HOUSE, Chawton, Hants. Tel: 01420-83262. Closed Mon.-Fri. in Jan. and Feb. Adm. £2.50. Jane Austen's home 1809–17

*KELMSCOTT MANOR, nr Lechlade, Oxon. Tel: 01367-252486. Open Wed., afternoon of third Sat. in April, May, June and Sept., first and third Sat. in July and Aug., Thurs. and Fri. by appointment. Adm. £6.00. Summer home of William Morris, with products of Morris and Co.

KENILWORTH CASTLE (EH), Warks. Tel: 01926-852078. Adm. £3.50. Castle with building styles from 1155 to 1649

KENSINGTON PALACE, London W8. Closed Mon. and Tues. in winter. Adm. £8.50. Built in 1605 and enlarged by Wren; bought by William and Mary in 1689. Birthplace of Queen Victoria. Royal Ceremonial Dress Collection

KENWOOD (EH), Hampstead Lane, London NW3. Tel: 0181-348 1286. Adm. free; exhibitions, £3.50. Adam villa housing the Iveagh bequest of paintings and furniture. Open-air concerts in summer

*KEW, Surrey. Tel: 0181-332 5189. *Queen Charlotte's Cottage,* weekends and Bank Holidays in May-Sept. Adm. free (but £5.00 adm. to Kew Gardens)

†KINGSTON LACY HOUSE (NT), Dorset. Tel: 01202-883402. Closed Thurs. and Fri.; grounds open daily except Mon. to Thurs. in Nov. and Dec. Adm. £6.00; grounds only, £2.50. A 17th-century house with 19th-century alterations; important art collection

†KNEBWORTH HOUSE, Herts. Tel: 01438-812661. Adm. £6.00; grounds only, £5.00. Tudor manor house concealed by 19th-century Gothic decoration; Lutyens gardens

*KNOLE (NT), Kent. Tel: 01732-462100. Closed Mon. (except Bank Holidays) and Tues.; park open daily; garden open first Wed. of each month. Adm. £5.00; garden, £1.00; park free to pedestrians. House dating from 1456 set in parkland; fine art treasures

LAMBETH PALACE, London SE1. Tel: 0171-928 8282. Visits by written application. Official residence of the Archbishop of Canterbury. A 19th-century house with parts dating from the 12th century

*LANERCOST PRIORY (EH), Cumbria. Tel: 01697-73030. Adm. £2.00. The nave of the Augustinian priory church, c.1166, is still used; remains of other claustral buildings

*LANHYDROCK (NT), Cornwall. Tel: 01208-73320. Closed Mon. (except Bank Holidays). Garden open all year. Adm. £6.40; garden and grounds only, £3.20. House dating from the 17th century; 45 rooms, including kitchen and nursery

LEEDS CASTLE, Kent. Tel: 01622-765400. Adm. £9.30; grounds only, £7.30. Castle dating from 9th century, on two islands in lake

†LEVENS HALL, Cumbria. Tel: 01539-560321. Closed Fri. and Sat. Adm. £5.30; grounds only, £3.90. Elizabethan house with unique topiary garden (1694). Steam engine collection

LINCOLN CASTLE. Tel: 01522-511068. Adm. £2.50. Built by William the Conqueror in 1068

LINDISFARNE PRIORY (EH), Northumberland. Tel: 01289-389200. Open all year, subject to tide times. Adm. £2.80. Bishopric of the Northumbrian kingdom destroyed by the Danes; re-established in the 11th century as a Benedictine priory, now ruined

LITTLE MORETON HALL (NT), Cheshire. Tel: 01260-272018. Closed Mon. (except Bank Holidays) and Tues. March – Oct.; closed Mon. – Fri. 6 Nov. – 19 Dec. Adm. £4.20; joint adm. with Biddulph Grange Garden £6.00; free 4 – 19 Dec. Timber-framed moated manor house with knot garden

LONGLEAT HOUSE, Warminster, Wilts. Tel: 01985-844400. Open daily; safari park closed winter. Adm. £13.00; house only, £6.00. Elizabethan house in Italian Renaissance style

LULLINGSTONE ROMAN VILLA (EH), Kent. Tel: 01322-863467. Adm. £2.50. Large villa occupied for much of the Roman period; fine mosaics

MANSION HOUSE, London EC4. Tel: 0171-626 2500. Group visits only, by prior arrangement. Adm. free. The official residence of the Lord Mayor of London

MARBLE HILL HOUSE (EH), Twickenham, Middx. Tel: 0181-892 5115. Closed Mon. and Tues. in winter. Adm. £3.00. English Palladian villa with Georgian paintings and furniture

*MICHELHAM PRIORY, E. Sussex. Tel: 01323-844224. Closed Mon. and Tues. except in Aug. Adm. £4.20. Tudor house built onto an Augustinian priory

MIDDLEHAM CASTLE (EH), N. Yorks. Tel: 01969-623899. Closed Mon. and Tues. in winter. Adm. £2.30. A 12th-century keep within later fortifications. Childhood home of Richard III

†MONTACUTE HOUSE (NT), Somerset. Tel: 01935-823289. Closed Tues; grounds open all year. Adm. £5.40; grounds only, £3.00. Elizabethan house with National Portrait Gallery portraits from period

MOUNT GRACE PRIORY (EH), N. Yorks. Tel: 01609-883494. Adm. £2.80. Carthusian monastery, with remains of monastic buildings

NETLEY ABBEY (EH), Hants. Tel: 01703-453076. Adm. free. Remains of Cistercian abbey, used as house in Tudor period

OLD SARUM (EH), Wilts. Tel: 01722-335398. Adm. £2.00. Earthworks enclosing remains of the castle and the 11th-century cathedral

ORFORD CASTLE (EH), Suffolk. Tel: 01394-450472. Closed Mon. and Tues. in winter. Adm. £2.50. Circular keep of c.1170 and remains of coastal defence castle built by Henry II

*OSBORNE HOUSE (EH), Isle of Wight. Tel: 01983-200022. Adm. £6.90; grounds only, £3.50. Queen Victoria's seaside residence

†OSTERLEY PARK HOUSE (NT), Isleworth, Middx. Tel: 0181-568 7714. Closed Mon. (except Bank Holidays), Tues. and Good Friday; grounds open all year. Adm. £4.10; grounds free. Elizabethan mansion set in parkland

PENDENNIS CASTLE (EH), Cornwall. Tel: 01326-316594. Adm. £3.80. Well-preserved coastal defence castle built by Henry VIII

†PENSHURST PLACE, Kent. Tel: 01892-870307. Closed Mon.-Fri. in Mar. Adm. £5.70; grounds only, £4.20. House with medieval Baron's Hall and 14th-century gardens

†PETWORTH (NT), W. Sussex. Tel: 01798-342207. Closed Thurs. and Fri. (except Good Friday); grounds open all year. Adm. £5.50; grounds free. Late 17th-century house set in deer park

PEVENSEY CASTLE (EH), E. Sussex. Tel: 01323-762604. Closed Mon. and Tues. in winter. Adm. £2.50. Walls of a 4th-century Roman fort; remains of an 11th-century castle

PEVERIL CASTLE (EH), Derbys. Tel: 01433-620613. Closed Mon. and Tues. in winter. Adm. £2.00. A 12th-century castle defended on two sides by precipitous rocks

†POLESDEN LACEY (NT), Surrey. Tel: 01372-458203. Closed Mon. (except Bank Holidays) and Tues.; grounds open daily all year. Adm. £6.00; grounds only, £3.00. Regency villa remodelled in the Edwardian era. Fine paintings and furnishings

PORTCHESTER CASTLE (EH), Hants. Tel: 01705-378291. Adm. £2.70. Walls of a late Roman fort enclosing a Norman keep and an Augustinian priory church

*POWDERHAM CASTLE, Devon. Tel: 01626-890243. Closed Sat. Adm. £5.45. Medieval castle with 18th- and 19th-century alterations

†RABY CASTLE, Co. Durham. Tel: 01833-660202. Closed Sat. (except Bank Holiday weekends); open Wed. and Sun. only in May and June. Adm. £4.00; grounds only, £1.50. A 14th-century castle with walled gardens

*RAGLEY HALL, Warks. Tel: 01789-762090. Closed Mon.-Wed. (except Bank Holidays); grounds open daily in July and Aug. Adm. £5.00. A 17th-century house with gardens, park and lake

RICHBOROUGH ROMAN FORT (EH), Kent. Tel: 01304-612013. Closed Mon. and Tues. in Nov. and March, Mon.-Fri. Dec.-Feb. Adm. £2.50. Landing-site of the Claudian invasion in AD 43, with 3rd-century stone walls

RICHMOND CASTLE (EH), N. Yorks. Tel: 01748-822493. Adm. £2.30. A 12th-century keep with 11th-century curtain wall and domestic buildings

RIEVAULX ABBEY (EH), N. Yorks. Tel: 01439-798228. Adm. £3.00. Remains of a Cistercian abbey founded c.1131

ROCHESTER CASTLE (EH), Kent. Tel: 01634-402276. Adm. £3.50. An 11th-century castle partly on the Roman city wall, with a square keep of c.1130

†Rockingham Castle, Northants. Tel: 01536-770240. Open Sun. and Thurs. only (and Bank Holiday Mon. and Tues., and Tues. in Aug.). Adm. £4.20; gardens only, £2.70. Built by William the Conqueror

Royal Pavilion, Brighton. Tel: 01273-290900. Adm. £4.50. Palace of George IV, in Chinese style with Indian exterior and Regency gardens

†Rufford Old Hall (NT), Lancs. Tel: 01704-821254. Closed Thurs. and Fri. Adm. £3.80; garden only, £2.00. A 16th-century hall with unique screen

St Augustine's Abbey (EH), Canterbury, Kent. Tel: 01227-767345. Adm. £2.50. Remains of Benedictine monastery, with Norman church, on site of abbey founded AD 598 by St Augustine

St Mawes Castle (EH), Cornwall. Tel: 01326-270526. Closed Thurs. in winter. Adm. £2.50. Coastal defence castle built by Henry VIII

St Michael's Mount (NT), Cornwall. Tel: 01736-710507. Opening times vary. Adm. £4.40. A 12th-century castle with later additions, off the coast at Marazion

*Sandringham, Norfolk. Tel: 01553-772675. Closed for two weeks in summer and when the Royal Family is in residence. Adm. £5.00; grounds only, £4.00. The Queen's private residence; a neo-Jacobean house built in 1870

Scarborough Castle (EH), N. Yorks. Tel: 01723-372451. Closed Mon. and Tues. in winter. Adm. £2.30. Remains of 12th-century keep and curtain walls

†Sherborne Castle, Dorset. Tel: 01935-813182. Open Tues., Thurs., Sat., Sun. and Bank Holiday Mon. Adm. £4.80. Sixteenth-century castle built by Sir Walter Raleigh

*Shugborough (NT), Staffs. Tel: 01889-881388. Open Sun. only in October; open for booked parties in winter. Adm. house, county museum and farm, £8.00; each site alone, £4.00. House set in 18th-century park with monuments, temples and pavilions in the Greek Revival style

Skipton Castle, N. Yorks. Tel: 01756-792442. Closed Sun. mornings. Adm. £4.00. D-shaped castle with six round towers and beautiful inner courtyard

†Smallythe Place (NT), Kent. Tel: 01580-762334. Closed Thurs. and Fri. (except Good Friday). Adm. £3.00. Half-timbered 16th-century house; home of Ellen Terry 1899-1928

†Stanford Hall, Leics. Tel: 01788-860250. Open Sat.-Sun.; also Bank Holiday Mon. and Tues. following. Adm. £4.00; grounds only, £2.20. William and Mary house with Stuart portraits. Motorcycle museum

Stonehenge (EH), Wilts. Tel: 01980-624715. Adm. £4.00. Prehistoric monument consisting of concentric stone circles surrounded by a ditch and bank

†Stonor Park, Oxon. Tel: 01491-638587. Opening days vary. Adm. £4.50; gardens only, £2.50. Medieval house with Georgian façade. Centre of Roman Catholicism after the Reformation

†Stourhead (NT), Wilts. Tel: 01747-841152. Closed Thurs. and Fri. Gardens open daily all year. Adm. £4.50; gardens only, £4.50 (Nov. – Feb. £3.50); combined ticket £8.00. English Palladian mansion with famous gardens

*Stratfield Saye House, Hants. Tel: 01256-882882. Closed Fri. June – Aug., Mon. – Fri. in Sept. Adm. £5.00. House built 1630-40; home of the Dukes of Wellington since 1817

Stratford-upon-Avon, Warks. Shakespeare's Birthplace with Shakespeare Centre; Anne Hathaway's Cottage, home of Shakespeare's wife; Mary Arden's House, home of Shakespeare's mother; Nash's House and New Place, where Shakespeare died; and Hall's Croft, home of Shakespeare's daughter. Tel: 01789-204016. Adm. £11.00 for all buildings; £7.50 for Shakespeare's Birthplace, Hall's Croft and Nash's House, and New Place. Also Grammar School attended by Shakespeare, Holy Trinity Church, where Shakespeare is buried, Royal Shakespeare Theatre (burnt down 1926, rebuilt 1932) and Swan Theatre (opened 1986)

*Sudeley Castle, Glos. Tel: 01242-602308. Adm. £6.00; grounds only, £4.50. Castle built in 1442; restored in the 19th century

Syon House, Brentford, Middx. Tel: 0181-560 0883. House closed Mon. (except Bank Holidays), Tues., Fri. and Sat. Adm. charges vary. Built on the site of a former monastery; Adam interior

Tilbury Fort (EH), Essex. Tel: 01375-858489. Closed Mon. and Tues. in winter. Adm. £2.50. A 17th-century coastal fort

Tintagel Castle (EH), Cornwall. Tel: 01840-770328. Adm. £2.80. A 12th-century cliff-top castle and Dark Age settlement site

Tower of London, London EC3. Tel: 0171-709 0765. Adm. £10.50. Royal palace and fortress begun by William the Conqueror in 1078. Houses the Crown Jewels

*Trerice (NT), Cornwall. Tel: 01637-875404. Closed Tues. and Sat. (except in Aug.). Adm. £4.00. Elizabethan manor house

Tynemouth Priory and Castle (EH), Tyne and Wear. Tel: 0191-257 1090. Closed Mon. and Tues. in winter. Adm. £1.80. Remains of a Benedictine priory, founded c.1090, on Saxon monastic site

†Uppark (NT), W. Sussex. Tel: 01730-825415. Closed Fri. and Sat. Adm. £5.50 by timed ticket. Late 17th-century house, completely restored after fire. Fetherstonhaugh art collection

Walmer Castle (EH), Kent. Tel: 01304-364288. Closed Mon. and Tues. in winter; closed Jan.-Feb. and when the Lord Warden is in residence. Adm. £4.50. One of Henry VIII's coastal defence castles, now the residence of the Lord Warden of the Cinque Ports

Waltham Abbey (EH), Essex. Tel: 01992-702200. Adm. free. Ruined abbey including the nave of the abbey church, 'Harold's Bridge' and late 14th-century gatehouse. Traditionally the burial place of Harold II (1066)

Warkworth Castle (EH), Northumberland. Tel: 01665-711423. Adm. £2.40. A 15th-century keep amidst earlier ruins, with 14th-century hermitage (open Wed., Sun. and Bank Holidays in summer, adm. £1.60) upstream

Warwick Castle. Tel: 01926-406600. Adm. £10.50. Medieval castle with Madame Tussaud's waxworks, in Capability Brown parkland

Whitby Abbey (EH), N. Yorks. Tel: 01947-603568. Adm. £1.70. Remains of Norman church on the site of a monastery founded AD 657

*Wilton House, Wilts. Tel: 01722-746720. Adm. £6.75. A 17th-century house on the site of a Tudor house and Saxon abbey

Windsor Castle, Berks. Tel: 01753-831118 for recorded information on opening times. Adm. £10.00, including the Castle precincts. Official residence of The Queen; oldest royal residence still in regular use. Also St George's Chapel

*WOBURN ABBEY, Beds. Tel: 01525-290666. Closed Mon.-Fri. in Oct. Adm. £7.50. Built on the site of a Cistercian abbey; seat of the Dukes of Bedford. Important art collection; antiques centre

WROXETER ROMAN CITY (EH), Shropshire. Tel: 01743-761330. Closed Mon. and Tues. in winter. Adm. £3.10. Second-century public baths and part of the forum of the Roman town of Viroconium

WALES

C Property of Cadw: Welsh Historic Monuments
NT National Trust property

BEAUMARIS CASTLE (C), Anglesey. Tel: 01248-810361. Adm. £2.20. Concentrically-planned castle

CAERLEON ROMAN BATHS AND AMPHITHEATRE (C), nr Newport. Tel: 01633-890104. Closed Sun. morning in winter. Adm. £2.00, joint ticket with Roman Legionary Museum £3.30. Rare example of a legionary bath-house and late 1st-century arena

CAERNARFON CASTLE (C). Tel: 01286-677617. Adm. £4.20. Important Edwardian castle built, with the town wall, between 1283 and 1330

CAERPHILLY CASTLE (C). Tel: 01222-883143. Adm. £2.50. Concentrically-planned castle (c.1270) notable for its scale and use of water defences

CARDIFF CASTLE. Tel: 01222-878100. Adm. charge. Castle built on the site of a Roman fort; spectacular towers and rich interior

CASTELL COCH (C), nr Cardiff. Tel: 01222-810101. Adm. £2.50. Rebuilt 1875-90 on medieval foundations

CHEPSTOW CASTLE (C). Tel: 01291-624065. Adm. £3.00. Rectangular keep amid extensive fortifications

CONWY CASTLE (C). Tel: 01492-592358. Adm. £3.50. Built by Edward I, 1283-7

*CRICCIETH CASTLE (C). Tel: 01766-522227. Adm. £2.20. Native Welsh 13th-century castle, altered by Edward I

DENBIGH CASTLE (C). Tel: 01222-500200. Adm. £2.00. Remains of the castle (begun 1282), including triple-towered gatehouse

HARLECH CASTLE (C). Tel: 01766-780552. Adm. £3.00. Well-preserved Edwardian castle, constructed 1283-90, on an outcrop above the former shoreline

PEMBROKE CASTLE. Tel: 01646-681510. Adm. £3.00. Castle founded in 1093; Great Tower built 1200; birthplace of King Henry VII

*PENRHYN CASTLE (NT), Bangor. Tel: 01248-353084. Closed Tues. Adm. £5.00; grounds only, £3.00. Neo-Norman castle built in the 19th century. Industrial railway museum

PORTMEIRION, Penrhyndeudraeth. Tel: 01766-770228. Adm. £4.00. Village in Italianate style

†POWIS CASTLE (NT), nr Welshpool. Tel: 01938-557018. Closed Mon. (except Bank Holidays) and Tues. (except July and Aug.). Adm. £7.50; garden only, £5.00. Medieval castle with interior in a variety of styles; 17th-century gardens and Clive of India museum

RAGLAN CASTLE (C). Tel: 01291-690228. Adm. £2.40. Remains of 15th-century castle with hexagonal keep

ST DAVIDS BISHOP'S PALACE (C), St Davids. Tel: 01437-720517. Closed Sun. mornings in winter. Adm. £2.00. Remains of bishops palace built 1328-47

TINTERN ABBEY (C), nr Chepstow. Tel: 01291-689251. Adm. £2.40. Remains of 13th-century church and conventual buildings of a Cistercian monastery

*TRETOWER COURT AND CASTLE (C), nr Crickhowell. Tel: 01874-730279. Adm. £2.20. Medieval house with remains of 12th-century castle nearby

SCOTLAND

HS Historic Scotland property
NTS National Trust for Scotland property

ANTONINE WALL, between the Clyde and the Forth. Adm. free. Built about AD 142, consists of ditch, turf rampart and road, with forts every two miles

BALMORAL CASTLE, nr Braemar. Tel: 013397-42334. Open mid-April to end July. Adm. £4.00. Baronial-style castle built for Victoria and Albert. The Queen's private residence

BLACK HOUSE, ARNOL (HS), Lewis, Western Isles. Tel: 01851-710395. Closed Sun.; also Fri. in winter. Adm. £2.00. Traditional Lewis thatched house

*BLAIR CASTLE, Blair Atholl. Tel: 01796-481207. Adm. £6.00. Mid 18th-century mansion with 13th-century tower; seat of the Dukes of Atholl

*BONAWE IRON FURNACE (HS), Argyll and Bute. Tel: 01866-822432. Adm. £2.50. Charcoal-fuelled ironworks founded in 1753

†BOWHILL, Selkirk. Tel: 01750-22204. House open July only; grounds open April—June, Aug. except Fri., daily in July. Adm. £4.50; grounds only, £2.00. Seat of the Dukes of Buccleuch and Queensberry; fine collection of paintings, including portrait miniatures

BROUGH OF BIRSAY (HS), Orkney. Adm. £1.00 June—Sept. Free other times of year. Remains of Norse church and village on Birsay

CAERLAVEROCK CASTLE (HS), nr Dumfries. Tel: 01387-770244. Adm. £2.50. Fine early classical Renaissance building

CALANAIS STANDING STONES (HS), Lewis, Western Isles. Tel: 01851-621422. Adm. £1.50. Standing stones in a cross-shaped setting, dating from 3000 BC

CATHERTUNS (BROWN AND WHITE) (HS), nr Brechin. Adm. free. Two large Iron Age hill forts

*CAWDOR CASTLE, Inverness. Tel: 01667-404615. Adm. £5.40; grounds only, £2.80. A 14th-century keep with 15th- and 17th-century additions

CLAVA CAIRNS (HS), Highland. Adm. free. Late Neolithic or early Bronze Age cairns

*CRATHES CASTLE (NTS), nr Banchory. Tel: 01330-844525. Garden and grounds open all year. Adm. castle, garden and grounds, £5.00; each site, £2.10. A 16th-century baronial castle

*CULZEAN CASTLE (NTS), S. Ayrshire. Tel: 01655-760274. Country park open all year. Adm. £7.00; country park only, £3.50. An 18th-century Adam castle with oval staircase and circular saloon

DRYBURGH ABBEY (HS), Scottish Borders. Tel: 01835-822381. Closed Sun. mornings in Winter. Adm. £2.50. A 12th-century abbey containing tomb of Scott

*DUNVEGAN CASTLE, Skye. Tel: 01470-521206. Adm. £5.20; gardens only, £3.70. A 13th-century castle with later additions; home of the chiefs of the Clan MacLeod; trips to seal colony

EDINBURGH CASTLE (HS). Tel: 0131-225 9846. Adm. £6.50; war memorial free. Includes the Scottish National War Memorial, Scottish United Services Museum and historic apartments

EDZELL CASTLE (HS), nr Brechin. Tel: 01356-648631. Closed Sun. mornings, Thurs. afternoons and Fri. in winter. Adm. £2.50. Medieval tower house

*EILEAN DONAN CASTLE, Wester Ross. Tel: 01599-555202. Adm. £3.75. A 13th-century castle with Jacobite relics

ELGIN CATHEDRAL (HS), Moray. Tel: 01343-547171. Closed Sun. mornings, Thurs. afternoons and Fri. in winter. Adm. £2.80. A 13th-century cathedral with fine chapterhouse

*FLOORS CASTLE, Kelso. Tel: 01573-223333. Adm. £5.00. Largest inhabited castle in Scotland

FORT GEORGE (HS), Highland. Tel: 01667-462800. Closed Sunday mornings in winter. Adm. £3.00. An 18th-century fort

*GLAMIS CASTLE, Angus. Tel: 01307-840393. Adm. £5.40; grounds only, £2.50. Seat of the Lyon family since 1372

GLASGOW CATHEDRAL (HS). Tel: 0141-552 6891. Closed Sun. mornings. Adm. free. Medieval cathedral with elaborately vaulted crypt

GLENELG BROCH (HS), Highland. Adm. free. Two broch towers with well-preserved structural features

*HOPETOUN HOUSE, nr Edinburgh. Tel: 0131-331 2451. Adm. £5.00. House designed by Sir William Bruce, enlarged by William Adam

HUNTLY CASTLE (HS). Tel: 01466-793191. Closed Sun. mornings, Thurs. afternoons and Fri. in winter. Adm. £2.50. Ruin of a 16th- and 17th-century house

*INVERARAY CASTLE, Argyll. Tel: 01499-302203. Adm. £3.60. Gothic-style 18th-century castle; seat of the Dukes of Argyll

IONA ABBEY, Inner Hebrides. Tel: 01828-640411. Adm. £2.00. Monastery founded by St Columba in AD 563

*JARLSHOF (HS), Shetland. Tel: 01950-460112. Adm. £2.50. Remains from Stone Age

JEDBURGH ABBEY (HS), Scottish Borders. Tel: 01835-863925. Adm. £3.00. Romanesque and early Gothic church founded c.1138

KELSO ABBEY (HS), Scottish Borders. Adm. free. Remains of great abbey church founded 1128

LINLITHGOW PALACE (HS). Tel: 01506-842896. Adm. £2.50. Ruin of royal palace in park setting. Birthplace of Mary, Queen of Scots

MAES HOWE (HS), Orkney. Tel: 01856-761606. Closed Sun. mornings, Thurs. afternoons and Fri. in winter. Adm. £2.50. Neolithic tomb

*MEIGLE SCULPTURED STONES (HS), Angus. Tel: 01828-640612. Adm. £1.80. Celtic Christian stones

MELROSE ABBEY (HS), Scottish Borders. Tel: 01896-822562. Adm. £3.00. Ruin of Cistercian abbey

MOUSA BROCH (HS), Shetland. Adm. free. Finest surviving Iron Age broch tower

NETHER LARGIE CAIRNS (HS), Argyll and Bute. Adm. free. Bronze Age and Neolithic cairns

NEW ABBEY CORN MILL (HS), nr Dumfries. Tel: 01387-850260. Closed Sun. mornings, Thurs. afternoons and Fri. in winter. Adm. £2.80. Water-powered mill

PALACE OF HOLYROODHOUSE, Edinburgh. Tel: 0131-556 7371. Closed when The Queen is in residence. Adm. £5.50. The Queen's official Scottish residence. Main part of the palace built 1671-9

RING OF BROGAR (HS), Orkney. Adm. free. Neolithic circle of upright stones with an enclosing ditch

RUTHWELL CROSS (HS), Dumfries and Galloway. Adm. free. Seventh-century Anglian cross

ST ANDREWS CASTLE AND CATHEDRAL (HS), Fife. Tel: 01334-477196 (castle); 01334-472563 (cathedral). Adm. £2.50 (castle); £1.80 (cathedral); £3.50 (combined ticket). Ruins of 13th-century castle and remains of the largest cathedral in Scotland

*SCONE PALACE, Perth. Tel: 01738-552300. Adm. £5.40. House built 1802-13 on the site of a medieval palace

SKARA BRAE (HS), Orkney. Tel: 01856-841815. Adm. £3.20 (winter); £4.00 (summer, joint ticket with Skaill House). Stone-Age village near 17th-century house

*SMAILHOLM TOWER (HS), Scottish Borders. Tel: 01573-460365. Adm. £1.80. Well-preserved tower-house

STIRLING CASTLE (HS). Tel: 01786-450000. Adm. £5.00. Great Hall and gatehouse of James IV, palace of James V, Chapel Royal remodelled by James VI

TANTALLON CASTLE (HS), E. Lothian. Tel: 01620-892727. Closed Sun. mornings, Thurs. afternoons and Fri. in winter. Adm. £2.50. Fortification with earthwork defences and a 14th-century curtain wall with towers

*THREAVE CASTLE (HS), Dumfries and Galloway. Tel: 0411-223101. Adm. £1.80, including ferry trip. Late 14th-century tower on an island reached by boat

URQUHART CASTLE (HS), Loch Ness. Tel: 01456-450551. Adm. £3.80. Castle remains with well-preserved tower

NORTHERN IRELAND

DE Property in the care of the Northern Ireland Department of the Environment
NT National Trust property

CARRICKFERGUS CASTLE (DE), Co. Antrim. Tel: 01960-351273. Closed Sun. mornings. Adm. £2.70. Castle begun in 1180 and garrisoned until 1928

†CASTLE COOLE (NT), Enniskillen. Tel: 01365-322690. Closed Thurs., also Mon.-Fri. in April and Sept. (except Bank Holidays). Adm. house, £2.80; estate, £2.00 per car. An 18th-century mansion by Wyatt

†CASTLE WARD (NT), Co. Down. Tel: 01396-881204. Closed Thurs.; also closed Mon.-Fri. in April, Sept. and Oct.; grounds open all year. Adm. £2.60. An 18th-century house with Classical and Gothic facades

*DEVENISH ISLAND (DE), Co. Fermanagh. Closed Sun. mornings and Mon. Adm. £2.25. Island monastery founded in the 6th century by St Molaise

DOWNHILL CASTLE (NT), Co. Londonderry. Tel: 01265-848728. Adm. free. Ruins of palatial house in landscaped estate including Mussenden Temple. Opening times of temple vary

DUNLUCE CASTLE (DE), Co. Antrim. Tel: 012657-31938. Closed Sun. morning (except July and Aug.). Adm. £1.50. Ruins of MacDonnells' 16th-century stronghold

†FLORENCE COURT (NT), Co. Fermanagh. Tel: 01365-348249. Closed Tues.; also closed Mon.-Fri. (except Bank Holidays) in April and Sept.; grounds open all year. Adm. £2.80; estate £2.00 per car. Mid 18th-century house with rococo plasterwork

*GREY ABBEY (DE), Co. Down. Tel: 01247-788585. Closed Sun. morning and Mon. Adm £1.00. Substantial remains of a Cistercian abbey founded in 1193

HILLSBOROUGH FORT (DE), Co. Down. Closed Sun. mornings and Mon. Adm. free. Built in 1650

†MOUNT STEWART (NT), Co. Down. Tel: 012477-88387. Closed Tues.; also closed Mon.-Fri. in April and Oct. Adm. £3.50; garden only, £3.00. An 18th-century house, childhood home of Lord Castlereagh

NENDRUM MONASTERY (DE), Mahee Island, Co. Down. Closed Sun. mornings and Mon.; also Mon.-Fri. in winter. Adm. 75p. Founded in the 5th century by St Machaoi

*TULLY CASTLE (DE), Co. Fermanagh. Closed Sun. mornings and Mon. Adm. £1.00. Fortified house and bawn built in 1613

*WHITE ISLAND (DE), Co. Fermanagh. Closed Sun. mornings and Mon. Adm. £2.25. Tenth-century monastery and 12th-century church. Access by ferry

Museums and Galleries

There are more than 2,500 museums and galleries in the United Kingdom. Over 1,700 are registered with the Museums and Galleries Commission (*see* page 320), which indicates that they have an appropriate constitution, are soundly financed, have adequate collection management standards and public services, and have access to professional curatorial advice. Museums must achieve full or provisional registration status in order to be eligible for grants from the Museums and Galleries Commission and from Area Museums Councils. Over 700 of the registered museums are run by a local authority.

The national museums and galleries receive direct government grant-in-aid. These are: British Museum; Imperial War Museum; National Army Museum; National Galleries of Scotland; National Gallery; National Maritime Museum; National Museums and Galleries on Merseyside; National Museum of Wales; National Museums of Scotland; National Portrait Gallery; Natural History Museum; RAF Museum; Royal Armouries; Science Museum; Tate Gallery; Ulster Folk and Transport Museum; Ulster Museum; Victoria and Albert Museum; Wallace Collection. An online art museum (http://www.24hourmuseum.org.uk) has also been awarded national collection status.

Local authority museums are funded by the local authority and may also receive grants from the Museums and Galleries Commission. Independent museums and galleries mainly rely on their own resources but are also eligible for grants from the Museums and Galleries Commission.

The Museums and Galleries Commission has identified 26 non-national museum bodies which have pre-eminent collections of more than local or regional importance. Some of those designated are museum services with a wide variety of collections; others are small and more focused in a particular field. Ten Area Museum Councils in the UK, which are independent charities that receive an annual grant from the Museums and Galleries Commission, give advice and support to the museums in their area and may offer improvement grants. They also circulate exhibitions and assist with training and marketing.

OPENING TO THE PUBLIC

The following is a selection of the museums and art galleries in the United Kingdom. The admission charges given are the standard charges for 1999–2000, where a charge is made; many museums have concessionary rates for children, etc. Where no charge is shown, admission is free. Opening hours vary. Most museums are closed on Christmas Eve, Christmas Day, Boxing Day and New Year's Day; many are closed on Good Friday, and some are closed on May Day Bank Holiday. Some smaller museums close at lunchtimes. Information about a specific museum or gallery should be checked by telephone.

* Local authority museum/gallery
† Museum/gallery contains a collection designated pre-eminent

ENGLAND

BARNARD CASTLE, Co. Durham – *†*The Bowes Museum*, Westwick Road. Tel: 01833-690606. Adm. £3.90. European art from the late medieval period to the 19th century; music and costume galleries; English period rooms from Elizabeth I to Victoria; local archaeology

BATH – *American Museum in Britain*, Claverton Manor. Tel: 01225-460503. Closed mornings and Mon. (except Bank Holidays); also closed in winter (except on application). Adm. £5.00 (including house); grounds and galleries only, £2.50. American decorative arts from the 17th to 19th century

Museum of Costume, Bennett Street. Tel: 01225-477752. Adm. £3.90. Fashion from the 16th century to the present day

Roman Baths Museum, Abbey Church Yard. Tel: 01225-477774. Adm. (excluding 18th-century Pump Room, which is free) £6.70. Museum adjoins the remains of a Roman baths and temple complex

Victoria Art Gallery, Bridge Street. Tel: 01225-477772. Closed Bank Holidays. European Old Masters and British art since the 18th century

BEAMISH, Co. Durham – *†*Beamish, The North of England Open Air Museum*. Tel: 01207-231811. Closed Mon. and Fri. in winter. Adm. charge. Recreated northern town *c.*1900, with rebuilt and furnished local buildings, colliery village, farm, railway station, tramway, Pockerley Manor and horse-yard (set *c.*1800)

BEAULIEU, Hants – †*National Motor Museum.* Tel: 01590-612345. Adm. charge. Displays of over 250 vehicles dating from 1895 to the present day

BIRMINGHAM – *†*Aston Hall*, Trinity Road. Tel: 0121-327 0062. Closed mornings and in winter. Jacobean house containing paintings, furniture and tapestries from 17th to 19th century

*†*Barber Institute of Fine Arts*, off Edgbaston Park Road. Tel: 0121-472 0962. Closed Sun. morning. Fine arts, including Old Masters

Birmingham Nature Centre, Edgbaston. Tel: 0121-472 7775. Closed Mon.-Fri. in winter. Adm. £1.50. Indoor and outdoor enclosures displaying wildlife, especially British and European

*†*City Museum and Art Gallery*, Chamberlain Square. Tel: 0121-303 2834. Closed Sun. mornings. Adm. free (except Gas Hall). Includes notable collection of Pre-Raphaelites

*†*Museum of the Jewellery Quarter*, Vyse Street, Hockley. Tel: 0121-554 3598. Closed Sun. Adm. £2.50. Built around a real jewellery workshop

*†*Soho House*, Soho Avenue. Tel: 0121-554 9122. Closed Sun. mornings and Mon. (except Bank Holidays). Adm. £2.50. Eighteenth-century home of industrialist Matthew Boulton

BOVINGTON CAMP, Dorset – †*Tank Museum.* Tel: 01929-405096. Adm. £6.50. Collection of 300 tanks from the earliest days of tank warfare to the present

BRADFORD – *Cartwright Hall Art Gallery*, Lister Park. Tel: 01274-493313. Closed Sun. mornings and Mon. (except Bank Holidays). British 19th- and 20th-century fine art

Industrial Museum and Horses at Work, Moorside Road. Tel: 01274-631756. Closed Sun. mornings and Mon. (except Bank Holidays). Engineering, textiles, transport and social history exhibits, including recreated back-to-back cottages, shire horses and horse tram-rides

National Museum of Photography, Film and Television. Tel: 01274-202030. Photography, film and television interactive exhibits. Features the UK's first IMAX cinema and the only public Cinerama screen in the world

BRIGHTON – *†Booth Museum of Natural History,* Dyke Road. Tel: 01273-292777. Closed Sun. mornings and Thurs. Zoology, botany and geology collections; British birds in recreated habitats

†Brighton Museum and Art Gallery, Church Street. Tel: 01273-290900. Closed Sun. mornings and Wed. Includes fine art and design, fashion, non-Western art, Brighton history

N.B. Rotational closure of galleries until 2001.

BRISTOL – *Arnolfini Gallery,* Narrow Quay. Tel: 0117-929 9191. Adm. free; charge for cinema and events. Contemporary visual arts, dance, performance, music, talks and workshops

†Blaise Castle House Museum, Henbury. Tel: 0117-950 6789. Closed Thurs. and Fri.; also closed 1 Nov. to 31 Mar. Agricultural and social history collections in an 18th-century mansion

†Bristol Industrial Museum, Prince Street. Tel: 0117-925 1470. Closed Thurs. and Fri.; closed Mon.-Fri. in winter. Industrial, maritime and transport collections

†City Museum and Art Gallery, Queen's Road. Tel: 0117-922 3571. Includes fine and decorative art, oriental art, Egyptology and Bristol ceramics and paintings

CAMBRIDGE – *Duxford Airfield,* Duxford. Tel: 01223-835000. Adm. £7.20. Displays of military and civil aircraft, tanks, guns and naval exhibits

†*Fitzwilliam Museum,* Trumpington Street. Tel: 01223-332900. Closed Mon. (except August Bank Holidays) and Sun. mornings. Antiquities, fine and applied arts, clocks, ceramics, manuscripts, furniture, sculpture, coins and medals, temporary exhibitions

† *Sedgwick Museum of Geology,* Downing Street. Tel: 01223-333456. Closed Sat. afternoons and Sun. Extensive geological collection

†*University Museum of Archaeology and Anthropology,* Downing Street. Tel: 01223-333516. Closed Sun., Mon. and mornings. Archaeology and anthropology from all parts of the world

†*University Museum of Zoology,* Downing Street. Tel: 01223-336650. Closed Sat., Sun. and mornings. Extensive zoological collection

†*Whipple Museum of the History of Science,* Free School Lane. Tel: 01223-330906. Closed mornings and weekends. Scientific instruments from the 14th century to the present day

CARLISLE – *Tullie House Museum and Art Gallery,* Castle Street. Tel: 01228-534781. Adm. £3.75 to Border galleries only; ground floor, Old Tullie House and Jacobean galleries, adm. free. Prehistoric archaeology, Hadrian's Wall, Viking and medieval Cumbria, and the social history of Carlisle; also British 19th- and 20th-century art and English porcelain

CHATHAM – *World Naval Base.* Tel: 01634-823800. Closed Mon., Tues., Thurs. and Fri. in Feb., Mar. and Nov., also closed Dec.-Jan. Adm. charge. Maritime attractions including HMS *Cavalier,* the UK's last World War II destroyer

†*Royal Engineers Museum,* Brompton Barracks. Tel: 01634-406397. Closed Fri. Adm. £3.00. Regimental history, ethnography, decorative art and photography

CHELTENHAM – *†Art Gallery and Museum,* Clarence Street. Tel: 01242-237431. Closed Sun. Paintings, arts and crafts

CHESTER – *Grosvenor Museum,* Grosvenor Street. Tel: 01244-321616. Closed Sun. mornings. Roman collections, natural history, art, Chester silver, local history and costume

CHICHESTER – †*Weald and Downland Open Air Museum,* Singleton. Tel: 01243-811348. Closed Mon., Tues., Thurs., Fri. in winter. Adm. £5.20. Rebuilt vernacular buildings from south-east England; includes medieval houses, agricultural and rural craft buildings and a working watermill

COLCHESTER – *†Colchester Castle Museum,* Castle Park. Tel: 01206-282931. Closed Sun. in winter, Sun. mornings in summer. Adm. £3.70. Largest Norman keep in Europe standing on foundations of roman Temple of Claudius; tours of the Roman vaults, castle walls and chapel with medieval and prison displays

COVENTRY – *Herbert Art Gallery and Museum,* Jordan Well. Tel: 01203-832381. Closed Sun. mornings. Local history, archaeology and industry, and fine and decorative art

†Museum of British Road Transport, Hales Street. Tel: 01203-832425. Hundreds of motor vehicles and bicycles

CRICH, nr Matlock, Derbys – †*National Tramway Museum.* Tel: 01773-852565. Closed Mon. to Sat. in winter. Adm. £6.50 summer, £3.00 winter. Open-air working museum with tram rides

DERBY – *Derby Museum and Art Gallery,* The Strand. Tel: 01332-716659. Closed Bank Holiday and Sun. mornings. Includes paintings by Joseph Wright of Derby and Derby porcelain

Industrial Museum, off Full Street. Tel: 01332-255308. Closed Bank Holiday and Sun. mornings. Rolls-Royce aero engine collection and a railway engineering gallery

DEVIZES – †*Devizes Museum,* Long Street. Tel: 01380-727369. Closed Sun. Adm. £2.00. Natural and local history, art gallery, archaeological finds from Bronze Age, Iron Age, Roman and Saxon sites

DORCHESTER – *Dorset County Museum,* High West Street. Tel: 01305-262735. Closed Sun. (except July and Aug.). Adm. charge. Includes a collection of Thomas Hardy's manuscripts, books, notebooks and drawings

ELLESMERE PORT – †*Boat Museum,* South Pier Road. Tel: 0151-355 5017. Closed Thurs. and Fri. in winter. Adm. £5.50. Craft and boating history

EXETER – *†Royal Albert Memorial Museum,* Queen Street. Tel: 01392-265858. Closed Sun. Natural history, archaeology, worldwide fine and decorative art including Exeter silver

GATESHEAD – *†Shipley Art Gallery,* Prince Consort Road. Tel: 0191-477 1495. Closed Sun. mornings. Contemporary crafts

GAYDON, Warwick – *British Motor Industry Heritage Trust,* Heritage Motor Centre, Banbury Road. Tel: 01926-641188. Adm. charge. History of British motor industry from 1895 to present; classic vehicles; engineering gallery; Corgi and Lucas collections

GLOUCESTER, – †*National Waterways Museum,* Llanthony Warehouse, The Docks. Tel: 01452-318054. Adm. £4.75. Two-hundred-year history of Britain's canals and inland waterways

GOSPORT, Hants – *Royal Navy Submarine Museum,* Haslar Jetty Road. Tel: 01705-529217. Adm. £3.75. Underwater warfare, including the submarine *Alliance;* historical and nuclear galleries; and first Royal Navy submarine

GRASMERE, Cumbria – †*Dove Cottage* and the *Wordsworth Museum* (*see* page 586)

HALIFAX – *Eureka! The Museum for Children*, Discovery Road. Tel: 01426-983191. Adm. £5.75 (over age 12), £4.75 (ages 3-12), free (under age 3). Hands-on museum designed for children up to age 12

HULL – *Ferens Art Gallery*, Queen Victoria Square. Tel: 01482-613902. Closed Sun. mornings. European art, especially Dutch 17th-century paintings, British portraits from 17th to 20th century, and marine paintings

Town Docks Museum, Queen Victoria Square. Tel: 01482-613902. Closed Sun. mornings. Whaling, fishing and navigation exhibits

HUNTINGDON – *Cromwell Museum*, Grammar School Walk. Tel: 01480-375830. Closed Mon., and mornings (except Sat.) in winter. Portraits and memorabilia relating to Oliver Cromwell

IPSWICH – *Christchurch Mansion and Wolsey Art Gallery*, Christchurch Park. Tel: 01473-253246. Closed Sun. mornings and Mon. (except Bank Holidays). Tudor house with paintings by Gainsborough, Constable and other Suffolk artists; furniture and 18th-century ceramics. Art gallery for temporary exhibitions

LEEDS – †*City Art Gallery*, The Headrow. Tel: 0113-247 8248. Closed Sun. mornings and Bank Holidays. British and European paintings including English watercolours, modern sculpture, Henry Moore gallery, print room

Leeds Industrial Museum at Armley Mills, Canal Road, Armley. Tel: 0113-263 7861. Closed Sun. mornings and Mon.; also closed Jan.-Feb.Adm. £2.00. Largest woollen mill in world

†Lotherton Hall, Aberford. Tel: 0113-281 3259. Closed Sun. mornings and Mon.; also closed Jan.-Feb. Adm. £2.00. Costume and oriental collections in furnished Edwardian house; deer park and bird garden

Royal Armouries Museum, Armouries Drive. Tel: 0990-106666. Adm. £7.95. National collection of arms and armour from BC to present; demonstrations of foot combat in museum's five galleries; falconry and mounted combat in the tiltyard

†Temple Newsam House. Tel: 0113-264 7321. Closed Sun. mornings and Mon.; also closed Jan.-Feb. Adm. £2.00. Old Masters and 17th- and 18th-century decorative art in furnished Jacobean/Tudor house

LEICESTER – *Jewry Wall Museum*, St Nicholas Circle. Tel: 0116-247 3021. Closed Sun. mornings. Archaeology, Roman Jewry Wall and baths, and mosaics

New Walk Museum and Art Gallery, New Walk. Tel: 0116-255 4100. Closed Sun. mornings. Natural history, geology, ancient Egypt gallery, European art and decorative arts

Snibston Discovery Park, Coalville. Tel: 01530-510851. Adm. £4.75. Open-air science and industry museum on site of a coal mine; country park with nature trail

LINCOLN – *Museum of Lincolnshire Life*, Burton Road. Tel: 01522-528448. Closed Sun. mornings in winter. Adm. charge. Social history and agricultural collection and Royal Lincs Regiment memorabilia

Usher Gallery, Lindum Road. Tel: 01522-527980. Closed Sun. mornings. Adm. £2.00, free on Fri. Watches, miniatures, porcelain, silver; collection of Peter de Wint works; Lincolnshire topography; Tennyson memorabilia

LIVERPOOL – *Lady Lever Art Gallery*, Wirral. Tel: 0151-478 4136. Closed Sun. mornings. Adm. £3.00 for an 'Eight Pass' which is valid for 12 months and for all National Museums and Galleries on Merseyside. Paintings, furniture and porcelain

Liverpool Museum, William Brown Street. Tel: 0151-478 4399. Closed Sun. mornings. Adm. 'Eight Pass' as above. Includes Egyptian mummies, weapons and classical sculpture; planetarium, aquarium, vivarium and natural history centre

Merseyside Maritime Museum, Albert Dock. Tel: 0151-478 4499. Adm. 'Eight Pass' as above. Floating exhibits, working displays and craft demonstrations; incorporates HM Customs and Excise National Museum

Museum of Liverpool Life, Mann Island. Tel: 0151-478 4080. Adm. 'Eight Pass' as above. The history of Liverpool

Sudley House, Mossley Hill Road. Tel: 0151-724 3245. Closed Sun. mornings. Adm. 'Eight Pass' as above. Late 18th- and 19th-century British paintings in former shipowner's home

Tate Gallery Liverpool, Albert Dock. Tel: 0151-709 3223. Twentieth-century painting and sculpture

Walker Art Gallery, William Brown Street. Tel: 0151-478 4399. Closed Sun. mornings. Adm. 'Eight Pass' as above. Paintings from the 14th to 20th century

LONDON: GALLERIES – *Barbican Art Gallery*, Barbican Centre, EC2. Tel: 0171-382 7105. Adm. £5.00 or £6.00 according to exhibition. Temporary exhibitions

†*Courtauld Gallery*, Somerset House, Strand, WC2. Tel: 0171-848 2526. Closed Sun. mornings. Adm. £4.00. The University of London galleries

†*Dulwich Picture Gallery*, College Road, SE21. Tel: 0181-693 5254. Closed for refurbishment until May 2000. Closed Mon. (except Bank Holidays). Adm. £3.00 (free on Fri.). Built by Sir John Soane to house 17th- and 18th-century paintings

Hayward Gallery, Belvedere Road, SE1. Tel: 0171-928 3144. Adm. £6.00. Temporary exhibitions

National Gallery, Trafalgar Square, WC2. Tel: 0171-839 3321. Western painting from the 13th to 20th century; early Renaissance collection in the Sainsbury wing

National Portrait Gallery, St Martin's Place, WC2. Tel: 0171-306 0055. Closed Sun. mornings and some Bank Holidays. Adm. free (except for some special exhibitions). Portraits of eminent people in British history

Percival David Foundation of Chinese Art, Gordon Square, WC1. Tel: 0171-387 3909. Closed weekends and Bank Holidays. Adm. free (charge for use of reference library). Chinese ceramics from tenth to 18th century

Photographers' Gallery, Great Newport Street, WC2. Tel: 0171-831 1772. Temporary exhibitions

The Queen's Gallery, Buckingham Palace, SW1. Tel: 0171-839 1377. Adm. £4.00. Closed from Oct. 1999 to Feb. 2002. Art from the Royal Collection

Royal Academy of Arts, Piccadilly, W1. Tel: 0171-300 8000. Adm. charge. British art since 1750 and temporary exhibitions; annual Summer Exhibition

Saatchi Gallery, Boundary Road, NW8. Tel: 0171-624 8299. Closed mornings and Mon.-Wed. Adm. £4.00. Contemporary art including paintings, photographs, sculpture and installations

Serpentine Gallery, Kensington Gardens, W2. Tel: 0171-298 1515. Temporary exhibitions of British and international contemporary art

Tate Gallery, Millbank, SW1. Tel: 0171-887 8000. Adm. free (charge for special exhibitions). British painting and 20th-century painting and sculpture. In 2000 the Millbank site will become the Tate Gallery of British Art, and the Tate Gallery of Modern Art will open on the South Bank, London SE1

Wallace Collection, Manchester Square, W1. Tel: 0171-935 0687. Closed Sun. mornings. Paintings and drawings, French 18th-century furniture, armour, porcelain, clocks and sculpture

Whitechapel Art Gallery, Whitechapel High Street, E1.
Tel: 0171-522 7878. Closed Mon. Adm. free to most
exhibitions. Temporary exhibitions of modern art
LONDON: MUSEUMS – *Bank of England Museum*,
Threadneedle Street, EC2 (entrance from Bartholomew
Lane). Tel: 0171-601 5545. Closed weekends and Bank
Holidays. History of the Bank since 1694
Bethnal Green Museum of Childhood, Cambridge Heath
Road, E2. Tel: 0181-983 5200. Closed Fri. Toys, games
and exhibits relating to the social history of childhood
British Museum, Great Russell Street, WC1. Tel: 0171-
636 1555. Closed Sun. mornings. Antiquities, coins,
medals, prints and drawings
Cabinet War Rooms, King Charles Street, SW1. Tel: 0171-
930 6961. Adm. £4.80. Underground rooms used by
Churchill and the Government during the Second
World War
Commonwealth Experience, Kensington High Street, W8.
Tel: 0171-603 4535. Exhibitions on Commonwealth
nations, visual arts and crafts; Interactive World
Cutty Sark, Greenwich, SE10. Tel: 0181-858 3445. Adm.
£3.50. Restored and rerigged tea clipper with exhibits
on board.
Design Museum, Shad Thames, SE1. Tel: 0171-378 6055.
Adm. £5.50. The development of design and the mass-
production of consumer objects
Geffrye Museum, Kingsland Road, E2. Tel: 0171-739
9893. Closed Mon.; also Sun. and Bank Holiday
mornings. English urban domestic interiors from 1600
to present day; also paintings, furniture, decorative arts,
walled herb garden and period garden rooms
HMS Belfast, Morgans Lane, Tooley Street, SE1. Tel:
0171-940 6300. Adm £4.70. Life on a warship,
illustrated on World War II warship
†*Horniman Museum and Gardens*, London Road, SE23. Tel:
0181-699 1872. Museum of ethnography, musical
instruments, natural history and aquarium; reference
library; sunken, water and flower gardens
Imperial War Museum, Lambeth Road, SE1. Tel: 0171-416
5000. Reference departments closed Sat. (except by
appointment) and Sun. Adm. £5.20. All aspects of the
two world wars and other military operations involving
Britain and the Commonwealth since 1914
†*Jewish Museum, Camden Town*, Albert Street, NW1. Tel:
0171-284 1997. Closed Fri., Sat., public and Jewish
holidays. Adm. £3.00. Jewish life, history and religion
† *Jewish Museum, Finchley*, East End Road, N3. Tel: 0181-
349 1143. Closed Fri., Sat., public and Jewish holidays.
Adm. £2.00. Jewish life in London and Holocaust
education
†*London Transport Museum*, Covent Garden, WC2. Tel:
0171-379 6344. Adm. £5.50. Vehicles, photographs and
graphic art relating to the history of transport in
London
MCC Museum, Lord's, NW8. Tel: 0171-289 1611. Open
match days (closed most Sun. mornings); also
conducted tours by appointment with Tours Manager.
Adm. charge. Cricket museum
Museum of Garden History, Lambeth Palace Road SE1.
Tel: 0171-401 8865. Closed Sat. and Dec.-Feb.
Exhibition of aspects of garden history and re-created
17th-century garden
†*Museum of London*, London Wall, EC2. Tel: 0171-600
3699. Adm. £5.00 (ticket valid for one year); free after
4.30 p.m. History of London from prehistoric times to
present day
National Army Museum, Royal Hospital Road, SW3. Tel:
0171-730 0717. Five-hundred-year history of the
British soldier; exhibits include model of the Battle of
Waterloo and *Army for Today* gallery

National Maritime Museum, Greenwich, SE10. Tel: 0181-
858 4422. Reference library closed Sat. (except by
appointment) and Sun. Adm. £7.50. Comprises the
main building, the Royal Observatory and the Queen's
House (*see page* 586). Maritime history of Britain;
collections include globes, clocks, telescopes and
paintings
Natural History Museum, Cromwell Road, SW7. Tel:
0171-938 9123. Adm. £6.50. Natural history collections
†*Petrie Museum of Egyptian Archaeology*, University College
London. Tel: 0171-504 2884. Closed Sun., Mon. and
mornings. Egyptian archaeology collection
Royal Air Force Museum, Colindale, NW9. Tel: 0181-205
2266. Adm. £6.50. National museum of aviation with
over 70 full-size aircraft; aviation from before the
Wright brothers to the present-day RAF; flight
simulator
Royal Mews, Buckingham Palace, SW1. Tel: 0171-839
1377. Open Mon.-Thurs. afternoons. Adm. £4.00.
Carriages, coaches, stables and horses
Science Museum, Exhibition Road, SW7. Tel: 0171-942
4454. Adm. £6.50. Science, technology, industry and
medicine collections
Shakespeare Globe Exhibition, Bankside, SE1. Tel: 0171-902
1500. Adm. £6.00. Recreation of Elizabethan theatre
using 16th-century techniques
Sherlock Holmes Museum, Baker Street, NW1. Tel: 0171-
935 8866. Adm. £5.00. Recreated rooms of the fictional
detective
Sir John Soane's Museum, Lincoln's Inn Fields, WC2. Tel:
0171-430 0175. Closed Sun. and Mon. Adm. free
(groups by appointment only). Art and antiques
Theatre Museum, Russell Street, WC2. Tel: 0171-836
2330. Closed Mon. Adm. £4.50. History of the
performing arts
Tower Bridge Experience, SE1. Tel: 0171-378 1928. Adm.
£6.15. History of the bridge and display of Victorian
steam machinery; panoramic views from walkways
Victoria and Albert Museum, Cromwell Road, SW7. Tel:
0171-938 8500. Adm. £5.00. Includes National Art
Library and Print Room (closed Sun. and Mon.). Fine
and applied art and design, including furniture, glass,
textiles, dress collections (British Galleries closed for
refurbishment)
Wellington Museum, Apsley House, W1 (*see* page 584)
Wimbledon Lawn Tennis Museum, Church Road, SW19.
Tel: 0181-946 6131. Closed Fri to Sun. before, middle
Sun. and Mon. following Championships. Adm. £4.00.
Tennis trophies, fashion and memorabilia; view of
Centre Court
MANCHESTER – *Gallery of Costume*, Rusholme. Tel: 0161-
224 5217. Exhibits from the 16th to 20th century
†*Manchester Museum*, Oxford Road. Tel: 0161-275 2634.
Closed Sun. Archaeology, archery, botany, Egyptology,
entomology, ethnography, geology, natural history,
numismatics, oriental and zoology collections
†*Museum of Science and Industry*, Castlefield. Tel: 0161-832
2244. Adm. £6.50. On site of world's oldest passenger
railway station; galleries relating to space, energy,
power, transport, aviation, textiles and social history;
interactive science centre
† *Pump House People's History Museum*, for *National Museum
of Labour History*, Left Bank. Tel: 0161-228 7212. Adm.
£1.00 (free on Fri.). Closed Mon. (except Bank
Holidays). Political and and working life history
†*Whitworth Art Gallery*, Oxford Road. Tel: 0161-275 7450.
Closed Sun. mornings. Watercolours, drawings, prints,
textiles, wallpapers and 20th-century British art
MONKWEARMOUTH – *†Monkwearmouth Station Museum*,
North Bridge Street. Tel: 0191-567 7075. Closed Sun.
mornings. Victorian train station

NEWCASTLE UPON TYNE – *†*Hancock Museum*, Barras Bridge. Tel: 0191-222 7418. Closed Sun. mornings. Adm. charge varies. Natural history
*†*Laing Art Gallery*, New Bridge Street. Tel: 0191-232 7734. Closed Sun. mornings. British and European art, ceramics, glass, silver, textiles and costume; *Art on Tyneside* display
*†*Newcastle Discovery Museum*, Blandford Square. Tel: 0191-232 6789. Closed Sun. mornings. Science and industry, local history, fashion and Tyneside's maritime history; *Turbinia* (first steam-driven vessel) gallery
NEWMARKET – *National Horseracing Museum*, High Street. Tel: 01638-667333. Closed Mon. (except July and Aug.) and Nov.-March. Adm. £3.50. The Essential Horse Millennium Exhibition, horseracing exhibits and tours of local trainers' yards and studs
NORTHAMPTON – *†*Central Museum and Art Gallery*, Guildhall Road. Tel: 01604-238548. Closed Sun. mornings. Boot and shoe collection
NORTH SHIELDS – †*Stephenson Railway Museum*, Middle Engine Lane. Tel: 0191-200 7144. Closed Mon. to Fri. Locomotive engines and rolling stock
NOTTINGHAM – *Brewhouse Yard Museum*, Castle Boulevard. Tel: 0115-915 3600. Adm. free (except weekends and Bank Holidays). Daily life from the 17th to 20th century
Castle Museum and Art Gallery. Tel: 0115-915 3700. Adm. free (except weekends and Bank Holidays). Paintings, ceramics, silver and glass; history of Nottingham
Industrial Museum, Wollaton Park. Tel: 0115-915 3910. Adm. free (except weekends and Bank Holidays). Lacemaking machinery, steam engines and transport exhibits
Museum of Costume and Textiles, Castle Gate. Tel: 0115-915 3500. Closed Mon. and Tues. Costume displays from 1790 to the mid-20th century in period rooms
Natural History Museum, Wollaton Park. Tel: 0115-915 3900. Adm. free (except weekends and Bank Holidays). Local natural history and wildlife dioramas
OXFORD – †*Ashmolean Museum*, Beaumont Street. Tel: 01865-278000. Closed Mon. (except Bank Holidays) and Sun. mornings. European and Oriental fine and applied arts, archaeology, Egyptology and numismatics
Museum of Modern Art, Pembroke Street. Tel: 01865-722733. Closed Mon. Adm. £2.50. Temporary exhibitions
†*Museum of the History of Science*, Broad Street. Tel: 01865-277280. Closed mornings and Sun.-Mon. Displays include early scientific instruments, chemical apparatus, clocks and watches
†*Oxford University Museum of Natural History*, Parks Road. Tel: 01865-272950. Closed mornings (except for school parties by appointment). Entomology, geology, mineralogy and zoology
†*Pitt Rivers Museum*, South Parks Road. Tel: 01865-270927. Closed mornings (except by appointment) and Sun. Ethnographic and archaeological artefacts. Check for periods of closure in 1999-2000
PLYMOUTH – *†*City Museum and Art Gallery*, Drake Circus. Tel: 01752-304774. Closed Mon. (except Bank Holidays) and Sun. Local and natural history, ceramics, silver, Old Masters, temporary exhibitions
The Dome, The Hoe. Tel: 01752-603300. Adm. £3.95. Maritime history museum

PORTSMOUTH – *Charles Dickens Birthplace Museum*, Old Commercial Road. Tel: 01705-827261. Closed 1 Oct. to 29 Nov. and 19 Dec. to 1 April, except 7 Feb. Adm. £2.00. Dickens memorabilia
D-Day Museum, Clarence Esplanade. Tel: 01705-827261. Closed Mon. morning Nov. to March. Adm. 4.75 (free Monday afternoon Nov. to March). Includes the Overlord Embroidery
Flagship Portsmouth, HM Naval Base. Incorporates the Royal Naval Museum (tel: 01705-727562), HMS *Victory* (tel: 01705-822034), HMS *Warrior* (tel: 01705-291379), the †*Mary Rose* (tel: 01705-750521) and the *Dockyard Museum*. Adm. charge to each (combined ticket available). History of the Royal Navy and of the dockyard and the trades in it
PRESTON – *Harris Museum and Art Gallery*, Market Square. Tel: 01772-258248. Closed Sun. and Bank Holidays. British art since the 18th century, ceramics, glass, costume and local history; also contemporary exhibitions
READING – †*Rural History Museum*, University of Reading. Tel: 0118-931 8660. Closed Sun. and Mon. Adm. £1.00. History of farming and the countryside over the last 200 years
ST ALBANS – *Verulamium Museum*, St Michael's. Tel: 01727-866100. Closed Sun. mornings. Adm. £3.00. Iron Age and Roman Verulamium, including wall plasters, jewellery, mosaics and room reconstructions
ST IVES, Cornwall – *Tate Gallery St Ives*, Porthmeor Beach. Tel: 01736-796226. Opening times vary seasonally; closed Mon. Oct.-March. Adm. £3.50. Painting and sculpture by artists associated with St Ives
SALISBURY – †*Salisbury and South Wiltshire Museum*, The Close. Tel: 01722-332151. Closed Sun., except July and Aug. Archaeology collection
SHEFFIELD – *City Museum and Mappin Art Gallery*, Weston Park. Tel: 0114-276 8588. Closed Mon. Includes applied arts, natural history, Bronze Age archaeology and ethnography, 19th- and 20th-century art
Graves Art Gallery, Surrey Street. Tel: 0114-273 5158. Closed Sun. Twentieth-century British art, Grice Collection of Chinese ivories
Kelham Island Industrial Museum, off Alma Street. Tel: 0114-272 2106. Closed Fri. and Sat. Adm. £3.50. Local industrial and social history
Ruskin Gallery and Ruskin Craft Gallery, Norfolk Street. Tel: 0114-273 5299/203 9416. Closed Sun.
SOUTHAMPTON – *†*City Art Gallery*, Civic Centre. Tel: 01703-832277. Fine art, especially 20th-century British
*†*Maritime Museum*, Town Quay. Tel: 01703-223941. Southampton maritime history
*†*Museum of Archaeology*, Town Quay. Tel: 01703-635904. Roman, Saxon and medieval archaeology
*†*Tudor House Museum and Garden*, Bugle Street. Tel: 01703-332513. Restored 16th century garden; social history exhibitions
All of the above are closed Sun. mornings and Mon.
SOUTH SHIELDS – *†*Arbeia Roman Fort*, Baring Street. Tel: 0191-456 6612. Closed Sun. in winter, Sun. mornings in summer. Excavated ruins
*†*South Shields Museum and Art Gallery*, Ocean Road. Tel: 0191-456 8740. Closed Sun. in winter, Sun. mornings in summer. South Tyneside history, including reconstructed street
STOKE-ON-TRENT – *Etruria Industrial Museum*, Etruria. Tel: 01782-233144. Closed Mon. and Tues. Adm. charge. Britain's sole surviving steam-powered potter's mill

Gladstone Pottery Museum, Longton. Tel: 01782-319232. Adm. charge. A working Victorian pottery.

*†*Potteries Museum and Art Gallery*, Hanley. Tel: 01782-232323. Closed Sun. mornings. Pottery, china and porcelain collections and a Mark XVI Spitfire. Pottery factory tours are available by arrangement Mon.-Fri., except during factory holidays, at the following: *Royal Doulton*, Burslem; *Spode*, Stoke; *Wedgwood*, Barlaston; *W. Moorcroft*, Cobridge; *H & R Johnson Tiles*, Tunstall; *Staffordshire Enamels*, Longton; *Royale Stratford China*, Fenton

STYAL, Cheshire – *Quarry Bank Mill*. Tel: 01625-527468. Closed Mon. in winter. Adm. £5.80. Working mill illustrating history of cotton industry; costumed guides at restored Apprentice House

SUNDERLAND – *†*Sunderland Art Gallery*, Borough Road. Tel: 0191-565 0723. Closed Sun. mornings. Fine and decorative art

WASHINGTON – †*Washington 'F' Pit Museum*, Albany Way. Tel: 0191-565 0723. Open Bank Holiday weekends only. Colliery-related collection

TELFORD – *†*Ironbridge Gorge Museums*. Tel: 01952-432166. Check opening times Nov. to March. Adm. charge £9.50 for all nine museums (ticket valid until all sites have been visited). Includes first iron bridge; Blists Hill (late Victorian working town); Museum of Iron; Jackfield Tile Museum; Coalport China Museum; Tar Tunnel; Broseley Pipeworks

TRING, Herts – *Tring Zoological Museum*, Akeman Street. Tel: 01442-824181. Closed Sun. mornings. Adm. £3.00. Display of more than 4,000 animal species

WAKEFIELD – *Yorkshire Sculpture Park*, West Bretton. Tel: 01924-830302. Open-air sculpture gallery including works by Moore, Hepworth, Frink and others in 300 acres of parkland

WORCESTER – *City Museum and Art Gallery*, Foregate Street. Tel: 01905-25371. Closed Thurs. and Sun. Includes a military museum, River Severn Gallery and changing art exhibitions
Museum of Worcester Porcelain and Royal Worcester Visitor Centre, Severn Street. Tel: 01905-23221. Factory tours

WROUGHTON, nr Swindon, Wilts – *Science Museum*, Wroughton Airfield. Tel: 01793-814466. Adm. charge. Aircraft displays and some of the Science Museum's transport and agricultural collection

YEOVIL, Somerset – *Fleet Air Arm Museum*, Royal Naval Air Station, Yeovilton. Tel: 01935-840565. Adm. £7.00. History of naval aviation; historic aircraft, including Concorde 002
Montacute House, Montacute (*see* page 587). Elizabethan and Jacobean portraits from the National Portrait Gallery

YORK – *Beningbrough Hall*, Shipton-by-Beningbrough. Tel: 01904-470666. Closed Thurs. and Fri. (except Good Friday and July-Aug.); also closed in winter. Adm. £4.75. Portraits from the National Portrait Gallery
*†*Castle Museum*. Tel: 01904-653611. Adm. £4.95. Reconstructed streets; costume and military collections
*†*City Art Gallery*, Exhibition Square. Tel: 01904-551861. European and British painting spanning seven centuries; modern pottery
Jorvik Viking Centre, Coppergate. Tel: 01904-643211. Adm. £5.35. Reconstruction of Viking York
National Railway Museum, Leeman Road. Tel: 01904-621261. Adm. £5.90. Includes locomotives, rolling stock and carriages
*†*Yorkshire Museum*, Museum Gardens. Tel: 01904-629745. Adm. £3.75. Yorkshire life from Roman to medieval times; geology gallery

WALES

BODELWYDDAN, Denbighshire – *Bodelwyddan Castle*. Tel: 01745-584060. Closed Fri. Adm. £4.30; grounds only £1.00. Portraits from the National Portrait Gallery, furniture from the Victoria and Albert Museum and sculptures from the Royal Academy

CAERLEON – *Roman Legionary Museum*. Tel: 01633-423134. Closed Sun. mornings. Adm. £3.30 museum and fortress, £2.10 museum only. Material from the site of the Roman fortress of Isca and its suburbs

CARDIFF – *National Museum and Gallery Cardiff*, Cathays Park. Tel: 01222-397951. Closed Mon. (except Bank Holidays). Adm. £4.50. Includes natural sciences, archaeology and Impressionist paintings
Museum of Welsh Life, St Fagans. Tel: 01222-573500. Adm. £5.50. Open-air museum with re-erected buildings, agricultural equipment and costume

DRE-FACH FELINDRE, nr Llandysul – *Museum of the Welsh Woollen Industry*. Tel: 01559-370929. Closed Sun., and Sat. in winter. Adm. £2.60. Exhibitions, a working woollen mill and craft workshops

LLANBERIS, nr Caernarfon – *Welsh Slate Museum*. Tel: 01286-870630. Closed in winter (except by appointment). Adm. £3.50. Former slate quarry with original machinery and plant; slate crafts demonstrations

LLANDRINDOD WELLS – *National Cycle Exhibition*, Automobile Palace, Temple Street. Tel: 01597-825531. Adm £2.50. Over 200 bicycles on display, from 1818 to the present day

SWANSEA – *Glynn Vivian Art Gallery and Museum*, Alexandra Road. Tel: 01792-655006. Closed Mon. (except Bank Holidays). Paintings, ceramics, Swansea pottery and porcelain, clocks, glass and Welsh art
Swansea Maritime and Industrial Museum, Museum Square. Tel: 01792-650351. Closed Mon. (except Bank Holidays). Includes a working woollen mill and historic boats afloat
Swansea Museum, Victoria Road. Tel: 01792-653763. Closed Mon. (except Bank Holidays). Archaeology, social history, Swansea pottery

SCOTLAND

ABERDEEN – *Aberdeen Art Gallery*, Schoolhill. Tel: 01224-523700. Closed Sun. mornings. Art from the 18th to 20th century
Aberdeen Maritime Museum, Shiprow. Tel: 01224-337700. Adm. £3.50. Maritime history, including shipbuilding and North Sea oil

EDINBURGH – *Britannia*, Leith docks. Tel: 0131-555 5566. Former royal yacht with royal barge and royal family picture gallery. Tickets must be pre-booked
City Art Centre, Market Street. Tel: 0131-529 3993. Closed Sun. Late 19th- and 20th-century art and temporary exhibitions
Huntly House Museum, Canongate. Tel: 0131-529 4143. Closed Sun. Local history, silver, glass and Scottish pottery
Museum of Childhood, High Street. Tel: 0131-529 4142. Closed Sun. Toys, games, clothes and exhibits relating to the social history of childhood
Museum of Flight, East Fortune Airfield, nr North Berwick. Tel: 01620-880308. Adm. £3.00. Display of aircraft

Museum of Scotland, Chambers Street. Tel: 0131-247 4422. Closed Sun mornings. Adm. £3.00. Scottish history from prehistoric times to the present
National Gallery of Scotland, The Mound. Tel: 0131-624 6200. Closed Sun. mornings. Paintings, drawings and prints from the 16th to 20th century, and the national collection of Scottish art
*The People's Story, Canongate. Tel: 0131-529 4057. Closed Sun. Edinburgh life since the 18th century
Royal Museum of Scotland, Chambers Street. Tel: 0131-225 7534. Closed Sun. mornings. Adm. £3.00. Scottish and international collections from prehistoric times to the present
Scottish Agricultural Museum, Ingliston. Tel: 0131-333 2674. Closed Sat. and Sun. in winter. History of agriculture in Scotland
Scottish National Gallery of Modern Art, Belford Road. Tel: 0131-624 6200. Closed Sun. mornings. Twentieth-century painting, sculpture and graphic art
Scottish National Portrait Gallery, Queen Street. Tel: 0131-624 6200. Closed Sun. mornings. Portraits of eminent people in Scottish history, and the national collection of photography
*The Writers' Museum, Lawnmarket. Tel: 0131-529 4901. Closed Sun. Robert Louis Stevenson, Walter Scott and Robert Burns exhibits
FORT WILLIAM – *West Highland Museum,* Cameron Square. Tel: 01397-702169. Closed Sun. Adm. £2.00. Includes tartan collections and exhibits relating to 1745 uprising .
GLASGOW – **Burrell Collection,* Pollokshaws Road. Tel: 0141-649 7151. Paintings, textiles, furniture, ceramics, stained glass and silver from classical times to the 19th century
*Gallery of Modern Art, Queen Street. Tel: 0141-229 1996. Collection of contemporary Scottish and world art
*Glasgow Art Gallery and Museum, Kelvingrove. Tel: 0141-287 2699. Includes Old Masters, 19th-century French paintings and armour collection
Hunterian Art Gallery, Hillhead Street. Tel: 0141-330 5431. Closed Sun. Rennie Mackintosh and Whistler collections; Old Masters, Scottish paintings and modern paintings, sculpture and prints
*McLellan Galleries, Sauchiehall Street. Tel: 0141-331 1854. Adm. charge. Temporary exhibitions
*Museum of Transport, Bunhouse Road. Tel: 0141-287 2720. Includes a reproduction of a 1938 Glasgow street, cars since the 1930s, trams and a Glasgow subway station
*People's Palace Museum, Glasgow Green. Tel: 0141-554 0223. History of Glasgow since 1175
*St Mungo Museum of Religious Life and Art, Castle Street. Tel: 0141-553 2557. Explores universal themes through objects of all the main world religions

NORTHERN IRELAND

BELFAST – *Ulster Museum,* Botanic Gardens. Tel: 01232-383000. Closed weekend mornings. Irish antiquities, natural and local history, fine and applied arts
HOLYWOOD, Co. Down – *Ulster Folk and Transport Museum,* Cultra. Tel: 01232-428428. Closed Sun. mornings. Adm. £4.00. Open-air museum with original buildings from Ulster town and rural life *c.* 1900; indoor galleries including Irish rail and road transport and *Titanic* exhibitions
LONDONDERRY – *The Tower Museum,* Union Hall Place. Tel: 01504-372411. Closed Sun. and Mon. except July and Aug. Adm. £3.75. Tells the story of Ireland through the history of Londonderry
OMAGH, Co. Tyrone – *Ulster American Folk Park,* Castletown. Tel: 01662-243292. Closed in winter. Adm. £4.00. Open-air museum telling the story of Ulster's emigrants to America; restored or recreated dwellings and workshops; ship and dockside gallery

Sights of London

For historic buildings and museums and galleries in London, *see* pages 584–89 and 593–4

ALEXANDRA PALACE, Alexandra Palace Way, Wood Green, London N22 7AY. Tel: 0181-365 2121. The Victorian Palace was severely damaged by fire in 1980 but was restored, and reopened in 1988. Alexandra Palace now provides modern facilities for exhibitions, conferences, banquets and leisure activities. There is an ice rink, open daily, and a boating lake.

BARBICAN CENTRE, Silk Street, London EC2Y 8DS. Tel: 0171-638 4141. Owned, funded and managed by the Corporation of London, the Barbican Centre opened in 1982 and houses the 1,156-seat Barbican Theatre, a 200-seat studio theatre (The Pit), and the 1,989-seat Barbican Hall. There are also three cinemas, two art galleries, a sculpture court, a lending library, conference, trade and banqueting facilities, conservatory, shops, restaurants, cafés and bars.

BRIDGES. The bridges over the Thames (from east to west) are:

The Queen Elizabeth II Bridge, opened 1991, from Dartford to Thurrock

Tower Bridge, opened 1894 (*see also* page 594)

London Bridge, opened after rebuilding by Rennie, 1831; the new London Bridge opened 1973

Alexandra Bridge (railway bridge), built 1863–6

Southwark Bridge (Rennie), built 1814–19; rebuilt 1912–21

Blackfriars Railway Bridge, completed 1864

Blackfriars Bridge, built 1760–9; rebuilt 1860–9; widened 1907–10

Waterloo Bridge (Rennie), opened 1817; rebuilt 1937–42

Hungerford Railway Bridge (Brunel), suspension bridge built 1841–5; replaced by present railway and footbridge 1863

Westminster Bridge (width 84 ft), opened 1750; rebuilt 1854–62

Lambeth Bridge, built 1862; rebuilt 1929–32

Vauxhall Bridge, built 1811–16; rebuilt 1895–1906

Grosvenor Bridge (railway bridge), built 1859–60; rebuilt 1963–7

Chelsea Bridge, built 1851–8; replaced by suspension bridge 1934; widened 1937

Albert Bridge, opened 1873; restructured (Bazalgette) 1884; strengthened 1971–3

Battersea Bridge (Holland), opened 1772; rebuilt (Bazalgette) 1890

Battersea Railway Bridge, opened 1863

Wandsworth Bridge, opened 1873; rebuilt 1940

Putney Railway Bridge, opened 1889

Putney Bridge, built 1727–9; rebuilt (Bazalgette) 1882–6; starting point of Oxford and Cambridge Boat Race

Hammersmith Bridge, built 1824–7; rebuilt (Bazalgette) 1883–7; closed in 1997 for safety work

Barnes Railway Bridge (also pedestrian), built 1846–9; restructured 1893

Chiswick Bridge, opened 1933

Kew Railway Bridge, opened 1869

Kew Bridge, built 1758–9; rebuilt and renamed King Edward VII Bridge 1903

Richmond Lock, lock, weir and footbridge opened 1894

Twickenham Bridge, opened 1933

Richmond Railway Bridge, opened 1848; restructured 1906–8

Richmond Bridge, built 1774–7; widened 1937

Teddington Lock, footbridge opened 1889; marks the end of the tidal reach of the Thames

Kingston Bridge, built 1825–8; widened 1914

Hampton Court Bridge, built 1753; replaced by iron bridge 1865; present bridge built 1933

Two new footbridges are under construction; the Millennium Bridge will link the City and the new Tate Gallery of Modern Art; and a second bridge is being constructed alongside the railway on Hungerford Bridge

CEMETERIES. *Abney Park*, Stamford Hill, N16 (35 acres), tomb of General Booth, founder of the Salvation Army, and memorials to many Nonconformist divines. *Brompton*, Old Brompton Road, SW10 (40 acres), graves of Sir Henry Cole, Emmeline Pankhurst, John Wisden. *City of London Cemetery and Crematorium*, Aldersbrook Road, E12 (200 acres). *Golders Green Crematorium*, Hoop Lane, NW11 (12 acres), with Garden of Rest and memorials to many famous men and women. *Hampstead*, Fortune Green Road, NW6 (36 acres), graves of Kate Greenaway, Lord Lister, Marie Lloyd. *Highgate*, Swains Lane, N6 (38 acres), tombs of George Eliot, Faraday and Marx; guided tours only, west side, £3.00. *Kensal Green*, Harrow Road, W10 (70 acres), tombs of Thackeray, Trollope, Sydney Smith, Wilkie Collins, Tom Hood, George Cruikshank, Leigh Hunt, I. K. Brunel and Charles Kemble. Churchyard of the former *Marylebone Chapel*, Marylebone High Street, W1, Charles Wesley and his son Samuel Wesley buried; chapel demolished in 1949, now Garden of Rest. *Nunhead*, Linden Grove, SE15 (26 acres), closed in 1969, recently restored and opened for burials. *St Marylebone Cemetery and Crematorium*, East End Road, N2 (47 acres). *West Norwood Cemetery and Crematorium*, Norwood High Street, SE27 (42 acres), tombs of Sir Henry Bessemer, Mrs Beeton, Sir Henry Tate and Joseph Whitaker (*Whitaker's Almanack*).

CENOTAPH, Whitehall, London SW1. The word 'cenotaph' means 'empty tomb'. The monument, erected 'To the Glorious Dead', is a memorial to all ranks of the sea, land and air forces who gave their lives in the service of the Empire during the First World War. Designed by Sir Edwin Lutyens and erected as a temporary memorial in 1919, it was replaced by a permanent structure unveiled by George V on Armistice Day 1920. An additional inscription was made after the Second World War to commemorate those who gave their lives in that conflict.

CHARTERHOUSE, Sutton's Hospital, Charterhouse Square, London EC1M 6AN. Tel: 0171-253 9503. A Carthusian monastery from 1371 to 1537, purchased in 1611 by Thomas Sutton, who endowed it as a hospital for aged men 'of gentle birth' and a school for poor scholars (removed to Godalming in 1872). Open to visitors on Wednesdays at 2.15 (April–July). Admission £3.00. *Registrar and Clerk to the Governors*, R. B. Heaton-Watson.

CHELSEA PHYSIC GARDEN, 66 Royal Hospital Road, London SW3 4HS. Tel: 0171-352 5646. A garden of general botanical research, maintaining a wide range of rare and unusual plants. The garden was established in 1673 by the Society of Apothecaries. Open Wednesday and Sunday p.m. during summer months. All enquiries to the Curator.

DOWNING STREET, London SW1. Number 10 Downing Street is the official town residence of the Prime Minister, No. 11 of the Chancellor of the Exchequer and No. 12 is the office of the Government Whips. The street was named after Sir George Downing, Bt., soldier and diplomatist, who was MP for Morpeth from 1660 to 1684.

Chequers, a Tudor mansion in the Chilterns near Princes Risborough, was presented by Lord and Lady Lee of Fareham in 1917 to serve, from 1921, as a country residence for the Prime Minister of the day.

GEORGE INN, Borough High Street, London SE1. The last galleried inn in London, built in 1677. Now run as an ordinary public house.

GREENWICH, London SE10. *The Royal Naval College* was until 1873 the Greenwich Hospital. It was built by Charles II, largely from designs by John Webb, and by Queen Anne and William III, from designs by Wren. It stands on the site of an ancient royal palace and of the more recent Palace of Placentia constructed by Humphrey, Duke of Gloucester (1391–1447), son of Henry IV. Henry VIII, Mary I and Elizabeth I were born in the royal palace (which reverted to the Crown in 1447) and Edward VI died there. *Greenwich Park* (196¼ acres) was enclosed by Humphrey, Duke of Gloucester, and laid out by Charles II from the designs of Le Nôtre. On a hill in Greenwich Park is the former Royal Observatory (founded 1675). Its buildings are now managed by the National Maritime Museum (*see* page 594) and the first observatory is named Flamsteed House, after John Flamsteed (1646–1719), the first Astronomer Royal (*see* page 586). *The Cutty Sark*, the last of the famous tea clippers, has been preserved as a memorial to ships and men of a past era. Sir Francis Chichester's round-the-world yacht, *Gipsy Moth IV*, can also be seen. *The Millennium Dome, see* Millennium Experience

HORSE GUARDS, Whitehall, London SW1. Archway and offices built about 1753. The mounting of the guard takes place at 11 a.m. (10 a.m. on Sundays) and the dismounted inspection at 4 p.m. Only those on the Lord Chamberlain's list may drive through the gates and archway into *Horse Guards' Parade* (230,000 sq. ft), where the Colour is 'trooped' on The Queen's official birthday.

THE HOUSES OF PARLIAMENT, Westminster, London SW1. The royal palace of Westminster, originally built by Edward the Confessor, was the normal meeting place of Parliament from about 1340. St Stephen's Chapel was used from about 1550 for the meetings of the House of Commons, which had previously been held in the Chapter House or Refectory of Westminster Abbey. The House of Lords met in an apartment of the royal palace.

The fire of 1834 destroyed much of the palace and the present Houses of Parliament were erected on the site from the designs of Sir Charles Barry and Augustus Welby Pugin between 1840 and 1867. The chamber of the House of Commons was destroyed by bombing in 1941 and a new Chamber designed by Sir Giles Gilbert Scott was used for the first time in 1950.

Lord Chancellor's Residence, Lord Chancellor's Office, House of Lords, London, SW1A 0PW. Tel: 0171-219 2394. Open 10.30 a.m.–12 noon, days vary. Postal requests in advance to 'Residence visit', Lord Chancellor's Office.

Westminster Hall was the only part of the old palace of Westminster to survive the fire of 1834. It was built by William Rufus (1097–9) and altered by Richard II (1394–9). The hammerbeam roof of carved oak dates from 1396–8. The Hall was the scene of the trial of Charles I.

The Victoria Tower of the House of Lords is about 330 ft high, and when Parliament is sitting the Union flag flies by day from its flagstaff. *The Clock Tower* of the House of Commons is about 320 ft high and contains 'Big Ben', the hour bell said to be named after Sir Benjamin Hall, First Commissioner of Works when the original bell was

cast in 1856. This bell, which weighed 16 tons 11 cwt, was found to be cracked in 1857. The present bell (13½ tons) is a recasting of the original and was first brought into use in 1859. The dials of the clock are 23 ft in diameter, the hands being 9 ft and 14 ft long (including balance piece). A light is displayed from the Clock Tower at night when Parliament is sitting.

For security reasons tours of the Houses of Parliament are available only to those who have made advance arrangements through an MP or peer. Admission to the Strangers' Gallery of the House of Lords is arranged by a peer or by queue via St Stephen's Entrance. Admission to the Strangers' Gallery of the House of Commons is by Members' order (Members' orders should be sought several weeks in advance), or by queue via St Stephen's Entrance. Queues are usually shorter after 6 p.m. Monday to Wednesday, on Wednesday mornings and on Thursdays after 2 p.m. The House does not always sit on Fridays. Overseas visitors may write to the Parliamentary Education Unit to obtain a permit to tour the Houses of Parliament, or obtain cards of introduction from their Embassy or High Commission to attend the public gallery.

INNS OF COURT. The *Inner* and *Middle Temple,* Fleet Street/Victoria Embankment, London EC4, have occupied since the early 14th century the site of the buildings of the Order of Knights Templars. *Inner Temple Hall* is open by appointment on application to the Treasurer's Office. *Middle Temple Hall* (1562–70) is open when not in use, Monday–Friday 10–12 and 3–4; closed on public holidays. In Middle Temple Gardens (open to the public May–July, Monday–Friday 12–3) Shakespeare (Henry VI, Part I) places the incident which led to the 'Wars of the Roses' (1455–85).

Temple Church, London EC4, has a nave which forms one of five remaining round churches in England. Open Wednesday–Friday 10–4. Services: 8.30 and 11.15 a.m. except in August and September. *Master of the Temple,* Revd R. Griffith-Jones

Lincoln's Inn, Chancery Lane/Lincoln's Inn Fields, London WC2, occupies the site of the palace of a former Bishop of Chichester and of a Black Friars monastery. The hall and library buildings are of 1845, although the library is first mentioned in 1474; the old hall (late 15th century) and the chapel were rebuilt *c.* 1619–23. Halls open by appointment, chapel and gardens, Monday–Friday 12–2.30. Chapel services Sunday 11.30 a.m. during law terms. *Lincoln's Inn Fields* (7 acres). The square was laid out by Inigo Jones.

Gray's Inn, Holborn/Gray's Inn Road, London WC1. Early 14th century; Hall 1556–8. Matins 11.15 a.m. (during dining term only). Holy Communion first Sunday in every month except January, August and September. Gardens open Monday–Friday 12–2.30 (except Public Holidays). Tel: 0171-458 7800.

No other 'Inns' are active, but there are remains of *Staple Inn,* a gabled front on Holborn (opposite Gray's Inn Road). *Clement's Inn* (near St Clement Danes Church), *Clifford's Inn,* Fleet Street, and *Thavies Inn,* Holborn Circus, are all rebuilt. *Serjeants' Inn,* Fleet Street, and another (demolished 1910) of the same name in Chancery Lane, were composed of Serjeants-at-Law, the last of whom died in 1922.

LLOYD'S, Lime Street, London EC3M 7HA. International insurance market which evolved during the 17th century from Lloyd's Coffee House. The present building was opened for business in May 1986, and houses the Lutine Bell. Underwriting is on three floors with a total area of 114,000 sq. feet.

LONDON PARKS, ETC.

Royal Parks

Bushy Park (1,099 acres), Surrey. Adjoining Hampton Court, contains avenue of horse-chestnuts enclosed in a fourfold avenue of limes planted by William III. 'Chestnut Sunday' (when the trees are in full bloom with their 'candles') is usually about 1 to 15 May

Green Park (49 acres), London w1. Between Piccadilly and St James's Park, with Constitution Hill leading to Hyde Park Corner

Greenwich Park (196½ acres), London se10

Hyde Park (341 acres), London w1/w2. From Park Lane to Kensington Gardens, containing the Serpentine. Fine gateway at Hyde Park Corner, with Apsley House, the Achilles Statue, Rotten Row and the Ladies' Mile. To the north-east is the Marble Arch, originally erected by George IV at the entrance to Buckingham Palace and re-erected in the present position in 1851

Kensington Gardens (275 acres), London w2/w8. From the western boundary of Hyde Park to Kensington Palace, containing the Albert Memorial and Peter Pan statue

Kew, Royal Botanic Gardens, see page 335

Regent's Park and *Primrose Hill* (464 acres), London nw1. From Marylebone Road to Primrose Hill surrounded by the Outer Circle and divided by the Broad Walk leading to the Zoological Gardens

Richmond Park (2,469 acres), Surrey

St James's Park (93 acres), London sw1. From Whitehall to Buckingham Palace. Ornamental lake of 12 acres. The original suspension bridge built in 1857 was replaced in 1957. The Mall leads from the Admiralty Arch to Buckingham Palace, Birdcage Walk from Storey's Gate to Buckingham Palace

Maintained by the Corporation of London

Ashtead Common (500 acres), Surrey

Burnham Beeches and *Fleet Wood* (540 acres), Bucks. Purchased by the Corporation for the benefit of the public in 1880, Fleet Wood (65 acres) being presented in 1921

Coulsdon Common (133 acres), Surrey

Epping Forest (6,000 acres), Essex. Purchased by the Corporation and opened to the public in 1882. The present forest is 12 miles long by 1 to 2 miles wide, about one-tenth of its original area

Farthing Downs (121 acres), Surrey

Hampstead Heath (789 acres), London nw3. Including Golders Hill (36 acres) and Parliament Hill (271 acres)

Highgate Wood (70 acres), London n6/n10

Kenley Common (138 acres), Surrey

Queen's Park (30 acres), London nw6

Riddlesdown (90 acres), Surrey

Spring Park (51 acres), Kent

West Ham Park (77 acres), London e15

West Wickham Common (25 acres), Kent

Woodredon and Warlies Park Estate (740 acres), Waltham Abbey

Also smaller open spaces within the City of London, including *Finsbury Circus Gardens*

Maintained by Historic Royal Palaces

Hampton Court Gardens (54 acres), Surrey

Hampton Court Green (17 acres), Surrey

Hampton Court Park (622 acres), Surrey

LONDON PLANETARIUM, Marylebone Road, London nw1 5lr. Tel: 0171-935 6861. Open daily (except Christmas Day), star show and interactive exhibits 12.20–5.00. Admission charge.

LONDON ZOO, Regent's Park, London nw1. Tel: 0171-722 3333. Opened in 1828. Open daily (except Christmas Day) 10–5.30 March–September, 10–4 in winter. Admission £9.00.

MADAME TUSSAUD'S, Marylebone Road, London nw1 5lr.

Tel: 0171-935 6861. Waxwork exhibition. Open daily (except Christmas Day) 9.30–5.30 (earlier at weekends and during school holidays). Admission charge.

MARKETS. The London markets are mostly administered by the Corporation of London. *Billingsgate* (fish), Thames Street site dating from 1875, a market site for over 1,000 years, moved to the Isle of Dogs in 1982. *Borough*, se1 (vegetables, fruit, flowers, etc.), established on present site 1756, privately owned and run. *Covent Garden* (vegetables, fruit, flowers, etc.), established in 1661 under a charter of Charles II, moved in 1973 to Nine Elms. *Leadenhall*, ec3 (meat, poultry, fish, etc.), built 1881, part recently demolished. *London Fruit Exchange*, Brushfield Street, built by Corporation of London 1928–9 as buildings for Spitalfields market; not connected with the market since it moved in 1991. *Petticoat Lane*, Middlesex Street, e1, a market has existed on the site for over 500 years, now a Sunday morning market selling almost anything. *Portobello Road*, w11, originally for herbs and horse-trading from 1870; became famous for antiques after the closure of the Caledonian Market in 1948; Saturdays. *Smithfield, Central Meat, Fish, Fruit, Vegetable and Poultry Markets*, built 1851–66, the site of St Bartholomew's Fair from 12th to 19th century, new hall built 1963, market refurbished 1993–4. *Spitalfields*, e1 (vegetables, fruit, etc.), established 1682, modernized 1928, moved to Leyton in 1991.

MARLBOROUGH HOUSE, Pall Mall, London sw1a 5hx. Built by Wren for the first Duke of Marlborough and completed in 1711, the house reverted to the Crown in 1835. In 1863 it became the London house of the Prince of Wales and was the London home of Queen Mary until her death in 1953. In 1959 Marlborough House was given by The Queen as a centre for Commonwealth government conferences and it was opened as such in 1962. The Queen's Chapel, Marlborough Gate, begun in 1623 from the designs of Inigo Jones for the Infanta Maria of Spain, and completed for Queen Henrietta Maria, is open to the public for services on Sundays at 8.30 a.m. and 11.15 a.m. between Easter Day and end July (*see* St James's Palace for winter services in The Chapel Royal).

MILLENNIUM EXPERIENCE (The Dome, Greenwich). Open to the public from 1 January 2000. The Dome's circumference is over one km, it is over 80,000 m² and the roof is 50 m high. It is divided into 15 zones: the Living Island, Global, Communication, Spirit, Rest, Mind, National Identity, Skyscape, Work, Learning, Money, Body, Play, Journey and Local. Web: http://www.dome2000.co.uk

LONDON MONUMENT (commonly called The Monument), Monument Street, London ec3. Built from designs of Wren, 1671–7, to commemorate the Great Fire of London, which broke out in Pudding Lane on 2 September 1666. The fluted Doric column is 120 ft high; the moulded cylinder above the balcony supporting a flaming vase of gilt bronze is an additional 42 ft; and the column is based on a square plinth 40 ft high (with fine carvings on the west face) making a total height of 202 ft. Splendid views of London from gallery at top of column (311 steps).

MONUMENTS (sculptor's name in parenthesis). *Albert Memorial* (Durham), Kensington Gore; *Royal Air Force* (Blomfield), Victoria Embankment; *Viscount Alanbrooke*, Whitehall; *Beaconsfield*, Parliament Square; *Beatty* (Macmillan), Trafalgar Square; *Belgian Gratitude* (setting by Blomfield, statue by Rousseau), Victoria Embankment; *Boadicea* (or Boudicca), Queen of the Iceni (Thornycroft), Westminster Bridge; *Brunel* (Marochetti), Victoria Embankment; *Burghers of Calais* (Rodin), Victoria Tower

Gardens, Westminster; *Burns* (Steel), Embankment Gardens; *Canada Memorial* (Granche), Green Park; *Carlyle* (Boehm), Chelsea Embankment; *Cavalry* (Jones), Hyde Park; *Edith Cavell* (Frampton), St Martin's Place; *Cenotaph* (Lutyens), Whitehall; *Charles I* (Le Sueur), Trafalgar Square; *Charles II* (Gibbons), South Court, Chelsea Hospital; *Churchill* (Roberts-Jones), Parliament Square; *Cleopatra's Needle* (68½ ft high, *c*.1500 BC, erected on the Thames Embankment in 1877–8; the sphinxes are Victorian); *Clive* (Tweed), King Charles Street; *Captain Cook* (Brock), The Mall; *Crimean*, Broad Sanctuary; *Oliver Cromwell* (Thornycroft), outside Westminster Hall; *Cunningham* (Belsky), Trafalgar Square; *Gen. Charles de Gaulle*, Carlton Gardens; *Lord Dowding* (Faith Winter), Strand; *Duke of Cambridge* (Jones), Whitehall; *Duke of York* (124 ft), Carlton House Terrace; *Edward VII* (Mackennal), Waterloo Place; *Elizabeth I* (1586, oldest outdoor statue in London; from Ludgate), Fleet Street; *Eros* (Shaftesbury Memorial) (Gilbert), Piccadilly Circus; *Marechal Foch* (Mallisard, copy of one in Cassel, France), Grosvenor Gardens; *Charles James Fox* (Westmacott), Bloomsbury Square; *George III* (Cotes Wyatt), Cockspur Street; *George IV* (Chantrey), riding without stirrups, Trafalgar Square; *George V* (Reid Dick), Old Palace Yard; *George VI* (Macmillan), Carlton Gardens; *Gladstone* (Thornycroft), Strand; *Guards'* (Crimea) (Bell), Waterloo Place; *(Great War)* (Ledward, figures, Bradshaw, cenotaph), Horse Guards' Parade; *Haig* (Hardiman), Whitehall; *Sir Arthur (Bomber) Harris* (Faith Winter), Strand; *Irving* (Brock), north side of National Portrait Gallery; *James II* (Gibbons and/or pupils), Trafalgar Square; *Jellicoe* (Wheeler), Trafalgar Square; *Samuel Johnson* (Fitzgerald), opposite St Clement Danes; *Kitchener* (Tweed), Horse Guards' Parade; *Abraham Lincoln* (Saint-Gaudens, copy of one in Chicago), Parliament Square; *Milton* (Montford), St Giles, Cripplegate; *The Monument* (*see* above); *Mountbatten*, Foreign Office Green; *Nelson* (170 ft 2 in), Trafalgar Square, with Landseer's lions (cast from guns recovered from the wreck of the *Royal George*); *Florence Nightingale* (Walker), Waterloo Place; *Palmerston* (Woolner), Parliament Square; *Peel* (Noble), Parliament Square; *Pitt* (Chantrey), Hanover Square; *Portal* (Nemon), Embankment Gardens; *Prince Consort* (Bacon), Holborn Circus; *Queen Elizabeth Gate*, Hyde Park Corner; *Raleigh* (Macmillan), Whitehall; *Richard I (Coeur de Lion)* (Marochetti), Old Palace Yard; *Roberts* (Bates), Horse Guards' Parade; *Franklin D. Roosevelt* (Reid Dick), Grosvenor Square; *Royal Artillery* (South Africa) (Colton), The Mall; *(Great War)*, Hyde Park Corner; *Captain Scott* (Lady Scott), Waterloo Place; *Shackleton* (Sarjeant Jagger), Kensington Gore; *Shakespeare* (Fontana, copy of one by Scheemakers in Westminster Abbey), Leicester Square; *Smuts* (Epstein), Parliament Square; *Sullivan* (Goscombe John), Victoria Embankment; *Trenchard* (Macmillan), Victoria Embankment; *Victoria Memorial*, in front of Buckingham Palace; *Raoul Wallenberg* (Phillip Jackson), Great Cumberland Place; *George Washington* (Houdon copy), Trafalgar Square; *Wellington* (Boehm), Hyde Park Corner, (Chantrey) riding without stirrups, outside Royal Exchange; *John Wesley* (Adams Acton), City Road; *William III* (Bacon), St James's Square; *Wolseley* (Goscombe John), Horse Guards' Parade.

PORT OF LONDON. The Port of London covers the tidal section of the River Thames from Teddington to the seaward limit (the outer Tongue buoy and the Sunk light vessel), a distance of 150 km. The governing body is the Port of London Authority (PLA). Each year 56 million tonnes of cargo is handled at privately operated riverside terminals between Fulham and Canvey Island, including the enclosed dock at Tilbury, 40 km below

London Bridge. Passenger vessels and cruise liners can be handled at moorings at Greenwich, Tower Bridge and Tilbury.

ROMAN REMAINS. The city wall of Roman *Londinium* was largely rebuilt during the medieval period but sections may be seen near the White Tower in the Tower of London; at Tower Hill; at Coopers' Row; at All Hallows, London Wall, its vestry being built on the remains of a semi-circular Roman bastion; at St Alphage, London Wall, showing a succession of building repairs from the Roman until the late medieval period; and at St Giles, Cripplegate. Sections of the great forum and basilica, more than 165 metres square, have been encountered during excavations in the area of Leadenhall, Gracechurch Street and Lombard Street. Traces of Roman activity along the river include a massive riverside wall built in the late Roman period, and a succession of Roman timber quays along Lower and Upper Thames Street. Finds from these sites can be seen at the Museum of London (*see* page 594).
Other major buildings are the amphitheatre at Guildhall; remains of bath-buildings in Upper and Lower Thames Street; and the temple of Mithras in Walbrook.

ROYAL ALBERT HALL, Kensington Gore, London SW7 2AP. Tel: 0171-589 3203. The elliptical hall, one of the largest in the world, was completed in 1871, and since 1941 has been the venue each summer for the Promenade Concerts founded in 1895 by Sir Henry Wood. Other events include pop and classical music concerts, dance, opera, sporting events, conferences and banquets.

ROYAL HOSPITAL, CHELSEA, Royal Hospital Road, London SW3 4SR. Tel: 0171-730 0161. Founded by Charles II in 1682, and built by Wren; opened in 1692 for old and disabled soldiers. Open Monday–Friday 10–12, daily 2–4. The extensive grounds include the former Ranelagh Gardens and are the venue for the Chelsea Flower Show each May. *Governor*, Gen. Sir Jeremy Mackenzie, GCB, OBE.

ROYAL OPERA HOUSE, Covent Garden, London WC2E 9DD. Home of The Royal Ballet (1931) and The Royal Opera (1946). The Royal Opera House is the third theatre to be built on the site, opening 1858; the first was opened in 1732. The theatre reopens in December 1999 after redevelopment.

ST JAMES'S PALACE, Pall Mall, London SW1. Built by Henry VIII; the Gatehouse and Presence Chamber remain; later alterations were made by Wren and Kent. The Chapel Royal is open for services on Sundays at 8.30 a.m. and 11.15 a.m. between the beginning of October and Good Friday (*see* Marlborough House for summer services in The Queen's Chapel). Representatives of foreign powers are still accredited 'to the Court of St James's'. *Clarence House* (1825) in the palace precinct is the home of The Queen Mother.

ST PAUL'S CATHEDRAL, London EC4M 8AD. Built 1675–1710, cost £747,660. The cross on the dome is 365 ft above the ground level, the inner cupola 218 ft above the floor. 'Great Paul' in the south-west tower weighs nearly 17 tons. The organ by Father Smith (enlarged by Willis and rebuilt by Mander) is in a case carved by Grinling Gibbons, who also carved the choir stalls. Open for sightseeing Monday–Saturday 8.30–4.00. Admission to cathedral and crypt: £4.00, children £2.00; galleries £3.50/£1.50. Services: Sundays, 8, 10, 11, 3.15 and 6; weekdays, 7.30, 8, 12.30 and 5; Saturday Matins 8.30 a.m.

SOMERSET HOUSE, Strand and Victoria Embankment, London WC2. The river façade (600 ft long) was built in 1776–86 from the designs of Sir William Chambers; the eastern extension, which houses part of King's College, was built by Smirke in 1829. Somerset House was the property of Lord Protector Somerset, at whose attainder in 1552 the palace passed to the Crown, and it was a royal residence until 1692.

SOUTH BANK, London SE1. The arts complex on the south bank of the River Thames which consists of the 2,903-seat *Royal Festival Hall* (opened in 1951 for the Festival of Britain), the adjacent 1,056-seat *Queen Elizabeth Hall*, the 368-seat *Purcell Room*, and the 77-seat Voice Box. Tel: 0171-960 4242.

The *National Film Theatre* (opened 1952), administered by the British Film Institute, has three auditoria showing over 2,000 films a year. The London Film Festival is held here every November. There is an IMAX cinema with 500 seats. Tel: 0171-928 3232.

The *Royal National Theatre* opened in 1976 and stages classical, modern, new and neglected plays in its three auditoria: the 1,160-seat Olivier theatre, the 890-seat Lyttelton theatre and the Cottesloe theatre which seats up to 400. Tel: 0171-452 3000.

SOUTHWARK CATHEDRAL, London SE1 9DA. Mainly 13th century, but the nave is largely rebuilt. The tomb of John Gower (1330–1408) is between the Bunyan and Chaucer memorial windows in the north aisle; Shakespeare's effigy, backed by a view of Southwark and the Globe Theatre, is in the south aisle; the tomb of Bishop Andrewes (died 1626) is near the screen. The lady chapel was the scene of the consistory courts of the reign of Mary (Gardiner and Bonner) and is still used as a consistory court. John Harvard, after whom Harvard University is named, was baptized here in 1607, and a chapel by the north choir aisle is his memorial chapel. Open 9–6, admission free (suggested donation £2.50). Services: Sundays, 9, 11, 3; weekdays, 8, 12.45, 5.30 (sung on Tuesdays and Fridays); Saturdays, 9, 4.

THAMES EMBANKMENTS. The *Victoria Embankment*, on the north side from Westminster to Blackfriars, was constructed by Sir Joseph Bazalgette (1819–91) for the Metropolitan Board of Works, 1864–70; the seats, of which the supports of some are a kneeling camel, laden with spicery, and of others a winged sphinx, were presented by the Grocers' Company and by W. H. Smith, MP, in 1874; the *Albert Embankment*, on the south side from Westminster Bridge to Vauxhall, 1866–9; the *Chelsea Embankment*, 1871–4. The total cost exceeded £2,000,000. Bazalgette also inaugurated the London main drainage system, 1858–65. A medallion (*Flumini vincula posuit*) has been placed on a pier of the Victoria Embankment to commemorate the engineer.

THAMES FLOOD BARRIER. Officially opened in May 1984, though first used in February 1983, the barrier consists of ten rising sector gates which span 570 yards from bank to bank of the Thames at Woolwich Reach. When not in use the gates lie horizontally, allowing shipping to navigate the river normally; when the barrier is closed, the gates turn through 90 degrees to stand vertically more than 50 feet above the river bed. The barrier took eight years to complete and can be raised within about 30 minutes.

THAMES TUNNELS. The *Rotherhithe Tunnel*, opened 1908, connects Commercial Road, London E14, with Lower Road, Rotherhithe; it is 1 mile 332 yards long, of which 525 yards are under the river. The first *Blackwall Tunnel* (northbound vehicles only), opened 1897, connects East India Dock Road, Poplar, with Blackwall Lane, East Greenwich. The height restriction on the northbound tunnel is 13ft 4in. A second tunnel (for southbound vehicles only) opened 1967. The lengths of the tunnels measured from East India Dock Road to the Gate House on the south side are 6,215 ft (old tunnel) and 6,152 ft. *Greenwich Tunnel* (pedestrians only), opened 1902,

connects the Isle of Dogs, Poplar, with Greenwich; it is 406 yards long. The *Woolwich Tunnel* (pedestrians only), opened 1912, connects North and South Woolwich below the passenger and vehicular ferry from North Woolwich Station, London E16, to High Street, Woolwich, London SE18; it is 552 yards long.

WALTHAM CROSS, Herts. At Waltham Cross is one of the crosses (partly restored) erected by Edward I to mark a resting place of the corpse of Queen Eleanor on its way to Westminster Abbey. Ten crosses were erected, but only those at Geddington, Northampton and Waltham survive; 'Charing' Cross originally stood near the spot now occupied by the statue of Charles I at Whitehall.

WESTMINSTER ABBEY, London SW1. Built between 1050 and 1745, it contains the chapel of Henry VII, chapter house and cloisters, Edward the Confessor's shrine, tombs of kings and queens and many other monuments, including the grave of 'The Unknown Warrior' and Poets' Corner. The Coronation Chair formerly enclosed the Stone of Scone, removed from Scotland by Edward I in 1296 and returned to Scotland in 1996. Open on weekdays 9.30–4.45. Admission £5.00. Last admission Monday–Friday 3.45 p.m., Saturday 1.45 p.m. No sightseeing on Sundays. Services: Sundays, 8, 10, 11.15, 3, 6.30 (generally preceded by an organ recital); Monday–Friday, 7.30, 8, 12.30, 5; Saturdays, 8, 9.30, 3.

WESTMINSTER CATHEDRAL, Ashley Place, London SW1P 1QW. Roman Catholic cathedral built 1895–1903 from the designs of J. F. Bentley. The campanile is 283 feet high. Cathedral open 6.50 a.m.–7 p.m. Masses: Sundays, 7, 8, 9, 10.30 (sung), 12, 5.30 and 7; Solemn Vespers and Benediction 3.30; Monday–Friday, 7, 8, 8.30, 9, 10.30, 12.30, 1.05 and 5.30 (sung), Morning Prayer 7.40, Vespers 5; Saturdays 8, 8.30, 9, 10.30 (sung), 12.30 and 6, Morning Prayer 10.00, Rosary, Benediction 7.00. Holy days of obligation, Low Masses 7, 8, 8.30, 9, 10.30, 12.30, 1.05, 5.30 (sung) and 7.

LONDON TOURIST BOARD AND CONVENTION BUREAU, Glen House, Stag Place, London, SW1E 5LT. Tourist information: 0839-123456

Hallmarks

Hallmarks are the symbols stamped on gold, silver or platinum articles to indicate that they have been tested at an official Assay Office and that they conform to one of the legal standards. With certain exceptions, all gold, silver or platinum articles are required by law to be hallmarked before they are offered for sale. Hallmarking was instituted in England in 1300 under a statute of Edward I.

MODERN HALLMARKS

Since 1 January 1999, UK hallmarks have consisted of three compulsory symbols – the sponsor's mark, the fineness (standard) mark and the assay office mark. Traditional marks such as the year date letter, the Britannia for 958 silver, the lion passant for 925 silver (lion rampant in Scotland) and the orb for 950 platinum may be added voluntarily. The distinction between UK and foreign articles has been removed, and more finenesses are now legal, reflecting the more common finenesses elsewhere in Europe.

SPONSOR'S MARK

Instituted in England in 1363, the sponsor's mark was originally a device such as a bird or fleur-de-lis. Now it consists of the initial letters of the name or names of the manufacturer or firm. Where two or more sponsors have the same initials, there is a variation in the surrounding shield or style of letters.

FINENESS (STANDARD) MARK

The fineness (standard) mark indicates that the content of the precious metal in the alloy from which the article is made, is not less than the legal standard. The legal standard is the minimum content of precious metal by weight in parts per thousand, and the standards are:

Gold	999	
	990	
	916.6	(22 carat)
	750	(18 carat)
	585	(14 carat)
	375	(9 carat)
Silver	999	
	958.4	(Britannia)
	925	(sterling)
	800	
Platinum	999	
	950	
	900	
	850	

ASSAY OFFICE MARK

This mark identifies the particular assay office at which the article was tested and marked. The British assay offices are:

LONDON, Goldsmiths' Hall, London EC2V 8AQ. Tel: 0171-606 8975

BIRMINGHAM, Newhall Street, Birmingham B3 1SB. Tel: 0121-236 6951

SHEFFIELD, 137 Portobello Street, Sheffield S1 4DS. Tel: 0114-275 5111

EDINBURGH, 24A Broughton Street, Edinburgh EH1 3RH. Tel: 0131-226 1122

Assay offices formerly existed in other towns, e.g. Chester, Exeter, Glasgow, Newcastle, Norwich and York, each having its own distinguishing mark.

DATE LETTER

The date letter shows the year in which an article was assayed and hallmarked. Each alphabetical cycle has a distinctive style of lettering or shape of shield. The date letters were different at the various assay offices and the particular office must be established from the assay office mark before reference is made to tables of date letters. Date letter marks became voluntary on 1 January 1999.

The table on page 604 shows specimen shields and letters used by the London Assay Office on silver articles in each period from 1498. The same letters are found on gold articles but the surrounding shield may differ. Since 1 January 1975, each office has used the same style of date letter and shield for all articles.

OTHER MARKS

FOREIGN GOODS

Foreign goods imported into the UK are required to be hallmarked before sale, unless they already bear a convention mark (*see* below) or a hallmark struck by an independent assay office in the European Economic Area which is deemed to be equivalent to a UK hallmark.

The following are the assay office marks used for gold until the end of 1998. For silver and platinum the symbols remain the same but the shields differ in shape.

 London

 Birmingham

 Sheffield

 Edinburgh

CONVENTION HALLMARKS

Special marks at authorized assay offices of the signatory countries of the International Convention on Hallmarking (Austria, the Czech Republic, Denmark, Finland, Ireland, the Netherlands, Norway, Portugal, Sweden, Switzerland and the UK) are legally recognized in the United Kingdom as approved hallmarks. These consist of a sponsor's mark, a common control mark, a fineness mark (arabic numerals showing the standard in parts per thousand), and an assay office mark. There is no date letter.

The fineness marks are:

Gold	750	(18 carat)
	585	(14 carat)
	375	(9 carat)
Silver	925	(sterling)
Platinum	950	

The common control marks are:

750 Gold (18 carat)

925 Silver

950 Platinum

DUTY MARKS

In 1784 an additional mark of the reigning sovereign's head was introduced to signify that the excise duty had been paid. The mark became obsolete on the abolition of the duty in 1890.

COMMEMORATIVE MARKS

There are three other marks to commemorate special events: the silver jubilee of King George V and Queen Mary in 1935, the coronation of Queen Elizabeth II in 1953, and her silver jubilee in 1977. During 1999 and 2000 there is a voluntary additional Millennium Mark.

LONDON (GOLDSMITHS' HALL) DATE LETTERS FROM 1498

		from	to
	Black letter, small	1498–9	1517–8
	Lombardic	1518–9	1537–8
	Roman and other capitals	1538–9	1557–8
	Black letter, small	1558–9	1577–8
	Roman letter, capitals	1578–9	1597–8
	Lombardic, external cusps	1598–9	1617–8
	Italic letter, small	1618–9	1637–8
	Court hand	1638–9	1657–8

		from	to
	Black letter, capitals	1658–9	1677–8
	Black letter, small	1678–9	1696–7
	Court hand	1697	1715–6
	Roman letter, capitals	1716–7	1735–6
	Roman letter, small	1736–7	1738–9
	Roman letter, small	1739–40	1755–6
	Old English, capitals	1756–7	1775–6
	Roman letter, small	1776–7	1795–6
	Roman letter, capitals	1796–7	1815–6
	Roman letter, small	1816–7	1835–6
	Old English, capitals	1836–7	1855–6
	Old English, small	1856–7	1875–6
	Roman letter, capitals [A to M *square* shield N to Z as shown]	1876–7	1895–6
	Roman letter, small	1896–7	1915–6
	Black letter, small	1916–7	1935–6
	Roman letter, capitals	1936–7	1955–6
	Italic letter, small	1956–7	1974
	Italic letter, capitals	1975	

Economic Statistics

The Budget 1999

GOVERNMENT RECEIPTS £ billion

	Outturn 1997–8	Estimate 1998–9	Forecast 1999–2000
Inland Revenue	117.5	127.3	128.9
Income tax (gross)	79.8	87.5	90.8
Income tax credits	−2.9	−2.0	−2.8
Corporation tax[1]	30.4	29.8	29.9
Windfall tax	2.6	2.6	—
Petroleum revenue tax	1.0	0.5	0.1
Capital gains tax	1.5	2.4	3.2
Inheritance tax	1.7	1.8	2.0
Stamp duties	3.5	4.7	5.7
Customs and Excise	89.8	93.4	96.2
Value added tax	50.6	51.7	54.0
Fuel duties	19.4	21.5	23.1
Tobacco duties	8.4	8.3	7.0
Spirits duties	1.5	1.6	1.6
Wine duties	1.4	1.5	1.6
Beer and cider duties	2.8	2.8	2.9
Betting and gaming duties	1.6	1.5	1.5
Air passenger duty	0.5	0.8	0.8
Insurance premium tax	1.0	1.2	1.4
Landfill tax	0.4	0.3	0.4
Customs duties and levies	2.3	2.0	1.8
Vehicle excise duties	4.5	4.6	4.6
Oil royalties	0.5	0.3	0.2
Business rates[2]	14.9	15.2	15.6
Social security contributions	51.1	54.9	55.7
Council tax	11.0	11.8	12.8
Other taxes and royalties	8.0	7.7	7.9
Net taxes and social security contributions	297.2	315.2	321.8
Interest and dividends	4.2	4.2	3.7
Gross operating surpluses and rent	17.6	18.3	18.4
Other receipts and accounting adjustments	−3.2	−3.5	−1.0
CURRENT RECEIPTS	315.7	334.2	344.3
North Sea revenues[3]	3.3	2.6	1.2

1. Includes advance corporation tax (net of payment). Also includes North Sea corporation tax after ACT set-off and corporation tax on gains
2. Includes district council rates in Northern Ireland
3. North Sea corporation tax (before ACT set-off), petroleum revenue tax and royalties
Source: The Stationery Office – *Budget 99*

GOVERNMENT EXPENDITURE

The Economic and Fiscal Strategy Report in June 1998 introduced changes to the public expenditure control regime. Three-year departmental expenditure limits (DELs) now apply to most government departments. Spending which cannot easily be subject to three-year planning is reviewed annually in the Budget as annually managed expenditure (AME). Current and capital expenditure are treated separately.

DEPARTMENTAL EXPENDITURE LIMITS
CURRENT BUDGET £ billion

	Outturn 1997–8	Estimate 1998–9	Plans 1999–2000
Education and Employment	14.0	13.7	14.5
Health	35.1	37.6	39.9
of which NHS	34.5	36.9	39.2
DETR – main programmes	4.1	4.1	4.4
DETR – local government and regional policy	31.1	32.4	33.9
Home Office	6.2	6.6	7.4
Legal departments[1]	2.6	2.6	2.7
Defence	20.1	20.9	20.8
Foreign and Commonwealth Office	1.0	1.0	1.0
International Development	1.9	2.1	2.0
Trade and Industry[2]	2.7	2.7	2.9
Agriculture, Fisheries and Food	1.4	1.2	1.1
Culture, Media and Sport	0.8	0.8	0.9
Social Security (administration)	3.4	3.5	3.3
Scotland[1]	11.5	11.7	12.2
Wales	5.6	5.9	6.3
Northern Ireland	4.9	5.2	5.3
Chancellor of the Exchequer's departments	2.7	2.9	3.0
Cabinet Office	0.8	1.2	1.2
Welfare to Work	0	0.4	1.2
Reserve[3]	0	0	1.1
Allowance for shortfall	0	−1.5	0
TOTAL CURRENT BUDGET	149.8	155.1	165.3

1. The Crown Office is included with the Legal Departments up to 1998–9 and thereafter with the Scotland figures
2. Including capital expenditure of the Export Credits Guarantee Department
3. Reserve arbitrarily apportioned between current (90 per cent) and capital (10 per cent) budgets. Figures for 1998–9 set to zero
Source: The Stationery Office – *Budget 99*

ANNUALLY MANAGED EXPENDITURE
(FORECASTS)   *£ billion*

	1998–9	1999–2000	2000–01
Departmental expenditure limits	168.0	179.2	189.7
Social security benefits	93.5	99.1	101.5
Housing revenue account subsidies	3.7	3.4	3.5
Common agricultural policy	2.6	2.4	2.7
Export Credits Guarantee Department	−0.2	0.5	0.8
Net payment to EC institutions	3.5	2.7	2.6
Self-financing public corporations	−0.2	−0.1	−0.2
Locally financed expenditure	16.1	17.0	18.3
Net public service pensions	5.1	6.2	6.1
National Lottery	1.4	2.6	2.7
Central government gross debt interest	29.5	26.0	27.6
Accounting and other adjustments	8.3	9.3	11.7
AME margin	0	1.0	2.0
Annually managed expenditure	163.4	170.0	179.1

Source: The Stationery Office – *Budget 99*

LOCAL AUTHORITY TRANSACTIONS
£ billion

	Outturn 1997–8	Estimate 1998–9	Forecast 1999–2000
Receipts			
Council tax[1]	10.8	11.8	12.8
Current grants from central government	59.9	60.1	62.2
Other receipts[2]	9.7	10.4	10.0
Capital grants from central government	2.7	3.0	2.8
Total receipts	83.1	85.4	87.9
Expenditure			
Current expenditure on goods and services	57.2	59.3	61.0
Current grants and subsidies	14.7	14.1	15.1
Interest	4.4	4.3	4.1
Capital expenditure before depreciation	6.5	7.2	7.6
Total expenditure	82.8	85.0	87.8[3]
Net borrowing	−0.3	−0.3	−0.1

1. Net of rebates and council tax benefit
2. Includes interest receipts, rent and gross trading surplus
3. Assumes no allocation from the reserve
Source: The Stationery Office – *Budget 99*

PUBLIC SECTOR FINANCES   *£ billion*

	Outturn 1997–8	Estimate 1998–9	Forecast 1999–2000
Current receipts	315.7	334.2	335.0
Current expenditure	304.3	313.5	329.0
Depreciation	14.0	14.6	15.0
Surplus on current budget*	−5.1	4.1	2.0
Net investment	4.0	3.4	5.0
Public sector net borrowing	9.1	−1.0	3.0

AS A PERCENTAGE OF GDP

	Outturn 1997–8	Estimate 1998–9	Forecast 1999–2000
Current receipts	38.9	39.4	39.2
Current expenditure	37.5	37.0	37.4
Depreciation	1.7	1.7	1.7
Surplus on current budget*	−0.6	0.5	0.3
Net investment	0.5	0.4	0.6
Public sector net borrowing	1.1	−0.1	0.3
Public sector net debt	42.5	40.6	39.4

* Excluding windfall tax receipts and associated spending
Source: The Stationery Office – *Budget 99*

GROSS VALUE ADDED AT BASIC PRICES BY INDUSTRY 1997*   *£ million*

Agriculture, hunting, forestry and fishing	10,820
Mining and quarrying, including oil and gas extraction	18,137
Manufacturing (revised definition)	146,522
Electricity, gas and water supply	16,227
Construction	36,491
Wholesale and retail trade	106,068
Transport and communication	59,694
Financial intermediation	185,851
Adjustment for financial services	−26,564
Public administration, defence	38,940
Education; health; social work	85,129
Other services	33,955
ALL INDUSTRIES	711,270

* At basic prices, not market prices, and excluding taxes on products
Source: The Stationery Office – *Annual Abstract of Statistics 1999* (Crown copyright)

BALANCE OF PAYMENTS 1996   *£ million*

CURRENT ACCOUNT
Trade in goods
Exports	167,403
Imports	180,489
Trade in goods balance	−13,086
Services balance	8,897
Investment income	9,652
Transfers balance	−4,522
CURRENT BALANCE	−402

Source: The Stationery Office − *Annual Abstract of Statistics 1999* (Crown copyright)

UK TRADE ON A BALANCE OF PAYMENTS BASIS
£ million

	Exports	Imports	Balance
1987	79,531	91,229	−11,698
1988	80,711	102,264	−21,553
1989	92,611	117,335	−24,724
1990	102,313	121,020	−18,707
1991	103,939	114,162	−10,223
1992	107,863	120,913	−13,050
1993	122,039	135,358	−13,319
1994	135,260	146,351	−11,091
1995	153,725	165,449	−11,724
1996	167,403	180,489	−13,086
1997	171,798	183,590	−11,792

Source: The Stationery Office − *Annual Abstract of Statistics 1999* (Crown copyright)

VALUE OF UK EXPORTS 1998
BY DESTINATION   *£ million*

European Community	95,054.2
Other western Europe	7,840.0
Eastern Europe	4,821.4
North America	24,714.0
Other America	3,102.3
Middle East and North Africa	8,874.7
Sub-Saharan Africa	3,811.8
Asia and Oceania	16,509.2
Low-value exports	514.5
Total non-EC exports	69,687.8
Total exports	164,742.0

Source: HM Customs and Excise

VALUE OF UK IMPORTS 1998
BY SOURCE   *£ million*

European Community	101,954.0
Other western Europe	10,290.5
Eastern Europe	4,604.7
North America	28,747.1
Other America	2,907.1
Middle East and North Africa	4,028.8
Sub-Saharan Africa	2,866.5
Asia and Oceania	34,423.0
Low-value imports	514.4
Total non-EC imports	88,382.2
Total imports	190,366.1

Source: HM Customs and Excise

EMPLOYMENT

LABOUR FORCE BY AGE 1997 (UK)

Age	Male	Female
16–24	2,400,000	2,000,000
25–44	8,100,000	6,400,000
45–59	4,500,000	3,700,000
60–64	700,000	400,000
65 and over	300,000	200,000
Total	16,000,000	12,700,000

Source: The Stationery Office − *Social Trends 29* (Crown copyright)

ECONOMIC STATUS OF PEOPLE OF WORKING AGE
(UK) *as at spring 1998*

	Male	Female
All in employment	14,600,000	11,500,000
Working full-time	11,300,000	6,100,000
Working part-time	900,000	4,600,000
Self-employed	2,300,000	800,000
Others in employment	100,000	100,000
Unemployed	1,100,000	700,000
All economically active	15,700,000	12,200,000
Economically inactive	3,000,000	4,900,000
TOTAL	18,700,000	17,100,000

Source: The Stationery Office − *Social Trends 29* (Crown copyright)

THE WORKFORCE IN EMPLOYMENT (UK)
SEASONALLY ADJUSTED, AT DECEMBER 1998

Employees in employment	23,880,000
Self-employed	3,465,000
*HM Forces	210,000
*Work-related government-supported training	112,000
Total workforce in employment	27,667,000

* not seasonally adjusted

EMPLOYEES IN EMPLOYMENT, BY MAIN SECTOR (UK)
SEASONALLY ADJUSTED, AT DECEMBER 1997

Service industries	20,749,000
Manufacturing industries	4,375,000
Energy and water supply	227,000
Other industries	2,315,000
Total employees in employment	27,667,000

AVERAGE GROSS WEEKLY EARNINGS OF EMPLOYEES
(GREAT BRITAIN) *as at April 1998*

	Full–time	Part–time
All adults	£384	£125
All men	427	150
Men, manual	328	—
Men, non-manual	506	—
All women	310	120
Women, manual	211	—
Women, non-manual	330	—

Source: Office for National Statistics

UNEMPLOYMENT BY REGIONS
December 1998 to February 1999

	Total	% of total economically active
United Kingdom	1,793,000	6.2
England:	1,459,000	6.0
Eastern	122,000	4.5
East Midlands	107,000	5.1
London	271,000	7.6
Merseyside	68,000	11.6
North East	116,000	9.9
North West	151,000	5.7
South East	158,000	3.8
South West	118,000	4.8
West Midlands	175,000	6.7
Yorkshire and the Humber	173,000	7.1
Wales	104,000	7.8
Scotland	179,000	7.2
Northern Ireland	51,000	6.8

Source: Office for National Statistics

UNEMPLOYMENT RATES BY AGE 1998 (UK)
Percentages

Age	Male	Female
16–17	18.0	15.2
18–24	13.0	9.3
25–44	5.8	5.2
45–54	4.8	3.1
55–59	6.7	3.5
60–64	7.0	—
60 and over	—	2.0
All ages	6.8	5.3

Source: The Stationery Office – *Social Trends 29* (Crown copyright)

INDUSTRIAL STOPPAGES 1997 (UK)

Duration
Not more than 5 days	184,000
6–10 days	15,000
11–20 days	8,000
21–30 days	2,000
31–50 days	6,000
More than 50 days	1,000
Total number of stoppages	216,000

Source: The Stationery Office – *Annual Abstract of Statistics 1999* (Crown copyright)

TRADE UNIONS (UK)

Year	No. of unions at end of year	Total membership at end of year
1970	543	11,187,000
1975	470	12,026,000
1980	438	12,947,000
1985	370	10,821,000
1990	287	9,947,000
1995	238	8,089,000
1997*	233	7,795,000

* Figures for Great Britain only
Source: Office for National Statistics; Department of Trade and Industry; Certification Office for Trade Unions and Employers' Associations

HOUSEHOLDS AND THEIR EXPENDITURE 1997–8[1]

NUMBER OF HOUSEHOLDS

SUPPLYING DATA	6,409
Total number of persons	15,430
Total number of adults[2]	11,429

DISTRIBUTION BY TENURE

Rented unfurnished	28.9%
Rented furnished	3.0%
Rent-free	1.5%
Owner-occupied	66.7%

AVERAGE NUMBER OF PERSONS
PER HOUSEHOLD

All persons	2.408
Males	1.152
Females	1.256
Adults[2]	1.783
Persons under 65	1.436
Persons 65 and over	0.348
Children[2]	0.624
Children under 2	0.069
Children 2 and under 5	0.113
Children 5 and under 18	0.442
Persons economically active	1.141
Persons not economically active	1.266
Men 65 and over, women 60 and over	0.375
Others	0.892

HOUSEHOLD EXPENDITURE ON COMMODITIES AND
SERVICES – WEEKLY AVERAGE

	£	As % of total
Housing[3]	51.53	15.7
Fuel and power	12.66	3.9
Food	55.92	17.0
Alcoholic drink	13.33	4.1
Tobacco	6.12	1.9
Clothing and footwear	19.96	6.1
Household goods	26.90	8.2
Household services	17.89	5.4
Personal goods and services	12.54	3.8
Motoring expenditure	46.63	14.2
Fares and other travel costs	8.12	2.5
Leisure goods	16.35	5.0
Leisure services	38.81	11.8
Miscellaneous	2.02	0.6
Total	328.78	100.0

1. Information derived from the Family Expenditure Survey; relates
to the UK
2. Adults = all persons 18 and over and married persons under 18
Children = all unmarried persons under 18
3. Includes interest element of mortgage payments
Source: The Stationery Office – *Annual Abstract of Statistics 1999*
(Crown copyright)

SOURCES OF HOUSEHOLD INCOME 1997–8*

AVERAGE WEEKLY INCOME BY SOURCE (£)

Wages and salaries	280.15
Self-employment	32.92
Investments	18.69
Annuities and pensions (other than social security benefits)	28.92
Social security benefits	54.97
Other sources	5.17
Total	420.82

SOURCES AS A PERCENTAGE OF TOTAL HOUSEHOLD
INCOME (%)

Wages and salaries	66.6
Self-employment	7.8
Investments	4.4
Annuities and pensions (other than social security benefits)	6.9
Social security benefits	13.1
Other sources	1.2
Total	100.0

* Information derived from the Family Expenditure Survey; relates
to the UK. Number of households supplying data, 6,409
Source: The Stationery Office – *Annual Abstract of Statistics 1999*
(Crown copyright)

AVAILABILITY OF CERTAIN DURABLE GOODS 1997–8*

	% of households
Car	69.8
One	43.9
Two	20.6
Three or more	5.2
Central heating, full or partial	88.6
Washing machine	90.6
Fridge/freezer or deep freezer	90.0
Refrigerator	51.0
Television	98.3†
Telephone	94.1
Home computer	29.0
Video recorder	84.1

* Information derived from the Family Expenditure Survey; relates
to the UK. Number of households supplying data, 6,409
† 1992 figure
Source: The Stationery Office – *Annual Abstract of Statistics 1999*
(Crown copyright)

Cost of Living and Inflation Rates

The first cost of living index to be calculated took July 1914 as 100 and was based on the pattern of expenditure of working-class families in 1914. The cost of living index was superseded in 1947 by the general index of retail prices (RPI), although the older term is still popularly applied to it.

GENERAL INDEX OF RETAIL PRICES

The general index of retail prices measures the changes month by month in the average level of prices of goods and services purchased by most households in the United Kingdom. The spending pattern on which the index is based is revised each year, mainly using information from the Family Expenditure Survey. The expenditure of certain higher income households and of households mainly dependent on state pensions is excluded.

The index is compiled using a selection of over 600 goods and services, and the prices charged for these items are collected at regular intervals in about 146 locations throughout the country. For the index, the price changes are weighted in accordance with the pattern of consumption of the average family.

INFLATION RATE

The twelve-monthly percentage change in the 'all items' index of the RPI is usually referred to as the rate of inflation. The percentage change in prices between any two months/years can be obtained using the following formula:

$$\frac{\text{Later date RPI} - \text{Earlier date RPI}}{\text{Earlier date RPI}} \times 100$$

e.g. to find the rate of inflation for 1988, using the annual averages for 1987 and 1988:

$$\frac{106.9 - 101.9}{101.9} \times 100 = 4.9\%$$

PURCHASING POWER OF THE POUND

Changes in the internal purchasing power of the pound may be defined as the 'inverse' of changes in the level of prices; when prices go up, the amount which can be purchased with a given sum of money goes down. To find the purchasing power of the pound in one month or year, given that it was 100p in a previous month or year, the calculation would be:

$$100p \times \frac{\text{Earlier month/year RPI}}{\text{Later month/year RPI}}$$

Thus, if the purchasing power of the pound is taken to be 100p in 1975, the comparable purchasing power in 1997 would be:

$$100p \times \frac{34.2}{157.5} = 21.71p$$

For longer term comparisons, it has been the practice to use an index which has been constructed by linking together the RPI for the period 1962 to date; an index derived from the consumers expenditure deflator for the period from 1938 to 1962; and the prewar 'cost of living' index for the period 1914 to 1938. This long-term index enables the internal purchasing power of the pound to be calculated for any year from 1914 onwards. It should be noted that these figures can only be approximate.

	Long-term index of consumer goods and services (Jan. 1987 = 100)	Comparable purchasing power of £1 in 1998	Rate of inflation (annual average)
1914	2.8	58.18	
1915	3.5	46.54	
1920	7.0	23.27	
1925	5.0	32.58	
1930	4.5	36.20	
1935	4.0	40.72	
1938	4.4	37.02	
There are no official figures for 1939–45			
1946	7.4	22.01	
1950	9.0	18.10	
1955	11.2	14.54	
1960	12.6	12.93	
1965	14.8	11.00	
1970	18.5	8.80	
1975	34.2	4.76	
1980	66.8	2.44	18.0
1981	74.8	2.18	11.9
1982	81.2	2.01	8.6
1983	84.9	1.92	4.6
1984	89.2	1.83	5.0
1985	94.6	1.72	6.1
1986	97.8	1.67	3.4
1987	101.9	1.60	4.2
1988	106.9	1.52	4.9
1989	115.2	1.41	7.8
1990	126.1	1.29	9.5
1991	133.5	1.22	5.9
1992	138.5	1.18	3.7
1993	140.7	1.16	1.6
1994	144.1	1.13	2.4
1995	149.1	1.09	3.5
1996	152.7	1.07	2.4
1997	157.5	1.03	3.1
1998	162.9	1.00	3.4

The RPI figures are published around the middle of each month. They are available as a recorded message which can be heard by telephoning 0171-533 5866. Each month an updated Consumer Price Indices bulletin is published by the Office of National Statistics.

OFFICE OF NATIONAL STATISTICS, 1 Drummond Gate, London SW1V 2QQ.
PUBLIC ENQUIRIES LINE: 0171-533 5874/6363/6364
WEB: http://www.ons.gov.uk

Lotteries and Gaming

Gaming and lotteries in the UK are officially regulated and may only be run by licensed operators or in licensed premises. Responsibility for policy and the laws on gaming and lotteries rests with the Home Secretary. The National Lottery (*see* below) is regulated by the National Lottery Commission, which replaced the Office of the National Lottery in April 1999. Supervision of other lottery operations and gaming and is mostly the responsibility of the Gaming Board of Great Britain.

Most betting is on horseracing and greyhound racing, and may take place at racecourses and greyhound tracks, or at off-course betting offices. The amount spent on on-course betting is estimated to be about 10 per cent of the figures for off-course betting.

OFF-COURSE BETTING (UK)

	£ million
1996–7	6,718
1997–8	6,838p
1998–9	7,108p

p provisional
Source: Horserace Totalisator Board

Other forms of gaming and lotteries include the following:

Number of casinos operating	119
Total drop (1997–8)	£2,720m
Bingo clubs holding gaming licences	818
Amount staked (1997–8)	£1,019m
Gaming machines licensed	over 250,000
Society lottery schemes registered	614
Local authority lottery schemes registered	9
On-line lotteries held under registered schemes	1,927
Number of lotteries held under registered schemes	5,070
Total ticket sales (£ million)	c.£125m

In 1997–8 sales of society lottery tickets increased by 9 per cent to £125 million. Of this, £41.4 million (33 per cent) was spent on prizes, £32.6 million (26 per cent) on expenses and £50.8 million (41 per cent) went to good causes.
Source: Report of the Gaming Board for Great Britain 1997–8

THE NATIONAL LOTTERY

The National Lottery is currently run by a private company, Camelot Group PLC. The seven-year licence granted to Camelot expires in 2001. It is expected that the successful bidder for the next licence will be appointed by autumn 2000.

The five-member National Lottery Commission regulates the National Lottery's operations, licenses games promoted as part of the lottery and will appoint the operator of the next licence.

The first National Lottery tickets draw was made on 19 November 1994 and Instants (scratchcards) were introduced on 21 March 1995. A second weekly draw was introduced on Wednesday 5 February 1997, and on 12 June 1999 Thunderball, a third weekly draw, was introduced. Tickets for the main lottery game cost £1. If the jackpot prize is not won, it is 'rolled over' to the next draw. The highest win on a single ticket to date was £22,590,829 on 10 June 1995. By June 1999, 802 millionaires had been created.

SALES 1998–9

Average number of tickets (on-line and instants) sold per week	c.94.8m
Average number of people playing weekly	c.30m
% of adult population buying tickets regularly	c.55%
Amount raised by ticket sales, 1994 to June 1999	c.£23,000m

Sources: Camelot, Oflot

DISTRIBUTION OF PROCEEDS
over the seven-year licence period

Allocated to:	%
Prize money	50
Tax	13
Retailer commission	5
Camelot (operating costs and profit)	4
Good causes	28

The 'good causes' originally benefiting from lottery funds were the arts, sport, heritage, charities and the Millennium Commission. In July 1998 the National Lottery Act created a sixth good cause, the New Opportunities Fund, to fund health, education and environmental initiatives. The New Opportunities Fund announced its first awards in summer 1999. The Act also created a National Endowment for Science, Technology and the Arts (NESTA), a non-departmental public body whose objectives are: to help talented individuals; to enable inventions and ideas to be commercially exploited; and to promote public knowledge of science, technology and the arts. NESTA received an initial £200 million from the New Opportunities Fund but thereafter is to generate its own income.

From October 1997 the percentage of all the funds allocated to the good causes received by each cause is as follows: the arts, sport, heritage and charities 16.66 per cent each; the Millennium Commission 20 per cent; and the New Opportunities Fund 13.33 per cent. From October 1999 the share going to the Millennium Commission will be reduced to 13.33 per cent and that going to the New Opportunities Fund will rise to 20 per cent.

The cumulative amount allocated to the good causes from November 1994 to March 1999 was £7,304 million.

AWARDS 1998–9

Most awards are conditional on partnership funding being obtained from other sources.

	Number	Total value £
Total	12,932	3,192,005,425
Arts, total	1,345	163,146,724
Arts Council of England	497	120,370,829
Arts Council of Wales	577	14,236,149
Scottish Arts Council	185	20,001,747
Arts Council of Northern Ireland	86	8,537,999
Millennium Commission		
awards to projects	187	1,260,000,000
awards to schemes funding individuals	57	56,058,751
Heritage Lottery Fund	2,738	1,283,321,186
National Lottery Charities Board	7,079	281,453,961
Sport, total	1,526	148,024,803
Sport England	289	103,331,000
Sports Council for Wales	58	5,326,106
Scottish Sports Council	980	28,904,282
Sports Council for Northern Ireland	199	10,463,415

Finance

British Currency

The unit of currency is the pound sterling (£) of 100 pence. The decimal system was introduced on 15 February 1971.

COIN

Gold Coins	‡*Bi-colour Coins*
*One hundred pounds	Two pounds £2
£100	
*Fifty pounds £50	*Nickel-Brass Coins*
*Twenty-five pounds £25	§Two pounds £2
*Ten pounds £10	One pound £1
Five pounds £5	
Two pounds £2	*Cupro-Nickel Coins*
Sovereign £1	Crown £5 (since 1990)
Half-Sovereign 50p	50 pence 50p
	Crown 25p (pre-1990)
Silver Coins	20 pence 20p
(*Britannia coins*)	10 pence 10p
Two pounds £2	5 pence 5p
One pound £1	
50 pence 50p	*Bronze Coins*
Twenty pence 20p	2 pence 2p
(†*Maundy Money*)	1 penny 1p
Fourpence 4p	
Threepence 3p	*Copper-plated Steel Coins*
Twopence 2p	2 penny 2p
Penny 1p	1 penny 1p

*Britannia coins: gold bullion coins introduced 1987; silver coins introduced 1997
†Gifts of special money distributed by the Sovereign annually on Maundy Thursday to the number of aged poor men and women corresponding to the Sovereign's own age
‡Cupro-nickel centre and nickel-brass outer ring
§Commemorative coins; not intended for general circulation

GOLD COIN

Gold ceased to circulate during the First World War. Since then controls on buying, selling and holding gold coin have been imposed at various times but subsequently have been revoked. Under the Exchange Control (Gold Coins Exemption) Order 1979, gold coins may now be imported and exported without restriction, except gold coins which are more than 50 years old and valued at a sum in excess of £8,000; these cannot be exported without specific authorization from the Department of Trade and Industry.

In 1982 the Government introduced VAT on sales of all gold coin.

SILVER COIN

Prior to 1920 silver coins were struck from sterling silver, an alloy of which 925 parts in 1,000 were silver. In 1920 the proportion of silver was reduced to 500 parts. From 1 January 1947 all 'silver' coins, except Maundy money, have been struck from cupro-nickel, an alloy of copper 75 parts and nickel 25 parts, except for the 20p, composed of copper 84 parts, nickel 16 parts. Maundy coins continue to be struck from sterling silver.

BRONZE COIN

Bronze, introduced in 1860 to replace copper, is an alloy of copper 97 parts, zinc 2.5 parts and tin 0.5 part. These proportions have been subject to slight variations in the past. Bronze was replaced by copper-plated steel in September 1992 and reintroduced in April 1997.

LEGAL TENDER

Gold (dated 1838 onwards, if not below least current weight)	to any amount
£5 (Crown since 1990)	to any amount
£2	to any amount
£1	to any amount
50p	up to £10
25p (Crown pre-1990)	up to £10
20p	up to £10
10p	up to £5
5p	up to £5
2p	up to 20p
1p	up to 20p

The £1 coin was introduced in 1983 to replace the £1 note.

These coins ceased to be legal tender on the following dates:

Farthing	31 December 1960
Halfpenny (¼d)	1 August 1969
Half-crown	1 January 1970
Threepence	31 August 1971
Penny (1d)	31 August 1971
Sixpence	30 June 1980
Halfpenny (½p)	31 December 1984
old 5 pence	31 December 1990
old 10 pence	30 June 1993
old 50 pence	28 February 1998

Since 1982 the word 'new' in 'new pence' displayed on decimal coins has been dropped.

The Channel Islands and the Isle of Man issue their own coinage, which are legal tender only in the island of issue. For denominations, *see* page 613.

	Metal	Standard weight (g)	Standard diameter (cm)
Penny	bronze	3.564	2.032
Penny	copper-plated steel	3.564	2.032
2 pence	bronze	7.128	2.591
2 pence	copper-plated steel	7.128	2.591
5p	cupro-nickel	3.25	1.80
10p	cupro-nickel	6.5	2.45
20p	cupro-nickel	5.0	2.14
25p Crown	cupro-nickel	28.28	3.861
50p	cupro-nickel	13.5	3.0
¶50p	cupro-nickel	8.00	2.73
£1	nickel-brass	9.5	2.25
£2	nickel-brass	15.98	2.84
‡£2	cupro-nickel, nickel-brass	12.00	2.84
£5 Crown	cupro-nickel	28.28	3.861

¶New 50p coin introduced on 1 September 1997

The 'remedy' is the amount of variation from standard permitted in weight and fineness of coins when first issued from the Mint.

The Trial of the Pyx is the examination by a jury to ascertain that coins made by the Royal Mint, which have been set aside in the pyx (or box), are of the proper weight, diameter and composition required by law. The trial is held annually, presided over by the Queen's Remembrancer (the Senior Master of the Supreme Court), with a jury of freemen of the Company of Goldsmiths.

BANKNOTES

Bank of England notes are currently issued in denominations of £5, £10, £20 and £50 for the amount of the fiduciary note issue, and are legal tender in England and Wales. No £1 notes have been issued since 1984 and in March 1998 the outstanding notes were written off.

The current E series of notes was introduced from June 1990, replacing the D series (*see* below). The historical figures portrayed in this series are:

£5	June 1990–	George Stephenson
£10	April 1992–	Charles Dickens
£20	June 1991–	Michael Faraday
£20	June 1999–	Sir Edward Elgar
£50	April 1994–	Sir John Houblon

NOTE CIRCULATION

Note circulation is highest at the two peak spending periods of the year, around Christmas and during the summer holiday period. The total value of notes in circulation at 23 December 1998 was £25,991 million, compared to £26,105 million at 24 December 1997.

The value of notes in circulation at end February 1998 and 1999 was:

	1998	1999
£5	£1,034m	£1,111m
£10	£5,960m	£5,966m
£20	£10,621m	£11,414m
£50	£3,636m	£3,962m
Other notes†	£2,242m	£2,339m
Total	£23,548m	£24,792m

† Includes higher value notes used internally in the Bank of England, e.g. as cover for the note issues of banks in Scotland and Northern Ireland in excess of their permitted issue

LEGAL TENDER

Banknotes which are no longer legal tender are payable when presented at the head office of the Bank of England in London.

The white notes for £10, £20, £50, £100, £500 and £1,000, which were issued until April 1943, ceased to be legal tender in May 1945, and the white £5 note in March 1946.

The white £5 note issued between October 1945 and September 1956, the £5 notes issued between 1957 and 1963 (bearing a portrait of Britannia) and the first series to bear a portrait of The Queen, issued between 1963 and 1971, ceased to be legal tender in March 1961, June 1967 and September 1973 respectively.

The series of £1 notes issued during the years 1928 to 1960 and the 10 shilling notes issued from 1928 to 1961 (those without the royal portrait) ceased to be legal tender in May and October 1962 respectively. The £1 note first issued in March 1960 (bearing on the back a representation of Britannia) and the £10 note first issued in February 1964 (bearing a lion on the back), both bearing a portrait of The Queen on the front, ceased to be legal tender in June 1979. The £1 note first issued in 1978 ceased to be legal tender on 11 March 1988. The 10 shilling note was replaced by the 50p coin in October 1969, and ceased to be legal tender on 21 November 1970.

The D series of banknotes was introduced from 1970 and ceased to be legal tender from the dates shown below.

The predominant identifying feature of each note was the portrayal on the back of a prominent figure from British history:

£1	Feb. 1978–March 1988	Sir Isaac Newton
£5	Nov. 1971–Nov. 1991	The Duke of Wellington
£10	Feb. 1975–May 1994	Florence Nightingale
£20	July 1970–March 1993	William Shakespeare
£50	March 1981–Sept. 1996	Sir Christopher Wren

The £1 coin was introduced on 21 April 1983 to replace the £1 note.

OTHER BANKNOTES

SCOTLAND – Banknotes are issued by three Scottish banks. The Royal Bank of Scotland issues notes for £1, £5, £10, £20 and £100. The Bank of Scotland and the Clydesdale Bank issue notes for £5, £10, £20, £50 and £100. Scottish notes are not legal tender in Scotland but they are an authorized currency and enjoy a status comparable to that of Bank of England notes.

NORTHERN IRELAND – Banknotes are issued by four banks in Northern Ireland. The Bank of Ireland, the Northern Bank and the Ulster Bank issue notes for £5, £10, £20, £50 and £100. The First Trust Bank issues notes for £10, £20, £50 and £100. Northern Ireland notes are not legal tender in Northern Ireland but they circulate widely and enjoy a status comparable to that of Bank of England notes.

CHANNEL ISLANDS – The States of Guernsey issues its own currency notes and coinage. The notes are for £1, £5, £10, £20 and £50, and the coins are for 1p, 2p, 5p, 10p, 20p, 50p, £1, £2 and £5. The States of Jersey issues its own currency notes and coinage. The notes are for £1, £5, £10, £20 and £50, and the coins are for 1p, 2p, 5p, 10p, 20p, 50p, £1 and £2.

THE ISLE OF MAN – The Isle of Man Government issues notes for £1, £5, £10, £20 and £50. Although these notes are only legal tender in the Isle of Man, they are accepted at face value in branches of the clearing banks in the UK. The Isle of Man issues coins for 1p, 2p, 5p, 10p, 20p, 50p, £1, £2 and £5.

Although none of the series of notes specified above is legal tender in the UK, they are generally accepted by the banks irrespective of their place of issue. At one time the banks made a commission charge for handling Scottish and Irish notes but this was abolished some years ago.

Banking

Deposit-taking institutions may be broadly divided into two sectors: the monetary sector, which is predominantly banks, and those institutions outside the monetary sector, of which the most important are the building societies (*see* pages 619–23) and National Savings (*see* pages 624–6). Both sectors are supervised by the Financial Services Authority. As a result of the conversion of several building societies into banks in recent years, the size of the banking sector, which was already substantially greater than the non-bank deposit-taking sector, has increased further.

The main institutions within the British banking system are the Bank of England (the central bank), the retail banks, the merchant banks and the overseas banks. In its role as the central bank, the Bank of England acts as banker to the Government and as a note-issuing authority; it also oversees the efficient functioning of payment and settlement systems.

Since May 1997, the Bank of England has had operational responsibility for monetary policy. At monthly meetings of its monetary policy committee the Bank sets the interest rate at which it will lend to the money markets.

OFFICIAL INTEREST RATES 1998–9

4 June 1998	7.50%
8 October 1998	7.25%
5 November 1998	6.75%
10 December 1998	6.25%
7 January 1999	6.00%
4 February 1999	5.50%
8 April 1999	5.25%
10 June 1999	5.00%

RETAIL BANKS

The major retail banks are Abbey National, Alliance and Leicester, Bank of Scotland, Barclays, Halifax, Lloyds/TSB, HSBC (formerly Midland), National Westminster, Northern Rock, Royal Bank of Scotland and the Woolwich.

Retail banks offer a wide variety of financial services to companies and individuals, including current and deposit accounts, loan and overdraft facilities, automated teller (cash dispenser) machines, cheque guarantee cards, credit cards and debit cards. Several banks also now offer telephone and Internet banking facilities.

The Banking Ombudsman scheme provides independent and impartial arbitration in disputes between a bank and its customer (*see also* page 636).

Banking hours differ throughout the UK. Many banks now open longer hours and some at weekends, and hours vary from branch to branch. Current core opening hours are:

ENGLAND AND WALES: Monday–Friday, 9.30–4.30
SCOTLAND: Monday–Friday, 9.00–5.00
NORTHERN IRELAND: Monday–Friday, 9.30–4.30
(Wednesdays 10.00–4.30, except Ulster Bank Ltd);
Northern Bank, 10.00–3.30, Saturdays 9.30–12.30

PAYMENT CLEARINGS

The Association for Payment Clearing Services (APACS) is an umbrella organization for payment clearings in the UK. It operates three clearing companies:
–BACS Ltd is the UK's automated clearing house for bulk clearing of electronic debits and credits (e.g. direct debits and salary credits)
–the Cheque and Credit Clearing Company Ltd operates bulk clearing systems for inter-bank cheques and paper credit items in Great Britain
–CHAPS Clearing Company Ltd provides same-day clearing for high-value electronic funds transfers throughout the UK in sterling and globally in euros
Membership of APACS and the clearing companies is open to any appropriately regulated financial institution providing payment services and meeting the relevant membership criteria. As at June 1999, APACS had 29 members, comprising the major banks and building societies.

ASSOCIATION FOR PAYMENT CLEARING SERVICES (APACS), Mercury House, Triton Court, 14 Finsbury Square, London EC2A 1LQ. Tel: 0171-711 6200. *Head of Public Affairs*, R. Tyson-Davies

BACS LTD, De Havilland Road, Edgware, Middx HA8 5QA. *Chief Executive*, G. Younger

CHEQUE AND CREDIT CLEARING COMPANY LTD, Mercury House, Triton Court, 14 Finsbury Square, London EC2A 1LQ

CHAPS CLEARING COMPANY LTD, Mercury House, Triton Court, 14 Finsbury Square, London EC2A 1LQ

MAJOR RETAIL BANKS: FINANCIAL RESULTS 1998

Bank Group	Profit before taxation £m	Profit after taxation £m	Total assets £m	Number of UK branches
Abbey National	1,520	1,105	177,800	793
Alliance and Leicester	455.2	317.9	27,579	316
Bank of Scotland	1,011.9	580.6	59,796	325
Barclays	1,918	1,380	219,494	1,950
Halifax	1,705	1,171	145,000	814
Lloyds/TSB Group	3,015	2,133	167,997	2,700
Midland	1,522	1,043	104,846	1,700
NatWest Group	2,142	1,641	185,993	1,727
Northern Rock	202.6	136.6	18,157	107
Royal Bank of Scotland Group	1,001	637	79,676	664
Woolwich	495.9	331.3	33,239	406

AUTHORIZED INSTITUTIONS

Banking in the UK is regulated by the Banking Act 1987 as amended by the European Community's Second Banking Co-ordination Directive, which came into effect on 1 January 1993. The Banking Act 1987 established a single category of banks eligible to carry out banking business; these are known as authorized institutions. Authorization under the Act is granted by the Bank of England; it is an offence for anyone not on its list of authorized institutions to conduct deposit-taking business, unless they are exempted from the requirements of the Act (e.g. building societies). The Government has announced that it will transfer responsibility for banking supervision to the Financial Services Authority. Once the necessary legislation has been passed (probably in 1999-2000) the FSA will be responsible for the authorization and supervision of banks and the supervision of clearing and settlement systems.

The implementation of the Second Banking Co-ordination Directive permits banks incorporated in one EU member state to carry on certain banking activities in another member state without the need for authorization by that state. Consequently, the Bank of England no longer authorizes banks incorporated in other EU states with branches in the UK; the authorization of their home state supervisor is sufficient provided that certain notification requirements are met.

As at 7 June 1999, a total of 594 institutions were authorized to carry out banking business in the UK, 335 authorized under the Banking Act 1987 and 259 recognized under the Second Banking Co-ordination Directive as European authorized institutions (EAIs):

UK-incorporated	200
Incorporated outside the EEA	135
EAIs with UK branches entitled to accept deposits in UK	106
EAIs entitled to accept deposits in UK on cross-border basis	114
Other EAIs	39

The following institutions were authorized or entitled to accept deposits through presences in the UK as at 7 June 1999.

AUTHORIZED BY THE FINANCIAL SERVICES AUTHORITY

UK-INCORPORATED

(Including partnerships formed under the law of any part of the UK)

ABC International Bank PLC
AMC Bank Ltd
AY Bank Ltd
Abbey National PLC
Abbey National Treasury Services PLC
Adam & COMPANY PLC
Afghan National Credit and Finance Ltd
Airdrie Savings Bank
Alliance and Leicester PLC
Alliance and Leicester Group Treasury PLC
Alliance Trust Savings Ltd
Allied Bank Philippines (UK) PLC
Allied Irish Bank (GB)/First Trust Bank – (AIB Group (UK) PLC)
Alpha Bank London Ltd
Anglo-Romanian Bank Ltd
Henry Ansbacher & Co. Ltd

Arbuthnot Latham & Co. Ltd
Assemblies of God Property Trust
Associates Capital Corporation PLC
Avco Trust PLC
Bank Leumi (UK) PLC
Bank of America International Ltd
Bank of China International (UK) Ltd
Bank of Cyprus (London) Ltd
Bank of Montreal Europe Ltd
Bank of Scotland
Bank of Scotland Treasury Services PLC
Bank of Wales PLC
Bankers Trust International PLC
Bankgesellschaft Berlin (UK) PLC
Banque Nationale de Paris PLC
Baptist Union Corporation Ltd
Barclays Bank PLC
Barclays Bank Trust Company Ltd
Barclays Private Bank Ltd
Baring Brothers Ltd
Beneficial Bank PLC
Bristol and West PLC
British Arab Commercial Bank Ltd
British Bank of the Middle East
British Linen Bank Ltd
Brown, Shipley & Co. LTD
CIBC World Markets PLC
Cafcash Ltd
Capital Bank PLC
Cater Allen Ltd
Chartered Trust PLC
Charterhouse Bank Ltd
Chase Manhattan International Ltd
Cheltenham and Gloucester PLC
Citibank International PLC
Close Brothers Ltd
Clydesdale Bank PLC
Consolidated Credits Bank Ltd
Co-operative Bank PLC
Coutts & Co.
Crédit Agricole Lazard Financial Products Bank
Credit Suisse Financial Products
Crown Agents Financial Services Ltd
Daiwa Europe Bank PLC
Dalbeattie Finance Co. Ltd
Dao Heng Bank (London) PLC
Dexia Municipal Bank PLC
Direct Line Financial Services Ltd
Dorset, Somerset and Wilts Investment Society Ltd
Dryfield Trust PLC
Dunbar Bank PLC
Duncan Lawrie Ltd
EFG Private Bank Ltd
Eccles Savings and Loans Ltd
FCE Bank PLC
FIBI Bank (UK) PLC
First National Bank PLC
Robert Fleming & Co. LTD
Forward Trust Group Ltd
Frizzell Bank Ltd
Gartmore Money Management Ltd
GE Capital Bank Ltd
Gerrard and King Ltd
Ghana International Bank PLC
Girobank PLC
Goldman Sachs International Bank
Granville Bank Ltd
Gresham Trust PLC

HFC Bank PLC
HSBC Equator Bank PLC
HSBC Investment Bank PLC
Habibsons Bank Ltd
Halifax PLC
Hampshire Trust PLC
Hardware Federation Finance Co. Ltd
Harrods Bank Ltd
Harton Bank Ltd
Havana International Bank Ltd
Heritable and General Investment Bank Ltd
C. Hoare & Co.
Julian Hodge Bank Ltd
3i PLC
3i Group PLC
IBJ International PLC
Investec Bank (UK) Ltd
Iran Overseas Investment Bank PLC
Jordan International Bank PLC
Leopold Joseph and Sons Ltd
KDB Bank (UK) Ltd
KEXIM Bank (UK) Ltd
Kleinwort Benson Ltd
Kleinwort Benson Investment Management Ltd
Kookmin Bank International Ltd
Lazard Brothers & Co. LTD
Legal and General Bank Ltd
Lloyds Bank PLC
Lloyds Bank (BLSA) Ltd
Lloyds Bowmaker Ltd
Lloyds Private Banking Ltd
Lombard and Ulster Ltd
Lombard Bank Ltd
Lombard North Central PLC
London Scottish Bank PLC
London Trust Bank PLC
MBNA International Bank Ltd
W. M. Mann & Co. (INVESTMENTS) LTD
Marks and Spencer Financial Services Ltd
Matheson Bank Ltd
Matlock Bank Ltd
Meghraj Bank Ltd
Merrill Lynch International Bank Ltd
Methodist Chapel Aid Association Ltd
Midland Bank Trust Company Ltd
Minster Trust Ltd
Samuel Montagu & Co. LTD
Morgan Grenfell & Co. LTD
Morgan Stanley Dean Witter Bank Ltd
Moscow Narodny Bank Ltd
National Bank of Egypt International Ltd
National Bank of Kuwait (International) PLC
National Westminster Bank PLC
NationsBank Europe Ltd
Nikko Bank (UK) PLC
Noble Grossart Ltd
Nomura Bank International PLC
Northern Bank Ltd
Northern Bank Executor and Trustee Company Ltd
Northern Rock PLC
PaineWebber International Bank Ltd
Philippine National Bank (Europe) PLC
Pointon York Ltd
Prudential-Bache International Bank Ltd
Prudential Banking PLC
RBS Trust Bank Ltd
R. Raphael and Sons PLC
Rathbone Bros & Co. LTD

Rea Brothers Ltd
Reliance Bank Ltd
Riggs Bank Europe Ltd
Riyad Bank Europe Ltd
N. M. Rothschild and Sons Ltd
Royal Bank of Canada Europe Ltd
Royal Bank of Scotland PLC
RoyScot Trust PLC
Ruffler Bank PLC
SBI European Bank PLC
SG Hambros Bank and Trust Ltd
Sabanci Bank PLC
Sainsbury's Bank PLC
Sanwa International PLC
Saudi American Bank (UK) Ltd
Saudi International Bank (Al-Bank Al-Saudi Al-Alami Ltd)
Schroder Leasing Ltd
J. Henry Schroder & Co. LTD
Scotiabank Europe PLC
Scottish Widows Bank PLC
Secure Trust Bank PLC
Singer and Friedlander Ltd
Smith and Williamson Investment Management Ltd
Southsea Mortgage and Investment Co. Ltd
Standard Bank London Ltd
Standard Chartered Bank
Standard Life Bank Ltd
State Street Bank Europe Ltd
Sun Bank PLC
TSB Bank PLC
TSB Bank Scotland PLC
Tesco Personal Finance Ltd
Tokai Bank Europe PLC
Toronto Dominion Bank Europe Ltd
Turkish Bank (UK) Ltd
Ulster Bank Ltd
Union Discount Company Ltd
United Bank of Kuwait PLC
United Trust Bank Ltd
Unity Trust Bank PLC
Weatherbys Bank Ltd
Wesleyan Savings Bank Ltd
West Merchant Bank Ltd
Whiteaway Laidlaw Bank Ltd
Wintrust Securities Ltd
Woolwich PLC
Yorkshire Bank PLC

INCORPORATED OUTSIDE THE EUROPEAN ECONOMIC
AREA
(Including partnerships or other unincorporated associ-
ations formed under the law of any member state of the
European Union other than the UK)
†Provisional liquidator appointed

ABSA Bank Ltd
Allied Bank of Pakistan Ltd
American Express Bank Ltd
Arab African International Bank
Arab Bank PLC
Arab National Bank
Asahi Bank Ltd
Australia and New Zealand Banking Group Ltd
BSI AG
Banca Serfin SA
Banco de la Nación Argentina
Banco do Brasil SA
Banco do Estado de São Paulo SA

Banco Mercantil Finasa SA São Paulo
Banco Nacional de Mexico SA
Banco Real SA
Bancomer SA
Bangkok Bank Public Company Ltd
Bank Julius Baer & Co. LTD
BankBoston NA
Bank Bumiputra Malaysia Berhad
PT Bank Ekspor Impor Indonesia (Persero)
Bank Handlowy w Warszawie SA
Bank Hapoalim BM
Bank Mellat
Bank Melli Iran
PT Bank Negara Indonesia (Persero) Tbk
Bank of America NT & SA
Bank of Baroda
Bank of Ceylon
Bank of China
Bank of Cyprus Ltd
Bank of East Asia Ltd
Bank of Fukuoka Ltd
Bank of India
Bank of Montreal
Bank of New York
Bank of Nova Scotia
Bank of Tokyo-Mitsubishi Ltd
Bank Saderat Iran
Bank Sepah-Iran
Bank Tejarat
Bankers Trust Company
Beirut Riyad Bank SAL

Canadian Imperial Bank of Commerce
Canara Bank
Capital One Bank
Chang Hwa Commercial Bank Ltd
Chase Manhattan Bank
Chiba Bank Ltd
Cho Hung Bank
Chuo Trust and Banking Co. Ltd
Citibank NA
Commonwealth Bank of Australia
Credit Suisse First Boston
Cyprus Popular Bank Ltd

Dai-Ichi Kangyo Bank Ltd
Development Bank of Singapore Ltd
Discount Bank and Trust Company

Emirates Bank International PJSC

First Bank of Nigeria PLC
First Commercial Bank
First National Bank of Chicago
First Union National Bank
Fuji Bank Ltd

Gulf International Bank BSC

Habib Bank AG Zurich
Habib Bank Ltd
Hanvit Bank
Hongkong and Shanghai Banking Corporation Ltd
Housing and Commercial Bank, Korea
Hua Nan Commercial Bank Ltd

Industrial Bank of Japan Ltd

Joyo Bank Ltd

KorAm Bank
Korea Development Bank
Korea Exchange Bank
Korea First Bank

Macquarie Bank Ltd
Malayan Banking Berhad
MashreqBank PSC
Mellon Bank NA
Mitsubishi Trust and Banking Corporation
Morgan Guaranty Trust Company of New York

Nacional Financiera SNC
National Australia Bank Ltd
National Bank of Abu Dhabi
National Bank of Canada
National Bank of Dubai Public Joint Stock Company
National Bank of Pakistan
NationsBank NA
Nedcor Bank Ltd
Norinchukin Bank
Northern Trust Company

Oversea-Chinese Banking Corporation Ltd
Overseas Trust Bank Ltd
Overseas Union Bank Ltd

People's Bank
Providian National Bank

Qatar National Bank SAQ

†Rafidain Bank
Republic National Bank of New York
Riggs Bank NA
Riyad Bank
Royal Bank of Canada

Sakura Bank Ltd
Sanwa Bank Ltd
Saudi American Bank
Saudi British Bank
SEOULBANK
Shanghai Commercial Bank Ltd
Shinhan Bank
Siam Commercial Bank Public Company Ltd
Sonali Bank
State Bank of India
State Street Bank and Trust Company
Sumitomo Bank Ltd
Sumitomo Trust and Banking Co. Ltd
Syndicate Bank

TC Ziraat Bankasi
Thai Farmers Bank Public Company Ltd
Tokai Bank Ltd
Toronto-Dominion Bank
Toyo Trust and Banking Company Ltd
Türkiye Iş Bankasi AŞ

UBS AG
Union Bancaire Privée UBP
Union Bank of Nigeria PLC
United Bank Ltd
United Mizrahi Bank Ltd
United Overseas Bank Ltd

Wachovia Bank NA
Westpac Banking Corporation

Zambia National Commercial Bank Ltd
Zivnostenská Banka AS

EUROPEAN AUTHORIZED INSTITUTIONS ENTITLED TO ESTABLISH UK BRANCHES

The following are entitled to establish branches in the UK for the purpose of accepting deposits in the UK. The country of the home state supervisory authority is in parenthesis.

ABN AMRO Bank NV (Netherlands)
AIB Capital Markets PLC (Republic of Ireland)
Allied Irish Banks PLC (Republic of Ireland)
Alpha Credit Bank AE (Greece)
Anglo Irish Bank Corporation PLC (Republic of Ireland)
Argentaria, Caja Postal y Banco Hipotecario SA (Spain)

BfG Bank AG (Germany)
BHF-Bank AG (Germany)
Banca Ambrosiano Veneto SpA (Italy)
Banca Cassa di Risparmio di Torino SpA (Italy)
Banca Commerciale Italiana (Italy)
Banca d'Intermediazione Mobiliare IMI SpA (Italy)
Banca di Napoli SpA (Italy)
Banca di Roma SpA (Italy)
Banca di Sicilia SpA (Italy)
Banca Monte dei Paschi di Siena SpA (Italy)
Banca Nazionale dell'Agricoltura SpA (Italy)
Banca Nazionale del Lavoro SpA (Italy)
Banca Popolare di Milano (Italy)
Banca Popolare di Novara (Italy)
Banco Bilbao-Vizcaya (Spain)
Banco Central Hispanoamericano SA (Spain)
Banco de Sabadell (Spain)
Banco Español de Crédito SA (Spain)
Banco Espirito Santo e Comercial de Lisboa (Portugal)
Banco March SA (Spain)
Banco Nacional Ultramarino SA (Portugal)
Banco Português do Atlântico (Portugal)
Banco Santander (Spain)
Banco Totta & Açores SA (Portugal)
Bank Austria AG (Austria)
Bank Austria Creditanstalt International AG (Austria)
Bank Brussels Lambert (Belgium)
Bankgesellschaft Berlin AG (Germany)
Bank of Ireland (Republic of Ireland)
Banque AIG (France)
Banque Arabe et Internationale d'Investissement (France)
Banque Banorabe (France)
Banque CPR (France)
Banque Française de l'Orient (France)
Banque Internationale à Luxembourg SA (Luxembourg)
Banque Nationale de Paris (France)
Bayerische Hypo-und Vereinsbank AG (Germany)
Bayerische Landesbank Girozentrale (Germany)
Belgolaise SA (Belgium)
Berliner Bank AG (Germany)
Byblos Bank Europe SA (Belgium)

CARIPLO (Cassa di Risparmio delle Provincie Lombarde SpA) (Italy)
Caisse Nationale de Crédit Agricole (France)
Cariverona Banca SpA (Italy)
Christiania Bank og Kreditkasse (Norway)
Commerzbank AG (Germany)
Compagnie Financière de CIC et de l'Union Européenne (France)
Confederación Española de Cajas de Ahorros (Spain)
Crédit Agricole Indosuez (France)
Crédit Commercial de France (France)
Crédit du Nord (France)
Crédit Lyonnais (France)

DG BANK, Deutsche Genossenschaftsbank AG (Germany)
De Nationale Investeringsbank NV (Netherlands)
Den Danske Bank Aktieselskab (Denmark)
Den norske Bank ASA (Norway)
DePfa Bank AG BauBoden (Germany)
Deutsche Bank AG (Germany)
Dexia Project and Public Finance International Bank (France)

Dresdner Bank AG (Germany)

Equity Bank Ltd (Republic of Ireland)
Ergobank SA (Greece)
Erste Bank der oesterreichischen Sparkassen AG (Austria)
Euro Hypo Aktiengesellschaft Europäische Hypothekenbank der Deutschen Bank (Germany)

FIMAT International Banque (France)
First Active PLC (Republic of Ireland)

Generale Bank (Belgium)

Hamburgische Landesbank Girozentrale (Germany)

ICC Bank PLC (Republic of Ireland)
ING Bank NV (Netherlands)
Ionian and Popular Bank of Greece SA (Greece)
Irish Nationwide Building Society (Republic of Ireland)
Irish Permanent PLC (Republic of Ireland)

Jyske Bank (Denmark)

KBC Bank NV (Belgium)
Kas-Associatie NV (Netherlands)

Landesbank Baden-Württemberg (Germany)
Landesbank Berlin Girozentrale (Germany)
Landesbank Hessen-Thüringen Girozentrale (Germany)
Lehman Brothers Bankhaus AG (Germany)
Leonia Bank PLC (Finland)

MeesPierson NV (Netherlands)
Merita Bank Ltd (Finland)

Natexis Banque (France)
National Bank of Greece SA (Greece)
Norddeutsche Landesbank Girozentrale (Germany)

Paribas (France)

Rabobank International (Coöperatieve Centrale Raiffeisen-Boerenleenbank BA) (Netherlands)
Raiffeisen Zentralbank Osterreich AG (Austria)

San Paolo-IMI SpA (Italy)
Skandinaviska Enskilda Banken AB (publ) (Sweden)
Société Générale (France)
Svenska Handelsbanken AB (publ) (Sweden)
SwedBank (FöreningsSparbanken AB (publ)) (Sweden)

Triodosbank NV (Netherlands)

Ulster Bank Markets Ltd (Republic of Ireland)
Unibank A/S (Denmark)
UniCredito Italiano SpA (Italy)

Westdeutsche ImmobilienBank (Germany)
Westdeutsche Landesbank Girozentrale (Germany)

Mutual Societies

In July 1997 the Government announced that responsibility for regulation of mutual societies would be transferred to a single new regulatory organization, since named Financial Services Authority (FSA).

On 1 January 1999 the staff of the Registry of Friendly Societies (RFS), which had supported the functions of the Building Societies Commission, the Friendly Societies Commission and (in relation to Credit Unions) the Chief Registrar, were transferred to FSA. The new organization provides services and support to the Commissions and Chief Registrar under agreements which will operate until their responsibilities are subsumed in those of FSA following the enactment of the Financial Services and Markets Bill, expected to be around summer 2000. It is currently planned that the registration and records work of the RFS, on which a decision had earlier been deferred, will now transfer the FSA with its supporting staff on enactment of the Bill.

FRIENDLY SOCIETIES IN BRITAIN

Friendly societies are voluntary mutual organizations, the main purposes of which are the provision of relief or maintenance during sickness, unemployment or retirement, and the provision of life assurance. Many of the older traditional societies complement their business activities by social activity and a general care for individual members in ways normally outside the scope of a purely commercial organization. There are three main categories of friendly societies: societies with separately registered branches, commonly called orders; centralized societies, which conduct business directly with members (having no separately registered branches); and collecting societies. Collecting societies conduct industrial assurance business and are subject to the requirements of the Industrial Assurance Acts in addition to the Friendly Societies Acts. Industrial assurance is life assurance for which the premiums are payable at intervals of less than two months and are received by means of collectors who make house-to-house visits for the purpose. Economic pressures have caused many 'home service assurance' providers to cease transacting this business. Following earlier consultations on the desirability of removing burdens imposed by the Industrial Assurance legislation, it was announced in June 1999 that the repeal, or substantial repeal, of the legislation would be dealt with in the Financial Services and Markets Bill.

The Friendly Societies Act 1974 allowed three other main classes of society to be registered: benevolent societies, working men's clubs and specially authorized societies. Benevolent societies are established for any charitable or benevolent purpose, to provide the same type of benefits as would be permissible for a friendly society, but in contrast the benefits must be for persons who are not members instead of, or in addition to, members. Working men's clubs provide social and recreational facilities for members. Specially authorized societies are registered for any purpose authorized by the Treasury as a purpose to which some or all of the provisions of the 1974 Act ought to be extended. Examples are societies for the promotion of science, literature and the fine arts, or to enable members to pursue an interest in sports and games. No new societies of any type may now be registered under this Act.

The most recent legislation, the Friendly Societies Act 1992, created a new legislative framework for friendly societies, enabling them to provide a wider range of services to their members and allowing them to compete on more equal terms with other financial institutions. At the same time it provided for more flexible prudential supervision to safeguard members of societies.

The Act enables friendly societies to incorporate and establish subsidiaries to provide various financial and other services to their members and the public. The activities which subsidiaries are able to conduct include those to establish and manage unit trust schemes and personal equity plans; to arrange for the provision of credit, whether as agents or providers; to carry on long-term or general insurance business; to provide insurance intermediary services; to provide fund management services for trustees of pension funds; to administer estates and execute trusts of wills; and to establish and manage sheltered housing, residential homes for the elderly, hospitals and nursing homes.

The Act established a new framework to oversee friendly societies, including a Friendly Societies Commission, whose principal functions are to regulate the activities of friendly societies, promote their financial stability and protect members' funds. All friendly societies carrying on insurance or non-insurance business require authorization by the Commission, which has a broad range of prudential powers. Friendly societies were also to be brought within the scope of the Policyholders Protection Act 1975, the statutory investor protection scheme covering insurance policyholders.

At the end of May 1999 there were 114 societies authorized to write new business. Thirty-seven societies had taken advantage of the 1992 Act to incorporate and 20 of them had established subsidiary companies providing a wide range of services. More than half the friendly societies on the register were not authorized to transact new business, many being small and with a declining membership.

At the end of 1997 there were 293 friendly societies on the register. The 40 societies carrying on long term insurance business accounted for 95 per cent of the total funds of the movement. Statistics for those societies are set out in the table below.

Life Directive and Incorporated Societies

	1997	1996
No. of societies	40	38
*Membership ('000s)	4,698	7,760
Contribution income (£'000s)	768,309	766,964
Investment income (£'000s)	1,059,216	746,966
Benefits paid (£'000s)	792,023	754,158
Management expenses (£'000s)	222,860	212,300
Total assets (£'000s)	11,716,427	10,452,884

* Some societies historically reported membership in terms of policies held and have estimated membership for 1997. Figure for 1996 and 1997 are therefore not comparable.

The numbers of the various types of bodies registered under the Friendly Societies Acts at the end of 1997 were:

FRIENDLY SOCIETIES
Orders*	15
Collecting societies	16
Other centralized societies	262

OTHER BODIES
Benevolent societies*	66
Working men's clubs	2,151
Specially authorized societies	122

* With 821 branches

INDUSTRIAL AND PROVIDENT SOCIETIES IN BRITAIN

The familiar 'Co-op' societies are amongst the wide variety which are registered under the Industrial and Provident Societies Act 1965. This consolidating Act, which is principally administered by the Central Office of the Registry of Friendly Societies (*see* below for credit unions), provides for the registration of societies and lays down the broad framework within which they must operate. Internal relations of societies are governed by their registered rules.

Registration under the Act confers upon a society corporate status by its registered name with perpetual succession and a common seal, and limited liability. A society qualifies for registration if it is carrying on an industry, business or trade, and it satisfies the Registrar either (a) that it is a bona fide co-operative society, or (b) that in view of the fact that its business is being, or is intended to be, conducted for the benefit of the community, there are special reasons why it should be registered under the Act rather than as a company under the Companies Act.

The Credit Unions Act 1979 added a new class of society registrable under the 1965 Act. It also made provision for the supervision of these savings and loan bodies. Unlike other classes, where the role of the Registry remains solely that of a registration authority, it was for credit unions the prudential supervisor, seeking to encourage the prudent safeguarding of members' money. On 1 January 1999 these responsibilities for credit unions were transferred to Financial Services Authority.

During 1997 the number of registered societies of all classes decreased by 17 to 10,584 but the number of credit unions again increased – by 51 during the year. The number of new credit unions has been growing steadily at an average rate in excess of 50 registrations a year since 1988. There were 624 by end September 1998. Assets of all industrial and provident societies totalled £47,031 million at the end of 1997. The principal statistics at the end of 1997 are given in the table below.

	No. of societies	No. of members 000s	Funds of members £000s	Total assets £000s
Retail	131	6,083	2,100,476	3,561,871
Wholesale and productive	122	45	664,478	1,461,872
Agricultural	939	249	220,650	731,561
Fishing	82	5	9,039	20,005
Clubs	3,656	3,072	352,677	592,225
General service	1,160	524	2,133,971	19,723,179
Housing	3,898	180	7,865,148	20,816,198
Credit unions	596	224	118,101	123,979
TOTAL	10,584	10,382	13,464,740	47,030,890

BUILDING SOCIETIES IN THE UK

The Building Societies Act 1997, which received royal assent on 21 March 1997, makes substantive amendments to, but does not replace, the Building Societies Act 1986. It liberalizes the statutory regime for building societies to enable them to compete on more level terms with other financial institutions without having to forego their mutual status.

The Building Societies Act 1986 gave building societies a completely new legal framework for the first time since the initial comprehensive building society legislation in 1874. The 1986 Act sets out detailed provisions in relation to:

– the constitution of building societies
– building societies' powers in relation to raising funds, advances, loans, other assets and the provision of services
– the powers of control of the Building Societies Commission
– protection of investors, and complaints and disputes
– management of building societies, accounts and audit
– mergers and transfers of business

The 1986 Act was prescriptive in respect of building societies' powers and the way in which they were exercised. However, it gave numerous powers to the Building Societies Commission and/or the Treasury to make statutory instruments which, subject to parliamentary approval, can amend, extend and supplement the provisions of the Act. Since it came into force on 1 January 1987 the Act had been amended and extended considerably, especially in respect of building societies' powers.

The main purposes of the Building Societies Act 1997 are:

– remove the prescriptive powers' regime relating to building societies and to replace it with a permissive regime with appropriately revised balance-sheet 'nature limits', thus increasing the commercial freedom of societies and allowing increased competition and wider choice for customers
– enhance the powers of control of the Building Societies Commission
– introduce a package of measures to enhance the accountability of building societies' boards to their members
– make changes to the provisions relating to the transfer of a building society's business to a company

The Act came fully into force on 21 October 1997. Under it a building society may pursue any activities set out in its memorandum, subject only to:

– principal purpose: its purpose or principal purpose must be that of making loans which are secured on residential properties and are funded substantially by its members
– lending limit: at least 75 per cent of its business assets must be loans fully secured on residential property
– funding limit: at least 50 per cent of its funds must be raised in the form of shares held by individual members
– restrictions: subject to certain exceptions, it must not act as a market maker in securities, commodities or currencies; trade in commodities or currencies; enter into transactions involving derivatives, except in relation to hedging; nor create a floating charge over its assets
– prudential: it must comply with the criteria of prudential management

All authorized building societies, after making the necessary changes to their memoranda and rules, are now operating under the more liberal statutory regime set out in the 1997 Act.

CONVERSIONS AND TAKE-OVERS

The Alliance and Leicester, Halifax, Northern Rock and Woolwich building societies completed their conversions to PLC status during 1997, whilst Bristol and West transferred to the Bank of Ireland and Greenwich transferred to the Portman.

The transfer of business of Birmingham Midshires Building Society to Halifax PLC was completed on 23 April 1999. Standard Building Society announced earlier in the year that it proposed to transfer its engagements to the Mercantile Building Society.

In the first half of 1999 seven of the largest remaining building societies received draft resolutions from their members proposing the demutualization of these societies. In six cases their Boards rejected the resolutions as invalid. A resolution put to the annual general meeting of Bradford and Bingley Building Society on 26 April 1999 was carried and the Board subsequently announced its decision to put a formal proposal for conversion to PLC status to its members.

OMBUDSMAN SCHEME

Societies must belong to an ombudsman scheme for the investigation of complaints. Matters to be covered by the scheme include operation of share and deposit accounts, loans (but not the making of new loans), money transmission services, foreign exchange services, agency payments and receipts, and the provision of credit. Grounds for complaint include breach of the Act or contract, unfair treatment or maladministration, and where the complainant has suffered pecuniary loss or expense or inconvenience. A society must

agree to be bound by decisions of the adjudicator unless it agrees to give notice to its members and the public of its reasons for not doing so. For address of the Building Societies Ombudsman scheme, *see* page 636.

BUILDING SOCIETIES 1997–8

	1997	1998
No. of societies – total	82	78
– authorized	71	71
No. of shareholders (000s)	19,234	21,195
No. of depositors (000s)	964	909
No. of borrowers (000s)	2,872	3,136
Share balances (£m)	90,092	103,290
Deposit balances (£m)	31,207	33,453
Mortgage balances (£m)	105,803	116,285
Total assets (£m)	137,864	156,014
Advances during year		
No. (000s)	522	521
Amount (£m)	22,730	24,244

MORTGAGE ARREARS AND REPOSSESSIONS

Economic recession resulted in a sharp rise in mortgage arrears and repossessions, with more than 75,000 properties repossessed in 1991. That total fell by 7,000 in 1992 as a result of a greater willingness by lenders to enter into arrangements with borrowers. The number continued to decline in the following four years. Under 33,000 properties

were taken into possession in 1997, the lowest figure since 1989. The 1998 figures do not, however, follow the declining trend, being very similar to those for 1997. Details of loans outstanding and properties repossessed for recent years, based on statistics of the largest building society and non-building society lenders, are shown below.

	1991	1992	1993	1994	1995	1996	1997	1998
No. of loans at end year (000s)	9,815	9,922	10,137	10,410	10,521	10,637	10,738	10,821
Properties repossessed in year								
Number	75,540	68,540	58,540	49,190	49,410	42,560	32,770	33,820
%	0.77	0.70	0.58	0.47	0.47	0.40	0.31	0.31

INTEREST RATES: MORTGAGE AND SHARE 1994–9

The interest rates prevailing on mortgage lending and share investment vary from society to society and in relation to the type or amount of loan or investment.

The interval between the payments or compounding of

interest is crucial in determining the competitiveness of particular societies' accounts. In order to make a true comparison of interest rates, the annual percentage rate or APR, which should appear in all advertisements and leaflets, must be used.

	1994	1995	1996	1997	1998	1999 1st quarter
Average bank base rate	5.46	6.70	5.96	6.56	7.24	5.69
Building societies average mortgage rate	7.68	7.84	6.72	7.03	7.76	6.76
Building societies average share rate	5.36	5.62	4.54	5.49	6.34	5.23

SOCIETIES WITH TOTAL ASSETS EXCEEDING £1 MILLION AT END OF FINANCIAL YEAR 1998

Name of Building Society* and head office address	Members	Total assets £'000
Barnsley, Regent Street, Barnsley, S. Yorks S70 2EH	51,713	236,791
Bath Investment, 20 Charles Street, Bath BA1 1HY	21,000	81,838
Beverley, 57 Market Place, Beverley, E. Yorks HU17 8AA	7,968	51,818
Birmingham Midshires, PO Box 81, Pendeford Business Park, Wobaston Road, Wolverhampton WV9 5HZ (transferred to Halifax PLC April 1999)	—	—
Bradford and Bingley, Crossflatts, Bingley, W. Yorks BD16 2UA	2,491,000	21,408,800
Britannia, Britannia House, Cheadle Road, Leek, Staffs ST13 5RA	1,857,189	12,665,124
Buckinghamshire, High Street, Chalfont St Giles, Bucks HP8 4QB	9,000	86,572
Cambridge, 51 Newmarket Road, Cambridge CB5 8FF	90,000	459,037
Catholic, 7 Strutton Ground, London SW1P 2HY	3,631	30,554
Century, 21 Albany Street, Edinburgh EH1 3QW	2,806	15,553
Chelsea, Thirlestaine Hall, Thirlestaine Road, Cheltenham, Glos GL53 7AL	309,896	4,041,610
Chesham, 12 Market Square, Chesham, Bucks HP5 1ER	17,897	134,242
Cheshire, Castle Street, Macclesfield, Cheshire SK11 6AF	278,263	2,059,345
Chorley and District, Key House, Foxhole Road, Chorley, Lancs PR7 1NZ	13,945	85,501
Clay Cross, Eyre Street, Clay Cross, Chesterfield S45 9NS	3,882	17,915
Coventry, PO Box 9, High Street, Coventry CV1 5QN	750,000	5,231,335
Cumberland, Cumberland House, Castle Street, Carlisle CA3 8RX	165,000	738,575
Darlington, Sentinel House, Lingfield Way, Darlington, Co. Durham DL1 4PR	74,897	366,585
Derbyshire, Duffield Hall, Duffield, Derby DE56 1AG	290,127	2,440,267
Dudley, Dudley House, Stone Street, Dudley DY1 1NP	26,552	97,820
Dunfermline, Caledonia House, Carnegie Avenue, Dunfermline, Fife KY11 8PJ	177,400	1,322,074
Earl Shilton, 22 The Hollow, Earl Shilton, Leicester LE9 7NB	13,232	65,643
Ecology, 18 Station Road, Cross Hills, Keighley, W. Yorks BD20 7EH	5,699	24,626
Furness, 51–55 Duke Street, Barrow-in-Furness LA14 1RT	95,693	419,846
Gainsborough, 9 Lord Street, Gainsborough, Lincs DN21 2DD	4,667	30,766
Hanley Economic, Granville House, Festival Park, Hanley, Stoke-on-Trent, Staffs ST1 5TB	33,874	214,689
Harpenden, 14 Station Road, Harpenden, Herts AL5 4SE	14,663	62,192
Hinckley and Rugby, Upper Bond Street, Hinckley, Leics LE10 1DG	83,000	412,880
Holmesdale, 43 Church Street, Reigate, Surrey RH2 0AE	7,410	91,603
Ilkeston Permanent, 3 South Street, Ilkeston, Derby DE7 5HQ	3,954	16,502
Ipswich, 44 Upper Brook Street, Ipswich IP4 1DP	25,570	226,063
Kent Reliance, Reliance House, Manor Road, Chatham, Kent ME4 6AF	58,400	319,621
Lambeth, 118–120 Westminster Bridge Road, London SE1 7XE	55,593	660,524
Leeds and Holbeck, 105 Albion Street, Leeds LS1 5AS	267,000	3,121,919
Leek United, 50 St Edward Street, Leek, Staffs ST13 5DH	60,908	445,490
Londonderry Provident, 31A Carlisle Road, Londonderry BT48 6JJ	1,386	12,039
Loughborough, 6 High Street, Loughborough, Leics LE11 2QB	23,757	146,537
Manchester, 24 Queen Street, Manchester M2 5AH	17,447	180,088
Mansfield, Regent House, Regent Street, Mansfield, Notts NG18 1SS	21,810	133,673
Market Harborough, Welland House, The Square, Market Harborough, Leics LE16 7PD	52,409	265,258
Marsden, 6–20 Russell Street, Nelson, Lancs BB9 7NJ	68,113	275,292
Melton Mowbray, 39 Nottingham Street, Melton Mowbray, Leics LE13 1NR	55,021	239,084
Mercantile, Mercantile House, Silverlink Business Park, Wallsend, Tyne and Wear NE28 9NY	33,788	157,643
Monmouthshire, John Frost Square, Newport, Gwent NP20 1PX	39,980	242,652
National Counties, National Counties House, Church Street, Epsom, Surrey KT17 4NL	23,488	587,497
Nationwide, Nationwide House, Pipers Way, Swindon SN38 1NW	7,980,146	52,953,000
Newbury, 17–20 Bartholomew Street, Newbury, Berks RG14 5LY	40,097	308,920
Newcastle, Portland House, New Bridge Street, Newcastle upon Tyne NE1 8AL	274,000	1,936,180
Norwich and Peterborough, Peterborough Business Park, Lynchwood, Peterborough PE2 6WZ	264,045	2,058,068
Nottingham, 5–13 Upper Parliament Street, Nottingham NG1 2BX	163,614	1,213,381
Nottingham Imperial, Imperial House, 72 Bridgford Road, West Bridgford, Nottingham NG2 6AP	9,071	56,916
Penrith, 7 King Street, Penrith, Cumbria CA11 7AR	5,932	54,673
Portman, Portman House, Richmond Hill, Bournemouth, Dorset BH2 6EP	1,176,000	5,560,712
Principality, PO Box 89, Principality Buildings, Queen Street, Cardiff CF10 1UA	300,000	1,869,029
Progressive, 33–37 Wellington Place, Belfast BT1 6HH	70,830	565,904
Saffron Walden, Herts and Essex, 1A Market Street, Saffron Walden, Essex CB10 1HX	67,931	303,642
Scarborough, Prospect House, PO Box 6, Scarborough, N. Yorks YO12 6EQ	131,780	895,968
Scottish, 23 Manor Place, Edinburgh EH3 7XE	27,357	139,634
Shepshed, Bull Ring, Shepshed, Loughborough, Leics LE12 9QD	8,419	40,405
Skipton, The Bailey, Skipton, N. Yorks BD23 1DN	423,951	4,376,759
Stafford Railway, 4 Market Square, Stafford ST16 2JH	11,624	64,093

Name of Building Society* and head office address	Members	Total assets £'000
Staffordshire, Jubilee House, PO Box 66, 84 Salop Street, Wolverhampton WV3 0SA	222,566	1,286,798
Standard, 64 Church Way, North Shields, Tyne and Wear NE29 0AF	2,500	17,369
Stroud and Swindon, Rowcroft, Stroud, Glos GL5 3BG	160,013	1,146,405
Swansea, 11 Cradock Street, Swansea SA1 3EW	4,058	32,911
Teachers, Allenview House, Hanham Road, Wimborne, Dorset BH21 1AG	15,816	160,298
Tipton and Coseley, 70 Owen Street, Tipton, W. Midlands DY4 8HG	17,016	151,400
Universal, Universal House, Kings Manor, Newcastle upon Tyne NE1 6PA	50,000	330,402
Vernon, 19 St Petersgate, Stockport, Cheshire SK1 1HF	31,820	155,943
West Bromwich, 374 High Street, West Bromwich, W. Midlands B70 8LR	445,132	2,408,800
Yorkshire, Yorkshire House, Yorkshire Drive, Bradford BD5 8LJ	1,100,000	9,395,980

* 'Building Society' are the last words in every society's name

National Savings

INVESTMENT AND ORDINARY ACCOUNTS

Interest is earned at 1.1 per cent per year on each ordinary account for every complete calendar month in which the balance is £500 or more, and becomes 1.0 per cent per year for other months. The minimum deposit is £10; maximum balance £10,000 plus interest credited.

The investment account pays a higher rate of interest depending on the account balance (the current rate can be found at any post office). The minimum deposit is £20; maximum balance £100,000 plus interest credited.

Since April 1999 Individual Savings Accounts (ISAs) have been offered by National Savings. An ISA can be opened with £10. Interest is calculated daily on balances of over £1 and is free of tax. The same regulations apply as for ISAs offered by all companies.

PREMIUM BONDS

Premium Bonds are a government security which were first introduced in 1956. Premium Bonds enable savers to enter a regular draw for tax-free prizes, while retaining the right to get their money back. A sum equivalent to interest on each bond is put into a prize fund and distributed by monthly prize draws. (The rate of interest is 3.25 per cent a year from 1 June 1999.) The prizes are drawn by ERNIE (electronic random number indicator equipment) and are free of all UK income tax and capital gains tax.

Bonds are in units of £1, with a minimum purchase of £100; above this, purchases must be in multiples of £10, up to a maximum holding limit of £20,000 per person. The scheme offers a facility to reinvest prize wins automatically. Upon completion of an automatic prize reinvestment mandate, holders receive new bonds which are immediately eligible for future prize draws. Bonds can only be held in the name of an individual and not by organizations.

Bonds become eligible for prizes once they have been held for one clear calendar month following the month of purchase. Each £1 unit can win only one prize per draw, but it will be awarded the highest for which it is drawn. Bonds remain eligible for prizes until they are repaid. When a holder dies, bonds remain eligible for prizes up to and including the twelfth monthly draw after the month in which the holder dies.

By July 1999 bonds to the value of over £12,500 million had been sold. By the July 1999 prize draw, 71 million prizes totalling £4,550 million had been distributed since the first prize draw in June 1957.

INCOME BONDS

National Savings Income Bonds were introduced in 1982. They are suitable for those who want to receive regular monthly payments of interest while preserving the full cash value of their capital. The bonds are sold in multiples of £1,000. The minimum holding is £2,000 and the maximum £250,000 (sole or joint holding).

Interest is calculated on a day-to-day basis and paid monthly. Interest is taxable but is paid without deduction of tax at source. The bonds have a guaranteed life of ten years, but may be repaid at par before maturity on giving three months' notice. Repayment is also possible without giving notice but incurs a penalty. If the sole or sole surviving holder dies, however, no fixed period of notice is required and there is no loss of interest for repayment made within the first year.

PENSIONERS GUARANTEED INCOME BONDS

Pensioners Guaranteed Income Bonds were introduced in January 1994 and are designed for people aged 60 and over

who wish to receive regular monthly payments with a rate of interest that is fixed for a five-year period whilst preserving the full cash value of their investment. A new two-year fixed rate term bond was introduced in May 1999.

The minimum limit for each purchase is £500. The maximum holding is £50,000 (£100,000 for a joint holding); within those limits bonds can be bought for any amount in pounds and pence. The rate of interest is fixed and guaranteed for the first two or five years, depending on term invested. Interest is taxable but is paid without deduction of tax at source.

Holders can apply for repayment (or part repayment of a bond subject to the minimum holding limits) by giving 60 days' notice (if repayment is before the fifth anniversary date). No interest is earned during the notice period. If repayment is requested within two weeks of any fifth anniversary of purchase, there is no formal period of notice. Repayment is possible without giving notice but a penalty is incurred. On the death of a holder or sole surviving investor in a joint holding, repayment will be made without notice. Interest will be paid in full up to the date of repayment.

CHILDREN'S BONUS BONDS

Children's Bonus Bonds were introduced in 1991. The latest issue, Issue O, was introduced in May 1999. They can be bought for any child under 16 and will go on growing in value until he or she is 21. The bonds are sold in multiples of £25. The minimum holding is £25. The maximum holding in Issue O is £1,000 per child. This is in addition to holdings of earlier issues of the bond (excluding interest and bonuses). Bonds for children under 16 must be held by a parent or guardian.

Children's Bonus Bonds (Issue O) earn 3.5 per cent a year over five years. A bonus (7.92 per cent) of the purchase price is added at the fifth anniversary. This is equal to 4.85 per cent a year compound. All returns are totally exempt from UK income tax. No interest is earned on bonds cashed in before the first anniversary of purchase. Bonuses are only payable if the bond is held until the next bonus date. Bonds over five years old continue to earn interest and bonuses until the holder is 21, when they should be cashed in. If bonds are not cashed in on the holder's 21st birthday, they earn no interest after that birthday.

FIRST OPTION BONDS

FIRST (Fixed Interest Rate Savings Tax-paid) Option Bonds were introduced in 1992. They offer guaranteed rates without the need for long-term commitment for personal savers over 16. They may be held indefinitely and will continue to grow in value at rates of interest fixed for 12 months at a time. Tax is deducted from the interest at source. The minimum purchase is £1,000 and the maximum holding is £250,000. Withdrawals can be made without penalty at any anniversary date and there is no formal notice period for repayment. No interest is earned on repayments before the first anniversary.

CAPITAL BONDS

National Savings Capital Bonds were introduced in 1989. The latest series, Series Q, was introduced in May 1999. Capital Bonds offer capital growth over five years with guaranteed returns at fixed rates. The interest is taxable each year (for those who pay income tax) but is not deducted at source. The minimum purchase is £100. There is a maximum holding limit of £250,000 from Series B onwards.

Capital Bonds will be repaid in full with all interest gained at the end of five years. No interest is earned on bonds repaid in the first year. Reinvestment or extension terms may also be available.

NATIONAL SAVINGS TREASURER'S ACCOUNT

The Treasurer's Account, introduced in September 1996, offers attractive rates and security to non-profit making organizations such as charities, friendly societies, clubs, etc. The minimum holding is £10,000 and the maximum is £2 million. Interest is paid at the rate of 4.05 per cent a year on holdings of £10,000 to £24,999, 4.3 per cent a year on holdings of £25,000 to £99,999, and 4.8 per cent a year on holdings of £100,000 and above.

NATIONAL SAVINGS CERTIFICATES

RECENT ISSUES

Interest, index-linked increase, bonus or other sum payable is free of UK income tax (including investment income surcharge) and capital gains tax.

From June 1982, savings certificates of the 7th to 41st Issues will be extended on general extension rates as they reach the end of their existing extension periods. The percentage interest rate is determined by the Treasury and any change in this general extension rate will be applicable from the first of the month following its announcement. Under the system, a certificate earns interest for each complete period of three months beyond the expiry of the previous extension terms. Within each three-month period, interest is calculated separately for each month at the rate applicable from the beginning of that month. The interest for each month is one-twelfth of the annual rate (i.e. it does not vary with the number of days in the month) and is capitalized annually on the anniversary of the date of purchase. The current rate of interest under the general extension rate is given in leaflets available at post offices.

ELEVENTH INDEX-LINKED ISSUE
25 July 1997–8 January 1998
Maximum holding: £10,000, plus special facility to reinvest an unlimited amount
Unit cost: certificates may be purchased for any amount, subject to a minimum purchase at any time of £100; reinvestment certificates are available for any amount and are not subject to a minimum or maximum requirement
Interest: the repayment value, subject to their being held for one year, is related to the movement of the UK General Index of Retail Prices. In addition, there is a guaranteed extra interest of 1.05 per cent for the first year, 1.3 per cent for the second year, 2.05 per cent for the third year, 3.07 per cent for the fourth year and 6.37 per cent for the fifth year. This is worth 2.75 per cent a year compound over the full five years. Reinvestment certificates repaid before the first anniversary date will earn RPI plus extra interest of 1 per cent a year for each complete month.

FORTY-FIFTH ISSUE
9 January–26 March 1998
Maximum holding: £10,000, plus special facility to reinvest an unlimited amount
Unit cost: certificates may be purchased for any amount, subject to a minimum purchase at any time of £100; reinvestment certificates are available for any amount and are not subject to a minimum or maximum requirement
Interest: after one year the repayment value increases by 3.6 per cent for ordinarily held 45th Issue. However, reinvestment certificates if encashed before the first anniversary earn interest at 3.6 per cent a year for each complete period of three months. During the second year the interest rate is 3.9 per cent; during the third year, 4.7 per cent; during the fourth year, 5.7 per cent; and during the fifth year, 7.14 per cent. The compound annual interest rate over the full five years is 5 per cent.

TWELFTH INDEX-LINKED ISSUE
9 January–26 March 1998
Maximum holding: £10,000, plus special facility to reinvest an unlimited amount
Unit cost: certificates may be purchased for any amount, subject to a minimum purchase at any time of £100; reinvestment certificates are available for any amount and are not subject to a minimum or maximum requirement
Interest: the repayment value, subject to their being held for one year, is related to the movement of the UK General Index of Retail Prices. In addition, there is a guaranteed extra interest of 1 per cent for the first year, 1.25 per cent for the second year, 2 per cent for the third year, 3 per cent for the fourth year and 5.31 per cent for the fifth year. This is worth 2.5 per cent a year compound over the full five years. Reinvestment certificates repaid before the first anniversary date will earn RPI plus extra interest of 1 per cent a year for each complete month.

FORTY-SIXTH ISSUE
27 March–15 October 1998
Maximum holding: £10,000, plus special facility to reinvest an unlimited amount
Unit cost: certificates may be purchased for any amount, subject to a minimum purchase at any time of £100; reinvestment certificates are available for any amount and are not subject to a minimum or maximum requirement
Interest: after one year the repayment value increases by 3.6 per cent for ordinarily held 46th Issue. However, reinvestment certificates if encashed before the first anniversary earn interest at 3.6 per cent a year for each complete period of three months. During the second year the interest rate is 3.8 per cent; during the third year, 4.4 per cent; during the fourth year, 5.2 per cent; and during the fifth year, 7.04 per cent. The compound annual interest rate over the full five years is 4.8 per cent.

THIRTEENTH INDEX-LINKED ISSUE
27 March–15 October 1998
Maximum holding: £10,000, plus special facility to reinvest an unlimited amount
Unit cost: certificates may be purchased for any amount, subject to a minimum purchase at any time of £100; reinvestment certificates are available for any amount and are not subject to a minimum or maximum requirement
Interest: the repayment value, subject to their being held for one year, is related to the movement of the UK General Index of Retail Prices. In addition, there is a guaranteed extra interest of 1 per cent for the first year, 1.2 per cent for the second year, 1.6 per cent for the third year, 2.6 per cent for the fourth year and 4.9 per cent for the fifth year. This is worth 2.25 per cent a year compound over the full five years. Reinvestment certificates repaid before the first anniversary date will earn RPI plus extra interest of 1 per cent a year for each complete month.

FORTY-SEVENTH ISSUE
16 October–30 December 1998
Maximum holding: £10,000, plus special facility to reinvest an unlimited amount
Unit cost: certificates may be purchased for any amount, subject to a minimum purchase at any time of £100; reinvestment certificates are available for any amount and are not subject to a minimum or maximum requirement
Interest: after one year the repayment value increases by 3.6 per cent for ordinarily held 47th Issue. However, reinvestment certificates if encashed before the first anniversary earn interest at 3.6 per cent a year for each complete period of three months. During the second year the interest rate is 3.76 per cent; during the third year, 4 per cent; during the fourth year, 4.2 per cent; and during the fifth year, 4.46 per cent. The compound annual interest rate over the full five years is 4 per cent.

FOURTEENTH INDEX-LINKED ISSUE
16 October–30 December 1998
Maximum holding: £10,000, plus special facility to reinvest an unlimited amount
Unit cost: certificates may be purchased for any amount, subject to a minimum purchase at any time of £100; reinvestment certificates are available for any amount and are not subject to a minimum or maximum requirement

Interest: the repayment value, subject to their being held for one year, is related to the movement of the UK General Index of Retail Prices. In addition, there is a guaranteed extra interest of 1 per cent for the first year, 1.25 per cent for the second year, 1.5 per cent for the third year, 2.3 per cent for the fourth year and 4 per cent for the fifth year. This is worth 2 per cent a year compound over the full five years. Reinvestment certificates repaid before the first anniversary date will earn RPI plus extra interest of 1 per cent a year for each complete month.

FORTY-EIGHTH ISSUE
31 December 1998–2 February 1999
Maximum holding: £10,000, plus special facility to reinvest an unlimited amount
Unit cost: certificates may be purchased for any amount, subject to a minimum purchase at any time of £100; reinvestment certificates are available for any amount and are not subject to a minimum or maximum requirement
Interest: after one year the repayment value increases by 1 per cent for ordinarily held 48th Issue. However, reinvestment certificates if encashed before the first anniversary earn interest at 1 per cent a year for each complete period of three months. During the second year the interest rate is 1.2 per cent; during the third year, 1.4 per cent; during the fourth year, 1.9 per cent; and during the fifth year, 2.76 per cent. The compound annual interest rate over the full five years is 3.5 per cent.

FIFTEENTH INDEX-LINKED ISSUE
31 December 1998–
Maximum holding: £10,000, plus special facility to reinvest an unlimited amount
Unit cost: certificates may be purchased for any amount, subject to a minimum purchase at any time of £100; reinvestment certificates are available for any amount and are not subject to a minimum or maximum requirement
Interest: the repayment value, subject to their being held for one year, is related to the movement of the UK General Index of Retail Prices. In addition, there is a guaranteed extra interest of 1 per cent for the first year, 1.2 per cent for the second year, 1.4 per cent for the third year, 1.9 per cent for the fourth year and 2.76 per cent for the fifth year. This is worth 1.65 per cent a year compound over the full five years. Reinvestment certificates repaid before the first anniversary date will earn RPI plus extra interest of 1 per cent a year for each complete month.

FORTY-NINTH ISSUE
3 February–18 March 1999
Maximum holding: £10,000, plus special facility to reinvest an unlimited amount
Unit cost: certificates may be purchased for any amount, subject to a minimum purchase at any time of £100; reinvestment certificates are available for any amount and are not subject to a minimum or maximum requirement
Interest: after one year the repayment value increases by 3 per cent for ordinarily held 49th Issue. However, reinvestment certificates if encashed before the first anniversary earn interest at 3 per cent a year for each complete period of three months. During the second year the interest rate is 3.1 per cent; during the third year, 3.2 per cent; during the fourth year, 3.3 per cent; and during the fifth year, 3.66 per cent. The compound annual interest rate over the full five years is 3.25 per cent.

FIFTIETH ISSUE
19 March–19 May 1999
Maximum holding: £10,000, plus special facility to reinvest an unlimited amount
Unit cost: certificates may be purchased for any amount, subject to a minimum purchase at any time of £100; reinvestment certificates are available for any amount and are not subject to a minimum or maximum requirement
Interest: after one year the repayment value increases by 3.2 per cent for ordinarily held 50th Issue. However, reinvestment certificates if encashed before the first anniversary earn interest at 3.2 per cent a year for each complete period of three months. During the second year the interest rate is 3.3 per cent; during the third year, 3.4 per cent; during the fourth year, 3.6 per cent; and during the fifth year, 4.01 per cent. The compound annual interest rate over the full five years is 3.5 per cent.

FIFTY-FIRST ISSUE
20 May 1999–
Maximum holding: £10,000, plus special facility to reinvest an unlimited amount

Unit cost: certificates may be purchased for any amount, subject to a minimum purchase at any time of £100; reinvestment certificates are available for any amount and are not subject to a minimum or maximum requirement
Interest: after one year the repayment value increases by 3.3 per cent for ordinarily held 51st Issue. However, reinvestment certificates if encashed before the first anniversary earn interest at 3.3 per cent a year for each complete period of three months. During the second year the interest rate is 3.4 per cent; during the third year, 3.5 per cent; during the fourth year, 3.75 per cent; and during the fifth year, 4.31 per cent. The compound annual interest rate over the full five years is 3.65 per cent.

Insurance

The Insurance Companies Act 1982 initially empowered the Department of Trade and Industry, Insurance Division to authorize corporate bodies to transact insurance in the United Kingdom provided they comply with the financial and other regulations detailed in the Act. In January 1998 an interim transfer of this function to the Insurance Directorate of HM Treasury was completed. This is prior to the eventual transfer to the Financial Services Authority.

At the end of 1998 there were over 800 insurance companies with authorization from the Treasury to transact one or more classes of insurance business. However, with the establishment of the single European insurance market on 1 July 1994 an insurer authorized in any of the European Union (EU) countries can now transact insurance in the UK without further formality; this creates a potential market of over 5,000 insurance companies.

REGULATION

Over 23,000 firms are authorized to conduct a wide variety of investment business in the UK. The overall regulator for investment business of any kind is the Financial Services Authority (FSA), (25 The North Colonade, London EI4 5HS).

The FSA does not undertake all the regulatory work itself. Instead it recognizes a number of specialist bodies to carry out the frontline regulation. The bulk of this work is undertaken by three Self Regulating Organizations (SROs).

The main regulator of firms advising on and arranging deals in life insurance and pensions, friendly society investments, unit trusts and investment trusts is one of the SROs, the Personal Investment Authority (PIA). (25 The North Colonade, Canary Wharf, London EI4 5HS).

Disputes between policyholders and life or general insurers that cannot be resolved by the two parties can be referred to the Insurance Ombudsman. The Insurance Ombudsman Bureau examines the facts of a complaint and delivers a decision which is binding on the insurer (but not the policy holder). The service is free. The Insurance Ombudsman is one of a number of schemes in the financial services industry. It is intended that by the end of 2000 all the financial services ombudsmen will merge their operations under the auspices of one Chief Ombudsman based at the Financial Services Authority.

ASSOCIATION OF BRITISH INSURERS

Over 96 per cent of the world-wide business of UK insurance companies is transacted by the 440 members of the Association of British Insurers (ABI) (51 Gresham Street, London EC2V 7HQ), a trade association which represents both life and general insurers. On general insurance (motor, household, holiday, etc.), ABI currently acts as a regulator for insurance intermediaries but this function will pass to the General Insurance Standards Council when its formation is complete.

INSURANCE BROKERS AND INTERMEDIARIES

In July 1998 The Economic Secretary to the Treasury confirmed that the Financial Services and Markets Bill, currently before parliament, will repeal the Insurance Brokers (Registration) Act 1977. This will end the statutory status of the Insurance Brokers Registration Council (IBRC) (Higham Business Centre, Midland Road, Higham Ferrers, Northants NN10 8DW) Until the Bill receives Royal Assent the IBRC remains in existence.

Intermediaries not registered under the IBRA are currently regulated by the Association of British Insurers. When it is established this will transfer to the General Insurance Standards Council (GISC), (107-112 Leadenhall Street, London EC3A 4AH).

BALANCE OF PAYMENTS

The overseas earnings of the UK insurance sector rose sharply from £4,976m in 1996 to £7,417m in 1997. The insurance industry remains the second largest contributor to the UK's balance of payments.

TAKE-OVERS AND MERGERS

The last two years has seen the beginning of a series of take-overs and mergers in the UK insurance company market. This was not unexpected as over-capacity has been a problem for a number of years and many commentators have held the view that even the largest UK insurers would need to expand if they were to compete on a global scale. The two main mergers have seen Royal Insurance and Sun Alliance merge to form Royal & SunAlliance and Commercial Union and General Accident join as CGU Insurance. Many more take-overs and acquisitions are expected in the UK insurance market.

GENERAL INSURANCE

The publication in July 1998 of the draft Financial Services and Markets Bill led to a re-opening of the debate about whether the current self-regulation system for general insurance was adequate. Unsurprisingly, the insurance company market, Lloyd's, and the intermediary sector were united in strongly opposing the inclusion of general insurance regulation by the Financial Services Authority in the Bill.

While this opposition proved successful, some form of additional safeguards was felt necessary. The market, therefore, moved to establish a new body to oversee the voluntary self-regulatory system. The result was the General Insurance Standards Council (GISC) which was established in November 1998. Chris Woodburn, formerly chief executive of the Securities and Futures Authority, was appointed the GISC's first chief executive.

Legal matters received much attention during the year with the Employers' Liability (Compulsory Insurance) Regulations 1998 being laid before Parliament in October and the completion of Lord Woolf's examination of the civil justice system. Both of these measures will have serious consequences for insurers. For many general insurers, however, it is the possible effects of the so-called 'millennium computer bug (Y2K)' that represent the most serious potential problem. This is on two levels. Firstly, as major users of IT and electronic commerce, insurers have had to test and, where required, update all their own internal IT systems. More importantly, insurers have also had to clarify whether damage directly attributable to 'Y2K' date problems in computer and other equipment will be covered by the policies in force. In most cases the insurers have argued that as the risk of damage of this kind was not taken into account when the premiums were calculated, they are not prepared to deal with claims.

Insurers have attempted to clarify the situation and give maximum publicity to loss prevention measures. Unfortunately this an issue where no one will know the extent of the problem until the turn of the millennium.

In the UK, the cost of most types of general insurance claims rose during 1998. The extent of these rises ranged from a 1.1 per cent increase in the cost of commercial theft claims to the 67.5 per cent increase recorded in weather damage claims. The only exception to the upward trend was the fall of 35.7 per cent in the cost of domestic subsidence, reflecting the wetter summer weather.

LONDON INSURANCE MARKET

The London Insurance Market is a distinct, separate sector of the UK insurance and reinsurance industry. It is the world's leading market for internationally traded insurances and reinsurance, its business comprising mainly overseas non-life large and high-exposure risks. The market is centred on the City of London, which provides the required international financial, banking, legal and other support services. Currently there are 139 Lloyd's syndicates, about 120 insurance companies and 39 Marine Protection and Indemnity Clubs active in the market. In 1996 the market had a written gross premium income of £14,000 million. Most of the business is brought to the market by the 201 firms of Lloyd's brokers.

The trade association for the international insurance and reinsurance companies writing primarily non-marine insurance and all classes of reinsurance business in the London Market is the London International Insurance and Reinsurance Market Association (LIRMA) (London Underwriting Centre, 3 Minster Court, Mincing Lane, London EC3R 7DD).

BRITISH INSURANCE COMPANIES

The following insurance company figures refer to members and certain non-members of the ABI.

CLAIMS STATISTICS (£ million)

	1997	1998
Domestic claims		
Theft	513	532
Fire	247	261
Weather	377	663
Subsidence	393	375
Business interruption	n/a	n/a
Total	1,530	1,831

Commercial claims		
Theft	167	171
Fire	492	601
Weather	171	255
Subsidence	n/a	n/a
Business interruption	270	236
Total	1,100	1,263

WORLD-WIDE GENERAL BUSINESS TRADING RESULT

	1996 £m	1997 £m
Net written premiums	35,177	34,911
Underwriting profit (loss) for one year account business	(1,888)	(1,773)
Transfer to profit and loss account for other business		
Marine, Aviation, Transport	(61)	(70)
Other	(60)	45
Total underwriting result	(1,888)	(1,773)
Net investment income	4,841	4,804
Overall trading profit	2,953	3,031
Profit as % of premium income	8.4	8.7

LLOYD'S OF LONDON

Lloyd's of London is an international market for almost all types of general insurance. Lloyd's currently has a capacity to accept insurance premiums of £10,000 million. Much of this business comes from outside Great Britain and makes a valuable contribution to the balance of payments.

A policy is underwritten at Lloyd's by a mixture of private and corporate members, corporate members having been admitted for the first time in 1992. Specialist underwriters accept insurance risks at Lloyd's on behalf of members (referred to as 'Names') grouped in syndicates. There are currently around 140 syndicates of varying sizes, some with up to 2,000 names, each managed by an underwriting agent approved by the Council of Lloyd's.

Individual members are still in the majority at Lloyd's with a total of 4,503 individuals as opposed to 668 corporate

WORLD-WIDE GENERAL BUSINESS UNDERWRITING RESULT

	1996					1997				
	UK	Other EU	USA	Other	Total	UK	Other EU	USA	Other	Total
Motor										
Premiums: £m	5,913	1,828	1,585	1,768	11,094	6,182	1,696	1,533	1,753	11,164
Profit (loss): £m	(698)	(173)	(67)	(49)	(987)	(1,135)	(244)	(66)	(44)	(1,489)
% of premiums	(11.8)	(9.4)	(4.2)	(2.8)	(8.89)	(18.4)	(14.4)	(4.3)	(2.5)	(13.33)
Non-motor										
Premiums: £m	12,519	2,389	1,995	2,218	19,121	13,018	2,389	1,890	2,075	19,372
Profit (loss): £m	74	(98)	(426)	(109)	(559)	80	(98)	(184)	(6)	(208)
% of premiums	0.6	(4.1)	(21.3)	(4.9)	(2.92)	0.6	(4.1)	(9.7)	(0.3)	(1.07)

NET PREMIUM INCOME BY TERRITORY 1997

	UK £m	Other EU £m	USA £m	Other £m	Total £m
Motor	6,182	1,696	1,533	1,753	11,165
Non-motor	13,018	2,351	1,890	2,075	19,333
Marine, Aviation and Transport	1,239	210	237	180	1,866
Non-MAT reinsurance	1,805	484	0	180	2,470
Other funded business	489	4	0	3	496
Total general business	22,734	4,745	3,660	4,191	35,330
Ordinary long-term	59,333	5,709	4,270	4,442	73,755
Industrial long-term	1,052	—	—	—	1,052
Total long-term business	60,385	5,709	4,270	4,442	74,807

members. In 1998 the market capacity of the corporate sector was £7,170 while individuals represented £2,700 million of capacity.

Lloyd's is incorporated by an Act of Parliament (Lloyd's Acts 1971 onwards) and is governed by a council of 19 members. Market management is handled by a Market Board of 18 members (comprising three working members and three external members of the Council, three Corporation executives (including the chief executive officer), eight additional market practitioners and one external member. Regulation is supervised by a Board of 14 members, comprising four nominated members of the Council, two external members of the Council, four appointed working members, two other appointed external members and the Director, Regulatory Division.

The Corporation is a non-profit making body chiefly financed by its members' subscriptions. It provides the premises, administrative staff and services enabling Lloyd's underwriting syndicates to conduct their business. It does not, however, assume corporate liability for the risks accepted by its members, who remain responsible to the full extent of their personal means for their underwriting affairs.

Lloyd's syndicates have no direct contact with the public. All business is transacted through insurance brokers accredited by the Corporation of Lloyd's. In addition, non-Lloyd's brokers in the UK, when guaranteed by Lloyd's brokers, are able to deal directly with Lloyd's motor syndicates, a facility which has made the Lloyd's market more accessible to the insuring public.

Lloyd's also provides the most comprehensive shipping intelligence service in the world. The shipping and other information received from Lloyd's agents, shipowners, news agencies and other sources throughout the world is collated and distributed to the media as well as to the maritime and commercial sectors in general. *Lloyd's List* is London's oldest daily newspaper and contains news of general commercial interest as well as shipping information. *Lloyd's Shipping Index*, also published daily, lists some 25,000 ocean-going vessels in alphabetical order and gives the latest known report of each.

DEVELOPMENTS IN 1998

The 1996 year of account produced a profit of £748m (£606m after deduction of expenses), representing a return of 15.6 per cent on net premiums of £4,794.

After three years of record market profits it was expected that the figure for 1996 would be lower. This and the deteriorating projections for 1997 and 1998 reflect the changing market conditions brought about by increased supply of capital and competition resulting in downward pressure on premium rates.

The result was better than some forecasters had expected as the major, insured catastrophe losses in 1996 decreased by 22 per cent over the previous year. The largest loss was caused by hurricane *Fran* in the USA, which resulted in claims of more than £1,000 million.

In the UK motor insurance rates continued to fall but claims costs increased over the previous year resulting in an underwriting loss of £696m (12 per cent of net written premiums). The non-motor sector remained in profit, although the underwriting result of £73m represented a reduction of 77 per cent on that of 1995. Reducing premiums and higher claims in the property insurance sector were blamed.

It has always been the intention of the Government that the Financial Services Authority should be responsible for the supervision of the Lloyd's market. This was confirmed by the Economic Secretary to the Treasury in January 1998 and in the draft Financial Services and Markets Bill, published in July. In November, the FSA issued a consultation paper outlining how it would use its powers for the protection of both Lloyd's policyholders and Names.

Chairman, M. Taylor
Chief Executive, R. Sandler

LLOYD'S MEMBERSHIP

	1996	1997	1998
Total no. of underwriting members participating			
Individuals	12,798	9,958	6,825
Corporate	162	202	435

TOTAL MARKET CAPACITY

	1996 £m	1997 £m	1998 £m
Individual	6,985	5,824	4,105
Corporate	3,009	4,500	6,064
Total	9,994	10,324	10,169

LLOYD'S GLOBAL ACCOUNTS
as at 31 December 1997

	1995 and prior years of account £m	1996 pure year result £m
Gross premiums written (net of brokerage)	8,027	6,687
Outward reinsurance premiums	2,155	1,893
Net premiums	5,872	4,794
Reinsurance to close premiums received from earlier years of account	2,595	—
Amounts retained to meet all known and unknown outstanding liabilities brought forward	261	—
	8,728	4,794
Gross claims paid	4,346	3,331
Reinsurers' share	1,069	798
Net claims	3,277	2,533
Other reinsurance premiums paid to close the year of account	3,713	1,675
Amounts retained to meet all known and unknown outstanding liabilities carried forward	136	11
	7,126	4,219
Underwriting result	1,602	575
Other profit (loss) on exchange	10	(5)
Syndicate operating expenses	(410)	(306)
Balance on technical account	1,202	264
Investment income	593	438
Investment expenses and charges	(10)	(8)
Investment gains less losses	16	54
Result before personal expenses	1,801	748
Personal expenses	(652)	(389)
Result after personal expenses	1,149	359

LLOYD'S RESULTS 1996

	Marine 1995 £m	1996 £m	Non-marine 1995 £m	1996 £m	Aviation 1995 £m	1996 £m	Motor 1995 £m	1996 £m
Net premiums	1,274	872	3,194	2,683	620	436	828	803
Pure year result	514	193	856	523	283	136	4	(104)

LIFE AND LONG-TERM INSURANCE AND PENSIONS

The total individual long-term new business (including collective investment schemes)in the UK rose by 31 per cent in 1998 to £3,588 million for annual contracts and by 15 per cent to £29,102 for single premium business. In addition 1998 saw the first year of strong growth of long term care policies. These contracts offer financial protection against the costs of nursing care for elderly people who are unable to carry out certain specified activities of daily living. Over 6.7 million of these policies were sold in 1998 representing £79 million in premiums.

REVIEW OF PENSIONS SELLING

The regulators' review of personal pensions continued throughout 1998. The pensions concerned were contracts sold between April 1988 and July 1994 to up to 1,500,000 people who were advised to take out a personal pension plan; in many cases this was in preference to remaining in a company pension scheme. The review began in late 1994 and because of the number of cases involved some were given higher priority and dealt with first. After an initially slow start, the pension providers largely completed the programme of dealing with these so-called 'phase one' cases in late 1998 after further threats of 'naming and shaming' from Treasury Ministers. The next stage, involving widespread advertising and publicity to encourage victims to come forward is now underway and should mean all potential victims of mis-selling will have been contacted by the FSA's deadline of 30 April 1999.

NET PREMIUM INCOME FOR WORLDWIDE LONG-TERM INSURANCE BUSINESS

	1996 £m	1997 £m
Ordinary Branch		
Business written in UK		
Annual premiums		
Life	11,977	12,604
Annuities	53	67
Pensions	10,283	11,176
Single premiums		
Life	12,545	13,970
Annuities	799	346
Pensions	15,389	20,369
Income protection	54	68
Business written overseas		
Annual premiums	5,392	4,966
Single premiums	8,317	9,471
Industrial Business	1,145	1,053
Total	66,546	74,849

PAYMENTS TO POLICYHOLDERS

	1996 £m	1997 £m
Payments to UK policyholders	40,469	47,674
Payments to overseas policyholders	8,957	10,042
Total	49,426	57,716

INVESTMENTS OF INSURANCE COMPANIES 1997

Investment of funds	Long-term business £m	General business £m
Index-linked British Government securities	16,461	1,795
Non-index-linked British Government securities	87,176	12,933
Other UK public sector debt securities	4,447	514
Overseas government, provincial and municipal securities	25,828	15,639
Debentures, loan shares, preference and guaranteed stocks and shares		
UK	49,083	6,347
Overseas	36,693	4,458
Ordinary stocks and shares		
UK	273,460	14,427
Overseas	68,591	8,809
Unit trusts		
Equities	48,688	864
Fixed interest	3,380	155
Loans secured on property	11,226	2,033
Real property and ground rents	42,234	3,871
Other invested assets	51,814	26,120
Total invested assets	711,766	84,156
Total	719,080	97,965
Net investment income	35,909	4,804

INDIVIDUAL PENSIONS: NEW BUSINESS 1997-8

	Yearly premium policies		Single premium policies	
	No. new policies	New premiums £m	No. new policies	New premiums £m
1997				
1st quarter	248,000	281	75,000	1,180
2nd quarter	310,000	375	120,000	1,818
3rd quarter	266,000	327	85,000	1,248
4th quarter	236,000	308	65,000	1,112
1998				
1st quarter	284,000	289	91,000	1,247
2nd quarter	311,000	284	88,000	1,159
3rd quarter	271,000	255	64,000	1,050
4th quarter	264,000	267	75,000	1,067

DIRECTORY OF INSURANCE COMPANIES

Classes of insurance undertaken		*Group membership*	
G	General	(CGU)	CGU
L	Life	(Z)	Zurich Financial Group
M	Marine	(A)	AXA Group
Re	Reinsurance	(NU)	Norwich Union
		(RSA)	Royal & SunAlliance

Nature of business	*Name of company*	*Head Office address*
L	Abbey Life	100 Holdenhurst Road, Bournemouth BH8 8AL
L	Abbey National Life	301 St Vincent Street, Glasgow G2 5NB
L	AIG Life (UK)	Alico House, 22 Addiscombe Road, Croydon CR9 5AZ
GM Re	Albion	Hill Place House, 55 High Street, London SW19 5BA
L	Alico	Alico House, 22 Addiscombe Road, Croydon CR9 5AZ
GL	Alliance & Leicester Insurance	Carlton Park, Narborough, LE9 5XX
GLM	Alliance Assurance (RSA)	30 Berkeley Square, London W1X 5HA
L	Allied Dunbar (Z)	Allied Dunbar Centre, Swindon SN1 1EL
G	Ansvar	31 St Leonards Road, Eastbourne BN21 3UR
L	Australian Mutual Provident	Spectrum, Bond Street, Bristol BS1 3AL
LGM	Avon Insurance	Arden Street, Stratford-upon-Avon CV37 6WA
L	AXA Equity and Law Life (A)	Amersham Road, High Wycombe HP13 5AL
G	AXA Insurance (A)	Meridian Gate, Bute Terrace, Cardiff CF1 2XA
G	AXA Provincial (A)	107 Cheapside, London EC2V 6DU
L	AXA Sun Life (A)	Sun Life Centre, PO Box 1810, Bristol BS99 5SN
G	Baptist	1 Merchant Street, London E3 4LY
L	Barclays Life	9 Fleetway House, 25 Farringdon Street, London EC4A 4JA
M	Bradford (RSA)	Bowling Mill, Dean Clough, Halifax HX3 5WA
L	Britannia Life	Britannia Court, 50 Bothwell Street, Glasgow G2 6HR
GL	Britannic Assurance	1 Wythall Green Way, Wythall, Birmingham B47 6WG
M	British and Foreign Marine (RSA)	New Hall Place, Liverpool
L	British Life Office	Reliance House, Mount Ephraim, Tunbridge Wells, Kent TN4 8BL
PM	BUPA	BUPA House, 15-19 Bloomsbury Way, London WC1A 2BA
L	Caledonian (A)	Royal Exchange, London EC3V 3LS
GM	Cambrian (A)	Royal Exchange, London EC3V 3LS
L	Canada Life	Canada Life House, Potters Bar EN6 5BA
L	Century Life	Century House, 5 Old Bailey, London EC4M 7BA
L	CGU Life	2 Rougier Street, York YO90 1UU
GL	CIGNA	PO Box 42, Greenock PA15 1AB
L	Clerical, Medical Group	Narrow Plain, Bristol BS2 0JH
L	Colonial	Colonial House, Chatham Maritime ME14 4YY
GLM Re	Commercial Union (CGU)	St Helen's, 1 Undershaft, London EC3P 3DQ
L	Confederation Life	Lytton Way, Stevenage SG1 2NN
G	Congregational and General	Currer House, Currer Street, Bradford BD1 5BA
GLM Re	Co-operative	Miller Street, Manchester M60 0AL
GLM Re	Cornhill	57 Ladymead, Guildford GU1 1DB
GL	Direct Line Insurance	3 Edridge Road, Croydon CR9 1AG
GLM Re	Eagle Star (Z)	60 St Mary Axe, London EC3A 8JQ
GL Re	Ecclesiastical	Beaufort House, Brunswick Road, Gloucester GL1 1JZ
G	Equine and Livestock	PO Box 100, Ouseburn, York YO5 9SZ
L	Equitable Life	Walton Street, Aylesbury HP21 7QW
L	Friends' Provident	Pixham End, Pixham Lane, Dorking RH4 1QA
L	Friends' Provident (London & Manchester)	Winslade Park, Exeter EX5 1DS
G	GAN	GAN House, 12 Arthur Street, London EC4R 9BT
GM Re	General Accident (CGU)	Pitheavlis, Perth PH2 0NH
G	Gresham Fire and Accident	11 Queen Victoria Street, London EC4N 4XP
GM	Guarantee Society (CGU)	42–47 Minories, London EC3N 1BX
GLMRe	Guardian Insurance (A)	Civic Drive, Ipswich IP1 2AN
GLM Re	Guardian Royal Exchange (A)	Civic Drive, Ipswich IP1 2AN
GLM Re	Hibernian	Haddington Road, Dublin 4, Republic of Ireland
L	Hill Samuel Life	NLA Tower, 12-16 Addiscombe Road, Croydon CR9 6DR
G	Hiscox Insurance Co.	52 Leadenhall Street, London EC3A 2BJ
GL	Ideal	Pitmaston, Moseley, Birmingham B13 8NG
L	Irish Life	Irish Life Centre, Victoria Street, St Albans AL1 5TS

Nature of business	Name of company	Head Office address
GF	Iron Trades	Iron Trades House, 21–24 Grosvenor Place, London SW1X 7JA
GLM Re	Legal and General	Temple Court, 11 Queen Victoria Street, London EC4N 4TP
L	Lincoln	Barnett Way, Barnwood, Gloucester, GL4 3RZ
GM	Liverpool Marine and General (RSA)	30 Berkeley Square, London W1X 5HA
GL	Liverpool Victoria Friendly	135 Poole Road, Bournemouth BH4 9BG
GM	Local Government Guarantee (A)	Royal Exchange, London EC3V 3LS
GM Re	Lombard General	Lombard House, 182 High Street, Tonbridge TN9 1BY
GM	London & Edinburgh (NU)	The Warren, Hill Barn Road, Worthing BN14 9QD
L	M and G Life	Three Quays, Tower Hill, London EC3R 6BQ
L	Manulife	Broadstreet House, 55 Old Broad Street, London EC2N 1TL
M	Marine (RSA)	1 Cornhill, London EC3V 3QR
M Re	Maritime	PO Box 6, Surrey Street, Norwich NR1 3NS
L	Medical Sickness Society	Colmore Circus, Birmingham B4 6AR
Re	Mercantile and General	Moorfields House, Moorfields, London EC4R 9BJ
L	Merchant Investors	St Bartholomew's House, Lewins Mead, Bristol BS1 2NH
G Re	Methodist	Brazennose House, Brazennose Street, Manchester M2 5AS
L	MGM Insurance	MGM House, Heene Road, Worthing BN11 2DY
L	National Mutual Life	The Priory, Hitchin SG5 2DW
GM	Navigators and General (Z)	Lanchester House, Trafalgar Place, Trafalgar Street, Brighton BN1 4DA
GL Re	NFU Mutual	Tiddington Road, Stratford-upon-Avon CV37 7BJ
G	NIG Skandia	Crown House, 145 City Road, London EC1V 1LP
L	NM Financial Management	Enterprise House, Isambard Brunel Road, Portsmouth PO1 2AW
GM	Norwich Union Insurance	PO Box 6, Surrey Street, Norwich NR1 3NS
L	NPI	NPI House, 55 Calverley Road, Tunbridge Wells TN1 2UE
GLM Re	Pearl	The Pearl Centre, Lynchwood, Peterborough PE2 6FY
L Sickness	Permanent	Pynes Hill House, Rydon Lane, Exeter EX2 5SP
GLM	Phoenix (RSA)	30 Berkeley Square, London W1X 5HA
Medical	PPP Healthcare (A)	PPP House, Vale Road, Tunbridge Wells TN1 1BJ
L	Property Growth (RSA)	Phoenix House, Redcliff Hill, Bristol BS1 6SX
GLM Re	Prudential	Laurence Pountney Hill, London EC4R 0EU
GL	Refuge	Refuge House, Alderley Road, Wilmslow, Cheshire SK9 1PF
L	Reliance Mutual	Reliance House, Mount Ephraim, Tunbridge Wells, Kent TN4 8BL
G	Road Transport and General (CGU)	Pitheavlis, Perth PH2 0NH
G	Royal Exchange (A)	Royal Exchange, London EC3V 3LS
L	Royal Heritage Life (RSA)	Royal Insurance House, Business Park, Peterborough PE2 6GG
GLM Re	Royal and SunAlliance (RSA)	30 Berkeley Square, London W1X 5HA
Engineering	Royal and SunAlliance Engineering (RSA)	17 York Street, Manchester M2 3RS
L	Royal Liver	Royal Liver Building, Pier Head, Liverpool L3 1HT
GL	Royal London	Royal London House, 27 Middleborough, Colchester CO1 1RA
L	Royal National Pension Fund for Nurses	Burdett House, 15 Buckingham Street, Strand, London WC2N 6ED
F	Salvation Army	117–121 Judd Street, London WC1H 9NN
L	Save and Prosper	Hexagon House, 28 Western Road, Romford RM1 3LB
L	Scottish Amicable	Craigforth, PO Box 25, Stirling FK9 4UE
Engineering	Scottish Boiler (CGU)	PO Box 131, 825 Wilmslow Road, Didsbury, Manchester M20 8GS
L	Scottish Equitable	28 St Andrew Square, Edinburgh EH2 2QZ
L	Scottish Friendly	16 Blythswood Square, Glasgow G2 6HJ
M	Scottish General (CGU)	PO Box 896, 103 Westerhill Road, Bishopbriggs, Glasgow G64 2QX
L	Scottish Legal Life	95 Bothwell Street, Glasgow G2 7HY
L	Scottish Life	19 St Andrew Square, Edinburgh EH2 1YE
L	Scottish Mutual	301 St Vincent Street, Glasgow G2 5HN
L	Scottish Provident Institution	6 St Andrew Square, Edinburgh EH2 2YA
GLM	Scottish Union and National (NU)	Surrey Street, Norwich NR1 3NS
L	Scottish Widows'	15 Dalkeith Road, Edinburgh EH16 5BU
GM	Sea (RSA)	1 Bartholomew Lane, London EC2N 2AB
L	Stalwart Assurance	Stalwart House, Station Road, Dorking RH4 1HL
L	Standard Life	30 Lothian Road, Edinburgh EH1 2DH
GLM	Sun Alliance (RSA)	30 Berkeley Square, London W1X 5HA
GM	Sun Insurance Office (RSA)	30 Berkeley Square, London W1X 5HA
L Re	Sun Life of Canada	Basing View, Basingstoke RG21 2DZ

Nature of business	Name of company	Head Office address
L	Swiss Life	Swiss Life House, South Park, Sevenoaks TN13 1BG
GL	Teacher's Assurance	Tringham House, Wessex Fields, Deansleigh Road, Bournemouth BH7 7DT
L	Tunstall Assurance	Station Chambers, The Boulevard, Tunstall, Stoke-on-Trent ST6 6DU
M	Ulster Marine (CGU)	Pitheavlis, Perth PH2 0NH
GL	UIA Insurance	Kings Court, London Road, Stevenage SG1 2TP
GM	Union Insurance Society of Canton (CGU)	Royal Exchange, London EC3V 3LS
L	United Friendly	Refuge House, Alderley Road, Wilmslow SK9 1PF
GL Re	Wesleyan Assurance	Colmore Circus, Birmingham B4 6AR
L	Windsor Life	Windsor House, Telford TF3 4NB
L	Winterthur Life	Winterthur Way, Basingstoke RG21 6SZ
GM Re	Zurich (Z)	Zurich House, Stanhope Road, Portsmouth PO1 1DU
L	Zurich Life (Z)	The Zurich Centre, 3000 Parkway, Whiteley, Fareham PO15 7JY

The London Stock Exchange

The London Stock Exchange Ltd serves the needs of government, industry and investors by providing facilities for raising capital and a central market-place for securities trading. This market-place covers government stocks (called gilts), UK and overseas company shares (called equities and fixed interest stocks), and traditional options.

PRIMARY MARKETS

The Exchange enables companies to raise capital for development and growth through the issue of securities. For a company entering the market for the first time there is a choice of Exchange markets, depending upon the size, history and requirements of the company. The first is the Official List, the main market, which exists for well-established companies; these must comply with stringent criteria relating to all aspects of their operations. At present, companies coming to this market require a minimum market capitalization of £700,000 and a three-year trading record with a minimum of 25 per cent of the shares held in public hands. The Alternative Investment Market (AIM) began trading in June 1995. It enables small, young and growing companies to raise capital, widen their investor base and have their shares traded on a regulated market without the expense of a full Exchange listing.

Once admitted to the Exchange, all companies are obliged to keep their shareholders informed of their progress, making announcements of a price-sensitive nature through the Exchange's company announcements department.

At the end of 1998 there were 2,087 UK companies listed on the London Stock Exchange; their equity capital had a total market value of £1,422,500 million. Also, 521 foreign companies were listed, with a total equity market value of £2,804,400 million. By the end of 1998 the Alternative Investment Market had attracted 307 companies, with a total capitalization of £4,400 million.

UK equity turnover in 1998 was £1,037,136.6 million, with an average 64,393 bargains and £4,115.6 million value a day. Foreign equity turnover in 1998 totalled £2,183,248.5 million.

BIG BANG

During 1986 the London Stock Exchange went through the greatest period of change in its 200-year history. In March 1986 it opened its doors for the first time to overseas and corporate membership of the Exchange, allowing banks, insurance companies and overseas securities houses to become members of the Exchange and to buy existing member firms. On 27 October 1986, three major reforms took place, changes which became known as 'Big Bang':

- the abolition of scales of minimum commissions, allowing clients to negotiate freely with their brokers about the charge for their services
- the abolition of the separation of member firms into brokers and jobbers: firms are now broker/dealers, able to act as agents on behalf of clients; to act as principals buying and selling shares for their own account; and to become registered market makers, making continuous buying and selling prices in specific securities
- the introduction of the Stock Exchange automated quotations (SEAQ) system

Since the introduction of SEAQ, dealing in stocks and shares takes place via the telephone in the firms' own dealing rooms, rather than face to face on the floor of the Exchange, or can be done through the Stock Exchange Electronic Trading Service (SETS), launched in 1997. The new systems also provide increased investor protection. All deals taking place via the Exchange's SEAQ system are recorded on a database which can be used to resolve disputes or to carry out investigations.

Members of the London Stock Exchange buy and sell shares on behalf of the public, as well as institutions such as pension funds or insurance companies. In return for transacting the deal, the broker will charge a commission, which is usually based upon the value of the transaction. The market makers, or wholesalers, in each security do not charge a commission for their services, but will quote the broker two prices, a price at which they will buy and a price at which they will sell. It is the middle of these two prices which is published in lists of Stock Exchange prices in newspapers.

REGULATORY BODIES

The London Stock Exchange Ltd and the Securities and Futures Authority are the two regulatory bodies (*see* pages 635–6). They were formed under the provisions of the Financial Services Act 1986, which requires investment businesses to be authorized and regulated by a self-regulating organization (SRO), of which the Securities and Futures Authority is one. The Act also requires business to be conducted through a recognized investment exchange (RIE). The London Stock Exchange is an RIE, regulating three main markets: UK equities, international equities and gilts. The changes to the financial regulatory system which are to be introduced in the next few years will affect the Stock Exchange's role as a regulatory body.

THE GOVERNING BOARD

The London Stock Exchange has its headquarters in London, and representative offices around the UK. At present there are about 264 member firms.

The governing board is responsible for overall policy and the strategic direction of the Exchange. The board consists of representatives drawn from listed companies, investors and other major users, elected at the annual general meeting, and the Government Broker, the Chief Executive and up to five senior executives of the Stock Exchange.

LONDON STOCK EXCHANGE LTD, Old Broad Street, London EC2N 1HP. Tel: 0171-797 1000
Chairman, Sir John Kemp-Welch
Chief Executive, G. Casey
Government Broker, I. Plenderleith (*Deputy Chairman*)
Other Board members, G. Allen, CBE; G. Allen; J. Bond; J. Howell; M. Marks; P. Meinertzhagen; S. Robertson; I. Salter; H. Sants; N. Sherlock; M. Wheatley

Financial Services Regulation

In May 1997 the Government announced plans to establish a new statutory single financial regulator responsible for the supervision of banks, building societies, insurance companies, investment firms and markets. It will replace the current supervisory framework, established under a number of different statutes. The new regulator is the Financial Services Authority (FSA), which in corporate and legal terms is the Securities and Investments Board (SIB) renamed.

The FSA is acquiring its full range of responsibilities in two stages. The first stage was completed on 1 June 1998 when the FSA acquired responsibility, under the Bank of England Act 1998, for supervising banks, listed money market institutions and related clearing houses; the Bank of England had previously exercised this responsibility. The majority of functions previously carried out by the Insurance Directorate of HM Treasury (including Lloyd's of London), has now been taken over by the FSA. The second stage will follow the enactment of the Financial Services and Markets Bill, introduced into Parliament in June 1999. When this bill is passed, a date commonly referred to as N2, the FSA will acquire its full range of powers and will take on responsibility for the regulation and registration functions of the following regulators and supervisors:

SELF-REGULATING ORGANIZATIONS

INVESTMENT MANAGEMENT REGULATORY
ORGANIZATION (IMRO)
PERSONAL INVESTMENT AUTHORITY (PIA)
SECURITIES AND FUTURES AUTHORITY LTD (SFA)

OTHERS

BUILDING SOCIETIES COMMISSION
FRIENDLY SOCIETIES COMMISSION
REGISTRY OF FRIENDLY SOCIETIES

All the above organizations are based at the FSA's offices in Canary Wharf (*see* below).

The FSA also supervises the recognized professional bodies and recognized clearing houses, ensuring that they continue to fulfil their regulatory responsibilities.

Until N2, the above organizations will continue to have legal responsibility for regulating their firms under the existing statutory or contractual arrangements. However, in order to facilitate speedy operational integration, the staff of the SROs have transferred contracts of employment to the FSA and now operate under a single management structure. Detailed contracts have been put in place providing the services of the FSA staff to these bodies to enable them to carry out their work.

The Government has said that the FSA will have statutory objectives in four main areas:
–maintaining confidence in the UK financial system
–promoting public understanding of the financial system, including awareness of the benefits and risks associated with different kinds of investment or other financial dealing
–securing the appropriate degree of protection for consumers, having regard to the differing degrees of risk involved in different kinds of investment or other transaction, the differing degrees of experience and expertise which different consumers may have, and the general principle that consumers should take responsibility for their decisions
–contributing to the reduction of financial crime

It is the Government's intention that the FSA should pursue its objectives in a way that is efficient and economic; facilitates innovation in financial services; balances restrictions on firms with the benefits of regulation; and takes account of the international nature of financial services business and the value of competition between firms. The FSA is currently preparing its policy, regulatory approach and rules. It is issuing consultation papers and feedback and policy statements. It has also established a Practitioner Forum and Consumer Panel and set up various advisory groups to look at specific topics.

CENTRAL REGISTER/PUBLIC ENQUIRIES

The FSA maintains the Central Register of all firms which are authorized to carry on investment business and authorized deposit takers. The entry for each firm gives its name, address and telephone number; a reference number; its authorization status; and states which organization regulates it; and whether it can handle client money. The FSA has issued a series of booklets aimed at providing generic advice to consumers and providing contact points for help and further information. These are also available on the FSA website.
PUBLIC ENQUIRIES OFFICE: 0845-606 1234

INVESTORS COMPENSATION SCHEME

The Investors Compensation Scheme is part of the overall investor protection system. This comes into play when a regulated investment firm becomes insolvent owing money to private investors. It is funded by a levy on all regulated firms. The maximum compensation that the scheme can pay to an investor is £48,000.

DEPOSIT PROTECTION SCHEME

This scheme provides investors with protection when a bank becomes insolvent. It provides protection for depositors of up to a maximum compensation payment of £18,000 (or ECU 20,000 if greater).

FINANCIAL SERVICES AUTHORITY, 25 The North Colonnade, Canary Wharf, London E14 5HS. Tel: 0171-676 1000. Web: http://www.fsa.gov.uk. *Chairman*, H. Davies

AUTHORIZED DEPOSIT-TAKING INSTITUTIONS

For deposit-taking institutions, *see* Banking

RECOGNIZED PROFESSIONAL BODIES

The FSA is empowered to recognize professional bodies (RPBs) which, as a result, can authorize their members to conduct investment business. Such business must not form the whole or main part of the total business undertaken by the firm.

INSTITUTE OF CHARTERED ACCOUNTANTS IN
ENGLAND AND WALES, Chartered Accountants' Hall, PO Box 433, Moorgate Place, London EC2P 2BJ. Tel: 0171-920 8100
INSTITUTE OF CHARTERED ACCOUNTANTS OF
SCOTLAND, 27 Queen Street, Edinburgh EH2 1LA. Tel: 0131-225 5673
THE ULSTER SOCIETY OF THE INSTITUTE OF
CHARTERED ACCOUNTANTS IN IRELAND, 11 Donegall Square South, Belfast BT1 5JE. Tel: 01232-321600

ASSOCIATION OF CHARTERED CERTIFIED ACCOUNTANTS, 29 Lincoln's Inn Fields, London WC2A 3EE. Tel: 0171-242 6855

INSTITUTE OF ACTUARIES, Staple Inn Hall, High Holborn, London WC1V 7QJ. Tel: 0171-242 0106

THE LAW SOCIETY, 113 Chancery Lane, London WC2A 1PL. Tel: 0171-242 1222

LAW SOCIETY OF NORTHERN IRELAND, Law Society House, 98 Victoria Street, Belfast BT1 3JZ. Tel: 01232-231614

LAW SOCIETY OF SCOTLAND, Law Society's Hall, 26 Drumsheugh Gardens, Edinburgh EH3 7YR. Tel: 0131-226 7411

RECOGNIZED INVESTMENT EXCHANGES

Investment exchanges are exempt from needing authorization under the Financial Services Act. To be a recognized investment exchange (RIE), it must fulfil the following requirements: adequate financial resources; proper conduct of business rules; a proper market in its products; procedures for recording transactions; effective monitoring and enforcement of rules; proper arrangements for the clearing and performance of contracts.

TRADEPOINT STOCK EXCHANGE, 35 King Street, London WC2E 8JD. Tel: 0171-240 8000

INTERNATIONAL PETROLEUM EXCHANGE (IPE), International House, 1 St Katharine's Way, London E1 9UN. Tel: 0171-481 0643

LONDON STOCK EXCHANGE (LSE), Old Broad Street, London EC2N 1HP. Tel: 0171-797 1000

LONDON INTERNATIONAL FINANCIAL FUTURES AND OPTIONS EXCHANGE (LIFFE), Cannon Bridge, London EC4R 3XX. Tel: 0171-623 0444

LONDON METAL EXCHANGE LTD (LME), 56 Leadenhall Street, London EC3A 2BJ. Tel: 0171-264 5555

THE LONDON SECURITIES AND DERIVATIVES EXCHANGE LTD (OM LONDON EXCHANGE LTD), 107 Cannon Street, London EC4N 5AF. Tel: 0171-283 0678

Following the implementation of the EC Investment Services Directive, recognition by the UK authorities is no longer required for exchanges within the European Economic Area (with certain exceptions).

RECOGNIZED CLEARING HOUSES

A recognized clearing house (RCH) must satisfy similar criteria to those which apply to be an RIE. There are two RCHs which act as clearing houses for some of the above RIEs. In addition, Crest also operates a system for dematerialized settlement of share transactions.

CRESTCO LTD, 33 Cannon Street, London EC4M 5SB. Tel: 0171-849 0000

LONDON CLEARING HOUSE LTD (LCH), Roman Wall House, 1–2 Crutched Friars, London EC3N 2AN. Tel: 0171-265 2000

DESIGNATED INVESTMENT EXCHANGES

The FSA has drawn up a list of 52 designated overseas investment exchanges. These are deemed to provide protection for investors of an equivalent standard to that provided by RIEs.

OMBUDSMAN SCHEMES

Independent ombudsman schemes have been set up for banks, building societies, insurance companies, financial institutions and independent financial advisers. They provide an independent and impartial method of resolving disputes that arise between a company and a customer. In most ombudsman schemes there is a council which appoints and supervises the Ombudsman. The Ombudsman Council is composed of people representing public and consumer interests and member companies. The schemes are funded in various ways: annual subscription from member companies, a levy on member companies according to the size of their assets, a charge for each complaint handled against a particular company, or a combination of these.

The Investment Ombudsman is responsible for resolving disputes that arise between a customer and a company regulated by IMRO. The Personal Investment Authority (PIA) Ombudsman is primarily responsible for resolving complaints against PIA members about personal investments.

The Pensions Ombudsman is appointed and operates under the Pension Schemes Act 1993 as amended by the Pensions Act 1995; he is responsible to Parliament. He investigates and decides complaints and disputes concerning occupational pension schemes, primarily alleged maladministration by the persons responsible for managing an occupational pension scheme. Personal pension complaints are normally dealt with only if outside the jurisdiction of the Personal Investment Authority.

THE OFFICE OF THE BANKING OMBUDSMAN, 70 Gray's Inn Road, London WC1X 8NB. Tel: 0171-404 9944. *Banking Ombudsman*, D. Thomas

THE OFFICE OF THE BUILDING SOCIETIES OMBUDSMAN, Millbank Tower, Millbank, London SW1P 4QU. Tel: 0171-931 0044. *Building Societies Ombudsman*, B. Murphy

THE INSURANCE OMBUDSMAN BUREAU, City Gate One, 135 Park Street, London SE1 9EA. Tel: 0171-928 4488. *Insurance Ombudsman*, W. Merricks

THE OFFICE OF THE INVESTMENT OMBUDSMAN, 6 Frederick's Place, London EC2R 8BT. Tel: 0171-796 3065. *Investment Ombudsman*, P. Dean, CBE

THE PENSIONS OMBUDSMAN, 6th Floor, 11 Belgrave Road, London SW1V 1RB. Tel: 0171-834 9144. *Pensions Ombudsman*, Dr J. T. Farrand

THE PIA OMBUDSMAN BUREAU, Hertsmere House, Hertsmere Road, London E14 4AB. Tel: 0171-216 0016. *Principal Ombudsman*, A. J. Holland; *Ombudsmen*, R. Prior; M. Thomas

THE TAKEOVER PANEL

The Takeover Panel was set up in 1968 in response to concern about practices unfair to shareholders in take-over bids for public and certain private companies. Its principal objective is to ensure equality of treatment, and fair opportunity for all shareholders to consider on its merits an offer that would result in the change of control of a company. It is a non-statutory body that operates the City code on take-overs and mergers.

The chairman, deputy chairmen and three lay members of the panel are appointed by the Bank of England. The remainder are representatives of the banking, insurance, investment, pension fund and accountancy professional bodies, the CBI, IMRO and the Stock Exchange.

THE TAKEOVER PANEL, PO Box 226, The Stock Exchange Building, London, EC2P 2JX. Tel: 0171-382 9026. *Chairman*, Sir David Calcutt, QC

Stamp Duties and Stamp Duty Reserve Tax

Stamp duty is a tax on documents; Stamp duty reserve tax is charged upon agreements for the sale of shares and securities where there is no stamped stock transfer form.

Where stamp duty is not paid or deposited with the Stamp Office within 30 days after execution, interest accrues. This applies where the instrument is executed offshore. For agreements for lease the interest commences from 30 days after the execution of the lease. A stampable instrument may be stamped without penalty if presented for stamping within 30 days after its date of first execution. Where first executed abroad, the period begins to run from the date of arrival in the UK.

Instruments presented after the proper time may be subject to a penalty which, subject to mitigation or reasonable excuse for the delay, is equal to:
(a) where presented within 12 months after execution, the lower of £300 or the amount of the duty;
(b) where presented after 12 months from execution, the higher of £300 or the amount of the duty

Agreement for Sale of Property
Charged with *ad valorem* duty as if an actual conveyance on sale, with certain exceptions, e.g. agreements for the sale of legal interests in land, stocks and shares, goods, wares or merchandise, a ship or foreign property (*see* s59 (1), Stamp Act 1891). If *ad valorem* duty is paid on an agreement in accordance with this provision, the subsequent conveyance or transfer is not chargeable with any *ad valorem* duty and the Commissioners will upon application either place a denoting stamp on such conveyance or transfer or will transfer the *ad valorem* duty thereto. Further, if such an agreement is not performed the *ad valorem* duty paid will be returned.

Bearer Instrument
Inland or Overseas bearer instrument, 1.5 per cent

Conveyance or Transfer on Sale
"Sale" includes transfers for cash, shares and debt and in the case of land exchanges, any other property.

Value not exceeding £60,000, *nil*
Value of £60,001–£250,000, 1 per cent
Value of £250,001–£500,000, 2.5 per cent
Value exceeding £500,000, 3.5 per cent
The rates are now decimalised and rounded up to £5.
Rates apply to conveyance or transfer on sale of any property except for shares and marketable securities where the rate is 0.5 per cent.

Conveyance or Transfer of Any Other Kind
Fixed duty, £5

However, under the Stamp Duty (Exempt Instruments) Regulations 1987, instruments which would otherwise fall under this head are exempt from stamp duty provided that the document is duly certified.

Covenant, for original creation and sale of any annuity, *see* Conveyance on Sale, above

Declaration of Trust
Not being a conveyance on sale, will or settlement, £5

Duplicate or Counterpart
£5

Leases (including Agreements for Leases)
Lease or tack for any definite term less than a year of any furnished dwelling-house or apartments where the rent for such term exceeds £500, £5

Of any lands, tenements etc. in consideration of any rent, according to the following:

† Term not exceeding seven years (and rent not exceeding £500 p.a.), *nil*
Term not exceeding seven years (and rent exceeding £500 p.a.), 1 per cent
Term not exceeding 35 years, 2 per cent
Term not exceeding 100 years, 12 per cent
Term exceeding 100 years, 24 per cent
†If the term is indefinite the same duty is payable as if the term did not exceed seven years.

Where a consideration other than rent is payable e.g. a premium in cash or other property, the same rule applies where the consideration does not exceed £60,000 as under conveyance or transfer on sale (except stock or marketable securities), provided that any rent payable does not exceed £600 a year and a certificate of value is included in the conveyance or transfer and the reduced rates of 1 per cent and 2.5 per cent for consideration not exceeding £500,000 apply.

Where a lease is granted pursuant to a prior written agreement for lease, the agreement itself is liable to duty. Credit for any duty paid on the agreement will be given against the duty payable on the lease and the Commissioners will place a denoting stamp on the lease. Where there is no prior written agreement for lease, the lease must contain a certificate that it has not been made in pursuance of such an agreement.

Stamp Duties

Unit Trust Instrument
Duty was abolished in the Finance Act 1988. Transfer of property to a unit trust or agreement to transfer units is generally subject to Conveyance on Sale duty or Stamp Duty Reserve Tax. By the Finance Act 1989, the transfer of units in certain authorised unit trusts is no longer subject to duty.

Voluntary Disposition, *inter vivos*
Fixed duty, £5

However, under the Stamp Duty (Exempt Instruments) Regulations 1987, instruments which would otherwise fall under this head are exempt provided that the document is certified as falling within category L in the schedule to the Regulations. *See* Conveyance or Transfer of Any Other Kind, above.

Stamp Duty Reserve Tax
This is charged where there is a contract for the transfer of chargeable securities unless the charge is cancelled. The tax is payable by or on behalf of the buyer who is required to report the transaction and pay the tax on the seventh day of the month following that in which the contract is made or becomes unconditional. Penalties and interest are imposed for late payment or reporting.

Taxation

INCOME TAX

Income tax is charged on the income of individuals for a year of assessment commencing on 6 April and ending on the following 5 April. Substantial changes have been introduced during recent years which affect both the calculation of income chargeable to tax and the rate or rates at which the amount of tax due must be determined. Some further changes being introduced in the future have also been announced. In view of these substantial changes the following information is confined to the year of assessment 1999–2000 ending on 5 April 2000 and has only limited application to earlier years. However, some changes affecting future years are also noted where the information is available.

An individual's liability to satisfy income tax for 1999–2000 is determined by establishing the level of taxable income for the year. This income must then be allocated between three different headings, namely: (a) all income excluding that arising from savings and dividends; (b) income from savings; (c) company dividends, including distributions.

Once this allocation has been completed the first calculation must be limited to taxable income excluding that arising from savings and dividends. This income will be reduced by an individual's personal allowance and other available allowances. The first £1,500 of taxable income remaining is assessed to income tax at the starting rate of 10 per cent. The next £26,500 is taxable at the basic rate of 23 per cent. Should any excess over £28,000 (£1,500 plus £26,500) remain, this will be taxable at the higher rate of 40 per cent.

The second calculation is limited to income from savings; if any. Liability arises at the lower rate of 20 per cent or the higher rate of 40 per cent only. The appropriate rate is determined by adding income from savings to other taxable income. To the extent that the addition does not increase taxable income above £28,000, income from savings is taxed at the lower rate of 20 per cent. If or to the extent that the level of £28,000 is exceeded, the excess income from savings will be taxed at 40 per cent.

Finally, any company dividends must be added to the list of taxable income. These dividends are taxed at either the Schedule F ordinary rate of 10 per cent or the Schedule F upper rate of 32.5 per cent. The amount of dividends must be added to taxable income comprising general income together with income from savings. If this addition does not increase total taxable income above £28,000 dividends remain taxable at the ordinary rate of 10 per cent only. However, if or to the extent that the addition discloses dividends exceeding the £28,000 level the excess is taxed at the upper rate of 32.5 per cent.

Trustees administering settled property and personal representatives dealing with the estate of a deceased person are chargeable to income tax at the basic rate of 23 per cent. Where trustees retain discretionary powers or income from settled property is accumulated, liability may be increased to 34 per cent. Companies residing in the UK are not liable to income tax but suffer corporation tax on income, profits and gains (*see* pages 648–9).

Income arising overseas will often incur liability to foreign taxation. If that income is also chargeable to UK income tax, excessive liability could arise. The UK has concluded double taxation agreements with the governments of many foreign countries and these ensure that the same slice of income is not doubly taxed.

HUSBAND AND WIFE

A husband and wife are separately taxed, with each entitled to his or her personal allowance. A married man 'living with' his wife can obtain a married couple's allowance. In the absence of any claim, this allowance must be used by the husband but where any balance remains the surplus may be transferred to the wife. It is possible for a married woman to claim half the basic married couple's allowance as of right. In addition, the entire basic allowance may be claimed by the wife, if her husband so agrees.

Each spouse may obtain other allowances and reliefs where the required conditions are satisfied. Income must be accurately allocated between the couple by reference to the individual beneficially entitled to that income. Where income arises from jointly-held assets, this must be apportioned equally between husband and wife. However, in those cases where the beneficial interests in jointly-held assets are not equal, a special declaration can be made to apportion income by reference to the actual interests in that income.

SELF-ASSESSMENT

Self-assessment affects individuals, trustees and personal representatives. Central to self-assessment is the requirement to deliver a completed tax return. This must normally be submitted by 31 January following the end of the year of assessment to which the return relates. In addition to completing the return, the taxpayer must calculate the amount of income tax due. If a taxpayer wishes the Inland Revenue to calculate the tax due, the return must be forwarded to the Inland Revenue not later than the previous 30 September.

It is the responsibility of the taxpayer to submit payments of income tax on time. There are three different dates on which payments may fall due:

(a) an interim payment due on 31 January in the year of assessment itself
(b) a second interim payment due on the following 31 July
(c) a balancing payment, or possibly a repayment, on the following 31 January

The two interim payments will be based on tax payable for the previous year of assessment but liability may be reduced where income has fallen or even avoided entirely where the amounts are not substantial.

The impact of self-assessment is largely restricted to some nine million persons receiving tax returns. These comprise self-employed individuals, those receiving income from the exploitation of land in the UK, company directors, others with investment income liable to higher rate income tax, trustees and personal representatives. Elderly persons receiving small amounts of untaxed income may be excluded from the need to complete a tax return. Separate tax return forms are issued to a husband and wife, where such forms are needed.

Failure to submit completed tax returns by 31 January or to discharge payments of income tax on time will incur a liability to interest, surcharges and penalties.

INCOME TAXABLE

Income tax is assessed under several Schedules. Each Schedule determines the extent of liability and establishes the amount to be included in taxable income. In some instances the actual income arising in a year of assessment will be charged to income tax for that year.

A different basis of assessment may be used for income taxable under Cases I to V of Schedule D. For many years income was assessed under these Cases on a 'preceding year' basis. This involved measuring income for the year by reference to that arising in a previous year or period but there were special rules where a new source was acquired or an existing source discontinued. The 'preceding year' basis has been replaced by a 'current year' basis of assessment. This requires that business profits assessable under Case I or Case II of Schedule D will be those for the accounting period ending in the year of assessment, with special adjustments for the opening and closing years of a business. Other income assessable under Schedule D will be that which arises in the actual year of assessment.

Following the withdrawal of income tax liability for most commercial woodlands in the UK, Schedule B no longer applies. Schedule C has also been withdrawn as the result of further changes. The contents of the remaining schedules are shown below.

Schedule A

Tax is charged under Schedule A on the annual profits or gains arising from a business carried on for the exploitation of land in the UK. As the result of recent amendments, the determination of profits from a Schedule A business adopts principles identical to those used when establishing the profits or gains of a trade, profession or vocation. Rents and other income from the exploitation of land are included in the calculation, and outgoings incurred wholly and exclusively for the purposes of the Schedule A business may be deducted from income.

Schedule A does not extend to profits from farming, market gardening or woodlands, nor does it apply to mineral rents and royalties. Premiums arising on the grant of a lease for a period not exceeding 50 years in duration are treated as rents. However, the amount of the taxable premium may be reduced by 2 per cent for each complete year, after the first 12 months, of the leasing period. Income arising from the provision of certain furnished holiday accommodation attracts a number of tax advantages not otherwise available for most income chargeable under Schedule A.

Receipts not exceeding £4,250 annually and accruing to an individual from letting property furnished in his or her own home are usually excluded from liability to income tax.

Schedule D

This Schedule is divided into six Cases:

Cases I and II – profits arising from trades, professions and vocations, including farming and market gardening. Capital expenditure incurred on assets used for business purposes will often produce an entitlement to capital allowances which reduce the profits chargeable. These profits may also be reduced by claims for loss relief and other matters.

Case III – interest on government stocks not taxed at source, interest on National Savings Bank deposits and discounts. Interest up to £70 on ordinary National Savings Bank deposits is exempt from income tax. The exemption applies to both husband and wife separately. Interest on National Savings Bank special investment accounts is not exempt. Interest and other items of savings income incur liability at the lower rate or the higher rate only.

Cases IV and V – interest from overseas securities, rents, dividends and all other income accruing outside the UK. Assessment is based on the full amount of income arising, whether remitted to the UK or retained overseas, but individuals who are either not domiciled in the UK or who are ordinarily resident overseas may be taxed on a remittance basis. Overseas pensions are taxable but the amount arising may be reduced by 10 per cent for assessment purposes. Interest received on most overseas investments is chargeable only at the lower rate of 20 per cent and the higher rate of 40 per cent, with overseas dividends usually taxed at 10 per cent or 32.5 per cent.

Case VI – sundry profits and annual receipts not assessed under any other Case or Schedule. These may include insurance commissions, post-cessation receipts and numerous other receipts specifically charged under Case VI.

Schedule E

All earnings from an office or employment are assessable under this Schedule. There are three Cases:

Case I – applies to all earnings of an individual resident and ordinarily resident in the UK.

Case II – of application where the individual is not resident or not ordinarily resident and extends to earnings for duties undertaken in the UK.

Case III – applies in rare situations to other earnings remitted to the UK.

A 'receipts basis' applies for determining the year of assessment in which earnings must be taxed. Where earnings are assessable under Case I or Case II, the date of receipt will comprise the earlier of the date of payment, or the date entitlement arises. In the case of company directors it is the earlier of these two dates, with the addition of the following three which establish the time of receipt: the date earnings are credited in the company's books; where earnings for a period are determined after the end of that period, the date of determination; where earnings for a period are determined in that period, the last day of that period.

The earnings assessable under Schedule E include all salaries, wages, director's fees and other money sums. In addition, the value of a wide range of benefits must be added to taxable earnings. These include the provision of living accommodation on advantageous terms and advantages arising from the use of vouchers.

Further taxable benefits accrue to directors and also to employees receiving earnings of £8,500 or more in the year of assessment. Such benefits include the reimbursement of expenses, the availability of motor cars for private motoring, the provision of petrol or other fuel for private motoring, the use of vans, the provision of interest-free loans, and other benefits provided at the employer's expense. The cost of providing a limited range of child care facilities may be excluded.

In arriving at the amount to be assessed under Schedule E, all expenses incurred wholly, exclusively and necessarily in the performance of the duties, together with the cost of business travel, may be deducted. Fees and subscriptions paid to certain professional bodies and learned societies may also be deducted. Fees paid to managers by entertainers, actors and others assessable under Schedule E may be deducted, up to a maximum of 17.5 per cent of earnings.

Compensation for loss of office and other sums received on the termination of an office or employment are assessable to tax. However, the first £30,000 may be excluded with only the balance remaining chargeable, unless the compensatory payment is linked with the retirement of the recipient.

For several years earnings received from an approved profit-related pay scheme have been exempt from income tax. However, this exemption is being phased out and will cease to apply entirely after 31 December 1999.

Schedule F

This Schedule is concerned with dividends and distributions received from a UK resident company.

Building society and bank interest

Many payments of interest by building societies and banks are received after the deduction of income tax at the lower rate of 20 per cent. However, investors not liable to income tax may arrange to receive interest gross, with no tax being deducted on payment. Others who suffer income tax by deduction can obtain a repayment in whole or in part if they are not fully liable at the lower rate. This income also comprises income from savings, which is taxable as outlined below.

INCOME FROM SAVINGS

Some forms of investment are taxable at special rates for 1999–2000. These rates are limited to 'income from savings', an expression which includes interest on bank and building society accounts together with interest on Government securities and the income element of purchased life annuities. In addition, 'income from savings' may extend to other income of a similar nature arising outside the United Kingdom. Not all forms of investment income are included in the list; notable exceptions comprise income from letting property and company dividends.

A great deal of interest will be received after deduction of income tax at the lower rate of 20 per cent. The significance of this rate is that income from savings will be taxed at 20 per cent where the income of the recipient is sufficiently substantial. It is not possible to take advantage of the reduced starting rate of 10 per cent and the basic rate of 23 per cent has no application. However, income from savings may incur liability at the higher rate of 40 per cent where total taxable income, excluding dividends, exceeds £28,000. As income tax will usually have been deducted at source at the rate of 20 per cent, higher rate liability arises at a further 20 per cent (40 per cent less 20 per cent).

DIVIDENDS

Dividends and other distributions paid by a UK resident company have a tax credit attached equal to one-ninth of the sum received in 1999–2000. Therefore a recipient shareholder also residing in the UK who receives a cash dividend of £90 will have a tax credit of £10. The gross dividend or distribution (sum received plus tax credit) is regarded as having suffered income tax, equal to the tax credit, at the rate of 10 per cent. Where the shareholder is not liable, or not fully liable, to income tax it is no longer possible to claim a repayment of the tax credit. However, for 1999–2000 dividends are taxed at the Schedule F ordinary rate of 10 per cent or the Schedule F upper rate of 32.5 per cent. Where the total income of an individual is not unduly substantial the amount of the tax credit, namely 10 per cent, will be offset against the Schedule F ordinary rate of income tax, which is also 10 per cent, leaving no further liability. Should the gross amount of dividends or distributions when added to other taxable income exceed £28,000 the excess is chargeable at the Schedule F upper rate of 32.5 per cent. The amount of the tax credit will then reduce tax otherwise payable at the upper rate. Although the rates of 10 per cent and 32.5 per cent apply to dividends and distributions from United Kingdom companies, they also extend to income of a similar nature arising outside the UK.

INCOME NOT TAXABLE

Income which is not taxable in 1999–2000 includes interest on National Savings certificates, most scholarship income, bounty payments to members of the armed services and annuities payable to the holders of certain awards. Dividend income arising from investments in personal equity plans (PEPs) and venture capital trusts may be exempt from tax, although tax credits on dividends from such trusts can no longer be recovered. Income received under most maintenance agreements and court orders made after 30 June 1988 will not be liable to tax. Nor will payments made under many deeds of covenant be recognized for tax purposes, unless the recipient is a charity. Interest arising on a tax exempt special savings account (TESSA) opened with a building society or bank will be exempt from tax if the account is maintained throughout a five-year period.

No new investments in PEPs can be made and no new TESSAs can be opened after 5 April 1999. A new vehicle, the individual savings account (ISA), became available on 6 April 1999 for investment by UK resident individuals aged 18 or over. The ISA may have three components: cash; stocks and shares; and life assurance. Interest on the cash component, usually comprising bank or building society deposits, is exempt from income tax. Dividends on most quoted holdings in the stocks and shares component are also immune from liability to income tax, with tax credits being repaid in the first five years. Income and gains accruing to the provider of the life assurance component will be free of all liability to taxation.

A maximum subscription of £7,000 can be made by an individual to an ISA during 1999–2000. Of this sum, no more than £3,000 can be allocated to the cash component and £1,000 to the life assurance component. For later years the maximum subscription is reduced to £5,000, with no more than £1,000 being allocated to each of the cash and life assurance components.

SOCIAL SECURITY BENEFITS

Many social security benefits are not liable to income tax. These include income support, family credit, maternity allowance, child benefit, war widow's pension and disability living allowance. The benefits which are taxable include the retirement pension, widow's pension, widowed mother's allowance and jobseeker's allowance. Short-term sick pay and maternity pay payable by an employer are also chargeable to tax. Incapacity benefit is chargeable to tax but no liability arises for the first 28 weeks of receiving benefit.

A new working families' tax credit system replaced family credit in October 1999 (*see* Social Welfare section).

PAY AS YOU EARN

The Pay As You Earn (PAYE) system is not an independent form of taxation but is designed to collect income tax by deduction from most earnings. When paying earnings to employees, an employer is usually required to deduct income tax and account for that tax to the Inland Revenue. In many cases this deduction procedure will fully exhaust the individual's liability to income tax, unless there is other income. The date of 'receipt' used for assessment purposes also identifies the date of 'payment' when establishing liability for PAYE.

The PAYE system is used to collect tax on certain payments made 'in kind'. The system is also used when collecting tax on many pensions.

ALLOWANCES

Allowances available to individuals for 1999–2000, together with any future changes are shown below.

Personal allowance

Basic personal allowance	£4,335
Those over 64 on 5 April 2000	£5,720
Those over 74 on 5 April 2000	£5,980

The increased allowance is available for those who died during the year of assessment but who would otherwise have achieved the appropriate age not later than 5 April 2000.

The amount of the increased personal allowance for older taxpayers will be reduced by one-half of total income in excess of £16,800. This reduction in the allowance will continue until it has been reduced to the basic personal allowance of £4,335.

The personal allowance is given as a deduction in calculating taxable income and may therefore produce relief at the rate of 10, 23 or 40 per cent, as appropriate.

This allowance remains and is not being withdrawn after 5 April 2000.

Married couple's allowance

A married man who was 'living with' his wife at any time in the year ending on 5 April 2000 is entitled to a married couple's allowance. The basic allowance is £1,970. This may be increased to £5,125 if either the husband or the wife is 65 years or over at any time in the year ending on 5 April 2000. A further increase to £5,195 can be obtained where either party to the marriage was 75 or over on 5 April 2000. Where an individual would otherwise have reached either age by 5 April 2000, but who died earlier in the year, the increased allowance is given.

The amount of the increased married couple's allowance may be reduced where the income of the husband (excluding the income of the wife) exceeds £16,800. The reduction will comprise:

(a) one-half of the husband's total income in excess of £16,800, less

(b) the amount of any reduction made when calculating the husband's increased personal allowance

This reduction in the married couple's allowance cannot reduce that allowance below the basic amount of £1,970.

If husband and wife were married during 1999–2000 the married couple's allowance of £1,970, or any increased sum, must be reduced by one-twelfth for each complete month commencing on 6 April 1999 and preceding the date of marriage.

Unlike the personal allowance, the married couple's allowance does not reduce taxable income. Relief is granted by reducing the tax payable by 10 per cent of the allowance. Should the allowance exceed taxable income, no tax will be due, nor will any repayment arise.

In the absence of any further action, the married couple's allowance will be given to the husband. If he is unable to utilize all or any part of that allowance due to an absence of income, the husband may transfer the unused portion to his wife. The decision whether or not to transfer remains at the discretion of the husband.

However, a wife may file an election to obtain one-half of the basic married couple's allowance as of right, leaving the husband with the balance of that allowance. Alternatively, the couple may jointly elect that the entire basic allowance should be allocated to the wife only. Should either spouse be unable to utilize his or her share of the married couple's allowance the unused part may be transferred to the other spouse.

The married couple's allowance will only be available for 2000–1 and future years if either the husband or wife, or both, was over the age of 64 on 5 April 2000.

Additional personal allowance

An allowance of £1,970 is available to a single person who has a qualifying child resident with him/her in 1999–2000.

The allowance can also be obtained by a married man or a married woman whose spouse is totally incapacitated by physical or mental infirmity throughout the year.

A 'qualifying child' for 1999–2000 must be born during the year, be under the age of 16 years at the commencement of the year, or be over the age of 16 at the commencement of the year and either receiving full-time instruction at a university, college, school or other educational establishment or undergoing training for a trade, profession or vocation throughout a minimum period of two years. It is also necessary that the child is the claimant's own, a stepchild of the claimant, an illegitimate child if the parents married after the child's birth, or an adopted child under the age of 18 at the time of adoption. Alternatively it must be shown that the child was either born during 1999–2000 or under the age of 18 at the commencement of the year and maintained by the claimant at his or her own expense during the whole of the succeeding 12-month period.

Only one additional personal allowance of £1,970 can be obtained by an individual notwithstanding the number of children involved. Where an unmarried couple are living together as husband and wife, it is not possible for both to obtain the additional personal allowance. The allowance is given by reducing tax payable at the rate of 10 per cent of £1,970. The allowance is not available for 2000–1 and future years.

Widow's bereavement allowance

For the year of assessment in which a husband dies his surviving widow may obtain a widow's bereavement allowance, which is £1,970 for 1999–2000. It is a requirement that the parties were 'living together' immediately before the husband's death. A similar allowance will be available in the year following death, unless the widow remarried in the year of death. No widow's bereavement allowance can be obtained for future years. Relief is granted by reducing tax payable at the rate of 10 per cent. The allowance will only be available for 2000–1 if the husband died in 1999–2000. Thereafter, no widows bereavement allowance can be obtained.

Blind person's allowance

An allowance of £1,380 is available to an individual if at any time during the year ending on 5 April 2000, he or she was registered as blind on a register maintained by a local authority. If the individual is 'living with' a wife or husband, any unused part of the blind person's allowance can be transferred to the other spouse. The allowance reduces taxable income and may therefore give rise to relief at the taxpayer's highest rate of tax suffered. It continues for 2000–1 and future years.

Transitional allowances

There are two remaining transitional allowances which are intended to ensure that the independent taxation of husband and wife, introduced on 6 April 1990, did not increase liability to income tax for subsequent years. These allowances comprise:

(a) an increased personal allowance available to a wife where the husband cannot fully use that allowance in 1999–2000

(b) a married couple's allowance available to a separated husband not 'living with' his wife if the separation occurred before 6 April 1990

These allowances are of limited application and cannot be obtained after 1999–2000.

Children's tax credit

A new allowance, the children's tax credit, is being introduced for 2001–2 and future years. This allowance will be available to a husband and wife 'living together' or a man and woman 'living together' as husband and wife. In both situations it is necessary that the couple have a qualifying child resident with them. Where these requirements are satisfied it is expected that an allowance of £4,160 will be available and given at the rate of 10 per cent as a deduction from income tax otherwise payable. Where the income of both members of the 'family' is insufficient to incur liability to income tax at the higher rate no further adjustments will be required. However, where one or both family members is liable to income tax at the higher rate the allowance will be allocated to the higher earner. It then becomes necessary to reduce the allowance of £4,160 by two-thirds of the higher earner's income chargeable at the higher rate.

INTEREST

Further reliefs may be available to an individual including payments of interest.

In some instances, interest paid by a business proprietor may be included when calculating profits chargeable to income tax under Case I or Case II of Schedule D. In addition, relief for interest paid on a loan applied to acquire or develop land and buildings for letting may be obtained by including the outlay in the calculation of income chargeable under Schedule A. However, many private individuals cannot obtain relief in this manner and must satisfy stringent requirements before relief will be forthcoming. In general terms it is a requirement that before interest can qualify for relief it must be paid for a qualifying purpose. Relief will not be available to the extent that interest exceeds a reasonable commercial rate and no relief is forthcoming for interest on an overdraft.

For 1999–2000 relief will be available on the following payments:

(a) Interest on a loan to purchase, develop or improve an interest in land owned by the individual and used as the only or main residence of that individual. 'Land' includes large houseboats and also caravans used for residential purposes. No relief is available for interest on loans applied after 5 April 1988 for the development or improvement of land, unless the work involves the construction of a new building. Relief is available for interest paid on a loan applied to acquire a property which is the only or main residence of a dependent relative, a separated spouse or a divorced former spouse, but only where that person occupied the property before 6 April 1988. Relief may also be forthcoming for interest on a loan used to acquire some other property, perhaps to be used as the only or main residence on retirement, by an individual who is compelled to occupy property by reason of his or her work. If the loan, or aggregate of several loans, exceeds £30,000, relief is restricted to interest on that amount. Where two or more persons apply loans after 31 July 1988 to acquire interests in a single building, those persons cannot, collectively, obtain relief for interest on more than £30,000 in relation to that building. Relief is given by reducing the income tax payable by 10 per cent of the qualifying interest paid in 1999–2000. However, the relief is being withdrawn and cannot be obtained for interest paid, or due, after 5 April 2000

(b) Interest on a loan made to acquire an interest in a close company or in a partnership, or to advance money to such a person

(c) Interest on a loan to a member of a partnership to acquire machinery or plant for use in the partnership business

(d) Interest on a loan to an employed person to acquire machinery or plant for the purposes of his/her employment

(e) Interest on a loan made for the purpose of contributing capital to an industrial co-operative

(f) Interest on a loan applied for investment in an employee-controlled company

(g) Interest on a loan made to elderly persons for the purchase of an annuity where the loan is secured on land. If the loan exceeds £30,000, relief is limited to interest on this amount. This relief is restricted to income tax at the basic rate of 23 per cent. Whilst the relief remains for existing borrowers, it cannot be obtained for interest on new loans taken out after 8 March 1999

(h) Interest on a loan to personal representatives to provide funds for the payment of inheritance tax

Relief for many payments of mortgage interest is obtained through MIRAS (mortgage interest relief at source). When making payments of this nature in 1999–2000 the payer will deduct and retain income tax at the rate of 10 per cent. This will provide the payer with full relief at that rate and no other relief will be necessary. Qualifying payments of interest outside the MIRAS scheme continue to produce relief by reducing tax payable at the rate of 10 per cent.

Other relief under headings (b) to (h) (but not (g)) is given by deducting interest from taxable income. This enables the taxpayer to obtain relief at his or her top rate suffered.

OTHER OUTGOINGS

Many employees pay contributions to an approved occupational pension scheme. The amount of their contributions may be deducted when calculating earnings assessable under Schedule E. Relief should also be available for any additional voluntary contributions paid.

Self-employed individuals and those receiving earnings not covered by an occupational pension scheme may contribute under personal pension scheme arrangements or perhaps under stakeholder schemes to be introduced shortly. Individuals may also pay premiums under retirement annuity schemes if the arrangements were concluded before 1 July 1988. Contributions paid under all headings and which do not exceed upper limits may obtain income tax relief by deduction from taxable income.

Subject to a maximum of £150,000 in 1999–2000, the cost of subscribing for shares in an unquoted trading company or companies may qualify for relief under the Enterprise Investment Scheme. Many requirements must be satisfied before this relief can be obtained, but a husband and wife may each take advantage of the £150,000 maximum. Relief is given by reducing tax payable at the rate of 20 per cent of the share subscription cost. Further relief, up to a maximum of £100,000 and also given at the rate of 20 per cent, is available for a subscription of shares in a venture capital trust company.

CAPITAL GAINS TAX

An individual is potentially chargeable to capital gains tax on chargeable gains which accrue to him/her during a year of assessment ending on 5 April. The application of the tax has been amended several times in recent years and further substantial alterations were made in spring 1998. The following information is largely confined to the year of assessment 1999–2000, ending on 5 April 2000.

Liability extends to individuals who are either resident or ordinarily resident for the year but special rules apply where a person permanently leaves the UK or comes to this territory for the purpose of acquiring residence. Non-residents are not usually liable to capital gains tax unless they carry on a business in the UK through a branch or agency. However, individuals who leave the UK after 16 March 1998 and who have been resident or ordinarily resident in at least four of the seven previous years may remain liable to capital gains tax unless they reside overseas throughout a period of five complete tax years. Exceptions from this liability may apply where there is a disposal of assets acquired in the period of absence.

Trustees residing in the UK, together with personal representatives are chargeable to capital gains tax at the rate of 34 per cent but chargeable gains accruing to companies are assessable to corporation tax.

For 1997–8 and earlier years, capital gains tax was chargeable on the net chargeable gains accruing to a person in a year of assessment after subtracting the annual exemption for that year. Net chargeable gains represented capital gains less capital losses arising from disposals carried out during the year. Unused losses brought forward from an earlier year could be offset against current net chargeable gains, but in the case of individuals were not to reduce the net gains for 1997–8 below £6,500. It was possible to utilize trading losses against chargeable gains where those losses had not been offset against income.

TAPER RELIEF

The calculation of net gains chargeable to capital gains tax for 1998–9 and future years is affected by the introduction of taper relief. The purpose of this relief, which replaces the indexation allowance, is to require that only a percentage of gains become chargeable to capital gains tax. The percentage is governed by the number of complete years of ownership falling after 5 April 1998, although one additional 'bonus year' can be obtained for most assets acquired before 17 March 1998.

Taper relief, which is limited to disposals made after 5 April 1998, draws a distinction between business assets and non-business assets. The expression 'business asset' broadly identifies an asset used for business purposes, in addition to some holdings of shares in trading companies. Where the nature of an asset has changed during the period of ownership from a business asset to a non-business asset, or vice versa, the asset must be effectively broken down into two parts. The percentages attributable to each type of asset are:

No. of whole years of ownership	Percentage of gain chargeable	
	Business assets	Non-business assets
	%	%
1	92.5	100
2	85.0	100
3	77.5	95
4	70.0	90
5	62.5	85
6	55.0	80
7	47.5	75
8	40.0	70
9	32.5	65
10	25.0	60

If only chargeable gains arise from disposals carried out in 1999–2000, the taper relief, if any, must be calculated by reference to each disposal. The aggregate sum will then be subtracted from the total chargeable gains and the net sum remaining reduced, or perhaps eliminated, by the annual exemption of £7,100.

Where disposals in 1999–2000 produce both gains and losses, the losses must be subtracted from the gains and taper relief calculated on the net sum remaining. It is necessary to allocate the losses between the gains where there are two or more disposals. Losses brought forward from an earlier year must also be subtracted when calculating the net gains qualifying for taper relief. However, losses brought forward are not to reduce the net gains below the annual exemption of £7,100.

RATES OF TAX

The net gains remaining, if any, after subtracting taper relief and the annual exemption incur liability to capital gains tax for 1999–2000. Although income tax rates are used for this purpose, the rates of tax differ from those which had to be used for earlier years. In the current year capital gains tax is due at the lower rate of 20 per cent, the higher rate of 40 per cent or a combination of the two rates. Unlike income tax commitments, there is no liability at the starting rate of 10 per cent or the basic rate of 23 per cent. The first step is to calculate the amount of taxable income chargeable to income tax. This will include income from savings, company dividends and all other forms of taxable income. The second step is to add the amount of net chargeable gains to the taxable income chargeable to income tax. To the extent that this does not increase the aggregate total above £28,000, capital gains tax will be charged at the rate of 20 per cent. If or to the extent that any part of the chargeable gains exceed the limit of £28,000 the excess is chargeable at 40 per cent and not at 20 per cent. Although some income tax rates are used, capital gains tax remains an entirely separate tax.

Capital gains tax for 1999–2000 falls due for payment in full on 31 January 2001. If payment is delayed beyond that date, interest or surcharges may be imposed.

HUSBAND AND WIFE

Independent taxation requires that a husband and wife 'living together' are separately assessed to capital gains tax. Each spouse must independently calculate his or her gains and losses, with each entitled to the benefit of taper relief, if any, and the annual exemption of £7,100 for 1999–2000. No liability to capital gains tax arises from the transfer of assets between husband and wife 'living together'.

DISPOSAL OF ASSETS

Before chargeable gains potentially liable to capital gains tax can arise, a disposal or deemed disposal of an asset must take place. This occurs not only where assets are sold or exchanged but applies on the making of a gift. There is also a disposal of assets where any capital sum is derived from assets, e.g. where compensation is received for loss or damage to an asset.

The date on which a disposal must be treated as having taken place will determine the year of assessment into which the chargeable gain or allowable loss falls. In those cases where a disposal is made under an unconditional contract, the time of disposal will be that when the contract was entered into and not the subsequent date of conveyance or transfer. A disposal under a conditional contract or option is treated as taking place when the contract becomes unconditional or the option is exercised. Disposals by way of gift are undertaken when the gift becomes effective.

VALUATION OF ASSETS

The amount actually received as consideration for the disposal of an asset will be the sum from which very limited outgoings must be deducted for the purpose of establishing the gain or loss. In cases where the consideration does not accurately reflect the value of the asset, a different basis must be used. This applies, in particular, where an asset is transferred by way of gift or otherwise than by a bargain made at arm's length. Such transactions are deemed to take place for a consideration representing market value, which will determine both the disposal proceeds accruing to the transferor and the cost of acquisition to the transferee.

Market value represents the price which an asset might reasonably be expected to fetch on a sale in the open market. In the case of unquoted shares or securities, it is to be assumed that the hypothetical purchaser in the open market would have available all the information which a prudent prospective purchaser of shares or securities might reasonably require if he/she were proposing to purchase them from a willing vendor by private treaty and at arm's length. The market value of unquoted shares or securities will often be established following negotiations with the Shares Valuation Division of the Capital Taxes Office. The valuation of land and interests in land in the UK will be dealt with by the District Valuer. Special rules apply to determine the market value of shares quoted on the Stock Exchange.

DEDUCTION FOR OUTGOINGS

Once the actual or notional disposal proceeds have been determined, it only remains to subtract eligible outgoings for the purpose of computing the gain or loss. There is the general rule that any outgoings deducted, or which are available to be deducted, when calculating income tax liability must be ignored. Subject to this, deductions will usually be limited to:

(a) the cost of acquiring the asset, together with incidental costs wholly and exclusively incurred in connection with the acquisition
(b) expenditure incurred wholly and exclusively on the asset in enhancing its value, being expenditure reflected in the state or nature of the asset at the time of the disposal, and any other expenditure wholly and exclusively incurred in establishing, preserving or defending title to, or a right over, the asset
(c) the incidental costs of making the disposal

Where the disposal concerns a leasehold interest having less than 50 years to run, any expenditure falling under (a) and (b) must be written off throughout the duration of the lease.

INDEXATION ALLOWANCE

In recent years an indexation allowance has been available when calculating a gain on the disposal of an asset. The allowance was based on percentage increases in the retail prices index between the month of March 1982, or the month in which expenditure was incurred if later, and the month of disposal. The indexation allowance calculated on this basis entered into the calculation of chargeable gain arising on the disposal of an asset. For several years it had not been possible to use the allowance to increase or to create an allowable loss.

Taper relief has largely replaced the indexation allowance for disposals made after 5 April 1998. However, where an asset was acquired before this date, the indexation allowance will be calculated to the month of April 1998 and then frozen. The frozen allowance will then enter into the calculation of chargeable gain, if any, when the asset is disposed of at some later date. The adjustment for the indexation allowance must be made before calculating taper relief on the net sum remaining.

EXEMPTIONS

There is a general exemption from liability to capital gains tax where the net gains of an individual for 1999–2000 do not exceed £7,100. This general exemption applies separately to a husband and wife whether or not the parties are 'living together'.

The disposal of many assets will not give rise to

chargeable gains or allowable losses and these assets include:

(a) private motor cars
(b) government securities
(c) loan stock and other securities (but not shares)
(d) options and contracts relating to securities within (b) and (c)
(e) National Savings Certificates, Premium Bonds, Defence Bonds and National Development Bonds
(f) currency of any description acquired for personal expenditure outside the UK
(g) decorations awarded for valour
(h) betting wins and pools, lottery or games prizes
(i) compensation or damages for any wrong or injury suffered by an individual in his/her person, profession or vocation
(j) life assurance and deferred annuity contracts where the person making the disposal is the original beneficial owner
(k) dwelling-houses and land enjoyed with a residence which is an individual's only or main residence
(l) tangible movable property, the consideration for the disposal of which does not exceed £6,000
(m) certain tangible movable property which is a wasting asset having a life not exceeding 50 years
(n) assets transferred to charities and other bodies
(o) works of art, historic buildings and similar assets
(p) assets used to provide maintenance funds for historic buildings
(q) assets transferred to trustees for the benefit of employees
(r) assets held in an Individual Savings Account

DWELLING-HOUSES

Exemption from capital gains tax will usually be available for any gain which accrues to an individual from the disposal of, or of an interest in, a dwelling-house or part of a dwelling-house which has been his/her only or main residence. The exemption extends to land which has been occupied and enjoyed with the residence as its garden or grounds. Some restriction may be necessary where the land exceeds half a hectare.

The gain will not be chargeable to capital gains tax if the dwelling-house, or part, has been the individual's only or main residence throughout the period of ownership, or throughout the entire period except for all or any part of the last three years. A proportionate part of the gain will be exempt in other cases if the dwelling-house has been the individual's only or main residence for part only of the period of ownership. In the case of property acquired before 31 March 1982, the period of ownership is treated as commencing on this date.

Where part of the dwelling-house has been used exclusively for business purposes, that part of the gain attributable to business use will not be exempt.

In those cases where part of a qualifying dwelling-house has been used to provide rented residential accommodation, this non-personal use may frequently be ignored when calculating exemption from capital gains tax, unless relatively substantial sums are involved.

Dwellings occupied by dependent relatives, separated spouses or divorced former spouses, may also qualify for the exemption, but only where occupation commenced before 6 April 1988.

ROLL-OVER RELIEF – BUSINESS ASSETS

Persons carrying on business will often undertake the disposal of an asset and use the proceeds to finance the acquisition of a replacement asset. Where this situation arises, a claim for roll-over relief may be available. The broad effect of such a claim is that all or part of the gain arising on the disposal of the old asset may be disregarded. The gain or part is then subtracted from the cost of acquiring the replacement asset. As this cost is reduced, any gain arising from the future disposal of the replacement asset will be correspondingly increased, unless a further roll-over situation then develops.

It remains a requirement that both the old and the replacement asset must be used for the purpose of the taxpayer's business. Relief will only be available if the acquisition of the replacement asset takes place within a period commencing twelve months before, and ending three years after, the disposal of the old asset, although the Inland Revenue retain a discretion to extend this period where the circumstances were such that it was impossible for the taxpayer to acquire the replacement asset before the expiration of the normal time limit.

Whilst many business assets qualify for roll-over relief there are exceptions.

DEFERRAL RELIEF

A form of roll-over relief enables gains arising on the disposal of an asset to be matched, in whole or in part, with a subscription for shares in a restricted range of unquoted companies, including certain companies whose shares are dealt in on the Alternative Investment Market. Where matching can be achieved any part of the gain arising on disposal, not exceeding the cost of the qualifying share subscription, may become the subject of a claim. Unlike the usual form of roll-over relief, this claim does not eliminate or reduce the chargeable gain. It has the effect of deferring that gain until the time of some future event, which will usually be identified by the disposal of the newly acquired shares or the loss of UK residential status. The relief, referred to as deferral relief, applied also to transactions taking place before 6 April 1998 but was limited to a subscription for shares qualifying for enterprise investment scheme income tax relief.

A similar form of deferral relief is available for gains arising on other disposals which are matched with a qualifying share investment in a venture capital trust company. To the extent of the gain arising, which must not exceed the amount of the investment qualifying for income tax relief, that gain is deferred until the time of a future event, which will normally comprise the disposal of shares in the venture capital trust or the loss of UK residential status.

HOLD-OVER RELIEF – GIFTS

The gift of an asset is treated as a disposal made for a consideration equal to market value, with a corresponding acquisition by the transferee at an identical value. In the case of gifts made by individuals and a limited range of trustees to a transferee resident in the UK, a form of hold-over relief may be available. Relief is limited to the transfer of certain assets, including the following:

(a) assets used for the purposes of a trade or similar activity carried on by the transferor or his/her personal company

(b) shares or securities of a trading company which is not listed on a stock exchange

(c) shares or securities of a trading company which is listed but which is the transferor's personal company

(d) many interests in agricultural property qualifying for agricultural property relief for inheritance tax purposes

(e) assets involved in transactions which are lifetime transfers for inheritance tax purposes, other than potentially exempt transfers

The effect of the claim is similar to that following a claim for roll-over relief on the disposal of business assets,

but adjustments may be necessary where some consideration is given for the transfer, the asset has not been used for business purposes throughout the period of ownership, or not all assets of a company are used for business purposes.

RETIREMENT RELIEF

Retirement relief is available to an individual who disposes by way of sale or gift of the whole or part of a business. The isolated disposal of assets used for the purpose of a business will not necessarily represent the disposal of the whole or part of a business. The main condition for granting this relief is that throughout a period of at least one year the business has been owned either by the individual or by a trading company in which the individual retained a sufficient shareholding interest. The relief extends also to cases where an individual disposes by way of sale or gift of shares or securities of a company. It must be demonstrated that the company was a trading company, that the individual retained a sufficient shareholding interest, and that he/she was engaged as a full-time working officer or employee.

An individual who has attained the age of 50 years at the time of a disposal may obtain substantial retirement relief which shelters gains from liability to capital gains tax. Full relief was available for disposals taking place not later than 5 April 1999. The amount of relief then reduces on an annual basis before being abolished entirely for disposals taking place on and after 6 April 2003.

No retirement relief will be forthcoming if the disposal occurs before the individual's 50th birthday, except where an individual is compelled to retire early on the grounds of ill-health.

Retirement relief must be subtracted from the net gains arising on disposal, leaving the balance, if any, chargeable to capital gains tax in the normal manner. Taper relief applies only to this balance of net gains and not to the calculation of gains eliminated by retirement relief.

DEATH

No capital gains tax is chargeable on the value of assets retained at the time of death. However, the personal representatives administering the deceased's estate are deemed to acquire those assets for a consideration representing market value on death. This ensures that any increase in value occurring before the date of death will not be chargeable to capital gains tax. If a legatee or other person acquires an asset under a will or intestacy no chargeable gain will accrue to the personal representatives, and the person taking the asset will also be treated as having acquired it at the time of death for its then market value.

INHERITANCE TAX

Liability to inheritance tax may arise on a limited range of lifetime gifts and other dispositions and also on the value of assets retained, or deemed to be retained, at the time of death. An individual's domicile at the time of any gift or on death is an important matter. Domicile will generally be determined by applying normal rules, although special considerations may be necessary where an individual was previously domiciled in the UK but subsequently acquired a domicile of choice overseas. In addition, individuals who have been resident in the UK for at least 17 of the previous 20 years at the time of an event are treated as domiciled in the UK for this purpose.

Where a person was domiciled, or treated as domiciled, in the UK at the time of a disposition or on death the location of assets is immaterial and full liability to inheritance tax arises. Individuals domiciled outside the UK are, however, chargeable to inheritance tax only on transactions affecting assets located in the UK.

The assets of husband and wife are not merged for inheritance tax purposes. Each spouse is treated as a separate individual entitled to receive the benefit of his or her exemptions, reliefs and rates of tax. Where husband and wife retain similar assets, e.g. shares in the same family company, special 'related property' provisions may require the merger of those assets for valuation purposes only.

LIFETIME GIFTS AND DISPOSITIONS

Gifts and dispositions made during lifetime fall under four broad headings, namely:
(a) dispositions which are not transfers of value
(b) exempt transfers
(c) potentially exempt transfers
(d) chargeable transfers

Dispositions which are not transfers of value

Several lifetime transactions are not treated as transfers of value and may be entirely disregarded for inheritance tax purposes. These include transactions not intended to confer gratuitous benefit, the provision of family maintenance, the waiver of the right to receive remuneration or dividends, and the grant of agricultural tenancies for full consideration.

Exempt transfers

Certain transfers are treated as exempt transfers and incur no liability to inheritance tax. The main exempt transfers are listed below:

Transfers between spouses – Transfers between husband and wife are usually exempt. However, if the transferor is, but the transferee spouse is not, domiciled in the UK, transfers will be exempt only to the extent that the total does not exceed £55,000. Unlike the requirement used for income tax and capital gains tax purposes, it is immaterial whether husband and wife are living together.

Annual exemption – The first £3,000 of gifts and other dispositions made in a year ending on 5 April is exempt. If the exemption is not used, or not wholly used, in any year the balance may be carried forward to the following year only. The annual exemption will only be available for a potentially exempt transfer if that transfer becomes chargeable by reason of the donor's subsequent death.

Small gifts – Outright gifts of £250 or less to any person in one year ending on 5 April are exempt.

Normal expenditure – A transfer made during lifetime and comprising normal expenditure is exempt. To obtain this exemption it must be shown that:
(a) the transfer was made as part of the normal expenditure of the transferor
(b) taking one year with another, the transfer was made out of income
(c) after allowing for all transfers of value forming part of normal expenditure the transferor was left with sufficient income to maintain his or her usual standard of living

Gifts in consideration of marriage – These are exempt if they satisfy certain requirements. The amount allowed will be governed by the relationship between the donor and a party to the marriage. The allowable amounts comprise:
(a) gifts by a parent, £5,000
(b) gifts by a grandparent, £2,500
(c) gifts by a party to the marriage, £2,500
(d) gifts by other persons, £1,000

Gifts to charities – These are exempt from liability.

Gifts to political parties – Gifts which satisfy certain requirements are generally exempt.

Gifts for national purposes – Gifts made to certain bodies are exempt from liability. These bodies include, among others, the National Gallery, the British Museum, the National Trust, the National Art Collections Fund, the National Heritage Memorial Fund, the Historic Buildings and Monuments Commission for England (English Heritage), any local authority, and any university or university college in the UK.

A number of other gifts made for the public benefit are also exempt.

Potentially exempt transfers

Lifetime gifts and dispositions which are neither to be ignored nor comprise exempt transfers incur possible liability to inheritance tax. However, relief is available for a range of potentially exempt transfers. These comprise gifts made by an individual to:
(a) a second individual
(b) trustees administering an accumulation and maintenance trust
(c) trustees administering a disabled person's trust

The accumulation and maintenance trust mentioned in (b) must provide that on reaching a specified age, not exceeding 25 years, a beneficiary will become absolutely entitled to trust assets or obtain an interest in possession in the income from those assets.

Additions to the above list affect settled property administered by trustees where an individual, or individuals, retain an interest in possession. The transfer of assets to, the removal of assets from, or the rearrangement of interests in such property comprise potentially exempt transfers if the person transferring an interest and the person benefiting from the transfer are both individuals.

No immediate liability to inheritance tax will arise on the making of a potentially exempt transfer. Should the donor survive for a period of seven years, immunity from liability will be confirmed. However, the donor's death within the seven-year *inter vivos* period produces liability if the amounts involved are sufficiently substantial (*see* below).

Chargeable transfers

Any remaining lifetime gifts or dispositions which are neither to be ignored nor represent exempt transfers or potentially exempt transfers, incur liability to inheritance tax.

GIFTS WITH RESERVATION

A lifetime gift of assets made at any time after 17 March 1986 may incur additional liability to inheritance tax if the donor retains some interest in the subject matter of the gift. This may arise, for example, where a parent transfers a dwelling-house to a son or daughter and continues to occupy the property or to enjoy some benefit from that property. The retention of a benefit may be ignored where it is enjoyed in return for full consideration, perhaps a commercial rent, or where the benefit arises from changed circumstances which could not have been foreseen at the time of the original gift. The gift with reservation provisions will not usually apply to most exempt transfers.

There are three possibilities which may arise where the donor reserves or enjoys some benefit from the subject matter of a previous gift and subsequently dies, namely:
(a) if no benefit is enjoyed within a period of seven years before death there can be no further liability
(b) if the benefit ceased to be enjoyed within a period of seven years before the date of death, the original donor is deemed to have made a potentially exempt transfer representing the value of the asset at the time of cessation

(c) if the benefit is enjoyed at the time of death, the value of the asset must be included in the value of the deceased's estate on death

It must be emphasized that the existence of a benefit enjoyed at any time within a period of seven years before death will establish liability to tax on gifts with reservation, notwithstanding that the gift may have been made many years earlier, providing it was undertaken after 17 March 1986.

DEATH

Immediately before the time of death an individual is deemed to make a transfer of value. This transfer will comprise the value of assets forming part of the deceased's estate after subtracting most liabilities. Any exempt transfers may, however, be excluded. These include transfers for the benefit of a surviving spouse, a charity and a qualifying political party, together with bequests to approved bodies and for national purposes.

Death may also trigger three additional liabilities:

(a) A potentially exempt transfer made within the period of seven years ending on death loses its potential status and becomes chargeable to inheritance tax

(b) The value of gifts made with reservation may incur liability if any benefit was enjoyed within a period of seven years preceding death

(c) Additional tax may become payable for chargeable lifetime transfers made within seven years before death

VALUATIONS

The valuation of assets establishes the value transferred for lifetime dispositions and also the value of a person's estate at the time of death. The value of property will represent the price which might reasonably be expected from a sale in the open market.

In some cases it may be necessary to incorporate the value of 'related property'. This will include property comprised in the estate of the transferor's spouse and certain property previously transferred to charities. The purpose of the related property valuation rules is not to add the value of the property to the estate of the transferor. Related property must be merged to establish the aggregate value of the respective interests and this value is then apportioned, usually on a *pro rata* basis, to the separate interests.

The value of shares and securities listed on the Stock Exchange will be determined by extracting figures from the daily list of official prices.

Where quoted shares and securities are sold or the quotation is suspended within a period of 12 months following the date of death, a claim may be made to substitute the proceeds or subsequent value for the value on death. This claim will only be beneficial if the gross proceeds realized are lower or the value has fallen below market value at the time of death. A similar claim may be available for interests in land sold within a period of four years following death.

RELIEF FOR SELECTED ASSETS

Special relief is made available for certain assets, notably:

Woodlands

Where woodlands pass on death the value will usually be included in the deceased's estate. However, an election may be made in respect of land in the UK on which trees or underwood is growing to delete the value of those assets. Relief is confined to the value of trees or underwood and does not extend to the land on which they are growing. Liability to inheritance tax will arise if and when the trees or underwood are sold.

Agricultural property

Relief is available for the agricultural value of agricultural property. Such property must be occupied and used for agricultural purposes and relief is confined to the agricultural value only.

The value transferred, either on a lifetime gift or on death, must be determined. This value may then be reduced by a percentage. For events taking place after 9 March 1992, a 100 per cent deduction will be available if the transferor retained vacant possession or could have obtained that possession within a period of 12 months following the transfer. In other cases, notably including land let to tenants, a lower deduction of 50 per cent is usually available. However, this lower deduction may be increased to 100 per cent if the letting was made after 31 August 1995.

It remains a requirement that the agricultural property was either occupied by the transferor for the purposes of agriculture throughout a two-year period ending on the date of the transfer, or was owned by him/her throughout a period of seven years ending on that date and also occupied for agricultural purposes.

Business property

Where the value transferred is attributable to relevant business property, that value may be reduced by a percentage. The reduction in value applies to:

(a) property consisting of a business or an interest in a business (i.e. a partnership)

(b) shares or securities of an unquoted company which provided the transferor with more than 25 per cent of voting rights

(c) other unquoted shares or securities

(d) shares or securities of a quoted company which provided the transferor with control

(e) any land, building, machinery or plant which, immediately before the transfer, was used wholly or mainly for the purposes of a business carried on by a company of which the transferor had control

(f) any land, building, machinery or plant which, immediately before the transfer, was used wholly or mainly for the purposes of a business carried on by a partnership of which the transferor was a partner

(g) any land, building, machinery or plant which, immediately before the transfer, was used wholly or mainly for the purposes of a business carried on by the transferor and was then settled property in which he/she retained an interest in possession

For events occurring after 9 March 1992, a deduction of 100 per cent is available for assets falling within (a) and (b). The deduction for unquoted shares in (c) is 100 per cent for events taking place after 5 April 1996. A deduction of 50 per cent remains for assets within (d) to (g).

It is a general requirement that the property must have been retained for a period of two years before the transfer or death and restrictions may be necessary if the property has not been used wholly for business purposes. The same property cannot obtain both business property relief and the relief available for agricultural property.

CALCULATION OF TAX PAYABLE

The calculation of inheritance tax payable adopts the use of a cumulative total. Each chargeable lifetime transfer is added to the total with a final addition made on death. The top slice added to the total for the current event determines the rate at which inheritance tax must be paid. However, the cumulative total will only include transfers made within a period of seven years before the current event and those undertaken outside this period must be excluded.

Lifetime chargeable transfers

The value transferred by the limited range of lifetime chargeable transfers must be added to the seven-year cumulative total to calculate whether any inheritance tax is due. Should the nil rate band be exceeded, tax will be imposed on the excess at the rate of 20 per cent. However, if the donor dies within a period of seven years from the date of the chargeable lifetime transfer, additional tax may be due. This is calculated by applying tax at the full rate or 40 per cent in substitution for the rate of 20 per cent previously used. The amount of tax is then reduced to a percentage by applying tapering relief. This percentage is governed by the number of years from the date of the lifetime gift to the date of death, as follows:

Period of years before death	
Not more than 3	100%
More than 3 but not more than 4	80%
More than 4 but not more than 5	60%
More than 5 but not more than 6	40%
More than 6 but not more than 7	20%

Should this exercise produce liability greater than that previously paid at the 20 per cent rate on the lifetime transfer, additional tax, representing the difference, must be discharged. Where the calculation shows an amount falling below tax paid on the lifetime transfer, no additional liability can arise nor will the shortfall become repayable.

Tapering relief will, of course, only be available if the calculation discloses a liability to inheritance tax. There can be no liability to the extent that the lifetime transfer falls within the nil rate band.

Potentially exempt transfers

Where a potentially exempt transfer loses immunity from liability due to the donor's death within the seven-year *inter vivos* period, the value transferred by that transfer enters into the cumulative total. Any liability to inheritance tax will be calculated by applying the full rate of 40 per cent, reduced to the percentage governed by tapering relief if the original transfer occurred more than three years before death. Liability can only arise to the extent, if any, that the nil rate band is exceeded.

Death

The final addition to the seven-year cumulative total will comprise the value of an estate on death. Inheritance tax will be calculated by applying the full rate of 40 per cent to the extent the nil rate band is exceeded. No tapering relief can be obtained.

RATES OF TAX

In earlier times there were several rates of inheritance tax which progressively increased as the value transferred grew in size. However, since 1988 there have been only three rates, namely:
(a) a nil rate
(b) a lifetime rate of 20 per cent
(c) a full rate of 40 per cent
The nil rate band usually changes on an annual basis and for events taking place after 5 April 1999 applies to the first £231,000. Any excess over this level is taxable at 20 per cent or 40 per cent as the case may be.

PAYMENT OF TAX

Inheritance tax usually falls due for payment six months after the end of the month in which the chargeable transaction takes place. Where a transfer other than that made on death occurs after 5 April and before the following 1 October, tax falls due on the following 30 April, although there are some exceptions to this.

Inheritance tax attributable to the transfer of certain land, controlling shareholding interests, unquoted shares, businesses and interests in businesses, together with agricultural property, may usually be satisfied by instalments spread over ten years. Except in the case of non-agricultural land, where interest is charged on outstanding instalments, no liability to interest arises where tax is paid on the due date. In all cases, delay in the payment of tax may incur as liability to discharge interest.

SETTLED PROPERTY

Complex rules apply to establish inheritance tax liability on settled property. Where a person is beneficially entitled to an interest in possession, that person is effectively deemed to own the property in which the interest subsists. It follows that where the interest comes to an end during the beneficiary's lifetime and some other person becomes entitled to the property or interest, the beneficiary is treated as having made a transfer of value. However, this will usually comprise a potentially exempt transfer. In addition, no liability will arise where the property vests in the absolute ownership of the previous beneficiary. The death of a person entitled to an interest in possession will require the value of the underlying property to be added to the value of the deceased's estate.

In the case of other settled property where there is no interest in possession (e.g. discretionary trusts), liability to tax will arise on each ten-year anniversary of the trust. There will also be liability if property ceases to be held on discretionary trusts before the first ten-year anniversary date is reached or between anniversaries. The rate of tax suffered will be governed by several considerations, including previous dispositions made by the settlor of the trust, transactions concluded by the trustees, and the period throughout which property has been held in trust.

Accumulation and maintenance settlements which require assets to be distributed, or interests in income to be created, not later than a beneficiary's 25th birthday may be exempt from any liability to inheritance tax.

CORPORATION TAX

Profits, gains and income accruing to companies resident in the UK incur liability to corporation tax. Non-resident companies are immune from this tax unless they carry on a trade in the UK through a permanent establishment, branch or office. Companies residing outside the UK may be liable to income tax at the basic rate on other income arising in the UK, perhaps from letting property. The following comments are confined to companies resident in the UK.

Liability to corporation tax is governed by the profits, gains or income for an accounting period. This is usually the period for which financial accounts are made up, and in the case of companies preparing accounts to the same accounting date annually will comprise successive periods of 12 months.

RATE OF TAX

The amount of profits or income for an accounting period must be determined on normal taxation principles. The special rules which apply to individuals where a source of income is acquired or discontinued are ignored and consideration is confined to the actual profits or income for an accounting period.

The rate of corporation tax is fixed for a financial year ending on 31 March. Where the accounting period of a company overlaps this date and there is a change in the rate of corporation tax, profits and income must be apportioned.

The full rate of corporation tax for recent years and that which applies for the immediate future is 31 March 1998 and 1999, 31 per cent; 31 March 2000 and 2001, 30 per cent.

SMALL COMPANIES' RATE

Where the profits of a company do not exceed stated limits, corporation tax becomes payable at the small companies' rate. It is the amount of profits and not the size of the company which governs the application of this rate.

In recent years and for the immediate future, the small companies' rate is 31 March 1998 and 1999, 21 per cent; 31 March 2000, 20 per cent.

The level of profits which a company may derive without losing the benefit of the small companies' rate is frequently changed. For each year ending on 31 March 1995 to 31 March 2000, the limit is £300,000. However, if profits exceed £300,000 but fall below £1,500,000, marginal small companies' rate relief applies. The effect of marginal relief is that the average rate of corporation tax imposed on all profits steadily increases from the lower small companies' rate to the full rate of 31 or 30 per cent, with tax being imposed on profits in the margin at an increased rate. Where the accounting period of a company overlaps 31 March, profits must be apportioned to establish the appropriate rate for each part of those profits.

The lower limit of £300,000 and the upper limit of £1,500,000 apply to a period of 12 months and must be proportionally reduced for shorter periods. Some restriction in the small companies' rate and the marginal rate may be necessary if there are two or more associated companies, namely companies under common control.

The small companies' rate is not available for close investment-holding companies.

COMPANIES' STARTING RATE

A new companies' starting rate is being introduced for the financial year commencing on 1 April 2000 and ending on 31 March 2001. Where profits of a twelve-month period do not exceed £10,000 a starting rate of 10 per cent will apply. Marginal relief will then be available where profits exceed £10,000 but do not exceed £50,000. Here also restrictions apply where there are associated companies or a company retains close investment-holding status.

PAYMENT OF TAX

Corporation tax charged on profits for an accounting period usually falls due for payment in a single lump sum nine months after the end of that period. Most companies discharge corporation tax on this basis but other arrangements concern large companies for accounting periods ending on or after 1 July 1999. These companies must discharge their liability by four instalments. The receipt of annual profits amounting to £1,500,000 or more is sufficient to identify a large company. Where a company is a member of a group the profits of the entire group must be merged to establish whether the company is large.

CAPITAL GAINS

Chargeable gains arising to a company are calculated in a manner similar to that used for individuals. However, the withdrawal of the indexation allowance after April 1998 and the introduction of taper relief have no application to companies. Nor are companies entitled to the annual exemption of £7,100. Companies do not suffer capital gains tax on chargeable gains but incur liability to corporation tax. Tax is suffered on the full chargeable gain of an accounting period after subtracting relief for losses, if any.

DISTRIBUTIONS

Dividends and other qualifying distributions made by a UK resident company on or after 6 April 1999 are not satisfied after deduction of income tax. Similar outgoings made by a company previously required the payment of advance corporation tax but this obligation no longer applies. The only effect which the payment of a dividend or the making of a distribution now has on a company is that the outlay cannot form an ingredient in the calculation of profits.

INTEREST

On making many payments of interest after 5 April 1996 a company is required to deduct income tax at the lower rate of 20 per cent and account for the tax deducted to the Inland Revenue. The gross amount of interest paid will usually be included in the calculation of profits on which corporation tax becomes payable.

GROUPS OF COMPANIES

Each company within a group is separately charged to corporation tax on profits, gains and income. However, where one group member realizes a loss, other than a capital loss, a claim may be made to offset the deficiency against profits of some other member of the same group.

Claims are also available to avoid the deduction of income tax on the payment of interest, for transactions between members of a group of companies. The transfer of capital assets from one member of a group to a fellow member will usually incur no liability to tax on chargeable gains.

COMPLIANCE

For several years a 'pay and file' system has affected all companies. A feature of this system required that tax should be payable nine months following the end of the accounting period involved with accounts and returns being submitted three months later. Failure to satisfy corporation tax or to submit documents within these time limits could result in a liability to discharge interest and penalties. This system is rapidly being replaced following the introduction of self-assessment which now extends to all companies for accounting periods ending after 30 June 1999.

VALUE ADDED TAX

Value added tax (VAT) is charged on the value of the supplies made by a registered trader and extends to both the supply of goods and the supply of services. It is administered by Customs and Excise.

Liability to account for VAT arises on the value of goods imported into the UK from sources outside the European Community. In contrast goods imported by a trader from a second trader in a member state of the European Community attract no VAT on importation. Instead there is an acquisition tax whereby a trader who acquires goods must include the acquisition in his normal VAT return and account for the tax due. A UK trader who exports goods to a member state will not be required to account for VAT on the supply, if that trader observes the requirements laid down by regulations.

REGISTRATION

All traders, including professional men and women and companies, making taxable supplies of a value exceeding stated limits are required to register for VAT purposes. Taxable supplies represent the supply of goods and services potentially chargeable with VAT. The limits which govern mandatory registration are amended periodically, and from 1 April 1999 an unregistered trader must register:

(a) at any time, if there are reasonable grounds for believing that the value of taxable supplies in the next 30 days will exceed £51,000

(b) at the end of any month if the value of taxable supplies in the 12 months then ending has exceeded £51,000.

Liability to register under (b) may be avoided if it can be shown that the value of supplies in the period of 12 months then beginning will not exceed £49,000. There may, however, be liability to register immediately where a business is taken over from another trader as a 'going concern'. Other limits apply where goods are acquired from within the European Community.

Where the limits governing mandatory registration have been exceeded, the trader must notify Customs and Excise. In the event of failure to provide prompt notification, the person concerned will be required to account for VAT from the proper registration date.

A trader whose taxable supplies do not reach the mandatory registration limits may apply for voluntary registration. This step may be thought advisable to recover input tax or to compete with other registered traders.

A registered trader may submit an application for deregistration if the value of taxable supplies subsequently falls. From 1 April 1999, an application for deregistration can be made if the value of taxable supplies for the year beginning on the application date is not expected to exceed £49,000.

INPUT TAX

A registered trader will both suffer tax (input tax) when obtaining goods or services for the purposes of his business and also become liable to account for tax (output tax) on the value of goods and services which he/she supplies. Relief can usually be obtained for input tax suffered, either by setting that tax against output tax due or by repayment. Most items of input tax can be relieved in this manner but there are exceptions, including the prohibition of relief for the cost of business entertaining. Where a registered trader makes both exempt supplies and taxable supplies to his customers or clients, there may be some restriction in the amount of input tax which can be recovered.

OUTPUT TAX

When making a taxable supply of goods or services, a registered trader must account for output tax, if any, on the value of the supply. Usually the price charged by the registered trader will be increased by adding VAT but failure to make the required addition will not remove liability to account for output tax.

The liability to account for output tax, and also relief for input tax, may be affected where a trader is using a special second-hand goods scheme.

EXEMPT SUPPLIES

No VAT is chargeable on the supply of goods or services which are treated as exempt supplies. These include the provision of burial and cremation facilities, insurance, finance and education. The granting of a lease to occupy land or the sale of land will usually comprise an exempt supply, but there are numerous exceptions. In particular, the sale of new non-domestic buildings or certain buildings used by charities cannot be treated as exempt supplies.

A taxable person may elect to tax rents and other supplies relating to buildings and agricultural land not used for residential or charitable purposes.

Exempt supplies do not enter into the calculation of taxable supplies which governs liability to mandatory registration. Such supplies made by a registered trader may, however, limit the amount of input tax which can be relieved. It is for this reason that the election may be useful.

RATES OF TAX

Two rates of VAT have applied since 1 April 1991, namely:
(a) a zero, or nil, rate
(b) a standard rate of 17.5 per cent

In addition, a special reduced rate of 8 per cent applied to supplies of domestic fuel after March 1994. This rate was reduced to 5 per cent for supplies made after 1 September 1997.

ZERO-RATING

A large number of supplies are zero-rated. The following list is not exhaustive but indicates the wide range of supplies which may be included under this heading:

(a) the supply of many items of food and drink for human consumption. This does not include ice creams, chocolates, sweets, potato crisps and alcoholic drinks. Nor does it extend to supplies made in the course of catering or to items supplied for consumption in a restaurant or café. Whilst the supply of cold items, e.g. sandwiches for consumption away from the supplier's premises, is zero-rated, the supply of hot food, e.g. fish and chips, is not

(b) animal feeding stuffs

(c) sewerage and water, unless for industrial purposes

(d) books, brochures, pamphlets, leaflets, newspapers, maps and charts

(e) talking books for the blind and handicapped, and wireless sets for the blind

(f) supplies of services, other than professional services, when constructing a new domestic building or a building to be used by a charity. The supply of materials for such a building is zero-rated, together with the sale or the grant of a long lease. Alterations to some protected buildings are zero-rated

(g) the transportation of persons in a vehicle, ship or aircraft designed to carry not less than 12 persons

(h) supplies of drugs, medicines and other aids for the handicapped

(i) supplies of clothing and footwear for young persons

(j) exports

Although no tax is due on a zero-rated supply, this does comprise a taxable supply which must be included in the calculation governing liability to register.

COLLECTION OF TAX

Registered traders submit VAT returns for accounting periods usually of three months duration but arrangements can be made to submit returns on a monthly basis. Very large traders must account for tax on a monthly basis but this does not affect the three-monthly return. The return will show both the output tax due for supplies made by the trader in the accounting period and also the input tax for which relief is claimed. If the output tax exceeds input tax the balance must be remitted with the VAT return. Where input tax suffered exceeds the output tax due the registered trader may claim recovery of the excess from Customs and Excise.

This basis for collecting tax explains the structure of VAT. Where supplies are made between registered traders the supplier will account for an amount of tax which will usually be identical to the tax recovered by the person to whom the supply is made. However, where the supply is made to a person who is not a registered trader there can be no recovery of input tax and it is on this person that the final burden of VAT eventually falls.

Where goods are acquired by a UK trader from a

supplier within a member state of the European Community, the trader must also account for the tax due on acquisition.

An optional scheme is available for registered traders having an annual turnover of taxable supplies not exceeding £300,000. Such traders may render returns annually. Nine interim payments of VAT will be made on account, with a final balancing payment accompanying submission of the return. The number of interim payments may be reduced if turnover does not exceed £100,000.

BAD DEBTS

Many retailers operate special retail schemes for calculating the amount of VAT due. These schemes are based on the volume of consideration received in an accounting period. Should a customer fail to pay for goods or services supplied, there will be no consideration on which to calculate VAT.

To avoid the problem of bad debts incurred by traders not operating a special retail scheme, an optional system of cash accounting is available. This scheme, confined to traders with annual taxable supplies not exceeding £350,000, enables returns to be made on a cash basis, in substitution for the normal supply basis. Traders using such a scheme will not include bad debts in the calculation of cash receipts.

Where neither the cash accounting arrangements nor the special retail scheme applies, output tax falls due on the value of the supply and liability is not affected by failure to receive consideration. However, where a debt is more than six months old, relief for bad debts will be forthcoming. The calculation of the six-month period commences from the date on which payment for the supply falls due.

In those cases where a supplier obtains relief for a bad debt, the person to whom the supply has been made must refund to Customs and Excise any input tax relief which may have been granted.

OTHER SPECIAL SCHEMES

In addition to the schemes for retailers, there are several special schemes applied to calculate the amount of VAT due and which also limit the ability to recover input tax. The supply of virtually all second-hand goods has now been brought within special margin schemes.

FARMERS

Farmers may elect to apply a special flat rate scheme. This scheme is available to farmers who are not registered traders. Under the scheme a flat-rate addition of 4 per cent may be made on sales, with the amount of the addition being retained by the farmer. Registered traders to whom such a supply is made may treat the 4 per cent as recoverable input tax.

Legal Notes

IMPORTANT

These notes outline certain aspects of the law as they might affect the average person. They are intended only as a broad guideline and are by no means definitive. The law is constantly changing so expert advice should always be taken. In some cases, sources of further information are given in these notes.

It is always advisable to consult a solicitor without delay; timely advice will set your mind at rest but sitting on your rights can mean that you lose them. Anyone who does not have a solicitor already can contact the Citizens' Advice Bureau, the Law Society of England and Wales (113 Chancery Lane, London WC2A 1PL) or the Law Society of Scotland (26 Drumsheugh Gardens, Edinburgh EH3 7YR) for assistance in finding one.

The legal aid and assistance schemes exist to make the help of a lawyer available to those who would not otherwise be able to afford one. Entitlement depends on an individual's means but a solicitor or Citizens' Advice Bureau will be able to advise about entitlement.

ADOPTION OF CHILDREN

In England and Wales the adoption of children is mainly governed by the Adoption Act 1976 and the Children Act 1989.

Anyone over 21 can legally adopt a child. Married couples must adopt 'jointly', unless one partner cannot be found, is incapable of making an application, or if a separation is likely to be permanent. Unmarried couples may not adopt 'jointly' although one partner in that couple may adopt. The only organizations allowed to arrange adoptions are the social services departments of local authorities or voluntary agencies which are registered with the local authorities.

Once an adoption has been arranged, a court order is necessary to make it legal. These are obtained from the High Court (Family Division) or from a county or family proceedings court. The child's natural parents (or guardians) must consent to the adoption, unless the court dispenses with the consent, e.g. where the natural parent has neglected the child or is incapable of giving consent. Once adopted, the child has the same status as a child born to the adoptive parents and the natural parents cease to have any rights or responsibilities where the child is concerned. The adopted child will be treated as the natural child of the adoptive parents for the purposes of intestate succession, national insurance, family allowances, etc. The adopted child ceases to have any rights to the estates of his/her natural parents.

REGISTRATION AND CERTIFICATES

All adoptions in England and Wales are registered in the Adopted Children Register kept by the Office of National Statistics, and by the General Register Office for Scotland. Certificates from the registers can be obtained in a similar way to birth certificates (*see* page 653).

TRACING NATURAL PARENTS OR CHILDREN WHO HAVE BEEN ADOPTED

An adult adopted person may apply to the Registrar-General for information to enable him/her to obtain a full birth certificate. For those adopted before 12 November 1975 it is obligatory to receive counselling services before this information is given; for those adopted after that date counselling services are optional. There is also an Adoption Contact Register (created after the 1989 Act) in which details of adult adopted people and of their relatives may be recorded. The BAAF (*see* below) can provide addresses of organizations which offer advice, information and counselling to adopted people, adoptive parents and people who have had their children adopted.

SCOTLAND

The relevant legislation is the Adoption (Scotland) Act 1978 (as amended by the Children (Scotland) Act 1995) and the provisions are similar to those described above. In Scotland, petitions for adoption are made to the Sheriff Court or the Court of Session.

Further information can be obtained from:
BRITISH AGENCIES FOR ADOPTION AND FOSTERING (BAAF), Skyline House, 200 Union Street, London SE1 0LX. Tel: 0171-593 2000
SCOTTISH ADOPTION ADVICE SERVICE
16 Sandyford Place, Glasgow G3 7NB
Tel: 0141-339 0772

BIRTHS (REGISTRATION)

The birth of a child must be registered within 42 days of birth at the register office of the district in which the baby was born. In England and Wales it is possible to give the particulars to be registered at any other register office. Responsibility for registering the birth rests with the parents, except in the case of an illegitimate child, when the mother is responsible for registration. Responsibility rests firstly with the parents (in Scotland, if the father of the child is not married to the mother and has not been married to her since the child's conception, the mother alone is responsible for registration) but if they fail, particulars may be given to the registrar by:
– a relative of either parent (in Scotland only)
– the occupier of the house in which the baby was born
– a person present at the birth
– the person having charge of the child
Failure to register the birth within 42 days without reasonable cause may leave the parents liable to a penalty in England and Wales and may lead to a court decree being granted by a sheriff in Scotland.

If the parents were married at the time of the birth, either parent may register the birth and details about both parents will be entered on the register. If the parents were unmarried at the time of the birth, the father's details are entered only if both parents attend or if the parents have made a statutory declaration confirming the identity of the father. Copies of the forms necessary to make such a declaration are available at the register offices. A short birth certificate is issued free when the birth is registered.

STILL BIRTHS

If a baby is stillborn, i.e. born dead after the 24th week of pregnancy, the birth must be registered. The doctor or midwife who attends the birth or afterwards examines the body of the child will issue a Medical Certificate of Stillbirth and this must be presented at the register office.

RE-REGISTRATION

In certain circumstances it may be necessary to re-register a birth, e.g. where the birth of an illegitimate child is legitimated by the subsequent marriage of the parents. It is also possible to re-register the birth of an illegitimate child so that the father's name is entered on the register.

BIRTH ABROAD

Births of British subjects occurring abroad are registered with consular officers and certificates of birth are subsequently available from the Registrar-General. The registration of births among members of the armed forces that occur abroad or on military ships or aircraft is governed by the Registration of Births, Deaths and Marriages (Special Provisions) Act 1957.

SCOTLAND

In Scotland the birth of a child must be registered within 21 days at the register office of either the district in which the baby was born or the district in which the mother was resident at the time of the birth.

If the child is born, either in or out of Scotland, on a ship, aircraft or land vehicle that ends its journey at any place in Scotland, the child, in most cases, will be registered as if born in that place.

CERTIFICATES OF BIRTHS, DEATHS OR MARRIAGES

Certificates of births, deaths or marriages that have taken place in England and Wales since 1837 can be obtained from the Office of National Statistics (General Register Office). Applications can be made:
- by a personal visit to the Family Records Centre, London
- by postal application to the General Register Office, Southport

Certificates are also available from the Superintendent Registrar for the district in which the event took place or, in the case of marriage certificates, from the minister of the church in which the marriage took place. Any register office can advise about the best way to obtain certificates. The fees for certificates (from 1 April 1999) are:

Obtained from Registrar who registered the birth, death or marriage
Standard certificate, £3.50
Special certificate for certain statutory purposes, £3.50
Short certificate of birth other than the first issued at the time of birth registration, £3.50

Obtained from Superintendent Registrar
Standard certificate, £6.50
Special certificate for certain statutory purposes, £6.50
Short certificate of birth, £5.00

From the Family Records Centre, London / by post from the General Register Office, Southport
Standard certificate of birth, death or marriage
Personal application, £6.50
Postal application, £12.00
Postal application and information from ONS Index supplied, £9.00
Standard certificate of adoption
Personal application, £6.50
Postal application, £10.50
Short certificate of birth
Personal application, £6.50
Postal application, £12.00

Postal application and information from ONS Index supplied, £9.00
Short certificate of adoption
Personal application, £3.50
Postal application, £9.00

Indexes prepared from the registers are available for searching by the public at the Family Records Centre in London or at a Superintendent Registrar's Office; indexes at the latter relate only to births, deaths and marriages which occurred in that registration district. There is no charge for searching the indexes in the Public Search Room at the Family Records Centre but a general search fee is charged for searches at a Superintendent Registrar's Office. A fee is charged for verifying index references against the records.

The Society of Genealogists has many records of baptisms, marriages and deaths prior to 1837.

SCOTLAND

Certificates of births, deaths or marriages that have taken place in Scotland since 1855 can be obtained from the General Register Office for Scotland or from the appropriate local registrar. The General Register Office for Scotland also keeps the Register of Divorces (including decrees of declaration of nullity of marriage), and holds parish registers dating from before 1855.

Fees for certificates (from 1 April 1999) are:
Certificates (full or abbreviated) of birth, death, marriage or adoption, £8.00
A priority service is available for an additional fee of £10.00
Particular search for each period of five years or part thereof, whether specified entry is traced or not:
Personal application, £3.00
Postal application, £5.00
General search in the indexes to the statutory registers and parochial registers, per day or part thereof:
Full day (i.e. 9a.m. to 4.30p.m.) search with payment being made not less than 14 days in advance, £13.00
Full day search in any other case, £17.00
Afternoon (i.e. 1p.m. to 4.30p.m.) search £10.00
One week search, £65.00

Further information can be obtained from:
THE GENERAL REGISTER OFFICE, Office for National Statistics, Smedley Hydro, Trafalgar Road, Birkdale, Southport, Merseyside PR8 2HH. Tel: 01704-569824
FAMILY RECORDS CENTRE, 1 Myddelton Street, London EC1R 1UW. Opens 9 a.m. on Monday, Wednesday, Thursday, Friday, 10 a.m. Tuesday, 9.30 a.m. Saturday. Closes 5 p.m. Monday, Wednesday, Friday, Saturday, 7 p.m. Tuesday, Thursday
THE GENERAL REGISTER OFFICE FOR SCOTLAND, New Register House, Edinburgh EH1 3YT. Tel: 0131-334 0380
THE SOCIETY OF GENEALOGISTS, 14 Charterhouse Buildings, Goswell Road, London EC1M 7BA. Tel: 0171-251 8799

BRITISH CITIZENSHIP

The British Nationality Act 1981 which came into force on 1 January 1983 established three types of citizenship to replace the single form of Citizenship of the UK and Colonies created by the British Nationality Act 1948. The three forms of citizenship are: British Citizenship; British Dependent Territories Citizenship; and British Overseas Citizenship. Three residual categories were created: British

Subjects; British Protected Persons; and British Nationals (Overseas).

BRITISH CITIZENSHIP

Almost everyone who was a citizen of the UK and colonies and had a right of abode in the UK prior to the 1981 Act became British citizens when the Act came into force. British citizens have the right to live permanently in the UK and are free to leave and re-enter the UK at any time.

A person born on or after 1 January 1983 in the UK (including, for this purpose, the Channel Islands and the Isle of Man) is entitled to British citizenship if he/she falls into one of the following categories:
– he/she has a parent who is a British citizen
– he/she has a parent who is settled in the UK
– he/she is a newborn infant found abandoned in the UK
– his/her parents subsequently settle in the UK
– he/she lives in the UK for the first ten years of his/her life and is not absent for more than 90 days in each of those years
– he/she is adopted in the UK and one of the adopters is a British Citizen

A person born outside the UK may acquire British citizenship if he/she falls into one of the following categories:
– he/she has a parent who is a British citizen otherwise than by descent, e.g. a parent who was born in the UK
– he/she has a parent who is a British citizen serving the Crown overseas
– the Home Secretary consents to his/her registration while he/she is a minor
– he/she is a British Dependent Territories citizen, a British Overseas citizen, a British subject or a British protected person and has been lawfully resident in the UK for five years
– he/she is a British Dependent Territories citizen who acquired that citizenship from a connection with Gibraltar
– he/she is adopted (*see* above) or naturalized (*see* below)

Where parents are married, the status of either may confer citizenship on their child. If a child is illegitimate, the status of the mother determines the child's citizenship.

Under the 1981 Act, Commonwealth citizens and citizens of the Republic of Ireland were entitled to registration as British citizens before 1 January 1988. In 1985 citizens of the Falkland Islands were granted British citizenship.

Renunciation of British citizenship must be registered with the Home Secretary and will be revoked if no new citizenship or nationality is acquired within six months. If the renunciation was required in order to retain or acquire another citizenship or nationality, the citizenship may be reacquired once.

BRITISH DEPENDENT TERRITORIES CITIZENSHIP

Under the 1981 Act, this type of citizenship was conferred on citizens of the UK and colonies by birth, naturalization or registration in British Dependent Territories. British Dependent Territories citizens may be entitled to registration as British citizens on completion of five years' legal residence in the UK.

On 1 July 1997 citizens of Hong Kong who did not qualify to register as British citizens under the British Nationality (Hong Kong) Act 1990 lost their British Dependent Territories citizenship on the handover of sovereignty to China; they may, however, have applied to register as British Nationals (Overseas).

Eligibility for British Dependent Territories citizenship is determined by similar rules to those for acquiring British citizenship, except that the connection is with the dependent territory rather than with the UK.

BRITISH OVERSEAS CITIZENSHIP

Under the 1981 Act, this type of citizenship was conferred on any UK and colonies citizens who did not qualify for British citizenship or citizenship of the British Dependent Territories. British Overseas citizenship may be acquired by the wife and minor children of a British Overseas citizen in certain circumstances. British Overseas citizens may be entitled to registration as British citizens on completion of five years' legal residence in the UK.

RESIDUAL CATEGORIES

British subjects, British protected persons and British Nationals (Overseas) may be entitled to registration as British citizens on completion of five years' legal residence in the UK.

Citizens of the Republic of Ireland who were also British subjects before 1 January 1949 can retain that status if they fulfil certain conditions.

EUROPEAN UNION CITIZENSHIP

British citizens (including Gibraltarians who are registered as such) are also EU citizens and are entitled to travel freely to other EU countries to work, study, reside and set up a business. EU citizens have the same rights with respect to the United Kingdom.

NATURALIZATION

Naturalization is granted at the discretion of the Home Secretary. The basic requirements are five years' residence (three years if the applicant is married to a British citizen), good character, adequate knowledge of the English, Welsh or Scottish Gaelic language, and an intention to reside permanently in the UK.

STATUS OF ALIENS

Aliens may not hold public office or vote in Britain and they may not own a British ship or aircraft. Citizens of the Republic of Ireland are not deemed to be aliens.

CONSUMER LAW

SALE OF GOODS

A sale of goods contract is the most common type of contract. It is governed by the Sale of Goods Act 1979 (as amended by the Sale and Supply of Goods Act 1994). The Act provides protection for buyers by implying terms into every sale of goods contract. These terms are:
– a condition that the seller will pass good title to the buyer (unless the seller agrees to transfer only such title as he/she has)
– where the seller sells goods by reference to a description, a condition that the goods will match that description and, where the sale is by sample and description, a condition that the bulk of the goods will correspond with such sample and description
– where goods are sold by a business seller, a condition that the goods will be of satisfactory quality if they meet the standard that a reasonable person would regard as satisfactory taking into account any description of the goods, the price, and all other relevant circumstances. The quality of the goods includes their state and condition, relevant aspects being whether they are suitable for their common purpose, their appearance and finish, freedom from minor defects and their safety and durability. This term will not be implied, however, if a buyer has examined the goods and should have noticed the defect or if the seller specifically drew the buyer's attention to the defect

– where goods are sold by a business seller, a condition that the goods are reasonably fit for any purpose made known to the seller by the buyer, unless the buyer does not rely on the seller's judgement, or it is not reasonable for him/her to do so

– where goods are sold by sample, conditions that the bulk of the sample will correspond with the sample in quality, that the buyer will have a reasonable opportunity of comparing the two and that the goods are free from any defect rendering them unsatisfactory which would not be obvious from the sample

Some of the above terms can be excluded from contracts by the seller. The seller's right to do this is, however, restricted by the Unfair Contract Terms Act 1977. The Act offers more protection to a buyer who 'deals as a consumer', that is where the sale is a business sale, the goods are of a type ordinarily bought for private use and the goods are bought by a buyer who is not a business buyer. In a sale by auction or competitive tender, a buyer never deals as consumer. Also, a seller can never exclude the implied term as to title mentioned above.

HIRE-PURCHASE AGREEMENTS

Terms similar to those implied in contracts of sales of goods are implied into contracts of hire-purchase, under the Supply of Goods (Implied Terms) Act 1973. The 1977 Act limits the exclusion of these implied terms as before.

SUPPLY OF GOODS AND SERVICES

Under the Supply of Goods and Services Act 1982, similar terms are also implied in other types of contract under which ownership of goods passes, e.g. a contract for 'work and materials' such as supplying new parts while servicing a car, and contracts for the hire of goods. These types of contracts have additional implied terms:
– that the supplier will use reasonable care and skill
– that the supplier will carry out the service in a reasonable time (unless the time has been agreed)
– that the supplier will make a reasonable charge (unless the charge has already been agreed)
The 1977 Act limits the exclusion of these implied terms in a similar manner as before.

UNFAIR TERMS

The Unfair Terms in Consumer Contracts Regulations 1994 apply to contracts between business sellers (or suppliers of goods and services) and consumers, where the terms have not been individually negotiated, i.e. where the terms were drafted in advance so that the consumer was unable to influence those terms. An unfair term is one which operates to the detriment of the consumer. An unfair term does not bind the consumer but the contract will continue to bind the parties if it is capable of existing without the unfair term. The regulations contain a non-exhaustive list of terms which are regarded as unfair. Whether a term is regarded as fair or not will depend on many factors, including the nature of the goods or services, the surrounding circumstances (such as the bargaining strength of both parties) and the other terms in the contract.

The 1994 Regulations will be replaced by The Unfair Terms in Consumer Contracts Regulations 1999 on 1 October 1999. These new Regulations give the same protection as the 1994 Regulations and stress the importance of plain English in contractual documents.

TRADE DESCRIPTIONS

It is a criminal offence under the Trade Descriptions Act 1968 for a business seller to apply a false trade description of goods or to supply or offer to supply any goods to which a false description has been applied. A 'trade description' includes descriptions of quality, size, composition, fitness for purpose and method, and place and date of manufacture of the goods. It is also an offence to give a false indication of the price of goods.

FAIR TRADING

The Fair Trading Act 1973 is designed to protect the consumer. It provides for the appointment of a Director-General of Fair Trading, one of whose duties is to review commercial activities in the UK relating to the supply of goods and services to consumers. An example of a practice which has been prohibited by a reference made under this Act is that of business sellers posing in advertisements as private sellers.

CONSUMER PROTECTION

Under the Consumer Protection Act 1987, producers of goods are liable for any injury or for any damage exceeding £275 caused by a defect in their product (subject to certain defences).

The Consumer Protection (Cancellation of Contracts Concluded Away from Business Premises) Regulations 1987 allow consumers a seven-day period in which to cancel contracts for the supply of goods and services, where the contracts were made during an unsolicited visit to the consumer's home or workplace. This only applies to contracts where the cost exceeds £35.

CONSUMER CREDIT

In matters relating to the provision of credit (or the supply of goods on hire or hire-purchase), consumers are also protected by the Consumer Credit Act 1974. Under this Act a licence, issued by the Director-General of Fair Trading, is required to conduct a consumer credit or consumer hire business or to deal in credit brokerage, debt adjusting, counselling or collecting. Any 'fit' person may apply to the Director-General of Fair Trading for a licence, which is normally renewable after ten years. A licence is not necessary if such types of business are only transacted occasionally, or if only exempt agreements are involved. The provisions of the Act only apply to 'regulated' agreements, i.e. those that are with individuals or partnerships, those that are not exempt (such as certain local authority and building society loans), and those where the total credit does not exceed £25,000. Provisions include:
– the terms of the regulated agreement can be altered by the creditor provided the agreement gives him/her the right to do so; in such cases the debtor must be given proper notice of this
– in order for a creditor to enforce a regulated agreement, the agreement must comply with certain formalities and must be properly executed. The debtor must also be given specified information by the creditor or his/her broker or agent during the negotiations which take place before the signing of the agreement. The agreement must state certain information such as the amount of credit, the annual interest rate, the amount and timing of repayments
– if an agreement is signed other than at the creditor's (or credit broker's or negotiator's) place of business and oral representations were made in the debtor's presence during discussions pre-agreement, the debtor has a right to cancel the agreement. Time for cancellation expires five clear days after the debtor receives a second copy of the agreement. The agreement must inform the debtor of his right to cancel and how to cancel
– if the debtor is in arrears (or otherwise in breach of the agreement), the creditor must serve a default notice before taking any action such as repossessing the goods
– if the agreement is a hire-purchase or conditional sale

agreement, the creditor cannot repossess the goods without a court order if the debtor has paid one-third of the total price of the goods
- in agreements where the debtor is required to make grossly exorbitant payments or where the agreement grossly contravenes the ordinary principles of fair trading, the debtor may request that the court alter or set aside some of the terms of the agreement. The agreement can also be reopened during enforcement proceedings by the court itself

Where a credit reference agency has been used to check the debtor's financial standing, the creditor must give the agency's name to the debtor, who is entitled to see the agency's file on him. A fee of £1 is payable to the agency.

SCOTLAND

The legislation governing the sale and supply of goods applies to Scotland as follows:
- the Sale of Goods Act 1979 applies with some modifications and it has been amended by the Sale and Supply of Goods Act 1994
- the Supply of Goods (Implied Terms) Act 1973 applies
- the Supply of Goods and Services Act 1982 does not extend to Scotland but some of its provisions were introduced by the Sale and Supply of Goods Act 1994
- only Parts II and III of the Unfair Contract Terms Act 1977 apply
- the Trade Descriptions Act 1968 applies with minor modifications
- the Consumer Credit Act 1974 applies

PROCEEDINGS AGAINST THE CROWN

Until 1947, proceedings against the Crown were generally possible only by a procedure known as a petition of right, which put the litigant at a considerable disadvantage. The Crown Proceedings Act 1947 placed the Crown (not the Sovereign in his/her private capacity, but as the embodiment of the State) largely in the same position as a private individual. The Act did not, however, extinguish or limit the Crown's prerogative or statutory powers, and it granted immunity to HM ships and aircraft. It also left certain Crown privileges unaffected. The Act largely abolished the special procedures which previously applied to civil proceedings by and against the Crown. Civil proceedings may be instituted against the appropriate government department or against the Attorney-General.

In Scotland proceedings against the Crown founded on breach of contract could be taken before the 1947 Act and no special procedures applied. The Crown could, however, claim certain special pleas. The 1947 Act applies in part to Scotland and brings the practice of the two countries as closely together as the different legal systems permit. Civil proceedings may be instituted against the Lord Advocate where proceedings are against the Scottish Administration of the Scottish Parliament or against the Advocate General for Scotland representing the appropriate government department in any other case.

DEATHS

When a Death Occurs

If the death was expected, the doctor who attended the deceased during their final illness should be contacted. If the death was sudden or unexpected, the family doctor (if known) and police should be contacted.   If the cause of death is quite clear the doctor will provide:

- a medical certificate that shows the cause of death (this will be in a sealed envelope, addressed to the registrar)
- a formal notice that states that the doctor has signed the medical certificate and that explains how to get the death registered

If the death was known to be caused by a natural illness but the doctor wishes to know more about the cause of death, he/she may ask the relatives for permission to carry out a post-mortem examination. This should not delay the funeral.

In England and Wales a coroner is responsible for investigating deaths occurring in the following circumstances:
- when no doctor has treated the deceased during his or her last illness or when the doctor attending the patient did not see him or her within 14 days before death, or after death; or
- when the death occurred during an operation or before recovery from the effect of an anaesthetic; or
- when the death was sudden and unexplained or attended by suspicious circumstances; or
- when the death might be due to an industrial injury or disease, or to accident, violence, neglect or abortion, or to any kind of poisoning; or
- the death occurred in prison or in police custody

The doctor will write on the formal notice that the death has been referred to the coroner; if the post mortem shows that death was due to natural causes, the coroner may issue a notification which gives the cause of death so that the death can be registered. If the cause of death was violent or unnatural, the coroner is obliged to hold an inquest.

In Scotland the office of coroner does not exist. The local procurator fiscal inquires into sudden or suspicious deaths. A fatal accident inquiry will be held before the sheriff where the death has resulted from an accident during the course of the employment of the person who has died, or where the person who has died was in legal custody, or where the Lord Advocate deems it in the public interest that an inquiry be held.

Registering a Death

In England and Wales the death must be registered by the registrar of births and deaths for the district in which it occurred; details can be obtained from the telephone directory (under registration of births and deaths and marriages), from the doctor or local council, or at a post office or police station. Since April 1997, information concerning a death can be given before any registrar of births and deaths in England and Wales. The registrar will pass the relevant details to the registrar for the district where the death occurred, who will then register the death or, if different in the registration district in which the death took place.

In England and Wales the death must normally be registered within five days; in Scotland it must be registered within eight days. If the death has been referred to the coroner/local procurator fiscal it cannot be registered until the registrar has received authority from the coroner/local procurator fiscal to do so. Failure to register a death involves a penalty in England and Wales and may lead to a court decree being granted by a sheriff in Scotland.

If the death occurred at a house, the death may be registered by:
- any relative of the deceased present at the death or in attendance during the last illness
- any relative of the deceased residing or being in the sub-district where the death occurred
- any person present at the death
- the occupier or any inmate of the house if he/she knew of the occurrence of the death

– any person causing the disposal of the body

The person registering the death should take the medical certificate of the cause of death with them; it is also useful, though not essential, to take the deceased's birth and marriage certificates, medical card (if possible), pension documents and life assurance details. The registrar will issue a certificate for burial or cremation and a certificate of registration of death; both are free of charge. A death certificate is a certified copy of the entry in the death register; these can be provided on payment of a fee and may be required for the following purposes:

– the will
– bank and building society accounts
– savings bank certificates and premium bonds
– insurance policies
– pension claims

If the death occurred abroad or on a foreign ship or aircraft, the death should be registered according to the local regulations of the relevant country and a death certificate should be obtained. The death can also be registered with the British Consul in that country and a record will be kept at the General Register Office. This avoids the expense of bringing the body back.

After 12 months of death or the finding of a dead body, no death can be registered without the consent of the Registrar-General.

BURIAL AND CREMATION

In most circumstances in England and Wales a certificate for burial or cremation must be obtained from the registrar before the burial or cremation can take place. If the death has been referred to the coroner, an order for burial or a certificate for cremation must be obtained. In Scotland a body may be buried (but not cremated) before the death is registered.

Funeral costs can normally be repaid out of the deceased's estate and will be given priority over any other claims. If the deceased has left a will it may contain directions concerning the funeral; however, these directions need not be followed by the executor.

The deceased's papers should also indicate whether a grave space had already been arranged. Most town churchyards and many suburban churchyards are no longer open for burial because they are full. Most cemeteries are non-denominational and may be owned by local authorities or private companies; fees vary.

If the body is to be cremated, an application form, two cremation certificates (for which there is a charge) or a certificate for cremation if the death was referred to the coroner, and a certificate signed by the medical referee must be completed in addition to the certificate for burial or cremation (the form is not required if the coroner has issued a certificate for cremation). All the forms are available from the funeral director or crematorium. Most crematoria are run by local authorities; the fees usually include the medical referee's fee and the use of the chapel. Ashes may be scattered, buried in a churchyard or cemetery, or kept.

The registrar must be notified of the date, place and means of disposal of the body within 96 hours (England and Wales) or three days (Scotland).

If the death occurred abroad or on a foreign ship or aircraft, a local burial or cremation may be arranged. If the body is to be brought back to England or Wales, a death certificate from the relevant country or an authorization for the removal of the body from the country of death from the coroner or relevant authority will be required. To arrange a funeral in England or Wales an authenticated translation of a foreign death certificate or a death certificate issued in Scotland or Northern Ireland which must show the cause of death, is needed, together with a certificate of no liability to register from the registrar in England and Wales in whose sub-district it is intended to bury or cremate the body. If it is intended to cremate the body a cremation order will be required from the Home Office or a certificate for cremation.

Further information can be obtained from:

THE GENERAL REGISTER OFFICE, Office for National Statistics, Smedley Hydro, Trafalgar Road, Birkdale, Southport, Merseyside PR8 2HH. Tel: 01704-569824

THE GENERAL REGISTER OFFICE FOR SCOTLAND, New Register House, Edinburgh EH1 3YT. Tel: 0131-334 0380

DIVORCE AND RELATED MATTERS

ENGLAND AND WALES

There are two types of matrimonial suit: those seeking the annulment of a marriage, and those seeking a judicial separation or divorce. To obtain an annulment, judicial separation or divorce in England and Wales, one or both of the parties must have their permanent home in England and Wales when the petition is started, or have been living in England and Wales for at least a year on the day the petition is started. All cases are commenced in divorce county courts or in the Divorce Registry in London. If a suit is defended it may be transferred to the High Court.

NULLITY OF MARRIAGE

Various circumstances will render a marriage invalid from the beginning including if: the parties were within the prohibited degrees of consanguinity, affinity or adoption; the parties were not male and female; either of the parties was already married; either of the parties was under the age of 16; the formalities of the marriage were defective, e.g. the marriage did not take place in an authorized building, and both parties knew of the defect. Declarations of nullity are sought in very few cases.

SEPARATION

A couple may enter into an agreement to separate by consent but for the agreement to be valid it must be followed by an immediate separation; a solicitor should be contacted.

Judicial separation does not dissolve a marriage and it is not necessary to prove that the marriage has irretrievably broken down. Either party can petition for a judicial separation at any time; the grounds listed below as grounds for divorce are also grounds for judicial separation.

DIVORCE

Neither party can petition for divorce until at least one year after the date of the marriage. The sole ground for divorce is the irretrievable breakdown of the marriage; this must be proved on one or more of the following grounds:

– the respondent has committed adultery and the petitioner finds it intolerable to live with him/her; however the petitioner cannot rely on an act of adultery by the other party if they have lived together for more than six months after the discovery that adultery had been committed
– the respondent has behaved in such a way that the petitioner cannot reasonably be expected to continue living with him/her
– the respondent deserted the petitioner for two years immediately before the petition. Desertion may be defined as a voluntary withdrawal from cohabitation by

the respondent without just cause and against the wishes of the petitioner; where one party is guilty of serious misconduct which forces the other party to leave, the party at fault is said to be guilty of constructive desertion
- the respondent and the petitioner have lived separately for two years immediately before the petition and the respondent consents to the decree
- the respondent and the petitioner have lived separately for five years immediately before the petition

A total period of less than six months during which the parties have resumed living together is disregarded in determining whether the prescribed period of separation or desertion has been continuous (but cannot be included as part of the period of separation).

The Matrimonial Causes Act 1973 requires the solicitor for the petitioner in certain cases to certify whether the possibility of a reconciliation has been discussed with the petitioner.

(The Family Law Act 1996 provides that irretrievable breakdown would be the sole ground for divorce; the partner initiating the divorce would be required to attend an information session about the nature of divorce and the options available; and divorce would be granted after one year, or 18 months if the couple have children, during which time the couple would have the chance to take part in mediation sessions. These changes may not be implemented at all as the pilot schemes have not been very successful).

THE DECREE NISI

A decree nisi does not dissolve or annul the marriage but must be obtained before a divorce or annulment can take place.

Where the suit is undefended, the evidence normally takes the form of a sworn written statement made by the petitioner which is considered by a district judge. If the judge is satisfied that the petitioner has proved the contents of the petition, he/she will set a date for the pronouncement of the decree nisi in open court; neither party need attend.

If the judge is not satisfied that the petitioner has proved the contents of the petition, or if the suit is defended, the petition will be heard in open court with the parties giving oral evidence.

THE DECREE ABSOLUTE

The decree nisi is usually made absolute after six weeks and on the application of the petitioner. If the judge thinks it may be necessary to exercise any of his/her powers under the Children Act 1989, he/she can in exceptional circumstances delay the granting of the decree absolute. The decree absolute dissolves or annuls the marriage.

CHILDREN

Neither parent is now awarded 'custody' of any children of the marriage in England and Wales. Both parents, if married, have 'parental responsibility'. Either parent can exercise this, independently of the other. Any dispute between the parents can be resolved by the courts. In all court cases concerning children, whether connected to a matrimonial suit or not, the welfare of the child is the paramount consideration.

MAINTENANCE, ETC.

Either party may be liable to pay maintenance to their former spouse. If there were any children of the marriage, both parents have a legal responsibility to support them financially if they can afford to do so. These so-called ancillary matters, including any property settlements, may be settled before the divorce goes through but currently can go on long after the marriage is dissolved.

The courts are responsible for assessing maintenance for the former spouse, taking into account each party's income and essential outgoings and other aspects of the case. The court also deals with any maintenance for a child which has been treated by the spouses as a 'child of the family', e.g. a stepchild, and any property settlements.

The Child Support Agency (CSA) was set up under the Child Support Act 1991 and is now responsible for assessing the maintenance that absent parents should pay for their natural or adopted children (whether or not a marriage has taken place). The CSA accepts applications only when all the people involved are habitually resident in the UK; the courts will continue to deal with cases where one of the people involved lives abroad. The CSA deals with all new cases, and is gradually taking on cases where the parent with care (or his/her new partner) was already receiving income support, family credit or disability working allowance before 5 April 1993. People with existing court orders or written maintenance agreements made before 5 April 1993 should continue to use the courts. Where it is already collecting child maintenance, the CSA has the power to offer a collection and enforcement service for certain other payments of maintenance.

A formula is used to work out how much child maintenance is payable. The formula ensures that after the payment of child maintenance the absent parent's income, and that of any second family he/she may now have, remains significantly above basic income support rates. Also, no absent parent will normally be assessed to pay more than 30 per cent of his/her net income in current child maintenance, or more than 33 per cent if he/she is also liable for any arrears. Absent parents are normally expected to pay at least a minimum amount of child maintenance (currently about £2.50 a week).

A scheme has begun to be introduced since the end of 1996 which allows departures from the formula in certain tightly defined circumstances, e.g. the high costs of travel to maintain contact with a child, or to have a property and capital transfer ('clean break' settlement) entered into before April 1993 taken into account; there will also be some additional grounds which may result in liability being increased.

Some cases involving unusual circumstances are treated as special cases and the assessment is modified. Where there is financial need (e.g. because of disability or continuing education), maintenance may be ordered by the court for children even beyond the age of 18.

The level of maintenance is reviewed automatically every two years. Either parent can report a change of circumstances and request a review at any time. An independent complaints examiner for the CSA was appointed in early 1997.

If the absent parent does not pay the child maintenance, the CSA may make an order for payments to be deducted directly from his/her salary or wages; if all other methods fail, the CSA may take court action to enforce the payment.

COURT ORDERS

Magistrates' courts used for domestic proceedings are now called family proceedings courts. A spouse can apply to the family proceedings court for a court order on the ground that the other spouse:
- has failed to pay reasonable maintenance for the applicant
- has failed to make a proper contribution towards the reasonable maintenance of a 'child of the family'
- has deserted the applicant
- has behaved in such a way that the applicant cannot reasonably be expected to live with the respondent

If the case is proved, the court can order:
– periodical payments for the applicant and/or a 'child of the family'
– a lump sum payment (not exceeding £1,000) to the applicant and/or a 'child of the family'

In deciding what orders (if any) to make, the court must consider guidelines which are similar to those governing financial orders in divorce cases. There are also special provisions relating to consent orders and separation by agreement. An order may be enforceable even if the parties are living together, but in some cases it will cease to have effect if they continue to do so for six months.

DOMESTIC VIOLENCE

If one spouse has been subjected to violence at the hands of the other, it is now possible to obtain a court order very quickly to restrain further violence and if necessary to have the other spouse excluded from the home. Such orders may also relate to unmarried couples and to a range of other relationships.

SCOTLAND

Although there is separate legislation for Scotland covering nullity of marriage, judicial separation, divorce and ancillary matters, the provisions are in most respects the same as those for England and Wales. The following is confined to major points on which the law in Scotland differs.

An action for 'declarator of nullity' can be brought only in the Court of Session. Where a spouse is capable of sexual intercourse but refuses to consummate the marriage, this is not a ground of nullity in Scots law, though it could be a ground for divorce. The fact that a spouse was suffering from venereal disease at the time of marriage and the other spouse did not know this is not a ground of nullity in Scots law, neither is the fact that a wife was pregnant by another man at the time of marriage and her husband did not know this.

An action for judicial separation or divorce may be raised in the Court of Session; it may also be raised in the Sheriff Court if either party was resident in the sheriffdom for 40 days immediately before the date of the action or for 40 days ending not more than 40 days before the date of the action. The fee for starting a divorce petition in the Sheriff Court is £74.

When adultery is cited as proof that the marriage has broken down irretrievably, it is not necessary in Scotland to prove also that it is intolerable for the pursuer to live with the defender. In the case of desertion, irretrievable breakdown is not established if, after the two year desertion period has expired, the parties resume living together at any time after the end of three months from the date when they first resume living together.

Where a divorce action has been raised, it may be sisted or put on hold for a variety of reasons.

If the parties do cohabit during such postponement, no account is taken of the cohabitation if the action later proceeds.

In actions for divorce and separation, the court has the power to award a residence order in respect of any children of the marriage. The welfare of the children is of paramount importance, and the fact that a spouse has caused the breakdown of the marriage does not in itself preclude him/her from being awarded residence.

A simplified procedure for 'do-it-yourself' divorce was introduced in 1983 for certain divorces. If the action is based on two or five years' separation and will not be opposed, and if there are no children under 16 and no financial claims, and there is no sign that the applicant's

spouse is unable to manage his or her affairs through mental illness or handicap, the applicant can write directly to the local sheriff court or to the Court of Session for the appropriate forms to enable him or her to proceed. The fee is £57, unless the applicant receives income support, family credit or legal advice and assistance, in which case there is no fee.

An extract decree, which dissolves or annuls marriage, will be made available 14 days after the divorce has been granted.

Further information can be obtained from any divorce county court, solicitor or Citizens' Advice Bureau, the Lord Chancellor's Department or the Lord Advocate's Department (for entries, *see* Index), or the following:

THE PRINCIPAL REGISTRY, First Avenue House, 42–49 High Holborn, London WC1V 6NP. Tel: 0171-936 6000

THE COURT OF SESSION, Parliament House, Parliament Square, Edinburgh EH1 1HQ. Tel: 0131-225 2595

THE CHILD SUPPORT AGENCY, Longbenton, Newcastle upon Tyne NE98 1YX. Tel: 0191-213 5000

EMPLOYMENT LAW

PAY AND CONDITIONS

The Employment Rights Act 1996 consolidates the statutory provisions relating to employees' rights. Employers must give each employee based in Great Britain and employed for more than one month a written statement containing the following information:
– names of employer and employee
– date when employment began
– remuneration and intervals at which it will be paid
– job title or description of job
– hours and place(s) of work
– holiday entitlement and holiday pay
– entitlement to sick leave and sick pay
– details of pension scheme(s)
– length of notice period that employer and employee need to give to terminate employment, or the end date for a fixed-term contract
– details of any collective agreement which affects the terms of employment
– details of disciplinary and grievance procedures
– if the employee is to work outside the UK for more than one month, the period of such work and the currency in which payment is made

This must be given to the employee within two months of the start of their employment. The Working Time Regulations 1998 and the National Minimum Wage Act 1998 now supplement the 1996 Act.

SICK PAY

Employees absent from work through illness or injury are entitled to receive Statutory Sick Pay (SSP) from the employer for a maximum period of 28 weeks in any three-year period. This applies to all employees, both men and women, up to the age of 65.

DEDUCTIONS FROM PAY

Employers may not make deductions from an employee's wages without the employee's prior written consent or unless authorized by statute (e.g. deductions for national insurance or tax).

SUNDAY TRADING

The Sunday Trading Act 1994 gave new rights to shop workers. They have the right not to be dismissed, selected for redundancy or to suffer any detriment (such as the denial of overtime, promotion or training) if they refuse to work on Sundays. This does not apply to those who, under their contracts, are employed to work on Sundays.

TRADE UNION MEMBERSHIP

Under employment legislation, employees or potential employees may not be penalized because they are or are not a member of a trade union.

DISPUTES

Where it has not been possible to settle a dispute in the workplace, it may be possible for employees to make a complaint to an industrial tribunal. ACAS (the Advisory, Conciliation and Arbitration Service; for entry, *see* Index) offers advice and conciliation in employment disputes.

TERMINATION OF EMPLOYMENT

An employee may be dismissed without notice if guilty of gross misconduct but in other cases a period of notice must be given by the employer. The minimum periods of notice specified in the Employment Rights Act 1996 are:
– at least one week if the employee has been continuously employed for one month or more but for less than two years
– at least two weeks if the employee has been continuously employed for two years or more. A week is added for every complete year of continuous employment up to 12 years
– at least 12 weeks for those who have been continuously employed for 12 years or more
– longer periods apply if these are specified in the contract of employment
If an employee is dismissed with less notice than he/she is entitled to, the employer is generally liable to pay wages for the period of proper notice (or for the period of the contract for those on fixed-term contracts). Generally, no notice needs to be given of the expiry of a fixed-term contract.

REDUNDANCY

An employee dismissed because of redundancy may be entitled to a lump sum. This applies if:
– the employee has at least two years' continuous service
– the employee is actually dismissed by the employer (even in cases of voluntary redundancy)
– dismissal is due to a reduction in the work force
An employee may not be entitled to a redundancy payment if offered a new job by the same employer. The amount of payment depends on the length of service, the salary and the age of the employee.

UNFAIR DISMISSAL

Complaints about unfair dismissal are dealt with by an employment tribunal. Since 1 June 1999 any employee, with one year's continuous service subject to exceptions, regardless of their hours of work, can make a complaint to the tribunal. For dismissals prior to that date, it is necessary for the employee to have two years' continuous service in order to bring a complaint (although this requirement has been referred by the House of Lords to the European Court of Justice). At the tribunal the employer must prove that the dismissal was due to one or more of the following reasons:
– the employee's capability for the job
– the employee's conduct
– redundancy
– a legal restriction preventing the continuation of the employee's contract
– some other substantial reason

If so, the tribunal must decide whether the employer acted reasonably in dismissing the employee for that reason. If the employee is found to have been unfairly dismissed, the tribunal can order that he/she be reinstated or compensated.

DISCRIMINATION

Discrimination in employment on the grounds of sex, race or (subject to wide exceptions) disability is unlawful. The following legislation applies to those employed in Great Britain but not to employees in Northern Ireland or (subject to EC exceptions) to those who work mainly abroad:
– The Equal Pay Act 1970 (as amended) entitles men and women to equality in matters related to their contracts of employment. Those doing like work for the same employer are entitled to the same pay and conditions regardless of their sex
– The Sex Discrimination Act 1975 (as amended by the Sex Discrimination Act 1986) makes it unlawful to discriminate on grounds of sex or marital status. This covers all aspects of employment, including advertising for recruits, terms offered, opportunities for promotion and training, and dismissal procedures
– The Race Relations Act 1976 gives individuals the right not to be discriminated against in employment matters on the grounds of race, colour, nationality, or ethnic or national origins. It applies to all aspects of employment
– The Disability Discrimination Act 1995 makes discrimination against a disabled person in all aspects of employment unlawful. Unlike sex and race discrimination, an employer may show that the treatment is justified and that the employer acted reasonably. Employers with fewer than 15 employees are exempt
The Equal Opportunities Commission, the Commission for Racial Equality and the Disablilty Rights Commission (for entries, *see* Index) have the function of eliminating such discriminations in the workplace and can provide further information and assistance.

In Northern Ireland like provisions exist but are constituted in separate legislation. The Fair Employment (Northern Ireland) Act 1989 adds specific provisions aimed at preventing religious discrimination.

IMPENDING LEGISLATION

The Employment Relations Act 1999 will make a number of important changes to the existing law when it comes into force. The main changes are:
– a right of accompaniment. A worker attending a serious disciplinary or grievance hearing will have a right to be accompanied by a trade union representative or co-worker of their choice
– a new scheme of compulsory trade union recognition following a workplace ballot
– greater protection for striking employees from dismissal
– more 'family friendly' measures, including greater rights to maternity leave and parental leave
– the maximum compensatory award in unfair dismissal cases is to be increased from £12,000 to £50,000.

ILLEGITIMACY AND LEGITIMATION

The Children Act 1989 gives the mother parental responsibility for the child when she is not married to the father. The father can acquire parental responsibility either by agreement with her (in prescribed form) or by applying to the court. If an illegitimate child is to be adopted, the father's consent is required only where he has been awarded parental rights by the court.

Every child born to a married woman during marriage is presumed to be legitimate, unless the couple are separated under court order when the child is conceived, in which case the child is presumed not to be the husband's child. It is possible to challenge the presumption of legitimacy or illegitimacy through civil proceedings.

In Scotland, the relevant legislation is the Children (Scotland) Act 1995, which also gives the mother parental responsibility for her child when she is not married to the child's father. The Act also provides that a father has no automatic parental rights when unmarried to the mother, but can acquire parental responsibility by applying to the court.

LEGITIMATION

Under the Legitimacy Act 1976, an illegitimate person automatically becomes legitimate when his/her parents marry. This applies even where one of the parents was married to a third person at the time of the birth. In such cases it is necessary to re-register the birth of the child. In Scotland, the relevant legislation is the Legitimation (Scotland) Act 1968.

RIGHTS OF ILLEGITIMATE PEOPLE

For the purposes of most legislation, illegitimate and legitimate people have the same rights and responsibilities. In particular, under the Family Law Reform Acts 1969 and 1987, legitimate and illegitimate children have broadly the same rights on an intestacy. Furthermore, in any will made after 31 December 1969, it is assumed that any reference to children or relatives will include those who are illegitimate and those related through another person who is illegitimate. In Scotland, illegitimate and legitimate people are given equal status under the Law Reform (Parent and Child) Scotland Act 1986.

JURY SERVICE

In England and Wales a person charged with any but the most minor offences is entitled to be tried by jury. No such right exists in Scotland, although more serious offences are heard before a jury. In England and Wales there are 12 members of a jury in a criminal case and eight members in a civil case. In Scotland there are 12 members of a jury in a civil case in the Court of Session (the civil jury being confined to the Court of Session and a restricted number of actions), and 15 in a criminal trial. Jurors are normally asked to serve for ten working days, although jurors selected for longer cases are expected to sit for the duration of the trial.

Every parliamentary or local government elector between the ages of 18 and 70 who has lived in the UK (including, for this purpose, the Channel Islands and the Isle of Man) for any period of at least five years since reaching the age of 13 is qualified to serve on a jury unless he/she is ineligible or disqualified.

ENGLAND AND WALES

Those ineligible for jury service include:
– those who have at any time been judges, magistrates or senior court officials
those who have within the previous ten years been concerned with the administration of justice
– priests of any religion and vowed members of religious communities
– certain sufferers from mental illness

Those disqualified from jury service include:
– those who have at any time been sentenced by a court in the UK (including, for this purpose, the Channel Islands and the Isle of Man) to a term of imprisonment or custody of five years or more
– those who have within the previous ten years served any part of a sentence of imprisonment, youth custody or detention, been detained in a young offenders' institution, received a suspended sentence of imprisonment or order for detention, or received a community service order
– those who have within the previous five years been placed on probation
– those who are on bail in criminal proceedings

Those who may be excused as of right from jury service include:
– persons over the age of 65
– members and officers of the Houses of Parliament
– members of the National Assembly for Wales
– representatives to the European Parliament
– full-time serving members of the armed forces
– registered and practising members of the medical, dental, nursing, veterinary and pharmaceutical professions
– those who have served on a jury in the previous two years

The court has the discretion to excuse a juror from service, or defer the date of service, if the service would be a hardship to the juror. If a person serves on a jury knowing himself/herself to be ineligible or disqualified, he/she is liable to be fined up to £5,000 if disqualified and up to £1,000 for all other offences. The defendant can object to any juror if he/she can show cause.

A juror may claim travelling expenses, a subsistence allowance and an allowance for other financial loss (e.g. loss of earnings or benefits, fees paid to carers or childminders) up to a stated limit.

It is an offence for a juror to disclose what happened in the jury room even after the trial is over. A jury's verdict must normally be unanimous, but if no verdict has been reached after two hours' consideration (or such longer period as the court deems to be reasonable) a majority verdict is acceptable if ten jurors agree to it.

SCOTLAND

Qualification criteria for jury service in Scotland are similar to those in England and Wales, except that the maximum age for a juror is 65, members of the judiciary are ineligible for ten years after ceasing to hold their post, and others concerned with the administration of justice are only eligible for service five years after ceasing to hold office. Ministers of religion, persons in holy orders and those who have served on a jury in the previous five years are excusable as of right.

The maximum fine for a person serving on a jury knowing himself/herself to be ineligible is £1,000. The maximum fine for failing to attend without good cause is also £1,000.

Further information can obtained from:
THE COURT SERVICE, Southside, 105 Victoria Street, London SW1E 6QT. Tel: 0171-210 2266
THE CLERK OF JUSTICIARY, High Court of Justiciary, Parliament House, Parliament Square, Edinburgh EH1 1HQ. Tel: 0131-225 2595

LANDLORD AND TENANT

When a property is rented to a tenant, the rights and responsibilities of the landlord and the tenant are determined largely by the tenancy agreement but also by statutory provisions. Some of the main provisions are outlined below but it is advisable to contact the Citizens' Advice Bureau or the local authority housing department for further information.

RESIDENTIAL LETTINGS

The provisions outlined here apply only where the tenant lives in a separate dwelling from the landlord and where the dwelling is the tenant's only or main home. It does not apply to licensees such as lodgers, guests or service occupiers.

The 1996 Housing Act radically changes certain aspects of the legislation referred to below, in particular the grant of assured and assured shorthold tenancies under the Housing Act 1988.

ASSURED SHORTHOLD TENANCIES

If a tenancy was granted on or after 15 January 1989 and before 28 February 1997, the tenant may have an assured tenancy giving that tenant greater rights. The tenant could, for example, stay in possession of the dwelling for as long as the tenant observed the terms of the tenancy. The landlord cannot obtain possession from such a tenant unless the landlord can establish a specific ground for possession (set out in the Housing Act 1988) and obtains a court order. The rent payable is that agreed with the landlord unless the rent has been fixed by the rent assessment committee of the local authority. The tenant or the landlord may request that the committee set the rent in line with open market rents for that type of property. Any rent increases that are to take place should be written into the agreement but failing that, the landlord must give advance notice of the increase.

Under the Housing Act 1996, most new lettings entered into on or after 28 February 1997 will be assured shorthold tenancies. This means that tenants are given limited rights. The landlord must obtain a court order, however, to obtain possession if the tenant refuses to vacate at the end of the tenancy.

REGULATED TENANCIES

Before the Housing Act 1988 came into force (15 January 1989) there were regulated tenancies; some are still in existence and are protected by the Rent Act 1977. Under this Act it is possible for the landlord or the tenant to apply to the local rent officer to have a 'fair' rent registered. The fair rent is then the maximum rent payable.

SECURE TENANCIES

Secure tenancies are generally given to tenants of local authorities, housing associations and certain other bodies. This gives the tenant lifelong tenure unless the terms of the agreement are broken by the tenant. In certain circumstances those with secure tenancies may have the right to buy their property. In practice this right is generally only available to council tenants.

AGRICULTURAL PROPERTY

Tenancies in agricultural properties are governed by the Agricultural Holdings Act 1986 and the Rent (Agricultural) Act 1976, which give similar protections to those described above, e.g. security of tenure, right to compensation for disturbance, etc. The Agricultural Holdings (Scotland) Act 1991 applies similar provisions to Scotland.

EVICTION

Under the Protection from Eviction Act 1977 (as amended by the Housing Act 1988), a landlord must give reasonable notice that he/she is to evict the tenant, and in most cases a possession order, granted in court, is necessary. Notice is generally to be at least four weeks and in prescribed statutory form (notices are available from law stationers). It is illegal for a landlord to evict a person by putting their belongings onto the street, by changing the locks and so on. It is also illegal for a landlord to harass a tenant in any way in order to persuade him/her to give up the tenancy.

LANDLORD RESPONSIBILITIES

Under the Landlord and Tenant Act 1985, where the term of the lease is less than seven years the landlord is responsible for maintaining the structure and exterior of the property and all installations for the supply of water, gas and electricity, for sanitation, and for heating and hot water.

LEASEHOLDERS

Legally leaseholders have bought a long lease rather than a property and in certain limited circumstances the landlord can end the tenancy. Under the Leasehold Reform Act 1967 (as amended by the Housing Acts 1969, 1974 and 1980), leaseholders of houses may have the right to buy the freehold or to take an extended lease for a term of 50 years. This applies to leases where the term of the lease is over 21 years and where the leaseholder has occupied the house as his/her main residence for the last three years, or for a total of three years over the last ten.

The Leasehold Reform, Housing and Urban Development Act came into force in 1993 and allows the leaseholders of flats in certain circumstances to buy the freehold of the building in which they live.

Responsibility for maintenance of the structure, exterior and interior of the building should be set out in the lease. Usually the upkeep of the interior of his/her part of the property is the responsibility of the leaseholder, and responsibility for the structure, exterior and common interior areas is shared between the freeholder and the leaseholder(s).

BUSINESS LETTINGS

The Landlord and Tenant Acts 1927 and 1954 (as amended) give security of tenure to the tenants of most business premises. The landlord can only evict the tenant on one of the grounds laid down in the 1954 Act, and in some cases where the landlord repossesses the property the tenant may be entitled to compensation.

SCOTLAND

In Scotland assured and short assured tenancies exist for lettings after 2 January 1989 and are similar to assured tenancies in England and Wales. The relevant legislation is the Housing (Scotland) Act 1988.

Most tenancies created before 2 January 1989 were regulated tenancies and the Rent (Scotland) Act 1984 still applies where these exist. The Act defines, among other things, the circumstances in which a landlord can increase the rent when improvements are made to the property. The provisions of the 1984 Act do not apply to tenancies where the landlord is the Crown, a local authority, the development corporation of a new town or a housing corporation.

The Housing (Scotland) Act 1987 and its provisions relate to local authority responsibilities for housing, the right to buy, and local authority secured tenancies. The provisions are broadly similar to England and Wales.

In Scotland, business premises are not controlled by statute to the same extent as in England and Wales, although the Shops (Scotland) Act 1949 gives some security to tenants of shops. Tenants of shops can apply to the sheriff for a renewal of tenancy if threatened with eviction. This application may be dismissed on various grounds including where the landlord has offered to sell the property to the tenant at an agreed price or, in the absence of agreement as to price, at a price fixed by a single arbiter appointed by the parties or the sheriff. The Act extends to properties where the Crown or government departments are the landlords or the tenants.

Under the Leases Act 1449 the landlord's successors (either purchasers or creditors) are bound by the agreement made with any tenants so long as the following conditions are met:

– the lease, if for more than one year, must be in writing
– there must be a rent
– there must be a term of expiry
– the tenant must have entered into possession

Many leases contain references to term and quarter days. The statutory dates of these are listed on page 9.

LEGAL AID

Under the Legal Aid Act 1988 (as amended) and the Legal Aid (Scotland) Act 1986 and subsequent Regulations, people on low or moderate incomes may qualify for help with the costs of legal advice or representation. The scheme is administered in England and Wales by the Legal Aid Board and in Scotland by the Scottish Legal Aid Board (for entries, *see* Index). There are three types of legal aid: civil legal aid, legal advice and assistance, and criminal legal aid.

CIVIL LEGAL AID

Applications for legal aid are made through a solicitor; the Citizens' Advice Bureau will have addresses for local solicitors. Franchised solicitors are those approved by the Legal Aid Boards, which can provide details.

Civil legal aid is available for proceedings in the following:

– the House of Lords
– the High Court
– the Court of Appeal
– county courts
– lands tribunals
– the Employment Appeal Tribunal
– the Restrictive Practices Court
– the Commons Commissioners
– civil proceedings in magistrates' courts
– family proceedings courts

It is not available for the following:

– tribunals other than those mentioned above
– defamation proceedings
– obtaining the decree in undefended divorce and judicial separation
– court cases outside England and Wales

ELIGIBILITY

The Legal Aid Board will only grant a civil legal aid certificate where:

– the applicant qualifies financially, and
– the applicant has reasonable grounds for taking or defending the action, and
– it is reasonable to grant legal aid in the circumstances of the case. For example, civil legal aid will not be granted where it appears that the applicant will gain only trivial advantage from the proceedings

In order to qualify for civil legal aid, a person's disposable income must be £7,940 a year or less and their disposable

capital must be £6,750 or less. (The financial limits are different for pensioners and in personal injury claims). Disposable income is the total income, less outgoings such as tax and national insurance contributions, rent, council tax, mortgage payments, etc., with allowances made for dependants. The income of a spouse or cohabitee is taken into account unless they are living apart or have a contrary interest in the proceedings. Disposable capital includes savings, insurances, any personal possessions of substantial value and property owned. For applications from 1 June 1996, the applicant's dwelling house is treated as follows:

– the capital value of the property (i.e. market value, less amount outstanding on any mortgage) will be taken into account in so far as it exceeds £100,000
– the capital amount allowed in respect of mortgage debt or charge over the property cannot exceed £100,000
– if the mortgage debt exceeds £100,000, the amount allowed against income for mortgage payments will be reduced in proportion
– the total amount of mortgage debt allowed for all properties (including second and subsequent dwellings) cannot exceed £100,000

CONTRIBUTIONS

Some of those who qualify for legal aid will have to contribute towards their legal costs:

– if in receipt of income support, no contributions are due
– if annual disposable income is between £2,680 and £7,940, a contribution must be made from disposable income
– if disposable capital is over £3,000, all disposable capital in excess of £3,000 must be paid as a contribution

Contributions from disposable income are paid monthly for as long as the person has legal aid. The amount of the contribution depends on the amount of disposable income in excess of £2,680; the greater the excess income, the greater the contribution. Contributions from capital are payable immediately.

STATUTORY CHARGES

A statutory charge is made if a person receives money or property in a case for which they have received legal aid. This means that the amount paid by the Legal Aid Fund on their behalf is deducted from the amount that the person receives. This does not apply if the court has ordered that the costs be paid by the other party or if the payments are for maintenance. In family proceedings cases, the first £2,500 is exempt and the statutory charge is taken from anything in excess of that.

In urgent cases, e.g. domestic violence, legal aid may be granted without the means test. This will be carried out later and the person will have to reimburse the Legal Aid Fund for any aid that they received which exceeded their entitlement.

SCOTLAND

Civil legal aid is available for cases in the following:

– the House of Lords
– the Court of Session
– the Lands Valuation Appeal Court
– the Scottish Land Court
– sheriff courts
– the Lands Tribunal for Scotland
– the Employment Appeal Tribunals
– the Restrictive Practices Court

Eligibility for civil legal aid is assessed in a similar way to that in England and Wales, though the financial limits differ in some respects and are as follows:

– a person is eligible if disposable income is £8,751 or less and disposable capital is £8,560 or less

– if disposable income is between £2,680 and £8,751, contributions are payable
– if disposable capital exceeds £3,000, contributions are payable

LEGAL ADVICE AND ASSISTANCE

The legal advice and assistance scheme (commonly referred to as the green form scheme) covers the costs of getting advice and help from a solicitor, and, in some cases, representation in court under the 'assistance by way of representation' scheme (*see* below).

A person is eligible for legal advice and assistance if:
– they have a disposable income of £83 a week or less and disposable capital of £1,000 or less (£1,335 if the person has one dependant, £1,535 if two dependants)
– they are eligible for income support, family credit, income-based jobseeker's allowance or disability working allowance (unless they have disposable capital of more than £1,000)

There are no contributions under this scheme.

If a person is eligible, the Legal Aid Board will pay for up to two hours' work by a solicitor on behalf of the person (three hours where drafting a petition for divorce). The solicitor must seek the approval of the Legal Aid Board to claim for longer periods of time. The work the solicitor does may include giving advice, writing letters, making an application for civil/criminal legal aid, seeking the advice of a barrister, etc. The scheme does not cover any form of proceedings before a court or tribunal.

Any money or property recovered with the help of legal advice and assistance will be subject to a 'solicitor's charge', which is similar to a statutory charge in civil legal aid but with some differences.

CONTINGENCY OR CONDITIONAL FEES

This system was introduced by the Courts and Legal Services Act 1990. It offers legal representation on a 'no win, no fee' basis. It provides an alternative form of assistance, especially to those who are ineligible for the Legal Aid schemes. The main area for such work is in the field of personal injuries. Not all solicitors offer such a scheme and different solicitors may well have different terms. The effect of the agreement is that solicitors will not make any charges until the case is concluded successfully. The charges are usually linked to a percentage of the amount recovered. The merits of a case are usually assessed before the scheme is offered to potential litigants. Should the case be accepted, then the percentage charges will be linked to the risks involved: the higher the risks, the higher the percentage. Any agreement should be in writing and set out the exact terms of the agreement and the effects of success and failure.

ASSISTANCE BY WAY OF REPRESENTATION

This type of assistance is available for most cases in a family proceedings court and to patients before a mental health review tribunal. It covers the cost of preparing a case and of legal representation in the court.

Under this scheme the two-hour limit does not apply and the approval of the Legal Aid Board is needed in all cases. The income and capital limits are different to legal advice and assistance. In order to qualify, a person's disposable income must be £178 a week or less and their savings must not exceed £3,000. There is no means test for patients due before a mental health review tribunal. Contributions may have to be made and a solicitor's charge will apply to money or property recovered.

DUTY SOLICITORS

The Legal Aid Act 1988 also provides free advice and assistance to anyone questioned by the police (whether under arrest or helping the police with their enquiries). No means test or contributions are required for this. The advice or assistance can be from the duty solicitor at the police station, from a person's own solicitor or from any local solicitor (a list is available at police stations).

Duty solicitors are usually available at the magistrates' court, in criminal cases, for advice and/or representation on first appearances. This assistance is not means-tested.

The Legal Aid Fund also covers the costs of a solicitor present in the buildings of family proceedings or county courts who may be requested by the court to advise or represent someone in need of help.

SCOTLAND

Legal advice and assistance operates in a similar way in Scotland. A person is eligible:
– if disposable income does not exceed £178 a week. If disposable income is between £75 and £178 a week, contributions are payable
– if disposable capital does not exceed £1,000 (£1,335 if the person has one dependant, £1,535 if two dependants with an additional £100 for every other dependant). There are no contributions from capital.

CRIMINAL LEGAL AID

The courts will grant criminal legal aid if it is desirable in the interests of justice (e.g. if there are important questions of law to be argued or the case is so serious that if found guilty the person may go to prison) and the person needs help to pay their legal costs.

Criminal legal aid covers the cost of preparing a case and legal representation (including the cost of a barrister) in criminal proceedings. It is also available for appeals against verdicts or sentences in magistrates' courts, the Crown Court or the Court of Appeal. It is not available for bringing a private prosecution in a criminal court.

If granted criminal legal aid, either the person may choose their own solicitor or the court will assign one. Contributions to the legal costs must be paid by anyone who has a disposable income of over £51 a week or disposable capital of over £3,000. These contributions are payable each month and will probably be returned to the person if they are acquitted. If the payments are not made, the legal aid order may be revoked.

SCOTLAND

The procedure for application for criminal legal aid depends on the circumstances of each case. In more serious cases, such as homicide, heard before a jury, a person is automatically entitled to criminal legal aid until they are given bail or placed in custody. Thereafter, it is for the court to decide whether to grant legal aid. The court will do this if the person accused cannot meet the expenses of the case without undue hardship on them or their dependants. In less serious cases the procedure depends on whether the person is in custody:
– anyone taken into custody has the right to free legal aid from the duty solicitor up to and including the first court appearance
– if the person is not in custody and wishes to plead guilty, they are not entitled to criminal legal aid but may be entitled to legal advice and assistance, including assistance by way of representation
– if the person is not in custody and wishes to plead not guilty, they can apply for criminal legal aid. This must be done within 14 days of the first court appearance at which they made the plea

The criteria used to assess whether or not criminal legal aid should be granted is similar to the criteria for England and Wales.

MARRIAGE

Any two persons may marry provided that:
- they are at least 16 years old on the day of the marriage (in England and Wales persons under the age of 18 must generally obtain the consent of their parents; if consent is refused an appeal may be made to the High Court, the county court or a court of summary jurisdiction)
- they are not related to one another in a way which would prevent their marrying (*see* below)
- they are unmarried (a person who has already been married must produce documentary evidence that the previous marriage has been ended by death, divorce or annulment)
- they are not of the same sex
- they are capable of understanding the nature of a marriage ceremony and of consenting to marriage
- the marriage would be regarded as valid in any foreign country of which either party is a citizen

DEGREES OF RELATIONSHIP

A marriage between persons within the prohibited degrees of consanguinity, affinity or adoption is void.

A man may not marry his mother, daughter, grandmother, granddaughter, sister, aunt, niece, great-grandmother, great-granddaughter, adoptive mother, former adoptive mother, adopted daughter or former adopted daughter. In some circumstances he may now be allowed to marry his former wife's daughter, former wife's granddaughter, father's former wife or grandfather's former wife.

A woman may not marry her father, son, grandfather, grandson, brother, uncle, nephew, great-grandfather, great-grandson, adoptive father, former adoptive father, adopted son or former adopted son. In some circumstances she may now be allowed to marry her former husband's son, former husband's grandson, mother's former husband or grandmother's former husband.

ENGLAND AND WALES

TYPES OF MARRIAGE CEREMONY

It is possible to marry by either religious or civil ceremony. A religious ceremony can take place at a church or chapel of the Church of England or the Church in Wales, or at any other place of worship which has been formally registered by the Registrar-General.

A civil ceremony can take place at a register office, a registered building or any other premises approved by the local authority.

An application for an approved premises licence must be made by the owners or trustees of the building concerned; it cannot be made by the prospective marriage couple. Approved premises must be regularly open to the public so that the marriage can be witnessed; the venue must be deemed to be a permanent and immovable structure. Open-air ceremonies are prohibited.

Non-Anglican marriages may also be solemnized following the issue of a Registrar-General's licence in unregistered premises where one of the parties is seriously ill, is not expected to recover, and cannot be moved to registered premises. Detained and housebound persons may be married at their place of residence.

MARRIAGE IN THE CHURCH OF ENGLAND OR THE CHURCH IN WALES

Marriage by banns

The marriage must take place in a parish in which one of the parties lives, or in a church in another parish if it is the usual place of worship of either or both of the parties. The banns must be called in the parish in which the marriage is to take place on three Sundays before the day of the ceremony; if either or both of the parties lives in a different parish the banns must also be called there. After three months the banns are no longer valid.

Marriage by common licence

The vicar who is to conduct the marriage will arrange for a common licence to be issued by the diocesan bishop; this dispenses with the necessity for banns. One of the parties must have lived in the parish for 15 days immediately before the issuing of the licence or must usually worship at the church. Affidavits are prepared from the personal instructions of one of the parties and the licence will be given to the applicant in person.

Marriage by special licence

A special licence is granted by the Archbishop of Canterbury in special circumstances for the marriage to take place at any place, with or without previous residence in the parish, or at any time. Application must be made to the Faculty Office of the Archbishop of Canterbury, 1 The Sanctuary, London SW1P 3JT. Tel: 0171-222 5381.

Marriage by certificate

The marriage can be conducted on the authority of the superintendent registrar's certificate, provided that the vicar's consent is obtained. One of the parties must live in the parish or must usually worship at the church.

MARRIAGE BY OTHER RELIGIOUS CEREMONY

One of the parties must normally live in the registration district where the marriage is to take place. In addition to giving notice to the superintendent registrar (*see* page 666), it may also be necessary to book a registrar to be present at the ceremony.

CIVIL MARRIAGE

A marriage may be solemnized at any register office, registered building or approved premises in England and Wales. The superintendent registrar of the district should be contacted, and, if the marriage is to take place at approved premises, the necessary arrangements at the venue must also be made.

NOTICE OF MARRIAGE

Unless it is to take place by banns or under common or special licence in the Church of England or the Church in Wales, a notice of the marriage must be given in person to the superintendent registrar. Notice of marriage may be given in the following ways:
- by certificate. Both parties must have lived in a registration district in England or Wales for at least seven days immediately before giving notice at the local register office. If they live in different registration districts, notice must be given in both districts. The marriage can take place in any register office in England and Wales 21 days after notice has been given
- by licence (often known as 'special licence'). One of the parties must have lived in a registration district in England or Wales for at least 15 days before giving notice at the register office; the other party need only be a resident of, or be physically in, England and Wales on the day notice is given. The marriage can take place one clear day (other than a Sunday, Christmas Day or Good Friday) after notice has been given

A notice of marriage is valid for 12 months. It is not therefore possible to give formal notice of a marriage more than three months before it is to take place, but it should be possible to make an advance (provisional) booking 12 months before the ceremony. In this case it is still necessary to give formal notice three months before the marriage. When giving notice of the marriage it is necessary to produce official proof, if relevant, that any previous marriage has ended in divorce or death by producing a decree absolute or death certificate; it is also useful, but not necessary, to take birth certificates or passports as proof of age and identity.

SOLEMNIZATION OF THE MARRIAGE

On the day of the wedding there must be at least two other people present who are prepared to act as witnesses and sign the marriage register. A registrar of marriages must be present at a marriage in a register office or at approved premises, but an authorized person may act in the capacity of registrar in a registered building.

If the marriage takes place at approved premises, the room must be separate from any other activity on the premises at the time of the ceremony, and no food or drink can be sold or consumed in the room during the ceremony or for one hour beforehand.

The marriage must be solemnized between 8 a.m. and 6 p.m., with open doors. At some time during the ceremony the parties must make a declaration that they know of no legal impediment to the marriage and they must also say the contracting words; the declaratory and contracting words may vary according to the form of service in use but the most basic forms are:

– (*declaratory words*) 'I declare that I know of no legal reason why I, A. B., may not be joined in marriage to C. D.' Alternatively, the couple may answer 'I am' to the question 'Are you, A. B., free lawfully to marry C. D.?'
– (*contracting words*) 'I, A. B., take you, C. D., to be my wedded wife [or husband]'

A civil marriage cannot contain any religious aspects, but it may be possible for non-religious music and/or poetry readings to be included. It may also be possible to embellish the marriage vows taken by the couple.

If both parties are Jewish, they may be married in a synagogue, in a private house or elsewhere. The wedding may take place at any time of day and must be registered by the secretary of the synagogue of which the man is a member. The presence of a registrar of marriages is not necessary.

If both parties are members of the Society of Friends (Quakers), they may be married in a Friends' meeting-house. The marriage must be registered by the registering officer of the Society appointed to act for the district in which the meeting-house is situated. The presence of a registrar of marriages is not necessary.

CIVIL FEES *from 1 April 1999*

Registrar
Attending a marriage at a register office, £32.00
Attending a marriage at a registered building/residence of a housebound person, £36.00
Attending a marriage by Registrar-General's licence, £2.00

Superintendent Registrar
Entering a notice of marriage in marriage notice book, £21.00
Entering notice of marriage by Registrar-General's licence in marriage notice book, £3.00
Attending outside office to be given notice of marriage of housebound/detained person, £40.00
Issuing licence for marriage, £46.50
Attending marriage at residence of housebound/detained person, £40.00
Attending a marriage by Registrar-General's licence, £2.00

Attending with a registrar a marriage on approved premises, fee set by local authority
Marriage certificate on day of marriage, £3.50

ECCLESIASTICAL FEES *from 1 April 1999*
(Church of England and Church in Wales*)
Marriage by banns
For publication of banns, £14.00
For certificate of banns issued at time of publication, £8.00
For marriage service, £127.00
Marriage by common licence
Fee for licence, £53.00
Marriage by special licence
Fee for licence, £120.00
Further fees may be payable for additional facilities at the marriage, e.g. the organist's fee.
*Some of these fees may not apply to the Church in Wales

SCOTLAND

REGULAR MARRIAGES

A regular marriage is one which is celebrated by a minister of religion or authorized registrar or other celebrant. Each of the parties must complete a marriage notice form and return it to the district registrar for the area in which they are to be married, irrespective of where they live, at least 15 days before the ceremony is due to take place. The district registrar must then enter the date of receipt and certain details in a marriage book kept for this purpose, and must also enter the names of the parties and the proposed date of marriage in a list which is displayed in a conspicuous place at the registration office until the date of the marriage has passed. All persons wishing to enter into a regular marriage in Scotland must follow the same preliminary procedure regardless of whether they intend to have a religious or civil ceremony.

A marriage schedule, which is prepared by the registrar, will be issued to one or both of the parties in person up to seven days before a religious marriage; for a civil marriage the schedule will be available at the ceremony. The schedule must be handed to the celebrant before the ceremony starts; it must be signed immediately after the wedding and the marriage must be registered within three days.

The authority to conduct a religious marriage is deemed to be vested in the authorized celebrant rather than the building in which it takes place; open-air religious ceremonies are therefore permissible in Scotland.

MARRIAGE BY COHABITATION WITH HABIT AND REPUTE

If two people live together constantly as husband and wife and are generally held to be such by the neighbourhood and among their friends and relations, there may arise a presumption from which marriage can be inferred. Before such a marriage can be registered, however, a decree of declarator of marriage must be obtained from the Court of Session.

CIVIL FEES *from 1 April 1999*

The basic statutory fee is £77.00, comprising a £12.00 per person fee for a statutory notice of intention to marry, a £45.00 fee for solemnization of the marriage in a register office, and an £8.00 fee for a copy of the marriage certificate.

Further information can be obtained from:
THE GENERAL REGISTER OFFICE, Office for National Statistics, Smedley Hydro, Trafalgar Road, Birkdale, Southport, Merseyside PR8 2HH. Tel: 01704-569824

THE GENERAL REGISTER OFFICE FOR SCOTLAND, New Register House, Edinburgh EHI 3YT. Tel: 0131-334 0380

TOWN AND COUNTRY PLANNING

The principal legislation governing the development of land and buildings in England and Wales is the Town and Country Planning Act 1990 (as amended by the Planning and Compensation Act 1991). The equivalent legislation in Scotland is the Town and Country Planning (Scotland) Act 1997. The uses of buildings are classified by the Town and Country Planning (Use Classes) Order 1987 (as amended) in England and Wales, and in Scotland by the Town and Country Planning (Use Classes) (Scotland) Order 1997. It is advisable in all cases to contact the planning department of the local authority to check whether planning or other permission is needed. Whilst the information below relates primarily to England and Wales, the position in Scotland is similar.

PLANNING PERMISSION

Planning permission is needed if the work involves:
- making a material change in use, such as dividing off part of the house so that it can be used as a separate home or dividing off part of the house for commercial use, e.g. for a workshop
- going against the terms of the original planning permission, e.g. there may be a restriction on fences in front gardens on an open-plan estate
- building, engineering for mining, except for the permissions below
- new or wider access to a main road
- additions or extensions to flats or maisonettes

Planning permission is not needed to carry out internal alterations or work which does not affect the external appearance of the building.

There are certain types of development for which the Secretary of State for the Environment, Transport and the Regions has granted general permissions. These include:
- house extensions and additions (including conservatories, loft conversions, garages and dormer windows). Up to 10 per cent or up to 50 cubic metres (whichever is the greater) can be added to the original house for terraced houses. Up to 15 per cent or 70 cubic metres (whichever is the greater) to other kinds of houses. The maximum that can be added to any house is 115 cubic metres
- buildings such as garden sheds and greenhouses so long as they are no more than 3 metres high (or 4 metres if the roof is ridged), are no nearer to a highway than the house, and at least half the ground around the house remains uncovered by buildings
- adding a porch with a ground area of less than 3 square metres and that is less than 3 metres in height
- putting up fences, walls and gates of under 1 metre in height if next to a road and under 2 metres elsewhere
- laying patios, paths or driveways for domestic use

OTHER RESTRICTIONS

It may be necessary to obtain other types of permissions before carrying out any development. These permissions are separate from planning permission and apply regardless of whether or not planning permission is needed, e.g.:
- building regulations will probably apply if a new building is to be erected, if an existing one is to be altered or extended, or if the work involves building over a drain or sewer The building control department of the local authority will advise on this

- any alterations to a listed building or the grounds of a listed building must be approved by the local authority
- local authority approval is necessary if a building (or, in some circumstances, gates, walls, fences or railings) in a conservation area is to be demolished; each local authority keeps a register of all local buildings that are in conservation areas
- many trees are protected by tree preservation orders and must not be pruned or taken down without local authority consent
- bats and other species are protected and English Nature, the Countryside Council for Wales or Scottish Natural Heritage (for entries, *see* Index) must be notified before any work is carried out that will affect the habitat of protected species, e.g. timber treatment, renovation or extensions of lofts
- any development in areas designated as a National Park, an Area of Outstanding National Beauty, a National Scenic Area or in the Norfolk or Suffolk Broads is subject to greater restrictions. The local planning authority will advise or refer enquirers to the relevant authority

VOTERS' QUALIFICATIONS

Those entitled to vote at parliamentary, European Union (EU) and local government elections are those who are:
- resident in the constituency or ward on the qualifying date i.e. 10 October in the year before the electoral register (*see* below) comes into effect; in Northern Ireland the qualifying date is 15 September and voters must have been resident in Northern Ireland for the three months leading up to that date
- over 18 years old
- Commonwealth (which includes British) citizens or citizens of the Republic of Ireland

British citizens resident abroad are entitled to vote, for 20 years after leaving Britain, as overseas electors in parliamentary and EU elections in the constituency in which they were last resident. Members of the armed forces, Crown servants and employees of the British Council who are overseas and their spouses are entitled to vote regardless of how long they have been abroad.

European Union citizens resident in the UK may vote in EU and local government elections.

The following people are not entitled to vote:
- peers, and peeresses in their own right, who are members of the House of Lords (except that they may vote in EU and local government elections and also in Scottish Parliamentary elections if resident in Scotland)
- patients detained under mental health legislation
- voluntary mental patients (unless they make a prescribed declaration)
- those serving prison sentences
- those convicted within the previous five years of corrupt or illegal election practices

REGISTERING TO VOTE

Voters must be entered on an electoral register, which runs from 16 February in one year to 15 February in the following year. The registration officer for each constituency is responsible for preparing and publishing the register. A registration form is sent to all households in the autumn of each year and the householder is required to provide details of all occupants who are eligible to vote, including ones who will reach their 18th birthday in the year covered by the register. Those who fail to give the required information or who give false information are liable to be fined. A draft register is usually published at the end of November. Any person whose name has been omitted may ask to be registered and should contact the registration officer. Anyone on the register may object to the inclusion of another person's name, in which case he/she should notify the registration officer, who will investigate that person's eligibility. Supplementary electors lists are published throughout the duration of the register.

Voting

Voting is not compulsory in the UK. Those who wish to vote must generally vote in person at the allotted polling station. Those who will be away at the time of the election, those who will not be able to attend in person due to physical incapacity or the nature of their occupation, and those who have changed address during the period for which the register is valid, may apply for a postal vote or nominate a proxy to vote for them. Overseas electors who wish to vote must do so by proxy.

Further information can be obtained from the local authority's electoral registration officer in England and Wales or the electoral registration office in Scotland, or the Chief Electoral Officer in Northern Ireland (3rd Floor, St Anne's House, 15 Church Street, Belfast BTI IER. Tel: 01232-245353).

WILLS AND INTESTACY

In a will a person leaves instructions as to the disposal of their property after they die. A will is also used to appoint executors (who will administer the estate), give directions as to the disposal of the body, appoint guardians for children and, for larger estates, can operate to reduce the level of inheritance tax. It is best to have a will drawn up by a solicitor but if a solicitor is not employed, the following points must be taken into account:

– if possible the will must not be prepared on behalf of another person by someone who is to benefit from it or who is a close relative of a major beneficiary

– the language used must be clear and unambiguous and it is better to avoid the use of legal terms where the same thing can be expressed in plain language

– it is better to rewrite the whole document if a mistake is made. If necessary, alterations can be made by striking through the words with a pen, and the signature or initials of the testator and the witnesses must be put in the margin opposite the alteration. No alteration of any kind should be made after the will has been executed

– if the person later wishes to change the will or part of it, it is better to write a new will revoking the old. The use of codicils (documents written as supplements or containing modifications to the will) should be left to a solicitor

– the will should be typed or printed, or if handwritten be legible and preferably in ink. Commercial will forms can be obtained from some stationers

The form of a will varies to suit different cases; the following is an example of how a will might be written. The notes after this example explain the terms used and procedures that need to be followed in drawing up a will.

This is the last will and testament of me [*Thomas Smith*] of [*Heather Cottage, Prospero Road, Manchester* MI 4DK] which I make this [*seventeenth*] day of [*May* 1999] and I revoke all previous wills and testamentary dispositions.
1. I appoint as my executors and trustees [*Ann Green of* _____ *and Richard Brown of* _____]. In my will the expression

'my Trustees' means any executors and trustees for the time being of my will and of any trust arising under it.
2. I give all my property to [*such of my children as shall survive me by 28 days and if more than one in equal shares* or as the case may be].
or
2. I give to [*Pamela Henderson of* _____] the sum of [£ _____] and to [*Michael Broadbent of* _____] the sum of [£ _____] and to [*Ruth Walker of* _____] all of my [*jewellery, books* or as the case may be]
and
3. I give everything not otherwise disposed of to [*Richard Black of* _____]
Signed by the testator in our joint presence and then by us in his.
Thomas Smith
[*Signature of the person making the will*]
Elizabeth Wall
[*Signature of witness*] of 67 Beatrice Lane, Manchester MI 4DK, journalist
William Jones
[*Signature of witness*] of 17 Paris Road, Manchester MI 4EN, tailor

Specific Gifts and Legacies

Gifts of specific items usually fail if the property is not owned by the person making the will on their death. This problem can be avoided by making a gift of any property fulfilling a particular description, e.g. a car, which is owned at the date of death. It is better in all cases where such gifts are made, to insert a clause which reads 'I give everything not otherwise disposed of to [*Richard Black of* _____], even if it seems that all property has already been disposed of in the will.

Lapsed Legatees

If a person who has been left property in a will dies before the person who made the will, the gift fails and will pass to the person entitled to everything not otherwise disposed of (the residuary estate).

If the person left the residuary estate dies before the person who made the will, their share will generally pass to the closest relative(s) of the person who made the will (as in intestacy) unless the will names a beneficiary such as a charity who will take as a 'long stop' if this gift is unable to take effect for any reason.

It is always better to draw up a new will if a beneficiary predeceases the person who made the will.

Executors

It is usual to appoint two executors, although one is sufficient. No more than four persons can deal with the estate of the person who has died. The name and address of each executor should be given in full (the addresses are not essential but including them adds clarity to the document).

Executors should be 18 years of age or over. An executor may be a beneficiary of the will.

Witnesses

A person who is a beneficiary of a will, or the spouse of a beneficiary at the time the will is signed, must not act as a witness or else he/she will be unable to take his/her gift. Husband and wife can both act as witnesses provided neither benefits from the will. It is better that a person does not act as an executor and as a witness, as he/she can take no benefit under a will to which he/she is witness. The identity of the witnesses should be made as explicit as possible.

EXECUTION OF A WILL

The person making the will should sign his/her name at the foot of the document, in the presence of the two witnesses. The witnesses must then sign their names while the person making the will looks on. If this procedure is not adhered to, the will will be considered invalid. There are certain exceptional circumstances where these rules are relaxed, e.g. where the person may be too ill to sign, and in these cases the attestation clause which normally reads 'signed by the testator in our joint presence and then by us in his/hers' should be reworded as follows:

'The will was read over to Thomas Smith in our presence when he stated that he understood it. It was then signed on his behalf by Thomas Brown in the presence of the testator and by his direction in our joint presence and then by us in his.'

CAPACITY TO MAKE A WILL

Anyone aged 18 or over can make a will. However, if there is any suspicion that the person making the will is not, through reasons of infirmity or age, fully in command of his/her faculties, it is advisable to arrange for a medical practitioner to examine the person making the will at the time it is to be executed to verify his/her mental capacity and to record that medical opinion in writing, and to ask the examining practitioner to act as a witness. If a person is not mentally able to make a will, the Court may do this for him/her by virtue of the Mental Health Act 1983.

REVOCATION

A will may be revoked or cancelled in a number of ways:
- a later will revokes an earlier one if it says so; otherwise the earlier will is impliedly revoked by the later one to the extent that it contradicts or repeats the earlier one
- a will is also revoked if the physical document on which it is written is destroyed by the person whose will it is. There must be an intention to revoke the will. It may not be sufficient to obliterate the will with a pen
- a will is revoked when the person marries, unless it is clear from the will that the person intended the will to stand after the marriage
- where a marriage ends in divorce or is annulled or declared void, gifts to the spouse and the appointment of the spouse as executor fail unless the will says that this is not to happen. A former spouse is treated as having predeceased the testator. A separation does not change the effect of a married person's will.

PROBATE AND LETTERS OF ADMINISTRATION

Probate is granted to the executors named in a will and once granted, the executors are obliged to carry out the instructions of the will. Letters of administration are granted where no executor is named in a will or is willing or able to act or where there is no will or no valid will; this gives a person, often the next of kin, similar powers and duties to those of an executor.

Applications for probate or for letters of administration can be made to the Principal Registry of the Family Division, to a district probate registry or to a probate sub-registry. Applicants will need the following documents: the original will (if any); a certificate of death; oath for executors or administrators; particulars of all property and assets left by the deceased; a list of debts and funeral expenses. Certain property, up to the value of £5,000, may be disposed of without a grant of probate or letters of administration.

WHERE TO FIND A PROVED WILL

Since 1858 wills which have been proved, that is wills on which probate or letters of administration have been granted, must have been proved at the Principal Registry of the Family Division or at a district probate registry. The Lord Chancellor has power to direct where the original documents are kept but most are filed where they were proved and may be inspected there and a copy obtained. The Principal Registry also holds copies of all wills proved at district probate registries and these may be inspected at Somerset House. An index of all grants, both of probate and of letters of administration, is compiled by the Principal Registry and may be seen either at the Principal Registry or at a district probate registry.

It is also possible to discover when a grant of probate or letters of administration is issued by requesting a standing search. In response to a request and for a small fee, a district probate registry will supply the names and addresses of executors or administrators, and the registry in which the grant was made, of any grant in the estate of a specified person made in the previous 12 months or following six months. This is useful for applicants under the Inheritance (Provision for Family and Dependants) Act 1975 (*see* Intestacy, page 670) and for creditors of the deceased.

SCOTLAND

In Scotland any person over 12 and of sound mind can make a will. The person making the will can only freely dispose of what is known as the 'dead's part' of the estate because:
- the spouse has the right to inherit one-third of the moveable estate if there are children or other descendants, and one-half of it if there are not
- children are entitled to one-third of the moveable estate if there is a surviving spouse, and one-half of it if there is not

The remaining portion is the dead's part, and legacies and bequests are payable from this. Debts are payable out of the whole estate before any division.

From August 1995, wills no longer needed to be 'holographed' and it is now only necessary to have one witness. The person making the will still needs to sign each page. It is better that the will is not witnessed by a beneficiary although the attestation would still be sound and the beneficiary would not have to relinquish the gift.

Subsequent marriage does not revoke a will but the birth of a child who is not provided for may do so. A will may be revoked by a subsequent will, either expressly or by implication, but in so far as the two can be read together both have effect. If a subsequent will is revoked, the earlier will is revived.

Wills may be registered in the sheriff court Books of the Sheriffdom in which the deceased lived or in the Books of Council and Session at the Registers of Scotland.

CONFIRMATION

Confirmation (the Scottish equivalent of probate) is obtained in the sheriff court of the sheriffdom in which the deceased was resident at the time of death. Executives are either 'nominate' (named by the deceased in the will) or 'dative' (appointed by the court in cases where no executor is named in a will or in cases of intestacy). Applicants for confirmation must first provide an inventory of the deceased's estate and a schedule of debts, with an affidavit. In estates under £17,000 gross, confirmation can be obtained under a simplified procedure at reduced fees. The local sheriff clerk's office can provide assistance.

Further information can be obtained from:
PRINCIPAL REGISTRY (FAMILY DIVISION), First Avenue House, 42–49 High Holborn, London, WC1V 6NP. Tel: 0171-936 6000

REGISTERS OF SCOTLAND, Meadowbank House, 153 London Road, Edinburgh, EH8 7AU. Tel: 0131-659 6111

INTESTACY

Intestacy occurs when someone dies without leaving a will or leaves a will which is invalid or which does not take effect for some reason. In such cases the person's estate (property, possessions, other assets following the payment of debts) passes to certain members of the family. The relevant legislation is the Administration of Estates Act 1925, as amended by various legislation including the Intestates Estates Act 1952, the Law Reform (Succession) Act 1995, and the Trusts of Land and Appointment of Trustees Act 1996 and Orders made there under. Some of the provisions of this legislation are described below. If a will has been written that disposes of only part of a person's property, these rules apply to the part which is undisposed of.

If the person (intestate) leaves a spouse who survives for 28 days and children (legitimate, illegitimate and adopted children and other descendants), the estate is divided as follows:

- the spouse takes the 'personal chattels' (household articles, including cars, but nothing used for business purposes), £125,000 free of tax (with interest payable at 6 per cent from the time of the death until payment) and a life interest in half of the rest of the estate (which can be capitalized by the spouse if he/she wishes)
- the rest of the estate goes to the children*

If the person leaves a spouse who survives for 28 days but no children:

- the spouse takes the personal chattels, £200,000 free of tax (interest payable as before) and full ownership of half of the rest of the estate
- the other half of the rest of the estate goes to the parents (equally, if both alive) or, if none, to the brothers and sisters of the whole blood*
- if there are no parents or brothers or sisters of the whole blood or their children, the spouse takes the whole estate

If there is no surviving spouse, the estate is distributed among those who survive the intestate as follows:

- to surviving children*, but if none to
- parents (equally, if both alive), but if none to
- brothers and sisters of the whole blood*, but if none to
- brothers and sisters of the half blood*, but if none to
- grandparents (equally, if more than one), but if none to
- aunts and uncles of the whole blood*, but if none to
- aunts and uncles of the half blood*, but if none to
- the Crown, Duchy of Lancaster or the Duke of Cornwall (*bona vacantia*)

* To inherit, a member of these groups must survive the intestate and attain 18, or marry under that age. If they die under 18 (unless married under that age), their share goes to others, if any, in the same group. If any member of these groups predeceases the intestate leaving children, their share is divided equally among their children.

In England and Wales the provisions of the Inheritance (Provision for Family and Dependants) Act 1975 may allow other people to claim provision from the deceased's assets. This Act also applies to cases where a will has been made and allows a person to apply to the Court if they feel that the will or rules of intestacy or both do not make adequate provision for them. The Court can order payment from the deceased's assets or the transfer of property from them if the applicant's claim is accepted. The application must be made within six months of the grant of probate or letters of administration and the following people can make an application:

- the spouse
- a former spouse who has not remarried

- a child of the deceased
- someone treated as a child of the deceased's family
- someone maintained by the deceased
- someone who has cohabited for two years before the death in the same household as the deceased and as the husband or wife of the deceased

SCOTLAND

Under the Succession (Scotland) Act 1964, no distinction is made between 'moveable' and 'heritable' property in intestacy cases.

A surviving spouse is entitled to 'prior rights'. This means that from 1 April 1999 the spouse has the right to inherit:

- the matrimonial home up to a value of £130,000, or one matrimonial home if there is more than one, or, in certain circumstances, the value of the matrimonial home
- the furnishings and contents of that home, up to the value of £22,000
- £35,000 if the deceased left children or other descendants, or £58,000 if not

These figures are increased from time to time by regulations.

Once prior rights have been satisfied, what remains of the estate is generally divided between the surviving spouse and children (legitimate and illegitimate) according to 'legal' rights. Legal rights are:

Jus relicti(ae) – the right of a surviving spouse to one-half of the net moveable estate, after satisfaction of prior rights, if there are no surviving children; if there are surviving children, the spouse is entitled to one-third of the net moveable estate

Legitim – the right of surviving children to one-half of the net moveable estate if there is no surviving spouse; if there is a surviving spouse, the children are entitled to one-third of the net moveable estate after the satisfaction of prior rights

Where there are no surviving spouse or children, half of the estate is taken by the parents and half by the brothers and sisters. Failing that, the lines of succession, in general, are:

- to descendants
- if no descendants, then to collaterals (i.e. brothers and sisters) and parents
- surviving spouse
- if no collaterals or parents or spouse, then to ascendants collaterals (i.e. aunts and uncles), and so on in an ascending scale
- if all lines of succession fail, the estate passes to the Crown

Relatives of the whole blood are preferred to relatives of the half blood. The right of representation, i.e. the right of the issue of a person who would have succeeded if he/she had survived the intestate, also applies.

Crime Statistics

ENGLAND AND WALES

NOTIFIABLE OFFENCES RECORDED 1997

Violence against the person	250,800
Sexual offences	33,200
Burglary	1,015,100
Robbery	63,100
Theft and handling stolen goods	2,165,000
Fraud and forgery	134,400
Criminal damage	877,000
Other offences	59,800
Total offences	4,598,300

Source: The Stationery Office – *Annual Abstract of Statistics 1999* (Crown copyright)

CRIMINAL JUSTICE STATISTICS 1997

*Number of arrests	1,920,000
Notifiable offences cleared up	1,258,000
Clear-up rate	27%
†Number of offenders cautioned	282,100
Defendants proceeded against at magistrates' courts	1,855,300
Defendants found guilty at magistrates' courts	1,312,500
Defendants tried at Crown Courts	91,300
Defendants found guilty at Crown Courts	73,500
Defendants sentenced at Crown Courts after summary conviction	6,200
Total offenders found guilty at both courts	1,386,000
†Total offenders found guilty or cautioned	1,668,100

*Increase of 10 per cent on 1996. The Metropolitan Police changed its reporting policy to include all arrests in 1997; when this is excluded the increase is 2 per cent
†Excludes motoring offences

OFFENDERS SENTENCED BY TYPE OF SENTENCE OR ORDER 1997

Absolute discharge	18,300
Conditional discharge	109,700
Fine	998,700
Probation order	54,100
Supervision order	11,200
Community service order	47,100
Attendance sentence order	7,600
Combination order	19,500
Curfew order	400
Young offender institution	22,100
Imprisonment:	
Suspended	3,500
Unsuspended	71,000
Otherwise dealt with	21,400
All sentences or orders: total	1,384,700

AVERAGE LENGTH OF SENTENCE 1997 *in months*

	Males aged 21 and over	Females aged 21 and over
Magistrates' courts	2.6	2.2
Crown court	24.0	19.5

Source: The Stationery Office – *Criminal Statistics England and Wales 1997* (Crown copyright)

SCOTLAND

CRIMES AND OFFENCES RECORDED 1997

Non-sexual crimes of violence against the person	19,164
Crimes involving indecency	7,147
Crimes involving dishonesty	267,207
Fire-raising, vandalism, etc.	81,000
Other crimes	46,124
Miscellaneous offences	155,900
Motor vehicle offences	330,983
Total crimes and offences	907,525

Source: The Scottish Office

CRIMINAL JUSTICE STATISTICS 1997

Number of persons proceeded against	172,556
Persons with charge proved	150,450

PERSONS WITH CHARGE PROVED BY MAIN PENALTY 1997

Absolute discharge	1,137
Remit to children's hearing	219
Admonition or caution	15,039
Compensation order	1,304
Fine	103,861
Probation	6,814
Community service order	5,707
Insanity or hospital order	162
Detention of child	29
Young offender institution	4,557
Prison	11,621
All penalties: total	150,450

Source: The Scottish Office

Intellectual Property

COPYRIGHT

Copyright protects all original literary, dramatic, musical and artistic works (including photographs, maps and plans), published editions of works, computer programs, sound recordings, films (including video), broadcasts (including satellite broadcasts) and cable programmes (including on-line information services). Under copyright the creators of these works can control the various ways in which their material may be exploited, the rights broadly covering copying, adapting, issuing (including renting and lending) copies to the public, performing in public, and broadcasting the material.

Copyright protection in the United Kingdom is automatic and there is no registration system. The main legislation is the Copyright, Designs and Patents Act 1988, which has been amended by other Acts and by Statutory Instrument to take account of EC Directives. As a result of an EC Directive effective from January 1996, the term of copyright protection for literary, dramatic, musical and artistic works lasts until 70 years after the death of the author, and for film now lasts for 70 years after the death of the last to survive of the director, author of the screenplay, author of the dialogue and composer of music specially created for the film. Sound recordings are protected for 50 years after their publication, and broadcasts and cable programmes for 50 years from the end of the year in which the first broadcast/transmission is made. Published editions remain under copyright protection for 25 years from the end of the year in which the edition was published. An EC Directive effective from January 1998 created a 15-year non-copyright called 'database right' to protect substantial investment in obtaining, verifying or presenting the contents of a database.

The main international treaties protecting copyright are the Berne Convention for the Protection of Literary and Artistic Works, the Rome Convention for the Protection of Performers, Producers of Phonograms and Broadcasting Organizations, and the Universal Copyright Convention (UCC); the UK is a signatory to these conventions. Copyright material created by UK nationals or residents is protected in each country which is a member of the conventions by the national law of that country. A list of participating countries may be obtained from the Patent Office. The World Trade Organization Trade-Related Aspects of Intellectual Property Agreement (TRIPS) also confers reciprocal obligations on signatory states to protect copyright works.

Two new treaties were agreed in December 1996, but have yet to enter into force. These are WIPO (World Intellectual Property Organization) Copyright Treaty, and the WIPO Performance and Phonograms Treaty.

LICENSING

Reproduction of copyright material without seeking permission in each instance may be permitted under licence. The International Federation of Reproduction Rights Organizations facilitates agreements between its member licensing agencies and on behalf of its members with organizations such as the WIPO, UNESCO, the European Union and the Council of Europe.

PATENTS

A patent is a document issued by the Patent Office relating to an invention and giving the proprietor monopoly rights, effective within the United Kingdom (including the Isle of Man).

To qualify for a patent an invention must be new, must exhibit an inventive step, and must be capable of industrial application. The patent is valid for a maximum of 20 years from the date on which the application was filed, subject to payment of annual fees from the end of the fourth year.

The Patent Office, established in 1852, is responsible for ensuring that all stages of an application comply with the Patents Act 1977, and that the invention meets the criteria for a patent. Patent Office Examiners check that the invention is new and innovative by searching previously published documents on the Patent Office databank, which contains details of some two million British patents, together with published international and European applications. The contents of the databank and of the Science Reference Library, which developed from the library established at the Patent Office, are available to the public.

The WIPO is responsible for administering many of the international conventions on intellectual property. The Patent Co-operation Treaty allows inventors to file a single application for patent rights in some or all of the 101 contracting states. This application is searched by an International Searching Authority and published by the International Bureau of WIPO. It may also be the subject of an (optional) international preliminary examination. Applicants must then deal directly with the patent offices in the countries where they are seeking patent rights.

The European Patent Convention, linked to the Patent Co-operation Treaty, allows inventors to obtain patent rights in all 19 contracting states by filing a single European patent application which is processed by the European Patent Office (EPO). Once granted, the patent is subject to national laws in each signatory country. To comply with security requirements, an applicant resident in the UK must file a European patent application with the UK Patent Office unless the Patent Office gives permission for it to be filed directly with the EPO.

TRADE MARKS

Registration of trade marks prevents other traders using the same or a similar trade mark for similar products or services for which the mark is registered.

In the UK trade marks are registered at the Trade Marks Registry in the Patent Office. In order to qualify for registration a mark must be capable of distinguishing the proprietor's goods or services from those of other undertakings. It should be non-deceptive and not easily confused with a mark that has already been registered for the same or similar goods or services. The relevant current legislation is the Trade Marks Act 1994.

It is possible to obtain an international trade mark registration, effective in 61 countries, under the Madrid Agreement. UK companies cannot take advantage of this because the UK is not a party to this agreement. Following revision of UK trade marks law, however, the UK has ratified the protocol to the Madrid Agreement, and British companies can now obtain international trade mark registration through a single application to WIPO in those countries party to the protocol.

EC trade mark regulation is now in force and is administered by the Office for Harmonization in the Internal Market (Trade Marks and Designs) in Alicante, Spain. The office registers EC trade marks, which are a unitary right valid throughout the European Union. The national registration of trade marks in member states is continuing in parallel with the EC trade mark.

DESIGN PROTECTION

Design protection covers the outward appearance of an article and takes two forms in the UK, registered design and design right, which are not mutually exclusive. Registered design protects the aesthetic appearance of an article, including shape, configuration, pattern or ornament, although artistic works such as sculptures are excluded, being generally protected by copyright. In order to qualify for protection, a design must be new and materially different from earlier UK published designs. The owner of the design must apply to the Designs Registry at the Patent Office. Initial registration lasts for five years and is extendible in five-yearly steps to a maximum of 25 years. The current legislation is the Registered Designs Act 1949 (as amended).

There is no international design registry currently available to UK applicants; in general, separate applications must be made in each country in which protection is sought. However, the EC Directive for the Legal Protection of Designs was adopted in 1998 to harmonize laws on certain aspects of design protection throughout the European Union. Member states are to amend their laws to comply with the Directive by 28 October 2001.

Design right is an automatic right which applies to the shape or configuration of articles and does not require registration. Unlike registered design, two-dimensional designs do not qualify for protection but designs of semiconductor chips (topographies) are protected by design right. Designs must be original and non-commonplace. The term of design right is ten years from first marketing of the design and the right is effective only in the UK. The current legislation is Part 3 of the Copyright, Designs and Patents Act 1988.

LEGAL DEPOSIT

Publishers are legally obliged to send one copy of a new publication to each of the legal deposit libraries within one month of publication. The aim of legal deposit is to keep a complete national archive of published works as a current reference and information source. The legal deposit libraries are the British Library, the Bodleian Library in Oxford, Cambridge University Library, the National Library of Scotland, the National Library of Wales, and Trinity College Library in Dublin.

All publications for the other four copyright libraries in the UK are dealt with by the Agent for the Copyright Libraries.

In 1998 the Report of the Working Party on Legal Deposit recommended that legislation should be introduced establishing legal deposit for certain electronically published materials (mainly CD-ROMs). The Government agreed in principle, but called for a voluntary scheme to be established first. In mid-1999 negotiations between publishers and the copyright libraries to agree a code of practice were still under way.

INTELLECTUAL PROPERTY ORGANIZATIONS

AGENT FOR THE COPYRIGHT LIBRARIES, 100 Euston Street, London NW1 2HQ. Tel: 0171-380 0240. *Agent*, A. T. Smail

CHARTERED INSTITUTE OF PATENT AGENTS, Staple Inn Buildings, London WC1V 7PZ. Tel: 0171-405 9450

DESIGNS REGISTRY, The Patent Office, Cardiff Road, Newport NP10 8QQ. Tel: 0645-500505

EUROPEAN PATENT OFFICE, *HQ*, Erhardtstrasse 27, D-8000, Munich 2, Germany. Tel: Munich 399 4538

INTERNATIONAL FEDERATION OF REPRODUCTION RIGHTS ORGANIZATIONS (IFRRO), rue du Prince Royal 87, B-1050 Brussels, Belgium. Tel: Brussels 551 0899

LEGAL DEPOSIT OFFICE, The British Library, Boston Spa, Wetherby, W. Yorks LS23 7BY. Tel: 01937-546267

NEWSPAPER LEGAL DEPOSIT OFFICE, The British Library Newspaper Library, Colindale Avenue, London NW9 5LF. Tel: 0171-412 7378

OFFICE FOR HARMONIZATION IN THE INTERNAL MARKET (TRADE MARKS AND DESIGNS), 20 Avenida de la Aguilera, 03080 Alicante, Spain. Tel: Alicante 139459

THE PATENT OFFICE, Cardiff Road, Newport NP10 8QQ. Tel: 0645-500505

SCIENCE REFERENCE LIBRARY, 96 Euston Road, London NW1 2DB. Tel: 0171-412 7494

STATIONERS' HALL REGISTRY LTD, The Registrar, Stationers' Hall, Ave Maria Lane, London EC4M 7DD. Tel: 0171-248 2934

TRADE MARKS REGISTRY, The Patent Office, Cardiff Road, Newport NP9 1RH. Tel: 0645-500505

WORLD INTELLECTUAL PROPERTY ORGANIZATION (WIPO), 34 chemin des Colombettes, 1211 Geneva 20, Switzerland. Tel: Geneva 338 9111

COPYRIGHT LICENSING/COLLECTING AGENCIES

AUTHORS' LICENSING AND COLLECTING SOCIETY, Marlborough Court, 14–18 Holborn, London EC1N 2LE. Tel: 0171-395 0600

CHRISTIAN COPYRIGHT LICENSING (EUROPE) LTD, PO Box 1339, Eastbourne, E. Sussex BN21 4YF. Tel: 01323-417711

COPYRIGHT LICENSING AGENCY LTD, 90 Tottenham Court Road, London W1P 0LP. Tel: 0171-631 5555

DESIGN AND ARTISTS COPYRIGHT AGENCY, Parchment House, 13 Northburgh Street, London EC1V 0AH. Tel: 0171-336 8811

EDUCATIONAL RECORDING AGENCY LTD, New Premier House, 150 Southampton Row, London WC1B 5AL. Tel: 0171-837 3222

INTERNATIONAL FEDERATION OF THE PHONOGRAPHIC INDUSTRIES, 54 Regent Street, London W1R 5PJ. Tel: 0171-878 7900

MCPS-PRS ALLIANCE, Copyright House, 29–33 Berners Street, London W1P 4AA. Tel: 0171-580 5544

NEWSPAPER LICENSING AGENCY, Lonsdale Gardens, Tunbridge Wells, Kent TN1 1NL. Tel: 01892-525274

PHONOGRAPHIC PERFORMANCE LTD, 1 Upper James Street, London W1R 3HG. Tel: 0171-534 1000

PUBLISHERS LICENSING SOCIETY, 5 Dryden Street, London WC2E 9NW. Tel: 0171-829 8486

VIDEO PERFORMANCE LTD, 1 Upper James Street, London W1R 3HG. Tel: 0171-534 1400

The Media

CROSS-MEDIA OWNERSHIP

There are rules on cross-media ownership to prevent undue concentration of ownership. These were amended by the Broadcasting Act 1996. Radio companies are now permitted to own one AM, one FM and one other (AM or FM) service; ownership of the third licence is subject to a public interest test. Local newspapers with a circulation under 20 per cent in an area are also allowed to own one AM, one FM and one other service, and may control a regional Channel 3 television service subject to a public interest test. Local newspapers with a circulation between 20 and 50 per cent in an area may own one AM and one FM service, subject to a public interest test, but may not control a regional Channel 3 service. Those with a circulation over 50 per cent may own one radio service in the area (provided that more than one independent local radio service serves the area) subject to a public interest test.

Ownership controls on the number of television or radio licences have been removed; holdings are now restricted to 15 per cent of the total television audience or 15 per cent of the total points available in the radio points scheme. Ownership controls on cable operators have also been removed. National newspapers with less than 20 per cent of national circulation may apply to control any broadcasting licences, subject to a public interest test. National newspapers with more than 20 per cent of national circulation may not have more than a 20 per cent interest in a licence to provide a Channel 3 service, Channel 5 or national and local analogue radio services.

Broadcasting

The British Broadcasting Corporation (*see* page 284) is responsible for public service broadcasting in the UK. Its constitution and finances are governed by royal charter and agreement. On 1 May 1996 a new royal charter came into force, establishing the framework for the BBC's activities until 2006.

The Independent Television Commission (*see* page 311) and the Radio Authority (*see* page 333) were set up under the terms of the Broadcasting Act 1990. The ITC is the regulator and licensing authority for all commercially-funded television services, including cable and satellite services. The Radio Authority is the regulator and licensing authority for all independent radio services.

COMPLAINTS

The Broadcasting Standards Commisson was set up in April 1997 under the Broadcasting Act 1996 and was formed from the merger of the Broadcasting Complaints Commission and the Broadcasting Standards Council. The Commission considers and adjudicates upon complaints of unfair treatment or unwarranted infringement of privacy in all broadcast programmes and advertisements on television, radio, cable, satellite and digital services. It also monitors the portrayal of violence and sex, and matters of taste and decency. Its new code of practice came into force on 1 January 1998.

BROADCASTING STANDARDS COMMISSION, 7 The Sanctuary, London SW1P 3JS. Tel: 0171-233 0544. *Chairman*, vacant; *Deputy Chairmen*, Ms J. Leighton, Mrs S. Warner; *Director*, S. Whittle

TELEVISION

All channels are broadcast in colour on 625 lines UHF from a network of transmitting stations. The BBC's transmission network was sold to the Castle Tower Consortium in February 1997; ITV transmission services are owned and operated by National Transcommunications Ltd. Transmissions are available to more than 99 per cent of the population.

The total number of receiving television licences in the UK at July 1999 was 22,274,792, of which 98.8 per cent were for colour televisions. Annual television licence fees are: monochrome £33.50; colour £101.00.

No overall statistics are available for subscriptions in the UK to satellite television services; British Sky Broadcasting had 7.75 million subscribers at March 1999 (7.2 million analogue and 551,000 digital), though an increasing number of these view through cable. At April 1999 there were 4,239,881 homes connected to cable television.

DIGITAL TELEVISION

Digital broadcasting will increase the number and quality of television channels. It uses digital modulation to improve reception and digital compression to make more effective use of the frequency channels available than PAL, the analogue system currently used.

The Broadcasting Act 1996 provided for the licensing of 20 or more digital terrestrial television channels (on six frequency channels or 'multiplexes'). Analogue broadcasting will eventually be discontinued, with the frequencies being sold to mobile telephone companies.

In June 1997 the licences to run the remaining digital multiplexes were awarded by the ITC to British Digital Broadcasting (now called ONdigital), a consortium led by Carlton Communications and Granada. The first digital services went on air in autumn 1998. A set-top digital decoder or an integrated digital television set is required to convert the digital signals into analogue sound and picture waves in order to watch the digital channels. Digital television services are also offered by cable and satellite companies.

ESTIMATED AUDIENCE SHARE *for 12 months to 31 March 1999*

	Percentage (rounded)
ITV companies	31.9
BBC 1	29.0
BBC 2	11.2
Cable, satellite and digital channels	13.4
Channel 4	9.9
Channel 5	4.6
S4C Wales	0.3

Source: Independent Television Commission

BBC TELEVISION

Television Centre, Wood Lane, London W12 7RJ
Tel 0181-743 8000

The BBC's experiments in television broadcasting started in 1929 and in 1936 the BBC began the world's first public service of high-definition television from Alexandra Palace.

The BBC broadcasts two UK-wide television services, BBC 1 and BBC 2; outside England these services are designated BBC Scotland on 1, BBC Scotland on 2, BBC 1 Northern Ireland, BBC 2 Northern Ireland, BBC Wales on 1 and BBC Wales on 2. On 9 November 1997 the BBC launched News 24, a 24-hour television news service broadcast by cable during the day and on BBC 1 at night.

BBC WORLDWIDE LTD
Woodlands, 80 Wood Lane, London W12 OTT
Tel 0181-576 2000

BBC Worldwide was formed in May 1994 to develop a co-ordinated approach to the BBC's international and commercial activities. BBC Worldwide Ltd provides commercial products and services in a range of media including television channels, books, CDs, videos, CD-ROMs and interactive media.

INDEPENDENT TELEVISION

The ITV franchises for the 15 regional companies and for breakfast television were allocated new ten-year licences from January 1993. Since 1998 licensees have had several opportunities to apply for renewal of their licence; the last such opportunity will be in early 2001. The ITC received bids for the licence for a new independent national television channel in May 1995. The winner was Channel 5 Broadcasting Ltd and the new channel was launched on 30 March 1997.

ITV NETWORK CENTRE/ITV ASSOCIATION
200 Gray's Inn Road, London WC1X 8HF
Tel 0171-843 8000

The ITV Network Centre is wholly owned by the ITV companies and undertakes the commissioning and scheduling of those television programmes which are shown across the ITV network. Through its sister organization, the ITV Association, it also provides a range of services to the ITV companies where a common approach is required. *Chief Executive*, R. Eyre

INDEPENDENT TELEVISION NETWORK COMPANIES

ANGLIA TELEVISION LTD (owned by United Broadcasting and Entertainment) (*eastern England*), Anglia House, Norwich NR1 3JG. Tel: 01603-615151

BORDER TELEVISION PLC (*the Borders*), The Television Centre, Carlisle CA1 3NT. Tel: 01228-25101

CARLTON UK TELEVISION (*London* (*weekdays*)), 101 St Martin's Lane, London WC2N 4AZ. Tel: 0171-240 4000

CENTRAL INDEPENDENT TELEVISION LTD (owned by Carlton Communications) (*the Midlands*), Central Court, Gas Street, Birmingham B1 2JT. Tel: 0121-643 9898

CHANNEL TELEVISION LTD (*Channel Islands*), The Television Centre, St Helier, Jersey JE2 3ZD. Tel: 01534-816816

GMTV LTD (*breakfast television*), The London Television Centre, Upper Ground, London SE19TT. Tel: 0171-827 7000

GRAMPIAN TELEVISION PLC (owned by Scottish Media) (*northern Scotland*), Queen's Cross, Aberdeen AB15 2XJ. Tel: 01224-846846

GRANADA TELEVISION LTD (owned by Granada Media) (*north-west England*), Quay Street, Manchester M60 9EA. Tel: 0161-832 7211

HTV GROUP PLC (owned by United Broadcasting and Entertainment) (*Wales and western England*), HTV Wales, The Television Centre, Culverhouse Cross, Cardiff CF5 6XJ. Tel: 01222-590590; HTV West, The Television Centre, Bath Road, Bristol BS4 3HG. Tel: 0117-977 8366

LONDON WEEKEND TELEVISION LTD (owned by Granada Media) (*London* (*weekends*)), The London Television Centre, Upper Ground, London SE1 9LT. Tel: 0171-620 1620

MERIDIAN BROADCASTING LTD (owned by United Broadcasting and Entertainment) (*south and south-east England*), The Television Centre, Southampton SO14 OPZ. Tel: 01703-222555

SCOTTISH TELEVISION PLC (owned by Scottish Media) (*central Scotland*), Cowcaddens, Glasgow G2 3PR. Tel: 0141-300 3000

TYNE TEES TELEVISION LTD (owned by Granada Media) (*north-east England*), The Television Centre, City Road, Newcastle upon Tyne NE1 2AL. Tel: 0191-261 0181

ULSTER TELEVISION PLC (*Northern Ireland*), Havelock House, Ormeau Road, Belfast BT7 1EB. Tel: 01232-328122

WESTCOUNTRY TELEVISION LTD (owned by Carlton Communications) (*south-west England*), Langage Science Park, Plymouth PL7 5BG. Tel: 01752-333333

YORKSHIRE TELEVISION LTD (owned by Granada Media) (*Yorkshire*), The Television Centre, Leeds LS3 1JS. Tel: 0113-243 8283

OTHER INDEPENDENT TELEVISION COMPANIES

CHANNEL 5 BROADCASTING LTD, 22 Long Acre, London WC2E 9LY. Tel: 0171-550 5555

CHANNEL FOUR TELEVISION CORPORATION, 124 Horseferry Road, London SW1P 2TX. Tel: 0171-396 4444. Provides a service to the UK except Wales and is charged to cater for interests under-represented by the ITV network companies. Channel 4 sells its own advertising

INDEPENDENT TELEVISION NEWS LTD, 200 Gray's Inn Road, London WC1X 8XZ. Tel: 0171-833 3000

TELETEXT LTD, 101 Farm Lane, London SW6 1QJ. Tel: 0171-386 5000. Provides teletext services for the ITV companies and Channel 4

WELSH FOURTH CHANNEL AUTHORITY (Sianel Pedwar Cymru), Parc Ty Glas, Llanishen, Cardiff CF4 5DU. Tel: 01222-747444. S4C schedules Welsh language and most Channel 4 programmes

DIRECT BROADCASTING BY SATELLITE TELEVISION

BRITISH SKY BROADCASTING LTD, Grant Way, Isleworth, Middx TW7 5QD. Tel: 0171-705 3000. Broadcasts 13 channels which are wholly owned by Sky (Sky One, Sky News, Sky Sports News, Sky Sports 1, Sky Sports 2, Sky Sports 3, Sky MovieMax, Sky Cinema (12 movie screens), Sky Box Office (48 pay-per-view channels), Sky Soap, Sky Premier, Sky Travel and .tv). Sky also broadcasts ten non-subscription channels, co-operates with ten joint venture channels and distributes 33 multi-channels for third parties.

RADIO

UK domestic radio services are broadcast across three wavebands: FM (or VHF), medium wave (also referred to as AM) and long wave (used by BBC Radio 4). In the UK the FM waveband extends in frequency from 87.5 MHz to 108 MHz and the medium wave band extends from 531 kHz to 1602 kHz. Some radios are still calibrated in wavelengths rather than frequency. To convert frequency to wavelength, divide 300,000 by the frequency in kHz.

DIGITAL RADIO

Digital radio allows more services to be broadcast to a higher technical quality and provides the data facility for text or pictures associated with sound programmes. It improves the robustness of high fidelity radio services, especially compared with current FM and AM radio transmissions. It was developed in a collaborative research project under the pan-European EUREKA initiative and has been adopted as a world standard for new digital radio systems. The frequencies allocated for terrestrial digital radio in the UK are 217.5 to 230 MHz.

The Broadcasting Act 1996 provided for the licensing of digital radio services (on seven frequency channels or 'multiplexes'). The BBC has been allocated a multiplex capable of broadcasting six to eight national stereo services; BBC digital broadcasts began in the London area in September 1995. A national digital multiplex has also been made available, on which the three independent national radio stations have a guaranteed place, and local and regional services (BBC and commercial) will use the remaining five multiplexes. The Radio Authority is responsible for awarding licences for capacity on the non-BBC multiplexes The first national independent radio digital licence was awarded in October 1998 to Digital One, a company owned by GWR Digital Radio, NTL Digital Radio and Talk Radio UK. Broadcasting will begin in October 1999. The first local multiplex licence was awarded in May 1999 (to CE Digital, for Birmingham) and will commence broadcasting in May 2000. Analogue services will eventually be discontinued. It is necessary to have a radio set with a digital decoder in order to receive digital radio broadcasts.

ESTIMATED AUDIENCE SHARE
January to March 1999

	Percentage
BBC Radio 1	9.8
BBC Radio 2	12.8
BBC Radio 3	1.4
BBC Radio 4	11.4
BBC Radio 5 Live	4.2
BBC Local/Regional	10.6
Atlantic 252	1.0
Classic FM	4.3
Talk Radio	1.8
Virgin Radio (AM only)	2.4
Local commercial	38.1
Other	2.2

Source: RAJAR/RSL

BBC RADIO
Broadcasting House, Portland Place, London WIA IAA
Tel 0171-580 4468

BBC Radio broadcasts five network services to the UK, Isle of Man and the Channel Islands. There is also a tier of national services in Wales, Scotland and Northern Ireland and 39 local radio stations in England and the Channel Islands. In Wales and Scotland there are also dedicated language services in Welsh and Gaelic respectively.

BBC NETWORK RadioServices

RADIO 1 (Contemporary pop music, social action campaigns and entertainment news) – 24 hours a day. *Frequencies:* 97.6–99.8 FM, coverage 99%

RADIO 2 (Popular music, entertainment, comedy and the arts) – 24 hours a day. *Frequencies:* 88–90.2 FM, coverage 99%

RADIO 3 (Classical music, classic drama, documentaries and features) – 24 hours a day. *Frequencies:* 90.2–92.4 FM, coverage 99%

RADIO 4 (News, documentaries, drama, entertainment, and cricket on long wave in season) – 5.55 a.m.–1.00 a.m. daily, with BBC World Service overnight. *Frequencies:* 94.6–96.1 FM and 103.5–105 FM, coverage 99%;1449 AM, plus eight local fillers on AM

RADIO 5 LIVE (News and sport) – 24 hours a day. *Frequencies:* 693 AM and 909 AM, plus one local filler

BBC NATIONAL RADIO SERVICES

RADIO SCOTLAND *Frequencies:* 810 AM plus two local fillers; 92.4–94.7 FM, coverage 99%. Local programmes on FM as above: HIGHLANDS; NORTH-EAST; BORDERS; SOUTH-WEST (also 585 AM); ORKNEY; SHETLAND

RADIO NAN GAIDHEAL (Gaelic service) *Frequencies:* 103.5–105 FM, 990 AM in Aberdeen, coverage 90%.

RADIO ULSTER *Frequencies:* 1341 AM (873 AM Enniskillen), plus two local fillers; 92.4–95.4 FM, coverage 96%. Local programmes on RADIO FOYLE *Frequencies:* 792 AM; 93.1 FM

RADIO WALES *Frequencies:* 882 AM plus two local fillers; 95.1 FM, 95.9 FM (*Gwent*), 103.9 FM (Cardiff), 95.4 FM (Wrexham), coverage 97%

RADIO CYMRU (Welsh-language) *Frequencies:* 92.4–94.6 FM, 95.7 FM (*Llanfyllin*), 96.1 FM (*Llandinam*), 96.8 FM and 103.5–105 FM, coverage 97%

BBC LOCAL RADIO STATIONS

There are 39 local stations serving England and the Channel Islands:

ASIAN NETWORK, Epic House, Charles Street, Leicester LEI 3SH. Tel: 0116-251 6688. *Frequencies:* 828/837/1458 AM

BRISTOL/SOMERSET SOUND, PO Box 194, Bristol BS99 7QT. Tel: 0117-974 1111; 14–15 Paul Street, Taunton TAI 3PF. Tel: 01823-252437. *Frequencies:* 1548 AM, 1323 AM 94.9/95.5/104.6 FM

CAMBRIDGESHIRE, Broadcasting House, 104 Hills Road, Cambridge CB2 ILD. Tel: 01223-259696. *Frequencies:* 96.0/95.7 FM

CLEVELAND, PO Box 95 FM, Newport Road, Middlesbrough TSI 5DG. Tel: 01642-225211. *Frequencies:* 95.0/95.8 FM

CORNWALL, Phoenix Wharf, Truro, Cornwall TRI IUA. Tel: 01872-275421. *Frequencies:* 95.2/96.0/103.9 FM

COVENTRY AND WARWICKSHIRE, Holt Court, 1 Greyfriars Road, Coventry CVI 2WR. Tel: 01203-860086. *Frequencies:* 94.8/103.7/104.0 FM

CUMBRIA, Annetwell Street, Carlisle CA3 8BB. Tel: 01228-592444. *Frequencies:* 95.6/96.1/104.1 FM

DERBY, PO Box 269, Derby DEI 3HL. Tel: 01332-361111. *Frequencies:* 1116 AM, 95.3/104.5 FM

DEVON, PO Box 5, Broadcasting House, Seymour Road, Plymouth PL3 5BD. Tel: 01752-260323. *Frequencies:* 103.4/96.0/95.8/94.8 FM

ESSEX, 198 New London Road, Chelmsford CM2 9XB. Tel: 01245-262393. *Frequencies:* 103.5/95.3 FM

GLOUCESTERSHIRE, London Road, Gloucester GLI ISW. Tel: 01452-308585. *Frequencies:* 1413 AM, 104.7 FM

GLR (GREATER LONDON RADIO), 35C Marylebone High Street, London WIA 4LG. Tel: 0171-224 2424. *Frequency:* 94.9 FM

GMR (GREATER MANCHESTER RADIO), PO Box 951, Oxford Road, Manchester M60 ISD. Tel: 0161-200 2000. *Frequencies:* 95.1/104.6 FM

GUERNSEY, Commerce House, Les Banques, St Peter Port, Guernsey GY1 2HS. Tel: 01481-728977. *Frequencies:* 1116 AM, 93.2 FM

HEREFORD AND WORCESTER, Hylton Road, Worcester WR2 5WW. Tel: 01905-748485. *Frequencies:* 104.6/104.0/94.7 FM

HUMBERSIDE, 9 Chapel Street, Hull HU1 3NU. Tel: 01482-323232. *Frequency:* 95.9 FM

JERSEY, 18 Parade Road, St Helier, Jersey JE2 3PL. Tel: 01534-870000. *Frequencies:* 1026 AM, 88.8 FM

KENT, Sun Pier, Chatham, Kent ME4 4EZ. Tel: 01634-830505. *Frequencies:* 96.7/97.6/104.2 FM

LANCASHIRE, 26 Darwen Street, Blackburn BB2 2EA. Tel: 01254-262411. *Frequencies:* 95.5/104.5/103.9 FM

LEEDS, Broadcasting House, Woodhouse Lane, Leeds LS2 9PN. Tel: 0113-244 2131. *Frequencies:* 774 AM, 92.4/95.3 FM

LEICESTER, Epic House, Charles Street, Leicester LE1 3SH. Tel: 0116-251 6688. *Frequency:* 104.9 FM

LINCOLNSHIRE, PO Box 219, Newport, Lincoln LN1 3XY. Tel: 01522-511411. *Frequencies:* 1368 AM, 94.9/104.7 FM

MERSEYSIDE, 55 Paradise Street, Liverpool L1 3BP. Tel: 0151-708 5500. *Frequency:* 95.8 FM

NEWCASTLE, Broadcasting Centre, Barrack Road, Newcastle upon Tyne NE99 1RN. Tel: 0191-232 4141. *Frequencies:* 95.4/104.4/96.0/103.7 FM

NORFOLK, Norfolk Tower, Surrey Street, Norwich NR1 3PA. Tel: 01603-617411. *Frequencies:* 95.1/104.4 FM

NORTHAMPTON, Broadcasting House, Abington Street, Northampton NN1 2BH. Tel: 01604-239100. *Frequencies:* 104.2/103.6 FM

NOTTINGHAM, London Road, Nottingham NG2 4UU. Tel: 0115-955 0500. *Frequencies:* 103.8/95.5 FM

SHEFFIELD, Ashdell Grove, 60 Westbourne Road, Sheffield S10 2QU. Tel: 0114-268 6185. *Frequencies:* 94.7/104.1/88.6 FM

SHROPSHIRE, 2–4 Boscobel Drive, Shrewsbury SY1 3TT. Tel: 01743-248484. *Frequencies:* 95.0/96.0 FM

SOLENT, Broadcasting House, Havelock Road, Southampton SO14 7PW. Tel: 01703-631311. *Frequencies:* 96.1/103.8 FM

SOUTHERN COUNTIES, Broadcasting Centre, Guildford GU2 5AP. Tel: 01483-306306. *Frequencies:* 95–95.3/104–104.8 FM

STOKE, Cheapside, Hanley, Stoke-on-Trent ST1 1JJ. Tel: 01782-208080. *Frequencies:* 94.6/104.1 FM

SUFFOLK, Broadcasting House, St Matthew's Street, Ipswich IP1 3EP. Tel: 01473-250000. *Frequencies:* 103.9/104.6/95.5 FM

THAMES VALLEY, 269 Banbury Road, Oxford OX2 7DW. Tel: 01865-311444. *Frequencies:* 95.2/95.4/104.0/104.1 FM

THREE COUNTIES RADIO, PO Box 3CR, Luton, Beds LU1 5XL. Tel: 01582-441000. *Frequencies:* 630 AM, 104.5/95.5/103.8 FM

WILTSHIRE SOUND, Broadcasting House, Prospect Place, Swindon SN1 3RW. Tel: 01793-513626. *Frequencies:* 103.6/104.3/103.5/104.9 FM

WM (WEST MIDLANDS), Pebble Mill Road, Birmingham B5 7SD. Tel: 0121-432 8484 *Frequency:* 95.6 FM.

YORK, 20 Bootham Row, York YO3 7BR. Tel: 01904-641351. *Frequencies:* 103.7/104.3/95.5 FM

BBC WORLD SERVICE

Bush House, Strand, London WC2B 4PH
Tel 0171-240 3456

The BBC World Service broadcasts over 1,000 hours of programmes a week in 44 languages including English. It has a weekly audience of 143 million globally, of whom 35 million listen to English language services. Many services are also available by satellite and on the internet. *UK frequencies:* 3955 AM (mornings and evenings only)/648 AM and on BBC Radio 4 at night.

The World Service is organized into five world regions, each responsible for programmes in English as well as regional languages.

AFRICA AND THE MIDDLE EAST, Arabic, French, Hausa, Kinyarwanda/Kirundi, Portuguese, Somali and Swahili; English programmes including *Network Africa* and *Focus on Africa*.

ASIA AND THE PACIFIC, Bengali, Burmese, Cantonese, Hindi, Indonesian, Mandarin, Nepali, Sinhala, Tamil, Thai, Urdu and Vietnamese; English programmes including *East Asia Today*.

EUROPE, Albanian, Bulgarian, Croatian, Czech, Greek, Hungarian, Macedonian, Polish, Romanian, Serbian, Slovak and Slovene; English programmes including *The World Today*.

FORMER SOVIET UNION AND SOUTH-WEST ASIA, Azeri, Kazakh, Kyrgyz, Pashto, Persian, Russian, Turkish, Ukrainian and Uzbek.

THE AMERICAS, Portuguese for Brazil, Spanish; English programmes including *The World* (a global news magazine for American listeners), *Caribbean Report* and *Calling the Falklands*.

BBC ENGLISH teaches English world-wide through radio, television and a wide range of published courses

BBC MARKET INTELLIGENCE carries out audience research and sells printed publications and data

BBC MONITORING supplies news and information from the output of overseas radio and television stations and news agency sources

BBC MPM (Marshall Plan of the Mind) makes programmes about business, democracy and management for countries of the former Soviet Union

BBC WORLD SERVICE TRAINING runs journalism, management and skills training courses for overseas broadcasters

INDEPENDENT RADIO

The Radio Authority began advertising new licences for the development of commercial radio in January 1991. Since then it has awarded three national licences, 101 new local radio licences (including ten regional licences) and one additional service licence (to use the spare capacity in an existing channel which is not used by the programme service). The Authority has also issued about 2,000 restricted service licences (for temporary low-powered radio services). In 1999–2000 the Authority will advertise one new analogue licence a month. It will also advertise one digital multiplex licence a month and re-advertise existing analogue licences.

COMMERCIAL RADIO COMPANIES ASSOCIATION, 77 Shaftesbury Avenue, London W1V 7AD. Tel: 0171-306 2603. *Chief Executive,* P. Brown

INDEPENDENT NATIONAL RADIO STATIONS

CLASSIC FM, Academic House, 24–28 Oval Road, London NW1 7DQ. Tel: 0171-343 9000. 24 hours a day. *Frequencies:* 99.9–101.9 FM

TALK RADIO, 76 Oxford Street, London W1N 0TR Tel: 0171-636 1089. 24 hours a day. *Frequencies:* 1053/1089 AM

VIRGIN RADIO, 1 Golden Square, London W1R 4DJ. Tel: 0171-434 1215. 24 hours a day. *Frequencies:* 1215/1197/1233/1242/1260 AM

INDEPENDENT REGIONAL LOCAL RADIO STATIONS

100.7 HEART FM (west Midlands), 1 The Square, 111 Broad Street, Birmingham B15 1AS. Tel: 0121-626 1007. Frequency: 100.7 FM

CENTURY 105 (north-west), Century House, Waterfront Quay, Salford Quays, Manchester M5 2XW. Tel: 0161-400 0105. Frequency: 105.4 FM

CENTURY 106 (east Midlands), City Link, Nottingham NG2 4NG. Tel: 0115-910 6100. Frequency: 106.0 FM

CENTURY RADIO (north-east), Century House, PO Box 100, Gateshead NE8 2YX. Tel: 0191-477 6666. Frequencies: 100.7/101.8/96.2/96.4 FM

GALAXY 101 (Severn estuary), Millennium House, 26 Baldwin Street, Bristol BS1 1SE. Tel: 0117-901 0101. Frequencies: 101.0/97.2 FM (Bristol)

GALAXY 105 (Yorkshire), Joseph's Well, Westgate, Leeds LS3 1AB. Tel: 0113-213 0105. Frequencies: 105.1 FM (Leeds); 105.6 FM (Bradford and Sheffield); 105.8 FM (Hull)

GALAXY 105—106 (north-east), Kingfisher Way, Silverlink Business Park, Tyne and Wear NE28 9ND. Tel: 0191-206 8000. Frequencies: 105.3/105.6/106.4 FM

JAZZ FM 100.4 (north-west), The World Trade Centre, Exchange Quay, Manchester M5 3EJ. Tel: 0161-877 1004. Frequency: 100.4 FM

SCOT FM (central Scotland), 1 Albert Quay, Leith EH6 7DN. Tel: 0131-554 6677. Frequencies: 100.3/101.1 FM

VIBE FM (east), Reflection House, The Anderson Centre, Olding Road, Bury St Edmunds, Suffolk IP33 3TA. Tel: 01284-718800. Frequencies: 107.7 FM (Peterborough); 105.6 FM (Cambridge); 106.1 FM (Norwich); 106.4 FM (Ipswich)

WAVE 105 FM (Solent), 5 Manor Court, Barnes Wallis Road, Segensworth East, Fareham, Hants PO15 5TH. Tel: 01489-481050. Frequencies: 105.2 FM (Solent); 105.8 FM (Poole)

INDEPENDENT LOCAL RADIO STATIONS

England

2-TEN FM, PO Box 2020, Reading RG31 7FG. Tel: 0118-945 4400. Frequencies: 97.0/102.9/103.4 FM

2CR FM, 5 Southcote Road, Bournemouth BH1 3LR. Tel: 01202-259259. Frequency: 102.3 FM

96 TRENT FM 29–31 Castle Gate, Nottingham NG1 7AP. Tel: 0115-952 7000. Frequencies: 96.2/96.5 FM

96.3 AIRE FM, 51 Burley Road, Leeds LS3 1LR. Tel: 0113-283 5500. Frequency: 96.3 FM

96.4 FM BRMB, Radio House, Aston Road North, Birmingham B6 4BX. Tel: 0121-359 4481. Frequency: 96.4 FM

96.4 THE EAGLE, Dolphin House, North Street, Guildford, Surrey GU1 4AA. Tel: 01483-300964. Frequency: 96.4 FM

96.6 OASIS FM, 9 Christopher Place Shopping Centre, St Albans, Herts AL3 5DQ. Tel: 01727-831966. Frequency: 96.6 FM

96.9 VIKING FM, Commercial Road, Hull HU1 2SG. Tel: 01482-325141. Frequency: 96.9 FM

97.2 STRAY FM, PO Box 972, Station Parade, Harrogate HG1 5YF. Tel: 01423-522972. Frequency: 97.2 FM

97.4 VALE FM, Longmead, Shaftesbury, Dorset SP7 8QQ. Tel: 01747-855711. Frequency: 97.4 FM

102.4 WISH FM, Orrell Lodge, Orrell Road, Orrell, Wigan WN5 8HJ. Tel: 01942-761024. Frequency: 102.4 FM

102.7 HEREWARD FM, PO Box 225, Queensgate Centre, Peterborough PE1 1XJ. Tel: 01733-460460. Frequency: 102.7 FM

103.2 POWER FM, Radio House, Whittle Avenue, Segensworth West, Fareham, Hants PO15 5SH. Tel: 01489-589911. Frequency: 103.2 FM

103.4 THE BEACH, PO Box 103.4, Lowestoft, Suffolk NR32 2TL. Tel: 07000-001035. Frequency: 103.4 FM

106 CTFM RADIO, 16 Lower Bridge Street, Canterbury, Kent CT1 2HQ. Tel: 01227-789106. Frequency: 106.0 FM

106.9 SILK FM, Radio House, Bridge Street, Macclesfield, Cheshire SK11 6DJ. Tel: 01625-268000. Frequency: 106.9 FM

107 OAK FM, 18 Jubilee Drive, Loughborough, Leics LE11 5TQ. Tel: 01509-217080. Frequency: 107.0 FM

107.2 WIRE FM, Warrington Business Park, Long Lane, Warrington WA2 8TX. Tel: 01925-445545. Frequency: 107.2 FM

107.4 TELFORD FM, PO Box 1074, Telford TF3 3WG. Tel: 01952-280011. Frequency:107.4 FM

107.5 CAT FM, Regent Arcade, Cheltenham, Glos GL50 1JZ. Tel: 01242-699555. Frequency: 107.5 FM

107.6 KESTREL FM, 2nd Floor, Paddington House, The Walks Shopping Centre, Basingstoke, Hants RG21 7LJ. Tel: 01256-694000. Frequency: 107.6 FM

107.7 CHELMER FM, Cater House, High Street, Chelmsford, Essex CM1 1AL. Tel: 01245-259400. Frequency: 107.7 FM

107.7 THE WOLF, 10th Floor, Mander House, Wolverhampton WV1 3NB. Tel: 01902-571070. Frequency: 107.7 FM

107.7 WFM, 11 Beaconsfield Road, Weston-super-Mare, Somerset BS23 1YE. Tel: 01934-624455. Frequency: 107.7 FM

107.8 ARROW FM, Priory Meadow Centre, Hastings, E. Sussex TN34 1PJ. Tel: 01424-461177. Frequency: 107.8 FM

107.8 FM THAMES RADIO, Brentham House, 45C High Street, Hampton Wick, Kingston upon Thames KT1 4DG. Tel: 0181-288 1300. Frequency: 107.8 FM

963/972 LIBERTY RADIO, 7th Floor, Trevor House, 100 Brompton Road, London SW3 1ER. Tel: 0171-893 8966. Frequency: 963/972 AM

1458 LITE AM, PO Box 1458, Quay West, Trafford Park, Manchester M17 1FL. Tel: 0161-872 1458. Frequency: 1458 AM

ACTIVE 107.5 FM, Lambourne House, 7 Western Road, Romford, Essex RM1 3LD. Tel: 01708-731643. Frequency: 107.5 FM

ALPHA 103.2, Radio House, 11 Woodland Road, Darlington DL3 7BJ. Tel: 01325-255552. Frequency: 103.2 FM

ASIAN SOUND RADIO, Globe House, Southall Street, Manchester M3 1LG. Tel: 0161-288 1000. Frequencies: 1377/963 AM

B97 Chiltern FM, 55 Goldington Road, Bedford MK40 3LT. Tel: 01234-272400. Frequency: 96.9 FM

BATH FM, 4 Queen Square, Bath BA1 2HA. Tel: 01225-339661. Expected on air November 1999. Frequency: to be announced

THE BAY, PO Box 969, St George's Quay, Lancaster LA1 3LD. Tel: 01524-848747. Frequencies: 96.9/102.3/103.2 FM

BEACON FM, 267 Tettenhall Road, Wolverhampton WV6 0DQ. Tel: 01902-838383. Frequencies: 97.2 FM (Wolverhampton and Black Country); 103.1 FM (Shrewsbury and Telford)

THE BREEZE, Radio House, Clifftown Road, Southend-on-Sea, Essex SS1 1SX. Tel: 01702-333711. Frequencies: 1359 AM (Chelmsford); 1431 AM (Southend)

BREEZE 1521, The Stanley Centre, Kelvin Way, Crawley, W. Sussex RH10 2SE. Tel: 01293-519161. Frequency: 1521 AM

BRISTOL COMMUNITY RADIO, PO Box 242, Springfield House, West Street, Bristol BS99 5BF. Expected on air late 1999. Frequency: to be announced

THE BUZZ 97.1, Media House, Claughton Road, Birkenhead CH41 6EY. Tel: 0151-650 1700. *Frequency:* 97.1 FM

BROADLAND 102, St George's Plain, 47–49 Colegate, Norwich NR3 1DB. Tel: 01603-630621. *Frequency:* 102.4 FM

CAMBRIDGE RED RADIO, PO Box 492, Cambridge CB1 2UW. Tel: 01223-722300. *Frequency:* 107.9 FM

CAPITAL FM AND GOLD, 30 Leicester Square, London WC2H 7LA. Tel: 0171-766 6000. *Frequencies:* 1548 AM (*Gold*), 95.8 FM

CAPITAL GOLD (1152), Radio House, Aston Road North, Birmingham B6 4BX. Tel: 0121-359 4481. *Frequency:* 1152 AM

CAPITAL GOLD (1170 AND 1557), Radio House, Whittle Avenue, Segensworth West, Fareham, Hants PO15 5SH. Tel: 01489-589911. *Frequencies:* 1170/1557 AM

CAPITAL GOLD (1242 AND 603), Radio House, John Wilson Business Park, Whitstable, Kent CT5 3QX. Tel: 01227-772004. *Frequencies:* 603 AM (East Kent); 1242 AM (Maidstone and Medway)

CAPITAL GOLD (1323 AND 945), Radio House, PO Box 2000, Brighton BN41 2SS. Tel: 01273-430111. *Frequencies:* 945/1323 AM

CENTRE FM, 5–6 Aldergate, Tamworth, Staffs B79 7DJ. Tel: 01827-318000. *Frequencies:* 101.6/102.4 FM

CFM, PO Box 964, Carlisle, Cumbria CA1 3NG. Tel: 01228-818964. *Frequencies:* 96.4 FM (Penrith); 102.5 FM (Carlisle); 102.2 FM (Workington); 103.4 FM (Whitehaven)

CHANNEL TRAVEL RADIO, Main Control Building, PO Box 2000, Eurotunnel UK Terminal, Folkestone, Kent CT18 8XY. Tel: 01303-283873. *Frequency:* 107.6 FM

CHILTERN FM, Chiltern Road, Dunstable, Beds LU6 1HQ. Tel: 01582-676200. *Frequency:* 97.6 FM

CHOICE FM, 291–299 Borough High Street, London SE1 1JG. Tel: 0171-378 3969. *Frequency:* 96.9 FM

RADIO CITY 96.7, 8–10 Stanley Street, Liverpool L1 6AF. Tel: 0151-227 5100. *Frequency:* 96.7 FM

CLASSIC GOLD 666/954, Hawthorn House, Exeter Business Park, Exeter EX1 3QS. Tel: 01392-444444. *Frequencies:*666/954 AM

CLASSIC GOLD 774, Bridge Studios, Eastgate Centre, Gloucester GL1 1SS. Tel: 01452-313200. *Frequency:* 774 AM

CLASSIC GOLD 792/828, Chiltern Road, Dunstable, Beds LU6 1HQ. Tel: 01582-676200. *Frequencies:* 792 AM (Bedford); 828 AM (Luton)

CLASSIC GOLD 828, 5 Southcote Road, Bournemouth, Dorset BH1 3LR. Tel: 01202-259259. *Frequency:* 828 AM

CLASSIC GOLD 936/1161 AM, PO Box 2000, Swindon SN4 7EX. Tel: 01793-842600. *Frequencies:* 936 AM (West Wilts); 1161 AM (Swindon)

CLASSIC GOLD RADIO 954/1530, 5 Barbourne Terrace, Worcester WR1 3JZ. Tel: 01905-612212. *Frequencies:* 954 AM (Hereford); 1530 AM (Worcester)

CLASSIC GOLD 1260, PO Box 2020, Watershed, Canons Road, Bristol BS99 7SN. Tel: 0117-984 3200. *Frequency:* 1260 AM

CLASSIC GOLD 1278/1530, Forster Square, Bradford BD1 5NE. Tel: 01274-203040. *Frequencies:* 1278/1530 AM

CLASSIC GOLD 1332 AM, PO Box 2020, Queensgate Centre, Peterborough PE1 1LL. Tel: 01733-460460. *Frequency:* 1332 AM

CLASSIC GOLD 1359, Hertford Place, Coventry CV1 3TT. Tel: 01203-868200. *Frequency:* 1359 AM

CLASSIC GOLD 1431/1485, PO Box 2020, Reading RG31 7FG. Tel: 0118-945 4400. *Frequencies:* 1431/1485 AM

CLASSIC GOLD 1557, 19–21 St Edmunds Road, Northampton NN1 5DY. Tel: 01604-795600. *Frequency:* 1557 AM

CLASSIC GOLD AMBER, St George's Plain, 47–49 Colegate, Norwich NR3 1DB. Tel: 01603-630321. *Frequency:* 1152 AM

CLASSIC GOLD AMBER (SUFFOLK), Radio House, Alpha Business Park, 6–12 White House Road, Ipswich IP1 5LT. Tel: 01473-461000. *Frequency:* 1170 AM (Ipswich); 1251 AM (Bury St Edmunds)

CLASSIC GOLD GEM, 29–31 Castle Gate, Nottingham NG1 7AP. Tel: 0115-952 7000. *Frequencies:* 945/999 AM

CLASSIC GOLD WABC, 267 Tettenhall Road, Wolverhampton WV6 0DQ. Tel: 01902-838383. *Frequencies:* 990 AM (Wolverhampton); 1017 AM (Shrewsbury and Telford)

CONNECT FM, Church Street, Wellingborough, Northants NN8 4XX. Tel: 01933-224972. *Frequency:* 97.2 FM

COUNTY SOUND RADIO 1476 AM, Dolphin House, North Street, Guildford GU1 4AA. Tel: 01483-300964. *Frequency:* 1476 AM

CRASH FM, 27 Fleet Street, Liverpool L1 4AR. Tel: 0151-707 3107. *Frequency:* 107.6 FM

DELTA FM 97.1, 65 Weyhill, Haslemere, Surrey GU27 1HN. Tel: 01428-651971. *Frequency:* 97.1 FM

DELTA FM 102, Prospect Place, Mill Lane, Alton, Hants GU34 2SY. Tel: 01420-544444. *Frequencies:* 102.0/101.6 FM

Dream 100 FM, Northgate House, St Peter's Street, Colchester, CO1 1HT. Tel: 01206-764466. *Frequency:* 100.2 FM

DUNE FM, The Power Station, Victoria Way, Southport PR8 1RR. Tel: 01704-502500. *Frequency:* 107.9 FM

ELEVEN SEVENTY, PO Box 1170, High Wycombe, Bucks HP13 6YT. Tel: 01494-446611. *Frequency:* 1170 FM

ESSEX FM, Radio House, Clifftown Road, Southend-on-Sea, Essex SS1 1SX. Tel: 01702-333711. *Frequencies:* 96.3 FM (Southend); 102.6 FM (Chelmsford)

FLR 107.3, Astra House, Arklow Road, London SE14 6EB. Tel: 0181-691 9202. *Frequency:* 107.3 FM

FM 102 – THE BEAR, The Guard House Studios, Banbury Road, Stratford-upon-Avon, Warks CV37 7HX. Tel: 01789-262636. *Frequency:* 102.0 FM

FM 103 HORIZON, The Broadcast Centre, Vincent Avenue, Crownhill Industry, Milton Keynes MK8 0AB. Tel: 01908-269111. *Frequency:* 103.3 FM

FM 107 THE FALCON, Brunel Mall, London Road, Stroud, Glos GL5 2BP. Tel: 01453-767369. *Frequency:* 107.2/107.9 FM

FOSSEWAY RADIO, PO Box 107, Hinckley, Leics LE10 1WR. Tel: 01455-614151. *Frequency:* 107.9 FM

Fox FM, Brush House, Pony Road, Oxford OX4 2XR. Tel: 01865-871000. *Frequencies:* 102.6/97.4 FM

GALAXY 102, 127–129 Portland Street, Manchester M1 6ED. Tel: 0161-228 0102. *Frequency:* 102.0 FM

GALAXY 102.2, 1 The Square, 111 Broad Street, Birmingham B15 1AS. Tel: 0121-695 0000. *Frequency:* 102.2 FM

GEMINI FM, Hawthorn House, Exeter Business Park, Exeter EX1 3QS. Tel: 01392-444444. *Frequencies:* 96.4/97.0/103.0 FM

GWR FM (BRISTOL AND BATH), PO Box 2000, Watershed, Canon's Road, Bristol BS99 7SN. Tel: 0117-984 3200. *Frequencies:* 96.3 FM (Bristol); 103.0 FM (Bath)

GWR FM (SWINDON AND WEST WILTSHIRE), PO Box 2000, Swindon SN4 7EX. Tel: 01793-842600. *Frequencies:* 97.2 FM (Swindon); 102.2 FM (West Wilts); 96.5 FM (Marlborough)

HALLAM FM, Radio House, 900 Herries Road, Sheffield
S6 IRH. Tel: 0114-285 3333. *Frequencies:* 97.4 FM
(Sheffield); 102.9 FM (Barnsley); 103.4 FM (Doncaster)

HEART 106.2 The Chrysalis Building, Bramley Road,
London W10 6SP. Tel: 0171-468 1062. *Frequency:* 106.2
FM

HUDDERSFIELD FM, The Old Stableblock, Brewery
Drive, Lockwood Park, Huddersfield HD1 3UR. Tel:
01484-321107. *Frequency:* 107.9 FM

INVICTA FM, Radio House, John Wilson Business Park,
Whitstable, Kent CT5 3QX. Tel: 01227-772004.
Frequencies: 103.1 FM (Maidstone and Medway); 102.8
FM (Canterbury); 95.9 FM (Thanet); 97.0 FM (Dover);
96.1 FM (Ashford)

ISLE OF WIGHT RADIO, Dodnor Park, Newport, Isle of
Wight PO30 5XE. Tel: 01983-822557. *Frequencies:*
102.0/107.0 FM

JAZZ FM 102.2, 26–27 Castlereagh Street, London
W1H 6DJ. Tel: 0171-706 4100. *Frequency:* 102.2 FM

KCBC, PO Box 1074, Centre 2000, Kettering, Northants
NN16 8PU. Tel: 07000-1074 1074. *Frequency:* 107.4 FM

KEY 103, Castle Quay, Castlefield, Manchester M15 4PR.
Tel: 0161-288 5000. *Frequency:* 103.0 FM

KFM, 1 East Street, Tonbridge, Kent TN9 1AR. Tel:
01732-369200. *Frequencies:* 96.2 FM (South); 101.6 FM
(North)

KISS 100 FM, Kiss House, 80 Holloway Road, London
N7 8JG. Tel: 0171-700 6100. *Frequency:* 100.0 FM

KIX 96, Watch Close, Spon Street, Coventry CV1 3LN. Tel:
01203-525656. *Frequency:* 96.2 FM

KL.FM 96.7, PO Box 77, 18 Blackfriars Street, King's
Lynn, Norfolk PE30 1NN. Tel: 01553-772777. *Frequency:*
96.7 FM

LANTERN FM, 17 Market Place, Bideford, N. Devon
EX39 2DR. Tel: 01237-424444. *Frequency:* 96.2 FM

LBC 1152 AM, 200 Gray's Inn Road, London WC1X 8XZ.
Tel: 0171-973 1152. *Frequency:* 1152 AM

LEICESTER SOUND, Granville House, Granville Road,
Leicester LE1 7RW. Tel: 0116-256 1300. *Frequency:* 105.4
FM

LINCS FM, Witham Park, Waterside South, Lincoln
LN5 7JN. Tel: 01522-549900. *Frequencies:* 102.2 FM/96.7
FM (Grantham Relay) 97.6 FM (Scunthorpe Relay)

LITE FM, 5 Church Street, Peterborough PE1 1XB. Tel:
01733-898106. *Frequency:* 106.8 FM

LONDON GREEK RADIO, Florentia Village, Vale Road,
London N4 1TD. Tel: 0181-800 8001. *Frequency:* 103.3
FM

LONDON TURKISH RADIO LTR, 185B High Road,
Wood Green, London N22 6BA. Tel: 0181-881 0606.
Frequency 1584 AM

MAGIC 105.4 FM, The Network Building, 97
Tottenham Court Road, London W1P 9HF. Tel: 0171-
504 6000. *Frequency:* 105.4 FM

MAGIC 828, 51 Burley Road, Leeds LS3 1LR. Tel: 0113-283
5500. *Frequency:* 828 AM

MAGIC 999, PO Box 999, Preston, Lancs PR1 1XR. Tel:
01772-556301. *Frequency:* 999 AM

MAGIC 1152, Castle Quay, Castlefield, Manchester
M15 4PR. Tel: 0161-288 5000. *Frequency:* 1152 AM

MAGIC 1152 AM, Newcastle upon Tyne NE99 1BB. Tel:
0191-420 3040. *Frequency:* 1152 AM

MAGIC 1161 AM, Commercial Road, Hull HU1 2SG. Tel:
01482-325141. *Frequency:* 1161 AM

MAGIC 1170, Radio House, Yales Crescent, Thornaby,
Stockton-on-Tees, Cleveland TS17 6AA. Tel: 01642-
888222. *Frequency:* 1170 AM

MAGIC 1548, 8–10 Stanley Street, Liverpool L1 6AF. Tel:
0151-227 5100. *Frequency:* 1548 AM

MAGIC AM, Radio House, 900 Herries Road, Sheffield
S6 IRH. Tel: 0114-285 2121. *Frequencies:* 990/1305/1548
AM

MANSFIELD 103.2, The Media Suite, Brunts Business
Centre, Samuel Brunts Way, Mansfield, Notts NG18
2AH. Tel: 01623-646666.. *Frequency:* 103.2 FM

MARCHER GOLD, The Studios, Mold Road, Wrexham
LL11 4AF. Tel: 01978-752202. *Frequency:* 1260 AM

MEDWAY FM, Berkeley House, 186 High Street,
Rochester ME1 1EY. Tel: 01634-841111. *Frequencies:*
107.9/100.4 FM

MERCIA FM, Hertford Place, Coventry CV1 3TT. Tel:
01203-868200. *Frequencies:* 97.0/102.9 FM

MERCURY FM, The Stanley Centre, Kelvin Way,
Crawley, W. Sussex RH10 2SE. Tel: 01293-519161.
Frequencies: 97.5/102.7 FM

METRO FM, Newcastle upon Tyne NE99 1BB. Tel: 0191-
420 0971. *Frequencies:* 97.1 FM (Northumberland, Tyne
and Wear, Durham); 103.0 FM (Tyne Valley); 102.6
FM (Alnwick); 103.2 FM (Hexham)

MFM 103.4, The Studios, Mold Road, Gwersyllt, Nr
Wrexham LL11 4AF. Tel: 01978-752202. *Frequency:* 103.4
FM

MILLENNIUM RADIO, Harrow Manor Way,
Thamesmead, London SE2 9XH. Tel: 0181-311 3112.
Frequency: 106.8 FM

MINSTER FM, PO Box 123, Dunnington, York YO1 5ZX.
Tel: 01904-488888. *Frequencies:* 104.7 FM (York); 102.3
FM (Thirsk)

MIX 96 Friars Square Studios, 11 Bourbon Street,
Aylesbury, Bucks HP20 2PZ. Tel: 01296-399396.
Frequency: 96.2 FM

NEPTUNE RADIO, PO Box 1068, Dover CT16 1GB; PO Box
964, Folkestone CT18 8GG. Tel: 01304-202505.
Frequencies: 96.4 FM (Folkestone); 106.8 FM (Dover)

NEWS DIRECT 97.3 FM, 200 Gray's Inn Road, London
WC1X 8XZ. Tel: 0171-973 1152. *Frequency:* 97.3 FM

NORTHANTS 96, 19–21 St Edmunds Road, Northampton
NN1 5DY. Tel: 01604-795600. *Frequency:* 96.6 FM

THE NRG, PO Box 1234, Bournemouth BH1 3YH. Tel:
01202-318100. *Frequency:* 107.6 FM

OCEAN FM, Radio House, Whittle Avenue, Segensworth
West, Fareham, Hants PO15 5SH. Tel: 01489-589911.
Frequencies: 96.7/97.5 FM

ORCHARD FM, Haygrove House, Taunton, Somerset
TA3 7BT. Tel: 01823-338448. *Frequencies:* 96.5 FM
(Taunton); 97.1 FM (Yeovil); 102.6 FM (Somerset)

OXYGEN 107.9 FM, Suite 41, Westgate Centre, Oxford
OX1 1PD. Tel: 01865-724442. *Frequency:* 107.9 FM

PEAK FM, Radio House, Foxwood Road,
Chesterfield, Derbys S41 9RF. Tel: 01246-269107.
Frequencies: 107.4 FM (Chesterfield and NE
Derbyshire); 102.0 FM (Matlock and Bakewell)

PIRATE FM 102, Carn Brea Studios, Wilson Way,
Redruth, Cornwall TR15 3XX. Tel: 01209-314400.
Frequencies: 102.2 FM (East Cornwall and West Devon);
102.8 FM (West Cornwall and Isles of Scilly)

PLYMOUTH SOUND AM AND FM, Earl's Acre, Plymouth
PL3 4HX. Tel: 01752-227272. *Frequencies:* 1152 AM,
96.6/97.0 FM

PREMIER CHRISTIAN RADIO, Glen House, Stag Place,
London SW1E 5AG. Tel: 0171-316 1300. *Frequencies:*
1305/1332/1413 AM

THE PULSE, Pennine House, Forster Square, Bradford
BD1 5NE. Tel: 01274-203040. *Frequencies:* 97.5 FM
(Bradford); 102.5 FM (Huddersfield and Halifax)

Q103 FM, Enterprise House, The Vision Park, Chivers
Way, Histon, Cambridge CB4 4WW. Tel: 01223-235255.
Frequencies: 103.0 FM (Cambridge); 97.4 FM
(Newmarket)

QUAY WEST RADIO, Harbour Studios, The Esplanade, Watchet, Somerset TA23 0AJ. Tel: 01984-634900. *Frequency:* 102.4 FM

RADIO VICTORY, Media House, Tipner Wharf, Twyford Avenue, Portsmouth PO2 8PE. Tel: 01705-358853. *Frequency:* 107.4 FM

RADIO XL 1296 AM, KMS House, Bradford Street, Birmingham BI2 0JD. Tel: 0121-753 5353. *Frequency:* 1296 AM

RAM FM, The Market Place, Derby DEI 3AA. Tel: 01332-292945. *Frequency:* 102.8 FM

REVOLUTION, PO Box 877, Oldham OL8 IUS. Tel: 0161-628 8787. *Frequency:* 96.2 FM

RIDINGS FM, PO Box 333, Wakefield WFI 5YN. Tel: 01924-367177. Expected on air late 1999. *Frequency:* 106.8 FM

RITZ 1035 AM, 33–35 Wembley Hill Road, London HA9 8RT. Tel: 0181-733 1300. *Frequency:* 1035 AM

ROCK FM, PO Box 974, Preston PRI IXS. Tel: 01772-556301. *Frequency:* 97.4 FM

RUTLAND RADIO, Rutland Business Centre, Gaol Street, Oakham, Rutland LEI5 6AQ. Tel: 01572-757868. *Frequency:* 107.2 FM (Rutland); 97.4 FM (Stamford)

SABRAS RADIO, Radio House, 63 Melton Road, Leicester LE4 6PN. Tel: 0116-261 0666. *Frequency:* 1260 AM

SEVERN SOUND FM, Bridge Studios, Eastgate Centre, Gloucester GLI ISS. Tel: 01452-313200. *Frequencies:* 103.0/102.4 FM

SGR COLCHESTER, Abbeygate Two, 9 Whitewell Road, Colchester CO2 7DE. Tel: 01206-575859. *Frequency:* 96.1 FM

SGR-FM, Radio House, Alpha Business Park, White House Road, Ipswich IPI 5LT. Tel: 01473-461000. *Frequencies:* 97.1 FM (Ipswich); 96.4 FM (Bury St Edmunds)

SIGNAL FM, Regent House, Heaton Lane, Stockport SK4 IBX. Tel: 0161-285 4545. *Frequencies:* 104.9 FM (Stockport); 96.4 FM (Cheshire)

SIGNAL ONE (FM) AND TWO (AM), Stoke Road, Stoke-on-Trent ST4 2SR. Tel: 01782-747047. *Frequencies:* 1170 AM, 102.6 FM/96.9 FM

SOUTHCITY FM, City Studios, Marsh Lane, Southampton, SOI4 3ST. Tel: 01703-233774. Expected on air late 1999. *Frequency:* 107.8 FM

SOUTHERN FM, Radio House, PO Box 2000, Brighton BN4I 2SS. Tel: 01273-430111. *Frequencies:* 102.0 FM (Hastings); 102.4 FM (Eastbourne); 96.9 FM (Newhaven); 103.5 FM (Brighton)

SOUTH HAMS RADIO, Brook House, South Milton, Kingsbridge, Devon TQ7 3JQ. Tel: 01548-561414. *Frequency:* 102.2 FM

SOVEREIGN RADIO, 14 St Mary's Walk, Hailsham, E. Sussex BN27 IAF. Tel: 01323-442700. *Frequency:* 107.5 FM

SPECTRUM INTERNATIONAL RADIO, International Radio Centre, 204–206 Queenstown Road, London SW8 3NR. Tel: 0171-627 4433. *Frequency:* 558 AM

SPIRE FM, City Hall Studios, Malthouse Lane, Salisbury, Wilts SP2 7QQ. Tel: 01722-416644. *Frequency:* 102.0 FM

SPIRIT FM, Dukes Court, Bognor Road, Chichester, W. Sussex PO19 2FX. Tel: 01243-773600. *Frequencies:* 96.6/102.3 FM

STAR FM, The Observatory Shopping Centre, Slough, Berks SLI ILH. Tel: 01753-551066. *Frequency:* 106.6 FM

SUN FM, PO Box 1034, Sunderland SR5 2YL. Tel: 0191-548 1034. *Frequency:* 103.4 FM

SUNRISE FM, Sunrise House, 30 Chapel Street, Little Germany, Bradford BDI 5DN. Tel: 01274-735043. *Frequency:* 103.2 FM

SUNRISE RADIO, Sunrise House, Sunrise Road, Southall, Middx UB2 4AU. Tel: 0181-574 6666. *Frequency:* 1458 AM

SUNSHINE 855, Sunshine House, Waterside, Ludlow, Shropshire SY8 IGS. Tel: 01584-873795. *Frequency:* 855 AM

SURF 107, PO Box 107, Brighton BNI IQG. Tel: 01273-386107. Frequency: 107.2 FM

TEN 17, Latton Bush Centre, Southern Way, Harlow, Essex CMI8 7BU. Tel: 01279-432415. *Frequency:* 101.7 FM

TFM, Radio House, Yale Crescent, Thornaby, Stockton-on-Tees TSI7 6AA. Tel: 01642-888222. *Frequency:* 96.6 FM

TLR, Imperial House, 2–14 High Street, Margate, Kent CT9 IDH. Tel: 01843-220222. *Frequency:* 107.2 FM

TOWER FM, The Mill, Brownlow Way, Bolton BLI 2RA. Tel: 01204-387000. *Frequency:* 107.4 FM

TRAX FM, PO Box 444, Worksop, Notts S8I 9YW. Tel: 01909-500611. *Frequency:* 107.9AM

TRAX FM, PO Box 444, Doncaster DN3 3GB. Tel: 01302-341166. Expected on air late 1999. *Frequency:* 107.1 FM

VIRGIN 105.8, 1 Golden Square, London WIR 4DJ. Tel: 0171-434 1215. *Frequency:* 105.8 FM

THE WAVE 96.5, 965 Mowbray Drive, Blackpool FY3 7JR. Tel: 01253-304965. *Frequency:* 96.5 FM

WESSEX FM, Radio House, Trinity Street, Dorchester DTI IDJ. Tel: 01305-250333. *Frequencies:* 97.2/96.0 FM

WIN 107.2, PO Box 1072, The Brooks, Winchester SO23 8FT. Tel: 01962-841071. *Frequency:* 107.2 FM

WYVERN FM, 5 Barbourne Terrace, Worcester WRI 3JZ. Tel: 01905-612212. *Frequencies:* 97.6 FM (Hereford); 102.8 FM (Worcester); 96.7 FM (Kidderminster)

X-CEL FM, 46 Camel Road, Littleport, Cambs CB6 IEW. Tel: 01353-861333. *Frequencies:* 107.1/107.5 FM

XFM, 30 Leicester Square, London WC2H 7LA. Tel: 0171-766 6600. *Frequency:* 104.9 FM

YORKSHIRE COAST RADIO, PO Box 962, Scarborough, N. Yorks YOI2 5YX. Tel: 01723-500962. *Frequencies:* 96.2/103.1 FM

YORKSHIRE DALES RADIO LTD, YDR House, Gargrave Road, Skipton, N. Yorks BD23 IYD. Tel: 01756-799991. *Frequencies:* 936 AM (Hawes); 1413 AM (Skipton)

Wales

CAPITAL GOLD, West Canal Wharf, Cardiff CFIO 5XL. Tel: 01222-237878. *Frequencies:* 1359 AM (Cardiff); 1305 AM (Newport)

CHAMPION FM, Llys y Dderwen, Parc Menai, Bangor LL57 4BN. Tel: 01248-671888. *Frequency:* 103.0 FM

COAST FM, 41 Conwy Road, Colwyn Bay LL28 5AB. Tel: 01492-533733. *Frequency:* 96.3 FM

RADIO CEREDIGION, Yr Hen Ysgol Gymraeg, Ffordd Alexandra, Aberystwyth SY23 ILF. Tel: 01970-627999. *Frequencies:* 96.6/97.4/103.3/FM

RADIO MALDWYN, The Studios, The Park, Newtown, Powys SYI6 2NZ. Tel: 01686-623555. *Frequency:* 756 AM

RED DRAGON FM, Radio House, West Canal Wharf, Cardiff CFIO 5XL. Tel: 01222-384041. *Frequencies:* 103.2 FM (Cardiff); 97.4 FM (Newport)

SWANSEA SOUND, PO Box 1170, Victoria Road, Gowerton, Swansea SA4 3AB. Tel: 01792-511170. *Frequency:* 1170 AM

VALLEYS RADIO, Festival Park, Victoria, Ebbw Vale NP3 6XW. Tel: 01495-301116. *Frequencies:* 999/1116 AM

THE WAVE 96.4 FM, PO Box 964, Victoria Road, Gowerton, Swansea SA4 3AB. Tel: 01792-511964. *Frequency:* 96.4 FM

Scotland

96.3 QFM, 26 Lady Lane, Paisley PAI 2LG. Tel: 0141-887 9630. *Frequency:* 96.3 FM

ARGYLL FM, Unit 6, Old Quay, Campbeltown, Argyll PA28 6ED. Tel: 01586-551800. Expected on air November 1999. *Frequency:* to be announced

BEAT 106, PO Box 25061, Glasgow G3 7WW. *Frequencies:* 105.7/106.1 FM

CENTRAL FM, 201 High Street, Falkirk FK1 1DU. Tel: 01324-611164. *Frequency:* 103.1 FM

CLAN FM, PO Box 9083, Dalziel Workspace, Motherwell ML1 1YU. Expected on air late 1999. *Frequency:* to be announced

CLYDE 1 (FM) AND 2 (AM), Clydebank Business Park, Clydebank, Glasgow G81 2RX. Tel: 0141-565 2200. *Frequencies:* 102.5 FM; 103.3 FM (Firth of Clyde); 97.0 FM (Vale of Leven); 1152 AM

DISCOVERY 102, 8 South Tay Street, Dundee DD1 1PA. Tel: 01382-901000. *Frequency:* 102.0 FM

FORTH AM AND FM, Forth House, Forth Street, Edinburgh EH1 3LF. Tel: 0131-556 9255. *Frequencies:* 1548 AM, 97.3/97.6/102.2 FM

HEARTLAND FM, Atholl Curling Rink, Lower Oakfield, Pitlochry, Perthshire PH16 5HQ. Tel: 01796-474040. *Frequency:* 97.5 FM

ISLES FM, PO Box 333, Stornoway, Isle of Lewis HS1 2PU. Tel: 01851-703333. *Frequency:* 103.0 FM

KINGDOM FM, Haig House, Haig Business Park, Markinch, Fife KY7 6AQ. Tel: 01592-753753. *Frequencies:* 95.2/96.1 FM

LOCHBROOM FM, Radio House, Mill Street, Ullapool, Wester Ross IV26 2UN. Tel: 01854-613131. *Frequency:* 102.2 FM

MORAY FIRTH RADIO, Scorguie Place, Inverness IV3 6SF. Tel: 01463-224433. *Frequencies:* 97.4 FM, 1107 AM; *local opt-outs:* MFR Speysound 96.6 FM, MFR Keith Community Radio 102.8 FM; MFR Kinnaird Radio 96.7 FM; MFR Caithness 102.5 FM

NECR (NORTH-EAST COMMUNITY RADIO), Town House, Kintore, Inverurie, Aberdeenshire AB51 0US. Tel: 01467-632909. *Frequencies:* 97.1 FM (Braemar); 102.1 FM (Meldrum and Inverurie); 102.6 FM (Kildrummy); 103.2 FM (Colpy)

NEVIS RADIO, Inverlochy, Fort William, Inverness-shire PH33 6LU. Tel: 01397-700007. *Frequencies:* 96.6 FM (Fort William); 97.0 FM (Glencoe); 102.3 FM (Skye); 102.4 FM (Loch Leven)

NORTHSOUND ONE (FM) AND TWO (AM), 45 Kings Gate, Aberdeen AB15 4EL. Tel: 01224-337000. *Frequencies:* 1035 AM, 96.9/97.6/103.0 FM

OBAN FM, 132 George Street, Oban, Argyll PA34 5NT. Tel: 01631-570057. *Frequency:* 103.3 FM

RADIO BORDERS, Tweedside Park, Galashiels TD1 3TD. Tel: 01896-759444. *Frequencies:* 96.8/97.5/103.1/103.4 FM

RADIO TAY AM AND TAY FM, 6 North Isla Street, Dundee DD3 7JQ. Tel: 01382-200800. *Frequencies:* 1161 AM, 102.8 FM (Dundee); 1584 AM, 96.4 FM (Perth)

RNA FM, Arbroath Infirmary, Rosemount Road, Arbroath, Angus DD11 2AT. Tel: 01241-879660. *Frequency:* 96.6 FM

SIBC, Market Street, Lerwick, Shetland ZE1 0JN. Tel: 01595-695299. *Frequencies:* 96.2/102.2 FM

SOUTH WEST SOUND, Campbell House, Bankend Road, Dumfries DG1 4TH. Tel: 01387-250999. *Frequencies:* 96.5/97.0/103.0 FM

WAVES RADIO PETERHEAD, Unit 2, Blackhouse Industrial Estate, Peterhead AB42 1BW. Tel: 01779-491012. *Frequency:* 101.2 FM

WEST SOUND AM AND WEST FM, Radio House, 54A Holmston Road, Ayr KA7 3BE. Tel: 01292-283662. *Frequencies:* 1035 AM, 96.7 FM (Ayr); 97.5 FM (Girvan)

Northern Ireland

CITY BEAT 96.7, Lamont Buildings, Stranmillis Embankment, Belfast BT9 5FN. Tel: 01232-205967. *Frequency:* 96.7 FM

COOL FM, PO Box 974, Belfast BT1 1RT. Tel: 01247-817181. *Frequency:* 97.4 FM

DOWNTOWN RADIO, Newtownards, Co. Down BT23 4ES. Tel: 01247-815555. *Frequencies:* 1026 AM (Belfast); 96.4 FM (Limavady); 96.6 FM (Enniskillen); 97.1 FM (Larne); 102.3 FM Ballymena; 102.4 FM (Londonderry); 103.1 FM (Newry); 103.4 FM (Newcastle)

Q102.9 FM, The Riverside Suite, Old Waterside Railway Station, Duke Street, Londonderry BT47 6DH. Tel: 01504-344449. *Frequency:* 102.9 FM

Channel Islands

104.7 ISLAND FM, 12 Westerbrook, St Sampsons, Guernsey GY2 4QQ. Tel: 01481-242000. *Frequencies:* 104.7 FM (Guernsey); 93.7 FM (Alderney)

CHANNEL 103 FM, 6 Tunnell Street, St Helier, Jersey JE2 4LU. Tel: 01534-888103. *Frequency:* 103.7 FM

PRESS AWARD WINNERS

WHAT THE PAPERS SAY AWARDS 1998
Journalist – Nick Davies, *The Guardian*
Columnist – Libby Purves, *The Times*
Editor – Simon Kelner, *The Independent*
Correspondent – David McKittrick, *The Independent*
Front Page – 'Zip Me Up Before You Go Go,' *The Sun*
Scoop – Peter Mandelson's home loan, *The Guardian*
Peter Black award (broadcasting writer) – Jaci Stephen, *Daily Mail*
Gerald Barry award (lifetime achievement) – Anthony Howard

BRITISH PRESS AWARDS 1999
National newspaper – *The Guardian*
Reporter – Mazher Mahmood, *News of the World*
Scoop – Michael Sean Gillard, Laurie Flynn, *The Guardian*, 'Exposed: the TV Drugs Fake'
Team reporting – *The Mirror*, Omagh bombing
Financial journalist – Alex Brummer, *The Guardian*
Business journalist – Neil Bennett, *Sunday Telegraph*
Foreign reporter – John Lichfield, *Independent on Sunday*
Sports reporter – Michael Calvin, *The Mail on Sunday*
Specialist reporter – Brian Deer, *The Sunday Times*
Feature writer – Deborah Ross, *The Independent*
Columnist – Rebecca Tyrrel, *The Sunday Telegraph*
Critic – Charles Spencer, *Daily Telegraph*
Cartoonist – Mac, *Daily Mail*
Young journalist – Burhan Wazir, *The Observer*
Photographer – Jeremy Selwyn, *The Evening Standard*
Sports photographer – Ian Rutherford, *The Scotsman*

REGIONAL PRESS AWARDS 1999
Regional newspaper – *Nottingham Evening Post*
Evening newspaper – *Nottingham Evening Post*
Weekly newspaper – *Westmorland Gazette*
Free newspaper – *Enfield Advertiser*
Daily or Sunday newspaper – *Sunday Life*
Campaign – *Evening Chronicle*, Newcastle, Free John Cairns
Reporter – Andrew Norfolk, *Yorkshire Post*
Scoop – Mikaela Sitford, *Manchester Evening News*
Feature writer – Rachel Lamb, *Southern Daily Echo*
Specialist reporter – Kathleen Nutt, *Edinburgh Evening News*
Sports journalist – Matthew Reeder, *Swindon Evening Advertiser*
Business and financial journalist – Bill Gleeson, *Liverpool Daily Post*
Columnist – Kate Ironside, *Western Morning News*
Young journalist – Clara Penn, *Western Morning News*
Photographer – Simon Dack, *Evening Argus* (Brighton)
Sports photographer – Kirsty Wigglesworth, *Birmingham Post and Mail*
Gold Award – Santha Rasaiah

MAGAZINE AWARDS 1999
Consumer magazine – *Men's Health*
Consumer specialist magazine – *Official UK PlayStation Magazine*
Editor (consumer) – Lindsay Nicholson, *Prima*
Writer (consumer) – Anthony Rowlinson, *Auto Express*
Specialist writer (consumer) – Ian Belcher, *Maxim*
International magazine (consumer) – *Hello!*
Business and professional magazine – *Building*
Editor (business and professional) – Sarah Woodhead, *Menswear*
Writer (business and professional) – Alistair Blair, *Real Business*
Columnist (business and professional) – Jane Salvage, *Nursing Times*
International magazine (business and professional) – *International Investment*
Editorial campaign – *Family Circle*

SERVICES BROADCASTING

The British Forces Broadcasting Service (BFBS), part of the Services Sound and Vision Corporation (SSVC) group of companies, provides HM Forces and their families with radio and television broadcasting. The broadcasting service covers Cyprus, Germany, Gibraltar, the Falkland Islands, Belize, Bosnia, Brunei, Kuwait, Saudi Arabia, Turkey, Macedonia and parts of Canada.

SSVC, Chalfont Grove, Gerrards Cross, Bucks SL9 8TN. Tel: 01494-874461. *Managing Director*, D. O. Crwys-Williams, CB

The Press

The newspaper and periodical press in the UK is large and diverse, catering for a wide variety of views and interests. There is no state control or censorship of the press, though it is subject to the laws on publication and the Press Complaints Commission (*see* below) was set up by the industry as a means of self-regulation.

The press is not state-subsidized and receives few tax concessions. The income of most newspapers and periodicals is derived largely from sales and from advertising; the press is the largest advertising medium in Britain.

SELF-REGULATION

The Press Complaints Commission was founded by the newspaper and magazine industry in January 1991 to replace the Press Council (established in 1953). It is a voluntary, non-statutory body set up to operate the press's self-regulation system following the Calcutt report in 1990 on privacy and related matters, when the industry feared that failure to regulate itself might lead to statutory regulation of the press. The performance of the Press Complaints Commission was reviewed after 18 months of operation (the *Calcutt Review of Press Self-Regulation*, presented to Parliament in January 1993) to determine whether statutory measures were required. No proposals for replacing the self-regulation system have been made to date.

The Commission is funded by the industry through the Press Standards Board of Finance.

COMPLAINTS

The Press Complaints Commission's objects are to consider, adjudicate, conciliate, and resolve complaints of unfair treatment by the press; and to ensure that the press maintains the highest professional standards with respect for generally recognized freedoms, including freedom of expression, the public's right to know, and the right of the press to operate free from improper pressure. The Commission judges newspaper and magazine conduct by a code of practice drafted by editors, agreed by the industry and ratified by the Commission.

Seven of the Commission's members are editors of national, regional and local newspapers and magazines, and nine, including the chairman, are drawn from other fields. One member has been appointed Privacy Commissioner with special powers to investigate complaints about invasion of privacy.

PRESS COMPLAINTS COMMISSION, 1 Salisbury Square, London EC4Y 8AE. Tel: 0171-353 1248. *Chairman*, Lord Wakeham, PC; *Director*, G. Black

---

NEWSPAPERS

Newspapers are usually financially independent of any political party, though most adopt a political stance in their editorial comments, usually reflecting proprietorial influence. Ownership of the national and regional daily newspapers is concentrated in the hands of large corporations whose interests cover publishing and communications. The rules on cross-media ownership, as amended by the Broadcasting Act 1996, limit the extent to which newspaper organizations (with over 20 per cent of national circulation) may become involved in broadcasting (*see* page 674).

There are 15 daily and about 17 Sunday national papers,

about 84 regional daily papers, and several hundred local papers that are published weekly or twice-weekly. Scotland, Wales and Northern Ireland all have at least one daily and one Sunday national paper.

Newspapers are usually published in either broadsheet or tabloid format. The 'quality' daily papers, i.e. those providing detailed coverage of a wide range of public matters, have a broadsheet format. The tabloid papers take a more popular approach and are more illustrated.

CIRCULATION

National Daily Newspapers

Daily Mail	2,346,000
Daily Sport	210,000
Daily Star	546,000
Daily Telegraph	1,044,000
The Express	1,092,000
Financial Times	385,000
The Guardian	401,000
The Independent	220,000
The Mirror	2,301,000
Racing Post	70,000
The Scotsman	80,000
The Sun	3,699,000
The Times	754,000

National Sunday Newspapers

Express on Sunday	1,010,000
Independent on Sunday	252,000
Mail on Sunday	2,326,000
News of the World	4,297,000
The Observer	407,000
The People	1,662,000
Scotland on Sunday	124,000
Sunday Mirror	1,985,000
Sunday Sport	250,000
Sunday Telegraph	817,000
Sunday Times	1,377,000

NATIONAL DAILY NEWSPAPERS

DAILY MAIL, Northcliffe House, 2 Derry Street, London w8 5TT. Tel: 0171-938 6000. Fax: 0171-937 3745

DAILY SPORT, 19 Great Ancoats Street, Manchester M60 4BT. Tel: 0161-236 4466. Fax: 0161-236 4535

DAILY STAR, Ludgate House, 245 Blackfriars Road, London SE1 9UX. Tel: 0171-928 8000. Fax: 0171-633 0244

DAILY TELEGRAPH, 1 Canada Square, Canary Wharf, London E14 5DT. Tel: 0171-538 5000. Fax: 0171-513 2506

THE EXPRESS, Ludgate House, 245 Blackfriars Road, London SE1 9UX. Tel: 0171-928 8000. Fax: 0171-633 0244

FINANCIAL TIMES, 1 Southwark Bridge, London SE1 9HL. Tel: 0171-873 3000. Fax: 0171-407 5700

THE GUARDIAN, 119 Farringdon Road, London ECIR 3ER. Tel: 0171-278 2332. Fax: 0171-837 2114

THE HERALD, 195 Albion Street, Glasgow G1 1QP. Tel: 0141-552 6255. Fax: 0141-552 1344

THE INDEPENDENT, 1 Canada Square, Canary Wharf, London E14 5DL. Tel: 0171-293 2000. Fax: 0171-293 2435

THE MIRROR, 1 Canada Square, Canary Wharf, London E14 5AP. Tel: 0171-293 3000. Fax: 0171-293 3405

MORNING STAR, 1–3 Ardleigh Road, London N1 4HS. Tel: 0171-254 0033. Fax: 0171-254 5950

RACING POST, 1 Canada Square, Canary Wharf, London E14 5AP. Tel: 0171-293 3000. Fax: 0171-293 3405
THE SCOTSMAN, 20 North Bridge, Edinburgh EH1 1YT. Tel: 0131-243 3207. Fax: 0131-226 7420
THE SUN, 1 Virginia Street, London E1 9XR. Tel: 0171-782 4000. Fax: 0171-583 9504
THE TIMES, 1 Pennington Street, London E1 9XN. Tel: 0171-782 5000. Fax: 0171-782 5988

REGIONAL DAILY NEWSPAPERS

BERKSHIRE

READING EVENING POST, 8 Tessa Road, Reading RG1 8NS

CAMBRIDGESHIRE

CAMBRIDGE EVENING NEWS, Winship Road, Milton, Cambridge CB4 6PP
PETERBOROUGH EVENING TELEGRAPH, New Priestgate House, 57 Priestgate, Peterborough PE1 1JW

CUMBRIA

NEWS AND STAR, Newspaper House, Dalston Road, Carlisle CA2 5UA
NORTH-WEST EVENING MAIL, Newspaper House, Abbey Road, Barrow-in-Furness LA14 5QS

DERBYSHIRE

DERBY EVENING TELEGRAPH, Northcliffe House, Meadow Road, Derby DE1 2DW

DEVON

EVENING HERALD, 17 Brest Road, Derriford Business Park, Plymouth PL6 5AA
EXPRESS AND ECHO, Heron Road, Sowton, Exeter EX2 7NF
HERALD EXPRESS, Harmsworth House, Barton Hill Road, Torquay TQ2 8JN
WESTERN MORNING NEWS, 17 Brest Road, Derriford Business Park, Plymouth PL6 5AA

DORSET

THE DAILY ECHO, Richmond Hill, Bournemouth BH2 6HH
DORSET EVENING ECHO, 57 St Thomas Street, Weymouth DT4 8EU

DURHAM

NORTHERN ECHO, Priestgate, Darlington DL1 1NF

EAST SUSSEX

THE ARGUS/EVENING ARGUS, Argus House, Crowhurst Road, Hollingbury, Brighton BN1 8AR

ESSEX

EVENING ECHO, Newspaper House, Chester Hall Lane, Basildon SS14 3BL
EVENING GAZETTE, Wickham House, 1 Northgate Street, Colchester CO1 1HA

GLOUCESTERSHIRE

THE CITIZEN, St John's Lane, Gloucester GL1 2AY
GLOUCESTERSHIRE ECHO, 1–3 Clarence Parade, Cheltenham GL50 3NZ

HAMPSHIRE

THE NEWS, The News Centre, Hilsea, Portsmouth PO2 9SX
SOUTHERN DAILY ECHO, Newspaper House, Test Lane, Retbridge, Southampton SO16 9JX

KENT

KENT TODAY, Messenger House, New Hythe Lane, Larkfield, Aylesford ME20 6SG

LANCASHIRE

BOLTON EVENING NEWS, Newspaper House, Churchgate, Bolton BL1 1DE
THE GAZETTE, Avroe House, Avroe Crescent, Blackpool FY4 2DP
LANCASHIRE EVENING POST, Oliver's Place, Fulwood, Preston PR2 9ZA
LANCASHIRE EVENING TELEGRAPH, Newspaper House, High Street, Blackburn BB1 1HT
MANCHESTER EVENING NEWS, 164 Deansgate, Manchester M60 2RD
OLDHAM EVENING CHRONICLE, 172 Union Street, Oldham OL1 1EQ
WIGAN EVENING POST, Oliver's Place, Fulwood, Preston PR2 9ZA

LEICESTERSHIRE

LEICESTER MERCURY, St George Street, Leicester LE1 9FQ

LINCOLNSHIRE

GRIMSBY EVENING TELEGRAPH, 80 Cleethorpe Road, Grimsby DN31 3EH
LINCOLNSHIRE ECHO, Brayford Wharf East, Lincoln LN5 7AT
SCUNTHORPE EVENING TELEGRAPH, Telegraph House, Doncaster Road, Scunthorpe DN15 7RE

LONDON

THE EVENING STANDARD, Northcliffe House, 2 Derry Street, London W8 5TT

MERSEYSIDE

DAILY POST, AND LIVERPOOL ECHO, PO Box 48, Old Hall Street, Liverpool L69 3EB

NORFOLK

EASTERN DAILY PRESS, AND EVENING NEWS, Prospect House, Rouen Road, Norwich NR1 1RE

NORTHAMPTONSHIRE

CHRONICLE AND ECHO, Upper Mounts, Northampton NN1 3HR
NORTHAMPTONSHIRE EVENING TELEGRAPH, Newspaper House, Ise Park, Rothwell Road, Kettering NN16 8GA

NOTTINGHAMSHIRE

NOTTINGHAM EVENING POST, Castle Wharf House, Nottingham NG1 7EU

OXFORDSHIRE

THE OXFORD MAIL, Newspaper House, Osney Mead, Oxford OX2 0EJ

SHROPSHIRE

SHROPSHIRE STAR, Ketley, Telford TF1 4HU

SOMERSET

THE BATH CHRONICLE, Windsor House, Windsor Bridge, Bath BA2 3AJ
BRISTOL EVENING POST, AND WESTERN DAILY PRESS, Temple Way, Bristol BS99 7HD

STAFFORDSHIRE

BURTON MAIL, 65–68 High Street, Burton on Trent DE14 1LE

THE SENTINEL, Sentinel House, Etruria, Stoke-on-Trent STI 5SS

SUFFOLK

EAST ANGLIAN DAILY TIMES, AND EVENING STAR, 30 Lower Brook Street, Ipswich IP4 IAN

TYNE AND WEAR

NEWCASTLE EVENING CHRONICLE, AND THE JOURNAL, Thomson House, Groat Market, Newcastle upon Tyne NEI IED
SHIELDS GAZETTE, Chapter Row, South Shields NE33 IBL
SUNDERLAND ECHO, Echo House, Pennywell, Sunderland SR4 9ER

WARWICKSHIRE

HEARTLAND EVENING NEWS, Newspaper House, 11–15 Newtown Road, Nuneaton CVII 4HP

WEST MIDLANDS

THE BIRMINGHAM POST, AND BIRMINGHAM EVENING MAIL, 28 Colmore Circus, Queensway, Birmingham B4 6AX
COVENTRY EVENING TELEGRAPH, Corporation Street, Coventry CVI IFP
EXPRESS AND STAR, 51–53 Queen Street, Wolverhampton WVI IES

WILTSHIRE

SWINDON EVENING ADVERTISER, Newspaper House, 100 Victoria Road, Swindon SNI 3BE

WORCESTERSHIRE

WORCESTER EVENING NEWS, Hylton Road, Worcester WR2 5JX

YORKSHIRE

EVENING GAZETTE, Gazette Buildings, Borough Road, Middlesbrough TSI 3AZ
HALIFAX EVENING COURIER, PO Box 19, Courier Buildings, King Cross Street, Halifax HXI 2SF
HUDDERSFIELD DAILY EXAMINER, PO Box A26, Queen Street South, Huddersfield HDI 2TD
HULL DAILY MAIL, Blundell's Corner, Beverley Road, Hull HU3 IXS
SCARBOROUGH EVENING NEWS, 17–23 Aberdeen Walk, Scarborough YOII IBB
SHEFFIELD STAR, York Street, Sheffield SI IPU
TELEGRAPH AND ARGUS, Hall Ings, Bradford BDI IJR
YORKSHIRE EVENING POST, PO Box 168, Wellington Street, Leeds LSI IRF
YORKSHIRE EVENING PRESS, PO Box 29, 76–86 Walmgate, York YOI 9YN
YORKSHIRE POST, PO Box 168, Wellington Street, Leeds LSI IRF

WALES

EVENING LEADER, Mold Business Park, Wrexham Road, Mold CH7 IXY
SOUTH WALES ARGUS, Cardiff Road, Maesglas, Newport NP9 IQW
SOUTH WALES ECHO, Thomson House, Havelock Street, Cardiff CFI IXR
SOUTH WALES EVENING POST, Adelaide Street, Swansea SAI IQT
WESTERN MAIL, Thomson House, Havelock Street, Cardiff CFI IXR

SCOTLAND

COURIER AND ADVERTISER, 2 Albert Square, Dundee DDI 9QJ

DAILY RECORD, 40 Anderston Quay, Glasgow G3 8DA
EDINBURGH EVENING NEWS, 20 North Bridge, Edinburgh EHI IYT
EVENING EXPRESS, PO Box 43, Lang Stracht, Mastrick, Aberdeen ABI5 6DF
EVENING TELEGRAPH AND POST, 2 Albert Square, Dundee DDI 9QJ
EVENING TIMES, 195 Albion Street, Glasgow GI IQP
GREENOCK TELEGRAPH, Pitreavie Business Park, Dunfermline KYII 8QS
PAISLEY DAILY EXPRESS, 1 Woodside Terrace, Glasgow G3 7UY
PRESS AND JOURNAL, PO Box 43, Lang Stracht, Mastrick, Aberdeen ABI5 6DF

NORTHERN IRELAND

BELFAST TELEGRAPH, 124–144 Royal Avenue, Belfast BTI IEB

CHANNEL ISLANDS

GUERNSEY EVENING PRESS AND STAR, PO Box 57, Guernsey GYI 3BW
JERSEY EVENING POST, PO Box 582, Five Oaks, St Saviour, Jersey JE4 8XQ

WEEKLY NEWSPAPERS

THE EXPRESS ON SUNDAY, Ludgate House, 245 Blackfriars Road, London SEI 9UX. Tel: 0171-928 8000. Fax: 0171-633 0244
INDEPENDENT ON SUNDAY, 1 Canada Square, Canary Wharf, London EI4 5DL. Tel: 0171-293 2000. Fax: 0171-293 2435
INDIA TIMES, Global House, 90 Ascot Gardens, Southall, Middx UBI 2SB. Tel: 0181-575 0151. Fax: 0181-575 5661
THE MAIL ON SUNDAY, Northcliffe House, 2 Derry Street, London W8 5TS. Tel: 0171-938 6000. Fax: 0171-937 7896
NEWS OF THE WORLD, 1 Virginia Street, London EI 9XR. Tel: 0171-782 4000. Fax: 0171-583 9504
THE OBSERVER, 119 Farringdon Road, London ECIR 3ER. Tel: 0171-278 2332. Fax: 0171-837 2114
SCOTLAND ON SUNDAY, 20 North Bridge, Edinburgh EHI IYT. Tel: 0131-243 3472. Fax: 0131-220 2443
SUNDAY BUSINESS, The Isis Building, 193 Marsh Wall, London EI4 5DT. Tel: 0171-418 9600. Fax: 0171-418 9655
THE SUNDAY HERALD, 195 Albion Street, Glasgow GI IQP. Tel: 0141-552 6255. Fax: 0141-552 1344
SUNDAY MAIL, 40 Anderston Quay, Glasgow G3 8DA. Tel: 0141-248 7000. Fax: 0141-242 3340
SUNDAY MIRROR, 1 Canada Square, Canary Wharf, London EI4 5AP. Tel: 0171-293 3000. Fax: 0171-293 3405
SUNDAY PEOPLE, 1 Canada Square, Canary Wharf, London EI4 5AP. Tel: 0171-293 3000. Fax: 0171-293 3405
SUNDAY POST, Courier Place, Dundee DDI 9QJ. Tel: 01382-223131. Fax: 01382-201064
SUNDAY SPORT, 848B Melton Road, Thurmaston, Leicester LE4 8BJ. Tel: 0116-269 4892. Fax: 0116-264 0948
THE SUNDAY TELEGRAPH, 1 Canada Square, Canary Wharf, London EI4 5DT. Tel: 0171-538 5000. Fax: 0171-512 2504
THE SUNDAY TIMES, 1 Pennington Street, London EI 9XN. Tel: 0171-782 5000. Fax: 0171-782 5988
WALES ON SUNDAY, Thomson House, Havelock Street, Cardiff CFI IXR. Tel: 01222-583583. Fax: 01222-583451

WEEKLY NEWS, Courier Place, Dundee DD1 9QJ. Tel: 01382-223131. Fax: 01382-201390

RELIGIOUS PAPERS

Alt. = Alternate; *M.* = Monthly; *Q.* = Quarterly; *W.* = Weekly

BAPTIST TIMES, PO Box 54, 129 The Broadway, Didcot, Oxon OX11 8XB. *W.*

CATHOLIC HERALD, Herald House, Lambs Passage, Bunhill Row, London EC1Y 8TQ. *W.*

CHALLENGE - THE GOOD NEWS PAPER, CPO, Garcia Estate, Canterbury Road, Worthing, W. Sussex BN13 1BW. *M.*

THE CHURCH OF ENGLAND NEWSPAPER, 10 Little College Street, London SW1P 3SH. *W.*

CHURCH OF IRELAND GAZETTE, 36 Bachelor's Walk, Lisburn, Co. Antrim BT28 1XN. *W.*

CHURCH TIMES, 33 Upper Street, London N1 OPN. *W.*

ENGLISH CHURCHMAN, 22 Lesley Avenue, Canterbury, Kent CT1 3LF. *Alt. W.*

THE FRIEND, Drayton House, 30 Gordon Street, London WC1H OBQ. *W.*

JEWISH CHRONICLE, 25 Furnival Street, London EC4A 1JT. *W.*

JEWISH TELEGRAPH, Telegraph House, 11 Park Hill, Bury Old Road, Prestwich, Manchester M25 OHH. *W.*

LIFE AND WORK, Church of Scotland, 121 George Street, Edinburgh EH2 4YN. *M.*

METHODIST RECORDER, 122 Golden Lane, London EC1Y OTL. *W.*

MIDDLE WAY, Buddhist Society, 58 Eccleston Square, London SW1V 1PH. *Q.*

ORTHODOX OUTLOOK, 42 Withens Lane, Wallasey, Merseyside L45 7NN. *Alt. M.*

PRESBYTERIAN HERALD, Church House, Fisherwick Place, Belfast BT1 6DW. *Ten times a year.*

QUAKER MONTHLY, Friends House, Euston Road, London NW1 2BJ. *M.*

REFORM, United Reformed Church, 86 Tavistock Place, London WC1H 9RT. *Eleven times a year.*

THE SIKH COURIER INTERNATIONAL, World Sikh Foundation, 33 Wargrave Road, Harrow, Middx HA2 8LL. *Q.*

THE SIKH MESSENGER, 43 Dorset Road, London SW19 3EZ. *Q.*

THE TABLET, 1 King Street Cloisters, Clifton Walk, London W6 OQZ. *W.*

THE UNIVERSE, 1st Floor, St James Building, Oxford Street, Manchester M1 6FP. *W.*

THE WAR CRY, 101 Newington Causeway, London SE1 6BN. *W.*

PERIODICALS

There are about 6,500 periodicals published in Britain. These are classified as consumer, i.e. general interest, or as trade, professional or academic.

CONSUMER PERIODICALS

Alt. = Alternate; *M.* = Monthly; *Q.* = Quarterly; *W.* = Weekly

AL MAJALLA, Arab Press House, 184 High Holborn, London WC1V 7AP. *W.*

AMATEUR GARDENING, Westover House, West Quay Road, Poole, Dorset BH15 1JG. *W.*

AMATEUR PHOTOGRAPHER, King's Reach Tower, Stamford Street, London SE1 9LS. *W.*

ANGLING TIMES, Bretton Court, Bretton, Peterborough PE3 8DZ. *W.*

ANTIQUE, 10–11 Lower John Street, London W1R 3PE. *Q.*

APOLLO, 1 Castle Lane, London SW1E 6DR. *M.*

ARENA, 3rd Floor, Block A, Exmouth House, Pine Street, London EC1R OJL. *M.*

ART MONTHLY, Suite 17, 26 Charing Cross Road, London WC2H ODG. *Ten times a year.*

ASTRONOMY NOW, PO Box 175, Tonbridge, Kent TN10 4ZY. *M.*

ATHLETICS WEEKLY, Bretton Court, Bretton, Peterborough PE3 8DZ. *W.*

AUTOCAR, 38–42 Hampton Road, Teddington, Middx TW11 OJE. *W.*

BBC GARDENER'S WORLD, Woodlands, 80 Wood Lane, London W12 OTT. *M.*

BBC GOOD FOOD MAGAZINE, Woodlands, 80 Wood Lane, London W12 OTT. *M.*

BBC HOMES AND ANTIQUES, Woodlands, 80 Wood Lane, London W12 OTT. *M.*

BBC TOP GEAR, Woodlands, 80 Wood Lane, London W12 OTT. *M.*

BBC VEGETARIAN GOOD FOOD, Woodlands, 80 Wood Lane, London W12 OTT. *M.*

BBC WILDLIFE MAGAZINE, Woodlands, 80 Wood Lane, London W12 OTT. *M.*

BELFAST GAZETTE (OFFICIAL), The Stationery Office, PO Box 276, London SW8 5DT. *W.*

BELLA, 2nd Floor, Shirley House, 25–27 Camden Road, London NW1 9LL. *W.*

BEST, 10th Floor, Portland House, Stag Place, London SW1E 5AU. *W.*

THE BIG ISSUE, 236–240 Pentonville Road, London N1 9JY. *W.*

BIKE, Bushfield House, Orton Centre, Peterborough PE2 5UW. *M.*

BIRDS, RSPB, The Lodge, Sandy, Beds SG19 2DL. *Q.*

BIRD WATCHING, Bretton Court, Bretton, Peterborough PE3 8DZ. *M.*

BOXING MONTHLY, 40 Morpeth Road, London E9 7LD. *M.*

BRIDES AND SETTING UP HOME, Vogue House, Hanover Square, London W1R OAD. *Alt. M.*

BRITISH PHILATELIC BULLETIN, 20 Brandon Street, Edinburgh EH3 5TT. *M.*

CAMPING AND CARAVANNING, Greenfields House, Westwood Way, Coventry CV4 8JH. *M.*

CAR, Bushfield House, Orton Centre, Peterborough PE2 5UW. *M.*

CARIBBEAN TIMES, 3rd Floor, Tower House, 141–149 Fonthill Road, London N4 3HF. *W.*

CAT WORLD, 10 Western Road, Shoreham-by-Sea, W. Sussex BN43 5WD. *M.*

CHAT, King's Reach Tower, Stamford Street, London SE1 9LS. *W.*

CLASSIC AND SPORTS CAR, 38–42 Hampton Road, Teddington, Middx TW11 OJE. *M.*

CLASSIC CARS, Bushfield House, Orton Centre, Peterborough PE2 5UW. *M.*

CLASSIC CD, Beauford Court, 30 Monmouth Street, Bath BA1 2BW. *Thirteen times a year.*

COARSE FISHERMAN, 67 Tyrrell Street, Leicester LE3 5SB. *M.*

COIN NEWS, PO Box 14, Honiton, Devon EX14 9YP. *M.*

COMPANY, National Magazine House, 72 Broadwick Street, London W1V 2BP. *M.*

COMPUTER AND VIDEO GAMES, Priory Court, 30–32 Farringdon Lane, London EC1R 3AU. *M.*

COMPUTER SHOPPER, 19 Bolsover Street, London W1P 7HJ. *M.*

COSMOPOLITAN, National Magazine House, 72 Broadwick Street, London W1V 2BP. *M.*

COUNTRY HOMES AND INTERIORS, King's Reach Tower, Stamford Street, London SE1 9LS. *M.*

COUNTRY LIFE, King's Reach Tower, Stamford Street, London SE1 9LS. *W.*

COUNTRY LIVING MAGAZINE, National Magazine House, 72 Broadwick Street, London W1V 2BP. *M.*

COUNTRY WALKING, Bretton Court, Bretton, Peterborough PE3 8DZ. *M.*

THE COUNTRYMAN, King's Reach Tower, Stamford Street, London SE1 9LS. *M.*

THE CRICKETER INTERNATIONAL, Beech Hanger, Ashurst, Tunbridge Wells, Kent TN3 9ST. *M.*

CYCLING WEEKLY, King's Reach Tower, Stamford Street, London SE1 9LS. *W.*

THE DALESMAN, Stable Courtyard, Broughton Hall, Skipton, N. Yorks BD23 3AE. *M.*

DALTONS WEEKLY, CI Tower, St George's Square, New Malden, Surrey KT3 4JA. *W.*

DANCE THEATRE JOURNAL, Laban Centre London, Laurie Grove, London SE14 6NH. *Three times a year.*

DANCING TIMES, Clerkenwell House, 45–47 Clerkenwell Green, London EC1R OEB. *M.*

DOG WORLD, Somerfield House, Wotton Road, Ashford, Kent TN23 6LW. *W.*

DOGS TODAY, Pankhurst Farm, Bagshot Road, West End, Woking, Surrey GU24 9QR. *M.*

THE ECOLOGIST, Unit 18, Chelsea Wharf, 15 Lots Road, London SW10 0QJ. *Alt. M.*

THE ECONOMIST, 25 St James's Street, London SW1A 1HG. *W.*

EDINBURGH GAZETTE (OFFICIAL), The Stationery Office, PO Box 276, London SW8 5DT. *Two times a week.*

ELLE, Victory House, 14 Leicester Place, London WC2H 7BP. *M.*

EMPIRE, Mappin House, 4 Winsley Street, London W1N 7AR. *M.*

ESQUIRE, National Magazine House, 72 Broadwick Street, London W1V 2BP. *M.*

ESSENTIALS, King's Reach Tower, Stamford Street, London SE1 9LS. *M.*

EXCHANGE AND MART, Link House, 25 West Street, Poole, Dorset BH15 1LL. *W.*

THE FACE, 3rd Floor, Block A, Exmouth House, Pine Street, London EC1R 0JL. *M.*

FAMILY CIRCLE, King's Reach Tower, Stamford Street, London SE1 9LS. *M.*

FHM, Mappin House, 4 Winsley Street, London W1N 7AR. *M.*

THE FIELD, King's Reach Tower, Stamford Street, London SE1 9LS. *M.*

FILM REVIEW, 9 Blades Court, Deodar Road, London SW15 2NU. *M.*

FORE!, Bretton Court, Bretton, Peterborough PE3 8DZ. *M.*

GARDEN NEWS, Apex House, Oundle Road, Peterborough PE2 9NP. *W.*

GAY TIMES, Ground Floor, Worldwide House, 116–134 Bayham Street, London NW1 0BA. *M.*

GEOGRAPHICAL JOURNAL, Royal Geographical Society, 1 Kensington Gore, London SW7 2AR. *Three times a year.*

GOLF WORLD, Bretton Court, Bretton, Peterborough PE3 8DZ. *M.*

GOOD HOLIDAY MAGAZINE, 3A High Street, Esher, Surrey KT10 9RP. *Q.*

GOOD HOUSEKEEPING, National Magazine House, 72 Broadwick Street, London W1V 2BP. *M.*

THE GOOD SKI GUIDE, 3A High Street, Esher, Surrey KT10 9RP. *Five times a year.*

GQ, Vogue House, Hanover Square, London W1R 0AD. *M.*

GRAMOPHONE, 135 Greenford Road, Sudbury Hill, Harrow, Middx HA1 3YD. *M.*

GRANTA, 2–3 Hanover Yard, Noel Road, London N1 8BE. *Q.*

THE GUARDIAN WEEKLY, 119 Farringdon Road, London EC1R 3ER. *W.*

GUIDING , 17–19 Buckingham Palace Road, London SW1W 0PT. *M.*

HANSARD, *see Parliamentary Debates*

HARPERS AND QUEEN, National Magazine House, 72 Broadwick Street, London W1V 2BP. *M.*

HAVING A BABY, National Magazine House, 72 Broadwick Street, London W1V 2BP. *Alt. M.*

HEALTH AND FITNESS MAGAZINE, Nexus House, Azalea Drive, Swanley, Kent BR8 8HU. *M.*

HELLO!, 69–71 Upper Ground, London SE1 9PQ. *W.*

HISTORY TODAY, 20 Old Compton Street, London W1V 5PE. *M.*

HOMES AND GARDENS, King's Reach Tower, Stamford Street, London SE1 9LS. *M.*

HORSE AND HOUND, King's Reach Tower, Stamford Street, London SE1 9LS. *W.*

HOUSE AND GARDEN, Vogue House, Hanover Square, London W1R 0AD. *M.*

HOUSE BEAUTIFUL, National Magazine House, 72 Broadwick Street, London W1V 2BP. *Eleven times a year.*

I-D MAGAZINE, Universal House, 251 Tottenham Court Road, London W1P 0AB. *M.*

IDEAL HOME, King's Reach Tower, Stamford Street, London SE1 9LS. *M.*

ILLUSTRATED LONDON NEWS, 20 Upper Ground, London SE1 9PF. *Twice a year.*

IN BRITAIN, Haymarket House, 1 Oxendon Street, London SW1Y 4EE. *M.*

INVESTORS CHRONICLE, Greystoke Place, Fetter Lane, London EC4A 1ND. *W.*

IRISH POST, Uxbridge House, 464 Uxbridge Road, Hayes, Middx UB4 0SP. *W.*

JAZZ JOURNAL INTERNATIONAL, 1–5 Clerkenwell Road, London EC1M 5PA. *M.*

JUST SEVENTEEN, Victory House, 14 Leicester Place, London WC2H 7BP. *W.*

LABOUR RESEARCH, 78 Blackfriars Road, London SE1 8HF. *M.*

THE LADY, 39–40 Bedford Street, London WC2E 9ER. *W.*

LAND AND LIBERTY, 177 Vauxhall Bridge Road, London SW1V 1EU. *Q.*

LITERARY REVIEW, 44 Lexington Street, London W1R 3LH. *M.*

LOADED, King's Reach Tower, Stamford Street, London SE1 9LS. *M.*

LONDON GAZETTE (OFFICIAL), The Stationery Office, PO Box 276, London SW8 5DT. *Five times a week.*

LONDON REVIEW OF BOOKS, 28–30 Little Russell Street, London WC1A 2HN. *Alt. W.*

M, National Magazine House, 72 Broadwick Street, London W1V 2BP. *Alt. M.*

MAJESTY, 26–28 Hallam Street, London W1N 6NP. *M.*

MARIE CLAIRE, King's Reach Tower, Stamford Street, London SE1 9LS. *M.*

MAX POWER, Bushfield House, Orton Centre, Peterborough PE2 5UW. *M.*

MELODY MAKER (MM), King's Reach Tower, Stamford Street, London SE1 9LS. *W.*

METEOROLOGICAL MAGAZINE, The Stationery Office, PO Box 276, London SW8 5DT. *M.*

MIZZ, King's Reach Tower, Stamford Street, London SE1 9LS. *Alt. W.*

MODEL BOATS, Nexus House, Azalea Drive, Swanley, Kent BR8 8HU. *M.*

MONEYWISE, 11 Westferry Circus, Canary Wharf, London E14 4HE. *M.*

MORE!, Victory House, 14 Leicester Place, London WC2H 7BP. *Alt. W.*

MOTHER AND BABY, Victory House, 14 Leicester Place, London WC2H 7BP. *M.*

MY WEEKLY, 80 Kingsway East, Dundee DD4 8SL. *W.*

NATURE, Porters South, Crinan Street, London N1 9SQ. *W.*

NEEDLECRAFT, Beauford Court, 30 Monmouth Street, Bath BA1 2BW. *Thirteen times a year.*

NEW INTERNATIONALIST, 55 Rectory Road, Oxford OX4 1BW. *M.*

NEW MUSICAL EXPRESS (NME), King's Reach Tower, Stamford Street, London SE1 9LS. *W.*

NEW SCIENTIST, 151 Wardour Street, London W1V 4BN. *W.*

NEW STATESMAN, 7th Floor, Victoria Station House, 191 Victoria Street, London SW1E 5NE. *W.*

NEWSWEEK, 18 Park Street, London W1Y 4HH. *W.*

NEW WOMAN, Victory House, 14 Leicester Place, London WC2H 7BP. *M.*

19, King's Reach Tower, Stamford Street, London SE1 9LS. *M.*

OK!, Northern and Shell Tower, City Harbour, London E14 9GL. *W.*

THE OLDIE, 45–46 Poland Street, London W1V 4AU. *M.*

OPERA, 1A Mountgrove Road, London N5 2LU. *M.*

OPERA NOW, 241 Shaftesbury Avenue, London WC2H 8EH. *Alt. M.*

OUR DOGS, 5 Oxford Road, Station Approach, Manchester M60 1SX. *W.*

PARENTS, Victory House, 14 Leicester Place, London WC2H 7BP. *M.*

PARLIAMENTARY DEBATES (COMMONS) (HANSARD), The Stationery Office, PO Box 276, London SW8 5DT. *Daily or weekly during parliamentary session.*

PARLIAMENTARY DEBATES (LORDS) (HANSARD), The Stationery Office, PO Box 276, London SW8 5DT. *Daily or weekly during parliamentary session.*

PEOPLE'S FRIEND, 80 Kingsway East, Dundee DD4 8SL. *W.*

PHILOSOPHY NOW, 226 Bramford Road, Ipswich IP1 4AS. *Q.*

POETRY REVIEW, 22 Betterton Street, London WC2H 9BU. *Q.*

PONY MAGAZINE, Haslemere House, Lower Street, Haslemere, Surrey GU27 2PE. *M.*

PRACTICAL BOAT OWNER, Westover House, West Quay Road, Poole, Dorset BH15 1JG. *M.*

PRACTICAL CARAVAN, 60 Waldegrave Road, Teddington, Middx TW11 8LG. *M.*

PRACTICAL HOUSEHOLDER, Nexus Hosue, Azalea Drive, Swanley, Kent BR8 8HU. *M.*

PRACTICAL PARENTING, King's Reach Tower, Stamford Street, London SE1 9LS. *M.*

PRACTICAL PHOTOGRAPHY, Apex House, Oundle Road, Peterborough PE2 9NP. *M.*

PRIMA, 10th Floor, Portland House, Stag Place, London SW1E 5AU. *M.*

PRIVATE EYE, 6 Carlisle Street, London W1V 5RG. *Alt. W.*

PROGRESS (BRAILLE TYPE), Deafblind UK, 100 Bridge Street, Peterborough PE1 1DY. *M.*

PROSPECT, 4 Bedford Square, London WC1B 3RA. *M.*

THE PUZZLER, Glenthorne House, Hammersmith Grove, London W6 0LG. *M.*

Q, Mappin House, 4 Winsley Street, London W1M 7AR. *M.*

THE RACING CALENDAR, British Horseracing Board Publications, c/o Weatherbys Group Ltd, Sanders Road, Wellingborough, Northants NN8 4BX. *W.*

RADIO TIMES, Woodlands, 80 Wood Lane, London W12 0TT. *W.*

THE RAILWAY MAGAZINE, King's Reach Tower, Stamford Street, London SE1 9LS. *M.*

RAILWAY MODELLER, Peco Publications and Publicity Ltd, Beer, Seaton, Devon EX12 3NA. *M.*

READER'S DIGEST, 11 Westferry Circus, Canary Wharf, London E14 4HE. *M.*

RIDE, Bushfield House, Orton Centre, Peterborough PE2 5UW. *M.*

RIDING, 164 Barkby Road, Leicester LE4 9LF. *M.*

RUGBY LEAGUER, Martland Mill, Martland Mill Lane, Wigan, Lancs WN5 0LX. *W.*

RUGBY WORLD, King's Reach Tower, Stamford Street, London SE1 9LS. *M.*

THE SCOTS MAGAZINE, 2 Albert Square, Dundee DD1 9QJ. *M.*

SCOTTISH FIELD, Royston House, Caroline Park, Edinburgh EH5 1QJ. *M.*

SCOUTING, Baden-Powell House, Queen's Gate, London SW7 5JS. *M.*

SEA ANGLER, Bretton Court, Bretton, Peterborough PE3 8DZ. *M.*

SHE, National Magazine House, 72 Broadwick Street, London W1V 2BP. *M.*

SHOOT, King's Reach Tower, Stamford Street, London SE1 9LS. *W.*

SHOOTING TIMES AND COUNTRY MAGAZINE, King's Reach Tower, Stamford Street, London SE1 9LS. *Alt. W.*

SKY MAGAZINE, 5th Floor, Mappin House, 4 Winsley Street, London W1N 7AR. *M.*

SLIMMING MAGAZINE, Victory House, 14 Leicester Place, London WC2H 7BP. *Ten times a year.*

SMASH HITS, Mappin House, 4 Winsley Street, London W1M 7AR. *Alt. W.*

THE SPECTATOR, 56 Doughty Street, London WC1N 2LL. *W.*

THE STRAD, 7 St John's Road, Harrow, Middx HA1 2EE. *M.*

TATLER, Vogue House, Hanover Square, London W1R 0AD. *Ten times a year.*

TENNIS WORLD, The Spendlove Centre, Enstone Road, Charlbury, Chipping Norton, Oxon OX7 3PQ. *Ten times a year.*

THIS ENGLAND, Alma House, 73 Rodney Road, Cheltenham, Glos GL50 1HT. *Q.*

TIME MAGAZINE, Brettenham House, Lancaster Place, London WC2E 7TL. *W.*

TIME OUT, Universal House, 251 Tottenham Court Road, London W1P 0AB. *W.*

THE TIMES EDUCATIONAL SUPPLEMENT, Admiral House, 66–68 East Smithfield, London E1 9XY. *W.*

THE TIMES HIGHER EDUCATION SUPPLEMENT, Admiral House, 66–68 East Smithfield, London E1 9XY. *W.*

THE TIMES LITERARY SUPPLEMENT, Admiral House, 66–68 East Smithfield, London E1 9XY. *W.*

TRIBUNE, 308 Gray's Inn Road, London WC1X 8DY. *W.*

TROUT AND SALMON, Bretton Court, Bretton, Peterborough PE3 8DZ. *M.*

TV TIMES, King's Reach Tower, Stamford Street, London SE1 9LS. *W.*

VACHER'S PARLIAMENTARY COMPANION, PO Box 3700, London SW1E 5NP. *Q.*

VANITY FAIR, Vogue House, Hanover Square, London W1R 0AD. *M.*

VIZ MAGAZINE, The New Boathouse, 136–142 Bramley Road, London W10 6SR. *Alt. M.*

VOGUE, Vogue House, Hanover Square, London W1R 0AD. *M.*

THE VOICE, 370 Coldharbour Lane, London SW9 8PL. *W.*

WEATHER, 104 Oxford Road, Reading RG1 7LL. *M.*

THE WEEKLY TELEGRAPH, 1 Canada Square, Canary Wharf, London E14 5DT. *W.*

WELSH NATION (PLAID CYMRU), 18 Park Grove, Cardiff CF1 3NB. *Q.*

WHAT CAR?, 38–42 Hampton Road, Teddington, Middx TW11 0JE. *M.*

WHICH?, 2 Marylebone Road, London NW1 4DF. *M.*

WOMAN, King's Reach Tower, Stamford Street, London SE1 9LS. *W.*

WOMAN AND HOME, King's Reach Tower, Stamford Street, London SE1 9LS. *M.*

WOMAN'S JOURNAL, King's Reach Tower, Stamford Street, London SE1 9LS. *M.*

WOMAN'S OWN, King's Reach Tower, Stamford Street, London SE1 9LS. *W.*

WOMAN'S REALM, King's Reach Tower, Stamford Street, London SE1 9LS. *W.*

WOMAN'S WEEKLY, King's Reach Tower, Stamford Street, London SE1 9LS. *W.*

THE WORLD OF INTERIORS, Vogue House, Hanover Square, London W1R 0AD. *M.*

YACHTING MONTHLY, King's Reach Tower, Stamford Street, London SE1 9LS. *M.*

YOUR GARDEN, Westover House, West Quay Road, Poole, Dorset BH15 1JG. *M.*

ZEST, National Magazine House, 72 Broadwick Street, London W1V 2BP. *M.*

ZM, National Magazine House, 72 Broadwick Street, London W1V 2BP. *Alt. M.*

TRADE, PROFESSIONAL AND ACADEMIC PERIODICALS

Alt. = Alternate; *M.* = Monthly; *Q.* = Quarterly; *W.* = Weekly

ACCOUNTANCY, Institute of Chartered Accountants, 40 Bernard Street, London WC1N 1LD. *M.*

ACCOUNTANCY AGE, VNU House, 32–34 Broadwick Street, London W1A 2HG. *W.*

THE ACTUARY, 6th Floor, 195 Albion Street, Glasgow G1 1QQ. *M.*

AGRICULTURE AND EQUIPMENT INTERNATIONAL, Nottingham Trent University, Library and Information Services, Dryden Street, Nottingham NG1 4FZ. *Alt. M.*

ANTIQUARIAN BOOK MONTHLY (ABM), PO Box 97, High Wycombe, Bucks HP10 8QT. *M.*

ANTIQUE DEALER AND COLLECTORS GUIDE, PO Box 805, London SE10 8TD. *M.*

ANTIQUES TRADE GAZETTE, 17 Whitcomb Street, London WC2H 7PL. *W.*

THE ARCHITECTS' JOURNAL, 151 Rosebery Avenue, London EC1R 4QX. *W.*

THE ARCHITECTURAL REVIEW, 151 Rosebery Avenue, London EC1R 4QX. *M.*

THE AUTHOR, Society of Authors, 84 Drayton Gardens, London SW10 9SB. *Q.*

THE BIOCHEMIST, The Biochemical Society, 59 Portland Place, London W1N 3AJ. *Alt. M.*

BIOLOGIST, Institute of Biology, 20–22 Queensberry Place, London SW7 2DZ. *Five times a year.*

THE BOOKSELLER, 12 Dyott Street, London WC1A 1DF. *W.*

BRAIN: A JOURNAL OF NEUROLOGY, Oxford University Press, Science, Medical and Journal Division, Great Clarendon Street, Oxford OX2 6DP. *M.*

BREWING AND DISTILLING INTERNATIONAL, Southbound House, 163 Burton Road, Branston, Burton on Trent, Staffs DE14 3DP. *M.*

BRITISH BAKER, Quantum House, 19 Scarbrook Road, Croydon CR9 1LX. *W.*

BRITISH DENTAL JOURNAL, BMA House, Tavistock Square, London WC1H 9JR. *Alt. W.*

BRITISH FOOD JOURNAL, 60–62 Toller Lane, Bradford, W. Yorks BD8 9BY. *Eleven times a year.*

BRITISH JOURNAL OF PHOTOGRAPHY, 39 Earlham Street, London WC2H 9LD. *W.*

BRITISH JOURNAL OF PSYCHIATRY, Royal College of Psychiatrists, 17 Belgrave Square, London SW1X 8PG. *M.*

BRITISH JOURNAL OF PSYCHOLOGY, British Psychological Society, St Andrews House, 48 Princess Road East, Leicester LE1 7DR. *Q.*

BRITISH MEDICAL JOURNAL, British Medical Association, BMA House, Tavistock Square, London WC1H 9JR. *W.*

BRITISH PRINTER, Miller Freeman House, Sovereign Way, Tonbridge, Kent TN9 1RW. *M.*

BRITISH TAX REVIEW, 100 Avenue Road, London NW3 3PF. *Alt. M.*

BUILDING, Exchange Tower, 2 Harbour Exchange Square, London E14 9GE. *W.*

BUILDING TRADE AND INDUSTRY, 131–133 Duckmoor Road, Ashton Gate, Bristol BS3 2BH. *M.*

BUSINESS EDUCATION TODAY, Pitman Publishing, 128 Long Acre, London WC2E 9AN. *Alt. M.*

CA MAGAZINE, Institute of Chartered Accountants of Scotland, 27 Queen Street, Edinburgh EH2 1LA. *M.*

CABINET MAKER, Miller Freeman House, Sovereign Way, Tonbridge, Kent TN9 1RW. *W.*

CAMPAIGN, 174 Hammersmith Road, London W6 7JP. *W.*

CARPET AND FLOORCOVERINGS REVIEW, Miller Freeman House, Sovereign Way, Tonbridge, Kent TN9 1RW. *Alt. W.*

CATERER AND HOTELKEEPER, Quadrant House, The Quadrant, Sutton, Surrey SM2 5AS. *W.*

CHEMIST AND DRUGGIST, Miller Freeman House, Sovereign Way, Tonbridge, Kent TN9 1RW. *W.*

CHEMISTRY AND INDUSTRY, 15 Belgrave Square, London SW1X 8PS. *Alt. W.*

CHEMISTRY IN BRITAIN, Royal Society of Chemistry, Burlington House, Piccadilly, London W1V 0BN. *M.*

CHILD EDUCATION, Villiers House, Clarendon Avenue, Leamington Spa, Warks CV32 5PR. *M.*

CLASSICAL MUSIC, 241 Shaftesbury Avenue, London WC2H 8EH. *Alt. W.*

COMMUNITY CARE, Quadrant House, The Quadrant, Sutton, Surrey SM2 5AS. *W.*

COMPUTER WEEKLY, Quadrant House, The Quadrant, Sutton, Surrey SM2 5AS. *W.*

COMPUTING, VNU House, 32–34 Broadwick Street, London W1A 2HG. *W.*

CONSTRUCTION NEWS, 151 Rosebery Avenue, London EC1R 4QX. *W.*

CONTAINER MANAGEMENT, 4th Floor, Regal House, 70 London Road, Twickenham, Middx TW1 3QS. *M.*

CONTRACT JOURNAL, Quadrant House, The Quadrant, Sutton, Surrey SM2 5AS. *W.*

CONTROL AND INSTRUMENTATION, City Reach, 5 Greenwich View Place, Millharbour, London E14 9NN. *M.*

COUNTRYSIDE FOCUS, The Countryside Agency, John Dower House, Crescent Place, Cheltenham, Glos GL50 3RA. *Q.*

CRAFTS MAGAZINE, Crafts Council, 44A Pentonville Road, London N1 9BY. *Alt. M.*

THE CRIMINOLOGIST, Tolley House, 2 Addiscombe Road, Croydon CR9 5AF. *Q.*

DAIRY FARMER AND DAIRY BEEF PRODUCER, 2 Wharfedale Road, Ipswich IP1 4LG. *M.*

DAIRY INDUSTRIES INTERNATIONAL, Apex House, London Road, Gravesend, Kent DA11 9JA. *M.*

THE DENTIST, Unit 2, Riverview Business Park, Walnut Tree Close, Guildford, Surrey GU1 4QT. *M.*

DESIGN WEEK, St Giles House, 49–50 Poland Street, London W1V 4AX. *W.*

THE DIRECTOR, (Journal of the Institute of Directors), 116 Pall Mall, London SW1Y 5ED. *M.*

DRAPERS RECORD, 67 Clerkenwell Road, London EC1R 5BH. *W.*

THE ECONOMIC JOURNAL, 108 Cowley Road, Oxford OX4 1JF. *Alt. M.*

EDUCATION TODAY, Datateam Publishing Ltd, Fairmeadow, Maidstone, Kent ME14 1NG. *Nine times a year.*

ELECTRICAL AND RADIO TRADING, Queensway House, 2 Queensway, Redhill, Surrey RH1 1QS. *W.*

ELECTRICAL REVIEW, Quadrant House, The Quadrant, Sutton, Surrey SM2 5AS. *Alt. W.*

ELECTRICAL TIMES, Quadrant House, The Quadrant, Sutton, Surrey SM2 5AS. *M.*

ELECTRONIC ENGINEERING, City Reach, 5 Greenwich View Place, Millharbour, London E14 9NN. *M.*

THE ENGINEER, City Reach, 5 Greenwich View Place, Millharbour, London E14 9NN. *W.*

ENGINEERING, Chester Court, High Street, Knowle, Solihull, W. Midlands B93 0LL. *Eleven times a year.*

THE ENGLISH HISTORICAL REVIEW, Pearson Education, Edinburgh Gate, Harlow, Essex CM20 2JE. *Five times a year.*

ENGLISH TODAY, Cambridge University Press, The Edinburgh Building, Shaftesbury Road, Cambridge CB2 2RU. *Q.*

EQUITY JOURNAL, Guild House, Upper St Martin's Lane, London WC2H 9EG. *Q.*

ESTATES GAZETTE, 151 Wardour Street, London W1V 4BN. *W.*

FAIRPLAY INTERNATIONAL SHIPPING WEEKLY, 20 Ullswater Crescent, Ullswater Business Park, Coulsdon, Surrey CR5 2HR. *W.*

FARMERS WEEKLY, Quadrant House, The Quadrant, Sutton, Surrey SM2 5AS. *W.*

FINANCIAL WORLD, 4–9 Burgate Lane, Canterbury, Kent CT1 2XJ. *M.*

FIRE, Queensway House, 2 Queensway, Redhill, Surrey RH1 1QS. *M.*

FIRE PREVENTION, Fire Protection Association, Melrose Avenue, Borehamwood, Herts WD6 2BJ. *Ten times a year.*

FISHING NEWS INTERNATIONAL, Meed House, 21 John Street, London WC1N 2BP. *M.*

FISH TRADER, Queensway House, 2 Queensway, Redhill, Surrey RH1 1QS. *M.*

FLIGHT INTERNATIONAL, Quadrant House, The Quadrant, Sutton, Surrey SM2 5AS. *W.*

FOOD TRADE REVIEW, Station House, Hortons Way, Westerham, Kent TN16 1BZ. *M.*

FORESTRY AND BRITISH TIMBER, Miller Freeman House, Sovereign Way, Tonbridge, Kent TN9 1RW. *M.*

FOUNDRY TRADE JOURNAL, Queensway House, 2 Queensway, Redhill, Surrey RH1 1QS. *Alt. W.*

FROZEN AND CHILLED FOODS, Queensway House, 2 Queensway, Redhill, Surrey RH1 1QS. *M.*

FUEL, The Boulevard, Langford Lane, Kidlington, Oxon OX5 1GB. *Fifteen times a year.*

GAS ENGINEERING AND MANAGEMENT, Institution of Gas Engineers, 21 Portland Place, London W1N 3AF. *Ten times a year.*

GEOGRAPHY, Geographical Association, 160 Solly Street, Sheffield S1 4BF. *Q.*

GEOLOGICAL MAGAZINE, Cambridge University Press, The Edinburgh Building, Shaftesbury Road, Cambridge CB2 2RU. *Alt. M.*

THE GROCER, Broadfield Park, Crawley, W. Sussex RH11 9RT. *W.*

GROWER, Nexus House, Azalea Drive, Swanley, Kent BR8 8HU. *W.*

HAIRDRESSERS' JOURNAL INTERNATIONAL, Quadrant House, The Quadrant, Sutton, Surrey SM2 5AS. *W.*

THE HEALTH SERVICE JOURNAL, Porters South, 4–6 Crinan Street, London N1 9XW. *W.*

HEATING, VENTILATING AND PLUMBING, Hereford House, Bridle Path, Croydon, Surrey CR9 4NL. *Ten times a year.*

HISTORY, 108 Cowley Road, Oxford OX4 1JF. *Q.*

INDEX ON CENSORSHIP, Writers and Scholars International Ltd, 33 Islington High Street, London N1 9LH. *Alt. M.*

INDUSTRIAL EXCHANGE AND MART, Link House, 25 West Street, Poole, Dorset BH15 1LL. *W.*

INDUSTRIAL RELATIONS JOURNAL, 108 Cowley Road, Oxford OX4 1JF. *Alt. M.*

INTERNATIONAL AFFAIRS, Cambridge University Press, The Edinburgh Building, Shaftesbury Road, Cambridge CB2 2RU. *Q.*

JANE'S DEFENCE WEEKLY, Sentinel House, 163 Brighton Road, Coulsdon, Surrey CR5 2YH. *W.*

THE JOURNALIST, National Union of Journalists, Acorn House, 314-320 Gray's Inn Road, London WC1X 8DP. *Alt. M.*

JOURNAL OF ALTERNATIVE AND COMPLEMENTARY MEDICINE, 9 Rickett Street, London SW6 1RU. *M.*

JOURNAL OF THE BRITISH ASTRONOMICAL ASSOCIATION, Burlington House, Piccadilly, London W1V 9AG. *Alt. M.*

JOURNAL OF THE CHEMICAL SOCIETY, Thomas Graham House, Science Park, Milton Road, Cambridge CB4 4WF. *Irregular.*

JUSTICE OF THE PEACE REPORTS, Tolley House, 2 Addiscombe Road, Croydon CR9 5AF. *Alt. W.*

THE LANCET, 42 Bedford Square, London WC1B 3SL. *W.*

LAW QUARTERLY REVIEW, 100 Avenue Road, London NW3 3PF. *Q.*

THE LAW REPORTS, 3 Stone Buildings, Lincoln's Inn, London WC2A 3XN. *M.*

LAW SOCIETY'S GAZETTE, 50 Chancery Lane, London WC2A 1SX. *W.*

LEATHER: THE INTERNATIONAL JOURNAL, Miller Freeman House, Sovereign Way, Tonbridge, Kent TN9 1RW. *M.*

LEISURE WEEK, St Giles House, 49–50 Poland Street, London W1V 4AX. *Alt. W.*

LIBRARY ASSOCIATION RECORD, 7 Ridgmount Street, London WC1E 7AE. *M.*

LLOYD'S LOADING LIST, Sheepen Place, Colchester, Essex CO3 3LP. *W.*

LLOYD'S SHIPPING INDEX, Sheepen Place, Colchester, Essex CO3 3LP. *W.*

LOCAL GOVERNMENT CHRONICLE, 33–39 Bowling Green Lane, London EC1R 0DA. *W.*

MACHINERY AND PRODUCTION ENGINEERING, Franks Hall, Franks Lane, Horton Kirby, Dartford DA4 9LL. *Alt. W.*

MACHINERY MARKET, 6 Blyth Road, Bromley, Kent BR1 3RX. *W.*

MANAGEMENT ACCOUNTING, Chartered Institute of Management Accountants, 63 Portland Place, London W1N 4AB. *M.*

MANAGEMENT TODAY, 174 Hammersmith Road, London W6 7JP. *M.*

MANAGING INFORMATION, ASLIB, Staple Hall, Stone House Court, London EC3A 7PB. *M.*

MANUFACTURING CHEMIST, City Reach, 5 Greenwich View Place, London EI4 9NN. *M.*

MARKETING, 174 Hammersmith Rd., London W6 7JP. *W.*

MARKETING WEEK, St Giles House, 49–50 Poland Street, London WIV 4AX. *W.*

MATERIALS RECYCLING WEEK, 19th Floor, Leon House, 233 High Street, Croydon, Surrey CRO 9XT. *W.*

MATERIALS WORLD, Institute of Materials, 1 Carlton House Terrace, London SWIY 5DB. *M.*

MEAT TRADES JOURNAL, Quantum House, 19 Scarbrook Road, Croydon, Surrey CR9 IQH. *W.*

MEDIA WEEK, Quantum House, 19 Scarbrook Road, Croydon, Surrey CR9 ILX. *W.*

METALS INDUSTRY NEWS, Queensway House, 2 Queensway, Redhill, Surrey RHI IQS. *Alt. M.*

MINING JOURNAL, 60 Worship St., London EC2A 2HD. *W.*

MOTOR TRANSPORT, Quadrant House, The Quadrant, Sutton, Surrey SM2 5AS. *W.*

MUNICIPAL JOURNAL, 32 Vauxhall Bridge Road, London SWIV 2SS. *W.*

MUSIC JOURNAL, Incorporated Society of Musicians, 10 Stratford Place, London WIN 9AE. *M.*

MUSIC WEEK, 8 Montague Close, London Bridge, London SEI 9UR. *W.*

MUSICIAN, 241 Shaftesbury Avenue, London WC2H 8EH. *Q.*

NUCLEAR ENGINEERING INTERNATIONAL, Wilmington House, Church Hill, Wilmington, Dartford, Kent DA2 7EF. *M.*

NURSING TIMES, Porters South, Crinan Street, London NI 9XW. *W.*

OFF-LICENCE NEWS, Broadfield Park, Crawley, W. Sussex RHII 9RT. *W.*

OPTICIAN, Quadrant House, The Quadrant, Sutton, Surrey SM2 5AS. *W.*

PACKAGING WEEK, Miller Freeman House, Sovereign Way, Tonbridge, Kent TN9 IRW. *W.*

PATENT WORLD, 69--77 Paul Street, London EC2A 4LQ. *Ten times a year.*

PC PLUS, Kingsgate House, 536 Kings Road, London SWIO OTE. *M.*

PEOPLE MANAGEMENT, Institute of Personnel and Development, 17 Britton St., London ECIM 9NQ. *Alt. W.*

PERSONAL COMPUTER WORLD, VNU House, 32–34 Broadwick Street, London WIA 2HG. *M.*

PHARMACEUTICAL JOURNAL, Royal Pharmaceutical Society of Great Britain, 1 Lambeth High Street, London SEI 7JN. *W.*

PHILOSOPHY (JOURNAL OF THE ROYAL INSTITUTE OF PHILOSOPHY), Cambridge University Press, The Edinburgh Building, Shaftesbury Road, Cambridge CB2 2RU. *Q.*

THE PHOTOGRAPHER, British Institute of Professional Photography, Fox Talbot House, Amwell End, Ware, Herts SGI2 9HN. *Ten times a year.*

PHYSICS WORLD, Dirac House, Temple Back, Bristol BSI 6BE. *M.*

POLICE REVIEW, 5th Floor, Celcon House, 289–293 High Holborn, London WCIV 7HZ. *W.*

THE PRACTITIONER, City Reach, 5 Greenwich View Place, Millharbour, London EI4 9NN. *M.*

PRESS GAZETTE, Quantum House, 19 Scarbrook Road, Croydon, Surrey CR9 ILX. *W.*

PRINTING WORLD, Miller Freeman House, Sovereign Way, Tonbridge, Kent TN9 IRW. *W.*

PROBATION JOURNAL, National Association of Probation Officers, 3–4 Chivalry Road, London SWII IHT. *Q.*

PROFESSIONAL CARE OF MOTHER AND CHILD, PO Box 100, Chichester, W. Sussex POI8 8HD. *Alt. M.*

THE PSYCHOLOGIST, British Psychological Society, St Andrews House, 48 Princess Road East, Leicester LEI 7DR. *M.*

QUARRY MANAGEMENT, 7 Regent Street, Nottingham NGI 5BS. *M.*

RAILWAY GAZETTE INTERNATIONAL, Quadrant House, The Quadrant, Sutton, Surrey SM2 5AS. *M.*

RATING AND VALUATION REPORTER, 4 Breams Buildings, London EC4A IAQ. *M.*

RETAIL NEWSAGENT, Robert Taylor House, 11 Angel Gate, City Road, London ECIV 2PT. *W.*

RETAIL WEEK, Maclaren House, PO Box 109, Croydon CR9 IQH. *W.*

RUSI JOURNAL, Royal United Services Institute for Defence Studies, Whitehall, London SWIA 2ET. *Alt. M.*

SCREEN INTERNATIONAL, 33–39 Bowling Green Lane, London ECIR ODA. *W.*

SHIPPING WORLD AND SHIPBUILDER, 1A Sutton Court Road, Sutton, Surrey SMI IHW. *M.*

SOCIOLOGICAL REVIEW, 108 Cowley Road, Oxford OX4 IJF. *Q.*

SOLICITORS JOURNAL, 21–27 Lamb's Conduit Street, London WCIN 3NJ. *W.*

THE STAGE, 47 Bermondsey Street, London SEI 3XT. *W.*

STRUCTURAL ENGINEER (INSTITUTION OF STRUCTURAL ENGINEERS), 11 Upper Belgrave Street, London SWIX 8BH. *Alt. W.*

THE SURVEYOR, 32 Vauxhall Bridge Road, London SWIV 2SS. *W.*

TAXATION PRACTITIONER (CHARTERED INSTITUTE OF TAXATION), 12 Upper Belgrave Street, London SWIX 8BB. *M.*

TAXI, Taxi House, 7–11 Woodfield Road, London W9 2BA. *Alt. W.*

THE TEACHER, National Union of Teachers, Hamilton House, Mabledon Place, London WCIH 9BD. *Eight times a year.*

TEACHING HISTORY, The Historical Association, 59A Kennington Park Road, London SEII 4JH. *Q.*

TELEVISION, Royal Television Society, Holborn Hall, 100 Gray's Inn Road, London WCIX 8AL. *Nine times a year.*

TEXTILE MONTH, Perkin House, 1 Longlands Street, Bradford, W. Yorks BDI 2TB. *M.*

TIMBER AND WOOD PRODUCTS, Miller Freeman House, Sovereign Way, Tonbridge, Kent TN9 IRW. *W.*

TOBACCO EUROPE, Queensway House, 2 Queensway, Redhill, Surrey RHI IQS. *Eight times a year.*

TOWN AND COUNTRY PLANNING, Town and Country Planning Association, 17 Carlton House Terrace, London SWIY 5AS. *M.*

TOWN PLANNING REVIEW, Liverpool University Press, Senate House, Abercromby Sq., Liverpool L69 3BX. *Q.*

TRADE MARKS JOURNAL, Patent Office, Cardiff Road, Newport, Gwent NP9 IRH. *W.*

THE TRADER, Link House, 25 West Street, Poole, Dorset BHI5 ILL. *W.*

TRAVEL TRADE GAZETTE (UK AND IRELAND), 1st Floor, City Reach, 5 Greenwich View Place, Mill Harbour, London EI4 9NN. *W.*

VETERINARY RECORD, British Veterinary Association, 24–28 Oval Road, London NWI 7DX. *W.*

WEEKLY LAW REPORTS, 3 Stone Buildings, Lincoln's Inn, London WC2A 3XN. *W.*

WOODCARVING, Castle Place, 166 High Street, Lewes, E. Sussex BN7 IXU. *Eight times a year.*

WORLD'S FAIR, 2 Daltry Street, Oldham, Lancs OLI 4BB. *W.*

Book Publishers

The following list is one comprising publishers whose names are most familiar to the general public.

ALLAN (IAN), Riverdene Business Park, Molesey Road, Hersham KT12 4RG. Tel: 01923-266600

ALLEN & UNWIN, 19 Compton Terrace, London N1 2UN. Tel: 0171-607 5050

ALLISON & BUSBY, 114 New Cavendish Street, London W1M 7FD. Tel: 0171-636 2942

APPLE PRESS, Fitzpatrick Building, 188–194 York Way, London N7 9QR. Tel: 0171-700 2929

ARNOLD, 338 Euston Road, London NW1 3BH. Tel: 0171-873 6000

ARROW BOOKS, 20 Vauxhall Bridge Road, London SW1V 2SA. Tel: 0171-840 8400

ASHGATE, Croft Road, Aldershot GU11 3HR. Tel: 01252-331551

ATHLONE PRESS, 1 Park Drive, London NW11 7SG. Tel: 0181-458 0888

AURUM PRESS, 25 Bedford Avenue, London WC1B 3AT. Tel: 0171-637 3225

BANTAM BOOKS, 61 Uxbridge Road, London W5 5SA. Tel: 0181-579 2652

BARRIE & JENKINS, 20 Vauxhall Bridge Road, London SW1V 2SA. Tel: 0171-840 8400

BARTHOLOMEW, 77 Fulham Palace Road, London W6 8JB. Tel: 0181-741 7070

BATSFORD (B. T.), 583 Fulham Road, London SW6 5BY. Tel: 0171-471 1100

BERLITZ PUBLISHING CO., Fourth Floor, 9 Grosvenor Street, London W1X 9FB. Tel: 0171-518 8300

BLACK (A. & C.), 35 Bedford Row, London WC1R 4JH. Tel: 0171-242 0946

BLACKWELL PUBLISHERS, 108 Cowley Road, Oxford OX4 1JF. Tel: 01865-791100

BLOOMSBURY PUBLISHING, 38 Soho Square, London W1V 5DF. Tel: 0171-494 2111

BOWKER-SAUR, Windsor Court, East Grinstead House, East Grinstead RH19 1XA. Tel: 01342-326972

BOXTREE, 25 Eccleston Place, London SW1W 9NF. Tel: 0171-881 8000

BOYARS (MARION), 24 Lacy Road, London SW15 1NL. Tel: 0181-788 9522

BRIMAX BOOKS, 2-4 Heron Quay, London E14 4JB. Tel: 0171-531 8400

BUTTERWORTH & CO., PO Box LB327, London WC2A 1ER. Tel: 0171-400 2500

CADOGAN BOOKS, Morris Communications, West End House, 11 Hills Place, London W1R 1AH. Tel: 0171-287 6555

CAMBRIDGE UNIVERSITY PRESS, The Edinburgh Building, Shaftesbury Road, Cambridge CB2 2RU. Tel: 01223-325566

CANONGATE BOOKS, 14 High Street, Edinburgh EH1 1TE. Tel: 0131-557 5111

CAPE (JONATHAN), 20 Vauxhall Bridge Road, London SW1V 2SA. Tel: 0171-840 8400

CASSELL, 125 Strand, London WC2R 0BB. Tel: 0171-420 5555

CAVENDISH PUBLISHING, The Glass House, Wharton Street, London WC1X 9PX. Tel: 0171-278 8000

CENTURY PUBLISHING CO., 20 Vauxhall Bridge Road, London SW1V 2SA. Tel: 0171-840 8400

CHAMBERS, 43–45 Annandale Street, Edinburgh EH7 4AZ. Tel: 0131-556 5929

CHATTO & WINDUS, 20 Vauxhall Bridge Road, London SW1V 2SA. Tel: 0171-840 8400

CHIVERS PRESS, Windsor Bridge Road, Bath BA2 3AX. Tel: 01225-335336

CHURCH HOUSE PUBLISHING, Church House, Great Smith Street, London SW1P 3NZ. Tel: 0171-898 1451

CHURCHILL LIVINGSTONE, 24–28 Oval Road, London NW1 7DX. Tel: 0171-267 4466

CLARK (T. & T.), 59 George Street, Edinburgh EH2 2LQ. Tel: 0131-225 4703

CONSTABLE & CO., 3 The Lanchesters, 162 Fulham Palace Road, London W6 9ER. Tel: 0181-741 3663

CORGI BOOKS, 61-63 Uxbridge Road, London W5 5SA. Tel: 0181-579 2652

DARTON, LONGMAN & TODD, 1 Spencer Court, 140–142 Wandsworth High Street, London SW18 4JJ. Tel: 0181-875 0134

DAVID & CHARLES, Brunel House, Newton Abbot, Devon TQ1 4PU. Tel: 01626-323200

DEAN & SON, 2-4 Heron Quay, London E14 4JB. Tel: 0171-531 8400

DENT (J. M.) & SONS, 5 Upper St Martin's Lane, London WC2H 9EA. Tel: 0171-240 3444

DEUTSCH (ANDRE), 76 Dean Street, London W1V 5HA. Tel: 0171-316 4450

DORLING KINDERSLEY, 9 Henrietta Street, London WC2E 8PS. Tel: 0171-836 5411

DOUBLEDAY, 61-63 Uxbridge Road, London W5 5SA. Tel: 0181-579 2652

DUCKWORTH & CO., 61 Frith Street, London W1V 5TA. Tel: 0171-434 4242

EBURY PRESS, 20 Vauxhall Bridge Road, London SW1V 2SA. Tel: 0171-840 8400

EDINBURGH UNIVERSITY PRESS, 22 George Square, Edinburgh EH8 9LF. Tel: 0131-650 4220

ELEMENT BOOKS, The Old School House, The Courtyard, Bell Street, Shaftesbury, Dorset SP7 8BP. Tel: 01747-851448

ELSEVIER SCIENCE, Oxford Spires, The Boulevard, Kidlington, Oxon OX5 1GB. Tel: 01865-843000

ENCYCLOPAEDIA BRITANNICA INTERNATIONAL, 12 Golden Square, London W1R 3AF. Tel: 0171-862 4000

EPWORTH PRESS, SCM Press, 9–17 St Albans Place, London N1 0NX. Tel: 0171-359 8033

EVANS BROS, 2A Portman Mansions, Chiltern Street, London W1M 1LE. Tel: 0171-935 7160

EVERYMAN'S LIBRARY, Fourth Floor, Gloucester Mansions, 140 Shaftesbury Avenue, London WC2H 8HD. Tel: 0171-539 7600

FABER & FABER, 3 Queen Square, London WC1N 3AU. Tel: 0171-465 0045

FOULIS (G. T.), Sparkford, Yeovil, Somerset BA22 7JJ. Tel: 01963-440635

FOULSHAM (W.) & CO., Bennetts Close, Cippenham, Slough SL1 5AP. Tel: 01753-526769

FOURTH ESTATE, 6 Salem Road, London W2 4BU. Tel: 0171-727 8993

FRENCH (SAMUEL), 52 Fitzroy Street, London W1P 6JR. Tel: 0171-387 9373

FT LAW & TAX, 100 Avenue Road, London NW3 3PF. Tel: 0171-449 1104

GIBBONS (STANLEY), 5 Parkside, Christchurch Road, Ringwood, Hants BH24 3SH. Tel: 01425-472363

GINN & CO., Linacre House, Jordan Hill, Oxford OX2 8DP. Tel: 01865-888000

GLOUCESTER PRESS, 96 Leonard Street, London EC2A 4XD. Tel: 0171-739 2929

GOWER PUBLISHING CO., Croft Road, Aldershot, Hants GU11 3HR. Tel: 01252-331551

GRANTA BOOKS, 2/3 Hanover Yard, Noel Road, London N1 8BE. Tel: 0171-704 9776

GUINNESS PUBLISHING, 338 Euston Road, London NW1 3BD. Tel: 0171-891 4567

HALE (ROBERT), 45 Clerkenwell Green, London EC1R 0HT. Tel: 0171-251 2661

HAMILTON (HAMISH), 27 Wrights Lane, London W8 5TZ. Tel: 0171-416 3000

HAMLYN, 2–4 Heron Quay, London E14 4JB. Tel: 0171-531 8400

HARCOURT BRACE, 24 Oval Road, London NW1 7DX. Tel: 0171-424 4200

HARPERCOLLINS PUBLISHERS, 77/85 Fulham Palace Road, London W6 8JB. Tel: 0181-741 7070

HARRAP, New Penderel House, 283–288 High Holborn, London, WC1V 7HZ. Tel: 0171-903 9999

HAYNES (J. H.), Sparkford, Yeovil, Somerset BA22 7JJ. Tel: 01963-440635

HEINEMANN (WILLIAM), (Adults' books), 20 Vauxhall Bridge Road, London SW1V 2SA. Tel: 0171-840 8400; (Children's books), 2–4 Heron Quay, London E14 4JB. Tel: 0171-531 8400

HERBERT PRESS, 35 Bedford Row, London WC1R 4JH. Tel: 0171-242 0946

HIPPO BOOKS, 1–19 New Oxford Street, London WC1A 1NU. Tel: 0171-421 9000

HMSO, see Stationery Office Books

HODDER HEADLINE, 338 Euston Road, London NW1 3BH. Tel: 0171-873 6000

INTERNATIONAL THOMSON PUBLISHING, 2–6 Boundary Row, London SE1 8HN. Tel: 0171-497 1422

ISIS LARGE PRINT BOOKS, 7 Centremead Road, Osney Mead, Oxford OX2 0ES. Tel: 01865-250333

JARROLD PUBLISHING, Whitefriars, Norwich NR3 1TR. Tel: 01603-763300

JORDAN PUBLISHING, 21 St Thomas Street, Bristol BS1 6JS. Tel: 0117-923 0600

JOSEPH (MICHAEL), 27 Wrights Lane, London W8 5TZ. Tel: 0171-416 3000

KEGAN PAUL INTERNATIONAL, PO Box 256, London WC1B 3SW. Tel: 0171-580 5511

KINGFISHER, New Penderel House, 283–288 High Holborn, London, WC1V 7HZ. Tel: 0171-903 9999

KINGSLEY (JESSICA) PUBLISHERS, 116 Pentonville Road, London N1 9JB. Tel: 0171-833 2307

KINGSWAY PUBLICATIONS, Lottbridge Drove, Eastbourne BN23 6NT. Tel: 01323- 437700

KOGAN PAGE, 120 Pentonville Road, London N1 9JN. Tel: 0171-278 0433

LADYBIRD BOOKS, Beeches Road, Loughborough LE11 2NQ. Tel: 01509-268021

LASCELLES (ROGER), 47 York Road, Brentford, Middx TW8 0QP. Tel: 0181-847 0935

LAW SOCIETY, 113 Chancery Lane, London WC2A 1PL. Tel: 0171-242 1222

LETTS EDUCATIONAL, Aldine House, 9–15 Aldine Street, London W12 8AW. Tel: 0181-740 2266

LINCOLN (FRANCES), 4 Torriano Mews, Torriano Avenue, London NW5 2RZ. Tel: 0171-284 4009

LION PUBLISHING, Sandy Lane West, Oxford OX4 5HG. Tel: 01865-747550

LITTLE, BROWN & CO., Brettenham House, Lancaster Place, London WC2E 7EN. Tel: 0171-911 8000

LUND HUMPHRIES, 1 Russell Gardens, London NW11 9NN. Tel: 0181-458 6314

LUTTERWORTH PRESS, PO Box 60, Cambridge CB1 2NT. Tel: 01223-350865

MACDONALD YOUNG BOOKS, 61 Western Road, Hove, E. Sussex BN3 1JD. Tel: 01273-722561

MCGRAW-HILL, Shoppenhangers Road, Maidenhead, Berks SL6 2QL. Tel: 01628- 623432

MACMILLAN PUBLISHERS, 25 Eccleston Place, London SW1W 9NF. Tel: 0171-881 8000

MAGNA LARGE PRINT BOOKS, Magna House, Long Preston, Skipton BD3 4ND. Tel: 01729-840225

MAINSTREAM PUBLISHING CO. (EDINBURGH), 7 Albany Street, Edinburgh EH1 3UG. Tel: 0131-557 2959

MAMMOTH, 239 Kensington High Street, London W8 6FA. Tel: 0171-761 3500

MANCHESTER UNIVERSITY PRESS, Oxford Road, Manchester M13 9NR. 0161-273 5539

METHUEN, 215 Vauxhall Bridge Road, London SW1V 1EL. Tel: 0171-828 2838

MILLS & BOON, 18–24 Paradise Road, Richmond, Surrey TW9 1SR. Tel: 0181-288 2800

MINERVA PRESS, Sixth Floor, Canberra House, 315-317 Regent Street, London W1R 7YB. Tel: 0171-580 4114

MURRAY (JOHN), 50 Albemarle Street, London W1X 4BD. Tel: 0171-493 4361

NELSON (THOMAS), Mayfield Road, Walton-on-Thames KT12 5PL. Tel: 01932-252211

NEW HOLLAND PUBLISHERS, 24 Nutford Place, London W1H 6DQ. Tel: 0171-724 7773

NEXUS SPECIAL INTERESTS, Nexus House, Azalea Drive, Swanley BR8 8HU. Tel: 01322-660070

NORTON (W.W.), 10 Coptic Street, London WC1A 1PU. Tel: 0171-323 1579

NOVELLO & CO., 8 Frith Street, London W1V 5TZ. Tel: 0171-434 0066

OCTOPUS PUBLISHING GROUP, 2-4 Heron Quay, London E14 4JB. Tel: 0171-531 8400

OLIVER & BOYD, Edinburgh Gate, Harlow, Essex CM20 2JE. Tel: 01279-623623

O'MARA (MICHAEL) BOOKS, 9 Lion Yard, Tremadoc Road, London SW4 7NQ. Tel: 0171-720 8643

OPEN UNIVERSITY PRESS, Celtic Court, 22 Ballmoor, Buckingham MK18 1XW. Tel: 01280-823388

ORION PUBLISHING GROUP, 5 Upper St Martin's Lane, London WC2H 9EA. Tel: 0171-240 3444

OSPREY PUBLISHING, First Floor, Elms Court, Chapel Way, Botley, Oxford OX2 9LP. Tel: 01865-727022

OWEN (PETER), 73 Kenway Road, London SW5 0RE. Tel: 0171-373 5628

OXFORD UNIVERSITY PRESS, Great Clarendon Street, Oxford OX2 6DP. Tel: 01865-556767

PAN BOOKS, 25 Eccleston Place, London SW1W 9NF. Tel: 0171-881 8000

PAVILION BOOKS, London House, Great Eastern Wharf, Parkgate Road, London SW11 4NQ. Tel: 0171-350 1230

PEARSON EDUCATION, Edinburgh Gate, Harlow CM20 2JE. Tel: 01279-623928

PENGUIN BOOKS, 27 Wrights Lane, London W8 5TZ. Tel: 0171-416 3000

PERGAMON PRESS, Oxford Spires, The Boulevard, Kidlington, Oxon OX5 1GB. Tel: 01865-843000

PHAIDON PRESS, Regent's Wharf, All Saints Street, London N1 9PA. Tel: 0171-843 1234

PHILIP (GEORGE), 2–4 Heron Quay, London E14 4JB. Tel: 0171-531 8400

PIATKUS BOOKS, 5 Windmill Street, London W1P 1HF. Tel: 0171-631 0710

PITKIN UNICHROME, Healey House, Dene Road, Andover, Hants SP10 2AA. Tel: 01264-409200

PITMAN PUBLISHING, 128 Long Acre, London WC2E 9AN. Tel: 0171-447 2000

PRENTICE HALL, Campus 400, Maylands Avenue, Hemel Hempstead HP2 7EZ. Tel: 01442-881900

QUARTET BOOKS, 27 Goodge Street, London WIP 2LD. Tel: 0171-636 3992

QUILLER PRESS, 46 Lillie Road, London SW6 ITN. Tel: 0171-499 6529

RANDOM HOUSE UK, 20 Vauxhall Bridge Road, London SWIV 2SA. Tel: 0171-840 8400

READER'S DIGEST, 11 West Ferry Circus, London EI4 4HE. Tel: 0171-715 8000

ROUGH GUIDES, 62–70 Shorts Gardens, London WC2H 9AB. Tel: 0171-556 5000

ROUTLEDGE, 11 New Fetter Lane, London EC4P 4EE. Tel: 0171-583 9855

SAGE PUBLICATIONS, 6 Bonhill Street, London EC2A 4PU. Tel: 0171-374 0645

ST ANDREW PRESS, 121 George Street, Edinburgh EH2 4YN. Tel: 0131-225 5722

SCM PRESS, 9–17 St Albans Place, London NI ONX. Tel: 0171-359 8033

SECKER & WARBURG, 20 Vauxhall Bridge Road, London SWIV 2SA. Tel: 0171-840 8400

SERPENT'S TAIL, 4 Blackstock Mews, London N4 2BT. Tel: 0171-354 1949

SEVERN HOUSE, 9 Sutton High Street, Sutton SMI IDF. Tel: 0181-770 3930

SIDGWICK & JACKSON, 25 Eccleston Place, London SWIW 9NF. Tel: 0171-881 8000

SIMON & SCHUSTER, Campus 400, Maylands Avenue, Hemel Hempstead HP2 7EZ. Tel: 01442-881900

SOUVENIR PRESS, 43 Great Russell Street, London WCIB 3PA. Tel: 0171-580 9307

SPCK, Holy Trinity Church, Marylebone Road, London NWI 4DU. Tel: 0171-387 5282

STATIONERY OFFICE BOOKS, PO Box 276, London SW8 5DT. Tel: 0171-873 0011

STEPHENS (PATRICK), Sparkford, Yeovil BA22 7JJ. Tel: 01963-440635

SUTTON PUBLISHING, Phoenix, Works, London Road, Stroud GL5 2BU. Tel: 01453-731114

SWEET & MAXWELL, 100 Avenue Road, London NW3 3PF. Tel: 0171-449 1104

TAYLOR & FRANCIS, 11 New Fetter Lane, London EC4P 4EE. Tel: 0171-583 0490

THAMES & HUDSON, 181A High Holborn, London WCIV 7QX. Tel: 0171-845 5000

THORSONS, 77 Fulham Palace Road, London W6 8JB. Tel: 0181-741 7070

TIMES BOOKS, 77 Fulham Palace Road, London W6 8JB. Tel: 0181-741 7070

TRANSWORLD PUBLISHERS, 61-63 Uxbridge Road, London W5 5SA. Tel: 0181-579 2652

UNIVERSITY OF WALES PRESS, 6 Gwennyth Street, Cardiff CF2 4YD. Tel: 01222-231919

USBORNE PUBLISHING, Usborne House, 83–85 Saffron Hill, London ECIN 8RT. Tel: 0171-430 2800

VIKING, 27 Wrights Lane, London W8 5TZ. Tel: 0171-416 3000

VIRAGO PRESS, Brettenham House, Lancaster Place, London WC2E 7EN. Tel: 0171-911 8000

VIRGIN PUBLISHING, Units 5 and 6, Thames Wharf, Rainville Road, London W6 9HT. Tel: 0171-386 3300

WALKER BOOKS, 87 Vauxhall Walk, London SEII 5HJ. Tel: 0171-793 0909

WARD LOCK EDUCATIONAL CO., 1 Christopher Road, East Grinstead, W. Sussex RHI9 3BT. Tel: 01342-318980

WATTS (FRANKLIN), 96 Leonard Street, London EC2A 4XD. Tel: 0171-739 2929

WAYLAND (PUBLISHERS), 61 Western Road, Hove, E. Sussex BN3 IJD. Tel: 01273-722561

WEIDENFELD & NICOLSON, 5 Upper St Martin's Lane, London WC2H 9EA. Tel: 0171-240 3444

WHICH? BOOKS, Consumer's Association, 2 Marylebone Road, London NWI 4DF. Tel: 0171-830 6000

WHITAKER (J.), Woolmead House West, Bear Lane, Farnham GU9 7LG. Tel: 01252-742500

WILEY (JOHN) & SONS, 1 Oldlands Way, Bognor Regis PO22 9SA. Tel: 01243-779777

YALE UNIVERSITY PRESS, 23 Pond Street, London NW3 2PN. Tel: 0171-431 4422

Annual Reference Books

If the address of the editorial office of a publication differs from the address to which orders should be sent, the address given is usually the one for orders.

AA HOTEL GUIDE, Distribution Centre, Colchester Road, Frating Green, Colchester CO7 7DW. (Oct.) £14.99

ADVERTISER'S ANNUAL, Windsor Court, East Grinstead House, London Road, East Grinstead, W. Sussex RH19 IXA. £210.00

AEROSPACE EUROPE, Riverbank House, Angel Lane, Tonbridge, Kent TN9 ISE. £97.00

ALLIED DUNBAR INVESTMENT AND SAVINGS HANDBOOK, PO Box 88, Harlow, Essex CM19 5SR. £27.99

ALLIED DUNBAR TAX HANDBOOK, PO Box 88, Harlow, Essex CM19 5SR. £25.99

ALMANACH DE GOTHA, PO Box 9, Woodbridge, Suffolk IP12 3DF. £60.00

ANNUAL ABSTRACT OF STATISTICS, PO Box 276, London SW8 5DT. (Jan.) £39.50

ANNUAL REGISTER: A RECORD OF WORLD EVENTS, 5 Five Mile Drive, Oxford OX2 8HT. £112.00

ANTIQUE SHOPS OF BRITAIN, GUIDE TO THE, Distribution Centre, Colchester Road, Frating Green, Colchester CO7 7DW. £14.95

ART SALES INDEX, 1 Thames Street, Weybridge, Surrey KT13 8JG. 2 vol. £110.00

ART YEAR REVIEW, 1 Stewarts Court, 220 Stewarts Road, London SW8 4UO. (Jan.) £9.99

ASLIB DIRECTORY OF INFORMATION SOURCES IN THE UNITED KINGDOM, Commerce Way, Colchester CO2 8HP. £295.00

ASSOCIATION OF CONSULTING ENGINEERS DIRECTORY OF MEMBERS FIRMS, Alliance House, 12 Caxton Street, London SW1H 0QL. £10.00

ASTRONOMICAL ALMANAC, PO Box 276, London SW8 5DT. (Dec.) £32.50

ATHLETICS: ASSOCIATION OF TRACK AND FIELD STATISTICIANS YEAR BOOK, Waldenbury, North Common, North Chailey, Lewes, E. Sussex BN8 4DR. (May) £14.95

AUTOMOBILE YEAR, Waldenbury, North Common, North Chailey, Lewes, E. Sussex BN8 4DR. £30.95

BAILY'S HUNTING DIRECTORY, Chesterton Mill, French's Road, Cambridge CB4 3NP. (Nov.) £34.95

BANKER'S ALMANAC, East Grinstead House, East Grinstead, W. Sussex RH19 IXA. (Feb.) 5 vol. £460.00

BENEDICTINE AND CISTERCIAN MONASTIC YEAR BOOK, Ampleforth Abbey, York YO6 4EN. (Dec.) £2.25

BENN'S MEDIA: UNITED KINGDOM, Riverbank House, Angel Lane, Tonbridge, Kent TN9 ISE. £145.00

BPIF PRINT BUYER'S DIRECTORY, 11 Bedford Row, London WC1R 4DX. £95.00

BRASSEY'S DEFENCE YEAR BOOK, Unit 1A Learoyd Road, Mountfield Industrial Estate, New Romney, Kent TN28 8XU. £45.00

BRITAIN: THE OFFICIAL HANDBOOK OF THE UNITED KINGDOM, PO Box 276, London SW8 5DT. (Jan.) £35.00

BRITANNICA BOOK OF THE YEAR, 1 Whittle Drive, Eastbourne, E. Sussex BN23 6QH. (May) £60.00

BRITISH CLOTHING INDUSTRY YEAR BOOK, 11 The Swan Courtyard, Charles Edward Road, Yardley, Birmingham B26 1BU. £50.00

BRITISH EXPORTS, East Grinstead House, East Grinstead, W. Sussex RH19 IXA. £185.00

BRITISH MUSIC YEAR BOOK, Albert House, Apex Business Centre, Boscombe Road, Dunstable, Beds LU5 4RL. £23.95

BRITISH PERFORMING ARTS YEAR BOOK, Albert House, Apex Business Centre, Boscombe Road, Dunstable, Beds LU5 4RL. (Jan.) £23.95

BRITISH PLASTICS AND RUBBER DIRECTORY, Catalyst House, 159 Clapham High Street, London SW4 7SS. £10.00

BRITISH THEATRE DIRECTORY, Douglas House, 3 Richmond Buildings, London W1V 5AE. (April) £34.95

BROWN'S NAUTICAL ALMANAC DAILY TIDE TABLES, 4–10 Darnley Street, Glasgow G41 2SD. (Sept.) £40.00

BUILDING AND CONSTRUCTION INDEX, Riverbank House, Angel Lane, Tonbridge, Kent TN9 ISE. (Jan.) £74.00

BUILDING SOCIETIES YEAR BOOK, Arnold House, 36-41 Holywell Lane, London EC2A 3SF. £52.25

BUSES YEAR BOOK, Columbia Building, Faraday Close, Durrington, Worthing BN13 3HD. £12.99

BUTTERWORTHS LAW DIRECTORY AND LEGAL SERVICES DIRECTORY, Windsor Court, East Grinstead House, Wood Street, East Grinstead, W. Sussex RH19 IXA. (Feb.) 2 vol. £59.00

CATHOLIC DIRECTORY OF ENGLAND AND WALES, St James's Buildings, Oxford Street, Manchester M1 6FP. £23.50

CBI SKILLS AND TRAINING HANDBOOK, Columbia Building, Faraday Close, Durrington, Worthing BN13 3HD. £30.00

CHARITIES CHOICE, Paulton House, 8 Shepherdess Walk, London N1 7LB. £69.95

CHEMICAL INDUSTRY EUROPE, Riverbank House, Angel Lane, Tonbridge, Kent TN9 ISE. £97.00

CHEMIST AND DRUGGIST DIRECTORY, Riverbank House, Angel Lane, Tonbridge, Kent TN9 ISE. £112.00

CHRISTIES' REVIEW OF THE YEAR, 1 Langley Lane, London SW8 1TH. (Nov.) £45.00

CHURCH OF ENGLAND YEARBOOK, St Mary's Works, St Mary's Plain, Norwich NR3 3BH. (Jan.) £24.00

CHURCH OF SCOTLAND YEAR BOOK, 121 George Street, Edinburgh EH2 4YN. (Oct.) £11.00

CITY OF LONDON DIRECTORY AND LIVERY COMPANIES GUIDE, Seatrade House, 42–48 North Station Road, Colchester CO1 1RB. £22.00, £20.00

CIVIL SERVICE YEAR BOOK, PO Box 276, London SW8 5DT. (Feb.) £40.00

COMMONWEALTH UNIVERSITIES YEAR BOOK, 36 Gordon Square, London WC1H 0PF. (July) 2 vol. £155.00

COMMONWEALTH YEAR BOOK, Jordan House, 47 Brunswick Place, London N1 6EB (May) £55.00

COMPUTER USERS' YEAR BOOK, Woodside, Hinksey Hill, Oxford OX1 5BE. 3 vol. £300.00

CONCRETE YEAR BOOK, 151 Rosebery Avenue, London EC1R 4GB. £66.00

CURRENT LAW STATUTES, Cheriton House, North Way, Andover, Hants SP10 5BE. £325.00

DEBRETT'S PEOPLE OF TODAY, Star Road, Partridge Green, W. Sussex RH13 8LD (March) £105.00

DIPLOMATIC SERVICE LIST, PO Box 276, London SW8 5DT. £27.50

DIRECTORY OF DIRECTORS, Windsor Court, East Grinstead House, East Grinstead, W. Sussex RH19 IXA. (Jan.) 2 vol. £235.00

DIRECTORY OF FURTHER EDUCATION, Plymbridge Distributors, Estover, Plymouth PL6 7PZ. (March) £76.50

DIRECTORY OF GRADUATE STUDIES, Plymbridge Distributors, Estover, Plymouth PL6 7PZ. (March) £109.99

DIRECTORY OF LOCAL AUTHORITIES AND PROPERTY SERVICES DIRECTORY, Cheriton House, North Way, Andover, Hants SP10 5BE. (June) £30.00

DIY TRADE BUYERS GUIDE, Riverbank House, Angel Lane, Tonbridge, Kent TN9 1SE. £75.00

DOD'S PARLIAMENTARY COMPANION, PO Box 3700, London SW1E 5NP. £105.00

EDUCATION AUTHORITIES' DIRECTORY AND ANNUAL, Derby House, Bletchingley Road, Merstham, Surrey RH1 3DN. (Jan.) £72.00, £60.00

EDUCATION YEAR BOOK, PO Box 88, Harlow, Essex CM19 5SR. £92.00

ELECTRICAL AND ELECTRONIC TRADES DIRECTORY, Michael Faraday House, Six Hills Way, Stevenage, Herts SG1 2AY. (Feb.) £82.00

ELECTRICITY SUPPLY HANDBOOK, PO Box 935, Finchingfield, Braintree, Essex CM7 4LN. (Feb.) £98.00

EUROPA WORLD YEAR BOOK, 18 Bedford Square, London WC1B 3JN. 2 vol. £425.00

EUROPEAN GLASS DIRECTORY AND BUYER'S GUIDE, 2 Queensway, Redhill, Surrey RH1 1QS. £156.00

FLIGHT INTERNATIONAL DIRECTORY, PO Box 1315, Potters Bar, Herts EN6 1PU. £68.00

FOOD TRADES DIRECTORY OF THE UK AND EUROPE, 32 Vauxhall Bridge Road, London SW1V 2SS. 2 vol. £160.00

FROZEN AND CHILLED FOODS YEAR BOOK, Queensway House, 2 Queensway, Redhill, Surrey RH1 1QS. £120.00

FURNITURE AND FURNISHINGS INDUSTRY, DIRECTORY OF THE, Riverbank House, Angel Lane, Tonbridge, Kent TN9 1SE. £107.00

GAS INDUSTRY DIRECTORY, Riverbank House, Angel Lane, Tonbridge, Kent TN9 1SE. (Oct.) £102.00

GIBBONS' SIMPLIFIED CATALOGUE OF STAMPS OF THE WORLD, 1 Whittle Drive, Eastbourne, E. Sussex BN23 6QH. (Oct.) 3 vol. £27.50, £27.50, £24.95

GOOD FOOD GUIDE, PO Box 11, West Drayton, Middx UB7 0DA. £14.99

GOOD GUIDE TO BRITAIN, Distribution Centre, Colchester Road, Frating Green, Colchester CO7 7DW. (Nov.) £14.99

GOOD HOTEL GUIDE, Distribution Centre, Colchester Road, Frating Green, Colchester CO7 7DW. £14.99

GUINNESS BOOK OF KNOWLEDGE, Brunel Road, Houndmills, Basingstoke, Hants RG21 2XS. (Oct.) £20.00

GUINNESS BOOK OF RECORDS, Brunel Road, Houndmills, Basingstoke, Hants RG21 2XS. (Oct.) £18.00

HEALTH AND SOCIAL SERVICES YEARBOOK, PO Box 88, Harlow, Essex CM19 5SR. £125.00

HEALTH CARE BUYERS GUIDE, Riverbank House, Angel Lane, Tonbridge, Kent TN9 1SE. £86.00

HISTORIC HOUSES, CASTLES AND GARDENS, Star Road, Partridge Green, Horsham, W. Sussex RH13 8LD. (March) £6.95

HOLLIS UK PRESS AND PR ANNUAL, Harlequin House, 7 High Street, Teddington TW11 8EY. (Oct.) £97.50

HOUSING AND PLANNING YEAR BOOK, PO Box 88, Harlow, Essex CM19 5SR. £110.00

INDEPENDENT SCHOOLS YEAR BOOK, PO Box 19, Huntingdon, Cambs PE19 3SF. £26.00

INSURANCE DIRECTORY, 39 Earlham Street, London WC2H 9LD (Feb.) £250.00

INTERNATIONAL PAPER DIRECTORY, PHILLIPS', Riverbank House, Angel Lane, Tonbridge, Kent TN9 1SE. £132.00

INTERNATIONAL WHO'S WHO, 18 Bedford Square, London WC1R 4JH. (July) £195.00

INTERNATIONAL YEARBOOK AND STATESMEN'S WHO'S WHO, Maypole House, Maypole Road, East Grinstead, W. Sussex RH19 1HU. (April) £185.00

JANE'S ALL THE WORLD'S AIRCRAFT, Sentinel House, 163 Brighton Road, Coulsdon, Surrey CR5 2NH. (Oct.) £280.00

JANE'S ARMOUR AND ARTILLERY, Sentinel House, 163 Brighton Road, Coulsdon, Surrey CR5 2NH. (Nov.) £280.00

JANE'S FIGHTING SHIPS, Sentinel House, 163 Brighton Road, Coulsdon, Surrey CR5 2NH. £280.00

JANE'S HIGH SPEED MARINE TRANSPORTATION, Sentinel House, 163 Brighton Road, Coulsdon, Surrey CR5 2NH. £265.00

JANE'S INFANTRY WEAPONS, Sentinel House, 163 Brighton Road, Coulsdon, Surrey CR5 2NH. (Aug.) £250.00

JANE'S NAVAL WEAPON SYSTEMS, Sentinel House, 163 Brighton Road, Coulsdon, Surrey CR5 2NH. £425.00

JANE'S WORLD RAILWAYS, Sentinel House, 163 Brighton Road, Coulsdon, Surrey CR5 2NH. £290.00

JEWISH YEAR BOOK, Star Road, Partridge Green, Horsham, W. Sussex RH13 8LD. (Feb.) £26.00

KELLY'S BUSINESS DIRECTORY, East Grinstead House, East Grinstead, W. Sussex RH19 1XA. £259.00

KEMPE'S ENGINEERS YEAR BOOK, Riverbank House, Angel Lane, Tonbridge, Kent TN9 1SE. £120.00

KIME'S INTERNATIONAL LAW DIRECTORY, PO Box 88, Harlow, Essex CM19 5SR. (Dec.) £77.00

LAXTON'S BUILDING PRICE BOOK, Halley Court, Jordan Hill, Oxford OX2 8EJ. 2 vol. £95.00

LIBRARY ASSOCIATION YEAR BOOK, 39 Milton Park, Abingdon, Oxon OX14 4TD. (June) £37.50

LLOYD'S LIST OF SHIPOWNERS, 100 Leadenhall Street, London EC3A 3BP (Sept.) £165.00

LLOYD'S MARITIME DIRECTORY, Sheepen Place, Colchester CO3 3LP. (Jan.) £245.00

LLOYD'S NAUTICAL YEAR BOOK, Sheepen Place, Colchester CO3 3LP. (Sept.) £48.00

LLOYD'S REGISTER OF SHIPS, 100 Leadenhall Street, London EC3A 3BP. (July) 3 vol. £595.00

LYLE OFFICIAL ANTIQUES PRICE GUIDE, Distribution Centre, Colchester Road, Frating Green, Colchester CO7 7DW. £18.99

MACMILLAN NAUTICAL ALMANAC, Brunel Road, Houndmills, Basingstoke, Hants RG21 2XS. £26.95

MAGISTRATES' COURT GUIDE, PO Box LB 327, London WC2A 1ER. £29.50

MEDICAL DIRECTORY, Maple House, 149 Tottenham Court Road, London W1P 9LL. (March) 2 vol. £175.00

MEDICAL REGISTER, 178 Great Portland Street, London W1N 6JE. (March) 4 vol. £110.00

MIDDLE EAST AND NORTH AFRICA, 18 Bedford Square, London WC1B 3JN. (Oct.) £235.00

MILLER'S ANTIQUES PRICE GUIDE, Exel Logistics, Shaw Close, Park Farm Industrial Estate, Wellingborough, Northants NN8 6BN. £22.50

MINING ANNUAL REVIEW AND METALS AND MINERALS ANNUAL REVIEW, PO Box 10, Edenbridge, Kent TN8 5NE. £85.00

MINING INTERNATIONAL YEAR BOOK, PO Box 88, Harlow, Essex CM19 5SR. (June) £175.00

MOTOR INDUSTRY OF GREAT BRITAIN WORLD AUTOMOTIVE STATISTICS, Forbes House, Halkin Street, London SW1X 7DS. (Oct.) £75.00

MOTOR SHIP DIRECTORY, PO Box 935, Finchingfield, Braintree, Essex CM7 4LN. £120.00

MUNICIPAL YEAR BOOK, 32 Vauxhall Bridge Road, London SW1V 2SS. (Dec.) £173.00

MUSEUMS AND GALLERIES IN GREAT BRITAIN AND IRELAND, Star Road, Partridge Green, Horsham, W. Sussex RH13 8LD. (Oct.) £8.95

NAUTICAL ALMANAC, PO Box 276, London SW8 5DT. (Oct.) £25.00

PACKAGING INDUSTRY DIRECTORY, Riverbank House, Angel Lane, Tonbridge, Kent TN9 1SE. £97.00

PEARS CYCLOPEDIA, PO Box 11, West Drayton, Middx UB7 0DA. £16.99

PHOTOGRAPHY YEAR BOOK, Fountain House, 2 Gladstone Road, Kingston-upon-Thames, Surrey KT1 3HD. £24.95

POLYMERS, PAINT AND COLOUR YEAR BOOK, Queensway House, 2 Queensway, Redhill, Surrey RH1 1QS. £130.00

PORTS OF THE WORLD, Sheepen Place, Colchester CO3 3LP. £230.00

PRINTING TRADES DIRECTORY, Riverbank House, Angel Lane, Tonbridge, Kent TN9 1SE. £112.00

PUBLIC AUTHORITIES DIRECTORY, 33-39 Bowling Green Lane, London EC1R 0DA. (Jan.) £110.00

PUBLIC SERVICES YEARBOOK, PO Box 88, Harlow, Essex CM19 5SR. (April) £28.00

PUBLISHING, DIRECTORY OF, Stanley House, 3 Fleets Lane, Poole, Dorset BH15 3AJ. (Oct.) £65.00

RAC EUROPE FOR THE INDEPENDENT TRAVELLER, Portland House, 4 Great Portland Street, London WIN 4AA. £8.99

RAC INSPECTED HOTELS, BRITAIN AND IRELAND, Portland House, 4 Great Portland Street, London WIN 4AA. £13.99

RAILWAY DIRECTORY, PO Box 935, Finchingfield, Braintree, Essex CM7 4LN. (Dec.) £95.00

REGIONAL TRENDS, PO Box 276, London SW8 5DT. (July) £39.50

RETAIL DIRECTORY OF THE UNITED KINGDOM, 32 Vauxhall Bridge Road, London SW1V 2SS. £148.00

RIBA DIRECTORY OF PRACTICES, 39 Moreland Street, London EC1V 8BB. (Oct.) £65.00

ROTHMAN'S FOOTBALL YEAR BOOK, 39 Milton Park, Abingdon, Oxon OX14 4TD. (Aug.) £30.00, £18.99

ROTHMAN'S RUGBY LEAGUE YEAR BOOK, 39 Milton Park, Abingdon, Oxon OX14 4TD. (Sept.) £17.99

ROTHMAN'S RUGBY UNION YEAR BOOK, 39 Milton Park, Abingdon, Oxon OX14 4TD. (Sept.) £17.99

ROYAL AND ANCIENT GOLFER'S HANDBOOK, Brunel Road, Houndmills, Basingstoke, Hants RG21 2XS. (April) £50.00, £19.99

ROYAL SOCIETY YEAR BOOK, 6 Carlton House Terrace, London SW1Y 5AG. (Feb.) £22.00

SALVATION ARMY YEAR BOOK, 117-121 Judd Street, London WC1H 9NN. (April) £10.50, £5.50

SCOTTISH LAW DIRECTORY, 59 George Street, Edinburgh EH2 2LQ. £34.00

SEABY STANDARD CATALOGUE OF BRITISH COINAGE, 5-7 King Street, London SW1Y 6QS. (Sept.) £15.00

SELL'S PRODUCTS AND SERVICES DIRECTORY, Riverbank House, Angel Lane, Tonbridge, Kent TN9 1SE. (June) £97.00

SHEET METAL INDUSTRIES YEAR BOOK, Queensway House, 2 Queensway, Redhill, Surrey RH1 1QS. £88.00

SHOWCASE INTERNATIONAL MUSIC BOOK, 38C The Broadway, London N8 9SU. £38.00

SOCIAL SERVICES YEAR BOOK, PO Box 88, Harlow, Essex CM19 5SR. (April) £125.00

SOCIAL TRENDS, PO Box 276, London SW8 5DT. (Jan.) £39.50

SOLICITORS AND BARRISTERS, DIRECTORY OF, PO Box 269, Abingdon, Oxon OX14 4YN. £54.95, £39.95

SPON'S ARCHITECTS' AND BUILDERS' PRICE BOOK, Cheriton House, North Way, Andover, Hants SP10 5BE. £75.00

SPON'S MECHANICAL AND ELECTRICAL SERVICES PRICE BOOK, Cheriton House, North Way, Andover, Hants SP10 5BE. £77.50

STATESMAN'S YEARBOOK, Brunel Road, Houndmills, Basingstoke, Hants RG21 2XS. (Aug.) £50.00

STOCK EXCHANGE YEARBOOK, Brunel Road, Houndmills, Basingstoke, Hants RG21 2XS. £259.00

STONE'S JUSTICES' MANUAL, PO Box LB327, London WC2A 1ER. 3 vol. (May) £250.00

STUDENT BOOK, Plymbridge Distributors, Estover, Plymouth PL6 7PZ. (April) £10.99

TANKER REGISTER, 12 Camomile Street, London EC3A 7BP. (April) £155.00

TIMBER TRADES ADDRESS BOOK, Riverbank House, Angel Lane, Tonbridge, Kent TN9 1SE. £72.00

TRAVEL TRADE GAZETTE DIRECTORY, Riverbank House, Angel Lane, Tonbridge, Kent TN9 1SE. (April) £57.00

UK KOMPASS REGISTER, East Grinstead House, East Grinstead, W. Sussex RH19 1XA. 2 vol. £420.00

UNITED KINGDOM MINERALS YEARBOOK, British Geological Survey, Keyworth, Nottingham NG12 5GG. £35.00

UNITED REFORMED CHURCH YEAR BOOK, 86 Tavistock Place, London WC1H 9RT. (Sept.) £17.50

UNIT TRUST YEAR BOOK, Maple House, 149 Tottenham Court Road, London W1P 9LL. £350.00

UNIVERSITY AND COLLEGE ENTRANCE, 14 Cooper's Row, London EC3N 2BH. (June) £19.95

VETERINARY ANNUAL, PO Box 269, Abingdon, Oxon. OX14 4YN. £59.50

WHITAKER DIRECTORY OF PUBLISHERS, 12 Dyott Street, London WC1A 1DF. (March) £25.00

WHITAKER'S ALMANACK, PO Box 276, London SW8 5DT. (Oct.) £65.00, £40.00

WHITAKER'S BOOKS IN PRINT, 12 Dyott Street, London WC1A 1DF. (Jan.) 4 vol. £449.00

WHITAKER'S CONCISE ALMANACK, PO Box 276, London SW8 5DT. (Oct.) £20.00

WHITAKER'S SCOTTISH ALMANACK, PO Box 276, London SW8 5DT. (Oct.) £14.99

WHO OWNS WHOM?, Holmers Farm Way, High Wycombe, Bucks HP12 4UL. 6 vol. £1,174.00

WHO'S WHO, PO Box 19, Huntingdon, Cambs PE19 3SF. £115.00

WILLING'S PRESS GUIDE, Harlequin House, 7 High Street, Teddington, Middx TW11 8EY. (Feb.) 2 vol. £205.00

WISDEN CRICKETERS' ALMANACK, PO Box 11, West Drayton, Middx UB7 0DA. (April) £28.00

WORLD HOTEL DIRECTORY, PO Box 88, Harlow, Essex CM19 5SR. £140.00

WORLD INSURANCE, PO Box 88, Harlow, Essex CM19 5SR. £195.00

WORLD MINERAL STATISTICS, British Geological Survey, Keyworth, Notts NG12 5GG. (Sept.) 2 vol. £85.00

WORLD OF LEARNING, 18 Bedford Square, London WC1B 3JN. (Jan.) 2 vol. £260.00

WORLD SHIPPING DIRECTORY, PO Box 96, Coulsdon, Surrey CR5 2TE. £99.00

WRITERS' AND ARTISTS' YEAR BOOK, PO Box 19, Huntingdon, Cambs PE19 3SF. (Sept.) £11.99

Employers' and Trade Associations

At 31 December 1998 there were 106 empoyers' associations listed by the Certification Officer (*see* page 288) and 101 which had not sought to be listed. Most national employers' associations are members of the Confederation of British Industry (CBI). For ACAS, the Certification Office, the Commission for Racial Equality, the Equal Opportunities Commission, the Health and Safety Commission, the Industrial Tribunals and Review Bodies, *see* Index.

CONFEDERATION OF BRITISH INDUSTRY

Centre Point, 103 New Oxford Street, London WCIA IDU
Tel 0171-379 7400

The Confederation of British Industry was founded in 1965 and is an independent non-party political body financed by industry and commerce. It exists primarily to ensure that the Government understands the intentions, needs and problems of British business. It is the recognized spokesman for the business viewpoint and is consulted as such by the Government.

The CBI represents, directly and indirectly, some 250,000 companies, large and small, from all sectors.

The governing body of the CBI is the 200-strong Council, which meets four times a year in London under the chairmanship of the President. It is assisted by 17 expert standing committees which advise on the main aspects of policy. There are 13 regional councils and offices, covering the administrative regions of England, Wales, Scotland and Northern Ireland. There is also an office in Brussels.

President, Sir Clive Thompson
Director-General, J. Adair Turner
Secretary, P. Forder
WALES: 3 Columbus Walk, Atlantic Wharf, Cardiff CFIO 4WW. Tel: 01222-453710. *Regional Director,* Ms E. Haywood
SCOTLAND: Beresford House, 5 Claremont Terrace, Glasgow G3 7XT. Tel: 0141-332 8661. *Regional Director,* I. McMillan
NORTHERN IRELAND: Fanum House, 108 Great Victoria Street, Belfast BT2 7PD. Tel: 01232-326658. *Regional Director,* N. Smyth

---

ASSOCIATIONS

ADVERTISING ASSOCIATION, Abford House, 15 Wilton Road, London SWIV INJ. Tel: 0171-828 2771. *Director-General,* A. Brown
AEROSPACE COMPANIES LTD, SOCIETY OF BRITISH, Duxbury House, 60 Petty France, London SWIH 9EU. Tel: 0171-227 1000. *Director-General,* D. Marshall
APPAREL AND TEXTILE CONFEDERATION LTD, BRITISH, 5 Portland Place, London WIN 3AA. Tel: 0171-636 7788. *Director-General,* J. R. Wilson
BAKERS, FEDERATION OF, 6 Catherine Street, London WC2B 5JW. Tel: 0171-420 7190. *Executive Director,* Mrs A. Linehan

BANKERS' ASSOCIATION, BRITISH, Pinners Hall, 105-108 Old Broad Street, London EC2N IEX. Tel: 0171-216 8800. *Director-General,* T. P. Sweeney
BLC LEATHER TECHNOLOGY CENTRE, Leather Trade House, Kings Park Road, Moulton Park, Northampton NN3 6JD. Tel: 01604-679999. *Chief Executive,* K. T. W. Alexander, PH.D
BREWERS AND LICENSED RETAILERS ASSOCIATION, 42 Portman Square, London WIH OBB. Tel: 0171-486 4831. *Chief Executive Officer,* R. Hayward, OBE
BRF (BRITISH ROAD FEDERATION), Pillar House, 194-202 Old Kent Road, London SEI 5TG. Tel: 0171-703 9769. *Director,* R. Diment
BUILDING MATERIAL PRODUCERS, NATIONAL COUNCIL OF, 26 Store Street, London WCIE 7BT. Tel: 0171-323 3770. *Director-General,* M. G. Ankers, FRSA
CHAMBER OF SHIPPING LTD, Carthusian Court, 12 Carthusian Street, London ECIM 6EZ. Tel: 0171-417 8400. *Director-General,* Vice-Adm. Sir Christopher Morgan, KBE
CHEMICAL INDUSTRIES ASSOCIATION LTD, Kings Buildings, Smith Square, London SWIP 3JJ. Tel: 0171-834 3399. *Director-General,* Dr E. G. Finer
CLOTHING INDUSTRY ASSOCIATION LTD, BRITISH, 5 Portland Place, London WIN 3AA. Tel: 0171-636 7788. *Director,* J. R. Wilson
CONSTRUCTION CONFEDERATION, Construction House, 56-64 Leonard Street, London EC2A 4JX. Tel: 0171-608 5000. *Chief Executive,* I. A. Deslandes
DAIRY INDUSTRY FEDERATION, 19 Cornwall Terrace, London NWI 4QP. Tel: 0171-486 7244. *Director-General,* J. Begg
ELECTROTECHNICAL AND ALLIED MANUFACTURERS' ASSOCIATIONS, FEDERATION OF BRITISH (BEAMA), Westminster Tower, 3 Albert Embankment, London SEI 7SL. Tel: 0171-793 3000. *Director-General,* A. A. Bullen
ENGINEERING EMPLOYERS' FEDERATION, Broadway House, Tothill Street, London SWIH 9NQ. Tel: 0171-222 7777. *Director-General,* M. J. Temple
FARMERS' UNION, NATIONAL (NFU), 164 Shaftesbury Avenue, London WC2H 8HL. Tel: 0171-331 7200. *Director-General,* R. Macdonald
FARMERS' UNION OF SCOTLAND, NATIONAL, Rural Centre, West Mains, Ingliston, Newbridge, Midlothian EH28 8LT. Tel: 0131-472 4000. *Chief Executive,* E. R. Brown
FARMERS' UNION, ULSTER, 475 Antrim Road, Belfast BTI5 3DA. Tel: 02890-370222. *Director-General,* A. MacLaughlin
FINANCE AND LEASING ASSOCIATION, 15-19 Imperial House, Kingsway, London WC2B 6UN. Tel: 0171-836 6511. *Director-General,* M. A. Hall, MVO
FOOD AND DRINK FEDERATION, 6 Catherine Street, London WC2B 5JJ. Tel: 0171-836 2460. *Director-General,* M. P. Mackenzie
FOREST PRODUCTS ASSOCIATION, UNITED KINGDOM, Office 14, John Player Building, Stirling Enterprise Park, Springbank Road, Stirling FK7 7RP. Tel: 01786-449029. *Executive Director,* D. J. Sulman
FREIGHT TRANSPORT ASSOCIATION LTD, Hermes House, 157 St John's Road, Tunbridge Wells, Kent TN4 9UZ. Tel: 01892-526171. *Director-General,* D. C. Green

INSURERS, ASSOCIATION OF BRITISH, 51 Gresham Street, London EC2V 7HQ. Tel: 0171-600 3333. *Director-General*, M. Francis

KNITTING INDUSTRIES' FEDERATION LTD, 53 Oxford Street, Leicester LE1 5XY. Tel: 0116-254 1608. *Director*, J. P. Harrison

LEATHER PRODUCERS' ASSOCIATION, Leather Trade House, Kings Park Road, Moulton Park, Northampton NN3 6JD. Tel: 01604-679999. *Chief Executive*, Dr K. Alexander

MANAGEMENT CONSULTANCIES ASSOCIATION, 11 West Halkin Street, London SW1X 8JL. Tel: 0171-235 3897. *Executive Director*, B. Petter

MARINE INDUSTRIES FEDERATION, BRITISH, Meadlake Place, Thorpe Lea Road, Egham, Surrey TW20 8HE. Tel: 01784-473377. *Executive Chairman*, A. V. Beechey

MARKET TRADERS' FEDERATION, NATIONAL, Hampton House, Hawshaw Lane, Hoyland, Barnsley S74 0HA. Tel: 01226-749021. *General Secretary*, D. E. Feeny

MASTER BUILDERS, FEDERATION OF, Gordon Fisher House, 14-15 Great James Street, London WC1N 3DP. Tel: 0171-242 7583. *Director-General*, I. Davis

MOTOR MANUFACTURERS AND TRADERS LTD, SOCIETY OF, Forbes House, Halkin Street, London SW1X 7DS. Tel: 0171-235 7000. *Chief Executive*, C. McGowan

NEWSPAPER PUBLISHERS ASSOCIATION LTD, 34 Southwark Bridge Road, London SE1 9EU. Tel: 0171-207 2200. *Director*, S. Oram

NEWSPAPER SOCIETY, Bloomsbury House, 74-77 Great Russell Street, London WC1B 3DA. Tel: 0171-636 7014. *Director*, D. Newell

OFFICE SYSTEMS AND STATIONERY FEDERATION, BRITISH, 6 Wimpole Street, London W1M 8AS. Tel: 0171-637 7692. *Chief Executive*, K. Davies

PAPER FEDERATION OF GREAT BRITAIN, Papermakers House, Rivenhall Road, Swindon SN5 7BD. Tel: 01793-889600. *Director-General*, W. J. Bartlett

PASSENGER TRANSPORT UK, CONFEDERATION OF, Imperial House, 15-19 Kingsway, London WC2B 6UN. Tel: 0171-240 3131. *Director-General*, Mrs V. Palmer, OBE

PLASTICS FEDERATION, BRITISH, 6 Bath Place, Rivington Street, London EC2A 3JE. Tel: 0171-457 5000. *Director-General*, P. Davis, OBE

PORTS ASSOCIATION, BRITISH, Africa House, 64-78 Kingsway, London WC2B 6AH. Tel: 0171-242 1200. *Director*, D. Whitehead

PRINTING INDUSTRIES FEDERATION, BRITISH, 11 Bedford Row, London WC1R 4DX. Tel: 0171-915 8300. *Chief Executive*, T. P. E. Machin

PRIVATE MARKET OPERATORS, ASSOCIATION OF, 4 Worrygoose Lane, Whiston, Rotherham S60 4AD. Tel: 01709-700072. *Secretary*, D. J. Glasby

PROPERTY FEDERATION, BRITISH, 7th Floor, 1 Warwick Row, London SW1E 5ER. Tel: 0171-828 0111. *Director-General*, W. A. McKee

PUBLISHERS ASSOCIATION, THE, 1 Kingsway, London WC2B 6XF. Tel: 0171-565 7474. *Chief Executive*, R. Williams, OBE

RADIO COMPANIES ASSOCIATION, COMMERCIAL, 77 Shaftesbury Avenue, London W1V 7AD. Tel: 0171-306 2603. *Chief Executive*, P. Brown

RETAIL CONSORTIUM, BRITISH, 5 Grafton Street, London W1X 3LB. Tel: 0171-647 1500. *Director-General*, Ms A. Robinson

RETAIL NEWSAGENTS, NATIONAL FEDERATION OF, Yeoman House, Sekforde Street, London EC1R 0HD. Tel: 0171-253 4225. *Chief Executive*, R. Clarke

ROAD HAULAGE ASSOCIATION LTD, Roadway House, 35 Monument Hill, Weybridge, Surrey KT13 8RN. Tel: 01932-841555. *Director-General*, S. J. Norris

RUBBER MANUFACTURERS' ASSOCIATION LTD, BRITISH, 90 Tottenham Court Road, London W1P 0BR. Tel: 0207-580 2794. *Director*, A. J. Dorken

SCOTCH WHISKY ASSOCIATION, 20 Atholl Crescent, Edinburgh EH3 8HF. Tel: 0131-222 9200. *Director-General*, H. Morison

SPORT INDUSTRIES FEDERATION, Federation House, National Agricultural Centre, Stoneleigh Park, Kenilworth, Warks CV8 2RF. Tel: 01203-414999. *Chief Executive*, M. Johnson

TIMBER GROWERS ASSOCIATION LTD, 5 Dublin Street Lane South, Edinburgh EH1 3PX. Tel: 0131-538 7111. *Executive Chairman*, L. Yull

TIMBER TRADE FEDERATION, Clareville House, 26-27 Oxendon Street, London SW1Y 4EL. Tel: 0171-839 1891. *Director-General*, P. G. Harris

UK OFFSHORE OPERATORS ASSOCIATION LTD, First Floor, 30 Buckingham Gate, London SW1E 6NN. Tel: 0171-802 2400. *Director-General*, J. May

UK PETROLEUM INDUSTRY ASSOCIATION LTD, 9 Kingsway, London WC2B 6XF. Tel: 0171-240 0289. *Director-General*, Dr M. A. Frend

Trade Unions

At 31 December 1998 there were 224 trade unions listed by the Certification Officer (*see* page 288). In 1997 7,795,289 people were members of listed trade unions, compared with 7,933,789 in 1996. Nearly 80 per cent of trade union members belong to unions affiliated to the TUC (*see* below).

The Central Arbitration Committee arbitrates in industrial disputes between trade unions and employers, and determines disclosure of information complaints.

The Commissioner for the Rights of Trade Union Members provides assistance to individuals taking action against their trade union when they have not been afforded their statutory rights or when specific union rules have been breached; these responsibilities will pass to the Certification Officer following the abolition of the office of the Commissioner under legislation expected to come into effect in September 1999. The Commissioner for Protection against Unlawful Industrial Action assists individuals who have been, or are likely to be, deprived of goods or services because of industrial action unlawfully organized by a trade union; the office of the Commissioner will be abolished under legislation expected to come into effect in September 1999; the functions of the Commissioner will not be replaced.

For ACAS, the Certification Office, the Commission for Racial Equality, the Equal Opportunities Commission, the Health and Safety Commission, the Industrial Tribunals and Review Bodies, *see* Index.

THE CENTRAL ARBITRATION COMMITTEE, Brandon House, 180 Borough High Street, London SE1 1LW. Tel: 0171-210 3737/8. *Chairman*, Prof. Sir John Wood, CBE; *Secretary*, S. Gouldstone
THE COMMISSIONER FOR THE RIGHTS OF TRADE UNION MEMBERS, 1st Floor, Bank Chambers, 2A Rylands Street, Warrington, Cheshire WA1 1EN. Tel: 01925-415771. *Commissioner*, G. Corless
THE COMMISSIONER FOR PROTECTION AGAINST UNLAWFUL INDUSTRIAL ACTION, 2nd Floor, Bank Chambers, 2A Rylands Street, Warrington, Cheshire WA1 1EN. Tel: 01925-414128. *Commissioner*, G. Corless

TUC-AFFILIATED TRADE UNIONS

TRADES UNION CONGRESS (TUC)
Congress House, 23-28 Great Russell Street, London WC1B 3LS
Tel 0171-636 4030

The Trades Union Congress, founded in 1868, is an independent association of trade unions. The TUC promotes the rights and welfare of those in work and helps the unemployed. It helps its member unions promote membership in new areas and industries, and campaigns for rights at work for all employees, including part-time and temporary workers, whether union members or not. TUC representatives sit on many public bodies at national and international level. It makes representations to government, political parties, employers and international bodies such as the European Union.

The governing body of the TUC is the annual Congress. Between Congresses, business is conducted by a General Council, which meets five times a year, and an Executive Committee, which meets monthly. The full-time staff is headed by the General Secretary who is elected by Congress and is a permanent member of the General Council.

Affiliated unions in 1998–9 totalled 76 with a total membership of nearly 6,800,000.
President (1998–9), H. McKenzie (UNISON).
(The President for 1999–2000 was elected in September 1999; *see* Stop-press)
General Secretary, J. Monks, *elected* 1993

SCOTTISH TRADES UNION CONGRESS
333 Woodlands Road, Glasgow G3 6NG
Tel 0141-337 8100

The Congress was formed in 1897 and acts as a national centre for the trade union movement in Scotland. In 1999 it consisted of 46 unions with a membership of 629,360 and 34 directly affiliated Trade Councils.

The Annual Congress in April elects a 38-member General Council on the basis of six industrial sections.
Chairman, M. Smith
General Secretary, B. Speirs

MERGERS
In 1998–9 the Banking, Insurance and Finance Union merged with UNiFI.

AFFILIATED UNIONS AS AT SEPTEMBER 1999
(Number of members in parenthesis)
AMALGAMATED ENGINEERING AND ELECTRICAL UNION (AEEU) (717,874), Hayes Court, West Common Road, Bromley, Kent BR2 7AU. Tel: 0181-462 7755. *General Secretary*, K. Jackson
ANSA (INDEPENDENT UNION FOR ABBEY NATIONAL STAFF) (7,468), 2nd Floor, 16-17 High Street, Tring, Herts HP23 5AH. Tel: 01442-891122. *General Secretary*, Ms L. Rolph
ASSOCIATED METALWORKERS UNION (AMU) (805), 92 Worsley Road North, Worsley, Manchester M28 5QW. Tel: 01204-793245. *General Secretary*, R. Marron
ASSOCIATED SOCIETY OF LOCOMOTIVE ENGINEERS AND FIREMEN (ASLEF) (14,721), 9 Arkwright Road, London NW3 6AB. Tel: 0171-317 8600. *General Secretary*, M. D. Rix
ASSOCIATION OF FIRST DIVISION CIVIL SERVANTS (10,627), 2 Caxton Street, London SW1H 0QH. Tel: 0171-343 1111. *General Secretary*, J. Baume
ASSOCIATION OF FLIGHT ATTENDANTS – COUNCIL 7 (867), United Airlines Cargo Centre, Shoreham Road East, Heathrow Airport, Hounslow TW6 3RD. Tel: 0181-750 9723. *President*, K. Creighan
ASSOCIATION OF MAGISTERIAL OFFICERS (6,015), 231 Vauxhall Bridge Road, London SW1 1EG. Tel: 0171-630 5455. *General Secretary*, Ms R. Eagleson
ASSOCIATION OF TEACHERS AND LECTURERS (113,760), 7 Northumberland Street, London WC2N 5DA. Tel: 0171-930 6441. *General Secretary*, P. Smith
ASSOCIATION OF UNIVERSITY TEACHERS (41,758), Egmont House, 25-31 Tavistock Place, London WC1H 9UT. Tel: 0171-670 9700. *General Secretary*, D. Triesman

BAKERS, FOOD AND ALLIED WORKERS' UNION
(29,962), Stanborough House, Great North Road,
Stanborough, Welwyn Garden City, Herts AL8 7TA.
Tel: 01707-260150. *General Secretary*, J. R. Marino

BRITISH ACTORS' EQUITY ASSOCIATION (36,563),
Guild House, Upper St Martin's Lane, London
WC2H 9EG. Tel: 0171-379 6000. *General Secretary*,
I. McGarry

BRITISH AIR LINE PILOTS ASSOCIATION (BALPA)
(6,555), 81 New Road, Harlington, Hayes, Middx
UB3 5BG. Tel: 0181-476 4000. *General Secretary*, C. Darke

BRITISH ASSOCIATION OF COLLIERY MANAGEMENT -
TECHNICAL, ENERGY AND ADMINISTRATIVE
MANAGEMENT (BACM-TEAM) (4,289), 17 South
Parade, Doncaster, S. Yorks DN1 2DR. Tel: 01302-
815551. *General Secretary*, P. M. Carragher

BRITISH DIETETIC ASSOCIATION (3,310), 5th Floor,
Elizabeth House, 22 Suffolk Street, Queensway,
Birmingham B1 1LS. Tel: 0121-616 4910. *National
Industrial Relations Officer*, D. Wood

BRITISH ORTHOPTIC SOCIETY (1,011), Tavistock House
North, Tavistock Square, London WC1H 9HX. Tel: 0171-
387 7992. *Executive Secretary*, Mrs S. Armour

BROADCASTING, ENTERTAINMENT, CINEMATOGRAPH
AND THEATRE UNION (BECTU) (28,128), 111
Wardour Street, London W1V 4AY. Tel: 0171-437 8506.
General Secretary, R. Bolton

CARD SETTING MACHINE TENTERS' SOCIETY (88), 48
Scar End Lane, Staincliffe, Dewsbury, W. Yorks
WF12 4NY. Tel: 01924-400206. *Secretary*, A. Moorhouse

CERAMIC AND ALLIED TRADES UNION (18,677),
Hillcrest House, Garth Street, Hanley, Stoke-on-Trent
ST1 2AB. Tel: 01782-272755. *General Secretary*, G. Bagnall

CHARTERED SOCIETY OF PHYSIOTHERAPY (31,351), 14
Bedford Row, London WC1R 4ED. Tel: 0171-306 6666.
Chief Executive, P. Gray

COMMUNICATION WORKERS UNION (287,732), 150 The
Broadway, Wimbledon, London SW19 1RX. Tel: 0181-
971 7200. *General Secretary*, D. Hodgson

COMMUNITY AND DISTRICT NURSING ASSOCIATION
(5,023), Thames Valley University, 8 University
House, Ealing Green, London W5 5ED. Tel: 0181-231
2776. *Hon. General Secretary*, Ms A. Keen

COMMUNITY AND YOUTH WORKERS UNION (3,315),
Unit 302, The Argent Centre, 60 Frederick Street,
Birmingham B1 3HS. Tel: 0121-244 3344. *General
Secretary*, D. Nicholls

ENGINEERING AND FASTENER TRADE UNION (150), 42
Galton Road, Warley, West Midlands B67 5JU. Tel:
0121-429 2594. *General Secretary*, J. Burdis

ENGINEERS' AND MANAGERS' ASSOCIATION (29,517),
Flaxman House, Gogmore Lane, Chertsey, Surrey
KT16 9JS. Tel: 01932-577007. *General Secretary*,
D. A. Cooper

FIRE BRIGADES UNION (57,654), Bradley House, 68
Coombe Road, Kingston upon Thames, Surrey KT2 7AE.
Tel: 0181-541 1765. *General Secretary*, K. Cameron

GENERAL UNION OF LOOM OVERLOOKERS (322), 9
Wellington Street, St Johns, Blackburn, Lancs BB1 8AF.
Tel: 01254-51760. *General Secretary*, D. J. Rishton

GMB (FORMERLY GENERAL, MUNICIPAL,
BOILERMAKERS AND ALLIED TRADES UNION)
(712,010), 22-24 Worple Road, London SW19 4DD. Tel:
0181-947 3131. *General Secretary*, J. Edmonds

GRAPHICAL, PAPER AND MEDIA UNION (203,229), 63-
67 Bromham Road, Bedford MK40 2AG. Tel: 01234-
351521. *General Secretary*, A. D. Dubbins

GUINNESS STAFF ASSOCIATION (585), Sun Works
Cottage, Park Royal Brewery, London NW10 7RR. Tel:
0181-963 5249. *Chairman*, J. Collins

HOSPITAL CONSULTANTS AND SPECIALISTS
ASSOCIATION (2,259), 1 Kingsclere Road, Overton,
Basingstoke, Hants RG25 3JA. Tel: 01256-771777. *General
Secretary*, S. Charkham

INDEPENDENT UNION OF HALIFAX STAFF (25,652),
Simmons House, 46 Old Bath Road, Charvil, Reading
RG10 9QR. Tel: 0118-934 1808. *General Secretary*,
G. Nichols

INSTITUTION OF PROFESSIONALS, MANAGERS AND
SPECIALISTS (73,329), 75-79 York Road, London
SE1 7AQ. Tel: 0171-902 6600. *General Secretary*, P. Noon

IRON AND STEEL TRADES CONFEDERATION (50,000),
Swinton House, 324 Gray's Inn Road, London
WC1X 8DD. Tel: 0171-837 6691. *General Secretary*,
M. J. Leahy

MANAGERIAL AND PROFESSIONAL OFFICERS (9,627),
Terminus House, The High, Harlow, Essex CM20 1TZ.
Tel: 01279-434444. *Chief Executive*, R. Newland

MANUFACTURING, SCIENCE AND FINANCE (MSF)
(416,000), MSF Centre, 33-37 Moreland Street,
London EC1V 8HA. Tel: 0171-505 3000. *General Secretary*,
R. Lyons

MILITARY AND ORCHESTRAL MUSICAL INSTRUMENT
MAKERS TRADE SOCIETY (57), 2 Whitehouse Avenue,
Borehamwood, Herts WD6 1HD. *General Secretary*,
F. McKenzie

MUSICIANS' UNION (30,811), 60-62 Clapham Road,
London SW9 0JJ. Tel: 0171-582 5566. *General Secretary*,
D. Scard

NASUWT (NATIONAL ASSOCIATION OF
SCHOOLMASTERS/UNION OF WOMEN TEACHERS)
(178,518), 5 King Street, London WC2E 8HN. Tel: 0171-
420 9670. *General Secretary*, N. de Gruchy

NATFHE (UNIVERSITY AND COLLEGE LECTURERS
UNION) (64,153), 27 Britannia Street, London WC1X 9JP.
Tel: 0171-837 3636. *General Secretary*, P. Mackney

NATIONAL ASSOCIATION OF COLLIERY OVERMEN,
DEPUTIES AND SHOTFIRERS (512), 19 Cadzow Street,
Hamilton, Lanarkshire. Tel: 01698-284981. *Secretary*,
P. McNestry

NATIONAL ASSOCIATION OF CO-OPERATIVE
OFFICIALS (3,012), Coronation House, Arndale Centre,
Manchester M4 2HW. Tel: 0161-834 6029. *General
Secretary*, L. W. Ewing

NATIONAL ASSOCIATION OF PROBATION OFFICERS
(6,174), 4 Chivalry Road, London SW11 1HT. Tel: 0171-
223 4887. *General Secretary*, Ms J. McKnight

NATIONAL LEAGUE OF THE BLIND AND DISABLED
(2,200), 2 Tenterden Road, London N17 8BE. Tel: 0181-
808 6030. *General Secretary*, J. Mann

NATIONAL UNION OF DOMESTIC APPLIANCES AND
GENERAL OPERATIVES (2,253), 7-8 Imperial
Buildings, Corporation Street, Rotherham, S. Yorks
S60 1PB. Tel: 01709-382820. *General Secretary*,
A. McCarthy

NATIONAL UNION OF INSURANCE WORKERS (7,822),
27 Old Gloucester Street, London WC1N 3AF. Tel: 0171-
405 6798. *General Secretary*, K. Perry

NATIONAL UNION OF JOURNALISTS (NUJ) (19,436),
Acorn House, 314-320 Gray's Inn Road, London
WC1X 8DP. Tel: 0171-278 7916. *General Secretary*, J. Foster

NATIONAL UNION OF KNITWEAR, FOOTWEAR AND
APPAREL TRADES (32,624), 55 New Walk, Leicester
LE1 7EB. Tel: 0116-255 6703. *General Secretary*, B. Morris

NATIONAL UNION OF LOCK AND METAL WORKERS
(4,021), Bellamy House, Wilkes Street, Willenhall, W.
Midlands WV13 2BS. Tel: 01902-366651. *General Secretary*,
R. Ward

NATIONAL UNION OF MARINE, AVIATION AND SHIPPING TRANSPORT OFFICERS (18,843), Oceanair House, 750-760 High Road, London E11 3BB. Tel: 0181-989 6677. *General Secretary*, B. D. Orrell

NATIONAL UNION OF MINEWORKERS (NUM) (5,000), Miners' Offices, 2 Huddersfield Road, Barnsley, S. Yorks S70 2LS. Tel: 01226-215555. *President*, A. Scargill

NATIONAL UNION OF RAIL, MARITIME AND TRANSPORT WORKERS (RMT) (56,476), Unity House, 205 Euston Road, London NW1 2BL. Tel: 0171-387 4771. *General Secretary*, J. Knapp

NATIONAL UNION OF TEACHERS (NUT) (194,259), Hamilton House, Mabledon Place, London WC1H 9BD. Tel: 0171-388 6191. *General Secretary*, D. McAvoy

NORTHERN CARPET TRADES' UNION (600), 22 Clare Road, Halifax HX1 2HX. Tel: 01422-360492. *General Secretary*, K. Edmondson

POWER LOOM CARPET WEAVERS' AND TEXTILE WORKERS' UNION (1,350), 148 Hurcott Road, Kidderminster, Worcs DY10 2RL. Tel: 01562-823192. *General Secretary*, G. Rudd

PRISON OFFICERS' ASSOCIATION (29,563), Cronin House, 245 Church Street, London N9 9HW. Tel: 0181-803 0255. *General Secretary*, D. Evans

PROFESSIONAL FOOTBALLERS ASSOCIATION (2,268), 20 Oxford Court, Bishopsgate, Manchester M2 3WQ. Tel: 0161-236 0575. *Chief Executive*, G. Taylor

PUBLIC AND COMMERCIAL SERVICES UNION (PCS) (254,350), 160 Falcon Road, London SW11 2LN. Tel: 0171-924 2727. *Joint General Secretaries*, B. Reamsbottom; J. Sheldon

SCOTTISH PRISON OFFICERS' ASSOCIATION (3,233), 21 Calder Road, Edinburgh EH11 3PF. Tel: 0131-443 8105. *General Secretary*, D. Turner

SCOTTISH UNION OF POWER-LOOM OVERLOOKERS (42), 88 Easterbank, Forfar DD8 2BN. Tel: 01307-463871. *Secretary*, D. Hunter

SHEFFIELD WOOL SHEAR WORKERS' UNION (10), 5 Collin Avenue, Sheffield S6 4ES. Tel: 0114-220 6748. *Secretary*, B. Bell

SOCIETY OF CHIROPODISTS AND PODIATRISTS (6,458), 53 Welbeck Street, London W1M 7HE. Tel: 0171-486 3381. *Chief Executive*, Ms H. B. De Lyon

SOCIETY OF RADIOGRAPHERS (13,725), 2 Carriage Row, 183 Eversholt Street, London NW1 1BU. Tel: 0171-391 4533. *General Secretary*, S. Evans

SOCIETY OF TELECOM EXECUTIVES (16,747), 30 St George's Road, London SW19 4BD. Tel: 0181-971 6000. *General Secretary*, S. Petch

TRANSPORT AND GENERAL WORKERS' UNION (TGWU) (881,625), Transport House, 16 Palace Street, London SW1E 5JD. Tel: 0171-828 7788. *General Secretary*, W. Morris

TRANSPORT SALARIED STAFFS' ASSOCIATION (28,940), Walkden House, 10 Melton Street, London NW1 2EJ. Tel: 0171-387 2101. *General Secretary*, R. A. Rosser

UNDEB CENEDLAETHOL ATHRAWON CYMRU (NATIONAL ASSOCIATION OF TEACHERS OF WALES) (3,666), Pen Roc, Rhodfa'r Môr, Aberystwyth, Ceredigion SY23 2AZ. Tel: 01970-615577. *General Secretary*, E. Williams

UNiFI (179,544), 1B Amity Grove, London SW20 0LG. Tel: 0181-946 9151. *Joint General Secretaries*, E. Sweeney, R. Murphy

UNION FOR BRADFORD AND BINGLEY STAFF (2,648), 18D Market Place, Malton, N. Yorks YO17 7LX. Tel: 01653-697634. *General Secretary*, D. Matthews

UNION OF CONSTRUCTION, ALLIED TRADES AND TECHNICIANS (UCATT) (111,804), UCATT House, 177 Abbeville Road, London SW4 9RL. Tel: 0171-622 2442. *General Secretary*, G. Brumwell

UNION OF SHOP, DISTRIBUTIVE AND ALLIED WORKERS (USDAW) (303,060), Oakley, 188 Wilmslow Road, Fallowfield, Manchester M14 6LJ. Tel: 0161-224 2804. *General Secretary*, W. Connor

UNION OF TEXTILE WORKERS (1,563), Foxlowe, Market Place, Leek, Staffs ST13 6AD. Tel: 01538-382068. *General Secretary*, A. Hitchmough

UNISON (1,272,330), 1 Mabledon Place, London WC1H 9AJ. Tel: 0171-388 2366. *General Secretary*, R. Bickerstaffe

WRITERS' GUILD OF GREAT BRITAIN (2,050), 430 Edgware Road, London W2 1EH. Tel: 0171-723 8074. *General Secretary*, vacant

NON-AFFILIATED TRADE UNIONS

BRITISH DENTAL ASSOCIATION (18,000), 64 Wimpole Street, London W1M 8AL. Tel: 0171-935 0875. *Chief Executive*, J. M. G. Hunt

INSTITUTE OF JOURNALISTS (1,100), 2 Dock Offices, Surrey Quays Road, London SE16 2XU. Tel: 0171-252 1187. *General Secretary*, C. Underwood

NATIONAL ASSOCIATION OF HEAD TEACHERS (NAHT) (32,500), 1 Heath Square, Boltro Road, Haywards Heath, W. Sussex RH16 1BL. Tel: 01444-472472. *General Secretary*, D. Hart, OBE

NATIONAL SOCIETY FOR EDUCATION IN ART AND DESIGN (2,148), The Gatehouse, Corsham Court, Corsham, Wilts SN13 0BZ. Tel: 01249-714825. *General Secretary*, Dr J. M. Steers

PRISON GOVERNORS ASSOCIATION (1,000), Room 718, Horseferry House, Dean Ryle Street, London SW1P 2AW. Tel: 0171-217 8591. *General Secretary*, D. Roddan

RETAIL BOOK, STATIONERY AND ALLIED TRADES EMPLOYEES' ASSOCIATION (6,000), 8-9 Commercial Road, Swindon SN1 5RB. Tel: 01793-615811. *President*, D. Pickles

ROYAL COLLEGE OF MIDWIVES (37,000), 15 Mansfield Street, London W1M 0BE. Tel: 0171-312 3535. *General Secretary*, Mrs K. Davis

SCOTTISH SECONDARY TEACHERS' ASSOCIATION (7,000), 15 Dundas Street, Edinburgh EH3 6QG. Tel: 0131-556 5919. *General Secretary*, D. H. Eaglesham

SECONDARY HEADS ASSOCIATION (9,000), 130 Regent Road, Leicester LE1 7PG. Tel: 0116-299 1122. *General Secretary*, Dr J. E. Dunford, OBE

SOCIETY OF AUTHORS (7,000), 84 Drayton Gardens, London SW10 9SB. Tel: 0171-373 6642. *General Secretary*, M. Le Fanu, OBE

UNITED ROAD TRANSPORT UNION (19,000), 76 High Lane, Chorlton-cum-Hardy, Manchester M21 9EF. Tel: 0161-881 6245. *General Secretary*, D. Higginbottom

National Academies of Scholarship

THE BRITISH ACADEMY (1901)
10 Carlton House Terrace, London SW1Y 5AH
Tel 0171-969 5200

The British Academy is an independent, self-governing learned society for the promotion of the humanities and social sciences. It supports advanced academic research and is a channel for the Government's support of research in those disciplines. The Humanities Research Board is responsible for the administration of the majority of the Academy's grant programmes.

The Fellows are scholars who have attained distinction in one of the branches of study that the Academy exists to promote. Candidates must be nominated by existing Fellows. At 1 June 1999 there were 686 Fellows, 15 Honorary Fellows, and 325 Corresponding Fellows overseas.

President, Sir Tony Wrigley, PBA
Vice-President, Prof. H. G. C. Matthew, FBA (second Vice-President to be appointed)
Treasurer, J. S. Flemming, FBA
Foreign Secretary, Prof. C. N. J. Mann, FBA
Publications Secretary, Prof. F. G. B. Millar, FBA
Chair, Committee on Academy Research Projects, Prof. R. R. Davies, FBA
Secretary, P. W. H. Brown, CBE

THE ROYAL ACADEMY (1768)
Burlington House, London W1V 0DS
Tel 0171-439 7438

The Royal Academy of Arts is an independent, self-governing society devoted to the encouragement and promotion of the fine arts.

Membership of the Academy is limited to 80 Royal Academicians, all being painters, engravers, sculptors or architects. Candidates are nominated and elected by the existing Academicians. There is also a limited class of honorary membership and there were 17 honorary members as at mid-1999.

President, Sir Philip Dowson, CBE, PRA
Treasurer, M. Kenny, RA
Keeper, B. Neiland, RA
Secretary, D. Gordon

THE ROYAL ACADEMY OF ENGINEERING (1976)
29 Great Peter Street, London SW1P 3LW
Tel 0171-222 2688

The Royal Academy of Engineering was established as the Fellowship of Engineering in 1976. It was granted a royal charter in 1983 and its present title in 1992. It is an independent, self-governing body whose object is the pursuit, encouragement and maintenance of excellence in the whole field of engineering, in order to promote the advancement of the science, art and practice of engineering for the benefit of the public.

Election to the Fellowship is by invitation only from nominations supported by the body of Fellows. Fellows are chosen from among chartered engineers of all disciplines. At July 1999 there were 1,125 Fellows, 19 Honorary Fellows and 77 Foreign Members. The Duke of Edinburgh is the Senior Fellow and the Duke of Kent is a Royal Fellow.

President, Sir David Davies, CBE, FRS, FREng
Senior Vice-President, Dr J. R. Forrest, FREng
Vice-Presidents, Prof. A. P. Dowling, FREng; B. V. George, CBE, FREng; Dr D. Michael, FREng
Hon. Treasurer, J. W. Herbert, FREng
Hon. Secretaries, Prof. J. M. Brady FRS, FREng (*Electrical Engineering*); Prof. P. Braiden, FREng (*Mechanical Engineering*); J. R. Darley, FREng (*Process Engineering*); Prof. R. W. E. Shannon, FREng (*International Activities*); Dr J. R. Forrest, FREng (*Education and Training*)
Executive Secretary, J. R. Appleton

THE ROYAL SCOTTISH ACADEMY (1838)
The Mound, Edinburgh EH2 2EL
Tel 0131-225 6671

The Scottish Academy was founded in 1826 to arrange exhibitions of contemporary paintings and to establish a society of fine art in Scotland. The Academy was granted a royal charter in 1838.

Members are elected from the disciplines of painting, sculpture, architecture and printmaking. Elections are from nominations put forward by the existing membership. At mid-1998 there were seven Senior Academicians, four Senior Associates, 34 Academicians, 45 Associates, four non-resident Associates and 22 Honorary Members.

President, W. J. L. Baillie, CBE, PRSA
Secretary, W. Scott, RSA
Treasurer, I. Metzstein, RSA
Librarian, P. Collins, RSA
Administrative Secretary, B. Laidlaw

ROYAL SOCIETY (1660)
6 Carlton House Terrace, London SW1Y 5AG
Tel 0171-839 5561

The Royal Society is the United Kingdom academy of science. It is an independent, self-governing body under a royal charter, promoting and advancing all fields of physical and biological sciences, of mathematics and engineering, medical and agricultural sciences, their applications and place in society.

Election to Fellowship of the Royal Society is limited to those distinguished for original scientific work. Each year up to 40 new Fellows and six Foreign Members are elected from the most distinguished scientists. In addition, the Council can recommend for election members of the royal family and, on average, one person each year for conspicuous service to the cause of science. At June 1998, there were 1,193 Fellows, 110 Foreign Members and six Royal Fellows or Patrons.

President, Sir Aaron Klug, OM, PRS
Treasurer, Prof. Sir Eric Ash, Kt., CBE, FRS, FREng
Biological Secretary, Prof. P. J. Lachmann, FRS

Physical Secretary, Prof. J. S. Rowlinson, FRS, FREng
Foreign Secretary, Prof. R. B. Heap, CBE, FRS
Executive Secretary, S. Cox

THE ROYAL SOCIETY OF EDINBURGH
(1783)
22–24 George Street, Edinburgh EH2 2PQ
Tel 0131-240 5000

The Royal Society of Edinburgh is Scotland's premier learned society. The Society was founded by royal charter in 1783 for 'the advancement of learning and useful knowledge', and its principal role is the promotion of scholarship in all its branches. It provides a forum for broadly-based interdisciplinary activity in Scotland, including organizing public lectures, conferences and specialist research seminars; providing advice to Parliament and government; administering a range of research fellowships held in Scotland; and publishing learned journals.

Fellows are elected by ballot after being nominated by at least four existing Fellows. At 31 May 1999 there were 1,159 Ordinary Fellows and 63 Honorary Fellows.

President, Prof. Sir William Stewart, Kt., FRS, FRSE
Treasurer, Prof. Sir Laurence Hunter, Kt., CBE, FRSE
General Secretary, Prof. P. N. Wilson, CBE
Executive Secretary, Dr W. Duncan

Royal Academicians

*Senior Academician
1989   Abrahams, Ivor
1988   Ackroyd, Prof. Norman
1967   Adams, Norman
1978   Aitchison, Craigie, CBE
1989   *Armfield, Diana
1994   *Armitage, Kenneth
1986   Bellany, John, CBE
1992   Berg, Adrian
1971   Blackadder, Elizabeth, OBE
1974   Blake, Peter, CBE
1970   *Blamey, Norman, OBE
1971   Blow, Sandra
1970   Bowey, Olwyn
1974   Bowyer, William
1968   Brown, Ralph
1964   Butler, James
1971   *Cadbury-Brown, Prof. H. T.,
        OBE
1974   *Camp, Jeffery
1962   *Casson, Sir Hugh, CH, KCVO
1993   Caulfield, Patrick, CBE
1980   Christopher, Ann
1970   Clarke, Geoffrey
1968   Clatworthy, Robert
1965   Coker, Peter
1965   Cooke, Jean
1994   Cragg, Prof. Tony
1993   *Craxton, John
1989   Cullinan, Edward, CBE
1969   Cuming, Frederick
1992   Cummins, Gus
1977   *Dannatt, Prof. Trevor
1998   Deacon, Richard
1970   Dickson, Jennifer
1979   Dowson, Sir Philip, CBE

1990   Draper, Kenneth
1959   *Dunstan, Bernard
1994   Durrant, Jennifer
1976   *Eyton, Anthony
1998   Farthing, Stephen
1992   *Fedden, Mary, OBE
1987   Flanagan, Barry, OBE
1983   Foster of Thames Bank,
        Baron, OM
1975   Fraser, Donald Hamilton
1990   Freeth, Peter
1992   *Frost, Sir Terry
1964   *Gore, Frederick, CBE
1971   Green, Anthony
1994   Grimshaw, Nicholas, CBE
1963   *Hayes, Colin
1990   *Herman, Josef, OBE
1985   Hockney, David, CH
1974   *Hogarth, Paul, OBE
1992   Hopkins, Sir Michael, CBE
1983   Howard, Ken
1983   Hoyland, John
1987   Huxley, Prof. Paul
1998   *Irvin, Albert
1996   *Irwin, Flavia
1989   Jacklin, Bill
1997   Jiricna, Eva, CBE
1981   Jones, Allen
1999   Kapoor, Anish
1976   Kenny, Michael
1989   Kiff, Ken
1977   King, Prof. Phillip, CBE
1984   Kitaj, R. B.
1970   Kneale, Bryan
1986   Koralek, Paul, CBE
1991   *Lasdun, Sir Dennis, CH, CBE

1982   Lawson, Sonia
1996   Le Brun, Christopher
1975   Levene, Ben
1987   McComb, Leonard
1993   MacCormac, Richard, CBE
1998   Mach, David
1995   Maine, John
1976   *Manasseh, Leonard, OBE
1994   Manser, Michael, CBE
1985   *Martin, Sir Leslie
1991   Mistry, Dhruva
1994   Moon, Mick
1999   Nash, David
1992   Neiland, Prof. Brendan
1995   Orr, Prof. Christopher
1979   Paolozzi, Sir Eduardo, CBE
1980   Partridge, John, CBE
1984   Phillips, Tom
1972   *Powell, Sir Philip, CH, OBE
1996   Procktor, Patrick
1996   Rae, Barbara, CBE
1998   Ritchie, Ian
1978   Rogers of Riverside, Lord
1990   Rooney, Michael
1960   *Rosoman, Leonard, OBE
1975   Stephenson, Ian
1977   Sutton, Philip
1985   Tilson, Joe
1973   Tindle, David
1992   Tucker, William
1980   Whishaw, Anthony
1970   *Williams, Sir Kyffin, OBE
1990   *Wilson, Sir Colin St J.
1983   Wragg, John

The Research Councils

The Government funds basic and applied civil science research, mostly through the seven research councils, which are supported by the Department of Trade and Industry. The councils support research and training in universities and other higher education establishments. They also receive income for research commissioned by government departments and the private sector. In July 1998, the Government announced additional funding for research of £1,100 million over the three years 1999–2002.

In addition to scientific research, the establishment of an Arts and Humanities Research Council was proposed by the National Committee of Inquiry into Higher Education (the Dearing Committee) in 1997. The Arts and Humanities Research Board was established in 1998 with the intention of becoming a Research Council in due course. It is supported by the British Academy, the Higher Education Funding Councils for England, Scotland and Wales and the Department of Education for Northern Ireland.

ARTS AND HUMANITIES RESEARCH BOARD, Northavon House, Coldharbour Lane, Bristol BS16 1QD. Tel: 0117-931 7317, *Chairman and Chief Executive*, Prof. P. Langford, D.Phil., FBA

The Government science budget for 1999–2000 was £1,372.568 million in total and included the following allocations:

	1998–9	1999–2000
	£m	£m
BBSRC	185.74	198.30
ESRC	65.99	69.75
EPSRC	382.98	397.58
MRC	290.21	304.54
NERC	171.77	178.53
PPARC	191.27	196.31
CCLRC	1.46	2.00
Pensions	12.30	12.00
Royal Society	22.62	23.85
Royal Academy of Engineering	3.44	3.71
OST initiatives	2.38	2.80
Joint Research Equipment Initiative	4.15	7.00
LINK/Foresight	1.00	1.00
University Challenge	–	10.00
Joint Infrastructure Fund	–	75.00
Science Enterprise Challenge	–	25.00

BIOTECHNOLOGY AND BIOLOGICAL SCIENCES RESEARCH COUNCIL (BBSRC)
Polaris House, North Star Avenue, Swindon SN2 1UH
Tel 01793-413200

The BBSRC promotes and supports research and postgraduate training relating to the understanding and exploitation of biological systems; advances knowledge and technology; provides trained scientists to meet the needs of biotechnological-related industries; and provides advice, disseminates knowledge, and promotes public understanding of biotechnology and the biological sciences.
Chairman, Dr P. Doyle, CBE, FRSE
Chief Executive, Prof. R. Baker, FRS

INSTITUTES

BABRAHAM INSTITUTE
Director, Dr R. G. Dyer, Babraham Hall, Babraham, Cambridge CB2 4AT. Tel: 01223-496000

INSTITUTE FOR ANIMAL HEALTH
Director, Dr C. J. Bostock, Compton, Newbury, Berks RG20 7NN. Tel: 01635-578411

BBSRC AND MRC NEUROPATHOGENESIS UNIT, Ogston Building, West Mains Road, Edinburgh EH9 3JF. Tel: 0131-667 5204/5.

COMPTON LABORATORY, Compton, Newbury, Berks RG20 7NN. Tel: 01635-578411.

PIRBRIGHT LABORATORY, Ash Road, Pirbright, Woking, Surrey GU24 0NF. Tel: 01483-232441. *Head*, Dr A. I. Donaldson

INSTITUTE OF ARABLE CROPS RESEARCH
Director, Prof. I. R. Crute, Rothamsted, Harpenden, Herts AL5 2JQ. Tel: 01582-763133

IACR – BROOM'S BARN, Higham, Bury St Edmunds, Suffolk IP28 6NP. Tel: 01284-812200. *Head*, Dr J. D. Pidgeon

IACR – LONG ASHTON RESEARCH STATION, Department of Agricultural Sciences, University of Bristol, Long Ashton, Bristol BS18 9AF. Tel: 01275-392181. *Head*, Prof. P. R. Shewry

IACR – ROTHAMSTED, Harpenden, Herts AL5 2JQ. Tel: 01582-763133. *Head*, Prof. I. R. Crute

INSTITUTE OF FOOD RESEARCH
Norwich Research Park, Colney Lane, Norwich NR4 7UA. Tel: 01603-255000. *Director*, Prof. P. Schroeder

INSTITUTE OF GRASSLAND AND ENVIRONMENTAL RESEARCH
Director, Prof. C. J. Pollock, Plas Gogerddan, Aberystwyth, Ceredigion SY23 3EB. Tel: 01970-828255

ABERYSTWYTH RESEARCH CENTRE, Plas Gogerddan, Aberystwyth, Ceredigion SY23 3EB. Tel: 01970-828255

BRONYDD MAWR RESEARCH STATION, Trecastle, Brecon, Powys LD3 8RD. Tel: 01874-636480

NORTH WYKE RESEARCH STATION, Okehampton, Devon EX20 2SB. Tel: 01837-82558. *Head*, Prof. R. J. Wilkins

TRAWSGOED RESEARCH FARM, Trawsgoed, Aberystwyth, Ceredigion SY23 4LL. Tel: 01974-261615

JOHN INNES CENTRE
Director (acting), Prof. M. Gale, FRS, Norwich Research Park, Colney, Norwich NR4 7UH. Tel: 01603-452571

ROSLIN INSTITUTE
Director, Prof. G. Bulfield, Roslin, Midlothian EH25 9PS. Tel: 0131-527 4200

SILSOE RESEARCH INSTITUTE
Director, Prof. B. J. Legg, Wrest Park, Silsoe, Bedford MK45 4HS. Tel: 01525-860000

SCOTTISH AGRICULTURAL AND BIOLOGICAL RESEARCH INSTITUTES

HANNAH RESEARCH INSTITUTE, Ayr KA6 5HL. Tel: 01292-674000. *Director*, Prof. M. Peaker, FRS

MACAULAY LAND USE RESEARCH INSTITUTE, Craigiebuckler, Aberdeen AB15 8QH. Tel: 01224-318611. *Director*, Prof. T. J. Maxwell, FRSE

MOREDUN RESEARCH INSTITUTE, Pentlands Science Park, Bush Loan, Penicuik, Midlothian EH26 0PZ.Tel: 0131-445 5111. *Director*, Prof. Q. A. McKellar

ROWETT RESEARCH INSTITUTE, Greenburn Road, Bucksburn, Aberdeen AB21 9SB. Tel: 01224-712751. *Director*, Dr P. J. Morgan

SCOTTISH CROP RESEARCH INSTITUTE (SCRI), Invergowrie, Dundee DD2 5DA. Tel: 01382-562731. *Director*, Prof. J. Hillman, FRSE

BIOMATHEMATICS AND STATISTICS SCOTLAND (BioSS) (administered by SCRI), University of Edinburgh, James Clerk Maxwell Building, The King's Buildings, Mayfield Road, Edinburgh EH9 3JZ. Tel: 0131-650 4901. *Director*, R. A. Kempton

COUNCIL FOR THE CENTRAL LABORATORY OF THE RESEARCH COUNCILS (CCLRC)
Chilton, Didcot, Oxon OX11 0QX
Tel 01235-821900

The CCLRC was set up in April 1995 and is responsible for the Daresbury and Rutherford Appleton Laboratories, which provide advanced facilities and specialist expertise to support academic and industrial research in the physical and life sciences. Eighty per cent of the CCLRC's programme supports academic research, funded mainly by the other research councils, and the remaining 20 per cent is research for industry, government and other institutions world-wide.
Chairman and Chief Executive, Dr A. R. C. Westwood, FREng.

DARESBURY LABORATORY, Daresbury, Warrington, Cheshire WA4 4AD. Tel: 01925-603000

RUTHERFORD APPLETON LABORATORY, Chilton, Didcot, Oxon OX11 0QX. Tel: 01235-821900

ECONOMIC AND SOCIAL RESEARCH COUNCIL (ESRC)
Polaris House, North Star Avenue, Swindon SN2 1UJ
Tel 01793-413000

The purpose of the ESRC is to promote and support research and postgraduate training in the social sciences; to advance knowledge and provide trained social scientists; to provide advice on, and disseminate knowledge and promote public understanding of, the social sciences.
Chairman, Dr B. Smith, OBE
Chief Executive, Prof. R. Amann

RESEARCH CENTRES

CAMBRIDGE GROUP FOR THE HISTORY OF POPULATION AND SOCIAL STRUCTURE, 27 Trumpington Street, Cambridge CB2 1QA. Tel: 01223-333181. *Director*, Prof. R. Smith

CENTRE FOR THE ANALYSIS OF SOCIAL EXCLUSION, London School of Economics, Houghton Street, London WC2A 2AE. Tel: 0171-955 7419. *Director*, Prof. J. Hills

CENTRE FOR BUSINESS RESEARCH, Department of Applied Economics, University of Cambridge, Sidgwick Avenue, Cambridge CB3 9DE. Tel: 01223-335248. *Director*, A. Hughes

CENTRE FOR ECONOMIC LEARNING AND SOCIAL EVOLUTION, Department of Economics, University College London, Gower Street, London WC1E 6BT. Tel: 0171-387 7050. *Research Director*, Prof. K. Binmore

CENTRE FOR ECONOMIC PERFORMANCE, London School of Economics, Houghton Street, London WC2A 2AE. Tel: 0171-955 7048. *Director*, Prof. R. Layard

CENTRE FOR FISCAL POLICY, Institute for Fiscal Studies, 7 Ridgmount Street, London WC1E 7AE. Tel: 0171-636 3784. *Director*, Prof. R. Blundell

CENTRE FOR INTERNATIONAL EMPLOYMENT RELATIONS RESEARCH, School of Industrial and Business Studies, University of Warwick, Coventry CV4 7AL. Tel: 01203-524265. *Director*, Prof. K. Sisson

CENTRE FOR ORGANIZATION AND INNOVATION, Institute of Work Psychology, University of Sheffield, Sheffield S10 2TN. Tel: 0114-222 3287. *Director*, Prof. T. Wall

CENTRE FOR RESEARCH IN DEVELOPMENT, INSTRUCTION AND TRAINING, Department of Psychology, University of Nottingham, Nottingham NG7 2RD. Tel: 0115-951 5312. *Director*, Prof. D. J. Wood

CENTRE FOR RESEARCH INTO ELECTIONS AND SOCIAL TRENDS, Social and Community Planning Research, 35 Northampton Square, London EC1V 0AX. Tel: 0171-250 1866. *Director*, Prof. R. Jowell

CENTRE FOR RESEARCH ON INNOVATION AND COMPETITION, Faculty of Economic and Social Studies, University of Manchester M13 9PL. Tel: 0161-275 2000. *Director*, Prof. S. Metcalfe; Manchester School of Management, UMIST, Manchester M60 1QD. Tel: 0161-236 3311. *Director*, Prof. R. Coombs

CENTRE FOR SOCIAL AND ECONOMIC RESEARCH ON THE GLOBAL ENVIRONMENT, School of Environmental Sciences, University of East Anglia, Norwich NR4 7TJ. Tel: 01603-593176. *Director*, Prof. K. Turner

CENTRE FOR THE STUDY OF AFRICAN ECONOMIES, Institute of Economics and Statistics, University of Oxford, St Cross Building, Manor Road, Oxford OX1 3UL. Tel: 01865-271084. *Director*, Prof. P. Collier

CENTRE FOR THE STUDY OF GLOBALIZATION AND REGIONALIZATION, Department of Political Science, University of Warwick, Coventry CV4 7AL. Tel: 01203-523916. *Directors*, Prof. R. Higgott, Prof. J. Whalley

COMPLEX PRODUCT SYSTEM INNOVATION CENTRE, SPRU, Mantell Building, University of Sussex, Brighton BN1 9RF. Tel: 01273-686758. *Director*, Dr M. Hobday; CENTRIM, University of Brighton, Brighton BN1 9PH. Tel: 01273-642188. *Director*, H. Rush

FINANCIAL MARKETS CENTRE, London School of Economics, Houghton Street, London WC2A 2AE. Tel: 0171-955 7002. *Director*, Prof. D. Webb

HUMAN COMMUNICATION RESEARCH CENTRE, University of Edinburgh, 2 Buccleuch Place, Edinburgh EH8 9LW. Tel: 0131-650 4444. *Director*, Prof. K. Stenning

RESEARCH CENTRE ON MICRO-SOCIAL CHANGE, University of Essex, Wivenhoe Park, Colchester, Essex CO4 3SQ. Tel: 01206-872957. *Director*, Prof. J. Gershuny

TRANSPORT STUDIES UNIT, Centre for Transport Studies, University College London, Gower Street, London WC1E 6BT. Tel: 0171-380 7009. *Director*, Dr P. Goodwin

RESOURCE CENTRES

BUSINESS PROCESS RESOURCE CENTRE, Warwick Manufacturing Group, University of Warwick, Coventry CV4 7AL. Tel: 01203-524173. *Director,* Prof. K. Bhattacharrya

CENTRE FOR APPLIED SOCIAL SURVEYS, Social and Community Planning Research, 35 Northampton Square, London ECIV OAX. Tel: 0171-250 1866. *Director,* R. Thomas

CENTRE FOR ECONOMIC POLICY RESEARCH, 90–98 Goswell Road, London ECIV 7DB. Tel: 0171-878 2900. *Director,* Prof. R. Portes

ESRC DATA ARCHIVE, University of Essex, Wivenhoe Park, Colchester, Essex CO4 3SQ. Tel: 01206-872006. *Director,* Dr S. Musgrave

INTERNATIONAL BIBLIOGRAPHY OF THE SOCIAL SCIENCES, British Library of Political and Economic Science, London School of Economics, Houghton Street, London WC2A 2AE. Tel: 0171-955 7000. *Director,* Ms J. Sykes

QUALITATIVE DATA ARCHIVAL RESOURCE CENTRE, Department of Sociology, University of Essex, Wivenhoe Park, Colchester, Essex CO4 3SQ. Tel: 01206-873333. *Director,* Prof. P. Thompson

RESOURCE CENTRE FOR ACCESS TO DATA IN EUROPE, Department of Geography, University of Durham, Durham DHI 3HP. Tel: 0191-374 7350. *Director,* Prof. R. Hudson

---

ENGINEERING AND PHYSICAL SCIENCES RESEARCH COUNCIL (EPSRC)

Polaris House, North Star Avenue, Swindon SN2 IET
Tel 01793-444000

The EPSRC promotes and supports basic, strategic and applied research and training in UK higher education institutions in the physical sciences and engineering.
Chairman, Prof. A. Ledwith, CBE, FRS
Chief Executive, Prof. R. Brook, OBE, FREng.

MEDICAL RESEARCH COUNCIL (MRC)

20 Park Crescent, London WIN 4AL
Tel 0171-636 5422

The purpose of the MRC is to promote medical and related biological research. The council employs its own research staff and funds research by other institutions and individuals, complementing the research resources of the universities and hospitals.
Chairman, Sir Anthony Cleaver
Chief Executive, Prof. G. K. Radda, CBE, D.Phil., FRS
Chairman, Neurosciences and Mental Health Board, Prof. T. W. Robbins
Chairman, Molecular and Cellular Medicine Board, Prof. L. K. Borysiewicz
Chairman, Physiological Medicine and Infections Board, Prof. A. M. McGregor, MD, FRCP
Chairman, Health Services and Public Health Research Board, Prof. R. Fitzpatrick, Ph.D.

NATIONAL INSTITUTE FOR MEDICAL RESEARCH, The Ridgeway, Mill Hill, London NW7 IAA. Tel: 0181-959 3666. *Director,* Prof. Sir John Skehel, Ph.D., FRS

CLINICAL SCIENCES CENTRE, Imperial College School of Medicine, Du Cane Road, London WI2 ONN. Tel: 0181-383 1000. *Director,* Prof. C. Higgins, Ph.D., FRSE

LABORATORY OF MOLECULAR BIOLOGY, Hills Road, Cambridge CB2 2QH. Tel: 01223-248011. *Director,* R. Henderson, Ph.D., FRS

RESEARCH UNITS

ANATOMICAL NEUROPHARMACOLOGY UNIT, Mansfield Road, Oxford OXI 3TH. Tel: 01865-271865. *Director,* Prof. P. Somogyi, Ph.D.

BBSRC/MRC NEUROPATHOGENESIS UNIT, Ogston Building, West Mains Road, Edinburgh EH9 3JF. Tel: 0131-667 5204. *Director,* C. Bostock, Ph.D.

BIOCHEMICAL AND CLINICAL MAGNETIC RESONANCE UNIT, Magnetic Resonance Spectroscopy, John Radcliffe Hospital, Headington, Oxford OX3 9DU. Tel: 01865-221111. *Hon. Director,* P. Styles, D.Phil.

BIOSTATISTICS UNIT, Institute of Public Health, University Forvie Site, Robinson Way, Cambridge CB2 2SR. Tel: 01223-330366. *Hon. Director,* Prof. N. E. Day, Ph.D.

BRAIN METABOLISM UNIT, University Department of Pharmacology, University of Edinburgh, 1 George Square, Edinburgh EH8 9JZ. Tel: 0131-650 3543. *Director,* Prof. G. Fink, MD, D.Phil., FRSE

CELL MUTATION UNIT, University of Sussex, Falmer, Brighton BNI 9RR. Tel: 01273-678123. *Director,* Prof. B. A. Bridges, Ph.D., FIBiol.

CELLULAR IMMUNOLOGY UNIT, Sir William Dunn School of Pathology, Oxford OXI 3RE. Tel: 01865-275594. *Director (acting),* D. W. Mason

CENTRE FOR BRAIN REPAIR, E. D. Adrian Building, University Forvie Site, Robinson Way, Cambridge CB2 2PY. Tel: 01223-331160. *Chairman,* Prof. D. A. S. Compston, MD, FRCP

CENTRE FOR MECHANISMS OF HUMAN TOXICITY, Hodgkin Building, University of Leicester, PO Box 138, Lancaster Road, Leicester LEI 9HN. Tel: 0116-252 5525. *Director,* Prof. G. C. K. Roberts, Ph.D.

CENTRE FOR PROTEIN ENGINEERING, MRC Centre, Hills Road, Cambridge CB2 2QH. Tel: 01223-248011. *Director,* Prof. A. Fersht, Ph.D., FRS

CHILD PSYCHIATRY UNIT, Institute of Psychiatry, De Crespigny Park, Denmark Hill, London SE5 8AF. Tel: 0171-703 5411. *Director (acting),* Prof. E. Taylor

CLINICAL TRIALS UNIT, University College London Medical School, Mortimer Market Centre, Mortimer Market (off Capper Street), London WCIE 6AU. Tel: 0171-380 9991. *Director,* Prof. J. H. Darbyshire

CLINICAL TRIALS UNIT (CANCER DIVISION), 5 Shaftesbury Road, Cambridge CB2 2BW. Tel: 01223-311110. *Head,* Dr M. Parmar

COGNITION AND BRAIN SCIENCES UNIT, 15 Chaucer Road, Cambridge CB2 2EF. Tel: 01223-355294. *Director,* Prof. W. Marslen-Wilson, FBA

COLLABORATIVE CENTRE, 1–3 Burtonhole Lane, Mill Hill, London NW7 IAD. Tel: 0181-906 3811. *Commercial Director,* Dr D. Copsey

COLLABORATIVE CENTRE (SCOTLAND), Western General Hospital, Crewe Road, Edinburgh EH4 2LF. Tel: 0131-623 5552. *Director,* Dr M. Dalrymple

CYCLOTRON UNIT, MRC Clinical Sciences Centre, RPMS Hammersmith Hospital, Du Cane Road, London WI2 ONN. Tel: 0181-383 3161. *Director,* Prof. C. Higgins, Ph.D., FRSE

DUNN HUMAN NUTRITION UNIT, Dunn Clinical Nutrition Centre, Hills Road, Cambridge CB2 2DH. Tel: 01223-415695. *Director,* Prof. Sir John Walker, D.Phil., FRS

ENVIRONMENTAL EPIDEMIOLOGY UNIT, Southampton General Hospital, Southampton SOI6 6YD. Tel: 01703-777624. *Director,* Prof. D. J. P. Barker, MD, Ph.D., FRCP, FRCOG

EPIDEMIOLOGY AND MEDICAL CARE UNIT, Wolfson Institute of Preventive Medicine, St Bartholomew's and the Royal London Hospital School of Medicine and Dentistry, Charterhouse Square, London ECIM 6BQ. Tel: 0171-982 6253. *Director*, Prof. T. W. Meade, CBE, DM, FRCP

HEALTH SERVICES RESEARCH CENTRE, University of Bristol, Canynge Hall, Whiteladies Road, Bristol BS8 2PR. Tel: 0117-928 7343. *Director,* Prof. P. Dieppe, MD, FRCP

HUMAN BIOCHEMICAL GENETICS UNIT, The Galton Laboratory, University College London, Wolfson House, 4 Stephenson Way, London NWI 2HE. Tel: 0171-380 7777. *Director*, Prof. D. A. Hopkinson, MD

HUMAN GENETICS UNIT, Western General Hospital, Crewe Road, Edinburgh EH4 2XU. Tel: 0131-322 2471. *Director*, Prof. N. D. Hastie, Ph.D., FRSE

HUMAN GENOME MAPPING PROJECT RESOURCE CENTRE, Hinxton Hall, Hinxton, Cambridge CBIO IRQ. Tel: 01223-494500. *Director*, D. Campbell, Ph.D.

HUMAN IMMUNOLOGY UNIT, John Radcliffe Hospital, Headington, Oxford OX3 9DU. Tel: 01865-222443. *Director*, Prof. A. McMichael

HUMAN MOVEMENT AND BALANCE UNIT, Institute of Neurology, National Hospital for Neurology and Neuro-surgery, Queen Square, London WCI 3BG. Tel: 0171-837 3611. *Hon. Director*, Dr J. C. Rothwell

IMMUNOCHEMISTRY UNIT, University Department of Biochemistry, South Parks Road, Oxford OXI 3QU. Tel: 01865-275354. *Director*, Prof. K. B. M. Reid, Ph.D.

INSTITUTE FOR ENVIRONMENT AND HEALTH, University of Leicester, 94 Regent Road, Leicester LEI 7DD. Tel: 0116-223 1600. *Director (acting)*, Dr P. Harrison

INSTITUTE OF HEARING RESEARCH, University of Nottingham, Nottingham NG7 2RD. Tel: 0115-922 3431. *Director*, Prof. M. P. Haggard, Ph.D.

INSTITUTE OF MOLECULAR MEDICINE, John Radcliffe Hospital, Headington, Oxford OX3 9DU. Tel: 01865-222359. *Director*, Prof. Sir David Weatherall, MD, FRCP, FRCPath., FRS

INTERDISCIPLINARY RESEARCH CENTRE FOR COGNITIVE NEURO-SCIENCE, Department of Experimental Psychology, University of Oxford, Oxford OXI 3UD. Tel: 01865-271444. *Director*, Prof. C. Blakemore, FRS

INTERDISCIPLINARY RESEARCH CENTRE IN CELL BIOLOGY, MRC Laboratory for Molecular Cell Biology, University College London, Gower Street, London WCIE 6BT. Tel: 0171-380 7806. *Director*, Prof. C. R. Hopkins, Ph.D.

MAMMALIAN GENETICS UNIT, Harwell Site, Chilton, Didcot, Oxon OXII ORD. Tel: 01235-834393. *Director*, Prof. S. Brown, Ph.D.

MOLECULAR HAEMATOLOGY UNIT, Institute of Molecular Medicine, John Radcliffe Hospital, Headington, Oxford OX3 9DS. Tel: 01865-222359. *Hon. Director*, Prof. Sir David Weatherall, MD, FRCP, FRCPath., FRS

MRC CENTRE, CAMBRIDGE, Hills Road, Cambridge CB2 2QH. Tel: 01223-248011. *Head of Centre*, M. B. Davies, Ph.D.

MRC CENTRE, OXFORD, Manor House, John Radcliffe Hospital, Headington, Oxford OX3 9DU. Tel: 01865-222124. *Head of Centre*, D. McLaren, Ph.D.

MRC LABORATORIES, THE GAMBIA, PO Box 273, Banjul, The Gambia, W. Africa. *Director*, Prof. K. McAdam, FRCP

MRC LABORATORIES, JAMAICA, University of the West Indies, Mona, Kingston 7, Jamaica. *Director*, Prof. G. R. Serjeant, CMG, MD, FRCP

MUSCLE AND CELL MOTILITY UNIT, Division of Biomedical Sciences, King's College London, 26–29 Drury Lane, London WC2B 5RL. Tel: 0171-836 8851. *Hon. Director*, Prof. R. M. Simmons, Ph.D.

NEUROCHEMICAL PATHOLOGY UNIT, Newcastle General Hospital, Westgate Road, Newcastle upon Tyne NE4 6BE. Tel: 0191-273 5251. *Director*, Prof. J. A. Edwardson, Ph.D.

PRION UNIT, Imperial College School of Medicine at St Mary's, Norfolk Place, London W2 IPG. Tel: 0171-594 3760. *Director*, Prof. J. Collinge

PROTEIN FUNCTION AND DESIGN UNIT, Department of Chemistry, University of Cambridge, Lensfield Road, Cambridge CB2 IEW. Tel: 01223-336341. *Hon. Director*, Prof. A. Fersht

PROTEIN PHOSPHORYLATION UNIT, Department of Biochemistry, Medical Sciences Institute, University of Dundee, Dundee DDI 4HN. Tel: 01382-344241. *Hon. Director*, Prof. Sir Philip Cohen, Ph.D., FRS, FRSE

RADIATION AND GENOME STABILITY UNIT, Harwell Site, Chilton, Didcot, Oxon OXII ORD. Tel: 01235-834393. *Director*, Prof. D. Goodhead, D.Phil.

REPRODUCTIVE BIOLOGY UNIT, Centre for Reproductive Biology, 37 Chalmers Street, Edinburgh EH3 9EW. Tel: 0131-229 2575. *Director*, Prof. R. P. Millar

RESOURCE CENTRE FOR HUMAN NUTRITION RESEARCH, Downhams Lane, Milton Road, Cambridge CB4 IXJ. Tel: 01223-426356. *Director*, Dr A. Prentice

SOCIAL AND PUBLIC HEALTH SCIENCES UNIT, 6 Lilybank Gardens, Glasgow GI2 8QQ. Tel: 0141-357 3949. *Director*, Prof. S. Macintyre, OBE, Ph.D.

SOCIAL, GENETIC AND DEVELOPMENTAL PSYCHIATRY RESEARCH CENTRE, Institute of Psychiatry, De Crespigny Park, Denmark Hill, London SE5 8AF. Tel: 0171-919 3873. *Director*, Prof. P. McGuffin

SYNAPTIC PLASTICITY CENTRE, Department of Anatomy, School of Medical Sciences, University of Bristol, University Walk, Bristol BS8 ITD. Tel: 0117-928 7420. *Director*, Prof. G. L. Collingridge

TOXICOLOGY UNIT, Hodgkin Building, University of Leicester, PO Box 138, Lancaster Road, Leicester LEI 9HN. Tel: 0116-252 5600. *Director (acting)*, Prof. G. Cohen

UK MOUSE GENOME CENTRE, Harwell Site, Chilton, Didcot, Oxon OXII ORD. Tel: 01235-834393. *Director*, Prof. S. Brown, Ph.D.

VIROLOGY UNIT, Institute of Virology, Church Street, Glasgow GII 5JR. Tel: 0141-330 4017. *Director*, Prof. D. J. McGeoch

---

NATURAL ENVIRONMENT RESEARCH COUNCIL (NERC)

Polaris House, North Star Avenue, Swindon SN2 IEU
Tel 01793-411500

The purpose of the NERC is to promote and support research, survey, long-term environmental monitoring and related postgraduate training in terrestrial, marine and freshwater biology, and Earth atmospheric, hydrological, oceanographic and polar sciences and Earth observation; to advance knowledge and technology, and to provide services and trained scientists and engineers; to provide advice, disseminate knowledge and promote public understanding in these fields.

Chairman, J. C. Smith, CBE, FREng., FRSE
Chief Executive, Prof. J. Lawton, CBE, FRS

CENTRES/SURVEYS

BRITISH ANTARCTIC SURVEY, High Cross, Madingley Road, Cambridge CB3 0ET. Tel: 01223-221400. *Director,* Dr C. Rapley

BRITISH GEOLOGICAL SURVEY, Kingsley Dunham Centre, Nicker Hill, Keyworth, Nottingham NG12 5GG. Tel: 0115-936 3100. *Director,* Dr D. Falvey

CENTRE FOR COASTAL AND MARINE SCIENCE *Director,* Prof. J. McGlade (based at Plymouth Marine Laboratory)
PLYMOUTH MARINE LABORATORY, Prospect Place, West Hoe, Plymouth PL1 3DH. Tel: 01752-633100. *Director,* Prof. R. F. Mantoura
PROUDMAN OCEANOGRAPHIC LABORATORY, Bidston Observatory, Birkenhead L43 7RA. Tel: 0151-653 8633. *Director (acting),* Dr J. Huthnance
DUNSTAFFNAGE MARINE LABORATORY, PO Box 3, Oban, Argyll PA34 4AD. Tel: 01631-562244. *Director,* Dr G. B. Shimmield

CENTRE FOR ECOLOGY AND HYDROLOGY *Director,* Prof. W. B. Wilkinson (based at Institute of Hydrology)
INSTITUTE OF FRESHWATER ECOLOGY, The Ferry House, Far Sawrey, Ambleside, Cumbria LA22 0LP. Tel: 015394-42468. *Director,* Prof. A. D. Pickering
INSTITUTE OF HYDROLOGY, Maclean Building, Crowmarsh Gifford, Wallingford, Oxon OX10 8BB. Tel: 01491-838800. *Director,* Dr J. Wallace
INSTITUTE OF TERRESTRIAL ECOLOGY, Monks Wood, Abbots Ripton, Huntingdon PE17 2LS. Tel: 01487-773381. *Director,* Prof T. M. Roberts
INSTITUTE OF VIROLOGY AND ENVIRONMENTAL MICROBIOLOGY, Mansfield Road, Oxford OX1 3SR. Tel: 01865-281630. *Director,* Dr P. Nuttall

SOUTHAMPTON OCEANOGRAPHY CENTRE, University of Southampton, Empress Dock, Southampton SO14 3ZH. Tel: 01703-596888. *Director,* Dr J. Shepherd

UNITS

ATMOSPHERIC CHEMISTRY MODELLING SUPPORT UNIT, University Chemical Laboratory, University of Cambridge, Lensfield Road, Cambridge CB2 1EP. Tel: 01223-336473. *Director,* Dr J. A. Pyle

CENTRE FOR GLOBAL ATMOSPHERIC MODELLING, Department of Meteorology, University of Reading, 2 Earley Gate, Whiteknights, Reading RG6 2AU. Tel: 0118-931 8315. *Director,* Prof. A. O'Neill

CENTRE FOR POPULATION BIOLOGY, Imperial College, Silwood Park, Ascot, Berks SL5 7PY. Tel: 01344-294346. *Director,* Prof. J. Lawton, CBE, FRS

ENVIRONMENTAL SYSTEMS SCIENCE CENTRE, Department of Geography, Reading University, Whiteknights, Reading RG6 2AB. Tel: 0118-931 8741. *Director,* Prof. R. Gurney

SEA MAMMAL RESEARCH UNIT, Gatty Marine Laboratory, University of St Andrews, St Andrews, Fife KY16 8LB. Tel: 01334-462630. *Head,* Dr. P. Hammond

PARTICLE PHYSICS AND ASTRONOMY RESEARCH COUNCIL (PPARC)

Polaris House, North Star Avenue, Swindon SN2 1SZ
Tel 01793-442000

The purpose of the PPARC is to support research into elementary particles and the fundamental forces of nature, planetary and solar research, including space physics, and astronomy, astrophysics and cosmology. It funds research in the universities and is responsible for funding both national and international facilities, including the European Laboratory for Particle Physics (CERN), the European Space Agency and the UK Astronomy Technology Centre (UKATC) at Edinburgh.
Chairman, Dr R. Hawley, CBE, FRSE, FREng.
Chief Executive, Prof. I. Halliday

ISAAC NEWTON GROUP OF TELESCOPES, Apartado de Coreos 321, Santa Cruz de la Palma, Tenerife 38780, Canary Islands. Tel: 00 3422-411048. *Director,* R. Rutten

JOINT ASTRONOMY CENTRE, 660 N A'ohoku Place, University Park, Hilo, Hawaii 96720. Tel: Hawaii 961 3756. *Head,* Prof. I. Robson

UK ASTRONOMY TECHNOLOGY CENTRE, Blackford Hill, Edinburgh EH9 3HJ.Tel: 0131-668 8100. *Director,* Dr A. Russell

Research and Technology Organizations

The following industrial and technological research bodies are members of the Association of Independent Research and Technology Organizations (AIRTO). Members' activities span a wide range of disciplines from life sciences to engineering. Their work includes basic research, development and design of innovative products or processes, instrumentation testing and certification, and technology and management consultancy. AIRTO publishes a directory to help clients identify the organizations which might be able to assist them.

AIRTO, PO Box 85, Leatherhead, Surrey KT22 7YG. Tel: 01372-802260. *President,* Dr B. Blunden, OBE

ADVANCED MANUFACTURING TECHNOLOGY RESEARCH INSTITUTE, Hulley Road, Macclesfield, Cheshire SK10 2NE. Tel: 01625-425421. *Managing Director,* D. Palethorpe

AIRCRAFT RESEARCH ASSOCIATION LTD, Manton Lane, Bedford MK41 7PF. Tel: 01234-350681. *Chief Executive,* B. Timmins

BHR GROUP LTD (*Fluid mechanics and process technology*), The Fluid Engineering Centre, Cranfield, Bedford MK43 0AJ. Tel: 01234-750422. *Chief Executive,* I. Cooper

BIBRA INTERNATIONAL (*Assessment of toxicity of food and chemicals to humans*), Woodmansterne Road, Carshalton, Surrey SM5 4DS. Tel: 0181-652 1000. *Director,* Dr S. E. Jaggers

BLC (THE LEATHER TECHNOLOGY CENTRE), Leather Trade House, Kings Park Road, Moulton Park, Northants NN3 6JD. Tel: 01604-679999. *Chief Executive,* Dr K. Alexander

BRITISH GLASS, Northumberland Road, Sheffield S10 2UA. Tel: 0114-268 6201. *Director-General,* Dr W. Cook

BRITISH MARITIME TECHNOLOGY LTD, Orlando House, 1 Waldegrave Road, Teddington, Middx TW11 8LZ. Tel: 0181-943 5544. *Chief Executive,* D. Goodrich

BREWING RESEARCH INTERNATIONAL (*Alcoholic beverages*), Lyttel Hall, Coopers Hill Road, Nutfield, Surrey RH1 4HY. Tel: 01737-822272. *Director-General,* Prof. R. Righelato

BRITISH TEXTILE TECHNOLOGY GROUP, Wira House, West Park Ring Road, Leeds LS16 6QL. Tel: 0113-259 1999; Shirley House, Wilmslow Road, Didsbury, Manchester M20 2RB. Tel: 0161-445 8141. *Chief Executive,* A. King

BUILDING RESEARCH ESTABLISHMENT, Garston, Watford WD2 7JR. Tel: 01923-664000. *Managing Director,* Dr. M. Wyatt

BUILDING SERVICES RESEARCH AND INFORMATION ASSOCIATION, Old Bracknell Lane West, Bracknell, Berks RG12 7AH. Tel: 01344-426511. *Chief Executive,* G. J. Baker

CAMBRIDGE REFRIGERATION TECHNOLOGY (CRT), 140 Newmarket Road, Cambridge CB5 8HE. Tel: 01223-365101. *Managing Director,* A. Robertson

CAMPDEN AND CHORLEYWOOD FOOD RESEARCH ASSOCIATION, Chipping Campden, Glos GL55 6LD. Tel: 01386-842000. *Director-General,* Prof. C. Dennis

CENTRE FOR MARINE AND PETROLEUM TECHNOLOGY, Exploration House, Offshore Technology Park, Aberdeen AB23 8GX. Tel: 01224-853400; 19 Buckingham Street, London WC2N 6EF. Tel: 0171-321 0674; Research Park North, Riccarton, Edinburgh EH14 4AP. Tel: 0131-451 5231. *Chief Executive,* R. Lane-Nott, CB

CERAM RESEARCH (BRITISH CERAMIC RESEARCH LTD), Queen's Road, Penkhull, Stoke-on-Trent ST4 7LQ. Tel: 01782-764444. *Chief Executive,* Dr N. E. Sanderson

CIRIA (CONSTRUCTION INDUSTRY RESEARCH AND INFORMATION ASSOCIATION), 6 Storey's Gate, London SW1P 3AU. Tel: 0171-222 8891. *Director-General,* Dr P. L. Bransby

CRL (*Specialist products, technology licences, research and development*), Dawley Road, Hayes, Middx UB3 1HH. Tel: 0181-848 9779. *Managing Director,* Dr J. White

EA TECHNOLOGY (*Use and distribution of electricity*), Capenhurst, Chester CH1 6ES. Tel: 0151-339 4181. *Chief Executive,* Dr S. F. Exell

ERA TECHNOLOGY LTD (*Electronic, electrical, materials and structural engineering*), Cleeve Road, Leatherhead, Surrey KT22 7SA. Tel: 01372-367000. *Managing Director and Chief Executive,* Prof. M. J. Withers

FIRA INTERNATIONAL LTD (FURNITURE INDUSTRY RESEARCH ASSOCIATION), Maxwell Road, Stevenage, Herts SG1 2EW. Tel: 01438-313433. *Managing Director,* H. Davies

HR WALLINGFORD GROUP LTD (*Hydroinformatics and engineering*), Howbery Park, Wallingford, Oxon OX10 8BA. Tel: 01491-835381. *Chief Executive,* Dr J. Weare, OBE

LABORATORY OF THE GOVERNMENT CHEMIST, Queens Road, Teddington, Middx TW11 OLY. Tel: 0181-943 7300. *Chief Executive and Government Chemist,* Dr R. Worswick

LEATHERHEAD FOOD RESEARCH ASSOCIATION, Randalls Road, Leatherhead, Surrey KT22 7RY. Tel: 01372-376761. *Director,* Dr M. P. J. Kierstan

LUCAS VARITY, Stratford Road, Solihull, W. Midlands B90 4GW. Tel: 0121-627 4141. *General Manager,* R. Tribe

MATERIALS ENGINEERING RESEARCH LABORATORY LTD, Tamworth Road, Hertford SG13 7DG. Tel: 01992-500120. *Managing Director,* Dr A. Stevenson

MINERAL INDUSTRY RESEARCH ORGANIZATION, Expert House, Sandford Street, Lichfield, Staffs WS13 6QA. Tel: 01543-262957. *Director,* N. Roberts

MOTOR INDUSTRY RESEARCH ASSOCIATION, Watling Street, Nuneaton, Warks CV10 0TU. Tel: 01203-355000. *Managing Director,* J. R. Wood

MOTOR INSURANCE REPAIR RESEARCH CENTRE, Colthorp Lane, Thatcham, Berks RG19 4NP. Tel: 01635-868855. *Chief Executive,* M. Smith

THE NATIONAL COMPUTING CENTRE LTD, Oxford House, Oxford Road, Manchester M1 7ED. Tel: 0161-228 6333. *Managing Director,* C. Pearse

NATIONAL PHYSICAL LABORATORY, Queens Road, Teddington, Middx TW11 OLW. Tel: 0181-977 3222. *Deputy Director,* Dr A. Wallard

PAINT RESEARCH ASSOCIATION, 8 Waldegrave Road, Teddington, Middx TW11 8LD. Tel: 0181-977 4427. *Managing Director,* J. A. Bernie

PERA GROUP (*Multi-disciplinary research, design, development and consultancy*), Middle Aston House, Middle Aston, Oxon OX6 3PT. Tel: 01869-347755. *Chief Executive,* R. A. Armstrong

PIRA INTERNATIONAL (*Paper and board, printing, publishing and packaging*), Randalls Road, Leatherhead, Surrey KT22 7RU. Tel: 01372-802000. *Managing Director,* M. Hancock

RAPRA TECHNOLOGY LTD (*Rubber and plastics*), Shawbury, Shrewsbury SY4 4NR. Tel: 01939-250383; North East Centre, 18 Belasis Court, Belasis Technology Park, Billingham TS23 4AZ. Tel: 01642-370406. *Chief Executive,* Dr P. Extance

SATRA TECHNOLOGY CENTRE (*Footwear, apparel, safety products and furniture*), Satra House, Rockingham Road, Kettering, Northants NN16 9JH. Tel: 01536-410000. *Chief Executive,* Dr R. E. Whittaker

SIRA LTD (*Measurement, instrumentation, control and optical systems technology*), South Hill, Chislehurst, Kent BR7 5EH. Tel: 0181-467 2636. *Managing Director,* Prof. R. A. Brook

SMITH INSTITUTE (*Mathematics and computing*), PO Box 183, Guildford, Surrey GU2 5GG. Tel: 01483-579108. *Director,* Dr L. Wallen

SPORTS TURF RESEARCH INSTITUTE, St Ives Estate, Bingley, W. Yorks BD16 1AU. Tel: 01274-565131. *Chief Executive,* Dr M. Canaway

STEEL CONSTRUCTION INSTITUTE, Silwood Park, Ascot, Berks SL5 7QN. Tel: 01344-623345. *Director,* Dr G. Owens

TRADA TECHNOLOGY LTD (*Timber and wood-based products*), Chiltern House, Stocking Lane, Hughenden Valley, High Wycombe, Bucks HP14 4ND. Tel: 01494-563091. *Managing Director,* A. Abbott

TRANSPORT RESEARCH LABORATORY, Old Wokingham Road, Crowthorne, Berks RG45 6AU. Tel: 01344-773131. *Chief Executive,* G. Clarke

TWI (*Welding*), Abington Hall, Abington, Cambridge CB1 6AL. Tel: 01223-891162. *Chief Executive,* A. B. M. Braithwaite, OBE

Sports Bodies

Sports Councils

CENTRAL COUNCIL OF PHYSICAL RECREATION, Francis House, Francis Street, London SW1P 1DE. Tel: 0171-828 3163. *General Secretary*, M. Denton

SPORT ENGLAND, 16 Upper Woburn Place, London WC1H 0QP. Tel: 0171-273 1500. *Chief Executive Officer*, D. Casey

SPORT SCOTLAND, Caledonia House, South Gyle, Edinburgh EH12 9DQ. Tel: 0131-317 7200. *Chief Executive*, F. A. L. Alstead, CBE

SPORTS COUNCIL FOR NORTHERN IRELAND, House of Sport, Upper Malone Road, Belfast BT9 5LA. Tel: 01232-381222. *Chief Executive*, E. McCartan

SPORTS COUNCIL FOR WALES, Sophia Gardens, Cardiff CF1 9SW. Tel: 01222-300500. *Chief Executive*, Dr H. Jones

UK SPORTS COUNCIL, Walkden House, 10 Melton Street, London NW1 2EB. Tel: 0171-380 8000. *Chief Executive*, R. Callicott

Angling

NATIONAL FEDERATION OF ANGLERS, Halliday House, Egginton Junction, Derbys DE65 6GU. Tel: 01283-734735. *Administration Manager*, Mrs J. A. Price

Archery

GRAND NATIONAL ARCHERY SOCIETY, National Agricultural Centre, 7th Street, Stoneleigh, Kenilworth, Warks CV8 2LG. Tel: 02476-696631. *Chief Executive*, J. S. Middleton

Association Football

THE FOOTBALL ASSOCIATION, 16 Lancaster Gate, London W2 3LW. Tel: 0171-262 4542. *Executive Director*, D. Davies

FOOTBALL ASSOCIATION OF WALES, Plymouth Chambers, 3 Westgate Street, Cardiff CF10 1DP. Tel: 01222-372325. *Secretary-General*, D. G. Collins

THE FOOTBALL LEAGUE LTD, Edward VII Quay, Navigation Way, Preston, Lancs PR2 2YF. Tel: 01772-325800. *Chief Executive*, R. C. Scudamore

IRISH FOOTBALL ASSOCIATION, 20 Windsor Avenue, Belfast BT9 6EE. Tel: 01232-669458. *General Secretary*, D. I. Bowen

IRISH FOOTBALL LEAGUE, 96 University Street, Belfast BT7 1HE. Tel: 01232-242888. *Secretary*, H. Wallace

SCOTTISH FOOTBALL ASSOCIATION, 6 Park Gardens, Glasgow G3 7YF. Tel: 0141-332 6372. *Chief Executive*, D. Taylor

SCOTTISH FOOTBALL LEAGUE, 188 West Regent Street, Glasgow G2 4RY. Tel: 0141-248 3844. *Secretary*, P. Donald

Athletics

ATHLETICS ASSOCIATION OF WALES, Morfa Stadium, Landore, Swansea SA1 7DF. Tel: 01792-456237. *Chairman*, Ms L. Harries

NORTHERN IRELAND ATHLETIC FEDERATION, Athletics House, Old Coach Road, Belfast BT9 5PR. Tel: 01232-602707. *Secretary*, J. Allen

SCOTTISH ATHLETICS FEDERATION, Caledonia House, South Gyle, Edinburgh EH12 9DQ. Tel: 0131-317 7320. *General Manager*, N. F. Park

UK ATHLETICS, 30A Harborne Road, Birmingham B15 3AA. Tel: 0121-456 5098. *Information Officer*, W. Adcocks

Badminton

BADMINTON ASSOCIATION OF ENGLAND LTD, National Badminton Centre, Bradwell Road, Loughton Lodge, Milton Keynes MK8 9LA. Tel: 01908-268400. *Chief Executive*, S. Baddeley

SCOTTISH BADMINTON UNION, Cockburn Centre, 40 Bogmoor Place, Glasgow G51 4TQ. Tel: 0141-445 1218. *Chief Executive*, Miss A. Smillie

WELSH BADMINTON UNION, Fourth Floor, 3 Westgate Street, Cardiff CF1 1ND. Tel: 01222-222082. *Coaching Development Manager*, L. Williams

Baseball

BRITISH BASEBALL FEDERATION, PO Box 45, Hessle, E. Yorks HU13 0YQ. Tel: 01482-643551. *Secretary*, Ms W. Macadam

Basketball

BASKETBALL ASSOCIATION OF WALES, Connies House, Rhymney River Bridge Road, Cardiff CF3 7YZ. Tel: 01222-454395. *Administrator*, F. M. Daw

ENGLISH BASKETBALL ASSOCIATION, 48 Bradford Road, Stanningley, Leeds LS28 6DF. Tel: 0113-236 1166. *Chief Executive*, S. Kirkland

SCOTTISH BASKETBALL ASSOCIATION, Caledonia House, South Gyle, Edinburgh EH12 9DQ. Tel: 0131-317 7260. *Chief Executive Officer*, Mrs S. F. E. Mason

Billiards

WORLD LADIES BILLIARDS AND SNOOKER ASSOCIATION, 27 Oakfield Road, Clifton, Bristol BS8 2AT. Tel: 0117-974 4491. *Company Secretary*, M. D. Blake

WORLD PROFESSIONAL BILLIARDS AND SNOOKER ASSOCIATION, 27 Oakfield Road, Clifton, Bristol BS8 2AT. Tel: 0117-974 4491. *Chief Executive*, M. D. Blake

Bobsleigh

BRITISH BOBSLEIGH ASSOCIATION, Albany House, 5 New Street, Salisbury, Wilts SP1 2PH. Tel: 01722-340014. *General Secretary*, Ms H. Alderman

Bowls

BRITISH ISLES BOWLS COUNCIL, 2 Pentland Avenue, Gowkshill, Gorebridge, Midlothian EH23 4PG. Tel: 01875-821105. *Hon. Secretary*, J. P. Darling

BRITISH ISLES INDOOR BOWLS COUNCIL, 9 Highlight Lane, Barry, Vale of Glam CF62 8AA. Tel: 01446-733978. *Hon. Secretary*, J. R. Thomas, MBE

BRITISH ISLES WOMEN'S BOWLING COUNCIL, 2 Case Gardens, Seaton, Devon EX12 2AP. Tel: 01297-21317. *Hon. Secretary*, Mrs N. Colling, MBE

BRITISH ISLES WOMEN'S INDOOR BOWLS COUNCIL, Hillcrest Villa, Tynewydd, Treorchy, Rhonda, Mid Glam. CF42 5LV. Tel: 01443-771618. *Hon. Secretary*, Mrs H. King

ENGLISH BOWLING ASSOCIATION, Lyndhurst Road, Worthing, W. Sussex BN11 2AZ. Tel: 01903-820222. *Secretary*, G. D. Shaw

ENGLISH INDOOR BOWLING ASSOCIATION, David Cornwell House, Bowling Green, Leicester Road, Melton Mowbray, Leics LE13 0DA. Tel: 01664-481900. *Secretary*, D. N. Brown

ENGLISH WOMEN'S BOWLING ASSOCIATION, 2 Case Gardens, Seaton, Devon EX12 2AP. Tel: 01297-21317. *Hon. Secretary*, Mrs N. Colling, MBE

ENGLISH WOMEN'S INDOOR BOWLING ASSOCIATION, 3 Scirocco Close, Moulton Park, Northampton NN3 6AP. Tel: 01604-494163. *Secretary*, Mrs M. E. Ruff

Boxing

THE AMATEUR BOXING ASSOCIATION OF ENGLAND LTD, Crystal Palace National Sports Centre, London SE19 2BB. Tel: 0181-778 0251. *General Secretary*, T. Collier

BRITISH AMATEUR BOXING ASSOCIATION, 96 High Street, Lochee, Dundee DD2 3AY. Tel: 01382-611412. *Chief Executive*, F. Hendry

BRITISH BOXING BOARD OF CONTROL LTD, Jack Petersen House, 52A Borough High Street, London SE1 1XW. Tel: 0171-403 5879. *General Secretary*, J. Morris

Canoeing

BRITISH CANOE UNION, John Dudderidge House, Adbolton Lane, West Bridgford, Nottingham NG2 5AS. Tel: 0115-982 1100. *Chief Executive*, P. Owen

Chess

BRITISH CHESS FEDERATION, 9A Grand Parade, St Leonard's-on-Sea, E. Sussex TN38 0DD. Tel: 01424-442500. *Manager*, Mrs G. White

Cricket

ENGLAND AND WALES CRICKET BOARD, Lord's Cricket Ground, London NW8 8QZ. Tel: 0171-432 1200. *Chief Executive*, T. Lamb

MCC, Lord's Cricket Ground, London NW8 8QN. Tel: 0171-289 1611. *Secretary*, R. D. V. Knight

Croquet

CROQUET ASSOCIATION, c/o The Hurlingham Club, Ranelagh Gardens, London SW6 3PR. Tel: 0171-736 3148. *Secretary*, P. W. P. Campion

Cycling

BRITISH CYCLING FEDERATION, National Cycling Centre, Stuart Street, Manchester M11 4DQ. Tel: 0161-230 2301. *Chief Executive*, P. King

ROAD TIME TRIALS COUNCIL, 77 Arlington Drive, Pennington, Leigh, Lancs WN7 3QP. Tel: 01942-603976. *National Secretary*, P. Heaton

Dance and Keep Fit

SCOTTISH DANCESPORT, 93 Hillfoot Drive, Bearsden, Glasgow G61 3QG. Tel: 0141-563 2001. *General Secretary and Administrator*, Mrs M. Fraser

SCOTTISH OFFICIAL BOARD OF HIGHLAND DANCING, 32 Grange Loan, Edinburgh EH9 2NR. Tel: 0131-668 3965. *Secretary*, Miss M. Rowan

Darts

BRITISH DARTS ORGANISATION, 2 Pages Lane, Muswell Hill, London N10 1PS. Tel: 0181-883 5544. *General Secretary*, O. A. Croft

Equestrianism

BRITISH EQUESTRIAN FEDERATION, National Agricultural Centre, Stoneleigh Park, Kenilworth, Warks CV8 2RH. Tel: 01203-698871. *Director-General*, D. Buck

BRITISH HORSE TRIALS ASSOCIATION, National Agricultural Centre, Stoneleigh Park, Kenilworth, Warks CV8 2RN. Tel: 01203-698856. *Managing Director*, D. C. Willis

Eton Fives

ETON FIVES ASSOCIATION, 3 Bourchier Close, Sevenoaks, Kent TN13 1PD. Tel: 01732-458775. *Secretary*, M. R. Fenn

Fencing

BRITISH FENCING ASSOCIATION, 1 Baron's Gate, 33-35 Rothschild Road, London W4 5HT. Tel: 0181-742 3032. *General Secretary*, Miss G. Kenneally

Gliding

BRITISH GLIDING ASSOCIATION, Kimberley House, Vaughan Way, Leicester LE1 4SE. Tel: 0116-253 1051. *Secretary*, B. Rolfe

Golf

LADIES' GOLF UNION, The Scores, St Andrews, Fife KY16 9AT. Tel: 01334-475811. *Secretary*, Mrs J. Hall

ROYAL AND ANCIENT GOLF CLUB OF ST ANDREWS, Golf Place, St Andrews, Fife KY16 9JD. Tel: 01334-472112. *Secretary*, P. Dawson

Greyhound Racing

NATIONAL GREYHOUND RACING CLUB LTD, Twyman House, 16 Bonny Street, London NW1 9QD. Tel: 0171-267 9256. *Chief Executive*, F. Melville

Gymnastics

BRITISH GYMNASTICS, Ford Hall, Lilleshall National Sports Centre, Newport, Shropshire TF10 9NB. Tel: 01952-820330. *General Secretary*, D. Minnery

Hockey

ENGLISH HOCKEY ASSOCIATION, The Stadium The Stadium, Silbury Boulevard, Milton Keynes MK9 1HA. Tel: 01908-544644. *Chief Executive*, R. F. Wyatt

SCOTTISH HOCKEY UNION, 34 Cramond Road North, Edinburgh EH4 6JD. Tel: 0131-312 8870. *Chairman*, P. Monaghan

WELSH HOCKEY UNION, 80 Woodville Road, Cathays, Cardiff CF2 4ED. Tel: 01222-233257. *Executive Secretary*, J. G. Williams

Horse-racing

BRITISH HORSERACING BOARD, 42 Portman Square, London W1H 0EN. Tel: 0171-396 0011. *Chief Executive*, T. Ricketts

THE JOCKEY CLUB, 42 Portman Square, London W1H 0EN. Tel: 0171-486 4921. *Senior Steward*, C. Spence

Ice Hockey

BRITISH ICE HOCKEY ASSOCIATION, The Galleries of Justice, Shire Hall, High Pavement, The Lace Market, Nottingham NG1 1HN. Tel: 0115-915 9204. *General Secretary*, M. Hudson

Ice Skating

NATIONAL ICE SKATING ASSOCIATION OF THE UK LTD, First Floor, 114-116 Curtain Road, London EC2A 3AH. Tel: 0171-613 1188. *Chief Executive*, R. Gordon

Judo

BRITISH JUDO ASSOCIATION, 7A Rutland Street, Leicester LE1 1RB. Tel: 0116-255 9669. *Office Manager*, Mrs S. Startin

Lacrosse

ENGLISH LACROSSE ASSOCIATION, 4 Western Court, Bromley Street, Digbeth, Birmingham B9 4AN. Tel: 0121-773 4422. *Chief Executive Officer*, D. Shuttleworth

Lawn Tennis

LAWN TENNIS ASSOCIATION, The Queen's Club, London W14 9EG. Tel: 0171-381 7000. *Secretary*, J. C. U. James

Lugeing

GREAT BRITAIN LUGE ASSOCIATION, 1 Highfield House, Hampton Bishop, Hereford HR1 4JN. Tel: 01432-271982. *General Secretary*, J. G. Evans

Martial Arts

MARTIAL ARTS DEVELOPMENT COMMISSION, PO Box 381, Erith, Kent DA8 ITF. Tel: 01322-431440. *Office Administrator*, Mrs E. Jewell

Motor Sports

AUTO-CYCLE UNION, ACU House, Wood Street, Rugby, Warks CV21 2YX. Tel: 01788-566400. *Chief Executive*, G. Wilson

MOTORCYCLE CIRCUIT RACING CONTROL BOARD, PO Box 72, Castle Donington, Derbys DE74 2ZQ. Tel: 01332-853822. *Manager*, D. R. Barnfield

THE MOTOR SPORTS ASSOCIATION, Motor Sports House, Riverside Park, Colnbrook, Slough SL3 OHG. Tel: 01753-681736. *Chief Executive*, J. Quenby

SCOTTISH AUTO CYCLE UNION LTD, Block 2, Unit 6, Whiteside Industrial Estate, Bathgate, W. Lothian EH48 2RX. Tel: 01506-630262. *Secretary*, G. Anderson

Mountaineering

BRITISH MOUNTAINEERING COUNCIL, 177-179 Burton Road, West Didsbury, Manchester M20 2BB. Tel: 0161-445 4747. *General Secretary*, R. Payne

Multi-Sport Bodies

BRITISH OLYMPIC ASSOCIATION, 1 Wandsworth Plain, London SW18 IEH. Tel: 0181-871 2677. *Chief Executive*, S. Clegg

BRITISH UNIVERSITIES SPORTS ASSOCIATION, 8 Union Street, London SE1 ISZ. Tel: 0171-357 8555. *Chief Executive*, G. Gregory-Jones

COMMONWEALTH GAMES COUNCIL FOR ENGLAND, Tavistock House South, Tavistock Square, London WC1H 9JZ. Tel: 0171-388 6643. *Chief Executive*, Miss A. Hogbin

COMMONWEALTH GAMES FEDERATION, Walkden House, 3-10 Melton Street, London NW1 2EB. Tel: 0171-383 5596. *Hon. Secretary*, D. Dixon, CVO

Netball

ALL ENGLAND NETBALL ASSOCIATION LTD, Netball House, 9 Paynes Park, Hitchin, Herts SG5 IEH. Tel: 01462-442344. *Chief Executive*, Mrs E. M. Nicholl

NORTHERN IRELAND NETBALL ASSOCIATION, House of Sport, Upper Malone Road, Belfast BT9 5LA. Tel: 01232-381222. *Secretary*, Mrs R. McWhinney

NETBALL SCOTLAND, 24 Ainslie Road, Hillington Business Park, Hillington, Glasgow G52 4RU. Tel: 0141-570 4016. *Administrator*, D. McLaughlan

WELSH NETBALL ASSOCIATION, 2nd Floor, 33-35 Cathedral Rd, Cardiff CF11 9HB. Tel: 01222-237048. *Chief Executive Officer*, Mrs S. J. Holvey

Orienteering

BRITISH ORIENTEERING FEDERATION, Riversdale, Dale Road North, Darley Dale, Matlock, Derbys DE4 2HX. Tel: 01629-734042. *Secretary-General*, D. Locke

Polo

THE HURLINGHAM POLO ASSOCIATION, Winterlake, Kirtlington, Kidlington, Oxon OX5 3HG. Tel: 01869-350044. *Secretary*, J. W. M. Crisp

Rackets and Real Tennis

TENNIS AND RACKETS ASSOCIATION, c/o The Queen's Club, Palliser Road, London W14 9EQ. Tel: 0171-386 3447/8. *Chief Executive*, Brig. A. D. Myrtle, CB, CBE

Rifle Shooting

NATIONAL RIFLE ASSOCIATION, Bisley Camp, Brookwood, Woking, Surrey GU24 OPB. Tel: 01483-797777. *Chief Executive*, Col. C. C. C. Cheshire, OBE

NATIONAL SMALL-BORE RIFLE ASSOCIATION, Lord Roberts House, Bisley Camp, Brookwood, Woking, Surrey GU24 ONP. Tel: 01483-485500. *Secretary*, Lt.-Col. J. D. Hoare

Rowing

AMATEUR ROWING ASSOCIATION LTD, The Priory, 6 Lower Mall, London W6 9DJ. Tel: 0181-748 3632. *National Manager*, Mrs R. Napp

HENLEY ROYAL REGATTA, Regatta Headquarters, Henley-on-Thames, Oxon RG9 2LY. Tel: 01491-572153. *Secretary*, R. S. Goddard

SCOTTISH AMATEUR ROWING ASSOCIATION, 71 Gillbrae Crescent, Georgetown, Dumfries DG1 4DJ. Tel: 01387-264233. *Secretary*, G. West

WELSH AMATEUR ROWING ASSOCIATION, Lyndhurst, 77 Hereford Road, Monmouth NP5 4JZ. Tel: 01600-714244. *Secretary*, M. C. Hargaden

Rugby Fives

RUGBY FIVES ASSOCIATION, The Old Forge, Sutton Valence, Maidstone, Kent ME17 3AW. Tel: 01622-842278. *General Secretary*, M. F. Beaman

Rugby League

BRITISH AMATEUR RUGBY LEAGUE ASSOCIATION, West Yorkshire House, 4 New North Parade, Huddersfield HD1 5JP. Tel: 01484-544131. *General Manager*, I. Cooper

THE RUGBY FOOTBALL LEAGUE, Red Hall, Red Hall Lane, Leeds LS17 8NB. Tel: 0113-232 9111. *Chief Executive*, J. N. Tunnicliffe

Rugby Union

IRISH RUGBY FOOTBALL UNION, 62 Lansdowne Road, Ballsbridge, Dublin 4. Tel: 00 353-1-668 4601. *Secretary*, P. R. Browne

IRISH WOMEN'S RUGBY UNION, 140 Georgian Village, Castleknock, Dublin 15. Tel: 00 353-1-821 4237. *Secretary*, Ms R. Hanley

RUGBY FOOTBALL UNION, Rugby House, Rugby Road, Twickenham TW1 IDS. Tel: 0181-892 2000. *Chief Executive*, F. Baron

RUGBY FOOTBALL UNION FOR WOMEN (ENGLAND), 33 Rice Mews, St Thomas, Exeter EX2 9AY. Tel: 01635-278177. *Secretary*, Ms. S. Eakers

SCOTTISH RUGBY UNION, Murrayfield, Roseburn Street, Edinburgh EH12 5PJ. Tel: 0131-346 5000. *Chief Executive*, W. Watson

SCOTTISH WOMEN'S RUGBY UNION, Flat 3, 108 Comiston Road, Edinburgh EH10 5QL. Tel: 0131-557 5663. *Chairperson*, Miss B. Wilson

WELSH RUGBY UNION, PO Box 22, Hodge House, St Mary Street, Cardiff CF1 IDY. Tel: 01222-781700. *Secretary*, D. Gethin

WELSH WOMEN'S RUGBY UNION, 40 Wolseley Street, Pilwenlly, Newport NP9 2HP. Tel: 01633-220249. *Secretary*, Ms. F. Margerison

Shooting

CLAY PIGEON SHOOTING ASSOCIATION LTD, Earlstrees Court, Earlstrees Road, Corby, Northants NN17 4AX. Tel: 01536-443566. *Director*, E. G. Orduna

Skiing

BRITISH SKI AND SNOWBOARD FEDERATION, 258 Main Street, East Calder, Livingston, W. Lothian EH53 OEE. Tel: 01506-884343. *Operations Director*, Ms F. McLean

Snooker

WORLD LADIES BILLIARDS AND SNOOKER ASSOCIATION, 27 Oakfield Road, Clifton, Bristol BS8 2AT. Tel: 0117-974 4491. *Company Secretary*, M. D. Blake

WORLD PROFESSIONAL BILLIARDS AND SNOOKER ASSOCIATION, 27 Oakfield Road, Clifton, Bristol BS8 2AT. Tel: 0117-974 4491. *Chief Executive*, M. D. Blake

Speedway

SPEEDWAY CONTROL BOARD LTD, ACU Headquarters, Wood Street, Rugby, Warks CV21 2YX. Tel: 01788-565603. *General Secretary*, L. Needman

Squash Rackets

SCOTTISH SQUASH, Caledonia House, South Gyle, Edinburgh EH12 9DQ. Tel: 0131-317 7343. *Secretary*, N. Brydon

SQUASH RACKETS ASSOCIATION, PO Box 1106, London W3 0ZD. Tel: 0181-746 1616. *Chief Executive*, S. H. Courtney

SQUASH WALES, PO Box 56, Penarth CF64 1XP. Tel: 01222-704096. *Administrator*, Ms D. Selley

Sub-Aqua

BRITISH SUB-AQUA CLUB, Telfords Quay, Ellesmere Port, Cheshire L65 4FY. Tel: 0151-350 6255. *Chief Executive Officer*, D. Roberts

Swimming

AMATEUR SWIMMING ASSOCIATION, Harold Fern House, Derby Square, Loughborough, Leics LE11 5AL. Tel: 01509-618700. *Chief Executive*, D. Sparkes

SCOTTISH AMATEUR SWIMMING ASSOCIATION, Holmhills Farm, Greenlees Road, Cambuslang, Glasgow G72 8DT. Tel: 0141-641 8818. *Administration Manager*, Miss G. Ross

WELSH AMATEUR SWIMMING ASSOCIATION, Roath Park House, Ninian Road, Cardiff CF2 5ER. Tel: 01222-488820. *Hon. General Secretary*, vacant

Table Tennis

ENGLISH TABLE TENNIS ASSOCIATION, Queensbury House, Havelock Road, Hastings, E. Sussex TN34 1HF. Tel: 01424-722525. *Chief Executive*, R. Yule

Volleyball

ENGLISH VOLLEYBALL ASSOCIATION, 27 South Road, West Bridgford, Nottingham NG2 7AG. Tel: 0115-981 6324. *Chief Executive Officer*, T. Ojasoo

SCOTTISH VOLLEYBALL ASSOCIATION, 48 The Pleasance, Edinburgh EH8 9TJ. Tel: 0131-556 4633. *Director*, N. S. Moody

WELSH VOLLEYBALL ASSOCIATION, 9 St Dennis Road, Heath, Cardiff CF4 4NA. Tel: 01222-758427. *Secretary*, Ms T. Shaw

Walking

RACE WALKING ASSOCIATION, Hufflers, Heard's Lane, Shenfield, Brentwood, Essex CM15 0SF. Tel: 01277-220687. *Hon. General Secretary*, P. J. Cassidy

Water Skiing

BRITISH WATER SKI FEDERATION, 390 City Road, London EC1V 2QA. Tel: 0171-833 2855. *Executive Officer*, Ms G. Hill

Weightlifting

BRITISH AMATEUR WEIGHTLIFTERS ASSOCIATION, 131 Hurst Street, Oxford OX4 1HE. Tel: 01865-200339. *Hon. Secretary*, W. Holland, OBE

Wrestling

BRITISH AMATEUR WRESTLING ASSOCIATION, 41 Great Clowes Street, Salford, Manchester M7 1RQ. Tel: 0161-832 9209. *Chairman*, M. Morley

Yachting

ROYAL YACHTING ASSOCIATION, RYA House, Romsey Road, Eastleigh, Hants SO50 9YA. Tel: 01703-627400. *Secretary-General*, R. Duchesne, OBE

Clubs

LONDON CLUBS

ALPINE CLUB (1857), 55 Charlotte Road, London
EC2A 3QF. Tel: 0171-613 0755. *Hon. Secretary*,
G. D. Hughes

AMERICAN WOMEN'S CLUB (1899), 68 Old Brompton
Road, London SW7 3LQ. Tel: 0171-589 8292. *Secretary*,
Mrs S. Byrnes

ANGLO-BELGIAN CLUB (1955), 60 Knightsbridge,
London SW1X 7LF. Tel: 0171-235 2121. *Secretary*,
Baronne van Havre

ARMY AND NAVY CLUB (1837), 36 Pall Mall, London
SW1Y 5JN. Tel: 0171-930 9721. *Secretary*, Cdr. J. A. Holt,
MBE

ARTS CLUB (1863), 40 Dover Street, London W1X 3RB.
Tel: 0171-499 8581. *Secretary*, Ms J. Macmillan

ARTS THEATRE CLUB (1927), 50 Frith Street, London
W1V 5TE. Tel: 0171-287 9236. *Hon. Secretary*, S. Labisko

THE ATHENAEUM (1824), 107 Pall Mall, London
SW1Y 5ER. Tel: 0171-930 4843. *Secretary*, J. G. F. Stoy

AUTHORS' CLUB (1892), 40 Dover Street, London
W1X 3RB. Tel: 0171-499 8581. *Secretary*,
Mrs A. de la Grange

BEEFSTEAK CLUB (1876), 9 Irving Street, London
WC2H 7AT. Tel: 0171-930 5722. *Secretary*, Sir John Lucas-
Tooth, Bt.

BOODLE'S (1762), 28 St James's Street, London SW1A 1HJ.
Tel: 0171-930 7166. *Secretary*, R. R. T. Smith

BROOKS'S (1764), St James's Street, London SW1A 1LN. Tel:
0171-493 4411. *Secretary*, G. Snell

BUCK'S CLUB (1919), 18 Clifford Street, London W1X 1RG.
Tel: 0171-734 6896. *Secretary*, Capt. P. G. J. Murison, RN

CALEDONIAN CLUB (1891), 9 Halkin Street, London
SW1X 7DR. Tel: 0171-235 5162. *Secretary*, P. J. Varney

CANNING CLUB (1910), 4 St James's Square, London
SW1Y 4JU. Tel: 0171-827 5757. *Secretary*,
T. M. Harrington

CARLTON CLUB (1832), 69 St James's Street, London
SW1A 1PJ. Tel: 0171-493 1164. *Secretary*, A. E. Telfer

CAVALRY AND GUARDS CLUB (1893), 127 Piccadilly,
London W1V 0PX. Tel: 0171-499 1261. *Secretary*,
Cdr. I. R. Wellesley-Harding, RN

CHELSEA ARTS CLUB (1891), 143 Old Church Street,
London SW3 6EB. Tel: 0171-376 3311. *Secretary*,
D. Winterbottom

CITY LIVERY CLUB (1914), 20 Aldermanbury, London
EC2V 7HP. Tel: 0171-814 0200. *Hon. Secretary*,
W. C. Hammond

CITY OF LONDON CLUB (1832), 19 Old Broad Street,
London EC2N 1DS. Tel: 0171-588 7991. *Secretary*,
G. Jones

CITY UNIVERSITY CLUB (1895), 50 Cornhill, London
EC3V 3PD. Tel: 0171-626 8571. *Secretary*,
Miss R. C. Graham

EAST INDIA CLUB (1849), 16 St James's Square, London
SW1Y 4LH. Tel: 0171-930 1000. *Secretary*, M. Howell

FARMERS CLUB (1842), 3 Whitehall Court, London
SW1A 2EL. Tel: 0171-930 3751. *Secretary*,
Gp Capt. G. P. Carson

FLYFISHERS' CLUB (1884), 69 Brook Street, London
W1Y 2ER. Tel: 0171-629 5958. *Secretary*,
Cdr. T. H. Boycott, OBE, RN

GARRICK CLUB (1831), 15 Garrick Street, London
WC2E 9AY. Tel: 0171-379 6478. *Secretary*, M. J. Harvey

GREEN ROOM CLUB (1877), 9 Adam Street, London
WC2N 6AA. Tel: 0171-836 7453. *Secretary*, D. Lamden

GROUCHO CLUB (1985), 45 Dean Street, London
W1V 5AP. Tel: 0171-439 4685. *Company Secretary*,
Miss Z. Noordin

HURLINGHAM CLUB (1869), Ranelagh Gardens, London
SW6 3PR. Tel: 0171-736 8411. *Secretary*, P. H. Covell

THE KENNEL CLUB (1873), 1-5 Clarges Street, London
W1Y 8AB. Tel: 0171-493 6651. *Chief Executive*, R. French

LANSDOWNE CLUB (1934), 9 Fitzmaurice Place, London
W1X 6JD. Tel: 0171-629 7200. *Secretary*, Lt.-
Cdr. T. P. Havers

LONDON ROWING CLUB (1856), Embankment, Putney,
London SW15 1LB. Tel: 0181-788 1400. *Hon. Secretary*,
N. A. Smith

MCC (MARYLEBONE CRICKET CLUB) (1787), Lord's
Cricket Ground, London NW8 8QN. Tel: 0171-289 1611.
Secretary, R. D. V. Knight

THE NATIONAL CLUB (1845), c/o Carlton Club, 69 St
James's Street, London SW1A 1PJ. Tel: 0171-493 1164.
Hon. Secretary, I. A. Sowton

NATIONAL LIBERAL CLUB (1882), Whitehall Place,
London SW1A 2HE. Tel: 0171-930 9871. *Secretary*,
S. J. Roberts

NAVAL AND MILITARY CLUB (1862), 4 St James's
Square, London SW1Y 4JU. Tel: 0171-827 5757. *Secretary*,
M. G. G. Ebbitt

NAVAL CLUB (1946), 38 Hill Street, London W1X 8DP.
Tel: 0171-493 7672. *Chief Executive*,
Cdr. J. L. L. Pritchard

NEW CAVENDISH CLUB (1984), 44 Great Cumberland
Place, London W1H 8BS. Tel: 0171-723 0391. *Secretary*,
J. P. Dauvergne

DEN NORSKE KLUB LTD (1924), 5 Wimbledon Close,
London SW20 8HW. Tel: 0181-879 3463. *Secretary*,
Ms J. P. Okkenhaug

ORIENTAL CLUB (1824), Stratford House, Stratford
Place, London W1N 0ES. Tel: 0171-629 5126. *Secretary*,
S. C. Doble

PORTLAND CLUB (1816), 69 Brook Street, London
W1Y 2ER. Tel: 0171-499 1523. *Secretary*, J. Burns, CBE

PRATT'S CLUB (1841), 14 Park Place, London SW1A 1LP.
Tel: 0171-493 0397. *Secretary*, G. Snell

THE QUEEN'S CLUB (1886), Palliser Road, London
W14 9EQ. Tel: 0171-385 3421. *Secretary*, J. A. S. Edwardes

RAILWAY CLUB (1899), Room 208, 25 Marylebone Road,
London NW1 5JS. Tel: 0171-781 2175. *Hon. Secretary*,
A. G. Wells

REFORM CLUB (1836), 104-105 Pall Mall, London
SW1Y 5EW. Tel: 0171-930 9374. *Secretary*, R. A. M. Forrest

ROEHAMPTON CLUB (1901), Roehampton Lane, London
SW15 5LR. Tel: 0181-480 4200. *Chief Executive*, M. Yates

ROYAL AIR FORCE CLUB (1918), 128 Piccadilly, London
W1V 0PY. Tel: 0171-399 1000. *Secretary*, P. N. Owen

ROYAL AUTOMOBILE CLUB (1897), 89-91 Pall Mall,
London SW1Y 5HS. Tel: 0171-930 2345. *Secretary*,
A. I. G. Kennedy

ROYAL OCEAN RACING CLUB (1925), 20 St James's
Place, London SW1A 1NN. Tel: 0171-493 2248. *General
Manager*, D. J. Minords, OBE

ROYAL OVER-SEAS LEAGUE (1910), Over-Seas House, Park Place, St James's Street, London SW1A 1LR. Tel: 0171-408 0214. *Director-General*, R. F. Newell

ROYAL THAMES YACHT CLUB (1775), 60 Knightsbridge, London SW1X 7LF. Tel: 0171-235 2121. *Secretary*, Capt. D. Goldson, RN

ST STEPHEN'S CONSTITUTIONAL CLUB (1870), 34 Queen Anne's Gate, London SW1H 9AB. Tel: 0171-222 1382. *Secretary*, L. D. Mawby

SAVAGE CLUB (1857), 1 Whitehall Place, London SW1A 2HD. Tel: 0171-930 8118. *Hon. Secretary*, The Ven. B. H. Lucas, CB

SAVILE CLUB (1868), 69 Brook Street, London W1Y 2ER. Tel: 0171-629 5462. *Secretary*, N. Storey

SKI CLUB OF GREAT BRITAIN (1903), The White House, 57-63 Church Road, Wimbledon SW19 5DQ. Tel: 0181-410 2000. *Managing Director*, Ms C. Stuart-Taylor

THAMES ROWING CLUB (1860), Embankment, Putney, London SW15 1LB. Tel: 0181-788 0798. *Hon. Secretary*, J. McConnell

TRAVELLERS CLUB (1819), 106 Pall Mall, London SW1Y 5EP. Tel: 0171-930 8688. *Secretary*, M. S. Allcock

TURF CLUB (1868), 5 Carlton House Terrace, London SW1Y 5AQ. Tel: 0171-930 8555. *Secretary*, Lt.-Col. O. R. StJ. Breakwell, MBE

UNITED OXFORD AND CAMBRIDGE UNIVERSITY CLUB (1972), 71 Pall Mall, London SW1Y 5HD. Tel: 0171-930 5151. *Secretary*, G. R. Buchanan

UNIVERSITY WOMEN'S CLUB (1886), 2 Audley Square, South Audley Street, London W1Y 6DB. Tel: 0171-499 2268. *Secretary*, J. Robson

VICTORY SERVICES CLUB (1907), 63-79 Seymour Street, London W2 2HF. Tel: 0171-723 4474. *General Manager*, G. F. Taylor

WHITE'S (1693), 37-38 St James's Street, London SW1A 1JG. Tel: 0171-493 6671. *Secretary*, D. A. Anderson

WIG AND PEN CLUB (1908), 229-230 Strand, London WC2R 1BA. Tel: 0171-583 7255. *Chairman*, B. Coral

CLUBS OUTSIDE LONDON

Bath: BATH AND COUNTY CLUB (1865), Queen's Parade, Bath BA1 2NJ. Tel: 01225-423732. *Secretary*, R. M. Lockert

Birmingham: THE BIRMINGHAM CLUB (1872), Winston Churchill House, 8 Ethel Street, Birmingham B2 4BG. Tel: 0121-643 3357. *Hon. Secretary*, T. R. Pepper

ST PAUL'S CLUB (1859), 34 St Paul's Square, Birmingham B3 1QZ. Tel: 0121-236 1950. *Hon. Secretary*, E. A. Fellowes

Bishop Auckland: THE CLUB (1868), Lightfoot Institute, Kingsway, Bishop Auckland, Co. Durham DL14 7JN. Tel: 01388-603219. *Hon. Secretary*, R. Kellett

Blackburn: DISTRICT AND UNION CLUB (1849), Northwood, 1 West Park Road, Blackburn BB2 6DE. Tel: 01254-51474. *Hon. Secretary*, R. W. Edge

Bristol: CLIFTON CLUB (1882), 22 The Mall, Clifton, Bristol BS8 4DS. Tel: 0117-973 5527. *Secretary*, M. G. M. Henry

Canterbury: KENT AND CANTERBURY CLUB (1868), The Elms, 17 Old Dover Road, Canterbury CT1 3JB. Tel: 01227-462181. *Secretary*, K. D. Bassey

Cheltenham: NEW CLUB (1874), 2 Montpellier Parade, Cheltenham GL50 1UD. Tel: 01242-523285. *Hon. Secretary*, N. S. Parrack

Chichester: REGNUM CLUB (1862), 45A South Street, Chichester, W. Sussex PO19 1DS. Tel: 01243-780219. *Hon. Secretary*, A. H. Murray

Durham: COUNTY CLUB (1890), 52 Old Elvet, Durham DH1 3HJ. Tel: 0191-384 8156. *Secretary*, Mrs C. Arnot

NORTH BAILEY CLUB (1842), 24 North Bailey, Durham DH1 3EU. Tel: 0191-384 3724. *Permanent Secretary*, Mrs E. M. Hardcastle

Guildford: THE COUNTY CLUB, 158 High Street, Guildford GU1 3HJ. Tel: 01483-560677. *Hon. Secretary*, R. W. D. Hemingway

Henley-on-Thames: LEANDER CLUB (1818), Henley-on-Thames, Oxon RG9 2LP. Tel: 01491-575782. *Hon. Secretary*, J. Beveridge

PHYLLIS COURT CLUB (1906), Marlow Road, Henley-on-Thames, Oxon RG9 2HT. Tel: 01491-570500. *Secretary*, R. Edwards

Hove: HOVE CLUB (1882), 28 Fourth Avenue, Hove, E. Sussex BN3 2PJ. Tel: 01273-730872. *Secretary*, G. J. L. Gordon

Leamington Spa: TENNIS COURT CLUB (1846), 50 Bedford Street, Leamington Spa, Warks CV32 5DT. Tel: 01926-424977. *Hon. Secretary*, P. J. Lloyd

Leeds: THE LEEDS CLUB (1849), 3 Albion Place, Leeds LS1 6JL. Tel: 0113-242 1591. *Administrator*, Mrs I. Sigsworth

Leicester: LEICESTERSHIRE CLUB (1873), 9 Welford Place, Leicester LE1 6ZH. Tel: 0116-254 0399. *Secretary*, T. M. Bedingfield

Liverpool: THE ATHENAEUM (1797), Church Alley, Liverpool L1 3DD. Tel: 0151-709 7770. *Secretary*, B. H. Denton

Macclesfield: OLD BOYS' AND PARK GREEN CLUB, 7 Churchside, Macclesfield, Cheshire SK10 1HG. Tel: 01625-423292. *Hon. Secretary*, J. G. P. van der Feltz

Newcastle upon Tyne: NORTHERN CONSTITUTIONAL CLUB (1882), 37 Pilgrim Street, Newcastle upon Tyne NE1 6QE. Tel: 0191-232 0884. *Hon. Secretary*, D. Blake

Northampton: NORTHAMPTON AND COUNTY CLUB (1873), George Row, Northampton NN1 1DF. Tel: 01604-632962. *Secretary*, J. Green

Norwich: THE NORFOLK CLUB (1770), 17 Upper King Street, Norwich NR3 1RB. Tel: 01603-610652. *Secretary*, G. G. Hardaker

Nottingham: THE NOTTINGHAM CLUB (1920), Newdigate House, Castle Gate, Nottingham NG1 6AF. Tel: 0115-912 6220. *Secretary*, R. Wileman

Oxford: FREWEN CLUB (1869), 98 St Aldate's, Oxford OX1 1BT. Tel: 01865-243816. *Hon. Secretary*, B. R. Boyt

VINCENT'S CLUB (1863), 1A King Edward Street, Oxford OX1 4HS. Tel: 01865-722984. *Steward*, H. Dean

Paignton: PAIGNTON CLUB (1882), The Esplanade, Paignton, Devon TQ4 6ED. Tel: 01803-559682. *Hon. Secretary*, P. Grafton

Shrewsbury: SALOP CLUB (1974), The Old House, Dogpole, Shrewsbury SY1 1EP. *Secretary*, J. W. Rouse

Stourbridge: STOURBRIDGE OLD EDWARDIAN CLUB (1898), Drury Lane, Stourbridge, W. Midlands DY8 1BL. Tel: 01384-395635. *Hon. Secretary*, Dr P. M. Mason

Teddington: ROYAL CANOE CLUB (1866), Trowlock Island, Teddington, Middx TW11 9QZ. Tel: 0181-977 5269. *Hon. Secretary*, Mrs J. S. Evans

WALES

Cardiff: CARDIFF AND COUNTY CLUB (1866), Westgate Street, Cardiff CF10 1DA. Tel: 01222-220846. *Hon. Secretary*, Cdr J. E. Payn, RD

SCOTLAND

Aberdeen: ROYAL NORTHERN AND UNIVERSITY CLUB (1854/1889, amal. 1979), 9 Albyn Place, Aberdeen AB10 1YE. Tel: 01224-583292. *Secretary*, Miss R. A. Black

Ayr: AYR COUNTY CLUB (1872), Savoy Park Hotel, Racecourse Road, Ayr KA7 2UT. Tel: 01292-266112. *Hon. Secretary,* G. A. Hay

Edinburgh: CALEDONIAN CLUB, 32 Abercromby Place, Edinburgh EH3 6QE. Tel: 0131-557 2675. *Secretary,* P. Walker

NEW CLUB (1787), 86 Princes Street, Edinburgh EH2 2BB. Tel: 0131-226 4881. *Secretary,* A. D. Orr Ewing

Glasgow: GLASGOW ART CLUB (1867), 185 Bath Street, Glasgow G2 4HU. Tel: 0141-248 5210. *Secretary,* L. J. McIntyre

ROYAL SCOTTISH AUTOMOBILE CLUB (1899), 11 Blythswood Square, Glasgow G2 4AG. Tel: 0141-221 3850. *Secretary,* J. C. Lord

WESTERN CLUB (1825), 32 Royal Exchange Square, Glasgow G1 3AB. Tel: 0141-221 2016. *Secretary,* D. H. Gifford

NORTHERN IRELAND

Belfast: ULSTER REFORM CLUB (1885), 4 Royal Avenue, Belfast BT1 1DA. Tel: 01232-323411. *General Manager,* A. W. Graham

Londonderry: NORTHERN COUNTIES CLUB (1880), 24 Bishop Street, Londonderry BT48 6PP. Tel: 01504-262012. *Hon. Secretary,* N. Dykes

CHANNEL ISLANDS

Guernsey: UNITED CLUB (1870), Pier Steps, St Peter Port, Guernsey GY1 2LF. Tel: 01481-725722. *Hon. Secretary,* J. J. L. Morgan

Jersey: VICTORIA CLUB (1853), Beresford Street, St Helier, Jersey JE2 4WN. Tel: 01534-23381. *Secretary,* W. A. F. Hurst

YACHT CLUBS

Bembridge: BEMBRIDGE SAILING CLUB (1886), Embankment Road, Bembridge, IOW PO35 5NR. Tel: 01983-872237. *Secretary,* Lt.-Col. M. J. Samuelson, RM

Birkenhead: ROYAL MERSEY YACHT CLUB (1844), Bedford Road East, Rock Ferry, Birkenhead, Merseyside L42 1LS. Tel: 0151-645 3204. *Hon. Secretary,* P. A. Bastow

Bridlington: ROYAL YORKSHIRE YACHT CLUB (1847), 1 Windsor Crescent, Bridlington, E. Yorks YO15 3HX. Tel: 01262-672041. *Secretary,* J. H. Evans

Burnham-on-Crouch: ROYAL CORINTHIAN YACHT CLUB (1872), The Quay, Burnham-on-Crouch, Essex CM0 8AX. Tel: 01621-782105. *Hon. Secretary,* D. Horn

Chichester: CHICHESTER YACHT CLUB (1965), Chichester Yacht Basin, Birdham, Chichester, W. Sussex PO20 7EJ. Tel: 01243-512918. *Secretary,* I. M. Clarke

Cowes: ROYAL YACHT SQUADRON (1815), The Castle, Cowes, IOW PO31 7QT. Tel: 01983-292191. *Secretary,* Maj. R. P. Rising, RM

Dover: ROYAL CINQUE PORTS YACHT CLUB (1872), 5 Waterloo Crescent, Dover, Kent CT16 1LA. Tel: 01304-206262. *Secretary,* Mrs C. A. Partridge

Fowey: ROYAL FOWEY YACHT CLUB (1881), Whitford Yard, Fowey, Cornwall PL23 1BH. Tel: 01726-833573. *Hon. Secretary,* P. J. Selbie

Ipswich: ROYAL HARWICH YACHT CLUB (1843), Woolverstone, Ipswich IP9 1AT. Tel: 01473-780319. *Secretary,* Cdr. J. A. Adams, RD

Dartmouth: ROYAL DART YACHT CLUB (1866), Priory Street, Kingswear, Dartmouth, Devon TQ6 0AB. Tel: 01803-752496. *Hon. Secretary,* J. Crozier

Leigh-on-Sea: ESSEX YACHT CLUB (1890), HQS Bembridge, Foreshore, Leigh-on-Sea, Essex SS9 1BD. Tel: 01702-478404. *Hon. Secretary,* Ms L. Kelly

London: THE CRUISING ASSOCIATION (1908), CA House, 1 Northey Street, Limehouse Basin, London E14 8BT. Tel: 0171-537 2828. *General Secretary,* Mrs. L. Hammett

ROYAL THAMES YACHT CLUB (1775), 60 Knightsbridge, London SW1X 7LF. Tel: 0171-235 2121. *Secretary,* Capt. D Goldson, RN

Lowestoft: ROYAL NORFOLK AND SUFFOLK YACHT CLUB (1859), Royal Plain, Lowestoft, Suffolk NR33 0AQ. Tel: 01502-566726. *General Manager,* A. Donovan

Lymington: ROYAL LYMINGTON YACHT CLUB (1922), Bath Road, Lymington, Hants SO41 3SE. Tel: 01590-672677. *Secretary,* I. Gawn

Plymouth: ROYAL PLYMOUTH CORINTHIAN YACHT CLUB (1877), Madeira Road, Plymouth PL1 2NY. Tel: 01752-664327. *Hon. Secretary,*

ROYAL WESTERN YACHT CLUB OF ENGLAND (1827), Queen Anne's Battery, Plymouth PL4 0TW. Tel: 01752-660077. *Chief Executive,* J. Lewis

Poole: EAST DORSET SAILING CLUB (1875), 352 Sandbanks Road, Poole, Dorset BH14 8HY. Tel: 01202-706111. *Hon. Secretary,* Mrs T. Neely

PARKSTONE YACHT CLUB (1895), Pearce Avenue, Poole, Dorset BH14 8EH. Tel: 01202-743610. *General Manager,* M. Simms

POOLE HARBOUR YACHT CLUB (1949), 38 Salterns Way, Lilliput, Poole, Dorset BH14 8JR. Tel: 01202-707321. *Secretary,* J. N. J. Smith

THE POOLE YACHT CLUB (1865), New Harbour Road West, Hamworthy, Poole, Dorset BH15 4AQ. Tel: 01202-672687. *Secretary/Manager,* Miss L. Clark

Portsmouth: ROYAL NAVAL CLUB AND ROYAL ALBERT YACHT CLUB (1867), 17 Pembroke Road, Portsmouth PO1 2NT. Tel: 01705-824491. *Secretary,* J. McDermott, MBE

Ramsgate: ROYAL TEMPLE YACHT CLUB (1857), 6 Westcliff Mansions, Ramsgate, Kent CT11 9HY. Tel: 01843-591766. *Hon. Secretary,* Maj. B. A. Cook

Southampton: ROYAL AIR FORCE YACHT CLUB (1932), Riverside House, Rope Walk, Hamble, Southampton SO31 4HD. Tel: 01703-452208. *Secretary,* W. J. Oakley

ROYAL SOUTHAMPTON YACHT CLUB, 1 Channel Way, Ocean Village, Southampton SO14 3QF. Tel: 01703-223352. *Secretary,* A. M. Paterson

ROYAL SOUTHERN YACHT CLUB (1837), Rope Walk, Hamble, Southampton SO31 4HB. Tel: 01703-450300. *Secretary,* M. G. Long, TD

Torquay: ROYAL TORBAY YACHT CLUB (1863), 12 Beacon Terrace, Torquay, Devon TQ1 2BH. Tel: 01803-292006. *Secretary,* R. M. Porteous

Westcliff-on-Sea: THAMES ESTUARY YACHT CLUB (1895), 3 The Leas, Westcliff-on-Sea, Essex SS0 7ST. Tel: 01702-345967. *Hon. Secretary,* D. G. Brown

Weymouth: ROYAL DORSET YACHT CLUB (1875), 11 Custom House Quay, Weymouth, Dorset DT4 8BG. Tel: 01305-786258. *Secretary,* Mrs M. Tye

Windermere: ROYAL WINDERMERE YACHT CLUB (1860), Fallbarrow Road, Bowness-on-Windermere, Windermere, Cumbria LA23 3DJ. Tel: 015394-43106. *Hon. Secretary,* Mrs F. Bentley

Yarmouth: ROYAL SOLENT YACHT CLUB (1878), Yarmouth, IOW PO41 0NS. Tel: 01983-760256. *Secretary,* Mrs S. Tribe

WALES

Beaumaris: ROYAL ANGLESEY YACHT CLUB (1802), 5-6 Green Edge, Beaumaris, Anglesey LL58 8BY. Tel: 01248-810295. *Hon. Secretary,* J. E. de Leyland-Berry

Caernarfon: ROYAL WELSH YACHT CLUB (1847), Porth-
Yr-Aur, Caernarfon LL55 1SN. Tel: 01286-672599. *Hon.
Secretary,* J. H. Long

Penarth: PENARTH YACHT CLUB (1880), The Esplanade,
Penarth, Vale of Glam CF64 3AU. Tel: 01222-708196.
Hon. Secretary, R. S. McGregor

Swansea: BRISTOL CHANNEL YACHT CLUB (1875), 744
Mumbles Road, Mumbles, Swansea SA3 4EL. Tel:
01792-366000. *Hon. Secretary,* R. L. Morgan

SCOTLAND

Dundee: ROYAL TAY YACHT CLUB (1885), 34 Dundee
Road, West Ferry, Dundee DD5 1LX. Tel: 01382-477516.
Hon. Secretary, M. B. Hackney

Edinburgh: ROYAL FORTH YACHT CLUB (1868), Middle
Pier, Granton Harbour, Edinburgh EH5 1HF. Tel: 0131-
552 8560. *Hon. Secretary,* C. D. Hurn

Helensburgh: ROYAL WESTERN YACHT CLUB (1875),
Braidhurst Cottage, Shandon, Helensburgh, Argyll and
Bute G84 8NP. Tel: 01436-820256. *Hon. Secretary,*
T. J. Henderson

Slockavullin: ROYAL HIGHLAND YACHT CLUB (1881),
Raslie House, Slockavullin, Argyll PA31 8QG. Tel:
01546-510261. *Secretary,* Mrs A. Wood

Helensburgh: ROYAL NORTHERN AND CLYDE YACHT
CLUB (1824, amal. 1978), Rhu, Helensburgh, Argyll
and Bute G84 8NG. Tel: 01436-820322. *General Manager,*
Capt. A. T. Lightoller

NORTHERN IRELAND

Bangor: ROYAL ULSTER YACHT CLUB (1866), 101 Clifton
Road, Bangor, Co. Down BT20 5HY. Tel: 01247-270568.
Secretary, Mrs V. F. M. Boyd

CHANNEL ISLANDS

Jersey: ROYAL CHANNEL ISLANDS YACHT CLUB (1862),
Le Mont du Boulevard, St Aubin, Jersey JE3 8AD. Tel:
01534-45783. *Hon. Secretary,* B. Murray

Societies and Institutions

Although this section is arranged in alphabetical order, organizations are usually listed by the keyword in their title. The date in parenthesis after the organization's title is the year of its foundation.

ABBEYFIELD SOCIETY (1956), Abbeyfield House, 53 Victoria Street, St Albans, Herts AL1 3UW. Tel: 01727-857536. *Chief Executive*, F. Murphy

ACCOUNTANTS, ASSOCIATION OF CHARTERED CERTIFIED (1904), 29 Lincoln's Inn Fields, London WC2A 3EE. Tel: 0171-242 6855. *Chief Executive*, Mrs A. L. Rose

ACCOUNTANTS IN ENGLAND AND WALES, INSTITUTE OF CHARTERED (1880), Chartered Accountants' Hall, PO Box 433, Moorgate Place, London EC2P 2BJ. Tel: 0171-920 8100. *Secretary-General*, J. Collier

ACCOUNTANTS, INSTITUTE OF COMPANY (1974), 40 Tyndalls Park Road, Bristol BS8 1PL. Tel: 0117-973 8261. *Director-General*, B. T. Banks

ACCOUNTANTS, INSTITUTE OF FINANCIAL (1916), Burford House, 44 London Road, Sevenoaks, Kent TN13 1AS. Tel: 01732-458080. *Chief Executive*, J. M. Dean

ACCOUNTANTS OF SCOTLAND, INSTITUTE OF CHARTERED (1854), 27 Queen Street, Edinburgh EH2 1LA. Tel: 0131-225 5673. *Chief Executive*, P. W. Johnston

ACCOUNTING TECHNICIANS, ASSOCIATION OF (1980), 154 Clerkenwell Road, London EC1R 5AD. Tel: 0171-837 8600. *Chief Executive*, Ms J. Scott Paul

ACE STUDY TOURS (formerly Association for Cultural Exchange), Babraham, Cambridge CB2 4AP. Tel: 01223-835055. *General Secretary*, P. B. Barnes

ACTION RESEARCH (1952), Vincent House, Horsham, W. Sussex RH12 2DP. Tel: 01403-210406. *Director-General*, Mrs A. Luther

ACTORS' BENEVOLENT FUND (1882), 6 Adam Street, London WC2N 6AA. Tel: 0171-836 6378. *General Secretary*, Mrs J. Skerrett

ACTORS' CHARITABLE TRUST (1896), 255-256 Africa House, 64-78 Kingsway, London WC2B 6BD. Tel: 0171-242 0111. *General Secretary*, B. Batchelor

ACTORS' CHURCH UNION (1899), St Paul's Church, Bedford Street, London WC2E 9ED. Tel: 0171-836 5221. *Senior Chaplain*, Canon W. Hall

ACTUARIES IN SCOTLAND, FACULTY OF (1856), 18 Dublin Street, Edinburgh EH2 3PP. Tel: 0131-240 1300. *Secretary*, W. W. Mair

ACTUARIES, INSTITUTE OF (1848), Staple Inn Hall, High Holborn, London WC1V 7QJ. Tel: 0171-632 2100. *Secretary-General*, G. B. L. Campbell

ADAM SMITH INSTITUTE (1977), 23 Great Smith Street, London SW1P 3BL. Tel: 0171-222 4995. *President*, Dr M. Pirie

ADMINISTRATIVE MANAGEMENT, INSTITUTE OF (1915), 40 Chatsworth Parade, Petts Wood, Orpington, Kent BR5 1RW. Tel: 01689-875555. *Chief Executive*, Prof. G. Robinson

ADULT SCHOOL ORGANIZATION, NATIONAL (1899), Riverton, 370 Humberstone Road, Leicester LE5 0SA. Tel: 0116-253 8333. *General Secretary*, Mrs P. C. Dean, BSc

ADVERTISING, INSTITUTE OF PRACTITIONERS IN (1927), 44 Belgrave Square, London SW1X 8QS. Tel: 0171-235 7020. *Deputy Director-General*, J. Read

ADVERTISING STANDARDS AUTHORITY (1962), 2 Torrington Place, London WC1E 7HW. Tel: 0171-580 5555. *Director-General*, Mrs M. Alderson

AERONAUTICAL SOCIETY, ROYAL (1866), 4 Hamilton Place, London W1V 0BQ. Tel: 0171-499 6230. *Director*, K. Mans

AFRICAN INSTITUTE, INTERNATIONAL (1926), SOAS, Thornhaugh Street, Russell Square, London WC1H 0XG. Tel: 0171-323 6035. *Hon. Director*, Prof. P. Spencer

AFRICAN MEDICAL AND RESEARCH FOUNDATION, 4 Grosvenor Place, London SW1X 7HJ. Tel: 0171-201 6070. *Executive Director*, A. Heroys

AGE CONCERN CYMRU, 4th Floor, 1 Cathedral Road, Cardiff CF1 9SD. Tel: 01222-371566. *Director*, R. W. Taylor

AGE CONCERN ENGLAND (1940), Astral House, 1268 London Road, London SW16 4ER. Tel: 0181-765 7200. *Director-General*, Lady S. Greengross, OBE

AGE CONCERN NORTHERN IRELAND (1976), 3 Lower Crescent, Belfast BT7 1NR. Tel: 01232-245729. *Director*, C. J. Common

AGE CONCERN SCOTLAND (1943), 113 Rose Street, Edinburgh EH2 3DT. Tel: 0131-220 3345. *Director*, Ms M. O' Neill

AGEING, CENTRE FOR POLICY ON (1947), 25-31 Ironmonger Row, London EC1V 3QP. Tel: 0171-253 1787. *Director*, Dr G. Dalley

AGEING, RESEARCH INTO (1978), Baird House, 15-17 St Cross Street, London EC1N 8UW. Tel: 0171-404 6878. *Director*, Mrs E. Mills

AGRICULTURAL BENEVOLENT INSTITUTION, ROYAL (1860), Shaw House, 27 West Way, Oxford OX2 0QH. Tel: 01865-724931. *Chief Executive*, Air Cdre R. B. Duckett, CVO, AFC

AGRICULTURAL BENEVOLENT INSTITUTION, ROYAL SCOTTISH (1897), Ingliston, Edinburgh EH28 8NB. Tel: 0131-333 1023. *Director*, I. C. Purves-Hume

AGRICULTURAL ENGINEERS ASSOCIATION (1875), Samuelson House, Paxton Road, Orton Centre, Peterborough PE2 5LT. Tel: 01733-371381. *Director-General*, J. Vowles

AGRICULTURAL SOCIETY, EAST OF ENGLAND, East of England Showground, Peterborough PE2 6XE. Tel: 01733-234451. *Chief Executive*, T. Gibson, OBE

AGRICULTURAL SOCIETY OF ENGLAND, ROYAL (1838), National Agricultural Centre, Stoneleigh Park, Kenilworth, Warks CV8 2LZ. Tel: 01203-696969. *Chief Executive*, C. Runge

AGRICULTURAL SOCIETY OF THE COMMONWEALTH, ROYAL (1957), 2 Grosvenor Gardens, London SW1W 0DH. Tel: 0171-259 9678. *Hon. Secretary*, J. Anderson, FRICS

AGRICULTURAL SOCIETY, ROYAL ULSTER (1826), The King's Hall, Balmoral, Belfast BT9 6GW. Tel: 01232-665255. *Chief Executive*, W. H. Yarr, OBE

AIR LEAGUE (1909), Broadway House, Tothill Street, London SW1H 9NS. Tel: 0171-222 8463. *Director*, E. Cox

ALCOHOLICS ANONYMOUS (1947), PO Box 1, Stonebow House, Stonebow, York YO1 2NJ. Tel: 01904-644026. *General Secretary,* J. Keeney

ALEXANDRA ROSE DAY (1912), 2A Ferry Road, Barnes, London SW13 9RX. Tel: 0181-748 4824. *National Director,* Mrs G. Greenwood

ALLIANCE PARTY OF NORTHERN IRELAND (1970), 88 University Street, Belfast BT7 1HE. Tel: 01232-324274. *Party Leader,* S. Neesan

ALLOTMENT AND LEISURE GARDENERS LTD, NATIONAL SOCIETY OF (1930), O'Dell House, Hunters Road, Corby, Northants NN17 5JE. Tel: 01536-266576. *National Secretary,* G. W. Stokes

ALMSHOUSES, NATIONAL ASSOCIATION OF (1946), Billingbear Lodge, Carter's Hill, Wokingham, Berks RG40 5RU. Tel: 01344-52922. *Director,* Maj.-Gen. A. deC. L. Leask

ALZHEIMER'S DISEASE SOCIETY (1979), Gordon House, 10 Greencoat Place, London SW1P 1PH. Tel: 0171-306 0606. *Chief Director,* H. Cayton

AMNESTY INTERNATIONAL UNITED KINGDOM (1961), 99-119 Rosebery Avenue, London EC1R 4RE. Tel: 0171-814 6200. *Director,* D. Bull

ANAESTHETISTS OF GREAT BRITAIN AND IRELAND, ASSOCIATION OF (1932), 9 Bedford Square, London WC1B 3RA. Tel: 0171-631 1650. *Hon. Secretary,* Dr. P. G. M. Wallace

ANCIENT BUILDINGS, SOCIETY FOR THE PROTECTION OF (1877), 37 Spital Square, London E1 6DY. Tel: 0171-377 1644. *Secretary,* P. Venning, FSA

ANCIENT MONUMENTS SOCIETY (1924), St Ann's Vestry Hall, 2 Church Entry, London EC4V 5HB. Tel: 0171-236 3934. *Secretary,* M. J. Saunders, MBE

ANGLO-ARAB ASSOCIATION (1961), The Arab British Centre, 21 Collingham Road, London SW5 0NU. Tel: 0171-373 8414. *Executive Director,* A. C. W. Lee

ANGLO-BELGIAN SOCIETY (1982), 5 Hartley Close, Bickley, Kent BR1 2TP. Tel: 0181-467 8442. *Hon. Secretary,* P. R. Bresnan

ANGLO-BRAZILIAN SOCIETY (1943), 32 Green Street, London W1Y 3FD. Tel: 0171-493 8493. *Secretary,* J. Wright

ANGLO-DANISH SOCIETY (1924), 25 New Street Square, London EC4A 3LN. *Chairman,* H. Castenskiold, OBE

ANGLO-NORSE SOCIETY (1918), 25 Belgrave Square, London SW1X 8QD. Tel: 0171-591 5500. *Chairman,* Sir John Robson, KCMG

ANIMAL CONCERN (1988), PO Box 3982, Glasgow G51 4WD. Tel: 0141-445 3570. *Organizing Secretary,* Dr M. Daly

ANIMAL HEALTH TRUST (1942), Lanwades Park, Kentford, Newmarket, Suffolk CB8 7UU. Tel: 01638-751000. *Chief Executive,* Dr. R. Pellew, BSc, MSc, Ph.D

ANTHROPOLOGICAL INSTITUTE, ROYAL (1843), 50 Fitzroy Street, London W1P 5HS. Tel: 0171-387 0455. *Director,* J. C. M. Benthall

ANTHROPOSOPHICAL SOCIETY IN GREAT BRITAIN (1923), Rudolf Steiner House, 35 Park Road, London NW1 6XT. Tel: 0171-723 4400. *General Secretary,* N. C. Thomas

ANTIQUARIES OF LONDON, SOCIETY OF (1717), Burlington House, Piccadilly, London W1V 0HS. Tel: 0171-734 0193. *General Secretary,* D. Morgan Evans, FSA

ANTIQUARIES OF SCOTLAND, SOCIETY OF (1780), Royal Museum of Scotland, Chambers Street, Edinburgh EH1 1JF. Tel: 0131-247 4115/4133. *Director,* Mrs F. Ashmore, FSA

ANTIQUE DEALERS' ASSOCIATION, BRITISH (1918), 20 Rutland Gate, London SW7 1BD. Tel: 0171-589 4128. *Secretary-General,* Mrs E. J. Dean

ANTI-SLAVERY INTERNATIONAL (1839), Thomas Clarkson House, The Stableyard, Broomgrove Road, London SW9 9TL. Tel: 0171-924 9555. *Director,* M. Dottridge

ANTI-VIVISECTION: BRITISH UNION FOR THE ABOLITION OF VIVISECTION (1898), 16A Crane Grove, London N7 8NN. *Chief Executive,* Ms M. Thew

ANTI-VIVISECTION SOCIETY, NATIONAL (1875), 261 Goldhawk Road, London W12 9PE. Tel: 0181-846 9777. *Director,* Ms J. Creamer

APOSTLESHIP OF THE SEA (1920), Stella Maris, 66 Dock Road, Tilbury, Essex RM18 7BX. Tel: 01375-850801. *National Director,* T. J. MacGuire

APOTHECARIES OF LONDON, SOCIETY OF (1617), 14 Black Friars Lane, London EC4V 6EJ. Tel: 0171-236 1189. *Clerk,* R. J. Stringer

ARBITRATORS, CHARTERED INSTITUTE OF (1915), 24 Angel Gate, City Road, London EC1V 2RS. Tel: 0171-837 4483. *Secretary-General,* K. Harding

ARCHAEOLOGICAL ASSOCIATION, CAMBRIAN (1846), Halfway House, Pont y Pandy, Bangor, Gwynedd LL57 3DG. Tel: 01248-364865. *General Secretary,* P. Llewellyn

ARCHAEOLOGICAL INSTITUTE, ROYAL (1843), c/o Society of Antiquaries of London, Burlington House, Piccadilly, London W1V 0HS. Tel: 0171-479 7092. *Secretary,* J. G. Coad, FSA

ARCHAEOLOGY, COUNCIL FOR BRITISH (1944), Bowes Morrell House, 111 Walmgate, York YO1 9WA. Tel: 01904-671417. *Director,* R. K. Morris

ARCHITECTS BENEVOLENT SOCIETY (1850), 43 Portland Place, London W1N 3AG. Tel: 0171-580 2823. *Secretary,* K. Robinson

ARCHITECTS IN SCOTLAND, ROYAL INCORPORATION OF (1922), 15 Rutland Square, Edinburgh EH1 2BE. Tel: 0131-229 7545. *Secretary,* S. Tombs

ARCHITECTS REGISTRATION BOARD (1931), 73 Hallam Street, London W1N 6EE. Tel: 0171-580 5861. *Registrar,* A. Finch

ARCHITECTS, ROYAL INSTITUTE OF BRITISH (1834), 66 Portland Place, London W1N 4AD. Tel: 0891-234400. *Director-General,* A. Reid, Ph.D.

ARCHITECTURAL ASSOCIATION (1847), 34-36 Bedford Square, London WC1B 3ES. Tel: 0171-887 4000. *Secretary,* E. Le Maistre

ARCHITECTURAL HERITAGE FUND (1976), Clareville House, 26-27 Oxendon Street, London SW1Y 4EL. Tel: 0171-925 0199. *Secretary,* Lady Weir

ARCHITECTURE AND SURVEYING INSTITUTE (1926), St Mary House, 15 St Mary Street, Chippenham, Wilts SN15 3WD. Tel: 01249-444505. *Chief Executive,* I. N. Norris

ARCHIVISTS, SOCIETY OF (1947), 40 Northampton Road, London EC1R 0HB. Tel: 0171-278 8630. *Executive Secretary,* P. S. Cleary

ARK ENVIRONMENTAL FOUNDATION (1988), Suite 640-643, Linen Hall, 162-168 Regent Street, London W1R 5TB. Tel: 0171-439 4567. *Co-ordinator,* R. Boorer

ARLIS/UK AND IRELAND (THE ART LIBRARIES SOCIETY) (1969), 18 College Road, Bromsgrove, Worcs B60 2NE. Tel: 01527-579298. *Administrator,* Ms S. French

ARMY BENEVOLENT FUND (1944), 41 Queen's Gate, London SW7 5HR. Tel: 0171-591-2000. *Controller,* Maj.-Gen. M. D. Regan, CB, OBE

ARMY CADET FORCE ASSOCIATION (1930), E Block, Duke of York's HQ, London SW3 4RR. Tel: 0171-730 9733. *General Secretary,* Brig. J. E. Neeve

ART COLLECTIONS FUND, NATIONAL (1903), Millais House, 7 Cromwell Place, London SW7 2JN. Tel: 0171-225 4800. *Director,* D. Barrie

ARTHRITIS CARE (1949), 18 Stephenson Way, London NW1 2HD. Tel: 0171-916 1500. *Chief Executive,* R. Gutch

ARTHRITIS RESEARCH CAMPAIGN (1936), Copeman House, St Mary's Court, St Mary's Gate, Chesterfield, Derbys S41 7TD. Tel: 01246-558033. *Chief Executive,* F. Logan

ARTISTS, FEDERATION OF BRITISH, 17 Carlton House Terrace, London SW1Y 5BD. Tel: 0171-930 6844. *Chairman,* T. Muir

ARTISTS' GENERAL BENEVOLENT INSTITUTION (1814) and ARTISTS' ORPHAN FUND (1871), Burlington House, Piccadilly, London W1V 0DJ. Tel: 0171-734 1193. *Secretary,* Ms A. Connett-Dance

ARTS, ROYAL CAMBRIAN ACADEMY OF (1882), Crown Lane, Conwy LL32 8AN. Tel: 01492-593413. *Curator and Secretary,* Ms V. Macdonald

ARTS, NATIONAL CAMPAIGN FOR THE (1984), Francis House , Francis Street , London SW1P 1DE . Tel: 0171-333 0375. *Director,* Miss V. Todd

ASIAN FAMILY COUNSELLING SERVICE (1985), 74 The Avenue, London W13 8LB. Tel: 0181-997 5749. *Director,* R. Atma

ASLIB (THE ASSOCIATION FOR INFORMATION MANAGEMENT) (1924), Staple Hall, Stone House Court, London EC3A 7PB. Tel: 0171-903 0000. *Chief Executive,* R. Bowes

ASTHMA CAMPAIGN, NATIONAL (1927), Providence House, Providence Place, London N1 0NT. Tel: 0171-226 2260. *Chief Executive,* Ms A. Bradley

ASTRONOMICAL ASSOCIATION, BRITISH (1890), Burlington House, Piccadilly, London W1V 9AG. *Assistant Secretary,* Miss P. M. Barber

ATS/WRAC ASSOCIATION BENEVOLENT FUNDS (1964), AGC Centre, Worthy Down, Winchester, Hants SO21 2RG. *Secretaries,* Mrs A. H. S. Matthews; Mrs R. R. Watt

AUDIT BUREAU OF CIRCULATIONS LTD (1931), Saxon House, 211 High Street, Berkhamsted, Herts HP4 1AD. Tel: 01442-870800. *Chief Executive,* S. Devitt

AUTHORS, SOCIETY OF (1884), 84 Drayton Gardens, London SW10 9SB. Tel: 0171-373 6642. *General Secretary,* M. Le Fanu, OBE

AUTOMOBILE ASSOCIATION LTD, THE (1905), Norfolk House, Priestley Road, Basingstoke, Hants RG24 9NY. Tel: 0990-500600. *Director-General,* J. H. Maxwell

AYRSHIRE CATTLE SOCIETY OF GREAT BRITAIN AND IRELAND (1877), 1 Racecourse Road, Ayr KA7 2DE. Tel: 01292-267123. *Chief Executive,* S. J. Thomson

BACK PAIN ASSOCIATION, NATIONAL (1968), 16 Elmtree Road, Teddington, Middx TW11 8ST. Tel: 0181-977 5474. *Executive Director,* Ms E. Tait

BALTIC AIR CHARTER ASSOCIATION (1949), The Baltic Exchange, St Mary Axe, London EC3A 8BH. Tel: 0171-623 5501. *Chairman,* Capt. N. J. Harris

BALTIC EXCHANGE (1903), St Mary Axe, London EC3A 8BH. Tel: 0171-369 1621. *Chief Executive,* J. Buckley

BALTIC EXCHANGE CHARITABLE SOCIETY (1978), 38 St Mary Axe, London EC3A 8BH. Tel: 0171-369 1643. *Secretary,* D. A. Painter

BALZAN FOUNDATION, INTERNATIONAL (1956), Piazzetta U Giordano 4, Milan 20122, Italy. *Secretary-General,* Mrs P. Rognoni

BANKERS, CHARTERED INSTITUTE OF (1879), 90 Bishopsgate, London EC2N 4AS. Tel: 0171-444 7111. *Chief Executive,* G. Shreeve

BANKERS IN SCOTLAND, CHARTERED INSTITUTE OF (1875), Drumsheugh House, 38B Drumsheugh Gardens, Edinburgh EH3 7SW. Tel: 0131-473 7777. *Chief Executive,* C. W. Munn

BAPTIST MISSIONARY SOCIETY (1792), Baptist House, PO Box 49, 129 Broadway, Didcot, Oxon OX11 8XA. Tel: 01235-512077. *General Director,* Revd Dr A. Brown

BAR ASSOCIATION FOR LOCAL GOVERNMENT AND THE PUBLIC SERVICE (1945), c/o Assistant Director (Legal), Bolton MBC, Town Hall, Bolton BL1 1RU. Tel: 01204-522311 ext. 1111. *Chairman,* M. F. N. Ahmad

BARNARDO'S (1866), Tanners Lane, Barkingside, Ilford, Essex IG6 1QG. Tel: 0181-550 8822. *Senior Director,* R. Singleton

BARONETAGE, STANDING COUNCIL OF THE (1898), 3 Eastcroft Road, West Ewell, Epsom, Surrey KT19 9TX. *Chairman,* Sir Brian Barttelot, Bt.

BARRISTERS' BENEVOLENT ASSOCIATION (1873), 14 Gray's Inn Square, London WC1R 5JP. Tel: 0171-242 4761. *Secretary,* Mrs L. C. Carlier

BEE-KEEPERS' ASSOCIATION, BRITISH (1874), National Agricultural Centre, Stoneleigh Park, Kenilworth, Warks CV8 2LZ. Tel: 01203-696679. *General Secretary,* A. C. Waring

BELL RINGERS, CENTRAL COUNCIL OF CHURCH (1891), 50 Cramhurst Lane, Witley, Godalming, Surrey GU8 5QZ. Tel: 01428-682790. *President,* J. A. Anderson

BEVIN BOYS ASSOCIATION (1989), 33 Sussex Street, Winchester, Hants SO23 8TG. Tel: 01962-843056. *Public Relations,* W. H. Taylor

BI (BRITISH INVISIBLES) (1983), Windsor House, 39 King Street, London EC2V 8DQ. Tel: 0171-600 1198. *Chief Executive,* E. J. Seddon

BIBLE SOCIETY, BRITISH AND FOREIGN (1804), Stonehill Green, Westlea, Swindon SN5 7DG. Tel: 01793-418100. *Chief Executive,* N. Crosbie

BIBLIOGRAPHICAL SOCIETY (1892), c/o The Wellcome Institute, 183 Euston Road, London NW1 2BE. Tel: 0171-611 7244. *Hon. Secretary,* D. Pearson

BIBLIOGRAPHICAL SOCIETY, EDINBURGH (1890), c/o Rare Books Division, National Library of Scotland, George IV Bridge, Edinburgh EH1 1EW. Tel: 0131-226 4531. *Hon. Secretary,* R. Ovenden

BIOCHEMICAL SOCIETY (1911), 59 Portland Place, London W1N 3AJ. Tel: 0171-580 5530. *Executive Secretary,* G. D. Jones

BIOLOGY, INSTITUTE OF (1950), 20-22 Queensberry Place, London SW7 2DZ. Tel: 0171-829 9409. *Chief Executive,* Dr A. Malcolm

BIRDS, *see* ROYAL SOCIETY FOR THE PROTECTION OF and SCOTTISH SOCIETY FOR THE PROTECTION OF WILD

BIRMINGHAM AND MIDLAND INSTITUTE (1854) and LIBRARY (1779), Margaret Street, Birmingham B3 3BS. Tel: 0121-236 3591. *Administrator and General Secretary,* P. A. Fisher

BLIND, GUIDE DOGS FOR THE, *see* GUIDE DOGS FOR THE BLIND ASSOCIATION

BLIND, NATIONAL LIBRARY FOR THE (1882), Far Cromwell Road, Bredbury, Stockport, Cheshire SK6 2SG. Tel: 0161-355 2000. *Chief Executive*, Ms M. Bennett

BLIND PEOPLE, ACTION FOR (1857), 14-16 Verney Road, London SE16 3DZ. Tel: 0171-732 8771. *Chief Executive*, S. Remington

BLIND, ROYAL LONDON SOCIETY FOR THE (1838), Dorton House, Seal, Sevenoaks, Kent TN15 0ED. Tel: 01732-592500. *Chief Executive*, P. Talbot

BLIND, ROYAL NATIONAL COLLEGE FOR THE (1872), College Road, Hereford HR1 1EB. Tel: 01432-265725. *Principal*, Mrs R. Burge

BLIND, ROYAL NATIONAL INSTITUTE FOR THE, *see* ROYAL NATIONAL INSTITUTE FOR THE BLIND

BLIND, ROYAL SCHOOL FOR THE, *see* ABILITY

BLOOD AUTHORITY, NATIONAL (1948), Oak House, Reeds Crescent, Watford, Herts WD1 1QH. Tel: 01923-486800. *Chairman*, M. Fogden

BLOOD TRANSFUSION ASSOCIATION, SCOTTISH NATIONAL (1940), c/o Scottish National Blood Transfusion Service, Ellen's Glen Road, Edinburgh EH17 7QT. Tel: 0131-664 2317. *Secretary*, W. Mack

BLUE CROSS (1897), Shilton Road, Burford, Oxon OX18 4PF. Tel: 01993-822651. *Secretary and Chief Executive*, A. Kennard, MBE

BODLEIAN, FRIENDS OF THE (1925), Bodleian Library, Oxford OX1 3BG. Tel: 01865-277022/277234. *Secretary*, G. Groom

BOOK AID INTERNATIONAL (1954), 39-41 Coldharbour Lane, London SE5 9NR. Tel: 0171-733 3577. *Director*, Mrs S. Harrity, MBE

BOOKSELLERS ASSOCIATION OF GREAT BRITAIN AND IRELAND (1895), Minster House, 272 Vauxhall Bridge Road, London SW1V 1BA. Tel: 0171-834 5477. *Chief Executive*, T. E. Godfray

BOOK TRADE BENEVOLENT SOCIETY (1967), Dillon Lodge, The Retreat, Kings Langley, Herts WD4 8LT. Tel: 01923-263128. *Chief Executive*, D. Hicks

BOOK TRUST (1986), Book House, 45 East Hill, London SW18 2QZ. Tel: 0181-516 2977. *Executive Director*, B. Perman

BORN FREE FOUNDATION (1984), 3 Grove House, Foundry Lane, Horsham, W. Sussex RH13 5PL. Tel: 01403-240170. *Director*, W. Travers

BOTANICAL SOCIETY OF SCOTLAND, c/o Royal Botanic Garden, Inverleith Row, Edinburgh EH3 5LR. Tel: 0131-552 7171. *Hon. General Secretary*, R. Galt

BOTANICAL SOCIETY OF THE BRITISH ISLES (1836), c/o Department of Botany, The Natural History Museum, Cromwell Road, London SW7 5BD. Tel: 0171-938 8701. *Hon. General Secretary*, R. Gwynn Ellis

BOYS' AND GIRLS' CLUBS OF NORTHERN IRELAND (1940), 2nd Floor, 38 Dublin Road, Belfast BT2 7HN. Tel: 01232-241924. *Chief Executive*, D. Spence

BOYS' BRIGADE (1883), Felden Lodge, Hemel Hempstead, Herts HP3 0BL. Tel: 01442-231681. *Brigade Secretary*, S. Jones, OBE

BOY SCOUTS ASSOCIATION, *see* SCOUT ASSOCIATION

BREWING, INSTITUTE OF (1886), 33 Clarges Street, London W1Y 8EE. Tel: 0171-499 8144. *Chief Executive*, P. W. E. Istead

BRIDEWELL ROYAL HOSPITAL (1553), Witley, Godalming, Surrey GU8 5SG. Tel: 01428-686700. *Clerk*, D. W. Hanson

BRITAIN-NEPAL SOCIETY (1960), 3C Gunnersbury Avenue, London W5 3NH. Tel: 0181-992 0173. *Hon. Secretary*, Mrs P. Mellor

BRITAIN-RUSSIA CENTRE and BRITISH EAST WEST CENTRE (1959), 1 Nine Elms Lane, London SW8 5NQ. Tel: 0171-498 6640. *Director*, Dr I. Elliot

BRITISH AND FOREIGN SCHOOL SOCIETY (1808), Croudace House, Godstone Road, Caterham, Surrey CR3 6RE. Tel: 01883-331177. *Director*, J. Kidd

BRITISH EXECUTIVE SERVICE OVERSEAS (1976), 164 Vauxhall Bridge Road, London SW1V 4RB. Tel: 0171-630 0644. *Chief Executive*, G. Ramsey, CBE

BRITISH INSTITUTE IN EASTERN AFRICA (1959), 10 Carlton House Terrace, London SW1Y 5AH. Tel: 0171-969 5201. *London Secretary*, Mrs J. Moyo

BRITISH INSTITUTE OF ARCHAEOLOGY AT ANKARA (1948), 10 Carlton House Terrace, London SW1Y 5AH. Tel: 0171-969 5204. *Director*, Dr R. J. Matthews

BRITISH INSTITUTE OF PERSIAN STUDIES (1961), c/o The British Academy, 10 Carlton House Terrace, London SW1Y 5AH. Tel: 0171-969 5203. *Hon. Secretary*, Dr R. Gleave

BRITISH INTERPLANETARY SOCIETY (1933), 27-29 South Lambeth Road, London SW8 1SZ. Tel: 0171-735 3160. *Executive Secretary*, Ms S. A. Jones

BRITISH ISRAEL WORLD FEDERATION (1919), 8 Blades Court, Deodar Road, London SW15 2NU. Tel: 0181-877 9010. *Secretary*, A. E. Gibb

BRITISH LEGION, ROYAL (1921), 48 Pall Mall, London SW1Y 5JY. Tel: 0345-725725. *Secretary-General*, Brig. I. G. Townsend

BRITISH LEGION SCOTLAND, ROYAL (1921), New Haig House, Logie Green Road, Edinburgh EH7 4HR. Tel: 0131-557 2782. *General Secretary*, Maj.-Gen. J. D. MacDonald, CB, CBE

BRITISH MEDICAL ASSOCIATION (1832), BMA House, Tavistock Square, London WC1H 9JP. Tel: 0171-387 4499. *Secretary*, Dr E. M. Armstrong

BRITISH NATIONAL PARTY (1982), PO Box 117, Welling, Kent DA16 3DW. Tel: 0700-900 1493. *Chairman*, J. Tyndall

BRITISH RED CROSS (1870), 9 Grosvenor Crescent, London SW1X 7EJ. Tel: 0171-235 5454. *Director-General*, S. Younger

BRITISH RESEARCH IN THE LEVANT, COUNCIL FOR (1998), 29 The Walk, Southport, Merseyside PR8 4GB. Tel: 01704-569664. *Secretary*, Miss C. Middleton

BUDDHIST SOCIETY (1924), 58 Eccleston Square, London SW1V 1PH. Tel: 0171-834 5858. *General Secretary*, R. C. Maddox

BUDGERIGAR SOCIETY (1925), 49-53 Hazelwood Road, Northampton NN1 1LG. Tel: 01604-624549. *General Secretary*, D. Whittaker

BUILDING, CHARTERED INSTITUTE OF (1834), Englemere, King's Ride, Ascot, Berks SL5 7TB. Tel: 01344-630700. *Chief Executive*, K. Banbury

BUILDING ENGINEERS, ASSOCIATION OF (1925), Jubilee House, Billing Brook Road, Weston Favell, Northampton NN3 8NW. Tel: 01604-404121. *Chief Executive*, D. Gibson

BUILDING SERVICES ENGINEERS, CHARTERED INSTITUTION OF (1897), Delta House, 222 Balham High Road, London SW12 9BS. Tel: 0181-675 5211. *Chief Executive*, R. John

BUILDING SOCIETIES ASSOCIATION (1936), 3 Savile Row, London WIX IAF. Tel: 0171-437 0655. *Director-General*, A. Coles

BUSINESS AND PROFESSIONAL WOMEN UK LTD (1938), 23 Ansdell Street, London W8 5BN. Tel: 0171-938 1729. *General Secretary*, Ms C. Garnier

BUSINESS ARCHIVES COUNCIL (1934), The Clove Building, 4 Maguire Street, London SE1 2NQ. Tel: 0171-407 6110. *Secretary-General*, Ms W. S. Quinn

BUSINESS IN THE COMMUNITY (1982), 44 Baker Street, London WIM IDH. Tel: 0171-224 1600. *Chief Executive*, Ms J. Cleverdon, CBE

BUSINESS SOFTWARE ALLIANCE (1989), 79 Knightsbridge, London SW1X 7RB. Tel: 0171-245 0304. *Managing Director*, Mrs E. Knight

CADET FORCE ASSOCIATION, COMBINED (1952), E Block, The Duke of York's HQ, London SW3 4RR. Tel: 0171-730 9733. *Secretary*, Brig. J. E. Neeve

CAFOD (CATHOLIC FUND FOR OVERSEAS DEVELOPMENT) (1962), Romero Close, Stockwell Road, London SW9 9TY. Tel: 0171-733 7900. *Director*, J. Filochowski

CALOUSTE GULBENKIAN FOUNDATION (1956), 98 Portland Place, London WIN 4ET. *Director*, vacant

CAMBRIDGE PRESERVATION SOCIETY (1929), Wandlebury Ring, Gog Magog Hills, Babraham, Cambridge CB2 4AE. Tel: 01223-243830. *Director*, R. Whittaker

CAMERON FUND (1971), Tavistock House North, Tavistock Square, London WC1H 9HR. Tel: 0171-388 0796. *Secretary*, Mrs J. Martin

CAMPAIGN FOR COURTESY, *see* POLITE SOCIETY

CAMPAIGN FOR NUCLEAR DISARMAMENT (CND) (1958), 162 Holloway Road, London N7 8DQ. Tel: 0171-700 2393. *Chair*, D. Knight

CANCERBACUP (FORMERLY BRITISH ASSOCIATION OF CANCER UNITED PATIENTS (BACUP)) (1985), 30 Bell Street, London GI ILG. Tel: 0141-553 1553. *Chief Executive*, Mrs J. Mossman

CANCER CARE, MARIE CURIE, *see* MARIE CURIE CANCER CARE

CANCER CARE FOR CHILDREN, SARGENT (1968), 14 Abingdon Road, London W8 6AF. Tel: 0171-565 5100. *Chief Executive*, Mrs D. Yeo

CANCER RELIEF, MACMILLAN (1911), Anchor House, 15-19 Britten Street, London SW3 3TZ. Tel: 0171-351 7811. *Chief Executive*, N. Young

CANCER RESEARCH CAMPAIGN, 10 Cambridge Terrace, London NW1 4JL. Tel: 0171-224 1333. *Director-General*, Prof. J. G. McVie

CANCER RESEARCH FUND, IMPERIAL (1902), PO Box 123, Lincoln's Inn Fields, London WC2A 3PX. Tel: 0171-242 0200. *Director-General*, Sir Paul Nurse, FRS

CANCER RESEARCH: ROYAL CANCER HOSPITAL, INSTITUTE OF, 123 Old Brompton Road, London SW7 3RP. Tel: 0171-352 8133. *Chief Executive*, Dr P. W. J. Rigby

CARERS NATIONAL ASSOCIATION (1988), Ruth Pitter House, 20-25 Glasshouse Yard, London ECIA 4JT. Tel: 0171-490 8818. *Chief Executive*, Ms D. Whitworth

CARNEGIE DUNFERMLINE TRUST (1903), Abbey Park House, Dunfermline, Fife KY12 7PB. Tel: 01383-723638. *Secretary and Treasurer*, W. C. Runciman

CARNEGIE HERO FUND TRUST (1908), Abbey Park House, Dunfermline, Fife KY12 7PB. Tel: 01383-723638. *Secretary*, W. C. Runciman

CARNEGIE UNITED KINGDOM TRUST (1913), Comely Park House, Dunfermline, Fife KY12 7EJ. Tel: 01383-721445. *Secretary*, C. J. Naylor, OBE

CATHEDRALS FABRIC COMMISSION FOR ENGLAND (1949), Fielden House, 13 Little College Street, London SW1P 3SH. Tel: 0171-898 1863. *Secretary*, Dr R. Gem

CATHOLIC ENQUIRY OFFICE (1954), The Chase Centre, 114 West Heath Road, London NW3 7TX. Tel: 0181-458 3316. *Secretary*, Fr P. Billington

CATHOLIC RECORD SOCIETY (1904), c/o 12 Melbourne Place, Wolsingham, Co. Durham DL13 3EH. Tel: 01388-527747. *Hon. Secretary*, Dr L. Gooch

CATHOLIC TRUTH SOCIETY (1868), 40-46 Harleyford Road, London SE11 5AY. Tel: 0171-640 0042. *General Secretary*, F. Martin

CATHOLIC UNION OF GREAT BRITAIN (1872), St Maximilian Kolbe House, 63 Jeddo Road, London W12 9EE. Tel: 0181-749 1321 or 01474-702439. *Secretary*, P. H. Higgs

CATTLE ASSOCIATION, NATIONAL, 60 Kenilworth Road, Leamington Spa, Warks CV32 6JX. Tel: 01926-337378. *Secretary*, Miss K. S. Brake

CATTLE BREEDERS' CLUB LTD, BRITISH (1945), Hayleys Manor, Upland Road, Thornwood, Epping, Essex CM16 6PQ. Tel: 01992-572511. *Secretary*, Mrs J. Padfield

CENTRAL AND CECIL HOUSING TRUST (1926), 2 Priory Road, Kew, Richmond, Surrey TW9 3DG. Tel: 0181-940 9828. *Chief Executive*, G. Brighton

CENTRAL BUREAU FOR EDUCATIONAL VISITS AND EXCHANGES (1948), 10 Spring Gardens, London SWIA 2BN. Tel: 0171-389 4487. *Director*, P. Upton

CENTREPOINT (1969), Bewlay House, 2 Swallow Place, London WIR 7AA. Tel: 0171-544 5000. *Chief Executive*, V. O. Adebowale

CHADWICK TRUST (1895), Department of Civil and Environmental Engineering, University College, Gower Street, London WC1E 6BT. Tel: 0171-380 7327/7766. *Secretary to the Trustees*, I. K. Orchardson, PH.D.

CHANTREY BEQUEST (1875), Royal Academy of Arts, Burlington House, Piccadilly, London WIV ODS. Tel: 0171-300 8000. *Secretary*, D. Gordon

CHARITIES AID FOUNDATION (1974), Kings Hill, West Malling, Kent ME19 4TA. Tel: 01732-520000. *Chief Executive*, M. Brophy

CHEMICAL ENGINEERS, INSTITUTION OF (1922), Davis Building, 165-189 Railway Terrace, Rugby, Warks CV21 3HQ. Tel: 01788-578214. *Chief Executive*, Dr T. J. Evans

CHEMISTRY, ROYAL SOCIETY OF, Burlington House, Piccadilly, London WIV OBN. Tel: 0171-437 8656. *Secretary-General*, Dr T. D. Inch

CHESHIRE (LEONARD) FOUNDATION, *see* LEONARD CHESHIRE

CHESS FEDERATION, BRITISH (1904), 9A Grand Parade, St Leonards-on-Sea, E. Sussex TN38 ODD. Tel: 01424-442500. *Manager*, Mrs G. White

CHEST, HEART AND STROKE ASSOCIATION, *see* STROKE ASSOCIATION

CHILDBIRTH TRUST, NATIONAL (1956), Alexandra House, Oldham Terrace, London W3 6NH. Tel: 0181-992 2616. *Chief Executive*, Ms B. Phipps

CHILDREN 1ST (ROYAL SCOTTISH SOCIETY FOR PREVENTION OF CRUELTY TO CHILDREN) (1884), Melville House, 41 Polwarth Terrace, Edinburgh EH11 1NU. Tel: 0131-337 8539. *Chief Executive*, Ms M. McKay

CHILDREN'S SOCIETY, THE (1881), Edward Rudolf House, Margery Street, London WC1X 0JL. Tel: 0171-841 4000. *Chief Executive*, I. Sparks

CHINA ASSOCIATION (1889), Swire House, 59 Buckingham Gate, London SW1E 6AJ. Tel: 0171-821 3220. *Executive Director*, D. F. L. Turner

CHIROPODISTS AND PODIATRISTS, SOCIETY OF (1945), 53 Welbeck Street, London W1M 7HE. Tel: 0171-486 3381. *General Secretary*, J. G. C. Trouncer

CHIROPRACTIC ASSOCIATION, BRITISH (1925), Blagrave House, 17 Blagrave Street, Reading, Berks RG1 1QB. Tel: 0118-950 5950. *Executive Director*, Miss S. A. Wakefield

CHOIRS SCHOOLS ASSOCIATION (1921), The Minster School, Deangate, York YO1 7JA. Tel: 01904-624900. *Administrator*, Mrs W. Jackson

CHRISTIAN AID (1945), PO Box 100, London SE1 7RT. Tel: 0171-620 4444. *Director*, Dr D. Mukarji

CHRISTIAN EDUCATION COUNCIL, NATIONAL (1809), 1020 Bristol Road, Selly Oak, Birmingham B29 6LB. Tel: 0121-472 4242. *General Manager*, Mrs. S. Sharman

CHRISTIAN EDUCATION MOVEMENT (1965), Royal Buildings, Victoria Street, Derby DE1 1GW. Tel: 01332-296655. *Director*, Revd Dr S. Orchard

CHRISTIAN KNOWLEDGE, SOCIETY FOR PROMOTING (SPCK) (1698), Holy Trinity Church, Marylebone Road, London NW1 4DU. Tel: 0171-387 5282. *General Secretary*, P. Chandler

CHRISTIANS AND JEWS, COUNCIL OF (1942), Drayton House, 30 Gordon Street, London WC1H 0AN. Tel: 0171-388 3322. *Director*, Sr M. Shepherd

CHURCH ARMY (1882), Independents Road, London SE3 9LG. Tel: 0181-318 1226. *Chief Secretary*, Capt. P. Johanson

CHURCH BUILDING SOCIETY, INCORPORATED (1818), Fulham Palace, London SW6 6EA. Tel: 0171-736 3054. *Secretary*, M. W. Tippen

CHURCH EDUCATION CORPORATION, Bedgebury School, Goudhurst, Cranbrook, Kent TN17 2SH. Tel: 01580-211221. *Secretary*, N. Willoughby, FCIS

CHURCH HOUSE, THE CORPORATION OF (1888), Church House, Dean's Yard, London SW1P 3NZ. Tel: 0171-898 1310. *Secretary*, C. D. L. Menzies

CHURCH LADS' AND CHURCH GIRLS' BRIGADE (1891), 2 Barnsley Road, Wath upon Dearne, Rotherham, S. Yorks S63 6PY. Tel: 01709-876535. *General Secretary*, J. S. Cresswell

CHURCH MISSION SOCIETY (1799), Partnership House, 157 Waterloo Road, London SE1 8UU. Tel: 0171-928 8681. *General Secretary*, Canon D. K. Witts

CHURCH MONUMENTS SOCIETY (1979), c/o Society of Antiquaries, Burlington House, Piccadilly, London W1V 0HS. Tel: 0171-734 0193. *Hon. Secretary*, C. J. Easter

CHURCH MUSIC, ROYAL SCHOOL OF (1927), Cleveland Lodge, Westhumble, Dorking, Surrey RH5 6BW. Tel: 01306-872800. *Director-General*, Prof. J. Harper

CHURCH OF ENGLAND PENSIONS BOARD (1926), 7 Little College Street, London SW1P 3SF. Tel: 0171-898 1800. *Secretary*, R. G. Radford

CHURCH SOCIETY, INTERCONTINENTAL (1823), 1 Athena Drive, Tachbrook Park, Warwick CV34 6NL. Tel: 01926-430347. *International Director*, Revd Canon J. R. Moore

CHURCH UNION (1859), Faith House, 7 Tufton Street, London SW1P 3QN. Tel: 0171-222 6952. *House Manager*, Mrs J. Miller

CHURCHES, COUNCIL FOR THE CARE OF (1921), Fielden House, 13 Little College Street, London SW1P 3SH. Tel: 0171-898 1866. *Secretary*, Dr T. Cocke

CHURCHES, FRIENDS OF FRIENDLESS (1957), St Ann's Vestry Hall, 2 Church Entry, London EC4V 5HB. Tel: 0171-236 3934. *Hon. Director*, M. Saunders, MBE

CHURCHES MAIN COMMITTEE (1941), Fielden House, 13 Little College Street, London SW1P 3SH. Tel: 0171-222 4984. *Secretary*, D. Taylor Thompson, CB

CHURCHILL SOCIETY - LONDON (1990), c/o 18 Grove Lane, Ipswich, Suffolk IP4 1NR . Tel: 01473-413533. *General Secretary*, N. H. Rogers

CITIZEN'S ADVICE BUREAUX, NATIONAL ASSOCIATION OF (1931), Myddelton House, 115-123 Pentonville Road, London N1 9LZ. Tel: 0171-833 2181. *Chief Executive*, D. Harker

CITY BUSINESS LIBRARY, Brewers Hall Garden, London EC2V 5BX. Tel: 0171-332 1812

CITY PAROCHIAL FOUNDATION (1891), 6 Middle Street, London EC1A 7PH. Tel: 0171-606 6145. *Clerk*, B. Mehta

CIVIC TRUST (1957), 17 Carlton House Terrace, London SW1Y 5AW. Tel: 0171-930 0914. *Director*, M. Gwilliam

CIVIL ENGINEERS, INSTITUTION OF (1818), 1 Great George Street, London SW1P 3AA. Tel: 0171-222 7722. *Chief Executive*, M. Casebourne

CIVIL LIBERTIES, NATIONAL COUNCIL FOR, *see* LIBERTY

CLASSICAL ASSOCIATION (1903), Department of Classics, University of Keele, Keele, Newcastle under Lyme, Staffs ST5 5BG. Tel: 01782-583048. *Hon. Treasurer*, R. Wallace

CLEAR AIR AND ENVIRONMENTAL PROTECTION, NATIONAL SOCIETY FOR (1899), 136 North Street, Brighton BN1 1RG. Tel: 01273-326313. *Secretary-General*, R. Mills

CLERGY ORPHAN CORPORATION (1749), 1 Dean Trench Street, London SW1P 3HB. Tel: 0171-799 3696. *Registrar*, R. C. F. Leach

CLERKS OF WORKS OF GREAT BRITAIN, INSTITUTE OF (1882), 41 The Mall, London W5 3TJ. Tel: 0181-579 2917. *General Secretary*, A. P. Macnamara

CLUBS FOR YOUNG PEOPLE, NATIONAL ASSOCIATION OF (1925), 371 Kennington Lane, London SE11 5QY. Tel: 0171-793 0787. *National Director*, C. Groves, FIPD, FIMgt

COACHING CLUB (1871), Craigmore, 24 Barton View, Penrith, Cumbria CA11 8AX. *Secretary*, A. S. Cowdery

COLITIS AND CROHN'S DISEASE, NATIONAL ASSOCIATION FOR (1979), 4 Beaumont House, Sutton Road, St Albans, Herts AL1 5HH. Tel: 01727-844296/ 830038. *Director*, R. Driscoll

COMMERCE, BRITISH CHAMBERS OF (1860), Manning House, 22 Carlisle Place, London SW1P 1JA. Tel: 0171-565 2000. *Director-General*, C. Humphries, CBE

COMMERCE AND ENTERPRISE, EDINBURGH CHAMBER OF (1786), Conference House, The Exchange, 152 Morrison Street, Edinburgh EH3 8EB. Tel: 0131-477 7000. *Chief Executive*, P. Stillwell

COMMERCE AND INDUSTRY, LONDON CHAMBER OF, 33 Queen Street, London EC4R IAP. Tel: 0171-248 4444. *Chief Executive*, S. G. Sperryn

COMMERCE AND MANUFACTURES, GLASGOW CHAMBER OF (1783), 30 George Square, Glasgow G2 IEQ. Tel: 0141-204 2121. *Chief Executive*, P. V. Burdon

COMMERCE, CANADA-UNITED KINGDOM CHAMBER OF (1921), 38 Grosvenor Street, London WIX ODP. Tel: 0171-258 6576. *Executive Director*, M. Hall

COMMERCE, SCOTTISH CHAMBERS OF, Conference House, The Exchange, 152 Morrison Street, Edinburgh EH3 8EB. Tel: 0131-477 8025. *Director*, L. Gold

COMMERCIAL TRAVELLERS' BENEVOLENT INSTITUTION (1849), 54 Rothbury Avenue, Regent Farm Estate, Gosforth, Newcastle upon Tyne NE3 3HL. Tel: 0191-284 9100. *Secretary*, Mrs G. Tate

COMMISSIONAIRES, THE CORPS OF (1859), Market House, 85 Cowcross Street, London ECIM 6BP. Tel: 0171-490 1125. *Managing Director*, C. J. Salt

COMMUNICATORS IN BUSINESS, BRITISH ASSOCIATION OF (1949), 42 Borough High Street, London SEI IXW. Tel: 0171-378 7139. *Secretary-General*, Mrs. K. Jones

COMPLEMENTARY AND ALTERNATIVE MEDICINE, COUNCIL FOR (1985), 179 Gloucester Place, London NWI 6DX. Tel: 0171-724 9103. *Secretary*, Ms C. Daglish

COMPLEMENTARY MEDICINE, INSTITUTE FOR (1856), PO Box 194, London SEI6 IQZ. Tel: 0171-237 5165. *Director*, A. Baird

COMPOSERS AND SONGWRITERS, BRITISH ACADEMY OF (1945), The Penthouse, 4 Brook Street, London WIY IAA. Tel: 0171-629 0992. *Chief Executive*, C. Green

COMPUTER SOCIETY, BRITISH (1957), 1 Sanford Street, Swindon SNI IHJ. Tel: 01793-417417. *Chief Executive*, Ms J. M. Scott

CONSERVATION OF HISTORIC AND ARTISTIC WORKS, INTERNATIONAL INSTITUTE FOR (1950), 6 Buckingham Street, London WC2N 6BA. Tel: 0171-839 5975. *Secretary-General*, D. Bomford

CONSERVATION VOLUNTEERS, BRITISH TRUST FOR (BTCV) (1970), 36 St Mary's Street, Wallingford, Oxon OXIO OEU. Tel: 01491-839766. *Chief Executive*, T. O. Flood

CONSULTANTS BUREAU, BRITISH (1965), 1 Westminster Palace Gardens, 1-7 Artillery Row, London SWIP IRJ. Tel: 0171-222 3651. *Director*, C. Adams, CBE

CONSULTING ECONOMISTS' ASSOCIATION, INTERNATIONAL (1986), Capricorn Business Services, 52 London End, Beaconsfield, Bucks HP9 2JH. *Chairman*, G. Todd

CONSULTING ENGINEERS, ASSOCIATION OF (1913), Alliance House, 12 Caxton Street, London SWIH OQL. Tel: 0171-222 6557. *Chief Executive*, N. Bennett

CONSULTING SCIENTISTS, ASSOCIATION OF (1958), PO Box 4040, Thorpe-le-Soken, Clacton-on-Sea CO16 OEL. Tel: 01255-862526. *Hon. Secretary*, W. G. Simpson

CONSUMERS' ASSOCIATION (1957), c/o The Association for Consumer Research, 2 Marylebone Road, London NWI 4DF. Tel: 0171-830 6000. *Director*, Ms S. McKechnie, OBE

CONTEMPORARY APPLIED ARTS (1948), 2 Percy Street, London WIP 9FA. Tel: 0171-436 2344. *Director*, Ms M. La Trobe-Bateman

CONVENIENCE STORES, ASSOCIATION OF (1890), Federation House, 17 Farnborough Street, Farnborough, Hants GUI4 8AG. Tel: 01252-515001. *Chief Executive*, T. Dixon

CONVEYANCERS, COUNCIL FOR LICENSED (1986), 16 Glebe Road, Chelmsford, Essex CMI IQG. Tel: 01245-349599. *Director*, Mrs V. Eden

CO-OPERATIVE PARTY, Victory House, 10-14 Leicester Square, London WC2H 7QH. Tel: 0171-439 0123. *Secretary*, P. Hunt

CO-OPERATIVE UNION LTD (1869), Holyoake House, Hanover Street, Manchester M60 OAS. Tel: 0161-246 9200. *Chief Executive*, D. L. Wilkinson

CO-OPERATIVE WHOLESALE SOCIETY LTD (1863), PO Box 53, New Century House, Manchester M60 4ES. Tel: 0161-834 1212. *Chief Executive*, G. J. Melmoth

COPYRIGHT COUNCIL, BRITISH (1953), 29-33 Berners Street, London WIP 4AA. Tel: 01986-788122. *Secretary*, Ms J. Ibbotson

CORAM FAMILY (FORMERLY THOMAS CORAM FOUNDATION FOR CHILDREN) (1739), 49 Mecklenburgh Square, London WCIN 2QA. Tel: 0171-520 0300. *Director*, Dr G. Pugh, OBE

CORONERS' SOCIETY OF ENGLAND AND WALES (1846), 44 Ormond Avenue, Hampton, Middx TWI2 2RX. *Hon. Secretary*, M. J. C. Burgess

CORPORATE TREASURERS, ASSOCIATION OF (1979), Ocean House, 10-12 Little Trinity Lane, London EC4V 2DJ. Tel: 0171-213 9728. *Director-General*, Dr D. Creed

CORPORATE TRUSTEES, ASSOCIATION OF (1974), The Glen House, 43 Surrey Road, Westbourne, Bournemouth, Dorset BH4 9HR. Tel: 01202-765559. *Secretary*, R. J. Payne

CORRESPONDENCE COLLEGES, ASSOCIATION OF BRITISH (1955), PO Box 17926, London SWI9 3WB. Tel: 0181-544 9559. *Secretary*, Mrs H. Owen

CORRYMEELA COMMUNITY (1965), Corrymeela House, 8 Upper Crescent, Belfast BT7 INT. Tel: 01232-325008. *Leader*, Revd T. Williams

COTTON GROWING ASSOCIATION, BRITISH (1904), Knowle Hill Park, Fairmile Lane, Cobham, Surrey KTII 2PD. Tel: 01932-861000. *Managing Director*, P. R. Walters

COUNCIL FOR THE PROTECTION OF RURAL ENGLAND, *see* CPRE

COUNCIL SECRETARIES AND SOLICITORS, ASSOCIATION OF (1974, merged 1996), Foxcroft, Gill Lane, Longton, Preston PR4 4SR. Tel: 01772-611167. *Executive Officer*, N. Yates

COUNSEL AND CARE (1954), Twyman House, 16 Bonny Street, London NWI 9PG. Tel: 0171-485 1550. *Chief Executive*, M. Green

COUNTRY HOUSES ASSOCIATION (1955), Suite 10, Aynhoe Park, Aynhoe, Banbury, Oxon OXI7 3BQ. Tel: 01869-812800. *Chief Executive*, A. R. A. Bennett

COUNTRY LANDOWNERS ASSOCIATION (1907), 16 Belgrave Square, London SWIX 8PQ. Tel: 0171-235 0511. *Director-General*, J. A. Anderson

COUNTRYSIDE ALLIANCE (1930), Old Town Hall, 367 Kennington Road, London SEII 4PT. Tel: 0171-582 5432. *Chief Executive*, R. Burge

COUNTY CHIEF EXECUTIVES, ASSOCIATION OF (1974), Office of the Chief Executive, County Hall, West Bridgford, Nottingham NG2 7QP. Tel: 0115-977 3582. *Hon. Secretary*, P. Housden

COUNTY EMERGENCY PLANNING OFFICERS' SOCIETY, *see* EMERGENCY PLANNING SOCIETY

COUNTY SECRETARIES, SOCIETY OF, *see* COUNCIL SECRETARIES AND SOLICITORS, ASSOCIATION OF

COUNTY SURVEYORS' SOCIETY, *see* CSS

COUNTY TREASURERS, SOCIETY OF (1903), County Hall, West Bridgford, Nottingham NG2 7QP. Tel: 0115-977 3404. *Hon. Secretary*, R. Latham

CPRE (COUNCIL FOR THE PROTECTION OF RURAL ENGLAND) (1926), Warwick House, 25 Buckingham Palace Road, London SW1W 0PP. Tel: 0171-976 6433. *Director*, Ms K. Parminter

CRAFTS COUNCIL (1971), 44A Pentonville Road, London N1 9BY. Tel: 0171-278 7700. *Director*, Ms J. Barnes

CRISIS (1967), 1st Floor, Challenger House, 42 Adler Street, London E1 1EE. Tel: 0171-655 8300. *Chief Executive*, S. Ghosh

CROSSLINKS (1922), 251 Lewisham Way, London SE4 1XF. Tel: 0181-691 6111. *General Secretary*, Revd R. Bowen

CRUEL SPORTS, LEAGUE AGAINST (1924), 83-87 Union Street, London SE1 1SG. Tel: 0171-403 6155. *Chief Officer*, G. Sirl

CRUELTY TO ANIMALS, SOCIETY FOR THE PREVENTION OF, *see* ROYAL and SCOTTISH

CRUELTY TO CHILDREN, SOCIETY FOR THE PREVENTION OF, *see* CHILDREN 1ST and NATIONAL

CRUSE BEREAVEMENT CARE (1959), 126 Sheen Road, Richmond, Surrey TW9 1UR. Tel: 0181-940 4818. Helpline: 0181-332 7227. *Executive Director*, Dr C. Easton

CSS (formerly County Surveyors' Society) (1884), c/o Director of Environmental Services, County Offices, Matlock DE4 3AG. Tel: 01629-585730. *Hon. Secretary*, D. Harvey

CTC (CYCLISTS' TOURING CLUB) (1878), Cotterell House, 69 Meadrow, Godalming, Surrey GU7 3HS. Tel: 01483-417217. *Director*, K. Mayne

CURWEN INSTITUTE (1875), 5 Bigbury Close, Styvechale, Coventry CV3 5AJ. Tel: 01203-413010. *Director*, J. Dowding

CWMNI URDD GOBAITH CYMRU (1922), Swyddfa'r Urdd, Aberystwyth, Dyfed SY23 1EN. Tel: 01970-613100. *Chief Executive*, J. O'Rourke

CYCLISTS' TOURING CLUB, *see* CTC

CYMMRODORION, THE HONOURABLE SOCIETY OF (1751), 30 Eastcastle Street, London W1N 7PD. Tel: 0171-631 0502. *Hon. Secretary*, J. Samuel

CYSTIC FIBROSIS TRUST (1964), 11 London Road, Bromley, Kent BR1 1BY. Tel: 0181-464 7211. *Chief Executive*, Ms R. Barnes

DAIRY FARMERS, ROYAL ASSOCIATION OF BRITISH (1876), Dairy House, 60 Kenilworth Road, Leamington Spa, Warks CV32 6JX. Tel: 01926 887477. *Chief Executive*, P. M. Gilbert

DAIRY TECHNOLOGY, SOCIETY OF (1943), 72 Ermine Street, Huntingdon, Cambs PE18 6EZ. Tel: 01480-450741. *National Secretary*, Mrs R. Gale

DATA (DESIGN AND TECHNOLOGY ASSOCIATION), 16 Wellesbourne House, Walton Road, Wellesbourne, Warks CV35 9JB. Tel: 01789-470007. *Chairman*, Dr R. V. Peacock, OBE

D-DAY AND NORMANDY FELLOWSHIP (1968), 9 South Parade, Southsea, Hants PO5 2JB. Tel: 01705-812180. *Hon. Secretary*, Mrs L. R. Reed

DEAF, COMMONWEALTH SOCIETY FOR THE (SOUND SEEKERS) (1959), 34 Buckingham Palace Road, London SW1W 0RE. Tel: 0171-233 5700. *Chief Executive*, Brig. J. A. Davies

DEAF ASSOCIATION, BRITISH (formerly British Deaf and Dumb Association) (1890), 1 Worship Street, London EC2A 2AB. Tel: 0171-588 3520. *Chief Executive*, J. McWhinney

DEAF CHILDREN, ROYAL SCHOOL FOR (1792), Victoria Road, Margate, Kent CT9 1NB. Tel: 01843-227561. *Secretary*, J. C. Gunnell, OBE

DEAF PEOPLE, FOLEY HOUSE RESIDENTIAL HOME FOR (1851), Foley House, 115 High Garrett, Braintree, Essex CM7 5NU. Tel: 01376-326552. *Director*, J. Bethell

DEAF PEOPLE, ROYAL ASSOCIATION IN AID OF (1841), Centre for Deaf People, Walsingham Road, Colchester, Essex CO2 7BP. Tel: 01206-509509. *Chief Executive*, T. Fenton

DEAF PEOPLE, ROYAL NATIONAL INSTITUTE FOR (1911), 19-23 Featherstone Street, London EC1Y 8SL. Tel: 0171-296 8000. *Chief Executive*, J. Strachan

DEFENCE STUDIES, ROYAL UNITED SERVICES INSTITUTE FOR (1831), Whitehall, London SW1A 2ET. Tel: 0171-930 5854. *Director*, Rear-Adm. R. Cobbold, CB

DEMOCRATIC LEFT (1991), 6 Cynthia Street, London N1 9JF. Tel: 0171-278 4443. *Secretary*, Ms N. Temple

DENTAL ASSOCIATION, BRITISH (1880), 64 Wimpole Street, London W1M 8AL. Tel: 0171-935 0875. *Chief Executive*, J. M. G. Hunt

DENTAL COUNCIL, GENERAL (1956), 37 Wimpole Street, London W1M 8DQ. Tel: 0171-887 3800. *Chief Executive*, Mrs R. M. Hepplewhite

DENTAL HOSPITALS OF THE UNITED KINGDOM, ASSOCIATION OF (1942), Birmingham Dental Hospital, St Chad's Queensway, Birmingham B4 6NN. Tel: 0121-236 8611. *Hon. Secretary*, Mrs P. Harrington

DESIGN AND INDUSTRIES ASSOCIATION (1915), 11 St Gabriel's Manor, Cormont Road, Lambeth, London SE5 9RH. Tel: 0171-735 8661. *Chairman*, E. Pond

DESIGNERS, CHARTERED SOCIETY OF (1930), 32-38 Saffron Hill, London EC1N 8FH. Tel: 0171-831 9777. *President*, Ms A. Leman

DESIGNERS FOR INDUSTRY, FACULTY OF ROYAL (1936), RSA, 8 John Adam Street, London WC2N 6EZ. Tel: 0171-451 6801. *Administrator*, Ms J. Thackray

DIABETIC ASSOCIATION, BRITISH (1934), 10 Queen Anne Street, London W1M 0BD. Tel: 0171-323 1531. *Director-General*, M. Cooper

DIANA, PRINCESS OF WALES MEMORIAL FUND (1997), County Hall, Westminster Bridge Road, London SE1 7PB. Tel: 0171-902 5500. *Chief Executive*, Dr A. Purkis

DICKENS FELLOWSHIP (1902), Dickens House, 48 Doughty Street, London WC1N 2LF. Tel: 0171-405 2127. *Joint Hon. General Secretaries*, Mrs T. Grove, Dr T. Williams

DIRECTORS, INSTITUTE OF (1903), 116 Pall Mall, London SW1Y 5ED. Tel: 0171-839 1233. *Director-General*, T. Melville-Ross

DIRECTORS OF PUBLIC HEALTH, ASSOCIATION OF (1982), Walsall Health Authority, Lichfield House, 27-31 Lichfield Street, Walsall, West Midlands WS1 1TE. Tel: 01922-720255. *Hon. Secretary*, Dr S. Ramaiah

DIRECTORY AND DATABASE PUBLISHERS ASSOCIATION (1970), PO Box 23034, London W6 0RJ. Tel: 0171-846 9707. *Secretary*, Ms R. Pettit

DISPENSING OPTICIANS, ASSOCIATION OF BRITISH (1925), 6 Hurlingham Business Park, Sulivan Road, London SW6 3DU. Tel: 0171-736 0088. *Registrar*, D. S. Baker

DISTRICT SECRETARIES, ASSOCIATION OF, *see*
COUNCIL SECRETARIES AND SOLICITORS,
ASSOCIATION OF

DITCHLEY FOUNDATION, Ditchley Park, Enstone,
Chipping Norton, Oxon OX7 4ER. Tel: 01608-677346.
Director, Sir Nigel Broomfield, KCMG

DOWNS SYNDROME ASSOCIATION (1970), 155 Mitcham
Road, London SW17 9PG. Tel: 0181-682 4001. *Director,*
Ms C. Boys

DOWSERS, BRITISH SOCIETY OF (1933), Sycamore Barn,
Hastingleigh, Ashford, Kent TN25 5HW. Tel: 01233-
750253. *General Secretary,* M. D. Rust

DRAINAGE AUTHORITIES, ASSOCIATION OF (1937), The
Mews, 3 Royal Oak Passage, High Street, Huntingdon,
Cambs PE18 6EA. Tel: 01480-411123. *Chief Executive,*
D. Noble

DRINKING FOUNTAIN AND CATTLE TROUGH
ASSOCIATION, METROPOLITAN (1859), Oaklands, 5
Queensborough Gardens, Chislehurst, Kent BR7 6NP.
Tel: 0181-467 1261. *Secretary,* R. P. Baber

DRIVING SOCIETY, BRITISH (1957), 27 Dugard Place,
Barford, Warwick CV35 8DX. Tel: 01926-624420.
Secretary, Mrs J. M. Dillon

DRUG DEPENDENCE, INSTITUTE FOR THE STUDY OF
(1968), 32 Loman Street, London SE1 0EE. Tel: 0171-928
1211. *Directors,* N. Dorn, Ms L. Fielding

DUKE OF EDINBURGH'S AWARD (1956), Gulliver House,
Madeira Walk, Windsor, Berks SL4 1EU. Tel: 01753-
727400. *Director,* Vice-Adm. M. P. Gretton, CB

DYERS AND COLOURISTS, SOCIETY OF (1884), PO Box
244, Perkin House, 82 Grattan Road, Bradford BD1 2JB.
Tel: 01274-725138. *General Secretary,* K. M. McGhee

DYSLEXIA INSTITUTE (1972), 133 Gresham Road,
Staines, Middlesex TW18 2AJ. Tel: 01784-463851.
Executive Director, Mrs E. J. Brooks

EARL HAIG FUND SCOTLAND, New Haig House, Logie
Green Road, Edinburgh EH7 4HR. Tel: 0131-557 2782.
General Secretary, Maj.-Gen. J. D. MacDonald

EARLY CHILDHOOD EDUCATION, BRITISH
ASSOCIATION FOR (1923), 111 City View House, 463
Bethnal Green Road, London E2 9QY. Tel: 0171-739
7594. *Chief Executive,* Ms W. Scott

EATING DISORDERS ASSOCIATION (1989), First Floor,
Wensum House, 103 Prince of Wales Road, Norwich
NR1 1DW. Tel: 01603-619090. Helpline: 01603-621414.
Youthline: 01603-765050. *Chief Executive,* Mrs. N. Bryant

ECCLESIASTICAL HISTORY SOCIETY (1961), Department
of History (Medieval), University of Glasgow, Glasgow
G12 8QQ. Tel: 0141-330 4087. *Secretary,* M. J. Kennedy

ECCLESIOLOGICAL SOCIETY (1839), Underedge, Back
Lane, Hathersage, Sheffield S32 1AR. Tel: 01433-650833.
Hon. Secretary, Prof. K. H. Murta, FRIBA

ECONOMIC AFFAIRS, INSTITUTE OF (1955), 2 Lord
North Street, London SW1P 3LB. Tel: 0171-799 3745.
General Director, J. Blundell

EDITH CAVELL AND NATION'S FUND FOR NURSES
(1917), Flints, Petersfield Road, Winchester, Hants
SO23 0JD. Tel: 01962-860900. *Administrator,* Mrs A. Rich

EDITORS, SOCIETY OF (1946), University Centre, Granta
Place, Mill Lane, Cambridge CB2 1RU. Tel: 01223-
304080. *Director,* R. Satchwell

EDUCATION OFFICERS' SOCIETY, COUNTY (1889),
Education Department, Northamptonshire County
Council, PO Box 149, County Hall, Northampton
NN1 1AU. Tel: 01604-236250. *Secretary,* J. R. Atkinson

EDUCATION OFFICERS, SOCIETY OF (1971), Boulton
House, 17-21 Chorlton Street, Manchester M1 3HY. Tel:
0161-236 5766. *General Secretary,* A. Collier

EDUCATIONAL RESEARCH IN ENGLAND AND WALES,
NATIONAL FOUNDATION FOR (1946), The Mere,
Upton Park, Slough SL1 2DQ. Tel: 01753-574123.
Director, Dr S. Hegarty

EGYPT EXPLORATION SOCIETY (1882), 3 Doughty
Mews, London WC1N 2PG. Tel: 0171-242 1880. *Secretary,*
Dr P. A. Spencer

ELECTORAL REFORM SOCIETY, 6 Chancel Street,
London SE1 0UU. Tel: 0171-928 1622. *Chief Executive,*
Dr K. Ritchie

ELECTRICAL ENGINEERS, INSTITUTION OF (1871),
Savoy Place, London WC2R 0BL. Tel: 0171-240 1871.
Secretary, J. C. Williams, OBE, PH.D., FREng.

ELGAR FOUNDATION (1973), The Elgar Birthplace
Museum, Lower Broadheath, Worcester WR2 6RH. Tel:
01905-33324. *Secretary to the Trustees,*
Air Cdre B. W. Opie

ELGAR SOCIETY (1951), c/o 29 Van Diemens Close,
Chinnor, Oxon OX9 4QE. Tel: 01844-354096. *Hon.
Secretary,* Ms W. Hillary

EMERGENCY PLANNING SOCIETY (1966),
Northumberland House, 11 The Pavement, Popes
Lane, London W5 4NG. Tel: 0181-579 7971. *Hon.
Secretary,* I. Hoult

ENABLE (SCOTTISH SOCIETY FOR THE MENTALLY
HANDICAPPED) (1954), 7 Buchanan Street, Glasgow
G1 3HL. Tel: 0141-226 4541. *Director,* N. Dunning

ENERGY ASSOCIATION, BRITISH (1924), 34 St James's
Street, London SW1A 1HD. Tel: 0171-930 1211. *Director,*
M. Jefferson

ENERGY, INSTITUTE OF (1927), 18 Devonshire Street,
London W1N 2AU. Tel: 0171-580 7124. *Secretary,*
Ms L. Evans

ENERGY SAVING TRUST (1992), 21 Dartmouth Street,
London SW1H 9BP. Tel: 0171-222 0101. *Chief Executive,*
Dr E. Lees

ENGINEERING COUNCIL, THE (1981), 10 Maltravers
Street, London WC2R 3ER. Tel: 0171-240 7891. *Director-
General,* M. Shirley

ENGINEERING DESIGNERS, INSTITUTION OF (1945),
Courtleigh, Westbury Leigh, Westbury, Wilts BA13 3TA.
Tel: 01373-822801. *Secretary,* M. J. Osborne

ENGINEERING INDUSTRIES ASSOCIATION (1941),
Broadway House, Tothill Street, London SW1H 9NS.
Tel: 0171-222 2367. *Administrator,* R. Stubbs

ENGINEERS, INSTITUTION OF BRITISH (1928), Royal
Liver Building, 6 Hampton Place, Brighton BN1 3DD.
Tel: 01273-734274. *Secretary,* Ms J. Busby

ENGINEERS, SOCIETY OF (1854), Guinea Wiggs,
Nayland, Colchester, Essex CO6 4NF. Tel: 01206-
263332. *Secretary,* Mrs L. C. A. Wright

ENGLISH ASSOCIATION (1906), University of Leicester,
University Road, Leicester LE1 7RH. Tel: 0116-252 3982.
Chief Executive, Ms H. Lucas

ENGLISH FOLK DANCE AND SONG SOCIETY (1932),
Cecil Sharp House, 2 Regent's Park Road, London
NW1 7AY. Tel: 0171-485 2206. *Chief Executive,* M. Frost

ENGLISH PLACE-NAME SURVEY (1923), Grey College,
Durham DH1 3LG. Tel: 0191-374 2961. *Hon. Director,*
V. E. Watts, FSA

ENGLISH-SPEAKING UNION OF THE COMMONWEALTH
(1918), Dartmouth House, 37 Charles Street, London
W1X 8AB. Tel: 0171-493 3328. *Director-General,*
Mrs V. Mitchell

ENTOMOLOGICAL SOCIETY OF LONDON, ROYAL (1833), 41 Queen's Gate, London SW7 5HR. Tel: 0171-584 8361. *Registrar*, G. G. Bentley

ENVIRONMENTAL HEALTH, CHARTERED INSTITUTE OF (1883), Chadwick Court, 15 Hatfields, London SE1 8DJ. Tel: 0171-928 6006. *Chief Executive*, M. Cooke

ENVIRONMENT COUNCIL (1969), 212 High Holborn, London WC1V 7VW. Tel: 0171-836 2626. *Chief Executive*, S. Robinson

EPILEPSY ASSOCIATION, BRITISH (1949), Anstey House, 40 Hanover Square, Leeds LS3 1BE. Tel: 0113-210 8800. Helpline: 0808 800 5050. *Chief Executive*, P. Lee

EPILEPSY, NATIONAL SOCIETY FOR (1892), Chesham Lane, Chalfont St Peter, Gerrards Cross, Bucks SL9 0RJ. Tel: 01494-601300. Helpline: 01494-601400. *Chief Executive*, D. Bennett

EQUESTRIAN FEDERATION, BRITISH (1972), National Agricultural Centre, Stoneleigh Park, Kenilworth, Warks CV8 2RH. Tel: 01203-698871. *Director-General*, D. Buck

ERSKINE HOSPITAL (formerly Princess Louise Scottish Hospital) (1916), Bishopton, Renfrewshire PA7 5PU. Tel: 0141-812 1100. *Chief Executive*, Col. M. F. Gibson, OBE

ESPERANTO ASSOCIATION OF BRITAIN (1977), 140 Holland Park Avenue, London W11 4UF. Tel: 0171-727 7821. *Office Manager*, M. McClelland

ESTATE AGENTS, NATIONAL ASSOCIATION OF (1962), Arbon House, 21 Jury Street, Warwick CV34 4EH. Tel: 01926-496800. *Chief Executive*, H. Dunsmore-Hardy

ESTATE AGENTS, OMBUDSMAN FOR (1990), Beckett House, 4 Bridge Street, Salisbury, Wilts SP1 2LX. Tel: 01722-333306. *Ombudsman*, T. D. G. Quayle, CB

EUGENICS SOCIETY, *see* GALTON INSTITUTE

EVANGELICAL LIBRARY (1928), 78A Chiltern Street, London W1M 2HB. Tel: 0171-935 6997. *Librarian*, S. J. Taylor

EXPORT, INSTITUTE OF (1935), Export House, 64 Clifton Street, London EC2A 4HB. Tel: 0171-247 9812. *Director-General*, I. J. Campbell

EX-SERVICES LEAGUE, BRITISH COMMONWEALTH (1921), 48 Pall Mall, London SW1Y 5JG. Tel: 0171-973 7263. *Secretary-General*, Lt.-Col. S. Pope, OBE, RM

EX-SERVICES MENTAL WELFARE SOCIETY (1919), Broadway House, The Broadway, London SW19 1RL. Tel: 0181-543 6333. *Director*, Cdre T. Elliott, OBE

FABIAN SOCIETY (1884), 11 Dartmouth Street, London SW1H 9BN. Tel: 0171-222 8877. *General Secretary*, M. Jacobs

FAIR ISLE BIRD OBSERVATORY TRUST (1948), Fair Isle Bird Observatory, Fair Isle, Shetland ZE2 9JU. Tel: 01595-760258. *Administrator*, H. Craig

FALSE MEMORY SOCIETY, BRITISH (1993), Bradford on Avon, Wilts BA15 1NF. Tel: 01225-868682. *Director*, Ms M. Greenhalgh

FAMILY HISTORY SOCIETIES, FEDERATION OF (1974), The Benson Room, Birmingham and Midland Institute, Margaret Street, Birmingham B3 3BS. Tel: 07041-492032. *Administrator*, Mrs P. A. Saul

FAMILY MEDIATION, NATIONAL (1982), 9 Tavistock Place, London WC1H 9SN. Tel: 0171-383 5993. *Director*, Ms T. Fisher

FAMILY PLANNING ASSOCIATION (1939), 2-12 Pentonville Road, London N1 9FP. Tel: 0171-837 5432. *Chief Executive*, Ms A. Weyman

FAMILY WELFARE ASSOCIATION (1869), 501-505 Kingsland Road, London E8 4AU. Tel: 0171-254 6251. *Chief Executive*, Ms H. Dent

FANY (PRINCESS ROYAL'S VOLUNTEER CORPS) (1907), Mercury House, Duke of York's Headquarters, London SW3 4RX. Tel: 0171-730 2058. *Corps Commander*, Mrs L. Rose

FAUNA AND FLORA INTERNATIONAL (1903), Great Eastern House, Tenison Road, Cambridge CB1 2DT. Tel: 01223-571000. *Director*, M. Rose

FELLOWSHIP HOUSES TRUST (1937), Clock House, 192 High Road, Byfleet, Surrey KT14 7RN. Tel: 01932-343172. *Secretary*, Mrs A. J. Elliott

FIELD ARCHAEOLOGISTS, INSTITUTE OF (1982), University of Reading, PO Box 239, Reading RG6 6AU. Tel: 0118-931 6446. *Director*, P. Hinton

FIELD STUDIES COUNCIL (1943), Preston Montford, Montford Bridge, Shrewsbury SY4 1HW. Tel: 01743-850674. *Chief Executive*, A. D. Thomas

FILM CLASSIFICATION, BRITISH BOARD OF (1912), 3 Soho Square, London W1V 6HD. Tel: 0171-439 7961. *Director*, R. Duval

FIRE ENGINEERS, INSTITUTION OF (1918), 148 New Walk, Leicester LE1 7QB. Tel: 0116-255 3654. *General Secretary*, D. W. Evans

FIRE PROTECTION ASSOCIATION (1946), Melrose Avenue, Borehamwood, Herts WD6 2BJ. Tel: 0181-207 2345. *Director*, Dr J. Denney

FIRE SERVICES NATIONAL BENEVOLENT FUND (1943), Fund Headquarters, Marine Court, Fitzalan Road, Littlehampton, W. Sussex BN17 5NF. Tel: 01903-736062. *General Manager*, C. W. Pile

FLAG INSTITUTE (1971), 9 Laurel Grove, Chester CH2 3HU. Tel: 01244-351335. *General Secretary*, G. Bartram

FLEET AIR ARM OFFICERS' ASSOCIATION (1957), 4 St James's Square, London SW1Y 4JU. Tel: 0171-930 7722. *Administration Director*, Cdr. J. D. O. Macdonald

FOLKLORE SOCIETY, c/o University College, Gower Street, London WC1E 6BT. Tel: 0171-387 5894. *Hon. Secretary*, Dr J. Simpson

FOOD FROM BRITAIN (1983), 123 Buckingham Palace Road, London SW1W 9SA. Tel: 0171-233 5111. *Chief Executive*, P. Davis

FOOD SCIENCE AND TECHNOLOGY, INSTITUTE OF (1964), 5 Cambridge Court, 210 Shepherd's Bush Road, London W6 7NJ. Tel: 0171-603 6316. *Chief Executive*, Ms H. G. Wild

FORCES HELP SOCIETY AND LORD ROBERTS WORKSHOPS, *see* SSAFA FORCES HELP

FOREIGN PRESS ASSOCIATION IN LONDON (1888), 11 Carlton House Terrace, London SW1Y 5AJ. *Secretary*, Ms D. Crole

FORENSIC SCIENCE SOCIETY (1959), Clarke House, 18A Mount Parade, Harrogate, N. Yorks HG1 1BX. Tel: 01423-506068. *Hon. Secretary*, Dr A. R. W. Forrest

FORENSIC SCIENCES, BRITISH ACADEMY OF (1959), Anaesthetic Unit, The Royal London Hospital, Whitechapel, London E1 1BB. Tel: 0171-377 9201. *Secretary-General*, Dr P. J. Flynn

FORESTERS, INSTITUTE OF CHARTERED (1982), 7A St Colme Street, Edinburgh EH3 6AA. Tel: 0131-225 2705. *Executive Director*, Mrs M. W. Dick

FORESTRY ASSOCIATION, COMMONWEALTH (1921), c/o Oxford Forestry Institute, South Parks Road, Oxford OX1 3RB. Tel: 01865-271037. *Chairman*, Dr J. S. Maini

FORESTRY SOCIETY OF ENGLAND, WALES AND NORTHERN IRELAND, ROYAL (1882), 102 High Street, Tring, Herts HP23 4AF. Tel: 01442-822028. *Director*, Dr J. E. Jackson

FORESTRY SOCIETY, ROYAL SCOTTISH (1854), The Stables, Dalkeith Country Park, Dalkeith, Midlothian EH22 2NA. Tel: 0131-660 9480. *Director*, M. Osborne

FOUNDRYMEN, INSTITUTE OF BRITISH (1904), Bordesley Hall, The Holloway, Alvechurch, Birmingham B48 7QA. Tel: 01527-596100. *Secretary*, A. M. Turner

FRANCO-BRITISH SOCIETY (1924), Room 623, Linen Hall, 162-168 Regent Street, London W1R 5TB. Tel: 0171-734 0815. *Executive Secretary*, Mrs M. Clarke

FREEDOM ASSOCIATION (1975), 35 Westminster Bridge Road, London SE1 7JB. Tel: 0171-928 9925. *Administrator*, Mrs P. North

FREEMASONS: GRAND LODGE OF ANCIENT FREE AND ACCEPTED MASONS OF SCOTLAND (1736), Freemasons' Hall, 96 George Street, Edinburgh EH2 3DH. Tel: 0131-225 5304. *Grand Secretary*, C. M. McGibbon

FREEMASONS: UNITED GRAND LODGE OF ENGLAND (1717), Freemasons' Hall, Great Queen Street, London WC2B 5AZ. *Grand Master*, HRH The Duke of Kent, KG, GCMG, GCVO

FREEMEN OF ENGLAND AND WALES (1966), Glenrise, Churchfields, Stonesfield, Witney, Oxon OX8 8PP. Tel: 01993-891414. *President*, R. J. M. Bishop

FREEMEN OF THE CITY OF LONDON, GUILD OF (1908), PO Box 153, 40A Ludgate Hill, London EC4M 7DE. Tel: 0171-223 7638. *Clerk*, Col. D. Ivy

FREEMEN OF THE CITY OF YORK, GUILD OF (1953), 29 Albermarle Road, York YO23 1EW. *Hon. Clerk*, R. Lee

FREEMEN'S GUILD, CITY OF COVENTRY (1946), 47 Brownshill Green Road, Coventry CV6 2AP. Tel: 01203-333980. *Hon. Clerk*, K. Talbot

FRIENDLY SOCIETIES, ASSOCIATION OF (1887), Royex House, Aldermanbury Square, London EC2V 7HR. Tel: 0171-606 1881. *General Secretary*, Miss M. Poole

FRIENDS OF CATHEDRAL MUSIC (1956), Aeron House, Llangeitho, Tregaron, Ceredigion SY25 6SU. *Secretary*, M. J. Cooke

FRIENDS OF THE EARTH (1971), 26-28 Underwood Street, London N1 7JQ. Tel: 0171-490 1555. *Director*, C. Secrett

FRIENDS OF THE ELDERLY (1905), 40-42 Ebury Street, London SW1W 0LZ. Tel: 0171-730 8263. *Chief Executive*, Mrs S. Levett

FRIENDS OF THE NATIONAL LIBRARIES (1931), c/o Department of Manuscripts, The British Library, 96 Euston Road, London NW1 2DB. Tel: 0171-412 7559. *Hon. Secretary*, M. Borrie, OBE, FSA

FURNITURE HISTORY SOCIETY (1964), 1 Mercedes Cottages, St John's Road, Haywards Heath, W. Sussex RH16 4EH. Tel: 01444-413845. *Membership Secretary*, Dr B. Austen

GALLIPOLI ASSOCIATION (1915), Earleydene Orchard, Earleydene, Ascot, Berks SL5 9JY. *Hon. Secretary*, J. C. Watson Smith

GALTON INSTITUTE (1907), 19 Northfields Prospect, London SW18 1PE. *General Secretary*, Mrs B. Nixon

GAMBLERS ANONYMOUS (1954), PO Box 88, London SW10 0EU. Tel: 01709-553089

GAME CONSERVANCY TRUST (1969), Fordingbridge, Hants SP6 1EF. Tel: 01425-652381. *Director-General*, Dr G. R. Potts

GARDENERS' ASSOCIATION, THE GOOD (1968), Pinetum, Churcham, Glos GL2 8AD. Tel: 01452-750402. *Hon. Director*, D. Wilkin

GARDENERS' ROYAL BENEVOLENT SOCIETY (1839), Bridge House, 139 Kingston Road, Leatherhead, Surrey KT22 7NT. Tel: 01372-373962. *Chief Executive*, R. T. Capewell

GARDEN HISTORY SOCIETY (1965), 70 Cowcross Street, London EC1M 6EJ. Tel: 0171-608 2409. *Director*, Ms L. Wigley

GARDENS SCHEME CHARITABLE TRUST, NATIONAL (1927), Hatchlands Park, East Clandon, Guildford, Surrey GU4 7RT. Tel: 01483-211535. *Director*, C. Barham Carter

GAS CONSUMERS COUNCIL (1986), 6th Floor, Abford House, 15 Wilton Road, London SW1V 1LT. Tel: 0171-931 0977. *Director*, P. Hamer

GAS ENGINEERS, INSTITUTION OF (1863), 21 Portland Place, London W1N 3AF. Tel: 0171-636 6603. *Acting Deputy Chief Executive*, Ms. J. Sedgwick

GEMMOLOGICAL ASSOCIATION AND GEM TESTING LABORATORY OF GREAT BRITAIN (1931), 27 Greville Street, (Saffron Hill entrance), London EC1N 8SU. Tel: 0171-404 3334. *Director*, Dr R. R. Harding

GENEALOGICAL RESEARCH SOCIETY, IRISH (1936), c/o The Irish Club, 82 Eaton Square, London SW1W 9AJ. Tel: 0171-235 4164. *Hon. Librarian*, T. G. Chartres

GENEALOGISTS AND RECORD AGENTS, ASSOCIATION OF (1968), 29 Badgers Close, Horsham, W. Sussex RH12 5RU

GENEALOGISTS, SOCIETY OF (1911), 14 Charterhouse Buildings, Goswell Road, London EC1M 7BA. Tel: 0171-251 8799. *Director*, R. I. N. Gordon

GENERAL PRACTITIONERS, ROYAL COLLEGE OF (1952), 14 Princes Gate, London SW7 1PU. Tel: 0171-581 3232. *Hon. Secretary*, Dr W. Reith

GENTLEPEOPLE, GUILD OF AID FOR (1904), 10 St Christopher's Place, London W1M 6HY. Tel: 0171-935 0641

GEOGRAPHICAL ASSOCIATION, 160 Solly Street, Sheffield S1 4BF. Tel: 0114-296 0088. *Chief Executive*, M. Curry

GEOGRAPHICAL SOCIETY, ROYAL and THE INSTITUTE OF BRITISH GEOGRAPHERS (1830), 1 Kensington Gore, London SW7 2AR. Tel: 0171-591 3000. *Director*, Dr R. Gardner

GEOGRAPHICAL SOCIETY, ROYAL SCOTTISH (1884), Graham Hills Building, 40 George Street, Glasgow G1 1QE. Tel: 0141-552 3330. *Director*, Dr D. M. Munro

GEOLOGICAL SOCIETY (1807), Burlington House, Piccadilly, London W1V 0JU. Tel: 0171-434 9944. *Chief Executive Officer*, E. Nickless

GEOLOGISTS' ASSOCIATION (1858), Burlington House, Piccadilly, London W1V 9AG. Tel: 0171-434 9298. *Executive Secretary*, Mrs S. Stafford

GEORGIAN GROUP (1937), 6 Fitzroy Square, London W1P 6DX. Tel: 0171-387 1720. *Secretary*, N. Burton

GIFTED CHILDREN, NATIONAL ASSOCIATION FOR (1966), Elder House, Milton Keynes MK9 1LR. Tel: 01908-673677. *Executive Director*, P. Carey

GILBERT AND SULLIVAN SOCIETY (1924), 1 Nethercourt Avenue, London N3 1PS. *Hon. Secretary*, Ms M. Bowden

GINGERBREAD (1970), 16-17 Clerkenwell Close, London
ECIR OAN. Tel: 0171-336 8183. *Chief Executive,*
Ms L. Sewell

GIRL GUIDES, *see* GUIDE ASSOCIATION

GIRLS' BRIGADE, Girls' Brigade House, 62 Foxhall Road,
Didcot, Oxon OX11 7BQ. Tel: 01235-510425. *Brigade
Secretary,* Mrs S. P. Bunting

GIRLS' FRIENDLY SOCIETY IN ENGLAND AND WALES
(1875), 126 Queens Gate, London SW7 5LQ. Tel: 0171-
589 9628. *General Secretary,* Mrs H. Crompton

GIRLS' VENTURE CORPS AIR CADETS (1964), Redhill
Aerodrome, Kings Mill Lane, South Nutfield, Redhill
RH1 5JY. *Corps Director,* Mrs M. A. Rowland

GLASS ENGRAVERS, GUILD OF (1975), 35 Ossulton Way,
London N2 0JY. Tel: 0181-731 9352. *Secretary,*
Mrs C. Weatherhead

GLASS TECHNOLOGY, SOCIETY OF (1916), Don Valley
House, Savile Street East, Sheffield S4 7UQ. Tel: 0114-
263 4455. *Administration Manager,* Ms J. Costello

GLIDING ASSOCIATION, BRITISH (1930), Kimberley
House, Vaughan Way, Leicester LE1 4SE. Tel: 0116-253
1051. *Secretary,* B. Rolfe

GOAT SOCIETY, BRITISH (1879), 34-36 Fore Street,
Bovey Tracey, Newton Abbot, Devon TQ13 9AD. Tel:
01626-833168. *Secretary,* Ms S. Knowles

GRAPHOLOGISTS, BRITISH INSTITUTE OF (1983), 24-26
High Street, Hampton Hill, Hampton, Middx TW12 1PD.
Tel: 01753-891241. *Chairman,* E. Rees

GREEK INSTITUTE (1969), 34 Bush Hill Road, London
N21 2DS. Tel: 0181-360 7968. *Director,* Dr K. Tofallis

GREEN PARTY (1973), 1A Waterlow Road, London
N19 5NJ. Tel: 0171-272 4474. *Executive Chair,* Ms J. Jones

GREENPEACE UK (1971), Canonbury Villas, London
N1 2PN. Tel: 0171-865 8100. *Executive Director,*
P. Melchett

GUIDE ASSOCIATION (1910), 17-19 Buckingham Palace
Road, London SW1W 0PT. Tel: 0171-834 6242. *Chief
Executive,* Mrs T. Ryall

GUIDE DOGS FOR THE BLIND ASSOCIATION (1931),
Hillfields, Burghfield Common, Reading, Berks RG7 3YG.
Tel: 0118-983 5555. *Chief Executive,* Mrs G. Peacock

GULBENKIAN FOUNDATION, *see* CALOUSTE
GULBENKIAN FOUNDATION

GURKHA WELFARE TRUST (1969), 3rd Floor, 88 Baker
Street, London WIM 2AX. Tel: 0171-707 1925. *Director,*
E. D. Powell-Jones

HAEMOPHILIA SOCIETY (1950), Chesterfield House, 385
Euston Road, London NW1 3AU. Tel: 0171-380 0600.
Chief Executive, Ms K. Pappenheim

HAIG HOMES (1928), Alban Dobson House, Green Lane,
Morden, Surrey SM4 5NS. Tel: 0181-648 0335. *Director,*
A. N. Carlier

HAKLUYT SOCIETY (1846), c/o Map Library, The British
Library, 96 Euston Road, London NW1 2DB. Tel: 01986-
788359. *Hon. Secretary,* Dr A. Cook

HANSARD SOCIETY FOR PARLIAMENTARY
GOVERNMENT (1944), St Philips Building North,
Sheffield Street, London WC2A 2EX. Tel: 0171-955 7478.
Director, Mrs S. Diplock

HARD OF HEARING, BRITISH ASSOCIATION OF THE, *see*
HEARING CONCERN

HARVEIAN SOCIETY OF EDINBURGH (1782), Respiratory
Medicine Unit, Department of Medicine, The Royal
Infirmary, Edinburgh EH3 9YW. Tel: 0131-536 2351.
Joint Secretaries, A. B. MacGregor, Prof. N. J. Douglas

HARVEIAN SOCIETY OF LONDON (1831), Lettsom
House, 11 Chandos Street, London WIM 0EB. *Executive
Secretary,* Col. R. Kinsella-Bevan

HEALTH CARE ASSOCIATION, BRITISH (1931), 24A
Main Street, Garforth, Leeds LS25 1AA. *Chief Executive,*
Mrs C. Bell

HEALTH, GUILD OF (1904), Edward Wilson House, 26
Queen Anne Street, London WIM 9LB. Tel: 0171-580
2492. *General Secretary,* Revd A. Lynn

HEALTH PROMOTION AND EDUCATION, INSTITUTE
OF (1962), Department of Oral Health and
Development, University Dental Hospital, Higher
Cambridge Street, Manchester M15 6FH. Tel: 0161-275
6610. *Hon. Secretary,* Prof. A. S. Blinkhorn

HEALTH SERVICES MANAGEMENT, INSTITUTE OF
(1902), 7-10 Chandos Street, London WIM 9DE. Tel:
0171-460 7654. *Director,* Ms K. Caines

HEARING CONCERN (BRITISH ASSOCIATION OF THE
HARD OF HEARING) (1948), 7-11 Armstrong Road,
London W3 7JL. Tel: 0181-743 1110. Helpline: 01245-
344600. *Director,* C. J. Meyer, OBE

HEART FOUNDATION, BRITISH (1963), 14 Fitzhardinge
Street, London W1H 4DH. Tel: 0171-487 7186. *Director-
General,* Maj.-Gen. L. F. H. Busk, CB

HEDGEHOG PRESERVATION SOCIETY, BRITISH (1982),
Knowbury House, Knowbury, Ludlow, Shropshire
SY8 3LQ. Tel: 01584-890801. *Chief Executive/Founder,*
Maj. A. H. Coles, TD

HELLENIC STUDIES, SOCIETY FOR THE PROMOTION
OF (1879), Senate House, Malet Street, London
WC1E 7HU. Tel: 0171-862 8730. *Executive Secretary,*
R. W. Shone

HELP THE AGED (1960), St James's Walk, Clerkenwell
Green, London ECIR 0BE. Tel: 0171-253 0253. *Director-
General,* C. M. Lake, CBE

HERALDIC AND GENEALOGICAL STUDIES, INSTITUTE
OF (1961), 79-82 Northgate, Canterbury, Kent CT1 1BA.
Tel: 01227-768664. *Registrar,* J. Palmer

HERALDRY SOCIETY (1947), PO Box 32, Maidenhead,
Berks SL6 3FD. Tel: 0118-932 0210. *Secretary,*
Mrs M. Miles, MBE, RD

HERPETOLOGICAL SOCIETY, BRITISH (1947), c/o
Zoological Society of London, Regent's Park, London
NW1 4RY. Tel: 0181-452 9578. *Secretary,* Mrs M. Green

HISPANIC AND LUSO BRAZILIAN COUNCIL (1943),
Canning House, 2 Belgrave Square, London SW1X 8PJ.
Tel: 0171-235 2303. *Director-General,* J. Amey

HISTORICAL ASSOCIATION (1906), 59A Kennington Park
Road, London SE11 4JH. Tel: 0171-735 3901. *Chief
Executive,* Mrs M. Stiles

HISTORICAL SOCIETY, ROYAL (1868), University
College London, Gower Street, London WC1E 6BT. Tel:
0171-387 7532. *Executive Secretary,* Mrs J. N. McCarthy

HISTORIC HOUSES ASSOCIATION (1973), 2 Chester
Street, London SW1X 7BB. Tel: 0171-259 5688. *Director-
General,* R. Wilkin

HOME FARM TRUST (1962), Merchants House, Wapping
Road, Bristol BS1 4RW. Tel: 0117-927 3746. *Director-
General,* C. Carey

HOMEOPATHIC ASSOCIATION, BRITISH (1902), 27A
Devonshire Street, London WIN 1RJ. *General Secretary,*
Mrs E. Segall

HONG KONG ASSOCIATION (1961), Swire House, 59
Buckingham Gate, London SW1E 6AJ. Tel: 0171-821
3220. *Executive Director,* D. F. L. Turner

HOROLOGICAL INSTITUTE, BRITISH (1858), Upton Hall, Upton, Newark, Notts NG23 5TE. Tel: 01636-813795. *Secretary*, E. L. Slicer

HOROLOGICAL SOCIETY, ANTIQUARIAN (1953), New House, High Street, Ticehurst, Wadhurst, E. Sussex TN5 7AL. Tel: 01580-200155. *Secretary*, Mrs P. Hossbach

HORSE SOCIETY, BRITISH (1947), Stoneleigh Deer Park, Kenilworth, Warks CV8 2XZ. Tel: 01926-707700. *Chief Executive*, H. Davies

HOSPITAL FEDERATION, INTERNATIONAL (1947), 4 Abbot's Place, London NW6 4NP. Tel: 0171-372 7181. *Director-General*, Dr E. N. Pickering

HOSPITALITY ASSOCIATION, BRITISH (1907), Queens House, 55-56 Lincoln's Inn Fields, London WC2A 3BH. Tel: 0171-404 7744. *Chief Executive*, J. Logie, OBE

HOSPITAL SATURDAY FUND (1873), 24 Upper Ground, London SE1 9PD. Tel: 0171-928 6662. *Chief Executive*, K. R. Bradley

HOSPITAL SAVING ASSOCIATION, Hambleden House, Andover, Hants SP10 1LQ. Tel: 01264-353211. *Chief Executive*, J. A. Young

HOSTELLING INTERNATIONAL NORTHERN IRELAND (formerly Youth Hostels Association of Northern Ireland) (1931), 22-32 Donegall Road, Belfast BT12 5JN. Tel: 01232-324733. *Hon. Secretary*, D. Forsythe

HOTEL AND CATERING INTERNATIONAL MANAGEMENT ASSOCIATION (1971), 191 Trinity Road, London SW17 7HN. Tel: 0181-672 4251. *Chief Executive*, D. Wood

HOUSE OF ST BARNABAS-IN-SOHO (1846), 1 Greek Street, London W1V 6NQ. Tel: 0171-434 1846. *Director*, Ms W. Taylor

HOUSING AID SOCIETY, CATHOLIC (1956), 209 Old Marylebone Road, London NW1 5QT. Tel: 0171-723 7273. *Director*, Ms R. Rafferty

HOUSING, CHARTERED INSTITUTE OF, Octavia House, Westwood Business Park, Westwood Way, Coventry CV4 8JP. Tel: 01203-695110. *Chief Executive*, D. Butler

HOVERCRAFT SOCIETY (1971), 15 St Mark's Road, Alverstoke, Gosport, Hants PO12 2DA. Tel: 01705-601310. *Chairman*, S. Syrad, OBE

HOWARD LEAGUE FOR PENAL REFORM (1866), 708 Holloway Road, London N19 3NL. Tel: 0171-281 7722. *Director*, Ms F. Crook

HUGUENOT SOCIETY OF GREAT BRITAIN AND IRELAND (1885), The Huguenot Library, University College, Gower Street, London WC1E 6BT. Tel: 0171-380 7094. *Hon. Secretary*, Mrs M. A. Bayliss

HUMANE RESEARCH TRUST (1974), Brook House, 29 Bramhall Lane South, Bramhall, Stockport, Cheshire SK7 2DN. Tel: 0161-439 8041. *Chairman*, K. Cholerton

HUMANIST ASSOCIATION, BRITISH (1963), 47 Theobald's Road, London WC1X 8SP. Tel: 0171-430 0908. *Executive Director*, R. Ashby

HUMAN RIGHTS, BRITISH INSTITUTE OF (1970), 8th Floor, King's College London, 75-79 York Road, London SE1 7AW. Tel: 0171-401 2712. *Director*, Ms S. Cooke

HYDROGRAPHIC SOCIETY (1972), c/o University of East London, Longbridge Road, Dagenham, Essex RM8 2AS. Tel: 0181-597 1946. *Hon. Secretary*, P. J. H. Warden

HYMN SOCIETY OF GREAT BRITAIN AND IRELAND (1936), 7 Paganel Road, Minehead, Somerset TA24 5ET. Tel: 01643-703530. *Secretary*, Revd G. Wrayford

ICAN (INVALID CHILDREN'S AID NATIONWIDE) (1888), 4 Dyers Buildings, Holborn, London EC1N 2QP. Tel: 0870-101 4066. *Chief Executive*, Ms G. Edelman

IMMIGRATION ADVISORY SERVICE (1970), County House, 190 Great Dover Street, London SE1 4YB. Tel: 0171-357 6917. *Chief Executive*, K. Best

INDEPENDENT BRITAIN, CAMPAIGN FOR AN (1976), 81 Ashmole Street, London SW8 1NF. Tel: 0181-340 0314. *Hon. Secretary*, Sir Robin Williams, Bt.

INDEPENDENT SCHOOLS' BURSARS ASSOCIATION (1933), 5 Chapel Close, Old Basing, Basingstoke, Hants RG24 7BY. Tel: 01256-330369. *General Secretary*, M. J. Sant

INDEPENDENT SCHOOLS CAREERS ORGANIZATION (1942), 12A Princess Way, Camberley, Surrey GU15 3SP. Tel: 01276-21188. *National Director*, J. D. Stuart

INDEPENDENT SCHOOLS COUNCIL (1974), Grosvenor Gardens House, 35-37 Grosvenor Gardens, London SW1W 0BS. Tel: 0171-798 1590. *General Secretary*, Dr A. B. Cooke, OBE

INDEPENDENT SCHOOLS INFORMATION SERVICE (1972), 56 Buckingham Gate, London SW1E 6AG. Tel: 0171-630 8793. *Director*, D. J. Woodhead

INDEXERS, SOCIETY OF (1957), Globe Centre, Penistone Road, Sheffield S6 3AE. Tel: 0114-281 3060. *Secretary*, Ms L. Weinhove

INDUSTRIAL CHRISTIAN FELLOWSHIP (1877), c/o St Malthaus House, 100 George Street, Croydon CRO 1PE. Tel: 0181-656 1644. *Chairman*, Revd Canon G. Brown

INDUSTRIAL SOCIETY (1918), Robert Hyde House, 48 Bryanston Square, London W1H 7LN. Tel: 0171-479 2000. *Chief Executive*, T. Morgan

INDUSTRY AND PARLIAMENT TRUST, 1 Buckingham Place, London SW1E 6HR. Tel: 0171-976 5311. *Director*, F. R. Hyde-Chambers

INDUSTRY TRAINING ORGANIZATIONS, NATIONAL COUNCIL OF (1988), 10 Meadowcourt, Amos Road, Sheffield S9 1BX. Tel: 0114-261 9926. *Chief Executive*, Dr A. Powell

INFANT DEATHS, FOUNDATION FOR THE STUDY OF (1971), 14 Halkin Street, London SW1X 7DP. Tel: 0171-235 0965. Helpline: 0171-235 1721. *Secretary-General*, Mrs J. Epstein

INFORMATION SCIENTISTS, INSTITUTE OF (1958), 44-45 Museum Street, London WC1A 1LY. Tel: 0171-831 8003. *Director*, E. Hyams

INNER WHEEL CLUBS IN GREAT BRITAIN AND IRELAND, ASSOCIATION OF (1934), 51 Warwick Square, London SW1V 2AT. *Secretary/Administrator*, Ms C. Charlesworth

INSOLVENCY, SOCIETY OF PRACTITIONERS OF (1990), Halton House, 20-23 Holborn, London EC1N 2JE. Tel: 0171-831 6563. *General Secretary*, R. M. Stancombe

INSURANCE BROKERS' ASSOCIATION, BRITISH, BIIBA House, 14 Bevis Marks, London EC3A 7NT. Tel: 0171-623 9043. *Chief Executive*, R. M. Williams

INSURANCE BROKERS REGISTRATION COUNCIL, 63 St Mary Axe, London EC3A 8NB. Tel: 0171-621 1061. *Registrar*, Miss E. J. Rees

INSURANCE INSTITUTE, CHARTERED (1897), 20 Aldermanbury, London EC2V 7HY. Tel: 0181-989 8464. *Director-General*, D. E. Bland, OBE, PH.D.

INSURERS, ASSOCIATION OF BRITISH (1985), 51 Gresham Street, London EC2V 7HQ. Tel: 0171-600 3333. *Director-General*, Ms M. Francis

INTERNATIONAL AFFAIRS, ROYAL INSTITUTE OF (1920), Chatham House, 10 St James's Square, London SW1Y 4LE. Tel: 0171-957 5700. *Director*, C. Gamble, PH.D.

INTERNATIONAL FRIENDSHIP LEAGUE (1931), 3 Creswick Road, London W3 9HE. *Chairman*, M. J. A. Prowse

INTERNATIONAL POLICE ASSOCIATION (British Section) (1950), 1 Fox Road, West Bridgford, Nottingham NG2 6AJ. *Chief Executive Officer*, A. F. Carter

INTERNATIONAL STUDENTS HOUSE (1962), 229 Great Portland Street, London W1N 5HD. Tel: 0171-631 8300. *Executive Director*, P. Anwyl

INTERSERVE (1852), 325 Kennington Road, London SE11 4QH. Tel: 0171-735 8227. *National Director*, R. Clark

INTER VARSITY CLUBS, ASSOCIATION OF (1946), 2nd Floor, Grosvenor House, 94-96 Grosvenor Square, Manchester M1 7HL. Tel: 0161-273 2316. *Chairman*, R. J. Clifford

INVALIDS-AT-HOME (1966), 17 Lapstone Gardens, Kenton, Harrow, Middx HA3 0EB. Tel: 0181-907 1706. *Executive Officer*, Mrs S. Lomas

INVOLVEMENT AND PARTICIPATION ASSOCIATION (1884), 42 Colebrooke Row, London N1 8AF. Tel: 0171-354 8040. *Director*, W. Coupar

IRAN SOCIETY (1936), 2 Belgrave Square, London SW1X 8PJ. Tel: 0171-235 5122. *Hon. Secretary*, A. D. Ashmole

ITRI (formerly International Tin Research Institute) (1932), Kingston Lane, Uxbridge, Middx UB8 3PJ. Tel: 01895-272406. *Director*, R. Bedder

JACQUELINE DU PRÉ MUSIC BUILDING LTD (1988), St Hilda's College, Oxford OX4 1DY. Tel: 01865-276821. *Chairman*, B. M. Levick

JAPAN ASSOCIATION (1950), Swire House, 59 Buckingham Gate, London SW1E 6AJ. Tel: 0171-821 3221. *Executive Director*, D. F. L. Turner

JERUSALEM AND THE MIDDLE EAST CHURCH ASSOCIATION (1887), 1 Hart House, The Hart, Farnham, Surrey GU9 7HA. Tel: 01252-726994. *Secretary*, Mrs V. Wells

JEWISH HISTORICAL SOCIETY OF ENGLAND (1893), 33 Seymour Place, London W1H 5AP. Tel: 0171-723 5852. *Hon. Secretary*, C. M. Drukker

JEWISH PEOPLE, CHURCH'S MINISTRY AMONG (1809), 30C Clarence Road, St Albans, Herts AL1 4JJ. Tel: 01727-833114. *General Director*, Revd T. Higton

JEWISH YOUTH, ASSOCIATION FOR (part of Norwood Ravenswood) (1899), Norwood House, Harmony Way, Victoria Road, London NW4 2BZ. Tel: 0181-203 3030. *Head*, E. Finestone

JOURNALISTS, INSTITUTE OF (1883), 2 Dock Offices, Surrey Quays Road, London SE16 2XU. Tel: 0171-252 1187. *General Secretary*, C. J. Underwood

JUSTICE (British Section of the International Commission of Jurists) (1957), 59 Carter Lane, London EC4V 5AQ. Tel: 0171-329 5100. *Director*, Ms A. Owers

JUSTICES' CLERKS' SOCIETY (1839), The Magistrates' Court, 107 Dale Street, Liverpool L2 2JQ. Tel: 0151-255 0790. *Hon. Secretary*, M. Marsh

KING GEORGE'S FUND FOR SAILORS (1917), 8 Hatherley Street, London SW1P 2YY. Tel: 0171-932 0000. *Director-General*, Capt. M. J. Appleton, RN

KING'S FUND, THE (formerly King Edward's Hospital Fund for London) (1897), 11-13 Cavendish Square, London W1M 0AN. Tel: 0171-307 2400. *Chief Executive*, Rabbi J. Neuberger

KIPLING SOCIETY (1927), Tree Cottage, 2 Brownleaf Road, Brighton, E. Sussex BN2 6LB. Tel: 01273-303719. *Hon. Secretary*, J. W. M. Smith

LADIES IN REDUCED CIRCUMSTANCES, SOCIETY FOR THE ASSISTANCE OF (1886), Lancaster House, 25 Hornyold Road, Malvern, Worcs WR14 1QQ. Tel: 01684-574645

LANDSCAPE INSTITUTE (1929), 6-8 Barnard Mews, London SW11 1QU. Tel: 0171-738 9166. *Director-General*, S. Royston

LAND-VALUE TAXATION AND FREE TRADE, INTERNATIONAL UNION FOR, Room 427, London Fruit Exchange, Brushfield Street, London E1 6EL. Tel: 0171-377 8885. *Hon. Secretary*, Mrs B. P. Sobrielo

LANGUAGE LEARNING, ASSOCIATION FOR (1990), 150 Railway Terrace, Rugby CV21 3HN. Tel: 01788-546443. *Director*, Dr. B. Boyce

LAW REPORTING FOR ENGLAND AND WALES, INCORPORATED COUNCIL OF (1865), Megarry House, 119 Chancery Lane, London WC2A 1PP. Tel: 0171-242 6471. *Secretary*, J. Cobbett

LEAGUE OF THE HELPING HAND (1908), Petersham Hollow, 226 Petersham Road, Petersham, Richmond, Surrey TW10 7AL. Tel: 0181-940 7303. *Secretary*, Mrs I. Goodlad

LEAGUE, THE (1893), 119-133 Limekiln Lane, Liverpool L5 8SN. Tel: 0151-207 1984. *Chief Executive*, P. Rooney

LEATHER AND HIDE TRADES' BENEVOLENT INSTITUTION (1860), 60 Wickham Hill, Hurstpierpoint, Hassocks, W. Sussex BN6 9NP. Tel: 01273-843488. *Secretary*, Mrs G. M. Stapleton, MBE

LEGAL EXECUTIVES, INSTITUTE OF (1892), Kempston Manor, Kempston, Bedford MK42 7AB. Tel: 01234-841000. *Secretary-General*, Ms D. Burleigh

LEONARD CHESHIRE (1955), 30 Millbank, London SW1P 4QD. Tel: 0171-802 8200. *Director-General*, B. Dutton

LEPROSY MISSION (ENGLAND AND WALES) (1874), Goldhay Way, Orton Goldhay, Peterborough PE2 5GZ. Tel: 01733-370505. *Executive Director*, Revd J. A. Lloyd, PH.D.

LEUKAEMIA RESEARCH FUND (1962), 43 Great Ormond Street, London WC1N 3JJ. Tel: 0171-405 0101. *Executive Director*, D. L. Osborne

LIBERAL PARTY (1877; relaunched 1989), The Pine Grove Centre, 1A Pine Grove, Southport PR9 9AQ. Tel: 01704-500115. *Communications Director*, D. Green

LIBERTY (NATIONAL COUNCIL FOR CIVIL LIBERTIES) (1934), 21 Tabard Street, London SE1 4LA. Tel: 0171-403 3888. *Director*, J. Wadham

LIBRARY ASSOCIATION (1877), 7 Ridgmount Street, London WC1E 7AE. Tel: 0171-636 7543. *Chief Executive*, Dr. R. A. McKee

LIFEBOATS, *see* ROYAL NATIONAL LIFEBOAT INSTITUTION

LINGUISTS, INSTITUTE OF (1910), Saxon House, 48 Southwark Street, London SE1 1UN. Tel: 0171-940 3100. *Director*, H. Pavlovich

LINNEAN SOCIETY OF LONDON (1788), Burlington House, Piccadilly, London W1V 0LQ. Tel: 0171-434 4479. *President*, Prof. Sir Ghillean Prance, FRS

LIONS CLUBS INTERNATIONAL (BRITISH ISLES AND IRELAND) (1949), 257 Alcester Road South, Kings Heath, Birmingham B14 6DT. Tel: 0121-441 4544. *Office Manager*, Mrs J. Davis

LISTENING BOOKS (formerly The Listening Library), 12 Lant Street, London SEI 1QH. Tel: 0171-407 9417. *Chief Executive*, T. Taylor

LLOYD'S OF LONDON, 1 Lime Street, London EC3M 7HA. Tel: 0171-327 1000. *Chief Executive*, R. Sandler

LLOYD'S REGISTER OF SHIPPING, 100 Leadenhall Street, London EC3A 3BP. Tel: 0171-709 9166. *Chief Executive Officer*, T. Jones

LOCAL AUTHORITY CHIEF EXECUTIVES AND SENIOR MANAGERS, SOCIETY OF (1974), PO Box 21, Archway Road, Huyton, Knowsley, Merseyside L36 9YU. Tel: 0151-443 3733. *Hon. Secretary*, D. Henshaw

LOCAL COUNCILS, NATIONAL ASSOCIATION OF (1947), 109 Great Russell Street, London WC1B 3LD. Tel: 0171-637 1865. *Deputy Chief Executive*, Ms R. Lonsdowne

LOCAL GOVERNMENT ASSOCIATION (1974), Local Government House, Smith Square, London SW1P 3HY. Tel: 0171-664 3000. *Chief Executive*, B. Briscoe

LOCAL GOVERNMENT INTERNATIONAL BUREAU (1913); *also* Council of European Municipalities and Regions (British Section) and International Union of Local Authorities (British Section) (1951), 35 Great Smith Street, London SW1P 3BJ. Tel: 0171-664 3100. *Director*, J. Smith

LOCAL HISTORY, BRITISH ASSOCIATION FOR (1843), 24 Lower Street, Harnham, Salisbury, Wilts SP2 8EY. Tel: 01722-322158. *General Secretary*, M. Cowan

LONDON APPRECIATION SOCIETY (1932), 7-20 Hampden Gurney Street, London W1H 5AL. *Chairman*, Miss V. C. Colin-Russ

LONDON CITY MISSION (1835), 175 Tower Bridge Road, London SEI 2AH. Tel: 0171-407 7585. *General Secretary*, Revd J. McAllen

LONDON COURT OF INTERNATIONAL ARBITRATION (LCIA) (1892), 6th Floor, Hulton House, 161-166 Fleet Street, London EC4A 2DY. Tel: 0171-936 3530. *Executive Director*, Ms M. May, CBE

LONDON FLOTILLA (1937), 40 Endlesham Road, London SW12 8JL. Tel: 0181-673 1879. *Hon. Membership Secretary*, Lt.-Cdr. H. C. R. Upton, RD, RNR

LONDON GOVERNMENT, ASSOCIATION OF (1964), 36 Old Queen Street, London SW1H 9JF. Tel: 0171-222 7799. *Chief Executive*, M. Pilgrim

LONDON LIBRARY, THE (1841), 14 St James's Square, London SW1Y 4LG. Tel: 0171-930 7705. *Librarian*, A. S. Bell

LONDON MAGISTRATES' CLERKS' ASSOCIATION (1889), c/o South Western Magistrates' Court, 176A LAVENDER HILL, BATTERSEA, LONDON SW11. Tel: 0171-228 9201. *Hon. Chairman*, J. Mulreany

LONDON PLAYING FIELDS SOCIETY (1890), Fraser House, 29 Albemarle Street, London W1X 3FA. Tel: 0171-493 3211. *Chief Executive*, Dr C. Goodson-Wickes

LONDON SOCIETY (1912), 4th Floor, Senate House, Malet Street, London WC1E 7HU. Tel: 0171-580 5537. *Hon. Secretary*, Mrs B. Jones

LORD'S DAY OBSERVANCE SOCIETY (1831), 3 Epsom Business Park, Kiln Lane, Epsom, Surrey KT17 1JF. Tel: 01372-728300. *General Secretary*, J. G. Roberts

LOTTERIES COUNCIL (1979), Woodlands, High Grove Road, Grasscroft, Saddleworth OL4 4GH. Tel: 01457-872988. *Executive Officer*, Ms S. Brierley

LUNG FOUNDATION, BRITISH (1985), 78 Hatton Garden, London EC1N 8LD. Tel: 0171-831 5831. *Chief Executive*, B. Walden

MACA – PARTNERS IN MENTAL HEALTH (formerly Mental After Care Association) (1879), 25 Bedford Square, London WC1B 3HW. Tel: 0171-436 6194. *Chief Executive*, G. Hitchon

MAGISTRATES' ASSOCIATION (1920), 28 Fitzroy Square, London W1P 6DD. Tel: 0171-387 2353. *Secretary*, Ms S. Dickinson

MAILING PREFERENCE SERVICE (1983), 5th Floor, Haymarket House, 1 Oxendon Street, London SW1Y 4EE. *Director of Compliance Operations*, Ms T. Kelly

MAIL USERS' ASSOCIATION (1976), 70 Main Road, Hermitage, Near Emsworth, W. Sussex PO10 8AX. Tel: 0976-710315. *Chairman*, D. Thomas

MANAGEMENT, INSTITUTE OF (1992), Management House, Cottingham Road, Corby, Northants NN17 1TT. Tel: 01536-204222. *Director-General*, Mrs M. Chapman

MANAGEMENT AND PROFESSIONAL STAFFS, ASSOCIATION OF (1972), Parkgates, Bury New Road, Prestwich, Manchester M25 0JW. Tel: 0161-773 8621. *Executive Secretary*, A. J. Casey

MANAGEMENT SERVICES, INSTITUTE OF, 1 Cecil Court, London Road, Enfield, Middx EN2 6DD. Tel: 0181-363 7452. *Director-General*, P. Symes

MANIC DEPRESSION FELLOWSHIP (1983), 8-10 High Street, Kingston upon Thames, Surrey KT1 1EY. Tel: 0181-974 6550. *Chief Executive*, Ms K. Campbell

MANORIAL SOCIETY OF GREAT BRITAIN (1906), 104 Kennington Road, London SE11 6RE. Tel: 0171-735 6633. *Hon. Chairman*, R. A. Smith

MANPOWER SOCIETY LTD (1969), 39 Apple Tree Walk, Climping, Littlehampton, W. Sussex BN17 5QN. Tel: 01903-731728. *Administration Manager*, Mrs H. Gale

MARIE CURIE CANCER CARE (1948), 28 Belgrave Square, London SW1X 8QG. Tel: 0171-235 3325. *Chief Executive*, Sir Nicholas Fenn, GCMG

MARINE ARTISTS, ROYAL SOCIETY OF (1939), 17 Carlton House Terrace, London SW1Y 5BD. Tel: 0171-930 6844. *Secretary*, Ms S. Robinson

MARINE BIOLOGICAL ASSOCIATION OF THE UK (1884), Citadel Hill, Plymouth PL1 2PB. Tel: 01752-633100. *Director*, Prof S. Hawkins

MARINE ENGINEERS, INSTITUTE OF (1889), 80 Coleman Street, London EC2R 5BJ. Tel: 0171-382 2600. *Director-General*, K. F. Read

MARINE SCIENCE, SCOTTISH ASSOCIATION FOR (1914), PO Box 3, Oban, Argyll PA34 4AD. Tel: 01631-562244. *Director*, Dr G. B. Shimmield, FRSE

MARINE SOCIETY, THE (1756), 202 Lambeth Road, London SEI 7JW. Tel: 0171-261 9535. *Director*, Capt. J. J. Howard

MARIO LANZA EDUCATIONAL FOUNDATION (1976), 646 Portway, Avonmouth, Bristol BS11 9NZ. *Hon. Secretary*, Mrs C. Jacobs

MARKET AUTHORITIES, NATIONAL ASSOCIATION OF BRITISH (1948), 13 Moor Road, Orrell Post, Wigan, Lancs WN5 8ND. Tel: 01942-203797. *General Secretary*, J. Edwards

MARKETING, CHARTERED INSTITUTE OF (1911), Moor Hall, Cookham, Maidenhead, Berks SL6 9QH. Tel: 01628-427500. *Chief Executive*, J. Stubbs

MARK MASTER MASONS, GRAND LODGE OF (1856), Mark Masons' Hall, 86 St James's Street, London SW1A 1PL. Tel: 0171-839 5274. *Grand Secretary*, T. J. Lewis

MARRIAGE CARE (formerly the Catholic Marriage Advisory Council) (1946), Clitherow House, 1 Blythe Mews, Blythe Road, London W14 0NW. Tel: 0171-371 1341. *Chief Executive*, Mrs M. Corbett

MASONIC BENEVOLENT INSTITUTION, ROYAL (1842), 20 Great Queen Street, London WC2B 5BG. Tel: 0171-405 8341. *Chief Executive*, Miss J. Reynolds

MASONIC TRUST FOR GIRLS AND BOYS (1985), 31 Great Queen Street, London WC2B 5AG. Tel: 0171-405 2644. *Secretary*, Lt.-Col. J. C. Chambers

MASTERS OF WINE, INSTITUTE OF (1955), Five Kings House, 1 Queen Street Place, London EC4R 1QS. *Executive Director*, J. F. Casson

MATERIALS, INSTITUTE OF (1985), 1 Carlton House Terrace, London SW1Y 5DB. Tel: 0171-451 7300. *Chief Executive*, Dr B. A. Rickinson

MATERNAL AND CHILD WELFARE, NATIONAL ASSOCIATION FOR (1911), 1st Floor, 40-42 Osnaburgh Street, London NW4 3ND. Tel: 0171-383 4117. *Administrator*, Mrs V. A. Farebrother

MATERNITY ALLIANCE (1980), 45 Beech Street, London EC2P 2LX. Tel: 0171-588 8583. *Director*, Ms C. Gowdridge

MATHEMATICAL ASSOCIATION (1871), 259 London Road, Leicester LE2 3BE. Tel: 0116-270 3877. *Executive Secretary*, Ms H. Whitby

MATHEMATICS AND ITS APPLICATIONS, INSTITUTE OF (1964), Catherine Richards House, 16 Nelson Street, Southend-on-Sea, Essex SS1 1EF. Tel: 01702-354020. *Executive Secretary*, Dr A. M. Lepper

MCPS-PRS ALLIANCE, 29-33 Berners Street, London W1P 4AA. *Chief Executive*, J. Hutchinson

ME ASSOCIATION (1976), 4 Corringham Road, Stanford-le-Hope, Essex SS17 0AH. Tel: 01375-642466. *Chief Executive*, Ms M. Moore

MEASUREMENT AND CONTROL, INSTITUTE OF (1944), 87 Gower Street, London WC1E 6AA. Tel: 0171-387 4949. *Secretary*, M. J. Yates

MECHANICAL ENGINEERS, INSTITUTION OF (1847), 1 Birdcage Walk, London SW1H 9JJ. Tel: 0171-222 7899. *Director-General*, Sir Michael Moore, KBE, LVO

MEDICAL COUNCIL, GENERAL (1858), 178 Great Portland Street, London W1N 6JE. Tel: 0171-580 7642. *Chief Executive*, F. M. Scott, TD

MEDIC-ALERT FOUNDATION, 1 Bridge Wharf, 156 Caledonian Road, London N1 9UU. Tel: 0171-833 3034. *Chief Executive*, Miss J. Friend

MEDICAL FOUNDATION FOR THE CARE OF VICTIMS OF TORTURE (1986), 96-98 Grafton Road, London NW5 3EJ. Tel: 0171-813 7777. *Director*, Ms H. Bamber

MEDICAL SOCIETY OF LONDON (1773), Lettsom House, 11 Chandos Street, London W1M 0EB. *Registrar*, Col. R. Kinsella-Bevan

MEDICAL WOMEN'S FEDERATION (1917), Tavistock House North, Tavistock Square, London WC1H 9HX. Tel: 0171-387 7765. *Hon. Secretary*, Dr S. Glendinning

MENCAP (THE ROYAL SOCIETY FOR MENTALLY HANDICAPPED CHILDREN AND ADULTS) (1946), 123 Golden Lane, London EC1Y 0RT. Tel: 0171-454 0454. *Chief Executive*, F. Heddell, CBE

MENSA, BRITISH (1946), Mensa House, St Johns Square, Wolverhampton WV2 4AH. Tel: 01902-772771. *General Manager*, D. Chatten

MENTAL HEALTH FOUNDATION (1949), 20-21 Cornwall Terrace, London NW1 4QL. Tel: 0171-535 7400. *Director*, Ms J. McKerrow

MENTAL HEALTH, NATIONAL ASSOCIATION FOR, *see* MIND

MENTAL HEALTH, SCOTTISH ASSOCIATION FOR (1923), Cumbrae House, 15 Carlton Court, Glasgow G5 9JP. Tel: 0141-568 7000. *Chief Executive*, Ms. S. M. Barcus

MENTALLY HANDICAPPED, SCOTTISH SOCIETY FOR THE, *see* ENABLE

MERCHANT NAVY WELFARE BOARD (1948), 19-21 Lancaster Gate, London W2 3LN. Tel: 0171-723 3642. *General Secretary*, Capt. D. A. Parsons

METAL TRADES BENEVOLENT SOCIETY, ROYAL (1843), Brooke House, 4 The Lakes, Bedford Road, Northampton NN4 7YD. Tel: 01604-622023. *General Secretary*, A. G. Johnson

METEOROLOGICAL SOCIETY, ROYAL (1850), 104 Oxford Road, Reading, Berks RG1 7LJ. Tel: 01734-568500. *Executive Secretary*, R. P. C. Swash

METROPOLITAN HOSPITAL-SUNDAY FUND (1872), 45 Westminster Bridge Road, London SE1 7JB. Tel: 0171-922 0200. *Secretary*, H. F. Doe

MIDDLE EAST ASSOCIATION (1961), Bury House, 33 Bury Street, London SW1Y 6AX. Tel: 0171-839 2137. *Director-General*, B. P. Constant

MIDWIVES, ROYAL COLLEGE OF (1881), 15 Mansfield Street, London W1M 0BE. Tel: 0171-312 3535. *General Secretary*, Mrs K. Davis

MIGRAINE ACTION ASSOCIATION, (formerly British Migraine Association) (1858), 178A High Road, Byfleet, West Byfleet, Surrey KT14 7ED. Tel: 01932-352468. *Director*, Mrs A. Turner

MIGRAINE TRUST (1965), 45 Great Ormond Street, London WC1N 3HZ. Tel: 0171-831 4818. *Director*, Ms A. Rush

MILITARY HISTORICAL SOCIETY, National Army Museum, Royal Hospital Road, London SW3 4HT. Tel: 01980-615689. *The Secretary*, Lt.-Col. R. E. L. Hodges

MIND (NATIONAL ASSOCIATION FOR MENTAL HEALTH), Granta House, 15-19 Broadway, London E15 4BQ. Tel: 0181-519 2122. *Chief Executive*, Ms J. Clements

MINERALOGICAL SOCIETY (1876), 41 Queen's Gate, London SW7 5HR. Tel: 0171-584 7516. *General Secretary*, Ms F. Wall

MINIATURE PAINTERS, SCULPTORS AND GRAVERS, ROYAL SOCIETY OF (1895), 1 Knapp Cottages, Wyke, Gillingham, Dorset SP8 4NQ. Tel: 01747-825718. *Executive Secretary*, Mrs P. Henderson

MINING AND METALLURGY, INSTITUTION OF (1889), Danum House, 6A South Parade, Doncaster, S. Yorks DN1 2DY. Tel: 01302-320486. *Secretary*, Dr G. J. M. Woodrow

MISSING PERSONS HELPLINE, NATIONAL (1992), Roebuck House, 284-286 Upper Richmond Road West, London SW14 7JE. Tel: 0181-392 4545. Helpline: 0500-700700. *Co-Founders*, Mrs M. Asprey, OBE; Mrs J. Newman, OBE

MISSION TO DEEP SEA FISHERMEN, ROYAL NATIONAL (1881), 43 Nottingham Place, London W1M 4BX. Tel: 0171-487 5101. *Chief Executive*, A. D. Marsden

MISSIONS TO SEAMEN (1856), St Michael Paternoster Royal, College Hill, London EC4R 2RL. Tel: 0171-248 5202. *Secretary-General*, Revd Canon G. Jones

MODERN CHURCHPEOPLE'S UNION (1898), MCU Office, 25 Birch Grove, London W3 9SP. Tel: 0181-932 4379. *General Secretary*, Revd N. P. Henderson

MONUMENTAL BRASS SOCIETY (1887), Lowe Hill House, Stratford St Mary, Colchester, Essex CO7 6JX. Tel: 0181-520 5249. *Hon. Secretary,* H. M. Stuchfield

MORAVIAN MISSIONS, LONDON ASSOCIATION IN AID OF (1817), Moravian Church House, 5-7 Muswell Hill, London N10 3TJ. Tel: 0181-883 3409. *Secretary,* Ms J. Morten

MOTHERS' UNION (1876), Mary Sumner House, 24 Tufton Street, London SW1P 3RB. Tel: 0171-222 5533. *Chief Executive,* vacant

MOTOR INDUSTRY, INSTITUTE OF THE, Fanshaws, Brickendon, Hertford SG13 8PQ. Tel: 01992-511521. *Director-General,* R. Ward

MOUNTBATTEN MEMORIAL TRUST (1979), 1 Grosvenor Crescent, London SW1X 7EF. Tel: 0171-235 5231 ext 255. *Director,* J. Boyd-Brent

MOUNTBATTEN TRUST, THE EDWINA (1960), 1 Grosvenor Crescent, London SW1X 7EF. Tel: 0171-235 5231 ext 255. *Secretary,* J. Boyd-Brent

MULTIPLE SCLEROSIS SOCIETY (1953), 25 Effie Road, London SW6 1EE. Tel: 0171-610 7171. *Chief Executive,* P. Cardy

MUNICIPAL ENGINEERS, ASSOCIATION OF, Institution of Civil Engineers, Great George Street, London SW1P 3AA. Tel: 0171-222 7722. *Director,* A. Bhogal

MUSEUMS ASSOCIATION (1889), 42 Clerkenwell Close, London EC1R 0PA. Tel: 0171-608 2933. *Director,* M. Taylor

MUSIC HALL SOCIETY, BRITISH (1963), c/o Brodie and Middleton Ltd, 68 Drury Lane, London WC2B 5SP. Tel: 0171-836 3289. *Hon. Secretary,* Mrs D. Masterton

MUSICIANS BENEVOLENT FUND (1921), 16 Ogle Street, London W1P 8JB. Tel: 0171-636 4481. *Secretary,* Ms H. Faulkner

MUSICIANS, INCORPORATED SOCIETY OF (1882), 10 Stratford Place, London W1N 9AE. Tel: 0171-629 4413. *Chief Executive,* N. Hoyle

MUSICIANS OF GREAT BRITAIN, THE ROYAL SOCIETY OF (1738), 10 Stratford Place, London W1N 9AE. Tel: 0171-629 6137. *Secretary,* Mrs M. Gibb

MUSIC INFORMATION CENTRE, BRITISH (1967), 10 Stratford Place, London W1N 9AE. Tel: 0171-499 8567. *Director,* M. Greenall

MUSIC SOCIETIES, NATIONAL FEDERATION OF (1935), Francis House, Francis Street, London SW1P 1DE. Tel: 0171-828 7320. *Chief Executive,* R. Jones

NABS (formerly National Advertising Benevolent Society) (1913), 32 Wigmore Street, London W1H 9DF. Tel: 0171-299 2888. *Director,* Ms H. Tridgell

NACRO (NATIONAL ASSOCIATION FOR THE CARE AND RESETTLEMENT OF OFFENDERS) (1966), 169 Clapham Road, London SW9 0PU. Tel: 0171-582 6500. *Chief Executive,* Ms H. Edwards

NATIONAL BENEVOLENT INSTITUTION (1812), 61 Bayswater Road, London W2 3PG. Tel: 0171-723 0021. *Secretary,* Gp Capt. D. St J. Homer, MVO

NATIONAL COUNCIL FOR VOLUNTARY ORGANIZATIONS, *see* VOLUNTARY ORGANIZATIONS, NATIONAL COUNCIL FOR

NATIONAL COUNCIL OF WOMEN OF GREAT BRITAIN (1895), 36 Danbury Street, London N1 8JU. Tel: 0171-354 2395. *President,* Dr D. Glick

NATIONAL DEMOCRATS (formerly National Front) (1967), PO Box 2269, London E6 3RF. Tel: 0181-471 6872. *Chairman,* I. Anderson

NATIONAL EXTENSION COLLEGE (1963), 18 Brooklands Avenue, Cambridge CB2 2HN. Tel: 01223-450200. *Director,* Dr R. Morpeth

NATIONAL SOCIETY, THE (1811), Church House, Great Smith Street, London SW1P 3NZ. Tel: 0171-898 1518. *General Secretary,* Canon J. Hall

NATIONAL SOCIETY FOR THE PREVENTION OF CRUELTY TO CHILDREN (NSPCC) (1884), 42 Curtain Road, London EC2A 3NH. Tel: 0171-825 2500. *Director,* J. Harding

NATIONAL TRUST, THE (1895), 36 Queen Anne's Gate, London SW1H 9AS. Tel: 0171-222 9251. *Director-General,* M. Drury

NATIONAL TRUST FOR SCOTLAND (1931), 5 Charlotte Square, Edinburgh EH2 4DU. Tel: 0131-226 5922. *Director,* T. Croft

NATIONAL UNION OF STUDENTS (1922), Nelson Mandela House, 461 Holloway Road, London N7 6LJ. Tel: 0171-272 8900. *National President,* A. Pakes

NATIONAL VIEWERS' AND LISTENERS' ASSOCIATION (1964), All Saints House, High Street, Colchester CO1 1UG. Tel: 01206-561155. *Director,* J. C. Beyer

NATIONAL WOMEN'S REGISTER (1960), 3A Vulcan House, Vulcan Road North, Norwich NR6 6AQ. Tel: 01603-406767. *National Organizers,* Mrs M. Dodkins, Mrs E. Thorn

NATURALISTS' ASSOCIATION, BRITISH (1905), 1 Bracken Mews, London E4 7UT. *Hon. Membership Secretary,* Mrs Y. H. Griffiths

NAUTICAL RESEARCH, SOCIETY FOR (1911), c/o National Maritime Museum, Greenwich, London SE10 9NF. *Hon. Secretary,* Lt.-Cdr W. J. R. Gardner

NAVAL ARCHITECTS, ROYAL INSTITUTION OF (1860), 10 Upper Belgrave Street, London SW1X 8BQ. Tel: 0171-235 4622. *Chief Executive,* T. Blakeley

NAVAL, MILITARY AND AIR FORCE BIBLE SOCIETY (1780), Radstock House, 3 Eccleston Street, London SW1W 9LZ. Tel: 0171-463 1468. *General Secretary,* J. M. Hines

NAVIGATION, ROYAL INSTITUTE OF (1947), 1 Kensington Gore, London SW7 2AT. Tel: 0171-591 3130. *Director,* Gp Capt. D. W. Broughton, MBE

NAVY RECORDS SOCIETY (1893), c/o Department of War Studies, King's College, The Strand, London WC2R 2LS. *Hon. Secretary,* Dr A. D. Lambert

NCH ACTION FOR CHILDREN (1869), 85 Highbury Park, London N5 1UD. Tel: 0171-226 2033. *Chief Executive,* D. Mead

NEEDLEWORK, ROYAL SCHOOL OF (1872), Apartment 12A, Hampton Court Palace, Surrey KT8 9AU. Tel: 0181-943 1432. *Principal,* Mrs E. Elvin

NEWCOMEN SOCIETY (1920), The Science Museum, London SW7 2DD. Tel: 0171-371-4445. *Executive Secretary,* C. Armstrong

NEWSPAPER PRESS FUND (1864), Dickens House, 35 Wathen Road, Dorking, Surrey RH4 1JY. Tel: 01306-887511. *Director,* P. W. Evans

NEWSTRAID BENEVOLENT SOCIETY (1839), PO Box 306, Dunmow, Essex CM6 1HY. Tel: 01371-874198. *President,* A. Cameron

NHS CONFEDERATION (1974), 26 Chapter Street, London SW1P 4ND. Tel: 0171-233 7388. *Chief Executive,* S. Thornton

NOISE ABATEMENT SOCIETY (1959), PO Box 518, Eynsford, Dartford, Kent DA4 0LL. Tel: 01695-725121. *Chairman,* J. Connell, OBE

NON-SMOKERS, NATIONAL SOCIETY OF, *see* QUIT

NORWOOD RAVENSWOOD (formerly Norwood Childcare) (1795), Broadway House, 80-82 The Broadway, Stanmore, Middx HA7 4HB. Tel: 0181-954 4555. *Executive Directors*, Ms N. Brier, S. Brier

NOTARIES' SOCIETY (1907), 23 New Street, Woodbridge, Suffolk IP12 IDN. Tel: 01394-384134. *Secretary*, A. G. Dunford

NUCLEAR ENERGY SOCIETY, BRITISH (1962), 1-7 Great George Street, London SW1P 3AA. Tel: 0171-665 2241. *Executive Officer*, A. Tillbrook

NUFFIELD FOUNDATION (1943), 28 Bedford Square, London WC1B 3EG. Tel: 0171-631 0566. *Director*, A. Tomei

NUFFIELD TRUST (formerly the Nuffield Provincial Hospitals Trust) (1939), 59 New Cavendish Street, London WIM 7RD. Tel: 0171-631 8450. *Secretary*, J. Wyn Owen, CB

NURSES' NATIONAL HOME, RETIRED (1934), Riverside Avenue, Bournemouth BH7 7EE. Tel: 01202-396418. *Chairman*, Ms J. Deacon, SRN

NURSES, ROYAL NATIONAL PENSION FUND FOR, Burdett House, 15 Buckingham Street, London WC2N 6ED. Tel: 0171-839 6785. *General Manager*, V. G. West

NURSING, MIDWIFERY AND HEALTH VISITING, ENGLISH NATIONAL BOARD FOR, Victory House, 170 Tottenham Court Road, London W1P OHA. Tel: 0171-391 6229. *Chief Executive Officer*, A. P. Smith, CBE

NURSING, MIDWIFERY AND HEALTH VISITING FOR NORTHERN IRELAND, NATIONAL BOARD FOR, Centre House, 79 Chichester Street, Belfast BT1 4JE. Tel: 01232-238152. *Chief Executive*, Prof. O. D'A. Slevin

NURSING, MIDWIFERY AND HEALTH VISITING FOR SCOTLAND, NATIONAL BOARD FOR, 22 Queen Street, Edinburgh EH2 INT. Tel: 0131-226 7371. *Chief Executive*, D. C. Benton

NURSING, MIDWIFERY AND HEALTH VISITING, UK CENTRAL COUNCIL FOR, 23 Portland Place, London WIN 4JT. Tel: 0171-333 6557. *Chief Executive*, Ms S. Norman

NURSING, MIDWIFERY AND HEALTH VISITING, WELSH NATIONAL BOARD FOR, 2nd Floor, Golate House, 101 St Mary Street, Cardiff CF1O IDX. Tel: 01222-026400. *Chief Executive*, D. A. Ravey

NURSING, ROYAL COLLEGE OF (1916), 20 Cavendish Square, London WIM OAB. Tel: 0171-409 3333. *General Secretary*, Miss C. Hancock

NUTRITION FOUNDATION, BRITISH (1967), High Holborn House, 52-54 High Holborn, London WC1V 6RQ. Tel: 0171-404 6504. *Director-General*, Prof. R. S. Pickard, PH.D, CBiol, FIBiol

NUTRITION SOCIETY (1941), 10 Cambridge Court, 210 Shepherds Bush Road, London W6 7NJ. Tel: 0171-602 0228. *Hon. Secretary*, Dr J. D. Oldham

OBSTETRICIANS AND GYNAECOLOGISTS, ROYAL COLLEGE OF (1929), 27 Sussex Place, London NW1 4RG. Tel: 0171-772 6200. *Secretary*, P. A. Barnett

OCCUPATIONAL HEALTH AND SAFETY AGENCY, *see* OHSA

OCCUPATIONAL SAFETY AND HEALTH, INSTITUTION OF (1946), The Grange, Highfield Drive, Wigston, Leics LE18 INN. Tel: 0116-257 3100. *Chief Executive*, J. R. Barrell, OBE

OFFICERS' ASSOCIATION, THE (1920), 48 Pall Mall, London SW1Y 5JY. Tel: 0171-930 0125. *General Secretary*, Brig. J. M. A. Norton, OBE, MC

OFFICERS' PENSIONS SOCIETY (1946), 68 South Lambeth Road, London SW8 IRL. Tel: 0171-820 9988. *General Secretary*, Maj.-Gen. P. R. F. Bonnet, CB, MBE

OHSA (formerly Occupational Health and Safety Agency), 46 Wimpole Street, London WIM 7DG. Tel: 0171-222 1202. *Managing Director*, Ms W. Gill

OIL PAINTERS, ROYAL INSTITUTE OF (1883), 17 Carlton House Terrace, London SW1Y 5BD. Tel: 0171-930 6844. *Secretary*, B. Bennett

ONE-PARENT FAMILIES, NATIONAL COUNCIL FOR, 255 Kentish Town Road, London NW5 2LX. Tel: 0171-428 5400. *Director*, Ms M. Sherlock

OPAS (PENSIONS ADVISORY SERVICE) (1982), 11 Belgrave Road, London SW1V IRB. Tel: 0171-233 8080. *Chief Executive*, M. McLean, OBE

OPEN-AIR MISSION (1853), 19 John Street, London WC1N 2DL. Tel: 0171-405 6135. *Secretary*, A. J. Greenbank

OPEN SPACES SOCIETY (1865), 25A Bell Street, Henley-on-Thames, Oxon RG9 2BA. Tel: 01491-573535. *General Secretary*, Miss K. Ashbrook

OPERATIC AND DRAMATIC ASSOCIATION, NATIONAL (1899), NODA House, 1 Crestfield Street, London WC1H 8AU. Tel: 0171-837 5655. *Chief Executive*, M. Thorburn

OPSIS (National Association for the Education, Training and Support of Blind and Partially Sighted People) (1992), c/o Queen Alexandra College, Court Oak Road, Birmingham B17 9TG. Tel: 0121-428 5037. *Executive Manager*, C. Gregory

OPTICAL COUNCIL, GENERAL (1958), 41 Harley Street, London WIN 2DJ. Tel: 0171-580 3898. *Registrar*, R. Wilshin

OPTOMETRISTS, COLLEGE OF, 42 Craven Street, London WC2N 5NG. Tel: 0171-839 6000. *Secretary*, P. D. Leigh

ORDERS AND MEDALS RESEARCH SOCIETY (1942), 123 Turnpike Link, Croydon CRO 5NU. Tel: 0181-680 2701. *General Secretary*, N. G. Gooding

ORIENTAL CERAMIC SOCIETY (1921), 30B Torrington Square, London WC1E 7LJ. Tel: 0171-636 7985. *Hon. Secretary*, Dr. F. Wood

ORNITHOLOGISTS' CLUB, SCOTTISH (1936), 21 Regent Terrace, Edinburgh EH7 5BT. Tel: 0131-556 6042. *Secretary*, Miss S. Laing

ORNITHOLOGISTS' UNION, BRITISH (1858), c/o The Natural History Museum, Akeman Street, Tring, Herts HP23 6AP. Tel: 01442-890080. *Administrator*, S. P. Dudley

ORNITHOLOGY, BRITISH TRUST FOR (1932), National Centre for Ornithology, The Nunnery, Thetford, Norfolk IP24 2PU. Tel: 01842-750050. *Director*, Dr J. J. D. Greenwood

ORTHOPAEDIC ASSOCIATION, BRITISH (1918), c/o The Royal College of Surgeons, 35-43 Lincoln's Inn Fields, London WC2A 3PN. Tel: 0171-405 6507. *Chief Executive*, D. C. Adams

OSTEOPATHIC COUNCIL, GENERAL (formerly General Council and Register of Osteopaths) (1936), Osteopathy House, 176 Tower Bridge Road, London SE1 3LU. Tel: 0171-357 6655. *Registrar*, Miss M. J. Craggs

OSTEOPATHIC MEDICINE, LONDON COLLEGE OF, 8-10 Boston Place, London NW1 6QH. Tel: 0171-262 5250. *Clinic Manager*, Mrs A. Dalby

OSTEOPOROSIS SOCIETY, NATIONAL (1986), PO Box 10, Radstock, Bath BA3 3YB. Tel: 01761-471771. *Communications Manager*, Miss C. Chisholm

OUTWARD BOUND TRUST (1941), Award House, 7-11 St Matthew Street, London SW1P 2JT. Tel: 0171-222 3059. *Director*, Sir Michael Hobbs, KCVO, CBE

OVERSEAS DEVELOPMENT INSTITUTE (1960), Portland House, Stag Place, London SW1E 5DP. Tel: 0171-393 1600. *Director*, S. Maxwell

OVERSEAS SERVICE PENSIONERS' ASSOCIATION (1960), 138 High Street, Tonbridge, Kent TN9 1AX. Tel: 01732-363836. *Secretary*, D. F. B. Le Breton, CBE

OXFAM GB (1942), 274 Banbury Road, Oxford OX2 7DZ. Tel: 01865-311311. *Director*, D. Bryer, CMG

OXFORD PRESERVATION TRUST (1927), 10 Turn Again Lane, St Ebbes, Oxford OX1 1QL. Tel: 01865-242918. *Secretary*, Mrs D. Dance

OXFORD SOCIETY (1932), 41 Wellington Square, Oxford OX1 2JF. Tel: 01865-270088. *Secretary*, T. J. Lewis

PAEDIATRICS AND CHILD HEALTH, ROYAL COLLEGE OF (1928), 5 St Andrews Place, Regents Park, London NW1 4LB. Tel: 0171-486 6151. *Hon. Secretary*, Dr K. Dodd

PAINTER-PRINTMAKERS, ROYAL SOCIETY OF (1880), Bankside Gallery, 48 Hopton Street, London SE1 9JH. Tel: 0171-928 7521. *President*, Prof. D. Carpanini

PAINTERS IN WATER COLOURS, ROYAL INSTITUTE OF (1831), 17 Carlton House Terrace, London SW1Y 5BD. Tel: 0171-930 6844. *Secretary*, T. Hunt

PALAEONTOLOGICAL ASSOCIATION (1957), c/o Lapworth Museum, School of Earth Sciences, University of Birmingham, Birmingham B15 2TT. Tel: 0121-414 4173. *Secretary*, Dr P. Smith

PARENTS AT WORK (1985), 45 Beech Street, Barbican, London EC2Y 8AD. Tel: 0171-628 3578. *Joint Chief Executives*, Ms S. Jackson, Ms S. Monk

PARKINSON'S DISEASE SOCIETY OF THE UNITED KINGDOM (1969), 215 Vauxhall Bridge Road, London SW1V 1EJ. Tel: 0171-931 8080. Helpline: 0171-233 5373. *Chief Executive*, B. A. Brooking, MBE

PARLIAMENTARY AND SCIENTIFIC COMMITTEE (1939), 48 Westminster Palace Gardens, 1-7 Artillery Row, London SW1P 1RR. Tel: 0171-222 7085. *Administrative Secretary*, Dr A. Whitehouse

PASTORAL PSYCHOLOGY, GUILD OF (1936), PO Box 1107, London W3 6ZP. Tel: 0181-993 8366. *Administrator*, Mrs N. Stanley

PATENT AGENTS, CHARTERED INSTITUTE OF (1882), Staple Inn Buildings, High Holborn, London WC1V 7PZ. Tel: 0171-405 9450. *Secretary*, M. C. Ralph

PATENTEES AND INVENTORS, INSTITUTE OF (1919), Suite 505A, Triumph House, 189 Regent Street, London W1R 7WF. Tel: 0171-434 1818. *Secretary*, R. Magnus

PATHOLOGISTS, ROYAL COLLEGE OF, 2 Carlton House Terrace, London SW1Y 5AF. Tel: 0171-930 5861. *Secretary*, K. Lockyer

PATIENTS ASSOCIATION (1963), PO Box 935, Harrow, Middx HA1 3YJ. Tel: 0181-423 9111. Helpline: 0181-423 8999. *General Manager*, Ms E. Richardson

PDSA (PEOPLE'S DISPENSARY FOR SICK ANIMALS) (1917), Whitechapel Way, Priorslee, Telford, Shropshire TF2 9PQ. Tel: 01952-290999. *Director-General*, M. R. Curtis, MBE

PEACE COUNCIL, NATIONAL (1908), 88 Islington High Street, London N1 8EG. Tel: 0171-354 5200. *Chief Executive*, T. Milne-Wallis

PEAK AND NORTHERN FOOTPATHS SOCIETY (1894), 15 Parkfield Drive, Tyldesley, Manchester M29 8NR. Tel: 0161-790 4383. *Hon. General Secretary*, D. Taylor

PEARSON'S HOLIDAY FUND, PO Box 123, Bishops Waltham, Southampton SO32 1ZE. Tel: 01489-893260. *General Secretary*, R. Heasman

PEDESTRIANS ASSOCIATION, THE (1929), 3rd Floor, 31-33 Bondway, London SW8 1SJ. Tel: 0171-820 1010. *Director*, B. Plowden

PEN, INTERNATIONAL (1921), 9-10 Charterhouse Buildings, Goswell Road, London EC1M 7AT. Tel: 0171-253 4308. *International Secretary*, T. Carlbom

PENSION FUNDS LTD, NATIONAL ASSOCIATION OF (1923), 12-18 Grosvenor Gardens, London SW1W 0DH. Tel: 0171-730 0585. *Director-General*, Dr A. Robinson

PENSIONS ADVISORY SERVICE, *see* OPAS

PERFORMING RIGHT SOCIETY LTD (1914), Copyright House, 29-33 Berners Street, London W1P 4AA. Tel: 0171-580 5544. *Chief Executive*, J. Hutchinson

PERIODICAL PUBLISHERS ASSOCIATION LTD (1913), Queens House, 28 Kingsway, London WC2B 6JR. Tel: 0171-404 4166. *Chief Executive*, I. Locks

PESTALOZZI CHILDREN'S VILLAGE TRUST (1959), Sedlescombe, Battle, E. Sussex TN33 0RR. Tel: 01424-870444. *Director*, M. Phillips

PETROLEUM, INSTITUTE OF (1913), 61 New Cavendish Street, London W1M 8AR. Tel: 0171-467 7100. *Director-General*, I. Ward

PHARMACEUTICAL SOCIETY OF GREAT BRITAIN, ROYAL (1841), 1 Lambeth High Street, London SE1 7JN. Tel: 0171-735 9141. *Secretary*, J. Ferguson, OBE

PHARMACOLOGICAL SOCIETY, BRITISH (1931), 16 Angel Gate, City Road, London EC1V 2SG. *President*, Prof. N. G. Bowery

PHILOLOGICAL SOCIETY (1842), School of Oriental and African Studies, University of London, Thornhaugh Street, London WC1H 0XG. *Hon. Secretary*, Prof. N. Sims-Williams

PHILOSOPHY, ROYAL INSTITUTE OF (1925), 14 Gordon Square, London WC1H 0AG. Tel: 0171-387 4130. *Director*, Prof. A. O'Hear

PHOTOGRAPHY, BRITISH INSTITUTE OF PROFESSIONAL (1901), Fox Talbot House, Amwell End, Ware, Herts SG12 9HN. Tel: 01920-464011. *Chief Executive*, A. Mair

PHYSICAL RECREATION, CENTRAL COUNCIL OF (1935), Francis House, Francis Street, London SW1P 1DE. Tel: 0171-828 3163. *General Secretary*, M. Denton

PHYSICIANS, ROYAL COLLEGE OF (1518), 11 St Andrews Place, London NW1 4LE. Tel: 0171-935 1174. *Secretary*, P. Masterton-Smith

PHYSICIANS AND SURGEONS OF GLASGOW, ROYAL COLLEGE OF (1599), 232-242 St Vincent Street, Glasgow G2 5RJ. Tel: 0141-221 6072. *Hon. Secretary*, Dr C. Semple

PHYSICIANS OF EDINBURGH, ROYAL COLLEGE OF (1681), 9 Queen Street, Edinburgh EH2 1JQ. Tel: 0131-225 7324. *Secretary*, Dr A. C. Parker

PHYSICS AND ENGINEERING IN MEDICINE, INSTITUTE OF, Fairmount House, 230 Tadcaster Road, York YO24 1ES. Tel: 01904-610821. *General Secretary*, R. W. Neilson

PHYSICS, INSTITUTE OF (1874), 76 Portland Place, London W1N 3DH. Tel: 0171-470 4800. *Chief Executive*, Dr A. D. W. Jones

PHYSIOLOGICAL SOCIETY, THE (1876), PO Box 11319, London WC1E 7JF. Tel: 0171-631 1458. *Hon. Secretary,* Prof. C. Fry

PHYSIOTHERAPY, CHARTERED SOCIETY OF (1894), 14 Bedford Row, London WC1R 4ED. Tel: 0171-306 6666. *Chief Executive,* P. Gray

PIG ASSOCIATION, BRITISH (1884), 7 Rickmansworth Road, Watford WD1 7HE. Tel: 01923-234377. *Chief Executive,* vacant

PILGRIM TRUST (1930), Fielden House, Little College Street, London SW1P 3SH. Tel: 0171-222 4723. *Director,* Miss G. Nayler

PILGRIMS OF GREAT BRITAIN (1902), Allington Castle, Maidstone, Kent ME16 0NB. *Hon. Secretary,* M. P. S. Barton

PLAIN ENGLISH CAMPAIGN (1979), PO Box 3, New Mills, Stockport SK22 4QP. Tel: 01663-744409. *Director,* Ms C. Maher, OBE

PLANT ENGINEERS, INSTITUTION OF, 77 Great Peter Street, London SW1P 2EZ. Tel: 0171-233 2855. *Secretary,* P. F. Tye

PLAYING FIELDS ASSOCIATION, NATIONAL (1925), 25 Ovington Square, London SW3 1LQ. Tel: 0171-584 6445. *Director,* Ms E. Davies

PLUNKETT FOUNDATION (1919), 23 Hanborough Business Park, Long Hanborough, Oxford OX8 8LH. Tel: 01993-883636. *Director,* S. Rawlinson

POETRY SOCIETY (1909), 22 Betterton Street, London WC2H 9BU. Tel: 0171-420 9880. *Director,* C. Meade

POLICY STUDIES INSTITUTE (1978), 100 Park Village East, London NW1 3SR. Tel: 0171-468 0468. *Director,* Prof. J. Skea

POLIO FELLOWSHIP, BRITISH (1939), Ground Floor, Unit A, Eagle Office Centre, The Runway, South Ruislip, Middx HA4 6SE. Tel: 0800-018 0586. *Chief Executive,* A. Kemp, CQSW

POLITE SOCIETY and CAMPAIGN FOR COURTESY (1986), 6 Norman Avenue, Henley-on-Thames, Oxon RG9 1SG. Tel: 01491-572794. *Hon. Secretary,* Miss G. Mackenzie

PONY CLUB (1929), National Agricultural Centre, Stoneleigh Park, Kenilworth, Warks CV8 2RW. Tel: 01203-698300. *Chief Executive,* P. R. Lord

PORTRAIT PAINTERS, ROYAL SOCIETY OF (1891), 17 Carlton House Terrace, London SW1Y 5BD. Tel: 0171-930 6844. *Secretary,* P. Brason

POST OFFICE USERS' NATIONAL COUNCIL (1970), 6 Hercules Road, London SE1 7DN. Tel: 0171-928 9458. *Secretary,* J. Dodds

PRAYER BOOK SOCIETY (1975), St James Garlickhythe, Garlick Hill, London EC4V 2AF. Tel: 01923-824278. *Chairman,* C. A. A. Kilmister

PRE-SCHOOL LEARNING ALLIANCE, 69 Kings Cross Road, London WC1X 9LL. Tel: 0171-833 0991. *Chief Executive,* Ms M. Lochrie

PRESS UNION, COMMONWEALTH (1909), 17 Fleet Street, London EC4Y 1AA. Tel: 0171-583 7733. *Director,* M. Robinson

PREVENTION OF ACCIDENTS, ROYAL SOCIETY FOR THE (1916), ROSPA House, Edgbaston Park, 353 Bristol Road, Birmingham B5 7ST. Tel: 0121-248 2000. *Chief Executive,* Dr J. Hooper

PRINCESS LOUISE SCOTTISH HOSPITAL, *see* ERSKINE HOSPITAL

PRINCE'S SCOTTISH YOUTH BUSINESS TRUST (1989), 6th Floor, Mercantile Chambers, 53 Bothwell Street, Glasgow G2 6TS. Tel: 0141-248 4999. *Director,* D. W. Cooper

PRINCESS ROYAL TRUST FOR CARERS (1990), 142 Minories, London EC3N 1LB. Tel: 0171-480 7788. *Chief Executive (acting),* Ms V. Daybell

PRINCE'S TRUST (1976) and ROYAL JUBILEE TRUSTS (1935, 1977), 18 Park Square East, London NW1 4LH. Tel: 0800-842842. *Director,* T. Shebbeare, CVO

PRINCE'S YOUTH BUSINESS TRUST, *see* PRINCE'S TRUST

PRINTERS' CHARITABLE CORPORATION (1827), 7 Cantelupe Mews, Cantelupe Road, East Grinstead, W. Sussex RH19 3BG. Tel: 01342-318882. *Director,* Ms T. Searle

PRINTING HISTORICAL SOCIETY (1964), St Bride Institute, Bride Lane, London EC4Y 8EE. *Hon. Secretary,* P. Wickens

PRINTING, INSTITUTE OF (1961), 8A Lonsdale Gardens, Tunbridge Wells, Kent TN1 1NU. Tel: 01892-538118. *Secretary-General,* D. Freeland

PRISONERS ABROAD (1978), 72-82 Rosebery Avenue, London EC1R 4RR. Tel: 0171-833 3467. *Director,* C. Laurenzi

PRISON VISITORS, NATIONAL ASSOCIATION OF (1922), 29 Kimbolton Road, Bedford MK40 2PB. Tel: 01234-359763. *General Secretary,* Mrs A. G. McKenna

PRIVATE LIBRARIES ASSOCIATION (1957), Ravelston, South View Road, Pinner, Middx HA5 3YD. *Hon. Secretary,* F. Broomhead

PROCURATORS IN GLASGOW, ROYAL FACULTY OF (1600), 12 Nelson Mandela Place, Glasgow G2 1BT. Tel: 0141-331-0533. *General Manager,* I. C. Pearson

PROFESSIONAL CLASSES AID COUNCIL (1921), 10 St Christopher's Place, London W1M 6HY. Tel: 0171-935 0641

PROFESSIONAL FOOTBALLERS' ASSOCIATION, 2 Oxford Court, Bishopsgate, Manchester M2 3WQ. Tel: 0161-236 0575. *Chief Executive,* G. Taylor

PROFESSIONS SUPPLEMENTARY TO MEDICINE, COUNCIL FOR, Park House, 184 Kennington Park Road, London SE11 4BU. Tel: 0171-582 0866. *Registrar,* M. D. Hall

PROTECTION OF UNBORN CHILDREN, SOCIETY FOR THE (1967), Phyllis Bowman House, 5-6 St Matthew Street, London SW1P 2JT. Tel: 0171-222 5845. *National Director,* J. Smeaton

PROTESTANT ALLIANCE (1845), 77 Ampthill Road, Flitwick, Bedford MK45 1BD. Tel: 01525-712348. *General Secretary,* Dr S. J. Scott-Pearson

PSORIASIS ASSOCIATION (1968), 7 Milton Street, Northampton NN2 7JG. Tel: 01604-711129. *Chief Executive,* Mrs L. Henley

PSYCHIATRISTS, ROYAL COLLEGE OF (1971), 17 Belgrave Square, London SW1X 8PG. Tel: 0171-201 2601. *Secretary,* Mrs V. Cameron

PSYCHICAL RESEARCH, SOCIETY FOR (1882), 49 Marloes Road, London W8 6LA. Tel: 0171-937 8984. *Secretary,* Ms E. J. O'Keeffe

PSYCHOLOGICAL SOCIETY, BRITISH (1901), St Andrews House, 48 Princess Road East, Leicester LE1 7DR. Tel: 0116-254 9568. *Executive Secretary,* C. V. Newman, PH.D.

PUBLIC FINANCE AND ACCOUNTANCY, CHARTERED INSTITUTE OF (1885), 3 Robert Street, London WC2N 6BH. Tel: 0171-543 5600. *Chief Executive,* D. Adams

PUBLIC HEALTH AND HYGIENE, ROYAL INSTITUTE OF, and SOCIETY OF PUBLIC HEALTH (1937), 28 Portland Place, London WIN 4DE. Tel: 0171-580 2731. *Secretary*, Gp Capt. R. A. Smith

PUBLIC RELATIONS, INSTITUTE OF (1948), The Old Trading House, 15 Northburgh Street, London ECIV OPR. Tel: 0171-253 5151. *Executive Director*, J. B. Lavelle

PUBLIC TEACHERS OF LAW, SOCIETY OF (1908), School of Law, Kings College London, Strand, London WC2R 2LS. Tel: 0171-848 2849. *Hon. Secretary*, Prof. D. Hayton

PURCHASING AND SUPPLY, CHARTERED INSTITUTE OF (1967), Easton House, Easton on the Hill, Stamford, Lincs PE9 3NZ. Tel: 01780-756777. *Chief Executive*, C. Holden

QUAKER SOCIAL RESPONSIBILITY AND EDUCATION, Friends House, 173-177 Euston Road, London NWI 2BJ. Tel: 0171-663 1000. *The General Secretary*, vacant

QUALITY ASSURANCE, INSTITUTE OF, 12 Grosvenor Crescent, London SWIX 7EE. Tel: 0171-245 6722. *Secretary-General*, D. G. Campbell

QUARRIERS (formerly Quarriers Homes) (1871), Head Office, Quarriers Village, Bridge of Weir, Renfrewshire PAII 3SX. Tel: 01505-612224. *Director*, G. E. Lee

QUARRYING, INSTITUTE OF (1917), 7 Regent Street, Nottingham NGI 5BS. Tel: 0115-941 1315. *Secretary*, Mrs L. Bryden

QUEEN ELIZABETH'S FOUNDATION FOR DISABLED PEOPLE (1967), Leatherhead Court, Leatherhead, Surrey KT22 OBN. Tel: 01372-841100. *Director*, M. B. Clark, PH.D.

QUEEN'S ENGLISH SOCIETY, THE (1972), 20 Jessica Road, London SW18 2QN. Tel: 0181-874 2200. *Hon. Secretary*, Miss P. Raper

QUEEN'S NURSING INSTITUTE (1887), 3 Albemarle Way, London ECIV 4RQ. Tel: 0171-490 4227. *Director*, Mrs J. Hesketh

QUEEN VICTORIA CLERGY FUND (1897), Church House, Dean's Yard, London SWIP 3NZ. Tel: 0171-898 1310. *Secretary*, C. D. L. Menzies

QUEEN VICTORIA SCHOOL (1908), Dunblane, Perthshire FKI5 OJY. Tel: 01786-822288. *Headmaster*, B. Raine

QUEKETT MICROSCOPICAL CLUB (1865), Flat 3, Romagna, 101 Truro Road, London N22 4DL. *Hon. Business Secretary*, Miss P. Hamer

QUIT (NATIONAL SOCIETY OF NON-SMOKERS) (1926), Victory House, 170 Tottenham Court Road, London WIP OHA. Tel: 0171-388 5775. *Chief Executive*, P. McCabe

RADAR (ROYAL ASSOCIATION FOR DISABILITY AND REHABILITATION) (1977), 12 City Forum, 250 City Road, London ECIV 8AF. Tel: 0171-250 3222. *Director*, B. Massie, OBE

RADIOLOGISTS, ROYAL COLLEGE OF (1934), 38 Portland Place, London WIN 4JQ. Tel: 0171-636 4432. *General Secretary*, A. J. Cowles

RADIOLOGY, BRITISH INSTITUTE OF (1897), 36 Portland Place, London WIN 4AT. Tel: 0171-307 1406. *Chief Executive*, Ms M.A. Piggott

RAIL USERS' CONSULTATIVE COMMITTEE, CENTRAL (1948), Clements House, 14-18 Gresham Street, London EC2V 7NL. Tel: 0171-505 9090. *National Director*, P. Hadley

RAILWAY AND CANAL HISTORICAL SOCIETY, 3 West Court, West Street, Oxford OX2 ONP. Tel: 01865-240514. *Hon. Secretary*, M. Searle

RAILWAY BENEVOLENT INSTITUTION (1858), Foundation House, 7-11 Macon Court, Herald Drive, Crewe, Cheshire CWI 6WA. Tel: 01270-251316. *Director*, B. R. Whitnall

RAMBLERS' ASSOCIATION (1935), 1-5 Wandsworth Road, London SW8 2XX. Tel: 0171-339 8500. *Director*, A. Mattingly

RARE BREEDS SURVIVAL TRUST (1973), National Agricultural Centre, Stoneleigh Park, Kenilworth, Warks CV8 2LG. Tel: 01203-696551. *Executive Director*, G. L. H. Alderson

RATHBONE COMMUNITY INDUSTRY (1919), 4th Floor, Churchgate House, Oxford Street, Manchester MI 6EU. Tel: 0161-236 5358. *Chief Executive*, Ms A. Weinstock, CBE

RECORDS ASSOCIATION, BRITISH (1932), 40 Northampton Road, London ECIR OHB. Tel: 0171-833 0428. *Hon. Secretary*, Mrs E. Hughes

RECORD SOCIETY, SCOTTISH (1897), Department of Scottish History, University of Glasgow, Glasgow GI2 8QH. Tel: 0141-339 8855 ext 5682. *Hon. Secretary*, J. Kirk, PH.D.

RED CROSS SOCIETY, BRITISH, *see* BRITISH RED CROSS

RED POLL CATTLE SOCIETY (1888), The Market Hill, Woodbridge, Suffolk IPI2 4LU. Tel: 01394-380643. *Secretary*, Mrs T. J. Booker

REFRIGERATION, INSTITUTE OF (1899), Kelvin House, 76 Mill Lane, Carshalton, Surrey SM5 2JR. Tel: 0181-647 7033. *Secretary*, M. J. Horlick

REFUGEE COUNCIL, BRITISH (1981), Bondway House, 3-9 Bondway, London SW8 ISJ. Tel: 0171-820 3000. *Chief Executive*, N. Hardwick

REGIONAL STUDIES ASSOCIATION (1965), Wharfdale Projects, 15 Micawber Street, London NI 7TB. Tel: 0171-490 1128. *Director*, Mrs S. Hardy

REGULAR FORCES EMPLOYMENT ASSOCIATION LTD (1885), 49 Pall Mall, London SWIY 5JG. Tel: 0171-321 2011. *Chief Executive*, Maj.-Gen. M. F. L. Shellard, CBE

RELATE (1938), Herbert Gray College, Little Church Street, Rugby, Warks CV21 3AP. Tel: 01788-573241. *Chief Executive*, Ms S. Bowler

RENT OFFICERS AND RENTAL VALUERS, INSTITUTE OF (1966), Beaufort House, Hamble Lane, Bursledon, Southampton SO3I 8BR. Tel: 01703-403716. *General Secretary*, A. E. Corcoran, FRV

RESEARCH DEFENCE SOCIETY (1908), 58 Great Marlborough Street, London WIV IDD. Tel: 0171-287 2818. *Executive Director*, Dr M. Matfield

RESERVE FORCES ASSOCIATION (formerly Council of Territorial, Auxiliary and Volunteer Reserve Associations) (1908), Duke of York's HQ, London SW3 4SG. Tel: 0171-730 6122. *Secretary-General*, Maj.-Gen. W. A. Evans, CB

RETIREMENT PENSIONS ASSOCIATIONS, NATIONAL FEDERATION OF (1938), Thwaites House, Railway Road, Blackburn BBI 5AX. Tel: 01254-52606. *General Secretary*, R. Stansfield

REVENUES, RATING AND VALUATION, INSTITUTE OF (1882), 41 Doughty Street, London WCIN 2LF. Tel: 0171-831 3505. *Director*, C. Farrington

RICHARD III SOCIETY (1924), 4 Oakley Street, London SW3 5NN. *Secretary*, Miss E. M. Nokes

ROAD SAFETY OFFICERS, INSTITUTE OF (1971), 11 Parkside, Groby, Leicester LE6 OEB. Tel: 0870-0104442. *Chairman*, Mrs R. Duffield

ROAD TRANSPORT ENGINEERS, INSTITUTE OF (1945), 22 Greencoat Place, London SW1P 1PR. Tel: 0171-630 1111. *Chief Executive*, A. F. Stroud

ROMAN STUDIES, SOCIETY FOR THE PROMOTION OF (1910), Senate House, Malet Street, London WC1E 7HU. Tel: 0171-862 8727. *Secretary*, Dr H. M. Cockle

ROOM: THE NATIONAL COUNCIL FOR HOUSING AND PLANNING (1900), 14-18 Old Street, London EC1V 9BH. Tel: 0171-251 2363. *Director*, K. MacDonald

ROTARY INTERNATIONAL IN GREAT BRITAIN AND IRELAND (1914), Kinwarton Road, Alcester, Warks B49 6BP. Tel: 01789-765411. *Secretary*, R. Freeman

ROUND TABLES OF GREAT BRITAIN AND IRELAND, NATIONAL ASSOCIATION OF (1927), Marchesi House, 4 Embassy Drive, Edgbaston, Birmingham B15 1TP. Tel: 0121-456 4402. *General Secretary*, J. Handley

ROYAL AIR FORCE BENEVOLENT FUND (1919), 67 Portland Place, London W1N 4AR. Tel: 0171-580 8343. *Controller*, Air Chief Marshal Sir David Cousins, KCB, AFC

ROYAL AIR FORCES ASSOCIATION (1943), 43 Grove Park Road, London W4 3RX. Tel: 0181-994 8504. *Secretary-General*, J. G. Hargreaves, CBE

ROYAL ALEXANDRA AND ALBERT SCHOOL (1758), Gatton Park, Reigate, Surrey RH2 0TW. Tel: 01737-642576. *Secretary*, Wg Cdr N. J. Wright

ROYAL ALFRED SEAFARERS' SOCIETY (1865), Weston Acres, Woodmansterne Lane, Banstead, Surrey SM7 3HB. Tel: 01737-352231. *General Secretary*, A. R. Quinton

ROYAL ARMOURED CORPS WAR MEMORIAL BENEVOLENT FUND (1946), c/o RHQ RTR, Bovington Camp, Wareham, Dorset BH20 6JA. Tel: 01929-403331. *Secretary*, Maj. A. Henzie, MBE

ROYAL ARTILLERY ASSOCIATION, Artillery House, Front Parade, Royal Artillery Barracks, Woolwich, London SE18 4BH. Tel: 0181-781 3003. *General Secretary*, Lt-Col M. G. Felton

ROYAL ASIATIC SOCIETY (1823), 60 Queen's Gardens, London W2 3AF. Tel: 0171-724 4742. *Publications Officer*, A. P. A. Belloli

ROYAL BRITISH LEGION, *see* BRITISH LEGION, ROYAL

ROYAL CALEDONIAN SCHOOLS TRUST (1815), 80A High Street, Bushey, Watford, Herts WD2 3DE. Tel: 0181-421 8845. *Chief Executive*, J. Horsfield

ROYAL CELTIC SOCIETY (1820), 23 Rutland Street, Edinburgh EH1 2RN. Tel: 0131-228 6449. *Secretary*, J. G. Cameron

ROYAL CHORAL SOCIETY (1871), Unit 9, 92 Lots Road, London SW10 0QD. Tel: 0171-376 3718. *Administrator*, G. Tonge

ROYAL ENGINEERS ASSOCIATION, RHQ Royal Engineers, Brompton Barracks, Chatham, Kent ME4 4UG. Tel: 01634-822394. *Controller*, Lt-Col J. W. Ray (retd)

ROYAL ENGINEERS, INSTITUTION OF (1875), Brompton Barracks, Chatham, Kent ME4 4UG. Tel: 01634-842669. *Secretary*, Col M. R. Cooper

ROYAL HIGHLAND AND AGRICULTURAL SOCIETY OF SCOTLAND (1784), Royal Highland Centre, Ingliston, Edinburgh EH28 8NF. Tel: 0131-335 6200. *Chief Executive*, R. Jones

ROYAL HORTICULTURAL SOCIETY (1804), 80 Vincent Square, London SW1P 2PE. Tel: 0171-834 4333. *Director-General*, Dr A. Colquhoun

ROYAL HOSPITAL FOR NEURO-DISABILITY (1854), West Hill, Putney, London SW15 3SW. Tel: 0181-780 4500. *Chief Executive*, V. J. Beauchamp

ROYAL HUMANE SOCIETY (1774), Brettenham House, Lancaster Place, London WC2E 7EP. Tel: 0171-836 8155. *Secretary*, Maj.-Gen. C. Tyler, CB

ROYAL INSTITUTION OF GREAT BRITAIN (1799), 21 Albemarle Street, London W1X 4BS. Tel: 0171-409 2992. *Director*, Prof. S. Greenfield

ROYAL LIFE SAVING SOCIETY UK (1891), River House, High Street, Broom, Warks B50 4HN. Tel: 01789-773994. *Director-General*, S. Lear

ROYAL LITERARY FUND (1790), 3 Johnson's Court, off Fleet Street, London EC4A 3EA. Tel: 0171-353 7150. *General Secretary*, Ms E. M. Gunn

ROYAL MEDICAL BENEVOLENT FUND (1836), 24 King's Road, London SW19 8QN. *Chief Executive Officer*, M. Baber

ROYAL MEDICAL SOCIETY (1737), Students Centre, 5/5 Bristo Square, Edinburgh EH8 9AL. Tel: 0131-650 2672. *Senior President*, P. Mills

ROYAL MICROSCOPICAL SOCIETY (1839), 37-38 St Clements, Oxford OX4 1AJ. Tel: 01865-248768. *Administrator*, P. B. Hirst

ROYAL MUSICAL ASSOCIATION (1874), Department of Music, The University of Leeds, Leeds LS2 9JT. *President*, J. Rushton

ROYAL NATIONAL INSTITUTE FOR THE BLIND (1868), 224 Great Portland Street, London W1N 6AA. Tel: 0345-669999. *Director-General*, I. Bruce

ROYAL NATIONAL LIFEBOAT INSTITUTION (1824), West Quay Road, Poole, Dorset BH15 1HZ. Tel: 01202-663000. *Director*, A. Freemantle, MBE

ROYAL NAVAL AND ROYAL MARINES CHILDREN'S FUND (1834), HMS Nelson, Portsmouth PO1 3HH. Tel: 01705-817435. *Secretary*, Mrs M. Bateman

ROYAL NAVAL ASSOCIATION (1950), 82 Chelsea Manor Street, London SW3 5QJ. Tel: 0171-352 6764. *General Secretary*, Capt. R. McQueen, CBE, RN

ROYAL NAVAL BENEVOLENT SOCIETY FOR OFFICERS (1739), 1 Fleet Street, London EC4Y 1BD. Tel: 0171-353 4080. *Secretary*, Capt. I. B. Sutherland, RN (retd)

ROYAL NAVAL BENEVOLENT TRUST (1922), Castaway House, 311 Twyford Avenue, Portsmouth PO2 8PE. Tel: 01705-690112/660296. *Chief Executive*, Cdr J. Owens

ROYAL NAVY OFFICERS, ASSOCIATION OF (1920), 70 Porchester Terrace, London W2 3TP. Tel: 0171-402 5231. *Secretary*, Lt-Cdr I. M. P. Coombes

ROYAL OVER-SEAS LEAGUE (1910), Over-Seas House, Park Place, St James's Street, London SW1A 1LR. Tel: 0171-408 0214. *Director-General*, R. F. Newell

ROYAL PATRIOTIC FUND CORPORATION (1854), 40 Queen Anne's Gate, London SW1H 9AP. Tel: 0171-233 1894. *Secretary*, Brig. T. G. Williams, CBE

ROYAL PHILATELIC SOCIETY LONDON (1869), 41 Devonshire Place, London W1N 1PE. *Hon. Secretary*, D. Gurney

ROYAL PHOTOGRAPHIC SOCIETY (1853), The Octagon, Milsom Street, Bath BA1 1DN. Tel: 01225-462841. *Secretary-General*, B. Lane

ROYAL PINNER SCHOOL FOUNDATION, 110 Old Brompton Road, London SW7 3RA. Tel: 0171-373 6168. *Secretary*, D. Crawford

ROYAL SAILORS' RESTS (1876), 5 St Georges Business Centre, St Georges Square, Portsmouth PO1 1EY. Tel: 01705-296096. *Executive Director*, Revd J. Martin

ROYAL SOCIETY FOR ASIAN AFFAIRS (1901), 2 Belgrave Square, London SW1X 8PJ. Tel: 0171-235 5122. *Secretary*, D. J. Easton

ROYAL SOCIETY FOR THE ENCOURAGEMENT OF ARTS, MANUFACTURES AND COMMERCE (RSA) (1754), 8 John Adam Street, London WC2N 6EZ. Tel: 0171-930 5115. *Chairman*, R. Onians

ROYAL SOCIETY FOR THE PREVENTION OF CRUELTY TO ANIMALS (RSPCA) (1824), Causeway, Horsham, W. Sussex RH12 1HG. Tel: 01403-264181. *Director-General*, P. R. Davies, CB

ROYAL SOCIETY FOR THE PROMOTION OF HEALTH (formerly Royal Society of Health) (1876), RSH House, 38 St George's Drive, London SW1V 4BH. Tel: 0171-630 0121. *Secretary*, Mrs H. Brandon

ROYAL SOCIETY FOR THE PROTECTION OF BIRDS (RSPB) (1889), The Lodge, Sandy, Beds SG19 2DL. Tel: 01767-680551. *Chief Executive*, G. R. Wynne

ROYAL SOCIETY OF LITERATURE (1823), 1 Hyde Park Gardens, London W2 2LT. Tel: 0171-723 5104. *Secretary*, Mrs M. Fergusson

ROYAL SOCIETY OF MEDICINE (1805), 1 Wimpole Street, London W1M 8AE. Tel: 0171-290 2900. *Executive Director*, Dr A. Grocock

ROYAL SOCIETY OF ST GEORGE (1894), 127 Sandgate Road, Folkestone, Kent CT20 2BL. Tel: 01303-241795. *Chairman*, W. M. Firth

ROYAL STAR AND GARTER HOME FOR DISABLED SAILORS, SOLDIERS AND AIRMEN (1916), Richmond Hill, Richmond upon Thames, Surrey TW10 6RR. Tel: 0181-940 3314. *Chief Executive*, I. A. Lashbrooke

ROYAL STATISTICAL SOCIETY (1834), 12 Errol Street, London EC1Y 8LX. Tel: 0171-638 8998. *Executive Secretary*, I. J. Goddard

ROYAL TANK REGIMENT BENEVOLENT FUND (1919), RHQ RTR, Bovington Camp, Wareham, Dorset BH20 6JA. Tel: 01929-403331. *Regimental Secretary*, Maj. A. Henzie, MBE

ROYAL TELEVISION SOCIETY (1927), Holborn Hall, 100 Gray's Inn Road, London WC1X 8AL. Tel: 0171-430 1000. *Executive Director*, M. Bunce

ROYAL UNITED KINGDOM BENEFICENT ASSOCIATION (1863), 6 Avonmore Road, London W14 8RL. Tel: 0171-602 6274. *Director*, W. Rathbone

RURAL ENGLAND, COUNCIL FOR THE PROTECTION OF, *see* CPRE

RURAL SCOTLAND, ASSOCIATION FOR THE PROTECTION OF (1926), 3rd Floor, Gladstone's Land, 483 Lawnmarket, Edinburgh EH1 2NT. Tel: 0131-225 7012/3. *Director*, Mrs J. Geddes

RURAL WALES, CAMPAIGN FOR THE PROTECTION OF (1928), Ty Gwyn, 31 High Street, Welshpool, Powys SY21 7YD. Tel: 01938-552525. *Director*, M. Williams

SAFETY COUNCIL, BRITISH (1957), 70 Chancellor's Road, London W6 9RS. Tel: 0181-741 1231. *Director-General*, Sir Neville Purvis, KCB

SAILORS' FAMILIES' SOCIETY (1821), Newland, Hull HU6 7RJ. Tel: 01482-342331. *Chief Executive*, G. J. Powell

SAILORS' SOCIETY, BRITISH AND INTERNATIONAL (1818), 3 Orchard Place, Southampton SO14 3AT. Tel: 01703-337333. *General Secretary*, G. Chambers

ST DEINIOL'S RESIDENTIAL LIBRARY (1902), Hawarden, Deeside, Flintshire CH5 3DF. Tel: 01244-532350. *Warden and Chief Librarian*, Revd P. B. Francis

ST DUNSTAN'S (FOR MEN AND WOMEN BLINDED IN THE SERVICE OF THEIR COUNTRY), 12-14 Harcourt Street, London W1A 4XB. Tel: 0171-723 5021. *Chief Executive*, G. B. J. Frost

ST JOHN AMBULANCE (1887), 1 Grosvenor Crescent, London SW1X 7EF. Tel: 0171-235 5231. *Executive Director*, L. Martin

SALES AND MARKETING MANAGEMENT, INSTITUTE OF (1966), Romeland House, Romeland Hill, St Albans AL3 4ET. Tel: 01727-812500. *Chief Executive*, P. Joiner

SALMON AND TROUT ASSOCIATION (1903), Fishmongers' Hall, London Bridge, London EC4R 9EL. Tel: 0171-283 5838. *Director*, C. W. Poupard

SALTIRE SOCIETY (1936), 9 Fountain Close, 22 High Street, Edinburgh EH1 1TF. Tel: 0131-556 1836. *Administrator*, Mrs K. Munro

SAMARITANS (1953), 10 The Grove, Slough SL1 1QP. Tel: 01753-216500. *Chief Executive*, S. Armson

SANE (1986), 1st Floor, Cityside House, 40 Alder Street, London E1 1EE. Tel: 0171-375 1002. *Chief Executive*, Ms M. Wallace, MBE

SAVE BRITAIN'S HERITAGE (1975), 70 Cowcross Street, London EC1M 6EJ. Tel: 0171-253 3500. *Secretary*, R. Pollard

SAVE THE CHILDREN FUND (1919), 17 Grove Lane, London SE5 8RD. Tel: 0171-703 5400. *Director-General*, M. Aaronson

SCHIZOPHRENIA FELLOWSHIP, NATIONAL (1970), 28 Castle Street, Kingston upon Thames, Surrey KT1 1SS. Tel: 0181-547 3937. *Chief Executive*, C. Prior

SCHOOL LIBRARY ASSOCIATION (1937), Liden Library, Barrington Close, Liden, Swindon SN3 6HF. Tel: 01793-617838. *Executive Secretary*, Ms K. Lemaire

SCHOOLMASTERS AND SCHOOLMISTRESSES, SOCIETY OF (1798), The King's School, Canterbury, Kent CT1 2ES. Tel: 01227-595546. *Hon. Secretary*, Dr R. B. Mallion

SCHOOLMISTRESSES AND GOVERNESSES BENEVOLENT INSTITUTION (1843), Queen Mary House, Manor Park Road, Chislehurst, Kent BR7 5PY. Tel: 0181-468 7997. *Director*, L. I. Baggott

SCIENCE, BRITISH ASSOCIATION FOR THE ADVANCEMENT OF (1831), 23 Savile Row, London W1X 2NB. Tel: 0171-973 3500. *Chief Executive*, Dr P. Briggs

SCIENCE EDUCATION, ASSOCIATION FOR (1963), College Lane, Hatfield, Herts AL10 9AA. Tel: 01707-283000. *Chief Executive*, Dr D. S. Moore

SCOPE (formerly The Spastics Society) (1952), 6 Market Road, London N7 9PW. Tel: 0171-619 7100. *Chief Executive*, R. P. Brewster

SCOTTISH CHIEFS, STANDING COUNCIL OF (1952), Hope Chambers, 52 Leith Walk, Edinburgh EH6 5HW. Tel: 0131-554 6321. *General Secretary*, G. A. Way of Plean

SCOTTISH CHURCH HISTORY SOCIETY (1922), Crown Manse, 39 Southside Road, Inverness IV2 4XA. Tel: 01463-231140. *Hon. Secretary*, Revd Dr P. H. Donald

SCOTTISH COUNTRY DANCE SOCIETY, ROYAL (1923), 12 Coates Crescent, Edinburgh EH3 7AF. Tel: 0131-225 3854. *Secretary*, Miss G. S. Parker

SCOTTISH GENEALOGY SOCIETY (1953), Library and Family History Centre, 15 Victoria Terrace, Edinburgh EH1 2JL. Tel: 0131-220 3677. *Hon. Secretary*, Miss J. P. S. Ferguson

SCOTTISH HISTORY SOCIETY (1886), Department of Scottish History, 17 Buccleuch Place, University of Edinburgh, Edinburgh EH8 9LN. Tel: 0131-650 4030. *Hon. Secretary*, Dr S. Boardman

SCOTTISH LANDOWNERS' FEDERATION (1906), Stuart House, Eskmills Business Park, Musselburgh EH21 7PB. Tel: 0131-653 5400. *Director*, Dr. M. S. Hankey

SCOTTISH LAW AGENTS SOCIETY, 11 Parliament Square, Edinburgh EH1 1RD. Tel: 0131-225 5051

SCOTTISH NATIONAL INSTITUTION FOR THE WAR BLINDED (1915), PO Box 500, Gillespie Crescent, Edinburgh EH10 4HZ. Tel: 0131-229 1456. *Secretary*, J. B. M. Munro

SCOTTISH NATIONAL WAR MEMORIAL (1927), The Castle, Edinburgh EH1 2YT. Tel: 0131-226 7393. *Secretary*, Lt-Col H. D. R. Mackay

SCOTTISH SOCIETY FOR THE PREVENTION OF CRUELTY TO ANIMALS (1839), Braehead Mains, 603 Queensferry Road, Edinburgh EH4 6EA. Tel: 0131-339 0222. *Chief Executive*, J. Morris, CBE

SCOTTISH SOCIETY FOR THE PROTECTION OF WILD BIRDS (1927), Foremount House, Kilbarchan, Renfrewshire PA10 2EZ. Tel: 01505-702419. *Secretary*, Dr J. A. Gibson

SCOUT ASSOCIATION (1907), Baden-Powell House, Queen's Gate, London SW7 5JS. Tel: 0171-584 7030. *Chief Executive*, D. M. Twine

SCRIBES AND ILLUMINATORS, SOCIETY OF (1921), 6 Queen Square, London WC1N 3AR. *Hon. Secretary*, Mrs G. Guest

SCRIPTURE GIFT MISSION INCORPORATED (1888), Radstock House, 3 Eccleston Street, London SW1W 9LZ. Tel: 0171-730 2155. *International Director*, H. Q. Davies

SCRIPTURE UNION (1867), 207-209 Queensway, Bletchley, Milton Keynes MK2 2EB. Tel: 01908-856000. *Chief Executive*, P. Kimber

SEA CADET ASSOCIATION, THE (1895), 202 Lambeth Road, London SE1 7JF. Tel: 0171-928 8978. *Chief Executive*, Cdre R. M. Parker

SEAMEN'S BOY'S HOME, BRITISH (1863), Outdoor Educational Activity Centre, Grenville House, Berry Head Road, Brixham, Devon TQ5 9AF. Tel: 01803-852797. *Secretary*, R. M. Williams

SEAMEN'S CHRISTIAN FRIEND SOCIETY (1846), 48 South Street, Alderley Edge, Cheshire SK9 7ES. Tel: 01625-590010. *Director*, M. J. Wilson

SEAMEN'S PENSION FUND, ROYAL (1919), 2A/ WEST STREET, EWELL, EPSOM, SURREY KT17 1UU. Tel: 0181-393 5873. *Secretary*, D. C. Barker

SECRETARIES AND ADMINISTRATORS, INSTITUTE OF CHARTERED (1891), 16 Park Crescent, London W1N 4AH. Tel: 0171-580 4741. *Chief Executive*, M. J. Ainsworth

SECULAR SOCIETY LTD, NATIONAL (1866), 25 Red Lion Square, London WC1R 4RL. Tel: 0171-404 3126. *General Secretary*, K. P. Wood

SEE ABILITY (formerly Royal School for the Blind) (1799), 56-66 Highlands Road, Leatherhead, Surrey KT22 8NR. Tel: 01372-373086. *Chief Executive*, R. M. Perkins

SELDEN SOCIETY (1887), Faculty of Laws, Queen Mary and Westfield College, Mile End Road, London E1 4NS. Tel: 0171-975 5136. *Secretary*, V. Tunkel

SENSE (NATIONAL DEAFBLIND AND RUBELLA ASSOCIATION) (1955), 11-13 Clifton Terrace, London N4 3SR. Tel: 0171-272 7774. *Chief Executive*, R. Clark

SHAFTESBURY HOMES AND ARETHUSA (1843), The Chapel, Royal Victoria Patriotic Building, Trinity Road, London SW18 3SX. Tel: 0181-875 1555. *Chief Executive*, Ms A. Chesney

SHAFTESBURY SOCIETY (1844), 16 Kingston Road, London SW19 1JZ. Tel: 0181-239 5555. *Chief Executive*, Ms F. Beckett

SHELLFISH ASSOCIATION OF GREAT BRITAIN (1904), Fishmongers' Hall, London Bridge, London EC4R 9EL. Tel: 0171-283 8305. *Director*, E. Edwards, OBE, PH.D.

SHELTER (THE NATIONAL CAMPAIGN FOR HOMELESS PEOPLE) (1966), 88 Old Street, London EC1V 9HU. Tel: 0171-505 2000. Shelterline: 0808-800 4444. *Director*, C. Holmes, CBE

SHERLOCK HOLMES SOCIETY OF LONDON (1951), 13 Crofton Avenue, Orpington, Kent BR6 8DU. Tel: 01689-811314. *Membership Secretary*, R. J. Ellis

SHIPBROKERS, INSTITUTE OF CHARTERED (1911), 3 St Helen's Place, London EC3A 6EJ. Tel: 0171-628 5559. *Director*, Ms B. Fletcher

SHIRE HORSE SOCIETY (1878), East of England Showground, Peterborough PE2 6XE. Tel: 01733-234451. *Secretary*, T. Gibson, OBE

SHRIEVALTY ASSOCIATION (1971), Office of the High Sheriffs, Duncombe Place, York YO1 7DY. Tel: 01904-634771. *Secretary*, J. H. N. Towers

SIGHT SAVERS INTERNATIONAL (ROYAL COMMONWEALTH SOCIETY FOR THE BLIND) (1950), Grosvenor Hall, Bolnore Road, Haywards Heath, W. Sussex RH16 4BX. Tel: 01444-446600. *Executive Director*, R. Porter

SIMPLIFIED SPELLING SOCIETY (1908), Tailours, High Road, Chigwell, Essex IG7 6DL. *Chairman*, C. J. H. Jolly

SIR OSWALD STOLL FOUNDATION (1916), 446 Fulham Road, London SW6 1DT. Tel: 0171-385 2110. *Chief Executive*, R. C. Brunwin

SMALL BUSINESSES, FEDERATION OF (1974), 2 Catherine Place, London SW1E 6HF. Tel: 0171-233 7900. *Head of Parliamentary Affairs*, S. Alambritis

SOCIAL CONCERN, NATIONAL COUNCIL FOR, Montague Chambers, Montague Place, London SE1 9DA. Tel: 0171-403 0977. *Director*, P. Carlin

SOCIALIST PARTY, THE (formerly Socialist Party of Great Britain) (1904), 52 Clapham High Street, London SW4 7UN. Tel: 0171-622 3811. *General Secretary*, B. Johnson

SOCIAL WORKERS, BRITISH ASSOCIATION OF (1970), 16 Kent Street, Birmingham B5 6RD. Tel: 0121-622 3911. *Director*, I. Johnston

SOIL ASSOCIATION (1946), Bristol House, 40-56 Victoria Street, Bristol BS1 6BY. Tel: 0117-929 0661. *Director*, P. Holden

SOLDIERS' AND AIRMEN'S SCRIPTURE READERS ASSOCIATION (1838), Havelock House, Barrack Road, Aldershot, Hants GU11 3NP. Tel: 01252-310033. *General Secretary*, Lt-Col M. Hitchcott

SOLDIERS' WIDOWS, ROYAL CAMBRIDGE HOME FOR (1851), 82-84 Hurst Road, East Molesey, Surrey KT8 9AH. Tel: 0181-979 3788. *Superintendent*, Mrs I. O. Yarnell

SOLICITORS IN THE SUPREME COURT OF SCOTLAND, SOCIETY OF (1784), SSC Library, Parliament House, 11 Parliament Square, Edinburgh EH1 1RF. Tel: 0131-225 6268. *Secretary*, I. L. S. Balfour

SOROPTIMIST INTERNATIONAL OF GREAT BRITAIN AND IRELAND (1923), 127 Wellington Road South, Stockport SK1 3TS. Tel: 0161-480 7686. *Executive Officer,* Ms K. Heward

SOS SOCIETY, *see* 2CARE

SOUTH AMERICAN MISSION SOCIETY (1844), Allen Gardiner House, Pembury Road, Tunbridge Wells, Kent TN2 3QU. Tel: 01892-538647. *General Secretary,* Rt Revd D. R. J. Evans

SOUTH WALES INSTITUTE OF ENGINEERS (1857), 2nd Floor, Empire House, Mount Stuart Square, Cardiff CF10 5PN. Tel: 01222-481726. *Hon. Secretary,* T. H. Rhodes

SPEAKERS CLUBS, ASSOCIATION OF (1971), 28 High Street, Auchterarder, Perthshire PH3 1DF. Tel: 01764-662457. *National Secretary,* D. Williams

SPINA BIFIDA AND HYDROCEPHALUS, ASSOCIATION FOR (ASBAH), ASBAH House, 42 Park Road, Peterborough PE1 2UQ. Tel: 01733-555988. *Executive Director,* A. Russell

SPORT AND THE ARTS, FOUNDATION FOR (1991), PO Box 20, Liverpool L13 1HB. Tel: 0151-259 5505. *Secretary to the Trustees,* G. Endicott, OBE

SPORT HORSE BREEDING OF GREAT BRITAIN (1885), 96 High Street, Edenbridge, Kent TN8 5AR. Tel: 01732-866277. *General Secretary,* Mrs K. P. Hall

SPORTS MEDICINE, INSTITUTE OF (1963), 2nd Floor, Charles Bell House, University College London Medical School, 67-73 Riding House Street, London W1P 7LD. Tel: 0171-813 2832. *Hon. Secretary,* Dr W. T. Orton

SPURGEON'S CHILD CARE (1867), 74 Wellingborough Road, Rushden, Northants NN10 9TY. Tel: 01933-412412. *Chief Executive,* D. C. Culwick

SSAFA FORCES HELP (1885, merged 1997), 19 Queen Elizabeth Street, London SE1 2LP. Tel: 0171-403 8783. *Controller,* Maj.-Gen. P. Sheppard, CB, CBE

STANDING CONFERENCE OF NATIONAL AND UNIVERSITY LIBRARIES (SCONUL) (1950), 102 Euston Street, London NW1 2HA. Tel: 0171-387 0317. *Secretary,* A. J. C. Bainton

STATISTICIANS, INSTITUTE OF, *see* ROYAL STATISTICAL SOCIETY

STEWART SOCIETY (1899), 2 York Place, Edinburgh EH1 3EP. Tel: 0131-557 6824. *Hon. Secretary,* Mrs M. Walker

STRATEGIC PLANNING SOCIETY (1967), 17 Portland Place, London W1N 3AF. Tel: 0171-636 7737. *General Manager,* D. Lambert

STRATEGIC STUDIES, INTERNATIONAL INSTITUTE FOR (1958), 23 Tavistock Street, London WC2E 7NQ. Tel: 0171-379 7676. *Director,* Dr J. Chipman

STROKE ASSOCIATION (1899), Stroke House, Whitecross Street, London EC1Y 8JJ. Tel: 0171-566 0300. *Chief Executive Officer,* Miss M. Goose

STRUCTURAL ENGINEERS, INSTITUTION OF (1908), 11 Upper Belgrave Street, London SW1X 8BH. Tel: 0171-235 4535. *Chief Executive,* Dr K. J. Eaton

STUDENT CHRISTIAN MOVEMENT (1889), Westhill College, 14-16 Weoley Park Road, Selly Oak, Birmingham B29 6LL. Tel: 0121-471 2404. *Co-ordinator,* Mrs C. Styles

SUFFOLK HORSE SOCIETY (1878), The Market Hill, Woodbridge, Suffolk IP12 4LU. Tel: 01394-380643. *Secretary,* Mrs T. J. Booker

SURGEONS OF EDINBURGH, ROYAL COLLEGE OF (1505), Nicolson Street, Edinburgh EH8 9DW. Tel: 0131-527 1664. *Secretary,* Miss A. S. Campbell

SURGEONS OF ENGLAND, ROYAL COLLEGE OF (1800), 35-43 Lincoln's Inn Fields, London WC2A 3PN. Tel: 0171-405 3474. *Secretary,* C. Duncan

SURVEYORS, ROYAL INSTITUTION OF CHARTERED (1868), 12 Great George Street, London SW1P 3AD. Tel: 0171-222 7000. *Chief Executive,* Ms C. Makin

SURVIVAL INTERNATIONAL (1969), 11-15 Emerald Street, London WC1N 3QT. Tel: 0171-242 1441. *Director,* S. Corry

SUZY LAMPLUGH TRUST (1986), 14 East Sheen Avenue, London SW14 8AS. Tel: 0181-392 1839. *Executive Secretary,* P. Lamplugh

SWEDENBORG SOCIETY (1810), 20-21 Bloomsbury Way, London WC1A 2TH. Tel: 0171-405 7986. *Secretary,* Miss M. G. Waters

TAVISTOCK INSTITUTE, THE (1947), 30 Tabernacle Street, London EC2A 4DD. Tel: 0171-417 0407. *Secretary,* J. Margarson

TAXATION, CHARTERED INSTITUTE OF (1930), 12 Upper Belgrave Street, London SW1X 8BB. Tel: 0171-235 9381. *Secretary-General,* R. A. Dommett

TEACHERS, COLLEGE OF (formerly College of Preceptors) (1846), Coppice Row, Theydon Bois, Epping, Essex CM16 7DN. Tel: 01992-812727. *Chief Executive Officer,* R. Page

TEACHERS OF HOME ECONOMICS AND TECHNOLOGY, NATIONAL ASSOCIATION OF (1896), Hamilton House, Mabledon Place, London WC1H 9BJ. Tel: 0171-387 1441. *General Secretary,* G. Thompson

TEACHERS OF MATHEMATICS, ASSOCIATION OF (1952), 7 Shaftesbury Street, Derby DE23 8YB. Tel: 01332-346599. *Hon. Secretary,* J. Richardson

TEACHERS' UNION, ULSTER (1919), 94 Malone Road, Belfast BT9 5HP. Tel: 01232-662216. *General Secretary,* R. Calvin

TELECOMMUNICATION USERS' ASSOCIATION (1965), Woodgate Studios, 2-8 Games Road, Cockfosters, Barnet, Herts EN4 9HN. Tel: 0181-449 8844. *Executive Chairman,* W. E. Mieran

TEMPERANCE COUNCIL, NATIONAL UNITED (1880), Alliance House, 12 Caxton Street, London SW1H 0QS. Tel: 0181-444 5004. *General Secretary,* Mrs G. O. Stretton

TEMPERANCE FRIENDLY SOCIETY, ORDER OF THE SONS OF (1855), 176 Blackfriars Road, London SE1 8ET. Tel: 0171-928 7384. *Secretary,* Mrs M. C. Scroby

TEMPERANCE LEAGUE, BRITISH NATIONAL (1834), Westbrook Court, 2 Sharrow Vale Road, Sheffield S11 8YZ. Tel: 0114-267 9976. *Manager,* Mrs B. Briggs

TEMPERANCE SOCIETY, ROYAL NAVAL (1876), 5 St George's Business Centre, St George's Square, Portsmouth PO1 3EY. Tel: 01705-296096. *General Secretary,* Revd J. P. M. Martin

TEMPLETON FOUNDATION (1973), 18 Eastgate Gardens, Taunton, Somerset TA1 1RD. *UK Representative,* Mrs N. Pearse

TERRENCE HIGGINS TRUST (1982), 52-54 Grays Inn Road, London WC1X 8JU. Tel: 0171-831 0330. *Chief Executive,* N. Partridge, OBE

TEXTILE INSTITUTE, THE (1910), 4th Floor, St. James's Building, Oxford Street, Manchester M1 6FQ. Tel: 0161-237 1188. *Operations Manager,* Mrs. K. Smith

THEATRE RESEARCH, SOCIETY FOR (1948), c/o The Theatre Museum, 1E Tavistock Street, London WC2E 7PA. *Joint Hon. Secretaries*, Ms E. Cottis, Ms F. Dann

THEATRES TRUST, THE (1976), 22 Charing Cross Road, London WC2H 0HR. Tel: 0171-836 8591. *Director*, P. Longman

THEATRICAL FUND, ROYAL (1839), 11 Garrick Street, London WC2E 9AR. Tel: 0171-836 3322. *Secretary*, Mrs R. M. Foster

THEOSOPHICAL SOCIETY IN ENGLAND (1875), 50 Gloucester Place, London W1H 4EA. Tel: 0171-935 9261. *National President*, C. Price

THISTLE FOUNDATION (1945), Niddrie Mains Road, Edinburgh EH16 4EA. Tel: 0131-661 3366. *Director*, Ms J. Fisher

TIDY BRITAIN GROUP (1953), The Pier, Wigan WN3 4EX. Tel: 01942-824620. *Director-General*, Prof. G. Ashworth, CBE

TOC H (1915), 1 Forest Close, Wendover, Aylesbury, Bucks HP22 6BT. Tel: 01296-623911. *Director*, vacant

TOURIST BOARD, ENGLISH, Thames Tower, Black's Road, London W6 9EL. Tel: 0181-846 9000. *Chief Executive*, T. Bartlett

TOURIST BOARD, NORTHERN IRELAND, St Anne's Court, 59 North Street, Belfast BT1 1NB. Tel: 01232-231221. *Chief Executive*, I. G. Henderson

TOURIST BOARD, SCOTTISH (1969), 23 Ravelston Terrace, Edinburgh EH4 3EU. Tel: 0131-332 2433. *Chief Executive*, T. Buncle

TOURIST BOARD, WALES, Brunel House, 2 Fitzalan Road, Cardiff CF2 1UY. Tel: 01222-499909. *Chief Executive*, J. French

TOWN AND COUNTRY PLANNING ASSOCIATION (1899), 17 Carlton House Terrace, London SW1Y 5AS. Tel: 0171-930 8903/4/5. *Director*, vacant

TOWN PLANNING INSTITUTE, ROYAL (1914), 26 Portland Place, London W1N 4BE. Tel: 0171-636 9107. *Secretary-General*, R. Upton

TOWNSWOMEN'S GUILDS (1929), Chamber of Commerce House, 75 Harborne Road, Birmingham B15 3DA. Tel: 0121-456 3435. *National Secretary*, Mrs P. Wilkes

TOYNBEE HALL (1884), 28 Commercial Street, London E1 6LS. Tel: 0171-247 6943. *Chief Executive*, A. Prescott

TRADE MARK AGENTS, INSTITUTE OF (1934), Canterbury House, 2-6 Sydenham Road, Croydon CR0 9XE. Tel: 0181-686 2052. *Secretary*, Mrs M. J. Tyler

TRADING STANDARDS ADMINISTRATION, INSTITUTE OF (1881), 3-5 Hadleigh Business Centre, 351 London Road, Hadleigh, Essex SS7 2BT. Tel: 01702-559922. *Chief Executive*, A. J. Street

TRANSLATION AND INTERPRETING, INSTITUTE OF (1986), 377 City Road, London EC1V 1ND. Tel: 0171-713 7600. *Chairman*, G. Cross

TRANSPORT ADMINISTRATION, INSTITUTE OF (1944), 32 Palmerston Road, Southampton SO14 1LL. Tel: 01703-631380. *Director*, J. K. Millar

TRANSPORT, CHARTERED INSTITUTE OF (1919), 80 Portland Place, London W1N 4DP. Tel: 0171-467 9400. *Director*, Mrs D. de Carvalho

TRAVEL AGENTS, ASSOCIATION OF BRITISH (ABTA) (1950), 68-71 Newman Street, London W1P 4AH. Tel: 0171-637 2444. *Chief Executive*, I. Reynolds

TREE COUNCIL (1974), 51 Catherine Place, London SW1E 6DY. Tel: 0171-828 9928. *Director*, R. Osborne

TREE FOUNDATION, INTERNATIONAL (formerly Men of the Trees) (1922), Sandy Lane, Crawley Down, W. Sussex RH10 4HS. Tel: 01342-712536. *Chairman*, S. G. Keys

TROPICAL MEDICINE AND HYGIENE, ROYAL SOCIETY OF (1907), Manson House, 26 Portland Place, London W1N 4EY. Tel: 0171-580 2127. *Hon. Secretaries*, Dr D. C. Barker, Dr S. B. Squire

TURNER SOCIETY (1975), BCM Box Turner, London WC1N 3XX. *Chairman*, E. Joll

2CARE (formerly The SOS Society) (1929), 11 Harwood Road, London SW6 4QP. Tel: 0171-371 0118. *Chief Executive*, Miss E. C. R. O'Sullivan

UFAW (UNIVERSITIES FEDERATION FOR ANIMAL WELFARE) (1926), The Old School, Brewhouse Hill, Wheathampstead, Herts AL4 8AN. Tel: 01582-831818. *Director*, Dr J. K. Kirkwood

UK INDEPENDENCE PARTY, Triumph House, 189 Regent Street, London W1R 7WF. Tel: 0171-434 4559. *Secretary*, A. Scholefield

UNBORN CHILDREN, SOCIETY FOR THE PROTECTION OF, *see* PROTECTION OF UNBORN CHILDREN

UNITED KINGDOM ALLIANCE (1863), 176 Blackfriars Road, London SE1 8ET. Tel: 0171-928 1538. *General Secretary*, Revd B. Kinman

UNITED NATIONS ASSOCIATION OF GREAT BRITAIN AND NORTHERN IRELAND (1945), 3 Whitehall Court, London SW1A 2EL. Tel: 0171-930 2931. *Director*, M. C. Harper

UNITED REFORMED CHURCH HISTORY SOCIETY (1972), Westminster College, Madingley Road, Cambridge CB3 0AA. *Hon. Secretary*, Revd E. J. Brown

UNITED SOCIETY FOR CHRISTIAN LITERATURE (1799), Albany House, 67 Sydenham Road, Guildford, Surrey GU1 3RY. Tel: 01483-888580. *General Secretary*, Dr A. Marriage

UNITED SOCIETY FOR THE PROPAGATION OF THE GOSPEL (USPG) (1701), Partnership House, 157 Waterloo Road, London SE1 8XA. Tel: 0171-928 8681. *Secretary*, Rt Revd M. Rumalshah

UNIVERSITIES OF THE UNITED KINGDOM, COMMITTEE OF VICE-CHANCELLORS AND PRINCIPALS OF THE (1918), Woburn House, 20 Tavistock Square, London WC1H 9HQ. Tel: 0171-419 4111. *Chief Executive*, Ms D. Warwick

VALUERS AND AUCTIONEERS, INCORPORATED SOCIETY OF (1968), 3 Cadogan Gate, London SW1X 0AS. Tel: 0171-235 2282. *Chief Executive*, C. Evans

VEGAN SOCIETY (1944), Donald Watson House, 7 Battle Road, St Leonards-on-Sea, E. Sussex TN37 7AA. Tel: 01424-427393. *Information Officer*, Ms C. Grainger

VEGETARIAN SOCIETY OF THE UNITED KINGDOM, Parkdale, Dunham Road, Altrincham, Cheshire WA14 4QG. Tel: 0161-925 2000. *Chief Executive*, Ms T. Fox

VENEREAL DISEASES, MEDICAL SOCIETY FOR THE STUDY OF (1922), 1 Wimpole Street, London W1M 8AE. Tel: 0171-290 2968. *Hon. Secretary*, Dr A. J. Robinson

VERNACULAR ARCHITECTURE GROUP (1953), Ashley, Willows Green, Chelmsford, Essex CM3 1QD. Tel: 01245-361408. *Hon. Secretary*, Mrs B. A. Watkin

VETERINARY ASSOCIATION, BRITISH (1881), 7 Mansfield Street, London W1M 0AT. Tel: 0171-636 6541. *Chief Executive*, J. H. Baird

VETERINARY SURGEONS, ROYAL COLLEGE OF (1844), Belgravia House, 62-64 Horseferry Road, London SWIP 2AF. Tel: 0171-222 2001. *Registrar*, Miss J. C. Hern

VICTIM SUPPORT (NATIONAL ASSOCIATION OF VICTIMS SUPPORT SCHEMES) (1979), National Office, Cranmer House, 39 Brixton Road, London SW9 6DZ. Tel: 0171-735 9166. Helpline: 0845-3030900. *Chief Executive*, Mrs H. Reeves, OBE

VICTORIA CROSS AND GEORGE CROSS ASSOCIATION, Room 028, The Old War Office, London SWIA 2EU. *Secretary*, Mrs D. Grahame, MVO

VICTORIA INSTITUTE (PHILOSOPHICAL SOCIETY OF GREAT BRITAIN), 41 Marne Avenue, Welling, Kent DAI6 2EY. Tel: 0181-303 0465. *Chairman of Council*, T. C. Mitchell

VICTORIAN SOCIETY (1958), 1 Priory Gardens, Bedford Park, London W4 ITT. Tel: 0181-994 1019. *Director*, Dr W. Filmer-Sankey

VICTORY (SERVICES) ASSOCIATION LTD AND CLUB (1907), 63-79 Seymour Street, London W2 2HF. Tel: 0171-723 4474. *General Manager*, G. F. Taylor

VIKING SOCIETY FOR NORTHERN RESEARCH (1892), Department of Scandinavian Studies, University College, Gower Street, London WCIE 6BT. Tel: 0171-380 7176. *Hon. Secretaries*, Prof. M. P. Barnes, Dr J. Jesh

VOLUNTARY ORGANIZATIONS, NATIONAL COUNCIL FOR (1919), Regents Wharf, 8 All Saints Street, London NI 9RL. Tel: 0171-713 6161. *Chief Executive*, S. Etherington

VOLUNTARY ORGANIZATIONS, SCOTTISH COUNCIL FOR (1943), 18-19 Claremont Crescent, Edinburgh EH7 4QD. Tel: 0131-556 3882. *Director*, M. Sime

VSO (VOLUNTARY SERVICE OVERSEAS) (1958), 317 Putney Bridge Road, London SW15 2PN. Tel: 0181-780 7200. *Chief Executive*, M. Goldring

WAR ON WANT (1952), Fenner Brockway House, 37-39 Great Guildford Street, London SEI 0ES. Tel: 0171-620 1111. *Director*, Ms M. Lynch

WAR WIDOWS ASSOCIATION (1971), Northedge House Farm, Old Tupton, Chesterfield, Derbyshire S42 6AY. Tel: 01246-590302. *Chairman*, Ms M. Brailsford

WASTES MANAGEMENT, INSTITUTE OF (1898), 9 Saxon Court, St Peter's Gardens, Northampton NNI ISX. Tel: 01604-620426. *Chief Executive*, M. J. Philpott

WATER AND ENVIRONMENTAL MANAGEMENT, CHARTERED INSTITUTION OF (1987), 15 John Street, London WCIN 2EB. Tel: 0171-831 3110. *Executive Director*, N. Reeves

WATERCOLOUR SOCIETY, ROYAL (1804), Bankside Gallery, 48 Hopton Street, London SEI 9JH. Tel: 0171-928 7521. *Secretary*, Ms J. Dixey

WELLBEING (THE HEALTH RESEARCH CHARITY FOR WOMEN AND BABIES) (1964), 27 Sussex Place, Regent's Park, London NWI 4SP. Tel: 0171-262 5337

WELLCOME TRUST, THE (1936), The Wellcome Building, 183 Euston Road, London NWI 2BE. Tel: 0171-611 8888. *Director*, Dr T. M. Dexter, FRS

WESLEY HISTORICAL SOCIETY (1893), 34 Spiceland Road, Northfield, Birmingham B31 INJ. Tel: 0121-475 4914. *General Secretary*, Dr E. D. Graham

WEST LONDON MISSION (1887), 19 Thayer Street, London WIM 5LJ. Tel: 0171-935 6179. *Superintendent*, Revd D. S. Cruise

WESTMINSTER FOUNDATION FOR DEMOCRACY (1992), 2nd Floor, 125 Pall Mall, London SWIY 5EA. Tel: 0171-930 0408. *Chief Executive*, Ms A. Jones

WES WORLD-WIDE EDUCATION SERVICE LTD (1888), Canada House, 272 Field End Road, Eastcote, Ruislip, Middx HA4 9NA. Tel: 0181-582 0317. *Head of Consultancy*, Mrs T. Mulder-Reynolds

WILDFOWL AND WETLANDS TRUST (1946), The New Grounds, Slimbridge, Glos GL2 7BT. Tel: 01453-890333. *Managing Director*, A. E. Richardson

WILDLIFE TRUSTS, THE (1912), The Green, Witham Park, Waterside South, Lincoln LN5 7JR. Tel: 01522-544400. *Director-General*, Dr S. Lyster

WILDLIFE TRUST, SCOTTISH (1964), Cramond House, Kirk Cramond, Cramond Glebe Road, Edinburgh EH4 6NS. Tel: 0131-312 7765. *Chief Executive*, S. Sankey

WILLIAM MORRIS SOCIETY AND KELMSCOTT FELLOWSHIP (1918), Kelmscott House, 26 Upper Mall, London W6 9TA. Tel: 0181-741 3735. *Hon. Secretary*, P. Faulkner

WINE AND SPIRIT ASSOCIATION OF GREAT BRITAIN AND NORTHERN IRELAND (*c.* 1825), Five Kings House, 1 Queen Street Place, London EC4R IXX. Tel: 0171-248 5377. *Director*, Q. Rappoport

WOMEN, SOCIETY FOR PROMOTING THE TRAINING OF (1859), Meadowbrook, Carlby Road, Greatford, Stamford, Lincs PE9 4PR. Tel: 01778-560978. *Hon. Secretary*, Revd B. Harris

WOMEN ARTISTS, SOCIETY OF (1855), 1 Knapp Cottages, Wyke, Gillingham, Dorset SP8 4NQ. Tel: 01747-825718. *Executive Secretary*, Mrs P. Henderson

WOMEN GRADUATES, BRITISH FEDERATION OF (1907), 4 Mandeville Courtyard, 142 Battersea Park Road, London SWII 4NB. Tel: 0171-498 8037. *Secretary*, Mrs A. B. Stein

WOMEN'S ENGINEERING SOCIETY (1920), 2 Queen Anne's Gate Buildings, Dartmouth Street, London SWIH 9BP. Tel: 0171-233 1974. *Secretary*, Mrs C. MacGillivray

WOMEN'S INSTITUTES, NATIONAL FEDERATION OF (1915), 104 New Kings Road, London SW6 4LY. Tel: 0171-371 9300. *General Secretary*, Mrs J. Osborne

WOMEN'S INSTITUTES OF NORTHERN IRELAND, FEDERATION OF (1932), 209-211 Upper Lisburn Road, Belfast BTIO 0LL. Tel: 01232-301506/601781. *General Secretary*, Mrs I. A. Sproule

WOMEN'S NATIONWIDE CANCER CONTROL CAMPAIGN (1964), Suna House, 128-130 Curtain Road, London EC2A 3AQ. Tel: 0171-729 4688. *Office Manager*, Miss J. Harding

WOMEN'S ROYAL NAVAL SERVICE BENEVOLENT TRUST (1942), 311 Twyford Avenue, Portsmouth PO2 8PE. Tel: 01705-655301. *General Secretary*, Mrs S. Tarabella

WOMEN'S ROYAL VOLUNTARY SERVICE (WRVS), Milton Hill House, Milton Hill, Abingdon, Oxfordshire OX13 6AF. Tel: 01235-442900. *National Chairman*, Ms T. Tietjen

WOMEN'S RURAL INSTITUTES, SCOTTISH (1917), 42 Heriot Row, Edinburgh EH3 6ES. Tel: 0131-225 1724. *General Secretary*, Mrs A. Peacock

WOODLAND TRUST (1972), Autumn Park, Dysart Road, Grantham, Lincs NG31 6LL. Tel: 01476-581111. *Chief Executive*, M. J. Townsend

WOOD PRESERVING AND DAMP-PROOFING ASSOCIATION, BRITISH (1930), 6 The Office Village, 4 Romford Road, London E15 4EA. Tel: 0181-519 2588. *Director*, Dr C. R. Coggins

WORKERS' EDUCATIONAL ASSOCIATION, Temple House, 17 Victoria Park Square, London E2 9PB. Tel: 0181-983 1515. *General Secretary*, R. Lochrie

WORLD EDUCATION FELLOWSHIP (1921), International Headquarters, 58 Dickens Rise, Chigwell, Essex IG7 6NY. Tel: 0181-281 7122. *General Secretary*, G. John

WORLD ENERGY COUNCIL (1924), Regency House, 1-4 Warwick Street, London WIR 5WA. Tel: 0171-930 3966. *Secretary-General*, G. W. Doucet

WORLD MISSION, COUNCIL FOR (1977), IPALO House, 32-34 Great Peter Street, London 2DB. Tel: 0171-222 4214. *General Secretary*, D. P. Niles, PH.D.

WORLD SHIP SOCIETY (1946), 101 The Everglades, Hempstead, Gillingham, Kent ME7 3PZ. Tel: 01634-372015. *Secretary*, J. Poole

WORLD SOCIETY FOR THE PROTECTION OF ANIMALS (1981), 2 Langley Lane, London SW8 ITJ. Tel: 0171-793 0540. *Chief Executive*, A. Dickson

WRITERS TO HM SIGNET, SOCIETY OF (1532), Signet Library, Parliament Square, Edinburgh EH1 IRF. Tel: 0131-220 3426. *General Manager*, J. R. C. Foster

WWF-UK (WORLD WIDE FUND FOR NATURE) (1961), Panda House, Weyside Park, Godalming, Surrey GU7 IXR. Tel: 01483-426444. *Director*, Dr R. Pellew

YEOMANRY BENEVOLENT FUND (1902), 10 Stone Buildings, Lincoln's Inn, London WC2A 3TG. Tel: 0171-831 6727. *Secretary*, Mrs C. W. Chrystie

YORKSHIRE AGRICULTURAL SOCIETY (1837), Great Yorkshire Showground, Harrogate, N. Yorks HG2 8PW. Tel: 01423-541000. *Chief Executive*, R. T. Keigwin

YORKSHIRE SOCIETY (1812), 35 Waldorf Heights, Camberley, Surrey GU17 9JH. Tel: 01276-36342. *Secretary*, G. G. Prince, FCIS, TD

YOUNG FARMERS' CLUBS, NATIONAL FEDERATION OF, YFC Centre, National Agricultural Centre, Stoneleigh Park, Kenilworth, Warks CV8 2LG. Tel: 01203-696544. *Chief Executive*, B. Loughran

YOUNG MEN'S CHRISTIAN ASSOCIATION (YMCA) (1844), National Council of YMCAs, 640 Forest Road, London E17 3DZ. Tel: 0181-520 5599. *National Secretary*, E. Thomas

YOUNG WOMEN'S CHRISTIAN ASSOCIATION OF GREAT BRITAIN (YWCA) (1855), Clarendon House, 52 Cornmarket Street, Oxford OX1 3EJ. Tel: 01865-304200. *Chief Executive*, Ms G. Tishler

YOUTH ACTION, NORTHERN IRELAND (1944), Hampton, Glenmachan Park, Belfast BT4 2PJ. Tel: 01232-760067. *Director*, P. Graham

YOUTH CLUBS UK (1911), 2nd Floor, Kirby House, 20-24 Kirby Street, London ECIN 8TS. Tel: 0171-242 4045. *Chief Executive*, J. Bateman

YOUTH HOSTELS ASSOCIATION (ENGLAND AND WALES) (1930), Trevelyan House, 8 St Stephen's Hill, St Albans, Herts ALI 2DY. Tel: 01727-855215. *Chief Executive*, C. Logan

YOUTH HOSTELS ASSOCIATION, SCOTTISH (1931), 7 Glebe Crescent, Stirling FK8 2JA. Tel: 01786-891400. *General Secretary*, W. Forsyth

ZOOLOGICAL SOCIETY (CHESTER ZOO), NORTH OF ENGLAND (1934), Chester Zoo, Upton by Chester, Chester CH2 ILH. Tel: 01244-380280. *Director*, Prof. G. McGregor Reid

ZOOLOGICAL SOCIETY OF LONDON (1826), Regent's Park, London NW1 4RY. Tel: 0171-722 3333. *Director-General*, vacant

ZOOLOGICAL SOCIETY OF SCOTLAND, ROYAL (1913), Scottish National Zoological Park, Edinburgh Zoo, 134 Corstorphine Road, Edinburgh EH12 6TS. Tel: 0131-334 9171. *Director*, Dr D. Waugh, PH.D.

LOCAL HISTORY AND ARCHAEOLOGICAL SOCIETIES

ENGLAND

Berkshire: BERKSHIRE ARCHAEOLOGICAL SOCIETY. *Hon. Secretary*, L. J. Over, 43 Laburnham Road, Maidenhead, Berks SL6 4DE. Tel: 01628-631225.

Buckinghamshire: BUCKINGHAMSHIRE ARCHAEOLOGICAL SOCIETY. *Hon. Secretary*, G. J. Aylett, County Museum, Church Street, Aylesbury, Bucks HP20 2QP

Cambridgeshire: CAMBRIDGE ANTIQUARIAN SOCIETY. *Hon. Secretary*, Mrs S. Oosthuizen, Board of Continuing Education, Madingley Hall, Madingley, Cambs CB3 8AQ

Cheshire: CHESTER ARCHAEOLOGICAL SOCIETY. *Secretary*, Dr D. J. P. Mason, FSA, Ochr Cottage, Porch Lane, Hope Mountain, Caergwrle, Flintshire LL12 9HG. Tel: 01978-760834.

Cornwall: CORNWALL ARCHAEOLOGICAL SOCIETY. *Hon. Secretary*, Mrs P. M. Fryer, Little Pengelly Cottage, Lower Sticker, St Austell, Cornwall PL26 7JJ

Cumberland and Westmorland: CUMBERLAND AND WESTMORLAND ANTIQUARIAN AND ARCHAEOLOGICAL SOCIETY. *Hon. Secretary*, R. Hall, 2 High Tenterfell, Kendal, Cumbria LA9 4PG. Tel: 01539-773542.

Derbyshire: DERBYSHIRE ARCHAEOLOGICAL SOCIETY. *Hon. Secretary*, C. McGee, 25 Bridgeness Road, Heatherton, Littleover, Derby DE23 7UJ

Devonshire: DEVON ARCHAEOLOGICAL SOCIETY. *Hon. Secretary*, H. Bishop, RAM Museum, Queen Street, Exeter EX4 3RX. Tel: 01392-265858.

Dorset: DORSET NATURAL HISTORY AND ARCHAEOLOGICAL SOCIETY. *Secretary*, R. M. de Peyer, Dorset County Museum, Dorchester, Dorset DT1 IXA. Tel: 01305-262735.

Durham: DURHAM AND NORTHUMBERLAND ARCHITECTURAL AND ARCHAEOLOGICAL SOCIETY. *Hon. Secretary*, S. Cousins, 24 Toll House Road, Durham DHI 4HU. Tel: 0191-384 2724.

Essex: ESSEX SOCIETY FOR ARCHAEOLOGY AND HISTORY. *Secretary*, Dr C. Thornton, Hollytrees Museum, High Street, Colchester CO1 IUG. Tel: 01206-271458.

Gloucestershire: BRISTOL AND GLOUCESTERSHIRE ARCHAEOLOGICAL SOCIETY. *Hon. Secretary*, D. J. H. Smith, FSA, 22 Beaumont Road, Gloucester GL2 0EJ. Tel: 01452-302610.

Hampshire: HAMPSHIRE FIELD CLUB AND ARCHAEOLOGICAL SOCIETY. *Secretary*, R. Iles, Hyde Historic Resources Centre, 75 Hyde Street, Winchester SO23 7DW. Tel: 01962-848269.

Herefordshire: WOOLHOPE NATURALISTS' FIELD CLUB. *Hon. Assistant Secretary*, Mrs M. Tonkin, Chy an Whyloryon, Wigmore, Leominster, Herefordshire HR6 9UD. Tel: 01568-770356.

Hertfordshire: EAST HERTFORDSHIRE ARCHAEOLOGICAL SOCIETY. *Hon. Secretary*, Mrs M. C. Readman, 1 Marsh Lane, Stanstead Abbots, Ware, Herts SG12 8HH. Tel: 01920-870664.

ST ALBANS AND HERTFORDSHIRE ARCHITECTURAL
AND ARCHAEOLOGICAL SOCIETY. *Hon. Secretary,*
B. E. Moody, 24 Rose Walk, St Albans, Herts AL4 9AF.
Tel: 01727-853204.

Isle of Wight: ISLE OF WIGHT NATURAL HISTORY AND
ARCHAEOLOGICAL SOCIETY. *Hon. Secretary,*
Dr. M. Jackson, Island Countryside Centre, Rylstone
Gardens, Shanklin, Isle of Wight PO37 6RG. Tel: 01983-
867016.

Kent: KENT ARCHAEOLOGICAL SOCIETY. *Hon. General
Secretary,* A. I. Moffat, Three Elms, Woodlands Lane,
Shorne, Gravesend, Kent DA12 3HH

Leicestershire: LEICESTERSHIRE ARCHAEOLOGICAL AND
HISTORICAL SOCIETY. *Hon. Secretary,*
Dr A. D. McWhirr, The Guildhall, Leicester LE1 5FQ.
Tel: 0116-270 3031.

Lincolnshire: SOCIETY OF LINCOLNSHIRE HISTORY AND
ARCHAEOLOGY. *Hon. Secretary,* Mrs M. A. Birch, Jew's
Court, Steep Hill, Lincoln LN2 1LS

London and Middlesex: CITY OF LONDON
ARCHAEOLOGICAL SOCIETY. *Hon. Secretary,*
Ms M. Bowen, 34 College Cross, London N1 1PR. Tel:
0171-609 2930.

LONDON AND MIDDLESEX ARCHAEOLOGICAL
SOCIETY. *Hon. Secretary,* M. Curtis, 34 Alexandra Road,
Wimbledon, London SW19 7JZ. Tel: 0181-879 7109.

Norfolk: NORFOLK AND NORWICH ARCHAEOLOGICAL
SOCIETY. *Secretary,* R. Bellinger, 30 Brettingham
Avenue, Norwich NR4 6XG. Tel: 01603-455913.

Northumberland and Tyne and Wear: SOCIETY OF
ANTIQUARIES OF NEWCASTLE UPON TYNE. *Secretary,*
N. Hodgson, Black Gate, Castle Garth, Newcastle upon
Tyne NE1 1RQ. Tel: 0191-261 5390.

Northumberland: SUNDERLAND ANTIQUARIAN SOCIETY.
Hon. Secretary, Mrs V. M. Stevens, 16 Grizedale Court,
Seaburn Dene, Sunderland SR6 8JP. Tel: 0191-548 7541.

Oxfordshire: OXFORDSHIRE ARCHITECTURAL AND
HISTORICAL SOCIETY. *Hon. Secretary,* Dr A. J. Dodd, 53
Radley Road, Abingdon, Oxon OX14 3PN. Tel: 01235-
525960.

Shropshire: SHROPSHIRE ARCHAEOLOGICAL AND
HISTORICAL SOCIETY. *Chairman,* J. B. Lawson,
Westcott Farm, Pontesbury, Shrewsbury SY5 0SQ. Tel:
01743-790531.

Somerset: SOMERSET ARCHAEOLOGICAL AND NATURAL
HISTORY SOCIETY. *Hon. Secretary,* Dr I. J. Sinclair,
Taunton Castle, Taunton, Somerset TA1 4AD. Tel:
01823-320200.

Staffordshire: STOKE-ON-TRENT MUSEUM
ARCHAEOLOGICAL SOCIETY. *Chairman,* E. E. Royle,
The Potteries Museum and Art Gallery, Hanley,
Stoke-on-Trent ST1 3DW. Tel: 01782-232323.

Suffolk: SUFFOLK INSTITUTE OF ARCHAEOLOGY AND
HISTORY. *Hon. Secretary,* B. J. Seward, Roots, Church
Lane, Playford, Ipswich IP6 9DS. Tel: 01473-624556.

Surrey: SURREY ARCHAEOLOGICAL SOCIETY. *Hon.
Secretary,* Miss A. J. Monk, Castle Arch, Guildford,
Surrey GU1 3SX. Tel: 01483-532454.

Sussex: SUSSEX ARCHAEOLOGICAL SOCIETY. *Chief
Executive,* J. Manley, Bull House, 92 High Street, Lewes,
E. Sussex BN7 1XH. Tel: 01273-486260.

Warwickshire: COVENTRY AND DISTRICT
ARCHAEOLOGICAL SOCIETY. *Hon. Secretary,*
Mrs J. Smith, 1 Holloway Field, Coventry CV6 2DA. Tel:
01203-591078.

BIRMINGHAM AND WARWICKSHIRE
ARCHAEOLOGICAL SOCIETY. *Hon. Secretary,*
Miss S. Middleton, c/o Birmingham and Midland
Institute, Margaret Street, Birmingham B3 3BS

Wiltshire: WILTSHIRE ARCHAEOLOGICAL AND NATURAL
HISTORY SOCIETY. *Chief Executive,* Dr G. Chancellor,
Devizes Museum, 41 Long Street, Devizes, Wilts
SN10 1NS. Tel: 01380-727369.

Worcestershire: WORCESTERSHIRE ARCHAEOLOGICAL
SOCIETY. *Hon. Secretary,* Ms S. L. Lamb, c/o
Worcestershire County Museum, Hartlebury Castle,
Hartlebury, Nr Kidderminster, Worcs DY11 7XZ. Tel:
01299-250416.

Yorkshire: HALIFAX ANTIQUARIAN SOCIETY. *Hon.
Secretary and Editor,* Dr J. A. Hargreaves, 7 Hyde Park
Gardens, Haugh Shaw Road, Halifax, W. Yorks
HX1 3AH. Tel: 01422-250780.

THORESBY SOCIETY. *Hon. Secretary,* B. Harrison,
Claremont, 23 Clarendon Road, Leeds LS2 9NZ

YORKSHIRE ARCHAEOLOGICAL SOCIETY. *Hon.
Secretary,* Ms J. Heron, Claremont, 23 Clarendon Road,
Leeds LS2 9NZ. Tel: 0113-245 7910.

SCOTLAND

Ayrshire: AYRSHIRE ARCHAEOLOGICAL AND NATURAL
HISTORY SOCIETY. *Hon. Secretary,* Dr T. Mathews, 10
Longlands Park, Ayr KA7 4RJ. Tel: 01292-441915.

Dumfriesshire and Galloway: DUMFRIESSHIRE AND
GALLOWAY NATURAL HISTORY AND ANTIQUARIAN
SOCIETY. *Hon. Secretary,* M. White, Smithy Cottage,
Crocketford Road, Milton, Dumfries DG2 8QT

Roxburghshire: HAWICK ARCHAEOLOGICAL SOCIETY. *Hon.
Secretary,* I. W. Landles, Orrock House, Stirches Road,
Hawick, Roxburghshire TD9 7HF. Tel: 01450-375546.

Invernessshire: INVERNESS FIELD CLUB. *Hon. Secretary,*
Miss I. McLean, 6 Drumblair Crescent, Inverness
IV2 4RG

WALES

Dyfed: CEREDIGION ANTIQUARIAN SOCIETY. *Hon.
Secretary,* T. G. Davies, Henllys, Lôn Tyllwyd,
Llanfarian, Aberystwyth SY23 4UH. Tel: 01970-625818.

Powys: POWYSLAND CLUB. *Hon. Secretary,*
Miss P. M. Davies, Llygad y Dyffryn, Llanidloes, Powys
SY18 6JD. Tel: 01686-412277.

CHANNEL ISLANDS

SOCIÉTÉ JERSIAISE, ARCHAEOLOGICAL SECTION. *Hon.
Secretary,* Mrs D. Shute, La Hougue Bie Museum,
Grouville, Jersey

The Commonwealth Games

The Games were originally called the British Empire Games. From 1954 to 1966 the Games were known as the British Empire and Commonwealth Games, and from 1970 to 1974 as the British Commonwealth Games. Since 1978 the Games have been called the Commonwealth Games.

BRITISH EMPIRE GAMES

I	Hamilton, Canada	1930
II	London, England	1934
III	Sydney, Australia	1938
IV	Auckland, New Zealand	1950

BRITISH EMPIRE AND COMMONWEALTH GAMES

V	Vancouver, Canada	1954
VI	Cardiff, Wales	1958
VII	Perth, Australia	1962
VIII	Kingston, Jamaica	1966

BRITISH COMMONWEALTH GAMES

IX	Edinburgh, Scotland	1970
X	Christchurch, New Zealand	1974

COMMONWEALTH GAMES

XI	Edmonton, Canada	1978
XII	Brisbane, Australia	1982
XIII	Edinburgh, Scotland	1986
XIV	Auckland, New Zealand	1990
XV	Victoria, Canada	1994
XVI	Kuala Lumpur, Malaysia	1998
XVII	Manchester, England	2002

International Organizations

ASSOCIATION OF SOUTH EAST ASIAN NATIONS
70 A. Jl. Sisingamangaraja Kebayoran Baru, Jakarta Selatan, PO Box 2072, Jakarta, Indonesia

The Association of South East Asian Nations (ASEAN) was formed in 1967 with the aims of fostering economic growth, social progress and cultural development, and ensuring regional stability.

The heads of government meeting, which convenes every three years, is ASEAN's highest authority. Its main policy-making body is the annual meeting of foreign ministers of the member countries, which appoints the secretary-general. The founding members are Indonesia, Malaysia, the Philippines, Singapore and Thailand. Brunei and Vietnam joined in 1984 and 1995 respectively. Laos and Myanmar were admitted in July 1997. Cambodia was admitted on 30 April 1999.

The heads of government summit in 1992 agreed to set up the ASEAN Free Trade Area (AFTA), which is to be implemented by 2003, with Vietnam likely to join by 2006. A common preferential tariff was introduced in 1993. At the annual summit in 1995, a South East Asia nuclear weapon-free zone was declared by ASEAN, Cambodia, Laos and Myanmar.

Secretary-General, Rodolfo C. Severino (Philippines)

BANK FOR INTERNATIONAL SETTLEMENTS
Centralbahnplatz 2, CH-4002 Basel, Switzerland
Tel: Basel 280 8080; fax: Basel 280 9100
E-mail: EMAILMASTER@bis.org
Web: http://www.bis.org

The objectives of the Bank for International Settlements (founded in 1930) are to promote co-operation between central banks; to provide facilities for international financial operations; and to act as trustee or agent in international financial settlements entrusted to it. There are 45 members. The London agent is the Bank of England, and the Governor of the Bank of England is a member of the Board of Directors, in which administrative control is vested.

Chairman of the Board of Directors and President of the Bank for International Settlements, Urban Bäckström (Sweden)

CAB INTERNATIONAL
Wallingford, Oxon OX10 8DE
Tel: 01491-832111; fax: 01491-833508
E-mail: cabi@cabi.org
Web: http://www.cabi.org

CAB International (formerly the Commonwealth Agricultural Bureaux) was founded in 1929. It generates, disseminates and applies scientific knowledge in support of sustainable development, with an emphasis on agriculture, forestry and natural resources, and the needs of developing countries. The organization is owned and governed by its 40 member governments, each represented on an Executive Council. A Governing Board provides guidance to management on policy issues.

CABI has three divisions: bioscience, information and publishing. These undertake research and consultancy aimed at raising agricultural productivity, conserving biological resources, protecting the environment and controlling disease. The organization publishes books, journals and newsletters and produces bibliographic databases on agriculture, health and allied disciplines. It also undertakes contracted scientific research and provides consultancy services and information support to developing countries.

Director-General, James H. Gilmore

CARIBBEAN COMMUNITY AND COMMON MARKET
PO Box 10827, Georgetown, Guyana
Tel: Georgetown 69281; fax: Georgetown 67816
E-mail: carisec2@caricom.org
Web: http://www.caricom.org

The Caribbean Community and Common Market (CARICOM) was established in 1973 with three objectives: economic co-operation through the Caribbean Common Market, the co-ordination of member states' foreign policy, and the provision of common services and co-operation in health, education, culture, communications and industrial relations.

The supreme organ is the Conference of Heads of Government, which determines policy, takes strategic decisions and is responsible for resolving conflicts and all matters relating to the founding treaty. The Community Council of Ministers consists of ministers of government responsible for CARICOM affairs and any other ministers designated by member states and is responsible for strategic planning in the areas of economic integration, functional co-operation and external relations. The principal administrative arm is the Secretariat, based in Guyana. The Bureau of the Conference of Heads of Government is the executive body. It comprises the Chairman of the Conference, the outgoing Chairman and the Secretary-General, who are authorized to initiate proposals and to secure the implementation of CARICOM decisions.

The 14 member states are Antigua and Barbuda, The Bahamas (which is not a member of the Common Market), Barbados, Belize, Dominica, Grenada, Guyana, Jamaica, Montserrat, St Christopher and Nevis, St Lucia, St Vincent and the Grenadines, Suriname, and Trinidad and Tobago. The British Virgin Islands and the Turks and Caicos Islands are associate members. The Dominican Republic, Haiti, Mexico, Puerto Rico and Venezuela have observer status. At the 1997 annual summit, the member countries agreed to admit Haiti as a full member, subject to the successful conclusion of negotiations.

Secretary-General, Edwin W. Carrington

THE COMMONWEALTH

The Commonwealth is a voluntary association of 54 sovereign independent states together with their associated states and dependencies. All of the states were formerly parts of the British Empire or League of Nations (later

UN) mandated territories, except for Mozambique which was admitted as a unique case because of its history of co-operation with neighbouring nations.

The status and relationship of member nations were first defined by the Inter-Imperial Relations Committee of the 1926 Imperial Conference, when the six existing dominions (Australia, Canada, the Irish Free State, Newfoundland, New Zealand and South Africa) were described as 'autonomous Communities within the British Empire, equal in status, in no way subordinate one to another in any aspect of their domestic or external affairs, though united by a common allegiance to the Crown and freely associated as Members of the British Commonwealth of Nations'. This formula was given legal substance by the Statute of Westminster 1931.

This concept of a group of countries owing allegiance to a single Crown changed in 1949 when India decided to become a republic. Her continued membership of the Commonwealth was agreed by the other members on the basis of her 'acceptance of The King as the symbol of the free association of its independent member nations and as such the head of the Commonwealth'. This paved the way for other republics to join the association in due course. Member nations agreed at the time of the accession of Queen Elizabeth II to recognize Her Majesty as the new Head of the Commonwealth. However, the position is not vested in the British Crown.

THE MODERN COMMONWEALTH

As the UK's former colonies joined, initially with India and Pakistan in 1947, the Commonwealth was transformed from a grouping of all-white dominions into a multi-racial association of equal, sovereign nations. It increasingly focused on promoting development and racial equality and effectively expelled South Africa in 1961 over its policy of apartheid.

The new goals of advocating democracy, the rule of law, good government and social justice were enshrined in the Harare Commonwealth Declaration (1991), which formed the basis of new membership guidelines agreed in Cyprus in 1993. Following the adoption of measures in New Zealand in 1995 against serious or persistent violations of these principles, Nigeria and Sierra Leone were suspended for anti-democratic behaviour. Sierra Leone's suspension was revoked when the legitimate government was returned to power. Similarly, Nigeria's suspension was lifted on 29 May 1999, the day a newly elected civilian president took office. The heads of government meeting in Edinburgh in 1997 established a set of economic principles for the Commonwealth, promoting economic growth whilst protecting smaller member states from the negative effects of globalization.

MEMBERSHIP

Membership of the Commonwealth involves acceptance of the association's basic principles and is subject to the approval of existing members. There are 54 members at present. (The date of joining the Commonwealth is shown in parenthesis.)

*Antigua and Barbuda (1981)
*Australia (1931)
*The Bahamas (1973)
Bangladesh (1972)
*Barbados (1966)
*Belize (1981)
Botswana (1966)
Brunei (1984)
Cameroon (1995)
*Canada (1931)
Cyprus (1961)
Dominica (1978)
Fiji (1970, 1997)
The Gambia (1965)

Ghana (1957)
*Grenada (1974)
Guyana (1966)India (1947)
*Jamaica (1962)
Kenya (1963)
Kiribati (1979)
Lesotho (1966)
Malawi (1964)
Malaysia (1957)
The Maldives (1982)
Malta (1964)
Mauritius (1968)
Mozambique (1995)
Namibia (1990)
Nauru (1968)
*New Zealand (1931)
Nigeria (1960)
Pakistan (1947)
*Papua New Guinea (1975)
*St Christopher and Nevis (1983)

*St Lucia (1979)
*St Vincent and the Grenadines (1979)
Samoa (1970)
Seychelles (1976)
Sierra Leone (1961)
Singapore (1965)
*Solomon Islands (1978)
South Africa (1931)
Sri Lanka (1948)
Swaziland (1968)
Tanzania (1961)
Tonga (1970)
Trinidad and Tobago (1962)
*Tuvalu (1978)
Uganda (1962)
*United Kingdom
Vanuatu (1980)
Zambia (1964)
Zimbabwe (1980)

*Realms of Queen Elizabeth II

Tuvalu is a special member, with the right to participate in all functional Commonwealth meetings and activities, but not to attend meetings of Commonwealth heads of government. Nauru was also a special member until 1 May 1999, when it became a full member.

Countries which have left the Commonwealth
Fiji (1987, rejoined 1997)
Republic of Ireland (1949)
Pakistan (1972, rejoined 1989)
South Africa (1961, rejoined 1994)

Of the 54 member states, 16 have Queen Elizabeth II as head of state, 33 are republics, and five have national monarchies.

In each of the realms where Queen Elizabeth II is head of state (except for the UK), she is personally represented by a Governor-General, who holds in all essential respects the same position in relation to the administration of public affairs in the realm as is held by Her Majesty in Britain. The Governor-General is appointed by The Queen on the advice of the government of the state concerned.

INTERGOVERNMENTAL AND OTHER LINKS

The main forum for consultation is the Commonwealth heads of government meetings held biennially to discuss international developments and to consider co-operation among members. Decisions are reached by consensus, and the views of the meeting are set out in a communiqué. There are also annual meetings of finance ministers and frequent meetings of ministers and officials in other fields, such as education, health, women's affairs, agriculture, and science. Intergovernmental links are complemented by the activities of some 300 Commonwealth non-governmental organizations linking professionals, sportsmen and sportswomen, and interest groups, forming a 'people's Commonwealth'. The Commonwealth Games take place every four years.

Assistance to other Commonwealth countries normally has priority in the bilateral aid programmes of the association's developed members (Australia, Britain, Canada and New Zealand), who direct about 30 per cent of their aid to other member countries. Developing Commonwealth nations also assist their poorer partners, and many Commonwealth voluntary organizations promote development.

COMMONWEALTH SECRETARIAT

The Commonwealth has a secretariat, established in 1965 in London, which is funded by all member governments.

This is the main agency for multilateral communication between member governments on issues relating to the Commonwealth as a whole. It promotes consultation and co-operation, disseminates information on matters of common concern, organizes meetings including the biennial summits, co-ordinates Commonwealth activities, and provides technical assistance for economic and social development through the Commonwealth Fund for Technical Co-operation.

The Commonwealth Foundation was established by Commonwealth governments in 1966 as an autonomous body with a board of governors representing Commonwealth governments that fund the Foundation. It promotes and funds exchanges and other activities aimed at strengthening the skills and effectiveness of professionals and non-governmental organizations. It also promotes culture, rural development, social welfare and the role of women.

COMMONWEALTH SECRETARIAT, Marlborough House, Pall Mall, London SW1Y 5HX. Tel: 0171-839 3411; fax: 0171-839 9081.

Web: http://www.thecommonwealth.org. *Secretary-General*, Chief Emeka Anyaoku (Nigeria)

COMMONWEALTH FOUNDATION, Marlborough House, Pall Mall, London SW1Y 5HY. Tel: 0171-930 3783.

Director, Dr Humayun Khan (Pakistan)

COMMONWEALTH INSTITUTE, Kensington High Street, London W8 6NQ. Tel: 0171-603 4535. *Director-General*, David French

---

COMMONWEALTH OF INDEPENDENT STATES

Ul. Kirova 17, Minsk, Belarus
Web: http://www.cis.minsk.by

The Commonwealth of Independent States (CIS) is a multilateral grouping of 12 sovereign states which were formerly constituent republics of the USSR. It was formed by Russia, Ukraine and Belarus on 8 December 1991, the remaining republics, apart from the Baltic states and Georgia, joining on 21 December. Georgia joined in December 1993. The CIS charter, signed in 1993 by seven states (Armenia, Belarus, Kazakhstan, Kyrgyzstan, Russia, Tajikistan, Uzbekistan) and open for signing by the other states, formally established the functions of the organization and the obligations of its member states.

The CIS acts as a co-ordinating mechanism for foreign, defence and economic policies, and is a forum for addressing problems which have specifically arisen from the break-up of the USSR. These matters are addressed in more than 50 inter-state, intergovernmental co-ordinating and consultative statutory bodies. However, member states have criticized the CIS for operating ineffectively, and for failing to carry through decisions made by CIS organs.

STRUCTURE

The two supreme CIS bodies are the Council of Heads of State and the Council of Heads of Government. The Council of Heads of State is the highest organ of the CIS and meets not less than twice yearly. It is chaired by the heads of state of the members in (Russian) alphabetical order. The Council of Heads of Government meets not less than once every three months to co-ordinate military and economic activity. Other important bodies are the Council of Heads of Collective Security (defence ministers), the Joint Staff for Co-ordinating Military Co-operation, the CIS Inter-Parliamentary Assembly, the Economic Arbitration Court and the Co-ordinating Con-

sultative Committee. Administrative support is provided by the Executive Secretariat based in Minsk.

DEFENCE CO-OPERATION

On becoming member states of the CIS, the 11 original states agreed to recognize their existing borders, respect one another's territorial integrity and reject the use of military force or other forms of coercion to settle disputes between them. Agreement was also reached on fulfilling all the international treaty obligations of the former USSR, together with the establishment of CIS joint armed forces.

The members agreed on a central CIS command for all nuclear weapons, the control over which was passed to CIS commander-in-chief Marshal Shaposhnikov in December 1991. All tactical nuclear weapons had been transferred to Russia by May 1992. An agreement was reached with the USA in May 1992 by the four republics with strategic nuclear weapons (Russia, Ukraine, Belarus, Kazakhstan) on implementing the strategic arms reduction talks (START) treaty previously signed by the USA and USSR, and the START I treaty was ratified by the five parties between October 1992 and February 1994. Under this agreement Ukraine, Belarus and Kazakhstan agreed to eliminate all their strategic nuclear weapons over a seven-year period and Russia has agreed to reduce its strategic nuclear weapons.

A CIS high command and a joint conventional force were created in 1992 to operate in parallel with member states' own armed forces. In the same year, a Treaty on Collective Security was signed by six states and a joint peacemaking force, to intervene in CIS conflicts, was agreed upon by nine states. Deployment of these forces was made conditional on consensus in the Council of Heads of State. Fear of Russian domination by some states led to the downgrading of the high command into a Joint Staff for Co-ordinating Military Co-operation in 1993. Russia responded by concluding bilateral and multilateral agreements with other CIS states under the supervision of the Council of Heads of Collective Security (established 1993). These have been gradually upgraded into CIS agreements under the umbrella of the Treaty on Collective Security, enabling Russia to station troops in ten of the other 11 CIS states (not Ukraine), and giving Russian forces *de facto* control of virtually all of the former USSR's external borders. Only Ukraine and Moldova remain outside the defence co-operation framework and have not signed the Treaty on Collective Security, from which Georgia and Uzbekistan have announced its withdrawal. In November 1995, the ten agreed to recreate a joint air defence system.

ECONOMIC CO-OPERATION

In 1991, 11 republics signed a treaty forming an economic community. The principles of the treaty were embodied within the CIS and formed the basis of its economic co-operation. Members agreed to refrain from economic actions that would damage each other and to co-ordinate economic and monetary policies. A Co-ordinating Consultative Committee, an economic arbitration court and an inter-state bank were established. A single monetary unit, the rouble, was originally agreed upon by all member states, and the members recognized that the basis of recovery for their economies was private ownership, free enterprise and competition.

Russia effectively forced the collapse of the rouble zone in July 1993 by withdrawing all pre-1993 roubles and forcing the remaining states using roubles to accept Russian monetary control or introduce their own currencies, which all did apart from Tajikistan. The resulting economic collapse of the non-Russian economies led to renewed interest in economic co-operation and the signing of a

Treaty on Economic Union in September 1993. The 11 CIS members who have signed the Treaty (Ukraine is an associate member of the economic union) are committed to a common market without internal barriers to trade, common fiscal policies and an eventual currency union with currencies semi-fixed against the rouble. In order to facilitate faster economic integration 11 states (not Turkmenistan) agreed in October 1994 to establish an Inter-state Economic Committee, and in May 1995 a monetary committee to facilitate payments in different currencies was agreed. Belarus has withdrawn its currency and rejoined Russia and Tajikistan in the rouble zone. A treaty creating a common market was signed by Kazakhstan, Kyrgyzstan, Russia and Belarus in March 1996, with other CIS states originally excluded from membership, although Tajikistan has since joined.

Executive Secretary, Yuri Yarov

THE COUNCIL OF EUROPE

F-67075 Strasbourg, France
Tel: Strasbourg 8841 2000; fax: Strasbourg 8841 2781/2/3
E-mail: information.point@seddoc.coe.fr
Web: http://www.coe.fr

The Council of Europe was founded in 1949. Its aim is to achieve greater unity between its members, to safeguard their European heritage and to facilitate their progress in economic, social, cultural, educational, scientific, legal and administrative matters, and in the furtherance of pluralist democracy, human rights and fundamental freedoms.

The 41 members are Albania, Andorra, Austria, Belgium, Bulgaria, Croatia, Cyprus, Czech Republic, Denmark, Estonia, Finland, France, Georgia, Germany, Greece, Hungary, Iceland, the Republic of Ireland, Italy, Latvia, Liechtenstein, Lithuania, Luxembourg, Macedonia (Former Yugoslav Republic of), Malta, Moldova, the Netherlands, Norway, Poland, Portugal, Romania, Russia, San Marino, Slovakia, Slovenia, Spain, Sweden, Switzerland, Turkey, the UK and Ukraine. 'Special guest status' has been granted to Armenia, Azerbaijan, and Bosnia-Herce-govina. Turkey's membership was suspended from April 1995 to September 1996 over its military offensive against Kurdish guerrillas in northern Iraq.

The organs are the Committee of Ministers, consisting of the foreign ministers of member countries, who meet twice yearly, and the Parliamentary Assembly of 291 members, elected or chosen by the national parliaments of member countries in proportion to the relative strength of political parties. There is also a Joint Committee of Ministers and Representatives of the Parliamentary Assembly.

The Committee of Ministers is the executive organ. The majority of its conclusions take the form of international agreements (known as European Conventions) or recommendations to governments. Decisions of the Ministers may also be embodied in partial agreements to which a limited number of member governments are party. Member governments accredit Permanent Representatives to the Council in Strasbourg, who are also the Ministers' Deputies. The Committee of Deputies meets every month to transact business and to take decisions on behalf of Ministers.

The Parliamentary Assembly holds three week-long sessions a year. Its 13 permanent committees meet once or twice between each public plenary session of the Assembly. The Congress of Local and Regional Authorities of Europe each year brings together mayors and municipal councillors in the same numbers as the members of the Parliamentary Assembly.

One of the principal achievements of the Council of Europe is the European Convention on Human Rights (1950) under which was established the European Commission and the European Court of Human Rights, which were merged in 1993. The reorganized European Court of Human Rights sits in chambers of seven judges or exceptionally as a grand chamber of 17 judges. Litigants must exhaust legal processes in their own country before bringing cases before the court.

Among other conventions and agreements are the European Social Charter, the European Cultural Convention, the European Code of Social Security, the European Convention on the Protection of National Minorities, and conventions on extradition, the legal status of migrant workers, torture prevention, conservation, and the transfer of sentenced prisoners. Most recently, the specialized bodies of the Venice Commission and Demosthenes have been set up to assist in developing legislative, administrative and constitutional reforms in central and eastern Europe.

Non-member states take part in certain Council of Europe activities on a regular or *ad hoc* basis; thus the Holy See participates in all the educational, cultural and sports activities. The European Youth Centre is an educational residential centre for young people. The European Youth Foundation provides youth organizations with funds for their international activities.

Secretary-General, Daniel Tarschys (Sweden)
Permanent UK Representative, HE Andrew Carter, CMG, *apptd* 1997

THE ECONOMIC COMMUNITY OF WEST AFRICAN STATES

Secretariat Building, Asokoro, Abuja, Nigeria
Tel: Abuja 523 1858

The Economic Community of West African States (ECOWAS) was founded in 1975 and came into operation in 1977. It aims to promote the cultural, economic and social development of West Africa through mutual co-operation. A revised ECOWAS Treaty was signed in 1993 and came into effect in July 1995. It makes the prevention and control of regional conflicts an aim of ECOWAS and provides for the imposition of a community tax and for the establishment of a regional parliament, an economic and social council, and a court of justice.

The supreme authority of ECOWAS is vested in the annual summit of heads of government of all 16 member states. A Council of Ministers, two from each member state, meets biannually to monitor the organization and make recommendations to the summit. ECOWAS operates through a Secretariat, headed by the Executive Secretary. In addition there is a financial controller, an external auditor, the Disputes Tribunal and the Defence Council.

A Fund for Co-operation, Compensation and Development, situated at Lomé, Togo, finances development projects and provides compensation to member states who have suffered losses as a result of ECOWAS's policies, particularly trade liberalization.

An ECOWAS Monitoring Group (ECOMOG) peace-keeping force has been involved in attempts to restore peace in Liberia (1990–6) and in Sierra Leone since 1997.

Executive Secretary, Lansana Kouyate (Guinea)

THE EUROPEAN BANK FOR RECONSTRUCTION AND DEVELOPMENT
One Exchange Square, London EC2A 2EH
Tel: 0171-338 6000; fax: 0171-338 6100
Web: http://www.ebrd.com

The European Bank for Reconstruction and Development (EBRD), established in 1991, is an international institution with 60 members (58 countries, the European Union and the European Investment Bank).

The aim of the EBRD is to facilitate the transformation of the states of central and eastern Europe and the former USSR and former Yugoslavia from centrally planned to free-market economies, and to promote multi-party democracy, entrepreneurial initiative, respect for human rights and environmentally sound development.

The EBRD finances projects in both the private and public sectors, providing direct funding for financial institutions, infrastructure and other key sectors. The main forms of EBRD financing are loans, equity investments and guarantees. No more than 40 per cent of the EBRD's investment can be made in state-owned concerns. The bank is the largest foreign investor in the region's private sector. It works in co-operation with its members, private companies, and international organizations such as the OECD, the IMF, the World Bank and the UN specialized agencies.

The EBRD has a subscribed capital of Euro 20 billion . The EBRD is also able to borrow on world capital markets. Its major subscribers are the USA, 10 per cent; Britain, France, Germany, Italy and Japan, 8.5 per cent each. As of 31 December 1998, the EBRD has signed 551 projects with a total net value of Euro 10.2 billion.

The highest authority is the Board of Governors; each member appoints one Governor and one Alternate. The Governors delegate most powers to a 23-member Board of Directors; the Directors are responsible for the EBRD's operations and budget, and are elected by the Governors for three-year terms. The Governors also elect the President of the Board of Directors, who acts as the Bank's president, for a four-year term. A Secretary-General liaises between the Directors and EBRD staff.

President of the Board of Directors, Horst Koehler (Germany)
Chairman of the Board of Governors, Yannos Papantoniou (Greece)
Secretary-General, Antonio Maria Costa (Italy)

EUROPEAN FREE TRADE ASSOCIATION
Headquarters: 9–11 rue de Varembé, CH-1211 Geneva 20, Switzerland
Tel: Geneva 749 1111; fax: Geneva 733 9291
Web: http://www.efta.int
EEA matters: 74 rue de Trèves, B-1040 Brussels, Belgium
Tel: Brussels 286 1711; fax: Brussels 286 1750
E-mail: efta-mailbox@secrbru.efta.be

The European Free Trade Association (EFTA) was established in 1960 by Austria, Denmark, Norway, Portugal, Sweden, Switzerland and the UK, and was subsequently joined by Finland (associate member 1961, full member 1986), Iceland (1970) and Liechtenstein (1991). Six members have left to join the European Union: Denmark and the UK (1972), Portugal (1985), Austria, Finland and Sweden (1995). The existing members are Iceland, Liechtenstein, Norway and Switzerland.

The first objective of EFTA was to establish free trade in industrial products between members; this was achieved in 1966. Its second objective was the creation of a single market in western Europe and in 1972 EFTA signed free trade agreements with the EC covering trade in industrial goods; the remaining tariffs on industrial products were abolished in 1984.

An agreement on the creation of the European Economic Area (EEA), an extension of the EC single market to the EFTA states, was signed in 1992 and entered into force on 1 January 1994. Switzerland rejected EEA membership in a referendum in 1992 and Liechtenstein joined on 1 May 1995 after adapting its customs union with Switzerland.

EFTA has expanded its relations with other non-EU states in recent years, signing free trade agreements with Turkey (1991), Israel, Poland and Romania (1992), Bulgaria, the Czech Republic, Hungary and Slovakia (1993), Estonia, Latvia, Lithuania and Slovenia (1995), Morocco (1997), and the PLO (1998). In addition, EFTA has signed declarations of economic co-operation with Albania (1992), Egypt and Tunisia (1995), Macedonia, and Jordan and Lebanon (1997).

The EFTA Council is the principle organ of the Association. It generally meets twice a month at the level of heads of the permanent national delegations to the EFTA Secretariat in Geneva and twice a year at ministerial level.

Secretary-General, Kjartan Jóhannsson (Iceland)
Deputy Secretary-General (Geneva), Aldo Matteucci (Switzerland)
Deputy Secretary-General (Brussels), Guttorm Vik (Norway)

EUROPEAN ORGANIZATION FOR NUCLEAR RESEARCH (CERN)
CH-1211 Geneva 23, Switzerland
Tel: Geneva 767 4101; fax: Geneva 785 0247
Web: http://www.cern.ch

The Convention establishing the European Organization for Nuclear Research (CERN) came into force in 1954. CERN promotes European collaboration in high energy physics of a scientific, rather than a military nature.

The member countries are Austria, Belgium, the Czech Republic, Denmark, Finland, France, Germany, Greece, Hungary, Italy, the Netherlands, Norway, Poland, Portugal, Slovakia, Spain, Sweden, Switzerland and the UK. Israel, Japan, Russia, Turkey, the USA, the EU Commission and UNESCO have observer status.

The Council is the highest policy-making body and comprises two delegates from each member state. There is also a Committee of the Council comprising a single delegate from each member state (who is also a Council member) and the chairmen of the scientific policy and finance advisory committees. The Council is chaired by the President who is elected by the Council in Session. The Council also elects the Director-General, who is responsible for the internal organization of CERN. The Director-General heads a workforce of approximately 3,000, including physicists, craftsmen, technicians and administrative staff. At present over 6,500 physicists use CERN's facilities.

The member countries contribute to the budget in proportion to their net national revenue. The 1999 budget was SFr 939 million.

President of the Council, Hans Eschelbacher (Germany)
Director-General (1999–2004), Prof. Luciano Maiani (Italy)

EUROPEAN SPACE AGENCY
8–10 rue Mario Nikis, F-75738 Paris, France
Tel: Paris 5369 7654; fax: Paris 5369 7560
Web: http://www.esa.int

The European Space Agency (ESA) was created in 1975 by the merger of the European Space Research Organization (ESRO) and the European Launcher Development Organization (ELDO). Its aims include the advancement of space research and technology and the implementation of a long-term European space policy.

The member countries are Austria, Belgium, Denmark, Finland, France, Germany, the Republic of Ireland, Italy, the Netherlands, Norway, Spain, Sweden, Switzerland and the UK. Canada is a co-operating state.

The agency is directed by a Council composed of the representatives of the member states; its chief officer is the Director-General.

Director-General, Antonio Rodotà, *apptd* 1997

FOOD AND AGRICULTURE ORGANIZATION OF THE UNITED NATIONS
Viale delle Terme di Caracalla, I-00100 Rome, Italy
Tel: Rome 57051; fax: Rome 5705 3152
E-mail: fao-hq@fao.org
Web: http://www.fao.org

The Food and Agriculture Organization (FAO) is a specialized UN agency, established in 1945. It assists rural populations by raising levels of nutrition and living standards, and by encouraging greater efficiency in food production and distribution. It analyses and disseminates information on agriculture and natural resources. The FAO also advises governments on national agricultural policy and planning; its Investment Centre, together with the World Bank and other financial institutions, helps to prepare development projects. The FAO's field programme covers a range of activities, including strengthening crop production, rural and livestock development, and conservation.

The FAO's top priorities are sustainable agriculture, rural development and food security. The Organization attempts to ensure the availability of adequate food supplies, stability in the flow of supplies and the securing of access to food by the poor. The FAO monitors potential famine areas. The Special Relief Operations Service channels emergency aid from governments and other agencies, and assists in rehabilitation. The Technical Co-operation Programme provides schemes for countries facing agricultural crises.

The FAO had 176 members (175 states and the EU) as at May 1999. It is governed by a biennial conference of its members which sets a programme and budget. The budget for 1998–9 is US$650million, funded by member countries in proportion to their gross national products. The FAO is also funded by the UN Development Programme, donor governments and other institutions.

The Conference elects a Director-General and a 49-member Council which governs between conferences. The Regular and Field Programmes are administered by a Secretariat, headed by the Director-General. Five regional, five sub-regional and 80 national offices help administer the Field Programme.

Director-General, Jacques Diouf (Senegal)
UK Representative, Anthony Beattie, British Embassy, Rome

INMARSAT
99 City Road, London ECIY IAX
Tel: 0171-728 1000; fax: 0171-728 1044
E-mail: information@inmarsat.org
Web: http://www.inmarsat.org

Inmarsat (formerly the International Mobile Satellite Organization) was founded in 1979 as the International Maritime Satellite Organization and began operations in 1982. Inmarsat was an internationally owned co-operative, but became a private company in April 1999. It now comprises two entities: a two-tier private company, (Inmarsat Holdings and Inmarsat Ltd), and an intergovernmental body, the International Mobile Satellite Organization (IMSO), to oversee Inmarsat's delivery of its public service obligations. It operates a system of satellites to provide global mobile communications. Inmarsat satellite terminals are used world-wide on ships, aircraft and on land for telecommunications, as well as maritime safety, position reporting and distress communications.

Inmarsat comprises three bodies: the Assembly, the Council and the Directorate. The Assembly is composed of representatives of the 80 member countries, each having one vote. It meets every two years to review activities and objectives, and to make recommendations to the Council. The Council is the main decision-making body and consists of representatives of the 18 members with the largest investment shares, and four members representing the interests of developing countries who are elected to the Council on the basis of geographical representation. Members have voting powers equal to their investment shares. The Council meets at least three times a year and oversees the activities of the Directorate, the permanent staff of Inmarsat.

Director-General, Warren Grace (Australia)

INTERNATIONAL ATOMIC ENERGY AGENCY
Vienna International Centre, Wagramerstrasse 5, PO Box 100, A-1400 Vienna, Austria
Tel: Vienna 26000; fax: Vienna 26007
E-mail: Official.Mail@iaea.org
Web: http://www.iaea.org/worldatom

The International Atomic Energy Agency (IAEA) was established in 1957. It is an intergovernmental organization which reports to, but is not a specialized agency of, the UN.

The IAEA aims to enhance the contribution of atomic energy to peace, health and prosperity, and to ensure that any assistance that it provides is not used for military purposes. It establishes atomic energy safety standards and offers services to its member states for the safe operation of their nuclear facilities and for radiation protection. It is the focal point for international conventions on the early notification of a nuclear accident, assistance in the case of a nuclear accident, civil liability for nuclear damage, physical protection of nuclear material, nuclear safety and the safety of spent fuel and radioactive waste management. The IAEA also encourages research and training in nuclear power. It is additionally charged with drawing up safeguards and verifying their use in accordance with the Nuclear Non-Proliferation Treaty (NPT) 1968, the Treaty for the Prohibition of Nuclear Weapons in Latin America (Tlatelolco Treaty) 1968, the Treaty on a South Pacific Nuclear Free Zone (Rarotonga Treaty), and the African Nuclear Weapon-Free Zone Treaty (Pelindaba Treaty) 1996.

Together with the Food and Agriculture Organization and the World Health Organization, the IAEA established an International Consultative Group on Food Irradiation in 1983.

The IAEA concluded a safeguards agreement with North Korea in April 1992 and began inspections to verify that its nuclear programme was for peaceful purposes only. In 1993 the IAEA informed the UN Security Council that North Korea had violated its NPT obligations and all technical aid to North Korea was suspended. North Korea resigned from the IAEA in 1994, but permitted IAEA inspections under the terms of an agreement with the USA which enabled the IAEA to resume safeguards inspections.

The IAEA had 128 members as at May 1999. A General Conference of all its members meets annually to decide policy, a programme and a budget (1999, US$224.3 million), as well as electing a Director-General and a 35-member Board of Governors. The Board meets four times a year to formulate policy which is implemented by the Secretariat under a Director-General.

Director-General, Mohamed El Baradei (Egypt)
Permanent UK Representative, Dr John Freeman, Jaurèsgasse 12, A-1030 Vienna, Austria

INTERNATIONAL CIVIL AVIATION ORGANIZATION

999 University Street, Montreal, Quebec, Canada H3C 5H7
Tel: Montreal 954 8219; fax: Montreal 954 6077
E-mail: icaohq@icao.int
Web: http://www.icao.int

The International Civil Aviation Organization (ICAO) was founded with the signing of the Chicago Convention on International Civil Aviation in 1944, and became a specialized agency of the United Nations in 1947. It sets international technical standards and recommended practices for all areas of civil aviation, including airworthiness, air navigation, traffic control and pilot licensing. It encourages uniformity and simplicity in ground regulations and operations at international airports, including immigration and customs control. The ICAO also promotes regional air navigation, plans for ground facilities, and collects and distributes air transport statistics world-wide. It is dedicated to improving safety and to the orderly development of civil aviation throughout the world.

The ICAO had 185 members as at 3 June 1999. It is governed by an assembly of its members which meets at least once every three years. A Council of 33 members is elected, which represents leading air transport nations as well as less developed countries. The Council elects the President, appoints the Secretary-General and supervises the organization through subsidiary committees, serviced by a Secretariat.

President of the Council, Dr Assad Kotaite (Lebanon)
Secretary-General, R. C. Costa Pereira (Brazil)
UK Representative, D. S. Evans, CMG, 999 University Street, Montreal, Quebec, Canada H3C 5H7

INTERNATIONAL CONFEDERATION OF FREE TRADE UNIONS

Boulevard Emile Jacqmain 155 B1, B-1210 Brussels, Belgium
Tel: Brussels 224 0211; fax: Brussels 201 5815/224 0297
E-mail: internetpo@icftu.org
Web: http://www.icftu.org

The International Confederation of Free Trade Unions (ICFTU) was created in 1949. It aims to establish, maintain and promote free trade unions, and to promote peace with economic security and social justice.

Affiliated to the ICFTU are 213 individual unions and representative bodies in 143 countries and territories. There were 124 million members on 27 November 1998.

The Congress, the supreme authority of the ICFTU, convenes at least every four years. It is composed of delegates from the affiliated trade union organizations. The Congress elects an Executive Board of 53 members, including five nominated by the Women's Committee and one representing young workers, which meets not less than once a year. The Board establishes the budget and receives suggestions and proposals from affiliates as well as acting on behalf of the Confederation. The Congress also elects the General Secretary.

General Secretary, Bill Jordan (UK)
UK Affiliate, TUC, Congress House, 23–28 Great Russell Street, London WC1B 3LS. Tel: 0171-636 4030

INTERNATIONAL CRIMINAL POLICE ORGANIZATION

200 Quai Charles de Gaulle, F-69006 Lyon, France
Tel: Lyon 7244 7000; fax: Lyon 7244 7163
Web: http://www.interpol.com

The International Criminal Police Commission (Interpol) was set up in 1923 to establish an international criminal records office and to harmonize extradition procedures. As of 1 January 1998, the organization comprised 177 member states.

Interpol's aims are to promote co-operation between criminal police authorities, and to support government agencies concerned with combating crime, whilst respecting national sovereignty. It is financed by annual contributions from the governments of member states.

Interpol's policy is decided by the General Assembly which meets annually; it is composed of delegates appointed by the member states. The 13-member Executive Committee is elected by the General Assembly from among the member states' delegates, and is chaired by the President, who has a four-year term of office. The permanent administrative organ is the General Secretariat, headed by the Secretary-General, who is appointed by the General Assembly.

Secretary-General, Raymond Kendall, QPM (UK)
UK OFFICE, NCIS Interpol, PO Box 8000, London SE11 5EN. Tel: 0171-238 8000. *UK Representative*, J. M. Abbott, QPM

INTERNATIONAL ENERGY AGENCY
9 rue de la Fédération, F-75739 Paris Cedex 15, France
Tel: Paris 4057 6554; fax: Paris 4057 6559
Web: http://www.iea.org

The International Energy Agency (IEA), founded in 1974, is an autonomous agency within the framework of the Organization for Economic Co-operation and Development (OECD). The IEA had 24 member countries as at June 1999.

The IEA's objectives include improvement of energy co-operation world-wide, increased efficiency, development of alternative energy sources and the promotion of relations between oil producing and oil consuming countries. The IEA also maintains an emergency system to alleviate the effects of severe oil supply disruptions.

The main decision-making body is the Governing Board, composed of senior energy officials from member countries. Various standing groups and special committees exist to facilitate the work of the Board. The IEA Secretariat, with a staff of energy experts, carries out the work of the Governing Board and its subordinate bodies. The Executive Director is appointed by the Board.

Executive Director, Robert Priddle (UK)

INTERNATIONAL FUND FOR AGRICULTURAL DEVELOPMENT
107 Via del Serafico, I-00142 Rome, Italy
Tel: Rome 54591; fax: Rome 504 3463
E-mail: ifad@ifad.org/communications@ifad.org
Web: http://www.ifad.org

The establishment of the International Fund for Agricultural Development (IFAD) was proposed by the 1974 World Food Conference and IFAD began operations as a UN specialized agency in 1977. Its purpose is to mobilize additional funds for agricultural and rural development projects in developing countries that benefit the poorest rural populations; provide employment and additional income for poor farmers; reduce malnutrition; and improve food distribution systems.

IFAD had 161 members as at April 1998. Membership is divided into three lists: List A (OECD countries), List B (OPEC countries), and List C (developing countries) which is subdivided into C1 (Africa), C2 (Africa, Asia and the Pacific) and C3 (Latin America and the Caribbean). All powers are vested in a Governing Council of all member countries. It elects an 18-member Executive Board (with 17 alternate members) responsible for IFAD's operations. The Council meets annually and elects a President who is also chairman of the Board. He is assisted by a Vice-President and three Assistant Presidents.

Between 1978 and 1998, IFAD has committed a total of US$6.4 thousand million in loans and grants for 520 approved projects in 113 developing countries.

President, Fawzi H. Al-Sultan (Kuwait)

INTERNATIONAL LABOUR ORGANIZATION
4 route des Morillons, CH-1211 Geneva 22, Switzerland
Tel: Geneva 799 6111; fax: Geneva 798 8685
Web: http://www.ilo.org

The International Labour Organization (ILO) was established in 1919 as an autonomous body of the League of Nations and became the UN's first specialized agency in 1946. The ILO aims to increase employment, improve working conditions, raise living standards and encourage democratic development. It sets minimum international labour standards through the drafting of international conventions. Member countries are obliged to submit these to their domestic authorities for ratification, and thus undertake to bring their domestic legislation in line with the conventions. Members must report to the ILO periodically on how these regulations are being implemented. The ILO plays a major role in helping developing countries achieve economic stability and job expansion through its wide-ranging programme of technical co-operation. The ILO is also the world's principal resource centre for information, analysis and guidance on labour and employment. The organization aims to improve working and living conditions throughout the world and to support the transition to democracy and market economics under way in many states.

The ILO had 174 members as at June 1998. It is composed of the International Labour Conference, the Governing Body and the International Labour Office. The Conference of members meets annually, and is attended by national delegations comprising two government delegates, one worker delegate and one employer delegate. It formulates international labour conventions and recommendations, provides a forum for discussion of world employment and social issues, and approves the ILO's programme and budget (2000–1, US$481 million).

The 56-member Governing Body, composed of 28 government, 14 worker and 14 employer members, acts as the ILO's executive council. Ten governments, including Britain, hold seats on the Governing Body because of their industrial importance. There are also various regional conferences and advisory committees. The International Labour Office acts as a secretariat and as a centre for operations, publishing and research.

Director-General, Juan Somavia (Chile)
UK OFFICE, Millbank Tower, 21-24 Millbank, London SW1P 4QP. Tel: 0171-828 6401; fax: 0171-233-5925.
E-mail: london@ilo-london.org.uk

INTERNATIONAL MARITIME ORGANIZATION
4 Albert Embankment, London SE1 7SR
Tel: 0171-735 7611; fax: 0171-587 3210
E-mail: info@imo.org
Web: http://www.imo.org

The International Maritime Organization (IMO) was established as a UN specialized agency in 1948. Owing to delays in treaty ratification it did not commence operations until 1958. Originally it was called the Inter-Governmental Maritime Consultative Organization (IMCO) but changed its name in 1982.

The IMO fosters intergovernmental co-operation in technical matters relating to international shipping, especially with regard to safety at sea. It is also charged with preventing and controlling marine pollution caused by shipping and facilitating marine traffic. The IMO is responsible for convening maritime conferences and drafting marine conventions. It also provides technical aid to countries wishing to develop their activities at sea.

The IMO had 157 members as at April 1999. It is governed by an Assembly comprising delegates of all its members. It meets biennially to formulate policy, set a budget (1998–9, £36.6 million), vote on specific recommendations on pollution and maritime safety and elect the

Council. The Council fulfils the functions of the Assembly between sessions and appoints the Secretary-General. It consists of 32 members: eight from the world's largest shipping nations, eight from the nations most dependent on seaborne trade, and 16 other members to ensure a fair geographical representation. The Maritime Safety Committee, through its sub-committees, makes reports and recommendations to the Council and the Assembly. There are a number of other specialist subsidiary committees, including one for marine environmental protection.

The IMO acts as the secretariat for the London Convention (1972) which regulates the disposal of land-generated waste at sea.

Secretary-General, William A. O'Neil (Canada)

INTERNATIONAL MONETARY FUND

700 19th Street NW, Washington DC 20431, USA
Tel: Washington DC 623 7300; fax: Washington DC 623 6278
E-mail: publicaffairs@imf.org
Web: http://www.imf.org

The International Monetary Fund (IMF) was established in 1944, at the UN Monetary and Financial Conference held at Bretton Woods, New Hampshire. Its Articles of Agreement entered into force in 1945 and it began operations in 1947.

The IMF exists to promote international monetary co-operation, the expansion of world trade, and exchange stability. It advises members on their economic and financial policies; promotes policy co-ordination among the major industrial countries; and gives technical assistance in central banking, balance of payments accounting, taxation, and other financial matters. The IMF serves as a forum for members to discuss important financial and monetary issues and seeks the balanced growth of international trade and, through this, high levels of employment, income and productive capacity. As at March 1999 the IMF had 182 members.

Upon joining the IMF, a member is assigned a 'quota', based on the member's relative standing in the world economy and its balance of payments position, that determines its capital subscription to the Fund, its access to IMF resources, its voting power, and its share in the allocation of Special Drawing Rights (SDRs). Quotas are reviewed every five years and adjusted accordingly. Since the 11th General Review of quotas in 1999, total Fund quotas stand at SDR 212 billion. The SDR, an international reserve asset issued by the IMF, is calculated daily on a basket of usable currencies and is the IMF's unit of account; on 30 April 1999, SDR 1 equalled US$1.35123. SDRs are allocated at intervals to supplement members' reserves and thereby improve international financial liquidity.

IMF financial resources derive primarily from members' capital subscriptions, which are equivalent to their quotas. In addition, the IMF is authorized to borrow from official lenders. It may also draw on a line of credit of SDR 18.5 billion from various countries under the so-called General Arrangements to Borrow (GAB). Periodic charges are also levied on financial assistance. At the end of April 1999, total outstanding IMF credits amounted to SDR 67.2 billion.

The IMF is not a bank and does not lend money; it provides temporary financial assistance by selling a member's SDRs or other members' currencies in exchange for the member's own currency. The member can then use the purchased currency to alleviate its balance of payments difficulties. The IMF's credit under its regular facilities is made available to members in tranches or segments of 25 per cent of quota. For first credit tranche purchases, members are required to demonstrate reasonable efforts to overcome their balance of payments difficulties. There are no performance criteria. Upper credit tranche purchases are normally associated with stand-by arrangements and are aimed at overcoming balance of payment difficulties and are required to meet certain performance criteria. Repurchases are made in three and a quarter to five years.

The IMF supports long-term efforts at economic reform and transformation as well as medium-term programmes under the extended Fund facility, which runs for three to four years and is aimed at overcoming balance of payments difficulties stemming from macroeconomic and structural problems. Members experiencing a temporary balance of payments shortfall have access to the compensatory and contingency financing facility. The IMF also offers credits to low-income countries engaged in economic reform through its enhanced structural adjustment facility (ESAF). As at 28 February 1999, SDR 7.0 billion in ESAF loans is outstanding.

The IMF is headed by a Board of Governors, comprising representatives of all members, which meets annually. The Governors delegate powers to 24 Executive Directors, who are appointed or elected by member countries. The Executive Directors operate the Fund on a daily basis under a Managing Director, whom they elect.

Managing Director, Michel Camdessus (France)
UK Executive Director, Gus O'Donnell, Room 11-120, IMF, 700 19th Street NW, Washington DC 20431, USA

INTERNATIONAL RED CROSS AND RED CRESCENT MOVEMENT

17 avenue de la Paix, CH-1211 Geneva, Switzerland
Web: http://www.icrc.org

The International Red Cross and Red Crescent Movement is composed of three elements. The International Committee of the Red Cross (ICRC), the organization's founding body, was formed in 1863. It aims to negotiate between warring factions and to protect and assist victims of armed conflict. It also seeks to ensure the application of the Geneva Conventions with regard to prisoners of war and detainees.

The International Federation of Red Cross and Red Crescent Societies was founded in 1919 to contribute to the development of the humanitarian activities of national societies, to co-ordinate their relief operations for victims of natural disasters, and to care for refugees outside areas of conflict. There are Red Cross and Red Crescent Societies in 175 countries, with a total membership of 250 million.

The International Conference of the Red Cross and Red Crescent meets every four years, bringing together delegates of the ICRC, the International Federation and the national societies, as well as representatives of nations bound by the Geneva Conventions.

President of the ICRC, Jakob Kellenberger
BRITISH RED CROSS, 9 Grosvenor Crescent, London SW1X 7EJ. Tel: 0171-235 5454; fax: 0171-245 6315.
E-mail: information@redcross.org.uk Web: http://www.redcross.org.uk/vauxhall.htm *Director-General*, Sam Younger

INTERNATIONAL TELECOMMUNICATIONS SATELLITE ORGANIZATION
3400 International Drive NW, Washington DC
20008–3098, USA
Tel: Washington DC 944 6800; fax: Washington DC
944 7898
E-mail: customer.service@intelsat.int
Web: http://www.intelsat.int

The International Telecommunications Satellite Organization (Intelsat) was formed in 1964. It owns and operates the world-wide commercial communications satellite system which is composed of 20 satellites and more than 4,000 antennas which connect over 200 countries, territories and dependencies. Intelsat provides international and domestic voice/data and video services.

Each of the 142 member states contributes to the capital costs of the organization in proportion to its investment share, which is based on its relative usage of the system.

There is a four-tier hierarchy. The Assembly of Parties to the agreement meets every two years to consider long-term objectives and is composed of representatives of the member governments. The Meeting of Signatories annually considers the financial, technical and operational aspects of the system. The Board of Governors has 28 members; INTELSAT Management is the permanent staff of the organization and is headed by a Director-General who reports to the Board of Governors.

Director-General, Conny Kullman (Sweden)

INTERNATIONAL TELECOMMUNICATION UNION
Place des Nations, CH-1211 Geneva 20, Switzerland
Tel: Geneva 730 5111; fax: Geneva 733 7256
E-mail: intumail@itu.org
Web: http://www.itu.org

The International Telecommunication Union (ITU) was founded in Paris in 1865 as the International Telegraph Union and became a UN specialized agency in 1947. It promotes international co-operation and sets standards and regulations for the interconnection of telecommunications systems of all kinds. It assists the development of telecommunications in developing countries by providing technical assistance, management, investment financing and network installation. The ITU adopts international regulations and treaties to allocate the radio frequency spectrum and registers radio frequency assignments in order to avoid harmful interference between radio stations of different countries. It also governs and allocates the use of the geostationary-satellite orbit and collects and disseminates telecommunications information.

The ITU had 187 member states and 433 members (scientific and industrial companies, broadcasters, public and private operators, and international organizations) as at June 1997. The supreme authority is the Plenipotentiary Conference, composed of representatives of all the members, which meets once every four years. It elects the Administrative Council of 46 members which meets annually to supervise the Union and set the budget (1996–7, SFr 295 million). The Conference also elects the Secretary-General, who heads the General Secretariat. The ITU is structured into three sectors: the radiocommunication sector, including world and regional radiocommunication conferences, radiocommunication assemblies and the Radio Regulations Board; the telecommunication standardization sector; and the telecommunication development sector.

Secretary-General, Yoshio Utsumi (Japan)

LEAGUE OF ARAB STATES
Maidane Al-Tahrir, Cairo, Egypt
Tel: Cairo 750 511; fax: Cairo 574 0331

The purpose of the League of Arab States, founded in 1945, is to ensure co-operation among member states and protect their independence and sovereignty, to supervise the affairs and interests of Arab countries, to control the execution of agreements concluded among the member states, and to promote the process of integration among them. The League considers itself a regional organization and has observer status at the United Nations.

Member states are Algeria, Bahrain, the Comoros, Djibouti, Egypt, Iraq, Jordan, Kuwait, Lebanon, Libya, Mauritania, Morocco, Oman, Palestine, Qatar, Saudi Arabia, Somalia, Sudan, Syria, Tunisia, UAE and Yemen.

Member states participate in various specialized agencies of the League whose role is to develop specific areas of co-operation between Arab states. These include: the Arab Organization for Mineral Resources; the Arab Monetary Fund; the Arab Satellite Communications Organization; the Arab Academy of Maritime Transport; the Arab Bank for Economic Development in Africa; the Arab League Educational, Cultural and Scientific Organization and the Council of Arab Economic Unity.

Secretary-General, Dr Ahmed Esmat Abdul-Maguid
  (Egypt)
UK Office, 52 Green Street, London wiy 3rh. Tel: 0171-629 0044; fax: 0171-493 7943

THE NORDIC COUNCIL

The Nordic Council was established in March 1952 as an advisory body on economic and social co-operation, comprising parliamentary delegates from Denmark, Iceland, Norway and Sweden. It was subsequently joined by Finland (1956), and representatives from the Faröes (1970), the Åland Islands (1970), and Greenland (1984).

Co-operation is regulated by the Treaty of Helsinki signed in 1962. This was amended in 1971 to create the Nordic Council of Ministers, which discusses all matters except defence and foreign affairs. Matters are given preparatory consideration by a Committee of Co-operation Ministers' Deputies and joint committees of officials. Decisions of the Council of Ministers, which are taken by consensus, are binding, although if ratification by member parliaments is required, decisions only become effective following parliamentary approval. The Council of Ministers is advised by the Nordic Council, to which it reports annually. There are Ministers for Nordic Co-operation in every member government.

The Nordic Council, comprising 87 voting delegates nominated from member parliaments and about 80 non-voting government representatives, meets at least once a year in plenary sessions. The full Council chooses an 11-member Praesidium, comprising two delegates from each sovereign member and one party group-nominated delegate, which conducts business between sessions. A Secretariat, located in Stockholm and headed by a Secretary-General, liaises with the Council of Ministers and provides administrative support, as well as acting as a publishing house and information centre. The Council of Ministers has a separate Secretariat, based in Copenhagen.

SECRETARIAT OF THE PRAESIDIUM OF THE NORDIC
COUNCIL, Tyrgatan 7,
PO Box 19506, S-10432 Stockholm, Sweden. Tel:
Stockholm 786 4000; fax: Stockholm 786 6129. Web:
http://www.norden.org. *Secretary-General,* Anders
Wenström (Sweden)

SECRETARIAT OF THE NORDIC COUNCIL OF
MINISTERS, Store Strandstraede 18, DK-1255
Copenhagen K, Denmark. *Secretary-General,* Per
Stenback (Finland)

NORTH ATLANTIC TREATY ORGANIZATION
Brussels B-1110, Belgium
Tel: Brussels 707 4111; fax: Brussels 707 4579
E-mail: natodoc@hq.nato.int
Web: http://www.nato.int

The North Atlantic Treaty (Treaty of Washington) was
signed in 1949 by Belgium, Canada, Denmark, France,
Iceland, Italy, Luxembourg, the Netherlands, Norway,
Portugal, the UK and the USA. Greece and Turkey
acceded to the Treaty in 1952, the Federal Republic of
Germany in 1955 (the reunited Germany acceded in
October 1990), Spain in 1982, and the Czech Republic,
Hungary and Poland in 1999.

The North Atlantic Treaty Organization (NATO) is
the structural framework for a defensive political and
military alliance designed to provide common security for
its members through co-operation and consultation in
political, military and economic as well as scientific and
other non-military fields.

STRUCTURE

The North Atlantic Council (NAC), chaired by the
Secretary-General, is the highest authority of the Alliance
and is composed of permanent representatives of the 19
member countries. It meets at ministerial level (foreign
ministers) at least twice a year. The permanent representatives (ambassadors) head national delegations of advisers
and experts. The Defence Planning Committee (DPC),
composed of representatives of all member countries, deals
with defence matters. The DPC also meets at ministerial
level (defence ministers) at least twice a year. Nuclear
matters are dealt with in the Nuclear Planning Group
(NPG), composed of representatives of all countries except
for France. The NPG meets regularly at Permanent
Representative level and twice a year at ministerial level
(defence ministers). The NATO Secretary-General chairs
the Council, the DPC and the NPG.

The Council and DPC are forums for constant intergovernmental consultation and are the main decision-
making bodies within the Alliance. They are assisted by an
International Staff, divided into five divisions: political
affairs; defence planning and operations; defence support;
security investment, logistics and civil emergency planning;
scientific and environmental affairs.

The senior military authority in NATO, under the
Council and DPC, is the Military Committee composed of
the Chief of Defence Staffs of each member country except
Iceland, which has no military and may be represented by
a civilian. The Military Committee, which is assisted by
an integrated international military staff, also meets in
permanent session with permanent military representatives
and is responsible for making recommendations to the
Council and DPC on measures considered necessary for
the common defence of the NATO area and for supplying
guidance on military matters to the major NATO

commanders. The Chairman of the Military Committee,
elected for a period of two to three years, represents the
committee on the Council.

The strategic area covered by the North Atlantic Treaty
is divided between two major NATO commands (MNCs),
European and Atlantic; and three major subordinate
commands (MSCs) within Allied Command Europe, South,
Central and North-West. There is also a Regional Planning
Group (Canada and the United States).

The major NATO commanders are responsible for the
development of defence plans for their respective areas, for
the determination of force requirements and for the
deployment and exercise of the forces under their
command. The major NATO commanders report to the
Military Committee. The integrated military structure of
the Alliance has been reorganized. The new structure,
based on reduced numbers of permanent headquarters and
more flexible and mobile forces, is expected to be fully in
place by 2003.

POST-COLD WAR DEVELOPMENTS

In response to the new security environment arising from
the demise of the Warsaw Pact and the end of the Cold
War in 1990, NATO issued a Declaration of Peace and
Co-operation in 1991, and published a new strategic
concept which introduced organizational changes and force
reductions of around 30 per cent. The strategic concept
was subsequently revised and updated and a new edition
was published in April 1999.

The Euro-Atlantic Partnership Council (EAPC), which
was established in 1997 as a replacement for the North
Atlantic Co-operation Council (NACC), was formed to
develop closer security links with eastern European and
former Soviet states. It focuses on defence planning,
defence industry conversion, defence management and
force structuring, and the democratic concepts of civilian-
military relations. The EAPC provides the framework for
consultations and co-operation under the Partnership for
Peace (PFP) programme, a form of association with NATO
launched in 1994. NATO will consult with any PFP
partner that perceives a direct threat to its territorial
integrity, political independence or security. Most of the
27 PFP partners send liaison officers to NATO headquarters in Brussels and to the Partnership Co-ordination Cell
in Mons, Belgium, and participate in joint military exercises
co-ordinated by NATO. EAPC membership is open to all
former NACC members and PFP participants. It meets
monthly at ambassadorial level in Brussels and twice a year
at foreign minister and defence minister level.

In 1994, NATO announced that it would consider
admitting new members, and in March 1999, Poland, the
Czech Republic and Hungary acceded to the Treaty. The
NATO-Ukraine Charter, signed in July 1997, recognized
the importance to European security of a democratic and
independent Ukraine, and set up a programme for further
co-operation in the future. Russian opposition to NATO's
enlargement was tempered by the signing of a Founding
Act on Mutual Relations, Co-operation and Security in
May 1997, which provided for the creation of a Permanent
Joint Council. Russian participation was suspended in
March 1999 as a result of NATO's stance on the conflict
in Kosovo.

In 1996 the NAC proposed the creation of combined
joint task forces which would provide European NATO
members with a framework for operations without US
involvement, under the auspices of the Western Europe
Union. The strengthening of the European Defence
Identity was one of several objectives developed in the
new strategic concept issued by the Alliance at the
Washington summit.

From 1992 until the end of 1995, NATO provided

support for UN peacekeeping efforts in the former Yugoslavia. With the signing of the Bosnian peace agreement in 1995, a NATO-led multinational Implementation Force (IFOR) embarked on Operation Joint Endeavour to implement the peace accord; IFOR was replaced by the Sustaining Force (SFOR) in December 1996.

In March 1999, NATO began air operations against military and industrial targets in Yugoslavia following the repression and ethnic cleansing of ethnic Albanians in Kosovo.

Secretary-General and Chairman of the North Atlantic Council, of the DPC and of the NPG, Javier Solana (Spain)

UK Permanent Representative on the North Atlantic Council, Sir John Goulden, KCMG

Chairman of the Military Committee, Adm. Guido Venturoni (Italy)

Supreme Allied Commander, Europe, Gen. Wesley Clark (USA)

Supreme Allied Commander, Atlantic, Adm. Harold W. Gehman, Jnr. (USA)

ORGANIZATION FOR ECONOMIC CO-OPERATION AND DEVELOPMENT

2 rue André-Pascal, F-75116 Paris
Tel: Paris 4524 8200; fax: Paris 4524 8500
Web: http://www.oecd.org

The Organization for Economic Co-operation and Development (OECD) was formed in 1961 to replace the Organization for European Economic Co-operation. It is the instrument for international co-operation among industrialized member countries on economic and social policies. Its objectives are to assist its member governments in the formulation and co-ordination of policies designed to achieve high, sustained economic growth while maintaining financial stability, to contribute to world trade on a multilateral basis and to stimulate members' aid to developing countries.

The members are Australia, Austria, Belgium, Canada, the Czech Republic, Denmark, Finland, France, Germany, Greece, Hungary, Iceland, the Republic of Ireland, Italy, Japan, the Republic of Korea, Luxembourg, Mexico, the Netherlands, New Zealand, Norway, Poland, Portugal, Spain, Sweden, Switzerland, Turkey, the UK and the USA. The Council is the supreme body of the organization. It is composed of one representative for each member country and meets at permanent representative level under the chairmanship of the Secretary-General, and at ministerial level (usually once a year) under the chairmanship of a minister elected annually. Decisions and recommendations are adopted by the unanimous agreement of all members. Most of the OECD's work is undertaken in over 200 specialized committees and working parties. Five autonomous or semi-autonomous bodies are associated in varying degrees to the Organization: the Nuclear Energy Agency, the International Energy Agency, the Development Centre, the Centre for Educational Research and Innovation, and the European Conference of Ministers of Transport. These bodies, the committees and the Council are serviced by an international Secretariat headed by the Secretary-General.

Secretary-General, Donald J. Johnston (Canada)

UK Permanent Representative, HE Christopher Crabbie, 19 rue de Franqueville, Paris 75116

ORGANIZATION FOR SECURITY AND CO-OPERATION IN EUROPE

Kärntner Ring 5–7, A-1010 Vienna, Austria
Tel: Vienna 514 360; fax: Vienna 514 3696
E-mail: pm@osce.org
Web: http://www.osce.org

The Organization for Security and Co-operation in Europe (OSCE) was launched in 1975 (as the Conference on Security and Co-operation in Europe (CSCE)) under the Helsinki Final Act. This established agreements between NATO members, Warsaw Pact members, and neutral and non-aligned European countries covering security in Europe; economic, scientific, technological and environmental co-operation; and humanitarian principles. Further conferences were held at Belgrade (1977–8), Madrid (1980–3) and Vienna (1986–9).

With the end of the Cold War, it was decided that the CSCE should be institutionalized to provide a new security framework for Europe. The Charter of Paris for a New Europe, signed on 21 November 1990, committed members to support multi-party democracy, free-market economics, the rule of law, and human rights. The signatories also agreed to regular meetings of heads of government, ministers and officials. The first institutionalized heads of state and government summit was held in Helsinki in December 1992, at which the Helsinki Document was adopted. This declared the CSCE to be a regional organization and defined the structures of the organization. The summit also appointed a High Commissioner on National Minorities. At its December 1994 summit CSCE was renamed the Organization for Security and Co-operation in Europe.

Three structures have been established: the Ministerial Council of foreign ministers, the central decision-making and governing body, which meets at least once a year; the Senior Council, which prepares work for the Ministerial Council, carries out its decisions and is responsible for the overview, management and co-ordination of OSCE activities and meets at least three times a year; and the Permanent Council, which is responsible for the day-to-day operational tasks of the OSCE and is the regular body for political consultation, meeting weekly. The chairmanship of the Ministerial Council, Senior Council and Permanent Council rotates among participating states with the Senior Council meeting in Prague and the Permanent Council in Vienna.

The OSCE is also underpinned by five permanent institutions: a Secretariat (Vienna); a Forum for Security Co-operation (Vienna), which meets weekly to discuss arms control, disarmament and security-building measures; an Office for Democratic Institutions and Human Rights (Warsaw), which is charged with furthering human rights, democracy and the rule of law; an office of the High Commissioner on National Minorities (The Hague), which identifies ethnic tensions that might endanger peace and promotes their resolution; and a Representative on Freedom of the Media (Vienna), which is responsible for assisting governments in the furthering of free, independent and pluralistic media. There is also a documentation and conference centre in Prague, an OSCE Parliamentary Assembly with a secretariat based in Copenhagen, and a Court of Conciliation and Arbitration in Geneva.

In June 1991 the CSCE agreed upon new crisis prevention mechanisms to prevent or manage violent conflict between and within member countries. The OSCE has monitoring missions in ten OSCE countries, has sent an assistance group to Chechenia, co-ordinates the international presence in Albania, and has an advisory and monitoring group in Belarus. It is also organizing a peacekeeping force in Nagorno-Karabakh. The OSCE supervised all elections in Bosnia-Hercegovina between 1996 and 1998. A Joint Consultative Group of the OSCE promotes the objectives and implementation of the Conventional Armed Forces in Europe (CFE) Treaty (1990) which limits conventional ground and air forces.

The OSCE has 55 participating states: Albania, Andorra, Armenia, Austria, Azerbaijan, Belarus, Belgium, Bosnia-Hercegovina, Bulgaria, Canada, Croatia, Cyprus, the Czech Republic, Denmark, Estonia, Finland, France, Georgia, Germany, Greece, Hungary, Iceland, the Republic of Ireland, Italy, Kazakhstan, Kyrgyzstan, Latvia, Liechtenstein, Lithuania, Luxembourg, Macedonia (Former Yugoslav Republic of), Malta, Moldova, Monaco, the Netherlands, Norway, Poland, Portugal, Romania, Russia, San Marino, Slovakia, Slovenia, Spain, Sweden, Switzerland, Tajikistan, Turkey, Turkmenistan, the UK, Ukraine, the USA, Uzbekistan, the Vatican and Yugoslavia (suspended from activities July 1992).
Chair of the OSCE, Norway (1999); Austria (2000)
Secretary-General of the OSCE, Giancarlo Aragona (Italy)
Director of the Office for Democratic Institutions and Human Rights, Gérard Stoudmann (Switzerland)
OSCE High Commissioner on National Minorities, Max van der Stoel (Netherlands)
Representative on Freedom of the Media, Freimut Duve (Germany)

ORGANIZATION OF AFRICAN UNITY
PO Box 3243, Addis Ababa, Ethiopia
Tel: Addis Ababa 517700; fax: Addis Ababa 513036

The Organization of African Unity (OAU) was established in 1963 and has 53 members; Morocco suspended its participation in 1985 in protest at the Polisario-proclaimed Saharan Arab Democratic Republic (SADR), representing Western Sahara, being admitted as a member. The OAU aims to further African unity and solidarity, to co-ordinate political, economic, social and defence policies, and to eliminate colonialism in Africa.

The chief organs are the Assembly of heads of state or government, which is the supreme organ of the OAU and meets once a year to consider matters of common African concern and to co-ordinate the Organization's policies; the Council of foreign ministers, which is the Organization's executive body responsible for the implementation of the Assembly's policies, and which meets twice a year; and the Commission of Mediation, Conciliation and Arbitration which promotes the peaceful settlement of disputes between member countries. The main administrative body is the General Secretariat, based in Addis Ababa, headed by a Secretary-General who is elected by the Assembly for a four-year term.

Substantial budgetary arrears due to delays in the payment of national contributions has meant that the OAU continually faces difficulties in furthering its aims. Its budget for 1997–8 was set at US$30.85 million; several OAU programmes have been suspended since November 1994 when unpaid contributions reached US$77 million, although by June 1995 arrears had dropped to US$38.3 million. In June 1991 the Assembly adopted an African Economic Community Treaty which envisages establishment of the Economic Community after ratification by two-thirds of the OAU's membership. In June 1993 a mechanism was created for conflict prevention, management and resolution, and a peace fund was established.

Secretary-General, Salim Ahmed Salim (Tanzania)

ORGANIZATION OF AMERICAN STATES
17th Street and Constitution Avenue NW,
Washington DC 20006, USA
Tel: Washington DC 458 3000; fax: Washington DC 458 6421
E-mail: pi@oas.org
Web: http://www.oas.org

Originally founded in 1890 for largely commercial purposes, the Organization of American States (OAS) adopted its present name and charter in 1948. The charter entered into force in 1951 and was amended in 1967, 1985 and 1996; the 1992 Protocol of Washington will enter into force upon ratification by two-thirds of member states.

The OAS aims to strengthen the peace and security of the continent; to promote and consolidate representative democracy with due respect for the principle of non-intervention; to prevent possible causes of difficulties and to ensure the peaceful resolution of disputes arising among its member states; to provide for common action on the part of those states in the event of aggression; to seek the resolution of political, judicial and economic problems that may arise among them; to promote, by co-operative action, their economic, social and cultural development; and to achieve an effective limitation of conventional weapons so that resources can be devoted to economic and social development.

The Declaration of Principles and the Plan of Action resulting from the 1994 Miami summit and signed by all the members except Cuba, envisage the establishment of a free trade area, in which barriers to trade and investment will be progressively eliminated.

Policy is determined by the annual General Assembly, which is the supreme authority and elects the Secretary-General for a five-year term. The Meeting of Consultation of ministers of foreign affairs considers urgent problems on an *ad hoc* basis. The Permanent Council, comprising one representative from each member state, promotes friendly inter-state relations, acts as an intermediary in case of disputes arising between states and oversees the General Secretariat, the main administrative body. The Inter-American Council for Integral Development was created in 1996 by the ratification of the Protocol of Managua to promote sustainable development.

The 35 member states are Antigua and Barbuda, Argentina, Bahamas, Barbados, Belize, Bolivia, Brazil, Canada, Chile, Colombia, Costa Rica, Cuba, Dominica, Dominican Republic, Ecuador, El Salvador, Grenada, Guatemala, Guyana, Haiti, Honduras, Jamaica, Mexico, Nicaragua, Panama, Paraguay, Peru, St Christopher and Nevis, St Lucia, St Vincent and the Grenadines, Suriname, Trinidad and Tobago, Uruguay, the USA and Venezuela. The European Union and 39 non-American states have permanent observer status.
Secretary-General, Dr César Gaviria Trujillo (Colombia)

ORGANIZATION OF ARAB PETROLEUM EXPORTING COUNTRIES
PO Box 20501, Safat 13066, Kuwait
Tel: Kuwait 484 4500; fax: Kuwait 481 5747
E-mail: oapec@qualitynet.net
Web: http://www.kuwait.net/~oapec

The Organization of Arab Petroleum and Exporting Countries (OAPEC) was founded in 1968. Its objectives are to promote co-operation in economic activities, to safeguard members' interests, to unite efforts to ensure the flow of oil to consumer markets, and to create a favourable climate for the investment of capital and expertise.

The Ministerial Council is composed of oil ministers from the member countries and meets twice a year to determine policy and to approve the budgets and accounts of the General Secretariat and the Judicial Tribunal. The Judicial Tribunal is composed of seven part-time judges who rule on disputes between member countries and disputes between countries and oil companies. The executive organ of OAPEC is the General Secretariat.

The members are Algeria, Bahrain, Egypt, Iraq, Kuwait, Libya, Qatar, Saudi Arabia, Syria and the United Arab Emirates. Tunisia's membership has been inactive since 1987.

Secretary-General, Abdel-Aziz A. Al-Turki

ORGANIZATION OF THE ISLAMIC CONFERENCE
PO Box 178, Jeddah 21411, Saudi Arabia
Tel: Jeddah 680 0800; fax: Jeddah 687 3568

The Organization of the Islamic Conference (OIC) was established in 1971 with the purpose of promoting solidarity and co-operation between Islamic countries. It also has the specific aims of co-ordinating efforts to safeguard the Muslim holy places, supporting the formation of a Palestinian state, assisting member states to maintain their independence, co-ordinating the views of member states in international forums such as the UN, and improving co-operation in the economic, cultural and scientific fields.

The OIC has three central organs, supreme among them the Conference of the Heads of State which meets once every three years to discuss issues of importance to Islamic states. The Conference of Foreign Ministers meets annually to prepare reports for the Conference of Heads of State. The General Secretariat carries out administrative tasks. It is headed by a Secretary-General who is elected by the Conference of Foreign Ministers for a non-renewable four-year term.

In addition to this structure, the OIC has several subsidiary bodies and specialized bodies. These include the Islamic Solidarity Fund, to aid Islamic institutions in member countries, and the Islamic Development Bank, to finance development projects in poorer member states. An Islamic Court of Justice is planned. The OIC runs various offices to organize the economic boycott of Israel.

The achievement of the OIC's aims has often been prevented by political rivalry and conflicts between member states, such as the Iran-Iraq war and the Iraqi invasion of Kuwait. Egypt's membership was suspended from 1979 to 1984 because of its peace treaty with Israel. Saudi Arabia, the main source of funding, exercises great influence within the OIC. Since 1991 the OIC has become more united and has spoken out against violence against Muslims in India, the Occupied Territories and Bosnia-Hercegovina. From 1993 to 1995 the OIC co-ordinated the offering of troops to the UN by Muslim states to protect Muslim areas of Bosnia-Hercegovina.

The Organization has 55 members (54 sovereign Muslim states in Africa, the Middle East, central and south-east Asia and Europe, plus the Palestine Liberation Organization) and three observers, the Central African Republic, Turkish Northern Cyprus and Côte d'Ivoire. It has an annual budget of £5 million.

Secretary-General, Azzedine Laraki (Morocco)

ORGANIZATION OF THE PETROLEUM EXPORTING COUNTRIES
Obere Donaustrasse 93, A-1020 Vienna, Austria
Tel: Vienna 211 120; fax: Vienna 214 9827
E-mail: info@opec.org
Web: http://www.opec.org

The Organization of the Petroleum Exporting Countries (OPEC) was created in 1960 as a permanent intergovernmental organization with the principal aims of unifying and co-ordinating the petroleum policies of its members, determining ways of protecting their interests individually and collectively, and ensuring the stabilization of prices in international oil markets with a view to eliminating unnecessary fluctuations. Since 1982 OPEC has attempted (only partially successfully) to impose overall production limits and production quotas in an attempt to maintain stable oil prices. In March 1998, OPEC members and a number of the main non-OPEC producers agreed to reduce oil production by 1.5 million barrels per day to boost oil prices, which had fallen to their lowest level in real terms since 1973.

The supreme authority is the Conference of Ministers of oil, mines and energy of member countries, which meets at least twice a year to formulate policy. The Board of Governors, nominated by member countries, directs the management of OPEC and implements conference resolutions. The Secretariat carries out executive functions under the direction of the Board of Governors.

The member states are Algeria, Indonesia, Iran, Iraq, Kuwait, Libya, Nigeria, Qatar, Saudi Arabia, UAE and Venezuela. Ecuador withdrew in 1992 and Gabon in 1995.

Secretary-General, HE Dr Rilwanu Lukman (Nigeria)

THE PACIFIC COMMUNITY
BP D5, 98848 Nouméa Cedex, New Caledonia
Tel: Nouméa 262000; fax: Nouméa 263818
E-mail: spc@spc.org.nc
Web: http://www.spc.org.nc

The Pacific Community (formerly the South Pacific Commission) was established in 1947 by Australia, France, the Netherlands, New Zealand, the UK and the USA with the aim of promoting the economic and social stability of the islands in the region. The Community now numbers 27 member states and territories: the five remaining founder states (the Netherlands has withdrawn), in which no programmes are run, and the other 22 states and territories of Melanesia, Micronesia and Polynesia.

The Secretariat of the Pacific Community (SPC) is a technical assistance agency with programmes in agriculture and plant protection, fisheries and marine resources, community health, socio-economic and statistical services, and community education services.

The governing body is the Conference of the Pacific Community, which meets every two years. The Director-General is the chief executive.

Director-General, Bob Dun (Australia)
Deputy Directors-General, Jimmie Rodgers (Solomon Islands); Lourdes Pangelinan (Guam)

THE UNITED NATIONS
UN Plaza, New York, NY 10017, USA
Tel: New York 963 1234
Web: http://www.un.org

The United Nations (UN) is an intergovernmental organization of member states, dedicated through signature of the UN Charter to the maintenance of international peace and security and the solution of economic, social and political problems through international co-operation.

The UN was founded as a successor to the League of Nations and inherited many of its procedures and institutions. The name 'United Nations' was first used in the Washington Declaration 1942 to describe the 26 states which had allied to fight the Axis powers. The UN Charter developed from discussions at the Moscow Conference of the foreign ministers of China, the UK, the USA and the Soviet Union in 1943. Further progress was made at Dumbarton Oaks, Washington, in 1944 during talks involving the same states. The role of the Security Council was formulated at the Yalta Conference in 1945. The Charter was formally drawn up by 50 allied nations at the San Francisco Conference between April and 26 June 1945, when it was signed. Following ratification the UN came into effect on 24 October 1945, which is celebrated annually as United Nations Day. The UN flag is light blue with the UN emblem centred in white.

The principal organs of the UN are the General Assembly, the Security Council, the Economic and Social Council, the Trusteeship Council, the Secretariat and the International Court of Justice. The Economic and Social Council and the Trusteeship Council are auxiliaries, charged with assisting and advising the General Assembly and Security Council. The official languages used are Arabic, Chinese, English, French, Russian and Spanish. Deliberations at the International Court of Justice are in English and French only.

MEMBERSHIP

Membership is open to all countries which accept the Charter and its principle of peaceful co-existence. New members are admitted by the General Assembly on the recommendation of the Security Council. The original membership of 51 states has grown to 185:

Afghanistan
Albania
Algeria
Andorra
Angola
Antigua and Barbuda
*Argentina
Armenia
*Australia
Austria
Azerbaijan
The Bahamas
Bahrain
Bangladesh
Barbados
*Belarus
*Belgium
Belize
Benin
Bhutan
*Bolivia
Bosnia-Hercegovina
Botswana
*Brazil
Brunei

Bulgaria
Burkina Faso
Burundi
Cambodia (suspended)
Cameroon
*Canada
Cape Verde
Central African Rep.
Chad
*Chile
*China
*Colombia
The Comoros
Congo, Democratic Rep.
Congo, Rep. of
*Costa Rica
Côte d'Ivoire
Croatia
*Cuba
Cyprus
*Czech Republic
*Denmark
Djibouti
Dominica
*Dominican Republic

*Ecuador
*Egypt
*El Salvador
Equatorial Guinea
Eritrea
Estonia
*Ethiopia
Federated States of
   Micronesia
Fiji
Finland
*France
Gabon
Gambia
Georgia
Germany
Ghana
*Greece
Grenada
*Guatemala
Guinea
Guinea-Bissau
Guyana
*Haiti
*Honduras
Hungary
Iceland
*India
Indonesia
*Iran
*Iraq
Ireland, Republic of
Israel
Italy
Jamaica
Japan
Jordan
Kazakhstan
Kenya
Korea, D. P. Rep. (North)
Korea, Rep. of (South)
Kuwait
Kyrgyzstan
Laos
Latvia
*Lebanon
Lesotho
*Liberia
Libya
Liechtenstein
Lithuania
*Luxembourg
Macedonia (Former
   Yugoslav Republic of)
Madagascar
Malawi
Malaysia
Maldives
Mali
Malta
Marshall Islands
Mauritania
Mauritius
*Mexico
Moldova
Monaco
Mongolia
Morocco
Mozambique

Myanmar (Burma)
Namibia
Nepal
*Netherlands
*New Zealand
*Nicaragua
Niger
Nigeria
*Norway
Oman
Pakistan
Palau
*Panama
Papua New Guinea
*Paraguay
*Peru
*Philippines
*Poland
Portugal
Qatar
Romania
*Russian Federation
Rwanda
St Christopher and Nevis
St Lucia
St Vincent and the
   Grenadines
Samoa
San Marino
São Tomé and Príncipe
*Saudi Arabia
Senegal
Seychelles
Sierra Leone
Singapore
*Slovakia
Slovenia
Solomon Islands
Somalia
*South Africa
Spain
Sri Lanka
Sudan
Suriname
Swaziland
Sweden
*Syria
Tajikistan
Tanzania
Thailand
Togo
Trinidad and Tobago
Tunisia
*Turkey
Turkmenistan
Uganda
*Ukraine
United Arab Emirates
*United Kingdom
*United States of America
*Uruguay
Uzbekistan
Vanuatu
*Venezuela
Vietnam
Yemen
*Yugoslavia (suspended)
Zambia
Zimbabwe

*Original member (i.e. from 1945)

From 25 October 1971 'China' was taken to mean the People's Republic of China. Czechoslovakia was an original member in 1945 and a member until 31 December 1992; the successor states of the Czech Republic and Slovakia were admitted as members in January 1993.

The Russian Federation took over the membership of the Soviet Union in the Security Council and all other UN organs on 24 December 1991. Belarus (formerly Belorussia) and Ukraine on becoming independent sovereign states continued their existing memberships of the UN, both having been granted separate UN membership in 1945 as a concession to the Soviet Union.

OBSERVERS

Permanent observer status is held by the Holy See and Switzerland. The Palestine Liberation Organization has special observer status.

NON-MEMBERS

A number of countries are not members, usually due to their small size and limited financial resources. Notable exceptions include Switzerland, which follows a policy of absolute neutrality, and Taiwan, which was replaced by the People's Republic of China in 1971. The others are Kiribati, Nauru, Tonga, Tuvalu and the Holy See.

THE GENERAL ASSEMBLY

UN Plaza, New York, NY 10017, USA

The General Assembly is the main deliberative organ of the UN. It consists of all members, each entitled to five representatives but having only one vote. The annual session begins on the third Tuesday of September, when the President is elected, and usually continues until mid-December. Special sessions are held on specific issues and emergency special sessions can be called within 24 hours.

The Assembly is empowered to discuss any matter within the scope of the Charter, except when it is under consideration by the Security Council, and to make recommendations. Under the 'uniting for peace' resolution, adopted in 1950, the Assembly may also take action to maintain international peace and security when the Security Council fails to do so because of a lack of unanimity of its permanent members. Important decisions, such as those on peace and security, the election of officers, the budget, etc., need a two-thirds majority. Others need a simple majority. The Assembly has effective power only over the internal operations of the UN itself; external recommendations are not legally binding.

The work of the General Assembly is divided among six main committees, on each of which every member has the right to be represented: disarmament and international security; economic and financial; social, humanitarian and cultural; special political issues and decolonization (including non-self governing territories); administrative and budgetary; and legal. In addition, the General Assembly appoints *ad hoc* committees to consider special issues, such as human rights, peacekeeping, disarmament and international law. All committees consider items referred to them by the Assembly and recommend draft resolutions to its plenary meeting.

The Assembly is assisted by a number of functional committees. The General Committee co-ordinates its proceedings and operations, while the Credentials Committee verifies the credentials of representatives. There are also two standing committees, the Advisory Committee on Administration and Budgetary Questions and the Committee on Contributions, which suggests the scale of members' payments to the UN.

President of the General Assembly (1997), Hennadiy Udovenko (Ukraine)

The Assembly has created a large number of specialized bodies over the years, which are supervised jointly with the Economic and Social Council. They are supported by UN and voluntary contributions from governments, non-governmental organizations and individuals. These organizations include:

THE CONFERENCE ON DISARMAMENT (CD)

Palais des Nations, CH-1211 Geneva 10, Switzerland

Established by the UN as the Committee on Disarmament in 1962, the CD is the single multilateral disarmament negotiating forum. The present title of the organization was adopted in 1984. There were 40 members as at June 1994.

A Chemical Weapons Convention was agreed in Paris in 1993 and came into force in April 1997 after being ratified by 87 countries. It bans the use, production, stockpiling and transfer of all chemical weapons. All US and Russian weapons must be destroyed within 15 years of the Convention entering into force and all other states' weapons must be destroyed within ten years.

Secretary-General, Vladimir Petrovsky (Russia)

UK Representative, I. Soutar, 37–39 rue de Vermont, CH-1211 Geneva 20, Switzerland

THE UNITED NATIONS CHILDREN'S FUND (UNICEF)

3 UN Plaza, New York, NY 10017, USA

Established in 1947 to assist children and mothers in the immediate post-war period, UNICEF now concentrates on developing countries. It provides primary health-care and health education. In particular, it conducts programmes in oral hydration, immunization against leading diseases, child growth monitoring, and the encouragement of breast-feeding. Its operations are often conducted in co-operation with the World Health Organization (WHO).

Executive Director, Carol Bellamy (USA)

THE UNITED NATIONS DEVELOPMENT PROGRAMME (UNDP)

1 UN Plaza, New York, NY 10017, USA

Established in 1966 from the merger of the UN Expanded Programme of Technical Assistance and the UN Special Fund, UNDP is the central funding agency for economic and social development projects around the world. Much of its annual expenditure is channelled through UN specialized agencies, governments and non-governmental organizations.

Administrator, James G. Speth (USA)

THE UNITED NATIONS HIGH COMMISSIONER FOR REFUGEES (UNHCR)

Centre William Rappard, 154 rue de Lausanne, PO Box 2500, CH-1211 Geneva 2, Switzerland

Established in 1951 to protect the rights and interests of refugees, UNHCR organizes emergency relief and longer-term solutions, such as voluntary repatriation, local integration or resettlement.

High Commissioner, Sadako Ogata (Japan)

UK OFFICE, 76 Westminster Palace Gardens, London SWIP IRL. Tel: 0171-828 9191

THE UN RELIEF AND WORKS AGENCY FOR PALESTINE REFUGEES IN THE NEAR EAST (UNRWA)

Vienna International Centre, Wagramerstrasse 5, PO Box 100, A-1400 Vienna, Austria

Established in 1949 to bring relief to the Palestinians displaced by the Arab-Israeli conflict.

Commissioner-General, Ilter Turkman (Turkey)

THE UNITED NATIONS HIGH COMMISSIONER FOR HUMAN RIGHTS
Established in 1993 to secure respect for, and prevent violations of human rights by engaging in dialogue with governments and international organizations. Responsible for the co-ordination of all UN human rights activities.
High Commissioner, Mary Robinson (Ireland)

Other bodies include:

THE UN CENTRE FOR HUMAN SETTLEMENTS (Habitat), PO Box 30030, Nairobi, Kenya
THE UN CONFERENCE ON TRADE AND DEVELOPMENT (UNCTAD), Palais des Nations, CH-1211 Geneva 10, Switzerland
THE DEPARTMENT OF HUMANITARIAN AFFAIRS (DHA), Palais des Nations, CH-1211 Geneva 10, Switzerland
THE INTERNATIONAL SEABED AUTHORITY, Kingston, Jamaica
THE UN ENVIRONMENT PROGRAMME (UNEP), PO Box 30552, Nairobi, Kenya
THE UN POPULATION FUND (UNFPA), 220 East 42nd Street, New York, NY 10017, USA
THE UN INSTITUTE FOR THE ADVANCEMENT OF WOMEN (INSTRAW), PO Box 21747, Santo Domingo, Dominican Republic
THE UN UNIVERSITY (UNU), Toho Seimei Building, 15-1, Shibuya, 2-Chome, Shibuya-ku, Tokyo 150, Japan
THE WORLD FOOD COUNCIL (WFC), Via delle Terme di Caracalla, I-00100 Rome, Italy
THE WORLD FOOD PROGRAMME (WFP), Via delle Terme di Caracalla, I-00100 Rome, Italy

BUDGET OF THE UNITED NATIONS
The budget adopted for the biennium 1998–9 was US$2,387 million. The scale of assessment contributions of 88 UN members is set at the minimum 0.01 per cent. The ten largest assessments are: USA, 25 per cent; Japan, 12.45; Germany, 8.93; Russia, 6.91; France, 6.00; UK, 5.02; Italy, 4.29; Canada, 3.11; Spain, 1.98; Australia, 1.51.

THE SECURITY COUNCIL
UN Plaza, New York, NY 10017, USA

The Security Council is the senior arm of the UN and has the primary responsibility for maintaining world peace and security. It consists of 15 members, each with one representative and one vote. There are five permanent members, China, France, Russia, the UK and the USA, and ten non-permanent members. Each of the non-permanent members is elected for a two-year term by a two-thirds majority of the General Assembly and is ineligible for immediate re-election. Five of the elective seats are allocated to Africa and Asia, one to eastern Europe, two to Latin America and two to western Europe and remaining countries. Procedural questions are determined by a majority vote. Other matters require a majority inclusive of the votes of the permanent members; they thus have a right of veto. The abstention of a permanent member does not constitute a veto. The presidency rotates each month by state in (English) alphabetical order. Parties to a dispute, other non-members and individuals can be invited to participate in Security Council debates but are not permitted to vote. In 1999 the ten non-permanent members are: Bahrain, Brazil, Gabon, Gambia, Slovenia (*term expires 31 December 1999*), Argentina, Canada, Malaysia, Namibia, the Netherlands (*term expires 31 December 2000*).
The Security Council is empowered to settle or adjudicate in disputes or situations which threaten international peace and security. It can adopt political, economic and military measures to achieve this end. Any matter considered to be a threat to or breach of the peace or an act of aggression can be brought to the Security Council's attention by any member state or by the Secretary-General. The Charter envisaged members placing at the disposal of the Security Council armed forces and other facilities which would be co-ordinated by the Military Staff Committee, composed of military representatives of the five permanent members. The Security Council is also supported by a Committee of Experts, to advise on procedural and technical matters, and a Committee on Admission of New Members.
Owing to superpower disunity, the Security Council rarely played the decisive role set out in the Charter; the Military Staff Committee was effectively suspended from 1948 until 1990, when a meeting was convened during the Gulf Crisis on the formation and control of UN-supervised armed forces. However, at an extraordinary meeting of the Security Council in January 1992, heads of government laid plans to transform the UN in light of the changed post-Cold War world. The Secretary-General was asked to draw up a report on enhancing the UN's preventive diplomacy, peacemaking and peacekeeping ability. The report, *An Agenda for Peace,* was produced in June 1992 and centred on the establishment of a UN army composed of national contingents on permanent standby, as envisaged at the time of the UN's formation.

PEACEKEEPING FORCES
The Security Council has established a number of peacekeeping forces since its foundation, comprising contingents provided mainly by neutral and non-aligned UN members. Current forces include: the UN Truce Supervision Organization (UNTSO), Israel, 1948; the UN Military Observer Group in India and Pakistan (UNMO-GIP), 1949; the UN Peacekeeping Force in Cyprus (UNFICYP), 1964; the UN Disengagement Observer Force (UNDOF), Golan Heights, Syria, 1974; the UN Interim Force in Lebanon (UNIFIL), 1978; the UN Iraq-Kuwait Observation Mission (UNIKOM), 1991; the UN Mission for the Referendum in Western Sahara (MINURSO), 1991; the UN Observer Mission in Georgia (UNOMIG), 1993; the UN Observer Mission in Liberia (UNOMIL), 1993; the UN Observer Mission in Guatemala (MINUGA), 1994; the UN Observer Mission in Tajikistan (UNMOT), 1994; the UN Preventive Deployment Force (UNPREDEP), Former Yugoslav Republic of Macedonia, 1995; the UN Mission in Bosnia-Hercegovina (UNMIBH), 1995; the UN Mission of Observers in Prevlaka (UNMOP), 1996.

THE ECONOMIC AND SOCIAL COUNCIL
UN Plaza, New York, NY 10017, USA

The Economic and Social Council is responsible under the General Assembly for the economic and social work of the UN and for the co-ordination of the activities of the 15 specialized agencies and other UN bodies. It makes reports and recommendations on economic, social, cultural, educational, health and related matters, often in consultation with non-governmental organizations, passing the reports to the General Assembly and other UN bodies. It also drafts conventions for submission to the Assembly and calls conferences on matters within its remit.
The Council consists of 54 members, 18 of whom are elected annually by the General Assembly for a three-year term. Each has one vote and can be immediately re-elected on retirement. A President is elected annually and is also eligible for re-election. One substantive session is held annually and decisions are reached by simple majority vote of those present.

The Council has established a number of standing committees on particular issues and several commissions. Commissions include: Statistical, Human Rights, Social Development, Sustainable Development, Status of Women, Crime Prevention and Criminal Justice, Narcotic Drugs, Science and Technology for Development, and Population; and Regional Economic Commissions for Europe, Asia and the Pacific, Western Asia, Latin America and Africa.

THE TRUSTEESHIP COUNCIL
UN Plaza, New York, NY10017, USA

The Trusteeship Council supervised the administration of territories within the UN Trusteeship system inherited from the League of Nations. It consists of the five permanent members of the Security Council. With the independence of the Republic of Palau in October 1994, all eleven trusteeships have now progressed to independence or merged with neighbouring states and the Trusteeship Council suspended its operations on 1 November 1994.

THE SECRETARIAT
UN Plaza, New York, NY 10017, USA

The Secretariat services the other UN organs and is headed by a Secretary-General elected by a majority vote of the General Assembly on the recommendation of the Security Council. He is assisted by an international staff, chosen to represent the international character of the organization. The Secretary-General is charged with bringing to the attention of the Security Council any matter which he considers poses a threat to international peace and security. He may also bring other matters to the attention of the General Assembly and other UN bodies and may be entrusted by them with additional duties. As chief administrator to the UN, the Secretary-General is present in person or via representatives at all meetings of the other five main organs of the UN. He may also act as an impartial mediator in disputes between member states.

The power and influence of the Secretary-General has been determined largely by the character of the office-holder and by the state of relations between the superpowers. The thaw in these relations since the mid-1980s has increased the effectiveness of the UN, particularly in its attempts to intervene in international disputes. It helped to end the Iran-Iraq war and sponsored peace in Central America. Following Iraq's invasion of Kuwait in 1990 the UN took its first collective security action since the Korean War. UN action to protect the Kurds in northern Iraq has widened its legal authority by breaching the prohibition on its intervention in the essentially domestic affairs of states. Currently the UN is involved in peacekeeping, aid distribution and negotiations in the former Yugoslavia; and is addressing the global problems of Aids and environmental destruction.

Secretary-General, Kofi Annan, apptd 1996 (Ghana)
Deputy Secretary-General, Louise Frechette, apptd 1998 (Canada)

UNDER-SECRETARIES-GENERAL

Administration and Management, Joseph Connor (USA)
Chef de Cabinet, Iqbqal Riza (Pakistan)
Development Support and Management Services, Jin Yongjian (China)
Humanitarian Affairs, Sergio Vieira de Mello (Brazil)
Legal Affairs and UN Legal Counsel, Hans Corell (Sweden)
Peacekeeping Operations, Bernard Miyet (France)
Policy Co-ordination and Sustainable Development, Nitin Desai (India)
Political Affairs, Sir Kieran Prendergast (UK)

FORMER SECRETARIES-GENERAL

1946–53	Trygve Lie (Norway)
1953–61	Dag Hammarskjöld (Sweden)
1961–71	U Thant (Burma)
1971–81	Kurt Waldheim (Austria)
1981–91	Javier Pérez de Cuéllar (Peru)
1991–6	Boutros Boutros-Ghali (Egypt)

INTERNATIONAL COURT OF JUSTICE
The Peace Palace, NL-2517 KJ The Hague, The Netherlands

The International Court of Justice is the principal judicial organ of the UN. The Statute of the Court is an integral part of the Charter and all members of the UN are *ipso facto* parties to it. The Court is composed of 15 judges, elected by both the General Assembly and the Security Council for nine-year terms which are renewable. Judges may deliberate over cases in which their country is involved. If no judge on the bench is from a country which is a party to a dispute under consideration, that party may designate a judge to participate *ad hoc* in that particular deliberation. If any party to a case fails to adhere to the judgement of the Court, the other party may have recourse to the Security Council.

President, Mohammed Bedjaoui (Algeria) (2006)
Vice-President, Stephen M. Schwebel (USA) (2006)
Judges, Carl-August Fleischhauer (Germany) (2003); Gilbert Guillaume (France) (2000); Geza Herczegh (Hungary) (2003); Rosalyn Higgins (UK) (2000); Shi Jiuyong (China) (2003); Pieter H. Kooijmans (Netherlands) (2006); Abdul G. Koroma (Sierra Leone) (2003); Shigeru Oda (Japan) (2003); Gonzalo Parra-Aranguren (Venezuela) (2000); Raymond Ranjeva (Madagascar) (2000); José Francisco Rezek (Brazil) (2006); Vladlen S. Vereshchetin (Russia) (2006); Christopher G. Weeramantry (Sri Lanka) (2000)

INTERNATIONAL WAR CRIMES TRIBUNAL FOR THE FORMER YUGOSLAVIA
Churchill Plein 1, PO Box 13888, NL-2501 EW The Hague, The Netherlands

In February 1993, the Security Council voted to establish a war crimes tribunal for the former Yugoslavia to hear cases covering grave breaches of the Geneva Conventions and crimes against humanity. The Court was inaugurated in November 1993 in The Hague with 11 judges elected by the UN General Assembly from 11 states, divided into two trial chambers of three judges each and an appeal chamber of five judges. The court is unable to force suspects to stand trial but is empowered to pass verdicts in the absence of suspects and can put suspects under an 'act of accusation' which prevents them from leaving their own country.

In October 1995, the tribunal formally charged the Bosnian Serb leaders Radovan Karadzić and Gen. Ratko Mladić, and the Croatian Serb President Milan Martić and 21 others with genocide and crimes against humanity. As at January 1997 only one of the 75 suspected war criminals to be indicted has been imprisoned. In May 1999, the tribunal formally charged the Yugoslav president Slobodan Milošević, the Serbian president Milan Milutinović two other Serb politicians and the Yugoslav armed forces chief of staff Dragoljub Ojdanić

President, Antonio Cassese (Italy)
Chief Prosecutor, Louise Arbour (Canada)

INTERNATIONAL CRIMINAL TRIBUNAL FOR RWANDA

In November 1994, the UN Security Council voted to establish a tribunal to try those responsible for genocide and other violations of international humanitarian law in Rwanda between 1 January and 31 December 1994. The tribunal, based in Arusha, Tanzania, is empowered to try the most senior people responsible for the massacre. It formally opened in November 1995 to consider 463 indictments.

Chief Prosecutor, Louise Arbour (Canada)

SPECIALIZED AGENCIES

Fifteen independent international organizations, each with its own membership, budget and headquarters, carry out their responsibilities in co-ordination with the UN under agreements made with the Economic and Social Council. An entry for each appears elsewhere in the International Organizations section. They are: the Food and Agriculture Organization of the UN; International Civil Aviation Organization; International Fund for Agricultural Development; International Labour Organization; International Maritime Organization; the International Monetary Fund; International Telecommunications Union; UN Educational, Scientific and Cultural Organization; UN Industrial Development Organization; Universal Postal Union; World Bank (International Bank for Reconstruction and Development, International Development Agency, International Finance Corporation); World Health Organization; World Intellectual Property Organization; and World Meteorological Organization. The International Atomic Energy Agency and the World Trade Organization are linked to the UN but are not specialized agencies.

UK MISSION TO THE UNITED NATIONS
1 Dag Hammarskjöld Plaza, 885 Second Avenue, New York, NY 10017, USA
Tel: New York 745 9200; fax: New York 745 9316
E-mail: uk@un.int
Web: http://www.britain-info.org/ukmis/ukmis.htm
Permanent Representative to the United Nations and Representative on the Security Council, Sir Jeremy Greenstock, KCMG, *apptd* 1998
Deputy Permanent Representative, S. G. Eldon, CMG, OBE

UK MISSION TO THE OFFICE OF THE UN AND OTHER INTERNATIONAL ORGANIZATIONS IN GENEVA
37–39 rue de Vermont, CH-1211 Geneva 20, Switzerland
Permanent UK Representative, R. M. J. Lyne, CMG, *apptd* 1997
Deputy Permanent Representative, P. R. Jenkins

UK MISSION TO THE INTERNATIONAL ATOMIC ENERGY AGENCY, THE UN INDUSTRIAL DEVELOPMENT ORGANIZATION AND THE UN IN VIENNA
Jaurèsgasse 12, A-1030 Vienna, Austria
Permanent UK Representative, Dr J. P. Freeman, *apptd* 1997
Deputy Permanent Representative, M. R. Etherton

UN OFFICE AND INFORMATION CENTRE
Millbank Tower, 21–24 Millbank, London, SW1P 4QH
Tel: 0171-630 1981; fax: 0171-976 6478

UNITED NATIONS EDUCATIONAL, SCIENTIFIC AND CULTURAL ORGANIZATION
7 place de Fontenoy, F-75352 Paris 07 SP, France
Tel: Paris 4568 1000; fax: Paris 4567 1690
Web: http://www.unesco.org

The United Nations Educational, Scientific and Cultural Organization (UNESCO) was established in 1946. It promotes collaboration among its member states in education, science, culture and communication. It aims to further a universal respect for human rights, justice and the rule of law, without distinction of race, sex, language or religion, in accordance with the UN Charter.

UNESCO runs a number of programmes to improve education and extend access to it. It provides assistance to ensure the free flow of information and its wider and better balanced dissemination without any obstacle to freedom of expression, and to maintain cultural heritage in the face of development. It fosters research and study in all areas of the social and environmental sciences.

UNESCO had 186 member states as at July 1997. There are three associate members. The General Conference, consisting of representatives of all the members, meets biennially to decide the programme and the budget (1998–9, US$544,367,250). It elects the 51-member Executive Board, which supervises operations, and appoints a Director-General who heads a Secretariat responsible for carrying out the organization's programmes. In most member states national commissions liaise with UNESCO to execute its programme.

The UK withdrew from UNESCO in 1985; it rejoined on 1 July 1997.

Director-General, Federico Mayor Zaragoza (Spain)

UNITED NATIONS INDUSTRIAL DEVELOPMENT ORGANIZATION
Vienna International Centre, Wagramerstrasse 5, PO Box 300, A-1400 Vienna, Austria
Tel: Vienna 26026; fax: Vienna 269 2669
E-mail: unido-pinfo@unido.org
Web: http://www.unido.org

The United Nations Industrial Development Organization (UNIDO) was established in 1966 by the UN General Assembly to act as the central co-ordinating body for industrial activities within the UN. It became a UN specialized agency in 1985. UNIDO's mission is to improve living conditions and promote prosperity by providing technical assistance and advice, investment promotion and planning. To this end, it assists both public and private sectors and has made its services available to former centrally planned economies in transition to a market economy.

UNIDO had 168 members as at May 1999. It is funded by the UN, member states and non-governmental organizations. A General Conference of all the members meets biennially to discuss strategy and policy, approve the budget (1998–9, US$129.5 million) and elect the Director-General. The Industrial Development Board is composed of members from 53 member states and reviews implementation of the regular work programme and the budget, which is prepared by the Programme and Budget Committee.

Director-General, Carlos Magariños (Argentina)
Permanent UK Representative, Dr John Freeman, British Embassy, Vienna

UNIVERSAL POSTAL UNION
Weltpoststrasse 4, CH-3000 Bern 15, Switzerland
Tel: Bern 350 3111; fax: Bern 350 3110
E-Mail: info@upu.int
Web: http://www.upu.int

The Universal Postal Union (UPU) was established by the Treaty of Bern 1874, taking effect from 1875, and became a UN specialized agency in 1948. The UPU is an intergovernmental organization which exists to form and regulate a single postal territory of all member countries for the reciprocal exchange of correspondence without discrimination. It also assists and advises on the improvement of postal services.

The UPU had 189 members as at May 1999. A Universal Postal Congress of all its members is the UPU's supreme authority and meets every five years to review the Treaty. A Council of Administration composed of 41 members was established by the 1994 Congress. It meets annually to ensure continuity between congresses, study regulatory developments and broad policies, approve the budget and examine proposed Treaty changes. A Postal Operations Council also meets annually to deal with specific technical and operational issues. The three UPU bodies are served by the International Bureau, a secretariat headed by a Director-General.

Funding is provided by members according to a scale of contributions drawn up by the Congress. The Council sets the annual budget (1999, SFr35,700,000) within a five-year figure decided by the Congress.

Director-General, Thomas E. Leavey (USA)

WESTERN EUROPEAN UNION
4 rue de la Régence, B-1000 Brussels, Belgium
Tel: Brussels 500 4411; fax: Brussels 511 3270
E-mail: ueo.presse@skynet.be
Web: http://www.weu.int

The Western European Union (WEU) originated as the Brussels Treaty Organization (BTO) established under the Treaty of Brussels, signed in 1948 by Belgium, France, Luxembourg, the Netherlands and the UK, to provide collective self-defence and economic and social collaboration amongst its signatories. With the collapse of the European Defence Community and the decision of NATO to incorporate the Federal Republic of Germany into the Western security system, the BTO was modified to become the WEU in 1954 with the admission of West Germany and Italy. However, owing to the overlap with NATO and the Council of Europe, the Union became largely defunct.

From the late 1970s onwards efforts were made to add a security dimension to the EC's European Political Co-operation. Opposition to these efforts from Denmark, Greece and Ireland led the remaining EC countries, all WEU members, to decide to reactivate the Union in 1984. Members committed themselves to harmonizing their views on defence and security and developing a European security identity, while bearing in mind the importance of transatlantic relations. Portugal and Spain joined the WEU in 1988, and Greece became a full member in 1995.

After much debate about its future, the EU Maastricht Treaty designated the WEU as the future defence component of the European Union. WEU foreign ministers agreed in the Petersberg Declaration 1992 to assign forces to WEU command for 'peacemaking' operations. In November 1992 the WEU's role as the common security dimension of the EU was enhanced when WEU ministers signed a declaration with remaining European NATO members to give them various forms of WEU membership. Iceland, Norway and Turkey became associate members; the Republic of Ireland, Denmark, Austria, Finland and Sweden became observer members. In 1994 the WEU reached agreements with Estonia, Latvia, Lithuania, Poland, the Czech Republic, Slovakia, Hungary, Romania and Bulgaria, under which they all became associate partners; Slovenia became an associate partner in 1996.

The Czech Republic, Hungary and Poland became associate members in 1999, following their accession to NATO.

The WEU works in close co-operation with the Atlantic Alliance, and relations between the WEU and NATO are developing on the basis of transparency and complementarity. The 1993 Luxembourg Declaration states that the WEU is ready to participate in the future work of the NATO Alliance as its European pillar, and at the Atlantic Alliance summit in January 1994, NATO expressed its readiness to make Alliance assets and capabilities available for WEU operations. In June 1996, NATO foreign and defence ministers approved the Combined Joint Task Force (CJTF) concept and the elaboration of multinational European command arrangements for WEU-led operations.

The formation of a 'Eurocorps' based on the Franco-German brigade as a force answerable to the WEU was announced in 1992. The 'Eurocorps' was inaugurated in 1993 and became fully operational in 1995 with 60,000 troops comprising French, German, Belgian, Luxembourg and Spanish forces.

A Council of Ministers (foreign and defence) meets biannually in the capital of the presiding country; the presidency rotates biannually, and from 1999 the sequence of WEU presidencies has been harmonized with those of the EU Council of Ministers. A Permanent Council of the member states' permanent representatives meets weekly in Brussels. The Permanent Council is chaired by the Secretary-General and serviced by the Secretariat. A planning cell has been established to draw up contingency plans in the areas of humanitarian relief, peacekeeping and crisis management and a military committee was established in 1998. The Assembly of the WEU is composed of 115 parliamentarians of member states and meets twice annually in Paris to debate matters within the scope of the revised Brussels Treaty.

Presidency (1999) Germany, Luxembourg; (2000) Portugal, France

Secretary-General, José Cutileiro (Portugal)

UK Representative on the Permanent Council, Sir John Goulden, KCMG

ASSEMBLY, 43 avenue du Président Wilson, F-75775 Paris Cedex 16, France

---

THE WORLD BANK
1818 H Street NW, Washington DC 20433, USA
Tel: Washington DC 477 1234; fax: Washington DC 477 6391
Web: http://www.worldbank.org

The World Bank, more formally known as the International Bank for Reconstruction and Development (IBRD), is a specialized agency of the UN. It developed from the international monetary and financial conference held at Bretton Woods, New Hampshire, in 1944 and was established by 44 nations in 1945 to encourage economic growth in developing countries through the provision of loans and technical assistance to their respective governments. The IBRD now has 181 members.

The Bank is owned by the governments of member countries and its capital is subscribed by its members. It finances its lending primarily from borrowing in world capital markets, and derives a substantial contribution to its resources from its retained earnings and the repayment of loans. The interest rate on its loans is calculated in relation to its cost of borrowing. Loans generally have a grace period of five years and are repayable within 20 years. The loans made by the Bank since its inception to 30 June 1997 totalled US$295,263.9 million to 131 countries. Total capital is US$182,426 million.

Originally directed towards post-war reconstruction in Europe, the Bank has subsequently turned towards assisting less-developed countries with the establishment of two affiliates, the International Finance Corporation (IFC) in 1956 and the International Development Association (IDA) in 1960. The IFC promotes the growth of the private sector in developing member countries by mobilizing domestic and foreign capital. The IFC's subscribed share capital was US$2.36 million at 30 June 1997. It is also empowered to borrow up to two and a half times the amount of its unimpaired subscribed capital and accumulated earnings for use in its lending programme. At 30 June 1997, the IFC had committed financing totalling more than US$6.7 billion in 129 countries.

The IDA performs the same function as the World Bank but primarily to less-developed countries and on terms that bear less heavily on their balance of payments than IBRD loans. Eligible countries typically have a per capita gross national product of less than US$925 (1996). Funds (called credits to distinguish them from IBRD loans) come mostly in the form of subscriptions and contributions from the IDA's richer members and transfers from the net income of the IBRD. The terms for IDA credits, which bear no interest and are made to governments only, are ten-year grace periods and 35- or 40-year maturities. By 30 June 1997, the IDA had extended development credits totalling US$101,563.4 million to 100 countries.

The IBRD and its affiliates are financially and legally distinct but share headquarters. The IBRD is headed by a Board of Governors, consisting of one Governor and one alternate Governor appointed by each member country. Twenty-four Executive Directors exercise all powers of the Bank except those reserved to the Board of Governors. The President, elected by the Executive Directors, conducts the business of the Bank, assisted by an international staff. Membership in both the IFC (162 members) and the IDA (160 members) is open to all IBRD countries. The IDA is administered by the same staff as the Bank; the IFC has its own personnel but draws on the IBRD for administrative and other support. All share the same President.

In 1988 a third affiliate, the Multilateral Investment Guarantee Agency (MIGA) was formed. MIGA encourages foreign investment in developing states by providing investment guarantees to potential investors and advisory services to developing member countries. At 30 December 1994 128 countries were members of MIGA.

President (IBRD, IFC, IDA, MIGA), James D. Wolfensohn (USA)

UK Executive Director, A. O'Donnell, Room 11-120, IMF, 700 19th Street NW, Washington DC 20431

EUROPEAN OFFICE, 66 avenue d'Iéna, F-75116 Paris, France

JAPAN OFFICE, 10F, Fukoku Seimei Building, 2-2-2 Uchisaiwai-cho, Chiyoda-ku, Tokyo 100-0011, Japan

UK OFFICE, New Zealand House, Haymarket, London SW1Y 4TQ. Tel: 0171-930 8511; fax: 0171-930 8515

THE WORLD COUNCIL OF CHURCHES
PO Box 2100, CH-1211 Geneva 2, Switzerland
Tel: Geneva 791 6111; fax: Geneva 791 0361
E-mail: info@mail.wcc-coe.org
Web: http://www.wcc-coe.org

The World Council of Churches (WCC) was constituted in 1948 to promote unity among Christian churches. The 336 member churches have adherents in more than 100 countries. With the exception of Roman Catholicism, virtually all Christian traditions are represented.

The policies of the Council are determined by delegates of the member churches meeting in Assembly, roughly every seven years; the seventh Assembly was held in Canberra, Australia, in February 1991 and the eighth Assembly was held in Harare, Zimbabwe, in December 1998. More detailed decisions are taken by a 156-member Central Committee which is elected by the Assembly and meets, with the eight WCC Presidents, annually. The Central Committee in turn appoints a smaller Executive Committee and also nominates commissions to guide the various programmes.

General Secretary, Dr Konrad Raiser (Germany)

WORLD HEALTH ORGANIZATION
20 avenue Appia, CH-1211 Geneva 27, Switzerland
Tel: Geneva 791 2111; fax: Geneva 791 0746
E-mail: info@who.ch
Web: http://www.who.ch

The UN International Health Conference, held in 1946, established the World Health Organization (WHO) as a UN specialized agency, with effect from 1948. It is dedicated to attaining the highest possible level of health for all. It collaborates with member governments, UN agencies and other bodies to improve health standards, control communicable diseases and promote all aspects of family and environmental health. It seeks to raise the standards of health teaching and training, and promotes research through collaborating research centres world-wide. Its other services include the *International Pharma-copoeia*, epidemiological surveillance, and the collation and publication of statistics. WHO activities are orientated to achieving 'Health for All'.

WHO had 191 members as at April 1998. It is governed by the annual World Health Assembly of members which meets to set policy, approve the budget (1997–8, US$1,800 million), appoint a Director-General, and adopt health conventions and regulations. It also elects 32 members who designate one expert to serve on the Executive Board. The Board effects the programme, suggests initiatives and is empowered to deal with emergencies. A Secretariat, headed by the Director-General, supervises the activities of six regional offices.

Director-General, Gro Harlem Bruntland (Norway)

WORLD INTELLECTUAL PROPERTY ORGANIZATION
34 chemin des Colombettes, CH-1211 Geneva 20, Switzerland
Tel: Geneva 338 9111; fax: Geneva 733 5428
E-mail: publicinf.mail@wipo.int
Web: http://www.wipo.int

The World Intellectual Property Organization (WIPO) was established in 1967 by the Stockholm Convention, which entered into force in 1970. In addition to that Convention, WIPO administers 19 treaties, the principal ones being the Paris Convention for the Protection of Industrial Property and the Berne Convention for the Protection of Literary and Artistic Works. WIPO became a UN specialized agency in 1974.

WIPO promotes the protection of intellectual property throughout the world through co-operation among states, and the administration of various 'Unions', each founded on a multilateral treaty and dealing with the legal and administrative aspects of intellectual property.

Intellectual property comprises two main branches: industrial property (inventions, trademarks, industrial designs and appellations of origin); and copyright (literary, musical, photographic, audiovisual and artistic works, etc.). WIPO also assists creative intellectual activity and facilitates technology transfer, particularly to developing countries.

WIPO had 171 members as at April 1999. The biennial session of all its governing bodies sets policy, a programme and a budget (1998–9, SFr400 million). WIPO has three governing bodies: the General Assembly, composed of WIPO members who are also members of the Paris or Berne conventions; the Conference, composed of all WIPO members; and the Co-ordination Committee, composed of member states elected by members of WIPO and the Paris and Berne conventions. The General Assembly elects a Director-General, who heads the International Bureau (secretariat).

A separate International Union for the Protection of New Varieties of Plants (UPOV), established by convention in 1961, is linked to WIPO. It has 40 members.

Director-General, Dr Kamil Idris (Sudan)

WORLD METEOROLOGICAL ORGANIZATION
7 bis, avenue de la Paix, PO Box 2300, CH-1211 Geneva 2, Switzerland
Tel: Geneva 730 8111; fax: Geneva 730 8181

The World Meteorological Organization (WMO) was established in 1950 and became a UN specialized agency in 1951, succeeding the International Meteorological Organization founded in 1873. It facilitates co-operation in the establishment of networks for making meteorological, climatological, hydrological and geophysical observations, as well as their exchange, processing and standardization, and assists technology transfer, training and research. It also fosters collaboration between meteorological and hydrological services, and furthers the application of meteorology to aviation, shipping, environment, water problems, agriculture, etc.

The WMO had 179 member states and six member territories as at 30 May 1999. The supreme authority is the World Meteorological Congress of member states and member territories, which meets every four years to determine general policy, make recommendations and set a budget (2000–3, SFr252.3 million). It also elects 26 members of the 36-member Executive Council, the other members being the President and three Vice-Presidents of the WMO, and the Presidents of the six regional associations, who are ex-officio members. The Council supervises the implementation of Congress decisions, initiates studies and makes recommendations on matters needing international action. The WMO functions through six regional associations and eight technical commissions. Each of the regional associations has responsibility for co-ordinating meteorological activities within its region. The technical commissions study meteorological and hydrological problems, lay down the necessary methodologies and procedures, and make recommendations to the Executive Council and Congress. The Secretariat is headed by a Secretary-General, appointed by the Congress.

Secretary-General, G. O. P. Obasi (Nigeria)

WORLD TRADE ORGANIZATION
Centre William Rappard, 154 rue de Lausanne, 1211 CH-Geneva 21, Switzerland
Tel: Geneva 739 5111; fax: Geneva 739 5458
E-mail: enquiries@wto.org
Web: http://www.wto.org

The World Trade Organization was established on 1 January 1995 as the successor to the General Agreement on Tariffs and Trade (GATT). GATT was established in 1948 as an interim agreement until the charter of a new international trade organization could be drafted by a committee of the UN Economic and Social Council and ratified by member states. The charter was never ratified and GATT became the only regime for the regulation of world trade, evolving its own rules and procedures.

GATT was dedicated to the expansion of non-discriminatory international trade and progressively extended free trade via 'rounds' of multilateral negotiations. Eight rounds were concluded: Geneva (1947), Annecy (1948), Torquay (1950), Geneva (1956), Dillon (1960–1), Kennedy (1964–7), Tokyo (1973–9), and Uruguay (1986–94). By the time the measures of the Uruguay Round are fully implemented in 2002, the average duties on manufactured goods will have been reduced from 40 per cent in the 1940s to 3 per cent. The Final Act of the Uruguay Round was signed by trade ministers from the 128 GATT negotiating states and the EU in Marrakesh, Morocco, on 15 April 1994. It established the World Trade Organization (WTO) to supersede GATT and implement the Uruguay Round agreements.

The WTO is the legal and institutional foundation of the multilateral trading system. It provides the contractual obligations determining how governments frame and implement trade policy and provides the forum for the debate, negotiation and adjudication of trade problems. The WTO's principal aims are to liberalize world trade and place it on a secure basis, and it seeks to achieve this partly by an agreed set of trade rules and market access agreements and partly through further trade liberalization negotiations. The WTO also administers and implements a further 29 multilateral agreements in fields such as agriculture, textiles and clothing, services, government procurement, rules of origin and intellectual property.

The highest authority of the WTO is the Ministerial Conference composed of all members, which meets at least once every two years. The General Council meets as required and acts on behalf of the Ministerial Conference in regard to the regular working of the WTO. Composed of all members, the General Council also convenes in two particular forms: as the Dispute Settlement Body, dealing with disputes between members arising from the Uruguay Round Final Act; and as the Trade Policy Review Body, conducting regular reviews of the trade policies of members. A secretariat of 500 staff headed by a Director-General services WTO bodies and provides trade performance and trade policy analysis. As at May 1999 there were 134 WTO members, and a further 31 governments had applied to join. The WTO budget for 1998 was SFr115 million, with members' contributions calculated on the basis of their share of the total trade conducted by WTO members. The official languages of the WTO are English, French and Spanish.

Acting Director-General, David Hartridge
Permanent UK Representative, R. M. J. Lyne, 37–39 rue de Vermont, CH-1211 Geneva 20

The European Union

MEMBERS

State	Accession Date	Population (million)	GNP (US$ million)	GDP per head (ECU)	Council Votes	EP Seats
Austria	1 January 1995	8.11	225,373	22,516	4	21
Belgium	1 January 1958*	10.16	272,382	20,998	5	25
Denmark	1 January 1973	5.26	184,347	26,537	3	16
Finland	1 January 1995	5.13	127,398	20,368	3	16
France	1 January 1958*	58.38	1,541,630	20,869	10	87
Germany	1 January 1958*†	81.91	2,320,985	22,585	10	99
Greece	1 January 1981	10.48	122,430	10,051	5	25
Ireland	1 January 1973	3.63	65,137	18,169	3	15
Italy	1 January 1958*	57.34	1,160,444	17,276	10	87
Luxembourg	1 January 1958*	0.41	18,850	33,035	2	6
Netherlands	1 January 1958*	15.52	403,057	20,392	5	31
Portugal	1 January 1986	9.92	109,472	8,919	5	25
Spain	1 January 1986	39.27	569,637	11,887	8	64
Sweden	1 January 1995	8.84	231,905	22,803	4	22
UK	1 January 1973	58.78	1,231,269	19,234	10	87
Total		372.57	8,584,316		87	626

* Acceded to the European Coal and Steel Community (ECSC) on its formation in 1952
† Federal Republic of Germany (West) 1952/1958; German Democratic Republic (East) acceded on German reunification (3 October 1990)
EP European Parliament

DEVELOPMENT

1950 Robert Schuman (French foreign minister) proposes that France and West Germany pool their coal and steel industries under a supranational authority (Schuman Plan)
1951 Paris Treaty signed by France, West Germany, Belgium, Italy, Luxembourg and the Netherlands establishes the European Coal and Steel Community (ECSC)
1952 ECSC treaty enters into force
1957 25 March: Treaty of Rome signed by the six, establishes the European Economic Community (EEC) and the European Atomic Energy Authority (EURATOM). Treaty aims to create a customs union; remove obstacles to free movement of capital, goods, people and services; establish common external trade policy and common agricultural and fisheries policies; co-ordinate economic policies; harmonize social policies; promote co-operation in nuclear research
1958 1 January: EEC and EURATOM begin operation. Joint Parliament and Court of Justice established for all three communities, and the Commission, Council of Ministers, Economic and Social Committee and Investment Bank for the EEC
1962 Common Agricultural Policy (CAP) agreed (*see* page 777)
1967 EEC, ECSC and EURATOM merge to form the European Communities (EC), with a single Council of Ministers and Commission
1968 EEC customs union completed
      Implementation of CAP completed
1974 Regular heads of governments summits begin
1975 'Own resources' funding of EC budget introduced (*see* page 777)
      UK renegotiates its terms of accession
      European Regional Development Fund created
1979 European Monetary System (EMS) comes into operation (*see* page 778)
      First direct elections to European Parliament (June)
1984 Fontainebleau summit settles UK annual budget rebate and agrees first major CAP reform
1986 Single European Act (SEA) signed (*see* page 778)
      European Political Co-operation (EPC) established (*see* page 779)
1988 Second major CAP reform
1991 Maastricht Treaty agreed (*see* page 779)
1992 31 December: Single internal market programme completed
1993 September: the exchange rate mechanism (ERM) of the EMS effectively suspended
      1 November: The Maastricht Treaty enters into force, establishing the European Union (EU)
1994 1 January: European Economic Area (EEA) agreement comes into operation (*see* page 778)
      Norway rejects EU membership in referendum
1997 Amsterdam Treaty agreed
1998 11 states chosen to enter first round of EMU
      European Central Bank replaces European Monetary Institute
1999 1 January: Euro launched
      March: 'Agenda 2000' financial and policy reform agreed
      1 May: The Amsterdam Treaty enters into force

ENLARGEMENT AND EXTERNAL RELATIONS

The procedure for accession to the EU is laid down in the Treaty of Rome; states must be stable European democra-

cies governed by the rule of law with free market economies. A membership application is studied by the Commission, which produces an Opinion. If the Opinion is positive, negotiations may be opened leading to an Accession Treaty which must be approved by all member state governments and parliaments, the European Parliament, and the applicant state's government and parliament.

Applicants: Morocco (applied 1987/rejected 1987), Turkey (applied 1987/negative Opinion 1989), Cyprus (applied 1990/rejected 1993/negotiations begun 1998), Malta (applied 1990/negative Opinion 1993; reapplied 1998), Switzerland (applied 1992/no Opinion yet), Hungary (applied 1994/negotiations begun 1998), Poland (applied 1994/negotiations begun 1998), Bulgaria (applied 1995/offered partnership 1998), Estonia (applied 1995/negotiations begun 1998), Latvia (applied 1995/offered partnership 1998), Lithuania (applied 1995/offered partnership 1998), Romania (applied 1995/offered partnership 1998), Slovakia (applied 1995/offered partnership 1998), the Czech Republic (applied 1996/negotiations begun 1998), Slovenia (applied 1995/negotiations begun 1998).

Apart from the EEA Agreement (*see* page 778), the EU has three types of agreements with other European and CIS states. 'Europe' Agreements commit the EU and signatory states to long-term political and economic integration, a free trade zone (apart from agriculture and labour movement) and eventual EU membership. Government representatives from the signatory states are entitled to attend one summit and two finance and foreign council meetings a year. Association agreements include a commitment to EU financial aid and to eventual membership; agreements have been signed with Malta (1971), Cyprus (1972), Turkey (1974) and Slovenia (1996). Partnership and co-operation agreements are based on regulating and improving political and economic relations and mutual trade concessions but exclude any possibility of membership. Agreements have been signed with Ukraine, Russia, Moldova (1994), Kyrgyzstan and Belarus (1995).

In March 1998, formal accession negotiations were begun with Hungary, Poland, Estonia, the Czech Republic, Slovenia and Cyprus; full membership of the EU is not expected until 2002 at the earliest. Bulgaria, Romania, Latvia, Lithuania and Slovakia have been invited into partnerships with the EU to help speed up preparations for their eventual membership. The European Commission reports each year on the progress towards accession of all thirteen current applicants.

THE COUNCIL OF THE EUROPEAN UNION
175 rue de la Loi, B-1048 Brussels, Belgium

The Council of the European Union (Council of Ministers) consists of ministers from the government of each of the member states. It formally comprises the foreign ministers of the member states but in practice the minister depends on the subject under discussion, e.g. when EC environment matters are under discussion, the meeting is informally known as the Environment Council. Council decisions are taken by qualified majority vote (in which members' votes are weighted), by a simple majority, or by unanimity. Council meetings are prepared by the Committee of Permanent Representatives (COREPER) of the member states, which acts as the 'gatekeeper' between national governments and the supranational EC, often negotiating on proposals with the Commission during the legislative process.

Unanimity votes are taken on sensitive issues such as

taxation and constitutional matters; in preparation for an expanded Union, the Amsterdam Treaty extended areas where qualified majority votes may be taken, to areas such as Single Market laws and harmonization, environment policy, health and safety, transport policy, overseas aid, research and development, culture, consumer protection, education and training, the development of a single currency and social policy. Member states have weighted votes in the Council loosely proportional to their relative population sizes (*see* introductory table), with a total of 87 votes. For a proposal from the Commission to pass, it must receive 62 votes; 26 votes are necessary to block a proposal, and 23 votes constitute a temporary blocking minority. For other proposals to be passed they must receive 62 votes cast by at least ten member states.

The European Council, comprising the heads of government of the member states, meets twice a year to provide overall policy direction. The presidency of the EC is held in rotation for six-month periods, setting the agenda for and chairing all Council meetings. The presidency provides the incumbent nation with an opportunity to pursue its own policy priorities. The European Council holds a summit in the country holding the presidency at the end of its period in office. The holders of the presidency for the years 1999–2001 are:

1999 Germany, Finland
2000 Portugal, France
2001 Sweden, Belgium

OFFICE OF THE UNITED KINGDOM PERMANENT
REPRESENTATIVE TO THE EUROPEAN COMMUNITIES
avenue d'Auderghem, B-1040 Brussels, Belgium
Ambassador and UK Permanent Representative, HE Sir
Stephen Wall, KCMG, LVO, *apptd* 1995
Minister and Deputy Permanent Representative, D. Bostock

THE EUROPEAN COMMISSION
200 rue de la Loi, B-1049 Brussels, Belgium

The Commission consists of 20 Commissioners, two each from France, Germany, Italy, Spain and the UK, and one each from the remaining member states. The members of the Commission are appointed for five-year renewable terms by the agreement of the member states; the terms run concurrently with the terms of the European Parliament. The President and the other Commissioners are nominated by the governments of the Member States, and, under the terms of the Amsterdam Treaty, the appointments are approved by the European Parliament. The Commissioners pledge sole allegiance to the EC. The Commission initiates and implements EC legislation and is the guardian of the EC treaties. It is the exponent of Community-wide interests rather than the national preoccupations of the Council. Each Commissioner is supported by advisers and oversees whichever of the departments, known as Directorates-General (DGs), is assigned to him. Each Directorate-General is headed by a Director-General.

The present Commission came into office on 23 January 1995 but resigned en masse on 16 March 1999 after a committee of experts appointed by the European Parliament concluded that lax management had allowed fraud and nepotism in the Commission's services.

A new President was nominated by the governments of the member states, and approved by the European Parliament. The present Commission will remain in office in a caretaker capacity until a new commission is appointed. This process was delayed until autumn 1999 by European Parliament elections.

The Commission has a total staff of around 15,000 permanent civil servants.

COMMISSIONERS *as at June 1999 (all in a caretaker capacity)*
President
Secretariat-General; Forward Studies Unit; Inspectorate-General; Legal Service; Spokesman's Service; Joint Interpreting and Conference Service; Security Office; Overall responsibility for monetary matters, common foreign and security policy, institutional questions and intergovernmental conference,
Jacques Santer (Luxembourg)
Vice-Presidents
External Relations with North America, Australia, Japan, New Zealand, China, South Korea, Taiwan, Hong Kong, Macao, Common Commercial Policy, Relations with the OECD and WTO, Sir Leon Brittan (UK)
External Relations with the Mediterranean, the Middle East, Latin America and parts of Asia, Manuel Marin (Spain)
Members
Industrial Affairs, Information Technology and Telecommunications, Martin Bangemann (Germany)
Immigration, Interior and Judicial Affairs, Financial Control, Anti-Fraud Measures, Relations with the Ombudsman, Anita Gradin (Sweden)
Agriculture and Rural Development, Franz Fischler (Austria)
Budget, Personnel and Administration, Translation, Erkki Liikanen (Finland)
Economic and Financial Affairs, Monetary Matters, Credit and Investments, Statistical Office, Yves-Thibault de Silguy (France)
Energy and Euratom Supply Agency, Small and Medium Enterprises, Tourism, Christos Papoutis (Greece)
Institutional Questions, Intergovernmental Conference, Relations with the European Parliament, Culture and Audiovisual, Publications Office, Openness, Communications and Information, Marcelino Oreja (Spain)
Transport, Neil Kinnock (UK)
Regional Policy, Relations with the Committee of the Regions, Cohesion Fund, Monika Wulf-Mathies (Germany)
Science, Research and Development, Joint Research Centre, Human Resources, Education, Training and Youth, Edith Cresson (France)
Competition, Karel Van Miert (Belgium)
External Relations with Central and Eastern Europe, the former Soviet Union and other European states, Common Foreign and Security Policy, External Service, Hans van den Broek (Netherlands)
External Relations with African, Caribbean and Pacific States, Lomé Convention, João de Deus Pinheiro (Portugal)
Social Affairs and Employment, Relations with the Economic and Social Committee, Padraig Flynn (Ireland)
Fisheries, Consumer Policy, EC Humanitarian Office, Emma Bonino (Italy)
Environment, Nuclear Safety, Ritt Bjerregaard (Denmark)
Internal Market, Financial Services, Customs, Taxation, Mario Monti (Italy)
Secretary-General, Carlo Trojan (Netherlands)

THE EUROPEAN PARLIAMENT

The European Parliament (EP) originated as the Common Assembly of the ECSC; it acquired its present name in 1962. Members (MEPs) were initially appointed from the membership of national parliaments; direct elections to the Parliament were first held in 1979 and take place at five-year intervals. Elections to the Parliament are held on differing bases throughout the EC; in June 1999, British

EUROPEAN PARLIAMENT POLITICAL GROUPINGS

	PES	EPP	UFE	ELDR	EUL/NGL	Green	ERA	IEN	Ind.	Total
Austria	7	7	–			2	–	–	5	21
Belgium	5	6	–	5	–	5	2	–	2	25
Denmark	3	1	–	6	1	–	–	4	1	16
Finland	3	5	–	5	1	2	–	–	–	16
France	22	15	–	–	6	9	–	13	22	87
Germany	33	53	–	–	6	7	–	–	–	99
Greece	9	9	–	–	5	–	–	–	2	25
Ireland	1	4	6	1	–	2	–	–	1	15
Italy	17	32	9	1	6	2	7	–	13	87
Luxembourg	2	2	–	1	–	1	–	–	–	6
Netherlands	6	9	–	8	1	4	–	3	3	34
Portugal	12	9	2	–	2	–	–	–	–	25
Spain	24	29	–	2	4	–	2	–	–	61
Sweden	6	7	–	4	3	2	–	–	–	22
UK	30	36	–	10	–	2	2	1	6	87
TOTAL	180	224	17	43	35	38	13	21	55	626

PES   Party of European Socialists (including British Labour Party, Northern Ireland Social Democratic and Labour Party, Italian Democratic Left Party) Socialist, Social Democratic and Labour parties

EPP   European People's Party (including British Conservative Party, Northern Ireland Official Unionist Party, Spanish Popular Party, French UDF, Irish Fine Gael, Swedish Moderate Party) Christian Democrats and Conservatives

UFE   Union for Europe (including Forza Italia Party, French Gaullists, Irish Fianna Fáil, Portuguese People's Party)

ELDR   European Liberal Democratic and Reformist Group (including British Liberal Democratic Party, Portuguese Social Democrats) centre and liberal parties

EUL/NGL   Confederal Group of the European United Left/Nordic Green Left (French, Greek and Portuguese Communist Parties, Italian Refounded Communist Party, some Spanish regionalists, Danish, Swedish, Finnish, Greek, Italian and Spanish Green/Left parties)

Green   Green and Ecologist parties

ERA   European Radical Alliance (Scottish National Party, Italian Radical Party, Belgian Flemish and Spanish regionalists)

IEN   Independent Europe of the Nations Group (French Other Europe Group, Dutch and Danish Euro-sceptics)

Ind   Independents (Italian National Alliance, French National Front, Belgian Vlaams Blok, Northern Ireland Democratic Unionist Party)

MEPs were elected for the first time by a 'regional list' system of proportional representation. The Parliament comprises 626 seats. The most recent elections were held in June 1999. For total number of seats per member and political groupings, see table above. MEPs serve on 20 committees, which scrutinize draft EC legislation and the activities of the Commission. A minimum of 12 plenary sessions a year are held in Strasbourg and Brussels, committees meet in Brussels, and the Secretariat's headquarters is in Luxembourg.

The EP has gradually expanded its influence within the EU through the Single European Act, which introduced the co-operation procedure, the Maastricht Treaty, which extended the co-operation procedure and introduced the co-decision procedure (see Legislative Process), and the Amsterdam Treaty, which effectively extended co-decision to all areas except economic and monetary union. It has general powers of supervision over the Commission, and consultation and co-decision with the Council; it votes to approve a newly appointed Commission and can dismiss it at any time by a two-thirds majority (as it threatened to do in January 1999). Under the Maastricht Treaty it has the right to be consulted on the appointment of the new Commission and can veto its appointment. It can reject the EU budget as a whole, alter non-compulsory expenditure not specified in the EU primary legislation, and can question the Commission's management of the budget and call in the Court of Auditors. Although the EP cannot directly initiate legislation, its reports can spur the Commission into action. In accordance with the Maastricht Treaty the EP appointed an ombudsman in October 1995, to provide citizens with redress against maladministration by EU institutions.

The Parliament's organization is deliberately biased in favour of multi-national political groupings, recognition of a political grouping in the parliament entitling it to offices, funding, representation on committees and influence in debates and legislation. A political grouping with members from only one country needs a minimum of 29 members for recognition, whereas one with members from two countries needs 23 members, a grouping with members from three countries needs 18 members, and a grouping with members from four or more countries needs only 14 members.

PARLIAMENT, Palais de l'Europe, F-67006 Strasbourg Cedex, France; 97–113 rue Belliard, 1047 Brussels, Belgium

SECRETARIAT, Centre Européen, Kirchberg, L-2929 Luxembourg

President, José Maria Gil-Robles Gil-Delgado (Spain)

Ombudsman, Jacob Söderman (Finland), 1 avenue du Président Robert Schuman, BP403, F-67001, Strasbourg, France

(For a full list of British MEPs, see page 269)

THE LEGISLATIVE PROCESS

The core of the EU policymaking process is a dialogue between the Commission, which initiates and implements policy, and the Council of Ministers, which takes policy decisions. An increasing degree of democratic control is exercised by the European Parliament.

The original legislative process is known as the consultative procedure. The Commission drafts a proposal which it submits to the Council and to the Parliament. The Council then consults the Economic and Social Committee (ESC), the Parliament and the Committee of the Regions; the Parliament may request that amendments are made. With or without these amendments, the proposal is then adopted by the Council and becomes law.

Under the Single European Act (SEA), the role of the

Parliament was strengthened by the introduction of the co-operation procedure. The Parliament now has a second reading of proposals in some fields, and after the second reading its rejection of a proposal can only be overturned by a unanimous decision of the Council. The Maastricht Treaty extended the scope of the co-operation procedure, which now applies to Single Market laws and harmonization, trans-European networks, development policy, the social fund, and some aspects of transport, environment, research, social policy and competition policy.

The SEA introduced the assent procedure, whereby an absolute majority of the Parliament must vote to approve laws in certain fields before they are passed. Issues covered by the assent procedure include foreign treaties, accession treaties, international agreements with budgetary implications, citizenship, residence rights, the CAP, and regional and structural funds.

The Maastricht Treaty introduced the co-decision procedure; if, after the Parliament's second reading of a proposal, the Council and Parliament fail to agree, a conciliation committee of the two will reach a compromise. If a compromise is not reached, the Parliament can reject the legislation by the vote of an absolute majority of its members. The Amsterdam Treaty extended co-decision to all areas covered by qualified majority voting.

The Council issues the following legislation:
– Regulations, which are binding in their entirety and directly applicable to all member states; they do not need to be incorporated into national law to come into effect
– Directives, which are less specific, binding as to the result to be achieved but leaving the method of implementation open to member states; a directive thus has no force until it is incorporated into national law
– Decisions, which are also binding but are addressed solely to one or more member states or individuals in a member state
– Recommendations
– Opinions, which are merely persuasive

The Council also has certain budgetary powers, including the power to reject the budget as a whole and to increase expenditure or redistribute money within sectors.

THE COMMUNITY BUDGET

The principles of funding the European Community budget were established by the Treaty of Rome and remain with modifications to this day. There is a legally binding limit on the overall level of resources (known as 'own resources') that the Community can raise from its member states; this limit is defined as a percentage of gross national product (GNP). Budget revenue and expenditure must balance and there is therefore no deficit financing. The own resources decision, which came into effect in 1975, states that there are four sources of Community funding under which each member state makes contributions: levies charged on agricultural imports into the Community from non-member states; customs duties on imports from non-member states; contributions based on member states' shares of a notional Community harmonized VAT base; and contributions based on member states' shares of Community GNP. The latter is the budget-balancing item and covers the difference between total expenditure and the revenue from the other three sources. Since 1984 the UK has had an annual rebate equivalent to 66 per cent of the difference between what the UK contributes to the budget and what it receives. This was introduced to compensate the UK for disproportionate contributions caused by its high proportion of agricultural and non-agricultural imports from non-member states and its relatively small receipts from the Common Agricultural

Policy, the most important portion of Community expenditure.

BUDGET 1999

	Billion ECU*	As % of total
Agriculture	40.9	42.2
Regional and Social	39.2	40.5
External Action	6.2	6.4
Administration	4.5	4.6
Research and Technology	3.5	3.6
Consumer Protection, Industry, Internal Market	1.1	1.2
Energy and Environment	0.2	0.2
TOTAL	96.9	99.9

EC BUDGET BY MEMBER STATE 1997 (*billion ECU*)

	Contributions		Receipts	Net gain‡
Germany	21.22	(28.2%)	9.99	−11.23
France	13.19	(17.5%)	12.20	−0.99
UK	8.93	(11.9%)	7.09	−1.83
Italy	8.67	(11.5%)	8.34	−0.32
Netherlands	4.84	(6.4%)	2.49	−2.35
Spain	5.37	(7.1%)	11.22	+5.85
Belgium	2.97	(3.9%)	1.98	−0.99
Austria	2.11	(2.8%)	1.32	−0.79
Sweden	2.33	(3.1%)	1.10	−1.23
Denmark	1.51	(2.0%)	1.53	+0.02
Greece	1.18	(1.6%)	5.37	+4.19
Finland	1.06	(1.4%)	1.07	+0.01
Portugal	1.08	(1.4%)	3.69	+2.61
Ireland	0.69	(0.9%)	3.31	+2.62
Luxembourg	0.17	(0.2%)	0.11	−0.07
TOTAL	75.29	(100%)	70.81	—

* 1 ECU = £0.691 as at 17 September 1998
‡Net contributor (−)/net recipient (+)

Under the Edinburgh summit agreement (December 1992) the EC budget will rise in stages from 1.2 per cent of Community (Union) GNP in 1992 to a maximum of 1.27 per cent in 1999. The agreed budget for 2000–2006 will keep the 1.27 per cent ceiling, but resources devoted to the existing member states will fall to 0.98 per cent, with the remaining resources devoted to enlargement.

THE COMMON AGRICULTURAL POLICY

The Common Agricultural Policy (CAP) was established to increase agricultural production, provide a fair standard of living for farmers and ensure the availability of food at reasonable prices. This aim was achieved by a number of mechanisms:
– import levies
– intervention purchase
– export subsidies

These measures stimulated production but also placed increasing demands on the EC budget which were exacerbated by the increase in EC members and yields enlarged by technological innovation; CAP now accounts for over 40 per cent of EC expenditure. To surmount these problems reforms were agreed in 1984, 1988, 1992, 1997 and 1999.

REFORMS

The 1984 reforms created the system of co-responsibility levies: farm payments to the EC by volume of product sold. This system was supplemented by national quotas for particular products, such as milk. The 1988 reforms emphasized 'set-aside', whereby farmers are given direct grants to take land out of production as a means of reducing surpluses. The set-aside reforms were extended in 1993 for another five years and to every farm in the EC. The 1992 reforms were based on the reduction of target prices for cereals, beef and dairy produce, which were reduced by 29 per cent, 15 per cent and 5 per cent respectively. The 1999 reforms will further reduce surpluses of cereals, beef and milk by cutting the intervention prices by up to 20 per cent and compensating producers by making area payments. Under the reforms, CAP rules will also be simplified, eliminating inconsistencies between policies.

Under the Uruguay round agreement of GATT concluded in 1993, the EU must, over a six-year period from 1 January 1995, reduce its import levies by 36 per cent, reduce its domestic subsidies by 20 per cent, reduce its export subsidies by 36 per cent in value, and reduce its subsidized exports by 21 per cent in volume. Agenda 2000, the programme to overhaul the institutions of the EU and prepare it for the accession of Central European states, will increase the cost of the CAP by £1,000 million a year in compensation payments in the short term, in the hope of achieving savings on farm subsidies by 2006.

THE SINGLE MARKET

Even after the removal of tariffs and quotas between member states in the 1970s and 1980s, the EC was still separated into a number of national markets by a series of non-tariff barriers. It was to overcome these internal barriers to trade that the concept of the Single Market was developed. The measures to be undertaken were codified in the Single European Act (SEA) 1986, which came into force in 1987 with a target date of 31 December 1992 for completion.

The SEA includes articles removing obstacles that distort the internal market: the elimination of frontier controls; the mutual recognition of professional qualifications; the harmonization of product specifications, largely by the mutual recognition of national standards; open tendering for public procurement contracts; the free movement of capital; the harmonization of VAT and excise duties; and the reduction of state aid to particular industries. The SEA changed the legislative process within the EC, particularly with the introduction of qualified majority voting in the Council of Ministers for some policy areas, and the introduction of the assent procedure in the European Parliament. The SEA also extends EC competence into the fields of technology, the environment, regional policy, monetary policy and external policy. The Single Market came into effect on 1 January 1993 and is expected to result in at least a 5 per cent increase in the collective GNP of EC member states. The full implementation of the elimination of frontier controls and the harmonization of taxes have, however, been repeatedly delayed.

THE EUROPEAN ECONOMIC AREA (see also EFTA, page 755)

The EC Single Market programme spurred European non-member states to open negotiations with the EC on preferential access for their goods, services, labour and capital to the Single Market. Principal among these states were European Free Trade Association (EFTA) members who opened negotiations on extending the Single Market to EFTA by the formation of the European Economic Area (EEA) encompassing all 19 EC and EFTA states. Agreement was reached in May 1992 but the operation of the EEA was delayed by its rejection in a Swiss referendum, necessitating an additional protocol agreed by the remaining 18 states. The EEA came into effect on 1 January 1994 after ratification by 17 member states (Liechtenstein joined on 1 May 1995 after adapting its customs union with Switzerland).

Austria, Finland and Sweden joined the EU itself on 1 January 1995, leaving only Norway, Iceland and Liechtenstein as the non-EU EEA members. Under the EEA agreement, the three states are to adopt the EU's *acquis communautaire*, apart from in the fields of agriculture, fisheries, and coal and steel.

The EEA is controlled by regular ministerial meetings and by a joint EU-EFTA committee which extends relevant EU legislation to EEA states. Apart from single market measures, there is co-operation in education, research and development, consumer policy and tourism. An EFTA Court of Justice has been established in Luxembourg and an EFTA Surveillance Authority in Brussels to supervise the implementation of the EEA Agreement.

THE EUROPEAN MONETARY SYSTEM AND THE SINGLE CURRENCY

The European monetary system (EMS) began operation in March 1979 with three main purposes. The first was to establish monetary stability in Europe, initially in exchange rates between EC member state currencies through the exchange rate mechanism (ERM), and in the longer term to be part of a wider stabilization process, overcoming inflation and budget and trade deficits. The second purpose was to overcome the constraints resulting from the interdependence of EC economies, and the third was to aid the long-term process of European monetary integration.

The Maastricht Treaty set in motion timetables for achieving economic and monetary union (EMU) and a single currency (the euro). At the Brussels summit in May 1998, 11 member states were judged to fulfil or be close to fulfilling the necessary criteria for participation in the first stage of EMU: Austria, Belgium, Finland, France, Germany, Ireland, Italy, Luxembourg, the Netherlands, Portugal and Spain.

The criteria were that:
– the budget deficit should be 3 per cent or less of gross domestic product (GDP)
– total national debt must not exceed 60 per cent of GDP
– inflation should be no more than 1.5 per cent above the average rate of the three best performing economies in the EU
– long-term interest rates should be no more than 2 per cent above the average of the three best performing economies in the EU in the previous 12 months
– applicants must have been members of the ERM for two years without having realigned or devalued their currency

Under the terms of a growth and stability pact agreed in Dublin in December 1996, penalties may be imposed on EMU members with high budget deficits. Governments with deficits exceeding 3 per cent of GDP will receive a warning and will be obliged to pay up to 0.5 per cent of their GDP into a fund after ten months. This will become a fine if the budget deficit is not rectified within two years. A member state with negative growth will be allowed to apply for an exemption from the fine in 'exceptional circumstances', e.g. a recession whereby GDP had fallen by 0.75 per cent or more during one year.

On 1 January 1999, the qualifying member states irrevocably fixed their exchange rates against each other and against the euro (see table below), the European Central Bank (ECB) took charge of the single monetary policy, and the euro replaced the ECU. The euro is now the legal currency in the participating states. Euro notes and coins will be introduced from 1 January 2002 and will circulate alongside national currencies for a maximum of six months, after which time national currencies will be abolished.

THE CONVERSION RATES BETWEEN THE EURO AND THE CURRENCIES OF THE MEMBER STATES ADOPTING THE EURO ARE:

1 euro =		
	13.7603	Austrian Schillings
	40.3399	Belgian Francs
	2.20371	Dutch Gulden
	5.94573	Finnish Markka
	6.55957	French Francs
	1.95583	German Deutsche Mark
	0.787564	Irish Punts
	1,936.27	Italian Lire
	40.3399	Luxembourg Francs
	200.482	Portuguese Escudos
	166.386	Spanish Pesetas

Source: The Official Journal of the European Communities

The ECB (*see also* page 780) meets every two weeks to set interest rates for the countries participating in the euro. Its board has 17 members, six appointed by the ECB and 11 representing the national central banks of the participating states.

The UK, Denmark and Sweden chose not to take part in the first stage of EMU; Greece was unable to meet the criteria. With the advent of EMU, the ERM was revised and Denmark and Greece became members of ERM II, which requires them to maintain their currencies within set margins of the euro. Membership of ERM II is voluntary, although all member states outside the euro zone are encouraged to take part. Sweden and the UK are currently not members.

THE MAASTRICHT TREATY

The Treaty on European Union was agreed at a meeting of the European Council in Maastricht, the Netherlands, in December 1991. It came into effect in November 1993 following ratification by the member states.

Three 'pillars' formed the basis of the new treaty:
– the European Community with its established institutions and decision-making processes
– a Common Foreign and Security Policy (*see* below) with the Western European Union as the potential defence component of the EU
– co-operation in justice and home affairs, with the Council of Ministers to co-ordinate policies on asylum, immigration, conditions of entry, cross-border crime, drug trafficking and terrorism
The Treaty established a common European citizenship for nationals of all member states and introduced the principle of subsidiarity whereby decisions are taken at the most appropriate level: national, regional or local. It extended EC competency into the areas of environmental and industrial policies, consumer affairs, health, and education and training, and extended qualified majority voting in the Council of Ministers to cover areas which had previously required a unanimous vote. The powers of the European Parliament over the budget and over the Commission were also enhanced and a co-decision procedure enabled the Parliament to override decisions made by the Council of Ministers (*see* pages 774–5). A separate protocol to the Maastricht Treaty on social policy was adopted by 11 states and was incorporated into the Amsterdam Treaty in 1997 following adoption by the UK.

THE AMSTERDAM TREATY

The treaties of Rome and Maastricht were again amended through the Treaty of Amsterdam, which came into effect on 1 May 1999. It extends the scope of qualified majority voting and the powers of the European Parliament.

COMMON FOREIGN AND SECURITY POLICY

The Common Foreign and Security Policy (CFSP) was created as a pillar of the EU by the Maastricht Treaty (*see* above). It adopted the machinery of the European Political Co-operation (EPC) framework which it replaced and was charged with providing a forum for member states and EU institutions to consult on foreign affairs.

The CFSP system is headed by the European Council, which provides general lines of policy. Specific policy decisions are taken by the Council of Foreign Ministers, which meets at least four times a year to determine areas for joint action. The foreign minister of the state holding the EU presidency initiates action, manages the CFSP and represents it abroad.. The Council of Ministers is supported by the Political Committee which meets monthly, or within 48 hours if there is a crisis, to prepare for ministerial discussions. A group of correspondents, designated diplomats in each member's foreign ministry, provides day-to-day contact.

The Amsterdam Treaty introduced qualified majority voting for foreign affairs and created a high representative on CFSP to act as a spokesperson. It also established a new policy planning and early warning unit to monitor international developments. The unit is to consist of specialists from the member states, the Council and the Commission, as well as from the WEU.

THE SCHENGEN AGREEMENT

The Schengen Agreement was signed by France, Germany, Belgium, Luxembourg and the Netherlands in 1990 to replace an accord on border controls agreed in Schengen, Luxembourg, in 1985. The Agreement committed the five states to abolishing internal border controls and erecting external frontiers against illegal immigrants, drug traffickers, terrorists and organized crime.

Subsequently signed by Spain and Portugal, the Agreement was ratified by the seven signatory states and entered into force in March 1995 with the removal of frontier, passport, customs and immigration controls. Italy and Austria became full members in April 1998. Provisional agreement was reached in June 1995 between the signatory states and the Nordic Union on a merger of the two frontier-free zones, but Denmark, Finland and Sweden are not yet full members, nor is Greece, although all four have signed the Schengen Agreement. The UK and the Republic of Ireland have not signed the agreement, but have expressed their intention to join in some aspects of its work.

The Schengen Agreement originated as an intergovernmental agreement but became part of the EU following the signing of the Amsterdam Treaty.

COURT OF JUSTICE OF THE EUROPEAN COMMUNITIES
L–2925 Luxembourg

The European Court superseded the Court of Justice of the ECSC and is common to the three European Communities. It exists to safeguard the law in the interpretation and application of the Community treaties, to decide on the legality of decisions of the Council of Ministers or the Commission, and to determine infringements of the treaties. Cases may be brought to it by the member states, the Community institutions, firms or individuals. Its decisions are directly binding in the member countries, and the Maastricht Treaty enhanced the Court's powers by permitting it to impose fines on member states. The 15 judges and nine advocates-general of the Court are appointed for renewable six-year terms by the member governments in concert. During 1998, 485 new cases were lodged at the court, 420 cases were concluded and 254 judgments were delivered.

Composition of the Court, in order of precedence, with effect from 8 October 1998:

G. C. Rodríguez Iglesias (*President*); P. J. G. Kapteyn (*President of the 4th and 6th Chambers*); J.-P. Puissochet (*President of the 3rd and 5th Chambers*); P. Léger (*First Advocate General*); G. Hirsch (*President of the 2nd Chamber*); P. Jann (*President of the 1st Chamber*); G. F. Mancini (*Judge*); J. C. Moitinho de Almeida (*Judge*); F. G. Jacobs (*Advocate-General*); C. Gulmann (*Judge*); J. L. Murray (*Judge*); D. A. O. Edward (*Judge*); A. M. La Pergola (*Advocate-General*); G. Cosmas (*Advocate-General*); H. Ragnemalm (*Judge*); L. Sevón (*Judge*); N. Fennelly (*Advocate-General*); D. Ruiz-Jarabo Colomer (*Advocate-General*); M. Wathelet (*Judge*); R. Schintgen (*Judge*); K. M. Ioannou (*Judge*); S. Alber (*Advocate-General*); J. Mischo (*Advocate-General*); A. Saggio (*Advocate-General*); R. Grass (*Registrar*)

COURT OF FIRST INSTANCE
L-2925 Luxembourg

Established under powers conferred by the Single European Act, the Court of First Instance started to exercise its functions at the end of October 1989. It had jurisdiction to hear and determine certain categories of cases brought by natural or legal persons, in particular cases brought by European Community officials, or cases on competition law. By a Council decision of 1993 the court had its jurisdiction enlarged to hear and determine all actions brought by natural or legal persons. During 1998, 215 new cases were lodged at the court, 319 cases were concluded and 150 judgments were delivered.

Composition of the Court, in order of precedence, for the judicial year 1998–9:

B. Vesterdorf (*President of the Court of First Instance*); A. Potocki (*President of Chamber*); R. Moura Ramos (*President of Chamber*); J. D. Cooke (*President of Chamber*); M. Jaeger (*President of Chamber*); R. García-Valdecasas y Fernández (*Judge*); K. Lenaerts (*Judge*); C. W. Bellamy (*Judge*); V. Tiili (*Judge*); P. Lindh (*Judge*); J. Azizi (*Judge*); J. Pirrung (*Judge*); P. Mengozzi (*Judge*); A. Meij (*Judge*); M. Vilaras (*Judge*); H. Jung (*Registrar*)

THE COMMITTEE OF THE REGIONS
79 rue Belliard, B-1040 Brussels, Belgium

The Committee of the Regions (COR) is an advisory and consultative body established to redress the lack of a role for regional and local authorities in the EU democratic system. The COR is composed of 222 appointed and indirectly elected members, of whom half are from large regions and half are from small local authorities, who meet five times each year for two days. The COR delivers opinions on policies affecting regions, such as trans-border transport links, economic and social cohesion, education and training, social policy, culture and regional policy.
President, Manfred Dammeyer (Germany)

THE ECONOMIC AND SOCIAL COMMITTEE
Ravensteinstraat 2, B-1000 Brussels, Belgium

The Economic and Social Committee (ESC) is an advisory and consultative body. It has 222 members, nominated by member states, and is divided into three groups: employers, workers, and other interest groups such as consumers, farmers and the self-employed. It issues opinions on draft EC legislation and can bring matters to the attention of the Commission, Council and Parliament. Consultation of the ESC by the Parliament is enshrined in the Amsterdam Treaty, formally recognizing the importance of the opinions of the EU's economic and social partners.
President, Beatrice Rangoni Machiavelli (Italy)

THE EUROPEAN CENTRAL BANK
29 Kaiserstrasse, D-60311 Frankfurt-am-Main, Germany

The European Central Bank (ECB), which superseded the European Monetary Institute, was established on 1 July 1998. It consists of the President, the Vice-President and four members of the executive board, who are appointed by the governments of the participating states, from people with recognized standing and professional experience. The ECB is independent of national governments. It became fully operational on 1 January 1999, and defines and implements the single monetary policy necessary for EMU. It works with the European System of Central Banks (ESCB), which is made up of the governors of the central banks of member states.
President, Willem Duisenberg (Netherlands)
Vice-President, Christian Noyer (France)

THE EUROPEAN COURT OF AUDITORS
12 rue A. De Gasperi, L-1615 Luxembourg

The European Court of Auditors, established in 1977, is responsible for the audit of the legality and regularity as well as of the sound financial management of the resources managed by the European Communities and Community bodies. The Court of Auditors may also submit observations on specific questions and deliver opinions. The Court of Auditors draws up an annual report and a statement of assurance on the accounts and underlying operations of the Communities. The Maastricht Treaty designated the Court of Auditors as a full institution of the European Union, enabling it to take other institutions to the Court of Justice. It has 15 members appointed for six-year terms by the Council of Ministers following consultation with the European Parliament.
President, Jan Karlsson (Sweden)

THE EUROPEAN INVESTMENT BANK
100 boulevard Konrad Adenauer, L-2950 Luxembourg

The European Investment Bank (EIB) was set up in 1958 under the terms of the Treaty of Rome to finance capital investment projects promoting the balanced development of the European Community.

It grants long-term loans to private and public enterprises, public authorities and financial institutions, to finance projects which further the economic development of less advanced regions (Assisted Areas); improvement of European communications; environmental protection; attainment of the EU's energy policy objectives; modernization of enterprises, co-operation between undertakings in the different member states, and the activities of small and medium-sized enterprises.

EIB activities have also been extended outside member countries as part of the EU's development co-operation policy, under the terms of different association or co-operation agreements with 12 countries in the Mediterranean region, 11 in central and eastern Europe, 30 in Latin America and Asia, South Africa, and, under the Lomé Conventions, 70 in Africa, the Caribbean and the Pacific.

The Bank's total financing operations in 1998 amounted to 29,526 million euro, of which 25,116 million was for investment in the EU and 4,410 million for investment outside the EU. Between 1994 and 1998 the EIB made available a total of more than 120,000 million euro for investment.

The members of the EIB are the 15 member states of the EU, who have all subscribed to the Bank's capital of 100,000 billion euro. The bulk of the funds required by the Bank to carry out its tasks are borrowed on the capital markets of the EU and non-member countries, and on the international market.

As it operates on a non-profit-making basis, the interest rates charged by the EIB reflect the cost of the Bank's borrowings and closely follow conditions on world capital markets.

The Board of Governors of the EIB consists of one government minister nominated by each of the member countries, usually the finance minister, who lay down general directives on the policy of the Bank and appoint members to the Board of Directors (24 nominated by the member states, one by the European Commission), which takes decisions on the granting and raising of loans and the fixing of interest rates. A Management Committee, composed of the Bank's President and seven Vice-Presidents, also appointed by the Board of Governors, is responsible for the day-to-day operations of the Bank. The President and Vice-Presidents also preside as Chairman and Vice-Chairmen at meetings of the Board of Directors.

President, Sir Brian Unwin, KCB

Vice-Presidents, Wolfgang Roth; Panagiotis-Loukas Gennimatas; Massimo Ponzellini; Louis Martí; Ariane Obolensky; Rudolf de Korte; Claes de Neergaard
UK OFFICE: 68 Pall Mall, London SW1Y 5ES. Tel: 0171-343 1200

THE EUROPEAN POLICE OFFICE
Raamweg 47, NL-2596 HN The Hague, The Netherlands

The European Police Office (Europol), which came into being on 1 October 1998 superseding the European Drugs Agency, was created to improve police co-operation between member states and to combat terrorism, illicit traffic in drugs and other serious forms of international crime. Each member state has set up a national unit to liaise with Europol, and the units send at least one liaison officer to represent its interests at Europol headquarters. Europol maintains a computerized information system, designed to facilitate the exchange of information between member states; the system is maintained by the national units and may be consulted by Europol agents. The computerized database may contain both personal and non-personal data; individuals are entitled to request access to data concerning themselves. All Europol activities are monitored by an independent joint supervisory body, to ensure the rights of the individual are upheld.

Co-ordinator, Juergen Storbeck (Germany)

Other bodies:

THE EUROPEAN MEDICINE EVALUATION AGENCY, London
THE EUROPEAN TRADEMARK OFFICE, Alicante
THE EUROPEAN AGENCY FOR HEALTH AND SAFETY AT WORK, Bilbao
THE EUROPEAN DRUGS OBSERVATORY, Lisbon
THE EUROPEAN FOUNDATION FOR TRAINING, Turin
THE EUROPEAN CENTRE FOR THE DEVELOPMENT OF VOCATIONAL TRAINING, Thessaloniki
THE EUROPEAN ENVIRONMENT AGENCY, Copenhagen
THE EUROPEAN TRANSLATION AGENCY, Luxembourg

EUROPEAN COMMUNITY INFORMATION

EUROPEAN COMMISSION REPRESENTATIVE OFFICES
ENGLAND, 8 Storey's Gate, London SW1P 3AT. Tel: 0171-973 1992
WALES, 4 Cathedral Road, Cardiff CF1 9SG. Tel: 01222-371631
SCOTLAND, 9 Alva Street, Edinburgh EH2 4HP. Tel: 0131-225 2058
NORTHERN IRELAND, Windsor House, 9–15 Bedford Street, Belfast BT2 7EG. Tel: 01232-240708
REPUBLIC OF IRELAND, 39 Molesworth Street, Dublin 2
AUSTRALIA, 18 Alakana Street, Yarralumla, ACT 2600, and a number of other cities
CANADA, Inn of the Provinces, Office Tower (Suite 1110), 350 Sparks Street, Ottawa, Ontario K1R 7SA
USA, 2100 M Street NW (Suite 707), Washington DC 20037; 1 Dag Hammarskjöld Plaza, 254 East 47th Street, New York, NY 10017

UK EUROPEAN PARLIAMENT INFORMATION OFFICE
2 Queen Anne's Gate, London SW1H 9AA. Tel: 0171-227 4300

There are European Information Centres, set up to give information and advice to small businesses, in 25 British towns and cities. A number of universities maintain European Documentation Centres.

Travel Overseas

PASSPORT REGULATIONS

Applications for United Kingdom passports must be made on the forms obtainable from regional passport offices (*see* below), main post offices and WorldChoice travel agents.

LONDON – Passport Office, Clive House, 70–78 Petty France, London SWIH 9HD

LIVERPOOL – Passport Office, 5th Floor, India Buildings, Water Street, Liverpool L2 0QZ

NEWPORT – Passport Office, Olympia House, Upper Dock Street, Newport, Gwent NP9 IXA

PETERBOROUGH – Passport Office, Aragon Court, Northminster Road, Peterborough PEI 1QG

GLASGOW – Passport Office, 3 Northgate, 96 Milton Street, Cowcaddens, Glasgow G4 0BT

BELFAST – Passport Office, Hampton House, 47–53 High Street, Belfast BTI 2QS

Central telephone number: 0870-521 0410
Central fax number: 0171-271 8581
Web site: http://www.open.gov.ukpass/ukpass.htm

Telephone calls are normally routed automatically to the nearest office unless all lines are busy, when the call will be rerouted to other offices. Recorded messages to deal with routine enquiries operate 24 hours a day.

The passport offices are open Monday–Friday 9 a.m. to 4.30 p.m. (8.15 a.m. to 4 p.m. in London). The Passport Office in London is also open for cases of emergency (e.g. death or serious illness) arising outside normal office hours between 4 p.m. and 6 p.m. Monday to Friday, between 10 a.m. and 7 p.m. on Saturdays, and between 9.30 a.m. and 2.30 p.m. on Sundays and Bank Holidays.

Straightforward, properly completed applications are processed within 15 working days from April to August, the busiest period, and within ten working days for the rest of the year. Applying in person does not guarantee that an application will be given priority.

The completed application form should be posted, with the appropriate documents and fee, to the regional passport office indicated on the addressed envelope which is provided with each application form (an exception to this is the London office which is a calling-in office only). Accompanying cheques and postal orders should be crossed and made payable to 'The Passport Office'.

A passport cannot be issued or extended on behalf of a person already abroad; such persons should apply to the nearest British High Commission or Consulate.

UK passports are granted to:
(i)   British citizens
(ii) British Dependent Territories citizens
(iii) British Nationals (Overseas)
(iv) British Overseas citizens
(v)   British Subjects
(vi) British Protected Persons

UK passports are generally available for travel to all countries. The possession of a passport does not, however, exempt the holder from compliance with any immigration regulations in force in British or foreign countries, or from the necessity of obtaining a visa where required.

A new, machine-readable application form is being introduced from July 1998. This replaces the five different application forms previously used, and takes into account the fact that all children will require their own passports (*see* below). The new form also covers amendments and extensions.

ADULTS

A passport granted to a person over 16 will normally be valid for ten years and will not be renewable. Thereafter, or if at any time the passport contains no further space for visas, a new passport must be obtained.

The issue of passports including details of the holder's spouse has been discontinued, but existing family passports may be used until expiry. A spouse who is included in a family passport cannot travel on the passport without the holder.

CHILDREN

From 5 October 1998 all children under the age of 16 will be required to have their own passport, primarily to help prevent child abductions. They will normally be valid for five years, after which point a new passport application must be made. This replaces the system whereby children under the age of 16 could either have their own document or be added to their parents' passports.

A passport granted to a child prior to this date is still valid for five years, although the free, five-year extension option no longer exists. On expiry, a new application must be made. Children included in their parents' passports when the new regulations come into force will not be affected and, assuming that the documents do not expire, can continue to travel on them until they reach the age of 16 or the passport expires or is amended.

COUNTERSIGNATURES

The completed application form should be countersigned by an MP, justice of the peace, minister of religion, a professionally qualified person (e.g. doctor, engineer, lawyer, teacher), bank officer, established Civil Servant, police officer or a person of similar standing who has known the applicant for at least two years, and who is either a British citizen, British Dependent Territories citizen, British National (Overseas), British Overseas citizen, British Subject or a citizen of a Commonwealth country. A relative must not countersign the application.

If the application is for a child under the age of 16, the countersignature should be by someone of relevant standing who has known the parent or person with parental responsibility who signs the declaration of consent, rather than the child.

PHOTOGRAPHS

Two identical unmounted photographs of the applicant must be sent. These photographs should be printed on normal thin photographic paper. They should measure 45 mm×35 mm (1.77 in×1.38 in) and should be taken full face against a white background. One photograph should be certified as a true likeness of the applicant by the person who countersigns the application form.

DOCUMENTATION

The applicant's birth certificate or previous British passport, and other documents in support of the statements made in the application must be produced at the time of applying. Details of which documents are required are set out in the notes accompanying the application form.

If the applicant for a passport is a British national by naturalization or registration, the certificate proving this must be produced with the application, unless the applicant holds a previous UK passport issued after registration or naturalization.

48-PAGE PASSPORTS

The 48-page passport is intended to meet the needs of frequent travellers who fill standard passports well before the validity has expired. It is valid for ten years.

PASSPORT FEES* *from March 1998*

New adult passport	£21
New child passport	£11
Renewal of passport	£21
Amendment of passport	£11
48-page passport	£31

* postal applications only. A £10 charge is added for applications made in person at a passport office in the UK or made abroad

VISAS

British nationals planning to travel overseas should enquire about visa requirements at the Foreign and Commonwealth Office, or the high commission or consulate of their country of destination (*see* the Countries of the World section). Visa requirements may vary depending on the purpose or the length of the visit, and regulations are also liable to change, sometimes at short notice.

Overseas nationals who wish to enter the UK must satisfy the immigration officer at the port of arrival that they meet the requirements of the UK immigration rules. Separate rules apply to nationals of a member state of the European Economic Area (member states of the European Union and Iceland, Liechtenstein and Norway). Details are available from the nearest British mission (*see* the Countries of the World section).

Nationals from the following countries must have a valid visa issued prior to travel to the UK, unless they are settled in the UK or are in the UK for some long-term purpose (more than six months) and returning within the period of a permission to stay granted previously: Afghanistan; Albania; Algeria; Angola; Armenia; Azerbaijan; Bahrain; Bangladesh; Belarus; Benin; Bhutan; Bosnia-Hercegovina; Bulgaria; Burkina Faso; Burundi; Cambodia; Cameroon; Cape Verde; Central African Republic; Chad; China; Colombia; Comoros; Democratic Republic of Congo; Republic of Congo; Côte d'Ivoire; Cuba; Northern Cyprus ('Turkish Republic of Northern Cyprus'); Djibouti; Dominican Republic; Ecuador; Egypt; Equatorial Guinea; Eritrea; Ethiopia; Fiji; Gabon; Gambia; Georgia; Ghana; Guinea; Guinea-Bissau; Guyana; Haiti; India; Indonesia; Iran; Iraq; Jordan; Kazakhstan; Kenya; Korea (North); Kuwait; Kyrgyzstan; Laos; Lebanon; Liberia; Libya; Macedonia (Former Yugoslav Republic of); Madagascar; Maldives; Mali; Mauritania; Mauritius; Moldova; Mongolia; Morocco; Mozambique; Myanmar (Burma); Nepal; Niger; Nigeria; Oman; Pakistan; Palestinian Authority; Papua New Guinea; Peru; Philippines; Qatar; Romania; Russia; Rwanda; São Tomé and Princípe; Saudi Arabia; Senegal; Sierra Leone; Slovak Republic; Somalia; Sri Lanka; Sudan; Suriname; Syria; Taiwan; Tajikistan; Tanzania; Thailand; Togo; Tunisia; Turkey; Turkmenistan; Uganda; Ukraine; United Arab Emirates; Uzbekistan; Vatican City; Vietnam; Yemen; Yugoslavia (Federal Republic of); Zambia.

A valid entry clearance is also required by people who are stateless or who hold a non-national travel document or passport issued by an authority not recognized by the UK.

Nationals of any country not listed above do not need an entry clearance to visit or study in the UK but must obtain entry clearance to settle, work or set up business. Entry clearances take the form of an entry certificate for non-visa nationals.

UK entry clearances can be obtained from British embassies, consulates and high commissions overseas (*see* Countries of the World section).

HEALTH ADVICE

Health Advice for Travellers (booklet T6), published by the Department of Health, contains information on health precautions, reciprocal health agreements with other countries, and immunization. It is available from some travel agents, local post offices or the Department of Health, PO Box 777, London SE1 6XH. Tel: 0800-555777 (single copy orders).

IMMUNIZATION

In very general terms immunization against typhoid, polio and hepatitis A should be considered for all countries where standards of hygiene and sanitation may be less than ideal. Protection against malaria, in the form of tablets, as well as measures to avoid mosquito bites, is advised for visits to malarious areas.

Immunization against yellow fever is compulsory for entry into some countries, either for all travellers or for those arriving from a yellow fever-infected area, and is recommended for all travellers to infected areas.

A doctor should be consulted, preferably at least eight weeks before departure, and will advise travellers and arrange vaccinations. If children will be travelling outside Europe, North America, Australia and New Zealand, the doctor should be informed, especially if they have not completed their full course of childhood immunization.

Country-by-country guidance is set out in *Health Advice for Travellers*. Health care professionals can obtain up-to-date information about immunization recommendations from the Department of Health publication *Health Information for Overseas Travel* or from:

ENGLAND – Communicable Disease Surveillance Centre, 61 Colindale Avenue, London NW9 5EQ. Tel: 0181-200 6868

WALES – Welsh Office, Cathays Park, Cardiff CF1 3NQ. Tel: 01222-825111

SCOTLAND – Scottish Office Department of Health, St Andrew's House, Edinburgh EH1 3DG. Tel: 0131-556 8400; or The Scottish Centre for Infection and Environmental Health, Clifton House, Clifton Place, Glasgow G3 7LN. Tel: 0141-300 1130

NORTHERN IRELAND – DHSS, Castle Buildings, Stormont, Belfast BT4 3PP. Tel: 01232-520000

MEDICAL TREATMENT ABROAD

Details of free or reduced cost emergency medical treatment when visiting European countries, and countries with which the UK has reciprocal health arrangements, are set out in *Health Advice for Travellers*. It also contains Form E111, the certificate that entitles people to urgent medical treatment in the European Economic Area (EEA), as well as guidance on its completion.

For countries where the UK has no health care agreements, including Canada, the USA, India, the Far East, and the whole of Africa and Latin America, it is advisable to take out medical insurance. A certain amount of insurance is also needed in countries with which the UK has health care agreements.

BUSINESS ABROAD

WORKING ABROAD

A passport issued after 31 December 1982 showing the holder's national status as British citizen will secure for the holder the right to take employment or to establish himself/herself in business or other self-employed activity in another member state of the European Union. A passport bearing the endorsement 'holder has the right of abode in the United Kingdom' where the holder so qualifies will also secure the same right.

In most other countries, employment permits are required, even for casual labour. The nearest representative of the country concerned should be consulted. Local employment offices have a booklet entitled *Working Abroad*.

EXPORT BUSINESS

Those planning to export are advised to contact British Trade International, the joint Department of Trade and Industry (DTI) and Foreign and Commonwealth Office export operation. The aim of British Trade International is to encourage potential exporters to consider selling overseas and existing exporters to sell more, and its offices can offer advice and information about the markets to be visited. British Trade International can be contacted through the following:

ENGLAND – Local Business Links offices

WALES – Welsh Office Industry Department, Cathays Park, Cardiff CF1 3NQ. Tel: 01222-825097

SCOTLAND – Scottish Trade International, 120 Bothwell Street, Glasgow G2 7PJ. Tel: 0141-228 2808

NORTHERN IRELAND – Export Development Branch, IDB House, 64 Chichester Street, Belfast BT1 4JX. Tel: 01232-233233

Information about specific overseas markets is available from the country desks at the DTI's headquarters: 1 Victoria Street, London SW1H 0ET. Tel: 0171-215 5000.

For details of the nearest Business Link, contact the Business Links Network. Tel: 0345-567765

Countries of the World

WORLD AREA AND POPULATION

The total population of the world in mid-1990 was estimated at 5,292 million, compared with 3,019 million in 1960 and 2,070 million in 1930.

Continent, etc.	Area sq. miles '000	sq. km '000	Estimated population mid-1990
Africa	11,704	30,313	642,000,000
North America[1]	8,311	21,525	276,000,000
Latin America[2]	7,933	20,547	448,000,000
Asia[3]	10,637	27,549	3,113,000,000
Europe[4]	1,915	4,961	498,000,000
Former USSR	8,649	22,402	289,000,000
Oceania[5]	3,286	8,510	26,500,000
TOTAL	52,435	135,807	5,292,000,000

[1] Includes Greenland and Hawaii
[2] Mexico and the remainder of the Americas south of the USA
[3] Includes European Turkey, excludes former USSR
[4] Excludes European Turkey and former USSR
[5] Includes Australia, New Zealand and the islands inhabited by Micronesian, Melanesian and Polynesian peoples
Source UN Demographic Yearbook 1990 (pub. 1992)

A United Nations report *The Sex and Age Distribution of the World Populations* (revised 1994) puts the world's population in the late 20th and the 21st centuries at the following levels (medium variant data):

1995	5,716.4m	2030	8,670.6m
2000	6,158.0m	2040	9,318.2m
2010	7,032.3m	2050	9,833.2m
2020	7,887.8m		

The population forecast for the years 2000 and 2050 is:

Continent, etc.	Estimated population (million) 2000	2050
Africa	831.596	2,140.844
North America[1]	306.280	388.997
Latin America[2]	523.875	838.527
Asia	3,753.846	5,741.005
Europe	729.803	677.764
Oceania	30.651	46.070
TOTAL	6,158.051	9,833.207

[1] Includes Bermuda, Greenland, and St Pierre and Miquelon
[2] Mexico and the remainder of the Americas south of the USA

AREA AND POPULATION BY CONTINENT

No complete survey of many countries has yet been achieved and consequently accurate area figures are not always available. Similarly, many countries have not recently, or have never, taken a census. The areas of countries given below are derived from estimated figures published by the United Nations. The conversion factors used are:

(i) to convert square miles to square km, multiply by 2.589988

(ii) to convert square km to square miles, multiply by 0.3861022

Population figures for countries are derived from the most recent estimates available. Accurate and up-to-date data for the populations of capital cities are scarce, and definitions of cities' extent differ. The figures given below are the latest estimates available.

Ψ seaport

AFRICA

COUNTRY/TERRITORY	AREA sq. miles	sq. km	POPULATION	CAPITAL	POPULATION OF CAPITAL
Algeria	919,595	2,381,741	29,168,000	Ψ Algiers	1,740,461
Angola	481,354	1,246,700	11,185,000	Ψ Luanda	475,328
Benin	43,484	112,622	5,563,000	Ψ Porto Novo	179,138
Botswana	224,607	581,730	1,490,000	Gaborone	286,779
Burkina Faso	105,792	274,000	10,780,000	Ouagadougou	634,479
Burundi	10,747	27,834	6,088,000	Bujumbura	235,440
Cameroon	183,569	475,442	13,560,000	Yaoundé	653,670
Cape Verde	1,557	4,033	396,000	Ψ Praia	61,644
Central African Republic	240,535	622,984	3,344,000	Bangui	473,817
Chad	495,755	1,284,000	6,515,000	N'Djaména	179,000
Comoros	863	2,235	632,000	Moroni	17,267
Congo, Dem. Rep. of	905,355	2,344,858	46,812,000	Kinshasa	2,664,309
Congo – Brazzaville, Rep. of	132,047	342,000	2,668,000	Brazzaville	596,200
Côte d'Ivoire	124,504	322,463	14,781,000	Yamoussoukro	126,191
Djibouti	8,958	23,200	617,000	Ψ Djibouti	62,000
Egypt	386,662	1,001,449	60,603,000	Cairo	6,800,000
Equatorial Guinea	10,831	28,051	410,000	Ψ Malabo	30,418
Eritrea	45,406	117,600	3,280,000	Asmara	358,100
Ethiopia	426,373	1,104,300	58,506,000	Addis Ababa	2,084,588

Country/Territory	Area sq. miles	sq. km	Population	Capital	Population of Capital
Gabon	103,347	267,668	1,106,000	Ψ Libreville	251,000
Gambia	4,361	11,295	1,141,000	Ψ Banjul	109,986
Ghana	92,098	238,533	18,885,616	Ψ Accra	1,445,515
Guinea	94,926	245,857	7,518,000	Ψ Conakry	763,000
Guinea-Bissau	13,948	36,125	1,091,000	Ψ Bissau	109,214
Kenya	224,081	580,367	31,806,000	Nairobi	1,400,000
Lesotho	11,720	30,355	2,078,000	Maseru	288,951
Liberia	43,000	111,369	2,820,000	Ψ Monrovia	421,053
Libya	679,362	1,759,540	4,389,739	Ψ Tripoli	1,000,000
Madagascar	226,658	587,041	15,353,000	Antananarivo	1,052,835
Malawi	45,747	118,484	10,114,000	Lilongwe	233,973
Mali	478,841	1,240,192	11,134,000	Bamako	809,552
Mauritania	395,956	1,025,520	2,351,000	Nouakchott	850,000
Mauritius	788	2,040	1,160,000	Ψ Port Louis	146,499
Mayotte (Fr.)	144	372	94,410	Mamoudzou	12,000
Morocco	172,414	446,550	27,623,000	Ψ Rabat	1,220,000
Western Sahara	102,703	266,000	256,000	Laayoune	20,010
Mozambique	309,496	799,380	16,916,600	Ψ Maputo	1,039,700
Namibia	318,261	824,292	1,575,000	Windhoek	147,056
Niger	489,191	1,267,000	9,465,000	Niamey	392,169
Nigeria	356,669	923,768	115,120,000	Abuja	378,671
Réunion (Fr.)	969	2,510	664,000	St Denis	121,999
Rwanda	10,169	26,338	5,397,000	Kigali	116,227
St Helena (UK)	47	122	5,157	Ψ Jamestown	884
Ascension Island (UK)	34	88	1,051	Ψ Georgetown	—
Tristan da Cunha (UK)	38	98	288	Ψ Edinburgh of the Seven Seas	—
São Tomé and Princípe	372	964	135,000	Ψ São Tomé	5,714
Senegal	75,955	196,722	8,572,000	Ψ Dakar	1,641,358
Seychelles	176	455	76,000	Ψ Victoria	24,324
Sierra Leone	27,699	71,740	4,297,000	Ψ Freetown	469,776
Somalia	246,201	637,657	9,822,000	Ψ Mogadishu	230,000
South Africa	471,445	1,221,037	42,393,000 {	Pretoria Ψ Cape Town	822,925 1,911,521
Sudan	967,500	2,505,813	27,291,000	Khartoum	947,483
Swaziland	6,704	17,364	938,000	Mbabane	38,290
Tanzania	362,162	938,000	30,799,000	Dodoma	85,000
Togo	21,925	56,785	4,201,000	Ψ Lomé	366,476
Tunisia	62,592	162,155	9,092,000	Ψ Tunis	1,830,634
Uganda	93,065	241,038	19,848,000	Kampala	750,000
Zambia	290,587	752,618	8,275,000	Lusaka	982,362
Zimbabwe	150,872	390,757	11,908,000	Harare	1,189,103

AMERICA

North America

Country/Territory	Area sq. miles	sq. km	Population	Capital	Population of Capital
Canada	3,849,674	9,970,610	29,964,000	Ottawa	1,010,498
Greenland (Den.)	840,004	2,175,600	58,000	Ψ Godthåb (Nuuk)	12,483
Mexico	756,066	1,958,201	96,578,000	Mexico City	15,047,685
St Pierre and Miquelon (Fr.)	93	242	7,000	Ψ St Pierre	5,416
United States of America	3,536,278	9,158,960	270,298,524	Washington DC	7,051,495

Central America and the West Indies

Country/Territory	Area sq. miles	sq. km	Population	Capital	Population of Capital
Anguilla (UK)	37	96	12,394	The Valley	2,400
Antigua and Barbuda	171	442	66,000	Ψ St John's	22,342
Aruba (Neth.)	75	193	87,000	Ψ Oranjestad	25,000
Bahamas	5,358	13,878	284,000	Ψ Nassau	172,196
Barbados	166	430	265,000	Ψ Bridgetown	108,000
Belize	8,763	22,696	222,000	Belmopan	44,087
Bermuda (UK)	20	53	64,000	Ψ Hamilton	2,277
Cayman Islands (UK)	102	264	38,000	Ψ George Town	20,000
Costa Rica	19,730	51,100	3,398,000	San José	1,209,045
Cuba	42,804	110,861	11,019,000	Ψ Havana	2,175,888
Dominica	290	751	74,000	Ψ Roseau	16,243

Country/Territory	Area sq. miles	sq. km	Population	Capital	Population of Capital
Dominican Republic	18,816	48,734	8,052,000	Ψ Santo Domingo	2,134,779
Grenada	133	344	92,000	Ψ St George's	4,788
Guadeloupe (Fr.)	658	1,705	431,000	Ψ Basse Terre	29,522
Guatemala	42,042	108,889	10,928,000	Guatemala City	1,675,589
Haiti	10,714	27,750	7,336,000	Ψ Port-au-Prince	846,247
Honduras	43,277	112,088	6,140,000	Tegucigalpa	670,100
Jamaica	4,243	10,990	2,491,000	Ψ Kingston	524,638
Martinique (Fr.)	425	1,102	384,000	Ψ Fort de France	133,920
Montserrat (UK)	39	102	4,500	Ψ Plymouth	1,478
Netherlands Antilles (Neth.)	309	800	207,333	Ψ Willemstad	50,000
Nicaragua	50,193	130,668	4,663,000	Managua	608,020
Panama	29,157	75,517	2,674,000	Ψ Panama City	458,490
Puerto Rico (USA)	3,427	8,875	3,736,000	Ψ San Juan	1,222,316
St Christopher and Nevis	101	261	41,000	Ψ Basseterre	14,161
St Lucia	240	622	144,000	Ψ Castries	56,000
St Vincent and the Grenadines	150	388	113,000	Ψ Kingstown	33,694
Salvador, El	8,124	21,041	5,796,000	San Salvador	1,200,000
Trinidad and Tobago	1,981	5,130	1,297,000	Ψ Port of Spain	46,222
Turks and Caicos Islands (UK)	166	430	23,000	Ψ Grand Turk	3,691
Virgin Islands					
British (UK)	58	151	19,000	Ψ Road Town	3,983
US (USA)	134	347	106,000	Ψ Charlotte Amalie	11,842
South America					
Argentina	1,073,518	2,780,400	35,220,000	Ψ Buenos Aires	11,298,030
Bolivia	424,165	1,098,581	8,140,000	La Paz	1,480,000
Brazil	3,300,171	8,547,403	157,872,000	Brasilia	1,737,813
Chile	292,135	756,626	14,419,000	Santiago	5,257,937
Colombia	439,737	1,138,914	35,626,000	Bogotá	5,398,998
Ecuador	109,484	283,561	11,698,000	Quito	1,444,363
Falkland Islands (UK)	4,700	12,173	2,221	Ψ Stanley	1,636
French Guiana (Fr.)	34,749	90,000	153,000	Ψ Cayenne	41,164
Guyana	83,000	214,969	838,000	Ψ Georgetown	250,000
Paraguay	157,048	406,752	4,955,000	Asunción	718,690
Peru	496,225	1,285,216	25,015,000	Lima	6,483,901
South Georgia (UK)	1,580	4,092	—		—
Suriname	63,037	163,265	423,000	Ψ Paramaribo	265,000
Uruguay	68,500	177,414	3,203,000	Ψ Montevideo	1,383,660
Venezuela	352,145	912,050	22,710,000	Caracas	2,784,042

ASIA

Country/Territory	Area sq. miles	sq. km	Population	Capital	Population of Capital
Afghanistan	251,773	652,090	20,883,000	Kabul	1,424,400
Bahrain	268	694	599,000	Ψ Manama	140,401
Bangladesh	55,598	143,998	120,073,000	Dhaka	3,397,187
Bhutan	18,147	47,000	1,812,000	Thimphu	15,000
Brunei	2,226	5,765	300,000	Bandar Seri Begawan	49,902
Cambodia	69,898	181,035	10,273,000	Ψ Phnom Penh	832,000
China[1]	3,705,408	9,596,961	1,232,083,000	Beijing (Peking)	7,362,426
Hong Kong (China)	415	1,075	6,687,200	—	—
India	1,269,346	3,287,590	970,930,000	New Delhi	301,297
Indonesia	735,358	1,904,569	196,813,000	Ψ Jakarta	9,160,500
Iran	634,293	1,648,195	61,128,000	Tehran	6,750,043
Iraq	169,235	438,317	20,607,000	Baghdad	3,841,268
Israel[2]	8,130	21,056	6,100,000	Tel Aviv	1,880,200
West Bank and Gaza Strip	2,406	6,231	1,635,000	Gaza City	120,000
Japan	145,870	377,801	125,761,000	Tokyo	11,680,296
Jordan	37,738	97,740	5,581,000	Amman	1,270,000
Kazakhstan	1,049,156	2,717,300	15,671,000	Astana	292,000
Korea, Democratic People's Republic	46,540	120,538	22,466,000	Pyongyang	2,741,260
Korea, Republic	38,368	99,373	46,430,000	Seoul	10,289,000
Kuwait	6,880	17,818	1,866,104	Ψ Kuwait City	400,000
Kyrgyzstan	76,641	198,500	4,575,000	Bishkek	585,800
Laos	91,429	236,800	5,035,000	Vientiane	132,253

Country/Territory	Area sq. miles	sq. km	Population	Capital	Population of Capital
Lebanon	4,015	10,400	3,084,000	Ψ Beirut	1,500,000
Macao (*Port.*)	7	18	440,000	Ψ Macao	241,413
Malaysia	127,320	329,758	20,581,000	Kuala Lumpur	1,145,342
Maldives	115	298	263,000	Ψ Malé	62,973
Mongolia	604,829	1,566,500	2,354,000	Ulaanbaatar	515,100
Myanmar	261,228	676,578	45,922,000	Ψ Yangon (Rangoon)	2,513,023
Nepal	56,827	147,181	21,127,000	Kathmandu	421,258
Oman	119,498	309,500	2,302,000	Ψ Muscat	400,000
Pakistan	307,374	796,095	134,146,000	Islamabad	350,000
Philippines	115,831	300,000	71,899,000	Ψ Manila	8,594,150
Qatar	4,247	11,000	558,000	Ψ Doha	217,294
Saudi Arabia	830,000	2,149,690	18,836,000	Riyadh	1,800,000
Singapore	239	618	3,044,000	—	
Sri Lanka	25,332	65,610	18,354,000	Ψ Colombo	615,000
Syria	71,498	185,180	14,619,000	Damascus	1,549,000
Taiwan	13,800	35,742	21,854,273	Taipei	2,638,565
Tajikistan	55,251	143,100	5,919,000	Dushanbe	602,000
Thailand	198,115	513,115	60,206,000	Ψ Bangkok	5,882,000
Turkey[3]	299,158	774,815	62,697,000	Ankara	3,103,000
Turkmenistan	188,456	488,100	4,569,000	Ashgabat	407,000
United Arab Emirates	32,278	83,600	2,260,000	Abu Dhabi	450,000
Uzbekistan	172,742	447,400	24,000,000	Tashkent	2,200,000
Vietnam	128,066	331,689	75,181,000	Hanoi	3,056,146
Yemen	203,850	527,968	15,919,000	Sana'a	926,595

[1] Including Tibet
[2] Including East Jerusalem, the Golan Heights and Israeli citizens on the West Bank
[3] Including Turkey in Europe

EUROPE

Country/Territory	Area sq. miles	sq. km	Population	Capital	Population of Capital
Albania	11,099	28,748	3,670,000	Tirana	244,153
Andorra	175	453	65,877	Andorra la Vella	21,721
Armenia	11,506	29,800	3,893,000	Yerevan	1,254,400
Austria	32,378	83,859	8,106,000	Vienna	1,806,737
Azerbaijan	33,436	86,600	7,625,000	Ψ Baku	1,149,000
Belarus	80,155	207,600	10,203,000	Minsk	1,700,223
Belgium	11,783	30,519	10,159,000	Brussels	953,175
Bosnia-Hercegovina	19,735	51,129	4,510,000	Sarajevo	529,021
Bulgaria	42,823	110,912	8,356,000	Sofia	1,191,743
Croatia	21,824	56,538	4,501,000	Zagreb	867,717
Cyprus	3,572	9,251	756,000	Nicosia	188,800
Czech Republic	30,450	78,864	10,315,000	Prague	1,216,568
Denmark	16,639	43,094	5,262,000	Ψ Copenhagen	1,362,264
Faroe Islands	540	1,399	47,000	Ψ Tórshavn	16,218
Estonia	17,413	45,227	1,453,844	Tallinn	415,299
Finland	130,559	338,145	5,125,000	Ψ Helsinki	1,056,495
France	212,935	551,500	58,375,000	Paris	9,319,367
Georgia	26,911	69,700	5,411,000	Tbilisi	1,268,000
Germany	137,735	356,733	81,912,000	Berlin	3,472,009
Gibraltar (*UK*)	2.5	6.5	27,192	Ψ Gibraltar	—
Greece	50,949	131,957	10,475,000	Athens	3,072,922
Hungary	35,920	93,032	10,193,000	Budapest	2,002,121
Iceland	39,769	103,000	275,277	Ψ Reykjavík	107,764
Ireland, Republic of	27,137	70,284	3,626,087	Ψ Dublin	952,700
Italy	116,320	301,268	57,339,000	Rome	2,693,383
Latvia	24,942	64,600	2,491,000	Riga	805,997
Liechtenstein	62	160	31,320	Vaduz	4,975
Lithuania	25,174	65,200	3,701,300	Vilnius	581,500
Luxembourg	998	2,586	412,000	Luxembourg	77,400
Macedonia	9,928	25,713	2,174,000	Skopje	448,229
Malta	122	316	376,513	Ψ Valletta	7,146
Moldova	13,012	33,700	4,327,000	Chişinău	655,940
Monaco	0.4	1	32,000	Monaco	27,063
Netherlands	15,770	40,844	15,517,000	Ψ Amsterdam	1,101,629
Norway[1]	125,050	323,877	4,445,460	Ψ Oslo	499,693

Country/Territory	Area sq. miles	sq. km	Population	Capital	Population of Capital
Poland	124,808	323,250	38,628,000	Warsaw	1,643,203
Portugal[2]	35,514	91,982	9,920,760	Ψ Lisbon	2,561,225
Romania	92,043	238,391	22,520,000	Bucharest	2,027,500
Russia[3]	6,592,850	17,075,400	146,100,000	Moscow	8,598,896
San Marino	24	61	25,000	San Marino	4,357
Slovakia	18,928	49,035	5,374,000	Bratislava	452,278
Slovenia	7,821	20,256	1,991,000	Ljubljana	280,146
Spain[4]	195,365	505,992	39,270,000	Madrid	3,084,673
Sweden	173,732	449,964	8,843,000	Ψ Stockholm	1,148,953
Switzerland	15,940	41,284	7,076,000	Bern	321,932
Ukraine	233,090	603,700	51,094,000	Kiev	2,630,000
United Kingdom[5]	94,248	244,101	58,784,000	Ψ London	7,007,091
England	50,351	130,410	48,903,000	—	—
Wales	8,015	20,758	2,917,000	Ψ Cardiff	302,747
Scotland	30,420	78,789	5,137,000	Ψ Edinburgh	447,550
Northern Ireland	5,467	14,160	1,649,000	Ψ Belfast	296,700
Vatican City State	0.2	0.44	1,000	Vatican City	766
Yugoslavia	39,449	102,173	10,574,000	Belgrade	1,338,856

[1] Excludes Svalbard and Jan Mayen Islands (approx. 24,101 sq. miles (62,422 sq. km) and 3,000 population)
[2] Includes Madeira (314 sq. miles) and the Azores (922 sq. miles)
[3] Includes Russia in Asia
[4] Includes Balearic Islands, Canary Islands, Ceuta and Melilla
[5] Excludes Isle of Man (221 sq. miles (572 sq. km), 69,788 population), and Channel Islands (75 sq. miles (194 sq. km), 142,949 population)

OCEANIA

Country/Territory	Area sq. miles	sq. km	Population	Capital	Population of Capital
American Samoa (USA)	77	199	56,000	Ψ Pago Pago	3,519
Australia	2,988,902	7,741,220	18,871,800	Ψ Canberra	309,500
Norfolk Island (Aust.)	14	36	1,772	Ψ Kingston	—
Fiji	7,056	18,274	797,000	Ψ Suva	141,273
French Polynesia (Fr.)	1,544	4,000	223,000	Ψ Papeete	36,784
Guam (USA)	212	549	153,000	Agana	1,139
Kiribati	280	726	80,000	Tarawa	17,921
Marshall Islands	70	181	58,000	Dalap-Uliga-Darrit	20,000
Micronesia, Federated States of	271	702	109,000	Palikir	—
Nauru	8	21	11,000	Ψ Nauru	—
New Caledonia (Fr.)	7,172	18,575	189,000	Ψ Noumea	97,581
New Zealand	104,454	270,534	3,681,546	Ψ Wellington	326,900
Cook Islands	91	236	19,000	Rarotonga	9,281
Niue	100	260	2,000	Alofi	—
Ross Dependency[1]	175,000	453,248	—	—	—
Tokelau	5	12	2,000	—	—
Northern Mariana Islands (USA)	179	464	49,000	Saipan	52,706
Palau (USA)	177	459	17,000	Koror	10,493
Papua New Guinea	178,704	462,840	4,400,000	Ψ Port Moresby	173,500
Pitcairn Islands (UK)	2	5	54	—	—
Solomon Islands	11,157	28,896	391,000	Ψ Honiara	40,000
Tonga	288	747	99,000	Ψ Nuku'alofa	29,018
Tuvalu	10	26	10,000	Ψ Funafuti	2,856
Vanuatu	4,706	12,189	169,000	Ψ Port Vila	26,100
Wallis and Futuna Islands (Fr.)	77	200	15,000	Ψ Mata-Utu	—
Western Samoa	1,093	2,831	166,000	Ψ Apia	36,000

[1] Includes permanent shelf ice

THE ANTARCTIC

The Antarctic is generally defined as the area lying within the Antarctic Convergence, the zone where cold north-ward-flowing Antarctic sea water sinks below warmer southward-flowing water. This zone is at about latitude 50° S. in the Atlantic Ocean and latitude 55°–62° S. in the Pacific Ocean. The continent itself lies almost entirely within the Antarctic Circle, an area of about 13.66 million sq. km (5.3 million sq. miles), 99.67 per cent of which is permanently ice-covered. The average thickness of the ice is 2,450 m (7,100 ft) but in places exceeds 4,500 m (14,500 ft). Some mountains protrude, the highest being Vinson Massif, 4,897 m (16,067 ft). The ice amounts to some 30 million cubic km (7.2 million cubic miles) and represents more than 90 per cent of the world's fresh water.

Along 43 per cent of the Antarctic coastline, land-ice flowing outwards forms extensive ice shelves, fragments of which break off to form tabular icebergs, leaving ice-cliffs up to 50 m (150 ft) high. Much of the sea freezes in winter, forming fast ice which breaks up in summer and drifts north as pack ice.

The most conspicuous physical features of the continent are its high inland plateau (much of it over 3,000 m (10,000 ft)), the Transantarctic Mountains (which together with the large embayments of the Weddell Sea and Ross Sea mark the approximate boundary between East and West Antarctica), and the mountainous Antarctic Peninsula and off-lying islands which extend northwards towards South America.

CLIMATE

On land, summer temperatures range from just above freezing around the coast to −34° C (about −30° F) on the plateau, and in winter from −20° C (about −4° F) on the coast to −65° C (about −85° F) inland. Over a large area the maxima do not exceed −15° C (+5° F).

Precipitation is scant over the plateau but amounts to 25–76 cm (10–30 in) (water equivalent) along the coast and some scientific stations are permanently buried by snow. Some rain falls over the more northerly areas in summer. Gravity winds on the plateau slopes and cyclonic storms further north can both exceed 160 km/h (100 m.p.h.) and gusts have been known to reach 240 km/h (150 m.p.h.). Visibility can be reduced to zero in blizzards.

FLORA AND FAUNA

Although a small number of flowering plants, ferns and clubmosses occur on the sub-Antarctic islands, only two (a grass and a pearlwort) extend south of 60° S. Antarctic vegetation is dominated by lichens and mosses, with a few liverworts, algae and fungi. Most of these occur around the coast or on islands, but lichens and some mosses also occur inland.

The only land animals are tiny insects and mites with nematodes, rotifers, and tardigrades in the mosses, but large numbers of seals, penguins and other sea-birds go ashore to breed in the summer. The emperor penguin is the only species which breeds ashore throughout the winter. By contrast, the Antarctic seas abound with life, a wide variety of invertebrates (including krill) and fish providing food for the seals, penguins and other birds, and a residual population of whales.

In 1994 the International Whaling Commission agreed to establish a whale sanctuary around Antarctica in which commercial whaling will be banned for ten years. The sanctuary covers all sea areas south of 60°S. latitude, apart from the south-west Atlantic and south-east Pacific where it will be south of 40°S. latitude.

POTENTIAL RESOURCES

In the 180 years from Captain James Cook's circumnav-igation of the Antarctic in 1772–5 to the mid-1950s, expeditions to the Antarctic made major contributions to geographical and scientific knowledge of the area.

Increasing pressure on the world's food and mineral supplies has stimulated interest in the potential resources even in the extremely hostile polar environment. Minerals may be present in great variety but not in commercially exploitable concentrations in accessible localities. There are indications that off-shore hydrocarbons may be present but mostly below great depths of stormy, ice-infested seas. A 50-year ban on Antarctic mineral exploitation came into effect in January 1998 (*see* below).

Currently, the chief interest is in marine protein, including the shrimp-like krill already fished commercially by Japan and Poland. Research to ensure management of stocks of this organism is being continued by international groups, but it is estimated that they could sustain a yield equal to the present total annual world fish catch.

THE ANTARCTIC TREATY

The International Geophysical Year 1957–8 gave great impetus to Antarctic research, increasing the number of stations from 17 to 44 and the number of nations involved in research from four to 12 by 1957. The co-operative scientific effort proved so fruitful that the 12 nations involved (Argentina, Australia, Belgium, Chile, France, Japan, New Zealand, Norway, South Africa, the Soviet Union, the UK and the USA) pledged themselves to promote scientific and technical co-operation unhampered by politics, and the Antarctic Treaty was signed by the 12 states in 1959.

The 12 signatories to the treaty agreed to establish free use of the Antarctic continent for peaceful scientific purposes; to freeze all territorial claims and disputes in the Antarctic; to ban all military activities in the area; and to prohibit nuclear explosions and the disposal of radioactive waste. Since then additional agreements have been reached to promote conservation and regulate tourism, waste disposal and pollution.

The Antarctic Treaty was defined as covering areas south of latitude 60° S., excluding the high seas but including the ice shelves, and came into force in 1961. It has since been signed by a further 31 states, 14 of which are active in the Antarctic and have therefore been accorded consultative status, bringing the number of consultative parties to 26. In 1998 an extension to the treaty came into effect, placing a 50-year ban on mining, oil exploration and mineral extraction in Antarctica. Further-more, all tourists, explorers and expeditions will now need permission to enter the Antarctic.

TERRITORIAL CLAIMS

Under the provisions of the Antarctic Treaty all territorial claims and disputes were frozen without the acceptance or denial of the claims of the various claimants. The US and Soviet governments also made it clear that although they had not made any specific territorial claims, they did not relinquish the right to make such claims.

Seven states have made claims in the Antarctic: Argentina claims the part of Antarctica between 74° W. and 25° W.; Chile that part between 90° W. and 53° W.; Britain claims the British Antarctic Territory, an area of 1,709,340 sq. km (660,000 sq. miles) between 20° and 80° W. longitude; France claims Terre Adélie, 432,000 sq. km (166,800 sq.

miles) between 136° and 142° E.; Australia claims the Australian Antarctic Territory, 6,120,000 sq. km (2,320,000 sq. miles) between 160° and 45° E. longitude excluding Terre Adélie; Norway claims Queen Maud Land between 20° W. and 45° E.; and New Zealand claims the Ross Dependency, 450,000 sq. km (175,000 sq. miles) between 160° E. and 150° W. longitude. The Argentinian, British and Chilean claims overlap; the part of the continent between 90° W. and 150° W. is unclaimed by any state.

SCIENTIFIC RESEARCH

There were 35 permanently occupied stations in 1998–9 operated by the following nations: Argentina (6), Australia (3), Brazil (1), Chile (3), China (2), France (1), Germany (1), India (1), Japan (2), New Zealand (1), Poland (1), Russia (4), South Africa (1), South Korea (1), UK (2), Ukraine (1), Uruguay (1), USA (3, including one at the South Pole).

The staff of these stations and summer field-workers are the only people present on the continent and off-lying islands. There are no indigenous inhabitants.

Currencies of the World

AND EXCHANGE RATES AGAINST £ STERLING

Franc CFA = Franc de la Communauté financière africaine
Franc CFP = Franc des Comptoirs français du Pacifique

COUNTRY/TERRITORY	MONETARY UNIT	AVERAGE RATE TO £ 4 September 1998	AVERAGE RATE TO £ 31 August 1999
Afghanistan	Afghani (Af) of 100 puls	Af 7947.70	Af 7429.49
Albania	Lek (Lk) of 100 qindarka	Lk 251.231	Lk 211.892
Algeria	Algerian dinar (DA) of 100 centimes	DA 98.4813	DA 105.034
American Samoa	Currency is that of the USA	US$ 1.6732	US$ 1.5878
Andorra	French and Spanish currencies in use	—	—
Angola	Readjusted kwanza (Kzrl) of 100 lwei	Kzrl 430226.7	Kzrl 4081484.3
Anguilla	East Caribbean dollar (EC$) of 100 cents	EC$ 4.5177	EC$ 4.2871
Antigua and Barbuda	East Caribbean dollar (EC$) of 100 cents	EC$ 4.5177	EC$ 4.2871
Argentina	Peso of 10,000 australes	Pesos 1.6720	Pesos 1.5872
Armenia	Dram of 100 louma	Dram 840.583	Dram 851.474
Aruba	Aruban florin	Florins 2.9950	Florins 2.8104
Ascension Island	Currency is that of St Helena	*at parity with £ sterling*	
Australia	Australian dollar ($A) of 100 cents	$A 2.8507	$A 2.5102
Norfolk Island	Currency is that of Australia	$A 2.8507	$A 2.5102
Austria	Schilling of 100 Groschen	Schilling 20.4216	Schilling 20.8988
Azerbaijan	Manat of 100 gopik	Manat 6609.14	Manat 6259.11
The Bahamas	Bahamian dollar (B$) of 100 cents	B$ 1.6732	B$ 1.5878
Bahrain	Bahraini dinar (BD) of 1,000 fils	BD 0.6308	BD 0.5986
Bangladesh	Taka (Tk) of 100 poisha	Tk 78.8078	Tk 78.5962
Barbados	Barbados dollar (BD$) of 100 cents	BD$ 3.3653	BD$ 3.1756
Belarus	Rouble of 100 kopeks	Roubles 402404.7	Roubles 500157.2
Belgium	Belgian franc (or frank) of 100 centimes (centiemen)	Francs 59.8839	Francs 61.2671
Belize	Belize dollar (BZ$) of 100 cents	BZ$ 3.3464	BZ$ 3.1756
Benin	Franc CFA	Francs 973.140	Francs 996.250
Bermuda	Bermuda dollar of 100 cents	$ 1.6732	$ 1.5878
Bhutan	Ngultrum of 100 chetrum (Indian currency is also legal tender)	Ngultrum 71.2156	Ngultrum 69.0693
Bolivia	Boliviano ($b) of 100 centavos	$b 9.3365	$b 9.3204
Bosnia-Hercegovina	Convertible marka	—	Marka 2.9385
Botswana	Pula (P) of 100 thebe	P 7.8389	P 7.3374
Brazil	Real of 100 centavos	Real 1.9711	Real 3.0653
Brunei	Brunei dollar (B$) of 100 sen (fully interchangeable with Singapore currency)	$ 2.9256	$ 2.6802
Bulgaria	Lev of 100 stotinki	Leva 2894.22	Leva 2.9555
Burkina Faso	Franc CFA	Francs 973.140	Francs 996.250
Burundi	Burundi franc of 100 centimes	Francs 747.541	Francs 969.612
Cambodia	Riel of 100 sen	Riel 6241.04	Riel 6020.84
Cameroon	Franc CFA	Francs 973.140	Francs 996.250
Canada	Canadian dollar (C$) of 100 cents	C$ 2.5605	C$ 2.3721
Cape Verde	Escudo Caboverdiano of 100 centavos	Esc 166.795	Esc 150.381
Cayman Islands	Cayman Islands dollar (CI$) of 100 cents	CI$ 1.3858	CI$ 1.3231
Central African Republic	Franc CFA	Francs 973.140	Francs 996.250
Chad	Franc CFA	Francs 973.140	Francs 996.250
Chile	Chilean peso of 100 centavos	Pesos 793.515	Pesos 817.479
China	Renminbi Yuan of 10 jiao or 100 fen	Yuan 13.8534	Yuan 13.1427
Hong Kong	Hong Kong dollar (HK$) of 100 cents	HK$ 12.9481	HK$ 12.3284
Colombia	Colombian peso of 100 centavos	Pesos 2585.26	Pesos 3055.72
The Comoros	Comorian franc (KMF) of 100 centimes	Francs 729.663	Francs 781.147
Congo, Dem. Rep. of	Congolese franc	CFr 230065.1	CFr 7.1451
Congo, Rep. of	Franc CFA	Francs 973.140	Francs 996.250
Costa Rica	Costa Rican colón (₡) of 100 céntimos	₡ 437.793	₡ 461.066
Côte D'ivoire	Franc CFA	Francs 973.140	Francs 996.250
Croatia	Kuna of 100 lipa	Kuna 10.5468	Kuna 11.5632
Cuba	Cuban peso of 100 centavos	Pesos 38.4836	Pesos 33.3438
Cyprus	Cyprus pound (C£) of 100 cents	C£ 0.8558	C£ 0.8781
Czech Republic	Koruna (Kčs) of 100 haléřu	Kčs 51.6208	Kčs 55.6659
Denmark	Danish krone of 100 øre	Kroner 11.0523	Kroner 11.2892
Farøe Islands	Currency is that of Denmark	Kroner 11.0523	Kroner 11.2892

COUNTRY/TERRITORY	MONETARY UNIT	AVERAGE RATE TO £ 4 September 1998	AVERAGE RATE TO £ 31 August 1999
Djibouti	Djibouti franc of 100 centimes	Francs 297.361	Francs 282.184
Dominica	East Caribbean dollar (EC$) of 100 cents	EC$ 4.5177	EC$ 4.2871
Dominican Republic	Dominican Republic peso (RD$) of 100 centavos	RD$ 25.7673	RD$ 25.1190
Ecuador	Sucre of 100 centavos	Sucres 9283.75	Sucres 17735.7
Egypt	Egyptian pound (£E) of 100 piastres or 1,000 millièmes	£E 5.7203	£E 5.4462
Equatorial Guinea	Franc CFA	Francs 973.140	Francs 996.250
Eritrea	Nakfa	—	—
Estonia	Kroon of 100 sents	Kroons 23.4228	Kroons 23.7512
Ethiopia	Ethiopian birr (EB) of 100 cents	EB 11.6923	EB 11.9355
Falkland Islands	Falkland pound of 100 pence	*at parity with £ sterling*	
Fiji	Fiji dollar (F$) of 100 cents	F$ 3.4536	F$ 3.1631
Finland	Markka (Mk) of 100 penniä	Mk 8.8297	Mk 9.0302
France	Franc of 100 centimes	Francs 9.7314	Francs 9.9625
French Guiana	Currency is that of France	Francs 9.7314	Francs 9.9625
French Polynesia	Franc CFP	Francs 176.887	Francs 181.171
Gabon	Franc CFA	Francs 973.140	Francs 996.250
The Gambia	Dalasi (D) of 100 butut	D 17.0918	D 18.6885
Georgia	Lari of 100 tetri	—	—
Germany	Deutsche Mark (DM) of 100 Pfennig	DM 2.9023	DM 2.9705
Ghana	Cedi of 100 pesewas	Cedi 3890.20	Cedi 4125.12
Gibraltar	Gibraltar pound of 100 pence	*at parity with £ sterling*	
Greece	Drachma of 100 leptae	Drachmae 501.358	Drachmae 495.902
Greenland	Currency is that of Denmark	Kroner 11.0523	Kroner 11.2892
Grenada	East Caribbean dollar (EC$) of 100 cents	EC$ 4.5177	EC$ 4.2871
Guadeloupe	Currency is that of France	Francs 9.7314	Francs 9.9625
Guam	Currency is that of USA	US$ 1.6732	US$ 1.5878
Guatemala	Quetzal (Q) of 100 centavos	Q 10.9173	Q 12.4287
Guinea	Guinea franc of 100 centimes	Francs 2079.79	Francs 2166.96
Guinea-Bissau	Franc CFA	Francs 973.140	Francs 996.250
Guyana	Guyana dollar (G$) of 100 cents	G$ 271.561	G$ 274.690
Haiti	Gourde of 100 centimes	Gourdes 27.5488	Gourdes 26.2257
Honduras	Lempira of 100 centavos	Lempiras 22.7555	Lempiras 22.8485
Hungary	Forint of 100 fillér	Forints 372.505	Forints 384.184
Iceland	Icelandic króna (Kr) of 100 aurar	Kr 118.496	Kr 116.751
India	Indian rupee (Rs) of 100 paisa	Rs 71.2156	Rs 69.0693
Indonesia	Rupiah (Rp) of 100 sen	Rp 18321.6	Rp 12067.3
Iran	Rial	Rials 5019.60	Rials 4763.40
Iraq	Iraqi dinar (ID) of 1,000 fils	ID 0.5202	ID 0.4933
Republic of Ireland	Punt (IR£) of 100 pence	IR£ 1.1582	IR£ 1.1962
Israel	Shekel of 100 agora	Shekels 6.4222	Shekels 6.7438
Italy	Lira of 100 centesimi	Lire 2866.48	Lire 2940.75
Jamaica	Jamaican dollar (J$) of 100 cents	J$ 59.9006	J$ 62.7975
Japan	Yen	Yen 224.769	Yen 177.357
Jordan	Jordanian dinar (JD) of 1,000 fils	JD 1.1913	JD 1.1297
Kazakhstan	Tenge	Tenge 132.518	Tenge 209.669
Kenya	Kenya shilling (Ksh) of 100 cents	Ksh 99.8064	Ksh 119.284
Kiribati	Australian dollar ($A) of 100 cents	$A 2.8507	$A 2.5102
Democratic People's Republic of Korea	Won of 100 chon	Won 3.6811	Won 3.4932
Republic of Korea	Won	Won 2247.11	Won 1877.57
Kuwait	Kuwaiti dinar (KD) of 1,000 fils	KD 0.5094	KD 0.4845
Kyrgyzstan	Som	—	—
Laos	Kip (K) of 100 at	K 4353.67	K 12146.7
Latvia	Lats of 100 santims	Lats 0.9952	Lats 0.9423
Lebanon	Lebanese pound (L£) of 100 piastres	L£ 2539.08	L£ 2394.41
Lesotho	Loti (M) of 100 lisente	M 10.4153	M 9.6697
Liberia	Liberian dollar (L$) of 100 cents	L$ 1.6732	L$ 1.5878
Libya	Libyan dinar (LD) of 1,000 dirhams	LD 0.6454	LD 0.7145
Liechtenstein	Swiss franc of 100 rappen (or centimes)	Francs 2.3816	Francs 2.4322
Lithuania	Litas	Litas 6.6946	Litas 6.3536
Luxembourg	Luxembourg franc (LF) of 100 centimes (Belgian currency is also legal tender)	LF 59.8839	LF 61.2671
Macao	Pataca of 100 avos	Pataca 13.3943	Pataca 12.7353
Macedonia	Dinar of 100 paras	Dinars 90.8466	Dinars 93.1193
Madagascar	Franc malgache (FMG) of 100 centimes	FMG 9035.28	FMG 10420.7

Country/Territory	Monetary Unit	Average Rate to £ 4 September 1998	Average Rate to £ 31 August 1999
Malawi	Kwacha (K) of 100 tambala	K 69.6029	K 69.1568
Malaysia	Malaysian dollar (ringgit) (M$) of 100 sen	M$ 6.3582	M$ 6.7005
Maldives	Rufiyaa of 100 laaris	Rufiyaa 19.6936	Rufiyaa 17.9263
Mali	Franc CFA	Francs 973.140	Francs 966.250
Malta	Maltese lira (LM) of 100 cents or 1,000 mils	LM 0.6432	LM 0.6442
Marshall Islands	Currency is that of the USA	US$ 1.6732	US$ 1.5878
Martinique	Currency is that of France	Francs 9.7314	Francs 9.9625
Mauritania	Ouguiya (UM) of 5 khoums	UM 338.932	UM 334.781
Mauritius	Mauritius rupee of 100 cents	Rs 40.7843	Rs 40.0682
Mayotte	Currency is that of France	Francs 9.7314	Francs 9.9625
Mexico	Peso of 100 centavos	Pesos 16.9704	Pesos 14.8952
Federated States of Micronesia	Currency is that of the USA	US$ 1.6732	US$ 1.5878
Moldova	Leu	Leu 8.0565	Leu 17.5174
Monaco	French franc of 100 centimes	Francs 9.7314	Francs 9.9625
Mongolia	Tugrik of 100 möngö	Tugriks 1368.03	Tugriks 1653.28
Montserrat	East Caribbean dollar (EC$) of 100 cents	EC$ 4.5177	EC$ 4.2871
Morocco	Dirham (DH) of 100 centimes	DH 15.8718	DH 15.7153
Mozambique	Metical (MT) of 100 centavos	MT 19233.4	MT 20166.7
Myanmar	Kyat (K) of 100 pyas	K 10.4604	K 9.9265
Namibia	Namibian dollar of 100 cents	*at parity with SA Rand*	
Nauru	Australian dollar ($A) of 100 cents	$A 2.8507	$A 2.5102
Nepal	Nepalese rupee of 100 paisa	Rs 114.330	Rs 109.130
The Netherlands	Gulden (guilder) or florin of 100 cents	Guilders 3.2753	Guilders 3.3470
Netherlands Antilles	Netherlands Antilles guilder of 100 cents	Guilders 2.9950	Guilders 2.8104
New Caledonia	Franc CFP	Francs 176.887	Francs 181.171
New Zealand	New Zealand dollar (NZ$) of 100 cents	NZ$ 3.3058	NZ$ 3.0924
Cook Islands	Currency is that of New Zealand	NZ$ 3.3058	NZ$ 3.0924
Niue	Currency is that of New Zealand	NZ$ 3.3058	NZ$ 3.0924
Tokelau	Currency is that of New Zealand	NZ$ 3.3058	NZ$ 3.0924
Nicaragua	Córdoba (C$) of 100 centavos	C$ 17.9869	C$ 19.0700
Niger	Franc CFA	Francs 973.140	Francs 966.250
Nigeria	Naira (N) of 100 kobo	N 36.6197	N 156.414
Northern Mariana Islands	Currency is that of USA	US$ 1.6732	US$ 1.5878
Norway	Krone of 100 øre	Kroner 12.8929	Kroner 12.6111
Oman	Rial Omani (OR) of 1,000 baisas	OR 0.6442	OR 0.6113
Pakistan	Pakistan rupee of 100 paisa	Rs 83.5680	Rs 82.2878
Palau	Currency is that of the USA	US$ 1.6732	US$ 1.5878
Panama	Balboa of 100 centésimos (US notes are also in circulation)	Balboa 1.6732	Balboa 1.5878
Papua New Guinea	Kina (K) of 100 toea	K 3.9376	K 4.6362
Paraguay	Guaraní (Gs) of 100 céntimos	Gs 4718.43	Gs 5255.62
Peru	New Sol of 100 cénts	New Sol 5.0966	New Sol 5.3509
The Philippines	Philippine peso (P) of 100 centavos	P 76.1189	P 63.1151
Pitcairn Islands	Currency is that of New Zealand	NZ$ 3.3058	NZ$ 3.0924
Poland	Złoty of 100 groszy	Złotys 6.1658	Złotys 6.3266
Portugal	Escudo (Esc) of 100 centavos	Esc 297.403	Esc 304.487
Puerto Rico	Currency is that of USA	US$ 1.6732	US$ 1.5878
Qatar	Qatar riyal of 100 dirhams	Riyals 6.0913	Riyals 5.7804
Réunion	Currency is that of France	Francs 9.7314	Francs 9.9625
Romania	Leu (Lei) of 100 bani	Lei 15038.7	Lei 25714.4
Russia	New rouble of 100 kopeks	Roubles 33.0877	Roubles 39.3933
Rwanda	Rwanda franc of 100 centimes	Francs 522.708	Francs 537.931
St Christopher and Nevis	East Caribbean dollar (EC$) of 100 cents	EC$ 4.5177	EC$ 4.2871
St Helena	St Helena pound (£) of 100 pence	*at parity with £ sterling*	
St Lucia	East Caribbean dollar (EC$) of 100 cents	EC$ 4.5177	EC$ 4.2871
St Pierre and Miquelon	Currency is that of France	Francs 9.7314	Francs 9.9625
St Vincent and the Grenadines	East Caribbean dollar (EC$) of 100 cents	EC$ 4.5177	EC$ 4.2871
El Salvador	El Salvador colón (₡) of 100 centavos	₡ 14.6489	₡ 13.8155
San Marino	San Marino and Italian currencies are in circulation	Lire 2866.48	Lire 2940.75
São Tomé and Princípe	Dobra of 100 centavos	Dobra 3998.95	Dobra 3794.84
Saudi Arabia	Saudi riyal (SR) of 20 qursh or 100 halala	SR 6.2754	SR 5.9551
Senegal	Franc CFA	Francs 973.140	Francs 996.250

COUNTRY/TERRITORY	MONETARY UNIT	AVERAGE RATE TO £ 4 September 1998	AVERAGE RATE TO £ 31 August 1999
Seychelles	Seychelles rupee of 100 cents	Rs 8.7007	Rs 8.4749
Sierra Leone	Leone (Le) of 100 cents	Le 2526.53	Le 2817.08
Singapore	Singapore dollar (S$) of 100 cents	S$ 2.9253	S$ 2.6802
Slovakia	Koruna (Sk) of 100 halierov	Kčs 58.8113	Kčs 67.1847
Slovenia	Tolar (SIT) of 100 stotin	Tolars 273.541	Tolars 298.428
Solomon Islands	Solomon Islands dollar (SI$) of 100 cents	SI$ 8.0261	SI$ 7.8226
Somalia	Somali shilling of 100 cents	Shillings 4383.79	Shillings 4160.04
South Africa	Rand (R) of 100 cents	R 10.4153	R 9.6697
Spain	Peseta of 100 céntimos	Pesetas 246.396	Pesetas 252.702
Sri Lanka	Sri Lankan rupee of 100 cents	Rs 110.808	Rs 114.115
Sudan	Sudanese dinar (SD) of 10 pounds	SD 305.526	SD 403.301
Suriname	Suriname guilder of 100 cents	Guilders 670.953	Guilders 1098.01
Swaziland	Lilangeni (E) of 100 cents (South African currency is also in circulation)	E 10.4153	E 9.6697
Sweden	Swedish krona of 100 öre	Kronor 13.2891	Kronor 13.2296
Switzerland	Swiss franc of 100 rappen (or centimes)	Francs 2.3816	Francs 2.4322
Syria	Syrian pound (S$) of 100 piastres	S£ 66.9280	S£ 71.4510
Taiwan	New Taiwan dollar (NT$) of 100 cents	NT$ 58.0508	NT$ 50.5794
Tajikistan	Tajik rouble (TJR) of 100 tanga	—	—
Tanzania	Tanzanian shilling of 100 cents	Shillings 1102.97	Shillings 1261.51
Thailand	Baht of 100 satang	Baht 68.2415	Baht 60.8049
Togo	Franc CFA	Francs 973.140	Francs 996.250
Tonga	Pa'anga (T$) of 100 seniti	T$ 2.8507	T$ 2.5102
Trinidad and Tobago	Trinidad and Tobago dollar (TT$) of 100 cents	TT$ 10.4441	TT$ 9.7162
Tristan da Cunha	Currency is that of the UK	—	—
Tunisia	Tunisian dinar of 1,000 millimes	Dinars 1.8806	Dinars 1.9094
Turkey	Turkish lira (TL) of 100 kurus	TL 464062.1	TL 710651.8
Turkmenistan	Manat of 100 tenesi	—	—
Turks and Caicos Islands	US dollar (US$)	US$ 1.6732	US$ 1.5878
Tuvalu	Australian dollar ($A) of 100 cents	$A 2.8507	$A 2.5102
Uganda	Uganda shilling of 100 cents	Shillings 2098.19	Shillings 2322.16
Ukraine	Hryvna of 100 kopiykas	Hryvnas 5.1033	Hryvnas 7.0261
United Arab Emirates	UAE dirham (Dh) of 100 fils	Dirham 6.1457	Dirham 5.8316
United Kingdom	Pound sterling (£) of 100 pence	£1.00 £1.00	
United States of America	US dollar (US$) of 100 cents	US$ 1.6732	US$ 1.5878
Uruguay	Uruguayan peso of 100 centésimos	Pesos 17.9702	Pesos 18.5201
Uzbekistan	Sum of 100 tiyin	Sum 481.045	Sum 992.375
Vanuatu	Vatu of 100 centimes	Vatu 221.700	Vatu 207.288
Vatican City State	Italian currency is legal tender	Lire 2866.48	Lire 2940.75
Venezuela	Bolívar (Bs) of 100 céntimos	Bs 976.530	Bs 982.531
Vietnam	Dồng of 10 hào or 100 xu	Dồng 23270.0	Dồng 22168.1
Virgin Islands, British	US dollar (US$) (£ sterling and EC$ also circulate)	US$ 1.6732	US$ 1.5878
Virgin Islands, US	Currency is that of the USA	US$ 1.6732	US$ 1.5878
Wallis and Futuna Islands	Franc CFP	Francs 176.887	Francs 176.887
Samoa	Tala (S$) of 100 sene	S$ 5.1546	S$ 4.8931
Yemen	Riyal of 100 fils	Riyals 219.173	Riyals 235.233
Yugoslavia	New dinar of 100 paras	New Dinars 17.5608	New Dinars 17.8645
Zambia	Kwacha (K) of 100 ngwee	K 3363.15	K 3842.49
Zimbabwe	Zimbabwe dollar (Z$) of 100 cents	Z$ 41.4120	Z$ 60.8129

Time Zones

Standard time differences from the Greenwich meridian

+   hours ahead of GMT
−   hours behind GMT
*   may vary from standard time at some part of the year (Summer Time or Daylight Saving Time)
h   hours
m   minutes

	h m
Afghanistan	+ 4 30
*Albania	+ 1
Algeria	+ 1
*Andorra	+ 1
Angola	+ 1
Anguilla	− 4
Antigua and Barbuda	− 4
Argentina	− 3
*Armenia	+ 4
Aruba	− 4
Ascension Island	0
*Australia	+10
*Broken Hill area (NSW)	+ 9 30
*Lord Howe Island	+10 30
Northern Territory	+ 9 30
*South Australia	+ 9 30
Western Australia	+ 8
*Austria	+ 1
*Azerbaijan	+ 4
*Azores	− 1
*Bahamas	− 5
Bahrain	+ 3
Bangladesh	+ 6
Barbados	− 4
*Belarus	+ 2
*Belgium	+ 1
Belize	− 6
Benin	+ 1
*Bermuda	− 4
Bhutan	+ 6
Bolivia	− 4
*Bosnia-Hercegovina	+ 1
Botswana	+ 2
Brazil	
Acre	− 5
central states	− 4
N. and NE coastal states	− 3
*S. and E. coastal states, including Brasília	− 3
Fernando de Noronha Island	− 2
western states	− 5
British Antarctic Territory	− 3
British Indian Ocean Territory	+ 5
Diego Garcia	+ 6
British Virgin Islands	− 4
Brunei	+ 8
*Bulgaria	+ 2
Burkina Faso	0
Burundi	+ 2
Cambodia	+ 7
Cameroon	+ 1
Canada	
*Alberta	− 7
*British Columbia	− 8
*Labrador	− 4
*Manitoba	− 6

	h m
*New Brunswick	− 4
*Newfoundland	− 3 30
*Northwest Territories	
Nunavut	
east of 85° W.	− 7
85° W.–102° W.	− 5
west of 102° W.	− 6
*Nova Scotia	− 7
*Ontario	− 4
east of 90° W.	− 5
west of 90° W.	− 6
*Prince Edward Island	− 4
Quebec	
east of 63° W.	− 4
*west of 63° W.	− 5
Saskatchewan	− 6
*Yukon	− 8
*Canary Islands	0
Cape Verde	− 1
Cayman Islands	− 5
Central African Republic	+ 1
Chad	+ 1
*Chatham Islands	+12 45
*Chile	− 4
China	+ 8
Christmas Island (Indian Ocean)	+ 7
Cocos (Keeling) Islands	+ 6 30
Colombia	− 5
Comoros	+ 3
Congo (Dem. Rep.)	
east	+ 2
west	+ 1
Congo (Rep. of)	+ 1
Cook Islands	− 10
Costa Rica	− 6
Côte d'Ivoire	0
*Croatia	+ 1
*Cuba	− 5
*Cyprus	+ 2
*Czech Republic	+ 1
*Denmark	+ 1
Djibouti	+ 3
Dominica	− 4
Dominican Republic	− 4
Ecuador	− 5
Galápagos Islands	− 6
*Egypt	+ 2
El Salvador	− 6
Equatorial Guinea	+ 1
Eritrea	+ 3
*Estonia	+ 2
Ethiopia	+ 3
*Falkland Islands	− 4
*Faröe Islands	0
Fiji	+12
*Finland	+ 2
*France	+ 1
French Guiana	− 3
French Polynesia	−10
Marquesas Islands	− 9 30
Gabon	+ 1
The Gambia	0
Georgia	+ 3
*Germany	+ 1
Ghana	0
*Gibraltar	+ 1
*Greece	+ 2

	h m
*Greenland	− 3
Danmarkshavn	0
Mesters Vig	0
*Scoresby Sound	− 1
*Thule area	− 4
Grenada	− 4
Guadeloupe	− 4
Guam	+10
Guatemala	− 6
Guinea	0
Guinea-Bissau	0
Guyana	− 4
*Haiti	− 5
Honduras	− 6
*Hungary	+ 1
Iceland	0
India	+ 5 30
Indonesia	
Bali	+ 8
Flores	+ 8
Irian Jaya	+ 9
Java	+ 7
Kalimantan (south and east)	+ 8
Kalimantan (west and central)	+ 7
Molucca Islands	+ 9
Sulawesi	+ 8
Sumatra	+ 7
Sumbawa	+ 8
Tanimbar	+ 9
Timor	+ 8
*Iran	+ 3 30
*Iraq	+ 3
*Ireland, Republic of	0
*Israel	+ 2
*Italy	+ 1
Jamaica	− 5
Japan	+ 9
*Jordan	+ 2
*Kazakhstan	
western (Aktau)	+ 4
central (Atyrau)	+ 5
eastern	+ 6
Kenya	+ 3
Kiribati	+12
Line Islands	+14
Phoenix Islands	+13
Korea, North	+ 9
Korea, South	+ 9
Kuwait	+ 3
*Kyrgyzstan	+ 5
Laos	+ 7
*Latvia	+ 2
*Lebanon	+ 2
Lesotho	+ 2
Liberia	0
*Libya	+ 2
*Liechtenstein	+ 1
Line Islands not part of Kiribati	−10
*Lithuania	+ 1
*Luxembourg	+ 1
Macao	+ 8
*Macedonia (Former Yug. Rep. of)	+ 1
Madagascar	+ 3

	h m		h m
*Madeira	0	St Lucia	− 4
Malawi	+ 2	*St Pierre and Miquelon	− 3
Malaysia	+ 8	St Vincent and the	
Maldives	+ 5	Grenadines	− 4
Mali	0	Samoa	−11
*Malta	+ 1	Samoa, American	−11
Marshall Islands	+12	*San Marino	+ 1
Ebon Atoll	−12	São Tomé and Princípe	0
Martinique	− 4	Saudi Arabia	+ 3
Mauritania	0	Senegal	0
Mauritius	+ 4	Seychelles	+ 4
*Mexico	− 6	Sierra Leone	0
Nayarit, Sinaloa, Sonora,		Singapore	+ 8
S. Baja California	− 7	*Slovakia	+ 1
N. Baja California	− 8	*Slovenia	+ 1
Micronesia		Solomon Islands	+11
Caroline Islands	+10	Somalia	+ 3
Kosrae	+11	South Africa	+ 2
Pingelap	+11	South Georgia	− 2
Pohnpei	+11	*Spain	+ 1
*Moldova	+ 2	Sri Lanka	+ 6
*Monaco	+ 1	Sudan	+ 2
*Mongolia	+ 8	Suriname	− 3
Montserrat	− 4	Swaziland	+ 2
Morocco	0	*Sweden	+ 1
Mozambique	+ 2	*Switzerland	+ 1
Myanmar	+ 6 30	*Syria	+ 2
*Namibia	+ 1	Taiwan	+ 8
Nauru	+12	Tajikistan	+ 5
Nepal	+ 5 45	Tanzania	+ 3
*Netherlands	+ 1	Thailand	+ 7
Netherlands Antilles	− 4	Togo	0
New Caledonia	+11	Tonga	+13
*New Zealand	+12	Trinidad and Tobago	− 4
Nicaragua	− 6	Tristan da Cunha	0
Niger	+ 1	Tunisia	+ 1
Nigeria	+ 1	*Turkey	+ 2
Niue	−11	Turkmenistan	+ 5
Norfolk Island	+11 30	*Turks and Caicos Islands	− 5
Northern Mariana Islands	+10	Tuvalu	+12
*Norway	+ 1	Uganda	+ 3
Oman	+ 4	*Ukraine	+ 2
Pakistan	+ 5	United Arab Emirates	+ 4
Palau	+ 9	*United Kingdom	0
Panama	− 5	*United States of America	
Papua New Guinea	+10	Alaska	− 9
*Paraguay	− 4	Aleutian Islands, east of	
Peru	− 5	169° 30′ W.	− 9
Philippines	+ 8	Aleutian Islands, west	
*Poland	+ 1	of 169° 30′ W.	−10
*Portugal	0	eastern time	− 5
Puerto Rico	− 4	central time	− 6
Qatar	+ 3	Hawaii	−10
Réunion	+ 4	mountain time	− 7
*Romania	+ 2	Pacific time	− 8
*Russia		Uruguay	− 3
Zone 1	+ 2	Uzbekistan	+ 5
Zone 2	+ 3	Vanuatu	+11
Zone 3	+ 4	*Vatican City State	+ 1
Zone 4	+ 5	Venezuela	− 4
Zone 5	+ 6	Vietnam	+ 7
Zone 6	+ 7	Virgin Islands (US)	− 4
Zone 7	+ 8	Yemen	+ 3
Zone 8	+ 9	*Yugoslavia (Fed. Rep. of)	+ 1
Zone 9	+10	Zambia	+ 2
Zone 10	+11	Zimbabwe	+ 2
Zone 11	+12		
Rwanda	+ 2		
St Helena	0		
St Christopher and Nevis	− 4		

Source: reproduced with permission from data produced by HM Nautical Almanac Office

Countries of the World: A—Z

AFGHANISTAN
Da Afghanistan Jamhuriat

AREA – 251,773 sq. miles (652,090 sq. km). Neighbours: Iran (west), Pakistan (south), Tajikistan, Uzbekistan and Turkmenistan (north), Pakistan and China (east)
POPULATION – 20,883,000 (1994 UN estimate): Pushtuns (38 per cent) predominate in the south and west; Tajiks (25 per cent); Hazaras (19 per cent) in the centre; Uzbeks (6 per cent) in the north; Aimaqs (4 per cent); Baluchis (0.5 per cent). The principal languages are Dari (a form of Persian) and Pushtu
CAPITAL – Kabul (population, 1,424,400, 1988)
MAJOR CITIES – Herat (177,300); Jalalabad (55,000); Kandahar (225,500); Mazar-i-Sharif (130,600) (1988 UN estimates)
CURRENCY – Afghani (Af) of 100 puls
NATIONAL ANTHEM – Soroud-e-Melli
NATIONAL DAY – 19 August
NATIONAL FLAG – Three horizontal stripes of green, white, black with the national arms in the centre in gold
LIFE EXPECTANCY (years) – male 43.00; female 44.00
POPULATION DENSITY – 32 per sq. km (1996)

Mountains, chief among which are the Hindu Kush, cover three-quarters of the country. There are three great river basins, the Oxus, Helmand, and Kabul. The climate is dry, with extreme temperatures.

HISTORY AND POLITICS

The elected president, Mohammad Daoud, was overthrown in 1978 by the armed forces and power was handed to the People's Democratic Party of Afghanistan (PDPA). In December 1979 Soviet troops invaded Afghanistan and installed Babrak Karmal as head of state. Armed Islamic resistance groups, the Mujahidin, fought against Soviet and Afghan forces until the withdrawal of Soviet troops in 1988. Mujahidin opposition to the Homeland Party (formerly PDPA) government continued until the government collapsed in April 1992. Mujahidin forces overran Kabul bringing an end to the war, and declared an Islamic state.

The new government appointed Burhanuddin Rabbani as interim president, but infighting between factions of the Mujahidin resumed in December 1992. A cease-fire and power sharing agreement between them collapsed in October 1993. In the winter of 1994–5, divided Mujahidin forces suffered heavy defeats at the hands of the Taliban (armed Islamic students), which extended its power across half of the country. In March 1996, the Mujahidin agreed to combine their forces against the Taliban but failed to prevent the Taliban from seizing Kabul in September 1996. The forces of the former government were forced northwards. The United Islamic Front for the Salvation of Afghanistan (UIFSA) or Northern Alliance was formed by the four main Mujahidin factions which together controlled one-third of Afghanistan. The Taliban, thought to be backed by Pakistan and Saudi Arabia, imposed strict Sharia law in Kabul. In May 1997 the Taliban temporarily gained control of Mazar-i-Sharif after forming an alliance with Gen. Malik Pahlawan who had defected from the opposition.

During the recapture of Mazar-i-Sharif by Taliban militia in August 1998, nine Iranian diplomats were killed, leading to border clashes between the two countries in October 1998. Peace talks between the Taliban and UIFSA resumed in March 1999, but soon collapsed; fighting continues throughout the country.

POLITICAL SYSTEM
There are 29 provinces, 20 of which are under Taliban control and governed through an interim council (*shura*).

EMBASSY OF THE ISLAMIC STATE OF AFGHANISTAN
31 Prince's Gate, London SW7 1QQ
Tel 0171-589 8891
Ambassador Extraordinary and Plenipotentiary, new appointment awaited
Minister-Counsellor and Chargé d'Affaires, Ahmad Wali Masud

BRITISH EMBASSY
Karte Parwan, Kabul
Staff were withdrawn from post in February 1989.
Ambassador is now resident in Islamabad.

ECONOMY

The economy has been devastated by the political upheavals of the last 20 years. Traditional industries have diminished as the narcotics trade has grown. In 1995 heroin worth £50,000 million was produced. Afghanistan is also the world's second largest producer of opium; the Taliban impose a 10 per cent tax on opium sales. In November 1997, the UN Drug Control Programme brokered an agreement with the Taliban to limit poppy production, and to give UN inspectors access to opium-producing areas.

Agriculture and sheep raising were traditionally the principal industries. Silk, woollen and hair cloths and carpets were manufactured. Salt, silver, copper, coal, iron, lead, rubies, lapis lazuli, gold, chrome, barite, uranium, and talc are found.

There are thought be considerable fuel reserves. US and Saudi Arabian companies have attempted to negotiate with the Taliban and Mujahidin for permission to construct an oil pipeline from Pakistan to Turkmenistan crossing Afghanistan.
GDP – US$55,995 million (1995); US$2,848 per capita (1995)
ANNUAL AVERAGE GROWTH OF GDP – 26.2 per cent (1995)
INFLATION RATE – 56.7 per cent (1991); estimated to be 400 per cent in 1996

TRADE
Trade is now largely limited to narcotics, but in the past exports have been Persian lambskins (Karakul), dried fruits, nuts, cotton, raw wool, carpets, spice and natural gas, while the imports are chiefly oil, cotton yarn and piece goods, tea, sugar, machinery and transport equipment.

In 1995 imports totalled US$50 million and exports US$26 million. There was a current account deficit of US$143 million in 1989.

Trade with UK	1997	1998
Imports from UK	£9,579,000	£10,565,000
Exports to UK	2,948,000	2,535,000

COMMUNICATIONS

Main roads run from Kabul to Kandahar, Herat, Maimana via Mazar-i-Sharif and Faizabad via Khanabad. Roads cross the border with Pakistan at Chaman and via the Khyber Pass, and there are roads from Herat to the borders of Central Asia and Iran. Much of the country's road system has been damaged during the fighting.

In 1982 the Afghan and Uzbek shores of the River Oxus were linked by a road and rail bridge which joins the Afghan port of Hairatan and the Uzbek port of Termez.

EDUCATION

Education is free and nominally compulsory, elementary schools having been established in most centres; there are secondary schools in large urban areas and four universities, in Kabul (established 1932), Jalalabad (established 1962), Balkh and Herat (both established 1988). Kabul's 26 newspapers were closed by the Taliban and women were prohibited from teaching or studying at schools and universities.

ILLITERACY RATE – 68.5 per cent

ENROLMENT (percentage of age group) – primary 29 per cent (1993); tertiary 1.8 per cent (1990)

ALBANIA
Republika e Shqipërisë

AREA – 11,099 sq. miles (28,748 sq. km). Neighbours: Montenegro (north), Serbia and Macedonia (east), Greece (south)

POPULATION – 3,670,000 (1994 UN estimate). Muslim (70 per cent), Greek Orthodox (20 per cent), Roman Catholic (10 per cent). The language is Albanian

CAPITAL – Tirana (population, 244,153, 1990)

CURRENCY – Lek (Lk) of 100 qindarka

NATIONAL DAY – 28 November

NATIONAL FLAG – Black two-headed eagle on a red field

LIFE EXPECTANCY (years) – male 69.60; female 75.50

POPULATION GROWTH RATE – 2.0 per cent (1996)

POPULATION DENSITY – 128 per sq. km (1996)

URBAN POPULATION – 36.7 per cent (1991)

ENROLMENT (percentage of age group) – primary 96 per cent (1995); tertiary 11.1 per cent (1995)

HISTORY AND POLITICS

Albania was under Turkish suzerainty from 1468 until 1912, when independence was declared. After a period of unrest, a republic was declared in 1925, and in 1928 a monarchy. The King went into exile in 1939 when the country was occupied by the Italians; Albania was liberated in November 1944. Elections in 1945 resulted in a Communist-controlled Assembly; the King was deposed in absentia and a republic declared in January 1946.

From 1946 to 1991 Albania was a one-party, Communist state. In March 1991 multiparty elections took place. Rioting broke out in January 1997 following the collapse of several pyramid investment schemes. Anti-government protests, taking the form of armed rebellion, spread throughout the country. A state of emergency was declared in March, and an interim government held power until elections could take place. Legislative elections were held in June 1997 and were won by a Socialist-led coalition. President Berisha resigned following the announcement of the result and was replaced by Rexhep Mejdani.

Following the abandonment of the Rambouillet peace talks on the future of Kosovo, NATO commenced air operations against Yugoslavia in March 1999. Yugoslavia responded by actively expelling hundreds of thousands of Kosovar Albanians, with the majority fleeing to Albania. In

April 1999, Albania granted NATO unrestricted access to Albania's airspace, ports and military infrastructure. There were several incursions into Albanian territory by Serb troops who captured some border villages and set fire to homes before withdrawing. By mid-May 1999, over 400,000 Kosovar Albanians had taken refuge in Albania and over 10,000 NATO troops were stationed there. In June 1999 the refugees began returning home following the end of air operations and the entry of NATO forces.

HEAD OF STATE

President, Prof. Rexhep Mejdani, *elected by parliament* 24 July 1997

COUNCIL OF MINISTERS *as at May 1999*

Prime Minister, Pandeli Majko (SP)
Deputy PM, Government Co-ordination, Ilir Meta (SP)
Agriculture and Food, Lufter Xhuveli (AP)
Defence, Luan Hajdaraga (SP)
Economic Co-operation and Trade, Ermelinda Meksi (SP)
Education and Science, Et'hem Ruka (SP)
Finance, Anastas Angjeli (SP)
Foreign Affairs, Paskal Milo (SDP)
Health, Leonard Solis (HRUP)
Information, Musa Ulqini (SP)
Justice, Thimjo Kondi (Ind.)
Labour and Social Affairs, Kadri Rrapi (SP)
Legislative Reform and Parliamentary Relations, Arben Imami (DAP)
Local Government, Arben Demeti (DAP)
Public Economy and Privatization, Ylli Bufi (SP)
Public Order, Petro Koci (SP)
Public Works and Transport, Ingrid Shuli (SDP)

AP Agrarian Party; DAP Democratic Alliance Party; HRUP Human Rights Union Party; SP Socialist Party; SDP Social Democratic Party

EMBASSY OF THE REPUBLIC OF ALBANIA

4th Floor, 38 Grosvenor Gardens, London SW1W 0EB
Tel 0171-730 5709
Ambassador Extraordinary and Plenipotentiary, HE Agim Besim Fagu, apptd 1997

BRITISH EMBASSY

Rruga Skenderbeg 12, Tirana
Tel: Tirana 34973/4/5
Ambassador Extraordinary and Plenipotentiary, HE Dr Peter January, apptd 1999

DEFENCE

The Army has 859 main battle tanks, 103 armoured personnel carriers and 823 artillery pieces. The Navy has one submarine and 31 patrol and coastal combatant vessels at six bases. The Air Force has 98 combat aircraft.

MILITARY EXPENDITURE – 6.7 per cent of GDP (1997)

MILITARY PERSONNEL – Armed Forces yet to be reconstituted following civil unrest

ECONOMY

Much of the country is mountainous and nearly a half is covered by forest. The main crops are wheat, maize, sugar beet, potatoes and fruit. There are large chromium deposits. The principal industries are agricultural product processing, textiles, oil products and cement.

Since April 1992, the government has imposed austerity measures in an attempt to reduce the budget deficit and to cut inflation. Up to US$1,200 million worth of personal savings were lost in the collapse of several fraudulent pyramid savings schemes in January 1997, and the value of the lek fell heavily.

Remittances from 500,000 overseas workers remain an important source of revenue. Albania has received US$1 billion in aid from Western donors and was promised £2,800 million in food and medical aid by the EU in March 1997. An international donors' conference in October 1997 approved a US$600 million aid package dependent on the closure of all remaining pyramid schemes, and in November 1997, the IMF approved credit of approximately US$12 million.

GNP – US$2,540 million (1997); US$760 per capita (1997)
GDP – US$2,919 million (1995); estimated to be US$2,300 million (1996); US$863 per capita (1995)
Annual Average Growth of GDP – 13.4 per cent (1995)
Inflation Rate – 33.2 per cent (1997)
Unemployment – 9.1 per cent (1991)
Total External Debt – US$706 million (1997)

TRADE

Exports include crude oil, minerals (bitumen, chrome, nickel, copper), tobacco, fruit and vegetables. In 1996 imports totalled US$842 million and exports US$207 million. In 1997 Albania had a trade deficit of US$535 million and a current account deficit of US$272 million.

Trade with UK	1997	1998
Imports from UK	£9,076,000	£7,176,000
Exports to UK	2,124,000	529,000

ALGERIA
Al-Jumhuriya al-Jazairiya ad-Dimuqratiya ash-Shabiya

Area – 919,595 sq. miles (2,381,741 sq. km). Neighbours: Morocco and Western Sahara (west), Mauritania and Mali (south-west), Niger (south-east), Libya and Tunisia (east)
Population – 29,300,000 (1994 UN estimate); 22,971,558 (1987 census). Arabic is the official language although French and Berber are also spoken
Capital – ΨAlgiers (population, 1,740,461, 1977; now roughly 3,250,000). It is one of the principal ports of the Mediterranean
Major Cities – ΨAnnaba; ΨBejaia; Blida; Constantine; ΨMostaganem; ΨOran; Setif; Sidi-Bel-Abbès; ΨSkikda; Tizi Ouzou; Tlemcen
Currency – Algerian dinar (DA) of 100 centimes
National Anthem – Qassaman
National Day – 1 November
National Flag – Divided vertically green and white with a red crescent and star over all in the centre
Life Expectancy (years) – male 65.75; female 66.34
Population Growth Rate – 2.3 per cent (1996)
Population Density – 12 per sq. km (1995)
Illiteracy Rate – 38.4 per cent
Enrolment (percentage of age group) – primary 94 per cent (1996); secondary 56 per cent (1996); tertiary 12.0 per cent (1995)

HISTORY AND POLITICS

Algeria was annexed to France in 1842, with the departments of Algiers, Oran and Constantine forming an integral part of France. President de Gaulle declared Algeria independent in July 1962 following an eight-year armed rebellion by the (Arab) Front de Libération Nationale (FLN), whose leader, Ben Bella, was elected president in

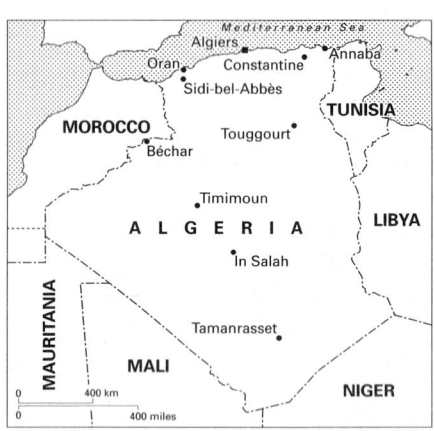

1963. Ben Bella was deposed in 1965 by a military junta presided over by Col. Boumediène, who was formally elected president in 1976. Boumediène died in 1978 and was succeeded by Chadli Bendjedid.

A new constitution agreed by referendum in 1988 moved Algeria towards pluralism. However, the 1991 legislative elections were abandoned in anticipation of the success of the opposition Islamic Salvation Front (FIS), which had campaigned on a radical 'Islamist' platform. The Army forced President Bendjedid to resign and a military-backed Higher Committee of State (HCS), headed by former FLN veteran Mohammed Boudiaf, took power. The HCS declared a state of emergency in 1992 which was extended indefinitely in 1993. The FIS was banned in 1992 but continued to operate covertly and was suspected of assassinating Boudiaf in June 1992.

A national reconciliation conference in January 1994 was boycotted by the FIS but nevertheless it appointed Brig.-Gen. Liamine Zeroual as president to replace the HCS, which disbanded itself. Zeroual was elected president for a five-year term in November 1995, but announced his intention to stand down from office in September 1998. Abdelaziz Bouteflika was elected president on 15 April 1999. The other candidates decided to boycott the election some days before it took place, saying that the military had intervened to rig the vote in his favour.

Multiparty elections on 5 June 1997 were won by a newly-formed pro-Zeroual party, National Democratic Rally (RND), which captured 155 seats. Hamas (Movement for a Society of Peace) (MSP) won 69 seats; the FLN 64 seats; Annahda (Renaissance Movement) 34; Rally for Culture and Democracy 19; Socialist Forces Front 19. Elections to the National Council (the upper house) took place in December 1997 and were dominated by RND, which won 80 of the 96 elected seats.

INSURGENCY

Since the abortive elections in 1992, the FIS-backed Islamic Salvation Army (AIS) and the more extreme Armed Islamic Group (GIA) have waged an armed campaign against the military regime in favour of an Islamic state. The two groups have targeted the military and security forces, their secular supporters in the population, and foreign expatriates. The FIS announced in June 1999 that it was renouncing the armed struggle following negotiations with the government. Up to 80,000 people have died in the fighting since 1992.

POLITICAL SYSTEM

The legislature is bicameral. The National Assembly (the lower chamber) has 380 members, directly elected for a five-year term. The *Majlis el-Umma* (Council of the Nation) is the upper chamber, with a third of its 144 members appointed by the president; two-thirds are indirectly elected for six-year terms.

HEAD OF STATE

President, Abdelaziz Bouteflika, *elected* April 1999

COUNCIL OF MINISTERS *as at June 1999*

Head of Government, Smail Hamdani
Agriculture and Fisheries, Belhouadjeb Benalia (FLN)
Commerce, Bakhti Belaib (RND)
Communications and Culture (interim), Tedjini Salaouanji
Energy and Mines, Youcef Yousfi (RND)
Equipment, National and Regional Development, Abderrahmane Belayat (FLN)
Finance, Abdelkrim Harchaoui (RND)
Foreign Affairs, Ahmed Attaf (RND)
Health and Population, Yahia Guidoum (RND)
Higher Education and Scientific Research, Amar Tou (FLN)
Housing, Abdelkader Bounekraf (FLN)
Industry and Restrucuturing, Abdelmajid Menasra (MSP)
Interior, Local Authorities, Environment, Abdelmalek Sellal
Justice, Ghaouti Mekamcha
National Education, Boubakeur Benbouzid (RND
Posts and Telecommunications, Mohamed Salah Youyou (RND)
Relations with Parliament, Mohamed Kechoud (RND)
Religious Affairs, Bouabdellah Ghlamallah (RND)
Small and Medium-sized Enterprises, Bouguerra Soltani (MSP)
Social Security and Vocational Training, Hacene Laskri (RND)
Tourism and Traditional Industries, Abdelkader Bengrina (MSP)
Transport, Sid Ahmed Boulil (MSP)
War Veterans, Mohamed Said Abadou (RND)
Youth and Sports, Mohammed Aziz Derouaz (RND)

ALGERIAN EMBASSY
54 Holland Park, London WII 3RS
Tel 0171-221 7800
Ambassador Extraordinary and Plenipotentiary, HE Ahmed Benyamina, apptd 1996

BRITISH EMBASSY
7 Chemin des Glycines,
BP 08, Alger-Gare 16000, Algiers
Tel: Algiers 230092
Ambassador Extraordinary and Plenipotentiary, HE William Sinton, apptd 1999

DEFENCE

The Army has 951 main battle tanks, 530 armoured personnel carriers and 416 artillery pieces. The Navy has two submarines, three frigates and 36 patrol and coastal vessels. The Air Force has 181 combat aircraft and 65 armed helicopters.

MILITARY EXPENDITURE – 4.6 per cent of GDP (1997)
MILITARY PERSONNEL – 268,200: Army 105,000, Navy 7,000, Air Force 10,000, Paramilitaries 146,200
CONSCRIPTION DURATION – 18 months

ECONOMY

The main industry is the hydrocarbons industry. Oil and natural gas are pumped from the Sahara to terminals on the coast before being exported; the gas is first liquefied at

liquefaction plants at Skikda and Arzew, although pipelines serve Libya and Italy direct. In November 1996 a 750-mile gas pipeline to Spain was opened, enabling Algeria to double its gas exports to Morocco, Spain, Germany and France. Its initial annual capacity of 8,000 million cubic metres is projected to rise to 20,000 million cubic metres a year by 2000.

Other major industries include a steel industry, motor vehicles, building materials, paper making, chemical products and metal manufactures. Most major industrial enterprises are still under state control.

Prior to 1989 the economy was centrally planned and state-controlled in most sectors. Economic reform, begun in 1987, was speeded up in 1988 and now includes industrial and financial sectors. In 1994 the government finally accepted full economic reform and liberalization under a reform programme agreed with the IMF. The government has cut the budget deficit, devalued the currency and freed price controls. The first stock exchange in Algiers opened on 15 December 1997.

GNP – US$43,927 million (1997); US$1,500 per capita (1997)
GDP – US$43,037 million (1995); US$1,531 per capita (1995)
ANNUAL AVERAGE GROWTH OF GDP – 3.9 per cent (1995)
INFLATION RATE – 21.6 per cent (1996)
UNEMPLOYMENT – 23.8 per cent (1992)
TOTAL EXTERNAL DEBT – US$30,921 million (1997)

TRADE

Export earnings come mainly from crude oil and liquefied natural gas sales. Algeria's main trading partners are France, Italy, USA, Spain and Germany.

In 1991 Algeria had a trade surplus of US$5,468 million and a current account surplus of US$2,367 million. In 1996 imports totalled US$8,840 million and exports US$12,620 million.

Trade with UK	1997	1998
Imports from UK	£91,094,000	£112,731,000
Exports to UK	85,239,000	82,128,000

ANDORRA
Principat d'Andorra

AREA – 175 sq. miles (453 sq. km). Neighbours: Spain and France
POPULATION – 65,877 (1998); less than one-quarter of the population are native Andorrans. The official language is Catalan, but French and Spanish (Castilian) are also spoken. The established religion is Roman Catholicism
CAPITAL – Andorra la Vella (population, 21,721, 1996)
CURRENCY – French and Spanish currencies in use
NATIONAL DAY – 8 September
NATIONAL FLAG – Three vertical bands, blue, yellow, red; Andorran coat of arms frequently imposed on central (yellow) band but not essential
POPULATION GROWTH RATE – 5.0 per cent (1996)
POPULATION DENSITY – 157 per sq. km (1996)
URBAN POPULATION – 95.6 per cent (1991)

HISTORY AND POLITICS

Andorra is a small, neutral principality formed by a treaty in 1278. The first elections under the new constitution were held in December 1993, and on 20 January 1994 the first sovereign government of Andorra took office.

POLITICAL SYSTEM

Under a new constitution promulgated in May 1993, Andorra became an independent, democratic parliamentary co-principality, with sovereignty vested in the people rather than in the two co-princes, as had previously been the case. The constitution enables Andorra to establish an independent judiciary and to carry out its own foreign policy, whilst its people may now join trade unions and political parties. The two co-princes, the President of the French Republic and the Spanish Bishop of Urgel, remain heads of state but now only have the power to veto treaties with France and Spain which affect the state's borders and security. The co-princes are represented by Permanent Delegates of whom one is the French Prefect of the Pyrénées Orientales department at Perpignan and the other is the Spanish Vicar-General of the diocese of Urgel.

Andorra has a unicameral legislature of 28 members known as the *Consell General de las Valls d'Andorra* (Valleys of Andorra General Council). Fourteen members are elected on a national list basis and 14 in seven dual-member constituencies based on Andorra's seven parishes. The Council appoints the head of the executive government, who designates the members of his government.

Permanent French Delegate, Jean Caullet
Permanent Episcopal Delegate, Nemesi Marqués Oste

EXECUTIVE GOVERNMENT *as at May 1999*

Prime Minister, Marc Forné Molné
Agriculture and the Environment, Olga Adellach Coma
Economy, Enric Casadevall Medrano
Education, Youth and Sports, Pere Cervos Cardona
Finance, Susagna Arasanz Serra
Foreign Affairs, Albert Pintat Santolària
Health and Social Security, Josep Maria Goicoechea Utrillo
Home Affairs, Estanislau Sangrà Cardona
Public Works, Candid Naudi Mora
Tourism and Culture, Enric Pujal Areny

ANDORRAN DELEGATION, 63 Westover Road, London SW18 2RF. Tel: 0181-874 4806
BRITISH AMBASSADOR – HE Peter Torry, resident at Madrid

ECONOMY

Potatoes are produced in the highlands and tobacco in the valleys. The economy is largely based on tourism, banking, commerce, tobacco, construction and forestry; a third of the country is classified as forest. Andorra has negotiated a customs union with the European Union which came into force in 1991. The economy is now diversifying rapidly into offshore financial services.
GDP – US$960 million (1995); US$14,111 per capita (1995)
ANNUAL AVERAGE GROWTH OF GDP – 3.0 per cent (1995)

Trade with UK	1997	1998
Imports from UK	£30,967,000	£15,488,000
Exports to UK	118,000	33,000

COMMUNICATIONS

A road into the valleys from Spain is open all year round, and that from France is closed only occasionally in winter. There are two radio stations in Andorra, one privately owned and Radio Andorra, operated by the government, as well as a state-owned television station.

ANGOLA
República de Angola

AREA – 481,354 sq. miles (1,246,700 sq. km). Neighbours: Democratic Republic of Congo (north and east), Zambia (east), Namibia (south). The enclave of Cabinda is separated from the rest of Angola by the Democratic Republic of Congo and also borders on the Republic of the Congo–Brazzaville
POPULATION – 11,185,000 (1994 UN estimate). The official language is Portuguese; Ovimbundu, Kimbundu, Bakongo and Chokwe are widely spoken
CAPITAL – ΨLuanda (population, 475,328, 1970; now estimated at 3,000,000)
CURRENCY – Readjusted kwanza (Kzrl) of 100 lwei
NATIONAL ANTHEM – Angola Avante
NATIONAL DAY – 11 November (Independence Day)
NATIONAL FLAG – Red and black with a yellow star, machete and cog-wheel
LIFE EXPECTANCY (years) – male 44.90; female 48.10
POPULATION GROWTH RATE – 1.8 per cent (1996)
POPULATION DENSITY – 9 per sq. km (1996)
ENROLMENT (percentage of age group) – tertiary 0.7 per cent (1991)

HISTORY AND POLITICS

After a Portuguese presence of five centuries, and an anti-colonial war since 1961, Angola became independent on 11 November 1975 in the midst of civil war. The Popular Movement for the Liberation of Angola (MPLA) took control early in 1976 with Soviet-Cuban military assistance, but remained under pressure from the National Union for the Total Independence of Angola (UNITA). Following a 1988 cease-fire, a peace agreement was signed between the government and UNITA in 1991 and foreign forces withdrew; multiparty legislative and presidential elections took place in 1992, and were won by the MPLA and its leader, José Eduardo dos Santos. UNITA refused to accept the results and the civil war resumed in 1993, with UNITA at one point controlling an estimated 75 per cent of the country.

UNITA and the MPLA government signed a peace agreement (the Lusaka Protocol) under UN mediation in November 1994. By September 1996 more than 70,000 UNITA troops had been confined by the UN peacekeeping force, UNAVEM III, although many subsequently fled. A government of national reconciliation was formed in April 1997 and 70 UNITA legislators took up their seats in parliament, although UNITA's leader, Dr Jonas Savimbi, rejected an offer of the vice-presidency and refused to enter Luanda. UNITA also refused to allow central state administration to be restored in key areas, and following the fall from power of Zaïre's President Mobutu (one of UNITA's key supporters), fighting resumed in May 1997.

On 31 October 1997 the UN Security Council ordered sanctions against UNITA for failing to meet its obligations under the Lusaka Protocol. UNITA returned much of its territory to government control in December, and in January 1998 a new schedule for implementation of the Lusaka Protocol was agreed; UNITA returned the Cuango valley diamond mines to the government, and in March UNITA became a legitimate political party. Three of its representatives were appointed governors of provinces of Angola.

Fighting continued and the UN Security Council adopted a resolution in September 1998 which urged the rejection of military force by all parties and named UNITA as 'the primary cause of the crisis in Angola'. In February 1999 the UN Security Council voted to withdraw the UN Observer Mission in Angola, the UN Secretary-General Kofi Annan having declared that the country was on the verge of a catastrophic breakdown and that there was no more peace to keep.

SECESSION

In the northern enclave of Cabinda, the Front for the Liberation of the Cabinda Enclave (FLEC) fought a 20-year war of independence until the signing of a cease-fire with the government in September 1995, which was followed by the initialling of a peace agreement in April 1996.

POLITICAL SYSTEM

The MPLA, formerly a Marxist-Leninist party, was the sole legal party until early 1991 when a multiparty system was adopted. The constitution declares Angola to be a democratic state and provides for a president, who appoints a Council of Ministers to assist him, and a 220-member National Assembly. In November 1996 the National Assembly adopted a constitutional amendment extending its mandate for between two and four years.

HEAD OF STATE

President, José Eduardo dos Santos, *re-elected* 30 September 1992

COUNCIL OF MINISTERS *as at February 1999*

Prime Minister, vacant
Agriculture and Rural Development, Gilberto Buta Lutukuta
Assistance and Social Reintegration, Albino Malungo
Defence, Gen. Kundi Paihama
Education and Culture, António Burity da Silva Neto
Energy and Water, Luis Felipe da Silva
Ex-Servicemen and War Veterans, Pedro José Van-Dúnem
Family and Women's Advancement, Cândida Celeste da Silva
Finance, Joaquim David
Fisheries and Environment, Maria de Fátima Monteiro Jardim
Foreign Affairs, João Bernardo de Miranda
Geology and Mines, Manuel Bunjo
Governor of the National Bank, Aguinaldo Jaime
Health, Adelino Manaças
Hotel Industry and Tourism, Jorge Alicerces Valentim
Industry, Albina Assis
Information, Pedro Hendrick Vaal Neto
Interior, Fernando Dias dos Santos
Justice, Paulo Tjipilica
Oil, José Maria Botelho de Vasconcelos
Planning, Ana Dias Lourenço
Posts and Telecommunications, Licinio Tavares
Public Administration, Employment and Social Security, António Pitra Neto
Public Works and Town Planning, António Henriques da Silva
Science and Technology, João Baptista Ngandagini
Territorial Administration, Fernando Faustino Muteka
Trade, Victorino Domingos Hossi
Transport, André Luis Brandão
Youth and Sports, José Marcos Barrica

EMBASSY OF ANGOLA
98 Park Lane, London W1Y 3TA
Tel 0171-495 1752
Ambassador Extraordinary and Plenipotentiary, HE Antonio da Costa Fernandes, apptd 1993

BRITISH EMBASSY
Rua Diogo Cão 4 (Caixa Postal 1244), Luanda
Tel: Luanda 334582

Ambassador Extraordinary and Plenipotentiary, HE Caroline Elmes, apptd 1998

DEFENCE

The Army has 100 main battle tanks, 100 armoured personnel carriers and 300 artillery pieces. The Navy has seven patrol vessels at three bases. The Air Force has 45 combat aircraft and 28 armed helicopters.
MILITARY EXPENDITURE – 8.8 per cent of GDP (1997)
MILITARY PERSONNEL – 129,000: Army 106,000, Navy 2,000, Air Force 6,000, Paramilitaries 15,000

ECONOMY

Angola has valuable oil and diamond deposits and exports of these two commodities account for over 90 per cent of total exports. Principal agricultural crops are cassava, maize, bananas, coffee, palm oil and kernels, cotton and sisal. Coffee, sisal, maize and palm oil are exported; exports also include mahogany and other hardwoods from the tropical rain forests in the north of the country.

The government is attempting to reform the socialist economy by free market reforms but is making little progress, with high inflation and a collapsing economy. Following implementation of the peace accord, UNITA transferred diamond mines in the Cuango valley back to the government in January 1998; the estimated annual revenue from the mines is US$400 million.

In 1994 Angola had a trade surplus of US$1,563 million and a current account deficit of US$340 million.
GNP – US$3,012 million (1997); US$260 per capita (1997)
GDP – US$3,838 million (1995); US$355 per capita (1995)
ANNUAL AVERAGE GROWTH OF GDP – 3.9 per cent (1995)
TOTAL EXTERNAL DEBT – US$10,160 million (1997)

Trade with UK	1997	1998
Imports from UK	£81,371,000	£41,481,000
Exports to UK	18,012,000	7,499,000

ANTIGUA AND BARBUDA
State of Antigua and Barbuda

AREA – 171 sq. miles (442 sq. km); Antigua 108 sq. miles (279 sq. km); Barbuda 62 sq.miles (160 sq. km); Redonda ½sq. mile (1.2 sq. km)
POPULATION – 66,000 (1994 UN estimate); 65,962, Antigua 64,562, Barbuda 1,400 (official census 1991); the official language is English
CAPITAL – ΨSt John's (population, 22,342, 1991)
MAJOR TOWNS – The town of Barbuda is Codrington
CURRENCY – East Caribbean dollar (EC$) of 100 cents
NATIONAL ANTHEM – Fair Antigua and Barbuda
NATIONAL DAY – 1 November (Independence Day)
NATIONAL FLAG – Red with an inverted triangle divided black over blue over white, with a rising gold sun on the white band
POPULATION GROWTH RATE – 0.5 per cent (1996)
POPULATION DENSITY – 149 per sq. km (1996)
MILITARY EXPENDITURE – 0.5 per cent of GDP (1997)
MILITARY PERSONNEL – 150: Army 125, Navy 25

Antigua is part of the Leeward Islands in the eastern Caribbean. It is distinguished from the rest of the Leeward group by its absence of high hills and forest, and a drier climate than most of the West Indies. Barbuda, formerly a possession of the Codrington family, is very flat, mainly scrub-covered, with a large lagoon.

HISTORY AND POLITICS

Antigua was first settled by the English in 1632, and was granted to Lord Willoughby by Charles II. It became internally self-governing in 1967 and fully independent on 1 November 1981.

The Antigua Labour party won the general election of 9 March 1999 and a sixth successive term of office with 12 seats in the House of Representatives compared to four seats for the United Progressive Party.

POLITICAL SYSTEM

Antigua and Barbuda is a constitutional monarchy with Queen Elizabeth II as Head of State, represented by the Governor-General. There is a Senate of 17 appointed members and a House of Representatives of 17 members elected every five years. The Attorney-General may be appointed.

Governor-General, HE Sir James Carlisle, GCMG

CABINET *as at June 1999*

Prime Minister, Foreign Affairs, Lester Bird
Agriculture, Lands and Fisheries, Vere Bird Jr
Commerce, Industry and Business Development, Hilroy Humphreys
Education, Culture and Technology, Dr Rodney Williams
Finance, John E. St Luce
Health and Social Development, Bernard Percival
Justice, Legal Affairs and Attorney-General, Dr L. Errol Cort
Labour, Home Affairs and Co-operatives, Steadroy Benjamin
Planning, Implementation and Public Service Affairs, Gaston Browne
Public Utilities, Housing, Transportation and Aviation, Robin Yearwood
Tourism and Environment, Molwyn Joseph
Youth Empowerment, Sports Carnival and Community Development, Guy Yearwood

HIGH COMMISSION FOR ANTIGUA AND BARBUDA
15 Thayer Street, London WIM 5LD
Tel 0171-486 7073/5
High Commissioner, HE Ronald Sanders, CMG, apptd 1995

BRITISH HIGH COMMISSION
11 Old Parham Road (PO 483), St John's
Tel: St John's 462 0008/9
High Commissioner, HE Gordon Baker, resident at Bridgetown, Barbados
Resident High Commissioner, M. Maxwell, MVO

ECONOMY

The economy is largely based on tourism and related services. For many years sugar was the dominant crop but is no longer produced. Agricultural production includes livestock, sea island cotton, mixed market gardening and fishing. An offshore banking centre has been developed.

In 1996 Antigua and Barbuda had a trade deficit of US$263 million and a current account deficit of US$40 million. Imports totalled US$314 million and exports US$30 million.
GNP – US$489 million (1997); US$7,380 per capita (1997)
GDP – US$460 million (1995); US$6,966 per capita (1995)
ANNUAL AVERAGE GROWTH OF GDP – 3.4 per cent (1995)

INFLATION RATE – 1.0 per cent (1985)

Trade with UK	1997	1998
Imports from UK	£42,825,000	£30,572,000
Exports to UK	3,449,000	1,161,000

ARGENTINA
República Argentina

AREA – 1,073,518 sq. miles (2,780,400 sq. km).
Neighbours: Bolivia (north), Paraguay, Brazil and Uruguay (north-east), Chile (west) from which it is separated by the Cordillera de los Andes
POPULATION – 35,220,000 (1994 UN estimate); 32,370,298 (1991 census). The language is Spanish
CAPITAL – ΨBuenos Aires (population, 11,298,030, 1991); metropolitan area 2,965,403
MAJOR CITIES – Córdoba (1,208,554); ΨLa Plata (642,979); ΨMar del Plata (512,880); Mendoza (773,113); ΨRosario (1,118,905); San Miguel de Tucumán (622,324)
CURRENCY – Peso of 10,000 australes
NATIONAL ANTHEM – ¡Oíd Mortales! (Hear, oh mortals!)
NATIONAL DAY – 25 May
NATIONAL FLAG – Horizontal bands of blue, white, blue; gold sun in centre of white band
LIFE EXPECTANCY (years) – male 68.17; female 73.09
POPULATION GROWTH RATE – 1.3 per cent (1996)
POPULATION DENSITY – 13 per sq. km (1996)

Argentina occupies the greater portion of the southern part of the South American continent, and extends from Bolivia to Cape Horn.

HISTORY AND POLITICS

The estuary of La Plata was discovered in 1515 by Juan Díaz de Solís and the region was subsequently colonized by the Spanish. Spain ruled the territory from the 16th century until 1810. In 1816, after a long campaign of liberation conducted by General José de San Martín, independence was declared by the Congress of Tucumán.

President Juan Domingo Perón was overthrown in 1955, and there followed 18 years of instability until 1973 when he was recalled from exile. Perón died within a year and was succeeded by his widow, Vice-President María Estela Martínez de Perón. A coup led to the establishment of a military junta in 1976. Following the Falkland Islands defeat in 1982, the President, Gen. Galtieri, resigned and the Army appointed Gen. Bignone. A civilian president was elected in 1983. Presidential elections in 1989 were won by the Justicialist Party (Perónist) candidate Carlos Menem. In the October 1997 elections, which followed widespread protests against the government's free market policies and a general strike in August 1997, the Justicialist Party lost its overall majority, holding 118 out of the 257 seats. It is still the largest single party in the Chamber of Deputies.

POLITICAL SYSTEM

The 1853 constitution was amended in 1994. Power is vested in the president who appoints the Cabinet and is directly elected for a once-renewable four-year term. A presidential candidate must win at least 45 per cent of the vote, or 40 per cent with a 10 per cent lead over the nearest challenger, to gain victory. The legislature consists of a 72-member (three for each province) Senate and a 259-member Chamber of Deputies. A third of the Senate is elected every three years and half of the Chamber of

Deputies is elected every two years. Senators serve for a nine-year term and Deputies for a four-year term.

FEDERAL STRUCTURE

The republic is divided into 23 provinces, each with an elected Governor and legislature, and one federal district (Buenos Aires), with an elected mayor and autonomous government.

Province	Area (sq. km)	Population (1991 census)	Capital
Buenos Aires	307,571	12,594,974	La Plata
Catamarca	102,602	264,234	Catamarca
Chaco	99,633	839,677	Resistencia
Chubut	224,686	357,189	Rawson
Córdoba	165,321	2,766,683	Córdoba
Corrientes	88,199	795,594	Corrientes
Entre Ríos	78,781	1,020,257	Paraná
Federal Capital	200	2,965,403	Buenos Aires
Formosa	72,066	398,413	Formosa
Jujuy	53,219	512,329	San Salvador de Jujuy
La Pampa	143,440	259,996	Santa Rosa
La Rioja	89,680	229,729	La Rioja
Mendoza	148,827	1,412,481	Mendoza
Misiones	29,801	788,915	Posadas
Neuquén	94,078	388,833	Neuquén
Rio Negro	203,013	506,772	Viedma
Salta	155,488	866,153	Salta
San Juan	89,651	528,715	San Juan
San Luis	76,748	286,458	San Luis
Santa Cruz	243,943	159,839	Rio Gallegos
Santa Fé	133,007	2,798,422	Santa Fé
Santiago del Estero	136,351	671,988	Santiago del Estero
Tierra del Fuego	21,571	69,369	Ushuaia
Tucumán	22,524	1,142,105	San Miguel de Tucumán

HEAD OF STATE

President, Dr Carlos Saúl Menem, *elected* May 1989, *re-elected* 14 May 1995
Vice-President, Dr Carlos Federico Ruckauf

CABINET *as at May 1999*

Cabinet Chief, Jorge Alberto Rodríguez
Defence, Jorge Domínguez
Economy and Public Works, Roque Fernández
Education and Culture, Susana Decibe
Environment, María Julia Alsogaray
Foreign Affairs, Guido di Tella
Interior, Carlos Corach
Justice, Raúl Granillo Ocampo
Labour and Social Security, Antonio Ermán González
Public Health and Social Action, Alberto José Mazza
Secretary-General of the Presidency, Alberto Kohan
Social Development, Ramón Ortega

EMBASSY OF THE ARGENTINE REPUBLIC
65 Brook Street, London WIY IYE
Tel 0171-318 1300
Ambassador Extraordinary and Plenipotentiary, HE Rogelio Pfirter, apptd 1995
Defence Attaché, Capt. Eduardo Rodríguez
Counsellor (Economic and Commercial Affairs), Gustavo Martino

BRITISH EMBASSY
Dr Luis Agote 2141/52, 1425 Buenos Aires
Tel: Buenos Aires 4803 7070
Ambassador Extraordinary and Plenipotentiary, HE William Marsden, CMG, apptd 1997

Deputy Head of Mission and Minister, Dominic Asquith
Defence and Air Attaché, Gp Capt. D. McDonnell, OBE
Naval and Military Attaché, Col. H. Massey
First Secretary (Commercial), H. Deas
Cultural Attaché and British Council Representative, M. Potter, OBE, Marcelo T. de Alvear 590, 1058 Buenos Aires

BRITISH CHAMBER OF COMMERCE, Av. Corrientes 457, 10 piso, 1043 Buenos Aires

DEFENCE

The Army has 326 main battle tanks, 846 armoured infantry fighting vehicles and armoured personnel carriers, 40 helicopters and 217 artillery pieces. The Navy has three submarines, six destroyers, seven frigates, 14 patrol and coastal vessels, 52 combat aircraft and 11 armed helicopters. The Air Force has 200 combat aircraft and 14 armed helicopters.
MILITARY EXPENDITURE – 1.7 per cent of GDP (1997)
MILITARY PERSONNEL – 104,240: Army 41,000, Navy 20,000, Air Force 12,000, Paramilitaries 31,240

ECONOMY

A large proportion of the land is still held in large estates devoted to cattle raising but the number of small farms is increasing. The principal crops are wheat, maize, oats, barley, rye, linseed, sunflower seed, alfalfa, sugar, fruit and cotton. Argentina is pre-eminent in the production of beef, mutton and wool. There is an oil refinery in San Lorenzo (Santa Fé province). Natural gas is also produced. Coal, lead, zinc, tungsten, iron ore, sulphur, mica and salt are the other chief minerals being exploited. There are small worked deposits of beryllium, manganese, bismuth, uranium, antimony, copper, kaolin, arsenate, gold, silver and tin. Coal is produced at the Rio Turbio mine in the province of Santa Cruz.

Meat-packing is one of the principal industries; flour-milling, sugar-refining, and the wine industry are also important. In recent years progress has been made by the textile, plastic and machine tool industries and engineering, especially in the production of motor vehicles and steel manufactures.

The Menem government introduced an economic reform programme in 1991 involving the privatization of most state-owned industries, widespread deregulation, exchange-rate stabilization and lower trade barriers. This led to economic growth, increased foreign investment and much lower inflation. Economic growth was 8 per cent in 1996–7. The IMF approved two credits of US$3 billion in November 1998. The peso has been pegged to the US dollar since 1991.
GNP – US$319,293 million (1997); US$8,950 per capita (1997)
GDP – US$280,070 million (1995); US$8,055 per capita (1995)
ANNUAL AVERAGE GROWTH OF GDP – –5.6 per cent (1995)
INFLATION RATE – 0.5 per cent (1997)
UNEMPLOYMENT – 18.8 per cent (1995)
TOTAL EXTERNAL DEBT – US$123,221 million (1997)

TRADE

The chief imports are machinery, industrial and transport equipment, chemicals, metals and plastics. The chief exports are vegetable products, processed foods, minerals, live animals and oils. Argentina's main trading partners are Brazil and the USA.

In 1997 Argentina had a trade deficit of US$3,195 million and a current account deficit of US$10,119 million. In 1997 imports totalled US$30,349 million and exports US$25,516 million.

Trade with UK	1997	1998
Imports from UK	£487,127,000	£469,077,000
Exports to UK	269,864,000	207,986,000

COMMUNICATIONS

The 25,386 miles of railway are state-owned. The combined national and provincial road network totals approximately 137,000 miles of which 23,180 miles are surfaced.

CULTURE AND EDUCATION

The literature of Spain is part of the culture. There is little indigenous literature before the break from Spain, but all branches have flourished since the latter half of the 19th century. About 450 daily newspapers are published in Argentina, including seven major ones in the city of Buenos Aires. The English language newspaper is the *Buenos Aires Herald* (daily).

Education is compulsory for the seven grades of primary school (six to 13). Secondary schools (14 to 17+) are available in and around Buenos Aires and in most of the important towns in the interior of the country. Most secondary schools are administered by the Central Ministry of Education in Buenos Aires, while primary schools are administered by the Central Ministry or by Provincial Ministries of Education. Private schools, of which there are many, are also loosely controlled by the Central Ministry. The total number of universities is over 50 with 24 national, 25 private and a small number of provincial universities.

ILLITERACY RATE – 3.8 per cent

ENROLMENT (percentage of age group) – primary 95 per cent (1991); secondary 59 per cent (1991); tertiary 41.8 per cent (1996)

ARMENIA
Hayastany Hanrapetoutioun

AREA – 11,506 sq. miles (29,800 sq. km). Neighbours: Azerbaijan (east and south-west), Georgia (north), Iran (south), Turkey (west)

POPULATION – 3,893,000 (1998). Armenians 93.8 per cent, Kurds 1.7 per cent and Russians 1.6 per cent. Azerbaijanis formed 2.6 per cent of the population, but most fled or were expelled after the outbreak of war with Azerbaijan. There are also Ukrainians, Greeks and Assyrians. The Armenian diaspora numbers some 5,300,000. Armenian is the official language, though Russian is widely spoken and understood. The main religion is Armenian Orthodox Christian (Armenian Church centred in Etchmiadzin). Armenia adopted Christianity as its official religion in AD 301, the first state in the world to do so

CAPITAL – Yerevan (population, 1,254,400, 1990)

CURRENCY – Dram of 100 louma

NATIONAL DAY – 21 September (Independence Day)

NATIONAL FLAG – Three horizontal stripes of red, blue and orange

LIFE EXPECTANCY (years) – male 68.66; female 75.51

POPULATION GROWTH RATE – 1.0 per cent (1996)

POPULATION DENSITY – 126 per sq. km (1996)

URBAN POPULATION – 68.5 per cent (1992)

Armenia lies between the Black and Caspian Seas, occupying the south-western part of the Caucasus region of the former Soviet Union. It is very mountainous, consisting of several vast tablelands surrounded by ridges. The climate is continental, dry and cold, but the Ararat valley has a long, hot and dry summer.

HISTORY AND POLITICS

Armenia was first unified in 95 BC but was divided between the Persian and Byzantine Empires in AD 387 and then conquered in the 11th century by the Seljuk Turks and the Mongols. In the 16th century most of Armenia was incorporated into the Ottoman Empire. In 1639 the country was divided again, the easternmost portions, now the republic of Armenia, becoming part of the Persian Empire. In 1828 eastern Armenia became part of the Russian Empire while western Armenia remained under Ottoman rule. The Ottomans launched pogroms against the Armenians from 1894 onwards, and in 1915 to 1918 massacred 1,500,000 Armenians.

Armenia declared its independence on 28 May 1918, but was crushed and divided between Turkish and Soviet forces in 1920, with the area under Soviet control proclaimed a Soviet Socialist Republic on 29 November 1920. The Soviet government was overthrown by a nationalist revolt in 1921 but reinstated by the Red Army a few months later. In early 1922 Armenia acceded to the USSR.

An Armenian nationalist movement swept to power in national elections in mid-1990. In a referendum in 1991, 99 per cent of the electorate voted for independence, which was declared on 21 September 1991.

FOREIGN RELATIONS

The dispute between the (ethnic Armenian) Nagorno-Karabakh forces supported by Armenia and the Azeri government over Nagorny-Karabakh erupted into all-out war in May 1992, when Nagorno-Karabakh forces breached Azerbaijan's defences to form a land bridge to Armenia. By the end of summer 1992 all of Nagorny-Karabakh was under Armenian control, and by the end of 1993 all Azeri territory that separated Nagorny-Karabakh from Armenia and all mountainous Azeri territory around Nagorny-Karabakh was under the control of Nagorny-Karabakh Armenians. Armenia claims this territory as historically Armenian land arbitrarily given to Azerbaijan by Stalin in 1921–2. A cease-fire agreement between Armenia, Azerbaijan and Nagorny-Karabakh was reached in May 1994, and talks mediated by the OSCE continue to seek a peaceful resolution to the dispute.

In August 1997 Armenia and Russia renewed a Treaty of Friendship, Co-operation and Mutual Assistance in effect since 1991.

POLITICAL SYSTEM

In April 1995, a law was passed creating a 190-member National Assembly, to be elected every four years by a combined constituency and party-list system. In the first elections to the new body in July 1995, the ruling Republican coalition led by the Pan-Armenian National Movement won a majority of seats. A new constitution was approved by a referendum in July 1995.

On 3 February 1998, President Levon Ter-Petrossian resigned after 40 deputies withdrew their support for his coalition government, in protest at his policy on Nagorny-Karabakh. Robert Kocharian, the Prime Minister and a former President of Nagorny-Karabakh, was elected to succeed him on 30 March.

Armenia is divided into 11 Administrative Regions.

HEAD OF STATE
President, Robert Kocharian, *sworn in* 9 April 1998

CABINET *as at May 1999*

Prime Minister, Armen Darbinian
Agriculture, Vladimir Movsisian
Communications, Artak Vardanian
Culture, Youth and Sport, Roland Sharoian
Defence, Vazgen Sarkissian
Economic Structural Reform, Vahram Avanessian
Education and Science, Levon Mkrtchian
Energy, Meruzhan Mikayelian
Environmental Protection, Gevork Vardanian
Finance and Economy, Edward Sandoyan
Foreign Affairs, Vardan Oskania
Health, Ayk Nikogosyan
Internal Affairs and National Security, Serge Sarkissian
Justice, David Haroutiounian
Local Government Affairs, David Zadoian
Mayor of Yerevan, Souren Abrahamian
Prime Minister's Chief of Staff, Eduard Tadevosian
Privatization, Pavel Khaltakchian
Production Infrastructures, Gagik Martirosian
Social Security, Gagik Yekanian
State Commission for Statistics and Data, Stepan
    Mnatsakanian
State Commission for Tax Inspection, Artashes Toumanian
Trade, Services, Tourism and Industry, Aik Kevorkian
Transport, Yervand Zakarian
Urban Planning and Construction, Feliks Pirumian

EMBASSY OF THE REPUBLIC OF ARMENIA
25A Cheniston Gardens, London W8 6TG
Tel 0171-938 5415
Ambassador Extraordinary and Plenipotentiary, HE Dr Armen
    Sarkissian, apptd 1998

BRITISH EMBASSY
28 Charents Street, Yerevan
Tel: Yerevan 151 841/2
Ambassador Extraordinary and Plenipotentiary, HE Dr John
    Mitchiner, apptd 1996

DEFENCE

The Army has 102 main battle tanks, 218 armoured infantry
fighting vehicles and armoured personnel carriers, 225
artillery pieces, six combat aircraft and 16 armed helicopters.

Russia maintains 4,100 army personnel in Armenia. An
agreement on military co-operation with Russia was signed
in 1996 which paved the way for joint military exercises. A
protocol was also signed on the establishment of coalition
troops in Transcaucasia and the planned use of Russian
and Armenian armed forces as part of coalition troops in
cases of mutual interest.
MILITARY EXPENDITURE – 8.9 per cent of GDP (1997)
MILITARY PERSONNEL – 53,000: Army 52,000,
    Paramilitaries 1,000
CONSCRIPTION DURATION – 18 months

ECONOMY

The Armenian economy has been badly affected by the
Azeri and Turkish economic embargoes which have been
in place since 1988. The main trade and transportation
routes now lie via Georgia and Iran.

Armenia has a strong agricultural sector in low-lying
areas, where industrial and fruit crops are grown. Grain is
grown in the hills and the country is also noted for its wine
and brandy. There are large copper ore and molybdenum
deposits and other minerals. The country also has

developed chemicals, industrial vehicles and textiles
industries.

The government introduced a programme of economic
reforms in November 1994 with IMF support, including
the liberalization of prices, stabilization of the currency
and privatization.

In 1996 Armenia had a trade deficit of US$469 million
and a current account deficit of US$291 million. In 1997
imports totalled US$892 million and exports US$233
million.
GNP – US$2,112 million (1997); US$560 per capita
    (1997)
GDP – US$1,287 million (1995); US$354 per capita
    (1995)
ANNUAL AVERAGE GROWTH OF GDP – 7.2 per cent
    (1998)
INFLATION RATE – 13.9 per cent (1997)
TOTAL EXTERNAL DEBT – US$666 million (1997)

Trade with UK	1997	1998
Imports from UK	£7,172,000	£4,533,000
Exports to UK	111,000	1,111,000

CULTURE AND EDUCATION

The Armenian alphabet was established in AD 405. Major
writers include the poets Narekatsi (10th century), Frick
(13th century), Nahapet Kuchak (16th century) and Sayat-
Nova (18th century). The composer Aram Khachaturian
(1903–78) was Armenian.
ILLITERACY RATE – 0.4 per cent
ENROLMENT (percentage of age group) – tertiary 12.0
    per cent (1996)

AUSTRALIA
The Commonwealth of Australia

AREA – 2,988,902 sq. miles (7,741,220 sq. km)
POPULATION – 18,871,800 (1998 estimate): 386,049 of
    Aboriginal and Torres Strait Islander origin (1996
    estimate). The language is English
CAPITAL – Canberra, in the Australian Capital Territory
    (population, 309,500, 1997 estimate). It has been the
    seat of government since 1927
MAJOR CITIES – Adelaide (1,083,100); Brisbane
    (1,548,346); Hobart (195,500); Melbourne (3,321,700;
    Perth, including Fremantle (1,319,000); Sydney
    (3,934,700)

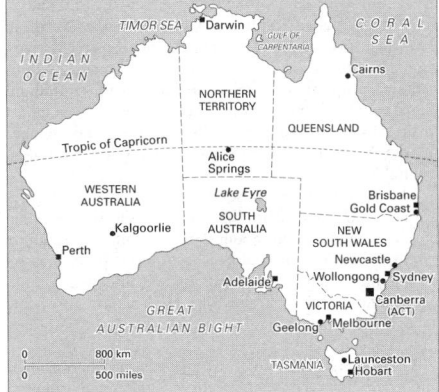

CURRENCY – Australian dollar ($A) of 100 cents
NATIONAL ANTHEM – Advance Australia Fair
NATIONAL DAY – 26 January (Australia Day)
NATIONAL FLAG – The British Blue Ensign with five
stars of the Southern Cross in the fly and the white
Commonwealth Star of seven points beneath the Union
Flag
LIFE EXPECTANCY (years) – male 75.04; female 80.94
POPULATION GROWTH RATE – 1.3 per cent (1998)
POPULATION DENSITY – 2 per sq. km (1996)
URBAN POPULATION – 85.4 per cent (1986)

Australia is a continent in the southern hemisphere. The
highest point is Mt. Kosciusko (2,228 m) and the lowest,
Lake Eyre (−15 m). Climatic conditions range from the
alpine to the tropical. Two-thirds of the continent is arid
or semi-arid although good rainfalls (over 800 mm annually) occur in the northern monsoonal belt and along
the eastern and southern highland regions.

HISTORY AND POLITICS

Australia was discovered in the 18th century and was
colonized by the British, initially as a penal colony. The
Commonwealth of Australia was inaugurated on 1 January
1901, at which time Australia gained dominion status
within the British Empire. Australia became independent
within the British Commonwealth by the 1931 Statute of
Westminster.

The general election in October 1998 was won by the
ruling Liberal-National Party coalition, though with a
much reduced majority.

POLITICAL SYSTEM

The government is that of a federal commonwealth within
the Commonwealth, the executive power being vested in
the Sovereign (through the Governor-General), assisted
by a federal government. Under the constitution the federal
government has acquired and may acquire certain defined
powers as surrendered by the states, residuary legislative
power remaining with the states. The right of a state to
legislate on any matter is not abrogated except in
connection with matters exclusively under federal control,
but where a state law is inconsistent with a law of the
Commonwealth the latter prevails to the extent of the
inconsistency.

Parliament consists of Queen Elizabeth II, the Senate
and the House of Representatives. The constitution
provides that the number of members of the House of
Representatives shall be, as nearly as practicable, twice the
number of senators. Members of the Senate are elected for
six years by universal suffrage, half the members retiring
every third year. Each of the six states returns 12 senators,
and the Australian Capital Territory and the Northern
Territory two each. The House of Representatives,
similarly elected for a maximum of three years, contains
members proportionate to the population, with a minimum
of five members for each state. There are now 148 members
in the House of Representatives, including one member
for the Northern Territory and two for the Australian
Capital Territory.

The High Court exercises jurisdiction over all matters
arising under the constitution, all matters arising between
the states and between residents of different states, matters
to which the Commonwealth of Australia is a party, matters
arising under any treaty, and matters affecting foreign
representatives in Australia. The High Court also hears
appeals from the Federal Court and from the Supreme
Courts of states and territories.

The Federal Court of Australia has jurisdiction over
important industrial, trade practices, intellectual property,

administrative law, admiralty law and bankruptcy matters.
It also acts as a court of appeal for decisions from the
Australian Capital Territory Supreme Court and certain
decisions of state Supreme Courts exercising federal
jurisdiction. Each state has its own judicature of supreme,
superior and minor courts for criminal and civil cases.

On 13 February 1998, the Constitutional Convention
voted by 89 votes to 52 to sever constitutional links with
the United Kingdom monarchy. A national referendum
will be held on the issue in November 1999.

FEDERAL STRUCTURE

In the states, executive authority is vested in a Governor
(appointed by the Crown), assisted by a Council of
Ministers or Executive Council. Each state has a legislature
comprising a Legislative Council and a Legislative Assembly or House of Assembly which are elected for four-year
terms, except Queensland, which has a Legislative Assembly only.

Administration of the Northern Territory became a
federal responsibility in 1911. Since 1978 Northern
Territory ministers have had responsibility for Territory
finances and administration.

GOVERNOR-GENERAL

Governor-General, HE The Hon. Sir William Deane, AC,
KBE, *assumed office* 16 February 1996

CABINET *as at May 1999*

Prime Minister, John Howard
Deputy Prime Minister, Trade, Tim Fischer
Agriculture, Fisheries and Forestry, Mark Vaile
Attorney-General, Daryl Williams
Communications, Arts, Information Technology, Sen. Richard
Alston
Defence, John Moore
Education, Training and Youth Affairs, David Kemp
Employment, Workplace Relations and Small Business, Peter
Reith
*Environment and Heritage, Leader of the Government in the
Senate*, Robert Hill
Family and Community Services, Jocelyn Newman
Finance and Administration, John Fahey
Foreign Affairs, Alexander Downer
Health and Aged Care, Dr Michael Wooldridge
Immigration and Multicultural Affairs, Philip Ruddock
Industry, Science and Resources, Nick Minchin
Transport and Regional Development, John Anderson
Treasurer, Peter Costello

President of the Senate, Sen. Kerry Sibraa
Speaker, House of Representatives, Stephen Martin

AUSTRALIAN HIGH COMMISSION
Australia House, Strand, London WC2B 4LA Tel 0171-379
4334
High Commissioner, HE Philip Flood, apptd May 1998
Deputy High Commissioner, R. McGovern
Minister-Counsellor, C. J. Walsh *(Industry, Science and
Technology)*
Head of Defence Staff, Air Cdre Gary Waters

NEW SOUTH WALES GOVERNMENT OFFICE, The
Australia Centre, Strand, London WC2B 4LG. Tel: 0171-
887 5871. *Agent-General*, Gary Offner
AGENT-GENERAL FOR QUEENSLAND, 392 Strand, London
WC2R 0LZ. Tel: 0171-836 1333. *Agent-General*, Dermot A.
McManus
AGENT-GENERAL FOR SOUTH AUSTRALIA, Australia
Centre, Strand, London WC2B 4LG Tel: 0171 836 3455.
Agent-General, Maurice de Rohan

STATES AND TERRITORIES

	Area (sq. km)	Resident population 31 December 1998p	Capital	Governor	Premier
Australian Capital Territory (ACT)	2,400	308,700	Canberra	—	Kate Carnell‡
New South Wales (NSW)	801,600	6,384,300	Sydney	HE Gordon Samuels, AC	Bob Carr
Northern Territory (NT)	1,346,200	191,400	Darwin*	Dr Neil Conn, AO†	Denis Burke‡
Queensland (Qld)	1,727,200	3,485,200	Brisbane	HE Maj.-Gen. Peter Arnison, AO	Peter Beattie
South Australia (SA)	984,000	1,490,400	Adelaide	HE Sir Eric Neal, AC, CVO	John Olsen
Tasmania (Tas.)	67,800	471,100	Hobart	HE Sir Guy Green, AC, KBE	Jim Bacon
Victoria (Vic.)	227,600	4,689,800	Melbourne	HE Sir James Gobbo, AC, KT	Jeff Kennett
Western Australia (WA)	2,525,500	1,847,800	Perth	HE Maj.-Gen. Philip Michael Jeffery, AC, MC	Richard Court

p preliminary
* Seat of administration
† Administrator
‡ Chief Minister

AGENT-GENERAL FOR VICTORIA, Victoria House, Melbourne Place, Strand, London WC2B 4LG. Tel: 0171 836 2656. *Agent-General*, Alan J. Brown
AGENT-GENERAL FOR WESTERN AUSTRALIA, Australia Centre, Strand, London WC2B 4LG. Tel: 0171 240 2881. *Agent-General*, Clive E. Griffiths

BRITISH HIGH COMMISSION
Commonwealth Avenue, Yarralumla, Canberra, ACT 2600 Tel: Canberra 6270 6666
High Commissioner, HE Alexander Allan, apptd 1997
Deputy High Commissioner, A. J. Pocock
First Secretary, B. J. Davidson *(Economic and Agricultural)*
Defence and Naval Adviser and Head of British Defence Liaison Staff, Cdre A. J. Lyall, MBE
Consuls-General, S. J. Hiscock (*Brisbane*); P. M. Innes (*Melbourne*); M. J. Horne, OBE (*Perth*); P. Morrice (*Sydney*)
Cultural Adviser and British Council Representative, J. Potts, OBE, Edgecliff Centre, 401/203 New South Head Road (PO Box 88), Edgecliff, Sydney, NSW 2027

DEFENCE

The Army has 71 main battle tanks, 620 armoured personnel carriers and armoured infantry fighting vehicles, 385 artillery pieces, four aircraft and 125 armed helicopters. The Navy has four submarines, three destroyers, eight frigates, 15 patrol and coastal vessels and 16 armed helicopters. There are bases at Sydney, Garden Island, Cairns and Darwin. The Air Force has 126 combat aircraft.
MILITARY EXPENDITURE – 2.2 per cent of GDP (1997)
MILITARY PERSONNEL – 57,400: Army 25,400, Navy 14,300, Air Force 17,700

ECONOMY

The wide range of climatic and soil conditions has resulted in a diversity of crops. Generally, cereal crops (excluding rice and sorghum) are widely grown, while other crops are confined to specific locations in a few states. However, scant or erratic rainfall, limited potential for irrigation and unsuitable soils or topography have restricted intensive agriculture.
Significant mineral resources include bauxite, coal, copper, crude petroleum, gems, gold, ilmenite, iron ore, lead, limestone, manganese, nickel, rutile, salt, silver, tin, tungsten, uranium, zinc and zircon. In 1997 277,190,000 tonnes of coal, 30,000,000 tonnes of crude oil, 29,950,000 cubic metres of natural gas, 157,766,000 tonnes of iron ore, 531,000 tonnes of lead, and 313,450 kilograms of gold were produced.
GNP – US$382,705 million (1997); US$20,650 per capita (1997)
GDP – US$358,147 million (1995); US$20,046 per capita (1995)
ANNUAL AVERAGE GROWTH OF GDP – 4.0 per cent (1996)
INFLATION RATE – 0.3 per cent (1997)
UNEMPLOYMENT – 8.5 per cent (1995)

TRADE

In 1996–7 the main exports were coal and gas (12.5 per cent); aluminium and aluminium oxide (6.3 per cent); iron, iron ore and steel (6.1 per cent); gold (6 per cent); wheat (5.5 per cent); petroleum oils and products (4.8 per cent). The major imports were motor vehicles and parts (10.1 per cent); computer technology (7.2 per cent); petroleum oils (6.1 per cent); telecommunications equipment (3.1 per cent); aircraft and spacecraft (2.3 per cent).
Australia's main trading partners are Japan, the USA, New Zealand, China, Korea, Germany and the UK.
In 1997 Australia had a trade surplus of US$1,807 million and a current account deficit of US$12,928 million. In 1997 imports totalled US$65,881 million and exports US$62,900 million.

Trade with UK	1997	1998
Imports from UK	£2,454,988,000	£2,260,308,000
Exports to UK	1,371,268,000	1,429,807,000

COMMUNICATIONS

There are six government-owned railway systems, operated by the State Rail Authority of NSW, Victorian Railways, Queensland Government Railways, Western Australian Government Railways, the State Transport Authority of Southern Australia, and the National Rail Corporation (NRC). The NRC incorporates the former Commonwealth Railways system, and the Tasmanian and non-metropolitan South Australian railways (urban rail services in Southern Australia remain the responsibility of the State Transport Authority).
The Northern Territory has three main ports: Darwin, and the private mining ports of Gove and Groote Eylandt. Most freight in the Territory is moved by road trains. These are massive trucks hauling two or three trailers, having a net capacity of about 100 tonnes and measuring up to 45 metres in length.

EDUCATION

Education is administered by the state governments and is compulsory between the ages of five or six and 15 years. It is available at government schools controlled by the state education department and at private or independent schools, some of which are denominational. Tertiary education is available through universities, and technical and further education colleges. There are 38 universities in Australia; the Australian Capital Territory has two universities, New South Wales 11, Queensland seven, Northern Territory one, South Australia three, Tasmania one, Victoria eight and Western Australia five.

ENROLMENT (percentage of age group) – primary 97 per cent (1996); secondary 92 per cent (1996); tertiary 75.6 per cent (1996)

EXTERNAL TERRITORIES

ASHMORE AND CARTIER ISLANDS

Ashmore Islands (known as Middle, East and West Islands) and Cartier Island are situated in the Indian Ocean 850 km and 790 km west of Darwin respectively. The islands are uninhabited. The territory has been administered by the Australian Government since 1933.

THE AUSTRALIAN ANTARCTIC TERRITORY

The Australian Antarctic Territory was established in 1933 and comprises all the islands and territories, other than Adélie Land, which are situated south of the latitude 60° S. and lying between 160° E. longitude and 45° E. longitude. The territory is administered by the Antarctic Division of the Department of the Environment. There are nine scientific research stations.

CHRISTMAS ISLAND

AREA – 52 sq. miles (135 sq. km)
POPULATION – 1,906 (1996 census)

Christmas Island is situated in the Indian Ocean about 1,408 km NW of North West Cape in Western Australia. The island became an Australian territory in 1958 and is managed by the Department of Transport and Regional Services. The Shire of Christmas Island (SOCI) has nine elected members. SOCI is responsible for municipal functions and services on the island.

Administrator, W. Taylor

COCOS (KEELING) ISLANDS

AREA – 5.4 sq. miles (14 sq. km)
POPULATION – 655 (1996 census)

The Cocos (Keeling) Islands are two separate atolls (North Keeling Island and, 24 km to the south, the main atoll) comprising some 27 small coral islands, situated in the Indian Ocean. The main islands of the southern atoll are West Island (about 9 km in length); Home Island, where the Cocos Malay community lives; Direction Island, Horsburgh and South Island.

The islands were declared a British possession in 1857. All land in the islands was granted to George Clunies-Ross and his heirs by Queen Victoria in 1886. In 1978 the Australian Government purchased all Clunies-Ross land and property interests except for the family home and grounds; the last of the remaining grounds were purchased in 1993. Between 1979 and 1984 most of the land was transferred to trusts with the Cocos (Keeling) Islands Council as trustee, the local government body established in 1979 which was replaced by the Shire of the Cocos (Keeling) Islands in July 1992.

On 6 April 1984 the Cocos community, in a UN-supervised Act of Self-Determination, chose to integrate with Australia. The islands are managed by the Australian Government through the Department of Transport and Regional Services.

Administrator, W. Taylor

CORAL SEA ISLANDS TERRITORY

The Coral Sea Islands Territory lies east of Queensland between the Great Barrier Reef and longitude 156° 06′ E., and between latitudes 12° and 24° S. It comprises scattered islands, spread over a sea area of 780,000 sq. km. The islands are formed mainly of coral and sand, and most are extremely small. There is a manned meteorological station in the Willis Group but the remaining islands are uninhabited.

The territory is managed by the Department of Transport and Regional Services.

HEARD ISLAND AND McDONALD ISLANDS

The Heard and McDonald islands, about 4,100 km south-west of Perth, comprise all the islands and rocks lying between 52° 30′ and 53° 30′ S. latitude and 72° and 74° 30′ E. longitude. The islands are administered by the Antarctic Division of the Department of the Environment.

NORFOLK ISLAND

AREA – 13.3 sq. miles (34.5 sq. km)
POPULATION – 1,772 (1996 census)
SEAT OF GOVERNMENT – Kingston

Norfolk Island is situated in the South Pacific Ocean. It is about 8 km long by 5 km wide. The climate is mild and subtropical.

The island, discovered by Captain Cook in 1774, served as a penal colony from 1788 to 1814 and 1825 to 1855. In 1856, 194 descendants of the *Bounty* mutineers accepted an invitation to leave Pitcairn and settle on Norfolk Island. Norfolk Island is an Australian external territory.

In 1979 Norfolk Island gained a substantial degree of self-government. Wide powers are exercised by a nine-member Legislative Assembly. The Administrator is responsible to the Australian Minister for Regional Services, Territories and Local Government.

Administrator, A. J. Messner

AUSTRIA
Republik Österreich

AREA – 32,378 sq. miles (83,859 sq. km). Neighbours: the Czech Republic and Slovakia (north), Italy and Slovenia (south), Hungary (east), Germany (north-west), Switzerland and Liechtenstein (west)

POPULATION – 8,106,000 (1995 estimate); 7,813,000 (1991 census). The language is German, but the rights of the Slovene- and Croat-speaking minorities in Carinthia, Styria and Burgenland are protected. The predominant religion is Roman Catholicism

CAPITAL – Vienna, on the Danube (population, 1,806,737, 1995 estimate)

MAJOR CITIES – Graz (237,810); Innsbruck (118,112); Klagenfurt (89,415); Linz (203,044); Salzburg (143,978)

CURRENCY – Schilling of 100 Groschen

NATIONAL ANTHEM – Land der Berge, Land am Strome (Land of mountains, land on the river)

NATIONAL DAY – 26 October
NATIONAL FLAG – Three equal horizontal stripes of red, white, red
LIFE EXPECTANCY (years) – male 73.34; female 79.73
POPULATION GROWTH RATE – 0.8 per cent (1996)
POPULATION DENSITY – 97 per sq. km (1996)
URBAN POPULATION – 64.6 per cent (1991)

HISTORY AND POLITICS

The Republic of Austria was established in 1918 on the break-up of the Austro-Hungarian Empire. In March 1938 Austria was incorporated into Nazi Germany under the name *Ostmark*. After the liberation of Vienna in 1945, the Republic of Austria was reconstituted within the 1937 frontiers and a freely-elected government took office in December 1945. The country was divided into four zones occupied respectively by the UK, USA, USSR and France, while Vienna was jointly occupied by the four Powers. In 1955 the Austrian State Treaty was signed by the foreign ministers of the four Powers and of Austria. This treaty recognized the re-establishment of Austria as a sovereign, independent and democratic state, having the same frontiers as on 1 January 1938. Austria acceded to the European Union on 1 January 1995.

After the general election of 17 December 1995 the Social Democrats and the People's Party formed a coalition government.

POLITICAL SYSTEM

There is a bicameral national assembly; the lower house (*Nationalrat*) has 183 members and the upper house (*Bundesrat*) has 64 members. There is a 4 per cent qualification for parliamentary representation.

FEDERAL STRUCTURE

There are nine provinces:

Provinces	Area (sq. km)	Population	Capital
Burgenland	3,965	274,334	Eisenstadt
Carinthia	9,533	560,994	Klagenfurt
Lower Austria	19,174	1,518,254	St Pölten
Salzburg	7,154	506,850	Salzburg
Styria	16,388	1,206,317	Graz
Tirol	12,648	658,312	Innsbruck
Upper Austria	11,980	1,385,769	Linz
Vienna	415	1,592,596	Vienna
Vorarlberg	2,601	343,109	Bregenz

HEAD OF STATE
President of the Republic of Austria, Dr Thomas Klestil, *took office* 8 July 1992, *re-elected* 19 April 1998

CABINET *as at May 1999*

Chancellor, Viktor Klima (SPÖ)
Vice Chancellor, Foreign Affairs, Wolfgang Schüssel (ÖVP)
Agriculture and Forestry, Wilhelm Molterer (ÖVP)
Defence, Werner Fasslabend (ÖVP)
Economic Affairs, Johann Farnleitner (ÖVP)
Education and Cultural Affairs, Elisabeth Gehrer (ÖVP)
Environment, Youth and Family, Martin Bartenstein (ÖVP)
Finance, Rudolf Edlinger (SPÖ)
Interior, Karl Schlögl (SPÖ)
Justice, Nikolaus Michalek (Ind.)
Labour, Health and Social Affairs, Eleonore Hostasch (SPÖ)
Science and Transport, Caspar Einem (SPÖ)
Women's Affairs and Consumer Protection, Barbara Prammer (SPÖ)

SPÖ Social Democratic Party; ÖVP People's Party; Ind. Independent

AUSTRIAN EMBASSY
18 Belgrave Mews West, London SWIX 8HU
Tel 0171–235 3731
Ambassador Extraordinary and Plenipotentiary, Eva Nowotny, apptd 1997
Minister, Brigitte Öppinger-Walchshofer
Defence Attaché, Brig. H. Rüdiger Sulzgruber
Consul-General, Hella Naumann
Commercial Counsellor and Trade Commissioner, Dr Rudolf Engel

BRITISH EMBASSY
Jaurèsgasse 12, 1030 Vienna
Tel: Vienna 716130
Ambassador Extraordinary and Plenipotentiary, HE Sir Anthony Figgis, KCVO, CMG, apptd 1996
Deputy Head of Mission, Counsellor and Consul-General, I. Cliffe, OBE
Defence Attaché, Lt.-Col. A. Manton
First Secretary (Economic), W. Brandon

BRITISH CONSULAR OFFICES – There is a consular office at Vienna, and Honorary Consulates at Bregenz, Graz, Innsbruck and Salzburg.

BRITISH COUNCIL REPRESENTATIVE, M. Evans, Schenkenstrasse 4, A–1010 Vienna

DEFENCE

The Army has 169 main battle tanks, 533 armoured personnel carriers and 286 artillery pieces. The Air Force has 53 combat aircraft.

Women were permitted to join the army for the first time in February 1998.
MILITARY EXPENDITURE – 0.8 per cent of GDP (1997)
MILITARY PERSONNEL – 49,750: Army 45,500, Air Force 4,250
CONSCRIPTION DURATION – Seven to eight months plus refresher training

ECONOMY

Austria produces wheat, rye, barley, oats, maize, potatoes, sugar beet and turnips. Timber forms a valuable source of Austria's indigenous wealth, about 47 per cent of the total land area consisting of forest areas. Foreign exchange receipts from tourism were a major contribution to the balance of payments.

In 1997 Austria had a current account deficit of US$3,865 million and a trade deficit of US$4,043 million.
GNP – US$225,373 million (1997); US$27,920 per capita (1997)
GDP – US$233,352 million (1995); US$29,006 per capita (1995)
ANNUAL AVERAGE GROWTH OF GDP – 1.8 per cent (1995)
INFLATION RATE – 1.3 per cent (1997)
UNEMPLOYMENT – 4.5 per cent (1995)

TRADE

Main exports are processed goods (iron and steel, other metal goods, textiles, paper and cardboard products), machinery and transport equipment, other finished goods (including clothing), raw materials, chemical products and foodstuffs. Main imports are machinery and transport equipment, processed goods, chemical products, foodstuffs, fuel and energy. Austria's main trading partners are Germany, Italy, France and Switzerland.

In 1997, Austria had a trade deficit of US$4,040 million and a current account deficit of US$3,860 million. In 1997, imports totalled US$67,331 million and exports US$57,818 million.

Trade with UK	1997	1998
Imports from UK	£1,329,000,000	£1,124,600,000
Exports to UK	1,082,600,000	1,364,900,000

COMMUNICATIONS

Internal communications are partly restricted because of the mountainous nature of the country, although there is now a network of 1,567 km of *Autobahn* between major cities which also links up with the German and Italian networks. The railways are state-owned and in 1993 had 5,605 km of track, 58.8 per cent of which is electrified. Of the 425 km of waterways, 350 km are navigable and there is considerable trade through the Danube ports by both local and foreign shipping. There are six commercial airports catering for 5,527,600 passengers in 1995.

There are four national radio and two national television channels, together with three national and twelve regional newspapers.

EDUCATION

Education is free and compulsory between the ages of six and 15 and there are good facilities for secondary, technical and professional education. There are 12 state-maintained universities and six colleges of art.

ENROLMENT (percentage of age group) – primary 100 per cent (1995); secondary 88 per cent (1995); tertiary 46.6 per cent (1995)

AZERBAIJAN
Azarbaijchan Respublikasy

AREA – 33,436 sq. miles (86,600 sq. km). Neighbours: Iran (south), Armenia (west), Georgia and Russia (north)

POPULATION – 7,625,000 (1998): 83 per cent Azeri, 6 per cent Russian and 6 per cent Armenian. There are also Kurds, Jews, Georgians and Turks. There are more Azeris in Iran than in Azerbaijan. The population is predominantly Shia Muslim although it was heavily secularized during the Soviet era. The language is Azeri

CAPITAL – ΨBaku (population, 1,149,000, 1990)

CURRENCY – Manat of 100 gopik

NATIONAL DAY – 28 May (Independence Day)

NATIONAL FLAG – Three horizontal stripes of blue, red and green with a white crescent and eight-pointed star in the centre

LIFE EXPECTANCY (years) – male 66.60; female 74.20

POPULATION GROWTH RATE – 0.9 per cent (1996)

POPULATION DENSITY – 87 per sq. km (1996)

URBAN POPULATION – 54.2 per cent (1989)

Azerbaijan occupies the eastern part of the Caucasus region of the former Soviet Union, on the shore of the Caspian Sea. The north-eastern part of the republic is taken up by the south-eastern end of the main Caucasus ridge, its south-western part by the smaller Caucasus hills, and its south-eastern corner by the spurs of the Talysh Ridge. Its central part is a depression irrigated by the River Kura and the lower reaches of its tributary the Araks. Azerbaijan has a continental climate.

Azerbaijan has 64 administrative districts and also includes the Nakhichevan Autonomous Republic, which is geographically separated from the rest of Azerbaijan by Armenia and borders on Iran and Turkey, and the Nagorno-Karabakh Autonomous Province.

HISTORY AND POLITICS

The territory that is now Azerbaijan was successively part of the Assyrian, Persian, Median and Greek empires. With the influx of Huns and Khazars in the first century BC, the Turkic Azerbaijani people evolved and formed an independent state. This was invaded by the Arab Caliphates in the seventh century AD and under their 300-year rule Islam was introduced and became the dominant religion. In the 16th century Azerbaijan was again invaded by Persia and became a Persian province. The country was divided during the Russo-Persian wars of the early 19th century, the northern portion (the present-day Azerbaijan) becoming part of the Russian Empire and the southern portion remaining Persian and subsequently Iranian.

In 1918 the Azerbaijan Democratic Republic was established. It was overthrown by Communists in 1918 and Azerbaijan acceded to the USSR in 1922.

In January 1990, the Azerbaijani Popular Front took power from the local Communist Party and declared independence from the Soviet Union. Soviet troops overthrew the Popular Front and restored the Communist regime under President Ayaz Mutalibov. This government declared Azerbaijan's independence in August 1991. Mutalibov won the presidential election held in September 1991, but widespread civil unrest forced him to resign. At the presidential election in June 1992 the Popular Front leader Abulfaz Elchibey was elected.

Popular discontent at military defeats caused Elchibey to flee Baku in June 1993 and the former Azerbaijani Communist Party First Secretary Heydar Aliyev took over the presidency. The new regime was confirmed in office in a referendum in August 1993 and Aliyev won the presidential election in October 1993.

In November 1995, elections were held to the *Milli Majlis* (parliament), which had been increased to 125 seats: 100 directly elected and 25 allocated by proportional representation. The New Azerbaijan party, founded by Aliyev, won 70 per cent of the vote and a majority of seats. Presidential elections were held on 11 October 1998. The incumbent President Aliyev won 76.1 per cent of the vote, but the elections were criticized by the OSCE and other international monitoring groups.

SECESSION

In 1998 fighting broke out in the predominantly Armenian-populated region of Nagorny-Karabakh between Soviet Azerbaijani forces and ethnic Armenians demanding unification with Armenia. In late 1993 Nagorno-Karabakh forces captured all of the region, together with all Azeri territory separating the region from Armenia (20 per cent of Azeri territory). Azeri forces pushed back the Nagorno-Karabakh forces in early 1994 before a cease-fire agreement was signed in May 1994. Between 500,000 and one million Azeris have been displaced by the fighting, which briefly flared up again along the Azeri-Armenian border in April and May 1997. Peace talks, held under the auspices of the OSCE, have yet to yield any significant results, although both sides reaffirmed their commitment to finding a peaceful solution at a meeting in October 1997, in which both sides rejected the idea of full independence for Nagorny-Karabakh as 'unrealistic'.

POLITICAL SYSTEM

A new constitution was approved by a referendum in November 1995, which created a presidential republic with executive power to be exercised by the president and with legislative power vested in the *Milli Majlis*.

HEAD OF STATE
President, Heydar Aliyev, *assumed office* 18 June 1993, *elected*
3 October 1993, re-elected 11 October 1998

GOVERNMENT *as at June 1999*

Prime Minister, Artur Rasizade
Deputy Prime Ministers, Elchin Efendiyev, Abid Sharifov,
Ali Gasanov
Agriculture, Irshad Aliyev
Communications, Nadir Akhmedov
Defence, Lt.-Gen. Safar Abiyev
Economy, Namik Nasrullayev
Education, Misir Mardanov
Finance, Fikret Yusifov
Foreign Affairs, Tofik Zulfugarov
Interior, Ramil Usubov
Justice, Sudaba Hasanova
Media and Information, Siruz Tebrizli
National Security, Namig Abbasov
Trade, Farkhad Aliyev
Youth and Sports, Abdulfaz Karayev

AZERBAIJANI EMBASSY
4 Kensington Court, London W8 5DL
Tel 0171-938 3412
Ambassador Extraordinary and Plenipotentiary, HE Mahmud
Mamed-Kuliyev, apptd 1994

BRITISH EMBASSY
2 Izmir Street, Baku 370065
Tel: Baku 924813
Ambassador Extraordinary and Plenipotentiary, HE David R.
Thomas, apptd 1997

DEFENCE

The Army has 270 main battle tanks, 287 armoured infantry
fighting vehicles, 74 armoured personnel carriers and 301
artillery pieces. The Navy is based at Baku, with a share of
the former Soviet Caspian Fleet Flotilla, comprising two
frigates and 18 patrol and coastal vessels. The Air Force
has 37 combat aircraft and 15 attack helicopters.
MILITARY EXPENDITURE – 4.0 per cent of GDP (1997)
MILITARY PERSONNEL – 83,150: Army 55,600, Navy
2,200, Air Force 10,350, Paramilitaries 15,000
CONSCRIPTION DURATION – 17 months

ECONOMY

Azerbaijan was heavily industrialized as part of the Russian
Empire. Industry is dominated by oil and natural gas
extraction and related industries centred on Baku and
Sumgait and the large oil deposits in the Caspian Sea,
estimated at more than 6,000 million barrels. Five contracts
to explore and exploit oilfields in the Caspian Sea have
been signed since 1994.
The republic is also rich in mineral resources, with iron,
copper, lead and salt, and is important as a cotton-growing
area and a silkworm-breeding area.
The Azeri economy was devastated by the war although
it is now showing signs of recovery. There was a 45 per
cent growth in investment activity in 1998.
GNP – US$3,886 million (1997); US$510 per capita (1997)
GDP – US$2,417 million (1995); US$321 per capita (1995)
TOTAL EXTERNAL DEBT – US$504 million (1997)

Trade with UK	1997	1998
Imports from UK	£55,728,000	£56,191,000
Exports to UK	10,088,000	8,207,000

CULTURE AND EDUCATION

Azerbaijan was the birthplace of the prophet Zoroaster,
who founded one of the first monotheistic religions in the
world. The country has witnessed a succession of three
religions: Zoroastrianism, Christianity and Islam.
Azeri is one of the Turkic languages. Previously written
in the Russian script, Azeri in the Latin script was adopted
as the official language in December 1992. In the 18th and
19th centuries Azerbaijani literature produced the poets
and dramatists Vagif, Vazekhi, Zakir, Akhundov and
Vezirov.
ILLITERACY RATE – 0.4 per cent
ENROLMENT (percentage of age group) – tertiary 17.5
per cent (1996)

THE BAHAMAS
The Commonwealth of The Bahamas

AREA – 5,358 sq. miles (13,878 sq. km)
POPULATION – 284,000 (1996 estimate). The language is
English
CAPITAL – ΨNassau (population, 172,196, 1996 estimate)
CURRENCY – Bahamian dollar (B$) of 100 cents
NATIONAL ANTHEM – March on, Bahamaland
NATIONAL DAY – 10 July (Independence Day)
NATIONAL FLAG – Horizontal stripes of aquamarine,
gold and aquamarine, with a black equilateral triangle
on the hoist
LIFE EXPECTANCY (years) – male 68.32; female 75.28
POPULATION GROWTH RATE – 1.8 per cent (1996)
POPULATION DENSITY – 20 per sq. km (1996)
URBAN POPULATION – 83.5 per cent (1990)

The Bahamas extend from the coast of Florida on the
north-west almost to Haiti on the south-east. The group
consists of 700 islands, of which 30 are inhabited, and 2,400
cays. The principal islands include: Abaco, Acklins, Andros,
Berry Islands, Bimini, Cat Island, Crooked Island, Eleuthera, Exuma, Grand Bahama, Harbour Island, Inagua, Long
Island, Mayaguana, New Providence (on which is located
the capital, Nassau), Ragged Island, Rum Cay, San Salvador
and Spanish Wells. San Salvador was the first landfall in
the New World of Christopher Columbus on 12 October
1492.

HISTORY AND POLITICS

The Bahamas were settled by the British and became a
Crown colony in 1717. Taken over in 1782 by the Spanish,
the Treaty of Versailles in 1783 restored them to the
British. The Bahamas gained independence on 10 July
1973.
A general election held in March 1997 was won by the
Free National Movement which defeated the Progressive
Liberal Party. The Free National Movement hold 35 seats
in the House of Assembly and the Progressive Liberal
Party six seats.

POLITICAL SYSTEM

The head of state is Queen Elizabeth II who is represented
in the islands by a Governor-General. There is an appointed
Senate of 16 members and an elected House of Assembly
of 40 members.

Governor-General, HE Sir Orville Turnquest, GCMG, QC,
apptd 1994

CABINET *as at May 1999*

Prime Minister, Hubert Ingraham
Deputy Prime Minister, National Security, Frank Watson
Agriculture and Fisheries, Earl Deveaux
Attorney-General, Justice, Tennyson Wells
Consumer Welfare and Aviation, Pierre Dupuch
Education, Dame Ivy Dumont, DCMG

Finance and Planning, William Allen
Foreign Affairs, Janet Bostwick
Health and Environment, Ronald Knowles
Labour, Immigration and Training, Theresa Moxey-
Ingraham
Public Works, Orville Turnquest
Social Development and Housing, Algernon Allen
Tourism, Cornelius Smith
Transport, James Knowles

President of the Court of Appeal, Sir Joaquim Gonsalves-
Sabola, KCMG
Chief Justice, Dame Joan Sawyer

BAHAMAS HIGH COMMISSION
Bahamas House, 10 Chesterfield Street, London WIX 8AH
Tel 0171-408 4488
High Commissioner, HE Arthur A. Foulkes, apptd 1992

BRITISH HIGH COMMISSION
PO Box N-7516, Nassau
Tel: Nassau 325 7471
High Commissioner, HE Peter Young, OBE, apptd 1996

DEFENCE

The Navy has seven patrol and coastal vessels, six harbour
patrol units and four light aircraft.
MILITARY EXPENDITURE – 0.6 per cent of GDP (1997)
MILITARY PERSONNEL – 860: Navy

ECONOMY

Tourism employs about half of the labour force and
provides about half of government revenue and about half
the country's foreign exchange earnings. International
banking and trust business is also important. The absence
of direct taxation coupled with internal stability have
enabled the country to become one of the world's leading
offshore financial centres. In February 1998, Finance
Minister William Allen announced that regulations were
in place for the establishment of a stock exchange, which
was scheduled to start operating by the end of 1998.

Agricultural production is mainly of fresh vegetables,
fruit, meat and eggs for the domestic market, and crawfish,
mostly for export. Reserves of aragonite, limestone and salt
are being commercially exploited. Freeport is the country's
leading industrial centre, with a pharmaceutical and
chemicals plant, an oil trans-shipment and storage terminal,
and port and bunkering facilities. There are also a brewery
and a rum distillery on New Providence.
GNP – US$3,297 million (1995); US$11,940 per capita
(1995)
GDP – US$3,500 million (1995); US$12,545 per capita
(1995)
ANNUAL AVERAGE GROWTH OF GDP – 1.0 per cent
(1995)
INFLATION RATE – 0.5 per cent (1997)
UNEMPLOYMENT – 13.3 per cent (1994)

TRADE

The imports are chiefly foodstuffs, manufactured articles,
building materials, vehicles and machinery, chemicals and
petroleum. The chief exports are rum, petroleum, hor-
mones, salt, crawfish and aragonite.

In 1997 the Bahamas had a trade deficit of US$1,038
million and a current account deficit of US$462 million. In
1996, imports totalled US$1,262 million and exports
US$173 million.

Trade with UK	1997	1998
Imports from UK	£19,110,000	£42,461,000
Exports to UK	56,850,000	62,705,000

COMMUNICATIONS

The main ports are Nassau (New Providence), Freeport
(Grand Bahama) and Matthew Town (Inagua). International air services are operated from Abaco, Bimini,
Eleuthera, Exuma, Grand Bahama and New Providence.
About 50 smaller airports and landing strips facilitate
services between the islands, the services being mainly
provided by Bahamasair, the national carrier. There are
roads on the larger islands, and roads are under construction
on the smaller islands. There are no railways.

EDUCATION

Education is compulsory between the ages of five and 16.
More than 60,000 students are enrolled in Ministry of
Education and independent schools in New Providence
and the Family Islands.
ILLITERACY RATE – 1.8 per cent
ENROLMENT (percentage of age group) – primary 95 per
cent (1993); secondary 87 per cent (1993); tertiary 17.7
per cent (1985)

BAHRAIN
Dawlet al-Bahrein

AREA – 268 sq. miles (694 sq. km)
POPULATION – 599,000 (1994 UN estimate); about 70 per
cent are Bahraini; about 40 per cent of the Bahrainis are
Sunni Muslims, the remaining 60 per cent being Shias;
the ruling family and many of the most prominent
merchants are Sunnis. The official language is Arabic;
English is often used for business, and Farsi, Hindi and
Urdu are also spoken
CAPITAL – ΨManama (population, 140,401, 1991 census)
CURRENCY – Bahraini dinar (BD) of 1,000 fils
NATIONAL DAY – 16 December
NATIONAL FLAG – Red, with vertical serrated white bar
next to staff
LIFE EXPECTANCY (years) – male 66.83; female 69.43
POPULATION GROWTH RATE – 2.9 per cent (1996)
POPULATION DENSITY – 863 per sq. km (1996)
URBAN POPULATION – 88.4 per cent (1991)
ILLITERACY RATE – 14.8 per cent
ENROLMENT (percentage of age group) – primary 98 per
cent (1996); secondary 83 per cent (1996); tertiary 20.2
per cent (1993)

Bahrain consists of a group of low-lying islands situated
about half-way down the Gulf, some 20 miles off the east
coast of Saudi Arabia. The largest of these, Bahrain Island,
is about 30 miles long and 10 miles wide at its broadest,
with the capital, Manama, situated on the north shore. The
second largest, Muharraq, with the town and Bahrain
International Airport, is connected to Manama by a
causeway 1½ miles long.

INSURGENCIES

Since 1994 Shi'ite protestors demanding the re-establishment of the National Assembly have regularly clashed with
security forces and Shi'ite leaders have been detained.
Opponents of the government have engaged in a sustained
bombing campaign.

POLITICAL SYSTEM

Bahrain is a constitutional monarchy and has been fully
independent since 1971, when British protectorate status
was ended. The 1973 constitution provides for a National
Assembly but this was dissolved in 1975. A 40-member
Consultative Council was appointed in September 1996; it
is an advisory body with no legislative powers.

HEAD OF STATE
HH The Amir of Bahrain, , C.-in-C., Bahrain Defence Force,
Shaikh Hamad bin Isa al-Khalifa, KCMG

CABINET *as at May 1999*
Prime Minister, HH Shaikh Khalifa bin Salman Al-Khalifa
Agriculture and Public Works, HE Ali Ibrahim Al-Mahroos
Amiri Court Affairs, HH Shaikh Ali bin Isa bin Sulman Al-
   Khalifa
Cabinet Affairs and Information, HE Mohammed Ibrahim
   Al-Mutawa
Commerce, HE Ali Saleh Abdulla Al-Saleh
Consultative Council President, Ibrahim Mohammed
   Humaidan
Defence, HE Maj.-Gen. Shaikh Khalifa bin Ahmed Al-
   Khalifa
Education, HE Brig.-Gen. Abdul Aziz Mohammed Al-
   Fadhil
Finance and National Economy, HE Abdulla Hasan Saif
Foreign Affairs, HE Shaikh Mohammed bin Mubarak Al-
   Khalifa
Health, HE Faisal Radhi Al-Mosawi
Housing, Municipalities, Shaikh Khalid bin Abdulla Al-
   Khalifa
Interior, HE Shaikh Mohammed bin Khalifa Al-Khalifa
Justice and Islamic Affairs, HE Shaikh Abdulla bin Khalid
   Al-Khalifa
Labour and Social Affairs, HE Abdul-Nabi Al-Shu'la
Minister of States, HE Jawad Salim Al-Urrayedh, HE
   Majed Jawad Al-Jeshi
Oil and Industry, HE Shaikh Isa bin Ali Al-Khalifa
Power and Water, HH Shaikh Duaj bin Khalifa bin
   Mohammed Al-Khalifa
Transport, Civil Aviation, HH Shaikh Ali bin Khalifa Al-
   Khalifa

EMBASSY OF THE STATE OF BAHRAIN
98 Gloucester Road, London SW7 4AU
Tel 0171-370 5132
Ambassador Extraordinary and Plenipotentiary, HE Shaikh
   Abdul-Aziz bin Mubarak Al-Khalifa, apptd 1996

BRITISH EMBASSY
21 Government Avenue, Manama 306, PO Box 114
Tel: Manama 534404
Ambassador Extraordinary and Plenipotentiary, P. Ford

BRITISH COUNCIL REPRESENTATIVE, J. Shorter, AMA
   Centre, PO Box 452, Manama 356

DEFENCE

The Army has 106 main battle tanks, 340 armoured
personnel carriers and 49 artillery pieces. The Navy, based
at Mina Sulman, has one frigate and 12 patrol and coastal
vessels. The Air Force has 24 combat aircraft and 24 armed
helicopters.
MILITARY EXPENDITURE – 6.5 per cent of GDP (1997)
MILITARY PERSONNEL – 20,850: Army 8,500, Navy
   1,000, Air Force 1,500, Paramilitaries 9,850

ECONOMY

The largest sources of revenue are oil production and
refining. The Bahrain field, discovered in 1932, is wholly
owned by the Bahrain National Oil Co. The Sitra refinery
derives about 70 per cent of its crude oil by submarine
pipeline from Saudi Arabia. Bahrain also has a half share
with Saudi Arabia in the profits of the offshore Abu Sa'afa
field. A reservoir of unassociated gas has recently been
developed on Bahrain Island.
   There is some heavy industry on the islands and a
number of small to medium-sized industrial units.

The state has developed as a financial centre. Apart from
several commercial banks, many international banks have
been licensed as offshore banking units; there are also
money brokers and merchant banks.
GNP – US$4,525 million (1995); US$7,840 per capita
   (1995)
GDP – US$5,054 million (1995); US$9,073 per capita
   (1995)
ANNUAL AVERAGE GROWTH OF GDP – 2.2 per cent
   (1995)
INFLATION RATE – –0.2 per cent (1996)

TRADE

In 1997 imports totalled US$3,868 million and exports
US$4,321 million. In 1995 the government had a trade
surplus of US$769 million and a current account surplus
of US$557 million.

Trade with UK	1997	1998
Imports from UK	£157,936,000	£144,168,000
Exports to UK	33,397,000	67,466,000

COMMUNICATIONS

Bahrain International airport is one of the main air traffic
centres of the Gulf; it is the headquarters of Gulf Air, and
a stopping point on routes between Europe and Australia
and the Far East for other airlines. A causeway links
Bahrain to Saudi Arabia.
   A worldwide telephone and telex service, by satellite
and cable, is operated by Bahrain Telecommunications
Company.

BANGLADESH
Ghana Praja Tantri Bangladesh

AREA – 55,598 sq. miles (143,998 sq. km). Neighbours:
   India (west, north and east), Myanmar (east)
POPULATION – 120,073,000 (1994 UN estimate). The
   state language is Bengali. Use of Bengali is compulsory
   in all government departments. English is understood
   and is used widely as an unofficial second language.
   The faith of 88 per cent of the population is Islam and
   10.5 per cent Hinduism. Islam has been declared the
   state religion
CAPITAL – Dhaka (population, 3,397,187, 1991 census)
CURRENCY – Taka (Tk) of 100 poisha
NATIONAL ANTHEM – Amar Sonar Bangla
NATIONAL DAY – 26 March (Independence Day)
NATIONAL FLAG – Red circle on a bottle-green ground
LIFE EXPECTANCY (years) – male 56.91; female 55.97
POPULATION GROWTH RATE – 1.5 per cent (1996)
POPULATION DENSITY – 834 per sq. km (1996)
URBAN POPULATION – 13.8 per cent (1986)

The country is crossed by a network of rivers, including
the eastern arms of the Ganges, the Jamuna (Brahmaputra)
and the Meghna, flowing into the Bay of Bengal. The
climate is tropical and monsoon; hot and extremely humid
during the summer, and mild and dry during the short
winter.

HISTORY AND POLITICS

Prior to becoming East Pakistan, Bangladesh had been the
province of East Bengal and the Sylhet district of Assam of
British India. The territory acceded to Pakistan in August
1947, which became a republic on 23 March 1956.
Bangladesh achieved its independence from Pakistan on 16

December 1971, following the conclusion of the Indo-Pakistan war. Pakistan and Bangladesh accorded one another mutual recognition in 1974.

In 1975 a one-party presidential system was introduced, with Prime Minister Sheikh Mujibur Rahman assuming the presidency under martial law until his assassination in 1975. A presidential election in 1978 was won by Maj.-Gen. Zia Rahman, who introduced a multiparty presidential system of government. Zia was assassinated in 1981. His replacement, Justice Abdus Sattar, was overthrown in 1982 in a coup led by the then Chief of Army Staff, Gen. Ershad. Following parliamentary elections in 1986, a civilian Cabinet was appointed and Gen. Ershad was elected president. Popular unrest forced Gen. Ershad's resignation in December 1990; the Bangladesh Nationalist Party (BNP) won the subsequent parliamentary elections and its leader, Begum Khaleda Zia, was sworn in as prime minister. In August 1991 a constitutional amendment returned Bangladesh to parliamentary rule.

In December 1994, the opposition parties resigned from parliament and organized a series of mass rallies and strikes demanding fresh elections. Public disorder persisted despite a general election in February 1996 which was won by the BNP, although turnout was a mere five per cent. In March 1996, Prime Minister Zia agreed to new elections; these elections in June 1996 produced a majority for the Awami League under Prime Minister Sheikh Hasina Wajed. In November 1997, the BNP walked out of parliament, accusing the government of repression. They returned in March 1998 after signing a memorandum of understanding with the government. A series of nationwide general strikes, organized by the seven-party opposition alliance led by the BNP, began in October 1998 in an effort to oust the government.

POLITICAL SYSTEM

There is a unicameral parliament (*Jatiya Sangshad*) of 330 members which can amend the constitution by a two-thirds majority. The country is divided into six administrative divisions, sub-divided into 64 districts.

HEAD OF STATE
President, Shahabuddin Ahmed, *sworn in* 9 October 1996

CABINET *as at May 1999*

Prime Minister, Armed Forces Division, Cabinet Division, Special Affairs, Defence, Establishment, Energy, Shaikh Hasina Wajed
Agriculture and Food, Matia Choudhry
Civil Aviation and Public Works, Mosharraf Hossain
Commerce and Industry, Tofael Ahmed
Education, Science and Technology, A. S. H. K. Sadek
Environment and Forests, Syeda Sajeda Chowdhury
Finance, S. A. M. S. Kibria
Foreign Affairs, Abdus Samad Azad
Health and Family Welfare, Salahuddin Yousuf
Home Affairs, Post and Telecommunications, Mohammad Nasim
Labour and Manpower, Abdul Mannan
Law, Justice and Parliamentary Affairs, Abdul Matin Khasru
Local Government, Rural Development and Co-operatives, Mohammad Zillur Rahman
Shipping, A. S. M. Abdur Rab
Water Resources, Irrigation and Flood Control, Abdur Razzak
Without Portfolio, Kalpa Ranjan Chakma; Maj. (retd) Rafiqul Islam
There are 17 Ministers of State.

BANGLADESH HIGH COMMISSION
28 Queen's Gate, London SW7 5JA
Tel 0171-584 0081

High Commissioner, HE Mahmood Ali, apptd 1997
Defence Adviser, Brig. M. A. Yusuf Farazi

BRITISH HIGH COMMISSION
United Nations Road, Baridhara, Dhaka
PO Box 6079, Dhaka-12
Tel: Dhaka 882705
High Commissioner, HE David Walker, CMG, CVO, apptd 1996
Deputy High Commissioner, S. E. Turner
Defence Adviser, Col. J. M. Philips

BRITISH COUNCIL REPRESENTATIVE, T. Cowin, 5 Fuller Road (PO Box 161), Dhaka 1000

DEFENCE

The army has 80 main battle tanks, 20 armoured personnel carriers and 140 artillery pieces. The Navy, based at Chittagong, has four frigates and 41 patrol and coastal vessels. The Air Force has 49 combat aircraft.
MILITARY EXPENDITURE – 1.9 per cent of GDP (1997)
MILITARY PERSONNEL – 170,700: Army 101,000, Navy 10,500, Air Force 9,500, Paramilitaries 49,700

ECONOMY

Between 1991–5, the government implemented an IMF economic reform plan which delivered stable prices and inflation, and reduced the budget deficit. In November 1997, the Paris Club promised US$1.9 billion of aid.

Bangladesh is self-sufficient in food production. Agricultural products include rice, wheat, tobacco, tea, oil seeds, pulses and sugar cane. The chief industries are jute, cotton, tea, leather, pharmaceuticals, fertilizer, sugar, prawn fishing and natural gas. Garment manufacturing is the main export. Remittances sent home by Bangladeshis abroad are of considerable significance to the economy.

Heavy flooding during the summer of 1998 left 23 million people homeless and killed 1,500; two-thirds of the country was under water and 800,000 hectares of farmland was destroyed.
GNP – US$44,090 million (1997); US$360 per capita (1997)
GDP – US$33,127 million (1995); US$280 per capita (1995)
ANNUAL AVERAGE GROWTH OF GDP – 5.3 per cent (1996)
INFLATION RATE – 5.7 per cent (1997)
TOTAL EXTERNAL DEBT – US$15,125 million (1997)

TRADE

In 1996 Bangladesh had a current account deficit of US$962 million and a trade deficit of US$2,251 million. In 1996 imports totalled US$6,616 million and exports US$3,297 million.

Trade with UK	1997	1998
Imports from UK	£81,517,000	£87,031,000
Exports to UK	246,401,000	252,857,000

COMMUNICATIONS

Principal seaports are Chittagong and Mongla. The Bangladesh Shipping Corporation was set up by the Government to operate the Bangladesh merchant fleet. The principal airports are Dhaka (Zia International) and Chittagong. The international airline, Bangladesh Biman, serves Europe, the Middle East, South and South-East Asia, and an internal network.

EDUCATION

Primary education is free and planned to be universal by 2000. There are 11 universities.

ILLITERACY RATE – 61.9 per cent
ENROLMENT (percentage of age group) – primary 62 per cent (1990); secondary 20 per cent (1990); tertiary 4.4 per cent (1990)

BARBADOS

AREA – 166 sq. miles (430 sq. km); nearly 21 miles long by 14 miles broad
POPULATION – 265,000 (1994 UN estimate). The official language is English; Bajan is also spoken
CAPITAL – ΨBridgetown in the parish of St Michael (population, 108,000, 1990)
MAJOR TOWNS – Holetown in St James, Oistins in Christ Church and Speightstown in St Peter
CURRENCY – Barbados dollar (BD$) of 100 cents
NATIONAL ANTHEM – In Plenty and in Time of Need
NATIONAL DAY– 30 November (Independence Day)
NATIONAL FLAG – Three vertical stripes, dark blue, gold and dark blue, with a trident head on gold stripe
LIFE EXPECTANCY (years) – male 67.15; female 72.46
POPULATION GROWTH RATE – 0.5 per cent (1996)
POPULATION DENSITY – 615 per sq. km (1996)
MILITARY EXPENDITURE – 0.6 per cent of GDP (1997)
MILITARY PERSONNEL – 610: Army 500, Navy 110

Barbados is the most easterly of the Caribbean islands. The land rises in a series of terraced tablelands to the highest point, Mt Hillaby (1,116 ft). The annual average temperature is 26.6°C (79.8°F) with rainfall varying from a yearly average of 75 inches in the high central district to 50 inches in the low-lying coastal areas.

HISTORY AND POLITICS

The first inhabitants of Barbados were Arawak Indians but the island was uninhabited when first settled by the British in 1627. It was a Crown Colony from 1652 until it became an independent state within the Commonwealth on 30 November 1966.
    The last general election took place on 20 January 1999 and seats in the House of Assembly were distributed as follows: Barbados Labour Party 26, Democratic Labour Party 2.

POLITICAL SYSTEM

The head of state is the British sovereign. The legislature consists of the Governor-General, a Senate and a House of Assembly. The Senate comprises 21 Senators appointed by the Governor-General, of whom 12 are appointed on the advice of the prime minister, two on the advice of the Leader of the Opposition and seven by the Governor-General at his/her discretion to represent religious, economic or social interests. The House of Assembly comprises 28 members elected every five years by adult suffrage.
    There are 11 administrative areas (parishes): St Michael, Christ Church, St Andrew, St George, St James, St John, St Joseph, St Lucy, St Peter, St Philip and St Thomas.

Governor-General, HE Sir Clifford Husbands, GCMG, KA, apptd 1996

CABINET *as at May 1999*

Prime Minister, Defence and Security, Finance and Economic Affairs, Owen Arthur
Deputy Prime Minister, Foreign Affairs, Foreign Trade, Billie Miller
Agriculture and Rural Development, Anthony Wood

Attorney-General and Home Affairs, David Simmons, QC
Consumer Affairs and Business Development, Ronald Toppin
Education, Youth and Culture, Mia Mottley
Environment, Energy and Natural Resources, Rawle Eastmond
Health , Elizabeth Thompson
Housing and Lands, Gline Clarke
Industry and International Business, Reginald Farley
Labour, Sports and Public Sector Reform, Rudolph Greenidge
Minister of State, Prime Minister's Office, Glyne Murray
Public Works and Transport, Philip Goddard
Social Transformation, Hamilton Lashley
Tourism and International Transport, George Payne

BARBADOS HIGH COMMISSION
1 Great Russell Street, London WC1B 3JY
Tel 0171-631 4975
High Commissioner, HE Peter Simmons, apptd 1995
Deputy High Commissioner, Herbert Yearwood
First Secretary (Commercial), Kenneth Campbell

BRITISH HIGH COMMISSION
Lower Collymore Rock, PO Box 676, Bridgetown C
Tel: Bridgetown 430 7800
High Commissioner, HE Gordon Baker, apptd 1998
Deputy High Commissioner, M. J. E. Mayhew
Defence Adviser, Capt. P. Jackson
First Secretary, P. Curwen

ECONOMY

The economy is based on tourism, sugar and light manufacturing. In 1995, 442,107 tourists visited Barbados and 484,670 cruise ship passengers. Chief exports are sugar, chemicals, electronic components and clothing.
GNP – US$1,745 million (1995); US$6,560 per capita (1995)
GDP – US$1,872 million (1995); US$7,173 per capita (1995)
ANNUAL AVERAGE GROWTH OF GDP – 2.7 per cent (1995)
INFLATION RATE – 7.7 per cent (1997)
UNEMPLOYMENT – 19.7 per cent (1995)
TOTAL EXTERNAL DEBT – US$644 million (1997)

TRADE

In 1996 Barbados had a current account surplus of US$103 million and a trade deficit of US$456 million. In 1997 exports totalled US$281 million and imports US$987 million.

Trade with UK	1997	1998
Imports from UK	£37,182,000	£42,470,000
Exports to UK	30,897,000	28,295,000

COMMUNICATIONS

Barbados has some 965 miles of roads, of which about 917 miles are asphalted. The Grantley Adams International airport is situated at Seawell, 12 miles from Bridgetown. Bridgetown, the only port of entry, has a deep-water harbour with berths for eight ships; oil is pumped ashore at Spring Garden and at an Esso installation on the West Coast.

EDUCATION

Education is free in government schools. There are 105 primary schools, 22 government secondary schools and 15 approved government secondary schools.
ILLITERACY RATE – 2.6 per cent
ENROLMENT (percentage of age group) – primary 78 per cent (1991); secondary 75 per cent (1989); tertiary 29.4 per cent (1995)

BELARUS
Respublika Belarus

AREA – 80,155 sq. miles (207,600 sq. km). Neighbours: Latvia and Lithuania (north), Russia (east), Ukraine (south), Poland (west)

POPULATION – 10,179,000 (1999): 78 per cent Belarusian, 13 per cent Russian, 4 per cent Polish and 3 per cent Ukrainian, with smaller numbers of Jews and Lithuanians. Belarusian, a Slavonic language written in the Cyrillic script, and Russian have equal official language status. Most of the population are Belarusian Orthodox with a minority of Roman Catholics

CAPITAL – Minsk (population, 1,700,223, 1996 UN estimate); the administrative centre of the CIS

MAJOR CITIES – Brest (293,086); Gomel (511,600); Grodno (301,783); Mogilev (366,705); Vitebsk (356,417), 1996 estimates

CURRENCY – Rouble of 100 kopeks

NATIONAL ANTHEM – The former Soviet national anthem but with the words omitted

NATIONAL DAY – 3 July (Independence Day)

NATIONAL FLAG – Red with a green strip along the lower edge, and in the hoist a vertical red and white ornamental pattern

LIFE EXPECTANCY (years) – male 63.75; female 74.43

POPULATION GROWTH RATE – 0.0 per cent (1996)

POPULATION DENSITY – 49 per sq. km (1996)

URBAN POPULATION – 68.1 per cent (1993)

Belarus is situated in the western part of the European area of the former USSR. The main rivers are the upper reaches of the Dnieper, of the Niemen and of the Western Dvina. Much of the land is a plain, with many lakes, swamps and marshy areas. The climate is continental with mild, humid winters and relatively cool and rainy summers.

HISTORY AND POLITICS

In the ninth century AD the Kievan Rus state was a unified state encompassing all the Russian, Ukrainian and Belarusian populations. After being absorbed into Lithuania in the 13th and 14th centuries, the Belarusian nationality, language and culture flourished until it came under Polish rule in the mid-16th century. Two hundred years of Polish rule followed until Belarus was re-absorbed into the Russian Empire.

Western Belarus was ceded to Poland after the Soviet defeat in the Polish-Soviet war of 1919–20, and was not recovered until Soviet forces occupied the area under the 1939 Nazi-Soviet Pact. Belarus was devastated by the German invasion in the Second World War; 25 per cent of the population was killed and thousands deported.

Belarus issued a Declaration of State Sovereignty on 27 July 1990 and declared its independence from the Soviet Union after the failed coup in Moscow in August 1991. Stanislav Shuskevich became Belarusian leader at the head of a coalition of Communists and democrats. Until 1994, however, parliament and the government remained under the control of former Communists, who thwarted all attempts at economic and political reform. Shuskevich was forced to resign in January 1994 and was replaced by Gen. Mecheslav Grib who pursued closer political, economic and trade relations with Russia. The presidential election in July 1994 was won by Alexandr Lukashenka.

FOREIGN RELATIONS

An agreement was signed with Russia in April 1996 to form a Commonwealth of Sovereign Republics. In April 1997 a treaty of union was signed with Russia. It provided for the creation of a supreme council, chaired by the state presidents on a two-year rotating basis, which will co-ordinate foreign affairs and economic and defence co-operation. The presidents of Belarus and Russia signed documents in December 1998 which called for the adoption of a common budget and single currency and for joint defence and security policies.

POLITICAL SYSTEM

The president's term of office is five years, although a referendum in 1996 extended Lukashenka's term until 2002; the president has authority to appoint half the members of the constitutional court and the electoral commission. The legislature is the bicameral National Assembly, comprising a 110-member House of Representatives (lower chamber) and a 64-member Council of the Republic (upper chamber). Eight members of the upper chamber are appointed by the president, the rest are indirectly elected by members of the local soviets in each region.

The republic is divided into six regions (*oblasts*): Brest, Gomel, Grodno, Minsk, Mogilev and Vitebsk.

HEAD OF STATE
President, Aleksandr Lukashenka, *elected* 10 July 1994

COUNCIL OF MINISTERS *as at June 1999*
Prime Minister, Sergei Ling
First Deputy Prime Minister, Vasily Dogolev
Deputy Prime Ministers, Valeriy Kokarau; Uladzimir Zamyatalin; Genadz Navitsky; Ural Latypov; Leonid Kozik; Alexander Popkov
Agriculture and Food, Yury Moroz
Architecture and Construction, Genadz Kurachkin
Communications and Information Technology, Uladzimir Gancharenka
Culture, Aleksandr Sasnouski
Defence, Lt.-Gen. Aleksandr Chumakow
Economy, Uladzimir Shymow
Education, Vasil Strazhau
Emergency Situations, Valery Astapov
Enterprise and Investments, Aleksandr Sazonau
Finance, Nikolai Korbut
Foreign Affairs, Ural Latypov
Forestry, Valentsin Zorin
Fuel and Energy, Valentin Gerasimov
Health, Igor Zelenkevich
Housing and Municipal Services, Boris Batura
Industry, Anatol Kharlap
Internal Affairs, Yury Sivakov
Justice, Genadz Varantsou
Labour, Ivan Lyakh
Natural Resources and Environmental Protection, Mikhail Rusy
Social Security, Volga Dargel
Sport and Tourism, Yawhen Vorsin
State-owned Property and Privatization, Vasil Novak
Statistics and Analysis, Vladimir Zinavsky
Trade, Pyotr Kazlou
Transport, Aleksandr Lukashou

EMBASSY OF THE REPUBLIC OF BELARUS
6 Kensington Court, London W8 5DL
Tel 0171-937 3288
Ambassador Extraordinary and Plenipotentiary, HE Uladzimir Shchasny, apptd 1995

BRITISH EMBASSY
37 Karl Marx Street, Minsk 220030
Tel: Minsk 292303/4/5
Ambassador Extraordinary and Plenipotentiary, HE Iain Kelly, apptd 1999

DEFENCE

The Army has 1,778 main battle tanks, 930 armoured personnel carriers and 1,519 artillery pieces. The Air Force has 230 combat aircraft and 74 armed helicopters.

MILITARY EXPENDITURE – 2.9 per cent of GDP (1997)
MILITARY PERSONNEL – 73,000: Army 43,000, Air Force 22,000, Paramilitaries 8,000
CONSCRIPTION DURATION – 18 months

ECONOMY

Agricultural productivity was severely affected by nuclear fallout from the Chernobyl disaster in 1986 although Belarus is now self-sufficient in the production of foodstuffs. As a result of the collapse of the Soviet centrally planned economic system, the country lost cheap supplies of energy and raw materials. Energy from Russia is still the largest import.

Economic reform and privatization have been introduced and in May 1995 a customs union agreement with Russia took effect. A treaty was signed with Kazakhstan, Kyrgyzstan and Russia in March 1996 aimed at the establishment of a single customs territory. In 1997 investment activity rose by 20 per cent; trade with Russia rose by 40 per cent during 1997, and in December 1997 the first Russia-Belarus joint budget was endorsed, with projects estimated to cost US$100 billion.

In 1996 the government had a budget deficit equivalent to 1.9 per cent of GDP. In 1997 imports totalled US$8,644 million and exports US$7,147 million. GDP increased by 8 per cent in 1998.

GNP – US$22,082 million (1997); US$2,150 per capita (1997)
GDP – US$10,293 million (1995); US$994 per capita (1995)
INFLATION RATE – 63.9 per cent (1997)
UNEMPLOYMENT – 2.7 per cent (1995)
TOTAL EXTERNAL DEBT – US$1,162 million (1997)

Trade with UK	1997	1998
Imports from UK	£35,242,000	£32,853,000
Exports to UK	15,615,000	20,433,000

EDUCATION

The national system comprises pre-school, general secondary, out-of-school, vocational training and trade schools, secondary specialized and higher education. General secondary education begins at the age of six. There are also 22 private educational institutions.

ILLITERACY RATE – 0.5 per cent
ENROLMENT (percentage of age group) – primary 86 per cent (1994); tertiary 44.0 per cent (1996)

BELGIUM
Royaume de Belgique

AREA – 11,783 sq. miles (30,519 sq. km). Neighbours: the Netherlands (north), France (south), Germany and Luxembourg (east)
POPULATION – 10,159,000 (1994 UN estimate). Greater Brussels 949,070; Flanders 5,847,022; Wallonia 3,304,539, of whom 68,741 are German-speaking. Roman Catholicism is the religion of 86 per cent of the population. The official languages are Flemish, French and German
CAPITAL – Brussels (population, 953,175, 1998 estimate)

MAJOR CITIES – ΨAntwerp, the chief port (931,718); Bruges (269,158); Charleroi (424,515); ΨGhent (493,329); Liège (588,312); Leuven (453,772); Mons (250,748); Namur (279,675)
CURRENCY – Belgian franc (or frank) of 100 centimes (centiemen)
NATIONAL ANTHEM – La Brabançonne
NATIONAL DAY – 21 July (Accession of King Leopold I, 1831)
NATIONAL FLAG – Three vertical bands, black, yellow, red
LIFE EXPECTANCY (years) – male 72.43; female 79.13
POPULATION GROWTH RATE – 0.3 per cent (1996)
POPULATION DENSITY – 333 per sq. km (1996)

The Meuse and its tributary, the Sambre, divide Belgium into two distinct regions, that in the west being generally level and fertile, while the tableland of the Ardennes, in the east, has mostly poor soil. The polders near the coast, which are protected by dykes against floods, cover an area of 193 sq. miles. The principal rivers are the Scheldt and the Meuse.

Belgium is divided between those who speak Dutch (the Flemings) and those who speak French (the Walloons). Dutch is recognized as the official language in the northern areas and French in the southern (Walloon) area and there are guarantees for the respective linguistic minorities. Brussels is officially bilingual. There is a small German-speaking area (Eupen and Malmédy) along the German border, east of Liège.

HISTORY AND POLITICS

The kingdom formed part of the Low Countries (Netherlands) from 1815 until 14 October 1830, when a National Congress proclaimed its independence. On 4 June 1831, Prince Leopold of Coburg was chosen as the hereditary king. The neutrality and inviolability of Belgium were guaranteed by a Conference of the European powers, and by the Treaty of London 1839. On 4 August 1914 the Germans invaded Belgium, in violation of the terms of the treaty, and this led the Allies to declare war. Eupen and Malmédy were ceded by Germany under the Versailles Treaty of 1919. The kingdom was again invaded by Germany in 1940 and was occupied by Nazi troops until liberated by the Allies in September 1944.

The last general election was held on 13 June 1999. The results were as follows (seats):

Chamber of Deputies: Christian Social Party (CVP) (Flemish) 22; Socialist Party (PS) (Francophone) 19; Flemish Liberals and Democrats (VLD) 23; Socialist Party (SP) (Flemish) 14; Liberal Reform Party-Democratic Front (PRL-FDF) (Francophone) 18; Christian Social Party (PSC) (Francophone) 10; Vlaams Blok (Flemish Nationalist Party) 15; Ecolo (Francophone Ecology Party) 11; Agalev (Flemish Environmental Party) 9; Flemish People's Union (VU) 8; Front National (FN) 1.

Senate: of the 40 seats directly elected, CVP 6; SP 4; VLD 6; PRL-FDF 5; PS 4; PSC 3; Vlaams Blok 4; VU 2; Ecolo 3; Agalev 3. A further 31 Senators are indirectly elected or co-opted (*see* below).

POLITICAL SYSTEM

Belgium is a constitutional representative and hereditary monarchy with a bicameral legislature, consisting of the King, the Senate and the Chamber of Deputies. The parliamentary term is four years. Amendments to the constitution enacted since 1968 have devolved power to the regions. The national government retains competence only in foreign and defence policies, the national budget and monetary policy, social security, and the judicial, legal and penal systems. The Senate has 71 seats, of which 40 are directly elected, 21 indirectly elected and ten co-opted by the Flemish and Francophone Communities. The Chamber of Deputies has 150 seats. There are four levels of sub-national government: community, regional, provincial, and communal.

FEDERAL STRUCTURE

There are three communities: Flemish; Francophone; Germanophone. Each community has its own assembly, which elects the community government. At this level, Flanders is covered by the Flemish Community Assembly; most of Wallonia is covered by the Francophone Community Assembly, and the areas of Wallonia in the German-speaking communities of Eupen and Malmédy are covered by the Germanophone Community Assembly; Brussels is covered by a Joint Community Commission of the Flemish and Francophone Community Assemblies.

At regional level, Belgium is divided into the three regions of Wallonia, Brussels and Flanders. Each region has its own assembly and government.

There are ten provinces; five French-speaking in Wallonia (Hainaut, Liège, Luxembourg, Namur and French Brabant); and five Dutch-speaking in Flanders (Antwerp, East Flanders, West Flanders, Limbourg and Flemish Brabant). In addition, Belgium has 589 communes as the lowest level of local government.

Minister-President of the Flemish Government, Luc van den Brande (CVP)
Minister-President of the Walloon Regional Government, Robert Collignon (PS)

Head of City Government in Brussels, Charles Picqué

HEAD OF STATE

HM *The King of the Belgians,* King Albert II, *born* 6 June 1934; *succeeded* 9 August 1993; *married* 2 July 1959, Donna Paola Ruffo di Calabria, and has *issue* Prince Philippe (*see* below); Princess Astrid, *b.* 5 June 1962; Prince Laurent, *b.* 20 October 1963
Heir, HRH Prince Philippe Léopold Louis Marie, *born* 15 April 1960

CABINET *as at July 1999*

Prime Minister, Guy Verhofstadt (VLD)
Deputy PM, Budget, Johan Vande Lanotte (SP)
Deputy PM, Elio di Rupo (PS)
Deputy PM, Finance, Foreign Trade, Philippe Maystadt (PSC)
Deputy PM, Mobility and Transport, Isabelle Dúrant (Ecolo)
Agriculture and Small and Medium-sized Enterprises, Jaak Gabriels (VLD)
Civil Service, Luc Van Den Bossche (SP)
Consumer Affairs, Public Health and Environment, Magda Aelvoet (Agalev)
Defence, André Flahaut (PS)
Economic Affairs and Scientific Research, Rudy Demotte (SP)
Employment, Laurette Onkelinx (PS)
Finance, Didier Reynders (PRL)
Foreign Affairs, Louis Michel (PRL)
Interior Affairs, Antoine Duquesne (PRL)
Justice, Mark Verwilghen (VLD)
Social Affairs and Pensions, Frank Vandenbroucke (SP)
Telecommunication and Public Enterprises, Rik Daems (VLD)

Agalev Green Party (Flemish); Ecolo Green Party (Francophone); PS Socialist Party (Francophone); SP Socialist Party (Flemish); PRL Reforming Liberals (Francophone); VLD Liberal Democrats (Flemish)

BELGIAN EMBASSY
103-105 Eaton Square, London SW1W 9AB
Tel 0171-470 3700
Ambassador Extraordinary and Plenipotentiary, HE Lode Willems, apptd 1997
Minister-Counsellors, M. Vanherk (*Political*); F. De Sutter (*Economic*)
Defence Attaché, Col. J. Bouzette

BRITISH EMBASSY
rue d'Arlon 85, B-1040 Brussels Tel: Brussels 287 6211
Ambassador Extraordinary and Plenipotentiary, HE David Colvin, CMG, apptd 1993
Deputy Head of Mission, Counsellor and Consul-General, M. T. Jones
Counsellor (Commercial), J. S. Smith
Defence and Military Attaché, Col. T. E. Hall

Province	Area (sq. km)	Population (1998)	Main Town	Population (1998)
FLANDERS				
Antwerp	2,867	1,637,857	Antwerp	931,718
East Flanders	2,982	1,357,576	Ghent	493,329
Flemish Brabant	2,106	1,007,882	Leuven	453,772
Limbourg	2,422	783,927	Hasselt	67,456
West Flanders	3,144	1,125,140	Bruges	269,158
WALLONIA				
Hainaut	3,786	1,282,783	Mons	92,260
Liège	3,862	1,016,762	Liège	588,312
Luxembourg	4,440	243,790	Arlon	15,000
Namur	3,666	438,864	Namur	279,675
Walloon Brabant	1,091	344,508	Wavre	27,000

There are British Consular Offices at Brussels, Antwerp and Liège.

British Council Representative to Belgium and Luxembourg – Dr Ken Churchill, obe, Liefdadigheidstraat 15, B–1210 Brussels

British Chamber of Commerce for Belgium and Luxembourg (Inc.), rue Egmont 15, 1000 Brussels

DEFENCE

The Army has 155 main battle tanks, 309 armoured personnel carriers, 230 armoured infantry fighting vehicles, 243 artillery pieces and 78 helicopters. The Navy is based at Ostend and Zeebrugge and has three frigates and three helicopters. The Air Force has 100 combat aircraft.

The headquarters of NATO, SHAPE and the Western European Union Military Planning Cell are in Belgium; 800 US personnel are stationed in the country.

Military Expenditure – 1.6 per cent of GDP (1997)

Military Personnel – 43,700: Army 28,250, Navy 2,600, Air Force 11,600, Medical Service 1,250

ECONOMY

With no natural resources except coal, production of which has now ceased, industry is based largely on the processing for re-export of imported raw materials. Principal industries are steel and metal products, chemicals and petrochemicals, textiles, glass, and foodstuffs.

On 1 May 1998, it was announced that Belgium had satisfied the convergence criteria and would be one of 11 countries to participate in the European Single Currency from 1 January 1999.

In 1997 there was a budget deficit of 2.0 per cent of GDP and public debt was 122.1 per cent of GDP.

GNP – US$272,382 million (1997); US$26,730 per capita (1997)

GDP – US$269,199 million (1995); US$26,582 per capita (1995)

Annual Average Growth of GDP – 1.9 per cent (1995)

Inflation Rate – 1.6 per cent (1997)

Unemployment – 9.3 per cent (1995)

TRADE

External trade figures relate to Luxembourg as well as Belgium since the two countries formed an economic union in 1921. The main trading partners are Germany, France and the Netherlands.

In 1997 Belgium and Luxembourg had a trade surplus of US$8,343 million and a current account surplus of US$13,954 million. In 1997 exports totalled US$170,259 million and imports US$156,436 million.

Trade with UK (Belgium and Luxembourg)

Trade with UK	1997	1998
Imports from UK	£8,005,500,000	£7,987,700,000
Exports to UK	8,716,000,000	9,074,100,000

COMMUNICATIONS

The railways are operated by the Belgian National Railways. Ship canals include Ghent-Terneuzen (18 miles, half in the Netherlands) by which ships up to 60,000 tons reach Ghent; Willebroek Rupel-Brussels (20 miles, by which ships drawing 18 ft reach Brussels from the sea); Bruges (from Zeebrugge on the North Sea to Bruges, 6¼ miles); and Albert (79 miles), Liège to Antwerp for barges up to 1,350 tons. The River Meuse from the Dutch to the French frontiers, the River Sambre between Namur and Monceau, the River Scheldt from Antwerp to Ghent and the Brussels-Charleroi Canal are being widened or deepened to take barges up to 1,350 tons. Most maritime trade is carried in foreign shipping.

In 1986 there were 14,260 km of trunk road, of which about 1,550 km were motorways. The Belgian national airline Sabena operates regular services between Brussels and European centres, as well as intercontinental services worldwide.

CULTURE AND EDUCATION

The literature of France and the Netherlands is supplemented by an indigenous Belgian literary activity in both French and Dutch. Maurice Maeterlinck (1862–1949) was awarded the Nobel Prize for Literature in 1911. Emile Verhaeren (1855–1916) was a poet of international standing. Of contemporary Belgian writers, the most celebrated was Georges Simenon (1903–89).

Nursery schools provide free education for children from two and a half to six years. There are over 4,000 primary schools (6 to 12 years), more than 1,000 secondary schools offering a general academic education slightly over half of which are free institutions (predominantly Roman Catholic but subsidized by the state) and the remainder official institutions. The official school-leaving age is 18.

Enrolment (percentage of age group) – primary 98 per cent (1994); secondary 99 per cent (1994); tertiary 54.4 per cent (1994)

BELIZE

Area – 8,763 sq. miles (22,696 sq. km). Neighbours: Mexico (north and north-west), Guatemala (west and south)

Population – 222,000 (1994 UN estimate): 44 per cent Mestizo (Maya-Spanish); 30 per cent Creole; 11 per cent Maya; plus a number of East Indian and Spanish descent. The races are now inter-mixed. The majority of the population is Christian, about 58 per cent Catholic and 34 per cent Protestant. The official language and language of instruction is English. Spanish is also widely spoken and English Creole is the vernacular. There are also Garifuna and Maya speakers

Capital – Belmopan (population, 44,087, 1991)

Major Cities – ΨBelize City (1993 census 46,342), the former capital; Corozal (7,420); Dangriga (6,761); Orange Walk (11,573); San Ignacio (9,417)

Currency – Belize dollar (BZ$) of 100 cents. The Belize dollar is tied to the US dollar, BZ$2 = US$1

National Anthem – Land of the Free

National Day – 21 September (Independence Day)

National Flag – Blue ground with red band along top and bottom edges, and in centre a white disc containing the coat of arms surrounded by a green garland

Life Expectancy (years) – male 69.95; female 74.07

Population Growth Rate – 2.7 per cent (1996)

Population Density – 10 per sq. km (1996)

Urban Population – 47.5 per cent (1994)

Military Expenditure – 2.6 per cent of GDP (1997)

Military Personnel – 1,000: Army

The coastal areas are mostly flat and swampy with many islets but the country rises gradually towards the interior, which is mainly forest. The northern and western districts are hilly, and in the south the Maya Mountains and the Cockscombs form the backbone of the country, reaching a height of 3,700 feet at Victoria Peak. The climate is subtropical.

HISTORY AND POLITICS

Numerous ruins in the area indicate that Belize was heavily populated by the Maya Indians. The first British settlement was established in 1638 but was subject to repeated attacks by the Spanish, who claimed sovereignty until defeated by the Royal Navy and settlers in 1798. In 1871 the area was recognized by Britain as a colony and called British Honduras. In 1973 the colony was renamed Belize, and was granted independence on 21 September 1981.

The 1998 elections were won by the People's United Party, who took 26 out of the 29 seats in the House of Representatives.

FOREIGN RELATIONS

A long-standing territorial dispute with Guatemala was provisionally resolved in 1992 when the Guatemalan Congress and Supreme Court voted to recognize Belize and establish diplomatic relations. Guatemala still retains its claim, subject to arbitration by the International Court of Justice.

POLITICAL SYSTEM

Queen Elizabeth II is head of state, represented in Belize by a Governor-General. There is a National Assembly, comprising a House of Representatives (29 members elected for five years) and a Senate (eight members appointed by the Governor-General). Executive power is vested in the Cabinet, which is responsible to the National Assembly.

Governor-General, HE Sir Colville Norbert Young, GCMG, apptd 17 November 1993

CABINET *as at May 1999*

Prime Minister, Finance and Foreign Affairs, Said Musa
Deputy PM, Natural Resources and the Environment, John Briceno
Senior Minister, George Price
Attorney-General, Housing, Dickie Bradley
Agriculture and Fisheries, Daniel Silva
Budget Planning, Development and Investment, Ralph Fonseca
Cabinet Secretary, Robert Leslie
Chief of Staff in the PM's Office, Godfrey Smith
Education and Sports, Cordel Hyde
Health, Servulo Baeza
Human Development, Women's Affairs and Youth, Dolores Balderamos García
Industry, Commerce, Public Services and Labour, José Coye
National Security and Immigration, Jorge Espat
Public Utilities, Transport and Communications, Maxwell Samuels
Rural Development and Culture, Marcial Mes
Sugar Industy, Local Government and Latin American Affairs, Florencio Marín
Tourism, Mark Espat
Works, Henry Canton

BELIZE HIGH COMMISSION

22 Harcourt House, 19A Cavendish Square, London WIM 9AD
Tel 0171-499 9728
High Commissioner, HE Assad Shomas, apptd 1999

BRITISH HIGH COMMISSION

PO Box 91, Belmopan
Tel: Belmopan 22146/7
High Commissioner, HE Timothy David, apptd 1998

ECONOMY

About 30 per cent of the population is engaged in agriculture. The country is more or less self-sufficient in fresh beef, pork and poultry, but processed meat and dairy products are imported. About 25 per cent of timber production (mostly mahogany) is exported, and there is a large US market for lobster, conch and scale fish. Tourism is also a valuable source of income.

In 1995 Belize had a trade deficit of US$66 million and a current account deficit of US$17 million. In 1997 imports totalled US$286 million and exports US$159 million.

GNP – US$614 million (1997); US$2,670 per capita (1997)
GDP – US$547 million (1995); US$2,569 per capita (1995)
ANNUAL AVERAGE GROWTH OF GDP – 1.4 per cent (1996)
INFLATION RATE – 1.0 per cent (1997)
UNEMPLOYMENT – 11.1 per cent (1994)
TOTAL EXTERNAL DEBT – US$383 million (1997)

Trade with UK	1997	1998
Imports from UK	£13,561,000	£11,604,000
Exports to UK	36,291,000	33,553,000

COMMUNICATIONS

There is a government-operated radio service and three privately-owned radio stations but no official television service in the country. An automatic telephone service operated by Belize Telecommunications Ltd covers the whole country.

The principal airport is at Belize City and various airlines operate international flights to the USA and other Central American states. The main port is also Belize City, which has deep water quays. Several inland waterways are also navigable. There are 1,865 miles of road, including four main highways, but there is no railway system.

EDUCATION

Education is compulsory from six to 14 years of age. In 1992 primary education was provided by 241 schools, most of which are government-aided. Secondary education is provided by 40 secondary and post-secondary institutions. A University College of Belize has been established. There is an extra-mural faculty of the University of the West Indies, with a resident tutor.

ENROLMENT (percentage of age group) – primary 99 per cent (1994); secondary 36 per cent (1992)

BENIN
République du Benin

AREA – 43,484 sq. miles (112,622 sq. km). Neighbours: Togo (west), Burkina Faso and Niger (north), Nigeria (east)
POPULATION – 5,563,000 (1994 UN estimate). The official language is French
CAPITAL – ΨPorto Novo (population, 179,138, 1992)
MAJOR TOWNS – ΨCotonou (487,020, 1992) is the principal commercial town and port
CURRENCY – Franc CFA of 100 centimes
NATIONAL DAY – 30 November
NATIONAL FLAG – Two horizontal stripes of yellow over red with a vertical green band in the hoist
LIFE EXPECTANCY (years) – male 45.92; female 49.29
POPULATION GROWTH RATE – 2.7 per cent (1996)
POPULATION DENSITY – 49 per sq. km (1996)
URBAN POPULATION – 35.7 per cent (1992)
MILITARY EXPENDITURE – 1.3 per cent of GDP (1997)
MILITARY PERSONNEL – 7,300: Army 4,500, Navy 150, Air Force 150, Paramilitaries 2,500

CONSCRIPTION DURATION – 18 months
ILLITERACY RATE – 63.0 per cent
ENROLMENT (percentage of age group) – primary 62 per
cent (1996); tertiary 3.1 per cent (1996)

Benin (formerly known as Dahomey) has a short coastline
of 78 miles on the Gulf of Guinea but extends northwards
inland for 437 miles. The four main regions, running
horizontally, are a narrow sandy coastal strip, a succession
of inter-communicating lagoons, a clay belt and a sandy
plateau in the north.

HISTORY AND POLITICS

Benin was placed under French administration in 1892 and
became an independent republic within the French
Community in December 1958; full independence outside
the Community was proclaimed on 1 August 1960. Between
1963 and 1972 successive governments were overthrown
by the military until a coup d'état in 1972 brought to power
a Marxist-Leninist military government headed by Lt.-
Col. Kérékou.

The government dropped Marxism-Leninism as the
official ideology in 1989, revoked the constitution in March
1990 and changed the country's official name from the
People's Republic of Benin to the Republic of Benin. The
Revolutionary National Assembly (legislature) was replaced by a High Council of the Republic (HCR).

A pluralistic constitution was adopted in December 1990
and legislative and presidential elections were held in 1991.
Nicéphore Soglo was sworn in as president and appointed
a Benin Renaissance Party (PRB)-dominated provisional
government. He was defeated by Gen. Kérékou in a
presidential election in March 1996. Legislative elections
to the 83-seat National Assembly in March 1999 gave the
PRB and allies 27 seats and opposition parties 42 seats.

POLITICAL SYSTEM

The president is head of government as well as head of
state, and is directly elected for a five-year term, renewable
once only. The president appoints and presides over the
Council of Ministers. The National Assembly has 83
members, directly elected for a maximum of four years.

HEAD OF STATE
President and Head of the Armed Forces, HE Gen. Mathieu
Kérékou, *sworn in* 4 April 1996

CABINET *as at May 1999*

Prime Minister, vacant
Minister Designate to the Presidency, Defence, Pierre Osho
Civil Service, Labour and Administrative Reform, Ousmane
  Batoko
Culture and Communications, Séverin Adjovi
Environment, Housing and Urban Affairs, Adekpedjou Sylvain
  Akindes
Finance, Abdoulaye Bio Tchane
Foreign Affairs and Co-operation, Antoine Idji Kolawole
Health, Marina d'Almeida-Massougbodji
Industry, Small and Medium-sized Enterprises, John Igue
Interior, Security and Territorial Administration, Daniel
  Tawema
Justice, Legislation and Human Rights, Joseph Gnonlonfou
Mines, Energy and Water Resources, Félix Essou Dansou
National Education and Scientific Research, Conceptia
  Ouinsou
Planning, Economic Reconstruction and Employment Promotion,
  Albert Tevoedjre
Public Works and Transport, Joseph Attin
Rural Development, Saka Saley
Social Welfare and Women's Affairs, Ramatou Baba-Moussa

Trade, Tourism and Handicrafts, Marie Elyse Gbedo
Youth, Sports and Leisure, Damien Alahassa

EMBASSY OF THE REPUBLIC OF BENIN
87 Avenue Victor Hugo, 75116 Paris, France
Tel: Paris 4500 9882
Ambassador Extraordinary and Plenipotentiary, HE Andres
  Ologoudou, apptd 1998

HONORARY CONSULATE, 16 The Broadway, Stanmore,
  Middx HA7 4DW. Tel: 0181–954 8800. *Honorary Consul*,
  Lawrence Landau

BRITISH AMBASSADOR, HE Graham Burton, CMG,
  resident at Lagos, Nigeria

ECONOMY

The principal exports are cotton, palm products, groundnuts, shea-nuts, and coffee. Small deposits of gold, iron and
chrome have been found. Oil production started in 1983.

In 1994 Benin had a trade deficit of US$65 million and
a current account surplus of US$36 million. In 1997 imports
totalled US$658 million and exports US$400 million.

GNP – US$2,227 million (1997); US$380 per capita
  (1997)
GDP – US$2,117 million (1995); US$391 per capita
  (1995)
ANNUAL AVERAGE GROWTH OF GDP – 5.7 per cent
  (1995)
INFLATION RATE – 3.5 per cent (1997)
TOTAL EXTERNAL DEBT – US$1,624 million (1997)

Trade with UK	1997	1998
Imports from UK	£47,211,000	£42,275,000
Exports to UK	1,249,000	1,238,000

BHUTAN
Druk-yul

AREA – 18,147 sq. miles (47,000 sq. km). Neighbours:
  Tibet (north), India (west, south and east)
POPULATION – 1,812,000 (1994 UN estimate): about 80
  per cent are Buddhists, the remainder (mostly the
  Nepali Bhutanese) are Hindu. The official language, for
  administrative and religious purposes, is Dzongkha, a
  variant of Tibetan, which functions as a lingua franca
  amongst a variety of languages and dialects. Nepali
  remains a recognized language and English remains the
  medium of instruction and the working language of the
  administration
CAPITAL – Thimphu (population, 15,000, 1987 estimate)
CURRENCY – Ngultrum of 100 chetrum (Indian currency
  is also legal tender)
NATIONAL DAY – 17 December
NATIONAL FLAG – Saffron yellow and orange-red
  divided diagonally, with dragon device in centre
LIFE EXPECTANCY (years) – male 49.10; female 52.40
POPULATION GROWTH RATE – 1.6 per cent (1996)
POPULATION DENSITY – 39 per sq. km (1996)
ILLITERACY RATE – 57.8 per cent

There is a mountainous northern region which is infertile
and sparsely populated, a central zone of upland valleys
where most of the population and cultivated land is found,
and in the south the densely forested foothills of the
Himalayas, which are mainly inhabited by Nepalese settlers
and indigenous tribespeople.

INSURGENCIES

In January 1989 the King introduced a code of national
etiquette designed to protect the national culture and

language from Nepali encroachment. These measures, together with the granting of citizenship only to Nepalis settled in Bhutan before 1958, led to an exodus of ethnic Nepalis to Nepal, where about 80,000 live in camps. A low-level insurgency has been waged in the south of the country against the King's policies by ethnic Nepalis since 1990. Talks between the Nepali and Bhutan governments continue in an attempt to resolve the fate of the refugees.

FOREIGN RELATIONS

Under a 1949 treaty Bhutan is guided by the advice of India in regard to its external relations. It retains its own diplomatic representatives and is a member of the UN. It also receives from India an annual payment of Rs500,000 as compensation for portions of its territory annexed by the British Government in India in 1864.

POLITICAL SYSTEM

Bhutan has a 150-member National Assembly which meets twice a year. The ten-member Royal Advisory Council, nominated by the King and the National Assembly, acts as a consultative body when the National Assembly is not in session. The King is also assisted by the *Lhengyal Sgungtsog* (Cabinet). There are no political parties.

In July 1998 the King introduced reforms giving the legislature the right to dismiss the King and to nominate the members of the cabinet, although the King retains the right to assign their portfolios.

HEAD OF STATE

HM *The King of Bhutan*, Jigme Singye Wangchuk, *born* 11 November 1955; *succeeded his father* July 1972; *crowned* 2 June 1974
Heir, Crown Prince Jigme Gesar Namgyal Wangchuk, *designated* 31 October 1988

CABINET *as at May 1999*

Chair of the Royal Advisory Council, Kungang Tsangbi
Chair of the Third Committee, Ugyen Tsering
Agriculture, Education and Health, Kinzang Dorji
Cabinet Chairman, Foreign Affairs, Jigme Thinley
Finance, Hishey Zimba
Home Affairs, Thinley Gyamtsho
Law, Sonam Tobgye
Trade and Industry, Khandu Wangchuk

ECONOMY

The economy is based on agriculture and animal hus-bandry, which engage over 90 per cent of the workforce in what is largely a self-sufficient rural society. The principal food crops are rice, wheat, maize and barley. Vegetables and fruit are also produced. Bhutan is the world's largest producer of cardamom, which forms its principal export to countries other than India. Agriculture is, however, limited by the country's mountainous topography and 60 per cent forest cover.   The mountains contain rich deposits of limestone, gypsum, dolomite and graphite and small amounts of coal, which are exported to India. A modest industrial base is being developed. A distillery and cement, chemicals and food-processing plants are in production; a forestry industries complex is being expanded. Tourism and postage stamps are increasingly important sources of foreign exchange.

The government budget deficit was equivalent to 0.26 per cent of GDP in 1993. In 1995 imports totalled US$112 million and exports US103 million.

GNP – US$315 million (1997); US$430 per capita (1997)
GDP – US$294 million (1995); US$166 per capita (1995)
ANNUAL AVERAGE GROWTH OF GDP – 6.4 per cent (1996)

INFLATION RATE – 8.8 per cent (1996)
TOTAL EXTERNAL DEBT – US$89 million (1997)

TRADE

Over 90 per cent of foreign trade is with India. Principal exports are agricultural products, timber, cement and coal; main imports are textiles, cereals and consumer goods. Bhutan's airline, Druk Air, flies between Paro, New Delhi and Calcutta.

Trade with UK	1997	1998
Imports from UK	£1,491,000	£1,563,000
Exports to UK	964,000	1,206,000

BOLIVIA
República de Bolivia

AREA – 424,165 sq. miles (1,098,581 sq. km). Neighbours: Brazil (north and east), Paraguay and Argentina (south), Chile and Peru (west)
POPULATION – 8,140,000 (1999 estimate): 12 per cent is of white European descent, 30 per cent Mestizo (mixed European-Indian), 25 per cent Quechua Indian and 17 per cent Aymará Indian. The official language is Spanish; Quechua and Aymará are also spoken. Roman Catholicism was the state religion until disestablishment in 1961
CAPITAL – La Paz (population, 784,976, 1993 estimate)
MAJOR CITIES – Cochabamba (772,000); El Alto (446,189); Oruro (253,000); Potosí (252,000); Santa Cruz (1,265,000); Sucre, the legal capital and seat of the judiciary (184,000)
CURRENCY – Boliviano ($b) of 100 centavos
NATIONAL ANTHEM – Bolivianos, El Hado Propicio (Oh Bolivia, our long-felt desires)
NATIONAL DAY – 6 August (Independence Day)
NATIONAL FLAG – Three horizontal bands, red, yellow, green
LIFE EXPECTANCY (years) – male 57.74; female 61.00
POPULATION GROWTH RATE – 2.4 per cent (1996)
POPULATION DENSITY – 7 per sq. km (1996)
URBAN POPULATION – 57.5 per cent (1992)

The chief topographical feature is the great central plateau over 500 miles in length, at an average altitude of 12,500 feet above sea level, between the two great chains of the Andes, which traverse the country from south to north. The total length of the navigable rivers is about 12,000 miles, the principal rivers being the Itenez, Beni, Mamore and Madre de Dios.

HISTORY AND POLITICS

Bolivia won its independence from Spain in 1825 after a war of liberation led by Simon Bolivar (1783–1830), from whom the country derives its name. From 1964 to 1982 Bolivia was ruled by military juntas until civilian rule was restored.

Congressional and presidential elections were held in June 1997. No party won an outright majority in Congress and a multiparty government was formed.

POLITICAL SYSTEM

The constitution provides for a directly elected executive president who appoints the Cabinet. The legislature (Congress) consists of a 27-member Senate and a 130-member Chamber of Deputies; both chambers are elected for four-year terms, and the president for five years.

HEAD OF STATE
President of the Republic, Gen. (retd) Hugo Bánzer Suárez, *inaugurated* 6 August 1997
Vice-President, Jorge Quiroga Ramírez

CABINET *as at May 1999*

Agriculture, Oswaldo Antezana Vacadiez (ADN)
Economic Development, Jorge Pacheco (UCS)
Education, Tito Hoz de Vila (ADN)
Finance, Herbert Muller (Ind.)
Foreign Affairs, Javier Murillo de la Rocha (ADN)
Housing and Basic Services, Amparo Ballivian (ADN)
Human Development and Health, Guillermo Cuentas (MIR)
International Trade and Investment, Carlos Saavedra Bruno (MIR)
Justice, Carlos Alberto Subirana Suárez (ADN)
Labour, Adolfo Solis (MIR)
National Defence, Jorge Crespo Velasco (ADN)
Presidency, Franz Ondarza Linares (ADN)
Sustainable Development and Environment, Erick Reyes Villa (NFR)

ADN Democratic Nationalist Action; MIR Movement of the Revolutionary Left; NFR New Republican Force; UCS Civic Solidarity Union

BOLIVIAN EMBASSY
106 Eaton Square, London SW1W 9AD
Tel 0171-235 2257/4248
Ambassador Extraordinary and Plenipotentiary, Jaime Quiroga Matos, apptd 1998

BRITISH EMBASSY
Avenida Arce 2732, (Casilla 694) La Paz
Tel: La Paz 433424
Ambassador Extraordinary and Plenipotentiary, HE Graham Minter, apptd 1998
Deputy Head of Mission, J. Gardner

There is an Honorary Consulate at Santa Cruz.

DEFENCE

The Army has 108 armoured personnel carriers and 146 artillery pieces. The Navy has 18 patrol vessels. The Air Force has 50 combat aircraft and 10 armed helicopters.
MILITARY EXPENDITURE – 2.0 per cent of GDP (1997)
MILITARY PERSONNEL – 70,600: Army 25,000, Navy 4,500, Air Force 4,000, Paramilitaries 37,100
CONSCRIPTION DURATION – 12 months

ECONOMY

Mining, natural gas, petroleum and agriculture are the principal industries. The ancient silver mines of Potosí are now worked chiefly for tin, but gold is obtained on the Eastern Cordillera of the Andes. Tin output, together with other minerals (copper, tungsten, antimony, lead, zinc, asbestos, wolfram, bismuth salt and sulphur), provides over one-third of exports. Following a decline in the price of tin, many workers have taken to growing coca, which has become a significant export. A government plan to reduce coca production by offering growers alternative means of support has only been of limited success. Small quantities of oil are produced for internal consumption, and gas (currently providing about a quarter of export income) is piped to Argentina; in December 1997 the World Bank approved financing for the 3,150 km Bolivia-Brazil gas pipeline, estimated to cost around US$2 billion.

The economy deteriorated badly in the late 1970s and early 1980s; in the mid-1980s economic reforms were introduced with privatization of some state-owned firms and the encouragement of foreign investment. The peso was replaced in 1987 with the Boliviano of 1,000,000 old

pesos in a successful effort to stem hyperinflation. The economy and currency have stabilized.

In 1996 the government signed an agreement with the South American Common Market (Mercosur) to create a free trade zone within 18 years.
GNP – US$7,564 million (1997); US$970 per capita (1997)
GDP – US$6,737 million (1995); US$909 per capita (1995)
ANNUAL AVERAGE GROWTH OF GDP – 3.5 per cent (1995)
INFLATION RATE – 4.7 per cent (1997)
UNEMPLOYMENT – 3.6 per cent (1995)
TOTAL EXTERNAL DEBT – US$5,248 million (1997)

TRADE

Mineral exports represent about 40 per cent of total trade. Bolivia has now developed its own smelters and is exporting metals. The chief imports are wheat and flour, iron and steel products, machinery, vehicles and textiles.

In 1996 Bolivia had a trade deficit of US$189 million and a current account deficit of US$296 million. In 1997 imports totalled US$1,810 million and exports US$1,128 million.

Trade with UK	1997	1998
Imports from UK	£15,241,000	£15,305,000
Exports to UK	16,436,000	22,689,000

COMMUNICATIONS

There are 2,200 miles of railways in operation. Communication with Peru is by road from La Paz via Copacabana and thence to the railhead at Puno. In 1993 Bolivia and Peru signed an agreement granting Bolivia a concession of 162 hectares at the southern Peruvian port of Ilo for 98 years to construct a free trade zone.

Commercial aviation is conducted by the national airline, Lloyd Aereo Boliviano and Transporte Aereo Militar between the major towns; Lloyd Aereo Boliviano and a number of foreign airlines provide international flights to the USA, South and Central America and Europe.

Most towns have radio, telephone or telegraph communication with the main cities. There are 16 principal daily newspapers.

EDUCATION

Elementary education is compulsory and free and there are secondary schools in urban centres. Provision is also made for higher education; in addition to St Francisco Xavier's University at Sucre, founded in 1624, there are seven other universities, the largest being the University of San Andrés at La Paz, and ten private universities.
ILLITERACY RATE – 16.9 per cent
ENROLMENT (percentage of age group) – primary 91 per cent (1990); secondary 29 per cent (1990); tertiary 22.2 per cent (1990)

BOSNIA-HERCEGOVINA

AREA – 19,735 sq. miles (51,129 sq. km). Neighbours: Serbia (east), Montenegro (south-east), Croatia (north and west)
POPULATION – 4,510,000 (1994 UN estimate); 4.4 million (1991 census): 44 per cent Bosniac, 33 per cent Serbs and 17 per cent Croats. The languages are Bosnian (spoken by Bosniacs and written in the Latin script), Serbian (spoken by Serbs and written in the Cyrillic alphabet) and Croatian (spoken by Croats and written in the Latin script)

CAPITAL – Sarajevo (population, 529,021, 1991 estimate)
MAJOR CITIES – Banja Luka (195,994); Mostar (127,034); Tuzla (131,866); Zenica (145,837)
CURRENCY – Convertible marka
NATIONAL DAY – 1 March (anniversary of 1992 declaration of independence)
NATIONAL FLAG – Blue, bearing a yellow triangle above a line of white stars
LIFE EXPECTANCY (years) – male 69.55; female 75.11
POPULATION GROWTH RATE – 0.1 per cent (1996)
POPULATION DENSITY – 88 per sq. km (1996)
URBAN POPULATION – 39.6 per cent (1991)
MILITARY EXPENDITURE – 5.0 per cent of GDP (1997)
MILITARY PERSONNEL – Bosniac Army (BiH): 40,000; Croat Defence Council (HVO): 16,000; Bosnian Serb Army: 30,000
GDP – US$968 million (1995); US$271 per capita (1995)

HISTORY AND POLITICS

The country was settled by Slavs in the seventh century and conquered by the Ottoman Turks in 1463. Ruled by the Turks for over 400 years, the country came under Austro-Hungarian control in 1878. The assassination of the heir to the Austro-Hungarian throne in Sarajevo by an ethnic Serb precipitated the First World War, after which Bosnia-Hercegovina became part of the 'Kingdom of Serbs, Croats and Slovenes' (renamed Yugoslavia in 1929) under the Versailles Treaty (1919). It was occupied by German and Axis forces between 1941 and 1945. At the end of the war Bosnia-Hercegovina came under Communist rule as part of the Socialist Federal Republic of Yugoslavia, which eventually collapsed with the secession of Slovenia and Croatia in 1991.

The Bosnia-Hercegovina government issued a declaration of sovereignty in October 1991 against the wishes of the ethnic Serb Democratic Party. Independence was declared on 1 March 1992 following a referendum which was boycotted by the Bosnian Serbs. Bosnia-Hercegovina was recognized as an independent state by the EC and USA in April 1992 and admitted to UN membership in May 1992.

THE WAR

Fighting broke out in March 1992 between the pro-independence Muslims and Bosnian Serbs who wanted to merge with the Serbian republic to form a Greater Serbia. The Bosnian Serbs, assisted by the Serb-dominated Federal Yugoslav Army (JNA) rapidly gained control of 70 per cent of Bosnia and in August 1992 declared their own 'Republika Srpska' with its capital at Pale. International pressure eventually forced the JNA to withdraw but it handed over its weapons to the Bosnian Serb forces.

The Bosnian government (Muslim) forces formed an alliance with Bosnian Croat and Croat forces in early 1992 which collapsed in 1993. The Muslims then came under fire from both Bosnian Serb and Bosnian Croat forces. In January 1993 the UN and EU attempted to negotiate an end to the war but the Vance-Owen plan was rejected by the Bosnian Serb parliament and the fighting continued.

The Bosnian Serbs began to shell Sarajevo and government-held enclaves following the collapse of a three-month détente between the Serbs and the Muslims which prompted the UN to declare Srebrenica, Zepa, Goražde, Sarajevo, Tuzla and Bihac 'safe areas'.

In August 1993 the Bosnian Croats declared a 'Republic of Herceg-Bosna', with its capital in Mostar, and following a cease-fire in February 1994 joined the government forces in a Muslim-Croat Federation.

Bosnian Serb forces captured most of the enclave of Goražde in April 1994 despite NATO air strikes. NATO galvanized the USA, Britain, France, Germany and Russia to form the Contact Group (CG) to co-ordinate peace efforts. The CG brought about a cease-fire in June 1994 and presented a peace plan, proposing a 51:49 division of territory between the Muslim-Croat Federation and the Bosnian Serbs. The Bosnian Serbs rejected the plan and the CG attempted to isolate them, with the support of Serbia, which had agreed to blockade Bosnian Serb forces in exchange for a relaxation of sanctions.

NATO air strikes against Bosnian Serbs in December 1994 resulted in the seizure of 350 UN peacekeepers, who were released as part of a cease-fire agreement in January. Bosnian Serbs retaliating against a Federation offensive in March resumed artillery attacks on Sarajevo, prompting a NATO bombing campaign and a second hostage crisis.

Fighting intensified in 1995, climaxing in a land-grab during the final months of the war. Bosnian Serb forces overran the UN safe areas of Zepa and Srebrenica in July, allegedly massacring thousands of fleeing Muslims, and then laid siege to the Bihac 'safe area' together with Croatian Serbs and rebel Muslims. Bosnian government and Croatian forces lifted the siege of Bihac in August, enabling a joint attack on Serb-held central Bosnia.

A Serb artillery attack on Sarajevo on 28 August which killed 37 people prompted NATO to bomb military and infrastructure targets and to issue an ultimatum to the Bosnian Serbs to remove their heavy weapons from around Sarajevo. The ultimatum was met by 20 September, following coercion from President Milošević of Serbia.

The foreign ministers of Bosnia, Croatia and Serbia (rump Yugoslavia) met in Geneva in September 1995 and agreed to a US-sponsored peace accord. A cease-fire agreement was signed on 5 October and observed from 22 October, delayed by a Federation advance in the west and north-west, and Bosnian Serbs overrunning Tuzla.

THE PEACE AGREEMENT

The Presidents of Bosnia, Serbia and Croatia met in Dayton, Ohio, USA, for negotiations which culminated in an agreement on 21 November 1995. The Dayton Peace Treaty was signed in Paris on 14 December. It was agreed to preserve Bosnia as a single state with a 51:49 division of territory between the Bosnian and Croat Federation and the Republika Srpska (Bosnian Serbs). A Republican (national) government, presidency and democratically elected institutions, based in Federation-controlled Sarajevo, were provided for. The Bosnian Serbs agreed to return five Sarajevo suburbs to the Federation and were given access to the sea in a land-swap with Croatia. The Federation gained a land corridor between Sarajevo and Goražde but was obliged to return Mrkonjic Grad to the Bosnian Serbs.

The Dayton agreement provided for the deployment of a 60,000-strong NATO-led Peace Implementation Force (IFOR) which took over from UNPROFOR on 20 December 1995 and was mandated until December 1996. IFOR was replaced by a 31,000-strong, NATO-led Stabilization Force (SFOR), mandated until June 1998. SFOR in turn was replaced by a Dissuasion Force (DFOR) with no formal end date.

Mostar, which had been divided during the war between the Muslims and Croats of the Federation and administered by the EU, held elections in June 1996. The EU withdrew in December 1996, when the Bosnian Croat state of Herceg-Bosna ceased to exist. Following a decision by international arbitrators, the northern town of Brčko, which had been under Bosnian Serb control, was merged into a self-governing neutral district in March 1999.

The Dayton peace agreement uses the term 'Bosniac' to refer to Bosnian Muslims.

POLITICAL SYSTEM

Under the Dayton peace agreement, the Bosnian republican (national) government was made responsible for foreign affairs, currency, citizenship and immigration. Executive authority was vested in a democratically elected rotating presidential triumvirate comprising a representative from each community.

Legislative authority is vested in a bicameral parliament, the Assembly of Bosnia-Hercegovina, comprising a House of Peoples and a House of Representatives. Both houses have two-year terms. The House of Peoples has 15 members, five from each community, who are selected by the House of Representatives. The House of Representatives has 42 directly elected members; two-thirds of the members come from the Federation and one-third from Republika Srpska. Within the Bosniac-Croat Federation there is a 140-member House of Representatives and ten cantonal assemblies; in the Republika Srpska there is an 83-member People's Assembly.

HEADS OF STATE (FOR ALL BOSNIA)
Current President, Živko Radišić (Serb); *Presidency Members,* Alija Izetbegović (Bosniac); Ante Jelavić (Croat), *elected* 12/13 September 1998

HEAD OF THE FEDERATION
President, Ejup Ganić (Bosniac)
Vice-President, Vladimir Soljić (Croat)

HEAD OF REPUBLIKA SRPSKA
President, vacant
Vice-President, Dragljub Mirjanić

COUNCIL OF MINISTERS (FOR ALL BOSNIA) *as at June 1999*
Co-Prime Ministers, Haris Silajdžić (Bosniac); Svetozar Mihajlović (Serb)
Deputy Prime Minister, Neven Tomić (Croat)
Communications and Civilian Affairs, Spasoje Albijanic (Serb)
Foreign Affairs, Jadranko Prlić (Croat)
Foreign Trade and Economic Relations, Mirsad Kurtović (Bosniac)

FEDERATION CABINET *as at June 1999*
Prime Minister, Edhem Bicakcić (Bosniac)
Deputy P.M, Finance, Dragan Čović (Croat)
Agriculture, Water-power and Forestry, Ahmed Smajić (Bosniac)
Defence, Miroslav Prce (Croat)
Education, Science, Culture and Sport, Fahrudin Rizvanbegović (Bosniac)
Energy, Mining and Industry, Mirsad Salkić (Bosniac)
Environment and Urban Planning, Ramiz Mehmedagić (Bosniac)
Health, Bozo Ljubić (Croat)
Interior, Mehmed Zilić (Bosniac)
Justice, Ignjac Dodik (Croat)
Social Welfare, Displaced Persons and Refugees, Sulejman Garib (Bosniac)
Trade, Branko Ivković (Croat)
Transport and Communications, Besim Mehmedić (Bosniac)
Without Portfolio, Nikola Antunović (Croat); Nedeljko Despotović (Serb)

REPUBLIKA SRPSKA GOVERNMENT *as at May 1999*
Prime Minister, Milorad Dodik
Deputy P.Ms, Djuradj Banjac *(Industry and Technology);* Ostoja Kremenović *(Internal Administration);* Savo Loncar *(Foreign Economic Relations);* Tihomir Gligorić *(Labour, Veterans and War Casualties)*
Agriculture, Waterways and Forestry, Milenko Savić
Defence, Manojlo Milovanović
Education, Nenad Suzić
Energy and Mining, Vladimir Dokić
Finance, Novak Kondić
Health and Social Welfare, Zeljko Rodić
Information, Rajko Vasić
Interior, Sredoje Nović
Justice, Milan Trbojević
Refugees and Displaced Persons, Milorad Dragicević
Religion, Jovo Turanjanin
Science and Culture, Zivojin Erić
Sport and Youth, Milorad Karalić
Trade and Tourism, Nikola Kragulj
Transport and Communications, Marko Pavić
Urban Planning, Construction, Housing, Public Services and Environment, Jovo Basić

EMBASSY OF THE REPUBLIC OF BOSNIA-HERCEGOVINA
4th Floor, Morley House, 320 Regent Street, London WIR 5AB
Tel 0171-255 3758
Ambassador Extraordinary and Plenipotentiary, HE Osman Topcagic, apptd 1998

BRITISH EMBASSY
8 Tina Ujevica, Sarajevo
Tel: Sarajevo 204781/2/3
Ambassador Extraordinary and Plenipotentiary, HE Graham Hand, apptd 1998

BRITISH COUNCIL REPRESENTATIVE, Claire Newton, 2nd Floor, Obala Kulina Bana 4, Sarajevo 71000

ECONOMY

Wheat, maize, potatoes and cabbage are among the major crops; crude steel and lignite are among the principal mineral products. In 1990 exports totalled US$2,876 million and imports US$2,548 million.

Trade with UK	1997	1998
Imports from UK	£10,015,000	£13,366,000
Exports to UK	1,368,000	2,281,000

BOTSWANA
The Republic of Botswana

AREA – 224,607 sq. miles (581,730 sq. km). Neighbours: South Africa (south and east), Zimbabwe (north and north-east), Namibia (west)
POPULATION – 1,490,000 (1994 UN estimate). The national language is Setswana and the official language is English
CAPITAL – Gaborone (population, 286,779, 1994 UN estimate)
MAJOR CITIES – Francistown (55,244); Lobatse (26,052); Selebi-Phikwe (39,772)
CURRENCY – Pula (P) of 100 thebe
NATIONAL ANTHEM – Fatshe La Rona
NATIONAL DAY – 30 September
NATIONAL FLAG – Light blue with a horizontal black stripe fimbriated in white across the centre
LIFE EXPECTANCY (years) – male 52.32; female 59.70
POPULATION GROWTH RATE – 2.3 per cent (1996)
POPULATION DENSITY – 3 per sq. km (1996)
URBAN POPULATION – 48.1 per cent (1995)

A plateau at a height of about 4,000 feet divides Botswana into two main topographical regions. To the east of the plateau streams flow into the Marico, Notwani and Limpopo rivers; to the west lies a flat region comprising the Kgalagadi Desert, the Okavango Swamps and the Northern State Lands area. The climate is generally sub-tropical.

HISTORY AND POLITICS

The Tswana people were dominant in the area now known as Botswana from the 17th century. In 1885, at the request of indigenous chiefs fearing invasion by the Boers, Britain formally took control of Bechuanaland, and in 1895 the territory was formally declared a British protectorate. On 30 September 1966 the British Protectorate of Bechuanaland became a republic within the Commonwealth under the name Botswana.

The last general election on 15 October 1994 was won by the Botswana Democratic Party with 26 seats to the Botswana National Front's 13 seats.

POLITICAL SYSTEM
The president is head of state and is elected by an absolute majority in the National Assembly. He appoints as vice-president a member of the National Assembly who is leader of government business in the National Assembly. The Assembly consists of the president, 40 members elected on a basis of universal adult suffrage, four specially elected members, the Attorney-General (non-voting) and the Speaker. Presidential and legislative elections are held every five years. There is also a 15-member House of Chiefs which considers legislation affecting the constitution and chieftaincy matters. In August 1997 the minimum voting age was lowered from 21 to 18.

HEAD OF STATE
President, HE Festus Mogae, *sworn in* 2 April 1998

CABINET *as at May 1999*
The President
Vice-President, Minister for Presidential Affairs and Public Administration, Lt.-Gen. Ian Khama
Agriculture, Ronald Sebego
Assistant Ministers, Lesedi Mothibamele *(Agriculture)*; vacant *(Finance and Development Planning)*; Joy Phumaphi, Boometswe Mokgothu *(Local Government, Lands and Housing)*

Commerce and Industry, George Kgoroba
Education, Gaositwe Chiepe
Finance and Development Planning, Ponatshego Kedikilwe
Foreign Affairs, Lt.-Gen. Mompati Merafhe
Health, Chapson Butale
Labour and Home Affairs, Bahiti Temane
Local Government, Lands and Housing, Daniel Kwelagobe
Mineral Resources, Energy and Water Affairs, Margaret Nasha
Works, Transport and Communications, David Magang

BOTSWANA HIGH COMMISSION
6 Stratford Place, London WIN 9AE
Tel 0171–499 0031
High Commissioner, HE Roy Warren Blackbeard, apptd 1999

BRITISH HIGH COMMISSION
Private Bag 0023, Gaborone
Tel: Gaborone 352841/2/3
High Commissioner, HE J. Wilde, apptd 1998

BRITISH COUNCIL REPRESENTATIVE, P. Mitchell, British High Commission Building, Queen's Road, The Mall, PO Box 439, Gaborone

DEFENCE

The Army has 30 armoured personnel carriers and 40 artillery pieces. The Air Wing has 40 combat aircraft.
MILITARY EXPENDITURE – 6.5 per cent of GDP (1997)
MILITARY PERSONNEL – 10,000: Army 8,500, Air Wing 500, Paramilitaries 1,000

ECONOMY

Agriculture is predominantly pastoral. The national herd is around 2.2 million cattle and one million sheep and goats. Cattle rearing accounts for about 85 per cent of agricultural output, and livestock products, particularly beef, are a major source of foreign exchange earnings.

Mineral extraction and processing is now the major source of income following the opening of large mines for diamonds and copper-nickel. Botswana is one of the largest producers of diamonds in the world, with diamonds accounting for 80 per cent of export revenue. Large deposits of coal have been discovered and are now being mined. Manufacturing industry is growing but it is still a small sector of the economy. Tourism is the third largest industry, generating about 7 per cent of GDP.

In 1996 the government had a trade surplus of US$791 million and a current account surplus of US$609 million. In 1997 imports totalled US$2,262 million and exports US$2,942 million.
GNP – US$5,070 million (1997); US$3,310 per capita (1997)
GDP – US$5,278 million (1995); US$3,640 per capita (1995)
ANNUAL AVERAGE GROWTH OF GDP – 7.0 per cent (1996)
INFLATION RATE – 9.3 per cent (1997)
TOTAL EXTERNAL DEBT – US$562 million (1997)

Trade with UK	1997	1998
Imports from UK	£20,460,000	£19,757,000
Exports to UK	108,978,000	77,430,000

COMMUNICATIONS

The railway from Cape Town to Zimbabwe passes through eastern Botswana. The main roads are the north-south road, which closely follows the railway, and the road running east-west that links Francistown and Maun. Air services are provided on a scheduled basis between the main towns.

EDUCATION

There are 657 primary schools, 163 community junior secondary schools and 23 government and government-aided senior secondary schools. Total enrolment in the tertiary sector (teacher training establishments, colleges of education and the University of Botswana) numbers 6,923.
ILLITERACY RATE – 30.2 per cent
ENROLMENT (percentage of age group) – primary 84 per cent (1996); secondary 45 per cent (1995); tertiary 5.8 per cent (1996)

BRAZIL
República Federativa do Brasil

AREA – 3,300,171 sq. miles (8,547,403 sq. km).
Neighbours: Guyana, Suriname, French Guiana, Colombia and Venezuela (north), Peru, Bolivia, Paraguay and Argentina (west), Uruguay (south)
POPULATION – 157,872,000 (1994 UN estimate).
Portuguese is the national language but Italian, Spanish, German, Japanese and Arabic are also spoken
CAPITAL – Brasília (population, 1,737,813, 1994 estimate)
MAJOR CITIES – Belo Horizonte (2,097,311); ΨFortaleza (1,917,236); ΨRecife (1,329,768); ΨRio de Janeiro (5,606,497), the former capital; ΨSalvador (2,262,731); São Paulo (10,017,821)
CURRENCY – Real of 100 centavos
NATIONAL ANTHEM – Ouviram do Ipirangas às Margens Placidas (From peaceful Ypiranga's banks)
NATIONAL DAY – 7 September (Independence Day)
NATIONAL FLAG – Green with a yellow lozenge containing a blue sphere studded with white stars, and crossed by a white band with the motto *Ordem e Progresso*
LIFE EXPECTANCY (years) – male 63.81; female 70.38
POPULATION GROWTH RATE – 1.4 per cent (1996)
POPULATION DENSITY – 18 per sq. km (1996)
URBAN POPULATION – 75.6 per cent (1991)

The north is mainly wide, low-lying, forest-clad plains. The central areas are principally plateau land and the east and south are traversed by successive mountain ranges interspersed with fertile valleys. The principal ranges are the Serra do Mar, the Serra da Mantiqueira and the Serra do Espinhaco along the east coast. The River Amazon flows from the Peruvian Andes to the Atlantic.

HISTORY AND POLITICS

Brazil was discovered by the Portuguese navigator Pedro Alvares Cabral in 1500 and colonized by Portugal in the early 16th century. In 1822 it became independent under Dom Pedro, son of King João VI of Portugal, who had been forced to flee to Brazil during the Napoleonic Wars. In 1889, Dom Pedro II was dethroned and a republic was proclaimed. In 1985 Brazil returned to democratic rule after two decades of military government.

Fernando Cardoso of the Social Democratic Party, part of the Liberal Front coalition, won the presidential election of October 1994 and was returned for a second term on 4 October 1998. In simultaneous legislative elections, the five-party coalition which supported him won 377 seats in the Chamber of Deputies and 21 state governorships. The coalition currently holds 68 seats in the Senate.

POLITICAL SYSTEM

The Federative Republic of Brazil is composed of the federal district and 26 states. Under the 1988 constitution the president, who heads the executive, is directly elected for a four-year term; in June 1997 the constitution was amended to allow the president to stand for a second term. The Congress consists of an 81-member Senate (three senators per state elected for an eight-year term) and a 517-member Chamber of Deputies which is elected every four years; the number of deputies per state depends upon the state's population. Each state has a Governor, and a Legislative Assembly with a four-year term.

FEDERAL STRUCTURE

Federal Unit	Area (sq. km)	Population (1991)	Capital
Central west			
Distrito Federal	5,822	1,601,094	Brasília
Goiás	341,290	4,018,903	Goiânia
Matto Grosso	906,807	2,027,231	Cuiabá
Matto Grosso do Sul	358,159	1,780,373	Campo Grande
North			
Acre	153,150	417,718	Rio Branco
Amapá	143,454	289,397	Macapá
Amazonas	1,577,820	2,103,243	Manaus
Pará	1,253,165	4,950,060	Belém
Rondônia	238,513	1,132,692	Pôrto Velho
Roraima	225,116	217,583	Boa Vista
Tocantins	278,421	919,863	Palmas
North-east			
Alagoas	27,933	2,514,100	Maceió
Bahia	567,295	11,867,991	Salvador
Ceará	146,348	6,366,647	Fortaleza
Maranhão	333,366	4,930,253	São Luís
Paraíba	56,585	3,201,114	João Pessoa
Pernambuco	98,938	7,127,855	Recife
Piaui	252,378	2,582,137	Teresina
Rio Grande do Norte	53,307	2,415,567	Natal
Sergipe	22,050	1,491,876	Aracajú
South			
Paraná	199,709	8,448,713	Curitiba
Rio Grande do Sul	282,062	9,138,670	Pôrto Alegre
Santa Catarina	95,443	4,541,994	Florianópolis
South-east			
Espírito Santo	46,184	2,600,618	Vitória
Minas Gerais	588,384	15,743,152	Belo Horizonte
Rio de Janeiro	43,910	12,807,706	Rio de Janeiro
São Paulo	248,809	31,588,925	São Paulo

HEAD OF STATE

President, Fernando Henrique Cardoso, *sworn in* 1 January 1995
Vice-President, Marco Maciel

CABINET *as at May 1999*

Agriculture, Francisco Turra
Armed Forces Chief of Staff, Gen. Benedito Bezerra Leonel
Civilian Household of the Presidency, Clovis de Barros Cavalho
Communications, João Pimenta da Veiga
Culture, Francisco Correa Weffort
Defence, Elcio Alvares
Development, Industry and Commerce, Celso Lafer
Education, Paulo Renato de Souza
Energy and Mines, Rodolfo Tourinho
Environment, José Sarney Filho
Finance, Pedro Malan
Foreign Affairs, Luiz Felipe Lampreia
Health, José Serra
Justice, José Renan Calheiros

Labour and Employment, Francisco Dornelles
Land Reform, Raúl Jungmann
Military Household of the Presidency, Gen. Alberto Cardoso
Planning, Budget and Co-ordination, vacant
Regional Policies, Ovidio de Angeles
Science and Technology, Luiz Carlos Bresser Pereira
Social Security and Welfare, Waldeck Vieira Ornelas
Special Affairs, Ronaldo Sardenberg
Sports and Tourism, Raphael Grecca
Transport, Eliseu Padilha

BRAZILIAN EMBASSY
32 Green Street, London WIY 4AT
Tel 0171-499 0877
Ambassador Extraordinary and Plenipotentiary, HE Rubens
   Antonio Barbosa, GCVO, apptd 1994
Military Attachés, Capt. Gilberto Hirschfeld, Col. Paulo
   Chagas, Gp. Capt. Alberto Pires Rolla
Counsellor (Commercial Affairs), João de Mendonça Lima
   Neto

There is also a Brazilian Consulate-General in London
and honorary consular offices at Cardiff and Glasgow.

BRITISH EMBASSY
Setor de Embaixadas Sul, Quadra 801, Conjunto K, CEP
70.408–900, Brasilia DF
Tel: Brasilia 225 2710
Ambassador Extraordinary and Plenipotentiary, HE Keith
   Haskell, CMG, CVO, apptd 1995
Deputy Head of Mission, Consul-General, J. A. Penney
Defence Attaché, Col. J. M. Bowles, MBE
First Secretary, J. F. Jarvine

There are British Consulates-General at Rio de Janeiro
and São Paulo.

BRITISH COUNCIL REPRESENTATIVE, Howard
   Thompson, OBE, Edifício Morro Vermilho, Quadra 1.
   Bloco H, SCS, 70399–900, Brasilia. Regional directors
   in Recife, Rio de Janeiro and São Paulo

BRITISH AND COMMONWEALTH CHAMBER OF
   COMMERCE IN SÃO PAULO, Rua Barão de Itapetininga
   275, 7th Floor, 01042, São Paulo (*Postal Address,* PO Box
   1621, 01000 São Paulo) and Rua Real Grandeza 99,
   22281 Rio de Janeiro

DEFENCE

The Army has 60 main battle tanks, 803 armoured
personnel carriers, 593 artillery pieces and 76 helicopters.
The Navy has bases at Rio de Janeiro, Salvador, Recife,
Belém, Floriancholis, Ladario and Manaus. It is equipped
with six submarines, one aircraft carrier, 18 frigates and 36
patrol and coastal vessels. Naval aviation has 22 combat
aircraft and 54 armed helicopters, the Marines have 33
armoured personnel carriers and 39 artillery pieces. The
Air Force has 278 combat aircraft and 29 armed helicopters.

MILITARY EXPENDITURE – 2.3 per cent of GDP (1997)
MILITARY PERSONNEL – 313,250: Army 195,000, Navy
   68,250, Air Force 50,000
CONSCRIPTION DURATION – 12 months (can be extended
   to 18)

ECONOMY

There are large mineral deposits including iron ore
(hematite), manganese, bauxite, beryllium, chrome, nickel,
tungsten, cassiterite, lead, gold, monazite (containing rare
earths and thorium) and zirconium. Diamonds and precious
and semi-precious stones are also found. Brazil is the
world's largest producer of coffee; the other main agricul-

tural products are cassava, maize, soya, rice, wheat, black
beans, potatoes, cotton, cocoa, tobacco and peanuts.
   Successive governments have attempted to curb high
inflation and large budget deficits. A new, supposedly non-
inflationary currency, the real, was introduced in 1994, but
had to be devalued by nearly nine per cent in January 1999
as a result of the effects of the global financial crisis on the
Brazilian economy, which had resulted in the government
announcing a R$20 billion austerity package in November
1997. The plan doubled interest rates, increased taxes and
cut budgets. In March 1998, unemployment reached its
highest level since 1985 and in November, inflation hit 40
per cent. The IMF agreed a US$41.5 billion rescue package
in November 1998 and in March 1999 made the reduction
of inflation and overall public debt preconditions of the
loan.
GNP – US$784,044 million (1997); US$4,790 per capita
   (1997)
GDP – US$717,187 million (1995); US$4,510 per capita
   (1995)
ANNUAL AVERAGE GROWTH OF GDP – 4.2 per cent
   (1995)
INFLATION RATE – 6.9 per cent (1997)
UNEMPLOYMENT – 6.2 per cent (1993)
TOTAL EXTERNAL DEBT – US$193,663 million (1997)

TRADE

Principal imports are machinery, fuel and lubricants,
mineral products, transport equipment and chemicals.
Principal exports are industrial goods, coffee, iron ore and
soya. In 1994 the Brazilian automobile industry produced
1,400,000 vehicles. Of these, 374,000 vehicles were exported. The main trading partners are the USA, Argentina
and the EU.
   In 1995 Brazil had a trade deficit of US$3,157 million
and a current account deficit of US$18,136 million. In 1997
imports totalled US$65,007 million and exports US$52,987
million.

Trade with UK	1997	1998
Imports from UK	£1,027,974,000	£921,300,000
Exports to UK	954,936,000	928,961,000

COMMUNICATIONS

There are 1,670,148 km of highways and the route-length
of railways is 30,129 km. There are ten international
airports and internal air services are highly developed.
There are 21,944 miles of navigable inland waterways. Rio
de Janeiro and Santos are the two leading ports.

EDUCATION

The education system includes both public and private
institutions. Public education is free at all levels.
ILLITERACY RATE – 16.7 per cent
ENROLMENT (percentage of age group) – primary 90 per
   cent (1994); secondary 19 per cent (1994); tertiary 11.3
   per cent (1995)

BRUNEI
Negara Brunei Darussalam

AREA – 2,226 sq. miles (5,765 sq. km). Neighbour:
   Malaysia
POPULATION – 300,000 (1996 official estimate): 66.9 per
   cent Malay, 15.2 per cent Chinese, 5.9 per cent
   indigenous races and 12 per cent European, Indian and
   other races. The majority are Sunni Muslims. The
   official language is Malay; English and dialects of
   Chinese are also spoken

CAPITAL – Bandar Seri Begawan (population, 49,902, 1994 estimate)
CURRENCY – Brunei dollar (B$) of 100 sen (fully interchangeable with Singapore currency)
NATIONAL ANTHEM – Allah Peliharakan Sultan (God Bless His Majesty)
NATIONAL DAY – 23 February
NATIONAL FLAG – Yellow with diagonal stripes of white over black and the arms in red all over the centre
LIFE EXPECTANCY (years) – male 70.13; female 72.69
POPULATION GROWTH RATE – 2.8 per cent (1996)
POPULATION DENSITY – 52 per sq. km (1996)
URBAN POPULATION – 66.6 per cent (1991)
ILLITERACY RATE – 11.8 per cent
ENROLMENT (percentage of age group) – primary 91 per cent (1994); secondary 68 per cent (1994); tertiary 6.6 per cent (1996)

Brunei is situated on the north-west coast of the island of Borneo. It has a humid tropical climate.

HISTORY AND POLITICS

Formerly a powerful Muslim sultanate, Brunei was reduced to its present size by the mid-19th century and became a British Protectorate in 1888. In 1959 the Sultan promulgated the first written constitution, and on 1 January 1984 Brunei resumed full independence from Britain.

POLITICAL SYSTEM

Supreme executive authority rests with the Sultan, who presides over and is advised by the Privy Council, the Religious Council and the Council of Ministers. The Sultan effectively rules by decree as a state of emergency has been in effect since a revolt in 1962; there are no political parties and no elections.

HEAD OF STATE

HM The Sultan of Brunei, HM Sultan Haji Hassanal Bolkiah Mu'izzaddin Waddaullah, Sultan and Yang Di-Pertuan, GCB, *acceded* 1967, *crowned* 1 August 1968

COUNCIL OF MINISTERS *as at May 1999*

Prime Minister, Defence, Finance, HM The Sultan
Communications, Pehin Dato Zakaria
Development, Pengiran Dato Haji Ismail
Education; Health (acting), Pehin Dato Haji Abdul Aziz
Foreign Affairs, Prince Mohamed Bolkiah
Home Affairs, Special Adviser to the Sultan, Pehin Dato Haji Isa
Industry and Primary Resources, Pehin Dato Haji Abdul Rahman
Law, Pengiran Haji Bahrin
Religious Affairs, Pehin Dato Haji Mohammad Zain
Youth, Sports and Culture, Pehin Dato Haji Hussein

BRUNEI DARUSSALAM HIGH COMMISSION
19–20 Belgrave Square, London SW1X 8PG
Tel 0171-581 0521
High Commissioner, HE Pehin Dato Jaya Abdul Latif, apptd 1997

BRITISH HIGH COMMISSION
2/01 2nd Floor Block D, Komplexs Bangunan Yayasan, Sultan Haji Hassanal Bolkiah, Jalan Pretty, PO Box 2197, Bandar Seri Begawan 1921
Tel: Bandar Seri Begawan 222231
High Commissioner, Stuart Laing, apptd 1998

BRITISH COUNCIL REPRESENTATIVE, T. Walsh, 45 Simpang 100, Jalan Tungku Link, Gadong, Bandar Seri Begawan 3192

DEFENCE

The Army has 26 armoured personnel carriers. The Navy, based in Muara, has nine patrol and coastal vessels. The Air Force has six armed helicopters.
MILITARY EXPENDITURE – 6.7 per cent of GDP (1997)
MILITARY PERSONNEL – 9,050: Army 3,900, Navy 700, Air Force 400, Paramilitaries 4,050

ECONOMY

The economy is based on the production of oil and natural gas. Royalties and taxes from these operations form the bulk of government revenue and have enabled the construction of free health, education and welfare services. However, the Asian economic slump coupled with a 40 per cent drop in the price of oil have damaged the economy.

The country has eight hospitals, 350 schools and one university. Royal Brunei Airlines operates scheduled flights to the UK, Australia and throughout the Far East. Radio Television Brunei broadcasts one television and three radio channels from the capital.

In 1997 Brunei produced 8,052,000 tonnes of crude petroleum and 11,600 million cubic metres of natural gas. In 1994 imports totalled US$1,634 million and exports US$2,215 million.
GNP – US$3,975 million (1994); US$14,240 per capita (1994)
GDP – US$4,888 million (1995); US$16,683 per capita (1995)
ANNUAL AVERAGE GROWTH OF GDP – 1.8 per cent (1995)

Trade with UK	1997	1998
Imports from UK	£560,184,000	£257,197,000
Exports to UK	336,627,000	183,564,000

BULGARIA
Republika Bulgaria

AREA – 42,823 sq. miles (110,912 sq. km). Neighbours: Romania (north), Serbia and the Former Yugoslav Republic of Macedonia (west), Greece and Turkey (south)
POPULATION – 8,356,000 (1997 estimate). The language is Bulgarian, a Southern Slavonic tongue closely allied to Serbo-Croat and Russian with local admixtures of modern Greek, Albanian and Turkish words. The alphabet is Cyrillic. The predominant religion is the Bulgarian Orthodox Church
CAPITAL – Sofia (population, 1,191,743, 1994 estimate)
MAJOR CITIES – ΨBourgas (215,035); Dobritch (104,074); Plévène (156,950); Plovdiv (346,330); Roussé (185,002); Slivène (144,675); Stara Zagora (176,045); ΨVarna (310,408), 1994 estimates
CURRENCY – Lev of 100 stotinki
NATIONAL DAY – 3 March
NATIONAL FLAG – Three horizontal bands, white, green, red
LIFE EXPECTANCY (years) – male 67.71; female 74.72
POPULATION GROWTH RATE – –1.2 per cent (1996)
POPULATION DENSITY – 75 per sq. km (1996)
URBAN POPULATION – 67.4 per cent (1993)

HISTORY AND POLITICS

A principality of Bulgaria was created by the Treaty of Berlin in 1878, and in 1908 the country was declared an independent kingdom. A coup d'état in September 1944 gave power to the Fatherland Front, a coalition of Communists, Agrarians and Social Democrats. In August 1945, the main body of Agrarians and Social Democrats left the government. A referendum in September 1946 led to the abolition of the monarchy and the establishment of a republic.

The post-war period was dominated by the Communist Party (BCP), led by Todor Zhivkov. He was forced to resign in November 1989, and in January 1990 the National Assembly voted to abolish the BCP's constitutional guarantee of power. Multiparty elections to a Grand National Assembly (parliament) were held in June 1990 and won by the BCP, renamed the Bulgarian Socialist Party (BSP). This government lasted only two months, and in December 1990 a multiparty government was formed which began to implement a programme of economic and political reform.

After legislative elections in October 1991 a coalition government of the Union of Democratic Forces (UDF) and the Turkish Movement for Rights and Freedom Party (MRF) was formed. This government was replaced in December 1992 by a weak government of non-party technocrats which also collapsed. The BSP won the ensuing general election in December 1994 and formed a government with the Agrarian National Union (ANU). In November 1996 the UDF candidate, Petar Stoyanov, became president. The following month the BSP Prime Minister Jan Videnov resigned following protests about falling standards of living. The UDF won the resulting elections in April 1997.

POLITICAL SYSTEM

A new constitution enshrining democracy and the free market was adopted in 1991. It provides for a directly-elected president who serves for no more than two five-year terms. The chief executive is the prime minister who is appointed by the president, and is usually the leader of the largest party in the legislature. There is a unicameral National Assembly of 240 members who are directly elected by proportional representation for five-year terms.

HEAD OF STATE
President, Petar Stoyanov, *elected* 3 November 1996

COUNCIL OF MINISTERS *as at May 1999*
Prime Minister, Ivan Kostov
Deputy P.M, Education and Science, Vesselin Metodiev
Deputy P.M, Industry, Aleksander Bozhkov
Deputy P.M, Regional and Urban Development, Evgenii Bakurdjiev
Agriculture, Forestry and Land Reform, Ventsislav Vurbanov
Culture, Emma Moskova
Defence, Georgi Ananiev
Environment and Water, Evdokia Maneva
Finance, Mouravei Radev
Foreign Affairs, Nadezhda Mihailova
Health, Peter Boyadjiev
Interior, Bogomil Bonev
Justice and European Legal Integration, Vassil Gotsev
Labour and Social Affairs, Ivan Neikov
Secretary-General to the Cabinet, State Administration, Mario Tagarinski
Trade and Tourism, Valentin Vassilev
Transport, Wilhelm Kraus

EMBASSY OF THE REPUBLIC OF BULGARIA
186–188 Queen's Gate, London SW7 5HL
Tel 0171–584 9400
Ambassador Extraordinary and Plenipotentiary, HE Valentin Dobrev, apptd 1998

Counsellor (Commercial), Hrist Charenkov
Military, Air and Naval Attaché, Lt.-Gen. Anu Anguelov

BRITISH EMBASSY
38 Boulevard Vassil Levski, Sofia
Tel: Sofia 2980 1220
Ambassador Extraordinary and Plenipotentiary, HE Richard Stagg, apptd 1998
Deputy Head of Mission, Consul and First Secretary, M. Tatham
Defence Attaché, Col. R. E. Fielding
First Secretary (Commercial), M. J. Carbine

BRITISH COUNCIL REPRESENTATIVE, K. Lewis, 7 Tulovo Street, 1504, Sofia

DEFENCE

The Army has 1,475 main battle tanks, 214 armoured infantry fighting vehicles, 1,894 armoured personnel carriers and 1,744 artillery pieces. The Navy has two submarines, one frigate, 25 patrol and coastal vessels, and nine armed helicopters. The Air Force has 217 combat aircraft and 44 armed helicopters.

MILITARY EXPENDITURE – 3.4 per cent of GDP (1997)
MILITARY PERSONNEL – 109,800: Army 50,400, Navy 6,100, Air Force 19,300, Paramilitaries 34,000
CONSCRIPTION DURATION – 12 months

ECONOMY

The principal crops are wheat, maize, beet, tomatoes, tobacco, oleaginous seeds, fruit, vegetables and cotton. The livestock includes cattle, sheep, goats, pigs, horses, asses, mules and water buffaloes. Cadmium, coal, copper, pig iron, kaolin, lead, silver and zinc are produced.

The lack of radical economic reform has hampered economic development; in 1996, the value of the lev plummeted by 70 per cent and food shortages were commonplace. The government responded by adopting a radical reform package including the closure of 70 state companies, but interest rates and inflation reached 300 per cent a year.

The lev was pegged to the Deutsche Mark from 1 July 1997, at a rate of DM1 = 1,000 leva. Privatizations in 1997 were expected to raise 600 billion leva. Following the implementation of fiscal reforms, Bulgaria received some US$385 million in loans from the EU and the World Bank to help economic recovery. The World Bank agreed a further loan of US$275 million in April 1999.

GNP – US$9,750 million (1997); US$1,170 per capita (1997)
GDP – US$12,918 million (1995); US$1,518 per capita (1995)
ANNUAL AVERAGE GROWTH OF GDP – 2.5 per cent (1995)
INFLATION RATE – 1,082.3 per cent (1997)
UNEMPLOYMENT – 11.1 per cent (1995)
TOTAL EXTERNAL DEBT – US$9,858 million (1997)

TRADE

The principal imports are fuels, minerals and metals, engineering goods and industrial equipment. The principal exports are agricultural produce, engineering goods and industrial equipment, industrial consumer goods, chemicals and fuels, minerals and metals.

In 1993 Bulgaria signed an Association Agreement with the EU, and EU duties on many Bulgarian industrial goods were abolished by 1995 and levies on agricultural goods significantly lowered.

In 1997 Bulgaria had a trade surplus of US$395 million

and a current account surplus of US$444 million. The principal trading partners are Russia, Germany and Italy.

Trade with UK	1997	1998
Imports from UK	£77,181,000	£80,417,000
Exports to UK	91,029,000	78,160,000

EDUCATION

Education is free and compulsory for children from seven to 15 years inclusive. There are three universities (at Sofia, Plovdiv and Veliko Turnovo), an American University and 21 higher education establishments.
ILLITERACY RATE – 1.7 per cent
ENROLMENT (percentage of age group) – primary 92 per cent (1996); secondary 74 per cent (1996); tertiary 41.2 per cent (1996)

BURKINA FASO

AREA – 105,792 sq. miles (274,000 sq. km). Neighbours: Mali (west), Niger and Benin (east), Togo, Ghana and Côte d'Ivoire (south)
POPULATION – 10,780,000 (1994 UN estimate). The official language is French. Mossi, More, Dioula and Gourmantché are indigenous languages
CAPITAL – Ouagadougou (population, 634,479, 1991 estimate)
MAJOR CITIES – Bobo-Dioulasso (228,668); Koudougou (30,000)
CURRENCY – Franc CFA of 100 centimes
NATIONAL ANTHEM – Ditanyé
NATIONAL DAY – 11 December
NATIONAL FLAG – Equal bands of red over green, with a yellow star in centre
LIFE EXPECTANCY (years) – male 45.84; female 49.01
POPULATION GROWTH RATE – 3.0 per cent (1996)
POPULATION DENSITY – 39 per sq. km (1996)
URBAN POPULATION – 15.0 per cent (1995)
MILITARY EXPENDITURE – 2.2 per cent of GDP (1997)
MILITARY PERSONNEL – 10,000: Army 5,600, Air Force 200, Paramilitaries 4,200
ILLITERACY RATE – 80.8 per cent
ENROLMENT (percentage of age group) – primary 31 per cent (1994); secondary 7 per cent (1993); tertiary 1.0 per cent (1995)

Burkina Faso (formerly Upper Volta) is an inland savannah state in West Africa. The largest tribe is the Mossi whose king, the Moro Naba, still wields a certain moral influence.

HISTORY AND POLITICS

Burkina Faso was annexed by France in 1896 and between 1932 and 1947 was administered as part of the Colony of the Ivory Coast. It decided on 11 December 1958 to remain an autonomous republic within the French Community; full independence outside the Community was proclaimed on 5 August 1960.
  In 1966 the Army assumed power; a constitution allowing for a partial return to civilian rule was adopted in 1970, but was suspended in 1974. Full legislative and presidential elections were held again in 1978.
  Following a number of military coups, Capt. Blaise Compaoré seized power in 1987. A new constitution was adopted in 1991. Presidential elections were held in November 1998 and won by Compaoré in the face of a boycott by the opposition parties.

HEAD OF STATE
President, Capt. Blaise Compaoré, assumed office October 1987, elected December 1991, re-elected November 1998

COUNCIL OF MINISTERS as at May 1999
Prime Minister, Economy and Finance, Kadré Désiré Ouedraogo
Agriculture, Bongnessan Arsène Yé
Animal Resources, Alassane Seré
Basic and Mass Education, Baworo Seydou Sanou
Civil Service and Institutional Development, Paramanga Ernest Yonli
Communications and Culture, Mahamoudou Ouedraogo
Defence, Albert D. Millogo
Economy and Finance (government spokesman), Tertius Zongo
Employment, Labour, Social Security, Elie Sarré
Energy and Mines, Elie Ouedraogo
Foreign Affairs, Youssouf Ouedraogo
Health, Alain Ludovic Tou
Infrastructure, Housing, Urban Planning, Joseph Kaboré
Justice, Keeper of the Seals, Paul Kiemde
Presidency Representative, Pierre Tapsoba
Regional Integration, Bernadette Sanou
Relations with Parliament, Cyril Goungounga
Secondary and Higher Education, Scientific Research, Christophe Dabiré
Social Affairs and Family, Bana Ouandaogo
Territorial Administration and Security, Yéro Boly
Trade, Industry and Crafts, Idrissa Zampalegré
Transport and Tourism, Bédouma Alain Yoda
Water and Environment, Salif Diallo
Women's Promotion, Alice Tiendrebeogo
Youth and Sports, Joseph André Tiendrebeogo

EMBASSY OF BURKINA FASO
16 Place Guy d'Arezzo, 1060 Brussels, Belgium
Tel: Brussels 345 9912
Ambassador Extraordinary and Plenipotentiary, vacant
HONORARY CONSULATE, 5 Cinnamon Row, Plantation Wharf, London SW11 3TW. Tel: 0171-738 1800. Honorary Consul-General, S. G. Singer

BRITISH AMBASSADOR, HE Haydon Warren-Gash, CMG, resident at Abidjan, Côte d'Ivoire

ECONOMY

The principal industry is cattle and sheep rearing. Agriculture employs one fifth of the workforce and contributes 10 per cent of GDP. The chief exports are livestock, groundnuts, millet and sorghum. Small deposits of gold, manganese, copper, bauxite and graphite have been found.
  In 1994 Burkina Faso had a trade deficit of US$129 million and a current account surplus of US$15 million. In 1996 imports totalled US$700 million and exports US$305 million.
GNP – US$2,579 million (1997); US$250 per capita (1997)
GDP – US$1,726 million (1995); US$165 per capita (1995)
ANNUAL AVERAGE GROWTH OF GDP – 4.5 per cent (1995)
INFLATION RATE – 2.3 per cent (1997)
TOTAL EXTERNAL DEBT – US$1,297 million (1997)

Trade with UK	1997	1998
Imports from UK	£5,798,000	£5,149,000
Exports to UK	1,193,000	1,182,000

BURUNDI
République du Burundi

AREA – 10,747 sq. miles (27,834 sq. km). Neighbours: Rwanda (north), Tanzania (east and south), Democratic Republic of Congo (west)
POPULATION – 6,088,000 (1994 UN estimate): 83 per cent Hutu, 15 per cent Tutsi. The official languages are Kirundi, a Bantu language, and French. Kiswahili is also used
CAPITAL – Bujumbura (formerly Usumbura) (population, 235,440, 1994)
MAJOR CITIES – Kitega (18,000)
CURRENCY – Burundi franc of 100 centimes
NATIONAL DAY – 1 July
NATIONAL FLAG – Divided diagonally by a white saltire into red and green triangles; on a white disc in the centre three red six-pointed stars edged in green
NATIONAL ANTHEM – Uburundi Bwacu
LIFE EXPECTANCY (years) – male 48.42; female 51.92
POPULATION GROWTH RATE – 1.8 per cent (1996)
POPULATION DENSITY – 219 per sq. km (1996)
URBAN POPULATION – 5.0 per cent (1990)
MILITARY EXPENDITURE – 5.7 per cent of GDP (1997)
MILITARY PERSONNEL – 43,500: Army 40,000, Paramilitaries 3,500
ILLITERACY RATE – 64.7 per cent
ENROLMENT (percentage of age group) – primary 52 per cent (1992); secondary 5 per cent (1992); tertiary 0.9 per cent (1995)

HISTORY AND POLITICS

Formerly a Belgian trusteeship under the United Nations, Burundi became independent as a constitutional monarchy on 1 July 1962. However, the monarchy was overthrown in 1966 and the country became a republic. After a coup in 1987 the Military Committee of National Redemption came to power, led by Maj. Pierre Buyoya, a Tutsi.

Although most of the population is Hutu, political and military power has traditionally rested with the Tutsi minority. Since the 1960s, Hutu attempts to overthrow Tutsi rule have resulted in ethnic massacres. The Tutsi-dominated army attempted a coup in 1993 in which President Melchior Ndadaye was killed. The government regained control in December but two months of inter-racial fighting left more than 50,000 dead and 500,000 refugees.

The Front for Democracy in Burundi (FRODEBU) and the National Unity and Progress Party (UPRONA) agreed to form a coalition government in 1994 with a Tutsi prime minister and Hutu president. However, the government was unable to halt attacks by the Tutsi-dominated army and Hutu militias on each other's communities. The fighting claimed 200,000 lives in 1993–5.

In July 1996 the army again seized power and installed Maj. Buyoya as president. Political parties were banned and the National Assembly was suspended until October 1996 when fewer than half its deputies attended. A multi-ethnic government of national unity was formed in August 1996. Clashes between the army and Hutu militias, and massacres of civilians have continued, despite talks aimed at finding a peaceful solution. More than 300,000 refugees remain in camps in Tanzania and the Democratic Republic of Congo.

A new transitional constituton, designed to provide for a political partnership between Hutus and Tutsis, came into being in June 1998 and a 117-member Transitional National Assembly was inaugurated in July 1998.

HEAD OF STATE

President, Maj. Pierre Buyoya, *appointed* 25 July 1996 , *sworn in* 11 June 1998
Vice–Presidents, Frédéric Bamvunginyumvira; Mathias Sinamenye

COUNCIL OF MINISTERS *as at May 1999*

Agriculture and Livestock, Salvator Ntihabose
Communal Development and Handicrafts, Gaspard Ntirampeba
Defence, Lt.-Col. Alfred Nkurunziza
Development Planning and Reconstruction, Léon Nimbona
Education, Prosper Mpawenayo
Energy and Mines, Bernard Barandereka
External Relations and Co-operation, Séverin Ntahomvukiye
Finance, Astère Girukwigomba
Health, Juma Mohamed Kariburyo
Human Rights, Institutional Reforms and Relations with National Assembly, Eugéne Nindorera
Information and Government Spokesman, Luc Rukingama
Internal Affairs and Public Security, Col. Ascension Twagiramungu
Justice, Térence Sinunguruza
Labour, Civil Service and Professional Training, Emmanuel Tungamwese
Land and Environment, Jean-Pacifique Nsengiyumva
Peace Process, Ambroise Niyonsaba
Public Works and Housing, Denis Nshimirimana
Reintegration and Resettlement of Displaced Persons and Repatriates, Pascal Ngurunziza
Trade, Industry and Tourism, Nestor Nyabenda
Transport, Posts and Telecommunications, Col. Epitace Bayaganakandi
Women, Welfare and Social Affairs, Romaine Ndorimana
Youth, Sports and Culture, Gérard Nyamwiza

EMBASSY OF THE REPUBLIC OF BURUNDI
Square Marie Louise 46, 1040 Brussels, Belgium
Tel: Brussels 2304535
Ambassador Extraordinary and Plenipotentiary, HE Jonathas Niyungeko, resident in Brussels
BRITISH AMBASSADOR, HE Kaye Oliver, OBE, resident at Kigali, Rwanda

ECONOMY

The chief crops are coffee, tea and cotton, accounting for over 80 per cent of export earnings. Mineral, hide and skin exports are also important.

A total economic blockade was imposed by Cameroon, Ethiopia, Kenya, Rwanda, Tanzania, Uganda and Zaïre (now the Democratic Republic of Congo) following the 1996 coup. This was relaxed slightly in April 1997 to allow food and medicine into the country and removed in February 1999.

In 1997 there was a trade deficit of US$11 million and a current account surplus of US$4 million. In 1997 imports totalled US$121 million and exports US$86 million.

GNP – US$924 million (1997); US$140 per capita (1997)
GDP – US$1,241 million (1995); US$205 per capita (1995)
ANNUAL AVERAGE GROWTH OF GDP – 6.6 per cent (1995)
INFLATION RATE – 31.1 per cent (1997)
TOTAL EXTERNAL DEBT – US$1,066 million (1997)

Trade with UK	1997	1998
Imports from UK	£2,224,000	£2,296,000
Exports to UK	8,867,000	188,000

CAMBODIA

AREA – 69,898 sq. miles (181,035 sq. km). Neighbours:
Laos (north), Thailand (north and west), Vietnam (east)
POPULATION – 10,273,000 (1997 estimate). The language
is Khmer. Chinese and Vietnamese are also spoken
CAPITAL – ΨPhnom Penh (population, 832,000, 1997)
CURRENCY – Riel of 100 sen
NATIONAL ANTHEM – Nokoreach
NATIONAL DAY – 9 November (Independence Day)
NATIONAL FLAG – Three horizontal stripes of blue, red,
blue, with the blue of double width and containing a
representation of the temple of Angkor in white
LIFE EXPECTANCY (years) – male 50.10; female 52.90
POPULATION GROWTH RATE – 3.0 per cent (1996)
POPULATION DENSITY – 57 per sq. km (1996)
URBAN POPULATION – 14.4 per cent (1996)
ILLITERACY RATE – 34.7 per cent
ENROLMENT (percentage of age group) – primary 97 per
cent (1996); tertiary 1.4 per cent (1996)

HISTORY AND POLITICS

Cambodia became a French protectorate in 1863 and was
granted independence within the French Union as an
Associate State in 1949. Full independence was proclaimed
in 1953, and Prince Norodom Sihanouk became head of
state. In 1970 Prince Sihanouk was deposed and a Khmer
Republic was declared.

In 1975, Phnom Penh fell to the North Vietnamese-
backed Khmer Rouge. During Khmer Rouge rule hundreds
of thousands of Cambodians fled into exile and an estimated
two million were killed.

In 1978, Vietnamese troops invaded Cambodia and the
state was renamed The People's Republic of Kampuchea
(PRK); in 1989 it became the State of Cambodia (SOC).
Following the Vietnamese withdrawal in 1989, the resistance forces regained ground.

In September 1990, the government and the resistance
forces established a Supreme National Council and peace
agreements were signed in October 1991. In March 1992
the United Nations Transitional Authority for Cambodia
(UNTAC) assumed authority from the government in the
run-up to the May 1993 elections.

Multiparty elections were held in May 1993. Prince
Sihanouk brokered a coalition government agreement
under which he became head of state and the leaders of
the United Front for an Independent, Neutral, Peaceful
and Co-operative Cambodia (FUNCINPEC) and the
Cambodian People's Party (CPP) (the former SOC party),
Prince Ranariddh and Hun Sen, became co-prime ministers. In September 1993 a new constitution was adopted
under which Cambodia became a pluralist liberal democracy with a constitutional monarchy. Prince Sihanouk was
elected king and he appointed a new government.

Prince Ranariddh was ousted from power following a
coup by soldiers loyal to Hun Sen in July 1997, and armed
conflicts between the rival factions broke out throughout
the country. At the opening of the United Nations General
Assembly in September, a resolution was adopted that
prevented Cambodia from taking its seat until the merits
of the rival delegations, those of Prince Ranariddh and
Hun Sen, could be assessed. On 27 February 1998, both
sides declared a cease-fire under a Japanese-brokered peace
plan. Under the terms of the deal Prince Ranariddh was
tried by the Hun Sen government and unconditionally
pardoned after being found guilty; he then returned to the
country for democratic elections in July 1998.

In November 1998 a coalition government was formed
with Hun Sen as prime minister and Prince Ranariddh as
chairman of the National Assembly and on 7 December
1998, Cambodia reoccupied its seat at the United Nations.

INSURGENCIES

In July 1994 the Royal Government outlawed the Khmer
Rouge, which responded by declaring a provisional
government. Large numbers of Khmer Rouge defected to
the Royal Government including more than 2,500 led by
Ieng Sary, who formally joined the Royal Cambodian
Armed Forces in November 1996. Khmer Rouge leader
Pol Pot was captured by a group of defectors in June 1997
and died in captivity on 15 April 1998. The remaining
4,332 Khmer Rouge soldiers surrendered on 9 February
1999.

POLITICAL SYSTEM

Legislative power is vested in the National Assembly,
which has 122 members elected for five-year terms, and
the Senate, which has 61 appointed members and was
formed on 25 March 1999, following an amendment to the
constitution by the National Assembly. Executive power
rests in the Royal Government, with the King having the
power only to make appointments and declare a state of
emergency, in consultation with the government.

HEAD OF STATE

HM The King of Cambodia, Norodom Sihanouk, *elected by the
Council of the Throne* 24 September 1993

ROYAL GOVERNMENT OF CAMBODIA *as at May 1999*

Prime Minister, Hun Sen (CPP)
Deputy Prime Minister, Co-Minister of Interior, Sar Kheng
(CPP)
Deputy Prime Minister, Education, Youth and Sports, Tol Loah
(F)
Agriculture, Forestry and Fishing, Chhea Song (CPP)
Co-Minister of National Defence, Prince Sisowath Sereiroat
(F)
Commerce, Cham Prasit (CPP)

Culture and Fine Arts, Princess Norodom Bophadevi (F)
Environment, Mok Maret (CPP)
Foreign Affairs and International Co-operation, Hor Namhong (CPP)
Health, Hong Sun-huot (F)
Industry, Mines and Energy, Suy Sem (CPP)
Information and Press, Loe Laysreng (F)
Justice, Uk Vithun (F)
Landscaping, Urbanism and Construction, Im Chhunlim (CPP)
Planning, Chhay Than (CPP)
Post and Telecommunications, So Khun (CPP)
Public Works and Transport, Khi Tanglim (F)
Relations with National Assembly and Inspection, Khun Hang (F)
Religious Affairs, Chea Savoeun (F)
Rural Development, Chhim Siekleng (F)
Social Affairs, Labour, Vocational Training and Youth Rehabilitation, It Sam-heng (CPP)
State Minister, Co-minister of Interior, Yu Hokkri (F)
State Minister, Co-Minister of National Defence, Gen. Tie Banh (CPP)
State Minister, Economy and Finance, Keat Chong (CPP)
State Minister, Office of the Council of Ministers, Sok An (CPP)
State Ministers, Loe Laysreng (F); Hor Namhong (F)
Tourism, Veng Sereivut (F)
Water Resources, Lim Kean-hao (CPP)
Women's and Veteran's Affairs, Mu Sok-huo (F)

CPP Cambodian People's Party; F FUNCINPEC

BRITISH EMBASSY
29, Street 75, Phnom Penh
Tel: Phnom Penh 427124
Ambassador Extraordinary and Plenipotentiary, HE George Edgar, apptd 1997

DEFENCE

The Army has 100 main battle tanks, 240 armoured personnel carriers and 400 artillery pieces. The Navy has 33 patrol and coastal vessels. The Air Force has 20 combat aircraft.
MILITARY EXPENDITURE – 7.3 per cent of GDP (1997)
MILITARY PERSONNEL – 139,000: Army 90,000, Navy 2,000, Air Force 2,000, Provincial Forces 45,000
CONSCRIPTION DURATION – Not implemented since 1993

ECONOMY

The economy is based on agriculture, fishing and forestry. In addition to rice, which is the staple crop, the major products are rubber, livestock, maize, timber, pepper, palm sugar, fresh and dried fish, kapok, beans, soya and tobacco. Rice, rubber and wood used to be the main exports, though production was brought to a standstill by the hostilities.

Under the Khmer Rouge, the urban population was forced to work on the land, and re-establish plantations producing such crops as cotton, rubber and bananas. Following the Vietnamese invasion of 1978 the towns were repopulated and factories, in particular textile mills, iron smelting works and cement works, were put back in production.

In 1997 there was a trade deficit of US$328 million and a current account deficit of US$210 million.
GNP – US$3,162 million (1997); US$300 per capita (1997)
GDP – US$1,303 million (1995); US$130 per capita (1995)

ANNUAL AVERAGE GROWTH OF GDP – 7.6 per cent (1995)
INFLATION RATE – 8.0 per cent (1997)
TOTAL EXTERNAL DEBT – US$2,129 million (1997)

Trade with UK	1997	1998
Imports from UK	£2,454,000	£6,083,000
Exports to UK	24,582,000	24,039,000

COMMUNICATIONS

The country has about 34,100 kilometres of roads, although most are now in a state of disrepair. There are two railways, one from Phnom Penh to the Thai border, the other from Phnom Penh to Kampot and Sihanoukville (Kompong Som). Phnom Penh is on a river capable of receiving ships of up to 2,500 tons all the year round. The deep water port at Sihanoukville (Kompong Som) on the Gulf of Thailand can receive ships of up to 10,000 tons. The port is linked to Phnom Penh by a modern highway.

CAMEROON
République du Cameroun

AREA – 183,569 sq. miles (475,442 sq. km). Neighbours: Nigeria (north and west), Chad and Central African Republic (east), Republic of Congo-Brazzaville, Gabon and Equatorial Guinea (south)
POPULATION – 13,560,000 (1994 UN estimate). French and English are both official languages and enjoy equal status
CAPITAL – Yaoundé (population, 653,670, 1986 estimate)
MAJOR CITIES – ΨDouala (1,029,736) is the commercial centre
CURRENCY – Franc CFA of 100 centimes
NATIONAL ANTHEM – O Cameroun, Berceau de Nos Ancêtres (O Cameroon, thou cradle of our forefathers)
NATIONAL DAY – 20 May
NATIONAL FLAG – Vertical stripes of green, red and yellow with single five-pointed yellow star in centre of red stripe
LIFE EXPECTANCY (years) – male 54.50; female 57.50
POPULATION GROWTH RATE – 2.8 per cent (1996)
POPULATION DENSITY – 29 per sq. km (1996)
MILITARY EXPENDITURE – 2.9 per cent of GDP (1997)
MILITARY PERSONNEL – 22,100: Army 11,500, Navy 1,300, Air Force 300, Paramilitaries 9,000
ILLITERACY RATE – 36.6 per cent
ENROLMENT (percentage of age group) – secondary 15 per cent (1980); tertiary 3.3 per cent (1990)

HISTORY AND POLITICS

The German colony of the Cameroons, established in 1884, was captured by British and French forces in 1916 and divided into the League of Nations-mandated territories (later UN trusteeships) of East (French) and West (British) Cameroon. On 1 January 1960 East Cameroon became independent as the Republic of Cameroon. This was joined on 1 October 1961 by the southern part of West Cameroon after a plebiscite held under United Nations auspices; the northern part joined Nigeria. Cameroon became a federal republic with separate East and West Cameroon state governments. After a plebiscite held in 1972, Cameroon became a unitary republic and a one-party state.

After extensive unrest, multiparty elections were held in March 1992, although they were boycotted by two of the main opposition parties. The ruling People's Democratic Movement emerged short of a parliamentary majority but formed a coalition government with a small opposition party, the Movement for the Defence of the Republic.

Presidential elections were held in October 1992 and won by the incumbent Paul Biya. The results were disputed by opponents and foreign observers, who accused the authorities of malpractice. In November a new coalition government was formed with the addition of the Union for Democracy and Progress and the Union of Peoples of Cameroon. A legislative election held in May 1997 was dominated by the ruling Cameroon People's Democratic Movement (CPDM) which won 109 of the 180 seats, though Commonwealth observers reported widespread fraud and voter intimidation.

INTERNATIONAL RELATIONS

There have been armed clashes with Nigeria over the disputed Bakassi peninsula. The dispute is under consideration at the International Court of Justice.

POLITICAL SYSTEM

The president is directly elected for a seven-year term, and appoints the prime minister and Cabinet. The National Assembly comprises 180 members, directly elected for a five-year term. Under the 1995 constitutional amendments a Senate is to be created.

HEAD OF STATE

President and Commander-in-Chief of the Armed Forces, Paul Biya, *acceded* 6 November 1982, *elected* 14 January 1984, *re-elected* 24 April 1988, 10 October 1992, 12 October 1997

CABINET *as at May 1999*

Prime Minister, Peter Mafany Musonge
Agriculture, Zacharie Perevet; Aboubakari Abdoulaye
Animal Breeding, Fisheries and Animal Industries, Ajoudji Hamadjoda
City Affairs, Antoine Zanga
Civil Service and Administrative Reform, Sali Dairou
Communication, René Ze Nguele
Culture, Ferdinand Leopold Oyono
Defence and National Police Force, Emmanuel Edou
Delegate at the Foreign Ministry in charge of Commonwealth Relations, Joseph Dion Ngute
Delegate at the Foreign Ministry in charge of Islamic Relations, Gargoum Adoum
Delegate at the Ministry of Finance in charge of Budget, Roger Melingui
Delegate at the Ministry of Finance in charge of the Plan for Stability, Jean-Marie Gankou
Delegate at the Presidency in charge of Defence, Ali Amadou
Delegate at the Presidency in charge of Relations with the Assemblies, Grégoire Owona
Delegate at the Presidency in charge of State Control, Lucy Gwanmesia
Economy and Finance, Edouard Akame Mfoumdou
Education, Charles Etoundi
Employment, Labour and Social Causes, Pius Ondoua
Environment and Forests, Sylvester Naah Ondoua
Foreign Affairs, Augustin Kontchou Kouemegni
Health, Alim Hayatou
Higher Education, Jean-Marie Atangana Mebara
Industrial and Commercial Development, Maigari Bello Bouba (UNDP); Edmond Mouampea Mbio
Investment and National Development, Tsala Messi
Justice, Keeper of the Seals, Laurent Esso
Mines, Water Resources and Energy, Yves Mbelle
National Education, Joseph Yunga Teghen

Post and Telecommunications, Saidou Mountchipou; Denis Oumarou
Public Health, Gotlieb Monekosso
Public Investment and Regional Planning, Justin Ndioro a Yombo
Public Works, Jérome Etah; Emmanuel Bonde
Scientific and Technical Research, Henri Hogbe Nlend
Social Affairs, Madaleine Fouda
Special Duties at the Presidency, Peter Abety; Martin Okouda; Amadou Baba; Elvis Ngole Ngole
Territorial Administration, Samson Ename Ename; Antar Gassagaye
Tourism, Claude Joseph Mbafou
Town Planning and Housing, Pierre Hele; Shey Johnes Yembe
Transport, Joseph Tsanga Abanda; Nana Aboubakar Diallo
Women's Affairs, Aissatou Yaou
Youth and Sports, Joseph Owona

EMBASSY OF THE REPUBLIC OF CAMEROON
84 Holland Park, London WII 3SB
Tel 0171–727 0771/3
Ambassador Extraordinary and Plenipotentiary, HE Samuel Libock Mbei, apptd 1995

BRITISH HIGH COMMISSION
Avenue Winston Churchill, BP 547 Yaoundé
Tel: Yaoundé 220545
High Commissioner, HE Peter Boon, MBE, apptd 1998
There is also a British Consulate at Douala.

BRITISH COUNCIL DIRECTOR, Terence Humphreys, Avenue Charles de Gaulle (BP 818), Yaoundé

ECONOMY

Principal products are cocoa, coffee, bananas, cotton, timber, groundnuts, aluminium, rubber and palm products. Crude petroleum is also one of Cameroon's principal products.

France, Italy and other European Union states are Cameroon's main trading partners. In 1995 there was a trade surplus of US$627 million and a current account surplus of US$90 million. In 1995 exports totalled US$2,040 million and imports US$1,241 million.

GNP – US$8,610 million (1997); US$620 per capita (1997)
GDP – US$8,273 million (1995); US$627 per capita (1995)
ANNUAL AVERAGE GROWTH OF GDP – 3.1 per cent (1995)
INFLATION RATE – 4.4 per cent (1997)
TOTAL EXTERNAL DEBT – US$9,293 million (1997)

Trade with UK	1997	1998
Imports from UK	£30,264,000	£37,118,000
Exports to UK	42,025,000	42,543,000

CANADA

AREA – 3,849,674 sq. miles (9,970,610 sq. km).
Neighbours: USA (south), Alaska (USA) (west)
POPULATION – 29,964,000 (1994 UN estimate). The languages are English and French
CAPITAL – Ottawa (population, 1,010,498, 1996 census).
CURRENCY – Canadian dollar (C$) of 100 cents
NATIONAL ANTHEM – O Canada
NATIONAL DAY – 1 July (Canada Day)
NATIONAL FLAG – Red maple leaf with 11 points on white square, flanked by vertical red bars one-half the width of the square

FEDERAL STRUCTURE

Provinces or Territories (with official contractions)	Area (sq. kilometres)	Population, census 1996	Capital	Lieutenant-Governor	Premier
Alberta (AB)	638,233	2,696,826	Edmonton	H. A. Olson	Ralph Klein
British Columbia (BC)	892,677	3,724,500	ΨVictoria	Garde Gardom	Daniel Miller
Manitoba (MB)	547,703	1,113,898	Winnipeg	Peter Liba	Gary Filmon
New Brunswick (NB)	71,569	738,133	Fredericton	Marilyn Counsell	Bernard Lord
Newfoundland and Labrador (NF)	371,635	551,792	ΨSt John's	A. M. House	Brian Tobin
Nova Scotia (NS)	52,840	909,282	ΨHalifax	James Kinley	Russell MacLellan
Ontario (ON)	916,733	10,753,573	ΨToronto	Hilary Weston	Michael Harris
Prince Edward Island (PE)	5,660	134,557	ΨCharlottetown	Gilbert Clements	Patrick Binns
Quebec (QC)	1,357,812	7,138,795	ΨQuébec	Lise Thibeault	Lucien Bouchard
Saskatchewan (SK)	570,113	990,237	Regina	John Wiebe	Roy John Romanow
Yukon Territory (YT)	531,844	30,766	*Whitehorse	†Judy Gingell	‡John Otashek
Northwest Territories (NT) & Nunavut (NT)§	3,246,389	64,402	*Yellowknife *Iqaluit	†Helen Maksagak †Jack Anawak	‡Don Morin ‡Paul Okalik

Area figures include land and water area † Commissioner
* seat of government ‡ Government Leader
§ Nunavut was created in 1999 from the Northwest Territories; area and population figures given are for both territories

LIFE EXPECTANCY (years) – male 73.02; female 79.79
POPULATION GROWTH RATE – 1.3 per cent (1996)
POPULATION DENSITY – 3 per sq. km (1996)
URBAN POPULATION – 76.6 per cent (1991)

Canada occupies the whole of the northern part of the North American continent, with the exception of Alaska. In eastern Canada, the southernmost point is Middle Island in Lake Erie. Canada has six main physiographic divisions: the Appalachian-Acadian region, the Canadian shield, which comprises more than half the country, the St Lawrence-Great Lakes lowland, the interior plains, the Cordilleran region and the Arctic archipelago.

The climate of the eastern and central portions presents greater extremes than in corresponding latitudes in Europe, but in the south-western portion of the prairie region and the southern portions of the Pacific slope the climate is milder.

HISTORY AND POLITICS

Canada was originally discovered by Cabot in 1497 but its history dates from 1534, when the French took possession of the country. The first permanent settlement at Port Royal (now Annapolis), Nova Scotia, was founded in 1605, and Quebec was founded in 1608. In 1759 Quebec was captured by British forces under General Wolfe and in 1763 the whole territory of Canada became a possession of Great Britain by the Treaty of Paris 1763. Nova Scotia was ceded in 1713 by the Treaty of Utrecht, the provinces of New Brunswick and Prince Edward Island being subsequently formed out of it. British Columbia was formed into a Crown colony in 1858, having previously been a part of the Hudson Bay Territory, and was united to Vancouver Island in 1866.

The constitution of Canada has its source in the British North America Act of 1867 which formed a Dominion, under the name of Canada, of the four provinces of Ontario, Quebec, New Brunswick and Nova Scotia. To this federation the other provinces have subsequently been admitted: Manitoba (1870), British Columbia (1871), Prince Edward Island (1873), Alberta and Saskatchewan (1905) and Newfoundland (1949). In 1982, the constitution was patriated (severed from the British parliament) with the approval of all provinces except Quebec. In 1985, the federal prime minister and the provincial premiers concluded the Meech Lake Accord which provided for Quebec to be recognized as a distinct society within Canada. However, two provincial legislatures withheld approval and the accord did not come into force. In Quebec, a referendum calling for sovereignty and a new political and economic partnership was defeated in October 1995. In September 1997 Quebec was recognized as having a 'unique character' by leaders of the other provinces and territories. A new territory, Nunavut, which means 'our land' in the Inuit language of Inuktitut, was created on 1 April 1999 by partitioning the Northwest Territories. It comprises approximately 2.2 million square kilometres, but has a population of only 25,000, about 85 per cent of whom are Inuit.

In the federal election on 2 June 1997 the Liberal Party was returned to power. The state of parties in the House of Commons following the election was Liberals 155, Reform Party 60, Bloc Québécois 44, New Democrats 21, Progressive Conservatives 20, Independent 1.

POLITICAL SYSTEM

Executive power is vested in a Governor-General appointed by the Sovereign on the advice of the Canadian government.

Parliament consists of a Senate and a House of Commons. The Senate consists of 104 members, nominated by the Governor-General on the advice of the prime minister, the seats being distributed between the various provinces. The House of Commons has 301 members directly elected for a five-year term. Representation is proportional to the population of each province.

The judicature is administered by judges following the civil law in Quebec province and common law in other provinces. Each province has a Court of Appeal. All superior, county and district court judges are appointed by the Governor-General, the others by the Lieutenant-Governors of the provinces.

The highest federal court is the Supreme Court of Canada, which exercises general appellate jurisdiction throughout Canada in civil and criminal cases. There is one other federally constituted court, the Federal Court of Canada, which has jurisdiction on appeals from its trial division, from federal tribunals and reviews of decisions and references by federal boards and commissions.

GOVERNOR-GENERAL
Governor-General and Commander-in-Chief, HE Roméo LeBlanc, PC, CC, CMM, CD

CABINET *as at May 1999*
Prime Minister, Jean Chrétien
Deputy Prime Minister, Herbert Gray
Agriculture and Agri-Food, Lyle Vanclief
Citizenship and Immigration, Lucienne Robillard
Environment, Christine Stewart
Finance, Paul Martin
Fisheries and Oceans, David Anderson
Foreign Affairs, Lloyd Axworthy
Health, Allan Rock
Heritage, Sheila Copps
Human Resources Development, Pierre Pettigrew
Indian Affairs and Northern Development, Jane Stewart
Industry, John Manley

Infrastructure, President of the Treasury Board, Marcel Massé
Intergovernmental Affairs, President of the Privy Council, Stéphane Dion
International Co-operation and Francophonie, Diane Marleau
International Trade, Sergio Marchi
Justice and Attorney-General, Anne McLellan
Labour and the Homeless, Claudette Bradshaw
Leader of the Government in the House of Commons, Don Boudria
Leader of the Government in the Senate, Bernard Graham
National Defence, Arthur C. Eggleton
Natural Resources, Canadian Wheat Board, Ralph Goodale
Public Works and Government Services, Alfonso Gagliano
Secretary of State for Asia-Pacific, Raymond Chan
Secretary of State for Atlantic Canada Opportunities Agency; Veterans' Affairs, Fred Mifflin
Secretary of State for Children and Youth, Ethel Blondin-Andrews
Secretary of State for International Financial Institutions, James Scott Peterson
Secretary of State for Latin America and Africa, David Kilgour
Secretary of State for Multiculturalism and the Status of Women, Hedy Fry
Secretary of State for Parks, Andrew Mitchell
Secretary of State for Regional Development in Quebec, Martin Cauchon
Secretary of State for Science, Research and Development; Western Economic Diversification, Ronald Duhamel
Solicitor-General, Lawrence MacAulay
Transport, David Collenette

CANADIAN HIGH COMMISSION
1 Grosvenor Square, London WIX OAB
Tel 0171-258 6600
Canada House, 5 Trafalgar Square, London SWIY 5BJ
High Commissioner, HE Roy MacLaren, apptd 1996
Deputy High Commissioner, J. Bilodeau
Minister, T. MacDonald (*Commercial/Economic*)
Defence Adviser, Brig.-Gen. R. Bastien

BRITISH HIGH COMMISSION
80 Elgin Street, Ottawa KIP 5K7
Tel: Ottawa 237 1530
High Commissioner, HE Sir Anthony Goodenough, KCMG, apptd 1996
Deputy High Commissioner, L. J. Duffield
Counsellor, M. Uden (*Economic*)
Defence and Military Adviser, Brig. E. Springfield, CBE
CONSULATES-GENERAL – Montreal, Toronto, Vancouver
CONSULATES – Halifax/Dartmouth, St John's, Winnipeg
BRITISH COUNCIL DIRECTOR, Dr S. Lewis (*Cultural Counsellor*)
BRITISH COUNCIL REPRESENTATIVE IN QUEBEC, S. Dawbarn, 1000 ouest rue de La Gauchetière, Montreal, Quebec H3B 4W5

DEFENCE

The Canadian armed forces are unified and organized into three functional commands: Land Force Command; Maritime Command; Air Command.

The Army (Land Forces) has 114 main battle tanks, 1,858 armoured personnel carriers and 272 artillery pieces. The Navy (Maritime Forces) has three submarines, four destroyers, 12 frigates and 14 patrol and coastal vessels. The Air Force has 140 combat aircraft and 143 armed helicopters.

MILITARY EXPENDITURE – 1.3 per cent of GDP (1997)
MILITARY PERSONNEL – 60,600: Army 20,900, Navy 9,000, Air Force 15,000, Other 15,700

ECONOMY

About 7.3 per cent of the total land area is farmed. Over 60 per cent of this is under cultivation, the remainder being predominantly classified as unimproved pasture. More than 80 per cent of the cultivated land is in the prairie region of western Canada. In 1996, there were 274,955 farms in Canada, with a total land area of 168 million acres. The farm sector accounts for less than 2 per cent of GDP and employs about 3 per cent of the labour force.

Almost half of Canada's land area is forest, making it the world's largest exporter of timber, pulp and newsprint.

Canada produced agricultural goods to the value of C$12,184 million in 1997 and of fishing, trapping, logging and forestry contributed a further C$5,005 million.

In 1997, Canada was the world's largest producer of potash and uranium, the second largest of nickel, asbestos, cadmium, zinc and elemental sulphur. The country is also rich in gold, copper, lead, molybdenum, platinum group metals, gypsum, cobalt, titanium concentrates, and aluminium. The total value of mineral production in 1996 was C$49,171.8 million.

Production of gold was 168,061 kg in 1997 and of silver 1,222,367 kg. Uranium production in 1997 was 11,908 tonnes.

GNP – US$594,976 million (1997); US$19,640 per capita (1997)

GDP – US$561,008 million (1995); US$18,943 per capita (1995)

ANNUAL AVERAGE GROWTH OF GDP – 1.5 per cent (1996)

INFLATION RATE – 1.6 per cent (1997)

UNEMPLOYMENT – 9.5 per cent (1995)

TRADE

The main exports in 1996 were passenger automobiles and chassis, motor vehicle parts except engines, lumber and softwood, crude petroleum, trucks, truck tractors and chassis, newsprint paper, other telecommunication and related equipment, wood pulp and similar pulp, natural gas, petroleum and coal products. Trade with the USA accounts for about 80 per cent of Canada's exports and 75 per cent of its imports.

In 1997 imports totalled US$200,929 million and exports US$214,422 million. In 1997 Canada had a trade surplus of US$17,556 million and a current account deficit of US$9,261 million.

Trade with UK	1997	1998
Imports from UK	£2,155,968,000	£2,189,409,000
Exports to UK	2,553,935,000	2,604,232,000

COMMUNICATIONS

In 1991 there were 290,194 km of federal and provincial territorial roads and highways and 85,563 km of railway track in operation.

The registered shipping on 1 January 1991 including inland vessels, was 43,787 vessels with gross tonnage 4,956,845. The bulk of canal shipping in Canada is handled through the two sections of the St Lawrence Seaway, which provide access to the Great Lakes for ocean-going ships.

EDUCATION

Education is under the control of the provincial governments, the cost of the publicly controlled schools being met by local taxation, aided by provincial grants. Education is compulsory between the ages of five or six and fifteen or sixteen.

In 1995–6 there were 16,096 elementary and secondary schools with 5,899,943 pupils. There were 70 degree-granting universities.

ENROLMENT (percentage of age group) – primary 95 per cent (1994); secondary 93 per cent (1995); tertiary 90.2 per cent (1995)

CAPE VERDE

República de Cabo Verde

AREA – 1,557 sq. miles (4,033 sq. km). Comprising the Windward Islands (Santo Antão, São Vicente, Santa Luzia, São Nicolau, Boa Vista and Sal) and Leeward Islands (Maio, São Tiago, Fogo and Brava)

POPULATION – 396,000 (1995 estimate), the majority of whom are Roman Catholic. The official language is Portuguese; a creole is spoken by most of the population

CAPITAL – ΨPraia (population, 61,644, 1995 estimate)

CURRENCY – Escudo Caboverdiano of 100 centavos

NATIONAL DAY – 5 July (Independence Day)

NATIONAL FLAG – Blue with three horizontal stripes of white, red, white near the bottom; over all on these near the hoist a ring of ten yellow stars

LIFE EXPECTANCY (years) – male 63.53; female 71.33

POPULATION GROWTH RATE – 2.5 per cent (1996)

POPULATION DENSITY – 98 per sq. km (1996)

URBAN POPULATION – 44.1 per cent (1990)

MILITARY EXPENDITURE – 1.7 per cent of GDP (1997)

MILITARY PERSONNEL – 1,100: Army 1,000, Air Force 100

CONSCRIPTION DURATION – Selective conscription

ILLITERACY RATE – 28.4 per cent

ENROLMENT (percentage of age group) – primary 100 per cent (1989); secondary 22 per cent (1993)

HISTORY AND POLITICS

The islands, colonized c.1460, achieved independence from Portugal on 5 July 1975 under the Partido Africano da Independência da Guiné e Cabo Verde (PAIGC). A federation of the islands with Guinea Bissau was planned but this was dropped following the 1980 coup in Guinea Bissau.

The republic was a one-party state under the African Party for the Independence of Cape Verde (PAICV) until the constitution was amended in 1990. Multiparty elections, held in January 1991, were won by the opposition Movement for Democracy (MPD). The MPD government was re-elected in December 1995 with 50 of the 72 seats in the National Assembly. President António Mascarenhas Monteiro was re-elected unopposed in February 1996.

HEAD OF STATE

President, António Mascarenhas Monteiro, *assumed office 22 March 1991, re-elected 18 February 1996*

COUNCIL OF MINISTERS *as at May 1999*

Prime Minister, Carlos Veiga

Deputy Prime Minister, Economic Co-ordination, António Gualberto do Rosario

Assistant to the Prime Minister, José António dos Reis

Agriculture, Food, Supply and the Environment, José António Pinto Monteiro

Culture, António Jorge Delgado

Defence, Ulpio Napoleão Fernandes

Deputy Secretary of State for Finance, Olavo Correia Garcia

Education, Science, Youth and Sport, José Luis Livramento de Brito

Employment, Training and Social Integration, Orlanda Santos Ferreira
Finance, José Ulysses Correia Silva
Foreign Affairs and Communities, José Luis de Jesus
Health, João Baptista Medina
Infrastructure and Housing, António Fernandes
Justice and Internal Administration, Simão Gomes Monteiro Rodriguez
Minister of the Presidency of the Council of Ministers, Rui Figueiredo Silva
Secretary of State for Cape Verdeans Abroad, Marly Meneses Vicente
Secretary of State for Decentralization, Cesar Almeida
Secretary of State for the Fight Against Poverty, Manuela Teresa Silva Gomes
Secretary of State for Public Administration, Anna Paula Almeida
Secretary of State for Youth and Sports, Victor Osório
Speaker of the National Assembly, Antonio Espirito Santo Fonseca
Tourism, Transport and Marine Affairs, Maria Helena Semedo
Trade, Industry and Energy, Alexandre Dias Monteiro

EMBASSY OF THE REPUBLIC OF CAPE VERDE
Burgemeester Patijnlaan 1930, NL-2585 CB, The Hague, The Netherlands
Tel: The Hague 355 3651/78
Ambassador Extraordinary and Plenipotentiary, HE Julio Vasco de Sousa Lobo, apptd 1998

BRITISH AMBASSADOR, HE David Snoxell, resident at Dakar, Senegal
There is a British Consulate on São Vicente.

ECONOMY

The islands have little rain and agriculture is mostly confined to irrigated inland valleys. The chief products are bananas and coffee (for export), maize, sugar cane and nuts. Fish and shellfish are important exports. Salt is obtained on Sal, Boa Vista and Maio; volcanic rock is also mined for export.

In 1993 the government announced a programme of reform to institute a change to a market economy and to privatize most industry within four years. In 1995 there was a trade deficit of US$224 million and a current account deficit of US$39 million. In 1995 imports totalled US$252 million and exports US$9 million.

The main ports are Praia and Mindelo, and there is an international airport on Sal.

GNP – US$436 million (1997); US$1,090 per capita (1997)
GDP – US$384 million (1995); US$994 per capita (1995)
TOTAL EXTERNAL DEBT – US$220 million (1997)

Trade with UK	1997	1998
Imports from UK	£5,483,000	£4,088,000
Exports to UK	881,000	3,097,000

CENTRAL AFRICAN REPUBLIC
République Centrafricaine

AREA – 240,535 sq. miles (622,984 sq. km). Neighbours: Chad (north), Sudan (east), Democratic Republic of Congo and Republic of Congo-Brazzaville (south), Cameroon (west)
POPULATION – 3,344,000 (1994 UN estimate). French is the official language; the native language is Sango

CAPITAL – Bangui (population, 473,817, 1984 estimate)
CURRENCY – Franc CFA of 100 centimes
NATIONAL DAY – 1 December
NATIONAL FLAG – Four horizontal stripes, blue, white, green, yellow, crossed by central vertical red stripe with a yellow five-pointed star in top left-hand corner
LIFE EXPECTANCY (years) – male 46.87; female 51.88
POPULATION GROWTH RATE – 2.2 per cent (1996)
POPULATION DENSITY – 6 per sq. km (1996)
MILITARY EXPENDITURE – 4.0 per cent of GDP (1997)
MILITARY PERSONNEL – 4,950: Army 2,500, Air Force 150, Paramilitaries 2,300
CONSCRIPTION DURATION – Two years
ILLITERACY RATE – 66.4 per cent
ENROLMENT (percentage of age group) – primary 54 per cent (1990); tertiary 1.4 per cent (1991)

HISTORY AND POLITICS

In December 1958 the French colony of Ubanghi Shari elected to remain within the French Community and adopted the title of the Central African Republic. It became fully independent on 17 August 1960. The first president, David Dacko, was overthrown in 1966 by the then Col. Bokassa, who in 1976 proclaimed himself Emperor and renamed the country the Central African Empire. In 1979 Bokassa was deposed by Dacko in a bloodless coup and the country reverted to a republic. President Dacko surrendered power in 1981 to Gen. André Kolingba, who instituted military rule until 1985, when a civilian-dominated Cabinet was appointed. In November 1986 a referendum was held which approved a new constitution and the establishment of a one-party state.

Multiparty presidential and legislative elections were held in October 1992 but were annulled due to irregularities. President Kolingba formed a coalition government in February 1993. Presidential elections held in 1993 were won by Ange-Félix Patasse of the Central African People's Liberation Party (MLPC). Legislative elections were held on 22 November and 13 December 1998. The MLPC emerged as the largest party with 47 of 109 seats.

POLITICAL SYSTEM

Constitutional reforms were passed in a national referendum in December 1994 which created a constitutional court, introduced elected local assemblies, extended presidential mandate to a maximum of two six-year terms and subordinated the government to the president.

INSURGENCY

The army is divided between southerners loyal to former President Gen. Kolingba and northerners loyal to President Patasse. The 1,100 French troops stationed near Bangui have been called upon to quell frequent mutinies by Gen. Kolingba's supporters; in March 1998 the French troops were replaced by the UN MINURCA peacekeeping force.

HEAD OF STATE
President, Ange-Félix Patasse, *elected* 19 September 1993

COUNCIL OF MINISTERS *as at May 1999*
Prime Minister, Economy, Planning and International Co-operation, Anicet Georges Doleguele (MLPC)
Agriculture, Joseph Kalite
Commerce, Industry and Tourism, Germain Nadjibe (Ind.)
Culture, Marie-Joseph Songomali Toungovala
Deputy Ministers, Théodore Dabanga (*Finance and Budget*); Jacob Mbaitadjimp (*Economy Planning and International Co-operation*)
Employment, Civil Service and Training, Maj. Denis Wangao-Kizimale

Environment, Thierry Ynifolo Vanden-Boss
Family and Social Affairs, Anne-Marie Ngouyombo
Foreign and Francophone Affairs, Marcel Metefara (MLPC)
Interior, Security, Théodore Biko
Justice, Laurient Gomina-Pampali
Mines and Energy, Jean Serge Wafio
National Defence, War Veterans and War Victims, Pascal Kado (MLPC)
National Education and Scientific Research, Agba Otikpo Mezode
Parliamentary Relations, Juliette Nzekou Dongoya
Posts and Telecommunications, Desiré Pendemon (MLPC)
Public Health, Prosper Thimossat
Public Works, Jackson Madeck (MLPC)
Secretary of State for Disarmament, Lt.-Col. Evariste Konzale
Secretary of State for National Education and Scientific Research, Emery Dede
Secretary of State for Public Security, Abraham Espere Langou
Transport and Civil Aviation, Thimothé Aguene
Urban Development and Housing, Armand Sama (MDD)
Youth and Sports, Cyrus-Emmanuel Sandy (MLPC)
Ind. Independent; MDD Movement for Democracy and Development; MLPC Movement for the Liberation of the Central African People

EMBASSY OF THE CENTRAL AFRICAN REPUBLIC
30 rue des Perchamps, F-75016, Paris
Tel: Paris 4224 4256
Ambassador Extraordinary and Plenipotentiary, new appointment awaited
BRITISH AMBASSADOR, HE Peter Boon, resident at Yaoundé, Cameroon
Honorary Consul, J. Y. Lauge, BP 977, Bangui

ECONOMY

The IMF approved a US$23 million credit to support economic reform in 1994. Cotton, diamonds, coffee and timber are the major exports.

In 1994 there was a trade surplus of US$15 million and a current account deficit of US$25 million. In 1995 exports totalled US$171 million and imports US$174 million.
GNP – US$1,104 million (1997); US$320 per capita (1997)
GDP – US$1,239 million (1995); US$379 per capita (1995)
INFLATION RATE – 1.2 per cent (1997)
TOTAL EXTERNAL DEBT – US$885 million (1997)

Trade with UK	1997	1998
Imports from UK	£1,183,000	£569,000
Exports to UK	63,000	206,000

CHAD
République du Tchad

AREA – 495,755 sq. miles (1,284,000 sq. km). Neighbours: Niger, Nigeria and Cameroon (west), Libya (north), Sudan (east), Central African Republic (south)
POPULATION – 6,515,000 (1994 UN estimate); French and Arabic are the official languages; there are more than 50 indigenous languages, of which the most widely spoken is Sara
CAPITAL – N'Djaména (population, 179,000, 1972 estimate)
CURRENCY – Franc CFA of 100 centimes
NATIONAL DAY – 1 December
NATIONAL FLAG – Vertical stripes, blue, yellow and red
LIFE EXPECTANCY (years) – male 45.93; female 49.12

POPULATION GROWTH RATE – 2.3 per cent (1996)
POPULATION DENSITY – 5 per sq. km (1996)
URBAN POPULATION – 21.7 per cent (1993)
MILITARY EXPENDITURE – 4.1 per cent of GDP (1997)
MILITARY PERSONNEL – 29,850: Army 25,000, Air Force 350, Paramilitaries 4,500
ILLITERACY RATE – 51.9 per cent
ENROLMENT (percentage of age group) – primary 52 per cent (1996); secondary 6 per cent (1995); tertiary 0.6 per cent (1995)

HISTORY AND POLITICS

Chad became a member state of the French Community in 1958, and was proclaimed fully independent on 11 August 1960. The constitution was suspended in 1975 when President Tombalbaye was killed in a coup by Gen. Félix Malloum; following a succession of further coups, Idriss Déby came to power in 1990 and announced the adoption of a multiparty system, allowing the legalization of political parties in 1991 and 1992. A Higher Transitional Council (CST) was elected in 1993 to serve as the transitional legislature and appointed a transitional government in conjunction with President Déby. The CST has twice extended the transitional period by one year to allow sufficient time to organize elections. In March 1996, the government concluded the Franceville agreement with opposition parties which provided for a national cease-fire and an independent commission to oversee the election. A new constitution, establishing a unified, democratic state, was confirmed by a referendum. Déby won the first multiparty presidential elections in 1996. Elections to the 125-member National Assembly in January and February 1997 were won by the pro-Déby Patriotic Salvation Movement (MPS).

FOREIGN RELATIONS

The Aouzou strip was claimed by Libya, which occupied the area from 1973 to 1994. A war over the territory ended in 1987. In 1990 Chad and Libya presented their claims to the International Court of Justice, which in 1994 awarded jurisdiction over the whole of the strip to Chad.

HEAD OF STATE
President, Idriss Déby, *took power* December 1990, *elected* 3 July 1996

GOVERNMENT *as at May 1999*
Prime Minister, Nassour Owaido Guelendouksia
Agriculture, Moctar Moussa
Civil Service and Labour, Mahamout Hissene Mahamout
Communication, Sekimbaye Bessane
Culture, Youth and Sport, Daboulaï Koyo Maïboula
Defence, Oumar Kadjalami
Education, Abderahim Breme Hamid
Environment and Water, Pascal Yoadimnadji
Finance and Economy, Bichara Cherif Daoussa
Foreign Affairs and Co-operation, Mahamat Saleh Annadif
Government Secretary, Houdeingar David
Higher Education and Scientific Research, Adoum Goudja
Industrial Development, Djitangar Djibangar
Interior, Security and Decentralization, Oumarou Djibrillah
Justice, Limane Mahamat
Livestock, Mahamat Nouri
Mines, Energy and Oil, Abdoulaye Lamana
Planning and Territorial Improvement, Mahamat Ali Hassan
Posts and Telecommunications, Salibou Ngarba
Public Health, Kedallah Younouss Hamit
Public Works, Transport, Housing, Ahmat Lamine
Social Affairs, Agnes Alafi
Tourism, Moussa Dago

EMBASSY OF THE REPUBLIC OF CHAD
Boulevard Lambermont 52, B-1030 Brussels, Belgium
Tel: Brussels 215 1975
Ambassador Extraordinary and Plenipotentiary, new appointment awaited
BRITISH AMBASSADOR, HE Peter Boon, resident at Yaoundé, Cameroon
Honorary Consul, E. Abtour, BP877, Avenue Charles de Gaulle, N'Djaména

ECONOMY

About 90 per cent of the workforce is occupied in agriculture, fishing and forestry. There is an oilfield in Kanem and salt is mined around Lake Chad, but the most important activities are cotton growing and animal husbandry. Raw cotton and meat are the main exports. Chad's main trading partners are France and Nigeria.

In 1994 Chad had a trade deficit of US$77 million and a current account deficit of US$38 million. In 1995 imports totalled US$220 million and exports US$252 million.

GNP – US$1,629 million (1997); US$230 per capita (1997)
GDP – US$1,185 million (1995); US$187 per capita (1995)
ANNUAL AVERAGE GROWTH OF GDP – 1.1 per cent (1995)
INFLATION RATE – 5.7 per cent (1997)
TOTAL EXTERNAL DEBT – US$1,027 million (1997)

Trade with UK	1997	1998
Imports from UK	£1,182,000	£1,050,000
Exports to UK	479,000	369,000

CHILE
República de Chile

AREA – 292,135 sq. miles (756,626 sq. km). Neighbours: Peru (north), Bolivia and Argentina (east)
POPULATION – 14,419,000 (1994 UN estimate). The main groups are: indigenous Araucanian Indians, Fuegians, Rapanui and Changos; Spanish settlers and their descendants; mixed Spanish Indians; and European immigrants. Because of extensive intermarriage only a few indigenous Indians are racially separate. The language is Spanish, with admixtures of local words of Indian origin. The main religion is Roman Catholicism
CAPITAL – Santiago (population, 5,257,937, 1992)
MAJOR CITIES – ΨAntofagasta (239,854); Concepción (356,371); Puente Alto (340,639); Temuco (246,304); ΨValparaíso (282,850); ΨPunta Arenas (118,677), on the Straits of Magellan, is the southernmost city in the world
CURRENCY – Chilean peso of 100 centavos
NATIONAL ANTHEM – Canción Nacional de Chile
NATIONAL DAY – 18 September (National Anniversary)
NATIONAL FLAG – Two horizontal bands, white, red; in top sixth a white star on blue square, next staff
LIFE EXPECTANCY (years) – male 71.83; female 77.77
POPULATION GROWTH RATE – 1.6 per cent (1996)
POPULATION DENSITY – 19 per sq. km (1996)
URBAN POPULATION – 84.5 per cent (1995)

Chile lies between the Andes (5,000 to 15,000 feet above sea level) and the shores of the South Pacific, extending coastwise from the arid north around Arica to Cape Horn. The extreme length of the country is about 2,800 miles, with an average breadth, north of 41°, of 100 miles.

Island possessions include the Juan Fernández group (three islands) about 360 miles from Valparaíso; one of these islands is the reputed scene of Alexander Selkirk's (Robinson Crusoe) shipwreck. Easter Island, about 2,000 miles away in the South Pacific Ocean, contains stone platforms and hundreds of stone figures.

HISTORY AND POLITICS

Chile was discovered by Spanish adventurers in the 16th century and remained under Spanish rule until 1810, when the first autonomous government was established. Full independence was consolidated in 1818 after a revolutionary war.

A Marxist, Salvador Allende, was elected president in 1970, but was overthrown in a military coup in 1973. Gen. Pinochet, who led the coup, assumed the presidency until presidential and congressional elections were held in 1989, beginning the transition to full democracy. Gen. Pinochet retired as commander-in-chief of the Army but took up an unelected seat for life in the Senate, despite public protests and government attempts to prevent it. He was arrested in London on 16 October 1998 following a request by the Spanish government for his extradition.

Presidential and legislative elections were held in 1993. Eduardo Frei won the presidential election and his ruling Coalition for Democracy (CPD) (centre and centre-left parties) won 70 seats in the Chamber of Deputies and 22 in the Senate. In the 1997 legislative elections the CPD maintained its 70-seat majority in the Chamber of Deputies. Presidential elections are due to be held in December 1999.

POLITICAL SYSTEM

Executive power is held by the president. Legislative power is exercised by a Congress which comprises a Senate of 46 Senators (38 elected and eight appointed) and a Chamber of Deputies of 120 elected members. A joint session of Congress in 1994 reduced the presidential term from eight to six years with no possibility of re-election.

Chile is divided into 12 regions and the Metropolitan Area.

HEAD OF STATE
President of the Republic, Eduardo Frei Ruíz-Tagle, *elected* 11 December 1993, *sworn in* 11 March 1994

CABINET *as at June 1999*

Agriculture, Angel Sartori
Defence, Edmundo Pérez Yoma
Economy, Development and Reconstruction, Jorge Leiva (PPD)
Education, José Pablo Arellano (PDC)
Finance, Eduardo Aninat Ureta (PDC)
Foreign Affairs, Juan Gabriel Valdés
Health, Alex Figueroa (PDC)
Housing and Urban Development, Sergio Henríquez
Interior, Raúl Troncoso Castillo (PDC)
Justice, Soledad Alvear (PDC)
Labour and Social Security, Germán Molina (PDC)
Mining, Sergio Jiménez Moraga (PRSD)
National Resources, Jorge Heine
Planning and Co-operation, Germán Quintana (PDC)
Public Works, Jaime Tohá (PS)
Secretary-General of the Government, Carlos Mladinic (PPD)
Secretary-General of the Presidency, José Miguel Insulza (PS)
Transport and Telecommunications, Claudio Hohmann (PDC)
Women's Affairs, Josefina Bilbao (Ind.)

PDC Christian Democratic Party; PPD Party for Democracy; PS Socialist Party; Ind. Independent

EMBASSY OF CHILE
12 Devonshire Street, London WIN 2DS
Tel 0171-580 6392
Ambassador Extraordinary and Plenipotentiary, HE Mario
Artaza, apptd 1996

BRITISH EMBASSY
Avenida El Bosque Norte 0125
Casilla 72-D, Santiago 9
Tel: Santiago 231 3737
Ambassador Extraordinary and Plenipotentiary, HE Glynne
Evans, CMG, apptd 1997
Deputy Head of Mission, Counsellor and Consul-General, D.
Roberts
Defence Attaché, Capt. P. Ellis
First Secretary (Commercial), T. Torlot
CONSULAR OFFICES – Antofagasta, Arica, Concepción,
Santiago, Punta Arenas, Valparaíso.

BRITISH COUNCIL DIRECTOR, D. Stokes (*Cultural
Attaché*), Eliodoro Yañez 832, Casilla 115 Correa 55,
Santiago
British-Chilean Chamber of Commerce, Av. Suecia
155-C, Casilla 536, Santiago

DEFENCE

The Army has 130 main battle tanks, 20 armoured infantry
fighting vehicles, 438 armoured personnel carriers and 154
artillery pieces. The Navy has four submarines, four
destroyers, four frigates, 28 patrol and coastal vessels, 14
combat aircraft and 12 armed helicopters. The Air Force
has 92 combat aircraft.
MILITARY EXPENDITURE – 2.8 per cent of GDP (1997)
MILITARY PERSONNEL – 124,000: Army 51,000, Navy
30,000, Air Force 13,500, Paramilitaries 29,500
CONSCRIPTION DURATION – 12–22 months

ECONOMY

Economic reforms during the late 1970s and the 1980s,
with large-scale privatization and deregulation, have made
Chile one of the most successful economies in Latin
America. Cereals, vegetables, fruit, tobacco, hemp and
vines are grown extensively and livestock accounts for
nearly 40 per cent of agricultural production. Sheep
farming predominates in the extreme south. There are
large timber tracts in the central and southern zones which
produce timber, cellulose and wood for export. Fishing is
also a major industry.
Chile is rich in copper-ore, iron-ore and nitrates, and
has the only commercial production of nitrate of soda
(Chile saltpetre) from natural resources in the world. There
are large deposits of high grade sulphur. Oil and natural
gas are produced in the Magallanes area, but domestic
production is now declining.
In 1997 there was a trade deficit of US$1,296 million
and a current account deficit of US$4,062 million.
GNP – US$70,510 million (1997); US$4,820 per capita
(1997)
GDP – US$67,296 million (1995); US$4,736 per capita
(1995)
ANNUAL AVERAGE GROWTH OF GDP – 7.2 per cent
(1996)
INFLATION RATE – 6.1 per cent (1997)
UNEMPLOYMENT – 4.7 per cent (1995)
TOTAL EXTERNAL DEBT – US$31,440 million (1997)

TRADE

The principal exports are minerals, timber and metal
products, fish products and vegetables. The principal
imports are food products, industrial raw materials,
machinery, and equipment and spares. The main trade
partners are Japan and the USA; in 1996 Chile joined the
Mercosur Free Trade Zone, and in March 1998 signed an
extension to a free trade agreement with Mexico. In 1997
imports totalled US$19,660 million and exports US$16,923
million.

Trade with UK	1997	1998
Imports from UK	£210,516,000	£172,774,000
Exports to UK	393,731,000	346,308,000

COMMUNICATIONS

With the improvement of the roads an increasing share of
internal transportation is moving by road and rail, although
shipping is still important. The road system is about 80,000
km in length.
A railway line runs from Valparaíso through La Calera
and Santiago to Puerto Montt. With the completion of a
section of 435 miles from Corumba, Brazil, to Santa Cruz,
Bolivia, the Trans-Continental Line will link the Chilean
Pacific port of Arica with Rio de Janeiro on the Atlantic. A
line runs from Antofagasta to Salta (Argentina).
Domestic air traffic is carried by Linea Aerea Nacional
(LAN) and LADECO, which also operate internationally,
and smaller regional carriers.

CULTURE AND EDUCATION

Chilean Nobel Prize winners include the writers Gabriela
Mistral (1945) and Pablo Neruda (1971).
Elementary education is free and compulsory. There
are eight state universities (three in Santiago, two in
Valparaíso, one each in Antofagasta, Concepción and
Valdivia), and many private universities.
ILLITERACY RATE – 4.8 per cent
ENROLMENT (percentage of age group) – primary 88 per
cent (1996); secondary 58 per cent (1996); tertiary 30.3
per cent (1996)

CHINA
*Zhonghua Renmin Gongheguo – The People's Republic of
China*

AREA – 3,705,408 sq. miles (9,596,961 sq. km).
Neighbours: Russia and Mongolia (north), North Korea
(east), Vietnam, Laos, Myanmar, India, Bhutan and
Nepal (south), India, Pakistan, Afghanistan, Tajikistan,
Kyrgyzstan and Kazakhstan (west)
POPULATION – 1,232,083,000 (1994 UN estimate). A
census (the fourth) was held in 1990 and recorded a
total population of 1,130 million. About 6 per cent of
the population belong to around 55 ethnic minorities.
Among the largest are the Zhuang of Guangxi, the
Uygurs of Xinjiang, the Tibetans and the Mongols. The
indigenous religions are Confucianism, Taoism and
Buddhism. There are also Muslims (officially estimated
at about 12 million) and Christians (unofficially
estimated at about 50 million). The official language is
Mandarin Chinese; of the many local dialects the
largest are Cantonese, Fukienese, Xiamenhua and
Hakka. The autonomous regions of Mongolia, Tibet
and Xinjiang have their own languages
CAPITAL – Beijing (Peking) (population, 7,362,426, 1990)
MAJOR CITIES – Chengdu (3,483,834); Chongqing
(3,122,704); Dalian (3,473,832); Guangzhou (Canton)
(3,918,010); Harbin (3,597,404); Qingdo (5,124,868);
ΨShanghai (8,205,598); Shenyang (4,655,280); Tianjin
(5,804,023); Wuhan (3,832,536); Wuxi (3,181,985);
Yantai (3,204,669); Zaozhuang (3,191,974)

CURRENCY – Renminbi Yuan of 10 jiao or 100 fen
NATIONAL ANTHEM – March of the Volunteers
NATIONAL DAY – 1 October (Founding of People's
  Republic)
NATIONAL FLAG – Red, with large gold five-point star
  and four small gold stars in crescent, all in upper
  quarter next staff
LIFE EXPECTANCY (years) – male 66.70; female 70.45
POPULATION GROWTH RATE – 1.1 per cent (1996)
POPULATION DENSITY – 128 per sq. km (1996)
URBAN POPULATION – 26.2 per cent (1990)

HISTORY AND POLITICS

China was ruled by imperial dynasties for over 20 centuries until revolutionaries led by Sun Yat-sen forced the Emperor to abdicate on 10 October 1911. Neither the new Nationalist Party (Kuomintang (KMT)) government nor the emergent Chinese Communist Party (CCP) were able to unify China, or to agree on the basis for further reform. Warlord infighting rendered China weak, enabling Japan to occupy Manchuria and all the important northern and coastal areas of China by 1939. Japan's occupation was ended by its defeat by the allies in 1945.

The Communists established control over large areas of China in the early 1940s, seizing the territory abandoned by Japan in 1945. Civil war lasted until 1949 when the CCP, led by Mao Zedong (Mao Tse-tung), inaugurated the People's Republic of China (PRC), and the KMT under Chiang Kai-shek went into exile in Taiwan. The USA continued to recognize the Chiang Kai-shek regime as the rightful government of China until 1971, when the

PRC took over China's membership of the United Nations from Taiwan.

Under Mao Zedong China was ruled on the basis of four 'cardinal principles': Marxist–Leninist–Maoist thought, the Socialist Road, the dictatorship of the proletariat, and the leadership of the CCP. Mao's 'Great Leap Forward' (1958–61) was an attempt to industrialize rural areas which resulted in a famine in which 30–40 million people died. China was plunged into chaos during the Cultural Revolution (1966–70) when the Red Guards were used to rid the country of 'rightist elements'.

Following the death of Mao Zedong in 1976, the disgraced Deng Xiaoping was recalled. In 1977 he was elected Vice-Chairman of the CCP, becoming the dominant force within the party by eliminating leftist influence, rehabilitating fallen leaders and promoting an 'open door' policy of economic liberalization. The Congresses of 1982 and 1987 reaffirmed Deng's policies, and in 1987 most of the revolutionary generation were replaced in the top posts by younger, more liberal supporters of reform.

Student-led pro-democracy demonstrations in April and May 1989, centred on Tiananmen Square in Beijing, ended on 3–4 June when the army took control of Beijing, killing thousands of protesters. This strengthened the position of hardliners within the leadership, who readopted policies of centralization based on Marxist ideology. Deng retired from his last official post in November 1989 but retained effective control until late 1994.

At Deng's instigation during 1992 the emphasis switched back to economic reform and the power of the hardliners waned. The 14th Party Congress in 1992 endorsed Deng's calls for faster, bolder economic reforms and his 'socialist market economy'. Deng died on 19 February 1997 and Jiang Zemin assumed the mantle of leader.

In addition to continuing economic reforms, Jiang has sought to improve China's standing in the international community. In June 1998, President Clinton became the first US president to visit China since the 1989 Tiananmen Square massacre; he was followed in October 1998 by UK Prime Minister, Tony Blair, who visited Beijing and Hong Kong and became the first foreign leader to have an article published in the *People's Daily*.

INSURGENCIES

Separatists from the Uygur Muslim minority group in Xinjiang Autonomous Region have demonstrated against Han rule. They have claimed responsibility for bomb attacks in the provincial capital, Ürümqi, and in Beijing. Two Muslim separatists were executed in January 1999 as part of an effort to tighten control of the region.

POLITICAL SYSTEM

Under the 1982 constitution, the National People's Congress is the highest organ of state power. It is elected for a term of five years and is supposed to hold one session a year. It is empowered to amend the constitution, make laws, select the president and vice-president and other leading officials of the state, approve the national economic plan, the state budget and the final state accounts, and to decide on questions of war and peace. The State Council is the highest organ of the state administration. It is composed of the Premier, the Vice-Premiers, the State Councillors, heads of Ministries and Commissions, the Auditor-General and the Secretary-General. Command over the armed forces is vested in the Central Military Commission.

Deputies to Congresses at the primary level are 'directly elected' by the voters 'through a secret ballot after democratic consultation'. This is now extended to county level. These Congresses elect the deputies to the Congress at the next higher level. Deputies to the National People's Congress are elected by the People's Congresses of the provinces, autonomous regions and municipalities directly under the central government, and by the armed forces.

Local government is conducted through People's Governments at provincial, municipal and county levels. Autonomous regions, prefectures and counties exist for national minorities and are described as self-governing.

HEAD OF STATE

President of the People's Republic of China, Jiang Zemin, *elected* April 1993, *re-elected* 16 March 1998

Vice-President, Hu Jintao
Chairman of the Standing Committee of the National People's Congress, Li Peng
Chairman of the Central Military Committee, Jiang Zemin

STATE COUNCIL *as at May 1999*

Premier, Zhu Rongji
Vice-Premiers, Qian Qichen; Li Lanqing; Wen Jiabao; Wu Bangguo
State Councillors, Gen. Chi Haotian; Ismail Amat; Luo Gan; Wu Yi; Wang Zhongyu

MINISTERS

Agriculture, Chen Yaobang
Civil Affairs, Doje Cering
Communications, Huang Zhendong
Construction, Yu Zhengsheng
Culture, Sun Jiazheng
Defence, Gen. Chi Haotian

Education, Chen Zhili
Finance, Xiang Huaicheng
Foreign Affairs, Tang Jiaxuan
Foreign Trade and Economic Co-operation, Shi Guansheng
Health, Zhang Wenkang
Information Industry, Wu Jichuan
Justice, Gao Changli
Labour and Social Security, Zhang Zuoji
Land and Natural Resources, Zhou Yongkang
Personnel, Song Defu
Public Security, Jia Chunwang
Railways, Fu Zhihuan
Science and Technology, Zhu Lilan
State Security, Xu Yongyue
Supervision, He Yong
Water Resources, Wang Shucheng

MINISTERS IN CHARGE OF STATE COMMISSIONS

Development Planning, Zeng Peiyan
Economics and Trade, Sheng Huaren
Ethnic Affairs, Li Dezhu
Family Planning, Zhang Weiqing
Legislative Affairs, Yang Jingyu
Science, Technology and Industry for National Defence, Liu Jibin
Auditor-General, Li Jinhua

Governor of the People's Bank of China, Dai Xianglong

THE CHINESE COMMUNIST PARTY

General Secretary, Jiang Zemin
Politburo Standing Committee, Jiang Zemin; Li Peng; Zhu Rongji; Li Ruihuan; Hu Jintao; Wei Jiangxing; Li Lanqing
Politburo of the Central Committee, Tian Jiyun; Jiang Zemin; Li Tieying; Li Ruihuan; Zhu Rongji; Hu Jintao; Ding Guangen; Qian Qichen; Li Lanqing; Wei Jiangxing; Wu Bangguo; Xie Fei; Li Peng; Huang Ju; Wen Jiabao; Li Changchun; Wu Guanzheng; Chi Haotian; Zhang Wannian; Luo Gan; Jia Qinglin; Jiang Chunyun (*full members*); Zeng Qinghong; Wu Yi (*alternate members*)
Secretariat of the Central Committee, Ding Guangen; Hu Jintao; Wei Jiangxing; Wen Jiabao; Zhang Wannian; Luo Gan; Zeng Qinghong (*full members*)
Membership, 52,000,000 (1993)

EMBASSY OF THE PEOPLE'S REPUBLIC OF CHINA
49-51 Portland Place, London WIN 4JL
Tel 0171-636 9375/5726
Ambassador Extraordinary and Plenipotentiary, HE Ma Zhengang, apptd 1997
Minister-Counsellor, Lu Kexing (*Commercial*)
Defence Attaché, Maj.-Gen. Yan Kunsheng

BRITISH EMBASSY
11 Guang Hua Lu, Jian Guo Men Wai, Beijing 100 600
Tel: Beijing 6532 1961/2/3/4
Ambassador, HE Anthony Galsworthy, DCMG, apptd 1997
Minister, Consul-General and Deputy Head of Mission, A. D. Sprake
Counsellors, J. V. Everard (*Political and Economic*); C. Segar (*Commercial*); M. Davidson (*Cultural, and British Council Representative*)
Defence, Military and Air Attaché, Brig. J. G. Kerr

BRITISH CONSULATES-GENERAL – Shanghai and Guangzhou

DEFENCE

All three military arms are parts of the People's Liberation Army (PLA). China has at least 17 intercontinental and 46 intermediate range land-based, and 13 submarine-launched nuclear ballistic missiles. The Army has about 8,800 main battle tanks, 5,500 armoured personnel carriers and armoured infantry fighting vehicles, and more than 14,500 artillery pieces.

The Navy has 63 submarines, 18 destroyers, 35 frigates, 747 patrol and coastal vessels, 541 combat aircraft and 25 armed helicopters. The Air Force has 3,566 combat aircraft.
MILITARY EXPENDITURE – 5.7 per cent of GDP (1997)
MILITARY PERSONNEL – 3,820,000: Army 2,090,000, Navy 260,000, Air Force 470,000, Paramilitaries 1,000,000
CONSCRIPTION DURATION – Three to four years

ECONOMY

Economic liberalization in the early 1980s reduced central planning and broadened the role of the market, which led to an explosion in manufacturing, concentrated in China's coastal regions. Foreign direct investment, especially from Hong Kong and Taiwan, has enabled the construction of a significant industrial base and transport infrastructure. In the coastal regions the economy has become a free market in all but name, with several stock markets and Shanghai's emergence as a financial centre. Excessive investment in capital construction required austerity measures in 1993–5 in an attempt to control inflation. The measures caused widespread unemployment, with an estimated 50–100 million migrant workers unemployed in 1995–6. By 1994, 50–60 per cent of industrial output was produced by private or collective firms which employed a total of 120 million people.

Agriculture remains of great importance, with 70 per cent of the population still living in rural areas. Agricultural policies have devolved responsibility for agricultural production to individual households. Cereals, with peas and beans, are grown in the northern provinces, and rice, tea and sugar in the south. Rice is the staple food of the inhabitants. Cotton (mostly in valleys of the Yangtze and Yellow Rivers), tea (in the west and south), with hemp, jute and flax, are the most important crops. Livestock is raised in large numbers. Sericulture is one of the oldest industries. Cottons, woollens and silks are manufactured in large quantities.

Coal, iron ore, tin, antimony, wolfram, bismuth and molybdenum are abundant. Oil is produced in several northern provinces, particularly in Heilongjiang and Shandong, and off-shore deposits are being sought in co-operation with western and Japanese companies. In November 1997, a deal was reached with Russia over the construction of a US$12 billion liquefied natural gas (LNG) pipeline to take LNG from Siberia to China's Pacific coast. In March 1998, China announced the construction of a US$2.3 billion 1,875-mile oil pipeline along the Silk Road to Kazakhstan.

In January 1998, reforms of the banking sector were announced in response to the south-east Asian financial crisis. The reforms introduce stricter controls on loan management, increased competition in the banking sector, and the dropping of import duties to encourage foreign investment. China's refusal to devalue the yuan has helped restore a degree of stability to the region.
GNP – US$1,055,372 million (1997); US$860 per capita (1997)
GDP – US$697,614 million (1995); US$582 per capita (1995)
ANNUAL AVERAGE GROWTH OF GDP – 10.5 per cent (1995)
INFLATION RATE – 2.8 per cent (1997)
UNEMPLOYMENT – 2.8 per cent (1994)

TOTAL EXTERNAL DEBT – US$146,697 million (1997)

TRADE

Foreign trade and external economic relations have grown enormously since 1978. In 1995, import tariffs were cut to an average 23 per cent in line with China's attempts to join the World Trade Organization. The principal exports are animals and animal products, oil, textiles, ores, metals, tea, electronics and manufactured goods. The principal imports are motor vehicles, machinery, chemical fertilizer, plants, aircraft, books, paper and paper-making materials, chemicals, metals and ores, and dyes.

In 1997 China had a trade surplus of US$46,222 million and a current account surplus of US$29,718. Imports totalled US$142,189 million and exports US$182,877 million.

Trade with UK	1997	1998
Imports from UK	£920,261,000	£868,952,000
Exports to UK	2,494,987,000	2,960,661,000

COMMUNICATIONS

There are 56,700 km of railway lines and 1,185,800 km of highway (1996). In addition, internal civil aviation has been developed, with routes totalling more than 471,900 km.

In the past the principal means of communication east to west was by the rivers, the most important of which are the Yangtze (Changjiang) (3,400 miles), the Yellow River (Huanghe) (2,600 miles) and the West River (Xihe) (1,650 miles). These, together with the network of canals connecting them, are still much used but their overall importance has declined. Coastal port facilities are being improved and the merchant fleet expanded.

Postal services and telecommunications have developed in recent years and it is claimed that 95 per cent of all rural townships are on the telephone and that postal routes reach practically every production brigade headquarters.

EDUCATION

Primary education lasts five years and secondary education lasts five years (three years in junior middle school and two years in senior middle school). There are over 1,000 universities, colleges and institutes.
ILLITERACY RATE – 17.8 per cent
ENROLMENT (percentage of age group) – primary 100 per cent (1996); tertiary 5.7 per cent (1996)

CULTURE

The Chinese language has many dialects, notably Cantonese, Hakka, Amoy, Foochow, Changsha, Nanchang, Wu (Shanghai) and the northern dialect. The Common Speech or *putonghua* (often referred to as Mandarin) is based on the northern dialect. The Communists have promoted it as the national language and it is taught throughout the country. As *putonghua* encourages the use of the spoken language in writing, the old literary style and ideographic form of writing has fallen into disuse. Since 1956 simplified characters have been introduced to make reading and writing easier. In 1958 the National People's Congress adopted a system of romanization known as pinyin.

Chinese literature is one of the richest in the world. Paper has been employed for writing and printing for nearly 2,000 years. The Confucian classics which formed the basis of traditional Chinese culture date from the Warring States period (fourth to third centuries BC), as do the earliest texts of Taoism. Histories, philosophical and scientific works, poetry, literary and art criticism, novels and romances survive from most periods.

Important newspapers and magazines include the *People's*

Daily and the twice-monthly *Qiushi*, which replaced *Red Flag* as the CCP's mouthpiece in 1989.

TIBET

AREA – 463,000 sq. miles (1,199,164 sq. km)
POPULATION – 2,260,000 (1993)
CAPITAL – Lhasa

Tibet is a plateau seldom lower than 10,000 feet, which forms the northern frontier of India (boundary imperfectly demarcated), from Kashmir to Myanmar, but is separated therefrom by the Himalayas.

From 1911 to 1950, Tibet was virtually an independent country though its status was never officially so recognized. In 1950 Chinese Communist forces invaded eastern Tibet. In 1951 an agreement was reached whereby the Chinese army was allowed entry into Tibet, and a Communist military and administrative headquarters was set up. A series of revolts against Chinese rule culminated in 1959 in a rising in Lhasa, the capital. Fighting continued for several days before the rebellion was crushed and military rule was imposed. The Dalai Lama fled to India where he and his followers were granted political asylum and established a government in exile.

In 1964 the Dalai Lama and the Panchen Lama were dismissed, marking the end of co-operation between the Chinese government and the traditional religious authorities. Tibet became an Autonomous Region of China in 1965. Martial law was declared in Tibet in 1989 after serious unrest, and sporadic outbursts of unrest continue.

The Panchen Lama died in 1989. China rejected the Dalai Lama's choice of successor, who is believed to have been executed, and enthroned its own candidate.

In December 1997, the International Commission of Jurists issued a report declaring that Tibet was 'under alien subjugation' and called for a UN-managed referendum to decide its future status. China contested that the report failed to acknowledge its historical claims to the region.

HONG KONG

AREA – 415 sq. miles (1,075 sq. km)
POPULATION – 6,687,200 (1998)
CURRENCY – Hong Kong dollar (HK$) of 100 cents
FLAG – Red, with a white bauhinia flower of five petals each containing a red star
LIFE EXPECTANCY (years) – male 75.84; female 81.16
POPULATION GROWTH RATE – 1.7 per cent (1996)
POPULATION DENSITY – 5,871 per sq. km (1996)
URBAN POPULATION – 93.1 per cent (1986)

Hong Kong, consisting of more than 230 islands and of a portion of the mainland (Kowloon and the New Territories) on the south-east coast of China, is situated at the eastern side of the mouth of the Pearl River. Hong Kong Island is about 11 miles (18 km) long and from two to five miles (three to eight km) broad. It is separated from the mainland by a narrow strait.

The climate is sub-tropical, tending towards the temperate for nearly half the year. The mean monthly temperature ranges from 16° C to 29° C. The average annual rainfall is 2,214 mm, of which nearly 80 per cent falls between May and September. Tropical cyclones occur between May and November, causing high winds and heavy rain.

HISTORY AND POLITICS

Hong Kong Island was first occupied by Great Britain in 1841 and formally ceded by the Treaty of Nanking in 1842. Kowloon was acquired by the Peking Convention of 1860 and the New Territories, consisting of a peninsula in the

southern part of the Guangdong province together with adjacent islands, by a 99-year lease signed on 9 June 1898.

On 19 December 1984 the UK and China signed a Joint Declaration in which it was agreed that China would resume sovereignty over Hong Kong on 1 July 1997. In the run-up to the 1997 handover, the Chinese government's insistence on a greater say in the running of the colony and Governor Patten's plan for an extension of democracy prompted acrimonious disputes. The Chinese government refused to accept the reforms and replaced the Legislative Council.

Hong Kong became, with effect from 1 July 1997, a Special Administrative Region (SAR) of the People's Republic of China.

The Joint Declaration which took effect in May 1985 guarantees: the free movement of goods and capital; the retention of Hong Kong's free port status, separate customs territory and freely convertible currency; the protection of property rights and foreign investment; the right of free movement to and from Hong Kong; Hong Kong's autonomy in the conduct of its external commercial relations and its own monetary and financial policies; and judicial independence. Hong Kong's constitution is the Basic Law which was passed by China's National People's Congress in 1990 and guarantees that the SAR's social and economic systems will remain unchanged for 50 years.

POLITICAL SYSTEM

Hong Kong is administered by the Hong Kong government, headed by the Chief Executive, who is aided by an Executive Council and a Legislative Council. The Executive Council consists of three ex-officio members (the Chief Secretary, the Financial Secretary and the Attorney-General) together with ten other members.

The Legislative Council consists of 60 members. Both the Chief Executive and the Legislative Council were elected by a 400-strong committee which in turn was chosen by a 150-member Preparatory Committee, headed by the Chinese foreign minister, from a shortlist drawn up by China. The President of the Legislative Council is elected by the members. Legislative elections in May 1998 used a proportional representation system in five geographical constituencies, each with three to five seats. Thirty members were elected in functional constituencies and ten more from a committee.

The Urban Council provides services relating to public health and sanitation, culture and recreation in the urban area. A Regional Council was set up in 1986 to provide similar services in the New Territories. There are also 18 district boards (nine in the urban areas and nine in the New Territories) which are statutory bodies that provide a forum for public consultation and participation in the administration of the districts.

Chief Executive, Tung Chee-hwa, *sworn in* 1 July 1997

EXECUTIVE COUNCIL *as at May 1999*

Non-official Members, Leung Chun-ying *(convenor)*; Dr Raymond Ch'ien; Chung Shui-ming; Nellie Fong Wong; Charles Lee; Antony Leung; Tam Yiu-chung; Henry Tang; Rosanna Wong; Yang Ti-liang
Ex-officio Members, Anson Chan; Donald Tsang; Elsie Leung

GOVERNMENT SECRETARIAT *as at May 1999*

Administrative Secretary, Anson Chan
Financial Secretary, Donald Tsang
Justice, Elsie Leung
Civil Service, Lam Woon-kwong
Constitutional Affairs, Michael Suen

Economic Services, Stephen Ip
Education and Manpower, Joseph Wong
Financial Services, Rafael Hui
Health and Welfare, Katherine Fok, OBE
Home Affairs, David Lan
Housing, Dominic Wong
Information, Technology and Broadcasting, Kwong Ki-chi
Planning, Environment and Lands, Gordon Siu
Security, Regina Ip
Trade and Industry, Chau Tak-hay
Transport, Nicholas Ng
Treasury, Denise Yue
Works, Kwong Hon-sang
President of the Legislative Council, Rita Fan

CONSUL-GENERAL, Sir Andrew Burns, KCMG, 1 Supreme Court Road, Central, (PO Box 528), Hong Kong. Tel: Hong Kong 2901 3000
BRITISH COUNCIL REPRESENTATIVE, D. Lauder
HONG KONG ECONOMIC AND TRADE OFFICE, 6 Grafton Street, London WIX 3LB. Tel: 0171-499 9821. *Commissioner,* Sandra Lee, apptd 1999

ECONOMY

The main economic sector is the services industry, especially financial services. It employs roughly two thirds of the workforce and contributed 84 per cent to GDP in 1996. The manufacturing sector contributed 8.8 per cent to GDP. Principal exports are clothing, electrical machinery and apparatus, and textiles.

Diversification in terms of products and markets continues to be the main feature of recent industrial development, as are industrial partnerships with overseas companies. The economy is based on export rather than the domestic market. Tourism is very important to the economy; over 12 million people visited Hong Kong in 1996.

In October 1997, the financial crisis in south-east Asia reached Hong Kong, causing the Hang Seng index to fall by 33.4 per cent in two weeks. The Hong Kong Monetary Authority used its foreign exchange reserves to fend off speculators and preserve the Hong Kong currency's peg to the US dollar, which stabilized the currency. In January 1998, the region's largest investment bank, Peregrine Investment Holdings, filed for liquidation, plunging the financial market back into turmoil; between September 1997 and January 1998 the Hang Seng index lost half its value. GDP declined throughout 1998, the result of falling government and consumer spending, property prices and exports. By January 1999, unemployment was 5.8 per cent and deflation had set in.
GNP – US$163,834 million (1997); US$25,200 per capita (1997)
GDP – US$140,201 million (1995); US$22,898 per capita (1995)
ANNUAL AVERAGE GROWTH OF GDP – 5.8 per cent (1995)
INFLATION RATE – 5.8 per cent (1997)

TRADE

In 1997 imports totalled US$208,616 million and exports US$188,063 million. Hong Kong's principal customers for its domestic products, in order of value of trade, were China, USA, Japan and Germany. China was its principal supplier.

Trade with UK	1997	1998
Imports from UK	£3,210,841,000	£2,699,885,000
Exports to UK	4,348,846,000	4,614,388,000

COMMUNICATIONS

Hong Kong has one of the world's finest natural harbours, and it is the busiest container port in the world, with eight terminals, as well as large modern cargo and liner terminals. Dockyard facilities include eight floating drydocks, the largest being capable of docking vessels up to 150,000 tonnes deadweight. A new 17-berth container port will open in stages between 1997 and 2003.

An international airport built on reclaimed land at Chek Lap Kok opened in July 1998. When fully operational, it will be capable of handling 35 million passengers and 1.5 million tonnes of cargo annually.

EDUCATION

Free education for children up to the age of 15 is compulsory. Post-secondary education is provided by six universities and one college. The Open Learning Institute of Hong Kong provides university education. There are also seven technical institutes and the Hong Kong Institute of Education.
ILLITERACY RATE – 7.8 per cent
ENROLMENT (percentage of age group) – primary 91 per cent (1995); secondary 71 per cent (1995); tertiary 21.9 per cent (1993)

COLOMBIA
República de Colombia

AREA – 439,737 sq. miles (1,138,914 sq. km). Neighbours: Venezuela (north and east), Brazil (south-east), Peru (south), Ecuador (south-west), Panama (north-west)
POPULATION – 35,626,000 (1994 UN estimate). The language is Spanish. Roman Catholicism is the established religion
CAPITAL – Bogotá (population, 5,398,998, 1993)
MAJOR CITIES – ΨBarranquilla (1,328,833), the major port on the Caribbean; Bucaramanga (759,651); ΨBuenaventura (227,478), the major port on the Pacific; Cali (2,063,867); ΨCartagena (656,632); Medellín (2,556,357)
CURRENCY – Colombian peso of 100 centavos
NATIONAL ANTHEM – Oh gloria inmarcesible
NATIONAL DAY – 20 July (National Independence Day)
NATIONAL FLAG – Broad yellow band in upper half, surmounting equal bands of blue and red
LIFE EXPECTANCY (years) – male 66.36; female 72.26
POPULATION GROWTH RATE – 1.6 per cent (1996)
POPULATION DENSITY – 31 per sq. km (1996)
URBAN POPULATION – 71.0 per cent (1993)

Colombia lies in the extreme north-west of South America, having a coastline on both the Caribbean Sea and Pacific Ocean.

The country is divided by the Cordillera de los Andes into a coastal region in the north and west and extensive plains in the east. The eastern range of the Colombian Andes is a series of vast tablelands. This temperate region is the most densely peopled portion of the country. The principal rivers are the Magdalena, Guaviare, Cauca, Atrato, Caquetá, Putumayo and Patia.

HISTORY AND POLITICS

The Colombian coast was visited in 1502 by Columbus, and in 1536 a Spanish expedition penetrated the interior and established a government. The country remained under Spanish rule until 1819 when Simón Bolívar established the Republic of Colombia, consisting of the territories now known as Colombia, Panama, Venezuela and Ecuador. In 1829–30 Venezuela and Ecuador withdrew, and in 1831 the remaining territories formed the Republic of New Granada. The name was changed to the Granadine Confederation in 1858, to the United States of Colombia in 1861 and to the Republic of Colombia in 1866. Panama seceded in 1903.

During the early 1950s Colombia suffered a period of virtual civil war between the supporters of the Conservative and the Liberal parties. From 1957 to 1974 the country was governed under the 'National Front' agreement with an alternating presidency and equal numbers of ministerial posts. The alternation of the presidency ended in 1974 and parity in appointments in 1978.

A new constitution was promulgated in 1991. In the 1994 presidential election the Liberal candidate Ernesto Samper narrowly defeated the Social Conservative Party (PSC) candidate. President Samper appointed a Liberal–PSC coalition government in August 1994. The March 1998 legislative elections were won by the Liberal Party, but some of its members defected to join the Great Alliance for Change, a Conservative-led coalition which now commands an overall majority in the House of Representatives. The presidential election in June 1998 was won by the PSC candidate Andrés Pastrana Arango, who swore in a cabinet which includes members of GAC coalition on 7 August 1998.

INSURGENCIES

Colombia is dogged by insurgency from left-wing guerrillas and from the drugs cartels centred on Cali. The main active guerrilla factions are the Revolutionary Armed Forces of Colombia (FARC) and the National Liberation Army (ELN). Preliminary discussions regarding peace talks were held in June 1997. Formal peace talks finally began on 6 May 1999.

POLITICAL SYSTEM

The Congress is a bicameral legislature. The lower house (the House of Representatives) has 161 members elected for a four-year term. The upper house (the Senate) has 102 members, 99 of whom are directly elected for four years; three seats are reserved for representatives of indigenous people. The president, who appoints the Cabinet, is directly elected for a four-year term.

HEAD OF STATE
President, Andrés Pastrana Arango, *elected* 21 June 1998
Vice-President, Gustavo Bell

CABINET *as at May 1999*
Agriculture and Rural Development, Carlos Murgas
Communications, Claudia de Francisco (PSC)
Culture, Alberto Casas
Defence, Rodrigo Lloreda Caicedo (PSC)
Economic Development, Fernando Araujo (PSC)
Education, Germán Bula (LP)
Environment, Juan Mayr (Ind.)
Finance, Juan Camilo Restrepo (PSC)
Foreign Affairs, Guillermo Fernández de Soto (PSC)
Foreign Trade, Marta Lucia Ramírez (LP)
Health, Virgilio Galvis (LP)
Interior, Néstor Humberto Martínez (LP)
Justice, Parmiento Cuéllar (LP)
Labour and Social Welfare, Hernando Yepes (PSC)
Mines and Energy, Luis Carlos Valenzuela (PSC)
Planning, Jaime Ruiz
Transport, Mauricio Cárdenas Santamaría (PSC)

COLOMBIAN EMBASSY
Flat 3A, 3 Hans Crescent, London SWIX OLN
Tel 0171-589 9177/5037

Ambassador Extraordinary and Plenipotentiary, HE Humberto de la Calle-Lombana, apptd 1998

BRITISH EMBASSY
Edificio Ing Barings, Carrera 9 No 76-49 Piso 9, Bogotá
Tel: Bogotá 317 6690/6310/6321
Ambassador Extraordinary and Plenipotentiary, HE Jeremy Thorp, apptd 1998
BRITISH CONSULAR OFFICES – Barranquilla, Bogotá, Cali and Medellín

BRITISH COUNCIL DIRECTOR, K. Board, OBE, Calle 87 No. 12–79, Bogotá DE
COLOMBO-BRITISH CHAMBER OF COMMERCE, Apartado Aereo 054 728, Av. 39 No. 13–62, Bogotá DE

DEFENCE

The Army has 12 light tanks, 160 armoured personnel carriers, and 130 artillery pieces. The Navy has two submarines, four frigates, 104 patrol and coastal vessels, six aircraft and two helicopters at nine bases. The Air Force has 72 combat aircraft and 72 armed helicopters.
MILITARY EXPENDITURE – 4.0 per cent of GDP (1997)
MILITARY PERSONNEL – 146,300: Army 121,000, Navy 18,000, Air Force 7,300
CONSCRIPTION DURATION – 12–18 months

ECONOMY

Coal, natural gas and hydroelectricity resources are largely unexploited, although development of coal is being given priority. The hydrocarbon sector accounts for over half of the mining output, precious metals (gold, platinum and silver) and iron ore accounting for the remainder. Other mineral deposits include nickel, bauxite, copper, gypsum, limestone, phosphates, sulphur and uranium. Colombia is also the world's largest producer of emeralds.

Major cash crops are coffee, sugar, bananas, cut flowers and cotton. Cattle are raised in large numbers, and meat and cured skins and hides are also exported.

The government has encouraged diversification to reduce dependence on coffee as the major export and this has led to the growth of new export-orientated industries, particularly textiles, paper products and leather goods. Stimulus to the economy has been provided by loans from the World Bank and IADB for project development.

Since the late 1980s the government has introduced trade liberalization and privatization measures which have effectively freed foreign exchange transactions, increased foreign competition, ended protectionism and reduced inflation.

In 1996 there was a trade deficit of US$2,133 million and a current account deficit of US$4,754 million. In 1996 and 1997 Colombia was blacklisted by the USA for failing to curb levels of drug production sufficiently. These sanctions were ended in March 1998 in recognition of new efforts made by the Colombian government in the fight against drugs; however, Colombia was not included on the USA's list of countries whose co-operation over narcotics was deemed to be 'satisfactory'
GNP – US$87,125 million (1997); US$2,180 per capita (1997)
GDP – US$79,322 million (1995); US$2,215 per capita (1995)
ANNUAL AVERAGE GROWTH OF GDP – 2.1 per cent (1996)
INFLATION RATE – 18.5 per cent (1997)
TOTAL EXTERNAL DEBT – US$31,777 million (1997)

TRADE

Principal exports are petroleum and derivatives, coffee, bananas, cut flowers, clothing and textiles, ferro-nickel and coal. Principal trading partners are the USA, the EU and Latin America.

In 1997 imports totalled US$15,378 million and exports US$11,522 million.

Trade with UK	1997	1998
Imports from UK	£170,503,000	£179,744,000
Exports to UK	185,657,000	208,520,000

COMMUNICATIONS

The Andes make surface transport difficult so air transport is used extensively. There are daily air services between Bogotá and all the principal towns, as well as frequent services to other countries. The 'Atlantic Railway' links the departmental lines running down to the River Magdalena, and completes the connection between Bogotá and Santa Marta. Although the railways are in a poor state, there are about 3,386 km of rail in use at present. The road network consists of 106,600 km of roads of all types, of which 21,800 km are classified as main trunk and transversal roads. A canal to link the Pacific Ocean and the Caribbean Sea has been planned.

There are three national television channels.

CULTURE AND EDUCATION

There is a flourishing press in urban areas and a national literature supplements the rich inheritance from the time of Spanish colonial rule. State education is free.

ILLITERACY RATE – 8.7 per cent

ENROLMENT (percentage of age group) – primary 89 per cent (1996); secondary 50 per cent (1995); tertiary 18.6 per cent (1996)

THE COMOROS
République Fédérale Islamique des Comores

AREA – 863 sq. miles (2,235 sq. km). The Comoro archipelago includes the islands of Great Comoro, Anjouan, Mayotte and Moheli and certain islets in the Indian Ocean

POPULATION – 632,000 (1994 UN estimate), mostly Muslim. French and Arabic are the official languages; the majority of the population speak Comoran, a blend of Arabic and Swahili

CAPITAL – Moroni (population, 17,267, 1980 estimate), on Great Comoro

CURRENCY – Comorian franc (KMF) of 100 centimes. The Franc CFA of 100 centimes is also used

NATIONAL DAY – 6 July (Independence Day)

NATIONAL FLAG – Green ground, with a white crescent and four white stars, horns towards the fly. The name of *Allah,* in Arabic script in the upper fly and the name of *Mohammed* in the lower hoist

LIFE EXPECTANCY (years) – male 55.50; female 56.50

POPULATION GROWTH RATE – 3.2 per cent (1996)

POPULATION DENSITY – 283 per sq. km (1996)

URBAN POPULATION – 28.5 per cent (1991)

ILLITERACY RATE – 42.7 per cent

ENROLMENT (percentage of age group) – primary 53 per cent (1993); tertiary 0.6 per cent (1995)

HISTORY AND POLITICS

The islanders voted for independence from France in December 1974 and three islands became independent on 6 July 1975. The island of Mayotte opposed independence and has remained under French administration.

An election in 1993 brought President Djohar's PDR party to power. Djohar was temporarily ousted in a coup in 1995 which was thwarted by French troops. While Djohar was abroad for medical attention, the Prime Minister of the newly installed unity government, Caabiel Yachrou-tou, declared himself interim president and refused to acknowledge Djohar's authority, resulting in the formation of a rival government. Djohar returned to the Comoros in January 1996 but was prohibited from contesting the March 1996 presidential election, which was won by Mohammad Taki Abdoulkarim of the National Union for Democracy in the Comoros. Taki dissolved the National Assembly and legislative elections were held in December 1996 although boycotted by the opposition FAR.

In August 1997 separatists on the islands of Anjouan and Moheli demanded independence from the Comoros and a return to French rule. Following a failed attempt to resolve the situation by force, President Taki assumed absolute power and established a State Transition Commission to function as a Cabinet. In a referendum in October, the inhabitants of Anjouan voted overwhelmingly for independence. Talks mediated by the OAU began in December 1997 and are continuing.

In March 1998, Anjouan's self-proclaimed President Abdallah Ibrahim appointed a prime minister and Cabinet, though their legitimacy has not been recognized internationally. Fighting broke out between President Ibrahim's forces and those of a previous Anjouan prime minister, Chamassi Said Omar, on 5 December 1998. Negotiations to secure peace between the two sides began on 17 December.

President Taki died in office on 6 November 1998 and Tajiddine Ben Said Massonde took over as interim president. He and the government he had appointed were deposed in a coup on 30 April 1999 by Col. Azali Assoumani, who was sworn in as president on 6 May.

POLITICAL SYSTEM

In October 1996 a new constitution was approved by referendum. The president may be elected for an unlimited number of six-year terms and has the authority to appoint a prime minister and Governors, and reports to the Federal Assembly.

Each island is administered by a Governor, assisted by up to four Commissioners whom he appoints, and has an elected Legislative Council.

HEAD OF STATE
President, Col. Azali Assoumani

COUNCIL OF MINISTERS *as at May 1999*
Prime Minister, Defence, Col. Azali Assoumani

EMBASSY OF THE FEDERAL ISLAMIC REPUBLIC OF THE COMOROS
20 rue Marbeau, 75016 Paris, France
Tel Paris 4067 9054

BRITISH AMBASSADOR, HE Robert Dewar, resident at Antananarivo, Madagascar

ECONOMY

The most important products are vanilla, copra, cloves and essential oils, which are the principal exports; cacao, sisal and coffee are also cultivated. Great Comoro is well forested and produces some timber.

GNP – US$209 million (1997); US$400 per capita (1997)

GDP – US$225 million (1995); US$367 per capita (1995)

TOTAL EXTERNAL DEBT – US$197 million (1997)

Trade with UK	1997	1998
Imports from UK	£457,000	£790,000
Exports to UK	35,000	229,000

DEMOCRATIC REPUBLIC OF CONGO

AREA – 905,355 sq. miles (2,344,858 sq. km). Neighbours:
Central African Republic (north), Sudan (north-east),
Uganda, Rwanda, Burundi and Tanzania (east), Zambia
(south), Angola (south-west), Republic of Congo-
Brazzaville (north-west)
POPULATION – 46,812,000 (1994 UN estimate). The
population was 34,671,607 at the 1985 census,
composed almost entirely of Bantu groups, divided into
roughly 300 semi-autonomous tribes. Minorities
include Sudanese, Nilotes, Pygmies and Hamites, as
well as refugees from Angola. Swahili, a Bantu dialect
with an admixture of Arabic, is the nearest approach to
a common language in the east and south, while
Lingala is the language of a large area along the river
and in the north, and Kikongo of the region between
Kinshasa and the sea. French is the language of
administration
CAPITAL – Kinshasa (population, 2,664,309, 1984)
MAJOR CITIES – Kananga (601,239); Kisangani (310,705);
Likasi (146,394); Lubumbashi (403,623); ΨMatadi
(143,598); Mbandaka (134,495)
CURRENCY – Congolese franc
NATIONAL DAY – 24 November
NATIONAL FLAG – Blue with a large yellow five-pointed
star in the centre and five small yellow five-pointed
stars in a vertical line down the hoist
LIFE EXPECTANCY (years) – male 50.40; female 53.66
POPULATION GROWTH RATE – 4.6 per cent (1996)
POPULATION DENSITY – 20 per sq. km (1996)
URBAN POPULATION – 39.5 per cent (1985)
MILITARY EXPENDITURE – 5.3 per cent of GDP (1997)
MILITARY PERSONNEL – 50,090: Army 50,000, Navy 90
ILLITERACY RATE – 22.7 per cent
ENROLMENT (percentage of age group) – primary 61 per
cent (1994); secondary 23 per cent (1994); tertiary 2.3
per cent (1994)

The Democratic Republic of Congo (formerly Zaïre) is
Africa's third largest state. Apart from the coastal district
in the west which is fairly dry, the rainfall averages between
60 and 80 inches. The average temperature is about 27°C,
but in the south the winter temperature can fall nearly to
freezing point. Extensive forest covers the central districts.

HISTORY AND POLITICS

The state of the Congo, founded in 1885, became a Belgian
colony in 1908 and was administered by Belgium until
independence in 1960. Mobutu Sésé Seko, formerly
commander-in-chief of the Congolese National Army,
came to power in a coup in 1965 and was elected president
in 1970. Legislative power was vested in a unicameral
National Legislative Council, with candidates proposed by
the sole legal political party, Mouvement Populaire de la
Révolution (MPR).

Political reforms were announced in April 1990 and
President Mobutu called a National Conference to draft a
new constitution although the government refused to grant
it sovereign status. Mobutu accepted an opposition-
dominated government under Prime Minister Etienne
Tshisekedi in October 1991. His attempts to replace this
with MPR-dominated governments failed and the National
Conference confirmed the Tshisekedi government as
legitimate in August 1992.

From 1992 to 1995 the president and the opposition
were locked in a power struggle. In January 1994 President

Mobutu dissolved the government and on 9 April 1994
promulgated a Transitional Constitutional Act which
regulated a 15-month period of transition to democracy. In
July 1995 the transition period was extended by a further
two years.

In October 1996 fighting broke out between Zaïrean
Tutsis (*Banyamulenge*) and the Zaïrean army in North and
South Kivu provinces which had received an influx of
Hutu refugees from Rwanda. The pro-Hutu army at-
tempted to expel the Tutsis from the region but found
themselves outgunned by the rebels, under the leadership
of Laurent Kabila, who were backed by the Rwandan and
Ugandan governments. Kabila's Alliance of Democratic
Forces for the Liberation of Congo-Zaïre (AFDL) captured
Kinshasa in May 1997 and President Mobutu fled. Zaïre
was renamed the Democratic Republic of Congo.

A rebellion against the government of Laurent Kabila
began in Kivu on 2 August 1998 and by the end of the
month the rebels had seized large areas in the east and
west of the country. Angola, Chad, Kenya, Namibia and
Zimbabwe promised President Kabila military support.
The Angolan army quickly recaptured several towns in the
south-west, but the rebels maintained their grip on the
eastern regions. The rebel movement, the Congolese
Democratic Rally (RCD), was supported by Uganda and
Rwanda. Uganda signed a unilateral peace agreement in
April 1999 after a meeting with President Kabila, but was
reported to have trained rebel troops. On 17 May 1999,
Ernest Wamba dia Wamba, the RCD leader, was ousted,
splitting the movement into two distinct factions.

POLITICAL SYSTEM

A Constituent Council was set up to draft a new
constitution. Political parties have been banned.

There are 11 regions, each under a Governor and
provincial administration: Bas-Zaïre (provincial capital,
Matadi); Bandundu (Bandundu); Equateur (Mbandaka);
Haut-Zaïre (Kisangani); Kinshasa (Kinshasa); Maniema
(Kindu); North Kivu (Goma); South Kivu (Bukavu); Shaba
(Katanga) (Lubumbashi); East Kasai (Mbuji-Mayi); West
Kasai (Kananga).

HEAD OF STATE

President and Minister of Defence, Laurent Désiré Kabila,
sworn in 29 May 1997

CABINET *as at May 1999*

Agriculture and Animal Husbandry, Etienne Kikanga Shima Musebo
Civil Service, Paul-Gabriel Kapita Shabanga
Culture, Juliana Lumumba
Economy and Industry, Bemba Saolona
Energy, Dabi Mbaye
Finance and State Enterprises, Ferdinand Mawapanga Mwananga
Foreign Affairs, Abdoulaye Yerodia Ndombasi
Health, Machako Mambai
Human Rights, Leonard Okitundu
Information and Tourism, Didier Mumengi
Interior, Gaetan Kakudji
Justice, Mwenze Kongolo
Land Affairs, Environment, Fisheries and Forest Resources, Anatole Bisikwabo Tshiumbaka
Mines, Frederic Kibassa-Maliba
National Education, Kamara Rwakaikara
Oil Development, Pierre-Victor Mpoyo
Planning and Trade, Badimani Bilembo Mulumba
Post and Telecommunications, Drosper Kibue Molambo
Public Works, Yagi Sitholo
Social Affairs, Moleko Moliwa
Transport and Communications, Odette Babandoya Etowa
Youth and Sports, Vincent Mutomb Tshibal

EMBASSY OF THE DEMOCRATIC REPUBLIC OF CONGO
26 Chesham Place, London SW1X 8HH
Tel 0171-235 6137
Chargé d'Affaires, Nsangolo Iwula

BRITISH EMBASSY
Avenue le Mera, Kinshasa
Tel: Kinshasa 1447752
Ambassador Extraordinary and Plenipotentiary, HE Douglas Scrafton, apptd 1996
CONSULATE – Kisangani

ECONOMY

Palm oil is the most important agricultural cash product though it is no longer exported. Coffee, rubber, cocoa and timber are the most important agricultural exports. The production of cotton, pyrethrum and copal is increasing. Copper is widely exploited, and industrial diamonds and cobalt are also produced. Oil deposits are exploited off the Zaïre estuary and reef-gold is mined in the north-east of the country.

The main industrial products are foodstuffs, beverages, tobacco, textiles, leather, wood products, cement and building materials, metallurgy, small river craft and bicycles. There are reserves of hydroelectric power and the Inga dam on the river Zaïre supplies electricity to Matadi, Kinshasa and Shaba.

Rampant hyperinflation and corruption have left the economy and the state's finances in a parlous state. Multilateral and bilateral aid were greatly reduced because of President Mobutu's refusal to leave office.

In 1993 the government had a budget deficit equivalent to 13.72 per cent of GDP.
GNP – US$5,201 million (1997); US$110 per capita (1997)
GDP – US$5,337 million (1995); US$117 per capita (1995)
ANNUAL AVERAGE GROWTH OF GDP – –0.7 per cent (1995)
INFLATION RATE – 175.5 per cent (1997)
TOTAL EXTERNAL DEBT – US$12,330 million (1997)

TRADE

The chief exports are copper, crude oil, coffee, diamonds, rubber, cobalt, gold, zinc and other metals.

In 1996 imports totalled US$424 million and exports US$592 million.

Trade with UK	1997	1998
Imports from UK	£14,827,000	£5,905,000
Exports to UK	5,073,000	4,129,000

COMMUNICATIONS

There are approximately 20,500 km of roads (earth-surfaced) of national importance, and 6,000 km of railways. The country has four international and 40 principal airports.

REPUBLIC OF CONGO-BRAZZAVILLE
République du Congo-Brazzaville

AREA – 132,047 sq. miles (342,000 sq. km). Neighbours: Gabon (west), Cameroon and Central African Republic (north), Angola (Cabinda) (south-west), the Democratic Republic of Congo (east and south)
POPULATION – 2,668,000 (1994 UN estimate). The official language is French; Lingala and Kikongo are widely spoken
CAPITAL – Brazzaville (population, 596,200, 1984)
MAJOR CITIES – ΨPointe Noire (350,000), the main commercial centre
CURRENCY – Franc CFA of 100 centimes
NATIONAL DAY – 15 August
NATIONAL FLAG – Divided diagonally into green, yellow and red bands
LIFE EXPECTANCY (years) – male 48.91; female 53.77
POPULATION GROWTH RATE – 3.0 per cent (1996)
POPULATION DENSITY – 8 per sq. km (1996)
MILITARY EXPENDITURE – 2.5 per cent of GDP (1997)
MILITARY PERSONNEL – 12,000: Army 8,000, Navy 800, Air Force 1,200, Paramilitaries 2,000
ILLITERACY RATE – 25.1 per cent
ENROLMENT (percentage of age group) –primary 96 per cent (1980); tertiary 5.3 per cent (1990)

HISTORY AND POLITICS

Formerly the French colony of Middle Congo, the Congo became a member state of the French Community on 28 November 1958 and fully independent on 17 August 1960.

In 1968, a National Council of army officers took power and created the Parti Congolais du Travail (PCT) and the People's Republic of the Congo. After popular pressure, the PCT abandoned its monopoly of power and renounced Marxism in 1990. In 1992 the country adopted a new multiparty constitution with a directly elected president and a bicameral parliament. The lack of a parliamentary majority forced President Lissouba to call fresh elections in 1993. These were won by the Pan-African Union for Social Democracy (UPADS) but the results were disputed by opposition groups and violence broke out between rival parties. A new UPADS-dominated government was appointed in January 1995. In June 1997, fighting broke out between forces of President Lissouba and followers of former president Sassou-Nguesso, who was reinstalled as president in October 1997. Elections scheduled for July 1997 were called off and a National Forum for Unity and Democracy was set up to schedule legislative elections. It declared a three-year transition period after which democratic elections will be held. A constitutional committee was inaugurated on 19 November 1998, charged with drafting a constitution to be approved by referendum in 1999.

Supporters of Bernard Kolelas, who had briefly been prime minister in 1997, were thought to be responsible for a wave of killings in the Pool region close to Brazzaville, which began in November 1998. In April 1999, they formed themselves into a political party, the Patriotic Union of Ninja Forces.

HEAD OF STATE
President, Denis Sassou-Nguesso, *sworn in* 25 October 1997

CABINET *as at May 1999*
Agriculture and Livestock, Nkoua Celestin Gongara
Civil Service, Administrative Reform and Women's Affairs,
  Jeanne Dambenze
Commerce, Small and Medium-sized Enterprises, Pierre
  Damien Boussoukou Boumba
Communication and Government Spokesman, François Ibovi
Culture and Tourism, Mambou Elie Niamy
Energy and Water Resources, Jean-Marie Tassoua
Finance and Budget, Mathias Dzon
Foreign Affairs and Co-operation, Rodolphe Adada
Forestry, Henri Djombo
Health and National Solidarity, Leon Alfred Opimba
Industrial Development, Alphonse Mbamba
Industry and Mines, Michel Mampoya
Interior, Security and Territorial Administration, Col. Pierre
  Oba
Keeper of the Seals, Justice, Jean-Martin M'bemba
Labour and Social Security, Lambert Ndouane
Minister in the President's Office in charge of Defence, Itihi
  Lekounzou Ossetoumba
Petroleum Affairs, Jean-Baptiste Taty-Loutard
Posts and Telecommunications, Jean-Félix Demba Delo
Primary and Secondary Education, Pierre Tsiba
Reconstruction and Urban Development, Martin Mberi
Social Amenities and Public Works, Col. Florent Tsiba
Technical Education and Vocational Training, André Okombi
  Salissan
Territorial and Regional Development, Pierre Moussa
Transport, Civil Aviation and Merchant Navy, Isidore
  Mvouba

EMBASSY OF THE REPUBLIC OF CONGO
37 bis rue Paul Valéry, F-75116 Paris, France
Tel: Paris 4500 6057
Ambassador Extraordinary and Plenipotentiary, vacant

HONORARY CONSULATE, 4 Wendle Court, 131–137
  Wandsworth Road, London SW8 2LH. Tel: 0171-622
  0419. *Honorary Consul,* L. Muzzu

BRITISH AMBASSADOR, HE Douglas Scrafton, resident at
  Kinshasa, Democratic Republic of Congo
HONORARY CONSULATE – Brazzaville

ECONOMY

Congo has its own oil deposits, producing about 9 million tonnes annually. It also produces lead, zinc and gold. The principal agricultural products are timber, cassava and yams. Imports are mainly of machinery.

In 1997 Congo had a trade surplus of US$941 million and a current account deficit of US$252 million. Imports in 1996 totalled US$1,551 million and exports US$1,345 million. In 1996 the UN approved a three-year loan of US$100 million and the Paris Club cancelled 67 per cent of the debt owed to it by Congo.

GNP – US$1,827 million (1997); US$670 per capita
  (1997)

GDP – US$2,614 million (1995); US$1,008 per capita
  (1995)
ANNUAL AVERAGE GROWTH OF GDP – –0.4 per cent
  (1995)
INFLATION RATE – –0.2 per cent (1996)
TOTAL EXTERNAL DEBT – US$5,071 million (1997)

Trade with UK	1997	1998
Imports from UK	£28,472,000	£21,512,000
Exports to UK	4,918,000	6,943,000

COSTA RICA
República de Costa Rica

AREA – 19,730 sq. miles (51,100 sq. km). Neighbours:
  Nicaragua, Panama
POPULATION – 3,398,000 (1994 UN estimate), mainly of
  European origin. The language is Spanish
CAPITAL – San José (population, 1,209,045, 1994
  estimate)
MAJOR CITIES – Alajuela (173,470); Cartago (119,299)
CURRENCY – Costa Rican colón (₡) of 100 céntimos
NATIONAL ANTHEM – Himno Nacional de Costa Rica
NATIONAL DAY – 15 September
NATIONAL FLAG – Five horizontal bands, blue, white,
  red, white, blue (the red band twice the width of the
  others with emblem near staff)
LIFE EXPECTANCY (years) – male 72.89; female 77.60
POPULATION GROWTH RATE – 3.2 per cent (1996)
POPULATION DENSITY – 66 per sq. km (1996)
URBAN POPULATION – 41.4 per cent (1994)
MILITARY EXPENDITURE – 0.7 per cent of GDP (1997)
MILITARY PERSONNEL – 8,400: Paramilitaries
ILLITERACY RATE – 5.2 per cent
ENROLMENT (percentage of age group) – primary 94 per
  cent (1996); secondary 43 per cent (1996); tertiary 31.9
  per cent (1994)

The coastal lowlands have a tropical climate but the interior plateau, with a mean elevation of 4,000 feet, enjoys a temperate climate.

HISTORY AND POLITICS

For nearly three centuries (1530–1821) Costa Rica was under Spanish rule. In 1821 the country obtained its independence, although from 1824 to 1839 it was one of the United States of Central America.

In 1948 the Army was abolished, the President declaring it unnecessary. The main political parties are the Social Christian Unity Party (PUSC) and the National Liberation Party (PLN). The last presidential and legislative elections were held on 1 February 1998, when PUSC candidate Miguel Angel Rodríguez won the presidential election, and the PUSC won 27 seats in the Legislative Assembly.

POLITICAL SYSTEM

Executive power is vested in the president, who is head of state and government, with legislative power vested in the 57-member Legislative Assembly. Under the constitution both the president and the members of the Legislative Assembly are elected for a single four-year term and may not be re-elected.

HEAD OF STATE
President, Miguel Angel Rodríguez , *elected* 1 February
  1998

CABINET *as at May 1999*

Vice-President, Minister of Culture, Astrid Fischel
Vice-President, Minister of Environment, Elizabeth Odio
Agriculture and Livestock, Esteban Brenes
Economy and Foreign Trade, Samuel Guzowski
Finance, Leonel Baruch
Foreign Affairs, Roberto Rojas
Health, Rogelio Pardo
Housing, José Antonio Lobo
Justice, Mónica Nágel
Labour and Social Security, Victor Morales
Presidency and Planning, Roberto Tovar
President of the Central Bank, Eduardo Lizano
Public Education, Claudio Gutiérrez
Public Security, Juan Rafael Lizano
Public Works and Transport, Rodolfo Mendez
Women's Affairs, Yolanda Ingianna

COSTA RICAN EMBASSY
Flat 1, 14 Lancaster Gate, London W2 3LH
Tel 0171-706 8844
Ambassador Extraordinary and Plenipotentiary, HE Rodolfo
   Gutierez, apptd 1998

BRITISH EMBASSY
Apartado 815, Edificio Centro Colón (Eleventh Floor),
San José 1007
Tel: San José 258 2025
*Ambassador Extraordinary and Plenipotentiary and Consul-
General,* HE Peter Spiceley, apptd 1998

ECONOMY

Tourism is the largest single industry, with ecotourism a growing area; one third of the country is national parkland or nature reserve. Industrial activity is principally in the manufacturing sector and manufactured goods include computer components, foodstuffs, textiles and clothing, plastic goods and pharmaceuticals. The principal agricultural products are coffee, bananas, sugar and cattle (for meat).

GNP – US$9,275 million (1997); US$2,680 per capita
   (1997)
GDP – US$9,233 million (1995); US$2,696 per capita (1995)
ANNUAL AVERAGE GROWTH OF GDP – –0.7 per cent
   (1996)
INFLATION RATE – 13.2 per cent (1997)
UNEMPLOYMENT – 5.2 per cent (1995)
TOTAL EXTERNAL DEBT – US$3,548 million (1997)

TRADE

The chief exports are manufactured goods, coffee, bananas, cocoa and sugar. The chief imports are machinery, including transport equipment, manufactures, chemicals, fuel and mineral oils and foodstuffs. In 1995 there was a trade deficit of US$474 million and a current account deficit of US$143 million. In 1997 imports totalled US$4,088 million and exports US$3,281 million.

Trade with UK	1997	1998
Imports from UK	£38,845,000	£38,381,000
Exports to UK	71,585,000	174,414,000

COMMUNICATIONS

The chief ports are Limón on the Atlantic coast, through which passes most of the coffee exported, and Caldera on the Pacific coast. LACSA is the national airline, operating flights throughout Central and South America, the Caribbean and the USA, besides internal flights to local airports by SANSA.

CÔTE D'IVOIRE
République de la Côte d'Ivoire

AREA – 124,504 sq. miles (322,463 sq. km). Neighbours:
   Guinea and Liberia (west), Mali and Burkina Faso
   (north), Ghana (east)
POPULATION – 14,781,000 (1994 UN estimate): 39 per
   cent Muslim, 28 per cent Christian (mainly Roman
   Catholic) and 17 per cent maintain traditional beliefs.
   The official language is French, but Agni, Baoulé,
   Dioula, Senoufo and Yacouba are spoken
CAPITAL – Yamoussoukro (population, 126,191, 1988),
   the political and administrative capital since 1983
MAJOR CITIES – ΨAbidjan (2,700,000), the economic and
   financial centre
CURRENCY – Franc CFA of 100 centimes
NATIONAL ANTHEM – L'Abidjanaise
NATIONAL DAY – 7 August
NATIONAL FLAG – Three vertical stripes, orange, white
   and green
LIFE EXPECTANCY (years) – male 49.69; female 52.38
POPULATION GROWTH RATE – 3.9 per cent (1996)
POPULATION DENSITY – 46 per sq. km (1996)
URBAN POPULATION – 45.6 per cent (1993)
MILITARY EXPENDITURE – 0.9 per cent of GDP (1997)
MILITARY PERSONNEL – 15,400: Army 6,800, Navy 900,
   Air Force 700, Paramilitaries 7,000
CONSCRIPTION DURATION – Six months
ILLITERACY RATE – 59.9 per cent
ENROLMENT (percentage of age group) – primary 55 per
   cent (1996); tertiary 4.5 per cent (1994)

The climate is equatorial in the south and west, which are mainly forested; tropical in the centre and east, which are savannah regions with trees; dry and tropical in the north, which is a grassy savannah region.

HISTORY AND POLITICS

Although French contact was made in the first half of the 19th century, Côte d'Ivoire became a colony only in 1893 and was finally pacified in 1912. It decided on 5 December 1958 to remain an autonomous republic within the French Community; full independence outside the Community was proclaimed on 7 August 1960.

The Democratic Party of Côte d'Ivoire (PDCI) won multiparty elections held in November 1990 amid allegations of electoral fraud. After having been president since independence in 1960, President Houphouët-Boigny died in December 1993 and was replaced by the parliamentary speaker Henri Konan-Bédié. Konan-Bédié was elected by an overwhelming majority following an opposition party boycott in the October 1995 presidential election. The PDCI won 148 of the 175 seats in the November 1995 elections to the National Assembly.

POLITICAL SYSTEM

Côte d'Ivoire has a presidential system of government and a single-chamber National Assembly of 175 members, directly elected for a five-year term. It has been a multiparty system since 1990. In May 1998, the president's term of office was increased from five to seven years.

HEAD OF STATE
President, Henri Konan Bédié, *took office* 7 December 1993,
   elected 22 October 1995

CABINET *as at May 1999*
Prime Minister, Daniel Kablan Duncan

Agriculture and Animal Resources, Lambert Kouassi Konan
Culture, Bernard Zadi Zaourou
Defence, Vincent Bandama N'Gatta
Economic Infrastructure, Jean Michel Moulod
Economy and Finance, Niamien N'Goran
Employment and Civil Service, Social Welfare, Achi Atsain
Energy, Safiatou Françoise Ba-N'daw
Environment and Forestry, Jean-Claude Kovassi
Family and Women's Promotion, Léopoldine Coffie
Foreign Trade, Guy-Alain Emmanuel Gauze
High Commissioners, Tchere Seka *(Development of Western Areas);* Ahmadou Ahmed Timite *(Development of Central and Northern Areas);* Sekou Toure *(Water Resources)*
Higher Education and Scientific Research, Francis Wodie
Housing and Urban Planning, Albert Kacou Tiapani
Industrial Development, Small and Medium-sized Enterprises, Théophile Ahova N'doli
Information, Danielle Boni-Claverie
Interior and Decentralization, Emile Constant Bombet
Justice and Human Rights, Jean Kouakou Brou
Mines and Petroleum Resources, Lamine Mohamed Fadika
National Education and Basic Training, Pierre Kipre
National Integration, Laurent Dona-Fologo
Planning and Development Programmes, Tidiane Thiam
President of the National Assembly, Emile Brou
Presidential Affairs, Government Spokesman, Paul Akoto Yao
Promotion of Internal Trade, Adou Kouadio
Public Health, Maurice Kacou Guikahue
Relations with Institutions, Timothée Ahoua N'Guetta
Security, Marcel Dibona Koné
Technical Education and Professional Training, Koné Dossongui
Tourism and Handicrafts, Kablan Norbert Anet
Transport, Adama Coulibaly
Youth and Sports, Sidigue Soumahoro

EMBASSY OF THE REPUBLIC OF CÔTE D'IVOIRE
2 Upper Belgrave Street, London SW1X 8BJ
Tel 0171-235 6991
Ambassador Extraordinary and Plenipotentiary, HE Kouadio Adjoumani, apptd 1997

BRITISH EMBASSY
Immeuble Les Harmonies, 01 BP 2581, Abidjan 01
Tel: Abidjan 226850
Ambassador Extraordinary and Plenipotentiary, HE Haydon Warren-Gash

ECONOMY

Côte d'Ivoire became wealthy in the 1970s because of the high prices of its two principal export earners, coffee and cocoa. In the late 1980s the economy contracted considerably as its exports deteriorated in competitiveness and its rivals devalued their currencies while the franc CFA remained pegged to the French franc. An economic reform and stabilization programme began in 1989 under IMF auspices and has brought down inflation, increased investment and led to GDP growth. The devaluation of the CFA franc in January 1994 has increased exports considerably and restored a trade surplus. In February 1998 a further economic reform programme began, aided by a US$385 million loan from the IMF. Under the terms of the loan, the government will liberalize the economy and introduce tighter fiscal controls.

The principal exports are coffee, cocoa, timber, palm oil, sugar, rubber, pineapples, bananas, and cotton. There are a few deposits of diamonds and minerals including manganese and iron. Oil and gas deposits began to be exploited in 1995.

There was a trade surplus of US$1,860 million in 1996

and a current account deficit of US$203 million. In 1997 imports totalled US$2,918 million and exports US$4,070 million.

GNP – US$10,152 million (1997); US$710 per capita (1997)
GDP – US$10,078 million (1995); US$736 per capita (1995)
ANNUAL AVERAGE GROWTH OF GDP – 6.5 per cent (1995)
INFLATION RATE – 5.6 per cent (1997)
TOTAL EXTERNAL DEBT – US$15,609 million (1997)

Trade with UK	1997	1998
Imports from UK	£58,844,000	£49,574,000
Exports to UK	68,451,000	74,801,000

CROATIA

AREA – 21,824 sq. miles (56,538 sq. km). Neighbours: Slovenia, Hungary (north), the rump Federal Yugoslav state (east), Bosnia-Hercegovina (south, and east of Adriatic coastal strip)
POPULATION – 4,501,000 (1994 UN estimate); 4,784,265 (1991 census): 78 per cent Croat, 12 per cent Serb, 2 per cent Yugoslav; also Hungarians, Italians, Albanians, Czechs, Ukrainians and Jews. Roman Catholic 76.5 per cent, Eastern Orthodox 11.1 per cent, Protestant 1.4 per cent, Muslim 1.2 per cent. The language is Croatian in the Latin script
CAPITAL – Zagreb (population, 867,717, 1991)
MAJOR CITIES – Osijek (129,792); Rijeka (167,964); Split (200,459), 1991
CURRENCY – Kuna of 100 lipa
NATIONAL ANTHEM – Lijepa naša domovina (Our Beautiful Homeland)
NATIONAL DAY – 30 May (Statehood Day)
NATIONAL FLAG – Three horizontal stripes of red, white, blue, with the national arms over all in the centre
LIFE EXPECTANCY (years) – male 68.29; female 75.63
POPULATION GROWTH RATE – –1.0 per cent (1996)
POPULATION DENSITY – 80 per sq. km (1996)
URBAN POPULATION – 54.3 per cent (1991)
ILLITERACY RATE – 2.4 per cent
ENROLMENT (percentage of age group) – primary 82 per cent (1994); secondary 66 per cent (1994); tertiary 27.9 per cent (1996)

Croatia is divided into three major geographic regions: the Pannonian region in the north, the central mountain belt, and the Adriatic coast region of Istria and Dalmatia which has 1,185 islands and islets and 1,104 miles (1,778 km) of coastline.

HISTORY AND POLITICS

Croatia was part of the Austro-Hungarian Empire from 1526 to 1918. On 29 October 1918 the Croatian parliament declared Croatia independent and soon after Croatia joined with Slovenia, Bosnia-Hercegovina, Serbia and Montenegro to form the 'Kingdom of Serbs, Croats and Slovenes' (renamed Yugoslavia in 1929). From 1941 to 1945 Yugoslavia was occupied by the Axis powers, with Italy and Hungary annexing parts of Croatia and a pro-Nazi Croat puppet state being established in the remainder of Croatia and Bosnia-Hercegovina. The armed extremists of this state (Ustashe) engaged in fierce fighting with Serbian royalists, Communist partisans and pro-Allied Croat partisans.

At the end of the war Yugoslavia was re-established as a federal republic under Communist rule but gradually disintegrated following the death of the wartime partisan leader Josep Tito in 1980.

In April and May 1990 Croatia's first free, democratic elections were won by the Croatian Democratic Union (HDZ) of Dr Franjo Tudjman. A new constitution was adopted by parliament in December 1990 and a referendum in May 1991 backed independence from Yugoslavia. Croatia declared its independence on 30 May 1991. The Federal Yugoslav Army (JNA) intervened against local defence forces to prevent the disintegration of the federation. Croatia's ethnic Serb minority, which rejected Croatia's independence, began fighting with the Croat defence forces. By September 1991 this had escalated into war between Croatia and Serbia, which had assumed control of the JNA.

The war in Croatia continued until January 1992 when a cease-fire was declared. The JNA and Serb forces had secured control of virtually all ethnic Serb areas in Croatia. Four UN protected areas, Northern and Southern Krajina and Eastern and Western Slavonia, were created from the Serb-controlled areas in Croatia and UN troops arrived to police the areas. The JNA withdrew from Croatia but the ethnic Serb forces refused to disarm.

The HDZ won a majority of seats in the 1995 elections to the Chamber of Representatives and in the April 1997 elections to the Chamber of Districts. Tudjman was re-elected in June 1997 with 61 per cent of the vote, although OSCE observers declared that the elections had not met the minimum standards for democracies. In January 1999, the chief prosecutor of the UN International Criminal Tribunal for the Former Yugoslavia criticized the Croatian government for its lack of co-operation in securing the capture of war crimes suspects.

SECESSION

Croatia's ethnic Serbs voted to establish a Republic of Serbian Krajina (RSK) in 1993 and elected Milan Martić as president in January 1994.   The government seized Western Slavonia in May 1995 and the whole of Krajina in August 1995 prompting the withdrawal of 10,000 UNCRO peacekeepers and the flight of 150,000 Serbs. The last Croatian Serb-held area of Eastern Slavonia agreed in November 1995 to its eventual reintegration into Croatia. A 5,000-strong UN force was dispatched to the area in 1996 to oversee the formation of a two-year transitional government. On 15 January 1998, the UN pulled out of Eastern Slavonia and Croatia resumed full control of the territory.

FOREIGN RELATIONS

An agreement to normalize relations with Yugoslavia was signed in August 1996. Croatia was sworn in as a member of the Council of Europe in November 1996.

POLITICAL SYSTEM

Executive power is vested in a president and government. The president is directly elected for five-year terms. Legislative power is vested in the bicameral parliament, comprising the 68-member Chamber of Counties and the 127-member Chamber of Representatives (Sabor).

Croatia is divided into 21 counties; each county elects three members to the Chamber of Counties. Counties are composed of groups of districts and function both as units of local government and as regional offices for the central administration. There are 102 districts.

HEAD OF STATE

President, Franjo Tudjman, elected May 1990, re-elected 2 August 1992, 15 June 1997, sworn in 5 August 1997

CABINET as at May 1999

Prime Minister, Zlatko Matesa
Deputy PMs, Jure Radić (Development and Reconstruction); Borislav Skegro (Finance); Mate Granić (Foreign Affairs); Ljerka Mintas-Hodak (European Integration)
Agriculture and Forestry, Ivan Djurkić
Croatian Homeland War Veterans, Juraj Njauro
Culture, Bozo Biskupić
Defence, Pavao Miljavac
Economy, Nenad Porges
Education and Sport, Bozidar Pugelnik
Government Secretary, Jagoda Premuzić
Health, Zeljko Rajner
Internal Affairs, Ivan Penić
Justice, Zvonimir Separović
Labour and Social Welfare, Joso Skara
Maritime Affairs, Transport and Communications, Zeljko Luzavec
Return and Immigration, Marijan Petrović
Science and Technology, Milena Zic-Fuchs
Tourism, Ivan Herak
Urban Planning, Construction and Housing, Marko Sirac
Without Portfolio, Milan Kovac

EMBASSY OF THE REPUBLIC OF CROATIA
21 Conway Street, London WIP 5HL
Tel 0171-387 2022
Ambassador Extraordinary and Plenipotentiary, HE Andrija Kojaković, apptd 1997

BRITISH EMBASSY
Vlaska 121/III Floor, PO Box 454, 10000 Zagreb
Tel: Zagreb 455 5310
Ambassador Extraordinary and Plenipotentiary, HE Colin Munro, apptd 1997
BRITISH CONSULATES – Split and Dubrovnik
BRITISH COUNCIL DIRECTOR, R. Evans, PO Box 55, 10000 Zagreb

DEFENCE

The Army has 298 main battle tanks, 44 armoured personnel carriers, 109 armoured infantry fighting vehicles and 979 artillery pieces. The Air Force has 40 combat aircraft and 15 armed helicopters. The Navy has one submarine and 13 patrol and coastal combatants at five bases.
MILITARY EXPENDITURE – 5.7 per cent of GDP (1997)
MILITARY PERSONNEL – 96,180: Army 50,000, Navy 3,000, Air Force 3,180, Paramilitaries 40,000
CONSCRIPTION DURATION – Ten months

ECONOMY

Production was severely hampered during the conflict in 1991–5; the material damage was estimated by the government to be US$27 billion, with the loss of 13,583 lives. Large areas of farmland were destroyed and the tourist industry, which provided one third of total foreign exchange earnings in 1990, was decimated.

Shipbuilding and fishing are major industries on the Adriatic coast. Inland there is a light manufacturing sector, food-processing industries, bauxite deposits, thermal mineral springs, hydroelectric potential, and agriculture based on grain, horticulture, livestock and tobacco. Textiles is one of the most important industries employing more than 17 per cent of the population. In April 1996, Croatia agreed to pay 29.5 per cent of Yugoslavia's debt, totalling US$1.45 billion.

In 1997 Croatia had a trade deficit of US$5,225 million and a current account deficit of US$2,435 million. In 1997

imports totalled US$9,313 million and exports US$4,341 million.
GNP – US$19,343 million (1997); US$4,060 per capita (1997)
GDP – US$18,081 million (1995); US$4,014 per capita (1995)
INFLATION RATE – 4.1 per cent (1997)
UNEMPLOYMENT – 16.8 per cent (1993)
TOTAL EXTERNAL DEBT – US$6,842 million (1997)

TRADE

Trade with UK	1997	1998
Imports from UK	£107,136,000	£105,867,000
Exports to UK	35,830,000	42,532,000

CUBA
República de Cuba

AREA – 42,804 sq. miles (110,861 sq. km)
POPULATION – 11,019,000 (1994 UN estimate). The language is Spanish
CAPITAL – ΨHavana (population, 2,175,888, 1992 estimate)
MAJOR CITIES – Camagüey (294,332); Guantánamo (207,796); Holguín (242,085); Santa Clara (205,400); ΨSantiago (430,494)
CURRENCY – Cuban peso of 100 centavos
NATIONAL ANTHEM – Al Combate, Corred Bayameses (To battle, men of Bayamo)
NATIONAL DAY – 1 January (Day of Liberation)
NATIONAL FLAG – Five horizontal bands, blue and white (blue at top and bottom) with red triangle, close to staff, charged with five-point star
LIFE EXPECTANCY (years) – male 72.89; female 76.80
POPULATION GROWTH RATE – 0.6 per cent (1996)
POPULATION DENSITY – 99 per sq. km (1996)
URBAN POPULATION – 74.4 per cent (1993)

HISTORY AND POLITICS

The island was visited by Columbus in 1492. Early in the 16th century the island was conquered by the Spanish, and for almost four centuries remained under Spanish rule. Separatist agitation culminated in the closing years of the 19th century in open warfare. In 1898 the USA intervened and demanded the evacuation of Cuba by Spanish forces. The Spanish–American war led to the abandonment of the island, which came under American military rule from 1899 until 1902, when an autonomous government was inaugurated with an elected president, and bicameral legislature.
A revolution led by Dr Fidel Castro overthrew the government of Gen. Batista in 1959. In 1965 the Communist Party of Cuba (PCC) was formed to succeed the United Party of the Socialist Revolution; it is the only authorized political party. A new Socialist constitution came into force in 1976 and indirect elections to the National Assembly of People's Power were subsequently held. The first direct elections to the 589-member National Assembly were held in February 1993; all candidates were officially approved by the Communist Party and ran for election unopposed. The 14 provincial assemblies were elected in the same manner. The fifth congress of the PCC was held in October 1997. At the election of deputies to the National Assembly in January 1998, all 601 PCC candidates received the required 50 per cent of the vote, and in February the National Assembly confirmed Dr Castro as president for a further five-year term.

HEAD OF STATE
President of Council of State and Council of Ministers, Dr Fidel Castro Ruz, *appointed* 2 November 1976, *re-elected* 15 March 1993, 24 February 1998

COUNCIL OF STATE *as at May 1999*
President, Dr Fidel Castro Ruz
First Vice-President, Gen. Raúl Castro Ruz
Vice-Presidents, Carlos Lage Dávila; Juan Almeida Bosque; Abelardo Colomé Ibarra; Esteban Lazo Hernández; José Ramón Machado Ventura
Secretary, José Miyar Barrueco

COUNCIL OF MINISTERS *as at May 1999*
President, Dr Fidel Castro Ruz
First Vice-President, Revolutionary Armed Forces, Gen. Raúl Castro Ruz
Vice-Presidents, Dr Carlos Rafael Rodríguez Rodríguez; Osmani Cienfuegos Gorriarán; Pedro Miret Prieto; José Ramón Fernández Alvárez; Jaime Crombet Hernández Baquero; Adolfo Diaz Suárez
Secretary, Carlos Lage Dávila

Ministers, Alfredo Jordán Morales (*Agriculture*); Gen. Silvano Colás Sánchez (*Communications*); Juan Mario Junco del Pino (*Construction*); vacant (*Construction Materials Industry*); Abel Prieto Jiménez (*Culture*); Barbara Castillo Cuesta (*Domestic Trade*); José Luis Rodríguez García (*Economy and Planning*); Luís Ignacio Gómez Gutiérrez (*Education*); Manuel Millares Rodríguez (*Finance and Prices*); Orlando Felipe Rodríguez Romay (*Fishing Industry*); Alejandro Rocas Iglesias (*Food Industry*); Ibrahim Farradaz (*Foreign Investment and Economic Co-operation*); Roberto Robaina González (*Foreign Relations*); Ricardo Cabrisas Ruíz (*Foreign Trade*); Marcos J. Portal León (*Heavy Industries*); Fernando Vecino Alegret (*Higher Education*); Gen. Abelardo Colomé Ibarra (*Interior*); Roberto Díaz Sotolongo (*Justice*); Salvador Valdez Mesa (*Labour and Social Security*); Jesús Pérez Othon (*Light Industry*); Roberto Ignacio González Planas (*Metalworking and Electronics Industries*); Carlos Dotres Martínez (*Public Health*); Rosa Eleana Simeón Negrín (*Science, Technology and Environment*); Div.-Gen. Ulises Rosales del Toro (*Sugar Industry*); Osmani Cienfuegos Gorriarán (*Tourism*); Alvaro Pérez Morales (*Transport*); Wilfredo López Rodríguez (*Without Portfolio*)

EMBASSY OF THE REPUBLIC OF CUBA
167 High Holborn, London WC1V 6PA
Tel 0171-240 2488
Ambassador Extraordinary and Plenipotentiary, HE Rodney Alejandro López Clemente, apptd 1995

BRITISH EMBASSY
Calle 34 No. 702/4 entre 7ma Avenida y 17, Miramar, Havana.
Tel: Havana 241 771
Ambassador Extraordinary and Plenipotentiary, HE David Ridgeway, OBE, apptd 1998

DEFENCE

The Army has 1,500 main battle tanks, 400 armoured infantry fighting vehicles, 700 armoured personnel carriers and 740 artillery pieces. The Navy has one submarine, two frigates and five patrol and coastal vessels at six bases. The Air Force has 130 combat aircraft and 45 armed helicopters.
The last former Soviet combat personnel left Cuba in 1993, but 810 Russian military advisers remain to operate military intelligence facilities. The United States has 1,420

naval personnel at Guantánamo Bay Naval Base, which has been leased since before the 1959 revolution.
MILITARY EXPENDITURE – 5.2 per cent of GDP (1997)
MILITARY PERSONNEL – 72,000: Army 38,000, Navy 5,000, Air Force 10,000, Paramilitaries 19,000
CONSCRIPTION DURATION – Two years

ECONOMY

After the revolution virtually all land and industrial and commercial enterprises were nationalized. Following the curtailing of Cuba's privileged trading relationships with the Soviet bloc in 1989, the economy deteriorated sharply. GDP fell by 75 per cent between 1989 and 1994, and the government was forced to introduce reforms. Since 1993, the government has legalized the holding of US dollars by private individuals, permitted private enterprise, cut subsidies to loss-making state industries, allowed prices for some goods and services to rise, and introduced income tax. State farms have been transformed into co-operatives run by private individuals and permitted to sell 20 per cent of produce on the open market, but remain relatively unproductive. In 1995, foreign investors were permitted to buy property and own Cuban-based companies, with British and Canadian firms becoming involved in the oil and mining industries.

Following austerity measures imposed in 1993, the economy has slowly started to grow. Sugar is still the mainstay of the economy and the principal source of foreign exchange; production dropped from 8.04 million tons in 1989–90 to 4.4 million tons in 1996–7. Domestic oil production is rising and reached 1,400,000 tonnes in 1997. Lack of external finance has been a major obstacle to economic recovery, as has the long-standing trade and economic embargo imposed by the USA, which has been criticized repeatedly by the UN and was condemned by the European Parliament in November 1998.

The tourism industry has expanded since 1986 to become the country's largest foreign exchange earner. In 1995 738,200 tourists visited Cuba, generating some US$1,100 million.
GDP – US$21,737 million (1995); US$1,983 per capita (1995)
ANNUAL AVERAGE GROWTH OF GDP – 2.5 per cent (1995)

TRADE

Cuba's exports dropped from US$8.1 billion in 1989 to US$1.7 billion in 1993 while imports declined by 73 per cent. Trade between Cuba and the former socialist economies of Europe is now less than 10 per cent of pre-1989 levels. A trade deal was signed with Russia in 1995 providing for the exchange of sugar for oil. The US trade and economic embargo remains in force, though it was relaxed in March 1998 to allow food and medicine into the country. Principal exports are sugar, nickel, seafood, citrus fruits, tobacco and rum.

Trade with UK	1997	1998
Imports from UK	£19,484,000	£33,641,000
Exports to UK	15,093,000	15,798,000

COMMUNICATIONS

There are 12,700 km of railway track, of which 5,000 km are in public service. In 1986 there were 13,247 km of road. Scheduled international air services run to Central and South American countries and Europe. In March 1998 the ban on direct flights between Cuba and the USA was lifted.

CULTURE AND EDUCATION

The press and broadcasting are under the control of the government. Education is compulsory and free. In 1964 illiteracy was officially declared to be eliminated.

ILLITERACY RATE – 4.3 per cent
ENROLMENT (percentage of age group) – primary 100 per cent (1996); secondary 59 per cent (1993); tertiary 12.4 per cent (1996)

CYPRUS
Kypriaki Dimokratia/Kibris Çumhuriyeti

AREA – 3,572 sq. miles (9,251 sq. km)
POPULATION – 756,000 (1994 UN estimate): 85 per cent Greek, 12 per cent Turkish. Greek and Turkish are official languages
CAPITAL – Nicosia (Lefkosia) (population in the government-controlled area, 188,800)
MAJOR CITIES – ΨFamagusta; ΨLarnaca; ΨLimassol; Paphos
CURRENCY – Cyprus pound (C£) of 100 cents
NATIONAL ANTHEM – Ode to Freedom
NATIONAL DAY – 1 October (Independence Day)
NATIONAL FLAG – White with a gold map of Cyprus above a wreath of olive
LIFE EXPECTANCY (years) – male 74.64; female 79.05
POPULATION GROWTH RATE – 1.8 per cent (1996)
POPULATION DENSITY – 82 per sq. km (1996)
URBAN POPULATION – 67.7 per cent (1992)
ENROLMENT (percentage of age group) – primary 96 per cent (1995); secondary 93 per cent (1995); tertiary 20.0 per cent (1995)

The climate is Mediterranean, with a hot dry summer and a variable warm winter.

HISTORY AND POLITICS

Cyprus came under British administration from 1878, and was formally annexed to Britain in 1914 on the outbreak of war with Turkey. From 1925 to 1960 it was a Crown Colony. Following the launching in 1955 of an armed campaign by EOKA in support of union with Greece, a state of emergency was declared which lasted for four years. An agreement was signed on 19 February 1959 between the United Kingdom, Greece, Turkey, and the Greek and Turkish Cypriots which provided that Cyprus would be an independent republic.

The island became independent on 16 August 1960. The constitution provided for a Greek Cypriot president and a Turkish Cypriot vice-president. The constitution proved unworkable and led to intercommunal trouble. The UN Peacekeeping Force in Cyprus (UNFICYP) was set up in 1964.

A general election was held for the House of Representatives (56 Greek Cypriot and 24 vacant Turkish Cypriot seats) on 26 May 1996, resulting in the parties gaining the following seats: Democratic Rally-Liberal Party 20; AKEL (Left-wing) 19; Democratic Party (DIKO) 10; EDEK (Socialist) 5; Free Democrats 2. In February 1998, Glafcos Clerides of the Democratic Rally-Liberal Party was re-elected president with 51 per cent of the vote. On 30 March 1998, formal accession talks with the EU began.

HEAD OF STATE
President, Glafcos Clerides, *elected* 14 February 1993, *re-elected* 15 February 1998

COUNCIL OF MINISTERS *as at June 1999*
Agriculture, Environment and Natural Resources, Costas Themistocleous
Commerce, Industry and Tourism, Nicos Rolandis
Communications and Works, Leontios Ierodiaconou
Defence, Yiannakis Chrysostomis
Education and Culture, Ouranios Ioannides
Finance, Takis Klerides
Foreign Affairs, Ioannis Kasoulides
Health, Christos Solomis
Interior, Christodoulos Christodoulou
Justice and Public Order, Nicos Koshis
Labour and Social Insurance, Andreas Moushouttas

CYPRUS HIGH COMMISSION
93 Park Street, London WIY 4ET
Tel 0171-499 8272
High Commissioner, HE Michalis Attalides, apptd 1998
Counsellors, P. Kyriakou (*Consular Affairs*); K. Avgoustinos (*Cultural Affairs*); A. Georgiades (*Commerce*), S. Georgiades (*Press Counsellor*)

BRITISH HIGH COMMISSION
Alexander Pallis Street (PO Box 21978), 1587 Nicosia
Tel: Nicosia 2-861100
High Commissioner, HE Edward Clay, CMG, apptd May 1999
Counsellor and Deputy High Commissioner, J. S. Buck
Defence Adviser, Col. C. S. Wakelin, OBE
First Secretary (Commercial), W. Preston

BRITISH COUNCIL DIRECTOR, Robert Ness, PO Box 25654, 3 Museum Street, 1097 Nicosia

BRITISH SOVEREIGN AREAS
The UK retained full sovereignty and jurisdiction over two areas of 99 square miles in all: Akrotiri–Episkopi–Paramali and Dhekelia–Pergamos–Ayios Nicolaos–Xylophagou. The British Administrator of these areas is appointed by The Queen and is responsible to the Secretary of State for Defence. The combined total of army and RAF personnel stationed in the areas is 5,000.
Administrator of the British Sovereign Areas, Air Vice-Marshal P. Millar

DEFENCE

The National Guard has 102 main battle tanks, 70 armoured infantry fighting vehicles, 402 armoured personnel carriers and 134 artillery pieces. Turkey has 30,000 troops in northern Cyprus.

In January 1998, a military airfield in Paphos was completed. It is intended to provide a base for Greek military aircraft, as Cyprus does not possess its own air force.
MILITARY EXPENDITURE – 5.8 per cent of GDP (1997)
MILITARY PERSONNEL – 10,000 National Guard, Northern Cyprus Army 4,500
CONSCRIPTION DURATION – 26 months

ECONOMY

Agriculture employs 10 per cent of the workforce. Main products are citrus fruits, grapes and vine products, meat, milk, potatoes and other vegetables. Manufacturing, construction, distribution and other service industries are other major employers. Tourism is the main growth industry with over two million tourists producing C£878 million in foreign exchange earnings in 1998; 1,055 foreign firms were registered as offshore companies in Cyprus in 1998, and 20 per cent of the world's ships are Cypriot registered.
GDP – US$8,537 million (1995); US$11,459 per capita (1995)
ANNUAL AVERAGE GROWTH OF GDP – 5.0 per cent (1995)
INFLATION RATE – 3.6 per cent (1997)
UNEMPLOYMENT – 2.6 per cent (1995)

The UK is the main trading partner, taking 15 per cent of exports in 1998 and supplying 11 per cent of imports. In 1998 there was a trade deficit of US$2,490 million and a current account deficit of US$600 million. In 1998 imports totalled US$4,650 million and exports US$3,940 million.

Trade with UK	1997	1998
Imports from UK	£265,959,000	£259,990,000
Exports to UK	122,413,000	170,127,000

TURKISH REPUBLIC OF NORTHERN CYPRUS

In 1974, mainland Greek officers under instructions from the military junta in Athens launched a coup and installed a former EOKA member, Nikos Sampson, as president. Turkey invaded northern Cyprus and occupied over a third of the island. In 1975 a 'Turkish Federated State of Cyprus' under Rauf Denktaş was declared in this area and in 1983 a 'Declaration of Statehood' was issued which purported to establish the 'Turkish Republic of Northern Cyprus'. The declaration was condemned by the UN Security Council and only Turkey has recognized the new 'state'. In 1985, Denktaş was elected president and a general election was held. Denktaş was re-elected in 1990 and 1995. A UN plan for the reunification of the island was formally rejected by him on 31 August 1998. On 6 December 1998, elections to the 50-seat Republican Assembly resulted in a coalition government between the National Unity Party, who gained 24 seats, and the Democrat Party, who gained 13 seats.

CZECH REPUBLIC
Česká Republika

AREA – 30,450 sq. miles (78,864 sq. km). Neighbours: Poland (north-east), Germany (west and north-west), Austria (south), Slovakia (south-east)

POPULATION – 10,315,000 (1994 UN estimate), 10,302,000 (1991 census): 95 per cent Czech, 3 per cent Slovak. Czech is the official language. The majority of the population is Roman Catholic, with a small Protestant minority

CAPITAL – Prague (Praha) on the Vltava (Moldau) (population, 1,216,568, 1994 estimate)

MAJOR CITIES – Brno (Brünn) (390,073); Ostrava (326,049); Plzeň (Pilsen) (172,055)

CURRENCY – Koruna (Kčs) of 100 haléřu

NATIONAL ANTHEM – Kde Domov Můj (Where is my Motherland)

NATIONAL DAY – 28 October

NATIONAL FLAG – White over red horizontally with a blue triangle extending from the hoist to the centre of the flag

LIFE EXPECTANCY (years) – male 69.53; female 76.55

POPULATION GROWTH RATE – –0.1 per cent (1996)

POPULATION DENSITY – 131 per sq. km (1996)

URBAN POPULATION – 74.7 per cent (1993)

The Czech Republic is composed of Bohemia and Moravia. Bohemia is surrounded by mountain ranges while Moravian land stretches to the Danubian basin.

HISTORY AND POLITICS

The area which is now the Czech Republic came under the rule of the Habsburg dynasty in 1526 and remained part of the Austro-Hungarian Empire until 1918. The rise of Czech nationalism in the late 19th century led to the proclamation of the independence of Czechoslovakia on 28 October 1918 following an amalgamation of Bohemia, Moravia, Slovakia and Ruthenia and was confirmed by the Versailles Peace Conference in 1919.

Czechoslovakia was forced to cede the ethnic German Sudetenland to Nazi Germany in 1938 after the Munich Agreement. German forces invaded the Czech Republic in March 1939 and incorporated it into Germany while Slovakia became a puppet state. The Czech Republic was liberated by Soviet and American forces in May 1945. The pre-war democratic Czechoslovak state was re-established in 1945, having ceded Ruthenia to the Soviet Union. The Communists took power in a coup in 1948 and remained in power until 1989.

In 1968 the Communist Party under Alexander Dubček embarked on a political and economic reform programme (the Prague Spring). The reforms were suppressed following an invasion by Warsaw Pact troops on the night of 20 August 1968, and were abandoned when Gustáv Husák became leader of the Communist Party in 1969.

Mass protests in November 1989 led to the resignation of the Communist Party Central Committee. The Party was forced to concede its monopoly of power and on 10 December a new government was appointed in which only half the ministers were Communists. Husák resigned as president and was replaced by the dissident writer Václav Havel. Free elections were held in June 1990 in which the Communist Party was defeated.

In late 1992 the leaders of the Czech and Slovak republics agreed to dissolve the federation and form two sovereign states; this took effect on 1 January 1993.

The elections of June 1992 had returned the Civil Democratic Party (ODS) as the largest party in the Czech parliament, and it formed a coalition government with three other centre-right parties. The former federal President Havel was elected president. Following the general election of 31 May 1996, the ODS and its coalition partners, two seats short of a majority, agreed to slow the rate of privatization in return for support from the opposition Social Democrats. The general election in June 1998 produced no outright winner. Miloš Zeman, leader of the Czech Social Democratic Party (CSSD), formed a coalition government; all ministers are members of the CSSD except the Justice Minister, who is non-partisan.

POLITICAL SYSTEM

The constitution vests legislative power in the bicameral parliament, comprising a 200-member Chamber of Deputies elected for a four-year term and an 81-member Senate elected for a six-year term, one-third being renewed every two years. The president is elected by parliament for a five-year term. Executive power is held by the prime minister and Council of Ministers. A two-thirds majority in parliament is necessary to amend the constitution, and federal laws remain in place unless superseded by Czech ones. A Constitutional Court has been established comprising 15 judges nominated by the president for ten-year terms with Senate approval.

HEAD OF STATE

President, Václav Havel (ODS), *elected* 26 January 1993, *re-elected* 20 January 1998

COUNCIL OF MINISTERS *as at May 1999*

Prime Minister, Miloš Zeman

Deputy Prime Minister, Employment and Social Affairs, Vladimír Špidla

Deputy Prime Ministers, Pavel Mertlík; Pavel Rychetsky; Egon Lánsky

Agriculture, Jan Fencl
Culture, Pavel Dostál
Defence, Vladimír Vetchy
Education, Youth and Sports, Eduard Zeman
Environment, Miloš Kužvart
Finance, Ivo Svoboda
Foreign Affairs, Jan Kavan
Health, Ivan David
Interior, Václav Grulich
Justice, Otakar Motejl
Regional Development, Jaromir Cisař
Trade and Industry, Miroslav Grégr
Transport and Communications, Antonín Peltrám
Without Portfolio, Jaroslav Bašta

EMBASSY OF THE CZECH REPUBLIC
26–30 Kensington Palace Gardens, London W8 4QY
Tel 0171-243 1115
Ambassador Extraordinary and Plenipotentiary, HE Pavel
    Seifter, apptd 1998
Minister-Counsellor, Ivo Silhav
Military Attaché, Col. Milan Skalick

BRITISH EMBASSY
Thunovská 14, 11800 Prague 1
Tel: Prague 5732 0355
Ambassador Extraordinary and Plenipotentiary, HE David
    Broucher, apptd 1997
Deputy Head of Mission, D. E. P. P. Keefe
Defence Attaché, Col. A. F. Davidson, MBE
First Secretary (Commercial), M. L. Connor
Cultural Attaché, M. O'Neill *(British Council Director)*

DEFENCE

The army has 938 main battle tanks, 945 armoured infantry
fighting vehicles, 422 armoured personnel carriers and 754
artillery pieces. The Air Force has 109 combat aircraft and
36 attack helicopters. The Czech Republic became a
member of NATO on 1 April 1999.
MILITARY EXPENDITURE – 2.2 per cent of GDP (1997)
MILITARY PERSONNEL – 45,900: Army 25,300, Air Force
    15,000, Paramilitaries 5,600
CONSCRIPTION DURATION – 12 months

ECONOMY

Under Communist rule industry and most agricultural land
was state-owned. An economic reform programme began
in 1990 to produce a free-market economy, and the
government of the Czech Republic has continued to follow
the policies of the former federal government. This has
necessitated a restrictive monetary policy to stem inflation
and a restructuring of industry to be competitive, and these
were major reasons for the break with Slovakia. As a result,
foreign investment (US$4,000 million in 1989–94) and
private enterprises have grown and reliance on trade with
the former Soviet bloc countries has ended. By late 1995
over 90 per cent of the economy had been privatized, with
two-thirds of the population owning shares.
    A trade-liberalizing association agreement with the EU
is in operation, and formal EU accession talks began in
March 1998.
    A customs union between the Czech and Slovak
Republics is in place but separate currencies were
introduced in February 1993 following speculation. The
Koruna was made fully convertible in October 1995.
    Principal agricultural products are sugar beet, potatoes
and cereal crops; the timber industry is also very important.
Having been the major industrial area of the Austro-
Hungarian Empire, the country has long been industrial-
ized, and machinery, industrial consumer goods and raw
materials are major exports.
    In 1994 the government had a budget surplus equivalent
to 0.88 per cent of GDP. In 1997 there was a trade deficit
of US$4,639 million and a current account deficit of
US$3,207 million. Imports totalled US$29,102 million in
1996 and exports totalled US$22,792 million in 1997.
GNP – US$53,952 million (1997); US$5,240 per capita
    (1997)
GDP – US$45,667 million (1995); US$4,450 per capita
    (1995)
ANNUAL AVERAGE GROWTH OF GDP – 4.4 per cent
    (1996)
INFLATION RATE – 8.4 per cent (1997)
UNEMPLOYMENT – 3.4 per cent (1995)
TOTAL EXTERNAL DEBT – US$21,456 million (1997)

Trade with UK	1997	1998
Imports from UK	£709,754,000	£714,866,000
Exports to UK	465,478,000	576,520,000

EDUCATION

Education is compulsory and free for all children from the
ages of six to 15. There are nine universities of which the
oldest and most famous is Charles University in Prague
(founded 1348).
ENROLMENT (percentage of age group) – primary 87 per
    cent (1995); secondary 87 per cent (1995); tertiary 21.9
    per cent (1995)

CULTURE

The Reformation gave a widespread impetus to Czech
literature, the writings of Jan Hus (martyred in 1415 as a
religious and social reformer) familiarizing the people with
Wyclif's teaching. This lasted until the close of the 17th
century when Jan Amos Komensky or Comenius (1592–
1670) was expelled from the country. There was a period
of stagnation until the national revival in the 19th century.
Authors of international reputation include Jaroslav Hašek
(1883–1923), Jaroslav Seifert (1901–86, Nobel Prize for
Literature, 1985), Václav Havel (b. 1936) and Milan
Kundera (b. 1929).

DENMARK
Kongeriget Danmark

AREA – 16,639 sq. miles (43,094 sq. km). Neighbour:
    Germany (south)
POPULATION – 5,262,000 (1996 estimate). The majority
    of the population is Lutheran. The language is Danish
CAPITAL – ΨCopenhagen (population, 1,362,264, 1996
    estimate)
MAJOR CITIES – ΨÅlborg 116,567; ΨÅrhus 209,404;
    Esbjerg 73,149; ΨOdense 143,029; Randers 55,515
CURRENCY – Danish krone of 100 øre
NATIONAL ANTHEMS – Kong Kristian; Det er et yndigt
    land
NATIONAL DAY – 5 June (Constitution Day)
NATIONAL FLAG – Red, with white cross
LIFE EXPECTANCY (years) – male 72.49; female 77.76
POPULATION GROWTH RATE – 0.4 per cent (1996)
POPULATION DENSITY – 122 per sq. km (1996)

Denmark is a kingdom, consisting of the islands of Zealand,
Funen, Lolland, etc., the peninsula of Jutland, the outlying
island of Bornholm in the Baltic, and the Farøes and
Greenland.

HISTORY AND POLITICS

Denmark derives its name from the Dan people of southern Sweden who invaded the area of present-day Denmark and established a unified state under Gorm the Old in the tenth century. The Danes were at the forefront of Viking expansionism and briefly united England and Scandinavia under Knut (Canute) (995– 1035).

From the 12th to 19th centuries the Danes contended for domination in Scandinavia and the Baltic region. The Union of Kalmar (1397) brought Norway and Sweden (including Finland) under Danish rule. Danish power waned during the 16th century, however, enabling Sweden to re-establish its independence in 1523. Sweden achieved ascendancy in the following two centuries, subjecting Denmark to defeat in the Thirty Years' War (1618–48) and the Great Northern War (1700–21). In the 19th century Norway was ceded to Sweden under the Treaty of Kiel (1814) and both Schleswig and Holstein, which had been subsumed in 1460, were surrendered to Germany.

Denmark remained neutral during the First World War, and in a plebiscite held in accordance with the Versailles Treaty (1919), northern Schleswig voted to return to Danish sovereignty. In 1939 Denmark signed a non-aggression pact with Germany but was invaded on 9 April 1940 and coerced into contributing to the German war effort. Iceland declared its independence from Denmark in 1944. Social Democrat-led coalitions dominated the post-war era until 1982 when a right-wing government was elected. Denmark joined the European Community in 1973.

On 21 September 1994, a new coalition government of the Social Democrat, Social Liberal and Centre Democrat parties was formed. On 12 March 1998, Poul Nyrop Rasmussen's centre-left coalition was re-elected, winning 90 of the 179 seats in the parliament, giving a majority of a single seat.

POLITICAL SYSTEM

The legislature consists of one chamber, the *Folketing*, of not more than 179 members, including two for the Farøes and two for Greenland, which is elected for a four-year term. The voting age is 18 with voting based on a proportional representation system with a 2 per cent threshold for parliamentary representation.

HEAD OF STATE

HM The Queen of Denmark, Queen Margrethe II, KG, *born* 16 April 1940, *succeeded* 14 January 1972, *married* 10 June 1967, Count Henri de Monpezat (Prince Henrik of Denmark), and *has issue* Crown Prince Frederik (*see* below); Prince Joachim, *born* 7 June 1969; *married* 18 November 1995, Miss Alexandra Manley (Princess Alexandra of Denmark)

Heir, HRH Crown Prince Frederik, *born* 26 May 1968

CABINET *as at May 1999*

Prime Minister, Poul Nyrup Rasmussen (S)
Culture, Elsebeth Gerner Nielsen (RV)
Defence, Hans Haekkerup (S)
Development Co-operation, Poul Nielson (S)
Economic Affairs and Nordic Co-operation, Marianne Jelved (RV)
Education and Ecclesiastical Affairs, Margrethe Vestager (RV)
Environment and Energy, Svend Auken (S)
Finance, Mogens Lykketoft (S)
Food, Agriculture and Fisheries, Henrik Dam Christensen (S)
Foreign Affairs, Niels Helveg Petersen (RV)
Health, Carsten Koch (S)
Interior, Thorkild Simonsen (S)
Justice, Frank Jensen (S)
Labour, Ove Hygum (S)
Research, Jan Trøjborg (S)
Social Affairs, Karen Jespersen (S)
Taxation, Ole Stavad (S)
Trade and Industry, Pia Gjellerup (S)
Transport, Sonja Mikkelsen (S)
Urban Affairs and Housing, Jytte Andersen (S)

S Social Democrat Party; RV Social Liberal Party

ROYAL DANISH EMBASSY

55 Sloane Street, London SW1X 9SR
Tel 0171-333 0200
Ambassador Extraordinary and Plenipotentiary, HE Ole Lønsmann Poulsen, apptd 1996
Counsellor (Commercial), Gunner Tetler
Defence Attaché, Capt. Uffe Haagen Olsen

BRITISH EMBASSY

36–40 Kastelsvej, DK-2100 Copenhagen Ø
Tel: Copenhagen 3544 5200
Ambassador Extraordinary and Plenipotentiary, HE Andrew Bache, CMG, apptd 1996
Counsellor and Deputy Head of Mission, P. B. Yaghmourian
Defence Attaché, Cmdr. A. Gordon-Lennox, RN
First Secretary (Commercial), F. J. Martin
BRITISH CONSULATES – Åbenrå, Ålborg, Århus, Esbjerg, Fredericia, Herning, Odense, Rønne (Bornholm); Tórshavn (Farøe Islands)

BRITISH COUNCIL REPRESENTATIVE, Dr M. Sørensen-Jones, Gammel Mont 12.3, 1117 Copenhagen K

DEFENCE

The Army has 337 main battle tanks, 50 armoured infantry fighting vehicles, 592 armoured personnel carriers, 503 artillery pieces and 12 attack helicopters. The Navy has five submarines, three frigates and 41 patrol and coastal vessels at two bases. The Air Force has 69 combat aircraft.
MILITARY EXPENDITURE – 1.7 per cent of GDP (1997)
MILITARY PERSONNEL – 32,100: Army 22,900, Navy 3,700, Air Force 5,500
CONSCRIPTION DURATION – Four to 12 months

ECONOMY

Of the labour force in 1996, 45 per cent was employed in the professional services and administration; 18 per cent in commerce; 19 per cent in manufacturing and 5 per cent in agriculture. The chief agricultural products are pigs, dairy products, poultry and eggs, seeds and cereals; manufactures are mostly based on imported raw materials but there are also considerable imports of finished goods. Denmark is self-sufficient in oil and natural gas.

GNP – US$184,347 million (1997); US$34,890 per capita (1997)

GDP – US$173,357 million (1995); US$ 33,191 per capita (1995)

ANNUAL AVERAGE GROWTH OF GDP – 2.4 per cent (1996); forecast to be 2.9 per cent in 1997

INFLATION RATE – 2.2 per cent (1997)

UNEMPLOYMENT – 7.0 per cent (1995)

TRADE

The principal imports are industrial raw materials, consumer goods, construction inputs, machinery, raw materials, vehicles and textile products. The chief exports are manufactured articles, and agricultural and dairy products. Germany and Sweden are Denmark's main trading partners.

In 1996 Denmark had a trade surplus of US$7,532 million and a current account surplus of US$2,865 million. In 1997 imports totalled US$44,219 million and exports US$48,035 million.

Trade with UK	1997	1998
Imports from UK	£1,986,300,000	£1,934,100,000
Exports to UK	2,223,000,000	2,067,300,000

COMMUNICATIONS

In 1996, the Danish mercantile fleet numbered 584 ships of more than 100 gross tonnage. There were 3,000 km of railway, 85 per cent of which belonged to the state and 15 per cent to privately-owned companies. A rail tunnel and bridge linking the islands of Zealand and Funen was opened in 1997.

CULTURE AND EDUCATION

The Danish language is akin to Swedish and Norwegian. Danish literature, ancient and modern, embraces all forms of expression, familiar names being Hans Christian Andersen (1805–75), Søren Kierkegaard (1813–55) and Karen Blixen (1885–1962). Some 38 newspapers are published in Denmark; eight daily papers are published in Copenhagen.

Education is free and compulsory. Special schools are numerous, commercial, technical and agricultural predominating. There are universities at Copenhagen (founded in 1479), Århus (1928), Odense (1966), Roskilde (1972) and Ålborg (1974).

ENROLMENT (percentage of age group) – primary 97 per cent (1995); secondary 87 per cent (1995); tertiary 45.0 per cent (1995)

THE FARØE ISLANDS

AREA – 540 sq. miles (1,399 sq. km)

POPULATION – 47,000 (1995)

CAPITAL – Tórshavn (population, 16,218, 1992)

Since 1948 the Farøes or Sheep Islands have had a degree of home rule. The islands are governed by a *Lagting* of 32 members and a *Landsstyret* of four members which deals with special Farøes affairs, and send two representatives to the *Folketing* at Copenhagen. The Farøes are not part of the EU.

Prime Minister, Edmund Joensen

Trade with UK	1997	1998
Imports from UK	£8,551,000	£7,533,000
Exports to UK	109,790,000	90,285,000

GREENLAND

AREA – 840,004 sq. miles (2,175,600 sq. km) of which about 16 per cent is ice-free

POPULATION – 58,000 (1995)

CAPITAL – Godthåb (Nuuk) (population, 12,483, 1995)

Greenland attained a status of internal autonomy in May 1979 and a government (*Landsstyret*) was established. It has a *Landsting* (parliament) of 31 members and sends two representatives to the *Folketing* at Copenhagen. Greenland negotiated its withdrawal from the EU, without discontinuing relations with Denmark, and left on 1 February 1985.

The USA has acquired certain rights to maintain air bases in Greenland.

Prime Minister, Jonathan Motzfeldt

Trade with UK	1997	1998
Imports from UK	£672,000	£1,909,000
Exports to UK	8,525,000	1,707,000

DJIBOUTI
Jumhouriyya Djibouti

AREA – 8,958 sq. miles (23,200 sq. km). Neighbours: Eritrea (north), Ethiopia (west and south), Somalia (south-east)

POPULATION – 617,000 (1994 UN estimate), 520,000 (1991 census), mostly Afar or Issas. The official languages are Arabic and French; Afar and Somali are also spoken

CAPITAL – ΨDjibouti (population, 62,000, 1991)

CURRENCY – Djibouti franc of 100 centimes

NATIONAL DAY – 27 June (Independence Day)

NATIONAL FLAG – Blue over green with white triangle in the hoist containing a red star

LIFE EXPECTANCY (years) – male 46.72; female 50.00

POPULATION GROWTH RATE – 2.9 per cent (1996)

POPULATION DENSITY – 27 per sq. km (1996)

MILITARY EXPENDITURE – 5.0 per cent of GDP (1997)

MILITARY PERSONNEL – 11,400: Army 8,000, Navy 200, Air Force 200, Paramilitaries 3,000

GDP – US$537 million (1995); US$893 per capita (1995)

ANNUAL AVERAGE GROWTH OF GDP – 0.2 per cent (1995)

TOTAL EXTERNAL DEBT – US$284 million (1997)

ILLITERACY RATE – 53.8 per cent

ENROLMENT (percentage of age group) – primary 32 per cent (1996); secondary 12 per cent (1996); tertiary 0.3 per cent (1996)

The climate is harsh and much of the country is semi-arid desert.

HISTORY AND POLITICS

Formerly French Somaliland and then the French Territory of the Afars and the Issas, the Republic of Djibouti became independent on 27 June 1977. A multiparty constitution was adopted by referendum in 1992 and subsequent multiparty elections held in December 1992 were won by the *Rassemblement Populaire pour le Progrès* (RPP, the Popular Rally for Progress). President Aptidon was re-elected for a fourth six-year term in 1993. However, less than half the electorate voted in either election and the Front for the Restoration of Unity and Democracy (FRUD) boycotted both. In December 1997, in the first elections since the 1994 peace accord, the RPP and the FRUD formed an alliance and won all 65 seats in the Chamber of Deputies. On 9 April 1999, President Ismael Omar Guelleh was elected, gaining approximately three-quarters of the votes cast; about 60 per cent of the electorate were estimated to have voted.

HEAD OF STATE
President, Ismael Omar Guelleh, *elected* 9 April 1999

COUNCIL OF MINISTERS *as at May 1999*

Prime Minister, National and Regional Development, Barkat Gourad Hamadou
Agriculture, Farming, Fisheries and Hydraulic Resources, Ibrahim Idriss Djibril
Civil Service and Administrative Reform, Ougoure Kifle Ahmed
Defence, Abdallah Chirwa Djibril
Economy, Finance, Planning and Privatization, Yacin Elmi Bouh
Energy and Natural Resources, Ali Abdi Farah
Environment, Tourism and Handicrafts, Osman Robleh Daach
Foreign Affairs and International Co-operation, Mohamed Moussa Chehem
Interior, Decentralization, Elmi Obsieh Farah
Justice, Islamic Affairs and Prisons, Mohamed Dini Farah
Labour and Vocational Training, Muhummad Ali Muhammad
National Education, Ahmed Guirreh Waberi
Public Health and Social Affairs, Ali Muhammad Daoud
Public Works, Town Planning and Housing, Hassan Farah Miguil
Trade and Industry, Mohamed Barkat Abdillahi
Transport and Telecommunications, Abdallah Abdillahi Miguil
Youth, Sport and Cultural Affairs, Rifki Abdoulkader Bamakhrama

EMBASSY OF THE REPUBLIC OF DJIBOUTI
26 rue Emile Ménier, F-75016 Paris, France
Tel: Paris 4727 4922
Ambassador Extraordinary and Plenipotentiary, HE Djama Omar Idleh, apptd 1998

BRITISH AMBASSADOR, HE Gordon Wetherell, resident at Addis Ababa, Ethiopia

BRITISH CONSULATE
PO Box 81, 9–11 Rue de Genève, Djibouti
Honorary Consul, P. Lambrecht

The French continue to maintain army, navy and air force bases in Djibouti, with a total strength of 1,500 personnel. Djibouti has an excellent port, an international airport, and a railway line runs to Addis Ababa. In 1995 Djibouti had a trade deficit of US$171 million and a current account deficit of US$23 million.

Trade with UK	1997	1998
Imports from UK	£15,380,000	£17,027,000
Exports to UK	411,000	235,000

DOMINICA
The Commonwealth of Dominica

AREA – 290 sq. miles (751 sq. km)
POPULATION – 74,000 (1994 UN estimate). English is the official language although Creole French is more commonly used
CAPITAL – ΨRoseau (population, 16,243, 1991)
MAJOR TOWNS – Portsmouth (3,620)
CURRENCY – East Caribbean dollar (EC$) of 100 cents
NATIONAL ANTHEM – Isle of Beauty
NATIONAL DAY – 3 November (Independence Day)
NATIONAL FLAG – Green ground with a cross overall of yellow, black and white stripes, and in the centre a red disc charged with a Sisserou parrot in natural colours within a ring of ten green stars
POPULATION GROWTH RATE – 0.6 per cent (1996)
POPULATION DENSITY – 99 per sq. km (1996)

Dominica, in the Lesser Antilles, lies in the Windward Islands group 95 miles south of Antigua. It is about 29 miles long and 16 miles wide. The island is of volcanic origin and very mountainous, and the soil is very fertile. The temperature varies, according to the altitude, from 13° to 29°C.

HISTORY AND POLITICS

The island was discovered by Columbus in 1493, when it was a stronghold of the Caribs, who remained virtually the sole inhabitants until the French established settlements in the 18th century. It was captured by the British in 1759 but passed back and forth between France and Britain until 1805, after which British possession was not challenged. From 1871 to 1939 Dominica was part of the Leeward Islands Colony, then from 1940 the island was a unit of the Windward Islands group. Internal self-government from 1967 was followed on 3 November 1978 by independence as a republic.

The most recent general election was held in June 1995 and won by the Dominica United Workers' Party, which captured 11 seats, with five seats each going to the Dominica Freedom Party and the Dominica Labour Party.

POLITICAL SYSTEM

Executive authority is vested in the president, who is elected by the House of Assembly for not more than two terms of five years. Parliament consists of the president and the House of Assembly (21 representatives elected by universal adult suffrage for a five-year term) and nine senators, five of whom are appointed on the advice of the prime minister and the other four on the advice of the Leader of the Opposition.

HEAD OF STATE
President, HE Vernon Shaw, *elected* 2 October 1998, *took office* 6 October 1998

CABINET *as at July 1999*

Prime Minister, Legal Affairs and Immigration, Edison James
Agriculture and Environment, Peter Carbon
Communications, Works and Housing, Earl Williams
Community Development and Women's Affairs, Gertrude Roberts
Education, Sports and Youth Affairs, Ronald Green
Finance, Industry and Planning, Julius Timothy
Foreign Affairs, Trade and Marketing, Norris Charles
Health and Social Security, Doreen Paul
Tourism, Ports and Employment, Norris Prevost

High Commission for the Commonwealth of Dominica
1 Collingham Gardens, London SW5 0HW
Tel 0171-370 5194/5
High Commissioner, HE George Williams, apptd 1996

British High Commissioner, HE Gordon Baker, resident at Bridgetown, Barbados

British Consulate
PO Box 2269, Roseau
Honorary Consul, P. Fletcher

ECONOMY

Agriculture is the principal occupation, with tropical and citrus fruits the main crops. Products for export are bananas, fruit juices, lime oil, bay oil, copra and rum. Forestry, fisheries and agro-processing are being encouraged. The only commercially exploitable mineral is pumice, used chiefly for building purposes. Manufacturing consists largely of the processing of agricultural products although there have been attempts to diversify into light industry.
GNP – US$225 million (1997); US$3,040 per capita (1997)
GDP – US$201 million (1995); US$2,831 per capita (1995)
Annual Average Growth of GDP – –1.5 per cent (1995)
Inflation Rate – 2.4 per cent (1997)
Total External Debt – US$98 million (1997)

Trade with UK	1997	1998
Imports from UK	£11,575,000	£10,982,000
Exports to UK	19,933,000	14,943,000

DOMINICAN REPUBLIC
República Dominicana

Area – 18,816 sq. miles (48,734 sq. km). Neighbour: Haiti (west)
Population – 8,052,000 (1994 UN estimate). The language is Spanish
Capital – ΨSanto Domingo (population, 2,134,779, 1993)
Major Cities – Duarte (272,227); La Vega (335,140); Puerto Plata (255,061); San Cristóbal (409,381); San Juan (247,029); Santiago de los Caballeros (690,458), 1993 UN estimates
Currency – Dominican Republic peso (RD$) of 100 centavos
National Flag – Divided into blue and red quarters by a white cross
National Anthem – Quisqueyanos Valientes, Alcemos (Brave men of Quisqueya, let's raise our song)
National Day – 27 February (Independence Day 1844)
Life Expectancy (years) – male 67.63; female 71.69
Population Growth Rate – 1.9 per cent (1996)
Population Density – 165 per sq. km (1996)
Urban Population – 61.7 per cent (1995)
Military Expenditure – 1.2 per cent of GDP (1997)
Military Personnel – 39,500: Army 15,000, Navy 4,000, Air Force 5,500, Paramilitaries 15,000
Illiteracy Rate – 17.9 per cent
Enrolment (percentage of age group) – primary 81 per cent (1994); secondary 22 per cent (1994); tertiary 18.0 per cent (1985)

The Dominican Republic, the eastern part of the island of Hispaniola (Haiti is the western part), is the oldest

European settlement in America. The climate is tropical in the lowlands and semi-tropical to temperate in the higher altitudes.

HISTORY AND POLITICS

Santo Domingo was discovered by Columbus in 1492, and was a Spanish colony until 1797, when it passed to France. It was restored to Spanish rule in 1809. Independence was proclaimed in 1821, but in 1822 it was subjugated by the neighbouring Haitians who remained in control until 1844, when the Dominican Republic was proclaimed. The country was occupied by American marines from 1916 until 1924. Gen. Rafael Trujillo ruled from 1930 until 1961.
President Juan Bosch held office from December 1962 to September 1963, when he was deposed by a military junta. A left-wing revolt in favour of ex-President Bosch in April 1965 developed into civil war lasting until September the same year, when Bosch's supporters were defeated by the arrival of US troops, a provisional president was elected and democracy was restored. A presidential election in May 1994 was won by the incumbent President Balaguer. Balaguer was replaced by opposition Dominican Liberation Party (PLD) candidate, Leonel Fernández, who defeated the ruling Christian Social Reform Party (PRSC) candidate, Jacinto Peynado, in a run-off election on 30 June 1996.

POLITICAL SYSTEM

Executive power is vested in the president, who is directly elected for a single four-year term and appoints the Cabinet. Legislative power is exercised by the Congress, which has a term of four years concurrent with the presidency. The Congress comprises the Senate of 30 senators, one for each province and one for Santo Domingo, and the 149-member Chamber of Deputies.

Head of State
President, Leonel Fernández Reyna, *elected* 30 June 1996
Vice-President, Jaime David Fernández Mirabal

Cabinet *as at May 1999*
Agriculture, Amílcar Romero
Chief Minister, Danilo Medina
Defence, Rear-Adm. Rubén Paulino Alvárez
Education and Culture, Ligia Amada Melo de Cardona
Finance, Daniel Toribio
Foreign Affairs, Eduardo Latorre Rodríguez
Health, Altagracia Guzmán
Industry and Commerce, Luís Manuel Bonetti
Interior, Ramón Blanco Fernández
Labour, Rafael Albuquerque
Public Works and Communications, Diandino Peña
Tourism, Felix Jiménez
Without Portfolio, Lidio Cadet; Ramón Ventura Camejo

Embassy of the Dominican Republic
139 Inverness Terrace, London, W2 6JF
Tel 0171-727 6285
Ambassador Extraordinary and Plenipotentiary, HE Dr Pedro Padilla Tonos, apptd 1997

British Embassy
Edificio Corominas Pepin, Ave 27 de Febrero No 233, Santo Domingo
Tel: Santo Domingo 472 7111
Ambassador Extraordinary and Plenipotentiary, HE David Ward, apptd 1999
British Consular Offices – Santo Domingo, Puerto Plata

ECONOMY

Since 1990 the government has successfully reduced inflation and increased output. Large amounts of foreign debt have been paid off but unemployment remains high. State subsidies were ended in 1995 in an attempt to reduce the budget deficit.

Sugar, cocoa, coffee, bananas, rice and tobacco are the most important crops. Other products are maize, molasses, beans, tomatoes, cement, ferro-nickel, gold, silver and cattle. Light industry produces beer, tinned foodstuffs, glass products, textiles, soap, cigarettes, construction materials, plastic articles, paint, rum, matches and peanut oil.

GNP – US$14,148 million (1997); US$1,750 per capita (1997)

GDP – US$11,801 million (1995); US$1,508 per capita (1995)

ANNUAL AVERAGE GROWTH OF GDP – 7.3 per cent (1996)

INFLATION RATE – 8.3 per cent (1997)

TOTAL EXTERNAL DEBT – US$4,239 million (1997)

TRADE

The chief imports are machinery, foodstuffs, iron and steel, cotton textiles and yarns, mineral oils (including petrol), motor vehicles, chemical and pharmaceutical products, electrical equipment and accessories, construction materials, paper and paper products, and rubber and rubber products. The chief exports are ferro-nickel, sugar, coffee, cocoa, tobacco, chocolate, molasses and gold.

In 1996 there was a trade deficit of US$1,765 million and a current account deficit of US$110 million. In 1997 imports totalled US$4,120 million and exports US$882 million.

Trade with UK	1997	1998
Imports from UK	£38,857,000	£43,854,000
Exports to UK	34,665,000	24,861,000

COMMUNICATIONS

There are over 4,000 miles of roads and a direct road from Santo Domingo to Port-au-Prince, the capital of Haiti, but that part of it in the border area has fallen into disuse. The frontier has been closed since 1967, except for the section crossed by the main road linking the two capitals. A telephone system connects all the principal towns. There are more than 90 commercial broadcasting stations and six television stations.

ECUADOR
República del Ecuador

AREA – 109,484 sq. miles (283,561 sq. km). Neighbours: Colombia (north), Peru (east and south)

POPULATION – 11,698,000 (1994 UN estimate), descendants of the Spanish, aboriginal Indians, and Mestizos. Spanish is the principal language but Quechua is also a recognized language and is spoken by most Indians

CAPITAL – Quito (population, 1,444,363, 1996 estimate)

MAJOR CITIES – Cuenca (247,421); ΨGuayaquil (1,925,479), the chief port

CURRENCY – Sucre of 100 centavos

NATIONAL DAY – 10 August (Independence Day)

NATIONAL FLAG – Three horizontal bands, yellow, blue and red (the yellow band twice the width of the others); emblem in centre

LIFE EXPECTANCY (years) – male 67.32; female 72.49

POPULATION GROWTH RATE – 2.2 per cent (1996)

POPULATION DENSITY – 41 per sq. km (1996)

URBAN POPULATION – 61.3 per cent (1996)

MILITARY EXPENDITURE – 3.5 per cent of GDP (1997)

MILITARY PERSONNEL – 57,370: Army 50,000, Navy 4,100, Air Force 3,000, Paramilitaries 270

CONSCRIPTION DURATION – 12 months

Ecuador is an equatorial state of South America. It extends across the Western Andes, the highest peaks being Chimborazo (20,408 ft) and Ilinza (17,405 ft) in the Western Cordillera; and Cotopaxi (19,612 ft) and Cayambe (19,160 ft) in the Eastern Cordillera. Ecuador is watered by the Upper Amazon, and by the rivers Guayas, Mira, Santiago, Chone, and Esmeraldas on the Pacific coast. There are extensive forests.

HISTORY AND POLITICS

The former kingdom of Quito was conquered by the Incas of Peru in the 15th century. Early in the 16th century Pizarro's conquests led to the inclusion of the present territory of Ecuador in the Spanish Vice-royalty of Quito. Independence was achieved in a revolutionary war which culminated in the battle of Mount Pichincha (1822).

After seven years of military rule, Ecuador returned to democracy in 1979. In the 1992 legislative election a loose coalition of parties enabled President Ballén to introduce a programme of economic reform, financial liberalization and privatization. This, together with reductions in state spending, caused social unrest in 1992–4 and led to the government's defeat in the May 1994 legislative elections. In the July 1996 elections the ruling Social Christian Party (PSC) won a majority of seats. Abdala Bucaram was elected president in July 1996, and appointed a coalition government. Bucaram was ousted by the legislature on the grounds of insanity and replaced firstly by Vice-President Arteaga and then by the Speaker of the National Congress Fabián Alarcón. The presidential elections in July 1998 were won by Jamil Mahaud, the former Mayor of Quito, who gained 51 per cent of the vote.

FOREIGN RELATIONS

The border with Peru was demarcated by a 1942 treaty which was partly revoked by Ecuador in 1960 in relation to a disputed 50-mile stretch. An inconclusive four-week border war was fought with Peru in February 1995 until a cease-fire was signed on 1 March 1995. A 54-mile demilitarized zone was agreed in July 1995. An agreement was signed on 26 October 1998 by the presidents of the two countries formally ending the territorial dispute after mediation by Argentina, Brazil, Chile and the USA.

POLITICAL SYSTEM

The 1978 constitution provides for an elected president and vice-president who serve for a single four-year term. There is a unicameral National Congress which meets for two months a year and has 121 members, 20 of whom are elected on a national basis every four years and 101 on a provincial basis every two years. Voting is compulsory for all literate and voluntary for all illiterate citizens over the age of 18. The republic is divided into 21 provinces.

HEAD OF STATE
President, Jamil Mahaud, *elected* 20 July 1998
Vice-President, Gustavo Noboa Bejarano

CABINET *as at May 1999*

Agriculture, Emilio Gallardo González
Defence, José Gallardo Roman
Education, Rosa Angela Adoum
Energy and Mines, René Ortiz
Environment, Yolanda Kakabadse
Finance, Ana Lucía Armijos

Foreign Affairs, Benjamin Ortiz
Foreign Trade, Héctor Plaza Saavedra
Health, Edgar Rodas
Home Affairs, Wladimiro Alvarez Grau
Housing, Teodoro Peño
Labour, Angel Polibio Chávez
Public Works, Raúl Samaniego
Social Welfare, Guillermo Celi
Tourism, Rocío Vásquez
General Secretaries, Jaime Durán (*Administration*); Ramón Yulee (*Presidency*)

EMBASSY OF ECUADOR
Flat 3B, 3 Hans Crescent, London SWIX OLS
Tel 0171-584 1367/2648/8084
Ambassador Extraordinary and Plenipotentiary, HE Osvaldo Ramírez-Landázuri

BRITISH EMBASSY
Calle González Suárez 111, Casilla 314, Quito
Tel: Quito 560670
Ambassador Extraordinary and Plenipotentiary, HE John Forbes-Meyler, OBE, apptd 1997
BRITISH CONSULAR OFFICES – Cuenca, Galápagos and Guayaquil

BRITISH COUNCIL REPRESENTATIVE, Anthony Deyes, Av. Amazonas 1646, Casilla 17-07-8829, Quito

ECONOMY

Agriculture is the most important sector of the economy. The main products for export are fish, bananas, which provide a third of agricultural exports, cocoa and coffee. Other important crops are sugar, soya, rice, cotton, African palm, vegetables, fruit and timber. The main imports are manufactured goods and machinery.

The economy was transformed by the discovery in 1972 of major oil fields in the Oriente area.

In March 1999, the sucre fell in value by 38 per cent, causing panic withdrawing of deposits which forced the government to close all banks for seven days. A state of emergency was declared following a two-day general strike, and an austerity programme, which included limiting bank withdrawals, tax increases and privatization of state enterprises, was introduced.

The 'Ecuador 2000' plan, unveiled by the president in April 1999, is intended to stimulate the economy and repair the country's infrastructure with a range of works programmes and development schemes.

In 1997 there was a trade surplus of US$598 million and a current account deficit of US$743 million. Imports totalled US$4,945 million and exports US$5,221 million.
GNP – US$18,785 million (1997); US$1,570 per capita (1997)
GDP – US$17,939 million (1995); US$1,565 per capita (1995)
ANNUAL AVERAGE GROWTH OF GDP – 2.9 per cent (1996)
INFLATION RATE – 30.6 per cent (1997)
UNEMPLOYMENT – 7.1 per cent (1994)
TOTAL EXTERNAL DEBT – US$14,918 million (1997)

Trade with UK	1997	1998
Imports from UK	£45,501,000	£40,275,000
Exports to UK	36,184,000	41,221,000

COMMUNICATIONS

There are 23,256 km of permanent roads and 5,044 km of roads which are only open during the dry season. Ten commercial airlines operate international flights and there are internal services between all important towns. Two daily newspapers are published at Quito and four at Guayaquil.

EDUCATION

Elementary education is free and compulsory. There are ten universities (three at Quito, three at Guayaquil, and one each at Cuenca, Machala, Loja and Portoviejo), polytechnic schools at Quito and Guayaquil and eight technical colleges in other provincial capitals.
ILLITERACY RATE – 9.9 per cent
ENROLMENT (percentage of age group) – primary 97 per cent (1996); tertiary 20.0 per cent (1990)

GALÁPAGOS ISLANDS

The Galápagos (Giant Tortoise) Islands, forming the province of the Archipelago de Colón, were annexed by Ecuador in 1832. The archipelago lies in the Pacific, about 500 miles from the mainland. There are 12 large and several hundred smaller islands with a total area of about 3,000 sq. miles and an estimated population (1982) of 6,119. The capital is Puerto Baquerizo Moreno, on San Cristobal Island. Although the archipelago lies on the equator, the temperature of the surrounding water is well below equatorial average owing to the Humboldt current. The province consists for the most part of National Park Territory, where unique marine birds, iguanas, and the giant tortoises are conserved. There is some local subsistence farming; the main industry, apart from tourism, is tuna and lobster fishing.

EGYPT
Al-Jumhuriyat Misr al-Arabiya

AREA – 386,662 sq. miles (1,001,449 sq. km). Neighbours: Sudan (south), Libya (west), Gaza Strip and Israel (east)
POPULATION – 60,603,000 (official estimate 1995). The largest, or 'Egyptian' element, is a Hamito-Semite race. A second element is the *Bedouin*, or nomadic Arabs of the Western and Eastern deserts, who are now mainly semi-sedentary tent-dwellers. The third element is the *Nubian* of the Nile Valley of mixed Arab and Negro blood. Over 90 per cent of the population are Muslims of the Sunni denomination, and most of the rest are Coptic Christians. Arabic is the official language
CAPITAL – Cairo (population, 6,800,000, 1994 estimate) stands on the Nile about 14 miles from the head of the delta
MAJOR CITIES – ΨAlexandria (3,328,196, 1997 estimate), founded 332 BC by Alexander the Great, was the capital for over 1,000 years; Asyût (2,802,185); Faiyûm (1,989,881); Ismailia (715,009); ΨPort Said (469,533); ΨSuez (417,610)
CURRENCY – Egyptian pound (£E) of 100 piastres or 1,000 millièmes
NATIONAL DAY – 23 July (Anniversary of Revolution in 1952)
NATIONAL FLAG – Horizontal bands of red, white and black, with an eagle in the centre of the white band
LIFE EXPECTANCY (years) – male 62.86; female 66.39
POPULATION GROWTH RATE – 2.1 per cent (1996)
POPULATION DENSITY – 61 per sq. km (1996)
URBAN POPULATION – 44.0 per cent (1996)
ILLITERACY RATE – 48.6 per cent
ENROLMENT (percentage of age group) – primary 80 per cent (1996); secondary 68 per cent (1996); tertiary 20.3 per cent (1995)

Egypt comprises Egypt proper, the peninsula of Sinai and a number of islands in the Gulf of Suez and Red Sea, of which the principal are Jubal, Shadwan, Gafatin and Zeberged (or St John's Island).

The country is mainly flat but there are mountainous areas in the south-west, along the Red Sea coast and in the south of the Sinai peninsula; the highest peak is Mt Catherina (8,668 ft). Most of the land is desert and the Nile valley and delta were the only fertile areas until the opening of the Aswan Dam allowed areas of desert to be reclaimed. West of the Nile Valley is the Western Desert, containing some depressions whose springs irrigate oases. The Eastern Desert between the Nile and the mountains along the Red Sea coast is mostly plateaux dissected by wadis (dry water-courses).

HISTORY AND POLITICS

The unification of the kingdoms of Lower and Upper Egypt under the Pharaohs *c.*3100 BC marked the establishment of the Egyptian state, with Memphis as its capital. Egypt was ruled for nearly 2,800 years by a succession of 31 Pharaonic dynasties which built the pyramids at Gizeh. A period of Hellenic rule began in 332 BC, followed by a period of rule by Rome (30 BC to AD 324) and then by the Byzantine Empire. In AD 640 Egypt was subjugated by Arab Muslim invaders. In 1517 the country was incorporated in the Ottoman Empire, under which it remained until the early 19th century. A British Protectorate over Egypt lasted from 1914 to 1922, when Sultan Ahmed Fuad was proclaimed King of Egypt. In 1953 the monarchy was deposed and Egypt became a republic.

In 1956, as a result of Egypt's trade agreements with Communist countries, Britain and the USA withdrew offers of financial aid and in retaliation President Nasser seized the assets of the Suez Canal Company. Egyptian occupation of the Canal Zone while repulsing an Israeli attack was used as a pretext for military action by Britain and France in support of their Suez Canal Company interests. A ceasefire and Anglo-French withdrawal were negotiated by the UN.

The Israeli invasion of 1956 overran the Sinai peninsula but six months later Israel withdrew. However, mounting tension culminated in a second invasion of Sinai (the Six Day War in June 1967) and occupation of the peninsula by Israel. Egypt's attempt to recapture the territory (the Yom Kippur War in October 1973) was unsuccessful but Sinai was returned to Egypt in 1982 under the treaty of 1979 which resulted from the Camp David talks and formally terminated a 31-year-old state of war between the two countries.

The ruling National Democratic Party won the general election held in November and December 1995. President Mubarak was nominated by the legislature to run unopposed for a third six-year term in July 1993, and was elected in October.

INSURGENCY

Militant Islamist fundamentalists re-emerged in 1992, carrying out attacks on tourists, Coptic Christians, government ministers, civil servants and the security forces. Attacks are concentrated in Upper Egypt and the Cairo area. The government has reacted vigorously to the armed campaign with the arrest of 20,000 militants.   On 27 March 1999, the largest fundamentalist organization, Gamaat-i-Islamiya, announced that it had given up its violent campaign to overthrow the government.

POLITICAL SYSTEM

The constitution of 1971 provides for an executive president who appoints the Council of Ministers and determines government policy. The president is elected by the legislature every six years. The legislature is the People's Assembly which has 454 members, 444 of whom are elected, the remaining ten nominated by the president. The Shura Council or Consultative Assembly (210 members) has an advisory role.

HEAD OF STATE
President, Muhammad Hosni Mubarak, *elected* 1981, *re-elected* 1987, 13 October 1993

COUNCIL OF MINISTERS *as at May 1999*
Prime Minister, Planning, International Co-operation, Kamal Ahmed al-Ganzuri
Deputy PM, Agriculture and Land Reclamation, Yousef Amin Wali
Administrative Development, Mahmoud Zaki Abu Amer
Cabinet Affairs and Follow-up of Economic Affairs, Tala'at Sayyed Ahmed Hammad
Culture, Farouk Hosni Abdel Aziz
Defence and Military Production, Field Marshal Mohammad Hussein Tantawi
Economy, Yussef Boutros Ghali
Education, Hussein Kamel Bahaeddin
Electricity and Energy, Mohamed Maher Othman Abaza
Environment, Nadia Makram Obeid
Finance, Mohieddin Abu Bakr al Ghareeb
Foreign Affairs, Amr Mahmoud Moussa
Health and Population, Ismail Awadallah Sallam
Higher Education and Scientific Research, Mufid Shehab
Housing, Utilities and New Urban Communities, Mohammed Ibrahim Soliman
Industry and Mineral Resources, Soliman Reda Ali Soliman
Information, Safwat El-Sherif
Interior, Brig. Habib al-Adli
Justice, Farouk Seif El-Nasr
Labour and Emigration, Ahmed al-Amawi
Military Production, Mohammad al-Ghamrawi Daoud Hasan
People's National Assembly and Consultative Council Affairs, Kamal Mohammed Al Shazli
Petroleum, Hamdi Abdel Wahab al-Banbi
Planning and International Co-operation, Zafir Selim Al-Beshri
Public Business Sector, Atef Mohammad Obeid
Public Works and Water Resources, Mahmoud Abdul Halim Abu Zaid
Religious Endowments (Wakfs), Mahmoud Hamdi Zakzouk
Rural Development, Mahmoud El-Sherif Sayeed Ahmed
Scientific Research, Venise Kamel Gouda
Social Insurance and Social Affairs, Marwat al-Tilawi
Tourism, Mamdouh Ahmed Al-Beltagui
Trade and Supply, Ahmed Ahmed Gowaili
Transport and Communications, Soliman Mutwalli

EMBASSY OF THE ARAB REPUBLIC OF EGYPT
12 Curzon Street, London WIY 7FJ
Tel 0171-499 2401/3304
Ambassador Extraordinary and Plenipotentiary, HE Abdel El-Gazzar, apptd 1997
Ministers Plenipotentiary, Samiha Abou Steit (*Consul-General*); Ismail Roushdy (*Commercial*)
Defence Attaché, Cdre. Mohamed F. E. Genina
Cultural Counsellor, Mohamed A. El-Sharkawy

BRITISH EMBASSY
Ahmed Ragheb Street, Garden City, Cairo
Tel: Cairo 354 0850
Ambassador Extraordinary and Plenipotentiary, HE Graham Boyce, CMG, apptd 1999
Counsellor and Deputy Head of Mission, G. D. Adams

Defence and Military Attaché, Col. A. Snook, OBE
First Secretaries, P. Byrde (*Consul*); D. G. Reader
(*Commercial*)
BRITISH CONSULAR OFFICES – *Consulate-General*,
Alexandria; *Consulates*, Luxor, Suez, Port Said, Aswan

BRITISH COUNCIL DIRECTOR, D. Marler OBE (*Cultural
First Secretary*), 192 Sharia el Nil, Agouza, Cairo

DEFENCE

The Army has 3,700 main battle tanks, 790 armoured
infantry fighting vehicles, 3,904 armoured personnel
carriers and 1,247 artillery pieces. The Navy has one
destroyer, eight frigates, four submarines, 42 patrol and
coastal vessels and 24 armed helicopters at six bases. The
Air Force has 585 combat aircraft and 125 armed
helicopters.
MILITARY EXPENDITURE – 4.3 per cent of GDP (1997)
MILITARY PERSONNEL – 680,000: Army 320,000, Navy
20,000, Air Force 30,000, Air Defence Command
80,000, Paramilitaries 230,000
CONSCRIPTION DURATION – Three years

ECONOMY

Despite increasing industrialization, agriculture remains
the most important economic activity, employing 35 per
cent of the labour force and producing 22 per cent of GDP
in 1995. Egypt is still a net importer of foodstuffs, especially
grain, and a food security programme has been set up with
the aim of achieving self-sufficiency. The main cash crop
is cotton, of which Egypt is one of the world's main
producers. Other important crops are maize, rice, sugar
cane, wheat and potatoes. Other fruits and vegetables are
also grown.

With its considerable reserves of petroleum and natural
gas, and the hydroelectric power produced by the Aswan
and High Dams, Egypt is self-sufficient in energy. The
major manufacturing industries are food processing, motor
cars, electrical goods, steel, chemical products, yarns and
textiles. In 1996 more than two million tourists visited
Egypt, though in 1997 the tourism industry was badly
affected following attacks on foreign tourists by Islamist
militants.

In 1996 the government had a trade deficit of US$8,390
million and a current account deficit of US$192 million.
GNP – US$72,164 million (1997); US$1,200 per capita
(1997)
GDP – US$60,436 million (1995); US$973 per capita
(1995)
ANNUAL AVERAGE GROWTH OF GDP – 5.1 per cent
(1996)
INFLATION RATE – 4.6 per cent (1997)
UNEMPLOYMENT – 11.0 per cent (1994)
TOTAL EXTERNAL DEBT – US$29,849 million (1997)

TRADE

The main imports are wheat, maize, chemicals and motor
vehicles and parts. The main exports are crude petroleum,
cotton, cotton yarn, oranges, rice and cotton textiles.

In 1996 Egypt's imports totalled US$13,019 million and
exports US$3,535 million.

Trade with UK	1997	1998
Imports from UK	£498,582,000	£510,246,000
Exports to UK	270,027,000	291,114,000

COMMUNICATIONS

There are international airports at Cairo and Luxor. The
road and rail networks link the Nile valley and delta with
the main development areas east and west of the river. The
Suez Canal was reopened in 1975 and a two-stage
development project begun to widen and deepen the canal
to allow the passage of larger shipping and to permit two-
way traffic. Port Said and Suez have been reconstructed
and the port of Alexandria is being improved.

EQUATORIAL GUINEA
República de Guinea Ecuatorial

AREA – 10,831 sq. miles (28,051 sq. km). Neighbours:
Cameroon (north), Gabon (east and south)
POPULATION – 410,000 (1994 UN estimate). The official
languages are Spanish and French
CAPITAL – ΨMalabo on the island of Bioko (population,
30,418, 1983 estimate)
MAJOR TOWN – ΨBata is the principal town and port of
Rio Muni
CURRENCY – Franc CFA of 100 centimes
NATIONAL DAY – 12 October
NATIONAL FLAG – Three horizontal bands, green over
white over red; blue triangle next staff; coat of arms in
centre of white band
LIFE EXPECTANCY (years) – male 44.86; female 47.78
POPULATION GROWTH RATE – 2.7 per cent (1996)
POPULATION DENSITY – 15 per sq. km (1996)
URBAN POPULATION – 37.0 per cent (1996)
MILITARY EXPENDITURE – 1.3 per cent of GDP (1997)
MILITARY PERSONNEL – 1,320: Army 1,100, Navy 120,
Air Force 100
ILLITERACY RATE – 21.5 per cent

Equatorial Guinea consists of the island of Bioko, in the
Bight of Biafra about 20 miles from the west coast of Africa,
Annonbón Island in the Gulf of Guinea, the Corisco Islands
(Corisco, Elobey Grande and Elobey Chico), and Rio
Muni, a mainland area between Cameroon and Gabon.

HISTORY AND POLITICS

Formerly colonies of Spain, the territories now forming
Equatorial Guinea were constituted as two provinces of
Metropolitan Spain in 1959, became autonomous in 1963
and fully independent in 1968.

In 1979 President Macias was deposed by a revolutionary
military council headed by Col. Obiang Nguema. Constitutional amendments in 1982 provided for legislative
elections, which were held in 1983 and 1988, but all
candidates were chosen by the president.

A multiparty political system under a new constitution
was approved by a referendum in 1991 and ten opposition
parties have been legalized, operating alongside the ruling
Equatorial Guinea Democratic Party (PDGE). A National
Pact was agreed and signed in March 1993 but legislative
elections in November, which were won by the PDGE,
were boycotted by most of the electorate and opposition
parties. In the February 1996 election, the president
claimed to have won more than 99 per cent of the vote.
Most opposition parties boycotted the ballot. In June 1997
the Progress Party, the largest opposition party, was banned
by the government, and in February 1998 opposition party
coalitions were deemed illegal. The PDGE won 75 of the
80 seats in the National Assembly elections on 7 March
1999 amid allegations of electoral malpractice.

HEAD OF STATE
*President of the Supreme Military Council and Minister of
Defence*, Brig.-Gen. Teodoro Obiang Nguema Mbasogo,
took office August 1979, *re-elected* June 1989, 25 February
1996

MINISTERS *as at May 1999*

Prime Minister, Angel Serafín Dougan
Deputy PM, Foreign Affairs, Miguel Oyono Ndong Mifumu
Deputy PM, Interior, Demetrio Elo Ndong
Minister of State, Health and Social Welfare, Salomón
  Nguema Owono
Minister of State, Labour and Social Security, Carmelo Modu
  Akune
Minister of State, Missions, Alejandro Evuna Owono
  Asangono
*Minister of State, Planning, Economic Development, Government
  Spokesman,* Antonio Fernando Nve Ngu
Minister of State, Public Works and Urban Affairs, Francisco
  Pascual Eyegue Obama Asue
Minister of State, Secretary-General at the Presidency, Ricardo
  Mangue Obama Nfue
Minister of State, Transport and Communication, Marcelino
  Oyono Ntutumu
Agriculture, Fisheries and Animal Husbandry, Constantine Eko
  Nsue
Civil Service and Administrative Reform, Fernando Mabale
  Mba
Economy and Finance, Baltazar Engonga Edjo
Education, Science and Francophonie, Santiago Ngua Nfumu
Forestry and Environment, Nguema Teodoro Obiang
Industry, Commerce, Small and Medium-sized Enterprises, Vidal
  Djoni Becoba
Information, Tourism and Culture, Lucas Nguema Esono
Interior and Local Corporations, Angel Esono Abaga
Justice and Religious Affairs, Rubén Mye Nsue
Mines and Energy, Juan Olo Mba Nseng
Social Affairs, Women's Affairs, Margarita Alene Mba
Youth and Sports, Ignacio Minlane Ntang

EMBASSY OF THE REPUBLIC OF EQUATORIAL GUINEA
6 rue Alfred de Vigny, F-75008, Paris
Tel: Paris 4766 4433
Ambassador Extraordinary and Plenipotentiary, HE Lino-Sima
  Ekua Avomo

BRITISH AMBASSADOR, HE Peter Boon, resident at
  Yaoundé, Cameroon

ECONOMY

The chief products are cocoa, coffee and wood. Production
has declined and except for cocoa there is little commercial
agriculture. The economy is heavily dependent on outside
aid, principally from Spain. Oil and gas production is
increasing. Equatorial Guinea entered the 'franc zone' in
1985.

In 1996, there was a trade deficit of US$117 million and
a current account deficit of US$344. Imports totalled
US$292 million and exports US$175 million.

GNP – US$444 million (1997); US$1,060 per capita
  (1997)
GDP – US$155 million (1995); US$388 per capita (1995)
ANNUAL AVERAGE GROWTH OF GDP – 1.2 per cent
  (1995)
INFLATION RATE – 4.0 per cent (1993)
TOTAL EXTERNAL DEBT – US$283 million (1997)

Trade with UK	1997	1998
Imports from UK	£10,594,000	£9,134,000
Exports to UK	626,000	7,969,000

ERITREA

AREA – 45,406 sq. miles (117,600 sq. km). Neighbours:
  Sudan (north and north-west), Ethiopia (south and
  south-west), Djibouti (south-east)
POPULATION – 3,280,000 (1994 UN estimate), roughly
  half Coptic Christian (mainly highlanders) and half
  Muslim (mainly lowlanders). Arabic and Tigrinya are
  official languages, but English and Italian are widely
  spoken. There are nine indigenous language groups:
  Afar; Bilen; Hadareb; Kunama; Nara; Rashida; Saho;
  Tigre; Tigrinya
CAPITAL – Asmara (population, 358,100, 1990 estimate)
MAJOR TOWNS – ΨAssab; ΨMassawa
CURRENCY – Nakfa
NATIONAL DAY – 24 May (Independence Day)
NATIONAL FLAG – Divided into three triangles; the one
  based on the hoist is red and bears a gold olive wreath;
  the upper triangle is green and the lower one light blue
LIFE EXPECTANCY (years) – male 48.85; female 52.06
POPULATION GROWTH RATE – 2.2 per cent (1996)
POPULATION DENSITY – 28 per sq. km (1996)
MILITARY EXPENDITURE – 8.3 per cent of GDP (1997)
MILITARY PERSONNEL – 47,100: Army 46,000, Navy
  1,100
CONSCRIPTION DURATION – Two years
ENROLMENT (percentage of age group) – primary 31 per
  cent (1996); secondary 16 per cent (1996); tertiary 1.0
  per cent (1996)

HISTORY AND POLITICS

Eritrea was colonized by Italy in the late 19th century and
was the base for the 1936 Italian invasion of Abyssinia
(Ethiopia). After the Italian defeat in East Africa in 1941
by British and Commonwealth forces, Eritrea became a
British protectorate. This lasted until 15 September 1952
when Eritrea was federated with Ethiopia. The Ethiopian
Emperor Haile Selassie incorporated Eritrea as a province
of Ethiopia in 1962. An armed campaign for independence
began in the 1970s, first against Emperor Haile Selassie's
forces and from 1974 against the Mengistu regime.

In 1991 the Mengistu government was overthrown by
the Eritrean People's Liberation Front (EPLF) and the
Ethiopian People's Revolutionary Democratic Front
(EPRDF). The new EPRDF-led government in Ethiopia
agreed to an Eritrean referendum on independence which
was held in April 1993 and recorded a 99 per cent vote in
favour. Independence was declared on 24 May 1993.

FOREIGN RELATIONS

Eritrea had claimed the Hanish and Mohabaka Islands in
the Red Sea, which they seized from Yemen in December
1995; however, on 9 October 1998, the International Court
of Justice ruled that the Hanish Islands belonged to Yemen
and Eritrea formally handed them over to Yemen on 1
November 1998. The land border with Djibouti is also
disputed.

In May 1998 sporadic fighting flared up on the border
with Ethiopia, with both countries accusing the other of
sending troops across the border. Proposals for a resolution
of the conflict drawn up by a special mediation committee
meeting of the Organization for African Unity (OAU) held
on 7–8 November 1998, which called on Eritrea to hand
back the disputed town of Badme pending adjudication,
were rejected by Eritrea. Full-scale fighting broke out on 6
February 1999 and Ethiopia had recaptured the town by
28 February. Eritrea accepted the OAU's proposals on 9
March, but fighting continues.

POLITICAL SYSTEM

Under the 1997 constitution, the head of state is the president, elected for a five-year term by the National Assembly, of which he is chair. The 150-member unicameral legislature (the *Hagerawi Baito*) is directly elected for four years. The president is head of government and presides over a State Council.

HEAD OF STATE
President, Chairman of the National Assembly, Issaias Afewerki, elected by National Assembly 22 May 1993

STATE COUNCIL *as at May 1999*

Chairman, The President
Agriculture, Arefaine Berhe
Defence, Sebhat Efraim
Education, Osman Salih Muhammad
Energy and Mining, Tesfay Gebreselassie
Environment and Water, Tesfaye Ghirmatsion
Eritrean Relief, Refugee Commission, Werku Tesfamichael
Finance and Development, Ghebresellsie Yossief
Fisheries, Petros Solomon
Foreign Affairs, Haile Weldetensae
Health, Saleh Mekki
Industry and Trade, Ali Said Abdella
Information, Beraki Gebreselassie
Justice, Fozia Hashim
Labour and Social Security, Okbe Abraha
Local Government, Mahammud Ahmed Sharifo
Public Works, Abraha Asfeha
Tourism, Ahmed Haji Ali
Transport and Communications, Saleh Kekia

EMBASSY OF THE STATE OF ERITREA
15–17 avenue de Wolvendael, B-1180 Brussels, Belgium
Tel: Brussels 374 4434/4500
Ambassador Extraordinary and Plenipotentiary, HE Andebrhan Weldegiorgis, apptd 1996
HONORARY CONSULATE, 96 White Lion Street, London NI 9PF. Tel: 0171–713 0096. *Honorary Consul,* Afewerki Abraha

BRITISH AMBASSADOR, HE Gordon Wetherell, resident at Addis Ababa, Ethiopia

BRITISH CONSULATE
Emperor Yohannes Avenue, House no 24, PO Box 5584, Asmara
Tel: Asmara 120145
Honorary Consul, vacant
BRITISH COUNCIL DIRECTOR – Dr Negusse Araya, PO Box 997, Asmara

ECONOMY

Since 1991 the government has attempted to rebuild industry, agriculture and infrastructure which were devastated by the war of independence. The rebuilding programme has focused on the ports of Massawa and Assab, the roads from the ports to Ethiopia, and the railway from Massawa to Sudan via Asmara. Before 1962 Eritrea was one of the most industrialized areas of Africa and some industry remains, producing textiles and footwear. The government hopes to base the rebuilding of the economy on the return of well-educated exiles, international aid and investment, the development of tourism along the coast, and the diversification of the economy away from agriculture.
GNP – US$852 million (1997); US$230 per capita (1997)
GDP – US$304 million (1995); US$96 per capita (1995)
ANNUAL AVERAGE GROWTH OF GDP – 7.7 per cent (1995)
TOTAL EXTERNAL DEBT – US$76 million (1997)

Trade with UK	1997	1998
Imports from UK	£7,042,000	£9,179,000
Exports to UK	84,000	189,000

ESTONIA
The Republic of Estonia

AREA – 17,413 sq. miles (45,227 sq. km). Neighbours: Russia (east), Latvia (south)
POPULATION – 1,453,844 (1998): 65 per cent Estonian, 28 per cent Russian, 2.5 per cent Ukrainian, 1.5 per cent Belarusian, 1 per cent Finnish, others 2 per cent. The majority religion is Lutheran, with Russian Orthodox and Baptist minorities. Estonian is the first language of 64.2 per cent and Russian of 28.7 per cent
CAPITAL – Tallinn (population, 415,299, 1998 estimate)
MAJOR TOWNS AND CITIES – Kohtla-Järve (70,800); Narva (80,300); Tartu (109,100)
CURRENCY – Kroon of 100 sents
NATIONAL ANTHEM – Mu Isamaa, mu õnn ja rõõm (My Native Land, My Joy, Delight)
NATIONAL DAY – 24 February (Independence Day)
NATIONAL FLAG – Three horizontal stripes of blue, black, white
LIFE EXPECTANCY (years) – male 64.05; female 75.03
POPULATION GROWTH RATE – –1.1 per cent (1996)
POPULATION DENSITY – 33 per sq. km (1996)
URBAN POPULATION – 70.1 per cent (1994)
MILITARY EXPENDITURE – 2.5 per cent of GDP (1997)
MILITARY PERSONNEL – 7,136: Army 3,980, Navy 320, Air Force 36, Paramilitaries 2,800
CONSCRIPTION DURATION – 12 months

Estonia includes 1,500 islands in the Baltic Sea and the Gulf of Riga. Forests cover roughly 20 per cent of the country, which also has many lakes. The climate is mild and maritime.

HISTORY AND POLITICS

Estonia, a former province of the Russian Empire, declared its independence on 24 February 1918. A war of independence was fought against the German army until November 1918, and then against Soviet forces until the peace treaty of Tartu was signed in 1920. By this treaty the Soviet Union recognized Estonia's independence.

The Soviet Union annexed Estonia in 1940 under the terms of the Molotov-Ribbentrop pact with Germany. Estonia was occupied when Germany invaded the Soviet Union during the Second World War. In 1944 the Soviet Union recaptured the country from Germany and confirmed its annexation.

The Estonian Supreme Soviet in November 1989 declared the republic to be sovereign and its 1940 annexation by the Soviet Union to be illegal. In February 1990 the leading role of the Communist Party was abolished, and following multiparty elections in March 1990 a period of transition to independence was inaugurated. Independence was declared on 20 August 1991.

Presidential and legislative elections were held in September 1992 on the basis of special provisions different from the 1992 constitution. The president was directly elected for a four-year term and the Riigikogu for a three-year term. A radical right-wing coalition government was elected which held power until September 1994. At the legislative election of March 1995 a centre-right government of the Coalition Party and Rural People's Union (KMÜ) and the Centre Party was formed; the government collapsed in October 1995. A new coalition government formed by the KMÜ and the Reform Party (R) lasted until the withdrawal of the Reform Party in November 1996, after which the KMÜ formed a minority government. After legislative elections held on 7 March 1999, a centre-right coalition government of the Pro Patria Union (I), the Mõõdukad Party (M) and the Reform Party was formed.

POLITICAL SYSTEM

Legislative power is exercised by the unicameral *Riigikogu* of 101 members elected by proportional representation every four years. The president is elected for a five-year term by the Riigikogu by a two-thirds majority or, if no candidate receives this majority after three rounds of voting, by an electoral body composed of Riigikogu members and local government officials. Executive authority is vested in a prime minister who is nominated by the president and who forms a government. Members of the government need not be members of the Riigikogu.

Estonia is divided into 46 towns and 15 districts for local administration purposes.

HEAD OF STATE

President, Lennart Meri, *elected* 5 October 1992, *re-elected* 20 September 1996

GOVERNMENT *as at May 1999*

Prime Minister, Mart Laar (I)
Agriculture, Ivari Padar (M)
Culture, Signe Kivi (R)
Defence, Jüri Luik (I)
Economics, Mihkel Pärnoja (M)
Education, Tõnis Lukas (I)
Environment, Heiki Kranich (R)
Finance, Siim Kallas (R)
Foreign Affairs, Toomas Hendrik Ilves (M)
Interior, Jüri Mõis (I)
Justice, Märt Rask (R)
Social Affairs, Eiki Nestor (M)
Transport and Communications, Toivo Jürgenson (I)
Without Portfolio, Toivo Asmer (R); Katrin Saks (M)

EMBASSY OF THE REPUBLIC OF ESTONIA

16 Hyde Park Gate, London SW7 5DG
Tel 0171-589 3428
Ambassador Extraordinary and Plenipotentiary, HE Raul Mälk, apptd 1996

BRITISH EMBASSY

Wismari 6, EE-10136 Tallinn
Tel: Tallinn 677 4700
Ambassador Extraordinary and Plenipotentiary, HE Timothy Craddock, apptd 1997

ECONOMY

Since 1992 the government has introduced free-market reforms, privatization and restructuring. Privatization has gained momentum with foreign direct investment quadrupling in 1994. Estonia is still dependent on Russian natural gas supplies.

Agriculture and dairy-farming are a major sector of the economy, the main products being rye, oats, barley, flax, potatoes, meat, milk, butter and eggs.

Light industry is the other major sector, concentrating on textiles, clothing and footwear, forestry, wood and paper products, and food and fish processing. Some heavy industry exists, mostly chemicals and the manufacture of power equipment.

The kroon is pegged to the Deutsche Mark.

GNP – US$4,899 million (1997); US$3,360 per capita (1997)
GDP – US$3,620 million (1995); US$2,433 per capita (1995)
ANNUAL AVERAGE GROWTH OF GDP – 2.5 per cent (1995)
INFLATION RATE – 11.2 per cent (1997)
UNEMPLOYMENT – 8.9 per cent (1994)
TOTAL EXTERNAL DEBT – US$658 million (1997). The IMF approved a stand-by credit of US$22 million in December 1997

TRADE

Although Estonia signed a free trade deal with Russia in 1992, it has greatly reduced its trade with the former Soviet states. In 1994 over 70 per cent of trade was with EU and EFTA states and Estonia's trade rose by 50 per cent. Free trade and association agreements with the EU came into effect in 1995; Estonia has a partnership agreement with the EU with a view to becoming a full member at a future date.

In 1997 there was a trade deficit of US$1,124 million and a current account deficit of US$562 million. Imports totalled US$4,282 million and exports US$2,832 million.

Trade with UK	1997	1998
Imports from UK	£63,728,000	£66,650,000
Exports to UK	154,680,000	158,471,000

COMMUNICATIONS

Freedom of the press is guaranteed in the constitution, and the state monopoly on television and radio ended soon after independence. All newspapers have been privatized and broadcasting channels are in the process of being privatized. Russian-language news and programmes are provided on Estonian Television. There are five Estonian- and three Russian-language daily newspapers.

EDUCATION

Estonia has a three-tier education system, consisting of primary level (four years), secondary level (six years) and university level (four to six years). Primary- and secondary-level education is compulsory.

ILLITERACY RATE – 0.2 per cent
ENROLMENT (percentage of age group) – primary 87 per cent (1995); secondary 83 per cent (1995); tertiary 41.8 per cent (1996)

ETHIOPIA
Federal Democratic Republic of Ethiopia

AREA – 426,373 sq. miles (1,104,300 sq. km). Neighbours: Sudan (west), Kenya (south), Djibouti and Somalia (east), Eritrea (north)
POPULATION – 58,506,000 (1994 UN estimate). About one-third are of Semitic origin (Amharas and Tigreans) and the remainder mainly Oromos (40 per cent), Somalis (6 per cent) and Afar (4 per cent). Amharas, Tigreans and many Oromos are Ethiopian Orthodox Christians. The Afar people in the north and the Somalis in the south-east, as well as some Oromos, are Muslim. Amharic is the most widely used of the 70 languages
CAPITAL – Addis Ababa (population, 2,084,588, 1994 estimate)
MAJOR CITIES – Dire Dawa (population, 194,587, 1994 estimate)
CURRENCY – Ethiopian birr (EB) of 100 cents
NATIONAL ANTHEM – Ityopya, Ityopya Kidemi
NATIONAL DAY – 28 May
NATIONAL FLAG – Three horizontal bands: green, yellow, red; in the centre a blue disc, containing a yellow pentagram
LIFE EXPECTANCY (years) – male 45.93; female 49.06
POPULATION GROWTH RATE – 3.2 per cent (1996)
POPULATION DENSITY – 53 per sq. km (1996)
URBAN POPULATION – 15.7 per cent (1996)

MILITARY EXPENDITURE – 2.1 per cent of GDP (1997)
MILITARY PERSONNEL – 120,000: Army 100,000, Others 20,000

HISTORY AND POLITICS

The Hamitic culture was heavily influenced by Semitic immigration from Arabia at about the time of Christ. Christianity was introduced in the fourth century. The empire attained its zenith in the sixth century under the Axum rulers but was checked by Islamic expansion from the east. Modern Ethiopia dates from 1855 when Theodore established supremacy over the various tribes. The last emperor was Haile Selassie who reigned from 1930 until 1974, when he was deposed by the armed forces. After ten years of military rule, a Workers' Party on the Soviet model was formed with Lt.-Col. Mengistu Haile Mariam as General Secretary. The People's Democratic Republic of Ethiopia was established under a new constitution in 1987 with Lt.-Col. Mengistu as president. Armed insurgencies by the Eritrean People's Liberation Front (EPLF) and the Ethiopian People's Revolutionary Democratic Front (EPRDF), originating in Tigre, brought down Mengistu's government in May 1991.

A transitional administration comprising the EPRDF and other opposition groups formed a Council of Representatives which governed until 1995 under President Meles Zenawi. In 1994, the Council agreed on a draft federal constitution which was adopted by an elected Constituent Assembly on 8 December 1994. Multiparty elections in May and June 1995 were won by the EPRDF, which gained 80 per cent of the seats in the newly-created 526-seat Council of People's Representatives; a 117-member Federal Council to represent the 22 ethnic groups was also created. The Council of People's Representatives elected Dr Negaso Gidada to the non-executive office of president and Meles Zenawi as prime minister. The Federal Democratic Republic of Ethiopia was proclaimed on 22 August 1995.

FOREIGN RELATIONS

Eritrea, which since 1962 had been a province of Ethiopia, seceded and became independent on 24 May 1993. Relations between the two countries had been good until fighting broke out along the border in June 1998, with each side accusing the other of sending troops across the border. American and Italian mediators are attempting to resolve the dispute peacefully.

POLITICAL SYSTEM

The constitution provides for a federal government responsible for foreign affairs, defence and economic policy, and for nine regional administrations (Tigre, Afar, Amara, Oromia, Somai, Benshangui, Gambela, Harer and Southern), with a degree of autonomy and the right to secede.

HEAD OF STATE

President, Dr Negaso Gidada, *elected by the Council of People's Representatives* 22 August 1995

COUNCIL OF MINISTERS *as at May 1999*

Prime Minister, Meles Zenawi
Deputy PMs, Tefera Walwa *(Defence)*; Kassu Ylala *(Economic Affairs)*
Agriculture, Seifu Ketema
Commerce and Industry, Kasahun Ayele
Economic Development and Co-operation, Giram Biru
Education, Genet Zewdie
Finance, Sufyan Ahmad

Foreign Affairs, Seyoum Mesfin
Health, Adem Ibrahim
Information and Culture, Wolde Mikael Chamo
Justice, Werede Woldemichael
Mines and Energy, Ezedin Ali
Revenue Collectors' Board, Desta Amare
Speaker, Council of People's Representatives, Davit Yohanes
Transport and Communications, Abdulmejid Hussein
Water Resources, Shiferaw Jarso
Works and Urban Development, Haile Asegde

EMBASSY OF ETHIOPIA
17 Prince's Gate, London SW7 1PZ
Tel 0171-589 7212/3/4/5
Ambassador Extraordinary and Plenipotentiary, HE Dr Beyene
  Negewo, apptd 1999
Counsellor, Osman Imam Beshir (*Commercial*)

BRITISH EMBASSY
Fikre Mariam Abatechan Street (PO Box 858), Addis
Ababa
Tel: Addis Ababa 161 2354
Ambassador Extraordinary and Plenipotentiary, HE Gordon
  Wetherell, apptd 1997
Deputy Head of Mission and First Secretary, F. Guy

BRITISH COUNCIL REPRESENTATIVE, M. Sargent, OBE,
  Artistic Building, Adwa Avenue (PO Box 1043), Addis
  Ababa

ECONOMY

The post-Mengistu government implemented a programme of free-market economic reform which reduced
government spending and inflation. The currency was
devalued, the civil service reduced and the army cut by
two-thirds. Western states have responded with debt relief
and loans. An agreement waiving customs levies was
concluded with Eritrea in April 1995.

  Agriculture accounts for approximately 50 per cent of
GDP and employs around 80 per cent of the workforce.
The major food crops are teff, maize, barley, sorghum,
wheat, pulses and oil seeds. Famine conditions in 1984–5
recurred to a lesser extent in 1992 and 1997. However,
agricultural liberalization has led to dramatic progress in
food production.

  Manufacturing industry accounts for less than 9 per cent
of GDP and is heavily dependent on agriculture. Ethiopia's
known, but as yet largely unexploited, natural resources
include gold, platinum, copper and potash. Traces of oil
and natural gas have been found.

  In 1996 there was a trade deficit of US$817 million and
a current account deficit of US$102 million.
GNP – US$6,507 million (1997); US$110 per capita
  (1997)
GDP – US$5,408 million (1995); US$96 per capita (1995)
ANNUAL AVERAGE GROWTH OF GDP – 7.7 per cent
  (1995)
INFLATION RATE – –3.7 per cent (1997)
TOTAL EXTERNAL DEBT – US$10,079 million (1997)

TRADE

The chief imports by value are machinery and transport
equipment, manufactured goods and chemicals; the principal exports by value are coffee, oil seeds, hides and skins,
and pulses. In 1995 imports totalled US$145 million and
exports US$423 million.

Trade with UK	1997	1998
Imports from UK	£58,070,000	£44,178,000
Exports to UK	16,686,000	14,202,000

COMMUNICATIONS

A network of roads in rural areas links the major cities with
each other, with the Sudanese and Kenyan borders and
through Eritrea to the Red Sea coast.

  There is a railway link from Addis Ababa to Djibouti.
Ethiopian Airlines maintains regular services from Addis
Ababa to many provincial towns, throughout Africa and to
Europe.

EDUCATION

Elementary and secondary education are provided by
government schools in the main centres of population;
there are also mission schools. The National University
(founded 1961) co-ordinates the institutions of higher
education. There is a separate university at Alemaya
(agricultural).
ILLITERACY RATE – 64.5 per cent
ENROLMENT (percentage of age group) – primary 24 per
  cent (1994); tertiary 0.7 per cent (1995)

FIJI
Matanitu Ko Viti – Republic of Fiji

AREA – 7,056 sq. miles (18,274 sq. km)
POPULATION – 797,000 (1994 UN estimate), 715,373
  (1986 census): 48.6 per cent Indians, 46.2 per cent
  Fijians, and 5.2 per cent other races. Since the 1987
  coup many ethnic Indians have left and by 1994
  Melanesian Fijians formed the largest population
  group. The main languages are Fijian and Hindi
CAPITAL – ΨSuva (population, 141,273, 1986), on the
  island of Viti Levu
CURRENCY – Fiji dollar (F$) of 100 cents
NATIONAL ANTHEM – God Bless Fiji
NATIONAL DAY – 10 October (Fiji Day)
NATIONAL FLAG – Light blue ground with Union flag in
  top left quarter and the shield of Fiji in the fly
LIFE EXPECTANCY (years) – male 60.72; female 63.87
POPULATION GROWTH RATE – 1.5 per cent (1997)
POPULATION DENSITY – 44 per sq. km (1996)
URBAN POPULATION – 38.7 per cent (1987)
MILITARY EXPENDITURE – 2.6 per cent of GDP (1997)
MILITARY PERSONNEL – 3,500: Army 3,200, Navy 300
ILLITERACY RATE – 8.4 per cent
ENROLMENT (percentage of age group) – primary 99 per
  cent (1992); tertiary 11.9 per cent (1991)

Fiji is composed of roughly 332 islands (about 100
permanently inhabited) and over 500 islets in the South
Pacific, about 1,100 miles north of New Zealand. The
group extends 300 miles from east to west and 300 miles
north to south. The International Date Line has been
diverted to the east of the island group. The largest islands
are Viti Levu and Vanua Levu. The main groups of islands
are Lomaiviti, Lau and Yasawas. The climate is tropical
without extremes of heat.

HISTORY AND POLITICS

Fiji was a British colony from 1874 until 10 October 1970
when it became an independent state and a member of the
Commonwealth.

  A coalition under Dr Timoci Bavadra won a general
election in April 1987, but was overthrown by the military
on 14 May by Lt.-Col. Sitiveni Rabuka. An Advisory
Council was set up as an interim government, but it too
was overthrown on 25 September 1987. On 7 October

Rabuka declared Fiji a republic; the Governor-General resigned on 15 October; Fiji's Commonwealth membership lapsed and another interim government was formed.

The constitution was changed in 1990 to give greater power to indigenous Melanesian Fijians at the expense of the Indian community. The Fijian Political Party led by Rabuka won the general elections in May 1992 and February 1994 and formed a coalition government. Following constitutional reform in July 1997, Fiji was readmitted to the Commonwealth on 1 October 1997. In the general election on 8–15 May 1999, the Fijian Political Party was swept from power by a coalition of parties led by the Fiji Labour Party. Its leader, Mahendra Chaudhry, became Fiji's first ethnic Indian prime minister.

POLITICAL SYSTEM

The 1990 constitution was reformed in July 1997 to reduce the political dominance of Melanesians within the government. The parliament is bicameral; the upper house or Senate has 32 members appointed by the president, of which 14 seats are reserved for Melanesian Fijians, one for the Polynesian island of Rotuma and nine for other races. The House of Representatives has 71 seats, of which 23 are reserved for Melanesians, 19 for Indians, one for Rotuma, and three for other races. The president is elected by the (Melanesian) Great Council of Chiefs, and appoints a prime minister who must establish a multiparty government.

HEAD OF STATE
President, Ratu Sir Kamisese Mara, *inaugurated* 18 January 1994

CABINET *as at July 1999*
Prime Minister, Finance, Public Enterprises, Sugar Industry and Information, Mahendra Chaudhry
Deputy Prime Minister, Foreign Affairs, Tupeni Baba
Deputy Prime Minister, Fijian Affairs, Adi Kuini Vuikaba Speed
Agriculture, Fisheries and Forests, Poseci Bune
Attorney-General, Justice, Anand Kumar Singh
Commerce, Business Development and Investment, Anup Kumar
Communications and Civil Aviation, Meli Bogileka
Education, Pratap Chand
Health, Isimeli Cokanasiga
Labour and Industrial Relations, Tevita Momeodonu
Lands, The Agricultural Landlords and Tenants Act and Mineral Resources, Mosese Volavola
National Planning, Local Government, Housing and Environment, Ganeshwar Chand
Regional Development and Multi-Ethnic Affairs, Manoa Bale
Tourism and Transport, Koila Mara Nailatikau
Women, Culture and Social Welfare, Lavenia Padarath
Works and Energy, Shiu Sharan Sharma
Youth, Employment and Sports, Ponipate Lesavua

EMBASSY OF THE REPUBLIC OF FIJI
34 Hyde Park Gate, London sw7 5DN
Tel 0171-584 3661
Ambassador Extraordinary and Plenipotentiary, HE Filimone Jitoko, apptd 1996

BRITISH EMBASSY
Victoria House, 47 Gladstone Road, PO Box 1355, Suva
Tel: Suva 311033
Ambassador Extraordinary and Plenipotentiary, HE Michael Dibben, apptd 1997

ECONOMY

The economy is primarily agrarian. The principal cash crop is sugar cane, which is the main export, followed by coconuts, ginger and copra. A variety of other fruit, vegetables and root crops are also grown, and self-sufficiency in rice is a major aim. Forestry, fishing and beef production are being encouraged in order to diversify the economy. The processing of agricultural, marine and timber products are the main industries, along with gold mining and textiles. Tourism is second only to sugar as a money-earner.

In January 1998 the Reserve Bank of Fiji devalued the Fijian dollar by 20 per cent in response to poor growth in 1997 and anxieties about the Asian financial crisis.
GNP – US$2,007 million (1997); US$2,460 per capita (1997)
GDP – US$2,033 million (1995); US$2,593 per capita (1995)
ANNUAL AVERAGE GROWTH OF GDP – minus 1.6 per cent (1997)
INFLATION RATE – 3.4 per cent (1997)
UNEMPLOYMENT – 5.4 per cent (1995)
TOTAL EXTERNAL DEBT – US$213 million (1997)

TRADE

The chief imports are foodstuffs, machinery, mineral fuels, chemicals, beverages, tobacco and manufactured articles. Chief exports are sugar, coconut oil, fish, lumber, molasses and ginger.

In 1996 there was a trade deficit of US$182 million and a current account surplus of US$10 million. In 1996 imports totalled US$980 million; in 1997 exports totalled US$591 million.

Trade with UK	1997	1998
Imports from UK	£10,560,000	£6,777,000
Exports to UK	60,281,000	65,203,000

COMMUNICATIONS

Fiji is one of the main aerial crossroads in the Pacific, providing services to New Zealand, Australia, Tonga, Western Samoa, Vanuatu, the Solomon Islands, Kiribati, Tuvalu, New Caledonia and American Samoa. Fiji has three ports of entry, at Suva, Lautoka and Levuka. There are 5,100 km of roads.

FINLAND
Suomen Tasavalta

AREA – 130,559 sq. miles (338,145 sq. km). Neighbours: Norway (north-west and north), Russia (east), Sweden (west)
POPULATION – 5,125,000 (1994 UN estimate). Finnish and Swedish are both official languages, 93.6 per cent speaking Finnish as their first language and 6.2 per cent Swedish. Lapp is spoken by the 2,500 Lapps who live in the far north. The population is predominantly Lutheran
CAPITAL – ΨHelsinki (Helsingfors) (population, 1,056,495, 1993 estimate)
MAJOR CITIES – Espoo (Esbo) (200,834); ΨOulu (Uleåborg) (113,567); Tampere (Tammerfors) (188,726); ΨTurku (Åbo) (168,772); Vantaa (Vanda) (171,297), 1997 estimates
CURRENCY – Markka (Mk) of 100 penniä
NATIONAL DAY – 6 December (Independence Day)
NATIONAL FLAG – White with blue cross
LIFE EXPECTANCY (years) – male 72.82; female 80.15
POPULATION GROWTH RATE – 0.4 per cent (1997)
POPULATION DENSITY – 15 per sq. km (1996)

Deputy PM, Finance, Sauli Niinistö (NCP)
Agriculture and Forestry, Kalevi Hemilä (Ind.)
Culture, Youth, Universities, Science, Suvi Lindén (NCP)
Defence, Jan-Erik Enestam (SPP)
Education, Maija Rask (SDP)
Environment, Development Co-operation, Satu Hassi (Greens)
European Affairs and Foreign Trade, Kimmo Sasi (NCP)
Finance, Taxation, Suvi-Anne Siimes (LA)
Foreign Affairs, Tarja Halonen (SDP)
Health, Eva Biaudet (SPP)
Interior, Kari Häkämies (NCP)
Justice, Johannes Koskinen (SDP)
Labour, Sinikka Mönkäre (SDP)
Local Communities and Regional Policy, Martti Korhonen
   (LA)
Social Affairs and Health, Maija Perho (NCP)
Trade and Industry, Erkki Tuomioja (SDP)
Transport, Olli-Pekka Heinonen (NCP)

SDP Social Democratic Party; NCP National Coalition
Party; LA Left-wing Alliance; SPP Swedish People's
Party

EMBASSY OF FINLAND
38 Chesham Place, London SW1X 8HW
Tel 0171-838 6200
Ambassador Extraordinary and Plenipotentiary, HE Pertti
   Salolainen, apptd 1996
Minister, Kirsti Eskelinen
Counsellor (Commercial), Marcus Moberg
Defence Attaché, Col. Ilpo Eerik Bergholm

BRITISH EMBASSY
Itäinen Puistotie 17, SF-00140 Helsinki
Tel: Helsinki 2286 5100
Ambassador Extraordinary and Plenipotentiary, HE Gavin
   Hewitt, CMG, apptd 1997
Deputy Head of Mission and Counsellor, R. A. Cambridge
First Secretary (Commercial), H. B. Formstone, OBE
Defence Attaché, Lt.-Col. G. A. B. Grant

BRITISH CONSULAR OFFICES – Helsinki, Jyväskylä,
   Kotka, Kuopio, Oulu, Pori, Tampere, Turku, Vaasa,
   Mariehamn

BRITISH COUNCIL REPRESENTATIVE, Tuija Talvitie,
   Hakaniemenkatu 2, SF-00530 Helsinki

URBAN POPULATION – 64.4 per cent (1995)

The Åland archipelago (Ahvenanmaa), a group of small
islands at the entrance to the Gulf of Bothnia, covers about
572 square miles, with a population (1994) of 25,158 (95.2
per cent Swedish-speaking). The islands have semi-
autonomous status.

HISTORY AND POLITICS

Finland was part of the Swedish Empire from the Middle
Ages until it was ceded to Russia in 1809 and became an
autonomous grand duchy of the Russian Empire. Finland
became independent after the Russian revolution of 1917,
but was forced to cede around one-tenth of its land to the
Soviet Union and to resettle 10 per cent of its population
under the Treaty of Paris (1947). A Soviet-Finnish Co-
operation Treaty forced Finland to demilitarize its Soviet
border, to enter into a barter trade agreement and to adopt
a stance of neutrality. These terms lasted until the demise
of the Soviet Union in 1991.
   Finland joined the European Union on 1 January 1995
following a referendum in October 1994.
   The present government took office in April 1999. The
five parties in the ruling coalition are the Social Democratic
Party, the National Coalition Party (conservative), the
Left-wing Alliance, the Swedish People's Party, and the
Greens, with a total of 150 out of 200 seats.

POLITICAL SYSTEM

Under the constitution there is a unicameral legislature,
the *Eduskunta*, composed of 200 members elected by
universal suffrage for a four-year term. The highest
executive power is held by the president who is directly
elected for a period of six years. The first direct elections
for the presidency were held in 1994, the president having
previously been elected by an electoral college.

HEAD OF STATE
President, Martti Ahtisaari, *inaugurated* 1 March 1994

CABINET *as at July 1999*

Prime Minister, Paavo Lipponen (SDP)

DEFENCE

The Army has 230 main battle tanks, 273 armoured infantry
fighting vehicles, 790 armoured personnel carriers, and
1,100 artillery pieces. The Navy has 14 patrol and coastal
vessels. The Air Force has 91 combat aircraft.
MILITARY EXPENDITURE – 1.7 per cent of GDP (1997)
MILITARY PERSONNEL – 35,100: Army 24,000, Navy
   5,000, Air Force 2,700, Paramilitaries 3,400
CONSCRIPTION DURATION – Six to 12 months

ECONOMY

Finland produces a wide range of capital and consumer
goods. Metal-working, electronics and engineering now
account for around half of exports, and timber and timber-
based products account for a third. The glass, ceramics and
furniture industries enjoy international reputations. Other
important industries are mobile phones, rubber, plastics,
chemicals and pharmaceuticals, footwear, foodstuffs and
shipbuilding.
   The markka joined the ERM in August 1996, and on 1
May 1998 it was announced that Finland had satisfied the
convergence criteria and would be one of the 11 countries
to participate in the European Single Currency from
January 1999.

In 1997 the budget deficit was equivalent to 4.5 per cent of GDP, and public debt was 67.7 per cent of GDP.
GNP – US$127,398 million (1997); US$24,790 per capita (1997)
GDP – US$124,881 million (1995); US$24,453 per capita (1995)
Annual Average Growth of GDP – 6.0 per cent (1997)
Inflation Rate – 1.2 per cent (1997)
Unemployment – 17.4 per cent (1995); estimated to be 15.3 per cent in 1997

TRADE

The principal imports are raw materials, machinery and manufactured goods. The barter-trade relationship with the former Soviet Union collapsed in 1991 and exports to the countries of the former Soviet Union fell from 20 per cent of the total in the early 1980s to 5 per cent in 1994. Trade with EU countries accounts for more than half of Finland's total trade.

In 1997 there was a trade surplus of US$11,590 million and a current account surplus of US$6,022 million. Imports totalled US$29,784 million and exports US$39,316 million.

Trade with UK	1997	1998
Imports from UK	£1,485,300,000	£1,363,000,000
Exports to UK	2,449,000,000	2,250,600,000

COMMUNICATIONS

There are 5,859 km of railroad, railway connections with Russia, and passenger boat connections with Sweden, Germany, Poland, Russia and the Baltic states. There are also passenger/cargo services between Britain and Helsinki, Kotka and other Finnish ports. External air services are maintained by most European airlines.

CULTURE AND EDUCATION

Newspapers, books, plays and films appear in both Finnish and Swedish. There is a vigorous modern literature. F. E. Sillanpää, who died in 1964, was awarded the Nobel Prize for Literature in 1939. In 1999 there were 56 daily newspapers.

Primary education (co-educational comprehensive school) is free and compulsory for children from seven to 16 years.
Enrolment (percentage of age group) – primary 99 per cent (1995); secondary 93 per cent (1995); tertiary 70.3 per cent (1995)

FRANCE
La République Française

Area – 212,935 sq. miles (551,500 sq. km). Neighbours: Belgium and Luxembourg (north-east), Germany, Switzerland and Italy (east), Spain and Andorra (south-west)
Population – 58,375,000 (1994 UN estimate); 57,218,000 (Metropolitan France), and 58,745,000 including overseas departments (1992 official estimate): 72 per cent Catholic, 8 per cent Muslim, 2 per cent Jewish. The language is French; there are several regional languages including Basque, Breton, Catalan, Corsican, Dutch, German and Provençal.
Capital – Paris (population, 9,319,367, 1990), on the Seine

Major Cities – ΨBordeaux (696,819); Grenoble (404,837); Lille (959,433); Lyon (1,262,342); ΨMarseille (1,230,871); Nantes (495,229); Nice (517,291); Strasbourg (388,466); Toulon (437,825); Toulouse (650,311). The chief towns of Corsica are ΨAjaccio (58,315) and ΨBastia (52,446)
Currency – Franc of 100 centimes
National Anthem – La Marseillaise
National Day – 14 July (Bastille Day 1789)
National Flag – The tricolour, three vertical bands, blue, white, red (blue next to flagstaff)
Life Expectancy (years) – male 72.94; female 81.15
Population Growth Rate – 0.5 per cent (1997)
Population Density – 106 per sq. km (1996)
Urban Population – 73.8 per cent (1993)

HISTORY AND POLITICS

There are dolmens and menhirs in Brittany, prehistoric remains and cave drawings in Dordogne and Ariège, and throughout France various megalithic monuments erected by primitive tribes, predecessors of Iberian invaders from Spain (now represented by the Basques), Ligurians from northern Italy and Celts or Gauls from the valley of the Danube. Gaul, the area which is now France, was conquered by Julius Caesar in the 1st century BC and remained a part of the Roman Empire until Germanic tribes drove out the Romans in the 3rd and 4th centuries. Roman remains are plentiful throughout France in the form of aqueducts, arenas, triumphal arches, etc.

France established itself as the dominant country in Europe in the 17th century. As a result of the French Revolution, a republic was declared in 1792 and the king, Louis XVI, was executed. The republic was overthown by Napoleon Bonaparte, who established the first French Empire, which ended in 1815.

In 1940, Germany invaded France, occupying most of the country and establishing a pro-German government in the south. France was liberated in 1944.

The state of the parties in the Senate at August 1996 was: Rassemblement pour la République (RPR) 102; Socialist Party (PS) 78; Centrist Union (UDC) 64; Republican and Independent Union (RI) 47; Democratic and European Rally (RDE) 26; Communists (PCF) 15; Independents 9.

In the last elections to the National Assembly in May and June 1997 the PS won 241 seats, the Gaullist RPR 134, Union pour la Démocratie Française (UDF) 108, PCF 38, Independent Left 21, Independent Right 14, Radical

Socialist Party 12, Green Party 7, National Front 1, Independent 1.

POLITICAL SYSTEM

The legislature consists of the National Assembly of 577 deputies (555 for Metropolitan France and 22 for the overseas departments and territories) and the Senate of 321 Senators (296 for Metropolitan France, 13 for the overseas departments and territories and 12 for French citizens abroad). Deputies in the National Assembly are directly elected for a five-year term. One-third of the Senate is indirectly elected every three years.

The prime minister is appointed by the president, as is the Council of Ministers on the prime minister's recommendation. They are responsible to the legislature, but as the executive is constitutionally separate from the legislature, ministers may not sit in the legislature and must hand over their seats to a substitute.

France is divided into 95 departments, including the island of Corsica, in the Mediterranean off the west coast of Italy.

HEAD OF STATE

President of the French Republic, Jacques Chirac, *elected* 7 May 1995, *took office* 17 May 1995

COUNCIL OF MINISTERS *as at July 1999*

Prime Minister, Lionel Jospin
Agriculture and Fisheries, Louis Le Pensec
Capital Works, Transport and Housing, Jean-Claude Gayssot
Civil Service, Administrative Reform and Decentralization, Emile Zuccarelli
Culture and Communications, Catherine Trautmann
Defence, Alain Richard
Economy, Finance and Industry, Dominique Strauss-Kahn
Employment and Solidarity, Martine Aubry
Foreign Affairs, Hubert Vedrine
Interior, Jean-Pierre Chevènement
Justice, Keeper of the Seals, Elisabeth Guigou
National Education, Research and Technology, Claude Allegre
Relations with Parliament, Daniel Vaillant
Town and Country Planning and the Environment, Dominique Voynet
Youth and Sport, Marie-George Buffet

FRENCH EMBASSY

58 Knightsbridge, London SW1X 7JT
Tel 0171-201 1000
Ambassador Extraordinary and Plenipotentiary, HE Daniel Bernard, apptd 1998
Minister-Counsellor, P. Andreani
Defence Attaché, Contre-Amiral J. Gheerbrant
Cultural Counsellor, X. North
Minister-Counsellor (Economic and Commercial Affairs), P. O'Quin

BRITISH EMBASSY

35 rue du Faubourg St Honoré, F-75383 Paris Cedex 08
Tel: Paris 4451 3100
Ambassador Extraordinary and Plenipotentiary, HE Sir Michael Jay, KCMG, apptd 1996
Minister, S. F. Howarth
Defence and Air Attaché, Air Cdre D. N. Adams
Counsellor, V. Caton (*Finance and Economic*)
First Secretary and Consul-General, K. C. Moss

BRITISH CONSULAR OFFICES – Amiens, Biarritz, Bordeaux, Boulogne, Calais, Cherbourg, Dunkirk, Le Havre, Lille, Lyon, Marseille, Montpellier, Nantes, Nice, Paris, Perpignan, St Malo, Saumur, Toulouse; overseas in Cayenne (French Guiana), Noumea (New Caledonia), Papeete (French Polynesia), Fort de France (Martinique), Pointe à Pitre (Guadeloupe) and St Denis (Réunion)

BRITISH COUNCIL DIRECTOR, C. Gamble, 9/11 rue de Constantine, F-75007 Paris
FRANCO-BRITISH CHAMBER OF COMMERCE, 8 rue Cimarosa, F-75116 Paris. *President,* R. Lyon. *Vice-President,* B. Cordery, OBE

DEFENCE

The Army has 1,210 main battle tanks, 4,533 armoured personnel carriers and armoured infantry fighting vehicles, 1,055 artillery pieces, two aircraft and 518 helicopters.

The Navy has 14 submarines, one aircraft carrier, one cruiser, four destroyers, 35 frigates and 40 patrol and coastal vessels, 61 combat aircraft and 25 armed helicopters. The Navy has four domestic and five overseas bases.

The Air Force has 505 combat aircraft including 45 short-range nuclear attack aircraft and 15 strategic bombers, and 18 intermediate-range ballistic missiles.

France deploys 44,083 armed forces personnel abroad; 11,700 in Germany; 20,300 in French Overseas Departments and Territories; 4,700 in former French colonies in Africa; and 4,180 on UN and peacekeeping duties.

MILITARY EXPENDITURE – 3.0 per cent of GDP (1997)
MILITARY PERSONNEL – 446,700: Army 203,200, Strategic Nuclear Forces 8,700, Navy 63,300, Air Force 78,100, Paramilitaries 93,400
CONSCRIPTION DURATION – Ten to 24 months. Conscription is to be phased out over six years, beginning in 1997

ECONOMY

Viniculture is extensive, regions famous for their wines including Bordeaux, Burgundy and Champagne. Production of wine in 1995 was 5,300,000 tonnes. Cognac, liqueurs and cider are also important products.

Oil is produced from fields in the Landes area, but France is a net importer of crude oil, for processing by its important oil-refining industry. Natural gas is produced in the foothills of the Pyrenees.

Heavy industries include oil-refining and the production of iron and steel, and aluminium. In 1995 production of pig iron was 13,154,000 tonnes and steel 18,104,000 tonnes. Other important industries produce chemicals, tyres, aluminium, textiles, paper products and processed food. Engineering products include motor vehicles, and television and radio sets.

In 1993 the government announced the privatization of most public-sector companies, which was expected to generate F300,000 million over five years.

The Banque de France was made independent in 1994 with the formation of a nine-member monetary policy council to define and implement monetary policy independent of the government.

In 1995–6, the government introduced austerity measures to enable France to meet the Maastricht criteria for European monetary union. Cost-cutting reforms targeted the welfare budget, provoking a series of strikes by public-sector workers in December 1995 and early 1996. On 1 May 1998 it was announced that France would participate in the European Single Currency from January 1999.

GNP – US$1,541,630 million (1997); US$26,300 per capita (1997)
GDP – US$1,536,475 million (1995); US$26,444 per capita (1995)
ANNUAL AVERAGE GROWTH OF GDP – 2.3 per cent (1997)
INFLATION RATE – 1.2 per cent (1997)
UNEMPLOYMENT – 11.6 per cent (1995); forecast to be 12.1 per cent in 1997

The principal imports are raw materials for the heavy and manufacturing industries (e.g. oil, minerals, chemicals), machinery and precision instruments, agricultural products, chemicals and vehicles. Raw materials, semi-manufactured and manufactured goods, chemicals and vehicles are also the principal exports. Most of France's trade is done with other EU countries.

In 1997 there was a trade surplus of US$28,069 million and a current account surplus of US$39,475 million. Imports totalled US$269,216 million and exports US$289,842 million.

Trade with UK	1997	1998
Imports from UK	£15,721,300,000	£15,559,300,000
Exports to UK	16,971,200,000	16,829,400,000

COMMUNICATIONS

The length of roads in 1996 was 964,356 km, of which 7,396 km were motorways.

The railroad system is extensive. The length of lines open for traffic in 1996 was 31,940 km.

The French mercantile marine consisted in 1995 of 208 ships of a total of 4,300,000 tonnes which transported 91,500,000 tonnes of freight.

CULTURE AND EDUCATION

French is the official language. The work of the French Academy, founded in 1635, has established le bon usage, equivalent to 'The Queen's English' in Britain. French authors have been awarded the Nobel Prize for Literature on 12 occasions and include R. F. A. Sully-Prudhomme (1901), Anatole France (1921), André Gide (1947), François Mauriac (1952), Albert Camus (1957), Jean-Paul Sartre (1964) and Claude Simon (1985).

Education is compulsory, free and secular from six to 16. Schools may be single-sex or co-educational. Primary education is given in nursery schools, primary schools and collèges d'enseignement général (four-year secondary modern course); secondary education in collèges d'enseignement technique, collèges d'enseignement secondaire and lycées (seven-year course leading to one of the five baccalauréats). Special schools are numerous.

There are many grandes écoles in France which award diplomas in many subjects not taught at university, especially applied science and engineering. Most of these are state institutions but have a competitive system of entry, unlike universities. There are universities in 24 towns including 13 in Paris and the immediate area.

In 1993 the government gave German official parity with French in Alsace schools.

ENROLMENT (percentage of age group) – primary 100 per cent (1995); secondary 94 per cent (1995); tertiary 51.0 per cent (1995)

OVERSEAS DEPARTMENTS

Greater powers of self-government were granted to French Guiana, Guadeloupe, Martinique and Réunion in 1982. These former colonies had enjoyed departmental status since 1946 and the status of regions since 1974. Their directly elected Assemblies operate in parallel with the existing, indirectly constituted Regional Councils. The French government is represented by a Prefect in each.

FRENCH GUIANA

AREA – 34,749 sq. miles (90,000 sq. km)
POPULATION – 153,000 (1994)
CAPITAL – ΨCayenne (41,164)

Situated on the north-eastern coast of South America, French Guiana is flanked by Suriname on the west and by Brazil on the south and east. Under the administration of French Guiana is a group of islands (St Joseph, Île Royal and Île du Diable), known as Îles du Salut.

Prefect, P. Dartout

Trade with UK	1995	1996
Imports from UK	£3,734,000	£11,713,000
Exports to UK	591,000	1,149,000

GUADELOUPE

AREA – 658 sq. miles (1,705 sq. km)
POPULATION – 431,000 (1994)
CAPITAL – ΨBasse Terre (29,522) on Guadeloupe
A number of islands in the Leeward Islands group of the West Indies, consisting of the two main islands of Guadeloupe (or Basse-Terre) and Grande-Terre, with the adjacent islands of Marie-Galante, La Désirade and Îles des Saintes, and the islands of St Martin and St Barthélemy over 150 miles to the north-west. The main towns are ΨPointe à Pitre (26,000) in Grande-Terre and ΨGrand Bourg (6,611) in Marie-Galante.

Prefect, M. Diefenbacher

Trade with UK	1995	1996
Imports from UK	£6,896,000	£10,029,000
Exports to UK	211,000	68,000

MARTINIQUE

AREA – 425 sq. miles (1,102 sq. km)
POPULATION – 384,000 (1994)
CAPITAL – ΨFort de France (133,920)

An island situated in the Windward Islands group of the West Indies, between Dominica in the north and St Lucia in the south. The main towns are ΨTrinité (11,214) and ΨMarin (6,104).

Prefect, J.-F. Cordet

Trade with UK	1995	1996
Imports from UK	£13,839,000	£16,422,000
Exports to UK	14,000	196,000

RÉUNION

AREA – 969 sq. miles (2,510 sq. km)
POPULATION – 664,000 (1994)
CAPITAL – St Denis (121,999)

Réunion, which became a French possession in 1638, lies in the Indian Ocean, about 569 miles east of Madagascar and 110 miles south-west of Mauritius. Other towns are Saint-Paul (71,669) and Saint-Pierre (58,846). The smaller, uninhabited islands of Bassas da India, Europa, Îles Glorieuses, Juan de Nova and Tromelin are administered from Réunion.

Prefect, H. Fournier

Trade with UK	1995	1996
Imports from UK	£15,345,000	£15,374,000
Exports to UK	2,278,000	2,910,000

TERRITORIAL COLLECTIVITIES

MAYOTTE

AREA – 144 sq. miles (372 sq. km)
POPULATION – 94,410 (1991 census)
CAPITAL – Mamoudzou (12,000)

Part of the Comoros Islands group, Mayotte remained a French dependency when the other three islands became independent as the Comoros Republic in 1975. Since 1976 the island has been a *collectivité territoriale*, an intermediate status between Overseas Department and Overseas Territory.

Prefect, P. Boisadam

Trade with UK	1997	1998
Imports from UK	£6,294,000	£3,427,000
Exports to UK	427,000	201,000

ST PIERRE AND MIQUELON

AREA – 93 sq. miles (242 sq. km)
POPULATION – 7,000 (1994)
CAPITAL – ΨSt Pierre (5,416)

These two small groups of islands off the coast of Newfoundland became a *collectivité territoriale* in 1985.

Prefect, R. Thuau

Trade with UK	1997	1998
Imports from UK	£708,000	£547,000
Exports to UK	—	—

OVERSEAS TERRITORIES

FRENCH POLYNESIA

AREA – 1,544 sq. miles (4,000 sq. km)
POPULATION – 223,000 (1994)
CAPITAL – ΨPapeete (36,784), in Tahiti

Five archipelagos in the south Pacific, comprising the Society Islands (Windward Islands group includes Tahiti, Moorea, Makatea, Mehetia, Tetiaroa, Tubuai Manu; Leeward Islands group includes Huahine, Raiatea, Tahaa, Bora-Bora, Maupiti), the Tuamotu Islands (Rangiroa, Hao, Turéia, etc.), the Gambier Islands (Mangareva, etc.), the Tubuai Islands (Rimatara, Rurutu, Tubuai, Raivavae, Rapa, etc.) and the Marquesas Islands (Nuku-Hiva, Hiva-Oa, Fatu-Hiva, Tahuata, Ua Huka, etc.).

High Commissioner, P. Roncière

Trade with UK	1997	1998
Imports from UK	£5,622,000	£4,796,000
Exports to UK	124,000	69,000

NEW CALEDONIA

AREA – 7,172 sq. miles (18,575 sq. km)
POPULATION – 189,000 (1994)
CAPITAL – ΨNoumea (97,581)

New Caledonia is a large island in the western Pacific, 700 miles east of Queensland. Dependencies are the Isles of Pines, the Loyalty Islands (Mahé, Lifou, Urea, etc.), the Bélep Archipelago, the Chesterfield Islands, the Huon Islands and Walpole.
    New Caledonia was discovered in 1774 and annexed by France in 1854; from 1871 to 1896 it was a convict settlement. In 1995, the territory was divided into three provinces, each with a provincial assembly which combined to form the Territorial Assembly. In elections in July 1995, Kanaks won majorities in North province and the Loyalty Islands, whereas pro-French settlers won a majority in the South province.

A referendum in 1987 on the question of independence was boycotted by the indigenous Kanaks, and New Caledonia therefore voted to remain French. In April 1998 an agreement was reached between the pro-independence Kanak Socialist National Liberation Front, the anti-independence Rally for Caledonia in the Republic and the French government to hold a referendum on independence in 15–20 years' time, and for greater autonomy for the indigenous people in the intervening period. A referendum on the agreement, the Noumea Accord, was held on 8 November 1998. It was supported by 71.9 per cent of voters; more than 74 per cent of registered voters took part.

High Commissioner, D. Bur

Trade with UK	1997	1998
Imports from UK	£16,558,000	£9,564,000
Exports to UK	5,209,000	1,855,000

SOUTHERN AND ANTARCTIC TERRITORIES

Created in 1955 from former Réunion dependencies, the territory comprises the islands of Amsterdam (25 sq. miles) and St Paul (2.7 sq. miles), the Kerguelen Islands (2,700 sq. miles) and Crozet Islands (116 sq. miles) archipelagos and Adélie Land (116,800 sq. miles) in the Antarctic continent. The only population are members of staff of the scientific stations.

WALLIS AND FUTUNA ISLANDS

AREA – 77 sq. miles (200 sq. km)
POPULATION – 15,000 (1994)
CAPITAL – Mata-Utu on Uvea, the main island of the Wallis group

Two groups of islands (the Wallis Archipelago and the Îles de Hoorn) in the central Pacific, north-east of Fiji.

Prefect, L. Legrand

Trade with UK	1997	1998
Imports from UK	£45,000	£43,000
Exports to UK	—	—

THE FRENCH COMMUNITY

The constitution of the Fifth French Republic, promulgated in 1958, envisaged the establishment of a French Community of States. A number of the former French states in Africa have seceded from the Community but for all practical purposes continue to enjoy the same close links with France as those that remain formally members. Most former French African colonies are closely linked to France by financial, technical and economic agreements.

GABON
République Gabonaise

AREA – 103,347 sq. miles (267,668 sq. km). Neighbours: Equatorial Guinea and Cameroon (north), Republic of Congo-Brazzaville (east and south)
POPULATION – 1,106,000 (1994 UN estimate). The official language is French; Fang is widely spoken
CAPITAL – ΨLibreville (population, 251,000)
CURRENCY – Franc CFA of 100 centimes
NATIONAL ANTHEM – La Concorde
NATIONAL DAY – 17 August
NATIONAL FLAG – Horizontal bands, green, yellow and blue

LIFE EXPECTANCY (years) – male 51.86; female 55.18
POPULATION GROWTH RATE – 2.6 per cent (1997)
POPULATION DENSITY – 4 per sq. km (1996)
URBAN POPULATION – 73.2 per cent (1993)
MILITARY EXPENDITURE – 1.9 per cent of GDP (1997)
MILITARY PERSONNEL – 9,500: Army 3,200, Navy 500,
Air Force 1,000, Paramilitaries 4,800
ILLITERACY RATE – 36.8 per cent

HISTORY AND POLITICS

The first Europeans to visit the region were the Portuguese in the 15th century, and Dutch, French and English traders arrived over the following decades. In 1849 a slave ship was captured by the French, and the freed slaves formed a settlement which they called Libreville, the current capital. The territory was annexed to French Congo in 1888.

Gabon elected on 28 November 1958 to remain an autonomous republic within the French Community and gained full independence on 17 August 1960.

Multiparty elections held in autumn 1990 were won by the ruling Parti Démocratique Gabonais (PDG), amid allegations of fraud. The PDG formed a coalition government, although the other parties left the government in 1991 in protest at PDG domination. A presidential election in 1993 was won by the incumbent, President Bongo of the PDG, amid accusations of corruption, which led to riots in Libreville. In September 1994, the government and opposition parties signed the Paris Agreement, which provided for a new coalition government and parliamentary elections. The elections, held in December 1996, returned the PDG to power.

POLITICAL SYSTEM

The constitution provides for an executive president, directly elected for a seven-year term, who appoints the Council of Ministers. There is a 120-member National Assembly and a 91-member Senate.

HEAD OF STATE
President, El Hadj Omar Bongo, *assumed office* December 1967, *re-elected* 1973, 1979, 1986, 1993 and 6 December 1998
Vice-President, Didjob Divungi-Di-Ndinge

COUNCIL OF MINISTERS *as at July 1999*
Prime Minister, Housing, Lands and Urban Planning and Welfare, Jean-François Ntoutoume-Emane
Deputy Prime Minister, Justice, Keeper of the Seals, Emmanuel Ondo Methogo
Minister of State, Communications, Posts and Information Technology, Jean-Rémy Pendy-Bouyiki
Minister of State, Equipment and Construction, Zacharie Myboto
Minister of State, Foreign Affairs, Co-operation and Francophone Affairs, Jean Ping
Minister of State, Housing, Urban Affairs, Land Survey, Welfare and Cities, Jacques Adiahénot
Minister of State, Interior, Public Security, Decentralization, Antoine Mboumbou-Miyakou
Minister of State, Labour, Employment, Professional Training, Paulette Moussavou Missambo
Minister of State, National Unity, Social Affairs, Paulin Obame-Nguéma
Minister of State, Planning, Development, Regional Development, Casimir Oyé Mba
Agriculture, Livestock and Rural Development, Noël Mboumbou-Ngoma
Civil Service, Administrative Reform and Modernization of the State, Patrice Nziengui

Commerce and Industrial Development, Marcel Doupambi Matoka
Culture, Art, Mass Education, Daniel Ona-Ondo
Defence, Ali Bongo
Family and the Advancement of Women, Victoire Lassény-Duboze
Finance, Economy, Budget and Privatization, Émile Doumba
Higher Education, Scientific Research, André Dieudonné Berre
Human Rights, Relations with Parliament and the Assemblies, Pierre Claver Zeng-Ebome
Mines, Energy and Oil, Paul Toungui
National Education, Government Spokesperson, André Mba-Obame
Public Health and Population, Faustin Boukoubi
Small and Medium-sized Enterprises and Industries, Handicrafts, Paul Biyoghe-Mba
Tourism Environment and Protection of Nature, Martin-Fidèle Magnaga
Transport and Merchant Marine, Gen. Idriss Ngari
Water, Forests, Fishing and Re-afforestation, Richard Onouviet
Youth, Civic Culture, Sports and Leisure, Pierre Emboni

EMBASSY OF THE REPUBLIC OF GABON
27 Elvaston Place, London SW7 5NL
Tel 0171–823 9986
Ambassador Extraordinary and Plenipotentiary, HE Honorine Dossou-Naki, apptd 1996

BRITISH AMBASSADOR, HE Peter Boon, OBE, resident at Yaoundé, Cameroon

ECONOMY

The economy is heavily dependent on oil and, to a lesser extent, other mineral resources, including manganese and uranium. Gabon has considerable timber reserves with 80 per cent of the country still forested, although production has stagnated in recent years.

France and the USA are the main trading partners. In 1995 there was a trade surplus of US$1,744 million and a current account surplus of US$100 million. In 1995 imports totalled US$882 million and exports US$2,713 million.

GNP – US$4,752 million (1997); US$4,120 per capita (1997)
GDP – US$5,387 million (1995); US$5,007 per capita (1995)
ANNUAL AVERAGE GROWTH OF GDP – 1.0 per cent (1995)
INFLATION RATE – 3.7 per cent (1996)
TOTAL EXTERNAL DEBT – US$4,285 million (1997)

Trade with UK	1997	1998
Imports from UK	£27,191,000	£21,512,000
Exports to UK	6,965,000	5,034,000

THE GAMBIA
The Republic of the Gambia

AREA – 4,361 sq. miles (11,295 sq. km). Neighbour: Senegal, which surrounds the Gambia except at the coast
POPULATION – 1,141,000 (1994 UN estimate), mainly Wollof, Mandinka and Fula peoples who originally migrated from the north and east. The official language is English; Fula, Jola, Mandinka, Serahule and Wollof are indigenous languages
CAPITAL – ΨBanjul (population, 109,986, 1980 estimate)
CURRENCY – Dalasi (D) of 100 butut

NATIONAL ANTHEM – For The Gambia, Our Homeland
NATIONAL DAY – 18 February (Independence Day)
NATIONAL FLAG – Horizontal stripes of red, blue and
green, separated by narrow white stripes
LIFE EXPECTANCY (years) – male 43.41; female 46.63
POPULATION GROWTH RATE – 3.6 per cent (1997)
POPULATION DENSITY – 101 per sq. km (1996)
MILITARY EXPENDITURE – 3.7 per cent of GDP (1997)
MILITARY PERSONNEL – 800: Army

The Gambia is named after the Gambia River, which it
straddles for over 200 miles inland from the west coast of
Africa. The climate is Sahelian, with a dry season between
October and May and heavy rainfall in July and August.

HISTORY AND POLITICS

The Gambia River basin was part of the region dominated
in the tenth to 16th centuries by the Songhai and Mali
kingdoms centred on the upper Niger. The Portuguese
reached the Gambia River in 1447; English merchants
began to trade along the river from 1588. Merchants from
France, Courland (now Latvia) and the Netherlands also
established trading posts. In 1816 the British stationed a
garrison on an island at the river mouth which became the
capital of a small British-administered colony. In 1889
France agreed that the British rights along the upper river
should extend to 10 km from the river on either bank.
British administration was extended from the Colony to
this Protectorate. The Gambia became independent within
the Commonwealth on 18 February 1965, and a republic
on 24 April 1970.

In July 1994 junior army officers launched a coup which
ousted the president and the government, and a military
council was formed. The coup leader, Lt. (later Capt.)
Jammeh, assumed the presidency, the constitution was
suspended and a civilian-military government was formed
to rule in conjunction with the Ruling Military Council. A
referendum approved a new constitution in August 1996,
Jammeh was elected president the following month and
the Ruling Military Council was dissolved. A pro-
presidential party won 33 of the 49 seats in the new
parliament in a legislative election in January 1997.

FOREIGN RELATIONS

The relationship with Senegal remains an important factor
in political and economic policy. Moves towards a closer
association were accelerated after an abortive coup in 1981
was put down with the help of Senegalese troops. In 1982
the Senegambia Confederation was instituted but following
disagreements it was dissolved in 1989. A treaty of
friendship and co-operation was signed with Senegal in
1991.

POLITICAL SYSTEM

The constitution gives enhanced powers to the president
who is elected for an indefinite term.

HEAD OF STATE

President, Defence, Capt. Yahya Jammeh, *took power* 23 July
1994, *elected* 26 September 1996
Vice-President, Health and Social Affairs, Isatou Njie-Saidy

CABINET *as at July 1999*

Agriculture, Fasaieney Dumbuya
Education, Thérèse Ndong-Jatta
External Affairs, Lamine Sedat Jobe
Finance and Economic Affairs, Famara Jatta
Interior, Ousman Badjie
Justice, Attorney-General, Fatou Bensouda
Presidency, National Assembly, Fisheries and Natural Resources,
Capt. Edward Singhateh

Public Works, Communications, Information, Sarjo Jallow
Territorial Administration, Capt. Lamin Bayo
Tourism and Culture, Susan Ogoo
Trade, Industry and Employment, Musa Sillah
Youth and Sports, Capt. Yankouba Touray

GAMBIA HIGH COMMISSION
57 Kensington Court, London W8 5DG
Tel 0171-937 6316/7/8
High Commissioner, HE John P. Bojang, apptd 1997

BRITISH HIGH COMMISSION
48 Atlantic Road, Fajara (PO Box 507), Banjul
Tel: Banjul 495133
High Commissioner, HE Tony Millson, apptd 1998

ECONOMY

Agriculture accounts for 75 per cent of employment and
contributes roughly 20 per cent of GDP. The chief product,
groundnuts, also forms over 80 per cent of domestic
exports. Other crops are cotton, rice, millet, sorghum and
maize. Fishing and livestock industries are being developed.

Manufactures are limited to groundnut processing,
minor metal fabrications, paints, furniture, soap and
bottling. Tourism is developing quickly with more than
80,000 visitors in 1996–7. Trade through the Gambia, re-
exporting imported goods to neighbouring countries, is an
important element in the economy. In 1996 there was a
trade deficit of US$98 million and a current account deficit
of US$48 million. Imports in 1997 totalled US$252 million
and exports US$11 million.

GNP – US$407 million (1997); US$340 per capita (1997)
GDP – US$357 million (1995); US$321 per capita (1995)
ANNUAL AVERAGE GROWTH OF GDP – 3.0 per cent
(1995)
INFLATION RATE – 2.8 per cent (1997)
TOTAL EXTERNAL DEBT – US$430 million (1997)

Trade with UK	1997	1998
Imports from UK	£19,182,000	£14,417,000
Exports to UK	3,104,000	2,904,000

COMMUNICATIONS

There is an international airport at Yundum, 17 miles from
Banjul, with scheduled services flying to other West African
states and to the UK and Belgium. Banjul is the main port.
Internal communication is by road and river. There are
five broadcasting stations and a UHF telephone service
linking Banjul with the principal towns in the provinces.
There is one television station.

EDUCATION

There are 24 secondary schools (eight high and 16
technical). Two high schools provide A-level education.
Gambia College provides post-secondary courses in education, agriculture, public health and nursing. There are
seven vocational training institutions. Higher education
and advanced training courses are taken outside The
Gambia, currently by over 200 students.
ILLITERACY RATE – 61.4 per cent
ENROLMENT (percentage of age group) – primary 65 per
cent (1995); secondary 18 per cent (1992); tertiary 1.7
per cent (1994)

GEORGIA
Sakartvelos Respublika

AREA – 26,911 sq. miles (69,700 sq. km). Neighbours: Russia (north), Azerbaijan (south-east), Armenia (south), Turkey (south-west)

POPULATION – 5,411,000 (1998 estimate): 70 per cent Georgian, 8 per cent Armenian, 6 per cent Russian, 6 per cent Azerbaijani, 3 per cent Ossetian and 2 per cent Abkhazian, with smaller groups of Greeks, Ukrainians, Jews and Kurds. The majority religion is the Georgian Orthodox Church. There is also a small Muslim minority. Georgian, Russian and Armenian are the most commonly used languages. Georgian is one of the oldest languages in the world to have been continually in use, the alphabet having emerged in the third century BC

CAPITAL – Tbilisi (population, 1,268,000, 1990 estimate)

MAJOR CITIES – Batumi (137,000); Kutaisi (236,000); Rustavi (160,000); Sukhumi (capital of Abkhazia) (122,000)

CURRENCY – Lari of 100 tetri

NATIONAL DAY – 26 May (Independence Day)

NATIONAL FLAG – Cherry red with a canton in the upper hoist divided black over white

LIFE EXPECTANCY (years) – male 68.10; female 75.70

POPULATION GROWTH RATE – –0.1 per cent (1997)

POPULATION DENSITY – 78 per sq. km (1996)

URBAN POPULATION – 55.4 per cent (1989)

MILITARY EXPENDITURE – 2.9 per cent of GDP (1997)

MILITARY PERSONNEL – 17,600: Army 12,600, Navy 2,000, Air Force 3,000

CONSCRIPTION DURATION – Two years

ILLITERACY RATE – 0.5 per cent

ENROLMENT (percentage of age group) – primary 83 per cent (1996); secondary 72 per cent (1996); tertiary 39.9 per cent (1996)

Georgia occupies the north-western part of the Caucasus region of the former Soviet Union. It contains the two autonomous republics of Abkhazia and Adjaria and the disputed region of South Ossetia (Tskhinvali).

Georgia is mountainous, with the Greater Caucasus in the north and the Lesser Caucasus in the south. Western Georgia has a mild and damp climate, eastern Georgia is more continental and dry. The Black Sea shore and the Rioni lowland are subtropical.

HISTORY AND POLITICS

The Georgians formed two states, Colchis and Iberia, on the edge of the Black Sea around 1000 BC. After centuries of invasions by Arabs, Turks and Khazars, Georgia entered its 'Golden Age' in the 12th century AD when trade, irrigation and communications were developed. Invasions by the Khazars and Mongols led to the division of Georgia into several states. These struggled against the Turkish and the Persian empires from the 16th to the 18th centuries, gradually turning to the Russian Empire for protection and support. Eastern Georgia signed a treaty of alliance with Russia which recognized Russian supremacy in 1783 and joined the Russian Empire in 1801, followed soon after by Western Georgia.

In the late 19th century, nationalist and Marxist movements competed for limited political influence under autocratic Russian rule. One of the most prominent Marxist activists was Iosif Dzhugashvili (Josef Stalin). After the Russian revolution of 1917, a nationalist government came to power in Georgia supported by allied intervention

forces. In 1921 Soviet forces occupied Tbilisi, and in 1922 Georgia joined the Soviet Union as part of the Transcaucasian Soviet Socialist Republic.

In March 1990 the Georgian Supreme Soviet declared illegal the treaties of 1921–2 by which Georgia had joined the Soviet Union. The Communist Party's monopoly on power was abolished and in multiparty elections held in October and November 1990 the nationalist leader Zviad Gamsakhurdia was elected president. Georgia declared its independence from the Soviet Union in May 1991 and was admitted to UN membership on 31 July 1992.

Gamsakhurdia's government faced armed opposition from 1991 onwards. Defeat in the ensuing civil war in Tbilisi led to Gamsakhurdia's overthrow in January 1992, and in March 1992 a state council was appointed with the former Soviet foreign minister Eduard Shevardnadze as chairman. Fighting continued throughout 1992 and 1993. In October 1992 Shevardnadze was elected head of state and Chairman of the Parliament, and a loose alliance of pro-Shevardnadze parties formed a government.

Gamsakhurdia returned to western Georgia in September 1993, a month after economic chaos had forced the government to resign. President Shevardnadze assumed full executive powers at the head of an emergency council, but failed to prevent the advance of Gamsakhurdia's rebels as most government forces were engaged in Abkhazia. Shevardnadze was forced to accept Russian armaments and troops to defeat the rebellion and in return agreed to join the CIS. Presidential and legislative elections, held on 5 November 1995, were won by President Shevardnadze and his Citizens' Union of Georgia party. A military revolt launched in the west of the country in October 1998 was quickly suppressed by forces loyal to the government. Georgia rescinded its participation in the CIS Collective Security treaty in February 1999 and Russian troops, who had been guarding Georgia's frontier with Turkey, began to withdraw.

SECESSION

In late 1990 the South Ossetians took up arms against Georgian rule in an attempt to join North Ossetia, itself part of Russia. The South Ossetian provincial parliament voted in November 1992 to secede from Georgia and join Russia. Fighting ceased in June 1992 and a joint Russian-Georgian-Ossetian peacekeeping force was dispatched. Representatives of the South Ossetian and Georgian governments met in April 1996 to agree security and confidence-building measures. South Ossetia was renamed Tskhinvali under Georgia's 1995 constitution. Presidential elections in South Ossetia were won by Ludvig Chibirov, the chair of the Supreme Council, in November 1996. Legislative elections were held in May 1999.

In July 1992 the Abkhazian republican parliament declared Abkhazia independent. Fighting broke out between Georgian forces and Abkhazian separatists supported by Russian arms and irregulars; Georgian forces were defeated and were forced to withdraw in September 1993. Negotiations under Russian auspices led to an Abkhaz-Georgian cease-fire and separation of forces agreement being signed in May 1994 and the deployment of 2,500 Russian UN peacekeepers on the Abkhaz-Georgian border. In November 1994 the Abkhaz Supreme Soviet declared Abkhazia's independence again and elected Vladislav Ardzinba as president. Abkhazia was given autonomous republic status under the 1995 constitution; this was rejected by the republican parliament. Elections to the self-declared Abkhaz People's Assembly were held in November 1996. Following a guarantee of security from President Ardzinba, ethnic Georgians who had fled Abkhazia during the fighting began returning in March 1999.

FOREIGN RELATIONS

In September 1997, President Shevardnadze signed an accord with President Maskhadov of Chechnya, calling for closer co-operation between the two states. In October 1997, a Georgian-Ukrainian declaration was signed, promising a development of co-operation with NATO within the framework of the Partnership for Peace programme. Georgia has signed a Partnership and Co-operation Agreement with the European Union.

POLITICAL SYSTEM

The 1995 constitution provides for a federal republic with a unicameral legislature, to become bicameral 'following the creation of appropriate conditions'; and a popularly elected president who serves a maximum of two five-year terms.

HEAD OF STATE

President, Eduard Shevardnadze, *elected* 11 October 1992, *re-elected* 5 November 1995

CABINET *as at July 1999*

Minister of State, Head of Chancellery, Vaja Lortkipanidze
Agriculture and Food, Bakur Gulua
Communications and Posts, Sergo Esakia
Culture, Valeri Asatiani
Defence, Maj.-Gen. David Tevzadze
Economy, Vladimir Papava
Education, Alexandre Kartozia
Finance, David Onoprishvili
Foreign Affairs, Irakli Menagarishvili
Fuel and Energy, Teimur Giorgadze
Health, Avtandil Jorbenadze
Industry, Badri Shoshitaishvili
Internal Affairs, Kakha Targamadze
Justice, Vladimir Chanturia
Natural Resources and Environment, Nino Chkobadze
Refugees and Accommodation, Valeri Vashakidze
Social Security, Labour, Employment, Tengiz Gazdeliani
State Property Management, Michael Ukleba
State Security, Vakhtang Kutateladze
Trade, Foreign Economic Relations, Tamara Beruchasvili
Transport, Merab Adeishvili
Urban Planning and Construction, Merab Chkhenkeli

EMBASSY OF THE REPUBLIC OF GEORGIA
3 Hornton Place, London, W8 4LZ
Tel 0171–937 8233
Ambassador Extraordinary and Plenipotentiary, HE Teimuraz Mamatsashvili, apptd 1995

BRITISH EMBASSY
Metechi Palace Hotel, 380003 Tbilisi
Tel: Tbilisi 955497
Ambassador Extraordinary and Plenipotentiary, HE Richard Jenkins, OBE, apptd 1997

ECONOMY

The economy was brought to the brink of collapse by civil and secessionist wars and the ending of former Soviet trading relationships. Industrial production fell by 70 per cent between 1991 and 1995. Although Georgia has deposits of coal, they have not been exploited and it is desperately short of energy supplies. A large proportion of production is stolen by black marketeers, whilst the tourist industry on the Black Sea coast has been destroyed by the fighting. The only productive sector of the economy is agriculture, with a concentration on viniculture, tea and tobacco-growing and citrus fruits.

Economic performance improved in 1995 with inflation dropping from 7,500 per cent in 1994 to 2 per cent per month in 1995. Reforms included the introduction of a new currency in October 1995, and new legislation permitting the private ownership of arable land and stricter bank regulation. GDP has grown gradually in the past two years, and in 1997 investment activity grew by 87 per cent. In May 1998, a co-operation agreement was signed with US company Enron to build a trans-Caspian pipeline for transporting oil and gas.

GNP – US$4,656 million (1997); US$860 per capita (1997)
GDP – US$1,869 million (1995); US$343 per capita (1995)
ANNUAL AVERAGE GROWTH OF GDP – 2.5 per cent (1995)
TOTAL EXTERNAL DEBT – US$1,446 million (1997)

Trade with UK	1997	1998
Imports from UK	£12,100,000	£20,991,000
Exports to UK	1,257,000	3,222,000

GERMANY
Bundesrepublik Deutschland – Federal Republic of Germany

AREA – 137,735 sq. miles (356,733 sq. km). Neighbours: Denmark (north), Poland (east), Czech Republic (east and south-east), Austria (south-east and south), Switzerland (south), France, Luxembourg, Belgium and the Netherlands (west)
POPULATION – 81,912,000 (1995 UN estimate). Approximately 80 per cent of the population live in the former West Germany. In 1994 there were 28,197,000 Protestants, 27,909,797 Roman Catholics, 2,700,000 Muslims and 53,797 Jews. The language is German; there are Danish- and Frisian-speaking minorities in Schleswig-Holstein and a Sorbian-speaking minority in Saxony
CAPITAL – Berlin (population, 3,472,009, 1996). The seat of government and parliament is to be transferred from Bonn to Berlin by 2000
MAJOR CITIES – Bremen (549,182); Cologne (963,817); Dortmund (600,918); Dresden (474,443); Duisburg (536,106); Düsseldorf (572,638); Essen (617,955); Frankfurt am Main (652,412); Hamburg (1,705,872); Hannover (524,823); Leipzig (481,121); Munich (1,244,676); Nuremberg (495,845); Stuttgart (588,482)
CURRENCY – Deutsche Mark (DM) of 100 Pfennig
NATIONAL ANTHEM – Einigkeit und Recht und Freiheit (Unity and right and freedom)
NATIONAL DAY – 3 October (Anniversary of 1990 Unification)
NATIONAL FLAG – Horizontal bars of black, red and gold
LIFE EXPECTANCY (years) – male 72.77; female 79.30
POPULATION GROWTH RATE – 0.5 per cent (1997)
POPULATION DENSITY – 230 per sq. km (1996)
URBAN POPULATION – 76.3 per cent (1990)

HISTORY AND POLITICS

The term 'deutsch' (German) was probably first used in the eighth century and described the language spoken in the eastern part of the Frankish realm. The first German realm was the Holy Roman Empire, established in AD 962 when Otto I of Saxony was crowned Emperor. The Empire endured until 1806, but the achievement of a national state was prevented by fragmentation into small principalities and dukedoms.

Treaty of Versailles (1919) returned Alsace-Lorraine to France, and large areas in the east were lost to Poland. The world economic crisis of 1929 contributed to the collapse of the Weimar Republic and the subsequent rise to power of the National Socialist movement of Adolf Hitler, who became Chancellor in 1933.

After concluding a Treaty of Non-Aggression with the Soviet Union in August 1939, Germany invaded Poland (1 September 1939), precipitating the Second World War, which lasted until 1945. Hitler committed suicide on 30 April 1945. On 8 May 1945, Germany unconditionally surrendered.

THE POST-WAR PERIOD

Germany was divided into American, French, British and Soviet zones of occupation. Supreme authority was exercised by the respective Commanders-in-Chief, and jointly through the Control Council of the four Commanders, with Berlin under joint administration. The USSR withdrew from the Control Council in 1948 and the rift divided Germany *de facto* into east and west.

The Federal Republic of Germany (FRG) was created out of the three western zones in 1949. A Communist government was established in the Soviet zone (henceforth the German Democratic Republic (GDR)). In 1961 the Soviet zone of Berlin was sealed off, and the Berlin Wall was built along the zonal boundary, partitioning the western sectors of the city from the eastern.

Soviet-initiated reform in eastern Europe during the late 1980s led to unrest in the GDR, culminating in the opening of the Berlin Wall in November 1989 and the collapse of Communist government. The 'Treaty on the Final Settlement with Respect to Germany', concluded between the FRG, GDR and the four former occupying powers in September 1990, unified Germany with effect from 3 October 1990 as a fully sovereign state. Economic and monetary union preceded formal union on 1 July 1990. Unification is constitutionally the accession of Berlin and the five reformed *Länder* of the GDR to the FRG, which remains in being. The first government of the new Germany took office in January 1991 following all-German elections on 2 December 1990. Berlin was declared to be the capital

The Empire was replaced by a loose association of sovereign states known as the German Confederation, which was dissolved in 1866 and replaced by the Prussian-dominated North German Federation. Prussia had translated its earlier economic predominance into political hegemony by the annexation of the duchies of Schleswig and Holstein from Denmark in 1864 and a decisive defeat of Austria in 1866 (the Seven Weeks' War). After the Franco-Prussian War of 1870–1, which resulted in the defeat of France and the cession of Alsace and part of Lorraine, the south German principalities united with the northern federation to form a second German Empire, the King of Prussia being proclaimed Emperor in 1871.

Defeat in the First World War led to the abdication of the Emperor, and the country became a republic. The

Land	Area (sq. km)	Population (1995)	Capital	Minister-President (June 1999)
Baden-Württemberg	35,752	10.3m	Stuttgart	Erwin Teufel (CDU)
Bavaria	70,554	12.0m	Munich	Dr Edmund Stoiber (CSU)
Berlin	889	3.5m	—	Eberhard Diepgen (CDU)*
Brandenburg	29,479	2.6m	Potsdam	Dr Manfred Stolpe (SPD)
Bremen	404	0.7m	—	Dr Henning Scherf (SPD)*
Hamburg	755	1.7m	—	Ortwin Runde (SPD)*
Hesse	21,114	5.8m	Wiesbaden	Roland Koch (CDU)
Lower Saxony	47,338	7.8m	Hannover	Gerhard Glogowski (SPD)
Mecklenburg-Western Pomerania	23,170	1.8m	Schwerin	Dr Harald Ringstorff (SPD)
North Rhine-Westphalia	34,078	18.0m	Düsseldorf	Wolfgang Clement (SPD)
Rhineland-Palatinate	19,849	4.0m	Mainz	Kurt Beck (SPD)
Saarland	2,570	1.1m	Saarbrücken	Reinhard Klimmt (SPD)
Saxony	18,341	4.6m	Dresden	Prof. Kurt Biedenkopf (CDU)
Saxony-Anhalt	20,455	2.7m	Magdeburg	Dr Reinhard Höppner (SPD)
Schleswig-Holstein	15,729	2.7m	Kiel	Heide Simonis (SPD)
Thuringia	16,251	2.5m	Erfurt	Dr Bernhard Vogel (CDU)

*Berlin, *Governing Mayor*; Bremen, *Mayor*; Hamburg, *First Mayor*

CDU Christian Democratic Union; CSU Christian Social Union; SPD Social Democratic Party

of the unified Germany and arrangements to transfer parliament and government departments from Bonn were drawn up. The transfer began in November 1998 and the process is due to be completed during 2000.

The distribution of seats following the last election for the Bundestag on 27 September 1998 was: Social Democrats, 298; Christian Democratic Union, 198 Christian Social Union, 47; The Greens, 47; Free Democrats, 44; Democratic Socialists, 35. A coalition of Social Democrats and Greens forms the present government.

POLITICAL SYSTEM

The Basic Law provides for a president, elected by a Federal Convention (electoral college) for a five-year term, a lower house (*Bundestag*) of 672 members elected by direct universal suffrage for a four-year term of office, and an upper house (*Bundesrat*) composed of 69 members appointed by the governments of the *Länder* in proportion to *Länder* populations, without a fixed term of office.

Judicial authority is exercised by the Federal Constitutional Court, the federal courts provided for in the Basic Law and the courts of the Länder.

FEDERAL STRUCTURE

Germany is a federal republic composed of 16 states (*Länder*) (ten from the former West, five from the former East and Berlin). Each *Land* has its own directly elected legislature and government led by Minister-Presidents (prime ministers) or equivalents. The 1949 Basic Law vests executive power in the *Länder* governments except in those areas reserved for the federal government.

HEAD OF STATE
Federal President, Johannes Rau, *elected* 23 May 1999

CABINET *as at July 1999*
Federal Chancellor, Gerhard Schröder (SPD)
Federal Vice-Chancellor, Foreign Affairs, Joschka Fischer (Greens)

Defence, Rudolf Scharping (SPD)
Economic Co-operation and Development, Heidemarie Wieczorek-Zeul (SPD)
Economics and Technology, Werner Müller (Ind.)
Education and Research, Edelgard Bulmahn (SPD)
Environment, Nature Conservation and Nuclear Safety, Jürgen Trittin (Greens)
Family, Pensioners, Women and Youth, Dr Christine Bergmann (SPD)
Finance, Hans Eichel (SPD)
Food, Agriculture and Forestry, Karl-Heinz Funke (SPD)
Head of Chancellory, Bodo Hombach (SPD)
Health, Andreas Fischer (Greens)
Interior, Otto Schily (SPD)
Justice, Herta Däubler-Gmelin (SPD)
Labour and Social Affairs, Walter Riester (SPD)
Minister Delegate for Culture, Michael Naumann (Ind.)
Minister Delegate for East Germany, Rolf Schwanitz (SPD)
Ministers Delegate for Foreign Affairs, Günter Verheugen (SPD); Ludger Volemer (Greens)
Public Works and Transport, Franz Müntefering (SPD)

CDU Christian Democratic Union; CSU Christian Social Union; FDP Free Democratic Party; Ind. Independent

EMBASSY OF THE FEDERAL REPUBLIC OF GERMANY
23 Belgrave Square, London SW1X 8PZ
Tel 0171-824 1300
Ambassador Extraordinary and Plenipotentiary, HE Gebhardt von Moltke, GCVO apptd 1997

Minister, Peter von Butler
Minister-Counsellor, Paul von Maltzahn, CVO
Counsellors, F. Burbach (*Cultural Affairs*); R. Lüdeking (*Economic Affairs*)
Defence Attaché, Cd. H. W. Fritz

BRITISH EMBASSY
Unter den Linden 32/34, D-10117 Berlin
Tel: Berlin 201 840
Ambassador Extraordinary and Plenipotentiary, HE Sir Paul Lever, KCMG, apptd 1997
Deputy Head of Mission, Minister, A. Charlton, CMG *Defence Attaché,* Brig. B. R. Isbell, MBE
Counsellor (Economic), R. L. Turner

BRITISH EMBASSY, COMMERCIAL, ENVIRONMENT AND MANAGEMENT SECTIONS
Friedrichstrasse 79/80, D-10117 Berlin
Tel: Berlin 201 840
Counsellor, Deputy Head of Mission, G. Whitaker
Minister, A. Ford, CMG
First Secretary (Commercial), D. S. Schroeder

BRITISH CONSULATES-GENERAL – Düsseldorf, Frankfurt, Hamburg, Munich, Stuttgart
BRITISH CONSULATES – Bremen, Hannover, Kiel and Nuremberg

BRITISH COUNCIL REPRESENTATIVE, K. Dobson, OBE, Hahnenstrasse 6, D-50667 Köln. Offices at Berlin, Hamburg, Leipzig and Munich

BRITISH CHAMBER OF COMMERCE, Neumarkt 14, D-5000 Köln 1. *Director,* Herr Heumann

DEFENCE

The Army has 2,716 main battle tanks, 3,455 armoured personnel carriers, 2,464 armoured infantry fighting vehicles, 2,040 artillery pieces, and 204 attack helicopters. The Navy has 14 submarines, three destroyers, 12 frigates, 30 patrol and coastal vessels, 52 combat aircraft and 17 armed helicopters. The Air Force has 451 combat aircraft.

There remain 102,567 NATO personnel in Germany (USA 57,700; UK 28,167; Belgium 2,000; France 11,700; Netherlands 3,000).

During 1993 both the Constitutional Court and the Bundestag agreed that German armed forces may operate outside Germany and the NATO area in UN and other peacekeeping operations for the first time since 1945. In 1994 the Constitutional Court ruled that German forces could serve in armed peacemaking missions.

MILITARY EXPENDITURE – 1.6 per cent of GDP (1997)
MILITARY PERSONNEL – 333,500: Army 230,600, Navy 26,700, Air Force 76,200. Under the terms of the Treaty of Unification, the German armed forces have been limited to 370,000 active personnel since the end of 1994
CONSCRIPTION DURATION – Ten to 23 months

ECONOMY

Germany has a predominantly industrial economy. Principal industries are coal mining, iron and steel production, machine construction, the electrical industry, the manufacture of steel and metal products, chemicals, automobile production, electronics, textiles and the processing of foodstuffs.

In 1997, Germany produced 223,950,000 tonnes of coal and 2,820,000 tonnes of crude petroleum. A government plan to abolish all 19 of Germany's nuclear power stations was abandoned after protests from France and the UK, who have nuclear waste processing agreements with Germany.

After a mini-boom generated by new East German demand in 1990 and 1991, Germany entered its most severe recession since the war induced by the costs of reunification. In 1993 a 'Solidarity Pact' was agreed by federal and Länder governments, opposition parties, and employers and trade unions, to take effect from 1995. The pact lays down the basis of future funding transfers to the East based on a 5.5 per cent rise in income taxes, wage restraint in the West, more private investment in the East, and the distribution of the funding burden between the federal and Länder governments. The government was forced to make spending cuts in order to meet the criteria for European monetary union. In November 1998, the government announced that it would double investment in research over its five-year term.

In 1997 there was a trade surplus of US$74,701 million and a current account deficit of US$1,186 million. Imports totalled US$441,742 million and exports US$512,427 million.

GNP – US$2,320,985 million (1997); US$28,280 per capita (1997)
GDP – US$2,417,762 million (1995); US$29,632 per capita (1995)
ANNUAL AVERAGE GROWTH OF GDP – 2.0 per cent (1997)
INFLATION RATE – 1.8 per cent (1997)
UNEMPLOYMENT – 12.9 per cent (1995); expected to be 10 per cent in 1997

Trade with UK	1997	1998
Imports from UK	£19,501,400,000	£19,453,500,000
Exports to UK	24,546,900,000	24,063,000,000

COMMUNICATIONS

In 1995 the state-owned railways measured 40,209 km of which 17,054 km were electrified, and the privately owned railways totalled approximately 2,807 km. Classified roads measured 228,860 km in 1996, of which motorways were 11,190 km. Merchant shipping under the German flag in 1994 amounted to 5,696,088 tonnes gross. Inland waterways are 6,929 km long.

EDUCATION

School attendance is compulsory between the ages of six and 18 and comprises nine years of full-time education at primary and main schools and three years of vocational education on a part-time basis. The secondary school leaving examination (*Abitur*) entitles the holder to a place of study at a university or another institution of higher education.

Children below the age of 18 who are not attending a general secondary or a full-time vocational school have compulsory day-release at a vocational school.

The largest universities are in Munich, Berlin, Hamburg, Bonn, Frankfurt and Cologne.

ENROLMENT (percentage of age group) – primary 100 per cent (1995); secondary 87 per cent (1995); tertiary 44.4 per cent (1995)

CULTURE

Modern (or New High) German has developed from the time of the Reformation to the present day, with differences of dialect in Austria, Alsace, Luxembourg, Liechtenstein and the German-speaking cantons of Switzerland.

The literary language is usually regarded as having become fixed by Luther and Zwingli at the Reformation, since which time many great names occur in all branches, notably philosophy, from Leibnitz (1646–1716) to Kant (1724–1804), Schelling (1775–1854) and Hegel (1770–

1831); drama, from Goethe (1749–1832) and Schiller (1759–1805) to Gerhart Hauptmann (1862–1946); and poetry, Heine (1797–1856). Seven German authors have received the Nobel Prize for Literature: Theodor Mommsen (1902), R. Eucken (1908), P. Heyse (1909), Gerhart Hauptmann (1912), Thomas Mann (1929), N. Sachs (1966) and Heinrich Böll (1972).

GHANA
The Republic of Ghana

AREA – 92,098 sq. miles (238,533 sq. km). Neighbours: Burkina Faso (north), Côte d'Ivoire (west), Togo (east)
POPULATION – 18,885,616 (1998 estimate); most are Sudanese Negroes, although Hamitic strains are common in the north. The official language is English. The principal indigenous language group is Akan, of which Twi and Fanti are the most commonly used. Ga, Ewe and languages of the Mole-Dagbani group are common in certain regions. Most Ghanaians are Christians, although there is a substantial Muslim minority in the north
CAPITAL – ΨAccra (population, 1,445,515, 1998), Greater Accra Region (including Tema) 2,384,753 (1998 estimate)
MAJOR CITIES – Koforidua (81,378); Kumasi (577,878); Ψ Takoradi (96,897); Tamale (228,827); CURRENCY – Cedi of 100 pesewas
NATIONAL FLAG – Equal horizontal bands of red over gold over green; five-point black star on gold stripe
NATIONAL ANTHEM – God Bless our Homeland Ghana
NATIONAL DAY – 6 March (Independence Day)
LIFE EXPECTANCY (years) – male 54.22; female 57.84
POPULATION GROWTH RATE – 2.7 per cent (1997)
POPULATION DENSITY – 75 per sq. km (1996)
MILITARY EXPENDITURE – 1.5 per cent of GDP (1997)
MILITARY PERSONNEL – 7,000: Army 5,000, Navy 1,000, Air Force 1,000
ILLITERACY RATE – 35.5 per cent
ENROLMENT (percentage of age group) – tertiary 1.4 per cent (1990)

HISTORY AND POLITICS

First reached by Europeans in the 15th century, the constituent parts of Ghana came under British administration at various times, the original Gold Coast Colony being constituted in 1874, and Ashanti and the Northern Territories Protectorate in 1901. Trans-Volta-Togoland, part of the former German colony of Togo, was mandated to Britain by the League of Nations after the First World War, and became a United Nations Trusteeship under British administration after the Second World War. After a plebiscite in 1956, the territory was integrated with the Gold Coast Colony. The former Gold Coast Colony and associated territories became the independent state of Ghana on 6 March 1957 and became a republic in 1960.

Since 1966, Ghana has experienced long periods of military rule interspersed with short-lived civilian governments. A coup in 1979 led to the formation of an Armed Forces Revolutionary Council chaired by Flt. Lt. Jerry Rawlings. Civilian rule was restored in 1979 but another coup in December 1981 brought Rawlings back to power.

A referendum in 1992 approved a new multiparty constitution and the legalization of political parties. The National Democratic Congress (NDC) was established as a political party from the ruling Provisional National Defence Council. The presidential and parliamentary elections in late 1992 were won by Rawlings and the NDC, following a boycott by most opposition parties and most of the electorate. The Fourth Republic was declared on 7 January 1993 and a new government nominated by the president took office in March 1993. In legislative elections in December 1996, the NDC retained its absolute majority; President Rawlings was also re-elected.

POLITICAL SYSTEM

The head of state is an executive president elected for a four-year term, renewable only once. The president appoints the Council of Ministers. The unicameral legislature, the Parliament, has 200 members directly elected for a four-year term.

For political and administrative purposes Ghana is divided into ten regions, each headed by a Regional Minister who is the representative of the central government.

HEAD OF STATE

President, Flt. Lt. (retd) Jerry John Rawlings, *took power* 31 December 1981, *elected* 3 November 1992, *re-elected* 7 December 1996
Vice-President, John Evans Mills

COUNCIL OF MINISTERS *as at July 1999*

Communications, John Mahama
Defence, Lt. Col. E. K. T. Donkoh
Education, Ekwow Spio-Garbrah
Employment and Social Welfare, Alhaji Mohammed Mumuni
Environment, Science and Technology, Cletus Avoka
Finance, Kwame Peprah
Food and Agriculture, J. H. Owusu-Acheampong
Foreign Affairs, Victor Gbeho
Health, Eunice Brookman-Amissah
Interior, Nii Okaidja Adamafio
Justice and Attorney-General, Obed Asamoah
Lands and Forestry, Christine Amoako-Nuamah
Local Government and Rural Development, Kwamena Ahwoi
National Security, Kofi Totobi-Quakyi
Parliamentary Affairs, Kwabena Adjei
Roads and Transport, Edward Salia
Tourism, Mike Gizo
Trade and Industry, John Abu
Works and Housing, Isaac Adjei-Mensah
Youth and Sports, E. T. Mensah

GHANA HIGH COMMISSION
13 Belgrave Square, London SW1 8PN
Tel 0171-235 4142
High Commissioner, HE James E. K. Aggrey-Orleans
Defence Adviser, Brig. Nii Coleman
Minister-Counsellor, Eric Amenuvor (*Trade*)

BRITISH HIGH COMMISSION
PO Box 296, Osu Link, Accra
Tel: Accra 221665/669585
High Commissioner, HE Ian Mackley, CMG, apptd 1996
Deputy High Commissioner, C. Murray
Defence Adviser, Lt.-Col. E. Glover
First Secretary (Commercial), M. A. Ives

BRITISH COUNCIL DIRECTOR, C. Stevenson, 11 Liberia Road (PO Box 771), Accra. There is also an office in Kumasi.

ECONOMY

Agriculture is the basis of the economy, employing 70 per cent of the workforce. Crops include cocoa, the largest single source of revenue, rice, cassava, plantains, oranges and pineapples, groundnuts, corn, millet, oil palms, yams, maize and vegetables. Livestock is raised in uncultivated areas. Fishing is important in coastal areas and in the Volta lake and river system.

Manganese production ranks among the world's largest, with 332,443 tonnes of ore being produced in 1997; diamonds, gold and bauxite are also produced. Some 30,000 persons are employed by the mining companies.

Small-scale traditional industries include tailoring, goldsmithing and carpentry. Priority has been given in recent years to establishing manufacturing industries and a modern industrial complex has developed in the Accra-Tema area. In 1995, 335,000 tourists visited Ghana.

Since 1966 the Volta Dams at Akosombo and Kpong have generated hydroelectric power for the processing of bauxite and fed a power transmission network for most of Ghana, Togo and Benin.

In 1998 there was a trade deficit of US$384 million and a current account deficit of US$502 million. Imports in 1998 totalled US$2,214 million and exports US$1,830 million.

GNP – US$6,982 million (1997); US$390 per capita (1997)
GDP – US$6,875 million (1995); US$397 per capita (1995)
ANNUAL AVERAGE GROWTH OF GDP – 6.9 per cent (1995)
INFLATION RATE – 27.9 per cent (1997)
TOTAL EXTERNAL DEBT – US$6,202 million (1996)

TRADE

Principal exports are cocoa, timber, minerals and gold. Principal imports are road vehicles, manufacturing equipment, petroleum, raw materials and food.

Trade with UK	1997	1998
Imports from UK	£270,189,000	£222,202,000
Exports to UK	134,978,000	155,160,000

COMMUNICATIONS

The Kotoka Airport at Accra is an international airport and Ghana Airways is the national airline. There are also internal airports at Takoradi, Kumasi, Sunyani, and Tamale.

There are more than 20,000 miles of motorable roads. There are 600 miles of railway, linking Accra and the principal ports of Takoradi and Tema with their hinterlands, the mining centres and with each other.

Takoradi Harbour consists of seven quay berths: one is leased specially for manganese exports. Tema Harbour has ten berths for larger ocean-going vessels and the largest dry dock on the West African coast. An oil berth has also been built to serve the refinery at Tema.

GREECE
Elliniki Dimokratia

AREA – 50,949 sq. miles (131,957 sq. km). Neighbours: Albania, Bulgaria and Macedonia (north), Turkey (east)
POPULATION – 10,475,000 (1994 UN estimate), 10,256,464 (1991 census): 98 per cent Greek Orthodox, 1 per cent Catholic, 1 per cent Muslim. The language is Greek
CAPITAL – Athens (population 3,072,922, 1991); including ΨPiraeus and suburbs, 3,096,775 (1991 census)
MAJOR CITIES – ΨCanea (Crete) (65,519); ΨHeraklion (Crete) (127,600); ΨKavalla (58,576); Larissa (113,426); ΨPatras (172,763); ΨRhodes (43,619); ΨThessaloniki (Salonika) (739,998); ΨVolos (115,732)

CURRENCY – Drachma of 100 leptae
NATIONAL ANTHEM – Imnos Eis Tin Eleftherian
  (Hymn to Freedom)
NATIONAL DAY – March 25 (Independence Day)
NATIONAL FLAG – Blue and white stripes with a white
  cross on a blue field in the canton
LIFE EXPECTANCY (years) – male 74.61; female 79.96
POPULATION GROWTH RATE – 0.5 per cent (1997)
POPULATION DENSITY – 79 per sq. km (1996)
URBAN POPULATION – 58.9 per cent (1991)

The main areas are: Macedonia (which includes Mt Athos and the island of Thasos), Thrace (including the island of Samothrace), Epirus, Thessaly, Continental Greece (which includes the island of Euboea and the Sporades), Crete and the Peloponnese. The main island groups are the Sporades (of which the largest is Skyros), the Dodecanese or Southern Sporades (Rhodes, Astypalaia, Karpathos, Kassos, Nisyros, Kalymnos, Leros, Patmos, Kos, Symi, Khalki, Tilos), the Cyclades (about 200, including Syros, Andros, Tinos, Mykonos, Naxos, Paros, Santorini, Milos and Serifos), the Ionian Islands (Corfu, Paxos, Levkas, Ithaca, Cephalonia, Zante and Cerigo), and the Aegean Islands (Chios, Lesbos, Limnos and Samos). In Crete from about 3000 to 1400 BC a civilization flourished which spread its influence throughout the Aegean, and the ruins of the palace of Minos at Knossos afford evidence of astonishing comfort and luxury.

HISTORY AND POLITICS

Greece was under Turkish rule from the mid-15th century until a war of independence (1821–7) led to the establishment of a Greek kingdom in the Peloponnese in 1829. The remainder of Greece gradually became independent until the Dodecanese were returned by Italy in 1947. After the Nazi German occupation of 1941–4, a civil war between monarchist and Communist groups lasted from 1946 to 1949, and tension between right-wing and radical groups continued after 1949. In 1967 right-wing elements in the army seized power and established a military regime (the 'Greek Colonels'). The King went into voluntary exile in 1967; in 1974 the monarchy was abolished and a republic established. Unrest in Athens in 1973–4 intensified after the government was involved in the overthrow of President Makarios of Cyprus in July 1974, and led the Colonels to surrender power. Konstantinos Karamanlis (prime minister 1955–63) returned from exile to form a provisional

government, and the first elections for ten years were held in 1974. The restoration of the monarchy was rejected by referendum on 8 December 1974 and Greece became a republic.

The most recent general election was held on 22 September 1996 with the Panhellenic Socialist Party (PASOK) winning 162 seats, the New Democracy Party (Christian Democrats) 108 seats, the Communist Party 11 seats, the Coalition of the Left and Progress ten seats, and the Democratic Social Movement nine seats.

POLITICAL SYSTEM

In 1986 most executive power was transferred from the president to the government. The unicameral 300-member Chamber of Deputies (*Vouli*) is elected for a four-year term by universal adult suffrage under a system of proportional representation, with a three per cent threshold for parliamentary representation.

HEAD OF STATE
President of the Hellenic Republic, Constantine
  Stephanopoulos, *elected by parliament* 8 March 1995

CABINET *as at July 1999*
Prime Minister, Costas Simitis
Aegean, Stavros Benos
Agriculture, George Anomeritis
Culture, Elisabeth Papazoi
Development, Evangelos Venizelos
Education and Religion, Gerasimos Arsenis
Environment, Town Planning and Public Works, Costas
  Laliotis
Foreign Affairs, George Papandreou
Health and Welfare, Lambros Papadimas
Interior, Public Administration and Decentralization, Vasso
  Papandreou
Justice, Evangelos Yiannopoulos
Labour and Social Security, Miltiadis Papaioannou
Macedonia and Thrace, Yiannis Magriotis
Merchant Marine, Stavros Soumakis
Minister of State, Costas Geitonas
National Defence, Akis Tsohatzopoulos
National Economy and Finance, Yiannos Papantoniou
Press and Media, Government Spokesman, Dimitris Reppas
Public Order, Michaelis Chrysohoidis
Transport and Communications, Tassos Mantelis

EMBASSY OF GREECE
1A Holland Park, London W11 3TP
Tel 0171-229 3850
Ambassador Extraordinary and Plenipotentiary, HE Christos
  Zacharakis, apptd 1999
Defence Attaché, Capt. N. Kostakis
Minister-Counsellor, C. Bitsios

HONORARY CONSULATES – Belfast, Birmingham,
  Edinburgh, Falmouth, Glasgow, Leeds and
  Southampton

BRITISH EMBASSY
1 Ploutarchou Street, GR-10675 Athens
Tel: Athens 727 2600
Ambassador Extraordinary and Plenipotentiary, HE David C.
  A. Madden, CMG, apptd 1999
Deputy Head of Mission, Counsellor and Consul-General, P. J.
  Millett
Defence and Military Attaché, Brig. S. W. J. Saunders
First Secretary (Commercial), G. G. Thomas

BRITISH CONSULAR OFFICES – Athens, Corfu,
  Heraklion (Crete), Kos, Patras, Rhodes, Thessaloniki,
  Syros and Zakynthos

BRITISH COUNCIL DIRECTOR, P. Chenery, 17 Kolonaki Square, Athens GR-10673. There is also an office at Thessaloniki.

BRITISH-HELLENIC CHAMBER OF COMMERCE, 25 Vas. Sofias Avenue, GR-10674 Athens. Tel: 721 0361

DEFENCE

The Army has 1,735 main battle tanks, 2,477 armoured personnel carriers and armoured infantry fighting vehicles, and 1,886 artillery pieces. The Navy has seven submarines, four destroyers, 12 frigates, 42 patrol and coastal vessels, six combat aircraft and 15 armed helicopters. The Air Force has a total of 402 combat aircraft.

Greece maintains 1,250 army personnel in Cyprus. There are 419 US military personnel stationed in Greece.

MILITARY EXPENDITURE – 4.6 per cent of GDP (1997)
MILITARY PERSONNEL – 172,500: Army 116,000, Navy 19,500, Air Force 33,000, Paramilitaries 4,000
CONSCRIPTION DURATION – Up to 21 months

ECONOMY

The principal minerals are nickel, bauxite, iron ore, iron pyrites, manganese magnesite, chrome, lead, zinc and emery. The chief industries are textiles (cotton, woollen and synthetics), chemicals, cement, glass, metallurgy, shipbuilding, domestic electrical equipment and footwear, the production of aluminium, nickel, iron and steel products, tyres, chemicals, fertilizers and sugar (from locally-grown beet). Food processing and ancillary industries are also growing.

The development of the country's electric power resources, irrigation and land reclamation schemes, and the exploitation of lignite resources for fuel and industrial purposes are continuing. Tourism is also a major industry, with over 10 million visitors in 1995.

Though there has been substantial industrialization, agriculture still employs about a fifth of the working population and contributes 12 per cent of GDP. The most important agricultural products are tobacco, wheat, cotton, sugar, rice, fruit (olives, peaches, vines, oranges, lemons, figs, almonds and currant-vines). Exports of fresh fruit, currants and vegetables are an important contributor to the economy.

The IMF austerity programme of privatization and reduction of the public sector has been partially reversed by the current government, which has slowed privatization. Further austerity measures imposed in an attempt to meet the EU's economic and monetary union criteria have prompted strikes. In March 1998 the drachma was devalued by 14 per cent and admitted to the ERM; Greece intends to participate in EMU in 2001, subject to meeting the economic criteria.

In 1996 there was a trade deficit of US$15,505 million and a current account deficit of US$4,554 million. In 1994 imports totalled US$21,466 million and in 1997 exports totalled US$8,626 million.

GNP – US$122,430 million (1997); US$11,640 per capita (1997)
GDP – US$90,785 million (1995); US$8,684 per capita (1995)
ANNUAL AVERAGE GROWTH OF GDP – 1.9 per cent (1995)
INFLATION RATE – 5.5 per cent (1997)
UNEMPLOYMENT – 10.0 per cent (1995)

Trade with UK	1997	1998
Imports from UK	£996,600,000	£987,900,000
Exports to UK	375,200,000	344,100,000

COMMUNICATIONS

The 2,650 km of railways are state-owned, with the exception of the Athens–Piraeus Electric Railway. Roads total over 38,500 km, of which about 25 per cent are national highways and just under 30,000 km are provincial roads. The Greek mercantile fleet numbers 1,864 ships over 100 tons gross with a total tonnage of 53,778,128 tons gross. Athens has direct airline links with Australasia, North America, most countries in Europe, Africa and the Middle East.

EDUCATION

Education is free and compulsory from the age of six to 15 and is maintained by state grants. There are eighteen universities and several other institutes of higher learning.

ILLITERACY RATE – 4.8 per cent
ENROLMENT (percentage of age group) – primary 91 per cent (1995); secondary 87 per cent (1995); tertiary 42.5 per cent (1995)

CULTURE

Greek civilization emerged c.1300 BC and the poems of Homer, which were probably current c.800 BC, record the struggle between the Achaeans of Greece and the Phrygians of Troy (1194 to 1184 BC).

The spoken language of modern Greece is descended from the Common Greek of Alexander the Great's empire. *Katharevousa*, a conservative literary dialect evolved by Adamantios Corais (Diamant Coray) (1748–1833) and used for official and technical matters, has been phased out. Novels and poetry are mostly in *dimotiki*, a progressive literary dialect which owes much to John Psycharis (1854–1929). The poets Solomos, Palamas, Cavafy and Sikelianos have won a European reputation. George Seferis (1963) and Odysseus Elytis (1979) have won the Nobel Prize for Literature.

GRENADA
The State of Grenada

AREA – 133 sq. miles (344 sq. km)
POPULATION – 92,000 (1994 UN estimate), 95,000 (1992 census). The language is English
CAPITAL – ΨSt George's (population, 4,788, 1981)
CURRENCY – East Caribbean dollar (EC$) of 100 cents
NATIONAL DAY – 7 February (Independence Day)
NATIONAL FLAG – Divided diagonally into yellow and green triangles within a red border containing six yellow stars, a yellow star on a red disc in the centre and a nutmeg on the green triangle in the hoist
POPULATION GROWTH RATE – 0.3 per cent (1997)
POPULATION DENSITY – 267 per sq. km (1996)

The island is about 21 miles long and 12 miles wide. Also a part of Grenada are some of the Grenadines islets, the largest of which is Carriacou, 13 square miles in area.

HISTORY AND POLITICS

Discovered by Columbus in 1498, and named Concepción, Grenada was originally colonized by France and was ceded to Great Britain by the Treaty of Versailles in 1783. It became an Associated State in 1967 and an independent nation within the Commonwealth on 7 February 1974.

The government was overthrown in 1979 by the New Jewel Movement and a People's Revolutionary Government was set up. In October 1983 disagreements within the

PRG led to the death of Prime Minister Maurice Bishop, whose government was replaced by a Revolutionary Military Council. These events prompted the intervention of Caribbean and US forces. The Governor-General installed an advisory council to act as an interim government until a general election was held in December 1984. A phased withdrawal of US forces was completed by June 1985.

The general election held on 18 January 1999 was won by the New National Party led by Dr Keith Mitchell. They won all 15 seats in the House of Representatives.

POLITICAL SYSTEM

Queen Elizabeth II is head of state and is represented by a Governor-General. Legislative power is vested in a bicameral parliament consisting of an elected 15-member House of Representatives and a 13-member Senate appointed by the Governor-General.

Governor-General, HE Sir Daniel Williams, GCMG, QC, apptd 1996

CABINET *as at July 1999*

Prime Minister, Finance, National Security, Mobilization, Finance, Trade, Industry, Foreign Affairs, Keith Mitchell
Minister of State, Agriculture, Forestry, Lands and Fisheries, Michael Baptiste
Communications, Works and Public Utilities, Gregory Bowen
Education, Augustine John
Health and Environment, Clarise Modest
Housing, Social Security, Women's Affairs, National Insurance, Laurina Waldron
Legal Affairs, Labour, Local Government, Carriacou and Petit Martinique Affairs, Elvin Nimrod
Tourism, Civil Aviation, Co-operatives, Joslyn Whiteman
Youth, Sports, Culture and Community Development, Adrian Mitchell

GRENADA HIGH COMMISSION
1 Collingham Gardens, London SW5 0HW
Tel 0171-373 7809
High Commissioner, HE Ruth Elizabeth Rouse, apptd 1999

BRITISH HIGH COMMISSION
14 Church Street, St George's
Tel: Grenada 440 3536/440 3222
High Commissioner, HE G. M. Baker, resident at Bridgetown, Barbados

ECONOMY

The economy is principally agrarian, with cocoa, nutmegs and bananas the major crops. Fruit and vegetables are grown and livestock raised for domestic consumption. The fishing industry is being developed. Manufacturing consists of processing agricultural products and the production of textiles, concrete, aluminium and handicrafts. Tourism is the main foreign exchange earner. In 1996 there were 386,013 tourists.

GNP – US$300 million (1997); US$3,140 per capita (1997)
GDP – US$229 million (1995); US$2,485 per capita (1995)
ANNUAL AVERAGE GROWTH OF GDP – –0.5 per cent (1995)
INFLATION RATE – 1.2 per cent (1997)
TOTAL EXTERNAL DEBT – US$105 million (1997)

TRADE

In 1996 there was a trade deficit of US$123 million and a current account deficit of US$58 million. Imports totalled US$152 million and exports US$21 million.

Trade with UK	1997	1998
Imports from UK	£7,010,000	£8,508,000
Exports to UK	1,050,000	744,000

GUATEMALA
República de Guatemala

AREA – 42,042 sq. miles (108,889 sq. km). Neighbours: Mexico (north and west), El Salvador, Honduras and Belize (east)
POPULATION – 10,928,000 (1994 UN estimate). The language is Spanish, but 40 per cent of the population speak an Indian language
CAPITAL – Guatemala City (population, 1,675,589, 1990 estimate)
MAJOR CITIES – Antigua (30,000); Mazatenango (21,000); ΨPuerto Barrios (23,000); Quezaltenango (100,000)
CURRENCY – Quetzal (Q) of 100 centavos
NATIONAL ANTHEM – Guatemala Feliz (Guatemala be praised)
NATIONAL DAY – 15 September
NATIONAL FLAG – Three vertical bands, blue, white, blue; coat of arms on white stripe
LIFE EXPECTANCY (years) – male 55.11; female 59.43
POPULATION GROWTH RATE – 2.6 per cent (1997)
POPULATION DENSITY – 100 per sq. km (1996)
URBAN POPULATION – 38.7 per cent (1995)
MILITARY EXPENDITURE – 1.5 per cent of GDP (1997)
MILITARY PERSONNEL – 41,200: Army 29,200, Navy 1,500, Air Force 700, Paramilitaries 9,800
CONSCRIPTION DURATION – 30 months
ILLITERACY RATE – 35.8 per cent
ENROLMENT (percentage of age group) – primary 58 per cent (1980); secondary 13 per cent (1980); tertiary 8.1 per cent (1995)

Guatemala is traversed from west to east by mountains containing volcanic summits rising to 13,000 feet above sea level; earthquakes are frequent. There are numerous rivers. The climate is hot and malarial near the coast, temperate in the higher regions.

HISTORY AND POLITICS

Guatemala was under Spanish rule from 1524 until gaining independence in 1821. It formed part of the Confederation of Central America from 1823 to 1839.

After a series of military coups, civilian rule was restored with the election of a Constituent Assembly in 1984 and the promulgation of a new constitution in 1985. In May 1993 President Serrano partially suspended the constitution and attempted to rule by decree but was effectively ousted by the army on 1 June. Ramiro de León Carpio was elected president by Congress to serve out Serrano's term to January 1996.

President de León continued attempts to curb political corruption and in November 1993 forced Congress and the Supreme Court to dissolve themselves and to agree to constitutional changes, including reducing the presidential term to four years, which were ratified by a referendum in January 1994. Legislative elections to a smaller 80-seat National Congress were held in August 1994. Elections to the National Congress in November 1995 were won by the National Advancement Party (PAN) which won 43 seats to the Guatemalan Republican Front's 21. The presidential election in January 1996 was won by Alvaro Arzú of the PAN.

INSURGENCY

Since 1960 the armed forces have been fighting insurgency by the left-wing, mainly Mayan Indian, guerrillas of the Guatemalan Revolutionary National Unity Movement (URNG). Some 200,000 have been killed in the fighting. Government–URNG negotiations began in 1991 and have continued since, leading to a reduction in fighting and agreements in 1993. In March 1994 a human rights accord was reached under which a 300-strong UN Observer Mission (MINUGUA) was established in November 1994 to supervise the implementation of government–URNG accords. An accord recognizing the rights of the indigenous population was signed in March 1995, but in a referendum held on 16 May 1999, constitutional reforms which would have recognized the rights of the majority indigenous population and limited the powers of the military were rejected. Representatives of the four rebel groups comprising the URNG signed a peace treaty with the government in December 1996; an independent commission into the 36-year civil war, set up under the 1996 peace treaty, published a report on 25 February 1999 which concluded that the army had committed acts of genocide against the indigenous Mayan population.

POLITICAL SYSTEM

Executive power is vested in the president, who is directly elected for a single four-year term. He appoints the Cabinet. Legislative authority is vested in the National Congress, whose 80 members are directly elected for a four-year term.

The republic is divided into 22 departments.

HEAD OF STATE

President, Alvaro Arzú Irigoyen, *sworn in* 14 January 1996
Vice-President, Luís Alberto Flores Asturias

GOVERNMENT *as at July 1999*

Agriculture, Livestock and Food, Mariano Ventura
Communications, Fritz García Gallont
Culture, Augusto Vela
Defence, Gen. Héctor Mario Barrios Zelada
Economy, Juan Wurmser
Education, Arabella Castro
Energy, Leonel López
Foreign Affairs, Eduardo Stein
Interior, Rodolfo Mendoza
Labour and Social Security, Luis Linares
Public Finance, Peter Lamport
Public Health, Marco Tulio Sosa
Secretary-General of the Presidency, Carlos García

EMBASSY OF GUATEMALA

13 Fawcett Street, London SW10 9HN
Tel 0171-351 3042
Ambassador Extraordinary and Plenipotentiary, HE Fernando Andrade Díaz-Duran, apptd 1996

BRITISH EMBASSY

Avenida La Reforma 16–00, Zona 10, Edificio Torre Internacional, Nivel 11, Guatemala City
Tel: Guatemala City 367 5425/6/7/8/9
Ambassador Extraordinary and Plenipotentiary, HE Andrew Caie, apptd 1998

ECONOMY

Agriculture provides 25 per cent of GDP and employs nearly two thirds of the workforce. The principal export is coffee, other articles being manufactured goods, sugar, bananas and cardamom. The chief imports are petroleum, vehicles, machinery and foodstuffs.

The chief seaports are San José de Guatemala and Champerico on the Pacific and Santo Tomás de Castilla and Puerto Barrios on the Atlantic side.

In 1996 there was a trade deficit of US$643 million and a current account deficit of US$452 million. In 1997 imports totalled US$3,852 million and exports US$2,344 million.

GNP – US$16,582 million (1997) (1996); US$1,580 per capita (1997)
GDP – US$14,783 million (1995); US$1,392 per capita (1995)
ANNUAL AVERAGE GROWTH OF GDP – 4.1 per cent (1997)
INFLATION RATE – 9.2 per cent (1997)
TOTAL EXTERNAL DEBT – US$4,086 million (1997)

Trade with UK	1997	1998
Imports from UK	£33,052,000	£38,701,000
Exports to UK	15,893,000	23,740,000

GUINEA
République de Guinée

AREA – 94,926 sq. miles (245,857 sq. km). Neighbours: Guinea-Bissau (east), Senegal and Mali (north), Côte d'Ivoire (west), Sierra Leone and Liberia (south)
POPULATION – 7,518,000 (1994 UN estimate); the official language is French; Fullah, Malinké and Soussou are indigenous languages
CAPITAL – ΨConakry (population, 763,000)
MAJOR CITIES – Kankan; Kindia; Labé; Mamou; N'Zérékoré; Siguiri
CURRENCY – Guinea franc of 100 centimes
NATIONAL DAY – 2 October (Anniversary of Proclamation of Independence)
NATIONAL FLAG – Three vertical stripes of red, yellow and green
LIFE EXPECTANCY (years) – male 44.00; female 45.00
POPULATION GROWTH RATE – 2.6 per cent (1997)
POPULATION DENSITY – 31 per sq. km (1996)
MILITARY EXPENDITURE – 1.6 per cent of GDP (1997)
MILITARY PERSONNEL – 12,300: Army 8,500, Navy 400, Air Force 800, Paramilitaries 2,600
CONSCRIPTION DURATION – Two years
ILLITERACY RATE – 64.1 per cent
ENROLMENT (percentage of age group) – primary 37 per cent (1993); secondary 9 per cent (1985); tertiary 1.2 per cent (1995)

HISTORY AND POLITICS

Guinea was separated from Senegal in 1891 and administered by France as a separate colony. On 2 October 1958 Guinea became an independent republic.

M. Sékou Touré assumed office as head of the new government, and was elected president in 1961. His death in 1984 was followed by a military coup. Guinea was ruled by a military government directed by a Military Committee for National Recovery (CMRN). A new constitution, providing for the end of military rule, was approved by referendum in 1990.

In January 1991 the CMRN was dissolved and a mixed civilian-military Transitional Committee for National Recovery (CTRN) was established which appointed a new government. Civil disturbances in 1991 caused the government to introduce a full multiparty system in April 1992, since when 40 opposition parties have been legalized. Legislative elections in June 1995 were won by President

Conté's Party of Unity and Progress (PUP), which gained 71 of the 114 National Assembly seats. A presidential election held on 14 December 1998 was won by the incumbent President Conté with 54 per cent of the vote.

HEAD OF STATE
President, Maj.-Gen. Lansana Conté, took power 3 April 1984, elected 19 December 1993, re-elected 14 December 1998

COUNCIL OF MINISTERS as at July 1999
Prime Minister, Co-ordinator of Government Actions, Lamine Sidime
Agriculture and Animal Husbandry, Jean-Paul Sarr
Communication, Alpha Abdoulaye Mongo Diallo
Commerce, Industry and Small and Medium-sized Enterprises, Madi Kaba Camara
Defence, Assifat Dorank Diasseny
Economic Affairs, Finance, Ibrahima Kassory Fofana
Employment and Civil Service, Lamine Kamara
Fishing and Marine Resources, Mansa Moussa Sidibe
Foreign Affairs, Zaïnoul Abidine Sanoussy
Higher Education and Scientific Research, Eugène Camara
Interior, Decentralization, Moussa Solano
Justice, Keeper of the Seals, Maurice Zogbélémou Togba
Mines, Geology and Environment, Facinet Fofana
Planning and International Co-operation, Thierno Mamadou Cellou Diallo
Pre-University Teaching and Civil Education, Germain Doualamou
Public Health, Dr Kandjoura Drame
Public Works, Transport, Cellou Dalen Diallo
Secretary-General to the Government, El Hadj Ousmane Sanoko
Secretary-General to the President, El Hadj Fodé Bangoura
Security, Sékou Goureissy Conde
Social Affairs, Promotion of Women and Children, Mariama Aribot
Technical Education and Vocational Training, Almamy Fodé Sylla
Tourism, Hotels and Handicrafts, Kozo Zoumanigui
Urbanization and Housing, Alpha Ousmane Diallo
Water Resources and Energy, Fassou Niankoye Sagno
Youth, Sports and Culture, Sylla Koumba Diakite

EMBASSY OF THE REPUBLIC OF GUINEA
51 rue de la Faisanderie, F-75016 Paris, France
Tel: Paris 4704 8148
Ambassador Extraordinary and Plenipotentiary, HE Ibrahima Sylla, apptd 1998

BRITISH CONSULATE
BP 834 Conakry, Guinea
British Ambassador, HE David Snoxell, resident at Dakar, Senegal

ECONOMY

The principal products are bauxite, alumina, palm kernels, millet, cassava, bananas, plantains and rubber. Deposits of iron ore, gold, diamonds and uranium have been discovered. Principal imports are cotton goods, petroleum products, sugar, flour and salt; exports, bauxite, alumina, iron ore, diamonds, coffee, bananas, palm kernels and pineapples.

In 1996 there was a trade surplus of US$111 million and a current account deficit of US$177 million.
GNP – US$3,830 million (1997); US$550 per capita (1997)
GDP – US$3,245 million (1995); US$442 per capita (1995)
ANNUAL AVERAGE GROWTH OF GDP – 4.0 per cent (1995)

TOTAL EXTERNAL DEBT – US$3,520 million (1997)

Trade with UK	1997	1998
Imports from UK	£17,091,000	£10,684,000
Exports to UK	1,017,000	2,191,000

GUINEA–BISSAU
República da Guiné-Bissau

AREA – 13,948 sq. miles (36,125 sq. km). Neighbours: Senegal (north), Guinea (east and south)
POPULATION – 1,091,000 (1994 UN estimate). The main ethnic groups are the Balante, Malinké, Fulani, Mandjako and Pepel. The official language is Portuguese; most of the population speak Guinean Creole
CAPITAL – ΨBissau (population, 109,214, 1979)
CURRENCY – Franc CFA
NATIONAL DAY – 24 September (Independence Day)
NATIONAL FLAG – Horizontal bands of yellow over green with vertical red band in the hoist charged with a black star
LIFE EXPECTANCY (years) – male 41.92; female 45.12
POPULATION GROWTH RATE – 2.2 per cent (1997)
POPULATION DENSITY – 30 per sq. km (1996)
MILITARY EXPENDITURE – 2.6 per cent of GDP (1997)
MILITARY PERSONNEL – 9,250: Army 6,800, Navy 350, Air Force 100, Paramilitaries 2,000
CONSCRIPTION DURATION – Selective conscription conscription
ILLITERACY RATE – 73.5 per cent
ENROLMENT (percentage of age group) – primary 46 per cent (1986); secondary 3 per cent (1980); tertiary 0.5 per cent (1988)

HISTORY AND POLITICS

Guinea-Bissau, formerly Portuguese Guinea, achieved independence on 24 September 1974. Following a coup led by Maj. (now Brig.-Gen.) Vieira in 1980, a Revolutionary Council was established. Under a new constitution adopted in 1984, the Revolutionary Council became a 15-member Council of State and an Assembly of 150 members was set up. The ruling African Party for the Independence of Guinea and Cape Verde (PAIGC) introduced a multiparty system in January 1991. Ten opposition parties have been legalized since November 1991. Elections to a new 100-seat legislature were held in July 1994; the PAIGC won 64 seats. Brig.-Gen. Vieira won the second round of the presidential election in August 1994 with 52 per cent of the vote.

In June 1998, several hundred people were killed when fighting broke out in Bissau between troops loyal to President Vieira and supporters of the sacked army chief Ansumane Mane. Guinea and Senegal sent in troops to support Vieira, and a peace agreement was signed on 1 November, which promised legislative and presidential elections in March 1999. On 27 November, the National Assembly called on Vieira to resign, but he refused. A government of national unity was formed in February 1999 and Guinean and Senegalese troops withdrew in March in accordance with the peace agreement, but no elections took place. Fighting resumed in May 1999, and the government was overthrown on 7 May by rebels loyal to Gen. Mane, who appointed the Speaker of the National Assembly as acting president.

HEAD OF STATE
Acting President, Malam Bacai Sanha, appointed 14 May 1999

COUNCIL OF MINISTERS *as at May 1999*
Prime Minister, Francisco Fadul

EMBASSY OF THE REPUBLIC OF GUINEA-BISSAU
94 rue St Lazare, Paris F-75009, France
Tel: Paris 4526 1851
Chargé d'Affaires, Maria Filomena Araujo Vieira

HONORARY CONSULATE
Flat 5, 8 Palace Gate, London W8 5NF
Tel: 0171-589 5253
Honorary Consul, Raja Makarem

BRITISH CONSULATE
Mavegro Int., CP100, Bissau
British Ambassador, HE David Snoxell, resident at Dakar,
   Senegal

ECONOMY

Guinea-Bissau produces rice, coconuts, groundnuts and plantains. Cattle are raised, and there are bauxite and phosphate deposits. In May 1997 Guinea-Bissau joined the French Franc Zone, and the CFA Franc replaced the peso as currency.

In 1995 there was a trade deficit of US$35 million and a current account deficit of US$41 million. In 1996 imports totalled US$87 million and exports US$27 million.

GNP – US$264 million (1997); US$230 per capita (1997)
GDP – US$141 million (1995); US$131 per capita (1995)
ANNUAL AVERAGE GROWTH OF GDP – 1.0 per cent
   (1995)
INFLATION RATE – 49.1 per cent (1997)
TOTAL EXTERNAL DEBT – US$921 million (1997)

Trade with UK	1997	1998
Imports from UK	£1,348,000	£722,000
Exports to UK	168,000	17,000

GUYANA
The Co-operative Republic of Guyana

AREA – 83,000 sq. miles (214,969 sq. km). Neighbours: Venezuela (west), Brazil (west and south), Suriname (east)
POPULATION – 838,000 (1994 UN estimate): 51 per cent East Indian (mainly rural), 30 per cent African (mainly urban), Amerindians, Europeans, Chinese and people of mixed descent; 50 per cent Christian, 35 per cent Hindu, less than 10 per cent Muslim. Guyana is the only English-speaking country in South America
CAPITAL – ΨGeorgetown (population, 250,000)
MAJOR TOWNS – Corriverton (24,000); Linden (35,000); ΨNew Amsterdam (25,000)
CURRENCY – Guyana dollar (G$) of 100 cents
NATIONAL ANTHEM – Dear Land of Guyana
NATIONAL DAYS – 26 May (Independence Day); 23 February (Republic Day)
NATIONAL FLAG – Green with a yellow, white-bordered triangle based on the hoist and surmounted by a red, black-bordered triangle
LIFE EXPECTANCY (years) – male 62.44; female 68.02
POPULATION GROWTH RATE – 0.9 per cent (1997)
POPULATION DENSITY – 4 per sq. km (1996)
MILITARY EXPENDITURE – 1.0 per cent of GDP (1997)
MILITARY PERSONNEL – 1,517: Army 1,400, Navy 17, Air Force 100

HISTORY AND POLITICS

Guyana (formerly British Guiana) became independent on 26 May 1966, with a Governor-General appointed by Queen Elizabeth II. It became a republic on 23 February 1970.

Elections were held in October 1992 after voter registration lists and electoral machinery had finally been established after many years. In the presidential election Dr Cheddi Jagan defeated the incumbent Desmond Hoyte and in the legislative election Jagan's People's Progressive Party (PPP) defeated the People's National Congress (PNC) which had governed since independence. Jagan died in March 1997 and was replaced by former Prime Minister Samuel Hinds. In the December 1997 election, Janet Jagan (who had previously served as prime minister and was the widow of the late president) was elected president and the PPP returned to power. The PNC claimed the result was fixed and their demonstrations against the government became violent; in January 1998 an agreement was reached between the PNC and the PPP whereby the constitution would be reviewed within 18 months and new elections would be held within three years rather than five.

POLITICAL SYSTEM

The 1980 constitution provides for an executive president who serves a five-year term, and a National Assembly of 65 members, of which 53 are elected nationally by proportional representation and 12 are regional representatives.

HEAD OF STATE
President, Janet Jagan, *elected* 15 December 1997
First Vice-President, Finance, Bharrat Jagdeo

CABINET *as at July 1999*

Prime Minister,Home Affairs and Public Works, Sam Hinds
Agriculture, Reepu Daman Persaud
Amerindian Affairs, Vibert de Souza
Attorney-General, Legal Affairs, Charles Ramson
Education, Ramnauth Bisnauth
Foreign Affairs, Clement Rohee
Forestry, Fisheries, Crops and Livestock, Satyadeow Sawh
Housing and Water, Shaik Baksh
Human Services, Social Security, Indranie Chandarpal
Information, Moses Nagamootoo
Labour, Health, Henry Jeffrey
Local Government, Harripersaud Nokta;
   Clinton Collymore
Presidential Secretariat, Roger Luncheon
Public Service, George Fung-on
Trade, Tourism and Industry, Michael Shree Chan
Transport and Hydraulics, Carl Anthony Xavier
Youth, Sport and Culture, Gail Teixeira

GUYANA HIGH COMMISSION
3 Palace Court, Bayswater Road, London W2 4LP
Tel 0171-229 7684
High Commissioner, HE Laleshwar Singh, apptd 1993

BRITISH HIGH COMMISSION
44 Main Street (PO Box 10849), Georgetown
Tel: Georgetown 65881/4
High Commissioner, HE Edward Glover, MVO, apptd 1998

ECONOMY

Agriculture is the principal economic activity. The economy is based almost entirely on the main export items of Demerara sugar, rice, shrimps, gold and rum. Diamonds are also mined. There is some cattle ranching in the savanna country, and oil deposits have been found there. Industry is fairly small-scale. Much emphasis is now being placed on eco-tourism. Foreign aid covers much of the government deficit.

In 1995 there was a trade deficit of US$41 million and a current account deficit of US$135 million. In 1997 exports totalled US$596 million.

GNP – US$677 million (1997); US$800 per capita (1997)
GDP – US$603 million (1995); US$726 per capita (1995)
ANNUAL AVERAGE GROWTH OF GDP – 5.5 per cent (1995)
INFLATION RATE – 2.6 per cent (1992)
TOTAL EXTERNAL DEBT – US$1,671 million (1997)

Trade with UK	1997	1998
Imports from UK	£25,774,000	£23,282,000
Exports to UK	81,852,000	71,895,000

COMMUNICATIONS

Georgetown and New Amsterdam are the principal ports, though bauxite ships also sail to Linden, on the Demerara, and Everton, on the Berbice. The few roads are confined mainly to the coastal areas. Paved roads total about 571 km out of a total network of 7,820 km. Air transport is the easiest form of communication between the coast and the interior. The state-owned national airline is called Guyana Airways.

There is a state-owned radio broadcasting station which operates two channels and a fledgling television service.

EDUCATION

Education is compulsory between the ages of five and 14; nursery, primary and secondary schooling are free. The government assumed total control of the education system in 1976 and made education free. The government instituted fees for study at the University of Guyana in 1994.

There are several technical and vocational institutions, as well as some 30 adult education schools. There are also a number of technical and vocational institutions not under the aegis of the Ministry of Education.

ILLITERACY RATE – 1.9 per cent
ENROLMENT (percentage of age group) – primary 87 per cent (1995); secondary 66 per cent (1992); tertiary 9.7 per cent (1995)

HAITI
République d'Haiti

AREA – 10,714 sq. miles (27,750 sq. km). Neighbour: Dominican Republic (east)
POPULATION – 7,336,000 (1994 UN estimate) of which 90 per cent are black and 10 per cent mulatto (mixed race). Both French and Creole are regarded as official languages. French is the language of government and the press but it is only spoken by the educated mulatto minority. The usual language is Creole
CAPITAL – ΨPort-au-Prince (population, 846,247, 1990 estimate)
MAJOR CITIES – ΨCap Haitien (54,691); Gonaives (36,736); Jérémie (25,117); Les Cayes (27,222)
CURRENCY – Gourde of 100 centimes
NATIONAL ANTHEM – La Dessalinienne
NATIONAL DAY – 1 January
NATIONAL FLAG – Horizontally blue over red
LIFE EXPECTANCY (years) – male 54.95; female 58.34
POPULATION GROWTH RATE – 2.1 per cent (1997)
POPULATION DENSITY – 264 per sq. km (1996)
URBAN POPULATION – 33.2 per cent (1996)

MILITARY EXPENDITURE – 5.2 per cent of GDP (1997)
ILLITERACY RATE – 55.0 per cent
ENROLMENT (percentage of age group) – primary 26 per cent (1990); tertiary 1.1 per cent (1985)

The Republic of Haiti occupies the western third of the Caribbean island of Hispaniola. The climate is tropical with high humidity and an almost constant temperature.

HISTORY AND POLITICS

Haiti was a French slave colony under the name of Saint-Domingue from 1697 until 1791, when French rule was overthrown in a revolt led by Toussaint L'Ouverture. French rule was restored by Napoleon in 1802 but in 1803 French forces surrendered to a British naval blockade and on 1 January 1804 the colony was declared independent as Haiti by Jean Jacques Dessalines. Dessalines became Emperor of Haiti but was assassinated in 1806.

Haiti was under US military occupation from 1915 to 1934. Dr François 'Papa Doc' Duvalier was elected in 1957 and became life president in 1964. He was succeeded in 1971 by his son Jean-Claude 'Baby Doc' Duvalier who fled to France in 1986 in the face of sustained popular unrest. Five years of military government followed until Father Jean-Bertrand Aristide, leader of the National Front for Change and Democracy, won a free presidential election in 1990.

Aristide fled to the USA following a military coup in September 1991. The UN and OAS imposed an oil and arms embargo and froze the military élite's foreign assets, forcing the regime to negotiate the Governor's Island Agreement in July 1993, which provided for Aristide's return. In September 1993, the military reneged on the agreement and the UN imposed a naval blockade and a total economic, trade and travel ban. In September 1994, an agreement was reached on President Aristide's return and the flight of the military junta members abroad. Sanctions were lifted and Aristide returned on 15 October to appoint a new government. Forces of the UN Mission in Haiti (UNMIH) took over responsibility for internal security and retraining Army personnel on 31 March 1995. At the expiration of the UNMIH peacekeeping mandate in November 1997, the UN Security Council agreed to establish a civilian police mission to continue training the Haitian police force for a further 12 months.

Elections to the 27-member Senate and 83-member Chamber of Deputies in June to August 1995 were won by the pro-Aristide Lavalas party. The presidential election in December 1995 was won by Lavalas candidate René Préval. Following the resignation of Prime Minister Rosny Smarth in October 1997, the President and the legislature were unable to agree on a successor and Haiti had no prime minister until 12 January 1999, when the appointment of Jacques Édouard Alexis was confirmed by a presidential decree, after the Senate but not the Chamber of Deputies had approved the appointment.

POLITICAL SYSTEM

The head of state is a president, directly elected for a five-year term that may not be renewed immediately. The National Assembly is the bicameral legislature; the lower house, the Chamber of Deputies, has 83 members directly elected for four years. The upper house or Senate has 27 members elected for six years; one third of the senators are elected every two years. The president appoints the prime minister, who must be approved by the National Assembly. The prime minister chooses the Cabinet.

HEAD OF STATE
President, René Préval, *sworn in* 7 February 1996

CABINET *as at July 1999*

Prime Minister, Interior, Territorial Communities, Jacques Édouard Alexis
Agriculture, Natural Resources and Rural Development, François Severin
Commerce and Industry, Gerald Germain
Culture, Jean-Robert Vaval
Economy and Finance, Fred Joseph
Environment, Yves Cadet
Foreign Affairs, Emmanuel Fritz Longchamp
Haitians Abroad, Jean Geneus
Justice and Public Safety, Camille Leblanc
National Education, Youth and Sport, Paul André Bien-Aimé
Labour and Social Affairs, Mathilde Flambert
Planning and External Co-operation, Antony Dessources
Public Health and Population, Michaelle Amede Gedeon
Public Works, Transport and Communications, Max Alce
Women's Affairs and Rights, Nemy Mathieu

BRITISH AMBASSADOR, HE David Ward, resident at Santo Domingo, Dominican Republic

ECONOMY

Coffee accounts for about one third of total exports. Cocoa is the second largest export earner. Corn, sorghum and rice are also grown. Increased production of tropical fruits and vegetables is being encouraged.

Leather goods, textiles, electronic components and sports equipment are manufactured, using imported raw materials, for re-export. Principal imports are raw materials for the export assembly sector, foodstuffs, machinery, vehicles, mineral oils and textiles.

In 1996 Haiti had a trade deficit of US$416 million and a current account deficit of US$138 million. In 1997 imports totalled US$648 million and exports US$120 million.

GNP – US$2,864 million (1997); US$380 per capita (1997)
GDP – US$2,750 million (1995); US$386 per capita (1995)
ANNUAL AVERAGE GROWTH OF GDP – 1.1 per cent (1997)
INFLATION RATE – 20.6 per cent (1997)
TOTAL EXTERNAL DEBT – US$1,057 million (1997)

Trade with UK	1997	1998
Imports from UK	£8,746,000	£8,254,000
Exports to UK	1,359,000	979,000

COMMUNICATIONS

There are more than 4,000 km of roads. Air services are maintained between the capital and the principal provincial towns and to the USA and Caribbean and South American countries. The principal towns and villages are connected by telephone and/or telegraph. There are several commercial radio stations and two television stations at Port-au-Prince.

HOLY SEE, *see* VATICAN CITY STATE

HONDURAS
República de Honduras

AREA – 43,277 sq. miles (112,088 sq. km). Neighbours: Guatemala (north-west), El Salvador (south-west), Nicaragua (south)
POPULATION – 6,140,000 (1996 UN estimate) of mixed Spanish and Indian blood. The Garifunas in the north are of West Indian origin. The language is Spanish, although English is the first language of many in the islands and on the north coast

CAPITAL – Tegucigalpa (population, 670,100, 1991 estimate)
MAJOR CITIES – Choluteca (63,200); ΨLa Ceiba (77,100); ΨPuerto Cortés (32,500); San Pedro Sula (325,900); ΨTela (24,000)
CURRENCY – Lempira of 100 centavos
NATIONAL ANTHEM – Tu Bandera Es Un Lampo De Cielo (Your flag is a heavenly light)
NATIONAL DAY – 15 September
NATIONAL FLAG – Three horizontal bands, blue, white, blue (with five blue stars on white band)
LIFE EXPECTANCY (years) – male 65.43; female 70.06
POPULATION GROWTH RATE – 2.9 per cent (1997)
POPULATION DENSITY – 55 per sq. km (1996)
URBAN POPULATION – 48.3 per cent (1996)
MILITARY EXPENDITURE – 2.1 per cent of GDP (1997)
MILITARY PERSONNEL – 14,300: Army 5,500, Navy 1,000, Air Force 1,800, Paramilitaries 6,000

The country is mountainous, being traversed by the Cordilleras, with peaks rising to 1,500 and 2,400 metres above sea level. Rainfall is seasonal, May to October being wet and November to April dry.

HISTORY AND POLITICS

Discovered and settled by the Spanish in the 16th century, Honduras formed part of the Spanish American dominions until 1821 when independence was proclaimed. Under military government from 1972, Honduras returned to civilian rule in 1981 with an executive presidency, a 128-seat unicameral Congress, and a multiparty system. The most recent legislative elections were held on 30 November 1997 and won by the Liberal Party. In October 1997, Congress approved a constitutional amendment reducing the legislature to 80 members. The amendment must also be ratified by the current session of Congress before it becomes law.

The country is divided into 18 departments.

HEAD OF STATE
President of the Republic, Carlos Roberto Flores (Liberal), *elected* 30 November 1997

CABINET *as at July 1999*

Agriculture and Livestock, Guillermo Alvarado
Culture, Arts and Sports, Herman Allan Padget
Director of the National Agrarian Institute, Anibal Delgado Fiallos
Education, Ramón Calix Figueroa
Finance, Gabriela Nuñez López
Foreign Affairs, Roberto Flores Bermúdez
Government and Justice, Enrique Flores Valeriano
Health, Plutarco Castellanos
Industry, Commerce, Reginaldo Panting
Labour and Social Security, Rosa America de Galo
Ministers without Portfolio, Jorge Arturo Reina; Nahum Valladares; Roberto Leiva
National Defence and Public Security, Edgardo Dumas Rodríguez
Natural Resources and Environment, Xiomara Gómez
Presidential Office, Gustavo Alfaro
Public Works, Transport and Housing, Tomás Lozano Reyes
Security, Elizabeth Chiuz Sierra
Social Investment Fund, Manuel Zelaya Rosales
Technical and International Co-operation Secretariat, Moises Starkman
Tourism, Norman García

EMBASSY OF HONDURAS
115 Gloucester Place, London WIH 3PJ
Tel 0171-486 4880

Ambassador Extraordinary and Plenipotentiary, HE Iván
Romero-Nasser, apptd 1999

BRITISH EMBASSY
Apartado Postal 290, Tegucigalpa
Tel: Honduras 232 0612/18
Ambassador Extraordinary and Plenipotentiary, HE David
Osbourne, apptd 1998
BRITISH CONSULATE – San Pedro Sula

ECONOMY

Three-quarters of the country is covered by pine forests.
Agriculture and cattle raising is mainly confined to the
fertile coastal plain on the Caribbean and the extensive
valleys in the Comayagua and Olancho regions of the
interior. The Mosquitia tropical forest covers the area from
the coast to the border with Nicaragua and provides
valuable reserves of timber. Lead, zinc and silver are mined
on a small scale.

The chief exports are coffee, bananas, frozen meat,
shrimps, lobsters and timber, the most important woods
being pine, mahogany and cedar. The main imports are
machinery and electrical equipment, industrial chemicals
and lubricants.

In October 1998 Hurricane Mitch devastated Honduras,
killing an estimated 6,500 people and wrecking Tegucigalpa. The cost of repairing the damage was estimated at
US$4 billion.

In 1995 Honduras had a trade deficit of US$141 million
and a current account deficit of US$201 million. In 1997
imports totalled US$2,048 million and exports US$1,443
million.

GNP – US$4,426 million (1997); US$740 per capita
(1997)
GDP – US$3,944 million (1995); US$697 per capita
(1995)
ANNUAL AVERAGE GROWTH OF GDP – 4.5 per cent
(1997)
INFLATION RATE – 20.2 per cent (1997)
UNEMPLOYMENT – 3.2 per cent (1995)
TOTAL EXTERNAL DEBT – US$4,698 million (1997)

Trade with UK	1997	1998
Imports from UK	£13,677,000	£18,074,000
Exports to UK	35,596,000	33,785,000

COMMUNICATIONS

There are about 595 km of railway in operation, chiefly to
serve the banana plantations and the Caribbean ports.
There are 15,100 km of roads, of which 3,050 km are paved.
There are over 80 smaller airstrips and four international
airports, Tegucigalpa, San Pedro Sula, La Ceiba and
Roatún (Bay Island).

The chief ports are Puerto Cortés, Tela and Puerto
Castilla on the north coast, through which passes the bulk
of the trade with the USA and Europe. Puerto Castilla is
being developed as a deep-water container port, and San
Lorenzo is also experiencing rapid growth.

EDUCATION

Primary and secondary education is free, primary education
being compulsory from the age of seven to 12, and the
government has launched a campaign to eradicate illiteracy.
ILLITERACY RATE – 27.3 per cent
ENROLMENT (percentage of age group) – primary 90 per
cent (1993); secondary 21 per cent (1991); tertiary 10.0
per cent (1994)

HUNGARY
Magyar Köztársaság

AREA – 35,920 sq. miles (93,032 sq. km). Neighbours:
Slovakia (north), Ukraine and Romania (east), the rump
Yugoslav Federal state and Croatia (south), Slovenia
and Austria (west)
POPULATION – 10,193,000 (1994 UN estimate). There
are minorities of gypsies (4 per cent), ethnic Germans
(3 per cent), Serbs (2 per cent), Romanians (1 per cent)
and Slovaks (1 per cent). About two-thirds of the
population are Roman Catholic and the remainder
mostly Calvinist. The language is Hungarian (Magyar)
CAPITAL – Budapest, on the Danube (population,
2,002,121, 1993 estimate)
MAJOR CITIES – Debrecen (214,245); Miskolc (185,877);
Pécs (167,772); Szeged (173,860)
CURRENCY – Forint of 100 fillér
NATIONAL ANTHEM – Isten Aldd Meg A Magyart (God
Bless the Hungarians)
NATIONAL DAYS – 15 March, 20 August, 23 October
NATIONAL FLAG – Red, white, green (horizontally)
LIFE EXPECTANCY (years) – male 64.84; female 74.23
POPULATION GROWTH RATE – –0.3 per cent (1997)
POPULATION DENSITY – 110 per sq. km (1996)
URBAN POPULATION – 63.0 per cent (1995)

HISTORY AND POLITICS

The Hungarians settled the Danube basin in 896 AD and in
1000, King Istvan (Stephen) adopted Roman Catholicism
and received a crown from the Pope. The Turks invaded
Hungary in 1526; the Austrians finally succeeded in
expelling them in 1699. Following nationalist unrest, the
Ausgleich (compromise) of 1867 created the Dual Monarchy
of Austria-Hungary, giving Hungary internal autonomy.
The defeat of Austria-Hungary in the First World War led
to the declaration of Hungarian independence in November
1918.

Hungary joined the Anti-Comintern Pact in February
1939 and entered the Second World War on the side of
Germany in 1941. On 20 January 1945 a Hungarian
provisional government of liberation signed an armistice
under the terms of which the frontiers of Hungary were
withdrawn to the 1937 limits.

After the liberation, a coalition of parties carried out
land reform and nationalization. By 1949 the Communists
had succeeded in gaining a monopoly of power and by
1952 practically the entire economy had been 'socialized'.

Divisions within the Communist Party and popular
demand for free elections and Soviet troop withdrawals
grew. An uprising on 23 October 1956 was quelled by
Soviet forces the following morning. But a reformist all-
party coalition government under Imre Nagy was formed
which declared Hungary's withdrawal from the Warsaw
pact. This government was suppressed by a renewed attack
by Soviet forces on Budapest on 4 November and a new
Communist government under János Kádár was announced
the same day.

From 1968 the government gradually introduced economic reforms and some political liberalization. Kádár was
forced to resign in May 1989. In October 1989 the National
Assembly (*Országgyülés*) approved an amended constitution
which described Hungary as an independent, democratic
state. The 386-seat National Assembly is elected on a
mixed first past the post and proportional representation
basis with a 5 per cent threshold for representation. The
first free multiparty elections took place in March and

April 1990 and were won by the (conservative) Hungarian Democratic Forum.

In the legislative elections in May 1998, no party won an overall majority. The Federation of Young Democrats-Hungarian Civic Party (Fidesz-MPP) won the largest number of seats and its leader, Viktor Orbán, was asked by President Göncz to form a coalition government. The composition of the National Assembly in June 1998 was: Fidesz-MPP 147, Hungarian Socialist Party (HSP) 134, Independent Smallholders Party (FKGP) 48, Alliance of Free Democrats (AFD) 24, Hungarian Democratic Forum (MDF) 18, Hungarian Justice and Life Party 14, others 1.

HEAD OF STATE

President, Árpád Göncz, *sworn in* 3 August 1990, *re-elected by parliament* 19 June 1995

CABINET *as at July 1999*

Prime Minister, Viktor Orbán (F)
Agriculture and Rural Development, József Torgyán (FKGP)
Defence, János Szabó (FKGP)
Economic Affairs, Attila Chikán (F)
Education, Zoltán Pokorni (F)
Environmental Protection, Pál Pepó (FKGP)
Finance, Zsigmond Járai (F)
Foreign Affairs, János Martonyi (F)
Health, Árpád Gógl (F)
Home Affairs, Sándor Pintér (F)
Justice, Ibolya Dávid (MDF)
National Cultural Heritage, József Hámori (F)
Social and Family Affairs, Péter Harrach (F)
Transport, Telecommunications and Water Management, Kálmán Katona (F)
Without Portfolio, László Kövér (F) *(Civil Security Services)*; Imre Boros (FKGP) *(PHARE Programme);* István Stumpf (F) *(Prime Minister's Office, Privatization)*
Youth and Sports, Tamás Deutsch (F)

F Fidesz-MPP; FKGP Independent Smallholders Party; MDF Hungarian Democratic Forum

EMBASSY OF THE REPUBLIC OF HUNGARY
35 Eaton Place, London SW1X 8BY
Tel 0171-235 5218
Ambassador Extraordinary and Plenipotentiary, HE Gábor Szentiványi, apptd 1997
Minister Plenipotentiary, Sándor Juhász
Counsellor and Consul-General, Dr Péter Kallós
Commercial Counsellor, Dr Jenó Hámori
Defence and Military Attaché, Col. István Lakatos

BRITISH EMBASSY
Harmincad Utca 6, H–1051 Budapest
Tel: Budapest 266-2888
Ambassador Extraordinary and Plenipotentiary, HE Nigel Thorpe, CVO, RCDS, apptd 1998
Counsellor and Deputy Head of Mission, G. B. Reid
Defence Attaché, Col. A. T. B. Kimber
First Secretary (Commercial), S. C. Martin
First Secretary (Management) and Consul, I. H. Davies

BRITISH COUNCIL DIRECTOR, P. Dick, OBE, Benczur Utca 26, H–1068 Budapest

DEFENCE

The Army has 835 main battle tanks, 527 armoured infantry fighting vehicles, 789 armoured personnel carriers and 840 pieces of artillery. The Air Force has 114 combat aircraft and 59 attack helicopters. Hungary became a member of NATO in March 1999.

MILITARY EXPENDITURE – 1.4 per cent of GDP (1997)

MILITARY PERSONNEL – 49,290: Army 23,400, Army Maritime Wing 290, Air Force 11,500, Paramilitaries 14,100

CONSCRIPTION DURATION – Nine months

ECONOMY

Agriculture accounts for around 8 per cent of GDP and employs 8 per cent of the workforce. Production is concentrated on maize, wheat, sugar beet, barley, rye and oats.

Industry is mainly based on imported raw materials but Hungary has its own coal, bauxite, considerable deposits of natural gas, some iron ore and oil. Output figures in 1995 were: coal 14,461,000 tonnes; aluminium 34,900 tonnes; rolled steel 1,865,000 tonnes; crude petroleum 1,669,000 tonnes. Natural gas production totalled 5,365 million cubic metres.

The economy has suffered from the loss of export markets in the Soviet Union and the former Yugoslavia, and the transition to a market economy. With the exception of the engineering sector, industrial output declined in 1996.

Privatization and the establishment of small businesses proved successful in 1990–4, aided by large-scale foreign investment. Some 40 per cent of state enterprises have been privatized. Hungary joined the OECD in March 1996. In February 1998, the IMF announced its decision not to renew Hungary's stand-by credit arrangement, on the basis that the Hungarian economy was now strong enough to operate without outside assistance.

In 1996 Hungary had a trade deficit of US$2,652 million and a current account deficit of US$1,689 million. Imports totalled US$15,896 million and exports US$12,686 million.

GNP – US$45,760 million (1997); US$4,510 per capita (1997)
GDP – US$43,712 million (1995); US$4,325 per capita (1995)
ANNUAL AVERAGE GROWTH OF GDP – 2.0 per cent (1995); estimated to be 3.2 per cent in 1997
INFLATION RATE – 18.3 per cent (1997)
UNEMPLOYMENT – 10.3 per cent (1995)
TOTAL EXTERNAL DEBT – US$24,373 million (1997)

Trade with UK	1997	1998
Imports from UK	£435,817,000	£500,190,000
Exports to UK	485,383,000	558,095,000

EDUCATION

There are five types of schools under the Ministry of Education: kindergartens for age three to six, general schools for age six to 14 (compulsory), vocational schools (15–18), secondary schools (15–18), universities and adult training schools (over 18).

ILLITERACY RATE – 0.8 per cent
ENROLMENT (percentage of age group) –
primary 97 per cent (1995); secondary 87 per cent (1995); tertiary 23.8 per cent (1995)

CULTURE

Magyar, or Hungarian, is one of the Finno-Ugrian languages. Hungarian literature began to flourish in the second half of the 16th century. Among the greatest writers of the 19th and 20th centuries are Mihály Vörösmarty (1800–55), Sándor Petöfi (1823–49), János Arany (1817–82), Imre Madách (1823–64), Kálmán Mikszáth (1847–1910), Endre Ady (1877–1918), Attila József (1905–37), Mihály Babits (1883–1941), Dezsö Kosztolányi (1885–1936), Gyula Illyes (1902–83), János Pilinszky (1921–81) and Sándor Weöres (1913–89).

ICELAND
Island

AREA – 39,769 sq. miles (103,000 sq. km)
POPULATION – 275,277 (1998). Some 92.2 per cent of the
population are members of the (Lutheran) Church of
Iceland. The language is Icelandic
CAPITAL – ΨReykjavík (population, 107,764, 1998)
MAJOR CITIES – Akranes; ΨAkureyri; Ψ Egilsstaðir;
    ΨHafnarfjörður; Isafjörður; Keflavík; Kópavogur;
    ΨSiglufjörður
CURRENCY – Icelandic króna (Kr) of 100 aurar
NATIONAL ANTHEM – O Gud Vors Lands (Our
    Country's God)
NATIONAL DAY – 17 June
NATIONAL FLAG – Blue, with white-bordered red cross
LIFE EXPECTANCY (years) – male 76.85; female 80.75
POPULATION GROWTH RATE – 0.9 per cent (1997)
POPULATION DENSITY – 3 per sq. km (1996)
URBAN POPULATION – 91.3 per cent (1993)
MILITARY PERSONNEL – 120 Paramilitaries

HISTORY AND POLITICS

Iceland was uninhabited before the ninth century, when
settlers came from Norway. For several centuries a form
of republican government prevailed, with an annual
assembly of leading men called the *Alþingi (Althingi)*, but in
1262 Iceland became subject to Norway, and later to
Denmark. During the colonial period, Iceland maintained
its cultural integrity but a deterioration in the climate,
together with frequent volcanic eruptions and outbreaks of
disease, led to a serious drop in living standards and to a
decline in the population to little more than 40,000. In the
19th century a struggle for independence led to home rule
in 1918 and to independence as a republic in 1944.

The parliamentary (*Althingi*) elections on 9 May 1999
gave the Independence Party 26 seats, Unified Left 17,
Progressives 12, Left-Green Alliance 6 and Liberals 2. A
coalition government of the Independence Party and the
Progressive Party was formed after the election.

HEAD OF STATE
President, Ólafur Ragnar Grímsson, *elected* 29 June 1996

CABINET *as at July 1999*
Prime Minister, Statistical Bureau of Iceland, David Oddsson
    (IP)
Agriculture, Gudni Ágústsson (PP)
Communications, Sturla Bödvarsson (IP)
Education and Culture, Björn Bjarnason (IP)
Environment, Siv Fridleifsdóttir (PP)
Finance, Geir Haarde (IP)
Fisheries, Árni Mathiesen (IP)
Foreign Affairs and External Trade, Halldór Ásgrímsson (PP)
Health and Social Security, Ingibjörg Pálmadóttir (PP)
Justice and Ecclesiastical Affairs, Sólveig Pétursdóttir (IP)
Social Affairs, Páll Pétursson (PP)
Trade and Industry, Finnur Ingólfsson (PP)

IP Independence Party; PP Progressive Party

EMBASSY OF ICELAND
1 Eaton Terrace, London SWIW 8EY
Tel 0171-590 1100
Ambassador Extraordinary and Plenipotentiary, HE
    Thorsteinn Pálsson, apptd 1999

BRITISH EMBASSY
Laufásvegur 31, 101 Reykjavík
Tel: Iceland 550 5100/1/2

*Ambassador Extraordinary and Plenipotentiary and Consul-
General,* HE James McCulloch, apptd 1996
CONSULATE – Akureyri

ECONOMY

Iceland has considerable resources of hydroelectric and
geothermal energy. Heavy industry includes an aluminium
smelter, a nitrogen fertilizer factory, a cement factory, a
diatomite plant and a ferro-silicon plant.

The major sectors of the economy are fishing and fish
processing, manufacturing, agriculture, energy production
and tourism, which is of growing importance with 232,219
visitors in 1998.

As a member of the European Free Trade Association
(EFTA), Iceland has become a member of the European
Economic Area (EEA) which extends most of the provisions
of the EU's single market to EFTA states.

In 1998 Iceland had a trade deficit of US$544 million
and a current account deficit of US$472 million. In 1998
imports totalled US$2,470 million and exports US$1,926
million.

GNP – US$7,175 million ; US$26,580 per capita
GDP – US$7,052 million (1995); US$26,217 per capita
    (1995)
ANNUAL AVERAGE GROWTH OF GDP – 5.0 per cent
    (1997)
INFLATION RATE – 1.7 per cent (1997)
UNEMPLOYMENT – 3.9 per cent (1997)

TRADE
The principal exports are fish and fish products, ferro-
silicon and aluminium; the chief imports are consumer
durables, petroleum products, transport equipment, textiles, foodstuffs, animal feeds and timber.

Trade with UK	1997	1998
Imports from UK	£158,329,000	£163,158,000
Exports to UK	242,664,000	264,829,000

COMMUNICATIONS

At 1 January 1998, the mercantile marine consisted of 978
registered vessels (271,116 gross tons). There are regular
shipping services between Reykjavík and Felixstowe,
Humber ports, Europe and the USA.

A regular air service is maintained by Icelandair between
Glasgow and London and Reykjavík. There are also air
services to Scandinavia, USA, Germany, France, the
Netherlands and Canada.

Road communications are adequate in summer but
greatly restricted by snow in winter. Only roads in town
centres and key highways are metalled, the rest being of
gravel, sand and lava dust. The climate and terrain make
first-class surfaces for highways out of the question. There
are no railways.

There are three television channels (one public, two
private) and several private and public radio stations.

CULTURE

The ancient Norraena (or Northern tongue) has close
affinities to Anglo-Saxon and as spoken and written in
Iceland today differs little from that introduced into the
island in the ninth century. There is a rich literature with
two distinct periods of development, from the mid-11th to
the late 13th century and from the early 19th century to
the present.

ENROLMENT (percentage of age group) – primary 98 per
    cent (1995); secondary 87 per cent (1995); tertiary 35.6
    per cent (1995)

INDIA
The Republic of India

AREA – 1,269,346 sq. miles (3,287,590 sq. km).
Neighbours: Pakistan (north-west), China, Tibet,
Nepal and Bhutan (north), Myanmar (east), Bangladesh
POPULATION – 970,930,000 (1998 estimate), 846,302,688
(1991 census): Hindu (82.41 per cent), the rest being
Muslim (11.67 per cent), Christian (2.32 per cent), Sikh
(1.99 per cent), Buddhist (0.77 per cent) and Jain (0.41
per cent). The official languages are Hindi in the
Devanagari script and English, though 17 regional
languages also are recognized for adoption as official
state languages
CAPITAL – New Delhi (population, 301,297; 8,419,084
including Delhi/Dilli), 1991
MAJOR CITIES – Ahmedabad (3,312,216); Bangalore
(4,130,288); ΨBombay/Mumbai (12,596,243);
ΨCalcutta/Kolkata (11,021,918); Hyderabad
(4,344,437); Kanpur (2,029,889); Lucknow (1,669,204);
ΨMadras/Chennai (5,421,985); Pune (2,493,987) (1991
figures)
CURRENCY – Indian rupee (Rs) of 100 paisa
NATIONAL ANTHEM – Jana-gana-mana
NATIONAL DAY – 26 January (Republic Day)
NATIONAL FLAG – A horizontal tricolour with bands of
deep saffron, white and dark green in equal
proportions. In the centre of the white band appears an
Asoka wheel in navy blue
LIFE EXPECTANCY (years) – male 57.70; female 58.10
POPULATION GROWTH RATE – 1.8 per cent (1997)
POPULATION DENSITY – 285 per sq. km (1996)
URBAN POPULATION – 26.3 per cent (1993)
ILLITERACY RATE – 48.0 per cent
ENROLMENT (percentage of age group) – tertiary 6.9 per
cent (1996)

India has three well-defined regions: the mountain range
of the Himalayas, the Indo–Gangetic plain, and the
southern peninsula. The main mountain ranges are the
Himalayas (over 29,000 feet) and the Western and Eastern
Ghats (over 8,000 feet). Major rivers include the Ganges,
Indus, Krishna, Godavari and Mahanadi.

Temperatures vary over the country between averages
of about 10°C and 33°C, reaching over 38°C in some parts
during the hot season. There are similar variations in
rainfall, from only a few inches a year falling in the western
Thar Desert to over 400 inches in Meghalaya.

HISTORY AND POLITICS

The Indus civilization was fully developed by *c*.2500 BC
but collapsed *c*.1750 BC, and was replaced by an Aryan
civilization from the west. Arab invasions of the north-west
began in the seventh century and Muslim, Hindu and
Buddhist states developed until the establishment of the
Mogul dynasty in 1526. The British East India Company
established settlements throughout the 17th century;
clashes with the French and native princes led to the
British government taking control of the company in 1784
and gradually extending sovereignty over the whole
subcontinent. The separate dominions of India and Pakistan
became independent within the Commonwealth on 15
August 1947 and India became a republic in 1950.

Between 1947 and 1996, India was ruled by the Congress
(I) Party for all but four times (March 1977–January 1980,
November 1989–June 1991). Congress (I) has been led by
members of the Nehru-Gandhi dynasty for most of the
post-independence period: Prime Ministers Jawaharlal

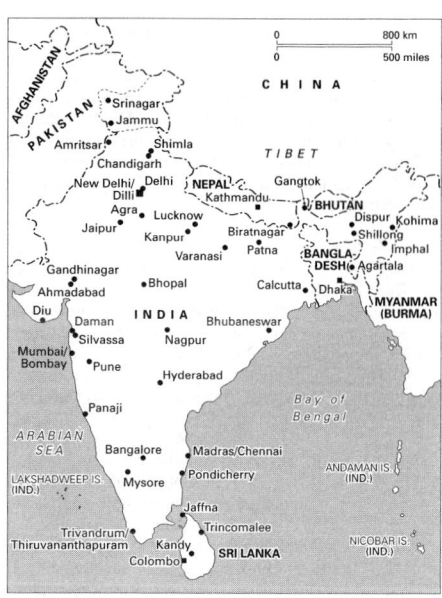

Nehru (1947–64), Indira Gandhi (1966–1977, 1980–84)
and Rajiv Gandhi (1984–89). Indira Gandhi was assassinated by Sikh extremists seeking an independent Sikh state
in Punjab; her son Rajiv was assassinated by Sri Lankan
Tamils.

In November 1997, the United Front government (a
coalition of Communist and low-caste parties) collapsed
after Congress (I) withdrew its support. The parliamentary
elections in February 1998 produced no outright winner;
in March 1998, the BJP formed a coalition government
under Atal Bihari Vajpayee, which collapsed following the
loss of a confidence motion on 17 April 1999. The
opposition parties were unable to form a majority government and parliament was dissolved on 26 April 1999 by
President Narayanan.

SECESSION

The Hindu Maharaja of Kashmir signed his state's
instrument of accession to India in October 1947, two
months after India and Pakistan became independent. This
was disputed by Pakistan, on the basis that the majority of
the state's population was Muslim. After three Indian-
Pakistani wars, a line of control was agreed under the 1972
Simla agreement (China has also occupied some of Kashmir
since the 1962 Sino-Indian war). The line was rejected by
armed groups which have waged a campaign of violence
against the Hindu population and against Indian security
forces. Kashmir was placed under direct rule in 1990 but
state assembly elections, held in September 1996, were
won by Jammu and Kashmir National Conference.

FOREIGN RELATIONS

India and Pakistan have fought three major wars since
independence, in 1947–8, 1965 and 1971. Since 1985 they
have continued a low-level war at altitude for control of
the Siachen glacier in Kashmir.

In May 1998, India conducted five underground nuclear
tests, confirming its status as a nuclear power. The tests
were condemned by the international community. Within
three weeks, Pakistan had conducted its own nuclear tests,
leading to fears that border confrontations between the two
countries could escalate into nuclear conflict.

On 20 May 1999 the Indian Air Force launched air attacks on Muslim insurgents who had occupied mountainous areas within Indian-controlled Kashmir; the Indian government accused Pakistan of sending more than 500 Islamist militants into Indian territory. Much of the lost territory was quickly recovered by the Indian Army; following mediation by the USA's President Clinton, on 9 July 1999, the Pakistani government asked the insurgents to withdraw.

POLITICAL SYSTEM

Executive power is vested in the president, elected for a five-year term by an electoral college consisting of the elected members of the Union and State legislatures. The president appoints the prime minister and, on the latter's advice, the ministers, and can dismiss them. The Council of Ministers is collectively responsible to the *Lok Sabha* (lower house). The vice-president is ex-officio chairman of the *Rajya Sabha* (upper house).

Legislative power rests with the president, the Rajya Sabha (245 members serving six-year terms) and the Lok Sabha (545 members). Twelve members of the Rajya Sabha are presidential nominees, the rest are indirectly elected representatives of the State and Union Territories. The 530 members of the Lok Sabha representing the States are directly elected by universal adult franchise, and 15 representatives of the Union Territories are chosen, for a maximum term of five years.

The Supreme Court consists of the Chief Justice and not more than 25 other judges, appointed by the president. It is the highest court in respect of all constitutional matters and the final Court of Appeal and is situated in New Delhi. Each state or group of states also has a High Court with a hierarchy of subordinate courts. The judges of the High Court of a state are appointed by the president.

FEDERAL STRUCTURE

There are 25 States and seven Union Territories. Each state is headed by a Governor, who is appointed by the president and holds office for five years, and by a Council of Ministers. All states have a Legislative Assembly, and some have also a Legislative Council, elected directly by adult suffrage for a maximum period of five years.

The Union Territories are administered, except where otherwise provided by Parliament, by the president acting through an Administrator or Lieutenant-Governor, or other authority appointed by him.

	Area (sq. km)	Population (1998 estimate)	Capital
STATES			
Andhra Pradesh	275,100	74,170,000	Hyderabad
Arunachal Pradesh	83,700	1,130,000	Itanagar
Assam	78,400	25,650,000	Dispur
Bihar	173,900	96,960,000	Patna
Goa	3,700	1,510,000	Panaji
Gujarat	196,000	47,100,000	Gandhinagar
Haryana	44,200	19,340,000	Chandigarh
Himachal Pradesh	55,700	6,420,000	Shimla
Jammu and Kashmir*	222,200	9,530,000	Srinagar/Jammu
Karnataka	191,800	50,980,000	Bangalore
Kerala	38,900	31,780,000	Trivandrum (Thiruvananthapuram)
Madhya Pradesh	443,500	77,400,000	Bhopal
Maharashtra	307,700	89,410,000	Bombay (Mumbai)
Manipur	22,300	2,390,000	Imphal
Meghalaya	22,400	2,310,000	Shillong
Mizoram	21,100	900,000	Aizawl

	Area (sq. km)	Population (1998 estimate)	Capital
Nagaland	16,600	1,590,000	Kohima
Orissa	155,700	35,300,000	Bhubaneswar
Punjab	50,400	23,100,000	Chandigarh
Rajasthan	342,200	52,010,000	Jaipur
Sikkim	7,100	530,000	Gangtok
Tamil Nadu	130,100	60,880,000	Madras (Chennai)
Tripura	10,500	3,580,000	Agartala
Uttar Pradesh	294,400	164,040,000	Lucknow
West Bengal	88,800	77,250,000	Calcutta (Kolkata)
UNION TERRITORIES			
Andaman and Nicobar Is.	8,200	370,000	Port Blair
Chandigarh	114	840,000	
Dadra and Nagar Haveli	500	180,000	Silvassa
Daman and Diu	112	130,000	
Delhi/Dilli	1,500	13,040,000	
Lakshadweep	30	70,000	Kavaratti
Pondicherry	500	1,050,000	

* The figures include those parts occupied by Pakistan and China, which are claimed by India. The state's capital is at Srinagar in summer and Jammu in winter.

HEAD OF STATE

President of the Republic of India, Kocheril Raman Narayanan, *elected* 14 July 1997
Vice-President, Krishan Kant, *elected* 16 August 1997

CARETAKER CABINET *as at May 1999*

Prime Minister, Agriculture, Atal Bihari Vajpayee (BJP)
Chemicals, Fertilizers and Food, Surjit Singh Barnala (SAD)
Civil Aviation, Anant Kumar (BJP)
Commerce, Ram Krishna Hegde (LS)
Defence, George Fernandes (SP)
Environment, Suresh Prabhakar Prabhu (SS)
External Affairs, Jaswant Singh (BJP)
Finance, Yashwant Sinha (BJP)
Home Affairs, Lal Krishna Advani (BJP)
Human Resource Development, Science and Technology, Murli Manohar Joshi (BJP)
Industry, Sikander Bakht (BJP)
Information, Broadcasting, Communications, Pramod Mahajan (BJP)
Labour, Satynarayan Jatiya (BJP)
Law, Ram Jethmalani (Ind.)
Petroleum and Natural Gas, K. Ramamurthy (TRC)
Power, Parliamentary Affairs, R. Kumaramangalam (BJP)
Railways, Nitish Kumar (SP)
Steel, Mines, Naveen Patnaik (BJD)
Surface Transport, R Muthiah
Textiles, Kashi Ram Rana (BJP)
Urban Development, Communications, Jagmohan Malhotrae (BJP)

BJP Bharatiya Janata Party; SAD Sikh Akali Dal; LS Lok Shakti (People's Power); SP Samta (Equality) Party; SS Shivaji's Army; TRC Tamil Rajiv Congress; BJD Biju Janata Dal; Ind. Independent

INDIAN HIGH COMMISSION

India House, Aldwych, London WC2B 4NA
Tel 0171-836 8484
High Commissioner, HE Lalit Mansingh, apptd 1998
Deputy High Commissioner, H. S. Puri
Ministers, S. K. Mandal *(Political)*; C. D. Sahay *(Consular)*; Prof. I Choudhury *(Culture)*; Counsellor *(Economic)*, M. S. Grover

Military Adviser, Brig. S. Sharma
CONSULATES-GENERAL – Birmingham, Glasgow

BRITISH HIGH COMMISSION
Chanakyapuri, New Delhi 1100021
Tel: New Delhi 687 2161
High Commissioner, HE Rob Young, KCMG, apptd 1998
Deputy High Commissioner and Minister, T. T. Macan
Deputy High Commissioners, M. C. Bates, OBE
(*Bombay/Mumbai*); S. M. Scaddan (*Calcutta/Kolkata*); M.
E. J. Herridge (*Madras/Chnnai*)
Defence and Military Adviser, Brig. S. M. A. Lee, OBE
Counsellor (Economic and Commercial), G. C. Gillham
Minister for Cultural Affairs and British Council Representative,
C.W. Perchard, OBE, CVO

BRITISH COUNCIL – offices at New Delhi,
Bombay/Mumbai, Calcutta/Kolkata and
Madras/Chennai. British Council libraries at these four
centres and British libraries at Ahmedabad, Bangalore,
Bhopal, Hyderabad, Lucknow, Patna, Pune and
Trivandrum/Thiruvananthapuram

DEFENCE

The Army has 3,414 main battle tanks, 1,350 armoured
infantry fighting vehicles, 157 armoured personnel carriers
and 4,175 artillery pieces. The Navy has 19 submarines,
one aircraft carrier, six destroyers, 18 frigates, 49 patrol
and coastal vessels, 67 combat aircraft and 83 armed
helicopters. It has nine bases including one under construction. The Air Force has 772 combat aircraft and 32 armed
helicopters.

India exploded its first nuclear weapon in 1974 and is
since believed to have acquired a stockpile of nuclear arms.
It conducted further nuclear tests in May 1998. In 1993–4
India successfully test-fired its intermediate-range 'Agni'
and 'Prithvi' ballistic missiles, and the latter went into
production in September 1997.
MILITARY EXPENDITURE – 3.3 per cent of GDP (1997)
MILITARY PERSONNEL – 2,265,000: Army 980,000, Navy
55,000, Air Force 140,000, Paramilitaries 1,090,000

ECONOMY

Agriculture supports about 64 per cent of the population,
and contributes nearly 27.4 per cent of GDP. Production
has grown by 2.67 per cent each year since 1951, remaining
slightly ahead of the 2 per cent increase necessary to keep
pace with the rising population. Food crops occupy three-
quarters of the total cultivated area. The main food crops
are rice, cereals (principally wheat) and pulses. The major
cash crops include sugar cane, jute, cotton and tea. Other
products include oil seeds, spices, groundnuts, soya bean,
tobacco, rubber and coffee. Livestock is raised, principally
for dairy purposes or for the hides.

Industry is based on the exploitation and processing of
mineral resources, principally coal, oil and iron, and on the
production of textiles. The coal industry reached an output
in 1997 of 320,900,000 tonnes; production of crude
petroleum was 33,000,000 tonnes. Steel production is
mainly in the hands of the public sector, with five public
and one private sector integrated steel plants producing
24,579,000 tonnes of ingot steel in 1997. The engineering
industry, heavy and light, is increasingly being privatized.

The manufacture of paper, cement, pharmaceuticals,
chemicals, fertilizers, petrochemicals, motor vehicles and
commercial vehicles has been expanded. Other principal
manufactures are those derived from agricultural products,
textiles, jute goods, sugar and leather, which along with
tea, tobacco, rubber, fish and iron ore are major exports.

India introduced free market reforms in 1991. Subsidies

were cut, state corporations privatized and the economy
opened up to foreign competition and investment. To
integrate India into the international trading system proper,
the 1993–5 budgets floated the rupee, cut interest rates and
duties on imports, reduced subsidies to farmers, restructured the taxation system, removed industrial controls and
dismantled protectionist structures.

The reforms have been successful, encouraging high
levels of foreign investment, a fall in inflation, a 24 per cent
increase in exports, a rise in foreign currency reserves from
US$1,000 million to US$16,000 million in 1996, improved
agricultural efficiency and an increase in the average
annual industrial growth rate from 1 per cent to 12 per
cent.

In 1996 there was a trade deficit of US$9,462 million
and a current account deficit of US$5,299 million. In 1997
imports totalled US$40,356 million and exports US$33,898
million.
GNP – US$357,391 million (1997); US$370 per capita
(1997)
GDP – US$338,785 million (1995); US$365 per capita
(1995)
ANNUAL AVERAGE GROWTH OF GDP – 7.4 per cent
(1996)
INFLATION RATE – 7.2 per cent (1997)
TOTAL EXTERNAL DEBT – US$94,404 million (1997)

Trade with UK	1997	1998
Imports from UK	£1,575,431,000	£1,255,370,000
Exports to UK	1,622,330,000	1,453,908,000

COMMUNICATIONS

The International Airports Authority manages five international airports: Indira Gandhi (Delhi/Dilli), Sahar
(Bombay/Mumbai), Dum Dum (Calcutta/Kolkata), Meen-
ambakkam (Madras/Chennai) and Thiruvananthapuram.
The other 88 aerodromes are controlled and operated by
the Civil Aviation Department of the government. The
national airlines are Indian Airlines (internal) and Air India
(international).

The railways are grouped into nine administrative zones,
Southern, Central, Western, Northern, North-Eastern,
North-East Frontier, Eastern, South-Eastern and South-
Central; there is also the Konkan Railway which links
Bombay/Mumbai and Mangalore. The total track length
is 63,675 km, of which 12,795 km is electrified. The total
length of the road network is about 3,290,000 km of which
1,440,000 km is surfaced.

The chief seaports are Bombay/Mumbai, Calcutta-
/Kolkata, Haldia, Madras/Chennai, Mormugao, Cochin,
Visakhapatnam, Kandla, Paradip, Mangalore and Tuti-
corin; these handled a cargo of 179.3 million tonnes in
1993–4. There are 139 minor working ports with varying
capacity.

INDONESIA
Republik Indonesia

AREA – 735,358 sq. miles (1,904,569 sq. km). Indonesia
shares borders with Malaysia (on Borneo) and Papua
New Guinea (on New Guinea)
POPULATION – 196,813,000 (1994 UN estimate): 87 per
cent Muslim, with Christian, Buddhist, Hindu and
Animist minorities. Bahasa Indonesian, a variant of
Malay, is the national language, although more than
250 dialects are spoken

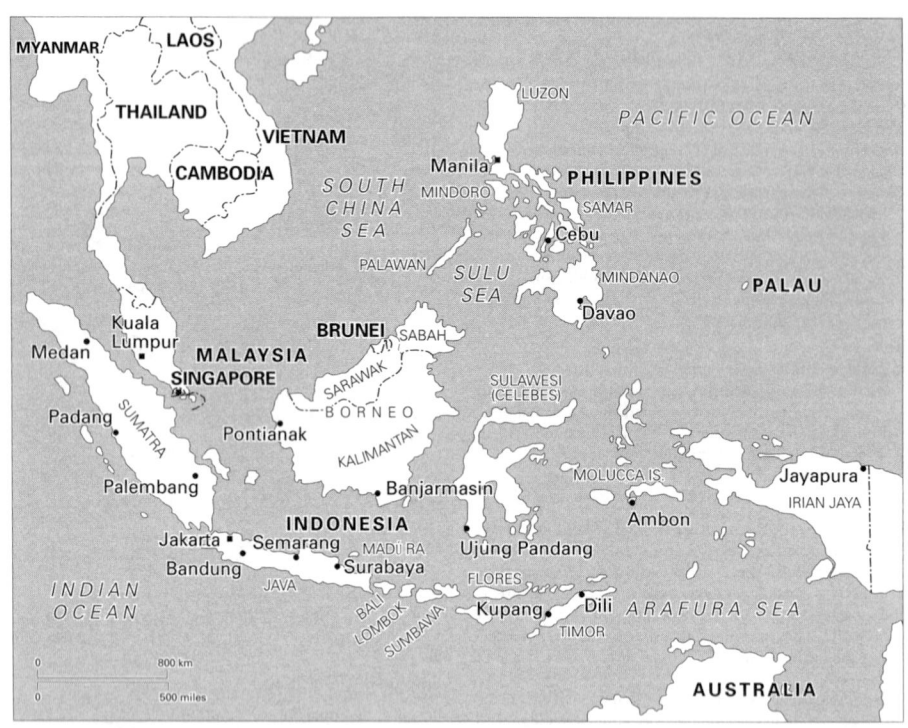

CAPITAL – ΨJakarta (population, 9,160,500)

MAJOR CITIES – (Irian Jaya) Jayapura (180,400); (Java) Bandung (2,368,200), ΨSemarang (1,366,500), ΨSurabaya (2,701,300); (Kalimantan) Banjarmasin (534,600), ΨPontianak (449,100); (Moluccas) Ambon (313,100); (Sulawesi) ΨUjung Pandang (1,091,800); (Sumatra) Medan (1,909,700), Palembang (1,352,300)

CURRENCY – Rupiah (Rp) of 100 sen

NATIONAL ANTHEM – Indonesia Raya (Great Indonesia)

NATIONAL DAY – 17 August (Anniversary of Proclamation of Independence)

NATIONAL FLAG – Equal bands of red over white

LIFE EXPECTANCY (years) – male 61.00; female 64.50

POPULATION GROWTH RATE – 1.7 per cent (1997)

POPULATION DENSITY – 103 per sq. km (1996)

URBAN POPULATION – 36.6 per cent (1996)

ILLITERACY RATE – 16.2 per cent

ENROLMENT (percentage of age group) – primary 97 per cent (1994); secondary 42 per cent (1994); tertiary 11.1 per cent (1994)

Indonesia comprises the islands of Java, Madura, Sumatra, the Riouw-Lingga archipelago, Bangka and Billiton, part of the island of Borneo (Kalimantan), Sulawesi (formerly Celebes), the Molucca Islands, the islands of Bali, Lombok, Sumbawa, Sumba, Flores, Timor and others comprising the provinces of East and West Nusa Tenggara and the western half of the island of New Guinea (Irian Jaya).

HISTORY AND POLITICS

From the early part of the 17th century much of the Indonesian archipelago was under Dutch rule. Following the Second World War, during which the archipelago was occupied by the Japanese, a strong nationalistic movement formed and after sporadic fighting all the former Dutch

East Indies except western New Guinea became independent as Indonesia on 27 December 1949. Western New Guinea became part of Indonesia in 1963 under the name West Irian (now Irian Jaya), this interpretation being confirmed in an 'Act of Free Choice' in July 1969.

The Army Minister Gen. Suharto assumed effective political power in March 1966. Gen. Suharto was appointed president in 1968 and was reappointed by the People's Consultative Assembly at every subsequent presidential election. The House of People's Representatives is composed of 425 elected members and 75 military appointees. The military has effectively ruled since 1966 through its political organization Golkar, which won 74 per cent of the votes cast in the general election on 29 May 1997.

Following the imposition of austerity measures, as a result of the Asian economic crisis in 1997, there was widespread ill-feeling towards Suharto and his family, many of whom had amassed large personal fortunes presiding over state businesses. Rampant inflation and high food and fuel prices provoked civil unrest, and by April 1998 riots and protests calling for Suharto's resignation were frequent. On 21 May 1998, he announced he would step down. He was replaced by his deputy B. J. Habibie.

In January 1999 the House of Representatives passed a number of liberalizing reforms to the country's political system, under which the next president was to be chosen in November 1999 by a joint assembly of MPs and representatives of the armed forces, regional legislatures and professional groups.

The Golkar party were defeated in the general election of 7 June 1999, in which the Indonesian Democratic Struggle Party led by Megawati Sukarnoputri, daughter of Indonesia's first president, won the greatest number of seats. A new government had not been appointed at the time of going to press.

INSURGENCIES

There are two armed secessionist movements based on ethnic and nationalist groups, which are fighting perceived Javanese domination. In Irian Jaya government forces are fighting the Papua Independent Organization (OPM) guerrillas who claim the 1969 referendum was rigged and oppose Indonesian settlement. In northern Sumatra the Free Aceh Movement is active.

See also East Timor, page 906

HEAD OF STATE

President, Bacharuddin Jusuf Habibie, *sworn in* 21 May 1998

CARETAKER CABINET *as at July 1999*

Co-ordinating Ministers, Hartarto Sastrosoenarto (*Development Supervision, State Administrative Reform*); Air Vice-Marshal (retd) Ginajar Kartasasmita (*Economy, Finance, Industry, National Development Planning Agency*); Haryono Suyono (*People's Welfare, Poverty Eradication, National Family Planning Board*); Feisal Tanjung (*Defence and Security Affairs, Attorney General* (*acting*))

Ministers, Akbar Tanjung (*State Secretary*); Budiono (*National Development Planning*); Zuhal (*Research, Science and Technology*); A. M. Saefuddin (*Food Affairs*); Ida Bagus Oka (*Population, National Family Planning Board*); Hamzah Haz (*Investment Affairs, National Investment Co-ordinating Board*); Hasan Basri Durin (*Land Affairs*); Tanri Abeng (*State Enterprises*); Panagian Siregar (*Environment*); Theo Sambuaga (*Public Housing*); Agung Laksono (*Youth and Sports Affairs*); Tutty Alawiyah (*Women's Affairs*); Lt.-Gen. Syarwan Hamid (*Home Affairs*); Ali Alatas (*Foreign Affairs*); Lt.-Gen. Wiranto (*Defence and Security, Commander-in-Chief of the Armed Forces, Head of Co-ordinating Agency for Reinforcement of National Stability*); Muladi (*Justice, State Secretary*); Lt.-Gen. Yunus Yosfiah (*Information*); Bambang Subianto (*Finance*); Rahardi Ramelan (*Trade and Industry*); Adi Sasono (*Co-operatives, Guidance of Small Business*); Soleh Solahuddin (*Agriculture*); Muslimin Nasution (*Forestry and Plantation*); Kuntoro Mangkusubroto (*Mines and Energy*); Yustika Baharsyah (*Social Affairs*); Rahmadi Bambang Sumadhyo (*Public Works*); Malik Fajar (*Religious Affairs*); Marzuki Usman (*Tourism, Arts and Culture, Investment Affairs*); Fahmi Idris (*Manpower*); Abdullah Makhmud Hendropriyono (*Transmigration*); Juwono Sudarsono (*Education and Culture*); Farid Anfasa Muluk (*Health*); Lt.-Gen. Muhammad Andi Ghalib (*Attorney-General*); Giri Suseno Hadihardjono (*Transport*)

Leading Members of the Armed Forces, Lt.-Gen. Wiranto (*Commander-in-Chief of Armed Forces*); Lt.-Gen. Subagio Hadiswoyo (*Army Chief of Staff*); Rear-Adm. Widodo (*Navy Chief of Staff*); Air Vice-Marshal Hanafie Asnan (*Air Force Chief of Staff*); Maj.-Gen. Jamari Chaniago (*Commander of Army Strategic Command*)

INDONESIAN EMBASSY

38 Grosvenor Square, London WIX 9AD
Tel 0171-499 7661
Ambassador Extraordinary and Plenipotentiary, HE Nana Sutresna, apptd 1999
Minister, R. R. Siahaan (*Deputy Chief of Mission*)
Commercial Attaché, Andreas Anugerah

BRITISH EMBASSY

Jalan M. H. Thamrin 75, Jakarta 10310
Tel: Jakarta 315 6264
Ambassador Extraordinary and Plenipotentiary, HE Robin Christopher, CMG, apptd 1997
Deputy Head of Mission and Consul-General, A. J. Sparkes

Counsellor (Commercial/Development), A. Godson
Defence Attaché, Col. D. S. MacFarlane
BRITISH CONSULAR OFFICES – Jakarta, Medan, Surabaya
BRITISH COUNCIL DIRECTOR, Dr N. Kemp, S Widjojo Centre, Jalan Jenderal Sudirman 71, Jakarta 12190

DEFENCE

The Army has 446 armoured personnel carriers, 180 artillery pieces and 32 aircraft. The Navy has two submarines, 17 frigates, 57 patrol and coastal vessels, 49 combat aircraft and 21 armed helicopters. There are five principal naval bases. The Air Force has 91 combat aircraft.
MILITARY EXPENDITURE – 2.2 per cent of GDP (1997)
MILITARY PERSONNEL – 476,000: Army 235,000, Navy 43,000, Air Force 21,000; Paramilitaries 177,000
CONSCRIPTION DURATION – Two years

ECONOMY

Nearly 70 per cent of the population is engaged in agriculture and related production. Copra, nutmeg, pepper, palm oil, sugar, fibres, rubber, tea, coffee and tobacco are produced. Rice is a staple food and Java, Sulawesi and Sumatra are important producers.

Oil and liquefied natural gas are the most important assets. Timber is the second largest foreign exchange earner after oil. Indonesia is rich in minerals, particularly tin, of which the country is the world's third biggest producer; coal, nickel and bauxite are the other principal mineral products. There are also considerable deposits of gold, silver, manganese phosphates and sulphur.

Principal exports are petroleum, textiles and clothing, timber, natural gas and rubber. Principal imports are machinery and transport equipment, electrical equipment and chemicals.

Indonesia was one of the countries worst affected by the Asian economic crisis, which began in the latter half of 1997; the ensuing high unemployment and inflation and the worsening standard of living have led to widespread political and interethnic unrest.

In 1997 there was a trade surplus of US$10,090 million and a current account deficit of US$4,816 million. Imports totalled US$41,694 million and exports US$53,443 million.
GNP – US$221,533 million (1997); US$1,110 per capita (1997)
GDP – US$201,183 million (1995); US$1,019 per capita (1995)
ANNUAL AVERAGE GROWTH OF GDP – 4.6 per cent (1997)
INFLATION RATE – 11.6 per cent (1997)
TOTAL EXTERNAL DEBT – US$136,174 million (1997)

Trade with UK	1997	1998
Imports from UK	£701,496,000	£379,118,000
Exports to UK	1,028,914,000	967,484,000

COMMUNICATIONS

There are railway systems in Java and Sumatra linking the main towns. There are about 137,060 km of roads.

Sea communications are maintained by the state-run shipping companies Jakarta-Lloyd (ocean-going) and PELNI (coastal and inter-island) and other small concerns. Transport by small craft on the rivers of the larger islands plays an important part in trade.

Air services are operated by Garuda Indonesian Airways and other local airlines, and Jakarta is served by various international services.

EAST TIMOR

East Timor was a Portuguese colony from 1702 until Portuguese control collapsed following the 1974 coup in Portugal. An independence war waged by the Marxist Fretilin (Revolutionary Front for an Independent East Timor) developed into a civil war between Fretilin and local conservative forces in 1975. After gaining control, Fretilin declared East Timor independent on 27 November 1975 and this was recognized by Portugal. Indonesian forces invaded East Timor on 7 December 1975 and declared East Timor Indonesia's 27th province.

Since 1975 Fretilin has waged an armed campaign for independence; resistance has left 200,000 East Timorese dead. About 150,000 Muslims have been settled in East Timor alongside the predominantly Roman Catholic population (80 per cent in 1975). The UN does not recognize the annexation and considers Portugal to exercise sovereignty still. A massacre of pro-independence demonstrators in the capital, Dili, in 1991 provoked international outrage. Following negotiations between Indonesia and Portugal, an agreement was reached to conduct a plebiscite on 30 August 1999, which would offer East Timor autonomy within Indonesia or independence.

IRAN
Jomhuri-e-Islami-e-Iran

AREA – 634,293 sq. miles (1,648,195 sq. km). Neighbours: Armenia, Azerbaijan, Turkmenistan (north), Afghanistan (north-east), Pakistan (south-east), Iraq (south-west), Turkey (north-west)

POPULATION – 61,128,000 (1996 census): 99 per cent Muslims (Shia 91 per cent and Sunni 8 per cent) with small minorities of Zoroastrians, Jews, and Armenian and Assyrian Christians. The official language is Persian (Farsi). Turkish, Kurdish, Arabic, Lori, Guilani, Mazandarani and Baluchi are also spoken

CAPITAL – Tehran, (population 6,750,043, 1994 estimate)

MAJOR CITIES – Ahwaz (828,380); Esfahan (1,220,595); Mashhad (1,964,489); Qom (780,453); Shiraz (1,042,801); Tabriz (1,166,203), 1994

CURRENCY – Rial

NATIONAL ANTHEM – Sorood-e Jomhoori-e Eslami

NATIONAL DAY – 11 February

NATIONAL FLAG – Three horizontal stripes of green, white, red, with the slogan *Allahu Akbar* repeated 22 times along the edges of the green and red stripes, and the national emblem in the centre

LIFE EXPECTANCY (years) – male 58.38; female 59.70

POPULATION GROWTH RATE – 1.6 per cent (1997)

POPULATION DENSITY – 37 per sq. km (1996)

URBAN POPULATION – 58.1 per cent (1994)

Iran is mostly an arid tableland, encircled, except in the east, by mountains, the highest in the north rising to 18,934 ft. The central and eastern portion is a vast salt desert.

HISTORY AND POLITICS

Iran was ruled from the end of the 18th century by Shahs of the Qajar dynasty. In 1925 the last of the dynasty, Sultan Ahmed Shah, was deposed in his absence by the National Assembly, which handed executive power to Prime Minister Reza Khan. Reza Khan was elected Shah as Reza Shah Pahlavi by the Constituent Assembly in December 1925. In 1941 Reza Shah abdicated in favour of the Crown Prince, who ascended the throne as Mohammed Reza Shah Pahlavi.

In January 1979, the Shah left Iran, handing over power to the Prime Minister, who was ousted by Ayatollah Khomeini, the spiritual leader of the Shia Muslims, on his return from exile. Following a national referendum, an Islamic Republic was declared on 1 April 1979. A new constitution, providing for a president, prime minister, Consultative Assembly, and leadership by Ayatollah Khomeini, was approved by referendum in December 1979. In June 1989 Khomeini died and President Khamenei was appointed Leader of the Islamic Republic. Rafsanjani was elected president in July 1989, and the post of prime minister was abolished. The 1997 presidential election was won by Mohammad Khatami, leader of a centre-left coalition. He was seen as a moderate, and following his election has pursued reformist policies, including calling for 'a thoughtful dialogue with the American people'. Iran and the UK re-established full diplomatic relations in May 1999.

FOREIGN RELATIONS

Iran was at war with Iraq following the Iraqi invasion of Iran in September 1980. International efforts to end the fighting resulted in a cease-fire in August 1988. In August 1990 Iraq accepted Iran's conditions for settling the conflict, including a return to the 1975 border, but a formal peace treaty has not been signed.

Following the murder of nine Iranian diplomats in August 1998 by Taliban militia forces in Afghanistan, Iran held large-scale military manoeuvres on the Afghan frontier. There were border skirmishes on 8 October 1998.

POLITICAL SYSTEM

The leader of the republic is elected by the Council of Experts whose 86 members are popularly elected every eight years. The president, who is the chief executive, is directly elected for a four-year term, renewable once. Ministers are nominated by the president and must obtain a vote of confidence in the Majlis. The Majlis comprises 270 representatives who are directly elected for a four-year term. Laws passed by the Majlis must be approved by the 12-member Guardian Council. In November 1997, President Khatami announced the establishment of the Committee for the Implementation and Supervision of the Constitution, a five-member body to ensure the constitution was abided by and that people's rights were respected.

Leader of the Islamic Republic, Ayatollah Seyed Ali Khamenei, *appointed* June 1989
President, Seyed Mohammad Khatami, *elected* 23 May 1997
First Vice-President, Hassan Ebrahim Habibi

COUNCIL OF MINISTERS *as at July 1999*

Vice-Presidents, Gholamreza Aqazadeh (*Atomic Energy*); Abdollah Nouri (*Development and Social Affairs*); Masoumeh Ebtekar (*Environmental Protection*); Mohammad Hashemi (*Executive Affairs*); Mohammad Ali Sadooqi (*Legal and Parliamentary Affairs*); Mostafa Hashemi-Taba (*Physical Education*); Mohammad Ali Najafi (*Planning and Budget*); Mohammad Baqerian (*State Employment and Administrative Affairs*)
Agriculture and Rural Affairs, Isa Kalantari
Commerce, Mohammad Shariatmadari
Co-operatives, Morteza Hajji
Culture and Islamic Guidance, Ataollah Mohajerani
Defence and Logistics, Ali Shamkhani
Economic Affairs and Finance, Hossain Namazi
Education, Hossain Mozafar
Energy, Habibollah Bitaraf
Foreign Affairs, Kamal Kharrazi

Health, Mohammad Farhadi
Higher Education, Mostafa Moin
Housing and Urban Development, Ali Abdol-Alizadeh
Industries, Gholamreza Shafei
Information, Ali Yunesi
Interior, Abdolvahed Mussavi-Lari
Jihad for Reconstruction, Mohamad Saidi Kya
Justice, Hojjatolislam Ismail Shoushtari
Labour and Social Affairs, Hossein Kamali
Mines and Metals, Eshaq Jahangiri
Oil, Bijan Namdar Zanganeh
Posts, Telephones and Telegraphs, Mohammad Reza Aref
Roads and Transport, Mahmoud Hojjati

EMBASSY OF THE ISLAMIC REPUBLIC OF IRAN
16 Prince's Gate, London SW7 IPT
Tel 0171-225 3000
Ambassador Extraordinary and Plenipotentiary, HE
    Gholamreza Ansari

BRITISH EMBASSY
143 Ferdowsi Avenue, PO Box 11365–4474, Tehran
11344
Tel: Tehran 675011
Ambassador Extraordinary and Plenipotentiary, HE Nicholas
    W. Browne, CMG
First Secretary (Commercial), A. F. Bedford

DEFENCE

The Army has around 1,400 main battle tanks, 550
armoured personnel carriers, 440 armoured infantry fighting vehicles, 2,170 artillery pieces, 77 aircraft and 100
attack helicopters. The Navy has three submarines, three
frigates, 65 patrol and coastal vessels, eight combat aircraft
and nine armed helicopters. There are six naval bases. The
Air Force has some 307 combat aircraft, of which about
60–80 per cent are serviceable.
MILITARY EXPENDITURE – 6.6 per cent of GDP (1997)
MILITARY PERSONNEL – 585,600: Army 350,000,
    Revolutionary Guard Corps 125,000, Navy 20,600, Air
    Force 50,000, Paramilitaries 40,000
CONSCRIPTION DURATION – Two years

ECONOMY

Iran's alleged support for international terrorism and its
suspected nuclear weapons programme prompted the USA
to impose a full trade and investment embargo in June
1995.
    Agricultural output rose following the end of the Iran–
Iraq war and an attempt is being made to reduce
dependence on food imports. Wheat is the principal crop;
other important crops are barley, rice, cotton, sugar beet,
fruit, nuts and vegetables. Wool is also a major product.
    The oilfields, which lie in south-western Iran, were
nationalized in 1951. In 1979, the National Iranian Oil
Company assumed control of the production, refining and
sale of oil. Oil production was 184,200,000 tonnes in 1997.
    Apart from oil, the principal industrial products are
carpets, textiles, sugar, cement and other construction
materials, ginned cotton, vegetable oil and other food
products, leather and shoes, metal manufactures, pharmaceuticals, motor vehicles, fertilizers and plastics. Privatization began in 1991.
    In 1996 there was a trade surplus of US$7,402 million
and a current account surplus of US$5,232 million. Imports
totalled US$ 16,274 million and exports totalled US$
22,391 million.
GNP – US$108,614 million (1997); US$1,780 per capita
(1997)

GDP – US$105,545 million (1995); US$1,544 per capita
(1995)
ANNUAL AVERAGE GROWTH OF GDP – 5.9 per cent
(1996)
INFLATION RATE – 17.2 per cent (1997)
TOTAL EXTERNAL DEBT – US$11,816 million (1997)

TRADE

Imports are mainly industrial and agricultural machinery,
motor vehicles and components for assembly, iron and
steel, electrical machinery and goods, foodstuffs and certain
textile fabrics and yarns. The principal exports, apart from
oil and gas, are carpets and fruit. Japan, Germany, France,
the UAE and Italy are Iran's main trading partners.

Trade with UK	1997	1998
Imports from UK	£395,845,000	£330,860,000
Exports to UK	36,158,000	36,123,000

COMMUNICATIONS

Tehran is the centre of a network of highways linking the
major towns, ports, the Caspian Sea and the national
frontiers; there are 156,507 km of roads.
    The Trans-Iranian Railway runs from Bandar Turco-
man, on the Caspian Sea, via Tehran to Bandar Khomeini,
on the Persian Gulf. Other lines link Tehran with Tabriz
and Mashhad; Tabriz to Julfa; Zahedan to Quetta; Ahvaz
to Khorramshahr; Qom to Kerman; and Bandar Turcoman
to Gorgan. The rail system is linked to the Turkish system
via Van. A track between Mashhad and Tedzhen in
Turkmenistan, opened in May 1996, has re-established the
ancient Silk Road between China and the Mediterranean;
there are 5,612 km of railway track.
    There is an international airport at Tehran (Mehrabad),
and airports at all the major provincial centres. The national
airline, Iranair, is government-owned and operates international and domestic routes.

EDUCATION AND CULTURE

Since 1943 primary education has been compulsory and
free. There are 74 universities in Iran. The educational
system has been reformed following the revolution.
    Persian or Farsi is an Indo-European language with
many Arabic elements added; the alphabet is mainly Arabic,
with writing from right to left. Among the great names in
Persian literature are those of Abu'l Kásim Mansúr, or
Firdausi (AD 939–1020), Omar Khayyám, the astronomer-
poet (died AD 1122), Muslihu'd-Din, known as Sa'di (born
AD 1184), and Shems-ed-Din Muhammad, or Hafiz (died
AD 1389).
ILLITERACY RATE – 27.7 per cent
ENROLMENT (percentage of age group) – primary 82 per
    cent (1996); secondary 69 per cent (1996); tertiary 17.1
    per cent (1996)

IRAQ
Al-Jumhouriya al-'Iraqia

AREA – 169,235 sq. miles (438,317 sq. km). Neighbours:
    Iran (east), Saudi Arabia, Kuwait (south), Jordan (west),
    Syria (north-west), Turkey (north)
POPULATION – 20,607,000 (1994 UN estimate),
    16,278,316 (1987 census). The official language is
    Arabic. Minority languages include Kurdish (about 15
    per cent), Turkic and Aramaic
CAPITAL – Baghdad (population, 3,841,268, 1987)
MAJOR CITIES – ΨBasra (406,296); Kirkuk (418,624);
    Mosul (664,221)

CURRENCY – Iraqi dinar (ID) of 1,000 fils
NATIONAL DAY – 17 July (Revolution Day)
NATIONAL FLAG – Three horizontal stripes of red,
   white, black; on the white stripe three stars and the
   slogan *Allahu Akbar* all in green
LIFE EXPECTANCY (years) – male 77.43; female 78.22
POPULATION GROWTH RATE – 2.7 per cent (1997)
POPULATION DENSITY – 47 per sq. km (1996)
URBAN POPULATION – 69.9 per cent (1990)
ILLITERACY RATE – 29.2 per cent
ENROLMENT (percentage of age group) – primary 76 per
   cent (1995); secondary 37 per cent (1992); tertiary 11.2
   per cent (1995)

In 1993 the border between Iraq and Kuwait was formally
demarcated, moving a few hundred metres northwards and
giving part of the port of Umm Qasr to Kuwait. The rivers
Euphrates (1,700 miles) and Tigris (1,150 miles) rise in
Turkey and traverse Iraq to their junction at Qurna, from
where the Euphrates flows the 70 miles to the Gulf.

HISTORY AND POLITICS

Iraq is the site of the remains of several ancient civilizations:
one site at Tel Hassuna, near Shura, dates back to 5000 BC;
Tel Abu Shahrain near 'Ur of the Chaldees' is the site of
the Sumerian city of Eridu; the ancient city of Hillah, 70
miles south of Baghdad, is near the site of Babylon and the
Tower of Babel. Mosul governorate covers a great part of
the ancient kingdom of Assyria, the ruins of Nineveh, the
Assyrian capital, being visible on the banks of the Tigris,
opposite Mosul. Qurna, at the junction of the Tigris and
Euphrates, is traditionally supposed to be the site of the
Garden of Eden.

Iraq was part of the Ottoman empire from 1534 until it
was captured by British forces in 1916. A provisional
government was set up in 1920, and in 1921 the Emir Faisal
was elected King of Iraq. The country was a monarchy
until July 1958, when King Faisal II was assassinated. From
1958 Iraq has been under the rule of the Ba'ath Party.

The Arab Ba'ath Socialist Party held a majority of
Assembly seats following the 1989 elections; no party
affiliations were ascribed in the results of the most recent
election, held on 24 March 1996.

FOREIGN RELATIONS

Iraq invaded Iran in September 1980 and was at war until
the August 1988 cease-fire. In 1990 Iraq accepted Iran's
conditions for peace, including a return to the 1975 border,
but a formal peace treaty has not been signed.

Iraq invaded Kuwait on 2 August 1990 and declared
Kuwait a province of Iraq. The UN Security Council
declared the annexation void. After months of diplomatic
attempts to secure an Iraqi withdrawal from Kuwait, an
alliance of NATO and Middle East countries launched an
offensive in January 1991 and liberated Kuwait in February
1991.

A United Nations Special Committee (UNSCOM),
charged with securing Iraq's full nuclear, biological and
chemical disarmament, has frequently been hindered in its
task by Iraqi officials. A military conflict was averted in
February 1998 when UN Secretary-General Kofi Annan
signed an agreement with the Iraqi government allowing
unlimited access for UN weapons inspectors. In October
1998, the Iraqi government announced that it was
suspending all co-operation with UNSCOM officials in
protest at the continuing sanctions; the USA and the UK
began to increase their military presence in the region and
emphasized that they were prepared to use military force
to· enable the UNSCOM mission to continue; on 15
November, the Iraqi regime agreed to allow UNSCOM
officials to resume operations.

INSURGENCIES

Following the allied victory in Kuwait in February 1991,
rebellion broke out in the Kurdish north and the Shi'ite
south. Although the revolt was quickly suppressed, Iraqi
attacks on Kurdish civilians led to the setting up of a UN
safe haven in northern Iraq to protect them. An air
exclusion zone north of the 36th parallel was also
established.   Although the Shi'ite revolt in southern Iraq
was defeated in April 1991, a low-level insurgency
continued in the southern marshlands. Since then the Iraqi
regime has systematically drained the southern marshes by
canal construction and river diversion; with continued
ground offensives, this had effectively ended the Shi'ite
rebellion by late 1994.

Iraqi aircraft have frequently violated the air exclusion
zones; allied forces have responded by attacking Iraqi air
defence installations.

POLITICAL SYSTEM

According to the provisional constitution, the highest state
authority is the Revolutionary Command Council (RCC),
which elects the president from among its members. A
constitutional amendment approved in September 1995
provided for the confirmation of the RCC's choice of
president by the National Assembly and by a popular
referendum.   The president appoints the Council of
Ministers. Legislative authority is shared by the RCC and
the 250-member National Assembly, which is elected
every four years by universal adult suffrage. Following the
amendment to the constitution, a referendum on a further
seven-year term for President Saddam was approved by a
claimed 99.96 per cent of voters on 15 October 1995.

HEAD OF STATE

President, Saddam Hussein, *assumed office* 16 July 1979,
   reappointed 17 October 1995
Vice Presidents, Taha Mohieddin Maarouf; Taha Yassin
   Ramadan

REVOLUTIONARY COMMAND COUNCIL

Chairman, The President
Vice-Chairman, Izzat Ibrahim
Secretary-General, Khaled Abdel-Moneim Rasheed
Members, Taha Yassin Ramadan; Sa'adoun Shaker; Tariq
   Aziz; Taha Mohieddin Maarouf; Mohammad Hamzah
   al-Zubaydi; Mizban Khader Hadi

CABINET *as at July 1999*

The President

Deputy Prime Ministers, Tariq Aziz; Taha Yassin Ramadan; Mohammad Hamzah al-Zubaydi

Agriculture, Abd al-Ilah Hamid Muhammad Salih

Defence, Gen. Abd al-Jabbar Shanshal

Education, Fahd Salem al-Shaqra

Finance, Hikmat Mizban Ibrahim al-Azzawi

Foreign Affairs, Muhammad Said Kazim al-Sahhaf

Health, Umid Midhat Mubarak

Higher Education and Scientific Research, Abd al-Jabbar Tawfiq Muhammad

Housing and Reconstruction, Ma'n Abdullah al-Sarsam

Industry, Minerals, Adnan Abd al Majid Jasim al-Ani

Information and Culture, Humam Abd al-Khaliq abd al-Ghafur

Interior, Muhammad Ziman Abd al-Razzaq

Irrigation, Mahmud Dhiyab al-Ahmad

Justice, Shabib Lazim al-Maliki

Labour and Social Affairs, Staff Gen. Sa'di Tu'mah Abbas

Ministers of State, Gen. Abdel-Jabbar Khalil Shanshal *(Military Affairs)*; Abdel Wahhab Omar Mirza al-Atrushi *(Without Portfolio)*; Arshad Muhammad Ahmad al-Zibari *(Without Portfolio)*

Oil, Lt.-Gen. Amir Muhammad Rashid al-Ubaydi

Religious Endowments and Religious Affairs, Abd al-Munim Ahmad Salih

Trade, Mohammad Mehdi Salih

Transport and Communications, Ahmad Murtada Khalil

IRAQI DIPLOMATIC MISSION IN LONDON

Since Iraq's breach of diplomatic relations with Britain in February 1991, the Jordanian Embassy has handled Iraqi interests in the UK.

Minister/Head of Interests Section, vacant

BRITISH DIPLOMATIC REPRESENTATION

The British Embassy was closed in January 1991. The Russian Embassy has since handled British interests in Iraq.

DEFENCE

The Army has roughly 2,700 main battle tanks, 2,900 armoured personnel carriers and armoured infantry fighting vehicles, 1,800 artillery pieces and 120 armed helicopters. The Navy has two frigates and six patrol and coastal vessels at two bases.

In 1991, the UN demanded the destruction of all weapons of mass destruction and their means of production as a prerequisite for the lifting of sanctions. By mid-1995 it was believed that most of these weapons had been destroyed and a long-term monitoring operation was under way to ensure production did not restart. In late 1995, evidence of a ballistic missile programme and large biological weapons stockpiles was discovered; in 1997 evidence of further Iraqi chemical weapons, including missiles loaded with VX gas, was discovered.

MILITARY EXPENDITURE – 7.4 per cent of GDP (1997)

MILITARY PERSONNEL – 479,000: Army 375,000, Navy 2,000, Air Force 35,000, Air Defence Force 17,000, Paramilitaries 50,000

CONSCRIPTION DURATION – 18–24 months

ECONOMY

Increasing industrialization is taking place but production has been hampered by war damage and sanctions. Iraq's major industry is oil production which was nationalized in 1972 and usually accounts for approximately 98 per cent of the total government revenue and 45 per cent of GNP. Production was 53,300,000 tonnes in 1997.

Agricultural production is important, with two harvests usually gathered in a year, depending on rainfall. Salinity and soil erosion limit productivity.

The UN imposed economic sanctions and a world-wide ban on Iraqi oil exports in August 1990. In May 1996, Iraq agreed to a UN-proposed 'oil-for-food' deal, permitting the sale of oil to buy food and medicine. Limited oil exports resumed in December 1996. Thirty per cent of the revenue will pay for reparations to Gulf War victims, and up to 15 per cent will provide aid to Iraqi Kurds.

GDP – US$227,229 million (1995); US$11,308 per capita (1995)

ANNUAL AVERAGE GROWTH OF GDP – –4.0 per cent (1995)

TRADE

The principal imports are normally iron and steel, military equipment, building materials, mechanical and electrical machinery, motor vehicles, textiles and clothing, essential foodstuffs and raw industrial materials. The chief exports are normally crude petroleum, dates, raw wool, raw hides and skins and raw cotton.

Trade with UK	1997	1998
Imports from UK	£6,431,000	£25,644,000
Exports to UK	29,000	21,481,000

COMMUNICATIONS

The port of Basra has not been used since the outbreak of hostilities with Iran in 1980. Continuous dredging of the Shatt-al-Arab has also been suspended by hostilities and the channel has seriously silted. The port of Umm Qasr on the Kuwaiti border, which was developed for freight and sulphur handling and includes a container terminal, was opened in late 1993. All external borders, except that of Jordan, are closed to Iraqi traffic.

There is an international airport at Baghdad. Iraqi Airways provided flights between Baghdad and London, and other international airlines operated to Europe. Iraqi Republican Railways provided regular passenger and goods services between Basra, Baghdad and Mosul. There is also a metre gauge rail line connecting Baghdad with Khanaqin, Kirkuk and Arbil.

Iraqi communications were greatly affected by the Gulf War; large numbers of bridges were destroyed and the railway system extensively disrupted.

REPUBLIC OF IRELAND

Poblacht Na hEireann

AREA – 27,137 sq. miles (70,284 sq. km). Neighbour: Northern Ireland (north)

POPULATION – 3,626,087 (1996 census). At the 1991 census religious adherence was: Roman Catholic, 3,228,327; Church of Ireland, 89,187; Presbyterians, 13,199; Methodists, 5,037; others, 189,969. Irish is the first official language; English is recognized as a second official language, but is more commonly used

CAPITAL – ΨDublin (*Baile Atha Cliath*), (population, 952,700, 1996 census)

MAJOR CITIES – ΨCork (180,000); ΨGalway (57,400); ΨLimerick (79,100); Waterford (44,200), 1996 census

CURRENCY – Punt (IR£) of 100 pence

NATIONAL ANTHEM – Amhrán na BhFiann (The Soldier's Song)

NATIONAL DAY – 17 March (St Patrick's Day)

NATIONAL FLAG – Equal vertical stripes of green, white and orange

LIFE EXPECTANCY (years) – male 72.30; female 77.87
POPULATION GROWTH RATE – 0.6 per cent (1997)
POPULATION DENSITY – 52 per sq. km (1996)
URBAN POPULATION – 57.0 per cent (1991)
MILITARY EXPENDITURE – 1.0 per cent of GDP (1997)
MILITARY PERSONNEL – 11,500: Army 9,300, Navy
   1,100, Air Force 1,100

Ireland is separated from Scotland by the North Channel
and from England and Wales by the Irish Sea and St
George's Channel. The greatest length of the island, from
north-east to south-west (Torr Head to Mizen Head), is
302 miles, and the greatest breadth, from east to west
(Dundrum Bay to Annagh Head), is 174 miles. On the
north coast of Achill Island (Co. Mayo) are the highest
cliffs in the British Isles, 2,000 feet sheer above the sea.

The highest point is Carrantuohill (3,414 ft). The
principal river is the Shannon (240 miles), which drains the
central plain. The Slaney flows into Wexford Harbour, the
Liffey to Dublin Bay, the Boyne to Drogheda, the Lee to
Cork Harbour, the Blackwater to Youghal Harbour, and
the Suir, Barrow and Nore to Waterford Harbour.

The principal hydrographic feature is the loughs; the
Shannon chain of Allen, Boderg, Forbes, Ree and Derg,
and the Erne chain of Gowna, Oughter, Lower Erne, and
Erne; Melvin, Gill, Gara and Conn in the north-west; and
Corrib and Mask (joined by a hidden channel) in the west.

The Republic of Ireland is divided into four provinces
of 26 counties: Leinster (Carlow, Dublin, Kildare, Kilkenny,
Laoighis, Longford, Louth, Meath, Offaly, Westmeath,
Wexford and Wicklow); Munster (Clare, Cork, Kerry,
Limerick, Tipperary and Waterford); Connacht (Galway,
Leitrim, Mayo, Roscommon and Sligo); and part of Ulster
(Cavan, Donegal and Monaghan).

HISTORY AND POLITICS

The first inhabitants of Ireland, hunters from mainland
Britain, arrived in 7,000 BC, and were joined by Celts from
central Europe from the sixth century BC until about the
time of Christ. The introduction of Christianity in the fifth

century is traditionally associated with St Patrick and
inspired 300 years of rich cultural achievements. The
Vikings, who established most of the major towns, including
Dublin and Cork, invaded around AD 800 and controlled
Ireland until their defeat at the Battle of Clontarf (1014)
by Brian Boru, who had become king of all Ireland in 1002.

In the 12th century the Norman English invaded at the
invitation of Dermod MacMurrough, the deposed king of
Leinster, and established feudal control over most of the
island; this lasted for 300 years. King Henry VIII of England
reconquered Ireland and in 1541 declared himself king of
Ireland, the first English monarch to do so. Protestantism
was introduced but failed to take root, except in Ulster
where English and Scottish Presbyterians settled during
the reign of James I (1603–25). A rebellion initiated by
Ulster Catholics in 1641 was ruthlessly crushed by Oliver
Cromwell's army. Catholicism was repressed and further
Protestant colonization encouraged. Following the abdication of the Catholic King James II in 1688, Irish
Protestants supported William of Orange's accession to the
throne. James II was defeated in Ireland, most famously at
the Battle of the Boyne (1690), and Protestant ascendancy
was restored, enduring throughout the 18th century.

The Irish parliament was granted independence in 1782,
although the Dublin administration was still appointed by
the king. The parliament was abolished by the Act of
Union in 1801 following a rebellion by the Society of the
United Irishmen in 1798, and subsequently Irish MPs sat
at Westminster. Demands for the restoration of the Irish
parliament and home rule for Ireland were successful in
1914, but were delayed when World War I broke out. A
rebellion, the Easter Rising of 1916, was suppressed by the
British, fuelling support for the Sinn Féin party, which won
the 1918 election in Ireland and withdrew from the British
parliament to form a legislature in Dublin under the
leadership of Éamon de Valera. The resulting two-year
war of independence between the Irish Republican Army
and British forces ended in a truce, followed by negotiations
leading to the signing of the Anglo-Irish Treaty in
December 1921. The island was partitioned, the 26 counties
of the Irish Free State accepting dominion status within
the British Empire, while six of the nine counties of Ulster,
where the majority Protestant population opposed home
rule, remained part of the United Kingdom, governed by a
Northern Ireland parliament.

Civil war broke out between the new Irish government
and opponents of the treaty until a truce was reached in
May 1923. Constitutional links between the Irish Free
State and the UK were gradually removed by the Irish
parliament and a new constitution enacted in 1937 declared
the Irish Free State a sovereign, independent state with a
republican government. However, it continued in association with the states of the British Commonwealth until
1949, when constitutional links with Britain were severed
and the state was renamed the Republic of Ireland.

Under the terms of the 1998 Belfast Agreement, the Irish
Republic gave up its territorial claim to the six counties of
Northern Ireland. Additionally, a North-South Ministerial
Council, comprising officials from both countries, would
meet to regulate areas of common interest.

The presidential election in October 1997 was won by
Mary McAleese with almost 59 per cent of second-round
votes. The composition of the Dáil Eireann as of July 1999
was: Fianna Fáil 76; Fine Gael 54; Labour 16; Democratic
Left 4; Progressive Democrats 4; Green Party 2; Sinn Fein
1; Socialist 1; others 6. Fianna Fail and the Progressive
Democrats formed a coalition government.

POLITICAL SYSTEM

The president (Uachtarán na hEireann) is directly elected
for a term of seven years, and is eligible for a second term.
The president is aided and advised by a Council of State.

The National Parliament (*Oireachtas*) consists of the president, House of Representatives (*Dáil Éireann*) and Senate (*Seanad Éireann*). Dáil Éireann is composed of 166 members elected for a five-year term on a basis of proportional representation by means of the single transferable vote. Seanad Éireann is composed of 60 members, of whom 11 are nominated by the prime minister (*Taoiseach*) and 49 are elected, six by institutions of higher education and 43 from panels of candidates established on a vocational basis.

Executive power is vested in the government subject to the constitution. The government is responsible to the Dáil. The taoiseach is appointed by the president on the nomination of the Dáil. The other members of the government are appointed by the president on the nomination of the taoiseach with the previous approval of the Dáil. The taoiseach appoints a member of the government to be his deputy (the *tánaiste*).

The judicial system comprises courts of first instance and a court of final appeal called the Supreme Court (*Cúirt Uachtarach*). The courts of first instance include a High Court (*Ard-Chúirt*) and courts of local and limited jurisdiction, with a right of appeal as determined by law. The High Court alone has original jurisdiction to consider the question of the validity of any law having regard to the provisions of the constitution. The Supreme Court has appellate jurisdiction from decisions of the High Court.

HEAD OF STATE

President, Mary McAleese, *elected* 30 October 1997, *sworn in* 11 November 1997

CABINET *as at July 1999*

Taoiseach (PM), Bertie Ahern

Tánaiste (Deputy PM), Enterprise, Trade and Employment, Mary Harney

Agriculture and Food, Joe Walsh

Arts, Heritage, Gaeltachta and Islands, Síle de Valera

Attorney-General, Michael McDowell

Defence and European Affairs, Michael Smith

Education and Science, Michael Martin

Environment and Local Government, Noel Dempsey

Finance, Charlie McCreevy

Foreign Affairs, David Andrews

Government Chief Whip, Seamus Brennan

Health and Children, Brian Cowen

Justice and Equality, Law Reform, John O'Donoghue

Marine and Natural Resources, Michael Woods

Public Enterprise, Mary O'Rourke

Social, Community and Family Affairs, Dermot Ahern

Tourism, Sport and Recreation, Jim McDaid

IRISH EMBASSY

17 Grosvenor Place, London SW1X 7HR

Tel 0171-235 2171

Ambassador Extraordinary and Plenipotentiary, HE Edward Barrington, apptd 1995

Counsellor, E. Carey (*Economic*)

BRITISH EMBASSY

29 Merrion Road, Dublin 4

Tel: Dublin 205 3700

Ambassador Extraordinary and Plenipotentiary, HE Ivor Roberts, CMG, apptd 1998

Counsellor and Deputy Head of Mission, D. M. Holt

Defence Attaché, Col. J. D. Wilson

First Secretary (Commercial), R. N. J. Baker

BRITISH COUNCIL REPRESENTATIVE, Harold Fish, OBE, Newmount House, 22/24 Lower Mount Street, Dublin 2

ECONOMY

Although industry has expanded greatly since Ireland's entry into the European Community in 1973, agriculture remains important; in 1998, 9 per cent of the workforce was employed in agriculture, forestry and fisheries. The main crops are wheat, barley, oats, potatoes and sugar beet. Agriculture has benefited considerably from the EU Common Agricultural Policy and support funds but has suffered from the drift of the rural population to urban areas and abroad.

Industry accounted for about 38 per cent of GNP and about 28.9 per cent of employment in 1997. The traditional brewing, spirits and food-processing sectors have expanded and have been joined by the manufacture of textiles, chemicals, pharmaceuticals, electronics, office machinery and transportation equipment. The services sector is currently the fastest-growing sector of the economy and accounted for 58 per cent of GNP and 68.8 per cent of employment in 1997. Tourism is the most important part of the service sector and in recent years has provided substantial revenue, with 5,716,000 visitors in 1998.

The Kinsale gas field off the south coast provides 50 per cent of Ireland's gas needs, with the rest coming via an undersea pipeline from Moffat, Scotland. There are seven government-funded milled peat power-generating stations. Hydroelectric power from the Shannon barrage and other schemes is also important but Ireland still imports 55 per cent of oil and coal for power generation. Metal content of ores raised (1998) was lead, 36,528 tonnes; zinc, 180,951 tonnes; silver 10,824,000 grammes.

Computer equipment and organic chemicals are the main exports. The UK, USA, Germany, France and the Netherlands are Ireland's main trading partners.

Having satisfied the Maastricht convergence criteria, Ireland participates in the European Single Currency.

In 1997 Ireland had a trade surplus of US$18,646 million and a current account surplus of US$1,934 million. In 1998 imports totalled US$44,434 million and exports US$64,091 million.

GNP – US$65,137 million (1997); US$17,790 per capita (1997)

GDP – US$61,769 million (1995); US$17,419 per capita (1995)

ANNUAL AVERAGE GROWTH OF GDP – 9.8 per cent (1997)

INFLATION RATE – 1.4 per cent (1997)

UNEMPLOYMENT – 12.15 per cent (1995)

Trade with UK	1997	1998
Imports from UK	£8,829,500,000	£9,026,600,000
Exports to UK	7,047,800,000	7,426,400,000

COMMUNICATIONS

In 1998 there was 1,945 km of railway operated by *Iarnród Éirann*. In 1997 the number of ships with cargo which arrived at Irish ports was 16,463 (165,925,000 net registered tons), with a total weight of goods handled of 36.3 million tonnes.

Shannon Airport, Co. Clare, is on the main transatlantic air route. In 1998 the airport handled 1,840,008 passengers. Dublin Airport serves the cross-channel and European services operated by the Irish national airline Aer Lingus and other airlines. In 1998 the airport handled 11,641,100 passengers. In 1998 Cork Airport handled 1,315,224 passengers.

EDUCATION

Primary education is directed by the state, with the exception of 49 private primary schools. There were 3,186 state-aided primary schools in 1997–8.

In 1997–8 there were 435 recognized secondary schools under private management (mainly religious orders), and 246 vocational schools. There were 16 state comprehensive schools and 65 community schools.

Third-level education is catered for by seven university colleges and 13 Institutes of Technology and a number of other third-level institutions.

ENROLMENT (percentage of age group) – primary 100 per cent (1995); secondary 86 per cent (1995); tertiary 38.5 per cent (1995)

ISRAEL
Medinat Israel

AREA – 8,130 sq. miles (21,056 sq. km). Neighbours: Lebanon (north), Syria (north-east), Jordan and the West Bank (east), the Gaza Strip and the Egyptian province of Sinai (south-west)

POPULATION – 6,100,000 (1999 estimate): roughly 82 per cent Jewish, 14 per cent Arab Muslims, 2.5 per cent Christians of which 90 per cent are Arab, and 2 per cent Druze. Since independence Israel has had a policy of granting an immigration visa to every Jew who expresses a desire to settle in Israel. Between 1948 and 1992, 2.3 million immigrants had entered Israel from over 100 different countries. Hebrew and Arabic are the official languages. Arabs are entitled to transact all official business with government departments in Arabic

CAPITAL – Most of the government departments are in Jerusalem, population 662,700 (1995 estimate). A resolution proclaiming Jerusalem as the capital of Israel was adopted by the *Knesset* in 1950. It is not, however, recognized as the capital by the UN because East Jerusalem is part of the Occupied Territories captured in 1967. The UN and international law continues to reject the Israeli annexation of East Jerusalem and considers the pre-1950 capital Tel Aviv (population, 1,880,200) to be the capital

MAJOR CITIES – Beersheba (and district 122,000); ΨHaifa (and district 491,000); Rishon Le'Zion (178,000)

CURRENCY – Shekel of 100 agora

NATIONAL ANTHEM – Hatikvah (The Hope)

NATIONAL FLAG – White, with two horizontal blue stripes, the Shield of David in the centre

LIFE EXPECTANCY (years) – male 75.33; female 79.10

POPULATION GROWTH RATE – 3.2 per cent (1997)

POPULATION DENSITY – 271 per sq. km (1996)

URBAN POPULATION – 89.7 per cent (1994)

Israel comprises the hill country of Galilee and parts of Judea and Samaria, rising to heights of nearly 4,000 ft; the coastal plain from the Gaza strip to north of Acre, including the plain of Esdraelon running from Haifa Bay to the south-east which divides the hill region; the Negev, a semi-desert triangular-shaped region, extending from a base south of Beersheba, to an apex at the head of the Gulf of Aqaba; and parts of the Jordan valley, including the Hula region, Tiberias and the south-western extremity of the Dead Sea.

The principal river is the Jordan, which rises from three main sources in Israel, the Lebanon and Syria, and flows through the Hula valley, Lake Tiberias/Kinneret (Sea of Galilee) and the Jordan Valley into the Dead Sea, falling 1,517 ft from Hulata to the Dead Sea. The other principal rivers are the Yarkon and Kishon. The Dead Sea is a lake (shared between Israel, the West Bank and Jordan), 1,286

ft below sea-level; it has no outlet, the surplus being carried off by evaporation.

The climate is variable, modified by altitude and distance from the sea, with hot summers and rainy winters.

HISTORY AND POLITICS

The Ottoman Empire province of Palestine was captured by British forces in 1917, the same year that the British Government issued the Balfour Declaration which 'viewed with favour the establishment of a national home for the Jewish people in Palestine'. The Balfour Declaration's terms were enshrined in Britain's League of Nations mandate over Palestine, leading to steady Jewish immigration in the inter-war years and a post-1945 flood by Nazi concentration camp survivors. The Arab Palestinian population revolted against Jewish immigration from 1936 onwards, while Jewish groups conducted a terrorist campaign against the British administration from 1945 onwards.

In 1947 Britain announced its withdrawal from Palestine with effect from May 1948, handing over to the UN responsibility for resolving the conflict between Arabs and Jews. Both sides ignored the UN partition plan; on the withdrawal of British forces on 14 May 1948 the State of Israel was proclaimed and the first Arab-Israeli war began. By the time of the January 1949 cease-fire Israeli forces controlled all of the former mandate territory apart from the West Bank (and East Jerusalem) and the Gaza Strip, which had come under Jordanian and Egyptian control respectively.

During the 1967 Six-Day War Israel captured the West Bank and the Gaza Strip, together with Sinai from Egypt and the Golan Heights from Syria, and annexed East Jerusalem. Israel held on to its gains in the 1973 Yom

Kippur War. The Golan Heights were annexed in 1981; Sinai was returned to Egypt in 1982 in accordance with the 1979 Israeli–Egyptian peace treaty, and the South Lebanon Security Zone was established after the 1982–5 invasion of Lebanon. The annexations of East Jerusalem and the Golan Heights remain unrecognized internationally.

The Labour leader of the coalition government formed after the 1992 general election, Yitzhak Rabin, was assassinated by a Jewish extremist on 4 November 1995, and was replaced by Foreign Minister Shimon Peres. A general election on 29 May 1996, the first to have separate ballots for the prime minister and legislature, was won by Likud leader Binyamin Netanyahu, who formed an eight-party coalition government which commanded 66 seats in the Knesset. Ehud Barak, leader of the One Israel Party, was elected prime minister on 17 May 1999 and formed a six-party coalition government which held 70 of the 120 seats in the Knesset.

FOREIGN RELATIONS

A peace process, started in October 1991 in Madrid, led to agreements with the Palestine Liberation Organization (*see* page 914), and with Jordan on 14 September 1993. A full peace agreement with Jordan was signed on 26 October 1994 and provides for the return to Jordan of land occupied by Israel since 1967 in the southern Araba valley (completed 9 February 1995).

POLITICAL SYSTEM

Israel is a sovereign democratic republic with executive power vested in a prime minister and Cabinet, and legislative power in a unicameral legislature (*Knesset*) of 120 members elected by proportional representation for a maximum term of four years. The prime minister is elected separately from the legislature. The president is head of state and is elected by the Knesset for a maximum of two five-year terms.

HEAD OF STATE

President of Israel, Ezer Weizman, *elected* 24 March 1993, *re-elected* 4 March 1998

CABINET *as at July 1999*

Prime Minister, Defence, Agriculture and Rural Development, Science, Tourism and Absorption, Ehud Barak (OI)
Communications, Benjamin Ben-Eliezer (OI)
Education, Yossi Sarid (M)
Environment, Dalia Itzik (OI)
Finance, Avraham Shochat (OI)
Foreign Affairs, David Levy (OI)
Health, Shlomo Benizri (Shas)
Housing, Yitzhak Levy (NRP)
Industry, Trade, Ran Cohen (M)
Interior, Natan Sharansky (YB)
Justice, Yossi Beilin (OI)
Labour and Social Affairs, Eliyahu Yishai (Shas)
National Infrastructure, Eli Suissa (Shas)
PM's Office, Jerusalem Affairs, Haim Ramon (OI)
Public Security, Shlomo Ben-Ami (OI)
Regional Co-operation, Shimon Peres (OI)
Religious Affairs, Yitzhak Cohen (Shas)
Transport, Yitzhak Mordechai (Centre)

OI One Israel; M Meretz; NRP National Religious Party; YB Yisrael B'Aliya;

EMBASSY OF ISRAEL
2 Palace Green, Kensington, London W8 4QB
Tel 0171-957 9500
Ambassador Extraordinary and Plenipotentiary, HE Dror Zeigerman, apptd 1998

Minister Plenipotentiary, A. Magid
Defence Attaché, Brig.-Gen. Y. Chen
Minister, M. Bar-On (*Consular*)
Counsellor, R. Kan (*Commercial*)

BRITISH EMBASSY
192 Hayarkon Street, Tel Aviv 63405
Tel: Tel Aviv 524 9171
Ambassador Extraordinary and Plenipotentiary,
HE Francis Cornish, CMG, LVO, apptd 1998
Counsellor, Consul-General and Deputy Head of Mission, S. Pease
Defence and Military Attaché, Col. E. Houstoun, OBE
First Secretary (Commercial), W. W. Magor
CONSULATES – Tel Aviv, Eilat

BRITISH COUNCIL DIRECTOR, D. Elliot, 140 Hayarkon Street, PO Box 3302, Tel Aviv 61032
ISRAEL-BRITISH CHAMBER OF COMMERCE, 76 IBN Guirol Street, Tel Aviv 64162

DEFENCE

Israel is believed to have a nuclear capacity of around 100 warheads which could be delivered by aircraft or Jericho I and II missiles.

The Army has 4,300 main battle tanks, around 9,700 armoured personnel carriers and 1,550 artillery pieces. The Navy has three submarines and 51 patrol and coastal vessels at three bases. The Air Force has 474 combat aircraft and 137 armed helicopters.

MILITARY EXPENDITURE – 11.5 per cent of GDP (1997)
MILITARY PERSONNEL – 181,050: Army 134,000, Navy 9,000, Air Force 32,000, Paramilitaries 6,050
CONSCRIPTION DURATION – 21–48 months (Jews and Druze only)

ECONOMY

The country is generally fertile although water supply for irrigation restricts production. Agriculture accounts for 2 per cent of GNP and 3.5 per cent of exports.

The 'Jaffa' orange is produced in large quantities for export, along with other summer fruits, seasonal vegetables and glasshouse crops. Olives are cultivated, mainly for the production of oil. The main winter crops are wheat, barley and various kinds of pulses, while in summer sorghum, millet, maize, sesame and summer pulses are grown. Beef, cattle and poultry farming have been developed. Tobacco and cotton are now grown.

Polished diamonds account for about 22.5 per cent of total exports. Amongst the most important industries are textiles, foodstuffs and chemicals (mainly fertilizers and pharmaceuticals). Metal-working and science-based industries are sophisticated and technologically advanced and include the aircraft and military industries. Other important manufacturing industries include plastics, rubber, cement, glass, paper and oil refining. Industry accounts for 66.7 per cent of GNP.

GNP – US$94,402 million (1997); US$16,180 per capita (1997)
GDP – US$92,480 million (1995); US$16,738 per capita (1995)
ANNUAL AVERAGE GROWTH OF GDP – 1.9 per cent (1997)
INFLATION RATE – 9.0 per cent (1997)
UNEMPLOYMENT – 6.9 per cent (1995)

TRADE

The principal imports are foodstuffs, crude oil, machinery and vehicles, iron, steel and chemicals. The principal exports are metal machinery, electronic goods, chemicals, rubber, plastics, textiles, food and beverages, minerals, citrus produce and polished diamonds.

In 1997 Israel had a trade deficit of US$6,523 million and a current account deficit of US$14,600 million. Imports totalled US$30,781 million and exports totalled US$22,503 million.

Trade with UK	1997	1998
Imports from UK	£1,178,664,000	£1,089,247,000
Exports to UK	879,922,000	918,911,000

COMMUNICATIONS

Israel State Railways serves Haifa, Tel Aviv, Jerusalem, Lod, Nahariya, Beersheba, Dimona, Ashdod and intermediate stations with a network of 526 km. There were 14,700 km of paved road in 1995. A major road building programme has been underway in the West Bank since 1992.

The chief ports are Haifa and Ashdod on the Mediterranean, and Eilat on the Red Sea; Acre has an anchorage for small vessels. The chief international airport is Ben Gurion between Tel Aviv and Jerusalem.

EDUCATION

Education from five to 16 years is free and compulsory. The law also provides for working youth aged 16–18, who for some reason have not completed their education, to be exempted from work in order to do so. There are seven universities including two engineering and technological institutes.

ILLITERACY RATE – 4.4 per cent
ENROLMENT (percentage of age group) – tertiary 41.1 per cent (1995)

CULTURE

Important historic sites in Israel include: *Jerusalem* – the Church of the Holy Sepulchre, the Al Aqsa Mosque and Dome of the Rock standing on the remains of the Temple Mount of Herod the Great of which the Western (wailing) Wall is a fragment, the Church of the Dormition and the Coenaculum on Mount Zion, Ein Karem, Church of the Visitation, Church of St John the Baptist; *Galilee* – the Sea, Church and Mount of the Beatitudes, ruins of Capernaum and other sites connected with the life of Christ; *Mount Tabor* – Church of the Transfiguration; *Nazareth* – Church of the Annunciation, and other Christian shrines associated with the childhood of Christ; there are also numerous sites dating from biblical and medieval days, such as Ascalon, Caesarea, Atlit, Massada, Megiddo and Hazor.

PALESTINIAN AUTONOMOUS AREAS

AREA – The total area is 2,406 sq. miles (6,231 sq. km). The area which is fully autonomous is 159 sq. miles (412 sq. km), of which the Gaza Strip is 136 sq. miles (352 sq. km) and the Jericho enclave 23 sq. miles (60 sq. km). The partially autonomous area is the remainder of the West Bank, some 2,247 sq. miles (5,819 sq. km). The UN and the international community also recognize East Jerusalem as part of the Occupied Territories
POPULATION – 2,920,454 (1998 census), of whom 210,209 live in East Jerusalem. In addition there are 141,000 Jewish settlers in the West Bank and 4,000 in the Gaza Strip who remain under Israeli administration and jurisdiction. Some 90 per cent of Palestinians are Muslim (the vast majority Sunni) and 10 per cent are Christians
CAPITAL – Although Palestinians claim East Jerusalem as their capital, the administrative capital has been established in Gaza City (population 120,000)

MAJOR TOWNS – Khan Yunis, Rafah in the Gaza Strip; Nablus, Hebron, Jericho, Ramallah and Bethlehem on the West Bank
FLAG – Three horizontal stripes of black, white, green with a red triangle based on the hoist (the PLO flag)
NATIONAL ANTHEM – Fidai, Fidai (Freedom Fighter, Freedom Fighter)

HISTORY AND POLITICS

Israel captured the Gaza Strip, East Jerusalem and the West Bank during the 1967 Six-Day War and annexed East Jerusalem. After the war the Israeli government began to establish settlements in the Occupied Territories. Palestinian resistance to Israeli rule was led by the Palestine Liberation Organization (PLO) which was established in 1964. Frustration at continued Israeli occupation led to the start of the *intifada*, a campaign of sustained unrest, in 1987. When the 1991 Madrid peace process stalled, Israeli and PLO officials engaged in secret negotiations in Norway which led to the signing of the 'Declaration of Principles on Interim Self-Government Arrangements' on 13 September 1993. Under this agreement the PLO renounced terrorism and recognized Israel's right to exist in secure borders, while Israel recognized the PLO as the legitimate representative of the Palestinian people.

The Declaration of Principles established a timetable for progress towards a final settlement: negotiations leading to an Israeli military withdrawal from the Gaza Strip and Jericho by 13 April 1994, when power was to be transferred to a nominated Palestinian National Authority (PNA); elections to a new Palestinian Council, which would also exercise control over six policy areas in the rest of the West Bank (culture, tourism, health, education, social welfare, direct taxation), and the Israeli military administration dissolved by 13 July 1994; negotiations on a permanent settlement, including Jewish settlers and East Jerusalem, to begin by 13 April 1996; and a permanent settlement to be in place by 13 April 1999.

The timetable has slipped, with the Israeli military not finally redeploying in the Gaza Strip and withdrawing from Jericho until 18 May 1994, when the five-year period of interim self-government under the PNA began.

Israel and the Palestinians struggled to reach agreement on the extension of self-rule until 28 September 1995, when the 'Oslo B' or Taba Accord was signed which provided for Israeli withdrawal from six towns and 85 per cent of Hebron; the extension of self-rule to most of the West Bank by 1998; the release of 5,300 Palestinian prisoners; and the striking out of the demand for Israel's destruction from the PLO's charter. On 29 December 1995 an agreement was reached on the transfer of 17 areas of civilian power to the PNA in Hebron.

Implementation of the agreement began with the release of 1,100 Palestinian prisoners in October 1995; Israeli troops left Ramallah, the last of the six West Bank towns, on 27 December 1995 and the inaugural Palestinian National Council meeting on 23 April 1996 voted to amend the PLO charter. The final element of the Declaration of Principles, the 'final status talks' opened in Taba, Egypt, on 5 May 1996 to decide the final status of the West Bank, Gaza and Jerusalem. The election of a Likud-led government opposed to the establishment of a Palestinian state resulted in a deadlock in negotiations in 1997 and delays in the withdrawal of Israeli troops from Hebron.

Legislative elections on 20 January 1996 were won by the mainstream al-Fatah faction of the PLO, with its leader Yasser Arafat winning 88.1 per cent of the vote to become the president of the Palestinian National Authority.

Talks between the Palestinians and Israelis continued intermittently throughout 1997, but little of substance was achieved. Yasser Arafat and Binyamin Netanyahu met separately with American diplomats in London in May 1998, but talks broke down over the precise extent of Israeli troop withdrawals.

Yasser Arafat had planned to declare an independent Palestinian state on 4 May 1999, the end of the five-year transitional period which had been agreed in the 1993 Oslo peace accords, but the announcement was postponed in the hope that talks with the new Israeli government would lead to a negotiated settlement.

POLITICAL SYSTEM

The Oslo B accord laid down the political structure of the nascent Palestinian state. Executive authority is vested in the Palestinian National Authority which is headed by a popularly elected leader (*rais*). Legislative authority is vested in the 88-member Palestinian Council which is directly elected by means of a first-past-the-post system, and itself elects the four-fifths of the PNA not appointed by the leader.

PALESTINIAN NATIONAL AUTHORITY *as at July 1999*

Leader, Yasser Arafat
Agriculture, Hikmet Zeid
Civil Affairs, Jamil al-Tarifi
Culture and Arts, Information, Yassir Abd ar-Rabbuh
Economy and Trade, Mahir al-Masri
Education, vacant
Environment, vacant
Finance, Muhammad Zuhdi al-Nashashibi
Higher Education, Dr Munther Salah
Housing, Dr Abd al-Rahman Hamad
Industry, Dr Saad al-Karnaz
Interior, vacant
Justice, Furayh Abu Middayn
Labour, Rafiq al-Natshe
Local Government, Dr Sa'ib 'Urayqat
Parliament, Nabil Amr
Planning, International Co-operation, Dr Nabil Sha'ath
Prisoners' Affairs, Hisham Abdul Razeq
Public Works, Azzam al-Ahmad
Religious Affairs, vacant
Social Affairs, Intisar al-Wazir
Supply, Abd al-Aziz Shahin
Telecommunications, Imad al-Faluji
Tourism and Archaeology, Mitri Abu Ayta
Transport, Dr Ali al-Qawasmi
Youth and Sport, vacant

BRITISH CONSULATE-GENERAL
19 Nashashibi Street, PO Box 19690, East Jerusalem 97200
Consul-General, R. A. Kealy

BRITISH COUNCIL DIRECTOR, P. Skelton, OBE (*Cultural Attaché*), Al-Nuzha Building, 2 Abu Obeida Street, PO Box 19136, Jerusalem

---

ITALY
Repubblica Italiana

AREA – 116,320 sq. miles (301,268 sq. km). Neighbours: Switzerland and Austria (north), Slovenia (east), France (west)

POPULATION – 57,339,000 (1994 UN estimate): 83 per cent Catholic. The language is Italian, a Romance language derived from Latin. German and Ladin in the South Tyrol, French in the Valle d'Aosta and Slovene in parts of Gorizia

CAPITAL – Rome (population, 2,693,383, 1991). The Eternal City was founded, according to legend, by Romulus in 753 BC. It was the centre of Latin civilization and capital of the Roman Republic and Roman Empire

MAJOR CITIES – Bologna (404,322); Florence (402,316); ΨGenoa (675,659); Milan (1,371,008); ΨNaples (1,054,601); Turin (961,916); *Sicily*, ΨPalermo (697,162); *Sardinia*, ΨCagliari (203,254), 1991 census

CURRENCY – Lira of 100 centesimi

NATIONAL ANTHEM – Inno di Mameli

NATIONAL DAY – 2 June

NATIONAL FLAG – Vertical stripes of green, white and red

LIFE EXPECTANCY (years) – male 73.79; female 80.36

POPULATION GROWTH RATE – –0.1 per cent (1997)

POPULATION DENSITY – 191 per sq. km (1996)

URBAN POPULATION – 96.6 per cent (1991)

Italy consists of a peninsula, the islands of Sicily, Sardinia, Elba and about 70 other small islands. The peninsula is for the most part mountainous, but between the Apennines, which form its spine, and the eastern coastline are two large fertile plains: Emilia-Romagna in the north and Apulia in the south. The Alps divide Italy from France, Switzerland, Austria and Slovenia. Partly within the Italian borders are Monte Rosa (15,217 ft), the Matterhorn (14,780 ft) and several peaks from 12,000 to 14,000 ft. The chief rivers are the Po (405 miles), flowing through Piedmont, Lombardy and the Veneto; the Adige (Trentino and Veneto); the Arno (Florentine plain); and the Tiber (flowing through Rome to Ostia).

HISTORY AND POLITICS

Italian unity was accomplished under the House of Savoy after a struggle from 1848 to 1870 in which Mazzini (1805–72), Garibaldi (1807–82) and Cavour (1810–61) were the principal figures. It was completed when Lombardy was ceded by Austria in 1859 and Venice in 1866, and through the evacuation of Rome by the French in 1870. In 1871 the King of Italy entered Rome, and that city was declared to be the capital.

A fascist regime came to power in 1922 under Benito Mussolini, known as *Il Duce* (The Leader), who was prime minister from 1922 until 25 July 1943, when the regime was abolished. Mussolini was captured by Italian partisans while attempting to escape across the Swiss frontier and killed on 28 April 1945.

In fulfilment of a promise given in April 1944 that he would retire when the Allies entered Rome, a decree was signed in June 1944 by King Victor Emmanuel III under which Prince Umberto, his son, became Lieutenant-General of the Realm. The King remained head of the House of Savoy and retained the title King of Italy until his abdication in May 1946, when he was succeeded by the Crown Prince. A referendum on the future of the monarchy was held in June 1946, in which a majority favoured a republic, and the royal family left the country.

Political instability and corruption led to public disenchantment with the major political parties, whose support collapsed in the 1992 general election. The so-called 'clean hands' investigation into corruption and Mafia links that began in 1992 has led to the arrest by magistrates of thousands of politicians and businessmen.

The first general election under the new electoral system, in March 1994, resulted in victory for the right-wing Freedom Alliance, who formed a government led by millionaire businessman Silvio Berlusconi in May 1994, which collapsed in December 1994 following Berlusconi's indictment on charges of bribery and corruption. The independent Treasury minister Lamberto Dini formed a government of technocrats in January 1995. Dini resigned in January 1996 and a general election on 21 April 1996 was won by the left-wing Olive Tree alliance led by the Democratic Party of the Left, whose leader, Romano Prodi, became prime minister. The government won 157 seats in the Senate and 284 seats in the Chamber of Deputies where it required the support of the Communist Refoundation (RC) to win a vote of confidence. In October 1997, the RC refused to support the government budget and Prodi offered his resignation. President Scalfaro refused to accept the resignation and after negotiations Prodi and the RC signed a one-year agreement, but on 9 October 1998, the government collapsed after the RC refused to support the 1999 budget. Prodi lost the confidence motion and was forced to resign. Massimo D'Alema was invited by the president to form a new government on 20 October.

POLITICAL SYSTEM

The constitution provides for the election of the president for a seven-year term by an electoral college which consists of the two houses of the parliament (the Chamber of Deputies and the Senate) sitting in joint session, together with three delegates from each region (one in the case of the Valle d'Aosta). The president, who must be over 50 years of age, has the right to dissolve one or both houses after consultation with the Speakers. Members of both houses were elected wholly by proportional representation until 1993. Now 75 per cent (232) of the 315 elected seats in the Senate are elected on a first-past-the-post basis and the remaining elected seats are filled by proportional representation. There are 11 life senators, who are past presidents and prime ministers. In the Chamber of Deputies 75 per cent (472) of seats are elected on a first-past-the-post basis, and 25 per cent (158) by proportional representation, with a 4 per cent threshold for parliamentary representation. A referendum on 18 April 1999 on abolishing the seats elected by proportional representation foundered when less than the required 50 per cent of the electorate participated.

HEAD OF STATE

President, Carlo Azeglio Ciampi, *elected by electoral college* 13 May 1999

COUNCIL OF MINISTERS *as at July 1999*

Prime Minister, Massimo D'Alema (DPL)
Deputy P.M, Sergio Mattarella (IPP)
Agriculture, Paolo De Castro (Ind.)
Communications, Salvatore Cardinale (DUR)
Culture, Giovanna Melandri (DPL)
Defence, Carlo Scognamiglio (DUR)
Education, Luigi Berlinguer (DPL)
Employment and Social Welfare, Antonio Bassolino (DPL)
Environment, Edo Ronchi (Green)
Equal Opportunities, Laura Balbo (Green)
European Policies, Enrico Letta (IPP)
Finance, Vincenzo Visco (DPL)
Foreign Affairs, Lamberto Dini (IR)
Foreign Trade, Piero Fassino (DPL)
Health, Rosaria Bindi (IPP)
Industry and Tourism, Pierluigi Bersani (DPL)
Institutional Reforms, Giuliano Amato (Ind.)
Interior, Rosa Russo Jervolino (IPP)
Justice, Oliviero Diliberto (PIC)
Public Administration, Angelo Piazza (DPL)
Public Works, Enrico Micheli (IPP)
Regional Affairs, Katia Belillo (PIC)
Relations with Parliament, Guido Folloni (IPP)
Social Solidarity, Livia Turco (DPL)
Transport and Navigation, Tiziano Treu (IR)
Treasury and Budget, Carlo Azeglio Ciampi (Ind.)
University and Scientific Research, Ortensio Zecchino (IPP)

DPL Democratic Party of the Left; DUR Democratic Union for the Republic; Green Green Party; IPP Italian People's Party; IR Italian Renewal; ISD Italian Social Democrats; PIC Party of Italian Communists; Ind. Independent

ITALIAN EMBASSY
14 Three Kings Yard, Davies Street, London WIY 2EH
Tel 0171-312 2200
Ambassador Extraordinary and Plenipotentiary,
HE Dr Paolo Galli, apptd 1995
Minister-Counsellor, Dr A. D'Andria
Defence Attaché, Rear-Admr. A. Campregher
Cultural Attaché, Prof. B. Abruzzese
Consul-General, L. Savoia
First Counsellor, A. Cevese (*Commercial*)
CONSULAR OFFICES – Bedford, Edinburgh, Manchester

BRITISH EMBASSY
Via XX Settembre 80A, I-00187 Rome
Tel: Rome 482-5441
Ambassador Extraordinary and Plenipotentiary,
HE Thomas L. Richardson, CMG, apptd 1996
Deputy Head of Mission, A. M. Leslie
Defence and Military Attaché, Brig. J. A. Anderson
Director-General for British Trade Development in Italy and
   Consul-General, C. De Chassiron (*Milan*)
Counsellor (Economic and Commercial), M. A. Hatfull
CONSULATES-GENERAL – Milan, Naples
CONSULATES – Rome, Bari, Florence, Genoa, Trieste, Turin, Venice, Messina, Brindisi, Palermo, Cagliari

BRITISH COUNCIL REPRESENTATIVE, R. Alford, OBE, Palazzo del Drago, Via Quattro Fontane 20, I-00184 Rome. There are British Council Offices at Milan, Bologna, Naples and Turin

BRITISH CHAMBER OF COMMERCE, Via San Paolo 7, I-20121 Milan

DEFENCE

The Army has 1,299 main battle tanks, 2,703 armoured personnel carriers and 1,567 artillery pieces. The Navy has eight submarines, one aircraft carrier, one cruiser, four destroyers, 24 frigates, 17 patrol and coastal vessels, 18 combat aircraft and 80 armed helicopters. There are ten naval bases. The Air Force has 253 combat aircraft.

MILITARY EXPENDITURE – 1.9 per cent of GDP (1997)
MILITARY PERSONNEL – 524,900: Army 165,600, Navy 40,000, Air Force 63,600, Paramilitaries 255,700
CONSCRIPTION DURATION – Ten months

ECONOMY

Deposits of natural methane gas and oil have been discovered, mainly south of Sicily, and have been rapidly exploited. Production of lignite has also increased. Other minerals include iron ores and pyrites, mercury (over one-quarter of the world production), lead, zinc and aluminium. Rich gold veins were discovered in Sardinia in 1996. Marble is a traditional product of the Massa Carrara district.

Agricultural production is concentrated in Tuscany, Emilia-Romagna, Sicily and the whole of the southern third of the country. The principal products are wine, tobacco, citrus fruits, tomatoes, almonds, sugar beet, wheat and maize.

Tourism is a major contributor to the economy; in 1996, more than 56 million people visited Italy. The commercial and banking services are concentrated in Rome and in Milan, where the stock market is located.

The state-owned sector of Italian industry is still important, dominated by the holding companies IRI (mechanical, steel, airlines), ENI (petrochemicals), and ENEL (electricity). Industry is centred around Milan (steel, machine tools, motor cars), Turin (motor cars, steel, roller bearings, textiles), Rome (light industries), Venice (ship-building, paper, mechanical equipment, electrical goods, woollens), Bologna/Florence (food industry, footwear and textiles, reproduction furniture, glassware, pottery, ceramics), Naples, Bari (valves, vehicle bodies, tyres), Taranto (steel, oil refining), Trieste (shipbuilding) and Cagliari (aluminium production, petrochemicals).

Following a programme of severe austerity measures, Italy satisfied the convergence criteria and participated in the European Single Currency from 1 January 1999.

In 1997 there was a trade surplus of US$46,785 million and a current account surplus of US$33,425 million. Imports totalled US$208,272 million and exports US$238,240 million.

Italy's chief exports are industrial and agricultural machinery, textiles and clothing, electrical equipment and chemicals. Chief imports are chemicals, motor vehicles and metals. Italy's main trading partners are Germany, France, the UK and the USA.

GNP – US$1,160,444 million (1997); US$20,170 per capita (1997)
GDP – US$1,093,799 million (1995); US$19,121 per capita (1995)
ANNUAL AVERAGE GROWTH OF GDP – 1.5 per cent (1997)
INFLATION RATE – 2.0 per cent (1997)
UNEMPLOYMENT – 12 per cent (1995); forecast to be 11.5 per cent in 1997

Trade with UK	1997	1998
Imports from UK	£7,786,400,000	£8,140,000,000
Exports to UK	9,106,900,000	9,273,700,000

COMMUNICATIONS

The main railway system is state-run by the *Ferrovia dello Stato*. There are 19,527 km of railway track. A network of motorways (*autostrade*) covers the country, built and operated mainly by the IRI state holding company and ANAS, the state highway authority. There are 306,445 km

of roads. Alitalia, the principal international and domestic airline, is also state-controlled by the IRI group. Other smaller companies, including ATI (an Alitalia subsidiary) and Air Mediterranea, operate on domestic routes. Genoa is the major port, handling about one-third of Italy's foreign trade.

EDUCATION

Education is free and compulsory between the ages of six and 14; this comprises five years at primary school and three in 'middle school', of which there are 9,215. Pupils who obtain the middle school certificate may seek admission to any 'senior secondary school', which may be a lyceum with a classical or scientific or artistic bias, or an institute directed at technology (of which there are eight different types), trade or industry (including vocational schools), or teacher-training. Courses at the lyceums and technical institutes usually last for five years and success in the final examination qualifies for admission to university.

There are 62 universities, some of ancient foundation; those at Bologna, Modena, Parma and Padua were started in the 12th century. University education is not free, but entrants with higher qualifications are charged reduced fees according to a sliding scale.

In general, schools, lyceums and universities are financed by local taxation and central government grants.

ILLITERACY RATE – 1.9 per cent
ENROLMENT (percentage of age group) – primary 98 per cent (1995); tertiary 41.4 per cent (1995)

CULTURE

Florence, the capital of Tuscany, was one of the greatest cities in Europe from the 11th to the 16th centuries, and the cradle of the Renaissance. Under the Medici family in the 15th century flourished many of the greatest names in Italian art, including Filippo Lippi, Botticelli, Donatello and Brunelleschi, and in the 16th century Michelangelo and Leonardo da Vinci.

Italian literature (in addition to Latin literature, which is the common inheritance of western Europe) is one of the richest in Europe, particularly in its golden age (Dante, 1265–1321; Petrarch, 1304–74; Boccaccio, 1313–75) and in the Renaissance (Ariosto, 1474–1533; Machiavelli, 1469–1527; Tasso, 1544–95). Notable in modern Italian literature are Manzoni (1785–1873), Carducci (1835–1907) and Gabriele d'Annunzio (1864–1938). The Nobel Prize for Literature has been awarded to Italian authors on six occasions: G. Cariducci (1906), Signora G. Deledda (1926), Luigi Pirandello (1934), Salvatore Quasimodo (1959), Eugenio Montale (1975) and Dario Fo (1997).

ISLANDS

CAPRI, in the Bay of Naples; area 4 sq. miles (10 sq. km); population 12,000
EOLIAN ISLANDS, including Lipari; area 45 sq. miles (116 sq. km); population 18,636
FLEGREAN ISLANDS, including Ischia; area 23 sq. miles (60 sq. km); population 51,883
PANTELLERIA ISLAND (part of Trapani Province) in the Sicilian Narrows; area 31 sq. miles (80 sq. km); population 9,601
THE PELAGIAN ISLANDS (Lampedusa, Linosa and Lampione) are part of the province of Agrigento; area 8 sq. miles (21 sq. km); population 4,811
PONTINE ARCHIPELAGO, including Ponza; area 4 sq. miles (10 sq. km); population 2,515
TREMITI ISLANDS; area 1 sq. mile (3 sq. km); population 426
THE TUSCAN ARCHIPELAGO (including Elba); area 113 sq. miles (293 sq. km); population 31,861

JAMAICA

AREA – 4,243 sq. miles (10,990 sq. km)
POPULATION – 2,491,000 (1994 UN estimate). The
official language is English; a local patois is also spoken
CAPITAL – ΨKingston (population, 524,638, 1991)
MAJOR CITIES – Mandeville; May Pen; ΨMontego Bay;
Ocho Rios; Spanish Town
CURRENCY – Jamaican dollar (J$) of 100 cents
NATIONAL ANTHEM – Jamaica, Land We Love
NATIONAL DAY – 6 August (Independence Day)
NATIONAL FLAG – Gold diagonal cross forming triangles
of green at top and bottom, triangles of black at hoist
and in fly
LIFE EXPECTANCY (years) – male 71.41; female 75.82
POPULATION GROWTH RATE – 0.9 per cent (1997)
POPULATION DENSITY – 227 per sq. km (1996)
MILITARY EXPENDITURE – 0.6 per cent of GDP (1997)
MILITARY PERSONNEL – 3,320: Army 3,000, Coast
Guard 150, Air Wing 170
ILLITERACY RATE – 15.0 per cent
ENROLMENT (percentage of age group) – primary 100
per cent (1992); secondary 64 per cent (1992); tertiary
8.1 per cent (1996)

Jamaica is divided into three counties (Surrey, Middlesex
and Cornwall) and 14 parishes. The island consists mainly
of coastal plains, divided by the Blue Mountain range in
the east and the hills and limestone plateaux in the central
and western areas of the interior. The central chain of the
Blue Mountains is over 6,000 feet above sea level, and the
Blue Mountain Peak is 7,402 feet.

HISTORY AND POLITICS

The island was discovered by Columbus in 1494, and
occupied by Spain from 1509 until 1655 when an English
expedition under Admiral Penn and General Venables
captured the island. In 1670 it was formally ceded to
England by the Treaty of Madrid. Jamaica became an
independent state within the Commonwealth on 6 August
1962.

At the general election of 18 December 1997, the
People's National Party won 50 out of a total of 60 seats,
securing a third term as prime minister for Percival
Patterson.

POLITICAL SYSTEM

Queen Elizabeth II is the head of state, represented by the
Governor-General. The legislature consists of a Senate of
21 nominated members and a House of Representatives
consisting of 60 members elected by universal adult
suffrage for a five-year term. The prime minister is the
leader of the majority party in the House.

Governor-General, HE Sir Howard Felix Hanlon Cooke,
GCMG, GCVO, apptd 1991

CABINET *as at July 1999*

Prime Minister, Percival J. Patterson, QC
Deputy PM, Foreign Affairs and Foreign Trade, Seymour
Mullings
Agriculture, Roger Clarke
Commerce and Technology, Phillip Paulwell
Education, Youth and Culture, Burchel Whiteman
Environment and Housing, Easton Douglas
Finance and Planning, Omar Davies
Health, John Archbald Junor
Industry, Investments and Commerce, Paul Robertson
Labour, Social Security and Sports, Portia Simpson

Legal Affairs, Attorney-General, Arnold Nicholson
Local Government and Community Development, Arnold
Bertram
Mining and Energy, Robert Pickersgill
National Security and Justice, Keith Desmond Knight
Tourism, Francis Tulloch
Transportation and Works, Peter Phillips
Water, Enoch Carl Blythe
Without Portfolio, Maxine Henry-Wilson

JAMAICAN HIGH COMMISSION
1–2 Prince Consort Road, London SW7 2BZ
Tel 0171-823 9911
High Commissioner, HE David Muirhead, apptd 1999
Deputy High Commissioners, O. Singh; J. K. Pringle, CBE, OJ
(*Trade*)
Minister-Counsellor, K. Hamilton (*Consular Affairs*)
Defence Adviser, Col. B. Blake

BRITISH HIGH COMMISSION
PO Box 575, Trafalgar Road, Kingston 10
Tel: Kingston 926 9050
High Commissioner, HE A. F. Smith, apptd 1999
Deputy High Commissioner, J. Malcolm, OBE
Defence Adviser, Col. A. Moorby
First Secretary (Management/Consular), P. Duffy

BRITISH COUNCIL REPRESENTATIVE IN THE
CARIBBEAN, J. Day, 4th Floor, PCMB Building, 64
Knutsford Boulevard, PO Box 235, Kingston 5

ECONOMY

Alumina, bananas, bauxite and sugar are the main exports.
Other exports include garments, processed food products,
limestone and horticultural products.

Since 1989 the PNP government has abolished price
subsidies, removed foreign exchange controls and introduced a 10 per cent consumption tax. Jamaica is a popular
tourist resort, attracting 1,900,000 visitors in 1998.

The introduction on 16 April 1999 of a 30 per cent tax
on fuel led to three days of violent protests. The
controversial tax was halved on 27 April 1999.

In 1997 Jamaica had a trade deficit of US$1,110 million
and a current account deficit of US$376 million. Imports
totalled US$3,026 million and exports US$1,352 million.
GNP – US$3,956 million (1997); US$1,550 per capita
(1997)
GDP – US$4,391 million (1995); US$1,779 per capita
(1995)
ANNUAL AVERAGE GROWTH OF GDP – minus 2.4 per
cent (1997)
INFLATION RATE – 9.7 per cent (1997)
UNEMPLOYMENT – 15.9 per cent (1992)
TOTAL EXTERNAL DEBT – US$3,913 million (1997)

Trade with UK	1997	1998
Imports from UK	£59,888,000	£68,277,000
Exports to UK	138,379,000	114,683,000

COMMUNICATIONS

There are several excellent harbours, Kingston being the
principal port. The island has 2,944 miles of main roads
and 7,264 miles of subsidiary roads.

There are two international airports, the Norman
Manley International Airport on the south coast serving
Kingston, and Sangster Airport on the north coast serving
the major tourist areas. In addition there are licensed
aerodromes at Port Antonio, Ocho Rios, Mandeville and
Negril. There are 16 privately owned, seven public and
two military airstrips. Air Jamaica, the national airline,
operates international services.

JAPAN
Nihon Koku – Land of the Rising Sun

AREA – 145,870 sq. miles (377,801 sq. km)
POPULATION – 125,761,000 (1994 UN estimate). The
principal religions are Mahayana Buddhism and Shinto.
About 1 per cent of Japanese are Christians. The
language is Japanese
CAPITAL – Tokyo (population, 11,680,296, 1993 estimate)
MAJOR CITIES – ΨFukuoka (1,284,795); ΨKobé
(1,423,792); Kyoto, the ancient capital (1,463,822);
ΨNagoya (2,152,184); ΨOsaka (2,602,421); Sapporo
(1,757,025); ΨYokohama (3,307,136), 1995
CURRENCY – Yen
NATIONAL ANTHEM – Kimigayo
NATIONAL DAY – 11 February (National Foundation
Day)
NATIONAL FLAG – White, charged with sun (red)
LIFE EXPECTANCY (years) – male 76.57; female 82.98
POPULATION GROWTH RATE – 0.3 per cent (1997)
POPULATION DENSITY – 333 per sq. km (1996)
URBAN POPULATION – 78.1 per cent (1995)

Japan consists of four large islands: *Honshu* (or Mainland)
88,839 sq. miles (230,448 sq. km), *Shikoku*, 7,231 sq. miles
(18,757 sq. km), *Kyushu*, 16,170 sq. miles (42,079 sq. km),
Hokkaido, 30,265 sq. miles (78,508 sq. km), and many small
islands (including Okinawa).

The interior is very mountainous, and crossing the
mainland from the Sea of Japan to the Pacific is a group of
volcanoes, mainly extinct or dormant. Mount Fuji, the
most sacred mountain of Japan, is 12,370 ft high and has
been dormant since 1707, but volcanoes which are active
include Mount Aso in Kyushu. There are frequent
earthquakes, mainly along the Pacific coast near the Bay of
Tokyo. The climate varies from sub-tropical in the south
to cool temperate in the north.

HISTORY AND POLITICS

According to tradition, Jimmu, the first Emperor of Japan,
ascended the throne on 11 February 660 BC. Under the
Meiji constitution (1889), the monarchy is hereditary in the
male heirs of the Imperial house.

After the unconditional surrender to the Allied nations
(14 August 1945), Japan was occupied by Allied forces
under General MacArthur. A Japanese peace treaty became
effective on 28 April 1952. Japan then resumed her status
as an independent power.

The (conservative) Liberal Democratic Party (LDP)
governed Japan almost without interruption from the
Second World War until 1993. During the 1990s public
disenchantment at political corruption led to a loss of
support for the LDP and the formation of several splinter
parties. Support for the new parties caused the LDP to lose
its majority at the 1993 election, following which a seven-
party coalition formed a government.

The government led by Morihiro Hosokawa (JNP)
reached a compromise with the LDP-controlled House of
Councillors to phase out corporate donations to individual
MPs by 2000. State funding for political parties was
introduced and the electoral system altered. The LDP
returned to power in June 1994 in coalition with the SDPJ
and Sakigake parties, with SDPJ leader Tomiichi
Murayama becoming Japan's first socialist prime minister.
Five reformist opposition parties (JNP, JRP, Komeito,
DSP, USDP) merged in November 1994 to form the New
Frontier Party (NFP) (Shinshinto) as a rival centre-right
conservative party to the LDP. Murayama resigned in

January 1996 and was replaced by LDP leader Ryutaro
Hashimoto. The NFP disbanded in December 1997. In
March 1998 four opposition parties merged to form the
Democratic Party of Japan.

Hashimoto was elected to a second term as prime
minister, but resigned in July 1998 following a heavy defeat
for the LDP in the upper house elections, seen as largely
due to his handling of the economic crisis. He was replaced
as prime minister and leader of the LDP by Foreign
Minister Keizo Obuchi. The LDP have 263 seats in the
House of Representatives. The standing of the other parties
is: Democratic Party 91; Heiwa Kaikaku 47; Liberal Party
40; Japan Communist Party 26; SDP 14; Sakigake 2;
Independent 10.

POLITICAL SYSTEM

Legislative authority rests with the bicameral *Diet*, which
comprises a 500-member House of Representatives, and a
252-member House of Councillors. The House of Representatives chooses the prime minister from among its ranks,
ratifies treaties and passes budget bills. Since 1996, 200 of
its members are elected by proportional representation in
11 regional blocks and 300 in single-member, first-past-
the-post constituencies. All members serve four-year terms.
The House of Councillors elects half its members every
three years for six-year terms. Unlike the lower House it
cannot be dissolved by the prime minister. Executive
authority is vested in the Cabinet which is responsible to
the legislature.

HEAD OF STATE

His Imperial Majesty The Emperor of Japan, Emperor
Akihito, *born* 23 December 1933; *succeeded* 8 January
1989; *enthroned* 12 November 1990; *married* 10 April
1959, Miss Michiko Shoda, and has *issue*: the Crown
Prince (*see* below); Prince Fumihito, *born* 30 November
1965; and Princess Sayako, *born* 18 April 1969
Heir, HRH Crown Prince Naruhito Hironomiya, *born* 23
February 1960, *married* 9 June 1993 Miss Masako
Owada

CABINET *as at July 1999*

Prime Minister, Keizo Obuchi
Agriculture, Forestry and Fisheries, Shoichi Nakagawa
Chief Cabinet Secretary, Hiromu Nonaka
Construction, National Land Agency, Katsutsugu Sekiya
Defence Agency, Hosei Norota
Economic Planning Agency, Taichi Sakaiya
Education, Science and Technology Agency, Akito Arima
Environment Agency, Kenji Manabe

Finance, Kiichi Miyazawa
Foreign Affairs, Masahiko Koumura
Health and Welfare, Sohei Miyashita
Home Affairs, Takeshi Noda
International Trade and Industry, Kaoru Yosano
Justice, Takao Jinnouchi
Labour, Akira Amari
Management and Co-ordination Agency, Seiichi Ota
National Banking System, Hakuo Yanagisawa
Post and Telecommunications, Seiko Noda
Transport, Hokkaido Development Agency, Jiro Kawasaki

EMBASSY OF JAPAN
101–104 Piccadilly, London WIV 9FN
Tel 0171-465 6500
Ambassador Extraordinary and Plenipotentiary, HE Sadayuki
    Hayashi, apptd 1997
Ministers, I. Umezu (*Plenipotentiary*); S. Nakamura (*Consul-
    General*); M. Amano (*Commercial*); C. Harada; K. Monji;
    T. Uranishi

BRITISH EMBASSY
No. 1 Ichiban-cho, Chiyoda-ku, Tokyo 102-8381
Tel: Tokyo 5211-1100
Ambassador Extraordinary and Plenipotentiary, HE Stephen
    Gommersall, CMG, apptd 1999
Chargé d'Affaires, C. T. W. Humfrey, CMG
Counsellors, P. Bateman (*Commercial*); R. R. Hoggard
    (*Management and Consul-General*)
Defence and Naval Attaché, Capt. N. D. V. Robertson
CONSULATES-GENERAL – Tokyo, Osaka
HONORARY CONSULATES – Fukuoka, Hiroshima,
    Nagoya, Sapporo

BRITISH COUNCIL REPRESENTATIVE, M. Barrett, OBE
    (*Cultural Attaché*), 2 Kagurazaka 1-Chome, Shinjuku-ku,
    Tokyo 162
BRITISH CHAMBER OF COMMERCE, No. 16 Kowa
    Building, 1–9–20 Akasaka, Minato-ku, Tokyo 107

DEFENCE

The constitution prohibits the maintenance of armed
forces, although internal security forces were created in
the 1950s and their mission was extended in 1954 to
include the defence of Japan against aggression. In the
1990s legislation was passed permitting the armed forces
limited participation in UN peacekeeping missions and
allowing them to enter foreign conflicts in order to protect
Japanese nationals. A revision to the USA–Japan defence
co-operation guidelines agreed in 1997 permits Japan to
play a supporting role in US military operations in areas
surrounding Japan.

The Ground Self-Defence Force (GSDF) has 1,090
main battle tanks, around 870 armoured personnel carriers,
60 infantry fighting vehicles, 790 artillery pieces, 20 aircraft
and 90 attack helicopters. The Maritime Self-Defence
Force (MSDF) has 16 submarines, nine destroyers, 48
frigates, 100 combat aircraft and 106 armed helicopters at
five bases. The Air Self-Defence Force (ASDF) has 329
combat aircraft.

The USA has 39,100 personnel stationed in Japan.
Following an agreement in December 1996 the USA is due
to vacate 21 per cent of the land it occupies in Japan and
close part or all of 11 military facilities.
MILITARY EXPENDITURE – 1.0 per cent of GDP (1997)
MILITARY PERSONNEL – 253,200: Army 151,800, Navy
    43,800, Air Force 45,600, Paramilitaries 12,000

ECONOMY

Owing to the mountainous nature of the country less than
20 per cent of its area can be cultivated and only 14 per

cent is used for agriculture; 67 per cent is wooded. The
soil is only moderately fertile but intensive cultivation
secures good crops. Tobacco, tea, potatoes, rice, maize,
wheat and other cereals are all cultivated. Rice is the staple
food of the people. Fruit is abundant and pigs and chickens
are widely reared.

Mineral resources include gold, silver, copper, lead, zinc,
iron chromite, white arsenic, coal, sulphur, petroleum, salt
and uranium. However, iron ore, coal and crude oil are
among the principal imports.

Japan is one of the most highly industrialized nations in
the world, with the whole range of modern light and heavy
industries, including steel, aerospace, computers, office
machinery, motor vehicles, electronics, metals, machinery,
chemicals, textiles (cotton, silk, wool and synthetics),
cement, pottery, glass, rubber, lumber, paper, oil refining
and shipbuilding.

Japan's economy has been severely affected by the
financial crisis in Asia. Its banks have made loans totalling
some US$200 billion to tiger economies, and following
widespread economic collapse in the region, Japan's
financial institutions have suffered; Yamaichi Securities
became Japan's largest ever commercial failure when it
folded in November 1997. The Nikkei Dow lost a quarter
of its value in 1997. Emergency measures announced by
the government were perceived by the markets as
inadequate. Japan's economy contracted in 1998; GDP fell
by 2.8 per cent. The economy showed signs of recovery in
1999, although unemployment reached 4.8 per cent, the
highest level since the Second World War.
GNP – US$4,812,103 million (1997); US$38,160 per
    capita (1997)
GDP – US$5,217,573 million (1995); US$41,718 per
    capita (1995)
ANNUAL AVERAGE GROWTH OF GDP – 0.9 per cent
    (1997)
INFLATION RATE – 1.7 per cent (1997)
UNEMPLOYMENT – 3.2 per cent (1995)

TRADE

Being deficient in natural resources, Japan has had to
develop a complex foreign trade. Principal imports include
mineral fuels, food, raw materials and metal ores. Principal
exports include machinery, transport equipment, chemicals, metal products and textiles.

In 1997 Japan had a trade surplus of US$101,600 million
and a current account surplus of US$94,354 million.
Imports totalled US$338,754 million and exports
US$420,957 million. The USA, China, Australia, Hong
Kong, South Korea, Taiwan and Singapore are Japan's
main trading partners.

Trade with UK	1997	1998
Imports from UK	£4,177,609,000	£3,222,587,000
Exports to UK	9,409,949,000	9,548,786,000

COMMUNICATIONS

There are 27,258 km of railway track and 1,142,308 km of
roads. Japan National Railways was privatized in 1987 and
is known as Japan Railways (JR). There are six regional
companies and one goods company. Shinkansen (bullet
train) tracks are currently being expanded. The opening in
1988 of the Seikan rail tunnel and the Seto Ohashi rail
bridge means that the four major islands are now linked for
the first time. There are six international airports.

EDUCATION

Education at elementary (six-year course) and lower
secondary (three-year course) schools is free, compulsory

and co-educational. The (three-year) upper secondary schools are attended by 96.7 per cent of the age group.

There are two- or three-year colleges and four-year universities. Some of the universities have graduate schools. In 1996 there were 576 universities and colleges, most of which are privately maintained. The most prominent universities are the seven state universities of Tokyo, Kyoto, Tohoku (Sendai), Hokkaido (Sapporo), Kyushu (Fukuoka), Osaka and Nagoya, and the two private universities of Keio and Waseda.

ENROLMENT (percentage of age group) – primary 100 per cent (1994); secondary 98 per cent (1994); tertiary 40.3 per cent (1994)

CULTURE

Japanese is said to be one of the Ural-Altaic group of languages and remained a spoken tongue until the fifth to seventh centuries AD, when Chinese characters came into use. Japanese who have received school education can read and write the Chinese characters in current use (about 1,800) and also the syllabary characters called Kana.

JORDAN
Al-Mamlaka al Urduniya al-Hashemiyah

AREA – 37,738 sq. miles (97,740 sq. km). Neighbours: Syria (north), Israel and the West Bank (west), Saudi Arabia (south and east), Iraq (east)

POPULATION – 5,581,000 (1994 UN estimate); 4,095,579 (1994 census). The majority are Sunni Muslims and Islam is the religion of the state; however, freedom of belief is guaranteed by the constitution

CAPITAL – Amman (population, 1,270,000, 1994)

MAJOR CITIES – Irbid (216,000); Zarqa (359,000), 1991

CURRENCY – Jordanian dinar (JD) of 1,000 fils

NATIONAL ANTHEM – Long Live the King

NATIONAL DAY – 25 May (Independence Day)

NATIONAL FLAG – Three horizontal stripes of black, white, green and a red triangle based on the hoist, containing a seven-pointed white star

LIFE EXPECTANCY (years) – male 66.16; female 69.84

POPULATION GROWTH RATE – 4.8 per cent (1997)

POPULATION DENSITY – 57 per sq. km (1996)

ILLITERACY RATE – 14.3 per cent

ENROLMENT (percentage of age group) – primary 89 per cent (1992); secondary 42 per cent (1989); tertiary 24.5 per cent (1989)

HISTORY AND POLITICS

After the defeat of Turkey in the First World War, the Amirate of Transjordan was established in the area east of the River Jordan as a state under British mandate. The mandate was terminated after the Second World War and the Amirate, still ruled by its founder the Amir Abdullah, became the Hashemite Kingdom of Jordan. Following the 1948–9 war between Israel and the Arab states, that part of Palestine remaining in Arab hands (the West Bank and East Jerusalem, but excluding Gaza) was, with Palestinian agreement, incorporated into the Hashemite Kingdom. King Abdullah was assassinated in 1951; his son Talal ruled briefly but abdicated in favour of King Hussein in 1952.

The West Bank has been under Israeli occupation since its capture from Jordan in the 1967 war, and East Jerusalem was annexed by Israel in 1967. In 1988 Jordan severed its legal and administrative ties with the occupied West Bank, but did not formally renounce sovereignty over the area.

As a result of the wars of 1948–9 and 1967 there are about one million Palestinian refugees and displaced persons living in East Jordan, about 200,000 of whom live in refugee and displaced persons camps established by the UN Relief and Works Agency (UNRWA). In addition there are 300,000 self-supporting Palestinians in East Jordan.

In 1993, multiparty parliamentary elections were held for the first time since 1956. In the most recent elections, held on 4 November 1997, pro-government candidates won 62 out of 80 seats; the main opposition parties boycotted the elections.

FOREIGN RELATIONS

The Middle East peace process begun in 1991 led to Jordan signing an agreement on a 'common agenda' for peace with Israel in 1993. On 25 July 1994 King Hussein and the Israeli Prime Minister signed a framework agreement for peace which ended the state of war existing since 1948. The first Israeli–Jordanian border crossing was opened between Eilat and Aqaba in August 1994. A full peace treaty was signed on 26 October 1994 which established full diplomatic and economic relations between the two states. It included agreements on sharing water from the Jordan and Yarmouk rivers; co-operating in the fields of commerce, transport, tourism, communications, energy and agriculture; and granted King Hussein custodianship of Islamic holy sites in Jerusalem. Israeli forces completed their withdrawal from Jordanian land in the Arava valley on 9 February 1995.

On 25 January 1999, King Hussein signed a decree naming his eldest son, Abdullah ibn al-Hussein, as his new heir, in place of his youngest brother, Prince Hassan; Prince Abdullah became King following the death of King Hussein on 7 February 1999.

Jordan and Kuwait re-established full diplomatic relations on 3 March 1999, which had been broken off following the 1990 Gulf War.

POLITICAL SYSTEM

The constitution provides for a Senate of 40 members (all appointed by the King) and an elected House of Representatives which has 80 members.

The King appoints the members of the Council of Ministers. In 1991 a new national charter was formulated which lifted the ban on political parties, imposed in 1957.

HEAD OF STATE

His Majesty The King of the Jordan, Abdullah ibn al-Hussein, born 30 January 1962, succeeded 7 February 1999

Crown Prince, Hamzeh ibn al-Hussein, born 29 March 1982, son of King Hussein of Jordan

COUNCIL OF MINISTERS *as at July 1999*

Prime Minister, Defence, Abdel Rauf Rawabdeh

Deputy PM, Marwan Hmoud

Deputy PM, Planning, Rima Khalaf

Deputy PM, Ayman Majali

Agriculture, Hashem Shbul

Education, Higher Education, Ezzat Jaradat

Energy and Mineral Resources, Suleiman Abu Alim

Finance, Michel Marto

Foreign Affairs, Abdul Illah al-Khatib

Health, Ishak Maraka

Information, Nasser Lawzi

Interior, Nayef al-Qadi

Justice, Hamzeh Haddad

Labour, Eid Fayez

Municipal, Rural, Environmental and Parliamentary Affairs, Tawliq Kreishan

Public Works and Housing, Hosni Abu Ghida
Religious Endowments (Waqfs), Islamic Affairs, Abdul Salam
al-Abbadi
Social and Administrative Development, Faisal al-Rafua
Tourism and Antiquities, Aqel Biltaji
Trade, Industry and Supply, Mohammed Asfur
Transport and Communications, Jamal Sarayreh
Water and Irrigation, Kamel Mahadin
Youth and Sport, vacant

EMBASSY OF THE HASHEMITE KINGDOM OF JORDAN
6 Upper Phillimore Gardens, London W8 7HB
Tel 0171-937 3685
Ambassador Extraordinary and Plenipotentiary, HE Fouad
Ayoub, apptd 1991
Defence Attaché, Brig. Ahmad Bataineh

BRITISH EMBASSY
Abdoun (PO Box 87), Amman
Tel: Amman 592 3100
Ambassador Extraordinary and Plenipotentiary, HE
Christopher Battiscombe, CMG, apptd 1997
Counsellor, S. P. Collis (*Deputy Head of Mission and Consul-
General*)
Defence Attaché, Col. R. J. Sandy
First Secretary, R. Leadbeater (*Consul and Management*)
BRITISH COUNCIL DIRECTOR, Dr D. Burton, Rainbow
Street (PO Box 634), Amman 11118

DEFENCE

The Army has 1,217 main battle tanks, 1,100 armoured
personnel carriers, 35 armoured infantry fighting vehicles,
and 521 artillery pieces. The Navy has three patrol and
coastal vessels at its base at Aqaba. The Air Force has 93
combat aircraft and 16 armed helicopters.
MILITARY EXPENDITURE – 6.4 per cent of GDP (1997)
MILITARY PERSONNEL – 113,980: Army 90,000, Navy
480, Air Force 13,500, Paramilitaries 10,000

ECONOMY

The main agricultural areas are the Jordan valley, the hills
overlooking the valley, and the flatter country to the south
of Amman and around Madaba and Irbid. However, several
large farms, which depend for irrigation on water pumped
from deep aquifers, have been established in the southern
desert area. The rest of the country is desert and semi-
desert. The principal crops are wheat, barley, vegetables,
olives and fruit. Agricultural production has increased
considerably in recent years due to improvements in
production and irrigation techniques.
  Important industrial products are raw phosphates (1997,
5,895,600 tonnes) and potash (1997, 849,400 tonnes), most
of which is exported, together with fertilizers and pharmaceuticals. The Trans-Arabian oil pipeline (Tapline)
runs through north Jordan from Saudi Arabia to the
Lebanese port of Sidon. A branch pipeline, together with
oil trucked by road from Iraq, feeds a refinery at Zerqa
(production 1994, 2.9 million tons) which meets most of
Jordan's requirements for refined petroleum products.
Sufficient reserves of natural gas have been discovered in
the north-east to produce electricity for the national grid
since 1989.
  The peace with Israel, including a preferential trade
agreement signed in October 1995, has created a mini-
boom, with a 40 per cent rise in tourism and 25 per cent
rise in exports. Tourism has developed, principally in
Amman, Aqaba, Zerka Ma'in and on the shores of the Dead
Sea. In 1995, Jordan had more than 800,000 visitors.
  In 1996 there was a trade deficit of US$2,001 million

and a current account deficit of US$222 million. In 1997
imports totalled US$4,102 million and exports US$1,845
million.
GNP – US$6,755 million (1997); US$1,520 per capita
(1997)
GDP – US$6,598 million (1995); US$1,228 per capita
(1995)
ANNUAL AVERAGE GROWTH OF GDP – 5.2 per cent
(1996)
INFLATION RATE – 3.0 per cent (1997)
TOTAL EXTERNAL DEBT – US$8,234 million (1997)

Trade with UK	1997	1998
Imports from UK	£147,603,000	£124,879,000
Exports to UK	23,369,000	27,045,000

COMMUNICATIONS

Amman is linked to Aqaba, Damascus, Baghdad and Jeddah
by roads which are of considerable importance in the
overland trade of the Middle East.
  The former Hejaz Railway runs from Syria through
Jordan, and is used mainly for freight between Amman and
Damascus. The Aqaba railway carries phosphate rock from
the mines of al Hasa and al Abiad to Aqaba.   The Royal
Jordanian Airline operates from Amman to Aqaba and has
an extensive network of routes to the Middle East, Europe,
North America and the Far East.

KAZAKHSTAN
Kazak Respublikasy

AREA – 1,049,156 sq. miles (2,717,300 sq. km).
  Neighbours: Russia (north and west), Turkmenistan,
  Uzbekistan and Kyrgyzstan (south), China (east)
POPULATION – 15,671,000 (1999 estimate): Kazakhs (43
  per cent), Russians (36 per cent), Ukrainians (5 per
  cent) and ethnic Germans (4 per cent), with smaller
  numbers of Tatars, Uzbeks, Koreans and Belarusians.
  The Russian population is concentrated in the north of
  the country, where it forms a significant majority, and
  in Almaty. The majority of ethnic Kazakhs are Sunni
  Muslims, and this is the main religion of the republic.
  Kazakh (one of the Turkic languages) became the
  official language in 1993; a law passed in July 1997
  decreed Kazakh as the language of state administration;
  Russian has a special status as the 'social language
  between peoples'. Otherwise each ethnic group uses its
  own language
CAPITAL – Astana (population, 292,000, 1993 estimate.
  Known as Akmola until May 1998). The capital was
  moved from Alma-Ata (Almaty) in December 1997
MAJOR CITIES – Almaty (1,198,000); Karaganda
  (596,000); Pavlograd (367,000); Shimkent (447,000),
  1993 estimates
CURRENCY – Tenge
NATIONAL DAY – 25 October (Republic Day)
NATIONAL FLAG – Dark blue with a sun and a soaring
  eagle in the centre all in gold, and a red vertical
  ornamentation stripe near the hoist
LIFE EXPECTANCY (years) – male 63.83; female 73.06
POPULATION GROWTH RATE – –0.5 per cent (1997)
POPULATION DENSITY – 6 per sq. km (1996)
URBAN POPULATION – 56.7 per cent (1993)
ILLITERACY RATE – 2.5 per cent
ENROLMENT (percentage of age group) – tertiary 32.7
  per cent (1995)

Kazakhstan occupies the northern part of what was Soviet Central Asia. It stretches from the Volga and the Caspian Sea in the west to the Altai and Tienshan mountains in the east. The country consists of arid steppes and semi-deserts, flat in the west, hilly in the east and mountainous in the south-east (Southern Altai and Tienshan mountains). The main rivers are the Irtysh, the Ural, the Syr-Darya and the Ili. The climate is continental and very dry.

HISTORY AND POLITICS

Kazakhstan was inhabited by nomadic tribes before being invaded by Ghenghiz Khan and incorporated into his empire in 1218. After his empire disintegrated, feudal towns emerged based on large oases. These towns affiliated and established a Kazakh state in the late 15th century which engaged in almost continuous warfare with the marauding Khanates on its southern border. After appealing to Russia for aid and protection, in 1731 Kazakhstan acceded to the Russian Empire under a voluntary act of accession.

The First World War brought privation to Kazakhstan, leading to an uprising in 1916 against the conscription of male Kazakhs. After the 1917 Russian revolution, Kazakhstan came under the control of White Russian forces until 1919. On 26 August 1920 a constitution was signed under which Kazakhstan became a Soviet Socialist Republic. Under Soviet rule in the 1920s and 1930s there was rapid industrial development and the traditional nomadic way of life disappeared. The Kazakhs suffered greatly in the Stalinist purges, the merchant and religious classes being murdered and thousands dying in the desert on collective farms. Other nationalities, such as Tatars and Germans, were forcibly transported to Kazakhstan by Stalin. Kazakhstan was the last of the former USSR republics to declare its independence (16 December 1991).

The Communist-derived Congress of People's Unity of Kazakhstan (SNEK) won the March 1994 legislative elections which were ruled invalid by the Constitutional Court. The President responded by dissolving the Supreme Kenges (the bicameral legislature) in March 1995. Elections to the new legislature were held in December 1995; the requirement for candidates to achieve an absolute majority made run-offs necessary. A referendum on 29 April 1995 extended President Nazarbayev's term until 2000, but constitutional changes unanimously agreed by the Kenges brought forward presidential elections to 10 January 1999.

POLITICAL SYSTEM

Executive power is vested in the president and government. The president must be a Kazakh speaker and has the power to appoint the prime minister, other senior ministers and all ambassadors. The parliament does not have the power to impeach the president but the president can dissolve parliament.

A new constitution approved by referendum on 30 August 1995 granted the president the power to dissolve the legislature and to rule by decree. It also nominated Kazakh as the sole official language; prohibited dual citizenship; and created a new bicameral legislature composed of a 47-member Senate and a 67-member Majlis (lower house of the legislature). The Constitutional Court, which opposed the new constitution, was replaced by a Constitutional Council which was made subject to presidential veto.

HEAD OF STATE

President, Nursultan Nazarbayev, *elected* 1 December 1991, *confirmed in office by referendum* 29 April 1995, *re-elected* 10 January 1999

GOVERNMENT *as at July 1999*
Prime Minister, Nurlan Balgymbayev
Deputy PM, Alexander Pavlov
Deputy PM, Agriculture, Zhanybek Karibzhanov
Deputy PM, Finance, Uraz Jandosov
Deputy PM, Foreign Affairs, Kasymzhomart Tokayev
Chairman of the Majlis, Marat Ospanov
Chairman of the Senate, Omirbek Baigeldi
Defence, Lt. Gen. Mukhtar Altynbayev
Ecology and Natural Resources, Serikbek Daukeyev
Education, Health and Sport, Kyrymbek Kusherbayev
Family and Women's Affairs, Aitkul Samakova
Information, Culture and Public Accord, Altynbek Sarsenbayev
Internal Affairs, Lt. Gen. Kairbek Suleymenov
Justice, Baurzhan Mukhamedzhanov
Labour and Social Security, Natalia Korzhova
Power, Industry and Trade, Mukhtar Ablyazov
Science and Higher Education, Vladimir Shkolnik
State Revenue, Zeinolla Kakimzhanov
Transport, Communications and Tourism, Serik Burkitbayev

EMBASSY OF THE REPUBLIC OF KAZAKHSTAN
33 Thurloe Square, London SW7 2SD
Tel 0171-581 4646
Ambassador Extraordinary and Plenipotentiary,
HE Kanat Saudabaev, apptd 1997

BRITISH EMBASSY
Ul. Furmanova 173, Almaty
Tel: Almaty 506191
Ambassador Extraordinary and Plenipotentiary,
HE Richard Lewington, apptd 1999

BRITISH COUNCIL DIRECTOR, L. Biglou, Panfilova 158, Almaty 480091

DEFENCE

In 1993–4 Kazakhstan established its own armed forces from forces that were formerly under joint CIS control with Russia. An agreement signed with Russia in January 1995 provides for eventual reunification of the two states' armed forces. The CIS mutual defence treaty of 1993, to which Kazakhstan is a signatory, retains a common air defence force, while Kazakh forces also take part in the CIS peacekeeping force along the Tajikistan–Afghanistan border. A military union with a joint staff is being formed in co-operation with Kyrgyzstan and Uzbekistan. Kazakhstan ratified the Start 1 Treaty in 1992 and signed the Nuclear Non-Proliferation Treaty in December 1994. By 1996, all nuclear warheads had been returned to Russia although Kazakhstan retained 48 SS-18 intercontinental ballistic missiles. Kazakhstan participates in the NATO Partnership for Peace programme.

The Army has 630 main battle tanks and 700 artillery pieces. The Caspian Sea Flotilla, which Kazakhstan shares with Russia and Turkmenistan, operates under Russian command. The Air Force has 123 combat aircraft.
MILITARY EXPENDITURE – 2.3 per cent of GDP (1997)
MILITARY PERSONNEL – 89,600: Army 40,000, Navy 100, Air Force 15,000, Paramilitaries 34,500
CONSCRIPTION DURATION – 31 months

ECONOMY

Kazakhstan is rich in minerals, with copper, lead, gold, uranium, chromium, silver, zinc, iron ore, coal, oil and natural gas. In 1997 production of coal was 72,647,000 tonnes and of iron ore was 26,309,400 tonnes. The oil and gas industry, concentrated in the west of the country, has been expanded by foreign investment, which is also being used to explore the Karachaganak (gas) and Tengiz (oil) fields in the Caspian Sea. In November 1997, a deal was signed with the USA that provided for a US$26 billion investment in the energy sector.

An oil pipeline between Russia and Kazakhstan is due to be completed in 2001. Further pipelines to China and Turkey are under consideration. Oil production in 1997 was 25.8 million tonnes and gas output was 8.1 billion cubic metres. Industry is dominated by food processing and mining and metals production; textiles, steel and tractors are also produced. The main centres of the metal industry are in the Altai mountains, in Shimkent, north of Lake Balkhash and in central Kazakhstan.

Agriculture, including stock-raising, is highly developed, particularly in the central and south-west of the republic. Grain is grown in the north and north-east, and cotton and wool produced in the south and south-east. 12.3 million tonnes of grain crop was grown in 1997 and 1.5 million tonnes of meat produced in 1993.

In 1993 the government announced a privatization programme under which most state-owned enterprises were to be sold. The economy was weakened by the ending of preferential trading links to other CIS states at the break-up of the Soviet Union although a single market was formed with Kyrgyzstan and Uzbekistan in 1994. A treaty on further economic and humanitarian co-operation, as well as a customs union, was signed with Belarus, Kyrgyzstan and Russia in March 1996. A treaty of economic co-operation for 1998–2007 was signed with Russia in October 1998. The tenge was floated on 5 April 1999 in a bid to reduce the trade deficit.

In 1997 the trade deficit was US$385 million and the current account deficit US$954 million. Imports totalled US$4,275 million and exports US$6,366 million.

GNP – US$21,317 million (1997); US$1,350 per capita (1997)
GDP – US$16,730 million (1995); US$995 per capita (1995)
ANNUAL AVERAGE GROWTH OF GDP – –8.9 per cent (1995)
UNEMPLOYMENT – 1.0 per cent (1993)
INFLATION RATE – 17.4 per cent (1997)
TOTAL EXTERNAL DEBT – US$4,278 million (1997)

Trade with UK	1997	1998
Imports from UK	£53,847,000	£95,792,000
Exports to UK	10,391,000	40,456,000

KENYA
Jamhuri ya Kenya

AREA – 224,081 sq. miles (580,367 sq. km). Neighbours: Somalia (east), Ethiopia (north), Sudan (north-west), Uganda (west), Tanzania (south)
POPULATION – 31,806,000 (1994 UN estimate). The main tribal groups are the Kikuyu, Luhya, Luo, Kalenjin, Kamba and Masai. The official languages are Swahili, which is generally understood throughout Kenya, and English; numerous indigenous languages are also spoken
CAPITAL – Nairobi (population, 1,400,000, 1989 estimate)
MAJOR CITIES –ΨKisumu (192,733); ΨMombasa (461,753); Nakuru (163,927), 1989 estimates
CURRENCY – Kenya shilling (Ksh) of 100 cents
NATIONAL DAY – 12 December (Independence Day)
NATIONAL FLAG – Horizontally black, red and green with the red fimbriated in white, and with a shield and crossed spears all over in the centre
LIFE EXPECTANCY (years) – male 54.18; female 57.29

POPULATION GROWTH RATE – 2.8 per cent (1997)
POPULATION DENSITY – 55 per sq. km (1996)
MILITARY EXPENDITURE – 2.4 per cent of GDP (1997)
MILITARY PERSONNEL – 29,200: Army 20,500, Navy 1,200, Air Force 2,500, Paramilitaries 5,000
ILLITERACY RATE – 21.9 per cent
ENROLMENT (percentage of age group) – primary 91 per cent (1980); tertiary 1.6 per cent (1990)

HISTORY AND POLITICS

Kenya became an independent state and a member of the British Commonwealth on 12 December 1963 and a republic in 1964. In 1982 the government introduced amendments to the constitution making the country a one-party state, with the Kenya African National Union (KANU) as the ruling party. In December 1991, the government yielded to internal and international pressure and introduced a multiparty democracy.

Multiparty presidential and legislative elections were held in December 1992 and were won by President Moi and KANU respectively, though Commonwealth observers declared that the elections were not free and fair. KANU formed a new government in January 1993. In July and August 1997, pro-democracy rallies were violently broken up by police and 14 demonstrators were killed, provoking outrage at home and abroad. In November 1997, Moi responded to pressure and granted limited reforms, repealing laws suppressing political debate, and granting equal media access to all parties. On 29 December 1997, in elections hampered by heavy flooding and marred by allegations of electoral malpractice, KANU won 109 out of 210 seats in the National Assembly, and Moi won just over 40 per cent of the vote to win a fifth term in office.

Following the elections, fighting broke out in the Rift Valley; by April 1998, more than 100 people had died and 300,000 had been driven from their homes. The victims were mainly from the Kikuyu tribe, and the perpetrators appeared to be members of Moi's Kalenjin tribe. The army was sent into the area to confiscate weapons and end the conflict in May 1998.

The country is divided into eight provinces (Central, Coast, Eastern, Nairobi, Nyanza, North Eastern, Rift Valley, Western).

HEAD OF STATE
President and C.-in-C. Armed Forces, Daniel T. arap Moi (KANU), *took office* 14 October 1978, *re-elected* 1979, 1983, 1988, 1992 and 29 December 1997
The Vice-President, Planning and National Development, George Saitoti

CABINET *as at July 1999*
The President
The Vice-President
Agriculture, Musalia Mudavadi
Attorney-General, Amos Wako
Co-operative Development, Chris Obure
East African and Regional Co-operation, Nicholas Kipyator Biwott
Education and Human Resource Development, Stephen Kalonzo Musyoka
Energy, Chrysanthus Okemo
Finance, Yekoyada Masakhalia
Foreign Affairs, Bonaya Godana
Health, Jackson Kalweo
Home Affairs, Shariff Nassir
Industrial Development, Andrew Kiptoon
Information and Broadcasting, Joseph Nyagah
Labour, Joseph Kimen Ngutu
Lands and Settlement, Gideon Ndambuki

Local Government, Samson Ongeri
Ministers of State in the President's Office, Frederick
    Amukowa Amangwe; Marsden Madoka; Julius Sunkuli
Natural Resources, Francis Lotodo
Public Works and Housing, Katana Ngala
Regional Development, Hussein Maalim Mohammed
Research, Technical Training and Technology, Kipkalya Kones
Secretary-General of the Government, Civil Service, Richard
    Leakey
Tourism, Henry Kiprono Kosgei
Trade, Joseph Kamotho
Transport and Communications, William ole Ntimama
Water Resources, Kipng'eno arap Ng'eny
Women and Youth Affairs, Mohammud Mohammed

KENYA HIGH COMMISSION
45 Portland Place, London WIN 4AS
Tel 0171-636 2371/5
High Commissioner, HE Mwanyengela Ngali, apptd 1996
Defence Adviser, Col. G. L. Okanga
Commercial Attaché, D. Mbugua

BRITISH HIGH COMMISSION
Upper Hill Road, PO Box 30465 Nairobi
Tel: Nairobi 714699
High Commissioner, HE Jeffrey James, CMG, apptd 1997
Deputy High Commissioner, A. Tucker
Defence Adviser, Col. T. Merritt, OBE
First Secretary (Commercial), J. Chandler
First Secretary (Consular), D. Levoir
CONSULAR OFFICES – Nairobi, Mombasa, Malindi

BRITISH COUNCIL REPRESENTATIVE, B. Harvey, (PO
    Box 40751) ICEA Building, Kenyatta Avenue, Nairobi.
    There are offices at Kisumu and Mombasa

ECONOMY

Agriculture provides about 30 per cent of GDP. The great
variation in altitude and ecology provides conditions under
which a wide range of crops can be grown. These include
wheat, barley, pyrethrum, coffee, tea, sisal, coconuts,
cashew nuts, cotton, maize and a wide variety of tropical
and temperate fruits and vegetables. The total area of well-
farmed land on which concentrated mixed farming can be
practised is small and the remainder is arid or semi-arid
country but population pressure and the need to increase
agricultural production for export has led to attempts to
develop such areas.

Mineral production consists of soda ash, salt and
limestone. Hydroelectric power has been developed,
particularly on the Upper Tana River, and Kenya is now
almost self-sufficient in electric power generation.

There has been considerable industrial development
over the last 15 years and Kenya has a variety of industries
processing agricultural produce and manufacturing products from local and imported raw materials. New industries
are steel, textile mills, dehydrated vegetable processing
and motor tyre manufacture. Smaller schemes have added
to the country's consumer goods manufacturing base.
There is an oil refinery in Mombasa supplying both Kenya
and Uganda, and a fuel pipeline now connects Mombasa
and Nairobi. Tourism generates some US$400 million per
year.
GNP – US$9,654 million (1997); US$340 per capita
    (1997)
GDP – US$8,960 million (1995); US$330 per capita
    (1995)
ANNUAL AVERAGE GROWTH OF GDP – 2.1 per cent
    (1997)
INFLATION RATE – 12.0 per cent (1997)
TOTAL EXTERNAL DEBT – US$6,486 million (1997)

TRADE

Principal exports are coffee and tea, which account for
roughly a third of total export earnings. Also exported are
fruit, vegetables, and crude animal and vegetable material.
Industrial machinery is the largest single import; other
imports are transport equipment, petroleum and petroleum
products, metals, pharmaceuticals and chemicals.

In 1996 Kenya had a trade deficit of US$510 million and
a current account deficit of US$166 million. In 1997
imports totalled US$3,273 million and exports US$2,054
million.

Trade with UK	1997	1998
Imports from UK	£238,190,000	£224,417,000
Exports to UK	195,731,000	214,975,000

COMMUNICATIONS

The Kenya Railways Corporation has 2,506 km of railway
open to traffic. There are also 67,000 km of road, of which
8,900 km are bitumen surfaced.

The principal port is Mombasa, operated by the Kenya
Ports Authority. International air services operate from
airports at Nairobi and Mombasa. The national airline is
Kenya Airways.

KIRIBATI
Ribaberikin Kiribati – Republic of Kiribati

AREA – 280 sq. miles (726 sq. km)
POPULATION – 80,000 (1994 UN estimate):
    predominantly Christian. The languages are I-Kiribati
    and English
CAPITAL – Tarawa (population, 17,921, 1978)
CURRENCY – Australian dollar ($A) of 100 cents
NATIONAL ANTHEM – Teirake Kain Kiribati (Stand
    Kiribati)
NATIONAL DAY – 12 July (Independence Day)
NATIONAL FLAG – Red, with blue and white wavy lines
    in base, and in the centre a gold rising sun and a flying
    frigate bird
POPULATION GROWTH RATE – 2.0 per cent (1997)
POPULATION DENSITY – 110 per sq. km (1996)

Kiribati (pronounced Kiribas) comprises 36 islands: the
Gilberts Group (17) including Banaba (formerly Ocean
Island), the Phoenix Islands (8), and the Line Islands (11),
which are situated in the south-west central Pacific around
the point at which the International Date Line cuts the
Equator. The total land area is spread over some 2 million
square miles of ocean. Few of the atolls are more than half
a mile in width or more than 12 feet high. The vegetation
consists mainly of coconut palms, breadfruit trees and
pandanus.

HISTORY AND POLITICS

The Gilbert and Ellice Islands were proclaimed a British
protectorate in 1892 and annexed as the Gilbert and Ellice
Islands Colony on 10 November 1915 (taking effect 12
January 1916). The Gilbert Islands were occupied by the
Japanese army during World War II. Nuclear tests were
carried out by the British off Kiritimati (Christmas Island)
in 1957. In October 1975 the Ellice Islands seceded to
become the independent state of Tuvalu. The Gilbert
Islands achieved independence on 12 July 1979 as the
Republic of Kiribati.

Legislative elections were held on 23 September 1998
and presidential elections held on 27 November 1998 were

won by Teburoro Tito. There are no formal political parties.

POLITICAL SYSTEM

The president is head of state as well as head of government and is elected nationally. There is a House of Assembly of 41 members (39 elected members, the Attorney-General and a representative of Banaba Island). Executive authority is vested in the Cabinet.

HEAD OF STATE

President, Foreign Affairs, Teburoro Tito, *sworn in* 1 October 1994, *re-elected* 27 November 1998

Vice-President, Home Affairs, Rural Development, Tewareka Tentoa

CABINET *as at July 1999*

The President
The Vice-President
Commerce, Industry and Tourism, Teaiwa Tenieu
Education, Training and Technology, Teambo Keariki
Environment, Social Development, Kataotika Tekee
Finance and Economic Planning, Beniamina Tinga
Health and Family Planning, Baraniko Mooa
Labour, Employment and Co-operatives, Teiraoi Tetabea
Line and Phoenix Islands, Tim Taekiti
Natural Resources Development, Emile Schutz
Transport, Communications and Information, Willie Tokataake
Works and Energy, Manraoi Kaiea

HIGH COMMISSION

c/o Office of the President, P.O Box 68, Bairiki, Tarawa, Kiribati
High Commissioner, vacant
Acting High Commissioner, Peter Timeon

BRITISH HIGH COMMISSIONER, HE Michael Dibben, apptd 1998, resident at Suva, Fiji

ECONOMY

Many people still practise a semi-subsistence economy, the main staples of their diet being coconuts and fish.

The principal imports are foodstuffs, consumer goods, machinery and transport equipment. The principal exports are copra and fish.

In 1994 there was a trade deficit of US$21 million and a current account surplus of US$1 million.

GNP – US$76 million (1997); US$910 per capita (1997)
GDP – US$51 million (1995); US$654 per capita (1995)

Trade with UK	1997	1998
Imports from UK	£174,000	£106,000
Exports to UK	13,000	—

COMMUNICATIONS

Air communication exists between most of the islands and is operated by Air Kiribati, a statutory corporation. Air Marshall Islands operates a weekly service between Majuro, Tarawa, Funafuti and Nadi, and Air Nauru between Tarawa, Nauru and Nadi. Inter-island shipping is operated by a statutory corporation, the Shipping Corporation of Kiribati.

EDUCATION AND SOCIAL WELFARE

There are 104 primary schools, eight secondary schools and one high school. There is a teacher training college, a technical institute and a marine training centre.

There is a general hospital at Tarawa. The other inhabited islands have dispensaries.

KOREA

Korea's southern and western coasts are fringed with innumerable islands, of which the largest, forming a province of its own, is Cheju. The Korean language is of the Ural-Altaic Group. Its script, Hangul, was invented in the 15th century; prior to this Chinese characters alone were used. Despite the great cultural influence of the Chinese, Koreans have developed and preserved their own cultural heritage.

HISTORY

The Korean peninsula was first unified in AD 668 when Shilla, having emerged as the dominant tribal state, conquered Koguryo and Paekche. The Koryo dynasty ruled from 912 until 1392 and was succeeded by the Choson dynasty, who ruled from 1392 until 1910 when Japan formally annexed Korea. The country remained part of the Japanese Empire until the defeat of Japan in 1945, when it was occupied by troops of the USA and the USSR, the 38th parallel being fixed as the boundary between the two zones of occupation.

Attempts to reunite Korea failed and the issue was referred to the UN General Assembly. The UN in November 1947 resolved that elections should be held for a National Assembly which, when elected, should set up a government. The Soviet government refused to comply and a UN commission was only allowed to operate south of the 38th parallel.

A general election was held on 10 May 1948, and the first National Assembly met in Seoul on 31 May. The Assembly passed a constitution on 12 July and on 15 August 1948 the republic was formally inaugurated and American military government came to an end. Meanwhile, in the Soviet-occupied zone north of the 38th parallel the Democratic People's Republic had been established with its capital at Pyongyang. A Supreme People's Soviet was elected in September 1948, and a Soviet-style constitution adopted.

THE KOREAN WAR

Korea remained divided along the 38th parallel until June 1950, when North Korean forces invaded South Korea. In response to Security Council recommendations, 16 nations, including the USA and the UK, came to the aid of the Republic of Korea. China entered the war on the side of North Korea in November 1950. The fighting was ended by an armistice agreement signed on 27 July 1953. By this agreement (which was not signed by the Republic of Korea), the line of division between North and South Korea remained close to the 38th parallel, and a Military Armistice Commission (MAC) was established to monitor the cease-fire. North Korea and China withdrew from the MAC in 1994.

Talks between North and South Korea on the reunification of the country have taken place intermittently. A non-aggression accord was signed between the North and South in 1991 and an agreement on the denuclearization of the Korean peninsula was reached in 1992. A summit of North and South Korean presidents was scheduled for July 1994 but Kim Il-sung died before it could take place. Four-party talks between China, the USA and the two Koreas took place in December 1997 and again in March 1998, but no new agreements were reached.

DEMOCRATIC PEOPLE'S REPUBLIC OF KOREA
Chosun Minchu-chui Inmin Kongwa-guk

AREA – 46,540 sq. miles (120,538 sq. km). Neighbours: China, Russia (north), Republic of Korea (south)
POPULATION – 22,466,000 (1994 UN estimate). The language is Korean
CAPITAL – Pyongyang (approximate population, 2,741,260)
CURRENCY – Won of 100 chon
NATIONAL ANTHEM – A Chi Mun Bin No Ra I Gang San (Shine bright, oh dawn, on this land so fair)
NATIONAL DAY – 16 February (Kim Jong Il's birthday)
NATIONAL FLAG – Red with white fimbriations and blue borders at top and bottom; a large red star on a white disc near the hoist
LIFE EXPECTANCY (years) – male 67.70; female 73.95
POPULATION GROWTH RATE – 1.6 per cent (1997)
POPULATION DENSITY – 186 per sq. km (1996)

POLITICAL SYSTEM

The constitution of the Democratic People's Republic of Korea provides for a Supreme People's Assembly, presently consisting of 687 deputies, which is elected every five years by universal suffrage. The Assembly elects a president for a five-year term, and the Central People's Committee. In turn, the Central People's Committee directs the Administrative Council which implements the policy formulated by the Committee. The Administrative Council (51 members), the government of North Korea, includes the prime minister and various ministers. In practice, however, the country is ruled by the Korean Workers' Party which elects a Central Committee; this in turn appoints a Politburo. The senior ministers of the Administrative Council are all members of the Communist Party Central Committee and the majority are also members of the Politburo. Kim Il Sung, who had been head of the state, party and military since the country's inception in 1948, died on 8 July 1994, but was declared the eternal president in September 1998. His son Kim Jong Il, who had been party general secretary since October 1997, became chair of the National Defence Committee, which is now *de facto* the highest office.

HEAD OF STATE

Eternal President, Kim Il Sung (deceased)
Chair of the National Defence Committee, General Secretary, Korean Workers' Party, Member of Presidium, Kim Jong Il
Chair of the Standing Committee of the Supreme People's Assembly, Kim Yong Nam

SPA STANDING COMMITTEE

Chairman, Kim Yong Nam
Vice-Chairmen, Yang Hyong Sop; Im Yong Tae
Secretary-General, Kim Yun Hyok
Honorary Vice-Chairmen, Yi Chong Ok; Pak Song Chol; Kim Yong Chu; Chon Mun Sop
Members, Yu Mi Yong; Kang Yong Sop; Yi Kil Song; Yi Chol Pong; Yi Il Hwan; Song Sam Sop

ADMINISTRATIVE COUNCIL *as at July 1999*

Prime Minister, Hong Song Nam
Deputy Prime Ministers, Kwak Pon Ki; Cho Chang Tok
Foreign Affairs, Paek Nam Sun

MINISTERS

Agriculture, Yi Ha Sop
Chair, State Planning Committee, Pak Nam Ki
Chemical Industry, Pak Pong Chu
City Management, Choe Chong Kon
Commerce, Yi Yong Son
Construction and Building Materials Industry, Cho Yun Hui
Culture, Choe Chae Yon
Director of the Central Statistics Bureau, Kim Chang Su
Director of the Secretariat and State Administration Council, Chong Mun Sang
Education, Choe Ki Chong
Finance, Yim Kyong Suk
Fisheries, Yi Song Un
Forestry, Yi Sang Mu
Labour, Yi Won Il
Land and Maritime Transport, Kim Yong Il
Land Environmental Protection, Chang Il Son
Light Industry, Yi Yong Su
Metal and Machine Industry, Chon Sung Hun
Mining Industry, Kim Sung Nam
People's Armed Forces, Vice-Marshall Kim Il Chol
Posts and Telecommunications, Yi Kun Pom
Power and Coal Industry, Sin Tae Nok
President of the Academy of Sciences, Yi Kwang Ho
President of the Central Bank, Chong Song Taek
Procurement and Food Administration, Paek Chang Yong
Public Health, Kim Su Hak
Public Security, Lt.-Gen. Paek Hak Nim
Railways, Kim Yong San
Sports, Pak Myong Chol
State Construction Commission, Pae Tal Chun
State Inspection, Kim Ui Sun
Trade, Kang Chong Mo

Full Members of the Politburo,
Kim Jong Il; Pak Son Chol; Yi Chong Ok; Yon Hyong Muk; Kang Song San; So Yun Sok; Ho Dam; Kim Yong Nam; Kye Ung Tae; Han Song Yong; Kim Yong Ju

DEFENCE

The Army has 3,000 main battle tanks, 2,500 armoured personnel carriers and 10,600 artillery pieces. The Navy has 26 submarines, three frigates and about 424 patrol and coastal vessels at 15 bases. The Air Force has 607 combat aircraft.

Between 1992 and 1994 North Korea embarked on a clandestine nuclear weapons programme despite being a signatory of the Nuclear Non-Proliferation Treaty (NPT). North Korea withdrew from the NPT following an International Atomic Energy Authority (IAEA) report that the country was attempting to reprocess plutonium for use in nuclear weapons. An agreement was signed with the USA on 21 October 1994 under which North Korea vowed to remain a party to the NPT; to permit IAEA inspections; and to switch to light-water reactors unsuitable for plutonium production. In return the USA agreed to establish diplomatic and economic relations and to pay for interim energy requirements. The IAEA verified the halting of North Korea's nuclear programme in November 1994 although a final settlement was only achieved in June 1995.
MILITARY EXPENDITURE – 27.0 per cent of GDP (1997)
MILITARY PERSONNEL – 1,243,000: Army 923,000, Navy 46,000, Air Force 85,000, Paramilitaries 189,000
CONSCRIPTION DURATION – Three to ten years

ECONOMY

North Korea is rich in minerals and industry was developed, but the economy has stagnated owing to poor planning and a shortage of foreign exchange. The current economic crisis was precipitated by the curtailment of barter trade with the Soviet Union after 1991, and the end of subsidized oil and grain from China. Industrial output has collapsed, with industry operating at one-third of capacity. The economy has been sustained by foreign exchange sent by ethnic Koreans in Japan. In April 1998, South Korea lifted its ban on investment in North Korea, allowing South Koreans to send money to their relatives in the north.

In 1995–8, a slump in agricultural production was exacerbated by widespread flooding which devastated the rice harvest. A North Korean survey quoted by South Korean security services stated that up to three million people had died as a result of famine between 1995 and 1998. In January 1998, the UN World Food Programme launched a food aid operation to provide 658,000 tonnes of food to North Korea. The USA increased food aid to North Korea in May 1999.

GDP – US$5,997 million (1995); US$271 per capita (1995)
ANNUAL AVERAGE GROWTH OF GDP – 4.6 per cent (1995)

Trade with UK	1997	1998
Imports from UK	£24,800,000	£10,769,000
Exports to UK	442,000	765,000

REPUBLIC OF KOREA
Taehanminguk

AREA – 38,368 sq. miles 99,373 sq. km). Neighbour: Democratic People's Republic of Korea (north)
POPULATION – 46,430,000 (1998 estimate). The largest religions are Buddhism (10.3 million) and Christianity (8.8 million Protestants, 2.9 million Roman Catholics). The language is Korean
CAPITAL – Seoul (population, 10,289,000, 1998 estimate)
MAJOR CITIES – ΨInchon (2,390,000); ΨPusan (3,865,000); Taegu (2,490,000)
CURRENCY – Won
NATIONAL ANTHEM – Aegukka (Love for the Mother Country)
NATIONAL DAY – 15 August (Liberation Day)
NATIONAL FLAG – White with a red and blue yin-yang symbol in the centre, surrounded by four black trigrams
LIFE EXPECTANCY (years) – male 67.66; female 75.67
POPULATION GROWTH RATE – 1.0 per cent (1997)
POPULATION DENSITY – 459 per sq. km (1996)
URBAN POPULATION – 78.5 per cent (1995)

HISTORY AND POLITICS

The Republic of Korea was not officially recognized by any former Communist bloc country until 1989, and not by the People's Republic of China until 1992.

The most recent elections to the National Assembly in April 1996 produced no outright majority although the ruling New Korea Party (formerly Democratic Liberal Party) was able to form a government following defections from opposition parties. In the most recent presidential election of 18 December 1997, Kim Dae-jung of the National Congress for New Politics was elected president with just over 40 per cent of the vote. He nominated Kim Jong-pil as prime minister, but this was rejected by the National Assembly. Kim Jong-pil was nevertheless appointed acting prime minister and formed a government.

POLITICAL SYSTEM

A new constitution was adopted in 1988 following a year of political unrest. The president, who is head of state, chief of the executive and commander-in-chief of the armed forces, is directly elected for a single term of five years. He appoints the prime minister with the consent of the National Assembly, and members of the State Council (Cabinet) on the recommendation of the prime minister. The president is also empowered to take wide-ranging measures in an emergency, including the declaration of martial law, but must obtain the agreement of the National Assembly. The National Assembly of 299 members is directly elected for a four-year term.

HEAD OF STATE
President, Kim Dae-jung, *elected* 18 December 1997, *sworn in* 25 February 1998

CABINET *as at July 1999*
Prime Minister, Kim Jong-pil
Agriculture and Forestry, Kim Sung-hoon
Construction and Transportation, Lee Kun-choon
Culture and Tourism, Park Jie-won
Defence, Cho Seong-tae
Education, Kim Duk-choong
Environment, Kim Myung-ja
Finance and Economy, Kang Bong-kyun
Foreign Affairs, Trade, Hong Soon-young
Government Administration, Home Affairs, Kim Kie-jai
Health and Welfare, Cha Heung-bong
Information and Communications, Namgoong Suek
Justice, Kim Jung-kil
Labour, Lee Sang-ryong
Legislation, Kim Hong-dae
Maritime Affairs and Fisheries, Jung Sang-chun
National Unification, Lim Dong-won
Patriots' and Veterans' Affairs, Choi Kyu-hak
Science and Technology, Seo Jung-uck
Trade, Industry and Energy, Chung Duck-koo

EMBASSY OF THE REPUBLIC OF KOREA
60 Buckingham Gate, London SW1E 6AJ
Tel 0171-227 5500
Ambassador Extraordinary and Plenipotentiary, HE Choi Sung-hong
Defence Attaché, Capt. Lee Byung-moon
Consul, Lee Jong-kug
Counsellor, Kim Chil-doo *(Commercial Affairs)*

BRITISH EMBASSY
No. 4, Chung-dong, Chung-gu, Seoul 100
Tel: Seoul 735-7341/3
Ambassador Extraordinary and Plenipotentiary, HE Stephen Brown, KCVO, apptd 1997
Counsellor (Economic) and Deputy Head of Mission, D. R. Marsh
Defence and Military Attaché, Brig. J. G. Baker, MBE
First Secretary (Commercial), D. F. Graham

There is a Trade Office and an Honorary British Consul at Pusan.

BRITISH COUNCIL REPRESENTATIVE, M. Baumfield, 1st and 2nd Floor, Joonghoo Building, 61–21, 1-ka Taepyung Ro, Chung-gu, Seoul 100–101

BRITISH CHAMBER OF COMMERCE, 2nd Floor, Joonghoo Building, 61–21, 1-ka Taepyung Ro, Chung-gu, Seoul 100–101

DEFENCE

The Army has 2,130 main battle tanks, 2,500 armoured personnel carriers, 4,540 artillery pieces and 143 armed helicopters. The Navy has 14 submarines, seven destroyers, 33 frigates, 105 patrol and coastal vessels, 23 combat aircraft, 47 armed helicopters, 60 main battle tanks and 60 armoured personnel carriers. There are eight naval bases. The Air Force has 488 combat aircraft.

The USA maintains 36,120 personnel in the country.
MILITARY EXPENDITURE – 3.3 per cent of GDP (1997)
MILITARY PERSONNEL – 676,500: Army 560,000, Navy 60,000, Air Force 52,000, Paramilitaries 4,500
CONSCRIPTION DURATION – 26–30 months

ECONOMY

Land redistribution and US aid (US$6,000 million from 1945 to 1978) enabled the rapid industrialization of South Korea in the 1950s and 1960s. Former land owners formed *chaebols* (industrial conglomerates) which benefited from a highly-educated workforce and import substitution policies. From 1961 to 1979 exports increased by an average of 10 per cent a year. From 1985 to 1994, economic growth averaged 7.8 per cent and 6.7 per cent between 1995 and 1997; it fell by 5.8 per cent during 1998.

In January 1997, the steel and construction firm Hanbo, one of Korea's largest companies, collapsed amid allegations of corruption and incompetence. Several other major Korean companies also collapsed in 1997, putting enormous strain on the Korean financial sector that had loaned money to the failed enterprises. Following economic problems elsewhere in Asia, the South Korean stock market fell heavily in October 1997. The value of the won also fell, raising the cost of borrowing for the already troubled banking sector exposed to bad loans in other Asian economies. On 3 December 1997, a record IMF rescue package totalling US$57 billion was announced. In January 1998, the government began implementing economic reforms required by the IMF, and in March 1998 negotiated an agreement to restructure US$21 billion of its short-term debt. By the end of the first quarter of 1999, the economy was growing, industrial production was rising rapidly and the won had stabilized.

Major industries include shipbuilding, construction, iron and steel, textiles, electrical and electronic goods, footwear, passenger vehicles and railway rolling stock.

The soil is fertile but arable land is limited by the mountainous nature of the country. Staple agricultural products are rice, barley and other cereals, beans and potatoes. Fruit-growing, sericulture and the growing of the medicinal root ginseng are also practised. The fishing industry is a major contributor to both food supply and exports.

Korea is deficient in mineral resources, except for deposits of coal on the east coast and tungsten. There are some prospects of discovering oil in the sea between Korea and Japan.

In 1997 there was a trade deficit of US$3,179 million and a current account deficit of US$8,167 million; imports totalled US$144,636 million and exports US$136,617 million.
GNP – US$485,209 million (1997); US$10,550 per capita (1997)
GDP – US$437,233 million (1995); US$9,736 per capita (1995)
ANNUAL AVERAGE GROWTH OF GDP – 7.1 per cent (1996)
INFLATION RATE – 4.4 per cent (1997)
UNEMPLOYMENT – 2.0 per cent (1995)

Trade with UK	1997	1998
Imports from UK	£1,223,293,000	£684,269,000
Exports to UK	2,238,623,000	2,304,934,000

COMMUNICATIONS

There are international airports in Seoul (Kimpo), Kimhae (near Pusan), Taegu and Cheju city. Korean Air and Asiana

Airlines operate regular flights to Europe, the USA, the Middle East and south-east Asia. In 1999, 29 foreign airlines operated services to Seoul. Pusan and Inchon are the major ports with Pusan serving the industrial areas of the south-east. Inchon, 28 miles from Seoul, serves the capital, but development and operation at Inchon are hampered by a tidal variation of 9–10 metres.

EDUCATION

Primary education is compulsory for six years from the age of six. Secondary and higher education is extensive with the option of middle school to age 15 and high school to age 18.
ILLITERACY RATE – 2.0 per cent
ENROLMENT (percentage of age group) – primary 92 per cent (1996); secondary 97 per cent (1996); tertiary 60.3 per cent (1996)

KUWAIT
Dowlat al- Kuwait

AREA – 6,880 sq. miles (17,818 sq. km). Neighbours: Iraq (north and west); Saudi Arabia (south and south-west)
POPULATION – 1,866,104 (1998 estimate): 41.6 per cent were Kuwaiti citizens, the remainder being other Arabs, Iranians, Indians and Pakistanis. The total Western population was 14,240. Islam is the official religion, though religious freedom is constitutionally guaranteed. The official language is Arabic, and English is widely spoken as a second language
CAPITAL – ΨKuwait City (population, 400,000, 1975)
CURRENCY – Kuwaiti dinar (KD) of 1,000 fils
NATIONAL DAY – 25 February
NATIONAL FLAG – Three horizontal stripes of green, white and red, with black trapezoid next to staff
LIFE EXPECTANCY (years) – male 71.77; female 73.32
POPULATION GROWTH RATE – 2.3 per cent (1997)
POPULATION DENSITY – 95 per sq. km (1996)
MILITARY EXPENDITURE – 11.4 per cent of GDP (1997)
MILITARY PERSONNEL – 20,300: Army 11,000, Navy 1,800, Air Force 2,500, Paramilitaries 5,000
CONSCRIPTION DURATION – Two years

In 1993 the UN settled the dispute between Kuwait and Iraq, moving the border some few hundred metres northwards. Kuwait has since completed a 130-mile ditch, sand wall and barbed wire system along its border.

Kuwait has a dry, desert climate with summer extending from April to September. The mean temperature varies between 29–45°C in summer, and 8–18°C in winter. Humidity rarely exceeds 60 per cent except in July and August.

HISTORY AND POLITICS

Although Kuwait had been independent for some years, the 'exclusive agreement' of 1899 between the Sheikh of Kuwait and the British government was formally abrogated by an exchange of letters dated 19 June 1961. Iraq invaded Kuwait on 2 August 1990 and it was liberated on 26 February 1991 by an alliance of Western and Arab forces. Iraq built up its armed forces on Kuwait's border in October 1994, until it was deterred by the arrival of US and British forces. Iraq formally recognized the sovereignty and territorial integrity of Kuwait as well as the UN-demarcated border in November 1994. Roughly 600 Kuwaitis are still held in Iraq.

The Amir dissolved the National Assembly on 4 May

1999; elections were held on 3 July 1999. Opposition Liberals won 16 and Islamists won 20 of the 50 seats.

In May 1999, the government adopted a decree allowing Kuwaiti women to vote and stand for public office from 2003.

POLITICAL SYSTEM

Under the constitution legislative power is vested in the Amir and the 50-member National Assembly, and executive power in the Amir and the Cabinet. Following popular pressure after the liberation, elections for the National Assembly were held in October 1992. The electorate consists of all Kuwaiti male nationals over 21 whose families have lived in the Emirate since before 1921.

There are five governorates: Capital, Hawally, Ahmadi, Jara and Al Farwaniya.

HEAD OF STATE

HH The Amir of Kuwait, Shaikh Jabir al-Ahmad al-Jabir al-Sabah, born 1928, acceded 31 December 1977
Crown Prince, HH Shaikh Saad al-Abdullah al-Salim al-Sabah

CABINET as at August 1999

Prime Minister, HH The Crown Prince
First Deputy PM, Foreign Affairs, Shaikh Sabah al-Ahmed al-Jaber al-Sabah
Deputy PM, Cabinet Affairs, National Assembly Affairs, Mohammad Deifallah Sharar
Deputy PM, Defence, Shaikh Salem Sabah al-Salem al-Sabah
Communications, Finance, Ahmad Abdallah al-Ahmad al-Sabah
Education and Higher Education, Dr Youssef Hamad al-Ibrahim
Electricity and Water, Awqaf and Islamic Affairs, Minister of State for Housing Affairs, Dr Adel Khalid al-Subaih
Health, Dr Mohammad Ahmad al-Jarallah
Information, Dr Saad Mohammad bin Teflah al-Ajmi
Interior, Mohammad Khaled al-Hamad al-Sabah
Justice, Dr Saad Jassem Youssef al-Hashel
Minister of State for Foreign Affairs, Sulaiman Majed al-Shaheen
Oil, Saud Nasser al-Sabah
Planning, Minister of State for Administrative Development Affairs, Dr Mohammad Bteihan al-Dweihees
Public Works, Eid Hathal Saud al-Rashidi
Trade and Industry, Labour and Social Affairs, Abdel Wahhab Mohammad al-Wazzan

EMBASSY OF THE STATE OF KUWAIT
2 Albert Gate, London SWIX 7JU
Tel 0171-590 3400
Ambassador Extraordinary and Plenipotentiary, HE Khaled al-Duwaisan, GCVO, apptd 1993
Cultural Attaché, Dr Ajeel al-Zaher

BRITISH EMBASSY
PO Box 2 Safat, 13001 Safat, Kuwait
Tel: Kuwait 240 3334/5/6
Ambassador Extraordinary and Plenipotentiary, HE Richard Muir, CMG, apptd 1999
Counsellor and Deputy Head of Mission, B. E. Stewart
First Secretaries, J. Francis (Management and Consul); M. Hurley (Commercial)
Defence Attaché, Col. Hon. A. J. C. Campell

BRITISH COUNCIL REPRESENTATIVE, C. Reuter, 2 Al Arabi Street (PO Box 345), 13004 Safat, Mansouriyah, Kuwait City

ECONOMY

Despite the desert terrain, 8.4 per cent of land is under cultivation; tomatoes, onions, melons and dates are the main crops. Shrimp fishing has declined through oil pollution of coastal waters.

The oil industry was brought into government ownership in 1975. Since reorganization in 1980, the national industry has been run by the Kuwait Petroleum Corporation. Oil installations were extensively damaged when Iraqi forces set light to oil wells prior to their retreat. Oil production was 104,100,000 tonnes in 1997.

There are four power stations capable of generating almost 7,000 MW of electricity. The country depends on desalination plants for its water supply. Both water and power facilities were heavily damaged during the war, although electricity and water distillation capacity were restored to pre-invasion levels in 1995.

GDP – US$26,645 million (1995); US$15.757 per capita (1995)
ANNUAL AVERAGE GROWTH OF GDP – 4.1 per cent (1995)
INFLATION RATE – 3.6 per cent (1996)

TRADE

Oil is the major export. Non-oil exports, mainly to Asian countries and the Indian sub-continent, have included chemical fertilizers, ammonia and other chemicals, metal pipes, shrimps and building materials. Re-exports to neighbouring states traditionally accounted for a major proportion of non-oil exports but were brought to a halt by the Iraqi invasion. Major trading partners are Japan, the USA, the UAE, Saudi Arabia and Western Europe.

In 1997 Kuwait had a trade surplus of US$6,296 million and a current account surplus of US$7,671 million. In 1996 imports totalled US$8,374 million and exports US$14,858 million.

Trade with UK	1997	1998
Imports from UK	£503,529,000	£334,825,000
Exports to UK	201,064,000	185,736,000

COMMUNICATIONS

There is a network of dual-carriageway roads and more are under construction; there are 4,741 km of roads. Telecommunications and postal services are conducted by the government.

SOCIAL WELFARE

The government invested its considerable oil revenues in comprehensive social services. Medical services are free to all residents. Education is free and compulsory from six to 14 years.
ILLITERACY RATE – 21.4 per cent
ENROLMENT (percentage of age group) – primary 65 per cent (1995); secondary 22 per cent (1995); tertiary 25.4 per cent (1995)

KYRGYZSTAN
Kyrgyz Respublikasy

AREA – 76,641 sq. miles (198,500 sq. km). Neighbours: Kazakhstan (north), China (east), Tajikistan (south and south-west), Uzbekistan (west)

POPULATION – 4,575,000 (1998 estimate): 52.4 per cent Kirghiz (Turkic origin), 21.5 per cent Russian and 12.9 per cent Uzbek, with smaller numbers of Ukrainians, Germans, Tatars and Kazakhs. Islam is the main religion. Kirghiz, the official language since independence, is a Turkic language, written in the Roman alphabet since 1992. Russian is an equal official language in the fields of science, industry and the health service, and in all regions where there is a large Russian population.

CAPITAL – Bishkek (population, 585,800, 1991 estimate; 616,000, 1989 census)

CURRENCY – Som of 100 tyin (introduced on 10 May 1993 at rate of 1:200 against the rouble)

NATIONAL DAY – 31 August (Independence Day)

NATIONAL FLAG – Red with a rayed sun containing a representation of a yurt, all in gold

LIFE EXPECTANCY (years) – male 64.23; female 72.23

POPULATION GROWTH RATE – 0.8 per cent (1997)

POPULATION DENSITY – 23 per sq. km (1996)

URBAN POPULATION – 34.9 per cent (1995)

MILITARY EXPENDITURE – 2.5 per cent of GDP (1997)

MILITARY PERSONNEL – 17,200: Army 9,800, Air Force 2,400, Paramilitaries 5,000

CONSCRIPTION DURATION – 18 months

Kyrgyzstan (formerly Kirghizia) is mountainous, the major part being covered by the ridge of the Central Tienshan, while the Pamir-Altai system occupies its southern part. There are a number of spacious mountain valleys, the Alai, Susamyr and others. Kyrgyzstan is divided into six administrative regions.

HISTORY AND POLITICS

The Kirghiz people were first mentioned in Chinese chronicles in the second millennium BC. They are a merger of two ethnic groups, a Turkic-speaking people driven into the area by the Mongols from the River Yenisei area of Central Asia, and indigenous peoples. After a long period under Mongol, Chinese and Persian rule, the Kirghiz became part of the Russian Empire in the 1860s and 1870s. Kyrgyzstan became part of the Soviet Union in 1920 and underwent some industrialization.

Kyrgyzstan declared independence just after the failed Moscow coup on 31 August 1991.

Ethnic tensions between the rural nomadic Kirghiz, the urban Russians and the wealthy Uzbeks who own many businesses and form the majority in the second largest town of Osh, are never far from the surface.

President Akayev had difficulty in introducing economic reforms because of obstruction by the bureaucracy and the *Uluk Kenesh* (parliament) over the reforms enshrined in the constitution. The president won a referendum on his plans for greater economic reform in January 1994. Elections to the new parliament, the *Zhogorku Kenesh*, were held in February 1995. A new government was appointed by the president in February 1996 in the wake of the referendum increasing his powers. On 23 December 1998, President Akayev dismissed the government for economic misjudgements and appointed Jumabek Ibraimov as prime minister and died in April 1999. Ibraimov was replaced by Amangeldy Muraliyev.

A referendum on amendments to the constitution was held on 17 October 1998, which introduced private ownership of land.

POLITICAL SYSTEM

The head of state is a president directly elected for a five-year term. There is a bicameral legislature composed of a 35-member Legislative Assembly and a 70-member People's Assembly, both of which are elected for five-year terms. The president appoints the prime minister and the other members of the government. The Assembly of the People of Kyrgyzstan, which comprises the leaders of the republic's ethnic communities, was designated a consultative body in January 1997.

HEAD OF STATE

President, Askar Akayev, *elected* 12 October 1991, *re-elected* 24 December 1995

GOVERNMENT *as at July 1999*

Prime Minister (acting), Amangeldy Muraliyev
Deputy PM, Boris Silayev
Agriculture and Water Resources, Emilbek Uzakbayev
Chair, Assembly of People's Representatives, Abdygany Erkrbayev
Chair, Legislative Assembly, Usup Mukambayer
Chair, State Property Fund, Sultan Mederov
Chair, Social Fund, Roza Uhkempirova
Defence, Col.-Gen. Myrzakan Subanov
Education, Science and Culture, Sovetbek Toktomyshev
Emergency Situations and Civil Defence, Sultan Urmanayev
Environmental Protection, Tynybek Alykulov
Finance, Marat Sultanov
Foreign Affairs, Muratbek Imanaliyev
Foreign Trade and Industry, Essengul Omuraliyev
Health, Naken Kasiyev
Interior, Maj.-Gen. Omurbek Kutuyev
Justice, Nelya Beishenaliyeva
Labour and Social Security, Mira Jangaracheva
National Security, Misir Ashirkulov
Transport and Communications, Zhantoro Satybaldiev

EMBASSY OF THE KYRGYZ REPUBLIC
Ascot House, 119 Crawford Street, London WIH IAF
Tel 0171-935 1462
Ambassador Extraordinary and Plenipotentiary, HE Roza Otunbayeva, apptd 1997

BRITISH AMBASSADOR, HE Richard Lewington, resident at Almaty, Kazakhstan

ECONOMY

Agriculture is the main sector of the economy, with sugar beet, grain and sheep the main products. Private ownership of land was legalized in 1997. Industry is concentrated in the food-processing, textiles, timber and mining fields. Since 1992, some 60 per cent of state-owned enterprises have been privatized. Hydroelectric power is abundant and Kyrgyzstan has reserves of gold, coal, mercury and uranium, although only gold has so far been exploited and is the country's largest export. In 1997, industry grew by 47 per cent and agriculture by 10 per cent.

The government introduced the som in May 1993 to break the link with the depreciating rouble, the cause of high inflation in 1992 and early 1993. The president and government have also made the Central Bank independent of government and parliamentary control. However, the country needs direct foreign investment desperately and has had most of its trading links with other Central Asian republics reduced because of their refusal to accept payments in soms, although this has been ameliorated by the signing of an economic union agreement with Kazakhstan and Uzbekistan in February 1994. Subsidized goods supplies from Russia have also been reduced. In March 1996, a treaty was signed with Belarus, Kazakhstan and Russia enhancing economic co-operation and working towards a single customs territory. In 1998 industrial production slumped by 5.6 per cent. In 1996 there was a trade deficit of US$252 million and a current account deficit of US$425 million. Imports totalled US$838 million and exports US$505 million.

GNP – US$2,211 million (1997); US$480 per capita (1997)

GDP – US$1,475 million (1995); US$331 per capita (1995)

ANNUAL AVERAGE GROWTH OF GDP – –6.2 per cent (1995)

INFLATION RATE – 25.5 per cent (1997)

TOTAL EXTERNAL DEBT – US$928 million (1997)

Trade with UK	1997	1998
Imports from UK	£3,056,000	£2,735,000
Exports to UK	2,722,000	2,654,000

CULTURE AND EDUCATION

Until the 1930s the Kirghiz language had an oral tradition of literature which included the epic poem *Manas*, which tells the history of the Kirghiz people. Internationally, one of the best-known writers of the former Soviet Union is the Kirghiz writer Chingiz Aitmatov (1928–).

ILLITERACY RATE – 3.0 per cent

ENROLMENT (percentage of age group) – primary 97 per cent (1995); tertiary 12.2 per cent (1995)

LAOS

Satharanarath Pasathipatai Pasason Lao

AREA – 91,429 sq. miles (236,800 sq. km). Neighbours: China (north), Vietnam (north-east and east), Cambodia (south), Thailand (west), Myanmar (north-west)

POPULATION – 5,035,000 (1995 census). Lao is the official language; French and English are spoken

CAPITAL – Vientiane (population, 132,253, 1966; 120,000, 1984 estimate)

CURRENCY – Kip (K) of 100 at

NATIONAL DAY – 2 December

NATIONAL FLAG – Blue background with a central white circle, framed by two horizontal red stripes

LIFE EXPECTANCY (years) – male 49.50; female 52.50

POPULATION GROWTH RATE – 2.6 per cent (1997)

POPULATION DENSITY – 21 per sq. km (1996)

MILITARY EXPENDITURE – 3.9 per cent of GDP (1997)

MILITARY PERSONNEL – 129,100: Army 25,000, Navy 600, Air Force 3,500, Paramilitaries 100,000

CONSCRIPTION DURATION – 18 months minimum

ILLITERACY RATE – 43.4 per cent

ENROLMENT (percentage of age group) – primary 71 per cent (1996); secondary 18 per cent (1993); tertiary 2.8 per cent (1996)

HISTORY AND POLITICS

The kingdom of Lane Xang, the Land of a Million Elephants, was founded in the 14th century but broke up at the beginning of the 16th century into the separate kingdoms of Luang Prabang and Vientiane and the principality of Champassac, which together came under French protection in 1893. In 1945 the Japanese staged a coup and suppressed the French administration. In 1947 Laos became a constitutional monarchy under King Sisvang Vong, and an independent sovereign state in 1953. The next 22 years in Laos were marked by power struggles and civil war, eventually won by the North Vietnamese-backed Pathet Lao, a Communist-dominated organization.

The Lao People's Democratic Republic was proclaimed in December 1975 following victory by the Pathet Lao and the abdication of the King. A president and Council of Ministers were installed, and a 45-member Supreme People's Council was appointed to draft a constitution, which was approved in 1991. The Lao People's Revolutionary Party (LPRP) is the sole legal political organization. A general election to the enlarged 99-member National Assembly was held on 21 December 1997; all the candidates were approved by the LPRP. The president, prime minister and Council of Ministers were confirmed in their posts by the National Assembly on 24 February 1998.

HEAD OF STATE

President, Gen. Khamtay Siphandone, *elected by the National Assembly* 24 February 1998

Vice-President, Oudom Khatti-Gna

COUNCIL OF MINISTERS *as at July 1999*

Prime Minister, Gen. Sisavat Keobounphanh

Deputy PMs, Boungnang Vorachith; Khamphoui Keoboualapha (*Finance*); Somsavat Lengsavad (*Foreign Affairs*); Gen. Choumaly Sayasone (*National Defence*);

Agriculture and Forestry, Siene Saphangthong

Commerce and Tourism, Phoumy Thipphavone

Communications, Transport, Posts and Construction, Phao Bounnaphol

Education, Phimmasone Leuangkhamma

Governor of the State Bank, Cheuang Sombounekhanh

Industry and Handicrafts, Soulivong Daravong

Information and Culture, Sileua Bounkham

Interior, Gen. Asang Laoly

Justice, Khamouane Boupha

Labour and Social Welfare, Somphan Phengkhammy

National Economic Institute, Minister attached to Prime Minister, Khamxay Souphanouvong

Public Health, Ponemek Daraloy

State Planning Committee, Bouathong Vonglokham

EMBASSY OF THE LAO PEOPLE'S DEMOCRATIC REPUBLIC

74 Avenue Raymond-Poincaré F-75116 Paris

Tel: Paris 4553 0298

Ambassador Extraordinary and Plenipotentiary, HE Kamphan Simmalavong, apptd 1996

BRITISH AMBASSADOR, HE Sir James Hodge, KCVO, CMG, resident at Bangkok, Thailand

ECONOMY

A 'new economic mechanism' programme was introduced in 1986 which began the liberalization of the economy, with greater autonomy for state enterprises, the relaxation of price controls and the encouragement of private business and investors. These reforms have produced a market-orientated economic system which has increased growth and reduced inflation. The economy is dominated by the agricultural sector, which contributed 55 per cent of real GDP in 1996. Laos is a major producer of opium.

Although Laos is one of the poorest states in the world, there is potential for increased hydroelectric power exports to Thailand and there are deposits of coal, tin, iron ore, gold, bauxite and lignite. Foreign capital investment in infrastructure began with the 1994 opening of the Friendship Bridge over the Mekong river border with Thailand which links road routes from Singapore to China. Hydroelectric power is the main export, followed by wood.

In 1997 Laos had a trade deficit of US$282 million and a current account deficit of US$316 million. In 1996 imports totalled US$690 million and exports US$323 million.

GNP – US$1,924 million (1997); US$400 per capita (1997)

GDP – US$1,755 million (1995); US$359 per capita (1995)

ANNUAL AVERAGE GROWTH OF GDP – 6.8 per cent (1996)

INFLATION RATE – 13.0 per cent (1996)

TOTAL EXTERNAL DEBT – US$2,320 million (1997)

Trade with UK	1997	1998
Imports from UK	£3,069,000	£5,117,000
Exports to UK	6,030,000	1,907,000

LATVIA
Latvijas Republika

AREA – 24,942 sq. miles (64,600 sq. km). Neighbours: Estonia (north), Lithuania and Belarus (south), the Russian Federation (east)

POPULATION – 2,491,000 (1997): 55.3 per cent Latvian, 32.5 per cent Russian, 4.0 per cent Belarusian, with small Ukrainian and Polish minorities. The main religions are Lutheran, Roman Catholic and Russian Orthodox. The official language is Latvian; Russian is also spoken. Education is in Latvian and Russian. Public sector employees must pass language tests in Latvian to a level commensurate with the nature of their employment. The right of minorities to use their mother tongue has been acknowledged

CAPITAL – Riga (population, 805,997, 1998)

MAJOR CITIES – Daugavpils (117,502); Jelgava (70,962); Jūrmala (58,977); Liepāja (97,278); Ventspils (46,564)

CURRENCY – Lats of 100 santims

NATIONAL ANTHEM – Dievs, svētī Latviju (God bless Latvia)

NATIONAL DAY – 18 November (Independence Day 1918)

NATIONAL FLAG – Crimson, with a white horizontal stripe across the centre

LIFE EXPECTANCY (years) – male 60.72; female 72.87

POPULATION GROWTH RATE – 1.1 per cent (1997)

POPULATION DENSITY – 39 per sq. km (1996)

URBAN POPULATION – 69.0 per cent (1995)

HISTORY AND POLITICS

Latvia came under the control of the German Teutonic Knights at the end of the 13th century. During the next few centuries the country endured sporadic invasions by the Swedes, Poles and Russians. By 1795 Latvia was entirely under Russian control. On 18 November 1918, Latvia declared its independence, but was annexed by the Soviet Union in 1940 under the terms of the Molotov–Ribbentrop pact with Germany. Latvia was invaded and occupied when Germany invaded the Soviet Union during the Second World War but recaptured by the Soviet Union in 1944.

In 1988 the Popular Front of Latvia was formed to campaign for greater sovereignty and democracy for Latvia. It won the elections to the Supreme Council in 1989, and on 4 May 1990 the Supreme Council declared the

independent republic of Latvia to be, *de jure*, still in existence. Agitation in Latvia against Soviet rule led to clashes between independence supporters and Latvian Communists and the Soviet military which reached a peak in January 1991. A national referendum was held in March 1991 in which 73 per cent voted in favour of independence, and this was declared on 21 August 1991. The State Council of the Soviet Union recognized the independence of Latvia on 10 September 1991.

The general election of 3 October 1998 resulted in the People's Party gaining the most seats, but a coalition of Latvia's Way, the Union for Fatherland and Freedom and the New Party formed a government on 26 November. The Latvian Social Democratic Union joined the coalition on 4 February 1999.

POLITICAL SYSTEM

Executive authority is vested in a prime minister and Cabinet of Ministers. Legislative power is exercised by the unicameral parliament (*Saeima*), which comprises 100 deputies elected for four-year terms by proportional representation, with a 5 per cent threshold for parliamentary representation. The deputies elect a president of state, serving for three years, who in turn appoints the prime minister. The prime minister appoints, and the Saeima approves, the Cabinet of Ministers.

The electorate and citizenship had been restricted to descendants of Latvian citizens before the 1940 Soviet occupation and to those who could pass the required Latvian language tests, until 1994 when a law was passed enabling naturalization of long-term residents. In October 1998 a referendum to amend the citizenship law was passed which granted citizenship to those children born in Latvia after Latvian independence if their parents requested it and provided for simpler language tests for older residents.

HEAD OF STATE
President, Vaira Vīķe-Freiberga, *elected* 17 June 1999, *sworn in* 8 July 1999

COUNCIL OF MINISTERS *as at August 1999*
Prime Minister, Latvian Privatization Agency, Andris Šķēle (TP)
Agriculture, Andris Kalvītis (TP)
Culture, Karīna Pētersone (LC)
Defence, Ģirts Kristovskis (TB)
Economy, Vladimirs Makarovs (TB)
Education and Science, Silva Golde (TP)
Environment and Regional Development, Vents Balodis (TB)
Finance, Edmunds Krastiņš (TP)
Foreign Affairs, Indulis Bērziņš (LC)
Interior, Mareks Segliņš (TP)
Justice, Valdis Birkavs (LC)
Special Tasks Minister for Co-operation with International Financial Institutions, Roberts Zīle (TB)
Transport, Anatolijs Gorbunovs (LC)
Welfare, Robert Jurdžs (TB)

TB Union For Fatherland and Freedom; LC Latvia's Way; TP People's Party

EMBASSY OF THE REPUBLIC OF LATVIA
45 Nottingham Place, London WIM 3FE
Tel 0171-312 0040
Ambassador Extraordinary and Plenipotentiary, HE Normans Penke, apptd 1997

BRITISH EMBASSY
5, Alunana Iela Street, Riga LV-1010
Tel: Riga 733 8126
Ambassador Extraordinary and Plenipotentiary, HE Stephen Nash, apptd 1999

BRITISH COUNCIL DIRECTOR, I. Stewart, 5a Blaumana
iela 3, Riga LV-1010

DEFENCE

The Army has 13 armoured personnel carriers and 24
artillery pieces, the Navy has 12 patrol craft at three bases
and the Air Force has three aircraft and five helicopters.

Russian forces withdrew from Latvia in 1994.

MILITARY EXPENDITURE – 4.6 per cent of GDP (1997)

MILITARY PERSONNEL – 7,080: Army 2,350, Navy 880,
Air Force 130, Paramilitaries 3,720

CONSCRIPTION DURATION – 12 months

ECONOMY

Attempts to move from a command economy to a market
economy resulted in low growth and high unemployment
in the early 1990s, though economic reforms have begun
to show results. The government has initiated a privatization process which has made many industrial facilities
available for purchase both by Latvian and foreign private
investors. The privatization of state industries was completed by the end of 1998.

Latvia is an agricultural exporter, specializing in cattle
and pig breeding, dairy farming and crops, including sugar
beet, flax, cereals and potatoes. In 1996, 13.6 per cent of the
population were employed in agriculture. Natural resources include limestone, gypsum, peat and timber.

Industry is specialized in certain areas including the
production of food and beverages, motor vehicles, textiles
and timber and paper products.

Tourism is being developed, capitalizing on Latvia's
beach resorts, nature reserves and parks. Latvia is also
geographically well-placed for the development of transport services.

GNP – US$5,995 million (1997); US$2,430 per capita
(1997)

GDP – US$4,474 million (1995); US$1,764 per capita
(1995)

ANNUAL AVERAGE GROWTH OF GDP – 6.5 per cent
(1997)

INFLATION RATE – 2.8 per cent (1998)

UNEMPLOYMENT – 6.6 per cent (1995)

TOTAL EXTERNAL DEBT – US$503 million (1997)

TRADE

In 1997, 48.9 per cent of Latvia's exports were to EU states,
compared to 19.7 per cent to the CIS. In 1996, a free trade
regime was agreed with the EU and EFTA. The main
imports are oil and energy, and the main exports are wood
and wood products, artificial fibres, meat and dairy products.

In 1997 there was a trade deficit of US$937 million and
a current account deficit of US$441 million. Imports
totalled US$2,718 million and exports US$1,664 million.

Trade with UK	1997	1998
Imports from UK	£86,828,000	£87,172,000
Exports to UK	346,686,000	296,471,000

COMMUNICATIONS

Latvia has 2,413 km of railways and some 20,400 km of
roads. Many of the exports from former CIS states are
transported to Western Europe via Latvia. Latvia is also
being developed as a transportation route from Scandinavia
to central and southern Europe. Several warm-water ports
exist, of which three, Riga, Ventspils and Liepaja, are
developed for commercial transport. The national airline,
Latvijas Aviolinijas, operates regular flights to Russia,
Scandinavia and Europe. 531,000 people came through the
international airport in Riga in 1997.

CULTURE AND EDUCATION

The Latvian language belongs to the Baltic branch of the
Indo-European languages. The Latin alphabet is used.
Latvian literature appeared in the 19th century and played
a role in the fight for independence in 1918.

There are 27 higher education institutions, of which five
are universities.

ILLITERACY RATE – 0.3 per cent

ENROLMENT (percentage of age group) – primary 90 per
cent (1996); secondary 79 per cent (1996); tertiary 33.3
per cent (1996)

LEBANON

Al-Jumhouriya al-Lubnaniya

AREA – 4,015 sq. miles (10,400 sq. km). Neighbours: Syria
(north and east), Israel (south)

POPULATION – 3,084,000 (1994 UN estimate): 34 per
cent Shi'ite Muslim, 21 per cent Sunni Muslim, 38 per
cent Christian, 7 per cent Druze. Arabic is the official
language, and French and English are also widely used

CAPITAL – ΨBeirut (population, 1,500,000, 1991)

MAJOR CITIES – ΨSidon (100,000); ΨTripoli (200,000);
ΨTyre (70,000)

CURRENCY – Lebanese pound (L£) of 100 piastres

NATIONAL ANTHEM – Kulluna Lil Watan Lil'ula
Lil'alam (We all belong to the homeland)

NATIONAL DAY – 22 November

NATIONAL FLAG – Horizontal bands of red, white and
red with a green cedar of Lebanon in the centre of the
white band

LIFE EXPECTANCY (years) – male 66.60; female 70.50

POPULATION GROWTH RATE – 1.9 per cent (1997)

POPULATION DENSITY – 297 per sq. km (1996)

HISTORY AND POLITICS

Lebanon has some important historical remains, notably
Baalbek (Heliopolis) which contains the ruins of first- to
third-century Roman temples and Jbeil (Byblos), one of
the oldest continuously inhabited towns in the world, and
ancient Tyre.

Lebanon became an independent state in 1920, admin-
istered under French mandate until 22 November 1943.
Powers were transferred to the Lebanese government from
January 1944 and French troops were withdrawn in 1946.

In 1975, fighting broke out in Beirut between Maronite,
Sunni and Shia factions, the latter supported by Palestinian
guerrillas based in Lebanon. In 1976 the Arab Deterrent
Forces, composed mainly of Syrian troops, imposed a
cease-fire but fighting resumed and continued until the
end of the civil war in 1990. In 1978 Israeli forces invaded
but withdrew some months later. In 1982 Israeli forces
again invaded, penetrating as far as Beirut; they withdrew
in 1985, but a buffer zone controlled by the Israeli-backed
South Lebanon Army (SLA), a Christian militia, was
established along the Israeli–Lebanon border. Syrian forces
are deployed in west Beirut and in the north and the east
of the country.

A new government incorporating the main militia
leaders was formed in December 1990. Since then the
government has attempted to clear the militias from the
Greater Beirut area and restore its authority throughout
most of the country. The Beqa'a valley remains under
Syrian control and the South Lebanon Security Zone under
Israeli control. All militias have been disarmed apart from
Hezbollah and the SLA. Since 1993 the Lebanese Army

has deployed in southern villages alongside UNIFIL forces but has not disarmed Hezbollah forces, who are financed, armed and trained by Syria and Iran to continue fighting against Israel and the SLA.

Low-level fighting continued throughout 1993–9. In April 1996, Israel began a two-week missile bombardment of Hezbollah targets in Beirut and southern Lebanon. The mission, code-named 'Grapes of Wrath', was in retaliation for suicide attacks and Hezbollah strikes against Israel's northern cities. An agreement was reached on 15 April to confine hostilities to southern Lebanon. Israel warned in January 1999 that it would respond to any further attacks by striking at infrastructure targets in central and northern Lebanon, thereby ending the agreement.

The first parliamentary elections since 1972 were held between August and October 1992. The 128-seat National Assembly was directly elected by universal suffrage and divided equally between Christians and Muslims. The polls were widely boycotted in Christian areas because of the continuing presence of Syrian troops. National Assembly elections were held in August and September 1996, and the first local elections for 35 years were held in May and June 1998.

Salim al-Hoss was appointed prime minister by President Lahoud on 2 December 1998, pledging himself to continue with the reconstruction programmes initiated by his predecessor, along with a programme of fiscal austerity to cut the budget deficit.

POLITICAL SYSTEM

The National Covenant (1943) is characterized by the division of power between the religious communities. The executive comprises the president, prime minister and Cabinet. The president is elected by the National Assembly for a non-renewable term of six years and must be a Maronite Christian. The prime minister is appointed following consultation between the president and National Assembly and must be a Sunni Muslim. The 128-member unicameral National Assembly comprises equal numbers of Christians and Muslims although the speaker must be a Shia Muslim. Political parties are banned. There are six governorates divided into 26 districts.

The constitution was amended on 15 October 1998 to allow the election of Gen. Lahoud. Serving state officials had previously been prohibited from standing for the presidency.

HEAD OF STATE

President of the Republic of Lebanon, Gen. Émile Lahoud, *elected* 15 October 1998, *sworn in* 24 November 1998

CABINET *as at July 1999*

Prime Minister, Foreign Affairs, Expatriates' Affairs, Salim al-Hoss
Deputy PM, Interior, Municipal and Rural Affairs, Michel al-Murr
Agriculture, Housing and Co-operatives, Soleiman Franjieh
Economy and Trade, Industry, Nasir al-Sa'idi
Finance, Georges Qurum
Hydroelectric Resources, Oil, Soleiman Trabulsi
Information, Displaced Persons' Affairs, Anwar al-Khalil
Justice, Joseph Shaoul
Labour, Social Affairs, Michel Musa
Minister of State for Administrative Reform, Hassan Shalaq
National Defence, Ghazi Zu'aytar
National Education, Youth and Sports, Vocational and Technical Education, Culture and Higher Education, Muhammad Yusuf Baydun
Post and Telecommunications, Isam Nu'man
Public Health, Karam Karam
Public Works, Transport, Najib Miqati
Speaker of the National Assembly, Nabi Berri
Tourism, Environment, Artur Nazarian

LEBANESE EMBASSY

21 Kensington Palace Gardens, London w8 4QM
Tel 0171–229 7265/6
Ambassador Extraordinary and Plenipotentiary, HE Jihad Mortada, apptd 1999

BRITISH EMBASSY

Autostrade Jal El Dib, Coolrite Building (PO Box 60180), Beirut
Tel: Beirut 406330
Ambassador Extraordinary and Plenipotentiary,
HE David MacLennan, apptd 1996
BRITISH COUNCIL DIRECTOR, A. Malamah-Thomas, MBE, Sidani Street, Fawzi Azar Building, Beirut

DEFENCE

The Army has 315 main battle tanks, 895 armoured personnel carriers and 203 artillery pieces. The Navy has 14 patrol and coastal vessels at three bases. The Air Force has three combat aircraft and four armed helicopters.

There are a 4,473-strong UN peacekeeping force, 30,000 Syrian troops and 150 Iranian Revolutionary Guards operating in Lebanon.
MILITARY EXPENDITURE – 4.5 per cent of GDP (1997)
MILITARY PERSONNEL – 68,100: Army 53,300, Navy 1,000, Air Force 800, Paramilitaries 13,000
CONSCRIPTION DURATION – 12 months

ECONOMY

Fruits are the most important products and include citrus fruit, apples, grapes, bananas and olives. There is some light industry, mostly for the production of consumer goods, but most factories are still in need of reconstruction because of the civil war.

A ten-year plan has been initiated to repair war damage and to restore Lebanon's position as a regional financial services and light industrial centre. The 1993–2002 reconstruction plan is estimated to cost US$12,900 million, of which US$7,600 million is to come from foreign loans and grants and US$5,300 million from budget surpluses. It is to concentrate on rebuilding housing, transport, services, education and health services, and aiding industry and agriculture.

A plan to reconstruct the commercial centre of Beirut has been started, with the issue in January 1994 of US$650 million of shares in the US$1,800 million Solidère company which will reconstruct the 400-acre site. The government has also obtained US$1,600 million in loans and grants for its national reconstruction programme, mainly from Arab states and international agencies.
GNP – US$13,900 million (1997); US$3,350 per capita (1997)
GDP – US$9,371 million (1995); US$3,114 per capita (1995)
ANNUAL AVERAGE GROWTH OF GDP – 7.0 per cent (1995)
INFLATION RATE – 6.8 per cent (1994)
TOTAL EXTERNAL DEBT – US$5,036 million (1997)

TRADE

Principal imports are gold and precious metals, machinery and electrical equipment, textiles and yarns, vegetable products, iron and steel goods, and motor vehicles. There had been a gradual decline in the overall amount of imports as a result of continued instability. A free trade agreement with Syria will be phased in from 1999.

Principal exports include gold and precious metals, fruits and vegetables, textiles, building materials, furniture, plastic goods, foodstuffs, tobacco and wine.

At one time there was a considerable transit trade through Beirut into the Arab hinterland. Lebanon is the terminal for two oil pipelines, one formerly belonging to the Iraq Petroleum Company, debouching at Tripoli, the other belonging to the Trans Arabian Pipeline Company, at Sidon. These lines have not functioned for some years.

In 1996 imports totalled US$7,582 million and exports US$1,017 million.

Trade with UK	1997	1998
Imports from UK	£191,206,000	£180,160,000
Exports to UK	16,876,000	21,502,000

COMMUNICATIONS

There are 7,370 km of roads, of which 6,265 are paved; there is 222 km of railway track. There is an international airport at Beirut, served by the national carrier Middle East Airlines and other airlines. An internal service operates from Beirut to Tripoli.

EDUCATION

There are 13 universities in Lebanon, among them the American and the French universities, and the Lebanese National University, the Beirut University College, the Kaslik Saint Esprit University and the Arab University in Beirut, with the University of Balamand situated near Tripoli. There are also ten other institutions of higher education and an Academy of Fine Arts. There are several institutions for vocational training, and there is a good provision throughout the country of primary and secondary schools, among which are a great number of private schools.

ILLITERACY RATE – 7.6 per cent

ENROLMENT (percentage of age group) – primary 76 per cent (1996); tertiary 27.0 per cent (1995)

LESOTHO

'Muso oa Lesotho

AREA – 11,720 sq. miles (30,355 sq. km). Neighbour: South Africa, which completely surrounds Lesotho

POPULATION – 2,078,000 (1994 UN estimate). The languages are Sesotho and English

CAPITAL – Maseru (population, 288,951, 1986)

CURRENCY – Loti (M) of 100 lisente. The South African rand is also legal tender

NATIONAL ANTHEM – Pina ea Sechaba

NATIONAL DAY – 4 October (Independence Day)

NATIONAL FLAG – Diagonally white over blue over green with the white of double width, and an assegai and knobkerrie on a Basotho shield in brown in the upper hoist

LIFE EXPECTANCY (years) – male 58.00; female 63.00

POPULATION GROWTH RATE – 2.2 per cent (1997)

POPULATION DENSITY – 68 per sq. km (1996)

MILITARY EXPENDITURE – 4.6 per cent of GDP (1997)

MILITARY PERSONNEL – 2,000 Army

HISTORY AND POLITICS

Lesotho (formerly Basutoland) became a constitutional monarchy within the Commonwealth on 4 October 1966. The independence constitution was suspended in 1970 and the country was governed by a Council of Ministers headed by Leabua Jonathan until the establishment of a National Assembly in 1974.

Jonathan's government was overthrown in 1986, and executive and legislative powers were conferred on the King, to be advised by the Military Council and Council of Ministers led by Maj.-Gen. Justin Lekhanya. In March 1990, King Moshoeshoe II's powers were formally revoked and in November the King was deposed and replaced by his son, who assumed the title of Letsie III. Maj.-Gen. Lekhanya was overthrown in 1991 in a coup led by Col. Elias Ramaema. Elections were held in March 1993 and the Basotho Congress Party (BCP) won all 65 seats in the new National Assembly. A BCP government led by Ntsu Mokhele was formed, King Letsie III swore allegiance to a new multiparty democratic constitution and the Military Council was dissolved.

On 17 August 1994 King Letsie III and sections of the military mounted a coup attempt and announced the dismissal of the government and the dissolution of parliament. After mediation, the government, which had refused to leave office, was restored by the King. King Letsie also announced his intention to abdicate in favour of his father, Moshoeshoe II, who was restored on 25 January 1995. When King Moshoeshoe II died in a car crash on 15 January 1996, King Letsie III again ascended to the throne.

At the last legislative elections in May 1998, the Lesotho Congress for Democracy won 78 of the 80 seats in the National Assembly. Allegations of electoral fraud, later confirmed by an investigation which said that the election had been marred by irregularities, but that there were insufficient grounds to annul the poll, led to violent protests, which began in August; there were also reports of an alleged army mutiny. The deteriorating situation led to the intervention of South African and Botswanan military forces on 22 September to restore order after a request by the prime minister, Bethuel Pakalitha Mosisili; they withdrew in May 1999.

The country is divided into ten administrative districts. In each district there is a district secretary who co-ordinates all government activity in the area, working in co-operation with hereditary chiefs.

HEAD OF STATE
HM The King of Lesotho, King Letsie III, *acceded* February 1996, *crowned* 31 October 1997

COUNCIL OF MINISTERS *as at July 1999*
Prime Minister, Defence, Public Service, Bethuel Pakalitha Mosisili
Deputy Prime Minister, Agriculture, Kelebone Albert Maope
Broadcasting, Post and Telecommunications, Nyane Mphafi
Education, Lesao Lehohla
Environment, Women, Youth Affairs, Mamoshebi Kabi
Finance and Development Planning, Leketekete Victor Ketso
Foreign Affairs, Motsoahae Thomas Thabane
Health and Social Welfare, Vova Bulane
Home Affairs, Local Government, Mopshatla Mabitle
Industry, Trade and Marketing, Mpho Malie
Justice, Human Rights, Law and Constitutional Affairs, Rehabilitation, Sephiri Motanyane
Labour and Employment, Not'si Molopo
Natural Resources, Monyane Moleleki
Prime Minister's Office, Mofelehetsi Moerane
Tourism, Sport and Culture, Hlalele Motaung
Works and Transport, Shakhane Robong Mokhehle

HIGH COMMISSION FOR THE KINGDOM OF LESOTHO
7 Chesham Place, London SW1 8HN
Tel 0171-235 5686
High Commissioner, HE Benjamin Masilo, apptd 1996

BRITISH HIGH COMMISSION
PO Box 521, Maseru 100
Tel: Maseru 313961
High Commissioner, HE Kaye Oliver, OBE, apptd 1999

BRITISH COUNCIL REPRESENTATIVE, S. Cweba,
Hobson's Square, PO Box 429, Maseru 100

ECONOMY

The economy is based on agriculture and animal husbandry, and the adverse balance of trade (mainly consumer and capital goods) is offset by the earnings of the large numbers of the population who work in South Africa. Apart from some diamonds, Lesotho has few natural resources. Agriculture contributes 15 per cent of GDP and the main crops are maize, sorghum and vegetables. The Lesotho National Development Corporation was set up to promote the development of industry, mining, trade and tourism; a number of light manufacturing and processing industries have recently been established. The main sources of revenue are customs and excise duty.

In 1994 Lesotho had a trade deficit of US$667 million and a current account surplus of US$108 million.

GNP – US$1,368 million (1997); US$680 per capita (1997)
GDP – US$984 million (1995); US$486 per capita (1995)
ANNUAL AVERAGE GROWTH OF GDP – 7.4 per cent (1995)
TOTAL EXTERNAL DEBT – US$660 million (1997)

Trade with UK	1997	1998
Imports from UK	£4,847,000	£1,041,000
Exports to UK	105,000	15,000

COMMUNICATIONS

A tarred road links Maseru to several of the main lowland towns, and this is being extended in the south of the country. The mountainous areas are linked by tarred, gravelled and earth roads and tracks. Roads link border towns in South Africa with the main towns in Lesotho. Maseru is also connected by rail with the main Bloemfontein–Natal line of the South African Railways. Scheduled international air services are operated daily between Maseru and Johannesburg, and other scheduled international flights are to Gaborone, Harare, Manzini and Maputo. There are around 30 airstrips. Internal scheduled services are operated by the Lesotho Airways Corporation.

The telephone network is fully automated in all urban centres. Radio telephone communication is used extensively in the remote rural areas.

EDUCATION

Most schools are mission-controlled, the government providing grants for salaries and buildings. There are over 1,200 primary and over 180 secondary schools, with emphasis being laid on agricultural and vocational education. The National University of Lesotho at Roma was established as a university in 1975.

ILLITERACY RATE – 28.7 per cent
Enrolment (percentage of age group) – primary 63 per cent (1996); secondary 17 per cent (1996); tertiary 2.4 per cent (1996)

LIBERIA
Republic of Liberia

AREA – 43,000 sq. miles (111,369 sq. km). Neighbours: Guinea (north), Côte d'Ivoire (east), Sierra Leone (north-west)
POPULATION – 2,820,000 (1994 UN estimate). The official language is English. The main African languages are Bassa, Kpelle and Kru, though some 16 ethnic languages are spoken
CAPITAL – ΨMonrovia (population, 421,053, 1984)
MAJOR CITIES – ΨBuchanan (Grand Bassa); ΨGreenville (Sinoe); ΨHarper (Cape Palmas)
CURRENCY – Liberian dollar (L$) of 100 cents
NATIONAL ANTHEM – All Hail, Liberia, Hail
NATIONAL DAY – 26 July
NATIONAL FLAG – Alternate horizontal stripes (five white, six red), with five-pointed white star on blue field in upper corner next to flagstaff
LIFE EXPECTANCY (years) – male 45.80; female 44.00
POPULATION GROWTH RATE – 2.4 per cent (1997)
POPULATION DENSITY – 25 per sq. km (1996)
URBAN POPULATION – 45.0 per cent (1996)
MILITARY EXPENDITURE – 3.9 per cent of GDP (1997)
MILITARY PERSONNEL – 14,000
ILLITERACY RATE – 61.7 per cent

HISTORY AND POLITICS

Liberia was founded by the American Colonization Society in 1822 as a colony for freed American slaves, and has been recognized since 1847 as an independent state.

William V. S. Tubman, President since 1944, died in 1971 and was succeeded by Dr Tolbert. The constitution was suspended following a military coup in 1980 during which Tolbert was killed. M/Sgt. Samuel Doe assumed power as chairman of a military council. A new constitution was endorsed by a referendum in 1984. Doe and his party, the National Democratic Party of Liberia (NDPL) won the elections held in 1985, amid allegations of electoral fraud, and a civilian government was formally installed in 1986.

CIVIL WAR

A rebel incursion in 1989 by the National Patriotic Front of Liberia (NPFL) led by Charles Taylor developed into a full-scale civil war in 1990. A five-nation Economic Community of West African States (ECOWAS) peacekeeping force (known as ECOMOG) landed in Monrovia in an effort to end the conflict but in September 1990 President Doe was killed, having refused to step down.

The Interim Government of National Unity (IGNU) was formed in August 1990. A cease-fire under ECOMOG supervision broke down in October 1992 when the NPFL attempted to seize Monrovia. In response ECOMOG assumed a more offensive role. By March 1993 the NPFL had been driven into eastern parts of Liberia and peace negotiations between the warring factions had begun. A peace agreement was signed by the IGNU, NPFL and another rebel group, ULIMO, on 25 July 1993 which brought about a cease-fire on 1 August.

Continued fighting and the fracturing of the three factions led to further negotiations and an agreement in December 1994 on a new Council of State. A Council of State comprising the faction leaders was inaugurated on 1 September 1995 and a transitional government formed. Fighting resumed briefly in April 1996, although a cease-fire in July 1996 enabled elections to be held in July 1997.

Legislative elections were won by the NPFL, and Charles Taylor was elected president with 75 per cent of the vote in elections deemed free and fair by international observers. The ECOMOG mandate expired in February 1998.

President Taylor dismissed 11 Cabinet ministers in May 1999 for their failure to attend an official church service; they were later reinstated.

HEAD OF STATE

President, Charles Taylor, *elected* 19 July 1997, *inaugurated* 3 August 1997

Vice-President, Enoch Dogolea Junior

CABINET *as at July 1999*

Agriculture, Roland Massaquoi
Commerce, Ibrahim Kaba
Defence, Daniel Chea
Education, Evelyne Kandakai
Finance, John Bestman
Foreign Affairs, Monie Captan
Forestry Development Authority, Bob Taylor
Health and Social Welfare, Peter Coleman
Information, Culture and Tourism, Joe Mulbah
Interior, Edward Sackor
Junior Legal Adviser to the President, James Teah
Justice, Eddington Varmah
Labour, Thomas Woewiyu
Land, Mines, Energy, Jenkins Dunbar
Liberia Electricity Corporation, Samuel Burnette
Liberia Telecommunications Corporation, Charles Roberts
Maritime Affairs Commissioner, Benoni Uray
Minister of State for Economic Affairs, Amelia Ward
Minister of State for Presidential Affairs, Jonathan Taylor
Minister of State Without Portfolio, Augustine Zayzay
National Bank Governor, Charles Bright
Planning and Economic Affairs, Wesseh McClain
Post and Telecommunications, Maxwell Kaba
Press Secretary, Reginald Goodrich
Public Works, Alvin Coleman
Rural Development, Roosevelt Johnson
Transport, Larmin Kawah
Youth and Sports, François Massaquoi

EMBASSY OF THE REPUBLIC OF LIBERIA
2 Pembridge Place, London W2 4XB
Tel 0171-221 1036
Ambassador Extraordinary and Plenipotentiary, HE William V. S. Bull, apptd 1998

BRITISH AMBASSADOR, HE Haydon Warren-Gash, resident at Abidjan, Côte d'Ivoire

ECONOMY

Before the civil war began principal exports were iron ore, crude rubber, timber, uncut diamonds, palm kernels, cocoa and coffee, but the civil war has resulted in the suspension of most economic activity.

GDP – US$2,385 million (1995); US$1,124 per capita (1995)

ANNUAL AVERAGE GROWTH OF GDP – 2.7 per cent (1995)

INFLATION RATE – 9.1 per cent (1989)

TOTAL EXTERNAL DEBT – US$2,012 million (1997)

Trade with UK	1997	1998
Imports from UK	£12,677,000	£7,818,000
Exports to UK	318,000	1,906,000

COMMUNICATIONS

The artificial harbour and free port of Monrovia was opened in 1948. There are 10,300 km of roads, of which 628 km are paved, and 490 km of railway track. There are nine ports of entry, including three river ports. Robertsfield International Airport is under NPFL control and not yet in use. Spriggs Payne airfield, on the outskirts of Monrovia, normally used for internal flights, is currently being used for flights to other West African countries.

LIBYA
Al-Jamahiriya Al-Arabiya
Al-Libiya Al-Shabiya Al-Ishtirakiya Al-Uthma

AREA – 679,362 sq. miles (1,759,540 sq. km). Neighbours: Egypt and Sudan (east), Chad and Niger (south), Algeria and Tunisia (west)

POPULATION – 4,389,739 (1995 census). The people of Libya are principally Arab with some Berbers in the west and some Tuareg tribesmen in the Fezzan. Islam is the official religion but other religions are tolerated. The official language is Arabic

CAPITAL – ΨTripoli (population, 1,000,000, 1991 estimate)

MAJOR CITIES – ΨBenghazi (500,000); ΨMisurata (200,000); Sirte (100,000)

CURRENCY – Libyan dinar (LD) of 1,000 dirhams

NATIONAL DAY – 1 September

NATIONAL FLAG – Libya uses a plain emerald green flag

LIFE EXPECTANCY (years) – male 61.58; female 65.00

POPULATION GROWTH RATE – 2.3 per cent (1997)

POPULATION DENSITY – 3 per sq. km (1996)

ILLITERACY RATE – 23.8 per cent

ENROLMENT (percentage of age group) – primary 97 per cent (1992); secondary 62 per cent (1980); tertiary 18.4 per cent (1992)

Vast sand and rock deserts, almost completely barren, occupy the greater part of Libya. The southern part of the country lies within the Sahara Desert. There are few rivers and as rainfall is irregular outside parts of Cyrenaica and Tripolitania, good harvests are rare.

The ancient ruins in Cyrenaica, at Cyrene, Ptolemais (Tolmeta) and Apollonia, are outstanding, as are those at Leptis Magna, 70 miles east, and at Sabratha, 40 miles west of Tripoli. An Italian expedition found in the south-west of the Fezzan a series of rock-paintings more than 5,000 years old.

HISTORY AND POLITICS

From the 16th century Libya was dominated by the Ottoman Empire, until occupied by Italy in 1911–12 in the course of the Italo-Turkish War. Under the 1912 Treaty of Ouchy, sovereignty over the province was transferred by Turkey to Italy, and in 1939 the four provinces of Libya (Tripoli, Misurata, Benghazi and Derna) were incorporated in the national territory of Italy as *Libia Italiana*. After the Second World War Tripolitania and Cyrenaica were placed provisionally under British and the Fezzan under French administration, and in conformity with a resolution of the UN General Assembly in 1949, Libya became on 24 December 1951 the first independent state to be created by the UN. The monarchy was overthrown by a revolution in 1969 and the country was declared a republic. It was ruled by the Revolutionary Command Council (RCC) under the leadership of Col. Muammar al-Gadhafi.

In 1977, a new form of direct democracy, the 'Jamahiriya' (state of the masses) was promulgated and the official name of the country was changed to Socialist People's Libyan Arab Jamahiriya. Since a reorganization in 1979, neither

Col. Gadhafi nor his former RCC colleagues have held formal posts in the administration. Gadhafi continues to hold the ceremonial title 'Leader of the Revolution'.

POLITICAL SYSTEM

At local level authority is vested in about 1,500 Basic and 14 Municipal People's Congresses which appoint Popular Committees to execute policy. Officials of these congresses and committees, together with representatives from unions and other organizations, form the General People's Congress, which normally meets twice each year. In addition, a number of extraordinary sessions are held throughout the year. This is the highest policy-making body in the country.

The General People's Congress appoints its own General Secretariat and the General People's Committee, whose members head the government departments which execute policy at national level. The Secretary of the General People's Committee has functions similar to those of a prime minister.

Leader of the Revolution and Supreme Commander of the Armed Forces, Col. Muammar al-Gadhafi

SECRETARIAT OF THE GENERAL PEOPLE'S CONGRESS *as at August 1999*

Secretary, Zenati Mohammad Zenati
Secretary, Affairs of People's Committees, Dr Albagdai Ali Mahmoudi
Secretary Affairs of People's Congresses, Ahmed Mohamed Ibrahim
Secretary, Foreign Affairs, Abdel Rahman Shalgam
Secretary, Trade Unions, Abdallah Idriss Ibrahim
Assistant Secretary, Abdulhamid Seid A al- Zenati
Assistant Secretary, Women's Affairs, Nuara Ramadan Busfreta

GENERAL PEOPLE'S COMMITTEE (CABINET)

Secretary (Premier), Mohammad Ahmed al-Mangoush
Agriculture, Ali ben Ramadan
Animal Resources, Massoud Said Abousawa
Arab Unity, Jomma Mahdi Alfazzani
Economy and Trade, Dr. Abdulhafid Zletni
Education and Scientific Research, Dr Mahdi Abdalla Emberish
Energy, Abdalla Salem Albadri
Finance, Dr Mohammed Beit Elmal
Foreign Liaison and International Co-operation, Omar Almuntaser
Formation and Training, Maatoug Mohamed Maatoug
Health and Social Security, Sleman Alghamari
Housing and Services, Moubarak Abdallah Shamekh
Industry and Mines, Moftah Azouz
Information, Culture and Jamahiri Mobilization, Faouzia Shalabi
Justice, Mohamed Belgasem Zouei
Marine Resources, Bashir Ramadan Abougenah
Planning, Jadallah Azouz al-Talhi
Public Security, Mohamed Mahmoud al-Hejiazi
Transport and Marine Carriage, Ezzeddine Henshiri

LIBYAN DIPLOMATIC MISSION IN LONDON

Since the break of diplomatic relations with Libya in April 1984, the Royal Embassy of Saudi Arabia has handled Libyan interests in Britain.
Head of Interests Section, Isa Baruni Edaeki

BRITISH EMBASSY

British interests are currently handled by the British Interests Section of the Italian Embassy, Sharia Uahran 1 (PO Box 4206), Tripoli.
Head of Interests Section, D. G. Ward

DEFENCE

The Army has 2,210 main battle tanks, 1,000 armoured infantry fighting vehicles, 990 armoured personnel carriers, and 1,170 artillery pieces. The Navy has four submarines, three frigates, 33 patrol and coastal vessels, and 32 armed helicopters at six bases. The Air Force has 420 combat aircraft and 52 armed helicopters.

Libya is alleged to have built at least one chemical weapons plant. The USA claims that a plant at Rabta, closed in 1990, was reopened in 1995, and that a plant has been constructed near Tahunah, south of Tripoli.

As part of the UN economic sanctions imposed in April 1992, there is a total embargo on arms sales to Libya.
MILITARY EXPENDITURE – 4.7 per cent of GDP (1997)
MILITARY PERSONNEL – 65,000: Army 35,000, Navy 8,000, Air Force 22,000
CONSCRIPTION DURATION – Selective conscription, one to two years

ECONOMY

Economic sanctions were imposed on Libya in April 1992 by the UN Security Council following Libya's failure to hand over two suspects in the bombing of Pan-Am flight 103 over Lockerbie, Scotland, in 1988, in which 270 people were killed. The UN imposed additional sanctions in December 1993, including freezing assets abroad and restricting imports of spare parts and equipment for the oil and aviation sectors. The sanctions were suspended in April 1999, following mediation by President Mandela of South Africa in March 1999, which led to the extradition in April of the two suspects to the Netherlands to stand trial.

Agriculture is confined mainly to the coastal areas of Tripolitania and Cyrenaica, where barley, wheat, olives, citrus fruits and livestock are produced, and to the areas of the oases, many of which are well supplied with springs supporting small fertile areas. Among the important oases are Jaghbub, Ghadames, Jofra, Sebha, Murzuq, Brak, Ghat, Jalo and the Kufra group in the south-east.

The main industry is oil and gas production. There are pipelines from Zelten to the terminal at Mersa Brega, from Dahra to Ras-es-Sider, from Amal to Ras Lanuf, and from the Intisar field to Zuetina. In 1995, 66.6 million tonnes of crude oil was produced. A major petrochemical complex has been built at Ras Lanuf. The construction of an iron and steel plant at Misurata has been completed. Cement, construction materials and textiles are also produced. Economic constraints have delayed some projects, particularly since Libya decided in 1983 to go ahead with a major irrigation scheme, the 'Great Man-Made River'.

Libya has technical assistance agreements with a number of countries, and also employs large numbers of foreign labourers and experts.
GDP – US$29,727 million (1995); US$5,498 per capita (1995)
ANNUAL AVERAGE GROWTH OF GDP – 1.2 per cent (1995)

TRADE

Exports are dominated by crude oil, but some wool, cattle, sheep and horses, olive oil, and hides and skins are also exported. Principal imports are machinery and transport equipment, foodstuffs, livestock, and most construction materials and consumer goods. After the revolution the private sector was virtually eliminated and Libya became a state trading country with imports controlled by state monopolies. Since reforms in 1988, however, a small private sector has been re-established.

Trade with UK	1997	1998
Imports from UK	£268,959,000	£237,386,000
Exports to UK	231,403,000	149,114,000

COMMUNICATIONS

There are 25,675 km of roads; the coastal road running from the Tunisian frontier through Tripoli to Benghazi, Tobruk and the Egyptian border serves the main population centres. Main roads also link the provincial centres, and the oil-producing areas of the south with the coastal towns.

There are airports at Tripoli and Benghazi (Benina), Kufra, Labrag, Misurata and Tobruk. Since April 1992 a UN embargo on air links with Libya has been in force.

LIECHTENSTEIN
Fürstentum Liechtenstein

AREA – 62 sq. miles (160 sq. km). Neighbours: Austria, Switzerland

POPULATION – 31,320 (1997). The language of the principality is German

CAPITAL – Vaduz (population, 4,975, 1997)

CURRENCY – Swiss franc of 100 rappen (or centimes)

NATIONAL ANTHEM – Oben am Jungen Rhein (Up on the young Rhine)

NATIONAL DAY – 15 August

NATIONAL FLAG – Equal horizontal bands of blue over red; gold crown on blue band near staff

LIFE EXPECTANCY (years) – male 66.07; female 72.94

POPULATION GROWTH RATE – 1.1 per cent (1996)

POPULATION DENSITY – 194 per sq. km (1996)

HISTORY AND POLITICS

The Principality of Liechtenstein was established by Emperor Charles VI in 1719. Following the First World War, Liechtenstein severed its ties with Austria and began its association with Switzerland, taking up the Swiss currency in 1921.

There is a threshold of 8 per cent for parties to gain representation in the 25-member *Landtag*, the unicameral parliament. The Patriotic Union and Progressive Citizens' parties governed the country in coalition from 1938 until March 1997. At the general election on 31 January and 2 February 1997 the Patriotic Union won 13 seats, Progressive Citizens' Party 10, and Free List 2. The Patriotic Union formed a government which took office in April 1997.

HEAD OF STATE

HSH The Prince of Liechtenstein, Hans Adam II, *born* 14 February 1945; *succeeded* 13 November 1989; *married* 30 July 1967, Countess Marie Kinsky; and has *issue*: Prince Alois (*see* below); Prince Maximilian, *b.* 16 May 1969; Prince Constantin, *b.* 15 March 1972; Princess Tatjana, *b.* 10 April 1973

Heir, HSH Prince Alois, *b.* 11 June 1968, *married* 1993 Duchess Sophie of Bavaria; and has *issue*: Prince Wenzel, *b.* 24 May 1995; Princess Marie, *b.* 17 October 1996; Prince Georg, *b.* 20 April 1999

MINISTRY *as at July 1999*

Prime Minister, Finance, Construction, General Government Affairs, Mario Frick

Education, Environment, Transport, Norbert Marxer

Foreign Affairs, Family and Equal Rights, Culture and Sport, Andrea Willi

Interior, Health and Social Matters, Economy, Michael Ritter

Justice, Heinz Frommelt

DIPLOMATIC REPRESENTATION

Liechtenstein is represented in diplomatic and consular matters in the United Kingdom by the Swiss Embassy.

BRITISH AMBASSADOR, Christopher Hulse, CMG, resident at Berne, Switzerland

ECONOMY

The main industries are high and ultra-high vacuum engineering, the semiconductor industry, roller bearings, artificial teeth, heating equipment, synthetic fibres, woollen and homespun fabrics.

In 1991 Liechtenstein became a member of the European Free Trade Association, and as such is a party to the European Economic Area (EEA) Agreement with the EU which came into force on 1 January 1994. In December 1992 in separate referenda, Switzerland voted against EEA membership while Liechtenstein voted in favour. After adapting its customs union with Switzerland, and again voting in favour of joining the EEA in a referendum in April 1995, Liechtenstein joined the EEA on 1 May 1995.

In 1998, imports from the UK totalled £6,125,000, and exports to the UK £20,575,000.

GDP – US$1,315 million (1995); US$42,416 per capita (1995)

ANNUAL AVERAGE GROWTH OF GDP – 0.7 per cent (1995)

LITHUANIA
Lietuva

AREA – 25,174 sq. miles (65,200 sq. km). Neighbours: Latvia (north), Belarus (east and south), Poland and the Kaliningrad region of the Russian Federation (south-west)

POPULATION – 3,701,300 (1998): 81.6 per cent Lithuanian, 8.2 per cent Russian, 6.9 per cent Polish, 1.5 per cent Belarusian, 1 per cent Ukrainian. The majority are Roman Catholic, with Russian Orthodox and Lutheran minorities. Lithuanian is the state language

CAPITAL – Vilnius (population, 581,500, 1997)

MAJOR CITIES – Kaunas (421,600); Klaipėda (204,300), 1993 estimates

CURRENCY – Litas, pegged to the dollar, US$1 = 4 litas

NATIONAL ANTHEM – Tautiška Giesmė (The National Song)

NATIONAL DAY – 16 February (Independence Day)

NATIONAL FLAG – Three horizontal stripes of yellow, green, red

LIFE EXPECTANCY (years) – male 63.27; female 75.04

POPULATION GROWTH RATE – –0.1 per cent (1997)

POPULATION DENSITY – 57 per sq. km (1996)

URBAN POPULATION – 68.1 per cent (1996)

Lithuania lies in the middle and lower basin of the river Nemunas. Along the coast is a lowland plain which rises inland to form uplands in east and central Lithuania. These uplands, the Middle Lowlands, give way to the Baltic Highlands in east and south-east Lithuania; the highest point is 294 m (965 ft). There is a network of rivers and over 2,800 lakes, which mainly lie in the east of the country. The climate varies between maritime and continental.

HISTORY AND POLITICS

The first independent Lithuanian state emerged as the Kingdom of Lithuania in 1251. After forming a joint

Commonwealth and Kingdom with Poland in 1561, Lithuania was taken over by the Russian Empire in the partitions of Poland that occurred in 1772, 1792 and 1795.

Lithuania declared its independence from the Russian Empire on 16 February 1918 and signed a peace treaty with the Soviet Union on 12 July 1920. The Soviet Union annexed Lithuania in 1940 under the terms of the Molotov–Ribbentrop pact with Germany. Lithuania was invaded and occupied when Germany invaded the Soviet Union during the Second World War. In 1944, the Soviet Union recaptured the country and confirmed its annexation.

In December 1989, public pressure forced the Lithuanian Communist Party to agree to multiparty elections, which were held in February 1990. These were won by the nationalist Sajudis movement, and the Supreme Council (parliament) declared the restoration of independence on 11 March 1990. Over 90 per cent of the population voted for independence in a referendum in February 1991. The Soviet Union recognized the independence of Lithuania on 10 September 1991.

The ruling Lithuanian Democratic Labour Party (former Communist Party) was defeated in a legislative election in October and November 1996. The Homeland Union (Conservative Party) and the Christian Democratic Party formed a coalition government. On 4 January 1998, the independent candidate Valdas Adamkus won the presidential election with 50.3 per cent of the vote.

FOREIGN RELATIONS

Lithuania applied for membership of the EU in December 1995; a treaty of association with the EU entered into force on 1 February 1998.

POLITICAL SYSTEM

Under the 1992 constitution, executive authority is vested in the government, consisting of the prime minister, who is appointed by the president with the approval of the *Seimas*, and ministers appointed upon the recommendation of the prime minister. The government is accountable to the Seimas, and presidential powers are subject to strict parliamentary control.

Legislative power is exercised by the Seimas, a unicameral parliament of 141 members elected for four-year terms. Seventy-one members are elected in first-past-the-post constituencies and 70 by proportional representation, with a 5 per cent threshold for representation. The constitution bans an alignment of Lithuania with any post-Soviet eastern alliance.

Lithuania is divided into 11 cities and 44 rural districts. Each has a municipal council elected by the local population for a period of three years.

HEAD OF STATE
President, Valdas Adamkus, *inaugurated* 26 February 1998

GOVERNMENT *as at July 1999*
Prime Minister, Rolandas Paksas (HU)
Agriculture and Forestry, Edvardas Makelis (Ind.)
Culture, Arūnas Békšta (Ind.)
Defence, Česlovas Stankevičius (CD)
Economy, Eugenijus Maldeikis (Ind.)
Education and Science, Kornelijus Platelis (Ind.)
Environment, Danius Lygis (HU)
Finance, Jonas Lionginas (Ind.)
Foreign Affairs, Algirdas Saudargas (CD)
Health, Raimundas Alekna (HU)
Interior, Česlovas Blažys (Ind.)
Justice, Gintaras Balčiūas (CU)
Public Administration Reforms and Local Authorities, Sigitas Kaktys (HU)

Social Welfare and Labour, Irena Degutiene (HU)
Transport, Rimantas Didžiokas (HU)
HU Homeland Union; CU Centre Union; CD Christian Democrat; Ind. Independent

EMBASSY OF LITHUANIA
84 Gloucester Place, London WiH 3HN
Tel 0171-486 6401
Ambassador Extraordinary and Plenipotentiary, HE Justas Paleckis, apptd 1996

BRITISH EMBASSY
2 Antakalnio, LT-2055 Vilnius
Tel: Vilnius 222 2070
Ambassador Extraordinary and Plenipotentiary, HE Christopher Robbins, apptd 1998
BRITISH COUNCIL REPRESENTATIVE, L. Balenaite, Vilniaus 39/6, LT-2600 Vilnius

DEFENCE

The Army has 27 armoured personnel carriers; the Navy has two frigates and four patrol and coastal vessels based at Klaipėda; the Air Force has eight helicopters. The last Russian troops withdrew in 1993.
MILITARY EXPENDITURE – 4.4 per cent of GDP (1997)
MILITARY PERSONNEL – 12,940: Army 6,750, Navy 1,320, Air Force 970, Paramilitaries 3,900
CONSCRIPTION DURATION – 12 months

ECONOMY

The economy was largely agricultural prior to rapid industrialization during the Soviet era. A privatization programme began in 1991 and progress in the sale of small enterprises has been quick and successful. In 1997, the privatization of communication, energy and transport companies was begun.

In 1998, agriculture and forestry accounted for 10 per cent of GDP, mining and manufacturing industry 19 per cent, construction 8 per cent and transport and communications 10 per cent.. The main industries are chemicals and petrochemicals, food processing, wood products, textiles, leather goods, machinery, machine tools and household appliances.
GNP – US$8,360 million (1997); US$2,260 per capita (1997)
GDP – US$5,957 million (1995); US$1,595 per capita (1995)
ANNUAL AVERAGE GROWTH OF GDP – 5.7 per cent (1997)
INFLATION RATE – 8.9 per cent (1997)
UNEMPLOYMENT – 7.3 per cent (1995)
TOTAL EXTERNAL DEBT – US$1,541 million (1997)

TRADE

Lithuania's main trading partners are Russia, Germany and Belarus. The Lithuanian economy is still heavily dependent on Russian supplies of oil, gas and metals. In 1998, total foreign investment in Lithuania reached US$1.6 billion.

In 1997 there was a trade deficit of US$1,147 million and a current account deficit of US$981 million. Imports totalled US$5,644 million and exports US$3,860 million.

Trade with UK	1997	1998
Imports from UK	£106,240,000	£116,743,000
Exports to UK	147,649,000	146,974,000

COMMUNICATIONS

There are 45,340 km of surfaced roads; there is a relatively well-developed railway system of 2,898 km running east-west and north-south and linking the major towns with Vilnius and Klaipėda, the main international port. Vilnius has an international airport and there are smaller ones at Kaunas, Palanga and Siauliai.

CULTURE AND EDUCATION

Lithuanian culture and literature are closely linked to the national liberation movements of the 19th and early 20th centuries, and the literature of Lithuanians who went into exile during the Soviet era.

Lithuania re-established a national education system in 1990. Education is free and compulsory from seven to 16 years, with the system comprising elementary schools (four years), nine-year schools (five years), and secondary schools (three years). The language of instruction is predominantly Lithuanian, but there are also Russian and Polish schools. There are 105 vocational schools and 65 colleges. Lithuania has eight universities and seven other institutes of higher education. Vilnius University, founded in 1579, is one of the oldest universities in eastern Europe.

ILLITERACY RATE – 0.5 per cent

ENROLMENT (percentage of age group) – secondary 80 per cent (1994); tertiary 31.4 per cent (1996)

LUXEMBOURG
Grand-Duché de Luxembourg

AREA – 998 sq. miles (2,586 sq. km). Neighbours: Germany (east), Belgium (west and north), France (south)

POPULATION – 412,000 (1997), nearly all Roman Catholic. The officially designated 'national language' is Lëtzebuergesch (Luxembourgish), a mainly spoken language. French and German are the official languages for written purposes, and French is the language of administration

CAPITAL – Luxembourg (population, 77,400, 1996)

CURRENCY – Luxembourg franc (LF) of 100 centimes (Belgian currency is also legal tender). The Luxembourg franc is linked in a currency union with the Belgian franc

NATIONAL ANTHEM – Ons Hémécht (Our homeland)

NATIONAL DAY – 23 June

NATIONAL FLAG – Three horizontal bands, red, white and blue

LIFE EXPECTANCY (years) – male 70.61; female 77.87

POPULATION GROWTH RATE – 1.4 per cent (1997)

POPULATION DENSITY – 159 per sq. km (1996)

ENROLMENT (percentage of age group) – primary 81 per cent (1985); secondary 64 per cent (1994); tertiary 2.6 per cent (1985)

HISTORY AND POLITICS

Established as an independent state under the sovereignty of the King of the Netherlands as Grand Duke by the Congress of Vienna in 1815, Luxembourg formed part of the Germanic Confederation from 1815 to 1866, and was included in the German 'Zollverein'. In 1867 the Treaty of London declared it a neutral territory. On the death of the King of the Netherlands in 1890 it passed to the Duke of Nassau.

The territory was invaded and overrun by the Germans at the beginning of the war in 1914 but was liberated in 1918. By the Treaty of Versailles (1919), Germany renounced its former agreements with Luxembourg and in

1921 an economic union was formed with Belgium. The Grand Duchy was again invaded and occupied by Germany in 1940, and liberated in 1944.

FOREIGN RELATIONS

The constitution was modified in 1948 and the stipulation of permanent neutrality was abandoned. Luxembourg is now a signatory of the Brussels and North Atlantic treaties, and also a member of the EU. Luxembourg is a member of the Belgium-Netherlands-Luxembourg Customs Union (Benelux 1960).

POLITICAL SYSTEM

There is a Chamber of 60 deputies, elected by universal suffrage for five years. Legislation is submitted to the Council of State. The last general election was held on 12 June 1994 and a coalition government was installed. In March 1998, Grand Duke Jean passed certain constitutional powers on to his son and heir, Prince Henri.

HEAD OF STATE

HRH The Grand Duke of Luxembourg, Grand Duke Jean, KG, *born* 5 January 1921; *succeeded* (on the abdication of his mother) 12 November 1964; *married* 9 April 1953, Princess Joséphine-Charlotte of Belgium, and has *issue*, three sons and two daughters

Heir, HRH Prince Henri, *born* 16 April 1955, *married* 14 February 1981, Maria Teresa Mestre, and has *issue*, Prince Guillaume, *b.* 11 November 1981; Prince Felix, *b.* 3 June 1984; Prince Louis, *b.* 3 August 1986; Princess Alexandra, *b.* 2 February 1991; Prince Sébastien, *b.* 16 April 1992, Princess Gabriella, *b.* 26 March 1994

CABINET *as at August 1999*

Prime Minister, Minister of State, Finance, Jean-Claude Juncker

Deputy P.M, Foreign Affairs, Trade, Civil Service and Administrative Reform, Lydie Polfer

Agriculture, Viticulture, Rural Development, Small Businesses, Housing and Tourism, Fernand Boden

Co-operation, Humanitarian Aid and Defence, Environment, Charles Goerens

Culture, Higher Education and Research, Public Works, Erna Hennicot-Schoepges

Economy, Transport, Henri Grethen

Family, Social Solidarity and Youth, Promotion of Women, Marie-Josée Jacobs

Health and Social Security, Carlo Wagner

Home Affairs, Michel Wolter

Labour and Employment, Religion, Parliamentary Relations, Communications, François Biltgen

National Education, Vocational Training and Sport, Anne Brasseur

Secretaries of State, Joseph Schaack; Eugène Berger

Treasury and Budget, Justice, Luc Frieden

EMBASSY OF LUXEMBOURG

27 Wilton Crescent, London SW1X 8SD

Tel 0171-235 6961

Ambassador Extraordinary and Plenipotentiary, HE Joseph Weyland, apptd 1993

BRITISH EMBASSY

14 Boulevard F. D. Roosevelt, L-2450 Luxembourg Ville

Tel: Luxembourg 229864/5/6

Ambassador Extraordinary and Plenipotentiary, HE William Ehrmann, apptd 1998

DEFENCE

For legal reasons, NATO's squadron of 18 E-3A Sentry airborne early warning aircraft is registered in Luxembourg.

MILITARY EXPENDITURE – 0.8 per cent of GDP (1997)
MILITARY PERSONNEL – 1,371: Army 811, Paramilitaries 560

ECONOMY

The country has an important iron and steel industry and is an important financial centre. In 1996, 667,000 tourists visited Luxembourg.
GDP – US$14,289 million (1995); US$35,109 per capita (1995)
ANNUAL AVERAGE GROWTH OF GDP – 3.2 per cent (1995)
INFLATION RATE – 1.4 per cent (1997)
UNEMPLOYMENT – 2.8 per cent (1995)

TRADE WITH UK
(Belgium and Luxembourg)

Trade with UK	1997	1998
Imports from UK	£8,005,500,000	£7,987,700,000
Exports to UK	8,716,000,000	9,047,100,000

MACEDONIA
Republika Makedonija

AREA – 9,928 sq. miles (25,713 sq. km). Neighbours: Federal Republic of Yugoslavia (north), Bulgaria (east), Greece (south), Albania (west)
POPULATION – 2,174,000 (1994 UN estimate); 1,936,877 (1994 census): 66.5 per cent Macedonian, 22.9 per cent Albanian, 4.0 per cent ethnic Turks, 2.3 per cent gypsies, 2.3 per cent Serbs and 0.4 per cent Vlachs. The census results are disputed by the ethnic Albanians and Serbs. Macedonian Orthodox Christianity is the majority religion, with a Muslim minority. The main language is Macedonian (a south Slavic language), which is written in the Cyrillic script
CAPITAL – Skopje (population, 448,229, 1991)
MAJOR CITIES – Bitola (84,002); Kumanov (69,231); Prilep (70,152)
CURRENCY – Dinar of 100 paras
NATIONAL ANTHEM – Denes nad Makedonija se radja novo sonce na slobodata (Today a new sun of liberty appears over Macedonia)
NATIONAL FLAG – Red with an eight-rayed sun displayed over the whole field
LIFE EXPECTANCY (years) – male 68.80; female 74.95
POPULATION GROWTH RATE – 0.7 per cent (1997)
POPULATION DENSITY – 85 per sq. km (1996)
URBAN POPULATION – 58.1 per cent (1991)
MILITARY EXPENDITURE – 10.2 per cent of GDP (1997)
MILITARY PERSONNEL– 27,500: Army 20,000, Paramilitaries 7,500
CONSCRIPTION DURATION – Nine months
ENROLMENT (percentage of age group) – primary 85 per cent (1996); secondary 51 per cent (1996); tertiary 18.1 per cent (1996)

HISTORY AND POLITICS

From the ninth to the 14th centuries AD Macedonia was ruled alternately by the Bulgars and the Byzantine Empire. In the middle of the 14th century the area was conquered by the Turks and remained under the Ottoman Empire for over 500 years. After the defeat of Turkey in the two Balkan wars of 1912–13 the geographical area of Macedonia was divided, the major part becoming Serbian (the areas of the present-day Macedonia) and the remainder given to Greece and Bulgaria. In 1918 on the formation of the Kingdom of the Serbs, Croats and Slovenes (later Yugoslavia), Serbian Macedonia was incorporated into Serbia as South Serbia. When Yugoslavia was reconstituted in 1944 as a Communist federal republic under President Tito, Macedonia became a constituent republic.

Multiparty elections for the 120-seat assembly held in November and December 1990 produced the first non-Communist government since the Second World War. The electorate overwhelmingly approved Macedonian sovereignty and independence in a referendum and independence was declared on 18 September 1991.

The presidential election in October 1994 was won by the incumbent, Kiro Gligorov. In elections to the *Sobranje* (National Assembly) held on 18 October and 1 November 1998, the coalition of the Internal Macedonian Revolutionary Organization-Democratic Party for Macedonian National Unity and the Democratic Alternative won 62 of the 120 seats. It invited the National Democratic Party, an ethnic Albanian party, to join the coalition.

FOREIGN RELATIONS

A new constitution was adopted in November 1991 and then amended at the EC's request to make it clear that Macedonia had no territorial claim on its neighbours. Macedonia applied for EC recognition in December 1991 but was refused because of Greece's objections to the state's name, flag and currency which, according to the Greek government, amounted to a territorial claim on the Greek province of Macedonia. The peaceful withdrawal of the Yugoslav Army (JNA) from Macedonia was completed in April 1992.

Tensions between Macedonia and its neighbours grew in late 1992, with Greece imposing a virtual economic blockade and Albania alleging discrimination against ethnic Albanians. Fearing conflict, the UN sent 1,000 peacekeepers in 1992–3 to man border posts with Serbia and Albania. A full UN peacekeeping force, the UN Preventive Deployment Force (UNPREDEP) was established in March 1995; its mandate expired on 1 March 1999.

Macedonia gained UN membership on 8 April 1993 following a compromise with Greece by which it is temporarily known as the 'Former Yugoslav Republic of Macedonia' (FYROM). Greece subsequently reopened its border to Macedonian trade in September 1993, but reimposed its economic blockade in February 1994 after the majority of EU states established diplomatic relations with Macedonia. An agreement was signed in September 1995 under which Greece agreed to lift the embargo on 15 October 1995 in exchange for Macedonia removing the contentious Star of Vergina from its flag.

The Federal Republic of Yugoslavia began forcibly expelling Kosovo's ethnic Albanian population following the outbreak of hostilities between Yugoslavia and NATO forces on March 24 1999, which resulted in an exodus of refugees; by early June, some 300,000 had sought sanctuary in Macedonia. The refugees began to return when the conflict ended on 9 June 1999.

HEAD OF STATE

President, Kiro Gligorov, *elected* 27 January 1991, *re-elected* 16 October 1994
Vice-Presidents, Dosta Dimovska (RO-DP);Radmila Kiprijanova Radovanovik (RO-DP); Bedredin Ibrahimi (DPA) (*Labour and Social Policy*)

CABINET *as at August 1999*

Prime Minister, Ljubčo Georgievski (RO-DP)
Agriculture, Forestry and Water Resources Management, Marjan Gjorcev (RO-DP)
Culture, Dimitar Dimitrov (RO-DP)

Defence, Nikola Kljusev (RO-DP)
Development, Milijana Danevska (RO-DP)
Economy, Mihajlo Tolevski (RO-DP)
Education and Physical Culture, Nenad Novkovski (RO-DP)
Emigration, Martin Trenevski (RO-DP)
Environment, Toni Popovski (RO-DP)
Finance, Boris Stojmenov (RO-DP)
Foreign Affairs, Aleksander Dimitrov (RO-DP)
Health, Dragan Danilovski (DA)
Information, Redzep Zlatku (DPA)
Internal Affairs, Pavle Trajanov (RO-DP)
Justice, Vlado Kambovski (RO-DP)
Local Self-Government, Dzevdet Nasufi (DPA)
Science, Merie Rusani (DPA)
Trade, Nikola Gruevski (RO-DP)
Transport and Communications, Bobi Spirkovski (RO-DP)
Urban Planning and Construction, Dusko Kadievski (RO-DP)
Without Portfolio, Adnan Klahil (RO-DP); Ernad Fejzulahu (DPA)
Youth and Sport, Georgi Boev (RO-DP)

DA Democratic Alternative; DPA Democratic Party of Albanians; RO-DP Internal Macedonian Revolutionary Organization-Democratic Party for Macedonian National Unity

EMBASSY OF THE REPUBLIC OF MACEDONIA
10 Harcourt House, 19A Cavendish Square, London
WIM 9AD
Tel 0171-499 5152
Ambassador Extraordinary and Plenipotentiary, HE Stevo Crvenkovski, apptd 1997

BRITISH EMBASSY
Veljko Vlahovíc 26, 9100 Skopje
Tel: Skopje 116772
Ambassador Extraordinary and Plenipotentiary, HE Mark Dickinson, apptd 1997

ECONOMY

The economy was decimated by the UN trade sanctions against the rump Yugoslavia (from May 1992 until November 1995), with which Macedonia had conducted 60 per cent of its trade. The Greek economic blockade (from February 1994 until October 1995) deprived Macedonia of most of its oil supplies and industry survived on imports from Turkey and Bulgaria. In February 1998 the World Bank approved a US$35 million loan to modernize six power plants. Macedonia is attempting to transform its economy to a market-orientated one and to introduce privatization. Foreign investment has been minimal because of the lack of international recognition.

In 1991 41.2 per cent of GDP was produced by industry and mining and 14 per cent by agriculture. Mineral resources include lead, zinc, copper, manganese and iron ore. The main industrial sectors are basic metal industries, chemicals, textiles and food processing. Important agricultural products are wheat, grapes, tomatoes and potatoes.

In 1997 there was a trade deficit of US$388 million and a current account deficit of US$275 million. In 1995 imports totalled US$1,719 million and exports US$1,204 million.

GNP – US$2,187 million (1997); US$1,100 per capita (1997)
GDP – US$3,579 million (1995); US$1,660 per capita (1995)
ANNUAL AVERAGE GROWTH OF GDP – –3.0 per cent (1995)
INFLATION RATE – 3.8 per cent (1996)
UNEMPLOYMENT – 35.6 per cent (1995)

TOTAL EXTERNAL DEBT – US$1,453 million (1997)

Trade with UK	1997	1998
Imports from UK	£15,618,000	£23,962,000
Exports to UK	10,043,000	14,027,000

MADAGASCAR
Repoblika n'i Madagaskar

AREA – 226,658 sq. miles (587,041 sq. km)
POPULATION – 15,353,000 (1994 UN estimate). The people are of mixed Malayo-Polynesian, Arab and African origin. There are sizeable French, Chinese and Indian communities. The official languages are Malagasy and French
CAPITAL – Antananarivo (population, 1,052,835, 1993 census)
MAJOR CITIES – ΨAntsiranana (942,410); Fianarantsoa (2,671,150); ΨMahajanga (100,807); ΨToamasina (127,441), the chief port
CURRENCY – Franc malgache (FMG) of 100 centimes
NATIONAL DAY – 26 June (Independence Day)
NATIONAL FLAG – Equal horizontal bands of red (above) and green, with vertical white band by staff
LIFE EXPECTANCY (years) – male 55.00; female 58.00
POPULATION GROWTH RATE – 2.8 per cent (1997)
POPULATION DENSITY – 26 per sq. km (1996)
MILITARY EXPENDITURE – 0.8 per cent of GDP (1997)
MILITARY PERSONNEL – 28,500: Army 20,000, Navy 500, Air Force 500, Paramilitaries 7,500
CONSCRIPTION DURATION – 18 months
ILLITERACY RATE – 54.3 per cent
ENROLMENT (percentage of age group) – primary 48 per cent (1995); tertiary 2.1 per cent (1995)

Madagascar lies 240 miles off the east coast of Africa and is the fourth largest island in the world.

HISTORY AND POLITICS

Madagascar (known from 1958 to 1975 as the Malagasy Republic) became a French protectorate in 1895, and a French colony in 1896 when the former queen was exiled. Republican status was adopted on 14 October 1958, and independence was proclaimed on 26 June 1960.

The post-independence civilian government was replaced by a military government in 1975 and martial law was declared. A Supreme Council of the Revolution under Capitaine de Frégate (subsequently Admiral) Didier Ratsiraka was established.

In November 1991, after six months of agitation against his one-party socialist rule, President Ratsiraka relinquished executive power to a new prime minister, Guy Razanamasy. However, the president retained his official position and the main opposition grouping, the *Forces Vives*, established a rival government led by Albert Zafy. In December 1991 a transitional government including Forces Vives and Razanamasy supporters was formed to draft a new constitution, approved by referendum in August 1992. Presidential elections were held in two rounds in November 1992 and February 1993, Albert Zafy emerging victorious with 67 per cent of the vote. He became the first president of the Third Republic, which came into being at the same time.

President Zafy was impeached in September 1996 and defeated in a presidential election in November and December 1996 by former president Ratsiraka. Following legislative elections held in May 1998, Ratsiraka's *Avant-garde de la révolution malgache* (AREMA) party became the largest party in the National Assembly.

HEAD OF STATE
President, Adm. Didier Ratsiraka, *elected* 29 December 1996, *inaugurated* 9 February 1997

COUNCIL OF MINISTERS *as at July 1999*

Prime Minister, Finance and Economy, Tantely Andrianarivo
Deputy PM, Budget, Development of Autonomous Provinces, Pierrot Rajaonarivelo
Agriculture, Marcel Raveloarijaona
Armed Forces, Maj.-Gen. Marcel Ranjeva
Civil Service, Labour and Social Legislation, Alice Razafinakanga
Energy and Mines, Charles Rasoja
Environment, M. Alphonse
Fishing and Marine Resources, Abdallah Houssene
Foreign Affairs, Lila Ratsifandrihamanana
Health, Rahantalalao Ratsimbazafimahefa
Higher Education, Joseph Sydson
Industrialization and Cottage Industry, Mamy Ratovomalala
Information, Culture and Communications, Fredo Betsimifira
Interior, Brig.-Gen. Jean-Jacques Rasolondraibe
Justice, Keeper of the Seals, Anaclet Imbiky
Livestock, M. Rakotondrasoa
Population, Women's Affairs and Childhood, Noëline Jaotody
Posts and Telecommunications, Ny Hasina Andriamanjato
Private Sector and Privatization, Constant Horace
Public Works, Col. Jean Emile Tsaranazy
Regional and Town Planning, Herivelona Ramanantsoa
Scientific Research, Soalahy Rakotonirainy
Secondary and Basic Education, Nivoson Simon
Secretaries of State, Maj.-Gen. Jean-Paul Bory *(Gendarmerie)*; Marofo Azaly Ben *(Public Security)*
Technical Education and Vocational Training, Boniface Levelo
Tourism, Blandin Razafimanjato
Trade and Consumption, Alphonse Randrianambinina
Transport and Meteorology, Charles Rasolonahy
Water and Forests, Rija Rajohnson
Youth and Sports, Cdr. Ndrianasolo

EMBASSY OF THE REPUBLIC OF MADAGASCAR
4 avenue Raphael, F- 75016 Paris, France
Tel: Paris 4504 6211
Ambassador Plenipotentiary and Extraordinary, HE Malala zo Raolison, apptd 1998

HONORARY CONSULATE OF THE REPUBLIC OF MADAGASCAR
16 Lanark Mansions, Pennard Road, London W12 8DT
Tel 0181-746 0133
Honorary Consul, Stephen Hobbs

BRITISH EMBASSY
1st Floor, Immeuble 'Ny Havana', Cite de 67 Ha, BP 167, Antananarivo
Tel: Antananarivo 27749
Ambassador Extraordinary and Plenipotentiary, HE C. F. Mochan, apptd 1999

ECONOMY

The economy is still largely based on agriculture, which employs more than 80 per cent of the workforce. The main products are rice, cassava, sugar cane and sweet potatoes. Development plans have placed emphasis on improving communications, the exploitation of mineral deposits and the creation of small industries.

In 1996 there was a trade deficit of US$120 million and a current account deficit of US$291 million. In 1997, imports totalled US$477 million and exports US$170 million.

GNP – US$3,575 million (1997); US$250 per capita (1997)
GDP – US$3,198 million (1995); US$215 per capita (1995)
ANNUAL AVERAGE GROWTH OF GDP – 3.6 per cent (1997)
INFLATION RATE – 4.5 per cent (1997)
TOTAL EXTERNAL DEBT – US$4,105 million (1997)

Trade with UK	1997	1998
Imports from UK	£8,191,000	£5,982,000
Exports to UK	24,432,000	20,783,000

MALAWI

Dziko La Malawi

AREA – 45,747 sq. miles (118,484 sq. km). Neighbours: Tanzania (north-east), Zambia (west), Mozambique (south)
POPULATION – 10,114,000 (1994 UN estimate). The official languages are Chichewa and English
CAPITAL – Lilongwe (population, 233,973, 1987)
MAJOR CITIES – Blantyre (331,588), incorporating Blantyre and Limbe, the major commercial and industrial centre; Mzuzu (44,238); Zomba (42,878), the former capital
CURRENCY – Kwacha (K) of 100 tambala
NATIONAL ANTHEM – O God Bless Our Land of Malawi
NATIONAL DAY – 6 July (Independence Day)
NATIONAL FLAG – Horizontal stripes of black, red and green, with rising sun in the centre of the black stripe
LIFE EXPECTANCY (years) – male 43.51; female 46.75
POPULATION GROWTH RATE – 2.7 per cent (1997)
POPULATION DENSITY – 85 per sq. km (1996)
URBAN POPULATION – 19.6 per cent (1996)
MILITARY EXPENDITURE – 1.1 per cent of GDP (1997)
MILITARY PERSONNEL – 6,000: Army 5,000, Paramilitaries 1,000
ILLITERACY RATE – 43.6 per cent
ENROLMENT (percentage of age group) – primary 100 per cent (1994); secondary 2 per cent (1994); tertiary 0.6 per cent (1995)

Malawi lies in south-eastern Africa. Much of the eastern border of Malawi is formed by Lake Malawi (formerly Lake Nyasa), which covers nearly half of the north of the country. The valley of the River Shire runs south from the lake, its watershed with the Zambezi lying on the western border with Mozambique and its tributary, the Ruo, with lakes Chinta and Chirwa, lying on the eastern border with Mozambique. The north and centre are plateaux, and the south highlands.

HISTORY AND POLITICS

Malawi (formerly Nyasaland) assumed internal self-government on 1 February 1963, and became independent on 6 July 1964. It became a republic on 6 July 1966.

In 1991–2 Life President Hastings Banda, who had ruled since independence, came under increasing pressure to introduce a multiparty democratic system of government. In May 1992 aid donors tied new loans to improvements in the human rights record and moves to multiparty democracy. A referendum was held on the adoption of a multiparty democracy in June 1993 and approved by 63 per cent of voters. President Banda and the Malawi Congress Party refused to resign but parliament passed a law to amend the constitution to allow multiparty politics and Banda announced a political amnesty to allow exiles to return. Multiparty presidential and legislative elections held in May 1994 were won by Bakili Muluzi and the United Democratic Front (UDF) respectively. Foreign and multilateral aid has since been restored. Former President Banda died on 25 November 1997. Presidential and legislative elections were due to be held on 25 May 1999, but were delayed until 15 June; they were won by the UDF, who won 93 seats. President Muluzi was also re-elected.

POLITICAL SYSTEM

There is a Cabinet consisting of the president and ministers. The National Assembly, which usually meets three times a year, consists of 192 members elected by universal suffrage.

HEAD OF STATE
President, Defence, Bakili Muluzi, *elected* 17 May 1994, *sworn in* 21 May 1994, *re-elected* 15 June 1999
Vice-President, Privatization, Justin Malewezi

CABINET *as at July 1999*
The President
The Vice-President
Agriculture and Irrigation Development, Aleke Banda
Attorney-General, Justice, Peter Fachi
Commerce and Industry, Kaliyoma Phumisa
Education, Sports and Culture, Ken Lipenga
Finance, Cassim Chilumpha
Foreign Affairs, Brown Mpinganjira
Health and Population, Lilian Patel
Home Affairs and Internal Security, Patrick Mbewe
Information, Clement Stambuli
Labour and Vocational Training, Leonard Mangulama
Lands, Housing, Physical Planning and Surveys, Thengo Maloya
Minister of State for Presidential Affairs, Rodwell Munyenyembe
Ministers of State in the President's Office, Ulada Musa (*Districts and Local Government Administration*); George Claver (*Persons with Disabilities*); Bob Kamisa (*Statutory Corporations*)
Natural Resources and Environmental Affairs, Harry Thomson
Tourism, National Parks and Wildlife, George Mtafu
Transport and Public Works, Peter Chupa
Water Development, Yusuf Mwawa
Women, Youth and Community Services, Mary Banda

MALAWI HIGH COMMISSION
33 Grosvenor Street, London WIX ODE
Tel 0171-491 4172/7
High Commissioner, Bright Msaka, apptd 1998

BRITISH HIGH COMMISSION
PO Box 30042, Lilongwe 3
Tel: Lilongwe 782400
High Commissioner, George Finlayson, apptd 1998

BRITISH COUNCIL REPRESENTATIVE, J. Kennedy, Plot No. 13/20, City Centre, PO Box 30222, Lilongwe 3

ECONOMY

The economy is largely agricultural, providing 90 per cent of export earnings; maize is the main subsistence crop, and tobacco, cassava, millet and rice are the main cash crops and principal exports. There are two sugar mills. A number of light manufacturing industries have been established, mainly in agricultural processing, clothing/textiles and building materials.

In 1994 there was a trade deficit of US$276 million and a current account deficit of US$450 million. In 1996

imports totalled US$624 million and exports US$481 million.
GNP – US$2,129 million (1997); US$210 per capita (1997)
GDP – US$1,369 million (1995); US$142 per capita (1995)
ANNUAL AVERAGE GROWTH OF GDP – 6.4 per cent (1997)
INFLATION RATE – 37.6 per cent (1996)
TOTAL EXTERNAL DEBT – US$2,206 million (1997)

Trade with UK	1997	1998
Imports from UK	£18,188,000	£13,066,000
Exports to UK	13,241,000	10,550,000

COMMUNICATIONS

A single-track railway runs from Mchinji on the Zambian border, through Lilongwe and Salima on Lake Malawi (itself served by two passenger and a number of cargo boats) through to Blantyre. The route south to the Mozambique port of Beira was severed by the Mozambican civil war, but the route to Nacala in Mozambique is open again; there are 797 km of railway track. There are 14,594 km of roads in Malawi of which 2,849 km are bituminized. There is an international airport 26 km from Lilongwe, which handles regional and intercontinental flights, and another airport at Chileka.

EDUCATION

The Ministry of Education and Culture is responsible for secondary schools, technical education and primary teacher training. Religious bodies, with government assistance, still play an important part in these fields. The University of Malawi was opened in 1965; there are also four colleges and one polytechnic.

MALAYSIA
Persekutuan Tanah Malaysia

AREA – 127,320 sq. miles (329,758 sq. km). Thailand borders the Malay peninsula to the north. On Borneo, Malaysia (Sarawak and Sabah) borders Indonesia to the south, and surrounds Brunei to the north
POPULATION – 20,581,000 (1995); 16,921,300 (1988 census): Malays (53 per cent), Chinese (35 per cent), and those of Indian and Sri Lankan origin, as well as the indigenous races of Sarawak and Sabah. Bahasa Malaysia (Malay) is the official language, but English, various dialects of Chinese, and Tamil are also widely spoken. There are a few indigenous languages widely spoken in Sabah and Sarawak. Islam is the official religion of Malaysia, each ruler being the head of religion in his state (except in Sabah and Sarawak). The Yang di-Pertuan Agong is the head of religion in Melaka and Penang. The constitution guarantees religious freedom
CAPITAL – Kuala Lumpur (population, 1,145,342, 1991)
MAJOR CITIES – Ipoh (382,633); Johore Bharu (328,646); Petaling Jaya (254,849)
CURRENCY – Malaysian dollar (ringgit) (M$) of 100 sen
NATIONAL ANTHEM – Negara-Ku
NATIONAL DAY – 31 August (*Hari Kebangsaan*)
NATIONAL FLAG – Equal horizontal stripes of red (seven) and white (seven); 14-point yellow star and crescent in blue canton
LIFE EXPECTANCY (years) – male 68.68; female 73.04

POPULATION GROWTH RATE – 2.5 per cent (1997)
POPULATION DENSITY – 62 per sq. km (1996)
URBAN POPULATION – 54.7 per cent (1995)
ILLITERACY RATE – 15.4 per cent
ENROLMENT (percentage of age group) – primary 91 per
cent (1994); tertiary 10.6 per cent (1994)

Malaysia comprises the 11 states of peninsular Malaya plus
Sabah and Sarawak. It occupies two distinct regions, the
Malay peninsula which extends from the isthmus of Kra to
the Singapore Strait, and the north-western coastal area of
the island of Borneo. Each is separated from the other by
the South China Sea.

The year is commonly divided into the south-west and
north-west monsoon seasons. Rainfall averages about 100
inches throughout the year. The average daily temperature
varies from 21° C to 32° C, though in higher areas
temperatures are lower and vary widely.

HISTORY AND POLITICS

The Federation of Malaya became an independent country
within the Commonwealth on 31 August 1957. On 16
September 1963 the federation was enlarged by the
accession of the states of Singapore, Sabah (formerly British
North Borneo) and Sarawak, and the name of Malaysia
was adopted from that date. On 9 August 1965 Singapore
seceded from the federation.

The National Front (Barisan Nasional) Coalition led by
Dr Mahathir Mohamed won a fourth term in office in a
general election held on 25 April 1995, winning 162 of the
192 seats.

POLITICAL SYSTEM

The constitution provides for a strong federal government
and a degree of autonomy for the state governments. It
created a constitutional Supreme Head of the Federation
(HM the *Yang di-Pertuan Agong*) and a Deputy Supreme
Head (HRH *Timbalan Yang di-Pertuan Agong*) to be elected
for a term of five years by the rulers from among their
number. The Malay rulers are either chosen or succeed to
their position in accordance with the custom of the
particular state. In other states of Malaysia, choice of the
head of state is at the discretion of the Yang di-Pertuan
Agong after consultation with the Chief Minister of the
state.

The Federal Parliament consists of two houses, the
Senate and the House of Representatives. The Senate
(*Dewan Negara*) consists of 69 members who serve a six-
year term, 26 being elected by the Legislative Assemblies
of the states (two from each) and 43 appointed by the Yang
di-Pertuan Agong. The House of Representatives (*Dewan
Rakyat*) consists of 192 members elected for a five-year
term by universal adult suffrage with a common electoral
roll.

The judicial system consists of a Federal Court and two
High Courts, one in peninsular Malaysia and one for Sabah
and Sarawak. The Federal Court comprises a president,
the two Chief Justices of the High Courts and other judges.
It possesses appellate, original and advisory jurisdiction.
Each of the High Courts consists of a Chief Justice and not
less than four other judges.

FEDERAL STRUCTURE

According to the constitution, each state shall have its own
constitution not inconsistent with the federal constitution,
with the ruler or governor acting on the advice of an
Executive Council appointed on the advice of the Chief
Minister and a single-chamber Legislative Assembly. The
Legislative Assemblies are fully elected on the same basis
as the federal parliament.

State	Area (sq. km)	Population (1997 estimate)	Main Town
Johore	18,986	2,554,100	ΨJohore Bahru
Kedah	9,426	1,530,100	Alor Setar
Kelantan	14,943	1,447,000	Kota Bahru
Melaka	1,650	582,000	ΨMelaka
Negri Sembilan	6,643	810,500	Seremban
Pahang	35,965	1,239,000	ΨKuantan
Penang	1,031	1,222,100	ΨGeorgetown
Perak	21,005	2,094,800	Ipoh
Perlis	795	217,400	Kangar
Sabah	73,711	2,593,400	ΨKota Kinabalu
Sarawak	124,449	1,954,300	ΨKuching
Selangor	7,956	2,999,800	ΨShah Alam
Terengganu	12,955	975,800	ΨKuala Terengganu

Federal Territories
Kuala Lumpur
Labuan } 1,231,500

HEAD OF STATE

Supreme Head of State, HM Salehuddin Abdul Aziz ibni al-
Marhum Hisamuddin Alam (Yang di-Pertuan Agong of
Selangor), *sworn in* 26 April 1999

CABINET *as at July 1999*

Prime Minister, Datuk Seri Dr Mahathir Mohamed
Deputy PM, Home Affairs, Datuk Abdullah Ahmad Badawi
Agriculture, Datuk Dr Sulaiman bin Daud
Culture, Arts and Tourism, Abdul Kadir Sheikh Fadzir,
  Datuk Sabbaruddin Chik
Defence, Datuk Abang Abu Bakar Mustapha
Domestic Trade and Consumer Affairs, Dato Megat Junid
  Ayob
Education, Datuk Seri Najib Tun Razak
Energy, Telecommunications and Posts, Datuk Leo Moggie
  Anak Irok
Entrepreneurial Development, Second Minister of Finance,
  Datuk Mustapha Mohamad
Finance, Special Functions, Tun Daim Zainuddin
Foreign Affairs, Datuk Seri Hamid Albar
Health, Datuk Chua Jui Meng
Housing and Local Government, Datuk Ting Chew Peh
Human Resources, Datuk Lim An Lek
Information, Mohamad Khalil Yaakob
International Trade and Industry, Datuk Seri Rafidah Aziz
Lands and Co-operative Development, Dato Osu Sukam
National Unity and Social Development, Datin Paduka Zaleha
  Ismail
Primary Industries, Datuk Seri Dr Lim Keng Yaik
Prime Minister's Department, Datuk Tajol Rosli Ghazali
  (*Legal and Justice Affairs*); Pandikar Amin Muliah (*Sabah
  Affairs*); Dato Dr Haji Abdul Hamid Osman; Dato
  Ibrahim Saad; Datuk Nazri Abdul Aziz; Siti Zahara
  Sulaiman
Public Works, Datuk Seri S. Samy Vellu
Rural Development, Dato Haji Anuar bin Musa
Sabah Affairs, Datuk Chong Kah Kiet
Science, Datuk Law Hieng Ding
Transport, Datuk Seri Dr Ling Liong Sik
Youth and Sports, Tan Sri Dato Muhyiddin Yasin

NOTE: Tunku/Tengku, Tun, Tan Sri, and Datuk/Dato
are titles. Tunku/Tengku is equivalent to Prince. Tun
denotes membership of the highest order of Malaysian
chivalry. Tan Sri and Datuk/Dato (Datuk Seri in Perak
and Datu in Sabah) are the equivalent of a knighthood.
The wife of a Tun is styled Toh Puan, that of a Tan Sri is
styled Puan Sri and of a Datuk, Datin. Tuan or Encik is
equivalent to Mr and Puan is equivalent to Mrs.

MALAYSIAN HIGH COMMISSION
45 Belgrave Square, London SW1X 8QT
Tel 0171-235 8033
High Commissioner, HE Dato Mohamad Amir bin Ja'afar,
apptd 1998
Deputy High Commissioner, Husni Zai Yaacob
Defence Adviser, Col. Kamaruddin Mattan

BRITISH HIGH COMMISSION
185 Jalan Ampang (PO Box 11030), 50450 Kuala Lumpur
Tel: Kuala Lumpur 248 2122
High Commissioner, HE G. Fry, apptd 1998
Deputy High Commissioner, R. J. Wildash, LVO
Counsellor (Commercial/Economic), H. Parkinson, CVO
Defence Adviser, Col. M. B. Cooper

BRITISH COUNCIL DIRECTOR, T. Edmundson, PO Box
10539, Jalan Bukit Aman, Kuala Lumpur 50916. There
are also offices at Penang, Kota Kinabalu (Sabah) and
Kuching (Sarawak).

DEFENCE

The Army has 816 armoured personnel carriers and 127
artillery pieces. The Royal Malaysian Navy has six frigates,
39 patrol and coastal vessels and 12 armed helicopters at
five bases. The Royal Malaysian Air Force has 89 combat
aircraft.
Australia maintains an infantry company and an air force
detachment in Malaysia.
MILITARY EXPENDITURE – 3.7 per cent of GDP (1997)
MILITARY PERSONNEL – 130,100: Army 85,000, Navy
12,500, Air Force 12,500, Paramilitaries 20,100

ECONOMY

From being an agriculturally-based economy reliant on
raw materials exports at independence, Malaysia has
undergone an industrialization programme and now produces clothing, textiles, rubber goods, electronics, office
equipment, cars, household appliances, semi-conductors,
food processing and chemicals. Under the New Economic
Policy of 1970–90, the economy grew at an average rate of
6.7 per cent a year. The National Development Policy
1990–2000 is seen as the second stage in making Malaysia
a fully-developed industrial state by 2020; it aims for GDP
growth of 8 per cent.per year. There are extensive
privatization programmes involving telecommunications,
railways, airports, electricity and shipping. In 1995 44 per
cent of GDP was produced by services, 35 per cent by
manufacturing and 14 per cent by agriculture.
Malaysia has been severely affected by the economic
crisis in Asia. The crisis was to some extent exacerbated by
sudden policy changes by the government, though austerity
measures and economic reforms averted the need to apply
for IMF assistance. In January 1998 the government
announced that it would deport all foreign workers except
Indonesians.
GNP – US$98,195 million (1997); US$4,530 per capita
(1997)
GDP – US$86,856 million (1995); US$4,313 per capita
(1995)
ANNUAL AVERAGE GROWTH OF GDP – 7.8 per cent
(1997)
INFLATION RATE – 2.7 per cent (1997)
UNEMPLOYMENT – 2.8 per cent (1995)
TOTAL EXTERNAL DEBT – US$47,228 million (1997)

TRADE

Malaysia is the largest exporter of natural rubber, tin, palm
oil and tropical hardwoods. Other major export commodities are manufactured and processed products, petroleum,
oil and other minerals, palm kernel oil, tea and pepper.
Imports consist mainly of machinery and transport equipment, manufactured goods, foods, consumer durables and
metal products. Japan, the USA and Singapore are the main
trading partners.
In 1995 Malaysia had a trade deficit of US$100 million
and a current account deficit of US$7,362 million. In 1997
imports totalled US$78,553 million and exports US$78,696
million.

Trade with UK	1997	1998
Imports from UK	£1,205,390,000	£683,186,000
Exports to UK	2,025,491,000	1,990,744,000

MALDIVES
Dhivehi Jumhooriyya

AREA – 115 sq. miles (298 sq. km)
POPULATION – 263,000 (1996). The people are Sunni
Muslims and the Maldivian (Dhivehi) language is akin
to Elu or old Sinhalese
CAPITAL – ΨMalé (population, 62,973, 1995)
CURRENCY – Rufiyaa of 100 laaris
NATIONAL DAY – 26 July
NATIONAL FLAG – Green field bearing a white crescent,
with wide red border
LIFE EXPECTANCY (years) – male 67.15; female 66.60
POPULATION GROWTH RATE – 2.6 per cent (1997)
POPULATION DENSITY – 883 per sq. km (1996)
URBAN POPULATION – 25.9 per cent (1990)
ILLITERACY RATE – 4.0 per cent

The Maldives are a chain of coral atolls 400 miles to the
south-west of Sri Lanka, stretching north for about 600
miles from just south of the Equator. There are about 19
coral atolls comprising over 1,200 islands, 198 of which are
inhabited. No point in the entire chain of islands is more
than eight feet above sea-level.

HISTORY AND POLITICS

Until 1952 the islands were a sultanate under the protection
of the British Crown. Internal self-government was
achieved in 1948 and full independence in 1965. The
Maldives became a special member of the Commonwealth
in 1982 and a full member in 1985.
The Maldives form a republic which is elective. The
legislature, the Citizens' Assembly (*Majlis*), has 40 representatives elected from all the atolls, and eight appointed
by the president, for a five-year term. The government
consists of a Cabinet, which is responsible to the Majlis.
Under the 1998 constitution, the president is elected by
the Majlis and confirmed by a referendum.

HEAD OF STATE
President, HE Maumoon Abdul Gayoom, *elected* 1978, *re-
elected* 1983, 1989, 1993, 16 October 1998

CABINET *as at July 1999*
Atolls Administration, Speaker of the Majlis, Abdullah Hameed
Attorney-General, Mohamed Munnawwar
*Chief Justice, President of the Supreme Council on Islamic
Affairs*, Mohamed Rashid Ibrahim
Construction and Public Works, Umar Zahir
Defence, National Security, Finance and Treasury, The
President
Education, Dr Mohamed Latheef
Fisheries and Agriculture, Abdul Rasheed Hussain
Foreign Affairs, Fathullah Jameel

Health, Ahmed Abdulla
Home Affairs, Housing and Environment, Ismail Shafeeu
Human Resources, Employment and Labour, Abdullah
  Kamaaludheen
Information, Arts and Culture, Ibrahim Manik
Justice, Ahmed Zahir
Minister at the President's Office, Abdullah Jameel
Ministers of State, Maj.-Gen. Ambaree Abdul Sattar *(Defence
  and National Security);* Arif Hilmy *(Finance and Treasury);*
  Mohamed Hussain *(Presidential Affairs);* Ismail Fathy
Mustashaaru of the Supreme Council on Islamic Affairs, Moosa
  Fathuhy
Planning and National Development, Ibrahim Hussain Zaki
Tourism, Hassan Sobir
Trade and Industry, Abdulla Yameen
Transport and Civil Aviation, Ilyas Ibrahim
Women's Affairs and Social Welfare, Rashida Yoosuf
Youth and Sports, Mohamed Zahir Hussain

HIGH COMMISSION OF THE REPUBLIC OF MALDIVES
22 Nottingham Place, London WIM 3FB
Tel 0171–224 2135
Acting High Commissioner, Adam Hassan

BRITISH HIGH COMMISSIONER, HE Linda Duffield,
  resident at Colombo, Sri Lanka

ECONOMY

The vegetation of the islands is coconut palms with some
scrub. Hardly any cultivation of crops is possible and
nearly all food to supplement the basic fish diet has to be
imported. Tourism is expanding rapidly (338,733 visitors
in 1996). The principal industry is fishing, which together
with tourism accounts for about 30 per cent of GDP. The
Maldives National Ship Management Ltd (MNSML) has
a fleet of nine merchant ships. There is an international
airport at Malé.

In 1996 the Maldives had a trade deficit of US$174
million and a current account surplus of US$9 million. In
1997 imports totalled US$349 million and exports US$73
million.

GNP – US$301 million (1997); US$1,180 per capita
  (1997)
GDP – US$274 million (1995); US$1,079 per capita
  (1995)
ANNUAL AVERAGE GROWTH OF GDP – 6.2 per cent
  (1997)
INFLATION RATE – 7.6 per cent (1997)
TOTAL EXTERNAL DEBT – US$160 million (1997)

Trade with UK	1997	1998
Imports from UK	£7,394,000	£4,538,000
Exports to UK	9,658,000	11,159,000

MALI
République du Mali

AREA – 478,841 sq. miles (1,240,192 sq. km). Neighbours:
  Senegal (west), Mauritania (north-west), Algeria
  (north-east), Niger (east), Burkina Faso and Côte
  d'Ivoire (south), Guinea (south-west)
POPULATION – 11,134,000 (1994 UN estimate). The
  official language is French; Bambara is the largest local
  language
CAPITAL – Bamako (population, 809,552, 1987)
MAJOR CITIES – Gao; Kayes; Mopti; Ségou; Sikasso;
  Timbuktu (all regional capitals)
CURRENCY – Franc CFA of 100 centimes

NATIONAL ANTHEM – A ton appel, Mali (At your call,
  Mali)
NATIONAL DAY – 22 September
NATIONAL FLAG – Vertical stripes of green (by staff),
  yellow and red
LIFE EXPECTANCY (years) – male 55.24; female 58.66
POPULATION GROWTH RATE – 2.8 per cent (1997)
POPULATION DENSITY – 9 per sq. km (1996)
URBAN POPULATION – 22.0 per cent (1987)
MILITARY EXPENDITURE – 1.7 per cent of GDP (1997)
MILITARY PERSONNEL – 12,150: Army 7,350,
  Paramilitaries 4,800
CONSCRIPTION DURATION – Two years
ILLITERACY RATE – 69.0 per cent
ENROLMENT (percentage of age group) – primary 26 per
  cent (1995); secondary 5 per cent (1990); tertiary 0.8
  per cent (1990)

HISTORY AND POLITICS

Formerly the French colony of Soudan, the territory
elected on 24 November 1958 to remain an autonomous
republic within the French Community. It associated with
Senegal in the Federation of Mali, which was granted full
independence on 20 June 1960. The Federation was
effectively dissolved in August 1960 by the secession of
Senegal. The title of the Republic of Mali was adopted in
September 1960.

The regime of Modibo Keita was overthrown in 1968
by a group of army officers who formed a National
Liberation Committee and appointed a prime minister.
Moussa Traoré assumed the functions of head of state. A
civil constitution came into being in 1979.

President Traoré was overthrown in March 1991 by
troops led by Lt.-Col. Touré. A military National Reconciliation Committee joined with democratic parties to form
a Transitional Committee for the Salvation of the People
which suspended the constitution and dissolved the Mali
People's Democratic Union (UPDM), formerly the sole
party. A transitional government was formed in April 1991
and a new constitution was approved by referendum in
January 1992. The new constitution provided for a
multiparty political system, and legislative elections were
held in February and March 1992 with the Alliance for
Democracy in Mali (ADEMA) emerging victorious. Alpha
Konaré, the ADEMA leader, won the presidential elections
in April 1992 and was re-elected in May 1997. In legislative
elections in July and August 1997, ADEMA won 129 out
of 147 seats in the National Assembly. Ex- President
Traoré was found guilty of embezzlement in January 1999
and sentenced to death.

HEAD OF STATE
President, Alpha Oumar Konaré, *elected* 1992, *re-elected* 11
  May 1997

CABINET *as at July 1999*
Prime Minister, Ibrahim Boubacar Keita
Armed Forces and Veterans, Mohamed Salia Sokona
Basic Education, Government Spokesperson, Adama
  Samassekou
Communications, Ascofaré Ouleymatou
Culture and Tourism, Aminata Dramane Traoré
Economy, Planning and Integration, Ahmed El Madani Diallo
Employment, Civil Service and Labour, Ousmane Oumarou
  Sidibé
Environment, Mohamed Ag Erlaf
Finance, Soumaila Cissé
Foreign Affairs, Malians Abroad, Maj. Modibo Sidibé
Health, Solidarity and the Elderly, Diakité Fatoumata
  N'Diayé

Industry, Commerce, Cottage Industries, Fatou Haidara
Justice and Keeper of the Seals, Hamidou Diabaté
Mines and Energy, Yoro Diakité
Public Works and Transport, Ibréhima Siby
Relations with Political Institutions and Parties, Hassane Barry
Rural Development and Water, Modibo Traoré
Secondary and Higher Education and Scientific Research,
   Younous Hamaye Dicko
Sports, Adama Koné
Territorial Administration and Security, Lt.-Col. Sada Samaké
Urban Development and Housing, Sy Kadiatou Sow
Women, Children and the Family, Diarra Afsata Thiero
Youth Promotion, Boubacar Karamoko Coulibaly

EMBASSY OF THE REPUBLIC OF MALI
Avenue Molière 487, B-1050 Brussels, Belgium
Tel: Brussels 345 7432
Ambassador Extraordinary and Plenipotentiary, HE Mohamed
   Ag Hamani; apptd 1999
BRITISH AMBASSADOR, HE David Snoxell, resident at
   Dakar, Senegal
BRITISH CONSULATE – Bamako

ECONOMY

Mali's principal exports are gold, groundnuts, cotton fibres,
meat and dried fish. Principal imports include petroleum,
textiles and machinery. Mali rejoined the CFA Franc Zone
in 1984.

In 1994 Mali had a trade deficit of US$102 million and
a current account deficit of US$164 million. In 1997
imports totalled US$812 million and exports US$519
million.
GNP – US$2,656 million (1997); US$260 per capita
   (1997)
GDP – US$2,403 million (1995); US$223 per capita
   (1995)
ANNUAL AVERAGE GROWTH OF GDP – 6.0 per cent
   (1995)
INFLATION RATE –0.4 per cent (1997)
TOTAL EXTERNAL DEBT – US$2,945 million (1997)

Trade with UK	1997	1998
Imports from UK	£24,051,000	£15,396,000
Exports to UK	613,000	468,000

MALTA
Repubblika ta' Malta

AREA – 122 sq. miles (316 sq. km)
POPULATION – 376,513 (1997). The Maltese are mainly
   Roman Catholic. The Maltese language is of Semitic
   origin and held by some to be derived from the
   Carthaginian and Phoenician tongues. Maltese and
   English are the official languages of administration.
   Maltese is the official language in all the courts of law
   and the language of general use in the islands
CAPITAL – ΨValletta (population, 7,146, 1997)
CURRENCY – Maltese lira (LM) of 100 cents or 1,000 mils
NATIONAL ANTHEM – L-Innu Malti
NATIONAL DAYS – 31 March (Freedom Day); 8
   September (Our Lady of Victories); 7 June (Sette
   Giugno Riots); 21 September (Independence Day); 13
   December (Republic Day)
NATIONAL FLAG – Two equal vertical stripes, white at
   the hoist and red at the fly. A representation of the
   George Cross is carried edged with red in the canton of
   the white stripe
LIFE EXPECTANCY (years) – male 74.86; female 79.11

POPULATION GROWTH RATE – 0.8 per cent (1997)
POPULATION DENSITY – 1,181 per sq. km (1996)
MILITARY EXPENDITURE – 0.9 per cent of GDP (1997)
MILITARY PERSONNEL – Armed Forces 1,900

Malta lies in the Mediterranean Sea, 93 km (58 miles) from
Sicily and about 288 km (180 miles) from the African coast.
It is about 27 km (17 miles) in length and 14.5 km (9 miles)
in breadth. Malta also includes the islands of Gozo (area
67 sq. km (25.9 sq. miles)), Comino and minor islets.

HISTORY AND POLITICS

Malta was in turn held by the Phoenicians, Carthaginians,
Romans and Arabs. In 1090 it was conquered by Count
Roger of Normandy and in 1530 handed over to the
Knights of St John. In 1565 it sustained the famous siege,
when the Turks were successfully withstood by Grand-
master La Valette. The Knights fortified the islands and
built Valletta before being expelled by Napoleon in 1798.
The Maltese rose against the French garrison soon
afterwards and the island was subsequently blockaded by
the British fleet. The Maltese people requested the
protection of the British Crown in 1802 on condition that
their rights would be respected. The islands were finally
annexed to the British Crown by the Treaty of Paris in
1814.

Malta was again besieged during the Second World
War. From June 1940 to the end of the war, 432 members
of the garrison and 1,540 civilians were killed by enemy
aircraft. The island was awarded the George Cross for
gallantry on 15 April 1942.

On 21 September 1964 Malta became an independent
state within the Commonwealth, and on 13 December
1974 a republic within the Commonwealth.

Elections to the unicameral parliament of 65 members
are held every five years by a system of proportional
representation; extra seats may be allocated to the party
with the most votes.

Early elections were called when the Malta Labour Party
lost its one-seat majority in August 1998; elections held in
September were won by the Nationalist Party, who gained
35 seats; Eddie Fenech-Adami, a strong supporter of
Malta's accession to the European Union, was appointed
prime minister.

FOREIGN RELATIONS

Malta applied for EC membership in 1990 and in June
1993 the Commission issued its Opinion that Malta should
be accepted as a member subsequent to the implementation
of a series of economic reforms. In October 1996 the
Labour government announced its intention to withdraw
Malta's EU application and its participation in NATO's
Partnership for Peace programme. Following the elections
of September 1998, the new government immediately re-
activated Malta's application for EU membership.

HEAD OF STATE
President, Guido de Marco, *took office* 4 April 1999

CABINET *as at July 1999*

Prime Minister, Dr Edward Fenech-Adami
Deputy PM, Social Policy, Environment, Dr Lawrence Gonzi
Agriculture and Fisheries, Ninu Zammit
Economic Services, Prof. Josef Bonnici
Education, Dr Louis Galea
Environment, Dr Francis Zammit Dimech
Finance, John Dalli
Foreign Affairs, Dr Joe Borg
Gozo, Giovanna Debono
Health, Dr Louis Deguara

Home Affairs, Dr Tonio Borg
Justice and Local Government, Dr Austin Gatt
Tourism, Dr Michael Refalo
Transport and Communications, Censu Galea

MALTA HIGH COMMISSION
Malta House, 36–38 Piccadilly, London WIV OPQ
Tel 0171-292 4800
High Commissioner, HE George Bonello du Puis, apptd
1999

BRITISH HIGH COMMISSION
7 St Anne Street, Floriana (PO Box 506), Malta
Tel: Floriana 233134/7
High Commissioner, HE Howard John Pearce, apptd 1999
BRITISH COUNCIL REPRESENTATIVE, A. Bradley, c/o
British High Commission

ECONOMY

Tourism has assumed primary importance, with more than
940,000 tourists visiting the island in 1998. In 1998 2.7
million passengers passed through Malta International
Airport.

Agriculture and fisheries are also important. Principal
products are potatoes, tomatoes, animal products, fruit,
flowers and cuttings.

The island's leading industry is the state-owned Malta
Drydocks, employing about 3,350 people. Malta Freeport
was opened in 1990 in the southern port of Marsaxlokk
and comprises a container distribution centre, an oil
products terminal and warehouse facilities. A second
container terminal is being built.

In 1998 manufacturing employed 29.4 per cent of the
workforce and accounted for 20 per cent of GDP. Industries
include food processing, textiles, footwear and clothing,
plastics and chemical products, electronic equipment,
machinery and components. Value Added Tax was reintroduced in January 1999.

In 1997 there was a trade deficit of US$703 million and
a current account deficit of US$205 million. In 1997
imports totalled US$2,556 million and exports US$1,642
million.

GNP – US$3,498 million (1997); US$9,330 per capita
(1997)
GDP – US$3,227 million (1995); US$8,793 per capita
(1995)
ANNUAL AVERAGE GROWTH OF GDP – 2.9 per cent
(1997)
INFLATION RATE – 3.3 per cent (1997)
UNEMPLOYMENT – 4.5 per cent (1993)
TOTAL EXTERNAL DEBT – US$1,034 million (1997)

TRADE

The principal imports are foodstuffs (mainly wheat, meats,
milk and fruit), fodder, beverages and tobacco, fuels,
chemicals, textiles and machinery (industrial, agricultural
and transport). The chief exports are processed food,
electronics, textiles, and other manufactures.

Trade with UK	1997	1998
Imports from UK	£253,777,000	£192,469,000
Exports to UK	85,753,000	85,974,000

EDUCATION

Education is compulsory between the ages of five and 16
and is free at all levels. Secondary education in state
schools is provided in secondary schools, junior lyceums
and trade schools. There are ten junior lyceums, 18
secondary schools and five centres catering for low
achievers.

A Junior College, administered by the University of
Malta, prepares students specifically for a university course.
Tertiary education is available at the University of Malta.
There are also schools administered by the Catholic
Church and other private schools.
ILLITERACY RATE – 8.7 per cent
ENROLMENT (percentage of age group) – primary 100 per
cent (1996); secondary 84 per cent (1995); tertiary 21.8
per cent (1994)

MARSHALL ISLANDS
Republic of the Marshall Islands

AREA – 70 sq. miles (181 sq. km)
POPULATION – 58,000 (1994 UN estimate): 99 per cent
are Micronesian. Over half the population is under 15.
About 60 per cent of the population is concentrated on
the two atolls of Majuro and Kwajalein. The population
is Christian, primarily Protestant but with a substantial
Catholic minority. Marshallese and English are the
official languages
CAPITAL – Dalap-Uliga-Darrit, on Majuro Atoll
(population, 20,000)
MAJOR TOWN – Ebeye (9,200)
CURRENCY – Currency is that of the USA
NATIONAL DAY – 1 May (Independence Day)
NATIONAL FLAG – Blue with a diagonal ray divided
white over orange running from the lower hoist to the
upper fly; in the canton a white sun
LIFE EXPECTANCY (years) – male 59.06; female 62.96
POPULATION GROWTH RATE – 3.9 per cent (1996)
POPULATION DENSITY – 323 per sq. km (1996)

The Republic of the Marshall Islands consists of 29 atolls
and five islands in the central Pacific. The islands and atolls
form two parallel chains running north-west to south-east:
the Ratak (Sunrise) chain and the Ralik (Sunset) chain.
The largest atoll is Kwajalein in the Ralik chain. The atolls
are coral and the islands are volcanic. None of the islands
rises more than a few metres above sea level. The climate
is hot and humid with little seasonal variation in temperature.

HISTORY AND POLITICS

The Marshall Islands were claimed by Spain in 1592 but
were left undisturbed by the Spanish Empire for 300 years.
In 1886 the Marshall Islands formally became a German
protectorate. On the outbreak of the First World War in
1914, Japan took control of the islands on behalf of the
Allied powers, and after the war administered the territory
as a League of Nations mandate. During the Second World
War US armed forces seized the islands from the Japanese
after intense fighting. In 1947 the USA entered into
agreement with the UN Security Council to administer
the Micronesia area, of which the Marshall Islands are a
part, as the UN Trust Territory of the Pacific Islands.

The islands became internally self-governing in 1979,
and the US Trusteeship administration came to an end on
21 October 1986, when a Compact of Free Association
between the USA and the Republic of the Marshall Islands
came into effect. By this agreement the USA recognized
the Republic of the Marshall Islands as a fully sovereign
and independent state. The UN Security Council terminated the UN Trust Territory of the Pacific in relation to
the Marshall Islands and recognized its independence in
December 1990.

FOREIGN RELATIONS

The Republic of the Marshall Islands has no defence forces. The Compact of Free Association places full responsibility for defence of the Marshall Islands on the USA. The US Department of Defense retains control of islands within Kwajalein Atoll where it has a missile test range.

POLITICAL SYSTEM

The republic is a democracy based on a parliamentary system of government. The executive is headed by the president, who is elected by the *Nitijela* from among its members. The president serves for a four-year term. The legislature has two chambers, the Council of Chiefs (*Iroij*) of 12 members and the Nitijela of 33 members. The Nitijela is the law-making chamber, to which the president and government are accountable. The Iroij has an advisory role.

There are 24 local government districts, each of which usually consists of an elected council, a mayor and appointed local officials.

HEAD OF STATE

President, Imata Kabua, *elected* 14 January 1997

GOVERNMENT *as at July 1999*

The President
Education, Justin DeBrum
Finance, Anton DeBrum
Foreign Affairs, Trade, Phillip Muller
Health and Environment, Tom Kijiner
Interior and Social Welfare, Brenson Wase
Justice, Hemos Jack
Resources and Development, Johnsay Riklon
Transportation and Communication, Kunio Lemari

BRITISH AMBASSADOR, HE Vernon Scarborough, resident at Suva, Fiji

ECONOMY

The economy is a mixture of subsistence and a service-based sector. About half the working population is engaged in agriculture and fishing, with coconut oil and copra production comprising 90 per cent of total exports. Imports include oil, food and machinery. The service sector is based in Majuro and Ebeye and concentrated in banking and insurance, construction, transportation and tourism. Direct US aid under the Compact accounts for two-thirds of the islands' budget. The islands charge foreign fishing fleets licences for fishing tuna in the waters around the islands. Japanese fleets pay some US$3 million a year. The USA, Japan and Australia are the main trading partners. GNP – US$97 million (1997); US$1,610 per capita (1997); GDP – US$91 million (1995); US$1,649 per capita (1995)

Trade with UK	1997	1998
Imports from UK	£15,635,000	£3,143,000
Exports to UK	441,000	223,000

COMMUNICATIONS

Air Marshall Islands provides air services within the islands and to Hawaii. Continental Air Micronesia serves Majuro and Kwajalein with flights to Hawaii and Guam. Majuro also has shipping links to Hawaii, Australia, Japan and throughout the Pacific.

SOCIAL WELFARE

Majuro and Ebeye have hospitals run by the government with aid from the US Public Health Service. Each outer island community has a health assistant.

The state school system provides education up to age 18, but only 25 per cent of students proceed beyond elementary level because of inadequate resources.

MAURITANIA
République Islamique de Mauritanie

AREA – 395,956 sq. miles (1,025,520 sq. km). Neighbours: Senegal (south-west), Mali (east and south), Algeria and Western Sahara (north)
POPULATION – 2,351,000 (1994 UN estimate). The official language is Arabic. Pulaar, Soninke, Wolof and French are also spoken
CAPITAL – Nouakchott (population, 850,000)
CURRENCY – Ouguiya (UM) of 5 khoums
NATIONAL DAY – 28 November
NATIONAL FLAG – Yellow star and crescent on green ground
LIFE EXPECTANCY (years) – male 49.90; female 53.10
POPULATION GROWTH RATE – 2.8 per cent (1997)
POPULATION DENSITY – 2 per sq. km (1996)
MILITARY EXPENDITURE – 2.2 per cent of GDP (1997)
MILITARY PERSONNEL – 20,650: Army 15,000, Navy 500, Air Force 150, Paramilitaries 5,000
CONSCRIPTION DURATION – Two years
ILLITERACY RATE – 62.3 per cent
ENROLMENT (percentage of age group) – primary 60 per cent (1995); tertiary 3.9 per cent (1995)

HISTORY AND POLITICS

Mauritania elected on 28 November 1958 to remain within the French Community as an autonomous republic. It became fully independent on 28 November 1960. In 1972 Mauritania left the Franc Zone.

Mauritania and Morocco occupied the Western Sahara territory in February 1976 when Spain formally relinquished it and in April 1976 agreed on a new frontier dividing the territory between them. In August 1979, Mauritania relinquished all claim to the southern sector of the Western Sahara after a three-year war against Polisario Front guerrillas.

After a military coup in 1978, Mauritania was ruled by a Military Committee for National Salvation. In April 1991 President ould Taya announced a political amnesty, followed by multiparty elections for a reconvened Senate and National Assembly. The constitution was approved by referendum in July 1991. Multiparty legislative elections were held in March 1992 and won by the Republican Democratic and Social Party (PRDS) led by President ould Taya. The president appointed a Cabinet of PRDS members in April 1992 but the legitimacy of the new government was undermined by the boycott of the elections by the main opposition grouping, the Union of Democratic Forces (UDF).

Legislative elections in October 1996 were won by the PRDS after the UDF pulled out after the first round accusing the government of fraud. In presidential elections in December 1997, President ould Taya was re-elected following a boycott by opposition parties.

HEAD OF STATE

President, Col. Moaouia ould Sidi Ahmed Taya (PRDS), *took power* 12 December 1984, *elected* 17 January 1992, *re-elected* 12 December 1997

COUNCIL OF MINISTERS *as at July 1999*

Prime Minister, Cheik El-Avia ould Mohamed Khouna
Civil Service, Labour, Youth, Sports, Baba ould Sidi

Communications and Relations with Parliament, Rachid ould Saleh
Culture, Islamic Orientation, Salmou ould Sidi Moustaph
Defence, Kaba ould Elewa
Economic and Development Affairs, Mohamed ould Annai
Education, Sghair ould M'bareck
Equipment and Transport, N'gaide Lamine Gayou
Finance, Kamara Ali Gueladio
Fisheries and Marine Economy, Mohamed El-Moctar ould Zamel
Foreign Affairs and Co-operation, Ahmed ould Sid Ahmed
Health and Social Affairs, Dia Ba
Interior, Post and Telecommunications, Dah ould Abdeljalil
Justice, Mohamed Salem ould Marzoug
Mines and Industry, Ishagh ould Rajel
Rural Development and Environment, Col. Mohamed ould Sid'Ahmed Lekhal
Trade, Handicrafts and Tourism, Ahmed ould Hamadi
Water Power, Energy, Cheik Ahmed ould Ezzahaf

EMBASSY OF THE ISLAMIC REPUBLIC OF MAURITANIA
5 rue de Montevideo, Paris XVIe, France
Tel: Paris 45048854
Ambassador Extraordinary and Plenipotentiary, Dah ould Abdi, apptd 1996

BRITISH AMBASSADOR, HE Anthony M. Layden, resident at Rabat, Morocco

ECONOMY

The main source of potential wealth lies in rich deposits of iron ore around Zouérate, in the north of the country, and rich fishing grounds off the coast.

In 1995 Mauritania had a trade surplus of US$184 million and a current account surplus of US$22 million. In 1994 imports totalled US$403 million and exports US$487 million.
GNP – US$1,093 million (1997); US$440 per capita (1997)
GDP – US$912 million (1995); US$401 per capita (1995)
ANNUAL AVERAGE GROWTH OF GDP – 4.7 per cent (1995)
INFLATION RATE – 4.6 per cent (1997)
TOTAL EXTERNAL DEBT – US$2,453 million (1997)

Trade with UK	1997	1998
Imports from UK	£8,555,000	£7,702,000
Exports to UK	16,357,000	8,542,000

MAURITIUS

AREA – 788 sq. miles (2,040 sq. km)
POPULATION – 1,160,000 (1998 estimate): Asiatic races (Hindus 51.8 per cent, Muslims 16.5 per cent, Chinese 2.8 per cent), and persons of European (mainly French) extraction, mixed and African descent (28.6 per cent). English is the official language but French may be used in the National Assembly and lower law courts. Creole is the most commonly used language and several Asian languages are also used
CAPITAL – ΨPort Louis (population, 146,499, 1997 estimate)
MAJOR TOWNS – Beau Bassin-Rose Hill (99,562); Curepipe (78,892); Quatre Bornes (75,967); Vacoas-Phoenix (97,417), 1997 estimates
CURRENCY – Mauritius rupee of 100 cents
NATIONAL ANTHEM – Glory to thee, Motherland
NATIONAL DAY – 12 March

NATIONAL FLAG – Red, blue, yellow and green horizontal stripes
LIFE EXPECTANCY (years) – male 66.44; female 73.95
POPULATION GROWTH RATE – 1.2 per cent (1997)
POPULATION DENSITY – 556 per sq. km (1996)
URBAN POPULATION – 43.6 per cent (1995)
MILITARY EXPENDITURE – 2.1 per cent of GDP (1997)
MILITARY PERSONNEL – 1,800 Paramilitaries

Mauritius is an island group lying in the Indian Ocean, 550 miles east of Madagascar. The climate is sub-tropical and maritime, with a wide range of rainfall and temperature resulting from the mountainous nature of the island. Humidity is high throughout the year.

HISTORY AND POLITICS

Mauritius was discovered in 1511 by the Portuguese; the Dutch visited it in 1598 and named it Mauritius after Prince Maurice of Nassau. From 1638 to 1710 it was held as a Dutch colony; the French took possession in 1715 but did not settle it until 1721. Mauritius was taken by a British force in 1810 and became a Crown Colony. It became an independent state within the Commonwealth on 12 March 1968 and a republic on 12 March 1992.

The last general election was held on 20 December 1995. The present government was formed by the Parti des Travailleurs Mauricien - Mauritius Labour Party (PTM).

POLITICAL SYSTEM

The president is head of state and is elected by the National Assembly. The prime minister, appointed by the president, is the member of the National Assembly who appears to the president best able to command the support of the majority of members of the Assembly. Other ministers are appointed by the president acting on the advice of the prime minister.

The National Assembly has a five-year term and consists of 62 elected members (the island of Mauritius is divided into 20 three-member constituencies and Rodrigues returns two members), and eight specially-elected members. Of the latter, four seats go to the 'best loser' of whichever communities in the island are under-represented in the Assembly after the general election and the four remaining seats are allocated on the basis of both party and community.

HEAD OF STATE

President, Cassam Uteem, *elected* June 1992, *re-elected* 28 June 1997
Vice-President, Angidi Veeriah Chettiar

COUNCIL OF MINISTERS *as at July 1999*

Prime Minister, Defence and Home Affairs, External Communications and Outer Islands, Dr Navinchandra Ramgoolam
Deputy PM, Foreign Affairs and International Trade, Rajkeswur Purryag
Agriculture, Food Technology and Natural Resources, Arvin Boolell
Arts and Culture, Tsang Fan Hin Tsang Mang Kin
Attorney-General, Justice, Human Rights and Corporate Affairs, Labour and Industrial Relations, Abdool Razack Mohamed Ameen Peeroo
Civil Service Affairs and Administrative Reform, Sachindev Mahess Kumar Soonarane
Economic Development, Productivity and Regional Development, Rundheersing Bheenick
Education and Scientific Research, Ramsamy Chedumbarum Pillay
Environment, Human Resource Development and Employment, Mohummud Siddick Chady

Finance, Vasant Kumar Bunwaree
Fisheries and Co-operatives, Dhaneshwar Beeharry
Health and Quality of Life, Nankeswarsingh Deerpalsingh
Housing and Lands, Satish Faugoo
Industry and Commerce, Sathiamoorthy Sunassee
Land Transport, Shipping and Port Development, Clarel Désiré
　Malherbe
Local Government, Urban and Rural Development, James Burty
　David
Public Infrastructure and Public Safety, Devanand
　Virahsawmy
Public Utilities, Dr Ahmed Rashid Beebeejaun
Rodrigues Island, Joseph Bénoit Jolicoeur
Social Security and National Solidarity, Ved Prakash
　Bundhun
Telecommunications and Information Technology, Sarat Dutt
　Lallah
Tourism and Leisure, Marie Joseph Jacques Chasteau de
　Balyon
Women, Family Welfare and Child Development, Indira
　Savitree Thacoor-Sidaya
Youth and Sports, Marie Claude Arouff-Parfait

MAURITIUS HIGH COMMISSION
32–33 Elvaston Place, London SW7 5NW
Tel 0171-581 0294/5
High Commissioner, HE Sir Satcam Boolell, QC, apptd 1996

BRITISH HIGH COMMISSION
Les Cascades Building, Edith Cavell Street, Port Louis
(PO Box 1063)
Tel: Port Louis 211 1361
High Commissioner, HE James Daly, CVO, apptd 1997

BRITISH COUNCIL DIRECTOR, S. Ponnapa, PO Box 111,
　Rose Hill

ECONOMY

The major cash crop is sugar cane. Tea and tobacco are grown commercially on a smaller scale. Production in 1998 was: sugar, 628,588 tonnes; tea (manufactured), 1,488 tonnes; tobacco (leaves), air cured 60,892 kg and Virginia flue-cured 640,815 kg. In 1998 production of molasses, mainly for export, was 168,891 tonnes. Other products include alcohol, rum, denatured spirits, perfumed spirits and vinegar.

The bulk of the island's requirements in manufactured products still has to be imported. However, the Mauritius Export Processing Zone (MEPZ) Scheme has attracted investment from overseas and the number of export-orientated enterprises had risen from ten in 1971 to 486 in 1998. The biggest firms are in clothing manufacture, particularly woollen knitwear, but the range of goods produced includes toys, plastic products, leather goods, diamond cutting and polishing, watches, television sets and telephones.

Tourism is a major source of income, with an estimated 558,195 tourists in 1998. France is the most important source of tourists, followed closely by the neighbouring French island of Réunion.

GNP – US$4,444 million (1997); US$3,870 per capita
　(1997)
GDP – US$3,919 million (1995); US$3,508 per capita
　(1995)
ANNUAL AVERAGE GROWTH OF GDP – 5.5 per cent
　(1996)
INFLATION RATE – 6.8 per cent (1997)
TOTAL EXTERNAL DEBT – US$2,472 million (1997)

TRADE

Most foodstuffs and raw materials have to be imported from abroad. Apart from local consumption (about 36,500

tonnes a year), the sugar produced is exported, mainly to Britain.

In 1997 Mauritius had a trade deficit of US$458 million and a current account deficit of US$115 million. In 1996 imports totalled US$2,278 million and exports US$1,751 million.

Trade with UK	1997	1998
Imports from UK	£65,751,000	£68,527,000
Exports to UK	339,214,000	329,201,000

COMMUNICATIONS

Port Louis, on the north-west coast, handles the bulk of the island's external trade. A bulk sugar terminal capable of handling the total crop began operating in 1980. The international airport is located at Plaisance, about five miles from Mahébourg. There are five daily newspapers and 15 weeklies, mostly in French. The Mauritius Broadcasting Corporation operates television and radio broadcasting in the country.

EDUCATION

Primary and secondary education are free and primary education is compulsory. There are a number of training facilities offering vocational training. The Institute of Education is responsible for training primary and secondary school teachers and for curriculum development. The University of Mauritius had 3,718 students in 1998–9.
ILLITERACY RATE – 17.1 per cent
ENROLMENT (percentage of age group) – primary 98 per
　cent (1996); tertiary 6.5 per cent (1996)

RODRIGUES AND DEPENDENCIES

Rodrigues, formerly a dependency but now part of Mauritius, is about 350 miles east of Mauritius, with an area of 40 square miles. Population (1996) 35,019. Cattle, salt fish, sheep, goats, pigs, maize and onions are the principal exports. The island is administered by an Island Secretary.
Island Secretary, B. Juggoo

The islands of Agalega and St Brandon are dependencies of Mauritius. Total population (1996) 170.

MEXICO
Estados Unidos Mexicanos

AREA – 756,066 sq. miles (1,958,201 sq. km). Neighbours:
　USA (north), Guatemala and Belize (south-east)
POPULATION – 96,578,000 (1994 UN estimate). Spanish
　is the official language and is spoken by about 95 per
　cent of the population. There are five main groups of
　Indian languages (Náhuatl, Maya, Zapotec, Otomí,
　Mixtec) and 59 dialects derived from them
CAPITAL – Mexico City (population, 15,047,685, 1990)
MAJOR CITIES – Ciudad Juárez (797,679); Guadalajara
　(2,846,000); León (956,070); Monterrey (2,521,697);
　Puebla (1,454,526); Tijuana (742,686); Toluca
　(827,339); Torreón (876,456), 1990 census
CURRENCY – Peso of 100 centavos
NATIONAL ANTHEM – Mexicanos, Al Grito De Guerra
　(Mexicans, to the war cry)
NATIONAL DAY – 16 September (Proclamation of
　Independence)
NATIONAL FLAG – Three vertical bands in green, white,
　red, with the Mexican emblem (an eagle on a cactus
　devouring a snake) in the centre

LIFE EXPECTANCY (years) – male 62.10; female 66.00
POPULATION GROWTH RATE – 1.8 per cent (1997)
POPULATION DENSITY – 49 per sq. km (1996)
ILLITERACY RATE – 10.4 per cent
ENROLMENT (percentage of age group) – primary 100 per cent (1995; secondary 51 per cent (1995); tertiary 15.3 per cent (1995)

The Sierra Nevada, known in Mexico as the Sierra Madre, and Rocky Mountains continue south from the northern border with the USA, running parallel to the west and east coasts. The interior consists of an elevated plateau between the two ranges. In the west is the peninsula of Lower California, separated from the mainland by the Gulf of California. The main rivers are the Rio Grande (Rio Bravo) del Norte, which forms part of the northern boundary and is navigable for about 70 miles from its mouth in the Gulf of Mexico, and the Rio Grande de Santiago, the Rio Balsas and Rio Papaloapan.

HISTORY AND POLITICS

Present-day Mexico and Guatemala were once the centre of a civilization which flowered in the periods from AD 500 to 1100 and 1300 to 1500 and collapsed before the army of Spanish adventurers under Hernán Cortés in the years following 1519. Pre-Columbian Mexico was divided between different Indian cultures, each of which has left distinctive archaeological remains, most notably the Mayan, Teotihuacáno, Zapotec, Totonac and Toltec cultures. The last and most famous Indian culture, the Aztec, based on Tenochtitlán, suffered more than the others at the hands of the Spanish and very few Aztec monuments remain.

After the conquest, the Spanish appointed a Viceroy to rule their new dominions, which they called New Spain. The country was largely converted to Christianity and a distinctive colonial civilization, representing a marriage of Indian and Spanish traditions, developed. In 1810 a revolt began against Spanish rule. This was finally successful in 1821, when a precarious independence was proclaimed.

Friction with the USA led to the war of 1845–8, at the end of which Mexico was forced to cede the northern provinces of Texas, California and New Mexico. In 1862 Mexican insolvency led to invasion by French forces which installed Archduke Maximilian of Austria as Emperor. The empire collapsed with the execution of the Emperor in 1867 and the austere reformer Juárez restored the republic. Juárez's death was followed by the dictatorship of Porfirio Díaz, which saw an enormous increase in foreign, particularly British and American, investment in the country. In 1910 began the Mexican Revolution which reformed the social structure and the land system, curbed the power of foreign companies and ushered in the independent industrial Mexico of today.

There are nine registered political parties, of which the largest is the Partido Revolucionario Institucional (PRI) which has constituted the governing party for more than 60 years. The main opposition parties are the Partido de Acción Nacional (PAN) and the Partido de la Revolución Democrática (PRD). On 6 July 1997 voting took place in the first fully democratic elections for the Chamber of Deputies, a quarter of the Senate, six state governorships and the Mayor of Mexico. Though still the largest party, the PRI no longer has an overall majority in the Chamber of Deputies.

INSURGENCIES

An armed revolt of Zapatista peasant Indians in the southern state of Chiapas in January 1994 highlighted continuing charges against the PRI of corruption, and these continued up to the August 1994 elections.

A further armed revolt by the Zapatista National Liberation Army (ZNLA) in Chiapas from December 1994 to February 1995 caused a political and economic crisis. President Zedillo introduced political reforms agreed with the PAN and PRD, making the electoral commission fully independent and providing for the re-examination of contentious elections by impartial observers. Negotiations with the Zapatistas produced a preliminary agreement on indigenous rights in February 1996, but talks broke down and were suspended in September 1996. Further talks took place in November 1998.

New guerrilla groups, the People's Revolutionary Army (EPR) and the Popular Insurgency Revolutionary Army (ERIP), emerged in 1996. There were nationwide protests after the police and senior officials were implicated in the massacre of 45 Indians in Chiapas on 22 December 1997. There were renewed calls for the Army to withdraw from the province, and discussions over new peace talks resumed in February 1998.

POLITICAL SYSTEM

Congress consists of a Senate (*Cámara de Senadores*) of 128 members, elected for six years, and of a Chamber of Deputies (*Cámara de Diputados*), at present numbering 500, elected for three years. The chief executive of the government is the president, who is elected for a six-year term and may not be re-elected.

FEDERAL STRUCTURE

State	Area (sq. km)	Population (1995)	Capital
Federal District	1,499	8,489,007	Mexico City
Aguascalientes	5,589	862,720	Aguascalientes
Baja California	70,113	2,112,140	Mexicali
Baja California Sur	73,677	375,494	La Paz
Campeche	51,833	642,516	Campeche
Coahuila	151,571	2,173,775	Saltillo
Colima	5,455	488,028	Colima
Chiapas	73,887	3,584,786	Tuxtla Gutiérrez
Chihuahua	247,087	2,793,537	Chihuahua
Durango	119,648	1,431,748	Victoria de Durango
Guanajuato	30,589	4,406,568	Guanajuato
Guerrero	63,794	2,916,567	Chilpancingo
Hidalgo	20,987	2,112,473	Pachuca de Soto
Jalisco	80,137	5,991,176	Guadalajara
México	21,461	11,707,964	Toluca de Lerdo
Michoacán	59,864	3,870,604	Morelia
Morelos	4,941	1,442,662	Cuernavaca
Nayarit	27,621	896,702	Tepic
Nuevo Léon	64,555	3,550,114	Monterrey
Oaxaca	95,364	3,228,895	Oaxaca de Juárez
Puebla	33,919	4,624,365	Puebla de Zaragoza
Querétaro	11,769	1,250,476	Querétaro
Quintana Roo	50,350	703,536	Chetumal
San Luis Potosí	62,848	2,200,763	San Luis Potosí
Sinaloa	58,092	2,425,675	Culiacán Rosales
Sonora	184,934	2,085,536	Hermosillo
Tabasco	24,661	1,748,769	Villahermosa
Tamaulipas	79,829	2,527,328	Ciudad Victoria
Tlaxcala	3,914	883,924	Tlaxcala
Veracruz	72,815	6,737,324	Jalapa Enríquez
Yucatán	39,340	1,556,622	Mérida
Zacatecas	75,040	1,336,496	Zacatecas

HEAD OF STATE

President, Dr Ernesto Zedillo Ponce de León, *elected* August 1994, *took office* 1 December 1994

CABINET *as at July 1999*

Agrarian Reform, Arturo Warman Gryj
Agriculture, Livestock and Rural Development, Románico
Arroyo Marroquin
Attorney-General, Jorge Madrazo Cuéllar
Communications and Transport, Carlos Ruiz Sacristan
Comptroller-General, Arsenio Farell Cubillas
Defence, Gen. Enrique Cervantes Aguirre
Education, Miguel Limón Rojas
Energy, Luis Téllez Kuenzler
Environment, Natural Resources and Fisheries, Julia Carabias
Lillo
Finance and Public Credit, José Ángel Gurría Treviño
Foreign Affairs, Rosario Green Macias
Health, Juan Ramón de la Fuente Ramírez
Interior, Diódoro Carrasco
Labour and Social Welfare, Mariano Palacios Alcocer
Mayor of Mexico City, Cuauhtémoc Cárdenas Solórzano
Naval Affairs, Adm. José Ramón Lorenzo Franco
Social Development, Esteban Moctezuma Barragan
Tourism, Oscar Espinosa Villareal
Trade and Industry, Herminio Blanco Mendoza

MEXICAN EMBASSY

42 Hertford Street, London WIY 7TF
Tel 0171-499 8586
Ambassador Extraordinary and Plenipotentiary, HE Santiago
Oñate, apptd 1997
Minister, Deputy Ambassador, J. Brito-Moncada
Military Attaché, Col. F. A. Espitia-Hernández
Minister, Consul-General, R. Xilótl-Ramírez
Minister, Economic Affairs, C. Ramos

BRITISH EMBASSY

Calle Río Lerma 71, Colonia Cuauhtémoc,
06500 Mexico City
Tel: Mexico City 207 2089
Ambassador Extraordinary and Plenipotentiary, HE Adrian
Thorpe, KCMG, apptd 1999
*Deputy Head of Mission, Minister-Counsellor and Consul-
General,* Dr P. Tibber
Defence Attaché, Col. J. Watson
First Secretary (Commercial), A. Stephens

CONSULAR OFFICES – Mexico City, Acapulco, Cancun,
Ciudad Juárez, Guadalajara, Mérida, Monterrey,
Oaxaca, Tampico, Tijuana, Veracruz

BRITISH COUNCIL DIRECTOR, A. Curry, Maestro
Antonio Caso 127, Col. San Rafael, Delegación
Cuauhtémoc, (PO Box 30-588), Mexico 06470

BRITISH CHAMBER OF COMMERCE, British Trade
Centre, Rio de la Plata 30, Col. Cuauhtémoc, CP
06500, Mexico City DF. *Manager,* Stephen Grant

DEFENCE

The Army has 762 armoured personnel carriers and 194
artillery pieces. The Navy has three destroyers, six frigates,
106 patrol and coastal vessels, and nine combat aircraft.
There are 20 naval bases. The Air Force has 125 combat
aircraft and 95 armed helicopters.

MILITARY EXPENDITURE – 1.0 per cent of GDP (1997)
MILITARY PERSONNEL – 175,000: Army 130,000, Navy
37,000, Air Force 8,000
CONSCRIPTION DURATION – 12 months (four hours per
week) by lottery

ECONOMY

The principal crops are maize, beans, sorghum, rice, wheat,
barley, sugar cane, coffee, cotton, tomatoes, chillies,
tobacco, chick-peas, groundnuts, cocoa and many kinds of
fruit. The maguey, or Mexican cactus, yields several
fermented drinks, mezcal and tequila (distilled) and pulque
(undistilled). Another species of the plant supplies sisal-
hemp (henequen). The forests contain mahogany, rose-
wood, ebony and chicle trees. Agriculture employs an
estimated 20 per cent of the working population.

The principal industries are mining and petroleum,
although there has been considerable expansion of both
light and heavy industries; exports of manufactured goods
now average more than 85 per cent of total exports. The
steel industry expanded steadily until recently and current
production is around 5.8 million tons. More than one
million vehicles are exported annually, along with more
than two million automotive engines and six million
television sets.

The mineral wealth is great, and principal minerals are
gold, silver, copper, fluorspar, lead, zinc, quicksilver, iron
and sulphur. Substantial reserves of uranium have been
found.

Oil production was 160 million tonnes in 1997. Oil
reserves have increased substantially due to discoveries in
the Gulf of Campeche. A refinery at Tula is the nation's
largest; and new refineries in Monterrey, State of Nuevo
León, and Salina Cruz, State of Oaxaca, are under
construction.

Following economic difficulties in late 1994, the government introduced austerity measures in January 1995. In
June 1997 the government announced a three-year
National Programme for the Financing of Development
intended to stimulate the economy.

In November 1997 the stock market and the peso fell as
a result of the economic crisis in south-east Asia. In
response, the government secured a contingency loan of
US$2.5 billion, which successfully halted the slide. The
currency and the stock market quickly recovered to their
pre-November levels. In 1998 the Mexican economy grew
by 4.8 per cent. The 1999 budget, presented in November
1998, contained US$2.5 billion of spending cuts and raised
some income and fuel taxes.

Mexico joined GATT in 1986 and the OECD in 1994.

GNP – US$348,627 million (1997); US$3,700 per capita
(1997)
GDP – US$246,126 million (1995); US$2,700 per capita
(1995)
ANNUAL AVERAGE GROWTH OF GDP – 7.0 per cent
(1997)
INFLATION RATE – 20.6 per cent (1997)
UNEMPLOYMENT – 4.7 per cent (1995)
TOTAL EXTERNAL DEBT – US$149,690 million (1997)

TRADE

Major imports include computers, auto assembly material,
electrical parts, auto and truck parts, powdered milk, corn
and sorghum, transport, sound-recording and power-
generating equipment, chemicals, industrial machinery,
pharmaceuticals and specialized appliances. Principal exports include oil, automobiles, auto engines, fruits and
vegetables, shrimps, coffee, computers, cattle, glass, iron
and steel pipes, and copper. The main trading partners are
the USA, EU, Latin America and Japan. The North
American Free Trade Agreement, to which Mexico is a
signatory, came into effect on 1 January 1994; trade
between Mexico, Canada and the USA rose by 17 per cent
per year. Mexico has free trade deals with Bolivia, Chile,
Colombia, Costa Rica, Nicaragua and Venezuela, and
negotiations are under way to create free trade agreements
with other South American countries as well as the EU;
negotiations with the EU began in November 1998.

In 1996 Mexico had a trade surplus of US$6,531 million
and a current account deficit of US$1,923 million. In 1996

imports totalled US$61,160 million and in 1997 exports totalled US$65,268 million.

Trade with UK	1997	1998
Imports from UK	£429,254,000	£536,775,000
Exports to UK	382,321,000	337,688,000

COMMUNICATIONS

Veracruz, Tampico and Coatzacoalcos are the chief ports on the Atlantic, and Guaymas, Mazatlán, Puerto Lázaro Cárdenas and Salina Cruz on the Pacific. Work is proceeding on the reorganization and re-equipment of the whole rail system. There were 307,142 km of roads in 1994; total track length of the railways was 20,445 km. Mexico City may be reached by at least three highways from the USA, and from the south from Yucatán as well as on two principal highways from the Guatemalan border.

There are 50 international airports and 33 national airports in Mexico. There are many airline companies, including two major, now private, national airlines, Mexicana de Aviación and Aeroméxico.

Teléfonos de México, now privatized, controls about 98 per cent of all telephone services.

FEDERATED STATES OF MICRONESIA

AREA – 271 sq. miles (701 sq. km)
POPULATION – 109,000 (1994 UN estimate). Pohnpei: population, 31,000; capital, Kolonia; Chuuk (Truk): population, 52,000; capital, Moen; Yap: population, 12,000; capital, Colonia; Kosrae: population, 6,500; capital, Lelu. The population is Micronesian and predominantly Christian. English (official) and eight other languages are used in different parts of the Federated States: Yapese, Ulithian, Woleaian, Ponapean, Nukuoran, Kapingamarangi, Trukese and Kosraen
FEDERAL CAPITAL – Palikir, on Pohnpei
CURRENCY – Currency is that of the USA
NATIONAL FLAG – United Nations blue with four white stars in the centre
POPULATION GROWTH RATE – 2.1 per cent (1997)
POPULATION DENSITY – 155 per sq. km (1996)

The Federated States of Micronesia comprise more than 600 islands extending 2,900 km (1,800 miles) across the archipelago of the Caroline Islands in the western Pacific Ocean. The islands vary geologically from mountainous islands to low coral atolls. The climate is tropical. Storms are common between August and December, and typhoons between July and November.

HISTORY AND POLITICS

The Spanish Empire claimed sovereignty over the Caroline Islands until 1899, when Spain withdrew from her Pacific territories and sold her possessions in the Caroline Islands to Germany. The Caroline Islands became a German protectorate until the outbreak of the First World War in 1914, when Japan took control of the islands on behalf of the Allied powers. After the war Japan continued to administer the territory under a League of Nations mandate. During the Second World War, US armed forces took control of the islands from the Japanese. In 1947 the USA entered into agreement with the UN Security Council to administer the Micronesia area, of which the Federated States of Micronesia were a part, as the UN Trust Territory of the Pacific Islands.

The US Trusteeship administration came to an end on 3 November 1986, when a Compact of Free Association between the USA and the Federated States of Micronesia came into effect. By this agreement the USA recognized the Federated States of Micronesia as a fully sovereign and independent state. The independence of the Federated States of Micronesia was recognized by the UN in December 1990.

POLITICAL SYSTEM

The constitution separates the executive, legislative and judicial branches. There is a bill of rights and provision for traditional rights. The executive comprises a federal president and vice-president, both of whom must be chosen from amongst the four nationally-elected senators. There is a single-chamber Congress of 14 members, four members elected on a nation-wide basis and ten members elected from congressional districts apportioned by population.

The Compact of Free Association places full responsibility for the defence of the Federated States of Micronesia on the USA.

The judiciary is headed by the Supreme Court, which is divided into trial and appellate divisions. Below this, each state has its own judicial system.

FEDERAL STRUCTURE

The Federated States of Micronesia is a federal republic of four constituent states: Chuuk, Kosrae, Pohnpei and Yap. Each of the constituent states has its own government and legislative system.

State	Area (sq. km)	Population (1994)	Headquarters
Chuuk	127	52,870	Weno
Kosrae	109	7,354	Tofol
Pohnpei	344	33,372	Kolonia
Yap	119	11,128	Colonia

HEAD OF STATE

President, Leo Falcam
Vice President, Redley Killian

CABINET *as at May 1999*

Administrative Services, Kapilly Capelle
Budget, Aloysius Tuuth
External Affairs, Asterio Takesy
Finance, Patrick MacKenzie
Health, Eliuel Pretrick
National Planning, Bermin Weilbacher
Resources and Development, Sabastian Anefel
Transportation and Communications, Lukner Weilbacher

BRITISH AMBASSADOR, HE Vernon Scarborough, resident at Suva, Fiji

ECONOMY

The economy is dependent mainly on subsistence agriculture and government spending. Copra and fish are the two main exports. The majority of the working population is engaged in government administration, subsistence farming, fishing, copra production and the tourist industry. In 1990, there were 20,475 visitors.
GNP – US$213 million (1997); US$1,920 per capita (1997)
GDP – US$259 million (1995); US$2,104 per capita (1995)

Trade with UK	1997	1998
Imports from UK	£95,000	£18,000
Exports to UK	1,000	—

MOLDOVA
Republica Moldova

AREA – 13,012 sq. miles (33,700 sq. km). Neighbours:
Ukraine (north, east and south-east), Romania (west)
POPULATION – 4,327,000 (1996 official estimate): 65 per
cent are Moldovan, 14.2 per cent Ukrainian and 13 per
cent Russian, together with smaller numbers of Gagauz
(ethnic Turks), Jews and Bulgarians. Most of the
population are adherents of the Moldovan Orthodox
Church. Moldovan was made the official language
(written in the Latin script) in 1989 but the use of
Russian in official business is permitted
CAPITAL – Chişinău (population, 655,940)
CURRENCY – Leu (plural lei)
NATIONAL DAY – 27 August (Independence Day)
NATIONAL FLAG – Vertical stripes of blue, yellow, red,
with the national arms in the centre
LIFE EXPECTANCY (years) – male 64.28; female 70.99
POPULATION GROWTH RATE – –0.2 per cent (1997)
POPULATION DENSITY – 128 per sq. km (1996)
URBAN POPULATION – 46.7 per cent (1995)
MILITARY EXPENDITURE – 4.4 per cent of GDP (1997)
MILITARY PERSONNEL – 14,450: Army 10,000, Air Force
1,050, Paramilitaries 3,400
CONSCRIPTION DURATION – Up to 18 months
ILLITERACY RATE – 3.6 per cent
ENROLMENT (percentage of age group) – tertiary 26.1
per cent (1996)

HISTORY AND POLITICS

In the 15th century a Moldovan principality was formed
which entered into military and political alliances with
Muscovy before being absorbed into the Turkish Empire
in the 16th century. Moldova became the site of many
Russo-Turkish battles and skirmishes in the 18th century
before the area between the Dniester and Prut rivers (later
known as Bessarabia) was annexed to the Russian Empire
by the Bucharest Peace Treaty of 1812.

After the Russian Revolution in 1917, Bessarabia came
under the control of White Russian forces and was annexed
to Romania under the Versailles Peace Treaty (1919). In
1924 the Moldavian Autonomous Soviet Socialist Republic
(ASSR) was established on the east bank of the Dniester
river as part of Soviet Ukraine. In August 1940 the Soviet
Union forced Romania to cede Bessarabia and the
Moldavian Soviet Socialist Republic was formed from the
majority of Bessarabia (the southernmost parts were
incorporated into the Ukraine) and the Moldavian ASSR.

Moldova (formerly Moldavia) declared its independence
from the USSR in August 1991. Reunification with Romania
was rejected in a referendum on 6 March 1994, following
which the Moldovan parliament voted to join the CIS. In
July 1994 the Moldovan parliament adopted a new
constitution which defines Moldova as a 'presidential
parliamentary republic' based on political pluralism. It also
provides for autonomous status for the Gagauz and
Transdniester regions, with the Gagauz region having its
own elected National Assembly.

Parliament now has 101 seats and is elected by
proportional representation for a four-year term. President
Petru Lucinschi replaced former Communist president
Mircea Snegur in presidential elections in November–
December 1996. In legislative elections in March 1998, no
party won an overall majority, and a right-wing coalition
government under Ion Ciubuc was formed. Ciubuc resigned
on 1 February 1999 and a new government led by Ion
Sturza was sworn in on 12 March.

A referendum in May 1999 on the introduction of a
presidential system of government was declared invalid
because less than the required 60 per cent of the electorate
voted.

INSURGENCIES

After independence was declared, the majority ethnic
Romanian (Moldovan) population expressed a wish to
rejoin Romania. This alienated the ethnic Ukrainian and
Russian populations, who formed a majority east of the
Dniester, and they declared their independence from
Moldova as the Transdniester republic in December 1991.
The Moldovan government refused to recognize this and
in 1992 a war was waged between government forces and
Transdniester forces, who were supported by the former
Soviet 14th Army stationed in Transdniester and by
Cossack volunteers from Russia.

A mainly Russian CIS peacekeeping force (later changed
to a joint Russian-Moldovan-Transdniester force) was
deployed in July 1992 and a cease-fire has held since
August 1992. Although no political solution has been
finalized and a state of armed truce remains, the Moldovan
government in February 1994 agreed to an OSCE plan for
the Transdniester area to have a high degree of autonomy
within Moldova but no independent or federal status. A
memorandum of understanding on the normalization of
relations between the two sides was signed in May 1997,
which committed both parties to hold further talks within
'the framework of a single state'.

A referendum in Transdniester on 24 December 1995
approved independence. President Igor Smirnov was re-
elected in presidential elections in Transdniester in
December 1996.

HEAD OF STATE
President, Petru Lucinschi, *elected* 1 December 1996

GOVERNMENT *as at July 1999*
Prime Minister, Ion Sturza
First Deputy PM, Nicolae Andronic
Deputy PMs, Oleg Stratulater, Alexander Muravschi
  (Economy and Reform)
Agriculture, Food Industry and Forestry, Valeriu Bulgari
Culture, Ghenadie Ciobanu
Defence, Brig.-Gen. Boris Gamurar
Education and Science, Anatol Grimalschi
Environmental Protection, Arcadie Capcelea
Finance, Anatol Arapu
Foreign Affairs, Nicolae Tabacaru
Health, Eugen Gladun
Industry and Trade, Alexander Can
Interior, Victor Catan
Justice, Ion Paduraru
Labour, Social Security and Family Affairs, Vladimir
  Guritenco
Minister of State, Vladimir Filat
National Security, Valeriu Pasat
Territorial Development, Public Utilities and Construction,
  Mihai Severovan
Transport and Communications, Victor Chibiş

EMBASSY OF THE REPUBLIC OF MOLDOVA
175 Avenue Emile Max, B-1040 Brussels, Belgium
Tel: Brussels 732 9659
Ambassador Extraordinary and Plenipotentiary, HE Ion
  Capatina

BRITISH AMBASSADOR, HE R. Ralph, CVO, CMG, resident
  at Bucharest, Romania

ECONOMY

The main sector is agriculture, especially viniculture, fruit-growing and market gardening. Industry is small and concentrated east of the Dniester. Severe drought in 1992, the severance of most trading ties with former Soviet republics, war damage and reductions in Russian fuel deliveries paralysed the economy from 1992 to 1994. An economic reform programme aiming to attract foreign investment began in summer 1993; a privatization programme, completed in November 1995, sold off 1,132 large enterprises. In 1998, telecommunications, power and heating companies were privatized. Moldova is dependent on Russia for energy supplies and owes roughly US$6,000 million. In September 1997 the World Bank approved a US$100 million loan to aid structural reform of the economy.

In 1996 there was a trade deficit of US$285 million and a current account deficit of US$214 million. Imports totalled US$1,079 million and exports US$805 million.

GNP – US$1,974 million (1997); US$460 per capita (1997)
GDP – US$1,699 million (1995); US$383 per capita (1995)
ANNUAL AVERAGE GROWTH OF GDP – –3.0 per cent (1995)
UNEMPLOYMENT – 1.0 per cent (1995)
TOTAL EXTERNAL DEBT – US$1040 million (1997)

Trade with UK	1997	1998
Imports from UK	£4,458,000	£5,644,000
Exports to UK	1,031,000	1,241,000

MONACO
Principauté de Monaco

AREA – 0.4 sq. miles (1 sq. km). Neighbour: France
POPULATION – 32,000 (1994 UN estimate). Only 6,000 residents have full Monégasque citizenship and thus the right to vote. The official language is French. Monégasque, a mixture of Provençal and Ligurian, is also spoken
CAPITAL – Monaco
CURRENCY – French franc of 100 centimes
NATIONAL ANTHEM – Hymne Monégasque
NATIONAL DAY – 19 November
NATIONAL FLAG – Two equal horizontal stripes, red over white
POPULATION GROWTH RATE – 1.1 per cent (1996)
POPULATION DENSITY – 21,477 per sq. km (1996)

A small principality on the Mediterranean, with land frontiers joining France at every point, Monaco is divided into the districts of Monaco-Ville, La Condamine, Font-vielle and Monte Carlo.

HISTORY AND POLITICS

The principality, ruled by the Grimaldi family since 1297, was abolished during the French Revolution and re-established in 1815 under the protection of the kingdom of Sardinia. In 1861 Monaco came under French protection.

The 1962 constitution, which can be modified only with the approval of the National Council, maintains the traditional hereditary monarchy and guarantees freedom of association, trade union freedom and the right to strike. Legislative power is held jointly by the Prince and a unicameral, 18-member National Council elected by universal suffrage. Executive power is exercised by the

Prince and a four-member Council of Government, headed by a Minister of State. The judicial code is based on that of France.

HEAD OF STATE
HSH The Prince of Monaco, Prince Rainier III Louis-Henri-Maxence Bertrand, *born* 31 May 1923, *succeeded* 9 May 1949; *married* 19 April 1956, Miss Grace Patricia Kelly (died 14 September 1982) and *has issue* Prince Albert (*see* below); Princess Caroline Louise Marguerite, *born* 23 January 1957; and Princess Stephanie Marie Elisabeth, *born* 1 February 1965
Heir, HRH Prince Albert Alexandre Louis Pierre, *born* 14 March 1958

President of the Crown Council, Charles Ballerio
President of the National Council, Dr Jean-Louis Campora
Minister of State, Michel Lévêque
Finance and Economy, Henri Fissore
Interior, Philippe Deslandes
Public Works and Social Affairs, Michel Sosso

CONSULATE-GENERAL OF MONACO
4 Cromwell Place, London sw7 2JE
Tel 0171-225 2679
Consul-General, I. B. Ivanovic

BRITISH CONSULATE-GENERAL
33 Boulevard Princesse Charlotte, BP 265, MC-98005 Monaco CEDEX
Tel: Monaco 93 50 99 66
Consul-General, I. Davies, apptd 1997, resident at Marseilles, France

ECONOMY

The whole available ground is built over so that there is no cultivation, though there are some notable public and private gardens. The economy is based on real estate revenues, the financial sector and tourism (226,421 visitors in 1996). Monaco has a small harbour (30 ft alongside quay) and the import duties are the same as in France.

GDP – US$847 million (1995); US$26,470 per capita (1995)

MONGOLIA
Mongol Uls

AREA – 604,829 sq. miles (1,566,500 sq. km). Neighbours: Russia (north), China (south)
POPULATION – 2,354,000 (1994 UN estimate). Mongolians also live in China and in the neighbouring regions of Russia, especially the Mongolian Buryat Autonomous Region. The official language is Khalkha Mongolian
CAPITAL – Ulaanbaatar (population, 515,100, 1987 estimate)
CURRENCY – Tugrik of 100 möngö
NATIONAL DAY – 11 July
NATIONAL FLAG – Vertical tricolour red, blue, red and in the hoist the traditional Soyombo symbol in gold
LIFE EXPECTANCY (years) – male 62.32; female 65.00
POPULATION GROWTH RATE – 2.0 per cent (1997)
POPULATION DENSITY – 2 per sq. km (1996)
URBAN POPULATION – 57.1 per cent (1989)
MILITARY EXPENDITURE – 2.0 per cent of GDP (1997)
MILITARY PERSONNEL – 16,000: Army 8,000, Air Defence 800, Paramilitaries 7,200
CONSCRIPTION DURATION – 12 months
ILLITERACY RATE – 1.3 per cent

ENROLMENT (percentage of age group) – primary 82 per cent (1996); secondary 53 per cent (1996); tertiary 17.0 per cent (1996)

Mongolia, which is almost entirely at least 1,000 metres above sea level, forms part of the central Asiatic plateau and rises towards the west in the mountains of the Mongolian Altai and Hangai ranges. The Hentai range, situated to the north-east of the capital Ulaanbaatar, is lower. The Gobi region covers much of the southern half of the country and contains sand deserts interspersed with semi-desert. There are several long rivers and many lakes but good water is scarce as much of the lake water is salty. The climate is harsh, with a short mild summer giving way to a long winter when temperatures can drop as low as −50°C.

HISTORY AND POLITICS

Mongolia, under Genghis Khan the conqueror of China and much of Asia, was for many years a buffer state between Tsarist Russia and China, although it was under general Chinese suzerainty. The Chinese Revolution in 1911 led to a declaration of autonomy under Chinese suzerainty which was confirmed by the Sino-Russian Treaty of Kiakhta (1915) but cancelled by a unilateral Chinese declaration in 1919. Later the country became a battleground of the Russian civil war, and Soviet and Mongolian troops occupied Ulaanbaatar in 1921; this was followed by another declaration of independence. In 1924 the Soviet Union in a treaty with China again recognized the latter's sovereignty over Mongolia, but this was never properly exercised because of China's preoccupation with internal affairs and later with the war with Japan. The Mongolian People's Republic was formally established in 1924. Under the Yalta Agreement, President Chiang Kai-shek of China agreed to a plebiscite, held in 1945, in which the Mongolians declared their desire for independence and this was formally recognized by China.

The Mongolian People's Revolutionary Party (MPRP) was the sole political party from 1924 to 1990. Demonstrations in favour of political and economic reform began in December 1989 and led to changes in the MPRP leadership in March 1990. The MPRP's constitutionally guaranteed monopoly of power was subsequently relinquished, and the introduction of a multiparty system was approved by the Great People's Hural (parliament). The MPRP won the first multiparty elections, held in July 1990. Since then, and following Moscow's lead, Mongolia has embarked on a programme of political and economic reforms.

The most recent legislative election, held on 30 June 1996, was won by the Democratic Union Coalition (Mongolian National Democratic Party and Mongolian Social Democratic Party) which won 50 seats. The country's first direct presidential election was held in 1993 and won by the incumbent Punsalmaagiyn Ochirbat, who stood as an opposition candidate after the MPRP refused to endorse him as its candidate. Ochirbat was ousted in May 1997 by the leader of the MPRP, Natsagyn Bagabandi. Prime Minister Mendsayhany Enhsayhan resigned in April 1998 and was replaced by Tsahiagiyn Elbegdorj, whose government lost a motion of no confidence in July 1998. Agreement was finally reached on a successor in December, when Janlaviin Narantsatsralt was appointed prime minister.

The country and three city districts (Ulanbaatar, Darkhan and Erdenet) are divided into 21 *aimaks* (provinces) and beneath these into 258 *somons* (districts), and these form the basis of the state organization of the country. The last remaining former Soviet armed forces personnel were withdrawn in late 1992.

POLITICAL SYSTEM

A new constitution was approved in January 1992 which enshrines the concepts of democracy, a mixed economy, free speech and neutrality in foreign affairs. The Great and Little Hurals were abolished, and a new unicameral Great Hural became the legislative body of the country. There are 76 members of the Great Hural, elected for four-year terms by a simple majority amounting to at least 25 per cent of the votes cast.

HEAD OF STATE
President, Natsagyn Bagabandi, *elected* 18 May 1997

CABINET *as at July 1999*
Prime Minister, Janlaviin Narantsatsralt
Agriculture and Industry, Choizangiin Sodnomtseren
Chief of the General Police, Dashdorjiyn Muren
Chief of the General Staff, Tserenbaljdyn Dashzeveg
Defence, Sh. Tuvdendorj
Education, Culture and Science, A. Battur
Finance, Ya. Ochirsuh
Foreign Affairs, Nyam-Osorin Tuya
Health and Welfare, S. Sonin
Infrastructure Development, Gavaagiin Bathuu
Justice, Logiyn Tsog
Nature and Environment Protection, Sonomtserengiin Mendsayhan
Secretary of the National Security Council, Ravdangiyn Bold

EMBASSY OF MONGOLIA
7 Kensington Court, London W8 5DL
Tel 0171-937 0150
Ambassador Extraordinary and Plenipotentiary, HE Tsedenjavyn Suhbaatar, apptd 1997

BRITISH EMBASSY
30 Enkh Taivny Gudamzh (PO Box 703), Ulaanbaatar 13
Tel: Ulaanbaatar 458133
Ambassador Extraordinary and Plenipotentiary, HE John Durham, apptd 1997

ECONOMY

Traditionally the Mongolians led a nomadic life tending flocks of sheep, goats, horses, cows and camels. With the coming of the Communist regime, and especially after 1952, great efforts were made to settle the population but a proportion still live nomadically or semi-nomadically in the traditional *ger* (circular tent). Collectivization at the end of the 1950s into huge *negdels* (co-operatives) and state farms hastened the process of settlement, but within these the herdsmen and their families still move with their *gers* from pasture to pasture as the seasons change. Total livestock was 25 million in 1993.

The semi-desert areas of the Gobi region provide pasture for sheep, goats, camels, horses and some cattle. In the steppe areas to the north of the Gobi pasturage is better and livestock more abundant. Even further north, in the better-watered provinces, grain, fodder and vegetable crops are grown.

Although the economy remains predominantly pastoral, factories have started up, coal, copper and molybdenum are mined and the electricity industry has been developed. Ulaanbaatar and Darkhan are the main seats of industry, which includes lime, cement and building materials, a flour mill and a power station. Choibalsan is also being developed industrially.

Communication is still difficult as there are only 1,185 km of surfaced roads and horses are still the characteristic means of transport for the rural population. The trans-Mongolian railway links Mongolia with both China and

World Physical

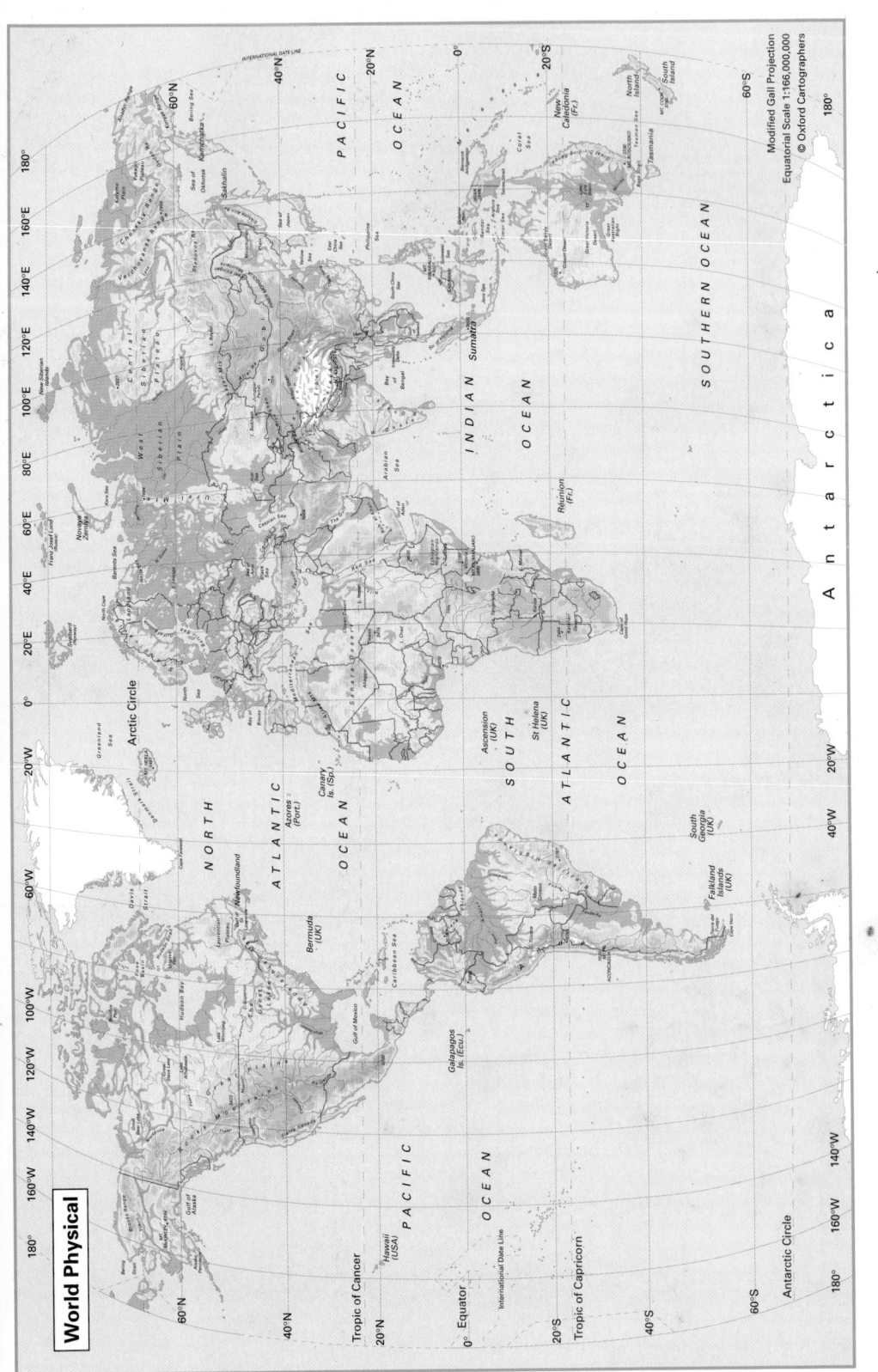

Modified Gall Projection
Equatorial Scale 1:166,000,000
© Oxford Cartographers

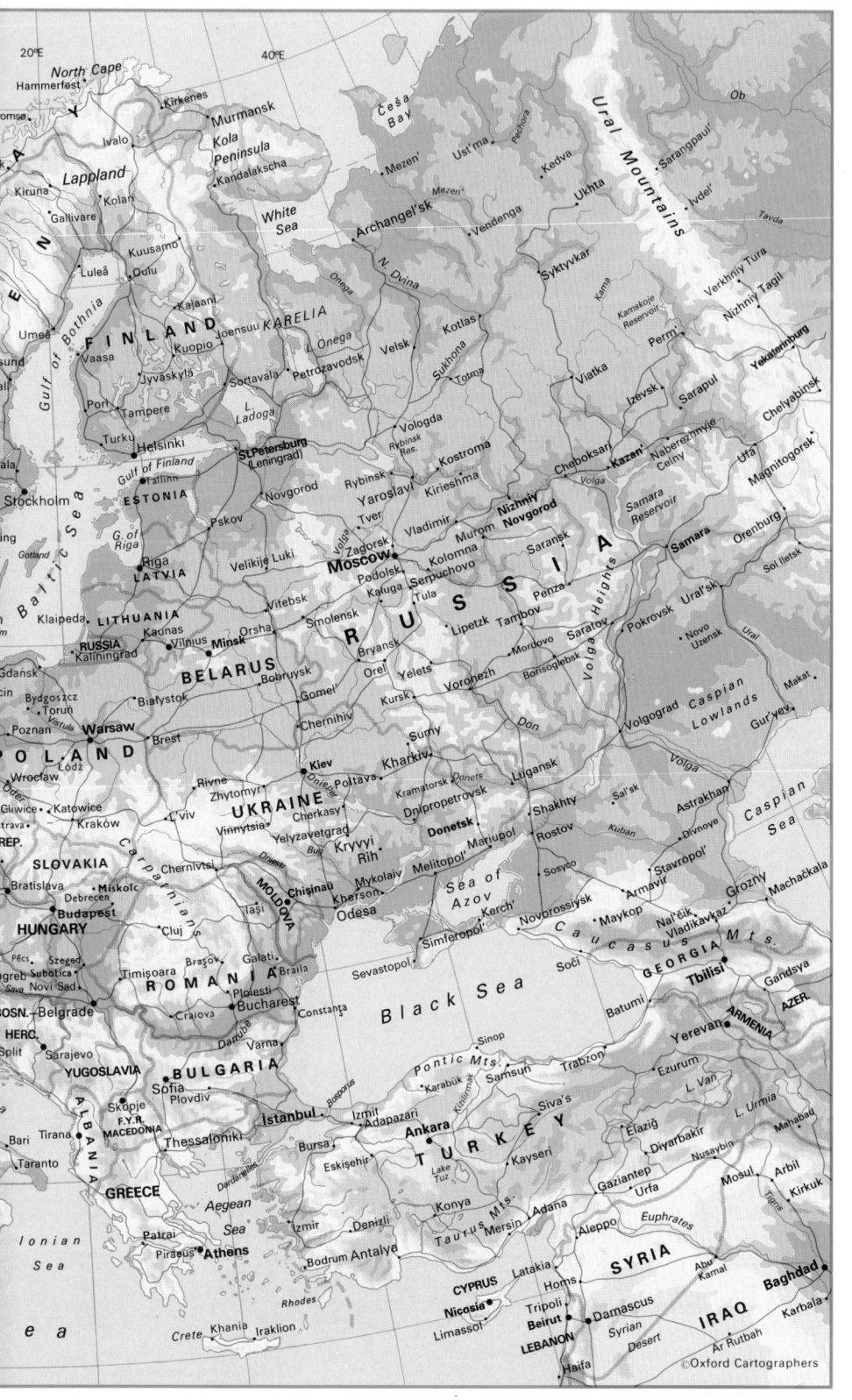

20°E North Cape
Hammerfest
Kirkenes
romsø
Murmansk
Ivalo
Kola
Kiruna
Kolari Peninsula
Gallivare Kandalakscha
 40°E
Ceša
Bay
Ob

Mezen' Ust'ma
Ust'ma
Pecsora
Sarangpaul'
Kuusamo
Luleå
Oulu
Vendenga
Ukhta
Ivdel'
Ural Mountains
N. Dvina Archangel'sk
Tavda
Verkhniy Tura

Lappland

White
Sea

Mezen'
Kedva
Syktyvkar
Nizhniy Tagil
Yekaterinburg

Umeå
sund
al

Kajaani
Joensuu KARELIA
Kuopio
L. Onega
Velsk
Sukhona
Totma
Viatka
Izevsk
Sarapul
Perm'
Chelyabinsk

FINLAND
Jyvaskylä
Sortavala Petrozavodsk
Kama
Kamskoje
Reservoir
Kotlas
Onega
L Ladoga

Pori
Tampere
Vaasa

Turku
Helsinki

Stockholm
ing

Gotland

Gulf of Finland
Tallinn
(Leningrad)
St.Petersburg
Novgorod

Vologda
Rybinsk Res.
Rybinsk
Kostroma
Yaroslavl
Kirieshma
Cheboksari
Kazan
Naberezhnyje
Celny
Ufa
Magnitogorsk

Volga
Samara
Reservoir
Samara
Orenburg
Sol Iletsk

ESTONIA
G. of
Riga
Riga
LATVIA

Pskov
Velikije Luki
Tver
Vladimir
Murom
Nizhniy
Novgorod
Saransk

sala
Baltic Sea
Klaipeda
LITHUANIA
Kaunas
Vilnius
Minsk

Vitebsk
Orsha
Smolensk
Zagorsk
Moscow
Podolsk
Kaluga
Tula
Serpuchovo
Kolomna

RUSSIA
Penza
Ural'sk
Pokrovsk
Novo
Uzensk
Ural
Makat

Gdańsk
cin
RUSSIA
Kaliningrad

BELARUS
Bobruysk
Bryansk
Orel
Yelets
Lipetzk Tambov
Mordovo Saratov
Volga Heights

Bydgoszcz
Toruń
Poznan
Warsaw
Brest
Gomel'
Kursk
Voronezh
Borisoglebsk
Volgograd Caspian
Lowlands
Gur'yev

POLAND
Łódź
Białystok
Chernihiv
Sumy
Don
Volga
Astrakhan

Wrocław
Oder
Gliwice
strava
Katowice
Kraków
REP.
Rivne
Zhytomyr
L'viv
Kiev
Poltava
Dnipro
Kharkiv
Kramatorsk Donets
Lugansk
Sal'sk
Caspian
Sea

SLOVAKIA
Bratislava
Miskolc
Debrecen
Budapest
HUNGARY
Cluj

Chernivtsi
Vinnytsia
Cherkasy
Yelyzavetgrad
Kryvyi
Rih
Dnipropetrovsk
Donetsk
Mariupol
Shakhty
Rostov
Kuban
Divnoye

UKRAINE
Chişinău
MOLDOVA
Iaşi
Mykolaiv
Melitopol
Kherson
Odesa
Sea of
Azov
Kerch'
Novorossiysk
Armavir
Stavropol'
Maykop
Nal'čik
Vladikavkaz
Grozny
Machačkala

Pécs
Szeged
agreb Subotica
Novi Sad
Timişoara
Braşov Galati
Braila
ROMANIA
Ploieşti
Bucharest
Constanta
Sevastopol
Simferopol'
Caucasus Mts.
GEORGIA
Tbilisi
Gandsya
AZER

BOSN. Belgrade
HERC.
Split Sarajevo
Craiova
Danube
Varna
Black Sea
Soči
Batumi
Yerevan
ARMENIA

YUGOSLAVIA
BULGARIA
Sofia
Plovdiv
Sinop
Pontic Mts.
Trabzon
Ezurum
L. Van
L. Urmia
Mahabad

ALBANIA
Tirana
Bari
Taranto
F.Y.R.
MACEDONIA
Skopje
Thessaloniki
Istanbul
Izmit
Adapazari
Ankara
Karabük
Samsun
Siva's
Elaziğ
Diyarbakir
Nusaybin
Arbil
Kirkuk

GREECE
Ionian
Sea
Patrai
Piraeus
Athens
Aegean
Sea
Izmir
Bursa
Eskişehir
Lake
Tuz
TURKEY
Konya
Kayseri
Taurus Mts.
Gaziantep
Urfa
Adana
Mersin
Aleppo
Euphrates
Tigris
Mosul

Denizli
Bodrum Antalya
Rhodes
CYPRUS
Nicosia
Latakia
Homs
SYRIA
Abu
Kamal
Baghdad

e a
Crete
Khania
Iraklion
Limassol
Tripoli
Beirut
LEBANON
Damascus
Syrian
Desert
IRAQ
Karbala
Ar Rutbah
Haifa
©Oxford Cartographers

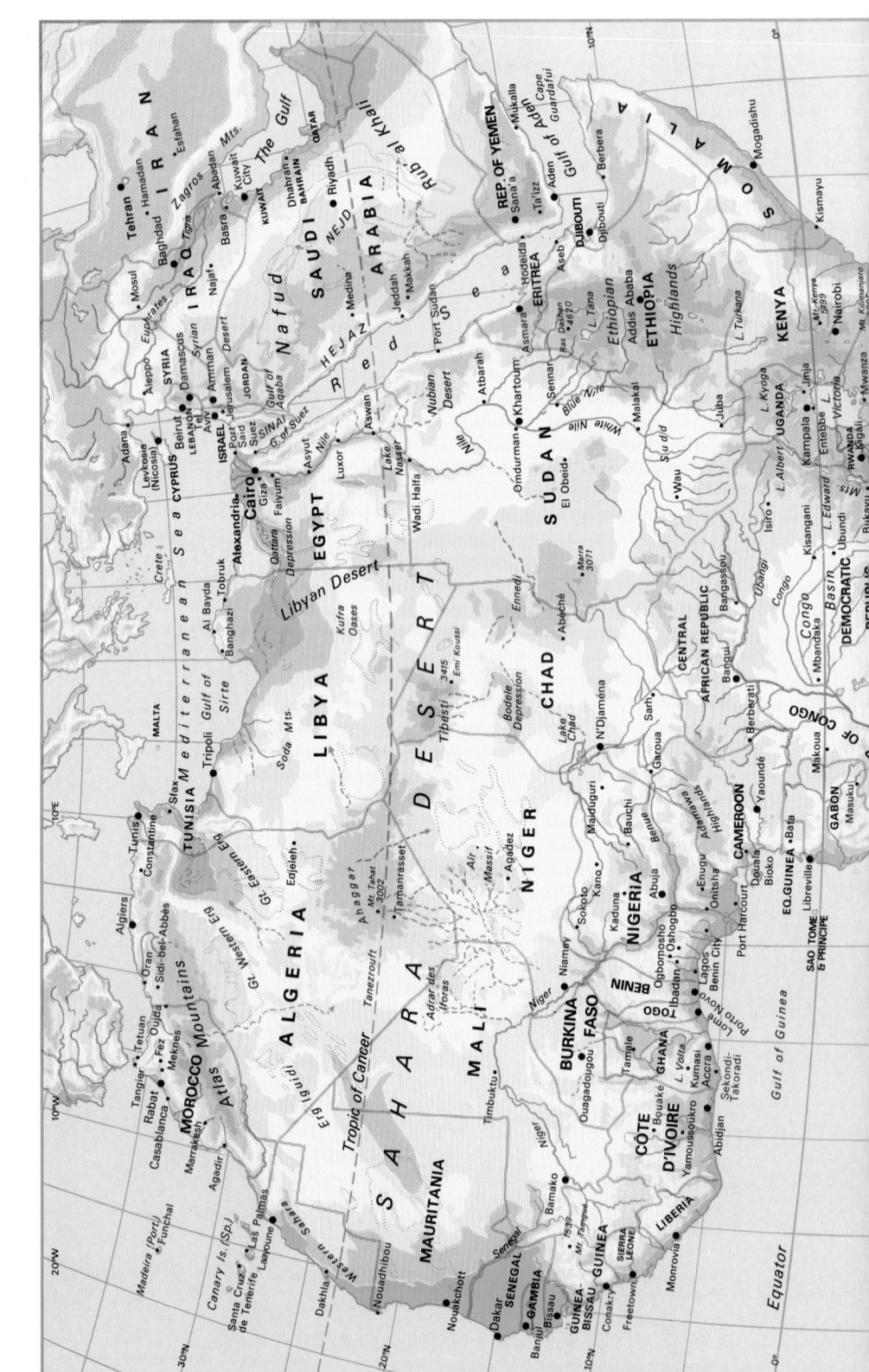

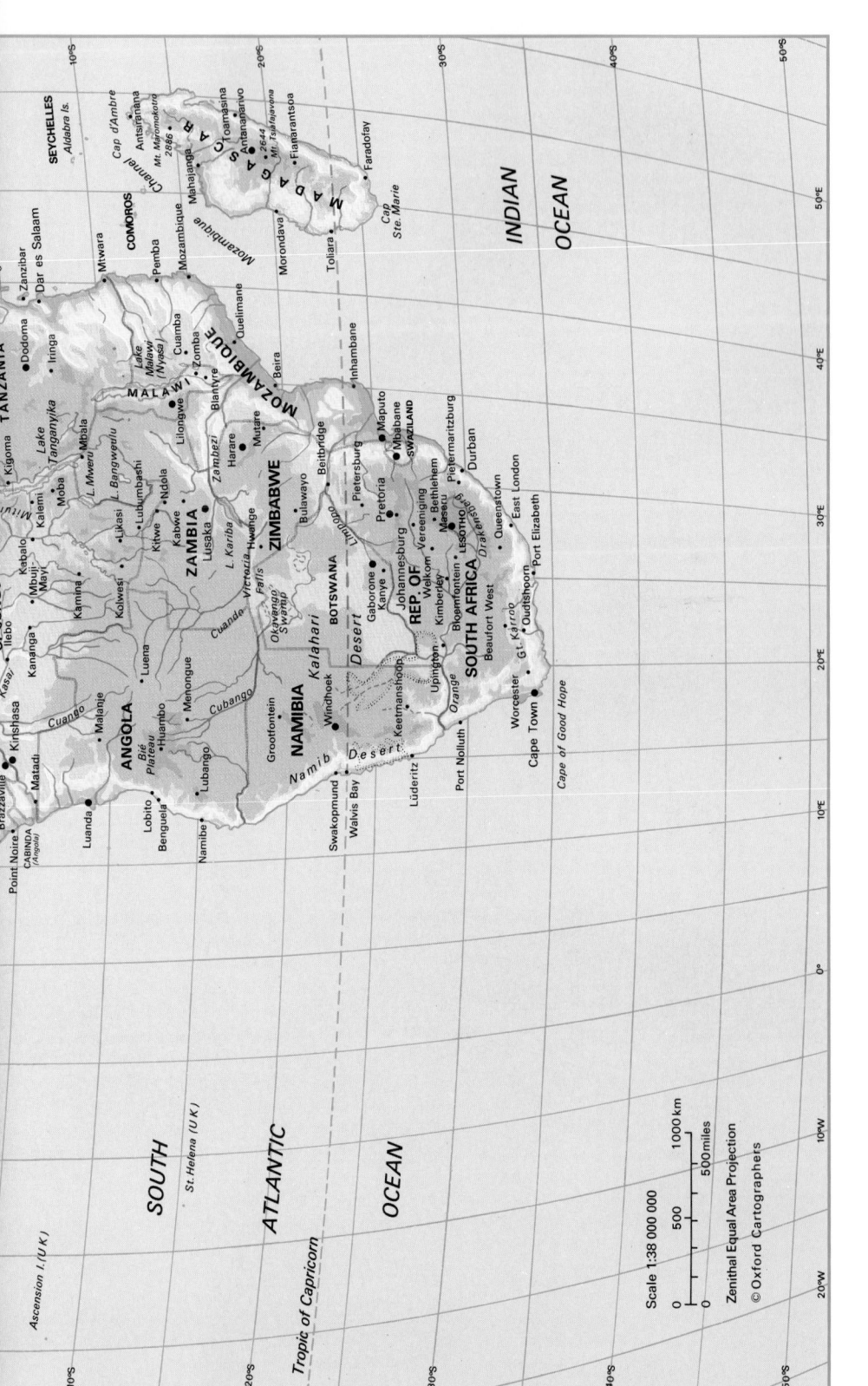

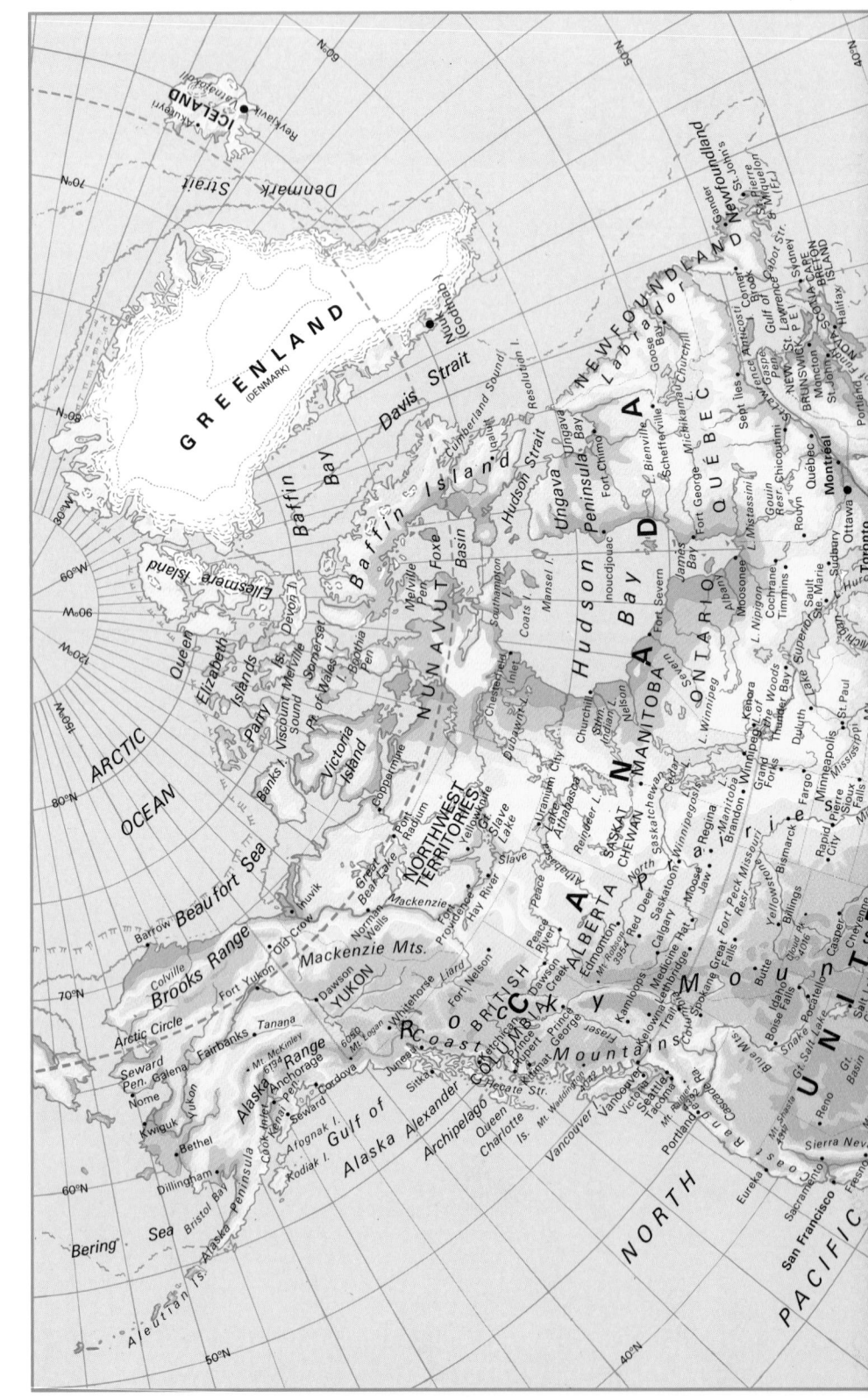

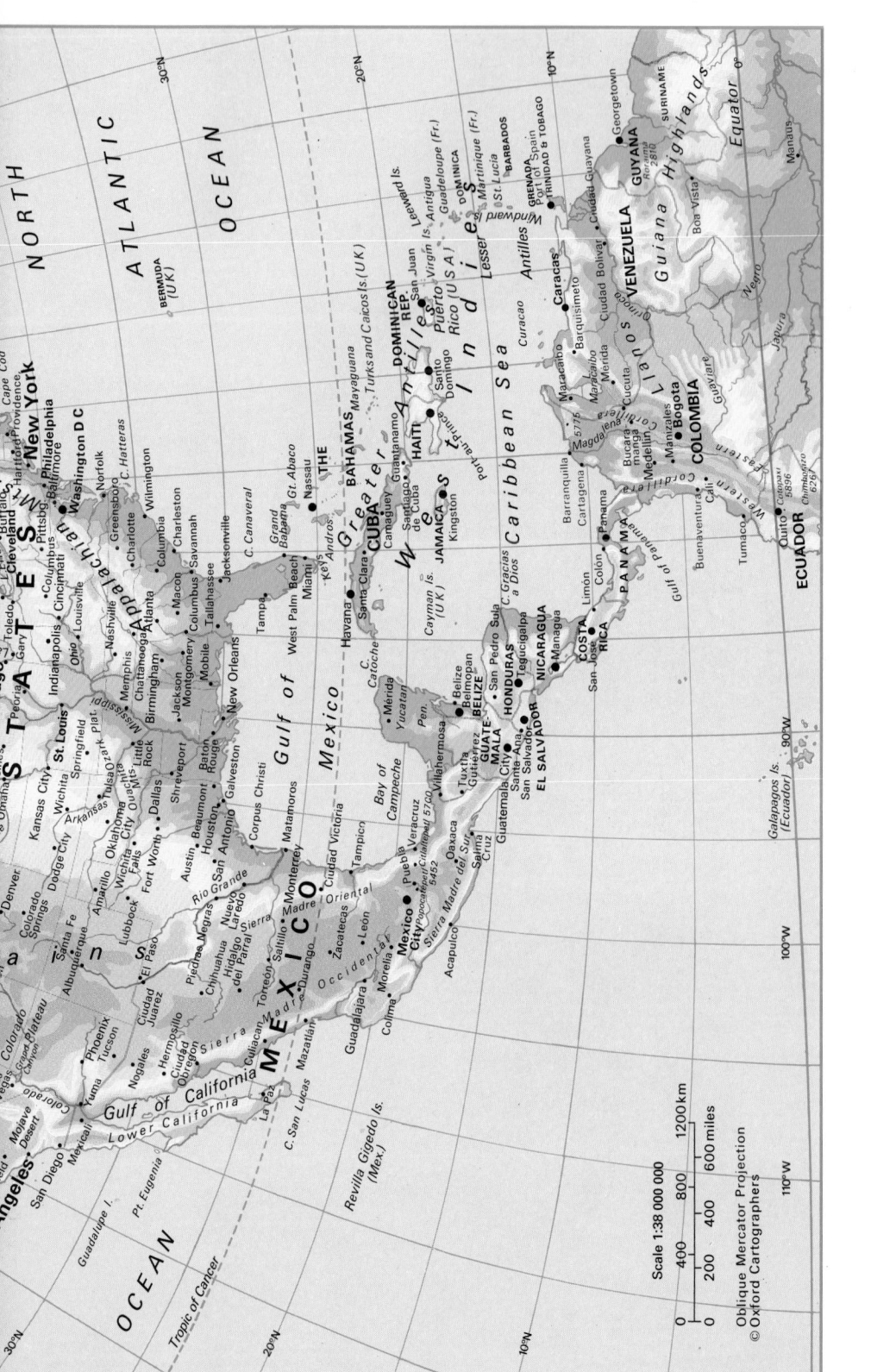

CUBA
Santa Clara
Camaguey
Santiago de Cuba
Guantanamo
JAMAICA
Kingston
HAITI
Port-au-Prince
Santo Domingo
DOMINICAN REP.
San Juan
Puerto Rico (USA)
Virgin Is.
Leeward Is.
Antigua (UK)
Guadeloupe (Fr.)
DOMINICA
Martinique (Fr.)
St.Lucia
BARBADOS
GRENADA
Lesser
Antilles
Windward Is.

Turks and Caicos Is.(UK)

Caribbean Sea

ATLANTIC

OCEAN

10°N

Limón
Colón
PANAMA
Panama
Gulf of Panama
Buenaventura
Cali

Barranquilla
Cartagena
Maracaibo
Maracaibo
Mérida
5775
Barquisimeto
Caracas
Curacao
Port of Spain
TRINIDAD & TOBAGO
Ciudad Bolívar
Ciudad Guayana
Georgetown
Paramaribo
Cayenne
FR.
GUIANA
SURINAME
GUYANA
VENEZUELA
Llanos
Guiana
Highlands
Roraima 2810
Boa Vista

Bucaramanga
Medellín
Manizales
Bogotá
COLOMBIA
Guaviare
Cúcuta

Tumaco

Quito
Cotopaxi 5896
ECUADOR
Guayaquil
Chimborazo 6267
Cuenca
Iquitos
Leticia

Sullana
Chiclayo
Cajamarca
Trujillo
Chimbote
PERU
Huánuco
Pucallpa
Cruzeiro do Sul
Río Branco
Pôrto Velho

0°

Equator

Marañón
Ucayali
Juruá
Purus
Madeira
Selvas
Napo
Amazon
Negro
Japurá
Manaus
Santarém
Belém
São Luís
Bacabal
Teresina
Fortaleza
C. São Roque
Natal
Mossoró
Juazeiro do Norte
João Pessoa
Recife
Maceió
Campina Grande
Caruaru
Paulo Afonso
Aracaju
Feira de Santana
Salvador
Ilhéus
Tapajós
Xingu
Tocantins
Teles pires
Paranaíba
São Francisco
Juazeiro
Barreiras
Montes Claros
Diamantina
Governador Valadares
Caratinga
Vitória
Campos

BRAZIL

10°S

La Oroya
Lima
Callao
Huancayo
Cuzco
Santa Ana
Trinidad
Mamoré
Serra dos Parecis
Mato Grosso
Mato
Grosso
Cuiabá
Goiás
Brasília
Goiânia
Uberlândia
Uberaba
Ribeirão Preto
Belo Horizonte
Juiz de Fora
Brazilian
Highlands
Campos
Pirapora
Plateau

Arequipa
Puno
L. Titicaca
La Paz
BOLIVIA
Cochabamba
Santa Cruz
Sucre
Oruro
L. Poopó
Potosí
Mollendo
Arica
Salt Flat
Iquique
Tarija
Corumba
Gran Chaco
Campo Grande
Marília
Paraná
Campinas
São Paulo
Volta Redonda
Niterói
Rio de Janeiro
Santos
Curitiba
Londrina

20°S

Tropic of Capricorn

Antofagasta
San Salvador de Jujuy
Salta
Taltal
Copiapó
Tucuman
Catamarca
La Rioja
Formosa
PARAGUAY
Concepción
Asunción
Villarrica
Pilcomayo
Bermejo
Resistencia
Corrientes
Posadas
Passo Fundo
Florianópolis
Pôrto Alegre

San Felix I.
San Ambrosio I.
(Chile)

30°S

SOUTH

ATLANTIC

OCEAN

La Serena
Santiago del Estero
Córdoba
Santa Fé
Paraná
Rosario
Mercedes
Santa Maria
Livramento
Tacuarembó
Paysandú
URUGUAY
Durazno
Salado
Salinas Grandes
Juan Fernández Is. (Chile)
Aconcagua 6960
Valparaíso
Santiago
Rancagua
San Juan
Mendoza
San Luis
Santa Rosa
Bolívar
Azul
Pelotas

Concepción
Chillán
Talca
Curicó
Córdoba
Buenos Aires
Montevideo
Rocha
Plate
Mar del Plata
Uruguay
Paraná
Entre Ríos

Valdivia
Osorno
Puerto Montt
Chiloé
Neuquén
Negro
Colorado
Bahía Blanca
Carmen de Patagones
Viedma
Chubut
Valdés Peninsula
Rawson

ARGENTINA
Pampas
Andes

40°S

Taitao Pen.
Chonos
Patagonia
L. Viedma
L. Argentino
Comodoro Rivadavia
Gulf of S. Jorge
Deseado
Bahía Grande

Falkland Is. (UK)
Port Stanley

Puerto Natales
Punta Arenas
Río Gallegos
Strait of Magellan
Tierra del Fuego
Ushuaia
Cape Horn

South Georgia (UK)

50°S

Scale 1:44 000 000

0   400   800   1200   1600 km

0   500   1000 miles

Oblique Mercator Projection

© Oxford Cartographers

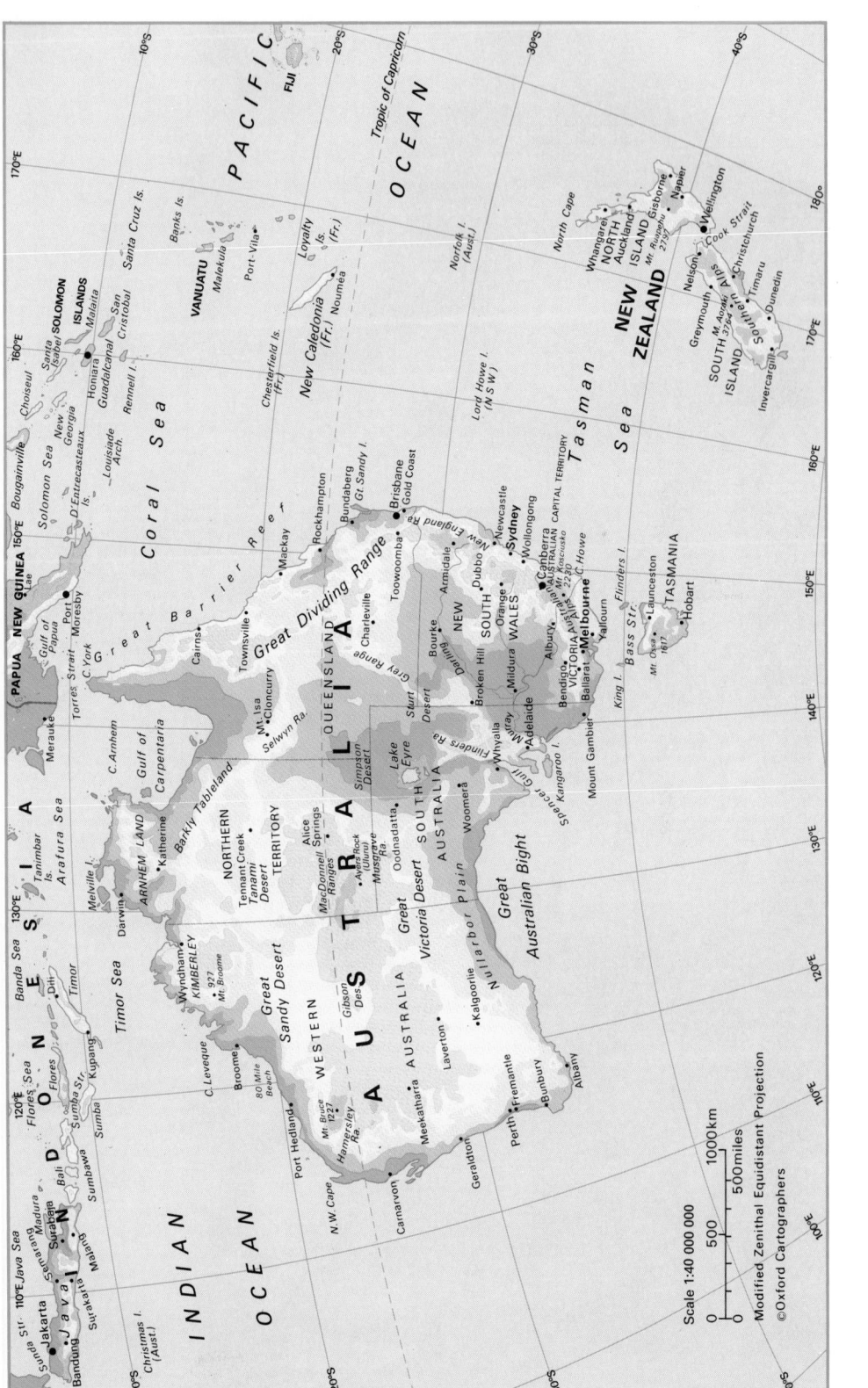

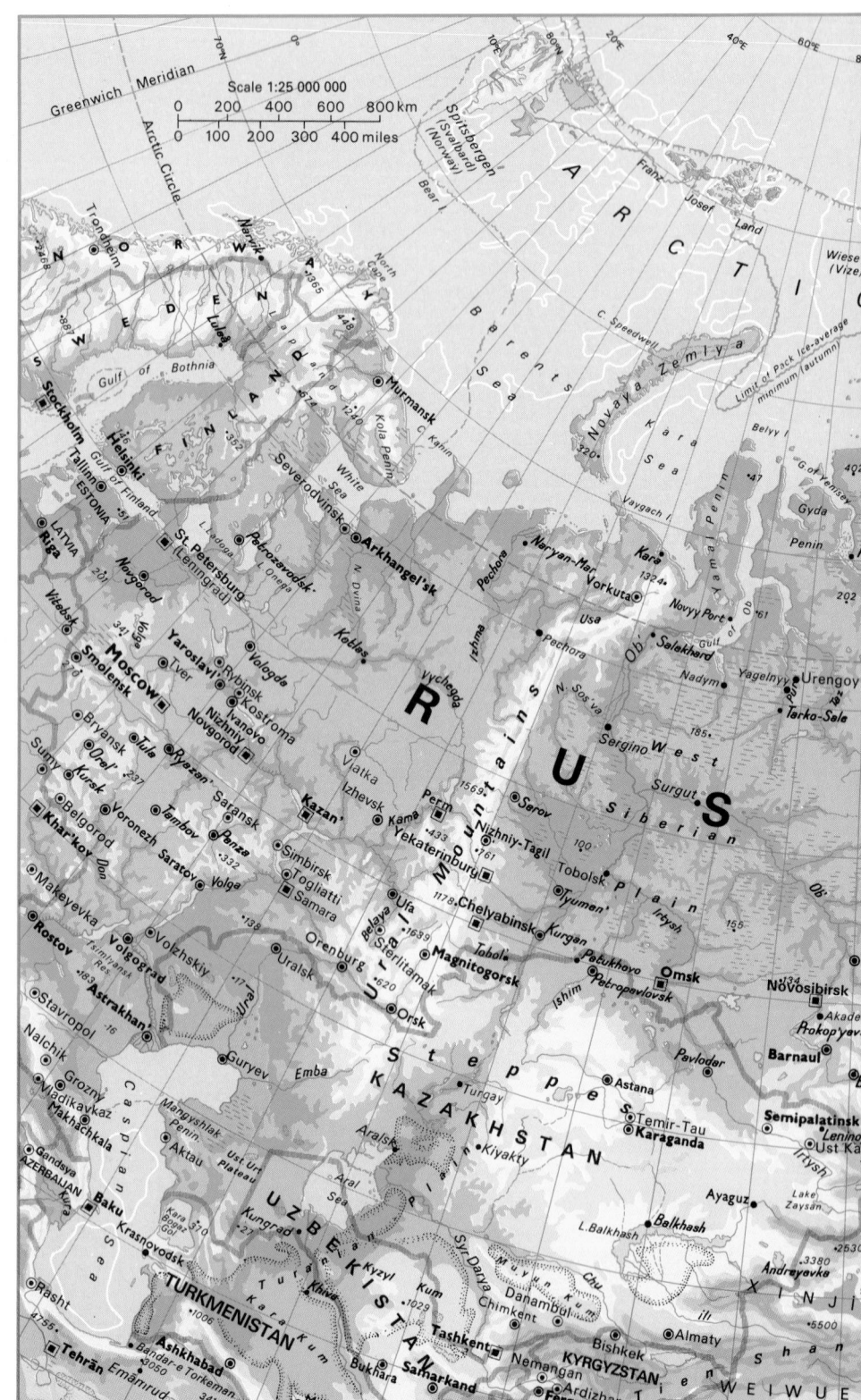

Greenwich Meridian

Scale 1:25 000 000

0   200   400   600   800 km

0   100   200   300   400 miles

Arctic Circle

A R C T I C

Spitsbergen (Svalbard) (Norway)

Franz Josef Land

Bear I.

Wiese I. (Vize)

Novaya Zemlya

Barents Sea

C. Speedwell

Limit of Pack Ice-average minimum (autumn)

Belyy I.

G.of Yenisey

402

•47

Gyda Penin.

Ka

202

Kara Sea

Vaygach I.

Yamal Penin.

320·

Murmansk

Kola Penin.

Kanin

Novyy Port

Gulf of Ob

•61

Trondheim

·3468

N O R W A Y

Narvik

•3365

•1418

North

Troms

Luleå

S W E D E N

·887

Stockholm

F I N L A N D

Helsinki

Tallinn

ESTONIA

Gulf of Bothnia

Gulf of Finland

•351

Lapland

·332

White Sea

Severodvinsk

Arkhangel'sk

N. Dvina

Kotlas

·340

Naryan-Mar

Vorkuta

1324·

Kara

Pechora

Usa

Pechora

Salekhard

Nadym

Yagelnyy

Urengoy

Tarko-Sale

185·

Riga

LATVIA

Vitebsk

L.Ladoga

St. Petersburg (Leningrad)

L.Onega

Petrozavodsk

Izhma

Vychegda

N. Sos'va

Sergino

West

Surgut

S i b e r i a n

Ob

Novgorod

·341

Vologda

Yaroslavl'

Rybinsk

Smolensk

Moscow

Tver

Kostroma

Ivanovo

Nizhniy Novgorod

Bryansk

Sumy

Tula

Orel'

Ryazan'

Vyatka

Izhevsk

Kazan

Kama

Perm

·1569

Serov

Nizhniy-Tagil

·761

U

S

Plain

100·

155·

Ob

Kursk

Belgorod

Voronezh

Tambov

Saransk

Penza

·237

·332

Simbirsk

Togliatti

Samara

Yekaterinburg

·433

M

Tobolsk

Tyumen

Irtysh

Khar'kov

Don

Saratov

Volga

Volga

·138

Belaya

Ufa

·1178

Chelyabinsk

Kurgan

Tobol

Petukhovo

Omsk

·134

Tс

Makeyevka

Volgograd

Tsimlyansk Res.

·183

Rostov

Stavropol

·16

Astrakhan

Guryev

Uralsk

Orenburg

·620

Sterlitamak

Magnitogorsk

·17

Ural

Orsk

U

r

a

l

Ishim

Petropavlovsk

Ishim

Pavlodar

Novosibirsk

Akadem

Prokop'yevsk

Barnaul

Biy

Nalchik

Grozny

Vladikavkaz

Makhachkala

Gandsva

AZERBAIJAN

Baku

Caspian Sea

Emba

Mangyshlak Penin.

Aktau

Kara Bogaz

·370

S t e p p e s

Turgay

Astana

Temir-Tau

Karaganda

Kiyakty

K A Z A K H S T A N

Aral Sea

Aralsk

Semipalatinsk

Leninog

Ust Kam

32

Ayaguz

Lake Zaysan

·3380

Andreyevka

·2530

Rasht

Krasnovodsk

Ust Urt Plateau

Kungrad

·27

UZBEKISTAN

Syr Darya

Muynak

Chu

L.Balkhash

Belkhash

Ili

X I N J I

·5500

Tehrān

Emānrud

Bandar-e Torkeman

·2050

TURKMENISTAN

·1006

Ashkhabad

Bukhara

·3414

Mary

Khiva

·1029

Kyzyl Kum

Karakum

Tashkent

Samarkand

Chimkent

Danambul

Nemangan

Bishkek

Ardizhan

Fergana

KYRGYZSTAN

Almaty

T i e n

WEIWUER

S h a n

·4755·

·8399

·3414

©Oxford Cartographers

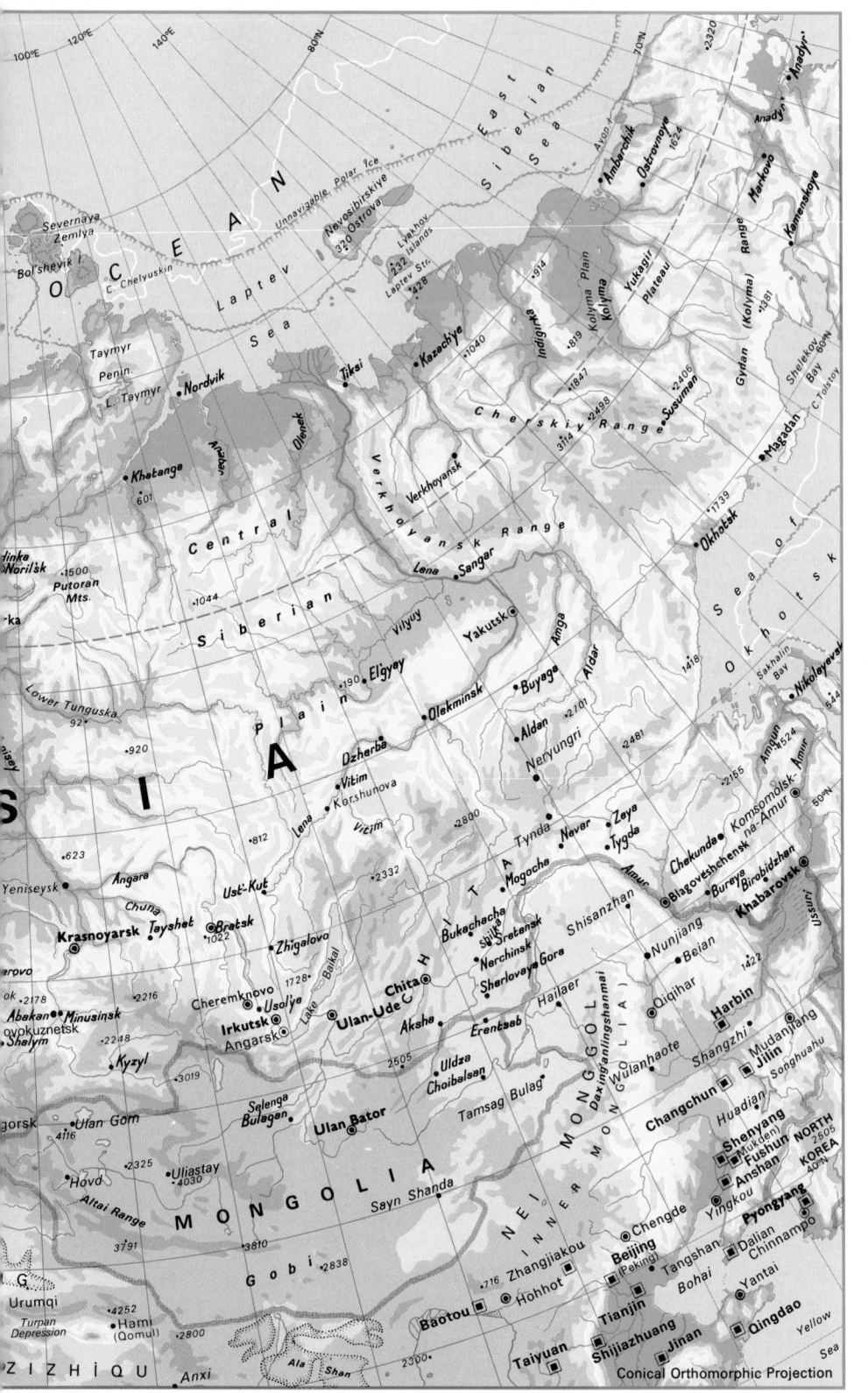

Conical Orthomorphic Projection

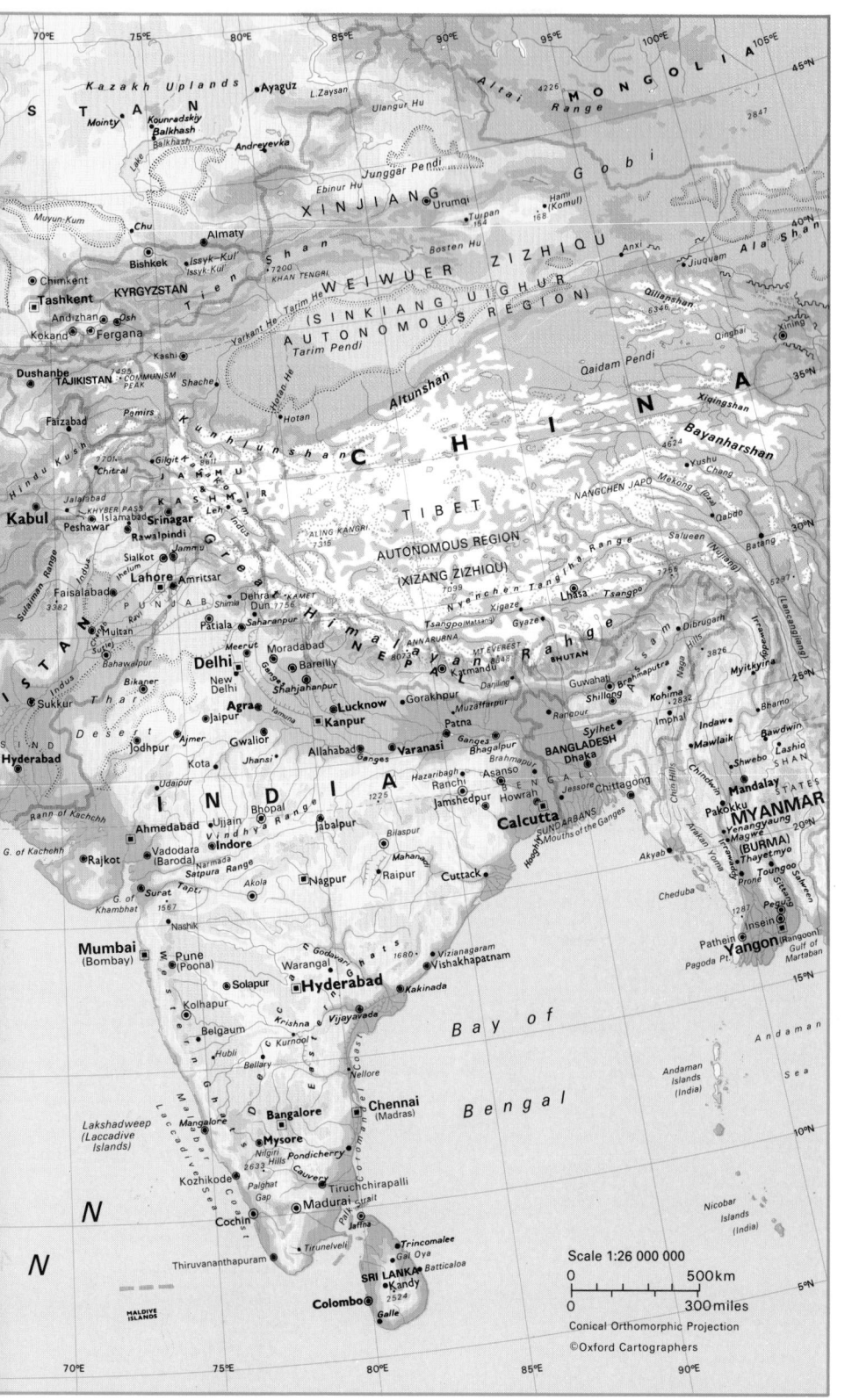

© Oxford Cartographers

Beaufort Sea

McClure Strait
Viscount Melville
Sound

Banks
Island

Melville Island

Devon Island

Baffin
Bay

Amundsen Gulf

Victoria
Island

Somerset I.

Gulf of Boothia

Baffin Island

70°N

Brooks Range

Alaska
(USA)

philip Smith Mts.

Great Bear Lake

Foxe
Basin

Arcle Crole

Cumberland Sound

Frobisher Bay

Yukon

Mackenzie Mts.

60°N

Alaska Range

Mt. McKinley
6194

Anchorage

Mt.
Logan
5951

Coast Mountains

Gt.
Slave Lake

Caribou
Mts.

L. Athabasca

Peace

Reindeer
Lake

Hudson
Bay

James
Bay

Ungava
Peninsula

Ungava
Bay

Labrador

Gulf of
Alaska

Queen
Charlotte
Islands

Rocky Mountains

Edmonton

Mt.
Robson
3954

Calgary

Saskatoon

C A N A D A

Lake
Winnipeg

Manitoba

Regina

Winnipeg

L.
Nipigon

Vancouver I.

Vancouver

Thunder
Bay

Lake
Superior

50°N

St. Lawrence

Québec

Gulf of
St.
Lawrence

Tacoma
Seattle

Portland

Mt. Rainier
4392

Boise

Minneapolis

St. Paul

Milwaukee

Lake
Michigan

Chicago

Detroit

Lake
Huron

Sudbury

Ottawa

L. Ontario

Toronto

L. Erie

Cleveland

Buffalo

Montréal

Boston

Nova Scotia

Halifax

H

Salt Lake
City

U S A

Omaha

Denver

Kansas
City

Indianapolis

Cincinnati

Pittsburgh

New York

Philadelphia

Baltimore

Washington DC

Appalachian Mts.

40°N

Oakland
San Francisco
San José

Mt. Whitney
4418

Colorado
Plateau

Las Vegas

Alberquerque

St. Louis

Memphis

Oklahoma
City

Raleigh

Norfolk

ATLANTIC

Los Angeles
San Diego
Tijuana

Phoenix

Tucson

Ciudad
Juárez

Fort
Worth

Dallas

Baton
Rouge

Atlanta

Columbus

Tallahassee

Bermuda
(UK)

Hermosillo

Chihuahua

Gulf of California

R. Grande

Colorado

Houston

Corpus Christi

New
Orleans

St. Petersburg

Orlando

Tampa

OCEAN

M E X I C O

Durango

Mazatlán

Monterrey

Ciudad Victoria

Tampico

Gulf of
Mexico

Bay of
Campeche

Miami

Havana

Nassau

CUBA

Tropic of Cancer

Revilla Gigedo Is.
(Mex.)

Guadalajara

Mexico City

Popocatepetl
5465

Veracruz

Acápulco

Campeche

Mérida

Cienfuegos

Camaguey

Port-au-
Prince

HAITI

JAMAICA

Kingston

DOMINICAN
REPUBLIC

Santo Domingo

20°N

Greater

Antilles

ST. KITTS
AND NEVIS

DOMINICA

BELIZE

Belmopan

GUATEMALA

HONDURAS

Guatemala City

Tegucigalpa

San Salvador

NICARAGUA

Managua

Caribbean

Sea

ST. VINCENT
& THE GRENADINES

TRINIDAD &
TOBAGO

EL SALVADOR

COSTA RICA

San José

PANAMA

Panama City

Cartegena

Maracaibo

Caracas

VENEZUELA

10°N

Medellin

Montería

S. Cristóbal

Guiana
Highlands

Orinoco

Buenaventura

Bogotá

Cali

COLOMBIA

Galapagos Is.
(Ecuador)

Esmeraldas

Quito

ECUADOR

Pico da
Neblina
3014

Equator

Cuenca

Iquitos

Amazon

Piura

Chiclayo

Trujillo

Selvas

B R A Z I L

Marquesas Is.
(Fr.)

Tuamotu Arch.

Lima

Ica

PERU

La Paz

Oruro

BOLIVIA

10°S

Society Islands
(Fr.)

French
Polynesia

Gambier Is.
(Fr.)

Pitcairn Is.
(UK)

Arica

Sucre

Potosí

ok Is.
(NZ)

Tubuai Is.
(Fr.)

Easter I.
(Chile)

Antofagasta

Gran

Chaco

Tropic of Capricorn

Salta

20°S

Catamarca

S O U T H   P A C I F I C

Juan Fernández Is.
(Chile)

Córdoba

Aconcagua
6960

Valparaíso
Santiago

Bahia
Blanca

CHILE

30°S

ARGENTINA

Concepción

O C E A N

Puerto Montt

Comodoro
Rivadavia

40°S

Equatorial Scale 1:82 600 000

0   500   1000   1500 miles

0   500   1000   1500   2000   2500 kms

50°S

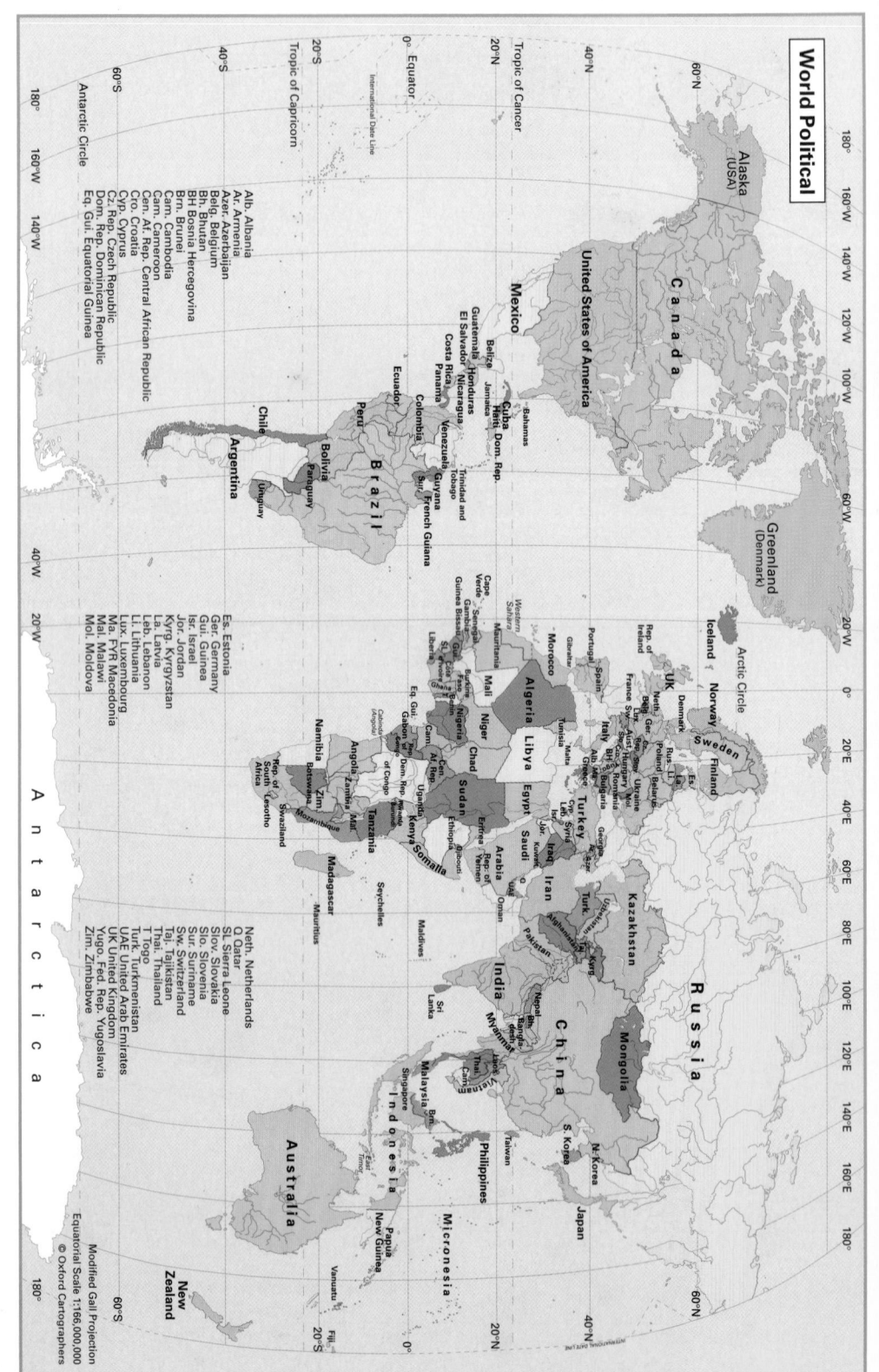

World Political

Alaska
(USA)

United States of America

C a n a d a

Greenland
(Denmark)

Iceland

Arctic Circle

Norway

Sweden

Finland

UK

Rep. of
Ireland

Mexico

Belize
Guatemala
El Salvador
Costa Rica
Panama

Honduras
Nicaragua

Cuba
Haiti Dom. Rep.
Jamaica

Bahamas

Portugal Spain

France

Denmark

Neth.
Belg. Ger.

Sw.

Aust. Hungary

Poland Belarus

Ukraine

Italy
Mal. Greece

Alb. Mac.

Bulgaria

Romania

Mol.

R u s s i a

Ecuador

Colombia

Venezuela

Guyana
Sur. French Guiana
Trinidad and
Tobago

Gibraltar

Morocco

Tunisia

Malta

Cro. Syria

Turkey

Georgia

Azer.

Kazakhstan

Mongolia

Peru

B r a z i l

Cape
Verde

Western
Sahara

Mauritania

Mali

Algeria

Libya

Egypt

Leb.
Isr.
Jor. Kuwait

Iraq

Cyp.

Iran

Turk.

Uzbekistan

Kyrg.

N. Korea

Bolivia

Chile

Argentina

Paraguay

Uruguay

Senegal
Gambia
Guinea Bissau
Gui.
SL
Liberia

Burkina
Faso

Ghana
Togo

Niger

Nigeria

Cam.

Chad

Sudan

Cen.
Af. Rep.

Eritrea

Rep. of
Yemen

Saudi
Arabia

Oman

Pakistan

Afghanistan

India

C h i n a

S. Korea

Japan

Eq. Gui.

Cabinda
(Angola)

Gabon Congo

Dem. Rep.
of Congo

Uganda

Rwanda
Burundi

Kenya

Ethiopia

Djibouti

Somalia

Nepal
Bh.
Bangla-
desh

Myanmar

Taiwan

Namibia

Angola

Zambia

Mal.

Tanzania

Seychelles

Sri
Lanka

Laos

Thai.
Cam.

Vietnam

Botswana

Zim.

Rep. of
South
Africa

Swaziland

Lesotho

Mozambique

Madagascar

Maldives

Mauritius

Malaysia

Brn.

Singapore

I n d o n e s i a

Philippines

M i c r o n e s i a

Papua
New Guinea

A u s t r a l i a

Vanuatu

Fiji

New
Zealand

East
Timor

A n t a r c t i c a

180°   160°W   140°W   120°W   100°W   80°W   60°W   40°W   20°W   0°   20°E   40°E   60°E   80°E   100°E   120°E   140°E   160°E   180°

60°N

40°N

Tropic of Cancer
20°N

0° Equator

20°S
Tropic of Capricorn

40°S

60°S

Antarctic Circle

International Date Line

Alb. Albania
Ar. Armenia
Azer. Azerbaijan
Belg. Belgium
Bh. Bhutan
BH Bosnia Hercegovina
Brn. Brunei
Cam. Cambodia
Cam. Cameroon
Cen. Af. Rep. Central African Republic
Cro. Croatia
Cyp. Cyprus
Cz. Rep. Czech Republic
Dom. Rep. Dominican Republic
Eq. Gui. Equatorial Guinea

Es. Estonia
Ger. Germany
Gui. Guinea
Isr. Israel
Jor. Jordan
Kyrg. Kyrgyzstan
La. Latvia
Leb. Lebanon
Li. Lithuania
Lit. Lithuania
Lux. Luxembourg
Mac. FYR Macedonia
Mal. Malawi
Mol. Moldova

Neth. Netherlands
Q. Qatar
SL Sierra Leone
Slo. Slovenia
Slov. Slovakia
Sur. Suriname
Sw. Switzerland
Taj. Tajikistan
Thai. Thailand
Togo
Turk. Turkmenistan
UAE United Arab Emirates
UK United Kingdom
Yugo. Fed. Rep. Yugoslavia
Zim. Zimbabwe

Modified Gall Projection
Equatorial Scale 1:166,000,000
© Oxford Cartographers

INTERNATIONAL DATE LINE

Russia; total track length is 1,928 km. All trade barriers were abolished in May 1997. In October 1997, the Mongolian Assistance Group pledged US$250 million in aid for 1998.

GNP – US$998 million (1997); US$390 per capita (1997)
GDP – US$957 million (1995); US$388 per capita (1995)
ANNUAL AVERAGE GROWTH OF GDP – 2.6 per cent (1996)
INFLATION RATE – 44.6 per cent (1997)
TOTAL EXTERNAL DEBT – US$718 million (1997)

TRADE

Foreign trade was formerly dominated by the Soviet Union and other Eastern bloc countries. Following the collapse of the COMECON trading system, trade with Western countries, Japan and South Korea is increasing. Since January 1991, trade has been in hard currency, causing particular strain. The principal exports are animal by-products (especially wool, hides and furs) and cattle.

In 1995 there was a trade surplus of US$25 million and a current account surplus of US$39 million. In 1996 imports totalled US$439 million and exports US$423 million.

Trade with UK	1997	1998
Imports from UK	£3,872,000	£2,594,000
Exports to UK	9,847,000	4,938,000

MOROCCO
Al-Mamlaka Al-Maghrebia

AREA – 172,414 sq. miles (446,550 sq. km). Neighbours: Algeria (east and south-east), Western Sahara (south-west)

POPULATION – 27,623,000 (1994 UN estimate). Arabic is the official language. Berber is the vernacular, mainly in the mountain regions. French and Spanish are also spoken, mainly in the towns. Islam is the state religion

CAPITAL – ΨRabat (population, 1,220,000, 1993 estimate)

MAJOR CITIES – ΨAgadir (923,000); ΨCasablanca (3,100,000); Fez (554,000); Marrakesh (878,000); Meknès (614,000); Oujda (430,000), 1997 estimates

CURRENCY – Dirham (DH) of 100 centimes

NATIONAL DAY – 3 March (Anniversary of the Throne)

NATIONAL FLAG – Red, with green pentagram (the Seal of Solomon)

LIFE EXPECTANCY (years) – male 61.58; female 65.00

POPULATION GROWTH RATE – 1.8 per cent (1997)

POPULATION DENSITY – 62 per sq. km (1996)

URBAN POPULATION – 52.1 per cent (1996)

Morocco is traversed in the north by the Rif mountains and, in a south-west to north-east direction, by the Middle Atlas, the High Atlas, the Anti-Atlas and the Sarrho ranges. Much of the country is desert. The north-westerly point of Morocco is the peninsula of Tangier dominated by the Jebel Mousa which, with the rocky eminence of Gibraltar, was known to the ancients as the Pillars of Hercules, the western gateway of the Mediterranean.

HISTORY AND POLITICS

Morocco became an independent sovereign state in 1956, following joint declarations made with France on 2 March 1956 and with Spain on 7 April 1956. The Sultan of Morocco, Sidi Mohammad ben Youssef, adopted the title of King Mohammad V.

Elections were held on 14 November 1997 to the new House of Representatives; no party won an overall majority, but Abderrahmane El Youssoufi was appointed prime

minister as the leader of the Socialist Union of Popular Forces, the largest party in the House of Representatives. On 5 December 1997, elections to the Chamber of Councillors were held. The pro-government *Wifaq* bloc and centre parties won 166 seats; the opposition *Koutla* bloc won 44 seats.

POLITICAL SYSTEM

The King nominates the prime minister and, on the latter's recommendation, appoints the members of the Council of Ministers. The government is responsible both to parliament and to the King. There is a bicameral legislature. The Chamber of Representatives (*Majlis an-Nuwab*) has 325 members elected by universal suffrage using a first-past-the-post system. The Chamber of Councillors (*Majlis al-Mustashareen*) has 270 members, 60 per cent of whom are elected by local councils, 20 per cent by employers' associations and 20 per cent by trade unions. One third of its members are elected every three years.

HEAD OF STATE
HM The King of Morocco, King Mohamed VI (Sidi Mohamed Ben Hassan), *born* 21 August 1963 *acceded* 23 July 1999

COUNCIL OF MINISTERS *as at August 1999*
Prime Minister, Abderrahmane El Youssoufi
Agriculture, Development, Maritime Fishing, Habib Malki
Communications, Larbi Messari
Country Planning, Environment, Town Planning, Housing, Mohamed El Yazghi
Cultural Affairs, Mohamed Achaari
Economy and Finance, Fathallah Oualalou
Energy and Mining, Youssef Tahiri
Equipment, Bouamar Tighouane
Foreign Affairs and Co-operation, Mohamed Ben Aissa
General Secretary of the Government, Abdessadek Rabii
Health, Abdelouahed El Fassi
Higher Education, Executive Training, Scientific Research, Najib Zerouali
Human Rights, Mohamed Aoujar
Industry, Commerce and Handicrafts, Alami Tazi
Justice, Omar Azziman
Minister of State for the Interior, Driss Basri
National Education, Ismail Alaoui
Public Sector and Privatization, Rachid Filali
Public Service and Administrative Development, Aziz Hocine
Relations with Parliament, Mohamed Bouzoubaa
Social Development, Solidarity, Employment, Vocational Training, Government Spokesman, Khalid Alioua
Tourism, Hassan Sebbar
Transport and Merchant Navy, Mustapha Mansouri
Waqf and Islamic Affairs, Abdelkebir M'Daghri Alaoui
Youth and Sports, Ahmed Moussaoui

EMBASSY OF THE KINGDOM OF MOROCCO
49 Queen's Gate Gardens, London SW7 5NE
Tel 0171-581 5001/4
Ambassador Extraordinary and Plenipotentiary, HE Khalil Haddaoui, apptd 1991

BRITISH EMBASSY
17 Boulevard de la Tour Hassan (BP 45), Rabat
Tel: Rabat 720905/6
Ambassador Extraordinary and Plenipotentiary, HE Anthony Layden, apptd 1999
CONSULATE-GENERAL – Casablanca
CONSULATES - Agadir, Marrakesh, Tangier

BRITISH COUNCIL DIRECTOR, P. Wingate-Saul, BP 427, 36 rue de Tanger, Rabat

BRITISH CHAMBER OF COMMERCE, 1st Floor, 185 Boulevard Zerktouni, Casablanca. Tel: 256920

DEFENCE

The Army has 524 main battle tanks, 100 light tanks, 115 armoured infantry fighting vehicles, 785 armoured personnel carriers, and 190 artillery pieces.

The Navy has one frigate and 27 patrol and coastal combatant vessels at five bases. The Air Force has 89 combat aircraft and 24 armed helicopters.

The UN has some 363 personnel in Western Sahara pending the referendum (*see* below). Polisario deploys 3,000–6,000 troops in Western Sahara with Algerian-supplied and captured Moroccan tanks, armoured personnel carriers, anti-tank and anti-aircraft weapons.

MILITARY EXPENDITURE – 4.2 per cent of GDP (1997)
MILITARY PERSONNEL – 238,300: Army 175,000, Navy 7,800, Air Force 13,500, Paramilitaries 42,000
CONSCRIPTION DURATION – 18 months

ECONOMY

Morocco's main sources of wealth are agricultural and mineral. The latest development plan (1987 onwards) emphasizes social improvement, industrial development, agriculture, fisheries and tourism. Economic reform has also been implemented to reduce debt and inflation. A large-scale privatization programme has attracted substantial foreign investment.

Agriculture contributes roughly four-fifths of GDP. The main agricultural exports are fruit and vegetables, with cereals and sugar beet produced and sheep reared for domestic consumption. Cork and wood pulp are the most important commercial forest products. Esparto grass is also produced. There is a fishing industry and substantial quantities of canned fish are exported.

For a developing country Morocco has a large industrial sector. The main sectors are chemicals, textiles and leather goods, food processing and cement production. Manufacturing industries are centred in Casablanca, Fez, Tangier and Safi.

Morocco's mineral exports are phosphates, fluorite, barite, manganese, iron ore, lead, zinc, cobalt, copper and antimony. Morocco possesses nearly three-quarters of the world's estimated reserves of phosphates. There are oil refineries at Mohammedia and Sidi Kacem handling about four million tonnes of crude oil a year.

Tourism is of increasing importance to the economy, with development concentrated in Agadir and Marrakesh. In 1994, 2,293,744 foreign tourists visited Morocco. Workers' remittances, US$1,959 million in 1993, are also important to the economy.

GNP – US$34,380 million (1997); US$1,260 per capita (1997)
GDP – US$33,561 million (1995); US$1,265 per capita (1995)
ANNUAL AVERAGE GROWTH OF GDP – minus 2.0 per cent (1996)
INFLATION RATE – 0.9 per cent (1997)
UNEMPLOYMENT – 16.0 per cent (1992)
TOTAL EXTERNAL DEBT – US$19,321 million (1997)

TRADE

The main imports are petroleum products, motor vehicles, building materials, agricultural and other machinery, chemical products, sugar, green tea and other foodstuffs. The EU, with which an association agreement was signed in November 1995, is Morocco's largest trading partner and in May 1998 awarded Morocco grants totalling US$98 million. The main exports are textiles, phosphates and

phosphoric acid, fertilizers, citrus fruits, and fish and seafoods.

In 1996 Morocco had a trade deficit of US$2,111 million and a current account deficit of US$627 million. In 1997 imports totalled US$9,525 million and exports US$7,030 million.

Trade with UK	1997	1998
Imports from UK	£356,677,000	£353,572,000
Exports to UK	346,992,000	637,237,000

COMMUNICATIONS

Railroads cover 1,907 km, linking the major towns. There are 60,449 km of roads; an extensive network of 30,374 km of surfaced roads covers all the main towns. There are air services between Casablanca, Tangier, Agadir (seasonal), Marrakesh and London, and also between Tangier and Gibraltar connecting with London. Royal Air Maroc is the national airline.

EDUCATION

Education is compulsory between the ages of seven and 16. There are government primary, secondary and technical schools. In 1991 there were 4,890 government schools. At Fez there is a theological university of great repute in the Muslim world. There is a secular university at Rabat. Schools for special denominations, Jewish and Catholic, are permitted and may receive government grants. American schools operate in Rabat and Casablanca. There is an English-language university in Ifrane.

ILLITERACY RATE – 56.3 per cent
ENROLMENT (percentage of age group) – primary 72 per cent (1996); secondary 20 per cent (1980); tertiary 11.1 per cent (1994)

WESTERN SAHARA

Formerly the Spanish Sahara, the territory was split between Morocco and Mauritania in 1976 after Spain withdrew in December 1975. In 1976 the Polisario Front (Frente Popular para la Liberación de Saguia y Río de Oro) declared Western Sahara to be an independent state, the Sahrawi Arab Democratic Republic, and formed a government which remains in exile. The Polisario Front has been recognized as the legitimate government of Western Sahara by over 70 states and the Organization of African Unity. In 1979 Mauritania renounced its claim to its share of the territory, which was added by Morocco to its area.

In 1988, Morocco and the Polisario Front accepted a UN peace plan under which a cease-fire came into effect in September 1991. A referendum to determine the future of the area was to have been held in January 1992 but has not yet taken place because the Moroccan government and Polisario have not agreed on the referendum terms or voter eligibility. Voter identification began in August 1994 but the failure to agree on eligibility prompted the UN to threaten the suspension of the UN Mission for the Referendum in Western Sahara (MINURSO), which had been deployed since 1991. The date for the referendum on the future of Western Sahara has now been set for March 2000, with MINURSO responsible for identifying voters.

Legislative elections to the National Assembly were held in 1995; President Mohamed Abdelaziz, who had been elected president since 1982 by the party congress of the Polisario Front, was re-elected by the National Assembly in 1995. Following a vote of no confidence in the previous incumbent, Bouchraya Hamoudi Bayoun was named prime minister on 10 February 1999.

MOZAMBIQUE
República de Moçambique

AREA – 309,496 sq. miles (799,380 sq. km). Neighbours: Swaziland (south), South Africa (south and west), Zimbabwe (west), Zambia and Malawi (north-west), Tanzania (north)
POPULATION – 16,916,600 (1998 census). The official language is Portuguese
CAPITAL – ΨMaputo (population, 1,039,700, 1998 census)
MAJOR CITIES – ΨBeira (264,202); ΨNacala (182,505), 1986 estimates
CURRENCY – Metical (MT) of 100 centavos
NATIONAL DAY – 25 June (Independence Day)
NATIONAL FLAG – Horizontally green, black, yellow with white fimbriations; a red triangle based on the hoist containing the national emblem
LIFE EXPECTANCY (years) – male 44.88; female 48.01
POPULATION GROWTH RATE – 2.3 per cent (1997)
POPULATION DENSITY – 22 per sq. km (1996)
MILITARY EXPENDITURE – 3.9 per cent of GDP (1997)
MILITARY PERSONNEL – 6,100: Army 5,000, Navy 100, Air Force 1,000
CONSCRIPTION DURATION – Two to three years
ILLITERACY RATE – 59.9 per cent
ENROLMENT (percentage of age group) – primary 40 per cent (1995); secondary 6 per cent (1995); tertiary 0.4 per cent (1995)

HISTORY AND POLITICS

Mozambique, discovered by Vasco da Gama in 1498 and colonized by Portugal, achieved independence on 25 June 1975. It was a Marxist one-party (Frelimo) state until a multiparty system was adopted in 1990. The legislative assembly has 250 members.

Following two years of negotiations, the Frelimo government and the rebel Mozambican National Resistance (Renamo) signed a peace agreement in October 1992 which ended 16 years of civil war. Under the peace agreement, demobilization of government and Renamo troops was due to begin within one month of parliamentary ratification of the peace accord (which occurred on 9 October 1992) although the belated arrival of the UN Operation for Mozambique (ONUMOZ) delayed demobilization until 1994.

Presidential and legislative elections were held on 27–29 October 1994. The incumbent, Joaquim Chissano of Frelimo, won the presidential election in the first round with 53 per cent of the vote. Frelimo also won the legislative election, gaining 129 seats to Renamo's 112 seats and the Democratic Union's 9 seats. Mozambique was admitted to the Commonwealth on 12 November 1995 as a special case, because of its close links with Commonwealth countries.

HEAD OF STATE
President, Joaquim Alberto Chissano, *sworn in* November 1986, *elected* 29 October 1994

COUNCIL OF MINISTERS *as at July 1999*
Prime Minister, Pascoal Mocumbi
Agriculture and Fisheries, Carlos Rosario
Culture, Youth and Sports, Mateus Kathupa
Education, Arnaldo Nhavoto
Environmental Action Co-ordination, Bernardo Ferraz
Foreign Affairs and Co-operation, Leonardo Simão
Health, Aurelio Zihao

Industry, Trade and Tourism, Oldemiro Baloi
Justice, José Abudo
Labour, Guilherme Mavila
Mineral Resources and Energy, John Katchamila
Ministers in the President's Office, Almerino da Cruz Manhenje (*Defence, Security Affairs and Interior*); Eneias da Conceiçao Comiche (*Economic and Social Affairs*); Francisco Madeira (*Parliamentary Affairs*); Isaac Murargy (*Secretary-General*)
National Defence, Aguiar Real Mazula
Planning and Finance, Tomas Salomao
Public Construction and Housing, Roberto White
Secretary-General of the Council of Ministers, Carlos Taju
Social Co-ordination, Acucena Duarte
State Administration, Alfredo Gamito
Transport and Communications, Paulo Muxanga

HIGH COMMISSION FOR THE REPUBLIC OF MOZAMBIQUE
21 Fitzroy Square, London WIP 5HJ
Tel 0171–383 3800
High Commissioner, HE Dr Eduardo José Baciao Koloma, apptd 1996

BRITISH HIGH COMMISSION
Av. Vladimir I Lenine 310, CP 55, Maputo
Tel: Maputo 420111/2/5/6/7
High Commissioner, HE Bernard J. Everett, apptd 1996

BRITISH COUNCIL DIRECTOR, P. Woods, PO Box 4178, Maputo

ECONOMY

The basis of the economy is subsistence agriculture, but there is an industrial sector based mainly in Beira and Maputo. There are substantial coal deposits in Tete province and an offshore gas field at Pande. Economic subsidies have been removed and an IMF reform programme is being implemented. The economy is still heavily dependent on aid. A five-year plan has been launched with the priorities of rural development, education, health and land reform.
GNP – US$2,405 million (1997); US$140 per capita (1997)
GDP – US$1,326 million (1995); US$77 per capita (1995)
ANNUAL AVERAGE GROWTH OF GDP – 2.0 per cent (1995)
INFLATION RATE – 5.5 per cent (1997)
TOTAL EXTERNAL DEBT – US$5,991 million (1997)

TRADE

The main exports are shellfish, cotton, sugar, cashew nuts, copra, tea and sisal. Mozambique's main trading partners are South Africa, Portugal, Spain and Japan.

In 1996 Mozambique had a trade deficit of US$478 million and a current account deficit of US$359 million. In 1995 imports totalled US$784 million and exports US$168 million.

Trade with UK	1997	1998
Imports from UK	£14,183,000	£10,968,000
Exports to UK	3,350,000	3,675,000

MYANMAR
Pyidaungsu Myanmar Naingngandaw – Union of Myanmar

AREA – 261,228 sq. miles (676,578 sq. km). Neighbours: Bangladesh (west), India (north-west), China (north-east), Laos and Thailand (east)

POPULATION – 45,922,000 (1994 UN estimate).The indigenous inhabitants are of similar racial types and speak languages of the Tibeto-Burman, Mon-Khmer and Thai groups. The three significant non-indigenous elements are Indians, Chinese and those from Bangladesh. Burmese is the official language, but minority languages include Bamar, Chin, Kachin, Kayah, Kayin (Karen), Mon, Rakhine and Shan. English is spoken in educated circles. Buddhism is the religion of 89.5 per cent of the people, with 4.9 per cent Christians , 3.8 per cent Muslims, 1.3 per cent Animists and 0.05 per cent Hindus

CAPITAL – ΨYangon (Rangoon) (population, 2,513,023, 1983)

MAJOR CITIES – Mandalay (532,949); Mawlamyine/Moulmein (219,961); Pathein/Bassein (144,096)

CURRENCY – Kyat (K) of 100 pyas

NATIONAL DAY – 4 January

NATIONAL FLAG – Red, with a canton of dark blue, inside which are a cogwheel and two rice ears surrounded by 14 white stars

LIFE EXPECTANCY (years) – male 57.89; female 63.14

POPULATION GROWTH RATE – 1.1 per cent (1997)

POPULATION DENSITY – 68 per sq. km (1996)

HISTORY AND POLITICS

The Union of Burma (the name was officially changed to the Union of Myanmar in 1989) became an independent republic outside the British Commonwealth on 4 January 1948 and remained a parliamentary democracy for 14 years. In 1962 the army took power, suspended the parliamentary constitution and instituted a socialist state.

After months of popular demonstrations and a series of presidents during 1988, Gen. Saw Maung, leader of the armed forces, assumed power in September 1988. The People's Assembly, the Council of State and the Council of Ministers were abolished and replaced by the State Law and Order Restoration Council (SLORC). The constitution was effectively abrogated.

A People's Assembly Election Law was published in 1989 and multiparty elections were held on 27 May 1990, resulting in a majority for the National League for Democracy (NLD) even though its leader Aung San Suu Kyi had been under house arrest since July 1989. The SLORC refused to transfer power to a civilian government and large numbers of NLD MPs and supporters were detained or fled to Thailand where an exile government was set up. However, following the replacement of Saw Maung by Than Shwe as SLORC chairman and prime minister in April 1992, the government began a dialogue with some elements of the opposition. A Constitutional Convention appointed by the SLORC to discuss a future constitution convened in January 1993 and has continued fitfully since, but with minimal progress. The SLORC released Aung San Suu Kyi (who won the Nobel Peace Prize in 1991) on 10 July 1995, although on several occasions subsequently she has been forcibly prevented from attending political meetings by government troops. Many other opposition figures remain in detention or under house arrest. In November 1997, the SLORC was renamed the State Peace and Development Council (SPDC).

The SPDC detained several hundred NLD members in September 1998 to thwart the NLD's plan to convene a 'People's Parliament' representing the assembly which would have resulted from the 1990 general election; most were released in October and November. Instead, the NLD set up an interim representation committee to act on behalf of the 'People's Parliament', which declared all laws and orders issued by the military government since the general election to be invalid.

Myanmar is comprised of seven states (Chin, Kachin, Kayin (Karen), Kayah, Mon, Rakhine, Shan) and seven divisions (Ayeyarwady (Irrawaddy), Magway (Magwe), Mandalay, Bago (Pegu), Yangon (Rangoon), Sagaing, Tanintharyi (Tenasserim)).

INSURGENCIES

Since independence in 1948 the government has fought various armed insurgent groups, the largest of which were derived from the Kachin, Kayin (Karen), Karenni, and Wa ethnic groups but the Shan, Mon, Arakan and Chin ethnic minorities have also formed armed groups.

Since 1992, as a result of government offensives, 15 ethnic groups have signed cease-fire agreements with the government, including the Kachin Independence Army, the Karenni National People's Liberation Front and the Shan State Liberation Organization in 1994, and Mon rebels in July 1995. In 1995–6, government forces launched successful offensives against the Kayin (Karen) National Union, the Karenni National Progressive Party and the Mong Tai army, whose leader, the drugs warlord Khun Sa, surrendered in January 1996. It was reported in May 1999 that 300,000 Shan had been forced out of their villages into resettlement camps close to army bases and that thousands more had fled to Thailand.

STATE PEACE AND DEVELOPMENT COUNCIL *as at July 1999*

Chairman, Senior Gen. Than Shwe
Vice-Chairman, Gen. Maung Aye
Members, Rear-Adml Nyunt Thein; Maj.-Gen. Kyaw Than; Maj.-Gen. Aung Htwe; Maj.-Gen. Ye Myint; Maj.-Gen. Khin Maung Than; Maj.-Gen. Kyaw Win; Maj.-Gen. Thein Sein; Maj.-Gen. Thura Thiha Thura Sit Maung; Brig.-Gen. Thura Shwe Mahn; Brig.-Gen. Myint Aung; Brig.-Gen. Maung Bo; Brig.-Gen. Thiha Thura Tin Aung Myint Oo; Brig.-Gen. Soe Win; Brig.-Gen. Tin Aye
Secretaries, Lt.-Gen. Khin Nyunt; Lt.-Gen. Tin Oo; Lt.-Gen. Win Myint

CABINET *as at July 1999*

Prime Minister, Defence, Senior Gen. Than Shwe
Deputy PMs, Vice-Adm. Maung Maung Khin (*Myanmar Investment Commission*); Lt. -Gen. Tin Hla (*Military Affairs*); Lt.-Gen. Tin Tun
Agriculture and Irrigation, Maj.-Gen. Nyunt Tin
Commerce, Maj.-Gen. Kyaw Than
Construction, Maj.-Gen. Saw Tun
Co-operatives, U Aung San
Culture, U Win Sein
Education, U Than Aung
Electric Power, Maj.-Gen. Tin Htut
Energy, Brig.-Gen. Lun Thi
Finance and Revenue, U Khin Maung Thein
Foreign Affairs, U Win Aung
Forestry, U Aung Phone
Health, Maj.-Gen. Ket Sein
Home Affairs, Col. Tin Hlaing
Hotels and Tourism, Maj.-Gen. Saw Lwin
Immigration and Population, U Saw Tun
Industry, U Aung Thaung; Maj.-Gen. Saw Lwin
Information, Maj.-Gen. Kyi Aung
Labour, Maj.-Gen. Tin Ngwe
Livestock Breeding and Fisheries, Brig.-Gen. Maung Maung Thein

Mines, Brig.-Gen. Ohn Myint
Ministers in the Office of the SPDC Chairman, Lt.-Gen. Min
Thein; Brig.-Gen. Maung Maung; Brig.-Gen. David
Abel
National Planning and Economic Development, U Soe Tha
Prime Minister's Office, Brig.-Gen. Lun Maung; U Than
Shwe; Lt.-Gen. Tin Ngwe
Progress of Border Area and National Races, Development Affairs,
Col. Thein Nyunt
Rail Transport, U Pan Aung
Religious Affairs, Maj.-Gen. Sein Htwa
Science and Technology, U Thaung
Social Welfare, Relief and Resettlement, Brig.-Gen. Pyi Sone
Sports, Col. Sein Win
Telecommunications, Posts and Telegraphs, Brig.-Gen. Win Tin
Transport, Maj.-Gen. Hla Myint Swe

EMBASSY OF THE UNION OF MYANMAR
19A Charles Street, Berkeley Square, London WIX 8ER
Tel 0171-499 8841
Ambassador Extraordinary and Plenipotentiary, Dr Kyaw Win,
apptd 1999

BRITISH EMBASSY
80 Strand Road (Box No. 638), Yangon
Tel: Yangon 295300
Ambassador Extraordinary and Plenipotentiary, HE Dr J
Jenkins, LVO, apptd 1999
Cultural Attaché and British Council Director, C. Henning, OBE

DEFENCE

The Army has some 130 main battle tanks, 270 armoured
personnel carriers and 246 artillery pieces. The Navy has
65 patrol and coastal vessels at six bases.
MILITARY EXPENDITURE – 7.7 per cent of GDP (1997)
MILITARY PERSONNEL – 435,050: Army 325,000, Navy
15,800, Air Force 9,000, Paramilitaries 85,250

ECONOMY

The chief sources of revenue are profits on state trading,
taxes and duties; the chief heads of expenditure are defence,
education and police.
Agriculture remains the main sector of the economy;
measures are being taken to increase productivity, promote
crop diversification and increase agricultural exports.
Three-quarters of the population depend on agriculture;
the chief products are rice, oilseeds (sesame and groundnut),
maize, millet, cotton, beans, wheat, grain, tea, sugar cane,
tobacco, jute and rubber.
Myanmar is rich in minerals, including petroleum, zinc,
nickel, lead, silver, tungsten, wolfram and gemstones.
Production of crude petroleum in 1997 totalled 635,000
tonnes. There are refineries at Chauk, the main oilfield,
Syriam and Mann. Major reserves of natural gas have been
discovered in the Martaban Gulf. Timber production is an
important industry and timber is a major export. Fisheries
produce pearls and oyster shells in addition to significant
quantities of fish.
A new ministry was established in 1992 with the task of
attracting more tourists; less than 10,000 visited in 1991
but visitors and revenues are increasing and in 1995 there
were over 105,000 visitors.
Since 1988, Myanmar has moved from a centrally
planned economy to a market-oriented economy and has
liberalized domestic and external trade, promoted the
development of the private sector and encouraged foreign
investment.
Myanmar is thought to be the world's leading producer
of opium with an estimated annual output of 2,600 tons,
although the government claimed to have destroyed 3,800

hectares of opium poppies between November 1998 and
March 1999.
In July 1997, Myanmar became a member of ASEAN.
In 1997 the EU stripped Myanmar of trading privileges
and the USA imposed economic sanctions.
In 1997 imports totalled US$2,261 million and exports
US$866 million.
GDP – US$108,199 million (1995); US$2,399 per capita
(1995)
ANNUAL AVERAGE GROWTH OF GDP – 5.7 per cent
(1996)
INFLATION RATE – 29.7 per cent (1997)
TOTAL EXTERNAL DEBT – US$5,074 million (1997)

Trade with UK	1997	1998
Imports from UK	£15,363,000	£12,571,000
Exports to UK	19,450,000	17,278,000

COMMUNICATIONS

The Irrawaddy and its chief tributary, the Chindwin, are
important waterways, the main stream being navigable 900
miles from its mouth and carrying much traffic. The chief
seaports are Yangon (Rangoon), Mawlamyine (Moulmein),
Akyab (Sittwe) and Pathein (Bassein).
The railway network covers 3,955 km, extending to
Myitkyina on the Upper Irrawaddy. There are 2,452 miles
of highways and 14,318 miles of other main roads. The
airport at Mingaladon, about 13 miles north of Yangon
(Rangoon), handles limited international air traffic.

EDUCATION

Most children attend primary school, and about six million
are currently enrolled; in middle and high schools,
enrolment is about two million. There are universities at
Yangon (Rangoon), Mandalay, Taunggyi, Sagaing and
Mawlamyine (Moulmein). Under the universities are three
affiliated degree colleges and the Workers' College, Yangon.
Vocational training is provided at 17 teachers' training
institutes and schools, 11 technical institutes, 17 technical
high schools, 17 agricultural institutes and schools, and 41
vocational schools.
ILLITERACY RATE – 16.9 per cent
ENROLMENT (percentage of age group) – tertiary 5.4 per
cent (1994)

NAMIBIA

The Republic of Namibia

AREA – 318,261 sq. miles (824,292 sq. km). Neighbours:
Angola (north), South Africa (south), Botswana (east),
Zambia and Zimbabwe (north-east)
POPULATION – 1,575,000 (1994 UN estimate). The main
population groups are: Ovambo (587,000), Kavango
(110,000), Damara (89,000), Herero (89,000), whites
(78,000), Nama (57,000), coloured (48,000), Caprivians
(44,000), Bushmen (34,000), Rehoboth Baster (29,000),
Tswana (7,000). English is the official language, with
Afrikaans, German and local languages also in use
CAPITAL – Windhoek (population, 147,056, 1995)
MAJOR TOWNS – Ondangwa (33,000); Oshakati (37,000);
Rehoboth (21,500); Swakopmund (18,000); Walvis Bay
(50,000), 1995
CURRENCY – Namibian dollar of 100 cents at parity to
South African rand
NATIONAL DAY – 21 March (Independence Day)
NATIONAL FLAG – Divided diagonally blue, red and
green with the red fimbriated in white; a gold twelve-
rayed sun in the upper hoist

LIFE EXPECTANCY (years) – male 57.50; female 60.00
POPULATION GROWTH RATE – 2.6 per cent (1997)
POPULATION DENSITY – 2 per sq. km (1996)
URBAN POPULATION – 27.1 per cent (1991)
MILITARY EXPENDITURE – 3.5 per cent of GDP (1997)
MILITARY PERSONNEL – 9,100: Army 9,000, Coast
Guard 100
ENROLMENT (percentage of age group) – primary 91 per
cent (1996); secondary 36 per cent (1996); tertiary 8.1
per cent (1995)

HISTORY AND POLITICS

The German protectorate of South West Africa from 1884
to 1915, Namibia was administered until the end of 1920
by the Union of South Africa. Under the terms of the
Treaty of Versailles, the territory was entrusted to South
Africa with full powers of administration and legislation
over the territory. After the dissolution of the League of
Nations and in the absence of a trusteeship agreement,
South Africa informed the UN that it would continue to
administer South West Africa. The UN terminated South
Africa's mandate in 1967.

An administrator-general was appointed in 1977 to
govern the territory until independence; he began repealing
all legislation based on racial discrimination. Elections
were held in 1978 for a Constituent Assembly, which was
dissolved in 1983. A transitional government was installed
in 1985. Elections for 72 seats in Namibia's National
Assembly took place under UN supervision on 7–11
November 1989. The South West Africa People's Organization (SWAPO) won 41 seats. Independence was declared
on 21 March 1990. Namibia joined the Commonwealth on
independence.

Previously a British and South African colony separate
from German South West Africa/Namibia, Walvis Bay
was governed from August 1992 by the joint South African-
Namibian Walvis Bay Administrative Body until 28
February 1994, when South Africa renounced its claim to
sovereignty over the enclave and it became part of Namibia.

Presidential and legislative elections were held on 7–8
December 1994 and won by the incumbent, Sam Nujoma,
and by SWAPO respectively. In the 72-seat National
Assembly SWAPO has 53 seats, the Democratic Turnhalle
Alliance 15 seats, and other parties four seats.

INSURGENCIES

Government officials claimed to have uncovered a plot by
Mishake Muyongo, a former leader of the opposition
Democratic Turnhalle Alliance, and Mishake Boniface
Mamili, a Mafwe chief, to launch a secessionist rebellion
in the Caprivi strip in November 1998. An attempted
uprising on 9 August 1999, believed to have been led by
the Caprivi Liberation Army, was quickly quashed by
government forces.

POLITICAL SYSTEM

Namibia has an executive president as head of state who
exercises the functions of government with the assistance
of a Cabinet headed by a prime minister. The president is
directly elected for a maximum of two five-year terms.
There is a bicameral legislature consisting of the 72-
member National Assembly, elected for a five-year term,
and the National Council, whose 26 members are indirectly
elected by the regional councils from among their own
members. The National Council is elected for a six-year
term, and its main function is to review and consider
legislation from the National Assembly. The constitution
can only be changed by a two-thirds majority in the
National Assembly.

HEAD OF STATE
President, Dr Sam Nujoma, elected 16 February 1990,
re-elected 8 December 1994

CABINET as at July 1999
Prime Minister, Hage Geingob
Deputy PM, Revd Hendrik Witbooi
Agriculture, Water and Rural Development, Helmut Angula
Attorney-General, Vekui Rukoro
Basic Education and Culture, John Mutorwa
Defence, Erikki Nghimtina
Environment and Tourism, Philemon Malima
Finance, Nangolo Mbumba
Fisheries and Marine Resources, Abraham Iyambo
Foreign Affairs, Theo-Ben Gurirab
Health and Social Services, Dr Libertine Amathila
Home Affairs, Jerry Ekandjo
Information and Broadcasting, Ben Amathila
Justice, Ngarikutuke Tjiriange
Labour and Manpower Development, Andimba Toivo ja
Toivo
Lands, Resettlement, Rehabilitation, Pendukeni Ithana
Mines and Energy, Jesaya Nyamu
National Planning Council, Saara Kuugongelwa
Prisons and Correctional Services, Marco Hausiku
Regional and Local Government and Housing, Dr Nick Iyambo
Special Advisers, Gert Hanekom (Economics); Kanana
Hishoono (Political Matters); Peter Tsheehama (Security)
Tertiary Education and Vocational Training, Nahas Angula
Trade and Industry, Hidipo Hamutenya
Without Portfolio, Hifikepunye Pohamba
Women's Affairs, Netumbo Ndaitwah
Works, Transport and Communication, Hampie Plichta
Youth and Sport, Richard Kapelwa-Kabajani

HIGH COMMISSION OF THE REPUBLIC OF NAMIBIA
6 Chandos Street, London WIM OLQ
Tel 0171-636 6244
High Commissioner, HE Monica Ndiliawike Nashandi,
apptd 1999

BRITISH HIGH COMMISSION
116 Robert Mugabe Avenue, PO Box 222022, Windhoek
Tel: Windhoek 223022
High Commissioner, HE Brian Donaldson, apptd 1999

BRITISH COUNCIL REPRESENTATIVE, G. Belben, PO
Box 24224, 74 Bülowstrasse, Windhoek

ECONOMY

Manufacturing contributes around 12 per cent of GDP,
with food production, metals and wooden products the
most important areas. Around 15 per cent of the population
are engaged in agriculture, primarily livestock. Guano is
also exported. Deposits of diamonds along the coast and
offshore along the sea bed are estimated at between 1,500
and 3,000 million carats; Namibia accounts for roughly 8
per cent of world diamond production. Walvis Bay and
Lüderitz are the main ports. There are 41,815 km of roads,
of which 4,572 km are surfaced; there are 2,382 km of
railway track.

In 1995 there was a trade deficit of US$112 million and
a current account surplus of US$31 million. In 1994 imports
totalled US$1,196 million and exports US$1,321 million.
GNP – US$3,428 million (1997); US$2,110 per capita
(1997)
GDP – US$3,162 million (1995); US$2,059 per capita
(1995)
ANNUAL AVERAGE GROWTH OF GDP – 3.0 per cent
(1996)
INFLATION RATE – 8.8 per cent (1997)

Trade with UK	1997	1998
Imports from UK	£4,045,000	£16,103,000
Exports to UK	17,916,000	26,987,000

NAURU
The Republic of Nauru

AREA – 8 sq. miles (21 sq. km)
POPULATION – 11,000 (1994 UN estimate); 8,042 (1983 census): Nauruans 4,964; other Pacific Islanders 2,134; Asians 682; Caucasians 262. About 43 per cent of Nauruans are adherents of the Nauruan Protestant Church and there is a Roman Catholic mission on the island. The main languages are English and Nauruan
CAPITAL – ΨNauru
CURRENCY – Australian dollar ($A) of 100 cents
NATIONAL DAY – 31 January (Independence Day)
NATIONAL FLAG – Twelve-point star (representing the 12 original Nauruan tribes) below a gold bar (representing the Equator), all on a blue ground
POPULATION GROWTH RATE – 1.6 per cent (1996)
POPULATION DENSITY – 524 per sq. km (1996)

HISTORY AND POLITICS

From 1888 until the First World War Nauru was administered by Germany. In 1920 it became a British Empire-mandated territory under the League of Nations, administered by Australia. A trusteeship superseding the mandate was approved in 1947 by the UN and Nauru continued to be administered by Australia until it became independent on 31 January 1968. It was announced in November 1968 that a special form of membership of the Commonwealth had been devised for Nauru at the request of its government. Rene Harris was elected president in April 1999 after his predecessor, Bernard Dowiyogo, lost a vote of confidence.

POLITICAL SYSTEM

Parliament has 18 members including the Cabinet and Speaker. Voting is compulsory for all Nauruans over 20 years of age, except in certain specified instances. Elections are held every three years. The Cabinet is chosen by the president, who is elected by the parliament from amongst its members, and comprises not fewer than five nor more than six members including the president.

A Supreme Court of Nauru is presided over by the Chief Justice. The District Court, which is subordinate to the Supreme Court, is presided over by a Resident Magistrate. Both the Supreme Court and the District Court are courts of record. The Supreme Court exercises both original and appellate jurisdiction.

HEAD OF STATE

President, Public Service, Foreign Affairs, Health, Island Development and Industry, the Nauru Phosphate Royalties Trust and the Republic of Nauru Finance Corporation, Rene Harris, *elected by parliament* 21 April 1999

CABINET *as at July 1999*

Education, Internal Affairs, Remy Namaduk
Finance, Kinza Clodumar
Justice, Civil Aviation, Anthony Audoa
Sports, Youth Affairs, Aloysius Amwano
Tourism, Fisheries, Works, Community Affairs, Godfrey Thoma

BRITISH HIGH COMMISSIONER, HE Michael Dibben, resident at Suva, Fiji

ECONOMY

The only fertile areas are in the narrow coastal belt and local requirements of fruit and vegetables are mostly met by imports. The economy is heavily dependent on the extraction of phosphate, of which the island has one of the world's richest deposits. In 1995, 190,100 tonnes of phosphate rock was exported. Considerable investments have been made abroad with the royalties on phosphate exports to provide for a time when production declines. In 1993 an agreement was signed with Australia for compensation to cover damage caused by phosphate mining during the Australian mandate and trusteeship periods. The compensation package is worth some £50 million (a portion of which will be paid by the UK and New Zealand governments), composed of a £33 million payment and a 20-year package of health and education programmes.

Air Nauru operates air services throughout the Pacific region and to Australia, New Zealand, Japan, Singapore and the Philippines.

GDP – US$368 million (1995); US$33,476 per capita (1995)
ANNUAL AVERAGE GROWTH OF GDP – 7.0 per cent (1995)

Trade with UK	1997	1998
Imports from UK	£1,132,000	£1,251,000
Exports to UK	29,000	90,000

SOCIAL WELFARE

Nauru has a hospital service and other medical and dental services. There is also a maternity and child welfare service.

Education is compulsory between the ages of six and 17. There are 10 infant and primary and two secondary schools on the island with a total enrolment of about 2,707 pupils.

NEPAL

AREA – 56,827 sq. miles (147,181 sq. km). Neighbours: China (north), India (south, west and east)
POPULATION – 21,127,000 (1994 UN estimate). The inhabitants are of mixed stock, with Tibetan characteristics prevailing in the north and Indian in the south. The official religion is Hinduism; 87 per cent of the population are Hindus, 8 per cent Buddhist and 3 per cent Muslim. Gautama Buddha was born in Nepal. The official language is Nepali
CAPITAL – Kathmandu (population, 421,258, 1991)
MAJOR CITIES – Bhadgaon (61,122); Biratnagar (130,129); Patan (117,023), 1991
CURRENCY – Nepalese rupee of 100 paisa
NATIONAL ANTHEM – May Glory Crown Our Illustrious Sovereign
NATIONAL DAYS – 18 February (National Democracy Day); 28 December (The King's Birthday)
NATIONAL FLAG – Double pennant of crimson with blue border on peaks; white moon with rays in centre of top peak; white quarter sun, recumbent in centre of bottom peak
LIFE EXPECTANCY (years) – male 50.88; female 48.10
POPULATION GROWTH RATE – 2.5 per cent (1997)
POPULATION DENSITY – 144 per sq. km (1996)
MILITARY EXPENDITURE – 0.9 per cent of GDP (1997)
MILITARY PERSONNEL – 86,215: Army 46,000, Air Force 215, Paramilitaries 40,000
ILLITERACY RATE – 62.2 per cent
ENROLMENT (percentage of age group) –tertiary 5.2 per cent (1993)

Nepal lies between India and the Tibet Autonomous Region of China on the slopes of the Himalayas, and includes Mount Everest (29,028 ft).

The southern region, the Terai, was covered with jungle but has been more widely cultivated recently. It forms about 23 per cent of the total land area and nearly 44 per cent of the population live there. The central belt is hilly, but with many fertile valleys, leading up to the snowline at about 16,000 feet. The hills account for 42 per cent of the area and about 48 per cent of the population. The remainder of the country, the Himalayan region, consists of high mountains which are sparsely inhabited. The country is drained by three great river systems rising within and beyond the Himalayan mountain ranges and eventually flowing into the Ganges in India.

HISTORY AND POLITICS

Nepal was originally divided into numerous hill clans and petty principalities but emerged as a nation in the middle of the 18th century when it was unified by the warrior Raja of Gorkha, Prithvi Narayan Shah, who founded the present Nepalese dynasty. In 1846 power was seized by Jung Bahadur Rana after a massacre of nobles, and he was the first of a line of hereditary Rana prime ministers who ruled Nepal for 104 years. During this time the role of the monarchs was mainly ceremonial.

In 1950–1 a revolutionary movement broke the hereditary power of the Ranas and restored the monarchy to its former position. After ten years, during which various parties and individuals tried their hand at government, King Mahendra proscribed all political parties and assumed direct powers in 1960, with the object of leading a united country to democracy. In 1962 he introduced a new constitution embodying a tiered, partyless system of panchyat (council) democracy.

Mass agitation for political reform led in April 1990 to the lifting of the ban on political parties and the abolition of the panchyat system. A new constitution was promulgated in November 1990 establishing a multiparty, parliamentary system of government and a constitutional monarchy. Elections in May 1991 were won by the Nepali Congress Party.

In October 1997 the government was brought down by a vote of no confidence and several coalition governments ruled until a general election held on 3 and 17 May 1999 gave an absolute majority to the Nepali Congress Party (NCP) who won 110 seats.

INSURGENCIES

Maoist guerrillas from the Communist Party of Nepal, who are opposed to the monarchy, began an armed rebellion in 1996; they organized a campaign to boycott the general election in May 1999 which involved strikes and attacks on government and industrial targets.

POLITICAL SYSTEM

The King retains joint executive power with the Council of Ministers. The bicameral legislature consists of a 205-member House of Representatives and a 60-member National Council, including ten royal nominees.

HEAD OF STATE

HM *The King of Nepal*, King Birendra Bir Bikram Shah Dev, *born* 28 December 1945; *succeeded* 31 January 1972; *crowned* 24 February 1975; *married* February 1970, HM Queen Aishwatya Rajya Laxmi Devi Shah

Heir, HRH Crown Prince Dipendra Bir Bikram Shah Dev, *born* 27 June 1971

CABINET *as at May 1999*

Prime Minister, Royal Palace Affairs, Home Affairs, Foreign Affairs, Defence, Women, Social Welfare, Krishna Prasad Bhattarai
Agriculture, Chakra Prasad Bastola
Education, Yog Prasad Upadhyaya
Finance, Mahesh Acharya
Forest and Soil Conservation, Mahanta Thakur
General Administration, Labour, Bal Bahadur Kesi
Health, Ram Baran Yadav
Housing and Physical Planning, Local Development, Khum Bahadur Khadka
Information and Communication, Industry, Purna Bahadur Khadka
Land Reforms and Management, Commerce, Chiranjibi Wagle
Law and Justice, Parliamentary Affairs, Tara Nath Ranabhat
Population and Environment, Works and Transport, Science and Technology, Omkar Shrestha
Supplies, Prakash Man Singh
Tourism and Civil Aviation, Bijaya Kumar Gachhadar
Water Resources, Govinda Raj Joshi
Youth, Sports and Culture, Sarat Singh Bhandari

ROYAL NEPALESE EMBASSY
12A Kensington Palace Gardens, London W8 4QU
Tel 0171–229 1594/6231
Ambassador Extraordinary and Plenipotentiary, HE Dr Singha B. Basnyat, apptd 1997

BRITISH EMBASSY
Lainchaur Kathmandu, PO Box 106
Tel: Kathmandu 410583
Ambassador Extraordinary and Plenipotentiary, HE R. P. Nash, LVO, apptd 1999

BRITISH COUNCIL REPRESENTATIVE, B. Wickham, (PO Box 640), Kantipath, Kathmandu

ECONOMY

Over 80 per cent of the population are dependent on agriculture. Nepal exports jute, handicrafts, carpets, hides and skins, medicinal herbs, cardamom, potatoes, tea, etc., and imports textiles, machinery and parts, transport equipment, medicine, petroleum products etc. Tourism is the single largest commercial earner of foreign exchange. Nepal's main trading partners are India, Germany and the USA.

In 1997 Nepal had a trade deficit of US$1,308 million and a current account deficit of US$418 million. In 1996 imports totalled US$1,442 million and exports US$385 million.

GNP – US$4,863 million (1997); US$220 per capita (1997)

GDP – US$4,351 million (1995); US$203 per capita (1995)

ANNUAL AVERAGE GROWTH OF GDP – 3.9 per cent (1997)

INFLATION RATE – 2.9 per cent (1997)

TOTAL EXTERNAL DEBT – US$2,398 million (1997)

Trade with UK	1997	1998
Imports from UK	£8,676,000	£8,745,000
Exports to UK	5,127,000	4,211,000

COMMUNICATIONS

The total length of roads is 9,933 km, of which 3,421 km are paved. Kathmandu is connected by road with India and Tibet. Internally, the road network links Kathmandu to Kodari and Pokhara, and Pokhara to Sunauli. There are 155 km of railway track.

Royal Nepal Airlines operates an extensive network of domestic flights, and there are international flights to Europe, the Middle East and throughout Asia. There is an international airport at Kathmandu.

Telecommunication services, both domestic and international, are available. Television was introduced in 1984.

THE NETHERLANDS
Koninkrijk der Nederlanden

AREA – 15,770 sq. miles (40,844 sq. km). Neighbours: Belgium (south), Germany (east)

POPULATION – 15,517,000 (1996): 36 per cent Catholic, 27 per cent Reformed Church, 8 per cent Muslim. The language is Dutch, a West Germanic language of Frankish origin closely akin to Old English and Low German. It is spoken in the Netherlands and the northern part of Belgium (Flanders). Frisian is spoken in Friesland. Dutch is the official language in the Netherlands Antilles and Aruba; Papiamento, a mixture of Dutch and Spanish, is the vernacular

CAPITAL – ΨAmsterdam (population, 1,101,629, 1995 estimate)

SEAT OF GOVERNMENT – The Hague (Den Haag or, in full, 's-Gravenhage), population 694,572, 1995 estimate

MAJOR CITIES – Eindhoven (396,986); Groningen (210,101); Haarlem (211,885); ΨRotterdam (1,077,813); Tilburg (238,301); Utrecht (547,767), 1995 estimates

CURRENCY – Gulden (guilder) or florin of 100 cents

NATIONAL ANTHEM – Wilhelmus

NATIONAL FLAG – Three horizontal bands of red, white and blue

LIFE EXPECTANCY (years) – male 74.21; female 80.20

POPULATION GROWTH RATE – 0.6 per cent (1997)

POPULATION DENSITY – 374 per sq. km (1996)

URBAN POPULATION – 60.9 per cent (1995)

The Kingdom of the Netherlands is a maritime country of western Europe, situated on the North Sea, consisting of 12 provinces (Eastern and Southern Flevoland being amalgamated to form the twelfth province). The land is generally flat and low, intersected by numerous canals and connecting rivers. The principal rivers are the Rhine, Maas, IJssel and Schelde.

HISTORY AND POLITICS

The country was fragmented until the 16th century when, led by William (the Silent) of Orange, the Low Countries fought the Eighty Years' War (1568–1648) against Spanish rule. The Union of Utrecht (1579) united the northern provinces and in 1581 independence was declared. Dutch economic and military power flourished in the 17th and 18th centuries but the country also came into conflict with Britain and France.

In 1688 William III of Orange acceded to the English throne, reigning jointly with his wife Mary, following the abdication and flight of James II, Mary's father. The Netherlands was overrun by French Revolutionary troops in the late 18th century, becoming part of the French Empire until 1814. In 1830 the southern provinces seceded to form Belgium. The Duchy of Luxembourg was made an independent state in 1867.

The Netherlands remained neutral during the First World War but were invaded by Germany during the Second World War and occupied until the war ended. The Netherlands joined the Benelux economic union with Belgium and Luxembourg in 1948 and became a member

of NATO in 1949. Most of the former Dutch colonies gained independence as Indonesia in 1949.

The most recent election to the Second Chamber was held on 6 May 1998 and resulted in a centre-left coalition of the Labour Party, People's Party for Freedom and Democracy, and Democrats 66. The state of the parties as at May 1998 was: Labour Party (PvdA) 45; People's Party for Freedom and Democracy (VVD) 38; Christian Democratic Appeal (CDA) 29; Democrats 66 (D66) 14; Green Left 11; others 13.

POLITICAL SYSTEM

The States-General consists of the *Eerste Kamer* (First Chamber) of 75 members, elected for four years by the Provincial Council; and the *Tweede Kamer* (Second Chamber) of 150 members, elected for four years by voters of 18 years and upwards. Members of the *Tweede Kamer* are paid.

HEAD OF STATE

HM The Queen of the Netherlands, Queen Beatrix Wilhelmina Armgard, KG, GCVO, *born* 31 January 1938; *succeeded* 30 April 1980, upon the abdication of her mother Queen Juliana; *married* 10 March 1966, HRH Prince Claus George Willem Otto Frederik Geert of the Netherlands, Jonkheer van Amsberg; and has *issue*, Prince Willem (*see* below); Prince Johan Friso, *b.* 25 September 1968; Prince Constantijn Christof, *b.* 11 October 1969

Heir, HRH Prince Willem Alexander, *b.* 27 April 1967

CABINET *as at July 1999*

Prime Minister, Wim Kok (PvdA)

Deputy PM, Economic Affairs, Annemarie Jorritsma (VVD)

Deputy PM, Health, Welfare and Sport, Dr Els Borst (D66)

Agriculture, Nature Management and Fisheries, Laurens Jan Brinkhorst (D66)

Defence, Frank de Grave (VVD)

Development Co-operation, Evelien Herfkens (PvdA)

Education, Cultural Affairs and Science, Loek Hermans (VVD)

Finance, Gerrit Zalm (VVD)

Foreign Affairs, Jozias van Aartsen (VVD)

Housing, Spatial Planning and Environment, Jan Pronk (PvdA)

Interior and Kingdom Relations, Dr Bram Peper (PvdA)
Justice, Benk Korthals (VVD)
Major Cities and Integration Policy, Roger van Boxtel
Social Affairs and Employment, Klaas de Vries (PvdA)
Transport and Public Works and Water Management, Tineke
   Netelenbos (PvdA)

VVD People's Party for Freedom and Democracy;
D66 Democrats 66; PvdA Labour Party

ROYAL NETHERLANDS EMBASSY
38 Hyde Park Gate, London SW7 5DP
Tel 0171–590 3200
Ambassador Extraordinary and Plenipotentiary, HE Baron
   Willem Oswald Bentinck van Schoonheten, apptd 1999
Ministers Plenipotentiary, G. C. M. van Pallandt; R. Brouwer
   (*Economic*)
Consul-General, P. W. A. Bas Backer
Defence, Naval and Air Attaché, Capt. W. T. Lansink

BRITISH EMBASSY
Lange Voorhout 10, The Hague, NL-2514 ED
Tel: The Hague 427 0427
Ambassador Extraordinary and Plenipotentiary, HE Rosemary
   Spencer, CMG, apptd 1996
Counsellors, T. C. Holmes (*Deputy Head of Mission*);
   C. Bradley (*Commercial and Consul-General*)
Defence and Naval Attaché, Capt. R. St J. S. Bishop, RN

CONSULATE-GENERAL – Amsterdam
CONSULATE – Willemstad (Curaçao); Vice-Consulate –
   Philipsburg (St Maarten) (both Netherlands Antilles)

BRITISH COUNCIL DIRECTOR, T. Butchard,
   Keizersgracht 269, NL-1016 ED Amsterdam

NETHERLANDS-BRITISH CHAMBER OF COMMERCE,
   The Dutch House, 307–308 High Holborn, London
   WC1V 7LS

UK OFFICE IN THE HAGUE, Holland Trade House,
   Bezuidenhoutseweg 181, NL-2594 AH The Hague

DEFENCE

The Army has 600 main battle tanks, 383 armoured infantry
fighting vehicles, 269 armoured personnel carriers, and 439
artillery pieces. The Navy has four submarines, four
destroyers, 12 frigates, 13 combat aircraft and 22 armed
helicopters. The Air Force has 170 combat aircraft and 42
armed helicopters.
MILITARY EXPENDITURE – 1.9 per cent of GDP (1997)
MILITARY PERSONNEL – 56,380: Army 27,000, Navy
   13,800, Air Force 11,980, Paramilitaries 3,600
CONSCRIPTION DURATION – abolished in August 1996

ECONOMY

The chief agricultural products are potatoes, wheat, rye,
barley, sugar beet, cattle, poultry, pigs, dairy products,
vegetables, fruit, flower bulbs, plants and cut flowers and
there is an important fishing industry.
   Among the principal industries are engineering, electronics, nuclear energy, petrochemicals and plastics, road
vehicles, aircraft and defence equipment, shipbuilding
repair, steel, textiles of all types, electrical appliances,
metal ware, furniture, paper, cigars, sugar, liqueurs, beer,
clothing etc.
GNP – US$403,057 million (1997); US$25,830 per capita
   (1997)
GDP – US$396,881 million (1995); US$25,635 per capita
   (1995)
ANNUAL AVERAGE GROWTH OF GDP – 3.7 per cent
   (1997)
INFLATION RATE – 2.2 per cent (1997)
UNEMPLOYMENT – 7.1 per cent (1995)

TRADE

The Dutch are traditionally a trading nation. Trade,
banking and shipping are of particular importance to the
economy. The geographical position of the Netherlands,
at the mouths of the Rhine, Maas and Schelde, brings a
large volume of transit trade to and from the interior of
Europe to Dutch ports. Principal trading partners are
Germany, Belgium/Luxembourg, the UK and France.
   In 1997 the Netherlands had a trade surplus of US$17,752
million and a current account surplus of US$21,242 million.
Imports totalled US$177,373 million and exports
US$194,008 million.

Trade with UK	1997	1998
Imports from UK	£13,157,000,000	£12,237,700,000
Exports to UK	11,794,600,000	12,858,800,000

COMMUNICATIONS

There are 58,133 km of inter-urban roads, of which 2,207
km are motorways. The total extent of navigable rivers
including canals is 5,046 km. The total length of the railway
system is 2,739 km, of which 1,991 km are electrified. The
mercantile marine in 1996 consisted of 379 ships of total
2,795,000 gross registered tons.
   There are 64 daily newspapers.

EDUCATION

Primary and secondary education is given in both
denominational and state schools and is compulsory.
   The principal universities are at Leiden, Utrecht,
Groningen, Amsterdam (two), Nijmegen, Maastricht and
Rotterdam, and there are technical universities at Delft,
Eindhoven, Enschede and Wageningen (agriculture).
ENROLMENT (percentage of age group) – primary 99 per
   cent (1995); secondary 91 per cent (1995); tertiary 48.6
   per cent (1995)

OVERSEAS TERRITORIES

ARUBA

AREA – 75 sq. miles (193 sq. km)
POPULATION – 87,000 (1996)
CAPITAL – ΨOranjestad (population 25,000); and Sint
   Nicolaas (17,000)
CURRENCY – Aruban florin

The island of Aruba was from 1828 part of the Dutch West
Indies and from 1845 part of the Netherlands Antilles. On
1 January 1986 it became a separate territory within the
Kingdom of the Netherlands. The 1983 Constitutional
Conference agreed that Aruba's separate status would last
for ten years from 1986, after which the island would
become fully independent. In 1994 this decision was
changed and it was decided that Aruba will retain its
separate status within the Kingdom of the Netherlands.

Governor, Olindo Koolman
Prime Minister, J. H. Eman

Trade with UK	1997	1998
Imports from UK	£59,094,000	£56,033,000
Exports to UK	306,000	682,000

NETHERLANDS ANTILLES

AREA – 309 sq. miles (800 sq. km)
POPULATION – 207,333 (1995), Curaçao 151,448, Bonaire
   14,218, St Martin 38,567, St Eustatius 1,900, Saba 1,200
CAPITAL – ΨWillemstad (on Curaçao) (pop. 50,000)
CURRENCY – Netherlands Antilles guilder of 100 cents

The Netherlands Antilles comprise the islands of Curaçao, Bonaire, part of St Martin, St Eustatius, and Saba in the West Indies. The Netherlands Antilles, which have a 22-member federal parliament, are largely self-governing under the terms of the Realm Statute which took effect in 1954.

Governor, Dr Jaime Saleh
Prime Minister, S. F. Camelia-Römer

Trade with UK	1997	1998
Imports from UK	£19,579,000	£25,697,000
Exports to UK	4,557,000	3,047,000
*Curaçao		

NEW ZEALAND

AREA – 104,454 sq. miles (270,534 sq. km)
POPULATION – 3,681,546 (1996): 79 per cent European stock, 13 per cent Maori, 5 per cent other Pacific Islanders. The main religion is Christianity. In 1991 the principal denominations were Anglican 22.1 per cent, Presbyterian 16.3 per cent, Roman Catholic 15 per cent, Methodist 4.2 per cent, Baptist 2.1 per cent. The official languages are English and Maori

Islands	Area (sq. miles)	Population (census 1996)
North Island	44,281	2,749,788
South Island	58,093	930,824
Other islands	1,362	934
Total	103,736	3,681,546
Territories		
Tokelau	5	1,487
Niue	100	1,708 (a)
Cook Islands	93	18,008
Ross Dependency	175,000	—

(a) 1997 estimate

CAPITAL – ΨWellington (population, 326,900, 1992 estimate)
MAJOR CITIES – ΨAuckland (929,300); ΨChristchurch (318,100); ΨDunedin (112,400); Hamilton (153,800); Ψ Napier-Hastings (110,200)
CURRENCY – New Zealand dollar (NZ$) of 100 cents
NATIONAL ANTHEM – God Save The Queen/God Defend New Zealand
NATIONAL DAY – 6 February (Waitangi Day)
NATIONAL FLAG – Blue ground, with Union Flag in top left quarter, four five-pointed red stars with white borders on the fly
LIFE EXPECTANCY (years) – male 72.86; female 78.74
POPULATION GROWTH RATE – 1.6 per cent (1997)
POPULATION DENSITY – 13 per sq. km (1996)
URBAN POPULATION – 84.9 per cent (1991)

New Zealand consists of a number of islands in the South Pacific Ocean, and also has administrative responsibility for the Ross Dependency in Antarctica. The two larger islands, North Island and South Island, are separated by a relatively narrow strait. The remaining islands are much smaller and widely dispersed.

Much of the North and South Islands is mountainous. The principal range is the Southern Alps, extending the entire length of the South Island and having its culminating

point in Mount Cook/Mount Aoraki (12,349 ft). The North Island mountains include several volcanoes, two of which are active. Of the numerous glaciers in the South Island, the Tasman (18 miles long by 1¼ wide), the Franz Josef and the Fox are the best known. The more important rivers include the Waikato (270 miles in length), Wanganui (180), and Clutha (210) and lakes include Taupo, 234 sq. miles in area; Wakatipu, 113; and Te Anau, 133.

New Zealand includes, in addition to North and South Islands: Chatham Islands (Chatham, Pitt, South East Islands and some rocky islets, combined area, 965 sq. km (373 sq. miles), largely uninhabited; Stewart Island (area 1,746 sq. km (674 sq. miles), largely uninhabited); the Kermadec Group (Raoul or Sunday, Macauley, Curtis Islands, L'Esperance, and some islets; population 9–10, all government employees at a meteorological station); Campbell Island, used as a weather station; the Three Kings (discovered by Tasman on the Feast of the Epiphany); Auckland Islands; Antipodes Group; Bounty Islands; Snares Islands and Solander.

New Zealand has a temperate marine climate, but with abundant sunshine. The mean temperature ranges from 15°C in the north to about 9°C in the south. Rainfall in the North Island ranges from 35 to 70 inches and in the South Island from 25 to 45 inches.

HISTORY AND POLITICS

The discoverers and first colonists of New Zealand were Polynesian people, ancestors of the modern-day Maori. The ninth century is generally considered to be the date of the first settlement; by the 13th or 14th century there were well-established settlements. The first European to discover New Zealand was a Dutch navigator, Abel Tasman, who sighted the coast in 1642 but did not land. It was the British explorer James Cook who circumnavigated New Zealand and landed in 1769. Largely as a result of increased British emigration, the country was annexed by the British government in 1840. The British Lieutenant-Governor, William Hobson, proclaimed sovereignty over the North Island by virtue of the Treaty of Waitangi, signed by him and many Maori chiefs, and over the South Island and Stewart Island by right of discovery.

In 1841 New Zealand was created a separate colony distinct from New South Wales. In 1907 the designation was changed to 'The Dominion of New Zealand'. The constitution rests upon the Constitution Act 1852 and other imperial statutes. A 1986 Constitution Act brought a number of statutory constitutional provisions. The Statute of Westminster was formally adopted by New Zealand in 1947.

Following the general election of 12 October 1996, the state of the parties in the House of Representatives was: National Party (NP) 44 seats, Labour 37, New Zealand First (NZF) 17, The Alliance 13, Association of Consumers and Tax Payers (ACT) 8, United Party 1. The National Party and New Zealand First formed a coalition government. Jim Bolger stepped down as prime minister on 8 December 1997 and was replaced by Jenny Shipley, who became New Zealand's first female prime minister.

POLITICAL SYSTEM

The executive authority is entrusted to a Governor-General appointed by the Crown and aided by an Executive Council, within a unicameral legislature, the House of Representatives. The House of Representatives consists of 120 members elected for three-year terms. 55 members are elected by the first-past-the-post system and 60 by proportional representation on a party list basis. There are five Maori electorates.

The judicial system comprises a High Court, a Court of Appeal and district courts having both civil and criminal jurisdiction.

GOVERNOR-GENERAL

Governor-General and Commander-in-Chief, HE Sir Michael Hardie Boys, KCMG, *sworn in* March 1996

THE EXECUTIVE COUNCIL *as at July 1999*

The Governor-General
Prime Minister, New Zealand Security Intelligence Service, Jenny Shipley (NP)
Deputy PM, Health, Wyatt Creech (NP)
Accident Rehabilitation and Compensation Insurance, Sport, Fitness and Leisure, Associate Minister of Immigration, Murray McCully (NP)
Agriculture and Forestry, Fisheries, Land Information, Customs Service, Associate Minister for Immigration and International Trade, John Luxton (NP)
Attorney-General, Treaty of Waitangi Negotiations, Sir Douglas Graham (NP)
Business Development, Consumer Affairs, Associate Minister of Social Services, Work and Income, Peter McCardle
Courts, Women's Affairs, Associate Minister of Health and Treaty of Waitangi Negotiations, Georgina te Heuheu
Cultural Affairs, Associate Minister for Accident Rehabilitation and Compensation Insurance, Environment and Radio New Zealand, Marie Hasler
Education, Conservation, Nick Smith (NP)
Enterprise and Commerce, Defence, Tertiary Education, Max Bradford (NP)
Finance, Revenue, Bill English (NP)
Foreign Affairs and Trade, Disarmament and Arms Control, War Pensions, Don McKinnon (NP)
Immigration, Pacific Island Affairs, Public Trust Office, Associate Minister of Finance and Health, Tuariki John Delamere
Internal Affairs, Civil Defence, Associate Minister of Local Government, Jack Elder
International Trade, Contact Energy Ltd, Tourism, Associate Minister of Finance, Lockwood Smith (NP)
Justice, State-owned Enterprises, Housing, Youth Affairs, Tony Ryall
Maori Affairs, Associate Minister of Education and Corrections, Tau Henare
Police, Corrections, Racing, Audit Affairs, Clem Simich
Senior Citizens, Associate Minister of Revenue and Food, Fibre, Biosecurity and Border Control, David Carter
Social Services, Work and Income, Leader of the House, Roger Sowry (NP)
State Services, Environment, Crown Research Institutes, Associate Minister of Foreign Affairs and Trade, Simon Upton (NP)
Transport, Research, Science and Technology, Communications, Local Government, Statistics, Information Technology, Associate Minister of State Services, Maurice Williamson (NP)
Treasurer, Bill Birch (NP)

NEW ZEALAND HIGH COMMISSION
New Zealand House, Haymarket, London SW1Y 4TQ
Tel 0171-930 8422
High Commissioner, HE Paul Clayton East, QC, apptd 1999
Deputy High Commissioner, C. J. Seed
Minister, J. Waugh (*Commercial*)
Head, Defence Staff, Brig. R. Ottaway, MBE

BRITISH HIGH COMMISSION
44 Hill Street (PO Box 1812), Wellington 1
Tel: Wellington 472 6049

High Commissioner, HE Martin Williams, CVO, OBE, apptd 1998
Deputy High Commissioner, C. H. Salvesen
Defence Adviser, Capt. D. A. Wines, RN
First Secretary, M. A. Capes (*Commercial*)
Consul-General and Director of Trade Promotion, T. N. Byrne; resident at Auckland
CONSULATE-GENERAL – Auckland
CONSULATE – Christchurch

BRITISH COUNCIL DIRECTOR, M. Willson (Acting)

BRITISH CHAMBER OF COMMERCE FOR AUSTRALIA AND NEW ZEALAND, PO Box 141, Manuka, ACT 2603, Australia; UK OFFICE, Suite 615, 6th Floor, The Linen Hall, 162–168 Regent Street, London WIR 5TB

DEFENCE

The Army has 78 armoured personnel carriers and 43 artillery pieces. The Navy has three frigates, four patrol and coastal vessels and four armed helicopters. The Air Force has 42 combat aircraft.
MILITARY EXPENDITURE – 1.6 per cent of GDP (1997)
MILITARY PERSONNEL – 9,550: Army 4,400, Navy 2,100, Air Force 3,050

ECONOMY

Finance market and labour market deregulation, privatization, VAT reform, the introduction of private sector principles in the civil service, health service and education, the ending of agricultural subsidies and the near elimination of import tariffs have all occurred. The Reserve Bank has been made independent, with a contract to keep inflation below 2 per cent. Agricultural production is dominated by cattle- and sheep-rearing, for meat, wool, dairy products and other by-products, such as skins, leather, etc.

Non-metallic minerals such as coal, clay, limestone and dolomite are more important than metallic ones. Coal output in 1997 was 3,664,034 tonnes. Of the metals, the most important are gold and ironsand. Natural gas deposits in the offshore Taranaki Maui field and onshore fields are increasingly being exploited and used for electricity generation and as a premium fuel. Energy use is dominated by oil (46 per cent), electricity (26 per cent), coal and gas (9 per cent each).

Manufacturing is based on food processing, machinery production, motor vehicle assembly, chemicals, electrical and electronic goods, and paper and printing. Tourism is the fastest growing sector of the economy, with 1,441,828 visitors in 1996.

In 1997 New Zealand had a trade surplus of US$387 million and a current account deficit of US$5,206 million. Imports totalled US$14,519 million and exports US$14,071 million.
GNP – US$59,539 million (1997); US$15,830 per capita (1997)
GDP – US$60,060 million (1995); US$16,866 per capita (1995)
ANNUAL AVERAGE GROWTH OF GDP – 2.9 per cent (1996)
INFLATION RATE – 1.2 per cent (1997)
UNEMPLOYMENT – 6.3 per cent (1995)

TRADE

New Zealand's largest trading partners are Australia, Japan, USA and the UK. Main exports include dairy products, meat, timber and metal and metal products. Imports include machinery, petroleum and petroleum products, plastics and motor vehicles.

Trade with UK	1997	1998
Imports from UK	£407,550,000	£348,078,000
Exports to UK	577,803,000	542,427,000

*Includes Niue, Tokelau and Cook Islands

COMMUNICATIONS

The national railway system is owned and operated by the privately-owned Tranz Rail Ltd. There are 4,439 km of railway track .

In December 1995 there were 2,977 ships registered in New Zealand (gross tonnage 482,180).

There are international airports at Auckland, Christchurch and Wellington. Air New Zealand is the national carrier.

There are 91,864 km of maintained roads.

EDUCATION

Schools are free and attendance is compulsory between the ages of six and 15. There are 2,240 state and 61 private primary schools and 320 state secondary schools. There are seven universities and 25 polytechnics.

ENROLMENT (percentage of age group) – primary 100 per cent (1996); secondary 97 per cent (1996); tertiary 58.5 per cent (1996)

TERRITORIES

TOKELAU (OR UNION ISLANDS)

Tokelau is a group of atolls, Fakaofo, Nukunonu and Atafu. It was proclaimed part of New Zealand as from 1 January 1949. A Council of Faipule, composed of one elected representative from each atoll, was established in August 1992 to govern Tokelau when the council of elders (General Fono) was not in session. The position of *Ulu-o-Tokelau* (leader) was also established in 1992 and is rotated among the three Faipule members annually. Administrative responsibility for Tokelau lies with the Administrator but in January 1994 his powers were delegated to the General Fono and Council of Faipule. The Tokelau Amendment Act, passed by the New Zealand Parliament in 1996, conferred legislative power on the General Fono. New Zealand provides substantial aid (NZ$5.0 million in year ended 30 June 1994).

Administrator, Lindsay Watt
Ulu-o-Tokelau (1998), Kuresa Nasau

THE ROSS DEPENDENCY

The Ross Dependency, placed under the jurisdiction of New Zealand in 1923, is defined as all the Antarctic islands and territories between 160° E. and 150° W. longitude which are situated south of the 60° S. parallel, including Edward VII Land and portions of Victoria Land. Since 1957 a number of research stations have been established in the Dependency.

ASSOCIATED STATES

COOK ISLANDS

Included in the realm of New Zealand since June 1901, the Cook Islands group consists of the islands of Rarotonga, Aitutaki, Mangaia, Atiu, Mauke, Mitiaro, Manuae, Takutea, Palmerston, Penrhyn or Tongareva, Manihiki, Rakahanga, Suwarrow, Pukapuka or Danger, and Nassau.

Queen Elizabeth II has a representative on the islands, as does the New Zealand government. Since 1965 the islands have been in free association with New Zealand

and enjoyed complete internal self-government, executive power being in the hands of a Cabinet consisting of a prime minister and eight other ministers. There is a 25-member Legislative Assembly. New Zealand has an obligation to assist with foreign affairs and defence if requested. The New Zealand citizenship of the Cook Islanders is embodied in the constitution.

HM Representative, Apenera Short, OBE
Prime Minister, Sir Geoffrey Henry, KBE
New Zealand High Commissioner, Rob Moore-Jones

NIUE

A New Zealand High Commissioner is stationed at Niue, which since 1974 has been self-governing in free association with New Zealand. New Zealand is responsible for external affairs and defence, and continues to give financial aid. Executive power is in the hands of a premier and a Cabinet of three drawn from the Assembly of 20 members. The Assembly is the supreme legislative body.

New Zealand High Commissioner, Michael Pointer

NICARAGUA
República de Nicaragua

AREA – 50,193 sq. miles (130,668 sq. km). Neighbours: Honduras (north), Costa Rica (south)

POPULATION – 4,663,000 (1997 estimate): three-quarters are of mixed blood, another 15 per cent are white, mostly of pure Spanish descent, and the remaining 10 per cent are West Indians or Indians. The latter group includes the Misquitos, who live on the Atlantic coast. The official language is Spanish and the majority are Roman Catholic, although the English language and the Moravian Church are widespread on the Atlantic coast

CAPITAL – Managua (population, 608,020, 1979 estimate)

MAJOR CITIES – Chinandega (144,291); Granada (72,640); León (158,577); Masaya (78,308)

CURRENCY – Córdoba (C$) of 100 centavos

NATIONAL ANTHEM – Salve A Tí Nicaragua (Hail, Nicaragua)

NATIONAL DAY – 15 September

NATIONAL FLAG – Horizontal stripes of blue, white and blue, with the Nicaraguan coat of arms in the centre of the white stripe

LIFE EXPECTANCY (years) – male 64.80; female 67.71

POPULATION GROWTH RATE – 2.9 per cent (1997)

POPULATION DENSITY – 33 per sq. km (1996)

URBAN POPULATION – 63.3 per cent (1995)

ILLITERACY RATE – 34.3 per cent

ENROLMENT (percentage of age group) – primary 83 per cent (1995); secondary 27 per cent (1993); tertiary 11.9 per cent (1995)

HISTORY AND POLITICS

Spanish colonization of Nicaragua began in 1523. Independence was secured in 1838, but the country was subject to frequent American intervention. In 1927 Augusto Cesar Sandino began a guerrilla war against the occupation of Nicaragua by US Marines, which continued until they were expelled in 1933. Sandino was assassinated by Anastasio Somoza, director of the National Guard, and in 1936 Somoza assumed the presidency. He was succeeded by his sons Luis and Anastasio Somoza, until 1979 when the government was overthrown by guerrillas of the Sandinista National Liberation Front (FSLN).

After ten years in power and a ten-year civil war against US-backed Contra guerrillas, the Sandinistas lost their parliamentary majority in elections held in February 1990. A coalition of former opposition parties, the Unión Nacional de Opositora (UNO), formed a government, with UNO leader Violeta Chamorro as president. With the defeat of the Sandinistas, the civil war came to an end.

President Chamorro and the UNO were forced to compromise with the Sandinistas, who controlled the trade unions, and to leave the armed forces and police under Sandinista control. In December 1992 UNO deputies tried to oust Chamorro from power. Chamorro ordered the police to seize the National Assembly and negotiated a new governing majority in the National Assembly of 39 Sandinistas and nine loyal UNO deputies. A further 19 UNO deputies formed the Democratic Christian Union (UDC) in January 1994, which joined the governing coalition. The Liberal Alliance won the legislative election in October 1996 although the Nationalist Liberal Party left the Alliance in May 1997.

POLITICAL SYSTEM

The head of government is the president, elected for a five-year term, not immediately renewable. The president appoints the Cabinet. There is a unicameral legislature, the National Assembly, with 90 members elected for a six-year term.

HEAD OF STATE

President, Arnoldo Alemán Lacayo *sworn in* 10 January 1997
Vice-President, Enrique Bolanos

CABINET *as at July 1999*

Agriculture and Livestock, Mario de Franco
Attorney-General, Julio Centeno Gómez
Construction and Transport, Edgard Quintana
Defence, Pedro Joaquin Chamorro
Development, Trade and Industry, Noel Sacasa
Education, Dr José Antonio Alvarado
Environment and Natural Resources, Roberto Stadhagen
Finance, Estebán Duque-Estrada
Foreign Affairs, Eduardo Montealegre
Foreign Co-operation, David Robleto Lang
Health, Lombardo Martinez Cabezas
Labour, Wilfredo Navarro Moreira
Social Action, Jamilet Bonilla
Tourism, Lorenzo Guerrero

EMBASSY OF NICARAGUA

Suite 31, Vicarage House, 58-60 Kensington Church Street, London W8 4DB.
Tel: 0171-938 2373
Ambassador Extraordinary and Plenipotentiary, HE Nora Campos de Lankes, apptd 1998

BRITISH EMBASSY

PO Box A-169, Plaza Churchill, Reparto 'Los Robles', Managua
Tel: Managua 780014
Ambassador and Consul-General, HE Roy Osbourne, apptd 1997

DEFENCE

The Army has 127 main battle tanks, 166 armoured personnel carriers and 142 artillery pieces. The Navy has 13 patrol and coastal vessels at three bases. The Air Force has 15 armed helicopters.
MILITARY EXPENDITURE – 1.4 per cent of GDP (1997)

MILITARY PERSONNEL – 17,000: Army 15,000, Navy 800, Air Force 1,200
CONSCRIPTION DURATION – 18–36 months

ECONOMY

The country is mainly agricultural. The major crops are maize, sugar cane, rice, sorghum, beans, bananas and coffee; livestock and timber production are also important. Nicaragua possesses deposits of gold and silver. There were 358,400 tourists in 1997.

In 1997 there was a trade deficit of US$742 million and a current account deficit of US$671 million. Imports totalled US$1,211 million and exports US$629 million.
GNP – US$1,907 million (1997); US$410 per capita (1997)
GDP – US$1,912 million (1995); US$464 per capita (1995)
ANNUAL AVERAGE GROWTH OF GDP – 5.0 per cent (1997)
INFLATION RATE – 11.6 per cent (1996)
UNEMPLOYMENT – 14.0 per cent (1991)
TOTAL EXTERNAL DEBT – US$5,677 million (1997)

TRADE

Considerable quantities of foodstuffs are imported as well as cotton goods, jute, iron and steel, machinery and petroleum products. The chief exports are cotton, coffee, beef and sugar.

Trade with UK	1997	1998
Imports from UK	£3,834,000	£5,740,000
Exports to UK	12,688,000	6,201,000

COMMUNICATIONS

The Inter-American Highway runs between the Honduras and the Costa Rican borders; the inter-oceanic highway runs from Corinto on the Pacific coast via Managua to Rama, where there is a natural waterway to Bluefields on the Atlantic; there are 15,478 km of roads. The main airport is at Managua. The chief port is Corinto on the Pacific. There are 252 miles of railway, all on the Pacific side of the country. There are 51 radio stations and seven television stations in Managua. An automatic telephone system has been installed in major cities.

There are four daily newspapers published at Managua, apart from the official Gazette (*La Gaceta*). There are 5,251 primary schools, 203,962 secondary schools and five universities.

NIGER
République du Niger

AREA – 489,191 sq. miles (1,267,000 sq. km). Neighbours: Algeria and Libya (north), Chad (east), Nigeria and Benin (south), Mali and Burkina Faso (west). Apart from a small region along the Niger Valley in the south-west near the capital, the country is entirely savannah or desert
POPULATION – 9,465,000 (1994 UN estimate): Hausa (54 per cent) in the south, Songhai and Djerma in the south-west, Fulani, Beriberi–Manga, and nomadic Tuareg in the north. 95 per cent of the population are Muslims, with Christian and Animist minorities. The official language is French. Hausa, Djerma and Fulani are also spoken
CAPITAL – Niamey (population, 392,169, 1988 census)
CURRENCY – Franc CFA of 100 centimes

NATIONAL DAY – 18 December
NATIONAL FLAG – Three horizontal stripes, orange, white and green with an orange disc in the middle of the white stripe
LIFE EXPECTANCY (years) – male 44.90; female 48.14
POPULATION GROWTH RATE – 3.4 per cent (1997)
POPULATION DENSITY – 7 per sq. km (1996)
URBAN POPULATION – 15.3 per cent (1988)
MILITARY EXPENDITURE – 1.4 per cent of GDP (1997)
MILITARY PERSONNEL – 10,700: Army 5,200, Air Force 100, Paramilitaries 5,400
CONSCRIPTION DURATION – Two years
ILLITERACY RATE – 86.4 per cent
ENROLMENT (percentage of age group) – primary 24 per cent (1996); secondary 6 per cent (1996); tertiary 0.7 per cent (1990)

HISTORY AND POLITICS

The first French expedition arrived in 1891 and the country was fully occupied by 1914. It decided on 18 December 1958 to remain an autonomous republic within the French Community; full independence outside the Community was proclaimed on 3 August 1960.

In 1974 Lt.-Col. Seyni Kountché seized power and set up a Supreme Military Council with himself as president. President Kountché died in 1987 and was succeeded by his cousin, Col. Ali Saibou. Legislative elections were held in February 1993. The Alliance of Forces for Change (AFC) formed the government. Mahamane Ousmane of the AFC won the presidential election in March.

The defection of one of the main AFC parties from the government in late 1994 led to a parliamentary election in January 1995 which was won by the National Movement for a Development Society (MNSD) and allied parties. The president and government were overthrown in a military coup led by Col. Ibrahim Barre Mainassara on 27 January 1996. Power was assumed by a National Salvation Council, which suspended the constitution, appointed a civilian Cabinet and created a transitional legislature until presidential and parliamentary elections could be held. A new constitution was promulgated on 12 May 1996 and the ban on political parties was lifted. Brig.-Gen. Mainassara was elected president on 8 July 1996. The pro-Mainassara National Union of Independents for Democratic Renewal won the largest number of seats in legislative elections in November 1996, though these were boycotted by main opposition groups. On 24 November 1997, President Mainassara dismissed the government led by Prime Minister Amadou Boubacar Cisse on grounds of incompetence, and appointed a new government under Ibrahim Hassane Mayaki. President Mainassara was assassinated on 9 April 1999. On 11 April Major Daouda Mallam Wanke, head of the presidential guard unit responsible for the assassination, was named as the country's new president and appointed head of a newly-created National Council for Reconciliation (CRN); he lifted the ban on political parties and announced that Ibrahim Hassane Mayaki would remain in post as prime minister until new elections could be held. In May, President Wanke established a Consultative Council which drafted a new constitution; it was approved by representatives of political groups in June and submitted to a national referendum in July. Legislative and presidential elections were due to be held in November 1999.

INSURGENCY

An ethnic Tuareg-based insurgency began in the north of Niger in November 1991; the Front for the Liberation of Aïr and Azawad (FLAA) aimed to gain greater local autonomy for the Tuaregs, a change to regional boundaries, the demilitarization of the north and the teaching of the Tuareg language, Tamashek. In 1993 two groups split from the FLAA in protest at its entry into negotiations with the government. A peace accord ending the conflict and providing for a peace process was signed in April 1995. In November 1997, the remaining active Tuareg groups agreed a cease-fire, and in March 1998, the National Assembly voted unanimously to grant an amnesty to all rebel groups representing the Tuareg and Toubou peoples. All rebel groups had been disarmed by June 1998.

HEAD OF STATE

President, Chairman of the National Reconciliation Council, Maj. Daouda Mallam Wanke, *took office* 11 April 1999

NATIONAL RECONCILIATION COUNCIL *as at May 1999*

Deputy Chairman, Maj. Soumana Zanguina
Permanent Secretary and CRN spokesman, Capt. Djibril Hami Mahamidou
Members of the Permanent Secretariat, Maj. Daouda Mallam Wanke; Lt.-Col. Moumouni Bouraima; Lt.-Col. Lawal Sheikou Kore; Maj. Soumana Zanguina; Maj. Ahmed Mohamed; Maj. Amadou Diallo ; Maj. Abdoulaye Mounkeila; Maj. Salifou Modi; Capt. Boubacar Amadou Sanda; Capt. Adamou Garba; Capt. Hamanou Salia, Capt. Soumana Fobo Kalkoye

CABINET *as at July 1999*

Prime Minister, Ibrahim Hassane Mayaki
Agriculture and Animal Breeding, Tassiou Aminou
Civil Service, Labour and Employment, Ousmane Mahamane
Communication, Culture, Youth and Sports, Government Spokesman, Mahamadou Danda
Equipment and Transport, Ousmane Ahmed Abani
Finance and Economic Reform, Ide Niandou
Foreign Affairs and Co-operation, Aichatou Mindaoudou
Higher Education, Research and Technology, Ibrahim Konate
Interior and Territorial Development, Lt.-Col. Boureima Moumouni
Justice and Keeper of the Seals, Lawali Mahamane Danda
Mines and Energy, Yahaya Bare
Minister Delegate to the Minister of Finance in Charge of the Budget, Sidibe Seydou
Minister Delegate to the Prime Minister in Charge of Planning, Adamou Salaou
National Defence, Col. Moussa Moumouni Djermakoye
National Education, Baringaye Ahmed Akilou
Public Health, Sani Mamane
Social Development, Population, Women's Promotion and the Protection of Children, Aissatou Foumakoye
Tourism and Crafts, Rissa ag Boula
Trade and Industry, Seyni Omar
Water Resources and Environment, Ali Seyni Gado

EMBASSY OF THE REPUBLIC OF NIGER
154 rue de Longchamp, F-75116, Paris
Tel: Paris 4504 8060
Ambassador Extraordinary and Plenipotentiary, HE Mariama Hima, apptd 1999

BRITISH AMBASSADOR, HE Haydon Warren-Gash, resident at Abidjan, Côte d'Ivoire

ECONOMY

The cultivation of groundnuts and the production of livestock are the main industries and provide two of the main exports. Other agricultural products include millet, cassava and sugar cane. There are large uranium deposits at Arlit and Akouta, and this is the main export. Gold deposits exist north-west of Niamey. France and Nigeria are the main trading partners.

In 1995 Niger had a trade deficit of US$18 million and a current account deficit of US$152 million. In 1997 imports totalled US$425 million and exports US$269 million.

GNP – US$1,962 million (1997); US$200 per capita (1997)

GDP – US$1,898 million (1995); US$207 per capita (1995)

ANNUAL AVERAGE GROWTH OF GDP – 3.3 per cent (1996)

INFLATION RATE – 2.9 per cent (1997)

TOTAL EXTERNAL DEBT – US$1,579 million (1997)

Trade with UK	1997	1998
Imports from UK	£2,957,000	£2,239,000
Exports to UK	11,445,000	7,883,000

NIGERIA
Federal Republic of Nigeria

AREA – 356,669 sq. miles (923,768 sq. km). Neighbours: Benin (west), Niger (north), Chad (north-east), Cameroon (east)

POPULATION – 115,120,000 (1994 UN estimate); 88,514,501 (1991 census). The main ethnic groups are Hausa/Fulani, Yoruba and Ibo, and the principal languages are English, Hausa, Yoruba and Ibo. Over half the population are Muslim, these being concentrated in the north and west. In the southern areas in particular there are many Christians

CAPITAL – Abuja (population, 378,671), declared the federal capital in 1991

MAJOR CITIES – Ibadan (1,295,000); Kaduna (309,600); Kano (699,900); Lagos, the former capital (1,347,000); Ogbomosho (660,600); ΨPort Harcourt (371,000)

CURRENCY – Naira (N) of 100 kobo

NATIONAL ANTHEM – Arise, O Compatriots

NATIONAL DAY – 1 October (Independence Day)

NATIONAL FLAG – Three equal vertical bands, green, white and green

LIFE EXPECTANCY (years) – male 48.81; female 52.01

POPULATION GROWTH RATE – 2.9 per cent (1997)

POPULATION DENSITY – 125 per sq. km (1996)

URBAN POPULATION – 16.1 per cent (1988)

ILLITERACY RATE – 42.9 per cent

ENROLMENT (percentage of age group) – tertiary 4.1 per cent (1993)

A belt of mangrove swamp forest lies along the entire coastline. North of this there is a zone of tropical rain forest and oil-palms. North of the rain forest, the country rises and the vegetation changes to open woodland and savannah. In the extreme north the country is semi-desert. The Niger, Benue, and Cross are the main rivers. The climate is tropical. The rainy season is from about April to October. During the dry season the cool *harmattan* wind blows from the desert.

HISTORY AND POLITICS

The Federation of Nigeria attained independence as a member of the Commonwealth on 1 October 1960 and became a republic in 1963. Originally regional in structure, the Federation is now divided into 36 states and the Federal Capital Territory.

In 1966 the military took power; in 1979 civil rule was restored after elections at national and state level. The administration was overthrown by the military in December 1983, this regime itself being overthrown in August 1985. An Armed Forces Ruling Council (AFRC) was sworn in and governed until January 1993, when it was replaced by a National Defence and Security Council (NDSC) and a civilian Transitional Council respectively to govern the country until a handover to civilian government. A presidential election on 11 June was declared invalid. The military government resigned on 26 August, handing power to the Transitional Council.

Continued instability led Defence Minister Gen. Sanni Abacha to launch a military coup on 17 November 1993 and install himself as head of state. A (military) Provisional Ruling Council and (civilian) Federal Executive Council were established to govern the country. Strikes and pro-democracy demonstrations continued.

The National Constitutional Conference (NCC) convened by Gen. Abacha in June 1994 announced in January 1995 that Gen. Abacha should have an open-ended term of office. An attempted coup was defeated in March 1995 and political activity was restored in June, when the NCC presented the draft of a new constitution to Gen. Abacha. The military regime vowed to hand over power to an elected government in October 1998. In June 1998 Gen. Abacha died of a heart attack and was replaced by Gen. Abdulsalami Abubakar, who promised to continue with the handover to civilian rule and began the release of political prisoners. It was expected that Chief Abiola would be released, but in July he died of a heart attack while still in prison. News of his death prompted widespread rioting across the country. Gen. Abubakar announced that all elections held under Gen. Abacha's rule would be considered invalid and that fresh legislative and presidential elections would be held. A general election was held on 20 February 1999 in which the People's Democratic Party (PDP) won a majority in both houses of parliament; a presidential election was held on 27 February, in which Gen. Olusegun Obasanjo, the PDP candidate, was elected president. President Obasanjo and the civilian administration took office on 29 May 1999.

FOREIGN RELATIONS

Nigeria was suspended from the Commonwealth on 11 November 1995, following the execution of nine human rights activists. It was readmitted on 29 May 1999, following the assumption of power by the democratically elected government.

FEDERAL STRUCTURE

State	Population (1991)	Capital
Sokoto ⎤ *Zamfara⎦	4,392,391	Sokoto Gusau
Kebbi	2,062,226	Birnin-Kebbi
Niger	2,482,367	Minna
Kwara	1,566,469	Ilorin
Kogi	2,099,046	Lokoja
Benue	2,780,398	Makurdi
Plateau ⎤ *Nassarawa⎦	3,283,704	Jos Lafia
Taraba	1,480,590	Jalingo
Adamawa	2,124,049	Yola
Borno	2,596,589	Maiduguri
Yobe	1,411,481	Damaturu
Bauchi ⎤ *Gombe⎦	4,294,413	Bauchi Gombe
Jigawa	2,829,929	Dutse
Kano	5,632,040	Kano
Katsina	3,878,344	Katsina
Kaduna	3,969,252	Kaduna
Federal Capital Territory	378,671	Abuja
Oyo	3,488,789	Ibadan
Osun	2,203,016	Oshogbo
Ogun	2,338,570	Abeokuta
Lagos	5,685,781	Ikeja
Ondo ⎤ *Ekiti⎦	3,884,485	Akure Ado Ekiti
Edo	2,159,848	Benin City
Delta	2,570,181	Asaba
Rivers ⎤ *Bayelsa⎦	3,983,857	Port-Harcourt Yenagoa
Abia	2,297,978	Umuahia
Imo ⎤ *Ebonyi⎦	2,485,499	Owerri Abakaliki
Anambra	2,767,903	Awka
Enugu	3,161,295	Enugu
Cross River	1,865,604	Calabar
Akwa Ibom	2,359,736	Uyo

*New state, created on 1 October 1996 by dividing state immediately preceding it in list

HEAD OF STATE

President, Olusegun Obasanjo, elected 20 February 1999, *sworn in* 29 May 1999

FEDERAL EXECUTIVE COUNCIL *as at August 1999*

Agriculture and Rural Development, Alhaji Sani Zangon Daura
Aviation, Dr Segun Agagu
Commerce, Mustapha Bello
Communications, Alhaji Mohammed Arzika
Culture and Tourism, Chief Ojo Madueke
Defence, Gen. Yakubu Danjuma
Education, Prof. Tunde Adeniran
Environment, Dr Hassan Adamu
Federal Capital Territory, Ibrahim Bunu
Finance, Mallam Adamu Ciroma
Foreign Affairs, Alhaji Sule Lamido
Health, Dr Tim Menakaya
Industries, Chief Iyorchia Ayu
Information, Chief Dapo Sarumi
Internal Affairs, Chief S. M. Afolabi
Justice, Kanu Godwin Agabi
Labour and Productivity, Chief Tonye Graham-Douglas
Petroleum, vacant
Planning, vacant
Police Affairs, Maj.-Gen.David Jemibewon
Power and Steel, Chief Bola Ige
Presidency (Co-operation and Integration in Africa), Prof. Jerry Gana
Presidency (Economic Matters), Vincent Ogbuleafor
Presidency (Inter-Governmental Affairs), Ibrahim Umar Kida
Presidency (Special Projects), Dan Chuke
Science and Technology, Chief Ebitimi Banigo
Solid Minerals, Alhaji Musa Gwadabe
Sports and Social Development, Damiso Sango
Transport, Dr Kema Chikwe
Water Resources, Col. Mohammadu Bello Kaliel
Women and Youth, vacant
Works and Housing, Chief Tony Anenih

NIGERIA HIGH COMMISSION

9 Northumberland Avenue, London WC2N 5BX
Tel 0171-839 1244
High Commissioner, vacant
Deputy High Commissioner, M. Sanusi
Minister, A. A. Ella

BRITISH HIGH COMMISSION

Shehu Shangari Way (North), Maitama, Abuja
Tel: Abuja 523 2010
11 Louis Farrakhan Crescent, Victoria Island, Lagos
Tel: Lagos 261 9531
High Commissioner, HE Graham Burton, KCMG, apptd 1997
Deputy High Commissioner and Counsellor (Political), R. A. Pullen
Counsellor (Economic and Commercial), D. D. Pearey
LIAISON OFFICES – Ibadan, Kaduna, Kano, Port Harcourt

BRITISH COUNCIL DIRECTOR, C. Bruton, 11 Kingsway Road, Ikoyi (PO Box 3702), Lagos. Branch offices at Enugu, Ibadan, Kaduna and Kano

DEFENCE

The Army has 200 main battle tanks, 380 armoured personnel carriers and 431 artillery pieces. The Navy has one frigate, 35 patrol and coastal vessels and two helicopters at six bases. The Air Force has 91 combat aircraft and 15 armed helicopters.

MILITARY EXPENDITURE – 4.0 per cent of GDP (1997)
MILITARY PERSONNEL – 77,000: Army 62,000, Navy 5,500, Air Force 9,500

ECONOMY

Nigeria was a predominantly agricultural country until the early 1970s when oil became the principal source of export revenue (over 90 per cent). Since 1981 oil revenues have fallen to half their peak level. Recent governments have attempted to stimulate greater self-reliance by encouraging non-oil exports and the use of local rather than imported raw materials.

The government introduced economic reforms in January 1995, including lifting exchange controls and ending foreign investment controls in Nigerian or jointly-owned firms. Economic recovery has been hampered by the suspension of aid and development programmes following the execution of nine human rights activists in November 1995. An enabling decree was passed on 3 May 1999 to prepare for the privatization of 61 state companies, including electricity, oil and telecommunications companies.

Three oil refineries are in operation at Port Harcourt, Warri and Kaduna, and steel plants at Warri and Ajaokuta. Other projects include natural gas liquefaction, petrochemicals, fertilizers, power stations and irrigation schemes. Tin and calumbite mining on the Jos plateau, textiles and coal mining are also important.

GNP – US$33,393 million (1997); US$280 per capita (1997)

GDP – US$65,615 million (1995); US$587 per capita (1995)

ANNUAL AVERAGE GROWTH OF GDP – 2.9 per cent (1995)

INFLATION RATE – 8.2 per cent (1997)

TOTAL EXTERNAL DEBT – US$28,455 million (1997)

TRADE

The principal exports are oil, groundnuts, tin, cocoa, rubber, fish and timber. In 1996 there was a trade surplus of US$8,482 million and a current account surplus of US$3,092 million. Imports totalled US$7,996 million and exports US$18,613 million.

Trade with UK	1997	1998
Imports from UK	£426,212,000	£468,572,000
Exports to UK	122,395,000	140,531,000

COMMUNICATIONS

There are 142,837 km of roads. The Nigerian railway system, which is controlled by the Nigerian Railway Corporation, has 3,505 route km of lines. The principal international airlines operate from Lagos, Kano and Port Harcourt. A network of internal air services connects the main centres. The principal seaports are served by a number of shipping lines, including the Nigerian National Line. A nationwide television and radio network is being developed, and ten states have their own television and radio stations.

NORWAY
Kongeriket Norge

AREA – 125,050 sq. miles (323,877 sq. km) of which Svalbard and Jan Mayen have a combined area of 24,355 sq. miles (63,080 sq. km). Neighbours: Sweden, Finland, Russia (east)

POPULATION – 4,445,460 (1999 estimated). The language is Norwegian and has two forms: Bokmål and Nynorsk. Sami is spoken in the north of the country. The state religion is Evangelical Lutheran

CAPITAL – ΨOslo (population, 499,693, 1998)

MAJOR CITIES – ΨBergen (225,439); ΨKristiansand (70,640); ΨStavanger (106,858); ΨTrondheim (145,778)

CURRENCY – Krone of 100 øre

NATIONAL ANTHEM – Ja, vi elsker dette landet (Yes, we love this country)

NATIONAL DAY – 17 May (Constitution Day)

NATIONAL FLAG – Red, with white-bordered blue cross

LIFE EXPECTANCY (years) – male 74.24; female 80.25

POPULATION GROWTH RATE – 0.5 per cent (1997)

POPULATION DENSITY – 14 per sq. km (1997)

URBAN POPULATION – 72.0 per cent (1990)

The coastline is deeply indented with numerous fjords and fringed with rocky islands. The surface is mountainous, consisting of elevated and barren tablelands separated by deep and narrow valleys. At the North Cape the sun does not appear to set from about 14 May to 29 July, causing the phenomenon known as the Midnight Sun; conversely, there is no apparent sunrise from about 18 November to 24 January. During the long winter nights are seen the Northern Lights or Aurora Borealis.

HISTORY AND POLITICS

Norway was unified under Harald I Fairhair c.AD 900 and participated in the Viking expansion from the ninth to the 11th centuries. The accession of Magnus VII (1319) unified the Norwegian and Swedish crowns until his son became King Haakon VI of Norway in 1343. The Norwegian and Danish crowns were united in 1380 and confirmed by the Union of Kalmar (1397) which also brought Sweden under the rule of Queen Margrethe of Denmark. Norway remained a Danish province until transferred to Sweden under the Treaty of Kiel (1814). The union with Sweden was dissolved on 7 June 1905 when Norway regained complete independence.

Norway remained neutral during the First World War and on the outbreak of the Second World War but was invaded by Germany in 1940. Neutrality was abandoned when Norway joined NATO in 1949. The Labour Party governed from 1945 to 1965 when the extensive welfare state system was built. A referendum in 1972 rejected membership of the EC.

The ruling centre-right coalition collapsed in October 1990 over the question of EC membership and was replaced by a minority Labour government. This was returned to power in the general election held on 13 September 1993. A general election was held on 15 September 1997, in which no party won an outright majority. The Labour Party has the largest number of seats (65) but the government is a minority coalition of the Christian Democratic People's Party, the Centre Party and the Liberal Party.

FOREIGN RELATIONS

The Storting voted in November 1992 to apply to join the European Community. Negotiations with the EU concluded on 1 March 1994 with a proposed accession date of 1 January 1995, subject to parliamentary and national referendum ratifications. However, in a national referendum on 28 November 1994 the electorate voted against joining the EU by 52.4 per cent to 47.6 per cent.

POLITICAL SYSTEM

Under the 1814 constitution, the 165-member *Storting* elects one-quarter of its members to constitute the *Lagting* (Upper Chamber), the other three-quarters forming the *Odelsting* (Lower Chamber).

HEAD OF STATE

HM The King of Norway, King Harald V, GCVO, *born* 21 February 1937; *succeeded* 17 January 1991, on the death of his father King Olav V; *married* 29 August 1968, Sonja Haraldsen, and has *issue*, Prince Haakon Magnus (*see* below), and Princess Martha Louise, *born* 22 September 1971

Heir, HRH Crown Prince Håkon Magnus, *born* 20 July 1973

CABINET *as at July 1999*

Prime Minister, Kjell Magne Bondevik (KrF)
Agriculture, Kåre Gjønnes (KrF)
Children and Family Affairs, Valgerd Svarstad Haugland (KrF)
Cultural Affairs, Anne Enger Lahnstein (SP)
Defence, Eldbjørg Løwer (V)
Education, Research and Church Affairs, Jon Lilletun (KrF)
Environment, Guro Fjellanger (V)
Finance and Customs, Gudmund Restad (SP)
Fisheries, Peter Angelsen (SP)
Foreign Affairs, Knut Vollebæk (KrF)
Health, Dagfinn Høybråten (KrF)
Industry and Trade, Lars Sponheim (V)
International Development and Human Rights, Hilde Frafjord Johnson (KrF)
Justice and Police, Odd Einar Dørum (V)

Labour and Government Administration, Laila Dåvøy
Local Government and Regional Development, Odd Roger
 Enoksen (SP)
Petroleum and Energy, Marit Arnstad (SP)
Social Affairs, Magnhild Melteveit Kleppa (SP)
Transport, Communications, Dag Jostein Fjæroll

KrF Christian Democratic Party; SP Centre Party; V
Liberal Party

ROYAL NORWEGIAN EMBASSY
25 Belgrave Square, London SW1X 8QD
Tel 0171-591 5500
Ambassador Extraordinary and Plenipotentiary, HE Kjell
 Colding, CMG, apptd 1996
Defence Attaché, Col. P. Bærøy
First Secretary, R. Øverjordet (*Consular*)
Counsellor, S. Lindtvedt (*Commercial*)

BRITISH EMBASSY
Thomas Heftyesgate 8, N-0244 Oslo
Tel: Oslo 2313 2700
Ambassador Extraordinary and Plenipotentiary, HE Richard
 Dales, CMG, apptd 1998
Counsellor, D. G. Blunt, LVO (*Deputy Head of Mission and
 Consul-General*)
First Secretary, Dr C. M. Sweeney (*Economic and Commercial*)
*Defence and Naval Attaché,*Cdr. D. L. Stanesby, RN

BRITISH CONSULAR OFFICES – Oslo; Honorary
 Consulates at Ålesund, Bergen, Harstad, Kristiansand
 (South), Kristiansund (North), Stavanger, Tromsø,
 Trondheim

BRITISH COUNCIL REPRESENTATIVE , R. Olsen, Fridtjof
 Nansens Plass 5, N-0160, Oslo 1

DEFENCE

Norway is a member of NATO. The Army has 170 main
battle tanks, 71 armoured infantry fighting vehicles, 212
armoured personnel carriers, and 222 artillery pieces. The
Navy has 12 submarines, four frigates and 22 patrol and
coastal vessels at three bases. The Air Force has 79 combat
aircraft.
MILITARY EXPENDITURE – 2.3 per cent of GDP (1997)
MILITARY PERSONNEL – 28,000: Army 15,200, Navy
 6,100, Air Force 6,700
CONSCRIPTION DURATION – 12 months

ECONOMY

The cultivated area is about 10,703 sq. km, 3.5 per cent of
the total surface area. Forests cover 23 per cent; the rest
consists of highland pastures or uninhabitable mountains.
The chief agricultural products are grain, vegetables, milk,
furs and timber.
 The Gulf Stream causes the sea temperature to be
higher than the average for the latitude, which brings
shoals of herring and cod into the fishing grounds. In 1997
the catch totalled more than 9 million tonnes.
 The chief industries are oil production and transport,
construction, electricity supply, manufactures, agriculture
and forestry, fisheries, mining, metal and ferro-alloy
production and shipping. Industries providing both manufactured products and services for the development of
North Sea energy resources have become increasingly
important. In 1997 156,215,000 tonnes of crude oil were
produced. Norway produces large amounts of hydroelectric
power.
GNP – US$158,973 million (1997); US$36,100 per capita
 (1997)
GDP – US$146,135 million (1995); US$33,734 per capita
 (1995)

ANNUAL AVERAGE GROWTH OF GDP – 3.5 per cent
 (1997)
INFLATION RATE – 2.6 per cent (1997)
UNEMPLOYMENT – 4.9 per cent (1995)

TRADE

The chief imports are motor vehicles, ships and machinery,
clothing, foods and textiles. Exports consist chiefly of crude
oil and gas, machinery and transport equipment and
manufactured goods.
 In 1997 Norway had a trade surplus of US$11,062
million and a current account surplus of US$8,112 million.
Imports totalled US$35,709 million and exports US$48,542
million.

Trade with UK	1997	1998
Imports from UK	£2,655,938,000	£2,066,273,000
Exports to UK	4,927,331,000	3,620,318,000

COMMUNICATIONS

The total length of railways open at the end of 1997 was
4,021 km, excluding private lines. There are 91,254 km of
public roads in Norway (including urban streets). Scheduled internal air services are operated by Scandinavian
Airlines System (SAS) on behalf of Det Norske Luftfart-
selskap (DNL), by Braathens South American and Far East
Airtransport (SAFE), and by Widerøes Flyveselskap AS.
There are international airports at Oslo, Bergen and
Stavanger. In 1996 there were 64 daily newspapers.

CULTURE AND EDUCATION

The Norwegian language in both its present forms is
closely related to other Scandinavian languages. Independence from Denmark (1814) and resurgent nationalism led
to the development of 'new Norwegian' based on dialects,
which now has equal official standing with 'bokmål', in
which Danish influence is more obvious. Ludvig Holberg
(1684–1754) is regarded as the father of Norwegian
literature, though the modern period begins with the
writings of Henrik Wergeland (1808–45). Some of the
famous names are Henrik Ibsen (1828–1906), Bjørnstjerne
Bjørnson (1832–1910), Nobel Prizewinner in 1903, and the
novelists Jonas Lie (1833–1908), Alexander Kielland (1849–
1906), Knut Hamsun (1859–1952) and Sigrid Undset
(1882–1949), the latter two also Nobel Prizewinners. Old
Norse literature is among the most ancient and richest in
Europe.
 Education from six to 16 is free and compulsory in the
'basic schools', and free from 16 to 19 years. The majority
of the pupils receive post-compulsory schooling at 'upper
secondary' schools, regional colleges akin to polytechnics,
and 11 universities and other university-level specialist
colleges.
ENROLMENT (percentage of age group) – primary 99 per
 cent (1995); secondary 96 per cent (1995); tertiary 58.5
 per cent (1995)

TERRITORIES

SVALBARD, area 24,295 sq. miles (62,923 sq. km);
 population 3,700; inhabitants mainly engaged in coal-
 mining. The Svalbard archipelago consists of the main
 island, Spitsbergen (15,200 sq. miles), North East Land,
 the Wiche Islands, Barents and Edge Islands, Prince
 Charles Foreland, Hope Island, Bear Island and many
 islands in the neighbourhood of the main group.
 Glaciers cover 60 per cent of the land area. The
 sovereignty of Norway over the archipelago was
 recognized by other nations in 1920 and in 1925
 Norway assumed sovereignty
JAN MAYEN ISLAND was joined to Norway by law in 1930

NORWEGIAN ANTARCTIC TERRITORIES

BOUVET ISLAND was declared a dependency of Norway in 1930

PETER THE FIRST ISLAND was declared a dependency of Norway in 1931

PRINCESS RAGNHILD LAND has been claimed as Norwegian since 1931

QUEEN MAUD LAND was declared Norwegian territory by the Norwegian government in 1939

OMAN
The Sultanate of Oman

AREA – 119,498 sq. miles (309,500 sq. km). Neighbours: Yemen, Saudi Arabia and the UAE (west)

POPULATION – 2,302,000 (1998 estimate). The official language is Arabic. Islam is the official religion. The majority of the population are Ibadhi Muslims; there is a large Sunni and a small Shia minority. Other religions are tolerated

CAPITAL – ΨMuscat (population, 400,000)

MAJOR CITIES – ΨBarka; ΨMutrah and Ruwi (the commercial centres); ΨSalalah (the main town of Dhofar); ΨSohar; ΨSur

CURRENCY – Rial Omani (OR) of 1,000 baisas

NATIONAL DAY – 18 November

NATIONAL FLAG – Red with a white panel in the upper fly and a green one in the lower fly; in the canton the national emblem in white

LIFE EXPECTANCY (years) – male 67.70; female 71.80

POPULATION GROWTH RATE – 4.7 per cent (1997)

POPULATION DENSITY – 11 per sq. km (1996)

Oman lies at the eastern corner of the Arabian peninsula. Sharjah and Fujairah (UAE) separate the main part of Oman from the northernmost part of the state, a peninsula extending into the Strait of Hormuz.

The north and the south of Oman are divided by nearly 400 miles of desert. The Batinah, the coastal plain, is fertile. The Hajjar is a mountain spine running from north-west to south-east and for the most part barren, but valleys penetrate the central massif which are irrigated by wells or a system of underground canals called *falajs* which tap the water table. The two plateaus leading from the western slopes of the mountains descend to the Empty Quarter of the Arabian Desert. Dhofar, the southern province, is the only part of the Arabian peninsula to be touched by the south-west monsoon. Temperatures are more moderate than in the north.

HISTORY AND POLITICS

Oman became part of the Islamic empire in the seventh century. From the ninth to 16th centuries the area was governed by a succession of religious leaders, or imams of the Ibadhi branch of Islam. The Portuguese established trading posts on the coast in 1507 but were expelled in 1650.

In 1744 Ahmad bin Said Al bu Said established the current ruling dynasty of sultans. The country was divided between the sultan's stronghold in the coastal Muscat-Matrah region and the imam in the interior. The sultan cultivated close relations with Britain and the Sultanate of Muscat and Oman became a British protectorate in 1798. In the late 19th century Dhofar was annexed.

In the 1950s the imam proclaimed an independent state in a revolt which was put down with British assistance. A seven-year-long Marxist uprising was crushed in 1975.

The current sultan ousted his father in a palace coup in 1970 and changed the state's name to the Sultanate of Oman. Dhofar is still governed as a separate province and Muscat has special status.

POLITICAL SYSTEM

A State Consultative Council established in 1981 was replaced by Sultanic decree in 1991 by a *Majlis al Shura*, or State Advisory Council. This body, meeting twice a year, consisted of representatives from each of the 59 wilayats, or governorates, of the Sultanate. The Council has the right to review legislation, question ministers and make policy proposals. Effective political power remains with the sultan, who rules by decree and is advised by the Cabinet, which he appoints.

In November 1996 the sultan decreed Oman to be a hereditary absolute monarchy. On 16 October 1997, elections were held to choose 164 people for a shortlist to the State Advisory Council; the sultan chose the 82 members of the Council from them. On 16 December 1997 the sultan appointed 41 members to the new *Majlis al-Dawla* (Council of State).

HEAD OF STATE

HM The Sultan of Oman, Sultan HM Qaboos bin Said al-Said, *succeeded* on deposition of Sultan Said bin Taimur, 23 July 1970

Council of Ministers *as at July 1999*

Prime Minister, Foreign Affairs, Defence and Finance, The Sultan

Personal Representative of HM The Sultan, HH Sayyid Thuwaini bin Shihab al Said

Deputy PM, HH Sayyid Fahad bin Mahmoud al Said

Minister of State and Governor of Dhofar, Sayyid Musallam bin Ali al Busaidi

Minister of State and Governor of Dhofar, Sayyid Musallam bin Ali al Busaidi

Minister of State and Governor of Muscat, Sayyid al Mutassim bin Hamoud al Busaidi

Agriculture and Fisheries, Dr Ahmed bin Khalfan bin Mohammed al Rowahi

Awqaf and Religious Affairs, Shaikh Abdullah bin Mohammed al Salimi

Civil Service, Shaikh Abdulaziz bin Matar bin Salim al Azizi

Commerce and Industry, Maqbool bin Ali bin Sultan

Communications, Salim bin Abdullah al Ghazali

Defence, Sayyid Badr bin Saud bin Hareb

Diwan of Royal Court, Sayyid Saif bin Hamed bin Saud

Education, Sayyid Saud bin Ibrahim al Busaidi

Electricity and Water, Shaikh Mohammed bin Ali al Qatabi

Foreign Affairs, Yusuf bin Alawi bin Abdullah

Health, Dr Ali bin Mohammed bin Moosa

Higher Education, Yahya bin Mahfudh al Mantheri

Housing, Malik bin Suleiman al Ma'amari

Information, Abdulaziz bin Mohammed al Rowas

Interior, Sayyid Ali bin Hamoud al Busaidi

Justice, Shaikh Mohammed bin Abdullah bin Zaher al Hinai

Legal Affairs, Mohammed bin Ali bin Nasir al Alawi

National Economy, Ministry of Finance, Ahmed bin Abdul-Nabi Macki

National Heritage and Culture, HH Sayyid Faisal bin Ali al Said

Oil and Gas, Dr Mohammed bin Hamad bin Saif al Romhi

Palace Office, Gen. Ali bin Majid al Ma'amari

Posts, Telegraphs and Telephones, Ahmed bin Suwaidan al Balushi

Regional Municipalities and Environment, Dr Khamis bin Mubarak bin Isa al Alawi

Social Affairs, Labour, Vocational Training, Shaikh Amer bin Shuwain al Hosni
Water Resources, Hamed bin Said al Aufi

EMBASSY OF THE SULTANATE OF OMAN
167 Queen's Gate, London SW7 5HE
Tel 0171-225 0001
Ambassador Extraordinary and Plenipotentiary, HE Hussain Ali Abdullatif, apptd 1995
Minister Plenipotentiary, Ghassan Ibrahim Shaker
Assistant Military Attachés, Lt.-Cdr. Qassim Al-Zadgali; Maj. Shabib bin Ibrahim bin Abdullah Al-Hajri

BRITISH EMBASSY
PO Box 300, Muscat, Postal Code 113
Tel: Muscat 693077
Ambassador Extraordinary and Plenipotentiary, HE Sir Ivan Callan, KCVO, CMG, apptd 1999
Counsellor, A. J. N. Tansley *(Deputy Head of Mission)*
Defence and Military Attaché, Brig. M. Smith, OBE, MC
First Secretary (Commercial), R. MacKenzie
Consul, P. Smith

BRITISH COUNCIL DIRECTOR, C. Hepburn, PO Box 73, Muscat. There are also offices at Salalah and Seeb

DEFENCE

The Army has 121 main battle tanks, 73 armoured personnel carriers and 91 artillery pieces. The Navy has two corvettes and 11 patrol and coastal vessels at five bases. The Air Force has 40 combat aircraft.
MILITARY EXPENDITURE – 10.9 per cent of GDP (1997)
MILITARY PERSONNEL – 44,200: Army 25,000, Navy 4,200, Air Force 4,100, Royal Household 6,500, Paramilitaries 4,400

ECONOMY

Although there is considerable cultivation in the fertile areas and cattle are raised on the mountains, the backbone of the economy is the oil industry, accounting for about 40 per cent of GDP. Petroleum Development (Oman) Ltd (owned 60 per cent by the Oman Government) began exporting oil in 1967. Concessions (off and on shore) are held by several major international companies. The current level of oil production is about 45,100,000 tonnes per year. The government is actively encouraging the diversification of the economy and private sector development. Tourism is also an expanding area.

A gas turbine power station operates at Rusail, where there is also a 200-plot industrial estate. There is a power station and a desalination plant near Muscat and flour, animal feed, cement and copper production facilities.

In 1996 there was a trade surplus of US$2,954 million and a current account deficit of US$265 million.
GDP – US$13,753 million (1995); US$6,232 per capita (1995)
ANNUAL AVERAGE GROWTH OF GDP – 3.5 per cent (1996)
TOTAL EXTERNAL DEBT – US$3,602 million (1997)

TRADE

Trade is mainly with the UAE, UK, Japan, South Korea and China. Chief imports are machinery, cars, building materials, food and telecommunications equipment.

In 1997 imports totalled US$5,026 million and exports US$7,630.

Trade with UK	1997	1998
Imports from UK	£370,422,000	£284,775,000
Exports to UK	105,089,000	92,026,000

COMMUNICATIONS

Port Qaboos at Matrah has eight deep-water berths which have been constructed as part of the harbour facilities; a new port is under construction at Sohar. A modern telecommunications service to the main population centres and an international service are operated by the General Telecommunications Organization. There are some 6,000 km of tarmac roads linking most main population centres of the country with the coast and with the towns of the UAE, though only a trunk road links the north and south of Oman. There are airports at Seeb, Salalah, Sur, Masirah, Khasab and Diba.

SOCIAL WELFARE AND EDUCATION

For many years the Sultanate was a poor country but the advent of oil revenues and the change of regime in 1970 led to the initiation of a wide-ranging development programme, especially concerned with health, education and communications. There are now 47 hospitals and 115 health centres. Mass immunization programmes have eradicated poliomyelitis and diphtheria; 1,069 schools, with 536,178 pupils, were in operation in 1998. There is one university.
ENROLMENT (percentage of age group) – primary 68 per cent (1996); secondary 56 per cent (1996); tertiary 6.4 per cent (1996)

PAKISTAN
Islami Jamhuriya-e-Pakistan

AREA – 307,374 sq. miles (796,095 sq. km). Neighbours: Iran (west), Afghanistan (north and north-west), China (north-east), the disputed territory of Kashmir, India (east)
POPULATION – 134,146,000 (1994 UN estimate); 95 per cent Muslim, 3.5 per cent Christian, about 1 per cent Hindu, and 0.5 per cent Buddhist. Urdu is the national language, but is only spoken by a small minority of the population. The most widely used language is Punjabi, followed by Sindi and Pushto. English is used in business, government and higher education
CAPITAL – Islamabad (population, 350,000)
MAJOR CITIES – ΨKarachi (7,183,000); Lahore (4,072,000)
CURRENCY – Pakistan rupee of 100 paisa
NATIONAL ANTHEM – Quami Tarana
NATIONAL DAYS – 23 March (Pakistan Day), 14 August (Independence Day)
NATIONAL FLAG – Green with a white crescent and star, and a white vertical strip in the hoist
LIFE EXPECTANCY (years) – male 59.04; female 59.20
POPULATION GROWTH RATE – 2.5 per cent (1997)
POPULATION DENSITY – 169 per sq. km (1996)
URBAN POPULATION – 28.2 per cent (1991)

Running through Pakistan are five great rivers, the Indus, Jhelum, Chenab, Ravi and Sutlej. The upper reaches of these rivers are in Kashmir, and their sources in the Himalayas.

HISTORY AND POLITICS

Pakistan was constituted as a Dominion under the Indian Independence Act 1947, becoming a republic on 23 March 1956. Until 1972 Pakistan consisted of two geographical units, West and East Pakistan, separated by about 1,100 miles of Indian territory. East Pakistan's insistence on complete autonomy led to civil war, which broke out on 25 March 1971 and continued until December 1971 when a cease-fire was arranged. The independence of East Pakistan as Bangladesh was proclaimed in April 1972. Under the 1972 Simla Agreement with India, a line of control was established in Kashmir; Pakistan controls an area of 33,653 sq. miles (87,159 sq. km) to the north and west of the line.

The armed forces under Gen. Zia-ul-Haq assumed power in 1977 and martial law was in force from July 1977 to March 1985. Gen. Zia declared himself president in September 1978, but was killed in a plane crash in August 1988. The Pakistan People's Party (PPP) won the election to the National Assembly and Benazir Bhutto became prime minister. In August 1990 the president dissolved the National Assembly and dismissed the Bhutto Cabinet. Elections were held in October 1990 and won by the Islamic Democratic Alliance, led by Mohammed Nawaz Sharif.

In July 1993, the Army intervened to end a power struggle between President Ishaq Khan and Prime Minister Sharif by replacing them with a caretaker administration until new elections were held in October. These were won by the PPP and Benazir Bhutto resumed the premiership. The PPP candidate Farooq Leghari was elected president by an electoral college of the National and provincial assemblies.

The Bhutto government was dismissed by the president in November 1996 for alleged corruption and economic mismanagement. Elections held in February 1997 were won by the Pakistan Muslim League with 134 seats; the PPP won only 18 seats. President Farooq Leghari resigned on 2 December 1997 following a dispute with Prime Minster Sharwaz. Muhammad Rafiq Tarar was subsequently elected president.

INSURGENCY

Since early 1994 there has been civil disorder in Sind province, especially in Karachi, in two conflicts: armed militants of the Mohajir Qaumi Movement (MQM) Party, which represents Urdu-speaking Indian Muslims who fled from India at partition and their descendants, are fighting for an autonomous Karachi province; and there is an armed conflict between Shia and Sunni fundamentalists.

POLITICAL SYSTEM

The legislature is bicameral. The *Majlis as-Shoora* (National Assembly) has a five-year term and comprises 237 members, of whom 207 are directly elected, 10 represent religious minorities and 20 are co-opted women. The Senate has 87 members, with a six-year term; half of the seats are renewed every three years. In January 1997 the interim government set up a Council for Defence and National Security including members of the Cabinet and armed forces to advise on foreign, defence and economic policies. The four provinces each have a provincial assembly and are represented in both legislative chambers.

The National Assembly amended the constitution in April 1997 to remove from the president the power to dismiss the government and dissolve parliament.

FEDERAL STRUCTURE

Province	Area (sq. km)	Population (1981)	Capital
Baluchistan	347,190	4,332,000	Quetta
Federal Capital Territory Islamabad	907	340,000	—
Federally Administered Tribal Areas	27,219	2,199,000	—
North-West Frontier Province	74,521	11,061,000	Peshawar
Punjab	205,344	47,292,000	Lahore
Sind	140,914	19,029	Karachi

HEAD OF STATE

President, Muhammad Rafiq Tarar, *sworn in* 1 January 1998

FEDERAL CABINET *as at August 1999*

Prime Minister, Muhammad Nawaz Sharif
Ministers of State, Ahmad Mahmood (*Environment, Local Government and Rural Development*); Muhammad Siddique Khan Kanju (*Foreign Affairs*); Azgar Ali Shah (*Housing and Construction*); Halim Siddiqui (*Water and Power*); Tahmina Daultana (*Women's Division, Social Welfare and Special Education*)
Attorney-General, Chaudary Farooq
Chair of the Prime Minister's Implementation and Inspection Commission, Lt.-Gen. Malik Abdul Majeed
Communications, Raja Nadir Parvez
Culture, Sports, Tourism and Youth Affairs, Labour, Manpower and Overseas Pakistanis, Sheikh Rashid Ahmed
Education, Ghous Ali Shah
Finance, Economic Affairs and Statistics, Commerce, Investment, Muhammad Ishaq Dar
Food and Agriculture, Abdul Sattar Laleka
Health, Javed Hashemi
Industries, Maqbool Siddiqui
Interior, Narcotics Control, Chaudary Shujat Hussain
Kashmir Affairs, Northern Areas, States and Frontier Regions, Abdul Majid Malik
Law and Justice, Khalid Anwar
Parliamentary Affairs, Mohammad Yasin Wattoo
Petroleum and Natural Resources, Chaudary Nissar Ali Khan
Planning and Development, Foreign Affairs, Sartaj Aziz
Population Welfare, Science and Technology, Social Welfare and Special Education, Environment, Local Government and Rural Development, Syeda Avida Hussain
Prime Minister's Adviser on Information and Mass Media Development, Mushahid Hussain
Railways, Sardar Mohammad Nasar
Religious Affairs, Minorities, Raja Zafarul Haq
Water, Power, Gohar Ayub Khan

HIGH COMMISSION FOR THE ISLAMIC REPUBLIC OF PAKISTAN

35–36 Lowndes Square, London SW1X 9JN
Tel 0171-664 9200
High Commissioner, HE Mian Riaz Samee
Consul-General, Syed Javed Hassan
Defence and Naval Adviser, Cdre Javed Ahmed Khan

BRITISH HIGH COMMISSION

Diplomatic Enclave, Ramna 5, PO Box 1122, Islamabad
Tel: Islamabad 822131/5
High Commissioner, HE Sir David Dain, KCVO, CMG, apptd 1994
Deputy High Commissioners, M. Forbes-Smith (*Islamabad*); D. B. Merry (*Karachi*)
Counsellor (Economic, Commercial, Development and Media), C. Smith
Counsellor, M. J. Crawford
Defence and Military Adviser, Brig. B. D. Wheelwright
DEPUTY HIGH COMMISSION – Karachi
CONSULATE – Lahore

BRITISH COUNCIL REPRESENTATIVE, P. Elwood, PO Box 1135, Islamabad. There are offices at Karachi, Lahore and Peshawar

DEFENCE

On 28 and 30 May 1998, Pakistan carried out six underground nuclear tests, less than a month after India had carried out its own nuclear tests. In doing so, it became the world's seventh declared nuclear power.

The Army has 2,120 main battle tanks, 850 armoured personnel carriers, 1,590 artillery pieces and 20 attack helicopters. The Navy has nine submarines, two destroyers, eight frigates, 10 patrol and coastal vessels, seven combat aircraft and 12 armed helicopters based at Karachi. The Air Force has 410 combat aircraft.

MILITARY EXPENDITURE – 5.8 per cent of GDP (1997)
MILITARY PERSONNEL – 834,000: Army 520,000, Navy 22,000, Air Force 45,000, Paramilitaries 247,000

ECONOMY

Agriculture employs half the workforce and contributes a quarter of GDP. The principal crops are cotton, rice, wheat and sugar cane. Pakistan has one of the longest irrigation systems in the world, irrigating 42.5 million acres. There are large deposits of rock salt.

Pakistan also produces hides and skins, leather, wool, fertilizers, paints and varnishes, soda ash, paper, cement, fish, carpets, sports goods, surgical appliances and engineering goods, including switchgear, transformers, cables and wires.

In 1996 foreign exchange reserves fell below the US$1,000 million floor decreed by the IMF and the economy went into a severe recession. Attempts to impose taxes resulted in industrial action and capital flight. The Sharif government announced an economic revival programme in March 1997 including tax and tariff reductions. In October 1997, the government devalued the rupee by 8.5 per cent, citing the strong US dollar and the currency crisis in south-east Asia. The IMF agreed a loan of more than US$1.5 billion to help finance economic reforms.

Following condemnation of Pakistan's nuclear tests in May 1998, the international community imposed economic sanctions. The government immediately announced a series of spending cuts and severe austerity measures to counteract the sanctions and protect the economy. In January 1999, the government committed itself to the continuation of financial reforms, trade liberalization and privatization in return for the resumption of IMF loans; the World Bank also agreed a loan for the reform of the banking and taxation systems and the public utilities.

In 1995 there was a trade deficit of US$2,878 million and a current account deficit of US$3,333 million.

GNP – US$64,638 million (1997); US$500 per capita (1997)
GDP – US$68,733 million (1995); US$504 per capita (1995)
ANNUAL AVERAGE GROWTH OF GDP – 3.4 per cent (1997)
INFLATION RATE – 11.4 per cent (1997)
UNEMPLOYMENT – 4.8 per cent (1994)
TOTAL EXTERNAL DEBT – US$29,665 million (1997)

TRADE

Principal imports are petroleum products, machinery, fertilizers, transport equipment, edible oils, chemicals and ferrous metals. Principal exports are cotton yarn and cloth, carpets, rice, petroleum products, textiles, leather and fish.

In 1997 imports totalled US$11,595 million and exports US$8,717 million.

Trade with UK	1997	1998
Imports from UK	£267,899,000	£234,572,000
Exports to UK	379,162,000	357,254,000

COMMUNICATIONS

There are major seaports at Karachi and Port Qasim. The main airports are at Karachi, Islamabad, Lahore, Peshawar and Quetta. Pakistan International Airlines operates air services between the principal cities as well as abroad. There are 86,597 km of roads and 7,344 km of rail track.

EDUCATION

Education consists of five years of primary education (five to nine years), three years of middle or lower secondary (general or vocational), two years of upper secondary, two years of higher secondary (intermediate) and two to five years of higher education in colleges and universities. Education is free to upper secondary level.

ILLITERACY RATE – 62.2 per cent
ENROLMENT (percentage of age group) – tertiary 3.0 per cent (1991)

PALAU
Republic of Palau

AREA – 177 sq. miles (459 sq. km)
POPULATION – 17,000 (1994 UN estimate); 15,122 (1990 census); 13,900 live on Koror and Babelthaup. The population is Micronesian, and predominantly Roman Catholic with a Protestant minority. Palauan and English are official languages
CAPITAL – Koror (population, 10,493, 1994)
CURRENCY – Currency is that of the USA
NATIONAL FLAG – Light blue with a yellow disc set near the hoist
POPULATION GROWTH RATE – 1.8 per cent (1997)
POPULATION DENSITY – 37 per sq. km (1996)

The Republic of Palau consists of 340 islands and islets in the western Pacific Ocean, of which eight are inhabited. Part of the Caroline Islands group, the Palau archipelago stretches over 400 miles (644 km) between 2° and 8°N., and 131° and 138°E. Koror island is about 810 miles (1,300 km) south-west of Guam and about 530 miles (852 km) south-east of Manila.

The islands vary in terrain from the highly mountainous to low coral atolls. The climate is tropical with a rainy season lasting from June to October; the average temperature is 27°C (81°F).

HISTORY AND POLITICS

Spain acquired sovereignty over the Caroline Islands, of which the Palau archipelago is part, in 1886. After defeat in the Spanish-American war of 1898, Spain sold its remaining Pacific possessions, including Palau, to Germany in 1899. On the outbreak of the First World War in 1914, Japan took control of Palau on behalf of the Allied powers, and Japanese administration was confirmed in a League of Nations mandate in 1921. During the Second World War Allied forces gained control of the archipelago after intense fighting. In 1947 the USA entered into agreement with the UN Security Council to administer the Micronesia area, including Palau, as the UN Trust Territory of the Pacific Islands.

In July 1978, the Palau electorate voted in a referendum not to join the new Federated States of Micronesia and instead became a separate part of the UN Trust Territory. A Compact of Free Association was signed with the USA in 1982, giving Palau internal sovereignty whilst leaving foreign policy to be decided by the USA. The compact only came into effect in November 1993, however, as successive referendums refused to allow US nuclear waste and weapons into Palau. The Compact was finally implemented on 1 October 1994. Under this agreement the USA recognized the Republic of Palau as a fully sovereign and independent state and assumed responsibility for its defence for 50 years; the UN Trust Territory of the Pacific Islands was terminated. Palau was admitted to UN membership in December 1994.

The last presidential and legislative elections were held in November 1996.

POLITICAL SYSTEM

Executive power is vested in the president and vice-president, who are elected for four-year terms; the president appoints the Cabinet. There is a bicameral legislature (*Olbiil era Kelulau*) composed of the 16-member House of Delegates (one member elected from each of the 16 constituent states) and the 14-member Senate. There is also a Council of Chiefs to advise the president on matters concerning traditional law and customs. Each of the 16 component states have their own elected governors and legislatures.

HEAD OF STATE

President, Kuniwo Nakamura, *elected* 4 November 1992, *re-elected* 6 November 1996
Vice-President, Administration, Tommy Remengesau

CABINET *as at June 1999*

Commerce and Trade, Okada Techitong
Community and Cultural Affairs, Rechucher Alexander Merep
Education, Billy Kuartei
Health, Masao Ueda
Justice, Elias Camsen Chin
Minister of State, Sabino Anastacio
Resources and Development, Marcelino Melairei
BRITISH AMBASSADOR, HE Vernon Scarborough, resident at Suva, Fiji

ECONOMY

The economy remains heavily dependent on US financial support, which the USA is committed to giving under the Compact. Fisheries, tourism, subsistence agriculture and government service are the main areas of employment. Agricultural products include coconuts and copra, and Palau earns significant revenue from the sale of fishing licences to foreign fleets fishing for tuna. Tourism is being developed; there are 40,000 visitors annually. On 17 December 1997, Palau joined the International Monetary Fund, becoming its 182nd member. Its initial quota was set at 2.25 million special drawing rights.

The USA carried out an infrastructure improvement programme in the 1970s and 1980s. There are now three airports on Koror, Peleliu and Angaur which have daily flights from Guam operated by Continental Micronesia. Ocean freight services to Palau are provided by two shipping lines to the port at Koror. There are 61 km of roads, of which 36 km are paved. A communications centre on Arakabesang Island handles international telephone, telex, cable and facsimile communications. There is a privately owned television station and a government-operated radio station.

GDP – US$109 million (1995); US$6,417 per capita (1995)

EDUCATION AND SOCIAL WELFARE

There is a free public school system which, together with independent missionary schools, provides primary and secondary education. A tertiary technical school has been established on Koror since 1969. General medical and dental care is provided by a public hospital.

PANAMA
República de Panamá

AREA – 29,157 sq. miles (75,517 sq. km). Neighbours: Colombia (east), Costa Rica (west)
POPULATION – 2,674,000 (1995 estimate). Spanish is the official language
CAPITAL – ΨPanama City (population, 458,490, 1995 estimate)
CURRENCY – Balboa of 100 centésimos (US notes are also in circulation)
NATIONAL ANTHEM – Alcanzamos Por Fin La Victoria (Victory is ours at last)
NATIONAL DAY – 3 November
NATIONAL FLAG – Four quarters; white with blue star (top, next staff), red (in fly), blue (below, next staff) and white with red star
LIFE EXPECTANCY (years) – male 70.85; female 75.00
POPULATION GROWTH RATE – 1.8 per cent (1997)
POPULATION DENSITY – 35 per sq. km (1996)
URBAN POPULATION – 55.2 per cent (1996)
MILITARY EXPENDITURE – 1.3 per cent of GDP (1997)
MILITARY PERSONNEL – 11,800 Paramilitaries
ILLITERACY RATE – 9.2 per cent
ENROLMENT (percentage of age group) – primary 91 per cent (1990); secondary 51 per cent (1990); tertiary 30.0 per cent (1995)

HISTORY AND POLITICS

After a revolt in 1903, Panama declared its independence from Colombia and established a separate government. After 1968, control of Panama was increasingly taken over by Gen. Omar Torrijos, commander of the National Guard, following a military coup. In 1978 Gen. Torrijos withdrew from the government, and Dr Aristides Royo was elected president by the Assembly of Representatives.

An attempt in February 1988 by President Delvalle to remove Gen. Noriega as Commander of the Defence Forces failed. Noriega ousted Delvalle and replaced him with Manuel Solis Palma. Presidential elections were held in May 1989 but Noriega annulled the results and on 15 December he assumed power formally as head of state. On 20 December US troops invaded Panama to oust Noriega. Guillermo Endara, believed to have won the May elections, was installed as president. In December 1991 the Legislative Assembly approved a change to the constitution which abolished the armed forces.

The most recent presidential election, on 2 May 1999, was won by Mireya Elisa Moscoso de Gruber of the Union for Panama coalition. Simultaneous legislative elections were won by the New Nation coalition with 46 of the 71 contested seats.

POLITICAL SYSTEM

Legislative power is vested in a unicameral Legislative Assembly of 72 members; executive power is held by the president, assisted by two elected vice-presidents and an appointed Cabinet. Elections are held every five years under a system of universal and compulsory adult suffrage.

HEAD OF STATE

President, Mireya Elisa Moscoso de Gruber, *elected* 2 May 1999, *sworn in* 1 September 1999

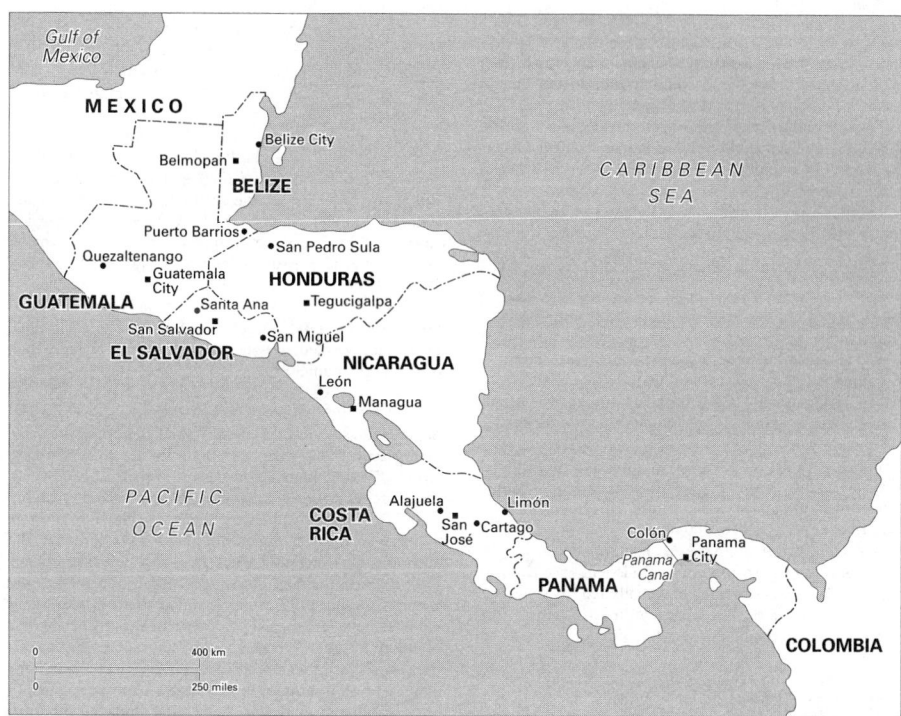

First Vice-President, Arturo Vallarino
Second Vice-President, Dominador Kaiser Bazan

PROVISIONAL CABINET *as at September 1999*
Agricultural Development, Alejandro Posse Martín
Canal Affairs, Ricardo Martinelli Berrocal
Commerce and Industry, Joaquin Jacome Diez
Education, Doris Rosas de Mata
Finance and Treasury, Victor Juliao
Foreign Relations, José Miguel Alemán
Health, Dr José Manuel Teran Sitton
Housing, Miguel Cardenas
Interior and Justice, Dr Winston Spadafora
Labour and Social Welfare, Joaquin José Vallarino III
Presidency, Ivonne Young Valdez
Public Works, Moises Castillo
Women, Youth and Family, Alma Ester Tejada de Rolla

EMBASSY OF THE REPUBLIC OF PANAMA
48 Park Street, London WIY 3PD
Tel 0171-493 4646
Chargé d'Affaires, Alberto Watson Fabrega

BRITISH EMBASSY
Torre Swiss Bank, Calle 53 (Apartado 889) Zona 1,
Panama City
Tel: Panama City 269 0866
Ambassador Extraordinary and Plenipotentiary, HE Glyn
    Davies, apptd 1999

ECONOMY

The soil is moderately fertile, but nearly one-half of the land is uncultivated. The chief crops are bananas, sugar, coconuts, coffee and cereals. Over 13,000 foreign ships are registered in Panama. The shrimping industry plays an important role in the economy. Tourism is the principal foreign currency earner. There are 547 km of railway track and 10,792 km of roads.

GNP – US$8,373 million (1997); US$3,080 per capita (1997)
GDP – US$7,719 million (1995); US$2,934 per capita (1995)
ANNUAL AVERAGE GROWTH OF GDP – 4.4 per cent (1997)
INFLATION RATE – 1.3 per cent (1997)
UNEMPLOYMENT – 13.7 per cent (1995)
TOTAL EXTERNAL DEBT – US$6,338 million (1997)

TRADE

Imports are mostly manufactured goods, machinery, lubricants, chemicals and foodstuffs. Exports are bananas, petroleum products, shrimps, sugar, meat, coffee and fishmeal.

In 1996 Panama had a trade deficit of US$630 million and a current account deficit of US$60 million. Imports totalled US$2,780 million and exports US$629 million.

Trade with UK	1997	1998
Imports from UK	£79,453,000	£82,822,000
Exports to UK	7,783,000	6,452,000

†Including Colón Free Zone

THE PANAMA CANAL ZONE

With effect from 1 October 1979 the Canal Zone (647 sq. miles) was disestablished, with all areas of land and water within the Zone reverting to Panama. By the 1977 treaty with the USA, the USA is allowed the use of operating bases for the Panama Canal, together with several military bases, but the Republic of Panama is sovereign in all such areas. Control of the Canal will revert to Panama at noon on 31 December 1999.

DEPENDENCIES

Taboga Island (area 4 sq. miles) is a popular tourist resort some 12 miles from the Pacific entrance to the Panama Canal.

Tourist facilities have also been developed in the Las Perlas Archipelago in the Gulf of Panama, particularly on the island of Contadora, as well as on the San Blas Islands in the Atlantic.

There is a penal settlement at Guardia on the island of Coiba (area 19 sq. miles) in the Gulf of Chiriqui.

PAPUA NEW GUINEA

AREA – 178,704 sq. miles (462,840 sq. km). Neighbour: Indonesia (west, on New Guinea)
POPULATION – 4,400,000 (1994 UN estimate). English is the official language; Hiri Motu and Neo-Melanesian are widely used
CAPITAL – ΨPort Moresby (population, 173,500, 1990)
MAJOR CITIES – Goroka; Lae; Madang; Mount Hagen; Rabaul; Wewak
CURRENCY – Kina (K) of 100 toea
NATIONAL ANTHEM – Arise All You Sons
NATIONAL DAY – 16 September (Independence Day)
NATIONAL FLAG – Divided diagonally red (fly) and black (hoist); on the red a soaring Bird of Paradise in yellow and on the black five white stars of the Southern Cross
LIFE EXPECTANCY (years) – male 55.16; female 56.68
POPULATION GROWTH RATE – 2.3 per cent (1997)
POPULATION DENSITY – 10 per sq. km (1996)
MILITARY EXPENDITURE – 1.2 per cent of GDP (1997)
MILITARY PERSONNEL – 4,300: Army 3,800, Navy 400, Air Force 100
ILLITERACY RATE – 27.8 per cent
ENROLMENT (percentage of age group) – tertiary 3.2 per cent (1995)

The country has many island groups, principally the Bismarck Archipelago, a portion of the Solomon Islands, the Trobriands, the D'Entrecasteaux Islands and the Louisade Archipelago. The main islands of the Bismarck Archipelago are New Britain, New Ireland and Manus. Bougainville is the largest of the Solomon Islands within Papua New Guinea.

Papua New Guinea lies within the tropics and has a typically monsoonal climate. Temperature and humidity are uniformly high throughout the year.

HISTORY AND POLITICS

New Guinea was sighted by Portuguese and Spanish navigators in the early 16th century, but remained largely isolated from the rest of the world. In 1884 a British protectorate, British New Guinea, was proclaimed over the southern coast of New Guinea (Papua) and the adjacent islands, which were annexed outright in 1888. In 1906 the Territory of British New Guinea was placed under the authority of Australia.

In 1884 Germany had formally taken possession of certain northern areas, later known as the Trust Territory of New Guinea. In 1914 the German areas were occupied by Australian troops and remained under military administration until 1921, when they became a League of Nations mandate administered by Australia. New Guinea was administered under the mandate and Papua under the Papua Act until the invasion by the Japanese in 1942 when the civil administration was suspended until the Japanese surrendered in 1945.

From 1970 there was a gradual assumption of powers by the Papua New Guinea government, culminating in formal self-government in December 1973. Papua New Guinea achieved full independence within the Commonwealth on 16 September 1975.

Following elections in June 1997, a coalition government was formed by Pangu, the People's Progress Party (PPP) and the People's National Congress, under Prime Minister Bill Skate. The PPP left the coalition in October 1998, but some PPP ministers joined the PNG First party formed in April 1998 by Bill Skate, who resigned as prime minister in July 1999; he was succeeded by Sir Mekere Morauta on 14 July 1999.

In July 1998, the north coast of Papua New Guinea was devastated by a tidal wave that killed more than 1,600 people and washed away entire villages, leaving more than 6,000 people homeless.

INSURGENCIES

Separatist aspirations, dormant since independence, re-emerged in 1989 when the Bougainville Revolutionary Army (BRA) mounted a successful insurrection. Government security forces withdrew from the island, enabling the BRA to declare an independent republic in May 1990. A peace accord was signed in January 1991, although the question of Bougainville's status was left unresolved. Fighting resumed and government forces returned to the island in October 1992, subsequently capturing 90 per cent of rebel-held territory. The government launched a new offensive in June 1996 after peace talks failed to produce a breakthrough. At least 7,000 people, mostly civilians, have died as a result of the insurrection.

A permanent cease-fire came into effect on 30 April 1998, bringing to an end the nine-year civil war. A small group of rebels led by Francis Ona vowed to continue the armed campaign for an independent Bougainville. An interim Bougainville Reconciliation Government was established on 1 January 1999, which renamed itself the Bougainville People's Congress in April. Elections were held in early May. Joseph Kabui, a former rebel leader, was elected president.

POLITICAL SYSTEM

Elections are held every five years. The National Parliament comprises 109 elected members, 20 from regional electorates, the remainder from open electorates. The Governor-General is appointed by parliament for a six-year term. Provincial governments were abolished in August 1995, and replaced with councils combining local and national politicians and headed by an appointed governor.

Governor-General, HE Silas Atopare, GCMG, *appointed* 14 November 1997

NATIONAL EXECUTIVE COUNCIL *as at July 1999*
Prime Minister, National Executive Council, National Security, Finance and Treasury, Bougainville Affairs, Health, Sir Mekere Morauta, KBE
Deputy PM, Home Affairs, John Pundari
Agriculture and Livestock, Ted Diro
Corporatization and Privatization, Vincent Auali
Defence, Alfred Pogo
Education, John Waiko
Fisheries and Marine Resources, Ron Ganarafo
Foreign Affairs, Sir Michael Somare, KCMG
Forests, Michael Ogio
Housing, John Kamb
Justice, Kilroy Genia
Labour, Employment, Culture and Tourism, Herowa Agiwa

Lands and Physical Planning, Fabian Pok
Mining, Sir John Kaputin, KBE
Minister of State assisting the PM, Peter Waieng
Petroleum and Energy, Tommy Tomscoll
Planning and Implementation, Moi Avei
Policy and Correctional Institutional Services, Mathias Karani
Provincial and Local Government, Andrew Kumbakor
Public Services and Communication, Philemon Embel
Rural Development and Environment and Conservation,
   William Ebenosi
Trade and Industry, Michael Nali
Transport, Bart Philemon
Works, Mao Zeming

PAPUA NEW GUINEA HIGH COMMISSION
3rd Floor, 14 Waterloo Place, London SW1R 4AR
Tel 0171-930 0922/7
High Commissioner, HE Sir Kina Bona, KBE, apptd 1995

BRITISH HIGH COMMISSION
PO Box 212, Waigani NCD 131, Port Moresby
Tel: Port Moresby 325 1643
High Commissioner, HE Charles Drace-Francis, CMG, apptd
1997

ECONOMY

Until the 1970s the economy was based almost entirely on agriculture, principally copra, cocoa, tea, coffee, palm oil, rubber, groundnuts, spices and timber. A variety of commercial agricultural developments co-exist with the traditional rural economy. In 1995, the government initiated an austerity programme intended to reduce the budget deficit, privatize state assets and eliminate trade tariffs. Following prolonged drought and the financial crisis in south-east Asia, the country is facing its worst financial crisis since independence, with debt servicing amounting to a quarter of government spending.

There are extensive mineral deposits throughout Papua New Guinea, including copper, gold, silver, nickel, bauxite and commercial deposits of oil. The Bougainville copper mine closed indefinitely in 1989 because of the unrest on the island. It had provided more than 15 per cent of the country's annual revenue.

Industry includes processing of primary products, and brewing, packaging, paint, plywood, and metal manufacturing and the construction industries.

In 1996 there was a trade surplus of US$1,017 million and a current account surplus of US$313 million. In 1997 imports totalled US$1,697 million and exports US$2,142 million.

GNP – US$4,185 million (1997); US$930 per capita
(1997)
GDP – US$4,657 million (1995); US$1,083 per capita
(1995)
ANNUAL AVERAGE GROWTH OF GDP – –4.8 per cent
(1995)
INFLATION RATE – 3.9 per cent (1997)
TOTAL EXTERNAL DEBT – US$2,273 million (1997)

Trade with UK	1997	1998
Imports from UK	£11,476,000	£6,572,000
Exports to UK	93,201,000	53,618,000

COMMUNICATIONS

Air Niugini operates regular air services to other countries in the region, as well as internal air services. Several shipping companies operate cargo services to Australia, Europe, the Far East and USA. There are very limited cargo and passenger services between Papua New Guinea main ports, outports, plantations and missions. There are

21,433 km of roads, the most important road being that linking Lae with the populous highlands. Papua New Guinea is linked by international cable to Australia, Guam, Hong Kong, Kota Kinabalu, the Far East and USA. Telecommunications are widely available.

PARAGUAY
República del Paraguay

AREA – 157,048 sq. miles (406,752 sq. km). Neighbours: Bolivia (north-west), Brazil (north-east and east), Argentina (south)
POPULATION – 4,955,000 (1994 UN estimate). Spanish is the official language of the country but outside the larger towns Guaraní, the language of the largest single group of original Indian inhabitants, is widely spoken, and is also an official language
CAPITAL – Asunción (population, 718,690)
MAJOR CITIES – Ciudad del Este (133,881); San Lorenzo (133,395)
CURRENCY – Guaraní (Gs) of 100 céntimos
NATIONAL ANTHEM – Paraguayos, República O Muerte (Paraguayans, republic or death)
NATIONAL DAY – 15 May
NATIONAL FLAG – Three horizontal bands, red, white, blue with the National seal on the obverse white band and the Treasury seal on the reverse white band
LIFE EXPECTANCY (years) – male 66.30; female 70.83
POPULATION GROWTH RATE – 2.7 per cent (1997)
POPULATION DENSITY – 12 per sq. km (1996)
URBAN POPULATION – 50.3 per cent (1992)
MILITARY EXPENDITURE – 1.5 per cent of GDP (1997)
MILITARY PERSONNEL – 35,000: Army 14,900, Navy 3,600, Air Force 1,700, Paramilitaries 14,800
CONSCRIPTION DURATION – One to two years

Paraguay is an inland subtropical state of South America, situated between Argentina, Bolivia and Brazil. It is a country of grassy plains and forested hills. In the angle formed by the Paraná-Paraguay confluence are extensive marshes, one of which, known as Neembucú (or endless) is drained by Lake Ypoa, a large lagoon south-east of the capital. The Chaco, lying between the rivers Paraguay and Pilcomayo and bounded on the north by Bolivia, is a flat plain, rising uniformly towards its western boundary to a height of 1,140 feet; it suffers much from floods and still more from drought, but the building of dams and reservoirs has converted part of it into good pasture for cattle.

HISTORY AND POLITICS

Paraguay was settled as a Spanish possession in 1537 and became independent in 1811.

Gen. Alfredo Stroessner, dictator from 1954, was overthrown in February 1989 by Gen. Andrés Rodríguez, who was elected president in May 1989. In May 1991, the first free municipal elections were held, and elections to the parliament were held in December 1991. Amendments to the constitution came into effect in June 1992. The last presidential and legislative elections were held on 10 May 1998. The presidential election was won by Raúl Cubas Grau of the Colorado Party, after its original candidate Gen. Lino Oviedo was banned from standing in elections for his part in a failed coup in 1996. In the legislative election, the distribution of seats in the Senate was: Colorado Party (CP) 24; Democratic Alliance (DA) 20; Blanco Party 1. In the Chamber of Deputies, the CP won 45 seats and the DA 35.

Vice-President Luis María Argaña was assassinated on 23 March 1999, following a power struggle between his supporters and those of President Cubas Grau and Gen. Ovieda. Supporters of Argaña demanded the resignation of the president and an indefinite general strike was called. The Chamber of Deputies voted to initiate impeachment proceedings against President Cubas Grau. He resigned on 28 March and was granted asylum in Brazil. The president of the Senate, Luis González Macchi, was immediately sworn in as the new president.

POLITICAL SYSTEM

The constitution provides for a two-chamber legislature consisting of a 45-member Senate and an 80-member Chamber of Deputies, both elected for five-year terms. Deputies are elected on a regional basis, the number of seats allocated to each regional department being directly proportional to the department's population. Voting is compulsory for all citizens over 18. The president is elected for a five-year term and may not be re-elected. The vice-president may only contest the presidency if he resigns his post six months before the election. The president appoints the Cabinet, which exercises all the functions of government.

HEAD OF STATE
President, Luis González Macchi, *sworn in* 28 March 1999
Vice-President, vacant

CABINET *as at May 1999*
Agriculture and Livestock, Luis Alberto Wagner *Defence*, Nelson Argaña
Education and Culture, Nicanor Duarte Frutos
Finance, Federico Zayas Chirife
Foreign Affairs, Miguel Abdon Saguier
Health and Social Welfare, Martin Chiola
Industry and Commerce, Guillermo Caballero Vargas
Interior, Walter Bower
Justice and Labour, Silvio Ferreira
Public Works, Communications, José Alberto Planas

EMBASSY OF PARAGUAY
Braemar Lodge, Cornwall Gardens, London SW7 4AQ
Tel 0171-937 1253
Ambassador Extraordinary and Plenipotentiary, Raúl Dos Santos, apptd 1998

BRITISH EMBASSY
Avda. Boggiani 4858, C/R 16 Boqueron, Asunción
Tel: Asunción 612611
Ambassador Extraordinary and Plenipotentiary and Consul-General, HE Andrew George, apptd 1998

ECONOMY

President Rodríguez introduced an economic liberalization programme which has been continued by subsequent governments. This has reduced foreign debt and attracted foreign investment, notably from Brazil. About half of the population are engaged in agriculture and cattle raising. Cassava, sugar cane, soya, cotton and wheat are the main agricultural products. The forests contain many varieties of timber which find a good market abroad.

Paraguay's rivers give it considerable hydroelectric capacity. There is a hydroelectric power station at Acaray which exports surplus power to Argentina and Brazil. Joint projects have been undertaken with Brazil, on a hydroelectric dam at Itaipú (the largest in the world), and with Argentina, at Yacyretá.

GNP – US$10,183 million (1997); US$2,000 per capita (1997)

GDP – US$8,982 million (1995); US$1,860 per capita (1995)
ANNUAL AVERAGE GROWTH OF GDP – 1.3 per cent (1996)
INFLATION RATE – 7.0 per cent (1997)
UNEMPLOYMENT – 4.4 per cent (1994)
TOTAL EXTERNAL DEBT – US$2,053 million (1997)

TRADE
The chief imports are machinery, fuels and lubricants, vehicles, drinks and tobacco. The chief exports are soya, cotton fibres, meat, timber and coffee. The main trading partners are Brazil, Argentina and the USA.

In 1994 Paraguay had a trade deficit of US$1,277 million and a current account deficit of US$749 million. In 1995 imports totalled US$3,144 million and exports US$919 million.

Trade with UK	1997	1998
Imports from UK	£64,147,000	£42,859,000
Exports to UK	4,785,000	1,547,000

COMMUNICATIONS

There are direct shipping services from Asunción to Europe and the USA, and river steamer services for internal transport. Eight airlines operate services from Asunción. There are 28,900 km of roads in Paraguay, connecting Asunción with São Paulo via the Bridge of Friendship and Foz de Yguazú, and with Buenos Aires via Puerto Pilcomayo. Many earth roads are liable to be closed or to become impassable in wet weather. There are 441 km of railway track. Rail services, with train ferries, provide internal and international links. Five daily and six weekly newspapers are published in Asunción.

EDUCATION

Education is free and compulsory. There are 11 universities and one institute of education.
ILLITERACY RATE – 7.9 per cent
ENROLMENT (percentage of age group) – primary 91 per cent (1996); secondary 38 per cent (1996); tertiary 11.4 per cent (1996)

PERU
República del Peru

AREA – 496,225 sq. miles (1,285,216 sq. km). Neighbours: Ecuador and Colombia (north), Brazil and Bolivia (east), Chile (south)
POPULATION – 25,015,000 (1999 estimate). The official languages are Spanish and Quechua.
CAPITAL – Lima (including ΨCallao, population, 6,483,901, 1993 census)
MAJOR CITIES – Arequipa (624,500); Chiclayo (448,400); Chimbote (314,700); Trujillo (521,200)
CURRENCY – New Sol of 100 cénts
NATIONAL ANTHEM – Somos Libres, Seámoslo Siempre (We are free, let us remain so forever)
NATIONAL DAY – 28 July (Anniversary of Independence)
NATIONAL FLAG – Three vertical stripes of red, white, red
LIFE EXPECTANCY (years) – male 62.74; female 66.55
POPULATION GROWTH RATE – 1.7 per cent (1997)
POPULATION DENSITY – 19 per sq. km (1996)
URBAN POPULATION – 71.2 per cent (1995)

The country is traversed throughout its length by the

Andes, running parallel to the Pacific coast. There are three main regions, the Costa, west of the Andes, the Sierra or mountain ranges of the Andes, which include the Punas or mountainous wastes below the region of perpetual snow, and the Montaña or Selva, which is the vast area of jungle stretching from the eastern foothills of the Andes to the eastern frontiers of Peru. The coastal area, lying upon and near the Pacific, is not tropical though close to the Equator, being cooled by the Humboldt Current.

HISTORY AND POLITICS

Peru was conquered in the early 16th century by Francisco Pizarro (1478–1541). He subjugated the Incas (the ruling caste of the Quechua Indians), who had started their rise to power some 500 years earlier, and for nearly three centuries Peru remained under Spanish rule. A revolutionary war of 1821–4 established its independence, declared on 28 July 1821. A military junta ruled Peru from 1968 until 1980 when civilian government was restored.

In April 1992 President Fujimori, faced with increasing terrorist violence, suspended the constitution, dissolved Congress and began to govern by decree. In November 1992 a legislative election was held to an 80-seat Democratic Constituent Congress (CCD) which was installed as an interim legislature and constituent assembly to write a new constitution. Parties supporting Fujimori's suspension of the constitution gained a majority in the CCD. In January 1993, the 1979 constitution was re-established and the CCD declared Fujimori constitutional head of state. The CCD produced a new constitution which was endorsed in a national referendum in October 1993.

Parliamentary and presidential elections were held on 9 April 1995, with President Fujimori winning the first round of the presidential election outright and his Cambio 90-Nueva Mayoría Party winning 67 out of 120 seats in the new *Congreso de la República* (Congress of the Republic).

FOREIGN RELATIONS

A 78 km stretch of the border with Ecuador has been in dispute since 1960. In 1995 an inconclusive border war was fought between the two countries, and in July 1995 a demilitarized zone was established around the disputed area. Four guarantor countries (Argentina, Brazil, Chile and the USA) adjudicated the claims of both countries and produced an agreement which was signed on 26 October 1998 by the presidents of Ecuador and Peru, formally ending the dispute.

INSURGENCIES

Since the late 1970s the government has faced violence from drug organizations and insurgencies from two leftist guerrilla movements, the Maoist Sendero Luminoso (Shining Path) and the Movimiento Revolucionario Túpac Amaru (MRTA), with fighting having left 30,000 dead.

Security forces captured the leader of the MRTA in November 1998 and the leader of Shining Path in December 1998.

POLITICAL SYSTEM

The constitution, promulgated in December 1993, provides for the president to be able to serve two terms rather than one, as previously; the introduction of the death penalty for treason; and the formation of a new 120-member unicameral Congress. A constitutional panel approved a Bill in August 1996, allowing President Fujimori to stand for a third term in office.

HEAD OF STATE

President of the Republic, Alberto Fujimori, *assumed office* 28 July 1990, *re-elected* 9 April 1995, *sworn in* 28 July 1995
First Vice-President, Ricardo Márquez Flores
Second Vice-President, César Paredes Canto

CABINET *as at July 1999*

Presidency, Edgardo Mosqueira Medina
President of the Council of Ministers, Economy and Finances, Victor Joy Way
Advancement of Women and Human Development, María Luisa Cuculiza Torres
Agriculture, Belisario de las Casas
Defence, Gen. Carlos Bergamino Cruz
Education, Dr Felipe Ignacio García Escudero
Energy and Mines, Daniel Hokama Tokashiki
Fisheries, Gustavo Caillaux Zazali
Foreign Affairs, Dr Fernando de Trazegnies
Health, Dr Alejandro Aguinaga Recuenco
Industry, Tourism, Integration and International Trade, Dr César Luna Victoria León
Interior, Gen. José Villanueva Ruesta
Justice, Dr Jorge Bustamante Romero
Labour and Social Promotion, Pedro Flores
Transport, Communication, Housing and Construction, Alberto Pandolfi

EMBASSY OF PERU

52 Sloane Street, London SWIX 9SP
Tel 0171-235 1917/2545/3802
Ambassador Extraordinary and Plenipotentiary, HE Eduardo Ponce-Vivanco, apptd 1995

BRITISH EMBASSY

Edificio El Pacifico Washington, Piso 12, Plaza Washington (PO Box 854), Lima 100
Tel: Lima 334738
Ambassador Extraordinary and Plenipotentiary, HE John Illman, CMG, apptd 1995

CONSULAR OFFICE – Lima
HONORARY CONSULATES – Arequipa, Cusco, Iquitos, Piura, Trujillo

BRITISH COUNCIL DIRECTOR, C. Brown, Calle Alberto Lynch 110, San Isidro, Lima 27

DEFENCE

The Army has 300 main battle tanks, 276 armoured personnel carriers, 276 artillery pieces, 29 aircraft and 59 helicopters. The Navy has eight submarines, two cruisers, one destroyer, four frigates, 11 patrol and coastal vessels, seven combat aircraft and nine armed helicopters at seven bases. The Air Force has 118 combat aircraft and 23 armed helicopters.
MILITARY EXPENDITURE – 2.2 per cent of GDP (1997)
MILITARY PERSONNEL – 203,000: Army 85,000, Navy 25,000, Air Force 15,000, Paramilitaries 78,000
CONSCRIPTION DURATION – Two years

ECONOMY

The chief products of the coastal belt are cotton, sugar and petroleum. There are large tracts of land suitable for cultivation and stock-raising (cattle, sheep, llamas, alpacas and vicuñas) on the eastern slopes of the Andes, and in the mountain valleys maize, potatoes and wheat are grown. The jungle area is a source of timber and petroleum. Other major crops are fruit, vegetables, rice, barley, grapes and coffee. The mountains contain rich mineral deposits and mineral exports include lead, zinc, copper, iron ore and silver. Peru is normally the world's largest exporter of fishmeal.

Since 1990 the government has launched a radical free-market restructuring programme which has rebuilt the foreign exchange reserves, reduced inflation from 7,600 per cent a year in 1990 to 11.5 per cent in 1996, cut subsidies and import tariffs, freed interest rates and privatized most state firms. Foreign investment has been encouraged and has grown dramatically. The economic recovery has increased the gap between rich and poor.

GNP – US$63,672 million (1997); US$2,610 per capita (1997)

GDP – US$58,750 million (1995); US$2,497 per capita (1995)

ANNUAL AVERAGE GROWTH OF GDP – 7.2 per cent (1997)

INFLATION RATE – 8.6 per cent (1997)

UNEMPLOYMENT – 7.1 per cent (1995)

TOTAL EXTERNAL DEBT – US$30,496 million (1997)

TRADE

The principal imports are machinery, chemicals and pharmaceutical products. The chief exports are minerals and metals, fishmeal, sugar, cotton and coffee.

In 1996 Peru had a trade deficit of US$2,000 million and a current account deficit of US$3,607 million. In 1997, imports totalled US$10,263 million and exports US$6,814 million.

Trade with UK	1997	1998
Imports from UK	£85,700,000	£66,433,000
Exports to UK	147,561,000	119,105,000

COMMUNICATIONS

There are 73,766 km of roads, of which 16,876 km are unsurfaced. The Andean Highway forms a link between the Pacific, the Amazon and the Atlantic. The Pan-American Highway runs along the Peruvian coast connecting it with Ecuador and Chile.

The railway is administered by the government. There are 1,992 km of railway track. There is also steam navigation on the Ucayali and Huallaga, and in the south on Lake Titicaca. Air services are maintained throughout Peru, and there is an international airport at Lima.

EDUCATION

Education is compulsory and free between seven and 16. There are 51 universities.

ILLITERACY RATE – 11.3 per cent

ENROLMENT (percentage of age group) – primary 91 per cent (1994); secondary 53 per cent (1994); tertiary 31.1 per cent (1994)

THE PHILIPPINES

Repúblika ng Pilipinas

AREA – 115,831 sq. miles (300,000 sq. km)

POPULATION – 71,899,000 (1994 UN estimate). The inhabitants are of Malay stock, with admixtures of Spanish and Chinese blood in many localities. The Chinese minority is estimated at 500,000, with smaller numbers of Spanish, American and Indian. About 90 per cent are Christian, predominantly Roman Catholics. Most of the remainder are Muslims or indigenous animists. The official languages are Filipino and English. Filipino is based on Tagalog, one of the Malay–Polynesian languages. English, the language of government, is spoken by at least 44 per cent of the population. Spanish is now spoken by a very small minority

CAPITAL – ΨManila (population, 8,594,150, 1994)

MAJOR CITIES – Bacolod (402,345); ΨCebu (662,299); ΨDavao (1,008,640); ΨIloilo (334,539); ΨZamboanga (511,139), 1995 UN estimates

CURRENCY – Philippine peso (P) of 100 centavos

NATIONAL ANTHEM – Lupang Hinirang

NATIONAL DAY – 12 June (Independence Day 1898)

NATIONAL FLAG – Equal horizontal bands of blue (above) and red; gold sun with three stars on a white triangle next staff

LIFE EXPECTANCY (years) – male 63.10; female 66.70

POPULATION GROWTH RATE – 2.3 per cent (1997)

POPULATION DENSITY – 240 per sq. km (1996)

URBAN POPULATION – 42.7 per cent (1990)

There are eleven larger islands and 7,079 other islands. The principal islands (area in sq. km) are: Luzon (104,688); Mindanao (94,630); Samar (13,080); Negros (12,710); Palawan (11,785); Panay (11,515); Mindoro (9,735); Leyte (7,214); Cebu (4,422); Bohol (3,865); Masbate (3,269). Other groups are the Sulu islands (capital, Jolo), Babuyanes and Batanes; the Calamian islands; and Kalayaan Islands.

HISTORY AND POLITICS

The Portuguese navigator Magellan came to the Philippines in 1521 and was killed by the natives of Mactan, a small island near Cebu. In 1565 Spain undertook the conquest of the country, which was named Filipinas after Philip II of Spain. In 1896 the Filipinos revolted against Spanish rule and declared their independence on 12 June 1898. In the Spanish–American War of 1898, Manila was captured by American troops with the help of Filipinos and the islands were ceded to the USA by the Treaty of Paris in 1898. Despite a rebellion against US rule between 1899 and 1902, the Americans remained in control of the country until 1946. The Republic of the Philippines came into existence on 4 July 1946.

Ferdinand Marcos was president from 1965 to 1986. Although he gained a majority of votes in the official count of a presidential election in February 1986, the election was marred by widespread electoral abuse and his rival, Mrs Corazón Aquino, launched a campaign of non-violent civil disturbance which gained wide support. On 25 February Marcos fled to Hawaii. Mrs Aquino took over as president and survived seven coup attempts.

Fidel Ramos was elected president in May 1992 and managed to overcome the attempted coups and legislative obstructiveness that had plagued President Aquino. The presidential election in May 1998 was won by the former vice-president, Joseph Estrada.

Legislative elections were held on 11 May 1998. The coalition of the Lakas ng EDSA/National Union of Christian Democrats won a majority in the House of Representatives.

INSURGENCIES

On 2 September 1996, the government signed an agreement with the Moro National Liberation Front (MNLF) on the creation of an autonomous Muslim region in Mindanao, Palawan, Sulu and Basilan, ending a 24-year rebellion which had left more than 120,000 people dead. The Moro Islamic Liberation Front (MILF), a radical breakaway group, threatened to disrupt the agreement. The Communist New People's Army (NPA) maintains a presence in eastern Mindanao, Negros, Samar, Bicol, the mountains of northern Luzon and Bataan. The NPA signed a cease-fire agreement with the government in December 1993; peace talks were suspended in February 1999. MILF immediately announced that its forces would come to the aid of NPA rebels should they be attacked by government forces.

POLITICAL SYSTEM

A new constitution came into force in July 1987. Legislative authority is vested in a bicameral Congress. The House of Representatives has 250 members, of whom 204 are directly elected and 46 appointed by the president for a three-year term. The Senate has 24 members, of whom 12 are re-elected every three years.

The Autonomous Region of Mindanao consists of four provinces: Sulu, Tawitawi, Lanao del Sur and Maguinadanao. There is a 24-member regional assembly and a Governor.

HEAD OF STATE

President, Minister of the Interior, Joseph Ejercito Estrada, *assumed office* 30 June 1998
Vice-President, Social Welfare, Gloria Macapagal Arroyo

CABINET *as at July 1999*

Agrarian Reform, Horacio Morales
Agriculture, William Dollente Dar
Budget and Management, Benjamin Diokno
Chief of Staff, Roberto Aventajado
Defence, Orlando Mercado
Economic Planning, Director-General of the National Economic Development Agency, Felipe Medalla
Education, Culture and Sport, Andrew Gonzales
Energy, Mario Tiaoque
Environment and Natural Resources, Antonio Cerilles
Executive Secretary, Ronaldo Zamora
Finance, Edgardo Espíritu
Foreign Affairs, Domingo Siazon
Governor of the Central Bank, Gabriel Singson
Health, Alberto Romualdez
Justice, Serafin Cuevas
Labour and Employment, Bienvenido Laguesma
National Security Adviser, Alexander Aguirre
Presidential Legal Counsel, Henrietta Demetriou
Presidential Press Secretary, Rodolfo Reyes
Public Works and Highways, Gregorio Vigilar
Science and Technology, William Padolina
Tourism, Gemma Cruz-Araneta
Trade and Industry, José Pardo
Transportation and Communications, Vicente Rivera

EMBASSY OF THE PHILIPPINES
9A Palace Green, London W8 4QE
Tel 0171-937 1600
Ambassador Extraordinary and Plenipotentiary, HE César Bautista, apptd 1999
Defence Attaché, Col. P. Inserto
Commercial Attaché, V. Casim

BRITISH EMBASSY
Floors 15–17 LV Locsin Building, 6752 Ayala Avenue, Corner Makati Avenue, 1226 Makati, Metro Manila (PO Box 2927 MCPO)
Tel: Manila 816 7116
Ambassador Extraordinary and Plenipotentiary, HE Alan Collins, CMG, apptd 1998
Deputy Head of Mission, M. Reilly
Defence Attaché, Capt. C. C. Peach, RN
First Secretary, E. McEvoy *(Commercial)*

BRITISH COUNCIL DIRECTOR, R. Bell, 10F Taipan Place, Emerald Avenue, Ortigas Business Centre, Pasig City 1605, Manila

DEFENCE

The Army has 85 armoured infantry fighting vehicles, 375 armoured personnel carriers, and 242 artillery pieces. The Navy has one frigate, 67 patrol and coastal vessels and eight combat aircraft at three bases. The Air Force has 39 combat aircraft and 99 armed helicopters.
MILITARY EXPENDITURE – 1.7 per cent of GDP (1997)
MILITARY PERSONNEL – 160,300: Army 74,500, Navy 25,900, Air Force 17,400, Paramilitaries 42,500

ECONOMY

The Philippines is predominantly agricultural, the chief products being rice, coconuts, sugar cane, bananas, maize and pineapples. There are an increasing number of manufacturing industries and it is the policy of the government to diversify the economy. There are also deposits of copper, coal, gold, silver, chromium, iron and nickel.

The Philippines has been bypassed by the economic growth of most of the rest of south-east Asia since the 1960s, mainly because of the incompetence and corruption of the Marcos regime. Recently, however, an economic reform programme of liberalization, privatization and deregulation has been put in place and has led to increased exports, increased foreign investment, and a reduction in inflation. In July 1998, the Bank of the Philippines effectively devalued the peso following attacks from speculators, prompted by the devaluation of the Thai baht. In December 1997, the government unveiled an austerity plan cutting spending by 25 per cent. Prompt and firm measures from the government are credited with limiting the damage caused by the regional economic crisis.
GNP – US$88,372 million (1997); US$1,200 per capita (1997)
GDP – US$74,134 million (1995); US$1,093 per capita (1995)
ANNUAL AVERAGE GROWTH OF GDP – 9.7 per cent (1997)
INFLATION RATE – 5.1 per cent (1997)
UNEMPLOYMENT – 8.4 per cent (1995)
TOTAL EXTERNAL DEBT – US$45,433 million (1997)

TRADE

Principal exports are electronic products, clothing, coconut oil, and wooden handicrafts and furniture. Principal imports are electronic components, fuels, machinery and telecommunications and transport equipment. The major trading partners are the USA, Japan, Singapore and Hong Kong.

In 1997 the Philippines had a trade deficit of US$11,127 million and a current account deficit of US$4,303 million. In 1996 imports totalled US$34,122 million and exports US$20,417 million.

Trade with UK	1997	1998
Imports from UK	£600,112,000	£304,129,000
Exports to UK	761,177,000	898,956,000

COMMUNICATIONS

The highway system covers about 187,000 kilometres. The Philippine National Railway operates 429 km of track. There are 415 ports. There are 82 national airports and 137 privately operated airports. Philippine Airlines has regular flights throughout the Far East, to the USA and Europe, in addition to inter-island services.

EDUCATION

Secondary and higher education is extensive and there are 21 public and 53 private universities recognized by the government, including the Dominican University of Santo

Tomás (founded in 1611). There are also 530 other institutions of higher education.

ILLITERACY RATE – 5.4 per cent

ENROLMENT (percentage of age group) – primary 100 per cent (1995); secondary 60 per cent (1995); tertiary 29.7 per cent (1995)

POLAND
Rzeczpospolita Polska

AREA – 124,808 sq. miles (323,250 sq. km). Neighbours: the Russian Federation (Kaliningrad) (north), Germany (west), the Czech Republic and Slovakia (south), Belarus, Ukraine and Lithuania (east)

POPULATION – 38,628,000 (1995). Roman Catholicism is the religion of 95 per cent of the inhabitants. The language is Polish; there are German, Ukrainian and Belarusian minorities

CAPITAL – Warsaw (population, 1,643,203, 1993), on the Vistula

MAJOR CITIES – Bydgoszcz (384,101); Gdańsk (Danzig) (462,239); Katowice (359,776); Kraków (744,203); Łódź (835,807); Poznań (582,839); Szczecin (Stettin) (417,115); Wrocław (Breslau) (641,386)

CURRENCY – Złoty of 100 groszy

NATIONAL ANTHEM – Jeszcze Polska Nie Zginela (Poland has not yet been destroyed)

NATIONAL DAY – 3 May

NATIONAL FLAG – Equal horizontal stripes of white (above) and red

LIFE EXPECTANCY (years) – male 67.37; female 76.00

POPULATION GROWTH RATE – 0.2 per cent (1997)

POPULATION DENSITY – 107 per sq. km (1996)

URBAN POPULATION – 61.9 per cent (1995)

HISTORY AND POLITICS

The Polish Commonwealth ceased to exist in 1795 after three successive partitions in 1772, 1793 and 1795 in which Prussia, Russia and Austria shared. The Republic of Poland was proclaimed at Warsaw in November 1918, and its independence guaranteed by the signatories of the Treaty of Versailles.

German forces invaded Poland on 1 September 1939; on 17 September, Russian forces invaded eastern Poland, and on 21 September 1939 Poland was declared by Germany and Russia to have ceased to exist. At the end of the war, its frontiers were redrawn; eastern Poland was ceded to the Soviet Union in return for the German territory east of the rivers Oder and Neisse. A coalition government was formed in which the Polish Workers' Party played a large part. In December 1948, the Polish Workers' Party and the Polish Socialist Party merged to form the Polish United Workers' Party (PUWP). A new constitution modelled on the Soviet constitution was adopted in 1952, and was modified in 1976.

Steep price rises in 1980 prompted strikes which forced the government to allow independent trade unions, including 'Solidarity' led by Lech Wałęsa. The unions agitated for further reforms although their activities were suspended when martial law was in force from December 1981 until July 1983.

A wave of strikes resulted in talks between Wałęsa and the PUWP early in 1989. Multiparty parliamentary elections were held in the summer of 1989, following which the PUWP ceased to be the ruling party. The post-Communist governments have introduced a market economy but economic difficulties and a fragmented parliament have led to a succession of short-lived governments.

Elections held on 21 September 1997 were won by the right-wing Solidarity Electoral Alliance (AWS), a group of 36 parties, which formed a government with Freedom Union (UW). The AWS won 201 seats in the *Sejm* and 51 in the Senate; the UW won 60 seats in the *Sejm* and 8 in the Senate.

FOREIGN RELATIONS

In July 1997, Poland was invited to join NATO. It has also been approved by the European Commission for membership of the EU, and formal accession talks began in March 1998.

POLITICAL SYSTEM

A new constitution came into effect on 16 October 1997. The president, directly elected for a maximum of two five-year terms, appoints the prime minister and has the right to be consulted over the appointment of the foreign, defence and interior ministers. The National Assembly is the bicameral legislature, comprising a 460-member *Sejm* (Diet) and a Senate of 100 members. Both houses have a four-year term. The Senate is elected on a provincial basis.

HEAD OF STATE

President, Aleksander Kwaśniewski, *elected* 19 November 1995, *sworn in* 23 December 1995

COUNCIL OF MINISTERS *as at July 1999*

Prime Minister, Jerzy Buzek (AWS)
Deputy PM, Finance, Leszek Balcerowicz (UW)
Deputy PM, Internal Affairs and Administration, Janusz Tomaszewski (AWS)
Agriculture and Food Economy, Artur Balazs (AWS)
Culture and Arts, Andrzej Zakrzewski (SKL)
Economy, Janusz Steinhoff (AWS)
Environmental Protection, Natural Resources and Forestry, Jan Szyszko (AWS)
European Integration Committee, Maria Karasińska-Fendler (AWS)
Foreign Affairs, Bronislaw Geremek (UW)
Health and Social Security, Franciszka Cegielska (AWS)
Justice, Hanna Suchocka (UW)
Labour and Social Policy, Longin Komolowski (AWS)
National Defence, Janusz Onyszkiewicz (UW)
National Education, Mirosław Handke (AWS)
National Security Bureau, Marek Siwiec (AWS)
Scientific Research Committee, Andrzej Wiszniewski (AWS)
Telecommunications, Maciej Srebro (AWS)
Transport and Maritime Economy, Tadeusz Syryjczyk
Treasury, Emil Wasacz (AWS)
Without Portfolio, Ryszard Czarnecki *(European Integration Affairs)*; Kazimierz Kapera *(Family Affairs)*; Jerzy Widzyk *(Floods)*; Jerzy Kropiwnicki *(Government Centre for Strategic Studies)*; Teresa Kamińska *(Social Reforms)*; Janusz Palubicki *(Security Services)*

AWS Solidarity Electoral Alliance; UW Freedom Union

EMBASSY OF THE REPUBLIC OF POLAND
47 Portland Place, London WIN 3AG
Tel 0171-580 4324/9
Ambassador Extraordinary and Plenipotentiary, HE Ryszard Stemplowski, apptd 1994
Defence Attaché, Capt. I. Goreczny

BRITISH EMBASSY
No. 1 Aleje Róz, PL-00-556 Warsaw
Tel: Warsaw 628 1001/5
Ambassador Extraordinary and Plenipotentiary, HE John Macgregor, CVO, apptd 1998
Counsellor, R. A. Barnett *(Deputy Head of Mission)*
Defence and Air Attaché, Gp Capt. M. Mitchell

Counsellor (Commercial and Consul-General), S. D. Pattison
Honorary Consulates – Gdańsk, Katowice, Poznań,
Szczecin, Wrocław (Breslau)

British Council Director, J. Eyres, Al. Jerozolimskie
59, PL-00–697 Warsaw

DEFENCE

The Army has 1,727 main battle tanks, 1,405 armoured
infantry fighting vehicles, 35 armoured personnel carriers,
and 1,580 artillery pieces. The Navy has three submarines,
one destroyer, one frigate, 33 patrol and coastal vessels, 28
combat aircraft and 11 armed helicopters at five bases. The
Air Force has 297 combat aircraft and 32 attack helicopters.
Military Expenditure – 2.3 per cent of GDP (1997)
Military Personnel – 238,300: Army 142,500, Navy
17,100, Air Force 55,300, Paramilitaries 23,400
Conscription Duration – 12 months

ECONOMY

Poland is well endowed with mineral resources; there are
large reserves of brown coal in central and south-western
Poland and hard coal in Upper Silesia and the Wałbrzych
and Lublin regions; sulphur, copper, zinc, lead, natural gas
and salt are also produced.

In 1990, the government embarked upon a series of
measures designed to introduce a free-market economy.

The transition to a market economy has been painful,
with unemployment doubling between 1990 and 1995.
Industrial output has improved and the rate of growth of
GDP has increased although inflation remains high.

The government has committed itself to reform the
health and education services, pension regulations and
local government. A campaign of strikes and blockades
began in December 1998 and continued until March 1999
in protest at the reforms and the refusal of the government
to impose import tariffs to protect farmers.

Poland's major imports are petroleum, chemicals, textiles, and industrial and electrical equipment. Its major
exports are fruits and vegetables, clothing, coal, non-
ferrous metals, iron, steel, furniture and transport equipment. Germany is Poland's main trading partner.

In 1996 there was a trade deficit of US$7,287 million
and a current account deficit of US$3,264 million. In 1997
imports totalled US$42,308 million and exports US$25,751
million.
GNP – US$138,909 million (1997); US$3,590 per capita
(1997)
GDP – US$117,906 million (1995); US$3,058 per capita
(1995)
Annual Average Growth of GDP – 7.0 per cent
(1995)
Inflation Rate – 15.9 per cent (1997)
Unemployment – 13.1 per cent (1995)
Total External Debt – US$39,890 million (1997)

Trade with UK	1997	1998
Imports from UK	£1,354,407,000	£1,213,416,000
Exports to UK	621,175,000	684,035,000

EDUCATION

Elementary education (ages seven to 15) is compulsory
and free. Secondary education is optional and free. There
are 179 institutions of higher education, including universities at Kraków, Warsaw, Poznan, Łódź, Wrocław, Lublin
and Toruń and a number of other towns.
Enrolment (percentage of age group) – primary 95 per
cent (1995); secondary 84 per cent (1994); tertiary 24.7
per cent (1995)

CULTURE

Polish is a western Slavonic tongue, the Latin alphabet
being used. Major writers include Henryk Sienkiewicz
(1846–1916), Nobel Prizewinner for Literature in 1905;
Bolesław Prus (1847–1912); Stanisław Reymont (1868–
1925), Nobel Prizewinner in 1924; Czesław Miłosz, Nobel
Prizewinner in 1980; and Wisława Szymborska, Nobel
Prizewinner in 1996.

PORTUGAL
República Portuguesa

Area – 35,514 sq. miles (91,982 sq. km). Neighbour: Spain
(north and east)
Population – 9,920,760 (1995); 9,833,014 (excluding the
Azores and Madeira). 94 per cent of the population are
Catholic. The language is Portuguese
Capital – ΨLisbon (population, 2,561,225, 1991)
Major Cities – ΨOporto (1,683,000)
Currency – Escudo (Esc) of 100 centavos
National Anthem – A Portuguesa
National Day – 10 June
National Flag – Divided vertically into unequal parts
of green and red with the national emblem over all on
the line of division
Life Expectancy (years) – male 71.18; female 78.23
Population Growth Rate – 0.1 per cent (1997)
Population Density – 107 per sq. km (1996)
Urban Population – 48.2 per cent (1991)

HISTORY AND POLITICS

Portugal was a monarchy from the 12th century until 1910,
when an armed rising in Lisbon drove King Manuel II into
exile and a republic was set up. A period of political
instability ensued until the military stepped in and
abolished political parties in 1926. The constitution of 1933
gave formal expression to the corporative 'Estado Novo'
(New State) which was personified by Dr Antonio Salazar,
prime minister 1932–68. Dr Caetano succeeded Salazar as
prime minister in 1968 but his failure to liberalize the
regime or to conclude the wars in the African colonies
resulted in his government's overthrow by a military coup
on 25 April 1974. There was great political turmoil between
April 1974 and July 1976, a period in which most of the
colonies gained their independence, but with the failure of
an attempted coup by the extreme left in November 1975
the situation stabilized. Full civilian government was
restored in 1982.

In the general election held on 1 October 1995, the
Socialist Party (PS) won 112 seats, the Social Democrats
(PSD) 88 seats, the Christian Democrats (CDS/PP) 15
seats, and the Communist Coalition (CDU) 15 seats. The
Socialist candidate, Jorge Sampaio, won the January 1996
presidential election.

POLITICAL SYSTEM

Under the 1976 constitution, amended in 1982 and 1989,
the president is elected for a five-year term by universal
adult suffrage. The prime minister is designated by the
largest party in the legislature. Legislative authority is
vested in the 230-member Assembly of the Republic,
elected by a system of proportional representation every
four years. The president retains certain limited powers to
dismiss the government, dissolve the Assembly or veto
laws.

President of the Republic, Jorge Sampaio, elected 14 January
1996, inaugurated 9 March 1996

COUNCIL OF MINISTERS as at July 1999
Prime Minister, António Guterres
Deputy PM, Foreign Affairs, Jaime Gama
Agriculture, Food and Fisheries, Luis Capoulas Santos
Culture, Manuel Maria Carrilho
Defence, vacant
Economy, Joaquim Pina Moura
Education, Eduardo Marçal Grilo
Environment, Elisa Ferreira
Finance, António Sousa Franco
Health, Maria de Belém Roseira
Interior, Jorge Coelho
Justice, José Vera Jardim
Parliamentary Affairs, Antonio Costa
Planning, Public Works and Territorial Administration, João
   Cravinho
Science and Technology, José Mariano Gago
Secretary of State to the Prime Minister, Antonio José Seguro
Secretary of State to the Prime Minister for Youth, Sport and
   Drug Addiction, José Socrates
Solidarity, Social Security, Employment, Eduardo Ferro
   Rodrigues

PORTUGUESE EMBASSY
11 Belgrave Square, London SW1X 8PP
Tel 0171-235 5331
Ambassador Extraordinary and Plenipotentiary, José Gregório
   Faria, apptd 1997
Minister-Counsellor and Consul-General, A. de Almeida
   Ribeiro
Minister-Counsellor, J. Ramos Pinto
Defence Attaché, Capt. J. de Mendonca

BRITISH EMBASSY
Rua de S. Bernardo 33, PT-1200 Lisbon
Tel: Lisbon 392 4000
Ambassador Extraordinary and Plenipotentiary, HE Sir John
   Holmes, apptd 1999
Counsellor, R. M. Publicover (Deputy Head of Mission)
Defence Attaché, Cdr. R. Goddard
First Secretary, P. Sinkinson (Commercial)

CONSULATES – Oporto, Portimão, Funchal (Madeira),
   Ribeira Grande (Azores), Macao

BRITISH COUNCIL DIRECTOR, R. S. Pryde, Rua de São
   Marçal 174, PT-1294 Lisbon. There are also offices at
   Cascais, Coimbra, Oporto and Parede
BRITISH PORTUGUESE CHAMBER OF COMMERCE, Rua
   da Estrela 8, PT-1200 Lisbon and Rua Sa de Bandeira
   784–20E, Frente, PT-4000 Oporto

DEFENCE

The Army has 180 main battle tanks, 361 armoured
personnel carriers and 290 artillery pieces. The Navy has
three submarines, ten frigates and 27 patrol and coastal
vessels at four bases. The Air Force has 68 combat aircraft.
   Lisbon is the base of the NATO Iberian Atlantic
Command and the USA maintains 1,050 personnel in
mainland Portugal and on the Azores.
MILITARY EXPENDITURE – 2.6 per cent of GDP (1997)
MILITARY PERSONNEL – 89,850: Army 24,800, Navy
   16,850, Air Force 7,300, Paramilitaries 40,900
CONSCRIPTION DURATION – Four to 12 months

ECONOMY

The chief agricultural products are wines, dairy products,
potatoes, tomatoes, maize, meat, fruits, olives, wheat, fish,
cork and rice. There are extensive forests of pine, cork,
eucalyptus and chestnut covering about 38 per cent of the
country. The principal mineral products are limestone,
granite, marble, copper, coal, kaolin and wolframite.
   The country is moderately industrialized. The principal
manufactures are motor vehicle components, clothing and
footwear, textiles, machinery, pulp and paper, pharmaceuticals, foodstuffs, chemicals, fertilizers, wood, cork, furniture, cement, glassware and pottery. There are a modern
steelworks and large shipbuilding and repair yards at
Lisbon and Setúbal, working mainly for foreign shipowners.
There are several hydroelectric power stations and two
thermal power stations.
   Since joining the EC (EU) in 1986 Portugal has been
adjusting its economy to the European single market, and
to the economic and monetary union criteria laid down in
the Maastricht Treaty. The escudo joined the ERM in
April 1992; having satisfied the convergence criteria,
Portugal was one of 11 states to adopt the European single
currency on 1 January 1999.
GNP – US$109,472 million (1997); US$11,010 per capita
   (1997)
GDP – US$102,352 million (1995); US$10,428 per capita
   (1995)
ANNUAL AVERAGE GROWTH OF GDP – 3.0 per cent
   (1996)
INFLATION RATE – 2.2 per cent (1997)
UNEMPLOYMENT – 5.5 per cent (1993)

TRADE

The principal imports are machinery, vehicles, agricultural
products, chemicals, oil, metals and textiles. The principal
exports are automobile parts, vehicles, clothing, minerals,
pulp and paper, cork and timber, and foodstuffs and
beverages.
   In 1997 Portugal had a trade deficit of US$9,551 million
and a current account deficit of US$1,877 million. In 1996
imports totalled US$34,104 million and exports US$23,824
million.

Trade with UK	1997	1998
Imports from UK	£1,661,700,000	£1,620,700,000
Exports to UK	1,690,600,000	1,695,800,000

COMMUNICATIONS

There are 3,072 km of railway track, of which 461 km are
electrified. There are international airports at Lisbon,
Oporto, Faro and Santa Maria and Lages (Azores) and
Funchal (Madeira). There are 23 daily newspapers.

EDUCATION

Education is free and compulsory for nine years from the
age of six. Secondary education is mainly conducted in
state general unified schools, lyceums, technical and
professional schools, but there are also private schools.
There are also military, naval, polytechnic and other
special schools. There are 17 public and private universities
including those at Coimbra (founded in 1290), Oporto,
Lisbon, Braga, Aveiro, Vila Real, Faro, Evora and in the
Azores.
ILLITERACY RATE – 10.4 per cent
ENROLMENT (percentage of age group) – primary 100 per
   cent (1994); secondary 78 per cent (1994); tertiary 36.8
   per cent (1994)

AUTONOMOUS REGIONS

Madeira and The Azores are two administratively autonomous regions of Portugal, having locally elected assemblies and governments.

MADEIRA is a group of islands in the Atlantic Ocean about 520 miles south-west of Lisbon, and consists of Madeira, Porto, Santo and three uninhabited islands (Desertas). Total area is 300 sq. miles (779 sq. km); population, 257,290 (1995). ΨFunchal in Madeira, the largest island (270 sq. miles), is the capital (population 44,111)

THE AZORES are a group of nine islands (Flores, Corvo, Terceira, São Jorge, Pico, Faial, Graciosa, São Miguel and Santa Maria) in the Atlantic Ocean; area 895 sq. miles (2,330 sq. km); population, 241,490 (1995). ΨPonta Delgada, on São Miguel, is the capital (population, 137,700). Other ports are ΨAngra, in Terceira (55,900) and ΨHorta (16,300)

OVERSEAS TERRITORY

MACAO

AREA – 6 sq. miles (15.5 sq. km)
POPULATION – 415,850 (1997)

Macao, situated at the mouth of the Pearl River, comprises a peninsula and the islands of Coloane and Taipa.

Macao became a Portuguese colony in 1557; in a Sino-Portuguese treaty of 1887 China recognized Portugal's sovereignty over Macao. An agreement to transfer the administration of Macao to the Chinese authorities was signed on 13 April 1987. Macao will become a 'special administrative region' (SAR) of China when transferred on 20 December 1999. The final session of the Macao SAR Basic Law Drafting Committee was held in Beijing in January 1993 and approved the Basic Law which will serve as Macao's constitution after 1999.

On 10 April 1999, a 200-member committee of Macao residents was established to determine the composition of the first government of the Macao SAR. They elected Edmund Ho Hau Wah to be its first chief executive.

Governor, Gen. Vasco Rocha Vieira (until 20 December 1999)
Chief Executive, Edmund Ho Hao Wah (from 20 December 1999)

Trade with UK	1997	1998
Imports from UK	£21,163,000	£31,029,000
Exports to UK	70,809,000	53,697,000

QATAR
Dawlat Qatar

AREA – 4,247 sq. miles (11,000 sq. km). Neighbours: United Arab Emirates (south), Saudi Arabia (south-west)

POPULATION – 558,000 (1994 UN estimate). Most of the population is concentrated in the urban district of Doha. Arabic is the official language. Islam is the religion of 95 per cent of the population

CAPITAL – ΨDoha (population, 217,294, 1986)
MAJOR CITIES – Dukhan; Khor; ΨUmm Said; Wakra
CURRENCY – Qatar riyal of 100 dirhams
NATIONAL DAY – 3 September
NATIONAL FLAG – White and maroon, white portion nearer the mast; vertical indented line comprising 17 angles divides the colours
LIFE EXPECTANCY (years) – male 68.75; female 74.20
POPULATION GROWTH RATE – 5.6 per cent (1997)
POPULATION DENSITY – 51 per sq. km (1996)
MILITARY EXPENDITURE – 13.7 per cent of GDP (1997)

MILITARY PERSONNEL – 11,800: Army 8,500, Navy 1,800, Air Force 1,500
ILLITERACY RATE – 20.6 per cent
ENROLMENT (percentage of age group) – primary 80 per cent (1993); secondary 70 per cent (1993); tertiary 27.6 per cent (1995)

The state of Qatar covers the peninsula of Qatar in the Gulf from approximately the northern shore of Khor al Odaid to the eastern shore of Khor al Salwa.

HISTORY AND POLITICS

Qatar was one of nine independent emirates in the Gulf in special treaty relations with the UK until 1971. On 2 April 1970, a provisional constitution for Qatar was proclaimed, providing for the establishment of a Council of Ministers and for the formation of a Consultative Council to assist the Council of Ministers in running the affairs of the state. There are no political parties or legislature; ministers are chosen by the Amir.

The Amir, who had ruled since 22 February 1972, was overthrown on 27 June 1995 by his son and heir, who assumed power as Amir the same day. A coup attempt was thwarted in February 1996.

The Amir announced in November 1998 that a committee of experts would be formed to draft a new constitution and that an elected National Assembly would be established. Municipal elections were held on 8 March 1999, the first in which women were allowed to vote and contest seats.

HEAD OF STATE
HH Amir of Qatar, Minister of Defence and Commander-in-Chief of Armed Forces, Sheikh Hamad bin Khalifa Al-Thani, KCMG, *assumed power* 27 June 1995
Crown Prince, HH Sheikh Jassem bin Khalifa Al-Thani

COUNCIL OF MINISTERS *as at July 1999*

Prime Minister, Interior, HH Sheikh Abdulla bin Khalifa Al-Thani
Deputy PM, Sheikh Mohammed bin Khalifa Al-Thani
Awqaf (Religious Endowments) and Islamic Affairs, Ahmed Abdulla Al-Merri
Civil Service Affairs and Housing, Sheikh Falah bin Jassim Al-Thani
Communications and Transport, Sheikh Ahmed bin Nasser Al-Thani
Education, Higher Education and Culture, Dr Mohammed Abdulrahim Kafoud
Energy and Industry, Electricity and Water, Abdulla bin Hamad Al-Attiyah
Finance, Economy and Trade, Yousef Hussein Kamal
Foreign Affairs, Sheikh Hamad bin Jassem bin Jabr Al-Thani
Justice, Hassan bin Abdulla Al-Ghanim
Minister of State, Cabinet Affairs, Ali bin Saad al-Kawari
Minister of State, Foreign Affairs, Ahmed Abdulla Al-Mahmoud
Minister of State, Internal Affairs, Sheikh Abdullah bin Khalid Al-Thani
Ministers of State, Sheikh Mohammad bin Khalid Al-Thani; Sheikh Hamad bin Suhaim Al-Thani; Sheikh Ahmed bin Saif Al-Thani; Sheikh Hamad bin Abdulla Al-Thani; Sheikh Hasan bin Abdulla Al-Thani
Municipal Affairs, Agriculture, Ali Mohammad Al-Khater
Public Health, Dr Hajar bin Ahmed Hajar

EMBASSY OF THE STATE OF QATAR
1 South Audley Street, London W1Y 5DQ
Tel 0171-493 2200

Ambassador Extraordinary and Plenipotentiary, HE Ali M. Jaidah, apptd 1993

BRITISH EMBASSY
PO Box 3, Doha
Tel: Doha 421991
Ambassador Extraordinary and Plenipotentiary, HE D. Wright, OBE, apptd 1997

BRITISH COUNCIL DIRECTOR, J. Gildea, 93 Al Sadd Street, (PO Box 2992), Doha

ECONOMY

Although Qatar is a desert country, there are gardens and smallholdings near Doha and to the north, and agriculture is being developed, with self-sufficiency an aim.

The Qatar General Petroleum Corporation is the state-owned company controlling Qatar's interests in oil, gas and petrochemicals. The corporation is responsible for Qatar's oil production onshore and offshore. The large reserves of natural gas in the North Field came into production in September 1991.

Current industries include a steel mill, a fertilizer plant, a cement factory, a petrochemical complex and two natural gas liquids plants. With the exception of the cement works at Umm Bab, all these industries are at Umm Said, about 30 miles south of Doha. Qatar is also expanding its infrastructure, including electrical generation and water distillation, roads, houses, and government buildings. The recent drop in demand for crude oil has slowed the economy considerably.

In 1994 imports totalled US$1,927 million.

GDP – US$7,679 million (1995); US$14,013 per capita (1995)

INFLATION RATE – 7.4 per cent (1996)

Trade with UK	1997	1998
Imports from UK	£584,335,000	£293,104,000
Exports to UK	15,747,000	29,971,000

COMMUNICATIONS

There are 1,210 km of roads, of which 1,089 km are surfaced. Regular air services provided by Gulf Air and Qatar Airways connect Qatar with the other Gulf states, the Middle East, the Indian sub-continent, Africa and Europe. The Qatar Broadcasting Service transmits on medium wave, shortwave and VHF.

ROMANIA
România

AREA – 92,043 sq. miles (238,391 sq. km). Neighbours: Ukraine (north and east), Moldova (east), Bulgaria (south), Yugoslavia (south-west), Hungary (north-west)
POPULATION – 22,520,000 (1998 estimate); 22,810,035 (1992 census): 89.4 per cent Romanian, 7.1 per cent Hungarian, 1.7 per cent gypsy, 0.5 per cent German, 0.3 per cent Ukrainian, 0.04 per cent Jews and others. Religious affiliation: Orthodox 86.8 per cent, Roman Catholic 5 per cent, Reformed 3.5 per cent, Greek Catholic 1 per cent. Romanian is a Romance language with many archaic forms and with admixtures of Slavonic, Turkish, Magyar and French words
CAPITAL – Bucharest (population, 2,027,500, 1997)
MAJOR CITIES – ΨBraşov (318,000); Constanţa (345,000); Cluj-Napoca (333,000); Craiova (313,000); ΨGalaţi (331,000); Iaşi (348,000); Oradea (222,994); Ploieşti (254,386); Timişoara (334,000), UN 1997
CURRENCY – Leu (Lei) of 100 bani

NATIONAL ANTHEM – Deşteaptă, române, din somnul cel de moarte (Awake ye, Romanians, from your deadly slumber)
NATIONAL DAY – 1 December
NATIONAL FLAG – Three vertical bands, blue, yellow, red
LIFE EXPECTANCY (years) – male 65.88; female 73.32
POPULATION GROWTH RATE – –0.4 per cent (1997)
POPULATION DENSITY – 95 per sq. km (1996)
URBAN POPULATION – 54.9 per cent (1996)

HISTORY AND POLITICS

Romania has its origin in the union of the Danubian principalities of Wallachia and Moldavia in 1859 when Alexandru Ioan Cuza was elected ruler of both territories. The name Romania was adopted in 1862. Full independence was proclaimed on 9 May 1877 and was formally recognized under the Treaty of Berlin (1878) which awarded part of the territory of Dobrogea to Romania. In 1881 Romania was recognized as a kingdom.

In 1918 the populations of Bessarabia, Bukovina, Transylvania and Banat voted in favour of union with Romania, these additions being confirmed by the Versailles Treaty (1919). In 1940 the Soviet government compelled Romania to cede Bessarabia and Northern Bukovina. In the same year north-western Transylvania was ceded to Hungary and southern Dobrogea to Bulgaria.

In 1947 King Michael was forced to abdicate and Romania became 'The Romanian People's Republic'. The leading political force from the Second World War until 1989 was the Romanian Communist Party. A revolution in December 1989 led to the overthrow of Nicolae Ceauşescu, president since 1965. A provisional government abolished the leading role of the Communist Party and held free elections in May 1990.

In the elections held in November 1996 the Romanian Democratic Convention (CDR) candidate, Prof. Emil Constantinescu, was elected president and three alliances (the CDR, the Social Democratic Union (USD), and the Democratic Union of the Romanian Magyars (UDMR)) combined to form a coalition government. Following disagreements in the ruling coalition over the speed of economic reforms, Victor Ciorbea of the Christian Democratic National Peasants' Party (PNTCD) resigned as prime minister on 30 March 1998 and was replaced by Radu Vasile, also of the PNTCD.

POLITICAL SYSTEM

The constitution of 1991 formally makes Romania a multiparty democracy and endorses human rights and a market economy. The parliament comprises the Chamber of Deputies with 341 seats, of which 15 are reserved for ethnic minorities. Both houses are elected for four-year terms.

HEAD OF STATE
President of the Republic, Prof. Emil Constantinescu, *elected* 17 November 1996

CABINET *as at July 1999*

Prime Minister, acting Minister for Privatization, Radu Vasile (PNTCD)
Culture, Ion Caramitru (PNTCD)
Education, Andrei Marga (PNTCD)
Finance, Decebal Traian Remeş (PNL)
Food and Agriculture, Ioan Avram Muresan (PNTCD)
Foreign Affairs, Andrei Plesu (Ind.)
Health, Gábor Hajdu (UDMR)
Industry and Trade, Radu Berceanu (PD)
Interior, Constantin Dudu Ionescu (PNTCD)
Labour, Social Protection, Alexandru Athanasiu (Ind.)

Minister-Delegate, European Integration, attached to the Prime Minister, Alexandru Ion Herlea (PNTCD)
Minister-Delegate, National Minorities, attached to the Prime Minister, Peter Eckstein-Kovacs (UDMR)
Minister of State, Justice, Valeriu Stoica (PNL)
Minister of State, National Defence, Relations with Parliament, Victor Babiuc (PD)
Public Works and Physical Planning, Nicolae Noica (PNTCD)
Secretary-General of the Government, Radu Stroe (PNL)
Transport, Traian Basescu (PD)
Water, Forestry and Environmental Protection, Romulus Tomescu (PNTCD)

PNTCD Christian Democratic National Peasants' Party; PNL National Liberal Party; PD Democratic Party; UDMR Democratic Union of Romanian Magyars; Ind. Independent

EMBASSY OF ROMANIA
Arundel House, 4 Palace Green, London W8 4QD
Tel 0171-937 9666
Ambassador Extraordinary and Plenipotentiary, HE Radu Onofrei, apptd 1997
Defence Attaché, Col. Vasile Palcău
Minister-Counsellor, G. Moloşaga

BRITISH EMBASSY
24 Strada Jules Michelet, 70154 Bucharest
Tel: Bucharest 312 0303
Ambassador Extraordinary and Plenipotentiary, HE R. Ralph, CVO, CMG, apptd 1999
Counsellor, Deputy Head of Mission, E. A. Galves
Defence Attaché, Col. R. D. Shaw-Brown
First Secretary (Commercial), R. J. Cork

BRITISH COUNCIL DIRECTOR, H. Meixner, Calea Dorobantilor 14, Bucharest

DEFENCE

The Army has 1,254 main battle tanks, 2,100 armoured personnel carriers and armoured infantry fighting vehicles, and 1,291 artillery pieces. The Navy has one submarine, one destroyer, six frigates, 65 patrol and coastal vessels, seven helicopters, 120 main battle tanks and 144 artillery pieces at six bases. The Air Force has 341 combat aircraft and 16 attack helicopters.
MILITARY EXPENDITURE – 2.3 per cent of GDP (1997)
MILITARY PERSONNEL – 255,600: Army 111,300, Navy 22,100, Air Force 46,300, Paramilitaries 75,900
CONSCRIPTION DURATION – 12–18 months

ECONOMY

Agriculture employs 30 per cent of the workforce and contributes 18.7 per cent of GDP. The principal crops are cereals, vegetables, flax and hemp. Vines and fruits are also grown. The forests of the mountainous regions are extensive, and the timber industry is important.
    There are plentiful supplies of natural gas, together with various mineral deposits including coal, iron ore, bauxite, chromium and uranium in quantities which allow a substantial part of the requirements of industry to be met from local resources. Production of crude oil was 6,500,000 tonnes in 1997.
    The economy inherited from the totalitarian regime was characterized by state-owned and co-operative ownership, excessive centralization, rigid planning and low efficiency. After the revolution the government opted for a slow pace of reform with subsidized production resulting in budget and trade deficits, high inflation and currency depreciation. The government elected in 1996 vowed to accelerate

the restructuring and privatization of state-owned companies, reduce subsidies and liberalize prices. Nevertheless, the economy faced severe difficulties. GDP fell by 7.3 per cent in 1998 and the leu fell sharply in early 1999. A package of reforms designed to accelerate the pace of privatization was introduced in May 1999.
GNP – US$31,787 million (1997); US$1,741 per capita (1997)
GDP – US$35,686 million (1995); US$1,570 per capita (1995)
ANNUAL AVERAGE GROWTH OF GDP – 6.9 per cent (1995)
INFLATION RATE – 154.8 per cent (1997)
UNEMPLOYMENT – 8.0 per cent (1995)
TOTAL EXTERNAL DEBT – US$10,442 million (1997)

TRADE

The main imports are machines and equipment, mineral fuels, textiles, chemicals and plastics. The main exports are textiles, clothing, metallurgical products, minerals and food products. Italy, Germany, Russia and France are Romania's most important trading partners.
    In 1996 Romania had a trade deficit of US$2,470 million and a current account deficit of US$2,579 million. In 1997 imports totalled US$11,280 million and exports US$8,431 million.

Trade with UK	1997	1998
Imports from UK	£212,127,000	£235,552,000
Exports to UK	205,360,000	232,742,000

COMMUNICATIONS

In 1996 there were 11,385 km of railway track, 34 per cent of which was electrified, and 73,160 km of public roads. The main national roads largely follow the railway lines and almost all lead to the capital. The principal ports are Constanţa (on the Black Sea), Sulina (on the Danube Estuary), Galaţi, Brăila, Giurgiu and Drobeta-Turnu Severin. The Danube and the Black Sea are linked by a canal completed in 1984.

EDUCATION

Education is free and primary and secondary education are compulsory. There are state universities in seven cities, 66 private universities, six polytechnics, two commercial academies, and five agricultural colleges.
ILLITERACY RATE – 2.1 per cent
ENROLMENT (percentage of age group) – primary 96 per cent (1996); secondary 73 per cent (1996); tertiary 22.5 per cent (1996)

RUSSIA
Rossiiskaya Federatsiya – Russian Federation

AREA – 6,592,850 sq. miles (17,075,400 sq. km).
    Neighbours: Norway, Finland, Estonia, Latvia, Belarus and Ukraine (west),Georgia, Azerbaijan, Kazakhstan, China, Mongolia and North Korea (south). The Kaliningrad enclave borders Lithuania and Poland
POPULATION – 146,100,000 (1999 estimate): 87.5 per cent Russian, 3.5 per cent Tatar, 2.7 per cent Ukrainian, 1.3 per cent ethnic German, 1.1 per cent Chavash, 0.9 per cent Bashkir, 0.7 per cent Belarusian and 0.7 per cent Mordovian. There are another six minorities with populations of over half a million and more than 130 nationalities in total. The Russian Orthodox Church is the predominant religion, though the Tatars are Muslims and there are Jewish communities in Moscow and St Petersburg. The language is Russian

CAPITAL – Moscow (population, 8,598,896, 1998 estimate), founded about 1147, became the centre of the rising Moscow principality and in the 15th century the capital of the whole of Russia (Muscovy). In 1325 it became the seat of the Metropolitan of Russia. In 1703 Peter the Great transferred the capital to St Petersburg, but on 14 March 1918 Moscow was again designated as the capital

MAJOR CITIES – ΨSt Petersburg (4,778,900, 1998), from 1914 to 1924 Petrograd and from 1924 to 1991 Leningrad. Other cities: Chelyabinsk (1,143,000); Kazan (1,094,000); Nizhny-Novgorod/Gorky (1,438,000); Novosibirsk/Novonikolayevsk (1,436,000); Omsk (1,148,000); Perm/Molotov (1,091,000); Rostov-on-Don (1,020,000); Samara/Kuibyshev (1,257,000); Ufa (1,083,000); Yekaterinburg/Sverdlovsk (1,367,000), 1990

CURRENCY – New Rouble of 100 kopeks
NATIONAL ANTHEM – The Patriotic Song
NATIONAL DAY – 12 June (Independence Day)
NATIONAL FLAG – Three horizontal stripes of white, blue, red
LIFE EXPECTANCY (years) – male 57.59; female 71.18
POPULATION GROWTH RATE – 0.1 per cent (1997)
POPULATION DENSITY – 9 per sq. km (1996)
URBAN POPULATION – 72.9 per cent (1995)
ILLITERACY RATE – 2.0 per cent
ENROLMENT (percentage of age group) – primary 93 per cent (1994); tertiary 42.9 per cent (1994)

Russia occupies three-quarters of the land area of the former Soviet Union.

The Russian Federation comprises 89 members: 49 regions (*oblast*) – Amur, Arkhangelsk, Astrakhan, Belgorod, Bryansk, Chelyabinsk, Chita, Irkutsk, Ivanovo, Kaliningrad, Kaluga, Kamchatka, Kemerovo, Kirov, Kostroma, Kurgan, Kursk, Leningrad, Lipetsk, Magadan, Moscow, Murmansk, Nizhny-Novgorod, Novgorod, Novosibirsk, Omsk, Orel, Orenburg, Penza, Perm, Pskov, Rostov, Ryazan, Sakhalin, Samara, Saratov, Smolensk, Sverdlovsk, Tambov, Tomsk, Tula, Tver, Tyumen, Ulyanovsk, Vladimir, Volgograd, Vologda, Voronezh, Yaroslavl; six autonomous territories (*krai*) – Altai, Khabarovsk, Krasnodar, Krasnoyarsk, Primorye, Stavropol; 21 republics – Adygeia, Altai, Bashkortostan, Buryatia, Chechnya, Chuvash, Daghestan, Ingush,

Kabardino-Balkar, Kalmykia, Karachai-Circassian, Karelia, Khakassia, Komi, Mari-El, Mordovia, North Ossetia (Alania), Sakha, Tatarstan, Tyva, Udmurt; ten autonomous areas – Aga-Buryat, Chuckchi, Evenki, Khanty-Mansi, Komi-Permyak, Koryak, Nenets, Taimyr, Ust-Orda-Buryat, Yamal-Nenets; two cities of federal status – Moscow, St Petersburg; and one autonomous Jewish region, Birobijan.

There are three principal geographic areas: a low-lying flat western area stretching eastwards up to the Yenisei and divided in two by the Ural ridge; the eastern area between the Yenisei and the Pacific, consisting of a number of tablelands and ridges; and a southern mountainous area. Russia has a very long coastline, including the longest Arctic coastline in the world (about 17,000 miles).

The most important rivers are the Volga, the Northern Dvina and the Pechora, the Neva, the Don and the Kuban in the European part, and in the Asiatic part, the Ob, the Irtysh, the Yenisei, the Lena and the Amur, and, further north, Khatanga, Olenek, Yana, Indigirka, Kolyma and Anadyr. Lake Baikal in eastern Siberia is the deepest lake in the world.

HISTORY AND POLITICS

The Gregorian calendar was not introduced until 14 February 1918. For the events surrounding the 1917 revolutions the dates given here are the Gregorian calendar dates in use in the rest of the world at the time, with the dates in the Julian calendar (OS) in parenthesis.

Russia was formally created from the principality of Muscovy and its territories by Tsar Peter I (The Great) (1682–1725), who initiated its territorial expansion, introduced Western ideas of government and founded St Petersburg. By the end of Peter the Great's reign, the Baltic territories (modern-day Estonia and Latvia) had been annexed from Sweden, and Russia had become the dominant military power of north-eastern Europe. In the 18th century the partitions of Poland and wars with Turkey brought the territories of modern-day Lithuania, Belarus, Ukraine and the Crimea under Russian control, and the colonization of Siberia east of the Urals began in earnest. Russia overran the Caucasus region (modern-day Armenia, Azerbaijan and Georgia) in the early 19th century, seized Finland from Sweden in 1809 and Bessarabia from Turkey in 1812. Throughout the remainder of the 19th century Russia subdued and annexed the independent Muslim states which later formed the five Central Asian republics.

Discontent caused by autocratic rule, the poor conduct of the military in the First World War and wartime privation led to a revolution which broke out on 12 March (27 February OS) 1917. Tsar Nicholas II abdicated three days later and a provisional government was formed; a republic was proclaimed on 14 September (1 September OS) 1917. A power struggle ensued between the provisional government and the Bolshevik Party which controlled the Soviets (councils) set up by workers, soldiers and peasants. This led to a second revolution on 7 November (25 October OS) 1917 in which the Bolsheviks, led by Lenin, seized power.

The Bolshevik (Communist) Party withdrew from the First World War under the Treaty of Brest-Litovsk (March 1918), surrendering large areas of territory. Armed resistance to Communist rule developed into an all-out civil war between 'red' Bolshevik forces and 'white' monarchist and anti-Communist forces which lasted until the end of 1922. During the civil war, Russia had been declared a Soviet Republic and other Soviet republics had been formed in Ukraine, Byelorussia and Transcaucasia. These four republics merged to form the Union of Soviet Socialist Republics (USSR) on 30 December 1922.

The Nazi–Soviet pact of August 1939 and the Second World War resulted in further territorial expansion, regaining much of the territory lost in or after 1918, as well as extending Soviet influence to the countries of eastern Europe liberated by Soviet troops. The USSR lost 26 million combatants and civilians in the war.

Joseph Stalin emerged as the undisputed party leader in 1928. He introduced a policy of rapid industrialization under a series of five-year plans, brought all sectors of industry under government control, abolished private ownership and enforced the collectivization of agriculture. He eliminated potential political opponents through purges and show trials, and total political repression lasted until his death in 1953.

Repression lessened under Khrushchev and Brezhnev, but the Communist Party remained dominant in all walks of life. This was the state of affairs when Mikhail Gorbachev became Soviet leader in March 1985. Gorbachev introduced the policies of *perestroika* (complete restructuring) and *glasnost* (openness) in order to revamp the economy, which had stagnated since the 1970s, to root out corruption and inefficiency, and to end the Cold War and its attendant arms race. The retreat from total control by the Communist Party unleashed ethnic and nationalist tensions.

On 19 August 1991 a coup was attempted by hardline elements of the Communist Party, the armed forces and the state security service (KGB) in an attempt to reimpose Communist control on the USSR. The coup was defeated by reformist and democratic political groups under the leadership of Russian President Yeltsin. Mikhail Gorbachev returned to Moscow although it became clear that effective political power was in the hands of the republican leaders, especially Russian President Yeltsin, and the Soviet Union began to break up as the constituent republics declared their independence. Gorbachev resigned as Soviet President on 25 December 1991 and on 26 December 1991 the USSR formally ceased to exist.

Russia was recognized as an independent state by the EC and USA in January 1992; it took over the Soviet Union's seat at the UN in December 1991.

A new Russian Federal Treaty was signed on 13 March 1992 between the central government and the autonomous republics. Tatarstan refused to sign the Treaty and in April 1992 declared its 'independence'. In February 1994

Tatarstan signed its own agreement with the federal government on the basis of being a 'state united with Russia'. Similarly, after declaring its 'independence' in March 1992, Bashkortostan signed a treaty with the Federation in August 1994 giving it considerable legislative and economic autonomy.

The state of the parties in the State *Duma* following the January 1996 election was: Communist Party 157 seats; Our Home is Russia 55; Liberal Democratic Party 51; Yabloko 45; Agrarian Party 20; Russia's Democratic Choice 9; Power to the People 9; Congress of Russian Communities 5; Independents 77; others 22. Boris Yeltsin was elected president on the second ballot on 3 July 1996, ahead of Communist Party candidate Gennadi Zyuganov.

A brief period of economic growth was followed by instability in the financial markets in early 1998. President Yeltsin dismissed the cabinet in March 1998, and appointed Sergei Kiriyenko, a little-known banker, to replace Viktor Chernomyrdin as prime minister. This did little to restore confidence in the economy and following a major collapse on the Russian stock exchange, Yeltsin once more dismissed the cabinet in August 1998. He nominated Chernomyrdin as prime minister but the *Duma* twice rejected the appointment. To avert a constitutional crisis, Yeltsin then nominated Foreign Minister Yevgeni Primakov, seen as a compromise candidate whose appointment as prime minister would appease all factions in the *Duma*. Although Primakov was successful in stabilizing the economy and improving relations with the *Duma*, President Yeltsin ordered his dismissal on 12 May 1999 and appointed Sergei Stepashin as prime minister, but dismissed him also on 9 August 1999 and replaced him with Vladimir Putin, whose appointment was confirmed by the *Duma* on 16 August.

POLITICAL SYSTEM

The 1993 constitution enshrines the right to private ownership and the freedoms of press, speech, association, worship and travel, and states that Russia is a multiparty democracy. The president is head of state and of government, head of the Security Council and commander-in-chief of the armed forces and may declare war or declare a state of emergency or martial law, subject to confirmation by the Federation Council. He may chair Cabinet meetings, determine basic government policy, veto legislation, issue decrees and directives, call referendums, dismiss the government, and nominate senior judges, the prosecutor-general and the Central Bank Governor. The president nominates the prime minister and deputy prime ministers, who must be approved by the State *Duma*.

The president is directly elected for a maximum of two four-year terms, and may only be impeached on the grounds of treason or serious crime after rulings in both the Supreme and Constitutional Courts and two-thirds majorities in both houses of parliament. The prime minister takes over from the president in the event that he is unable to fulfil his duties.

Legislative power is vested in the Federal Assembly, comprising the Federation Council (upper house) of 178 members, two elected by each of the 89 members of the Russian Federation; the State *Duma* (lower house) of 450 members, of which 225 are elected by constituencies on a first-past-the-post basis and 225 by proportional representation, with a 5 per cent threshold for representation. State *Duma* deputies may not serve as ministers. The Council is composed of two representatives from each constituent territory of the Federation: the head of the legislative and the head of the executive body.

The State *Duma*, elected for four-year terms, oversees government appointments, has the power to reject the government's fiscal and monetary policies, may pass votes of no confidence in the government (which the president may ignore on the first vote), and cannot be dissolved less than one year after its election.

The judicial system consists of a Constitutional Court of 19 members appointed for a 12-year term which protects and interprets the constitution and decides if laws are compatible with it. The Supreme Court adjudicates in criminal and civil laws cases. The Arbitration Court deals with commercial disputes between companies. The new code of civil law came into force in January 1995.

INSURGENCIES

The Chechen republic declared its 'independence' in November 1991 after a nationalist coup in the republic which brought former Soviet Air Force General Dudayev to power as republican president. Chechnya refused to sign the Russian Federal Treaty in March 1992 and a constitutional stalemate ensued. Civil war began in early 1994 between Gen. Dudayev's forces and armed opposition forces of the 'Provisional Chechen Council', tacitly supported by the Russian government. On 9 December 1994 President Yeltsin ordered the Russian military to retake the republic. Chechen forces were finally forced out of Grozny in early February 1995.

A peace accord was signed on 30 July 1995 which provided for the disarming of rebels and the withdrawal of Russian troops. The agreement collapsed in October 1995, however, and a state of emergency was declared by the Russian government. The Russian-approved candidate was elected head of state of Chechnya on 17 December 1995 and concluded an autonomy accord with Russia giving the region autonomous status within the Federation. The rebels rejected the accord, and attacked Grozny in March 1996. President Yeltsin's new National Security Adviser, Gen. Lebed, resumed negotiations with the rebels in August 1996, reaching an agreement to end hostilities and to delay a decision on Chechnya's final status until 2001. The last Russian troops were withdrawn in January 1997 when presidential and legislative elections were also held in Chechnya. A treaty renouncing the use of force to resolve Chechnya's status was signed between Presidents Maskhadov and Yeltsin in May 1997. In September 1997, Chechnya introduced *Sharia* law, leading to public executions which were strongly criticized by Russia. A state of emergency was declared and a curfew imposed in June 1998 following an increase in serious criminal activity.

In November 1992 President Yeltsin imposed direct rule in the autonomous republics of Ingush and North Ossetia after Ingush forces attacked North Ossetia; a state of emergency was declared in the two autonomous republics in March 1993; it remains in place.

On 10 August 1999, Islamic rebels led by Shamil Basayev, a Chechen warlord, launched an incursion into Dagestan, declaring it to be an independent Islamic state. The Russian government immediately dispatched troops to the mountainous frontier region of Dagestan to quell the insurgency; a state of emergency was declared in Chechnya after Russia threatened to attack rebel bases located there.

FOREIGN RELATIONS

A union treaty was signed by the presidents of Russia and Belarus in April 1997. Both countries will retain sovereignty and territorial integrity although citizens of the two countries will also be citizens of the Union. The presidents of the two countries decided in December 1998 to effect a currency union.

A Founding Act was signed by Russia and NATO in May 1997 which lays down the principles of post-Cold War co-operation. A joint permanent council is to be set up.

HEAD OF STATE
President, Boris Yeltsin, *elected* 12 June 1991, *re-elected* 3 July 1996, *inaugurated* 9 August 1996

GOVERNMENT *as at August 1999*
Prime Minister, Vladimir Putin
First Deputy PMs, Nikolai Aksenenko; Viktor Khristenko
Deputy PMs, Vladimir Shcherbak *(Agriculture and Foodstuffs)*; Ilya Klebanov *(Military/Industrial Complex)*; Valentina Matviyenko *(Social Issues)*
Anti-Monopoly Policy and Support for Entrepreneurship, Ilya Yuzhanov
Chair of Commission on Co-operation with the G8, Alexander Livschitz
CIS Affairs, Leonid Drachevsky
Culture, Vladimir Yegorov
Economy, Andrei Shapovalyants
Education, Vladimir Filippov
Federation and Nationalities Affairs, Vyacheslav Mikhailov
Finance, Mikhail Kasyanov
Foreign Affairs, Igor Ivanov
Fuel and Energy, Viktor Kalyuzhny
Health, Yuri Shevchenko
Interior, Vladimir Rushailo
Justice, Pavel Krasheninnikov
Labour and Social Development, Sergei Kalashnikov
Nationalities and Regional Policy, Ramazan Abdulatipov
Natural Resources, Viktor Orlov
Physical Culture, Sport and Tourism, Boris Ivanyuzhenkov
Press, Television, Radio and Other Mass Media, Mikhail Lesin
Railways, Vladimir Starostenko
Russian Federation, Chief of Staff, Andrei Chernenko
Science and Technology, Mikhail Kirpichnikov
State Property, Farit Gazizullin
Taxes and Duties, Alexander Pochinok
Trade, Mikhail Fradkov

EMBASSY OF THE RUSSIAN FEDERATION
13 Kensington Palace Gardens, London W8 4QX
Tel 0171-229 2666
Ambassador Extraordinary and Plenipotentiary, HE Yuri Fokine, apptd 1997
Minister-Counsellor, G. Gventsadze
Defence and Air Attaché, Maj.-Gen. V. E. Glagolev
Counsellor and Consul-General, A. L. Prosvirkin

BRITISH EMBASSY
Sofiyskaya Naberezhnaya 14, Moscow 109072
Tel: Moscow 956 7200
Ambassador Extraordinary and Plenipotentiary, HE Sir Andrew Wood, KCMG, apptd 1995
Minister and Deputy Head of Mission, A. J. Longrigg, CMG
Defence and Air Attaché, Air Cdre J. C. Jarron
Counsellor (Commercial), S. J. M. Smith
Consuls-General: P. A. McDermott, MVO (Moscow); J. W. Guy, OBE (St Petersburg); S. T. Harrison (Yekaterinburg)
CONSULATE-GENERAL – St Petersburg

BRITISH COUNCIL DIRECTOR, A. Andrews, VGBIL, Ulitsa Nikoloyamskaya 1, Moscow 109189. There are also offices at St Petersburg and Yekaterinburg

DEFENCE

Since the demise of the Soviet Union the Russian armed forces have been considerably reduced but remain among the most powerful in the world. In July 1998 it was announced that the armed forces would be reduced to 1.2 million personnel.

The Strategic Nuclear Forces have 26 nuclear-powered ballistic missile submarines with 412 missiles, 756 intercontinental ballistic missiles, 66 long-range bomber aircraft and 100 anti-ballistic missiles.

The Army has 15,500 main battle tanks, 9,839 armoured personnel carriers and armoured infantry fighting vehicles, 5,999 artillery pieces and 2,300 helicopters. The Navy has 195 submarines, one aircraft carrier, 34 cruisers, 26 destroyers, two anti-submarine vessels, 26 frigates, 233 patrol and coastal vessels, 535 combat aircraft and 607 armed helicopters. The Air Force has 1,855 combat aircraft.

Russia deploys forces in Armenia (4,100), Georgia (9,200), Moldova (2,500) and Tajikistan (8,200). Russia is the world's third largest contributor to peacekeeping operations. An agreement with Ukraine on the division on the Black Sea Fleet was signed in May 1997.

MILITARY EXPENDITURE – 5.8 per cent of GDP (1997)

MILITARY PERSONNEL – 1,502,000: Strategic Nuclear Forces 149,000, Army 420,000, Navy 180,000, Air Force 210,000, Paramilitaries 543,000

CONSCRIPTION DURATION – 18–24 months. Due to be ended by 2000

ECONOMY

Under the Soviet regime, an essentially agrarian economy in 1917 was transformed by the early 1960s into the second strongest industrial power in the world. However, by the early 1970s the concentration of resources on the military-industrial complex was causing the civilian economy to stagnate. This was exacerbated by the bureaucratic inefficiency of the centrally planned economic system and the poor distribution system. It was in an attempt to solve these problems that Gorbachev introduced economic restructuring (*perestroika*). Free market reforms were introduced, including the legalization of small private businesses, the reduction of state control over the economy, and denationalization and privatization. In May 1992 most state subsidies were abolished and price liberalization was introduced. The first stage of mass privatization of state industries began in October 1992 and the central distribution system was abolished with effect from 1 January 1993.

However, the abolition of central planning before a fully free market system was in place resulted in economic confusion. By the end of the first stage of mass privatization in June 1994 an estimated 35–40 per cent of enterprises had been privatized. On 27 October 1993 President Yeltsin issued a decree allowing the unrestricted buying and selling of land for the first time since 1917. The second stage of mass privatization was launched on 1 July 1994 and consists of the sale of residual government shares in most companies. By February 1996, 80 per cent of the economy had been privatized.

The restructuring of state enterprises has not been successful. In January 1992 economic 'shock therapy' was introduced to end hyperinflation and restore government reserves by liberalizing prices and restructuring firms to end their reliance on state subsidies. The policy was only partially implemented in 1992–4 due to parliamentary resistance. As a result industrial production declined (15.5 per cent in 1993), hyperinflation continued (900 per cent in 1993) and the rouble tumbled.

From 1994 to 1996, the economy began to stabilize with economic reforms judged to have become irreversible. Industrial output and GDP fell by 3 per cent and 4 per cent respectively in 1995, compared with 21 per cent and 18.6 per cent in 1994, a result of the government having finally gained control of the money supply. Agricultural

production declined by more than 10 per cent in 1995, whereas arms sales grew by 62 per cent, rising to US$6,000 million from US$3,700 million in 1994.

Russia has received considerable international aid since 1993. The G7 summit in Tokyo in April 1994 pledged aid of US$43 billion for structural reform and rouble stabilization, conditional on political and economic reforms. In 1995 the IMF provided US$6,800 million in stand-by credit to cover part of the budget deficit. A further three-year credit of US$10,087 million, granted in February 1996, was made conditional on the government maintaining spending limits.

In 1997, for the first time since economic reforms were introduced, Russian GDP grew by 0.4 per cent.   In May 1998 the Russian stock market went into steep decline, and interest rates were tripled to 150 per cent to avoid a devaluation of the currency. The IMF pledged US$13.7 billion to support the rouble, but in August, trading on the Russian stock exchange was suspended twice in a week after shares lost 15 per cent of their value. On 17 August, the central bank announced it was relaxing control of the rouble, in effect a *de facto* devaluation of 50 per cent, triggering panic selling of roubles, and prompting widespread fears that Russia would default on its loans. Western governments and financial institutions refused to pledge any more money to support the rouble, raising fears of hyperinflation and economic collapse.

A package of measures approved by the government in October 1998 included a state monopoly on alcohol sales and measures aimed at reducing inflation. The budget for 1999 increased military spending and allocated US$9.5 billion to servicing foreign debt, although US$17.5 billion of repayments were due. The IMF agreed in March 1999 to lend US$4.8 billion to enable Russia to restructure its debt; in April, it agreed a further loan of US$4.5 billion subject to reforms of banking laws, the relaxation of exchange controls and increases in indirect taxation.

Russia has some of the richest mineral deposits in the world. Coal is mined in the Kuznetsk area, in the Urals, south of Moscow, in the Donets basin and in the Pechora area in the north. Oil is produced in the northern Caucasus, between the Volga and the Urals, and in western Siberia, which also has large deposits of natural gas. A pipeline to bring Caspian oil into Russia via Dagestan and North Ossetia is under construction. Coal and gas deposits in Siberia and the far east (especially Yakutia) are being developed. The Ural mountains contain high-quality iron ore, manganese, copper, aluminium, platinum, precious stones, salt, asbestos, pyrites, coal, oil, etc. Iron ore is also mined near Kursk, Tula, Lipetsk, in several areas in Siberia and in the Kola Peninsula. Non-ferrous metals are found in the Altai, in eastern Siberia, in the northern Caucasus, in the Kuznetsk basin, in the far east and in the far north. 106 tonnes of gold were produced in 1997.

The vast area and the great variety in climatic conditions are reflected in the structure of agriculture. In the far north reindeer breeding, hunting and fishing are predominant. Further south, timber industry is combined with grain growing. In the southern half of the forest zone and in the adjacent forest-steppe zone, the acreage under grain crops is larger and the structure of agriculture more complex. Between the Volga and the Urals cericulture is predominant (particularly summer wheat), followed by cattle breeding. Beyond the Urals is another important grain-growing and stock-breeding area in the southern part of the western Siberian plain. The southern steppe zone is the main wheat granary of Russia, containing also large acreages under barley, maize and sunflowers. In the extreme south cotton is cultivated. Vine, tobacco and other southern crops are grown on the Black Sea shore of the Caucasus.

Moscow and St Petersburg are still the two largest industrial centres in the country, but new industrial areas have been developed in the Urals, the Kuznetsk basin, in Siberia and the far east. Most of the oil produced in the former USSR came from Russia; half the annual output comes from Tyumen Oblast in western Siberia. All industries are represented in Russia, including iron and steel and engineering.

GNP – US$394,861 million (1997); US$2,680 per capita (1997)
GDP – US$363,881 million (1995); US$2,451 per capita (1995)
ANNUAL AVERAGE GROWTH OF GDP – –4.2 per cent (1995)
INFLATION RATE – 14.6 per cent (1997)
UNEMPLOYMENT – 8.3 per cent (1995)
TOTAL EXTERNAL DEBT – US$125,645 million (1997)

TRADE

Russia's main trading partners are Germany, the USA, Italy, China and the former Soviet states. In 1997 there was a trade surplus of US$17,326 million and a current account surplus of US$3,345 million. Imports totalled US$67,619 million and exports US$87,368 million.

Trade with UK	1997	1998
Imports from UK	£1,232,581,000	£937,124,000
Exports to UK	1,476,772,000	1,465,886,000

COMMUNICATIONS

The European area of Russia is well served by railways, St Petersburg and Moscow being the two main focal points of rail routes. The centre and south have a good system of north-south and east-west lines, but the eastern part (the Volga lands), traversed by trunk lines between Europe and Asia, lacks north-south routes. In Asia, there are still large areas, notably in the far north and Siberia, with few or no railways. In the northern part of European Russia, the North Pechora Railway has been completed, while in the far east a second Trans-Siberian line (the Baikal-Amur Railway) is partially in use; it follows a more northerly alignment than the earlier Trans-Siberian and terminates in the Pacific port of Sovetskaya Gavan.

The most important ports (Taganrog, Rostov and Novorossiisk) lie around the Black Sea and the Sea of Azov. The northern ports (St Petersburg, Murmansk and Arkhangelsk) are, with the exception of Murmansk, icebound during winter. Several ports have been built along the Arctic Sea route between Murmansk and Vladivostok and are in regular use every summer. The far eastern port of Vladivostok, the Pacific naval base of Russia, is kept open by icebreakers all the year round.

Inland waterways, both natural and artificial, are of great importance in the country, although some of them are icebound in winter (from two and a half months in the south to six months in the north). The great rivers of European Russia flow outwards from the centre, linking all parts of the plain with the chief ports, an immense system of navigable waterways which carried about 690 million tons of freight in 1988. They are supplemented by a system of canals which provide a through traffic between the White, Baltic, Black and Caspian Seas. The most notable are the White Sea-Baltic Canal, the Moscow-Volga Canal and the Volga-Don Canal linking the Baltic and the White Seas in the north to the Caspian Sea, the Black Sea and the Sea of Azov in the south.

CULTURE

Russian is a branch of the Slavonic family of languages and is written in the Cyrillic script.

Before the westernization of Russia under Peter the Great (1682–1725), Russian literature consisted mainly of folk ballads (byliny), epic songs, chronicles and works of moral theology. The 18th and 19th centuries saw the development of poetry and fiction. Poetry reached its zenith with Alexander Pushkin (1799–1837), Mikhail Lermontov (1814–41), Alexander Blok (1880–1921), the 1958 Nobel Prize laureate Boris Pasternak (1890–1960), Vladimir Mayakovsky (1893–1930) and Anna Akhmatova (1888–1966). Fiction is associated with the names of Nikolai Gogol (1809–52), Ivan Turgenev (1818–83), Fyodor Dostoevsky (1821–81), Leo Tolstoy (1828–1910), Anton Chekhov (1860–1904), Maxim Gorky (1868–1936), Ivan Bunin (1870–1953), Mikhail Bulgakov (1891–1940), Mikhail Sholokhov (1905–84) and Alexander Solzhenitsyn (b. 1918).

Great names in music include Glinka (1804–57), Borodin (1833–87), Mussorgsky (1839–81), Rimsky-Korsakov (1844–1908), Rubinstein (1829–94), Tchaikovsky (1840–93), Rachmaninov (1873–1943), Skriabin (1872–1915), Prokofiev (1891–1953), Stravinsky (1882–1971), Shostakovich (1906–75) and Alfred Schnittke (b. 1934).

RWANDA
Republika y'u Rwanda

AREA – 10,169 sq. miles (26,338 sq. km). Neighbours: Burundi (south), Democratic Republic of Congo (west), Uganda (north), Tanzania (east)
POPULATION – 5,397,000 (1994 UN estimate): Hutus 90 per cent, Tutsis 9 per cent, Twa (pygmy) 1 per cent. Kinyarwanda, French and English are the official languages. Swahili is also spoken
CAPITAL – Kigali (population, 116,227)
CURRENCY – Rwanda franc of 100 centimes
NATIONAL DAY – 1 July
NATIONAL FLAG – Three vertical bands, red, yellow and green with letter R on yellow band
LIFE EXPECTANCY (years) – male 45.10; female 47.70
POPULATION GROWTH RATE – 1.8 per cent (1997)
POPULATION DENSITY – 205 per sq. km (1996)
URBAN POPULATION – 5.4 per cent (1991)
MILITARY EXPENDITURE – 5.5 per cent of GDP (1997)
MILITARY PERSONNEL – 47,000: Army 40,000, Paramilitaries 7,000
ILLITERACY RATE – 39.5 per cent
ENROLMENT (percentage of age group) – primary 76 per cent (1991); secondary 8 per cent (1991); tertiary 0.5 per cent (1990)

HISTORY AND POLITICS

The majority Hutu population rebelled against Tutsi feudal rule (under the Belgian colonial authority) in 1959–61, leading to the massacre of thousands of Tutsis. Large numbers fled into exile in Uganda. Rwanda became an independent republic on 1 July 1962, with Grégoire Kayibanda as head of state. He was deposed in 1973 and replaced by a military government under Maj.-Gen. Juvénal Habyarimana, who established a one-party state.

Armed Tutsi exiles repeatedly attempted to invade Rwanda in the 1960s and 1970s but were defeated by the predominantly Hutu army. Continued Hutu-Tutsi conflict left thousands dead over a period of 30 years. In October 1990 Rwanda was invaded by the Rwandan Patriotic Front (RPF) of exiled Tutsis and moderate Hutus, who forced the one-party MRND (National Revolutionary Movement for Development) government to introduce a multiparty constitution in 1991. After the government reneged on a 1992 peace agreement, the RPF advanced on Kigali and forced the government to restart negotiations, which led to the August 1993 Arusha peace accord. The accord provided for a transitional period under a broad-based government including the RPF until the 1995 elections, with UN forces in the country throughout the period.

President Habyarimana, who had retained the interim presidency, died on 6 April 1994 in a plane crash widely believed to have been caused by a rocket attack by extremist sections of the Hutu army. The Hutu army and armed militia, the *interahamwe*, then carried out a pre-planned act of genocide against the Tutsi minority and moderate Hutus; 500,000 people were massacred in three months. The civil war restarted and the RPF gradually re-established its control over the country, forcing the defeated government forces and two million Hutu refugees into exile. On 18 July 1994 the RPF declared victory and established a broad-based government of national unity in which moderate Hutus were given the presidency and premiership and the RPF took eight of the 22 seats.

Some 50,000–60,000 Hutu refugees died of disease in refugee camps in eastern Zaïre (now the Democratic Republic of Congo) in August–September 1994. French troops withdrew from their 'safe zone' in the south-west of Rwanda in September 1994 and were replaced by RPF forces who gradually returned most refugees in the zone to their homes. UN forces (UNAMIR II) were deployed to deter revenge attacks by Tutsis on Hutus.

In November 1994 the UN Security Council established the International Criminal Tribunal for Rwanda (ICTR) to prosecute those responsible for genocide and other international humanitarian law violations between 1 January and 31 December 1994. An estimated 200,000 Tutsi refugees who fled to Uganda in the 1960s and 1970s have returned to Rwanda. By December 1995, 500,000 refugees remained in Tanzania, and one million in Zaïre.

The 70-member Transitional National Assembly provided for by the Arusha agreement began operation on 12 December 1994 with the extremist Hutu MRND excluded. However, tensions between Tutsis and moderate Hutus in the government remain, with Prime Minister Twagiramungu and four other ministers being dismissed in August 1995 after criticizing the lack of power-sharing by the RPF and the security situation in the country.

UN forces left the country in March 1996. Killings by both Hutu militia and government forces continued, and Hutu attacks in central and western Rwanda were frequent in the first half of 1998.

At the ICTR in May 1998, former Prime Minister Jean Kambanda pleaded guilty to charges of genocide, the first admission by a senior Hutu official that genocide had taken place. His admission may be used to implicate other officials who had denied that genocide was taking place.

Rwanda has supported a rebellion in the Democratic Republic of Congo led by the Congolese Democratic Rally, a Congolese Tutsi group. Rwandan troops have also been deployed in the Democratic Republic of Congo.

Local elections took place on 29–31 March 1999, the first since 1994. The Transitional National Assembly was extended for four further years on 9 June 1999.

HEAD OF STATE
President, Pasteur Bizimungu, *sworn in* 19 July 1994
Vice-President, Defence, Maj-Gen. Paul Kagame

GOVERNMENT *as at July 1999*

The President (FPR)
The Vice-President (FPR)
Prime Minister, Pierre-Célestin Rwigyema (MDR)

Agriculture, Livestock, Environment and Rural Development, Ephraim Kabayija
Civil Service and Labour, Jean-Nepomunce Nayinzira (PDC)
Commerce, Industry and Tourism, Marc Rugenera (PSD)
Education, Emmanuel Mudidi
Energy, Water and Natural Resources, Bonaventure Niyibizi
Finance and Economic Planning, Donat Kaberuka
Foreign Affairs and Regional Co-operation, Amri Sued
Gender and Women's Promotion, Angeline Muganza
Health, Ezechias Rwabuhihi
Information, Augustin Iyamuremye
Internal Affairs, Communal Development and Resettlement, Sheikh Abdul Karim Harerimana (FPR)
Justice, Jean-de Dieu Mucyo
Lands, Resettlement and Environmental Protection, Joseph Nsengimana
Ministers of State, Laurien Ngirabanzi *(Agriculture, Livestock, and Forestry);* Col. Emmanuel Habyarimana *(Defence and National Security);* Jean-Damascene Ntawukuriryayo *(Education);* Emmanuel Ndahimana *(Finance and Economic Planning);* Sylvie Zainab Kayitesi *(Lands, Resettlement and Environmental Protection)*
President's Office, Patrick Mazimpaka (FPR)
President's Office, Institutional Relations, Anastase Gasana (MDR)
Public Works, Transport and Communications, Vincent Biruta
Social Affairs, Charles Ntakirutinka (PSD)
Territorial Administration, Désiré Nyandwi
Youth, Culture and Sports, François Ngarambe

FPR Rwandan Patriotic Front; MDR Republican Democratic Movement; PSD Social Democratic Party; PDC Christian Democratic Party

EMBASSY OF THE REPUBLIC OF RWANDA
Uganda House, 58-59 Trafalgar Square, London WC2N 5DX
Tel: 0171-930 2570
Ambassador Extraordinary and Plenipotentiary, Dr Zac Nsenga, apptd 1996

BRITISH EMBASSY
Parcelle No. 1131, Blvd de l'Umuganda, Kacyira-Sud, BP 576 Kigali
Tel: Kigali 84098/85771/85773
Ambassador Extraordinary and Plenipotentiary, HE Graeme Loten, apptd 1998

ECONOMY

Coffee, tea and sugar are grown. Tin, hides, bark of quinine and extract of pyrethrum flowers are also exported.

In 1996 there was a trade deficit of US$148 million and a current account surplus of US$1 million. In 1997 imports totalled US$300 million and exports US$88 million.

GNP – US$1,680 million (1997); US$210 per capita (1997)
GDP – US$1,235 million (1995); US$238 per capita (1995)
ANNUAL AVERAGE GROWTH OF GDP – 60.7 per cent (1995)
INFLATION RATE – 11.5 per cent (1997)
TOTAL EXTERNAL DEBT – US$1,111 million (1997)

Trade with UK	1997	1998
Imports from UK	£4,944,000	£2,848,000
Exports to UK	1,212,000	610,000

ST CHRISTOPHER AND NEVIS
The Federation of St Christopher and Nevis

AREA – 101 sq. miles (261 sq. km)
POPULATION – 41,000 (1994 UN estimate). The language is English
CAPITAL – ΨBasseterre (population, 14,161, 1980)
MAJOR TOWNS – ΨCharlestown (1,200), the chief town of Nevis
CURRENCY – East Caribbean dollar (EC$) of 100 cents
NATIONAL ANTHEM – Oh Land of Beauty
NATIONAL DAY – 19 September (Independence Day)
NATIONAL FLAG – Three diagonal bands, green, black and red; each colour separated by a stripe of yellow. Two white stars on the black band
LIFE EXPECTANCY (years) – male 65.10; female 70.08
POPULATION GROWTH RATE – 0.4 per cent (1997)
POPULATION DENSITY – 157 per sq. km (1996)

The state of St Christopher and Nevis is located at the northern end of the eastern Caribbean. It comprises the islands of St Christopher (St Kitts) (68 sq. miles) and Nevis (36 sq. miles). The central area of St Christopher is forest-clad and mountainous, rising to the 3,792 ft Mount Liamuiga. Nevis is separated from the southern tip of St Christopher by a strait two miles wide and is dominated by Nevis Peak, 3,232 ft.

HISTORY AND POLITICS

St Christopher was the first island in the British West Indies to be colonized (1623). The Territory of St Christopher and Nevis became a State in Association with Britain in 1967. The State of St Christopher and Nevis became an independent nation on 19 September 1983.

In the July 1995 election to the National Assembly, the Labour Party won seven seats, and the People's Action Movement won one seat. Of the three seats reserved for Nevis, the Concerned Citizens' Movement won two seats and the Nevis Reformation Party won one seat. On 10 August 1998 a referendum was held in Nevis on the question of independence from St Christopher; although 61.8 per cent voted in favour of secession, it fell short of the two-thirds majority needed for independence.

POLITICAL SYSTEM

Under the constitution, Queen Elizabeth II is head of state, represented in the islands by the Governor-General. There is a central government with a ministerial system, the head of which is the prime minister of St Christopher and Nevis, and a National Assembly located on St Christopher. The National Assembly is composed of the Speaker, three senators (nominated by the prime minister and the Leader of the Opposition) and 11 elected representatives. On Nevis there is a Nevis Island Administration, the head being styled Premier of Nevis, and a Nevis Island Assembly of five elected and three nominated members.

Governor-General, HE Sir Cuthbert Montraville Sebastian, GCMG, OBE, apptd 1996

CABINET *as at July 1999*

Prime Minister, Finance, National Security, Planning, Information, Foreign Affairs, Dr Denzil Douglas
Deputy PM, Trade, Industry and Caricom Affairs, Youth, Sports and Community Affairs, Sam Condor
Agriculture, Lands and Housing, Timothy Harris
Attorney-General, Delano Bart
Communications, Works, Utilities and Ports, Cedric Liburd
Culture, Environment and Tourism, Dwyer Astaphan
Education, Labour and Social Security, Rupert Herbert
Health and Women's Affairs, Dr Earl Asim Martin

HIGH COMMISSION FOR ST CHRISTOPHER AND NEVIS
10 Kensington Court, London w8 5DL
Tel 0171-937 9522
High Commissioner for St Christopher and Nevis, HE Aubrey Hart, apptd 1994

BRITISH HIGH COMMISSIONER, HE G. M. Baker, resident at Bridgetown, Barbados

ECONOMY

The economy of the islands has been based on sugar for over three centuries. Tourism (214,000 visitors in 1995) and light industry, concentrating on distilling, food processing, clothing and electronics, are now being developed. The economy of Nevis centres on small peasant farmers, but a sea-island cotton industry is being developed for export.

The main exports are sugar, lobsters, beverages and electrical equipment. Foodstuffs, energy, machinery and transport equipment are the main imports.

About 70 per cent of homes on St Christopher were damaged by Hurricane Georges in September 1998.

In 1994 St Christopher and Nevis had a trade deficit of US$69 million and a current account deficit of US$26 million.
GNP – US$256 million (1997); US$6,260 per capita (1997)
GDP – US$198 million (1995); US$4,819 per capita (1995)
ANNUAL AVERAGE GROWTH OF GDP – 4.9 per cent (1995)
INFLATION RATE – 8.6 per cent (1997)
TOTAL EXTERNAL DEBT – US$62 million (1997)

Trade with UK	1997	1998
Imports from UK	£9,976,000	£12,649,000
Exports to UK	9,049,000	5,918,000

COMMUNICATIONS

Basseterre is a port of registry and has deep water harbour facilities. Golden Rock airport, on St Kitts, can take most large jet aircraft; Newcastle airstrip on Nevis can take small aircraft and has night landing facilities. The sea ferry route from Basseterre to Charlestown is 11 miles.

ST LUCIA

AREA – 240 sq. miles (622 sq. km)
POPULATION – 144,000 (1994 UN estimate). The official language is English. A French creole is spoken by most of the population
CAPITAL – ΨCastries (population, 56,000, 1989)
CURRENCY – East Caribbean dollar (EC$) of 100 cents
NATIONAL ANTHEM – Sons and Daughters of Saint Lucia
NATIONAL DAY – 22 February (Independence Day)
NATIONAL FLAG – Blue, bearing in centre a device of yellow over black over white triangles having a common base
LIFE EXPECTANCY (years) – male 68.00; female 74.80
POPULATION GROWTH RATE – 0.9 per cent (1997)
POPULATION DENSITY – 232 per sq. km (1996)

St Lucia, the second largest of the Windward group, is 27 miles in length, with an extreme breadth of 14 miles. It is mountainous, its highest point being Mt Gimie (3,145 ft) and for the most part it is covered with forest and tropical vegetation.

HISTORY AND POLITICS

Possession of St Lucia was fiercely disputed and it constantly changed hands between the British and the French until 1814 when it was ceded to Britain by the Treaty of Paris. It became independent within the Commonwealth on 22 February 1979.

The St Lucia Labour Party defeated the ruling United Workers' Party in a general election on 23 May 1997, winning all but one of the seats in the House of Assembly.

POLITICAL SYSTEM

The head of state is Queen Elizabeth II, represented in the island by a St Lucian Governor-General, and there is a bicameral legislature. The Senate has 11 members, six appointed by the ruling party, three by the Opposition and two by the Governor-General. The House of Assembly, which has a life of five years, has 17 elected members and a Speaker, who may be elected from outside the House.

Governor-General, HE Perlette Louisy, apptd 1997

CABINET *as at July 1999*

Prime Minister, Finance, Planning, Information, Public Service, Kenny Anthony
Agriculture, Fisheries, Environment, Cassius Elias
Commerce, Industry, Consumer Affairs, Walter François
Communications, Works, Transport and Public Utilities, Calixte George
Community Development, Culture, Local Government and Co-operatives, Damian Greaves
Education, Human Resources Development, Youth and Sport, Mario Michel
Foreign Affairs, International Trade, George Odlum
Health, Human Services, Family Affairs, Women, Sarah Flood
Legal Affairs, Labour, Home Affairs, Velon John
Parliamentary Secretaries, Petrus Compton *(Attorney-General)*; Menissa Rambally *(Civil Aviation, Financial Services)*; Cyprian Lansiquot *(Communications, Works, Transport and Public Utilities)*; Kenneth John *(Education, Human Resources Development, Youth and Sport)*
Tourism, Civil Aviation, Phillip Pierre

HIGH COMMISSION FOR ST LUCIA
10 Kensington Court, London w8 5DL
Tel 0171-937 9522
High Commissioner for St Lucia, HE Emmanuel Cotter, apptd 1998

OFFICE OF THE BRITISH HIGH COMMISSION
PO Box 227, Castries
Tel: Castries 452 2484
High Commissioner, HE G. M. Baker, resident at Bridgetown, Barbados

ECONOMY

The economy is mainly agrarian, with manufacturing based on the processing of agricultural products. Principal crops are bananas, coconuts, cocoa, mangoes, breadfruit, yams and citrus fruit. Attempts are being made to increase industrialization. There were 394,000 visitors to the island in 1994.
GNP – US$558 million (1997); US$3,510 per capita (1997)
GDP – US$452 million (1995); US$3,183 per capita (1995)
ANNUAL AVERAGE GROWTH OF GDP – 3.0 per cent (1995)

INFLATION RATE – –6.2 per cent (1996)
TOTAL EXTERNAL DEBT – US$152 million (1997)

TRADE

The principal exports are bananas, coconut products (copra, edible oils, soap), cardboard boxes, beer, and textile manufactures. The chief imports are flour, meat, machinery, building materials, motor vehicles, manufactured goods, petroleum and fertilizers.

In 1996 St Lucia had a trade deficit of US$184 million and a current account deficit of US$80 million.

Trade with UK	1997	1998
Imports from UK	£15,134,000	£13,929,000
Exports to UK	34,029,000	37,889,000

ST VINCENT AND THE GRENADINES

AREA – 150 sq. miles (388 sq. km)
POPULATION – 113,000 (1994 UN estimate). The language is English
CAPITAL – ΨKingstown (population, 33,694)
CURRENCY – East Caribbean dollar (EC$) of 100 cents
NATIONAL ANTHEM – St Vincent, Land So Beautiful
NATIONAL DAY – 27 October (Independence Day)
NATIONAL FLAG – Three vertical bands, of blue, yellow and green, with three green diamonds in the shape of a 'V' mounted on the yellow band
POPULATION GROWTH RATE – 0.7 per cent (1997)
POPULATION DENSITY – 291 per sq. km (1996)

The territory of St Vincent includes certain of the Grenadines, a chain of small islands stretching 40 miles across the Caribbean Sea between Grenada and St Vincent, some of the larger of which are Bequia, Canouan, Mayreau, Mustique, Union Island, Petit St Vincent and Prune Island.

HISTORY AND POLITICS

St Vincent was discovered by Christopher Columbus in 1498. It was granted by Charles I to the Earl of Carlisle in 1627 and after subsequent grants and a series of occupations alternately by the French and English, it was finally restored to Britain in 1783. St Vincent achieved full independence within the Commonwealth as St Vincent and the Grenadines on 27 October 1979.

The governing New Democratic Party won eight seats and the United Labour Party seven seats at the election held on 15 June 1998.

POLITICAL SYSTEM

Queen Elizabeth II is head of state, represented by a Governor-General. The House of Assembly consists of 15 elected members and four Senators appointed by the government and two by the Opposition. It is presided over by a Speaker elected by the House from within or without it.

Governor-General, HE Sir Charles Antrobus, GCMG, OBE, *sworn in* 15 October 1996

CABINET *as at July 1999*

Prime Minister, National Security and Home Affairs, Sir James Mitchell, KCMG
Agriculture, Lands and Surveys, Jeremiah Scott
Attorney-General, Justice, Carl Joseph
Communications and Works, Glenford Stewart
Education, Alpian Allen
Finance, Public Service, Arnhim Eustace
Foreign Affairs, Tourism, Allan Cruickshank

Health, St Clair Thomas
Housing, Community Development, Youth and Sports, Monty Roberts
Trade, Industry and Consumer Affairs, John Horne

HIGH COMMISSION FOR ST VINCENT AND THE
GRENADINES
10 Kensington Court, London W8 5DL
Tel 0171-565 2874
High Commissioner for St Vincent and the Grenadines, HE
Carlyle Dougan, QC, apptd 1998

BRITISH HIGH COMMISSION
Granby Street (PO Box 132), Kingstown
Tel: St Vincent 457 1701
High Commissioner, HE G. M. Baker, resident at
Bridgetown, Barbados
Acting High Commissioner, B. Robertson

ECONOMY

This is based mainly on agriculture but tourism (218,000 visitors in 1995) and manufacturing industries have been expanding. The main products are bananas, arrowroot, coconuts, cocoa, spices and various kinds of food crops. The main imports are foodstuffs, textiles, lumber, chemicals, motor vehicles and fuel.

In 1996 St Vincent and the Grenadines had a trade deficit of US$75 million and a current account deficit of US$35 million. In 1996 imports totalled US$132 million and exports US$46 million.

GNP – US$272 million (1997); US$2,420 per capita (1997)
GDP – US$258 million (1995); US$2,305 per capita (1995)
ANNUAL AVERAGE GROWTH OF GDP – 0.9 per cent (1996)
INFLATION RATE – 0.4 per cent (1997)
TOTAL EXTERNAL DEBT – US$258 million (1997)

Trade with UK	1997	1998
Imports from UK	£7,992,000	£7,462,000
Exports to UK	15,346,000	19,531,000

EL SALVADOR
República de El Salvador

AREA – 8,124 sq. miles (21,041 sq. km). Neighbours: Guatemala (north-west), Honduras (north-east and east)
POPULATION – 5,796,000 (1994 UN estimate). The language is Spanish
CAPITAL – San Salvador (population, 1,200,000, 1998)
MAJOR CITIES – San Miguel (225,000); Santa Ana (270,000)
CURRENCY – El Salvador colón (₡) of 100 centavos
NATIONAL ANTHEM – Saludemos La Patria Orgullosos (Let us proudly hail the Fatherland)
NATIONAL DAY – 15 September
NATIONAL FLAG – Three horizontal bands, sky blue, white, sky blue; coat of arms on white band
LIFE EXPECTANCY (years) – male 50.74; female 63.89
POPULATION GROWTH RATE – 2.1 per cent (1997)
POPULATION DENSITY – 275 per sq. km (1996)
URBAN POPULATION – 50.4 per cent (1992)
MILITARY EXPENDITURE – 1.9 per cent of GDP (1997)
MILITARY PERSONNEL – 36,600: Army 22,300, Navy 700, Air Force 1,600, Paramilitaries 12,000
CONSCRIPTION DURATION – 12 months

El Salvador extends along the Pacific coast of Central America for 160 miles. The surface of the country is very mountainous, many of the peaks being extinct volcanoes. Much of the interior has an average altitude of 2,000 feet. The climate varies from tropical to temperate. There is a wet season from May to October, and a dry season from November to April. Earthquakes are frequent, the most recent being in October 1986.

HISTORY AND POLITICS

El Salvador was conquered in 1526 by Pedro de Alvarado, and formed part of the Spanish viceroyalty of Guatemala until 1821. It is divided into 14 Departments.

Decades of military rule ended in October 1979 when a Constituent Assembly was elected. Subsequent presidential and parliamentary elections were boycotted by the FMLN (Farabundo Martí National Liberation Front) guerrilla movement. Conflict between the guerrillas and the government continued throughout the 1980s until negotiations culminated in a peace plan signed in January 1992. In December 1992 the FMLN disarmed and became a political party.

The UN Observer Mission in El Salvador (ONUSAL) monitored the 1992–4 transition process, overseeing the final destruction of FMLN arms in August 1993 and the presidential, parliamentary and local elections held in March and April 1994. ARENA won 28 of the Legislative Assembly's 84 seats and formed a government with other right-wing parties in legislative elections in March 1999; the FMLN won 27 seats. On 7 March 1999, Francisco Flores of the ruling right-wing ARENA party won the presidential election; he took office on 1 June.

HEAD OF STATE
President, Francisco Flores Perez, *elected* 7 March 1999, *took office* 1 June 1999
Vice-President, Minister of the Presidency, Carlos Quintanilla Schmidt
Secretary of the Presidency, Juan José Daboub

COUNCIL OF STATE *as at July 1999*
Agriculture and Livestock, Salvador Urrutia Loucel
Defence, Gen. Antonio Martínez Varela
Economy, Miguel E. Lacayo
Education, Ana Evelyn Jacir de Lovo
Environment, Ana María Majano
Foreign Affairs, María Eugenia Brizuela de Avila
Home Affairs, Mario Acosta Oertel
Justice and Public Security, Francisco Bertrand Galindo
Labour and Social Security, Jorge Nieto Menéndez
Public Health, José López Beltrán
Public Works, José Angel Quiroz
Treasury, José Luis Trigueros

EMBASSY OF EL SALVADOR
Tennyson House, 159 Great Portland Street, London
W1N 5FD
Tel 0171-436 8282
Ambassador Extraordinary and Plenipotentiary, HE Mauricio Castro-Aragón, apptd 1999

BRITISH EMBASSY
PO Box 1591, San Salvador
Tel: San Salvador 263 6527
Ambassador Extraordinary and Plenipotentiary, HE Patrick Morgan, apptd 1999

ECONOMY

The principal agricultural products are coffee, cotton, sugar cane, maize, shrimps and balsam. In the lower altitudes towards the east, sisal is produced and used in the manufacture of coffee and cereal bags. The Salvadorean Coffee Company and the banking system are being privatized.

Existing factories make textiles, clothing, constructional steel, furniture, cement and household items.

GNP – US$10,704 million (1997); US$1,810 per capita (1997)

GDP – US$9,398 million (1995); US$1,660 per capita (1995)

ANNUAL AVERAGE GROWTH OF GDP – 4.0 per cent (1997)

INFLATION RATE – 4.5 per cent (1997)

UNEMPLOYMENT – 7.7 per cent (1995)

TOTAL EXTERNAL DEBT – US$3,282 million (1997)

TRADE

Chief exports are coffee, cotton, sugar, shrimps, sisal, balsam, meat, towels, hides and skins. The chief imports are chemicals, petroleum, manufactured goods, industrial and electronic machinery, pharmaceutical goods, vehicles and consumer goods.

In 1997 there was a trade deficit of US$1,107 million and a current account surplus of US$96 million; imports totalled US$2,973 million and exports US$1,359 million.

Trade with UK	1997	1998
Imports from UK	£22,399,000	£18,647,000
Exports to UK	13,236,000	85,400,000

COMMUNICATIONS

The principal ports are Cutuco, La Unión and Acajutla. There are more than 12,000 km of roads and 600 km of railways. The Pan-American Highway from the Guatemalan frontier passes through San Salvador and Santa Ana, and continues to the Honduran frontier. Comalapa international airport has daily flights to other Central American capitals, Mexico and the USA. There are 100 broadcasting stations and nine television stations. Five daily newspapers are published in San Salvador.

EDUCATION

Primary education is free and compulsory. There are 38 universities.

ILLITERACY RATE – 28.5 per cent

ENROLMENT (percentage of age group) – primary 79 per cent (1995); secondary 21 per cent (1995); tertiary 16.7 per cent (1996)

SAMOA
Ole Malo Tutoatasi o Samoa – Independent State of Samoa

AREA – 1,093 sq. miles (2,831 sq. km)

POPULATION – 166,000 (1994 UN estimate); 162,000 (1989 census), the largest numbers being on Upolu (114,980) and Savai'i (43,150). The Samoans are a Polynesian people, though the population also includes other Pacific Islanders, Euronesians, Chinese and Europeans. The main languages are Samoan and English. The islanders are Christians of different denominations

CAPITAL – ΨApia (population, 36,000, 1989), on Upolu. Robert Louis Stevenson died and was buried at Apia in 1894

CURRENCY – Tala (S$) of 100 sene

NATIONAL ANTHEM – The Banner of Freedom

NATIONAL DAY – 1 June (Independence Day)

NATIONAL FLAG – Red with a blue canton bearing five white stars of the Southern Cross

LIFE EXPECTANCY (years) – male 61.00; female 64.30

POPULATION GROWTH RATE – 1.2 per cent (1997)

POPULATION DENSITY – 59 per sq. km (1996)

Samoa consists of the islands of Savai'i, Upolu, Apolima, Manono, Fanuatapu, Namua, Nuutele, Nuulua and Nuusafee. All the islands are mountainous. Upolu, the most fertile, contains the harbours of Apia and Mulifanua, and Savai'i the harbour of Salelologa.

HISTORY AND POLITICS

Formerly administered by New Zealand (latterly with internal self-government), Western Samoa became fully independent on 1 January 1962. The state was treated as a member country of the Commonwealth until its formal admission on 28 August 1970. A constitutional amendment came into effect on 4 July 1997 changing the state's name to the Independent State of Samoa.

Suffrage was made universal following a referendum held in 1990. After elections held on 26 April 1996, the seats in the Fono were: Human Rights Protection Party 26; Samoan National Development Party 13; Independents 10.

POLITICAL SYSTEM

The 1962 constitution provides for a head of state to be elected by the 49-member legislative assembly, the Fono, for a five-year term. Initially two of the four Paramount chiefs jointly held the office of head of state for life. When one of the chiefs died in April 1963, Susuga Malietoa Tanumafili II became head of state for life. The head of state's functions are analogous to those of a constitutional monarch. Executive government is carried out by a Cabinet of Ministers.

HEAD OF STATE

Head of State for Life, HH Susuga Malietoa Tanumafili II, GCMG, CBE, *since* 15 April 1963

CABINET *as at July 1999*

Prime Minister, Foreign Affairs, Broadcasting, Police and Prisons, Internal Affairs, Finance, Tourism, Trade, Commerce and Industry, Customs, Audit, Tuilaepa Sailele Malielegaoi

Agriculture, Forestry, Fisheries and Meteorological Services, Molioo Teofilo

Education, Fiame Naomi Mata'afa

Health, Misa Telefoni

Justice, Solia Papu Vaai

Labour, Polataivao Fosi

Lands, Survey and Environment, Tuala Sale Tagaloa

Posts and Telecommunications, Electric Power Corporation, Leafa Vitale

Public Works, Luagalau Levaula Kamu

Senior Minister without Portfolio, Tofilau Eti Alesana

Transport and Shipping, Hans Joachim Kell

Women's Affairs, Statistics, Leniu Tofaeono Avamagalo

Youth, Sports and Culture, Leota Lu II

EMBASSY OF THE INDEPENDENT STATE OF SAMOA
Avenue Franklin D. Roosevelt 123, B-1050 Brussels
Tel: Brussels 660 8454

Ambassador Extraordinary and Plenipotentiary, HE Tau'ili'ili Meredith, appt'd 1998

BRITISH HIGH COMMISSIONER, HE Martin Williams, CVO, CBE, resident at Wellington, New Zealand

HONORARY CONSULATE – PO Box 2029, Apia

ECONOMY

Agriculture is the basis of the economy, the principal cash crops (and exports) being coconuts (copra), cocoa and bananas. Efforts are being made to develop fishing on a commercial scale. Manufacturing is very small in scope and concerned largely with processing agricultural products, but is being encouraged by the government. There were over 60,000 visitors in 1995.

In 1996 Samoa had a trade deficit of US$81 million and a current account surplus of US$12 million. In 1997 imports totalled US$96 million and exports US$15 million.

GNP – US$199 million (1997); US$1,140 per capita (1997)
GDP – US$183 million (1995); US$1,106 per capita (1995)
ANNUAL AVERAGE GROWTH OF GDP – 12.6 per cent (1995)
INFLATION RATE – 10.5 per cent (1997)
TOTAL EXTERNAL DEBT – US$156 million (1997)

Trade with UK	1997	1998
Imports from UK	£890,000	£708,000
Exports to UK	8,000	14,000

SAN MARINO
Repubblica di San Marino

AREA – 24 sq. miles (61 sq. km). Neighbour: Italy
POPULATION – 25,000 (1996). The official language is Italian and the religion is Roman Catholic
CAPITAL – San Marino (population, 4,357, 1994), on the slope of Monte Titano
CURRENCY – San Marino and Italian currencies are in circulation
NATIONAL DAY – 3 September
NATIONAL FLAG – Two horizontal bands, white, blue (with coat of arms of the republic in centre)
LIFE EXPECTANCY (years) – male 73.16; female 79.12
POPULATION GROWTH RATE – 1.5 per cent (1996)
POPULATION DENSITY – 416 per sq. km (1996)
URBAN POPULATION – 89.4 per cent (1995)
GDP – US$478 million (1995); US$19,121 per capita (1995)
ANNUAL AVERAGE GROWTH OF GDP – 3.0 per cent (1995)
UNEMPLOYMENT – 39 per cent (1995)

HISTORY AND POLITICS

San Marino is a small republic in the hills near Rimini, on the Adriatic, founded, it is said, by a pious stonecutter of Dalmatia in the fourth century. The republic resisted Papal claims and those of neighbouring dukedoms during the 15th to 18th centuries, and its integrity and sovereignty is recognized and respected by Italy.

A coalition government of the Christian Democratic Party and the Socialist Party was returned in the general elections of May 1998.

The principal products are wine, cereals and fruits, and the main industries are tourism, metals, machinery, textiles and food.

POLITICAL SYSTEM

Executive power is vested in the Congress of State composed of ten ministries under the presidency of the two heads of state, who are elected at six-monthly intervals (every April and October). Legislative power is exercised by the 60-member Great and General Council which is elected for a term of five years. A Council of Twelve forms in certain cases a Supreme Court of Justice.

HEADS OF STATE
Regents, Two 'Capitani Reggenti'

CONGRESS OF STATE *as at July 1999*
Education, Social Affairs, Justice and Culture, Sante Canducci (PDCS)
Finance, Budget, Philatelic and Numismatic Agency, Clelio Galassi (PDCS)
Foreign and Political Affairs, Gabriele Gatti (PDCS)
Health and Social Security, Luciano Ciavatta (PSS)
Industry, Handicrafts and Economic Co-operation, Post and Telecommunications, Fiorenzo Stolfi (PSS)
Internal Affairs, Antonio Lazzaro Volpinari (PSS)
Labour and Co-operation, Romeo Morri (PDCS)
Relations with Municipal Authorities, Production, Services, Cesare Antonio Gasperoni (PDCS)
Territory, Environment and Agriculture, Augusto Casali (PSS)
Tourism, Commerce and Sport, Claudio Podeschi (PDCS)

PDCS Christian Democratic Party; PSS San Marino Socialist Party

BRITISH AMBASSADOR, HE Thomas Richardson, CMG, resident at Rome, Italy

TRADE

Trade with UK	1997	1998
Imports from UK	£15,037,000	£13,772,000
Exports to UK	6,560,000	7,900,000

SÃO TOMÉ AND PRINCÍPE
República Democrática de São Tomé e Príncipe

AREA – 372 sq. miles (964 sq. km)
POPULATION – 135,000 (1994 UN estimate). The official language is Portuguese
CAPITAL – ΨSão Tomé (population, 5,714, 1991)
CURRENCY – Dobra of 100 centavos
NATIONAL DAY – 12 July (Independence Day)
NATIONAL FLAG – Horizontal stripes of green, yellow, green, the yellow of double width and bearing two black stars; and a red triangle in the hoist
POPULATION GROWTH RATE – 2.7 per cent (1997)
POPULATION DENSITY – 140 per sq. km (1996)

The islands of São Tomé and Príncipe are situated in the Gulf of Guinea, off the west coast of Africa.

HISTORY AND POLITICS

The islands were first settled by the Portuguese in 1493. In 1951 they became an overseas province of Portugal, and gained full independence on 12 July 1975. A multiparty constitution was approved by referendum in August 1990. The Movement for the Liberation of São Tomé and Príncipe-Social Democratic Party (MLSTP-PSD), which had been the sole legal party since independence, was defeated by the opposition Democratic Convergence Party (PCD) in legislative elections held on 20 January 1991. Miguel Trovoada, an independent, was elected president on 3 March 1991. On 15 August 1995 five junior army officers launched a bloodless military coup, arrested the president and suspended parliament and the constitution. Following Angolan mediation and an EU threat to suspend all aid, the officers relinquished power on 21 August. The president, government, parliament and constitution were restored and the officers were granted an amnesty.

A government of national unity incorporating opposition party members was appointed on 5 January 1996. President Trovoada was re-elected in July 1996. In September 1996 the government lost a vote of confidence in the National Assembly and a coalition government was installed. Legislative elections were held on 8 November 1998, in which the MLSTP-PSD won 31 of the 55 seats in the National Assembly. Guilherme Posser da Costa was confirmed as prime minister by the president on 23 December; the Cabinet was sworn into office on 5 January 1999.

HEAD OF STATE
President and Commander-in-Chief of the Armed Forces, Miguel Trovoada, *elected* 3 March 1991, *re-elected* July 1996, *inaugurated* 3 September 1996

CABINET *as at May 1999*
Prime Minister, Guilherme Posser da Costa
Defence, Maj. João Quaresma Viegas Bexigas
Economy, Maria das Neves Ceita Batista de Sousa
Education and Culture, Peregrino do Sacramento da Costa
Foreign Affairs, Alberto Paulino
Health, Antonio Soares Marques de Lima
Infrastructure and Natural Resources, Luis Alberto Carneiro dos Prazeres
Interior, Manuel da Cruz Marcal Lima
Justice and Parliamentary Affairs, Paulo Jorge Rodrigues do Espirito Santo
Planning, Finance and Co-operation, Adelino Castelo David
Youth, Sport and Professional Training, Emilio Guadalupe Fernandes Lima

EMBASSY OF THE DEMOCRATIC REPUBLIC OF SÃO TOMÉ AND PRÍNCIPE
Square Montgomery, 175 avenue de Tervuren, B-1150 Brussels
Tel: Brussels 734 8966
Chargé d'Affaires, Antonio de Lima Viegas

BRITISH CONSULATE
Residencial Avenida, Av. Da Independencia CP 257, São Tomé
British Ambassador, HE Roger D. Hart, resident at Luanda, Angola
Honorary Consul, J. Gomes

ECONOMY

The economy is heavily dependent on tourism and agriculture, with cocoa being the main product.

In 1997 imports totalled US$16 million and exports US$5 million.
GNP – US$40 million (1997); US$290 per capita (1997)
GDP – US$7 million (1995); US$49 per capita (1995)
ANNUAL AVERAGE GROWTH OF GDP – 2.6 per cent (1995)
TOTAL EXTERNAL DEBT – US$261 million (1997)

Trade with UK	1997	1998
Imports from UK	£2,706,000	£1,427,000
Exports to UK	38,000	198,000

SAUDI ARABIA
Al Mamlaka al Arabiya as-Sa'udiyya

AREA – 830,000 sq. miles (2,149,690 sq. km). Neighbours: UAE and Qatar (east), Jordan, Iraq and Kuwait (north), Yemen and Oman (south)

POPULATION – 18,836,000 (1994 UN estimate); 16,929,294 (1992 census). Islam is the only permitted religion. The language is Arabic
CAPITAL – Riyadh (population, 1,800,000, 1991)
MAJOR CITIES – Jeddah (1.5 million); Buraydah; Dammam; Hofuf; Mecca; Medina; Tabuk
CURRENCY – Saudi riyal (SR) of 20 qursh or 100 halala
NATIONAL ANTHEM – Long live our beloved King
NATIONAL DAY – 23 September (proclamation and unification of the Kingdom, 1932)
NATIONAL FLAG – Green oblong, white Arabic device in centre: 'There is no God but God and Muhammad is the Prophet of God', and a white scimitar beneath the lettering
LIFE EXPECTANCY (years) – male 68.39; female 71.41
POPULATION GROWTH RATE – 3.4 per cent (1997)
POPULATION DENSITY – 9 per sq. km (1996)

Saudi Arabia comprises almost the whole of the Arabian peninsula, with the exception of Yemen, Oman, the UAE and Qatar. The Nejd ('plateau') extends over the centre of the peninsula, including the Nafud and Dahna deserts. The Hejaz ('the boundary') extends along the Red Sea coast to Asir and contains the holy towns of Mecca (Makkah) and Medina (Madinah). Asir ('inaccessible') is so named for its mountainous terrain, and, with the coastal plain of the Tihama, lies along the southern Red Sea coast from the Hejaz to the border with Yemen. It is the only region to enjoy substantial rainfall. The east and south-east of the country are lower-lying and largely desert.

Mecca (Al-Makkah), about 60 km east of Jeddah, is the birthplace of the Prophet Muhammad, and contains the Great Mosque, within which is the Kaaba (*Ka'abah*) or sacred shrine of the Muslim religion. This is the focus of the annual Hajj ('pilgrimage'). Medina (Al-Madinah) Al Munawwarah ('The City of Light'), some 300 km north of Mecca, is celebrated as the first city to embrace Islam and as the Prophet Muhammad's burial place.

HISTORY AND POLITICS

In the 18th century Nejd was an independent state governed from Diriya. It subsequently fell under Turkish rule; in 1913 Abdul Aziz ibn Saud threw off Turkish rule and captured the Turkish province of Al Hasa. In 1920 he captured the Asir and in 1921 the Jebel Shammar territory of the Rashid family. In 1925 he completed the conquest of the Hejaz. Great Britain recognized Abdul Aziz ibn Saud as an independent ruler, King of the Hejaz and of Nejd and its Dependencies, in 1927. The name was changed to the Kingdom of Saudi Arabia in September 1932.

INSURGENCIES

Opposition to the al Saud regime has been growing, fuelled by the economic downturn. Attacks on government and US military targets, including a bomb which killed 19 people at a US Air Force base in June 1996, have been blamed on Islamic militants.

POLITICAL SYSTEM

Saudi Arabia is a hereditary monarchy, ruled by the sons and grandsons of Abdul Aziz ibn Saud, in accordance with the Islamic Sharia law. The line of succession passes from brother to brother according to age, although several sons of Ibn Saud renounced their right to the throne. All sons and grandsons of Ibn Saud must be consulted before a new king accedes the throne.

In 1992 King Fahd announced a new Basic Law for the system of government based on Sharia law and including rules to protect personal freedoms. The constitution is defined as the Holy Koran (*Qur'an*) and the *Sunnah* (the teachings and sayings of the Prophet Muhammad). The King and the Council of Ministers (established in 1953) retain executive power. A consultative council (*Majlis-ash-Shoura*) of a chairman and 90 members appointed by the King was set up to share power with, and question, the government and to make recommendations to the King. The Majlis-ash-Shoura began meeting in December 1993 and debates government policy in the areas of the budget, defence, foreign and social affairs. Members of the ruling al Saud family are excluded from membership of the Council, which has a four-year term and takes decisions by majority vote. Cabinet ministers have terms of four years, with the possibility of a two-year extension.

In 1993 the country was reorganized into 13 provinces: Riyadh; Mecca (Makkah); Medina (Madinah); Al Qasim; Eastern; Asir; Tabuk; Hail; Northern Border; Jizan; Najran; Baha; Jouf. Each province has a governor appointed by the King and a council of prominent local citizens to advise the governor on local government, budgetary and planning issues.

The judicial system is based on Sharia law, administered by the Justice Ministry through the Sharia courts: general courts, courts of first instance, the High Sharia Court and the Appeals Court. The highest court of appeal is the Council of Ministers whose decision, signed by the King, is final and absolute.

HEAD OF STATE

Custodian of the Two Holy Mosques and HM The King of Saudi Arabia, King Fahd ibn Abdul Aziz al Saud, *born* 1923, *ascended the throne* 1 June 1982
HRH Crown Prince, Prince Abdullah ibn Abdul Aziz al Saud

COUNCIL OF MINISTERS *as at July 1999*

Prime Minister, HM The King
First Deputy PM, Commander of the National Guard, HRH The Crown Prince
Second Deputy PM, Defence and Civil Aviation, HRH Prince Sultan ibn Abdul Aziz al Saud
Agriculture and Water Resources, Abdullah ibn Abdul Aziz ibn Muammar
Civil Service, Muhammad ibn Ali al-Fayiz
Commerce, Osama ibn Jaafar ibn Ibrahim al-Faqih
Consultative Council, Muhammad ibn Ibrahim ibn Jubair *(Chairman)*; Shaikh Abdullah Omar Naseef *(Vice-Chairman)*
Education, Mohammad ibn Ahmad al-Rashid
Finance and National Economy, Ibrahim ibn Abdel Aziz al-Assaf
Foreign Affairs, HRH Prince Saud al-Faisal ibn Abdul Aziz al Saud
Health, Osama ibn Abdul-Majid Shobokshi
Higher Education, Khalid ibn Muhammad al-Anqari
Industry and Electricity, Hashem ibn Abdullah ibn Hashem Yamani
Information, Fouad ibn Abdul-Salam Mohammad Farisi
Intelligence Services, HRH Prince Saud ibn Fahd *(Deputy Director)*
Interior, HRH Prince Nayef ibn Abdul Aziz al Saud
Islamic Affairs, Religious Endowments, Call and Guidance, Shaikh Saleh ibn Abdul-Aziz ibn Muhammad ibn Ibrahim al-Shaikh
Justice, Abdullah ibn Muhammed al-Shaikh
Labour and Social Affairs, Ali ibn Ibrahim al-Namlah
Municipal and Rural Affairs, Mohammad ibn Ibrahim al-Jarallah
Oil and Mineral Resources, Ali Ibrahim al-Naimi
Pilgrimage Affairs, Iyyad ibn Amin Madani
Planning, Khaled ibn Muhammad al-Qusaybi

Public Works and Housing, HRH Prince Miteb ibn Abdul Aziz al Saud
Supreme Judicial Council Chairman, Shaikh Salih ibn Muhammad al-Lihaydan
Telegraphs, Ali ibn Talal al-Jehani
Transport, Nasir ibn Muhammad al-Sallum
Without Portfolio, HRH Prince Abdel Aziz ibn Fahd

ROYAL EMBASSY OF SAUDI ARABIA
30 Charles Street, London WIX 7PM
Tel 0171-917 3000
Ambassador Extraordinary and Plenipotentiary, HE Dr Ghazi Algosaibi, apptd 1992
Defence Attaché, Brig.-Gen. B. F. al-Othman
Cultural Attaché, A. M. al-Nasser
Commercial Attaché, M. A. al-Sheddi

BRITISH EMBASSY
PO Box 94351, Riyadh 11693
Tel: Riyadh 488 0077
Ambassador Extraordinary and Plenipotentiary, HE Sir Andrew F. Green, KCMG, apptd 1996
Counsellors, S. G. McDonald *(Deputy Head of Mission and Consul-General)*; R. Northern, MBE *(Commercial)*
Defence and Military Attaché, Brig. R. I. Talbot
First Secretary and Consul, S. J. Lovett
CONSULATE-GENERAL – PO Box 393, Jeddah 21411.
Consul-General, I. Rae, OBE
TRADE OFFICE – Dhahran/Al Khobar, PO Box 88, Dhahran Airport 31932
BRITISH COUNCIL DIRECTOR, A. Lewis, OBE, Al Mousa Centre, Tower B (PO Box 58012), Olaya Street, Riyadh 11594. There are also offices in Jeddah, Dammam and Jubail

DEFENCE

The Army has 1,055 main battle tanks, 1,850 armoured personnel carriers, 970 armoured infantry fighting vehicles, 448 artillery pieces and 55 helicopters. The Navy has eight frigates, 29 patrol and coastal vessels and 21 armed helicopters at eight bases. The Air Force has 432 combat aircraft.

Saudi Arabia is base to the Gulf Co-operational Council Peninsula Shield Force of 7,000 troops. The USA, UK and France station aircraft and support units in the country to patrol the air exclusion zone in southern Iraq.
MILITARY EXPENDITURE – 12.4 per cent of GDP (1997)
MILITARY PERSONNEL – 198,000: Army 70,000, Navy 13,500, Air Force 18,000, Air Defence Force 4,000, National Guard 77,000, Paramilitaries 15,500

ECONOMY

Saudi Arabia's revenue has been lower since the drop in world oil prices from the mid-1980s onwards, and financial reserves have been used up to meet budget deficits.

Outside the manufacturing centres which have grown up around many towns, most of the population are engaged in agriculture. The productivity of traditional dryland farming is supplemented by extensive irrigation, desalination and use of aquifers, so that agricultural production has increased greatly over the past 20 years.

The principal industry is oil extraction and processing; 415,900,000 tonnes were produced in 1997. Oil was first found in commercial quantities in 1938. About 97 per cent of the total is extracted by Saudi Aramco, formerly the Arabian–American Oil Company, which was effectively nationalized in 1980. Proven oil reserves of 260,100 million barrels account for about one-quarter of the world's proven reserves. The country is the world's largest oil exporter and supplied 12 per cent of world demand in 1993. Recoverable gas reserves of 190 trillion cubic feet, in fields associated with crude oil and those separate from it, are beginning to be exploited; production in 1997 was 43,900 million cubic metres. Mineral exploitation of gold, silver, copper and other minerals is also beginning, with gold production of 7.2 tonnes in 1997.

The government, in a series of five-year development plans begun in 1970, has actively encouraged the establishment of manufacturing industry. Industries have developed in the fields of construction materials, metal fabrication, simple machinery and electrical equipment, food and beverages, textiles, chemicals and plastics. Investment in industrial gases, intermediate petrochemicals, light engineering and machinery is encouraged.

Eight industrial centres have been established, the principal ones at Jubail and Yanbu, financed by the state agency Saudi Arabian Basic Industries Corporation. Linked by gas and oil pipelines, both have petrochemical complexes producing ethylene and methanol; six of the seven plants on-stream are joint ventures with American and Japanese companies.

A steep reduction in oil revenues in 1998 led to an austere 1999 budget, which aimed to reduce government expenditure by 12.6 per cent.
GNP – US$143,430 million (1997); US$7,150 per capita (1997)
GDP – US$120,168 million (1995); US$6,583 per capita (1995)
ANNUAL AVERAGE GROWTH OF GDP – –0.8 per cent (1995)
INFLATION RATE – 0.1 per cent (1997)

TRADE

Oil remains the main source of receipts in the balance of payments. The leading suppliers of imports are the USA, the UK, Germany and Japan, and the chief customers for exports are Japan, the USA, South Korea and Singapore. There is a total ban on the importation of alcohol, pork products, firearms, and items regarded as non-Islamic or pornographic.

In 1997 there was a trade surplus of US$33,530 million and a current account surplus of US$254 million. In 1995 imports totalled US$28,091 million and exports totalled US$50,040 million.

Trade with UK	1997	1998
Imports from UK	£3,800,465,000	£2,690,207,000
Exports to UK	£996,907,000	£891,959,000

COMMUNICATIONS

There is one railway line from Dammam to Riyadh, which was opened in 1951 and is operated by the Saudi Government Railway Organization. It carries around 450,000 passengers and 1.9 million tons of goods per year. The line is being extended to the port of Jubail on the Gulf. A network of 139,200 km of roads, including an expressway system, connects all the cities and main towns. There are 21 ports, of which the major ones are Dammam and Jubail (Gulf) and Jeddah, Yanbu and Jizan (Red Sea). The 15.5 mile-long King Fahd Causeway completed in 1986 connects the Eastern Province to the state of Bahrain and is the world's second longest causeway.

The government-owned Saudi Arabian Airlines (Saudia) operates scheduled services to 22 domestic airports. There are international airports at Dhahran (King Fahd), Jeddah (King Abdul Aziz), and Riyadh (King Khalid). Saudia has an extensive overseas operation, and a large number of international airlines operate into the country.

Telecommunications are being rapidly expanded with 1.78 million telephone lines in 1995 and seven earth stations linked to the Intelsat system, allowing direct dialling to 185 countries.

EDUCATION

With the exception of a few schools for expatriate children, all schools are government-supervised and are segregated for boys and girls. There are universities in Jeddah, Mecca, Riyadh (branches in Abha and Qassim), Dammam (branch at Hofuf) and Dhahran, and there are Islamic universities in Medina and Riyadh together with 83 tertiary colleges. There is great emphasis on vocational training, provided at literacy and artisan skill training centres and more advanced industrial, commercial and agricultural education institutes. Education from kindergarten to university is free, with more than 22,000 schools in 1996.
ILLITERACY RATE – 29.2 per cent
ENROLMENT (percentage of age group) – primary 61 per cent (1996); secondary 42 per cent (1996); tertiary 16.3 per cent (1996)

SENEGAL
République du Sénégal

AREA – 75,955 sq. miles (196,722 sq. km). Neighbours: Mauritania (north), Mali (east), Guinea-Bissau and Guinea (south), the Gambia
POPULATION – 8,572,000 (1994 UN estimate), 94 per cent Muslim, 4 per cent Christian, 1 per cent Animist. The official language is French; the principal local language is Wolof. Fulani, Serer, Mandingo, Jola and Sarakole are also spoken
CAPITAL – ΨDakar (population, 1,641,358, 1994)
MAJOR CITIES – Kaolack (193,115), ΨSaint-Louis (132,499), Thies (216,381), ΨZinqunichor (161,680)
CURRENCY – Franc CFA of 100 centimes
NATIONAL DAY – 4 April
NATIONAL FLAG – Three vertical bands, green, yellow and red; a green star on the yellow band
LIFE EXPECTANCY (years) – male 48.30; female 50.30
POPULATION GROWTH RATE – 2.6 per cent (1997)
POPULATION DENSITY – 44 per sq. km (1996)
URBAN POPULATION – 41.7 per cent (1996)
MILITARY EXPENDITURE – 1.6 per cent of GDP (1997)
MILITARY PERSONNEL – 16,800: Army 10,000, Navy 600, Air Force 400, Paramilitaries 5,800
CONSCRIPTION DURATION – Two years
ILLITERACY RATE – 66.9 per cent
ENROLMENT (percentage of age group) – primary 59 per cent (1996); tertiary 3.4 per cent (1994)

HISTORY AND POLITICS

Formerly a French colony, Senegal elected in 1958 to remain within the French Community as an autonomous republic. It became independent as part of the Federation of Mali in June 1960 and seceded to form the Republic of Senegal in September 1960.

President Diouf was re-elected in the first round of presidential elections in February 1993 with 58.4 per cent of the vote. The legislative election in May 1998 was won by the ruling Parti Socialiste (PS), which secured 93 seats, with the Parti Démocratique Sénégalais (PDS) winning 23 seats, and the Union for Democratic Renewal 11 seats.

POLITICAL SYSTEM

In 1963 a new constitution was approved giving executive powers to the president. In August 1998 the National

Assembly voted to remove the restriction which limited the president to two consecutive seven-year terms. A general election for the National Assembly of 140 seats is held every five years. An upper house, the Senate, was established in January 1999. It comprises 45 members chosen by a 14,000-member electoral college, three elected by overseas representatives and 12 appointed by the president.

HEAD OF STATE
President, Abdou Diouf, *installed* 1981, *re-elected* 1988, 21 February 1993

COUNCIL OF MINISTERS *as at July 1999*

Prime Minister, Mamadou Lamine Loum (PS)
Ministers of State, Robert Sagna (PS) (*Agriculture*); Jacques Baudin (PS) (*Foreign Affairs and Senegalese Abroad*); Ousmane Tanor Dieng (PS) (*Presidential Services and Affairs*)
Animal Husbandry, Sanghe Mballo
Armed Forces, Cheikh Hamidou Kane (PS)
Communications, Aissatou Tall Sall
Culture, Abdoulaye Elimane Kane (PS)
Economy, Finance and Planning, Mouhamed El Moustapha Diagne (PS)
Energy, Mines and Industry, Magued Diouf (PS)
Environment and Protection of Nature, Souty Toure (PS)
Equipment and Land Transport, Landing Sané (PS)
Family, Social Welfare and National Solidarity, Aminata Mbengue Ndiaye (PS)
Fisheries and Maritime Transport, Alassane Dialy N'diaye (PS)
Health, Assane Diop
Interior, Gen. Lamine Cisse (PS)
Justice, Keeper of the Seals, Serigne Diop (PS)
Labour and Employment, Marie-Louise Corea (PS)
Modernization of the State, Abdoulaye Makhtar Diop
National Education, André Sonko (PS)
Scientific Research and Technology, Balla Moussa Daffe
Tourism and Air Transport, Tidiane Sylla (PS)
Trade and Handicrafts, Khalifa Ababacar Sall (PS)
Urban Planning and Housing, Abdourahmane Sow (PS)
Water Resources, Mamadou Faye (PS)
Youth and Sports, Iba Gueye

PS Socialist Party

EMBASSY OF THE REPUBLIC OF SENEGAL
39 Marloes Road, London w8 6LA
Tel 0171-930 7237
Ambassador Extraordinary and Plenipotentiary, HE Gabriel Alexandre Sar, apptd 1993

BRITISH EMBASSY
20 rue du Docteur Guillet (BP 6025), Dakar
Tel: Dakar 823 7392/9971
Ambassador Extraordinary and Plenipotentiary, HE David Snoxell, apptd 1997

BRITISH COUNCIL DIRECTOR, S. McNulty, 34–36 Blvd. de la République, Immeuble Sonatel, BP 6232, Dakar

ECONOMY

Around 60 per cent of the workforce are employed in agriculture. Senegal's principal exports are fish, groundnuts (raw and processed) and phosphates. Tourism is also of growing importance as a revenue earner. Principal imports are food, machinery, fuel oils and transport equipment. There are 13,850 km of roads, of which nearly one third are paved, and 1,225 km of railway track.

In 1995 there was a trade deficit of US$250 million and a current account deficit of US$58 million. In 1997 imports totalled US$1,190 million and exports US$870 million.
GNP – US$4,777 million (1997); US$540 per capita (1997)
GDP – US$4,756 million (1995); US$572 per capita (1995)
ANNUAL AVERAGE GROWTH OF GDP – 4.5 per cent (1995)
INFLATION RATE – 1.7 per cent (1997)
TOTAL EXTERNAL DEBT – US$3,671 million (1997)

Trade with UK	1997	1998
Imports from UK	£24,950,000	£27,093,000
Exports to UK	10,969,000	9,007,000

SEYCHELLES
The Republic of Seychelles

AREA – 176 sq. miles (455 sq. km)
POPULATION – 76,000 (1994 UN estimate). The languages are English, French and Creole
CAPITAL – ΨVictoria (population, 24,324, 1987), on Mahé
CURRENCY – Seychelles rupee of 100 cents
NATIONAL ANTHEM – Koste Seselwa (Seychellois Unite)
NATIONAL DAY – 18 June
NATIONAL FLAG – Five rays extending from the lower hoist over the whole field, coloured blue, yellow, green, white and red
LIFE EXPECTANCY (years) – male 65.26; female 74.05
POPULATION GROWTH RATE – 1.5 per cent (1997)
POPULATION DENSITY – 168 per sq. km (1996)
MILITARY EXPENDITURE – 2.9 per cent of GDP (1997)
MILITARY PERSONNEL – 450: Army 200, Paramilitaries 250

Seychelles, in the Indian Ocean, consists of 115 islands spread over 400,000 sq. miles of ocean. There is a relatively compact granitic group, 32 islands in all, with high hills and mountains (highest point about 2,972 ft), of which Mahé is the largest and most populated (90 per cent of the population live on Mahé); and the outlying coralline group, for the most part only a little above sea-level. Although only 4° S. of the Equator, the climate is pleasant though tropical.

HISTORY AND POLITICS

Proclaimed French territory in 1756, the Mahé group was settled as a dependency of Mauritius from 1770, was captured by a British ship in 1794, and changed hands several times between 1803 and 1814, when it was finally assigned to Great Britain. In 1903 these islands, together with the coralline group, were formed into a separate colony. On 29 June 1976, the islands became an independent republic within the Commonwealth. A coup d'état took place in 1977. Seychelles was a one-party state from 1979 until 1991, when a multiparty democratic system was proposed by President René.

In presidential and legislative elections held in March 1998, President René was re-elected with 67 per cent of the vote, and the Seychelles People's Progressive Front formed a government after winning 30 seats in the National Assembly.

POLITICAL SYSTEM

Under the constitution adopted in 1993, multiparty politics was institutionalized, a National Assembly of 33 members

(22 elected by constituencies, 11 by proportional representation) was established and the presidential mandate was set at five years, renewable three times.

HEAD OF STATE

President, Commander-in-Chief of the Armed Forces, Defence, Interior, France-Albert René, *assumed office* 5 June 1977; *elected* 1979; *re-elected* 1984, 1989, 1993, 22 March 1998
Vice-President, Finance, Economic Planning, Communications, James Michel

COUNCIL OF MINISTERS *as at July 1999*

Administration, Noellie Alexander
Agriculture and Marine Resources, Ronny Jumeau
Attorney-General, Francis Chang-Sam
Education, Danny Faure
Employment and Social Affairs, William Herminie
Foreign Affairs, Jeremie Bonnelame
Health, Jacquelin Dugasse
Industries and International Business, Joseph Belmont
Land Use and Environment, Dolor Ernesta
Local Government and Sports, Sylvette Pool
Tourism and Civil Aviation, Simone de Commarmond
Youth and Culture, Patrick Pillay

SEYCHELLES HIGH COMMISSION
Box No. 4PE, 2nd Floor, Eros House, 111 Baker Street, London WIM IFE
Tel 0171-224 1660
High Commissioner, HE Callixte d'Offay, apptd 1998, resident at Paris, France
Chargé d'Affaires, Susie Williamson

BRITISH HIGH COMMISSION
Oliaji Trade Centre, PO Box 161 Victoria, Mahé
Tel: Victoria 225225
High Commissioner, HE John Yapp, apptd 1997

ECONOMY

The economy is based on tourism, fishing, small-scale agriculture and manufacturing, and the re-export of fuel for aircraft and ships. Deep sea tuna fishing by foreign fleets under licence, improved port facilities at Victoria and exports from a tuna canning factory attract growing revenues. The government is attempting to reduce the reliance on tourism, which generates 70 per cent of foreign exchange earnings, by promoting the country as an offshore haven for financial services.
GNP – US$537 million (1997); US$6,910 per capita (1997)
GDP – US$531 million (1995); US$7,272 per capita (1995)
ANNUAL AVERAGE GROWTH OF GDP – 2.8 per cent (1997)
INFLATION RATE – 0.6 per cent (1997)
TOTAL EXTERNAL DEBT – US$149 million (1997)

TRADE

Principal exports include fish, coconuts and cinnamon. The principal imports are foodstuffs, beverages, tobacco, mineral fuels, manufactured items, building materials, machinery and transport equipment.
In 1997 there was a trade deficit of US$188 million and a current account deficit of US$63 million. In 1995 imports totalled US$233 million and exports US$53 million.

Trade with UK	1997	1998
Imports from UK	£21,415,000	£19,536,000
Exports to UK	4,256,000	20,009,000

SIERRA LEONE
The Republic of Sierra Leone

AREA – 27,699 sq. miles (71,740 sq. km). Neighbours: Guinea (north, north-east), Liberia (south-east)
POPULATION – 4,297,000 (1994 UN estimate). The south is inhabited by peoples whose languages fall into the Mende group; the north by the Temne and smaller groups such as the Limba, Loko, Koranko and Susu
CAPITAL – ΨFreetown (population, 469,776, 1985)
CURRENCY – Leone (Le) of 100 cents
NATIONAL ANTHEM – High We Exalt Thee, Realm of the Free
NATIONAL DAY – 27 April (Independence Day)
NATIONAL FLAG – Three horizontal stripes of leaf green, white and cobalt blue
LIFE EXPECTANCY (years) – male 37.47; female 40.58
POPULATION GROWTH RATE – 2.5 per cent (1997)
POPULATION DENSITY – 60 per sq. km (1996)
MILITARY EXPENDITURE – 6.9 per cent of GDP (1997)
MILITARY PERSONNEL – 200: (Army disbanded - to reform with strength of c. 5,000) Navy 200

HISTORY AND POLITICS

In the late 18th century a project was begun to settle destitute Africans from England on Freetown peninsula. In 1808 the settlement was declared a Crown colony and became the main base in West Africa for enforcing the 1807 Act outlawing the slave trade. Africans from North America and the West Indies, and Africans rescued from slave ships also settled there. In 1896 a Protectorate was declared over the hinterland.
In 1951 a new constitution was set up that united the colony of Freetown and the Protectorate and on 27 April 1961 Sierra Leone became a fully independent state within the Commonwealth. In 1971 a republican constitution was adopted and Dr Siaka Stevens became the first executive president. In 1978 Sierra Leone became a one-party state, following approval by Parliament and a referendum.
In September 1991 a new multiparty constitution was adopted and an interim government formed until a general election could be held. This government was overthrown by a coup on 29 April 1992. Captain Valentine Strasser became head of state, the House of Representatives was dissolved and all political activity was suspended. Strasser was ousted on 16 January 1996 in a bloodless coup by his deputy, Brig.-Gen. Julius Maada Bio. The military government surrendered power to a civilian government on 29 March 1996, following legislative elections on 26–27 February and a run-off election for the presidency on 15 March.
The Sierra Leone People's Party (SLPP) won 27 seats in the 68-member National Assembly and formed a government with the support of the People's Democratic Party and the Democratic Centre Party. The SLPP's candidate, Ahmad Tejan Kabbah, won the presidential contest, attracting 59.4 per cent of the vote.
In May 1997 army officers led by Major Johnny Koroma seized power. President Kabbah fled and a 20-member Armed Forces Revolutionary Council was set up with Koroma as chairman and Revolutionary United Front (RUF) leader Foday Sankoh as vice-chairman. In July 1997, a Nigerian-led ECOMOG force was sent to oust Koroma and restore the legitimate government. On 24 October 1997, a peace agreement was reached which provided for Kabbah to return to power within six months and granted immunity from prosecution to Koroma. There

was renewed fighting in February 1998 with both sides accusing the other of breaking the cease-fire. ECOMOG troops gained control of Freetown on 12 February 1998, and ousted the Koroma regime. President Kabbah returned to Freetown on 10 March 1998. Public executions of some of those responsible for the 1997 military coup took place in October 1998. Death sentences were also passed in November on some who had collaborated with the military government.

INSURGENCY

Since May 1991 government forces have been fighting the RUF whose aim is to force all foreigners out of the country and to nationalize the mining sector. Attacks by the RUF intensified in December 1998 and on 6 January 1999 the RUF attacked Freetown, brutalizing civilians, looting and burning many official buildings and forcing President Kabbah to flee the capital. ECOMOG troops launched a counter-attack on 9–10 January, recapturing the city. President Kabbah and Foday Sankoh signed a cease-fire agreement on 18 May 1999 and it was agreed in July 1999 that Sankoh would be appointed vice-president and head the Mineral Resources Commission. Attacks by various rebel splinter groups continued.

HEAD OF STATE
President, Minister of Defence, Ahmad Tejan Kabbah, *elected* 15 March 1996
Vice-President, Foday Sankoh

CABINET *as at July 1999*
Agriculture and Environment, Harry Will
Attorney-General, Justice, Solomon Berewa
Deputy Minister of Defence, Hinga Norman
Education, Alpha Wurie
Energy, Power and Works, Thaimu Bangura
Finance, Development and Economic Planning, James Jonah
Foreign Affairs, Sama Banya
Government Spokesman, Septimus Kaikai
Health, Sulaiman Tejan Jalloh
Information, Julius Spencer
Information, Broadcasting, Tourism, Charles Spencer
Internal Affairs, Local Government, Charles Magai
Labour, Social Welfare and Sports, Abass Collier
Lands, Housing and Gender Affairs, Shirley Gbujama
Mineral Resources, Alhaji Mohamed Deen
Presidential Affairs, vacant
Trade, Industry and State Enterprises, Allieu Bangura

SIERRA LEONE HIGH COMMISSION
33 Portland Place, London WIN 3AG
Tel 0171-287 9884
High Commissioner, HE Prof. Cyril Foray, apptd 1996

BRITISH HIGH COMMISSION
Spur Road, Freetown
Tel: Freetown 232563/4/5
High Commissioner, HE Peter Penfold, CMG, OBE, apptd 1997

BRITISH COUNCIL DIRECTOR, Dr R. Bendre, PO Box 124, Tower Hill, Freetown

ECONOMY

On the Freetown peninsula, farming is largely confined to the production of cassava and crops such as maize and vegetables for local consumption. In the hinterland the principal agricultural product is rice, which is the staple food of the country, and cash crops such as cocoa, coffee, palm kernels and ginger. Cattle production is also important.

The economy depends largely on mineral exports, mainly diamonds, gold and bauxite, although mineral production has been disrupted by the insurgency.

In 1995 there was a trade deficit of US$127 million and a current account deficit of US$127 million. In 1996 imports totalled US$211 million and exports US$47 million.
GNP – US$762 million (1997); US$160 per capita (1997)
GDP – US$1,229 million (1995); US$293 per capita (1995)
ANNUAL AVERAGE GROWTH OF GDP – –2.8 per cent (1995)
INFLATION RATE – 23.2 per cent (1996)
TOTAL EXTERNAL DEBT – US$1,149 million (199)

Trade with UK	1997	1998
Imports from UK	£30,135,000	£21,909,000
Exports to UK	4,528,000	3,944,000

COMMUNICATIONS

Since the phasing out of the railway system in 1974 the road network has been developed considerably; there are now 7,000 miles of roads in the country, 2,000 miles being surfaced. A bridge has been constructed over the Mano River linking Sierra Leone and Liberia.

The Freetown international airport is situated at Lungi. The main port is Freetown, which has one of the largest natural harbours in the world. There are smaller ports at Pepel, Bonthe and Niti.

Radio is operated by the government. Broadcasts are made in several of the indigenous languages, in addition to English and French.

EDUCATION

Technical education is provided in the two government technical institutes, situated in Freetown and Kenema, in two trade centres and in the technical training establishments of the mining companies. Teacher training is carried out at the University of Sierra Leone, six colleges in the provinces and in the Milton Margai Training College near Freetown.
ILLITERACY RATE – 68.6 per cent
ENROLMENT (percentage of age group) – tertiary 1.3 per cent (1990)

SINGAPORE

AREA – 239 sq. miles (618 sq. km)
POPULATION – 3,044,000 (1996): Chinese 77.3 per cent, Malays 14.1 per cent, Indians (including those of Pakistani, Bangladeshi and Sri Lankan origin) 7.3 per cent and 1.3 per cent from other ethnic groups. Malay, Mandarin, Tamil and English are the official languages. At least eight Chinese dialects are used. Malay is the national language and English is the language of administration. The religions are Buddhism 31.9 per cent, Taoism 21.9 per cent, Islam 14.9 per cent, Hinduism 3.3 per cent
CURRENCY – Singapore dollar (S$) of 100 cents
NATIONAL ANTHEM – Majulah Singapura
NATIONAL DAY – 9 August
NATIONAL FLAG – Horizontal bands of red over white; crescent with five-point stars on red band near staff
LIFE EXPECTANCY (years) – male 74.20; female 78.50
POPULATION GROWTH RATE – 2.0 per cent (1997)
POPULATION DENSITY – 4,926 per sq. km (1996)
MILITARY EXPENDITURE – 4.3 per cent of GDP (1997)
MILITARY PERSONNEL – 180,500: Army 50,000, Navy 9,000, Air Force 13,500, Paramilitaries 108,000

CONSCRIPTION DURATION – 24–30 months
ILLITERACY RATE – 8.7 per cent
ENROLMENT (percentage of age group) – primary 94 per cent (1995); tertiary 38.5 per cent (1996)

Singapore consists of the island of Singapore and 59 islets. Singapore island is 26 miles long and 14 miles in breadth and is situated just north of the Equator off the southern extremity of the Malay peninsula, from which it is separated by the Straits of Johore. A causeway crosses the three-quarters of a mile to the mainland. The climate is hot and humid. Rainfall averages 240 cm a year and temperature ranges from 24° to 32° C (76°–89° F).

HISTORY AND POLITICS

Singapore, where Sir Stamford Raffles first established a trading post under the East India Company in 1819, was incorporated with Penang and Malacca to form the Straits Settlements in 1826. The Straits Settlements became a Crown colony in 1867. Singapore fell into Japanese hands in 1942 and civil government was not restored until 1946, when it became a separate colony. Internal self-government was introduced in 1959. Singapore became a state of Malaysia in September 1963, but left Malaysia and became an independent sovereign state within the Commonwealth on 9 August 1965. Singapore adopted a republican constitution from that date.

After the general election of 2 January 1997 the People's Action Party (PAP) had 81 seats in Parliament. S. R. Nathan became president of Singapore on 1 September 1999; no election was held as he was the sole candidate.

POLITICAL SYSTEM

The president is directly elected for a six-year term, and can veto government decisions relating to internal security, the budget, financial reserves and the appointment of senior civil servants. The president appoints the prime minister and, on his advice, the members of the Cabinet. There is a Parliament of 83 directly elected members, with up to three further members appointed by the president.

HEAD OF STATE

President, Sellapan Ramanathan Nathan, *took office* 1 September 1999

CABINET *as at July 1999*

Prime Minister, Goh Chok Tong
Senior Minister, PM's Office, Lee Kuan Yew
Deputy PM, Defence, Dr Tony Tan
Deputy PM, PM's Office, Lee Hsien Loong
Communications, Mah Bow Tan
Community Development, Muslim Affairs, Abdullah Tarmugi
Education, Defence, Rear-Adm. Teo Chee Hean
Finance, Dr Richard Hu Tsu Tau
Foreign Affairs and Law, Shanmugam Jayakumar
Health and Environment, Yeo Cheow Tong
Home Affairs, Wong Kan Seng
Information and the Arts, Trade and Industry, Brig.-Gen. George Yeo
Labour, Dr Lee Boon Yang
National Development, Foreign Affairs, Lim Hng Kiang
Trade and Industry, Finance, Lee Yock Suan
Without Portfolio, PM's Office, Lim Boon Heng

HIGH COMMISSION FOR THE REPUBLIC OF SINGAPORE

9 Wilton Crescent, London SW1X 8RW
Tel 0171-235 8315
High Commissioner, HE J. Y. Pillay, apptd 1996
Counsellor, Jimmy Tin Chew Chua
First Secretary, Kheng Hian Philip Ho (*Commercial*)

BRITISH HIGH COMMISSION

Tanglin Road, Singapore 247919
Tel: Singapore 473 9333
High Commissioner, HE Alan Hunt, CMG, apptd 1997
Deputy High Commissioner, A. Gooch
Defence Adviser, Gp Capt. C. B. LeBas

BRITISH COUNCIL DIRECTOR, Dr J. Grote, OBE, 30 Napier Road, Singapore 258509

ECONOMY

Historically Singapore's economy was based on the sale and distribution of raw materials from surrounding countries and on entrepôt trade in finished products. An industrialization programme launched in 1968 has established a wide range of manufacturing industries, including shipbuilding, iron and steel, micro-electronics, electrical goods, telecommunications equipment, office machinery, scientific instruments, pharmaceuticals, etc. Singapore has also become an important financial services centre with significant insurance and foreign exchange markets, a stock exchange, 149 commercial banks and 79 merchant banks and an oil-refining centre. In February 1998 the government announced substantial liberalizing reforms of the financial sector, aimed at allowing the country to compete more competitively with other financial sectors in the region. Singapore has not been as badly affected as its neighbours by the economic crisis in south-east Asia, due in part to currency reserves estimated at US$118 billion; it was praised by the IMF for its adroit response to the crisis, which included wage cuts.

By late 1999, every household was to have been connected to a cable network providing television, telephone and Internet access.

Singapore's major trading partners are the USA, Malaysia, the EU, Hong Kong and Japan.

In 1997 Singapore had a trade surplus of US$1,145 million and a current account surplus of US$14,803 million. In 1997 imports totalled US$132,437 million and exports US$124,986 million.

GNP – US$101,834 million (1997); US$32,810 per capita (1997)
GDP – US$85,107 million (1995); US$25,581 per capita (1995)
ANNUAL AVERAGE GROWTH OF GDP – 7.3 per cent (1996)
INFLATION RATE – 2.0 per cent (1997)
UNEMPLOYMENT – 2.7 per cent (1995)

Trade with UK	1997	1998
Imports from UK	£2,042,966,000	£1,614,891,000
Exports to UK	2,713,666,000	2,462,773,000

COMMUNICATIONS

Singapore is one of the largest and busiest seaports in the world, with six terminals, deep water wharves and ship repairing facilities. Ships also anchor in the roads, unloading into lighters. In 1994, the total volume of cargo handled was 290,100,000 tonnes. There were 127,242 ship arrivals in 1996.

The international airport is at Changi, in the east of the island, with Singapore Airlines operating flights to 43 countries and 24,500,000 passengers using the airport in 1996. There are 25.8 km of railway connected to the Malaysian rail system by the causeway across the Straits of Johore, and 3,027 km of roads.

There are 19 radio and four television channels operated by the Singapore Broadcasting Corporation in the four official languages, and three private broadcasting stations.

SLOVAKIA
Slovenská Republika – *The Republic of Slovakia*

AREA – 18,928 sq. miles (49,035 sq. km). Neighbours: Poland (north), Ukraine (east), Hungary (south), Austria (west), the Czech Republic (north-west)
POPULATION – 5,374,000 (1995 estimate): 87.7 per cent are ethnic Slovaks, 10.6 per cent ethnic Hungarians, 1.4 per cent Romany, 1 per cent Czech, with smaller numbers of Ruthenians, Ukrainians and Germans. The population is mainly Christian, some 60 per cent Roman Catholic and 8 per cent Protestant. Slovak is the official language, while Hungarian and Czech are also spoken
CAPITAL – Bratislava (population, 452,278, 1993), on the Danube
MAJOR CITIES – Košice (239,927); Žilina (86,373); Prešov (92,013); Banská Bystríca (88,390)
CURRENCY – Koruna (Sk) of 100 halierov
NATIONAL ANTHEM – Nad Tatrou sa blýska (Storm over the Tatras)
NATIONAL DAYS – 1 January (Establishment of Slovak Republic); 5 July (Day of the Slav Missionaries); 29 August (Slovak National Uprising); 1 September (Constitution Day)
NATIONAL FLAG – Three horizontal stripes of white, blue, red with the arms all over near the hoist
LIFE EXPECTANCY (years) – male 68.34; female 76.48
POPULATION GROWTH RATE – 0.3 per cent (1997)
POPULATION DENSITY – 110 per sq. km (1996)
URBAN POPULATION – 57.0 per cent (1995)
ENROLMENT (percentage of age group) – tertiary 22.1 per cent (1996)

The Tatry (Tatras) mountains in the centre and north of Slovakia reach heights of 2,655 m. The major river is the Váh which flows from the Tatry mountains to join the Danube at the Hungarian border. The climate is continental.

HISTORY AND POLITICS (*see also* Czech Republic)

At the end of the 11th century Slovakia became part of the Hungarian state when the Magyars gained control of the area. After the Hungarians were defeated in 1526, most of Hungary (including part of Slovakia) was occupied by the Turks, with the remainder of Hungary and Slovakia being incorporated into the Austrian Empire. With the establishment of the Austro-Hungarian monarchy in 1867, Slovakia again came under Hungarian control. The attempted Magyarization of Slovakia gave impetus to the national revival which had begun in 1848–9, and when the First World War came many Slovaks fought with the allies. Amalgamated into the republic of Czechoslovakia on 28 October 1918, Slovakia became independent in March 1939 as a Nazi puppet state when Germany invaded the Czech lands. Slovakia was liberated by Soviet forces in 1945 and returned to Czechoslovakia. The formation of a federal republic between the Czech lands and Slovakia was the only Prague Spring reform to survive the Soviet invasion of 1968. Following the collapse of Communist rule in 1989, the Czech and Slovak republics began to negotiate the dissolution of the federation into two sovereign states in 1992. Dissolution took effect on 1 January 1993.

A coalition government led by the Movement for a Democratic Slovakia (HZDS) was sworn in on 12 January 1993 but lost its majority in the National Council when the Slovak National Party (SNS) left the government. Increasing criticism of the economic policy and authoritarian style of the government led ten HZDS members to form a new party which, in alliance with three other parties, brought down the government by a no-confidence vote in March 1994.

Legislative elections on 30 September and 1 October 1994 returned the HZDS to power at the head of a three-party coalition which took office on 13 December 1994.

Following the legislative elections on 25–26 September 1998, the HZDS remained the largest party, but a four-party coalition government led by the Slovak Democratic Coalition (SDK) was formed.

The number of seats held by each of the parties in the National Council following the 1998 election was: HZDS 43; SDK 42; Party of the Democratic Left (SDL) 23; Hungarian Coalition Party (SMK) 15; Slovak National Party (SNS) 14; Party of Civic Understanding (SOP) 13. President Kováč's term of office ended on 2 March 1998. The presidential elections were not contested by the ruling HZDS, who were accused by opposition parties of trying to create a constitutional vacuum; since no president was elected by the end of Kováč's term, certain presidential powers were transferred to the prime minister. After the 1998 legislative elections, the National Council voted on 14 January 1999 for direct presidential elections, which were held on 29 May 1999.

POLITICAL SYSTEM

The constitution vests legislative power in the National Council of 150 members elected for a four-year term by proportional representation with a five per cent threshold for parliamentary representation. The president is elected for a five-year term, renewable only once, by direct election; executive power is held by the prime minister and Cabinet.

HEAD OF STATE
President, Rudolf Schuster, *elected* 29 May 1999, *sworn in* 15 June 1999

CABINET *as at July 1999*
Prime Minister, Mikuláš Dzurinda (SDK)
Deputy PMs, Ivan Mikloš (SDK) *(Economy)*; Pavol Hamžík (SOP) *(European Integration)*; Pál Csáky (SMK) *(Human and Minority Rights and Regional Development)*; L'ubomír Fogaš (SDL) *(Legislature and Media Policy)*
Agriculture, Pavel Koncoš (SDL)
Construction and Public Works, István Harna (SMK)
Culture, Milan Kňažko (SDK)
Defence, Pavol Kanis (SDL)
Economy, L'udovít Černák (SDK)
Education, Milan Ftáčnik (SDL)
Environment, László Miklós (SMK)
Finance, Brigita Schmögnerová (SDL)
Foreign Affairs, Eduard Kukan (SDK)
Health, Tibor Šagát (SDK)
Interior, Ladislav Pittner (SDK)
Justice, Ján Čarnogurský (SDK)
Labour, Social Affairs and the Family, Peter Magvaši (SDL)
Privatization, Mária Machová (SOP)
Transport, Posts and Telecommunications, Gabriel Palacka (SDK)

EMBASSY OF THE SLOVAK REPUBLIC
25 Kensington Palace Gardens, London w8 4QY
Tel 0171-243 0803
Ambassador Extraordinary and Plenipotentiary, HE Igor Slobodník, apptd 1997

BRITISH EMBASSY
Panská 16, 81101 Bratislava
Tel: Bratislava 531 9632
Ambassador Extraordinary and Plenipotentiary, HE David
Lyscom, apptd 1998
BRITISH COUNCIL DIRECTOR, J. McGrath, PO Box 68,
Panská 17, 81499 Bratislava

DEFENCE

The Army has 478 main battle tanks, 207 armoured
personnel carriers, 476 armoured infantry fighting vehicles,
and 382 artillery pieces. The Air Force has 121 combat
aircraft and 19 attack helicopters.
MILITARY EXPENDITURE – 2.1 per cent of GDP (1997)
MILITARY PERSONNEL – 38,400: Army 23,800, Air Force
12,000, Paramilitaries 2,600
CONSCRIPTION DURATION – 12 months

ECONOMY

From independence until mid-1994 Slovakia faced economic difficulties because of the structure of its centrally-
planned and inefficiently managed economy, reliant on
state-subsidized heavy industries with low productivity,
and because of the ambivalent attitude to reform of the
HZDS government. In mid-1994 the economic situation
stabilized as the Moravčik government implemented a
second round of privatization. The election of an HZDS-
led government in October 1994 slowed the pace of reform.
Following severe depreciation of the Koruna and the
failure of the economy to achieve the anticipated growth
targets, the government introduced a package of austerity
measures on 20 May 1999; the basic rate of VAT was
raised, there were increases in energy, water, telecommunications and housing prices, and import taxes were
reintroduced.
    Natural resources include brown coal, natural gas, iron
ore, antimony, lead, zinc and magnesite.
    In 1997 Slovakia had a trade deficit of US$1,481 million
and a current account deficit of US$1,359 million. In 1996
imports totalled US$11,445 million and exports US$8,829
million.
GNP – US$19,801 million (1997); US$3,680 per capita
(1997)
GDP – US$17,435 million (1995); US$3,266 per capita
(1995)
ANNUAL AVERAGE GROWTH OF GDP – 6.5 per cent
(1997)
INFLATION RATE – 6.1 per cent (1997)
UNEMPLOYMENT – 13.1 per cent (1995)
TOTAL EXTERNAL DEBT – US$9,989 million (1997)

Trade with UK	1997	1998
Imports from UK	£132,250,000	£104,766,000
Exports to UK	73,317,000	75,165,000

SLOVENIA
Republika Slovenija

AREA – 7,821 sq. miles (20,256 sq. km). Neighbours:
    Austria (north), Hungary (north-east), Croatia (east and
    south), Italy (west)
POPULATION – 1,991,000 (1994 UN estimate). The
    population is mostly Slovenian. There are small
    Hungarian (0.5 per cent) and Italian (0.1 per cent)
    minorities, together with a Romany population. The
    main religion is Roman Catholicism. Slovene is the
    official language, together with Hungarian and Italian
    in ethnically mixed regions

CAPITAL – Ljubljana (population, 280,146)
MAJOR CITIES – Maribor (103,113); Celje (39,782); Kranj
    (36,770); ΨKoper (24,495), the only port, 1994
CURRENCY – Tolar (SIT) of 100 stotin
NATIONAL ANTHEM – Zdravljica (A Toast)
NATIONAL DAY – 25 June (Statehood Day)
NATIONAL FLAG – Three horizontal stripes of white,
    blue, red, with the arms in the upper hoist
LIFE EXPECTANCY (years) – male 69.58; female 77.38
POPULATION GROWTH RATE – –0.1 per cent (1997)
POPULATION DENSITY – 98 per sq. km (1996)
URBAN POPULATION – 50.0 per cent (1995)
MILITARY EXPENDITURE – 1.7 per cent of GDP (1997)
MILITARY PERSONNEL – 14,050: Army 9,550,
    Paramilitaries 4,500
CONSCRIPTION DURATION – Seven months

Slovenia is a small mountainous state which is the most
northerly of the former Yugoslav republics. The two major
rivers are the Sava and the Drava. There is a short coastline
in the south-west 29 miles (46 km) in length on the Adriatic.
The climate is a mixture of Mediterranean, continental
and alpine.

HISTORY AND POLITICS

The area that is now Slovenia came under the control of
the Habsburg Empire in the 13th and 14th centuries and
remained so until the defeat of the Austro-Hungarian
Empire in 1918. On 27 October 1918 Slovenia became part
of the state of Slovenes, Croats and Serbs (later Yugoslavia)
and this was confirmed by the Versailles Treaty (1919). In
1941 German forces invaded Yugoslavia and Slovenia was
divided between Germany, Italy and Hungary. Slovenia
was reformed as a constituent republic of the federal
Yugoslav state in May 1945. After a dispute with Italy and
nine years of international administration, the Adriatic
coast and hinterland were returned to Slovenia in 1954 and
Italy retained Trieste.
    Slovenian fears of Serbian dominance led the Slovene
Assembly in 1989 to amend the republican constitution to
lay the basis of a sovereign state. The first democratic
elections, held in April 1990, were won by the pro-
independence 'Demos' coalition. In a referendum in
December 1990, 88 per cent of the electorate voted for
independence, which was declared on 25 June 1991. A ten-
day war with the Yugoslav National Army followed before
the Army called off hostilities and withdrew.
    Legislative elections were held on 10 November 1996.
Liberal Democracy of Slovenia won the most seats and
formed a coalition government. President Kučan was re-
elected on 23 November 1997.

FOREIGN RELATIONS

Slovenia signed an association agreement and applied for
membership of the EU in June 1996. The EU began formal
accession negotiations with Slovenia on 10 November
1998. Slovenia has a temporary seat on the UN Security
Council.

POLITICAL SYSTEM

The head of state is the president, elected for a five-year
term. Executive power is vested in the prime minister and
Cabinet of Ministers. The lower house of the legislature,
the National Assembly, has 90 members directly elected
for a four-year term. The upper house, the 40-member
National Council, has an advisory role. The National
Assembly is elected on a proportional representation basis,
with one seat each reserved for the Italian and Hungarian
minorities.

HEAD OF STATE
President, Milan Kučan, *elected* April 1990, *re-elected*
    December 1992, 23 November 1997

CABINET *as at August 1999*

Prime Minister, Janez Drnovšek (LDS)
Deputy PM, Co-ordination, Marjan Podobnik (SLS)
Agriculture and Forestry, Ciril Smrkolj (SLS)
Co-ordination of Social Activities, Janko Kušar (DeSUS)
Culture, Josef Školjc (LDS)
Defence, Dr Franci Demšar (SLS)
Economic Affairs, Dr Tea Petrin (LDS)
Economic Relations and Development, Marjan Senjur (SLS)
Education and Sports, Pavel Zgaga (LDS)
Environment and Physical Planning, Dr Pavel Gantar (LDS)
European Affairs, Igor Bavcar (LDS)
Finance, Mitja Gaspari (Ind.)
Foreign Affairs, Boris Frlec (LDS)
Health, Marjan Jereb (SLS)
Internal Affairs, Borut Šuklje (LDS)
Justice, Tomaž Marušič (SLS)
Labour, Family and Social Affairs, Tone Rop (LDS)
Local Government, Božo Grafenauer (SLS)
Science, Technology, Alojzij Marinček (SLS)
Small Enterprises, Tourism, Janko Razgoršek (LDS)
Transport and Communications, Anton Bergauer (SLS)

LDS Liberal Democracy of Slovenia; SLS Slovene People's
Party; DeSUS Democratic Party of Pensioners of Slovenia;
Ind. Independent

EMBASSY OF THE REPUBLIC OF SLOVENIA
11–15 Wigmore Street, London WIH 9LA
Tel 0171-495 7775
Ambassador Extraordinary and Plenipotentiary, HE Marjan
    Setinc, apptd 1998

BRITISH EMBASSY
4th Floor, Trg Republike 3, SI-61-000 Ljubljana
Tel: Ljubljana 125 7191
Ambassador Extraordinary and Plenipotentiary, HE David
    Lloyd, OBE, apptd 1997

BRITISH COUNCIL DIRECTOR, F. King, Cankarjevo
    nabrezje 27, SI-1000 Ljubljana

ECONOMY

Slovenia's economy has emerged as the most stable of the
former Yugoslav economies and the least affected by the
end of central planning. Although it has lost its captive
export market and cheap supplies of raw materials from
other parts of the former Yugoslavia, Slovenia is one of the
richest ex-Communist countries. It has successfully re-
orientated its exports towards Western markets, its main
trading partners being Germany, Italy and France. The
privatization process was completed in 1998.

In 1998 agriculture contributed 4.5 per cent to the total
value of GDP, industry 32 per cent and services 58 per
cent. The main agricultural products are potatoes, wheat,
corn, sugar beet and wine. The major manufacturing sectors
are metalworking, electronics, textiles, automotive parts,
chemicals, glass products and food-processing. Tourism
and transport are major export earners, with 1,400,000
tourists visiting in 1991.

In 1998 Slovenia had a trade deficit of US$775 million
and a current account deficit of US$4 million. Imports
totalled US$10,098 million and exports US$9,095 million.
GNP – US$19,550 million (1997); US$9,840 per capita
    (1997)
GDP – US$18,579 million (1995); US$9,652 per capita
    (1995); estimated to be US$20,294 million and
    US$10,248 per capita in 1999

ANNUAL AVERAGE GROWTH OF GDP – 3.9 per cent
    (1995); forecast to be 4 per cent in 1997
INFLATION RATE – 9.1 per cent (1997)
UNEMPLOYMENT – 7.4 per cent (1995)
TOTAL EXTERNAL DEBT – US$4,762 million (1997)

Trade with UK	1997	1998
Imports from UK	£149,494,000	£136,308,000
Exports to UK	98,204,000	103,527,000

COMMUNICATIONS

There are 14,810 km of roads and 1,201 km of rail track.
Important road and rail communications cross the country
from west to east (Milan–Ljubljana–Budapest), and north
to south (Munich–Ljubljana–Zagreb–Belgrade–Athens).
There are international airports at Ljubljana, Maribor and
Portorož (Adriatic Coast). Koper is an important shipment
point for goods from Austria, Hungary, the Czech Republic
and Slovakia.

EDUCATION

Education is compulsory and free between the ages of
seven and 14. There are 821 primary schools (age seven–
14), 153 secondary or middle schools (age 14–19), 44
colleges and two universities (Ljubljana and Maribor).
ENROLMENT (percentage of age group) – primary 100
    per cent (1996); tertiary 36.4 per cent (1996)

SOLOMON ISLANDS

AREA – 11,157 sq. miles (28,896 sq. km)
POPULATION – 391,000 (1995 estimate); 328,723 (1991
    census). English is the official language; there are over
    80 local languages
CAPITAL – ΨHoniara (population, 40,000, 1991)
CURRENCY – Solomon Islands dollar (SI$) of 100 cents
NATIONAL ANTHEM – God Bless our Solomon Islands
NATIONAL DAY – 7 July (Independence Day)
NATIONAL FLAG – Blue over green divided by a
    diagonal yellow band, with five white stars in the top
    left quarter
LIFE EXPECTANCY (years) – male 59.90; female 61.40
POPULATION GROWTH RATE – 3.2 per cent (1997)
POPULATION DENSITY – 14 per sq. km (1996)

Forming a scattered archipelago of mountainous islands
and low-lying coral atolls, the Solomon Islands stretches
about 900 miles in a south-easterly direction from the
Shortland Islands to the Santa Cruz islands. The six biggest
islands are Choiseul, New Georgia, Santa Isabel, Guadalcanal, Malaita and Makira. They are characterized by
thickly-forested mountain ranges intersected by deep,
narrow valleys.

HISTORY AND POLITICS

The origin of the present Melanesian inhabitants is
uncertain. European interest in the islands began in the
mid-16th century and continued intermittently for about
300 years, when the inauguration of sugar plantations in
Queensland and Fiji (which created a need for labour) and
the arrival of missionaries and traders led to increased
European interest in the region. Great Britain declared a
Protectorate in 1893 over the Southern Solomons, adding
the Santa Cruz group in 1898 and 1899. The islands of the
Shortland groups were transferred from Germany to Great
Britain by treaty in 1900. The Solomon Islands achieved
internal self-government in 1976, and became independent
in July 1978.

Following legislative elections held on 6 August 1997, the National Unity group was the largest party in the National Parliament, winning 21 seats. Bartholomew Ulufa'alu, the Liberal Party leader, was elected prime minister.

INSURGENCY

In late 1998 tension between the indigenous inhabitants of Guadalcanal and settlers from other parts of the country, chiefly Malaita, led to violent attacks on the settlers. On 28 June 1999, a peace agreement was signed by representatives of the national and provincial governments and the Isatambu Freedom Fighters, a local militant group, following mediation by the Commonwealth special envoy Sitiveni Rabuka.

POLITICAL SYSTEM

The Solomon Islands is a constitutional monarchy. Queen Elizabeth II is represented locally by the Governor-General. Executive authority is exercised by the Cabinet. Legislative power is vested in a unicameral National Parliament of 50 members, elected for a four-year term.

Governor-General, HE John Lapli, apptd 1999

CABINET *as at July 1999*

Prime Minister, Finance (acting),, Bartholomew Ulufa'alu
Deputy PM, Minister of Transport, Works and Communications, Sir Baddeley Devesi
Agriculture and Fisheries, Steve Auman
Commerce and Tourism, Enele Kwainirara
Development Planning, Fred Fono
Education, Roni Mani
Foreign Affairs, John Patteson Oti
Forests, Environment and Conservation, Hilda Kari
Health and Medical Services, Dick Warakohia
Home Affairs, Revd Leslie Boseto
Indigenous Business Development Department, vacant
Justice and Legal Affairs, Edmond Andresen
Lands and Housing, Jackson Piesi
Mines and Energy, Walter Naezon
Police and National Security, Roben Mesipitu
Provincial Government, Japhet Waipora
Women, Youth and Sports, Gordon Mara

HIGH COMMISSION OF THE SOLOMON ISLANDS
Boulevard Saint Michel 28, Box 23, B-1040 Brussels
Tel: Brussels 2732 7085
High Commissioner, HE Robert Sisilo, apptd 1996

BRITISH HIGH COMMISSION
Telekom House, Mendana Avenue (PO Box 676), Honiara
Tel: Honiara 21705/6
High Commissioner, HE Alan Waters, apptd 1998

ECONOMY

The main imports are foodstuffs, consumer goods, machinery and transport materials. Principal exports are timber, fish, palm oil, copra and cocoa. In 1995 imports totalled US$154 million and exports totalled US$168 million.
GNP – US$350 million (1997); US$870 per capita (1997)
GDP – US$259 million (1995); US$686 per capita (1995)
ANNUAL AVERAGE GROWTH OF GDP – 7.0 per cent (1995)
INFLATION RATE – 8.1 per cent (1997)
TOTAL EXTERNAL DEBT – US$135 million (1997)

Trade with UK	1995	1996
Imports from UK	£2,111,000	£776,000
Exports to UK	6,573,000	9,101,000

COMMUNICATIONS

Solomon Airlines operates international services to other Pacific states and Australia. Air Niugini flies from Port Moresby to Honiara. There are about 2,100 km of roads, including those in private plantations, forestry areas and roads built and maintained by councils; only 32 km of roads are paved. Telekom, a company jointly owned by Cable and Wireless and the Solomon Islands government, operates the international and domestic telephone circuits from a ground station in Honiara via the Intelsat Pacific Ocean communication satellite.

SOMALIA
Jamhuuriyadda Diimoqraadiga ee Soomaaliya

AREA – 246,201 sq. miles (637,657 sq. km). Neighbours: Djibouti, Ethiopia and Kenya (west)
POPULATION – 9,822,000 (1994 UN estimate). Somali and Arabic are the official languages. English and Italian are also spoken
CAPITAL – ΨMogadishu (population, 230,000, 1987 estimate)
MAJOR CITIES – ΨBerbera (15,000); Boroma (65,000); Burao (15,000); Hargeisa (20,000); ΨKisimayu (60,000)
CURRENCY – Somali shilling of 100 cents
NATIONAL DAY – under review
NATIONAL FLAG – Five-pointed white star on blue ground
LIFE EXPECTANCY (years) – male 45.41; female 48.60
POPULATION GROWTH RATE – 1.7 per cent (1997)
POPULATION DENSITY – 15 per sq. km (1996)
URBAN POPULATION – 23.5 per cent (1987)
ENROLMENT (percentage of age group) – primary 8 per cent (1985); secondary 3 per cent (1985); tertiary 2.1 per cent (1985)

HISTORY AND POLITICS

British rule in Somaliland lasted from 1887 until 1960, except for a short period in 1940–1 when the Protectorate was occupied by Italian forces. Somalia, formerly an Italian colony, was occupied by British forces in 1941. In 1950 the UN placed it under Italian administration; this trusteeship lasted until the British protectorate and the trust territory became independent on 1 July 1960. In 1969, the armed forces seized power and established a ruling Revolutionary Council under Siad Barre's leadership.

Siad Barre was overthrown by rebels in January 1991, sparking civil war between rival clan-based movements. The United Somali Congress (USC) seized control in Mogadishu and formed an interim administration under Ali Mahdi Muhammad. In the north, the Somali National Movement formed a rival administration under its leader, Abourahman Ahmed Ali. Fighting between the USC and supporters of the Somali National Alliance (SNA) of Gen. Mohammed Aideed devastated Mogadishu and large parts of the south, exacerbating famine conditions. The UN Operation in Somalia proved ineffective in securing aid distribution routes and was replaced on 9 December 1992 by a UN-approved, US-led, United Task Force (UNITAF).

On 4 May 1993, UNITAF handed over to a 28,000-strong UN force (UNOSOM). Clashes between the UN force, attempting to broker a settlement, and the SNA left 90 UN troops and 2,000 Somalis dead between June and November 1993. Western troops withdrew from the UN operation in March 1994, leaving UN troops from India, Pakistan and Egypt, which were easily overrun by the Somali factions.

The UN withdrew its troops in March 1995, enabling Gen. Aideed's militia to take control of the city's port and airport. On 12 June 1995, Gen. Aideed was ousted as SNA leader by a joint USC-SNA congress which nominated Osman Ali Ato as its leader. Gen. Aideed responded by declaring himself president on 15 June 1995. Gen. Aideed died of gunshot wounds in July 1996 and was replaced by his son, Hussein Aideed. Fighting between the factions continued in 1996–7 despite a brief cease-fire in October 1996.

On 22 December 1997, 26 out of the 28 factions signed the Cairo Declaration, an agreement aimed at establishing a cross-factional 13-member Presidential Council and a 189-member Council of Deputies in preparation for full elections to be held no later than 2003. The declaration was approved by both Aideed and Ali Mahdi Muhammad, although the conference to organize the composition of the new bodies has been repeatedly postponed. Since the signing of the declaration, fighting has continued. Following the capture of Baidoa by militiamen loyal to Aideed on 2 May 1999, Ethiopian forces assisted the Rahawein Resistance Army (RRA), a rival militia, to recapture the town on 6 June.

INSURGENCIES

Civil war broke out in May 1988 between the government and the opposition Somali National Movement (SNM) in the north of the country. With the downfall of Siad Barre, the SNM took control of the north-west (the former British Somaliland Protectorate) and in May 1991 declared unilateral independence as the 'Somaliland Republic'. A government and legislature was formed which elected Mohammed Ibrahim Egal as president in May 1993; he was re-elected in February 1997.

An autonomous administration was proclaimed in north-eastern Somalia on 23 July 1998. Col. Ahmed Abdullahi Yusuf was named as president of the region, calling itself Puntland, and a Cabinet was appointed. On 15 September 1998, a 69-member parliament was inaugurated.

SOMALI DIPLOMATIC REPRESENTATION
The Embassy closed in January 1992.

BRITISH DIPLOMATIC REPRESENTATION
The British Embassy in Mogadishu closed in January 1991.

ECONOMY

Livestock raising is the main occupation and there is a modest export trade in livestock, skins and hides. Italy, the Gulf States and Saudi Arabia import the bulk of the banana crop, the second biggest export. Due to UN aid and pacification of the countryside, the harvest improved from 10 per cent of normal in 1992 to 50 per cent in 1993.
GDP – US$1,132 million (1995); US$119 per capita (1995)
ANNUAL AVERAGE GROWTH OF GDP – 0.0 per cent (1995)
INFLATION RATE – 81.9 per cent (1988)
TOTAL EXTERNAL DEBT – US$2,561 million (1997)

Trade with UK	1997	1998
Imports from UK	£1,682,000	£1,601,000
Exports to UK	36,000	920,000

SOUTH AFRICA
Republiek van Suid-Afrika – Republic of South Africa

AREA – 471,445 sq. miles (1,221,037 sq. km). Neighbours: Namibia (north-west), Botswana and Zimbabwe (north), Mozambique and Swaziland (north-east), Lesotho, which is completely surrounded by South Africa
POPULATION – 42,393,000 (1994 UN estimate); 40,583,573 (1996 census): 76.7 per cent African, 10.9 per cent White, 8.9 per cent Coloured, 2.6 per cent Asian. The interim constitution designates 11 official languages: Afrikaans; English; IsiNdebele; IsiXosa; IsiZulu, Sepedi; Sosetho; SiSwati; Setswana; Tshivenda; Xitsonga. Afrikaans and English are to remain the languages of record although any citizen may correspond official business in his own language. Afrikaans is descended from Dutch and is the language of the Afrikaner and Coloured populations
CAPITAL – The seat of the government is Pretoria (population 2,341,000, 1995 estimate); the seat of the legislature is Cape Town (population, 2,279,000, 1995 estimate)
MAJOR CITIES – ΨDurban (3,215,000); ΨEast London (611,000); Johannesburg (4,247,360); Pietermaritzburg (519,000); ΨPort Elizabeth (1,015,000), 1995 estimates
CURRENCY – Rand (R) of 100 cents
NATIONAL ANTHEMS – Die Stem Van Suid-Afrika (The Call of South Africa); Nkosi Sikelel' iAfrika (God Bless Africa)
NATIONAL DAY – 27 April (Freedom Day)
NATIONAL FLAG – Divided red over blue by a horizontal white-fimbriated green Y; in the hoist a black triangle fimbriated in yellow
LIFE EXPECTANCY (years) – male 60.01; female 66.00
POPULATION GROWTH RATE – 2.0 per cent (1997)
POPULATION DENSITY – 35 per sq. km (1996)
URBAN POPULATION – 53.7 per cent (1996)
ILLITERACY RATE – 18.2 per cent
ENROLMENT (percentage of age group) – primary 94 per cent (1996); secondary 51 per cent (1996); tertiary 17.3 per cent (1995)

South Africa occupies the southernmost part of the African continent from the courses of the Limpopo, Marico, Molopo, Nosop and Orange Rivers to the Cape of Good Hope, with the exception of Lesotho, Swaziland and the extreme south of Mozambique. To the west, east and south lie the south Atlantic and southern Indian Oceans. Some 1,192 miles (1,920 km) to the south-east of Cape Town lie Prince Edward and Marion Islands, part of South Africa since 1947.

The Orange, with its tributary the Vaal, is the principal river, rising in the Drakensberg and flowing into the Atlantic near the border with Namibia. The Limpopo, or Crocodile River, in the north, rises in North-West Province and flows into the Indian Ocean through Mozambique.

The climate is subtropical, dry and sunny, moderated by the temperate winds from the Atlantic and Indian Oceans. Moist hot air masses from the Indian Ocean are the chief source of rainfall for most of the country.

HISTORY AND POLITICS

Hunter-gatherers, the San (Bushmen) and Khoikhoi (Hottentots) inhabited southern Africa from c.8,000 BC. Their descendants, and those of Bantu-speaking peoples who had migrated south, occupied the area when the Portuguese navigator Bartolomeu Dias charted the coast in 1488.

The colony of the Cape of Good Hope was founded by the Dutch at Cape Town in 1652 and remained a Dutch colony until Britain took possession of it in 1795. Restored to Dutch rule in 1803, it was again taken by Britain in 1806 and this was confirmed by the London Convention of 1814. A rejection of British liberalism and the desire to keep slaves led to the movement of large numbers of Boers (the descendants of Dutch settlers) north-eastwards in the years following 1834. This 'Great Trek' led to the foundation of the Orange Free State and Transvaal republics by the Boers, which were recognized by Britain in 1853–4. Natal was annexed to Cape Colony by the British in 1844 and then formed as a separate colony in 1856, to which Zululand was added in 1897 after the British victory in the Zulu wars. Transvaal and the Orange Free State (renamed the Orange River Colony) became British colonies after the Boer defeat in the Second Boer War 1899–1902. The self-governing colonies of the Cape of Good Hope, Natal, Transvaal and the Orange River Colony became united in 1910 under the name of the Union of South Africa. Independence within the Commonwealth was gained in 1931 under the Statute of Westminster. South Africa left the Commonwealth and became a republic on 31 May 1961, largely as a result of international condemnation of apartheid and of the Sharpeville massacre.

From 1948, when the Afrikaner National Party came to power, South Africa's social and political structure was based on apartheid, a policy of racial segregation. Opposition protests culminated in the Sharpeville massacre in 1960; the African National Congress (ANC) and other opposition groups were subsequently banned. A new wave of opposition climaxed in 1976 with uprisings in Soweto, in which hundreds were shot dead. In 1984 renewed rioting in the black townships and continuing unrest led to the declaration of a state of emergency in July 1985 in 36 districts, and nationwide from 12 June 1986; it was renewed annually until 1990.

As part of its policy of apartheid, the government established a number of black 'homelands'. Six areas (Gazankulu, Lebowa, KwaNdebele, KaNgwane, Qwaqwa and KwaZulu) were designated as self-governing states. A further four (Bophuthatswana, Ciskei, Transkei and Venda) were regarded as independent republics by the South African government but never recognized as such by the UN.

MOVES TO DEMOCRACY

The first moves to reform apartheid came into effect in 1984, when a new constitution extended the franchise to the Coloured and Indian populations. However, whites retained effective political power and blacks remained excluded.

In 1989, F. W. de Klerk became president of South Africa and accelerated the process of reform. In 1990, the ban on the ANC and restrictions on other anti-apartheid groups were lifted; Nelson Mandela, the main ANC political detainee, was released. In 1991 the laws implementing apartheid were effectively abolished. In 1992 a referendum amongst the white electorate on continued political reform and a new constitution reached by negotiation was approved by 69 per cent to 31 per cent.

On 20 December 1991, the Convention on a Democratic South Africa (CODESA) talks between the government, ANC, Inkatha Freedom Party and other political, business and church groups, opened. CODESA reached agreement on the establishment of an inter-racial administration and the formation of a five-year coalition government following a multiracial election. An interim constitution was agreed on 17 November and adopted by parliament on 22 December.

In the country's first multiracial general election held on 26–29 April 1994 the ANC gained 252 seats in the 400-seat National Assembly with 62.7 per cent of the votes cast. In the 90-seat Senate the ANC gained 60 seats.

The parliament has passed two significant pieces of legislation to settle the legacy of the apartheid era. In November 1994 the Restitution of Land Rights Act was passed which established a Commission and a Court to restore the rights of those dispossessed of their land since the 1913 Land Act. In June 1995 the Promotion of National Unity and Reconciliation Act was passed which established a Truth Commission covering the apartheid era, with a remit to assess confessions, grant amnesties for political crimes and set compensation for victims. The first hearing opened on 15 April 1996.

In legislative and provincial elections held on 2 June 1999, the ANC gained 266 seats in the National Assembly with 66.4 per cent of votes cast, the Democratic Party (DP) 38 seats (9.6 per cent), the Inkatha Freedom Party (IFP) 34 seats (8.58 per cent), the New National Party (NNP) 28 seats (6.87 per cent), the United Democratic Movement 14 seats (3.42 per cent) and the African Christian Democratic Party 6 seats (1.43 per cent). Of parties who obtained less than 1 per cent of the vote, the Freedom Front, the United Christian Democratic Party and the Pan African Congress (PAC) gained three seats each, the Federal Alliance two seats and the Minority Front, the Afrikaner Eenheidsbeweging (Afrikaner Unity Movement) and the Azanian People's Organization each gained one seat. In the provincial elections, the ANC retained an absolute majority in seven out of the nine provinces and formed a coalition government with the IFP in KwaZulu-Natal. In Western Cape, the ANC was the largest party, but a coalition was formed between the NNP and the DP.

On 9 June 1999 the ANC, being one seat short of the two-thirds majority required to amend the constitution, entered into a coalition with the Minority Front, which held just one seat in the National Assembly.

On 14 June 1999 the National Assembly met to select a new president. Thabo Mbeki was elected unopposed and was formally sworn in on 16 June 1999.

POLITICAL SYSTEM

The final constitution, which came into effect in 1999, retains the existing political structure but replaces the Senate with a National Council of Provinces, rejects the representation of minority parties in the Cabinet and incorporates a Bill of Rights.

Under the interim constitution the ten homelands had been reincorporated in South Africa. Executive power is vested in a president and Cabinet, with the president elected by parliament. Legislative power is vested in a bicameral parliament, a directly elected member National Assembly elected by proportional representation, and an indirectly elected member National Council of Provinces composed of ten members elected by each of the nine regional legislatures.

The four former provinces (Cape Province, Natal, Orange Free State, Transvaal) have been replaced by nine new regions (Western Cape, Northern Cape, Eastern Cape, Free State, North-West, KwaZulu/Natal, Gauteng, Northern Province, Mpumalanga). Each region has its own prime minister, a legislature of between 30 and 100 seats elected by proportional representation, and its own constitution.

HEAD OF STATE

President, Commander-in-Chief of the Armed Forces, Thabo Mbeki (ANC), *elected by parliament* 14 June 1999, *sworn in* 16 June 1999

Executive Deputy President, Jacob Zuma (ANC)

CABINET *as at July 1999*

Agriculture and Land Affairs, Angela Didiza (ANC)
Arts, Culture, Science and Technology, Ben Ngubane (IFP)
Communications, Ivy Matsepe-Cassburi (ANC)
Correctional Services, Ben Skosana (IFP)
Defence, Patrick Lekota (ANC)
Education, Kader Asmal (ANC)
Environmental Affairs and Tourism, Mohammed Valli
   Moosa (ANC)
Finance, Trevor Manuel (ANC)
Foreign Affairs, Nkosazana Dlamini-Zuma (ANC)
Health, Mantombazana Tshabalala-Msimang (ANC)
Home Affairs, Chief Mangosuthu Buthelezi (IFP)
Housing, Sankie Mthembi-Mahanyele (ANC)
Intelligence Service, Joseph Nhlanhla (ANC)
Justice and Constitutional Development, Penuell Maduna
   (ANC)
Labour, Membathisis Mdladlana (ANC)
Mineral and Energy Affairs, Phumzile Mlambo-Ncguka
   (ANC)
Minister, Office of the President, Essop Pahad (ANC)
Parliamentary Counsellor, Charles Nqakula (ANC)
Provincial and Local Government, Sydney Mufamadi (ANC)
Public Enterprises, Jeffrey Radebe (ANC)
Public Service and Administration, Geraldine Fraser-
   Moleketi (ANC)
Public Works, Stella Sigcua (ANC)
Safety and Security, Steve Tshwete (ANC)
Sports and Recreation, Balfour Ngconde (ANC)
Trade and Industry, Alec Erwin (ANC)
Transport, Dullah Omar (ANC)
Water Affairs and Forestry, Ronnie Kasrils (ANC)
Welfare and Population Developmen,, Zola Skweyiya (ANC)

HIGH COMMISSION FOR THE REPUBLIC OF SOUTH
AFRICA
South Africa House, Trafalgar Square, London WC2N 5DP
Tel 0171-451 7299
High Commissioner, HE Cheryl Carolus, apptd 1998
Deputy High Commissioner, vacant
Minister (Economic), S. Pretorius
Counsellors, S. van Heerden; G. Johannes
Air Adviser, Col. M. Venter
Defence and Naval Adviser, Rear-Adm. J. Vorster

BRITISH HIGH COMMISSION
255 Hill Street, Arcadia 0083
Tel: Pretoria 483 1200
91 Parliament Street, Cape Town 8001
Tel: Cape Town 461 7220
High Commissioner, HE Dame Maeve Fort, DCMG, apptd
   1996
Counsellor, Deputy High Commissioner, S. Gass, KCMG
Counsellor (Political), D. Woods
Defence and Military Adviser, Brig. M. Raworth
Consul-General and Director of Trade Promotion
   (Johannesburg), N. McInnes
CONSULATES-GENERAL – Cape Town and
   Johannesburg
CONSULATE – Durban
HONORARY CONSULS – Port Elizabeth, East London

Cultural Attaché and British Council Director, L. T. Phillips,
   OBE, 8th Floor, 76 Juta Street, (PO Box 30637),
   Braamfontein 2017, Johannesburg. There are also
   offices in Cape Town and Durban

DEFENCE

The new South African National Defence Force (SANDF)
was created from the merger of the South African Defence

Forces (SADF), the Umkhonto we Sizwe (MK) armed
wing of the ANC, the Azanian People's Liberation Army
(APLA) of the PAC, and the defence forces of the four
former independent homelands.
   The Army has 124 main battle tanks, 974 armoured
personnel carriers, 1,200 armoured infantry fighting vehicles, and 285 artillery pieces. The Navy has three
submarines and eight patrol and coastal vessels at two
bases. The Air Force has 116 combat aircraft and 14 armed
helicopters.
MILITARY EXPENDITURE – 1.8 per cent of GDP (1997)
MILITARY PERSONNEL – 75,000: Army 58,600, Navy
   5,500, Air Force 10,900

ECONOMY

Mining is of great importance, employing more than half a
million people in 1996. It is the largest source of foreign
exchange. The principal minerals produced are gold, coal,
diamonds, copper, iron ore, manganese, lime and limestone,
uranium, platinum, fluorspar, andalusite, zinc, zirconium,
vanadium, titanium and chrome. South Africa is the world's
largest producer of gold, platinum, diamonds, manganese,
chrome and vanadium, and has the world's largest reserves
of chrome ore, manganese, vanadium and andalusite.
   Agriculture, forestry and fishing accounted for 4.8 per
cent of GDP in 1996. Over 70 per cent of land is pasture
so livestock farming is widespread and meat and wool
important products. Principal crops are maize, sugar cane,
fruits and vegetables, wheat, sorghum, sunflower seeds and
groundnuts. Cotton is widely grown, and viticulture is also
widespread.
   Industries, concentrated most heavily around Johannesburg, Pretoria and the major ports, process foodstuffs,
metals and non-metallic mineral products, produce oil
from coal, and also produce beverages and tobacco, motor
vehicles, chemicals and chemical products, machinery,
textiles and clothing, and paper and paper products.
Manufacturing industry contributed 24 per cent of GDP
in 1996.
   Energy production is based upon coal and natural gas
and the production of synthetic liquid fuel from coal. One
nuclear power station is in operation and others are
planned. South Africa exports electricity through its electric
grid connections to all states in southern Africa.
   In 1997 there was a trade surplus of US$1,992 million
and a current account deficit of US$1,931 million; imports
totalled US$32,938 million and exports US$31,020 million.
GNP – US$130,151 million (1997); US$3,210 per capita
   (1997)
GDP – US$133,924 million (1995); US$3,230 per capita
   (1995)
ANNUAL AVERAGE GROWTH OF GDP – 1.7 per cent
   (1997)
INFLATION RATE – 8.5 per cent (1997)
UNEMPLOYMENT – 4.5 per cent (1995)
TOTAL EXTERNAL DEBT – US$25,222 million (1997)

TRADE

Principal exports are gold, base metals and metal products,
coal, diamonds, food (especially fruit) and wool. Principal
imports are machinery, chemicals, motor vehicles, metals
and metal products, food, inedible raw materials and
textiles.
   South Africa's main trading partners are Germany, the
USA, the UK, Italy and Japan.

Trade with UK	1997	1998
Imports from UK	£1,633,911,000	£1,541,813
Exports to UK	1,389,338,000	1,421,675

COMMUNICATIONS

There are international airports at Johannesburg, Durban and Cape Town. South African Airways operates international services to Europe, South America, the Far East, Africa, Australia and the USA, and it is the principal operator of domestic flights. Durban is the largest seaport. Other major ports are Cape Town, Port Elizabeth, East London, Saldanha Bay, Mossel Bay and Richards Bay. The national railway system, and most long-distance passenger and freight road transport are run by independent companies. The six landlocked states of Botswana, Lesotho, Swaziland, Zimbabwe, Zambia and Malawi make extensive use of *Spoornet*, the South African rail freight and long-distance passenger carrier, for foreign trade.

SPAIN
España

AREA – 195,365 sq. miles (505,992 sq. km). Neighbours: Portugal (west), France (north)

POPULATION – 39,270,000 (1996 census): 96 per cent Catholic, 1 per cent Muslim. Castilian Spanish is the official language, although Basque, Catalan, Galician and Valencian, a dialect of Catalan, are spoken and have official status in the autonomous regions where they are spoken

CAPITAL – Madrid (population, 3,084,673, 1996)

MAJOR CITIES – ΨBarcelona (4,748,236); Ψ Valencia (2,200,319); Málaga (1,224,959); Sevilla (1,719,446); Zaragoza (852,332), 1995

CURRENCY – Peseta of 100 céntimos

NATIONAL ANTHEM – Marcha Real Española

NATIONAL DAY – 12 October

NATIONAL FLAG – Three horizontal stripes of red, yellow, red, with the yellow of double width

LIFE EXPECTANCY (years) – male 73.40; female 80.49

POPULATION GROWTH RATE – 0.2 per cent (1997)

POPULATION DENSITY – 78 per sq. km (1996)

URBAN POPULATION – 64.1 per cent (1991)

The interior of the Iberian peninsula consists of an elevated tableland surrounded and traversed by mountain ranges: the Pyrenees, the Cantabrian Mountains, the Sierra de Guadarrama, Sierra Morena, Sierra Nevada, Montes de Toledo, etc. The principal rivers are the Duero, the Tajo, the Guadiana, the Guadalquivir, the Ebro and the Miño.

HISTORY AND POLITICS

The kingdoms of Castile and Aragón were united in 1479; they captured Granada, the last region of Spain under Moorish rule, in 1492 and conquered Navarra in 1512. In 1492 Columbus reached the Americas on behalf of Spain and began the process of colonization which led to most of central and south America coming under Spanish rule until their independence in the 19th century. A republic was proclaimed in 1931 and in February 1936 the Popular Front, a left-wing coalition, was elected. In July 1936 a counter-revolution broke out in military garrisons in Spanish Morocco and spread throughout Spain. Civil war ensued until March 1939, when the Popular Front governments in Madrid and Barcelona surrendered to the Nationalists (as Gen. Franco's followers were then named). Gen. Franco became president and ruled the country until his death in 1975, when, according to his wishes, he was succeeded as head of state by Prince Juan Carlos of Bourbon (grandson of Alfonso XIII) and Spain again became a monarchy. The first free election was held on 15 June 1977.

The general election of 3 March 1996 was won by the Popular Party (PP), which won 156 seats in the Congress of Deputies. The PP formed a minority government with the support of the Basque and Catalan nationalists and the Canary Islands Coalition.

INSURGENCIES

The Basque separatist terrorist organization ETA (*Euzkadi ta Azkatasuna* – Basque Nation and Liberty) has since its formation in 1959 carried out a terrorist campaign of bombings, shootings and kidnappings against the Spanish state and its security forces in an attempt to gain independence for the Basque country. ETA rejected regional autonomy for the Basque country in 1979 as insufficient and continued its campaign, but increased co-operation between French and Spanish security forces and an alleged illegal anti-terrorist campaign organized by the Spanish state under the acronym GAL (*Grupos Antiterroristas de Liberación*) had greatly weakened ETA by the early 1990s. Most of its leaders were caught and jailed in 1992; the conflict has left 700–800 dead and 600 ETA members in jail. On 16 September 1998, ETA announced an indefinite truce, which was to begin the following day.

POLITICAL SYSTEM

Under the 1978 constitution there is a bicameral *Cortes Generales* comprising a 350-member Congress of Deputies (*Congreso de los Diputados*) elected for a maximum term of four years, which elects the prime minister; and a Senate (*Senado*) consisting of 208 directly elected representatives and 48 representatives appointed by the assemblies of the autonomous regions.

Since the promulgation of the 1978 constitution, 19 autonomous regions have been established, with their own parliaments and governments. These are Andalucía, Aragón, Asturias, Balearics, the Basque country, Canaries, Cantabria, Castilla-La Mancha, Castilla y León, Catalunya, Ceuta, Extremadura, Galicia, Madrid, Melilla, Murcia, Navarra, La Rioja and Valencia.

HEAD OF STATE

HM *The King of Spain*, King Juan Carlos I de Borbón, KG, GCVO, *born* 5 January 1938, *acceded to the throne* 22 November 1975, *married* 14 May 1962, Princess Sophie of Greece *and has issue* Infante Felipe (*see* below); Infanta Elena Maria Isabel Dominga, *born* 20 December 1963; and Infanta Cristina Federica Victoria Antonia, *born* 13 June 1965

Heir, HRH The Prince of the Asturias (Infante Felipe Juan Pablo Alfonso y Todos los Santos), *born* 30 January 1968

CABINET *as at July 1999*

Prime Minister, José María Aznar López

Deputy PMs, Rodrigo de Rato y Figaredo (*Economy and Finance*); Francisco Alvárez-Cascos Fernández (*Presidency*)

Agriculture, Food and Fisheries, Jesús Posada Moreno

Defence, Eduardo Serra Rexach

Development, Rafael Arias-Salgado y Montalvo

Education and Culture, Mariano Rajoy Brey

Environment, Isabel Tocino Biscarolasaga

Foreign Affairs, Abel Matutes Juan

Health and Consumer Affairs, José Manuel Romay Beccaría

Industry and Energy, Josep Piqué i Camps

Interior, Jaime Mayor Oreja

Justice, Margarita Maríscal de Gante

Labour and Social Affairs, Manuel Pimentel Siles

Public Administration, Angel Acebes Paniagua

SPANISH EMBASSY
39 Chesham Place, London SW1X 8SB
Tel 0171-235 5555
Ambassador Extraordinary and Plenipotentiary, HE The
Marqués de Tamarón, apptd 1999
Minister Counsellor, Don Pablo Barrios
Defence and Naval Attaché, Capt. Don Angel Cabrera
Counsellors, Don Juan Calabozo (*Commercial*); Don Federico
Torres (*Consular*); Don Ramón Abaroa (*Cultural*)

BRITISH EMBASSY
Calle de Fernando el Santo 16, E-28010 Madrid
Tel: Madrid 700 8200
Ambassador Extraordinary and Plenipotentiary, HE Peter
Torry, apptd 1998
Minister, Deputy Head of Mission, J. A. Dew
Counsellors, M. H. Conner (*Commercial*); E. A. Oakden
(*Economic and Community Affairs*); M. Ramscar
Defence and Naval Attaché, Capt. P. Pacey
Consuls-General, J. Thomas (*Madrid*); J. R. Cowling
(*Barcelona*); I. Lewis (*Bilbao*)
CONSULATES-GENERAL – Madrid, Barcelona, Bilbao
CONSULATES – Alicante, Málaga, Palma de Mallorca, Las
Palmas, Seville, Tenerife
VICE-CONSULATES – Ibiza, Menorca
HONORARY CONSULATES – Santander, Vigo

BRITISH COUNCIL DIRECTOR, P. Sandiford, Paseo del
General Martínez, Campos 31, E-28010 Madrid. There
are offices in Barcelona, Bilbao, Las Palmas, Murcia,
Palma, Seville and Valencia

BRITISH CHAMBER OF COMMERCE, Plaza de Santa
Barbara 10, 1st Floor, E-28004 Madrid; Paseo de
Gracia 11, Barcelona 7; Alameda de Mazarredo 5,
Bilbao 1

DEFENCE

The Army has 725 main battle tanks, 1,995 armoured
personnel carriers, 1,260 artillery pieces and 28 attack
helicopters. The Navy has eight submarines, one aircraft
carrier, 17 frigates, 32 patrol and coastal vessels, 18 combat
aircraft and 25 armed helicopters at seven bases. The Air
Force has 193 combat aircraft.

The USA maintains 2,200 naval and 230 air force
personnel in Spain.

MILITARY EXPENDITURE – 1.4 per cent of GDP (1997)
MILITARY PERSONNEL – 269,710: Army 127,000, Navy
36,950, Air Force 30,000, Paramilitaries 75,760
CONSCRIPTION DURATION – Nine months

ECONOMY

The expansion of the economy and accession to the EU
have led to changes in Spanish agriculture. It accounted
for 5 per cent of GDP in 1994 and employs over 10 per
cent of the working population. The country is generally
fertile, and olives, oranges, lemons, almonds, pomegranates,
bananas, apricots, tomatoes, peppers, cucumbers and grapes
are cultivated. Other agricultural products include wheat,
barley, oats, rice, hemp and flax. The vine is cultivated
widely; in the south-west, around Jerez, sherry and tent
wines are produced. Spain has one of Europe's largest
fishing industries.

Spain's mineral resources of coal, iron, wolfram, copper,
zinc, lead and iron ores are exploited. The principal
industrial goods are cars, steel, ships, manufactured goods,
textiles, chemical products, footwear and other leather
goods. Tourism is a major industry with 62 million tourists
visiting Spain in 1996.

Spain successfully met the convergence criteria laid
down for EU economic and monetary union and was a
participant in the European single currency, the euro, on 1
January 1999.

In 1997 Spain had a trade deficit of US$13,347 million
and a current account surplus of US$2,486 million. Imports
totalled US$122,717 million and exports US$104,363
million.

GNP – US$569,637 million (1997); US$14,490 per capita
(1997)
GDP – US$559,163 million (1995); US$14,111 per capita
(1995)
ANNUAL AVERAGE GROWTH OF GDP – 3.6 per cent
(1997)
INFLATION RATE – 2.0 per cent (1997)
UNEMPLOYMENT – 22.9 per cent (1995)

TRADE

The principal imports are cotton, tobacco, timber, coffee
and cocoa, food products, fertilizers, dyes, machinery,
motor vehicles and agricultural tractors, wool and petroleum products. The principal exports include cars, petroleum products, iron ore, cork, salt, vegetables, fruits, wines,
olive oil, potash, mercury, pyrites, tinned fruit and fish,
tomatoes and footwear.

Trade with UK	1997	1998
Imports from UK	£6,385,200,000	£6,756,800,000
Exports to UK	4,879,500,000	5,513,400,000

EDUCATION

Education is free for those aged six to 18, and compulsory
up to the age of 15. Private schools (30 per cent of primary
and 60 per cent of secondary schools) have to fulfil certain
criteria to receive government maintenance grants. There
are 33 public sector universities, the oldest of which,
Salamanca, was founded in 1218. Other ancient foundations
are Valladolid (1346), Barcelona (1430), Zaragoza (1474),
Santiago (1495), Valencia (1500), Seville (1505), Madrid
(1508), Granada (1531), Oviedo (1604). Private universities
are Deusto in Bilbao, Navarra in Pamplona, Carlos III in
Madrid and one in Salamanca.

ILLITERACY RATE – 2.9 per cent
ENROLMENT (percentage of age group) – primary 100 per
cent (1995); secondary 94 per cent (1994); tertiary 48.6
per cent (1995)

CULTURE

Castilian is the language of more than three-quarters of
the population of Spain. Basque, said to have been the
original language of Iberia, is spoken in Vizcaya, Guipúzcoa
and Álava. Catalan is spoken in Provençal Spain, and
Galician, spoken in the north-western provinces, is akin to
Portuguese. The governments of these regions actively
encourage use of their local languages.

The literature of Spain is one of the oldest and richest
in the world, the *Poem of the Cid,* the earliest of the heroic
songs of Spain, having been written about 1140. The
outstanding writings of its golden age are those of Miguel
de Cervantes Saavedra (1547–1616), Lope Felix de Vega
Carpio (1562–1635) and Pedro Calderón de la Barca (1600–
81). The Nobel Prize for Literature has five times been
awarded to Spanish authors: J. Echegaray (1904), J.
Benavente (1922), Juan Ramón Jiménez (1956), Vicente
Aleixandre (1977) and Camilo José Cela (1989).

ISLANDS AND ENCLAVES

THE BALEARIC ISLES form an archipelago off the east coast of Spain. There are four large islands (Majorca, Minorca, Ibiza and Formentera), and seven smaller (Aire, Aucanada, Botafoch, Cabrera, Dragonera, Pinto and El Rey). Area 1,935 sq. miles (5,011 sq. km); population 685,088. The archipelago forms a province of Spain, the capital is ΨPalma in Majorca, population 323,138

THE CANARY ISLANDS are an archipelago in the Atlantic, off the African coast, consisting of seven islands and six islets. Area 2,807 sq. miles (7,270 sq. km); population 1,444,626. The Canary Islands form two provinces of Spain: Las Palmas, comprising Gran Canaria, Lanzarote (38,500), Fuerteventura (19,500) and the islets of Alegranza, Roque del Este, Roque del Oeste, Graciosa, Montaña Clara and Lobos, with seat of administration at ΨLas Palmas (373,772) in Gran Canaria; and Santa Cruz de Tenerife, comprising Tenerife, La Palma (76,000), Gomera (31,829), and Hierro (10,000), with seat of administration at ΨSanta Cruz in Tenerife, population estimate 204,948

ISLA DE FAISANES is an uninhabited Franco-Spanish condominium, at the mouth of the Bidassoa in La Higuera bay

ΨCEUTA is a fortified post on the Moroccan coast, opposite Gibraltar. Area 5 sq. miles (13 sq. km); population 70,864. ΨMelilla is a town on a rocky promontory of the Rif coast, connected with the mainland by a narrow isthmus. Population 58,449. Ceuta and Melilla are autonomous regions of Spain

OVERSEAS TERRITORIES

The following territories are Spanish settlements on the Moroccan seaboard.

PEÑÓN DE ALHUCEMAS is a bay including six islands; population 366

PEÑÓN DE LA GOMERA (or Peñón de Velez) is a fortified rocky islet; population 450

THE CHAFFARINAS (or Zaffarines) is a group of three islands near the Algerian frontier; population 610

SRI LANKA
Sri Lanka Prajatantrika Samajawadi Janarajaya

AREA – 25,332 sq. miles (65,610 sq. km)
POPULATION – 18,354,000 (1994 UN estimate): 74 per cent Sinhalese, 12.6 per cent Sri Lankan Tamils, 5.6 per cent Indian Tamils, 7.1 per cent Sri Lankan Moors, 0.7 per cent Burghers, Malays and others. The religion of the majority is Buddhism (69.3 per cent), then Hinduism (15.5 per cent), Islam (7.6 per cent), and Christianity (7.5 per cent). The national languages are Sinhala and Tamil

CAPITAL – ΨColombo (population, 615,000, 1993)
MAJOR CITIES – ΨGalle (971,000); ΨJaffna (879,000); Kandy (1,269,000); ΨTrincomalee (323,000)
CURRENCY – Sri Lankan rupee of 100 cents
NATIONAL ANTHEM – Namo Namo Matha (We all stand together)
NATIONAL DAY – 4 February (Independence Day)
NATIONAL FLAG – On a dark red field, within a golden border, a golden lion passant holding a sword in its right paw, and a representation of a *bo*-leaf, issuing from each corner; and to its right, two vertical stripes of saffron and green also placed within a golden border, to represent the minorities of the country

LIFE EXPECTANCY (years) – male 67.78; female 71.66
POPULATION GROWTH RATE – 1.3 per cent (1997)
POPULATION DENSITY – 279 per sq. km (1996)
ILLITERACY RATE – 9.8 per cent
ENROLMENT (percentage of age group) – tertiary 5.1 per cent (1995)

Sri Lanka (formerly Ceylon) is an island in the Indian Ocean, off the southern tip of India and separated from it by the narrow Palk Strait. Forests, jungle and scrub cover the greater part of the island. In areas over 2,000 ft above sea level grasslands (*patanas* or *talawas*) are found. One of the highest peaks in the central massif is Adam's Peak (7,360 ft), a place of pilgrimage for Buddhists, Hindus and Muslims.

The climate is warm throughout the year, with a high relative humidity. The two main monsoon seasons are mid-May to September (south-west) and November to March (north-east).

HISTORY AND POLITICS

The Portuguese landed in Ceylon in the early 16th century and founded settlements, eventually conquering much of the country. Portuguese rule lasted 150 years; in 1658 it gave way to that of the Dutch East India Company until 1796. The maritime provinces of Ceylon were ceded by the Dutch to the British in 1798, becoming a British Crown Colony in 1802. With the annexation of the Kingdom of Kandy in 1815, all Ceylon came under British rule. Ceylon became a self-governing state and a member of the British Commonwealth on 4 February 1948. A republican constitution was adopted in 1972 and the country was renamed Sri Lanka (meaning 'Resplendent Island').

Eight provincial councils were set up in 1988 under the Indo-Sri Lankan peace accord in an attempt to diffuse ethnic tension. Since then, except for the temporarily merged North-East province, all provinces have had elected provincial councils.

In the general election of 16 August 1994 the ruling United National Party (UNP) was defeated by the People's Alliance led by Chandrika Bandaranaike Kumaratunga. The People's Alliance, a coalition of seven parties, won 105 seats; the UNP 94 seats; and other parties, mainly Muslim and moderate Tamils, 26 seats. The People's Alliance formed a government with the support of the Sri Lankan Muslim Congress and moderate Tamil parties. Prime Minister Kumaratunga won the presidential election on 9 November 1994 with 62 per cent of the vote after the UNP candidate Gamini Dissanayake was assassinated by Tamil Tiger terrorists. President Kumaratunga handed over the premiership to her mother, the former Prime Minister Sirimavo Bandaranaike.

In August 1995 the government proposed constitutional changes intended to form a federal state with eight autonomous regions (one covering the Tamil north-east). Each region would have its own elected legislature, executive and judicial branch of government, a police force, and powers devolved from the central government.

Provincial elections were due to be held on 28 August 1998, but were delayed by a national state of emergency declared on 5 August. The elections were held on 6 April 1999 in five of the eight provinces; the People's Alliance won control of all five contested provincial legislatures. Elections in Southern Province were held on 10 June 1999.

INSURGENCIES

The Liberation Tigers of Tamil Eelam (LTTE) guerrilla group has been fighting Sri Lankan forces for control of the Tamil majority areas in the north and east of the country since 1983.

The People's Alliance government came to power on a platform of negotiating a peaceful settlement, to include full autonomy for the Tamil-majority areas. Peace negotiations in 1994, led to a formal cease-fire in January 1995. Fighting resumed in April 1995 after the LTTE had unilaterally broken the cease-fire and negotiations had broken down. A government offensive in April 1996 gained control over almost the entire northern Jaffna peninsula. A second government offensive in May 1997 to take control of a strategic highway on the Jaffna peninsula resulted in losses for the LTTE, though fighting continues in the area. Because of the deteriorating security situation, a nationwide state of emergency was announced on 5 August 1998; on 1 October the government admitted that the LTTE had captured the town of Kilinochchi.

POLITICAL SYSTEM

The 1978 constitution introduced a system of proportional representation. Legislative power is vested in the parliament, whose 225 members are directly elected for a six-year term. Executive power is exercised by the president, elected for six years, and the Cabinet.

HEAD OF STATE

President, Buddha Sasana, Defence, Finance, Chandrika Bandaranaike Kumaratunga, *elected* 9 November 1994, *sworn in* 12 November 1994

CABINET *as at July 1999*

The President
Prime Minister, Sirimavo Bandaranaike (SLFP)
Agriculture and Land, D. M. Jayaratna (SLFP)
Co-operative Development, D. P. Wickremasinghe (SLFP)
Cultural and Religious Affairs, Buddhist Affairs, Lakshman Jayakody (SLFP)
Education and Higher Education, Richard Pathirana (SLFP)
External Trade, Kingsley Wickremaratna (SLFP)
Foreign Affairs, Lakshman Kadirgamar (SLFP)
Forestry and Environment, Nandimitra Ekanayake (SLFP)
Health and Indigenous Medicine, Nimal Siripala De Silva (SLFP)
Housing and Urban Development, Indika Gunawardena (CPSL)
Industrial Development, C. V. Gunaratna (SLFP)
Justice and Constitutional Affairs, G. L. Peiris (SLFP)
Labour, John Seneviratne (SLFP)
Livestock Development and Estates Infrastructure, S. Thondaman (SLWC)
Mahaweli Development, Maithripala Sirisena (SLFP)
Media, Posts and Telecommunications, Mangala Samaraweera (SLFP)
Planning, Implementation and Parliamentary Affairs, Jeyaraj Fernandopulle (SLFP)
Power, Irrigation, Gen. Anuruddha Ratwatte (SLFP)
Provincial Councils and Local Government, Alavi Maulana (SLFP)
Public Administration, Home Affairs, Plantation Industries, Ratnasiri Wickramanayaka (SLFP)
Science and Technology, Bernard Soysa (LSSP)
Shipping, Ports, Rehabilitation of Eastern Provinces, M. H. M. Ashraff (SLMC)
Social Services, Berty Premanand Dissanayake (SLFP)
Tourism and Aviation, Dharmasiri Senanayake (SLFP)
Transport and Highways, A. H. M. Fowzie (SLFP)
Vocational Training and Rural Industries, Amarasiri Dodangoda (SLFP)
Welfare, Youth and Sport, S. B. Dissanayake (SLFP)
Women's Affairs, Hema Ratnayake (SLFP)

SLFP Sri Lanka Freedom Party; CPSL Communist Party of Sri Lanka; SLWC Sri Lanka Workers' Congress; LSSP Lanka Sama Samaja Party; SLMC Sri Lanka Muslim Congress

HIGH COMMISSION FOR THE DEMOCRATIC SOCIALIST REPUBLIC OF SRI LANKA
13 Hyde Park Gardens, London W2 2LU
Tel 0171-262 1841/7
High Commissioner, HE Lal Jayawardena, apptd 1999
Deputy High Commissioner, C. Wagiswara
Ministers, A. Karunaratne *(Consular);* T. Ariyaratne *(Commercial)*

BRITISH HIGH COMMISSION
190 Galle Road, Kollupitiya, PO Box 1433, Colombo 3
Tel: Colombo 437336
High Commissioner, HE Linda Duffield, apptd 1999
Deputy High Commissioner, M. H. P. Hill
Defence Adviser, Lt.-Col. R. N. Kendell, MBE
First Secretary (Commercial and Economic), A. Madeley

BRITISH COUNCIL DIRECTOR, S. Maingay, 49 Alfred House Gardens, PO Box 753, Colombo 3

DEFENCE

The Army has 25 main battle tanks, 153 armoured personnel carriers, 16 armoured infantry fighting vehicles, and 50 artillery pieces. The Navy has 54 patrol and coastal vessels at seven bases. The Air Force has 22 combat aircraft and 15 armed helicopters.
MILITARY EXPENDITURE – 6.1 per cent of GDP (1997)
MILITARY PERSONNEL – 225,200: Army 95,000, Navy 10,000, Air Force 10,000, Paramilitaries 110,200

ECONOMY

The staple products are tea, rubber, copra, spices and gems. There is increasing emphasis on local production of food, especially rice, and plans for the large-scale production of sugar cane, cotton and citrus fruits.
   The manufacturing sector has grown considerably over the past few years and in addition to processing agricultural products, it produces ceramics, paper, leather goods, plywood, cement, chemicals, textiles, garments, ilmenite, hardware, fertilizers, jewellery and tyres. There is a petroleum refinery. Tourism attracts roughly 400,000 visitors annually.
   In 1997 there was a trade deficit of US$628 million and a current account deficit of US$388 million. Imports totalled US$5,839 million and exports US$4,633 million.
GNP – US$14,781 million (1997); US$800 per capita (1996)
GDP – US$12,840 million (1995); US$716 per capita (1995)
ANNUAL AVERAGE GROWTH OF GDP – 6.4 per cent (1997)
INFLATION RATE – 9.6 per cent (1997)
UNEMPLOYMENT – 12.5 per cent (1995)
TOTAL EXTERNAL DEBT – US$7,638 million (1997)

Trade with UK	1997	1998
Imports from UK	£210,624,000	£136,948,000
Exports to UK	274,795,000	295,877,000

COMMUNICATIONS

There are 25,952 km of roads in Sri Lanka, of which 11,077 km are surfaced, and a government-run railway system with 1,459 km of lines. A satellite earth station at Padukka provides telecommunication links world-wide. The principal airport is at Katunayake, north of Colombo. Air Lanka operates 69 flights weekly to the Gulf States, the Maldives, western Europe and the Far East.

SUDAN
Al-Jamhuryat es-Sudan Al-Democratia

AREA – 967,500 sq. miles (2,505,813 sq. km). Neighbours: Egypt (north), Eritrea and Ethiopia (east), Kenya, Uganda and the Democratic Republic of Congo (south), Central African Republic, Chad, and Libya (west)

POPULATION – 27,291,000 (1994 UN estimate). Arab and Nubian peoples populate the north and centre, Nilotic and Negro peoples the south. Arabic is the official language and Islam the state religion, although the Nilotics of the Bahr el Ghazal and Upper Nile valleys are generally Animists or Christians

CAPITAL – Khartoum (population, 947,483, 1994). The combined population of Khartoum, Khartoum North and Omdurman (excluding refugees and displaced people) is estimated at 3,000,000

MAJOR CITIES – El Obeid (228,096); Nyala (1,267,077); ΨPort Sudan (305,385); Sharg el nil (879,105), 1993 estimate

CURRENCY – Sudanese dinar (SD) of 10 pounds

NATIONAL ANTHEM – Nahnu Djundullah (We are the army of God)

NATIONAL DAY – 1 January (Independence Day)

NATIONAL FLAG – Three horizontal stripes of red, white and black with a green triangle next to the hoist

LIFE EXPECTANCY (years) – male 51.58; female 54.37

POPULATION GROWTH RATE – 2.0 per cent (1997)

POPULATION DENSITY – 11 per sq. km (1996)

URBAN POPULATION – 27.1 per cent (1994)

MILITARY EXPENDITURE – 5.6 per cent of GDP (1997)

MILITARY PERSONNEL – 109,700: Army 90,000, Navy 1,700, Air Force 3,000, Paramilitaries 15,000

CONSCRIPTION DURATION – Three years

The White Nile, as the Bahr el Jebel, flows through Sudan from Nimule to Wadi Halfa. The Blue Nile flows from Lake Tana on the Ethiopian plateau through Sudan to join the White Nile at Khartoum. The next confluence of importance is at Atbara where the main Nile is joined by the River Atbara. Between Khartoum and Wadi Halfa lie five of the six cataracts.

HISTORY AND POLITICS

The Anglo-Egyptian Condominium over Sudan was established in 1899 and ended when the Sudan House of Representatives, on 19 December 1955, declared Sudan a fully independent sovereign state. A republic was proclaimed on 1 January 1956, and was recognized by Great Britain and Egypt. Sudan was under military rule from 1958 to 1964; under the rule of a revolutionary council headed by Col. Gaafar Mohamed El Nimeri from 1969 until April 1985 when the army command deposed Nimeri; and experienced a third military coup in June 1989 when the civilian government, in power since 1986, was overthrown by Brig.-Gen. Omar Hassan Ahmad al-Bashir. The constitution was suspended and parliament was replaced by a 15-member ruling junta (Revolutionary Command Council) who exercised control over a Cabinet. The ruling junta appointed Gen. al-Bashir as head of state on 16 October 1993 and then dissolved itself. Presidential and legislative elections were held in March 1996. President al-Bashir was elected with 75.7 per cent of the vote having faced no serious contender. Hassan al-Tourabi of the fundamentalist National Islamic Front (NIF) was elected president of the 400-member National Assembly, although political parties had officially been banned from contesting

the elections. The founding of political parties was legalized on 1 January 1999. In early January 1999, the voting age was lowered to 17 and a new dress code was imposed on women, requiring them to wear headscarves. In March 1999, the UN Children's Fund (UNICEF) asked the government of Sudan to investigate the continued existence of slavery in Sudan; the Foreign Ministry denied institutionalized slavery, but admitted that tribal kidnappings were commonplace.

INSURGENCIES

Nearly 17 years of insurrection in the southern provinces ended in 1972 with the signing of an agreement recognizing southern regional autonomy within the Sudanese state. However, insurrection resumed in 1983 and since then there has been civil war in the regions of Eastern and Western Equatoria in the south of the country between government forces and the Christian and Animist majority in the area, organized into the Sudan People's Liberation Army (SPLA).

Between 1991 and 1994 the SPLA was split into four factions based on tribal groups. The two principal factions were SPLA-Torit led by the original SPLA leader John Garang, and SPLA-United led by Riek Machar. Garang's SPLA-Torit faction made considerable advances against government forces in late 1995 and early 1996. In April 1996, the government signed a peace treaty with the South Sudan Independence Movement and SPLA-United who agreed to relinquish any hope of independence. SPLA-Torit rejected the agreement and made advances in the south. In May 1998, the government and SPLA agreed to hold a referendum on self-determination for the south, though no date for this was set.

The warfare has left an estimated 1.4 million dead, including 300,000 who died in the war-induced famine in 1988 and thousands in a similar situation in 1994. Some three million refugees have fled the fighting, either to the north, to neighbouring states or to the far south near the Ugandan border. The fighting has left large areas of the south desolate and uninhabitable.

FOREIGN RELATIONS

The government has developed close relations with Iran and is believed by Western states to support international terrorism and have Iranian Revolutionary Guards' bases on its territory. Supported and dominated by the NIF, the government has since 1989 turned Sudan into an Islamic state. In 1995 Sudan's relations with its neighbours, notably Egypt, Eritrea and Uganda, deteriorated as they consider that Sudan is arming Islamic and insurgent groups in their states. On 2 May 1999 a peace agreement was signed with Eritrea. Sudan and the UK agreed to resume full diplomatic representation in June 1999.

HEAD OF STATE

President, Prime Minister, Lt.-Gen. Omar Hassan Ahmad al-Bashir, *appointed* 16 October 1993, *elected* 17 March 1996

First Vice-President, Maj.-Gen. Ali Osman Mohamad Taha

Vice-President, Gen. George Kongor

Assistant President, Riek Machar

CABINET *as at July 1999*

Agriculture and Forestry, Uthman al-Hadi Ibrahim

Aviation, Makki Ali Bilayl

Cabinet Affairs, Muhammad al-Amin Khalifah

Defence, Lt.-Gen. Abd al-Rahman Sirr al-Khatim

Education, Hamid Muhammad Ali Turayn

Energy and Mining, Awad Ahmad al-Jaz

Environment and Tourism, Muhammad Tahir Ila

External Relations, Mustapha Osman Ismail

External Trade, Adam al-Tahir Hamdun
Federal Relations, Ahmad Ibrahim al-Tahir
Finance, National Economy, Abd al-Wahhab Uthman
Health, Gen. (retd) Mahdi Babu Nimir
Higher Education and Scientific Research, Ibrahim Ahmed Omer
Information and Culture, Ghazi Salah al-Din
Internal Affairs, Maj.-Gen. Abd al-Rahim Muhammad Husayn
International Co-operation and Investment, Abdalla Hassan Ahmed
Irrigation and Water Resources, Kamal Ali Muhammad
Justice, Ali Mohammad Uthman Yassin
Khartoum State Governor, Majzoub al-Khalifa
Livestock, Joseph Malwal
National Industry, Badr al-Din Sulayman
Planning, Hassan Uthman
Presidential Adviser on Legal Affairs, Abd al-Basit Salih Sabdarat
Presidential Adviser on Peace Affairs, Nafi Ali Nafi
Presidential Affairs, Brig. Bakri Hasan Salih
Public Service, Agnes Lukudo
Relations in the National Assembly, Abul al-Qasim Muhammad Ibrahim
Roads, Communications, Maj.-Gen. (retd) Hadi Bushra
Social Planning, Brig. Tayyib Ibrahim Muhammad Khayr
State Minister for National Defence, Ibrahim Shamseddin
State Minister, Presidential Adviser on Economic Affairs, Isam Siddiq
Transport, Lam Akol

EMBASSY OF THE REPUBLIC OF THE SUDAN
3 Cleveland Row, London SW1A 1DD
Tel 0171-839 8080
Ambassador Extraordinary and Plenipotentiary, vacant

BRITISH EMBASSY
PO Box 801, Khartoum East
Tel: Khartoum 777105
Ambassador Extraordinary and Plenipotentiary, HE Alan Goulty, CMG, apptd 1995

BRITISH COUNCIL DIRECTOR, D. Sloan, 14 Abu Sin Street (PO Box 1253), Khartoum.

ECONOMY

Agriculture provides employment for over half the labour force and contributes over one-third of GDP. It is based on large and medium-sized public sector irrigation projects. Mechanized and traditional agriculture is practised in areas of sufficient rainfall. The principal grain crops are *dura* (great millet) and wheat, the staple food of the population. Sesame and groundnuts are other important food crops, which also yield an exportable surplus, and a promising start has been made with castor seed. The principal export crops are cotton and sugar, and Sudan also produces the bulk of the world's supply of gum arabic. Sudan still has to achieve self-sufficiency in its production.

In 1996 Sudan had a trade deficit of US$719 million and a current account deficit of US$827 million. In 1995 imports totalled US$1,185 million and exports US$556 million.

GNP – US$7,917 million (1997); US$290 per capita (1997)
GDP – US$975 million (1995); US$36 per capita (1995)
INFLATION RATE – 101.4 per cent (1993)
TOTAL EXTERNAL DEBT – US$16,326 million (1997)

TRADE

The principal exports are cotton, sesame, gum arabic, livestock, sugar and other agricultural produce. The chief imports are petroleum goods and other raw materials, machinery and equipment, foodstuffs, medicines and chemicals.

Trade with UK	1997	1998
Imports from UK	£50,722,000	£72,281,000
Exports to UK	7,961,000	10,985,000

COMMUNICATIONS

The railway system, adversely affected by the civil war, has a route length of about 5,516 km. There are 11,610 km of roads, of which 4,203 km are paved. Nile river services between Khartoum and Juba have been interrupted by the southern insurrection. Port Sudan is the country's main seaport. Sudan Airways flies services from Khartoum to other parts of Sudan and to other African states, Europe and the Middle East.

EDUCATION

School education is free for most children but not compulsory, beginning with six years of primary education, followed by three years of secondary education at general secondary schools, the more academic higher secondary schools or vocational schools. The medium of instruction is Arabic. English has not been taught in schools since new Arabization legislation came into effect in 1991.

In addition to 20 universities there are various technical post-secondary institutes as well as professional and vocational training establishments.

ILLITERACY RATE – 49.4 per cent
ENROLMENT (percentage of age group) – tertiary 3.0 per cent (1990)

SURINAME
Republiek Suriname

AREA – 63,037 sq. miles (163,265 sq. km). Neighbours: French Guiana (east), Brazil (south), Guyana (west)
POPULATION – 423,000 (1994 UN estimate). The official language is Dutch, the native language is Sranang Tongo, and other widely-used languages are Hindustani and Javanese
CAPITAL – ΨParamaribo (population, 265,000, 1993)
CURRENCY – Suriname guilder of 100 cents
NATIONAL DAY – 25 November
NATIONAL FLAG – Horizontal stripes of green, white, red, white, green, with a five-pointed yellow star in the centre
LIFE EXPECTANCY (years) – male 67.80; female 72.78
POPULATION GROWTH RATE – 0.3 per cent (1997)
POPULATION DENSITY – 3 per sq. km (1996)
MILITARY EXPENDITURE – 4.4 per cent of GDP (1997)
MILITARY PERSONNEL – 1,800: Army 1,400, Navy 240, Air Force 160
ILLITERACY RATE – 7.0 per cent

HISTORY AND POLITICS

Formerly known as Dutch Guiana, Suriname remained part of the Netherlands West Indies until 25 November 1975, when it achieved complete independence. The civilian government was ousted in 1980 by the military who appointed a predominantly civilian government in 1982.

The New Front won the most seats in the elections to the National Assembly on 23 May 1996 but failed to win a majority sufficient to appoint the president, and a coalition government headed by the National Democratic Party was formed.

POLITICAL SYSTEM

The unicameral legislature, the National Assembly, has 51 members, directly elected for a five-year term. The president is elected by a two-thirds majority in the National Assembly, or if the required majority cannot be achieved, by a specially convened United Peoples' Conference, including district and local council representatives, for a five-year term of office.

HEAD OF STATE

President, Jules Wijdenbosch, *inaugurated* 14 September 1996
Vice-President, Pretaapnarain Radhakishun

COUNCIL OF MINISTERS *as at August 1999*

Agriculture, Animal Husbandry and Fisheries, Saimin Redjosentono (KTPI)
Defence, Ramon Dwarka Panday (KTPI)
Education, Karan Ramsundersingh (NDP)
Finance, Tjan Gobardhan (BVD)
Foreign Affairs, Errol Snijders (NDP)
Internal Affairs, Sonny Kertowidjojo (KTPI)
Justice and Police, Paul Sjak-Shie (NDP)
Labour, Public Health, Social Affairs and Housing, Soewarto Moestadja (KTPI)
Natural Resources, Errol Alibux (NDP)
Planning and International Co-operation, Waldi Nain (Pendawalima)
Public Works, Rudolf Mangal (BVD)
Regional Development, Yvonne Raveles-Resida (NDP)
Trade and Industry, Robby Dragman (KTPI)
Transportation, Communications and Tourism, Dick de Bie (NDP)

KTPI Party for Unity and Harmony; BVD Movement for Renewal and Change; NDP National Democratic Party; HPP Hindustani Progressive Party

EMBASSY OF THE REPUBLIC OF SURINAME
Alexander Gogelweg 2, NL-2517 JH The Hague, The Netherlands
Tel: The Hague 365 0844
Ambassador Extraordinary and Plenipotentiary, HE Evert Guillaume Azimullah, apptd 1994

BRITISH AMBASSADOR, HE Edward Glover, MVO, resident at Georgetown, Guyana
BRITISH CONSULATE, c/o VSH United Buildings, Van 't Hogerhuystraat, PO Box 1860, Paramaribo. *Honorary Consul,* J. J. Healy, MBE

ECONOMY

Suriname has large timber resources. Rice and sugar cane are the main crops. Bauxite is mined, and is the principal export. Principal trading partners are the Netherlands, the USA and Norway.
In 1995 Suriname had a trade surplus of US$123 million and a current account surplus of US$73 million.
GNP – US$544 million (1997); US$1,320 per capita (1997)
GDP – US$413 million (1995); US$967 per capita (1995)
ANNUAL AVERAGE GROWTH OF GDP – 7.0 per cent (1994)
INFLATION RATE – 7.1 per cent (1997)
UNEMPLOYMENT – 12.7 per cent (1994)

Trade with UK	1997	1998
Imports from UK	£12,514,000	£12,728,000
Exports to UK	17,015,000	16,528,000

SWAZILAND
Umbuso we Swatini

AREA – 6,704 sq. miles (17,364 sq. km). Neighbours: South Africa (north, west and south), Mozambique (east)
POPULATION – 938,000 (1994 UN estimate). The languages are English and Swazi
CAPITAL – Mbabane (population, 38,290, 1986)
MAJOR TOWNS – Manzini (30,000); Big Bend; Mhlume; Nhlangano; Pigg's Peak
CURRENCY – Lilangeni (E) of 100 cents (South African currency is also in circulation). Swaziland is a member of the Common Monetary Area and its unit of currency *Emalangeni* (singular *Lilangeni*) has a par value with the South African rand
NATIONAL ANTHEM – Ingoma Yesive
NATIONAL DAY – 6 September (Independence Day)
NATIONAL FLAG – Blue with a wide crimson horizontal band bordered in yellow across the centre, bearing a shield and two spears horizontally
LIFE EXPECTANCY (years) – male 42.90; female 49.50
POPULATION GROWTH RATE – 3.1 per cent (1997)
POPULATION DENSITY – 54 per sq. km (1996)
URBAN POPULATION – 25.3 per cent (1996)
ILLITERACY RATE – 23.3 per cent
ENROLMENT (percentage of age group) – primary 95 per cent (1996); secondary 37 per cent (1996); tertiary 6.0 per cent (1996)

The broken mountainous Highveld along the western border, with an average altitude of 4,000 ft, is densely forested, mainly with conifers and eucalyptus; the Middleveld, averaging about 2,000 ft, is a mixed farming area including cotton and pineapples; and the Lowveld in the east was mainly scrubland until the introduction of large sugar-cane plantations. Four rivers, the Komati, Usutu, Mbuluzi and Ngwavuma, flow from west to east.

HISTORY AND POLITICS

The Kingdom of Swaziland came into being on 25 April 1967 under a self-government constitution and became an independent kingdom, headed by HM Sobhuza II, in membership of the Commonwealth on 6 September 1968.

POLITICAL SYSTEM

The King, assisted by his appointed Cabinet, holds considerable executive, legislative and judicial authority. There is a bicameral legislative body comprising a Senate and a House of Assembly. Each of the 55 traditional *Tinkhundla* (chieftaincies) are directly elected and become members of the House of Assembly. The King appoints ten members to the House of Assembly, making 65 in all, who then elect ten members of their own number to the Senate. To these are added 20 senators appointed by the King, bringing the full membership of the Senate to 30. In addition, the King appoints Commissions, who assess public opinion. There are also public gatherings, where any citizen can express an opinion. All political parties are banned.
A Constitutional Review Commission is due to report its conclusions by the end of 1999. Legislative elections to the House of Assembly were held on 16–24 October 1998. The members of the Senate were elected and appointed in November 1998.

HEAD OF STATE
King of Swaziland, HM King Mswati III, *inaugurated* 25 April 1986

CABINET *as at July 1999*

Prime Minister, Dr Barnabas Sibusiso Dlamini
Deputy PM, Arthur Khoza
Agriculture, Co-operatives, Roy Fanourakis
Economic Planning and Development, Majozi Sithole
Education, Revd Abednego Ntshangase
Enterprise and Employment, Lutfo Dlamini
Finance, John Carmichael
Foreign Affairs and Trade, Albert Shabangu
Health and Social Welfare, Dr Phetsile Dlamini
Home Affairs, Prince Sobandla Dlamini
Housing and Urban Development, Stella Lukhele
Justice and Constitutional Development, Chief Maweni
    Simelane
Natural Resources and Energy, Prince Guduza
Public Service and Information, Ephraim Magwagwa Mdluli
Public Works and Transport, Peter Dlamini
Tourism, Environment and Communications, Soze Vilakazi

KINGDOM OF SWAZILAND HIGH COMMISSION
20 Buckingham Gate, London SW1E 6LB
Tel 0171-630 6611
High Commissioner, HE Revd Percy Mngomezulu, apptd
    1994

BRITISH HIGH COMMISSION
Allister Miller Street, Mbabane
Tel: Mbabane 4042581/4
High Commissioner, HE Neil Hook, MVO, apptd 1999

BRITISH COUNCIL DIRECTOR, B. Gallagher

ECONOMY

Manufacturing has replaced agriculture as the dominant
sector, with timber, textiles and footwear the main products.
Agricultural products include sugar cane and fruit.

In 1997 Swaziland had a trade deficit of US$212 million
and a current account deficit of US$49 million. In 1996
imports totalled US$1,174 million and exports US$893
million.

GNP – US$1,458 million (1997); US$1,520 per capita
    (1997)
GDP – US$1,190 million (1995); US$1,389 per capita
    (1995)
ANNUAL AVERAGE GROWTH OF GDP – 3.8 per cent
    (1996)
INFLATION RATE – 12.2 per cent (1996)
TOTAL EXTERNAL DEBT – US$368 million (1997)

Trade with UK	1997	1998
Imports from UK	£3,679,000	£3,844,000
Exports to UK	43,069,000	41,469,000

COMMUNICATIONS

Swaziland's railway is 301 km long and connects with the
Mozambique port of Maputo and the South African railway
network to Richards Bay. A rail line to the north-west
border provides a link to Komatipoort. There are 2,886 km
of roads, of which 828 km are paved. Most passenger and
goods traffic is carried by privately-owned motor transport
services. There is an international airport at Manzini. Royal
Swazi National Airways provides scheduled air services to
southern and eastern Africa. International telecommunications and television services are provided through a
satellite earth station.

SWEDEN
Konungariket Sverige

AREA – 173,732 sq. miles (449,964 sq. km). Neighbours:
    Norway (west), Finland (east)
POPULATION – 8,843,000 (1994 UN estimate); 8,745,109
    (1993 census). The state religion is Lutheran
    Protestant, to which over 95 per cent officially adhere.
    The language is Swedish; in the north there are both
    Finnish- and Lapp-speaking communities
CAPITAL – ΨStockholm (population, 1,148,953, 1995)
MAJOR CITIES – ΨGothenburg (Göteborg) (480,839);
    ΨMalmö (234,599); Uppsala (119,979), 1995
CURRENCY – Swedish krona of 100 öre
NATIONAL ANTHEM – Du Gamla, Du Fria (Thou
    ancient, thou freeborn)
NATIONAL DAY – 6 June (Day of the Swedish Flag)
NATIONAL FLAG – Yellow cross on a blue ground
LIFE EXPECTANCY (years) – male 76.08; female 81.38
POPULATION GROWTH RATE – 0.5 per cent (1997)
POPULATION DENSITY – 20 per sq. km (1996)
URBAN POPULATION – 83.4 per cent (1990)

HISTORY AND POLITICS

Sweden takes its name from the Svear people who inhabited
the region during the seventh century AD. The Swedes
participated in the Viking expansion during the ninth to
11th centuries but focused on the east; sovereignty over
Finland was established in the 13th century. The Union of
Kalmar (1397) brought Sweden and Norway under the
rule of Queen Margrethe of Denmark. Northern Sweden
regained its independence following a rebellion by noble-
men in 1521 which resulted in the election to the Swedish
throne of Gustav I of the house of Vasa.

Swedish influence burgeoned under the Vasa kings
despite frequent wars with Denmark. Control over Estonia
was achieved in 1561 and marriage brought Poland briefly
into the Swedish sphere of influence. Sweden's power
climaxed in the 17th century under Gustavus II Adolf. The
Danes were driven out of southern Sweden, the Baltic
coast of Russia was seized and the Swedish army pushed
into Germany after vanquishing the Catholic League. The
Treaty of Westphalia (1648) confirmed Sweden's great
power status. Swedish power waned in the 17th and 18th
centuries. Finland was lost to Russia in 1809; Norway was
ceded to Sweden under the Congress of Vienna (1814–5)
but seceded in 1905.

Sweden remained neutral during both World Wars.
Post-war party politics was dominated by Social Democrat-
led coalitions which established a mixed economy and a
generous welfare state. Right-wing and centrist parties held
power from 1976–82 and 1991–4.

In the general election held on 20 September 1998 the
Social Democrats remained the largest party in the
legislature with 131 seats and formed a minority government.

FOREIGN RELATIONS

Sweden applied for EU membership in July 1991 and
acceded to the EU on 1 January 1995.

POLITICAL SYSTEM

Sweden is a constitutional monarchy, with the monarch
retaining purely ceremonial functions as head of state.
Under the Act of Succession 1810 (with amendments) the
throne is hereditary in the House of Bernadotte. The
constitution is based upon the Instrument of Government

1974, which amended the 1810 Act and removed from the monarch the roles of appointing the prime minister and signing parliamentary bills into law. A 1979 amendment vested the succession in the monarch's eldest child irrespective of sex.

Executive power is vested in the prime minister and Council of Ministers. There is a unicameral legislature (*Riksdag*) of 349 members elected by universal suffrage on a proportional representation basis (with a 4 per cent threshold for representation) for four years. The Council of Ministers (*Statsråd*) is responsible to the *Riksdag*.

Sweden is divided into 24 counties (*län*) and 288 municipalities (*kommun*).

HEAD OF STATE

HM The King of Sweden, Carl XVI Gustaf, KG, *born* 30 April 1946, *succeeded* 15 September 1973, *married* 19 June 1976 Fräulein Silvia Renate Sommerlath and has *issue,* Crown Princess Victoria (*see* below); Prince Carl Philip Edmund Bertil, Duke of Värmland, *born* 13 May 1979; Princess Madeleine Thérèse Amelie Josephine, Duchess of Hälsingland and Gästrikland, *born* 10 June 1982

Heir, HRH Crown Princess Victoria Ingrid Alice Désirée, Duchess of Västergötland, *born* 14 July 1977

CABINET *as at July 1999*

Prime Minister, Göran Persson
Deputy Prime Minister, Lena Hjelm-Wallén
Agriculture, Food and Fisheries, Margareta Winberg
Culture, Marita Ulvskog
Defence, Björn von Sydow
Education and Science, Thomas Östros
Environment, Kjell Larsson
Finance, Bo Ringholm
Foreign Affairs, Anna Lindh
Health and Social Affairs, Lars Engqvist
Industry and Commerce, Björn Rosengren
International Development Co-operation, Migration and Asylum Policy, Pierre Schori
Justice, Laila Freivalds
Trade and Nordic Co-operation, Leif Pagrotsky

EMBASSY OF SWEDEN
11 Montagu Place, London WIH 2AL
Tel 0171-917 6400
Ambassador Extraordinary and Plenipotentiary, HE Mats Bergquist, CMG, apptd 1997
Minister (Economic), T. Rosander
Naval and Air Attaché, Col. N. Eklund
Consul-General, G. Dannerljung

BRITISH EMBASSY
Skarpögatan 6–8, S-115 93 Stockholm
Tel: Stockholm 671 9000
Ambassador Extraordinary and Plenipotentiary, HE John Grant, apptd 1999
Counsellor, Consul-General and Deputy Head of Mission, M. Raven
Counsellor (Economic and Commercial), P. J. Mathers, LVO
Naval and Military Attaché, Cmdr. G. Bateman

CONSULAR OFFICES – Stockholm, Gothenburg
HONORARY CONSULATES – Gothenburg, Malmö, Sundsvall

BRITISH COUNCIL DIRECTOR , Dr P. Spaven, PO Box 27819, S-115 93 Stockholm
BRITISH-SWEDISH CHAMBER OF COMMERCE, Grevgatan 34, S-114 53 Stockholm

DEFENCE

The Army has 350 main battle tanks, 1,500 armoured personnel carriers and armoured infantry fighting vehicles,

740 artillery pieces and 70 helicopters. The Navy has nine submarines, 33 patrol and coastal vessels and one combat aircraft at four bases. The Air Force has 294 combat aircraft.

Sweden has a policy of non-alignment in peace and neutrality in war, and it maintains a 'total defence' which includes peacetime organizations for civil, economic and psychological defence.

It was announced in March 1999 that the size of the armed forces was to be reduced by about 50 per cent in line with budget cuts and the perceived diminished threat to Sweden's security.

MILITARY EXPENDITURE – 2.4 per cent of GDP (1997)
MILITARY PERSONNEL – 53,700: Army 35,100, Navy 9,200, Air Force 8,800, Paramilitaries 600
CONSCRIPTION DURATION – Seven to 15 months

ECONOMY

Less than 10 per cent of the land area is farmland and less than 3 per cent of the labour force is employed in farming, although Sweden is more than 80 per cent self-sufficient in food.

Industrial prosperity is based on natural resources: forests, mineral deposits and water power. The forests cover about half the total land surface and sustain timber, finished wood products, pulp and paper milling industries. The mineral resources include iron ore, lead, zinc, sulphur, granite, marble, precious and heavy metals (the latter not exploited) and extensive deposits of low-grade uranium ore. Industries based on mining are important but it is the general engineering industry that provides 80 per cent of Sweden's exports, especially specialized machinery and systems, motor vehicles, aircraft, electrical and electronic equipment, pharmaceuticals, plastics and chemical industries.

Hydroelectricity supplies 15 per cent of energy needs. Sweden has no significant indigenous resources of conventional hydrocarbon fuels and relies for 50 per cent of its energy needs upon imported oil and coal. Around half of Sweden's electricity is generated by nuclear power but as a result of a referendum in 1980 the nuclear programme is to be phased out by 2010. Small supplies of natural gas are imported from Denmark into southern Sweden, with the pipeline being extended to Gothenburg.

Sweden experienced a deep recession between 1990 and 1993. The centre-right government, elected in 1991, introduced austerity measures and free market economic policies of privatization, deregulation, the ending of state subsidies, trade union legislation, a floating exchange rate, central bank independence and tax reform. Further budget cuts and reductions in the public sector, local government, and the welfare state, together with tax increases, have been implemented by the Social Democratic government. In October 1997 Sweden decided not to join European economic and monetary union (EMU) at the first stage.

In 1997 there was a trade surplus of US$17,921 million and a current account surplus of US$7,301 million. Imports totalled US$65,483 million and exports US$82,739 million.

GNP – US$231,905 million (1997); US$26,210 per capita (1997)
GDP – US$230,713 million (1995); US$26,253 per capita (1995)
ANNUAL AVERAGE GROWTH OF GDP – 1.8 per cent (1997)
INFLATION RATE – 0.5 per cent (1997)
UNEMPLOYMENT – 7.7 per cent (1995)

TRADE

About 45 per cent of industrial output is exported, mainly in the form of cars, trucks, machinery, and electrical and communications equipment. Sweden conducts 70 per cent of its trade with EFTA and the rest of the EU.

Trade with UK	1997	1998
Imports from UK	£4,201,800,000	£4,153,900,000
Exports to UK	4,569,700,000	4,213,900,000

COMMUNICATIONS

The total length of railroads is 10,939 km. The road network is about 210,000 km in length. The mercantile marine amounted in 1996 to 2,950,000 gross tonnage. Regular domestic air traffic is maintained by the Scandinavian Airlines System and by Malmö Aviation. Regular European and intercontinental air traffic is maintained by the Scandinavian Airlines System.

EDUCATION

The state system provides nine years' free and compulsory schooling from the age of seven to 16 in the comprehensive elementary schools. 95 per cent continue into further education of two to four years' duration in the upper secondary schools and a unified higher education system administered in six regional areas containing one of the universities: Uppsala (founded 1477); Lund (1668); Stockholm (1878); Gothenburg (1887); Umeå (1963) and Linköping (1967). There are 40 institutions of higher education including three technical universities in Stockholm, Gothenburg and Luleå.

ENROLMENT (percentage of age group) – primary 100 per cent (1995); secondary 98 per cent (1995); tertiary 46.0 per cent (1995)

CULTURE

Swedish belongs, with Danish and Norwegian, to the North Germanic language group. Swedish literature dates back to King Magnus Eriksson, who codified the old Swedish provincial laws in 1350. With his translation of the Bible, Olaus Petri (1493–1552) formed the basis for the modern Swedish language. Literature flourished during the reign of Gustavus III, who founded the Swedish Academy in 1786. Notable Swedish writers include Almquist (1795–1866), Strindberg (1849–1912) and Lagerlöf (1858–1940), Nobel Prizewinner in 1909. Contemporary authors include Lagerquist (1891–1974), Nobel Laureate in 1951, Martinson (1904–78) and Johnson (1900–76), Nobel Laureates jointly in 1974. The Swedish scientist Alfred Nobel (1833–96) founded the Nobel Prizes for literature, science and peace.

SWITZERLAND

Schweizerische Eidgenossenschaft – Confédération Suisse – Confederazione Svizzera

AREA – 15,940 sq. miles (41,284 sq. km). Neighbours: France (west and north-west), Germany (north), Austria and Liechtenstein (east), Italy (south)

POPULATION – 7,076,000 (1994 UN estimate): 46.1 per cent Roman Catholic, 40 per cent Protestant, 5 per cent other religions and 8.9 per cent without religion. The official languages are German (the first language of 63.7 per cent), French (19.2 per cent), Italian (7.6 per cent) and Romansh (0.6 per cent). German is the dominant language in 19 of the 26 cantons; French in Fribourg, Jura, Geneva, Neuchâtel, Valais and Vaud; Italian in Ticino; and Romansch in parts of the Grisons

CAPITAL – Bern (population, 321,932, 1994)

MAJOR CITIES – Geneva (438,819); Lausanne (283,631); Lucerne (180,050); Winterthur (115,994); Zürich (921,446), 1994

CURRENCY – Swiss franc of 100 rappen (or centimes)

NATIONAL ANTHEM – Trittst im Morgenrot Daher (Radiant in the morning sky)

NATIONAL DAY – 1 August

NATIONAL FLAG – Square and red, bearing a couped white cross

LIFE EXPECTANCY (years) – male 75.10; female 81.60

POPULATION GROWTH RATE – 0.8 per cent (1997)

POPULATION DENSITY – 171 per sq. km (1996)

URBAN POPULATION – 67.7 per cent (1995)

Switzerland is the most mountainous country in Europe. The Alps, from 1,700 to 4,634 m (5,000 to 15,217 ft) in height, occupy its southern and eastern frontiers and the chief part of its interior; the Jura mountains rise in the north-west. The Alps occupy 61 per cent, and the Jura mountains 12 per cent of the country. The highest peak, Mont Blanc, Pennine Alps (4,807 m/15,782 ft) is partly in France and partly in Italy; Monte Rosa (4,634 m/15,217 ft) and Matterhorn (4,478 m/14,780 ft) are partly in Switzerland and partly in Italy. The highest wholly Swiss peaks are Finsteraarhorn (4,274 m/14,026 ft), Aletschhorn (4,195/13,711), Jungfrau (4,158/13,671), Mönch (4,099/13,456), Eiger (3,970/13,040), Schreckhorn (4,078/13,385) and Wetterhorn (3,701/12,150) in the Bernese Alps, and Dom (4,545/14,918), Weisshorn (4,506/14,803) and Breithorn (4,165/13,685). The Swiss lakes include Lakes Maggiore, Zürich, Lucerne, Neuchâtel, Geneva, Constance, Thun, Zug, Lugano, Brienz and the Walensee.

HISTORY AND POLITICS

The Romans invaded the area populated by Helvetii tribes in the first century BC and named the region Helvetia. The Roman Empire was overrun in the fifth century AD by Germanic tribes who are the ancestors of the modern Swiss.

The Swiss confederation achieved full independence under the Peace of Westphalia (1648), having been a province of the Holy Roman Empire since 1033. French Revolutionary forces seized Switzerland in 1789 and named it the Helvetic Republic. Independence was not restored until the Congress of Vienna (1815), which also joined Geneva and Valais to the confederation and instituted perpetual neutrality in foreign affairs. In 1847 a war broke out between the Protestant and Roman Catholic cantons, the latter being defeated. A new constitution was adopted in 1848 which enhanced the powers of the central government.

Proportional representation was introduced in 1919 and has ensured coalition governments throughout the 20th century. Women were given the vote in 1971.

On 22 October 1995, the ruling coalition, comprising the Social Democrats, the Swiss People's Party, the Radical Democratic Party and the Christian Democrats, in power since 1959, was re-elected with 162 of the 200 seats in the National Council.

FOREIGN RELATIONS

The Federal Council voted in 1992 to apply for European Community membership. The European Economic Area (EEA) Treaty between the EC and EFTA, which extends the provisions of the EC single internal market to EFTA states, was rejected in a national referendum on 6 December 1992. Switzerland is consequently the only EFTA state outside the EEA. Switzerland has observer status at the UN.

POLITICAL SYSTEM

The federal government consists of the Federal Assembly of two chambers, a National Council (*Nationalrat*) of 200 members, and a States Council (*Ständerat*) of 46 members (two from each canton and one from each demi-canton). Members of the National Council are elected for four years, elections taking place in October. The executive power is in the hands of a Federal Council (*Bundesrat*) of seven members, elected for four years by the Federal Assembly and presided over by the president of the Confederation. Each year the Federal Assembly elects from the Federal Council the president and the vice-president. Not more than one person from the same canton may be elected a member of the Federal Council; however, there is a tradition that Italian- and French-speaking areas should between them be represented on the Federal Council by at least two members.

CONFEDERAL STRUCTURE

There are 23 cantons, three of which are subdivided, making 26 in all. Each canton has its own government. The main language in 19 of the cantons is German; in the others it is French (*) or Italian (†).

Canton	Area (sq. km)	Population (1994)
Aargau (Argovie)	1,404	524,100
Appenzell-Inner Rhoden	173	14,700
Appenzell-Outer Rhoden	243	54,400
Basel-Country (Bâle-Campagne)	428	251,400
Basel-Town (Bâle-Ville)	37	197,700
Bern	6,050	943,600
*Fribourg (Freiburg)	1,671	222,100
*Geneva	282	391,100
Glarus (Glaris)	685	39,300
Graubünden (Grisons)	7,105	184,300
*Jura	836	69,000
Lucerne	1,493	337,700
*Neuchâtel (Neuenburg)	803	164,500
Nidwalden	276	36,000
Obwalden	490	31,100
St Gallen (St Gall)	2,026	440,700
Schaffhausen (Schaffhouse)	299	74,000
Schwyz	908	120,600
Solothurn (Soleure)	791	237,100
Thurgau (Thurgovie)	991	220,400
†Ticino (Tessin)	2,812	302,400
Uri	1,077	35,900
*Valais (Wallis)	5,225	269,600
*Vaud (Waadt)	3,212	601,600
Zurich	1,729	1,167,600
Zug	239	90,300

FEDERAL COUNCIL *as at August 1999*

President of the Swiss Confederation (1999), *Home Affairs*, Ruth Dreifuss (SPS)
Vice-President (1999), *Defence, Civil Protection and Sports*, Adolf Ogi (SVP)
Federal Chancellor, François Couchepin
Economic Affairs, Pascal Conchepin (FDP)
Environment, Transport, Energy and Communications, Moritz Leuenberger (SPS)
Finance, Kaspar Villiger (FDP)
Foreign Affairs, Joseph Deiss (CVP)
Justice and Police, Ruth Metzler (CVP)

CVP Christian Democratic People's Party; SPS Social Democratic Party; FDP Radical Democratic Party; SVP Swiss People's Party

EMBASSY OF SWITZERLAND
16–18 Montagu Place, London WIH 2BQ
Tel 0171-616 6000
Ambassador Extraordinary and Plenipotentiary, HE François Nordmann, apptd 1994
Minister, R. Reich
Defence Attaché, Col. W. Knüsli
Consul-General, R. Müller
Counsellor, D. Furgler (*Economic and Financial*)
CONSULATE-GENERAL – Manchester

BRITISH EMBASSY
Thunstrasse 50, CH-3005 Bern
Tel: Bern 359 7700
Ambassador Extraordinary and Plenipotentiary, HE Christopher Hulse, CMG, OBE, apptd 1997
Counsellor, Deputy Head of Mission and Director of Trade Promotion, J. Nichols
Commercial Attachés, B. Hässig, S. Valdettaro, H. Küpfer
Defence Attaché, Lt.-Col. E. J. Gould
CONSULATE – Geneva
CONSULAR OFFICES – Bern (at Embassy), Lugano, Montreux, Valais, Zürich

BRITISH COUNCIL DIRECTOR, C. Morrissey, Sennweg 2, PO Box 532, CH-3000 Bern 9

BRITISH-SWISS CHAMBER OF COMMERCE, Freiestrasse 155, CH-8032 Zürich
SWISS-BRITISH SOCIETIES: Bern, *President*, Dr H. Beriger; Zürich, *President*, J.-P. Müller; Basel, *President*, Dr C. Grey

DEFENCE

The Army has 769 main battle tanks, 958 armoured personnel carriers, 513 armoured infantry fighting vehicles, 796 artillery pieces and 60 helicopters. The Air Force has 171 combat aircraft.
MILITARY EXPENDITURE – 1.5 per cent of GDP (1997)
MILITARY PERSONNEL – 3,300 active (390,060 to be mobilized: Army 357,460, Air Force 32,600)
CONSCRIPTION DURATION – 15 weeks, then ten refresher courses

ECONOMY

Agriculture is followed chiefly in the valleys and the central plateau, where cereals, flax, hemp, wine and tobacco are produced, and fruits and vegetables are grown. Dairying and stock-raising are the principal industries; there are 308,924 hectares of open arable land, 111,133 ha of cultivated grassland and 628,976 ha of natural grassland and pasture. The forests cover about 28 per cent of the whole surface.

The chief manufacturing industries comprise engineering and electrical engineering, metalworking, chemicals and pharmaceuticals, textiles, watchmaking, woodworking, foodstuffs, publishing and footwear. Banking, insurance and tourism are major industries. 4 per cent of the workforce is employed in agriculture, 48 per cent in industry and 48 per cent in services.
GNP – US$305,238 million (1997); US$43,060 per capita (1997)
GDP – US$303,950 million (1995); US$42,416 per capita (1995)
ANNUAL AVERAGE GROWTH OF GDP – 1.1 per cent (1997)
INFLATION RATE – 0.5 per cent (1997)
UNEMPLOYMENT – 3.3 per cent (1995)

TRADE

The principal imports are machinery, electrical and electronic equipment, textiles, motor vehicles, non-ferrous metals, clothing, food and pharmaceutical products. The principal exports are machinery, chemical elements, non-ferrous metals, watches, electrical and electronic equipment and textiles.

In 1996 Switzerland had a trade surplus of US$1,836 million and a current account surplus of US$20,470 million. In 1997 imports totalled US$71,064 million and exports US$72,493 million.

Trade with UK	1997	1998
Imports from UK	£3,008,297,000	£2,982,711
Exports to UK	4,894,966,000	5,025,776,000

COMMUNICATIONS

There were in 1995, 5,041 km of railway tracks and 70,975 km of roads, of which 1,540 km were national highways. The merchant marine consisted in 1995 of 174 vessels with a total gross tonnage of 4.36 million tonnes. Goods handled at Basel Rhine ports amounted to 13 million tonnes. Swissair, the national airline, flies to and from the airports at Zürich, Geneva and Basel.

The Swiss electorate voted in a February 1994 referendum for a ban on foreign lorries using alpine roads, which will be phased in over ten years. From 2005 onwards foreign lorries will have to use two new north-south road-rail tunnels.

EDUCATION

Education is controlled by cantonal and communal authorities. Primary education is free and compulsory. School age varies, generally seven to 14, with secondary education from age 12 to 15. Special schools make a feature of commercial and technical instruction. Universities are Basel (founded 1460), Bern (1834), Fribourg (1889), Geneva (1873), Lausanne (1890), Zürich (1832), and Neuchâtel (1909), the technical universities of Lausanne and Zürich and the economics university of St Gall.

ENROLMENT (percentage of age group) – primary 100 per cent (1993); secondary 79 per cent (1990); tertiary 32.9 per cent (1995)

CULTURE

Modern authors who have achieved international fame include Karl Spitteler (1845–1924) and Hermann Hesse (1877–1962), awarded the Nobel Prize for Literature in 1919 and 1946 respectively.

In 1993 there were 96 daily newspapers published (76 German, 16 French, four Italian).

SYRIA
Al-Jamhouriya Al-Arabia as-Souriya

AREA – 71,498 sq. miles (185,180 sq. km). Neighbours: Lebanon (west), Israel and Jordan (south-west), Iraq (east), Turkey (north)

POPULATION – 14,619,000 (1994 UN estimate): mostly Muslim. Arabic is the principal language, but Kurdish, Turkish and Armenian are spoken among significant minorities and a few villages still speak Aramaic, the language spoken by Christ and the Apostles. English has taken over from French as the main foreign language

CAPITAL – Damascus (population, 1,549,000, 1994)

MAJOR CITIES – Aleppo (1,542,000); Hama (273,000); Homs (558,000); ΨLatakia, the principal port (303,000), 1994 estimates

CURRENCY – Syrian pound (S$) of 100 piastres

NATIONAL DAY – 17 April

NATIONAL FLAG – Red over white over black horizontal bands, with two green stars on central white band

LIFE EXPECTANCY (years) – male 64.42; female 68.05

POPULATION GROWTH RATE – 2.9 per cent (1997)

POPULATION DENSITY – 79 per sq. km (1996)

URBAN POPULATION – 51.4 per cent (1995)

The Orontes flows northwards from the Lebanon range across the northern boundary to Antakya (Antioch, Turkey). The Euphrates crosses the northern boundary near Jerablus and flows through north-eastern Syria to the boundary of Iraq.

The region is rich in historical remains. Damascus (Dimishq ash-Sham) is said to be the oldest continuously inhabited city in the world (although Aleppo disputes this claim), having existed as a city for over 4,000 years. The city contains the Omayed Mosque, the Tomb of Saladin, and the 'street which is called Straight' (Acts 9:11), while to the north-east is the Roman outpost of Dmeir and further east is Palmyra. On the Mediterranean coast at Amrit are ruins of the Phoenician town of Marath, and also ruins of Crusaders' fortresses at Markab, Sahyoun, and Krak des Chevaliers. At Tartous the cathedral of Our Lady of Syria, built by the Knights Templars in the 12th and 13th centuries, has been restored as a museum. One of the oldest alphabets in the world has been discovered at Ugarit (Ras Shamra), a Phoenician village near the port of Latakia. Hittite cities dating from 2000 to 1500 BC, have been explored on the west bank of the Euphrates at Jerablus and Kadesh.

HISTORY AND POLITICS

Once part of the Ottoman Empire, Syria came under French mandate after the First World War. Syria became an independent republic during the Second World War; the first independently elected parliament met in August 1943, but foreign troops were in occupation until April 1946. Syria remained an independent republic until 1958, when it became part, with Egypt, of the United Arab Republic. It seceded from the United Arab Republic in September 1961.

Elections to the 250-seat People's Council in November 1998 resulted in the National Progressive Front retaining all of its 167 seats unchallenged. This seven-party bloc is dominated by the Ba'ath Party, its allies being the Arab Socialist Union, Socialist Unionist Party, Arab Socialist Movement, Syrian Communist Party and Socialist Unionist Democratic Party. Independents, who are predominantly businessmen, won 83 seats.

POLITICAL SYSTEM

The constitution promulgated in 1973 declares that Syria is a democratic, popular socialist state, and that the Arab Socialist Renaissance (Ba'ath) Party, which has been the ruling party since 1963, is the leading party in the state and society. The president is head of state and is elected by parliament for a seven-year term. The legislature, the *Majlis al-Chaab* (People's Council) has 250 members directly elected for a four-year term.

HEAD OF STATE

President, Lt.-Gen. Hafez al-Assad, *assumed office* 14 March 1971, *re-elected* 1978, 1985, 1991, 14 January 1999

Vice-Presidents, Abdel Halim Khaddam, Zuheir Masharqa

CABINET *as at July 1999*

Prime Minister, Mahmoud Zubi
Deputy P.M, Defence, 1st Lt.-Gen. Mustafa Tlass
Deputy P.M, Economic Affairs, Salim Yassin
Deputy P.M, Service Affairs, Rashid Akhtarini
Agriculture and Agrarian Reform, Asad Mustafa
Assistant Secretary-General, Abdullah al-Ahmar
Awqaf (Religious Endowments), Mohammed Abd al-Rauf
    Ziyadah
Communications, Radwan Martini
Construction and Building, Majid Izzu Ruhaybani
Culture, Najah al-Attar
Economy and Foreign Trade, Mohammad al-Imadi
Education, Ghassan Halabi
Electricity, Mounib Saaem Aldaher
Finance, Khaled al-Mahayni
Foreign Affairs, Farouk al-Shara
Health, Iyad al-Shatti
Higher Education, Salihah Sanqar
Housing and Utilities, Husam al-Safadi
Industry, Ahmad Nizam al-Din
Information, Mohammad Salman
Interior, Mohammad Harbah
Irrigation, Abd ar-Rahman Madani
Justice, Husayn Hassun
Local Administration, Yahya Abu Asaleh
Ministers of State, Musallam Mohammed Hawwa *(Cabinet
    Affairs);* Abd al-Hamid Munajjid *(Environment Affairs);*
    Nasser Qaddur *(Foreign Affairs);* Abd al-Rahim Subayi
    (Planning Affairs); Nabil Mallah; Hanna Murad; Yusuf
    al-Ahmad; Abdullah Tulbah
Petroleum and Mineral Resources, Mohamed Maher Jamal
Presidential Affairs, Wahib Fadel
Social Affairs and Labour, Ali Khalil
Supply and Internal Trade, Nadim Akkash
Tourism, Danhu Dawud
Transport, Mufid Abd al-Karim

EMBASSY OF THE SYRIAN ARAB REPUBLIC
8 Belgrave Square, London SW1X 8PH
Tel 0171-245 9012
Chargé d'Affaires, Dr Sami Glaiel

BRITISH EMBASSY
Kotob Building, 11 Mohammad Kurd Ali Street, Malki,
Damascus (PO Box 37)
Tel: Damascus 371 2561/2/3
Ambassador Extraordinary and Plenipotentiary, HE Basil
    Eastwood, CMG, apptd 1996
CONSULATE – Aleppo

BRITISH COUNCIL DIRECTOR, D. Baldwin, Al Jala'a, Abu
    Rumaneh, PO Box 33105, Damascus

DEFENCE

The Army has 4,600 main battle tanks, 1,500 armoured
personnel carriers and 2,310 armoured infantry fighting
vehicles. The Navy has three submarines, two frigates, 21
patrol and coastal vessels and 24 armed helicopters at three
bases. The Air Force has 589 combat aircraft and 72 armed
helicopters.

Syria maintains a force of some 30,000 men in Lebanon;
1,045 UN troops are deployed on the Golan Heights.
MILITARY EXPENDITURE – 6.3 per cent of GDP (1997)
MILITARY PERSONNEL – 328,000: Army 215,000, Navy
    5,000, Air Force 40,000, Air Defence Command 60,000,
    Paramilitaries 8,000
CONSCRIPTION DURATION – 30 months

ECONOMY

Agriculture is the principal source of production; wheat
and barley are the main cereal crops, but the cotton crop is
the highest in value. Tobacco is grown in the maritime
plain in Sahel, the Sahyoun and the Djebleh district of
Latakia. Large areas are coming under cultivation in the
north-east of the country as a result of irrigation from the
Thawra dam. There are an increasing number of light
assembly plants as Syria's industrialization programme
develops. Leather goods, wool and silk, textiles, vegetable
oil, soap, sugar, plastics and metal utensils are produced.
Oil has been found in the north-eastern corner of the
country and production of high quality reserves is
proceeding in the region of Deir ez Zor. A pipeline has
been built to the Mediterranean port of Banias, via Homs.
Two oil refineries are in production at Homs and Banias.
Syria also has gas reserves, deposits of phosphate and rock
salt, and produces asphalt.
GNP – US$16,643 million (1997); US$1,120 per capita
    (1997)
GDP – US$50,749 million (1995); US$3,573 per capita
    (1995)
ANNUAL AVERAGE GROWTH OF GDP – 5.5 per cent
    (1996)
INFLATION RATE – 1.9 per cent (1997)
UNEMPLOYMENT – 6.8 per cent (1991)
TOTAL EXTERNAL DEBT – US$20,865 million (1997)

TRADE

The principal imports are foodstuffs (fruit, vegetables,
cereals, tea, coffee), mineral and petroleum products,
textiles, iron and steel manufactures, pharmaceuticals,
machinery, chemicals and timber. Exports include raw
cotton, oil, cereals, fruit, phosphates, cement, livestock,
other foodstuffs, textiles and raw wool.

In 1997 Syria had a trade surplus of US$454 million and
a current account surplus of US$564 million. In 1996
imports totalled US$5,380 million and exports US$3,999
million.

Trade with UK	1995	1996
Imports from UK	£84,382,000	£84,191,000
Exports to UK	39,079,000	26,620,000

COMMUNICATIONS

Although railway lines run from Damascus to both Beirut
and Amman, train services go only to Amman as much of
the Lebanese line has been dismantled. A track has been
opened connecting Homs with Damascus. A track links
Homs, Hamah, Aleppo, Deir ez Zor and Qamishliye to the
Iraqi frontier. There are 2,750 km of rail track. All the
principal towns in the country are connected by roads
which vary from modern dual carriageways to narrow
country lanes. There are 39,333 km of roads, of which
11,564 km are unpaved. An internal air service operates
between all major towns. The main international airport is
at Damascus and there are also flights from Aleppo, Al-
Kamishli, Lattakia and Deir Ez-Zor.

There are eight national daily newspapers.

EDUCATION

Education is under state control and although a few of the
schools are privately owned, they all follow a common
syllabus. Elementary education is free at state schools and
is compulsory from the age of seven. Secondary education
is not compulsory and is free only at the state schools.
There are universitites at Damascus, Aleppo, Tishrin,
Latakia and the Ba'ath University, Homs.
ILLITERACY RATE – 20.1 per cent
ENROLMENT (percentage of age group) – primary 91 per
    cent (1996); secondary 38 per cent (1996); tertiary 15.7
    per cent (1994)

TAIWAN
Chung-hua Min-kuo – Republic of China

AREA – 13,800 sq. miles (35,742 sq. km)
POPULATION – 21,854,273 (1998). Mandarin Chinese has been the official language since 1949. Now Taiwanese, spoken by 85 per cent of the population, is growing in importance
CAPITAL – Taipei (population, 2,638,565, 1998)
MAJOR CITIES – ΨKaohsiung (1,461,996); ΨKeelung (381,695), Taichung (916,279); Tainan (721,264), 1998
CURRENCY – New Taiwan dollar (NT$) of 100 cents
NATIONAL DAY – 10 October
NATIONAL FLAG – Red, with blue quarter at top next staff, bearing a 12-point white sun

An island in the China Sea, Taiwan, formerly Formosa, lies 90 miles east of the Chinese mainland. The eastern part of the main island is mountainous and forested. Mt Morrison (Yu Shan) (13,035 ft) and Mt Sylvia (Tz'ukaoshan) (12,972 ft) are the highest peaks. The western plains are watered by many rivers.

Territories include the Pescadores Islands (50 sq. miles), some 35 miles west of Taiwan, as well as Quemoy (68 sq. miles) and Matsu (11 sq. miles) which are only a few miles from mainland China.

HISTORY AND POLITICS

Settled for centuries by the Chinese, the island was ceded by China to Japan in 1895 and remained part of the Japanese empire until Japan's defeat in 1945. Nationalist Kuomintang (KMT) leader Gen. Chiang Kai-shek withdrew to Taiwan in 1949, towards the end of the war against the Communist regime in mainland China, after which the territory continued under his presidency until his death in 1975. He was succeeded as president by his son Gen. Chiang Ching-kuo who ruled until his death in 1988, when Vice-President Lee Teng-hui was appointed president. Martial law was lifted in 1987 after 38 years.

In 1991, President Lee announced that the 'period of Communist rebellion' on the Chinese mainland was over, recognizing *de facto* the People's Republic of China. The announcement also ended emergency measures which had frozen political life on Taiwan since 1949. In 1991–2 power shifted away from mainlanders to native Taiwanese with the forcible retirement of the 'Senior Parliamentarians' who had retained their seats since being elected on the mainland in 1948. The new parliament, the Legislative Yuan, gained control of the budget, of law-making and of the appointment of the prime minister. A general election to the Legislative Yuan on 5 December 1998 was won by the KMT with 123 of the 225 seats; the pro-independence Democratic Progressive Party won 70 seats; the pro-reunification New Party won 11 seats; independents and minor parties won 21 seats.

The incumbent, President Lee, won the first democratic presidential election in March 1996, with 54 per cent of the vote. On 1 September 1997, following a reshuffle of the Executive Yuan, Vincent Siew was named as prime minister.

FOREIGN RELATIONS

Taiwan (Nationalist China) held China's seat on the UN Security Council until 25 October 1971 when it was replaced by the People's Republic of China. The Republic of China is recognized by less than 40 states.

POLITICAL SYSTEM

The legislature is bicameral. The National Assembly has 334 members (106 delegates and 228 regional representa-

tives) elected for a four-year term. The Legislative Yuan has 225 members, 176 elected and 49 appointed proportionately by party, and serves a three-year term. Constitutional reforms passed by the Legislative Yuan in 1994 provide for the president and vice-president to be directly elected for four-year terms (previously the president was elected by parliament).

HEAD OF STATE
President, Lee Teng-hui, *appointed* 13 January 1988, *elected by parliament* 21 March 1990, *elected* 23 March 1996
Vice-President, Lien Chan

EXECUTIVE YUAN *as at September 1999*
Prime Minister, Vincent Siew
Vice-PM, Liu Chao-shiuan
Chair, Central Election Commission, Lin Feng-cheng
Chair, Fair Trade Commission, Chao Yang-ching
Chair, Mongolian and Tibetan Affairs Commission, Kao Koong-lian
Chair, National Youth Commission, Lee Chi-chu
Chair, Overseas Chinese Affairs Commission, Chiao Jen-ho
Chair, Public Construction Commission, Tsai Chao-yang
Chair, Research, Development and Evaluation Commission, Yang Chao-shin
Chair, Vocational Assistance for Retired Servicemen Commission, Gen. Lee Chen-lin
Director, National Palace Museum, Chin Hsiao-yi
Director-General of Budget, Accounting and Statistics, Wei Duan
Director-General, Central Personnel Administration, Clement Wea
Director-General, Government Information Office; Government Spokesman, Chen Chien-jen
Director-General, Health, Chan Chi-sheah
Economic Affairs, Wang Chih-kang
Education, Lin Ching-chiang
Environmental Protection Administration, Tsai Hsung-hsiung
Finance, Paul Chiu
Foreign Affairs, Jason Hu
Interior, Huang Chu-wen
Justice, Yeh Chin-fong
National Defence, Gen. Tang Fei
Transport and Communications, Lin Feng-cheng
Without Portfolio, Chao Shou-po; Shirley Kuo Wan-jung; Huang Ta-chou; Yang Shih-chien; Chen Chien-min

Chairs of Councils:
Agriculture, Peng Tso-kuei
Atomic Energy, Hu Ching-piao
Cultural Planning and Development, Lin Cheng-chi
Economic Planning and Development, Chiang Ping-kung
Labour Affairs, Chan Huo-sheng
Mainland Affairs, Su Chi
Science, Huang Chen-tai

TAIPEI REPRESENTATIVE OFFICE, 50 Grosvenor Gardens, London, SWIW OEB

BRITISH COUNCIL REPRESENTATIVE, Dr Patrick Hart, 7th Floor, British Trade and Cultural Office, 99 Jen Ai Road, Section 2, Taipei 10625

DEFENCE

The Army has 719 main battle tanks, 950 armoured personnel carriers, 225 armoured infantry fighting vehicles, 20 aircraft and 221 helicopters. The Navy has four submarines, 18 destroyers, 18 frigates, 101 patrol and coastal vessels, 31 combat aircraft and 21 armed helicopters at four bases. The Air Force has 529 combat aircraft.
MILITARY EXPENDITURE – 4.7 per cent of GDP (1997)

MILITARY PERSONNEL – 402,650: Army 240,000, Navy 68,000, Air Force 68,000, Paramilitaries 26,650
CONSCRIPTION DURATION – Two years

ECONOMY

Taiwan has transformed itself from a mainly agricultural country to a highly developed industrial economy. The industrial base has expanded to include steel, shipbuilding, chemicals, cement, machinery, electrical equipment and textiles. In 1997 agriculture contributed 3.5 per cent of GDP, manufacturing 36.3 per cent and services 60.2 per cent. Continued trade surpluses have led to one of the largest foreign exchange reserves of any country in the world. Direct shipping between Taiwan and China, which had been suspended in 1949, resumed in April 1997.

The soil is very fertile, producing sugar, rice, sweet potatoes, tea, fruit and tobacco. Livestock provided a third of the value of Taiwan's agricultural produce in 1996. Mineral resources are meagre. Taiwan produces one-tenth of its coal needs and some natural gas. There are important fisheries. The principal seaports are ΨKeelung and ΨKaohsiung situated in the north and south of the island respectively.

TRADE

The principal exports are electronic goods, machinery, metal goods, textiles, plastic products, and toys and games. The main imports are oil, chemicals, machinery and natural resources. The main trading partners are the USA, Japan, Hong Kong and Germany.

In 1997 imports totalled US$113,930 million and exports US$121,301 million.

Trade with UK	1997	1998
Imports from UK	£1,033,670,000	£878,292,00000
Exports to UK	2,341,812,000	2,328,940,000

TAJIKISTAN
Respublika i Tojikiston

AREA – 55,251 sq. miles (143,100 sq. km). Neighbours: Uzbekistan (north-west), Kyrgyzstan (north-east), China (east), Afghanistan (south)
POPULATION – 5,919,000 (1998): 62 per cent Tajik, 23 per cent Uzbek and 8 per cent Russian, with smaller numbers of Tatars, Kirghiz, Germans and Ukrainians. The people are predominantly Sunni Muslim. The main languages are Tajik, Uzbek and Russian. Tajik is close to the Farsi spoken in Iran
CAPITAL – Dushanbe (population, 602,000, 1990)
CURRENCY – Tajik rouble (TJR) of 100 tanga
NATIONAL DAY – 9 September (Independence Day)
NATIONAL FLAG – Three horizontal stripes of red, white and green with the white of double width and charged with a crown and seven stars, all in gold
LIFE EXPECTANCY (years) – male 65.40; female 71.10
POPULATION GROWTH RATE – 1.8 per cent (1997)
POPULATION DENSITY – 41 per sq. km (1996)
URBAN POPULATION – 28.4 per cent (1994)
MILITARY EXPENDITURE – 12.1 per cent of GDP (1997)
MILITARY PERSONNEL – 8,200: Army 7,000, Paramilitaries 1,200
CONSCRIPTION DURATION – Two years
ILLITERACY RATE – 2.3 per cent
ENROLMENT (percentage of age group) – tertiary 19.9 per cent (1996)

The republic includes the Gorno-Badakhstan Autonomous

Province and the Kulyab, Kurgan-Tyubinsk and Khodzhent Provinces. The country is mountainous with the Pamir highlands in the east and the high ridges of the Pamir-Altai system in the centre. Plains are formed by wide stretches of the Syr-Darya valley in the north and of the Amu-Darya in the south. The country has areas prone to earthquakes, and a continental climate.

HISTORY AND POLITICS

The area that is now Tajikistan was conquered by Alexander the Great in the fourth century BC and remained under Greek and Greco-Persian rule for 200 years, until the Kingdom of Kusha was established, based on Bacharia (Bukhara). Tajikistan was invaded by both the Arabs and the Samanid Persians between the seventh and ninth centuries AD. The cities of Bukhara and Samarkand were two of the most important cultural and educational centres in the Islamic world.

The Tajiks lived under the control of various feudal emirates until the area was subsumed within the Russian Empire in 1868. At the time of the Russian revolution in 1917 the central Asian emirates attempted to re-establish their independence. Soviet power was re-established in northern Tajikistan by 1 April 1918, when the Turkestan Soviet Socialist Republic was formed, and the Bukhara emirate was overthrown by Soviet forces in 1920. In 1924 the Tajikistan Autonomous Soviet Socialist Republic was formed as part of the Uzbek Republic before Tajikistan was given full republican status within the Soviet Union in 1929. Stalin deprived the Tajiks of Bukhara and Samarkand, which remained in Uzbekistan, and during Soviet rule 1,000,000 Uzbeks and 800,000 Russians were settled in Tajikistan.

Tajikistan declared independence from the Soviet Union on 9 September 1991 and became a UN member on 2 March 1992. Tension between President Nabiev's supporters and the opposition Islamic and democratic groups led to armed clashes in 1992 and Nabiev was forced to resign on 7 September 1992. The Islamic-Democratic alliance formed a government in September but civil war broke out as forces loyal to the former Communist regime rebelled against the new government. By early November, pro-Communist forces controlled virtually all the country and the Supreme Soviet installed Imamali Rakhmonov as its Speaker and head of state.

Fighting resumed in July, leading to the establishment of a CIS peacekeeping force on the Tajik-Afghan border to contain the rebel attacks. Negotiations between the government and opposition brought about a cease-fire in October 1994 to allow for presidential and parliamentary elections. The elections were won by acting head of state Imamali Rakhmonov and the ruling (former Communist) People's Party of Tajikistan, although the elections were boycotted by most opposition groups and were condemned as undemocratic by the OSCE monitoring team. Fighting restarted along the Afghan border in early 1995. A peace agreement was signed in December 1996 which provided for the formation of a National Reconciliation Commission (NRC), a general amnesty and an exchange of prisoners. The agreement has held, although there have been sporadic outbreaks of violence since it was signed. In June 1999, following complaints by the opposition, the NRC announced that opposition armed forces would be integrated into government forces by August 1999, that a timetable would be drawn up for assigning 30 per cent of government posts to the opposition and that a referendum would be held to decide on constitutional amendments demanded by the opposition and aimed at creating a bicameral legislature.

Presidential elections are scheduled for 6 November 1999 and legislative elections are to take place early in 2000.

A new democratic constitution which re-established the presidency was approved in a referendum in November 1994. The legislature is the 181-seat Supreme Council (*Majlisi Oli*) which serves a five-year term. Administratively Tajikistan is divided into two regions and one autonomous region.

HEAD OF STATE
President, Imamali Rakhmonov, *elected by Supreme Soviet* 19 November 1992, *elected* 6 November 1994

COUNCIL OF MINISTERS *as at July 1999*
Prime Minister, Yahya Azimov
First Deputy PM, Khodzhi Turadzhorzoda
Deputy PMs, Abdurakhmon Azimov; Bazgul Dodkhudoyeva; Ismat Eshmirzoyev; Zakir Vazirov
Administrator to the Council of Ministers, Ramazan Mirzoyev
Agriculture and Land Reform, Shodi Kobirov
Chair of State Committee for Construction and Architecture, Bahavaddin Zuhuruddinov
Chair of State Property Committee, Davlatov Matlubkhon
Communications, Nuriddin Mukhitdinov
Construction, Odil Ochilov
Culture and Information, Bobokohon Mahmadov
Defence, Lt.-Gen. Sherali Khayrulloyev
Economics and Foreign Economic Relations, Davlat Ismonov
Education, Munira Inoyatova
Emergency Situations and Civil Defence, Mirzo Ziyoev
Environmental Protection, Usmonkul Shokirov
Finance, Anvarsho Muzaffurov
Foreign Affairs, Talbak Nazarov
Grain, Bekmurod Urokov
Health, Alamkhon Ahmedov
Industry, Shavkat Umarov
Interior, Homiddin Sharipov
Justice, Shavkat Ishmoilov
Labour and Employment, Khudoiberdy Kholiknazarov
Land Improvement and Water Conservancy, Davlatbek Makhsudov
Oil and Gas, Salomsho Muhabbatov
Precious Metals, Muhammadjon Davlatov
Security, Maj.-Gen. Saidamin Zuhurov
Social Security, Abdusattor Jabborov
Trade and Material Resources, Hakim Soliyev
Transport, Fariddun Muhiddinov

HONORARY CONSULATE
33 Ovington Square, London SW3 1LJ
Honorary Consul, Benjamin Brahms

BRITISH AMBASSADOR, HE Christopher Ingham, apptd 1998, resident at Tashkent, Uzbekistan

ECONOMY

In January 1994 Tajikistan entered into a monetary union with Russia, effectively handing over monetary control to Russia in exchange for a US$100 million loan needed to prevent an economic collapse following the civil war. The Tajik rouble replaced the Russian rouble in May 1995. The economy is being reformed and privatization undertaken in order to attract foreign investment. In 1997 GDP grew by 1.7 per cent and industry grew by 9 per cent.

Agriculture is the major sector of the economy, concentrating on cotton-growing and cattle-breeding. Tajikistan also has rich mineral deposits of mercury, lead, zinc, oil, gold and uranium. Industry specializes in the production of clothing and textiles. In November 1997 and May 1998, donor conferences pledged loans totalling US$340 million to help stabilize the economic and political situation in Tajikistan.

GNP – US$2,010 million (1997); US$330 per capita (1997)
GDP – US$713 million (1995); US$122 per capita (1995)
TOTAL EXTERNAL DEBT – US$901 million (1997)

Trade with UK	1997	1998
Imports from UK	£1,425,000	£1,763,000
Exports to UK	1,501,000	2,372,000

TANZANIA
Jamhuri ya Muungano wa Tanzania – United Republic of Tanzania

AREA – 362,162 sq. miles (938,000 sq. km). Neighbours: Kenya and Uganda (north), Mozambique (south), Malawi and Zambia (south-west), Rwanda, Burundi and the Democratic Republic of Congo (west)
POPULATION – 30,799,000 (1994 UN estimate). Africans form a large majority, with European, Asian, and other non-African minorities. The African population consists mostly of tribes of mixed Bantu race. The official languages are Swahili and English
CAPITAL – Dodoma (population, 85,000, 1988)
MAJOR CITIES – ΨDar es Salaam (1,096,000), the economic and administrative centre; Mbeya (194,000); Mwanza (252,000); ΨTanga (172,000), 1985 estimates
CURRENCY – Tanzanian shilling of 100 cents
NATIONAL ANTHEM – Mungu Ibariki Afrika (God Bless Africa)
NATIONAL DAY – 26 April (Union Day)
NATIONAL FLAG – Green (above) and blue; divided by diagonal black stripe bordered by gold, running from bottom (next staff) to top (in fly)
LIFE EXPECTANCY (years) – male 47.00; female 50.00
POPULATION GROWTH RATE – 3.0 per cent (1997)
POPULATION DENSITY – 35 per sq. km (1996)
URBAN POPULATION – 20.8 per cent (1990)
MILITARY EXPENDITURE – 3.4 per cent of GDP (1997)
MILITARY PERSONNEL – 35,400: Army 30,000, Navy 1,000, Air Force 3,000, Paramilitaries 1,400
CONSCRIPTION DURATION – Two years

Tanzania comprises Tanganyika, on the mainland of east Africa, and the island of Zanzibar. The greater part of the country is occupied by the central African plateau from which rise, among others, Mt Kilimanjaro (19,340 ft), the highest point on the continent of Africa, and Mt Meru (14,974 ft). The Serengeti National Park covers an area of 6,000 sq. miles in the Arusha, Mwanza and Mara Regions.

HISTORY AND POLITICS

Tanganyika became an independent state and a member of the British Commonwealth on 9 December 1961, and a republic within the Commonwealth on 9 December 1962. Zanzibar, comprising the islands of Zanzibar, Pemba and Mafia, was formerly ruled by the Sultan of Zanzibar and was a British Protectorate until 10 December 1963 when it became an independent state within the Commonwealth. On 26 April 1964 Tanganyika united with Zanzibar to form the United Republic of Tanzania.

The sole legal political party from 1977 to 1992 was the Chama Cha Mapinduzi – the Revolutionary Party of Tanzania (CCM). The constitution was amended in 1992 to allow multiparty politics, with the stipulation that all parties must be active in both the mainland and in Zanzibar and that parties must not be formed on regional, religious, tribal or racial grounds.

The first multiparty presidential and parliamentary elections were held in October and November 1995. The CCM's candidate, Salmin Amour, was elected president of Zanzibar and his party won 26 seats in the Zanzibar House of Representatives. The Civic United Front gained 24 seats. Benjamin Mkapa of the CCM was elected Union president. The CCM won 186 of the 232 elected seats in the National Assembly.

POLITICAL SYSTEM

The president is directly elected and may serve two terms. The National Assembly contains 275 members, of whom 182 are elected from mainland constituencies and 50 from Zanzibar, 37 seats are reserved for women and are distributed to parties in ratio to their share of seats, five are nominated by the Zanzibar government and one is reserved for the Attorney-General. Constituency members are elected at a general election held at a maximum of five-yearly intervals.

Although Zanzibar has its own president, government and 60-member House of Representatives, Tanganyika is governed by the government of the Union. The president of Zanzibar is also a member of the Union Cabinet.

HEAD OF STATE

President of the United Republic, Benjamin Mkapa, *elected* 29 October 1995
Vice-President, President of Zanzibar, Salmin Amour

CABINET *as at July 1999*

The President
The Vice-President
Prime Minister, Frederick Sumaye
Agriculture and Co-operatives, William Kusila
Communications and Transport, Ernest Nyanda
Community Development, Women's Affairs and Children, Mary Nagu
Defence, Edgar Maokola Majogo
Education, Prof. Juma Athumani Kapuya
Energy and Mineral Resources, Dr Abdalla Kigoda
Foreign Affairs and International Co-operation, Jakaya Kikwete
Health, Dr Aaron Chiduo
Home Affairs, Ali Amer Mohammed
Justice and Constitutional Affairs, Harith Bakari Mwapachu
Labour and Youth Development, Paul Kimiti
Land, Housing and Urban Development, Gideon Cheyo
Ministers of State in the President's Office, Mateo Karesi
  (Cabinet Affairs); Jackson Makweta *(Civil Service)*; Daniel Yona Ndhiwa *(Finance)*; Nasoro Maloche *(Planning and Sector Reform)*; Wilson Masilingi *(Security)*
Minister of State in the Vice-President's Office, Edward Lowassa
Ministers of State in the Prime Minister's Office, Bakari Mbonde *(Information and Policy)*; Mohammed Seif Khatib
Natural Resources, Tourism and Environment, Zakia Meghji
Regional Administration and Local Government, Kingunge Ngombare Mwiru
Science, Technology and Higher Education, Pius Ng'wandu
Trade and Industry, Iddi Simba
Water and Livestock Development, Mussa Nkhangaa
Works, Anna Abdallah

HIGH COMMISSION FOR THE UNITED REPUBLIC OF TANZANIA
43 Hertford Street, London WIY 8DB
Tel 0171-499 8951/4
High Commissioner, HE Dr Abdul-kader Shareef, apptd 1995

BRITISH HIGH COMMISSION
Social Security House, Samora Avenue (PO Box 9200), Dar es Salaam
Tel: Dar es Salaam 117659/64
High Commissioner, HE Bruce Dinwiddy, apptd 1998

BRITISH COUNCIL DIRECTOR, R. Hilhorst, Samora Avenue (PO Box 9100), Dar es Salaam

ECONOMY

90 per cent of the workforce are employed in agriculture and agricultural produce accounts for 57 per cent of GDP. The islands of Zanzibar and Pemba produce a large part of the world's supply of cloves and clove oil; coconuts, coconut oil and copra are also produced. The mainland's chief exports are coffee, manufactured goods, cotton, minerals, tea, tobacco, cashew nuts and petroleum products. Industry, which accounts for 17 per cent of GDP, is largely concerned with the processing of raw material for export or local consumption; secondary manufacturing industries include factories for the manufacture of leather and rubber footwear, knitwear, razor blades, cigarettes and textiles, and a wheat flour mill.

In 1997 Tanzania had a trade deficit of US$449 million and a current account deficit of US$567 million. Imports totalled US$1,337 million and exports US$719 million.

GNP – US$6,632 million (1997); US$210 per capita (1997)
GDP – US$4,188 million (1995); US$139 per capita (1995)
ANNUAL AVERAGE GROWTH OF GDP – 27.5 per cent (1995)
INFLATION RATE – 16.1 per cent (1997)
TOTAL EXTERNAL DEBT – US$7,177 million (1997)

Trade with UK	1997	1998
Imports from UK	£77,008,000	£63,732,000
Exports to UK	33,148,000	29,089,000

COMMUNICATIONS

The main ports are Dar es Salaam, Tanga, Mtwara, Zanzibar, Mkoani and Wete, in addition to Mwanza, Musoma and Bukoba on Lake Victoria and Kigoma on Lake Tanganyika. Coastal shipping services connect the mainland to Zanzibar, and lake services are operated on Lake Tanganyika and Lake Malawi with neighbouring countries. The principal international airports are Dar es Salaam, Kilimanjaro and Zanzibar. There are two railway systems; one connecting Dar es Salaam to Zambia, and the second having two main lines running from Dar es Salaam, one to northern Tanzania and Kenya and the other to Lakes Tanganyika and Victoria. There are more than 3,000 km of rail track.

EDUCATION

The school system is administered in Swahili but the government is making efforts to improve English standards for the purposes of secondary and higher education. All Tanzanian secondary schools are expected to include practical subjects in the basic course. There are three institutes of higher education: the University of Dar es Salaam, Sokoine University of Agriculture in Morogoro and an open university.
ILLITERACY RATE – 32.2 per cent
ENROLMENT (percentage of age group) – primary 48 per cent (1996); tertiary 0.5 per cent (1995)

THAILAND
Prathes Thai – Kingdom of Thailand

AREA – 198,115 sq. miles (513,115 sq. km). Neighbours: Malaysia (south), Myanmar (west), Laos and Cambodia (east)

POPULATION – 60,206,000 (1997 census). The principal language is Thai, a monosyllabic, tonal language of the Indo-Chinese linguistic family, with a vocabulary strongly influenced by Sanskrit and Pali. It is written in an alphabetic script derived from ancient Indian scripts. Significant minorities speak Chinese (in urban areas), Lao (in the north-east), Khmer (in the east) and Malay (in the far south). The principal religion is Buddhism (94.37 per cent), with Muslim and Christian minorities

CAPITAL – ΨBangkok (population, 5,882,000, 1993)

MAJOR CITIES – Chiang Mai (167,000); Chon Buri (187,000); Muang Khon Kaen (206,000); Nakhon Ratchasima (278,000); Songkhla (243,000)

CURRENCY – Baht of 100 satang

NATIONAL ANTHEM – Pleng Chart

NATIONAL DAY – 5 December (The King's Birthday)

NATIONAL FLAG – Five horizontal bands, red, white, dark blue, white, red (the blue band twice the width of the others)

LIFE EXPECTANCY (years) – male 63.82; female 68.85

POPULATION GROWTH RATE – 1.2 per cent (1996)

POPULATION DENSITY – 117 per sq. km (1996)

URBAN POPULATION – 18.7 per cent (1990)

Thailand, formerly known as Siam, is divided geographically into four: the centre is a plain; to the north-east there is a plateau area and to the north-west mountains. The south of Thailand consists of a narrow mountainous peninsula. The principal rivers are the Chao Phraya in the central plains, and the Mekong on the northern and north-eastern borders.

HISTORY AND POLITICS

The Thai nation was founded in the 13th century. Although occupied by Burma in the 18th century, Thailand is the only country in the region not to have been colonized by a European power.

Following a revolution in 1932, Thailand became a constitutional monarchy. After a military coup in February 1991, a new constitution was approved under which the military would have significant political power. Parties aligned with the military won the general election in March 1992, but opposition to the government grew and mass demonstrations held in Bangkok, with the help of the King, forced the government from power. Military power was curbed, the 1978 constitution was restored and the interim government sacked military chiefs.

Parliamentary elections in September 1992 resulted in a majority for those parties not allied with the military. Chuan Leekpai became prime minister at the head of a coalition which implemented a number of reforms. Some 600,000 families were granted land title rights, the voting age was reduced to 18, the appointed Senate was reduced to a maximum of two-thirds of the number of House of Representatives' seats and anti-corruption laws were introduced. In a general election on 17 November 1996, New Aspiration became the largest party in the House of Representatives and formed a six-party coalition government. As a result of the economic crisis in Asia, the government resigned in November 1997, and a new eight-party coalition government was formed under Chuan Leekpai.

POLITICAL SYSTEM

The amended 1978 constitution provides for a National Assembly consisting of a 262-member Senate appointed by the King and a 393-member House of Representatives elected by universal adult suffrage for a term of four years.

In September 1997, the House of Representatives approved a number of constitutional reforms, including making the Senate a directly-elected body instead of one appointed by the King, and changing the House of Representatives to comprise 400 MPs from single constituencies and 100 from party lists.

HEAD OF STATE

HM The King of Thailand, King Bhumibol Adulyadej, *born* 1927; *succeeded his brother* 9 June 1946; *married* 28 April 1950 Princess Sirikit Kitiyakara; *crowned* 5 May 1950; and has *issue*, Princess Ubolratana, *born* 6 April 1951; Crown Prince Vajiralongkorn (*see* below); Princess Maha Chaki Sirindhorn, *born* 2 April 1955; Princess Chulabhorn, *born* 4 July 1957

Heir, HRH Crown Prince Vajiralongkorn, *born* 28 July 1952; *married* 3 January 1977 Soamsawali Kitiyakra

CABINET *as at July 1999*

Prime Minister, Defence, Chuan Leekpai (DP)

Deputy PMs, Phichai Rattakun (DP) ; Suphachai Phanitchaphak (DP) *(Commerce)*; vacant *(Education)*; Maj.-Gen Sanan Khachonprat (DP) *(Interior)*; Kon Thappharangsi (CP) *(Public Health)*; vacant *(Science, Technology and Environment)*

Ministers to the Prime Minister's Office, Suphattra Matsadit (DP); Sawit Phothiwihok (DP); Churin Laksanawisit (DP); Aphisit Wetchachiwa (DP); Air Chief Marshal Sombun Rahong (PT); Chaiyot Somsap (E); Phitak Intharawitthayanan

Agriculture and Co-operatives, Pongphon Adireksan (CT)

Finance, Tharin Nimmanhemin (DP)

Foreign Affairs, Surin Phitsuwan (DP)

Industry, Suwat Liptaphanlop (CP)

Justice, Suthat Ngoenmun (DP)

Labour and Social Welfare, Somphong Amonwiwat (CP)

State University Bureau, Prachuap Chaiyasan

Transport and Communications, Suthep Thuaksuban (DP)

CP Chart Pattana; CT Chart Thai; DP Democrat Party; E Ekkaparb; PT Prakachakorn Thai

ROYAL THAI EMBASSY

29–30 Queen's Gate, London SW7 5JB

Tel 0171-589 2944

Ambassador Extraordinary and Plenipotentiary, HE Sir Vidhya Rayananonda, KCVO, apptd 1994

Minister and Deputy Head of Mission, A. Manasvanich

Defence Attaché, Capt. S. Pruksa

Minister Counsellor, P. Siripanich *(Commercial)*

BRITISH EMBASSY

Wireless Road, Bangkok 10330

Tel: Bangkok 2530 1919

Ambassador Extraordinary and Plenipotentiary, HE Sir James Hodge, KCVO, CMG, apptd 1996

Deputy Ambassador and Counsellor, P. Sizeland

Defence Attaché, Col. J. H. Thoyts

Counsellor (Commercial), P. J. W. Hardman

Consul, B. P. Kelly

CONSULATE – Chiang Mai

BRITISH COUNCIL DIRECTOR, Dr J. Richards, OBE, 254 Chulalongkorn Soi 64, Siam Square, Phayathai Road, Pathumwan, Bangkok 10330. There is also an office in Chiang Mai

BRITISH CHAMBER OF COMMERCE, BP Building 18th Floor, Unit 1810, 54 Asoke Road (Sukhumvit 21), Bangkok 10110

DEFENCE

The Army has 277 main battle tanks, 970 armoured personnel carriers, 574 artillery pieces and four attack helicopters. The Navy has one aircraft carrier, 14 frigates, 87 patrol and coastal vessels, 54 combat aircraft and five armed helicopters at five bases. The Air Force has 206 combat aircraft.

MILITARY EXPENDITURE – 2.1 per cent of GDP (1997)

MILITARY PERSONNEL – 377,300: Army 190,000, Navy 73,000, Air Force 43,000, Paramilitaries 71,000

ECONOMY

Thailand was one of the countries worst affected by the economic crisis in south-east Asia. Many Thai banks had borrowed heavily to finance the booming property market, and suffered when the market collapsed. In May 1997 it was announced that, despite emergency budget cuts, Thailand was heading for its first fiscal deficit in over a decade, and as a result the stock market fell to an eight-year low. In July 1997 the government allowed the currency to float freely, resulting in a *de facto* devaluation of 20 per cent and triggering a currency crisis throughout south-east Asia. On 5 August 1997, an IMF loan of US$16.7 billion was announced, in return for emergency financial reforms. However, these reforms were only implemented after a delay and were seen by the markets as inadequate, further damaging economic confidence. The government resigned on 3 November 1997, and was replaced by an eight-party coalition. In January 1998 the prime minister approved a move to repatriate foreign workers, in order to provide more jobs for native Thais. The Thai economy contracted by about 8 per cent in 1998. In March 1999, the government announced a package of tax cuts and increased spending designed to stimulate the economy.

The agricultural sector employs around half of the labour force. In 1997 it contributed 11 per cent of GDP. Rice remains the most important crop; other main crops are sugar, maize, sorghum, cassava, rubber, tobacco, kenaf and jute. In recent years fishing and livestock production have gained importance. There are reserves of oil, natural gas and lignite; mineral resources include tin, tungsten, lead and iron.

Important industrial sectors include textiles, transportation vehicles and equipment, construction materials, brewing, petroleum refining, electrical appliances, plastics, computers and parts, and integrated circuits. In 1996, manufacturing contributed 30.5 per cent of GDP. Since 1982 tourism has been the main foreign exchange earner. In 1996, there were 7.2 million foreign visitors.

GNP – US$165,759 million (1997); US$2,740 per capita (1997)

GDP – US$168,637 million (1995); US$2,896 per capita (1995)

ANNUAL AVERAGE GROWTH OF GDP – –0.4 per cent (1995)

INFLATION RATE – 5.6 per cent (1997)

UNEMPLOYMENT – 1.5 per cent (1993)

TOTAL EXTERNAL DEBT – US$93,416 million (1997)

TRADE

Thailand's main exports are computers and parts, cars, integrated circuit boards, precious stones, rice, maize, canned sea food, fabrics, sugar and tin. Main imports are crude oil, chemicals, electrical goods, industrial machinery, iron, steel and transport equipment.

In 1997 Thailand had a trade surplus of US$1,564 million and a current account deficit of US$2,917 million. Imports totalled US$61,353 million and exports US$57,619 million.

Trade with UK	1997	1998
Imports from UK	£861,736,000	£391,119,000
Exports to UK	1,222,138,000	1,329,084,000

COMMUNICATIONS

The road network, totalling 56,903 km in 1993, reaches all parts of the country. Navigable waterways have a length of about 1,100 km in the dry season and 1,600 km in the wet season. There are 4,600 km of state-owned railways. Main lines run from Bangkok to the Cambodian border, the ferry terminal on the River Mekong opposite Vientiane, Chiang Mai and to Hat Yai, whence lines run down both sides of the Malay peninsula to Singapore. A new line to Sattahip on the east coast is being constructed. Bangkok is the international airport, though airports at Chiang Mai, Phuket and Hat Yai also receive international flights. Most major provincial towns have airports. A mass transit system has been planned for Bangkok.

There are two important ports in the country. Bangkok, which is a river port, can serve vessels up to 27 ft draught. The deep-sea port at Sattahip caters for larger vessels. Phuket and Songkhla deep-water ports have already been completed and are the first to be managed privately under a ten-year concession.

EDUCATION

Primary education is compulsory and free, and secondary education in government schools is free. Private universities and colleges are playing an increasing role in higher education. Out of 43 universities and other similar higher institutes of learning, 21 are private.

ILLITERACY RATE – 6.2 per cent

ENROLMENT (percentage of age group) – tertiary 20.1 per cent (1995)

TOGO
République Togolaise

AREA – 21,925 sq. miles (56,785 sq. km). Neighbours: Ghana (west), Burkina Faso (north), Benin (east)

POPULATION – 4,201,000 (1994 UN estimate). The official language is French; Ewe, Watchi and Kabiyé are the main indigenous languages

CAPITAL – ΨLomé (population, 366,476, 1983)

CURRENCY – Franc CFA of 100 centimes

NATIONAL DAY – 13 January (National Liberation Day)

NATIONAL FLAG – Five alternating green and yellow horizontal stripes; a quarter in red at top next staff bearing a white star

LIFE EXPECTANCY (years) – male 53.23; female 56.82

POPULATION GROWTH RATE – 3.0 per cent (1997)

POPULATION DENSITY – 74 per sq. km (1996)

MILITARY EXPENDITURE – 2.1 per cent of GDP (1997)

MILITARY PERSONNEL – 7,700: Army 6,500, Navy 200, Air Force 250, Paramilitaries 750

CONSCRIPTION DURATION – Two years

ILLITERACY RATE – 48.3 per cent

ENROLMENT (percentage of age group) – primary 81 per cent (1996); secondary 18 per cent (1990); tertiary 3.6 per cent (1996)

HISTORY AND POLITICS

The first president of Togo, Sylvanus Olympio, was assassinated in 1963. His successor was overthrown by an army coup d'état in 1967 and the army commander Lt.-Col. (later Gen.) Eyadéma named himself president. President Eyadéma came under increasing popular pressure to introduce reforms in 1990 and in October the *Rassemblement du peuple togolais* (RPT), the sole legal party, approved plans for a new constitutional conference after pro-democracy riots. Riots broke out again in March 1991 in protest at the slow pace of reform, and in April the government was forced to concede a political amnesty, the introduction of a multiparty constitution and a national conference. In August 1991 the national conference stripped President Eyadéma of all powers, banned the RPT and elected Kokou Koffigoh as prime minister of an interim government. The national conference set a date of 9 February 1992 for a referendum on a new constitution.

From the second half of 1991 onwards the political situation became progressively more unstable. Troops loyal to President Eyadéma three times attempted to overthrow Koffigoh (in October, November and December 1991) but were frustrated by pro-democracy supporters. Continued violence in 1992 between the army and pro-democracy groups and among rival opposition parties forced the postponement of the referendum until September 1992, when a new multiparty constitution was agreed. In November, Eyadéma, who had regained the position of head of state in August 1992, ordered the Army to crush civil unrest and a general strike against his rule. In February 1993, as violence continued, Koffigoh and Eyadéma agreed on the formation of a crisis government, which the national conference and the Collective Democratic Opposition-2 (COD-2) declared illegal.

The presidential election of 21 June 1998 was won by Gen. Eyadéma. Opposition politicians and EU observers expressed serious doubts over the conduct of the election.

Legislative elections to the 81-seat National Assembly were held on 21 March 1999. Opposition parties, who had refused to accept the results of the presidential election in 1998, boycotted the election, with the result that the ruling RPT gained 79 seats, the remaining two seats being won by independents. Eugene Koffi Adoboli was appointed prime minister on 22 May 1999 and a new Cabinet was appointed on 18 June.

HEAD OF STATE

President, Gen. Gnassingbé Eyadéma, *assumed office* 14 April 1967 *re-elected* 1986, 1993, 21 June 1998

GOVERNMENT *as at July 1999*

Prime Minister, Eugene Koffi Adoboli
Agriculture, Livestock and Fisheries, Komikpine Bamenante
Civil Service and Labour, Biossey Kokou Tozoun
Communication and Civic Education, Koffi Panou
Defence, Brig.-Gen. Assani Tidjani
Economic Affairs, Finance and Privatization, Abdoul-Hamid Segoun Tidjani Dourodjaye
Environment and Forest Resources, Koffi Adade
Health, Kondi Charles Agba
Industry, Commerce and Development of Free Zone, Rudolph Kossivi Osseyi
Interior, Security and Decentralization, Gen. Sizing Akawilou Walla
Justice and Keeper of the Seals, Brig.-Gen. Séyi Memene
Mines, Energy, Posts and Telecommunications, Tchamdja Andjo
Minister Delegate at the Prime Minister's Office, Relations with Parliament and the European Union, Devo Hodeminou

Minister of State, Foreign Affairs and Co-operation, Kokou Joseph Koffigoh
National Education and Research, Koffi Sama
Planning and Development, Sinfeitcheou Pre
Promotion of Democracy and the Rule of Law, Harry Octavianus Olympio
Secretary of State to the Prime Minister, Private Sector, Saibou Samarou
Social Affairs, National Solidarity and the Promotion of Women, Irene Ashir Aissah
Special Adviser to the President, Barry Moussa Barque
Technical Education, Professional Training and Cottage Industry, Edo Kodjo Maurille Agbobli
Town Planning and Housing, Hope Agboli
Tourism and Leisure, Tankpadja Lalle
Transport and Water Resources, Dama Dramani
Youth, Sports and Culture, Horatio Freitas

EMBASSY OF THE REPUBLIC OF TOGO
8 rue Alfred-Roll, F-75017 Paris, France
Ambassador Extraordinary and Plenipotentiary, HE Kondi Charles

BRITISH AMBASSADOR, HE Ian Mackley, CMG, resident at Accra, Ghana
There is a Consulate (BP 20050) and a Commercial Office (BP 60958 BE) in Lomé.

ECONOMY

Although the economy remains largely agricultural, exports of phosphates have superseded agricultural products as the main source of export earnings. Other exports include palm kernels, copra and manioc.

In December 1998 the EU announced that it would not resume developmental aid to Togo following irregularities in the country's election process.

In 1994 Togo had a trade deficit of US$37 million and a current account deficit of US$63 million. In 1997 imports totalled US$374 million and exports US$237 million.

GNP – US$1,485 million (1997); US$340 per capita (1997)
GDP – US$1,316 million (1995); US$322 per capita (1995)
ANNUAL AVERAGE GROWTH OF GDP – 6.7 per cent (1995)
INFLATION RATE – 15.7 per cent (1995)
TOTAL EXTERNAL DEBT – US$1,339 million (1997)

Trade with UK	1997	1998
Imports from UK	£13,046,000	£18,777,000
Exports to UK	2,302,000	1,630,000

TONGA
Kingdom of Tonga

AREA – 288 sq. miles (747 sq. km)
POPULATION – 99,000 (1994 UN estimate). The languages are Tongan and English
CAPITAL – Ψ Nuku'alofa (population, 29,018, 1986), on Tongatapu
CURRENCY – Pa'anga (T$) of 100 seniti
NATIONAL ANTHEM – E, 'Otua Mafimafi (Oh, Almighty God Above)
NATIONAL DAY – 4 June (Emancipation Day)
NATIONAL FLAG – Red with a white canton containing a couped red cross
POPULATION GROWTH RATE – 0.3 per cent (1997)
POPULATION DENSITY – 132 per sq. km (1996)

URBAN POPULATION – 30.7 per cent (1986)

Tonga, or the Friendly Islands, comprises a group of islands situated in the southern Pacific some 450 miles east-south-east of Fiji. The largest island, Tongatapu, was discovered by Tasman in 1643. Most of the islands are of coral formation, but some are volcanic (Tofua, Kao and Niuafoou or 'Tin Can' Island).

HISTORY AND POLITICS

The Kingdom of Tonga is an independent constitutional monarchy within the Commonwealth. Prior to 4 June 1970 it had been a British-protected state for 70 years. The constitution provides for a government consisting of the Sovereign, an appointed privy council which functions as a Cabinet, a legislative assembly and a judiciary. The 30-member legislative assembly comprises the King, the 11-member privy council, nine hereditary nobles elected by their peers, and nine popularly elected representatives who hold office for three years. The most recent election took place on 12 March 1999.

HEAD OF STATE
King of Tonga, HM King Taufa'ahau Tupou IV, GCMG, GCVO, KBE, *born* 4 July 1918, *acceded* 16 December 1965
Heir, HRH Crown Prince Tupouto'a

CABINET *as at July 1999*
Prime Minister, Agriculture, Forestry, Fisheries, Marine Affairs, Baron Vaea of Houma
Deputy PM, Education and Civil Aviation, Dr S. Langi Kavaliku
Finance, Tutoatosi Fakafanua
Foreign Affairs and Defence, HRH Prince Lavaka Ata
Governor of Ha'apali, Fielakepa
Governor of Vava'u, Capt. S. M. Tuita
Health, Vailami Tangi
Justice, Tevita Tupou
Labour, Commerce and Industries, Masaso Paunga
Lands, Survey, and Natural Resources, Tu'i'afitu
Police, Prisons and Fire Services, Immigration, Clive Edwards
Works and Disaster Relief, Cecil Cocker

TONGA HIGH COMMISSION
36 Molyneux Street, London WIH 6AB
Tel 0171-724 5828
High Commissioner, HE 'Akosita Fineanganofo, apptd 1996

BRITISH HIGH COMMISSION
PO Box 56, Nuku'alofa
Tel: Nuku'alofa 24285
High Commissioner, HE Brian Connelly, apptd 1998

ECONOMY

The economy is primarily agricultural; the main crops are coconuts, vanilla, yams, taro, cassava, groundnuts, squash pumpkins and other fruits. Fish is an important staple food, though recent shortfalls have led to canned fish being imported. Industry is based on the processing of agricultural produce, and the manufacture of foodstuffs, clothing and sports equipment.
GNP – US$177 million (1997); US$1,810 per capita (1997)
GDP – US$175 million (1995); US$1,787 per capita (1995)
ANNUAL AVERAGE GROWTH OF GDP – 5.4 per cent (1995)
INFLATION RATE – 2.1 per cent (1997)
TOTAL EXTERNAL DEBT – US$61 million (1997)

TRADE

The principal exports are squash, vanilla, kava, copra, other coconut products, fruit and vegetables, knitwear, leather goods and fibreglass boats.
In 1996 imports totalled US$75 million and exports US$10 million.

Trade with UK	1997	1998
Imports from UK	£4,892,000	£1,205,000
Exports to UK	193,000	17,000

TRINIDAD AND TOBAGO
The Republic of Trinidad and Tobago

AREA – 1,981 sq. miles (5,130 sq. km)
POPULATION – 1,297,000 (1994 UN estimate). The language is English. Roman Catholicism, Protestantism, Hinduism and Islam are all practised
CAPITAL – ΨPort of Spain (population, 46,222, 1994)
MAJOR CITIES – San Fernando (55,784); ΨScarborough, the main town of Tobago
CURRENCY – Trinidad and Tobago dollar (TT$) of 100 cents
NATIONAL DAY – 31 August (Independence Day)
NATIONAL FLAG – Black diagonal stripe bordered with white stripes, running from top by staff, all on a red field
LIFE EXPECTANCY (years) – male 68.06; female 73.03
POPULATION GROWTH RATE – 0.8 per cent (1997)
POPULATION DENSITY – 253 per sq. km (1996)
MILITARY EXPENDITURE – 1.4 per cent of GDP (1997)
MILITARY PERSONNEL – 7,400: Army 1,900, Coast Guard 700, Paramilitaries 4,800

Trinidad, the most southerly of the West Indian islands, lies seven miles off the north coast of Venezuela. The island is about 50 miles in length by 37 miles in width. Two mountain systems, the Northern and Southern Ranges, stretch across almost its entire width and a third, the Central Range, lies diagonally across its middle portion; otherwise the island is mostly flat.
Tobago lies 19 miles north-east of Trinidad. The island is 32 miles long at its widest point, and 11 miles wide.
Corozal Point and Icacos Point, the north-west and south-west extremities of Trinidad, enclose the Gulf of Paria. West of Corozal Point lie several islands, of which Chacachacare, Huevos, Monos and Gaspar Grande are the most important.
The climate is tropical. There is a dry season from December to May, and a wet season from June to November broken by a short dry season (the *Petite Careme*) in September and October.

HISTORY AND POLITICS

Trinidad was discovered by Columbus in 1498, was colonized in 1532 by the Spaniards, capitulated to the British in 1797, and was ceded to Britain under the Treaty of Amiens (1802). Tobago was discovered by Columbus in 1498. Dutch colonists arrived in 1632; Tobago subsequently changed hands numerous times until it was ceded to Britain by France in 1814 and amalgamated with Trinidad in 1888. The Territory of Trinidad and Tobago became an independent state and a member of the British Commonwealth on 31 August 1962, and a republic in 1976.
The most recent general election on 6 November 1995 produced 17 seats each for the ruling People's National Movement (PNM) and the United National Congress (UNC). The UNC formed a coalition government with

the National Alliance for Reconstruction (NAR) which held the remaining two seats.

POLITICAL SYSTEM

The president is elected for five years by all members of the Senate and the House of Representatives. The House of Representatives has 36 members, directly elected for a five-year term, and the Senate has 31, of whom 16 are appointed on the advice of the prime minister, six on the advice of the Leader of the Opposition and nine at the discretion of the president. Legislation was passed in September 1980 which afforded Tobago a degree of self-administration through the 15-member Tobago House of Assembly.

HEAD OF STATE

President, HE Arthur N. Robinson, *elected* 14 February 1997

CABINET *as at July 1999*

Prime Minister, Basdeo Panday
Agriculture, Lands and Marine Resources, Dr Reeza Mohammed
Attorney-General, Leader of the House of Representatives, Ramesh Lawrence Maharaj
Community Development, Culture and Women's Affairs, Daphne Phillips
Education, Dr Adesh Nanan
Energy and Energy Industries, Finbar Ganga
Finance and Tourism, Brian Kuei Tung
Foreign Affairs, Ralph Maraj
Health, Dr Hamza Rafeeq
Housing and Settlements, John Humphrey
Information, Communications, Training and Distance Learning, Dr Rupert Griffith
Labour and Co-operatives, Harry Partrap
Legal Affairs, Kamla Persad-Bissessar
Local Government, Dhanraj Singh
National Security, Joseph Theodore
Planning and Development, Trevor Sudama
Public Administration, Wade Mark
Public Utilities, Ganga Singh
Social Development, Manohar Ramsaran
Sport and Youth Affairs, Pamela Nicholson
Tobago Affairs, Morgan Job
Trade, Tourism, Industry and Consumer Affairs, Mervyn Assam
Works and Transport, Sadeeq Baksh

HIGH COMMISSION OF THE REPUBLIC OF TRINIDAD AND TOBAGO
42 Belgrave Square, London SW1X 8NT
Tel 0171-245 9351
High Commissioner, HE Sheelagh de Osuna, apptd 1996

BRITISH HIGH COMMISSION
19 St Clair Ave, St Clair, Port of Spain
Tel: Port of Spain 622 2748
High Commissioner, HE P. G. Harborne, apptd 1999

ECONOMY

Trinidad and Tobago's main source of revenue is from oil. Production of domestic crude was 6.4 million tonnes in 1997. Trinidad has large reserves of natural gas, and reserves are estimated to be in the region of 45 years at the current rates of production. An integrated steel plant, two anhydrous ammonia plants, four methanol plants, one urea plant and one iron carbide plant have been constructed at Point Lisas. An industrial complex, including an iron and steel production plant, is developing around San Fernando.

Fertilizers, tyres, clothing, soap, furniture and foodstuffs are manufactured locally while motor vehicles, radios, TV sets, and electro-domestic equipment are assembled from parts, mainly from Japan. The main agricultural products are sugar, cocoa, coffee, horticultural products and teak. There were more than 250,000 tourists in 1996.

In 1995 Trinidad and Tobago had a trade surplus of US$588 million and a current account surplus of US$294 million. In 1997 imports totalled US$2,990 million and exports US$2,542 million.

GNP – US$5,553 million (1997); US$4,250 per capita (1997)
GDP – US$5,255 million (1995); US$4,083 per capita (1995)
ANNUAL AVERAGE GROWTH OF GDP – 3.1 per cent (1996)
INFLATION RATE – 5.6 per cent (1998)
UNEMPLOYMENT – 16.1 per cent (1996)
TOTAL EXTERNAL DEBT – US$2,162 million (1997)

Trade with UK	1997	1998
Imports from UK	£94,311,000	£94,177,000
Exports to UK	63,328,000	39,274,000

COMMUNICATIONS

There are some 9,586 km of roads in Trinidad and Tobago. The three main ports are Scarborough (Tobago), Port of Spain and Point Lisas where new industries powered by local natural gas are located. The national airline is International Trinidad and Tobago Airways (BWIA), and the international airport, Piarco, is at Port of Spain. Air Caribbean flies between Trinidad and Tobago.

EDUCATION

Education is free at all state-owned and government-assisted denominational schools and certain faculties at the University of the West Indies. Attendance is compulsory for children aged six to 12 years, after which attendance at free secondary schools is determined by success in the common entrance examination at 11 years. There are three technical institutes, two teachers' training colleges, and one of the three branches of the University of the West Indies is located in Trinidad. A medical teaching complex at Mt Hope operates in collaboration with the University of the West Indies.

ILLITERACY RATE – 2.1 per cent
ENROLMENT (percentage of age group) – primary 88 per cent (1995); secondary 64 per cent (1992); tertiary 7.8 per cent (1996)

TUNISIA
Al-Djoumhouria Attunusia

AREA – 62,592 sq. miles (162,155 sq. km). Neighbours: Algeria (west), Libya (south)
POPULATION – 9,092,000 (1994 UN estimate). Arabic is the official language
CAPITAL – ΨTunis (population, 1,830,634, 1994)
MAJOR CITIES – ΨBizerte (484,250); ΨSfax (732,865); ΨSousse (435,075), 1996
CURRENCY – Tunisian dinar of 1,000 millimes
NATIONAL ANTHEM – Himat Al Hima
NATIONAL DAY – 20 March
NATIONAL FLAG – Red with a white disc containing a red crescent and star
LIFE EXPECTANCY (years) – male 66.85; female 68.68
POPULATION GROWTH RATE – 1.7 per cent (1997)
POPULATION DENSITY – 56 per sq. km (1996)

URBAN POPULATION – 61.0 per cent (1994)
MILITARY EXPENDITURE – 1.8 per cent of GDP (1997)
MILITARY PERSONNEL – 47,000: Army 27,000, Navy 4,500, Air Force 3,500, Paramilitaries 12,000
CONSCRIPTION DURATION – 12 months
ILLITERACY RATE – 33.3 per cent
ENROLMENT (percentage of age group) – primary 96 per cent (1996); secondary 23 per cent (1980); tertiary 13.7 per cent (1996)

HISTORY AND POLITICS

A French Protectorate from 1881 to 1956, Tunisia became an independent sovereign state on 20 March 1956. In 1957 the Constituent Assembly abolished the monarchy and elected M. Bourguiba president of the Republic. In March 1975 the National Assembly proclaimed M. Bourguiba as president for life. He was deposed on 7 November 1987 and succeeded by President Zine el-Abidine Ben Ali. Presidential and legislative elections were held in April 1989. The *Rassemblement constitutionnel démocratique* (RCD) won all 141 seats in the National Assembly *(Majlis al-Nuwaab)* and President Ben Ali was elected with 99 per cent of the vote, although the elections were boycotted by the main opposition parties.

Electoral changes enacted in September 1993 provide for opposition parties to be represented in the National Assembly; the Assembly has been expanded to 163 seats, 19 of which are reserved, on a proportional basis, for those parties not winning any of the 144 first-past-the-post seats. Presidential and legislative elections held in March 1994 were won by President Ben Ali, the only candidate, and the RCD, which won all 144 constituency seats. Presidential and legislative elections are due to be held on 24 October 1999.

The country is divided into 23 regions *(gouvernorats)* each administered by a governor.

HEAD OF STATE
President, Gen. Zine el-Abidine Ben Ali, *took office* 7 November 1987, *elected* 2 April 1989, *re-elected* 20 March 1994

CABINET *as at July 1999*
Prime Minister, Hamed Karoui
Agriculture, Sadok Rabah
Communications, Ahmed Friaa
Culture, Abdelbaki Hermassi
Defence, Habib Ben Yahia
Economic Development, Abdellatif Saddam
Education, Abderrahim Zouari
Environment and Land Development, Faiza Kefi
Finance, Taoufik Baccar
Foreign Affairs, Said Ben Mustapha
Higher Education, Dali Jazi
Industry, Moncef Ben Abdallah
Interior, Ali Chaouch
International Co-operation and Foreign Investment, Mohammed Ghannouchi
Justice, Abdallah Kallel
Minister-Delegate to the Prime Minister in charge of Women and the Family, Neziha Zarrouk
Minister-Director of the Presidential Office, Mohammed Jegham
Minister of State, Special Adviser to the President, Abdullah Kallel
Public Health, Hedi Mhenni
Public Works and Housing, Slaheddine Belaid
Religious Affairs, Ali Chebbi
Secretary-General of the Government, Slaheddine Ben Cherif
Social Affairs, Chedli Neffati
State Property, Real Estate Affairs, Ridha Grira
Tourism and Handicrafts, Slaheddine Maaouia
Trade, Mondher Zenaidi
Transport, Hassine Chouk
Vocational Training and Employment, Moncer Rouissi
Youth and Childhood, Raouf Najar

TUNISIAN EMBASSY
29 Prince's Gate, London SW7 1QG
Tel 0171-584 8117
Ambassador Extraordinary and Plenipotentiary, HE Khemaies Jhinaoui, apptd 1999

BRITISH EMBASSY
5 Place de la Victoire, Tunis 1015 RP
Tel: Tunis 134 1444
Ambassador Extraordinary and Plenipotentiary, HE Ivor Rawlinson, OBE, apptd 1998
Consul, B. Bennett (*Deputy Head of Mission*)
HONORARY CONSULATE – Sfax

BRITISH COUNCIL DIRECTOR, J. McKenzie (*Cultural Attaché*)

ECONOMY

The valleys of the northern region support large flocks and herds and contain rich agricultural areas in which cereal crops, citrus fruits, dates, melons and tomatoes are grown. Vines and olives are extensively cultivated. Crude oil production in 1997 was 4.3 million tonnes. Gas has also been discovered off the east coast but is only exploited in small quantities. Tourism is the main foreign exchange earner and there were more than 3.5 million visitors in 1994.

In 1996 Tunisia had a trade deficit of US$1,804 million and a current account deficit of US$536 million. In 1997 imports totalled US$7,914 million and exports US$5,559 million.
GNP – US$19,433 million (1997); US$2,110 per capita (1997)
GDP – US$18,247 million (1995); US$2,030 per capita (1995)
ANNUAL AVERAGE GROWTH OF GDP – 5.4 per cent (1997)
INFLATION RATE – 3.7 per cent (1997)
TOTAL EXTERNAL DEBT – US$11,323 million (1997)

TRADE

The chief exports are crude oil, phosphates, olive oil, textiles and fruit. The chief imports are machinery and equipment, foodstuffs and petroleum products. France remains the main trading partner.

Tunisia became an associate of the EC in 1969. In July 1995 a new EU-Tunisian partnership agreement was signed which aims to modernize Tunisia's economy and improve its competitiveness with a view to creating a future free trade zone with the EU.

Trade with UK	1997	1998
Imports from UK	£108,303,000	£101,387,000
Exports to UK	59,496,000	77,024,000

TURKEY
Türkiye Cumhuriyeti

AREA – 299,158 sq. miles (774,815 sq. km). Neighbours: Greece (west), Bulgaria (north), Georgia, Armenia and Iran (east), Syria and Iraq (south)

POPULATION – 62,697,000 (1994 UN estimate);
56,473,035 (1990 census). Islam ceased to be the state
religion in 1928 but 98.99 per cent of the population are
Muslim. The main religious minorities, which are
concentrated in Istanbul and on the Syrian frontier, are
Greek Orthodox, Armenian, Syrian Christian, and
Jewish. The language is Turkish; Kurdish is widely
spoken in the south-east of the country.
CAPITAL – Ankara (Angora), in Asia (population,
3,103,000, 1994). Ankara (or Ancyra) was the capital of
the Roman Province of *Galatia Prima*, and a marble
temple (now in ruins), dedicated to Augustus, contains
the *Monumentum* (*Marmor*) *Ancyranum*, inscribed with a
record of the reign of Augustus Caesar
MAJOR CITIES – Adana (1,519,800); Bursa (1,381,300);
Gaziantep (973,800); ΨIstanbul (7,784,100); ΨIzmir
(2,411,500); Konya (1,069,400), 1994 estimates. Istanbul,
in Europe, is the former capital. The Roman city of
Byzantium, it was selected by Constantine the Great as
the capital of the Roman Empire about AD 328 and
renamed Constantinople. Istanbul contains the
celebrated church of St Sophia, which, after becoming a
mosque, was made a museum in 1934. It also contains
Topkapi, former palace of the Ottoman Sultans, which
is also a museum
CURRENCY – Turkish lira (TL) of 100 kurus
NATIONAL ANTHEM – Istiklal Marşi (The Independence
March)
NATIONAL DAY – 29 October (Republic Day)
NATIONAL FLAG – Red, with white crescent and star
LIFE EXPECTANCY (years) – male 63.26; female 66.01
POPULATION GROWTH RATE – 1.8 per cent (1997)
POPULATION DENSITY – 81 per sq. km (1996)
URBAN POPULATION – 63.3 per cent (1996)

Turkey lies partly in Europe and partly in Asia. Turkey in
Europe consists of Eastern Thrace, including the cities of
Istanbul and Edirne, and is separated from Asia by the
Bosporus at Istanbul and by the Dardanelles (about 40
miles in length with a width varying from one to four
miles). Turkey in Asia comprises the whole of Asia Minor
or Anatolia.

HISTORY AND POLITICS

On 29 October 1923 the National Assembly declared
Turkey a republic and elected Gazi Mustafa Kemal (later
known as Kemal Atatürk) president. In 1945 a multiparty
system was introduced but in 1960 the government was
overthrown by the armed forces. A new constitution was
adopted in 1961 and a civilian government took office.
Civilian governments remained in power until September
1980 when mounting problems with the economy and
terrorism led to a military takeover.
    Following the general election in November 1983 the
military leadership handed over power to a civilian
government.
    Following elections on 18 April 1999, the Democratic
Left Party (DSP) won the most seats and formed a coalition
with the Nationalist Action Party (MHP) and the Motherland Party (ANAP). The MHP, a right-wing nationalist
organization, became the second biggest party in the Grand
National Assembly, having not been represented in the
previous parliament as it had not managed to secure the
necessary 10 per cent of the vote. Hadep, the pro-Kurdish
People's Democracy Party, failed to obtain the necessary
10 per cent of the vote, but won control of several towns
in south-eastern Turkey in simultaneous local elections.

INSURGENCIES

Since 1984 Turkey has been fighting armed guerrillas of
the Marxist Kurdistan Workers' Party (PKK) in the south-
east of the country where Kurds are the majority population.
The PKK has an estimated strength of 10,000 operating
from bases in Lebanon, northern Iraq and Syria, with the
latter giving tacit support and finance. The south-east
remains under martial law. Since May 1993 the Turkish
army has attempted to destroy the PKK by launching land
and air raids against PKK bases in Syria and northern Iraq.
Tension rose between Turkey and Syria in September
1998 when Turkey mobilized its troops on its southern
border with Syria and threatened to bomb Kurdish bases
in Syria and Lebanon. Egyptian and Iranian mediation
secured an agreement by Syria not to offer support to the
PKK, The leader of the PKK. Abdullah Öcalan, left Syria
in October 1998 and was captured by Turkish authorities
in February 1999 in Kenya and returned to Turkey to
stand trial, where he was found guilty of treason on 31
May and sentenced to death on 29 June 1999.

POLITICAL SYSTEM

A new constitution, extending the powers of the president,
was approved in 1982. It provided for the separation of
powers between the legislature, executive and judiciary,
and the holding of free elections to the unicameral Grand
National Assembly, which now has 550 members elected
every five years.
    Turkey is divided for administrative purposes into 76 *il*
with subdivisions into *ilçe* and *nahiye*. Each *il* has a governor
(*vali*) and elective council.

HEAD OF STATE

President, Süleyman Demirel, *elected by parliament for a
    seven-year term* 16 May 1993

CABINET *as at July 1999*

Prime Minister, Bülent Ecevit (DSP)
Deputy PMs, Ministers of State, Devlet Bahceli (MHP);
    Hasan Husamettin Ozkan (DSP)
Ministers of State, Mustafa Yilmaz (DSP); Sükrü Sina
    Gürel (DSP); Fikret Unlu (DSP); Hasan Gemici (DSP);
    Mehmet Kececiler (ANAP); Yuksel Yalova (ANAP);
    Rüstü Kazim Yücelen (ANAP); Tunca Toskay (MHP);
    Sadi Somuncuoglu (MHP); Ramazan Mirzaoglu
    (MHP); Edip Safter Gaydali (ANAP); Suayip Usenmez
    (MHP); Mehmet Ali Irtemcelik (ANAP); Abdulhaluk
    Cay (MHP)
Agriculture and Village Affairs, Husnu Yusuf Gokalp (MHP)
Culture, Mustafa Istemihan Talay (DSP)
Economy, Recep Onal (DSP)
Education, Metin Bostancioglu (DSP)

Energy and Natural Resources, Cumhur Ersümer (ANAP)
Environment, Fevzi Aytekin (DSP)
Finance, Sumer Oral (ANAP)
Foreign Affairs, Ismail Cem (DSP)
Forestry, Ibrahim Nami Cagan (DSP)
Health, Osman Durmus (MHP)
Interior, Saadettin Tantan (ANAP)
Justice, Hikmet Sami Türk (DSP)
Labour and Special Security, Yasan Okuyan (ANAP)
National Defence, Sabahattin Cakmakoglu (MHP)
Public Works, Koray Aydin (MHP)
Tourism, Erkan Mumcu (ANAP)
Trade and Industry, Ahmet Kenan Tanrikulu (MHP)
Transport, Enis Oksuz (MHP)

ANAP Motherland Party; DSP Democratic Left Party;
MHP Nationalist Action Party

TURKISH EMBASSY
43 Belgrave Square, London SW1X 8PA
Tel 0171-393 0202
Ambassador Extraordinary and Plenipotentiary, HE Özdem
Sanberk, apptd 1995
Minister Counsellor, Meli Mehmet Akat

BRITISH EMBASSY
Sehit Ersan Caddesi 46/A, Cankaya, Ankara
Tel: Ankara 468 6230/42
Ambassador Extraordinary and Plenipotentiary, HE David
Logan, CMG, apptd 1997
Counsellor, Deputy Head of Mission, H. Mortimer
First Secretary, J. Macpherson *(Commercial)*
Defence and Military Attaché, Brig. A. V. Twiss
Consul-General (Istanbul), P. Hunt
CONSULATE-GENERAL – Istanbul
VICE-CONSULATE – Izmir
HONORARY CONSULATES – Antalya, Bodrum, Bursa,
Iskenderun, Marmaris, Mersin

BRITISH COUNCIL DIRECTOR, C. Gobby, Esat Caddesi
No:41, Kucukesat, Ankara 06660

BRITISH CHAMBER OF COMMERCE OF TURKEY INC.,
Mesrutiyet Caddessi No. 34, Tepebasi Beyoğlu,
Istanbul *(postal address,* PO Box 190 Karaköy, Istanbul)

DEFENCE

The Army has 4,205 main battle tanks, 3,618 armoured
personnel carriers, 280 armoured infantry fighting vehicles,
4,274 artillery pieces and 37 attack helicopters. The Navy
has 16 submarines, two destroyers, 19 frigates, 50 patrol
and coastal vessels and 13 armed helicopters at eight bases.
The Air Force has 440 combat aircraft.

Between 150,000 and 200,000 troops are stationed in the
south-east of the country fighting Kurdish guerrillas.

Since its invasion of Cyprus in 1974, Turkey has
maintained forces in the north of the island and at present
has about 30,000 men stationed there.

As a member of NATO, Turkey is host to the
Headquarters Allied Land Forces South-Eastern Europe
and the Sixth Allied Tactical Air Force Headquarters. US
(1,440 personnel) and UK (230 personnel) air force
detachments are based at Incirlik air base in southern
Turkey to patrol the air exclusion zone over northern Iraq.
MILITARY EXPENDITURE – 4.2 per cent of GDP (1997)
MILITARY PERSONNEL – 821,200: Army 525,000, Navy
51,000, Air Force 63,000, Paramilitaries 182,200
CONSCRIPTION DURATION – 18 months

ECONOMY

Agricultural production accounts for some 15 per cent of
GDP. About 50 per cent of the working population are in
the rural sector. The principal crops are wheat, barley, rice,
tobacco, sugar beet, tea, olives, grapes, figs and hazelnuts.
Most of the crops are grown on the fertile littoral. Tobacco,
sultana and fig cultivation is centred around Izmir, where
substantial quantities of cotton are also grown. The main
cotton area is in the Cukurova plain around Adana. The
forests which lie between the littoral plain and the Anatolian
plateau contain beech, pine, oak, elm, chestnut, lime, plane,
alder, box, poplar and maple.

After agriculture, Turkey's most important industry is
based on the considerable mineral wealth which is, however,
relatively unexploited. The main export minerals are
chromite and boron. Tourism is a major industry, with
over 8.5 million visitors in 1996.

The bulk of the country's requirements in sugar, cotton,
woollen and silk textiles, and cement, is produced locally.
Other industries include vehicle assembly, paper, glass and
glassware, iron and steel, leather and leather goods, sulphur
refining, canning and rubber goods, soaps and cosmetics,
pharmaceutical products, and prepared foodstuffs.

A customs union with the EU came into force on 1
January 1996 which was expected to boost the economy,
although Greece has managed to suspend EU aid packages.
A gas deal worth £14,800 million was signed with Iran in
August 1996 which provided for a 20-year supply of Iranian
gas.
GNP – US$199,307 million (1997); US$3,130 per capita
(1997)
GDP – US$171,225 million (1995); US$2,814 per capita
(1995)
ANNUAL AVERAGE GROWTH OF GDP – 7.4 per cent
(1996)
INFLATION RATE – 85.7 per cent (1997)
UNEMPLOYMENT – 6.6 per cent (1995)
TOTAL EXTERNAL DEBT – US$91,205 million (1997)

TRADE

The main imports are machinery, crude oil and petroleum
products, iron and steel, vehicles, medicines, chemicals and
electrical appliances. Agricultural commodities (cotton,
tobacco, fruits, nuts, livestock) represent 47 per cent of
total exports. Other exports are minerals, textiles, glass and
cement. Germany, the USA and Italy are the main trading
partners.

In 1997 Turkey had a trade deficit of US$15,466 million
and a current account deficit of US$2,750 million. In 1997
imports totalled US$48,585 million and exports US$26,245
million.

Trade with UK	1997	1998
Imports from UK	£1,766,992,000	£1,630,709
Exports to UK	1,043,429,000	1,164,664

COMMUNICATIONS

The rail network is run by the State Railways Administration. There are 8,549 km of railway track and 31,422 km of
state highways, including 125 km of motorways. The
Bosporus is spanned by two bridges; plans are being drawn
up for a third fixed link between the two continents. The
state airline (THY) operates all internal services and has
services to Europe, the Far East, Africa, North America
and the Middle East. Most of the leading European airlines
operate services to Istanbul and some also to Ankara.

EDUCATION

Education is free and secular, and since August 1997,
compulsory from the ages of six to 14. There are elementary,
secondary and vocational schools. There are 54 universities
in Turkey.

ILLITERACY RATE – 17.7 per cent
ENROLMENT (percentage of age group) – primary 96 per cent (1994); secondary 50 per cent (1994); tertiary 18.2 per cent (1994)

CULTURE

Turkish was written in Arabic script until 1926 when a version of the Roman alphabet reflecting Turkish phonetics was substituted for use in official correspondence and in 1928 for universal use, with Arabic numerals as used throughout Europe. The revolution of 1908 led to the introduction of native literature free from foreign influences and adapted to the understanding of the people.

TURKMENISTAN
Turkmenostan Respublikasy

AREA – 188,456 sq. miles (488,100 sq. km). Neighbours: Iran and Afghanistan (south), Uzbekistan (east and north), Kazakhstan (north-west)
POPULATION – 4,569,000 (1998 estimate); 4,483,000 (1996 census): 77 per cent Turkmen, 9.2 per cent Uzbek, 6.7 per cent Russian, together with smaller numbers of Kazakhs, Tatars, Ukrainians and Armenians. Most of the population are Sunni Muslims. The main languages are Turkmen (72 per cent), Russian (9 per cent), Uzbek (9 per cent). Turkmen is one of the Turkic languages
CAPITAL - Ashgabat(population, 407,000, 1990)
MAJOR CITIES – Chardzhou (164,000), Tashauz (114,000), 1990
CURRENCY – Manat of 100 tenesi
NATIONAL DAY – 27–28 October (Independence Day)
NATIONAL FLAG – Green with a vertical carpet pattern near the hoist in black, white and wine-red; and in the lower part of the carpet design two laurel branches; in the upper hoist a crescent and five stars, all in white
LIFE EXPECTANCY (years) – male 61.80; female 68.40
POPULATION GROWTH RATE – 3.4 per cent (1997)
POPULATION DENSITY – 9 per sq. km (1996)
URBAN POPULATION – 45.2 per cent (1989)
MILITARY EXPENDITURE – 2.7 per cent of GDP (1997)
MILITARY PERSONNEL – 19,000: Army 16,000, Air Force 3,000
CONSCRIPTION DURATION – 24 months
ILLITERACY RATE – 2.3 per cent
ENROLMENT (percentage of age group) – tertiary 21.7 per cent (1990)

The republic comprises five regions: Ashgabat; Chardzhou; Krasnovodsk; Mary; and Tashauz. The country is a low-lying plain fringed by hills in the south. Ninety per cent of the plain is taken up by the Obe Kara-Kum (Black Sands) desert. The climate is hot and dry.

HISTORY AND POLITICS

Situated at the crossroads of Central Asia, the area that is now Turkmenistan has been invaded and occupied by many empires: Persian; Greek under Alexander the Great; Parthian; Mongol. From the early 19th century until 1886 Turkmenistan was gradually incorporated into the Russian Empire. Soviet control over Turkmenistan was established on 30 April 1918 when it became an Autonomous Soviet Socialist Republic. The banks, cotton refineries and oil and gas fields were nationalized before a civil war broke out in July 1918, sparked by the intervention of British troops from Iran and India. The war ended in 1920 with the withdrawal of the interventionist forces; Turkmenistan

became a full republic of the Soviet Union in February 1925.

Turkmenistan declared its independence from the Soviet Union on 27 October 1991 and gained UN membership on 2 March 1992.

The autocratic government of President Niyazov has prevented any effective political opposition or free press through harassment and the continuation of authoritarianism. The political leadership has rejected political pluralism and instead a cult of personality has developed around President Niyazov. The Supreme Soviet voted on 30 December 1993 to extend the term of President Niyazov to 2002 and this was confirmed by a 99.99 per cent vote in a referendum on 15 January 1994. The Communist Party, renamed the Democratic Party, remains in power. Legislative elections to the *Khalk Maslakhaty* were won by the Democratic Party.

FOREIGN RELATIONS

In 1992 joint Turkmen–Russian armed forces of 34,000 army and air force personnel were established and remain in operation. In late 1993 Turkmen–Russian agreements were signed allowing Russian troops to protect the borders with Iran and Afghanistan; Russian citizens to undergo military training in Turkmenistan; Turkmen officers to train in Russia; and Turkmenistan to bear the cost of Russian forces in the country. Agreement on dual citizenship for ethnic Russians in Turkmenistan was also reached. In December 1993 Turkmenistan signed the CIS charter to become a full CIS member and in January 1994 became a member of the CIS economic union.

POLITICAL SYSTEM

The 1992 constitution declares the president head of state and government. The legislature is the 50-member *Majlis* (formerly the Supreme Soviet). The *Khalk Maslakhaty* (People's Council) is a supervisory body with no legislative powers.

HEAD OF STATE

President, Saparmurad Niyazov, *elected* 27 October 1990, *re-elected* 21 June 1992, *appointed head of government* 18 May 1992, *elected by referendum for an eight-year term* 15 January 1994

COUNCIL OF MINISTERS *as at July 1999*

Prime Minister, The President
Deputy PMs, Serdar Babayev (*Agriculture and Water Industry*); Orazgeldi Aydogdiyev (*Culture*); Saparmurad Nuryev (*Energy and Industry*); Rejep Saparov (*Foreign Economic Activity*); Yolly Gurbanmuradov (*Foreign Investment, Chair of State Bank Council on Foreign Economic Activity*); Khudaikuli Orazov (*Interbank Council*); Batyr Sarjayev (*Oil and Gas, Defence*); Djamal Geklenova (*Textile Industry*); Khudaykuli Khalykov (*Transport*)
Chairmen, Muhamed Nazarov (*Committee for National Security*); Tirkish Tyrmyev (*State Border Service*); Seyitguly Chareyev (*State Committee for Land Use and Land Reform*); Ishankuli Gulmuradov (*State Commodity and Raw Materials Exchange*); Ovezgeldy Atayev (*Supreme Court*)
Communications, Rovshan Kerkavov
Construction Materials Industry, Mukhammetnazar Khudaygulyyev
Economy, Matkarim Rajapov
Education, Abat Ryzayeva
Foreign Affairs, Boris Shikhmuradov
General Public Prosecutor, Kurbanbibi Atadjanova
Health and the Pharmaceutical Industry, Gurbanguli Berdymuhamedov

Interior, Poran Berdiev
Justice, Gen. Gurbanmuhamed Kasimov
Natural Resources and Environmental Protection, Pirdjan
   Kurbanov
Oil and Gas Industry and Mineral Resources, Rejapbay Arazov
Social Security, Eylaman Shikhiev
Trade and Foreign Economic Relations, Dortguly Aidogdyev
Transport, Senakuly Rakhmonov

EMBASSY OF TURKMENISTAN
2nd Floor South, St George's House, 14/17 Wells Street,
London WIP 3FP
Tel: 0171-255 1071
Ambassador Extraordinary and Plenipotentiary, HE Chary
   Babaev, apptd 1999

BRITISH EMBASSY
3rd Floor, Office Building, Ak Altin Plaza Hotel, Ashgabat
Tel Ashgabat 5106161/510861/510862
Ambassador Extraordinary and Plenipotentiary, HE Fraser
   Wilson, MBE, apptd 1998

ECONOMY

The large reserves of natural gas and the foreign revenue
that they earn make the country economically viable and
have enabled the government to maintain low stable prices
for basic commodities and utilities.

The principal industries are cotton cultivation, stock-
raising and mineral extraction, together with natural gas
production and the long-established silk industry. Some
fisheries exist along the Caspian Sea coast. Arable land is
irrigated by the Niyazov canal, which cuts through the
Kara Kum desert. There are estimated reserves of some
700 million tonnes of oil and 8,000,000 million cubic metres
of natural gas. Natural gas is exported by pipeline to
Ukraine and western Europe. A pipeline through Iran and
Turkey was opened in December 1997, and a pipeline to
Pakistan is under construction. A further pipeline is to be
built under the Caspian Sea, through Azerbaijan and
Georgia, to supply gas to Turkey.
GNP – US$2,987 million (1997); US$640 per capita
   (1997)
GDP – US$1,308 million (1995); US$321 per capita
   (1995)
TOTAL EXTERNAL DEBT – US$1,771 million (1997)

Trade with UK	1997	1998
Imports from UK	£10,679,000	£10,155,000
Exports to UK	1,912,000	554,000

TUVALU

AREA – 10 sq. miles (26 sq. km)
POPULATION – 10,000 (1994 UN estimate). About 1,500
   Tuvaluans work overseas, mostly in Nauru, or as
   seamen. The people are almost entirely Polynesian.
   The principal languages are Tuvaluan and English. A
   large majority of the population is Christian,
   predominantly Protestant
CAPITAL – ΨFunafuti (population, 2,856)
CURRENCY – The Australian dollar ($A) of 100 cents is
   legal tender. In addition there are Tuvalu dollar and
   cent coins in circulation
NATIONAL ANTHEM – Tuvalu Mo Te Atua (Tuvalu for
   the Almighty)
NATIONAL DAY – 1 October (Independence Day)
NATIONAL FLAG – Light blue ground with Union flag in
   top left quarter and nine five-pointed gold stars in the
   fly

POPULATION GROWTH RATE – 1.8 per cent (1996)
POPULATION DENSITY – 385 per sq. km (1996)

Tuvalu comprises nine coral atolls situated in the south-
west Pacific around the point at which the International
Date Line cuts the Equator. Few of the atolls are more
than 12 ft above sea level or more than half a mile in width.
The vegetation consists mainly of coconut palms.

HISTORY AND POLITICS

Tuvalu, formerly the Ellice Islands, formed part of the
Gilbert and Ellice Islands Colony until 1 October 1975,
when separate constitutions came into force. Separation
from the Gilbert Islands was implemented on 1 January
1976. On 1 October 1978 Tuvalu became a fully independent state within the Commonwealth.

In April 1998, Prime Minister Bikenibeu Paeniu was
sworn in for a second term of office; he was forced to resign
following his defeat in a motion of no confidence on 15
April 1999 and on 27 April was succeeded by Ionatana
Ionatana.

POLITICAL SYSTEM

The constitution provides for a prime minister and four
other ministers, who must be members of the 12-member
parliament. The prime minister presides at meetings of the
Cabinet, which consists of the five Ministers and is attended
by the Attorney-General. Local government services are
provided by elected Island Councils.

Governor-General, Sir Tomasi Puapua

CABINET *as at July 1999*

Prime Minister, Foreign Affairs, Tourism, Trade, Commerce,
   Ionatana Ionatana
Deputy PM, Finance and Economic Planning, Langi Tupu
   Tuilima
Attorney-General, Teleti Teo
Education, Sports and Culture, Health, Women's and Community
   Affairs, Teagai Esekia
Home Affairs and Rural Development, Natural Resources and
   Environment, Faimalanga Luka
Works, Energy and Communications, Samuelu Penitala Teo
BRITISH HIGH COMMISSIONER, HE M. Dibben, resident
   at Suva, Fiji

ECONOMY

Most people still practise a subsistence economy, the main
staples of the diet being coconuts and fish. The main
imports are foodstuffs, consumer goods and building
materials. The only export is copra, though philatelic sales
provide a major source of revenue and handicraft sales are
increasing. However, Tuvalu is almost entirely dependent
on foreign aid. In August 1998, Tuvalu signed a deal worth
several million US dollars with a Canadian media company,
granting rights to use the country's internet suffix of ".tv".

Funafuti has an airfield from which a service operates
regularly to Fiji and Kiribati, and is also the only port.
GDP – US$9 million (1995); US$914 per capita (1995)

Trade with UK	1996	1997
Imports from UK	£210,000	£306,000
Exports to UK	3,000	584,000

SOCIAL WELFARE

All islands are served by a dispensary and a primary school.
A maritime training school caters for 60 boys a year. There
is a 30-bed hospital at Funafuti.

UGANDA
Republic of Uganda

AREA – 93,065 sq. miles (241,038 sq. km). Neighbours: Democratic Republic of Congo (west), Sudan (north), Kenya (east), Tanzania and Rwanda (south)
POPULATION – 19,848,000 (1994 UN estimate). The official language is English. The main local vernaculars are of Bantu, Nilotic and Hamitic origins. Ki-Swahili is generally understood
CAPITAL – Kampala (population, 750,000, 1990)
MAJOR CITIES – Jinja (45,000); Masaka (29,000); Mbale (28,000)
CURRENCY – Uganda shilling of 100 cents
NATIONAL ANTHEM – Oh Uganda
NATIONAL DAY – 9 October (Independence Day)
NATIONAL FLAG – Six horizontal stripes of black, yellow, red, with a white disc in the centre containing the badge of a crested crane
LIFE EXPECTANCY (years) – male 43.57; female 46.19
POPULATION GROWTH RATE – 3.1 per cent (1997)
POPULATION DENSITY – 82 per sq. km (1996)
URBAN POPULATION – 13.9 per cent (1996)
MILITARY EXPENDITURE – 2.4 per cent of GDP (1997)
MILITARY PERSONNEL – 40,600: Ugandan People's Defence Force 40,000, Paramilitaries 600

Large parts of Lakes Victoria, Edward and Albert (Mobuto) are within Uganda's boundaries, as are Lakes Kyoga, Kwania, George and Bisina (formerly Salisbury) and the course of the River Nile from its outlet from Lake Victoria to the Sudan border at Nimule.

Despite its tropical location, the climate is tempered by its situation some 3,000 ft above sea level, and well over that altitude in the highlands of the Western and Eastern Regions. Uganda has three National Parks and a fourth (Lake Mburo) has been designated.

HISTORY AND POLITICS

Uganda became an independent state within the Commonwealth on 9 October 1962, after some 70 years of British rule. A republic was instituted in 1967, under an executive president assisted by a Cabinet of Ministers.

Early in 1971 an army coup took place and Maj.-Gen. Idi Amin, the army commander, proclaimed himself head of state. In 1979, following uprisings and military intervention by Tanzania, President Amin was overthrown. Dr Milton Obote became president in 1980 but was ousted by a military coup in 1985. A military council was installed but the National Resistance Movement led by Yoweri Museveni captured Kampala in January 1986, securing control of the rest of the country in the following few months. Yoweri Museveni was sworn in as president in January 1986.

President Museveni won the first direct presidential election on 9 May 1996. Supporters of the president won a majority of seats in legislative elections on 27 June. The ban on political party activity will continue until 2000.

POLITICAL SYSTEM

A Constituent Assembly was elected in March 1994 to draft a new constitution. The constitution, promulgated on 8 October 1995, endorsed the existing non-party political system. The legislature, the 276-seat National Assembly, is elected for a four-year term.

HEAD OF STATE
President, Yoweri Museveni, *sworn in* 29 January 1986, *elected* 9 May 1996

Vice-President, Specioza Wandira Kazibwe

CABINET *as at July 1999*
The President
The Vice-President
Prime Minister, Apolo Nsibambi
First Deputy PM, Foreign Affairs, Eriya Kategaya
Second Deputy PM, Tourism, Trade and Industry, Brig. Moses Ali
Ministers in the Office of the President, Kweronda Ruhemba (*Economic Monitoring*); Miria Matembe (*Ethics and Integrity*); Basoga Nsadhu (*Information*); Elizabeth Okwir (*Office of the Vice-President*); Ruhakana Rugunda (*Presidency*); Wilson Muruli Mukasa (*Security*)
Agriculture, Animal Industry and Fisheries, Kisamba Mugwera
Attorney-General, Bart Katureebe
Disaster Preparedness and Refugees, Maj. Tom Butiime
Education and Sports, Kiddu Makubuya
Energy and Minerals, Syda Bbumba
Finance, Planning and Economic Development, Gerald Sendawula
Gender, Labour and Social Development, Janet B. Mukwaya
General Duties, vacant
Health, Dr Crispus W. C. B. Kiyonga
Internal Affairs, vacant
Justice and Constitutional Affairs, Joshua Mayanja-Nkangi
Local Government, Jaberi Bidandi-Ssalli
Parliamentary Affairs, Rebecca Kadaga
Public Service, Amanya Mushega
Water, Lands and Environment, Henry Muganwa Kajura
Works, Housing and Communications, John Nassasira

UGANDA HIGH COMMISSION
Uganda House, 58–59 Trafalgar Square, London WC2N 5DX
Tel 0171–839 5783
High Commissioner, HE Prof. George Kirya, apptd 1990
Deputy High Commissioner, D. Ssozi
Financial Attaché, A. Bamweyana

BRITISH HIGH COMMISSION
10–12 Parliament Avenue, PO Box 7070, Kampala
Tel: Kampala 257054/9
High Commissioner, HE Michael Cook, apptd 1997
Deputy High Commissioner, P. Rouse, MBE
Defence Adviser, Lt.-Col. C. Thom, OBE

BRITISH COUNCIL DIRECTOR, S. Beaumont *(First Secretary)*

ECONOMY

Since 1988 the government has been successful in implementing an IMF recovery programme that has reduced the army and civil service, encouraged foreign investment, and returned property to Asians expelled by Idi Amin. In April 1998 the IMF and the World Bank agreed to grant Uganda debt relief totalling some US$360 million. In December 1998, the IMF pledged US$2.2 billion in economic assistance over a three-year period.

The principal export earners are coffee, tobacco, cotton and tea. Hydroelectricity is produced from the Owen Falls power station, some of which is exported to Kenya. The principal food crops are plantains, sugar cane, cassava, maize and sorghum; livestock raising and inshore fishing are also important.

In 1997 Uganda had a trade deficit of US$467 million and a current account deficit of US$388 million. Imports totalled US$1,313 million and exports US$558 million.
GNP – US$6,608 million (1997); US$330 per capita (1997)

GDP – US$6,000 million (1995); US$305 per capita (1995)

ANNUAL AVERAGE GROWTH OF GDP – 5.9 per cent (1996)

INFLATION RATE – 7.0 per cent (1997)

TOTAL EXTERNAL DEBT – US$3,708 million (1997)

Trade with UK	1997	1998
Imports from UK	£52,121,000	£45,643,000
Exports to UK	20,147,000	16,453,000

COMMUNICATIONS

There is an international airport at Entebbe, and eight other airfields around the country. Having no sea coast, Uganda is dependent upon rail and road links to Mombasa and Dar es Salaam for its trade. There are more than 27,000 km of roads. A railway network joins the capital to the western, eastern and northern centres.

EDUCATION

Education is a joint undertaking by the government, local authorities and voluntary agencies. In 1995 Uganda had an estimated 7,905 primary schools, 774 secondary schools, and various technical training institutions and universities.

ILLITERACY RATE – 38.2 per cent

ENROLMENT (percentage of age group) – tertiary 1.7 per cent (1995)

UKRAINE
Ukraina

AREA – 233,090 sq. miles (603,700 sq. km). Neighbours: Belarus (north), Russia (north and east), Romania and Moldova (south-west), Hungary, Slovakia and Poland (west)

POPULATION – 51,094,000 (1998 estimate); 51,471,000 (1989 census): 73 per cent Ukrainian, 22 per cent Russian, with smaller numbers of Jews, Belarusians, Moldovans, Tatars, Poles, Hungarians and Greeks. The majority religion is Orthodox Christianity, which is divided between the Ukrainian Orthodox Church (which owes obedience to the Russian Orthodox Church), the Autocephalous Ukrainian Orthodox Church and the Kiev Patriarchate Ukrainian Orthodox Church. There are also large numbers of Uniates and Reformed Protestants in the Transcarpathian region and a sizeable Jewish community in Kiev. The sole official language is Ukrainian, which is an Eastern Slavonic language related to Russian and Belarusian; Russian is the language of 22 per cent of the population

CAPITAL – Kiev (population, 2,630,000, 1996 estimate)

MAJOR CITIES – Dnipropetrovsk (1,147,000); Donetsk (1,088,000); Kharkiv (1,555,000); ΨOdesa (1,046,000), 1996 estimates

CURRENCY – Hryvna of 100 kopiykas

NATIONAL DAY – 24 August (Independence Day)

NATIONAL FLAG – Two horizontal stripes of blue over yellow

LIFE EXPECTANCY (years) – male 63.50; female 73.70

POPULATION GROWTH RATE – −0.3 per cent (1997)

POPULATION DENSITY – 85 per sq. km (1996)

URBAN POPULATION – 67.6 per cent (1995)

ILLITERACY RATE – 1.2 per cent

ENROLMENT (percentage of age group) – tertiary 40.6 per cent (1993)

The area of the present Ukraine is larger than that of the

Ukrainian Soviet Republic formed in 1917–19 because of the westward territorial expansion of the former Soviet Union in the 1939–45 period and the addition of the Crimea from Russia in 1954. Ukraine now consists of 25 regions: Cherkasy, Chernihiv, Chernivtsi, Crimea, Dnipropetrovsk, Donetsk, Ivano-Frankivsk, Kharkiv, Kherson, Khmelnytsky, Kiev, Kirovohrad, Luhansk, Lviv, Mykolaïv, Odesa, Poltava, Rivne, Sumy, Ternopil, Transcarpathia, Vinnitsa, Volhynia, Zaporizhya and Zhytomyr.

Most of Ukraine forms a plain with small elevations. The Carpathian mountains lie in the south-western part of the republic. The main rivers are the Dnieper with its tributaries, the Southern Bug and the Northern Donets (a tributary of the Don). The climate is moderate with relatively mild winters (particularly in the south-west) and hot summers.

HISTORY AND POLITICS

The earliest Russian state was formed in the middle reaches of the Dnieper River with its capital at Kiev in the ninth century AD. The state united the two large Slav states of Kiev and Novgorod and established the first common Russian language and nationality. The state lasted until Kiev fell to the Mongols in 1240. For the next four centuries Ukraine was invaded and ruled by Tatars, Turks, Poles, Hungarians and Lithuanians. In 1648 the Ukrainians threw off Polish rule to become independent and increasingly allied with Russia (formerly Muscovy). During the reign of Catherine the Great of Russia (1763–96) Ukraine and the Crimea came under Russian control.

Ukraine became a battleground in the Russian civil war before the imposition of Soviet rule in 1922. Ukraine became a constituent republic of the USSR on 30 December 1922.

Ukraine declared itself independent of the Soviet Union, subject to a referendum, after the failed Moscow coup in August 1991. The referendum was held on 1 December 1991 and 90 per cent of the electorate voted for independence.

Political power in Ukraine in 1991–4 rested with the former Communists, led by President Leonid Kravchuk, in loose alliance with the Rukh nationalist party.

In the June 1994 presidential election Leonid Kuchma defeated President Kravchuk. A power struggle soon developed between President Kuchma and the Supreme Council. Kuchma's reformist government lost a no confidence vote in the Supreme Council but the president refused to dismiss it, and in June 1995 secured the passing of a 'constitutional treaty' by the Supreme Council. This gives the president the power to appoint the government without reference to the Supreme Council and allows greater presidential power to rule by decree. These changes were incorporated into a new constitution adopted in June 1996. The constitution also provides for the Supreme Council to be renamed the People's Council (*Narodna Rada*) and for the creation of a Constitutional Court. Following a constitutional amendment in September 1997, half of the 450 Supreme Council seats are to be elected from single-seat constituencies by a simple majority, and the other 225 are to be filled by proportional representation from party lists, with a 4 per cent barrier for representation.

In legislative elections held in March 1998, the Communist Party of Ukraine won 119 seats, well short of an overall majority, but making it the largest party in the legislature. The Popular Democratic Party won 84 seats, and the People's Movement of Ukraine 46. OSCE observers noted serious shortcomings in the electoral process, including violence and discrimination against certain candidates that 'raise[d] questions about the neutrality of the state apparatus in the election'.

INSURGENCIES

The Crimean parliament voted to make Crimea an autonomous republic in September 1991, which was accepted by Kiev, but then voted for independence in May 1992, which was not accepted, and was suspended. A Russian nationalist, Yuri Meshkov, was elected President of Crimea in January 1994 and the Crimean parliament in May 1994 restored the suspended 1992 constitution declaring sovereignty. A constitutional and political crisis in Crimea caused by a power struggle between President Meshkov and the Crimean parliament from September 1994 onwards was resolved by Ukrainian intervention in March 1995. Direct presidential rule over Crimea was imposed in April 1995, to be lifted in August following elections to the Crimean parliament which saw a dramatic drop in support for pro-Russian parties. Arkady Demydenko was appointed Prime Minister of Crimea on 26 February 1996. A new constitution, which gave Crimea property and budget rights, came into effect in January 1999.

A referendum in June 1994 in the Donbass region of eastern Ukraine in favour of closer economic ties with Russia and making Russian an official language was overwhelmingly passed, as was one in the Crimea in favour of dual Russian–Ukrainian citizenship.

FOREIGN RELATIONS

Since the demise of the Soviet Union, Russia and Ukraine have clashed over defence issues. All strategic nuclear weapons were placed under a central CIS command in December 1991, but on the abolition of the central command in July 1993 the government claimed possession of all nuclear weapons on its territory. Despite international pressure, the Supreme Council only ratified the START I Treaty in February 1994 and the Nuclear Non-Proliferation Treaty in November 1994.

Under a January 1994 USA–Russia–Ukraine Treaty, Ukraine agreed to transfer its nuclear arsenal to Russia for dismantling over a seven-year period. This was completed in May 1996. In return Ukraine has received a territorial guarantee from Russia, a cancellation of a large part of its debt to Russia, and nuclear security guarantees from Russia and the USA. Ukraine will also receive low-grade uranium from Russia for use in its power stations; and economic and technical aid from the USA.

In May 1997, a treaty of friendship and co-operation was signed with Russia. Agreement was also reached over the division of the former Soviet Black Sea Fleet. Russia is to gain four-fifths of the fleet and will rent most of the port of Sevastopol. The rent will be used to pay off part of Ukraine's debt to Russia.

In February 1998, a treaty on economic co-operation was signed between Ukraine and Russia which will increase trade between them by up to US$2 billion. It was announced in September 1997 that there would be annual summits for EU–Ukraine relations.

HEAD OF STATE

President, Leonid Kuchma, elected 10 July 1994, sworn in 19 July 1994

CABINET as at July 1999

Prime Minister, Valery Pustovoitenko
First Deputy PM, Volodymyr Kuratchenko
Deputy PMs, Serhiy Tyhypko; Valery Smoly; Mykola Bilobotskyy; Mykhaylo Hladiy (Agro-Industrial Complex)
Agro-Industrial Complex, Borys Supikhanov
Chairman, Supreme Soviet, Alexander Tkachenko
Coal Industry, Serhiy Tulub
Culture and Art, Dmytro Ostapenko

Defence, Gen. Oleksandr Kuzmuk
Economy, vacant
Education, Valentyn Zaychuk
Emergency Situations and Protection of the Population from the aftermath of Chernobyl, vacant
Energy, Ivan Plachkov
Environmental Protection and Nuclear Safety, Vasyl Shevchuk
Finance, Ihor Mityukov
Foreign Affairs, Boris Tarasyuk
Foreign Economic Relations and Trade, Andriy Honcharuk
Head of the Security Service, Volodymyr Radchemko
Health, Rayisa Bohatyryova
Industrial Policy, Vasyl Hureyev
Interior, Yurii Kravchenko
Justice, Syuzanna Stanik
Labour and Social Policy, Ivan Sakhan
Transport, Ivan Dankevich
Without Portfolio, Anatoly Tolstoukhov

There are also 11 heads of state committees.

UKRAINIAN EMBASSY
60 Holland Park, London WII 3SJ
Tel 0171-727 6312
Ambassador Extraordinary and Plenipotentiary, HE Volodymyr Vassylenko, apptd 1998
Minister Plenipotentiary, Y. Kyrylenko

BRITISH EMBASSY
252025 Kiev Desyatinna 9
Tel: Kiev 462 0011/2/4
Ambassador Extraordinary and Plenipotentiary, HE Roland Smith, CMG, apptd 1999
Consul-General and Deputy Head of Mission, S. Butt
Defence Attaché, Capt. M. Littleboy
First Secretary (Commercial), R. Cook

BRITISH COUNCIL DIRECTOR – M. Bird, Ploscha 9, 252004 Kiev Bessarabska

DEFENCE

The Army has 4,014 main battle tanks, 1,823 armoured personnel carriers, 3,079 armoured infantry fighting vehicles, 3,749 artillery pieces and 236 attack helicopters. The Navy has four submarines, nine principal surface combat vessels and 11 patrol and coastal vessels at six bases. The Air Force has 786 combat aircraft and 24 attack helicopters.
MILITARY EXPENDITURE – 2.7 per cent of GDP (1997)
MILITARY PERSONNEL – 340,200: Army 171,300, Navy 12,500, Air Force 124,400, Paramilitaries 32,000
CONSCRIPTION DURATION – 18 months to two years

ECONOMY

The Communist-led government of 1991–4 was characterized by economic mismanagement and opposition to economic reforms. The economy came close to collapse because of hyperinflation caused by the printing of money to support uneconomic enterprises, industrial output and GDP fell dramatically, and Russia threatened to cut all oil and gas supplies as Ukraine could not pay in hard currency. Ukraine has joined the CIS economic union as an associate member and is likely to seek full membership for access to better trading relations with Russia.

President Kuchma has introduced a wide-ranging economic reform programme. Ukraine has received large amounts of foreign aid in support of this programme and for the closure of the Chernobyl nuclear plant which suffered a partial meltdown in 1986; however, the G-8 summit in June 1999 failed to agree to further financial assistance for the completion of two nuclear reactors to replace Chernobyl. An aid package worth US$3 billion was approved by international donors in October 1996 and in August 1997 the IMF approved a stand-by credit of more than US$500 million, subject to the implementation of economic austerity measures. A further IMF loan of US$2.2 billion was agreed in September 1998. Continuing economic difficulties led to the devaluation of the hryvna in February 1999.

Ukraine is still in disagreement with Russia over the division of assets and debts of the former Soviet Union. A large proportion of Ukraine's debt to Russia has been paid by granting Russian enterprises shares in Ukrainian firms which are to be privatized; the remainder of the debt has been rescheduled. Russia accounts for 40 per cent of Ukraine's trade turnover and supplies all its oil needs and more than half of its industrial raw materials and components. Agreement was reached with Turkey in June 1997 to build an oil pipeline which will reduce Ukraine's dependence on Russia. In May 1998 Ukraine signed an agreement with the USA allowing it to import the technology necessary to modernize its nuclear power industry.

The southern part of the country contains a coal-mining and iron and steel industrial area which was the largest in the former Soviet Union. Ukraine also contains engineering and chemical industries and ship-building yards on the Black Sea coast. Ukrainian agricultural production is good with large areas under cultivation with wheat, cotton, flax and sugar beet; stock-raising is very important. There are large deposits of coal and salt in the Donets Basin, of iron ore in Kryvyi Rih and near Kerch in the Crimea, of manganese in Nikopol, and of quicksilver in Nikitovka.

The major ports are Odesa, Mykolaïv, Kerch and Sevastopol.

In 1997 there was a trade deficit of US$4,205 million and a current account deficit of US$1,335 million. In 1996, imports totalled US$18,639 million and exports US$14,441 million.

GNP – US$52,625 million (1997); US$1,040 per capita (1997)
GDP – US$35,933 million (1995); US$694 per capita (1995)
INFLATION RATE – 15.9 per cent (1997)
TOTAL EXTERNAL DEBT – US$10,091 million (1997)

Trade with UK	1997	1998
Imports from UK	£164,777,000	£168,821,000
Exports to UK	38,777,000	50,762,000

UNITED ARAB EMIRATES
Al-Imarat Al-Arabiya Al-Muttahida

AREA – 32,278 sq. miles (83,600 sq. km) approximately.
  Neighbours: Oman (north-east and east), Saudi Arabia (south and west), Qatar (north-west)
POPULATION – 2,260,000 (1997 estimate), of which 75 per cent are expatriates. The official language is Arabic, and English is widely spoken. The established religion is Islam
CAPITAL – Abu Dhabi (population, 450,000)
CURRENCY – UAE dirham (Dh) of 100 fils
NATIONAL DAY – 2 December
NATIONAL FLAG – Horizontal stripes of green over white over black with vertical red stripe in the hoist
LIFE EXPECTANCY (years) – male 72.95; female 75.27
POPULATION GROWTH RATE – 4.8 per cent (1997)
POPULATION DENSITY – 27 per sq. km (1996)

The United Arab Emirates is situated in the south-east of the Arabian peninsula. Six of the emirates lie on the shore of the Gulf between the Musandam peninsula in the east and the Qatar peninsula in the west while the seventh, Fujairah, lies on the Gulf of Oman. The climate varies between hot and humid in May to September and mild with erratic rainfall in October to April.

HISTORY AND POLITICS

The United Arab Emirates (formerly the Trucial States) is composed of seven emirates (Abu Dhabi, Ajman, Dubai, Fujairah, Ras al-Khaimah, Sharjah and Umm al-Qaiwain) which came together as an independent state on 2 December 1971 when they ended their individual special treaty relationships with the British government (Ras al-Khaimah joined the other six on 10 February 1972). On independence, the Union Government assumed full responsibility for all internal and external affairs apart from some internal matters that remained the prerogative of the individual emirates.

FOREIGN RELATIONS

Relations with Iran remain strained over Iran's illegal occupation of three UAE islands in the Gulf (Abu Musa and the Two Tunbs).

POLITICAL SYSTEM

Overall authority lies with the Supreme Council of the seven emirate rulers, each of whom also governs in his own territory. The president and vice-president are elected every five years by the Supreme Council from among its members. The Supreme Council appoints the Council of Ministers. A 40-member Federal National Council, drawn proportionately from each emirate and composed of appointees of the rulers, studies draft laws referred to it by the Council of Ministers.

The legal system consists of both secular and religious courts guided by the Islamic philosophy of justice. Individual emirates retain their own penal codes and courts alongside a federal court system and penal code.

FEDERAL STRUCTURE

Each emirate has its separate government, with Abu Dhabi having an executive council chaired by the Crown Prince.

Emirate	Area (sq. km)	Population (1997)
Abu Dhabi	80,000	1,017,000
Ajman	259	137,000
Dubai	3,900	757,000
Fujairah	1,300	83,000
Ras al-Khaimah	1,700	152,000
Sharjah	2,600	439,000
Umm al-Qaiwain	777	39,000

HEAD OF STATE

President, HH Sheikh Zayed bin Sultan al-Nahyan (*Abu Dhabi*), *elected* 1971, *re-elected* 1976, 1981, 1986, 1991, October 1996
Vice-President, Prime Minister, HH Sheikh Maktoum bin Rashid al-Maktoum (*Dubai*)

SUPREME COUNCIL

The President
The Vice-President
HH Sheikh Sultan bin Mohammed al-Qassimi (*Sharjah*)
HH Sheikh Saqr bin Mohammed al-Qassimi (*Ras Al-Khaimah*)
HH Sheikh Hamad bin Mohammed al-Sharqi (*Fujairah*)
HH Sheikh Humaid bin Rashid al-Nuaimi (*Ajman*)
HH Sheikh Rashid bin Ahmad al-Mualla (*Umm al-Qaiwain*)

Council of Ministers *as at July 1999*
The Vice-President
Deputy PM, Sheikh Sultan bin Zayed al-Nahyan
Agriculture and Fisheries, Saeed Mohammed al-Raqabani
Communications, Ahmed Humaid al-Tayir
Defence, HH Gen. Sheikh Mohammed bin Rashid al-Maktoum
Economy and Commerce, HH Sheikh Fahim bin Sultan al-Qassimi
Education and Youth, Ali Abd al-Aziz al-Sharhan
Electricity and Water, Humaid bin Nasir al-Uways
Finance and Industry, HH Sheikh Hamdan bin Rashid al-Maktoum
Foreign Affairs, Rashid Abdullah al-Nuaimi
Health, Hamad Abdul Rahman al-Madfa
Higher Education and Scientific Research, HH Sheikh Nahyan bin Mubarak al-Nahyan
Information and Culture, HH Sheikh Abdullah bin Zayed al-Nahyan
Interior, Lt.-Gen. Mohammed Saeed al-Badi
Justice, Islamic Affairs and Awqaf (Religious Endowments), Mohammed Nakhira al-Dhahiri
Labour and Social Affairs, Matar Humaid al-Tayir
Minister of State for Cabinet Affairs, Saeed Khalfan al-Ghaith
Minister of State for Finance and Industrial Affairs, Dr Mohammed Khalfan bin Kharbash
Minister of State for Foreign Affairs, HH Sheikh Hamdan bin Zayed al-Nahyan
Minister of State for Supreme Council Affairs, HH Sheikh Majid bin Saeed al-Nuaimi
Petroleum and Mineral Resources, Ubayd bin Sayf al-Nasiri
Planning, HH Sheikh Humaid bin Ahmed al-Mualla
Public Works and Housing, Rakadh bin Salem al-Rakadh

Embassy of the United Arab Emirates
30 Princes Gate, London SW7 1PT
Tel 0171-581 1281
Ambassador Extraordinary and Plenipotentiary, HE Easa Saleh Al-Gurg, CBE, apptd 1991
Military Attaché, Col. M. K. S. Al-Hamadi
Cultural Attaché, A. Al-Marri

British Embassies
PO Box 248, Abu Dhabi
Tel: Abu Dhabi 326600
Ambassador Extraordinary and Plenipotentiary, HE Patrick Nixon, CMG, OBE, apptd 1998
Counsellor and Deputy Head of Mission, G. Pirnie
Defence and Military Attaché, Col. T. Dumas, OBE

PO Box 65, Dubai
Tel: Dubai 521070
Counsellor and Consul-General, N. Armour
Deputy Head of Post, H. Dunnachie, MBE

British Council Representatives
Abu Dhabi – R. Sykes, PO Box 46523, Abu Dhabi
Dubai – T. Gore (*Cultural Attaché*)

DEFENCE

The Army has 231 main battle tanks, 570 armoured personnel carriers and 433 armoured infantry fighting vehicles. The Navy has 19 patrol and coastal vessels. The Air Force has 99 combat aircraft and 49 armed helicopters.
Military Expenditure – 5.5 per cent of GDP (1997)
Military Personnel – 64,500: Army 59,000, Navy 1,500, Air Force 4,000

ECONOMY

The UAE is the Gulf's third largest oil producer after Saudi Arabia and Iran, with oil reserves of 200,000 million

barrels and gas reserves of 200,000,000 million cubic feet. Oil production in 1998 accounted for 30.5 per cent of GDP. Other important sectors of the economy are manufacturing (aluminium, cement, chemicals, fertilizers, ship repair), government services, construction, transport, communications and financial services. Tourism is growing in importance, with 1,919,000 visitors in 1994. Agricultural production (vegetables, dates, fruit, eggs, flowers, olives, animal husbandry) has increased due to large-scale water desalination and irrigation projects, with 250,000 hectares of agricultural land in 1996. There is no personal or corporate taxation apart from on oil companies and foreign banks. There are several free zones, where overseas companies can trade tax-free.

Fifteen major ports, of which nine are modern container terminals, handled 35 million tonnes of cargo in 1993. Six international airports (Dubai, Abu Dhabi, Sharjah, Ras al-Khaimah, Fujairah, Al Ain) are in operation.

Oil revenues over the past 30 years have enabled the government to invest heavily in education, health and social services, housing, transport and communications infrastructure, and agriculture, and enabled the UAE's citizens to have one of the highest GDPs per capita in the world.
GDP – US$39,096 million (1995); US$17,690 per capita (1995)
Annual Average Growth of GDP – 5.2 per cent (1995)

Trade with UK	1997	1998
Imports from UK	£1,546,747,000	£1,562,540,000
Exports to UK	515,698,000	459,111,000

EDUCATION AND SOCIAL WELFARE

In 1997 there were 668 government schools, where education is free; and 400 private schools. There are five universities. There were 41 hospitals in 1997.
Illiteracy Rate – 20.8 per cent
Enrolment (percentage of age group) – primary 78 per cent (1996); secondary 71 per cent (1996); tertiary 11.9 per cent (1996)

UNITED STATES OF AMERICA

Area – 3,536,278 sq. miles (9,158,960 sq. km).
Neighbours: Canada (north), Mexico (south)
Population – 270,298,524 (1998 estimate). The language is English. There is a significant Spanish-speaking minority
Capital – Washington DC (population, 7,051,495, 1992). The area of the District of Columbia (with which the City of Washington is considered co-extensive) is 61 sq. miles, with a resident population (1998 estimate) of 523,124. The District of Columbia is governed by an elected mayor and City Council
Major Cities –ΨChicago (2,802,079); Dallas (1,075,894); ΨDetroit (970,196); ΨHouston (1,786,691); ΨLos Angeles (3,597,556); ΨNew York (7,420,166); ΨPhiladelphia (1,436,287); Phoenix (1,198,064); San Antonio (1,114,130); ΨSan Diego (1,220,666), 1998 estimates
Currency – US dollar (US$) of 100 cents
National Anthem – The Star-Spangled Banner
National Day – 4 July (Independence Day)
National Flag – Thirteen horizontal stripes, alternately red and white, with blue canton in the hoist showing 50 white stars in nine horizontal rows of six and five alternately (known as the Star-Spangled Banner)

LIFE EXPECTANCY (years) – male 72.20; female 78.80
POPULATION GROWTH RATE – 1.0 per cent (1997)
POPULATION DENSITY – 28 per sq. km (1996)
URBAN POPULATION – 75.2 per cent (1990)

The coastline has a length of about 2,069 miles on the Atlantic, 7,623 miles on the Pacific, 1,060 miles on the Arctic, and 1,631 miles on the Gulf of Mexico.

The principal river is the Mississippi-Missouri-Red (3,710 miles long), traversing the whole country to its mouth in the Gulf of Mexico; its main affluents are the Yellowstone, Platte, Arkansas, and Ohio rivers. The chain of the Rocky Mountains separates the western portion of the country from the remainder. West of these, bordering the Pacific coast, the Cascade Mountains and Sierra Nevada form the outer edge of a high tableland, consisting in part of stony and sandy desert and partly of grazing land and forested mountains, and including the Great Salt Lake, which extends to the Rocky Mountains. In the eastern states large forests still exist, the remnants of the forests which formerly extended over all the Atlantic slope. The highest point is Mount McKinley (20,320 ft) in Alaska, and the lowest point of dry land is in Death Valley (Inyo, California), 282 ft below sea level.

AREA AND POPULATION

	Total land area 1990 (sq. km)	Population census 1990
The United States (a)	9,159,116	248,709,873
Outlying areas under US jurisdiction	10,929	3,862,431
Territories	10,888	3,862,238
Puerto Rico	8,875	3,522,037
Guam	544	133,152
US Virgin Islands	346	101,809
American Samoa	200	46,773
Northern Mariana Is.	464	43,345
Other US possessions	41	193
Population abroad (b)	–	925,845
TOTAL	9,170,045	253,498,149

(a) the 50 states and the Federal District of Columbia
(b) excludes US citizens temporarily abroad on business

RESIDENT POPULATION BY RACE 1998 ESTIMATE
(Thousands)

White	233,001
Black	34,431
*American Indian	2,360
Asian and Pacific Islanders	10,507
†Hispanic origin	30,250
Total	270,299

*Includes Eskimo and Aleut
†Persons of Hispanic origin may be of any race

IMMIGRATION

From 1820 to 1996, 63,140,227 immigrants were admitted to the United States. Total number of immigrants in 1996 was 915,900, of which 402,309 came from North and South America (163,572 from Mexico), 307,807 from Asia and 141,581 from Europe.

HISTORY AND POLITICS

The area which is now the USA was first inhabited by nomadic hunters who probably arrived from Asia c.30,000 BC. The first (failed) European colony was founded by Sir Walter Raleigh in 1585. By 1733 there were 13 British colonies, composed largely of religious non-conformists

who had left Britain to escape persecution; the French and Spanish had also founded colonies. Relations between the colonies reflected tensions and conflicts between the European powers in the 17th and 18th centuries; from 1689 to 1763 the French, with native Indians, frequently attacked British settlements. In accordance with the Peace of Paris (1763) Britain returned Cuba and the Philippines to Spain and received Florida in return and France ceded New Orleans and (until 1800) Louisiana to Spain.

The War of Independence broke out in 1775 largely because of the colonists' objection to being taxed by, but having no representation in, the British Parliament. The forces of the British government were defeated with French, Spanish and Dutch assistance. The Declaration of Independence which inaugurated the United States of America was signed on 4 July 1776; Britain recognized American sovereignty in 1783. The first federal constitution was drawn up in 1787; ten amendments, termed the Bill of Rights, were added in 1791. The 13 original states of the Union ratified the constitution between 1787 and 1790. Vermont, Kentucky and Tennessee were admitted in the 1790s but most of the states acceded in the 19th century as the opening up of the centre and west led to the creation of new states and European or neighbouring countries ceded or sold their territories to the USA.

The Civil War (1861–5) was fought over the issue of slavery, which was integral to the economy of the southern states but was opposed by the northern states. The northern states defeated the Confederacy of southern states (South Carolina, Georgia, Alabama, Florida, Mississippi, Louisiana), all of which had seceded from the Union between 1860 and 1861; they all re-entered the Union by 1870.

The USA emerged as a world economic and military superpower in the 20th century and played a decisive role in the two world wars, in which it was engaged between 1917 and 1918, and between 1941 and 1945. Its economic and military (including nuclear) supremacy gave the USA a key role in shaping the post-war world. The USA facilitated the rebuilding of Europe through the Marshall Plan, oversaw the creation of the United Nations, the International Monetary Fund and the International Bank for Reconstruction and Development, and underpinned the new liberal world economy. The USA contended for global supremacy with the USSR and the two superpowers engaged in a costly arms race and 'cold war' fought by proxy in the Third World. The USA's opposition to communism led it into wars in Korea (1950–3) and Vietnam (1964–73). President Richard Nixon initiated détente with Russia and China in the early 1970s but was forced to resign in 1974 over corruption allegations (Watergate).

POLITICAL SYSTEM

By the constitution of 17 September 1787 (to which amendments were added in 1791, 1798, 1804, 1865, 1868, 1870, 1913, 1920, 1933, 1951, 1961, 1964, 1967, 1971 and 1992), the government of the United States is entrusted to three separate authorities: the executive (the president and Cabinet), the legislature (Congress) and the judicature.

The president is indirectly elected by an electoral college every four years. There is also a vice-president, who, should the president die, becomes president for the remainder of the term. The tenure of the presidency is limited to two terms.

The president, with the consent of the Senate, appoints the Cabinet officers and all the chief officials. He makes recommendations of a general nature to Congress, and when laws are passed by Congress he may return them to Congress with a veto. But if a measure so vetoed is again passed by both Houses of Congress by two-thirds majority in each House, it becomes law, notwithstanding the

objection of the president. The president must be at least 35 years of age and a native citizen of the United States.

Presidential elections

Each state elects (on the first Tuesday after the first Monday in November of the year preceding the year in which the presidential term expires) a number of electors (members of the electoral college), equal to the whole number of Senators and Representatives to which the state may be entitled in the Congress. The electors for each state meet in their respective states on the first Monday after the second Wednesday in December following, and vote for a president by ballot. The ballots are then sent to Washington, and opened on 6 January by the President of the Senate in the presence of Congress. The candidate who has received a majority of the whole number of electoral votes cast is declared president for the ensuing term. If no one has a majority, then from the highest on the list (not exceeding three) the House of Representatives elects a president, the votes being taken by states, the representation from each state having one vote. A presidential term begins at noon on 20 January.

HEAD OF STATE
President of the United States, William Jefferson Blythe IV Clinton, *born* 19 August 1946, *elected* 1992, *re-elected* 5 November 1996, *sworn in* 20 January 1997. Democrat
Vice-President, Albert Gore, jun., *born* 31 March 1948

THE CABINET *as at July 1999*
Agriculture, Daniel Glickman
Attorney-General, Janet Reno
Commerce, William Daley
Defence, William Cohen
Education, Richard Riley
Energy, Bill Richardson
Health and Human Services, Donna Shalala
Housing and Urban Development, Andrew Cuomo
Interior, Bruce Babbitt
Labour, Alexis Herman
Secretary of State, Madeleine Albright

Transportation, Rodney Slater
Treasury, Lawrence Summers
Veterans' Affairs, Jesse Brown
Other senior positions:
Permanent Representative to the UN, Bill Richardson
Chair, Council of Economic Advisers, Janet Yellin
White House Chief of Staff, Erskine Bowles
National Security Adviser, Samuel Berger
Environmental Protection Agency, Carol Browner
Director, National Economic Council, Gene Sperling
Director, Office of Management and Budget, Franklin Raines
Director, Small Business Administration, Aida Alvarez
Director, US Information Agency, Joseph Duffey
Trade Representative, Charlene Barshefsky
Director of CIA, George Tenet
Director of FBI, Louis Freeh
Chairman, Federal Reserve Board of Governors, Alan Greenspan

UNITED STATES EMBASSY
24 Grosvenor Square, London WIA IAE
Tel 0171-499 9000
Ambassador Extraordinary and Plenipotentiary, HE Philip Lader, apptd 1997
Deputy Chief of Mission, R. Bradtke
Defence and Naval Attaché, Capt. J. Mader
Minister-Counsellors, L. A. Lohman (*Administrative*); C. A. Ford (*Commercial*); W. G. Griffith (*Consular*)

BRITISH EMBASSY
3100 Massachusetts Avenue NW, Washington DC 20008
Tel: Washington DC 588 6500
Ambassador Extraordinary and Plenipotentiary, HE Sir Christopher Meyer, KCMG, apptd 1997
Ministers, M. A. Arthur, CMG; S. J. Pickford (*Economic*); J. C. Taylor (*Defence Material*)
Head of British Defence Staff and Defence Attaché, Maj.-Gen. C. Vyvyan, CBE
Counsellor, R. French (*Management and Consul-General*)
Consul-General (*New York*) *and Director-General of Trade and Investment*, T. Harris, CMG

THE STATES OF THE UNION

The United States of America is a federal republic consisting of 50 states and the federal District of Columbia and of organized territories. Of the present 50 states, 13 are original states, seven were admitted without previous organization as territories, and 30 were admitted after such organization.

STATE (with date and *order* of admission)	LAND AREA sq. km	POPULATION (1998 estimate)	CAPITAL	GOVERNOR (end of term in office)	
Alabama (Ala.) (1819) (*22*)	131,443	4,351,999	Montgomery	Don Siegelman (*D*)	(2002)
Alaska (1959) (*49*)	1,477,268	614,010	Juneau	Tony Knowles (*D*)	(2002)
Arizona (Ariz.) (1912) (*48*)	294,333	4,668,631	Phoenix	Jane Dee Hull (*R*)	(2002)
Arkansas (Ark.) (1836) (*25*)	134,875	2,538,303	Little Rock	Mike Huckabee (*R*)	(2002)
California (Calif.) (1850) (*31*)	403,971	32,666,550	Sacramento	Gary Davis (*D*)	(2002)
Colorado (Colo.) (1876) (*38*)	268,658	3,970,971	Denver	Bill Owens (*R*)	(2002)
Connecticut (Conn.) § (1788) (*5*)	12,550	3,274,069	Hartford	John Rowland (*R*)	(2002)
Delaware (Del.) § (1787) (*1*)	5,063	743,603	Dover	Tom Carper (*D*)	(2000)
Florida (Fla.) (1845) (*27*)	139,853	14,915,980	Tallahassee	Jeb Bush (*R*)	(2002)
Georgia (Ga.) § (1788) (*4*)	150,010	7,642,207	Atlanta	Roy Barnes (*D*)	(2002)
Hawaii (1959) (*50*)	16,637	1,193,001	Honolulu	Ben Cayetano (*D*)	(2002)
Idaho (1890) (*43*)	214,325	1,228,684	Boise	Dirk Kempthorne (*R*)	(2002)
Illinois (Ill.) (1818) (*21*)	143,987	12,045,326	Springfield	George Ryan (*R*)	(2002)
Indiana (Ind.) (1816) (*19*)	92,904	5,899,195	Indianapolis	Frank O'Bannon (*D*)	(2000)
Iowa (1846) (*29*)	144,716	2,862,447	Des Moines	Tom Vilsack (*D*)	(2002)
Kansas (Kan.) (1861) (*34*)	211,922	2,629,067	Topeka	Bill Graves (*R*)	(2002)
Kentucky (Ky.) (1792) (*15*)	102,907	3,936,499	Frankfort	Paul Patton (*D*)	(1999)
Louisiana (La.) (1812) (*18*)	112,836	4,368,967	Baton Rouge	M. J. Mike Foster (*R*)	(1999)
Maine (Me.) (1820) (*23*)	79,939	1,244,250	Augusta	Angus King (*I*)	(2002)
Maryland (Md.) § (1788) (*7*)	25,316	5,134,808	Annapolis	Parris Glendening (*D*)	(2002)
Massachusetts (Mass.) § (1788) (*6*)	20,300	6,147,132	Boston	Argeo Paul Cellucci (*R*)	(2002)
Michigan (Mich.) (1837) (*26*)	147,136	9,817,242	Lansing	John Engler (*R*)	(2002)
Minnesota (Minn.) (1858) (*32*)	206,207	4,725,419	St Paul	Jesse Ventura (*Reform*)	(2002)
Mississippi (Miss.) (1817) (*20*)	121,506	2,752,092	Jackson	Kirk Fordice (*R*)	(1999)
Missouri (Mo.) (1821) (*24*)	178,446	5,438,559	Jefferson City	Mel Carnahan (*D*)	(2000)
Montana (Mont.) (1889) (*41*)	376,991	880,453	Helena	Marc Racicot (*R*)	(2000)
Nebraska (Neb.) (1867) (*37*)	199,113	1,662,719	Lincoln	Mike Johanns (*R*)	(2002)
Nevada (Nev.) (1864) (*36*)	284,396	1,746,898	Carson City	Kenny Guinn (*R*)	(2002)
New Hampshire (NH) § (1788) (*9*)	23,231	1,185,048	Concord	Jeanne Shaheen (*D*)	(2000)
New Jersey (NJ) § (1787) (*3*)	19,215	8,115,011	Trenton	Christine Whitman (*R*)	(2002)
New Mexico (NM) (1912) (*47*)	314,334	1,736,931	Santa Fé	Gary Johnson (*R*)	(2002)
New York (NY) § (1788) (*11*)	122,310	18,175,301	Albany	George Pataki (*R*)	(2002)
North Carolina (NC) § (1789) (*12*)	126,180	7,546,493	Raleigh	James B. Hunt, jun. (*D*)	(2000)
North Dakota (ND) (1889) (*39*)	178,695	638,244	Bismarck	Edward Schafer (*R*)	(2000)
Ohio (1803) (*17*)	106,067	11,209,493	Columbus	Bob Taft (*R*)	(2002)
Oklahoma (Okla.) (1907) (*46*)	177,877	3,346,713	Oklahoma City	Frank Keating (*R*)	(2002)
Oregon (Ore.) (1859) (*33*)	248,646	3,281,974	Salem	John Kitzhaber (*D*)	(2002)
Pennsylvania (Pa.) § (1787) (*2*)	116,083	12,001,451	Harrisburg	Tom Ridge (*R*)	(2002)
Rhode Island (RI) § (1790) (*13*)	2,707	988,480	Providence	Lincoln Almond (*R*)	(2002)
South Carolina (SC) § (1788) (*8*)	77,988	3,835,962	Columbia	Jim Hodges (*D*)	(2002)
South Dakota (SD) (1889) (*40*)	196,571	738,171	Pierre	William Janklow (*R*)	(2002)
Tennessee (Tenn.) (1796) (*16*)	106,759	5,430,621	Nashville	Don Sundquist (*R*)	(2002)
Texas (1845) (*28*)	678,358	19,759,614	Austin	George W. Bush (*R*)	(2002)
Utah (1896) (*45*)	212,816	2,099,758	Salt Lake City	Mike Leavitt (*R*)	(2000)
Vermont (Vt.) (1791) (*14*)	23,956	590,883	Montpelier	Howard Dean (*D*)	(2000)
Virginia (Va.) § (1788) (*10*)	102,558	6,791,345	Richmond	James Gilmore (*R*)	(2002)
Washington (Wash.) (1889) (*42*)	172,445	5,689,263	Olympia	Gary Locke (*D*)	(2000)
West Virginia (W. Va.) (1863) (*35*)	62,384	1,811,156	Charleston	Cecil Underwood (*R*)	(2000)
Wisconsin (Wis.) (1848) (*30*)	140,672	5,223,500	Madison	Tommy Thompson (*R*)	(2002)
Wyoming (Wyo.) (1890) (*44*)	251,501	480,907	Cheyenne	Jim Geringer (*R*)	(2002)
Dist. of Columbia (DC) (1791)	159	523,124	—	Anthony Williams (*D*) (*Mayor*)	

OUTLYING TERRITORIES AND POSSESSIONS

American Samoa	200	62,093	Pago Pago	Tauese Pita Sunia (*D*)	(2000)
Guam	544	149,101	Hagatna	Carl Gutierrez (*D*)	(2002)
Northern Mariana Islands	464	66,611	Saipan	Pedro P. Tenorio (*R*)	(1998)
Puerto Rico	8,875	3,860,091	San Juan	Dr Pedro J. Rossello (*D*)	(2000)
US Virgin Islands	346	118,382	Charlotte Amalie	James Turnbull (*D*)	(2002)

§The 13 original states
D Democratic Party; *I* Independent; *R* Republican Party

Cultural Attaché and British Council Director, D. Blagbrough
BRITISH CONSULATES-GENERAL – Atlanta, Boston, Chicago, Houston, Los Angeles, New York and San Francisco
BRITISH CONSULATES – Anchorage, Charlotte, Cleveland, Dallas, Denver, Kansas City, Miami, Minneapolis, Nashville, New Orleans, Philadelphia, Phoenix, Pittsburgh, Portland, St Louis, Salt Lake City, San Diego, Seattle and Puerto Rico
BRITISH-AMERICAN CHAMBER OF COMMERCE, 275 Madison Avenue, New York 10016; UK OFFICE, Suite 201, High Holborn, London WCIV 6RR

THE CONGRESS

Legislative power is vested in two houses, the Senate and the House of Representatives. The Senate has 100 members, two Senators from each state, elected for the term of six years, and each Senator has one vote. Representatives are chosen in each state, by popular vote, for two years.

The House of Representatives consists of 435 Representatives, a resident commissioner from Puerto Rico and a delegate each from American Samoa, the District of Columbia, Guam and the Virgin Islands.

Members of the 106th Congress were elected on 3 November 1998. The 106th Congress is constituted as follows:

Senate – Republicans 55; Democrats 45; total 100
House of Representatives – Republicans 223; Democrats 211; Independent 1; total 435

President of the Senate, The Vice-President
Senate Majority Leader, Trent Lott (*R*), *Mississippi*
Speaker of the House of Representatives, J. Dennis Hastert (*R*), *Illinois*
Secretary of the Senate, Gary Sisco
Clerk of the House of Representatives, Jeff Trandahl

THE JUDICATURE

The federal judiciary consists of three sets of federal courts: the Supreme Court at Washington DC, consisting of a Chief Justice and eight Associate Justices, with original jurisdiction in cases where a state is a party to the suit, and with appellate jurisdiction from inferior federal courts and from the judgments of the highest courts of the states; the United States Courts of Appeals, dealing with appeals from district courts and from certain federal administrative agencies, and consisting of 168 circuit judges within 13 circuits; the 94 United States district courts served by 575 district court judges.

THE SUPREME COURT
US Supreme Court Building, Washington DC 20543

Chief Justice, William H. Rehnquist, *Arizona,* apptd 1986

Associate Justices
John Paul Stevens, *Illinois,* apptd 1975
Sandra Day O'Connor, *Arizona,* apptd 1981
Antonin Scalia, *Virginia,* apptd 1986
Anthony M. Kennedy, *California,* apptd 1988
David H. Souter, *New Hampshire,* apptd 1990
Clarence Thomas, *Georgia,* apptd 1991
Ruth Bader Ginsburg, *New York,* apptd 1993
Stephen Breyer, *Massachusetts,* apptd 1994

Clerk of the Supreme Court, William K. Suter

In 1997 there were 13,175,070 recorded offences: murder and non-negligent manslaughter 18,210; forcible rape 96,120; robbery 497,950; aggravated assault 1,022,490;

burglary 2,461,100; larceny-theft 7,725,500; motor vehicle theft 1,353,700.

DEFENCE

Each military department is separately organized and functions under the direction, authority and control of the Secretary of Defence. The Air Force has primary responsibility for the Department of Defence space development programmes and projects.

Under strategic command the USA has 432 submarine-launched ballistic missiles, 680 inter-continental ballistic missiles, 174 heavy nuclear-capable bombers and 90 strategic defence interceptor aircraft together with multiple intelligence satellites, radars and early warning systems throughout the world.

The Army has 7,836 main battle tanks, 6,720 armoured infantry fighting vehicles, 17,800 armoured personnel carriers, 5,680 artillery pieces, 269 aircraft and 1,489 armed helicopters.

The Navy has 18 strategic submarines, 66 tactical submarines, 12 aircraft carriers, 29 cruisers, 57 destroyers, 40 frigates, 21 patrol and coastal vessels, 352 amphibious and support ships, 1,510 combat aircraft and 506 armed helicopters.

The Marine Corps has 403 main battle tanks, 1,322 amphibious armoured vehicles and 954 artillery pieces.

The Air Force has 206 long-range strike aircraft, 2,398 tactical combat aircraft and 220 helicopters.

The major deployments of US personnel overseas are: Germany (57,740); South Korea (36,128); Japan (39,180); Italy (10,380); UK (10,540); Panama (3,500); Turkey (2,430).
MILITARY EXPENDITURE – 3.4 per cent of GDP (1997)
MILITARY PERSONNEL – 1,443,600: Army 479,400, Navy 380,600, Marine Corps 171,300, Coast Guard 42,000, Air Force 370,300

Secretary of Defence (*in the Cabinet*), William Cohen
Chairman, Joint Chiefs of Staff, Gen. Henry Shelton

ECONOMY AND FINANCE

In 1998 central government budget receipts totalled US$1,721.4 billion and outlays US$1,651.4 billion. The largest items of expenditure were: defence US$270.4 billion; social security US$379.2 billion, income security US$232.9 billion, debt interest US$243.4 billion. Social welfare expenditure was US$1,363,884 million in 1993 including US$657,328 million (US$2,515 per capita) spent on social insurance, US$331,910 million (US$1,274 per capita) spent on education and US$74,503 million (US$286 per capita) spent on health.

At the end of September 1992 the total gross federal debt stood at US$4,002,062 million.
GNP – US$7,783,092 million (1997); US$29,080 per capita (1997)
GDP – US$6,954,787 million (1995); US$26,037 per capita (1995)
ANNUAL AVERAGE GROWTH OF GDP – 3.8 per cent (1997)
INFLATION RATE – 2.3 per cent (1997)
UNEMPLOYMENT – 4.5 per cent (1998)

GROSS DOMESTIC PRODUCT BY INDUSTRY 1997

	US$ millions
Private industries	7,083,258
Agriculture, forestry, fisheries	131,745
Mining	120,515
Construction	328,806
Manufacturing	1,378,869
Transportation and public utilities	676,313

Wholesale trade	562,755
Retail trade	712,890
Finance, insurance, and real estate	1,570,308
Services	1,656,849
Government and government enterprises	1,027,639
Statistical discrepancy	−55,792
TOTAL	8,110,897

AGRICULTURE

The total number of farms in 1998 was 2,191,510 with a total area of land in farms of 953,765,000 acres, and an average acreage per farm of 435 acres. Principal crops are corn for grain, soybeans, wheat, hay, cotton, tobacco, grain sorghums, potatoes, oranges and barley. Gross income from farming in 1997 was US$228 billion. Cash receipts from all crops in 1997 was US$112 billion and from livestock and livestock products US$97 billion.

MINERALS

The value of non-fuel raw mineral production in 1997 totalled an estimated US$39 billion. Mineral exports in 1997 were valued at US$37 billion, and imports at US$58 billion. In 1997 the following quantities of minerals were produced: iron ore 62,750,000 tons; marketable phosphate rock 45,100,000 tons; copper 1,910,000 tons; zinc 573,000 tons; lead 415,000 tons.

ENERGY

Production in 1997 was 72.51 quadrillion BTU, principally coal, natural gas and crude oil. Coal accounted for almost half of energy exports of 4.63 quadrillion BTU. Imports were 20.89 quadrillion BTU, of which crude oil was 17.65 quadrillion BTU, to meet consumption of 94.37 quadrillion BTU (quadrillion = 10^{15}).

TRADE

In 1997 the USA had a trade deficit of US$197,001 million and a current account deficit of US$166,803 million. Imports totalled US$899,020 million and exports US$688,697 million.

Trade with UK	1997	1998
Imports from UK	£20,967,631,000	£21,614,472,000
Exports to UK	25,028,913,000	25,614,472,000

COMMUNICATIONS

In 1997 there were 3.96 million miles of public roads and streets, of which 3.12 million miles were in rural areas and 0.84 million miles were in urban areas. Surfaced roads and streets account for 60.9 per cent of the total. An estimated total of US$101,256 million was spent in 1997 on public roads in the United States.

The ocean-going merchant marine on 1 January 1999 consisted of 29,827 vessels with a capacity of 73.7 million tonnes, of which 508 privately engaged in foreign trade. There were 189 ships in the National Defense Reserve Fleet of inactive government-owned vessels.

According to preliminary figures, US domestic and international scheduled airlines in 1998 carried 613,376,849 passengers over 619,296,949 revenue passenger miles. Operating revenues of all US scheduled airlines were US$113,857,190,132 in 1998. Total operating expenses rose to US$104,595,516,809 in 1998. Scheduled operations showed an operating profit of US$9,261,673,323 and a net profit of US$4,828,037,584 in 1998.

EDUCATION

All the states and the District of Columbia have compulsory school attendance laws. In general, children are obliged to attend school from seven to 16 years of age.

Most of the revenue for public elementary and secondary school purposes comes from federal, state, and local governments. Less than three per cent comes from gifts and from tuition and transportation fees.

Among the better-known universities are: Harvard, founded at Cambridge, Mass. in 1636, and named after John Harvard of Emmanuel College, Cambridge, England, who bequeathed to it his library and a sum of money in 1638; Yale, founded at New Haven, Connecticut, in 1701; Princeton, NJ, founded 1746.

ILLITERACY RATE – 0.5 per cent

ENROLMENT (percentage of age group) – primary 94 per cent (1995); secondary 90 per cent (1995); tertiary 81.0 per cent (1995)

US TERRITORIES, ETC

Responsibility within the federal government for the United States insular areas other than Puerto Rico and Kingman Reef lies with the United States Department of the Interior, either the Office of Insular Affairs (for American Samoa, Guam, the Northern Mariana Islands, the United States Virgin Islands, Navassa Island (3 sq. miles), Palmyra Atoll (1.56 sq. miles) and Wake Atoll (2.5 sq. miles) (shared with the United States Army Space and Missile Defense Command)) or the United States Fish and Wildlife Service (for Baker Island (0.59 sq. miles), Howland Island (1 sq. mile) and Jarvis Island (1.66 sq. miles), Midway Atoll (2 sq. miles) and Johnston Atoll (0.98 sq. miles) (shared with the Defense Special Weapons Agency)). Four of the eight populated insular areas are represented in the United States House of Representatives, Puerto Rico by a resident commissioner and American Samoa, Guam and the United States Virgin Islands each by a delegate. Although represented in the United States House of Representatives by a delegate, the District of Columbia was an incorporated territory for only three years, from 21 February 1871 to 20 June 1874.

THE COMMONWEALTH OF PUERTO RICO

AREA – 3,427 sq. miles (8,875 sq. km)

POPULATION – 3,827,038 (1997 estimate); 3,522,037 (1990 census). The majority of the inhabitants are of Spanish descent, and Spanish and English are the official languages

CAPITAL – ΨSan Juan, population of the municipality (1997 estimate), 436,334. Other major towns are: Bayamón (233,784); Carolina (189,853); ΨPonce (189,900)

Puerto Rico (Rich Port) is an island of the Greater Antilles group in the West Indies.

Puerto Rico was discovered in 1493 by Columbus and explored by Ponce de León in 1508. It was a Spanish possession until 1898, when the USA took formal possession as a result of the Spanish-American War.

The 1952 constitution establishes the Commonwealth of Puerto Rico with full powers of local government. The Legislative Assembly consists of two elected houses: the Senate of 27 members and the House of Representatives of 51 members. The term of the Legislative Assembly is four years. The Governor is popularly elected for a term of four years. Residents of Puerto Rico are US citizens. Puerto Rico is represented in Congress by a resident commissioner, elected for a term of four years, who has a seat in the House of Representatives but not a vote, although he has a right to vote on those committees of which he is a member. A plebiscite on the future constitutional status of Puerto Rico was held on 14 November 1993 in which 48 per cent voted to maintain the existing Commonwealth status, 46 per cent voted for full US statehood and 4 per cent for independence.

Principal crops are sugar cane, coffee, vegetables, fruits and tobacco. Most valuable areas of manufacturing are chemicals and allied products, metal products and machinery, and food processing.

Governor, Dr Pedro J. Rossello

Trade with UK	1997	1998
Imports from UK	£392,732,000	£349,400,000
Exports to UK	93,106,000	148,963,000

GUAM

AREA – 212 sq. miles (549 sq. km)
POPULATION – 145,780 (1997 estimate): 43 per cent Chamorro stock mingled with Filipino and Spanish blood. The Chamorro language belongs to the Malayo-Polynesian family, but with considerable admixture of Spanish. Chamorro and English are the official languages; most Chamorro residents are bilingual
CAPITAL – Hagatna. Port of entry, ΨApra

Guam is the largest of the Mariana Islands, in the north Pacific Ocean.

Guam was occupied by the Japanese in December 1941 but was recaptured by US forces in 1944. Under the Organic Act of Guam 1950, Guam has statutory powers of self-government, and any person born in Guam is a US citizen. A 21-member unicameral legislature is elected biennially. The Governor and Lieutenant-Governor are popularly elected. There is also a District Court of Guam, with original jurisdiction in cases under federal law.

Guam's two main sources of revenue are tourism and US military spending.

Governor, Carl Gutierrez
Lt.-Governor, Frank Blas

AMERICAN SAMOA

AREA – 77 sq. miles (199 sq. km)
POPULATION – 60,383 (1997 estimate)
CAPITAL – ΨPago Pago (population, 3,519)

American Samoa consists of the islands of Tutuila, Aunu'u, Ofu, Olesega, Ta'u, Rose and Swains Islands. Tutuila, the largest of the group, has an area of 52 sq. miles and a magnificent harbour at Pago Pago. The remaining islands have an area of about 24 sq. miles. Tuna and copra are the chief exports.

Those born in American Samoa are US non-citizen nationals, but some have acquired citizenship through service in the United States armed forces or other naturalization procedure. The 1960 constitution grants American Samoa a measure of self-government, with certain powers reserved to the US Secretary of the Interior. There is a bicameral legislature with popularly elected representatives and traditionally elected senators, and a popularly elected Governor.

Governor, Tauese Pita Sunia
Lt.-Governor, Togiola Tulafo

THE UNITED STATES VIRGIN ISLANDS

AREA – 134 sq. miles (347 sq. km)
POPULATION – 114,483 (1997 estimate)
CAPITAL – ΨCharlotte Amalie (population, 12,331, 1990), on St Thomas

The US Virgin Islands were purchased from Denmark and came under US sovereignty in 1917. There are three main islands, St Thomas (28 sq. miles), St Croix (84 sq. miles), St John (20 sq. miles) and about 50 small islets or cays, mostly uninhabited.

Under the provisions of the Revised Organic Act of the Virgin Islands 1954, legislative power is vested in the Legislature, a unicameral body composed of 15 senators popularly elected for two-year terms. The Governor is popularly elected. Those born in the US Virgin Islands are US citizen nationals. A referendum is to take place at a future date to determine the future political status of the islands.

Governor, Roy Schneider
Lt.-Governor, Kenneth E. Mapp

Trade with UK	1997	1998
Imports from UK	£11,184,000	£18,488,000
Exports to UK	1,078,000	11,682,000

NORTHERN MARIANA ISLANDS

AREA – 179 sq. miles (464 sq. km)
POPULATION – 63,763 (1997 estimate)
SEAT OF GOVERNMENT – Saipan (population, 52,706, 1995 census)

The USA administered the Northern Mariana Islands as part of a UN Trusteeship until the trusteeship agreement was terminated in 1986, bringing fully into effect a 1976 congressional law establishing the Northern Mariana Islands as a Commonwealth under US sovereignty. Most of the then residents became US citizens. Those born subsequently in the Northern Mariana Islands are US citizen nationals. There is a popularly elected bicameral legislature and a popularly elected Governor.

Governor, Pedro P. Tenorio
Lt.-Governor, Jesus Sablan

THE PANAMA CANAL

As a result of the Panama Canal Treaty 1977, the Canal Zone was disestablished, with all jurisdiction over the former Canal Zone reverting to Panama with effect from 1 October 1979. Under the treaty, the United States is allowed the use of operating areas for the Panama Canal, together with several military bases, although the Republic of Panama is sovereign in all such areas. The Panama Canal Commission, an arm of the US Government, will continue to operate the canal until noon on 31 December 1999. The Panama Canal Authority, a Panama government agency, will then assume administration of the waterway.

In the fiscal year 1998, the total number of transits by ocean-going commercial traffic was 13,025; canal net tons totalled 221,634,400; cargo tons totalled 192,091,000.

URUGUAY
República Oriental del Uruguay

AREA – 68,500 sq. miles (177,414 sq. km). Neighbours: Argentina (west), Brazil (north and east)
POPULATION – 3,203,000 (1994 UN estimate): predominantly of Spanish and Italian descent. Spanish is the official language. Many Uruguayans are Roman Catholics. There is no established church
CAPITAL – ΨMontevideo (population, 1,383,660, 1992)
MAJOR CITIES – Melo; Mercedes; Minas; ΨPaysandú; Punta del Este; Rivera; Salto
CURRENCY – Uruguayan peso of 100 centésimos

NATIONAL ANTHEM – Orientales, La Patria O La Tumba (Uruguayans, the fatherland or death)
NATIONAL DAY – 25 August (Declaration of Independence, 1825)
NATIONAL FLAG – Four blue and five white horizontal stripes surcharged with sun on a white ground in the top corner, next flagstaff
LIFE EXPECTANCY (years) – male 68.43; female 74.88
POPULATION GROWTH RATE – 0.7 per cent (1997)
POPULATION DENSITY – 18 per sq. km (1996)
URBAN POPULATION – 90.3 per cent (1996)
MILITARY EXPENDITURE – 2.3 per cent of GDP (1997)
MILITARY PERSONNEL – 26,520: Army 17,600, Navy 5,000, Air Force 3,000, Paramilitaries 920

The country consists mainly of undulating grassy plains. The principal river is the Rio Negro (with its tributary the Yi), flowing from north-east to south-west into the Rio Uruguay. The climate is temperate.

HISTORY AND POLITICS

Uruguay (or the *Banda Oriental*, as the territory lying on the eastern bank of the Uruguay River was then called) resisted all attempted invasions of the Portuguese and Spanish until the early 17th century; 100 years later the Portuguese settlements were captured by the Spanish. From 1726 to 1814 the country formed part of Spanish South America. In 1814 the armies of the Argentine Confederation captured the capital and annexed the province; afterwards it was annexed by Portugal and became a province of Brazil. In 1825, the country threw off Brazilian rule. This action led to war between Argentina and Brazil which was also settled by the mediation of the UK, Uruguay being declared an independent state in 1828. In 1830 a republic was inaugurated.

General elections held in 1984 marked the return to civilian rule after 11 years of presidential rule with military support. The first fully free presidential and legislative elections since 1971 were held in 1989, and were won by the *Partido Nacional Blanco*. After the 1994 elections a coalition government of the Colorado Party (CP), the Partido Nacional Blanco (PNB), the Party for the Government of the People (PGP) and the Civic Union (CU) was appointed by President Sanguinetti (CP). Legislative and presidential elections are due to be held in November 1999.

POLITICAL SYSTEM

Under the constitution the president (who may serve only a single term of five years) appoints a council of ministers and a Secretary (Planning and Budget Office), and the vice-president presides over Congress. The Congress consists of a Chamber of 99 deputies and a Senate of 30 members (plus the vice-president), elected for five years by proportional representation.

The republic is divided into 19 Departments, each with an elected governor and legislature.

HEAD OF STATE

President, Dr Julio María Sanguinetti, *elected* 27 November 1994, *took office* 1 March 1995
Vice-President, Hugo Fernández Faingold

COUNCIL OF MINISTERS *as at July 1999*

Economy and Finance, Luis Mosca (CP)
Education and Culture, Samuel Lichtensztein (PGP)
Foreign Relations, Didier Operti (CP)
Health, José Raúl Busto (CP)
Housing and Environment, Juan Chiruchi (PNB)
Industry, Energy and Mines, Dr Julio Herrera (CP)

Interior, Luis Hierro López (CP)
Labour and Social Security, Ana Lía Piñeyrúa (PNB)
Livestock, Agriculture and Fisheries, Sergio Chiesa (PNB)
National Defence, Dr Raúl Iturria (PNB)
Planning and Budget, Ariel Davrieux (CP)
Tourism, Benito Stem (CP)
Transport and Works, Lucio Caceres (CP)

CP Colorado Party; PNB Partido Nacional Blanco; PGP Party for the Government of the People

EMBASSY OF THE ORIENTAL REPUBLIC OF URUGUAY
2nd Floor, 140 Brompton Road, London SW3 1HY
Tel 0171-584 8192
Ambassador Extraordinary and Plenipotentiary, HE Dr Agustín Espinosa-Lloveras, apptd 1998

BRITISH EMBASSY
Calle Marco Bruto 1073, 11300 Montevideo (PO Box 16024)
Tel: Montevideo 622 3650
Ambassador Extraordinary and Plenipotentiary, HE Andrew Murray, apptd 1998

BRITISH-URUGUAYAN CHAMBER OF COMMERCE, Avenida Labertador Brig. Gen., Lavalleja 1641, P2-OF 201, Montevideo

ECONOMY

The economy is based on agriculture, primarily livestock. There are 10 million cattle and 25 million sheep. Rice, wheat, barley, linseed and sunflower seed are cultivated. Other foodstuffs (citrus, wine, beer), fishing and textile industries are also of importance.

Industrial development continues and, in addition to the greatly augmented textile industry, includes tyres, sheet-glass, three-ply wood, cement, leather-curing, beet-sugar, plastics, household consumer goods, edible oils and the refining of petroleum and petroleum products. There are some ferrous minerals, not extracted at present. Non-ferrous exploited minerals include clinker, dolomite, marble and granite.
GNP – US$20,035 million (1997); US$6,130 per capita (1997)
GDP – US$17,847 million (1995); US$5,602 per capita (1995)
ANNUAL AVERAGE GROWTH OF GDP – 5.1 per cent (1997)
INFLATION RATE – 19.8 per cent (1997)
UNEMPLOYMENT – 10.2 per cent (1995)
TOTAL EXTERNAL DEBT – US$6,652 million (1997)

TRADE

The major exports are meat and by-products, textiles, hides and bristle and agricultural products. The principal imports are raw materials, construction materials, oils and lubricants, automotive vehicles and machinery. Principal trading partners are Brazil, Argentina, the USA and Canada.

In 1997 Uruguay had a trade deficit of US$723 million and a current account deficit of US$321 million. Imports totalled US$3,716 million and exports US$2,726 million.

Trade with UK	1997	1998
Imports from UK	£77,446,000	£70,191,000
Exports to UK	74,582,000	53,643,000

COMMUNICATIONS

There are over 50,000 km of roads, including 12,000 km of national highways, and over 2,000 km of standard gauge railway in use. A state-owned airline, PLUNA, provides international services, and internal passenger and limited freight services are provided by TAMU, a branch of the Uruguayan Air Force. The international airport of Carrasco lies 12 miles outside Montevideo. The River Uruguay is navigable from its estuary to Salto, 200 miles north, and the Negro is also navigable as far as Mercedes. In December 1998, the Senate approved the construction of a 45-km bridge across the River Plate, linking Uruguay and Argentina.

EDUCATION

Primary and secondary education is compulsory and free, and technical and trade schools and evening courses for adult education are state controlled. The university at Montevideo (founded in 1849) has ten faculties and a new university has been built at Salto.

ILLITERACY RATE – 3.2 per cent
ENROLMENT (percentage of age group) – primary 96 per cent (1996); tertiary 29.4 per cent (1996)

UZBEKISTAN
O'zbekiston Respublikasy

AREA – 172,742 sq. miles (447,400 sq. km). Neighbours: Kazakhstan (north and west), Kyrgyzstan and Tajikistan (east), Afghanistan and Turkmenistan (south)

POPULATION – 24,000,000 (1998 estimate): 72 per cent Uzbek, 8 per cent Russian, 5 per cent Tajik and 4 per cent Kazakh, with smaller numbers of Tatars, Kara-Kalpaks, Koreans, Ukrainians and Kirghiz. The predominant religion is Sunni Muslim. Islam is tolerated within strict bounds; it is allowed to play no part in politics. The official language is Uzbek (72 per cent). Russian (8 per cent), Tajik (5 per cent) and Kazakh (4 per cent) are also spoken. Uzbek is one of the Turkic group of languages. In 1994 the government approved a six-year programme for the transfer of the Uzbek language to a Latin script

CAPITAL – Tashkent (population, 2,200,000, 1998 estimate)

MAJOR CITIES – Samarkand (370,000), which contains the Gur-Emir (Tamerlane's Mausoleum); Bukhara (228,000), which contains the Samanid Mausoleum and the Ulughbek Madrassah

CURRENCY – Soum of 100 tiyin

NATIONAL DAY – 1 September (Independence Day)

NATIONAL FLAG – Three horizontal stripes of blue, white, green, with the white fimbriated in red; on the blue near the hoist a crescent and twelve stars, all in white

LIFE EXPECTANCY (years) – male 66.00; female 72.10

POPULATION GROWTH RATE – 2.0 per cent (1997)

POPULATION DENSITY – 51 per sq. km (1996)

URBAN POPULATION – 38.8 per cent (1994)

MILITARY EXPENDITURE – 3.9 per cent of GDP (1997)

MILITARY PERSONNEL – 74,000: Army 50,000, Air Force 4,000, Paramilitaries 20,000

CONSCRIPTION DURATION – 18 months

ILLITERACY RATE – 2.8 per cent

ENROLMENT (percentage of age group) – tertiary 32.9 per cent (1992)

Uzbekistan occupies the south-central part of former Soviet Central Asia, lying between the high Tienshan Mountains and the Pamir highlands in the east and south-east and sandy lowlands in the west and north-west, in the basin of the Amudarya and Syrdarya rivers. Uzbekistan consists of the Republic of Karakalpakstan and 12 regions: Andijan, Bukhara, Jizak, Fergana, Kashka-Darya, Khorezm, Naman-ghan, Navoi, Samarkand, Surhan-Darya, Syr-Darya and Tashkent. Most of the country is a plain with huge waterless deserts, and several large oases which form the main centres of population and economic life. The climate is hot, continental and dry.

HISTORY AND POLITICS

The ancient kingdoms of Khorazmshahs, Afrosiyab and Sogdiana flourished during the first millennium BC. Between the sixth and fourth centuries BC the area that is now Uzbekistan was under the control of the Persians and then Alexander the Great. In the 13th century the area became the centre of a great Muslim empire under Amir Timur (Tamerlane), with its capital at Samarkand. By the beginning of the 19th century three independent Khanates, Khiva, Kokand and Bukhara, existed in what is now Uzbekistan. These were annexed to the Russian Empire in the second half of the 19th century. In November 1917 a Communist revolution broke out in Tashkent and parts of Uzbekistan were included in the Turkestan Soviet Republic at its formation in 1918. The remainder of Uzbekistan was under the rule of the independent states of Khiva and Bukhara, which had re-emerged in 1918, until they were defeated by the Red Army and Soviet rule was established throughout the area in 1921. Under Soviet rule a massive land irrigation programme was implemented to allow the cultivation of cotton.

Uzbekistan declared its independence from the Soviet Union on 1 September 1991. Its independence was confirmed in a referendum on 29 December and recognized internationally. Elections to the new *Oliy Majlis* were held on 25 December 1994 and won by the ruling People's Democratic Party (PDP) and its allies with a total of 205 seats. Legislative elections are due to be held in December 1999.

The government of President Karimov is formed by the People's Democratic Party. Despite the constitutionally guaranteed freedom of religion and thought, and respect for human rights and multiparty democracy, censorship is still widely used and little political opposition is tolerated. The main opposition parties, Erk (Freedom) and Birlik (Unity) nationalist parties, have been continually banned since the introduction of the multiparty constitution in December 1992. In March 1995 President Karimov's hold on power was confirmed when his term of office was extended to 2000 by a national referendum.

FOREIGN RELATIONS

Uzbekistan has actively supported international efforts to resolve the conflict in Afghanistan. It was announced in February 1999 that Uzbekistan was to withdraw from the collective security treaty of the Commonwealth of Independent States. Uzbekistan is a member of the UN, OSCE, UNESCO, WHO and many other international organizations.

POLITICAL SYSTEM

Under the constitution of December 1992, the president and government hold executive power. The president may serve a maximum of two five-year terms and has the power to dissolve the 250-member unicameral Supreme Assembly (*Oliy Majlis*), which may not remove or impeach the president.

HEAD OF STATE

President, Islam Karimov, *elected* 29 December 1991, *elected by referendum for a five-year term* 26 March 1995

CABINET *as at August 1999*
Chairman of the Cabinet, The President
Prime Minister, Utkur Sultanov
Deputy PMs, Bakhtiyar Khamidov; Khamidulla
  Karamatov; Dilbar Ghulomova; Mirabror Usmanov;
  Rustam Junusov; Anatoliy Isaev; Bakhtiyor Alimjanov;
  Viktor Chjen; Lerik Ahmetov; Valery Ataev
Agriculture, Islam Babadjanov
Chairman, National Parliament, Erkin Khalilov
Communications, Abduwahid Djurabaev
Cultural Affairs, Khairulla Djuraev
Defence, Maj.-Gen. Khikmatulla Tursunov
Education, Djura Yuldashev
Emergency Situations, Bakhodir Kasimov
Finance, Rustam Azimov
Foreign Affairs, Abdulaziz Kamilov
Foreign Economic Relations, Elyor Majidovich Ganiev
Health, Feruz Nazirov
Higher and Secondary Specialized Education, Saidahror
  Ghulomov
Interior, Zokirzhon Almatov
Justice, Sirojiddin Mirsafaev
Labour, vacant
Municipal Economy, Gafurjan Mukhamedov
Power and Electrification, Valeriy Ataev
Social Security, Akildjon Abidov
Water Resources and Land Improvement, Marks Djumaniasov

EMBASSY OF THE REPUBLIC OF UZBEKISTAN
41 Holland Park, London WII 2RP
Tel: 0171-229 7679
Ambassador Extraordinary and Plenipotentiary, HE Fatih
  Teshabaev, apptd 1997

BRITISH EMBASSY
Ul. Gogolya 67, Tashkent 700000
Tel: Tashkent 1206822
Ambassador Extraordinary and Plenipotentiary, HE
  Christopher Ingham, apptd 1998

ECONOMY

Uzbekistan signed an economic agreement with Kazakhstan in January 1994 to allow the free circulation of goods, services and capital and the co-ordination of credit and finance policies, budgets, taxation and customs duties. Uzbekistan is also a member of the CIS economic union and in 1994 signed an economic treaty with Russia to provide for mutually convertible currencies and to enhance private business links. In 1994–5 the government embarked on an economic reform programme under which subsidies on foodstuffs and transport were abolished and those on public utilities reduced. Peasant farmers have been granted private plots of land and inflation has been reduced.

Uzbekistan's economy is based on intensive agricultural production, which accounts for over 20 per cent of GDP. Cotton production is approximately 4 million tonnes per year, made possible by extensive irrigation schemes. Textile manufacture, silk production and leather goods are also important. Wheat, potatoes and rice are widely grown. In 1997 agricultural output increased by 4 per cent. In addition there are some agricultural and textile machinery plants and several chemical combines. Uzbekistan possesses extensive mineral deposits. Copper, uranium, oil, gold and many other metals are extracted. In 1997 oil output was 7.9 million tonnes, and gas production was 50 billion cubic metres. The Muruntao mine is the largest open-cast gold mine in the world; in 1997, 85 tonnes of gold were produced.

Foreign direct investment exceeds US$6.2 billion. South Korea, the USA, Japan, Turkey and the UK are the main investors.

GNP – US$24,236 million (1997); US$1,020 per capita (1997)
GDP – US$9,908 million (1995); US$435 per capita (1995)
UNEMPLOYMENT – 0.4 per cent (1995)
TOTAL EXTERNAL DEBT – US$2,761 million (1997)

Trade with UK	1997	1998
Imports from UK	£91,001,000	£35,709,000
Exports to UK	17,377,000	7,413,000

VANUATU
Ripablik Blong Vanuatu

AREA – 4,706 sq. miles (12,189 sq. km)
POPULATION – 169,000 (1994 UN estimate). About 95
  per cent are Melanesian, the rest being mostly
  Micronesian, Polynesian and European. The national
  language is Bislama, but English and French are also
  official languages
CAPITAL – ΨPort Vila (population, 26,100, 1993), on
  Efate
MAJOR TOWN – Luganville (8,800, 1993), on Espiritu
  Santo
CURRENCY – Vatu of 100 centimes
NATIONAL ANTHEM – Nasonal sing sing blong Vanuatu
NATIONAL DAY – 30 July (Independence Day)
NATIONAL FLAG – Red over green with a black triangle
  in the hoist, the three parts being divided by
  fimbriations of black and yellow, and in the centre of
  the black triangle a boar's tusk overlaid by two crossed
  fern leaves
LIFE EXPECTANCY (years) – male 63.48; female 67.34
POPULATION GROWTH RATE – 2.7 per cent (1996)
POPULATION DENSITY – 14 per sq. km (1996)
URBAN POPULATION – 18.4 per cent (1989)
ENROLMENT (percentage of age group) – primary 74 per
  cent (1989); secondary 17 per cent (1991)

Vanuatu is situated in the South Pacific Ocean. It includes 13 large and some 70 small islands, of coral and volcanic origin, including the Banks and Torres Islands in the north. The principal islands are Vanua Lava, Espiritu Santo, Maewo, Pentecost, Ambae, Malekula, Ambrym, Epi, Efate, Erromango, Tanna and Aneityum. Most islands are mountainous and there are active volcanoes on several. The climate is oceanic tropical, moderated by the southeast trade winds which blow between May and October. At other times winds are variable and cyclones may occur.

HISTORY AND POLITICS

Vanuatu, the former Anglo-French Condominium of the New Hebrides, became an independent republic within the Commonwealth on 30 July 1980. Parliament consists of 50 members elected for a term of four years. A Council of Chiefs advises on matters of custom. Executive power is held by the prime minister (elected from and by parliament) and a Council of Ministers who are responsible to parliament. The president is elected for a five-year term by the presidents of the six provincial governments and the members of parliament.

HEAD OF STATE
President, HE Fr John Bani, *elected* 24 March 1999

COUNCIL OF MINISTERS *as at July 1999*
Prime Minister, Agriculture, Forestry and Fisheries, Donald
  Kalpokas (VP)
Deputy PM, Trade and Commerce, Willie Jimmy (UMP)
Education, Youth and Sports, Joe Natuman (VP)
Finance, Sela Molisa (VP)
Health, Jean Keasipai (JFM)
Infrastructure, Public Utilities, Henri Taga (UMP)
Internal Affairs, Vincent Boulekone (UMP)
Lands, Geology and Mines, John Morrison Willy (VP)
Ministerial Assistants, Steven Iatika (Ind.) (*Economic
  Development*); Daniel Bangtor (VP) (*Economic Reforms*);
  Willie Ollie Varasmaite (VP) (*Education*); Clement Leo
  (VP) (*Foreign Affairs*); Paul Telukluk (UMP) (*Local
  Business Development*)

VP Vanuaaku Pati; JFM John Frum Movement; Ind.
Independent; UMP Union of Moderate Parties

HIGH COMMISSIONER TO GREAT BRITAIN, vacant,
  resident at Port Vila, Vanuatu

BRITISH HIGH COMMISSION
KPMG House, Rue Pasteur, PO Box 567, Port Vila
Tel: Vila 23100
High Commissioner, HE Malcolm Hilson, apptd 1997

ECONOMY

Most of the population is employed on plantations or in
subsistence agriculture. Subsistence crops include yams,
taro, manioc, sweet potato and breadfruit; principal cash
crops are copra, cocoa and coffee. Cattle are kept on the
plantations and beef is the second largest export. Principal
exports are copra, meat (frozen, tinned and chilled), timber
and cocoa.
  There were 46,000 tourists in 1996. The absence of
direct taxation has led to growth in the finance and
associated industries.
  In 1995 Vanuatu had a trade deficit of US$51 million
and a current account deficit of US$18 million. In 1996
imports totalled US$97 million and exports totalled US$30
million.
GNP – US$238 million (1997); US$1,340 per capita
  (1997)
GDP – US$218 million (1995); US$1,289 per capita
  (1995)
ANNUAL AVERAGE GROWTH OF GDP – 3.2 per cent
  (1995)
INFLATION RATE – 2.8 per cent (1997)
TOTAL EXTERNAL DEBT – US$47 million (1996)

Trade with UK	1997	1998
Imports from UK	£158,000	£206,000
Exports to UK	677,000	25,000

VATICAN CITY STATE
Stato della Città del Vaticano

AREA – 0.2 sq. miles (0.44 sq. km). Neighbour: Italy
POPULATION – 1,000 (1994 UN estimate). The language
  is Italian
CAPITAL – Vatican City (population, 766, 1988)
CURRENCY – Italian currency is legal tender
NATIONAL DAY – 22 October (Inauguration of present
  Pontiff)
NATIONAL FLAG – Square flag; equal vertical bands of
  yellow (next staff), and white; crossed keys and triple
  crown device on white band
POPULATION GROWTH RATE – 0.0 per cent (1996)

POPULATION DENSITY – 2,273 per sq. km (1996)
GDP – US$19 million (1995); US$19,121 per capita
  (1995)

The office of the ecclesiastical head of the Roman Catholic
Church (Holy See) is vested in the Pope, the Sovereign
Pontiff. For many centuries the Sovereign Pontiff exercised
temporal power but by 1870 the Papal States had become
part of unified Italy. The temporal power of the Pope was
in suspense until the treaty of 1929 which recognized the
full and independent sovereignty of the Holy See in the
City of the Vatican.

Sovereign Pontiff, His Holiness Pope John Paul II (Karol
  Wojtyła), *born* at Wadowice (Kraków, Poland), 18 May
  1920, *elected* Pope in succession to Pope John Paul I, 16
  October 1978
Secretary of State, Cardinal Angelo Sodano, *apptd* December
  1990

APOSTOLIC NUNCIATURE
54 Parkside, London SW19 5NF
Tel 0181-946 1410/7971
Apostolic Nuncio, HE Archbishop Pablo Puente, apptd 1997

BRITISH EMBASSY TO THE HOLY SEE
91 Via Condotti, I–00187 Rome
Tel: Rome 6992 3561
Ambassador Extraordinary and Plenipotentiary, HE Mark
  Pellew, LVO, apptd 1997

Trade with UK	1997	1998
Imports from UK	£1,497,000	£1,469,000
Exports to UK	139,000	105,000

VENEZUELA
República de Venezuela

AREA – 352,145 sq. miles (912,050 sq. km). Neighbours:
  Colombia (west), Guyana (east), Brazil (south)
POPULATION – 22,710,000 (1994 UN estimate): 67 per
  cent Mestizo, 21 per cent white, 10 per cent black and 2
  per cent Indian. The language is Spanish. 96 per cent of
  the population is Roman Catholic
CAPITAL – Caracas (population, 2,784,042, 1990)
MAJOR CITIES – Barquisimeto (793,565); ΨMaracaibo
  (1,660,233); Maracay (449,180); Valencia (1,225,342),
  1997 estimates
CURRENCY – Bolívar (Bs) of 100 céntimos
NATIONAL ANTHEM – Gloria Al Bravo Pueblo (Glory to
  the brave people)
NATIONAL DAY – 5 July
NATIONAL FLAG – Three horizontal stripes of yellow,
  blue, red with an arc of seven white stars on the blue
  stripe
LIFE EXPECTANCY (years) – male 66.68; female 72.80
POPULATION GROWTH RATE – 2.7 per cent (1996)
POPULATION DENSITY – 25 per sq. km (1996)
URBAN POPULATION – 84.1 per cent (1990)
ILLITERACY RATE – 6.5 per cent
ENROLMENT (percentage of age group) – primary 84 per
  cent (1996); secondary 22 per cent (1996); tertiary 28.5
  per cent (1991)

Included in the area of the South American republic of
Venezuela are 72 islands off the coast, with a total area of
about 14,650 sq. miles, the largest being Margarita (area,
about 400 sq. miles), which is politically associated with
Tortuga, Cubagua and Coche to form the state of Nueva
Esparta.

The mountains are the Eastern Andes and Maritime Andes, running south-west to north-east. The main range is known as the Sierra Nevada de Mérida, and contains Pico Bolivar (16,411 ft) and Picacho de la Sierra (15,420 ft). The principal river is the Orinoco, with innumerable affluents, the main river exceeding 1,600 miles in length. The upper waters of the Orinoco are united with those of the Rio Negro (a Brazilian tributary of the Amazon) by a natural river or canal, known as the Casiquiare. The coastal regions contain many lagoons and lakes, of which Maracaibo (area 8,296 sq. miles) is the largest lake in South America.

The climate is tropical, except where modified by altitude or tempered by sea breezes.

HISTORY AND POLITICS

The first Spanish settlement was established at Cumaná in 1520. During the 18th century there were a number of uprisings against Spanish rule, and troops led by Simón Bolívar finally defeated the Spanish in 1823. Venezuela became an independent republic in 1830.

Carlos Andrés Pérez and the (Social Democratic) Democratic Action (AD) party came to power in December 1988. They successfully introduced a series of free market economic reforms which led to impressive economic growth but increasing social problems. Two military coup attempts in 1992 were defeated. Former President Rafael Caldera won the ensuing presidential election in December 1993. Legislative elections were held on 8 November 1998 and were won by the Patriotic Front movement (PF), a coalition of 14 minor parties led by the Fifth Republic Movement. Hugo Chávez Frías of the PF was elected president on 6 December 1998. On 25 April 1999, a referendum on convening a constituent assembly to rewrite the constitution was passed, with more than 85 per cent of voters in favour; however only a minority of those eligible cast their vote. An election to decide the members of the constituent assembly was held on 25 July 1999.

POLITICAL SYSTEM

Under the 1961 constitution, executive power is held by the president, who also appoints the Council of Ministers. Legislative power is exercised by a bicameral National Congress, comprising a 201-member Chamber of Deputies and a Senate of 46 elected members plus the former presidents of constitutional governments as life members. The president and National Congress are directly elected for concurrent five-year terms.

FEDERAL STRUCTURE

Venezuela is divided into 22 states and two federal districts.

State	Area (sq. km)	Population (1990)	Capital
Amazonas	175,750	60,207	Puerto Ayacucho
Anzoátegui	43,300	924,074	Barcelona
Apure	76,500	305,132	San Fernando
Aragua	7,014	1,194,982	Maracay
Barinas	35,200	456,246	Barinas
Bolívar	238,000	968,695	Ciudad Bolívar
Carabobo	4,650	1,558,608	Valencia
Cojedes	14,800	196,526	San Carlos
Delta Amacuro	40,200	91,085	Tucupita
Falcón	24,800	632,513	Coro
Federal District	1,930	2,265,874	Caracas
Federal Dependen- cies	120	2,245	—
Guárico	64,986	525,737	San Juan
Lara	19,800	1,270,196	Barquisimeto
Mérida	11,300	615,503	Mérida
Miranda	7,950	2,026,229	Los Teques
Monagas	28,900	503,176	Maturín
Nueva Esparta	1,150	280,777	La Asunción
Portuguesa	15,200	625,576	Guanare
Sucre	11,800	722,707	Cumaná
Táchira	11,100	859,861	San Cristóbal
Trujillo	7,400	520,292	Trujillo
Yaracuy	7,100	411,980	San Felipe
Zulia	63,100	2,387,208	Maracaibo

HEAD OF STATE
President, Hugo Chávez Frías , *elected* 6 December 1998, *sworn in* 2 February 1999

COUNCIL OF MINISTERS *as at July 1999*
Agriculture and Livestock, Juan Jesús Montilla
Co-ordination and Planning, Jorge Giordani
Defence, Gen. Raúl Salazar
Education, Héctor Navarro
Energy and Mines, Alí Rodríguez Araque
Environment and Renewable Natural Resources, Jesús Arnaldo Pérez
Family, Labour and Social Development, Lino Martínez
Federal District Governor, Clemente Scotto
Finance, José Rojas
Foreign Relations, José Vicente Rangel
Health, Gilberto Rodriguez
Industry and Commerce, Gustavo Márquez
Information, Freddy Balzan
Interior and Justice, Ignacio Arcaya
Secretary of the Presidency, Gen. Lucas Rincón
Superintendent of Taxation, Col. Humberto Prieto
Transport and Communications, Julio Montés

VENEZUELAN EMBASSY
1 Cromwell Road, London SW7 2HW
Tel 0171-584 4206/7
Ambassador Extraordinary and Plenipotentiary, HE Roy Chaderton-Matos, apptd 1996
Defence Attaché, Capt. L. E. Vargas-Lander

BRITISH EMBASSY
Apartado 1246, Caracas 1010–A
Tel: Caracas 993 4111/4224
Ambassador Extraordinary and Plenipotentiary, HE Richard Wilkinson, CVO, apptd 1997
Deputy Head of Mission, Donald Maclaren of Maclaren
Defence Attaché, Col. P. A. Reynolds
First Secretary (Commercial), A. Goodworth

CONSULAR OFFICES – Caracas, Maracaibo, Margarita, Mérida, San Cristobal, Valencia

BRITISH COUNCIL DIRECTOR, G. Liesching, Apartado 65131, Caracas 1065

BRITISH-VENEZUELAN CHAMBER OF COMMERCE, Apartado 5713, Caracas 1010. Torre Británica, Piso 10, Letra E, Av. José Félix Sosa, Altamira Sur, Caracas 1060

DEFENCE

The Army has 70 main battle tanks, 290 armoured personnel carriers, 107 artillery pieces and five attack helicopters. The Navy has two submarines, six frigates, six patrol and coastal vessels, seven combat aircraft and eight armed helicopters at nine bases. The Air Force has 116 combat aircraft and 27 armed helicopters.
MILITARY EXPENDITURE – 1.1 per cent of GDP (1997)
MILITARY PERSONNEL – 79,000: Army 34,000, Navy 15,000, Air Force 7,000, National Guard 23,000
CONSCRIPTION DURATION – 30 months

ECONOMY

Following a recession in 1993–4, the government announced a two-year economic stabilization programme in September 1994, raising taxes, attracting foreign investment, reactivating the privatization programme and reducing government spending. In April 1996, foreign exchange controls were dismantled.

President Hugo Chávez Frías pledged in December 1998 that his government would cut public spending and tackle tax evasion and corruption.

Products of the tropical forest region include orchids, wild rubber, timber, mangrove bark, balata gum and tonka beans. Agricultural products include corn, bananas, cocoa beans, coffee, cotton, rice, maize, sugar, sesame, groundnuts, potatoes, tomatoes, other vegetables, sisal and tobacco. There is an extensive beef and dairy farming industry.

The principal industry is that of petroleum, although daily production in the oilfields (nationalized 1976) has steadily declined since 1973 in line with Venezuela's conservation policies. There are eight refineries. The Orinoco heavy oil belt is being developed; estimates put recoverable resources at 73,000 million barrels in 1996.

Aluminium is the second highest source of foreign exchange after petroleum. Rich iron ore deposits in eastern Venezuela have been developed. The government-owned steel mill at Matanzas uses local iron ore and obtains its electric power from hydroelectric installations on the Caroni River. A mill at Ciudad Guayana produces centrifugally-cast iron pipe. Other industry includes a wide variety of manufacturing and component assembly, principally petrochemicals, gold, diamonds and foodstuffs.

GNP – US$79,317 million (1997); US$3,480 per capita (1997)
GDP – US$76,363 million (1995); US$3,496 per capita (1995)
ANNUAL AVERAGE GROWTH OF GDP – –1.6 per cent (1996)
INFLATION RATE – 50.0 per cent (1997)
UNEMPLOYMENT – 10.3 per cent (1995)
TOTAL EXTERNAL DEBT – US$35,344 million (1996)

TRADE

Apart from oil, the main exports are bauxite, iron ore, agricultural products and basic manufactures. The main imports are machinery and transport equipment, chemicals and foodstuffs. Over 40 per cent of trade is conducted with the USA.

In 1997 Venezuela had a trade surplus of US$11,592 million and a current account surplus of US$5,999 million. In 1996 imports totalled US$9,880 million and exports US$23,070 million.

Trade with UK	1997	1998
Imports from UK	£203,825,000	£245,004,000
Exports to UK	157,025,000	122,568,000

COMMUNICATIONS

There are about 62,000 km of roads, some 24,000 km of them paved. Road and river communications have made railways of negligible importance in Venezuela except for carrying iron ore in the south-east, though the government is expanding the network, and there are now some 336 km of railway lines.

The Orinoco is navigable for ocean-going ships (up to 40 ft draught) for 150 miles upstream, by large steamers for 700 miles, and by smaller vessels some 900 miles upstream. There are seven Venezuelan airlines which between them have a comprehensive network of internal and international flights. There is an international airport at Caracas.

VIETNAM
Công Hòa Xã Hôi Chu Nghĩa Viêt Nam

AREA – 128,066 sq. miles (331,689 sq. km). Neighbours: China (north), Laos and Cambodia (west)
POPULATION – 75,181,000 (1994 UN estimate). The language is Vietnamese
CAPITAL – Hanoi (population, 3,056,146, 1989)
MAJOR CITIES – Hai Phong (1,447,523); Ho Chi Minh City (3,924,435)
CURRENCY – Dông of 10 hào or 100 xu
NATIONAL ANTHEM – Tien Quan Ca (The troops are advancing)
NATIONAL DAY – 2 September
NATIONAL FLAG – Red, with yellow five-point star in centre
LIFE EXPECTANCY (years) – male 63.66; female 67.89
POPULATION GROWTH RATE – 2.1 per cent (1996)
POPULATION DENSITY – 227 per sq. km (1996)
URBAN POPULATION – 19.5 per cent (1994)
ILLITERACY RATE – 6.3 per cent
ENROLMENT (percentage of age group) – primary 95 per cent (1980); tertiary 4.1 per cent (1995)

HISTORY AND POLITICS

Vietnam became a unified state at the end of the 18th century, with the assistance of France, whose influence on the region grew. In 1899 the Indo-Chinese Union was proclaimed, uniting Vietnam with Cambodia and Laos under French rule. Vietnam was under Japanese occupation from 1940-1945; insurrection by Communist, Nationalist and Revolutionary forces led to a French withdrawal in 1954 and the division of the country into Communist North Vietnam and non-communist South Vietnam. War broke out between the two countries in 1961, which lasted until 1975. North and South Vietnam were reunified in 1976 under the name of the Socialist Republic of Vietnam. The national flag, anthem and capital of North Vietnam were adopted, and Saigon was renamed Ho Chi Minh City.

POLITICAL SYSTEM

Effective power lies with the Vietnamese Communist Party (VCP), its highest executive body being the Central Committee, elected by a Party Congress on a national basis. The Politburo and the Secretariat of the Central Committee exercise the real power.

The constitution of 1992 reaffirmed Communist Party rule but also formalized free market economic reforms.

A new National Assembly (*Quoc-Hoi*) was elected on 20 July 1997; the VCP holds 384 of the 450 seats. The president is elected for a five-year term by the members of the National Assembly.

HEAD OF STATE
President, Tran Duc Luong, *elected* 25 September 1997
Vice-President, Nguyen Thi Binh

POLITBURO
Secretary-General of the VCP, Le Kha Phieu
Politburo Standing Board, Le Kha Phieu; Nong Duc Manh; Phan Van Khai; Pham The Duyet; Tran Duc Luong.

COUNCIL OF MINISTERS *as at July 1999*
Prime Minister, Phan Van Khai
Deputy PMs, Pham Gia Khiem *(Culture, Education and the Environment)*; Nguyen Manh Cam *(Foreign Affairs)*; Nguyen Tan Dzung *(Governor of the State Bank)*; Ngo Xuan Loc *(Industry, Transportation and Construction)*; Nguyen Cong Tan *(Rural Development, Agriculture and Waterworks)*

Agriculture and Rural Development, Le Huy Ngo
Aquatic Resources, Ta Quang Ngoc
Child Protection and Care, Tran Thi Thanh Thanh
Construction, Nguyen Manh Kiem
Culture and Information, Nguyen Khoa Diem
Education and Training, Nguyen Minh Hien
Ethnic Minorities and Mountain Regions, Hoang Duc Nghi
Finance, Nguyen Sinh Hung
Government Personnel and Organization, Do Quang Trung
Government Secretariat, Lai Van Cu
Industry, Dang Vu Chu
Interior, Le Minh Huong
Justice, Nguyen Dinh Loc
Labour, War Invalids and Social Affairs, Tran Dinh Hoan
National Defence, Gen. Pham Van Tra
Physical Training and Sports, Ha Quang Du
Planning and Investment, Tran Xuan Gia
Population Activities and Family Planning, Tran Thi Trung
Chien
Public Health, Do Nguyen Phuong
Science, Technology and Environment, Chu Tuan Nha
State Inspectorate, Ta Huu Thanh
Trade, Truong Dinh Tuyen
Transport, Le Ngoc Hoan

EMBASSY OF THE SOCIALIST REPUBLIC OF VIETNAM
12–14 Victoria Road, London W8 5RD
Tel 0171-937 1912/8564
Ambassador Extraordinary and Plenipotentiary, HE Vuong
Thua Pong, apptd 1998

BRITISH EMBASSY
Central Building, 31 Hai Ba Trung, Hanoi
Tel: Hanoi 825 2510
Ambassador Extraordinary and Plenipotentiary, HE David
Fall, apptd 1997

CONSULATE-GENERAL – Ho Chi Minh City

BRITISH COUNCIL DIRECTOR, I. Simm (*Cultural Attaché*)

DEFENCE

The Army has 1,315 main battle tanks, 1,100 armoured
personnel carriers, 300 armoured infantry fighting vehicles,
and 2,330 artillery pieces. The Navy has seven frigates and
44 patrol and coastal vessels at seven principal bases. The
Air Force has 201 combat aircraft and 43 armed helicopters.
MILITARY EXPENDITURE – 4.1 per cent of GDP (1997)
MILITARY PERSONNEL – 524,000: Army 412,000, Navy
42,000, Air Force 15,000, Air Defence Force 15,000,
Paramilitaries 40,000
CONSCRIPTION DURATION – Two to three years

ECONOMY

Vietnam experienced economic difficulties following the
imposition of socialist reforms in the south after 1975.
However, economic reforms, known as 'Doi Moi' liberalization, were instituted in 1986 and have had significant
success. The state's share of control has been greatly
reduced in most sectors, leading to significant improvement
in agricultural production, with Vietnam becoming a major
rice exporter. Industry has grown and now contributes 30
per cent of GDP. Building materials, chemicals, machinery
and foodstuffs are the main products.
Foreign investment has been actively encouraged.
Investment was further boosted by the US decision in 1995
to establish full diplomatic and economic relations and by
Vietnam's accession to ASEAN in August 1995. Oil
production has increased and large natural gas reserves
have been found offshore, though these are also claimed
by China. Under an agreement between Vietnam and

Russia worth US$800 million which was agreed in
November 1998, an oil refinery is to be built at Dung Quat.
In response to the regional financial crisis, in February
1998 the dông was officially devalued from 11,175 to the
US dollar to 11,800 to the US dollar. In February 1999 it
was announced that the dông would be allowed to
depreciate daily by up to 0.1 per cent. International donors
have pledged US$2.7 billion of development aid to Vietnam
for 1999.
In 1997 imports totalled US$11,271 million and exports
US$8,900 million.
GNP – US$24,008 million (1997); US$310 per capita
(1997)
GDP – US$19,912 million (1995); US$270 per capita
(1995)
TOTAL EXTERNAL DEBT – US$26,764 million (1996)

Trade with UK	1997	1998
Imports from UK	£94,746,000	£67,987,000
Exports to UK	194,425,000	243,729,000

YEMEN
Al-Jamhuriya Al-Yamaniya

AREA – 203,850 sq. miles (527,968 sq. km). Neighbours:
Saudi Arabia (north), Oman (east)
POPULATION – 15,919,000 (1995 census). The language is
Arabic
CAPITAL – Sana'a (population, 926,595, 1995)
MAJOR CITIES – ΨAden (400,783), the former capital of
South Yemen; Hodeidah (246,068); Taiz (290,107),
1993 estimates
CURRENCY – Riyal of 100 fils
NATIONAL DAY – 22 May
NATIONAL FLAG – Horizontal bands of red, white and
black
LIFE EXPECTANCY (years) – male 49.90; female 50.40
POPULATION GROWTH RATE – 5.7 per cent (1996)
POPULATION DENSITY – 30 per sq. km (1996)
URBAN POPULATION – 26.4 per cent (1994)
ENROLMENT (percentage of age group) – tertiary 4.2 per
cent (1996)

Included in the state of Yemen are the offshore islands of
Perim and Kamaran in the Red Sea, and Socotra in the
Gulf of Aden. The border with Saudi Arabia is unclear and
remains in dispute; only the north-west corner of it is
delineated, by the 1934 Taif Accord. The highlands and
central plateau, and the highest portions of the maritime
range in the south, form the most fertile part of Arabia,
with abundant but irregular rainfall. The north is largely
composed of mountains and desert, and rainfall is generally
scarce.

HISTORY AND POLITICS

Turkish occupation of North Yemen (1872–1918) was
followed by the rule of the Hamid al-Din dynasty until a
revolution in 1962 overthrew the monarchy and the Yemen
Arab Republic was declared. The People's Republic of
South Yemen was set up in 1967 when the British
government ceded power to the National Liberation Front,
bringing to an end 129 years of British rule in Aden and
some years of protectorate status in the hinterland.
Negotiations towards merging the two states began in 1979
and unification was proclaimed on 22 May 1990. The
constitution was approved by referendum in May 1991,
and a five-member Presidential Council comprising former
senior government figures of the separate states was formed
for the period of transition.

Following the general election in April 1993, the General People's Congress (GPC, former ruling party in the North), the Islamic Islah (Alliance for Reform) party and the Yemeni Socialist Party (YSP, former ruling party in the South) formed a coalition government and the House of Representatives asked the Presidential Council to remain in office.

Continued political tensions and a power struggle between the former Northern and Southern Yemen elites in mid-1993 led YSP leaders to withdraw to Aden in August 1993. A reconciliation pact signed in February 1994 by President Saleh and Vice-President al-Beedh was never implemented and, after sporadic clashes, a civil war broke out on 5 May 1994 between the unmerged Northern and Southern forces. The Southern leadership declared secession on 20 May but fled when Aden was captured by victorious Northern forces on 7 July, ending the civil war.

After the war a coalition government of the General People's Congress and the Islamic Islah was formed, an amnesty for the secessionists declared (with the exception of key YSP leaders) and the constitution amended. Gen. Saleh was elected president by the House of Representatives for a five-year term; presidential elections were due to be held on 28 September 1999. Multiparty democracy, a free market economy and Sharia law are enshrined in the constitution.

A general election in April 1997 was won by the ruling General People's Congress. In December 1997, the House of Representatives endorsed the promotion of President Saleh to the rank of Field Marshal.

HEAD OF STATE

President, Field Marshal Ali Abdullah Saleh, took office 22 May 1990, elected 1 October 1994
Vice-President, Maj.-Gen. Abd Rabbah Mansur Hadi

COUNCIL OF MINISTERS AS AT AUGUST 1999

Prime Minister, Abd al-Karim al-Iryani
Deputy PM, Foreign Affairs, Abd al-Qadir Abd al-Rahman Bajammal
Agriculture and Irrigation, Ahmad Salim al-Jabali
Awqaf (Religious Endowments) and Guidance, Sheikh Nasser al-Shaibani
Civil Service and Administrative Reform, Muhammad Ahmad al-Junayd
Construction, Housing and Urban Planning, Abdullah Husayn al-Daf'i
Culture and Tourism, Abd al-Malik Mansur
Defence, Maj.-Gen. Muhammad Dayfallah Muhammad
Education, Yahya Muhammad Abdullah al-Shu'aybi
Finance, Alawi Salih al-Salami
Fisheries, Ahmad Musa'id Husayn
Industry, Abd al-Rahman Muhammad Ali Uthman
Information, Abd al-Rahman Muhammad al-Akwa
Interior, Maj.-Gen. Husayn Muhammad Arab
Justice, Ismael Ahmed Al-Wazir
Labour and Vocational Training, Muhammad Muhammad al-Tayyib
Legal and Parliamentary Affairs, Abdullah Ahmad Ghanim
Local Administration, Sadiq Amin Abu Ra's
Ministers of State, Mutahhar al-Sa'idi (*Affairs of the Council of Ministers*); Faysal Mahmud Hasan Ali (Council of Ministers); Ahmad Ali al-Bishari (*Expatriate Affairs*)
Oil and Mineral Resources, Muhammad al-Khadim al-Wajih
Planning and Development, Ahmad Muhammad Sufan
Power and Water, Ali Hamid Sharaf
Public Health, Abdullah Abd al-Wali Nashir
Social Security and Social Affairs, Muhammad Abdullah al-Batani
Telecommunications, Ahmad Muhammad al-Ansi
Trade and Supply, Abd al-Aziz al-Kumaym

Transport, Brig.-Gen. Abd al-Malik Sayyani
Youth and Sport, Abd al-Wahhab Rawih

EMBASSY OF THE REPUBLIC OF YEMEN
57 Cromwell Road, London SW7 2ED
Tel 0171-584 6607
Ambassador Extraordinary and Plenipotentiary, HE Dr Hussein Abdullah Al-Amri, apptd 1995

BRITISH EMBASSY
129 Haddah Road, PO Box 1287, Sana'a
Tel: Sana'a 264 081/2/3/4
Ambassador Extraordinary and Plenipotentiary, HE Victor Henderson, apptd 1997

British Council Director, B. McSharry, MBE, As-Sabain Street No. 7 (PO Box 2157), Sana'a

DEFENCE

The Army has 1,320 main battle tanks, 60 armoured personnel carriers, 300 armoured infantry fighting vehicles, and 452 artillery pieces. The Navy has 15 patrol and coastal vessels at two bases. The Air Force has 49 combat aircraft and eight attack helicopters.
Military Expenditure – 7.0 per cent of GDP (1997)
Military Personnel – 136,300: Army 61,000, Navy 1,800, Air Force 3,500, Paramilitaries 70,000
Conscription Duration – Three years

ECONOMY

The economy has been seriously damaged by the civil war. However, the war had little effect on oil production, which averages roughly 400,000 barrels per day (bpd). The refinery at Aden was damaged in the civil war and is working at reduced capacity. An agreement was signed with the French oil company Total in September 1995 for the exploitation of liquefied natural gas over a 25-year period and the construction of a gas liquefication plant by 2000. Despite the production of oil Yemen remains one of the poorest states in the world. Tourism has been hampered by the prevalence of kidnapping.

Agriculture is the main occupation of the inhabitants. This is largely of a subsistence nature, sorghum, sesame, millet, wheat and barley being the chief crops. Exports include cotton, coffee, fruit, vegetables and hides. Imports include food and animals

In 1995 Yemen had a trade deficit of US$11 million and current account surplus of US$183 million.
GNP – US$4,405 million (1997); US$270 per capita (1997)
GDP – US$11,001 million (1995); US$732 per capita (1995)
Total External Debt – US$6,356 million (1996)

Trade with UK	1997	1998
Imports from UK	£72,053,000	£77,923,000
Exports to UK	5,067,000	3,249,000

YUGOSLAVIA
Federativna Republika Jugoslavije – Federal Republic of Yugoslavia

AREA – 39,449 sq. miles (102,173 sq. km). Neighbours: Hungary (north), Romania and Bulgaria (east), the Former Yugoslav Republic of Macedonia and Albania (south), Bosnia-Hercegovina and Croatia (west)

POPULATION – 10,574,000 (1994 UN estimate): 66 per cent Serb and Montenegrin, 18 per cent Albanian, 8 per cent Muslim Slavs, 4 per cent Hungarian, with smaller numbers of Yugoslavs (no ethnic group), Croats and Bulgarians. The majority religion is Serbian Orthodox, with significant Muslim and small Roman Catholic minorities. The main language is Serbian (Serbo-Croat) (74 per cent), with Albanian and Hungarian minorities. Serbo-Croat is a South Slav language written in the Cyrillic script

CAPITAL – Belgrade (population, 1,136,786, 1991)

MAJOR CITIES – Kragujevac (146,607); Niš (175,555); Novi Sad (178,896); Podgorica (117,875), the capital of Montenegro; Priština (108,083); Subotica (100,219), 1991

CURRENCY – New dinar of 100 paras

NATIONAL ANTHEM – Hej, Slaveni, Jošte Živi Reč Naših Dedova (Oh! Slavs, our ancestors' words still live)

NATIONAL DAY – 27 April

NATIONAL FLAG – Three horizontal stripes of blue, white, red

LIFE EXPECTANCY (years) – male 69.50; female 74.49

POPULATION GROWTH RATE – 0.1 per cent (1996)

POPULATION DENSITY – 103 per sq. km (1996)

MILITARY EXPENDITURE – 7.8 per cent of GDP (1997)

MILITARY PERSONNEL – 114,200: Army 90,000, Navy 7,500, Air Force 16,700

CONSCRIPTION DURATION – 12–15 months

ILLITERACY RATE – 6.7 per cent

ENROLMENT (percentage of age group) – primary 69 per cent (1990); secondary 62 per cent (1990); tertiary 22.5 per cent (1996)

The climate is continental. Montenegro and southern Serbia are extremely mountainous, while the north is dominated by the low-lying plains of the Danube. The major rivers are: the Danube, which flows through the north of Serbia to Romania and Bulgaria; the Sava, which flows eastwards from Bosnia to join the Danube at Belgrade; the Drina, which flows along most of the Serbian–Bosnian border to join the Sava; and the Morava, which flows from the extreme south to join the Danube in the north.

HISTORY AND POLITICS

Serbia emerged from the rule of the Byzantine Empire in the 13th century to form a large and prosperous state in the Balkans. Defeat by the Turks in 1389 led to almost 500 years of Turkish rule. After gaining autonomy within the Ottoman Empire in 1815, Serbia became fully independent in 1878 and a kingdom in 1881. Montenegro was part of the Serbian state before it was conquered by the Turks in 1355; it became independent in 1851. At the end of the First World War Serbia and Montenegro joined with the former Austro-Hungarian provinces of Slovenia, Croatia and Bosnia-Hercegovina to form the 'Kingdom of Serbs, Croats and Slovenes' which was proclaimed on 1 December 1918 under the rule of the Serbian royal house. The state was renamed Yugoslavia in 1929. In 1941–5 Yugoslavia was occupied by Axis forces which were fought by Communist and royalist Četnik partisans supplied by Allied forces. In 1945 with the defeat of Nazi Germany, Yugoslavia was reformed as a Communist federal republic under the presidency of partisan leader Josip Tito.

Tito died in 1980 and the delicate political balance of a rotating federal presidency was unable to contain the growing nationalist movements after his death. Efforts by the six republican presidents to negotiate a new federal or confederal structure for the country failed in 1991. On 25

June 1991 Slovenia and Croatia declared their independence from Yugoslavia..

In Croatia the ethnic Serb minority refused to accept Croatia's independence and fighting began in July 1991 between Croat Defence Forces and Serbian guerrillas backed by the JNA. By September 1991 this had escalated into war between Croatia and Serbia. The war in Croatia continued until January 1992 when the EU and the UN were able to bring about a cease-fire (*see* Croatia).

Bosnia-Hercegovina adopted a memorandum on state sovereignty on 15 October 1991 and independence was affirmed in a referendum on 1 March 1992. Independence was supported by the Bosniacs (Muslims) and Croats but rejected by the ethnic Serbs and fighting between Bosniacs and Serbs broke out in March 1992. The JNA intervened against the Bosniacs but in May 1992 withdrew to Serbia and Montenegro.

On 27 April 1992 the two remaining republics of the former Socialist Federal Republic of Yugoslavia, Serbia and Montenegro, announced the formation of a new Yugoslav federation, which they invited Serbs in Croatia and Bosnia-Hercegovina to join.

Federal legislative elections were held in November 1996. The Serbian Socialist Party emerged as the largest party in the federal legislature and formed a coalition government with Yugoslav United Left and New Democracy. Legislative elections were held in Montenegro in May 1998 and were won by reformists led by President Djukanović. Kosovo has been under UN administration since June 1999.

INSURGENCY

The province of Kosovo in the south of Serbia is more than 90 per cent ethnically Albanian. In defiance of the Serbian authorities, presidential and parliamentary elections were held in Kosovo in May 1992, and were won by the Democratic League of Kosovo and its leader Ibrahim Rugova. Following clashes between ethnic Albanians and Serbian police in February and March 1998, the Serbian military attacked civilians in the province on the pretext of eliminating support for the Kosovo Liberation Army (KLA), an ethnic Albanian organization fighting for independence for the province. The international community condemned the brutality of the Serbian forces and a UN arms embargo was imposed on Yugoslavia, but the situation deteriorated with clashes between the KLA and security forces becoming commonplace. The civil unrest deteriorated into a state of open war. Following early gains by the KLA, Serbian forces fought back, sending tanks and artillery to engage in the systematic destruction of entire villages in the region in order to drive out KLA troops. International organizations detailed widespread human rights abuses by the security forces; NATO and Russia ordered both sides to attend a peace conference in Paris on 6 February 1999, which was unsuccessful. Talks resumed on 15 March and the Kosovar Albanian delegation signed the internationally mediated agreement that offered Kosovo autonomy within Serbia and provided for the deployment of a NATO peacekeeping force. The Yugoslav authorities refused to sign and peace talks were abandoned. Tens of thousands of Kosovar Albanians fled when Yugoslav forces began to attack Kosovar villages. Following warnings to the Yugoslav authorities, NATO commenced air strikes against military targets in Yugoslavia on 24 March 1999. Hundreds of thousands of people fled or were forced to leave their homes and sought refuge in Albania, Macedonia or Montenegro, which, although part of the Yugoslav Federation, had refused to become involved in the fighting. NATO intensified its bombing campaign, now targeting industrial, communications and power links.

On 27 May 1999, the UN War Crimes Tribunal indicted President Milošević of Yugoslavia, President Milutinović of Serbia, and other senior Yugoslav officials for crimes against humanity.

On 3 June President Milošević accepted a peace plan agreed by NATO and Russia and on 10 June Yugoslav forces began to withdraw; NATO air operations were immediately suspended and NATO and Russian forces entered Kosovo the following day. By 20 June all Yugoslav forces had been withdrawn from Kosovo and the Kosovar refugees had begun to return.

POLITICAL SYSTEM

The Federal Republic has a bicameral parliament with a directly elected 138-seat (108 Serbian, 30 Montenegrin) lower house, the Chamber of Citizens, and an indirectly elected 40-seat (20 Serbian, 20 Montenegrin) upper house, the Chamber of Republics. Both houses serve four-year terms. Executive power is vested in a federal president and government.

HEAD OF STATE

Federal President, Slobodan Milošević, *elected by parliament* 15 July 1997

FEDERAL GOVERNMENT *as at July 1998*

Prime Minister, Momir Bulatović
Deputy PMs, Jovan Zebić; Danilo Vuksanović; Nikola Sainović; Zoran Lilić; Vladan Kutlesić
Agriculture, Nedeljko Sipovac
Defence, Pavle Bulatović
Development, Science and the Environment, Jagos Zelenović
Economy, Rade Filipović
External Trade, Borislav Vuković
Finance, Dragisa Pesić
Financial Aid, Nenad Djokić
Foreign Affairs, Zivadin Jovanović
Information, vacant
Internal Affairs, Zoran Sokolović
Internal Trade, vacant
Labour, Miodrag Kovac
Sports, Zoran Bingulac
Telecommunications, Dojcilo Radojević
Transport, Dejan Drobnjaković

MONTENEGRO

AREA – 5,331 sq. miles (13,812 sq. km)
POPULATION – 615,000: 62 per cent Montenegrin, 14.5 per cent Bosniac, 6.5 per cent Albanian and 3 per cent Serb

CAPITAL – Podgorica (population, 117,875, 1991)

The Montenegrin Social Democrat Party (former Communists) won multiparty elections in November 1996 for the 85-seat republican assembly and formed a government. The most recent presidential election was won by Milo Djukanović, a reformist candidate favouring greater independence for the province.

President, Milo Djukanović, *elected* 19 October 1997
Prime Minister, Filip Vujanović

SERBIA

AREA – 34,175 sq. miles (88,538 sq. km)
POPULATION – 9,300,000, of whom 66 per cent are Serbs
CAPITAL – Belgrade (population, 1,338,856, 1991)

Serbia includes the provinces of Kosovo (population 1.6 million), of great historic importance to Serbs, and Vojvodina (population 2 million); the autonomy of both was ended in September 1990. Vojvodina, with its capital at Novi Sad, has a large Hungarian minority (21 per cent). Kosovo, with its capital at Priština, is predominantly Albanian (90 per cent). Following the conflict in Kosovo, more than 200,000 people have been left homeless and entire villages have been destroyed.

The Socialist Party of Serbia (SPS) (formerly the Communists) emerged as the largest party in multiparty elections for the 250-seat National Assembly, held in November 1996, although the results of the election were disputed.

President, Milan Milutinović
Prime Minister, Mirko Marjanović

ECONOMY

Since 1991 the economy has been devastated by the wars in Croatia and Bosnia-Hercegovina, by the UN economic sanctions and trade embargo, and because of the lack of free-market reforms. Most factories have closed. Only the evasion of UN sanctions and the country's agricultural self-sufficiency have kept it afloat. By 1993 inflation had reached 21,000 per cent a month, following continued over-printing of currency to finance war and subsidize industries. The tax system collapsed, output was one-third of pre-war levels, industry was working at one-quarter of capacity and the dinar had been devalued ten times. In January 1994 an economic stabilization package was introduced with a new superdinar pegged at one-to-one parity with the Deutsche Mark.

The UN voted to lift economic sanctions on 22 November 1995 following the conclusion of the Dayton Peace Accord. Industrial production remains extremely low. In April 1998 the dinar was devalued by 45 per cent against the Deutsche Mark. Following the conflict in Kosovo, the USA and EU froze all Yugoslav assets within their jurisdiction and banned all investment in the country.
GDP – US$15,243 million (1995); US$1,487 per capita (1995)
ANNUAL AVERAGE GROWTH OF GDP – 6.0 per cent (1995)
INFLATION RATE – 117.4 per cent (1991)
TOTAL EXTERNAL DEBT – US$13,439 million (1996)

Trade with UK	1997	1998
Imports from UK	£37,777,000	£42,596,000
Exports to UK	31,147,000	30,876,000

ZAMBIA
Republic of Zambia

AREA – 290,587 sq. miles (752,618 sq. km). Neighbours: Democratic Republic of Congo and Tanzania (north), Malawi (east), Mozambique, Zimbabwe and Namibia (south), Angola (west)
POPULATION – 8,275,000 (1994 UN estimate)
CAPITAL – Lusaka (population, 982,362, 1990)
MAJOR CITIES – Chingola (162,954); Kabwe (166,519); Kitwe (338,207); Luanshya (146,275); Mufulira (152,944); Ndola (376,311)
CURRENCY – Kwacha (K) of 100 ngwee
NATIONAL ANTHEM – Stand and Sing of Zambia, Proud and Free
NATIONAL DAY – 24 October (Independence Day)
NATIONAL FLAG – Green with three small vertical stripes, red, black and orange (next fly); eagle device on green above stripes
LIFE EXPECTANCY (years) – male 50.70; female 53.00
POPULATION GROWTH RATE – 0.4 per cent (1996)
POPULATION DENSITY – 11 per sq. km (1996)
URBAN POPULATION – 39.4 per cent (1990)
MILITARY EXPENDITURE – 1.7 per cent of GDP (1997)
MILITARY PERSONNEL – 23,000: Army 20,000, Air Force 1,600, Paramilitaries 1,400
ILLITERACY RATE – 21.8 per cent
ENROLMENT (percentage of age group) – primary 75 per cent (1995); secondary 16 per cent (1994); tertiary 2.5 per cent (1994)

Zambia lies on the plateau of Central Africa. With the exception of the valleys of the Zambezi, the Luapula, the Kafue and the Luangwa rivers, and the Luano valley, elevations vary from 3,000 to 5,000 feet above sea level, but in the north-east the plateau rises to occasional altitudes of over 6,000 feet. Although Zambia lies within the tropics, and fairly centrally in the African land mass, its elevation relieves it from extremely high temperatures and humidity.

HISTORY AND POLITICS

Northern Rhodesia came under British rule in 1889. It achieved internal self-government when the Federation of Rhodesia and Nyasaland was dissolved in 1963 and became an independent republic within the Commonwealth on 24 October 1964 under the name of Zambia.

Zambia was a one-party state (the United National Independence Party) from 1973 until 1990, when pressure from opposition groups led to a new constitution (August 1991) and multiparty legislative and presidential elections in October 1991. The Movement for Multiparty Democracy (MMD) won 125 of the 150 seats in parliament, and the MMD candidate Frederick Chiluba defeated Kenneth Kaunda, who had ruled since independence, in the presidential election; Kaunda was later stripped of his Zambian citizenship.

Following an abortive coup attempt in October 1997, the president declared a state of emergency. 90 people were subsequently arrested in connection with the coup, including former President Kaunda. The state of emergency was lifted in March 1998.

HEAD OF STATE

President, Frederick J. Chiluba, *elected* October 1991, *re-elected* 18 November 1996
Vice-President, Lt.-Gen. (retd) Christon Tembo

CABINET *as at July 1999*
Agriculture, Food and Fisheries, Suresh Desai
Commerce, Trade and Industry, David Mapamba
Communications and Transport, David Saviye *Community Development and Social Services,* Dawson Lupunga
Defence, Chitalu Sampa
Education, Brig.-Gen. Godfrey Miyanda
Energy and Water Development, Ben Mwila
Environment and Natural Resources, William Harrington
Finance and Economic Development, Katele Kalumba
Foreign Affairs, Keli Walubita
Health, Prof. Nkandu Luo
Home Affairs, Peter Machungwa
Information and Broadcasting Services, Newstead Zimba
Labour and Social Security, Edith Nawakwi
Lands, Samuel Miyanda
Legal Affairs, Vincent Malambo
Local Government and Housing, Bennie Mwiinga
Mines and Mineral Development, Syamukayumbu Syamujaye
Presidential Affairs, Eric Silwamba
Science, Technology and Vocational Training, Alfeyo Hambayi
Sport, Youth, and Child Development, A. M. Chambeshi
Tourism, Rev. Anoshi Chipawa
Without Portfolio, Michael Sata
Works and Supply, Gilbert Mandandi

HIGH COMMISSION FOR THE REPUBLIC OF ZAMBIA
2 Palace Gate, London W8 5NG
Tel 0171-589 6655
High Commissioner, HE Prof. Moses Musonda, apptd 1997
Deputy High Commissioner, Geoffrey P. Alikipo
Defence Adviser, Brig.-Gen. M. G. Lisita

BRITISH HIGH COMMISSION
Independence Avenue (PO Box 50050), 15101, Lusaka
Tel: Lusaka 251133
High Commissioner, HE Thomas Young, apptd 1997
Deputy High Commissioner, P. W. D. Nessling
First Secretary (Development and Economic), M. T. Murray

BRITISH COUNCIL DIRECTOR, M. Fryars, Heroes Place, Cairo Road (PO Box 34571), Lusaka

ECONOMY

In 1991, the MMD government began the transition from a state-controlled economy to a free market system. Privatization has been encouraged, foreign exchange controls have been removed and the Kwacha has been floated. Price subsidies and tariffs have been lowered or abolished, but increased imports have affected manufacturing. Principal agricultural products are maize, sugar, groundnuts, cotton, livestock, vegetables and tobacco.

In 1997 imports totalled US$807 million and exports US$902 million.
GNP – US$3,536 million (1997); US$370 per capita (1997)
GDP – US$3,085 million (1995); US$382 per capita (1995)
ANNUAL AVERAGE GROWTH OF GDP – 6.4 per cent (1996)
INFLATION RATE – 18.6 per cent (1997)
TOTAL EXTERNAL DEBT – US$6,571 million (1996)

Trade with UK	1997	1998
Imports from UK	£45,620,000	£35,387,000
Exports to UK	32,067,000	24,582,000

ZIMBABWE
Republic of Zimbabwe

AREA – 150,872 sq. miles (390,757 sq. km). Neighbours: Zambia (north), Mozambique (east), South Africa (south), Botswana and Namibia (west)
POPULATION – 11,908,000 (1994 UN estimate); 10,400,000 (1992 census). The official language is English, with Shona the largest indigenous language group
CAPITAL – Harare (population, 1,189,103, 1992)
MAJOR CITIES – Bulawayo (621,742), the largest town in Matabeleland; Chitungwiza (274,912)
CURRENCY – Zimbabwe dollar (Z$) of 100 cents
NATIONAL ANTHEM – Ngaikomberarwe Nyika Ye Zimbabwe (Blessed be the country of Zimbabwe)
NATIONAL DAY – 18 April (Independence Day)
NATIONAL FLAG – Seven horizontal stripes of green, yellow, red, black, red, yellow, green; a white, black-bordered, triangle based on the hoist containing the national emblem
LIFE EXPECTANCY (years) – male 58.00; female 62.00
POPULATION GROWTH RATE – 4.0 per cent (1996)
POPULATION DENSITY – 30 per sq. km (1996)
MILITARY EXPENDITURE – 4.7 per cent of GDP (1997)
MILITARY PERSONNEL – 60,800: Army 35,000, Air Force 4,000, Paramilitaries 21,800

HISTORY AND POLITICS

European colonization of Zimbabwe began in 1890 when settlers forcibly acquired Shona lands, followed by the seizure of Ndebele lands in 1893. It became a self-governing colony under the name of Southern Rhodesia in 1923. A unilateral declaration of independence on 11 November 1965, which resulted in UN sanctions against the country, was finally terminated on 12 December 1979. Following elections in February 1980 the country became independent on 18 April 1980 as the Republic of Zimbabwe, a member of the British Commonwealth.

The independence constitution was amended in 1987, making the presidency an executive post. The president is popularly elected for a six-year term, appoints the Cabinet and can veto parliamentary bills. The House of Assembly has 150 members: 120 elected, eight provincial governors, ten traditional chiefs and 12 others appointed by the president. A commission was appointed in April 1999 to consider amending the constitution. A merger agreement between the ZANU (PF) and ZAPU parties was signed in 1987 with a view to the eventual creation of a one-party state. The new party is known as ZANU-PF. The most recent general election was held in April 1995 and ZANU-PF won 118 of the 120 elective seats, although it lost a by-election in November 1995. President Mugabe was re-elected for a six-year term in March 1996, following the withdrawal of the other two contenders.

The country is divided into eight provinces: Manicaland, Masvingo, Matabeleland North, Matabeleland South, Midlands, Mashonaland West, Mashonaland Central and Mashonaland East.

HEAD OF STATE
Executive President, C.-in-C. of the Defence Forces, Robert Gabriel Mugabe, *elected* 30 December 1987, *re-elected* March 1990, March 1996
Vice-President, Simon Vengesai Muzenda

CABINET *as at July 1999*

Defence, Moven Mahachi
Education, Sports and Culture, Gabriel Machinga
Finance, Dr Herbert Murerwa
Foreign Affairs, Dr Stanislaus Mudenge
Health and Child Welfare, Dr Timothy Stamps
Higher Education and Technology, Ignatius Chombo
Home Affairs, Dumiso Dabengwa
Industry and Commerce, Dr Nathan Shamuyarira
Information, Posts and Telecommunications, Chenhamo Chimutengwende
Justice, Legal and Parliamentary Affairs, Emmerson Mnangagwa
Lands and Agriculture, Kumbirai Kangai
Local Government and National Housing, John Nkomo
Mines, Environment and Tourism, Simon Moyo
National Affairs, Employment Creation and Co-operatives, Virginia Lesabe
National Security, Dr Sidney Sekeramayi
Planning, Richard Hove
President's Office, Cephas Msipa
Public Service, Labour and Social Welfare, Florence Chitauro
Rural Resources and Water Development, Joyce Mujuru
Transport and Energy, Enos Chikowore
Without Portfolio, Dr Eddison Zvobgo; Joseph Msika;

HIGH COMMISSION OF THE REPUBLIC OF ZIMBABWE
Zimbabwe House, 429 Strand, London WC2R 0SA
Tel 0171-836 7755
Acting High Commissioner, Pavelyn Tendai Musaka
    Minister-Counsellor, T. Jamu
Defence Adviser, Col. J. J. Murozvi
Senior Commercial Attaché, J. Foroma

BRITISH HIGH COMMISSION
Corner House, Samora Machel Avenue (PO Box 4490), Harare
Tel: Harare 772990
High Commissioner, HE Peter Longworth, apptd 1998
Deputy High Commissioner, T. Hay-Campbell, LVO
Defence Adviser, Col. J. S. Field, CBE
First Secretaries, D. Seddon (*Commercial*); J. Lidell (*Consular*)

BRITISH COUNCIL DIRECTOR, Dr J. Taylor, 23 Jason Moyo Avenue (PO Box 664), Harare

ECONOMY

Ten years of socialism and central planning in 1980–90 brought the economy to crisis point before free-market economic reforms were introduced in 1990. Reforms have included the floating of the currency, opening the market to imports, and a reduction in subsidies. The programme has been partially implemented but the economy remains highly regulated and weak. Inflation remains high and the rises in the prices of basic commodities and fuel resulted in widespread strike action and protests.

The Supreme Court approved government plans to seize 12 million acres of predominantly white-owned farmland in June 1996, though controversy over the repossession and the question of compensation payments, mean that the future of the plan is unclear. After announcing the appropriation of 841 white-owned farms in November 1998; it was announced in January 1999 that only 118, which were already on the market, would be acquired over a two-year period.

The country is endowed with minerals, water, forests, wildlife and other resources. The agricultural sector is well-developed and employs 68 per cent of the workforce. Tobacco remains the most important crop in terms of export (Zimbabwe is the largest exporter in the world), and maize the most important for domestic consumption. Other crops include wheat, cotton, sugar, horticultural products, fruit and vegetables. Beef is exported to the EU.

The manufacturing sector is very dependent on the

agricultural sector for raw materials. Industry is also dependent on imports e.g. fuel oil, steel products and chemicals, as well as heavy machinery and items of transport. The mining sector, although contributing a relatively small portion to GDP, is important to the economy as a foreign exchange earner. Almost all mineral production is exported. Gold is the most important product; others are asbestos, diamonds, silver, nickel, copper, platinum, chrome ore, tin, iron ore and cobalt. There is a successful ferro-chrome industry and a substantial steel works which has been heavily subsidized by government.

The value of the Zimbabwean dollar fell by 65 per cent in 1998 and the prices of basic foodstuffs and petrol rose dramatically. In September 1998, foreign exchange restrictions were imposed and import duties on luxury goods were doubled in an attempt at currency stabilization. The 1999 budget raised duties on alcohol, tobacco and fuel and reformed the income tax system, raising taxation for those on higher salaries.

Tourism is of growing importance, with more than 1,000,000 visitors in 1995.

In 1994 Zimbabwe had a trade surplus of US$158 million and a current account deficit of US$425 million. In 1995 imports totalled US$2,660 million and exports US$2,119 million.

GNP – US$8,208 million (1997); US$720 per capita (1997)

GDP – US$8,800 million (1995); US$786 per capita (1995)

ANNUAL AVERAGE GROWTH OF GDP – 2.7 per cent (1995)

INFLATION RATE – 18.3 per cent (1997)

TOTAL EXTERNAL DEBT – US$5,005 million (1996)

Trade with UK	1997	1998
Imports from UK	£97,531,000	£77,603,000
Exports to UK	128,361,000	122,784,000

EDUCATION

Education is compulsory, and the language of instruction is English. Over 80 per cent of schools are government-aided. There are four universities; the University of Zimbabwe was founded in 1955.

ILLITERACY RATE – 14.9 per cent

ENROLMENT (percentage of age group) – tertiary 6.5 per cent (1996)

UK Overseas Territories

AREA – 37 sq. miles (96 sq. km)
POPULATION – 12,394 (1998 estimate)
CAPITAL – The Valley (population, 2,400, 1994)
CURRENCY – East Caribbean dollar (EC$) of 100 cents
FLAG – British blue ensign with the coat of arms and three dolphins in the fly
POPULATION GROWTH RATE – 8.6 per cent (1998)
POPULATION DENSITY – 83 per sq. km (1996)
GDP – US$88 million (1997); US$7,383 per capita (1997)
ILLITERACY RATE – 4.6 per cent
ENROLMENT (percentage of age group) –primary per cent; secondary per cent; tertiary per cent

Anguilla is a flat coralline island in the Caribbean, about 16 miles in length, three and a half miles in breadth at its widest point and its area is about 37 sq. miles (96 sq. km). The island is covered with low scrub and fringed with white coral-sand beaches. The climate is pleasant, with temperatures in the range of 24-30° C throughout the year.

HISTORY AND POLITICS

Anguilla has been a British colony since 1650. For much of its history it was linked administratively with St Christopher, but three months after the Associated State of Saint Christopher (St Kitts)-Nevis-Anguilla came into being in 1967, the Anguillans repudiated government from St Kitts. A Commissioner was installed in 1969 and in 1976 Anguilla was given a new status and separate constitution. Final separation from St Kitts and Nevis was effected on 19 December 1980 and Anguilla reverted to a British dependency. A new constitution was introduced in 1982, providing for a Governor, an Executive Council comprising four elected Ministers and two ex-officio members (the Attorney-General and Deputy Governor), and an 11-member legislative House of Assembly presided over by a Speaker.

The 1982 Constitution (Amendment) Order 1990 came into operation on 30 May 1990. Among the new constitutional provisions are a Deputy Governor , a Parliamentary Secretary, Leader of Opposition and Deputy Speaker.

Governor, HE Robert Harris, *apptd* 1997
Deputy Governor, Roger Cousins

EXECUTIVE COUNCIL *as at June 1999*

Chairman, The Governor
Chief Minister, Finance and Economic Development, Hubert Hughes
Attorney-General, Ronald Scipio
Infrastructure, Communications and Utilities, Albert Hughes
Social Services, Edison Baird
Member, The Deputy Governor

ECONOMY

Low rainfall limits agricultural output and export earnings are mainly from sales of fish and lobsters. Tourism has developed rapidly in recent years and accounts for most of the island's economic activity. In 1998 there were 43,874 tourists and a further 69,922 day visitors.

TRADE WITH UK	1997	1998
Imports from UK	£5,137,000	£5,697,000
Exports to UK	13,000	24,000

— *see* St Helena

AREA – 20 sq. miles (53 sq. km)
POPULATION – 64,000 (1994 UN estimate)
CAPITAL – ΨHamilton (population, 2,277, 1994)
CURRENCY – Bermuda dollar of 100 cents
FLAG – British red ensign with the shield of arms in the fly
LIFE EXPECTANCY (years) – male 70.23; female 78.01
POPULATION GROWTH RATE – 0.9 per cent (1996)
POPULATION DENSITY – 1,208 per sq. km (1996)
GDP – US$2,047 million (1995); US$32,495 per capita (1995)

The Bermudas, or Somers Islands, are a cluster of about 100 small islands (about 20 of which are inhabited) situated in the west of the Atlantic Ocean, the nearest point of the mainland being Cape Hatteras in North Carolina, about 570 miles distant.

HISTORY AND POLITICS

The colony derives its name from Juan Bermudez, a Spaniard, who sighted it before 1515. No settlement was made until 1609 when Sir George Somers, who was shipwrecked there on his way to Virginia, colonized the islands.

Internal self-government was introduced in 1968. There is a Senate of 11 members and an elected House of Assembly of 40 members. The Governor retains responsibility for external affairs, defence, internal security and the police, although administrative matters for the police service have been delegated to the Minister of Labour, Home Affairs and Public Safety. Independence from the UK was rejected in a referendum in August 1995.

The last general election was held on 9 November 1998. The Progressive Labour Party won 26 of the 40 seats.

Governor and Commander-in-Chief, HE Thorold Masefield, CMG, *apptd* 1997
Deputy Governor, Tim Gurney

CABINET *as at June 1999*

Premier, Jennifer Smith
Deputy Premier, Minister of Finance, C. Eugene Cox
Development, Opportunity and Government Services, Terry E. Lister
Education, L. Milton Scott
Environment, Arthur D. O. Hodgson
Health and Family Services, Nelson Bascombe Jr
Labour, Home Affairs and Public Safety, Paula A. Cox
Tourism, David H. Allen
Transport, Ewart Brown
Works and Engineering, W. Alex Scott
Youth, Sport, Parks and Recreation, P. Lister

President of the Senate, Alfred J. Oughton, MBE
Speaker of the House of Assembly, Stanley Lowe
Chief Justice, Austin Ward, QC

ECONOMY

The islands' economic structure is based on tourism, the major industry, and international company business, attracted by the low level of taxation and sophisticated telecommunications system. In 1996 a total of 576,628 visitors arrived by air and cruise ship.

Locally manufactured concentrates, perfumes, cut flowers and pharmaceuticals are the islands' leading exports. Little food is produced except vegetables and fish, other foodstuffs being imported.

In November 1995, the US, UK and Canadian governments handed over 1,500 acres of land (roughly 10 per cent of the colony), to the government. The land, which had been used for military bases, included an airport on St David's Island.

TRADE WITH UK	1997	1998
Imports from UK	£55,366,000	£40,214,000
Exports to UK	54,203,000	3,701,000

COMMUNICATIONS

One daily and two weekly newspapers are published in Bermuda. Three commercial companies operate radio and television services, including a cable-television system. The Bermuda Telephone Company and Cable and Wireless provide telecommunications links to more than 140 countries.

EDUCATION

Free elementary education was introduced in 1949. Free secondary education was introduced in 1965 for those children in the aided and maintained schools who were below the upper limit of the statutory school age of 18 (from 1969 onwards).

THE BRITISH ANTARCTIC TERRITORY

AREA – 660,000 sq. miles (1,709,340 sq. km.)
POPULATION – No permanent population
FLAG – British white ensign, without the cross of St George, with the coat of arms of the Territory in the fly

The British Antarctic Territory was designated in 1962 and consists of the areas south of 60°S. latitude and bounded by longitudes 20°W. and 80°W. The territory includes the South Orkney Islands, the South Shetland Islands, the mountainous Antarctic Peninsula (highest point Mount Jackson, 10,443 ft above sea level) and all adjacent islands, and the land mass extending to the South Pole. The territory has no indigenous inhabitants and the British population consists of the scientists and technicians at the British Antarctic Survey stations. These numbered 42 during the 1998–9 winter, but this number increases considerably in the southern hemisphere's summer months with the arrival of field scientists. Argentina, Brazil, Bulgaria, Chile, China, Korea (South), Poland, Russia, Spain, Ukraine, Uruguay and the USA also have scientific stations in the territory.

The first two British Antarctic Survey stations were established in the South Shetland Islands in 1944, and by 1956 the number of stations had risen to 12. Due to the completion of field work in some areas and increased

mobility, this number has now been reduced to four: Rothera (Adelaide Island), Halley (Brunt Ice Shelf, Caird Coast) and, in summer only, Fossil Bluff (Alexander Island) and Signy Island (South Orkney Islands). Four other stations are at present unoccupied.

The territory is administered by a Commissioner, resident in London.

Commissioner (non-resident), Charles John Branford White, *apptd* 1997

THE BRITISH INDIAN OCEAN TERRITORY

AREA – 23 sq. miles (59 sq. km.)
POPULATION – No permanent population
FLAG – Divided horizontally into blue and white wavy stripes, with the Union Flag in the canton and a crowned palm-tree over all in the fly

The British Indian Ocean Territory was established by an Order in Council in 1965 and included islands formerly administered from Mauritius and the Seychelles. The islands of Farquhar, Desroches and Aldabra became part of the Seychelles when it became independent in 1976; since then the Territory has consisted of the Chagos Archipelago only.

The Chagos Archipelago consists of six main groups of islands situated on the Great Chagos Bank and covering some 21,000 sq. miles (54,389 sq. km). The largest and most southerly of the Chagos Islands is Diego Garcia, a sand cay with a land area of about 17 sq. miles approximately 1,100 miles east of Mahé, used as a joint naval support facility by Britain and the USA.

The other main island groups of the archipelago, Peros Banhos (29 islands with a total land area of 4 sq. miles) and Salamon (11 islands with a total land area of 2 sq. miles) are uninhabited. The islands have a tropical maritime climate, with average temperatures between 25°C and 29°C in Diego Garcia, and rainfall in the whole archipelago of 90–100 inches a year.

Commissioner, John White, *apptd* 1998
Administrator, Louise Savill, *apptd* 1996

TRADE WITH UK	1997	1998
Imports from UK	£1,406,000	£561,000
Exports to UK	2,000	14,000

BRITISH VIRGIN ISLANDS

AREA – 58 sq. miles (151 sq. km)
POPULATION – 19,000 (1997 estimate; by island: Tortola 15,687; Virgin Gorda 2,885; Anegada 191; Jost Van Dyke 170; other islands 172)
CAPITAL – ΨRoad Town (population, 3,983, 1994)
CURRENCY – US dollar (US$) (£ sterling and EC$ also circulate)
FLAG – British blue ensign with the shield of arms in the fly
POPULATION GROWTH RATE – 2.9 per cent (1996)
POPULATION DENSITY – 126 per sq. km (1996)
GDP – US$268 million (1995); US$14,122 per capita (1995)

The Virgin Islands, divided between the UK and the USA, are situated at the eastern extremity of the Greater Antilles. Those of the group which are British number 46, of which

11 are inhabited, and have a total area of about 58 sq. miles (151 sq. km). The principal islands are Tortola, the largest (area, 21 sq. miles), Virgin Gorda (8¼ sq. miles), Anegada (15 sq. miles) and Jost Van Dyke (3½ sq. miles).

Apart from Anegada, which is a flat coral island, the British Virgin Islands are hilly, being an extension of the Puerto Rico and the US Virgin Islands archipelago. The highest point is Sage Mountain on Tortola which rises to a height of 1,780 feet.

The islands lie within the trade winds belt and possess a sub-tropical climate. The average temperature varies from 22°–28° C in winter to 26°–31° C in summer. Average annual rainfall is 53 inches.

HISTORY AND POLITICS

Under the 1977 constitution the Governor, appointed by the Crown, remains responsible for defence and internal security, external affairs and the civil service but in other matters acts in accordance with the advice of the Executive Council. The Executive Council consists of the Governor as Chairman, one ex-officio member (the Attorney-General), the Chief Minister and three other ministers. The Legislative Council consists of a Speaker chosen from outside the Council, one ex-officio member (the Attorney-General), and 13 elected members returned from ten electoral districts.

Governor, HE Frank Savage, CMG, OBE, LVO, *apptd* 1998
Deputy Governor, Elton Georges, OBE

EXECUTIVE COUNCIL *as at June 1998*

Chairman, The Governor
Chief Minister and Minister of Finance, Ralph O'Neal, OBE
Attorney-General, Dancia Penn
Communications and Works, Alvin Christopher
Health, Education and Welfare, Eileene L. Parsons
Natural Resources and Labour, Julian Frazer

Puisne Judge (resident), Justice Stanley Moore; Justice Kenneth Benjamin

ECONOMY

Tourism is the main industry but the financial centre is growing steadily in importance. Other industries include a rum distillery, three stone-crushing plants and factories manufacturing concrete blocks and paint. The major export items are fresh fish, gravel, sand, fruit and vegetables; exports are largely confined to the US Virgin Islands. Chief imports are building materials, machinery, cars and beverages.

TRADE WITH UK	1997	1998
Imports from UK	£4,906,000	£10,477,000
Exports to UK	2,953,000	3,654,000

COMMUNICATIONS

The principal airport is on Beef Island, linked by bridge to Tortola, and an extended runway of 3,600 ft enables larger aircraft to call. There is a second airfield on Virgin Gorda and a third on Anegada. There are direct shipping services to the UK and the USA and fast passenger services connect the main islands by ferry.

CAYMAN ISLANDS

AREA – 102 sq. miles (264 sq. km)
POPULATION – 38,000 (1998 estimate)
CAPITAL – ΨGeorge Town (population, 20,000, 1994)

CURRENCY – Cayman Islands dollar (CI$) of 100 cents
FLAG – British blue ensign with the arms on a white disc in the fly
POPULATION GROWTH RATE – 4.4 per cent (1998)
POPULATION DENSITY – 144 per sq. km (1998)
GDP – US$1,095 million (1998); US$30,476 per capita (1998)

The Cayman Islands consist of three islands, Grand Cayman, Cayman Brac, and Little Cayman. About 150 miles south of Cuba, the islands are divided from Jamaica, 180 miles to the south-east, by the Cayman Trench, the deepest part of the Caribbean. The nearest point on the US mainland is Miami in Florida, 450 miles to the north. Cooled by trade winds, the annual average temperature and rainfall are 28.5° C and 50.7 inches respectively.

HISTORY AND POLITICS

The colony derives its name from the Carib word for the crocodile, 'caymanas', which appeared in the log of the first English visitor to the islands, Sir Francis Drake. Although tradition has it that the first settlers arrived in 1658, the first recorded settlers arrived in 1666–71. The first recorded permanent settlers followed the first land grant by Britain in 1734. The islands were placed under direct control of Jamaica in 1863. When Jamaica became independent in 1962, the islands opted to remain under the British Crown.

The constitution provides for a Governor, a Legislative Assembly and an Executive Council, and effectively allows a large measure of self-government. Unless there are exceptional reasons, the Governor accepts the advice of the Executive Council, which comprises three official members and five ministers elected from the 15 elected members of the Assembly. The official members also sit in the Assembly. The Governor has responsibility for the police, civil service, defence and external affairs. The Governor handed over the presidency of the Legislative Assembly to the Speaker in 1991. The normal life of the Assembly is four years, with a general election next due in November 2000.

Governor, HE Peter Smith, CBE, *apptd* 1999

EXECUTIVE COUNCIL *as at June 1999*

President, The Governor
Chief Secretary, James Ryan, MBE
Agriculture, Environment, Communications and Natural Resources, John McLean, OBE
Attorney-General, David Ballantyne
Community Development, Sports, Women's Affairs, Youth and Culture, Juliana O'Connor-Connolly
Education, Aviation and Planning, Truman Bodden, OBE
Financial Secretary, George McCarthy, OBE
Health, Social Welfare, Drug Abuse Prevention and Rehabilitation, Anthony Eden, OBE
Tourism, Commerce, Transport and Works, Thomas Jefferson, OBE
Speaker of Legislative Assembly, Capt. Mabry Kirkconnell, MBE

CAYMAN ISLANDS GOVERNMENT OFFICE, 6 Arlington Street, London SWIA IRE. Tel: 0171-491 7772.
Government Representative, T. Russell, CMG, CBE

ECONOMY

With a complete absence of direct taxation, the Cayman Islands has become successful over the past 30 years as an offshore financial centre. With representation from 62 countries, there were, at the end of 1998, 587 banks and trust companies, of which local offices were maintained by

107. In addition, there were 516 licensed insurance companies and 45,169 registered companies. The Cayman Islands stock exchange opened in January 1997. Tourism, with an emphasis on scuba diving, has also been developed successfully. There were 404,205 visitors by air and 850,000 cruise ship callers in 1998.

The two industries support a heavy imbalance in trade resulting from the need to import most of what is consumed and used on the islands, and have created a thriving local economy. Import duty and fees from financial centre operations have provided revenue enabling the government to undertake heavy investment in education (which is provided free to all four- to 16-year olds), health and other social programmes.

TRADE WITH UK	1997	1998
Imports from UK	£11,407,000	£9,762,000
Exports to UK	35,860,000	324,000

FALKLAND ISLANDS

AREA – 4,700 sq. miles (12,173 sq. km)
POPULATION – 2,221 (1996)
CAPITAL – ΨStanley (population, 1,636, 1994)
CURRENCY – Falkland pound of 100 pence
FLAG – British blue ensign with the arms on a white disc in the fly
POPULATION GROWTH RATE – 0.0 per cent (1996)
URBAN POPULATION – 76.0 per cent (1991)

The Falkland Islands, the only considerable group in the South Atlantic, lie about 300 miles east of the Straits of Magellan. They consist of East Falkland (area 2,610 sq. miles; 6,759 sq. km), West Falkland (2,090 sq. miles; 5,413 sq. km) and over 700 small islands. Mount Usborne (E. Falkland), the loftiest peak, rises 2,312 feet above sea level. The islands are chiefly moorland.

The climate is cool. At Stanley the mean monthly temperature varies between 24° C in January and –5° C in July.

HISTORY AND POLITICS

The Falklands were sighted first by Davis in 1592, and then by Hawkins in 1594; the first known landing was by Strong in 1690. A settlement was made by France in 1764; this was subsequently sold to Spain, but the latter country recognized Great Britain's title to a part at least of the group in 1771. The first British settlement was established in 1765. After Argentina declared independence from Spain, the Argentine government in 1820 proclaimed its sovereignty over the Falklands and a settlement was founded in 1826. The settlement was destroyed by the Americans in 1831. In 1833 occupation was resumed by the British for the protection of the seal-fisheries, and the islands were permanently colonized. Argentina continued to claim sovereignty over them as *las Islas Malvinas*), and in pursuance of this claim invaded the islands on 2 April 1982 and also occupied South Georgia. A naval and military force dispatched from Great Britain recaptured South Georgia on 25 April and after landing at San Carlos Bay on 21 May, recaptured the islands from the Argentines, who surrendered on 14 June 1982. A British naval and military garrison of 1,700 personnel remains in the area. A military zone of 55 miles (previously 80) remains around the islands within which Argentinian naval and air forces may not intrude.

Under the 1985 constitution, the Governor is advised by an Executive Council consisting of three elected members of the Legislative Council and two ex-officio members, the Chief Executive and the Financial Secretary. The Legislative Council consists of eight elected members and the same two ex-officio members.

Governor and Chairman of the Executive Council, HE Donald Lamont, *apptd* 1999
Chief Executive, Andrew M. Gurr
Attorney-General, David G. Lang, CBE, QC
Commander, British Forces, Falkland Islands, Brigadier David V. Nicholls RM
Financial Secretary, Derek F. Howatt
FALKLAND ISLANDS GOVERNMENT OFFICE, Falkland House, 14 Broadway, London SW1H OBH. Tel: 0171-222 2542. *Government Representative,* Miss S. Cameron

ECONOMY

The economy was formerly based solely on agriculture, principally sheep farming with a little dairy farming for domestic requirements and crops for winter fodder. Since the establishment of an interim conservation and management fishing zone around the islands in 1987 and the consequent introduction of a licensing regime for vessels fishing within the 200-mile zone, the economy has diversified. Income from the associated fishing activities, mainly for illex squid, is now the largest source of revenue. The increase in government revenue from fishing licences has led to the establishment of a substantial health, education and welfare system. The islands are now self-financing except for defence. Chief imports are provisions, alcoholic beverages, timber, clothing and hardware. Tourism is a small but expanding industry.

In 1993 the Falkland Islands government announced a 200-mile oil exploration zone around the islands. In September 1995 the UK and Argentina signed an agreement which provided for a joint commission to co-ordinate exploration of the oil field. Exploration licences were issued in October 1996, and exploratory drilling began in April 1998. In 1995–6 the government had a budget deficit of £5 million.

TRADE WITH UK	1997	1998
Imports from UK	£18,082,000	£42,237,000
Exports to UK	9,949,000	12,635,000

GIBRALTAR

AREA – 2.5 sq. miles (6.5 sq. km)
POPULATION – 27,192 (1997 estimate)
CAPITAL – ΨGibraltar
CURRENCY – Gibraltar pound of 100 pence
FLAG – White with a red stripe along the lower edge; over all a red castle with a key hanging from its gateway
POPULATION GROWTH RATE – 1.6 per cent (1996)
POPULATION DENSITY – 4,667 per sq. km (1996)

Gibraltar is a rocky promontory which juts southwards from the south-east coast of Spain, with which it is connected by a low isthmus. It is about 20 miles (32 km) from the opposite coast of Africa. The town stands at the foot of the promontory on the west side.

HISTORY AND POLITICS

Gibraltar was captured in 1704, during the War of the Spanish Succession, by a combined Dutch and English force, and was ceded to Great Britain by the Treaty of Utrecht (1713). Several attempts have been made to retake it, the most celebrated being the great siege of 1779 to 1783, when General Eliott held it for three years and seven months against a combined French and Spanish force. The Treaty of Utrecht stipulates that if Britain ever relinquishes its colonial rights over Gibraltar the colony would return to Spain. In a 1967 referendum on the colony's status, 12,138 people voted to remain a British Dependent Territory and 44 voted to join Spain. Spain closed the border with Gibraltar from 1969 to 1985 and refused to engage in any trade.

The 1969 constitution makes provision for certain domestic matters to devolve on a local government of ministers appointed from among elected members of the House of Assembly. The House of Assembly consists of an independent Speaker, 15 elected members, the Attorney-General and the Financial and Development Secretary.

The Governor retains responsibility for external affairs, defence, internal security and financial security, while the local government is responsible for other domestic matters. The Gibraltar government has recently been pressing for more local autonomy especially in its relations with the EU, and this has led to tension with the UK and Spanish governments. Gibraltar is part of the EU (with the UK government responsible for enforcing EU directives affecting Gibraltar) but is not a fully-fledged member. The Gibraltar Social Democrats won the last election in May 1996.

Governor and Commander-in-Chief, HE the Rt. Hon. Sir Richard Luce
Commander British Forces, HM Naval Base, Gibraltar, Cdre A. J. S. Taylor
Deputy Governor, M. Robinson, CMG
Attorney-General, R. Rhoda
Chief Justice, Derek Schofield
Chief Minister, Peter Caruana
Deputy Chief Minister, Trade and Industry, Peter Montegriffo
Education, Training, Culture and Youth, Dr Bernard Linares
Employment and Buildings and Works, Jaime Netto
Environment and Health, Keith Azzopardi
Government Services and Sport, Ernest Britto
Social Affairs, Hubert Corby
Speaker, John Alcantara, CBE
Tourism and Transport, Joe Holliday

ECONOMY

Gibraltar has an extensive shipping trade and is a popular shopping centre and tourist resort. The chief sources of revenue are the port dues, the rent of the Crown estate in the town, and duties on consumer items. The free port tradition of Gibraltar is still reflected in the low rates of import duty. A financial services industry is expanding, based on Gibraltar's status as an offshore financial centre. However, many jobs have been lost as a result of reductions in the British naval and military presence.

A total of 5,164 merchant ships (97.9 million gross registered tons aggregate) entered the port during 1998. There are 53 km of roads.

TRADE WITH UK	1997	1998
Imports from UK	£82,351,000	£81,077,000
Exports to UK	5,680,000	10,075,000

EDUCATION

Education is compulsory and free for children between the ages of five and 15 whose parents are ordinarily resident in Gibraltar. Scholarships are available for higher education in Britain. The total enrolment in government schools was 4,777 in September 1998.

MONTSERRAT

AREA – 39 sq. miles (102 sq. km)
POPULATION – 4,500 (1998 estimate)
CAPITAL – ΨPlymouth (destroyed by volcanic activity)
CURRENCY – East Caribbean dollar (EC$) of 100 cents
FLAG – British blue ensign with the shield of arms in the fly
POPULATION GROWTH RATE – 0.0 per cent (1996)
POPULATION DENSITY – 108 per sq. km (1996)
GDP – US$70 million (1995); US$6,400 per capita (1995)

Montserrat is about 11 miles long and seven miles wide. It is volcanic with several hot springs. About two-thirds of the island is mountainous, the rest capable of cultivation but volcanic activity has covered two-thirds of the island with ash and lava, destroying the economy.

HISTORY AND POLITICS

Discovered by Columbus in 1493, Montserrat became a British colony in 1632. The first settlers were predominantly Irish indentured servants from St Christopher. Montserrat was captured by the French in 1664, 1667 and 1782 but the island reverted to Britain within a few years on each occasion and was finally assigned to Great Britain in 1783.

A ministerial system was introduced in Montserrat in 1960. The Executive Council is presided over by the Governor and is composed of four elected members (the Chief and three other Ministers) and two ex-officio members (the Attorney-General and the Financial Secretary). The four Ministers are appointed from the members of the political party or coalition holding the majority in the Legislative Council. The Legislative Council consists of the Speaker, two ex-officio members (the Attorney-General and the Financial Secretary), two nominated members and seven elected members. Following elections in November 1996 the elected element of the legislature comprised the following parties: Movement for National Reconstruction (MNR) 2; People's Progressive Alliance (PPA) 2; National Progressive Party 1; Independents 2.

Governor, HE Anthony Abbott, OBE, *apptd* 1997

EXECUTIVE COUNCIL *as at June 1999*
President, The Governor
Chief Minister and Minister of Finance and Economic Development, David Brandt
Agriculture, Trade and the Environment, P. Austin Bramble
Attorney-General, Charles Ekins
Communications and Works, Rupert Weekes
Education, Health, Community Services and Labour, Adelina Tuitt
Financial Secretary, Charles. T. John, OBE

Speaker of the Legislative Council, Dr Howard. A. Fergus, CBE

ECONOMY

The economy, which consists of tourism, related construction activities, offshore business services and agriculture, has been seriously affected by relocation to the north of the island due to volcanic activity.

TRADE WITH UK	1997	1998
Imports from UK	£3,109,000	£2,000,000
Exports to UK	1,167,000	56,000

PITCAIRN ISLANDS

AREA – 2 sq. miles (5 sq. km)
POPULATION – 54 (1999 estimate). Since 1887 the
islanders have generally been adherents of the Seventh-
day Adventist Church
CURRENCY – Currency is that of New Zealand
FLAG – British blue ensign with the arms in the fly.

Pitcairn is the chief of a group of islands situated about
midway between New Zealand and Panama in the South
Pacific Ocean. The island rises in cliffs to a height of 1,100
feet and access from the sea is possible only at Bounty Bay,
a small rocky cove, and then only by surf boats. The other
three islands of the group (Henderson, lying 105 miles
east-north-east of Pitcairn, Oeno, lying 75 miles north-
west, and Ducie, lying 293 miles east) are all uninhabited.
   Mean monthly temperatures vary between 66° F (19° C)
in August and 75° F (24° C) in February and the average
annual rainfall is 80 inches. With an equable climate, the
island is very fertile and produces both tropical and sub-
tropical trees and crops.

HISTORY AND POLITICS

First settled in 1790 by the Bounty mutineers and their
Tahitian companions, Pitcairn was left uninhabited in 1856
when the entire population was resettled on Norfolk Island.
The present community are descendants of two parties
who, not wishing to remain on Norfolk, returned to Pitcairn
in 1859 and 1864 respectively.
   Pitcairn became a British settlement under the British
Settlement Act 1887, and was administered by the
Governor of Fiji from 1952 until 1970, when the
administration was transferred to the British High Commission in New Zealand and the British High Commissioner was appointed Governor. The local Government
Ordinance of 1964 provides for a Council of ten members
of whom six are elected.

Governor of Pitcairn, Henderson, Ducie and Oeno Islands, HE
   Martin J. Williams, CVO, MBE (*British High Commissioner
   to New Zealand*)
Island Magistrate, J. Warren

ECONOMY

The islanders live by subsistence gardening and fishing.
Wood carvings and other handicrafts are sold to passing
ships and to a few overseas customers. Other than small
fees charged for gun and driving licences there are no taxes
and government revenue is derived almost solely from the
sale of postage stamps and income from investments.
Communication with the outside world is maintained by
cargo vessels travelling between New Zealand and Panama
which call at irregular intervals, and by means of a satellite
service providing telephone, telex and fax facilities.

TRADE WITH UK	1997	1998
Imports from UK	£909,000	£1,459,000
Exports to UK	228,000	—

EDUCATION

Education is compulsory between the ages of five and 15.
Secondary education in New Zealand is encouraged by
the administration, which provides scholarships and bursaries. Medical care is provided by a registered nurse when
a doctor is not present.

ST HELENA

AREA – 47 sq. miles (122 sq. km)
POPULATION – 5,157 (1994 UN estimate)
CAPITAL – ΨJamestown (population, 884, 1998)
CURRENCY – St Helena pound (£) of 100 pence
FLAG – British blue ensign with the shield of arms in the
   fly
POPULATION GROWTH RATE – 0.8 per cent (1996)
POPULATION DENSITY – 40 per sq. km (1996)
URBAN POPULATION – 39.2 per cent (1998)
ILLITERACY RATE – 3.6 per cent (1998)

St Helena is situated in the South Atlantic Ocean, 955
miles south of the Equator, 702 miles south-east of
Ascension, 1,140 miles from the nearest point of the African
continent, 1,800 miles from the coast of South America and
1,694 miles from Cape Town. It is 10.5 miles long and 6.5
broad.
   St Helena is of volcanic origin, and consists of numerous
rugged mountains, the highest rising to 2,700 feet (820 m),
interspersed with picturesque ravines. Although within the
tropics, the south-east trade winds keep the temperature
mild and equable.

HISTORY AND POLITICS

St Helena was probably discovered by the Portuguese
navigator, João da Nova in 1502. It was used as a port of
call for vessels of all nations trading to the East until it was
annexed by the Dutch in 1633. It was never occupied by
them, however, and the English East India Company seized
it in 1659. From 1815 to 1821 the island was lent to the
British government as a place of exile for the Emperor
Napoleon Bonaparte who died in St Helena on 5 May
1821, and in 1834 it was annexed to the British Crown.
   The government of St Helena is administered by a
Governor, with the aid of a Legislative Council, consisting
of a Speaker, three ex-officio members (Chief Secretary,
Financial Secretary and Attorney-General) and 12 elected
members. Five committees of the Legislative Council are
responsible for the overseeing of the activities of the five
biggest government departments and have in addition a
wide range of statutory and administrative functions. The
Governor is also assisted by an Executive Council of the
three ex-officio members and the chairmen of the Council
committees.

Governor, HE David Hollamby, *apptd* 1999
Attorney-General, Kurt de Freitas, OBE
Chief Administrative Health Officer, Robert Essex
Chief Agriculture and Natural Resources Officer, Roderick J.
   Steele
Chief Auditor, Rupert Bladon
Chief Development Officer, Mrs Corinda S. S. Essex
Chief Education Officer, John Price
Chief Employment and Social Services Officer, John
   MacDonald
Chief Engineer, vacant
Chief Finance Officer, Desmond H. Wade
Chief Justice, Geoffrey W. Martin, OBE
Chief Personnel Officer, Mrs Sylvia I. Ellick
Chief Secretary, Michael J. Clancy
Chief of Police, G. G. Yon
Deputy Secretary, Ms Ethel C. Yon
Financial Secretary, Matthew J. Young
Postmistress, Mrs Iva I. Henry

ECONOMY

St Helena receives an annual grant from the UK which
amounted to £3.184 million in 1999. The only significant

export is canned and frozen fish. The other exports are a small amount of high quality coffee and cottage industry products (including lace, decorative woodwork and beadwork). James's Bay, on the north-west of the island, possesses a good anchorage. There is as yet no airport or airstrip.

TRADE WITH UK	1997	1998
Imports from UK	£8,879,000	£6,993,000
Exports to UK	594,000	654,000

ASCENSION ISLAND

AREA – 34 sq. miles (88 sq. km)
POPULATION – 1,049 (1999 census)
CAPITAL – ΨGeorgetown
CURRENCY – Currency is that of St Helena or the UK

The small island of Ascension lies in the South Atlantic some 750 miles north-west of the island of St Helena. It is a rocky peak of purely volcanic origin. The highest point (Green Mountain), some 2,817 ft, is covered with lush vegetation and has a farm of some ten acres, producing vegetables and livestock. The island is a breeding area for green turtles and for the sooty tern, or wideawake. Other wildlife includes feral donkeys and cats, nine varieties of sea birds and five of land birds.

Ascension Island's residents consist of the employees and families of the British organizations, of the contractors of the US Air Force and RAF and of the St Helena government.

British forces returned to the island in April 1982 in support of operations in the Falkland Islands. At present there are about 25 RAF personnel on the island supporting the air link to the Falklands.

HISTORY AND POLITICS

Ascension is said to have been discovered by João da Nova in 1501 and two years later was visited on Ascension Day by Alphonse d'Albuquerque, who gave the island its present name. It was uninhabited until the arrival of Napoleon in St Helena in 1815 when a small British naval garrison was stationed on the island. As HMS *Ascension* it remained under the supervision of the Board of Admiralty until 1922, when it was made a dependency of St Helena.

The British Foreign Secretary appoints the Administrator who is responsible to the Governor resident in St Helena. There is a small police force, bank and post office. The British organizations through Ascension Island Services (AIS) provide and operate various common services for the island (school, hospital, public works etc).

Administrator, Geoffrey Fairhurst, *apptd* 1999

COMMUNICATIONS

Cable and Wireless PLC operates the international telephone and cable services and maintains an internal telephone service. The BBC opened its Atlantic relay station broadcasting to Africa and South America in 1967. There is a monthly shipping service and two flights a week by RAF Tristars which transit Ascension en route to the Falkland Islands. US aircraft and ships service the American base.

TRISTAN DA CUNHA

AREA – 38 sq. miles (98 sq. km)
POPULATION – 288 (1994 UN estimate)
CAPITAL – ΨEdinburgh of the Seven Seas
CURRENCY – Currency is that of the UK

Tristan da Cunha is the chief island of a group of islands in the South Atlantic which lies some 1,260 nautical miles

(2,333 km) south-south-west of St Helena. Inaccessible Island lies 20 nautical miles south-west and has an area of 4 sq. miles (10 sq. km), and the three Nightingale Islands lie 20 nautical miles south of Tristan da Cunha and have an area of three-quarters of a sq. mile (2 sq. km). Gough Island lies some 230 nautical miles south-south-east of Tristan da Cunha and has an area of 35 sq. miles (91 sq. km).

All the islands are volcanic and steep-sided with cliffs or narrow beaches. Tristan itself has a single volcanic cone rising to 6,760 feet (2,060 m) and a narrow north-western coastal plain on which the settlement of Edinburgh is situated.

Inaccessible Island is a lofty mass of rock with sides two miles in length; the island is the resort of penguins and sea-birds. Cultivation was started in 1937 but has been abandoned.

The Nightingale Islands are three in number, of which the largest is one mile long and three-quarters of a mile wide, and rises in two peaks, 960 and 1,105 feet above sea level respectively. The smaller islands, Stoltenhoff and Middle Isle, are little more than huge rocks. Seals, penguins, and sea-birds visit these islands.

Gough Island is about eight miles long and four miles broad. It is a World Heritage Site, qualifying because of its unique temperate oceanic flora and fauna. It is the resort of penguins, sea-elephants, fur seals and sea-birds and has valuable guano deposits.

Gough and Inaccessible islands are nature reserves and access is strictly limited.

The islands have a warm-temperate oceanic climate which is damp and windy. Rainfall averages 66 inches a year on the coast of Tristan da Cunha.

Population is centred in the settlement of Edinburgh on Tristan da Cunha. In addition, there is a meteorological station maintained on Gough Island by the South African government. Inaccessible Island and the Nightingale Islands are uninhabited.

HISTORY AND POLITICS

Tristan da Cunha was discovered in 1506 by a Portuguese admiral (Tristão da Cunha) after whom it was named. In 1760 a British naval officer visited the islands and gave his name to Nightingale Island. In 1816 the group was annexed to the British Crown and a garrison was placed on Tristan da Cunha, but this force was withdrawn in 1817. Corporal William Glass remained at his own request with his wife and two children. This party, with two others, formed a settlement. In 1827 five women from St Helena, and afterwards others from Cape Colony, joined the party.

Due to its position on a main sailing route the colony thrived, with an economy based on trading with whalers, sealers and other passing ships. However, the replacement of sail by steam and the opening of the Suez Canal in the late 19th century led to decline.

In October 1961 a volcano, believed to have been extinct for thousands of years, erupted and the danger of further volcanic activity led to the evacuation of inhabitants to the UK. An advance party returned to Tristan da Cunha in 1963 and subsequently the main body of the islanders returned to the island.

GOVERNMENT

In 1938 Tristan da Cunha and the neighbouring islands of Inaccessible, Nightingale and Gough were made dependencies of St Helena. They are administered by the Governor of St Helena through a resident Administrator, with headquarters at Edinburgh. Under a constitution introduced in 1985, the Administrator is advised by an Island Council of eight elected members, of whom one must be a woman, and three appointed members. There is universal suffrage at 18. Elections are held every three years.

Administrator, Brian Baldwin, *apptd* 1998

ECONOMY

The island is financially self-sufficient. The main industries are crayfish fishing, fish-processing and agriculture, with the shore-based fishing industry having been developed with the construction of the boat harbour in 1967 and the re-establishment of the lobster factory in 1966. There are no taxes, income being derived from the royalties from the rock lobster fishery around the islands, interest from the reserve fund, and the sales of stamps and handicrafts, as well as vegetables, to passing ships. Tourism is increasing, the island being on the itinerary of several environmental tours. Apart from the fishing industry, the other main employer is the administration itself. There is one hospital with a resident medical officer, and a school catering for children up to age 15. Healthcare and education are free for the islanders.

COMMUNICATIONS

Scheduled visits to the island are restricted to about six calls a year by fishing vessels from Cape Town and annual calls of the RMS *St Helena* and the *SA Agulhas*, also from Cape Town. A wireless station on the island is in daily contact with Cape Town and a radio-telephone service was established in 1969, the same year that electricity was introduced to all the islanders' homes. A marine satellite system providing direct dialling telephone, telex and fax facilities was installed in 1992. Since 1998 the island has had internet and e-mail facilities, as well as a public telephone.

SOUTH GEORGIA AND THE SOUTH SANDWICH ISLANDS

AREA – 1,580 sq. miles (4,092 sq. km)
POPULATION – No permanent population

South Georgia is an island 800 miles east-south-east of the Falkland group. The population comprises a small military garrison and a civilian marine officer at King Edward Point, and staff of the British Antarctic Survey at Bird Island, to the north-west of South Georgia.

The South Sandwich Islands lie some 470 miles south-east of South Georgia. The group is a chain of uninhabited, actively volcanic islands about 150 miles long, with a wholly Antarctic climate.

The present constitution came into effect in 1985. It provides for a Commissioner who, for the time being, is the officer administering the government of the Falkland Islands.

In 1993 the UK government decreed an extension of Crown sovereignty and jurisdiction from 12 miles around South Georgia and the South Sandwich Islands to 200 miles around each in order to preserve marine stocks.

Commissioner for South Georgia and the South Sandwich Islands, Donald Lamont, *apptd* 1999

TURKS AND CAICOS ISLANDS

AREA – 166 sq. miles (430 sq. km)
POPULATION – 23,000 (1999 estimate)
CAPITAL – ΨGrand Turk (population, 3,691, 1994)
CURRENCY – US dollar (US$)
FLAG – British blue ensign with the shield of arms in the fly
POPULATION GROWTH RATE – 3.7 per cent (1996)
POPULATION DENSITY – 35 per sq. km (1996)

The Turks and Caicos Islands are about 50 miles south-east of the Bahamas of which they are geographically an extension. There are over 30 islands, of which eight are inhabited, covering an estimated area of 166 sq. miles (430 sq. km). The principal island and seat of government is Grand Turk.

The islands lie in the trade wind belt. The average temperature varies from 24°–27° C in the winter to 29°–32° C in the summer and humidity is generally low. Average rainfall is 21 inches a year.

HISTORY AND POLITICS

A constitution was introduced in 1988, and amended in 1993, which provides for an Executive Council and a Legislative Council. The Executive Council is presided over by the Governor and comprises the Chief Minister and five elected Ministers, together with the ex-officio Chief Secretary and Attorney-General.

At the general election of 4 March 1999, the People's Democratic Movement won nine seats and the Progressive National Party four seats in the Legislative Council.

Governor, HE John P. Kelly, LVO, MBE, *apptd* 1996

EXECUTIVE COUNCIL *as at June 1999*
President, The Governor
Attorney-General, David Jeremiah
Chief Minister, Derek H. Taylor
Chief Secretary, Cynthia Astwood, MBE
Ministers, Hilly Ewing (*Deputy Chief Minister*); Larry Coalbrooke; Noel Skippings; Oswald Skippings; Clarence Selver

ECONOMY

The most important industries are fishing, tourism and offshore finance. The islands were visited by 111,855 tourists in 1998.

TRADE WITH UK	1997	1998
Imports from UK	£2,192,000	£1,529,000
Exports to UK	727,000	30,000

COMMUNICATIONS

The principal airports are on the islands of Grand Turk and Providenciales. Air services link Providenciales and Grand Turk with Miami, the Bahamas, Haiti and the Dominican Republic. An internal air service provides a regular service between the principal islands. There are direct shipping services to the USA (Miami). A comprehensive telephone and telex service is provided by Cable and Wireless (WI) Ltd.

Events of the Year

1 September 1998 to 31 August 1999

SEPTEMBER 1998

2. Parliament was recalled from its summer recess (*see* Northern Ireland Affairs, below). 8. Sir David Rowland was appointed chairman of NatWest Group from April 1999. 9. The Labour MP for Renfrewshire West, Tommy Graham, was expelled from the Labour Party for misconduct and bringing the party into disrepute. 14. The TUC annual congress opened in Blackpool. 17. The Queen and the Duke of Edinburgh arrived in Brunei for a three-day state visit; on 20 September they arrived in Malaysia for a four-day state visit, during which The Queen closed the Commonwealth Games in Kuala Lumpur. 20. Camilla Carr and Jon James, British aid workers who were kidnapped by rebels in Chechenia in July 1997, were released from captivity. 21. The Liberal Democrat annual conference opened in Brighton. 24. Diplomatic relations between the UK and Iran were upgraded after the Iranian government said that it would not encourage or assist the murder of Salman Rushdie, the writer against whom Ayatollah Khomeini issued a *fatwa* in 1989 over his novel, *The Satanic Verses*. 27. The Labour Party conference opened in Blackpool.

OCTOBER 1998

1. The British embassy in Belgrade ordered Britons in Yugoslavia to leave the country because of the threat of UN air strikes over the massacre of Albanians in Kosovo. 4. Three Britons working in Chechenia were kidnapped. 5. The Prime Minister arrived in China for a five-day official visit. The Conservative Party conference opened in Bournemouth. The results of a ballot on party policy were announced: 58.9 per cent of members had voted, of which 84.4 per cent supported the policy of not joining a single European currency in the lifetime of this Parliament or the next. 13. The Committee on Standards in Public Life published a report which proposed reforms to the funding of political parties, a limit of £20 million on the amount a party can spend on a general election campaign, and new rules on the conduct of referendums. Phil Walker resigned as Editor of the *Daily Star* and was replaced by Peter Hill. 14. The Government announced that a Royal Commission would be set up on the second stage of reforming the House of Lords. 19. President Havel of the Czech Republic arrived in Britain at the start of a four-day official visit. 23–25. At least 12 people died as heavy rain caused severe flooding

in Wales and western England. 27. Ron Davies resigned as Secretary of State for Wales over a 'serious lapse of judgment' after being robbed at knifepoint on 26 October by a stranger he had met on Clapham Common, London; he was replaced by Alun Michael. On 29 October Mr Davies resigned as the Labour Party's prospective candidate for First Minister of the National Assembly for Wales, although he denied that he had done anything improper or illegal. On 20 November the Crown Prosecution Service said that there was insufficient evidence to proceed with charges against a man suspected of having committed the robbery. President Menem of Argentina arrived in Britain at the start of a six-day official visit, the first by an Argentine president since the Falklands Conflict. 28–31. Severe flooding hit the Severn Valley, the Welsh border country and south-west England. 29. The Independent Commission on the Voting System set up by the Government and headed by Lord Jenkins of Hillhead published its report; it proposed a new system of electing members of the House of Commons which would combine an alternative vote system with a list system of proportional representation.

NOVEMBER 1998

2. The Prince of Wales arrived in Ljubljana at the start of an eight-day visit to Slovenia and the Balkans. 6. The Prince of Wales issued a statement strongly denying reports in a television documentary that he wished his mother to abdicate. 7. Following revelations in the tabloid press by a former lover, the Agriculture Minister, Nick Brown, acknowledged that he was gay. 11. The Queen took part in ceremonies in France and Belgium to mark the 80th anniversary of the end of the First World War, and joined with President Chirac to unveil a statue of Winston Churchill in central Paris. 14. The Prime Minister joined President Clinton in calling off imminent air strikes on Iraq because of a promise from the Iraqi president, Saddam Hussein, that he would co-operate with UN weapons inspectors. The Prince of Wales celebrated his 50th birthday. 16. The Agriculture Minister announced a £120 million aid package for farmers to cushion the effects of a collapse in the price of almost all agricultural produce. 18. The House of Lords defeated the Government's European Parliamentary Elections Bill, under which a 'closed list' system of proportional representation would be introduced for the 1999 elections to the European Parliament, for the fifth time; the Government announced that the legislation would be re-introduced in the new

parliamentary session under the Parliament Acts. **22.** The Prince of Wales arrived in Greece for a two-day official visit. **23.** EU agriculture ministers voted, subject to certain conditions, to lift the global ban on exports of British beef. **24.** The state opening of parliament took place. **26.** Tony Blair addressed both Houses of the Irish Parliament, the first British prime minister to do so. The North-East Scotland European Parliament by-election took place (*see* page 271).

DECEMBER 1998

1. The president of Germany, Roman Herzog, arrived in Britain for a four-day state visit. **2.** The Leader of the Opposition (William Hague) sacked the Conservative leader in the House of Lords, Viscount Cranborne, for unilaterally reaching an agreement with the Government over an interim compromise arrangement for reform of the House of Lords, under which 91 hereditary peers would temporarily retain voting rights in the Upper House. Viscount Cranborne was replaced by the Earl of Strathclyde. On 3 December four Conservative peers (Lord Fraser of Carmyllie, Lord Bowness, Lord Pilkington and the Earl of Home) resigned as front-benchers in protest at the sacking of Lord Cranborne, and Baroness Strange and Baroness Flather resigned the Conservative whip. **8.** Four hostages, including three Britons, who had been kidnapped in Chechenia on 3 October, were found beheaded after a failed rescue mission by Chechen special forces. **15.** The House of Lords rejected the Government's European Parliamentary Elections Bill for the sixth time; it subsequently received royal assent under the Parliament Acts. The Government published a Green Paper outlining plans to abolish the State Earnings-Related Pension and encourage middle-income earners to take out personal pensions. **16.** Cruise missiles were launched by US forces at military and security installations in Iraq in a joint US/British operation code-named Operation Desert Fox. The Labour MP Brian Sedgemore said in the House of Commons that the editor of the *Sunday Telegraph*, Dominic Lawson, had been named as an MI6 agent; Mr Lawson said that he was not an agent of MI6 or any other government agency. **17.** An emergency debate on the crisis in Iraq was held in the House of Commons; RAF Tornado bombers later joined in the airstrikes on the country. **19.** The Prime Minister said that Operation Desert Fox was over and that serious damage had been caused to Iraq's military capabilities. **21.** The Trade and Industry Secretary (Peter Mandelson) admitted that he had borrowed £373,000 from the Paymaster-General (Geoffrey Robinson) in 1996 in order to buy a house; he denied that there was any conflict of interest since he had removed himself from involvement in the ongoing DTI investigation into Mr Robinson's financial affairs. On 23 December Peter Mandelson and Geoffrey Robinson both resigned from the Government and Stephen Byers was appointed

Trade and Industry Secretary. On 4 January 1999 Charlie Whelan, the Chancellor of the Exchequer's press secretary, resigned after denying persistent allegations that he had leaked information about Mr Mandelson's loan, and Dawn Primarolo was appointed Paymaster-General. **25.** Richard Branson was forced to abandon his attempt to fly around the world in a balloon after 12,000 miles when the balloon hit a trough of low pressure over the Pacific. **28.** Twelve Britons were among 16 tourists kidnapped by tribesmen in southern Yemen; on 29 December four of the hostages, including three Britons, were killed when government troops stormed the kidnappers' hideout.

JANUARY 1999

6. The Prince Edward announced his engagement to Sophie Rhys-Jones. The Prime Minister arrived in South Africa at the start of a three-day official visit. On 8 January in Cape Town police opened fire on armed Muslim demonstrators protesting against Britain's involvement in airstrikes against Iraq; four people were wounded. **9.** A Briton was kidnapped in Yemen; he was released unharmed on 13 January. **16.** A couple who had left their home in Ramsey, Cambs, with their two foster children in September 1998 because they had been told they would be unable to adopt the children returned home after Cambridgeshire social services agreed to put the matter in the hands of the courts. **17.** Two British aid workers were among six people kidnapped in Yemen. They were released unharmed on 2 February. **20.** The Government published a White Paper on reforming the House of Lords (*see* page 1171) and a Bill to remove the right of hereditary peers to sit and vote in the House of Lords. Paddy Ashdown announced that he would resign as leader of the Liberal Democrats after the elections to the European Parliament in June 1999. **26.** David Montgomery resigned as chief executive of the Mirror Group. **31.** Six RAF Tornado bombers were involved in an attack on an air defence site south of Baghdad after an Iraqi fighter breached a no-fly zone. Tom Spencer, a Conservative MEP who had been caught carrying drugs and homosexual pornography at Heathrow airport on 17 January, said that he would not stand in the European elections in June 1999.

FEBRUARY 1999

8. The Prince of Wales and the Prime Minister attended the state funeral of King Hussein of Jordan in Amman. **9.** The foreign affairs select committee of the House of Commons published a report highly critical of the role of Foreign Office officials in the 'arms to Sierra Leone' affair. **16.** Hundreds of Kurds demonstrated outside the Greek Embassy in London after the rebel leader Abdullah Öcalan was arrested outside the Greek Embassy in Nairobi; a 15-year-old girl was taken to hospital after setting fire to herself. The protest ended on 18 February when 77 demonstrators who had occupied the embassy surrendered to police. **20.** The Welsh Secretary Alun Michael was narrowly elected as Labour leader in Wales. **23.** The Prime Minister announced a 'national changeover plan' paving the way for the adoption of the euro in the UK.

MARCH 1999

1. Fourteen tourists, including five Britons, were kidnapped by Hutu rebels in the Bwindi Impenetrable National Park, Uganda; on 2 March eight of the tourists including four Britons were murdered. The Royal Commission on the Long-Term Care of the Elderly published its report, which recommended that the state should cover the costs of nursing and personal care for all elderly people who need it, and only those with assets above £60,000 should pay for the full costs of accommodation and food in residential and nursing homes. The Health Secretary (Frank Dobson) said that the recommendations would be put out to consultation until the end of 1999. **4.** An earthquake registering 4.0 on the Richter scale hit Arran, western Scotland. **7.** Four Britons were arrested in Kinshasa, Democratic Republic of Congo, and accused of espionage; on 10 March the Third Secretary at the British Embassy was also accused of spying and was expelled from the country. **8.** The Government announced plans to introduce a statutory 'right to roam' over millions of acres of private land in England and Wales. **9.** The Chancellor of the Exchequer (Gordon Brown) presented the Budget to the House of Commons (*see* page 275). The Prince of Wales arrived in Argentina at the start of a three-day official visit; he then visited Uruguay for two days before flying to the Falklands for a two-day visit. Heavy rain and melting snow caused the River Derwent to burst its banks, resulting in severe flooding in Malton and Norton, N. Yorks. **15.** Sir Leon Brittan and Neil Kinnock resigned as the UK's European Commissioners after the publication of a report detailing a culture of corruption and nepotism at the executive in Brussels; the other 18 Commissioners also resigned. **23.** The Prime Minister said that there was no alternative to military action by NATO forces against the Serbs in Kosovo. From 24 March British forces took part in bomb and missile attacks on Serb targets. **30.** Britain and other NATO leaders rejected an offer by President Milosević of Yugoslavia to start withdrawing troops from Kosovo and begin peace talks if NATO air strikes ceased.

APRIL 1999

6. An offer of an immediate cease-fire by President Milosević was rejected by NATO leaders. **10.** The Government announced that the aircraft carrier *Invincible* was to be deployed off the coast of Yugoslavia. **13.** The Prime Minister said in the House of Commons that a further 2,000 British troops, with tanks and artillery, would be sent to Macedonia to be part of an international force for eventual deployment in Kosovo; this brought the total number of British troops in Macedonia to

6,300. The House of Lords voted by a majority of 76 against giving a second reading to the Sexual Offences (Amendment) Bill, under which the gay age of consent would be reduced to 16; the Government said that it would reintroduce the Bill in the next session of Parliament and if necessary use the Parliament Acts to force the legislation through. **17.** About 50 people were injured when a nail bomb exploded in Brixton, London. **19.** The Queen and the Duke of Edinburgh arrived in Seoul, Republic of Korea, at the start of a four-day state visit. **22.** The Prime Minister held talks with President Clinton in Washington DC and said that NATO ground troops would be used in Yugoslavia if President Milosević did not accede to NATO's demands concerning Kosovo. **24.** Six people were injured when a nail bomb exploded in Brick Lane, London. **25.** The first refugees from the Balkan conflict to arrive in Britain landed at Leeds-Bradford airport. **27.** Michael Simmonds left his post as the Conservative Party's director of membership after details of a speech by the party's deputy leader, Peter Lilley, were leaked to the press; controversy continued within the party over whether the speech constituted a change of policy over the involvement of the market in the provision of public services. **30.** Three people were killed and 73 injured when a nail bomb exploded in a gay pub in Soho, London. On 2 May a man was charged with murder and causing explosions in relation to the bombs in Brixton, Brick Lane and Soho.

MAY 1999

3. The Prime Minister visited the border region between Kosovo and Macedonia. An American expedition on Mount Everest found the body of the British mountaineer George Mallory, who disappeared in 1924 less than 900 ft from the summit. **6.** Elections were held to the Scottish Parliament and the National Assembly for Wales; local elections were also held in Scotland, Wales and most parts of England except London. In Scotland the turnout was 59 per cent; Labour became the largest single party, with 56 seats, but failed to win an overall majority in the Parliament. In Wales the turnout was 46 per cent; Labour became the largest single party, with 28 seats, but failed to win an overall majority in the Assembly. In the local elections in England the turnout was 30 per cent; Labour won 36 per cent of the vote, the Conservatives 33 per cent and the Liberal Democrats 27 per cent. For full election results, *see* Local Government section. **8–9.** Demonstrators threw petrol bombs and bricks at the British embassy in Beijing in protest at the accidental bombing of the Chinese embassy in Belgrade by NATO planes on 7 May. **10.** Britain joined the USA and Germany in rejecting an offer by President Milosević to withdraw some of his forces from Kosovo. **11.** The House of Lords voted by 352 votes to 32 in favour of an amendment to the House of Lords Bill under which 92 hereditary peers would be allowed to remain in the House until the second stage of its reform. **12.** The Scottish Parliament sat for the first time; the Rt. Hon. Sir David Steel was elected Presiding Officer. The National Assembly for Wales met for the first time; Alun Michael was elected First Minister and named the eight other members of the Executive, and Lord Elis-Thomas was elected Presiding Officer. A list of serving MI6 agents was published illegally on the Internet. Chris Patten was appointed as one of Britain's two European Commissioners from September 1999. **13.** In the Scottish Parliament, Donald Dewar was elected First Minister; Labour and the Liberal Democrats agreed terms to form a coalition in the Parliament and the Liberal Democrat MSP Jim Wallace was named Deputy First Minister. **17.** Dr John Reid was appointed Scottish Secretary in place of Donald Dewar; Helen Liddell replaced Dr Reid as Transport Minister. Donald Dewar announced the members of the Scottish Executive. **20.** In the House of Commons 67 Labour MPs voted in favour of an amendment to the Welfare Reform and Pensions Bill aimed at blocking the Government's plans to means-test and restrict access to Incapacity Benefit. **25.** Cardinal Basil Hume was appointed by The Queen to the Order of Merit. **26.** The National Assembly for Wales was formally inaugurated by The Queen in Cardiff. **29.** The Prince of Wales represented The Queen at the inauguration of the first democratically elected president of Nigeria; the country also rejoined the Commonwealth.

JUNE 1999

9. Lt.-Gen. Sir Michael Jackson, in his role as NATO's commander in Kosovo, announced that the peace deal setting out terms for a Serb withdrawal from the area had been signed by Serb generals. On 12 June British troops entered Kosovo as part of the NATO-led peacekeeping operation. **10.** Elections were held to the European Parliament under the regional list system of proportional representation. The turnout was 23 per cent, with the Conservatives winning 36 seats, Labour 29, the Liberal Democrats 10, the UK Independence Party three, and the SNP, Plaid Cymru and the Green Party two each. For full results, *see* pages 269–271. The Leeds Central by-election was held; it was won by Labour with a reduced majority on a turnout of 19.6 per cent, the lowest in any post-war parliamentary election. **15.** William Hague reshuffled the Shadow Cabinet. John Prescott announced plans for Railtrack to control some London Underground lines. **16.** The Government published a series of hospital and health authority performance tables. **17.** The Public Health Minister (Tessa Jowell) said that tobacco advertising would be banned in the UK from December 1999. **18.** About 50 people were injured and 15 arrests were made during an anti-capitalist demonstration in the City of London. Thirty-six new life peers were created. **19.** The Queen conferred the earldom of Wessex and the viscountcy of Severn on the Prince Edward and said that he would be given the dukedom of Edinburgh

after the death of his parents. The Earl married Sophie Rhys-Jones at St George's Chapel, Windsor. **22.** President Göncz of Hungary began a four-day state visit to Britain. **25.** The funeral of Cardinal Basil Hume, the Archbishop of Westminster who died on 17 June, was held at Westminster Cathedral. **27.** The veteran Labour MP Tony Benn said that he would not stand for parliament at the next general election. **29.** The Home Secretary apologized for problems at the Passport Agency that were resulting in long delays in issuing passports. **30.** Janet Street-Porter was appointed editor of the Independent on Sunday.

JULY 1999

1. The Scottish Parliament was opened by The Queen. **7.** Britain resumed full diplomatic relations with Libya after the Libyan regime accepted responsibility for the murder of WPC Yvonne Fletcher outside the Libyan Embassy in London in 1984. **8.** The Government published proposals to reform the Post Office, including its conversion into a public limited company (*see* page 1174). **14.** The European Commission said that the ban on the export of British beef would be lifted on 1 August, but with severe restrictions still in force. **22.** The Conservatives won the Eddisbury by-election (*see* page 233). **28.** Paul Murphy was appointed Welsh Secretary in succession to Alun Michael, the First Secretary of the National Assembly for Wales; the Prime Minister also reshuffled a range of junior ministerial posts. **31.** The Prime Minister visited Priština, Kosovo.

AUGUST 1999

1. The European Union lifted its ban on the export of British beef; on 3 August the German health minister said that the ban would remain in place in Germany **4.** The Defence Secretary, George Robertson, was appointed secretary-general of NATO. Seven British soldiers acting as UN observers were taken hostage with 40 other people by rebels near Freetown, Sierra Leone; two of the soldiers were released in order to carry the rebel's demands to the Sierra Leonean government and the UN. On 8 August two more soldiers and 11 other hostages were released. On 9 August the remaining three soldiers were released. Queen Elizabeth the Queen Mother celebrated her 99th birthday. **9.** Charles Kennedy was elected leader of the Liberal Democrats. **11.** A total eclipse of the sun occurred at 11.11 a.m. over south-west England. Four British aid workers were abducted in Liberia; they were released on 13 August. **26.** John Stevens was appointed Commissioner of the Metropolitan Police from January 2000.

NORTHERN IRELAND AFFAIRS

1. The Sinn Fein president, Gerry Adams, said that for his party violence was 'a thing of the past'. 2. The British and Irish parliaments were recalled to debate anti-terrorist measures drawn up after the bombing at Omagh on 15 August. Sinn Fein agreed to appoint a delegate to the international body set up to oversee decommissioning of terrorist weapons. Two Scots Guardsmen who had been sentenced to life imprisonment for the murder of a teenager in Belfast in 1992 were released from prison. 3. President Clinton visited Northern Ireland. 5. A man who had been injured in the Omagh bombing on 15 August died, bringing the number of people killed to 29. 8. The Real IRA declared a permanent cease-fire. 11. The first seven prisoners to be released under the terms of the Belfast Agreement were freed from the Maze prison, Lisburn, and Magilligan prison, Londonderry. 12. Army patrols in Belfast ceased. 14. The New Northern Ireland Assembly met for the first time at Stormont.

OCTOBER 1998

6. A policeman who had been injured on 5 September in a bomb explosion during loyalist rioting in Portadown, Co. Armagh, died. 16. John Hume and David Trimble were awarded the Nobel peace prize. 20. Three INLA members were sentenced in Downpatrick to life imprisonment for the murder of Billy Wright, the leader of the LVF, at the Maze prison in December 1997. 31. A Roman Catholic man was shot dead by the dissident loyalist group the Red Hand Defenders.

NOVEMBER 1998

10. The Chief Inspector of Prisons (Sir David Ramsbotham) published a report highly critical of the regime at the Maze prison; the Government said that the prison would be closed by late 2000. 12. The Government formally recognized the cease-fire declared by the LVF in May 1998. 14. The Leader of the Opposition called for a halt to the release of terrorist prisoners until arms decommissioning had started.

DECEMBER 1998

18. Unionist and nationalist leaders reached agreement on new executive and cross-border bodies. The LVF surrendered some weapons to the Independent International Commission on Decommissioning.

JANUARY 1999

25. The Northern Ireland Secretary (Mo Mowlam) called for an end to punishment attacks by paramilitaries. 27. Eamon Collins, a former IRA terrorist turned informer, was found murdered in South Armagh.

FEBRUARY 1999

16. The New Northern Ireland Assembly voted for a 12-member executive on which Sinn Fein would be entitled to two seats, and ratified plans for a North-South ministerial council, six cross-border bodies, a civic forum and a British-Irish council.

MARCH 1999

8. In the face of continuing deadlock between the UUP and Sinn Fein over the issue of decommissioning weapons, the Government extended the deadline for the establishment of an executive from 10 March to 2 April. 11. The paratrooper Lee Clegg, who served four years in prison for the murder of a joyrider in Belfast in 1990 and who had his conviction quashed in the House of Lords in 1998, was acquitted of the murder at a retrial at Belfast Crown Court. 15. A leading nationalist lawyer, Rosemary Nelson, was killed by a bomb planted under her car in Lurgan, Co. Armagh. 17. A prominent loyalist, Frankie Curry, was shot dead in the Shankill Road area of Belfast. 22. The Home Secretary (Jack Straw) successfully sought a judicial review of the timing of the release from the Maze prison of four IRA prisoners under the terms of the Belfast Agreement; on 23 March the High Court in Belfast upheld the timing of their release. 30 March–1 April. The British and Irish Prime Ministers and Northern Ireland's political leaders held talks at Hillsborough Castle aimed at breaking the deadlock over the issue of decommissioning weapons. On 1 April the talks were suspended until 13 April after the two Prime Ministers had put forward a detailed plan for decommissioning. The plan was formally rejected by Sinn Fein when the talks resumed.

MAY 1999

12. Loyalist gunmen shot and wounded a Roman Catholic man in Carrickfergus, Co. Antrim. 14. The Prime Minister held talks at Downing Street with Northern Ireland's political leaders aimed at breaking the deadlock over the implementation of the Belfast Agreement. On 16 May the British and Irish prime ministers set a final deadline of 30 June for devolution of powers to the New Northern Ireland Assembly. 28. The IRA left the body of Eamon Molloy, an IRA member shot dead by the IRA in 1975, in a graveyard in Faughart, Co. Louth; his was the first of nine bodies that the IRA had agreed to return to their families. On 1 June the IRA said it had been unable to locate the burial sites of the remaining eight bodies.

JUNE 1999

5. A Protestant woman married to a Roman Catholic man was killed when a bomb was thrown into her house in Portadown, Co. Armagh; five men believed to be loyalist extremists were later arrested in connection with the attack. 15. The Prime Minister said that decommissioning of weapons was not a

prerequisite for Sinn Fein to participate in Northern Ireland's government but that the party should either bring about decommissioning or condemn those who failed to bring it about. **17.** The High Court ruled that the decision of the forthcoming Saville inquiry, that 16 soldiers should not be granted automatic anonymity before giving evidence concerning the 'Bloody Sunday' shootings in Londonderry in 1972, was flawed. Martin McGartland, an IRA informer, was shot and seriously wounded at his home in Whitley Bay, Tyne and Wear. **22.** Patrick Magee, who was given eight life sentences in 1986 for the bomb attack on the Grand Hotel in Brighton which killed five people during the 1984 Conservative Party conference, was released from prison under the terms of the Belfast Agreement. David Trimble said that Mo Mowlam had lost the confidence of the Protestant community in Northern Ireland. **23.** The Prime Minister said that if the Belfast Agreement could not be implemented, violence would return to Northern Ireland. A former soldier was charged with the murder of the Roman Catholic solicitor Patrick Finucane in Belfast in 1989. **25.** The Prime Minister proposed that the IRA should commit itself to a timetable for decommissioning all its weapons by May 2000 in return for the agreement of the Unionists to the participation of Sinn Fein in the Executive of the New Northern Ireland Assembly. **28.** The Parades Commission ruled that the Orange Order could not march down the Garvaghy Road in Portadown on 4 July. **30.** Talks continued in Belfast aimed at breaking the deadlock over the issue of decommissioning. The deadline for the devolution of power to the Assembly passed with no agreement being reached.

JULY 1999

2. The Prime Minister and the Taoiseach put forward a new set of proposals aimed at breaking the deadlock over decommissioning; they said that a power-sharing executive could be formed in the middle of July and that the IRA would begin the process of decommissioning within days of power being devolved, with actual decommissioning starting within weeks. If any stage of the decommissioning obligations was not met, or if the Unionists did not co-operate in the devolution of power, the executive would be suspended. The talks were adjourned. **4.** The Prime Minister said that if the proposed decommissioning obligations were not met, the executive could be re-formed by the other parties without Sinn Fein. **12.** Emergency legislation to devolve power to a power-sharing executive was introduced into the House of Commons; under the legislation, the Government could suspend the executive and review its future if its proposed conditions were not met. The Unionists largely voted against the legislation on the grounds that it did not incorporate a clear timetable for the decommissioning of weapons and did not allow for Sinn Fein to be expelled immediately from the executive should the IRA not disarm. **14.** The legislation was tabled in the House of Lords after the Prime Minister had introduced amendments to set out a timetable for decommissioning. The Unionists said that it was still party policy to refuse to sit on an executive with Sinn Fein unless the decommissioning process had begun. The legislation was therefore put on hold. **15.** The Unionists boycotted the session of the New Northern Ireland Assembly at which ministers were nominated for the power-sharing executive; the process therefore collapsed. The Deputy First Minister, Seamus Mallon, resigned in protest at the Unionists' actions. The Prime Minister announced a review of the implementation of the Belfast Agreement. **21.** The IRA said that the British government was responsible for the developing political crisis in Northern Ireland. **28.** The Court of Appeal ruled that the soldiers giving evidence to the forthcoming inquiry concerning the 'Bloody Sunday' shootings in Londonderry in 1972 should be granted anonymity.

AUGUST 1999

14. There were violent clashes between nationalist protesters and the RUC in Belfast and Londonderry as loyalist marches took place. **26.** Mo Mowlam said that in spite of the murder of a taxi driver in July 1999 and evidence of gun-running in the USA, in her judgement the IRA ceasefire was still intact; however she said that the continuing violence was deplorable and that the situation was deeply worrying. **28.** Four youths from Dungannon, Co. Tyrone, left Northern Ireland after receiving death threats from the IRA; a fifth youth left Belfast on 29 August.

ACCIDENTS AND DISASTERS

SEPTEMBER 1998

3. All 229 people on board a Swissair plane flying from New York to Geneva were killed when it crashed into the sea off Halifax, Nova Scotia. **13.** The death toll as a result of the flooding in Bangladesh rose to 950. **13–19.** Four hundred people died following torrential rains in Chiapas, Mexico. **18.** More than 120 people were missing feared drowned after a ferry sank near Manila, Philippines. **21–25.** Hurricane Georges hit the Caribbean and was reported to have left at least 300 people dead. **25.** Thirty-eight people were killed when an airliner bound for Melilla crashed into a mountain in Morocco.

OCTOBER 1998

8. At least 20 people drowned when a pleasure boat broke in two on Lake Banyoles, near Gerona, northeast Spain. **17.** Seven hundred people died when an oil pipeline in Nigeria caught fire. **23.** At least 82 people died and 250,000 were made homeless by typhoons in the Philippines. **28 October–**

2 November. Up to 20,000 people were killed in floods and mudslides and millions were left homeless when Hurricane Mitch hit central America. **30.** Sixty teenagers were killed and 190 were injured when fire broke out at a Hallowe'en discotheque in Gothenburg, Sweden.

NOVEMBER 1998

26. At least 205 people were killed in a train crash in the Punjab, India.

DECEMBER 1998

11. At least 100 people were killed when a Thai Airways airbus crashed in southern Thailand. **16.** Up to 40 people were killed when a five-storey block of flats collapsed in Rome, Italy.

JANUARY 1999

25. Up to 2,000 people were killed when an earthquake registering 6.0 on the Richter scale hit western Colombia.

FEBRUARY 1999

23–24. Thirty-eight people were killed when avalanches hit the ski resort of Galtür, Austria. **24.** All 64 people on board a China Southwest Airlines plane were killed when it exploded in mid-air near Wenzhou, eastern China.

MARCH 1999

16. At least 14 people were killed when a passenger train hit a lorry at Bourbonnias, USA. **24.** Forty people were killed after fire broke out in the Mont Blanc tunnel linking France and Italy. At least 32 people were killed when a train was derailed between Nairobi and Mombasa, Kenya. **29.** At least 85 people died when a series of earthquakes hit villages in northern India.

MAY 1999

4. At least 45 people were killed and hundreds injured when a tornado storm hit Oklahoma and Kansas, USA. **8.** At least 200 people were drowned when a ferry was sucked into a whirlpool in the Meghna River, Bangladesh. **21.** All 1,100 passengers and crew aboard a cruise liner were saved when the ship sank off the coast of Malaysia. **31.** Fifty-four people, mainly teenage girls, were killed in a stampede for shelter during a storm at a beer festival in Minsk, Belarus.

JUNE 1999

2. Nine people were killed and more than 80 injured when an American Airlines plane crashed and burst into flames on landing at Little Rock, Arkansas. **15.** At least 17 people were killed and hundreds were injured when an earthquake registering 6.7 on the Richter scale hit central Mexico. **23.** Thirty-one people were injured when a Virgin express train crashed into an empty commuter train on the West Coast main line route south of Winsford station, Cheshire. **30.** Twenty-three children were killed in a fire in a summer camp dormitory in Hwasong, S. Korea.

JULY 1999

1. Twenty people were killed when a cable car fell onto the mountainside in the Alps near Saint-Etienne-en-Dévoluy, France. **8.** More than 1,100 passengers were rescued when a Norwegian ferry caught fire off the coast of Sweden. **27.** Twenty-one people were killed while canyoning near Wilderswil, Switzerland.

AUGUST 1999

2. At least 250 people were killed when two trains crashed head-on at Gaisal, eastern India. **5.** It was reported that 725 people had been killed and 5.5 million left homeless by flooding after the Yangtze River in China broke its banks. **17.** An estimated 40,000 people were killed when an earthquake registering at least 7.5 on the Richter scale hit western Turkey. **25.** A container ship caught fire after colliding with a cruise liner carrying 2,340 people in the English Channel; 29 people were slightly injured. **31.** At least 64 people were killed when a Boeing 737 crashed on take-off at Buenos Aires airport, Argentina.

ARTS, SCIENCE AND THE MEDIA

SEPTEMBER 1998

2. ITV lodged proposals with the Independent Television Commission to move the main evening news bulletin from 10 p.m. to 6.30 p.m. **9.** The Royal Opera House announced plans to shut down the Royal Opera company for 11 months of 1999 in order to save money. **14.** The Health Secretary (Frank Dobson) said that the anti-impotence drug Viagra would not be available on the NHS. **16.** The National Year of Reading was launched by the Education Secretary (David Blunkett). Michael Kaiser, the executive director of American Ballet Theatre, was appointed executive director of the Royal Opera House. **23.** Surgeons in Lyon, France, carried out the first ever arm transplant.

OCTOBER 1998

1. The first digital televisions went on sale to the public. **10.** Bernard Haitink said that he had resigned as music director of the Royal Opera House. He withdrew his resignation in December 1998 when the Arts Council announced increased funding for the House. **12.** The new Sadler's Wells Theatre in Islington, London, opened. **13.** A Briton, Prof. John Pople, was jointly awarded the Nobel prize for chemistry. **18.** Richard Bacon, one of the presenters of the children's television programme *Blue Peter,* was sacked after he admitted taking cocaine. **21.** The restored Albert Memorial in London was unveiled by The Queen. **25.** A controversial new biography of the Prince of Wales by Penny Junor began to be serialized in the *Mail on Sunday*; the Prince and Camilla Parker Bowles issued a joint statement saying that the book was not authorized, solicited or approved by them. **30.** The Royal Greenwich Observatory closed.

NOVEMBER 1998

19. The ITC approved a request from ITV to move its main evening news bulletin from 10 p.m. to 6.30 p.m. **20.** Five leading male dancers resigned from the Royal Ballet to join a new London-based ballet company. **30.** The Queen opened the new Museum of Scotland in Edinburgh. The Royal Exchange Theatre, Manchester, which was badly damaged by the IRA bomb that exploded in the city in June 1996, reopened after a £31 million refurbishment.

DECEMBER 1998

1. Chris Ofili won the Turner Prize for modern art. **2.** The Royal Court Theatre announced that it had secured sponsorship worth £3 million from the Jerwood Foundation and that its two auditoriums would in future carry the sponsor's name. **20.** A woman in Houston, Texas, gave birth to octuplets; one baby later died. **11.** Ted Hughes was awarded the T. S. Eliot Prize for Poetry posthumously for his book *Birthday Letters*. On 12 January he won the Whitbread Poetry Award for the same work, and on 26 January he won the Whitbread Book of the Year Award for it, becoming the first writer ever to win the award twice.

JANUARY 1999

19. A major exhibition of late paintings by Monet opened at the Royal Academy, London. Amanda Platell was sacked as editor of the *Express on Sunday*.

FEBRUARY 1999

11. The BBC suspended two producers and a researcher from *The Vanessa Show* after it emerged that four guests on the daytime chat show had been fakes. **16.** At the Brit Awards in London, Robbie Williams won the awards for best male singer, best single and best video.

MARCH 1999

5. The News at Ten was broadcast for the last time on ITV before moving to the new time of 6.30 p.m. **23.** Antonio Pappano was appointed music director of the Royal Opera from 2002. **24.** The former editor of the *Sunday Express*, Amanda Platell, was appointed press secretary to the Leader of the Opposition, William Hague.

MAY 1999

10. Quentin Blake was appointed the first 'Children's Laureate' with the aim of attracting more children to reading and writing. At Sotheby's in New York, Cezanne's *Still life with curtain, pitcher and bowl of fruit* sold for £36.8 million, a record for a work by the artist, and Seurat's *Island of the Grande Jatte* sold for £21.4 million, a record for a work by Seurat. The

private papers of Christopher Isherwood were acquired by the Huntington Library, Los Angeles. **13.** A memorial service for the late Poet Laureate, Ted Hughes, was held at Westminster Abbey. **18.** The Canadian billionaire Garry Weston gave the British Museum £20 million to enable it to complete its Great Court project. Paul Muldoon was appointed professor of poetry at Oxford University. **19.** Andrew Motion was appointed poet laureate. **26.** Buckingham Palace made a formal complaint to the Press Complaints Commission (PCC) following the publication by the *Sun* of a photograph of Prince Edward's fiancée Sophie Rhys-Jones topless in 1988; the *Sun* published an apology on 27 May. **27.** Leonardo da Vinci's *Last Supper* was unveiled in Milan for the first time after 22 years of restoration.

JUNE 1999

1. William Hague said that he had written to the chairman of the BBC to say that the broadcaster Greg Dyke would be a 'totally unacceptable' choice as director-general of the BBC in view of his donations totalling £50,000 to the Labour Party. **2.** Sir Anthony Dowell announced his resignation as director of the Royal Ballet from August 2001. **17.** The art collector Sir Denis Mahon donated his collection of Old Masters to the nation. **22.** The Royal Opera House said that its financial crisis was over. **24.** Greg Dyke was appointed director-general of the BBC from April 2000. **28.** At Sotheby's in London a Degas pastel, *Dancer at Rest*, sold for £17.6 million, a record for a work by the artist.

JULY 1999

8. A collection of art and antiques stolen by the Nazis from the Rothschild family in Austria in 1938 and recovered in 1945 sold for more than £57 million in an auction at Christie's in London. **20.** The Government announced an immunization programme against the C strain of meningitis.

AUGUST 1999

4. The director Alan Parker was appointed chairman of the new Film Council to be established by the Government in April 2000.

CRIMES AND LEGAL AFFAIRS

OCTOBER 1998

13. In the High Court 11-year-old Sam Mansell, who developed cerebral palsy after being deprived of oxygen at birth, was awarded record damages of £3.29 million. **17.** The former Chilean dictator Augusto Pinochet was arrested at a hospital in London under a warrant issued by the Spanish government; the request for his extradition to face charges of murdering Spanish citizens in Chile during his regime was refused in the High Court on 28 October on the grounds that he was entitled to sovereign immunity in respect of acts committed while he was head of state. On 25 November five Law Lords ruled by a majority of three to two that Gen. Pinochet was not entitled as a former head of state to immunity from extradition. On 9 December the Home Secretary (Jack Straw) ruled that extradition proceedings against Gen. Pinochet could proceed. **23.** Michael Stone was sentenced in Maidstone to life imprisonment for the murders of Lin and Megan Russell and the attempted murder of Josie Russell near Chillenden, Kent, in July 1996. **31.** Twenty-two-year-old Jennifer King was reported missing after failing to return home from a nightclub in Bristol; her body was found in nearby woodland on 3 November.

NOVEMBER 1998

3. Patrizia Reggiani, the former wife of the fashion heir Maurizio Gucci, was sentenced in Rome to 29 years' imprisonment for arranging his murder in 1995. **5.** Two police dog instructors were each sentenced in Chelmsford to four months' imprisonment for cruelty to dogs at their training centre at Sandon, Essex. **11.** Two small oil paintings by John Constable which had been in storage were reported to have been stolen from the Victoria and Albert Museum, London. **16.** In the High Court 17-year-old Helen Edwards, who suffered brain damage after being deprived of oxygen during an operation to remove a birthmark in 1986, was awarded record damages of £3.9 million. **17.** Paul Seddon was sentenced in Preston to life imprisonment for the murder of five-year-old Dillon Hull, who was killed by a bullet intended for his stepfather in a drug feud in Bolton in August 1997. **18.** A French court rejected a request from Britain to extradite David Shayler, the former MI5 officer who was arrested in Paris in August 1998 and wanted for allegedly leaking secrets to a newspaper; the court ruled that Mr Shayler's motives for revealing secret information were political and that there were therefore no grounds for his extradition. **23.** A social worker was stabbed to death at a hostel in Balham, London; a 'care in the community' patient she had been looking after was charged with the murder.

DECEMBER 1998

1. The gay activist Peter Tatchell was fined £18.60 at a magistrates' court in London for interrupting the Archbishop of Canterbury's sermon in Canterbury Cathedral on Easter Sunday 1998 with a protest about the Archbishop's views on the gay age of consent. **2.** The Lord Chancellor published a White Paper on reforming legal services in Britain (*see* page 1171). **17.** Five law lords overturned the ruling by five other law lords on 25 November that the former Chilean dictator Gen. Pinochet did not enjoy immunity from extradition; they reached their decision on the grounds that one of the law lords involved in the earlier ruling, Lord Hoffmann, had failed to disclose his links with Amnesty International, one of the organizations which had made representations to the law lords during the case.

The conviction of Gilbert 'Danny' McNamee, who was sentenced in 1987 to 25 years' imprisonment for making IRA bombs and who was released in November 1998 under the terms of the Belfast Agreement, was quashed by the Court of Appeal. **21.** In the High Court Martijn Biesheuvel, who was left paralysed after a car crash in Bath in May 1994, was awarded record damages of £9.2 million.

JANUARY 1999

19. Jonathan Aitken, the former Conservative Cabinet minister, admitted at the Central Criminal Court charges of perjury and perverting the course of justice in relation to his unsuccessful libel action against the *Guardian* and Granada Television in June 1997. On 8 June he was sentenced to 18 months' imprisonment. **27.** Mary Chipperfield, the circus trainer, was convicted in Andover of 12 charges of cruelty to animals; on 9 April she was fined £7,500.

FEBRUARY 1999

2. Jenny Cupit was sentenced in Chester to life imprisonment for the murder of Kathryn Linaker, with whose husband she had been having an affair, in April 1998. Louise Sullivan, an Australian nanny, was sentenced at the Central Criminal Court to fifteen months' imprisonment, suspended for two years, for the manslaughter of a six-month-old baby in her care in April 1997. **4.** A case involving the alleged smuggling of £14 million worth of cannabis was halted in Bristol after the judge said that customs officers had displayed a 'reckless disregard for the law' which would have prevented the ten defendants from having a fair trial. Nicholas Mullen, who had been sentenced in 1990 to 30 years' imprisonment for conspiracy to cause IRA explosions on the mainland, was released from prison after the Court of Appeal quashed his conviction on the ground that his deportation from Zimbabwe to England had been illegal. **15.** John Drewe was sentenced in London to six years' imprisonment for tampering with the records of national archives in order to create false histories for hundreds of fake copies of 20th-century works of art. **20.** The Home Secretary (Jack Straw) obtained an injunction to prevent the *Sunday Telegraph* from publishing leaked extracts from the report of the inquiry led by Sir William Macpherson of Cluny into the murder of Stephen Lawrence in London in 1993. On 21 February Mr Straw agreed that extracts already in the public domain could be reprinted and commented on. The full report was published on 24 February; it accused the Metropolitan Police of 'racism, professional incompetence and bad leadership' and made a series of recommendations aimed at eradicating racism from the criminal justice system and other areas of public life (*see* page 1172). On 25 February Sir William apologized for releasing the names and addresses of police informants in the case as part of the report.

MARCH 1999

6. Seven people including three children were killed in an arson attack on a house in Chingford, north-east London. **9.** The Chief Constable of Sussex Police was suspended over a raid in January 1998 during which an unarmed suspect was shot dead. **12.** Kenneth Peatfield was sentenced in Sheffield to life imprisonment for the murder of his lover, whose head was found in a block of concrete in his garage, in March 1998. **15.** The Commission of the European Court of Human Rights ruled that Jon Venables and Robert Thompson, who were convicted in 1993 of the murder of two-year-old James Bulger, did not receive a fair trial; the case was referred to the court for a full judgment. **19.** Four IRA members were sentenced in Belfast to an aggregate total of 640 years' imprisonment and three life terms for terrorist activities which led to the deaths of nine people. The Labour MP for Newark, Notts, Fiona Jones, was convicted in Nottingham of election expenses fraud in relation to her campaign at the 1997 general election; she was therefore immediately disqualified as an MP. On 15 April her conviction was quashed in the Court of Appeal. **24.** Seven law lords ruled that the former Chilean dictator Gen. Pinochet did not enjoy immunity as a former head of state from extradition on charges of torture, but that he could only face trial in Spain in relation to alleged crimes committed after 29 September 1988 when torture became an 'extraterritorial' crime in the UK after being incorporated in the Criminal Justice Act; this reduced the number of charges against him from 32 to three, and so the law lords referred the case back to the Home Secretary for a new ruling as to whether or not Gen. Pinochet should be extradited. On 15 April the Home Secretary ruled that extradition proceedings could begin. The anti-apartheid activist Allan Boesak was sentenced in Johannesburg, South Africa, to six years' imprisonment for the theft of more than £100,000 from his charity, the Foundation for Peace and Justice. **25.** The Labour MP for Glasgow Govan, Mohammed Sarwar, was acquitted in Edinburgh of bribing a rival candidate in the 1997 general election; two further charges of electoral fraud and understating his election expenses had been dropped during the trial. **26.** Jack Kevorkian, a doctor who had admitted assisting the suicide of terminally ill patients many times, was convicted in Michigan, USA, of second degree murder. On 13 April he was sentenced to between ten and 25 years' imprisonment.

APRIL 1999

5. Two Libyans, Abdel Basset Ali al-Megrahi and Lamen Khalifa Fhimah, arrived in Holland to face charges of bombing Pan Am flight 103 which crashed over Lockerbie, Scotland, in 1988; the trial was to be conducted at a former military air base, Camp Zeist, under Scottish law before three High Court judges sitting without a jury. **7.** At the Central Criminal Court, Edgar Pearce pleaded guilty to 20 charges including blackmail, assault, causing an explosion and possession of firearms; he had been known as the Mardi Gra bomber after planting home-made explosives near branches of Barclay's Bank and Sainsbury's between 1994 and 1998. On 14 April he was sentenced to 21 years' imprisonment. **13.** Seventeen-year-old Ashleigh Robinson, a pupil at Millfield school, was found murdered in Guildford, Surrey. **20.** Fourteen students and a teacher were killed and 24 people were injured when two teenagers entered their school in Colorado, USA, exploding bombs and firing indiscriminately. **23.** Darren Vickers, a bus driver, was sentenced in Manchester to life imprisonment for the murder of Jamie Lavis, an eight-year-old boy he had befriended, in May 1997. **26.** The television presenter Jill Dando was shot dead outside her home in Fulham, London. **27.** Neil Sayers and Graham Wallis were convicted in Maidstone of the murder of a fellow student at Hadlow Agricultural College, Kent, in May 1998. **28.** A man was arrested after shooting at police, hijacking four cars and taking refuge in a house in Feltham, London. **30.** Dame Shirley Porter, the former leader of Westminster city council who was found guilty of wilful misconduct and gerrymandering by the district auditor in 1996 and faced a surcharge of millions of pounds, was cleared of wrongdoing by the Court of Appeal.

MAY 1999

3. A former Israeli paratrooper, Daniel Okev, was sentenced in Beersheba, Israel to 20 years' imprisonment for murdering a British tourist and badly wounding his girlfriend in the Negev desert in August 1997. **11.** Dr David Moor, a GP, was cleared in Newcastle upon Tyne of murdering a terminally ill patient to whom he gave a fatal dose of a painkiller. **18.** Craig Smith was sentenced in Chester to life imprisonment for the murder of 13-year-old Claire Hart in Congleton, Cheshire, in June 1998. **19.** The Home Secretary (Jack Straw) put forward proposals for defendants in 'either way' cases to have the right to elect for trial by jury to be withdrawn. **25.** Shakeela Naz and her son Shazad were each sentenced in Nottingham to life imprisonment for the murder of her daughter Rukhsana, who was deemed to have brought disgrace on the family by conceiving a child as a result of an adulterous affair, in March 1998. **28.** Alan Hopkinson was sentenced in Lewes to nine terms of life imprisonment for abducting, imprisoning and assaulting two ten-year-old girls from Hastings in January 1999.

JUNE 1999

4. Kim Galbraith was sentenced in Glasgow to life imprisonment for the murder of her husband, who she claimed had subjected her to sexual and mental abuse, in January 1999. **6.** A British woman, Kathleen Morgan, was cleared in Dubai of unlawfully killing a Russian tourist in a jet ski accident. **27.** Two children, their mother and their grandmother were murdered in Clydach, near Swansea.

JULY 1999

17. The mutilated body of a woman was found in a suitcase in the car park at Heathrow airport; a man was later charged with the murder. **18.** A Radio 1 disc jockey, Tim Westwood, was shot in the arm when a gunman opened fire on his car in Kennington, south London. **21.** The Treasurer of the Conservative Party, Michael Ashcroft, started a libel action against *The Times* over articles it had published on his business activities in Belize. **23.** The pilot of an All Nippon Airways flight was stabbed to death by a hijacker after taking off from Tokyo airport; the hijacker was then overpowered by other crew members and arrested when the plane had returned to Tokyo. **26.** Thirty Greenpeace protesters, including its executive director, Lord Melchett, were arrested after starting a field of genetically modified maize in Lyng, Norfolk. **27.** Two 15-year-old girls were ordered in Manchester to be detained at Her Majesty's pleasure for the murder in September 1998 of an elderly woman in Failsworth, Gtr Manchester, whose body they dumped in the Rochdale Canal. At the Central Criminal Court, a record fine of £1.5 million was imposed on Great Western Trains over safety failures that contributed to the Southall crash in September 1997 in which seven people died. **29.** Twelve people were shot dead in Atlanta, Georgia, by a man who had lost money selling stocks and shares on the Internet.

AUGUST 1999

9. Eight British men were convicted in Yemen of plotting an Islamic fundamentalist bombing campaign in December 1998. **23.** A man was charged with murder after a 16-year-old boy was shot dead during a burglary at a farm in Emneth, Norfolk.

ECONOMIC AND BUSINESS AFFAIRS

SEPTEMBER 1998

1. The Dow Jones industrial average rose 288.36 points, the second-biggest one-day rise in its history. Scottish Hydro and Southern Electric announced a £4.9 billion merger. **3.** Shell and Texaco announced a joint venture in marketing and refining European oil. **4.** The Japanese electronics company Fujitsu announced that it was ceasing production at its factory in Newton Aycliffe, Co. Durham, with the loss of 570 jobs. **8.** The Dow Jones industrial average rose 380.53 points, the biggest one-day rise in its history. **15.** Microsoft replaced General Electric as the world's biggest company when its market worth reached US$267 billion. **23.** The Trade and Industry Secretary (Peter Mandelson) blocked the planned take-over of Coral by Ladbroke on the advice of the Monopolies and Mergers Commission. **24.** The

sale of the RAC roadside rescue business to the American marketing group Cendant was referred to the Monopolies and Mergers Commission. On 4 February 1999 Cendant pulled out of the sale.

OCTOBER 1998

4. The Group of Seven industrialized countries called for immediate interest rate cuts and a co-ordinated response to the prevailing financial crisis. **5.** Sterling closed at DM2.7638, its lowest level since May 1997. **6.** The Chancellor of the Exchequer (Gordon Brown) said that the British economy would suffer a significant slowdown in 1999 as a result of the economic crisis in Asia. **8.** The Bank of England cut bank base rates by 0.25 per cent to 7.25 per cent. **12.** The FT-SE 100 index closed 214.2 points up, the biggest ever points rise in a single day, at 5,037.6. **21.** Rover confirmed that it was seeking cost-cutting measures including 2,400 job cuts at its Longbridge plant in Birmingham. **30.** The Group of Seven industrialized countries announced a package of measures designed to restore confidence in the world financial markets.

NOVEMBER 1998

2. The Office for National Statistics suspended publication of monthly average earnings figures amid growing doubts about their reliability. **3.** The Chancellor of the Exchequer said that he would increase borrowing to compensate for lower than projected growth in 1999 but that there would be a return to strong economic growth in 2000. **5.** The Bank of England cut bank base rates by 0.5 per cent to 6.75 per cent. **23.** The Dow Jones industrial average rose 214 points to close at a record high of 9,374.27. **24.** America Online (AOL) announced a $4.2 billion agreed take-over bid for the Internet software company Netscape. **26.** Sir Richard Greenbury resigned as chief executive of Marks & Spencer to become its non-executive chairman; he was replaced as chief executive by Peter Salsbury. The company's deputy chairman, Keith Oates, resigned. **27.** Martin Taylor resigned as chief executive of Barclays Bank; Sir Peter Middleton was appointed interim chief executive. **30.** Deutsche Bank announced an agreed $10.1 billion take-over of Bankers Trust.

DECEMBER 1998

1. Exxon announced an agreed $82 billion take-over of Mobil. **2.** Walter Hasselkus resigned as chairman of Rover after heavy losses at the business; he was replaced by Werner Sämann. **3.** European central banks of the 11 countries due to join the single European currency on 1 January 1999 took co-ordinated action to cut interest rates. **7.** The Trade and Industry Secretary (Peter Mandelson) announced a set of proposals aimed at giving the Post Office greater commercial freedom. **9.** The British drugs company Zeneca announced a merger with the Swedish company Astra. **10.** The Bank of England cut bank base rates by 0.5 per cent to 6.25 per cent.

JANUARY 1999

1. The euro replaced the existing currencies in 11 European countries. **7.** The Bank of England cut bank base rates by 0.25 per cent to 6 per cent. **8.** The FT-SE 100 index closed at a record high of 6,195.6. **11.** British American Tobacco and Rothmans International announced a £15 billion merger. **17.** Vodafone announced an agreed £7.5 billion merger with the American company AirTouch. **19.** British Aerospace announced a £7.7 billion merger with the Marconi Electronic Systems arm of GEC. The Internet service provider AtHome agreed to buy the Internet search company Excite for $6.7 billion. **21.** January Investments bought the retailing group Sears, subject to shareholders' approval, in a deal worth £548 million. **22.** International stock markets fell after Argentina confirmed that it was considering adopting the US dollar as its currency. **28.** Ford agreed a £3.9 billion deal to buy Volvo's passenger car division.

FEBRUARY 1999

1. The French insurance company AXA acquired Guardian Royal Exchange (GRE) for £3.4 billion. **2.** Pricewaterhouse Coopers, which as Coopers and Lybrand had acted as auditors to the group of companies controlled by the late Robert Maxwell, was fined £1.2 million and ordered to pay costs of £2.1 million by the accountancy Joint Disciplinary Tribunal for failures in its auditing of the companies. **4.** The Bank of England cut bank base rates by 0.5 per cent to 5.5 per cent. **5.** Bernd Pischetsrieder was ousted as chairman of BMW. **8.** Ladbroke announced a £1.16 billion agreed take-over of the hotelier Stakis. **20.** The flotation of the betting shop chain William Hill was cancelled after the company was bought by the venture capitalists Cinven and CVC Capital Partners in a deal worth £825 million. **24.** The FT-SE 100 index closed at a record high of 6,307.6.

MARCH 1999

8. The World Trade Organization met in emergency session in Geneva; it urged the EU and the USA to resolve their dispute over sanctions imposed by the USA against some EU goods because of the EU's alleged protectionism in favouring bananas from the Caribbean over those from Latin America. **11.** Prudential announced an agreed £1.9 billion take-over of M&G. **16.** The Dow Jones Industrial Average rose to over 10,000 points for the first time when it reached 10,001.12. On 29 March it closed at over 10,000 points for the first time, at 10,006.78. **31.** The future of the Rover car plant at Longbridge, Birmingham, was secured by a government aid package believed to be worth about £150 million.

APRIL 1999

6. The FT-SE 100 index closed at a record high of 6,415.3. **7.** Sears sold the mail-order business Freemans to the German retailer Otto Versand in a

deal believed to be worth £150–£200 million. The FT-SE 100 index closed at a record high of 6,473.2. **8.** The Bank of England cut bank base rates by 0.25 per cent to 5.25 per cent. **12.** The Ford Motor Company agreed to buy the Kwik-Fit car repair chain for about £1 billion. **13.** The Norwegian company Kvaerner put the Govan and Clydebank shipyards in Glasgow and engineering and construction operations in the north-east and in Sheffield up for sale; the Government set up a task force aimed at finding a new buyer and safeguarding jobs. Mike O'Neill resigned as chief executive of Barclays for health reasons on his first day in the job. **16.** The retail groups Kingfisher and Asda announced plans to merge (see 14 June below). **19.** The FT-SE 100 index closed at a record high of 6,513.3. **27.** The FT-SE 100 index closed at a record high of 6,593.6. **28.** Keith Henry resigned as chief executive of National Power. **30.** Lex Service announced an agreed £437 million take-over of the RAC's breakdown operation.

MAY 1999

3. The Dow Jones industrial average rose 225.65 points to close at a record high of 11,014.69. **4.** The US investment bank Goldman Sachs floated on the New York stock exchange. **7.** The Treasury said that the Bank of England would sell half of Britain's gold reserves over the medium term. **18.** Marks and Spencer announced that pre-tax profits had fallen from £1.16 billion in 1997 to £546.1 million in 1998. **20.** Barclays Bank announced 6,000 job losses. **24.** WH Smith announced an agreed £185 million bid for the publishing company Hodder Headline. **25.** British Airways announced that pre-tax profits had fallen by 61 per cent in the 1998–9 financial year. Allied Domecq sold its pubs business to Whitbread for £2.4 billion.

JUNE 1999

2. Sainsbury's announced pre-tax profits for 1998–9 of £756 million and said that it would cut 1,100 jobs. The euro fell to a new low against the pound of £0.6437. **10.** The Bank of England cut bank base rates by 0.25 per cent to 5.0 per cent. **14.** The American retailer Wal-Mart launched a £6.7 billion take-over bid for Asda. **17.** Prudential Corporation announced 4,000 job losses. **23.** Scottish Widows announced a £7 billion take-over by Lloyds TSB.

JULY 1999

1. The euro fell to a new low against the dollar of $1.0201. **5.** Centrica made a £1.1 billion offer for the AA. **6.** The price of gold fell to $257.60 per ounce, the lowest for 20 years, after the Government sold 25 tonnes of the UK's gold reserves at auction. **11.** The commercial law firm Clifford Chance announced a merger with the American firm Rogers & Wells; a further merger was planned with the German firm Pünder, Volhard, Weber & Axster. **12.** Kingston Communications, the telecoms business owned by Hull City Council, was floated on the

Stock Exchange; the Council retained a 49 per stake in the company. **13.** The Government announced plans to sell off 49 per cent of British Nuclear Fuels. About 1,200 jobs at the Govan shipyard, Glasgow, were safeguarded following a deal between its owners Kvaerner and the electronics company Marconi. **19.** Centrica announced the closure of its high street shops with the loss of 1,500 jobs. **26.** The Internet subsidiary of Dixons, Freeserve, floated on the Stock Exchange; its shares rose from 150p to close at 205p.

AUGUST 1999

4. The American congolomerate SFX Entertainment bought Apollo Leisure for £162 million. **6.** Deutsche Telekom bought the mobile phone operator One 2 One for £8.4 billion.

ENVIRONMENT

SEPTEMBER 1998

1. Government safety inspectors said that the Dounreay nuclear complex suffered from many chronic safety problems. **17.** Thousands of mink were released from a farm at Onneley, Staffs, by animal rights activists. **23.** The Environment Secretary (John Prescott) announced that the water companies would be required to treat all sewage discharged into the sea and to protect sites of special scientific interest (SSSIs).

OCTOBER 1998

1. The World Wide Fund for Nature published a report which said that a third of the Earth's natural resources had been lost in the previous 25 years.

NOVEMBER 1998

2. Researchers at the Institute of Terrestrial Ecology in Edinburgh said that billions of acres of tropical forests would turn into desert in the middle of the 21st century because of global warming. **11.** The Environment Secretary addressed a conference on climate change in Buenos Aires, Argentina.

JANUARY 1999

11. A large section of Beachy Head, E. Sussex, collapsed into the sea. **15.** The Milford Haven Port Authority was fined £4 million in Cardiff after admitting responsibility for the Sea Empress disaster in February 1996.

FEBRUARY 1999

12. The Prime Minister said that there was no scientific case for a moratorium on the sale of genetically modified foods in the UK. **19.** Greenabella Marsh, a Site of Special Scientific Interest in the Tees estuary, was contaminated by a major acid spill caused by a faulty drain at a company in Hartlepool.

MAY 1999

19. Environmentalists called for a five-year freeze on the planting of genetically modified (GM) crops in the UK. **27.** The Nuffield Council said that there was a 'compelling moral imperative' to develop GM foods.

JUNE 1999

7. A farmer in Wiltshire destroyed a test field of GM oil seed rape after pressure from the farm's trustees.

SPORT

For Sports results, *see* Sports section

SEPTEMBER 1998

5. Christian Gross was sacked as manager of Tottenham Hotspur FC. **7.** The satellite television group BskyB announced a £625 million agreement to buy Manchester United FC. On 9 April the Government accepted a recommendation by the Monopolies and Mergers Commission that the takeover should be blocked because it would damage the quality of British football. **26.** The Sheffield Wednesday striker Paolo Di Canio was suspended by his club for pushing over the referee after being sent off during a match against Arsenal at Hillsborough. On 23 October Di Canio was banned for 11 matches and fined £10,000 by the FA. **27.** Great Britain returned to the World Group of the Davis Cup after beating India 3–2 in Nottingham.

OCTOBER 1998

6. UEFA announced proposals to expand the European Champions' League and merge the UEFA Cup and the European Cup Winners' Cup. **14.** The first-class cricket counties and the MCC agreed changes to professional cricket in England and Wales from 1999–2000, including more international matches and the possible establishment of a two-division county championship. **15.** The BBC lost the right to televise Test and most one-day cricket matches. **27.** The England wicket-keeper Jack Russell announced his retirement from international cricket. **29.** The proposed take-over by BskyB of Manchester United FC was referred to the Monopolies and Mergers Commission.

NOVEMBER 1998

3. The West Indies cricket captain and vice-captain, Brian Lara and Carl Hooper, refused to join their team for a tour of South Africa because of a dispute over the fees to be paid to the players. On 4 November both players were dropped by the West Indies Cricket Board. On 5 November more players joined the protest. On 9 November the players reached agreement with the Board and Lara and Hooper were reinstated. **12.** Roy Evans resigned as joint manager of Liverpool FC, leaving Gerard

Houllier in sole charge. **14.** The England rugby union team set a new national record for the number of points scored in a match when they beat Holland 110–0 at Huddersfield; they also scored a record 16 tries during the match. **17.** David Hemery was elected the first president of Athletics UK. **21.** Roy Hodgson resigned as manager of Blackburn Rovers FC. **30.** Peter Johnson resigned as chairman of Everton FC.

DECEMBER 1998

3. The English county cricket clubs voted in favour of a two-division county championship from 2000. Brian Kidd was appointed manager of Blackburn Rovers FC. **8.** The Australian Cricket Board confirmed that Shane Warne and Mark Waugh had been fined in 1995 for giving information to an illegal Indian bookmaker in exchange for payment during a tour to Sri Lanka in late 1994. **13.** Michael Owen was named BBC Sports Personality of the Year. **15.** Graham Kelly resigned as chief executive of the FA for allegedly offering a £3.2 million loan to the Welsh FA without authorization. The FA's executive passed a unanimous vote of no confidence in its chairman, Keith Wiseman, over the same issue, but Mr Wiseman refused to resign. **22.** The Australian Open tennis champion Petr Korda was stripped of the prize-money and the world ranking points he won at Wimbledon in July 1998 because he had tested positive for steroids at the championships; he escaped being banned because an independent appeals committee accepted his evidence that he did not know he had taken the relevant substance. **27.** Six people, including the British Olympic yachtsman Glyn Charles, were missing presumed drowned when the Sydney-Hobart yacht race was hit by heavy storms. **29.** The Kent fast bowler Dean Headley took six wickets for 60 runs during the fourth Test between England and Australia at Melbourne; England won the match by 12 runs.

JANUARY 1999

2. Leeds United drew 0–0 with non-league Rushden and Diamonds in the third round of the FA Cup; Leeds United won the replay 3–1. On the first day of the fifth Test in Sydney, Darren Gough became the first England bowler for 100 years to take a hat-trick in an Ashes series. **7.** Supporters of Shiv Sena, a right-wing Hindu party, vandalized the pitch at New Delhi where the first Test between India and Pakistan was due to begin on 28 January. **15.** Terry Venables resigned as head coach of Crystal Palace FC. **17.** The former world heavyweight boxing champion Mike Tyson beat Francois Botha in his first fight since being banned for a year for biting off part of Evander Holyfield's ear in a fight in June 1997. **18.** England were expelled from the Five Nations Championship after a dispute over television rights; they were readmitted on 19 January. **23.** A row broke out after the Sri Lankan bowler Muttiah Muralitharan was no-balled by an umpire

during a one-day match against England in Adelaide; the Sri Lankan team walked to the edge of the pitch and a 15-minute delay ensued before the match resumed. **24.** An internal report by the International Olympic Committee acknowledged that members of the committee had accepted bribes in connection with the successful bid by Salt Lake City, Utah, to stage the 2002 Winter Olympics; three committee members had already resigned, and the report recommended that six more members be expelled. **26.** Dougie Walker, the European 200 metres champion, was revealed to have tested positive for drugs in December 1998; he denied having taking any banned substances but was suspended for two years by UK Athletics on 31 March. The new governing body for athletics in Britain, UK Athletics, was launched. **29.** On 2 February Glenn Hoddle was sacked after admitting a 'serious error of judgment' and Howard Wilkinson was appointed as acting coach.

FEBRUARY 1999

1. The Welsh Rugby Union rejected a proposal from the RFU to form an Anglo-Welsh league including five Welsh clubs. **7.** Amil Kumble, the India leg spinner, became only the second man in Test history to take ten wickets in an innings when he finished with figures of 10 for 74 in the second Test against Pakistan at Delhi. **13.** The Arsenal manager Arsène Wenger offered to replay an FA Cup tie against Sheffield United after his side won by a goal scored after breaking an unwritten rule that a ball put out of play because a player is injured should be returned to the opposition; the FA accepted the offer. The French solo yachtswoman Isabelle Autissier was rescued by a fellow competitor in the Around Alone single-handed round-the-world race after her boat had capsized in the South Pacific Ocean. **17.** Kevin Keegan was appointed England football coach on a part-time basis until June 1999.

MARCH 1999

1. The Government launched a £160 million regional network of sports facilities. **7.** Colin Prescot and Andy Elson set a new world record for a hot-air balloon flight when their balloon came down in the Pacific Ocean off Japan 18 days into an attempt to fly non-stop around the world. The London rugby league player Martin Offiah became the top English try-scorer in history when he scored his 447th try during a match against Huddersfield at the Stoop. **8.** West Indies were all out for 51, their lowest ever score, in the second Test against Australia in Port of Spain. **11.** Sir John Quinton resigned as chairman of the Premier League and Peter Leaver resigned as chief executive after allegedly exceeding their powers by giving lucrative consultancy contracts to two former BSkyB executives. Wembley Stadium was sold for £103 million to a consortium backed by the FA; the new owners said that the stadium would be demolished and rebuilt by 2003. **13.** The world heavyweight unification title fight between Evander Holyfield and Lennox Lewis in New York was declared a draw in spite of the widespread belief that it had been won by Lewis; on 15 March the three governing bodies involved said that a rematch should take place within six months. **20.** Brian Jones and Bertrand Piccard became the first people to fly non-stop round the world in a balloon when their British-made Breitling Orbiter 3 balloon reached Mauretania after 19 days in the air. The balloon landed in Egypt on 21 March. **23.** David Lloyd said that he would resign as the England cricket coach after the world cup in June 1999. **28.** The leading European rugby union countries and clubs agreed an eight-year format for European competition.

APRIL 1999

5. Richard Dunwoody became the most successful National Hunt jockey in history when he won the 1,679th race of his career in a meeting at Wincanton. **9.** The Liverpool striker Robbie Fowler was banned for six games and fined £32,000 by the FA for taunting the Chelsea defender Graeme Le Saux during a match in February, and for miming cocaine-sniffing after scoring a goal against Everton on 3 April. **25.** The seventh and final one-day cricket international between the West Indies and Australia in Bridgetown, Barbados, was disrupted by serious crowd trouble after the West Indies batsman Sherwin Campbell was controversially run out. David Ginola was named the Professional Footballers' Association Player of the Year.

MAY 1999

1. Leeds Rhinos won the rugby league Challenge Cup final with the biggest ever score and by the biggest ever margin when they beat London Broncos 52–16 at Wembley; Leroy Rivett became the first player ever to score four tries in a Challenge Cup final. **2.** The referee of a match between Celtic and Rangers at Celtic Park was injured by a coin thrown from the crowd; there were further crowd disturbances and three players were sent off during the match. **3.** Stephen Hendry became the first snooker player to win the world championship seven times when he beat Mark Williams in the final at Sheffield. **7.** The world motor cycling champion, Michael Doohan, was badly injured in a crash during qualifying for the Spanish Grand Prix in Jerez. **14.** The cricket world cup opened at Lord's. Kevin Keegan was confirmed as England football coach on a full-time basis. **16.** Manchester United won the football premiership for the fifth time in seven years. **23.** The *News of the World* published allegations that the England rugby union captain Lawrence Dallaglio had sold drugs as a teenager and had taken drugs while on a British Lions tour in 1997. On 24 May Dallaglio denied the allegations but resigned as England captain and was replaced by Martin Johnson. On 25 August Dallaglio was fined £15,000 by the RFU for bringing the game into disrepute.

26. Manchester United became the first English club ever to win the league, FA Cup and European Cup when they beat Bayern Munich 2–1 in the European Cup final in Barcelona. On 27 May hundreds of thousands of people lined the streets in Manchester to welcome the team back. **30.** England was knocked out of the cricket world cup.

JUNE 1999

2. The Irish government refused to grant entry visas to the Yugoslav football team, which was due to play a European Championship qualifying match against the Republic of Ireland in Dublin on 5 June; the match was therefore called off. **5.** The leading Italian cyclist Marco Pantani was suspended for 15 days after failing a drugs test during the Giro D'Italia. **6.** Andre Agassi became the fifth man to win all four Grand Slam titles when he beat Andrei Medvedev to win the French Open in Paris. **7.** The Irish swimmer and former Olympic gold medallist Michelle De Bruin lost her appeal against a four-year ban imposed by FINA, the sport's international governing body, in 1998 after she had tested positive for drugs. **10.** Kenny Dalglish was appointed director of football operations and John Barnes was appointed head coach at Celtic. Ford announced that it had bought Jackie Stewart's grand prix team. **16.** In Athens the American athlete Maurice Greene set a new world record of 9.79 for the men's 100 metres. The former world motor racing champion Damon Hill announced his retirement from the sport. **17.** Australia qualified for the cricket world cup final after tying with South Africa in a semi-final at Edgbaston. **20.** Australia beat Pakistan in the cricket world cup final at Lord's. **22.** The women's top seed at Wimbledon, Martina Hingis, was knocked out of the tournament in the first round by a 16-year-old Australian qualifier, Jelena Dokić. **24.** Nasser Hussain was appointed England cricket captain in place of Alec Stewart. **26.** Geoff Thompson was elected chairman of the FA. **27.** The FA offered to exempt Manchester United from the 1999–2000 FA Cup to facilitate the club's participation in the inaugural FIFA World Team Championship in Brazil. On 30 June the club agreed to withdraw from the FA Cup.

JULY 1999

4. Pete Sampras won the men's singles title at Wimbledon for the sixth time, more than any other player in the 20th century, when he beat Andre Agassi in straight sets in the final. In the women's final, Lindsay Davenport won the title for the first time by beating Steffi Graf in straight sets. **5.** Chelsea FC bought Chris Sutton from Blackburn Rovers for £10 million. **7.** In Rome, the Moroccan athlete Hicham El Guerrouj set a new world record of 3 minutes 43.13 seconds for the mile. **13.** Granada bought a 9.9 per cent stake in Liverpool FC for £22 million. **18.** Paul Lawrie became the first Scotsman to win The Open golf championship in Scotland for 68 years when he won the tournament at Carnoustie after a four-hole play-off against Jean Van de Velde and Justin Leonard. **27.** The champion jockey Kieren Fallon was sacked as first jockey of the trainer Henry Cecil. **28.** The European 200 metres champion, Doug Walker, who had been suspended after failing a drugs test in March 1999, was reinstated after UK Athletics dropped the charges against him. **29.** Plans for a new £475 million Wembley Stadium designed by a team of architects headed by Lord Foster were unveiled.

AUGUST 1999

2. The BBC sports presenter Desmond Lynam announced that he was moving to ITV to present its live football coverage. **4.** The former Olympic 100 metres champion Linford Christie was suspended from athletics by the IAAF after failing a drugs test. The world high jump record-holder Javier Sotomayor was stripped of the gold medal he won at the Pan American Games in Canada in July 1999 after testing positive for cocaine. **5.** The Arsenal striker Nicolas Anelka was sold to Real Madrid for £22.5 million. **13.** The tennis champion Steffi Graf announced her retirement from the sport. **18.** The Jamaican sprinter Merlene Ottey withdrew from her country's squad for the World Championships after failing a drugs test. **25.** Colin Jackson became the first Briton to regain a world championship title when he won the 110 metres hurdles in Seville. **26.** At the World Championships in Seville, Michael Johnson set a new world record of 43.18 seconds for the 400 metres. **27.** Maurice Greene became the first athlete in the history of the World Championships to win both the 100 metres and the 200 metres titles. **28.** Ruud Gullit resigned as manager of Newcastle United FC.

AFRICA

SEPTEMBER 1998

7. The seven countries involved in fighting in the Democratic Republic of Congo held talks on the conflict and the future of the country. **13.** President Zeroual of Algeria called early presidential elections for February 1999 and announced that he would not be standing for re-election. **19.** Twenty-six people were killed and 125 injured in a bomb explosion in Zaroura, Algeria. **20.** Thirty-three people died in fighting between government forces and the troops of warlord Roosevelt Johnson in Monrovia, Liberia. **22.** Rioting broke out in Maseru, Lesotho, following intervention by South African troops to put down an attempted coup. **28.** More than 1,000 rebel soldiers in Lesotho surrendered to the South African-led Intervention Force.

OCTOBER 1998

1. The South African Development Community declared that it would attempt to destroy the Angolan rebel group UNITA because of its destabilizing influence in the region. **10.** Forty people

were killed when rebel troops in the Democratic Republic of Congo shot down a Boeing 727. **18.** Fighting resumed in Guinea-Bissau between government forces and rebels. **19.** In Sierra Leone, 24 army officers were executed for their part in the 1997 coup. **20.** Sixteen Zimbabwean troops were captured by rebels in the Democratic Republic of Congo, the first evidence that Zimbabwe's forces were active in the country. **29.** The final report of South Africa's Truth and Reconciliation Commission was published; it blamed the successive white governments for years of atrocities but also criticized the African National Congress (ANC) for excessive violence.

NOVEMBER 1998

4. In Zimbabwe, thousands of protesters demonstrated against President Mugabe. **5.** The former president of Sierra Leone, Joseph Momoh, was sentenced to ten years' imprisonment for conspiracy in the 1997 coup. **6.** The Zambian opposition politician and possible presidential candidate, Ronald Penza, was shot dead. President Taki of the Comoros died. **10.** The family of the late Nigerian president, Sani Abacha, returned US$750 million of state funds he had illegally amassed. **11.** A one-day general strike was called in Zimbabwe to protest at price rises and the government's handling of the economy. **15.** Captain Blaise Compaoré was re-elected president of Burkina Faso; the election was boycotted by much of the opposition. **18.** A second one-day general strike was called in Zimbabwe. Following a compulsory purchase order by President Mugabe of Zimbabwe, 841 white farmers had their property seized.

DECEMBER 1998

5. The secretary-general of the UN, Kofi Annan, met Colonel Gaddafi of Libya to discuss the proposed trial of the Libyans suspected of the 1988 Lockerbie bombing. Four people died in heavy fighting on the island of Anjouan in the Comoros following a failed assassination attempt on the separatist leader Foundi Abdallah Ibrahim. In local elections in Nigeria, the People's Democratic Party won control of 459 of 751 councils. **6.** The presidential election in Gabon was won by the incumbent President Bongo. **7.** The death toll from fighting on Anjouan rose to between 30 and 40. **10.** Eighty-one people were killed by Muslim militants in the west of Algeria, bringing the number of deaths since the beginning of December to 200. **14.** Ahmed Ouyahia resigned as prime minister of Algeria. **16.** Civil war broke out again in Angola. **26.** A UN plane carrying 14 people crashed, possibly after being shot at, in Angola. **31.** Several hundred people died in the Republic of Congo following fighting between the army and the militia of Bernard Kolelas, the former prime minister.

JANUARY 1999

1. Five hundred civilians were killed by rebels in eastern areas of the Democratic Republic of Congo.

2. The UN suspended its flights to parts of Angola after a second UN plane was shot down. 9. State elections were held in Nigeria. 11. Nigerian troops launched a counter-offensive against rebel forces in Freetown, Sierra Leone. 12. The former president of Mali, Moussa Traoré, was sentenced to death by a court in Bamako, Mali, after being convicted of economic crimes. 13. Nigerian-led Economic Community of West African States' Monitoring Group (ECOMOG) troops drove rebel forces out of Freetown, Sierra Leone. 18. The UN announced that it would withdraw its personnel from Angola by 20 March, after fighting in the civil war escalated; Kofi Annan declared that 'there is no more peace to keep'. A cease-fire was declared in the Democratic Republic of Congo. The former president of Zimbabwe, Canaan Banana, was sentenced to ten years' hard labour for sodomy and assault. 23. Sifiso Nkabinde, the secretary-general of South Africa's United Democratic Movement, was murdered. 24. Eleven ANC supporters were murdered in a suspected revenge attack after Nkabinde's death. 27. In Angola, UNITA rebels captured the strategically important town of Mbanza-Congo. 28. At least 178 civilians were killed either by Hutu rebels or during clashes between rebels and government forces in Burundi. 31. Three of Zimbabwe's five judges of the Supreme Court wrote to President Mugabe asking him to condemn the illegal arrest and torture of two journalists, who had subsequently been freed.

FEBRUARY 1999

2. At least 35 people were killed in fighting between rebels and government forces in Guinea-Bissau. 6. Eritrean and Ethiopian forces clashed in renewed fighting along the border between the two countries. 8. President Kabbah of Sierra Leone announced that he would agree to talks with the rebel leader Foday Sankoh. 17. About 100 ECOMOG troops were arrested in Sierra Leone after allegations of 'summary executions'. 20. Parliamentary elections were held in Nigeria. 27. Presidential elections were held in Nigeria; they were won by General Olusegun Obasanjo, although independent observers identified 'many serious discrepancies' in the election process.

MARCH 1999

12. Britain recalled its ambassador in Kinshasa, Democratic Republic of Congo, after the arrest and subsequent expulsion of four British diplomats accused of espionage. 17. Eritrean troops claimed to have repelled a major attack by Ethiopian forces at Tsarona, 60 miles south of the Eritrean capital, Asmara. 21. Rebels massacred more than 250 civilians in the South Kivu region of the Democratic Republic of Congo. 26. Government and opposition parties in South Africa united to bid farewell to President Mandela when he addressed parliament for the last time before his retirement. Mr Mandela acknowledged the praise, but said that he was merely a product of his country's history.

APRIL 1999

5. UN sanctions against Libya were lifted after two suspected terrorists, Abdel Basset Ali al-Megrahi and Lamen Khalifa Fhimah, were deported to the Netherlands to face trial over the 1988 Lockerbie disaster. The appeal court in Abuja, Nigeria, upheld the victory of Olusegun Obasanjo in February's presidential election. 9. President Ibrahim Bare Mainassara of Niger was assassinated by members of his personal security guard. Five former Rwandan politicians pleaded not guilty to 11 charges of genocide and crimes against humanity before the International Criminal Tribunal for Rwanda. 15. In Algeria, the presidential election took place; Abdelaziz Bouteflika, who was backed by the military, was the only candidate after the other six withdrew in protest against fraud in early voting. 16. Abdelaziz Bouteflika was proclaimed president of Algeria with 73 per cent of the vote. 17. Three former Rwandan government ministers implicated in the 1994 genocide of 800,000 people were arrested in Cameroon. 18. President Laurent Kabila of the Democratic Republic of Congo signed a peace agreement with President Museveni of Uganda. Rebels later dismissed the agreement, saying they wanted to talk directly to President Kabila. In Egypt, 20 Islamic militants were sentenced to death or life with hard labour. 21. ECOMOG said that rebels had hacked and burned to death scores of civilians as they retreated from Song, 27 miles east of Freetown, Sierra Leone. 30. The Government of the Comoros was overthrown in a bloodless military coup after three days of rioting.

MAY 1999

2. Militiamen of the warlord Hussein Mohamed Aidid counterattacked and recaptured the town of Baidoa, Somalia, from the Rahanwein resistance Army, which had overrun it on 1 May. 7. A military junta overthrew President Vieira of Guinea-Bissau; at least 70 people were killed. 14. Five people were sentenced to death for the 1993 assassination of Burundi's first democratically elected President, Melchior Ndadaye. 22. The African National Congress (ANC) and the Inkatha Freedom Party (IFP) in South Africa signed a pre-election peace pact. In Algeria's Tiaret province, troops killed 19 Muslim rebels suspected of murdering nine villagers. 24. In Sierra Leone, a cease-fire came into effect between government and rebel forces. 29. Olusegun Obasanjo was sworn in as Nigeria's president, ending more than 15 years of military rule. President Mandela addressed ANC supporters in the final rally before South Africa's general election.

JUNE 1999

3. South African voters returned the ANC to power with 266 seats in the 400-seat National Assembly, one seat short of a two-thirds majority. The Democratic Party became the official opposition with 38 seats and the IFP won 34 seats. The ANC

also won clear control of seven provinces in the parallel provincial election. **10.** The new South African president, Thabo Mbeki, consolidated his power by downgrading the office of deputy president and allying the ANC with a tiny opposition party, the Minority Front, which had won one seat in the election. The pact meant that the ANC had the two-thirds majority necessary to change the constitution. Several hundred Algerians who lost members of their family at the hands of Islamic extremists protested in Algiers against a government entente with the Islamic Salvation Army, the armed wing of the banned Islamic Salvation Front. **16.** In South Africa, Nelson Mandela handed over power to the new president, Thabo Mbeki **17.** President Mbeki named his first cabinet. **22.** Millers and bakers went on strike in Zimbabwe after the government issued new price controls. **25.** Violent protests followed the announcement that Bakili Muluzi had been re-elected as president of Malawi. In a separate election for parliament, opposition parties claimed the largest number of seats.

JULY 1999

1. Joshua Nkomo, the vice-president of Zimbabwe since 1990 and founder of the Zimbabwean African People's Union (ZAPU), died at the age of 83. **7.** The Sierra Leonean government reached a peace deal with the main rebel movement, under which its leader, Foday Sankoh, would become vice-president and head of the Mineral Resources Commission. **8.** The Swiss-based charity Christian Solidarity International claimed to have freed a record 2,035 slaves in a week in southern Sudan, bringing the number it had saved since 1995 to more than 11,000. **12.** Zimbabwe offered compensation to thousands of victims of the widespread massacres of the Ndebele tribe in 1982, in which at least 5,000 people died. **14.** The Truth and Reconciliation Commission implicated P. W. Botha, the former president of South Africa, in the murder of eight black activists in the 1980's. **19.** In Nigeria, hundreds of Hausa residents of Sagamu fled after heavy fighting with members of the Yoruba tribe left at least 66 people dead. Ethnic clashes between the two communities took place in other locations on 25 July, when some 30 people were killed. **23.** King Hassan II of Morocco died. **24.** In Angola, the authorities issued a warrant for the arrest of UNITA leader Jonas Savimbi, blaming him for the return to civil war. The Natal Law Society tendered a posthumous apology to Mahatma Gandhi for rejecting his application to become a South African lawyer in 1894 on racial grounds. **29.** A strike by 500,000 South African public sector workers began, threatening the strained alliance between the ANC and its trade union and Communist Party allies. **30.** A group of Kenyan MPs, including some from the ruling party, filed a no-confidence motion against the government, quoting evidence of senior officials' corruption.

AUGUST 1999

2. More than 12 people were killed in the Caprivi Strip, Namibia, in fighting between Namibian forces and the Caprivi Liberation Army seeking independence for the region. Namibian human rights activists later attempted to force President Nujoma to bring to court at least 300 people who disappeared in a round-up of suspects by paramilitary police. **3.** At least 15 people died and more than 25 were hurt after fighting between rival militia groups in Mogadishu, Somalia. **5.** The Sudanese government declared a two-month cease-fire in its conflict with southern rebels in order to allow aid to reach the region. In Nigeria, at least 700 people were thought to have died in local or ethnic fighting since May. **9.** The Zimbabwean Congress of Trade Unions announced it was to launch a political party. **11.** A former Rwandan minister for family and women's affairs, Pauline Nyiramasuhuko, was indicted for incitement to rape at the international tribunal sitting in Tanzania. **12.** Burundian villagers accused the Tutsi-led army of killing 147 Hutu civilians in revenge for a Hutu rebel attack **16.** Islamic extremists killed 29 people at Beni Ounif, Algeria. **21.** A bomb killed 17 people and wounded five near Ouzra, south of Algiers. **27.** The Roman Catholic bishop of Gikongoro diocese in Rwanda went on trial accused of genocide and crimes against humanity. In Uganda, King Ronald Muwenda Mutebi II of the Baganda tribe married British-born Sylvia Nagginda Luswata in Kampala Anglican Cathedral. **29.** President Mugabe demanded compensation from Britain for its part in colonizing Zimbabwe, saying that colonialism was an international criminal offence.

THE AMERICAS

SEPTEMBER 1998

3. Forest fires in Brazil were said to have destroyed more than three million acres of the Amazon rainforest. **11.** In the USA, the report of the investigation by the independent prosecutor Kenneth Starr into charges against President Clinton was published; it put forward 11 acts that might constitute grounds for the impeachment of the president. Brazil raised its interest rates by 20 per cent to 49.75 per cent and spent US$1.9 billion defending its currency. **21.** President Clinton's videotaped testimony to the grand jury investigating his alleged affair with Monica Lewinsky was broadcast in its entirety on US television. **30.** The IMF announced a rescue package for the Brazilian economy.

OCTOBER 1998

5. Fernando Cardoso was re-elected president of Brazil. **8.** The US House of Representatives voted 258–176 to authorize impeachment hearings into President Clinton's alleged misdemeanours. **26.**

Ecuador and Peru signed an agreement demarcating 48 km of common border, an issue that had led to three wars between the countries.

NOVEMBER 1998

2. In mid-term elections in the USA, the Republican majority in the House of Representatives was halved, though its majority in the Senate remained unchanged. 13. Paula Jones settled her sexual harassment case against President Clinton in return for $850,000. 19. Impeachment hearings against President Clinton began in the USA. 20. Tobacco companies reached a US$206 billion settlement with US states to pay for the treatment of smoking-related diseases. 25. Admiral Emilio Massera, the most notorious member of Argentina's military junta between 1976 and 1983, was arrested on charges of abducting children. 30. In Canada, the Quebec provincial election was won by the separatist Parti Québécois, but by a margin insufficient to force an immediate referendum on independence.

DECEMBER 1998

6. Hugo Chávez won the presidential election in Venezuela. 14. Puerto Rico voted to retain its status as a commonwealth within the USA. 16. Argentina and Chile signed an agreement settling their last territorial dispute in the Andes. 19. The US House of Representatives voted 228–206 to impeach President Clinton on charges of perjury before a grand jury and obstruction of justice.

JANUARY 1999

5. The US relaxed its trade embargo on Cuba. The senior military leader of the Shining Path rebel group was captured by Peruvian anti-terrorist forces in Lima. 7. The impeachment trial of President Clinton began in Washington DC. President Pastrana of Colombia held talks with the country's largest left-wing guerrilla group. 12. President Préval of Haiti said that he would appoint a government by decree, bypassing the country's parliament. 13. Brazil devalued its currency by 10 per cent. 22. The governor of Argentina's central bank said that his country was holding talks with the USA aimed at replacing the peso with the US dollar.

FEBRUARY 1999

2. Hugo Chávez was sworn in as president of Venezuela. Brazil sacked the governor of its central bank for the second time in a month when Francisco Lopes was fired. 12. The US Senate acquitted President Clinton of perjury and obstruction of justice. A Californian woman was awarded US$51 million damages against a tobacco company for its failure to warn her that smoking was addictive.

MARCH 1999

7. Francisco Flores won the presidential election in El Salvador. 8. President Préval and opposition party leaders agreed to create a provisional electoral council to organize elections in Haiti 22. The USA stepped up its trade dispute with the EU by threatening to impose punitive tariffs on $900 million worth of European agricultural exports in retaliation for the ban on its beef treated with growth hormones. 23. The vice-president of Paraguay, Luis Maria Argana, was assassinated in Asunción. 26. Jacques-Edouard Alexis took office as prime minister of Haiti and promised that elections would be held. 28. President Raul Cubas of Paraguay resigned and was granted asylum in Brazil. The first major sporting event between the USA and Cuba for 40 years was held when the Baltimore Orioles played the Cuban national baseball squad in Havana.

APRIL 1999

1. Nunavut, the new self-governing region of Canada, officially came into being. 6. Cuba condemned the American plan to house 20,000 Kosovar Albanians in the US naval base at Guantánamo Bay, saying it was a European problem. 12. In Colombia, left-wing rebels hijacked an Aviance plane on a domestic flight, forced it to land and herded away the 46 people on board. Police later found the empty plane. 16. Alabama's state house voted to repeal its constitutional ban on interracial marriages. 21. Four people died in rioting over fuel tax increases in Jamaica. The government later decided to halve the increases. 23. All cigarette billboards in the USA were removed under the terms of an agreement reached in 1998 between states and the tobacco industry. 28. According to a report in the *New York Times*, a scientist suspected of spying for China transferred huge amounts of data concerning nuclear weapons in the USA from a secret computer system to an unclassified network. The House of Representatives voted to limit President Clinton's freedom to deploy ground troops in Kosovo by insisting that congressional approval would have to be obtained first.

MAY 1999

3. Mireya Moscoso was elected president of Panama. 9. In the USA, the Energy Secretary Bill Richardson admitted that China had obtained nuclear secrets from the USA over the previous six years . 25. An Argentine delegation met a group of four councillors from the Falklands, the first meeting since the end of the conflict in 1982. They agreed to work together to conserve fish stocks and to co-operate over oil exploration as well as a range of regional issues. 25. A congressional inquiry in the USA reported that China had spent 40 years stealing nuclear technology and had spread it to unstable regimes around the world. The report by the Cox committee detailed what it described as the worst security lapse in American history. 28. The Colombian defence minister resigned in protest at a government decision to allow left-wing guerrillas to remain in control of a large area of jungle territory. 31. In Colombia, left-wing rebels held more than 100 worshippers from a church hostage. Four hostages were killed and 79 were later released.

JUNE 1999

1. Cuba demanded $181.1 billion (£113 billion) compensation for the deaths of 3,478 Cubans and injuries to 2,099 in 40 years of 'war' by the USA. 16. The American Vice-President Al Gore formally announced his bid for the presidency. The Republican George W. Bush also announced his candidacy. 30. Kenneth Starr ended his five-year Whitewater investigation into President and Mrs Clinton's financial dealings in Arkansas.

JULY 1999

9. Argentina applied for associate membership of NATO. 12. In Colombia, left-wing guerrillas launched their biggest offensive in 35 years of civil war. 13. In Peru, the last remaining commander of the Shining Path, a Maoist guerrilla movement, was captured. 16. The head of the US Chamber of Commerce, Thomas Donahue, visited Cuba; it was the first such visit in 40 years. 20. Cuba announced that it would claim US$181 billion in damages for the alleged deaths and injuries suffered by its citizens in four decades of American aggression against Cuba. 30. Venezuelan voters gave candidates backed by President Hugo Chávez an overwhelming majority in a constituent assembly that will draft a new constitution for the country. The USA announced it would pay $4.5 million in compensation for the three killed and 17 wounded at the Chinese embassy in Belgrade on 7 May 1999.

AUGUST 1999

2. Rebels from the Revolutionary Armed Forces of Colombia killed 19 villagers in Narion. 8. The first group of Argentine tourists to be allowed to visit the Falkland Islands since the 1982 conflict were given a cool reception. Islanders protested in Port Stanley after an Argentine flag was laid at a memorial on 11 August. 11. Buford Furrow, a member of the Aryan Nations white supremacist group, gave himself up to the FBI after shooting three children and two teachers at a Jewish community centre in Los Angeles. 25. The US Congress announced that it would investigate allegations that American financial institutions had helped to launder billions of dollars from Russia, including funds loaned by the IMF. 27. In Venezuela, the Constituent Assembly placed the opposition-controlled Congress in indefinite recess. The president of the Supreme Court resigned after the assembly voted to grant itself powers to sack judges.

ASIA

SEPTEMBER 1998

2. Thousands of students in Myanmar protested against the country's military rulers. 6. Iran moved thousands of troops to its border with Afghanistan following the deaths of Iranian diplomats and journalists during fighting in Mazar-i-Sharif, Af-

ghanistan. 8. There were anti-government demonstrations in Jakarta, Indonesia and Phnom Penh, Cambodia. The Commonwealth Games opened in Malaysia. 11. The UN High Commissioner for Refugees confirmed that the Taleban militia in Afghanistan had massacred thousands of ethnic Hazara people during the battle for control of Mazar-i-Sharif in August 1998. Twelve people were killed when a bomb planted by Tamil Tiger rebels exploded in Jaffna, Sri Lanka. 20. Anwar Ibrahim, the former deputy prime minister of Malaysia, was arrested for demonstrating against the government. 27. More than 150,000 people demonstrated against the government in Kuala Lumpur, Malaysia. 28–29. More than 700 soldiers and Tamil Tigers were killed in fighting in northern Sri Lanka.

OCTOBER 1998

1. Tamil Tiger guerrillas captured the town of Kilinochi, northern Sri Lanka. 2. Sanjaasuregiin Zorig, the leader of Mongolia's transition to democracy and the man expected to be the country's next prime minister, was murdered. 8. Fighting was reported between Iranian and Taleban troops on the border between Iran and Afghanistan. Japan apologised to South Korea for the 'tremendous damage and suffering' caused during colonial rule. 9. Pakistan amended its constitution to make the Koran and the sayings of Muhammad supreme law. 10. Ten thousand Malaysians demonstrated in support of the imprisoned former deputy prime minister Anwar Ibrahim. 11. Presidential elections in Azerbaijan were won by the incumbent, Haidar Aliyev, although observers from the Organization for Security and Co-operation in Europe (OSCE) declared the election to be marred by fraud. 14. The Taleban militia in Afghanistan agreed to free all Iranian prisoners and to punish those responsible for killing Iranian diplomats and journalists. 14–19. China and Taiwan held their highest-level talks since 1949 when the semi-official Taiwanese envoy to the mainland met President Jiang Zemin in Beijing.

NOVEMBER 1998

2. The trial of Anwar Ibrahim opened in Malaysia. 4. Anti-government forces seized the airport and official buildings in Khodzhand, Tajikistan. 5. The Philippines complained to China after the latter had sent armed vessels to the disputed Spratly Islands in the South China Sea. 6. Talks between India and Pakistan opened with Pakistan rejecting a cease-fire offer. President Clinton agreed to further relax sanctions on India and Pakistan. 8. Fifteen former army officers and politicians in Bangladesh were sentenced to death for their involvement in the assassination of Sheikh Mujibir Rahman, Bangladesh's first president, in 1975. 12. Ninety people were injured in riots in Jakarta, Indonesia. 13. Hun Sen formed a coalition government in Cambodia. Fourteen protestors were killed following fighting in Indonesia. 20. China announced that it will open

all court trials to the public from December 1998. **25.** The IMF agreed a US$5.5 billion rescue package for Pakistan. President Jiang Zemin of China arrived in Tokyo for a state visit. **29.** The Congress Party in India won elections in three key states.

DECEMBER 1998

6. The ruling nationalist party Kuomintang increased its majority in Taiwan following parliamentary elections. **17.** South Korean troops sank a North Korean spy submarine during fighting in South Korean waters. One hundred and fifty students were injured in clashes with police in Jakarta, Indonesia. The Association of South-East Asian Nations (ASEAN) announced that Cambodia's membership would be delayed. The country's suspended UN membership was restored. **21.** Two Chinese dissidents, Xu Wenli and Wang Youcai, were jailed for more than ten years on charges of subversion. **22.** Qin Yongmin, a Chinese dissident who had attempted to set up the Chinese Democratic Party, was jailed for 12 years on charges of subversion.

JANUARY 1999

3. The prime minister of Pakistan, Nawaz Sharif, survived a suspected assassination attempt when a bridge was blown up shortly before he was due to cross it. **4.** Gunmen killed 16 Shi'ite Muslims at a mosque in Punjab province, Pakistan **10.** Nursultan Nazarbayev, the incumbent, won the presidential election in Kazakhstan, although the elections were described as 'grossly unfair' by human rights groups. **13.** Japan's ruling Liberal Democratic Party and an opposition group formed a coalition government. **16.** Afghan opposition forces captured the strategically important town of Yakaolang. **28.** Indonesia's House of Representatives passed a number of reforms liberalizing the country's political system. **31.** About 50 Tamil Tigers were killed in fighting in north-eastern Sri Lanka.

FEBRUARY 1999

2. Police in Pakistan attacked hundreds of journalists and press workers protesting at a government crackdown on the press. **5.** Leo Echegaray became the first person to be executed in the Philippines for 23 years after he was found guilty of raping his stepdaughter. **9.** The last remaining soldiers of the Khmer Rouge guerilla group formally joined the Cambodian army. **10.** The East Timorean leader Xanana Gusmão was moved from prison to house arrest to help shape the future of the disputed territory. **20.** The spiritual leader of Iraq's Shi'ite Muslims was shot dead in Najaf, Iraq. **21.** India and Pakistan agreed to inform each other of any future nuclear tests.

MARCH 1999

10. At least three people were killed and dozens injured as Muslims and Christians rioted in the Spice Islands, Indonesia, where religious violence had claimed 200 lives in the preceding two months.

14. The Taliban and the opposition in the north of Afghanistan reached an agreement to share power. **21.** Sri Lankan government forces captured the town of Madhu from Tamil Tiger control. Warring ethnic groups set fire to houses in Borneo after clashes in which at least 70 people were killed. **23.** Pakistan paraded long-range nuclear ballistic missiles capable of hitting targets deep inside India. **24.** Japanese ships fired shots for the first time in 46 years as two vessels, thought to be North Korean, were chased from Japanese waters.

APRIL 1999

11. India test-fired an Agni II ballistic missile, breaking a five-year period of restraint. **13.** Several million Sikhs gathered at Anandpur Sahib to celebrate the 300th anniversary of the formal founding of the Sikh brotherhood. **14.** Pakistan's successful test-firing of a Ghauri-II missile raised fears of a deterioration of security in South Asia. **15.** The former prime minister of Pakistan, Benazir Bhutto, and her husband were sentenced to five years' imprisonment and fined £5 million on corruption charges. Benazir Bhutto was absent. **17.** In India, Sonia Gandhi, the president of the Congress Party, tried to form a government after India's ruling coalition lost a confidence vote by one vote. **23.** More than 5,000 members of Nepal's Tibetan community demanded the release of the Panchen Lama, who was arrested by China in 1995. **25.** Mrs Gandhi met President Narayanan to tell him that she could not obtain a majority. **26.** Sultan Salahuddin Abdul Aziz Shah was installed as the 11th king of Malaysia under the system of rotating constitutional monarchs. President Narayanan dissolved India's lower house of parliament. **27.** Japan decided to legislate to allow military forces to provide support to US forces in case of emergency situations in areas surrounding Japan. Indonesia's President Habibie announced that he accepted the UN plan for a referendum to take place on 8 August giving East Timor a choice between autonomy and independence. **28.** China and Russia achieved a breakthrough in talks to map out their common 2,656-mile border, ending a 300-year-old dispute. An agreement was due to be signed later in 1999. The Congress Party announced that Sonia Gandhi would stand for election to parliament.

MAY 1999

1. Iran's culture minister, Ataollah Mohajerani, won a parliamentary vote of confidence after an attempt to unseat him by Islamic hard-liners **7.** China protested to the UN that the NATO bombing of the Chinese embassy in Belgrade was a war crime. Anti-Western demonstrations continued in Beijing for several days. **9.** Najam Sethi, the editor of Pakistan's *Friday Times*, was arrested on a sedition charge; he had called Pakistan a failed state and questioned the legitimacy of its creation. **17.** Mrs Gandhi resigned as president of India's Congress Party after three colleagues said that she was unfit to be a prime ministerial candidate because of her foreign origins. She retracted her resignation after they were expelled from the party. In Indonesia, the three leading reformist parties agreed to unite against President B. J. Habibie. **22.** Pakistan launched eight-day celebrations to mark the first anniversary of its nuclear weapons tests. Benazir Bhutto declared that she would not return to Pakistan to fight her conviction for corruption and that she intended instead to settle in the UK. **26.** Indian military officials said that MiG 21 and MiG 27 aircraft and helicopter gunships had inflicted 'heavy casualties' on about 500 separatist guerrillas who had infiltrated the disputed region of Kashmir from Pakistan. Squadrons of Pakistani aircraft were sent to front-line airfields in the first major confrontation involving aircraft since the war in 1971. **27.** The government of the Philippines agreed to allow the American navy to resume port calls after a three-year suspension, and to resume joint military exercises using ground troops. Pakistan shot down two Indian MiG fighters over the Pakistani-controlled area of Kashmir. India declared that it would continue its airstrikes in spite of the loss. Shamshad Ahmad, Pakistan's foreign secretary, appealed to Western ambassadors to increase the strength of the UN Military Observers Group in Kashmir. **28.** Pakistan-backed Muslim guerrillas in Kashmir shot down an Indian helicopter. India increased its troop numbers to more than 30,000, double the number of Pakistani troops in Kashmir. **29.** Pakistan said its Foreign Minister, Sartaj Aziz, would visit New Delhi in an attempt to resolve the conflict in Kashmir.

JUNE 1999

1. India renewed air strikes and ground operations against Muslim guerrillas in the mountains of northern Kashmir. **7.** Indonesians voted in the first democratic elections in the country in more than 40 years. Early poll returns showed that the main opposition party, Indonesian Democratic Struggle Party, had a commanding lead. **10.** Pakistan returned the mutilated bodies of six Indian soldiers in northern Kashmir; the soldiers, from a 14-man patrol that had been captured, had apparently been tortured. **11.** Pakistan claimed to have repulsed two major assaults by Indian troops in Kashmir. A four-day stand-off over fishing rights in the Yellow Sea was broken after South Korean Navy vessels rammed North Korean military boats; no shots were fired. **13.** India's prime minister, Atal Behari Vajpayee, warned his country to be prepared for war with Pakistan. **15.** North and South Korea fought a fierce naval battle at their disputed maritime border; five vessels on each side suffered damage. **18.** The Beijing-appointed Panchen Lama returned to the Tibetan capital, Lhasa, in what was seen as an attempt to secure his acceptance over a rival nominated by the Dalai Lama. **22.** The Indian Army began a huge offensive on a strategic peak and mountain range in Kashmir. **23.** A UN-supervised

vote on the future of East Timor was delayed for two weeks because of the poor security situation in the province. **26.** Pakistan's army chief, Pervez Musharraf, announced that Pakistan would not withdraw unilaterally from the battle zone of Kargil; this was the first admission by Pakistan that its forces had crossed the 1972 frontier. **27.** More than 200 mainland Chinese protested in front of Hong Kong's Immigration Tower against China's reinterpretation of the territory's constitution, which took away their right of abode in the territory. **29.** Amnesty International accused Myanmar's ruling military government of widespread abuses, including killings, torture and rape, against ethnic minorities.

JULY 1999

3. Pakistan called for UN mediation in the Kashmir conflict. Provisional results of the Indonesian general election were announced; the party of Megawati Sukarnoputri, daughter of Indonesia's founding president, gained the most votes **8.** Five people died and dozens disappeared when the police and Islamic vigilantes in Tehran, Iran, broke up a student march. **9.** The Pakistani Cabinet asked Muslim guerrillas fighting against Indian forces in Kashmir to withdraw. **12.** Iran's reformist President Mohammed Khatami vowed to put down student protests in Tehran, which had spread from the university to the main commercial area. In Lahore, 15,000 people demonstrated to denounce what they saw as a betrayal by the Pakistani government in Kashmir. **13.** Lee Teng-hui, the Taiwanese president, repudiated the One China policy, the pretence of a common goal of unification; he later declared that there would be one China only when the two sides had reunified as a democracy. Tens of thousands of Iranians marched through Tehran to show their support for the Islamic regime. **14.** China declared that it had the technology to make neutron bombs. **20.** Militants believed to be members of Laskar-i-Toiba (Army of the Pure) shot fifteen people dead in a Kashmiri village **28.** The UN-sponsored referendum in East Timor on independence or greater autonomy within Indonesia was deferred until 30 August because of difficulties in registering voters.

AUGUST 1999

3. President Habibie of Indonesia declared the results of the parliamentary election valid and binding, clearing the way for a presidential election in November 1999. Hundreds of thousands of civilians fled fierce fighting in northern Afghanistan after a series of military victories by the Taliban militia. **5.** South Korea and Japan conducted their first joint naval exercise. Afghan opposition forces launched a fierce counterattack against the Taliban, reversing its military gains. She Wanbao, a member of the China Democracy Party, was sentenced to 12 years' imprisonment for subversion; four other members of the banned party were given sentences of between eight and 13 years. **9.** Beijing vetoed a proposed papal visit to Hong Kong, citing the Vatican's diplomatic ties with Taiwan. A Yemeni court convicted eight British men and two Algerians of plotting a fundamentalist bombing campaign in December 1998. **10.** Indian forces were put on alert after two of their combat planes shot down a Pakistani Navy aircraft, killing all 16 people on board. **12.** Priests accused the army of killing at least 25 Christians in Ambon, Indonesia; the armed forces launched an investigation the following day. **13.** The Japanese Cabinet approved research into an anti-ballistic missile defence system, to be run jointly with the USA; on 18 July the Taiwanese president said that Taiwan wished to participate in the project. **16.** The Indian Prime Minister Atal Bihari Vajpayee said that he would legislate to prevent those not born in India from holding the highest state offices. **24.** Presidents Yeltsin of Russia and Jiang Zemin of China met in Bishkek, Kyrgyzstan, with leaders of three Central Asian countries to discuss combating separatism, religious extremism and the narcotics and arms trades. Calcutta was officially renamed Kolkata. **25.** The largest pro-independence rally staged during more than two decades of Indonesian rule was held in East Timor. **30.** In East Timor, more than 90 per cent of the 450,000 electorate voted in a referendum on independence.

AUSTRALASIA AND THE PACIFIC

OCTOBER 1998

3. The ruling Liberal-National coalition led by John Howard won the general election in Australia.

MARCH 1999

23. The proposed new preamble to Australia's constitution was announced by the prime minister, John Howard **28.** The Labour government won a second term with an increased majority in the parliament of New South Wales, Australia.

APRIL 1999

12. The Australian foreign minister, Alexander Downer, denounced the Yugoslav government's claim that Steve Pratt, a captured aid worker, had been a spy.

JUNE 1999

10. In Australia, legislation was introduced under which a referendum on becoming a republic would be held on 6 November. **24.** Sitiveni Rabuka, the former prime minister of Fiji and a Commonwealth envoy, was taken hostage briefly whilst he tried to bring an end to the increasingly bitter civil war in the Solomon Islands.

JULY 1999

9. Papua New Guinea established diplomatic relations with Taiwan. **13.** Sir Mekere Morauta was elected prime minister of Papua New Guinea; he suggested that the controversial recognition of Taiwan, which had led to the fall of the previous government, would be cancelled. **18.** Luagalau Levaula Kamu, the Samoan minister of Public Works, was shot dead.

AUGUST 1999

12. Prime Minister John Howard of Australia was accused by opposition politicians of trying to engineer the defeat of the referendum on a republic which was due to be held in November 1999.

EUROPE

SEPTEMBER 1998

27. The German federal elections were won by Gerhard Schröder's Social Democrats who said that they would govern in coalition with the Green Party. Opposition parties won 93 of the 150 seats in the Slovakian election and said they would attempt to form a coalition government. **28.** Fatos Nano resigned as prime minister of Albania. **30.** Pandeli Majko, the leader of the Socialist Party, began to form a new government in Albania.

OCTOBER 1998

7. In Moscow, tens of thousands of protesters called for President Yeltsin to resign. **9.** Romano Prodi resigned as prime minister of Italy after losing a vote of confidence. **13.** Romano Prodi was asked to form a new coalition government in Italy. **15.** Prodi announced that he had failed to form a government and proposed that Massimo D'Alema, the leader of the Left Democrats, be appointed prime minister. **27.** Gerhard Schröder was inaugurated as chancellor of Germany. **29.** At the International Criminal Tribunal in The Hague, Goran Jelisić admitted to killing at least 14 Bosnians and Croats and pleaded guilty to 15 counts of crimes against humanity.

NOVEMBER 1998

3. The Spanish government announced that it was prepared to hold talks with ETA, the terrorist group that had announced a cease-fire in September. A new left-right coalition government was formed in Slovakia under Mikulas Dzurinda. **13.** Abdullah Öcalan, the head of the Kurdish terrorist organization the PKK, was arrested at Rome airport. **19.** Turkish importers announced a boycott on Italian goods after Rome refused to extradite Öcalan to face charges of terrorism in Turkey. **20.** Galina Starovoitova, Russia's most prominent female politician, was shot dead in St Petersburg. **25.** The Turkish government lost a vote of confidence following a corruption scandal in which the prime minister was implicitly accused of having links with organized crime. **27.** In Dublin, Paul Ward was convicted of the murder of journalist Veronica Guerin in June 1996.

DECEMBER 1998

1. NATO troops arrested General Radislav Krstić, the most senior member of the Serbian military to face charges of genocide in The Hague. **2.** Bülent Ecevit was appointed prime minister-designate in Turkey. **9.** Ruth Dreifuss became Switzerland's first female president. **16.** An Italian court of appeal ruled that Abdullah Öcalan should not be detained, although the Italian government said that he would remain under observation and could not leave Italy; on 17 January 1999 he was allowed to leave the country. **29.** The Cypriot government announced that it would not deploy Russian-made anti-aircraft systems on its territory, defusing tensions on the divided island. **30.** Juan José Ibarratxe of the moderate Basque Nationalist Party was elected president of the Basque region of Spain. **31.** Brane Miljus, a moderate, was named prime minister-designate of Republika Srpska, Bosnia-Hercegovina.

JANUARY 1999

11. Bülent Ecevit formed a new government in Turkey. Turkey's chief prosecutor called for the abolition of the main Kurdish party, Hadep, claiming that it was acting as a front for the outlawed Kurdistan Workers' Party.

FEBRUARY 1999

16. Abdullah Öcalan was captured by Turkish special forces in Kenya. **17.** Kurds across Europe held violent protests following the arrest of Öcalan. Greenland's governing Siumut Social Democratic Party won the largest number of seats in elections to the island's home-rule parliament. **18.** Three Greek ministers were dismissed following an outcry against the country's alleged role in the capture of Abdullah Öcalan.

MARCH 1999

5. Boris Berezovsky was sacked as head of the CIS. Nikola Poplasen was sacked as president of Republika Srpska. **7.** In the Estonian general election, the Centre Party won most seats but a coalition of centre-right parties formed the new government. **11.** Oskar Lafontaine resigned as finance minister of Germany and chairman of the Social Democratic Party. **13.** Two Kurdish groups claimed responsibility for the fire-bombing of an Istanbul shopping complex in which 13 people died. **20.** A bomb in the city of Vladikavkaz, the North Ossetian capital, killed 51 people and injured 154. **21.** President Aslan Maskhadov of the rebel Russian republic of Chechnya was the target of an assassination attempt. Finland's governing Social Democratic Party lost ground but retained the largest share of parliamentary seats in national elections. **31.** Finland's prime minister, Paavo Lipponen, tendered his government's resignation.

APRIL 1999

12. Dario Kordić, a former ally of President Tudjman of Croatia, went on trial before the International War Crimes Tribunal in The Hague, charged with 22 counts of war crimes in Bosnia in 1992 and 1993. In Germany, the Social Democratic Party confirmed Gerhard Schröder, the German Chancellor, as its leader. **16.** The Swedish finance minister, Erik Asbrink, resigned two days before he was to present a budget. **18.** A referendum was held in Italy on abolishing proportional representation; 90 per cent voted in favour, but the referendum was declared invalid as the number voting fell short of the required 50 per cent. Swiss voters approved changes to the constitution giving workers the right to strike for the first time. **28.** In Turkey, prosecutors formally demanded the death penalty for Abdullah Öcalan.

MAY 1999

4. Merve Kavakci, an Islamist deputy, caused uproar by wearing a headscarf to the Turkish Parliament; President Suleyman Demirel later stripped her of her Turkish citizenship for having taken up American citizenship without approval. **9.** Monaco celebrated the 50th anniversary of the accession of Prince Rainier. **12.** President Yeltsin sacked the prime minister, Yevgeny Primakov, and the rest of the government. The Duma later confirmed his nominee, Sergei Stepashin, as prime minister. **13.** Carlo Azeglio Ciampi was elected Italy's tenth president by an overwhelming majority in the first round of voting by the Italian Parliament. **22.** The Social Democrat Johannes Rau was elected president of Germany.

JUNE 1999

1. In Belgium, the public health minister, Marcel Colla, and the farm minister, Karel Pinxten, resigned after criticism that they had failed to act over animal feed contaminated with dioxin. The sale of Belgian poultry, eggs, beef and pork were later banned throughout the EU. **5.** The Pope began a 13-day tour of Poland in the city of Gdańsk, where he was welcomed by President Aleksander Kwasniewski. **10.** The Romanian Parliament voted to allow public access to the confidential files of the Securitate, the secret police during the communist era. **14.** Belgium's prime minister, Jean-Luc Dehaene, resigned after losing an election marked by public anger over the handling of the contaminated food crisis. **15.** Rudolf Schuster was sworn in as president of Slovakia, after a ballot which ended more than a year in which the country had been without a head of state. **29.** Abdullah Öcalan was sentenced to hang after he was convicted of treason against the Turkish state. **30.** Militant Kurds were suspected of fire-bombing ten Turkish businesses and an Islamic cultural centre in Germany in protest against the death sentence passed on Abdullah Öcalan.

JULY 1999

1. In Germany, Johannes Rau, the first Social Democratic President for 30 years, took office and promised to guide the country towards a more multicultural society. Turkish troops backed by helicopter gunships fought rebels loyal to Abdullah Öcalan after army positions in Tunceli province were attacked. **4.** Thousands of Belgian farmers marched through Brussels to demand more government aid to overcome the dioxin contamination crisis. **6.** British special forces soldiers arrested Radislav Brdjanin, who was a close political associate of Radovan Karadzić, the former Bosnian Serb leader accused of genocide, in Banja Luka, Bosnia-Hercegovina. **7.** Russia deployed helicopter gunships and armoured vehicles in a border battle against guerrillas from Chechnya equipped with mortars and grenade launchers on a bridge linking Chechnya and Dagestan. **8.** Turkey was convicted at the European Court of Human Rights of 13 instances of violating Kurds' free speech, and of two concerning torture and missing persons. **11.** In Belgium, King Albert II announced a new government led by liberal Guy Verhofstadt. **12.** The Dutch government voted to decriminalize euthanasia. **19.** Bülent Ecevit, the Turkish prime minister, ruled out any form of compromise over Cyprus; he was taking part in the 25th anniversary celebrations of the Turkish Republic of Northern Cyprus. **21.** The entire former executive of ETA, the Basque terrorist organization, was freed after Spain's Constitutional Court overturned seven-year jail sentences against them; they had been in prison for 20 months. **26.** Turkish and Greek leaders launched a week of consultations on a range of issues from trade to terrorism in an attempt to ease tensions. **27.** In Turkey, the Ankara State Security Council, which had imposed the death sentence on Abdullah Öcalan, sent its decision to the High Court of Appeals for review. **29.** The Autonomous Republic of Ingushetia declared its intention to legalize polygamy in defiance of the Russian government.

AUGUST 1999

9. President Yeltsin of Russia sacked the prime minister, Sergei Stepashin and appointed Vladimir Putin in his place. The appointment was approved by parliament on 16 August. Vinko Martinović, a Bosnian Croat, was handed over to the International Criminal Tribunal for the former Yugoslavia by the Croatian government to face trial on charges of ethnic cleansing. **10.** Islamic rebels in the republic of Dagestan declared it an independent Islamic state. **13.** Russia launched an offensive against Islamic rebels in Dagestan. **15.** A state of emergency was declared in Chechnya after Russia threatened to attack Islamic guerrilla bases located there. **17.** In response to Turkey's worst earthquake in 20 years, Greece sent emergency supplies, medical teams and pharmaceutical aid to the stricken area. In Bosnia-Hercegovina, a report by the anti-fraud unit of the Office of the High Representative of the European Union revealed 220 cases of fraud, naming several officials linked to various political parties. The report claimed that up to US$1 billion (£625 million) had been stolen from public funds and international aid. **20.** The Danish Court of Appeal ordered the government to pay £44,000 in damages to Inuits who had been forced off land to expand the American airforce base at Thule, Greenland. **25.** Prime Minister Bülent Ecevit launched an appeal for the international community to come to Turkey's financial rescue. **26.** Russia claimed that it had recaptured all the villages seized by rebels in Dagestan. **29.** A Norwegian soldier with the NATO peacekeeping force was arrested by Macedonian authorities after his vehicle was involved in a crash in which Radovan Stojkoski, a government minister, was killed. **31.** A bomb blast in a Moscow shopping centre injured 29 people, five seriously. It was thought to be the work of Islamic militants from the Caucasus.

EUROPEAN UNION

OCTOBER 1998

1. The European Police Office (Europol) came into being in The Hague. **8.** The European Parliament voted by a large majority to lift the immunity of Jean-Marie Le Pen, the leader of the National Front in France, who was facing charges in Germany of trivializing the Holocaust. **27.** EU officials dropped non-military sanctions against Nigeria.

NOVEMBER 1998

10. The EU began formal enlargement talks with Hungary, Poland, the Czech Republic, Estonia, Slovenia and Cyprus. **13.** A report by the European Court of Auditors showed that 5 per cent of EU funds was misspent on schemes that were either mismanaged, poorly managed or fraudulent.

DECEMBER 1998

3. The European Parliament voted to end the process of allowing MEPs' salaries to be topped up by large expenses allowances. **11.** The Vienna summit opened. **17.** The European Parliament refused to clear the accounts of the European Commission.

JANUARY 1999

1. The euro became the standard currency of 11 European states, nicknamed 'Euroland'. Germany assumed the presidency of the EU. **14.** MEPs rejected a motion of censure against the European Commission. **17.** EU ambassadors returned to Belarus following a six-month dispute over their residences.

FEBRUARY 1999

22. Thirty thousand European farmers clashed with riot police in Belgium in protest against the proposed reform of the Common Agricultural Policy.

MARCH 1999

11. The euro rose strongly after the resignation of the German finance minister, Oskar Lafontaine, who had been criticized for political interference in the affairs of the European Central Bank. **13.** Britain asked to be allowed to opt into parts of the Schengen agreement, but to be excluded from the requirements relating to border controls. **15.** European finance ministers met in Brussels to consider a 'withholding tax', a measure proposed by the Commission as part of moves towards tax harmonization. **16.** All the members of the European Commission resigned after an auditors' report concluded that fraud and corruption in the Commission had passed unnoticed. **24.** Romano Prodi was unanimously nominated to succeed Jacques Santer as president of the European Commission. **29.** The euro fell to a record low against the pound and the dollar, undermined by the intensifying conflict in the Balkans and fresh signs of European economic weakness.

APRIL 1999

8. The prospect of EU membership for all countries in the Balkan region was held out by EU foreign ministers as part of a strategy to promote peace. **13.** The European Parliament voted for the harmonization of criminal law for a limited range of serious offences. Romano Prodi, the president-designate of the European Commissions promised to use his term to create a single European economy and accelerate moves toward political unity. **28.** The final meeting of Schengen ministers took place before the Schengen Agreement became part of general EU law following the ratification of the Amsterdam Treaty .

MAY 1999

1. The Amsterdam Treaty came into force. **9.** Romano Prodi said that the creation of a European army was the logical next step in the integration of EU foreign policy.

JUNE 1999

2. EU leaders agreed an ambitious common defence and security policy giving it the means to respond to international crises independently of NATO. **4.** Javier Solana was appointed to the new position of EU High Representative for foreign and security policy. The European Commission placed restrictions on a wide range of Belgian foodstuffs, following fears of contamination by dioxins. **14.** The European People's party (EPP), an umbrella centre-right bloc, won the most seats in the European Parliament election, which was marked by a low turnout of voters. **25.** Tougher controls on the commercial release of genetically modified crops were agreed by EU environment ministers. **29.** The European Commission threatened to launch proceedings against Spain over delays imposed on people crossing the frontier to and from Gibraltar.

JULY 1999

1. The outgoing Commission rebuked the Industry Commissioner, Martin Bangeman, who had resigned

and accepted an employment offer from a telecommunications company. **6.** Pauline Green resigned as leader of the Socialist group in the European Parliament amid criticism of her leadership. **9.** Romano Prodi announced his team of 20 commissioners. **13.** A confidential report from the European Central Bank warned that governments of the countries participating in the euro were in danger of undermining the single currency by failing to take action to curb their budget deficits. Jacques Santer stepped down from his caretaker role as president of the Commission.

AUGUST 1999

19. The Italian authorities reopened a criminal investigation into the activities of Romano Prodi; the case involved a consulting company jointly owned by him and his wife, which he had failed to declare during his term as Italy's prime minister. **30.** Socialist MEPs declared that they would oppose the appointment of Loyola de Palacio as vice-president of the Commission.

THE BALKAN CONFLICT

SEPTEMBER 1998

28. International observers found evidence of systematic torturing and killing of ethnic Albanians by Serb forces in Kosovo, Yugoslavia.

OCTOBER 1998

12. President Milošević of Yugoslavia allowed international observers into Kosovo and agreed to talks on greater autonomy for the province.

DECEMBER 1998

14. Thirty-eight people died in fighting in Kosovo.

JANUARY 1999

8. Eight Serb soldiers were taken hostage by separatist soldiers in Kosovo; they were released on 12 January. **11.** Enver Maloku, a senior aide to the moderate ethnic Albanian leader Ibrahim Rugova, was shot dead outside his house in Priština, Kosovo. **16.** Serbian police forces broke the existing ceasefire and killed 45 Kosovars near the town of Racak, Kosovo. **18.** President Milošević expelled the chief observer of the OSCE and barred the head UN war crimes prosecutor from Kosovo as Serbian troops continued their attack on Racak. **21.** Following international pressure President Milošević backed down over the expulsion of the OSCE chief observer. **29.** NATO and Russia ordered the warring factions in Kosovo to attend a peace conference in Paris in February 1999.

FEBRUARY 1999

6. Peace talks over Kosovo began in Paris. **23.** The Kosovo peace talks broke up without a deal being agreed.

MARCH 1999

12. President Milošević repeated his opposition to any deployment of foreign troops in Kosovo after talks with Richard Holbrooke, the US special envoy. NATO's supreme commander, Gen. Wesley Clark, warned President Milošević that the alliance was prepared to strike Serbia if he blocked peace talks on Kosovo. **17.** Kosovar Albanians signed an international peace agreement in Paris that offered Kosovo broad autonomy within Serbia and provided for the deployment of a 28,000-strong NATO peacekeeping force. **19.** Western monitors evacuated Kosovo after peace talks were abandoned. **20.** Western embassies withdrew non-essential staff from Belgrade. **21.** Thousands fled their homes as Serbian forces advanced against a Kosovo Liberation Army (KLA) stronghold in the Drenica region. **22.** Richard Holbrooke met President Milošević in a final effort to avert military conflict. **23.** The Yugoslav government declared a state of emergency. The Russian prime minister, Yevgeni Primakov, denounced plans for 'unjustified' NATO attacks on Serb military targets. **24.** NATO air strikes against targets in Yugoslavia commenced. The German Luftwaffe flew into combat for the first time since the Second World War. President Yeltsin ordered an end to Russia's co-operation with NATO. **25.** Yugoslavia formally broke off diplomatic relations with the UK, the USA, France and Germany. Journalists from countries linked to the NATO air strikes were ordered to leave Yugoslavia. **26.** NATO forces shot down two Yugoslav MiG 29 aircraft after they flew into Bosnia's UN no-fly zone. **27.** NATO began low-level bombing missions against Serbian forces after reports of hundreds of Kosovar Albanian civilians being massacred in Kosovo. **28.** Albania appealed for international help to deal with tens of thousands of Kosovar refugees. NATO launched more air attacks against Serb military targets. **30.** NATO ambassadors met to consider extending the range of targets for the air strikes to include ministries in Belgrade and other key targets. Yevgeni Primakov visited Belgrade with the Russian foreign and defence ministers in a diplomatic mission aimed at ending the conflict in Kosovo.

APRIL 1999

2. President Milošević asked Russia to provide weapons to combat NATO's air attacks. **5.** NATO targeted oil storage sites inside Serbia. **6.** An offer from the Yugoslav government to begin a unilateral cease-fire in Kosovo was rejected by NATO. **7.** Macedonian troops forcibly evicted 30,000 refugees into Albania. Simultaneously, Serbian troops closed the border with Macedonia and ordered thousands of Kosovar Albanians back to Kosovo. Tony Blair and President Clinton warned President Milošević that the cessation of Serbia's ethnic cleansing policy was a precondition of Nato calling off its assault against Yugoslavia. **9.** President Yeltsin warned NATO not to send ground troops into Kosovo,

saying it would force Russia to become involved and could cause a European or even a world war. **11.** Paskal Milo, the Albanian foreign minister, said that his government was ready to accept ground troops from NATO and had decided to give NATO the right to control Albania's airspace, ports and other military infrastructure. President Djukanović of Montenegro warned that any attempt by Serbia to overthrow his government would result in civil war in Montenegro. **12.** The Yugoslav parliament voted overwhelmingly to apply for membership of a confederation with Russia and Belarus. **13.** Up to 100 Serb infantry crossed into Albania, seizing the villages of Kamenica and Padesh and setting fire to homes before retreating when engaged by the Albanian army. The Vatican criticized the distribution by UN agencies of the 'morning after' pill to Kosovar refugees who had been raped. **18.** NATO bombed a combined petrochemicals, fertilizer and refinery complex on the banks of the Danube in the northern outskirts of Belgrade, releasing clouds of poisonous gases and polluting the waters of the Danube. **21.** Tony Blair spoke on Russian television, appealing for support for NATO's actions and likening events in Kosovo to those in Nazi Germany. Dragan Burzan, the deputy prime minister of Montenegro, described the killing of Kosovar refugees as a crime against humanity and called for the perpetrators to be tried for war crimes. **22.** Romania granted NATO unrestricted use of its airspace. **28.** Vuk Drasković was dismissed as deputy prime minister of Yugoslavia after he told the government that Russia would not help Yugoslavia militarily and that the world's public opinion was against Yugoslavia.

MAY 1999

1. Serbian authorities reported that more than 40 people, mainly Kosovar Albanians, had been killed when NATO accidentally hit a bus in Luzane, Kosovo, during an air strike. **4.** Bulgaria's parliament voted to allow NATO access to its airspace for strikes against Yugoslavia. **7.** NATO forces accidentally bombed the Chinese embassy in Belgrade, killing three people. The Serb regime launched a fierce attack against opposition leaders, calling them 'traitors' and 'agents of NATO'. **9.** Britain, Germany and the USA rejected an offer from Yugoslavia to pull back part of its forces from Kosovo, saying that the offer fell far short of NATO's demand for a complete withdrawal to allow refugees to return. **12.** The EU appointed President Ahtisaari of Finland to represent its interests in negotiations alongside Russia's Viktor Chernomyrdin with President Milošević. **13.** President Milošević refused to meet Mary Robinson, the UN High Commissioner for Human Rights, who had planned to challenge him about ethnic cleansing. **14.** Ibrahim Rugova, the Kosovar leader, said that he was in talks with other exiled politicians to prepare for control of their homeland. **17.** President Djukanović of Montenegro appealed to the EU for emergency food and refugee relief. **20.** Yugoslav soldiers blocked Montenegro's border with Croatia, confiscating Italian humanitarian aid. **22.** Yugoslav troops briefly occupied a buffer zone of Albanian territory. Hundreds protested in the Serbian town of Raska, near the Kosovar border, after dozens of soldiers from the area were reported to have been killed by NATO bombing. **24.** Serb forces launched a second wave of ethnic cleansing in Kosovo aimed at removing tens of thousands of Kosovar Albanians still living in Priština. **27.** The UN War Crimes Tribunal indicted President Milošević of Yugoslavia, President Milutinović of Serbia, the Yugoslav deputy prime minister Nikola Sainović, the Yugoslav armed forces chief of staff Dragoljub Ojdanić, and the Serbian minister of the interior and commander of police, Vlajko Stojiljković, for crimes against humanity. **28.** Viktor Chernomyrdin arrived in Belgrade for peace talks, saying the indictment of President Milošević had complicated his mission.

JUNE 1999

2. The EU and Russian negotiators met Slobodan Milošević, after the Yugoslav leader said that he accepted the general principles of the plan put forward by the G8 group of nations. The plan called for the withdrawal of all Serb military, police and paramilitary forces and the occupation of Kosovo by an international force. **3.** President Milošević accepted the peace plan agreed by NATO and Russia after having obtained the approval of the Serb Parliament, but NATO insisted that the bombing would go on until there was clear evidence that Yugoslav troops were leaving Kosovo. **5.** NATO commanders met Yugoslav generals on the Kosovo-Macedonia border to present them with a detailed military blueprint for the complete withdrawal of soldiers, police and paramilitary forces from Kosovo within seven days. **6.** NATO accused Yugoslavia's generals of stalling on the deal to end the conflict and issued a warning that unless they agreed the details by the following day, the talks would be called off and the military campaign intensified. **8.** Lt.-Gen. Sir Mike Jackson met Yugoslav officers at Kumanovo on the Kosovo-Macedonia border to obtain their formal acceptance of the withdrawal plan in line with the agreement reached a few hours earlier by the G8 foreign ministers in Cologne. **10.** Yugoslav generals signed a military pact setting out terms for their forces' withdrawal from Kosovo, so paving the way for an end to NATO airstrikes. Dr Javier Solana, the NATO secretary-general, ordered the suspension of air operations following confirmation that the full withdrawal of the Yugoslav security forces from Kosovo had begun. The UN Security Council voted 14–0, with China abstaining, to adopt the peace plan prepared by the G8 powers. Europe, Russia and the USA launched a Stability Pact, which would offer billions of pounds for investment, market access and economic reform to the Balkan countries. **11.** Russian troops, who had been based in Bosnia, seized control of Priština

airport. **13.** British forces entered Priština and were hailed as liberators by the Kosovar Albanian population. **14.** Three thousand refugees in Glogovac cheered the arrival of the first UN aid convoy to reach Kosovo. German and Italian forces arrived in their sector capitals, Pec and Prizren. Hungary and Bulgaria refused a Russian request for overflight rights, effectively cutting off the 200 Russian soldiers holding the airport in Priština. **15.** Serb security forces withdrew from Priština. Their departure triggered a wave of revenge attacks by Kosovar Albanians on local Serbs while British peacekeepers tried to keep control. The Holy Synod of the Serbian Orthodox Church demanded the resignation of President Milošević. **18.** Russia's defence and foreign ministers agreed with their American counterparts that Moscow would send about 3,000 soldiers to Kosovo. **20.** All Yugoslav soldiers and policemen were declared to have withdrawn from Kosovo. President Yeltsin agreed with Western leaders to refuse any reconstruction aid to Serbia while President Milošević remained in power. **26.** Patriarch Pavle, the head of the Serbian Orthodox Church travelled to Kosovo to persuade Serbs to remain in the province. **28.** Crown Prince Alexander of Yugoslavia returned from exile in London and called for Milošević's removal; he backed demands from the Orthodox Church for the formation of a government of national salvation. **29.** A crowd of 5,000 staged a demonstration in the Serbian town of Cacak, demanding the resignation of Slobodan Milošević and free elections in Serbia. Thousands of KLA troops rebels assembled at NATO-designated assembly points to hand in their weapons.

JULY 1999

1. The International Committee of the Red Cross claimed that thousands of Kosovar Albanians seized by Serb security forces were being held in Serbia and that the Serbian Ministry of Justice had refused to release a list of its detainees or their whereabouts. Tens of thousands of people poured onto the streets of Priština to celebrate the NATO Victory. **4.** The President of the International Red Cross arrived in Serbia for a four-day assessment of the refugee crisis caused by tens of thousands of Serbs fleeing their homes in Kosovo. **5.** Differences concerning the interpretation of the Helsinki agreement between Russia and NATO were resolved. The main contingent of the 3,600 Russian troops that were to take part in the KFOR peacekeeping force began arriving in Kosovo the day after differences between NATO and Russia were resolved. Zoran Djindjić, leader of the Democratic Party, returned to Belgrade from Montenegro. More than 20,000 people joined an anti-government march in the southern Serbian town of Leskovac. **7.** French gendarmes and troops fought to keep order in Kosovska Mitrovica after escorting 7,000 Kosovar Albanians through its Serb section in a bid to reopen the divided city. **8.** Kosovar Albanians demonstrated against the deployment of Russian troops in Ohorovac. **13.** Serbia and Montenegro began two days of talks on constitutional issues after Montenegro demanded control of the military and the economy in its territory. **19.** EU sanctions against Kosovo and Montenegro were lifted. **24.** NATO appealed for calm after 14 Serbian men were murdered in the British-run sector of Kosovo near Gracko; British forces arrested four suspects on 28 July.

AUGUST 1999

4. Serbs in Kosovo claimed that Russian peacekeepers had failed to protect them. **5.** Montenegro declared that it wanted to abolish the Yugoslav Federation in favour of a loose partnership with Serbia, each with its own army, foreign ministry and currency. **11.** The UN refugee agency claimed that the Serb population of Priština had shrunk from about 40,000 to less than 2,000. **12.** British troops clashed with Kosovar Albanian extremists when two patrols thwarted an attack by an armed group who had fired automatic weapons and rocket-propelled grenades at a Serb-populated village, Dornja Brnica. Four of the five were arrested. Slobodan Milošević reshuffled the Yugoslav government, increasing the representation of the ultra-nationalist Serbian Radical Party and the United Left. **15.** Bernard Kouchner, the head of the UN mission in Kosovo, warned the KLA that the UN was not prepared to see the Serbs driven out of Kosovo. The UN estimated that 170,000 of 200,000 Serbs had left the province. **18.** General Agim Ceku, the KLA's military commander, denied responsibility for murders and attacks by Albanians that had forced Serbs and Gipsies to flee Kosovo. **19.** More than 100,000 people demonstrated in Belgrade, calling on President Milošević to resign. **20.** French troops began escorting Albanian families back to their homes in the Serb sector of the divided city of Kosovska Mitrovica. **22.** Serbs in Kosovo demanded the division of the province into ethnic cantons to protect them from the Albanians.

INTERNATIONAL RELATIONS

SEPTEMBER 1998

2. President Clinton arrived in Russia for talks on the country's economic crisis.

OCTOBER 1998

1. The UN Security Council condemned the massacres of ethnic Albanians being carried out in Kosovo, Federal Republic of Yugoslavia. **17.** The former Chilean dictator General Augusto Pinochet was arrested in London at the request of the Spanish government in connection with the murders of Spanish citizens in Chile during his regime.

NOVEMBER 1998

7–14. The USA withdrew most of the sanctions imposed on India and Pakistan following their

nuclear tests. **12.** The USA became the last major industrialized country to sign the Kyoto Protocol on 'greenhouse' gas emissions.

DECEMBER 1998

23. At a special court in Brussels, Willy Claes, the former secretary-general of NATO, was found guilty of corruption.

JANUARY 1999

11. Officials from China and the USA met in Washington DC to discuss human rights.

FEBRUARY 1999

25. China exercised its Security Council veto to end the UN mandate for its peacekeeping mission in the Former Yugoslav Republic of Macedonia following that country's extension of diplomatic recogntion to Taiwan.

MARCH 1999

3. The USA imposed sanctions on a range of EU goods in the so-called 'Banana War'(*see* Economic and Business Affairs). **12.** Poland, Hungary and the Czech Republic became members of NATO at a ceremony in Independence, Missouri. **26.** The UN Security Council rejected a Russian resolution demanding an immediate halt to NATO bombing in Yugoslavia. **29.** The UN High Commissioner for Refugees, Sadako Ogata, appealed to the international community to assist the Kosovar refugees.

APRIL 1999

7. The World Trade Organization (WTO) ruled that EU import regulations had given preferential treatment to bananas from former colonies of member states and discriminated unfairly against Latin American producers. The decision cleared the way for the USA to impose £120 million of punitive tariffs against unrelated EU exports to the USA as damages for lost business. **25.** At its 50th anniversary gathering, NATO offered a formal defence guarantee to Albania and Macedonia. It also agreed to give the EU a direct role in military matters. **29.** A Commonwealth working group recommended that Nigeria be readmitted to full membership on 29 May, when the democratically elected president, Olusegun Obansajo, was due to take over from the military government.

MAY 1999

28. A three-man group led by the former Swedish prime minister, Carl Bildt, was appointed by Kofi Annan to investigate the role of the UN in Rwanda during the 1994 genocide.

JUNE 1999

2. A request by Yugoslavia for emergency court orders against the UK and nine other NATO countries to stop their bombing was rejected by the International Court of Justice. Judges ruled that it lacked the jurisdiction to grant the provisional measures. **17.** The International Labour Organization voted for the *de facto* expulsion of Myanmar for using forced labour.

JULY 1999

4. NATO blocked two Russian military aircraft from flying to Kosovo with reinforcements, declaring that Russia had ignored an agreement on the deployment and responsibilities of its troops. Bulgaria, Hungary and Romania refused permission for the aircraft to cross their airspace. **13.** The Organization of African Unity committed itself to greater democracy by declaring that governments which came to power by military force would not be allowed to attend the next summit. **30.** Brazil suspended trade talks with Argentina and called for an emergency meeting of Mercosur officials after Argentina announced unilateral quotas on Brazilian textiles and shoes.

AUGUST 1999

8. George Robertson was confirmed as the new secretary-general of NATO. **11.** The UN Security Council appointed Switzerland's attorney-general, Carla Del Ponte, prosecutor at the UN War Crimes Tribunals for the Former Yugoslavia and Rwanda.

THE MIDDLE EAST

OCTOBER 1998

9. Ariel Sharon was appointed Israeli foreign minister. **15.** General Emile Lahoud was elected president of Lebanon. **23.** The Wye River Agreement, an interim peace plan for Palestine, was signed by Yasser Arafat and Binyamin Netanyahu; Israel agreed to withdraw its troops from a further 13.1 per cent of the West Bank in exchange for security guarantees from the Palestinian National Authority. **31.** The president of Iraq, Saddam Hussein, announced that all Iraqi co-operation with UN weapons inspectors would cease.

NOVEMBER 1998

14. Saddam Hussein agreed to co-operate with UN weapons inspectors after the USA sent troops to the Gulf. **20.** Israel withdrew troops from 2 per cent of the West Bank.

DECEMBER 1998

2. Salim al-Hoss was appointed prime minister of Lebanon. **10.** The Palestinian Central Committee voted to change the Palestinian Charter to remove references to the need for Israel's destruction. **12–15.** President Clinton visited Israel and Palestine.

JANUARY 1999

25. King Hussein of Jordan signed a royal decree naming his eldest son, Prince Abdullah ibn al-Hussein, as his successor in place of his youngest brother, Prince Hassan.

FEBRUARY 1999

7. King Hussein of Jordan died.

MARCH 1999

4. Abdel-Raouf Rawabdeh was named prime minister of Jordan. **6.** The Emir of Bahrain, Sheikh Issa, died of a heart attack; he was succeeded by his son, Sheikh Hamad al-Khalifa.

APRIL 1999

15. In Israel, Arieh Deri, the leader of the ultra-orthodox Shas party and an ally of Prime Minister Netanyahu, was jailed for four years for corruption. **21.** An end to years of strained relations between Syria and Jordan was signalled when the new Jordanian ruler, King Abdullah II, received a warm welcome from President Assad. **26.** In Egypt, more than 1,000 Islamic militants, all members of al-Gamaa al-Islamiya, were released from prison; the group had announced in March that it was halting all armed operations.

MAY 1999

4. The Emir of Kuwait dissolved parliament. **17.** Ehud Barak was elected prime minister of Israel; he promised to withdraw troops from Lebanon within a year, and offered to return the Golan Heights to Syria in return for a comprehensive peace settlement. **27.** Prime Minister Binyamin Netanyahu announced he would stand down from parliament.

JUNE 1999

8. Four judges were killed and five bystanders wounded when two gunmen sprayed a courtroom with machine gun fire in Sidon, Lebanon; Esmat al-Ansar, a Muslim fundamentalist group, was suspected of the attack. **21.** A Hezbollah mortar attack on northern Israel forced 250,000 people into bomb shelters.

JULY 1999

1. Ehud Barak, the prime minister-elect of Israel, formed a broad coalition of seven parties. **4.** In Kuwait, opposition liberals won 16 of the 50 National Assembly seats. Islamists won 20 seats and pro-government candidates' numbers halved. **7.** Ehud Barak assumed the premiership of Israel. **11.** Israel announced it would withdraw from 10 per cent of the West Bank, fulfilling the conditions of the Wye River agreement. **19.** Syrian-based dissident Palestinian and militant Muslim groups were ordered by the government to end their armed struggle against Israel.

Obituaries

Abraham, Sir Edward, CBE, FRS, biochemist, aged 85 – 8 May 1999

Adams, Rt. Revd James, suffragan bishop of Barking 1975–83, aged 83 – 11 May 1999

Ali Haidar, Jemadar, VC, aged 85 – 15 July 1999

Alport, Lord (Cuthbert), PC, former Conservative MP, High Commissioner in the Federation of Rhodesia and Nyasaland 1961–3, aged 86 – 28 October 1998

Ambler, Eric, OBE, novelist and screenwriter, aged 89 – 22 October 1998

Archer, Gen. Sir John, KCB, OBE, Commander-in-Chief UK Land Forces 1978–9, aged 75 – 12 March 1999

Autry, Gene, American actor and singer known as the 'singing cowboy', aged 91 – 2 October 1998

Bart, Lionel, composer and songwriter, aged 68 – 3 April 1999

Beloff, Lord (Max), FBA, aged 85 – 22 March 1999

Beriosova, Svetlana, Lithuanian-born ballerina, aged 66 – 10 November 1998

Blanchflower, Jackie, former Manchester United and Northern Ireland footballer, survivor of the 1958 Munich air disaster, aged 65 – 2 September 1998

Bogarde, Sir Dirk, actor and author, aged 78 – 8 May 1999

Box, Betty, OBE, film producer, aged 83 – 15 January 1999

Boxcar Willie, American country music singer, aged 67 – 12 April 1999

Brandon of Oakbrook, Lord (Henry), MC, PC, Lord Justice of Appeal 1972–81, Lord of Appeal in Ordinary 1981–91, aged 78 – 24 March 1999

Bristol, 7th Marquess of, aged 44 – 10 January 1999

Brooksby, John, CBE, FRS, veterinary virologist, aged 83 – 17 December 1998

Brown, Dennis, Jamaican reggae singer, aged 42 – 1 July 1999

Buckley, Sir Denys, PC, MBE, a Lord Justice of Appeal 1970–81, aged 92 – 13 September 1998

Budgen, Nicholas, Conservative MP for Wolverhampton South-West 1974–97, aged 60 – 26 October 1998

Butler, Sir Clifford, FRS, physicist and educational administrator, aged 77 – 30 June 1999

Cairncross, Sir Alec, KCMG, economist, aged 87 – 21 October 1998

Carmichael, Stokely (Kwame Ture), American civil rights leader, aged 57 – 15 November 1998

Carter, Betty, American jazz singer, aged 69 – 26 September 1998

Casey, Rt. Revd Patrick, Roman Catholic bishop of Brentwood 1969–79, aged 85 – 26 January 1999

Casson, Sir Hugh, CH, KCVO, architect, designer and artist, president of the Royal Academy 1976–84, aged 89 – 15 August 1999

Cathcart, Maj.-Gen. The 6th Earl, CB, DSO, MC, aged 79 – 15 June 1999

Cayzer, Lord (Nicholas), aged 89 – 16 April 1999

Chaudhuri, Nirad C., Indian author and broadcaster, aged 101 – 1 August 1999

Chebrikov, Viktor, head of the KGB 1982–8, aged 76 – 2 July 1999

Cockerell, Sir Christopher, CBE, FRS, inventor of the hovercraft, aged 88 – 1 June 1999

Crewe, Quentin, writer, aged 72 – 14 November 1998

Crombie, Prof. Leslie, FRS, chemist, aged 76 – 3 August 1999

Crowder, Petre, QC, Conservative MP for Ruislip-Northwood 1950–74 and for Hillingdon, Ruislip-Northwood 1974–9, aged 79 – 16 February 1999

Dalhousie, 16th Earl of, KT, GCVO, GBE, MC, governor-general of the Federation of Rhodesia and Nyasaland 1957–63, aged 84 – 15 July 1999

Dando, Jill, television presenter, aged 37 – murdered 26 April 1999

Darling, Gen. Sir Kenneth, GBE, KCB, DSO, aged 89 – 31 October 1998

Dean of Beswick, Lord (Joe), Labour MP for Leeds West 1974–83, aged 76 – 26 February 1999

Denning, Lord, OM, PC, Lord Justice of Appeal 1948–57, Lord of Appeal in Ordinary 1957–62, Master of the Rolls 1962–82, aged 100 – 5 March 1999

Devon, 17th Earl of, aged 82 – 19 November 1998

DiMaggio, Joe, American baseball player, aged 84 – 8 March 1999

Dunnett, Sir Alastair, editor of the *Daily Record* 1946–55 and of the *Scotsman* 1956–73, aged 89 – 2 September 1998

Dunsany, Lt.-Col. The 19th Lord, aged 92 – 6 February 1999

Eccles, 1st Viscount, PC, CH, KCVO, Conservative MP for Chippenham 1943–62, President of the Board of Trade 1957–9, Minister of Education 1959–62, Paymaster-General 1970–73, aged 94 – 24 February 1999

Erlichman, John, American lawyer involved in Watergate scandal, aged 73 – 15 February 1999

Evans, Godfrey, CBE, cricketer, aged 78 – 3 May 1999

Fairgrieve, Sir Russell, CBE, Conservative MP for Aberdeenshire West 1974–83, aged 74 – 17 February 1999

Fatchett, Derek, PC, Minister of State at the Foreign and Commonwealth Office since 1997, Labour MP for Leeds South 1982–3 and Leeds Central since 1983, aged 53 – 9 May 1999

Fifield, Elaine, Australian ballerina, aged 68 – 11 May 1999

Flanagan, Sir Jamie, CBE, Chief Constable of the RUC 1973–6, aged 85 – 4 April 1999

Fleming, Amaryllis, cellist, aged 73 – 27 July 1999

Fletcher, Air Chief Marshal Sir Peter, KCB, OBE, DFC, AFC, aged 82 – 2 January 1999

Foyle, Christina, bookseller, aged 88 – 8 June 1999

Frankel, Sir Otto, FRS, agricultural scientist, aged 98 – 21 November 1998

French, Leslie, actor and director, aged 94 – 21 January 1999

Gable, Christopher, CBE, dancer and actor, founder of the Central School of Ballet, director of Northern Ballet Theatre since 1987, aged 58 – 23 October 1998

Gardner, Andrew, newscaster, aged 66 – 2 April 1999

Giant Haystacks (Martin Ruane), wrestler, aged 52 – 29 November 1998

Gillard, Frank, CBE, broadcaster, BBC radio war correspondent 1942–5, aged 89 – 21 October 1998

Gillmore of Thamesfield, Lord (David), GCMG, Permanent Secretary at the Foreign and Commonwealth Office and Head of the Diplomatic Service 1991–4, aged 64 – 20 March 1999

Godden, Rumer, OBE, writer, aged 90 – 8 November 1998

Golding, John, Labour MP for Newcastle-under-Lyme 1969–86, junior employment minister 1976–9, General Secretary of the National Communications Union 1986–8, aged 67 – 20 January 1999

Goodchild, Rt. Revd Ronald, suffragan bishop of Kensington 1964–80, aged 88 – 28 December 1998

Goring, Marius, actor, aged 86 – 30 September 1998

Goulding, Cathal, chief of staff of the IRA 1962–9 and of the Official IRA 1969–80, aged 76 – 26 December 1998

Gowing, Prof. Margaret, CBE, FRS, FBA, historian, aged 77 – 7 November 1998

Grade, Lord (Lew), Russian-born film and television producer, aged 91 – 13 December 1998

Gray, Rt. Revd Joseph, Roman Catholic Bishop of Shrewsbury 1980–95, aged 79 – 7 May 1999

Griffith-Joyner, Florence, American athlete, winner of three gold medals at the 1988 Olympics, aged 38 – 21 September 1998

Grotowski, Jerzy, Polish theatre director, aged 65 – 14 January 1999

Guilford, 9th Earl of, aged 65 – 26 March 1999

Hale, Sir John, FBA, historian, aged 75 – 12 August 1999

Hassan II, King of Morocco since 1961, aged 70 – 23 July 1999

Hayes, Patricia, OBE, actress, aged 88 – 19 September 1998

Haynes, Frank, Labour MP for Ashfield 1979–92, aged 72 – 11 September 1998

Heron, Patrick, CBE, artist and writer, aged 79 – 20 March 1999

Hickson, Joan, OBE, actress, aged 92 – 17 October 1998

Hill, Sir James, Conservative MP for Southampton Test 1970–4 and 1979–97, aged 72 – 16 February 1999

Hobson, Valerie, actress, aged 81 – 13 November 1998

Hodgkin, Prof. Sir Alan, OM, KBE, FRS, biophysicist, joint winner of the Nobel prize for medicine 1963, aged 84 – 20 December 1998

Hodson, H. V., editor of the *Sunday Times* 1950–61, aged 92 – 27 March 1999

Hollenden, 3rd Baron, aged 85 – 12 April 1999

Howard de Walden, 9th Lord, TD, aged 86 – 9 July 1999

Hughes, Ted, OM, Poet Laureate since 1984, aged 68 – 28 October 1998

Hull, Rod, entertainer, aged 63 – 17 March 1999

Hume, Cardinal George Basil, OM, Roman Catholic Archbishop of Westminster since 1976, aged 76 – 17 June 1999

Hunt, Lord (John), KG, CBE, DSO, leader of the British expedition that conquered Everest in 1953, aged 88 – 8 November 1998

Hussein, King of Jordan since 1952, aged 63 – 7 February 1999

Jackson, Air Chief Marshal Sir Brendan, GCB, aged 63 – 19 November 1998

Jackson, Gen. Sir William, GBE, KCB, OBE, MC and Bar, aged 81 – 12 March 1999

Jenkins, Meg, actress, aged 81 – 5 October 1998

John, Rosamund, actress, aged 85 – 27 October 1998

Kane, Bob, American cartoonist, creator of Batman, aged 83 – 3 November 1998

Kane, Sarah, playwright, aged 27 – 20 February 1999

Karekin I, Supreme Patriarch and Catholicos of All Armenians since 1994, aged 66 – 29 June 1999

Keller, Prof. Andrew, FRS, polymer scientist, aged 73 – 7 February 1999

Kelley, DeForest, American actor, aged 79 – 11 June 1999

Kemball, Prof. Charles, CBE, FRS, chemist, aged 75 – 4 September 1998

Kemsley, 2nd Viscount, aged 89 – 28 February 1999

Kendall, Prof. Henry, physicist and Nobel laureate, aged 72 – 2 February 1999

Kennedy, John F., Jr, son of the late president of the USA, aged 38, in a plane crash – 16 July 1999

Killanin, 3rd Baron, president of the International Olympic Committee 1972–80, aged 84 – 25 April 1999

Kubrick, Stanley, American film-maker, aged 70 – 7 March 1999

Kurosawa, Akira, Japanese film director, aged 88 – 6 September 1998

Kurti, Prof. Nicholas, CBE, FRS, Hungarian-born physicist, aged 90 – 24 November 1998

Lanesborough, 9th Earl, aged 80 – December 1998

Lansdowne, 8th Marquess of, PC, aged 86 – 25 August 1999

Latey, Sir John, MBE (MIL), PC, High Court judge 1965–89, aged 85 – 24 April 1999

Leontief, Wassily, Russian-born economist, winner of the Nobel Prize for Economics 1973, aged 92 – 5 February 1999

Lewin, Admiral of the Fleet Lord, KG, GCB, LVO, DSC, Chief of the Defence Staff 1979–82, aged 78 – 23 January 1999

Love, Adrian, radio DJ, aged 54 – 10 March 1999

Lowry, Lord (Robert), PC, Lord Chief Justice of Northern Ireland 1971–88, Lord of Appeal in Ordinary 1988–94, aged 79 – 15 January 1999

Machin, Arnold, OBE, RA, sculptor who designed the portrait of The Queen which has appeared on postage stamps since 1967, aged 87 – 9 March 1999

Marais, Jean, French actor, aged 84 – 8 November 1998

March, Elspeth, actress, aged 88 – 29 April 1999

Marks of Broughton, 2nd Baron, aged 78 – 9 September 1998

Mars, Forrest, American confectionery maker who built the Mars chocolate empire, aged 95 – 1 July 1999

Mars-Jones, Sir William, MBE, High Court judge 1969–90, aged 83 – 10 January 1999

Marsden, Prof. David, FRS, neurologist, aged 60 – 29 September 1998

Martineau, Rt. Revd Robert, Bishop of Blackburn 1972–81, aged 85 – 28 June 1999

Masters, Rt. Revd Brian, area bishop of Edmonton since 1984, aged 65 – 23 September 1998

Mature, Victor, American film actor, aged 86 – 4 August 1999

McAdoo, Most Revd Henry, Church of Ireland Archbishop of Dublin and Primate of Ireland 1977–85, aged 82 – 10 December 1998

McCann, Donal, Irish actor, aged 56 – 17 July 1999

McCrea, Sir William, FRS, mathematician and astrophysicist, president of the Royal Astronomical Society 1961–3, aged 94 – 25 April 1999

McCrindle, Sir Robert, Conservative MP for Billericay 1970–4 and for Brentwood and Ongar 1974–92, aged 69 – 8 October 1998

McDowall, Roddy, actor, aged 70 – 3 October 1998

McGahey, Mick, former Scottish miners' leader, aged 73 – 30 January 1999

Mellon, Paul, American philanthropist, aged 91 – 2 February 1999

Menuhin, Lord (Yehudi), OM, violinist, conductor and philanthropist, aged 82 – 12 March 1999

Merryfield, Buster, actor, aged 78 – 23 June 1999

Mitchison, Naomi, CBE, author, aged 101 – 11 January 1999

Moore, Archie, American boxer, world light-heavyweight champion 1952–62, aged 84 – 9 December 1998

Moore, Brian, novelist, aged 77 – 11 January 1999

Moro, Peter, CBE, architect, associate designer of the Royal Festival Hall, London, aged 87 – 10 October 1998

Morris, Johnny, OBE, children's broadcaster, presenter of *Animal Magic* for 21 years, aged 82 – 6 May 1999

Mosey, Don, cricket journalist and broadcaster, aged 74 – 11 August 1999

Murdoch, Dame Iris, DBE, novelist and philosopher, aged 79 – 8 February 1999

Musin, Ilya, Russian conductor and teacher, aged 95 – 6 June 1999

Nedwell, Robin, comedy actor, aged 52 – 2 February 1999

Newborough, 7th Lord, DSC, aged 81 – 11 October 1998

Newley, Anthony, actor, singer and songwriter, aged 67 – 14 April 1999

Nimmo, Derek, actor and comedian, aged 68 – 25 February 1999

Nkomo, Joshua, vice-president of Zimbabwe since 1987, aged 82 – 1 July 1999

Nutting, Sir Anthony, Bt., PC, aged 79 – 23 February 1999

Orr-Ewing, The Lord, OBE, life peer and 1st baronet, aged 87 – 19 August 1999

Owen, Bill, actor, aged 85 – 12 July 1999

Pakula, Alan J., American film director, aged 70, in a car accident – 19 November 1998

Papadopoulos, George, dictator of Greece 1967–73, aged 80 – 27 June 1999

Paterson, Jennifer, television cook, aged 71 – 10 August 1999

Paton, Sir Angus, CMG, FRS, civil engineer, aged 93 – 7 April 1999

Peck, Bob, actor, aged 53 – 4 April 1999

Perry, Ernest, Labour MP for Battersea South 1964–79, aged 90 – 28 December 1998

Peters, Jim, marathon runner, aged 80 – 9 January 1999

Phillips of Ellesmere, Lord, KBE, FRS, scientist, aged 74 – 23 February 1999

Pillar, Adm. Sir William, GBE, KCB, aged 75 – 18 March 1999

Playfair, Sir Edward, KCB, Permanent Secretary at the Ministry of Defence 1960–61, aged 89 – 21 March 1999

Pliatzky, Sir Leo, KCB, Permanent Secretary at the Department of Trade 1977–9 and at the Civil Service Department 1979–80, aged 79 – 4 May 1999

Portman, 9th Viscount, aged 67 – 2 May 1999

Price, William, Labour MP for Rugby 1966–79, aged 64 – 6 May 1999

Pulman, John, world professional snooker champion 1957 and 1964–8, aged 75 – 25 December 1998

Puzo, Mario, American novelist, aged 78 – 2 July 1999

Quarry, Jerry, American heavyweight boxer, aged 53 – 3 January 1999

Ramsey, Sir Alf, England football manager 1963–74, aged 79 – 28 April 1999

Ray, Robin, actor, broadcaster and writer, aged 63 – 29 November 1998

Reed, Oliver, film actor, aged 61 – 2 May 1999

Rhodes James, Sir Robert, historian, Conservative MP for Cambridge 1976–92, aged 66 – 20 May 1999

Richards, Gordon W., national hunt trainer, aged 68 – 29 September 1998

Riches, Rt. Revd Kenneth, Bishop of Lincoln 1956–74, aged 90 – 15 May 1999

Robens of Woldingham, The Lord (Alfred), PC, former Labour MP, chairman of the National Coal Board 1961–71, aged 88 – 27 June 1999

Robinson, Betty, American athlete, the first woman to win an Olympic gold medal, aged 87 – 18 May 1999

Rodrigo, Joaquín, Spanish composer, aged 97 – 6 July 1999

Roe, Rt. Revd Gordon, suffragan bishop of Huntingdon 1980–97, aged 67 – 19 July 1999

Rollason, Helen, MBE, sports reporter, aged 43 – 9 August 1999

Rosier, Air Chief Marshal Sir Frederick, GCB, CBE, DSO, aged 82 – 10 September 1998

Rossington, Norman, actor, aged 70 – 21 May 1999

Rothermere, 3rd Viscount, proprietor of the *Daily Mail*, the *Mail on Sunday* and the *Evening Standard*, aged 73 – 2 September 1998

Rutland, 10th Duke of, CBE, aged 79 – 3 January 1999

Rybakov, Anatoli, Russian author, aged 87 – 23 December 1998

Sainsbury, Lord (Alan), chairman of Sainsbury's 1956–67, aged 96 – 21 October 1998

Sarazen, Gene, American golfer, first to win all four Majors, aged 97 – 13 May 1999

Schawlow, Arthur, American physicist, co-inventor of the laser, aged 77 – 28 April 1999

Seaborg, Prof. Glenn, American nuclear chemist who discovered plutonium, winner of the Nobel Prize for Chemistry 1951, aged 86 – 25 February 1999

Shacklock, Constance, OBE, opera singer, aged 86 – 29 June 1999

Sheikh Isa bin Sulman al-Khalifa, Emir of Bahrain since 1961, aged 65 – 6 March 1999

Soper, The Revd Lord, Methodist minister, aged 95 – 22 December 1998

Springfield, Dusty, OBE, pop singer, aged 59 – 2 March 1999

St Oswald, 5th Baron, aged 79 – 18 March 1999

Steinberg, Saul, American artist, aged 84 – 12 May 1999

Stephenson, Sir John, PC, Lord Justice of Appeal 1971–85, aged 88 – 1 November 1998

Stone, Jesse, rhythm and blues pioneer, aged 97 – 1 April 1999

Stoph, Willi, Chairman of the Council of Ministers (Prime Minister) of the German Democratic Republic 1964–73 and 1976–89, aged 84 – 13 April 1999

Stott, Lord (George), Lord Advocate 1964–7, Senator of the College of Justice in Scotland 1967–84, aged 89 – 12 April 1999

Stott, Roger, CBE, Labour MP for Westhoughton 1973–83 and for Wigan since 1983, aged 56 – 8 August 1999

Sutch, Screaming Lord, founder of the Official Monster Raving Loony Party, aged 58 – committed suicide 16 June 1999

Thomas, Adm. Sir Richard, KCB, KCVO, OBE, Gentleman Usher of the Black Rod 1992–5, aged 66 – 13 December 1998

Tilberis, Liz, magazine editor, aged 51 – 21 April 1999

Toms, Carl, OBE, theatrical designer, aged 72 – 4 August 1999

Tormé, Mel, American jazz singer and songwriter, aged 73 – 5 June 1999

Torney, Thomas, Labour MP for Bradford South 1970–87, aged 83 – 21 October 1998

Turnbull, Sir Richard, GCMG, governor of Tanganyika 1958–61, aged 89 – 21 December 1998

Vanneck, Air Cdre Hon. Sir Peter, GBE, CB, AFC, Conservative MEP for Cleveland 1979–84 and Cleveland and Yorks North 1984–9, aged 77 – 2 August 1999

Vick, Sir Arthur, OBE, vice-chancellor of Queen's University, Belfast 1966–76, aged 87 – 2 September 1998

Viollet, Dennis, former Manchester United footballer, survivor of the 1958 Munich air disaster, aged 65 – 6 March 1999

Wallace, George, former governor of Alabama and US presidential candidate, aged 79 – 13 September 1998

Waller, Sir George, PC, OBE, High Court judge 1965–76, a Lord Justice of Appeal 1976–84, aged 87 – 5 February 1999

Washbrook, Cyril, CBE, cricketer, aged 84 – 27 April 1999

Welch, Rt. Revd Neville, suffragan bishop of Bradwell 1968–73, aged 92 – 3 February 1999

West, Rt. Revd Francis, suffragan bishop of Taunton 1962–77, aged 89 – 2 January 1999

Whitelaw, 1st Viscount, KT, CH, MC, PC, Conservative MP for Penrith and the Border 1955–83, Leader of the House of Commons 1970–72, Northern Ireland Secretary 1972–3, Employment Secretary 1973–4, Chairman of the Conservative Party 1974–5, Home Secretary 1979–83, Leader of the House of Lords 1983–8, aged 81 – 1 July 1999

Winchilsea and Nottingham, The Earl of (16th Earl of Winchilsea and 11th Earl of Nottingham), aged 62 – June 1999

Wise, Ernie, OBE, comedian, aged 73 – 21 March 1999

Woolf, Sir John, film and television producer, aged 86 – 28 June 1999

Yang Shangkun, president of China 1988-92, aged 91 – 14 September 1998

Young, Freddie, OBE, cinematographer, aged 96 – 1 December 1998

Archaeology

The hill fort of Cadbury Castle in Somerset is popularly associated with King Arthur, but excavations over the years have shown an occupation sequence stretching from Neolithic to Saxon times. In recent years researchers from the Universities of Birmingham and Glasgow have surveyed the area beyond the fort's defences and their findings are described by Richard Tabor in *Current Archaeology* (June 1999). The sequence of features revealed by the excavation at Milsoms Corner is reported, and of more general interest is the discovery of a late Bronze Age Shield lying face down in a ditch having, previous to deposition, been damaged by a blow to the rim and a small stake being driven through it twice. The account notes that: 'The shield exhibits the highest standard of Late Bronze Age craftsmanship. It was fashioned from a single sheet of bronze with a boss at the centre and concentric circles of decoration around the outside – alternate rows of ribs and bosses. Around 20 other shields of this period have been found in Britain mostly buried in bogs and marshes and Professor John Coles has classified them as the Yetholm type, dating to around 1000–800BC'. The shield is unique in being buried in dry ground: 'all other examples for which a context has been noted have a demonstrable link with wet contexts – lakes, bogs and rivers. This pattern of depositing broken weaponry in wet places is noted throughout northern Europe in this period.' There are interesting discussions as to the identity of the shield's owner and how the shield came to be placed where it was, with the suggestion that perhaps it was part of a burial ritual; possibly the shield was hung from a stake while its owner was posthumously cremated. 'At the end of the ceremony the stake would have been removed, and the shield placed face down, its boss in the cavity. There the symbol of the man's status became the symbol of his death as it was deliberately pierced by a stake.' In addition to discussing this very distinctive object, the article also reviews current work in the vicinity of the site.

An Early Iron Age Torc

Field walking along the route of a new water pipeline being installed between the village of Great Houghton and the Brackmills industrial estate in Northampton suggested that the line cut through a Middle Iron Age settlement. The discoveries made are described by Andy Chapman in *Current Archaeology* (September 1998) and include a particularly significant adult inhumation burial. 'As usual with such Iron Age pit burials, it was to our eyes buried in a somewhat unkind fashion, face down, with its head against the side of the pit, and all trussed up:

the arms lay crossed beneath the chest and the legs were flexed, pulled up so far towards the chest that they must have been bound in this position. The discovery of a fairly typical Iron Age pit burial added extra interest to the excavation, but this interest turned to astonishment when the excavator noticed a metal torc encircling the neck; as the torc lay in the ground it was almost identical in colour to the partially cleaned bones.' It was the composition of the torc, made in two parts, which occasioned particular interest: 'This lead neck-ring from Northamptonshire may be a poor object in comparison to the gold, electrum and silver torcs from East Anglia, but it does appear to be the only torc known made of lead, its form is unique, and it is well dated to the Middle Iron Age. It is certainly the first such object from Northamptonshire, a county with a long history of excavation of Iron Age settlement sites. Such torcs are usually considered to denote high status – the equivalent perhaps of a crown or a tiara in the modern world. However the burial was plebeian – the body was placed face downwards in a pit that was already half filled, crouched, with its legs so tightly drawn up that they must have been bound. Her arms were also crossed – possibly her wrists were bound too – and she was trussed arm and leg. What place then did this woman have in society? Iron Age pit burials are not uncommon, but they often give the impression that those buried were somehow outside the usual Iron Age disposal of the dead (whatever that was).'

Nor was this burial the only discovery of interest, as a possibly Christian cemetery of some 23 inhumation burials was also recorded. What is of special interest is that one of the main burials had an identical medical condition of the wristbone as the Iron Age woman. This particular condition 'occurs in only 1.4 per cent of the modern population, so its presence suggests a possible genetic link between these two individuals'. While the remains of the woman had been dated to the fourth or fifth century BC, the remains of the man have been dated by radiocarbon to the seventh century AD, leading to suggestions that this might be an isolated inbred community. 'We must be looking at an early Christian cemetery, located beyond an unknown settlement and occupying that transitional period prior to the appearance of churches and churchyards within settlements, a rare enough find on its own. If we accept the possible genetic link back to the Iron Age woman, then we can perhaps understand why we are seeing an inbred native population. The ancestors of the occupants of the cemetery may have occupied this hillside for over 1000 years, surviving through the coming of both the Romans and the Saxons: these possibilities all being raised by the odd shape of two wristbones!'

A STONE SARCOPHAGUS

Archaeologists have not been slow to adapt and take advantage of new scientific discoveries and procedures. A recent example is the process by which it is possible to reconstruct facial features from the skulls of the long departed. This facility has been particularly useful to police forces in reconstructing the faces of murder victims, and archaeologists have applied the same procedures to skeletons found in the course of archaeological investigations. There has been much public interest in the possibilities offered and a television series, *Meet the Ancestors*, presented by Julian Richards, a professional archaeologist, has brought the process to a much wider audience. Given this interest and the excellent public relation skills of Simon Thurley, the Director of the Museum of London, it was not surprising that the public opening of a Roman stone sarcophagus recently discovered in Spitalfields would occasion much media interest.

A report by Jenny Hall and Chris Thomas in *Minerva* (July/August 1999) puts the discovery in context as one made during excavations in Spitalfields by the Museum of London Archaeological Service, the staff of which investigated part of a Roman cemetery ahead of redevelopment. As the authors note, 'The site is adjacent to the former Ermine Street and is about 400 metres to the north of the Roman city wall. This cemetery lies beneath the extensive remains of the medieval Priory and Hospital of St Mary Spital.' After reviewing the results of past and current excavations, the authors come to the discovery of the intact stone sarcophagus which, although already cracked and broken, was complete with its lid and contained a lead coffin covered by soil. The sarcophagus had been put into an open grave and a number of artefacts were discovered near it. After the lid had been removed, in the earth covering the sarcophagus was found a complete glass vessel of fourth-century AD type and the authors note that 'It seems to be found in burials and was used for perfumed oils'. A similar example was found only some 40 metres away during earlier excavations on an adjoining site, also part of the Roman cemetery. After the accumulated soil had been removed it was seen that the lead coffin had a lid which 'was highly decorated with cable pattern dividing the lid into diamonds and triangles, with a rectangle intersected by diagonal cables at the tapering end. Within the diamonds were scallop shells in clusters of four and within each triangle, a single shell. Scallop shells are common motifs on the lids of lead coffins and a real shell would have been used in the mould when the lid was being cast. Such shells are associated with the pagan belief of the journey of the dead to the Underworld or Isles of the Blessed.'

The coffin was opened publicly on the evening of 14 April 1999 in the Museum of London by and in the presence of a number of specialists. 'When the coffin was opened all that could be seen was the skeleton laid out, held in place by a layer of muddy silt in the bottom of the coffin...the careful removal of the silt successfully produced evidence of leaves, fig seeds, and small fragments of textiles and thread.' Recovered from the area of the skull, the leaves are likely to be bay leaves, and some textile evidence suggests that there could have been a cushion or pillow supporting the head. A cloth may also have been laid on the bottom of the coffin before the body was received. The skeleton is of a woman in her early 20s who lived well and judging by the state of her teeth had access to sweeter foods, suggesting that she belonged to a wealthy family. There was no indication of cause of death and the authors note: 'It is most likely, therefore, that she died of an infectious disease that would have left no trace on the bones. The style of the burial, the expensive grave goods and the physical condition of the skeleton all indicate that the lady belonged to a wealthy family of fourth-century London. It also indicates a family with overseas connections who formed part of either the ruling class, the rich merchant, or land-owning classes. There was no inscription to indicate her name or social status and who she was is likely always to remain a mystery.'

A SMALL ROMAN DOG

John Musty in *Current Archaeology* (September 1998) reports on the work of Ian Baxter who has been researching small Roman dogs. In particular he had 'examined the skeleton of a dwarf hound found in a human-sized grave at York Road, Leicester. It is of fourth-century date. The dog's grave was one of four graves, the others containing human burials orientated east–west. The dog, too, seemed to be deliberately orientated, in its case north east–south west with the head to the north east.' Baxter's view is reported 'that the dog was a dwarf hound and, in life, would have resembled a dachshund. Remains of others of this size have been located, but complete skeletons are comparatively rare: small dogs such as this are not known before the Roman period.' There were three cut marks in the dog's skull which are interpreted as being the result of stabbing, suggesting 'that the burial of the dog was a sacrificial act. However, although dogs may be buried with humans there was no human buried with the York Road dog and it may be a substitute for a dead person's body or intended to summon a missing person to his grave.' In the course of his study Baxter has classified these small Roman dogs into three groups, the first two probably being lap-dogs while the dog found in the York Road grave was probably a member of that group of 'specialized hunting dogs, possibly used to hunt boar and other game in dense undergrowth.'

A ROMAN COIN HOARD

Large hoards of Roman coins always generate great interest and Edward Besly reports in *Minerva* (March/April 1999) on a particularly interesting example which was declared to be Treasure at a coroner's inquest on 10 December 1998, the first hoard in Wales to be subject to the Treasure Act 1996. The hoard consisted of some 3,778 Roman coins of late third-century AD date and had been found by a metal-detectorist 'not far from the site of a known Roman building in the Magor area, and a few miles from Caerwent, the *civitas* capital of the Silures.'

Of particular interest in this hoard from South Wales is that whereas most of the later third-century British coin hoards usually contain the most highly debased coinages of the period AD 260–274 with only small quantities of the reformed coinages of the Emperor Aurelian (270–275) and his successors, this 'new hoard is most unusual in a British context in comprising predominantly the latter category, with few of the most debased issues.' Besly reports that 'There are over 300 coins of Aurelian, 600 of Tacitus (275–276), and 1300 of Probus (276–282), as well as smaller number of Carus and family (282–285) and of Diocletian and Maximian (284–305); the western mint of Lyon predominates.' Particularly significant is the fact that the hoard contains 750 coins of Allectus; 'His coins are the latest in the hoard, which places its deposition in the years shortly after AD 293.' It is the small numbers of coins of Carausius (287–293) and Allectus (293–5), paralleled in the hoard found at Gloucester in 1960, that will be one of the topics for future study, it being noted that 'Conscious exclusion of these two British usurpers is a feature of an emerging group of hoards from the 290s, termed "legitimist", which have a fairly restricted distribution in the south and west of England.'

BLUNSDON RIDGE

With the help of £100,000 made available by Swindon Borough Council, English Heritage bought a field at Blunsdon Ridge near Swindon for £850,000 after it was threatened by redevelopment. The story is told in *Current Archaeology* (June 1999) of how the site was discovered by Bryn Walters, who, with a team of volunteers, opened a trial trench; 'Immediately they came down on "treasure" concealed in a back room of an aisled building, a deposit of silver all crushed together by some late-Roman looter in the form known by the German word of *Hacksilber*. In effect there is one large bowl, probably 18 inches in diameter, fluted and not unlike the fluted washing bowls found both at Sutton Hoo and in the Mildenhall treasure. There were also bits and pieces of 3–6 other vessels including the escutcheons of a situla or wine bowl.' Following the ruling out of various options by magnetometer survey, 'The current theory suggests that there might be a shrine of some sort, possibly connected with a water deity for there are several springs rising on the upper terrace. Not only did the single trench produce the silver hoard but it also produced 60 coins, which is far more than one would expect in any normal occupation site.'

ALFRED THE GREAT

One of the popular debates of the summer of 1999 was whose statue should be placed on the empty plinth in Trafalgar Square. Among the many contributions was one from Christopher Hudson writing in the London *Evening Standard* on 20 July 1999 suggesting that King Alfred the Great (AD 849–899) might be an appropriate candidate. He was answered by John Clark of the Museum of London, in a letter to the same newspaper of 23 July, suggesting that a more appropriate place for a memorial to King Alfred would be Queenhithe in the City of London, 'once the centre of Alfred's town. Recent excavations by the Museum of London nearby have confirmed the documentary evidence showing that it was in this area that a new planned town was first laid out during Alfred's reign.' In essence Alfred refounded London, moving the settlement which had spread outside the Roman town along the Strand back inside the old Roman walls, and refortifying the city against the Danish threat.

The year 1999 is the anniversary of the death of King Alfred in 899 and it is appropriate that the year sees important excavations in Winchester, where the King was buried, which hope to find some new evidence. Although universally remembered for 'burning the cakes', Alfred the Great deserved his epithet for the contribution he made in achieving a settlement with the Viking invaders, as well as his contribution to the establishment of a naval force, the revival of religion and the promotion of learning and literacy. The development of King Alfred's reputation down the ages will be reviewed in an exhibition at the Museum of London entitled *Alfred the Great: London's Forgotten King* which will run from 8 September 1999 until 9 January 2000.

ST MARY'S KEMPLEY

The Church of St Mary at Kempley in Gloucestershire is one of a small number in the care of English Heritage, and is fortunate in having preserved within it a splendid series of wall paintings, the earliest dating from the early 12th century. What is particularly interesting is that according to work reported in *Current Archaeology* (August 1999) investigations show 'that the nave roof can be dated between 1120 and 1150 AD', contemporary with the original scheme of the wall paintings. The west door of the church is also of much the same date. As John Musty writes: 'Surprise was expressed that the timbers (probably 70–80 years old when felled) should have survived but it was pointed out that these had been kept dry and well ventilated. As it is, the roof is one of the earliest timber roofs in Europe.'

SHREWSBURY

While the significance of field archaeology and excavation is widely understood, much less well known is the vital work being undertaken on compiling databases. A good example is given by Nigel Baker in *Current Archaeology* (September 1998) in which he describes the compilation of an Urban Archaeological Database (UAD) for Shrewsbury.

The background is explained, as is the method used to acquire the necessary information; it is noted that 'Rapid visits and selective recording in cellars and back yards could be a cheap and effective way of finding out what was there. The results exceeded expectations. Within the two-acre pilot study area, two monuments and thirty-odd pre-1700 listed buildings on the existing County Sites and Monuments Record were transformed into ninety or more records on the new Urban Archaeological Database.' Baker reports that 'Following the pilot study, a programme of rapid field visits was designed for the main database project. In all, some 254 properties were visited by a team of two, site visits varying in duration from two minutes to two hours, with selected follow-ups. The main aim was the identification of early cellars and terraces, resources not permitting an attic-by-attic survey, as fascinating and productive as this would certainly be.'

The results are certainly impressive: 'Underground, over 80 sandstone-built cellars, of various dates, were eventually recorded. Thirty of these appear to be medieval, of which only five were known previously. A further 18 are of probably late 16th or early 17th century date, generally associated with surviving contemporary buildings. But many masonry cellars turned out to be 18th-century or even later, built of reused salvaged masonry, in some instances incorporating medieval architectural fragments.' Amongst the latter were fragments of a late Saxon interlace-decorated frieze. It was also noted that many of Shrewsbury's cellars are distinctive in that they had 'simple timber ceilings – instead of being stone-vaulted, as is the norm elsewhere.' The UAD together with the dendro-dating of standing buildings as well as historical research allows new questions to be asked and comparisons made with other similar towns. The ability to pose questions and seek explanations will be greatly enhanced as new Urban Archaeological Databases are completed for a number of towns, ensuring that 'Local authorities and their officers in planning, conservation, museums, and tourism, will – like Shrewsbury's – have for the first time a comprehensive and accurate picture of the magnitude and potential of their archaeological resource.'

A Tudor Fish Farm

There was much media excitement in May 1999 over discoveries made by archaeologists from the Museum of London excavating a two-acre site near Tooley Street. The site is reported as a Tudor fish farm which fell into disuse at about the time of the Reformation, perhaps because there was no longer a requirement that fish be eaten on Fridays. The area then became a place where many items were dumped; objects discovered range from a 14th-century porcelain pig through to some 400 leather shoes by way of swords and cutlery, all of which will help archaeologists and curators to give a more detailed picture of social life especially in the late 15th to mid-16th centuries. In addition to this fill,

when the wall which lined the fish ponds was being removed the remains of an upside down 13th-century rowing galley was discovered, in effect holding up one side of the medieval ponds. Because of the cost of timber, this boat had been broken up and recycled. In the 13th and 14th centuries rowing galleys were naval vessels crewed by up to ten sailors. The surviving timbers from this vessel are about 18 feet long, but the galley could have been up to 100 feet long when in service. These remains are apparently the first of their kind to be discovered in Britain and will form the basis of extensive research in the years to come.

Although the site revealed important sequences of different categories of object, perhaps the most unusual, as reported in June 1999, was the discovery of a banana skin. It had previously been thought that bananas were not imported until the 19th century, and certainly there had been no indication that they formed a normal part of Tudor diet. The status of this Tudor banana skin will no doubt give pause for thought as the archaeologists work towards the final report on the excavations.

Post-Medieval Ships

Although the *Mary Rose* was raised in 1982, that was only the beginning of the long research and conservation project which has continued ever since. The latest media report in May 1999 concerned the work which had been done on identifying the galley in what had been Henry VIII's flagship. Rather than food being prepared on deck as previously thought, researchers have established that there were two 600-litre cauldrons which were situated in the hold of the ship. Each cauldron was set into a firebox on top of shingle ballast, with logs being used for fuel. The total weight was substantial and contributed to the ship's ballast. This research, proposing a solution to a fundamental question relating to the feeding of the crew, demonstrates clearly the time and resources necessary to understand fully the results of such a significant excavation as that of the *Mary Rose*.

The Great Storm of 1703 caused the loss of thousands of lives and the sinking of hundreds of ships, among which was the 70-gun Royal Navy warship the *Stirling Castle*. It was forced to ground on the Goodwin Sands off the coast of Kent but has now reappeared in a well preserved state in 70 feet of water, as reported in the press in July 1999. Divers have studied the wreck of the ship, which was built after the Restoration in 1660 for service with the Royal Navy and would have been familiar to the predecessors of Nelson's generation. The contents of the *Stirling Castle*, which provide a splendid cross-section of life in the 18th-century Royal Navy, are being recorded by divers; it is unlikely that the ship will be raised and more likely that the Goodwin Sands will reclaim her.

The rare discovery of river craft is described by John Buglass in *Current Archaeology* (June 1999) where he describes the complicated link between open cast coal-mining and the threat it posed to the remains of old river boats on the River Aire near Castleford, 14 miles upstream from Hull. The researchers 'have so far found eight river boats, a ferry crossing point, a 17th century lock, a watermill and a dry dock.' Among the most significant features of a very interesting site was Boat Site 4, the last to be identified, which consisted of a vessel sunk with a cargo of coal which had to be removed. It is reported that 'Some 5 tons of coal later, the hull started to appear. During the removal of the coal, finds also started to appear and more so than on any of the other sites. This was unexpected as at first it was thought that the vessel had been deliberately scuttled, so finds were not expected, particularly the range of material that was found. The majority of the artefacts were ceramic: porcelain, earthenware, transfer printing, hand painted, slipped, glazed, enamelled – coffee cans, storage vessels, plates, bowls and cups. There was a surprising number of complete vessels – eight at the last count and three found on a single day. In addition we have recovered shoes, a pewter spoon and a cast iron galley cauldron. Many of these were found in the bows of the boat and may represent part of the crew's belongings.' Like the other vessels this boat was clinker built and a possible late 17th or 18th-century date is suggested. 'Though these boats are not very old, they are interesting because there are very few river craft known from this date.'

One of the most famous of all ships, Captain James Cook's *Endeavour*, may still survive at the bottom of Newport Harbour, Rhode Island, where an appropriate wreck has been found and where local legend maintains the *Endeavour* sank. Painstaking work reported in March 1999 demonstrates that the *Endeavour* was renamed the *Lord Sandwich* in 1776 and was subsequently used to ship troops and convicts between Britain and America. It was reported that the *Lord Sandwich* had been sunk during the Siege of Newport in 1778 with two other transport ships. The detailed researches of Dr Kathy Abbass, Head of the Rhode Island Marine Archaeology Project, and the exploration of marine archaeologists in Newport Harbour suggest that the last resting place of the *Endeavour* may indeed have been found. If correct, clearly there would be enormous interest in investigating the vessel on which Captain Cook discovered Australia and New Zealand during his expedition of 1768–71.

ENGLISH HERITAGE

When English Heritage was set up in 1984 under the National Heritage Act of the previous year, it was intended that it would soon merge with the Royal Commission on the Historical Monuments of England (RCHME). Despite strong arguments both for and against the merger, serious lobbying prevented the amalgamation going ahead; however, in 1999 the Secretary of State for Culture, Media and Sport decided that the two bodies would finally merge, with English Heritage taking the lead role.

It may be that the reason for this decision was unrelated to function but more to a general government commitment to reduce the number of Non-Departmental Public Bodies (NDPBs) or 'quangos'. In any case it is appropriate to mark the passing of RCHME and its fine series of volumes on many aspects of the English land and townscapes. The success of Tom Hassall, the Secretary of RCHME, in moving the National Monuments Record to Swindon should also be recorded at this time.

The other important change, which is internal to English Heritage, is its intention to move the Ancient Monuments Laboratory from central London to Fort Cumberland near Portsmouth. The Laboratory is an important facility of English Heritage and as always there are arguments for and against the decision; certainly moving of the Ancient Monuments Laboratory alongside the Central Archaeology Service will provide a world class complex with a substantial increase in space; however, it is not thought that any but a minority of the specialist staff will make the move. There is little doubt that the plan will go ahead in 1999, and the relocation of this important service after so many years in central London is certainly worthy of note.

Architecture

MUSEUM OF SCOTLAND
Edinburgh, Scotland
Architect Benson and Forsyth

As Edinburgh acquires new political importance as the seat of the Scottish Parliament, the timing of the opening of this new museum ensured that it has assumed considerable importance in the debate about what it is to be Scottish. In 1991 a competition was organized to procure a design for a complementary building adjacent to the Royal Scottish Museum (designed in 1861 by Captain Francis Fowke), to house the collection of the Museum of Antiquities. Originally conceived as an annexe to the earlier building, policy changes eventually enabled the new museum to have its own entrance and identity. Benson and Forsyth's winning design has changed little in the process of realization, apart from the conversion of the prominent corner tower to accommodate the entrance, and adjustments to some of the display space.

The site is an important one in the heart of the Old Town, where Chambers Street meets George IV Bridge opposite the Greyfriars Church and at the confluence of four roads. The prominent corner is accentuated by the bold juxtaposition of a free-standing circular stone-clad tower. The building has something of a fortress character, its external walls being clad in Moray sandstone, whose sawn panels range from buff to pink and from plain textures to highly figured stones. The elevations are highly modelled and feature a wide range of window treatments, from narrow incised slots, both vertical and horizontal, to stone-mullioned arrangements and large picture windows.

The sandstone walls, which meet at an obtuse angle on the corner where the tower is positioned, enclose an inner core which rises to higher levels and is capped by a shallow concave roof. The highly sculptural shape of this capping feature acknowledges two functions, firstly to reflect light from its curving soffit down into the central galleries of the core, and secondly to enclose a roof garden from which can be gained superb views of the Edinburgh skyline. In contrast to the outer walls, the central core element is clad in white render and pre-cast concrete, a device which helps to break down the bulk of the total building and lighten the appearance of the highest sections.

The obtuse angle at which the outer walls meet is the key to the spatial organization of the building. The circular corner tower acts as an entrance vestibule with two heavily modelled entrances. A quasi-moat is formed with a tapering well area at basement level, so that access from the vestibule into the museum proper is across a narrow bridge. This gives access into a long narrow entrance hall which is set at an angle to the line of Chambers Street and which occupies the ground level of a three-storey wing. The juxtaposition of this wing with the orthogonal alignment of the rectangular block of the main central core establishes a huge triangular top lit void, Hawthornden Court, which soars through the building to establish a reference point at every level of the museum. In addition, the other two sides of the core structure are separated from the adjacent street frontages by a narrow vertiginous slot of space, crossed at different levels by narrow bridges and top lit, further reinforcing the castle concept of a central keep surrounded by its protecting walls.

Both internal and external walls have an exaggerated thickness, echoing the solid masonry character of the exterior, and are used to brilliant effect in housing some of the enormous variety of exhibits in specially created openings and niches. Great care has been taken in the detailed design of the interior to ensure that objects in the collection are housed in locations designed to enhance their meaning or significance. Exhibits and spaces are also considered in the wider city context, for example, in the gallery where the National Covenant is displayed, a window has been placed looking out over the Greyfriars Church, the place where the Covenant was signed in 1638. Elsewhere, windows are carved into the external walls in a range of shapes, sizes and forms to frame specific aspects of the surrounding city, bringing them into the museum almost as ersatz exhibits.

Internal views have received no less attention, with the grid of massive walls pierced with openings and relieved by projecting balcony features, and spaces opened up across galleries where the section steps back or where walls are replaced with slender columns. The simple aisle form of the central core is thus enlivened and given a spatial complexity that provides continual visual interest and a wide range of spaces. As a result there is no predetermined route through the building; each visitor can generate their own particular promenade through the ages. The primary internal wall finish is an unpainted white plaster applied in one coat. The finish requires a high standard of craftsmanship and attention to detail, but offers a natural material finish compatible with the other natural materials used in the building, and an appropriately neutral background to the colours and textures of the exhibits.

Construction work commenced on site in January 1996 and the completed building was opened by HM The Queen on St Andrew's Day (30 November) 1998. High praise is due to the architects for this highly romantic and picturesque, but equally refined, totally committed and culturally significant building.

BLUEWATER PARK RETAIL COMPLEX
Dartford, Kent
Concept Architect: Eric Kuhne
Executive Architect: Benoy Ltd.

Bluewater Shopping and Leisure Centre, which opened to the public on 16 March 1999, is the first stage in a linear urban development, to include some 30,000 dwellings, planned for the largely 'brownfield' land between the Thames estuary and the A2, east of Dartford. The centre occupies the floor of a huge worked-out chalk quarry, and a development of some 7,000 dwellings is planned for an adjacent quarry.

Bluewater will pose stiff competition for the Lakeside Shopping Centre north of the Dartford river crossing, and will be a huge draw for shoppers. It is the largest shopping centre in Europe, 155,000 m² in area, with some 320 shops and 13,000 car parking spaces to accommodate the needs of the 30 million visits per year anticipated by the developers. The centre is aimed firmly at the quality end of the market. About 10 million people live within an hour's drive, and the catchment population has an income spread and socio-economic rating far higher than the national average. This has been a major determining factor in the design approach, justifying standards in the quality of materials, finish and detailing unmatched by earlier generations of out-of-town shopping centres.

The centre's distinctive layout is based around a triangular circuit of two-storey malls, rather than the more typical linear pattern familiar elsewhere. This has the advantage for the developer of accommodating the maximum retail mass on to the smallest site area, and for the shoppers of being able to make a round trip without the need to retrace their steps. The three malls describe a bow-like shape, with two straight malls and one gently curved on plan, the intersections being marked by three major department stores fronting onto circular galleried nodal spaces.

Each of the malls has been given a particular identity in terms of its retail mix, and each has a differing architectural treatment to reflect this, although a common design theme runs through all three. A high level of natural lighting is provided, but the mall roofs are more solid than glazed and more architectonic in their forms than the ubiquitous fully glazed conservatory type mall roof, which often presents problems with solar gain and glare. The two straight malls are roofed with a series of shallow domes which derive their inspiration from the ceilings of Sir John Soane's Bank of England building. Clerestorey glazing in semicircular openings floods light down onto the malls from the sides, and a circular rooflight marks the centre of each bay. The curved south mall has a roof design in a sawtooth pattern of alternating triangular glazed and solid sections, the solid elements placed on the south side, the glazed sections facing north. Circular rooflights penetrate the solid sections on the centreline of the mall. Subtle differences in design

help to orientate the shoppers and provide visual interest and variety at the same time. Iconic elements sourced from Britain's heritage, including graphic presentations of famous literary and visual quotations, are used to reinforce the identity of the various spaces.

The west mall, known as Guild Hall, caters mainly for high fashion shops and 'lifestyle' retailing, with gourmet restaurants. More than 100 sculptured panels are set into the wall face over the upper level shopfronts, each featuring the practitioners and work of one of the medieval trades or guilds. The east mall, themed as the Rose Gallery, is aimed more at families, with children's wear, toy shops and fast-food restaurants, and features extensive use of natural and plant motifs. The curving south mall is called Thames Walk, and features the course of the River Thames laid out as a contrasting graphic pattern in the stone floor, with selected place names inlaid in polished metal. The sides of the triangulated roof panels are painted alternately blue and ochre, so that the mall is all blue seen from one end and all ochre seen from the other. The watery theme is reinforced with sail-like banners suspended over the mall.

The centre can be entered through each of the department stores and from the adjacent multistorey car parks. At the centre of each mall the space opens out to create a link with the external landscape via a specially themed feature space, supporting specialist retail or leisure facilities. The three main feature areas are named The Village, The Water Circus and The Wintergarden. The Water Circus features a central fountain feature overlooked by the solid metal-clad bulk of a 3,000-seat multiplex cinema. The Wintergarden features the largest greenhouse built in the UK this century and is home to an abundance of mature tropical trees, ponds and streams of running water. It opens out via an enormous glazed frontage and a generous timber decked terrace onto a substantial lake, one of seven around the complex, surrounded by expanses of luxurious and verdant landscaping

The external elevations of this enormous complex are perhaps less significant than is the case with more compact building types. The corner department stores are the dominant elements and are given individual styles, commonly featuring boldly modelled and articulated reconstituted limestone panels and split block masonry. There is an absence of strong colour, the pale buff and cream tones taking their cue from the enormous walls of chalk that surround the site. As all vehicular approaches to the centre descend from the surrounding land levels great emphasis has been placed on the external design of the mall roofs. Atop the centre of each domed bay, where the circular rooflights appear from the malls below, sits a conical aluminium fresh air ventilator, each with a projecting triangular vane to catch the direction of the wind and with its sharp pointed apex offset from the centre of the base. The vents are mounted on bearings to permit them to rotate at low wind speeds, and scoop fresh air into the malls below, via glass dampers which are automatically controlled by the building management system to suit the prevailing weather conditions. Their similarity to the distinctive cowls of Kentish oast-houses is unmistakable, and provides the centre with a unique identity; but the overriding impression of the futuristic silver and white building sitting in its white chalk chasm is far more that of a space station in a lunar landscape than a reflection of the cosy fields and orchards of Kent.

MEDIA CENTRE, LORD'S CRICKET GROUND
London
Architect: Future Systems

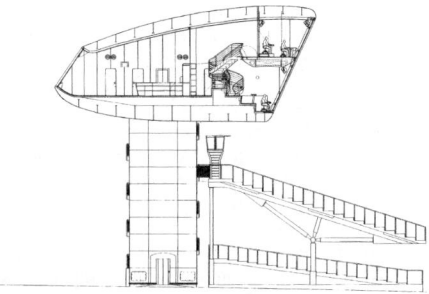

Media Centre, Lord's Cricket Ground. Future Systems.

This extraordinary new media centre, hovering high over the bowler's arm at the Nursery Ground end, is a revolutionary and dramatic piece of building construction that uses imagery and techniques from a diverse range of sources. The completed building, which opened in time for the inaugural match of the 1999 Cricket World Cup, is little different from the design which won a limited competition in 1995. This was based on the techniques employed by the boat building industry, and features a futuristic curved metal skinned pod, inspired by the geometry of boat hulls and aircraft fuselages, cantilevered forward over the lower tiers of the Compton and Edrich stands and supported on two concrete 'legs' in the form of access towers containing stairs and lifts. All the solid surfaces are in a glistening white finish, echoing the predominantly white surrounding stands.

The most dramatic feature is the west elevation, a huge 40-metre-long glazed window-wall, which slices through the subtly curving volume of the pod, and is set at an inclined angle of 25° to prevent solar reflections from disturbing the players' vision. From this hi-tech eyrie the journalists and broadcasters are blessed with a bird's-eye view of the playing area, some 15 metres below the bottom tier of desks. The leading edge is a full 21 metres above the ground. The viewing gallery is divided into upper and lower decks, the lower section comprising four

stepped tiers of worktops with stylish, white Arne Jacobsen-designed chairs. The white worktops are provided with cooling air jets set into the desk surface, and have ample socket outlets for electronic gadgetry. A spiral staircase at each end of the tiered section leads up to the mezzanine level, where 11 rooms provide facilities for radio commentary teams and television broadcast crews. A bar and restaurant area occupies the space to the rear between the two lift shafts and the accommodation includes lavatories and a kitchen, a locker room and two hospitality rooms, one placed at each of the outer ends of the lower tier.

The structural design of the pod is based on the use of aluminium as the primary material in a largely prefabricated semi-monocoque form of construction. Aluminium offered clear advantages in terms of cost, weight and corrosion resistance, while a monocoque form of construction enabled advantage to be taken of the structural performance of the outer skin working in conjunction with the underlying framework of structural ribs. The structural engineering consultants Ove Arup and Partners worked with the manufacturers of the pod envelope, Pendennis Shipyard, using three-dimensional computer techniques to model the curving forms and to develop the two-dimensional templates for cutting the flat aluminium sheeting prior to its rolling into three-dimensional shapes. The complete super-structure shell consists of 26 separate elements, the largest of them measuring 20 x 4.5 metres, which were prefabricated in the manufacturer's Falmouth shipyard and then transported to London for assembly. Craned into position, they were fixed one to another by continuous welded joints, and the whole supported off the concrete structure of the towers by bolted connections.

The allowances for thermal movement within the structure have given rise to particular structural devices. The mezzanine floor is suspended from the roof structure by concealed hangers and therefore moves up and down in relation to the lower floor level. The glass window wall bears on the lower level but is restrained by the mezzanine. The resulting complex differential movement in the inclined plane is accommodated by neatly designed movement joint fixings connecting the sloping panes of laminated and toughened glass to a series of glass stiffening ribs at the mid point and at roof level.

Internally, the walls, carpets and ceilings are all selected from a palette of pale powder-blue colours, said to be inspired by the décor of a 1957 Chevrolet. A blue suedette material is used on the walls, which also has good sound dampening properties. The interior is a fully enclosed environment, with comfort cooling and only a limited amount of natural ventilation. Services and air-handling ductwork are contained largely within the depth of the structural framing and floor zone, and no protrusions of pipework, vents or flues are allowed to interfere with the smooth white exterior skin. The one concession to tradition in all this hi-tech engineering was to accede to the request of the BBC's *Test Match Special* team for an opening window in order to gauge the atmosphere around the ground. This has been provided by the insertion of a framed inward-opening window in the centre of the enormous sheer glass wall.

This addition to the familiar Lord's scene is a most impressive technical achievement, seamlessly blending architecture and engineering to produce an instantly recognizable icon for the cricketing community. Although more expensive than initial estimates predicted, the final cost of £5.8 million will in time surely come to be seen as an excellent investment for the headquarters of the national summer game.

THE CONTACT THEATRE
Victoria University Campus, Manchester
Architect: Short and Associates

This radical overhaul and extension of the former University Theatre on the University of Manchester campus provides a vivid example of the potential that exists for dramatic and arresting styles of architecture that have a primarily environmental justification.

Opened in 1963, the original theatre was relatively sophisticated and was housed in a clean and simple modernist box very much of its time. Since 1972 it has been known as the Contact Theatre. The task recently completed by the architects was to reorder the principal auditorium, foyers, dressing rooms, bar, café and backstage areas, and to accommodate all the displaced functions such as production, administration and marketing, together with rehearsal space and room for the Young Person Theatre Company, in one new coherent structure. The extra accommodation required a significant expansion of the building footprint, and the university therefore consented to the realignment of the adjoining Brisbane Street in order to create the extended site required.

The existing auditorium, together with its 17-metre-wide stage, was retained but totally reworked, with a new design for the tiered seating incorporating open boxes at the sides defined by low beech-panelled partitions. These structure the auditorium space and enable the central curved rows of seating to be filled first, as well as facilitating events requiring a smaller opening width for the proscenium arrangement, which can be varied. Immediately to one side of the stage area, forming an L-shaped arrangement in relation to the auditorium, is a new block containing backstage areas, and a square studio theatre on the second floor set diagonally over the accommodation below and provided with a surrounding corridor giving access at all four corners. The extension is terminated by a circular brick tower which contains a winding stair up to the studio theatre from the entrance foyer which it partly frames. The new entrance has been relocated here, with much improved visibility from the nearby Oxford Road, a major thoroughfare

heading south from the city centre through the campus.

From the tower at one end, the entrance foyer wanders into the space contained by the wings of the L-shaped core through a series of loosely connected spaces defined by the sensuous curves of both brick and rendered walls. At the inner corner, the elbow of the L-shape, a staircase sweeps up to the main auditorium entry points and the bar. The colour scheme for these areas is exotic and 'hot', with red and yellow walls offsetting the buff brickwork, and a deep bright blue ground for the floors offset by a pattern of black squares and bright yellow lippings to the stair treads. The auditorium has deep blue floor and walls and red seats. In addition to the Studio Theatre on the second floor there is also a full-scale rehearsal room, larger than the main stage area, which opens up into the shallow pitched roof which caps it.

The really distinctive features of this project are those driven by the designers' commitment to the principle of natural ventilation and conditioning. The basis of natural ventilation is generally that fresh ambient air is drawn in at low level, passes through the various internal spaces and is exhausted through high level chimneys, utilizing the stack effect. One practical result of this modelling and wind-tunnel testing was that the proposed new stacks to the studio theatre were raised to a height of 40 metres, the same height as the parapet of the adjacent building. They consequently tower over the theatre complex in an exaggerated manner reminiscent of the most elaborate of Jacobean chimneys. A similar, but slightly lower set of chimneys, this time clad in zinc sheeting, emerges from the roof of the main auditorium. Both variants of the chimney terminate in complex 'multi-pots' formed by branching the air ducts into an intersecting double H-shape so that each rising shaft vents through four separate sub-chimneys. The lower metal-clad chimneys maintain the zinc cladding throughout.

The grander, brick-clad chimneys are developed into a complex trussed and braced composition of considerable expressive power. Each of four main brick shafts rises from the centre of the sides of the diagonally disposed studio theatre, whose surrounding brick wall steps up and down with a mixture of curving, stepped and inclined parapet sections. Once clear of the parapet detailing each shaft sprouts four pairs of spear-shaped metal struts, linked and jointed at their foot to the corners of the brickwork, angled apart at the tops so that the spear heads support a metal section box frame forming the square support for each of the branches of the intersecting H-shape brick terminations. It sounds, and looks, precarious and top-heavy, but is undeniably dramatic. Each of the inner series of sub-shafts has its steel support braced to the adjacent one of the next stack by a further restraining member, so that the whole combination of four shafts and sixteen 'pots' is interlinked and crossbraced, with additional pairs of tension wires connecting to the roof some way below.

These powerful features form the backdrop to the main entrance elevation facing Oxford Road. The entrance to the foyer is marked by a device that turns a complex section of the façade into the image of a stage curtain in the process of being raised, to reveal a vibrant red wall that guides the visitor sideways into the main foyer space. The recessed entry is flanked by blank zinc-clad towers that frame a series of overlapping curtains. Rows of windows illuminating the upper foyer levels peep out from beneath the ragged edges of these screens, whose effect is subtly enhanced by concealed top lighting at night. They also fulfil an environmental function by concealing air intake ducts for the bar areas behind. The outer wall of the foyer is marked by four projecting brick boxes, triangular on plan, with canted lid-like roofs and walls peppered with a grid of terracotta flue liners to act as fresh-air inlets.

The whole composition has an appropriately theatrical and melodramatic quality to it, and in making such a positive statement about the possibilities and benefits of a more sustainable approach to traditionally high energy consumption elements of building design, the designer is fulfilling his own manifesto for a 'greener' approach to building in the future.

THE MILLENNIUM DOME
Greenwich, London
Architect: Richard Rogers Partnership
Engineer: Buro Happold

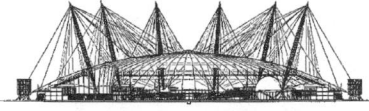

Architect's Line Drawing of the Millennium Dome. Richard Rogers/NMEC.

No review of architecture completed in the last two years of the 20th century would be complete without mention of the impressive £40 million structure that will be the focus of the nation's New Year celebrations as the clocks tick over to the year 2000. The essential design concept is very simple – a fabric-covered stressed-cable structure supported from a series of masts, but here constructed on the most gigantic scale. There were several advantages of the dome concept. Firstly, it provided a recognizable symbol for the Millennium Experience event, to be sited on the windswept and featureless tip of the Greenwich peninsula. Secondly, it enabled more time to be taken in developing the individual exhibition and event zones, which could be brought in nearer the final deadline. Finally, the exhibit structures would not need to be weatherproof (earlier concepts for the Experience had envisaged free-standing pavilions), and could therefore adopt more radical ideas and forms.

The final design for the dome involves a single ring of 12 masts which provide the necessary support for a dome 364 metres in diameter. The masts describe a circle 200 metres in diameter and the internal covered area, 320 metres in diameter, extends to 80,000 sq. metres. The apex of the dome reaches a height of 50 metres above the floor.

The fabric envelope is divided into panels by 72 paired radial cables, which intersect at node points with seven circumferential cable rings which are set out at intervals from the 30-metre diameter central ring at the apex to the lowest running around the perimeter on the line of the polycarbonate window screens that provide security and shelter at ground level. The envelope continues beyond this line as the radial cables are connected onto a final edge cable that follows a complex set of catenary curves sweeping up and down over the multiple entry points and bays of glazing, and concentrates the tensile forces into 24 sculpted cast concrete ground anchor blocks. The tension introduced into the cables keeps the dome relatively stiff, though wind forces inevitably create a degree of movement in the structure. The fabric itself is manufactured from teflon-coated glass fibre, a material which has a life expectancy in excess of twenty-five years and is largely self-cleaning. The fabric infill to each radial segment is installed in two pieces, the upper piece covering the 70 metres from the central to the fourth ring, the lower completing the distance to the edge cable.

The apparent length of the radial cables is misleading as they are in fact terminated and started again at each of the intersecting node points. The nodes are the points at which the supporting cable hangers from the masts are fixed, although a proportion of them are connected to internal tie-down cables, radiating from the bases of the masts, in order to resist the forces of wind uplift. These tie-down cables are kept away from the floor surface by the expedient of mounting the masts on top of a ten-metre high open pyramid of steel tubular sections springing from shaped concrete bases.

Each of the bright yellow masts is a cylindrical verendeel lattice of tubular and rectangular steel sections, 90 metres long and tapering at each end, set at an outward leaning angle more or less perpendicular to the slope of the roof. Their shape is very reminiscent of the famous 1951 Festival of Britain 'Skylon'. They are at their widest section where they penetrate the plane of the roof and at this point accommodate within their girth a large axial fan to assist the extraction of air. Additional air outlets are provided by opening the rooflights within the central cable ring, while supply air comes from the perimeter at low level. The fabric skin is a two-layer assembly to provide a measure of insulation and to guard against condensation. Inside the dome, six three-storey service blocks are spaced equally around the outer segment of the space beyond the masts. These will house mechanical plant as well as lavatory facilities and restaurants.

Associated with each of the service blocks, and ringing the perimeter of the dome, are pairs of cylindrical air-handling equipment towers which will supply ventilation air to selected central areas to compensate for their distance from the perimeter.

The Blackwall Tunnel, which passes underneath the dome, is served by a substantial air vent which is located within the circumference of the dome and which could not be relocated. Accordingly it emerges in all its sculptural white glory through a large circular opening in the dome roof, separated from the internal space by a fabric-clad steel framed sleeve.

Seen from afar, the huge white expanse of roof, which has a surface area of 10 hectares, and the coronet of leaning yellow masts, looks impressive and conveys something of the actual scale of the space within. The construction of the disarmingly simple but enormous umbrella that will house the Millennium Experience has answered all the sceptics who said it could never be done. It has been done, convincingly, on time, and at a cost that is said to equate to the average construction cost per square metre of a typical retail park shed.

Bequests to Charity

The list below represents some of the principal charitable bequests from wills published since the last edition. The exact values of residues of estates cannot be accurately assessed, since prior bequests and inheritance tax (on any personal bequests) have to be deducted from the net figures given. It is worth noting that there is still no inheritance tax payable on any charitable bequest, however large.

Undoubtedly the largest single charitable bequest this year comes from the will of Thomas Cookson, who survived his wife, the prolific authoress Catherine Cookson, by just 17 days. Catherine had left an estate of over £8 million, which mostly went to Thomas as the survivor, with the result that he thus left the bulk of his £20 million estate to the Catherine Cookson Trust. The list includes another prominent author, Hammond Innes, who left nearly £7 million. He left bequests of £100,000 to the Society of Authors, "to provide for authors of some note who have fallen on bad times due to no fault of their own", £50,000 to the World Ship Trust and £20,000 to his local church in Kersey, Suffolk, with the residue going to the Association of Sail Training Organisations.

Yorkshireman Fred Green left the bulk of his £8.4 million estate to Doncaster Health Authority, desiring that it gave priority to benefitting the Montagu Hospital in his home town of Mexborough. Margaret Hole, from East Grinstead in W. Sussex, left the residue of her £9 million estate between eight charities, and Kenneth Williams, who lived near Salisbury, left the income from his £6.7 million estate variously to seven charities over the next 79 years, with the remainder then going to such charities as his Trustees decided. The RNLI was a beneficiary in both these estates as well as figuring prominently in the list as a whole. In fact they were the sole residuary beneficiary in no less than seven other estates in the list – Ruth Scott (£2.3 million) for a lifeboat named after her late husband Richard, Evelyn Hunt (£1.4 million) for the provision of craft in Devon, and Florence Broadhead (£1.5 million), Stanley Clare (£1.2 million), Kenneth Shaw £959,839), Mercia Fisher (£962,730), and Anthony Lawson left all his £563,043 estate to them. Notably only two of them lived on or near the coast.

Three other people left their entire estate to a single charity – Norah Hecksher, of Chelsea, left the whole of her £7 million estate to the National Canine Defence League, which is the largest bequest this year to a named charity, while Enid Luxton, from Brecon, left her entire £837,505 estate to Save the Children, and Edward Winter, from Goole in E. Yorks, left all of his £649,808 estate to the RSPCA.

Jesus College, Oxford, received the residue of the £2.4 million estate of Myrtle Zeitlyn, of Sutton,

Surrey, in memory of her late father Elsley Zeitlyn, a barrister and former student there, while four Cambridge colleges feature in the list – Thomas Glynn Jones, who lived in nearby Coulsdon, left the residue of his £915,113 estate to Downing College, for scholarships for students "in the business management education field". Londoner Hubert Walker left the residue of his £1.6 million estate to Fitzwilliam College, and Wiltshire resident George Partridge left £80,000 and one-third of the residue of his £1.1 million estate equally between Peterhouse College, the Institute of Ophthalmology and Nottingham High School. Another Londoner, Christopher Evans, left the residue of his £2.1 million estate to Queen's College, Cambridge, for the repair and maintenance of the buildings. He also left a bequest of £50,000 to the Myra Hess Trust, "to help outstanding young pianists ordinarily resident in the UK". Musicians in the form of the Musicians Benevolent Fund also benefitted by receiving the residue of the £2 million estate of Joan Randall, of Bromley, Kent.

Alfred Wheeldon, of Hale Barns in Cheshire, left a pecuniary bequest of £800,000 to the Salvation Army, and the residue of his £2 million estate "to a registered charity or charities that will apply the funds for charitable purposes and will honour the memory of my wife Kitty to my Trustees' satisfaction". Others in the list who left large sums for charitable purposes also at their Trustees' discretion included Rachel Sharman, of Lymington, Hants, who left £100,000 and the residue of her £1.2 million estate in such a manner. Isabel Topping, of Dalston, Carlisle, and Ian Hay, of Camberley, Surrey, each left the residue of their estates (£1.6 million and £875,294 respectively) in similar fashion, while Gordon Mackay, of Shobley, Hants, left half the residue of his £1.5 million estate for such charitable objects as he had already directed by memorandum. George Tomkins, of Cardiff, also left the residue of his £1.2 million estate to his Trustees, but in this case to be given to charities involved in providing relief to cancer sufferers, and those involved in medical research, specialist training, and the provision of specialist nursing care and other support. The Charities Aid Foundation received the residue of the estates of John Sykes, of Esher, Surrey, who left £730,715, and Alec Barber, of Harrow Weald, Middx, who left £603,429. The former desired the Foundation to benefit those charities for which he had already made covenants or gifts, and the latter to benefit those according to his written wishes.

An unusually large number of people left the residues of their estates to named charitable trusts – Constance Taylor, of Halesowen, W. Midlands

(£5.9 million), Margaret Robertson, of Hexham, Northumberland (£3.6 million), Arthur Mason, of Albury, near Guildford (£3.4 million), John Bearder, of Holywell Green, near Halifax (£3.1 million), Carmen Butler-Charteris, of London (£2.7 million), Irene Lawton, of Watford, Herts (£1.3 million), Hettie Childs, of Eastbourne (£869,643), and Anne Kochan, of Tetford, Lincs (£537,452). One of the more unusual bequests was the £500,000 left to the Friends of Highgate Cemetery by Londoner Andrew Hardman, who gave no reason why he made a separate codicil for this gift.

Hilda Robinson, who lived near Wincanton in Somerset, left most of her £1.3 million estate to charity, as to 5 per cent to the Friends of Tewkesbury Abbey, and the remainder equally between the Methodist Missionary Society and the National Children's Homes. The reason this will made quite a stir in the national press was the clause which read "I love all my family very deeply, but noticing the great unhappiness that inherited wealth has brought to my family, I do not wish to leave my money directly to my children, as they have all received reasonable provision and first class education in my lifetime. I hope they will understand my wishes in this respect".

Anne Banks, of Chorley, Lancs, £1,615,220 (the residue equally between the National Canine Defence League, RSPB and RSPCA)

Alec Herbert Barber, of Harrow Weald, Middx, £603,429 (the residue to the Charities Aid Foundation, with the request that it be distributed in accordance with his written wishes)

John Alfred Bearder, of Holywell Green, Halifax, W. Yorks, £3,141,078 (the residue to the Bearder Charity)

Ethel Doreen Bettle, of Southborough, Tunbridge Wells, Kent, £1,413,200 (the residue to the National Trust, in memory of her husband Eric)

Neville Alfred Edmund Blackburne, of Nowton, Bury St. Edmunds, Suffolk, £872,149 (the residue to Ely Cathedral, for the fabric)

Muriel Louisa Bottell, of Chichester, W. Sussex, £2,653,012 (the residue equally between King Edward VII's Hospital for Officers, London, and the Royal Marsden Hospital, for cancer research in memory of her husband John)

Florence Barbara Ann Broadhead, of Bessacarr, S. Yorks, £1,574,006 (the residue to the RNLI)

Barbara Parkes-Buchanan, of Minchinhampton, Glos, £3,455,645 (£500,000 to the British Lung Foundation, £400,000 to the Hull and East Riding Charitable Trust and £20,000 each to Barnardo's, Royal Star and Garter Home, Richmond, Cancer Relief Macmillan Fund and Salvation Army)

Harold Butler, of Warminster, Wilts, £680,268 (the residue to Save the Children)

Hilda Adelaide Castang, of Hastings, E. Sussex, £1,716,600 (the residue to the H. and M. Castang Charitable Trust)

Margaret Frances Charlish, of Windsor, Berks, £2,187,697 (the residue equally between "the Cheshire Homes", the Sue Ryder Home, Nettlebed, Oxon, Cancer Research Campaign, Marie Curie Memorial Foundation and Ely Cathedral)

Carmen Butler-Charteris, of Grosvenor Square, London W1, £2,773,980 (the residue to the Carmen Butler-

Charteris Charitable Trust, desiring it be used for the benefit of the RNIB, Fight for Sight and other charities concerned with research into blindness or the treatment and care of blind people)

Jessie Catherine Cheek, of Brentwood, Essex, £988,881 (the residue to Scope, desiring it be used for the benefit of the Drummond Centre, Feering, Essex)

Hettie Violet Childs, of Eastbourne, E. Sussex, £869,643 (the residue to the Childs Charitable Trust, Eastbourne)

Stanley Benjamin Clare, of Napier Avenue, London SW6, £1,270,791 (the residue to the RNLI)

Margaret Coate, of Dormansland, Lingfield, Surrey, £3,122,405 (40 per cent of the residue each to the Imperial Cancer Research Fund and Dr. Margaret Spittle's Cancer Research Fund at Middlesex Hospital, and 10 per cent of the residue each to the Marie Curie Memorial Foundation and Malcolm Sargent Cancer Fund for Children)

Irene Steains Cook, of Haywards Heath, W. Sussex, £916,719 (the residue to the PDSA, desiring it be used to establish an auxiliary service in Cuckfield, Haywards Heath and Burgess Hill)

Thomas Henry Cookson, of Jesmond, Newcastle upon Tyne, £20,222,381 (the residue to the Catherine Cookson Trust)

Ernest George Cox, of Southsea, Hants, £1,553,018 (the residue to the RAF Benevolent Fund)

Howard Cragg, of Brighton, E. Sussex, £2,042,993 (the residue equally between the RNLI, Salvation Army and Cancer Relief Macmillan Fund)

Edna Maud Cross, of Colney, Norfolk, £810,947 (the residue to the RSPCA, for the Norwich and Norfolk District)

James William Davison, of South Shields, Tyne and Wear, £560,295 (the residue to the South Shields and Westoe Club, for the furtherance of amateur sport in the local community)

Percy Joseph William Dickins, of Caldecotte, Milton Keynes, £3,764,638 (the residue equally between the RNIB, British Heart Foundation and Milton Keynes General Hospital, for the purchase of equipment)

Josephine Anne Dodds, of Wilmslow, Cheshire, £917,212 (the residue to Action Aid)

Rethe Pearl Donald, of Welshpool, Powys, £958,414 (the residue to the League of Friends of Welshpool Victoria Memorial Hospital)

Bertha Joyce Eade, of Sidcup, Kent, £529,432 (the residue to the National Trust)

Christopher Chilcott Evans, of Rosslyn Hill, London NW3, £2,102,517 (£50,000 to the Myra Hess Trust, "to help outstanding young pianists ordinarily resident in the UK", and the residue to Queen's College, Cambridge, towards the repair and maintenance of the buildings)

Olga Hazel Evans, of Hagley, W. Midlands, £2,157,549 (the residue equally between the Stroke Association and the Mary Stevens Hospice, Stourbridge)

Henry Walter Fairey, of St Ives, Cambs, £1,100,953 (the residue to the British and Foreign Unitarian Association, London)

Audrey Carrick Feest, of Storrington, W. Sussex, £2,225,326 (25 per cent of the residue each to St. Barnabas Home, Worthing, the Salvation Army, for the Worthing Centre, and Centrepoint, London, 10 per cent of the residue each to the Raystede Animal Sanctuary, Ringmer, and Brooke Hospital for Animals, London, and 5 per cent of the residue to the Worthing Association for Mental Health)

Mercia Rosina Fisher, of Balcombe, W. Sussex, £962,730 (the residue to the RNLI)

Clarice Maud Garrett, of Bathford, Avon, £608,413 (£10,000 each to the RSPB and National Trust, and the residue to the Whitehaven Trust, Bath)

Marjorie Yewdall Gaunt, of Harrogate, N. Yorks, £2,286,627 (£50,000 to the British Heart Foundation and the residue equally between the Cats Protection League, DGAA Homelife, London, Parkinsons Disease Society and Yorkshire Cancer Research Campaign)

Harry Leslie Gill, of Warwick, £1,273,246 (£50,000 to the Salvation Army, and £50,000 and half the residue to the Myton Hamlet Hospice, Warwick)

Dorothea Gmelin, of Cookham Dean, Berks, £719,756 (the residue to the Postgraduate Teaching and Educational Fund of the Homoeopathic Trust, London)

Fred Stanley Green, of Mexborough, S. Yorks, £8,432,654 (the residue to Doncaster Health Authority, desiring it gives priority to benefitting the Montagu Hospital, Mexborough)

Leonard John Digby Halcrow, of Godalming, Surrey, £1,568,093 (£10,000 to the Watts Gallery, Guildford, two-thirds of the residue to Crusaid, and one-third of the residue to the Guildford Undetected Tumour Survey at the Royal Surrey County Hospital, Guildford)

Andrew Mark Hardman, of Murray Mews, London NW1, £1,129,075 (£500,000 to the Friends of Highgate Cemetery)

Ruby Kathleen Harwood, of Fradley, Lichfield, Staffs, £793,518 (the residue to St Giles Hospice, Whittingham, Lichfield)

Ian Charles Scott Hay, of Camberley, Surrey, £875,294 (the residue for such charitable institutions in England and Wales as his trustees determine)

Robin John Hayden, of Weybridge, Surrey, £670,901 (£10,000 to the London Weekend Charitable Trust, and the residue to Great Ormond Street Hospital for Children)

Norah Fielden Hecksher, of Mulberry Walk, London SW3, £7,070,206 (all her estate to the National Canine Defence League)

Alice Mary Hehir, of Cambridge, £1,256,032 (the residue to the NSPCC)

Hilda Frances Hicken, of Dorridge, W. Midlands, £3,564,312 (£50,000 to Knowle Parish Church, Solihull, £10,000 each to Solihull School, and Job's Close Old People's Home, Knowle, and the residue equally between the British Heart Foundation and RNIB)

Margaret Winifred Hole, of East Grinstead, W. Sussex, £9,052,860 (the residue equally between the British Diabetic Association, Imperial Cancer Research Fund, Barnardo's, National Trust, RNLI, RNIB, Children's Society, and the Royal British Legion, Tewkesbury, Glos)

Winifred Hughes, of Sketty, Swansea, £2,981,207 (the residue equally between the Yorkshire Cancer Research Campaign and RNIB)

Evelyn Mary Hunt, of Brixham, Devon, £1,418,215 (the residue to the RNLI, for the provision of craft in Devon)

Ralph Hammond Innes, of Kersey, Suffolk, £6,872,325 (£100,000 to the Society of Authors "to provide for authors of some note who have fallen on bad times due to no fault of their own", £50,000 to the World Ship Trust, for a paid secretariat, £20,000 to St. Mary's Church, Kersey, and the residue to the Association of Sail Training Organisations)

Lucy Anne Jones, of Sloane Avenue, London SW3,

£886,738 (£5,000 to the Royal Opera House, Covent Garden, and the residue to the Royal College of Music, for the endowment of a scholarship or scholarships to be known as "the L. A. Jones Scholarships")

Thomas Glynn Jones, of Coulsdon, Surrey, £915,113 (the residue to Downing College, Cambridge, to be used for scholarships in memory of Margaret and Thomas Glynn Jones, for Downing men and women "in the business and management education field")

Betty Thackwell King, of Bournemouth, Dorset, £2,330,898 (one quarter of the residue each to the Imperial Cancer Research Fund, British Heart Foundation and NSPCC)

Anne Kochan, of Tetford, Lincs, £537,452 (the residue to the Kochan Trust, instituted by her in 1993)

Maurice Lass, of Christchurch Avenue, London NW6, £1,428,531 (the residue to Jewish Care)

Anthony Newton Lawson, of Ivy Road, London N14, £563,043 (all his estate to the RNLI)

Irene Mary Lawton, of Watford, Herts, £1,304,307 (the residue to the William and Irene Lawton Charitable Trust)

Enid Luxton, of Brecon, Powys, £837,505 (all her estate to Save the Children)

Isobel Mack, of Goring by Sea, W. Sussex, £1,153,424 (the residue to the Multiple Sclerosis Society)

Gordon Cameron Mackay, of Shobley, Ringwood, Hants, £1,567,070 (half the residue for such charitable objects as he directed by memorandum)

Mary Margerison, of Fairhaven, Lancs, £1,427,653 (the residue equally between the Imperial Cancer Research Fund and RNIB)

Arthur Malcolm Mason, of Albury, Surrey, £3,416,383 (£10,000 to the Missions to Seamen, £10,000 each to St Joseph's Hospital, Chiswick, St Peter's Church Seaview, Isle of Wight, the Friends of Guildford Cathedral, Christ Church, Harrogate, and St. James the Less Church, Lancing, all for flowers, and the residue to the Mason Medical Research Trust)

Adelaide Moss, of Pinner, Middx, £1,042,055 (the residue to the Jewish Philanthropic Association for Israel and the Middle East, to be used for the works of the Max Moss Laboratory at the Bone Marrow Transplant Unit at the Hadassah Hospital, Jerusalem)

Robin Mugford, of Bournemouth, Dorset, £1,492,374 (half the residue to Save the Children, and one-tenth of the residue each to Help the Aged, MIND, War on Want, Mencap and the Royal London Society for the Blind)

Mary Mildred Neesham, of New Brancepeth, Co. Durham, £3,654,148 (the residue equally between the Little Sisters of the Poor, High Barnes, Sunderland, RNIB, Guide Dogs for the Blind Association, National Deaf Children's Society and Mencap)

Florence Saxbee Palmer, of Bury, Pulborough, W. Sussex, £1,387,330 (£10,000 to the Guide Dogs for the Blind Association and the residue to the Bury Health Care NHS Trust Endowment Fund, Bury, Lancs)

George Thomson Partridge, of Tisbury, Wilts, £1,104,003 (£80,000 and one–third of the residue each to Peterhouse College, Cambridge, the Institute of Ophthalmology, London, and Nottingham High School)

Walter Alfred Percival, of Whitstable, Kent, £542,299 (the residue to the League of Friends of Whitstable and Tankerton Hospital)

George Pollock, of Wellington, Salop, £720,612 (the residue to the Leonard Cheshire Foundation)

Winifred Storer Poynton, of Holbeach, Lincs, £688,740 (the residue to Barnardo's "in memory of my late mother who always took a keen interest in Barnardo's")

Joan Florence Randall, of Bromley, Kent, £2,045,366 (the residue to the Musicians Benevolent Fund)

Marjorie Riddle, of Shoreham by Sea, W. Sussex, £1,130,575 (the residue equally between the National Trust and the Sussex Cancer Treatment Fund at the Royal Sussex County Hospital, Brighton)

Margaret Maureen Robertson, of Hexham, Northumberland, £3,640,557 (the residue to the Michael Robertson Scholarship Fund)

Hilda Robinson, of Wincanton, Somerset, £1,320,210 (47.5 per cent of the residue each to the Methodist Missionary Society and National Children's Homes, and 5 per cent of the residue to the Friends of Tewkesbury Abbey, Glos)

Ann Sachs, of Lindfield Gardens, London NW3, £745,050 (£40,000 to Amnesty International, £30,000 to the AJR Charitable Trust, and £50,000 and the residue to Parkinsons Disease Society)

Ruth Marygold Dix Scott, of Mawnan Smith, Falmouth, Cornwall, £2,344,209 (£10,000 to the National Trust, £5,000 to Mount Edgcumbe Hospice, St Austell, some smaller charitable bequests, and the residue to the RNLI, with the wish that a lifeboat be named after her late husband Richard Cox Scott)

Rachel Dorothy Sharman, of Lymington, Hants., £1,277,774 (£100,000 and the residue for such charitable purposes as her Trustees select)

Kenneth Brian Shaw, of Reigate, Surrey, £959,839 (the residue to the RNLI)

Jared William Sinclair, of Brigsteer, Kendal, Cumbria, £620,479 (the residue to St John's Hospice, Lancaster)

Constance Annie Smith, of Frinton on Sea, Essex, £1,096,876 (the residue to the British Red Cross)

Phyllis Violet Smythe, of Bramley, Surrey, £3,324,376 (the residue equally between the RSPCA, NSPCC, British Red Cross, Salvation Army and Help the Aged)

Raymond Stockton, of Poynton, Cheshire, £901,697 (the residue to St Ann's Hospice, Heald Green, Stockport)

Eva Mary Sunley, of Truro, Cornwall, £1,603,059 (£10,000 to Truro Lions Club and the residue to the Bernard Sunley Charitable Foundation, for building homes in or near Truro for elderly people to be known as "The Sunley Homes for the Elderly")

John Sykes, of Esher, Surrey, £730,715 (the residue to the Charities Aid Foundation, to benefit any charities for which he had made covenants or gifts)

Louise Tapper, of Avenue Road, London NW8, £1,605,969 (three-quarters of the residue to the Society of Friends of the Federation of Women Zionists, and one-quarter of the residue to the Friends of the Hebrew University, London)

Constance Iris Taylor, of Halesowen, W. Midlands, £5,959,547 (the residue to the Connie and Albert Taylor Charitable Trust)

Margaret Anne Taylor, of Kirkella, E. Yorks, £588,614 (the residue to the North Humberside Hospice Project, Hull)

Clara Edith Teape, of Houndsfield Road, London N9, £600,438 (the residue to the National Kidney Research Fund)

Vera June Tiley, of Dinas Powys, Glamorgan, £532,840 (the residue to the National Museums and Galleries of Wales, requesting they use some to buy a picture by a British artist pre 1950 in her memory)

George Tomkins, of Cardiff, £1,218,283 (the residue among such charities involved in the relief of those suffering from cancer as his trustees think fit, to include those involved in medical research, specialist training and the provision of specialist nursing care or other support)

Isabel Topping, of Dalston, Carlisle, £1,681,375 (the residue for general charitable purposes as her Trustees think fit)

Lina Wachtel, of Kingston Hill, Surrey, £4,188,513 (£40,000 to the Wimbledon District Synagogue, and the residue equally between the Nightingale House for Aged Jews, London, Jewish Care, British Heart Foundation, Age Concern and Imperial Cancer Research Fund)

Hubert Park Walker, of Parkway, London SW20, £1,669,509 (the residue to Fitzwilliam College, Cambridge)

John Wallis, of Scarborough, N. Yorks, £1,568,521 (the residue to the USPG)

Robert Dudley West, of Braunston, Oakham, Rutland, £2,336,612 (the residue equally between the National Trust, PDSA, Council for the Protection of Rural England, National Society for Cancer Relief, Army Benevolent Fund and Barnardo's)

Alfred Leslie Davenport Wheeldon, of Hale Barns, Altrincham, Cheshire, £2,051,121 (£800,000 to the Salvation Army, which represents part of the cost of the sheltered accommodation in Sale known as Kitty Wheeldon Gardens, the remainder of the cost having been funded by him in his lifetime, and the residue to a registered charity or charities "that will apply the funds for charitable purposes and will honour the memory of my wife Kitty to my trustees' satisfaction")

Charles Henry Whiteley, of Edgbaston, Birmingham, £631,880 (the residue to Oxfam)

Kenneth Maurice Williams, of Salisbury, Wilts, £6,743,102 (the annual income from his residuary estate for 79 years after his death as to 25 per cent for the RNLI, to build or maintain a lifeboat named "The William Blannin", 20 per cent each for the Guide Dogs for the Blind Association and Battersea Dogs Home, 15 per cent for the PDSA, Bristol Branch, 10 per cent for the Princess Louise Scottish Hospital, Bishopton, Renfrewshire, and 5 per cent each for the Royal Masonic Hospital and St John Ambulance Brigade, Salisbury Divisional HQ, and then the remainder of his estate for such charities as his trustees decide)

Edward Winter, of Howden, Goole, E. Yorks, £649,808 (all his estate to the RSPCA)

Hilda Grace Wood, of Bicester, Oxon, £746,212 (the residue to the Imperial Cancer Research Fund)

Stanley Ellis Woodhouse, of Esher, Surrey, £1,186,533 (the residue to Parkinson Disease Society)

Myrtle Henriette Zeitlyn, of Sutton, Surrey, £2,490,539 (£50,000 to the British Academy, to establish "The Elsley Zeitlyn Annual Lecture on Chinese Archaeology and Culture" combined with the hosting of a related exhibition, and the residue to Jesus College, Oxford, in memory of her late father Elsley Zeitlyn, barrister at law and former student of the College)

Broadcasting

TELEVISION

The year 1998–9 was a period of sweeping changes and turmoil in British broadcasting, most noticeably in television. After years of lobbying and counter-lobbying one of the great institutions of British television, ITV's *News at Ten*, was finally abandoned, a sign of the intense competition for audiences. The move was designed to enable ITV to show non-stop entertainment throughout the evening and in the long term to compete effectively with the new digital offerings. Sky Digital and On Digital finally arrived in the autumn. During the year the BBC launched two new digital channels, Choice, and Knowledge, but much more relevant to most viewers was the never-ending drain of talent and sports rights from the BBC to rival networks. Barry Norman quit the Corporation to present a new film review show for Sky; Channel 4 snatched the rights to Test Match cricket, and most spectacularly of all, Des Lynam defected to ITV. Making matters worse for the beleaguered BBC was the contentious proposal that audiences with digital TV should pay a supplementary licence fee; a government committee, chaired by economist Gavyn Davies, recommended that the extra charge should be about £24 for seven years.

Critics and broadcasters argued endlessly over whether television was 'dumbing down' or – less frequently – 'braining up'. As usual the debate often amounted to little more than a smokescreen as the main channels struggled to come up with shows that pleased both audiences and reviewers, ideally at the same time. The growing disparity between cut-price shows and stale ideas, evident throughout terrestrial and non-terrestrial channels, and programmes of unquestionable high quality was more noticeable than ever. Regrettably, the latter were often shunted to the margins of the schedules – or tucked away from the mainstream on BBC2, which continued to sparkle, or the more erratic Channel 4.

Stephen Poliakoff's BBC2 serial, *Shooting the Past*, was hailed as a small screen masterpiece, far removed from the sinking standards of daytime talk shows, unimaginative lifestyle programmes, endless series featuring pets and vets, the perennial glut of middling drama, a surfeit of docu-soaps and an increasing coarseness. The latter was evident in an inappropriately scheduled Christmas episode of the BBC1 sitcom, *Men Behaving Badly*, when jokes about masturbation backfired. Family audiences were offended.

There was an increased emphasis on sex, hetero- and homosexual, as a way of enticing viewers to stay tuned. Channel 4, attempting to regain its reputation for cutting-edge fare, screened *Queer as Folk*, British television's first gay drama series. Wherever you looked, sex scenes were in plentiful supply. The second series of BBC1's *The Lakes* contained an especially brutal rape scene, screened too close to the 9 p.m. family viewing watershed for many people's taste. *The Vice* was yet another ITV crime drama set in the murky world of prostitution. Channel 4 had *Sex in the City*, an American import, and *Shanghai Vice*, the latest documentary from Phil Agland. But of the terrestrial networks it was the upstart Channel 5, two years old in March, that received the most criticism for its shameless exploitation of sex. But sex, even TV sex, cannot always be guaranteed to generate ratings. In the summer ITV's much-publicised *The Sexual Century* was shunted out of its peak-viewing slot after just two weeks because audience stayed away.

JILL DANDO IS SHOT

On a more sombre note, the saddest news of the broadcasting year was the murder of BBC presenter Jill Dando, who was shot outside her London home in April. The media reaction to her death may have been overblown; the *Sun* devoted 17 pages to the tragedy, the *Daily Mail* had 11. Meanwhile ITV screened an instant special, although she had never worked for the channel. But there was no denying the sense of outrage that such an obviously decent woman and gifted young presenter had met such an untimely and cruel end. Both the Queen and the Prime Minister paid tributes to Dando. Even the usually razor-tongued Julie Burchill had a good word for the women known to millions for her work hosting *Holiday* and *Crimewatch*. 'They'd managed to take out the one decent person in a profession full of rotters,' she wrote.

MILLIONAIRE HITS THE JACKPOT

Of the main channels ITV had the most successful year, but it was not without its setbacks. Its biggest hit, the Chris Tarrant-hosted quiz show, *Who Wants to Be a Millionaire?* was, strictly speaking, a variation on a theme almost as old as television itself – the big prize money quiz show. The format did feature an original audience participation element allowing contestants to phone a friend when they got into difficulties with the questions, plus the opportunity to win £1 million, the most money ever offered by a British TV quiz show. The closest anyone got was £125,000.

In another departure with tradition, *Who Wants to Be a Millionaire* was screened on consecutive nights. Once audiences were hooked, they came back for more the following evening to follow the progress of last night's competitor. It all added up to one of ITV's most successful series ever: more than 19 million people tuned in, an extraordinarily high audience in the multi-channel era.

News at Ten – The End of an Era

ITV's successful campaign to jettison *News at Ten* after 32 years provided more ammunition for those, including the BBC, who claimed the network was reneging on what remained of its public service responsibilities. The network had tried to ditch its flagship news programme once before, but opposition from the regulator, the Independent Television Commission (ITC), and the then Prime Minister John Major, had kept the programme on air. As ITV's plans became public in September, Tony Blair voiced his objections to moving the news. Surprisingly, the ITC rejected his argument.

After consulting the public, many of whom agreed with the Prime Minister, the watchdog said ITV could axe *News at Ten* provided 'its commitment to public service was undiminished'. The regulator argued that audiences for TV news were declining. Moreover, with rival stations all offering news bulletins during peak time and the growth of round-the-clock news channels, including the BBC's News 24, viewers would not be starved of news. To date the BBC has insisted it will continue to show its main evening news bulletin at 9 p.m. That the BBC was prepared to consider inviting show business celebrities, including Elizabeth Hurley and Peter Stringfellow, to participate in *Question Time* raises doubts about what might happen to news and current affairs in the future.

ITV's new-look, entertainment-led schedule (a 20-minute bulletin was shown at around 11 p.m.) was launched on 8 March. But after an initial flurry, due chiefly to a bumper helping of *Who Wants to Be a Millionaire?* and Hollywood films, the longed-for ratings bonanza did not materialise. Part of the problem was that ITV had not stockpiled enough tempting new programmes. Or maybe it was because most of the nation tends to go to bed around 10.30 p.m. and does not want to sit up watching TV until 11 o'clock.

ITV's timing could not have been worse. The demise of *News at Ten* came weeks before the Kosovo conflict, one of the most important European news stories since 1945. The excellence of the BBC's war reporting, featuring extended broadcasts only, highlighted ITV's diminished commitment to news. Those who believed the station was 'dumbing down' also pointed to the network's much-hyped new weekly current affairs show, *Tonight – with Trevor McDonald*. Screened at 10 p.m., critics thought that *Tonight* was trivial and soft-centred. They said it was not a worthy successor to the veteran investigative programme, *World in Action*, it had replaced. McDonald looked ill at ease in the programme's studio, with little sense of engagement in proceedings. *Tonight's* first edition did, however, contain a genuine scoop – interviews with the suspected murderers of Stephen Lawrence.

Applause for Drama

While news became an Achilles' heel for ITV in 1998–9, it fared better with its traditional strength,

drama, and not only with the usual star-studded vehicles that for years have given the network some of its highest audiences. In the winter, new series of such tried-and-tested favourites as *A Touch of Frost*, *Heartbeat*, now minus Nick Berry, and *Kavanagh* performed strongly, easily outpacing anything the BBC pitched against them. In addition to playing the rough-edged barrister John Thaw also starred in two other successful ITV dramas, *Goodnight, Mr Tom* and *Plastic Man*. In the former, set in the Second World War, he played curmudgeon Tom Oakley opposite child actor Nick Robinson. *Goodnight, Mr Tom* was easily the most popular single drama of the year, was watched by almost 14 million, ITV's best audience for a single drama since 1991. In *Plastic Man* Thaw played a plastic surgeon faced with a moral dilemma.

One of ITV's new hit series was *Grafters*, featuring the amorous adventures of Robson Green and Stephen Tompkinson cast as two itinerant builders. More than ten million tuned in. Less successful but more ambitious was an adaptation of C S Forester's *Hornblower* novels starring Ioan Gruffudd. The first of these films, hailed as the most expensive British TV drama ever made, was screened in October, attracting just over eight million viewers. ITV's £3 million investment in the programme and *Hornblower's* failure to attract a bigger audience led to hostile press comment. Over on BBC1, the home makeover show, *Changing Rooms*, costing only £60,000, achieved the same-sized audience.

Much of ITV's drama, and come to that, BBC1's, continued to exploit the audience's apparently endless appetite for crime and medical sagas. *Always and Everyone*, starring Martin Shaw, was a partially successful attempt to make a British version of *ER*, the slick American hospital series. The mix contained some surprises. Juliet Stevenson received praise for her role in a well-judged version of Laurie Lee's *Cider with Rosie*, made by Carlton and shown by ITV over Christmas. Another Yuletide treat was *Lost for Words*, a sentimental but honest portrayal of caring for an elderly parent starring Thora Hird and Pete Postlethwaite. Another successful departure was *Cold Feet*, Granada's romantic comedy shown in the autumn with a cast featuring Helen Baxendale.

The Bill Hits Back

The network's veteran soaps, *Coronation Street* and *Emmerdale* continued to perform consistently throughout the year, the former generally considered to be on better form than its BBC rival, *EastEnders*. Meanwhile another veteran series, *The Bill*, was back on top after a revamp that resulted in one-hour, instead of 30-minute, episodes and the introduction of photogenic new CID officer, detective constable Duncan Lennox.

ITV's peak-time documentaries were almost invariably in the docu-soap vein or sensational, frequently both. Their purpose was to offer instant gratification rather than provide insight into hidden worlds or investigations of public affairs. The titles said it all: *Full Frontal in Flip Flops, Neighbours from Hell* and *Infidelity*. One welcome exception was a film about Alzheimer's, *Malcolm and Barbara: A Love Story*, by veteran documentary maker Paul Watson. Despite the tough subject matter and a late night slot (9.30–11 p.m.) more than five million remained gripped by this touching story. Meanwhile Melvyn Bragg's epic history depicting the history of Christianity, *Two Thousand Years*, which debuted in April, went virtually unnoticed.

ITV's reputation for credible investigative documentaries took a battering when in December the ITC fined Carlton Television a record £2 million for its award-winning drug trafficking film, *The Connection*, originally shown in 1996, after it was found to have been largely faked.

In comedy perhaps the network's biggest embarrassment was what sounded like a promising attempt to hire American comedy producers, Carsey Werner, to make a British version of one of their hit shows. The resulting *Days Like These*, despite some authentic seventies costumes, was a spectacular flop.

BBC1 FALTERS

BBC1's performance during the year was more erratic than ITV's. In fact, the station had to soak up a steady stream of abuse, not least from inside the Corporation itself. Commenting in the BBC's annual report, published in June, the board of governors suggested that more work needed to be done to improve popular drama and entertainment. 'The BBC needs to work harder to find the successors to Basil Fawlty and Victor Meldrew'. Popular drama for the BBC has to be distinctive, creative and original. The scripts have to come first. The BBC makes a mistake if it simply apes a formula from the competition. The BBC can and should create more of its own successes.' The Davies Committee suggested that the Corporation had held onto audiences by 'cheapening or dumbing down the product'. BBC1's plight reached rock bottom in February following newspaper allegations that the high-profile daytime talk show, *Vanessa*, had used fake guests. Three members of the production team were sacked, and in the summer the BBC bowed to the inevitable and axed the programme.

There were, however, several undoubted high spots. The network's big autumn drama, Andrew Davies' adaptation of *Vanity Fair*, may not have pleased all the critics, but the serial was visually exciting and boasted a memorable soundtrack. Natasha Little, last seen in *This Life*, made her mark as the seductive social climber Becky Sharp and there was a strong supporting cast. David Attenborough's latest natural history blockbuster, *The Life of Birds*, maintained the standards of previous triumphs. Another outstanding BBC1 documentary, albeit one made by Granada, was *42 Up*, the latest instalment in Michael Apted's ambitious venture chronicling the lives of a disparate group of individuals on their passage through life. Also well received were The

Human Body and *The Life of Twins*, ably presented by Lord Winston. Perhaps the year's most unlikely new TV star was Charlie Dimmock, co-presenter of the gardening makeover series, *Ground Force*, which, along with DIY format *Changing Rooms*, successfully moved across from BBC2.

On the popular drama front, the inventive Saturday night crime series, *Jonathan Creek*, starring Alan Davis and Caroline Quentin, was praised by critics and won a loyal following. Less impressive was the new Nick Berry vehicle, *Harbour Lights*, and *Casualty* spin-off *Holby City*, starring Michael French. Lucy Gannon's *Hope and Glory* provided a welcome change of scene from police stations and hospitals. The setting was an inner-city comprehensive school on the brink of collapse. Lenny Henry starred as the heroic new head attempting to restore morale; Amanda Redman played his newly appointed deputy. BBC1's comic masterpiece of the year was *Dinnerladies*, the first ever sitcom penned by Victoria Wood. Despite its unlikely setting – a works canteen – *Dinnerladies* showed it was still possible to reinvent TV's most troublesome genre provided enough care was taken with the writing, acting and direction. Without it this would have been a dismal year for new comedy on the Corporation's flagship channel.

BBC2 GETS THE LAST LAUGH

Thankfully BBC2 fared better. The station screened the most inventive comedy of the year, *The Royle Family*, a merciless and cleverly observed portrait of a Northern working-class family co-written by and starring Caroline Aherne. Unfortunately for the BBC, Granada produced it. Two other well-received BBC2 comedies debuting in 1998–9 were *Big Train* and *The League of Gentlemen*. *Big Train*, created by *Father Ted* writers Arthur Matthews and Graham Linehan, was a sketch show with a difference; *The League of Gentlemen*, originally broadcast on Radio 4, contained echoes of *Monty Python* but still displayed considerable originality. It was quirky British TV comedy at its best, full of eccentric characters and a surreal edge.

The best of BBC2's drama came from reliable sources. Tony Garnett, the veteran producer behind hits such as *Cathy Come Home, Between the Lines* and *This Life*, brought his inimitable edge to a new police drama, the documentary-style *The Cops*. In a more polished, traditional style Andrew Davies' (him again!) adaptation of Angela Lambert's *A Rather English Marriage*, starring Albert Finney, Tom Courtney and Joanna Lumley, won great acclaim, as did the aforementioned *Shooting the Past*. Writing in the *Evening Standard*, Andrew Billen described the piece as 'a rebellious tribute to the recent past, albeit TV's, a time when original stories were allowed to be told and at their own pace, rather than in a hectic succession of short scenes.' The second series of Alan Bennett monologues, *Talking Heads 2*, delighted viewers and critics but some wanted to know why the programme had been relegated from BBC1 to 2.

Another high-profile BBC2 drama was Tony Marchant's interpretation of Dickens's *Great Expectations*. Dramatised in just two episodes, many felt the film was a wasted opportunity as it failed to take full advantage the novelist's extraordinary characters. But Charlotte Rampling was excellent as Miss Havisham. Documentary highlights included the ambitious *Earth Story*, employing state-of-the-art graphics to explain the world's geology, and Lucy Blakstad's *Naked*, which explored people's relationship with their own bodies. However, Jeremy Isaacs' blockbuster series, *Cold War*, failed to live up to the pre-transmission publicity.

CHANNEL 4 REPOSITIONS ITSELF

In an attempt, in the words of its chief executive Michael Jackson, 'to be ahead of the mainstream' Channel 4 tried to strike a new, more modern pose. The station was not without its successes, but some commentators felt it was rapidly losing touch with its roots as a challenging, risk-taking network and was becoming just another TV station or media company. They argued that too many of its programmes had little appeal to the over-35s.

C4's most widely admired initiative of the year was the launch, in November, of FilmFour, a digital subscription channel showcasing independent and art house films, plus its own impressive archive of self-financed movies. Critics agreed that FilmFour was one digital channel well worth paying for. But elsewhere, the once cutting-edge network sent out a confusing set of messages. By outbidding rivals for Test Match cricket coverage and paying £400,000 for an exclusive audience with Clinton aide Monica Lewinsky (interviewed by Jon Snow), C4 risked making itself appear conservative. Critics, however, liked the station's cricket programmes.

Certainly its consistently most successful programmes continued to be American imports: *ER*, *Frasier*, *Friends* and *South Park* accounted for much of the station's identity. At least one critic maintained that *The Sopranos*, a US comedy-drama about a New Jersey mobster suffering a mid-life crisis, shown during the summer, was the best new television drama she had seen all year.

With the demise of *Father Ted* and the last series of *Drop the Dead Donkey*, the station provided no new important sitcoms. There was praise for the debut series of an all-female sketch show, *Smack the Pony*. Factual and current affairs were the station's strongest suit. Channel 4 News also excelled; overall the network won praise for its Kosovo coverage. *The Clintons: A Marriage of Power* provided a timely portrait of the world's most powerful couple; the *Dispatches* strand continued to impress and a lengthy fly-on-the-wall portrait of ex-Spice Girl Geri Halliwell, *Geri*, made by Molly Dineen, caught the public's imagination. The film was a refreshing non-hagiographic portrait of a celebrity. The station also scored with its often revealing biographical series, *The Real...* in which *Peter Mandelson, Jonathan Aitken, Rupert Murdoch* and *Kaiser Bill* were all reassessed.

Meanwhile Channel 4's veteran Liverpudlian soap, *Brookside*, was showing signs of fatigue. Even its creator Phil Redmond confessed the serial 'had lost the plot' and needed overhauling to bring it up to date.

Throughout British television arts programmes were suffering from an identity crisis, not helped by the attention given to science in the media generally. Thankfully, Channel 4 attempted to redress the balance with an innovative Sunday series, *This Is Modern Art*.

FIVE FAILS TO COME ALIVE

Those waiting for something genuinely special from Channel 5 during 1998–9 went unrewarded. Most commentators agreed with veteran critic Christopher Dunkley who, writing in the *Financial Times* in May, opined: 'It does not seem unfair to suggest that Channel 5 has contributed nothing – literally nothing – to the total of high-quality programmes.' A month earlier the network had been ordered to smarten up by the ITC. The regulator found little of note on C5 although it did praise the documentary *Truckers*, but others, such as *The Real Monty* and *Swindon Superbabes*, were said to be 'overly voyeuristic', while the sexually explicit nature of *Sex and Shopping* was 'unacceptable'. Even its once innovative evening news bulletin had begun to look stale in the light of changes to news programme on the other, established networks. C5 risked further admonishment by bringing back the much-derided Miss World contest to terrestrial TV. However, its commercial success seemed assured.

RADIO

Compared with the convulsions affecting television, radio had a relatively quiet year. The 25th anniversary of commercial radio in October went unnoticed by the majority of listeners, digital radio looked further away than ever and when in June the BBC announced the appointment of a new director general, Greg Dyke, it was clear he was chosen because of his television expertise. Dyke, who is due to take over next April, admitted he had much to learn about radio. In fact, despite the arrival of ex-*Sun* editor Kelvin MacKenzie as the new chief executive of commercial station Talk Radio and the continued success of Classic FM, the BBC's radio services generally received more favourable comment than the organisation's television activities. Radio 2 remained far and away the nation's favourite station, while the setbacks that led to such negative publicity for Radios 1 and 4 in recent years began to recede as audience losses levelled off.

Radio 2 consolidated its position as Britain's foremost pop station and in March was voted station of the year at the Sony Radio Awards after increasing its audience for the third year running. As breakfast presenter Terry Wogan said: 'Radio 1 once set the popular music agenda. It made the hits that topped the charts. Now it's Radio 2, no question about it.' As if to reflect the outfit's new image, one of its DJs, the veteran Johnnie Walker, was suspended after the *News of the World* published allegations about cocaine use.

In the music industry, it was acknowledged that Radio 2's following with the under-44s was sufficient to make or break certain entertainers; the chart-topping success of Blondie's *Maria* owed much to extensive exposure on Radio 2. Other performers championed by the station included The Corrs, The Mavericks and LeAnn Rimes. The broadcaster's reinvention inevitably led to several high-profile changes and some concern by critics. Debbie Thrower resigned; Steve Wright took Ed Stewart's place; and the ubiquitous Jonathan Ross, Barry Norman's successor on BBC1, was given a new Saturday morning show. In the *Sunday Times* radio writer Paul Donovan wondered if the changes really marked an improvement. 'There is a price to be paid for turning Radio Wrinklie into Radio Rock, and that price is a perceptible coarsening.' Others wondered if the BBC was abandoning the over-55s.

If Radio 2 was beginning to look slightly tacky during the year under review, the outcry that greeted Radio 4 controller James Boyle's radical revamp of April 1998 began to subside. Not that it was all plain sailing for Britain's leading speech radio network. In fact the year got off to a bad start for the station when it emerged in 1998 autumn that Radio 4 had lost more than half a million listeners during the previous three months. This was a record low. However as the year progressed listening figures stabilised and in June the BBC claimed people were tuning in to Mr Boyle's network for an extra 17 minutes a week. Radio 4 certainly did well at the annual Sony awards, winning an impressive eight gold medals. Among the winners was John Peel's *Home Truths*, the Saturday morning sideways look at family life that audiences seemed to love and hate at the same time. Critics still insisted that Boyle needed to improve the quality of the lunchtime quizzes and early evening comedies, a complaint he and the BBC acknowledged. Yet there was plenty that was praiseworthy, not least a high-profile Reith lecture, on globalisation, from leading Blairite, Professor Anthony Giddens. Also hitting the intellectual high notes was an evening of debate coinciding with the 40th anniversary of C P Snow's 'Two Cultures' speech. Among newer shows, the early evening arts strand *Front Row* and *Bookclub*, where listeners discuss a specific work with its author, made an impact. In the summer the network's five-part series, *The Reference Library*, featured a programme relating the history of *Whitaker's Almanack*. Such Radio 4 staples as *Start the Week*, with new presenter Jeremy Paxman, *Desert Island Discs* and *In the Psychiatrist's Chair* continued to please. Meanwhile *Any Questions* celebrated its 50th anniversary with a special broadcast from the British Library. Disquiet, however, continued regarding the new extended edition of *Today*, while MPs forced Mr Boyle to reinstate *Yesterday in Parliament* to FM after 12 months in exile on long wave following a dramatic fall in listening.

Much of the station's drama received good notices, including a season of remastered works first heard on American radio in the 1930s and 1940s. Versions of Dickens' *Bleak House* and Graham Greene's *The End of the Affair* won acclaim. Yet there were worries that in its 75th anniversary year, radio drama risked being squeezed. The actor Martin Jarvis voiced concern that the once 40-strong BBC Radio Drama Company had been reduced to six actors, two of them students. 'It would be tragic,' he said, 'if, in the future, the only drama associated with radio was that of its demise.'

Arguably the biggest row to hit Radio 4 during the year was the highly publicised sacking after 13 years of Christopher Dunkley as the presenter of *Feedback*. Dunkley decided to walk out rather than present his final two shows. Producer Nick Utechin had to step in quickly to fill the gap. Dunkley claimed he had been dismissed because Mr Boyle disliked *Feedback* being used as a forum for listeners annoyed by his changes. Roger Bolton, the television producer and presenter of Channel 4's *Right to Reply*, was chosen as Dunkley's successor and the show was doubled in length from 15 minutes to half an hour.

In September Roger Wright, BBC's head of music, was appointed Nicholas Kenyon's successor as controller of Radio 3. Commentators reacted with relief interpreting his promotion as a sign that the station intended to put an even greater distance between itself and Classic FM. Wright indicated he wanted to see less chat, more music and less of the popular classical repertoire already broadcast on Radio 3's commercial rival.

ZOË BALL TRIUMPHS

The year saw Radio 1 start to reverse its recent audience decline. Its biggest success was adding half a million listeners to the early morning show when it was relaunched in September as *The Radio 1 Breakfast Show* with Zoë Ball. The presenter was rarely out of the headlines and her marriage, in the summer, to DJ Norman Cook, a.k.a. Fatboy Slim, made front-page news. Ball was the winner of a special Sony Gold Award. Another Radio 1 DJ in the news was hip hop presenter Tim Westwood, shot in a London street during July in a suspected gang attack. The network's desire to be in tune with its constituency was not always appreciated by everyone. A panel set up by the BBC to monitor Radio 1, whose members included Geri Halliwell, noted that the style of presentation was occasionally 'laddish'. The panel also regretted the lack of any black DJs on mainstream daytime programmes. Radio 5 continued to thrive with, according to the BBC, more listeners tuning in for news, rather than sport. Several new presenters joined the line-up during the year, including Julian Worricker and Victoria Derbyshire who took over the breakfast slot. The *Nicky Campbell Show* maintained its high profile helping to secure the presenter a stint on BBC2's *Newsnight*, scheduled to begin in the autumn.

In the commercial sector MacKenzie's arrival at Talk Radio led to several upheavals. Breakfast presenter Kirsty Young left in October. Other casualties of the new regime included Tommy Boyd and Nick Abbott. Meanwhile in typical MacKenzie style, the disgraced Geoff Boycott was signed as the station's chief cricket correspondent. Arguably a more impressive acquisition was winning the rights to England's winter cricket tour, snatched from the BBC.

Classic FM also received an injection of fresh blood during the year. New managing director Roger Lewis, who took over in September, attempted to make his mark on the station by introducing a new look in the spring. Out went Margaret Howard, who had been part of Classic's team since its launch in 1992, Mike Read and Alan Mann. Joining from the BBC was Radio 3 stalwart Natalie Wheen. The move sent out confusing signals over the station's future direction. But Lewis appeared single-minded. He said: 'The challenge of Classic FM is to be predictable to switch on for, but not so predictable that it becomes bland or boring.'

At least Classic had the merit of being distinctive. This was not a quality always evident in pop radio, especially in the commercial sector. With growing consolidation by the big radio owners, Capital and Emap, critics complained that an increasing number of stations were beginning to sound exactly alike. Capital was criticised for taming the once imaginative London station Xfm. This prompted a demonstration by protesters outside Xfm's HQ in the Capital building in London's Leicester Square and a presentation of a 4,000-strong petition. It remains to be seen whether this corporate sterilisation of radio can be curbed. Overall, broadcasting looked and sounded more homogeneous during 1998–9.

TELEVISION AWARD WINNERS

BAFTA Awards 1998

Best single drama – *A Rather English Marriage*
Best drama series – *The Cops*
Best drama serial – *Our Mutual Friend*
Best light entertainment – *Who Wants to Be a Millionaire?*
Best comedy – *Father Ted*
Best soap – *EastEnders*
Best actor – Tom Courtenay, *A Rather English Marriage*
Best actress – Thora Hird, *Waiting for the Telegram*
Best comedy performance – Dermot Morgan, *Father Ted*
Best light entertainment performance – Michael Parkinson, *Parkinson*
Best factual series – *The Human Body*
Best arts programme (Huw Wheldon award) – *Arena: The Brian Epstein Story*
Flaherty documentary award – *After Lockerbie*
Best news and current affairs journalism – *Dispatches: Inside the Animal Liberation Front*
Best live outside broadcast coverage – Channel 4: *Racing – Derby Day*
Best features: *Back to the Floor*
Originality Award – *The Human Body*

BAFTA Fellowship – Morecambe and Wise
Alan Clarke award (for outstanding creative contribution to television) – Jimmy Mulville, Denise O'Donoghue
Richard Dimbleby award (for most important personal contribution on screen in factual television) – Trevor McDonald
Lew Grade award (for a significant and popular programme) – *Goodnight Mister Tom*
Dennis Potter award – David Renwick
International Television Programme award – *The Larry Sanders Show*
Special Award – Richard Curtis

Royal Television Society Awards 1998

Entertainment – *Who Wants to Be a Millionaire?*
Situation comedy and comedy drama – *Cold Feet*
Single documentary – *Modern Times: Drinking for England*
Documentary series – *Windrush*
Presenter – David Attenborough: *Life of Birds*
Male actor – Ray Winstone, *Our Boy*
Female actor – Thora Hird, *Talking Heads: Waiting for the Telegram*
Single drama – *A Rather English Marriage*
Drama serial – *A Young Person's Guide to Becoming a Rock Star*
Drama series – *Jonathan Creek*
TV performance – Rory Bremner, *Rory Bremner...Who Else?*
Live sports coverage – Sky Sports, *The First Division Play-off*
Sports news – ITN News: *World Cup Trouble*
Sports documentary – BBC Wales/BBC One, *The Man Who Jumped to Earth*
Sports presenter – Desmond Lynam, BBC
International news – BBC News: *The Massacre at Drenica*
Home news – GMTV: *Drumcree: Portadown Divided*
News event – BBC News, *Good Friday Agreement*
Current affairs (international) – *Correspondent Special: The Serbs' Last Stand*
Current affairs (home) – *Dispatches: Inside the ALF*
Television journalist of the year – David Loyn, BBC News
Judges' Award for Television Journalism – *World In Action*
The Gold Medal – Roger Laughton

RADIO AWARD WINNERS

Sony Radio Awards 1999

Best event – *The Enthronement of the Seventh Bishop* (BBC Radio Merseyside)
Best comedy – *Old Harry's Game* (BBC Radio 4)
Best sports – *Metro Sport: Two Wembley Finals* (Metro FM)
Best drama – *Bleak House* (BBC Radio 4)
Best arts – *Landscape of Fear* (BBC Radio 4)
Best news – *Farming Today* (BBC Radio 4)
Best short form – *Home Truths Inserts* (BBC Radio 4)
Best feature: music – We Got the Funk (BBC Radio 1)
Best feature: speech – *Between the Ears: Out of the Blue* (BBC Radio 3)
Best special interest music – *Shake, Rattle and Roll* (BBC Radio 2)
Best talk/news broadcaster – Tim Hubbard (BBC Radio Cornwall)
Best Music Broadcaster – Mark Lamarr (BBC Radio 2)
Best Sports Broadcaster – Ian Payne (BBC Radio 5 Live)
Gold award (contribution to British radio 1998–9) – Zoë Ball (BBC Radio 1)
Station of the Year (up to 500,000 listeners) – Moray Firth Radio
Station of the Year (500,000–12 m listeners) – Clyde 2
UK Station of the Year (broadcasting primarily to the UK) – BBC Radio 2

Conservation and Heritage

THE NATURAL ENVIRONMENT

GENETICALLY-MODIFIED FOOD AND WILDLIFE

Despite all the news coverage of GM food during the year, relatively few facts are available about the impact of the new technology on the environment and on biodiversity. Most trials have been undertaken in the United States and other large continental countries where agriculture and natural habitats are not as closely integrated as they are in Britain. Here most of the public debate has focused on human health. The government intends to evaluate the ecological effects of GM crops by planting trial plots among conventional crops over the next four years. Anti-GM campaigners, led by Greenpeace, have illegally destroyed several of these plots, and some farmers have changed their minds about participating in the scheme. Some food manufacturers and supermarket chains claim to have refused to use or sell GM crops, and food writers and chefs have been outspoken in their condemnation of the new technology.

Wildlife campaigners, backed by English Nature, have called for a five year moratorium on the commercial release of GM crops, to give time for scientific evaluations on their effects on wildlife. This the government has turned down. One of their concerns is that crops with genetically modified resistance to broad-spectrum herbicides would remove virtually all the weeds necessary to sustain birds and insects on arable land. Another is the possible creation of herbicide-resistant 'superweeds' which might 'run amok' in the countryside, smothering native vegetation (as escaped oil-seed rape has already done). Yet another 'nightmare scenario' would be the evolution of new viruses, to correspond with the modified genes, which might cross from species to species in an uncontrolled way.

English Nature has proposed a series of tests which would have to be passed before GM crops could be released into the environment. They include 'rigorous risk analysis' of trail corps, a consideration of all the consequent changes in husbandry and agricultural practices, and a ban on the use of artificial genes.

RIGHT TO ROAM

In March 1999, the countryside minister, Michael Meacher, announced that the government would honour an election pledge by forming legislation to give the public the right of access on unenclosed land. This is defined as areas of mountain, moorland, registered commons, downs and heaths: about 1.8 million hectares or 10 per cent of the land surface of England and Wales. Scotland, with far more open land, would require separate legislation. Landowners will continue to have the discretion to close land temporarily for shooting, land management or where human safety or wildlife or historic interest may be threatened. The newly established Countryside Agency under the chairmanship of Ewen Cameron (a farmer and former president of the Country Landowner's Association) is charged with the responsibility for identifying these areas, organising local advisory forums and advising the public and landowners about their rights and responsibilities. The response of Wildlife bodies has been muted. English Nature, for example, voiced its concern that increased access might lead to 'unwitting damage to wild plants and animals'.

EC PROTECTION FOR TOP HABITATS

Britain has put forward a list of 340 sites for protection under the EC Habitats Directive. Most of them are already protected as Sites of Special Scientific Interest under home legislation. In 2000 they are likely to be scheduled as Special Areas of Conservation (SAC), as part of a Europe-wide network called Natura 2000. In September 1999, member states, conservation bodies and independent experts met in Ireland to discuss the sites lists.

Britain's list was criticized by the Worldwide Fund for Nature (WWF), which points out that we have proposed only 3.4 per cent of our land area for protection as SACs, whilst Spain and Greece have put forward 15 per cent of theirs'. Britain, however, has far less wild land than those countries, and our sites are smaller on average and more fragmented. Proposed British 'SACs' include the New Forest, Caledonian pure forests, ancient woods rich in mosses and lichens, peat bogs, limestone pavements, natural river systems such as the Spey, and shallow inshore water like the Wash.

BADGER CULL

In 1998 the government approved a £30 million programme to slaughter up to 20,000 badgers in an experiment to try to prove a link between badgers and tuberculosis in cattle. In each area the Ministry of Agriculture will compare the results of 'full culling' (all badgers to be killed), 'reactive culling' (badgers killed only on farms where a tuberculosis outbreak has been confirmed) and control zones where no badgers will be killed. The experiment will take place in 30 areas of up to 100 square kilometres each over the next five years.

Culling began in late 1998 in North Devon. Reportedly the Ministry trappers experienced some resistance from animal-lovers destroying the baited traps, and also from farmers refusing access, while some badgers evidently dispersed to outlying setts, making them difficult to locate. Moreover there are reports of farmers illegally killing badgers in the control areas. The experiment will lack scientific validity if badgers survive in the full culling area, whilst others are killed in a control area. These problems are expected to recur in the second area in the Wye Valley and Forest of Dean, where culling began in 1999. Later in the year the experiment was extended to parts of Cornwall, Dyfed and Gwent.

The experiment is opposed by conservation groups, who claim it breaches the Bern Convention on protected species and argue that the scheme is anyway impractical. They say the government would do better to spend money on developing vaccines and improving techniques of animal husbandry to minimise the risk of disease transmission. While many dairy farmers are in no doubt that cattle contract the disease from badgers, the senior scientist running the cull publicly admitted that badgers may be being blamed in cases where tuberculosis is in fact being passed from cattle to cattle.

SITES OF SPECIAL SCIENTIFIC INTEREST

The government is consulting landowning and conservation bodies about improvements in protecting Sites of Special Scientific Interest (SSSI). Figures produced by the government nature conservation agencies indicate an unacceptable rate of loss or erosion of interest of these protected sites, although the majority of this loss is attributed to 'neglect' or over-grazing rather than development. English Nature considered that 45 per cent of SSSIs are in a less than favourable condition. The government has promised a new Habitats Bill, but so far no Parliamentary time has been made available for it. Among the measures sought by conservationists are the right to enter sites to inspect them, for 'stop orders' to be made available on all SSSIs, and general legal tightening in line with EC legislation.

Within Britain, the approach to SSSI designation is diverging between England and Wales on the one hand and Scotland on the other. In 1998, the then Scottish Office published proposals to review existing SSSIs from a Scottish perspective, with the apparent intention of reducing their number. It has also suggested shifting the responsibility for designating SSSIs from government to local authorities. In parts of Scotland, these protected sites are widely perceived as being too restrictive and even unnecessary. Local authorities there are not charged, as English and Welsh ones are, with a duty to protect SSSIs.

DEVELOPMENT CASEWORK

Several wildlife-rich parts of the coast are under threat from development. The Royal Society for the Protection of Birds (RSPB) was concerned about the impact of proposals by Associated British Ports to develop coastal land and tidal mudflats at Dibden Bay in Southampton Water. These support passage wild fowl and waders such as brent geese, grey plover and dunlin as well as an interesting coastal flora. The developer has offered to create new habitats for birds, but conservationists are concerned that this would involve techniques which have never been tried and tested. There is no guarantee that the new habitats would be able to replace the destroyed old one; experience so far indicates otherwise.

After a public inquiry, the government overturned planning permission given by the local authority that would have allowed the dumping of dredgings on a 82-hectare area of wild marshland in the Medway estuary called Barksore Marshes. This is part of an internationally important area for breeding and wintering birds protected under EU Habitat Regulations. The issue involved the matter of compensation for landowners and operators affected by protective legislation; it was wrong, say the RSPB, to expect local authorities to foot the bill.

A conservation package was agreed between conservation bodies and the Harwich Haven Authority over dredging in the Stour and Orwell estuaries. This will include the creation of new mudflats from the dredgings needed to deepen the approaches to the ports.

A MOUNTAIN RAILWAY FOR CAIRNGORM

In October 1998 the Scottish Court of Session rejected the case, brought by the RSPB and WWF that a proposed funicular railway in the Cairngorms would have damaging consequences for the natural environment and wildlife. The organizations had contested that the railway breached European law on vulnerable habitats and rare species, such as the dotterel and golden eagle. They also proposed a less damaging alternative site. The development is now free to proceed. The railway, which is funded by the government and the European Union, will take visitors to the summit of Cairngorm, and is likely to result in increased use of the high plateau area, most of which is a National Nature Reserve.

BIRD FORTUNES

The wet summer of 1998 affected many species breeding success was below normal. Parts of northern Britain had another poor season in 1999. However some rare species did well, benefiting from conservation work on nature reserves and other protected sites. The stone curlew has increased from a low of 145 breeding pairs in 1993 to 215, partly as a result of enthusiasts rescuing chicks from the path of tractors and also due to more benevolent farm practices under the Ministry of Agriculture's set-aside and Environmentally Sensitive Area schemes. The reintroduced white-tailed or sea eagles also enjoyed their best year yet, with 15 breeding pairs, all in north-west Scotland, despite two incidents of nest-robbing.

There is concern for the lapwing, whose numbers have halved over the past 11 years, according to a survey by the RSPB and the British Trust for

Ornithology. The decline is believed to be related to intensified grassland management and autumn ploughing, and also the loss of mixed farming on which the birds depend. Other birds, whose decline is attributed to early ploughing include such familiar birds as grey partridge, linnet, skylark and even house sparrow.

Despite expensive schemes to help it by recreating wetlands and reedbeds, the bittern remains an endangered species in Britain. Only 13 'booming males' were heard in 1998 – locating calling birds is the only practicable way of censusing this elusive species. Most breeding bitterns rely on RSPB nature reserves at Leighton Moss in Cumbria and Minsmere in Suffolk; only one bird was heard in the bittern's former heartland in the Norfolk Broads. The underlying cause is probably a shortage of suitably sized fish, especially eels. On the other hand, there are hopeful signs that bitterns are investigating new sites, while one bird managed to rear a record two broods totalling seven chicks in 1998.

In England and Scotland reintroduced the red kite had mixed fortunes. As a result of the wet summer only three young were reared in the Midlands, but elsewhere some 94 pairs reared 187 young, despite reports of poisoned birds especially from northern Scotland.

UNWELCOME INVADERS

Animal-rights activists broke into two mink-farms in or near the New Forest and released an estimated 15,000 American mink into the countryside. Escaped mink have long been an ecological problem, and are believed to be the main agent behind the decline of the water vole as well as a threat to ground-nesting birds. In that sense, the government's decision to ban mink-farming came as a relief to the conservation world.

Other recent invaders had their own hour of glory in the press during the year. The large and colourful Asian longhorn beetle is a native of China, and reaches Britain in imported timber. Another invader from the Orient is the Chinese mitten-crab, which has started to spread from its base in the Thames estuary. Described as a voracious 'eating machine' it will probably make an impact on potential prey like native freshwater mussels and crayfish. The Environment Agency is also worried about its habit of burrowing into river banks.

In northern England and Scotland, the New Zealand flatworm continues to spread. Some areas in the path of its progress have been reportedly denuded of earthworms, which leads to poorer drainage and the loss of soil fertility. However, in other areas the invasion front earthworms and flatworms seem to co-exist.

RUDDY DUCKS

About 4,000 pairs of the North American ruddy duck breed in the wild in Britain, the descendent of birds that escaped from the then Wildfowl Trust's collections at Slimbridge in the 1950s. Although these attractive small ducks with blue beaks and upwardly pointed tails are harmless to native wildlife in Britain, they present a threat to the rare and closely related white-headed duck in Spain. Where they meet, the two species will cross-breed, and purebred white-headed ducks are likely to be replaced by hybrids. Since 1995, and under pressure from Spanish ornithologists, the RSPB and Wildfowl and Wetlands Trust have campaigned for a cull of British ruddy ducks. The then Environment Secretary, John Gummer, refused, as initially, did his Labour successors. In 1998, however, the government changed its mind, and set up a Task Force to organize a cull. This is currently taking place in West Midlands, Anglesey and Fife, all areas with strong populations of ruddy duck.

NEW BATS

Breeding colonies of two rare species of bat have been found for the first time. Beckstein's bat is occasionally found as adults and was assumed to breed, but colonies of it have eluded investigators. In 1998, however, a colony of 80 bats were found in a specially designed bat box at a wood in Dorset. This chance find soon was followed by the astonishing discovery of another colony of 52 Beckstein's Bats using a loft and airing cupboard in a house in Sussex.

The first confirmed nursery roost of Nathusius' Pipistrelle, only recently recorded from Britain, was reported from County Antrim in Northern Ireland, where some 150 individuals were found in farm buildings. This species is closely related to the Common Pipistrelle, and may have been overlooked. Equally, it could be a recent colonist, for this bat has been spreading westwards on the continental mainland.

FROG LOST

The last known Pool Frog has died. This species has been much confused with the Edible Frog, which was widely released by enthusiasts in the 19th century. However, a small population discovered in Norfolk in the 1980s was believed to have escaped genetic dilution with released Edible Frogs, and to have represented the last known colony of pure bred Pool Frogs. Fossil evidence indicates that Pool Frogs may have been an overlooked native species which suffered from the draining of fenland and the drying out of pools in its East Anglian haunts. The frog was captured and taken into captivity in 1993 as the possible last survivor of its kind, no more have been seen at the site. The University of Sussex is analysing the frog's DNA and preserved Pool Frog specimens in museums, and comparing it with frogs from mainland Europe. A pronounced difference in DNA would be strong evidence for a native origin.

PICKING MUSHROOMS

Demand for wild 'forest mushrooms' by restaurants has led to a much increased trade in edible wild fungi, especially bolekes and chantarelles. Scotland now exports large numbers of these species, all of them picked from the wild. In certain areas, like the New Forest, picking fungi is seen as a threat to wild stocks of these species. The Forestry Commission's response was to ban commercial picking in the Forest, except by local licence-holders, and in certain locations, all non-scientific picking of fungi. In 1998, English Nature entered the fray with a 'code of conduct' proposing limitations on the weight of fungi anyone should pick, and further restriction on SSSIs and other protected land. There is, however, no scientific evidence that picking causes permanent harm to fungi; on the contrary, experience in Europe indicates that fungi are a sustainable harvest, like nuts or berries. English Nature justified their approach by invoking 'the precautionary principle': that it is better to be safe than sorry.

THE BUILT ENVIRONMENT

The survey of 1997–8 in *Whitaker's Almanack* ended with brief notice of a consultation paper issued by the Department for Culture, Media and Sport (DCMS) as part of the Government's Comprehensive Spending Review. The far-ranging changes proposed in the paper were subsequently approved by the DCMS. The most fundamental in constitutional terms was the merger of English Heritage (EH) and the Royal Commission on the Historical Monuments of England, which was completed by April 1999. This united under one management structure the study and the conservation of historic buildings and archaeological sites. The paper also confirmed that 'heritage' would continue to be a 'good cause' under the National Lottery and pledged that the grant-in-aid offered to the National Heritage Memorial Fund, which has gradually been whittled down to £2 million, would be restored to £5 million. This relative generosity took place against the background of a financial settlement for the DCMS which found an extra £290 million between 1999 and 2002. Of this, museums and galleries were allocated £99 million, the performing arts £124 million, and 'heritage and the royal parks' a mere £10 million.

THE NATIONAL LOTTERY

Dr Eric Anderson succeeded Lord Rothschild as chairman of the Heritage Lottery Fund (HLF) in April 1999. His appointment coincided with the tentative exercise of HLF's new powers to go beyond the conservation of 'heritage things' to promote education and access, training and conservation skills. Although 20 per cent of Lottery income is now directed to the New Opportunities Fund, the HLF's Strategic Plan for 1999–2002 was still able to predict a modest enhancement of income: £305 million in 1999–2000, rising to £325 million

in 2001–2. The Plan allocated 24 per cent to museums and galleries, including acquisitions, 28 per cent to historic buildings, 22 per cent to land and countryside, 8 per cent to libraries and archives, 9 per cent to projects with an industrial, maritime or transport theme, and 9 per cent to revenue schemes. A Townscapes Heritage Initiative was launched in company with English Heritage, whilst the Joint Scheme for Places of Worship was relaunched early in 1999 with a budget of £20 million, having been overwhelmed by applications in its first incarnation. The eligibility of Grade II listed churches was limited to those falling within the 50 most socially and economically deprived local authority districts.

Up to 31 March 1999 the HLF had announced capital and revenue grants totalling £1,271,907,836 to 2,686 projects. These included £134,351,989 to 232 historic parks, £74,005,000 to 567 churches, and a total of £246,501,739 towards projects that involved some degree of repair to an historic building. Only representative examples can be cited: Moggerhanger Park, Beds (£3,035,000), to restore the house by Sir John Soane and the garden by Humphry Repton; Nunhead Cemetery, Southwark (£1,250,000); Dulwich Picture Gallery (£5,000,000); St Mary's Church, Preston, Lancs (£189,500), to provide an extension to the Museum of Lancashire in a redundant church of 1836; the Whitstable Road Jewish Cemetery, Canterbury (£42,000), to restore a Jewish cemetery of 1760; Queen's Square, Bristol (£3,670,600), to remove the road which cuts through the first landscaped square to be completed in England (*c.*1699); Brighton, West Pier (£10,650,000); Eltham Palace (£1,000,000), to facilitate the acquisition by English Heritage from the Crown Estate of the medieval Great Hall and the 1933 house immediately opposite; the Stanley Mills, Perth (£7,610,000), to guarantee the future of one of the country's largest group of textile mills; Rowntree Park, York (£1,304,000), one of scores of urban parks to benefit; Strathleven House, Dumbarton (£982,826), to facilitate the rescue of this long-derelict Grade A-listed building by the Scottish Historic Buildings Trust; a project in Scotland (£626,500) to catalogue and conserve 25 collections of important Scottish architects' papers, including those of Sir Basil Spence and Sir Robert Lorimer; and £174,000 to conserve and interpret the site of the Battle of Shrewsbury.

ENGLISH HERITAGE

English Heritage's Annual Report for 1997–8, the latest available at the time of writing, shows that in that year EH spent a total of £36.5 million in grants to buildings, conservation areas, churches, monuments, historic parks and landscapes and archaeological projects. In a new initiative known as Heritage Economic Regeneration Schemes, EH proposed to target £15 million over three years 'to support ordinary working historic buildings' in Britain's most deprived urban and rural communities. About 11.5 million visitors were welcomed to the 409 properties for which EH is responsible, whilst EH membership reached 384,000, a spectacular quadrupling over barely a decade. Income earned from non-governmental sources reached a record total of £25.6 million, an increase of more than 60 per cent over the previous five years, but government grant-in-aid is to remain effectively frozen in the period 1999–2002. The beneficiaries of EH's largest grants were Ightham Mote, Kent (£523,000), the Church of the Ascension, Lavender Hill, Wandsworth by James Brooks (£359,838), Stowe Landscape Gardens, Bucks (£274,000) and Staircase House, Stockport (£250,000). A further £9 million was allocated by EH towards its Conservation Area Partnership Schemes, the principal recipients being Brixton, Hove and Birkenhead. A total of £117,349 went to 12 historic gardens in 1997–8, half the figure for the previous year. The spectacular restoration of the Albert Memorial in London was completed to universal acclaim and under budget.

WALES

The equivalent of English Heritage in Wales is Cadw which, from 1 July 1999, became accountable to the new National Assembly for Wales in place of the old Welsh Office. Cadw's latest Annual Report, also that for 1997–8, revealed excellent progress in the updating of the lists of buildings of special architectural and historic interest and the scheduling of ancient monuments, both of which exceeded their target. In all, 1,134 buildings were listed, bringing the total as at 31 March 1998 to 20,295. A parallel thematic assessment of chapels should ensure that all such buildings worthy of listing have been so protected by the year 2000. Well over 100 historic buildings grants were offered to the value of nearly £2.5 million, and a total of £287,000 was offered to owners of 23 ancient monuments. Two significant and long-running conservation programmes to monuments in Pembrokeshire came to a conclusion – at Manorbier Castle, which received £125,000 over nine years, and Carew Castle, which received £75,000 over 15 years. Cadw's publishing programme expanded with a much praised account of the conservation and conversion of nonconformist chapels and an illustrated *Register of Landscapes of Outstanding Historic Interest in Wales*. In September 1998 the only course in Architectural and Building Conservation in Wales was launched at the University of Glamorgan.

SCOTLAND

In 1997–8 Historic Scotland awarded £12 million in grants to 135 projects. Its programme of Technical Advice Notes continued with publications on thatch and the associated subject of fire protection. The Society for the Protection of Ancient Buildings, the oldest conservation society in the world, reconfirmed its presence in Scotland by moving into shared offices with the Architectural Heritage Society of Scotland in Edinburgh. Apart from the

amenity societies, the main private activity was among Building Preservation Trusts (BPT). One of the most spectacular of those projects was that by the Glasgow BPT to restore and convert St Andrew's in the Square Church of 1739. On 1 April 1999 a pilot scheme lasting three years was introduced which will apply secular historic buildings legislation to ecclesiastical buildings but only, initially, to the exteriors. The effectiveness of the scheme and the possibilities for its expansion will be assessed after 31 December 2001.

LISTING

Britain has the most comprehensive system of protection of any country in the world, with the possible exception of Italy. In England alone by the end of 1998 nearly 453,000 buildings were listed. Among the additions in the course of the year were several hundred structures identified under the assessment of post-war design – ten bridges including the Severn Bridge (listed Grade I), and some theatres, such as the Chichester Festival Theatre of 1962, the Belgrave at Coventry of 1958 and the Congress at Eastbourne of the same year. About 30 churches also made it onto the lists, both traditional – for example All Saints, Bawdeswell, Norfolk of 1953–5 – and modern – for example the Roman Catholic Church of St Mary Leyland in Lancashire and the William Temple Memorial Church at Wythenshawe in Manchester. *Sui generis* buildings were also listed, including two 1962 structures at London Zoo: the Elephant and Rhino Pavilions by Sir Hugh Casson and Lord Snowdon's Aviary. Other additions outside the post-war period gave protection to a rare example in Chesterfield of a 19th-century purpose-built trade union office; a purpose-built photographic studio in Midland Road, Derby of 1867; the earliest known surviving Assembly Rooms, of *c*.1692, at Epsom in Surrey; the wash basin at Buckland Dinham in Somerset of 1876 paid for by the local rector to provide a shared facility for the villagers to wash their clothes; and a dentist's clinic designed by Baillie Scott at Sevenoaks in Kent.

Infinitely more select are the World Heritage Sites approved by UNESCO. In 1999 the Government put forward 25 sites for this prestigious accolade, with a pronounced emphasis on sites of social and industrial significance. The proposed sites included Chatham Naval Base, Charles Darwin's home at Down House in Kent, the Royal Botanic Gardens at Kew, the commercial centre and waterfront in Liverpool, the New Forest in Hampshire, Saltaire in West Yorkshire, the 19th-century model town laid out by Sir Titus Salt, Shakespeare's Birthplace and associated buildings in Stratford-on-Avon, the Forth Rail Bridge near Edinburgh, Robert Owen's settlement at New Lanark, the Blaenavon Industrial Landscape at Torfaen in the Welsh Valleys and Mount Stewart in Co. Down, Northern Ireland.

Listing circumscribes threats but it does not

prevent them. In 1998, 184 listed buildings in England and Wales were the subject of applications to demolish, of which the most prominent was perhaps the Roman Catholic Cathedral at Middlesbrough of 1878. The most outlandish threat was to the Free Trade Hall in Manchester of 1846, where only the front elevation was to be retained as part of a multi-storey hotel soaring skywards behind it. That scheme was rejected after a public inquiry. A record fine of £200,000 was handed down in 1998 for the illegal demolition of a listed late 19th-century villa at Newport in Gwent. Listing also cannot prevent the rampages of the vandal or the arsonist. The most distressing loss to fire in the course of the year was St Brandon's Church at Brancepeth in Co. Durham, where the elaborate fittings of 1626–40 were utterly destroyed at an arsonist's whim. English Heritage's decision to publish annual Buildings at Risk Lists, covering buildings listed Grade II* or I, concentrated attention on 1,500 such properties in 1998 and on 1,600 properties in 1999.

INNOVATIONS

A number of new bodies and initiatives were launched in 1998–9. These included a National Tile and Architectural Ceramics Location Database, a Centre for 18th-Century Studies based at York, an Association of European Historic Towns formed after a conference at Valletta in Malta, a new award for the repair of historic bridges co-ordinated by the Institution of Civil Engineers, and a Foundation for Architecture and the Built Environment to work alongside the Prince of Wales School of Architecture. The Government announced its intention to establish the Commission for Architecture and the Built Environment to succeed the Royal Fine Arts Commission, and it came into being in August 1999. Its primary brief is to promote good new architecture, but it is also given a role in the vetting of conservation schemes and new ventures in historic settings. It was also announced in the course of the year that the world's greatest collection of architectural drawings, belonging to the Royal Institute of British Architects, would be moved in June 2000 to new premises at the Victoria and Albert Museum.

Several properties opened their doors to the public for the first time in 1998–9: the new Museum of Scotland in November 1998, in a new building just below St Giles Cathedral in Edinburgh; the new museum on the site of Shakespeare's Rose Theatre on the South Bank in London; Eltham Palace in London, under its new owner, English Heritage; Chastleton in Oxfordshire and a modest late Victorian suburban villa called Sunnycroft in Wellington, Shropshire, both administered by the National Trust; Compton Verney House in Warwickshire; the National Glass Centre at Sunderland; and the library of the distinguished architectural historian and writer, Sir James Richards, which is now available for consultation at the Museum of Domestic Architecture and Design 1850–1950 at Middlesex University.

The period under review drew to a close with the publication of the report of the Urban Task Force headed by Lord Rogers in late June 1999. Whilst its main thrust was directed at new design, it acknowledged the importance of the historic environment and joined the calls of many for the reform of the VAT rules, which are weighted against the repair of listed buildings and serve to encourage alteration and demolition.

Dance

SADLER'S WELLS THEATRE

The new Sadler's Wells Theatre opened in Islington, London, on 12 October 1998. The theatre cost £48 million and took two years to build; on opening night it seemed that a few extra months were still needed. The performance, by Rambert Dance Company, had to be delayed pending the last-minute granting of a safety licence by Islington Council, and finishing touches were being added to the theatre throughout the season. It still seats about 1,500 people, but can also be adapted to a more intimate scale; a studio theatre will house more experimental work; the foyers are more spacious and there is a separate Education Centre. Most importantly, the stage is now 15 metres square and so offers a space big enough for large-scale companies to perform most of their repertoire, although the wing-space for elaborate scenery is still limited. The auditorium is grey, severe and uninspiring, and there are surprising inadequacies in the seating and lighting arrangements for a newly-built theatre. But it immediately took its place at the centre of London's dance world and offered an impressive range of companies, including welcome visits by the Frankfurt Ballet and Pina Bausch as well as seasons by most of the leading British companies.

The theatre's first season faced disaster when the Royal Opera cancelled more than 100 performances scheduled for 1999; in the event a compensation deal was agreed and Sadler's Wells remained open, although with continuing rumours of financial problems. The Royal Ballet did undertake its planned performances at the theatre, returning to the site of its foundation in 1931. The company survived another turbulent year. The season started with financial crises and threats of impending closure, but the appointment of Michael Kaiser, the executive director of American Ballet Theatre, to a similar position at the Royal Opera House in September 1998 inspired confidence in the theatre's backers. Agreement was eventually reached with the dancers on new contracts and working practices, and after the Arts Council announced increased funding for the Royal Opera House for three years following its reopening a period of comparative stability ensued. In addition to its Sadler's Wells seasons, the company performed at the Royal Festival Hall and in Belfast as well as staging its usual 'Dance Bites' tour to smaller venues in England. It also undertook an extensive tour to Japan and China in spring 1999.

THE ROYAL BALLET

The Royal Ballet dancers have maintained a superb level of dancing throughout the period of disruption.

Although no new works of substance were performed during the year, the company gave memorable performances in both one-act and full-length works and there were some very welcome revivals, notably MacMillan's *My Brother, My Sisters*, Ashton's *Ondine* and *Enigma Variations*, and Balanchine's *Serenade*. *Ondine* in particular was revealing as a work of real imagination and theatrical invention, very different in style from most modern productions. It was also graced by impressive performances in the title role, in particular by Sarah Wildor, who was promoted to principal dancer on the strength of her achievement in the ballet.

Wildor was partnered in *Ondine* by Adam Cooper (her real-life fiancé), who had returned to help out his former company. In October 1998 the company's Japanese star dancer Tetsuya Kumakawa had walked out without honouring his commitments to future performances, and a few months later five other male dancers also left to join Kumakawa in setting up his own company. The Royal Ballet was therefore left very short of experienced men, and Cooper's temporary return emphasized how valuable he is – or could be – to the company. The talented Cuban dancer Carlos Acosta had joined at the beginning of the season and several other men were recruited in the New Year, but it still remains a problem. Another leading Royal Ballet dancer, Deborah Bull, attracted increasing publicity during the year as much for her off-stage activities as for her dancing. She was appointed to the newly-constituted Arts Council, and was awarded a CBE in the Queen's Birthday Honours for her services to dance.

In May 1999 Sir Anthony Dowell, the company's director since 1986, announced that he would retire in August 2001 after seeing the company through its first two seasons back at the Royal Opera House. The announcement was greeted with a mixture of relief and sadness; Dowell is very well liked and enormously respected as a dancer, but his directorship has been marred by poor judgement and a lack of real artistic leadership. Speculation immediately started over his successor, with some obvious candidates and some fanciful names being mentioned; it is hoped that the appointment will be made in 2000 so that the new director can participate in planning future seasons.

As the Royal Ballet's situation stabilized and the search for a new director began, Scottish Ballet attempted to use the appointment of its new director, Robert North, to shore up its position and assert its future course during its planned merger with Scottish Opera. Scottish Ballet had been without an artistic director since the resignation of Galina Samsova in 1997, and its future had seemed increasingly under threat as arguments raged about its role and funding. Robert North has a contemporary dance background and is a former director of Ballet Rambert, but he has also choreographed for and directed classical companies and is committed to maintaining the breadth of Scottish Ballet's repertoire. The company mounted welcome revivals of Peter Darrell's production of *Cinderella* and MacMillan's *Diversions*, not performed by the Royal Ballet since 1979, and gave its first London season for 20 years at the new Sadler's Wells.

NORTHERN BALLET THEATRE

Northern Ballet Theatre also enters the new year with a new director. Christopher Gable, artistic director of the company since 1987, died of cancer in October 1998 at the age of 58. Gable had been a leading dancer with the Royal Ballet and created the role of Romeo in MacMillan's *Romeo and Juliet* in 1965, although the first performance was danced by Rudolf Nureyev. He left the company in 1967 and went on to become a successful actor before founding the Central School of Ballet in 1982, with the aim of encouraging young dancers to develop the dramatic side of their work. This led to the directorship of Northern Ballet Theatre, and Gable mounted a string of popular full-length ballets for the company, including reworkings of the classics and completely new works. The company premièred a new production of *Carmen*, which Gable had entrusted to the Rambert dancer Didy Veldman, after his death, and brought his adaptation of *Dracula*, with choreography by Michael Pink, to Sadler's Wells for its London première. The Italian dancer and choreographer Stefano Giannetti was appointed artistic director of Northern Ballet Theatre from May 1999.

RAMBERT DANCE COMPANY

The honour of opening the new Sadler's Wells Theatre went to Rambert Dance Company, which offered a new work by its director, Christopher Bruce, to celebrate the occasion. Set to Dave Heath's Violin Concerto, *Four Scenes* was an enjoyable but downbeat work, and the real joy of the evening was provided by Paul Taylor's memorable *Airs*. Rambert had a successful year and consolidated its reputation as a versatile and talented company.

BIRMINGHAM ROYAL BALLET

Birmingham Royal Ballet also made good use of the space offered by Sadler's Wells, as well as undertaking its usual programme of UK touring. The company was based for many years at the previous Sadler's Wells Theatre, and its return showed that the years since its move to Birmingham have been highly productive. It continues to offer excellent standards of dancing and a varied and usually interesting repertoire; unfortunately the only new work of the season, Stanton Welch's *Powder*, was disappointing.

ENGLISH NATIONAL BALLET

The UK's other big touring company, English National Ballet, continued to be very successful at attracting publicity and intermittently successful at maintaining artistic standards. Derek Deane adapted his in-the-round production of *Romeo and Juliet* from the previous season and toured it extensively; Michael Corder's exquisite *Cinderella* brought real style to the repertoire. Deane caused a stir in April 1999 by stating – not for the first time – that female British dancers (with the sole exception of Darcey Bussell) lacked the physical attributes to be true ballerinas. His preference is evidently for tall, thin, streamlined dancers (and so it is somewhat mystifying when he cites Margot Fonteyn as an ideal), but he fails to appreciate that ballet has developed in a range of interesting styles precisely because different countries produce different types of physiques that are used by different choreographers in different ways. It is also strange if Deane really thinks classical ballet is so limited an art form that it is suited to only one very specific type of body; and if he feels that that type of body is not available in England, it is tempting to ask why he wishes to direct English National Ballet.

DANCE UMBRELLA

Dance Umbrella celebrated its 20th anniversary in autumn 1998 and presented a wide range of companies and performers at venues throughout London. It culminated in a short but long-awaited season by Frankfurt Ballet at Sadler's Wells in November. Several popular works by William Forsythe, the director of Frankfurt Ballet, have entered the Royal Ballet's repertoire, and Forsythe has gained a reputation as the saviour of classical ballet who is marking out new territory for the art. He brought three works to London: *Hypothetical Stream 2*, *Enemy in the Figure* and *Quintett*. His style has moved on from the works already familiar to London audiences, and the classical roots of his work are now barely discernible. He has settled into patterns of creation already familiar in much modern dance, but his company dances with a sophistication and self-belief rarely to be found in contemporary troupes. The company won critical plaudits, and two Laurence Olivier awards for its season.

Dance Umbrella also brought the Merce Cunningham company to London for another well-received season, including one of Cunningham's now celebrated 'Events', at the Barbican Theatre. An Event involves excerpts from existing works linked by new choreography and designed for the venue in which it is to be performed. *Barbican Event* was joined in the repertoire by works including *Windows*, first performed in 1995, and the controversial, over-designed *Scenario* from 1997.

Richard Alston celebrated his 50th birthday with a new work for Dance Umbrella, entitled *Waltzes in Disorder* and set to Brahms's Liebeslieder Waltzer. Other highlights of Dance Umbrella were *Babel Index*, created by the American choreographer

Stephan Koplowitz and performed in the new British Library, Siobhan Davies's performances at the Barbican, Mark Baldwin and his company at the Queen Elizabeth Hall, and the return (again) of Michael Clark in a relatively low-key new work, *Current/SEE*.

Shobana Jeyasingh was also celebrating this year – it was the tenth anniversary of the founding of her company in 1989. She marked this with a tour of two works, one (*Memory and Other Props*) commissioned by Dance Umbrella but using elements from works created since 1989 to explore the process of remembering, and the other (*Fine Frenzy*) looking to the future, with an avant-garde jazz score by Django Bates.

ARC DANCE COMPANY

Another high-profile season at Sadler's Wells during the year was by Arc Dance Company. The company's director, Kim Brandstrup, once again created a leading role for the Royal Ballet's Russian star Irek Mukhamedov. *The Return of Don Juan*, to a commissioned score by the Danish composer Kim Helweg, was dominated by Mukhamedov, who made the most of Brandstrup's fairly limited choreographic language.

THE PLACE THEATRE

The Place theatre hosted the Spring Loaded festival of British contemporary dance, the Resolution! festival for emerging choreographers, and the tenth and last Turning World festival of international contemporary dance. The Place is about to undergo extensive refurbishment, having been awarded £750,000 by King's Cross Partnership to add to the £5 million already granted from the National Lottery. Work on the building began in summer 1999 and is due to be completed in spring 2001.

Siobhan Davies continues to produce quietly beautiful work. *Wild Air*, to music by Kevin Volans, was her first full-length work and was romantic, satisfying and expertly danced, especially by Sarah Warsop. Davies was also involved in an interesting but ultimately unrewarding experiment at the Atlantis Building, an old warehouse in east London. She choreographed a work, *13 Different Keys*, for two of her regular collaborators, including Gill Clarke, and three Royal Ballet dancers, including Deborah Bull. The work was intended to illustrate Davies's response to the specific architectural context of the building, and was a 'promenade' performance (i.e. the audience could wander around as the dancers danced). In fact the result was unfocused and frustrating precisely because of the physical setting, with the dancers often invisible to parts of the audience and unable to dominate the performing space. But the collaboration did prove, if proof were needed, the versatility of the Royal Ballet dancers.

Visitors to the UK during the year were more numerous and more varied than usual, partly because of the availability of the new Sadler's Wells. Pina Bausch brought her Dance Theatre of Wup-

pertal to the capital for the first time in 17 years, giving new audiences the chance to experience her extraordinary work. *Viktor*, lasting three-and-a-half hours, is a series of theatrical vignettes open to myriad interpretations and set between towering walls of earth. A former member of the Pina Bausch company, Meryl Tankard, brought her Australian Dance Theatre to Sadler's Wells in May 1999. Pacific Northwest Ballet gave the first London performances of Balanchine's *A Midsummer Night's Dream*, and the Martha Graham Dance Company performed in the city for the first time in 20 years, opening at the Barbican with the celebrated *Appalachian Spring*. Nederlands Dans Theater 1 gave its last London season under its director, Jiří Kylián. The American season at the Barbican also encompassed a season by Twyla Tharp, and Mikhail Baryshnikov once more performed with his White Oak Dance Project at Sadler's Wells. The year drew to a close with a mammoth season by the Bolshoi Ballet at the London Coliseum which provided welcome evidence that, at least in terms of its dancing, the company can once more be regarded as world-class.

PRODUCTIONS

ROYAL BALLET
Founded 1931 as the Vic-Wells Ballet
Royal Opera House, Covent Garden, London WC2E 9DD

World premières:
Sawdust and Tinsel (Ashley Page), 2 November 1998. A one-act ballet. Music, Poulenc; design, Jon Morrell. Cast led by Zenaida Yanowsky, Jonathan Cope, Edward Watson, Sarah Wildor and Michael Nunn
The Turn of the Screw (William Tuckett), 23 July 1999. A one-act ballet. Music, Andrzej Panufnik; set design, Steven Scott; costume design, Kandis Cook. Cast led by Zenaida Yanowsky, Irek Mukhamedov, Bruce Sansom, Monica Mason, Ricardo Cervera and Laura Morera

Company premières:
Room of Cooks (Ashley Page), 20 October 1998. A one-act ballet. Music, Orlando Gough; costume design, Jon Morrell; set design, Ashley Page after Stephen Chambers, sets realized by Susie Hickinbotham. Dancers, Laura Morera, Michael Nunn, Ricardo Cervera
Words Apart (Cathy Marston), 20 October 1998. A *pas de deux*. Music, Dylan Newcomb; design, Paul Andrews. Dancers, Deborah Bull and Jonathan Cope
Puirt-a-Beul (William Tuckett), 20 October 1998. A one-act ballet. Music, Celtic Mouth Music; design, Elizabeth Cook. Dancers, Mara Galeazzi, Sian Murphy, Ricardo Cervera, Matthew Dibble, Yohei Sasaki
Towards Poetry (Mark Baldwin), 9 July 1999. A one-act ballet. Music, Julian Anderson; design, Michael Howells. Cast led by Darcey Bussell, Inaki Urlezaga, Laura Morera and Campbell McKenzie
Love's Fool (William Tuckett), 10 July 1999. A one-act ballet. Music, Karl Jenkins; design, William Tuckett. Cast led by Zenaida Yanowsky, Luke Heydon and Christopher Saunders

Full-length ballets from the repertoire: *Mr Worldly Wise*

(Tharp, 1995), *Cinderella* (Ashton, 1948), *La fille mal gardée* (Ashton, 1960), *Romeo and Juliet* (MacMillan, 1965), *Giselle* (Coralli/Perrot, prod. Wright 1985), *Ondine* (Ashton, 1958).

One-act ballets from the repertoire: *Concerto* (MacMillan, 1966), *In the middle, somewhat elevated* (Forsythe, 1988), *Les Patineurs* (Ashton, 1937), *Enigma Variations* (Ashton, 1968), *Birthday Offering* (Ashton, 1956), *Las Hermanas* (MacMillan, 1963), *Raymonda Act III* (Nureyev after Petipa, 1964), *Fearful Symmetries* (Page, 1994), *Serenade* (Balanchine, 1934), *My Brother, My Sisters* (MacMillan, 1978), *Rhapsody* (Ashton, 1980).

Due to the closure of the Royal Opera House, the company gave seasons in London at Sadler's Wells Theatre (two seasons) and the Royal Festival Hall. The company toured to Belfast for the first time in November 1998, performing *Manon* (MacMillan, 1974), *Les Patineurs, Enigma Variations* and *Birthday Offering*. It also toured to Japan and China in April–May 1999, performing *Swan Lake* (Petipa/Ivanov, prod. Dowell 1987), *La fille mal gardée, Manon* and *Romeo and Juliet*.

Two groups of Royal Ballet dancers performed in Darlington, Cambridge, Truro, High Wycombe, Bath, Northampton, Dartford and Woking in March 1999 (the 'Dance Bites' tour), giving new works by William Tuckett (*Love's Fool*), Mark Baldwin (*Towards* Poetry), Cathy Marston (*Tidelines*) and Michael Corder (*Masquerade*) and works by Ashton (*Montones,* 1965), Page (*Walk and Talk,* 1990) and Bintley (*Galanteries,* 1986). Dancers from the Royal Ballet led the Royal Ballet School performance of *Giselle* at Sadler's Wells Theatre on 17 July 1999.

BIRMINGHAM ROYAL BALLET
Founded 1946 as the Sadler's Wells Opera Ballet
Birmingham Hippodrome, Thorp Street, Birmingham
B5 4AU

World première:
Powder (Stanton Welch), 7 October 1998. A one-act ballet. Music, Mozart; design, Kandis Cook. Cast led by Sabrina Lenzi and Yuri Zhukov

Company premières:
In the Upper Room (Twyla Tharp), 10 February 1999. A one-act ballet. Music, Philip Glass; set design, Santo Loquasto; costume design, Norma Kamali
The Four Seasons (members of Birmingham Royal Ballet), 13 May 1999. A one-act ballet. Music, Vivaldi; design, students of the University of Central England
The Dance House (David Bintley), 13 May 1999. A one-act ballet. Music, Shostakovich; design, Robert Heindel. Cast led by David Justin, Monica Zamora and Wolfgang Stollwitzer

Full length ballets from the repertoire: *Romeo and Juliet* (MacMillan, 1965), *Coppélia* (Petipa, Cecchetti and Wright, prod. Wright 1995), *The Nutcracker* (Ivanov, prod. Wright, additional choreography by Redmon, 1990) (including a special one-off performance, *The Cracked Nut,* on 16 December 1998 with guest artists from the world of television and entertainment and local celebrities), *Edward II* (Bintley, 1995), *Hobson's Choice* (Bintley, 1989).

One-act ballets from the repertoire: *The Protecting Veil* (Bintley, 1998), *Still Life at the Penguin Cafe* (Bintley, 1988), *The Prospect Before Us* (de Valois, 1940), *Choros* (Bintley, 1983), *Five Tangos* (Van Manen, 1977).

In addition to four seasons at the Birmingham Hippodrome, the company toured to Plymouth (two seasons), Bristol (two seasons), Bradford, Sunderland (two

seasons), London (Sadler's Wells Theatre) and Manchester.

ENGLISH NATIONAL BALLET
Founded 1950 as London Festival Ballet
Markova House, 39 Jay Mews, London SW7 2ES

Full-length ballets from the repertoire: *Cinderella* (Corder, 1996), *The Nutcracker* (Deane, 1997), *Romeo and Juliet* (Deane, 1998, originally created in the round), *Swan Lake* (Petipa/Ivanov, prod. Struchkova 1993).

The full company toured to Oxford (two seasons), Liverpool, Southampton (two seasons), Manchester (three seasons), Bristol, London (The Coliseum and the Royal Albert Hall), Glasgow, Sheffield and Birmingham. It also toured to Hong Kong and Australia in May–June 1999, performing *Swan Lake.*
In March–April 1999 the company split into two groups and went on two small-scale tours (called *Tour de Force*). One group toured *Country Garden* (Hampson, 1998) and *pas de deux* from *Don Quixote, The Sleeping Beauty, The Nutcracker* and *Raymonda* to Swindon, Woking, Blackpool, Richmond (Surrey), Crawley and Poole. The other group toured a new work by Christopher Hampson (*Concerto Grosso*), *Three Preludes* (Stevenson, 1969) and *pas de deux* from *Romeo and Juliet, Paquita* and *Le Corsaire* to Crewe, Scunthorpe, Cheltenham, Bexhill-on-Sea, Barrow-in-Furness and Cambridge.

RAMBERT DANCE COMPANY
Founded 1926 as the Marie Rambert Dancers
94 Chiswick High Road, London W4 1SH

World première:
Four Scenes (Christopher Bruce), 12 October 1998. Music, Dave Heath; design, Es Devlin

Company première:
The Golden Section (Twyla Tharp), 6 May 1999. Music, David Byrne; design, Santo Loquasto

Works from the repertoire: *Gaps, Lapse and Relapse* (James, 1998), *Three Gone, Four Left Standing* (Bonachela, 1998), *Rooster* (Bruce, 1991), *Embarque* (Davies, 1988), *Cruel Garden* (Bruce and Kemp, 1977), *Swansong* (Bruce, 1987), *Airs* (Taylor, 1978), *August Pace* (Cunningham, 1989), *Axioma 7* (Naharin, 1991), *No More Play* (Kylián, 1988), *Petite Mort* (Kylián, 1991), *Ghost Dances* (Bruce, 1981).

The company performed in Manchester, Bristol, London (three seasons at Sadler's Wells Theatre), Brighton, Sheffield, High Wycombe, Plymouth, Aberdeen, Truro, Woking, Mold, Northampton and Norwich. It also toured to Austria in January 1999, performing *Axioma 7, Swansong* and *Rooster,* and Italy in April 1999, performing *Cruel Garden.*

RICHARD ALSTON DANCE COMPANY
Founded 1994
Cecil Sharp House, 2 Regent's Park Road, London
NW1 7AY

All works danced by the company are choreographed by Richard Alston.

World premières:
Waltzes in Disorder, 30 October 1998. Music, Brahms. Cast led by Martin Lawrence and Christopher Tudor
Slow Airs Almost All of Them, 19 February 1999. Music, Bach arr. Mozart

Works from the repertoire: *Brisk Singing* (1997), *Light Flooding into Darkened Rooms* (1997), *Rumours, Visions* (1994),

Movements from Petrushka (1994), *Red Run* (1998), *Beyond Measure* (1996).

The company performed in High Wycombe, Northampton, London (the Queen Elizabeth Hall, including a special performance on 30 October 1998 to mark Richard Alston's 50th birthday), Manchester, Cambridge, Malvern, Brighton, Nottingham, Canterbury, Stevenage, Blackpool, Oxford, Horsham, Epsom, Norwich and Brecon. It also performed in Turkey (at the Eskisehir Festival) on 16 October 1998, and in Germany (Neuss) on 25 February 1999.

SCOTTISH BALLET
Founded 1956 as the Western Theatre Ballet
261 West Princes Street, Glasgow G4 9EE

World premières:
Mosaic (members of Scottish Ballet), 16 September 1998. Music, an anthology of 20th-century piano work; design, Scottish Ballet
First Movement (Micaela Greganti), 16 September 1998. Music, Prokofiev; design, Scottish Ballet. Dancers, Vladislav Bubnov, Campbell McKenzie, Ari Takahashi and Yi-Lei Cai
Bitter Destiny (Ivan Dinev), 16 September 1998. Music, Tchaikovsky; design, Scottish Ballet. Cast led by Linda Packer and Campbell McKenzie
Night Life (Tim Rushton), 15 April 1999. Music, Bach; design, Lez Brotherston

Company premières:
Light Fandango (Robert North), 27 April 1999. Music, traditional Scottish and Irish themes; design, Catherine Garnier
Rapture (Lila York), 15 April 1999. Music, Prokofiev; design, Anne C. Patterson
Diversions (Kenneth MacMillan), 15 April 1999. Music, Bliss; design, Philip Prowse. Cast led by Vladislav Bubnov and Sabine Chaland

Full-length ballets from the repertoire: *Cinderella* (Darrell, 1979), *La fille mal gardée* (Ashton, 1960), *La Sylphide* (Bournonville, prod. Brenaa 1973).

One-act ballets from the repertoire: *Faerie Feet* (Nicol, 1998), *Five Rückert Songs* (Darrell, 1978), *Just Scratchin' the Surface* (Cooper, 1998).

The company performed in Glasgow (three seasons), Edinburgh (three seasons), Falkirk, Greenock, Irvine, Motherwell (two seasons), Musselburgh (two seasons), Inverness (two seasons), Pitlochry, Kirkcaldy, Stirling, Aberdeen (two seasons), Nottingham, Hull and London (Sadler's Wells Theatre). It also toured to Spain in July 1999, performing *Giselle* (Petipa after Coralli/Perrot, prod. Darrell 1971).

Film

For the second year running, the fortunes of the film industry were inextricably tied to the performance of just one movie. In 1998, *Titanic* kept exhibitors afloat with its billion dollar box-office record. In 1999, the inelegantly-titled *Star Wars Episode 1: The Phantom Menace* played the same role, dominating film markets across the globe.

These titles share some interesting attributes. Both are 'signature films', written and directed by one man, though both James Cameron (*Titanic*) and George Lucas (*Star Wars*) are also their own producers, and regard themselves as businessmen as well as artists (in fact they are so powerful they can make films on their terms, a privilege that is limited to only a handful of people in Hollywood today). Both movies draw on old stories (*Titanic* on *A Night to Remember* and other accounts of the famous real-life naval disaster; the self-consciously mythic *Phantom Menace* assuming a familiarity with the other Star Wars films), but address a predominantly young audience. Neither relies on star power (Leonardo DiCaprio and Ewan McGregor had not had a US box-office hit before), yet both were hyped for months before their release, generating so much media interest that the frenzy fed on itself. Finally, both exploited the very latest in digital technology to create spectacular effects the like of which have never been seen before.

A few years ago, the influential critic David Thomson argued in an article that Hollywood had been transformed beyond recognition by the blockbuster phenomenon heralded by the original *Star Wars* and *Jaws*. According to Thomson, the studios gave up any aspirations to quality drama when they realised the vast profits that accrued to spectacular 'event' movies released on as many screens as possible. His thesis infuriates Lucas, who still sees himself as an independent film-maker, and indeed funded the estimated $120 million budget for *Phantom Menace* himself (in return, he receives 90 per cent of the profits).

ARTISTICALLY COMPROMISED

But it is true that the industry operates very differently 22 years after the first *Star Wars* film surprised everyone by attracting queues around the block. Today Lucas can release his film concurrently on more than 2,500 screens, insist that cinemas book it for a minimum of eight weeks, and demand the lion's share of ticket receipts (the exhibitors are allowed to milk the profits from soft drinks and popcorn). *The Phantom Menace* was well into profit before anyone had seen it, on the back of licensing deals with toy manufacturers and fast-food companies. This is how blockbusters really make their money, and it explains why most of them are so

artistically compromised. In 1999 the studios all belong to larger conglomerates. A company such as Sony, which owns Columbia, can afford to see the studio as a software ancillary to its core hardware operations – only 9.4 per cent of its revenue in 1998 came from film and television.

Small wonder that Hollywood movies are in a creative trough. Mega-budget movies vie for the lucrative holiday audiences, all intent on selling themselves in 30 second television advertising slots to as wide a population reach as possible. And that means to international audiences as well as Americans (after all they only represent 4 per cent of the world's 'eyeballs'). These extravaganzas have pushed the average cost of producing a Hollywood film from $26.1 million in 1993 to $52.7 million today, with marketing costs going through the roof to protect this increased investment, up 79 per cent to $25.3 million over the same period.

The 'tent-pole' movies – so called because they prop up the studios – will continue, but Hollywood is well aware that the market can only support so many of them. Profits are slowing, and the studios are beginning to cut back on the number of films in production. In 1998, stung by the successive disappointments of *Batman and Robin* and *The Avengers*, Warner Bros pulled the plug on two potential money-pits: Nicolas Cage as *Superman* and Arnold Schwarzengger in *I Am Legend*. Meanwhile, aside from *The Phantom Menace*, the most profitable movies of the year have all been relatively cheap pictures aimed at the youth market. Nearly half of the cinema-going audience in the USA and the UK is aged under 24. This age group tends to be impatient with drama and unimpressed with star prestige (they prefer to anoint their own stars, through television shows or teenage magazines: people like Adam Sandler and Sarah Michelle Gellar). They flock to outrageous, bad taste comedy and to horror, two genres in the ascendant over the last 12 months. Hits include the comedies *There's Something About Mary, Austin Powers: The Spy Who Shagged Me, American Pie*, and *South Park*; and the horror movies *The Blair Witch Project, The Haunting, Deep Blue Sea, The Faculty, The Mummy* and *I Still Know What You Did Last Summer*.

One, happier by-product of this tendency has been something of a renaissance in teen comedies. The likes of *Election*, a post-Lewinsky political satire that just happens to be set in high school, the strangely sophisticated *Rushmore, Cruel Intentions*, an elegant contemporary adaptation of *Les Liaisons Dangureuses*, and *10 Things I Hate About You*, a barbed up-dating of *The Taming of the Shrew*, were among the sharpest films of the year, from any source.

This polarisation between blank cheque movies

for all and cheap movies for teenagers has led the studios to cede the middle ground. They are no longer equipped to make adult dramas cost effectively. 'If we make high-end dramas intended for adults... then you're dealing with an audience that shows up only sporadically, and that requires great reviews,' Joe Roth, chairman of Walt Disney Studios, explained in the *New York Times*. 'And if I have it executed one degree short of perfection, I may lose it all.'

INDIES SWEEP OSCARS

Increasingly, distributors rely on mini-majors, so-called 'independent' studios, to keep the culture ticking over (though they're usually aligned to the same big corporations; Miramax with Disney, and so on). The extent to which this is true is underlined each year by the Academy Awards. Of the 15 nominees in the categories Best Picture, Best Actor and Best Actress, only four went to major studio releases (two for Dreamworks's *Saving Private Ryan*, one for Twentieth Century Fox's *The Thin Red Line* and one for Paramount's *One True Thing*, which looks like it will be released straight to video in the UK). Even more revealingly, of the eight nominees in the Best Actress and Best Supporting Actress categories, only three were American – and one of those, best actress Gwyneth Paltrow, was playing an English character.

Miramax was the big winner this year, with 13 nominations for its UK production, *Shakespeare in Love*, and a further seven for *Life Is Beautiful*, an Italian film it distributed in the USA. The former picked up the statuettes for Best Picture, Actress (Gwyneth Paltrow), Supporting Actress (Judi Dench), Screenplay (Marc Norman and Tom Stoppard), Art Direction, Comedy Score, and Costume. An exceptionally witty middle-brow entertainment which has young Will Shakespeare (Joseph Fiennes) falling in love half way through writing his latest play, *Romeo and Ethel, the Pirate's Daughter*, John Madden's film was a safe, rather soft choice for the Academy voters, against the more challenging, controversial movies *Saving Private Ryan, The Thin Red Line, Hilary and Jackie, American History X, Bulworth* and *The Truman Show*. In a year which saw US air strikes in the Middle East and in the Balkans, three Second World War films divided opinion. Although Steven Spielberg won the consolation of a Best Director prize and some technical awards for *Saving Private Ryan*, the voters clearly preferred the soft-soap represented by Roberto Benigni's sentimental Holocaust comedy, *Life Is Beautiful* (Best Actor/Best Foreign Language Film/Dramatic Score).

Terrence Malick's *The Thin Red Line* did not win anything, but it was by some margin the most ambitious of the films, a meditation on war, nature and transcendence in death based on James Jones' autobiographical novel about the Pacific campaign. Like George Lucas, Malick had not directed a film since the late 1970s. A doctor of philosophy who spent the intervening years living as a recluse in Paris, he re-emerged with such a legendary reputation that the best actors in Hollywood were falling over themselves to work for the man who made *Badlands* and *Days of Heaven*. The final cast of *The Thin Red Line* included Sean Penn, Woody Harrelson, John Travolta, George Clooney, John Cusack, Nick Nolte and Ben Chaplin, many in small roles they accepted for a token fee.

One can count the other Hollywood releases with any aspirations to seriousness on the fingers of one hand: Jonathan Demme's maligned adaptation of *Beloved*, Steve Zaillian's real-life courtroom drama *A Civil Action*, Gary Ross's allegory *Pleasantville*, and Steven Soderbergh's deft, romatic Elmore Leonard movie, *Out of Sight*. Perhaps this would not seem such a poor showing, if the independents were producing the goods, but they are also going through a bad spell, with too many careerist 'calling-card' films designed to attract studio talent-spotters, and little in the way of originality or conviction.

Two exceptions were Vincent Gallo's dazzling directorial début, *Buffalo 66*, and Todd Solondz's taboo-tackling *Happiness*. Gallo, an actor who is also a respected artist and musician, threw away the rule-book to create his very personal, touching but mordantly funny film about a man who kidnaps the first woman he comes across out of prison in order to show her off to his solipsistic parents (Anjelica Huston and Ben Gazzara). *Happiness* has a crueller sensibility. This third film by Todd Solondz is a suburban tragicomedy about three grown sisters (Jane Adams, Cynthia Stevenson and Lara Flynn Boyle), each living in denial of their own social and sexual dysfunction. With its frank, unsettlingly funny scenes of masturbation and the paedophilia theme, the film proved too contentious for its distributors, and the production company released it on its own, by-passing the Motion Picture Association of America (MPAA), the US ratings board; consequently, one of the best reviewed American movies of the year grossed a mere $3 million.

CALL FOR RESTRAINT

It was a difficult year for the censors. The massacre at Columbine High School in Colorado was immediately linked to the stylish techno-thriller *The Matrix*, in which Keanu Reeves sported raincoat and shades, the uniform of the teenage killers. Others pointed to Leonardo DiCaprio's 1997 film *The Basketball Diaries*, which features a fantasy scene of a schoolroom shoot-out. President Clinton, and ex-Presidents Bush and Ford all called for more restraint in the treatment of violence from Hollywood, although in truth, it is far less prevalent on today's movie screens that it was 20 years ago. On the other hand, perhaps as a consequence of the Lewinsky scandal and following the $100 million success of *There's Something About Mary*, sex comedies seem to be on the way back. *South Park: Bigger, Longer, and Uncut* was nothing less than a full-frontal assault on puritanism that set out to make a mockery of censorship; and it did just that, by escaping with 'R' rating, presumably because it was animated. In contrast, American critics were understandably outraged when Stanley Kubrick's last film *Eyes Wide Shut*, was only released in a digitally-neutered form.

As keenly awaited as *The Phantom Menace* in some quarters, especially after a prolonged 18-month shoot conducted in teasing secrecy, *Eyes Wide Shut* was only Kubrick's second film since *The Shining* back in 1980. A surprisingly faithful adaptation of Arthur Schnitzler's *Traumnovelle*, updated to contemporary Manhattan, it stars Tom Cruise as Doctor Bill Harford, and Nicole Kidman as his wife, Alice. They are happily married, or so they fondly imagine, but when Alice confides to her husband that she has been unfaithful – at least in her heart – he embarks on a nocturnal odyssey that culminates in a masked sex orgy; he returns a sadder, wiser man. Much less explicit than advanced speculation suggested, the film was nevertheless too risqué for the MPAA. Before he died in March 1999, Kubrick was prevailed upon to tone down the orgy sequence in order to meet his contractual obligation to deliver an 'R' rated film. The MPAA-approved version brought derision from some American audiences, but even uncensored, the film sometimes feels unbalanced, occasionally banal and at other times overblown. Most disappointingly, it exposes Kubrick's greatest failing as an artist, his incomprehension of women.

In the UK, there was no suggestion of tampering with Kubricks' last testament. Under the enlightened new regime of president Andreas Whittam Smith and director Robin Duval, the British Board of Film Classification (BBFC) maintained a hands-off policy on the vast majority of theatrical releases, and finally gave the green light to video releases of *The Exorcist* (refused a video certificate for 20 years under James Ferman's directorship), *The Texas Chainsaw Massacre* (ditto), and *The Driller Killer* (unavailable since the 'video nasty' tabloid scare of the early 1980s). At the same time, it should be noted that a video certificate was refused Sam Peckinpah's 1972 film *Straw Dogs*, when the distributors declined to censor the rape scene. Still, of the 393 cinema films submitted to the board in 1998, only 14 were cut, the lowest percentage on record – and these were mostly voluntary to secure a lower rating. Whittam Smith and Duval passed such potentially controversial titles as Catherine Breillat's explicit *Romance* and Lars Von Trier's *The Idiots* uncut, despite penetrative sex on camera. A similar more prolonged scene in *Seul Contre Tous* was rendered out of focus at the BBFC's insistence, although the same film's scenes of brutal violence (a man punching his pregnant wife in the stomach, for example) and racist diatribes were deemed acceptable.

BRITISH PRIDE

If American cinema is going through a fallow artistic period, there are still plenty of British films to be proud of. It may still be a cottage industry, but the cheaper overheads this implies have freed up British film-makers to tackle more eclectic, confrontational and intrepid projects. While *Shakespeare in Love* is technically an American production, it is overwhelmingly British in terms of tone and talent, both in front of and behind the camera. Another Tudor drama, *Elizabeth* also garnered Oscar attention, with seven nominations, and proved a significant international box-office draw. This Working Title production assembled a remarkable cast including the Australians Cate Blanchett (Elizabeth) and Geoffrey Rush (Walsingham), French stars Fanny Ardant, Vincent Cassel and Eric Cantona, as well as Brits Joseph Fiennes, Lord Attenborough, Kathy Burke and Chris Eccleston. Directed by Shekhar Kapur, *Elizabeth* combined the conspiratorial menace of *The Godfather* films and the energy and brio of *Trainspotting*, held together by a brilliant central performance from Blanchett.

Better yet, though much reviled by the musical establishment in the UK, was Anand Tucker's *Hilary and Jackie*, based on the autobiography *A Genius in the Family* by Hilary and Piers du Pré. This stylish and passionate film had the audacity to suggest that the illustrious cellist Jacqueline du Pré was emotionally needy and sometimes difficult to live with, especially after she began to develop multiple sclerosis. Emily Watson and Rachel Griffiths were both nominated for Academy Awards as Jackie and Hilary, respectively. There was a nomination too for Sir Ian McKellen, playing the ageing director of *Frankenstein*, James Whale, in *Gods and Monsters*, a crafty piece of invented biography that illuminates American attitudes to homosexuality in the 1950s, and pays worthy tribute to a flamboyant, witty director.

Whale worked at a time when any British film-maker worth his salt moved to Hollywood. That is no longer the case, and many of the more interesting directors and stars prefer the freedom and control they can only get on this side of the Atlantic. Besides, the lives they want to put on screen are inextricably British. Ken Loach has stayed the course since the 1960s, and in *My Name Is Joe* he came up with one of his most powerful proletarian melodramas, the story of an (ex-)alcoholic whose conscience only leads him to further trouble. Peter Mullan, who won the Best Actor award 1998 at Cannes for his performance as Joe went on to direct his own feature, *Orphans*, which married Loach's grasp of the bleakness of working class lives with a surreal black comic sensibility, quite at odds with what we have come to expect of British realism. More poetic, but just as impressive, was Lynne Ramsey's extraordinary début *Ratcatcher*, a hard-hitting Scottish drama about growing up in Glasgow in the late '70s.

None of these films found much of an audience, but there were a number of significant British successes at the box-office. Apart from *Shakespeare in Love* and *Elizabeth*, the roguish crime comedy *Lock, Stock and Two Smoking Barrels* proved very popular at home (£11.3 million), while *Notting Hill*, the follow-up to *Four Weddings and a Funeral*, was a huge hit everywhere ($214 million worldwide after ten weeks on release), relaunching Hugh Grant as a viable movie star after a lean period. Not surprisingly, Working Title, the production company responsible, easily found a new support structure when Polygram's film division was sold to Universal. With Miramax establishing closer ties with Film Four, British production continues to look healthy, even if 1998 saw a fractional fall in the domestic box-office, down to 135.2 million admissions from 139.5 in 1997.

A GENERATION DISADVANTAGED

Sadly, foreign language films make up less and less of that figure (under one per cent, compared with 7 per cent in 1984); fewer foreign films are being released in the UK and no inroads are being made into the new multiplex audience. As British television relegated subtitled cinema to post-midnight slots, an entire generation is growing up without access to non-English language film. It would also be true to say that European cinema is not the artistic force it once was, but any reasonable list of the movies of the year would have to include Pedro Almodóvar's *All About My Mother* (Spain), Eric Rohmer's *An Autumn Tale* and Eric Zonca's *The Dream Life of Angels* (France), Walter Salles' *Central Station* (Brazil), *Hana-Bi*, by Takeshi Kitano (Japan), Samira Makmalbaf's *The Apple* (Iran), and *Eternity and a Day* by Theo Angelopoulos (Greece). And to these one could add the first two films produced under the Danish manifesto 'Dogme 95': *The Idiots* by Lars Von Trier, and *Festen* ('The Celebration') by Thomas Vinterberg.

Dogme 95 is a series of rules governing the production of films: that they are shot in natural light, on 35mm in Academy ratio; that no extraneous props are supplied but only those items that already exist on location; that all sound (including music) is recorded live during the shooting, and so on. Taken literally, the manifesto is rather silly, yet the first films made under this banner represent a corrective to the exorbitant cost and decadent form of mainstream cinema at the end of this century. Shot on new digital video cameras (thus breaking one of the rules), *Festen*, in particular, has a spontaneity and immediacy which seem to have liberated the storytellers; the result is fresh, invigorating, and urgent.

With the booming new market in DVDs (digital versatile discs) looking to supplant video in the next year or two, pay-per-view transmission systems coming on line, and the news that George Lucas expects the second *Star Wars* instalment to be shot entirely digitally (*The Phantom Menace* was the first feature to be screened digitally in the USA by satellite broadcast at four experimental sites), it looks as if the writing is on the wall for celluloid. At both the high and the low end of cinema, during production, distribution and exhibition, the future is digital.

FILM AWARD WINNERS

ACADEMY AWARDS 1998

Best picture – *Shakespeare in Love*
Best director – Steven Spielberg, *Saving Private Ryan*
Best actor – Roberto Benigni, *Life is Beautiful*
Best actress – Gwyneth Paltrow, *Shakespeare in Love*
Best supporting actor – James Coburn, *Affliction*
Best supporting actress – Judi Dench, *Shakespeare in Love*
Best original screenplay – *Shakespeare in Love*
Best adapted screenplay – *Gods and Monsters*
Best foreign language film – *Life is Beautiful* (Italy)
Best original musical or comedy score – *Shakespeare in Love*
Best original dramatic score – *Life is Beautiful*
Best original song – *When You Believe*
Best cinematography – *Saving Private Ryan*
Best art direction – *Shakespeare in Love*
Best film editing – *Saving Private Ryan*
Best costume design – *Shakespeare in Love*
Best sound – *Saving Private Ryan*
Best sound effects editing – *Saving Private Ryan*
Best visual effects – *What Dreams May Come*
Best make-up – *Elizabeth*
Best animated short – *Bunny*
Best documentary feature – *The Last Days*
Best short documentary – *The Personals: Improvisations On Romance in the Golden Years*
Best live action short – *Election Night*
Lifetime achievement – Elia Kazan
Irving G. Thalberg Award – Norman Jewison

BAFTA AWARDS 1998

Best film – *Shakespeare in Love*
David Lean award (best achievement in direction) – Peter Weir, *The Truman Show*
Best actor – Roberto Benigni, *Life is Beautiful*
Best actress – Cate Blanchett, *Elizabeth*
Best supporting actor – Geoffrey Rush, *Shakespeare in Love*
Best supporting actress – Judi Dench, *Shakespeare in Love*
Alexander Korda award (British film of the year) – *Elizabeth*
Best foreign language film – *Central do Brasil*
Best original screenplay – Andrew Niccol, *The Truman Show*
Best adapted screenplay – Elaine May, *Primary Colours*
Academy Fellowship – Elizabeth Taylor

CANNES FESTIVAL 1999

Palme d'Or – *Rosetta*
Best director – Pedro Almodovar, *All About My Mother*
Best actor – Emmanuel Schotte, *L'Humanité*
Best actress (joint) – Emilie Dequenne, *Rosetta*; Severine Caneele, *L'Humanité*
Grand Jury prize – *L'Humanité*

GOLDEN GLOBE AWARDS 1999

Best drama – *Saving Private Ryan*
Best actress in drama – Cate Blanchett, *Elizabeth*
Best actor in drama – Jim Carrey, *The Truman Show*
Best musical or comedy – *Shakespeare in Love*
Best actress in musical or comedy – Gwyneth Paltrow, *Shakespeare in Love*
Best actor in musical or comedy – Michael Caine, *Little Voice*
Best foreign language film – *Ma Vie en Rose*
Best supporting actress – Lynn Redgrave, *Gods and Monsters*
Best supporting actor – Ed Harris, *The Truman Show*
Best director – Steven Spielberg, *Saving Private Ryan*
Best screenplay – Tom Stoppard, Marc Norman, *Shakespeare in Love*
Cecil B. De Mille Award for outstanding contribution to entertainment – Jack Nicholson

Literature

NATIONAL YEAR OF READING

September 1998 to August 99 was remarkable for being the National Year of Reading. This was launched by David Blunkett MP, Secretary of State for Education and Employment, as part of the DfEE's national literacy strategy, and was master-minded by the National Literacy Trust. The initiative was chaired by author Ken Follett, who enlisted the support of WH Smith, the BBC, and publishers Random House and HarperCollins. Project Director of the National Year of Reading was Liz Attenborough, a former director of Penguin Books, who worked from the London offices of the Trust. Other businesses were involved, as well as libraries, local authorities, schools, educational organisations, community services and the arts, and individual celebrities, from footballers to newsreaders, together aiming to 'change the national culture'.

Initiatives included the government's donation of £2,000 to all schools (a total allocation of some £60m) in order to buy books other than text books; a national campaign to stimulate parental involvement with their children's reading (called A Little Reading Goes a Long Way); supermarket chain Sainsbury's contribution of £6m to Bookstart ('Books for Babies'); Walker's snack foods and News International's joint 'Books for Schools' promotion (leading to around 1.5 million free books going to schools); Orange Talks Books at Work which encouraged companies, including Boots and Marks & Spencer, to introduce reading groups at work; the Yorkshire Literacy Challenge (Right to Read) in which companies trained staff as reading volunteers; and promotions such as Asda supermarket's Big Read fortnight, during which staff ran storytelling sessions in the stores, and the media- and business-led Dads and Lads and Kick Off!, which were designed to encourage fathers to read to sons. Tabloids and broadsheets, and both local and national press, backed the idea with regular articles and special supplements. Radio and television coverage included the introduction of literacy storylines to soap operas (Brookside and Hollyoaks). Brookside's story was supported by a free phoneline, which took over 10,000 calls. In July the Queen and the Duke of Edinburgh visited Liverpool's Central Library to meet people involved in National Year of Reading projects.

The National Year of Reading was felt to be successful enough to warrant a further three years, under the new banner, Read On, of building on the projects that worked during the year. Although there was general enthusiasm for the campaign, and research suggested that in several areas people's lives and attitudes had been altered, there were a few criticisms of the book trade itself for its 'sporadic' response, which left the organisers 'surprised and disappointed'.

WORLD BOOK DAY

One annual bookfest that was successfully repeated this year was World Book Day, hitherto celebrated on Shakespeare's birthday, 23 April (although in the year 2000 it will be moved to 16 March). Twelve million £1 vouchers were distributed, again thanks to the DfEE, to be spent on books – although the take-up was slightly less than last year because of a new rule that the voucher could only be used on books over a certain value. Unless, that is, it was spent on one of two specially produced volumes costing £1: the *Children's Book of Books* (as last year), in which celebrities chose extracts from their favourite children's books, or (new this year) the *Grown-Ups' Book of Books*, following the same formula. As in the previous year, however, there were myriad events in schools, libraries, and bookshops around the country, as well as in many public arenas, that consolidated the message of the National Year of Reading. Almost a quarter of a million adults were influenced by the day to buy a book, according to research by Chambers & Stoll for the World Book Day steering committee, so although there were a few of the usual isolated quibbles about organization and promotion, the day can only be regarded as a triumph. The search for more sponsorship outside the book trade for the year 2000 got off to a disappointing start, none the less.

THE WORD

The largest literary festival yet was launched this year, dreamt up by the London Arts Board, and orchestrated by Peter Florence, founder of the Hay-on-Wye Literature Festival. London's first Festival of Literature, The Word, linked activities around the metropolis for ten days in March, with varying degrees of success. The appearance at Westminster Hall, for instance, of Germaine Greer, whose latest feminist polemic *The Whole Woman* was published in March, (after earning a reported advance of nearly £500,000) and extracted in the press, was a sell-out. And many of the events held around the edges of London, in venues that were not accustomed to hosting big-name authors, were also strikingly popular. But a few of the central London bookings were overly ambitious – with venues, such as theatres and concert halls, that were too big to fill, and there were accusations that The Word ran up a large debt. The Word was, on the other hand, imaginatively programmed, multi-cultural, multi-media and innovative, and some of its teething problems will doubtless be resolved in the future.

The Word's most striking innovation was the

'adoption' by each of London's 33 local authorities, of two of 66 writers, invited from all over the world. These authors took part in four main events within their adoptive borough, and were encouraged nurture a relationship with its inhabitants involving libraries, schools, arts centres and the Internet. Some were also commissioned to create new work. The 66 writers included literary legends, such as Margaret Atwood, Seamus Heaney, Doris Lessing, Wole Soyinka and Derek Walcott; commercial writers such as Terry Pratchett, Wilbur Smith and Sue-Townsend; and relative newcomers including Giles Foden, Tony Hanania, Robert McLiam Wilson and Amanda Foreman. It included writers for stage and screen, biographers and poets, and some participants who did not originally write in English, such as Alice Vieira of Portugal and Edwar Al Kharrat of Egypt. Whatever the truth of the accusations of debt – and the organizers insisted that all that was owing would be paid off, the debut Festival certainly had its fans, among them Joseph Heller, who described it as 'The best literary festival I've been to.'

CHILDREN'S LAUREATESHIP

Another new literary development that got off the ground in 1999 was the Children's Laureateship, the brainchild of author Michael Morpurgo and the late Poet Laureate, Ted Hughes, who died in November 1998. Hughes was a children's author himself (his *The Iron Man* was made into an enthusiastically received animated film, as *The Iron Giant*, in 1999), and he and Morpurgo were concerned about the low status of writing for children in Britain. A children's laureateship would, they believe, reward merit and attract recognition, not only for individuals, but for writers of children's books in general. The two swiftly summoned a steering committee, and enlisted the support of Chris Smith, the Minister for the Arts; the government gave £10,000 to be given to the laureate. HRH the Princess Royal agreed to present the first biennial award. There was some debate about how much a laureate would be expected to be a champion of children's literature at large, but once it was agreed that the honour did not carry any ambassadorial obligation, it was generally welcomed. The first shortlist of candidates was: Anne Fine, Peter Dickinson and Quentin Blake, with Quentin Blake, author and illustrator, most famously of Roald Dahl's books, (and for many years a head of department at the Royal College of Art), receiving the honour at a ceremony at the National Theatre in May.

KID'S BOOKS RULE OK

It was a good year for children's books for other reasons, too. The out-and-out fastseller of the year was a children's book, the third volume of J. K. Rowling's *Harry Potter* series: *Harry Potter and the Prisoner of Azkaban*. Unprecedentedly published at a given time as well as on a given day, at 3.45pm – in order to allow young fans to race from school to the bookshops – the book went on to break records for sales in the first week. It sold 68,159 copies in the first two-and-a-half days following publication. This meant that it outstripped Thomas Harris's thriller, *Hannibal*, the sequel to *The Silence of the Lambs*, which itself had just broken all records by selling 60,000 copies in the first week of publication. (The nearest 1999 rival to either was Wilbur Smith's *Monsoon*, about 18th-century brothers seeking their fortune in Africa, which sold a mere 16,000 copies in the first week of publication.)

Harry Potter was showered with accolades in 1999. Volume two of the series, *Harry Potter and The Chamber of Secrets*, was voted Children's Book of the Year at the British Book Awards (as the first volume, *Harry Potter and the Philosopher's Stone* had been the previous year) and won the Smarties Prize Gold Medal. J. K. Rowling received *The Bookseller-/Bookseller's Association* award for Author of the Year. And there was unprecedented coverage in the media for a children's book when volume three came out: the front of the Books section of the *Sunday Times* was given over to a review of a children's book for the first time, for instance. Received as the darkest of the first three books – although no lesser in its inventiveness and readability – it was ubiquitously enjoyed.

Although volume two was shortlisted for the Whitbread Children's Book of the Year, it was pipped to the prize by David Almond's tale of a troubled boy's friendship with an unlikely angel, *Skellig*. Chair of the judges Raymond Seitz said in his speech at the prizegiving ceremony that both books could have been contenders in the novel categories, and so reinforced an idea that gained some currency in 1999 (partly thanks to the laureateship) that children's literature was an underrated genre in our society. Bloomsbury, publishers of *Harry Potter* (whose share price rose 19.2 per cent when volume three was published) had also set a trend by publishing an adult edition of the first two volumes, which sold spectacularly. *Skellig's* publisher, Hodder, followed suit – and *Skellig* also went on to win the Library Association prestigious Carnegie Medal, for which, controversially, *Harry Potter and the Chamber of Secrets* was not shortlisted. There was a feeling that the boundaries between adults' and children's literature were being broken down, not least because the UK book trade magazine *The Bookseller* (and, in the US, the *New York Times*), included *Harry Potter* on the adult bestseller lists, where it entered at number one. This consolidated the idea of a 'crossover' book – a book written ostensibly for children but which has a significant readership among adults. This also led to a change of policy for the Whitbread Prize. In 1996 the Children's Book of the Year category had been separated, with increased prize money, from the other categories of the award (novel, first novel, biography and poetry) which were in contention for an overall book of the year award. From 1999, the children's book was permitted once again to compete with other literary genres to be Book of the Year.

The overall winner of the Whitbread Prize for 1998 was Ted Hughes' moving tribute to Sylvia Plath, *Birthday Letters*, which had caused a stir on publication because it ended decades of silence about his first wife, and her suicide. This was the second year running that Hughes had won the Whitbread: the previous year he won for *Tales from Ovid*. *Birthday Letters* was the bestselling hardback of 1998, voted Book of the Year at the book trade's British Book Awards.

These same awards honoured Beryl Bainbridge as Author of the Year – a very popular win. Her intense and luminous novel about a surgeon in the Crimean War, *Master Georgie*, had been the favourite among the shortlisted for the Booker Prize (Bainbridge's third shortlisting), and had been beaten by Ian McEwan's satirical jeu d'esprit, *Amsterdam*. There were many in the literary world who believed that Bainbridge deserved the highest recognition.

A new award for non-fiction this year, the £30,000 Samuel Johnson Prize, went to Anthony Beevor's harrowing and generally acclaimed *Stalingrad*. Within 24 hours of this win, Beevor was also named winner of the £2,000 Hawthornden Prize and of Wolfson Literary Award for History. In the year since publication in April 1998, *Stalingrad* sold some 80,000 copies in hardback and more than 48,000 in paperback.

Also on the shortlist for the Samuel Johnson Prize was John Diamond's *C: Cowards Get Cancer Too*, a fine book (about his own diagnosis and treatment) in a genre that, thanks to at least one lesser instance, may have begun to burn itself out during the year. The genre is that of confessional writing by London journalists, the first obvious example of which was (a few years ago) Blake Morrison's memoir of his late father *'And When Did You Last See Your Father?'*. This was followed more recently by Linda Grant's account of her mother's Alzheimer's disease, *Tell Me Who I Am Again*, and the bestselling collection of the late Ruth Picardie's writing, *Before I Say Goodbye*, which all together seemed to constitute a trend. Although these books were all well received, one arrived which wasn't: journalist Kathryn Flett's account of her divorce, *The Heart-Shaped Bullet*. Personal, psychological and literary attacks ensued, and it became clear that pouring out your soul is not in enough to make a bestseller: the confession must be well-written too.

John Bayley's very well reviewed memoir of his marriage to the distinguished novelist Dame Iris Murdoch, including his account of her decline into Alzheimer's disease, found a large readership. Then in February 1999 Iris Murdoch died. Bayley's friend Peter Conradi has already been commissioned to write her official biography, for publication a few years hence.

The single book that received the most media attention in the past year was surely Andrew Morton's biography of Monica Lewinsky, *Monica's Story*, for which publisher Michael O'Mara paid him a reported $600,000. It was launched with a tour by Ms Lewinsky, whom a prurient public queued to meet, at bookshops around the country. Kenneth Starr's investigation into the sexual relationship between Ms Lewinsky and President Clinton (The Starr Report) had already been a huge bestseller in the US, and the subject of a record-breaking number of 'hits' when it was first released on the Internet. Morton's book sold 10,000 copies in the UK in the first five days after publication in March, but, though it attempted to be a sympathetic portrait of its subject, did little to inspire a general respect for its author.

Also controversial was *Mirror* journalist Paul Routledge's biography of Peter Mandelson, *Mandelson: The Unauthorised Biography*. One of its revelations, that Mandelson had been given a loan of £373,000 by the Paymaster General Geoffrey Robinson, was scooped by the *Guardian* (although the *Sunday Times* had won a battle for serial rights) and led to Mandelson's resignation. (The *Sunday Times* subsequently pulled its own serialisation, amid rumours that Mandelson's influence affected this decision.) Donald Macintyre, rival political journalist, from the *Independent*, who wrote the competing *Mandelson: The Biography*, had his own book recalled and pulped in July after a libel action by journalist John Booth.

Among the significant literary novels of the year were the third Bech book from John Updike, *Bech at Bay*, a satirical 'quasi-novel' about a septuagenarian writer who wins the Nobel prize for literature; David Lodge's *Home Truths* (evolved from a stage play) about a pair of writers' taking revenge on a 'rottweiler' interviewer; it got a mixed response from critics; Salman Rushdie's tale of love, death and rock 'n' roll in *The Ground Beneath Her Feet*, the life story of a singer who dies in an earthquake, which led to an unlikely alliance between Rushdie and pop group U2's lead singer Bono, who sang the song of the book; and Michael Frayn's *Headlong*, a 'nail-biting farce' about a painter's obsession with a lost Breughel painting, which was enthusiastically received. Tom Wolfe's first novel after many years, *A Man in Full*, was a notable bestseller, as were Robert Harris's *Archangel*, Sebastian Faulks' *Charlotte Gray*, Rebecca Wells' *Divine Secrets of the Ya-Ya Sisterhood*, John Le Carre's *Single & Single* and Jilly Cooper's *Score!* Sustained paperback bestsellers included Alex Garland's *The Tesseract*, Nick Hornby's *About a Boy*, and Joanna Trollope's *Other People's Children*. Delia Smith's *How to Cook* books topped the non-fiction bestseller lists for months.

1999 was the Year of the Tulip, in that several books were, coincidentally, published about the aesthetic and commercial history of the bulb, beginning with Anna Pavord's labour of love, *The Tulip*. Mike Dash's *Tulipomania* followed, and a novel by Debbie Moggach, *Tulip Fever*, set in the 17th-century house of a Dutch tulip speculator. The big business book of the year was Bill Gates' *Business at the Speed of Thought*, although Richard Branson's *Losing My Virginity* stayed airborne in the bestseller lists. A. N. Wilson's *God's Funeral*, a history of atheism, was one of the talked-about heavyweight books of the summer. Bloomsbury launched a huge investment, the *Encarta World English Dictionary*, which aspired to redress the empire-building British (or American) centricity of previous dictionaries of English. Carmen Callil and Colm Toibin caused a flutter in the press with their selection of the best 200 novels in English since 1950, *The Modern Library*, whose choices critics enjoyed taking issue with. And there was a small murmur of consternation when the publisher talked to the book trade about a biography of the Queen Mother, to be published posthumously.

CELEBRITY DEALS

More celebrity book deals made the news. Huge six-figure advances were paid to Geri Halliwell (formerly 'Ginger Spice' of the Spice Girls) for her autobiography (not yet published) and to Britain's most mercurial footballer, Paul 'Gazza' Gascoigne, for telling his own story. But it was not just celebrities who made fortunes out of book contracts. A few fortunate first novels earned huge advances for their authors, among them *HONEYmoon* by Amy Jenkins (writer of the sitcom *This Life*), bought (with a second book) for £600,000 on the basis of one chapter alone, and *Sunday Times* journalist Paul Eddy's *Flint*, introducing a new female detective, Grace Flint (also earning six figures for two books, with the US rights going for $1m).

ON LINE LITERATURE

1999 was also a year in which readers came by their books in a different way, as it saw the growth of Internet bookselling. Amazon.co.uk claimed that Christmas 1998 was the moment when Internet book sales took off in the UK, and the Internet Bookshop (which later began to trade as WH Smith Online) said that its sales had tripled since the same period of the previous year. Sales through both continued to rocket during the year. Amazon's main rival was newcomer Bol.com (the Bertelsmann's group's Internet bookselling service); Waterstone's and Ottakar's bookselling chains also established their own Internet bookshops. Competitive discounts between the different Internet booksellers reached a peak when Bol.com gave away 20,000 books free in two hours to customers who registered with the company.

At the same time, the face of high street bookshops continued to change. The arrival of the Borders chain last year had introduced the concept of 'destination shopping' in bookstores – which offered cafes, Internet terminals, and live piano music among their attractions. In 1999 Borders signed up for its sixth UK site and other chains, including Waterstone's, followed the formula.

LITERARY PRIZEWINNERS

Nobel Prize 1998 – José Saramago
Commonwealth Writers Prize 1999 – Murray Bail, *Eucalyptus*
First work – Kerri Sakamato, *The Electrical Field*
Prix Goncourt 1998 – Paul Constant – *Confidence pour confidence*
Booker Prize 1998 – Ian McEwan, *Amsterdam*
Whitbread Prize 1998: overall winner – Ted Hughes, *Birthday Letters*
  Novel – Justin Cartwright, *Leading the Cheers*
  First novel – Giles Foden, *The Last King of Scotland*
  Biography – Amanda Foreman, *Georgiana, Duchess of Devonshire*
  Poetry – Ted Hughes, *Birthday Letters*
  Children's novel – David Almond, *Skellig*
David Higham Prize 1998 – Gavin Kramer, *Shopping*
Forward Prize 1998 (poetry) – Ted Hughes, *Birthday Letters*
  First collection – Paul Farley, *The Boy From the Chemist is Here to See You*
  Single Poem – Sheenagh Pugh, *Envying Owen Beattie*
William Hill Sports Book of the Year 1998 – Robert Twigger, *Angry White Pyjamas*
Smarties Prize 1998 (children's books):
  Age 0–5 – Sue Heap, *Cowboy Baby*
  Age 6–8 – Harry Horse, *Last of the Gold Diggers*
  Age 9–11 – J. K. Rowling, *Harry Potter and the Chamber of Secrets*
Crime Writers Association 1998:
  Gold Dagger (fiction) – James Lee Burke, *Sunset Limited*
  Gold Dagger (non-fiction) – Gitta Sereny, *Cries Unheard*
  Silver Dagger (fiction) – Nicholas Blincoe, *Manchester Slingback*
  Short Story Dagger – Jerry Sykes, 'Roots' from *Mean Times*
British Book Awards 1998 – Ted Hughes, *Birthday Letters*
  Author of the Year – Beryl Bainbridge
  Children's – J. K. Rowling, *Harry Potter and the Chamber of Secrets*
Encore Award 1999 (second novel) – Christina Koning, *Undiscovered Country*
Orange Award 1998 (women writers) – Suzanne Berne, *A Crime in the Neighbourhood*
Somerset Maugham Awards 1999 – Andrea Ashworth, *Once in a House on Fire*; Paul Farley, *The Boy From the Chemist is Here to See You*; Giles Foden, *The Last King of Scotland*; Jonathan Freedland, *Bring Home the Revolution*
Betty Trask Prize 1999 (first novel by an author under 35) – Elliot Perlman, *Three Dollars*
McKitterick Prize 1999 (first novel by a writer over 40) – Magnus Mills, *The Restraint of Beasts*
W. H. Smith Prize 1999 – Beryl Bainbridge, *Master Georgie*
Mail on Sunday/John Llewellyn Rhys Prize 1999 – Peter Ho Davis, *The Ugliest House in the World*
Cholmondeley Awards 1999 (poetry) – Vicki Feaver, Geoffrey Hill, Elma Mitchell, Sheenagh Pugh
T.S. Eliot Prize (poetry) – Ted Hughes, *Birthday Letters*
Parker Romantic Novel of the Year 1999 – Clare Chambers, *Learning to Swim*
Carnegie Prize 1999 (children's) David Almond, *Skellig*
Kate Greenaway 1999 (children's illustrated) – Helen Cooper, *Pumpkin Soup*
Queen's Gold Medal for Poetry – Les Murray
David Cohen British Literature Prize (lifetime achievement) – William Trevor
Samuel Johnson Prize – Antony Beevor, *Stalingrad*

Opera

The season was dominated by the continuing managerial troubles of the Royal Opera at Covent Garden. Although the rebuilding of the Opera House remained on schedule for the reopening in December 1999, financial matters went from bad to worse. To save money, all but the first two productions of the season at Sadler's Wells Theatre were cancelled. This had the effect of goading the musical director, Bernard Haitink, into tendering his resignation – a decision that he fortunately later rescinded when the much-praised production of Benjamin Britten's *Paul Bunyan* was revived at Sadler's Wells, and several concert performances were given at the Royal Festival Hall. Haitink undertook to remain as musical director until the end of the 2001–2 season. He will be succeeded by Antonio Pappano, who will also act as artistic director. Elaine Padmore will become Director of Opera after seven extremely successful years at the Royal Opera, Copenhagen on 6 January 2000.

In an effort to improve the financial situation, an American administrator, Michael Kaiser, was brought in as executive director in November 1998. Kaiser's experience had been largely with ballet companies, but he had an enviable reputation for turning debt-ridden artistic institutions into solvent and successful ones. What was left of the season opened with a superlative, semi-staged performance of Wagner's *Der Ring des Nibelungen*, conducted by Haitink at the Royal Albert Hall. All involved, but most particularly the orchestra of the Royal Opera House, received torrents of praise from critics and public alike. The orchestra won both the 1998 *Evening Standard* Opera Award for Outstanding Artistic Achievement, and the 1999 Laurence Olivier Award for Outstanding Achievement in Opera, while Haitink received the Royal Philharmonic Society Award for his conducting; John Tomlinson, who sang *Wotan* in *Der Ring* and *Gurnemanz* in *Parsifal* at Covent Garden earlier in 1998, was given the RPS Outstanding Achievement of the Year Award. The orchestra and Tomlinson also won *Evening Standard* Awards, while baritone Thomas Allen, who first sang at Covent Garden in 1971, received a knighthood in the 1999 Birthday Honours.

ENO TAKES UP THE SLACK

Meanwhile English National Opera (ENO) took full advantage of the lack of competition in central London. With its new general director, Nicholas Payne, fully installed and joining music director Paul Daniel, with whom he had worked at Opera North so successfully, the future of the company looked good, despite the financial troubles that it too had to overcome. ENO embraced the sugges-

tions of the Eyre Review (delivered in July 1998), promising greater access through its education programmes. In return it sought the commitment of the Arts Council and the Department for Culture, Media and Sport to the restoration of its grant, eroded during the last three years, and to investment in the fabric of the Coliseum, which is in urgent need of repair.

Among the seven new productions of the season, the most successful were Donizetti's *Mary Stuart*, directed by Gale Edwards, which benefited from a superlative performance of the title role by Ann Murray; Wagner's *Parsifal*, conducted by ENO's previous music director, Mark Elder; Boito's *Mefistofele*, staged by Ian Judge; and, in celebration of the centenary of the birth of Francis Poulenc in January 1999, *Dialogues des Carmélites*. Perhaps the most enjoyable of all ENO's productions during the season was Robert Carsen's hilarious staging of Handel's *Semele*, first seen at the Aix-en-Provence Festival in 1996. Revivals during the year included Davis Pountney's much-loved stagings of Dvořák's *Rusalka* and Humperdinck's *Hansel and Gretel*, as well as Jonathan Miller's ever-popular 'Mafia' production of Verdi's *Rigoletto*.

A visit by Welsh National Opera (WNO) to London was particularly welcome owing to the dearth of opera in the capital. WNO brought two new productions to Sadler's Wells Theatre, Britten's *Peter Grimes*, staged by the famous German director, Peter Stein, and *Hansel and Gretel*, directed by Richard Jones. At home in Cardiff, there was a fine new staging of Janáček's *Jenůfa* by Katie Mitchell, conducted by Daniel Harding, the 22-year-old prodigy, currently assistant to Claudio Abbado in Berlin. Three of the late Göran Järvefelt's most popular productions, Mozart's *The Magic Flute*, Verdi's *Un ballo in maschera*, and Puccini's *La Bohème*, were successfully revived, as was the 20-year-old production of *Madama Butterfly*, originally staged by Joachim Herz. Welsh tenor Dennis O'Neill appeared in both Mascagni's *Cavalleria rusticana* and its inseparable twin, Leoncavallo's *Pagliacci*, conducted by WNO's music director Carlo Rizzi, who also conducted a revival of Wagner's *Tristan und Isolde*.

Opera North began the season well, with a new production of Smetana's *The Bartered Bride*, directed by Daniel Slater, and a revival of Tim Albery's impressive staging of Verdi's *Don Carlos*. Next came the world première of Simon Holt's *The Nightingale's to Blame*, performed in Huddersfield as part of the Huddersfield Contemporary Music Festival. Based on Lorca's play *The Love of Don Perlimplin for Belisa in the Garden*, this was Holt's first opera, and scored a critical as well as popular success. Unfortunately the new production of Strauss's *Arabella*, unveiled during the spring season, received possibly the worst reviews ever meted out to the staging of an opera by a reputable company; the performance did not escape criticism either, despite the fine conducting of Elgar Howarth. The return of Paul Daniel to conduct a revival of Britten's *Gloriana*, with Josephine Barstow in the title role, a superb performance of a work now recognised as a masterpiece, was some consolation. Meanwhile Opera North appointed Steven Sloane as its new music director from the beginning of the 1999–2000 season.

In June 1999 Scottish Opera announced that Ruth Mackenzie, the general director, had tendered her resignation after only two seasons with the company. This was received with dismay, as Scottish Opera had scored substantial successes during that period. David Pountney's production of Smetana's *Dalibor*, premièred at the 1998 Edinburgh Festival, was successfully presented in Glasgow later in the season, while Frederick Delius's *The Magic Fountain*, written in 1893 and hitherto heard only on BBC Radio in 1977, was given its first stage performance. Strauss's *Der Rosen-kavalier* scored a great success for its young Scottish director, David McVicar, whose work for Scottish Opera and Opera North has been greatly praised during the last few years. Verdi's *Macbeth*, Scottish Opera's contribution to the 1999 Edinburgh Festival, was staged by the internationally renowned Swiss director, Luc Bondy.

CHANGING SEATS AT GLYNDEBOURNE

Sir George Christie, son of the founder of Glyndebourne Opera, John Christie, announced his resignation as chairman of Glyndebourne Productions Ltd on the last day of 1999. He will be succeeded by his son Augustus. Nicholas Snowman, Glyndebourne's new general director, took up his appointment at the end of last season, but his plans to integrate the Touring Opera more fully into the festival led to the resignation of Sarah Playfair, the hugely successful and popular administrator of Glyndebourne Touring Opera (GTO), who had worked for Glyndebourne for ten years. As Snowman himself commented, 'her knowledge, commitment and expertise will be sorely missed'. Playfair was subsequently appointed consultant to Garsington Opera. In June 1999 the new opera house at Glyndebourne, opened in 1994, won the gold medal at the ninth Prague Quadrennial of Stage Design and Theatre Architecture for its 'theatrical quality, which perfectly fuses tradition with contemporary style'. Roy Henderson, the Scottish baritone who sang Count Almaviva in *Le nozze di Figaro* at the opening of Glyndebourne in 1934, and attended the first performance, also of *Le nozze di Figaro*, in the new theatre exactly 60 years to the day later, celebrated his 100th birthday on 4 July 1999. Meanwhile the first new production of the season, Debussy's *Pelléas et Mélisande*, directed by Graham Vick, split critical and public opinion down the

centre; the performance, though, was universally praised, in particular the conducting of Andrew Davis, Glyndebourne's music director, who received a knighthood in the New Year's Honours. Jonathan Dove's new opera *Flight*, premièred by GTO last season, was successfully taken into the Festival repertory.

Jonathan Dove had another new opera given its first performance by Almeida Opera. *Tobias and the Angel*, a church opera, staged in Christchurch, Highbury Grove, was basically a community effort, using an enormous amateur chorus with professional soloists and a small orchestral ensemble, conducted by David Parry. Both Dove's music and the libretto, by David Lan, received high praise. Almeida Opera, in conjunction with the Aldeburgh Festival, also performed a new production of *Powder Her Face* by Thomas Adès, who has become artistic director of the Aldeburgh Festival. *Powder Her Face*, which received its world première at the Cheltenham Festival in 1995, has since been performed in the USA, Germany and Australia. Conducted by the composer, the production was staged by David Alden.

In memory of the 50th anniversary of the death of Richard Strauss, Garsington Opera gave the first British production of *Die Liebe der Danae*, directed and designed by David Fielding. This opera had only been performed in London by the Bavarian State Opera, when the company from Munich visited Covent Garden in 1953. Another opera performed only once before in Britain was Gabriel Fauré's *Pénélope*, premièred in Monte Carlo in 1913; staged by the Royal Academy of Music in 1970, it was given a very fine performance by the Guildhall School of Music and Drama in 1999. The Guildhall had earlier staged Tchaikovsky's *Tcherevichki* (The Little Shoes) most enjoyably.

The Poulenc centenary was also celebrated in the Henry Wood Promenade Concerts at the Royal Albert Hall with a semi-staged performance of *Dialogues des Carmélites* given by the Opéra du Rhin from Strasbourg. Other operas included in the Proms were Rameau's *Les Boréades*, conducted by Simon Rattle with the Orchestra of the Enlightenment, with a fine cast headed by Barbara Bonney and Charles Workman. Glyndebourne's new production of *Pelléas et Mélisande* (semi-staged) scored a great success with the Prom audience, as did Leonard Bernstein's *Wonderful Town*, Rattle again conducted, while baritone Thomas Hampson obtained a personal triumph. Finally there was Rachmaninov's *Aleko*, conducted by Vassily Sinaisky and with a mainly Russian cast.

DISTINGUISHED PERFORMERS

Constance Shacklock, the mezzo-soprano who sang for more than ten years with Covent Garden Opera (as the Royal Opera was then called) from its foundation in 1946, died in July 1999 at the age of 86. She sang several Verdi roles, such as Amneris in *Aida* and Azucena in *Il trovatore*, as well as Marina in

Boris Godounov and the title role of *Carmen*, in 1953, the Coronation Year season, she alternated with Joan Cross (who created the role) as Queen Elizabeth I in Britten's *Gloriana*. However, her two finest interpretations were of Brangäne in Wagner's *Tristan und Isolde*, and Octavian in *Der Rosenkavalier*, both under the inspired conducting of Erich Kleiber. Olwen Price, a Welsh contralto who sang with Sadler's Wells Opera (which later became English National Opera) during the 1940s and 50s, died in April 1999, aged 95; her roles included Azucena in Verdi's *Il trovatore*, Mamma Lucia in Mascagni's *Cavalleria rusticana* and Tatiana's Nurse in Tchaikovsky's *Eugene Onegin*, as well as comic roles such as Mistress Quickly in Verdi's *Falstaff*, Marthe in Gounod's *Faust*, and Frugola in Puccini's *Il tabarro*.

Donald Smith, the Australian tenor who sang with Sadler's Wells Opera throughout the 1960s, died in December 1998 aged 76. A Verdi specialist, he sang the Duke of Mantua in *Rigoletto*, Foresto in *Attila*, Gustavus in *Un ballo in maschera*, Ernani, Manrico in *Il trovatore* and Don Alvaro in *La forza del destina* with great success. His other roles included Don José in *Carmen*, Jenik in Smetana's *The Bartered Bride* and, probably his most popular interpretation, Dick Johnson in Puccini's *La fanciulla del West*. At Covent Garden in 1965 he took the part of Calaf in Puccini's *Turandot*. Leonard Hancock, the repetiteur and conductor who died in March 1999, started his career at Covent Garden, where in 1951 he conducted the première of Vaughan Williams' *The Pilgrim's Progress*; later he worked with Sadler's Wells Opera and Scottish Opera; he made several excellent English translations of opera libretti from French, German and Italian.

PRODUCTIONS

In the summaries of company activities shown below, the dates in brackets indicate the year that the current productions entered the company's repertory.

ROYAL OPERA
Founded 1946
Royal Opera House, Covent Garden, London WC2E 9DD
Productions from the repertory: *Paul Bunyan* (1997)
New productions at the Royal Albert Hall:
Das Rheingold (Wagner), 28 September 1998. Conductor, Bernard Haitink; director, Andrew Sinclair; semi-staged. John Tomlinson (Wotan), Philip Langridge (Loge), Kristin Sigmundsson (Fasolt), Matthias Hölle (Fafner), Ekkehard Wlaschiha (Alberich), Robin Leggate (Mime), Michelle de Young (Fricka), Rita Cullis (Freia), Catherine Wyn-Rogers (Erda)
Die Walküre (Wagner), 29 September 1998. Conductor, Bernard Haitink; director, Andrew Sinclair; semi-staged. Kim Begley (Siegmund), Rita Cullis (Sieglinde), Matthias Hölle (Hunding), Hildegard Behrens (Brünnhilde), John Tomlinson (Wotan), Michelle de Young (Fricka)
Siegfried (Wagner), 1 October 1998. Conductor, Bernard Haitink; director, Andrew Sinclair; semi-staged. Stig Andersen (Siegfried), Graham Clark (Mime), John Tomlinson (Wanderer), Ekkehard Wlaschiha (Alberich),

Catherine Wyn-Rogers (Erda), Rosemary Joshua (Forest Bird), Sabine Hass (Brünnhilde)
Götterdämmerung (Wagner), 3 October 1998. Conductor, Bernard Haitink; director, Andrew Sinclair; semi-staged. Sabine Hass (Brünnhilde), Stig Andersen (Siegfried), Karl Rydl (Hagen), Alan Held (Gunther), Vivian Tierney (Gutrune), Petra Lang (Waltraute), Ekkehard Wlaschiha (Alberich)
New productions at Sadler's Wells Theatre:
The Bartered Bride (Smetana), 10 December 1998. Conductor, Bernard Haitink; director, Francesca Zambello; designer, Alison Chitty. Soile Isokoski (Mařenka), Jorma Silvasti (Jenik), Ian Bostridge (Vašek), Franz Hawlata (Kecal), Robert Tear (Ring Master), Colette Delahunt (Esmeralda), Heather Begg (Ludmila), Anne Howells (Hata), Gwynne Howell (Krušina), Jeremy White (Micha)
The Golden Cockerel (Zolotoy Petushok), 22 December 1998. Conductor, Vladimir Jurowski; director, Tim Hopkins; designer, Anthony Baker. Elena Kelessidi (Queen of Shemakha), Gillian Webster (Golden Cockerel), Jean-Paul Fouchécourt (Astrologer), Paata Burchuladze (King Dodon), Maxim Mikhailov (General Polkan), Alexandra Dourseneva (Amelfa)
Concert performance at the Royal Festival Hall:
Un giorno di regno (Verdi), 31 May 1999. Conductor, Maurizio Benini. Vladimir Chernov (Belfiore), John Del Carlo (Kelbar), Irene Tsirakidis (Marchesa del Poggio), Susanne Mentzer (Giulietta), Carlo Scibelli (Edoardo), Donald Maxwell (La Rocca)

ENGLISH NATIONAL OPERA
Founded 1931
London Coliseum, St Martin's Lane, London WC2N 4BS
Productions from the repertory: *Rusalka* (1983), *Madam Butterfly* (1984), *Hansel and Gretel* (1987), *La traviata* (1996), *Orpheus and Eurydice* (1997), *Salome* (1996), *Carmen* (1995), *Rigoletto* (1982).

New productions:
Otello (Verdi), 11 September 1998. Conductor, Paul Daniel; director, David Freeman; designer, Tom Phillips. David Rendall (Otello), Susan Bullock (Desdemona), Robert Hayward (Iago), Mark Le Brock (Cassio), Rebecca Du Pont Davies (Emilia), Mark Beesley (Lodovico), Richard Roberts (Roderigo)
Mary Stuart (Donizetti), 5 October 1998. Conductor, Jean-Yves Ossonce; director, Gale Edward; designers, Peter J. Davison (sets), Jasper Conran (costumes). Ann Murray (Mary Stuart), Susan Parry (Queen Elizabeth I), John Hudson (Leicester), Gwynne Howell (Talbot), Ashley Holland (Cecil), Sandra Ford (Hannah)
Boris Godunov (Mosorgsky), 11 November 1998. Conductor Paul Daniel; director, Francesca Zambello; designers, Hildegard Bechler (sets), Nicky Gillibrand (costumes). John Tomlinson (Boris), Robert Tear (Shuisky), John Connell (Pimen), John Daszak (Dimitri), Jeremy White (Varlaam), Mark Le Brocq (Missail), Della Jones (Innkeeper), Susan Gritton (Xenia), Timothy Webb (Fyodor)
Parsifal (Wagner), 13 February 1999. Conductor, Mark Elder; director, Nikolaus Lehnhoff; designers, Raimund Bauer (sets), Andrea Schmidt-Fulterer (costumes). Kim Begley (Parsifal), Gwynne Howell (Gurnemanz), Kathryn Harries (Kundry), Jonathan Summers (Amfortas), Peter Sidhom (Klingsor)
Mefistofele (Boito), 18 March 1999. Conductor, Oliver von Dohnanyi; director, Ian Judge; designer, John Gunter. Alastair Miles (Mefistofele), David Rendall (Faust), Susan Patterson (Margherita/Helen of Troy), Christine Rice (Martha)

Semele (Handel), 19 April 1999. Conductor, Harry Bicket; director, Robert Carsen; designer, Patrick Kinmonth. Rosemary Joshua (Semele), John Mark Ainsley (Jupiter), Sarah Connolly (Ino), Susan Bickley (Juno), John Connell (Cadmus/ Somnus), Janis Kelly (Iris), Stephen Wallace (Athamas)

Dialogues des Carmélites (Poulenc), 20 May 1999. Conductor, Paul Daniel; director, Phyllida Lloyd; designer, Anthony Ward. Joan Rodgers (Blanche de la Force), Elizabeth Vaughan (Old Prioress), Rita Cullis (New Prioress), Josephine Barstow (Mother Marie), Susan Gritton (Sister Constance), Neill Archer (Chevalier de la Force), Alan Opie (Marquis de la Force)

OPERA NORTH
Founded 1978
Grand Theatre, 46 New Briggate, Leeds LSI 6NU

Productions from the repertory: *Il re pastore* (1993), *Don Carlos* (1993), *The Thieving Magpie* (1993), *Gloriana* (1997).

New Productions:
The Bartered Bride (Smetana), 23 September 1998. Conductor, Oliver von Dohnányi; director, Daniel Slater; designer, Robert Innes Hopkins. Alwyn Mellor (Mařenka), Neill Archer (Jeník), Iain Paton (Vašek), Clive Bayley (Kecal), Carole Wilson (Ludmila), Glenville Hargreaves (Krušina), Colette Delahunt (Esmeralda)

The Nightingale's to Blame (Simon Holt), world première, 21 November 1998. Conductor, Nicholas Kok; director, Martin Duncan; designer, Neil Irish. Donald Maxwell (Don Perlimpin), Patricia Rozario (Belisa), Frances McCafferty (Belissa's Mother), Fiona Kimm (Marcolfa)

Carmen (Bizet), 19 December 1998. Ruby Philogene (Carmen), Susannah Glanville (Micaela), Antoni Garfield Henry (Don José), Mark Stone (Escamillo), Michael John Pearson (Zuniga), Denise Mulholland (Frasquita), Katherine Henderson (Mercédès), Nicholas Garrett (Dancairo), Peter Auty (Remendado)

Arabella (R. Strauss), 22 May 1999. Conductor, Elgar Howarth; director, Francisco Negrin. Susannah Glanville (Arabella), Isabel Monat (Zdenka), Robert Hayward (Mandryka), Carole Wilson (Adelaide), Richard Angas (Count Waldner), Jeffrey Lloyd-Roberts (Matteo), Nicole Tibbels (Fiakermilli)

Performances were given at the Grand Theatre, Leeds, and on tour at Manchester, Nottingham, Newcastle, Huddersfield, Sheffield and York.

SCOTTISH OPERA
Founded 1962
39 Elmbank Crescent, Glasgow G2 4PG

Productions from the repertory: *The Magic Flute* (1992), *Tristan und Isolde* (1994), *Dalibor* (1998), *Hansel and Gretel* (1996), *La Bohème* (1988), *Inez de Castro* (1996).

New productions:
Der Rosenkavalier (R. Strauss), 6 February 1999. Conductor, Richard Armstrong; director and set designer, David McVicar; costume designer, Tanya McCallin. Joan Rodgers (Princess von Werdenberg), Stella Doufexis (Octavian), Lisa Milne (Sophie), Peter Rose (Baron Ochs), Andrew Slater (Faninal), Wynne Evans (Italian tenor), Alasdair Elliot (Valzacchi), Joanna Campion (Annina), Phyllis Cannan (Marianne)

The Magic Fountain (Delius), 20 February 1999, first British stage performance. Conductor, Richard Armstrong; director, Aidan Lang; designer, Ashley Martin-Davis. Anne Mason (Watawa), Stephen Allen (Solano), Stafford Dean (Wapanacki), Jonathan Veira (Talum Hadjo)

Aida (Verdi), 5 May 1999. Conductor, Emmanuel Joel;

director/designer, Antony McDonald. Lada Biriucov (Aida), Rosalind Plowright (Amneris), Vladimir Kuzmenko (Radames), Vladimir Redkin (Amonasro), Michael Ryssov (Ramphis), Stafford Dean (King of Egypt)

Macbeth (Verdi), 29 August 1999, as part of the 1999 International Edinburgh Festival. Conductor, Richard Armstrong; director, Luc Bondy; designers, Rolf Glittenberg (sets), Rudy Sabounghi (costumes). Richard Zeller (Macbeth), Kathleen Broderick (Lady Macbeth), Carsten Stabell (Banquo), Marco Berti (Macduff)

Performances were given at the Theatre Royal, Glasgow, and on tour at Edinburgh, Aberdeen and Inverness.

WELSH NATIONAL OPERA
Founded 1946
John Street, Cardiff CFIO 5SP

Productions from the repertory: *Madama Butterfly* (1978), *Un ballo in maschera* (1982), *La Bohème* (1984), *The Magic Flute* (1979), *Cavalleria rusticana* (1996), *Pagliacci* (1996), *Tristan und Isolde* (1993).

New Productions:
Jenufa (Janacek), 12 September 1998. Conductor, Daniel Harding; director, Katie Mitchell; designer, Vicki Mortimer. Rosalind Sutherland (Jenufa), Suzanne Murphy (The Kostelnička), Nigel Robson (Laca), John Daszak (Števa), Susan Gorton (Grandmother Buryjovka), Adele Eikenes (Karolka), Simon Thorpe (Foreman)

Hansel and Gretel (Humperdinck), 10 December 1998. Conductor, Wladimir Jurowski; director, Richard Jones; designer, John MacFarlane. Imelda Drumm (Hansel), Linda Kitchen (Gretel), Nigel Rogson (The Witch), Mary Lloyd-Davies (The Mother), Robert Poulton (Peter), Mary-Louise Aitken (Sandman/Dew Fairy)

Peter Grimes (Britten), 15 February 1999. Conductor Carlo Rizzi; director, Peter Stein; designers, Stefan Mayer (sets), Moidele Bickel (costumes). John Daszak (Peter Grimes), Janice Watson (Ellen Orford), Donald Maxwell (Balstrode), Ann Howard (Auntie), Peter Bronder (Bob Boles), Andrew Greenan (Swallow), Susan Gorton (Mrs Sedley), Peter Savidge (Ned Keene), Neil Jenkins (Revd Adams)

Productions were performed at the New Theatre, Cardiff, and on tour at Sadler's Wells Theatre, London, and at Oxford, Birmingham, Liverpool, Swansea, Southampton, Bristol and Llandudno.

GLYNDEBOURNE FESTIVAL OPERA
Founded 1934
Glyndebourne, Lewes, East Sussex BN8 5UU

The Festival ran from 19 May to 29 August 1999. *La clemenza di Tito* (1991), *Rodelinda* (1998), *Manon Lescaut* (1997). *Flight* (1998, GTO) were revived.

New Productions:
Pelléas et Mélisande (Debussy), 21 May 1999. Conductor, Andrew Davis; director, Graham Vick; designer Paul Brown. Christiane Oelze (Mélisande), Jean Rigby (Geneviève), Richard Croft (Pelléas), John Tomlinson (Golaud), Gwynne Howell (Arkel)

The Bartered Bride (Smetana), 25 July 1999. Conductor, Jiři Kout; director, Nicholas Lehnhoff; designer, Tobias Hoheisel. Solveig Krinkelborn (Mařenka), Kim Begley (Jenik), Wolfgang Abinger-Sperrhacke (Vašek), Jonathan Veira (Kecal), Helga Dernesch (Ludmila), Anne Howells (Hata), Norman Bailey (Krušina), Richard Van Allan (Micha)

GLYNDEBOURNE TOURING OPERA
La clemenza di Tito, *The Bartered Bride* and *Pelléas et Mélisande* were performed at Glyndebourne, Milton

Keynes, Oxford, Stoke-on-Trent, Woking, Plymouth and
Norwich, from 11 October to 11 December 1999.

GARSINGTON OPERA
Founded 1989
Garsington Manor, Garsington, Oxford ox44 9DH
The season ran from 14 June to 11 July 1999.
New productions:
Die Entführung aus dem Serail (Mozart), 14 June 1999.
Conductor, Stephen Barlow; director, Stephen Unwin;
designer, Jackie Brooks. Cara O'Sullivan (Constanze),
Mary Hegarty (Blonde), Mark Le Brocq (Belmonte), Iain
Paton (Pedrillo), Stephen Richardson (Osmin), Rolf
Kanies (Pasha Selim)
    L'Italiana in Algeri (Rossini), 15 June 1999. Conductor,
Charles Peebles; director, Michael McCaffery; designer,
Paul Edwards. Silvia Tro Santafé (Isabella), Bradley
Williams (Lindoro), Jonathan Veira (Mustafa), Carlos
Marin (Taddeo), Kate Ladner (Elvira), Henry
Waddingron (Haly), Lora Lixenberg (Zulma)
    Die Liebe der Danae (R. Strauss), 26 June 1999.
Conductor, Elgar Howarth; director/designer, David
Fielding. Orla Boylan (Danae), Peter Coleman-Wright
(Jupiter), Adrian Thompson (Midas), Robin Leggate
(Pollux), Yvette Bonner (Semele), Lucy Schauffer
(Europa), Clarissa Meek (Alcmene), Rebecca Du Pont
Davies (Leda)

ENGLISH TOURING OPERA
Founded 1980 as Opera 80
Fidelio (Beethoven) and *The Daughter of the Regiment*
(Donizetti) were toured to Richmond, High Wycombe,
Dartford, Crewe, Southsea, Weston-super-Mare,
Canterbury, Bath, Basingstoke, Carlisle and Buxton
between 14 October and 4 November 1998.

The Daughter of the Regiment (Donizetti) and *Macbeth*
(Verdi) were toured to Cambridge, Preston, Cheltenham,
Brighton, Reading, Yeovil, Exeter, Truro, Poole, Ipswich,
Crawley, Lincoln, Leicester, Ulverstone and London
(Peacock Theatre) between 23 February and 5 June 1999.

Parliament

In the spill-over period from its first session of Parliament (1997–98), the Government completed the issues of constitutional reform in Scotland and Wales. The House of Lords continued to inflict defeats on the Government in the final passage of the Scotland Bill, introduced in December 1997. On 2 November, the third day of report stage, the Lords were defeated when an amendment moved by Lord McCluskey to remove the most senior Scottish judges in Scotland from the effects of Clause 90 was passed by 144 votes to 108, a majority against the Government of 36. When the bill returned to the Commons on 11 November, the Government was able to overturn comfortably the defeats it had suffered on the bill in committee in the Lords – that on schedule 1 (Size of the Parliament) by 303 votes to 173, a Government majority of 130, and on clause 31 (Scrutiny of Bills by Presiding Officer) by 350 votes to 119, a Government majority of 231. The Lords accepted these reverses and the bill gained Royal Assent on 19 November.

Thus on 1 July 1999 both the Scottish Parliament and Welsh Assembly assumed their powers, though in neither case did Labour have an overall majority following the elections on 6 May. On 12 July the Speaker had to make a statement to clarify how questions to the Secretaries of State for Wales and Scotland should be handled: in essence these had to relate to matters for which Ministers in Westminster are responsible, not on issues that had been clearly devolved.

In its second session, the Government continued with its plans for constitutional reform, tackling the issue of hereditary peers and the second chamber, with its plans for reform for the government of London and with attempts to make progress on a devolved Assembly for Northern Ireland. It also concentrated on its other election pledges concerning the National Health Service and education.

NORTHERN IRELAND

Events in Northern Ireland were brought into focus following the bomb explosion in Omagh on 15 August that killed 28 people. Parliament was recalled on 2 and 3 September 1998 (in parallel with the Dail in Dublin) to pass emergency measures to strengthen anti-terrorist laws. Prime Minister Tony Blair described the atrocity as 'a deliberate attempt...to wreck the Good Friday agreement'. The Criminal Justice (Terrorism and Conspiracy) Bill was introduced by the Home Secretary, Jack Straw. Although the measure had all party support, the bill was timetabled by a guillotine motion passed by 317 votes to 87 (drawn from across all the parties), a Government majority of 230. It received Royal Assent on 3 September. The Northern Ireland Bill,

setting up the powers of the newly elected Assembly and ending the use of Orders in Council by the Westminster Parliament, introduced in July 1998, completed its passage through the Lords in the spill-over period, getting Royal Assent on 19 November.

The Opposition kept the pressure on the Government over the decommissioning of terrorist arms and early release of prisoners convicted of terrorist offences, with a debate on 9 December, when the Conservative Northern Ireland spokesman (Andrew Mackay) stressed that 'wherever possible we seek to support the Government in the bipartisan policy, but I have always maintained clearly that I cannot give them a blank cheque'. In another debate, on 27 January 1999, the Leader of the Democratic Unionist Party, Revd Ian Paisley, used Parliamentary Privilege to name those whom he thought were associated with the Omagh bombing.

In an attempt to help the peace process the Government introduced the Northern Ireland (Location of Victims Remains) Bill on 28 April. Introducing the bill on second reading on 10 May, the Minister of State at the Northern Ireland Office (Adam Ingram) said that 'the overriding purpose of the Bill is to ensure that the remains of the "disappeared" can be located and that, for the sake of these victims and their families, funerals can finally take place'. For the Conservatives, Malcolm Moss said, 'frankly it sticks in the throat that we should have to bargain with terrorists to locate the bodies of people whom they have killed...but we shall do nothing to impede its passage'. The second reading was passed by 289 votes to 10, a Government majority of 279. The third reading was agreed by 324 votes to 5, a Government majority of 319, and the bill received Royal Assent on 26 May.

In June, the Government was embarrassed when Jack Straw had to admit that, after 18 months, technical defects had come to light in parts IVA and IVB of the Prevention of Terrorism (Temporary Provisions) Act 1989 annual renewal order. As a result the Government had to introduce the Prevention of Terrorism (Temporary Provisions) Act 1989 (Revival of parts IVA and IVB) Order 1999, which was passed the next day by both Houses.

Despite a peaceful marching season in the Province, negotiations on the peace process broke down. On 5 July Tony Blair came to the House of Commons to make a statement on the talks on the future of the Northern Ireland Assembly following deadlock over arms decommissioning and a proposal put forward by the British and Irish Governments on the previous Friday to resolve it. Northern Ireland Ministers would be nominated by the parties in the Assembly using the d'Hondt procedure, on 15 July; the devolution order would be laid before

Parliament on the following day and powers transferred on 18 July. The International Commission on Decommissioning under General John de Chastelain would require a start to the process of decommissioning within a matter of days. Mr. Blair said, 'If this agreement is put through we will know in days whether the paramilitaries are serious about decommissioning their weapons'. The Leader of the Opposition, William Hague, offered his support to the Prime Minster but warned, 'Let us make no mistake; the stumbling block is the failure of paramilitaries, loyalist and republican, to decommission weapons'. This led to the publication of the Northern Ireland Bill on 12 July making provision for the suspension, in certain circumstances, of the devolved government in Northern Ireland. Discussed under a guillotine motion, the bill completed all its Commons stages. The second reading was passed by 312 votes to 19, a Government majority of 293. No amendments were passed in Committee of the Whole House and the third reading was passed by 343 votes to 24, a Government majority of 319. The bill was introduced in the Lords the next day, but before any progress could be made on discussion the Northern Ireland Secretary, Mo Mowlam, came to the House of Commons on 15 July to announce a setback, the breakdown of the peace process with the failure of the Unionist and Alliance Parties to nominate Ministers for the new Assembly and the resignation of the Deputy Minister (designate), Seamus Mallon. The bill was not withdrawn but would 'not now proceed at emergency speed in the other place'. She announced a review of the implementation of the Good Friday agreement.

HOUSE OF LORDS

The Government was committed to the reform of the House of Lords by its manifesto. Having inflicted over 30 defeats on the Government in the 1997–98 session of Parliament, the Upper Chamber continued to express its views on Government legislation in this session. Most importantly perhaps, the Lords twice threw out Government bills, which had to be reintroduced under the procedure of the Parliament Acts 1911 and 1949 (this meant that the House of Lords would not be able to amend or delay any measure so introduced). At the tail end of the 1997–98 session, the Lords refused to compromise on their amendment to the European Parliamentary Elections Bill, and, on 4 November, insisted on their amendment to clause 1 (rejected by the Commons in October) allowing for the use of open rather than closed lists for the elections due to be held in June 1999 by 221 votes to 145, a majority against the Government of 76. The Commons again disagreed with the Lords (by 307 votes to 125, a Government majority of 182) on 10 November, when Jack Straw commented, 'The other place has now voted twice to amend the bill to change the nature of the list system for which it provides...there is now a

challenge to this democratically elected House by hereditary Conservative peers'.

With time running out, the Lords insisted yet again on their amendment, by 237 votes to 194, a majority against the Government of 42. Labour peer Lord Shore of Stepney said, 'We do not want a rubber stamp Chamber...the argument that it is simply a matter of elected Commons versus unelected Peers and that the unelected Peers, because they are dominated by hereditary Conservative Members, should always be brushed aside, is not in itself strong enough'. The Commons rejected these reasons. Again, the Lords insisted and again the Commons again rejected, with Jack Straw saying, 'If the other place persists in its stance, it must do so in the clear knowledge that it will cause the bill to fall in this session. The Government will have failed to achieve one of their manifesto commitments because of obstruction in another place–a clear breach of the doctrine established by Lord Salisbury'. When the Lords returned to the fray with their original version of the amendment on 18 November (212 votes to 183, a majority against the Government of 29) the Leader of the Lords, Baroness Jay of Paddington, announced that the Government was dropping the bill from the 1997–98 session, which ended on 19 November, but would reintroduce it in the next session under the Parliament Acts. The bill was duly reintroduced on 27 November, with a closed, proportional representation voting system; all stages were taken in the Commons under a guillotine motion on 2 December. Although the Lords refused a Second Reading on 15 December, the bill received Royal Assent on 14 January.

The Lords also caused the postponement of the Government's Sexual Offences (Amendment) Bill, intended to lower the age of consent for homosexuals to 16 and to introduce the concept of abuse of trust. This bill had a second reading in the Commons on 25 January by 313 votes to 130, a Government majority of 183. Jack Straw described it as 'a good measure that balances the need to ensure that young people are adequately protected with the right that all citizens should have to equality before the law', and clause 1 (Age of Consent) was approved by the Committee of the Whole House on 10 February by 330 votes to 126, a Government majority of 204; the third reading completed on 1 March. When the bill came for second reading in the Lords in April, a reasoned amendment moved by Baroness Young (Conservative) denying a second reading was passed by 222 votes to 146, a majority against the Government of 76. Baroness Young claimed that the bill was not part of the Labour Party's manifesto in 1997 and therefore not subject to the Salisbury Convention. The bill was therefore lost for this session and will be reintroduced under the Parliament Acts in the next session.

Other defeats to flagship legislation were inflicted by the Lords but with less drastic consequences. On the final day of the committee consideration of the

Access to Justice Bill (Lords) on 28 January, part of the Bill was defeated by 88 votes to 77, a majority against the Government of 11. On report the Government was again defeated when a new clause (Principles to Be Applied) was passed; on 16 February, an amendment moved by Liberal Democrat Peer Lord Thomas of Gresford to remove the right of the Legal Services Commission to provide advice, assistance and representation through salaried lawyers in the Commission's own employment was passed by 189 votes to 134, a majority against the Government of 55. When these were overturned during the Commons discussion, Lord Thomas insisted on his amendment by 141 votes to 85, a majority against the Government of 56, and the Lords amended a Commons amendment on Bar Practicing Certificates. The Commons accepted their reasons and inserted a new amendment in lieu; the bill received Royal Assent on 27 July.

The Lords also passed amendments against the will of the Government to other bills: to the Disability Rights Commission Bill (Lords); to the Youth Justice and Criminal Evidence Bill (Lords); to the Tax Credits Bill; and, to the Employment Relations Bill.

As a result the Government was glad to introduce its promised legislation to reform the Upper Chamber and remove hereditary peers. The White Paper '*Modernising Parliament: Reforming the House of Lords*' was published on 20 January, the day after the House of Lords Bill was introduced in the Commons. The Leader of the House, Margaret Beckett, said 'The bill will modernise the way in which we handle legislation, improve our Parliament and so lead to a better Britain'. During the two-day second reading debate on 1 and 2 February, the Conservative constitutional affairs spokesman, Dr Liam Fox, moved a reasoned amendment denying a second reading as no replacement for the House of Lords had yet been proposed. He called the bill 'small minded…piecemeal, incoherent and unsustainable…The debate is not about the democratic legitimacy in proposing a plan that was in their manifesto, but about the wisdom of doing it in the way they have'. The reasoned amendment was defeated by 383 votes to 137, a Government majority of 246 and the second reading passed by 381 votes to 185, a Government majority of 196. After much discussion on the constitutional issues involved the committee stage was taken on the floor of the House over four days in February and March but no amendments were made. The third reading on 16 March was passed by 340 votes to 132, a Government majority of 208.

In the Lords, Viscount Cranborne had been sacked as Leader of the Conservative Peers in December for holding secret negotiations with the Government on a compromise way ahead. The Lords had themselves debated a take note motion on the White Paper on 22 and 23 February when some 98 peers had spoken and an amendment moved by the new Leader of the Conservative Peers, Lord Strathclyde, urging that more thought be given to the future replacement of the Upper House. Moving to the Lords, the second reading debate was held over 29 and 30 March. While the second reading itself was unopposed an amendment moved by cross-bench peer Lord Cobbold, regretting that the bill radically altered the historic composition of the House for nothing more than party political advantage without consultation or consensus on its successor was also passed by 192 votes to 126, a majority against the Government of 70. The bill had eight days in committee. On the first day (20 April) Lord Campbell of Alloway (C.) was persuaded to withdraw a new clause demanding the holding of a referendum on the Government's manifesto commitment to remove all hereditary peers from the Lords. On the fourth day of committee (11 May) a new clause proposed as a compromise by cross-bench Peer Lord Weatherill (former Speaker of the House of Commons), to allow some 92 hereditary peers to remain in the Lords until the Chamber had been fully reformed, was passed by 351 votes to 32, a majority of 329. Lord Weatherill suggested that the purpose of his amendment was to 'provide a means of easing the transition from the present Chamber to a fully reformed second Chamber'. There was a row on the sixth day of committee (17 May) when the Conservative Chief Whip (Lord Henley) forced a division on the resumption of the House, passed by 145 votes to 136, a majority against the Government of nine as a protest at the slow progress being made.

On report the Government suffered the following defeats. On 22 June a new clause moved by Conservative constitutional affairs spokesman Lord Kingsland to establish an Appointments Commission to chose the future, independent, cross-bench peers was passed with a majority against the Government of 42. Earlier that day the Lord Chancellor, Lord Irvine of Lairg, had agreed to an amendment to clause 2 (Exception from section 1) to allow hereditary peers who are allowed to stay on in the Lords to be replaced by fellow hereditaries as necessary. On 30 June a new clause moved by Lord Mancroft (C.), to prevent peers from voting on a bill to postpone a General Election, if they had been appointed since the previous General Election, was passed with a majority against the Government of 106. On 27 July two motion were proposed by Conservative peers and accepted: Lord Mayhew of Twysden moved that the rights of certain hereditary peers to continue to sit during the Parliament during which the House of Lords Bill was enacted be referred to the Committee of Privileges; Lord Gray moved that the effect of the bill on the Treaty of Union between England and Scotland also be referred to the Committee of Privileges, which was approved by 275 votes to 185, a majority against the Government of 90. Baroness Jay felt this was an attempt to establish the role of the Committee of Privileges. When Parliament rose for the summer recess the bill was still awaiting its third reading in the Lords.

GOVERNMENT OF LONDON

After the referendum in May 1998, when Londoners endorsed the new Labour Government's plans for a mayor and assembly for London, the Government was committed to introducing a bill defining their powers. This was duly announced in the Queen's Speech opening the session of Parliament on 24 November and introduced in the Commons on 2 December. Introducing the second reading on 14 and 15 December, the Deputy Prime Minister, John Prescott, said the bill was about 'modernising the government of the capital, giving power to the people of London, stripping away the shadowy committees, burgeoning bureaucracies and quangos created by our predecessor'. The Conservatives continued to oppose the bill as drafted, voting against the third reading on 5 May (265 votes to 105, a Government majority of 160). Progress on the bill in the Lords was slow following the second reading on 20 May, but no defeats were inflicted by the Upper House. It will continue its progress after the summer recess but should be in place well in time for the elections to be held in the year 2000.

The other issue in Parliament over London was the possible candidates for Mayor. Tony Blair's reshuffle at the beginning of the summer recess freed up two former ministers (Glenda Jackson and Tony Banks) from their responsibilities to stand as possible Labour candidates against the London Labour MP Ken Livingstone. The leading Conservative candidates are not current MPs (Lord Archer of Weston-Super-Mare and Steve Norris). One of the leading Liberal Democrat contenders was a London MP (Simon Hughes).

ELECTION PLEDGES FULFILLED

Two of the early pledges of the Government were to bring down NHS waiting lists and to reduce class sizes in schools. Progress was made towards helping to achieve the former in this Parliamentary session. The Health Bill (Lords), introduced on 28 January in the Lords, had its second reading on 9 February. During its passage through the Lords, the Government were defeated three times. On Report an amendment moved by Earl Howe to clause 2 (Primary Care Trusts), asking for wider consultation with local doctors before establishing such a trust was passed by a majority against the Government of three; a new clause on Independent Hospitals also moved by Earl Howe was passed by a majority against the Government of 48; and on third reading on 25 March, an amendment moved by Baroness Masham of Ilton (C.) to clause 9 covering out-of-area transfers was passed by a majority against the Government of 27. In the Commons on 13 April a Conservative reasoned amendment declining a second reading because the bill removed choice was defeated by 368 votes to 127, a Government majority of 241. Health Secretary, Frank Dobson, pledged to overturn the defeats in the Lords. When the bill came back from committee for remaining stages in

the Commons on 14 June, the Government tabled some 85 amendments and new clauses for discussion. Slow progress on these caused the Leader of the House, Margaret Beckett, to introduce a guillotine motion the next day, timetabling further debate. Following an ill-tempered exchange this was passed by 325 votes to 145, a Government majority of 180, and the third reading itself by 373 votes to 112, a Government majority of 260. The Bill received Royal Assent on 30 June. Frank Dobson hailed this as 'an end to the competitive internal market…the creation of a new, modern and dependable NHS that can give easier and quicker access to the top quality treatment and care that the British people need'.

The issue of waiting list reduction and waiting times was a constant theme of questions to the Prime Minister, with little agreement on the statistics that either side chose to use. Although no legislation was introduced on schools in this session, class sizes dominated Prime Ministers Questions towards the summer recess. In a celebrated exchange on 21 July, for instance, William Hague and Tony Blair crossed swords over figures produced by Mr. Hague from the House of Commons Library, Mr. Hague claiming they showed a rise in the past two years in average class sizes, and Mr. Blair maintaining that there had been a reduction.

INTERNATIONAL CRISES

Tony Blair came to the Commons on 16 November to warn Saddam Hussein that unless the Iraqis complied fully with their obligations towards UN-SCOM under UN resolutions, both the UK and the USA remained ready to strike. On 17 December he announced that US-UK air raids had commenced. He said, 'The objectives of this military operation are clear and simple: to degrade the ability of Saddam Hussein to build and use weapons of mass destruction including command and control and delivery systems, and to diminish the threat that he poses to his neighbours by weakening his military capability'. The Conservatives and Liberal Democrats offered their full support for the action taken. This was followed by an emergency debate on the situation, when disaffected left wing Labour MPs expressed their doubts about he course of action taken.

The situation in Kosovo was first reported to Parliament by the Foreign Secretary (Robin Cook) on 18 January following reports of ethnic cleansing atrocities in Racak, south of Pristina, and again on 1 February after a meeting of the Contact Group had called on both sides to end hostilities. But the killings had continued. On 11 February, the Defence Secretary, George Robertson, made an evening statement to the Commons as the Contact Group continued its attempts to produce a peace package at Rambouillet, on the decision to make British forces available immediately in case a NATO force was required to deploy to Kosovo. Robin Cook reported back to the Commons on the outcome of the Rambouillet meeting and the work of the Contact Group on 24 February. He said, 'We did obtain consensus from both sides, for a democratic, self-governing Kosovo and agreement to the main elements in the detailed texts of its constitution...but I regret to inform the House that violent conflict continues...both sides have recognized the value of the Contact Group proposals. I urge them now to work with us in implementing them and to turn their commitment on paper into reality on the ground'. Tony Blair reported back on the deteriorating situation in Kosovo on 23 March and the increased likelihood of NATO air strikes, saying, 'We stand ready for action...for very clear reasons. We do so primarily to avert what would otherwise be a humanitarian disaster in Kosovo'. With the Prime Minister away at the European Union Summit in Berlin, the Deputy Prime Minister, John Prescott, confirmed that bombing raids had begun on targets in the Federal Republic of Yugoslavia in a late night statement to MPs on 24 March. For the Conservatives, Deputy Leader, Peter Lilley, expressed full support for the Government's actions as did Menzies Campbell for the Liberal Democrats. The Commons debated the situation the following day and again some voices were raised against the all-party consensus supporting the action. On 29 March, Tony Blair reported back on the outcome of the EU summit, where the situation in Kosovo had dominated events. He announced that further RAF aircraft would be sent to join the NATO operation.

Returning from the Easter recess on 13 April, Tony Blair announced that the UK would be sending an extra 1,800 troops to the area and repeated the Alliance's aims: a verifiable end to Serb military action and the immediate ending of violence and repression; withdrawal from Kosovo; the installation of an international peace-keeping force; safe return of all refugees and the willingness to work to establish a political framework agreement for Kosovo. The Commons debated the situation on 19 April, and again the majority of speakers supported the action, although the voices of concern were spreading to the Opposition benches.

On 26 April Tony Blair reported back on the NATO 50th anniversary summit in Washington where again Kosovo had dominated proceedings and NATO had decided that the air campaign should be intensified. Opposition leaders continued to give broad support, but the Liberal Democrat Leader, Paddy Ashdown, warned that 'unless we are prepared to make a decision on the reinforcement of our troops against the contingency that we may have to use them on the ground, against whatever opposition there is, we may find that we have left it too late'. On 5 May Jack Straw announced that the UK would start taking up to 1,000 refugees a week from Kosovo from the middle of the month. On 10 May Robin Cook reported to the Commons on the accidental bombing of the Chinese Embassy

in Belgrade by NATO aircraft. During another debate on the situation on 18 May, the Conservative Foreign Affairs spokesman, Michael Howard, reiterated the Opposition's support for the NATO objectives but said that William Hague had asked 'for the appointment of an inquiry...into the circumstances that led up to the conflict'. On 26 May George Robertson announced that more British and other NATO troops were being sent to the area. On 8 June Tony Blair reported back to the House on developments with the peace process brokered by President Ahtisaari of Finland and the Russian special envoy Viktor Chernomyrdin following the EU summit in Cologne, and on 9 June George Robertson was able to come to the House to make a late night statement on the breakthrough in the negotiations with the Serbs over the withdrawal of all their forces and the signing of the agreement by General Sir Michael Jackson on behalf of NATO and the Serb military commanders. The withdrawal was to begin at once.

On 14 June, Robin Cook reported on the developments in the military peace operation and a further debate was held on 17 June, when Mr Cook warned that 'it is the start of a new stage in which we must face the civilian challenge of rebuilding its shattered economy and its fractured society'. The newly appointed Conservative Foreign Affairs spokesman, John Maples, called for careful examination of the military lessons that had been learnt. Tony Blair, reporting back on the outcome of the G8 summit in Cologne on 21 June said that 'the progress made in the few days since Milosovic finally caved in has been extraordinary...This is a remarkable story and Britain and British forces can be very proud of their role in it'.

Robin Cook was also able to report to the House on 7 July on the restoration of full diplomatic relations with Libya, following acceptance by the Libyan Government of responsibility for the murder of WPC Yvonne Fletcher in 1984.

PARLIAMENTARY DISCIPLINE

The Government were continuously accused of trying to devalue the role of Parliament by allowing announcements to be made outside the House and letting spin doctors dominate. Prime Minister's Question time continued to see the rather fawning attitude of Labour back-benchers. Despite the size of the Labour majority (177) the Government did not tolerate back-bench dissent, though there were occasions when this broke out. During the 17 December debate on Iraq, disaffected left wing Labour MPs were annoyed that they could not vote against the motion on developments as the Government would not appoint anyone to act as a teller for the Aye Lobby. Labour back-bench MP Tam Dalyell therefore introduced a Private Member's Bill in January to require prior approval by a simple majority of the House of Commons before any military action could be taken against Iraq. Similarly, in the debate on Kosovo on 19 April, many of the same MPs failed to force a vote on the motion only 11 MPs voted for the closure motion when a quorum of 40 MPs were needed to vote.

In the Remaining stages debate of the Welfare Reform and Pensions Bill on 17 May, the Government Whips initially tried to postpone debate to avoid publicity over a threatened back-bench revolt by more than 60 Labour MPs concerned about the effect on disabled people of plans to means test and restrict access to incapacity benefit, but when debate had gone on until nearly 4 a.m. and the issue had still not been resolved they moved a closure motion, which was passed by 314 votes to 21, a Government majority of 293. When the issue was finally discussed on 20 May under a guillotine motion timetabling further discussion, a Labour back-bench amendment to clause 53 (Incapacity Benefit; restriction to recent contributors), was defeated by 310 votes to 270, a Government majority of 40; but some 67 Labour MPs voted against the Government and up to 15 abstained, despite the last minute offer of a review by the Social Security Secretary, Alistair Darling.

On the remaining stages debate on the Immigration and Asylum Bill on 16 June, also taken under a guillotine motion, seven Labour back-bench MPs voted against the Government over plans to reduce the amount of money available to all refugees and replace it with more vouchers.

Embarrassing moments came over the Stephen Lawrence Inquiry. In February, Jack Straw came to the House to explain why he had at first sought and then dropped an injunction in respect of prior publication of a leaked copy of the Macpherson Report in the weekend's newspapers; then, upon the publication of the report itself on 24 February Mr Straw had to defend his decision to allow the Commissioner of the Metropolitan Police (Sir Paul Condon) to remain in post to deliver the programme of reforms recommended in the report; and again on 26 February Mr Straw's deputy, Home Office Minister Paul Boateng had to apologise to the House for the inadvertent publication of informers' names in the annexes to the original report, which had now been withdrawn. There was a further row when it transpired that the Home Secretary had not come to the House to make this statement himself because he was on holiday abroad. A similar impression that the Government did not really have any time for the House of Commons was given when no minister for the Department for Education and Employment came to the Commons on 19 March to tell MPs about the Government's response to an OFSTED report on failing schools in Hackney. Jack Straw again had to apologise in June over the confusion with the renewal order for the Prevention of Terrorism (Temporary Provision) Act 1989.

The Prime Minister had some difficulties with his ministerial team. He accepted the resignation of his Welsh Secretary, Ron Davies, in October following what he referred to as 'a serious error of judgement on Clapham Common'. The session saw

a record number of personal statements made to the House, the majority of them by Labour MPs denting the sleaze-free impression that Tony Blair wanted to project for his party. In November the Paymaster General, Geoffrey Robinson, apologized to the House for a breach of the rules concerning registration of outside interests. The pressure on the Prime Minister to sack Mr Robinson over other issues grew and, on 22 December, he accepted the resignation of both Mr Robinson and the Trade and Industry Secretary, Peter Mandelson, to whom Mr Robinson had given a substantial loan in order to buy a house.

There were instances of leaks of draft select committee reports to Government, most notably that of the Foreign Affairs Committee on the Sandline/Arms for Sierra Leone affair. Robin Cook made a statement to the House on 24 February protesting that 'I did not obstruct or impede the work of the committee; I did not interfere with the deliberations of the committee; and I have fully respected the role of scrutiny of both the committee and the Chamber'. But when the Standards and Privileges Committee was able finally to investigate the affair it called for the suspension of the mole responsible for leaking an advance copy of the report to the Foreign Office, Labour back-bench MP Ernie Ross; this was approved by the Commons on 12 July and the MP made his personal apology to the House that day. The Labour chairman of Foreign Affairs Committee, Donald Anderson, also had to make a personal apology to the House in July for misleading members over the extent to which he had discussed the Sandline report with the Foreign and Commonwealth Office. On 20 May Teresa Gorman had apologised for failing to register an interest properly in the Register of Members' Interests. Following another report by the Standards and Privileges Committee into the leaking of a Social Security Select Committee document on child benefit, two back-bench Labour MPs made personal statements on 27 July: Don Touhig, the Parliamentary Private Secretary to the Chancellor, and Kali Mountford, a member of the Commons Social Security Committee. They had been recommended for suspension from the House for three days and five days respectively. Both resigned from their positions. The committee also criticized the Social Security Committee Chairman, Archy Kirkwood, for being more than forthcoming than was prudent about the report when briefing a journalist ahead of its publication. Then there was the case of the back-bench Labour MP Fiona Jones (Newark): she was originally convicted for false declaration over election expenses, which caused the Speaker to declare her seat vacated with effect from 19 March, but after a successful appeal against conviction, she re-took her seat on 29 April.

There was, too, growing criticism of the Government for the way in which it was handling legislation under guillotine motions, timetabling or restricting discussion. Of the major pieces of legislation in this session, the following were subject to a Parliamentary guillotine in the Commons: all stages of the re-introduced European Parliamentary Elections Bill (2 December), the remaining stages of the Local Government Bill (23 and 24 March); the remaining stages of the Welfare Reform and Pensions Bill (20 May); the remaining stages of the Health Bill (Lords) and of the Immigration and Asylum Bill (15 June); the remaining stages of the Access to Justice Bill (Lords) and the Consideration of Lords amendments to the Tax Credits Bill (22 June); the Northern Ireland Bill (13 July); the remaining stages of the Food Standards Bill and the Consideration of Lords amendments to the Employment Relations Bill (22 July); and the Consideration of Lords amendments to the Local Government Bill (26 July).

Following the decision in the previous session to alter the timing of Prime Minster's Question Time to one, half-hour session a week, the Government pressed ahead with other reforms through the Modernisation Committee. In December, the House agreed to the report of the Committee on the Parliamentary Calendar, which allowed for the sittings of the House of Commons on Thursdays to begin at 11.30 a.m. and finish at 7.30 p.m. (with the undertaking to avoid discussing controversial legislation) so that MPs from distant constituencies could get away at a reasonable hour. This procedure was adopted as an experiment from 14 January. It also agreed in principle to a week's recess in February to coincide with school half-terms. On 24 May, the House agreed with the recommendations of the second report on Sittings of the House in Westminster Hall, which proposed certain sittings to be held in Westminster Hall to allow for more back-bench debates. This would be adopted as an experiment in the next session.

Another innovation, which some saw as a threat to the Parliamentary position, was the use of pre-legislative scrutiny of bills and the proposal to carry over certain bills to the following session of Parliament as a result. Several bills were introduced this way including the Electronic Communications Bill, the draft Freedom of Information Bill and the Food Standards Bill, in which there was a major change from the first draft when the proposal for a blanket £90 levy on all food outlets to pay for the Food Standards Agency was dropped. Most controversy surrounded the Railways Bill (to set up a Strategic Railway Authority), introduced on 7 July and given a second reading on 19 July. The Conservatives tabled a reasoned amendment declining a second reading due to the lack of time in the present session to complete the passage of the Bill (which had not been singled out as one to be carried over) but this was defeated by 300 votes to 123, a Government majority of 207. The bill was then, unusually, committed to the Environment Select Committee for scrutiny by 12 November but no clarification was forthcoming as to whether a new bill and another second reading would be required in the next session. The row over this led to Opposition back-bench MPs forcing a series of divisions on issues that would have normally been nodded through in protest on 19 July.

The actions of certain Conservative back-bench MPs in respect of proceedings with Private Member's Bills did not escape criticism. Eric Forth (Bromley & Chislehurst) and David Maclean (Penrith & the Border) were accused of killing off several bills by their filibustering, most notably the Fur Farming (Prohibition) Bill, whose remaining stages were talked out on 14 May and 11 June.

The pundits claimed that by the time of the summer recess Tony Blair was looking in need of a holiday. His Government had kept up a brisk pace with continuing reform as promised in its manifesto and, as well as the international crises, he had also had to deal with such recurring issues as the Government's position on the euro, following its introduction on 1 January, European Commission fraud (which saw the resignation of the whole European Commission in 18 March and may have accounted for the very low turnout in the elections to the European Parliament in the UK in June) and the continuing disquiet over genetically modified food. The next session looks like being another crowded one. It sees a new Leader of the Liberal Democrat Party, Charles Kennedy, following the decision of Paddy Ashdown to stand down.

PUBLIC ACTS OF PARLIAMENT

This list commences with four Public Acts which received the royal assent before September 1998. Those Public Acts which follow received the royal assent after August 1998. The date stated after each Act is the date on which it came into operation; c. indicates the chapter number of each Act.

Crime and Disorder Act 1998, c. 37 various dates some to be appointed
creates certain racially aggravated offences, abolishes the rebuttable presumption that a child is doli incapax; provides for the effect of a child's failure to give evidence; abolishes the death penalty for treason and piracy and makes various other provisions with regard to crime and disorder, including the release and recall of prisoners.

Government of Wales Act 1998, c. 39 various dates, some to be appointed
establishes and makes provision about the National Assembly for Wales and the offices of the Auditor-General for Wales and Welsh Administration Ombudsman, and reforms certain other Welsh public bodies.

National Minimum Wage Act 1998, c. 39 various dates, some to be appointed
makes provision for and in connection with a national minimum wage; amends certain enactments relating to the remuneration of agricultural workers; and for connected purposes.

Criminal Justice (Terrorism and Conspiracy) Act 1998, c. 40 September 4, 1998
makes provision about procedure and forfeiture in relation to offences concerning proscribed organisations, and about conspiracy to commit offences outside the UK.

Competition Act 1998, c. 41 various dates, some to be appointed
makes provision about competition and abuse of a dominant position in the market; confers powers in relation to investigations conducted in connection with Arts 85 and 86 of the EC Treaty; amends the Fair Trading Act 1973; and for connected purposes. Inter alia, the Act provides for a new regime which will be applied and enforced by the Director of Fair Trading.

Human Rights Act 1999, c. 42 various dates, some to be appointed
gives further effect to rights and freedoms guaranteed under the European Convention on Human Rights; makes provision in connection with holders of certain judicial offices who become judges of the European Court of Human Rights. The Act is designed to incorporate the provisions of the Convention into the law of the UK, as opposed to hitherto being solely a signatory to it. It will enable the provisions to be enforced in the UK as well as the ECHR.

Statute Law Repeals Act 1998, c. 43 November 19, 1998
repeals certain enactments which are no longer of practical utility, in accordance with recommendations of the Law Commission and the Scottish Law Commission.

Waste Minimisation Act 1998, c. 44 November 19, 1998
amends the Environmental Protection Act 1990 to give certain local authorities powers to take steps to minimise the generation of waste in their area; and for related purposes.

Regional Development Agencies Act 1998, c. 45 various dates, some to be appointed
makes provision for the establishment, constitution, status, purpose, powers and strategy of regional development agencies in England, and for the transfer of property, rights and liabilities from the Development Commission and the Urban Regeneration Agency to agencies; and for connected purposes.

Scotland Act 1998, c. 46 various dates
provides for the establishment of a Scottish Parliament and Administration and other changes in the government of Scotland; for changes in the constitution and functions of certain public authorities, for the variation of the basic rate of income tax in relation to the income of Scottish taxpayers; and for the amendment of the laws relating to parliamentary constituencies in Scotland.

Northern Ireland Act 1998, c. 47 various dates, some to be appointed
makes provision for the government of Northern Ireland for the purpose of implementing the agreement (set out in Command Paper 3883 and known colloquially as the Good Friday Agreement) reached at multi-party talks on Northern Ireland.

Registration of Political Parties Act 1998, c. 48 various dates, some to be appointed
makes provision about the registration of political parties including, inter alia, the use of emblems for ballot purposes.

Consolidated Fund (No. 2) Act 1998, c. 49 December 17, 1998
applies certain sums out of the Consolidated Fund to the service of the years ending on March 31, 1999 and 2000.

European Parliamentary Elections Act 1999, c. 1 various dates, some to be appointed
amends the Act of 1978 so as to alter the method used in Great Britain for electing MEPs; and for connected purposes.

Social Security Contributions (Transfer of Functions, etc) Act 1999, c. 2 various dates, some to be appointed
transfers from the Secretary of State to the

Commissioners of Inland Revenue or the Treasury certain functions relating to NICs, the NI Fund, statutory sick pay, statutory maternity pay and other benefits; makes further provision in connection with the functions transferred, contracted out pension schemes, and for connected purposes.

Road Traffic (NHS Charges) Act, c. 3 April 5, 1999 (except in relation to military hospitals) makes provision about the recovery from insurers and certain other persons of charges in connection with the treatment of road traffic casualties in NHS and certain other hospitals; and for connected purposes.

Consolidated Fund Act 1999, c. 4 March 25, 1999. applies certain sums out of the Consolidated Fund to the service of the years ending on March 31, 1998 and 1999.

Scottish Enterprise Act 1999, c. 5 July 26, 1999 makes provision with respect to the financial limits in the Enterprise and New Towns (Scotland) Act 1990, s. 25(2).

Rating (Valuation) Act 1999, c. 6 May 26, 1999 makes provision in relation to valuation for the purposes of non-domestic rates in England and Wales.

Northern Ireland (Location of Victims' Remains) Act 1999, c. 7 May 26, 1999 makes provision connected with Northern Ireland about locating the remains of persons killed before April 10 1998 as a result of unlawful acts of violence committed on behalf of, or in connection with, proscribed organisations; and for connected purposes.

Health Act 1999, c. 8 various dates, some to be appointed amends the law about the NHS; makes provision in respect of arrangements and payments between health service bodies and local authorities with respect to health and health related functions; confers power to regulate any professions concerned with the physical or mental health of individuals; and for connected purposes.

Water Industry Act 1999, c. 9 various dates, some to be appointed makes further provision in England and Wales as to charges for the supply of water and provision of sewerage services; and in Scotland by establishing the Water Industry Commissioner for Scotland to promote the interests of customers; and for connected purposes.

Tax Credits Act 1999, c. 10 various dates provides for the administration and enforcement of the working families tax credit and the disabled person's tax credit which replace, respectively, family credit and disability working allowance; and for connected purposes.

Breeding and Sale of Dogs (Welfare) Act 1999, c. 11 December 30, 1999

amends and extends certain enactments relating to the commercial sale and breeding of dogs; regulates the welfare of dogs kept in commercial breeding establishments; extends powers of inspection; and establishes record keeping for dogs kept in such establishments; and for connected purposes.

Road Traffic (Vehicle Testing) Act 1999, c. 12 various dates, some to be appointed makes further provision for tests for the satisfactory condition of vehicles for the purposes of the Road Traffic Act 1988.

Appropriation Act 1999, c. 13 July 15, 1999 applies a sum out of the Consolidated Fund to the service of the year ending March 31, 2000; applies the supplies granted in this Session of Parliament; and repeals certain Consolidated Fund and Appropriation Acts.

Protection of Children Act 1999, c. 14 various dates, some to be appointed requires a list to be kept of persons considered unsuitable to work with children; enables the protection afforded to children to be afforded to persons suffering from mental impairment; and for connected purposes.

Trustee Delegation Act 1999, c. 15 day to be appointed amends the law relating to the delegation of trustee functions by a power of attorney and the exercise of such functions by the donee of a power of attorney; makes provision about the authority of the donee of a power of attorney to act in relation to land.

Finance Act 1999, c.16
Disability Right Commission Act 1999, c. 17
Adoption (Intercountry Aspects) Act 1999, c. 18
Company and Business Names (Chambers of Commerce, etc.) Act 1999, c. 19
Commonwealth Development Corporation Act 1999, c. 20
Football (Offences and Disorder) Act 1999, c. 21
Access to Justice Act 1999, c. 22
Youth Justice and Criminal Evidence Act 1999, c. 23
Pollution Prevention and Control Act 1999, c. 24
Criminal Cases Review (Insanity) Act 1999, c. 25
Employment Relations Act 1999, c. 26
Local Government Act 1999, c. 27

WHITE PAPERS, REPORTS, ETC.

Local Voices: Modernizing Local Government in Wales was presented to Parliament by the Welsh Secretary (Ron Davies) on 3 August 1998. It included the following main proposals:
– a code of conduct for councillors and council employees
– an independent Standards Commission to deal with allegations of wrong-doing
– a cabinet-style system of government for local councils, and directly-elected mayors if desired by the local population
– the abolition of universal capping
– the abolition of compulsory competitive tendering and its replacement by a duty on councils to achieve best value in service delivery

Conclusions of the Review of Energy Sources for Power Generation and Government Response to Fourth and Fifth Reports of the Trade and Industry Committee was presented to Parliament by the Trade and Industry Secretary (Peter Mandelson) on 8 October 1998. It included the following main proposals:
– the sale of coal-fired capacity by the major generators
– stricter consents on new gas-fired power stations
– a radical overhaul of the electricity pool
– full competition among electricity supply companies
– a regulatory framework separating monopoly (distribution) from competitive (supply) activities

Three White Papers on the Welfare State, *A New Contract for Welfare: Principles into Practice*, *A New Contract for Welfare: The Gateway to Work*, and *A New Contract for Welfare: Support for Disabled People* were presented to Parliament by the Social Security Secretary (Alistair Darling) on 28 October 1998. They included the following main proposals:
– all future benefit claimants of working age to attend compulsory job interviews
– a new employability test to be introduced for future claimants of incapacity benefit; the benefit to be available only to those who have made NI contributions in the previous two years
– severe disablement allowance to be abolished for new claimants aged over 20 and paid at a higher rate to new claimants aged under 20
– a disability income guarantee to be introduced for severely disabled people aged under 60

The Government's Response to the Children's Safeguard Review was presented to Parliament by the Health Secretary (Frank Dobson) on 5 November 1998. It included the following main proposals in response to the Utting report on children in residential care:
– a national register of people considered unsuitable to work with children
– the extension of local authorities' duty of care for young people to those aged 16 to 18
– better support and services for those leaving care

– a new national organization to voice the concerns of children in care or those who were formerly in care
– a campaign to increase the number of foster carers
– the extension of the regulatory system to all children's homes, residential schools and independent fostering agencies
– a requirement for councils to train staff working in children's homes
– a General Social Care Council to set standards for people working with or caring for children

Defence Diversification: Getting the Most out of Defence Technology was presented to Parliament by the Defence Secretary (George Robertson) on 5 November 1998. It outlined plans for a Defence Diversification Agency to be established within the Defence Evaluation and Research Agency by the beginning of 1999, under the oversight of a Defence Diversification Council.

A White Paper on the parliamentary scrutiny of European business was presented to Parliament by the Leader of the House of Commons (Margaret Beckett) on 12 November 1998. It included the following main proposals:
– measures in the fields of Common Foreign and Security Policy and Justice and Home Affairs to be subject to scrutiny in both Houses of Parliament
– European Select Committees in the House of Commons to scrutinize important institutional and procedural developments in the EU and important European legislation

Compact on Relations between Government and the Voluntary and Community Sector in England was presented to Parliament by the Home Secretary (Jack Straw) on 12 November 1998. The compact had been launched in Scotland on 23 October, and separate compacts were subsequently developed in Wales and Northern Ireland. It was intended as a general framework and an enabling mechanism to enhance the relationship between the Government and the voluntary and community sector and set out a series of shared principles underpinning the compact.

Details of cuts to the Territorial Army as part of the Government's Strategic Defence Review were announced by the Defence Secretary (George Robertson) on 17 November 1998. The main points were:
– the total strength to be cut from 59,000 to 41,200
– the Royal Armoured Corps to be cut from seven regiments to four regiments
– the Royal Engineers to be cut from nine regiments to five regiments
– the Infantry to be cut from 33 battalions to 15 battalions
– the Royal Logistic Corps to be cut from 19 regiments to 14 regiments

– TA Bands to be cut from 24 to 14

– 87 drill centres to close

– Army Medical Services to gain 2,000 posts

Modernizing Social Services – Promoting Independence, Improving Protection, Raising Standards was presented to Parliament by the Health Secretary (Frank Dobson) on 30 November 1998. It included the following main proposals:

– a Commission for Care Standards to be set up in each English region and to cover all care services, wherever provided

– new national performance standards to be set for local authorities

– regional children's rights officers to be appointed to inspect children's homes

– a General Social Care Council to be established to replace the Central Council for Education and Training in Social Work

– increased funding for social services in England

Modernizing Justice – the Government's Plans for Reforming Legal Services and the Courts was presented to Parliament by the Lord Chancellor (Lord Irvine of Lairg) on 2 December 1998. It included the following main proposals:

– the legal aid scheme to be replaced by a system of specialist lawyers working under contract

– a Community Legal Service (for civil and family cases) and a Criminal Defence Service (for criminal cases) to be established; a Legal Services Commission to be established to administer both services initially

– new tests to be introduced to identify cases suitable for legal aid

– changes to the legal insurance market to encourage 'no win, no fee' work

– all lawyers to have rights of audience in all courts

– the Court of Appeal and magistrates' courts to be reformed

– fixed up-front costs for advocacy in 'fast track' civil justice cases

Smoking Kills: a White Paper on Tobacco was presented to Parliament by the Health Secretary (Frank Dobson) on 10 December 1998. It included the following main proposals and targets:

– tobacco advertising on billboards to be banned by summer 1999

– courses and counselling to be available for people who wish to give up smoking

– most tobacco sponsorship of the arts and sport to be banned by 2003

– the tobacco industry to be encouraged to introduce a 'proof of age' card

– targets to be set for the provision of smoke-free areas in public places

– an Approved Code of Practice on smoking at work to be introduced

– a three-year anti-smoking campaign in the media

– the percentage of child smokers to be cut from 13 per cent to 9 per cent or less by 2010

– the percentage of adult smokers to be cut from 28 per cent to 24 per cent or less by 2010

– the percentage of women who smoke during pregnancy to be cut from 23 per cent to 15 per cent by 2010

Our Competitive Future: Building the Knowledge Driven Economy was presented to Parliament by the Trade and Industry Secretary (Peter Mandelson) on 16 December 1998. It included the following main proposals:

– an enterprise fund worth £150 million to be established to support high technology businesses

– up to eight enterprise centres to be created in universities

– the development of business 'clusters' to be encouraged

– insolvency laws and merger policy to be reviewed

– legislation to be introduced under which legal barriers to on-line trading would be removed

– a national strategy to meet the skills needs of the information and communication technologies sector

Public Services for the Future: Modernization, Reform, Accountability was presented to Parliament by the Chief Secretary to the Treasury (Stephen Byers) on 17 December 1998. It set out more than 500 performance targets in 31 public services agreements covering all government departments. The aim was to save more than £8 billion per year by 2001–2 and reinvest it in front-line services.

Modernizing Parliament: Reforming the House of Lords was presented to Parliament by the Leader of the House of Lords (Baroness Jay of Paddington) on 20 January 1999. It put forward a range of possibilities for the future powers and composition of the House of Lords, and included the following main proposals:

– the removal of the right of hereditary peers to sit and vote in the House

– the nomination of life peers through an independent Appointments Commission

– the establishment of a Royal Commission to consider longer-term reform of the House and to report by 31 December 1999

Targeting Excellence – Modernizing Scotland's Schools was presented to Parliament by the Scottish Secretary (Donald Dewar) on 27 January 1999. It included the following main proposals:

– the development of primary teachers' skills in teaching science

– measures to improve learning in the first two years of secondary school

– consultation on the machinery for determining teachers' pay and conditions and on new arrangements for the dismissal of ineffective teachers

– the Scottish Qualification for Headship to become mandatory for aspiring head teachers

– a new framework for addressing under-performance in schools

Towards a Healthier Scotland was presented to Parliament by the Scottish Office Health Minister (Sam Galbraith) on 17 February 1999. It outlined four 'demonstration projects':

- Starting Well, to focus on health promotion among children up to primary school age
- Healthy Respect, to promote good sexual health among young people and reduce the number of teenage pregnancies
- The Cancer Challenge, to reduce the number of people who smoke and to introduce a screening programme for the early detection of colorectal cancer
- The Heart of Scotland, to focus on the prevention of heart disease by promoting a healthier diet, exercise, giving up smoking and cutting alcohol intake

It also set new targets to assess the impact of these measures, including the following:

- 60 per cent of five-year-olds to have no experience of dental disease by 2010
- the number of women who smoke during pregnancy to be cut from 29 per cent to 20 per cent by 2010
- the pregnancy rate among 13 to 15 year-olds to be cut by 20 per cent by 2010
- the death rate of people under 75 to be cut by 20 per cent by 2010
- the number of young people who smoke to be cut by 20 per cent by 2010
- the number of adults dying from heart disease to be cut by 50 per cent by 2010

The report of the inquiry led by Sir William Macpherson of Cluny into the murder of Stephen Lawrence in London in 1993 was published by the Home Secretary (Jack Straw) on 24 February 1999. It was highly critical of the conduct of the investigation by the Metropolitan Police and made the following main recommendations:

- the Home Secretary to declare as a matter of priority the aim of 'eliminating racist prejudice and disadvantage and the demonstration of fairness in all aspects of policing'
- HM Inspectorate of Constabulary to conduct an immediate inspection of the Metropolitan Police
- the police and other public bodies no longer to be exempt from race relations legislation
- an incident to be defined as racist if it is perceived to be so by the victim or anyone else
- targets to be set for the recruitment, retention and progression of ethnic minority police staff
- procedures at the scene of incidents to be reviewed and first aid training to be improved
- family liaison officers, victim liaison officers and witness liaison officers to be available at local level
- police officers to be subject to disciplinary action up to at least five years after retirement
- a record to be kept of all 'stops' or 'stops and searches' by police officers
- investigation of serious complaints against the police not to be conducted by other police officers
- consideration to be given to abolishing 'double jeopardy' so that someone acquitted of a crime could be re-tried if 'fresh and viable' new evidence emerged

- consideration to be given to criminalizing the use of racist language or behaviour, or the possession of an offensive weapon, in private
- local government, the criminal justice system and other agencies to consider their race training
- consideration to be given to amending the National Curriculum to value cultural diversity and prevent racism; schools to publish details annually of racist incidents and the ethnic make-up of pupils who have been excluded

The 2001 Census of Population was published by the Government on 4 March 1999. It set out the reasons for holding a census in 2001 (on 29 April), the broad principles on which it was to be based, the reasons for including each proposed topic, the arrangements for collecting and processing the data and disseminating the results, and the measures to safeguard the confidentiality of the information collected.

Aiming for Excellence: Modernizing Social Work Services in Scotland was presented to Parliament by the Scottish Social Work Minister (Sam Galbraith) on 15 March 1999. It included the following main proposals:

- a Scottish Commission for the Regulation of Care to be established, to provide independent regulation of children's services, residential care homes, nursing homes and home care services
- a Consultancy Index of information on people considered unsuitable to work with children and young people to be introduced
- a Strategic Framework for Children's Services to be developed
- a Scottish Social Services Council to be established, to register the workforce, draw up a code of conduct for staff and raise professional training and service standards

Partnership for Progress and Prosperity: Britain and the Overseas Territories was presented to Parliament by the Foreign Secretary (Robin Cook) on 17 March 1999. It included the following main proposals:

- the title 'Overseas Territories' to replace 'Dependent Territories' and the change to be enshrined in legislation
- a Council of the Territories to be established to improve liaison with the overseas territories
- British citizenship to be offered to all residents of the territories, with their right of abode in the UK offered on a non-reciprocal basis
- the territories to be required to meet international standards in terms of financial regulation and human rights

The Future Management of Crown Copyright was presented to Parliament by the Minister for the Cabinet Office (Jack Cunningham) on 26 March 1999. It said that the guiding principles of the new regime for managing crown copyright material would be:

- coherence, transparency and consistency of approach
- ease of access

- increasing use of waiver of copyright
- a streamlined administrative process
- strengthened accountability
- clear co-ordination and control by HMSO

Modernizing Government was presented to Parliament by the Minister for the Cabinet Office (Jack Cunningham) on 30 March 1999. It included the following specific proposals:
- areas for joint working and budgeting between departments to be targeted
- best practice to be identified and disseminated
- unnecessary regulation to be removed
- central and local government to work together to assess how different local services can be located in one centre
- a major initiative to align boundaries of public bodies
- all basic dealings with the Government to be deliverable electronically by 2008
- public services to be available 24 hours a day, seven days a week, where there is a demand
- electronic signatures to be given the same force in law as paper signatures
- smartcards to be developed so that a range of services can be made available on one card
- government services to be available through one, easy-to-use gateway
- 90 per cent of low value purchases by central government to be carried out electronically by March 2001

Public Services for the Future: Modernization, Reform, Accountability was presented to Parliament by the Chief Secretary to the Treasury (Alan Milburn) on 31 March 1999. It outlined seven new Public Service Agreements setting targets for the quality and efficiency of a range of public services, and detailed the indicators to be used to monitor progress towards the targets. Some of the main targets included:
- child support assessments to be carried out within seven weeks by the end of 2002
- the number of lone parents dependent on Income Support to be reduced by 10 per cent by 2002
- losses from fraud and error in Income Support and Jobseekers' Allowance to be reduced by 30 per cent by March 2007
- at least 90 per cent of children to have normal speech and language development at 18 months and three years by 2001–2
- no BT residential customer to experience any real increase in charges annually to July 2001
- new water leakage targets to be set annually

Social Services: Building for the Future –A White Paper for Wales was presented to Parliament by the Welsh Secretary (Alun Michael) on 31 March 1999. It included the following main proposals:
- an independent Commission for Care Standards in Wales to regulate residential and nursing homes and care provided to people in their own homes
- statutory standards of service to ensure consistency in the quality of services

- a Care Council for Wales to regulate and train the workforce
- a strategy for children's services
- clear and consistent monitoring and inspection arrangements, to be outlined in a Performance Management framework
- the possible establishment of a children's commissioner

A Better Quality of Life: A Strategy for Sustainable Development for the United Kingdom was presented to Parliament by the Deputy Prime Minister (John Prescott) on 17 May 1999. It included the following main proposals:
- a new government strategy, *A Better Quality of Life*, aimed at making sustainable development a reality and outlining the priorities for the immediate future
- a national 'Are You Doing Your Bit?' advertising campaign
- a 'quality of life barometer', with indicators to measure progress
- a Sustainable Development Commission

Learning to Succeed – A New Framework for Post-16 Learning was presented to Parliament by the Education and Employment Secretary (David Blunkett) on 30 June 1999. It included the following main proposals:
- a national Learning and Skills Council and 40–50 local Learning and Skills Councils
- a youth programme, Connexions, including a new youth support service modernizing the Careers Service
- an independent inspectorate covering all work-related learning and training, with a new role for Ofsted in inspecting provision for 16–19 year-olds in schools and colleges
- responsibility for work-based learning for unemployed adults to transfer to the Employment Service

A New Contract for Welfare: Children's Rights and Parents' Responsibilities was presented to Parliament by the Social Security Secretary (Alistair Darling) on 1 July 1999. It included the following main proposals:
- a simpler system for calculating the maintenance an absent father should pay, amounting to 15 per cent of take-home pay for one child, 20 per cent for two children and 25 per cent for three or more children
- failure to provide information or to meet maintenance responsibilities to become a criminal offence
- mothers on Income Support to be allowed to keep up to £10 a week of the maintenance paid to their children

Saving Lives: Our Healthier Nation was presented to Parliament by the Health Secretary (Frank Dobson) on 6 July 1999. It set new targets for reductions in deaths from heart disease, cancer, suicide and accidents by 2010, with the following main proposals:
- deaths from cancer in those under 75 to be cut by 20 per cent by 2010

–deaths from heart disease in those under 75 to be cut by 40 per cent by 2010
–suicides to be cut by 20 per cent by 2010
–deaths from accidents to be cut by 20 per cent by 2010
–first-aid programmes to be set up for 11 year-olds and 16 year-olds
–new public health observatories to be set up to monitor health trends
–healthy eating and healthy lifestyles to be promoted
–NHS Direct to be extended
–a health development agency to replace the Health Education Authority

Post Office Reform: A World Class Service for the 21st Century was presented to Parliament by the Trade and Industry Secretary (Stephen Byers) on 8 July 1999. It included the following main proposals:
–the Post Office to become a public limited company; all shares initially to be owned by the Government
–the new company to be allowed to enter into a joint venture with another company, subject to parliamentary approval, and to be able to borrow up to £75 million a year
–the annual dividend to the Government to be reduced to 50 per cent of post-tax profits in 1999–2000 and 40 per cent in following years
–an independent regulator to be established to promote consumer interests
–a strengthened Post Office National Users' Council
–a Universal Service Obligation to be introduced
–the monopoly on letter deliveries to be reduced from £1 to 50 p or 150 g from 1 April 2000
–minimum criteria to be laid down for access to post office counter services

Modern Markets: Confident Customers was presented to Parliament by the Trade and Industry Secretary (Stephen Byers) on 22 July 1999. It included the following main proposals:
–a hallmark for consumers to identify those companies that have received the Office of Fair Trading's Seal of Approval
–a digital hallmark for Internet traders who guarantee security of payment and privacy of information
–the publication of international price comparisons
–new consumer protection powers for trading standards officers, the Office of Fair Trading and the courts

The Funding of Political Parties in the United Kingdom was presented to Parliament by the Home Secretary (Jack Straw) on 27 July 1999. It included the following main proposals:
–each political party fielding candidates in all seats to be subject to an expenditure limit of £19.77 million for a general election campaign
–expenditure limits also to be applied to campaigns before elections to the Scottish Parliament, the National Assembly for Wales and the New

Northern Ireland Assembly and before referendums
–details of all donations or sponsorship over £5,000 to be disclosed
–the Government to be required to remain neutral for the last 28 days of a referendum campaign
–foreign donations to be banned unless the donor appears on the UK electoral register
–the proposals to be policed by a new Electoral Commission

The Queen's Awards

The Queen's Award for Export Achievement and The Queen's Award for Technological Achievement were instituted by royal warrant in 1975. The two separate awards took the place of The Queen's Award to Industry, which had been instituted in 1965. In 1992 the scheme was extended with the launch of a third award, The Queen's Award for Environmental Achievement. In December 1998 it was announced that a review committee, chaired by the Prince of Wales, would examine all aspects of the awards and recommend any changes it felt necessary.

The export and technological awards are designed to recognize and encourage outstanding achievements in exporting goods or services from the United Kingdom and in advancing process or product technology. The purpose of the environmental award is to recognize and encourage product and process development which has major benefits for the environment and which is commercially successful.

The awards differ from a personal royal honour in that they are given to a unit as a whole, management and employees working as a team. They may be applied for by any organization within the United Kingdom, the Channel Islands or the Isle of Man producing goods or services which meet the criteria for the awards. Eligibility is not influenced in any way by the particular activities, location or size of the unit applying. Units or agencies of central and local government with industrial functions, as well as research associations, educational institutions and bodies of a similar character, are also eligible provided that they can show they have contributed to industrial efficiency.

Each award is formally conferred by a grant of appointment and is symbolized by a representation of its emblem cast in stainless steel and encapsulated in a transparent acrylic block.

Awards are held for five years and holders are entitled to fly the appropriate award flag and to display the emblem on the packaging of goods produced in this country, on the goods themselves, on the unit's stationery, in advertising and on certain articles used by employees. Units may also display the emblem of any previous current awards during the five years.

Awards are announced on 21 April (the birthday of The Queen) and published formally in a special supplement to the London Gazette.

AWARDS OFFICE

All enquiries about the scheme and requests for application forms (completed forms must be returned by 31 October) should be made to: The Secretary, The Queen's Awards Office, 151 Buckingham Palace Road, London SW1W 9SS. Tel: 0171-222 2277.

EXPORT ACHIEVEMENT

The criterion upon which recommendations for an award for export achievement are based is a substantial and sustained increase in export earnings to a level which is outstanding for the products or services concerned and for the size of the applicant unit's operations. Account will be taken of any special market factors described in the application. Applicants for the award will be expected to explain the basis of the achievement (e.g. improved marketing organization or new initiative to cater for export markets) and this will be taken into consideration. Export earnings considered will include receipts by the applicant unit in this country from the export of goods produced in this country, the provision of services to non-residents, merchant profit on re-export of foreign goods and/or trade arranged between overseas countries and royalties and fees from abroad. Account will be taken of the overseas expenses incurred other than marketing expenses. Income from profits (after overseas tax) remitted to this country from the applicant unit's direct investments in its overseas branches, subsidiaries or associates in the same general line of business will be taken into account, but not receipts from profits on other overseas investments or by interest on overseas loans or credits. Commissions or fees received by applicants for selling UK goods or services overseas as agents for other UK firms are also regarded as eligible export earnings.

In 1999, The Queen's Award for Export Achievement was conferred on the following concerns:

Aggreko UK Ltd, Dumbarton – *generators and oil-free air compressors*

Akos Healthcare Group Ltd, St Albans, Herts – *international healthcare consultancy and contract services*

Allen and Overy, London EC4 *legal services*

Beardow and Adams (Adhesives) Ltd, Milton Keynes – *hot melt adhesives*

Belleek Pottery Ltd, Belleek, Co. Fermanagh – *Parian china giftware*

British Aerospace Airbus, Filton, Bristol – *Airbus airliner wing design and manufacture*

BUPA International, Brighton – *private medical insurance*

CRP Print and Packaging Ltd, Corby, Northants – *flexographic printing of packaging items*

Cambrian Consultants Ltd, Usk, Monmouthshire – *geoscience, engineering, training and software expertise to the oil and gas industry*

Cambridge Pharma Consultancy Ltd, Cambridge – *international management consultancy to the pharmaceutical industry*

Caterpillar (UK) Ltd, Telehandler Division, Desford, Leics – *telehandlers*

H. Charlesworth and Co. Ltd, t/a The Charlesworth Group, Huddersfield – *typesetting and printing of scientific journals*

Colortrac Ltd, Huntingdon – *large format digital colour scanners*

Compugraphics International Ltd, Glenrothes, Fife – *photomasks for the semiconductor industry*

Corney and Barrow (Broker Services) Ltd, London EC1 – *fine and rare wines*

Crambeth Allen Publishing, Craven Arms, Shrops – *technical periodicals*

Crystalox Ltd, Wantage, Oxon – *crystal growth equipment*

Data Connection Ltd, Enfield, Middx – *communications and networking software products and software engineering*

Digital Engineering Ltd, Mallusk, Belfast – *apparatus for developing and testing telecommunications equipment*

Dorset Cereals Ltd, Dorchester – *breakfast cereals*

Druck Ltd, Groby, Leics – *electronic pressure measurement devices, pressure calibrators and aircraft ground support equipment*

Durham Associates Group Ltd, Castle Eden, Co. Durham – *training in business administration*

Dytech Corporation Ltd, Sheffield – *catalysts and ceramic materials*

Edinburgh Business School, Edinburgh – *MBA distance learning courses*

Element Communications Ltd, Shaftesbury, Dorset – *sale of books and intellectual rights*

Elmar Services Ltd, Aberdeen – *design, manufacture and rental of oilfield equipment*

Equisys PLC, London SE1 – *Zetafax corporate fax software*

EuroFinance Conferences Ltd, London EC3 – *conference, exhibition and training course organisers in international cash and treasury management*

Euromoney Publications PLC, London EC4 – *financial publishers and conference organisers*

Evans and Sutherland Computer Ltd, Horsham, W. Sussex – *visual flight simulators*

The Financial Times Ltd, London SE1 – *newspaper publishing and advertising*

Fine Fragrances and Cosmetics Ltd, Hampton, Middx – *toiletries and cosmetics*

GAC (UK) Ltd, Cwmbran, Gwent – *aerosols for parties, celebrations and decoration*

GE Aircraft Engine Services Ltd, London W6 – *repair and overhaul of aircraft engines*

GEW (EC) Ltd, Redhill, Surrey – *ultra-violet curing equipment for printing machines*

Getty Connections Ltd, Carrickfergus, Co. Antrim – *cable assemblies and general equipment wire*

Glenmorangie PLC, Broxburn, W. Lothian – *malt and blended Scotch whisky*

Güralp Systems Ltd, Aldermaston, Berks – *seismometers*

H. D. A. Forgings Ltd, Redditch, Worcs – *specialist forgings*

Heatric (a division of Meggitt (UK) Ltd), Poole, Dorset – *highly compact printed circuit heat exchangers*

Hill Price Davison Ltd, London SW15 – *computer software and services*

Holton Machinery Ltd, Bournemouth – Holton Conform™ *continuous rotary extrusion machines*

John Horsfall and Sons (Greetland) Ltd, Halifax, W. Yorks – *airline blankets*

Huthwaite International, Rotherham, S. Yorks – *sales and management training consultancy*

Hydrovision Ltd, Dyce, Aberdeen – *underwater remotely operated vehicles*

IAI International Ltd, London EC4 – *investment management*

Ilmor Engineering Ltd, Brixworth, Northants – *CART and Formula One Mercedes Benz racing engines*

Innovative Technology Ltd, Oldham, Lancs – *banknote validation equipment*

Innovative Tooling Solutions (a division of Forth Tool and Valve Ltd), Glenrothes, Fife – *specialised machine tooling for controlled boring operations*

London City Airport, London E16 – *airport services*

Lowe Refrigeration Co, Carryduff, Belfast – *rental and sale of refrigerated display and storage equipment*

M4 Data Ltd, Wells, Somerset – *data storage devices*

The Macallan Distillers Ltd, Craigellachie, Moray – *Highland malt Scotch whisky*

MacDuff Shellfish (Scotland) Ltd, MacDuff, Aberdeenshire – *fresh and frozen shellfish*

McCormick Europe, Condiment Division, Paisley, Renfrewshire – *condiments and seasonings*

Motorola Ltd, GSM Systems Division, Swindon, Wilts – *cellular radio telephone equipment*

Owen Mumford Ltd, Medical Division, Woodstock, Oxon – *sterile medical disposables for capillary blood sampling and delivery systems for self-administration of injectable pharmaceuticals*

Nikwax Ltd, Wadhurst, E. Sussex – *waterproofing preparations for footwear, clothing, outdoor and equestrian equipment*

Norton Rose, London EC3 – *legal services*

Partridge Films (a division of HTV Ltd), Bristol – *natural history films*

Penny and Giles Drives Technology Ltd, Christchurch, Dorset – *electronic motor controllers for invalid wheelchairs and electric scooters*

Pilkington Micronics Ltd, Deeside, Clwyd – *processed glass for data storage and display*

Powder Systems Ltd, Liverpool – *pharmaceutical processing equipment, high containment and product protection systems for pharmaceuticals*

L. E. Pritchitt and Co. Ltd, t/a Pritchitt Foods, Bromley, Kent – *dairy and dairy alternative products*

Rig Design Services Ltd, London W1 – *engineering and design services*

Scherer DDS Ltd, Zydis Division, Swindon, Wilts – *fast dispersing tablets for prescription pharmaceuticals*

SciMAT Ltd, Swindon, Wilts – *battery separator components and filtration products*

Sea Air and Land Forwarding Ltd, London NW10 – *general merchanting and freight forwarding*

Snell and Wilcox Ltd, Petersfield, Hants – *equipment for broadcasting television studios, multimedia and telecommunications*

Software 2000 Ltd, Sandford-on-Thames, Oxon – *computer software*

Sonardyne International Ltd, Yateley, Hants – *underwater acoustic navigation positioning and telemetry equipment*

Specialist Refractory Services Ltd, Riddings, Derbys – *refractory mould materials*

Stannah Stairlifts Ltd, Andover, Hants – *electrically powered stairlifts*

Charles F. Stead and Co. Ltd, Leeds – *high quality suede leather for the shoe trade*

Svitzer Ltd, Great Yarmouth, Norfolk – *seabed and subseabed surveys for the oil and gas communications industries*

Technical Absorbents Ltd, Grimsby, Lincs – *man-made super-absorbent fibre*

Thermatool Europe Ltd, Basingstoke, Hants – *high frequency welding and annealing equipment and high speed shears*

Trans Euro PLC, London NW10 – *global move management, worldwide corporate relocation services, fire-safe secure storage and freight forwarding*

UK Project Support Ltd, Norwich – *specialist technical contract personnel*

University of Manchester Institute of Science and Technology (UMIST), Manchester – *research, teaching and technology transfer*

Walkers Shortbread Ltd, Aberlour-on-Spey, Moray – *shortbread*
Woods Air Movement Ltd, Colchester, Essex – *mechanical ventilation equipment*

TECHNOLOGICAL ACHIEVEMENT

The criterion upon which recommendations for an award for technological achievement are based is a significant advance, leading to increased efficiency, in the application of technology to a production or development process in British industry or the production for sale of goods which incorporate new and advanced technological qualities. An award is only granted for production or development processes which have achieved commercial success.

In 1999 The Queen's Award for Technological Achievement was conferred on the following concerns:

Acordis Speciality Fibres, Coventry, W. Midlands – *AQUACEL® Hydrofibre™ wound dressing*
AirSense Technology Ltd, Hitchin, Herts – *Stratos-HSSD incipient fire/smoke detection system*
ALSTOM Energy Ltd, Rugby, Warwickshire – *advanced 3-D steam turbine blading with improved efficiency for high power density applications*
Brunton's Propellers Ltd, Clacton-on-Sea, Essex – *'Autoprop' automatic variable pitch marine propeller*
ConvaTec Ltd, Deeside, Clwyd – *AQUACEL® Hydrofibre™ wound dressing*
Digital Engineering Ltd, Mallusk, Belfast – *design/development of ISDN central office simulators that emulate different country variants of ISDN telecoms worldwide*
Glaxo Research and Development Ltd, Greenford, Middx – *Diskus™ multidose dry powder inhaler*
Telecom Systems (a division of Hewlett-Packard Ltd), South Queensferry, W. Lothian – *HP acceSS7, the standard for SS7-based network monitoring and data-mining in telecoms*
Immunodiagnostic Systems Ltd, Boldon, Tyne and Wear – *determination of vitamin D in human serum and plasma*
Marathon Belting Ltd, Rochdale, Lancs – *COPSIL™ (a press compensating mat)*
Exhaust Gas Cooling (a division of Serck Heat Transfer Ltd), Birmingham – *exhaust gas cooler (for diesel emissions improvement)*
Snell and Wilcox Ltd, Petersfield, Hants – *MPEG compression pre-processor for high quality noise reduction/digital decoding of video signals*
The Technology Partnership PLC, Royston, Herts – *ChemScan® RDI for microbial detection and identification*
Zeneca Agrochemicals, Haslemere, Surrey – *AMISTAR fungicide*

ENVIRONMENTAL ACHIEVEMENT

The criterion upon which recommendations for an award for environmental achievement are based is a significant advance in the application by British industry of the development of products, technology or processes which offer major benefits in environmental terms compared to existing products, technology or processes. An award is only granted for products, technology or processes which have achieved commercial success. Applicants are expected to show the significance and difficulty of the environmental problem addressed, the extent to which the product, technology or process addresses the problem's cause as opposed to its effect, and the potential for wider application or transfer.

In 1999 The Queen's Award for Environmental Achievement was conferred on the following concerns:

Jesse Brough Metals Group, Hixon, Staffs – *recycling of furnace waste*
Esmil Process Systems Ltd, High Wycombe, Bucks – *zero discharge wood pulp effluent and water recovery system*
Exotherm Products Ltd, Cardiff – *energy efficient electrical heaters, 'Insulwatt'*
Synetix (a member of the ICI Group), Billingham, Cleveland – *HYDECAT™, a fixed-bed catalytic destruction technology for waste sodium hypochlorite*
Zeneca Metal Extraction Products, Blackley, Manchester – *novel magnesium-based process used in the manufacture of copper mining chemical, P50*

Science and Discovery

MOON'S IRON CORE

Even the tremendous amount of data received from the Apollo days did not provide sufficient evidence to convince astronomers that the Moon had an iron rich core. But recent observations from three different experiments have provided data which has now convinced most scientists that the Moon has such a core.

Evidence from NASA's Lunar Prospector, a satellite in orbit round the Moon was designed to provide a detailed map of the Moon's gravity and hence information on the structure of its interior. Alex S. Konopliv of the Jet Propulsion Laboratory and others have analysed the data sent back and have confirmed earlier suspicions that the core contains about 1 to 4 per cent of the lunar mass. If it consists of iron this corresponds to a diameter of 440 to 900 km.

Information has also been collected by studying the effect of the magnetic field induced within the Moon when the Moon passes through the Earth's magnetosphere each month. This induced field is very weak and can only be detected from the lunar surface or a close orbiting spacecraft. Even so the effect can only be detected if the geomagnetic field is strong and steady. A favourable situation arose with the Lunar Prospector in the Spring of 1998. Lon Hood and colleagues at the University of Arizona have put forward a diameter of between 600 and 850 km.

A third approach involved a careful measurement of lunar libration using laser light bounced off the special reflectors left by astronauts during the Apollo missions and the automated Soviet landers. Work carried out by James G. Williams and colleagues suggests that there is a liquid core of maximum diameter of 700 km and consisting of a mixture of iron nickel and sulphur with a melting point lower than 1000°C.

These data suggest that the Moon was formed after a large object grazed the primordial Earth, the impact blasting some of the planet's iron poor outer layers into orbit where they formed the Moon.

STELLAR PLANETARY SYSTEMS

Planetary systems are now being identified by an entirely new technique. American astronomers estimate that about 8 per cent of all Sun-like stars are likely to have Jupiter-sized planets associated with them. This estimate is based on the information gleaned from the light emitted from a star during its "red giant" phase, which lasts on an average about a few hundred million years.

Mario Livio and Lionel Siess of the Space Telescope Science Institute in Baltimore, Maryland have argued that Sun-like stars currently in their red giant phase in which any planets present would be in the process of being absorbed into the star itself should reveal this in three ways. Firstly the star would glow with an excess of infrared light due to the gravitational energy of the planet being absorbed by the star causing it to expand and shed its outer layers as shells of dust. Also the angular momentum transferred by the planet would speed up the spin of a normally slow rotating red giant to about 10 per cent of the escape velocity. This increase in rotational speed should be readily observable. Thirdly, the planet would contaminate the star with the element lithium, which does not survive at normal star temperatures.

Livio and Siess claim that many of the red giants show these features, up to 8 per cent of those examined, a figure in line with estimates from other lines of investigations. It is suggested by other workers that this is the best explanation for the origin of the lithium rich giants.

MULTIPLE PLANETARY SYSTEM DISCOVERED

Recently the first case of a multiple system of Jupiter-sized planets has been discovered. Two independent planet hunting teams have identified a system of at least three planets orbiting the star Upsilon Andromedae. The teams, from the Harvard-Smithsonian Centre for Astrophysics, the Anglo-Australian Observatory and the San Francisco State University monitored the tiny changes in the star's radial (line of sight) velocity caused by the planets as they circled the star. The innermost of the planets has been known since 1996. It has a mass of 0.7 that of Jupiter and orbits the star in 4.6 days. However the observed changes in the radial velocity of the star could not be explained solely by this planet. The fluctuations however were finally explained by a second planet twice as massive as Jupiter orbiting the star in eight months in a fairly elliptical orbit and also a third planet having a mass of about 4.6 that of Jupiter circling the star in 3.5 years also in a highly elliptical orbit.

Computer simulations of the system indicate that the system is very stable and that it could last for billions of years. The important implication of the discovery and the identification that the system is stable indicates that planetary systems could be quite a common feature. It is therefore felt that it will not be long before further multiple systems are discovered. There is already a possibility that a second case has been identified. The star Rho Cancri (55 Cancri) has been known since 1996 to have a Jupiter-sized planet in close orbit round the star but preliminary data suggests the existence of a further planet taking 10 to 15 years to go round.

TECTONIC PLATES ON MARS

Presently, there is no magnetic field on Mars but this has not always been the case. The data sent back by the Mars Global Surveyor implies that when the planet was young it had moving tectonic plates like that existing on the Earth today. The probe showed that there existed on the ancient southern highlands a pattern of parallel strips of land about 200 km across and 2000 km long in which the rocks were magnetized in alternating directions.

On the Earth, magma issuing from the mid-ocean rifts is magnetized by the Earth's magnetic field and as the rocks cool the direction of this magnetic field is frozen. Approximately every 300,000 years, the direction of the Earth's field reverses (see *Reversals in the Earth's Magnetic Field*), producing strips of rock with alternating polarities. This provided the key evidence for the theory of plate tectonics. The fact that similar magnetization has been found on Mars shows conclusively that at the time the rocks were formed, tectonic plates existed and that Mars had a magnetic field. What is also surprising is that the strength of the magnetic field which produced the magnetism in the rocks was found to be more than ten times the magnitude found in any terrestrial rocks. Jack Connorney of NASA's Space Flight Center says that an internal dynamo must have generated the field that magnetized the rocks when the planet was young. He is of the opinion that this condition lasted for at least half a billion years but after this the internal conditions which existed in the planet altered and the dynamo died. Since then any rocks formed have not been magnetized. It is thought that the earlier rocks preserved their magnetization because they contain iron rich minerals.

THE CHANGING SURFACE OF MARS

Many of the surface features on Mars are, according to the information sent back by Hubble's Wide Field Planetary Camera 2, not permanent features. Over long timescales many of the larger bright and dark marking seem to be fairly permanent but much of the smaller features appear to change considerably.

One of the largest storm systems ever seen in the northern hemisphere was recorded on 27 April 1999. The storm consisted of water-ice clouds and not the usual sand storms. At least three spiral bands of cloud circled counter-clockwise around a hollow core or 'eye' and was nearly three times larger than any similar storms seen by Viking Orbiters a couple of decades ago. The storm measured 1,760 km from east to west and 1,440 km north to south. The eye of the storm was 320 km across and the overall size of the storm was comparable to a terrestrial hurricane. Three days after Hubble photographed the storm, the Mars Global Surveyor could find no trace of the storm.

During the time that Mars was closest to the Earth, at the end of April and the beginning of May, being only 87 million kilometres away, Hubble took a series of four photos which when combined cover the whole of the planet. They showed that there had been substantial changes in the bright and dark markings when compared with the maps produced by the Viking Orbiters. It showed that some of the regions that were dark 20 years ago were now quite bright red and some areas that are bright red are now dark. It is thought that these changes are due to sand and dust blown about by the severe sand storms that are known to occur from time to time. The four images were taken during the Martian northern summer and they showed a very reduced size of the residual polar cap consisting of water ice. The telescope could resolve details as small as 19 km.

DYNAMIC URANUS

Very little was known about the planet Uranus prior to 1986 except that its spin axis was tilted at 98 degrees to the plane of its orbit round the Sun, which produces a very complicated system of heating and illumination over the surface. When the spacecraft Voyager 2 flew passed the planet in 1986, very little was learned to alter the general picture that the planet was a bland blue ball. The most striking fact to emerge from studies in the last few decades was that the planet had its own ring system.

Erich Karkoschka of the University of Arizona in Tucson has made a detailed study of the photographs sent back by Voyager 2. On the image taken on 23 January 1986, when the probe was 1 million kilometres from Uranus, he discovered the 18th moon of the planet. Its presence was confirmed by seven subsequent photographs taken during the fly-by. It is about 40 km in diameter and circles the planet in 15 hours and 18 minutes at a height of 51,000km above the cloud tops of Uranus.

The Hubble Space Telescope has also taken a time-lapse series of photographs of the planet. Uranus is now in a position in its orbit for the Sun to begin heating the mid-latitudes of the northern hemisphere after decades of winter and darkness. This area of the planet is now experiencing waves of very large storms, several thousands of kilometres in diameter. The associated clouds are very bright, probably the brightest in the outer regions of the Solar System. It is thought they are made of methane crystals. The movie also recorded a wobbling of the ring system, caused by the flattening of the planet's poles and the gravitational effect of its moons.

The tilt of the planet's spin axis produces strange affects on the visibility of its moon system. For the last quarter century the ten innermost satellites have been in constant sunlight but within two years they will all be entering the planet's shadow on each orbit.

THE FUTURE OF THE UNIVERSE

After years of discussions and arguments in which theories about the future of the Universe have come and gone, this last year has seen announcements that at last the whole problem has been solved and that the Universe will go on expanding for ever. Cosmologists have come to that conclusion based on observations indicating that supernovae in the distant parts of the Universe appear to be fainter than expected. This has been explained by the idea that the expansion of the Universe is speeding up because of a mysterious force, represented by a cosmological constant in Einstein's equations of general relativity, which can be described in general terms, as an antigravity force.

If this force does exist, it will mean that the Universe will gradually become emptier and consequently lonelier much faster than expected. But it will overcome the embarrassment of having stars older than the age of the Universe, a weakness in most earlier theories. Although many cosmologists accepted these new ideas not all were satisfied that it was correct. But the theory holds only if the distant supernovae are behaving in a similar manner to those much closer to us. Recently doubt has been expressed that this is not true. Supernovae which are caused by matter from one star falling onto a companion white dwarf star which subsequently becomes unstable and explodes fall into a standard pattern brightening over about 20 days and then fading slowly but the peak intrinsic brightness remains the same. This gives a method for estimating the distance of the supernova. Studies of these events in the far distant parts of the Universe showed that they were consistently fainter than predicted. Hence it was concluded that the Universe was expanding at a faster rate than that occurring in the closer regions.

However this explanation is not as watertight as originally thought. Studies of the light curves of the distant explosions have shown that they behave in a different way and that they reach their peak brightness two days earlier. The data collected is sufficiently different to question the accuracy of the above theory. So until this has been sorted out, cosmologists are back at square one.

LARGEST IMPACT CRATER IN SOLAR SYSTEM

Over the last few decades, space probes to all the main bodies of the Solar System that have solid surfaces have shown that since their formation these bodies have been subjected to intense bombardment, producing impact craters over a large range in size from just a few centimetres across to those several thousands of kilometres in diameter. Until recently the largest impact and deepest crater known was the South Pole-Aitken basin, about 2,300 kilometres in diameter lying near to the south pole of the Moon but on the Moon's far side. It is not visible from the Earth's surface but was discovered using instruments on board the Clementine spacecraft in 1994.

However, this crater pales into insignificance when compared with a feature on the planet Mars known as the Hellas basin. The team leader of the Mars Orbiter Laser Altimeter (MOLA), David Smith, describes it as very impressive and says that we have nothing like it on the Earth. MOLA obtained the elevation data by sending flashes of infrared light on to the Martian surface and timing how long it took for the reflected beam to bounce back to the spacecraft. Maps of Mars were constructed from this data over a period of two years and it was possible to measure altitudes to an accuracy of 13 metres.

The new maps showed that what was thought to be Hellas' main ring with a diameter of 2,300 kilometres actually lies on the inner slope about 2 km below the Martian equivalent of sea level. It appears that the true diameter is roughly 4000 km across and the feature is some 9 km deep. Markings on the floor of the crater seem to indicate that something flowed there in the past, but there is no evidence to suggest what this was.

SURPRISE LEONID PEAK

The Leonid meteor stream has been formed by debris ejected from comet 55P/Tempel-Tuttle and every year on about November 17 the Earth in its orbit round the Sun passes through the orbit containing this debris. In most years very little is seen but roughly every 33 years there occurs a major display of meteors. The Leonid meteoroids and the Earth travel round the Sun in opposite directions and so they tend to meet each other head on. Generally in meteor streams the particles are distributed round the whole of the orbit but in the case of the Leonids these are still concentrated near to the responsible comet. The comet passed through perihelion in February 1998 and the Earth arrived at the descending node of the comet on November 17 and it is then that we see the meteors. In similar circumstances in 1966, observers on the western side of America saw a storm of meteors, estimated at 150,000 per hour and it was hoped that something similar would happen in 1998. Although it could not be described as a storm, a spectacular display was seen on the night before the predicted date, some 16 hours early and virtually little activity at the expected time.

The reason for this early display has been explained by David Asher and Mark Bailey of Armagh Observatory in Northern Ireland and a Russian astronomer Vacheslav Emelyanenko. They are of the opinion that the Earth passed through a dense stream of large dust particles released from the comet in September 1333. These particles did not disperse in the normal way because of an orbital resonance with Jupiter. The comet makes 5 orbits round the Sun for every 14 revolutions of the planet creating conditions that restrict the dispersion of the particles.

It has been calculated that in November 1998, most of the resonant arcs within the stream missed the Earth except that of the 1333 release. There are hopes that astronomers will see good displays in 1999, peaking at about 0200 UT on November 18.

A SUPERNOVA NEAR TO THE EARTH

If a supernova occurred near to the Sun, then the effect on the Earth would be catastrophic. Even at a distance of 100 light years, the protective ozone layer would be stripped with dire results to life on the Earth. Nevertheless it is only to be expected that at least one event should have occurred during the lifetime of the Earth and scientists think they have found the evidence for such an event.

Gunther Korschinek, a physicist at the Technical University at Munich argued that iron-60 should be the easiest substance to identify. It is produced in great quantities in a supernova explosion and it is thrown out into interstellar space but otherwise there are few local sources. Sediments laid down over the last 13 million years and currently at a depth of 1300 metres were dredged up from the sea bed near to Mona Pihoa in the South Pacific Ocean. Using a specially designed mass spectrometer, they separated traces of iron-60 from nickel-60 a terrestrial isotope. These two isotopes have the same mass but the latter has two more protons so that it was possible to separate them by passing through a magnetic field. Significant quantities of the iron-60 were found in two relatively recent layers of the sediment. The scientists claim that cosmic ray and other sources could only account for a few per cent of the amount found. Since this isotope has a half-life of 1.5 million years it is thought that they originated fairly recently, about 5 million years ago.

ETA CARINAE STILL A MYSTERY

Although it is being monitored continuously by many observatories, the southern hemisphere star Eta Carinae is still presenting problems. The star is amongst the biggest and is thought by some astronomers that it will soon explode as a supernova, 'soon' being interpreted in an astronomical time scale. It lies about 7,500 light years away in the extreme southern sky and is about 4 million times brighter than our Sun. Although its spectrum is frequently monitored, it is not certain whether or not it is a single or double star. In addition it has so far not been possible to explain variations in its X-ray emission or in its visual spectrum, with changes which seem to occur every 5 and-a-half years. Observations using the Hubble Space telescope's spectrographs show that the star doubled in brightness between December 1997 and February 1999. Kris Davidson and colleagues at the University of Minnesota reported in an IAU Circular that this was the largest and most rapid brightening in the last 50 years and that the star is now brighter than it has been since it faded after its famous outburst just over 150 years ago. It is currently a 5th magnitude object. In 1843 it underwent a 20 year outburst, outshining the brilliant southern hemisphere star Canopus (magnitude -0.7) even though it was some 30 times more distant. It is believed that several solar masses were ejected before fading to leave the central star intact.

Antonella Nota of the Space Telescope Science Institute has attempted to construct a three-dimensional picture for the Eta Carinae nebula and her results, although only provisional, may throw some light on to the understanding of the star's structure. An appeal has been made for as many observers as possible to monitor the star and it is felt that there will be many more surprises before Eta Carinae is fully explained.

GAMMA RAY BURSTS

Powerful bursts of gamma rays have been observed for some time but because of their relatively short life it has until recently been impossible to study the bursts at other wavelengths. Success was finally achieved on 23 January 1999 as a result of the setting up of a special organization designed to activate a network of observers at a very short notice.

The intensity of the gamma ray bursts indicated that they must have originated during the occurrence of one of the most powerful explosions in the Universe. During such events the energy released in a few seconds rivals that released by the rest of the Universe combined. Because such bursts occur with no warning and last only for a few seconds, it was necessary for the orbiting spacecraft to detect the outburst quickly and transmit the information rapidly to base and then alert the appropriate observatories as fast as possible.

On 23 January 1999, NASA's orbiting Compton gamma ray observatory detected the beginning of an outburst. Approximate position was then determined and the information relayed to the Gamma Ray Burst Co-ordinates Network at the Goddard Space Flight Center. The position was then relayed to observatories globally. Within 22 seconds the Robotic Optical Transient Search Experiment at Los Alamos in New Mexico was operational and took images of the sky in the region of Bootes. The first frames showed a brightening new star and within 5 seconds the star had brightened to magnitude 9. Within 8 minutes the brightness had faded by a factor of over a hundred.

The burst occurred about 9 billion light years away, roughly half way to the edge of the visible Universe. This was the first time that the actual explosion had been seen. The cause of the explosions and the emission of Gamma Rays is still questionable but it is thought that it may be due to the merger of two neutron stars or two black holes or a so-called hypernovae.

PREDICTING CORONAL MASS EJECTIONS

Coronal Mass Ejections (CMEs) are possibly the most powerful explosions that can occur on the Sun, when billions of tons of plasma are propelled outwards from the Sun's surface in less than a day. This plasma is ejected at speeds of about a million kilometres per hour and takes about three to four days to cover the Sun-Earth distance. Several of these ejections may occur each day and if these occur on the face of the Sun pointing to the Earth and if the Earth happens to intercept one of these jets, then its effect on the Earth's magnetosphere can be catastrophic. The larger events can, for example, disrupt power grids, disrupt flowmeters in oil pipelines, interrupt short wave communications and damage satellites in orbit round the Earth. Recent discoveries indicate that it may be possible to predict the occurrence of a CME and hence give advance warning so that electrical equipment can be protected etc.

It has been found that quite often an 'S' shaped pattern appears on the Sun's surface prior to an explosion and may take several days to develop. This 'S' shaped pattern, known as a sigmoid, is an indicator of a magnetic disturbance on the Sun and is now known to be the forerunner of an eruption in that locality. The link was first noticed on 7 April 1997 when the X-ray monitor on the Japanese Yohkoh satellite detected an 'S' shaped hot spot in the southeast quadrant of the solar disc closely followed by the detection of a CME by the white light coronograph on board the SOHO satellite. Four hours later when the ejection was more or less over, the sigmoid drastically altered shape and then faded.

Two years of study of the Yohkoh images and CMEs have shown a very strong statistical link between the two phenomena. The size of the CME has also been found to be directly linked to the size of sunspots in these magnetically disturbed regions.

REVERSALS IN THE EARTH'S MAGNETIC FIELD

One of the methods for determining the age of rocks involves an examination of the direction of the residual magnetic field and its relationship to the magnetic fields of the surrounding rocks. The magnetic poles of the Earth can drift as much as 45 degrees from an earlier position and then may gradually return to its original position. In addition, approximately every 300,000 years the Earth's magnetic field spontaneously reverses direction. Whilst these changes are taking place, the strength of the field experienced on the Earth's surface can vary considerably over a few thousand years. A geologist at the University of Leeds, David Gubbins, claims that the magnetic field has lost about 50 per cent of that existing in Roman times.

Gubbins has put forward a theory that it is caused by the interplay between the Earth's inner solid core and the outer liquid core. He thinks that the fluid iron in the outer core is responsible for the wandering of the magnetic field experienced on the Earth's surface. The flow of this iron is about 10 to 20 km per year. This movement is resisted by the inner core and tends to make the outer core return to its original state. Occasionally the outer core's magnetization becomes too strong and forces the inner core to respond. The field reverses in the inner core causing the magnetic field over the whole of the Earth to reverse direction.

Work carried out by Gary Glatzmaier of the University of California at Santa Cruz claims that this explanation falls in line with the computer simulations of the magnetic changes. He believes that most of the changes occur in the outer core and that it takes time for these changes to reach the inner core. Generally they die out before the inner core is reached.

THE LENGTHENING DAY

It has been known for years that the Earth has been slowing down in rather an irregular manner. That is why present-day accurate time measurements are based on the atomic clock. Work carried out during the last few decades has shown that there are at least two possible major causes for this variation.

Research on ocean currents associated with the El Niño, has shown that they make the equatorial winds blow faster and hence increase the angular momentum of the atmosphere. To keep the principle of the conservation of momentum this extra component must come from the Earth's rotation, making it spin more slowly. Observations from orbiting satellites have shown that the El Niño of 1998 lengthened the day by about 0.4 milliseconds.

It has recently been shown that global warming also lengthens the day. This has been suspected for some time but work carried out by Rodrigo Abarca del Rio of the French Space Agency at Toulouse has shown that over the past 50 years, the average temperature of the Earth has risen at a rate of $0.79°C$ per century. By using American data for the winds over the same period he calculated that the angular momentum of the atmosphere had risen in step with the temperature rise. The resulting loss in angular momentum for the solid Earth has slowed the Earth's rotation by a rate of 0.56 milliseconds per century, about one third of the total recorded by scientists.

There are many other effects which can affect the rotation spin of the Earth but the data suggest that the results for global warming are large enough for future predictions. Every $0.1°C$ rise should produce a slowing down of 0.7 milliseconds. This increase in the length of a day could provide an independent measure for global warming confirming data collected by the standard methods of recording surface air temperatures.

COMPLEX HISTORY OF MAN

Many of the latest discoveries have been made on the African continent, especially in the areas around the Great Rift valley. Fossils of a new species of hominids have recently been found by anthropologists working in Ethiopia, Australopithecus garhi, making the evolutionary family tree even more complex.

Limb bones and a partial skull and teeth have been uncovered by an international team and the team also found in the vicinity antelope bones bearing cut marks made by stone tools. This suggests that Australopithecus garhi was a meat eater, the earliest known carnivorous hominid.

The fossils were found in sediments 2.5 million

years old, indicating that this new hominid lived roughly half a million years earlier that the previously recognized earliest meat eating hominid. Tim White, from the University of California at Berkeley, estimates that if the skeletons come from the same species the males were about 1.5 metres tall and the females about half a metre smaller. Measurements of the brain indicate that the size was about a third of that of modern man. The skull had a projecting muzzle and very large back teeth with molars some 17 mm across.

How this new hominid fits into the overall evolutionary picture is unknown. It could have subsequently become extinct or it could have become a direct ancestor of modern man. An anthropologist at the George Washington University in Washington DC has commented that this new discovery highlights the complexity of human evolution two to three million years ago. He commented that human evolution was just like the evolution of every other large mammal in Africa, a species rich story.

Modern Humans and Neanderthals

It was not long ago that it was thought that our own evolutionary history was closely linked to the Neanderthals and that Neanderthal man was thought to be the first European. The fact that they had bigger brains than ours and that they made stone tools, cared for their injured and buried their dead strengthened these ideas but subsequent research showed that such direct descent was flawed and most palaeoanthropologists dismissed this theory in favour of the 'Out of Africa' theory, in which all modern humans can trace their origins to a single African population, whose descendants, Cro-Magnons, spread across Europe some 40,000 years ago killing off the Neanderthals.

Modern discoveries have shown that the Neanderthals were not wiped out but absorbed through centuries of interbreeding with the larger Cro-Magnon population. It has been found that Neanderthal populations existed in both eastern and western Europe long after modern humans arrived. In addition, the discovery in Portugal of the skeleton of a hybrid four year old boy strengthens these new ideas.

Chris Stringer of the Natural History Museum in London, accepts the idea of a long coexistence of the two races, in spite of the DNA research two years ago which seemed to indicate that the Neanderthals were clearly on a dead-end branch of the family tree. But the DNA differences have been shown not to be significant. It is not known the degree of hybridization between the two races but there is plenty of evidence to show that they existed side by side in Europe for a very long time. Neanderthals are known to have existed in southern Spain and Portugal as recently as 30,000 years ago. At Zafarraya in Spain Neanderthals were still around some 8,000 years after the arrival of the Cro-Magnons. In addition the discovery of a

Neanderthal fossil in Croatia dated only 29,000 years ago is the youngest date known at the present time. Currently there is much research being carried out. The fact that evidence for Neanderthal technology and the Cro-Magnon's artistic achievements exist side by side provides much ammunition.

Estimating the Age of Human Remains

Much concern has been expressed by archaeologists over the last few years about the dating of fossil remains based on the state of skeletal development and the wear on bones and teeth. Based on this dating technique errors of as much as 30 years have been suspected, and the idea has developed that in the 11th century very few people lived beyond the age of 55 and even farther back in time the remains of neolithic man at a site in the Orkneys suggest that the mean life span was about 25. In addition studies at sites where human remains have been linked to other techniques for age determination a strong conflict of opinion has arisen and it appears that death at an early age is just a myth.

Mark Pollard and colleagues at Bradford University, working with Robert Aykroyd, a statistician at the University of Leeds, have come up with an explanations that accounts for the above discrepancies. It appears that the problem lies with the statistical method used to handle the information. In a technique known as linear regression, a graph is plotted of the wear on a bone joint against the age and then a line of best fit is drawn and from this line an age is determined from the wear noted on bones from other sites. Unfortunately the technique can give erroneous results if the correlation between age and bone wear is not good.

Pollard said that if the correlation is low then, there is a tendency to underestimate the ages of the older people in the population that is being studied. It has been found that bones thought to be coming from a 40 year old were actually from a 70 year old. This realization has solved many problems. For example, the bones of the 7th-century Mayan king Hanab Pakal were originally thought to have come from someone in his 40s. Yet the inscriptions on the tomb indicated that the king was 80 when he died. This new work on regression techniques could have surprising results in other fields of study, for example the records of past climates.

Polynesian Colonization of the Pacific

Until recently it has not been possible to provide a satisfactory explanation for the way the Polynesians successfully navigated across thousands of miles of open water in small canoes. Two contrasting theories have been put forward, neither of which had much scientific evidence for support. One theory proposed that the colonization was a gradual process, lasting many thousands of years. The rival theory claims that it was a fairly rapid expansion to the islands, lasting just a couple of centuries, and involved a single stock of people from South-East Asia. Archaeological, linguistic and generic research of present day Polynesians has provided a range of dates when it is thought each island was first colonized.

An evolutionary biologist, Christopher Austin, from the South Australian Museum in Adelaide, has now provided evidence to suggest the latter of these two theories is correct. A generic analysis of a lizard found on the islands, Lipinia noctua, seems to have solved the mystery. It is about 5 cm in length, spends much of its time hiding under the bark of trees and it could easily have lived in the wood used for making the canoes. He studied 29 lizards from different islands in the pacific, covering an area from Palau in the west to Tuamotu in the east, and found that they were so similar to each other that they must have developed very recently from a common population. They were nearly genetically identical, demonstrating that there was a very rapid colonization in the Pacific. The outstanding mystery is still how did they manage to navigate over such huge distances?

The Early Australians

Until about 10 years ago, it was generally thought that the Aborigines first landed on the mainland of Australia about 40,000 years ago. However, in 1990 Bert Roberts of La Trobe University in Melbourne estimated the age of some manufactured pigment from Malakunanja in Arnhem Land and suggested that it was more likely to have been between 50,000 and 60,000 years ago. In 1996, David Price of the University of Woolongong in NSW gave a date of 176,000 years based on rock art at Jinmium in the Northern Territory. This has now been rejected and archaeologists appealed for dates based on human remains rather than artefacts.

A skeleton excavated in 1974, known as Mungo Man, from the Willandra Lakes of New South Wales has now been studied in detail. The original age of 30,000 years was based on radio carbon dating, which is very unreliable for samples of this age. Scientists at the Australian National University have now used three different techniques and all have come up with consistent results. One team led by Rainer Grun used the radioactive decay of uranium isotopes. They also used electron spin resonance to date the teeth of the skeleton. Electrons in buried teeth become excited into higher energy levels with time due to the radio active elements in the surrounding sediments. A result of 62,000 years was obtained with an accuracy of 6,000 years. Nigel Spooner, however, used an optically stimulated luminescence technique which measures the cumulative exposure to radiation of the buried sample, derived an age of 61,000 years with a possible error of 2,000 years.

Alan Thorne also of ANU, and who excavated the Mungo Man, is of the opinion that it would have taken several thousand years for people to adapt to the conditions in the interior of Australia and so he thinks that man arrived in Australia much earlier than the age indicated by Mungo Man.

Dinosaur Embryos

Scientists have discovered thousands of dinosaur eggs buried in an ancient flood plain at a site near to Auca Mahuida in Patagonia, Argentina. It is thought that a river of mud engulfed the dinosaur nesting site about 90 million years ago, the silt protecting the eggs from erosion and scavengers. About a dozen eggs were found intact which contained dinosaur embryos. The eggs are almost spherical with a diameter of about 15 centimetres. An examination of these embryos has shown that in addition to the skin of the animal a streak of scales appears to run down the back of the embryos.

Lowell Dingus, a research worker at the American Museum of Natural History in New York, is of the opinion that the scales ran down the animal's backbone. In addition this is the first time that scientists have been able to see what these animals looked like before being hatched. One specimen had at least 22 pencil-like teeth some 2 mm long. It is thought that these have the same shape as those of sauropod dinosaurs known as titanosaurs. Sauropods had very long necks and tails, a fully grown animal being about 15 metres in length from nose to tail and weighing several tons. Dr Dingus commented that at the time of hatching the dinosaur would have been about 40 cm in length.

Fish-Eating Dinosaur

A virtually complete skeleton of a fish-eating dinosaur has been found in fossil beds in the Tenere Desert, Niger. Its size rivals that of the largest carnivore, Tyranosaurus rex, but it had claws the size and shape of giant meat-hooks. This suggests that as well as size it rivalled T. rex in ferocity.

It has been given the name Suchomimus tenerensis, after its crocodile like skull and the place where it was found. It is a member of the piscivore group, the spinosaurids, which had long narrow jaws containing cone shaped teeth. They also had a sail-like fin running down their backs. This new species stood on its hind legs and was over 10 metres in length. Oliver Rauhut of the University of Bristol believes that the narrow snout enabled the animal to swim quickly and its teeth would have enabled it to hold the prey in a similar way to a modern crocodile. Together with the prominent thumb claws, this suggests that it was fish eating. The largest claws measured 35 cm along the outer curve and were attached to very strong forelimbs. He said that they were used for hunting slightly larger prey or slicing up carcasses.

The team leader, Paul Sereno, a palaeontologist at the University of Chicago says that it is one of the most significant discovery in the understanding of how dinosaurs spread round the world. The fossil was found in an area covered by swampy forests in the Cretaceous period, about 120 million years ago. At that time Africa and South America were merged together in a single supercontinent Gondwanaland and separated from the giant northern continent

Laurasia by the Tethys Sea. The finding will provide data on the traffic across the Tethys Sea during the Cretaceous period. Suchomimus appears to be more closely related to the northern fish eaters, the Baronyx, than to the southern spinosaurids found in Egypt and Brazil.

World's Oldest Whale

The discovery of a fossilized jawbone of what is thought to be the world's oldest whale has shed new light on the evolution of one of the most successful group of sea mammals. It was found in the foothills of the Himalayas. The fossil has been dated to about 53.5 million ago, at which time that part of the world which now contains the Himalayas was a sea separating two ancient continents.

This new whale, called Himalayacetus subathuensis, lived about 3.5 million years before the previous oldest known member of the whale family. These early members of the whale family lived a semi-aquatic life in river estuaries and shallow seas before evolving into a completely marine environment. It is thought that H. subathuensis lived in water but returned to dry land to rest and breed.

Philip Gingerich, of the University of Michigan, and Sunil Bajpai, of the University of Roorkee in northern India, have studied the jawbone and found that it contained teeth, indicating that the whale was adapted to eat fish. Of significance is the fact that the fossil was found in a layer of sediments associated with marine animals not those linked with fresh water species.

This new species is considerably older than Pakicetus which has also been linked with the Tethys Sea which separated Asia from the Indian subcontinent before they collided to form the Himalayas. Pakicetus is though to have been the ancestor of the first whale, archaeocetus, about the size of a modern porpoise, a fish eater and lived some 35 million years ago. This new discovery extends the fossil record of Cetacea further back in time but strengthens the belief that whales originated in the margins of the Tethys sea and also the theory that these early whales were amphibians entering the sea to feed.

Archaeocetus had two non-functional hind legs and it is thought that the earlier species had limbs which allowed them to move over land. It seems that evolutionary processes removed the need for these limbs allowing the whales to exploit the abundant food found in the oceans.

Europe Cooled by Melting Ice

At the end of the Ice Age some 10,000 years ago, two large lakes of fresh water formed in central Canada when the melting ice from the great North American ice sheet was trapped by ice in the Hudson Bay region of northern Canada. These lakes existed for about 2000 years but the build up of pressure of the water caused the ice to give way. The water rushed through the Hudson Strait into the Atlantic Ocean. Evidence for this surge exists as a half a metre of sediment still present on the sea bed of the Hudson Strait.

Donny Barber and colleagues of the University of Colorado have studied these sediments and also those lying immediately above. Plankton trapped in the sediment from that time show that the salinity of the water in the Labrador Sea between Greenland and Canada fell dramatically. From their calculations they estimate that some 200,000 cubic kilometres of water poured into the Atlantic Ocean raising sea levels world wide by about 30 centimetres. The volume of water can be compared with the total volume of the water currently in the North Sea. The outpouring disrupted the normal circulation of the oceans and caused a drop in temperature of about 3 degrees celsius in Europe. The theory is certainly in line with a puzzling fact that at that time there had been a sudden unexplained drop in temperature.

Under normal circumstances seawater in the North Atlantic freezes during the winter. This ice does not contain the salt so that the remaining water becomes increasingly saline and being denser sinks to the bottom of the ocean. The warmer water from the south pours in to replace it and in doing so has the effect of keeping Europe warmer. However the huge increase of fresh water upset this circulation and hence the temperature in Europe fell. It is estimated that it took about 350 years before conditions reverted back to normal.

Understanding Tornadoes

Each year tornadoes strike the Mid-west of the United States but 1999 seems to have produced the most devastating 'twisters' for many years. Oklahoma City was devastated by one of a series which tore through its residential areas killing 47 people and destroying 2,000 homes. Scientists have for years been trying to collect data from these storms so that eventually a prediction centre can be set up. This year they have been successful in getting the raw data and it is thought that a reliable warning service may be possible in the near future.

These tornadoes are caused when warm moist air from the Gulf of Mexico is drawn northwards over the plains of central America and meets and runs underneath dry cool air from the Arctic travelling in the opposite direction. This condition is highly unstable and the warm air rises through the cool dry air causing the moisture to condense forming hail or rain. The latent heat produced by this condensation makes the warm air rise high still, creating conditions leading to the formation of supercells, strongly rotating updrafts of air containing severe thunder storms. Meteorologists track these anticlockwise rotating clouds but cannot say whether they will produce tornadoes. Only 20 per cent of these supercells actually produce tornadoes and only when they have been seen reaching the ground can they give a definitive warning.

Joshua Wurman of the University of Oklahoma and colleagues took two trucks fitted with Doppler radars and intercepted the twister that hit Oklahoma City . They measured the highest wind speed ever recorded-512 kilometres per hour- and also collected data for nearly half an hour on a tornado measuring more than 1.5 km in diameter with peak wind speeds of about 320 km per hour. Another team headed by Howard Bluestein of the same University obtained data on the region where the tornado funnel actually reached the ground.

TURNING DIAMONDS INTO METAL

On the face of it, it does not seem sensible to destroy a valuable gem by turning it into metal, but the knowledge gained by understanding the processes involved in doing it may have important implications in the study of the interior of stars.

A diamond is chemically classed as a non-metal because its electrons cannot flow freely but by using a laser designed for nuclear weapon research it has been found possible to subject the diamond to a sufficiently high pressure to cause it to behave like a metal.

A team led by Gilbert Collins of the Lawrence Livermore National Laboratory in California, using the world's most powerful laser, have focused several blue light beams from the Nova laser on to an aluminium target holding a small diamond. The shock wave set up by the laser's energy penetrated the metal and the diamond subjecting them to pressures of millions of atmospheres. Suddenly the diamond was thought to have melted and it started to reflect light in a manner similar to that of a metal. It is thought that at this stage the diamond was compressed into a metallic state where its electrons could flow freely.

The behaviour of the diamond at these super high pressures may be similar to the behaviour of carbon at the centres of dense stars such as those existing in white dwarfs, which form when stars similar to the Sun run out of fuel. A study of the properties of melted diamonds might lead to a better understanding of the conditions existing in the cores of high density stars.

CODED MESSAGES USING DNA

The techniques for cracking a code is becoming exceedingly complex. The secret agent must be confident that his messages to base are getting through without being intercepted. Even during the last war the methods of transmitting messages became very sophisticated. The Germans used a microdot technique in which the text was contained in circular photographs roughly the size of a full stop placed at the end of a sentence.

This method appears crude compared with that currently being developed. A team headed by Carter Bancroft, a biophysicist at the Mount Sinai School of Medicine in New York have developed a technique for storing hidden messages in a tiny smear of DNA.

Each letter is assigned to a triplet of DNA bases. For example the letter A was represented by CGA

and Y by AAA. Hence the team converted the message 'June 6 invasion: Normandy' into a strand of DNA. They then put a 10 base-pair tag at each end of the message strand. The message carrying DNA strand is then mixed with ordinary human DNA and smeared on to a piece of paper. It is virtually impossible to detect the message as it hidden by the 'noise' of the ordinary DNA.

The intended recipient of the message will know the sequence of the tags at the end of the message and can use the polmerase chain reaction to copy and recopy several times the message carrying strands until the molecules with the message greatly outnumber the junk DNA and can then be read. At the moment the laboratory equipment needed to code and decode the messages have not been miniaturized sufficiently for practical use but it is fairly certain that this will not present too big a problem once the other practical difficulties have been sorted out.

RATIO OF THE BIRTHS OF THE SEXES

It has been thought for some time that there were seasonal variations in the ratio of boys to girls born in a given population but no satisfactory explanation had been put forward. Experiments carried out on rats has suggested that environmental temperatures may have an affect on the sex ratio of the offspring. Work carried out in Germany may have provided the explanation for this variation in humans.

Alexander Lerchl of the University of Munster examined the average monthly temperatures in Germany between 1946 and 1995 from data supplied by National Climatic Data Center in Asheville, North Carolina. He extracted the months when it was unseasonably hot and cold and compared these with the German records for births for the same fifty years to see if there was any correlation between temperature and the sex ratio of the births. He found that the sex ratio seemed to correlate with temperature about a month before conception. Cold weather seemed to favour girls and hot and unseasonably warm spells favour boys, with only just a few degrees centigrade producing the difference. Lerchl has suggested that the temperature may affect processes within the testes. He thinks that this is due to processes when the father-to-be's sperm starts maturing. He speculates that hot spells may damage sperm carrying an X chromosome more than that carrying the Y chromosome and hence more boys are conceived.

This small bias could have important implications in so far that global warming could increase the ratio of boys to girls even further. But Lerchl also pointed to the possibility that warm weather made people have sex more often which increases the woman's chance of conceiving as soon as she ovulates. Sperm carrying a Y-chromosome are faster although less robust than X-carriers which stand a better chance if they have to wait for ovulation.

HYPERICIN AND SUNLIGHT

Research workers in the United States have found that people taking St John's Wort as an antidepressant should avoid going into bright sunlight. It has been found that hypericin, the active ingredient in St John's Wort, reacts with visible and ultraviolet light to produce free radicals which may damage those proteins in the eye which give the eye its transparency. The damaged proteins precipitate out of solution and make the lens cloudy, producing a cataract. Fortunately this reaction does not take place when not exposed to bright light.

This limitation in the use of hypericin is of great importance for sufferers of seasonal affective disorders (SAD), who combine its use with light-box therapy. Joan Roberts of Fordham University in New York says that the use of the drug should never be used in conjunction with light-box therapy. She has also said that all users should be warned of the risks especially if taking the herb whilst at the beach or water skiing. Similar advice is also given by German researchers who also recommend that the use of tanning beds should be avoided whilst taking the herb. However a London based psychiatrist claims that he has received no complaints from his patients about the side effects while taking St John's Wort.

Geoffrey Bove, a neurophysiologist at the Harvard Medical School, in a report published in The Lancet describes how he has treated a patient who developed intense pain in areas exposed to the Sun whilst taking St John's Wort. He is of the opinion that the free radicals generated by the hypericin damage the patient's nerve cells.

Hypericin's reaction to sunlight is being investigated as a possible treatment for some forms of skin cancer. It may be possible to use the side-effect as a potential therapy for killing cancer cells, says Roberts.

TREES UNDER ATTACK FROM FUNGI

Many species of trees are being threatened by epidemics of fungal diseases the epidemics being usually caused by introduced pathogens which quickly wipe out native species which have no natural resistance to them. This was the case in the 1970s when the Dutch Elm disease virtually wiped out the elm from the British countryside. Until recently there was no evidence to support the idea that introduced species were exchanging genes with either resident fungi or even other exotic fungi. Now however it has been found that an unnatural union between two fungi has produced a very aggressive disease which is playing havoc with alders over most of Europe.

Two species of Phytophthora, relatives of the potato blight, have hybridized to produce lethal fungi which destroy the bark around the base of the alders and finally kill the trees. The disease was first noticed in 1993 and Clive Brasier and colleagues at the Scottish Crop Research Institute at Invergowrie used DNA techniques to identify the fungus. They found signatures from two distinct species, indicating that it was a hybrid. It is very rare for fungi to hybridize in nature because species that live in the same environment have evolved barriers to prevent it happening. But if they are geographically isolated then there are no barriers to prevent hybridization.

Subsequent research has identified the two parents of the responsible hybrid. One of them affects some trees but not alders. The other is similar to strawberry and raspberry blight. But the hybrids of these two parents vary considerably both in structure and behaviour in different parts of Europe and in some cases have reproductive abnormalities. Brasier is of the opinion that the pathogen is still evolving and is unsure of the way this will develop.

Currently the disease has claimed 10 per cent of the Alder population and is killing a further 2 per cent each year. Alders are a key species in wetlands and along river banks where they have a stabilizing function.

Theatre

Star power continued to fuel London theatres in 1998–9. This was most spectacularly true in the case of *The Blue Room* at the Donmar Warehouse, an adaptation by David Hare of Arthur Schnitzler's infamous turn-of-the-century play *Reigen*, better known as the film *La Ronde*. Schnitzler describes a merry-go-round of sexual encounters in which the men have little and the women much to lose. For Sam Mendes' chic production of Hare's lighter, contemporary version, the Hollywood star Nicole Kidman was paired with the Scottish actor Iain Glen. In an acting *tour de force*, they played all the parts from au pair to politician's wife and cab driver to playwright. The whole evening was memorably described by Charles Spencer, the *Daily Telegraph* critic, as 'pure theatrical Viagra'. The production transferred to Broadway although the critics there were less seduced.

STARRY STRUGGLE

For the Hampstead Theatre's production of *Little Malcolm and His Struggle against the Eunuchs*, tickets were reportedly changing hands for £200. The attention here was centred on Ewan McGregor, the star of films such as *Trainspotting*, *Velvet Goldmine* and, more recently, the new *Star Wars* prequel, playing Malcolm Scrawdyke in David Halliwell's play directed by McGregor's uncle Denis Lawson. First performed in 1965, the play anticipates the student rebellions that were to come in its story of Scrawdyke's plot to take revenge on the head of the art college in Huddersfield from which he has been expelled. Lawson's production and Rob Howell's design brilliantly recreated the early '60s world of bedsits, jazz, duffle coats and gas fires.

The Almeida Theatre in Islington had been the first to realize the potential of asking a new breed of young film stars to appear on London's stages when it cast Ralph Fiennes as Hamlet in the East End. It now invited Cate Blanchett, the Australian star of the film *Elizabeth*, to play the leading part of Susan Traherne in a revival of David Hare's *Plenty*. Hare's play explores the moral bankruptcy of post-war Britain leading up to the debacle of Suez. Traherne, an undercover agent working in France during the war, finds that life loses its meaning once the war is over. The production was one of a season of plays produced by the Almeida at the Albery Theatre in the West End. In the event, neither Blanchett nor Hare were seen at their best. Although the play is still of interest in its linking of Traherne's personal unhappiness with the political state of the country, her hysteria is so highly pitched that it is easier to feel sympathy for her long-suffering husband than for Traherne. Jonathan Kent's intense production needed a lighter touch. It was, however, beautifully designed by Maria Bjornson, flicking with filmic fluency through both time and Europe.

UNHAPPY COUPLE

The pitfalls of star casting were illustrated earlier in the year when *Antony and Cleopatra* opened at the Royal National Theatre with Helen Mirren and Alan Rickman in the title roles. Mirren had played the role twice before with great success and there was every reason to believe that this sensual actress would work well with Rickman's dishevelled Antony. Sean Mathias's ponderous production opened in October 1998; apart from faults in staging, inept verse speaking, and the fact that Rickman was barely audible, it was most noticeable that there was no chemistry between the two lovers at all. Significantly, Mirren's performance improved dramatically once Rickman's Antony died.

In the West End, older film fans were offered Richard Dreyfuss and Margery Mason making their London début at the Theatre Royal Haymarket, cracking the one-liners in Neil Simon's *The Prisoner of Second Avenue*. Both actors are still remembered for their performances in the film of Simon's *The Goodbye Girl*. Even older fans could enjoy Charlton Heston and his wife in the dreadfully static *Love Letters*.

At at the time of writing, almost every theatre in London is up for sale. Apollo Leisure, which owns the Lyceum in London and most of the major touring theatres in the provinces, was sold to the American giant SFX in August 1999. After a successful takeover bid, the Crescent Theatres (including Wyndhams, the Albery, the Comedy and the Donmar) were put up for sale for £20 million. This was followed by the shock announcement by Janet Holmes a Court, head of Heytesbury, that Stoll Moss was also going on the market, all ten theatres, including the Theatre Royal Drury Lane, Her Majesty's and the London Palladium, to be sold together for £100 million. It is thought that SFX will be prevented by the Competition Commission from also acquiring Stoll Moss.

Policy has changed in the West End as well as owners. More adventurous work was staged at the Albery, the New Ambassadors and the Whitehall. The Almeida took over the Albery and, as well as *Plenty*, daringly presented revivals of Racine's *Britannicus* and *Phèdre* and Gorky's *Vassa*. In a translation by Ted Hughes that matched grandeur with economy, Diana Rigg played the doomed *Phèdre*, guiltily in love with her stepson, Toby Stephens' Hippolytus. Later, Sheila Hancock played the monstrous mother in *Vassa*, a representative of the grasping merchant class living in a provincial town on the Volga. Determined to keep the family business going, she ruthlessly dominates her family including her son, a whining hunchback, played at the Albery by David Tennant.

NEW THEATRE

A new development was also seen at the Ambassadors, which was one of the homes of the Royal Court during its influential sojourn in the West End. During the Royal Court's tenancy, it refused to compromise its programming and consequently proved that it was possible to attract new, demanding audiences into theatres. Once the Royal Court left, Friedman renamed the theatre the New Ambassadors and opened with two productions: *Holy Mothers*, a scatological black comedy by Werner Schwab in a translation by Meredith Oakes; and *Sell Out*, a devised performance piece by Frantic Assembly. In Schwab's satirical feast of stools, three working-class women share their fears and fantasies in a hideous high-rise flat in Austria. The play gives verbal diarrhoea a whole new meaning, but Richard Jones' production was far too strained to be funny in spite of a moving performance from Paola Dionisotti as Greta. Frantic Assembly, an enormously popular company who probably never expected to play in the West End, followed with late night performances of their award-winning *Sell Out*, a highly physical, exciting account of the end of a love affair.

The Whitehall Theatre was occupied by the Oxford Stage Company under the direction of Dominic Dromgoole. Dromgoole, who produced new plays for Peter Hall when he was established at the Old Vic, was invited to run a season at the theatre under terms that allowed a certain degree of risk. The season opened with a revival of Robert Holman's 1986 tender, elegiac triptych *Making Noise Quietly* about the impact of war on those indirectly involved. Holman, already a highly regarded dramatist in subsidized theatre, made his début in the West End in a production headed by Eleanor Bron. Dromgoole's own fresh, spontaneous production of *Three Sisters* followed in an abrasive translation by Samuel Adamson and with a cast of young actresses who will surely be stars in the future. Claudie Blakley played Masha as a swearing, uninhibited, manic depressive; Kelly Reilly was a delicate Irina and Claire Rushbrook a sympathetic, wounded Olga.

Sir Peter Hall and the West End producer Bill Kenwright launched a season at the Piccadilly Theatre, opening with Eduardo de Filippo's comedy *Filumena* with Judi Dench both tough and touching as the ex-prostitute and mistress of Michael Pennington's Domenico for 25 years. Hall returned to the Old Vic, now run by a trust, and opened *Amadeus* with David Suchet and Michael Sheen as Salieri and Mozart respectively. The play did well at the box office, but Hall's plans for a company needed financial backing and he went to the Arts Council to ask for £500,000. He was turned down and later announced that he was leaving England to set up an American Shakespeare Company in Los Angeles and to teach over there. However, he did return later in the year to direct *Lenny*, a play about the life of Lenny Bruce with Eddie Izzard as the blistering comic who was always falling foul of the obscenity laws.

MONEY WORRIES

Frustratingly, although extra money was given to the arts, much of it has been held back for particular schemes dear to the Arts Council's heart such as new audiences and education, instead of being delivered to the theatres which desperately need to replenish their core funding. Hall and others set up a 'Shadow Arts Council' with the intention of representing the views of those who actually work in the theatre rather than the bureaucrats.

Two plays written by women made their mark this year. *The Memory of Water* by Shelagh Stephenson transferred from Hampstead to the Vaudeville with Samantha Bond, Alison Steadman and Julia Sawalha as three very different sisters reunited for their mother's funeral and raking over their very different perceptions of the past. This was followed by Liz Lochhead's comedy *Perfect Days* first seen at the Traverse in Edinburgh, then at Hampstead before it too moved into the Vaudeville with Siobhan Redmond, for whom it was written, as the Glaswegian celebrity hairdresser who at 39 is desperate to have a baby and increasingly willing to resort to extreme tactics.

The centenary of Noel Coward's birth was celebrated with a number of revivals around the country, most notoriously Declan Donnellan's of Coward's 1925 comedy *Hay Fever* which after a tour ended up at the Savoy. Donnellan, highly respected for his work with the touring company Cheek by Jowl, had two significant successes abroad during the year: firstly his production of *The Winter's Tale* for the Maly Theatre in St Petersburg which was also seen at the Lyric Hammersmith and which won a prestigious award in Russia; and secondly, his acclaimed production in France of Pierre Corneille's classic *Le Cid*. *Hay Fever*, however, with Geraldine McEwan as Judith Bliss, was less applauded. Donnellan took a number of liberties with the text including beginning, not with the Bliss's bohemian house in the country, but rather with a performance of the Victorian melodrama *Love's Whirlwind* in which Bliss is supposed to have made her name. The heavy-handed comedy that followed was hard to laugh at. Coward traditionalists were appalled and even those who didn't in principle feel that the text should be sacrosanct were not amused.

MUSICALS

Revivals and compilations dominated the scene. The lyricist Martin Charnin revived *Annie* at the Victoria Palace and *West Side Story* came into the Prince Edward in an over-faithful reproduction of the original production. More happily, Trevor Nunn's production of *Oklahoma!* moved from the

Lyttelton into the Lyceum and was just as popular in Covent Garden as it had been on the South Bank. Vivian Ellis and A.P. Herbert's 1947 musical *Bless the Bride* was revived at the tiny King's Head with the veteran actress Judy Campbell in the cast and also directed by Martin Charnin. The romantic nonsense of A.P. Herbert's story is redeemed by Vivian Ellis' songs.

Lloyd Webber closed *Starlight Express* and Cameron Mackintosh announced the impending closure of *Miss Saigon*. *Dr Doolittle* also folded after a respectable run. A rare new opening was that of *Mamma Mia!*, based on 22 hit songs by Abba woven into a story by the playwright Catherine Johnson and directed by Phyllida Lloyd. Catchy and enjoyable, *Mamma Mia!* wallows in the '70s with plenty of platform shoes and white lycra. Cleverly, it appeals to those who were Abba fans in the past and also manages to win over a whole new generation of fans. In complete contrast, *Jackie – An American Life*, based on the life of Jacqueline Onassis, was crucified by the critics and joined those London musicals that have become famous for the brevity of their run. A summer dominated by compilation musicals such as *4 Steps to Heaven, Oh What a Night* and *Soul Train* also, at last, welcomed into the West End *Forbidden Broadway*, the revue that has been sending up the musicals of Sondheim, Boublil-Schonberg and Andrew Lloyd Webber for years in America.

TEN OF THE BEST

The Royal National Theatre looked forward to the Millennium by asking more than 800 actors, directors, politicians and critics to select their ten best plays written in English in the last 100 years. Each playwright was allowed only one play, so that the final list covered a wide spectrum from *The Mousetrap* to *The Birthday Party* and included *The Weir*, currently running in the West End. Samuel Beckett's *Waiting for Godot* came out on top, with Arthur Miller's *Death of a Salesman* and Tennessee Williams' *A Streetcar Named Desire* behind. Throughout the year, early evening platform performances were devoted to each of the plays, including the reading of extracts and talks with many of the people who were involved in the original productions. *Look Back in Anger* came in at number four and was given a major revival at the National with Michael Sheen as Jimmy Porter and Emma Fielding as his long-suffering wife. Instead of focusing on Jimmy's confusing politics, Gregory Hersov's fine production and Sheen's gripping performance concentrated on Porter's despair, vulnerability and self-hatred; also on the misery of marital pain as Fielding revealed the aggression of Alison's silence as she soaks up his anger behind the ironing board. A play that has often seemed too wordy and old-fashioned in its structure and unworthy of its historical importance was once more hailed as a masterpiece.

Noel Coward's centenary was celebrated in the Lyttelton theatre with a production of *Private Lives*

by Philip Franks with Juliet Stevenson making a rare foray into comedy as Amanda and Anton Lesser as Elyot. Although Franks' production took no liberties with the text, it did reveal a darker, more Strindberg-like side to a comedy so often revived that audiences could probably prompt the actors if they forgot their lines. Earlier, on the same stage, Terry Johnson directed his own nostalgic tribute to the world of the *'Carry On'* comedies with Geoffrey Hutchings as Sid James, Adam Godley as Kenneth Williams, and Samantha Spiro as Barbara Windsor. All set in Sid James' trailer and full of wonderfully horrible jokes in the first half, it became darker and more elegiac in the second.

TROILUS AND CRESSIDA

Trevor Nunn, the new artistic director of the National, created a company of 40 actors contracted to the theatre for a year. He opened with *Troilus and Cressida* in the Olivier, a production in which the Trojans were all played by black actors and the Greeks by white actors. The circular stage was covered in red earth and lit by flickering flames. Roger Allam made a cynical, often cruelly funny Ulysses and Sophie Okonedo an astute and vulnerable Cressida. The production introduced alterations by John Napier to the theatre's space, bringing the seating closer to the action in an attempt to make the Olivier more intimate.

The company's next production was *Candide* with Simon Russell Beale as Voltaire and Daniel Evans as Candide who tries to keep his spirits up throughout a series of grisly adventures. *Candide*, with music by Leonard Bernstein, has been constantly re-worked ever since it was first performed in 1956 and this new version by the director John Caird was accounted as successful as the musical probably ever could be. A rare revival of Edward Bulwer Lytton's *Money* followed, and then *The Merchant of Venice* directed by Trevor Nunn in the Cottesloe and almost certainly the production of the year. Set in the traverse with the audience sitting on either side, the production was located between the last two wars and created a café society reminiscent of Germany or Austria rather than Venice and populated by arrogant, insensitive young blades who, as well as scorning Shylock, snigger at Antonio's depression. Henry Goodman's magnificent well-dressed Shylock was affable and good humoured on the street, only able to reveal his true feelings with Gabrielle Jourdan's Jessica at home. The Moor, played by Chu Omambala, was enormously attractive and Portia was swept off her feet in the suitor scenes at Belmont.

NEW AT THE NATIONAL

As richly detailed as a 19th-century classic novel, the production revealed Nunn's extraordinary talent for directing Shakespeare. His talent for choosing the National's repertoire is more in question; in particular, he does not share his predecessor's flair for choosing new plays. *The Darker Face of the Earth* was an unremarkable American piece, a re-working of the Oedipal story on a slave plantation. And although Olympia Dukakis was engrossing in *Rose*, sitting on a bench in mourning for Yiddish culture and for a Palestinian girl she had seen killed by Israelis on television, Martin Sherman's play was unsatisfactory, determinedly trawling through every aspect of Jewish history over the last 50 years .

The Royal Shakespeare Company had a good year: box office receipts increased when the old summer season was re-introduced in Stratford and there were a number of high-quality productions, not all of them written by the Bard. Robert Lindsay made his début with the company for a tour of *Richard III*, an old-fashioned production by Elijah Moshinsky in which Lindsay revelled in the hunchback's villainy. Antony Sher played Leontes in Gregory Doran's production of *The Winter's Tale* with Alexandra Gilbreath giving a heart-stopping performance as his much-wronged queen. Alan Bates and Frances de la Tour made the year's second attempt on *Antony and Cleopatra* with considerably more success than Rickman and Mirren at the National. Stephen Poliakoff's *Talk of the City* was a fascinating account of the BBC in the 1930s. The French playwright Bernard-Marie Koltes' *Roberto Zucco* finally made it to London in a cool, funny production by James Macdonald, and Neil Bartlett directed his own translation of Marivaux's *The Dispute*, a strange play in which an aristocrat whimsically has four babies isolated at birth and then brought together on their eighteenth birthdays to see whether the men or the women will be the first to be false in love. Beautifully performed by Hayley Carmichael and Martin Freeman, Bartlett's production was delightful and chilling at the same time.

The other Shakespearean company, Shakespeare's Globe, continued to be popular with tourists. Most unusual was yet another production of *Antony and Cleopatra* but this time with Cleopatra played as a berouged floozie by Mark Rylance. In a brave move, the company also commissioned its first new play from poetic playwright Peter Oswald, who wrote *Augustine's Oak*, an account of Britian's conversion to Christianity, in a very Shakespearean fashion.

Sarah Kane

The world of new plays in general and the Royal Court in particular was devastated by the suicide of the playwright, poet and director Sarah Kane. Aged 28, she had made a tremendous impact right from the notorious opening night of her play *Blasted* in which the multiple horrors of war invaded a British hotel room. This year saw two new plays by Kane: *Cleansed*, a love story set in a concentration camp, once again with shocking, brutal imagery, and *Crave*, presented by Paines Plough.

For the most of the year, the Royal Court was absorbed in raising the final £3 million it needed towards the £24 million cost of its new building in Sloane Square. Eventually the Jerwood Foundation came up with the money, but only on the understanding that the main theatre and the Theatre Upstairs should be renamed the Jerwood theatres at the Royal Court, to the dismay of some of the Royal Court playwrights. Most interestingly, David Hare made his début as an actor at the Duke of York's in his very personal account of his trip to Palestine and Israel. *Via Dolorosa* later went to Broadway and was part of a momentous year for the playwright, with three of his plays crossing the Atlantic: *Dolorosa*, *The Blue Room*, and *Amy's View* with Judi Dench for which she won a Tony award.

The Tricycle Theatre did more to probe our national conscience than any other theatre during the year, in particular with *The Colour of Justice*, a finely edited account of the inquiry into the death of Stephen Lawrence. The production moved to the West End as well as to the National and became a rallying call for the many people who felt that the police's ineptitude was prompted by racism. Less impressive was *Collateral Damage*, swiftly written by Tariq Ali and Howard Brenton and attempting to show a middle-class Britain divided by the NATO action in Serbia.

Regional theatre struggled to survive in the face of declining funding. Jude Kelly's West Yorkshire Playhouse was one of the few theatres to thrive. Like the National, she too set up a company and managed to lure Ian McKellen to Yorkshire; he provocatively declared at the press launch that he hoped to see audiences in Leeds who, unlike in London, would reflect the population as a whole and not a small middle-class minority. Later he acknowledged that there was little difference between the two audiences. The season was notable for being an ambitious mix of Chekhov, Coward and Shakespeare. The Royal Exchange in Manchester celebrated the reopening of its building, which had been damaged in the IRA bomb in 1996. The opening production was *Hindle's Wake* by local playwright Stanley Houghton, later followed by Richard Wilson as one of the tramps in *Waiting for Godot*, possibly the greatest English language play of this century.

PRODUCTIONS
September 1998 to August 1999

LONDON PRODUCTIONS

ADELPHI, WC2. *Chicago*, since November 1997

ALBERY, WC2 (9 September 1998) *Phèdre* (Racine, adapt. Ted Hughes) with Diana Rigg, Toby Stephens, Julian Glover; director, Jonathan Kent. (4 November) *Britannicus* (Racine, adapt. Robert David MacDonald) with Kevin McKidd, Toby Stephens, Diana Rigg; director, Jonathan Kent. (14 January 1999) *Vassa* (Maxim Gorky, adapt. Peter Gill) with Sheila Hancock, Ron Cook, David Tennant, Adrian Scarborough, Aisling O'Sullivan; director, Howard Davies. (27 April) *Plenty* (David Hare) with Cate Blanchett, Julian Wadham; director, Jonathan Kent. (29 July) *Forbidden Broadway* (Gerrard Alessandrini) with Sophie-Louise Dann, Christine Pedi, Mark O'Malley, Alistair Robins; director, Philip George. (8 September) *Quartet* (Ronald Harwood) with Stephanie Cole, Alec McCowen, Donald Sinden, Angela Thorne; director, Christopher Morahan.

ALDWYCH, WC2. *Whistle Down the Wind*, since July 1998

ALMEIDA, N1 (1 September 1998) *The Play About the Baby* (Edward Albee) with Frances de la Tour, Alan Howard; director, Howard Davies. (13 October) *Mr Puntila and his Man Matti* (Brecht, adapt. Lee Hall) with Hamish McColl, Sean Foley; director, Kathryn Hunter. (17 November) *The Storm* (Ostrovsky, trans. Frank McGuinness) with Susan Lynch, Paul Hilton, Richard Lynch, Maggie Steed; director, Hettie Macdonald. (27 January 1999) *Certain Young Men* (Peter Gill) with Jeremy Northam, John Light, Andrew Woodall, Alec Newman; director, Peter Gill. (9 March) *Speer* (Esther Vilar) with Klaus Maria Brandauer, Sven Eric Bechtolf; director, Klaus Maria Brandauer. (5 May) *Aunt Dan and Lemon* (Wallace Shawn) with Miranda Richardson, Glenne Headly; director, Tom Cairns. (20 July) *Chère Maître* (Peter Eyre) with and directed by Peter Eyre, Irene Worth. (31 August) *The Triumph of Love* with Helen McCrory.

AMBASSADORS, WC2 (10 September 1998) *Crave* (Sarah Kane), a Paines Plough production; director, Vicky Featherstone. (19 October) *A Real Classy Affair* (Nick Grosso) with Callum Dixon, Joseph Fiennes, Jason Hughes, Nick Moran, Liza Walker, Jake Wood; director, James Macdonald. (28 November) *About the Boy* (Ed Hime) with Lee Ingleby, Laura Sadler, Alex Pamer; director, Rufus Norris. (1 December) *B22* (Ranjit Khutan) with Sushil Chudasama, Rhydian Jai-Persad; director, Annabelle Comyn. *The Crutch* (Ruwanthie De Chickera) with Sumitra Bhagat, Daniel Cerqueira, Shelley King; director, Indhu Rubasingham. *Four* (Christopher Shinn) with Joseph Mydell, Fraser Ayres; director, Richard Wilson. (2 December) *When Brains Don't Count* (Simon Stephens). (plays shown in different combinations) *Bluebird* (Simon Stephens) with Chris Gascoyne, Jo McInnes; director, Gordon Anderson. *The Shining* (Leomi Walker). *Trade* (Richard Oberg) with Annabelle Apsion. *In the Family* (Sara Barr) with Amelia Lowdell. (14 January 1999) *The Glory of Living* (Rebecca Gilman) with Monica Dolan, Tony Curran; director, Kathryn Hunter. (15 February) *Toast* (Richard Bean) with Christopher Campbell, Ewan Hooper, Paul Wyett, Matthew Dunster, Mark Williams, Sam Kelly, Ian Dunn; director, Richard Wilson. (19 February) *Lift Off* (Roy Williams) with Michael Price, Alex Walkinshaw, Sid Mitchell, Ashley

Chin; director, Indhu Rubasingham. (11 March) *Trust* (Gary Mitchell) with Patrick O'Kane, Barnaby Kay; director, Mick Gordon. (27 March) *Sacred Heart* (Mick Mahoney) with Michael French, Doon MacKichan; director, Edward Hall.
In May 1999 the Ambassadors Theatre was renamed the New Ambassadors Theatre (*see* page 1189)

APOLLO, W1 (7 December 1998) *Jesus, My Boy* (John Dowie) with Tom Conti; director, Tom Kinninmont. (19 February 1999) *Defending the Caveman* (Rob Becker) with Mark Little.

APOLLO LABATTS, W6. *Doctor Dolittle*, since July 1998. (27 July 1999) *Oh! What a Night* (Kim Gavin, Christopher Barr, Stuart Littlewood) with John Altman, Kid Creole, Will Mellor, Lucy Moorby; director, Kim Gavin.

APOLLO VICTORIA, SW1. *Starlight Express*, since 1984

ARTS, WC2 (3 September 1998) *Dancing at Lughnasa* (Brian Friel), a National Youth Theatre production; director, Edward Wilson. (24 September) *Party* (David Dillon) with James Rochfort, Joe Hutton, John-Lloyd Stephenson, John Sackville, Stephen Giffin, David Ashley, Andrew Hallett; director, Andrew Neil. (12 November) *Ecstasy* (Mike Leigh), an About Face production; director, Patrick Davey. (5 January 1999) *Krapp's Last Tape* (Beckett) with Edward Petherbridge; directors, Edward Petherbridge, David Hunt. *Breath* (Beckett); directors, Edward Petherbridge, David Hunt.

BARBICAN, EC2 (10 September 1998) *Peony Pavilion*; director, Peter Sellars. (20 September) *Strike up the Band* (George Kaufman, George and Ira Gershwin) with David de Keyser, Barry Cryer, Sam Kelly, Thelma Ruby; director, Ian Marshall Fisher. (29 October) *The School for Scandal* transferred from the Royal Shakespeare Theatre, Stratford. (2 December) *The Merchant of Venice*, transferred from the Royal Shakespeare Theatre, Stratford. (5 January 1999) *The Tempest*, transferred from the Royal Shakespeare Theatre, Stratford. (20 January) *Measure for Measure*, transferred from the Royal Shakespeare Theatre, Stratford. (18 March) *The Lion, the Witch and the Wardrobe*, transferred from the Royal Shakespeare Theatre, Stratford. (25 March) *The Winter's Tale*, transferred from the Royal Shakespeare Theatre, Stratford. (9 June) *Platonov or the Play with no Name* (Chekhov), a Maly Theatre of St Petersburg production; director, Lev Dodin. (17 June) *The Game of Love and Chance* (Marivaux); director, Jean-Pierre Vincent. (9 July) *Shazam!*

THE PIT (16 September 1998) *Miss Evers's Boys* (David Feldshuh) with Craig Wroe, Charles Dumas, Lorey Hayes, Lee Simon Jr., Tab Baker; director, Martin L. Platt. (6 October) *A Huey P. Newton Story* with Roger Guenveur Smith. (28 October) *Troilus and Cressida* (Shakespeare) with William Houston, Jayne Ashbourne; director, Michael Boyd. (2 December) *Shadows* (*Riders to the Sea, Shadow of the Glen* (J. M. Synge)), *Purgatory* (W. B. Yeats) with Stella McCusker, Maíread McKinley, Lalor Roddy, Stephen Kennedy, Owen Sharpe; director, John Crowley. (21 December) *The Two Gentlemen of Verona*, transferred from The Swan, Stratford. (13 January 1999) *Bad Weather* (Robert Holman) with Susan Engel, Susan Brown, Ryan Pope, Paul Popplewell; director, Steven Pimlott. (18 February) *Goodnight Children Everywhere* (Richard Nelson), a Royal Shakespeare Company production; director, Ian Brown. (3 April) *Roberto Zucco* transferred from The Other Place, Stratford. (4 May) *A Month in the Country*, transferred from the Swan Theatre, Stratford. (May) *Yemayá, Goddess of the Sea* (Jan Blake) with Hopal Romans, Rodolfo Fournier, Jan Blake. (June) *City: Odessa Stories* (Isaac Babel, adapt. Yevgeny Arye), a Gesher

Theatre production; director, Yevgeny Arye. (1 July) *Tinka's New Dress*

BUSH, W12 (9 September 1998) *Love Upon the Throne*, a National Theatre of Brent production. (30 September) *Yard* (Kaite O'Reilly) with Peter Dineen, Kate Binchy; director, Julie-Anne Robinson. (13 November) *Shang-a-Lang* (Catherine Johnson) with Nicola Redmond, Ona McCracken, Joanne Pearce; director, Mike Bradwell. (13 January 1999) *In Flame* (Charlotte Jones) with Valerie Gogan, Emma Dewhurst; director, Anna Mackmin. (12 February) *Howie the Rookie* (Mark O'Rowe) with Aidan Kelly, Karl Shields; director, Mike Bradwell. (24 March) *Card Boys* (Mike Packer) with Albie Woodington, Willie Ross, Suzan Sylvester; director; Simon Usher. (5 May) *Dogs Barking* (Richard Zajdlic) with Tony Curran, Raquel Cassidy; director, Mike Bradwell. (18 June) *High Life* (Lee Macdougall) with Nigel Planer, Paul Barber, David Schofield, Joe McKay; director, Richard Bridges. (14 July) *The Backroom* (Adrian Pagan) with Ben Price, Justin Salinger; director, Jonathan Lloyd.

CAMBRIDGE, WC2. *Grease*, since 1996

COMEDY, WC2 (4 November 1998) *Love Upon the Throne*, transferred from the Bush. (21 January 1999) *Little Malcolm and his Struggle Against the Eunuchs*, transferred from the Hampstead. (10 April) *Suddenly Last Summer* (Tennessee Williams) with Sheila Gish, Rachel Weisz; director, Sean Mathias. (22 July) *I Love You, You're Perfect, Now Change* (Joe DiPietro, Jimmy Roberts) with Clive Carter, Shona Lindsay, Gillian Kirkpatrick, Russell Wilcox; director, Joel Bishoff.

CRITERION, WI. *The Complete Works of William Shakespeare (Abridged)* and *The Complete History of America (Abridged)*, since 1996

DOMINION, WC1. *Beauty and the Beast*, since May 1997

DONMAR WAREHOUSE, WC2 (10 September 1998) *The Blue Room* (based on *La Ronde*, Arthur Schnitzler, adapt. David Hare) with Nicole Kidman, Iain Glen; director, Sam Mendes. (16 November) *Into the Woods* (Stephen Sondheim, James Lapine) with Nick Holder, Sophie Thompson, Clare Burt; director, John Crowley. (16 February 1999) *Splash Hatch on the E Going Down* (Kia Corthron) with Shauna Shim; director, Roxana Silbert. (17 February) *Morphic Resonance* (Katherine Burger) with Joanna Roth, Lloyd Owen, Anastasia Hille; director, James Kerr. (1 March) *Three Days of Rain* (Richard Greenberg) with Colin Firth, Elizabeth McGovern; director, Robin Lefevre. (23 March) *Good* (C. P. Taylor) with Charles Dance, Ian Gelder, Jessica Turner, Emilia Fox; director, Michael Grandage. (27 May) *The Real Thing* (Stoppard) with Jennifer Ehle, Nigel Lindsay, Sarah Woodward, Stephen Dillane; director, David Leveaux.

DRURY LANE THEATRE ROYAL, WC2. *Miss Saigon*, since 1989

DUCHESS, WC2 (5 February 1999) *Copenhagen*, transferred from the Royal National.

DUKE OF YORK'S, WC2 (13 October 1998) *The Weir* (Conor McPherson) with Jim Norton, Brendan Coyle; director, Ian Rickson.

FORTUNE, WC2. *The Woman in Black*, since 1986. Also the 'Lost Musicals' series: (9 May 1999) *I'd Rather Be Right* (Richard Rogers, Lorenz Hart, Moss Hart, George S. Kaufman) with Kenneth Haigh, Clare Rayner; director, Ian Marshall Fisher. (4 July) *110 in the Shade* (Harvey Schmidt, Tom Jones, N. Richard Nash) with Louise Gold; director, Ian Marshall Fisher.

GARRICK, WC2. *An Inspector Calls*, the 1992 National Theatre production, since 1995

GATE, WII (22 October 1998) *Volunteers* (Brian Friel) with Colin Farrell, Partick O'Kane; director, Mick Gordon. (November) *Suppliants* (Aeschylus, trans. James Kerr) with David Oyelowo; director, James Kerr. (January 1999) *Intimate Death* (Marie de Hennezel, adapt. Mick Gordon) with Gillian Barge; director, Mick Gordon. (February) *El Quijote* (Cervantes, adapt. David Johnston); director, Marta Momblant Ribas. (March) *The Colonel Bird* (Hristo Boytchev) with Damian Myerscough; director, Rupert Gould. (10 May) *Svejk* (Jaroslav Hasek, adapt. Colin Teevan) with Martin Savage; director, Dalia Ibelhauptaite. (10 June) *Perdition* (Jim Allen) with Morris Perry, Osnat Schmool, Penny Bunton, Ian Flintoff; director, Elliot Levey. (6 July) *Tales from the Vienna Woods* (Von Horvath), a London Academy of Performing Arts production. (13 July) *The Comedy of Errors* (Shakespeare) director, Valery Petrov. (20 July) *The Trial* (Kafka), a CZKD production. (3 August) *The Tunnel*, a New Riga Theatre of Latvia production.

GIELGUD, WI (14 September 1998) *Alarms and Excursions* (Michael Frayn) with Felicity Kendal, Josie Lawrence, Nicky Henson, Robert Bathurst; director, Michael Blakemore. (22 March 1999) *Gross Indecency*, transferred from the Theatre Royal, Plymouth. (8 June) *Boyband* (Peter Quilter) with Bryan Murray, Damian Flood, Danny Crossley, Tom Ashton, Kevin Andrew; director, Peter Quilter.

GLOBE, SEI (26 May 1999) *Julius Caesar* (Shakespeare) with Mark Lewis Jones, Danny Sapani, Richard Bremmer; director, Mark Rylance. (3 June) *The Comedy of Errors* (Shakespeare) with Marcello Magni, Vincenzo Nicoli; director, Kathryn Hunter. (30 July) *Antony and Cleopatra* (Shakespeare) with Mark Rylance, Paul Shelley; director, Mark Rylance. (7August) *Augustine's Oak* (Peter Oswald) with Terry McGinity, Yolanda Vazquez, Martin Turner; director, Tim Carroll.

HAMPSTEAD, NW3 (October 1998) *An Experiment with an Air Pump* (Shelagh Stephenson) with Barbara Flynn, David Horovitch; director, Matthew Lloyd. (18 November) *Little Malcolm and his Struggle Against the Eunuchs* (David Halliwell) with Ewan McGregor, Sean Gilder; director, Denis Lawson. (8 January 1999) *Perfect Days* (Liz Lochhead) with Siobhan Redmond, Ann Scott-Jones, John Kazek; director, John Tiffany. (5 February) *Celaine* (Matt Parker) with Jackie Morrison, Paul Copley, Alison Fiske, Lee Oakes; director, Edward Hall. (19 February) *Falling* (David Eldridge) with Mark Aiken, Caroline Harker, Helen Gardiner, Julian Kerridge; director, John Dove. (6 March) *The Life and Loves of Edith Wharton* (Frank Barrie, Katrina Hendrey) with Gayle Hunnicut; director, Frank Barrie. (9 March) *No Exp. Req'd* (Simon Block) with Jay Simpson. (19 March) *Snake* (Rona Munro) with Terence Maynard, Linsdey Coulson; director, Gema Bodinetz. (6 April) *By Many Wounds* (Zinnie Harris) with Mark Hadfield, Suzanne Burden, Julia Malewski; director, Debbie Seymour. (16 April) *Hushabye Mountain* (Jonathan Harvey), an English Touring Company production; director, Paul Miller. (25 May) *The Death of Cool* (Alan Pollocks) with Susannah Doyle, Colin Tierney; director, Gemma Bodinetz. (13 June) *Shylock*, written, performed and directed by Gareth Armstrong. (8 July) *Disposing of the Body* (Hugh Whitemore) with Charlotte Cornwell, Gemma Jones, Stephen Moore; director, Robin Lefèvre.

HAYMARKET THEATRE ROYAL, SWI (3 November 1998) *The Invention of Love*, transferred from the Royal National. (30 March 1999) *The Prisoner of Second Avenue* (Neil Simon) with Richard Dreyfuss, Marsha Mason; director, David Taylor. (8 July) *Love Letters* (A. R. Gurney) with Charlton Heston, Lydia Clarke Heston. (4 August) *The*

Importance of Being Earnest, transferred from the Festival Theatre, Chichester.

HER MAJESTY'S, SW1. *The Phantom of the Opera,* since 1986

LONDON PALLADIUM, WC1. *Saturday Night Fever,* since May 1998

LYCEUM, WC2 (20 January 1999) *Oklahoma!,* transferred from the Royal National

LYRIC, W1 (3 November 1998) *An Ideal Husband,* transferred from the Haymarket Theatre Royal. (16 March 1999) *Animal Crackers* (Marx Brothers) with Ben Keaton, Joe Alessi, Toby Sedgwick; directors, Gregory Hersov, Emil Wolk.

LYRIC, W6 (16 September 1998) *Anna Karenina* (Tolstoy, adapt. Helen Edmindson), a Shared Experience production; director, Nancy Meckler. (December) *Cinderella* with Angela Clerkin, Richard Katz; directors, Julian Crouch, Phelim McDermott, Lee Simpson, Neil Bartlett. (14 January 1999) *Lord of the Flies* (William Golding, adapt. Nigel Williams), a Pilot Theatre Company production; director, Marcus Romer. (February) *The Kissing Dance* (Charles Hart, Howard Goodall, based on *She Stoops to Conquer* (Goldsmith)), a National Youth Music Theatre production. (17 February) *Shockheaded Peter* (based on *Struwwelpeter* (Heinrich Hoffman)), a Cultural Industry/Improbable Theatre/Tiger Lillies production; directors, Julian Crouch, Phelim McDermott. (22 February) *Barbers of Surreal,* a Forkbeard Fantasy production. (April) *The Dispute,* transferred from The Other Place, Stratford. (May) *The Cosmonaut's Last Message to the Woman he Once Loved in the Former Soviet Union* (David Greig), a Paines Plough production; director, Vicky Featherstone. (25 May) *The Winter's Tale* (Shakespeare) a Maly Theatre of St Petersburg production; director, Declan Donnellan.

LYRIC STUDIO (14 September 1998) *Handbag* (Mark Ravenhill), an Actors Touring Company production; director, Nick Philippou. (12 November) *Fourteen Songs, Two Weddings and a Funeral* (adapt. of film *Hum Aap Ke Hain Koun…!*), a Tamasha company production. (3 February 1999) *Fourplay* (Sergi Belbel), a Mammoth production; director, Hans-Peter Kellner. (10 March) *Take the Fire* (Jean Cocteau) with Amanda Harris; director, Paul Carrington. (April) *The Tempest* (Shakespeare), an Actor's Touring Company production; director, Nick Philippou. (29 June) *Sleeping Around* (Mark Ravenhill, Abi Morgan, Hilary Fannin, Stephen Greenhorn). (13 July) *Life During Wartime* (Keith Reddin); director, Toby Reisz.

NEW AMBASSADORS, WC2 (1 June 1999) *Holy Mothers* (Werner Schwab), a Frantic Assembly production; director, Richard Jones. (31 May) *Sell Out* (Michael Wynne), a Frantic Assembly production. (8 July) *Last Dance at Dum Dum* (Ayub Khan-Din) with Madhur Jaffrey, Nicholas le Prevost; director, Stuart Buge. (July) *East is East.*

NEW LONDON, WC2. *Cats,* since 1981

OLD VIC, SE1 (15 October 1998) *Amadeus* (Peter Shaffer) with Michael Sheen, David Suchet; director, Peter Hall. (27 July 1999) *Jeffrey Bernard is Unwell* (Keith Waterhouse) with Peter O'Toole; director, Ned Sherrin.

OPEN AIR, REGENT'S PARK (1 June 1999) *The Merry Wives of Windsor* (Shakespeare) with Robert Lang; director, Alan Strachan. (4 June) *Twelfth Night* (Shakespeare) with Emily Hamilton, Christopher Godwin; director, Rachel Kavanaugh. (26 July) *A Funny Thing Happened on the Way to the Forum* (Stephen Sondheim, Burt Shevelove, Larry Gelbart) with Roy Hudd, Susie Blake, Rhashan Stone; director, Ian Talbot. (6 August) *The*

Last Fattybottypuss in the World, a New Shakespeare Company production; director, Pete Harris.

PALACE, WC2. *Les Miserables,* since 1985

PHOENIX, WC1. *Blood Brothers,* since 1991

PICCADILLY, W1 (8 October 1998) *Filumena* (Eduardo de Filippo, trans. Timberlake Wertenbaker) with Judi Dench, Michael Pennington; director, Peter Hall. (9 October) *Pidgin Macbeth,* a Ken Campbell's Company production; directors, Ken Campbell, Daisy Campbell. (6 November) *Kafka's Dick* (Alan Bennett) with Julia McKenzie, John Gordon-Sinclair, Dennis Lil, Eric Sykes; director, Peter Hall. (20 April 1999) *The Birthday Party* (Pinter) with Timothy West, Prunella Scales, Steven Pacey, Nigel Terry; director, Joe Harmston. (2 August) *Four Steps to Heaven* (Bill Kenwright) with Peter Howarth, Reuven Gershon, Rebel Dean, Kludo White; director, Keith Strachan.

PLAYHOUSE, WC2 *Much Ado About Nothing,* since June 1998

PRINCE EDWARD, W1 (6 October 1998) *West Side Story* (Bernstein, Sondheim, Laurents) with Katie Knight-Adams, David Habbin; director, Alan Johnson. (6 April 1999) *Mamma Mia!* (Catherine Johnson, Benny Andersson, Bjorn Ulvaeus) with Siobhan McCarthy, Lisa Stokke; director, Phyllida Lloyd.

PRINCE OF WALES, W1 (15 October 1998) *Fame* (Adam Spiegel, Michael White). (18 January 1999) *West Side Story,* transferred from the Prince Edward.

QUEENS, W1 (12 October 1998) *Jackie* (Gip Hoppe) with Lysette Anthony, James Gaddas; director, Gip Hoppe. (18 December) *The Pirates of Penzance* (Gilbert and Sullivan), a D'Oyly Carte production; director, Stuart Maunder. (14 January 1999) *The Street of Crocodiles* (Bruno Schulz, adapt. Simon McBurney, Mark Wheatley), a Théâtre de Complicité production; director, Simon McBurney. (3 March) *Macbeth* (Shakespeare) with Rufus Sewell, Sally Dexter; director, John Crowley. (10 June) *Dreaming* (Peter Barnes) with Gerard Murphy, Christopher Ettridge; director, Peter Barnes. (27 July) *Lenny* (Julian Barry) with Eddie Izzard; director, Peter Hall.

ROYAL COURT and THEATRE UPSTAIRS, SW1. Closed for refurbishment 1998–9; performances at the Ambassadors and Duke of York theatres

ROYAL NATIONAL THEATRE, SE1, Cottesloe (25 September 1998) *Haroun and the Sea of Stories* (Salman Rushdie, adapt. Tim Supple, David Tushingham) with Nabil Shaban, Nitin Chandra Ganatra, Sam Dastor; director, Tim Supple. (26 October) *Copenhagen* (Michael Frayn) with David Burke, Sara Kestelman, Matthew Marsh; director, Michael Blakemore. (11 November) *Guiding Star* (Jonathan Harvey) with Colin Tierney, Tracey Wilkinson; director, Gemma Bodinetz. (February 1999) *The Riot* (Nick Darke), a Royal National Theatre/Kneehigh Theatre of Cornwall co-production; director, Mike Shepherd. (22 April) *Sleep with Me* (Hanif Kureishi) with Sean Chapman, Penny Downie, Jonathan Hyde, Sian Thomas; director, Anthony Page. (5 May) *The Two Gentlemen of Verona* (Shakespeare); director, Julie-Anne Robertson. (22 May) *Rose* (Martin Sherman) with Olympia Dukakis; director, Nancy Meckler. (12 June) *The Merchant of Venice* (Shakespeare) with Henry Goodman, Debra Crotty, David Bamber; director, Trevor Nunn. (5 August) *The Darker Face of the Earth* (Rita Dove), an NT Ensemble production; director, James Kerr.

LYTTELTON (September 1998) *Cleo, Camping, Emmanuelle and Dick* (Terry Johnson) with Geoffrey Hutchings, Adam Godley, Samantha Spiro; director, Terry Johnson. (20 November) *Betrayal* (Pinter) with Anthony Calf, Douglas

Hodge, Imogen Stubbs; director, Trevor Nunn. (22 January 1999) *The Forest* (Ostrovsky, adapt. Alan Ayckbourn) with Michael Feast, Frances de la Tour, Michael Williams; director, Anthony Page. (18 March) *The Colleen Bawn* (Dion Boucicault), a Dublin Abbey Theatre production; director, Conall Morrison. (13 May) *Private Lives* (Coward) with Juliet Stevenson, Anton Lesser; director, Philip Franks. (9 June) *Sparklesbark* (Philip Ridley) with Nitzan Sharron, Paul Sharma, Chiwetel Ejiofor, Maggie Lloyd-Williams; director, Terry Johnson. (15 July) *Look Back in Anger* (John Osborne) with Michael Sheen, Emma Fielding; director, Gregory Hersov.

OLIVIER (20 October 1998) *Antony and Cleopatra* (Shakespeare) with Alan Rickman, Helen Mirren; director, Sean Mathias. (17 December) *Peter Pan* (J. M. Barrie, adapt. John Caird, Trevor Nunn) with Justin Salinger, David Troughton, Rebecca Johnson; director, Fiona Laird. (18 February 1999) *Private Lives* (Coward) (6 March) *Troilus and Cressida* (Shakespeare) with Peter de Jersey, Sophie Okonedo, David Bamber, Roger Allam; directors, Trevor Nunn, John Caird. (13 April) *Candide* (Leonard Bernstein) with Daniel Evans, Alex Kelly, Simon Russell Beale; directors, John Caird, Trevor Nunn. (3 June) *Money* (Edward Bulmer-Lytton) with Simon Russell Beale, Denis Quilley, Michael Bryant, Sophie Okonedo; director, John Caird. (28 August) *Summerfolk* (Gorky), a New York Ensemble production; director, Trevor Nunn.

ST MARTINS, WC2. *The Mousetrap*, since 1974

SAVOY, WC2 (16 October 1998) *Boogie Nights* (Jon Conway, Shane Richie, Terry Morrison) with Shane Richie, Lisa Maxwell; director, Jon Conway. (18 January 1999) *Richard III*, transferred from the Royal Shakespeare Theatre, Stratford. (30 March) *The Gin Game* (D. L. Coburn) with Joss Ackland, Dorothy Tutin; director, Frith Banbury. (14 June) *Hay Fever* (Coward) with Geraldine McEwan, Peter Blythe, Stephen Mangan; director, Declan Donnellan.

SHAFTESBURY THEATRE, WC2 *Rent*, since 1998

STRAND, WC2. *Buddy*, since 1995

TRICYCLE, NW6 (2 November 1998) *Ugly Rumours* (Tariq Ali, Howard Brenton) with Neil Mullarkey, Gordon Kennedy, Sylvia Sims; directors, Christopher Morahan, Stephen Rayne. (1 December) *The Snow Palace* (Pam Gems) with Kathryn Pogson, Nigel Cooke, Mark Lewis Jones; director, Janet Suzman. (12 January 1999) *The Colour of Justice* (Richard Norton-Taylor) with Tyrone De Rizzio, Yvonne Pascal; director, Nicolas Kent. (9 February) *And the Brother Too* (Flann O'Brien, adapt. Eamon Morrissey) with and directed by Eamon Morrissey. (1 March) *Paddy Irishman, Paddy Englishman and Paddy…?*, a Birmingham Repertory Company production; director, Anthony Clark. (25 March) *Up Against the Wall* (Felix Cross, Paulette Randall), a Black Theatre Co-op production; director, Paulette Randall. (20 April) *The Garden of Habustan* (Rebecca Wolman), a Besht Tellers production. (11 May) *Catalpa* (Donal O'Kelly) with Donal O'Kelly; director, Baírbe Ní Chaoímh. (30 May) *Collateral Damage* (Tariq Ali, Howard Brenton, Andy de la Tour) with Jeremy Clyde, Susan Wooldridge; director, Andy de la Tour. (9 June) *Ubu and the Truth Commission* (Alfred Jarry) with Dawid Minaar; director, William Kentridge. (21 June) *The Story I'm About to Tell* (William Kentridge Handspring Puppet Company), a Mehlo Players production. (28 June) *Phakama – Be Yourself*. (5 July) *True Believers* (Joseph O'Connor) with Geraldine Plunkett, Enda Oates; director, Jim Culleton. (31 August) *Stones in his Pockets* (Marie Jones).

VAUDEVILLE, WC2 (11 January 1999) *The Memory of Water* (Shelagh Stephenson) with Alison Steadman, Samantha Bond, Julia Sawalha; director, Terry Johnson. (11 June) *Perfect Days*, transferred from the Hampstead.

VICTORIA PALACE, SW1 (22 September 1998) *Annie* (Charles Strouse and Martin Charnin) with Charlene Barton, Jenny Logan, Lesley Joseph, Kevin Colson; director, Martin Charnin. (3 March 1999) *The Colour of Justice*, transferred from the Tricycle. (14 April) *The New Rocky Horror Show* (Richard O'Brien) with Jason Donovan; director, Christopher Malcolm. (22 June) *Soul Train* (Mark Clements, Michael Vivian) with Sheila Ferguson, Danny John-Jules, Sharon Benson; director, Mark Clements.

WHITEHALL, SW1 (23 September 1998) *Dead Monkey* (Nick Darke) with David Soul, Alexa Hamilton, James Terry; director, Brennan Street. (14 April 1999) *Making Noise Quietly* (trilogy: *Being Friends, Lost, Making Noise Quietly* (Robert Holman)) with Eleanor Bron, Peter Hanly, John Lloyd Fillingham; director, Deborah Bruce. (27 May) *Three Sisters* (Chekhov) with Claire Rushbrook, Claudie Blakley, Kelly Reilly; director, Dominic Dromgoole. (8 July) *Eurydice* (Jean Anouilh), a Straydogs production; director, Simon Godwin.

WYNDHAM'S, WC2. *Art*, since 1996

YOUNG VIC, SE1 (September 1998) *Our Country's Good* (Timberlake Wertenbaker), a Young Vic and Out of Joint co-production; director, Max Stafford-Clark. (3 November) *Stranded* (adapt. of *Crime on Goat Island* (Ugo Betti)), a Scarlet Theatre production. (2 December) *Arabian Nights* (Dominic Cooke) with Sophie Okonedo, Chu Omambala; director, Dominic Cooke. (1 February 1999) *Talk of the City* (Stephen Poliakoff) with David Westhead, Angus Wright; director, Stephen Poliakoff. (18 February) *Bartholomew Fair*, transferred from the Swan Theatre, Stratford. (2 April) *Hamlet* (Shakespeare) with Paul Rhys, Megan Dodds, Donald Sumter, Suzanne Bertish; director, Laurence Boswell. (18 May) *The House of Bernarda Alba* (Lorca, trans. Rona Munro), a Shared Experience production; director, Polly Teale. (6 July) *The Maids* (Genet) with Anastasia Hille, Aisling O'Sullivan; director, Katie Mitchell. (31 August) *Demons and Dybbuks* (Isaac Bashevis Singer), a Method and Madness production.

OUTSIDE LONDON

BIRMINGHAM: REPERTORY (September 1998) *Hamlet* (Shakespeare) with Richard McCabe, Rakie Ayola, Gerard Murphy, Anna Nicholas; director, Bill Alexander. (November) *Three Sisters* with Susan Wooldridge, Felicity Dean, Rachel Pickup, Charles Dance; director, Bill Bryden. (23 December) *Cinderella* with Brian Conley, Danny La Rue; director, Paul Elliott. (12 January 1999) *Just, not Fair* (Jim Robinson), a Moving Theatre Company production; director, Jessica Dromgoole. (14 January) *De Profundis* (Wilde) with Corin Redgrave; a Moving Theatre production. (26 January) *Two Pianos, Four Hands* (Ted Dykstra, Richard Greenblatt) with Ted Dykstra, Richard Greenblatt; director, Jeremy Sams. (23 February) *The Four Alice Bakers* (Fay Weldon) with Diane Fletcher, Carol Royle, Paula Stockbridge, Flora Montgomery, David Hargreaves, Michael Cashman. (29 April) *The Pajama Game* (Richard Adler, Jerry Ross) with Ulrika Jonsson, Anita Dobson, John Hegley; director, Simon Callow. (22 June) *Jumpers* (Stoppard) with Samantha Spiro, Malcolm Tierney; director, Bill Alexander.

BRISTOL: OLD VIC (22 September 1998) *One for the Road* (Willy Russell) with Gary Wilmot; director, Andy Hay. (2

December) *Jack and the Beanstalk* (Chris Denys, Chris Harris) with Chris Harris; director, Elwyn Johnson. (January 1999) *Freebird* with William Ely; director, Ian Hastings. (6 February) *Blues Brother Soul Sisters* (Kwame Kwei-Armah) with Kwame Kwei-Armah, Ruby Turner, Paulette Ivory, Dawn Michael; director, Andy Hay. (9 March) *Hello Dolly* (Michael Stewart, Jerry Herman), a University of the West of England production. (18 March) *The Price* (Arthur Miller) with Clive Mantle, Malcolm Tierney; director, Jan Sargent. (4 April) *The Mystery Plays*, adapt. of mystery plays for Easter Sunday. (17 April) *Tons of Money* (Will Evans and Valentine, adapt. Alan Ayckbourn), a Bristol Old Vic production; director, Ian Hastings. (20 May) *Up 'N' Under* (John Godber) with Gareth Chilcott; director, Andy Hay. (17 June) *Mansfield Park* (Jane Austen, adapt. Willis Hall) a Bristol Old Vic Theatre School production. (6 July) *The Wiz* (adapt. from *The Wonderful Wizard of Oz* by Frank Baum), a BOS production. (13 July) *Iolanthe* (Gilbert and Sullivan). (20 July) *Oliver!* (Lionel Bart), a Bristol Musical Comedy Club production; director, Andrew D. Ford.

CHICHESTER: FESTIVAL (11 September 1998) *Katherine Howard* (William Nicholson) with Emilia Fox, Richard Griffiths, Julian Rhind-Tutt; director, Robin Lefèvre. (13 October) *John Buchan's The Thirty-Nine Steps* (John Buchan, adapt. Nobby Dimon, Simon Corble) with Simon Ward, George Sewell, Catherine Rabbett, Kern Falconer; director, Richard Baron. (15 March 1999) *Loot* (Orton) with Michael Elphick, Letitia Dean; director Paul Farrah. (13 April) *Brassed Off* (Mark Herman, adapt. Paul Allen). The Touring Partnership/Sheffield Theatres co-production; director, Joanna Reed. (18 May) *The Importance of Being Earnest* (Wilde) with Patricia Routledge, Adam Godley, Alan Cox, Rebecca Johnson; director, Christopher Morahan. (28 May) *Semi-Detached* (David Turner) with James Bolam, Anna Carteret; director, Christopher Morahan. (21 July) *Easy Virtue* (Coward) with Greta Scacchi, Wendy Craig, Michael Jayston; director, Maria Aitken. (13 August) *The Man Who Came to Dinner* (Moss Hart, George S. Kaufman) with Richard Griffiths, Issy van Randwyck, Sarah Crowden; director, Joe Dowling.

MINERVA (18 September 1998) *The Glass Menagerie* (Tennessee Williams) with Gemma Jones, Michael Mueller, Alexandra Lilley, Adam James; director, Jacob Murray. (30 October) *Song of Singapore* (book, Allan Katz; music and lyrics, Erik Frandsen, Robert Hipkens, Michael Garin, Paula Lockheart) with Ben Albu, Béatrice Grace, Issy van Randwyck, Simon Slater; director, Roger Redfarn. (3 December) *My Fair Lady* (music, Frederick Loewe, lyrics, Alan Jay Lerner), a Chichester Amateur Operatic Society production; director, Sally Davis. (15 June 1999) *The King of Prussia* (Nick Darke); director, Sean Holmes. (14 July) *Insignificance* (Terry Johnson) with Ron Cook, Alan Corduner, Martin Marquez, Sharon Small; director, Loveday Ingram. (5 August) *Nymph Errant* (Cole Porter, adapt. Steve Mackes, Michael Whaley) with Rae Baker, Mark Adams; director, Roger Redfarn.

EDINBURGH: ROYAL LYCEUM (11 September 1998) *Britannia Rules* (Liz Lochhead) with Billy Boyd, Mark Cox, Vicki Liddelle, Jenny Ryan; director, Tony Cownie. (9 October) *Thérèse Raquin* (Emile Zola, adapt. Stuart Paterson), a Royal Lyceum Theatre Company/Communicado Theatre Company production. (30 October) *The Collector* (John Fowles, adapt. Mark Healy) with Danielle Tilley, Mark Letheren; director, Mark Clements. (15 January 1999) *The Deep Blue Sea* (Terence Rattigan) (12 February) *The Anatomist* (James Bridie). (12 March) *An Experienced Woman Gives Advice*

(Iain Heggie). (16 April)   *Stiff!* (Forbes Masson) with Forbes Masson, Tom McGovern, Jennifer Black; director, Caroline Hall. (August) *The Speculator* (David Greig), a Traverse Theatre production. (August) *The Meeting* (Lluïsa Cunillé), a Traverse Theatre production.

GLASGOW: CITIZENS (24 September 1998) *The Fall of the House of Usher* (Poe, adapt. Jon Pope) with Jay Manley, James Duke, Lorna McDevitt; director, Jon Pope. (25 September) *Men Should Weep* (Ena Lamont Stewart) with Barbara Rafferty, Matt Costello; director, Giles Havergal. (28 October) *Oleanna* (David Mamet) with Peter Guinness, Lorna McDevitt; director, Kenny Miller. (30 October) *The Homecoming* (Pinter) with Stuart Bowman, Andrea Hart; director, Philip Prowse. (2 March 1999) *Phaedra's Love* (Sarah Kane), a Ghostown production; director, Peter Mackie Burns.

LEEDS: WEST YORKSHIRE PLAYHOUSE (10 September 1998) *Picasso at the Lapin Agile* (Steve Martin) with Ben Walden, Brian Shelley; director, Randall Arney. (October) *Trackers* (Tony Harrison) with Barrie Rutter; director, Barrie Rutter. (29 October) *The Seagull* (Chekhov) with Clare Higgins, Ian McKellen; director, Jude Kelly. (28 November) *Martin Guerre* (Alain Boublil, Claud-Michel Schönberg) with Stephen Weller, Joanna Riding, Matthew Cammelle, Stephen Weller; director, Cameron Mackintosh. (15 December) *Present Laughter* (Coward) with Ian McKellen, Susie Baxter, Clare Higgins; director, Malcolm Sutherland. (2 February 1999) *The Tempest* (Shakespeare) with Ian McKellen, Paul Bhattacharjee, Claudie Blakley; director, Jude Kelly. (26 February) *Wuthering Heights* (Emily Brontë, adapt. Malcolm Sutherland) with Jacqueline King, Elisabeth Dermot-Walsh, Chook Sibtain, David Groves, Ed Purver, Michelle Abrahams; director, Malcolm Sutherland. (10 April) *Kes* (Barry Hines, *A Kestrel for a Knave*, adapt. Lawrence Till) with Raymond Pickard, Joanna Bacon, Alan Cowan, Frank Moorey; director, Natasha Betteridge. (21 May) *Deadmeat* (Q) with Howard Saddler, Q, Ian McKellen; director, Jude Kelly. (28 May) *Enjoy* (Alan Bennett) with Bernard Gallagher, Thelma Barlow; director, Alan Dossor. (17 June) *Who's Boss?* (Ansell Broderick) with Anthony Warren, Charles Abomeli, Nigel Betts, Vanessa Bray; director, Ansell Broderick.

LEICESTER: HAYMARKET (4 September 1998) *The Rink* (Kander and Ebb) with Kathryn Evans and Linzi Hateley; director, Paul Kerryson. (3 November) *Richard III* (Shakespeare) with Ian Pepperell, Peter Forbes, Janet Henfrey; director, Paul Kerryson. (3 December) *Singin' in the Rain* (Nacio Herb Brown, Arthur Freed; adapt. Betty Comden, Adolph Green) with Gavin Lees, Samantha George, Helen Way; director, Paul Kerryson. (17 February 1999) *Unleashed* (John Godber), a Hull Truck Theatre production. (25 February) *A Passionate Woman* (Kay Mellor), a Haymarket Theatre production; director, Nona Shepphard. (23 March) *Vita and Virginia* (Eileen Atkins), a Sphinx Theatre Company/Palace Theatre, Watford production; director, Maria Aitken. (30 March) *Charlotte's Web* (E. B. White, adapt. Joseph Robinette), a Watershed production; director, Chris Wallis. (9 April) *The White Devil* (Webster) with Gabrielle Drake, Ian Pepperell, Richard Willis; director, Paul Kerryson. (7 May) *The Importance of Being Earnest* (Wilde), a Haymarket Theatre production; director, Paul Kerryson.

MANCHESTER: ROYAL EXCHANGE (8 December) *Hindle Wakes* (Stanley Houghton) with Claire Rushbrook, Pearce Quigley, Sue Johnston, Ewan Hooper; director, Helena Kaut-Howson. (19 January 1999) *Martin Yesterday* (Brad Fraser) with Ben Daniels, Ian Gelder, Ruth Lass; director, Marianne Elliott. (11 February) *Peer Gynt* (Ibsen, adapt.

Michael Meyer) with David Threlfall, Espen Skjønberg, Josette Bushell-Mingo; director, Braham Murray. (17 March) *Dreaming* (Peter Barnes) with Gerard Murphy, Richard Bremmer, Dilys Laye; director, Matthew Lloyd. (20 April) *Tobaccoland* (Alex Finlayson) with Trevor Peacock, Lisa Eichhorn, Joseph Mydell, James Clyde; director, Gergory Hersov. (18 May) *Waiting for Godot* (Beckett) with Richard Wilson, Brian Pettifer; director, Matthew Lloyd. (30 June) *Nude with Violin* (Coward) with Derek Griffiths, Marcia Warren; director, Marianne Elliott.

MOLD: CLWYD THEATR CYMRU, EMLYN WILLIAMS (19 October 1998) *Of Mice and Men* (Steinbeck), a Clwyd Theatr Cymru production; director, Tim Baker. (9 November) *Time of My Life* (Ayckbourn), a Volcano Theatre Company production. (24 November) *Bouncers* (John Godber), a Hull Truck Theatre production; director, John Godber. (14 January 1999) Under Milk Wood (Thomas) with Guy Masterson; director, Tony Boncza. (18 May) *Twelfth Night* (Shakespeare) with Kirsten Packer, Rachel Pickup; director, Terry Hands. ANTHONY HOPKINS. (8 September 1998) *They Offered Bob and Wilma Cash!* (Steven Froelich) with Sylvia Williams; director, Joel Santoni. (6 October) *Table Manners* (Alan Ayckbourn), a Clwyd Theatr Cymru production; director, Terry Hands. (6 October) *Living Together* (Alan Ayckbourn), a Clwyd Theatr Cymru production; director Terry Hands. (6 October) *Round and Round the Garden* (Alan Ayckbourn), a Clwyd Theatr Cymru production; director Terry Hands. (11 December) *Aladdin: The Wok 'n' Roll Pantomime* (Peter Rowe, Allan Ellis), a Clwyd Theatr Cymru production; director, Peter Rowe. (4 February 1999) *Hosts of Rebecca* (Alexander Cordell) a Clwyd Theatr Cymru production; director, Tim Baker. (8 April) *Happy End* (Dorothy Lane, adapt. Kurt Weill, Bertolt Brecht), a Clwyd Theatr Cymru production; director, Peter Rowe.

NOTTINGHAM: PLAYHOUSE (10 September 1998) *The Boy Friend* (Sandy Wilson), a York Theatre Royal/Mercury Theatre, Colchester co-production; director, Ultz. (22 October) *Who's Afraid of Virginia Woolf?* (Edward Albee), a York Theatre Royal/Mercury Theatre, Colchester co-production; director, Mark Wing-Davey. (5 December) *Jack and the Beanstalk* (Kenneth Alan Taylor) with Sarah Hadland, Jeremy Stroughair; director, Kenneth Alan Taylor. (24 February 1999) *Endgame* (Beckett) with James Bolam, Alistair McGowan, Steven Beard, Darlene Johnson; director, Martin Duncan. (13 March) *Krapp's Last Tape* (Beckett) with John Neville; director, Martin Duncan. (23 March) *A Clockwork Orange* (Anthony Burgess), a Northern Stage production; directors, Alan Lyddiard, Mark Murphy. (23 April) *Frogs* (Aristophanes, trans. Fiona Laird) with Jonjo O'Neill, Jonathan Kemp; director, Fiona Laird. (2 May) *Rats, Buckets and Bombs* (Barry Heath) with Mark Whiteley, Joseph Traynor, Claire Wilkie; director, Paul Jepson. (24 June) *Red Riding Hood* (Grimms brothers, adapt.), a Teatro Kismet production; director, Carlo Formigoni. (6 July) *Momo and the Time Thieves* (Michael Ende, adapt. Carlo Formigoni), a Teatro Kismet production; director, Carlo Formigoni.

SCARBOROUGH: STEPHEN JOSEPH (21 October 1998) *A Doll's House* (Ibsen) with Claire Carrie; director, Alan Ayckbourn. (3 December) *The Boy Who Fell into a Brook* (Ayckbourn) with Charlie Hayes, Richard Derrington, Nicola Sloane; director, Alan Ayckbourn. (29 May 1999) *Comic Potential* (Ayckbourn); director, Alan Ayckbourn. (17 June) *House and Garden* (Ayckbourn) with Robert Blythe, Janie Dee, Eileen Battye, Terence Booth. (2 July) *Perfect Pitch* (John Godber); director, John Godber. (21 July)

Knights in Plastic Armour (Robert Shearman), a Stephen Joseph Theatre production; director, Alan Ayckbourn. (6 August) *Love Songs for Shopkeepers* (Tim Firth); director, Alan Ayckbourn.

SHEFFIELD: CRUCIBLE (29 October 1998) *All Credit to the Lads* (Alan Plater) with Roy Marsden, Edward Peel, Lynn Farleigh, Polly Hemingway; director, Max Roberts. (17 November) *Twelfth Night* (Shakespeare) with Malcolm Sinclair, Una Stubbs, Daniel Flynn, Susannah Hitching; director, Michael Grandage. (18 December) *South Pacific* (Rodgers and Hammerstein) with Janie Dee, Mark Adams; director, Deborah Paige. (11 February 1999) *Mojo* (Jez Butterworth) with Jonathan McGuinness, Alan Westaway, Joshus Henderson; director, Deborah Paige. (8 June) *Angels in America Part I* (Tony Kushner) with Michael Mawby, David Gwillim, Stephen Bickett, Clare Francis; director, Phil Wilmott.

STRATFORD: ROYAL SHAKESPEARE THEATRE (9 October 1998) *The School for Scandal* (Sheridan) with Jason O'Mara, Matthew McFadyen, Emma Fielding; director, Declan Donnellan. (27 October) *Richard III* (Shakespeare) with Robert Lindsay, Sian Thomas, Anna Carteret, David Yelland; director, Elijah Moshinsky. (24 November) *The Lion, The Witch and the Wardrobe* (C. S. Lewis, adapt. Adrian Mitchell) with Patrice Naiambana, William Mannering, Estelle Kohler; director, Adrian Noble. (10 December) *The Winter's Tale* (Shakespeare) with Antony Sher, Estelle Kohler, Alexandra Gilbreath; director, Gregory Doran. (25 March 1999) *A Midsummer Night's Dream* (Shakespeare) with Josette Simon, Nicholas Jones; director, Michael Boyd. (21 April) *Othello* (Shakespeare) with Ray Fearon, Zoë Waites, Richard McCabe; director, Michael Attenborough. (23 June) *Antony and Cleopatra* (Shakespeare) with Alan Bates, Frances de la Tour; director, Steven Pimlott. (11 August) *Timon of Athens* (Shakespeare) with Michael Pennington, Richard McCabe; director, Gregory Doran.

SWAN (25 November 1998) *A Month in the Country* (Brian Friel, after Turgenev) with Sara Stewart, Catherine Walker, Jack Tarlton, Sam Graham; director, Michael Attenborough. (8 December) *Troilus and Cressida*, transferred from The Pit, London. (24 March 1999) *Volpone* (Jonson) with Malcolm Storry, Guy Henry; director, Lindsay Posner. (20 April) *Tales from Ovid* (Ted Hughes, adapt. Tim Supple, Simon Reade), a Royal Shakespeare Company production; directors, Tim Supple, Melly Still. (9 June) *The Family Reunion* (T. S. Eliot) with Margaret Tyzack, Lynn Farleigh, Greg Hicks; director, Adrian Noble.

THE OTHER PLACE (2 March 1999) *The Dispute* (Pierre Carlet de Marivaux, trans. Neil Bartlett), a Royal Shakespeare Company production; director, Neil Bartlett. (28 April) *Oroonoko* (Aphra Behn, adapt. Biyi Bandele) with Israel Aduramo, David Collings, Nadine Marshall, Nicholas Monu; director, Gergory Doran. (9 June) *Don Carlos* (Friedrich Schiller) with Rupert Penry-Jones, Josette Simon, John Woodvine; director, Gale Edwards. (12 August) *A Warwickshire Testimony* (April de Angelis) with Cherry Morris, Susan Dury; director, Alison Sutcliffe.

Weather

JULY 1998

Rainfall totals were slightly below normal. On the 1st 113.1 mm (4.5 in) of rain fell at Nant-y-Maen (Gwynedd). The 4th had rain over Scotland and northern England. Heavy rain fell in northern England on the 8th. The 10th brought heavy rain to Scotland which spread to most areas on the 11th when 54.6 mm (2.15 in) fell at Davidstow Moor (Cornwall). The 12th continued very wet in all areas and 36 mm (1.4 in) of rain fell at Salsburgh (Strathclyde). The 13th saw thunderstorms down the east coast and in the Irish Sea. Heavy rain fell over south-west England on the 15th, over East Anglia on the 16th and over many areas on the 17th. On the 18th some heavy rain fell in Scotland. Heavy rain fell in northern areas on the 19th when 57.4 mm (2.3 in) fell at Forest Lodge (Highland) and 65.2 mm (2.6 in) at Doune (Highland). Heavy rain fell in Northern Ireland, northern England and northern Wales on the 22nd when 33.6 mm (1.3 in) fell at Capel Curig (Gwynedd). A heavy thunderstorm occurred over Yorkshire on the 27th when 98.5 mm (3.9 in) of rain fell at Thislington Quarry. Rain fell over Scotland on the 28th and on the 29th, when 66 mm (2.6 in) fell at Mylnefield (Tayside). Thunderstorms were frequent over northern and south-west England on the 31st when 163.3 mm (6.4 in) of rain fell at Avon Dam (Devon), 116 mm (4.6 in) at Belstone (Devon) and 144.4 mm (5.7 in) at Parracombe (Devon).

Monthly mean temperatures were mostly below normal. The highest temperature recorded was 29.4°C (84.9°F) at Weybourne (Norfolk). The lowest temperature was 3.1°C (37.6°F) at Tulloch Bridge (Highland) on the 15th and at Aboyne (Grampian) on the 1st.

Sunshine totals were mostly below normal and the highest daily total was 14.9 hours at St Helier (Jersey) on the 19th.

AUGUST 1998

Rainfall totals were generally below normal. On the 1st there were heavy thunderstorms in the south when 76 mm (2.3 in) of rain fell at Broad Oak (Dorset) and 68 mm (2.7 in) fell at Beckenham (London), 48 mm (1.88 in) of which fell in just 30 minutes. The 2nd brought heavy rain to Northern Ireland and Scotland and 53.7 mm (2.1 in) of rain fell at Frizington (Cumbria). The 5th was wet in Scotland when 67.9 mm (2.7 in) of rain fell at Glendessary (Highland). The 10th brought thunderstorms over Scotland. Fog was persistent on western coasts on the 11th. The 13th brought rain to western areas which became heavier on the 14th. Heavy rain fell over East Anglia and south-east England on the 15th and over Northern Ireland and

Scotland on the 16th, when 72.1 mm (2.8 in) fell at Inverinan Mor (Central). The 17th to 19th were mainly dry, but 176.8 mm (7 in) of rain fell at Aberhosan (Powys). The 20th was very wet in many areas; 35.6 mm (1.4 in) of rain fell at Capel Curig (Gwynedd). The 22nd brought thunderstorms across East Anglia. The 23rd was the wettest day for at least six weeks, with strong winds over southern England; 45.6 mm (1.79 in) of rain fell at Nantmor (Gwynedd). Rain fell over England, Wales and Northern Ireland on the 25th. Rain fell in Scotland on the 28th. The 31st brought general rain and 85 mm (3.3 in) fell at Belstone (Dorset).

Monthly mean temperatures were generally around normal. The highest temperature recorded was 32.3°C (90.1°F) at Gravesend (Kent) on the 10th and the lowest was −0.1°C (31.8°F) at Eskdalemuir (Dumfries and Galloway) on the 27th.

Sunshine totals were mainly above normal and the highest daily total was 14.9 hours at Bastreet (Cornwall) on the 8th. The summer months (June, July and August) together were mostly cool and wet.

SEPTEMBER 1998

Rainfall totals were generally above normal. Heavy rain fell generally on the 1st with scattered thunderstorms; 130 mm (5.1 in) of rain fell at Nant-y-Maen (Dyfed) and 70 mm (2.8 in) fell at Sheffield (Yorkshire). The main feature of the 2nd was persistent fog, but 63.7 mm (2.5 in) of rain fell at Barcaldine (Strathclyde). The 3rd had fog in the north and heavy rain over southern England where 66.5 mm (2.6 in) fell at Slapton (Devon). Dense fog persisted on the 4th with heavy rain again in southern areas; 68.3 mm (2.7 in) fell at Cymmer (W.Glam). The 5th saw fog in northern areas; 40.4 mm (1.6 in) of rain fell at Bala Brook (Devon). The 6th was foggy with rain in the south-west while the 7th was windy over Northern Ireland and north-west Scotland; 77 mm (3 in) of rain fell at Honister Pass (Cumbria) and 66.5 mm (2.6 in) fell at Cymmer (W. Glam). The 8th was another generally wet day and 48.3 mm (1.9 in) of rain fell at Bentpath (Dumfries and Galloway). On the 9th there were widespread thunderstorms and strong winds over southern England. Tornadoes occurred between Ashbourne and Matlock in Derbyshire. On the 10th 67.5 mm (2.7 in) of rain fell at Venford Reservoir (Devon). On the 11th 84.4 mm (3.3 in) of rain fell at Aberhosan (Powys). The 15th brought heavy rain and gales to Scotland when 61 mm (2.4 in) of rain fell at Cassley (Highland) and a wind speed of 60 kt (69 mph) was recorded at Suleskerry (Orkney). The 16th was windy with gales in eastern parts of Scotland and England. Gusts in excess of 80 kt (92 mph) were recorded over the Cairngorms. The 19th, 20th and 21st were foggy. Dense fog was confined to northern areas on the 22nd but became widespread again on the 24th and more dense on the 25th. Heavy rain fell over south-east England on the 26th; 55.8 mm (2.2 in) of rain fell at Brizenorton (Oxon). There was further heavy rain on the 27th in southern areas but 62.2 mm (2.5 in) of rain fell at Sella Ness (Shetland). On the 28th 45 mm (1.8 in) of rain fell at Shefford Mill (Beds). Rain and showers, some extremely heavy, fell in many parts of England on the 30th when 218.4 mm (8.59 in) fell at Avon Dam (Devon) and 141.3 mm (5.6 in) at Parracombe (Devon).

Monthly mean temperatures were 1.1°C (2°F) above normal and it was the warmest September since 1961. The highest temperature recorded was 28.7°C (83.7°F) at Cardiff (S. Glam) on the 20th and the lowest was −15°C (5°F) at Aberfoyle (Central) on the 29th.

Sunshine totals were slightly below normal and the highest daily total was 13.2 hours at Salcombe (Devon) on the 19th.

OCTOBER 1998

Rainfall totals were well above normal. There was severe local flooding in southern Wales and the Severn Valley, and Coleshill near Birmingham had its wettest month on record. General rain or showers occurred on the 4th, and on the 5th when 86.5 mm (3.5 in) of rain fell at Princetown (Devon). Rain fell over south-east England on the 8th and almost everywhere on the 9th. The 13th was generally wet when 39.4 mm (1.5 in) of rain fell at Capel Curig (Gwynnedd). Scotland was very windy on the 15th and 34.8 mm (1.4 in) of rain fell at Port Ellen (Strathclyde). The 16th was a generally wet day and 63.6 mm (2.5 in) of rain fell at Waterstein (Highland). Waterspouts were seen off The Lizard on the 18th and thunderstorms occurred along the Devon and Dorset coasts. Heavy rain fell in many areas on the 20th when 63.6 mm (2.5 in) fell at Waterstein (Highland). The 21st brought gales around the coasts and a gust of 61 kt (70 mph) was reported near Anglesey. Rain was heavy in places and 75.3 mm (3 in) fell at Glenlee (Dumfries and Galloway). Rain fell in most places on the 22nd when 90.4 mm (3.5 in) fell at Ystradfelte (Powys). On the 23rd 54.6 mm (2.1 in) of rain fell at Trassey Slievenaman (Co. Down). Gales continued along the south coast with 58 kt (67 mph) being reported at Brixham (Devon). The 24th brought gales to south-western areas and 76 kt (87 mph) was recorded at Portland (Dorset). Heavy rain fell in many places and 150.4 mm (6.1 in) fell at Ballaculish (Highland). On the 25th 55.6 mm (2.2 in) of rain fell at Burrington (Devon) and on the 26th 49.8 mm (1.96 in) fell at Lake Vyrnwy (Powys). On the 27th 49.6 mm (1.95 in) fell at Coleshill (Warwick). There were gales in the west and along the English Channel. On the 29th 55.6 mm (2.2 in) of rain fell at Burrington (Devon) and a heavy shower in Manchester pro-

duced 2 in (5 cm) of marble-sized hail. On the 30th 49.8 mm (1.96 in) of rain fell at Lake Vyrnwy (Powys). Rain fell over southern counties on the 31st when 49.6 mm (1.95 in) fell at Coleshill (Warwick).

Monthly mean temperatures were mostly around normal and the highest temperature recorded was 20.2°C (68.4°F) at Cannington (Somerset) on the 21st and the lowest was −5.1°C (22.8°F) at Eskdalemuir (Dumfries and Galloway) on the 18th.

Sunshine totals were generally around normal and the highest daily total was 10 hours at Saunton Sands (Devon) on the 8th.

NOVEMBER 1998

Rainfall totals were generally below normal. On the 1st 135 mm (5.3 in) of rain fell at Forstal (Kent) and 59 mm (2.3 in) at Burrington (Devon). On the 2nd 72.6 mm (2.9 in) of rain fell at Kielder (Northumberland) and 58.6 mm (2.3 in) at Carterhouse (Border). Gales developed overnight in the English Channel. On the 3rd 225 mm (8.9 in) of rain fell at Sheffield (Yorks) and 141.7 mm (5.8 in) at Skockholm Island (Dyfed). The 5th and 6th brought snow to Scotland. Rain fell in most areas on the 8th but mainly over Scotland on the 9th when winds reached storm force over Northern Ireland and Scotland. Rain fell over south-east England and hail fell in western areas on the 10th. In squally winds in the south, a tornado hit Southampton. Heavy rain fell over southern England on the 13th when 50.3 mm (2 in) fell at Davidstow Moor (Cornwall). Snow fell over southern England on the 14th and in the north-east on the 15th. The 17th brought persistent fog to much of the country. Fog was confined to northern areas on the 18th with some rain in the east. Fog was again persistent over England and Wales on the 19th but some rain fell in the south-west. On the 21st 38.2 mm (1.5 in) of rain fell at Tulloch Bridge (Highland). Rain fell over northern Wales and northern England on the 22nd and over northern England, Northern Ireland and Scotland on the 23rd with fog in places. Rain fell in most areas on the 24th with fog at times. The fog became widespread on the 25th with rain and showers in the west; 279 mm (10.9 in) of rain fell at Grizedale (Cumbria). On the 27th 31.2 mm (1.2 in) of rain fell at Eskdalemuir (Dumfries and Galloway). On the 30th very heavy showers brought 258.2 mm (10.2 in) of rain to Belstone (Devon), 190.8 mm (7.8 in) to Avon Dam (Devon) and 151.6 mm (6 in) to Parracombe (Devon).

Monthly mean temperatures were 0.4 C (0.7°F) below normal over England and Wales. The highest temperature recorded was 20.1°C (68.1°F) at Altnahara (Highland) on the 24th and the lowest was −11.3°C (11.7°F) at Aviemore (Highland) on the 18th.

Sunshine totals were generally above normal and the highest daily total was 10.5 hours at Liscombe (Somerset) on the 19th.

DECEMBER 1998

Rainfall totals were generally below normal over England and Wales. Fog was widespread on the 3rd, freezing in places with rain later. Wintry showers fell in Scotland and the east of England on the 4th and sleet or snow fell as far south as the Thames Estuary on the 5th and 6th. The 7th was a generally foggy day with some rain in western areas; 73.5 mm (2.9 in) fell at Rydal Hall (Cumbria). Rain fell in most places on the 8th when 35.6 mm (1.4 in) fell at St Catherines Point (Isle of Wight). Fog became dense over the Midlands, the Vale of York, Lincolnshire and East Anglia on the 9th. Fog was persistent in places on the 11th with rain mostly in western areas. The 12th brought rain to most of England and Wales. Hail and tornadoes were reported across southern England. Heavy rain fell over much of the country on the 13th when 69 mm (2.7 in) fell at Glendessary (Highland) and 47.8 mm (1.9 in) fell at Skye (Western Isles). The 14th brought rain to most areas while the 15th had rain in the south. There were gales in north and west Scotland when a gust of 74 kt (85 mph) was recorded at Kirkwall (Orkney). The 16th was windy again in Northern Ireland and Scotland. On the 17th 30.9 mm (1.2 in) of rain fell at Dalmally (Strathclyde). On the 19th 39.2 mm (1.5 in) of rain fell at Jersey (Channel Islands). Snow fell over Scotland on the 20th and in Scotland, north-east England and northern Wales on the 21st. The 22nd was mainly foggy but some rain in most areas. Rain or showers fell almost everywhere on the 23rd. The 24th brought strong winds over Scotland and rain to most areas when 31.4 mm (1.2 in) fell at Capel Curig (Gwynedd). Winds were strong again over Scotland on the 25th which was a generally wet day; 34 mm (1.3 in) of rain fell at Mumbles Head (W. Glam). Gales swept northern areas on the 26th when gusts of 87 kt (100 mph) at Capel Curig (Gwynedd), 83 kt (94 mph) at Machrihanish (Strathclyde) and 81 kt (93 mph) at Boulmer (Northumberland) occurred. It was another wet day and 51 mm (2 in) of rain fell at Benmore (Highland). Rain fell in most areas on the 27th but mainly in the north and west on the 28th. Eskdalemuir recorded 7 cm (2.7 in) of snow lying early in the morning. Gales occurred on the 29th when 64 kt (74 mph) was recorded at South Uist (Hebrides). Rain fell mostly in the north and 33.6 mm (1.3 in) fell at Tulloch Bridge (Highland). Gales continued on the 30th in the north and west. There was heavy rain in Cornwall on the 31st when 213.4 mm (8.4 in) fell at Parracombe (Devon).

Monthly mean temperatures were 0.6°C (1.08°F) above normal; the highest temperature recorded was 16.3°C (61.3°F) at Hawarden Bridge (Clwyd) on the 14th and the lowest was −12.2°C (10°F) at Braemar (Grampian) on the 6th.

Sunshine totals were generally below normal and the highest daily total was 7.3 hours at St Mawgan and at Bastreet (Cornwall) on the 20th.

THE YEAR 1998

1998 was the wettest since 1966. January was wet but sunny and the mildest since 1994. February was the mildest since 1990 and the second mildest since 1869. March was a wet month and mainly dull but warm. April was the wettest since 1818 and the third wettest since 1766. It was the coldest April since 1989. May was the warmest since 1992 and the driest since 1991. June was the fourth wettest this century. July was the dullest since 1992. August was also dull but dry. September was the warmest since 1961 and the eighth warmest this century. It was yet another wet month. October saw record-breaking rainfall over southern Wales and the Severn Valley where severe flooding occurred. November was the driest since 1993 but mainly sunny with temperatures around normal. December was cold at first but then wet and windy with a severe gale in the north on Boxing Day. The year was generally very warm. Temperatures were 0.84°C (1.5°F) above normal over England and Wales and it was the eighth warmest year this century. Sunshine totals were generally below normal.

JANUARY 1999

Rainfall totals were generally well above normal. On the 1st 37 mm (1.5 in) of rain fell at Tulloch Bridge (Highland). Gales affected south-west England and a gust of 64 kt (74 mph) was recorded at Aberporth (Dyfed). On the 2nd 43.1 mm (1.7 in) of rain fell at Loch Venachar (Central) and on the 3rd 70.5 mm (2.8 in) fell at Wroughton Waterworks (Wilts). Gale-force winds swept across southern areas; Aberporth (Dyfed) recorded a gust of 68 kt (78 mph) and Manston (Kent) recorded 65 kt (75 mph). The gales moved north on the 4th when Tiree (Hebrides) recorded a gust of 76 kt (87 mph) and one of 72 kt (83 mph) was recorded at Glasgow (Strathclyde); 183 mm (7.2 in) of rain fell at Princetown (Devon) and 66.2 mm (2.6 in) fell at Capel Curig (Gwynedd). The 5th was wet in northern areas when 91.6 mm (3.6 in) of rain fell at Spadeadam (Cumbria). Rain was heavy for a time over England and Wales on the 7th. The 11th was foggy but 33 mm (1.3 in) of rain fell at Capel Curig (Gwynedd). Rain or showers fell almost everywhere on the 12th with snow in northern parts. The 13th brought gales to north-western areas when Tiree (Hebrides) recorded a gust of 65 kt (75 mph). It was a generally wet day and 41.8 mm (1.6 in) of rain fell at Sella Ness (Shetland). On the 14th 35.8 mm (1.4 in) of rain fell at Tulloch Bridge (Highland). A gust of 62 kt (71 mph) was recorded at Barra (Highland). Widespread rain fell on the 15th and was especially heavy in south-western areas where 104.2 mm (4.1 in) of rain fell at Llyn Fawr (Powys), 102.8 mm (4 in) fell at Venford Reservoir (Devon) and 70.6 mm (2.8 in) fell at Capel Curig (Gwynedd). Lerwick (Shetland) recorded a gust of 64 kt (74 mph) on the 16th. The 17th brought 39.7 mm (1.6 in) of rain to

Nantmor (Gwynedd). The 18th was a generally wet day and 81.4 mm (3.2 in) of rain fell at Tulloch Bridge (Highland). Ronaldsway (Isle of Man) recorded a gust of 60 kt (69 mph). The 19th was wet in southern England where 75.5 mm (3 in) of rain fell at Blackdown Reservoir (Devon) and 65.2 mm (2.6 in) fell at North Hessary Tor (Cornwall). The 20th was generally wet over England. The 21st brought dense fog to England and Wales. The 22nd was also foggy and 46.8 mm (1.8 in) of rain fell at Lussa (Isle of Skye). The 23rd started generally foggy. The 24th produced heavy rain mainly over northern England and southern Scotland and 42.4 mm (1.7 in) fell on Shap Fell (Cumbria). On the 25th 204.5 mm (8.1 in) of rain fell at Princetown (Devon). The 26th brought frequent thunderstorms to southern England. Rain was widely scattered on the 27th but 41.6 mm (1.6 in) fell at Capel Curig (Gwynedd). The 30th brought fog over central areas. Fog formed in parts of England and Wales on the 31st.

Monthly mean temperatures were 1.5°C (2.7°F) above normal and on the 6th London had its warmest January day on record with 16°C (60.8°F) while Gravesend (Kent) recorded 16.3°C (61.3°F), this being the highest temperature recorded for the month. The lowest temperature was –8.4°C (16.9°F) at Braemar (Grampian) on the 12th.

Sunshine totals were generally above normal. The highest daily total was 8.3 hours at Portland (Dorset) on the 22nd.

FEBRUARY 1999

Rainfall totals were mainly below normal but slightly above in northern Wales, Scotland and northern England. On the 4th Leeds (W. Yorks) recorded a gust of 73 kt (84 mph) while Fair Isle (Shetland) recorded one of 85 kt (98 mph) The gales continued on the 5th. The 8th brought snow to all areas which was more scattered on the 9th. Snow was mainly confined to eastern areas on the 10th and to northern areas on the 11th. It was windy in northern parts on the 15th. The gales continued in the north on the 16th when Tiree (Hebrides) reported a gust of 65 kt (75 mph). The 17th brought general snow to Scotland with rain elsewhere. Conditions were similar on the 18th but 143.2 mm (5.6 in) of rain fell at Machrihanish (Strathclyde) and 49 mm (1.9 in) fell at Dalmally (Strathclyde). On the 20th 30.7 mm (1.2 in) of rain fell at Dalmally. On the 21st Waddington (Lincs) recorded a gust of 60 kt (69 mph) and on the 22nd Aberporth (Dyfed) recorded a gust of 60 kt (69 mph). Rain fell over England, Wales and Northern Ireland on the 23rd and 24th but mainly over eastern areas on the 25th, when 159.6 mm (6.3 in) fell at Machrihanish (Highland). Rain was confined to southern areas on the 26th. On the 27th 69.6 mm (2.7 in) of rain fell at Doune (Highland) and on the 28th 141.5 mm (5.6 in) fell at Parracombe (Devon), 166.2 mm (6.5 in) at Machrihanish (Strathclyde) and 70.2 mm (2.8 in) at Capel Curig (Gwynedd).

Monthly mean temperatures were 1.1°C (2°F) above normal over England and Wales and the highest temperature recorded was 14.8°C (58.6°F) at Wittering (Cambs) on the 19th. The lowest temperature was –11°C (12.2°F) at Aboyne (Grampian) on the 8th.

Sunshine totals were generally above normal and the highest daily total was 9.4 hours at Abbotsinch (Strathclyde) on the 22nd. The winter months (December, January, February) as a whole had generally average rainfall but were very windy at times. Temperatures were 1.1°C (2°F) above normal and sunshine totals were well above normal.

MARCH 1999

Rainfall totals were mainly below normal in southern areas but above normal in the north. Rain fell generally on the 1st when 135 mm (5.3 in) fell at Nant-y-Maen (Dyfed) and 31.2 mm (1.2 in) at Capel Curig (Gwynedd). It was wintry in western areas. The 2nd was windy in western and southern regions with heavy rain; 63.6 mm (2.5 in) fell at Footholme (Lancs) and 43.2 mm (1.7 in) at Capel Curig (Gwynedd). On the 3rd Fair Isle (Shetland) recorded a gust of 75 kt (86 mph) and 98.8 mm (3.9 in) of rain fell at Machrihanish (Strathclyde). Rain or showers with snow in Scotland fell on the 4th and snow fell in all eastern areas on the 5th and 6th; 12 cm (4.7 in) of snow lay on Emley Moor (W. Yorks) on the 6th. Boltshope Park (Northumberland) had 21 cm (8.3 in) of snow lying on the 8th. The 9th brought snow to Scotland and eastern England. On the 14th 94 mm (3.7 in) of rain fell at Brockhampton (Hereford). The 15th was wet over Scotland when 78.6 mm (3.1 in) of rain fell at Blaran (Strathclyde) and 96.8 mm (3.8 in) fell at Skye (Western Isles). Fog was widespread over England and Wales on the 17th. Some heavy rain fell over Scotland on the 20th when 43.3 mm (1.7 in) fell at Dalmally (Strathclyde). On the 23rd 51.8 mm (2 in) fell at Ballykelly (Co. Londonderry). The 24th was wet only in Scotland but rain became widespread over England and Wales on the 25th. Rain fell mainly over south-east England on the 26th. The 28th brought heavy rain to Scotland and northern England when 59.3 mm (2.9 in) fell at Eskdalemuir (Dumfries and Galloway) and 108.4 mm (4.3 in) fell at Honister Pass (Cumbria). There were gales in northern areas. Rain fell in most places on the 29th but mostly over England and Wales on the 30th. On the 31st 96.5 mm (3.8 in) of rain fell at Nant-y-Maen (Dyfed).

Monthly mean temperatures were 1.2°C (2.2°F) above normal. The highest temperature recorded was 21.2°C (70.2°F) at Slobdon (Hereford and Worcester) on the 17th and the lowest was –6.4°C (20.5°F) at Aboyne (Grampian) on the 28th.

Sunshine totals were generally around normal and the highest daily total was 11.5 hours at Bristol (Avon) on the 27th.

APRIL 1999

Rainfall totals were generally above normal except in East Anglia. Heavy showers on the 1st produced 152.5 mm (6 in) of rain at Nant-y-Maen (Dyfed), 134 mm (5.3 in) at Teifi Reservoir (Dyfed) and 109 mm (4.3 in) at Inchlaggan (Highland). The 2nd brought thunderstorms to the Midlands while the 3rd had rain over southern England with fog in many areas. Rain affected most areas on the 4th but mostly northern and western areas on the 5th. Heavy rain fell over Scotland on the 6th. The 9th brought rain to Scotland. Heavy rain fell in the north-west and south-east on the 11th when 50.2 mm (2 in) of rain fell at Capel Curig (Gwynedd). The 12th brought gales round northern and western coasts and there were gales in Northern Ireland and along western coasts on the 13th. Heavy rain fell in Scotland on the 14th when 30.3 mm (1.2 in) fell at Aviemore (Highland). Snow fell in places and 8 cm (3.1 in) lay on Bristol Airfield. Thunderstorms with hail occurred in southern and eastern England on the 17th and 30.8 mm (1.2 in) of rain fell at Conningsby (Lincs) while heavy snow over the Pennines left 12-15 cm (5-6 in) lying in places. Thunderstorms were widespread on the 18th and some heavy rain fell over southern England on the 19th. The 20th was generally wet and 40 mm (1.56 in) of rain fell at Dundrennan (Dumfries and Galloway). On the 21st 41 mm (1.61 in) of rain fell at Lochranza (Strathclyde). The 22nd brought rain to Scotland. Heavy rain fell over England on the 23rd. Severe thunderstorms occurred in the south-west Midlands on the 26th when 49 mm (1.9 in) of rain fell at Barbourne (Worcs). The 27th to 30th were mainly dry but isolated heavy showers gave 221.6 mm (8.7 in) of rain at Avon Dam (Devon) and 153 mm (6 in) at Parracombe (Devon).

Monthly mean temperatures were 1.5 °C (2.7 °F) above normal. The highest temperature recorded was 22.4 °C (72.3 °F) at Dalmally (Strathclyde) on the 27th and the lowest was -6.7 °C (19.9 °F) at Redesdale (Northumberland) on the 14th.

Sunshine totals were mostly above normal. The highest daily total was 14.2 hours at Lyneham (Wilts) on the 30th.

MAY 1999

Rainfall totals were mainly below normal. On the 1st 65.1 mm (2.6 in) of rain fell at Barnby-on-the-Marsh (W. Yorks). The 2nd brought some rain in the north of Scotland. The 3rd had general fog and on the 4th 91.8 mm (3.6 in) of rain fell at Machrihanish (Highland). Rain fell over England and Wales on the 5th and more generally on the 6th. The rain became heavy on the 7th and 68 mm (2.7 in) fell at Overton (Lancs) and 47.4 mm (1.9 in) at Bingley (W. Yorks). Rain fell again on the 9th. Thunderstorms occurred in East Anglia on the 12th and 31 mm (1.2 in) of rain fell at Sunderland (Tyne and Wear). On the 13th 36 mm (1.4 in) of rain fell at Drumburgh (Cumbria). The 19th brought fre-

quent thunderstorms to southern England which moved to south-east England on the 20th. Rain fell in northern England and Scotland on the 25th. Heavy thunderstorms affected most of England and southern Wales on the 27th when 31.4 mm (1.2 in) of rain fell at Castledarg (Co. Tyrone). The thunderstorms moved northwards on the 28th and 36.3 mm (1.4 in) of rain fell at Kinloss (Grampian). The 29th brought rain to Scotland and thunderstorms to much of England and Wales. On the 30th 114.6 mm (4.5 in) of rain fell at Cassley (Highland). On the 31st 98 mm (3.9 in) of rain fell at Parracombe (Devon).

Monthly mean temperatures were generally above normal. The highest temperature recorded was 27.2 °C (81 °F) at Southampton (Hants) on the 29th and the lowest was -0.9 °C (30.4 °F) at Dalmally (Strathclyde) on the 1st.

Sunshine totals were generally below normal and the highest daily total was 16 hours at Lerwick (Shetland) on the 19th. The spring months (March, April and May) as a whole were warm; rainfall was slightly below normal and sunshine totals were slightly above normal.

JUNE 1999

Rainfall totals were generally above normal. The 1st brought severe thunderstorms to southern England and 70.3 mm (2.8 in) of rain fell at Ripon (N. Yorks), 66.1 mm (2.6 in) at Petworth Park (Sussex) and 44.6 mm (1.7 in) at Northolt (Gtr London). The thunderstorms spread to most of England and Wales on the 2nd when 22.2 mm (0.9 in) of rain fell in one hour at Southampton (Hants). On the 4th 120.9 mm (4.7 in) of rain fell at Aberhosan (Powys). The 5th brought 79.3 mm (3.1 in) of rain to Penzance (Cornwall). The 7th brought severe thunderstorms to southern England when 37.6 mm (1.5 in) of rain fell at Leeming (N. Yorks). There was rain over East Anglia on the 10th and in most eastern areas on the 11th and 12th. The 13th brought rain to northern areas and fog to the south. Rain fell generally on the 14th and over Scotland on the 16th and northern England on the 17th. Heavy rain fell generally on the 19th when 88 mm (3.5 in) fell at Honister Pass (Cumbria) and 48.1 mm (1.9 in) fell at Dalmally (Strathclyde). Rain fell over England and Wales on the 26th when 44.6 mm (1.7 in) fell at Walney Island (Cumbria). The 29th brought rain to southern England which spread to most areas on the 30th when 154 mm (6.1 in) fell at Avon Dam (Dorset) and 73.1 mm (2.9 in) fell at Parracombe (Devon).

Monthly mean temperatures were slightly below normal over England and Wales. The highest temperature recorded was 27.2 °C (80.9 °F) at Northolt (Gtr London) on the 26th and the lowest was -1.2 °C (29.8 °F) at Saughall (Strathclyde) on the 7th.

Sunshine totals were generally above normal and the highest daily total was 16.6 hours at Kirkwall (Orkney) on the 23rd.

AVERAGE AND GENERAL VALUES 1997–9 (June)

	Rainfall (mm)				Temperature (° C)				Bright Sunshine (hrs per day)			
	Average 1961–90	1997	1998	1999	Average 1961–90	1997	1998	1999	Average 1961–90	1997	1998	1999
England and Wales												
January	77	14	119	120	3.8	2.4	5.3	7.7	1.6	1.7	1.7	2.1
February	55	120	23	47	3.8	6.5	7.4	5.1	2.4	2.5	3.3	3.0
March	63	32	98	64	5.6	8.3	8.0	7.2	3.5	4.2	2.5	3.8
April	53	25	125	72	7.7	8.8	7.9	9.2	4.9	5.6	4.3	5.6
May	56	75	34	53	10.9	11.5	12.9	12.6	6.2	7.8	6.8	5.7
June	58	128	124	78	13.9	14.0	14.2	13.6	6.4	5.0	7.0	–
July	56	48	54	–	15.7	16.4	15.3	–	6.0	7.4	5.4	–
August	68	95	47	–	15.6	18.7	15.8	–	6.0	6.5	7.3	–
September	70	35	88	–	13.6	14.3	14.6	–	4.5	5.4	4.4	–
October	77	68	144	–	10.7	10.4	10.6	–	3.2	4.3	3.4	–
November	81	117	82	–	6.6	8.6	6.1	–	2.2	1.5	2.7	–
December	82	108	83	–	4.7	6.0	5.7	–	1.5	1.3	1.4	–
Year	796	865	1021	–	9.4	10.5	10.3	–	4.0	4.4	4.3	–
Scotland												
January	117	56	165	138	3.1	3.1	4.3	3.7	1.3	1.3	1.2	1.4
February	78	268	200	88	3.1	4.8	7.4	3.4	2.4	2.3	1.3	2.9
March	94	138	122	79	4.6	6.8	6.0	5.3	3.2	3.2	2.3	3.8
April	60	76	122	74	6.5	7.8	6.1	7.4	4.8	3.6	4.9	4.9
May	67	113	57	81	9.3	9.3	10.5	9.8	5.6	5.8	5.4	5.9
June	67	104	114	87	12.1	12.0	11.3	11.1	5.6	4.9	5.7	5.1
July	74	90	109	–	13.6	14.9	12.6	–	4.9	5.3	3.9	–
August	92	65	87	–	13.5	16.1	13.0	–	4.9	6.3	4.2	–
September	111	114	66	–	11.5	11.9	12.2	–	3.5	4.7	3.8	–
October	120	80	165	–	9.1	8.9	7.6	–	2.6	3.1	3.5	–
November	118	139	141	–	5.3	7.7	4.9	–	1.7	1.3	2.1	–
December	115	182	110	–	3.9	5.3	4.7	–	1.0	0.9	1.1	–
Year	1113	1425	1458	–	7.9	9.1	8.4	–	3.5	3.6	3.3	–

Source: Data provided by the Met Office

WEATHER RECORDS

World Records

Maximum air temperature	57.8°C/136°F
San Louis, Mexico, 11 August 1933	
Minimum air temperature	−89.2°C/−128.56°F
Vostok, Antarctica, 21 July 1983	
Greatest rainfall in one day	1870 mm/73.62 in
Cilaos, Ile de Réunion, 16 March 1952	
Greatest rainfall in one calendar month	9300 mm/366.14 in
Cherrapunji, Assam, July 1861	
Greatest annual rainfall total	22,990 mm/905.12 in
Cherrapunji, Assam, 1861	
Fastest gust of wind	201 knots/231 mph
Mt Washington Observatory, USA, 12 April 1934	

United Kingdom Records

Maximum air temperature	37.1°C/98.8°F
Cheltenham, Glos, 3 August 1990	
Minimum air temperature	−27.2°C/−17°F
Braemar, Grampian, 11 February 1895 and 10 January 1982	
Greatest rainfall in one day	280 mm/11 in
Martinstown, Dorset, 18 July 1955	
Greatest annual rainfall total	6528 mm/257 in
Sprinkling Tarn, Cumbria, 1954	
Fastest gust of wind	150 knots/173 mph
Cairngorm, Highland, 20 March 1986	
Fastest low-level gust*	123 knots/141.7 mph
Fraserburgh, Grampian, 13 February 1989	
Highest mean hourly speed	92 knots/106 mph
Great Dun Fell, Cumbria, December 1974	
Highest low-level mean hourly speed*	72 knots/83 mph
Shoreham-by-Sea, Sussex, 16 October 1987	

* below 200 m/656 ft

WIND FORCE MEASURES

The *Beaufort Scale* of wind force has been accepted internationally and is used in communicating weather conditions. Devised originally by Admiral Sir Francis Beaufort in 1805, it now consists of the numbers 0–17, each representing a certain strength or velocity of wind at 10 m (33 ft) above ground in the open.

Scale no.	Wind Force	mph	knots
0	Calm	1	1
1	Light air	1–3	1–3
2	Slight breeze	4–7	4–6
3	Gentle breeze	8–12	7–10
4	Moderate breeze	13–18	11–16
5	Fresh breeze	19–24	17–21
6	Strong breeze	25–31	22–27
7	High wind	32–38	28–33
8	Gale	39–46	34–40
9	Strong gale	47–54	41–47
10	Whole gale	55–63	48–55
11	Storm	64–72	56–63
12	Hurricane	73–82	64–71
13	–	83–92	72–80
14	–	93–103	81–89
15	–	104–114	90–99
16	–	115–125	100–108
17	–	126–136	109–118

TEMPERATURE, RAINFALL AND SUNSHINE
At selected climatological reporting stations, July 1998–June 1999 and calendar year 1998

Ht   height (in metres) of station above mean sea level
°C   mean air temperature
Rain   total monthly rainfall
Sun   mean daily bright sunshine (hours)
Source: data provided by the Met Office

		July 1998			August 1998			September 1998			October 1998		
	Ht m	°C	Rain mm	Sun hrs	°C	Rain mm	Sun hrs	°C	Rain mm	Sun hrs	°C	Rain mm	Sun hrs
Lerwick	82	11.2	75.9	2.7	11.2	79.3	2.8	11.5	116.5	2.1	7.4	182.3	2.7
Stornoway	15	12.7	94.9	3.4	12.9	53.4	3.9	12.8	54.6	4.1	8.2	152.3	3.3
Dyce	65	13.6	109.0	3.8	13.9	52.9	4.8	12.8	83.9	2.7	8.2	111.1	4.3
Eskdalemuir	242	12.9	183.7	3.2	13.0	154.6	4.1	12.3	120.0	3.4	7.4	276.1	3.1
Aldergrove	68	14.5	87.4	3.8	14.7	60.2	4.8	13.7	59.0	3.8	9.7	121.8	3.4
Leeds	64	15.9	28.2	5.3	16.3	29.4	5.9	14.9	44.9	3.5	10.5	93.7	3.7
Valley	10	14.9	39.1	5.0	15.6	50.8	6.6	14.8	44.5	5.1	11.3	120.8	3.6
Elmdon	98	15.6	40.8	4.9	15.8	39.0	6.6	14.6	66.4	4.0	10.2	119.4	3.1
Skegness	6	16.0	24.2	5.5	16.1	35.0	6.1	14.5	49.6	3.7	10.9	87.7	3.5
Bristol	42	16.4	54.3	5.6	17.4	53.8	7.9	16.2	85.4	5.1	12.0	163.6	3.0
St. Mawgan	103	15.1	96.6	5.0	16.0	41.0	8.3	15.3	99.8	5.0	12.3	154.2	3.8
Hastings	45	16.3	39.1	6.8	17.3	8.4	9.3	16.0	98.5	5.8	11.6	139.1	3.0

	November 1998			December 1998			The Year 1998			January 1999			February 1999		
	°C	Rain mm	Sun hrs	°C	Rain mm	Sun hrs	°C	Rain mm	Sun hrs	°C	Rain mm	Sun hrs	°C	Rain mm	Sun hrs
Lerwick	5.4	160.7	1.9	4.8	170.0	0.7	7.4	1457	3.0	4.0	139.2	1.1	2.6	202.8	2.4
Stornoway	6.3	158.3	2.1	5.9	165.8	0.8	8.7	1387	3.4	4.9	206.3	1.2	4.1	129.4	2.1
Dyce	4.6	86.1	3.0	4.2	66.9	1.7	8.7	869	3.3	4.1	50.0	2.1	3.4	48.3	4.0
Eskdalemuir	4.0	204.5	1.8	3.5	184.1	1.2	7.9	1960	2.8	2.9	291.3	1.1	3.3	119.5	2.9
Aldergrove	6.6	77.4	2.5	5.5	99.2	1.1	9.4	974	3.3	4.2	94.8	1.3	5.1	54.7	2.5
Leeds	6.3	56.0	2.4	5.8	46.5	1.5	10.6	740	3.7	5.9	59.5	2.5	5.8	27.2	3.5
Valley	8.2	128.3	2.3	7.6	90.2	0.8	10.8	923	4.1	6.7	139.2	1.7	6.4	47.3	2.6
Elmdon	5.8	51.6	2.3	4.9	72.2	1.4	9.9	—	—	5.1	125.8	2.2	4.9	41.2	2.6
Skegness	5.4	46.4	2.6	5.4	102.4	1.5	10.3	615	3.9	5.3	100.4	2.5	4.7	31.1	3.5
Bristol	8.1	74.2	2.5	7.2	96.4	1.5	11.7	928	4.3	7.4	174.4	1.8	6.6	51.0	2.9
St. Mawgan	8.9	158.4	2.8	7.6	148.0	2.1	11.2	1225	4.7	7.6	116.0	2.3	7.2	80.8	2.4
Hastings	7.1	44.1	3.9	6.5	92.3	1.5	10.7	770	4.9	6.8	80.3	2.8	5.5	34.2	3.6

	March 1999			April 1999			May 1999			June 1999		
	°C	Rain mm	Sun hrs	°C	Rain mm	Sun hrs	°C	Rain mm	Sun hrs	°C	Rain mm	Sun hrs
Lerwick	4.9	93.9	3.6	6.3	77.0	4.9	7.6	86.5	6.6	9.8	89.4	3.7
Stornoway	5.8	153.7	3.5	7.7	107.4	4.9	9.8	103.8	5.9	10.8	104.6	4.1
Dyce	6.0	37.8	4.2	8.2	53.8	4.9	10.2	44.2	6.4	12.1	74.4	5.2
Eskdalemuir	4.7	133.1	2.8	7.0	136.7	4.2	10.3	164.3	4.4	11.3	113.1	4.5
Aldergrove	6.7	48.0	4.2	9.1	63.2	5.4	12.0	46.2	5.2	12.8	61.6	5.2
Leeds	7.7	67.3	4.0	9.9	67.1	5.0	13.4	43.3	5.5	14.6	63.9	6.3
Valley	7.4	49.8	4.0	9.5	70.0	6.3	12.6	43.4	6.1	13.3	81.0	7.3
Elmdon	7.0	66.4	3.1	9.4	74.7	5.1	13.0	64.2	4.7	13.8	69.0	6.5
Skegness	7.7	69.1	3.7	9.8	41.8	6.2	12.8	35.6	7.0	14.1	67.9	6.3
Bristol	8.6	74.6	3.6	10.5	94.9	5.3	14.1	53.6	4.5	15.2	74.8	7.4
St. Mawgan	7.9	37.8	5.0	9.9	99.2	5.9	13.1	50.6	5.8	13.6	84.6	7.3
Hastings	8.0	43.6	4.5	10.0	54.7	6.2	13.8	24.4	7.8	15.0	64.5	8.8

METEOROLOGICAL OBSERVATIONS London (Heathrow)

Temperature maxima and minima cover the 24-hour period 9–9 h; mean wind speed is 10 m above the ground; rainfall is for the 24 hours starting at 9 h on the day of entry; sunshine is for the 24 hours 0–24 h; averages are for the period 1961–90. *Source:* Data provided by the Met Office

JULY 1998

Day	Temperature Max. °C	Min. °C	Wind knots	Rain mm	Sun hrs
1	19.9	12.9	5.4	0.0	9.4
2	17.0	11.0	5.5	0.0	0.1
3	19.6	10.1	3.0	0.0	3.7
4	19.1	11.3	3.5	0.0	0.8
5	23.3	12.1	5.6	0.0	9.1
6	19.3	15.9	2.5	0.6	0.0
7	20.5	12.6	3.2	0.0	5.2
8	22.7	8.9	5.4	0.2	5.9
9	21.9	14.4	4.6	0.0	0.4
10	21.0	15.8	4.1	0.2	2.2
11	18.2	14.6	6.5	7.4	0.1
12	19.1	14.6	10.8	3.9	0.4
13	19.8	11.6	7.3	0.2	12.8
14	20.2	11.1	7.5	0.0	7.6
15	20.0	12.3	6.8	2.2	3.4
16	22.3	13.1	3.3	0.2	5.9
17	22.8	14.0	8.3	0.0	8.1
18	21.9	13.1	7.5	0.0	10.3
19	23.2	11.6	4.6	0.0	9.2
20	26.3	14.4	4.6	0.6	10.6
21	21.8	15.8	8.3	0.0	8.5
22	22.5	13.0	8.6	2.2	9.3
23	23.5	14.8	7.2	0.2	8.6
24	21.9	11.4	3.1	0.0	11.5
25	22.7	12.0	2.0	0.0	10.6
26	21.0	12.1	3.0	2.0	3.0
27	23.1	13.1	3.5	Trace	4.5
28	21.7	13.9	4.1	0.8	1.8
29	22.3	15.0	7.3	0.4	7.3
30	22.5	13.1	9.2	1.6	8.5
31	22.6	12.8	4.0	4.2	7.1
Total	—	—	—	26.9	184.3
Mean	21.4	13.0	5.5	—	—
Temp °F	70.5	55.4	—	—	—
Average	22.5	13.1	7.4	46.0	194.5

AUGUST 1998

Day	Temperature Max. °C	Min. °C	Wind knots	Rain mm	Sun hrs
1	21.9	11.8	3.1	Trace	6.4
2	20.8	11.9	2.0	0.0	8.1
3	18.4	11.5	7.6	0.8	0.0
4	23.1	13.9	5.3	0.0	14.3
5	26.6	12.3	4.7	0.0	14.2
6	27.2	11.1	5.4	0.0	13.4
7	29.2	12.4	3.4	0.0	13.7
8	29.9	13.9	2.6	0.0	13.9
9	26.0	16.4	7.4	0.0	8.1
10	31.2	15.5	3.0	0.0	11.9
11	29.7	15.7	3.4	0.0	13.6
12	23.8	15.0	6.5	0.0	12.0
13	22.0	11.7	5.6	0.0	8.0
14	26.7	15.1	5.6	7.8	8.0
15	22.6	14.2	3.0	0.0	10.1
16	24.7	11.4	3.8	0.0	11.3
17	25.3	14.3	5.8	0.0	6.6
18	22.6	15.4	2.3	0.0	7.2
19	25.0	10.9	2.8	0.0	10.9
20	22.2	12.7	7.5	Trace	5.2
21	22.7	16.0	9.3	0.0	8.0
22	20.4	11.8	4.8	0.8	7.5
23	19.4	9.0	6.1	5.2	0.0
24	19.0	11.6	3.8	0.2	3.1
25	22.1	9.8	3.3	0.4	8.4
26	17.8	15.7	5.4	0.2	0.1
27	20.3	9.2	2.9	0.0	10.9
28	20.1	8.6	1.5	0.0	6.8
29	22.7	9.5	2.3	0.0	9.9
30	21.7	13.2	3.2	0.0	3.3
31	22.7	11.2	7.9	1.2	7.7
Total	—	—	—	16.6	262.6
Mean	23.5	12.7	4.6	—	—
Temp °F	59.7	32.3	—	—	—
Average	22.1	12.8	7.2	51.0	186.7

SEPTEMBER 1998

Day	Temperature Max. °C	Min. °C	Wind knots	Rain mm	Sun hrs
1	25.9	15.5	6.0	0.0	5.6
2	23.3	13.7	1.9	12.8	2.1
3	22.4	15.1	4.3	0.2	6.3
4	20.2	12.0	4.3	20.2	1.0
5	20.0	14.9	4.3	3.3	2.8
6	21.7	13.0	4.9	Trace	3.1
7	23.3	15.8	7.8	2.2	9.6
8	23.3	15.6	8.0	0.1	5.1
9	21.5	16.0	12.1	2.8	4.7
10	21.0	15.1	9.7	0.4	7.8
11	18.2	11.2	4.5	Trace	6.6
12	14.8	6.9	4.3	10.6	5.3
13	15.9	7.1	6.8	0.0	7.7
14	17.6	7.8	6.8	0.6	8.8
15	18.7	8.7	5.0	2.0	0.9
16	18.9	8.4	7.6	0.0	8.6
17	18.4	8.2	3.0	0.0	7.9
18	21.6	11.4	3.5	Trace	0.9
19	23.6	15.1	1.2	0.0	5.0
20	21.4	13.3	4.5	0.0	8.3
21	21.6	14.1	6.1	0.0	7.5
22	18.4	13.8	6.6	0.0	0.8
23	21.5	12.0	5.5	0.0	10.0
24	22.0	13.0	5.1	0.0	6.9
25	23.0	13.2	4.3	0.4	6.8
26	22.2	14.7	3.9	21.4	0.8
27	19.2	14.2	1.6	3.6	1.2
28	18.1	15.0	2.0	0.0	0.2
29	16.8	13.3	4.1	3.6	0.0
30	18.4	13.6	10.5	17.0	6.8
31	—	—	—	—	—
Total	—	—	—	101.2	149.1
Mean	20.4	12.7	5.3	—	—
Temp °F	68.7	54.9	—	—	—
Average	19.3	10.8	7.1	51.0	144.7

OCTOBER 1998

Day	Temperature Max. °C	Min. °C	Wind knots	Rain mm	Sun hrs
1	17.8	13.1	7.5	0.0	4.0
2	14.2	11.1	4.3	0.0	0.2
3	11.6	5.4	2.8	Trace	2.7
4	12.5	8.8	4.4	1.4	2.8
5	11.9	8.2	4.8	11.4	0.8
6	12.1	8.9	5.3	0.0	0.0
7	13.2	9.8	6.5	0.2	0.1
8	11.9	9.5	9.3	0.0	0.0
9	15.4	10.0	4.1	2.8	2.9
10	16.1	9.3	3.7	1.4	1.8
11	17.7	9.5	6.8	Trace	6.4
12	16.0	9.5	6.5	0.8	8.7
13	17.8	8.6	6.2	2.8	0.0
14	18.3	11.1	6.4	1.2	1.9
15	16.1	7.1	2.5	0.0	8.6
16	17.1	6.1	8.3	11.0	0.1
17	14.5	9.8	9.8	0.0	5.8
18	12.4	2.9	1.8	0.0	9.1
19	13.3	3.4	3.3	0.0	7.9
20	15.7	4.1	5.0	3.2	1.8
21	19.1	7.9	11.3	Trace	1.9
22	17.9	15.2	13.8	8.2	0.1
23	17.4	15.8	9.9	3.4	1.9
24	15.1	6.0	12.5	15.8	0.0
25	13.4	9.2	11.0	1.8	6.4
26	14.4	5.3	4.4	4.8	4.9
27	16.0	7.4	15.3	4.8	0.8
28	14.0	12.4	13.1	1.6	2.5
29	12.7	7.5	10.5	1.4	7.4
30	11.1	7.3	6.2	1.4	5.2
31	9.5	5.8	4.3	24.4	0.0
Total	—	—	—	103.8	96.7
Mean	14.7	8.6	7.1	—	—
Temp °F	58.5	47.5	—	—	—
Average	15.4	8.0	7.2	58.0	107.2

NOVEMBER 1998

		Temperature Max. °C	Min. °C	Wind knots	Rain mm	Sun hrs
Day	1	10.5	3.5	4.5	1.2	7.3
	2	10.6	4.5	5.1	9.8	0.0
	3	10.3	6.7	7.6	3.8	1.1
	4	8.1	2.1	3.8	0.0	3.2
	5	11.1	0.1	7.9	2.0	3.1
	6	12.7	5.9	3.7	0.0	4.6
	7	14.5	5.4	4.8	4.4	2.6
	8	16.6	9.5	6.6	5.6	1.1
	9	15.9	11.8	8.7	5.2	5.9
	10	12.0	8.9	5.0	0.0	8.1
	11	10.8	1.6	3.3	2.2	7.0
	12	10.8	4.0	7.5	0.0	1.9
	13	9.2	6.0	3.7	10.2	0.0
	14	8.9	3.2	6.0	0.2	2.5
	15	8.8	3.4	5.8	0.2	1.2
	16	7.1	1.0	2.8	0.0	6.1
	17	7.3	−0.8	0.8	0.2	6.5
	18	7.4	−0.2	1.5	0.0	2.5
	19	7.3	2.2	1.9	0.2	0.0
	20	6.4	−0.3	5.2	0.0	0.9
	21	6.9	0.0	4.6	0.0	1.2
	22	5.7	−0.4	5.2	0.0	1.2
	23	6.3	0.6	1.5	0.0	1.9
	24	8.6	1.2	4.0	7.8	0.0
	25	6.0	5.9	1.5	Trace	0.0
	26	10.6	1.3	4.3	0.4	0.0
	27	11.5	4.4	2.0	0.1	0.0
	28	12.5	7.1	3.8	3.5	0.0
	29	8.3	0.7	3.1	0.0	7.1
	30	6.5	2.8	3.5	0.0	1.5
	31					
Total		—	—	—	57.0	78.5
Mean		9.6	3.4	4.3	—	—
Temp °F		49.2	38.1	—	—	—
Average		10.4	4.1	8.0	55.0	68.1

DECEMBER 1998

		Temperature Max. °C	Min. °C	Wind knots	Rain mm	Sun hrs
Day	1	5.1	3.0	6.7	0.0	0.0
	2	4.3	2.8	8.8	0.0	3.5
	3	4.3	1.7	4.6	0.2	0.0
	4	5.5	−0.4	5.3	0.0	4.8
	5	5.7	−2.8	5.9	0.2	1.0
	6	4.3	−3.8	2.6	0.0	6.9
	7	9.1	−1.8	0.5	0.2	0.0
	8	10.5	2.3	4.3	2.2	0.0
	9	12.2	8.9	1.4	0.0	1.6
	10	10.6	6.7	4.9	5.4	0.5
	11	13.4	4.5	4.6	0.4	0.0
	12	14.1	6.5	7.4	2.0	0.3
	13	14.2	7.6	8.2	0.0	0.3
	14	14.8	8.0	10.5	0.4	0.1
	15	13.2	12.3	4.9	2.7	0.0
	16	12.1	5.3	4.2	0.0	3.2
	17	10.2	6.4	6.0	1.2	0.0
	18	10.8	7.1	6.4	3.9	2.3
	19	7.9	4.5	6.3	0.0	3.7
	20	5.2	2.6	6.7	0.0	6.0
	21	5.4	−3.1	3.3	0.4	0.8
	22	9.6	−0.8	1.8	0.6	0.0
	23	8.9	3.8	6.8	8.0	0.0
	24	11.6	−0.8	7.0	3.4	4.1
	25	12.2	1.3	14.5	4.8	0.0
	26	13.4	5.8	14.9	6.6	0.0
	27	10.5	7.4	9.9	0.4	0.0
	28	8.4	6.1	6.4	0.0	3.2
	29	11.4	1.6	10.5	0.0	0.0
	30	12.2	6.6	10.4	5.2	0.1
	31	10.1	9.1	9.1	1.0	0.0
Total		—	—	—	49.2	42.4
Mean		9.7	3.8	6.7	—	—
Temp °F		49.5	38.8	—	—	—
Average		8.0	2.3	8.1	57.0	46.2

JANUARY 1999

		Temperature Max. °C	Min. °C	Wind knots	Rain mm	Sun hrs
Day	1	10.5	8.0	9.0	3.4	3.6
	2	9.7	6.9	11.0	6.6	5.9
	3	13.6	4.0	9.3	3.6	2.7
	4	14.3	5.5	9.7	0.2	0.8
	5	14.7	10.0	9.8	0.0	2.5
	6	15.4	8.9	9.2	2.6	3.0
	7	8.9	3.2	5.5	3.8	1.2
	8	7.6	2.5	4.8	6.0	1.8
	9	4.5	1.6	3.0	0.0	1.4
	10	3.7	1.5	4.0	0.0	3.3
	11	3.2	0.6	3.0	1.2	0.9
	12	6.6	−3.8	6.0	7.2	0.0
	13	9.2	1.7	6.7	0.6	0.1
	14	10.0	3.4	9.4	0.8	6.0
	15	11.7	4.1	15.1	13.0	0.0
	16	7.9	6.4	8.5	0.0	1.1
	17	8.7	3.3	5.1	0.0	6.1
	18	11.5	3.5	9.9	2.9	2.9
	19	12.5	6.1	12.2	7.2	0.0
	20	11.7	11.2	8.2	0.4	0.0
	21	6.1	4.4	0.5	0.1	0.1
	22	4.6	−2.1	0.3	0.1	0.0
	23	9.4	−1.8	5.0	1.0	0.5
	24	12.5	4.5	5.3	Trace	1.1
	25	13.4	6.2	11.7	Trace	0.7
	26	8.9	3.2	8.4	5.0	1.3
	27	11.7	1.6	5.5	1.4	3.9
	28	10.8	3.0	7.6	0.2	2.8
	29	7.0	1.6	1.9	0.6	0.0
	30	4.8	3.7	4.4	0.8	0.0
	31	7.5	3.3	1.4	0.0	0.0
Total		—	—	—	68.7	53.7
Mean		9.4	3.7	6.8	—	—
Temp °F		48.9	38.7	—	—	—
Average		7.1	1.4	8.5	52.0	51.7

FEBRUARY 1999

		Temperature Max. °C	Min. °C	Wind knots	Rain mm	Sun hrs
Day	1	9.8	4.4	1.7	0.0	0.0
	2	9.8	5.4	1.8	0.0	4.4
	3	10.7	3.4	4.7	0.0	0.0
	4	11.1	7.3	10.3	0.0	2.1
	5	9.7	7.1	8.4	0.2	0.9
	6	9.0	6.4	7.8	4.8	0.7
	7	5.3	1.9	6.6	0.0	7.4
	8	2.9	−1.4	3.1	1.2	0.0
	9	3.3	−1.7	5.3	0.0	8.2
	10	4.7	−2.6	5.0	0.0	6.6
	11	6.0	−3.8	1.9	0.2	4.5
	12	7.7	−0.4	1.0	0.0	0.3
	13	7.0	1.9	3.6	0.0	8.7
	14	7.2	−2.8	2.6	0.9	0.7
	15	9.1	0.4	3.3	0.2	5.4
	16	9.3	3.5	7.5	0.0	5.7
	17	10.0	4.0	6.4	1.0	2.5
	18	11.5	4.8	6.5	1.4	0.4
	19	13.2	9.1	6.4	0.4	0.0
	20	10.2	4.6	4.2	0.4	6.6
	21	11.4	6.0	11.0	1.6	2.7
	22	8.1	2.7	12.8	0.6	7.3
	23	7.8	2.4	5.7	1.5	7.2
	24	6.4	2.5	5.4	0.0	0.1
	25	9.9	−1.3	4.6	Trace	0.0
	26	10.3	3.3	8.0	5.3	0.0
	27	10.6	7.2	5.9	0.0	4.2
	28	12.6	4.0	11.0	1.4	3.5
	29	—	—	—	—	—
	30	—	—	—	—	—
	31	—	—	—	—	—
Total		—	—	—	21.1	90.1
Mean		8.8	2.8	5.8	—	—
Temp °F		47.8	37.0	—	—	—
Average		7.5	1.5	8.8	35.0	67.3

MARCH 1999

Day	Temperature Max. °C	Min. °C	Wind knots	Rain mm	Sun hrs
1	13.4	7.1	11.2	0.6	0.1
2	15.1	11.1	11.1	7.8	0.5
3	11.4	7.3	13.6	4.8	4.3
4	7.8	4.9	2.3	0.2	0.7
5	5.6	1.5	6.4	Trace	0.5
6	6.9	2.3	5.2	1.4	2.2
7	5.4	2.6	5.4	3.0	0.0
8	8.3	4.0	3.8	0.0	3.2
9	9.0	3.9	1.7	0.2	4.8
10	7.2	−0.2	2.9	0.0	3.4
11	10.3	−0.3	5.9	0.0	0.2
12	14.0	3.5	2.4	3.8	2.1
13	13.8	9.0	3.6	0.0	6.1
14	13.6	2.7	1.3	0.0	9.6
15	14.7	3.8	0.9	0.0	7.7
16	15.7	2.8	1.0	0.0	9.3
17	19.7	6.1	1.3	0.0	9.8
18	13.4	6.3	5.3	0.0	4.3
19	11.4	4.8	4.6	0.0	1.8
20	11.3	2.9	2.8	1.0	3.6
21	11.8	6.8	10.3	0.6	2.6
22	10.8	5.9	7.5	Trace	6.4
23	15.1	6.4	6.9	0.0	6.3
24	12.0	8.6	6.3	0.0	0.0
25	12.9	4.1	3.7	1.4	0.3
26	11.8	5.5	3.3	Trace	2.1
27	13.9	1.5	0.8	0.0	11.1
28	15.4	2.2	5.1	0.0	9.7
29	14.8	9.1	8.4	0.6	0.2
30	12.9	9.9	2.7	0.2	0.0
31	19.4	9.9	7.2	0.0	9.6
Total	—	—	—	25.6	122.5
Mean	12.2	5.0	5.0	—	—
Temp °F	54.0	41.0	—	—	—
Average	10.3	2.7	8.9	47.0	110.1

APRIL 1999

Day	Temperature Max. °C	Min. °C	Wind knots	Rain mm	Sun hrs
1	20.4	8.6	9.0	0.0	10.4
2	17.9	9.6	5.1	0.0	6.0
3	13.4	5.9	3.0	0.0	0.0
4	17.4	8.5	5.4	0.4	1.6
5	15.3	11.1	8.5	Trace	0.2
6	17.3	10.4	10.4	0.4	4.2
7	12.6	6.5	6.3	0.0	1.1
8	16.5	4.4	3.4	0.0	6.7
9	16.0	9.9	4.7	Trace	2.8
10	15.9	8.0	7.3	0.0	1.7
11	14.4	3.7	9.0	6.8	10.2
12	12.4	7.3	10.2	3.4	3.1
13	9.3	5.2	9.6	1.6	7.5
14	8.5	−1.6	3.7	0.0	7.5
15	11.5	0.3	3.6	1.6	9.8
16	11.6	1.0	2.5	1.2	6.1
17	12.9	1.7	3.2	0.4	9.3
18	11.5	2.8	3.3	0.0	8.6
19	12.6	0.6	5.5	1.4	5.3
20	12.6	5.1	11.8	8.0	0.0
21	15.1	8.9	14.6	0.8	3.9
22	14.1	9.4	10.6	1.8	6.2
23	13.1	6.3	6.1	3.6	0.0
24	16.7	8.7	4.6	0.0	4.7
25	16.6	4.8	6.7	3.4	2.3
26	17.8	10.1	6.0	0.2	1.9
27	18.4	10.0	11.7	0.0	10.6
28	18.8	7.3	9.9	0.0	13.6
29	16.8	7.3	9.4	0.0	9.8
30	20.8	5.7	3.1	0.0	12.7
31					
Total	—	—	—	35.0	167.8
Mean	14.9	6.2	6.9	—	—
Temp °F	58.8	43.1	—	—	—
Average	13.1	4.7	8.5	45.0	146.9

MAY 1999

Day	Temperature Max. °C	Min. °C	Wind knots	Rain mm	Sun hrs
1	19.9	7.4	3.5	0.0	8.3
2	20.3	11.1	6.3	0.0	6.1
3	22.4	9.2	5.8	0.0	5.8
4	18.1	10.7	9.5	0.0	4.5
5	18.1	10.1	7.5	1.2	3.7
6	17.6	8.8	5.8	0.2	5.2
7	16.7	8.5	5.4	4.4	0.6
8	16.5	8.6	9.9	0.8	2.9
9	20.5	12.7	10.0	0.0	6.1
10	18.4	12.4	11.2	1.0	10.6
11	19.0	11.3	10.5	0.0	10.1
12	17.8	10.4	8.4	3.4	4.4
13	19.1	10.3	6.8	2.4	4.4
14	17.2	10.7	4.2	2.4	6.9
15	15.0	9.3	5.8	0.0	1.6
16	16.5	6.6	5.7	0.0	7.9
17	15.8	7.7	12.4	0.4	6.6
18	16.5	10.9	9.5	0.2	0.0
19	22.8	10.0	3.0	0.8	8.2
20	22.0	11.3	4.1	0.2	6.8
21	18.6	9.5	9.2	0.0	5.2
22	17.6	7.9	9.6	0.0	12.9
23	19.7	10.3	8.1	0.0	1.3
24	18.9	11.9	8.0	0.0	0.3
25	18.4	7.3	5.8	0.0	14.2
26	21.7	8.3	4.6	0.0	6.9
27	26.4	11.2	9.3	0.2	10.8
28	22.5	15.6	10.6	0.0	8.4
29	25.0	12.1	5.9	10.0	8.9
30	15.4	13.5	7.3	8.2	0.0
31	17.7	9.9	4.3	0.0	1.1
Total	—	—	—	35.8	184.9
Mean	19.1	10.2	7.4	—	—
Temp °F	66.3	50.4	—	—	—
Average	17.0	8.0	8.1	51.0	193.7

JUNE 1999

Day	Temperature Max. °C	Min. °C	Wind knots	Rain mm	Sun hrs
1	22.7	10.3	5.1	43.8	13.2
2	20.7	13.0	10.8	3.8	1.9
3	17.7	12.2	8.6	4.0	3.4
4	17.9	11.2	9.3	1.0	3.8
5	18.0	8.7	6.9	4.0	8.7
6	19.7	9.6	4.8	1.8	7.8
7	17.6	9.8	4.3	6.0	4.7
8	18.3	5.7	6.0	0.0	11.6
9	19.1	6.7	3.4	0.0	14.2
10	18.0	8.7	3.0	0.0	4.2
11	17.3	12.3	2.6	1.4	1.5
12	16.5	12.3	3.7	0.2	0.1
13	20.9	9.6	2.9	0.0	10.8
14	23.0	11.2	2.2	0.2	7.7
15	24.9	12.4	3.1	0.0	13.7
16	25.5	13.0	3.2	0.0	14.4
17	21.4	12.6	4.5	0.0	9.0
18	23.2	10.9	2.3	0.0	15.3
19	21.0	11.6	5.4	1.0	6.2
20	18.9	14.5	8.3	0.8	9.2
21	17.0	9.4	5.7	0.0	9.6
22	18.4	7.5	2.9	0.0	7.8
23	21.7	12.1	2.4	0.0	5.9
24	23.0	11.4	4.0	0.0	7.4
25	22.3	11.8	6.0	0.0	15.5
26	26.7	11.9	6.5	0.2	11.0
27	18.9	15.5	7.8	0.6	4.0
28	19.5	10.6	8.4	15.0	8.5
29	17.5	13.4	3.0	14.2	0.0
30	20.5	11.3	5.3	0.2	8.0
31					
Total	—	—	—	98.2	239.1
Mean	20.3	11.0	5.1	—	—
Temp °F	68.5	51.8	—	—	—
Average	20.4	11.0	7.6	51.0	198.5

Sports Results

For 2000 sports fixtures, *see* pages 12–13
For 1998–9 sporting events, *see* pages 1089–1092

ALPINE SKIING

WORLD CUP 1998–9

MEN
Downhill: Lasse Kjus (Norway), 760 points
Slalom: Thomas Stangassinger (Austria), 566 points
Giant Slalom: Michael von Grünigen (Switzerland), 483
points
Super Giant Slalom: Hermann Maier (Austria), 516 points
Overall: Lasse Kjus (Norway), 1,465 points

WOMEN
Downhill: Renate Götschl (Austria), 610 points
Slalom: Sabine Egger (Austria), 425 points
Giant Slalom: Alexandra Meissnitzer (Austria), 652 points
Super Giant Slalom: Alexandra Meissnitzer (Austria), 459
points
Overall: Alexandra Meissnitzer (Austria), 1,672 points

Nations Cup: Austria, 15,995 points

WORLD CHAMPIONSHIPS 1999

Vail, Colorado, February

MEN
Downhill: Hermann Maier (Austria)
Slalom: Kalle Palander (Finland)
Giant Slalom: Lasse Kjus (Norway)
Super Giant Slalom: = Hermann Maier (Austria) and Lasse
Kjus (Norway)
Combined Event: Kjetil Andre Aamodt (Norway)

WOMEN
Downhill: Renate Götschl (Austria)
Slalom: Zali Steggall (Australia)
Giant Slalom: Alexandra Meissnitzer (Austria)
Super Giant Slalom: Alexandra Meissnitzer (Austria)
Combined Event: Pernilla Wiberg (Sweden)

AMERICAN FOOTBALL

AFC Championship 1999: Denver Broncos beat New York
Jets 23–10
NFC Championship 1999: Atlanta Falcons beat Minnesota
Vikings 30–27
XXXIII American Superbowl 1999 (Miami, 31 January):
Denver Broncos beat Atlanta Falcons 34–19
World Bowl 1999: Frankfurt Galaxy beat Barcelona
Dragons 38–24
British National Division final 1999: London Os beat
Birmingham Bulls 9–7

ANGLING

NATIONAL COARSE CHAMPIONSHIPS 1998
Division: 1
Venue: River Thames; *no. of teams:* 81
Individual winner: M. Runacres (Suffolk County), 24.710 kg
Team winners: Southport and District, 701 points

Division: 2
Venue: Middle Trent; *no. of teams:* 82
Individual winner: J. Griffin (Beverley and District),
20.600 kg
Team winners: Royal Ordnance, 768 points

Division: 3
Venue: Grand Union Canal; *no. of teams:* 85
Individual winner: M. Ulyett (Aviesta Sheffield), 18.750 kg
Team winners: Lincs County, 839 points

Division: 4
Venue: Stainforth and Keadby Canal; *no. of teams:* 76
Individual winner: J. Berry (ASI Wigan), 4.210 kg
Team winners: Team ACE, 798 points

Division: 5
Venue: Bridgewater Canal; *no. of teams:* 43
Individual winner: P. Eyres (Farnworth and District),
3.070 kg
Team winners: Little Lever, 406 points

Ladies' Championship
Venue: Trent and Mersey Canal
Winner: Linda Cooke (Warrington)

ASSOCIATION FOOTBALL

LEAGUE COMPETITIONS 1998–9

ENGLAND AND WALES
Premiership
1. Manchester United, 79 points
2. Arsenal, 78 points
Relegated: Charlton Athletic, 36 points; Blackburn Rovers,
35 points; Nottingham Forest, 30 points

Division 1
1. Sunderland, 105 points
2. Bradford City, 87 points
Third promotion place: Watford
Relegated: Bury, 47 points; Oxford United, 44 points; Bristol
City, 42 points

Division 2
1. Fulham, 101 points
2. Walsall, 87 points
Third promotion place: Manchester City
Relegated: York City, 50 points; Northampton Town, 48
points; Lincoln City, 46 points; Macclesfield Town, 43
points

Division 3
1. Brentford, 85 points
2. Cambridge United, 81 points
3. Cardiff City, 80 points
Fourth promotion place: Scunthorpe United
Relegated: Scarborough, 48 points

Football Conference
Champions: Cheltenham Town, 80 points
Relegated: Barrow, 43 points (relegated instead of Welling
United, 41 points, because Barrow could not guarantee
its participation in the 1999-2000 Conference); Leek
Town, 32 points; Farnborough Town, 32 points

League of Wales: Barry Town, 76 points
Women's Premier League: Croydon

SCOTLAND

Premier Division
1. Rangers, 77 points
2. Celtic, 71 points
Relegated: Dunfermline Athletic, 28 points

Division 1
1. Hibernian, 89 points
2. Falkirk, 66 points
Relegated: Hamilton Academicals, 28 points; Stranraer, 17 points

Division 2
1. Livingston, 77 points
2. Inverness Caledonian Thistle, 72 points
Relegated: East Fife, 42 points; Forfar Athletic, 31 points

Division 3
1. Ross County, 77 points
2. Stenhousemuir, 64 points
Bottom: Montrose, 30 points

NORTHERN IRELAND

Irish League Championship: Glentoran, 78 points

CUP COMPETITIONS

ENGLAND

FA Cup final 1999 (Wembley, 22 May): Manchester United beat Newcastle United 2–0
Worthington (League) Cup final 1999: Tottenham Hotspur beat Leicester City 1–0
Auto Windscreens Shield final 1999: Wigan Athletic beat Millwall 1–0
FA Trophy final 1999: Kingstonian beat Forest Green Rovers 1–0
FA Vase final 1999: Tiverton Town beat Bedlington Terriers 1–0
Charity Shield 1999: Arsenal beat Manchester United 2–1
Women's FA Cup final 1999: Arsenal beat Southampton 2–0
Women's League Cup final 1999: Arsenal beat Everton 3–1

WALES

Welsh Cup final 1999: Barry Town beat Wrexham 2–1
League of Wales Cup final 1999: Carmarthen Town 1, Inter CableTel 1 a.e.t. Inter CableTel won 4–2 on penalties

SCOTLAND

Scottish Cup final 1999 (Hampden Park, 29 May): Rangers beat Celtic 1–0
League Cup final 1998 (Celtic Park, 29 November): Rangers beat St Johnstone 2–1

NORTHERN IRELAND

Irish Cup final 1999: not held because one of the finalists, Cliftonville, had fielded an ineligible player in a semi-final replay

EUROPE

European Champions' Cup final 1999 (Barcelona): Manchester United beat Bayern Munich 2–1
European Cup-Winners' Cup final 1999 (Villa Park): Lazio beat Real Mallorca 2–1
UEFA Cup final 1999: Parma beat Marseilles 3–0
European Super Cup final 1999: Lazio beat Manchester United 1–0
InterToto Cup final 1999: West Ham beat Metz 3–2 on aggregate

INTERNATIONALS

EUROPEAN CHAMPIONSHIPS QUALIFYING MATCHES
1998

10 Oct	Wembley	England 0, Bulgaria 0
	Edinburgh	Scotland 3, Estonia 2
	Windsor Park	N. Ireland 1, Finland 0
	Copenhagen	Denmark 1, Wales 2
14 Oct	Luxembourg	Luxembourg 0, England 3
	Aberdeen	Scotland 2, Faroe Islands 1
	Cardiff	Wales 3, Belarus 2
18 Nov	Windsor Park	N. Ireland 2, Moldova 2

1999

27 March	Wembley	England 3, Poland 1
	Belfast	N. Ireland 0, Germany 3
31 March	Glasgow	Scotland 1, Czech Republic 2
	Kishinev	Moldova 0, N. Ireland 0
	Zurich	Switzerland 2, Wales 0
5 June	Wembley	England 0, Sweden 0
	Toftir	Faroe Islands 1, Scotland 1
	Bologna	Italy 4, Wales 0
9 June	Sofia	Bulgaria 1, England 1
	Prague	Czech Republic 3, Scotland 2
	Anfield	Wales 0, Denmark 2
4 Sept	Wembley	England 6, Luxembourg 0
	Sarajevo	Bosnia 1, Scotland 2
	Minsk	Belarus 1, Wales 2
	Belfast	N. Ireland 0, Turkey 3
8 Sept	Warsaw	Poland 0, England 0
	Tallinn	Estonia 0, Scotland 0
	Dortmund	Germany 4, N. Ireland 0

FRIENDLIES
1998

18 Nov	Wembley	England 2, Czech Republic 0

1999

10 Feb	Wembley	England 0, France 2
27 April	Belfast	N. Ireland 1, Canada 1
28 April	Budapest	Hungary 1, England 1
	Bremen	Germany 0, Scotland 1
29 May	Dublin	Rep. of Ireland 0, N. Ireland 1
18 Aug	Belfast	N. Ireland 0, France 1

Women's World Cup final 1999: USA 0, China 0. USA won 5–4 on penalties

ATHLETICS

WORLD HALF MARATHON CHAMPIONSHIPS

Zürich, Switzerland, 27 September 1998
MEN
Individual: Paul Koech (Kenya), 60 min. 01 sec.
Team result: South Africa, 3 hr. 02 min. 21 sec.

WOMEN
Individual: Tegla Loroupe (Kenya), 1 hr. 08 min. 29 sec.
Team result: Kenya, 3 hr. 29 min. 43 sec.

EUROPEAN CROSS-COUNTRY CHAMPIONSHIPS

Ferrara, Italy, 13 December 1998
MEN
Individual: Sergei Lebed (Ukraine), 28 min. 07 sec.
Team: Italy, 53 points

WOMEN
Individual: Paula Radcliffe (GB), 18 min. 07 sec.
Team: Portugal, 16 points

AAA INDOOR CHAMPIONSHIPS

Birmingham, 30–31 January 1999

MEN

	min.	sec.
60 *metres:* Jason Gardener (Wessex and Bath)		6.57
200 *metres:* Marcus Adam (Haringey)		20.77
400 *metres:* Allyn Condon (Sale)		47.14
800 *metres:* Andy Hart (Coventry Godiva)	1	49.41
1,500 *metres:* Eddie King (Sale)	3	40.24
3,000 *metres:* Philip Tulba (Basingstoke)	8	07.46
60 *metres hurdles:* Colin Jackson (Brecon)		7.59
3,000 *metres walk:* Andi Drake (Coventry Godiva)	11	56.72

	metres
High jump: Ben Challenger (Belgrave)	2.25
Pole vault: Nick Buckfield (Crawley)	5.30
Long jump: Chris Davidson (Newham)	7.62
Triple jump: Julian Golley (TVH)	16.22
Shot: Gary Sollitt (Team Solent)	17.26
Heptathlon: Du'aine Ladejo (Belgrave)	5,607 points

WOMEN

	min.	sec.
60 *metres:* Christine Bloomfield (Essex Ladies)		7.40
200 *metres:* Shani Anderson (Shaftesbury Barnet)		23.90
400 *metres:* Sinead Dudgeon (Edinburgh)		53.51
800 *metres:* Paula Fryer (Sale)	2	08.99
1,500 *metres:* Rachel Jordan (Birchfield)	4	25.88
3,000 *metres:* Zahara Hyde-Peters (Havant)	9	30.76
60 *metres hurdles:* Keri Maddox (Sale)		8.36
3,000 *metres walk:* Sharon Tonks (Bromsgrove and Redditch)	14	29.44

	metres
High jump: Michelle Dunkley (Essex Ladies)	1.86
Pole vault: Janine Whitlock (Trafford)	4.13
Long jump: Jo Wise (Coventry Godiva)	6.32
Triple jump: Ashia Hansen (Shaftesbury Barnet)	14.23
Shot: Judy Oakes (Croydon)	17.36
Pentathlon: Diana Bennett (Epsom and Ewell)	4,110 points

* Held at Birmingham, 23–24 January 1999

WORLD INDOOR CHAMPIONSHIPS

Maebashi, Japan, 5–7 March 1999

MEN

	min.	sec.
60 *metres:* Maurice Greene (USA)		6.45
200 *metres:* Frankie Fredericks (Namibia)		20.10
400 *metres:* Jamie Baulch (GB)		45.73
800 *metres:* Johan Botha (S. Africa)	1	45.47
1,500 *metres:* Haile Gebrselassie (Ethiopia)	3	33.77
3,000 *metres:* Haile Gebrselassie (Ethiopia)	7	53.57
60 *metres hurdles:* Colin Jackson (GB)		7.38
4 × 400 *metres relay:* USA	3	02.83

	metres
High jump: Javier Sotomayor (Cuba)	2.36
Pole vault: Jean Galfione (France)	6.00
Long jump: Ivan Pedroso (Cuba)	8.62
Triple jump: Charles Friedek (Germany)	17.18
Shot: Alexander Bagach (Ukraine)	21.41
Heptathlon: Sebastian Chmara (Poland)	6,386 points

WOMEN

	min.	sec.
60 *metres:* Ekaterini Thanou (Greece)		6.96
200 *metres:* Ionela Tirlea (Romania)		22.39
400 *metres:* Grit Breuer (Germany)		50.80
800 *metres:* Ludmila Formanova (Czech Republic)	1	56.90
1,500 *metres:* Gabriela Szabo (Romania)	4	03.23
3,000 *metres:* Gabriela Szabo (Romania)	8	36.42
60 *metres hurdles:* Olga Shishigina (Kazakhstan)		7.86
4 × 400 *metres relay:* Russia	3	24.25

	metres
High jump: Khristina Kalcheva (Bulgaria)	1.99
Pole vault: Nastja Ryshich (Germany)	4.50
Long jump: Tatyana Kotova (Russia)	6.86
Triple jump: Ashia Hansen (GB)	15.02
Shot: Irina Korzhanenko (Russia)	20.56
Pentathlon: DeDee Nathan (USA)	4,753 points

NATIONAL CROSS-COUNTRY CHAMPIONSHIPS

Newark, 13 March 1999

MEN

Individual: Justin Pugsley (Birchfield), 38 min. 32 sec.

Team: Tipton Harriers, 102 points

WOMEN

Individual: Angela Newport (Basingstoke and Mid Hants), 29 min. 33 sec.

Team: Shaftesbury Barnet, 57 points

WORLD CROSS-COUNTRY CHAMPIONSHIPS

Belfast, 27–28 March 1999

MEN (12 KM)

Individual: Paul Tergat (Kenya), 38 min. 26 sec.

Team: Kenya, 12 points

MEN (4,236 M)

Individual: Benjamin Limo (Kenya), 12 min. 28 sec.

Team: Kenya, 14 points

WOMEN (8,012 M)

Individual: Gete Wami (Ethiopia), 28 min. 00 sec.

Team: Ethiopia, 18 points

WOMEN (4,236 M)

Individual: Jackline Maranga (Kenya), 15 min. 09 sec.

Team: France, 40 points

LONDON MARATHON

18 April 1999

Men: Abdelkader El Mouaziz (Morocco), 2 hr. 07 min. 57 sec.

Women: Joyce Chepchumba (Kenya), 2 hr. 23 min. 22 sec.

EUROPEAN CUP SUPER LEAGUE

Paris, France, 19–20 June 1999

MEN

	min.	sec.
100 *metres:* Dwain Chambers (GB)		10.21
200 *metres:* Marcin Urbas (Poland)		20.34
400 *metres:* Mark Richardson (GB)		44.96
800 *metres:* Yuri Borzakovsky (Russia)	1	48.53
1,500 *metres:* Giuseppe D'Urso (Italy)	3	46.01
3,000 *metres:* Salvatore Vincenti (Italy)	7	59.12
5,000 *metres:* Gennaro di Napoli (Italy)	13	53.37
3,000 *metres steeplechase:* Gael Pencreach (France)	8	27.78

	min.	sec.
110 *metres hurdles:* Falk Balzer (Germany)		13.21
400 *metres hurdles:* Fabrizio Mori (Italy)		48.68
4 × 100 *metres relay:* Great Britain		38.16
4 × 400 *metres relay:* Great Britain	3	00.61

	metres
High jump: Martin Buss (Germany)	2.34
Pole vault: Michael Stolle (Germany)	5.65
Long jump: Emmanuel Bangue (France)	7.97
Triple jump: Denis Kapustin (Russia)	17.40
Shot: Oliver-Sven Buder (Germany)	20.53
Discus: Jurgen Schult (Germany)	65.68
Hammer: Christos Polychroniou (Greece)	79.72
Javelin: Raymond Hecht (Germany)	86.05

Team points: Germany 122, Italy 98½, Great Britain 97, Russia 95, France 81½, Greece 80, Poland 79, Czech Republic 62

WOMEN

	min.	sec.
100 *metres:* Christine Arron (France)		10.97
200 *metres:* Svetlana Goncharenko (Russia)		22.59
400 *metres:* Ionela Tirlea (Romania)		50.69
800 *metres:* Natalya Tsyganova (Russia)	1	58.18
1,500 *metres:* Gabriela Szabo (Romania)	4	13.63
3,000 *metres:* Gabriela Szabo (Romania)	8	36.35
5,000 *metres:* Paula Radcliffe (GB)	14	48.79
100 *metres hurdles:* Patricia Girard (France)		12.96
400 *metres hurdles:* Silvia Rieger (Germany)		55.09
4 × 100 *metres relay:* France		42.90
4 × 400 *metres relay:* Russia	3	24.61

	metres
High jump: Yelena Gulyayeva (Russia)	1.99
Pole vault: Nicole Humbert (Germany)	4.35
Long jump: Fiona May (Italy)	6.88
Triple jump: Cristina Nicolau (Romania)	14.61
Shot: Krystyna Danilczyk (Poland)	18.58
Discus: Natalya Sadova (Russia)	66.84
Hammer: Mihaela Melinte (Romania)	74.48
Javelin: Tanja Damaske (Germany)	65.44

Team points: Russia 127, Romania 99, France 97, Germany 93½, Italy 71, Great Britain 68½, Poland 65, Czech Republic 62

AAA CHAMPIONSHIPS
Birmingham, 23–25 July 1999

MEN

	min.	sec.
100 *metres:* Jason Gardener (Wessex and Bath)		10.02
200 *metres:* John Golding (Blackheath)		20.20
400 *metres:* Jamie Baulch (Cardiff)		45.36
800 *metres:* Mark Sesay (Leeds)	1	48.03
1,500 *metres:* John Mayock (Cannock)	3	39.12
5,000 *metres:* Rob Denmark (Basildon)	13	34.17
*10,000 *metres:* Paul Evans (Belgrave)	28	34.62
3,000 *metres steeplechase:* Christian Stephenson (Cardiff)	8	44.42
110 *metres hurdles:* Colin Jackson (Brecon)		13.24
400 *metres hurdles:* Chris Rawlinson (Belgrave)		49.62
10,000 *metres walk:* Andi Drake (Coventry Godiva)	42	14.69

	metres
High jump: Steve Smith (Liverpool)	2.28
Pole vault: Kevin Hughes (Haringey)	5.50
Long jump: Steve Phillips (Rugby)	7.79
Triple jump: Larry Achike (Shaftesbury Barnet)	16.73
Shot: Carl Myerscough (Blackpool)	18.97
Discus: Rob Weir (Birchfield)	61.35
Hammer: Michael Jones (Belgrave)	74.25
Javelin: Steve Backley (Cambridge Harriers)	87.59

WOMEN

	min.	sec.
100 *metres:* Joice Maduaka (Essex Ladies)		11.37
200 *metres:* Joice Maduaka (Essex Ladies)		22.83
400 *metres:* Katherine Merry (Birchfield)		50.62
800 *metres:* Kelly Holmes (Ealing)	1	59.86
1,500 *metres:* Hayley Tullett (Swansea)	4	08.06
5,000 *metres:* Hayley Haining (City of Glasgow)	15	56.59
*10,000 *metres:* Bev Jenkins (Salford)	33	58.81
100 *metres hurdles:* Keri Maddox (Sale)		12.97
400 *metres hurdles:* Sinead Dudgeon (Edinburgh)		55.24
5,000 *metres walk:* Vicky Lupton (Sheffield)	23	37.47

	metres
High jump: Jo Jennings (Rugby)	1.87
Pole vault: Janine Whitlock (Trafford)	4.25
Long jump: Joanne Wise (Coventry Godiva)	6.62
Triple jump: Michelle Griffith (Windsor, Slough and Eton)	13.41
Shot: Myrtle Augee (Bromley)	17.32
Discus: Shelley Drew (Sutton)	55.16
Hammer: Lyn Spaules (Hounslow)	62.62
Javelin: Kirsty Morrison (Medway)	55.70

* Held at Watford, 3 July 1999

WORLD CHAMPIONSHIPS
Seville, Spain, 21–29 August 1999

MEN

	hr.	min.	sec.
100 *metres:* Maurice Greene (USA)			9.80
200 *metres:* Maurice Greene (USA)			19.90
400 *metres:* Michael Johnson (USA)			43.18
800 *metres:* Wilson Kipketer (Denmark)		1	43.30
1,500 *metres:* Hicham El Guerrouj (Morocco)		3	27.65
5,000 *metres:* Salah Hissou (Morocco)		12	58.13
10,000 *metres:* Haile Gebrselassie (Ethiopia)		27	57.27
Marathon: Abel Anton (Spain)	2	27	31
3,000 *metres steeplechase:* Chris Koskei (Kenya)		8	11.76
110 *metres hurdles:* Colin Jackson (GB)			13.04
400 *metres hurdles:* Fabrizio Mori (Italy)			47.72
4 × 100 *metres relay:* USA			37.59
4 × 400 *metres relay:* USA		2	56.45
20,000 *metres walk:* Ilya Markov (Russia)	1	23	34
50,000 *metres walk:* German Skurygin (Russia)	3	44	23

	metres
High jump: Vyacheslav Voronin (Russia)	2.37
Pole vault: Maksim Tarasov (Russia)	6.02
Long jump: Ivan Pedroso (Cuba)	8.56
Triple jump: Charles Friedek (Germany)	17.59
Shot: C. J. Hunter (USA)	21.79
Discus: Anthony Washington (USA)	69.08
Hammer: Karsten Kobs (Germany)	80.24
Javelin: Aki Parviainen (Finland)	89.52
Decathlon: Tomas Dvorak (Czech Republic)	8,744 points

Women

	hr.	min.	sec.
100 *metres:* Marion Jones (USA)			10.70
200 *metres:* Inger Miller (USA)			21.77
400 *metres:* Cathy Freeman (Australia)			49.67
800 *metres:* Ludmila Formanova (Czech Republic)		1	56.68
1,500 *metres:* Svetlana Masterkova (Russia)		3	59.53
5,000 *metres:* Gabriela Szabo (Romania)		14	41.82
10,000 *metres:* Gete Wami (Ethiopia)		30	24.56
Marathon: Song-ok Jong (N. Korea)	2	26	59
100 *metres hurdles:* Gail Devers (USA)			12.37
400 *metres hurdles:* Daimi Pernia (Cuba)			52.89
4 × 100 *metres relay:* Bahamas			41.92
4 × 400 *metres relay:* Russia		3	21.98
20,000 *metres walk:* Liu Hongyu (China)	1	30	50

	metres
High jump: Inga Babakova (Ukraine)	1.99
Pole vault: Stacy Dragila (USA)	4.60
Long jump: Niurka Montalvo (Spain)	7.06
Triple jump: Paraskevi Tsiamita (Greece)	14.88
Shot: Astrid Kimbernuss (Germany)	19.85
Discus: Franka Dietzsch (Germany)	68.14
Hammer: Mihaela Melinte (Romania)	75.20
Javelin: Mirela Manjani-Tzelili (Greece)	67.09
Heptathlon: Eunice Barber (France)	6,861 points

GB v. USA
Scotstoun, Glasgow, 4 September 1999

Men

	min.	sec.
100 *metres:* Maurice Green (USA)		10.16
200 *metres:* Kevin Little (USA)		20.51
400 *metres:* Antonio Pettigrew (USA)		45.70
800 *metres:* Rich Kenah (USA)	1	48.31
110 *metres hurdles:* Colin Jackson (GB)		13.35
400 *metres hurdles:* Joey Woody (USA)		49.09
4 × 100 *metres relay:* Great Britain		39.09
4 × 400 *metres relay:* United States	3	04.26

	metres
High jump: Charles Austin (USA)	2.20
Triple jump: Jonathan Edwards (GB)	17.07
Shot: Kevin Toth (USA)	20.96
Javelin: Steve Backley (GB)	85.74

Women

	min.	sec.
100 *metres:* Gail Devers (USA)		11.33
400 *metres:* Katharine Merry (GB)		51.11
800 *metres:* Kelly Holmes (GB)	1	59.85
1,500 *metres:* Regina Jacobs (USA)	4	04.30
400 *metres hurdles:* Joanna Hayes (USA)		55.56

	metres
Long jump: Jo Wise (GB)	6.66
Triple jump: Ashia Hansen (GB)	13.90
Hammer: Dawn Ellerbe (USA)	64.18
Team Points: United States 171, Great Britain 143	

GRAND PRIX 1999 FINAL
Munich, Germany, 11 September 1999

Men

	min.	sec.
200 *metres:* Claudinei da Silva (Brazil)		19.89
800 *metres:* Wilson Kipketer (Denmark)	1	43.55
1,500 *metres:* Noah Ngeny (Kenya)	3	28.93
3,000 *metres:* Benjamin Limo (Kenya)	7	36.32
3000 *metres steeplechase:* Bernard Barmasai (Kenya)	8	06.92
110 *metres hurdles:* Mark Crear (USA)		13.08

	metres
Pole vault: Maksim Tarasov (Russia)	6.84
Long jump: Ivan Pedroso (Cuba)	8.43
Discus: Lars Riedel (Germany)	68.61
Javelin: Konstadinos Gatsioudis (Greece)	89.84
Overall winner: Bernard Barmasai (Kenya)	

Women

	min.	sec.
200 *metres:* Sevatheda Fynes (Bahamas)		22.55
800 *metres:* Maria Mutola (Mozambique)	1	59.10
3,000 *metres:* Gabriela Szabo (Romania)	8	43.52
400 *metres hurdles:* Deon Hemmings (Jamaica)		53.41

	metres
High jump: Hestrie Storbeck-Cloete (South Africa)	1.96
Triple Jump: Ashia Hansen (Great Britain)	14.96
Shot: Nadine Kleinert (Germany)	19.16
Overall winner: Gabriela Szabo (Romania)	

BADMINTON

WORLD CHAMPIONSHIPS 1999
Copenhagen, May

Men's Singles: Sun Jun (China) beat Fung Permadi (Taiwan) 15–6, 15–13
Ladies' Singles: Camilla Martin (Denmark) beat Dai Yun (China) 11–6, 6–11, 11–10
Men's Doubles: Ha Tae-Kwon and Kim Dong-Moon (S. Korea) beat Lee Dong-Soo and Yoo Yong-Sung (S. Korea) 15–5, 15–5
Ladies' Doubles: Ge Fei and Gu Jun (China) beat Ra Kyung-Min and Chung Jae-Hee (China) 15–4, 15–5
Mixed Doubles: Ra Kyung-Min and Kim Dong-Moon (S. Korea) beat Joanne Goode and Simon Archer (GB) 15–10, 15–13
Sudirman Cup final (mixed team event): China beat Denmark 3–1

ENGLISH NATIONAL CHAMPIONSHIPS 1999
Haywards Heath, February

Men's Singles: Darren Hall beat Colin Haughton 6–15, 15–7, 15–5
Ladies' Singles: Julia Mann beat Tracey Hallam 11–2, 11–2
Men's Doubles: Simon Archer and Chris Hunt beat Julian Robertson and Nathan Robertson 17–15, 15–12
Ladies' Doubles: Ella Miles and Sara Sankey beat Joanne Goode and Donna Kellogg 15–11, 7–15, 15–10
Mixed Doubles: Joanne Goode and Simon Archer beat Donna Kellogg and Chris Hunt 15–6, 15–5

Scottish National Championships 1999
Edinburgh, February

Men's Singles: Bruce Flockhart beat David Gilmour 15–6, 15–7
Ladies' Singles: Gillian Martin beat Susan Hughes 11–10, 11–9
Men's Doubles: Russell Hogg and Kenny Middlemiss beat Alastair Gatt and Craig Robertson 15–1, 17–15
Ladies' Doubles: Kirsteen McEwan and Sandra Watt beat Alexis Blanchflower and Fiona Sneddon 15–2, 15–3
Mixed Doubles: Kirsteen McEwan and Kenny Middlemiss beat Jillian Haldane and Russell Hogg 15–7, 13–15, 15–11

Welsh National Championships 1999
Brecon, February

Men's Singles: Richard Vaughan beat Matthew Hughes 15–2, 15–7
Ladies' Singles: Kelly Morgan beat Kate Ridler 11–0, 11–0
Men's Doubles: Christopher Rees and Neil Cottrill beat Chris Davies and Matthew Hughes 15–2, 15–8
Ladies' Doubles: Kelly Morgan and Rachelle Edwards beat Gail Osborne and Katy Howell 15–6, 15–7
Mixed Doubles: Kelly Morgan and Richard Vaughan beat Robyn Ashworth and Chris Davies 15–7, 15–4

All-England Championships 1999
Birmingham, March

Men's Singles: Peter Gade Christensen (Denmark) beat Taufik Hidayat (Indonesia) 15–11, 7–15, 15–10
Ladies' Singles: Ye Zhaoying (China) beat Dai Yun (China) 9–11, 11–5, 11–1
Men's Doubles: Candra Wijaya and Tony Gunawan (Indonesia) beat Lee Dong-soo and Yoo Yong-sung (S. Korea) 15–7, 15–5
Ladies' Doubles: Chung Jae-hee and Ra Kyung-min (S. Korea) beat Huang Sui and Lu Ying (China) 15–6, 15–8
Mixed Doubles: Joanne Goode and Simon Archer (England) beat Chung Jae-hee and Ha Tae-kwan (S. Korea) 15–2, 15–13

BASEBALL

American League Championship Series winners 1998: New York Yankees
National League Championship Series winners 1998: San Diego Padres
World Series 1998: New York Yankees beat San Diego Padres 4–0

BASKETBALL

Men
Championship play-off final 1999: London Towers beat Thames Valley Tigers 82–71
League Trophy final 1999: Manchester Giants beat Derby Storm 90–69
National Cup final 1999: Sheffield Sharks beat Greater London Leopards 67–65
Premier League Championship 1999: Sheffield Sharks

Women
Championship play-off final 1999: Sheffield Hatters beat Thames Valley 63–60
National Cup final 1999: Sheffield Hatters beat Birmingham Q. C. 75–47
National League Championship 1999: Sheffield Hatters

BILLIARDS

World Professional Championship 1998: Geet Sethi (India) beat Mike Russell (England) 1,400–1,015
World Matchplay Championship 1999: Geet Sethi (India) beat David Causier (England) 1,405–1,195
British Open 1999: Mike Russell (England) beat Chris Shutt (England) 2,195–335
UK Professional Championship 1998: Mike Russell (England) beat Geet Sethi (India) 2,204–807
Women's World Championship 1999: Karen Corr (N. Ireland) beat Kelly Fisher (England) 354–276

BOWLS – INDOOR

MEN
World Championships 1999
Hopton-on-Sea, January–February

Singles: Alex Marshall (Scotland) beat David Gourlay (Scotland) 7–6, 7–2, 7–0
Pairs: John Price and Stephen Rees (Wales) beat Graham Robertson and Richard Corsie (Scotland) 7–6, 5–7, 3–7, 7–1, 7–1

UK Championships 1998
Hopton-on-Sea, November

Singles: David Corkill (Ireland) beat Paul Foster (Scotland) 7–0, 7–6, 5–7, 7–3

National Championships 1999
Melton Mowbray, April

Singles: Martin Pulling (Grantham) beat Simon Skelton (Scunthorpe) 21–18
Pairs: Blackpool Borough beat Five Rivers 20–13
Triples: Blackpool Borough beat Chipping Norton 19–11
Fours: Cumbria beat Chipping Norton 24–14

British Isles Championships 1999
Bournemouth, March

Singles: Paul Foster (Scotland) beat Jamie Mills (England) 21–2
Pairs: Scotland beat Wales 23–8
Triples: Scotland beat England 18–17
Fours: Wales beat England 22–11

Hilton Trophy (Home International Championship) 1999: Scotland
Liberty Trophy (Inter-County Championship) final 1999: Hampshire beat Durham 120–106

WOMEN
World Championships 1999
Prestwick, April

Singles: Caroline McAllister (Scotland) beat Kate Adams (Scotland) 3–2

National Championships 1999
Exeter, February–March

Singles: Chris Hiom (Boston) beat Sharon Rickman (King George High) 21–11
Pairs: North Walsham beat Oxford 24–15
Triples (two wood): Isca beat Tamworth 27–2
Triples (four wood): Preston beat Lincoln 17–12
Fours: Cherwell beat York 21–14

BRITISH ISLES CHAMPIONSHIPS 1999
Belfast, March

Singles: Chris Hiom (England) beat Aeres Davies (Wales)
21–19
Pairs: Scotland beat Ireland 17–12
Triples: Scotland beat Ireland 18–16
Fours: Scotland beat Ireland 20–19

Home International Championship 1999: Scotland
Atherley Trophy (Inter-County Championship) 1999: Yorkshire

BOWLS – OUTDOOR

MEN

NATIONAL CHAMPIONSHIPS 1999
Worthing, August

Singles: Nicky Brett (Warboys White Hart, Hunts) beat
Graham Ashby (Stoke Coventry, Warwicks) 21–18
Pairs: Wellingborough, Northants beat Sandwich, Kent
24–23
Triples: Boscombe Cliff beat Stoke Coventry 19–11
Fours: Gerrards Cross, Bucks, beat Blackheath and
Greenwich, Kent 21–5

BRITISH ISLES CHAMPIONSHIPS 1999
Le Creux Club, Jersey, July

Singles: Clifford Craig (Ireland) beat Raymond Logan
(Scotland) 21–20
Pairs: Scotland beat England 21–20
Triples: Ireland beat Channel Islands 23–11
Fours: Ireland beat England 19–18

Home International Championship 1999: Ireland
Middleton Cup (Inter-County Championship) final 1999:
Cumbria beat Kent 125–114

WOMEN

NATIONAL CHAMPIONSHIPS 1999
Royal Leamington Spa, August

Singles (four woods): Joyce Hadfield (Newquay Trenance,
Cornwall) beat Jayne Smith (Henlow Park, Beds) 21–
17
Singles (two woods): Elizabeth Messer (Southbourne, Hants)
beat Lynne Whitehead (Norfolk) 14–11
Pairs: Park, Lincoln beat Croydon 21–15
Triples: Temple, Surrey beat Wooler, Northumberland
17–16
Fours: Clevedon Promenade, Somerset beat Long Eaton
Silver Band, Derbyshire 23–12

BRITISH ISLES CHAMPIONSHIPS 1999
Belfast, June

Singles: Margaret Johnston (Ireland) beat Karina Horman
(Jersey) 25–8
Pairs: Ireland beat Scotland 18-13
Triples: Scotland beat Ireland 19–11
Fours: Wales beat England 24–9

Home International Championship 1999: Scotland
Johns Trophy (Inter-County Championship) final 1999: Essex
beat Durham 122–93

BOXING

PROFESSIONAL BOXING
as at 1 September 1999

WORLD BOXING COUNCIL (WBC) CHAMPIONS

Heavy: Lennox Lewis (GB)
Cruiser: Juan Carlos Gomez (Cuba)
Light-heavy: Roy Jones (USA)
Super-middle: Richie Woodhall (GB)
Middle: Keith Holmes (USA)
Super-welter: Javier Castillejo (Spain)
Welter: Oscar De La Hoya (USA)
Super-light: Konstantin Tszyu (Australia)
Light: Stevie Johnston (USA)
Super-feather: Floyd Mayweather (USA)
Feather: Cesar Soto (Mexico)
Super-bantam: Erik Morales (Mexico)
Bantam: Veeraphol Sahaprom (Thailand)
Super-fly: Cho In-joo (S. Korea)
Fly: Manny Pacquiao (Philippines)
Light-fly: Saman Sorjaturong (Thailand)
Straw: Ricardo Lopez (Mexico)

WORLD BOXING ASSOCIATION (WBA) CHAMPIONS

Heavy: Evander Holyfield (USA)
Cruiser: Fabrice Tiozzo (France)
Light-heavy: Roy Jones (USA)
Super-middle: Byron Mitchell (USA)
Middle: William Joppy (USA)
Junior-middle: David Reid (USA)
Welter: James Page (USA)
Super-light: Sharmba Mitchell (USA)
Light: Julien Jorcy (France)
Super-feather: Lakva Sim (Mongolia)
Feather: Freddie Norwood (USA)
Super-bantam: Nestor Garza (Mexico)
Bantam: Paulie Ayala (USA)
Super-fly: Jesus Rojax (Venezuela)
Fly: Leo Gamez (Venezuela)
Light-fly: Phichit Chor Siriwat (Thailand)
Straw: Ricardo Lopez (Mexico)

INTERNATIONAL BOXING FEDERATION (IBF)
CHAMPIONS

Heavy: Evander Holyfield (USA)
Cruiser: Vassily Jirov (Kazakhstan)
Light-heavy: Roy Jones (USA)
Super-middle: Sven Ottke (Germany)
Middle: Bernard Hopkins (USA)
Junior-middle: Fernando Vargas (USA)
Welter: Felix Trinidad (Puerto Rico)
Junior-welter: Terran Millett (USA)
Light: vacant
Junior-light: Roberto Garcia (USA)
Feather: Manuel Medina (Mexico)
Junior-feather: Lehlohonolo Ledwaba (S. Africa)
Bantam: Tim Austin (USA)
Junior-bantam: Mark Johnson (USA)
Fly: Irene Pacheco (Colombia)
Junior-fly: Will Grigsby (USA)
Mini-fly: Zolani Petelo (S. Africa)

BRITISH CHAMPIONS

Heavy: Julius Francis
Cruiser: vacant
Light-heavy: Clinton Woods
Super-middle: David Starie

Middle: Howard Eastman
Light-middle: Ensley Bingham
Welter: Derek Roche
Light-welter: Jason Rowland
Light: Bobby Vanzie
Super-feather: vacant
Feather: Jon Jo Irwin
Super-bantam: Drew Docherty
Bantam: Paul Lloyd
Fly: Keith Knox

EUROPEAN CHAMPIONS

Heavy: vacant
Cruiser: Alexei Iliin (Russia)
Light-heavy: Clinton Woods (GB)
Super-middle: Bruno Girard (France)
Middle: Erland Betare (France)
Light-middle: Mamadou Thiam (France)
Welter: Alessandro Duran (Italy)
Light-welter: Thomas Damgaard (Denmark)
Light: Billy Schwer (GB)
Junior-light: Dennis Holbek (Denmark)
Feather: Steve Robinson (GB)
Super-bantam: Michael Brodie (GB)
Bantam: Johnny Bredahl (Denmark)
Fly: vacant

COMMONWEALTH CHAMPIONS

Heavy: Julius Francis (GB)
Cruiser: Bruce Scott (GB)
Light-heavy: Clinton Woods (GB)
Super-middle: David Starie (GB)
Middle: vacant
Light-middle: Tony Bedea (Canada)
Welter: Kofi Jantuah (Ghana)
Light-welter: Paul Burke (GB)
Light: Bobby Vanzie (GB)
Super-feather: vacant
Feather: Paul Ingle (GB)
Super-bantam: Michael Brodie (GB)
Bantam: Paul Lloyd (GB)
Fly: Keith Knox (GB)

AMATEUR BOXING

AMATEUR BOXING ASSOCIATION (ABA)
CHAMPIONSHIP WINNERS 1999

Super-heavy (91+ kg): B. Bessey
Heavy (91 kg): S. St John
Cruiser (86 kg): M. Krence
Light-heavy (81 kg): J. Ainscough
Middle (75 kg): C. Froch
Light-middle (71 kg): C. Bessey
Welter (67 kg): A. Cessay
Light-welter (63.5 kg): D. Happe
Light (60 kg): S. Burke
Feather (57 kg): S. Miller
Bantam (54 kg): M. Hunter
Fly (51 kg): D. Robinson
Light-fly (48 kg): G. Jones

CHESS

PCA World Champion: Garry Kasparov (Russia)
WCF World Champion: Bobby Fischer (USA)
FIDE World Champion 1999: Alexander Khalifman (Russia)
British Champion 1999: Julian Hodgson
FIDE Women's World Champion 1999: Xye Jun (China)
British Women's Champion 1999: Harriet Hunt

CRICKET

TEST SERIES

AUSTRALIA V. ENGLAND

Brisbane (20–24 November 1998): Match drawn. Australia 485 and 237–3 dec.; England 375 and 179–6
Perth (28–30 November 1998): Australia beat England by 7 wickets. England 112 and 191; Australia 240 and 64–3
Adelaide (11–15 December 1998): Australia beat England by 205 runs. Australia 391 and 278–5 dec.; England 227 and 237
Melbourne (26–29 December 1998): England beat Australia by 12 runs. England 270 and 244; Australia 340 and 162
Sydney (2–5 January 1999): Australia beat England by 98 runs. Australia 322 and 184; England 220 and 188

ENGLAND V. NEW ZEALAND

Edgbaston (1–3 July 1999): England beat New Zealand by 7 wickets. New Zealand 226 and 107; England 126 and 211–3
Lord's (22–25 July 1999): New Zealand won by 9 wickets. England 186 and 229; New Zealand 358 and 60–1
Old Trafford (5–9 August 1999): Match drawn. England 199 and 181–2; New Zealand 496–9 dec.
The Oval (19–22 August 1999): New Zealand won by 83 runs. New Zealand 236 and 162; England 153 and 162

OTHER TEST SERIES

Pakistan v. Australia (October–November 1998): Australia won 1–0; two matches drawn
Zimbabwe v. India (October 1998): Zimbabwe won 1–0
Pakistan v. Zimbabwe (November–December 1998): Zimbabwe won 1–0; one match drawn, one match abandoned because of fog
South Africa v. West Indies (November 1998–January 1999): South Africa won 5–0
New Zealand v. India (December 1998–January 1999): New Zealand won 1–0; one match drawn, one match abandoned because of rain
India v. Pakistan (January–February 1999): Pakistan 1, India 1
Asian Test Championship (February–March 1999): Pakistan beat India, Sri Lanka drew with India, Pakistan drew with Sri Lanka; Pakistan beat Sri Lanka in the final
New Zealand v. South Africa (February–March 1999): South Africa won 1–0; two matches drawn
West Indies v. Australia (March– April 1999): West Indies 2, Australia 2

ONE-DAY INTERNATIONALS

THREE-NATION INTERNATIONAL SERIES (AUSTRALIA, ENGLAND AND SRI LANKA)

First final (Sydney, 10 February 1999): Australia beat England by 10 runs. Australia 232–8; England 222
Second final (Melbourne, 13 February 1999): Australia beat England by 162 runs. Australia 272–5; England 110

WORLD CUP 1999

FIRST ROUND

Group A

	P	W	L	Points	Net run-rate
South Africa	5	4	1	8	0.86
India	5	3	2	6	1.28
Zimbabwe	5	3	2	6	0.02
England	5	3	2	6	−0.33
Sri Lanka	5	2	3	4	−0.81
Kenya	5	0	5	0	−1.20

Group B

	P	W	L	Points	Net run-rate
Pakistan	5	4	1	8	0.53
Australia	5	3	2	6	0.73
New Zealand	5	3	2	6	0.58
West Indies	5	3	2	6	0.50
Bangladesh	5	2	3	4	−0.54
Scotland	5	0	5	0	−1.93

SUPER SIX ROUND

Australia beat India by 77 runs. Australia 282–6; India 205
South Africa beat Pakistan by 3 wickets. Pakistan 220–7;
    South Africa 221–7
New Zealand v. Zimbabwe – no result (match abandoned
    because of rain). Zimbabwe 175; New Zealand 70–3
India beat Pakistan by 47 runs. India 227–6; Pakistan 180
Australia beat Zimbabwe by 44 runs. Australia 303–4;
    Zimbabwe 259–6
South Africa beat New Zealand by 74 runs. South Africa
    287–5; New Zealand 213–8
Pakistan beat Zimbabwe by 148 runs. Pakistan 271–9;
    Zimbabwe 123
New Zealand beat India by 5 wickets. India 251–6; New
    Zealand 253–5
Australia beat South Africa by 5 wickets. South Africa
    271–7; Australia 272–5

	P	W	L	NR	Points	Net run-rate
Pakistan	5	3	2	0	6	0.65
Australia	5	3	2	0	6	0.36
South Africa	5	3	2	0	6	0.17
New Zealand	5	2	2	1	5	−0.52
Zimbabwe	5	2	2	1	5	−0.79
India	5	1	4	0	2	−0.15

SEMI-FINALS

Pakistan beat New Zealand by 9 wickets. New Zealand
    241–7; Pakistan 242–1
Australia tied with South Africa. Australia 213; South
    Africa 213. Australia qualified for the final because they
    finished above South Africa in the Super Six round

FINAL

Lord's, 20 June 1999
Australia beat Pakistan by 8 wickets. Pakistan 132;
    Australia 133–2

OTHER INTERNATIONAL CUPS

Wills International Cup final 1998: South Africa beat West
    Indies by 4 wickets. West Indies 245; South Africa 248–
    6
Sharjah Champions Trophy final 1998: India beat Zimbabwe
    by 10 wickets. Zimbabwe 196–9; India 197–0
Sharjah Champions' Cup final 1999: Pakistan beat India by 8
    wickets. India 125; Pakistan 129–2

AUSTRALIA v. ENGLAND 1998–9 (Test Averages)

AUSTRALIA BATTING

	I	NO	R	HS	Av.
S. R. Waugh	10	4	498	122*	83.00
M. E. Waugh	10	3	393	121	56.14
J. L. Langer	10	1	436	179*	48.44
M. J. Slater	10	0	460	123	46.00
I. A. Healy	8	1	221	134	31.57
D. W. Fleming	5	1	95	71*	23.75
M. A. Taylor	10	0	228	61	22.80
D. S. Lehmann	4	0	49	32	12.25
R. T. Ponting	4	0	47	21	11.75
S. C. G. MacGill	6	0	69	43	11.50
C. R. Miller	4	2	17	11	8.50
G. D. McGrath	7	0	15	10	2.14

Played in one match: J. N. Gillespie, 11; S. K. Warne, 2*,8;
    M. J. Nicholson, 5,9; M. S. Kasprowicz, 0
*Not out

AUSTRALIA BOWLING

	O	M	R	W	Av.
S. R. Waugh	11	3	28	2	14.00
J. N. Gillespie	22.2	2	111	7	15.85
S. C. G. MacGill	185.2	33	477	27	17.66
G. D. McGrath	196.4	53	492	24	20.50
D. W. Fleming	134.5	29	392	16	24.50
C. R. Miller	99	18	238	9	26.44
M. J. Nicholson	25	4	115	4	28.75
M. E. Waugh	26	2	90	3	30.00
S. K. Warne	39	7	110	2	55.00
M. S. Kasprowicz	37	10	111	2	55.50

Also bowled: R. T. Ponting, 4–1–10–0

ENGLAND BATTING

	I	NO	R	HS	Av.
M. R. Ramprakash	10	2	379	69*	47.37
N. Hussain	10	1	407	89*	45.22
A. J. Stewart	10	1	316	107	35.11
M. A. Butcher	10	0	259	116	25.90
G. A. Hick	8	0	205	68	25.62
J. P. Crawley	6	0	86	44	14.33
M. A. Atherton	8	0	110	41	13.75
D. G. Cork	4	1	39	21*	13.00
A. J. Tudor	4	1	35	18*	11.66
A. R. C. Fraser	3	2	8	7*	8.00
W. K. Hegg	4	0	30	15	7.50
D. W. Headley	6	0	41	16	6.83
D. Gough	9	1	43	11	5.37
A. D. Mullally	7	0	20	16	2.85
P. M. Such	4	1	2	2	0.66

Played in one match: G. P. Thorpe, 77,9; R. D. B. Croft,
    23,4*
*Not out

ENGLAND BOWLING

	O	M	R	W	Av.
D. W. Headley	121.3	20	423	19	22.26
A. J. Tudor	42.2	8	180	7	25.71
P. M. Such	116.5	24	323	11	29.36
A. D. Mullally	157.3	44	364	12	30.33
D. Gough	201.3	41	687	21	32.71
D. G. Cork	57	11	165	4	41.25
A. R. C. Fraser	69	8	229	4	57.25
R. D. B. Croft	43	8	126	2	63.00
M. R. Ramprakash	44	3	136	1	136.00

Also bowled: G. A. Hick, 1–0–1–0

ENGLAND v. NEW ZEALAND 1999 (Test Averages)

ENGLAND BATTING

	I	NO	R	HS	Av.
M. A. Atherton	4	0	133	64	33.25
N. Hussain	5	0	164	61	32.80
A. J. Stewart	8	1	215	83*	30.71
M. R. Ramprakash	6	1	127	69*	25.40
G. P. Thorpe	8	2	147	44	24.50
A. R. Caddick	6	0	126	45	21.00
M. A. Butcher	6	0	86	33	14.33
D. W. Headley	3	0	34	18	11.33
C. M. W. Read	4	0	38	37	9.50
A. Habib	3	0	26	19	8.66
P. C. R. Tufnell	6	3	14	6	4.66
A. D. Mullally	5	0	18	10	3.60

Played in one match: G. A. Hick, 12; D. L. Maddy, 14,5; R. C. Irani, 9,1; P. M. Such, 0; E. S. H. Giddins, 0,0*; A. J. Tudor, 99*,32*
* Not out

ENGLAND BOWLING

	O	M	R	W	Av.
E. S. H. Giddins	26	7	79	4	19.75
A. R. Caddick	174.1	62	412	20	20.60
P. C. R. Tufnell	132.2	36	317	14	22.64
A. D. Mullally	111.4	29	300	11	27.27
P. M. Such	41	11	114	4	28.50
R. C. Irani	11	3	38	1	38.00
M. A. Butcher	12	2	45	1	45.00
D. W. Headley	58	11	189	4	47.25
A. J. Tudor	16	4	59	1	59.00

Also bowled: M. R. Ramprakash, 1–0–1–0; G. A. Hick, 1–0–8–0

NEW ZEALAND BATTING

	I	NO	R	HS	Av.
M. D. Bell	5	1	151	83	37.75
C. D. McMillan	6	1	188	107*	37.60
S. P. Fleming	7	2	166	66*	33.20
N. J. Astle	6	0	193	101	32.16
C. L. Cairns	6	0	183	80	30.50
M. J. Horne	7	0	203	100	29.00
D. L. Vettori	6	1	114	54	22.80
D. J. Nash	6	1	81	26	16.20
A. C. Parore	6	0	96	73	16.00
R. G. Twose	6	0	73	52	12.16
G. I. Allott	3	3	8	7*	–

Played in one match: S. B. Doull, 46,11; S. B. O'Connor, 6,1; C. Z. Harris, 3
* Not out

NEW ZEALAND BOWLING

	O	M	R	W	Av.
D. J. Nash	135.1	52	297	17	17.47
S. B. O'Connor	24	6	62	3	20.66
C. L. Cairns	139	34	404	19	21.26
C. Z. Harris	26	10	46	2	23.00
D. L. Vettori	137	50	249	10	24.90
G. I. Allott	55.4	10	182	7	26.00
N. J. Astle	27	13	36	1	36.00
S. B. Doull	19	6	65	1	65.00

Also bowled: C. D. McMillan, 3.4–0–14–0

COUNTY CHAMPIONSHIP TABLE 1999

Order for 1998 in brackets	P	W	L	D	Bt	Bl	Pts
Surrey (5)	17	12	0	5	36	64	264
Lancashire (2)	17	8	4	5	37	55	208
Leicestershire (1)	17	5	3	9	43	61	200
Somerset (9)	17	6	4	7	38	56	194
Kent (11)	17	6	4	7	34	60	194
Yorkshire (3)	17	8	6	3	21	64	193
Hampshire (6)	17	5	5	7	45	58	191
Durham (14)	17	6	7	4	34	66	188
Derbyshire (10)	17	7	8	2	34	61	187
Warwickshire (8)	17	6	5	6	35	56	187
Sussex (7)	17	6	5	6	29	60	185
Essex (18)	17	5	5	5	38	63	181
Northamptonshire (15)	17	4	7	6	35	64	171
Glamorgan (12)	17	5	7	5	26	57	163
Worcestershire (13)	17	4	6	7	18	65	159
Middlesex (17)	17	4	5	8	24	53	157
Nottinghamshire (16)	17	4	11	2	27	57	140
Gloucestershire (4)	17	2	9	6	26	62	136

FIRST CLASS BATTING AVERAGES 1999

Qualifying requirement: 6 completed innings

	I	NO	R	HS	Av.
S. G. Law	29	4	1,833	263	73.32
T. M. Dilshan	10	1	562	127	62.44
J. L. Langer	22	4	1,048	241*	58.22
J. Cox	30	2	1,617	216	57.75
M. L. Hayden	15	2	745	170	57.30
R. J. Turner	27	4	1,217	138*	52.91
N. Hussain	20	1	988	143	52.00
D. J. Sales	29	4	1,291	303*	51.64
A. D. Brown	26	4	1,127	265	51.22
D. J. Nash	11	3	395	135*	49.37
P. D. Bowler	27	8	931	149	49.00
G. A. Hick	22	0	1,063	150	48.31
M. J. Powell	26	4	1,060	164	48.18
C. C. Lewis	13	2	520	139	47.27
G. M. Hamilton	20	8	567	94*	47.25
M. J. Horne	15	0	670	172	44.66
M. A. Atherton	15	2	578	268*	44.46
N. J. Astle	15	1	617	121	44.07
G. R. Loveridge	10	0	427	126	42.70
R. A. Smith	29	3	1,110	96	42.69

*Not out

FIRST CLASS BOWLING AVERAGES 1999

Qualifying requirement: 20 wickets taken

	O	M	R	W	Av.
Saqlain Mushtaq	290.5	90	660	58	11.37
M. Muralitharan	386.2	122	777	66	11.77
D. J. Nash	232	84	548	34	16.11
D. J. Millns	142.3	35	372	23	16.17
A. C. Morris	172	51	497	28	17.75
N. Killeen	411.3	114	1,070	58	18.44
M. P. Bicknell	545.4	157	1,346	71	18.95
G. M. Hamilton	277.1	64	825	43	19.18
T. M. Smith	162.4	29	561	29	19.34
J. B. D. Thompson	434.1	106	1,265	64	19.76
T. A. Munton	409.1	107	1,028	52	19.76
R. Herath	168	46	448	22	20.36
C. E. W. Silverwood	405.2	87	1,204	59	20.40
A. M. Smith	450.1	127	1,168	57	20.49
P. J. Martin	446.4	134	1,028	50	20.56
A. R. Caddick	763.5	249	1,900	91	20.87
R. C. Irani	395.2	101	1,084	51	21.25
P. Aldred	362.4	85	1,063	50	21.26
M. K. Davies	423.3	137	857	40	21.42
P. A. J. DeFreitas	477.2	123	1,284	59	21.76

Source for averages and county championship table: ECB/PA Cricket Record

OTHER RESULTS 1999

Super Cup final: Gloucestershire beat Yorkshire by 124 runs. Gloucestershire 291–9; Yorkshire 167
NatWest Trophy final: Gloucestershire beat Somerset by 50 runs. Gloucestershire 230–8; Somerset 180
National League Champions: Division 1, Lancashire; *Division 2,* Sussex
ECB County Cup final: Bedfordshire beat Cumberland by 8 wickets. Cumberland 153; Bedfordshire 154–2
Minor Counties Championship final: Cumberland beat Dorset by 6 wickets. Cumberland 315–7 and 214–4; Dorset 130 and 396
National Club Championship final: Wolverhampton beat Teddington by 4 wickets. Teddington 185–7; Wolverhampton 189–6
National Village Championship final: Linton Park beat Woodhouse Grange by 20 runs. Linton Park 195–4; Woodhouse Grange 175–8
Varsity Match (one-day): Oxford beat Cambridge by 7 wickets. Cambridge 175–9; Oxford 178–3
Varsity Match (three-day): Cambridge drew with Oxford. Oxford 259 and 203–6; Cambridge 411

CYCLING

World Cup series overall winner 1998: Andre Tchmil (Belgium)
Tour of Britain 1999: Marc Wauters (Belgium)
Tour of Italy 1999: Ivan Gotti (Italy)
Tour de France 1999: Lance Armstrong (USA)
Tour of Spain 1999: Jan Ullrich (Germany)
World Road Race Championship 1998: Oscar Camenzind (Switzerland)
World Cyclo-Cross Championship 1999: Mario de Clercq (Belgium)
World Cyclo-Cross Cup series overall winner 1999: Mario de Clercq (Belgium), 206 points
British Road Race Championship 1999: John Tanner (Pro Vision-Planet X)
British Cyclo-Cross Championship 1999: Steve Knight (Peugeot 406-Michelin)
Women's World Road Race Championship 1998: D. Ziliute (Lithuania)
Women's National Road Race Championship 1999: Nicole Cooke (MI Racing)

DARTS

Skol World Championship 1999: Phil Taylor (England) beat Peter Manley (England) 6–2
Embassy World Championship 1999: Ray Barneveld (Holland) beat Ronnie Baxter (England) 6–5

EQUESTRIANISM

SHOW JUMPING

World Championship 1998: Rodrigo Pessoa (Brazil)
World Cup final 1999: Rodrigo Pessoa (Brazil) on Baloubet du Rouet
European Championships 1999:
　Individual: Alexandra Lederman (France) on Rochet M
　Team: Germany
British Jumping Derby 1999 (Hickstead): Rob Hoekstra (GB) on Lionel

THREE-DAY EVENTING

World Championships 1998:
　Individual: Blyth Tait (New Zealand) on Ready Teddy
　Team: New Zealand
Badminton Horse Trials 1999: Ian Stark (GB) on Jaybee
British Open Horse Trials 1999 (Gatcombe Park): Mark Todd (New Zealand) on Word for Word
Burghley Horse Trials 1999: Mark Todd (New Zealand) on Diamond Hall Red

ETON FIVES

County Championship final 1999: Middlesex beat Berkshire 2–1
Amateur Championship (Kinnaird Cup) 1999: Robin Mason and Jonathan Mole beat James Toup and Matthew Wiseman, walk-over
Holmwoods Schools' Championship 1999: St Olave's I beat Eton I 3–1
Barber Cup final 1999: Old Salopians beat Old Cholmeleians 2–1
League Championship (Douglas Keeble Cup) 1999: Old Salopians I

FENCING

MEN

WORLD CHAMPIONS 1998

Foil: Sergei Golubitsky (Ukraine)
Epée: Hughes Obry (France)
Sabre: L. Tarantino (Italy)
Team foil: Poland
Team epée: Hungary
Team sabre: Hungary

BRITISH CHAMPIONS 1999

Foil: James Beevers (Cyrano)
Epée: Alex Agrenich (Haverstock)
Sabre: Robin Knight (London Thames)
Team Foil: Sussex House A
Corble Cup 1999 (international sabre tournament): Raffaello Caserta (Italy)

WOMEN

WORLD CHAMPIONS 1998

Epée: Laura Flessel (France)
Foil: S. Bau (Germany)
Team epée: France
Team foil: Italy

BRITISH CHAMPIONS 1999

Foil: Linda Strachan (Salle Boston)
Epée: Valerie Cramb
Sabre: Louise Bond-Williams (Shakespeare)
Team Foil: Salle Paul A
Ipswich Cup 1999 (international epée world cup series): I. Duplitzer (Germany)

GOLF (MEN)

THE MAJOR CHAMPIONSHIPS 1999

US Masters (Augusta, Georgia, 8–11 April): José María Olazábal (Spain), 280

US Open (Pinehurst, North Carolina, 17–20 June): Payne Stewart (USA), 279

The Open (Carnoustie, 15–18 July): Paul Lawrie (GB), 290*

US PGA Championship (Medinah Country Club, Illinois, 12–15 August): Tiger Woods (USA), 277

PGA EUROPEAN TOUR 1998

Belgacom Open (Knokke-Le-Zoute): Lee Westwood (GB), 268*

World Matchplay Championship (Wentworth): Mark O'Meara (USA) beat Tiger Woods (USA) by 1 hole

Volvo Masters (Jerez): Darren Clarke (N. Ireland), 271

European Tour Order of Merit 1998: 1. Colin Montgomerie (GB); 2. Darren Clarke (N. Ireland); 3. Lee Westwood (GB)

World Open Championship 1998 (Braselton, Georgia): Dudley Hart (USA), 272

PGA EUROPEAN TOUR 1999

South African PGA (Johannesburg): Ernie Els (S. Africa), 273

South African Open (Stellenbosch): David Frost (S. Africa), 279

Heineken Classic (Perth, Australia): Jarrod Moseley (Australia), 274

Dubai Desert Classic: David Howell (GB), 275

Qatar Masters (Doha): Paul Lawrie (GB), 268

Portuguese Open (Penina): Van Phillips (GB), 276*

Turespana Masters (Malaga): Miguel-Angel Jiménez (Spain), 264

Madeira Island Open: Pedro Linhart (Spain), 276

Estoril Open (Penha Longa): Jean-François Remesy (France), 286

Spanish Open (Barcelona): Jarmo Sandelin (Sweden), 267

Italian Open (Turin): Dean Robertson (GB), 271

French Open (Club de Médoc, near Bordeaux): Retief Goosen (S. Africa), 272*

International Open (The Oxfordshire): Colin Montgomerie (GB), 273

European Tournament Players' Championship (Heidelberg): Tiger Woods (USA), 273

PGA Championship (Wentworth): Colin Montgomerie (GB), 270

English Open (Hanbury Manor): Darren Clarke (N. Ireland), 268

German Open (Berlin): Jarmo Sandelin (Sweden), 274*

Moroccan Open (Agadir): Miguel Martin (Spain), 276*

European Grand Prix (Slaley Hall): David Park (GB), 274

Irish Open (Druid's Glen): Sergio García (Spain), 268

Loch Lomond Invitational: Colin Montgomerie (GB), 268

Dutch Open (Hilversum): Lee Westwood (GB), 269

European Open (K Club, Co. Kildare): Lee Westwood (GB), 271

Scandinavian Masters (Malmö): Colin Montgomerie (GB), 268

West of Ireland Classic (Galway): Costantino Rocca (Italy), 276

International Open (Munich): Colin Montgomerie (GB), 268

European Masters (Crans-sur-Sierre): Lee Westwood (GB), 270

British Masters (Woburn): Bob May (USA), 269

Lancôme Trophy (St-Nom-la-Bretèche): Pierre Fulke (Sweden), 270

World Matchplay Championship final 1999 (La Costa, San Diego): Jeff Maggert (USA) beat Andrew Magee (USA) at second extra hole

MAJOR TEAM EVENTS

Alfred Dunhill Cup final 1998 (St Andrews, 8–11 October): South Africa beat Spain 3–0

Ryder Cup 1999 (Brookline, 24–26 September): USA beat Europe 14½–13½

Walker Cup 1999 (Nairn, 11–12 September): Great Britain and Ireland beat USA 15–9

AMATEUR CHAMPIONSHIPS

British Amateur Championship 1999 (Royal County Down): Graeme Storm (Wynyard)

English Amateur Championship 1999 (St Mellion): Paul Casey (Burhill)

Welsh Amateur Championship 1999 (Tenby): Matthew Griffiths (Wood Lake Park)

Scottish Amateur Championship 1999 (Cruden Bay): Craig Heap (East Kilbride)

Brabazon Trophy (English Open Strokeplay) 1999 (Moortown): Mark Side (Shirley Park), 279

Welsh Open Strokeplay 1999 (Northop Country Park): Craig Williams (Creigiau), 288

Scottish Open Strokeplay 1999 (St Andrew's): Graham Rankin (Drumpellier), 286

Lytham Trophy 1999 (Royal Lytham and St Anne's): Tino Schuster (Germany), 283

Berkshire Trophy 1999 (The Berkshire): Darren Henley (Stoneham), 275

International Match 1999 (Walton Heath): England beat Spain 16–8

Home International Championship 1999 (Royal County Down): England

Eisenhower Trophy (world amateur team championship) 1998 (Santiago, Chile): Great Britain and Ireland, 852

European Amateur Championship 1999 (Newport): G. Havret (France), 207

European Amateur Team Championship 1999 (Como, Italy): Italy

President's Putter 1999 (Rye): Chris Dale (Cambridge) beat Richard Bisson (Oxford) 4 and 3

Halford Hewitt Cup 1999 (for public schools' old boys) (Deal): Watson's beat Tonbridge 3–2

Varsity Match 1999 (Royal Cinque Ports): Oxford beat Cambridge 9½–5½

* After a play-off

GOLF (WOMEN)

US Women's Open 1999 (Old Waverly, Mississippi): Juli Inkster (USA), 272

Women's World Championship 1998 (The Villages, Florida): Juli Inkster (USA), 275

EUROPEAN LPGA TOUR 1998

Air France Open (Deauville): Patricia Meunier Lebouc (France), 208

Marrakesh Open: Sophie Gustafson (Sweden), 201

European Open (Praia d'El Rey, Portugal): Men's Senior Tour 10, European LPGA Tour 10. Men's Senior Tour retained cup

European Tour Order of Merit 1998: 1. Helen Alfredsson (Sweden); 2. Sophie Gustafson (Sweden); 3. Maria Hjorth (Sweden)

EUROPEAN LPGA TOUR 1999

Royal Marie-Claire Open (Evian): Silvia Cavalleri (Italy), 215

Evian Masters: Catrin Nilsmark (Sweden), 279

Chrysler Open (Halmstad, Sweden): Laura Davies (GB), 273

French Open (Paris): Trish Johnson (GB), 282

Austrian Open (Frohnleiten): Marina Arruti (Spain), 203

German Open (Treudelberg): Anne-Marie Knight (Australia), 278

Championship of Europe (Gleneagles): Laura Davies (GB), 280*
British Open (Woburn): Sherri Steinhauer (USA), 283
Compaq Open (Stockholm, Sweden): Laura Davies (GB), 277
Laura Davies Invitational (Brocket Hall, Herts): Sofia Gronberg Whitmore (Sweden), 275*
Irish Open (Letterkenny): Sandrine Mendiburu (France), 286*
Expo 2000 Open (Hanover): Sandrine Mendiburu (France), 208
Italian Open (Florence): Sam Head (GB), 214

AMATEUR CHAMPIONSHIPS

British Open Championship 1999 (Royal Birkdale): Marine Monnet (France)
English Amateur Championship 1999 (Ganton): Fiona Brown (Heswall)
Welsh Amateur Championship 1999 (Conwy): Becky Brewerton (Abergele)
Scottish Amateur Championship 1999 (Nairn Dunbar): Jayne Smith (Gullane)
British Strokeplay 1999 (Huddersfield): Becky Brewerton (Wales)
English Strokeplay 1999 (Gog Magog): Clare Lipscombe (Cirencester), 300
Welsh Strokeplay 1999 (Celtic Manor): Anne Walker (Strathaven), 230
Scottish Strokeplay 1999 (Portland and Royal Troon): Lesley Nicholson (Edinburgh University)
Home International Championship 1999 (Royal Dornoch): Wales
European Amateur Championship 1999 (Karlovy Vary, Czech Republic): Sofia Sandolo (Italy), 284
European Amateur Team Championship 1999 (Saint-Germain, Paris): France beat England 4½–2½
* After a play-off

GREYHOUND RACING

1998
Gold Collar (Catford): Lenson Billy
Cesarewitch (Catford): Fourth Ace
St Leger (Wembley): Droopys Pacino
Oaks (Wimbledon): Sarah Dee
Grand Prix (Walthamstow): Dans Sport
Television Trophy (Wimbledon): Note Book
1999
Grand National (Wimbledon): Pottos Storm and Hello Buttons
Derby (Wimbledon): Chart King
Scurry Gold Cup (Catford): Lissenair Luke
The Masters (Reading): Torbal Piper
The Regency (Brighton): Honest Lord

GYMNASTICS

BRITISH MEN'S CHAMPIONSHIPS 1998

Stoke-on-Trent, November
British Champion: Craig Heap (North Tyne)
Individual Apparatus Champions:
Floor: John Smethurst (Manchester)
Pommel Horse: Chris Hanson (Manchester)
Rings: Craig Heap (North Tyne)
Vault: Julian Niven Reed (Woking)
Parallel Bars: Andrew Atherton (Park Wrekin)

High Bar: James Boys (Hinkley)
British Men's Team Champions 1998 (Adam Shield): Woking

BRITISH MEN'S CHAMPIONSHIPS 1999

Stoke-on-Trent, September
British Champion: Craig Heap (North Tyne)
Individual Apparatus Champions:
Floor: R. Brewer (Woking)
Pommel Horse: I. McDermot (Woking)
Rings: J. Mirceta (Stoke) and Craig Heap (North Tyne) =
Vault: K. Jackson (Harrow)
Parallel Bars: R. Brewer (Woking)
High Bar: R. Brewer (Woking)

BRITISH WOMEN'S CHAMPIONSHIPS 1998

Nottingham, November
British Champion: Lisa Mason (Huntingdon)
Individual Apparatus Champions:
Floor: Annika Reeder (S. Essex)
Beam: Annika Reeder (S. Essex)
Vault: Annika Reeder (S. Essex)
Assymetric Bars: Rochelle Douglas (Alderwood)

BRITISH WOMEN'S CHAMPIONSHIPS 1999

Guildford, July
British Champion: Annika Reeder (S. Essex)
Individual Apparatus Champions:
Floor: Lisa Mason (Huntingdon)
Beam: Annika Reeder (S. Essex)
Vault: Lisa Mason (Huntingdon)
Assymetric Bars: Lisa Mason (Huntingdon)
British Rhythmics Champion 1999: Rebecca Jose (Spelthorne)

HOCKEY

MEN
English Hockey League Premier Division 1999: Cannock
English Hockey League Premiership final 1999: Cannock 3, Reading 3 a.e.t. Cannock won 4–3 on penalties
Hockey Association Cup final 1999: Reading 4, Cannock 4. Reading won 5–4 on penalties
National Indoor Club Championship final 1999: Southgate 5, Old Loughtonians 5. Southgate won 3–2 on penalties
County Championship final 1999: Sussex beat Yorkshire 3–2
Champions Trophy final 1998: Holland beat Pakistan 3–1
Champions Trophy final 1999: Australia beat South Korea 3–1
European Club Championship final 1999: Den Bosch (Holland) beat Egara (Spain) 2–1
European Nations Cup final 1999: Germany 3, Holland 3. Germany won 5–4 on penalties
European Cup Winners' Cup final 1999: Amsterdam (Holland) 2, Athletic Terrassa (Spain) 2. Amsterdam won 3–1 after a penalty shoot-out
Varsity Match 1999: Oxford 2, Cambridge 2

WOMEN
English Hockey League Premier Division 1999: Slough
English Hockey League Premiership final 1999: Slough beat Clifton 4–2
EHA Cup final 1999: Slough beat Leicester 4–3
English Hockey Indoor League Premier Division 1999: Hightown
County Championship final 1999: Surrey beat Herefordshire 3–1
Champions Trophy final 1999: Australia beat Holland 3–2

European Nations Cup final 1999: Holland beat Germany 2–1

European Club Championship final 1999: Rot-Weiss Cologne (Germany) 2, Den Bosch (Holland) 2. Rot-Weiss Cologne won 3–1 after a penalty shoot-out

European Indoor Club Championship final 1999: Russelsheim (Germany) beat Slough (England) 7–1

European Cup Winners' Cup final 1999: Amsterdam (Holland) beat Berliner (Germany) 3–1

Varsity Match 1999: Cambridge beat Oxford 4–1

HORSE-RACING

RESULTS

CAMBRIDGESHIRE HANDICAP
(1839) Newmarket, 1 mile

1995	Cap Juluca (3y), (9st 10lb), R. Hughes
1996	Clifton Fox (4y), (8st 2lb), N. Day
1997	Pasternak (4y), (9st 1lb), G. Duffield
1998	Lear Spear (3y), (8st 4lb), N. Pollard

PRIX DE L'ARC DE TRIOMPHE
(1920) Longchamp, 1½ miles

1995	Lammtarra (3y), (8st 11lb), F. Dettori
1996	Helissio (3y), (8st 11lb), O. Peslier
1997	Peintre Célèbre (3y), (8st 11lb), O. Peslier
1998	Sagamix (3y), (8st 11lb), O. Peslier

CESAREWITCH
(1839) Newmarket, 2 miles and about 2 f

1995	Old Red (5y), (7st 11lb), L. Charnock
1996	Inchcailloch (7y), (7st 10lb), R. Ffrench
1997	Turnpole (6y), (7st 10lb), L. Charnock
1998	Spirit of Love (3y), (8st 8lb), O. Peslier

CHAMPION STAKES
(1877) Newmarket, 1 mile, 2 f

1995	Spectrum (3y), (8st 10lb), J. Reid
1996	Bosra Sham (3y), (8st 8lb), P. Eddery
1997	Pilsudski (5y), (9st 2lb), M. Kinane
1998	Alborada (3y), (8st 8lb), G. Duffield

*HENNESSY GOLD CUP
(1957) Newbury, 3 miles and about 2½ f

1995	Couldn't Be Better (8y), (10st 8lb), D. Gallagher
1996	Coome Hill (7y), (10st), J. Osborne
1997	Suny Bay (8y), (11st 8lb), G. Bradley
1998	Teeton Mill (9y), (10st 5lb), N. Williamson

*KING GEORGE VI CHASE
(1937) Kempton, about 3 miles

†1995	One Man (8y), (11st 10lb), R. Dunwoody
1996	One Man (8y), (11st 10lb), R. Dunwoody
1997	See More Business (7y), (11st 10lb), A. Thornton
1998	Teeton Mill (9y), (11st 10lb), N. Williamson

*CHAMPION HURDLE
(1927) Cheltenham, 2 miles and about ½ f

1996	Collier Bay (6y), (12st), G. Bradley
1997	Make A Stand (6y), (12st), A. McCoy
1998	Istabraq (6y), (12st), C. Swan
1999	Istabraq (7y), (12st), C. Swan

*QUEEN MOTHER CHAMPION CHASE
(1959) Cheltenham, about 2 miles

1996	Klairon Davis (7y), (12st), F. Woods
1997	Martha's Son (10y), (12st), R. Farrant
1998	One Man (10y), (12st), B. Harding
1999	Call Equiname (9y), (12st), M. Fitzgerald

*CHELTENHAM GOLD CUP
(1924) 3 miles and about 2½ f

1996	Imperial Call (7y), (12st), C. O'Dwyer
1997	Mr Mulligan (9y), (12st), A. McCoy
1998	Cool Dawn (10y), (12st), A. Thornton
1999	See More Business (9y), (12st), M. Fitzgerald

LINCOLN HANDICAP
(1965) Doncaster, 1 mile

1996	Stone Ridge (4y), (8st 12lb), D. O'Neill
1997	Kuala Lipis (4y), (8st 6lb), T. Quinn
1998	Hunters Of Brora (8y), (9st), J. Weaver
1999	Right Wing (5y), (9st 5lb), T. Quinn

*GRAND NATIONAL
(1837) Liverpool, 4 miles and about 4 f

1996	Rough Quest (10y), (10st 7lb), M. Fitzgerald
1997	Lord Gyllene (9y), (10st), A. Dobbin
1998	Earth Summit (10y), (10st 5lb), C. Llewellyn
1999	Bobbyjo (9y), (10st), P. Carberry

Record times: 8 minutes 47.8 seconds by Mr Frisk in 1990; 9 minutes 1.9 seconds by Red Rum in 1973

*WHITBREAD GOLD CUP
(1957) Sandown, 3 miles and about 5 f

1996	Life Of A Lord (10y), (11st 10lb), C. Swan
1997	Harwell Lad (8y), (10st), Mr R. Nuttall
1998	Call It A Day (8y), (10st 10lb), A. Maguire
1999	Eulogy (9y), (10st), B. Fenton

JOCKEY CLUB STAKES
(1894) Newmarket, 1½ miles

1996	Riyadian (4y), (8st 9lb), T. Quinn
1997	Time Allowed (4y), (8st 6lb), J. Reid
1998	Romanov (4y), (8st 9lb), J. Reid
1999	Silver Patriarch (5y), (9st), P. Eddery

KENTUCKY DERBY
(1875) Louisville, Kentucky, 1½ miles

1996	Grindstone, J. Bailey
1997	Silver Charm, G. Stevens
1998	Real Quiet, K. Desormeaux
1999	Charismatic, C. Antley

PRIX DU JOCKEY CLUB
(1836) Chantilly, 1½ miles

1996	Ragmar (9st 2lb), G. Mossé
1997	Peintre Célèbre (9st 2lb), O. Peslier
1998	Dream Well (9st 2lb), C. Asmussen
1999	Montjeu (9st 2lb), C. Asmussen

ASCOT GOLD CUP
(1807) Ascot, 2 miles and about 4 f

1996	Classic Cliché (4y), (9st), M. Kinane
1997	Celeric (5y), (9st 2lb), P. Eddery
1998	Kayf Tara (4y), (9st), F. Dettori
1999	Enzeili (4y), (9st), J. Murtagh

IRISH SWEEPS DERBY
(1866) Curragh, 1½ miles, for three-year-olds

1996	Zagreb (9st), P. Shanahan
1997	Desert King (9st), C. Roche
1998	Dream Well (9st), C. Asmussen
1999	Montjeu (9st), C. Asmussen

ECLIPSE STAKES
(1886) Sandown, 1 mile and about 2 f

1996	Halling (5y), (9st 7lb), J. Reid
1997	Pilsudski (5y), (9st 7lb), M. Kinane
1998	Daylami (4y), (9st 7lb), F. Dettori
1999	Compton Admiral (3y), (8st 10lb), D. Holland

THE CLASSICS
ONE THOUSAND GUINEAS
(1814) Rowley Mile, Newmarket, for three-year-old fillies

Year	Winner	Betting	Owner	Jockey	Trainer	No. of Runners
1996	Bosra Sham	10–11	Wafic Said	P. Eddery	H. Cecil	13
1997	Sleepytime	5–1	C. Wacker III	K. Fallon	H. Cecil	15
1998	Cape Verdi	100–30	Godolphin	F. Dettori	Saeed bin Suroor	16
1999	Wince	4–1	Prince K. Abdulla	K. Fallon	H. Cecil	22

Record time: 1 minute 36.71 seconds by Las Meninas in 1994

TWO THOUSAND GUINEAS
(1809) Rowley Mile, Newmarket, for three-year-olds

Year	Winner	Betting	Owner	Jockey	Trainer	No. of Runners
1996	Mark of Esteem	8–1	Godolphin	F. Dettori	Saeed bin Suroor	13
1997	Entrepreneur	11–2	M. Tabor	M. Kinane	M. Stoute	16
1998	King of Kings	7–2	Mrs J. Magnier/M. Tabor	M. Kinane	A. O'Brien	18
1999	Island Sands	10–1	Godolphin	F. Dettori	Saeed bin Suroor	16

Record time: 1 minute 35.08 seconds by Mister Baileys in 1994

THE DERBY
(1780) Epsom, 1 mile and about 4 f, for three-year-olds

The first winner was Sir Charles Bunbury's Diomed in 1780. The owners with the record number of winners are Lord Egremont, who won in 1782, 1804, 1805, 1807, 1826 (also won five Oaks); and the late Aga Khan, who won in 1930, 1935, 1936, 1948, 1952. Other winning owners are: Duke of Grafton (1802, 1809, 1810, 1815); Mr J. Bowes (1835, 1843, 1852, 1853); Sir J. Hawley (1851, 1858, 1859, 1868); the 1st Duke of Westminster (1880, 1882, 1886, 1899); and Sir Victor Sassoon (1953, 1957, 1958, 1960). Record times are: 2 min. 32.31 sec. by Lammtarra in 1995; 2 min. 33.80 sec. by Mahmoud in 1936; 2 min. 33.84 sec. by Kahyasi in 1988; 2 min. 33.88 by High-Rise in 1998; 2 min. 33.9 sec. by Reference Point in 1987.
The Derby was run at Newmarket in 1915–18 and 1940–5.

Year	Winner	Betting	Owner	Jockey	Trainer	No. of Runners
1996	Shaamit	12–1	Khalifa Dasmal	M. Hills	W. Haggas	20
1997	Benny The Dip	11–1	L. Knight	W. Ryan	J. Gosden	13
1998	High Rise	20–1	Sheikh Mohammed Obaidh Al Maktoum	O. Peslier	L. Cumani	15
1999	Oath	13–2	Prince Ahmed Salman	K. Fallon	H. Cecil	16

THE OAKS
(1779) Epsom, 1 mile and about 4 f, for three-year-old fillies

Year	Winner	Betting	Owner	Jockey	Trainer	No. of Runners
1996	Lady Carla	100–30	Wafic Said	P. Eddery	H. Cecil	11
1997	Reams of Verse	5–6	Prince K. Abdulla	K. Fallon	H. Cecil	12
1998	Shahtoush	12–1	Mrs D. Nagle/Mrs J. Magnier	M. Kinane	A. O'Brien	8
1999	Ramruma	3–1	Prince Fahd Salman	K. Fallon	H. Cecil	10

Record time: 2 minutes 34.19 seconds by Intrepidity in 1993

ST LEGER
(1776) Doncaster, 1 mile and about 6 f, for three-year-olds

Year	Winner	Betting	Owner	Jockey	Trainer	No. of Runners
1996	Shantou	8–1	Sheikh Mohammed	F. Dettori	J. Gosden	11
1997	Silver Patriarch	5–4	P. Winfield	P. Eddery	J. Dunlop	10
1998	Nedawi	5–2	Godolphin	J. Reid	Saeed bin Suroor	9
1999	Mutafaweq	11–2	Godolphin	R. Hills	Saeed bin Suroor	9

Record time: 3 minutes 1.60 seconds by Coronach in 1926 and Windsor Lad in 1934

KING GEORGE VI AND QUEEN ELIZABETH DIAMOND
STAKES
(1952) Ascot, 1 mile and about 4 f

1996	Pentire (4y), (9st 7lb), M. Hills
1997	Swain (5y), (9st 7lb), J. Reid
1998	Swain (6y), (9st 7lb), F. Dettori
1999	Daylami (5y), (9st 7lb), F. Dettori

GOODWOOD CUP
(1812) Goodwood, about 2 miles

1996	Grey Shot (4y), (9st), P. Eddery
1997	Double Trigger (6y), (9st), M. Roberts
1998	Double Trigger (7y), (9st 5lb), D. Holland
1999	Kayf Tara (5y), (9st 7lb), F. Dettori

*National Hunt
†Run on 6 January 1996 because of bad weather

STATISTICS

WINNING FLAT OWNERS 1998

Godolphin	£2,214,651
Hamdan Al-Maktoum	1,429,322
K. Abdulla	984,161
Sheikh Mohammed	800,274
Sheikh Mohammed Obaid Al-Maktoum	772,188
Maktoum Al-Maktoum	705,670
M. Tabor/Mrs J. Magnier	479,096
The Thoroughbred Corporation	454,221
HRH Prince Fahd Salman	431,607
J. C. Smith	428,987

WINNING FLAT TRAINERS 1998

Saeed bin Suroor	£2,214,651
H. R. A. Cecil	1,677,939
J. L. Dunlop	1,451,032
L. M. Cumani	1,402,201
M. Johnston	1,275,121
Sir Michael Stoute	1,274,558
B. W. Hills	1,126,539
J. H. M. Gosden	962,188
D. R. Loder	832,254
J. Berry	816,452

WINNING FLAT SIRES 1998

	Races won	Stakes
Nashwan by Blushing Groom	30	£910,595
Alzao by Lyphard	45	864,463
Sadler's Wells by Northern Dancer	34	838,177
Green Desert by Danzig	47	830,467
High Estate by Shirley Heights	14	811,039
Rainbow Quest by Blushing Groom	32	729,746
Generous by Caerleon	33	649,625
Night Shift by Northern Dancer	61	584,228
Warning by Known Fact	58	546,056
Darshaan by Shirley Heights	32	543,326

WINNING FLAT JOCKEYS 1998

	1st	2nd	3rd	Unpl.	Total mts
K. Fallon	204	146	136	487	974
F. Dettori	132	92	59	283	566
D. Holland	128	103	81	378	690
T. Quinn	108	99	87	518	812
J. Fortune	108	96	83	479	766
P. Eddery	104	98	77	454	733
J. Reid	101	84	97	492	774
K. Darley	94	85	92	463	734
A. Culhane	86	78	64	549	777
R. Hills	83	73	48	283	487

WINNING NATIONAL HUNT TRAINERS 1998–9

M. C. Pipe	£1,188,929
P. F. Nicholls	1,151,597
D. Nicholson	835,574
Miss V. Williams	583,896
N. J. Henderson	572,781
P. J. Hobbs	570,047
Mrs M. Reveley	507,528
N. A. Twiston-Davies	486,652
Mrs J. Pitman	312,592
O. Sherwood	298,711

WINNING NATIONAL HUNT JOCKEYS 1998–9

	1st	2nd	3rd	Unpl.	Total mts
A. P. McCoy	186	115	85	382	768
R. Johnson	133	132	128	403	796
M. A. Fitzgerald	121	68	78	308	575
N. Williamson	117	78	70	288	553
R. Dunwoody	108	80	63	240	491
J. Tizzard	91	62	53	211	417
C. Llewellyn	78	82	78	370	608
A. Maguire	73	59	66	305	503
T. J. Murphy	73	49	42	291	455
A. Dobbin	62	58	59	308	487

The above statistics have been provided by *Timeform*, publishers of
the *Racehorses* and *Chasers and Hurdlers* annuals

ICE HOCKEY

World Championship 1999: Czech Republic
Stanley Cup final 1999: Dallas beat Buffalo 4–2
Super League Championship play-off final 1999: Cardiff Devils
  beat Nottingham Panthers 2–1
Super League Championship 1999: Manchester Storm
Benson and Hedges Cup final 1998: Nottingham Panthers
  beat Ayr Scottish Eagles 2–1

ICE SKATING

BRITISH CHAMPIONSHIPS 1998
Milton Keynes, November

Men: Clive Shorten (Chelmsford)
Women: Stephanie Main (Murrayfield)
Pairs: Marsha Poluliaschenko and Andrew Seabrook
  (Swindon)
Ice Dance: Charlotte Clements and Gary Shortland
  (Slough)

EUROPEAN CHAMPIONSHIPS 1999
Prague, January

Men: Alexei Yagudin (Russia)
Women: Maria Butyrskaya (Russia)
Pairs: Maria Petrova and Alexei Tikhonov (Russia)
Ice Dance: Anjelika Krylova and Oleg Ovsyannikov
  (Russia)

WORLD CHAMPIONSHIPS 1999
Helsinki, March

Men: Alexei Yagudin (Russia)
Women: Maria Butyrskaya (Russia)
Pairs: Elena Berezhnaya and Anton Sikharulidze (Russia)
Ice Dance: Anjelika Krylova and Oleg Ovsyannikov
  (Russia)

JUDO

BRITISH NATIONAL CHAMPIONSHIPS 1998
Cardiff, December

MEN
Heavyweight (over 100 kg): Richard Blanes
Light-heavyweight (100 kg): Keith Davis
Middleweight (90 kg): Ryan Birch
Welter (81 kg): Graeme Randall
Lightweight (73 kg): Eric Bonti
Junior lightweight (66 kg): David Sommerville
Bantamweight (60 kg): John Buchanan

WOMEN
Heavyweight (over 78 kg): Simone Callender
Light-heavyweight (78 kg): Chloe Cowan
Middleweight (70 kg): Kate Howey
Welter (63 kg): Gemma Hutchins
Lightweight (57 kg): Nicola Fairbrother
Junior lightweight (52 kg): Georgina Singleton
Bantamweight (48 kg): Joyce Heron

LAWN TENNIS

MAJOR CHAMPIONSHIPS 1999
AUSTRALIAN OPEN CHAMPIONSHIPS
Melbourne, 18–31 January
Men's Singles: Yevgeny Kafelnikov (Russia) beat Thomas
   Enqvist (Sweden) 4–6, 6–0, 6–3, 7–6
Women's Singles: Martina Hingis (Switzerland) beat Amélie
   Mauresmo (France) 6–2, 6–3
Men's Doubles: Jonas Bjorkman (Sweden) and Patrick
   Rafter (Australia) beat Mahesh Bhupathi and Leander
   Paes (India) 6–3, 4–6, 6–4, 6–7, 6–4
Women's Doubles: Martina Hingis (Switzerland) and Anna
   Kournikova (Russia) beat Lindsay Davenport (USA)
   and Natasha Zvereva (Belarus) 7–5, 6–3
Mixed Doubles: Mariaan de Swardt and David Adams
   (South Africa) beat Serena Williams (USA) and Max
   Mirnyi (Belarus) 6–4, 4–6, 7–6

FRENCH OPEN CHAMPIONSHIPS
Paris, 24 May–6 June
Men's Singles: Andre Agassi (USA) beat Andrei Medvedev
   (Ukraine) 1–6, 2–6, 6–4, 6–3, 6–4
Women's Singles: Steffi Graf (Germany) beat Martina
   Hingis (Switzerland) 4–6, 7–5, 6–2
Men's Doubles: Mahesh Bhupathi and Leander Paes (India)
   beat Goran Ivanisevic (Croatia) and Jeff Tarango
   (USA) 6–2, 7–5
Women's Doubles: Venus Williams and Serena Williams
   (USA) beat Martina Hingis (Switzerland) and Anna
   Kournikova (Russia) 6–3, 6–7, 8–6
Mixed Doubles: Lisa Raymond (USA) and Leander Paes
   (India) beat Anna Kournikova (Russia) and Jonas
   Bjorkman (Sweden) 6–4, 3–6, 6–3

ALL-ENGLAND CHAMPIONSHIPS
Wimbledon, 21 June–4 July
Men's Singles: Pete Sampras (USA) beat Andre Agassi
   (USA) 6–3, 6–4, 7–5
Women's Singles: Lindsay Davenport (USA) beat Steffi Graf
   (Germany) 6–4, 7–5
Men's Doubles: Mahesh Bhupathi and Leander Paes (India)
   beat Paul Haarhuis (Holland) and Jared Palmer (USA)
   6–7, 6–3, 6–4, 7–6

Women's Doubles: Lindsay Davenport and Corina Morariu
   (USA) beat Mariaan de Swardt (South Africa) and
   Elena Tatarkova (Ukraine) 6–4, 6–4
Mixed Doubles: Lisa Raymond (USA) and Leander Paes
   (India) beat Anna Kournikova (Russia) and Jonas
   Bjorkman (Sweden) 6–4, 3–6, 6–3

US OPEN CHAMPIONSHIPS
New York, 30 August–12 September
Men's Singles: Andre Agassi (USA) beat Todd Martin
   (USA) 6–4, 6–7, 6–7, 6–3, 6–2
Women's Singles: Serena Williams (USA) beat Martina
   Hingis (Switzerland) 6–3, 7–6
Men's Doubles: Sebastien Lareau (Canada) and Alex
   O'Brien (USA) beat Mahesh Bhupathi and Leander
   Paes (India) 7-6, 6-4
Women's Doubles: Serena Williams and Venus Williams
   (USA) beat Sandrine Testud (France) and Chanda
   Rubin (USA) 6–4, 6–1, 6–4
Mixed Doubles: Ai Sugiyama (Japan) and Mahesh Bhupathi
   (India) beat Kimberly Po and Donald Johnson (USA)
   6–4, 6–4
ATP Tour World Championship final 1998: Alex Corretja
   (Spain) beat Carlos Moyà (Spain) 3–6, 3–6, 7–5, 6–3,
   7–5
Grand Slam Cup 1998:
   Men: Marcelo Rios (Chile) beat Andre Agassi (USA) 6–
   4, 2–6, 7–6, 5–7, 6–3
   Women (inaugural): Venus Williams (USA) beat Patty
   Schnyder (Switzerland) 6–2, 3–6, 6–2

TEAM CHAMPIONSHIPS
Davis Cup final 1998: Sweden beat Italy 4–1
Fed Cup final 1999: USA beat Russia 4–1
LTA County Cup 1999:
   Men: Hampshire and Isle of Wight
   Women: Leicestershire

NATIONAL CHAMPIONSHIPS 1998
Telford, November
Men's Singles: Danny Sapsford (Surrey) beat Nick Weal
   (Hants and Isle of Wight) 6–4, 2–6, 7–5
Women's Singles: Julie Pullin (Sussex) beat Sam Smith
   (Essex) 6–7, 6–2, 7–6
Men's Doubles: Andrew Richardson (Lincs) and Miles
   Maclagan (W. of Scotland) beat Tom Spinks (Norfolk)
   and Danny Sapsford (Surrey) 6–4, 6–2
Women's Doubles: Julie Pullin (Sussex) and Lorna
   Woodroffe (Surrey) beat Karen Cross (Devon) and Jo
   Ward (Middlesex) 6–4, 4–6, 6–2

MOTOR CYCLING

500 CC GRAND PRIX 1998
Argentinian (Buenos Aires): Michael Doohan (Australia),
   Honda
Australian (Phillip Island): Michael Doohan (Australia),
   Honda
Riders' Championship 1998: 1. Michael Doohan (Australia),
   Honda, 260 points; 2. Max Biaggi (Italy), Honda, 208
   points; 3. Alex Criville (Spain), Honda, 198 points

500 CC GRAND PRIX 1999
Malaysian (Kuala Lumpur): Kenny Roberts, jun. (USA),
   Suzuki
Japanese (Motegi): Kenny Roberts, jun. (USA), Suzuki
Spanish (Jerez): Alex Criville (Spain), Honda
French (Le Castelleton): Alex Criville (Spain), Honda

Italian (Mugello): Alex Criville (Spain), Honda
Catalunya (Barcelona): Alex Criville (Spain), Honda
Dutch (Assen): Tadayuki Okada (Japan), Honda
British (Donington Park): Alex Criville (Spain), Honda
German (Sachsenring): Kenny Roberts, jun. (USA), Suzuki
Czech (Brno): Tadayuki Okada (Japan), Honda
San Marino (Imola): Alex Criville (Spain), Honda
Valencia: Regis Laconi (France), Yamaha

Senior Manx Grand Prix 1999: Colin Breeze (Kawasaki)
Senior TT 1999, Isle of Man: David Jefferies (Yamaha)
Junior TT 1999, Isle of Man: Jim Moodie (Honda)

World Superbike Champion 1999: Carl Fogarty (GB), Ducati
British Superbike Champion 1999: Troy Bayliss (Ducati)
500cc World Motocross Champion 1999: Andrea Bartolini (Italy), Yamaha
British Open Motocross Champion 1998: Joakim Karlsson (Sweden), Honda

MOTOR RACING

FORMULA ONE GRAND PRIX 1998

Japanese (Suzuka): Mika Hakkinen (Finland), McLaren-Mercedes
Drivers' World Championship 1998: 1. Mika Hakkinen (Finland), McLaren-Mercedes, 100 points; 2. Michael Schumacher (Germany), Ferrari, 86 points; 3. David Coulthard (GB), McLaren-Mercedes, 56 points
Constructors' World Championship 1998: 1. McLaren-Mercedes, 156 points; 2. Ferrari, 133 points; 3. Williams-Mecachrome, 38 points

FORMULA ONE GRAND PRIX 1999

Australian (Melbourne): Eddie Irvine (GB), Ferrari
Brazilian (São Paulo): Mika Hakkinen (Finland), McLaren-Mercedes
San Marino (Imola): Michael Schumacher (Germany), Ferrari
Monaco (Monte Carlo): Michael Schumacher (Germany), Ferrari
Spanish (Barcelona): Mika Hakkinen (Finland), McLaren-Mercedes
Canadian (Montreal): Mika Hakkinen (Finland), McLaren-Mercedes
French (Magny-Cours): Heinz-Harald Frentzen (Germany), Jordan
British (Silverstone): David Coulthard (GB), McLaren-Mercedes
Austrian (Spielberg): Eddie Irvine (GB), Ferrari
German (Hockenheim): Eddie Irvine (GB), Ferrari
Hungarian (Budapest): Mika Hakkinen (Finland), McLaren-Mercedes
Belgian (Spa-Francorchamps): David Coulthard (GB), McLaren-Mercedes
Luxembourg: Mika Hakkinen (Finland), McLaren-Mercedes
Italian (Monza): Heinz-Harald Frentzen (Germany), Jordan
European (Nurburgring): Johnny Herbert (GB), Stewart
Indianapolis 500 1999: Kenny Brack (Sweden), Dallara Aurora
Le Mans 24-hour Race 1999: Pierluigi Martini (Italy), Joachim Winkelhock (Germany) and Yannick Dalmas (France), BMW

MOTOR RALLYING

1998

San Remo Rally: Tommi Makinen (Finland), Mitsubishi Lancer
Rally Australia: Tommi Makinen (Finland), Mitsubishi Lancer
RAC Rally: Richard Burns (GB), Mitsubishi Lancer
Drivers' World Championship 1998: Tommi Makinen (Finland), Mitsubishi Lancer, 58 points
Manufacturers' World Championship 1998: Mitsubishi, 91 points

1999

Dakar Rally: Jean-Louis Schlesser (France), Schlesser
Monte Carlo Rally: Tommi Makinen (Finland), Mitsubishi Lancer
Swedish Rally: Tommi Makinen (Finland), Mitsubishi Lancer
Safari Rally: Colin McRae (GB), Ford Focus
Rally of Portugal: Colin McRae (GB), Ford Focus
Catalunya Rally: Philippe Bugalski (France), Citroën Xsara
Corsica Rally: Philippe Bugalski (France), Citroën Xsara
Argentine Rally: Juha Kankunnen (Finland), Subaru
Acropolis Rally: Richard Burns (GB), Subaru
New Zealand Rally: Tommi Makinen (Finland), Mitsubishi Lancer
1,000 Lakes Rally (Jyvaskyla, Finland): Juha Kankunnen (Finland), Subaru
Chinese Rally (Huairou): Didier Auriol (France), Toyota
Rally of Wales 1999: David Higgins (Isle of Man), Subaru Impreza
Scottish Rally 1999: Tapio Laukkanen (Finland), Renault Megane
Ulster Rally 1999: Neil Wearden (England), Vauxhall Astra
British Champion 1999: Tapio Laukkanen (Finland), Renault Megane
Manx International Rally 1999: Martin Rowe (Isle of Man), Renault Megane

NETBALL

TESTS AND INTERNATIONALS

1999

31 Jan	Cardiff	Wales 26, England 55
22 Feb	Manchester	England 57, South Africa 54
25 May	Melbourne	Australia 69, England 31
28 May	Sydney	Australia 56, England 36
31 May	Adelaide	Australia 66, England 34
6 July	Newcastle upon Tyne	England 56, Jamaica 70
10 July	Wembley	England 49, Jamaica 57
14 July	Birmingham	England 48, Jamaica 53

Inter-County Championship final 1999: Bedfordshire beat Derbyshire 17–15
National Clubs Championship 1999: Lawn (Wilts)
English Counties League Championship 1999: Essex Metropolitan
National Clubs League Championship 1999: Linden

POLO

Prince of Wales's Trophy final 1999: Ellerston beat Pommery 14–9
Queen's Cup final 1999: Ellerston beat Jerudong Park 12–8
Warwickshire Cup final 1999: Pommery beat Woodchester 9–7
Gold Cup (British Open) final 1999: Pommery beat Ellerston 12–8
Coronation Cup 1999: England beat Australasia 11–10
Prince Philip Trophy 1999: Pommery beat Pasha 10–8
Arena Gold Cup 1999: Ashfronts beat Metropolitan 19–13
Arena European Nations 1999: Sweden beat Scotland 13–11
Varsity Match 1999: Cambridge beat Oxford 4–2

RACKETS

World Singles Challenge 1999: Neil Smith (GB) beat James Male (GB) 4–2 (Male retired through injury)
Professional Singles Championship final 1999: Toby Sawrey-Cookson beat Mark Hubbard 3–0
British Open Singles Championship final 1999: Neil Smith (GB) beat Willie Boone (GB) 4–3
British Open Doubles Championship final 1999: James Male and Mark Hue Williams (GB) beat Jonathan Larken and Toby Sawrey-Cookson (GB) 4–0
Amateur Singles Championship final 1998: James Male beat Willie Boone 3–0
Amateur Doubles Championship final 1999: Guy Barker and Alister Robinson beat Willie Boone and Mark Hue Williams 4–2
National League 1999: Old Wykehamists
Noel Bruce Cup final 1998 (public schools' old boys' doubles championship): Eton I (Willie Boone and Mark Hue Williams) beat Wellington I (Toby Sawrey-Cookson and Tim Cockroft) 4–1
Varsity Match 1999: Oxford beat Cambridge 3–0

REAL TENNIS

Professional Singles Championship final 1999: Steve Virgona (Australia) beat Mike Gooding (GB) 3–0
Professional Doubles Championship final 1999: Chris Bray and Mike Gooding (GB) beat Ruaraidh Gunn (GB) and Steve Virgona (Australia) 3–1
British Open Singles Championship final 1998: Julian Snow (GB) beat Steve Virgona (Australia) 3–2
British Open Doubles Championship final 1998: Julian Snow and James Male (GB) beat Ruaraidh Gunn (GB) and Steve Virgona (Australia) 3–0
Amateur Singles Championship final 1999: Julian Snow beat James Willcocks 3–0
Amateur Doubles Championship final 1999: Julian Snow and James Acheson-Gray beat Howard Angus and Nigel O'Hagan 3–0
Henry Leaf Cup final 1999 (public schools' old boys' doubles championship): Canford beat Cranleigh 2–0
Women's World Singles Championship final 1999: Penny Lumley (GB) beat Sue Haswell (GB) 2–1
Women's World Doubles Championship final 1999: Penny Lumley and Sue Haswell (GB) beat Sally Jones and Alex Garside (GB) 2–1
Women's British Open Singles Championship final 1999: Penny Lumley (GB) beat Kate Leeming (Australia) 2–0
Women's British Open Doubles Championship final 1999: Penny Lumley and Alex Garside (GB) beat Sally Jones (GB) and Kate Leeming (Australia) 2–0

ROAD WALKING

RWA Men's National 20 km Walk
Leamington, 21 March 1999
Individual: Chris Maddocks (Plymouth), 1 hr. 26 min. 22 sec.
Team: Road Hoggs, 38 points

RWA Women's National 20 km Walk
Leamington, 21 March 1999
Individual: Gillian O'Sullivan (Ireland), 1 hr. 36 min. 44 sec.
Team: Sheffield, 21 points

World Walking Cup
Mezidon, France, 1–2 May 1999
Men's 20 km: Bernardo Segura (Mexico), 1 hr. 20 min. 20 sec.
Team: Russia, 19 points
Men's 50 km: Sergei Korepanov (Kazakhstan), 3 hr. 39 min. 22 sec.
Team: Russia, 14 points
Women's 20 km: Hongyu Lu (China), 1 hr. 27 min. 32 sec.
Team: China, 13 points

RWA Men's National 35 km Walk
Stockport, 5 June 1999
Individual: Darrell Stone (Steyning), 2 hr. 49 min. 45 sec.
Team: Steyning, 10 points

RWA Women's National 5 km Walk
Stockport, 5 June 1999
Individual: Catherine Charnock (Barrow), 23 min. 09 sec.
Team: Sheffield, 13 points

RWA Men's National 50 km Walk
Leamington Spa, 11 September 1999
Individual: Chris Cheeseman (Surrey), 4 hr. 31 min. 08 sec.
Team: Coventry, 14 points

RWA Women's National 10 km Walk
Leicester, 5 September 1999
Individual: Catherine Charnock (Dudley), 47 min. 51 sec.
Team: Dudley and Stourbridge

ROWING

WORLD CHAMPIONSHIPS 1999
St Catherine's, Canada, 22–29 August

Men
Coxed pairs: USA
Coxless pairs: Australia
Coxed fours: USA
Coxless fours: Great Britain
Single sculls: Rob Waddell (New Zealand)
Double sculls: Slovenia
Quad sculls: Germany
Eights: USA

Women
Coxless pairs: Canada
Coxless fours: Belarus
Single sculls: E. Karsten (Belarus)
Double sculls: Germany
Quad sculls: Germany
Eights: Romania

NATIONAL CHAMPIONSHIPS 1999
Nottingham, July

MEN
Coxed pairs: Thames Tradesmen
Coxless pairs: Thames Tradesmen
Coxed fours: Notts County
Coxless fours: Oxford Brookes
Single sculls: Lazlo Szogi (Queen's Tower)
Double sculls: Auriol Kensington/Queen's Tower
Quad sculls: Thames
Eights: Castle Semple

WOMEN
Coxless pairs: Queen's Tower
Coxed fours: Kingston/Gloucester/Headington/LEH
Coxless fours: Kingston/Gloucester/Headington/LEH
Single sculls: Alison Watt (Clydesdale)
Double sculls: Thames
Quad sculls: Thames Tradesmen
Eights: Marlow/Molesey/NCR/Star/Tideway Scullers

THE 145th UNIVERSITY BOAT RACE
Putney–Mortlake, 4 miles 1 f, 180 yd, 3 April 1999

Cambridge beat Oxford by 3½ lengths; 16 min. 41 sec.
Cambridge have won 76 times, Oxford 68 and there has been one dead heat. The record time is 16 min. 19 sec., rowed by Cambridge in 1998

Women's Boat Race 1999 (Henley): Cambridge beat Oxford by 1 length; 6 min. 01 sec. (a record time)

HENLEY ROYAL REGATTA 1999
Grand Challenge Cup: Ruder Club Hansa von 1898 e.V. Dortmund and Berliner Ruder Club (Germany) beat Leander and Queen's Tower by ½ length
Ladies' Challenge Plate: Cambridge University and Queen's Tower beat University of California, Berkeley (USA) by 2¼ lengths
Thames Challenge Cup: Molesey A beat Crabtree by ¾ length
Temple Challenge Cup: Cambridge University beat Imperial College, London A by 3½ lengths
Princess Elizabeth Challenge Cup: St Edward's beat St Peter's College (Australia) by 2½ lengths
Stewards' Challenge Cup: Leander and Queen's Tower beat Danmarks Rocenter (Denmark) by 1 length
Prince Philip Challenge Cup: Nottinghamshire County beat Leander by ½ length
Queen Mother Challenge Cup: Allemannia Hamburg (Germany) beat Augusta A (USA) by 1¼ lengths
Visitors' Challenge Cup: Oxford Brookes University A beat Imperial College, London by 4½ lengths
Wyfold Challenge Cup: Holme Pierrepont A beat Llandaff by ½ length
Britannia Challenge Cup: Molesey beat Isis by 1 length
Fawley Challenge Cup: Leander and Tiffin beat Burway and Walton by 2¼ lengths
Silver Goblets and Nickalls' Challenge Cup: S. D. Williams and S. J. Dennis (GB) beat D. J. Weightman and R. G. Scott (Australia) by 3¼ lengths
Double Sculls Challenge Cup: I. M. McGowan and N. V. Peterson (USA) beat C. P. Groom and R. S. Tucker (USA) by 3 lengths
Diamond Challenge Sculls: Marcel Hacker (Germany) beat Jamie Koven (USA) by 4¾ lengths
Princess Royal Challenge Cup: Katrin Rutschow (Germany) rowed over Maria Brandin (Sweden)
Women's Eights: Marlow and Thames beat Thames and Marlow by 4½ lengths

OTHER ROWING EVENTS
Cambridge Lents 1999: Men, Caius; *Women,* Trinity Hall
Oxford Torpids 1999: Men, Pembroke; *Women,* Osler-Green
Oxford Summer Eights 1999: Men, Oriel; *Women,* Osler-Green
Cambridge Mays 1999: Men, Caius; *Women,* Emmanuel
Head of the River 1999: Men, Queen's Tower I; *Women,* Marlow A
Scullers Head of the River 1999: Giles Monnickendam (Notts County)
Doggett's Coat and Badge 1999: Thomas Woods (London)
Wingfield Sculls 1999: Greg Searle (Molesey)
London Cup 1999: no race due to bad weather
Thames World Sculling Challenge 1999: Men, Iztok Copp (Slovenia); *Women,* Miriam Batten-Luke (GB)

RUGBY FIVES
National Singles Championship final 1998: Ian Fuller beat Neil Roberts 15–8, 15–4
National Doubles Championship final 1999: Wayne Enstone and Neil Roberts beat Ian Fuller and David Hebden 2–15, 15–12, 15–13
National Club Championship final 1999: Alleyn Old Boys beat RFA Club 91–62
National Schools' Singles Championship final 1999: Giles Corner (St Paul's) beat James Toop (St Olave's) 11–3, 11–3
National Schools' Doubles Championship final 1999: St Paul's I beat St Paul's II 11–2, 11–5
Varsity Match 1999: Oxford beat Cambridge 284–159

RUGBY LEAGUE

TESTS
1998

31 Oct	Huddersfield	Great Britain 16, New Zealand 22
7 Nov	Bolton	Great Britain 16, New Zealand 36
14 Nov	Watford	Great Britain 23, New Zealand 23

COMPETITIONS
Super League Grand Final 1998 (Old Trafford, 24 October): Wigan beat Leeds 10–4
Challenge Cup final 1999 (Wembley, 1 May): Leeds Rhinos beat London Broncos 52–16
Division 1 Grand final 1999 (Headingly, 26 September): Hunslet beat Dewsbury 12–11
Varsity Match 1999: Cambridge beat Oxford 14–10

AMATEUR RUGBY LEAGUE 1998–9
County Championship: Lancashire
National Cup Open Age Competition: Skirlaugh
National Conference League Premier Division Champions: West Hull

RUGBY UNION

FIVE NATIONS' CHAMPIONSHIP 1999

6 Feb	Murrayfield	Scotland 33, Wales 20
	Dublin	Ireland 9, France 10
20 Feb	Twickenham	England 24, Scotland 21
	Wembley	Wales 23, Ireland 29
6 March	Dublin	Ireland 15, England 27
	Paris	France 33, Wales 34
20 March	Twickenham	England 21, France 10
	Murrayfield	Scotland 30, Ireland 13
10 April	Paris	France 22, Scotland 36
11 April	Wembley	England 31, Wales 32

	P	W	D	L	Points F	A	Total
Scotland	4	3	0	1	120	79	6
England	4	3	0	1	103	78	6
Wales	4	2	0	2	109	126	4
Ireland	4	1	0	3	66	90	2
France	4	1	0	3	75	100	2

WORLD CUP QUALIFYING MATCHES

1998
14 Nov	Huddersfield	England 110, Holland 0
	Lansdowne Road	Ireland 70, Georgia 0
21 Nov	Lansdowne Road	Ireland 53, Romania 35
22 Nov	Huddersfield	England 23, Italy 15
28 Nov	Murrayfield	Scotland 85, Portugal 11
5 Dec	Murrayfield	Scotland 85, Spain 3

OTHER INTERNATIONAL MATCHES

1998
14 Nov	Wembley	Wales 20, South Africa 28
21 Nov	Llanelli	Wales 43, Argentina 30
	Murrayfield	Scotland 10, South Africa 35
28 Nov	Twickenham	England 11, Australia 12
	Lansdowne Road	Ireland 13, South Africa 27
5 Dec	Twickenham	England 13, South Africa 7

1999
6 March	Murrayfield	Scotland 30, Italy 12
20 March	Treviso	Italy 21, Wales 60
10 April	Lansdowne Road	Ireland 39, Italy 30
5 June	Buenos Aires	Argentina 26, Wales 36
12 June	Buenos Aires	Argentina 16, Wales 23
	Brisbane	Australia 46, Ireland 10
19 June	Perth	Australia 32, Ireland 26
26 June	Sydney	Australia 22, England 15
	Cardiff	Wales 29, South Africa 19
21 Aug	Twickenham	England 106, USA 8
	Murrayfield	Scotland 22, Argentina 31
	Cardiff	Wales 33, Canada 19
28 Aug	Twickenham	England 36, Canada 11
	Cardiff	Wales 34, France 23
	Hampden Park	Scotland 60, Romania 19
	Lansdowne Road	Ireland 32, Argentina 24

European Club Cup final 1999 (Dublin, 30 January): Ulster beat Colomiers 21–6

Women's (Inaugural) Five Nations' Championship 1999: England

DOMESTIC COMPETITIONS

Premiership: Division 1, Leicester, 44 points; *Division 2,* Bristol, 44 points

National League: Division 1, Henley, 45 points; *Division 2 (north),* Preston Grasshoppers, 46 points; *Division 2 (south),* Bracknell, 47 points

County Championship final 1999: Cornwall beat Gloucestershire 24–15

Tetley's Bitter Cup final 1999: Wasps beat Newcastle Falcons 29–19

Scottish Premiership: Division 1, Heriot's F. P., 69 points; *Division 2,* Gala, 70 points; *Division 3,* Peebles, 62 points

Scottish Cup final 1999: Gala beat Kelso 8–3

Welsh National League: Premier Division, Group A, Llanelli, 64 points; *Premier Division, Group B,* Caerphilly, 34 points

Welsh Challenge (Swalec) Cup final 1999: Swansea beat Llanelli 37–10

Irish League: Division 1, Cork Constitution; *Division 2,* Dungannon; *Division 3,* University College Dublin; *Division 4,* Middleton

Ulster Cup 1999: Enstonians

Services Championship 1999: Army beat Royal Air Force 43–8; Royal Navy beat Royal Air Force 28–7; Army beat Royal Navy 24–13

Varsity Match 1998: Cambridge beat Oxford 16–12

Middlesex Sevens final 1999: Penguins beat Saracens 40–35

SHOOTING

130th NATIONAL RIFLE ASSOCIATION IMPERIAL MEETING
Bisley, July 1999

Queen's Prize: Danny Coleman, 294.37 v-bulls
Grand Aggregate: Paul Kent, 693.76 v-bulls
Prince of Wales Prize: Tom Rylands, 75.13 v-bulls
St George's Vase: Cmdt A. S. H. McCullough, 150.24 v-bulls
Allcomers Aggregate: Bill Richards, 371.50 v-bulls
National Trophy: England, 2,082.293 v-bulls
Kolapore Cup: Great Britain, 1,193.154 v-bulls
Chancellor's Trophy: Cambridge University, 1,143.107 v-bulls
Musketeers Cup: Edinburgh University A, 583.61 v-bulls
Vizianagram Trophy: House of Commons, 498.29 v-bulls
County Long-Range Championship: Cheshire, 572.55 v-bulls
Mackinnon Challenge Cup: England, 1,153.99 v-bulls
The Ashburton: Epsom, 491 points
The Elcho: England, 1,664.138 v-bulls
The Albert: Alexander Henderson, 216.25 v-bulls
Hopton Challenge Cup: Stuart Collings, 960.97 v-bulls

CLAY PIGEON SHOOTING 1999

World Sporting Championship: George Digweed (England), 194
British Open Sporting Championship: Stuart Clarke (England), 83
International Down-the-Line Cup: England, 5,807
World Down-the-Line Championship: John Winn (England), 892
British Open Down-the-Line Championship: John Bellamy (England), 298
British Open Skeet Championship: Neil Faulkner (England), 100

SNOOKER

1998
Grand Prix: Stephen Lee (England) beat Marco Fu (Hong Kong) 9–2
Regal Masters: Ronnie O'Sullivan (England) beat John Higgins (Scotland) 9–7
Benson and Hedges Championship: David Gray (England) beat Dave Harold (England) 9–6
UK Championship: John Higgins (Scotland) beat Matthew Stevens (Wales) 10–6
Malta Grand Prix: Stephen Hendry (Scotland) beat Ken Doherty (Rep. of Ireland) 7–6
German Masters: John Parrott (England) beat Mark Williams (Wales) 6–4
Irish Open: Mark Williams (Wales) beat Alan McManus (Scotland) 9–4

1999
Nations Cup: Wales beat Scotland 6–4
Welsh Open: Mark Williams (Wales) beat Stephen Hendry (Scotland) 9–8
Benson and Hedges Masters: John Higgins (Scotland) beat Ken Doherty (Rep. of Ireland) 10–8

Scottish Open: Stephen Hendry (Scotland) beat Graeme Dott (Scotland) 9–1
Thailand Masters: Mark Williams (Wales) beat Alan McManus (Scotland) 9–7
China International: John Higgins (Scotland) beat Billy Snaddon (Scotland) 9–3
Irish Masters: Stephen Hendry (Scotland) beat Stephen Lee (England) 9–8
British Open: Fergal O'Brien (Ireland) beat Anthony Hamilton (England) 9–7
World Championship: Stephen Hendry (Scotland) beat Mark Williams (Wales) 18–11
Champions' Cup: Stephen Hendry (Scotland) beat Mark Williams (Wales) 7–5

Women's UK Championship 1998: Tessa Davidson (England) beat Kelly Fisher (England) 4–1
Women's Welsh Open 1999: Lisa Quick (Weston-super-Mare) beat Tessa Davidson (Banbury) 4–1
Women's National Championship 1999: Kelly Fisher (Pontefract) beat Julie Gillespie (Stirling) 4–1
Women's World Championship 1999: Kelly Fisher (England) beat Karen Corr (N. Ireland) 4–2
Women's British Open 1999: Lynette Horsburgh (England) beat Tessa Davidson (England) 4–3

SPEEDWAY

Elite League Champions 1998: Ipswich
Elite League Riders' Championship 1998: Tony Rickardsson (Sweden)

GRAND PRIX 1999

Czech (Prague): Tomasz Gollob (Poland)
Swedish (Linkoping): Mark Loram (England)
Polish (Wroclaw): Tomasz Gollob (Poland)
British (Coventry): Tony Rickardsson (Sweden)
Polish (Bydgoszcz): Hans Nielsen (Denmark)
Danish (Vojens): Tony Rickardsson (Sweden)
World Champion 1999: Tony Rickardsson (Sweden)
World Championship, Overseas final 1999: Mark Loram (England)
World Championship, British final 1999: Mark Loram (Poole)
World Championship, Intercontinental final 1999: Todd Wiltshire

SQUASH RACKETS

MEN

World Open Championship final 1998: Jonathon Power (Canada) beat Peter Nicol (GB) 3–1
European Team Championship final 1999: England beat Scotland 3–1
European Club Championship 1999: Colets (GB)
National Championship final 1999: Paul Johnston (Kent) beat Simon Parke (Yorks) 3–2

WOMEN

World Open Championship final 1998: Sarah Fitz-Gerald (Australia) beat Michelle Martin (Australia) 3–2
World Team Championship final 1998: Australia beat England 3–0
European Team Championship final 1999: England beat Germany 3–0
National Championship final 1999: Cassie Jackman (Norfolk) beat Sue Wright (Kent) 3–2

SWIMMING

EUROPEAN CHAMPIONSHIPS 1999
Istanbul, July

MEN

50 metres freestyle: Pieter van den Hoogenband (The Netherlands)
100 metres freestyle: Pieter van den Hoogenband (The Netherlands)
200 metres freestyle: Pieter van den Hoogenband (The Netherlands)
400 metres freestyle: Paul Palmer (GB)
1,500 metres freestyle: I. Snitko (Ukraine)
50 metres backstroke: S. Theloke (Germany)
100 metres backstroke: S. Theloke (Germany)
200 metres backstroke: R. Bruan (Germany)
50 metres breaststroke: M. Warnecke (Germany)
100 metres breaststroke: D. Fioravanti (Italy)
200 metres breaststroke: S. Perrot (France)
100 metres butterfly: Lars Frolander (Sweden)
200 metres butterfly: Franck Esposit (France)
200 metres medley: Marcel Wouda (The Netherlands)
400 metres medley: F. Hviid (Spain)
4 x 100 metres freestyle relay: The Netherlands
4 x 200 metres freestyle relay: Germany
4 x 100 metres medley relay: The Netherlands

WOMEN

50 metres freestyle: Inge De Bruijn (The Netherlands)
100 metres freestyle: Susan Rolph (GB)
200 metres freestyle: Camelia Potec (Romania)
400 metres freestyle: Camelia Potec (Romania)
800 metres freestyle: H. Stockbayer (Germany)
50 metres backstroke: Sandra Voelker (Germany)
100 metres backstroke: Sandra Voelker (Germany)
200 metres backstroke: Roxana Maracineanu (France)
50 metres breaststroke: Agnes Kovacs (Hungary)
100 metres breaststroke: Agnes Kovacs (Hungary)
200 metres breaststroke: Agnes Kovacs (Hungary)
100 metres butterfly: Inge De Bruijn (The Netherlands)
200 metres butterfly: Mette Jacobsen (Denmark)
200 metres medley: J. Klochkova (Ukraine)
400 metres medley: J. Klochkova (Ukraine)
4 x 100 metres freestyle relay: Germany
4 x 200 metres freestyle relay: Germany
4 x 100 metres medley relay: Sweden

NATIONAL CHAMPIONSHIPS 1999
Sheffield, July

MEN

50 metres freestyle: Mark Foster (University of Bath)
100 metres freestyle: Gavin Meadows (City of Leeds)
200 metres freestyle: Paul Palmer (University of Bath)
400 metres freestyle: Paul Palmer (University of Bath)
1,500 metres freestyle: Graeme Smith (Stockport Metro)
50 metres backstroke: Martin Harris (Tower Hamlets)
100 metres backstroke: Martin Harris (Tower Hamlets)
200 metres backstroke: Adam Ruckwood (Stockport Metro)
50 metres breaststroke: Adam Whitehead (City of Coventry)
100 metres breaststroke: Adam Whitehead (City of Coventry)
200 metres breaststroke: Adam Whitehead (City of Coventry)
50 metres butterfly: Mark Foster (University of Bath)
100 metres butterfly: James Hickman (City of Leeds)
200 metres butterfly: James Hickman (City of Leeds)
200 metres medley: M. Racher (Hatfield)
400 metres medley: M. Halika (Israel)

4× 100 metres freestyle relay: University of Bath
4× 200 metres freestyle relay: University of Bath
4× 100 metres medley relay: University of Bath

WOMEN
50 metres freestyle: Alison Sheppard (Milngavie and Bearsden)
100 metres freestyle: Susan Rolph (City of Newcastle)
200 metres freestyle: Karen Pickering (Ipswich)
400 metres freestyle: N. Baranovskaia (Belarus)
800 metres freestyle: Sarah Collings (University of Bath)
50 metres backstroke: Katy Sexton (Portsmouth Northsea)
100 metres backstroke: Katy Sexton (Portsmouth Northsea)
200 metres backstroke: Helen Don-Duncan (Aston Central)
50 metres breaststroke: Zoë Baker (City of Sheffield)
100 metres breaststroke: Linda Hindmarsh (City of Leeds)
200 metres breaststroke: Linda Hindmarsh (City of Leeds)
50 metres butterfly: Nicola Jackson (Derwenside)
100 metres butterfly: M. Loots (S. Africa)
200 metres butterfly: Margaretha Pedder (Portsmouth Northsea)
200 metres medley: Susan Rolph (City of Newcastle)
400 metres medley: M. Loots (S. Africa)
4× 100 metres freestyle relay: University of Bath
4× 200 metres freestyle relay: City of Leeds
4× 100 metres medley relay: University of Bath

TABLE TENNIS

WORLD CHAMPIONSHIPS 1999
Eindhoven, August

Men's Singles: Liu Guoliang (China) beat Ma Lin (China) 3–2
Women's Singles: Wang Nan (China) beat Zhang Yining (China) 3–2
Men's Doubles: Liu Guoliang and Kong Linghui (China) beat Wang Liqin and Yan Sen (China) 3–2
Women's Doubles: Wang Nan and Li Ju (China) beat Yang Ying and Sun Jin (China) 3–0
Mixed Doubles: Zhang Yingying and Ma Lin (China) beat Sun Jin and Feng Zhe (China) 3–1
World Cup final 1998: J. Rosskopf (Germany) beat Kim Taek Soo (S. Korea) 3–2

ENGLISH NATIONAL CHAMPIONSHIPS 1999
Bath, January

Men's Singles: Alex Perry (Devon) beat Terry Young (Berks) 3–0
Women's Singles: Nicola Deaton (Derbys) beat Andrea Holt (Lancs) 3–0
Men's Doubles: Alex Perry (Devon) and Gareth Herbert (Bucks) beat Terry Young (Berks) and Darren Blake (Surrey) 2-0
Women's Doubles: Nicola Deaton (Derbys) and Helen Lower (Staffs) beat Andrea Holt (Lancs) and Kubrat Owolabi (Middx) 2–1
Mixed Doubles: Nicola Deaton (Derbys) and Alex Perry (Devon) beat Kubrat Owolabi (Middx) and Darren Blake (Surrey) 2–0

VOLLEYBALL

MEN
World Championship final 1998: Italy beat Yugoslavia 3–0
World League 1999: Italy
National League Championship 1999: London Malory
National Cup final 1999: London Malory beat City of Liverpool 3–1

WOMEN
World Championship final 1998: Cuba beat China 3–0
Grand Prix final 1999: Russia beat Brazil 3–0
National League Championship 1999: London Malory
National Cup final 1999: Loughborough beat London Malory 3–0

YACHTING

Around Alone Round-the-World Race (set off from Charleston, South Carolina, in September 1998; arrived Charleston, South Carolina, 8 May 1999): Giovanni Soldini (Italy), in Fila, 116 days, 20 hours, 7 minutes
Admiral's Cup 1999: The Netherlands (Innovision 7, Trust Computer and Mean Machine), 124 points
Fastnet Race 1999: Loïck Peyron (France) in Fujicolor II, 40 hours, 27 minutes

Sports Records

All the world records given below have been accepted by the International Amateur Athletic Federation except those marked with an asterisk* which are awaiting homologation. Fully automatic timing to 1/100th second is mandatory up to and including 400 metres. For distances up to and including 10,000 metres, records will be accepted to 1/100th second if timed automatically, and to 1/10th if hand timing is used.

MEN'S EVENTS

TRACK EVENTS	hr.	min.	sec.
100 metres			9.79*
Maurice Greene, USA, 1999			
200 metres			19.32
Michael Johnson, USA, 1996			
400 metres			43.18*
Michael Johnson, USA, 1999			
800 metres		1	41.11
Wilson Kipketer, Denmark, 1997			
1,000 metres		2	11.96*
Noah Ngeny, Kenya, 1999			
1,500 metres		3	26.00
Hicham El Guerrouj, Morocco, 1998			
1 mile		3	43.13*
Hicham El Guerrouj, Morocco, 1999			
2,000 metres		4	44.79*
Hicham El Guerrouj, Morocco, 1999			
3,000 metres		7	20.67
Daniel Komen, Kenya, 1996			
5,000 metres		12	39.36*
Haile Gebrselassie, Ethiopia, 1998			
10,000 metres		26	22.75*
Haile Gebrselassie, Ethiopia, 1998			
20,000 metres		56	55.6
Arturo Barrios, Mexico, 1991			
21,101 metres (13 miles 196 yards 1 foot)	1	00	00.0
Arturo Barrios, Mexico, 1991			
25,000 metres	1	13	55.8
Toshihiko Seko, Japan, 1981			
30,000 metres	1	29	18.8
Toshihiko Seko, Japan, 1981			
Marathon	2	06	05
Ronaldo da Costa, Brazil, 1998			
110 metres hurdles (3 ft 6 in)			12.91
Colin Jackson, GB, 1993			
400 metres hurdles (3 ft 0 in)			46.78
Kevin Young, USA, 1992			
3,000 metres steeplechase		7	55.72
Bernard Barmasai, Kenya, 1997			

RELAYS		min.	sec.
4×100 metres			37.40
USA, 1992, 1993			
4×200 metres		1	19.11
Santa Monica TC, 1992			
4×400 metres		2	54.20
USA, 1998			
4×800 metres		7	03.89
GB, 1982			
4×1,500 metres		14	38.8
Federal Republic of Germany, 1977			

FIELD EVENTS	metres	ft	in
High jump	2.45	8	0½
Javier Sotomayor, Cuba, 1993			
Pole vault	6.14	20	1¾
Sergei Bubka, Ukraine, 1994			
Long jump	8.95	29	4½
Mike Powell, USA, 1991			
Triple jump	18.29	60	0¼
Jonathan Edwards, GB, 1995			
Shot	23.12	75	10¼
Randy Barnes, USA, 1990			
Discus	74.08	243	0
Jürgen Schult, GDR, 1986			
Hammer	86.74	284	7
Yuriy Sedykh, USSR, 1986			
Javelin	98.48	323	1
Jan Zelezny, Czech Rep., 1996			
Decathlon†	8,994* points		
Tomas Dvorak, Czech Rep., 1999			

† Ten events comprising 100 m, long jump, shot, high jump, 400 m, 110 m hurdles, discus, pole vault, javelin, 1500 m

WALKING (TRACK)	hr.	min.	sec.
20,000 metres	1	17	25.6
Bernard Segura, Mexico, 1994			
29,572 metres (18 miles 660 yards)	2	00	00.0
Maurizio Damilano, Italy, 1992			
30,000 metres	2	01	44.1
Maurizio Damilano, Italy, 1992			
50,000 metres	3	40	57.9
Thierry Toutain, France, 1996			

WOMEN'S EVENTS

TRACK EVENTS	min.	sec.
100 metres		10.49
Florence Griffith-Joyner, USA, 1988		
200 metres		21.34
Florence Griffith-Joyner, USA, 1988		
400 metres		47.60
Marita Koch, GDR, 1985		
800 metres	1	53.28
Jarmila Kratochvilova, Czechoslovakia, 1983		
1,500 metres	3	50.46
Qu Yunxia, China, 1993		
1 mile	4	12.56
Svetlana Masterkova, Russia, 1996		
3,000 metres	8	06.11
Wang Junxia, China, 1993		
5,000 metres	14	28.09
Jiang Bo, China, 1997		
10,000 metres	29	31.78
Wang Junxia, China, 1993		
Marathon	2	20	47
Tegla Loroupe, Kenya, 1998		
100 metres hurdles (2 ft 9 in)		12.21
Yordanka Donkova, Bulgaria, 1988		
400 metres hurdles (2 ft 6 in)		52.61
Kim Batten, USA, 1995		

RELAYS		min.	sec.
4×100 metres			41.37
GDR, 1985			
4×200 metres		1	28.15
GDR, 1980			
4×400 metres		3	15.17
USSR, 1988			
4×800 metres		7	50.17
USSR, 1984			

FIELD EVENTS	metres	ft	in
High jump	2.09	6	10¼
Stefka Kostadinova, Bulgaria, 1987			
Pole vault	4.60	15	1
Emma George, Australia, 1999			
Stacy Dragila, USA, 1999			
Long jump	7.52	24	8¼
Galina Chistiakova, USSR, 1988			
Triple jump	15.50	50	10¼
Inessa Kravets, Ukraine, 1995			
Shot	22.63	74	3
Natalya Lisovskaya, USSR, 1987			
Discus	76.80	252	0
Gabriele Reinsch, GDR, 1988			
Hammer	75.97	249	2
Mihaela Melinte, Romania, 1999			
Javelin (new implement in 1999)	68.19*	223	8
Trine Hattestad, Norway, 1999			
Heptathlon†		7,291 points	
Jackie Joyner-Kersee, USA, 1988			

†Seven events comprising 100 m hurdles, shot, high jump, 200 m, long jump, javelin, 800 m

ATHLETICS NATIONAL (UK) RECORDS
AS AT 5 SEPTEMBER 1999

Records set anywhere by athletes eligible to represent Great Britain and Northern Ireland

MEN

TRACK EVENTS	hr.	min.	sec.
100 metres			9.87
Linford Christie, 1993			
200 metres			19.87
John Regis, 1994			
400 metres			44.36
Iwan Thomas, 1997			
800 metres		1	41.73
Sebastian Coe, 1981			
1,000 metres		2	12.18
Sebastian Coe, 1981			
1,500 metres		3	29.67
Sebastian Coe, 1985			
1 mile		3	46.32
Steve Cram, 1985			
2,000 metres		4	51.39
Steve Cram, 1985			
3,000 metres		7	32.79
David Moorcroft, 1982			
5,000 metres		13	00.41
David Moorcroft, 1982			
10,000 metres		27	18.14*
Jon Brown, 1998			
20,000 metres		57	28.7
Carl Thackery, 1990			
20,855 metres	1	00	00.0
Carl Thackery, 1990			

25,000 metres	1	15	22.6
Ron Hill, 1965			
30,000 metres	1	31	30.4
Jim Alder, 1970			
3,000 metres steeplechase		8	07.96
Mark Rowland, 1988			
110 metres hurdles			12.91
Colin Jackson, 1993			
400 metres hurdles			47.82
Kriss Akabusi, 1992			

RELAYS		min.	sec.
4×100 metres			37.73*
GB team, 1999			
4×200 metres		1	21.29
GB team, 1989			
4×400 metres		2	56.60
GB team, 1996			
4×800 metres		7	03.89
GB team, 1982			

FIELD EVENTS	metres	ft	in
High jump	2.37	7	9¼
Steve Smith, 1992, 1993			
Pole vault	5.80*	19	0¼
Nick Buckfield, 1998			
Long jump	8.23	27	0
Lynn Davies, 1968			
Triple jump	18.29	60	0¼
Jonathan Edwards, 1995			
Shot	21.68	71	1½
Geoff Capes, 1980			
Discus	66.64*	218	8
Perris Wilkins, 1998			
Hammer	77.54	254	5
Martin Girvan, 1984			
Javelin	91.46	300	1
Steve Backley, 1992			
Decathlon		8,847 points	
Daley Thompson, 1984			

WALKING (TRACK)	hr.	min.	sec.
20,000 metres	1	23	26.5
Ian McCombie, 1990			
30,000 metres	2	19	18
Christopher Maddocks, 1984			
50,000 metres	4	05	44.6
Paul Blagg, 1990			
26,037 metres (16 miles 315 yards)	2	00	00.0
Ron Wallwork, 1971			

WOMEN

TRACK EVENTS		min.	sec.
100 metres			11.10
Kathy Cook, 1981			
200 metres			22.10
Kathy Cook, 1984			
400 metres			49.43
Kathy Cook, 1984			
800 metres		1	56.21
Kelly Holmes, 1995			
1,500 metres		3	58.07
Kelly Holmes, 1997			
1 mile		4	17.57
Zola Budd, 1985			
3,000 metres		8	27.40*
Paula Radcliffe, 1999			
5,000 metres		14	43.54*
Paula Radcliffe, 1999			

10,000 metres	30	27.13*
Paula Radcliffe, 1999		
100 metres hurdles		12.80
Angela Thorp, 1996		
400 metres hurdles		52.74
Sally Gunnell, 1993		

RELAYS	min.	sec.
4×100 metres		42.43
GB team, 1980		
4×200 metres	1	31.57
GB team, 1977		
4×400 metres	3	22.01
GB team, 1991		
4×800 metres	8	23.8
GB team, 1971		

FIELD EVENTS	metres	ft	in
High jump	1.95	6	4¾
Diana Elliott, 1982			
Pole vault	4.31*	14	1¾
Janine Whitlock, 1998			
Long jump	6.90	22	7¾
Beverley Kinch, 1983			
Triple jump	15.15	49	8½
Ashia Hansen, 1997			
Shot	19.36	63	6¼
Judy Oakes, 1988			
Discus	67.48	221	5
Margaret Ritchie, 1981			
Hammer	67.10	220	2
Lorraine Shaw, 1999			
Javelin	77.44	254	1
Fatima Whitbread, 1986			
Heptathlon		6,736 points	
Denise Lewis, 1997			

*Awaiting ratification

SWIMMING WORLD RECORDS
AS AT 5 SEPTEMBER 1999

MEN	min.	sec.
50 metres freestyle		21.81
Tom Jager, USA		
100 metres freestyle		48.21
Alexander Popov, Russia		
200 metres freestyle	1	46.00
Ian Thorpe, Australia		
400 metres freestyle	3	41.80
Ian Thorpe, Australia		
800 metres freestyle	7	46.00
Kieren Perkins, Australia		
1,500 metres freestyle	14	41.66
Kieren Perkins, Australia		
100 metres breaststroke	1	00.60
Fred Deburghgraeve, Belgium		
200 metres breaststroke	2	10.16
Mike Barrowman, USA		
100 metres butterfly		52.15
Michael Klim, Australia		
200 metres butterfly	1	55.22
Denis Pankratov, Russia		
100 metres backstroke		53.86
Jeff Rouse, USA		
200 metres backstroke	1	55.87
Lenny Krayzelburg, USA		
200 metres medley	1	58.16
Jani Sievinen, Finland		

400 metres medley	4	12.30
Tom Dolan, USA		
4×100 metres freestyle relay	3	15.11
USA		
4×200 metres freestyle relay	7	08.79
Australia		
4×100 metres medley relay	3	34.84
USA		

WOMEN	min.	sec.
50 metres freestyle		24.51
Jingyi Le, China		
100 metres freestyle		54.01
Jingyi Le, China		
200 metres freestyle	1	56.78
Franziska van Almsick, Germany		
400 metres freestyle	4	03.85
Janet Evans, USA		
800 metres freestyle	8	16.22
Janet Evans, USA		
1,500 metres freestyle	15	52.10
Janet Evans, USA		
100 metres breaststroke	1	06.52
Penny Heyns, South Africa		
200 metres breaststroke	2	23.64
Rebecca Brown, Australia		
100 metres butterfly		57.88
Jenny Thompson, USA		
200 metres butterfly	2	05.96
Mary Meagher, USA		
100 metres backstroke	1	00.16
Cihong He, China		
200 metres backstroke	2	06.62
Krisztina Egerszegi, Hungary		
200 metres medley	2	09.72
Wu Yanyan, China		
400 metres medley	4	34.79
Chen Yan, China		
4×100 metres freestyle relay	3	37.91
USA		
4×200 metres freestyle relay	7	55.47
GDR		
4×100 metres medley relay	4	01.67
China		

Weights and Measures

The Système International d'Unités (SI) is an international and coherent system of units devised to meet all known needs for measurement in science and technology. The system was adopted by the eleventh Conférence Générale des Poids et Mesures (CGPM) in 1960. A comprehensive description of the system is given in *SI The International System of Units* (HMSO). The British Standards describing the essential features of the International System of Units are *Specifications for SI units and recommendations for the use of their multiples and certain other units* (BS 5555:1993) and *Conversion Factors and Tables* (BS 350, Part 1:1974).

The system consists of seven base units and the derived units formed as products or quotients of various powers of the base units. Together the base units and the derived units make up the coherent system of units. In the UK the SI base units, and almost all important derived units, are realized at the National Physical Laboratory and disseminated through the National Measurement System.

BASE UNITS

metre (m) = unit of length
kilogram (kg) = unit of mass
second (s) = unit of time
ampere (A) = unit of electric current
kelvin (K) = unit of thermodynamic temperature
mole (mol) = unit of amount of substance
candela (cd) = unit of luminous intensity

DERIVED UNITS

For some of the derived SI units, special names and symbols exist; those approved by the CGPM are as follows:

hertz (Hz) = unit of frequency
newton (N) = unit of force
pascal (Pa) = unit of pressure, stress
joule (J) = unit of energy, work, quantity of heat
watt (W) = unit of power, radiant flux
coulomb (C) = unit of electric charge, quantity of electricity
volt (V) = unit of electric potential, potential difference, electromotive force
farad (F) = unit of electric capacitance
ohm (Ω) = unit of electric resistance
siemens (S) = unit of electric conductance
weber (Wb) = unit of magnetic flux
tesla (T) = unit of magnetic flux density
henry (H) = unit of inductance
degree Celsius (°C) = unit of Celsius temperature
lumen (lm) = unit of luminous flux
lux (lx) = unit of illuminance
becquerel (Bq) = unit of activity (of a radionuclide)
gray (Gy) = unit of absorbed dose, specific energy imparted, kerma, absorbed dose index
sievert (Sv) = unit of dose equivalent, dose equivalent index
radian (rad) = unit of plane angle
steradian (sr) = unit of solid angle

Other derived units are expressed in terms of base units. Some of the more commonly-used derived units are the following:

Unit of area = square metre (m^2)
Unit of volume = cubic metre (m^3)
Unit of velocity = metre per second ($m\ s^{-1}$)
Unit of acceleration = metre per second squared ($m\ s^{-2}$)
Unit of density = kilogram per cubic metre ($kg\ m^{-3}$)
Unit of momentum = kilogram metre per second ($kg\ m\ s^{-1}$)
Unit of magnetic field strength = ampere per metre ($A\ m^{-1}$)
Unit of surface tension = newton per metre ($N\ m^{-1}$)
Unit of dynamic viscosity = pascal second (Pa s)
Unit of heat capacity = joule per kelvin ($J\ K^{-1}$)
Unit of specific heat capacity = joule per kilogram kelvin ($J\ kg^{-1}\ K^{-1}$)
Unit of heat flux density, irradiance = watt per square metre ($W\ m^{-2}$)
Unit of thermal conductivity = watt per metre kelvin ($W\ m^{-1}\ K^{-1}$)
Unit of electric field strength = volt per metre ($V\ m^{-1}$)
Unit of luminance = candela per square metre ($cd\ m^{-2}$)

SI PREFIXES

Decimal multiples and submultiples of the SI units are indicated by SI prefixes. These are as follows:

multiples	*submultiples*
yotta (Y)$\times 10^{24}$	deci (d)$\times 10^{-1}$
zetta (Z)$\times 10^{21}$	centi (c)$\times 10^{-2}$
exa (E)$\times 10^{18}$	milli (m)$\times 10^{-3}$
peta (P)$\times 10^{15}$	micro (μ)$\times 10^{-6}$
tera (T)$\times 10^{12}$	nano (n)$\times 10^{-9}$
giga (G)$\times 10^{9}$	pico (p)$\times 10^{-12}$
mega (M)$\times 10^{6}$	femto (f)$\times 10^{-15}$
kilo (k)$\times 10^{3}$	atto (a)$\times 10^{-18}$
hecto (h)$\times 10^{2}$	zepto (z)$\times 10^{-21}$
deca (da)$\times 10$	yocto (y)$\times 10^{-24}$

METRIC UNITS

The metric primary standards are the metre as the unit of measurement of length, and the kilogram as the unit of measurement of mass. Other units of measurement are defined by reference to the primary standards.

MEASUREMENT OF LENGTH

Kilometre (km) = 1000 metres
Metre (m) is the length of the path travelled by light in vacuum during a time interval of 1/299 792 458 of a second
Decimetre (dm) = 1/10 metre
Centimetre (cm) = 1/100 metre
Millimetre (mm) = 1/1000 metre

MEASUREMENT OF AREA

Hectare (ha) = 100 ares
Decare = 10 ares
Are (a) = 100 square metres
Square metre = a superficial area equal to that of a square each side of which measures one metre

Square decimetre = 1/100 square metre
Square centimetre = 1/100 square decimetre
Square millimetre = 1/100 square centimetre

MEASUREMENT OF VOLUME

Cubic metre (m^3) = a volume equal to that of a cube each edge of which measures one metre
Cubic decimetre = 1/1000 cubic metre
Cubic centimetre (cc) = 1/1000 cubic decimetre
Hectolitre = 100 litres
Litre = a cubic decimetre
Decilitre = 1/10 litre
Centilitre = 1/100 litre
Millilitre = 1/1000 litre

MEASUREMENT OF CAPACITY

Hectolitre (hl) = 100 litres
Litre (l or L) = a cubic decimetre
Decilitre (dl) = 1/10 litre
Centilitre (cl) = 1/100 litre
Millilitre (ml) = 1/1000 litre

MEASUREMENT OF MASS OR WEIGHT

Tonne (t) = 1000 kilograms
Kilogram (kg) is equal to the mass of the international prototype of the kilogram
Hectogram (hg) = 1/10 kilogram
Gram (g) = 1/1000 kilogram
*Carat (metric) = 1/5 gram
Milligram (mg) = 1/1000 gram

*Used only for transactions in precious stones or pearls

METRICATION IN THE UK

The European Council Directive 80/181/EEC, as amended by Council Directive 89/617/EEC, relates to the use of units of measurement for economic, public health, public safety or administrative purposes in the member states of the European Union. The provisions of the directives were incorporated into British law by the Weights and Measures Act 1985 (Metrication) (Amendment) Order 1994 and the Units of Measurement Regulations 1994; these instruments amended the Weights and Measures Act 1985. Parallel statutory rules amending Northern Ireland weights and measures legislation were made in May 1995.

The general effect of the 1994 and 1995 legislation is to end the use of imperial units of measurement for trade, replacing them with metric units – *see* below for timetable for UK metrication. Imperial units can, however, be used in addition to metric units, as supplementary indications.

IMPERIAL UNITS

The imperial primary standards are the yard as the unit of measurement of length and the pound as the unit of measurement of mass. Other units of measurement are defined by reference to the primary standards. Most of these units are no longer authorized for use in trade in the UK – *see* below.

MEASUREMENT OF LENGTH

Mile = 1760 yards
Furlong = 220 yards
Chain = 22 yards

Yard (yd) = 0.9144 metre
Foot (ft) = 1/3 yard
Inch (in) = 1/36 yard

MEASUREMENT OF AREA

Square mile = 640 acres
Acre = 4840 square yards
Rood = 1210 square yards
Square yard (sq. yd) = a superficial area equal to that of a square each side of which measures one yard
Square foot (sq. ft) = 1/9 square yard
Square inch (sq. in) = 1/144 square foot

MEASUREMENT OF VOLUME

Cubic yard = a volume equal to that of a cube each edge of which measures one yard
Cubic foot = 1/27 cubic yard
Cubic inch = 1/1728 cubic foot

MEASUREMENT OF CAPACITY

Bushel = 8 gallons
Peck = 2 gallons
Gallon (gal) = 4.546 09 cubic decimetres
Quart (qt) = 1/4 gallon
*Pint (pt) = 1/2 quart
Gill = 1/4 pint
*Fluid ounce (fl oz) = 1/20 pint
Fluid drachm = 1/8 fluid ounce
Minim (min) = 1/60 fluid drachm

MEASUREMENT OF MASS OR WEIGHT

Ton = 2240 pounds
Hundredweight (cwt) = 112 pounds
Cental = 100 pounds
Quarter = 28 pounds
Stone = 14 pounds
*Pound (lb) = 0.453 592 37 kilogram
*Ounce (oz) = 1/16 pound
*†Ounce troy (oz tr) = 12/175 pound
Dram (dr) = 1/16 ounce
Grain (gr) = 1/7000 pound
Pennyweight (dwt) = 24 grains
Ounce apothecaries = 480 grains
Drachm (ℨ) = 1/8 ounce apothecaries
Scruple (℈) = 1/3 drachm

*Units of measurement still authorized for use for trade in the UK
†Used only for transactions in gold, silver or other precious metals, and articles made therefrom

PHASING-OUT OF IMPERIAL UNITS IN THE UK

The Weights and Measures Act 1985 enacted the legal units for the United Kingdom. It was amended to implement the provisions of European Council Directive 80/181/EEC, as amended by Directive 89/617/EEC, by the Weights and Measures Act 1985 (Metrication) (Amendment) Order 1994 and the Units of Measurement Regulations 1994, and by parallel statutory rules in Northern Ireland in May 1995.

The effect of the amended legislation is to phase out the use of imperial units for trade, replacing them with metric units. With effect from 30 September 1995 imperial units ceased to be authorized for use in the UK for economic, public health, public safety and administrative purposes, with the following exceptions:

Units of measurement authorized for use in specialized fields between 1 October 1995 and 31 December 1999

Unit	Field of application
fathom	Marine navigation
fluid ounce ⎱ pint ⎰	Beer, cider, water, lemonade, fruit juice in returnable containers
ounce ⎱ pound ⎰	Goods for sale loose from bulk
therm	Gas supply

Units of measurement authorized for use in specialized fields from 1 October 1995, without time limit

Unit	Field of application
inch ⎫ foot ⎪ yard ⎬ mile ⎭	Road traffic signs, distance and speed measurement
pint ⎰	Dispense of draught beer or cider / Milk in returnable containers
acre	Land registration
troy ounce	Transactions in precious metals

MEASUREMENT OF ELECTRICITY

Units of measurement of electricity are defined by the Weights and Measures Act 1985 as follows:

ampere (A) = that constant current which, if maintained in two straight parallel conductors of infinite length, of negligible circular cross-section and placed 1 metre apart in vacuum, would produce between these conductors a force equal to 2×10^{-7} newton per metre of length

ohm (Ω) = the electric resistance between two points of a conductor when a constant potential difference of 1 volt, applied between the two points, produces in the conductor a current of 1 ampere, the conductor not being the seat of any electromotive force

volt (V) = the difference of electric potential between two points of a conducting wire carrying a constant current of 1 ampere when the power dissipated between these points is equal to 1 watt

watt (W) = the power which in one second gives rise to energy of 1 joule

kilowatt (kW) = 1000 watts

megawatt (MW) = one million watts

WATER AND LIQUOR MEASURES

1 cubic foot = 62.32 lb

1 gallon = 10 lb

1 cubic cm = 1 gram

1000 cubic cm = 1 litre; 1 kilogram

1 cubic metre = 1000 litres; 1000 kg; 1 tonne

An inch of rain on the surface of an acre (43560 sq. ft) = 3630 cubic ft = 100.992 tons

Cisterns: A cistern 4×2½ feet and 3 feet deep will hold brimful 186.963 gallons, weighing 1869.63 lb in addition to its own weight

WATER FOR SHIPS

Kilderkin = 18 gallons

Barrel = 36 gallons

Puncheon = 72 gallons

Butt = 110 gallons

Tun = 210 gallons

BOTTLES OF WINE

Traditional equivalents in standard champagne bottles:

Magnum = 2 bottles

Jeroboam = 4 bottles

Rehoboam = 6 bottles

Methuselah = 8 bottles

Salmanazar = 12 bottles

Balthazar = 16 bottles

Nebuchadnezzar = 20 bottles

A quarter of a bottle is known as a *nip*

An eighth of a bottle is known as a *baby*

ANGULAR AND CIRCULAR MEASURES

60 seconds (″) = 1 minute (′)

60 minutes = 1 degree (°)

90 degrees = 1 right angle or quadrant

Diameter of circle × 3.141 6 = circumference

Diameter squared × 0.7854 = area of circle

Diameter squared × 3.141 6 = surface of sphere

Diameter cubed × 0.523 = solidity of sphere

One degree of circumference × 57.3 = radius*

Diameter of cylinder × 3.141 6; product by length or height, gives the surface

Diameter squared × 0.7854; product by length or height, gives solid content

*Or, one radian (the angle subtended at the centre of a circle by an arc of the circumference equal in length to the radius) = 57.3 degrees

MILLION, BILLION, ETC.

Value in the UK		
Million	thousand × thousand	10^6
*Billion	million × million	10^{12}
Trillion	million × billion	10^{18}
Quadrillion	million × trillion	10^{24}
Value in USA		
Million	thousand × thousand	10^6
*Billion	thousand × million	10^9
Trillion	million × million	10^{12}
Quadrillion	million × billion US	10^{15}

*The American usage of billion (i.e. 10^9) is increasingly common, and is now universally used by statisticians

NAUTICAL MEASURES

DISTANCE

Distance at sea is measured in nautical miles. The British standard nautical mile was 6080 feet but this measure has been obsolete since 1970 when the international nautical mile of 1852 metres was adopted by the Hydrographic Department of the Ministry of Defence. The cable (600 feet or 100 fathoms) was a measure approximately one-tenth of a nautical mile. Such distances are now expressed in decimal parts of a sea mile or in metres.

Soundings at sea were recorded in fathoms (6 feet). Depths are now expressed in metres on Admiralty charts.

SPEED

Speed is measured in nautical miles per hour, called knots. A ship moving at the rate of 30 nautical miles per hour is said to be doing 30 knots.

knots	m.p.h.	knots	m.p.h.
1	1.1515	9	10.3636
2	2.3030	10	11.5151
3	3.4545	15	17.2727
4	4.6060	20	23.0303
5	5.7575	25	28.7878
6	6.9090	30	34.5454
7	8.0606	35	40.3030
8	9.2121	40	46.0606

TONNAGE

Under the Merchant Shipping Act 1854, the tonnage of UK-registered vessels was measured in tons of 100 cubic feet. The need for a universal method of measurement led to the adoption of the International Convention on Tonnage Measurements of Ships 1969, which measures, in cubic metres, all the internal spaces of a vessel for the gross tonnage and those of the cargo compartments for the net tonnage. The convention has applied since July 1982 to new ships, ships which needed to be remeasured because of substantial alterations, and ships whose owners requested remeasurement. On 18 July 1994 the convention became mandatory and all vessels should have been remeasured by that date; however, there is a backlog and some vessels have not yet been remeasured.

DISTANCE OF THE HORIZON

The limit of distance to which one can see varies with the height of the spectator. The greatest distance at which an object on the surface of the sea, or of a level plain, can be seen by a person whose eyes are at a height of five feet from the same level is nearly three miles. At a height of 20 feet the range is increased to nearly six miles, and an approximate rule for finding the range of vision for small heights is to increase the square root of the number of feet that the eye is above the level surface by a third of itself. The result is the distance of the horizon in miles, but is slightly in excess of that in the table below, which is computed by a more precise formula. The table may be used conversely to show the distance of an object of given height that is just visible from a point on the surface of the earth or sea. Refraction is taken into account both in the approximate rule and in the table.

Height in feet	range in miles
5	2.9
20	5.9
50	9.3
100	13.2
500	29.5
1,000	41.6
2,000	58.9
3,000	72.1
4,000	83.3
5,000	93.1
20,000	186.2

TEMPERATURE SCALES

The SI (International System) unit of temperature is the kelvin, which is defined as the fraction 1/273.16 of the temperature of the triple point of water (i.e. where ice, water and water vapour are in equilibrium). The zero of the Kelvin scale is the absolute zero of temperature. The freezing point of water is 273.15 K and the boiling point (as adopted in the International Temperature Scale of 1990) is 373.124 K.

The Celsius scale (formerly centigrade) is defined by subtracting 273.15 from the Kelvin temperature. The Fahrenheit scale is related to the Celsius scale by the relationships:

temperature °F = (temperature °C×1.8) + 32
temperature °C = (temperature °F−32)÷1.8

It follows from these definitions that the freezing point of water is 0°C and 32°F. The boiling point is 99.974°C and 211.953°F.

The temperature of the human body varies from person to person and in the same person can be affected by a variety of factors. In most people body temperature varies between 36.5°C and 37.2°C (97.7–98.9°F).

Conversion between scales

°C	°F		°C	°F		°C	°F
100	212		60	140		20	68
99	210.2		59	138.2		19	66.2
98	208.4		58	136.4		18	64.4
97	206.6		57	134.6		17	62.6
96	204.8		56	132.8		16	60.8
95	203		55	131		15	59
94	201.2		54	129.2		14	57.2
93	199.4		53	127.4		13	55.4
92	197.6		52	125.6		12	53.6
91	195.8		51	123.8		11	51.8
90	194		50	122		10	50
89	192.2		49	120.2		9	48.2
88	190.4		48	118.4		8	46.4
87	188.6		47	116.6		7	44.6
86	186.8		46	114.8		6	42.8
85	185		45	113		5	41
84	183.2		44	111.2		4	39.2
83	181.4		43	109.4		3	37.4
82	179.6		42	107.6		2	35.6
81	177.8		41	105.8		1	33.8
80	176		40	104		zero	32
79	174.2		39	102.2		− 1	30.2
78	172.4		38	100.4		− 2	28.4
77	170.6		37	98.6		− 3	26.6
76	168.8		36	96.8		− 4	24.8
75	167		35	95		− 5	23
74	165.2		34	93.2		− 6	21.2
73	163.4		33	91.4		− 7	19.4
72	161.6		32	89.6		− 8	17.6
71	159.8		31	87.8		− 9	15.8
70	158		30	86		−10	14
69	156.2		29	84.2		−11	12.2
68	154.4		28	82.4		−12	10.4
67	152.6		27	80.6		−13	8.6
66	150.8		26	78.8		−14	6.8
65	149		25	77		−15	5
64	147.2		24	75.2		−16	3.2
63	145.4		23	73.4		−17	1.4
62	143.6		22	71.6		−18	0.4
61	141.8		21	69.8		−19	−2.2

PAPER MEASURES

Printing Paper		*Writing Paper*	
516 sheets	= 1 ream	480 sheets	= 1 ream
2 reams	= 1 bundle	20 quires	= 1 ream
5 bundles	= 1 bale	24 sheets	= 1 quire

Brown Papers

	inches		*inches*
Casing	46×36	Imperial Cap	29×22
Double Imperial	45×29	Haven Cap	26×21
Elephant	34×24	Bag Cap	24×19½
Double Four Pound	31×21	Kent Cap	21×18

Printing Papers

	inches		*inches*
Foolscap	17×13½	Double Large Post	33×21
Double Foolscap	27×17	Demy	22½×17½
Quad Foolscap	34×27	Double Demy	35×22½
Crown	20×15	Quad Demy	45×35
Double Crown	30×20	Music Demy	20×15½
Quad Crown	40×30	Medium	23×18
Double Quad Crown	60×40	Royal	25×20
Post	19¼×15½	Super Royal	27½×20½
Double Post	31½×19½	Elephant	28×23
		Imperial	30×22

Writing and Drawing Papers

	inches		*inches*
Emperor	72×48	Copy or Draft	20×16
Antiquarian	53×31	Demy	20×15½
Double Elephant	40×27	Post	19×15¼
Grand Eagle	42×28¾	Pinched Post	18½×14¾
Atlas	34×26	Foolscap	17×13½
Colombier	34½×23½	Double Foolscap	26½×16½
Imperial	30×22	Double Post	30½×19
Elephant	28×23	Double Large Post	33×21
Cartridge	26×21	Double Demy	31×20
Super Royal	27×19	Brief	16½×13¼
Royal	24×19	Pott	15×12½
Medium	22×17½		
Large Post	21×16½		

INTERNATIONAL PAPER SIZES

The basis of the international series of paper sizes is a rectangle having an area of one square metre, the sides of which are in the proportion of $1:\sqrt{2}$. The proportions $1:\sqrt{2}$ have a geometrical relationship, the side and diagonal of any square being in this proportion. The effect of this arrangement is that if the area of the sheet of paper is doubled or halved, the shorter side and the longer side of the new sheet are still in the same proportion $1:\sqrt{2}$. This feature is useful where photographic enlargement or reduction is used, as the proportions remain the same.

Description of the A series is by capital A followed by a figure. The basic size has the description A0 and the higher the figure following the letter, the greater is the number of sub-divisions and therefore the smaller the sheet. Half A0 is A1 and half A1 is A2. Where larger dimensions are required the A is preceded by a figure. Thus 2A means twice the size A0; 4A is four times the size of A0.

Subsidiary Series

B sizes are sizes intermediate between any two adjacent sizes of the A series. There is a series of C sizes which is used much less. A is for magazines and books, B for posters, wall charts and other large items, C for envelopes particularly where it is necessary for an envelope (in C series) to fit into another envelope. The size recommended for business correspondence is A4.

Long sizes (DL) are obtainable by dividing any appropriate sizes from the two series above into three, four or eight equal parts parallel with the shorter side in such a manner that the proportion of $1:\sqrt{2}$ is not maintained, the ratio between the longer and the shorter sides being greater than $\sqrt{2}:1$. In practice long sizes should be produced from the A series only.

It is an essential feature of these series that the dimensions are of the trimmed or finished size.

A Series

	mm		*mm*
A0	841×1189	A6	105×148
A1	594×841	A7	74×105
A2	420×594	A8	52×74
A3	297×420	A9	37×52
A4	210×297	A10	26×37
A5	148×210		

B Series

	mm		*mm*
B0	1000×1414	B6	125×176
B1	707×1000	B7	88×125
B2	500×707	B8	62×88
B3	353×500	B9	44×62
B4	250×353	B10	31×44
B5	176×250		

C Series / DL

C Series	*mm*	DL	*mm*
C4	324×229	DL	110×220
C5	229×162		
C6	114×162		

BOUND BOOKS

The book sizes most commonly used are listed below. Approximate centimetre equivalents are also shown. International sizes are converted to their nearest imperial size, e.g. A4 = D4; A5 = D8.

		inches	*cm*
Crown 32mo	C32	2½×3¾	6×9
Crown 16mo	C16	3¾×5	9×13
Foolscap 8vo	F8	4¼×6¾	11×17
Demy 16mo	D16	4⅜×5⅝	11×14
Crown 8vo	C8	5×7½	13×19
Demy 8vo	D8	5⅝×8¾	14×22
Medium 8vo	M8	5¾×9	15×23
Royal 8vo	R8	6¼×10	16×25
Super Royal 8vo	suR8	6¾×10	17×25
Foolscap 4to	F4	6¾×8½	17×22
Crown 4to	C4	7½×10	19×25
Imperial 8vo	Imp8	7½×11	19×28
Demy 4to	D4	8¾×11¼	22×29
Royal 4to	R4	10×12½	25×31
Super Royal 4to	suR4	10×13½	25×34
Crown Folio	Cfol	10×15	25×38
Imperial Folio	Impfol	11×15	28×38

Folio = a sheet folded in half
Quarto (4to) = a sheet folded into four
Octavo (8vo) = a sheet folded into eight
Books are usually bound up in sheets of 16, 32 or 64 pages. Octavo books are generally printed 64 pages at a time, 32 pages on each side of a sheet of quad.

CONVERSION TABLES FOR WEIGHTS AND MEASURES

Bold figures equal units of either of the columns beside them; thus: 1 cm = 0.394 inches and 1 inch = 2.540 cm

LENGTH			AREA			VOLUME			WEIGHT (MASS)		
Centimetres		*Inches*	*Square cm*		*Square in*	*Cubic cm*		*Cubic in*	*Kilograms*		*Pounds*
2.540	1	0.394	6.452	1	0.155	16.387	1	0.061	0.454	1	2.205
5.080	2	0.787	12.903	2	0.310	32.774	2	0.122	0.907	2	4.409
7.620	3	1.181	19.355	3	0.465	49.161	3	0.183	1.361	3	6.614
10.160	4	1.575	25.806	4	0.620	65.548	4	0.244	1.814	4	8.819
12.700	5	1.969	32.258	5	0.775	81.936	5	0.305	2.268	5	11.023
15.240	6	2.362	38.710	6	0.930	98.323	6	0.366	2.722	6	13.228
17.780	7	2.756	45.161	7	1.085	114.710	7	0.427	3.175	7	15.432
20.320	8	3.150	51.613	8	1.240	131.097	8	0.488	3.629	8	17.637
22.860	9	3.543	58.064	9	1.395	147.484	9	0.549	4.082	9	19.842
25.400	10	3.937	64.516	10	1.550	163.871	10	0.610	4.536	10	22.046
50.800	20	7.874	129.032	20	3.100	327.742	20	1.220	9.072	20	44.092
76.200	30	11.811	193.548	30	4.650	491.613	30	1.831	13.608	30	66.139
101.600	40	15.748	258.064	40	6.200	655.484	40	2.441	18.144	40	88.185
127.000	50	19.685	322.580	50	7.750	819.355	50	3.051	22.680	50	110.231
152.400	60	23.622	387.096	60	9.300	983.226	60	3.661	27.216	60	132.277
177.800	70	27.559	451.612	70	10.850	1147.097	70	4.272	31.752	70	154.324
203.200	80	31.496	516.128	80	12.400	1310.968	80	4.882	36.287	80	176.370
228.600	90	35.433	580.644	90	13.950	1474.839	90	5.492	40.823	90	198.416
254.000	100	39.370	645.160	100	15.500	1638.710	100	6.102	45.359	100	220.464
Metres		*Yards*	*Square m*		*Square yd*	*Cubic m*		*Cubic yd*	*Metric tonnes*		*Tons (UK)*
0.914	1	1.094	0.836	1	1.196	0.765	1	1.308	1.016	1	0.984
1.829	2	2.187	1.672	2	2.392	1.529	2	2.616	2.032	2	1.968
2.743	3	3.281	2.508	3	3.588	2.294	3	3.924	3.048	3	2.953
3.658	4	4.374	3.345	4	4.784	3.058	4	5.232	4.064	4	3.937
4.572	5	5.468	4.181	5	5.980	3.823	5	6.540	5.080	5	4.921
5.486	6	6.562	5.017	6	7.176	4.587	6	7.848	6.096	6	5.905
6.401	7	7.655	5.853	7	8.372	5.352	7	9.156	7.112	7	6.889
7.315	8	8.749	6.689	8	9.568	6.116	8	10.464	8.128	8	7.874
8.230	9	9.843	7.525	9	10.764	6.881	9	11.772	9.144	9	8.858
9.144	10	10.936	8.361	10	11.960	7.646	10	13.080	10.161	10	9.842
18.288	20	21.872	16.723	20	23.920	15.291	20	26.159	20.321	20	19.684
27.432	30	32.808	25.084	30	35.880	22.937	30	39.239	30.481	30	29.526
36.576	40	43.745	33.445	40	47.840	30.582	40	52.318	40.642	40	39.368
45.720	50	54.681	41.806	50	59.799	38.228	50	65.398	50.802	50	49.210
54.864	60	65.617	50.168	60	71.759	45.873	60	78.477	60.963	60	59.052
64.008	70	76.553	58.529	70	83.719	53.519	70	91.557	71.123	70	68.894
73.152	80	87.489	66.890	80	95.679	61.164	80	104.636	81.284	80	78.737
82.296	90	98.425	75.251	90	107.639	68.810	90	117.716	91.444	90	88.579
91.440	100	109.361	83.613	100	119.599	76.455	100	130.795	101.605	100	98.421
Kilometres		*Miles*	*Hectares*		*Acres*	*Litres*		*Gallons*	*Metric tonnes*		*Tons (US)*
1.609	1	0.621	0.405	1	2.471	4.546	1	0.220	0.907	1	1.102
3.219	2	1.243	0.809	2	4.942	9.092	2	0.440	1.814	2	2.205
4.828	3	1.864	1.214	3	7.413	13.638	3	0.660	2.722	3	3.305
6.437	4	2.485	1.619	4	9.844	18.184	4	0.880	3.629	4	4.409
8.047	5	3.107	2.023	5	12.355	22.730	5	1.100	4.536	5	5.521
9.656	6	3.728	2.428	6	14.826	27.276	6	1.320	5.443	6	6.614
11.265	7	4.350	2.833	7	17.297	31.822	7	1.540	6.350	7	7.716
12.875	8	4.971	3.327	8	19.769	36.368	8	1.760	7.257	8	8.818
14.484	9	5.592	3.642	9	22.240	40.914	9	1.980	8.165	9	9.921
16.093	10	6.214	4.047	10	24.711	45.460	10	2.200	9.072	10	11.023
32.187	20	12.427	8.094	20	49.421	90.919	20	4.400	18.144	20	22.046
48.280	30	18.641	12.140	30	74.132	136.379	30	6.599	27.216	30	33.069
64.374	40	24.855	16.187	40	98.842	181.839	40	8.799	36.287	40	44.092
80.467	50	31.069	20.234	50	123.555	227.298	50	10.999	45.359	50	55.116
96.561	60	37.282	24.281	60	148.263	272.758	60	13.199	54.431	60	66.139
112.654	70	43.496	28.328	70	172.974	318.217	70	15.398	63.503	70	77.162
128.748	80	49.710	32.375	80	197.684	363.677	80	17.598	72.575	80	88.185
144.841	90	55.923	36.422	90	222.395	409.137	90	19.798	81.647	90	99.208
160.934	100	62.137	40.469	100	247.105	454.596	100	21.998	90.719	100	110.231

Abbreviations

A — Associate of
AA — Alcoholics Anonymous
Automobile Association
AAA — Amateur Athletic Association
AB — Able-bodied seaman
ABA — Amateur Boxing Association
abbr(ev) — abbreviation
ABM — Anti-ballistic missile
abr — abridged
ac — alternating current
a/c — account
AC — Aircraftman
(*Ante Christum*) Before Christ
Companion, Order of Australia
ACAS — Advisory, Conciliation and Arbitration Service
ACT — Australian Capital Territory
AD — (*Anno Domini*) In the year of our Lord
ADC — Aide-de-Camp
ADC (P) — Personal ADC to The Queen
adj — adjective
Adj — Adjutant
ad lib — (*ad libitum*) at pleasure
Adm — Admiral
Admission
adv — adverb
AE — Air Efficiency Award
AEEU — Amalgamated Engineering and Electrical Union
AEM — Air Efficiency Medal
AFC — Air Force Cross
AFM — Air Force Medal
AG — Adjutant-General
Attorney-General
AGM — air-to-ground missile
annual general meeting
AH — (*Anno Hegirae*) In the year of the Hegira
AI — Artificial intelligence
AIDS — Acquired immune deficiency syndrome
AIM — Alternative Investment Market
alt — altitude
am — (*ante meridiem*) before noon
AM — (*Anno mundi*) In the year of the world
amplitude modulation
Member of the Welsh Assembly
amp — ampere
amplifier
ANC — African National Congress
anon — anonymous
ANZAC — Australian and New Zealand Army Corps
AO — Air Officer
Officer, Order of Australia
AOC — Air Officer Commanding
AONB — Area of Outstanding Natural Beauty
AS — Anglo-Saxon
ASA — Advertising Standards Authority
Amateur Swimming Association
asap — as soon as possible
ASB — Alternative Service Book
ASEAN — Association of South East Asian Nations
ASH — Action on Smoking and Health
ASLEF — Associated Society of Locomotive Engineers and Firemen

ASLIB — Association for Information Management
ATC — Air Training Corps
AUC — (*ab urbe condita*) In the year from the foundation of Rome
(*anno urbis conditae*) In the year of the founding of the city
AUT — Association of University Teachers
AV — Audio-visual
Authorized Version (*of Bible*)
AVR — Army Volunteer Reserve
AWOL — Absent without leave

b — born
bowled
BA — Bachelor of Arts
BAA — British Airports Authority
British Astronomical Association
BAF — British Athletics Federation
BAFTA — British Academy of Film and Television Arts
Bart — Baronet
BAS — Bachelor in Agricultural Science
British Antarctic Survey
BBC — British Broadcasting Corporation
BBSRC — Biotechnology and Biological Sciences Research Council
BC — Before Christ
British Columbia
B Ch (D) — Bachelor of (Dental) Surgery
BCL — Bachelor of Civil Law
B Com — Bachelor of Commerce
BD — Bachelor of Divinity
BDA — British Dental Association
BDS — Bachelor of Dental Surgery
B Ed — Bachelor of Education
BEM — British Empire Medal
B Eng — Bachelor of Engineering
BFI — British Film Institute
BFPO — British Forces Post Office
BL — British Library
B Litt — Bachelor of Letters *or* of Literature
BM — Bachelor of Medicine
British Museum
BMA — British Medical Association
B Mus — Bachelor of Music
BOTB — British Overseas Trade Board
BpBishop — B Pharm
Bachelor of Pharmacy
B Phil — Bachelor of Philosophy
Br(it) — Britain
British
BR — British Rail
Brig — Brigadier
BSc — Bachelor of Science
BSE — Bovine spongiform encephalopathy
BSI — British Standards Institution
BST — British Summer Time
Bt — Baronet
BTEC — Business and Technology Education Council
B Th — Bachelor of Theology
Btu — British thermal unit
BVM — (*Beata Virgo Maria*) Blessed Virgin Mary
BVMS — Bachelor of Veterinary Medicine and Surgery

c — (*circa*) about
C — Celsius
Centigrade
Conservative
CA — Chartered Accountant (*Scotland*)
CAA — Civil Aviation Authority
CAB — Citizens' Advice Bureau
Cantab — (of) Cambridge
Cantuar: — of Canterbury (*Archbishop*)
CAP — Common Agricultural Policy
Capt — Captain
Caricom — Caribbean Community and Common Market
Carliol: — of Carlisle (*Bishop*)
CB — Companion, Order of the Bath
CBE — Commander, Order of the British Empire
CBI — Confederation of British Industry
CC — Chamber of Commerce
Companion, Order of Canada
City Council
County Council
County Court
CCC — County Cricket Club
CCF — Combined Cadet Force
C Chem — Chartered Chemist
CD — Civil Defence
compact disc
Corps Diplomatique
Cdr — Commander
Cdre — Commodore
CDS — Chief of the Defence Staff
CE — Christian Era
Civil Engineer
C Eng — Chartered Engineer
Cestr: — of Chester (*Bishop*)
CET — Central European Time
Common External Tariff
cf — (*confer*) compare
CF — Chaplain to the Forces
CFC — Chlorofluorocarbon
CFS — Chronic Fatigue Syndrome
CGC — Conspicuous Gallantry Cross
CGM — Conspicuous Gallantry Medal
CGS — Centimetre-gramme-second (*system*)
Chief of General Staff
CH — Companion of Honour
ChB/M — Bachelor/Master of Surgery
CI — Channel Islands
The Imperial Order of the Crown of India
CIA — Central Intelligence Agency
Cicestr: — of Chichester (*Bishop*)
CID — Criminal Investigation Department
CIE — Companion, Order of the Indian Empire
cif — cost, insurance and freight
C-in-C — Commander-in-Chief
CIPFA — Chartered Institute of Public Finance and Accountancy
CIS — Commonwealth of Independent States
CJD — Creutzfeld-Jakob disease
C Lit — Companion of Literature
CLJ — Commander, Order of St Lazarus of Jerusalem
CM — (*Chirurgiae Magister*) Master of Surgery

CMG	Companion, Order of St Michael and St George
CND	Campaign for Nuclear Disarmament
c/o	care of
CO	Commanding Officer conscientious objector
COD	Cash on delivery
C of E	Church of England
COI	Central Office of Information
Col	Colonel
Con	Conservative
cons	consecrated
Cpl	Corporal
CPM	Colonial Police Medal
CPRE	Council for the Protection of Rural England
CPS	Crown Prosecution Service
CPVE	Certificate of Pre-Vocational Education
CRE	Commission for Racial Equality
CSA	Child Support Agency
CSE	Certificate of Secondary Education
CSI	Companion, Order of the Star of India
CVO	Commander, Royal Victorian Order
d	(*denarius*) penny
DA	District Attorney (*USA*)
DBE	Dame Commander, Order of the British Empire
dc	direct current
DC	District Council District of Columbia
DCB	Dame Commander, Order of the Bath
D Ch	(*Doctor Chirurgiae*) Doctor of Surgery
DCL	Doctor of Civil Law
DCM	Distinguished Conduct Medal
DCMG	Dame Commander, Order of St Michael and St George
DCMS	Department for Culture, Media and Sport
DCVO	Dame Commander, Royal Victorian Order
DD	Doctor of Divinity
DDS	Doctor of Dental Surgery
DDT	dichlorodiphenyl-trichloroethane
del	(*delineavit*) he/she drew it
DETR	Department of the Environment, Transport and the Regions
DFC	Distinguished Flying Cross
DfEE	Department for Education and Employment
DFID	Department for International Development
DFM	Distinguished Flying Medal
DG	(*Dei gratia*) By the grace of God
DH	Department of Health
DHA	District Health Authority
Dip Ed	Diploma in Education
Dip HE	Diploma in Higher Education
Dip Tech	Diploma in Technology
DJ	Disc jockey
DL	Deputy Lieutenant
D Litt	Doctor of Letters *or* of Literature
DM	Deutsche Mark
D Mus	Doctor of Music
DNA	deoxyribonucleic acid
DNB	*Dictionary of National Biography*
do	(*ditto*) the same
DoE	Department of the Environment

DOS	Disk operating system (*computer*)
DP	Data processing
D Ph *or* D Phil	Doctor of Philosophy
DPP	Director of Public Prosecutions
Dr	Doctor
D Sc	Doctor of Science
DSC	Distinguished Service Cross
DSM	Distinguished Service Medal
DSO	Companion, Distinguished Service Order
DSS	Department of Social Security
DTI	Department of Trade and Industry
DTP	Desk-top publishing
Dunelm:	of Durham (*Bishop*)
DV	(*Deo volente*) God willing
E	East
Ebor:	of York (*Archbishop*)
EBRD	European Bank for Reconstruction and Development
EC	European Community
ECG	Electrocardiogram
ECGD	Export Credits Guarantee Department
ECSC	European Coal and Steel Community
ECU	European Currency Unit
ED	Efficiency Decoration
EEC	European Economic Community
EEG	Electroencephalogram
EFA	European Fighter Aircraft
EFTA	European Free Trade Association
eg	(*exempli gratia*) for the sake of example
EIB	European Investment Bank
EMS	European Monetary System
EMU	European Monetary Union
EOC	Equal Opportunities Commission
EPSRC	Engineering and Physical Sciences Research Council
ER	(*Elizabetha Regina*) Queen Elizabeth
ERD	Emergency Reserve Decoration
ERM	Exchange Rate Mechanism
ERNIE	Electronic random number indicator equipment
ESA	European Space Agency
ESP	Extra-sensory perception
ESRC	Economic and Social Research Council
ETA	*Euzkadi ta Askatasuna* (Basque separatist organization)
et al	(*et alibi*) and elsewhere (*et alii*) and others
etc	(*et cetera*) and the other things/ and so forth
et seq	(*et sequentia*) and the following
EU	European Union
Euratom	European Atomic Energy Commission
Exon:	of Exeter (*Bishop*)
f	(*forte*) loud
F	Fahrenheit Fellow of
FA	Football Association
FANY	First Aid Nursing Yeomanry
FAO	Food and Agriculture Organization (*UN*)

FBA	Fellow, British Academy
FBAA	Fellow, British Association of Accountants and Auditors
FBI	Federal Bureau of Investigation
FBIM	Fellow, British Institute of Management
FBS	Fellow, Botanical Society
FC	Football Club
FCA	Fellow, Institute of Chartered Accountants in England and Wales
FCCA	Fellow, Chartered Association of Certified Accountants
FCGI	Fellow, City and Guilds of London Institute
FCIA	Fellow, Corporation of Insurance Agents
FCIArb	Fellow, Chartered Institute of Arbitrators
FCIB	Fellow, Chartered Institute of Bankers Fellow, Corporation of Insurance Brokers
FCIBSE	Fellow, Chartered Institution of Building Services Engineers
FCII	Fellow, Chartered Insurance Institute
FCIPS	Fellow, Chartered Institute of Purchasing and Supply
FCIS	Fellow, Institute of Chartered Secretaries and Administrators
FCIT	Fellow, Chartered Institute of Transport
FCMA	Fellow, Chartered Institute of Management Accountants
FCO	Foreign and Commonwealth Office
FCP	Fellow, College of Preceptors
FD	(*Fidei Defensor*) Defender of the Faith
FE	Further Education
fec	(*fecit*) made this
ff	(*fecerunt*) made this (*pl*) folios following
ff	(*fortissimo*) very loud
FFA	Fellow, Faculty of Actuaries (*Scotland*) Fellow, Institute of Financial Accountants
FFAS	Fellow, Faculty of Architects and Surveyors
FFCM	Fellow, Faculty of Community Medicine
FFPHM	Fellow, Faculty of Public Health Medicine
FGS	Fellow, Geological Society
FHS	Fellow – Heraldry Society
FHSM	Fellow, Institute of Health Service Management
FIA	Fellow, Institute of Actuaries
FIBiol	Fellow, Institute of Biology
FICE	Fellow, Institution of Civil Engineers
FICS	Fellow, Institution of Chartered Shipbrokers
FIEE	Fellow, Institution of Electrical Engineers
FIERE	Fellow, Institution of Electronic and Radio Engineers
FIFA	International Association Football Federation
FIM	Fellow, Institute of Metals
FIMM	Fellow, Institution of Mining and Metallurgy
FInstF	Fellow, Institute of Fuel
FInstP	Fellow, Institute of Physics
FIQS	Fellow, Institute of Quantity Surveyors

FIS	Fellow, Institute of Statisticians	FRPharmS	Fellow, Royal Pharmaceutical Society	HGV	Heavy Goods Vehicle
FJI	Fellow, Institute of Journalists	FRPS	Fellow, Royal Photographic Society	HH	Her/His Highness Her/His Honour
fl	(*floruit*) flourished				His Holiness
FLA	Fellow, Library Association	FRS	Fellow, Royal Society	HIM	Her/His Imperial Majesty
FLS	Fellow, Linnaean Society	FRSA	Fellow, Royal Society of Arts	HIV	Human immunodeficiency
FM	Field Marshal	FRSC	Fellow, Royal Society of		virus
	frequency modulation		Chemistry	HJS	(*hic jacet sepultus*) here lies
fo	folio	FRSE	Fellow, Royal Society of		buried
FO	Flying Officer		Edinburgh	HM	Her/His Majesty('s)
fob	free on board	FRSH	Fellow, Royal Society of	HMAS	Her/His Majesty's Australian
FPhS	Fellow, Philosophical Society		Health		Ship
FRAD	Fellow, Royal Academy of Dancing	FRSL	Fellow, Royal Society of Literature	HMC HMI	Headmasters' Conference Her/His Majesty's Inspector
FRAeS	Fellow, Royal Aeronautical	FRTPI	Fellow, Royal Town Planning	HML	Her/His Majesty's Lieutenant
	Society		Institute	HMS	Her/His Majesty's Ship
FRAI	Fellow, Royal Anthropological	FSA	Fellow, Society of Antiquaries	HMSO	Her/His Majesty's Stationery
	Institute	FSS	Fellow, Royal Statistical		Office
FRAM	Fellow, Royal Academy of		Society	HNC	Higher National Certificate
	Music	FSVA	Fellow, Incorporated Society	HND	Higher National Diploma
FRAS	Fellow, Royal Asiatic Society		of Valuers and Auctioneers	HOLMES	Home Office Large Major
	Fellow, Royal Astronomical	FT	*Financial Times*		Enquiry System
	Society	FTI	Fellow, Textile Institute	Hon	Honorary
FRBS	Fellow, Royal Botanic Society	FTII	Fellow, Chartered Institute of		Honourable
	Fellow, Royal Society of		Taxation	hp	horse power
	British Sculptors	FZS	Fellow, Zoological Society	HP	Hire purchase
FRCA	Fellow, Royal College of			HQ	Headquarters
	Anaesthetists	G7	Group of Seven (Canada,	HR	Human resources
FRCGP	Fellow, Royal College of		France, Germany, Italy, Japan,	HRH	Her/His Royal Highness
	General Practitioners		UK, USA)	HSE	Health and Safety Executive
FRCM	Fellow, Royal College of	GATT	General Agreement on Tariffs		(*hic sepultus est*) here lies buried
	Music		and Trade	HSH	Her/His Serene Highness
FRCO	Fellow, Royal College of	GBE	Dame/Knight Grand Cross,	HWM	High water mark
	Organists		Order of the British Empire		
FRCOG	Fellow, Royal College of	GC	George Cross	I	Island
	Obstetricians and	GCB	Dame/Knight Grand Cross,	IAAS	Incorporated Association of
	Gynaecologists		Order of the Bath		Architects and Surveyors
FRCP	Fellow, Royal College of	GCE	General Certificate of	IAEA	International Atomic Energy
	Physicians, London		Education		Agency
FRCPath	Fellow, Royal College of	GCHQ	Government Communications	IATA	International Air Transport
	Pathologists		Headquarters		Association
FRCPE *or*	Fellow, Royal College of	GCIE	Knight Grand Commander,	ibid	(*ibidem*) in the same place
FRCPEd	Physicians, Edinburgh		Order of the Indian Empire	IBRD	International Bank for
FRCPI	Fellow, Royal College of	GCLJ	Knight Grand Cross, Order of		Reconstruction and
	Physicians, Ireland		St Lazarus of Jerusalem		Development
FRCPsych	Fellow, Royal College of	GCMG	Dame/Knight Grand Cross,	ICAO	International Civil Aviation
	Psychiatrists		Order of St Michael and St		Organization
FRCR	Fellow, Royal College of		George	ICBM	Inter-continental ballistic
	Radiologists	GCSE	General Certificate of		missile
FRCS	Fellow, Royal College of		Secondary Education	ICFTU	International Confederation of
	Surgeons of England	GCSI	Knight Grand Commander,		Free Trade Unions
FRCSE *or*	Fellow, Royal College of		Order of the Star of India	ICJ	International Court of Justice
FRCSEd	Surgeons of Edinburgh	GCVO	Dame/Knight Grand Cross,	ICRC	International Committee of the
FRCSGlas	Fellow, Royal College of		Royal Victorian Order		Red Cross
	Physicians and Surgeons of	GDP	Gross domestic product	id	(*idem*) the same
	Glasgow	Gen	General	IDA	International Development
FRCSI	Fellow, Royal College of	GHQ	General Headquarters		Association
	Surgeons in Ireland	GM	George Medal	IDD	International direct dialling
FRCVS	Fellow, Royal College of	GMB	General, Municipal,	ie	(*id est*) that is
	Veterinary Surgeons		Boilermakers and Allied	IEA	International Energy Agency
FREconS	Fellow, Royal Economic		Trades Union	IFAD	International Fund for
	Society	GMT	Greenwich Mean Time		Agricultural Development
FREng	Fellow, Royal Academy of	GNP	Gross national product	IFC	International Finance
	Engineering	GNVQ	General National Vocational		Corporation
FRGS	Fellow, Royal Geographical		Qualification	IHS	(*Iesus Hominum Salvator*) Jesus
	Society	GOC	General Officer Commanding		the Saviour of Mankind
FRHistS	Fellow, Royal Historical	GP	General Practitioner	ILO	International Labour Office/
	Society	Gp Capt	Group Captain		Organization
FRHS	Fellow, Royal Horticultural	GSA	Girls' Schools Association	ILR	Independent local radio
	Society			IMF	International Monetary Fund
FRIBA	Fellow, Royal Institute of	HAC	Honourable Artillery	IMO	International Maritime
	British Architects		Company		Organization
FRICS	Fellow, Royal Institution of	HB	His Beatitude	Inc	Incorporated
	Chartered Surveyors	HBM	Her/His Britannic Majesty('s)	incog	(*incognito*) unknown,
FRMetS	Fellow, Royal Meteorological	HCF	Highest common factor		unrecognized
	Society		Honorary Chaplain to the	INLA	Irish National Liberation
FRMS	Fellow, Royal Microscopical		Forces		Army
	Society	HE	Her/His Excellency	in loc	(*in loco*) in its place
FRNS	Fellow, Royal Numismatic		Higher Education	Inmarsat	International Maritime
	Society		His Eminence		Satellite Organization

INRI — (*Iesus Nazarenus Rex Iudaeorum*) Jesus of Nazareth, King of the Jews
inst — (*instant*) current month
Intelsat — International Telecommunications Satellite Organization
Interpol — International Criminal Police Commission
IOC — International Olympic Committee
IOM — Isle of Man
IOU — I owe you
IOW — Isle of Wight
IQ — Intelligence quotient
IRA — Irish Republican Army
IRC — International Red Cross
Is — Islands
ISBN — International Standard Book Number
ISO — Imperial Service Order; International Standards Organization
ISSN — International Standard Serial Number
ITC — Independent Television Commission
ITN — Independent Television News
ITU — International Telecommunication Union
ITV — Independent Television

JP — Justice of the Peace

K — Köchel numeration (*of Mozart's works*)
KBE — Knight Commander, Order of the British Empire
KCB — Knight Commander, Order of the Bath
KCIE — Knight Commander, Order of the Indian Empire
KCLJ — Knight Commander, Order of St Lazarus of Jerusalem
KCMG — Knight Commander, Order of St Michael and St George
KCSI — Knight Commander, Order of the Star of India
KCVO — Knight Commander, Royal Victorian Order
KG — Knight of the Garter
KGB — (*Komitet Gosudarstvennoi Besopasnosti*) Committee of State Security (*USSR*)
kHz — kiloHertz
KKK — Ku Klux Klan
KLJ — Knight, Order of St Lazarus of Jerusalem
ko — knock out (*boxing*)
KP — Knight, Order of St Patrick
KStJ — Knight, Order of St John of Jerusalem
Kt — Knight
KT — Knight of the Thistle
kV — Kilovolt
kW — Kilowatt
kWh — Kilowatt hour

L — Liberal
Lab — Labour
Lat — Latitude
lbw — leg before wicket
lc — lower case (*printing*)
LCJ — Lord Chief Justice
LCM — Least/lowest common multiple
LD — Liberal Democrat
LDS — Licentiate in Dental Surgery
LEA — Local Education Authority

LHD — (*Literarum Humaniorum Doctor*) Doctor of Humane Letters/ Literature
Lib — Liberal
Lic — (*Licenciado*) lawyer (*Spanish*)
Lic Med — Licentiate in Medicine
Lit — Literary
Lit Hum — (*Literae Humaniores*) Faculty of classics and philosophy, Oxford
Litt D — Doctor of Letters
LJ — Lord Justice
LLB — Bachelor of Laws
LLD — Doctor of Laws
LLM — Master of Laws
LM — Licentiate in Midwifery
LMS — Local management in schools
LMSSA — Licentiate in Medicine and Surgery, Society of Apothecaries
loc cit — (*loco citato*) in the place cited
log — logarithm
Londin: — of London (*Bishop*)
Long — Longitude
LS — (*loco sigilli*) place of the seal
LSA — Licentiate of Society of Apothecaries
Lsd — (*Librae, solidi, denarii*) £, shillings and pence
LSE — London School of Economics and Political Science
Lt — Lieutenant
LTA — Lawn Tennis Association
Ltd — Limited (liability)
LTh *or* L Theol — Licentiate in Theology
LVO — Lieutenant, Royal Victorian Order
LW — long wave
LWM — Low water mark

M — Member of; Monsieur
MA — Master of Arts
MAFF — Ministry of Agriculture, Fisheries and Food
Maj — Major
max — maximum
MB — Bachelor of Medicine
MBA — Master of Business Administration
MBE — Member, Order of the British Empire
MC — Master of Ceremonies; Military Cross
MCC — Marylebone Cricket Club
MCh(D) — Master of (Dental) Surgery
MD — Managing Director; Doctor of Medicine
MDS — Master of Dental Surgery
ME — Middle English; Myalgic Encephalomyelitis
MEC — Member of Executive Council
MEd — Master of Education
mega — one million times
MEP — Member of the European Parliament
MFH — Master of Foxhounds
Mgr — Monsignor
MI — Military Intelligence
micro — one-millionth part
milli — one-thousandth part
min — minimum
MIRAS — Mortgage Interest Relief at Source
MLA — Member of Legislative Assembly
MLC — Member of Legislative Council
MLitt — Master of Letters
Mlle — Mademoiselle

MLR — Minimum lending rate
MM — Military Medal
Mme — Madame
MN — Merchant Navy
MO — Medical Officer/Orderly
MoD — Ministry of Defence
MoT — Ministry of Transport
MP — Member of Parliament; Military Police
mph — miles per hour
M Phil — Master of Philosophy
MR — Master of the Rolls
MRC — Medical Research Council
MS — Master of Surgery; Manuscript (*pl* MSS); Multiple Sclerosis
MSc — Master of Science
MSF — Manufacturing, Science and Finance Union
MSP — Member of the Scottish Parliament
MTh — Master of Theology
Mus B/D — Bachelor/Doctor of Music
MV — Merchant Vessel; Motor Vessel
MVO — Member, Royal Victorian Order
MW — medium wave

N — North
n/a — not applicable; not available
NAAFI — Navy, Army and Air Force Institutes
NASA — National Aeronautics and Space Administration
NAS/UWT — National Association of Schoolmasters/Union of Women Teachers
NATO — North Atlantic Treaty Organization
NB — New Brunswick; (*nota bene*) note well
NCIS — National Criminal Intelligence Service
NCO — Non-commissioned officer
NDPB — Non-departmental public body
NEB — New English Bible
nem con — (*nemine contradicente*) no one contradicting
NERC — Natural Environment Research Council
nes — not elsewhere specified
NFT — National Film Theatre
NFU — National Farmers' Union
NHS — National Health Service
NI — National Insurance; Northern Ireland
NIV — New International Version (*of Bible*)
No — (*numero*) number
non seq — (*non sequitur*) it does not follow
Norvic: — of Norwich (*Bishop*)
NP — Notary Public
NRA — National Rifle Association
NS — New Style (*calendar*); Nova Scotia
NSPCC — National Society for the Prevention of Cruelty to Children
NSW — New South Wales
NT — National Theatre; National Trust; New Testament
NUJ — National Union of Journalists
NUM — National Union of Mineworkers
NUS — National Union of Students
NUT — National Union of Teachers

NVQ	National Vocational Qualification
NWT	Northwest Territory
NY	New York
NZ	New Zealand
OAPEC	Organization of Arab Petroleum Exporting Countries
OAS	Organization of American States
OAU	Organization of African Unity
Ob *or* obit	died
OBE	Officer, Order of the British Empire
OC	Officer Commanding
ODA	Overseas Development Administration
OE	Old English
	omissions excepted
OECD	Organization for Economic Co-operation and Development
OED	*Oxford English Dictionary*
Offer	Office of Electricity Regulation
Ofgas	Office of Gas Supply
OFM	Order of Friars Minor (*Franciscans*)
Ofsted	Office for Standards in Education
OFT	Office of Fair Trading
Oftel	Office of Telecommunications
Ofwat	Office of Water Services
OHMS	On Her/His Majesty's Service
OM	Order of Merit
OND	Ordinary National Diploma
ONO	or near offer
ONS	Office for National Statistics
op	(*opus*) work
OP	Opposite prompt side (*of theatre*)
	Order of Preachers (*Dominicans*)
	out of print (*books*)
op cit	(*opere citato*) in the work cited
OPCS	Office of Population Censuses and Surveys
OPEC	Organization of Petroleum Exporting Countries
OPRAF	Office of Passenger Rail Franchising
OPS	Office of Public Service
ORR	Office of the Rail Regulator
OS	Old Style (*calendar*) Ordnance Survey
OSA	Order of St Augustine
OSB	Order of St Benedict
OSCE	Organization for Security and Co-operation in Europe
O St J	Officer, Order of St John of Jerusalem
OT	Old Testament
OTC	Officers' Training Corps
Oxon	(of) Oxford Oxfordshire
p	page
p	(*piano*) softly
PA	Personal Assistant Press Association
PAYE	Pay as You Earn
pc	(*per centum*) in the hundred
PC	personal computer Police Constable politically correct Privy Counsellor
PCC	Press Complaints Commission
PDSA	People's Dispensary for Sick Animals

PE	Physical Education
PEP	Personal equity plan
Petriburg:	of Peterborough (*Bishop*)
PFI	Private Finance Initiative
PGA	Professional Golfers Association
PGCE	Postgraduate Certificate of Education
PhD	Doctor of Philosophy
pinx(it)	he/she painted it
pl	plural
PLA	Port of London Authority
PLC	Public Limited Company
PLO	Palestine Liberation Organization
pm	(*post meridiem*) after noon
PM	Prime Minister
PMRAFNS	Princess Mary's Royal Air Force Nursing Service
PO	Petty Officer Pilot Officer Post Office postal order
POW	Prisoner of War
PP	pages (*per procurationem*) by proxy
PPARC	Particle Physics and Astronomy Research Council
PPS	Parliamentary Private Secretary
PR	Proportional representation Public relations
PRA	President of the Royal Academy
Pro tem	(*pro tempore*) for the time being
Prox	(*proximo*) next month
PRS	President of the Royal Society
PRSE	President of the Royal Society of Edinburgh
PSpsalmPS	(*postscriptum*) postscript
PSBR	Public sector borrowing requirement
psc	passed Staff College
PSV	Public Service Vehicle
PTA	Parent-Teacher Association
Pte	Private
PTO	Please turn over
PVC	Polyvinyl chloride
QARANC	Queen Alexandra's Royal Army Nursing Corps
QARNNS	Queen Alexandra's Royal Naval Nursing Service
QB(D)	Queen's Bench (Division)
QC	Queen's Counsel
QED	(*quod erat demonstrandum*) which was to be proved
QGM	Queen's Gallantry Medal
QHC	Queen's Honorary Chaplain
QHDS	Queen's Honorary Dental Surgeon
QHNS	Queen's Honorary Nursing Sister
QHP	Queen's Honorary Physician
QHS	Queen's Honorary Surgeon
QMG	Quartermaster General
QPM	Queen's Police Medal
QS	Quarter Sessions
QSO	Quasi-stellar object (quasar) Queen's Service Order
quango	quasi-autonomous non-governmental organization
qv	(*quod vide*) which see
R	(*Regina*) Queen (*Rex*) King
RA	Royal Academy/Academician Royal Artillery
RAC	Royal Armoured Corps Royal Automobile Club

RADA	Royal Academy of Dramatic Art
RADC	Royal Army Dental Corps
RAE	Royal Aerospace Establishment
RAEC	Royal Army Educational Corps
RAeS	Royal Aeronautical Society
RAF	Royal Air Force
RAM	Random-access memory (*computer*) Royal Academy of Music
RAMC	Royal Army Medical Corps
RAN	Royal Australian Navy
RAOC	Royal Army Ordnance Corps
RAPC	Royal Army Pay Corps
RAVC	Royal Army Veterinary Corps
RBG	Royal Botanic Garden
RBS	Royal Society of British Sculptors
RC	Red Cross Roman Catholic
RCM	Royal College of Music
RCN	Royal Canadian Navy
RCT	Royal Corps of Transport
RD	Refer to drawer (*banking*) Royal Naval and Royal Marine Forces Reserve Decoration Rural Dean
RDI	Royal Designer for Industry
RE	Religious Education Royal Engineers
REME	Royal Electrical and Mechanical Engineers
Rep	Representative Republican
Rev(d)	Reverend
RFU	Rugby Football Union
RGN	Registered General Nurse
RGS	Royal Geographical Society
RHA	Regional Health Authority
RHS	Royal Horticultural Society
RI	Rhode Island Royal Institute of Painters in Watercolours Royal Institution
RIBA	Royal Institute of British Architects
RIP	(*Requiescat in pace*) May he/she rest in peace
RIR	Royal Irish Regiment
RL	Rugby League
RM	Registered Midwife Royal Marines
RMA	Royal Military Academy
RMN	Registered Mental Nurse
RMT	National Union of Rail, Maritime and Transport Workers
RN	Royal Navy
RNIB	Royal National Institute for the Blind
RNID	Royal National Institute for the Deaf
RNLI	Royal National Lifeboat Institution
RNMH	Registered Nurse for the Mentally Handicapped
RNR	Royal Naval Reserve
RNVR	Royal Naval Volunteer Reserve
RNXS	Royal Naval Auxiliary Service
RNZN	Royal New Zealand Navy
Ro	(*Recto*) on the right-hand page
ROC	Royal Observer Corps
Roffen:	of Rochester (*Bishop*)
ROI	Royal Institute of Oil Painters
ROM	Read-only memory (*computer*)
RoSPA	Royal Society for the Prevention of Accidents

RP	Royal Society of Portrait Painters
rpm	revolutions per minute
RRC	Lady of Royal Red Cross
RSA	Republic of South Africa
	Royal Scottish Academician
	Royal Society of Arts
RSC	Royal Shakespeare Company
RSCN	Registered Sick Children's Nurse
RSE	Royal Society of Edinburgh
RSM	Regimental Sergeant Major
RSPB	Royal Society for the Protection of Birds
RSPCA	Royal Society for the Prevention of Cruelty to Animals
RSV	Revised Standard Version (of *Bible*)
RSVP	(Répondez, s'il vous plaît) Please reply
RSW	Royal Scottish Society of Painters in Watercolours
RTPI	Royal Town Planning Institute
RU	Rugby Union
RUC	Royal Ulster Constabulary
RV	Revised Version (*of Bible*)
RVM	Royal Victorian Medal
RWS	Royal Water Colour Society
RYS	Royal Yacht Squadron
s	second
	(*solidus*) shilling
S	South
SA	Salvation Army
	South Africa
	South America
	South Australia
SAE	stamped addressed envelope
Salop	Shropshire
Sarum:	of Salisbury (*Bishop*)
SAS	Special Air Service Regiment
SBN	Standard Book Number
SBS	Special Boat Squadron
ScD	Doctor of Science
SCM	State Certified Midwife
SDLP	Social Democratic and Labour Party
SEAQ	Stock Exchange Automated Quotations system
SEN	State Enrolled Nurse
SERPS	State Earnings Related Pension Scheme
SFO	Serious Fraud Office
SHMIS	Society of Headmasters and Headmistresses of Independent Schools
SI	(*Système International d'Unités*) International System of Units
	Statutory Instrument
sic	so written
Sig	Signature
	Signor
SJ	Society of Jesus (*Jesuits*)
SLD	Social and Liberal Democrats
SMP	Statutory Maternity Pay
SNP	Scottish National Party
SOE	Special Operations Executive
SOS	Save Our Souls (*distress signal*)
sp	(*sine prole*) without issue
spgr	specific gravity
SPQR	(*Senatus Populusque Romanus*) The Senate and People of Rome
SRN	State Registered Nurse
SRO	Self Regulating Organizations
SS	Saints
	Schutzstaffel (Nazi paramilitary organization)
	Steamship

SSC	Solicitor before Supreme Court (*Scotland*)
SSF	Society of St Francis
SSN	Standard Serial Number
SSP	Statutory Sick Pay
SSSI	Site of special scientific interest
STD	(*Sacrae Theologiae Doctor*) Doctor of Sacred Theology
	Subscriber trunk dialling
stet	let it stand (*printing*)
stp	Standard temperature and pressure
STP	(*Sacrae Theologiae Professor*) Professor of Sacred Theology
Sub Lt	Sub-Lieutenant
SVQ	Scottish Vocational Qualification
TA	Territorial Army
TB	Tuberculosis
TCCB	Test and County Cricket Board
TD	Territorial Efficiency Decoration
TEC	Training and Enterprise Council
TEFL	Teaching English as a foreign language
temp	temperature
	temporary employee
TES	Times Educational Supplement
TGWU	Transport and General Workers' Union
THES	Times Higher Education Supplement
TLS	Times Literary Supplement
TNT	trinitrotoluene (*explosive*)
trans	translated
trs	transpose (*printing*)
TRH	Their Royal Highnesses
TT	Teetotal
	Tourist Trophy (*motorcycle races*)
	Tuberculin tested
TUC	Trades Union Congress
TVEI	Technical and Vocational Education Initiative
U	Unionist
UAE	United Arab Emirates
uc	upper case (*printing*)
UCAS	Universities and Colleges Admissions Service
UCATT	Union of Construction, Allied Trades and Technicians
UCL	University College London
UDA	Ulster Defence Association
UDI	Unilateral Declaration of Independence
UDM	Union of Democratic Mineworkers
UDR	Ulster Defence Regiment
UEFA	Union of European Football Associations
UFF	Ulster Freedom Fighters
UFO	Unidentified flying object
UHF	ultra-high frequency
UK	United Kingdom
UKAEA	UK Atomic Energy Authority
UN	United Nations
UNESCO	United Nations Educational, Scientific and Cultural Organization
UNHCR	United Nations High Commissioner for Refugees
UNICEF	United Nations Children's Fund
UNIDO	United Nations Industrial Development Organization

Unita	National Union for the Total Independence of Angola
UPU	Universal Postal Union
URC	United Reformed Church
US(A)	United States (of America)
USDAW	Union of Shop, Distributive and Allied Workers
USM	Unlisted Securities Market
USSR	Union of Soviet Socialist Republics
UTC	Co-ordinated Universal Time system
UVF	Ulster Volunteer Force
v	(*versus*) against
VA	Vicar Apostolic
	Victoria and Albert Order
VAD	Voluntary Aid Detachment
V and A	Victoria and Albert Museum
VAT	Value added tax
VC	Victoria Cross
VCR	video cassette recorder
VD	Venereal disease
	Volunteer Officers' Decoration
VDU	Visual display unit
Ven	Venerable
VHF	very high frequency
VIP	Very important person
Vo	(*Verso*) on the left-hand page
VRD	Royal Naval Volunteer Reserve Officers' Decoration
VSO	Voluntary Service Overseas
VTOL	Vertical take-off and landing (*aircraft*)
W	West
WCC	World Council of Churches
WEA	Workers' Educational Association
WEU	Western European Union
WFTU	World Federation of Trade Unions
WHO	World Health Organization
WI	West Indies
	Women's Institute
Winton:	of Winchester (*Bishop*)
WIPO	World Intellectual Property Organization
WMO	World Meteorological Organization
WO	Warrant Officer
WRAC	Women's Royal Army Corps
WRAF	Women's Royal Air Force
WRNS	Women's Royal Naval Service
WRVS	Women's Royal Voluntary Service
WS	Writer to the Signet
WTO	World Trade Organization
YMCA	Young Men's Christian Association
YWCA	Young Women's Christian Association

Ψ = seaport

Index

London *continued*
 City of, MP, 241
 civic dignitaries, 550
 clubs, 717–8
 Corporation of, 550–2
 distances by air from, 111
 education authorities, 441
 galleries, 593–4
 High Sheriff, 540
 Lord Lieutenant, 540
 Lord Mayor, 550
 markets, 600
 Museum of, 322, 594
 museums, 594
 parks, 600
 Passport Office, 782
 places of interest, 598–602
 police forces, 374, 377
 population, 785
 sights of, 598–602
 stipendiary magistrates, 362
 tourist board, 602
 Traffic Director, 299
 universities, 446–7, 448–9, 452
Londonderry, 566, 568
 East, MP, 268
London International Financial Futures
 and Options Exchange, 636
London Metal Exchange, 636
London Planetarium, 600
London Port Authority, 330
London Regional Transport, 318
London Zoo, 600
Lonsdale, Westmorland and, MP, 260
Lord, 150
Lord Advocate, 272, 318, 363
 Department, 318
Lord Chamberlain, Office, 119
Lord Chancellor, 220–1, 272, 318, 353
Lord Chancellor's Advisory Committee on
 Statute Law, 319
Lord Chancellor's Department, 318–9
 Visitors, 357
Lord Chief Justice:
 of England, 353, 355
 of Northern Ireland, 367
Lord Great Chamberlain, 138, 319
 Office, 319
Lord High Admiral, 388
Lord High Chancellor, 220–1, 272, 318,
 353
Lord High Commissioner, Church of
 Scotland, 414
Lord Justice Clerk, 364
Lord Justice General, 364
Lord Justices of Appeal, 354
 Northern Ireland, 367
Lord Lieutenants, 522–3
 England, 540
 Northern Ireland, 568
 Scotland, 563
 Wales, 558
Lord Lyon, Court of the, 280
Lord Mayor:
 London, 550
 office of, 523
Lord Mayor's Day, 9, 550
Lord Mayors, 543–9, 558, 568
Lord President of the Council, *see*
 President of the
Lord Privy Seal, 272, 319
 Office, 319
Lords-in-Waiting, 120, 273
Lords of Appeal in Ordinary, 157, 353
Lords of Parliament, 136, 147–56
Lords of Session, 364–5
Lord Steward, 119, 146
Lord Warden of the Stannaries, 294
Lothian:
 Education Authorities, 442
 West, 531, 564

Lothian and Borders Police Authority, 376
Lothian, East, 531, 564
 Lord Lieutenant, 563
 MP, 265
Lothian, West, Lord Lieutenant, 563
Lotteries and gaming, 611
Loudoun, Kilmarnock and, MP, 266
Loughborough:
 Archdeacon, 407
 MP, 250
 University, 449
Louisiana, 1057
Louth and Horncastle, MP, 250
Lower Saxony, 886
Luanda, 785, 802
Ludlow:
 Archdeacon, 407
 Bishop (Suffragan), 406
 MP, 250
Lunar cycle, 87
Lunar occultations (2000), 66–7
Lundy, 532
Lunesdale, Morecambe and, MP, 251
Lusaka, 786, 1071
Lutheran Church, 418–9
Luton, 527, 543
 airport, 504
 Education Authority, 440
 MPs, 250
 University, 449
Luxembourg, 788, 942–3
 city, 788, 942
 EU membership, 773
 map, 819
Luzon, 990
Lydd airport, 504
Lynn:
 Archdeacon, 408
 Bishop (Suffragan), 408

Maastricht, Treaty of, 774, 777, 779, 782
Macao, 788, 995
 map, 845
Macclesfield, 529, 546
 Archdeacon, 405
 MP, 250
McDonald Islands, 810
Macedonia, Republic of, 788, 943–4
Madagascar, 105, 786, 944–5
Madame Tussaud's Exhibition, 600
Madeira, 789, 995
Madrid, 789, 1023
Magazines, 687–92
 awards, 683
Magherafelt, 568
Magistrates:
 Courts' Service Inspectorate, 319
 lay, 353
 stipendiary, 361–2, 366
Magnetic storms, 77–8
Magnetism, terrestrial, 77–8
Mahé Island, 1012
Maidenhead, MP, 250
Maidenhead, Windsor and, 544
 Education Authority, 441
Maidstone, 529, 546
 Archdeacon, 402
 Bishop (Suffragan), 402
Maidstone and the Weald, MP, 250
Mail services, 513–5
 airmail zones, 518–9
Maine, 1057
Maintenance orders, legal notes, 658
Majorca, 1025
Majuro, 951
Makerfield, MP, 250
Malabo, 785, 870
Malawi, 786, 945–6
Malaysia, 788, 946–8
 map, 904

Maldives, 788, 948–9
Maldon, 529, 546
Maldon and Chelmsford East, MP, 250
Malé, 788, 948
Mali, 786, 949–50
 map, 976
Malling, Tonbridge and, 530, 548
 MP, 258
Malta, 788, 950–1
Malvern Hills, 529, 546
Mamoundzou, 786, 881
Management, qualifying bodies, 455
Managua, 787, 973
Manama, 787, 814
Manchester, 527, 537, 543
 airport, 504
 Archdeacon, 408
 Bishop, 164, 408
 Education Authority, 440
 MPs, 250
 universities, 449
Manchester, Greater, Police Authority, 375
Manila, 788, 990
Man, Isle of, 569, 789
 Archdeacon, 410
 currency, 613
 Education Authority, 442
 flag, 569
 Police Authority, 376
 population, 113
Man, Sodor and, Bishop, 410
Manitoba, 838
Mankind, development of, 94–6
Manpower Economics, Office of, 320
Mansfield, 529, 546
 MP, 250–1
Maputo, 786, 963
Mariana Islands, Northern, 789, 1055,
 1057, 1060
Marine Accidents Investigation Branch,
 298
Marine nature reserves, 578
Maritime and Coastguard Agency, 299
Maritime Museum, National, 322–3
Maritime Organization, International, 758–
 9
Maritime Satellite Organization,
 International, 756
Marlborough House, 600
Marquesses, 138–9
 courtesy titles, 165
 forms of address, 135, 138
 premier, 137, 138, 139
Marriage:
 certificates, 653, 665, 666
 legal notes, 665–7
 licences, 665, 666
 registration, 326, 339, 653, 665, 666
 statistics, 114
Mars, 72, 76
 discoveries, 1179
 monthly data (2000), 17, 18, 21, 22, etc.
 phenomena (2000), 16, 20, 24, etc.
 satellites, 76
Marshall Islands, 789, 951–2
Marshals of the Royal Air Force, 392
Martinique, 787, 880
 map, 859
Martinmas (term day), 9
Maryhill (Glasgow), MP, 265–6
Maryland, 1057
Maseru, 786, 936
Masonic year, 88
Mass, measurement, 1235
Massachusetts, 1057
Master of the Horse, 119
Master of The Queen's Music, 120
Master of the Rolls, 354
Mata-Utu, 789, 881
Materials studies, qualifying body, 459

Scotland *continued*
  geographical features, 560
  health boards, 479–80
  history, 561–2
  Inland Revenue, 312
  islands, 560–1
  judicature, 363–5
  kings and queens, 132–3
  local authorities, 525–6, 564
  local authority expenditure, 526
  local government, 521–31
  Local Health Care Co-operatives, 478
  lord lieutenants, 563
  map, 563
  MEPS, 271
  MPs, 263–7
  National Archives, 334
  national galleries, 282, 596–7
  National Health Service, 339, 478–84
  National Library, 316–7
  national museums, 323, 596–7
  parliament, 562–3, 565, 1161
  police authorities, 376
  political parties, 224–5
  population statistics, 112–5, 560
  prison service, 382–3
  Queen's household, 120
  Roman Catholic Church, 416
  Royal Commission on Ancient and
    Historical Monuments, 307
  state of parties, 565
  transport, 504–12
  universities, 434–5, 444–51
  Water Services, 498
Scotland Office, 336
  Ministers, 336
  Secretary of State, 336
Scottish Agricultural Museum, 323, 597
Scottish Agricultural Science Agency, 338
Scottish Arts Council, 281
  National Lottery awards, 611
Scottish Ballet, 1143–4, 1147
Scottish Borders, 531, 564
  Education Authority, 442
Scottish Criminal Cases Review
  Commission, 336
Scottish Enterprise, 336
Scottish Environment Protection Agency,
  337
Scottish Excecutive, Education
  Department, 338
Scottish Executive, 337–40
  Development Department, 338
  Enterprise and Lifelong Learning Exec-
    utive, 338–9
  Environmental Affairs Group, 337
  First Minister, 337
  Health Department, 339
  Pensions Agency, 338
  Rural Affairs Department, 337
Scottish Fisheries Protection Agency, 338
Scottish Homes, 340
Scottish Law Commission, 315
Scottish Legal Aid Board, 315
Scottish Legal Services Ombudsman, 316
Scottish National Gallery of Modern Art,
  282, 597
Scottish National Party, 225
  financial support, 223
Scottish National Portrait Gallery, 282,
  597
Scottish Natural Heritage, 340
Scottish Office:
  Ministers, 272
  Secretary of State, 272
Scottish Opera, 1159
Scottish Pariamentary Commissioner for
  Administration, 340
Scottish Prisons Complaints Commission,
  340

Scottish Prisons Service, 382–3
Scottish Record Office, 334
Scottish Records Advisory Council, 334
Scottish Solicitors Discipline Tribunal, 373
Scottish Sports Council, National Lottery
  awards, 611
Scottish Tourist Board, 343
Scottish United Services Museum, 323
Scottish Vocational Qualifications (SVQs),
  433
Scunthorpe, MP, 255
Sea Fisheries Inspectorate, 278
Sea Fish Industry Authority, 340
Seaport traffic, 512
Seas, areas and depths, 104
Seasons, defined, 15
Second, defined, 74
Secretaries of State, 272
  salaries, 276
Secret Intelligence Service, 341
Security and Intelligence Services, 340–1
Security Council, UN, 767
Security Service, 341
  Commissioner, 341
  Tribunal, 341
Sedgefield, 529, 547
  MP, 255
Sedgemoor, 529, 547
Sefton, 528, 543
  Education Authority, 440
  Knowsley North and, MP, 248–9
Selby, 529, 547
  Bishop (Suffragan), 402
  MP, 255
Select committees, 221
  House of Commons, 220
  House of Lords, 217
Selly Oak (Birmingham), MP, 237–8
Senegal, 786, 1011–2
  map, 976
Senior Salaries Review Body, 335
Sentence Review Commissioners, 341
Seoul, 787, 928
Separation, legal notes, 657
Serbia, 1070
  map, 1069
Serbian Orthodox Church, 420
Serious Fraud Office, 341
SERPS, 487–8
Services Broadcasting, 683
Sevenoaks, 529, 547
  MP, 255
Seventh-Day Adventist Church, 421–2
Severe disablement allowance, 491
Seychelles, 786, 1012–3
Shadow Cabinet, 224
Sharjah, 1053
Sheffield, 528, 538–9, 543
  airport, 504
  Archdeacon, 410
  Bishop, 164, 410
  Education Authority, 440
  MPs, 255
  universities, 451
Shepherd's Bush, Ealing Acton and, MP,
  243
Sheppey, Sittingbourne and, MP, 255
Shepway, 529, 547
Sherborne:
  Archdeacon, 410
  Bishop (Suffragan), 410
Sheriff Court of Chancery, 365
Sheriffs:
  Corporation of London, 550
  High, 522–3, 540, 558, 568
  Scotland, 365–6
Sherwood:
  Bishop (Suffragan), 411
  MP, 255
  Newark and, 529, 546

Shetland:
  airports, 504
  Education Authority, 442
  islands, 561
  Islands Council, 531, 564
  Lord Lieutenant, 563
  Orkney and, MP, 266
Shettleston (Glasgow), MP, 266
Shikoku, 919
Shipley, MP, 255
Shipping:
  British, 510–2
  lighthouse authorities, 317
  Lloyd's List, 629
  merchant fleets, 511
  passenger movement, 512
  UK seaborne trade, 512
Shooting:
  Bisley, 1228
  clay pigeon, 1228
  close seasons, 583
Shoreditch, Hackney South and, MP, 246
Shoreham:
  airport, 504
  Worthing East and, MP, 261
Shotts, Airdrie and, MP, 264
Show jumping, 1218
Shrewsbury:
  Bishop (RC), 416
  Bishop (Suffragan), 407
Shrewsbury and Atcham, 529, 547
  MP, 255
Shrivenham, Royal Military College, 456
Shropshire, 527, 541, 542
  Education Authority, 439
  MP, 255
  Shropshire North, 529, 547
  Shropshire South, 529, 547
Sicily, 915
Sickness benefit, 492
Sick Pay, Statutory, 490, 495, 659
Sidcup, Old Bexley and, MP, 252
Sidereal day, 73, 77
Sidereal time (2000), 17, 21, 25, etc., 69, 71,
  73–4
Sidereal year, 75
Sierra Leone, 786, 1013–4
  map, 976
Sikhism, 400
  calendar, 86
  organizations in UK, 400
Silver:
  coin, 612
  hallmarks, 603
Singapore, 788, 1014–5
  map, 904
Single European Act, 781
Single Market, 781
Single-parent benefit, 493
Sirius, 69, 81
Sites of Special Scientific Interest, 577
Sittingbourne and Sheppey, MP, 255
Skating, 1223
Skegness, Boston and, MP, 238
Skiing, 1208
Skipton and Ripon, MP, 255
Skopje, 788, 943
Skye, 561
  Ross, Inverness West and, MP, 267
Sleaford and North Hykeham, MP, 255
Slough, 528, 543
  Education Authority, 440
  MP, 255
Slovakia, 789, 1016–7
Slovenia, 789, 1017–8
  map, 1069
Small Heath, Sparkbrook and
  (Birmingham), MP, 238
Smoking statistics, 476
Snares Islands, 971

Stop-press

CHANGES SINCE PAGES WENT TO PRESS

THE YEAR 2000

Amendments to the Hindu religious calendar:

Chaitra	5 April
Janmashtami	23 August
Sarasvati-puja	2 October
Diwali, last day	28 October

PEERAGE

Died: 2nd Viscount Caldecote; Baron Oram

BARONETAGE AND KNIGHTAGE

Rt. Hon. John Morris, QC, MP became a Knight Bachelor
Died: Sir Melville Arnott; *Vice-Adm.* Sir Ronald Buckley; Sir Philip Haddon-Cave; Sir Wilfred Cockcroft; Sir Piers Jacobs; Sir Robert Southern; Sir Gerald Staples; Sir Colin Walker

PRIVY COUNCIL

John Morris made a Knight Bachelor
Alan Clark died

PARLIAMENT

MPs – Rt. Hon. John Morris, QC, MP made a Knight Bachelor
Died: Roger Stott, *Lab.* Wigan and Rt. Hon. Alan Clark, *C.* Kensington and Chelsea
Bill Tynan (*Lab.*) won the Hamilton South by-election
Neil Turner (*Lab.*) won the Wigan by-election

GOVERNMENT DEPARTMENTS AND PUBLIC OFFICES

British Railways Board and Shadow Strategic Rail Authority – Lew Adams, OBE; Baron Bradshaw; D. Jefferies, CBE; P. Kent, CBE and D. Quarmby appointed members
Commonwealth Development Corporation – Dr A. R. Gillespie appointed Chief Executive
Office of Gas and Electricity Markets – C. Coulthard to be Deputy Director-General, Scotland; Ms J. Whittington appointed a Director
Highways Agency – L. J. Haynes resigned as Chief Executive
Office for National Statistics – A. Goldsmith appointed Director of Finance and Corporate Services
Science Museum – Prof. A. Dowling and M. Smith appointed Trustees

LAW COURTS AND OFFICES

Circuit judges – A. J. Worthington and A. J. Mills appointed (SE circuit); Judge M. K. Lee (Midland and Oxford) died
Special Commissioners of Income Tax – Dr A. N. Brice appointed
VAT and Duties Tribunals – Dr A. N. Brice appointed Chairman

DEFENCE

RAF – Air Chief Marshal Sir Peter Squire, KCB, DFC, AFC, to be Chief of the Air Staff from 21 April 2000

CHURCH OF ENGLAND

P. A. Delaney appointed Archdeacon of London

EDUCATION

The Council for Dance Education and Training has not recognized the teacher registration system of the Association of American Dancing.

HEALTH

White Paper *Saving Lives: Our Healthier Nation* published. Measures include improving the health of people on low incomes and public health observatories to be set up in each NHS region. Targets include:
– cancer deaths among under-75s to be reduced by 20 per cent over ten years
– heart disease and stroke rates among under-75s to be reduced by 40 per cent over ten years
– accidental deaths and suicides to be reduced by 20 per cent over ten years

THE WATER INDUSTRY

Ofwat issued plans for average reductions in bills of 14 per cent over five years.

ENERGY

The Government announced a partial privatization of BNFL, with 49 per cent of shares to be sold.

COMMUNICATIONS

Cable and Wireless Communications' residential cable telephone system to be sold to NTL and its business telecommunications and data services to be taken over by Cable and Wireless during 2000
One-2-One bought by Deutsche Telekom
BT is now the sole owner of BT Cellnet

LOCAL GOVERNMENT

Lord Mayor of London 1999–2000 – Alderman Clive Martin, OBE, TD, elected 29 September

FINANCIAL SERVICES REGULATION

Financial Services Ombudsman Scheme – Ian Marshall appointed Chief Operating Officer

THE PRESS

Janet Street-Porter is Editor of *Independent on Sunday*

TRADE UNIONS

President of the TUC 1999–2000 – Rita Donaghy (UNISON)

EUROPEAN UNION COMMISSIONERS

President, Romano Prodi (Italy)
Vice-Presidents, Neil Kinnock (UK)(*Administrative Reform*); Loyola de Palacio (Spain)(*Transport, Energy*)
Members:
Franz Fischler (Austria) (*Agriculture*); Michaele Schreyer (Germany) (*Budget*); David Byrne (Ireland) (*Consumer Affairs*); Poul Nielson (Denmark) (*Development, Humanitarian Affairs*); Viviane Reding (Luxembourg) (*Education and Culture*); Anna Diamantopoulou (Greece) (*Employment, Social Affairs*); Günter Verheugen (Germany) (*Enlargement*); Margot Wallström (Sweden)(*Environment*); Chris Patten (UK) (*Foreign Affairs*); Erkki Liikanen (Finland) (*Information Society*); Frits Bolkestein (Netherlands) (*Internal Market*); Antonio Vitorino (Portugal)

(*Justice and Home Affairs*); Pedro Solbes (Spain) (*Monetary Affairs*); Michel Barnier (France) (*Regional Policy*); Philippe Busquin (Belgium) (*Research*); Pascal Lamy (France) (*Trade*); Mario Monti (Italy) (*Trade Policy*)

COUNTRIES OF THE WORLD

Comoros - Provisional government appointed
Ecuador - Ian Gerken to take over as British Ambassador in January 2000
Guinea-Bissau - new Council of Ministers appointed
Kazakhstan - Agriculture Minister Zhanibek Karibzhanov resigned July 1999
Mongolia - British Ambassador now Kay Coombs
Nepal - 15 additional members of the Cabinet named on 30 June 1999.
São Tomé and Príncipe - changes to the Cabinet announced on 17 July 1999
Solomon Islands - changes to the Cabinet announced
Thailand and Laos - Lloyd Barnaby Smith to take over as British Ambassador in early 2000

OBITUARIES

September 1999
5 Alan Clark, Conservative MP for Plymouth, Sutton 1974-92, for Kensington and Chelsea 1997-99; government minister 1983-92, aged 71
10 Alfredo Kraus, opera singer, aged 71
14 Rt Revd Cyril Bowles, Bishop of Derby 1969-87, aged 83
15 Rt Revd William Westwood, Bishop of Peterborough 1984-95, aged 73
17 Frankie Vaughan, singer and entertainer, aged 71
20 Raisa Gorbachev, wife of the USSR's last president, Mikhail Gorbachev, aged 67
22 George C. Scott, American actor, aged 71

EVENTS - SEPTEMBER 1999

1. In Serbia, two Australian aid workers detained on spying charges were released. **4.** An agreement between Israel and the PLO was signed, under which Israel agreed to withdraw from a further 11 per cent of the West Bank. The Final Status talks, to decide the boundaries of a Palestinian state, began on 13 September. **5.** In Russia, Islamic rebels launched a second invasion of Dagestan. **6.** Former US Senator George Mitchell, who chaired negotiations leading to the 1998 Good Friday Agreement, met with political parties in Belfast in an attempt to renew progress. **7.** At least 32 people were killed when an earthquake measuring 5.9 on the Richter scale struck Athens, Greece. **8.** The Bank of England raised bank base rates by 0.25 per cent to 5.25 per cent. **8-16.** Over 200 people were killed in a series of bombings in Russia. The Dagestan Liberation Army, a previously unknown group, later claimed responsibility. **9.** Chris Patten's commission on policing in Northern Ireland published its proposals, including re-naming the force the Northern Ireland Police Service and increasing the number of Roman Catholic officers. **14.** Hurricane Floyd caused extensive damage in the Bahamas before moving north to the eastern United States, where over three million people fled their homes by 16 September, although damage was less severe. **16.** Seven people, including four children, were killed when a man opened fire inside a church in Fort Worth, USA; the gunman also killed himself. In Bloomfontein, South Africa, an army officer killed seven colleagues before being shot dead himself. **17.** Fifty-nine soldiers were sentenced to death for taking part in a coup attempt against the democratically elected government of Zambia in October 1997. **20.** At least 2,000 people were killed when an earthquake measuring 7.6 on the Richter scale struck Taiwan. Powerful aftershocks caused more damage in subsequent days. UN Peacekeeping troops began to arrive in East Timor; violence had flared after the referendum on independence. The Agriculture Minister, Nick Brown, announced an extra £150m package to aid farmers. **22.** The political leader of Hamas, Khaled Meshaal, and two other senior Hamas officials were detained in Amman, Jordan.

Regional Government

Please see below listings of constituencies, regions, election results and members of the recently established Scottish Parliament and Welsh Assembly. (*see also* Local Government section)

ABBREVIATIONS

Alt LD	Alternative Liberal Democrat	Int. Ind.	International Independent
Anti-Corr.	Anti-Corruption, Mobile Home Scandal, Roads	LCP	Legalise Cannabis Party
Anti-Drug	Independent Anti-Drug Party	LD	Liberal Democrat
Bean	New Millennium Bean Party	Lab.	Labour
Beanus	Space Age Superhero from Planet Beanus	Lab. Co-op	Labour Co-operative
BNP	British National Party	Lib.	Liberal
Braveheart	Braveheart	Local Soc.	Local Socialist
C.	Conservative	Loony	Monster Raving Loony Party
CCP	Capital Circus Party	Mission	Scottish Peoples Mission
Celtic All.	Celtic Alliance	NLP	Natural Law Party
Ch. U.	Christian Unity	O. Lab.	Old Labour
Choice	People's Choice	PC	Plaid Cymru
Comm.	Communist	PRP	People's Representative Party
Comm. Brit.	Communist Party of Britain	ProLife	ProLife Alliance
Cvty.	Conservatory Party	Ref.	Referendum Party
D. Nat.	Democratic Nationalist	Rhuddlan	Rhuddlan Debt Protest Campaign
Dem. All.	Democrat Alliance of Wales	Rights	Civil Rights Movement
FP	Freedom Party	Rizz	Rizz Party
Falkirk W.	MP for Falkirk West	SCU	Scottish Conservative Unofficial
Green	Green	SEP	Socialist Equality Party
Highlands	Highlands and Islands Alliance	SFPP	Scottish Families and Pensioners Party
Humanist	Humanist Party	SLI	Scottish Labour Independent
Ind.	Independent	SLU	Scottish Labour Unofficial
Ind. You	Independent of London:Independent for You	SNP	Scottish National Party
Ind. Dem.	Independent Democrat	SPGB	Socialist Party of Great Britain
Ind. Ind.	Independent Independent	SSA	Scottish Socialist Alliance
Ind. Lab.	Independent Labour	SSP	Scottish Socialist Party
Ind. Matt.	Independent Mathias	SUP	Scottish Unionist Party
Ind. Noble	Independent Noble	SWP	Socialist Workers Party
Ind. Phill.	Independent Phillips	Soc.	Socialist Party
Ind. Prog.	Independent Progressive	Soc. Lab.	Socialist Labour Party
Ind. R.	Independent Robertson	TFPW	Tourism and Farmers Party of Wales
Ind. SB	Independent Sleaze-Buster	UK Ind.	UK Independence Party
Ind. Turner	Independent Turner	United Soc.	United Socialists
Ind. Voice	Independent Voice for Scottish Parliament	Value	Value Party
Ind. Water	Independent Labour Keep Scottish Water Public	WRP	Workers Revolutionary Party
Ind. Watt	Independent Watt	WWP	Worldly Wise Party
Individual	Independent Individual	Witchery	Witchery Tour Party

For other abbreviations, *see* Parliament section

CONSTITUENCIES - SCOTLAND

ABERDEEN CENTRAL
(Scotland North East region)
E. 52,715   *T.* 50.26%

L. Macdonald, *Lab.*	10,305
R. Lochhead, *SNP*	7,609
Ms E. Anderson, *LD*	4,403
T. Mason, *C.*	3,655
A. Cumbers, *SSP*	523

Lab. majority 2,696

ABERDEEN NORTH
(Scotland North East region)
E. 54,553   *T.* 51.00%

Ms E. Thomson, *Lab.*	10,340
B. Adam, *SNP*	9,942
J. Donaldson, *LD*	4,767
I. Haughie, *C.*	2,772

Lab. majority 398

ABERDEEN SOUTH
(Scotland North East region)
E. 60,579   *T.* 57.26%

N. Stephen, *LD*	11,300
M. Elrick, *Lab.*	9,540

Ms N. Milne, *C.*	6,993
Ms I. McGugan, *SNP*	6,651
S. Sutherland, *SWP*	206

LD majority 1,760

ABERDEENSHIRE WEST AND KINCARDINE
(Scotland North East region)
E. 60,702   *T.* 58.87%

M. Rumbles, *LD*	12,838
B. Wallace, *C.*	10,549
Ms M. Watt, *SNP*	7,699
G. Guthrie, *Lab.*	4,650

LD majority 2,289

AIRDRIE AND SHOTTS
(Scotland Central region)
E. 58,481   *T.* 56.79%

Ms K. Whitefield, *Lab.*	18,338
G. Paterson, *SNP*	9,353
P. Ross-Taylor, *C.*	3,177
D. Miller, *LD*	2,345

Lab. majority 8,985

ANGUS
(Scotland North East region)
E. 59,891   T. 57.66%
A. Welsh, *SNP*	16,055
R. Harris, *C.*	7,154
I. McFatridge, *Lab.*	6,914
R. Speirs, *LD*	4,413
SNP majority 8,901

ARGYLL AND BUTE
(Highlands and Islands region)
E. 49,609   T. 64.86%
G. Lyon, *LD*	11,226
D. Hamilton, *SNP*	9,169
H. Raven, *Lab.*	6,470
D. Petrie, *C.*	5,312
LD majority 2,057

AYR
(Scotland South region)
E. 56,338   T. 66.48%
I. Welsh, *Lab.*	14,263
P. Gallie, *C.*	14,238
R. Mullin, *SNP*	7,291
Ms E. Morris, *LD*	1,662
Lab. majority 25

BANFF AND BUCHAN
(Scotland North East region)
E. 57,639   T. 55.06%
A. Salmond, *SNP*	16,695
D. Davidson, *C.*	5,403
M. Mackie, *LD*	5,315
Ms M. Harris, *Lab.*	4,321
SNP majority 11,292

CAITHNESS, SUTHERLAND AND EASTER ROSS
(Highlands and Islands region)
E. 41,581   T. 62.60%
J. Stone, *LD*	10,691
J. Hendry, *Lab.*	6,300
Ms J. Urquhart, *SNP*	6,035
R. Jenkins, *C.*	2,167
J. Campbell, *Ind.*	554
E. Stewart, *Ind.*	282
LD majority 4,391

CARRICK, CUMNOCK AND DOON VALLEY
(Scotland South region)
E. 65,580   T. 62.66%
Ms C. Jamieson, *Lab. Co-op.*	19,667
A. Ingram, *SNP*	10,864
J. Scott, *C.*	8,123
D, Hannay, *LD*	2,441
Lab. Co-op. majority 8,803

CLYDEBANK AND MILNGAVIE
(Scotland West region)
E. 52,461   T. 63.55%
D. McNulty, *Lab.*	15,105
J. Yuill, *SNP*	10,395
R. Ackland, *LD*	4,149
Ms D. Luckhurst, *C.*	3,688
Lab. majority 4,710

CLYDESDALE
(Scotland South region)
E. 64,262   T. 60.61%
Ms K. Turnbull, *Lab.*	16,755
Ms A. Winning, *SNP*	12,875
C. Cormack, *C.*	5,814
Ms S. Grieve, *LD*	3,503
Lab. majority 3,880

COATBRIDGE AND CHRYSTON
(Scotland Central region)
E. 52,178   T. 57.87%
Ms E. Smith, *Lab.*	17,923
P. Kearney, *SNP*	7,519
G. Lind, *C.*	2,867
Ms J. Hook, *LD*	1,889
Lab. majority 10,404

CUMBERNAULD AND KILSYTH
(Scotland Central region)
E. 49,395   T. 61.97%
Ms C. Craigie, *Lab.*	15,182
A. Wilson, *SNP*	10,923
H. O'Donnell, *LD*	2,029
R. Slack, *C.*	1,362
K. McEwan, *SSP*	1,116
Lab. majority 4,259

CUNNINGHAME NORTH
(Scotland West region)
E. 55,867   T. 59.95%
A. Wilson, *Lab.*	14,369
Ms K. Ullrich, *SNP*	9,573
M. Johnston, *C.*	6,649
C. Irving, *LD*	2,900
Lab. majority 4,796

CUNNINGHAME SOUTH
(Scotland South region)
E. 50,443   T. 56.06%
Ms I. Oldfather, *Lab.*	14,936
M. Russell, *SNP*	8,395
M. Tosh, *C.*	3,229
S. Ritchie, *LD*	1,717
Lab. majority 6,541

DUMBARTON
(Scotland West region)
E. 56,090   T. 61.86%
Ms J. Baillie, *Lab.*	15,181
L. Quinan, *SNP*	10,423
D. Reece, *C.*	5,060
P. Coleshill, *LD*	4,035
Lab. majority 4,758

DUMFRIES
(Scotland South region)
E. 63,162   T. 60.93%
Ms E. Murray, *Lab.*	14,101
D. Mundell, *C.*	10,447
S.Norris, *SNP*	7,625
N. Wallace, *LD*	6,309
Lab. majority 3,654

DUNDEE EAST
(Scotland North East region)
E. 57,222   T. 55.33%
J. McAllion, *Lab.*	13,703
Ms S. Robison, *SNP*	10,849
I. Mitchell, *C.*	4,428
R. Lawrie, *LD*	2,153
H. Duke, *SSP*	530
Lab. majority 2,854

DUNDEE WEST
(Scotland North East region)
E. 55,725   T. 52.19%
Ms K. MacLean, *Lab.*	10,925
C. Cashley, *SNP*	10,804
G. Buchan, *C.*	3,345
Ms E. Dick, *LD*	2,998
J. McFarlane, *SSP*	1,010
Lab. majority 121

DUNFERMLINE EAST
(Scotland Mid and Fife region)
E. 52,087　*T.* 56.94%

Ms H. Eadie, *Lab. Co-op.*	16,576
D. McCarthy, *SNP*	7,877
Ms C. Ruxton, *C.*	2,931
F. Lawson, *LD*	2,275
Lab. Co-op. majority 8,699	

DUNFERMLINE WEST
(Scotland Mid and Fife region)
E. 53,112　*T.* 57.75%

S. Barrie, *Lab.*	13,560
D. Chapman, *SNP*	8,539
Ms E. Harris, *LD*	5,591
J. Mackie, *C.*	2,981
Lab. majority 5,021	

EAST KILBRIDE
(Scotland Central region)
E. 66,111　*T.* 62.49%

A. Kerr, *Lab.*	19,987
Ms L. Fabiani, *SNP*	13,488
C. Stevenson, *C.*	4,465
E. Hawthorn, *LD*	3,373
Lab. majority 6,499	

EAST LOTHIAN
(Scotland South region)
E. 58,579　*T.* 64.16%

J. Home Robertson, *Lab.*	19,220
C. Miller, *SNP*	8,274
Ms C. Richard, *C.*	5,941
Ms J. Hayman, *LD*	4,147
Lab. majority 10,946	

EASTWOOD
(Scotland West region)
E. 67,248　*T.* 67.51%

K. Macintosh, *Lab.*	16,970
J. Young, *C.*	14,845
Ms R. Findlay, *SNP*	8,760
Ms A. McCurley, *LD*	4,472
M. Tayan, *Ind.*	349
Lab. majority 2,125	

EDINBURGH CENTRAL
(Lothians region)
E. 65,945　*T.* 56.73%

Ms S. Boyack, *Lab.*	14,224
I. McKee, *SNP*	9,598
A. Myles, *LD*	6,187
Ms J. Low, *C.*	6,018
K. Williamson, *SSP*	830
B. Allingham, *Ind. Dem.*	364
W. Wallace, *Braveheart*	191
Lab. majority 4,626	

EDINBURGH EAST AND MUSSELBURGH
(Lothians region)
E. 60,167　*T.* 61.48%

Ms S. Deacon, *Lab.*	17,086
K. MacAskill, *SNP*	10,372
J. Balfour, *C.*	4,600
Ms M. Thomas, *LD*	4,100
D. White, *SSP*	697
M. Heavey, *Ind. You*	134
Lab. majority 6,714	

EDINBURGH NORTH AND LEITH
(Lothians region)
E. 62,976　*T.* 58.19%

M. Chisholm, *Lab.*	17,203
Ms A. Dana, *SNP*	9,467

J. Sempill, *C.*	5,030
S. Tombs, *LD*	4,039
R. Brown, *SSP*	907
Lab. majority 7,736	

EDINBURGH PENTLANDS
(Lothians region)
E. 60,029　*T.* 65.97%

I. Gray, *Lab.*	14,343
D. McLetchie, *C.*	11,458
S. Gibb, *SNP*	8,770
I. Gibson, *LD*	5,029
Lab. majority 2,885	

EDINBURGH SOUTH
(Lothians region)
E. 64,100　*T.* 62.61%

A. MacKay, *Lab.*	14,869
Ms M. MacDonald, *SNP*	9,445
M. Pringle, *LD*	8,961
I. Whyte, *C.*	6,378
W. Black, *SWP*	482
Lab. majority 5,424	

EDINBURGH WEST
(Lothians region)
E. 61,747　*T.* 67.34%

Ms M. Smith, *LD*	15,161
Lord J. Douglas-Hamilton, *C.*	10,578
Ms C. Fox, *Lab.*	8,860
G. Sutherland, *SNP*	6,984
LD majority 4,583	

FALKIRK EAST
(Scotland Central region)
E. 57,345　*T.* 61.40%

Ms C. Peattie, *Lab.*	15,721
K. Brown, *SNP*	11,582
A. Orr, *C.*	3,399
G. McDonald, *LD*	2,509
R. Stead, *Soc. Lab.*	1,643
V. MacGrain, *SFPP*	358
Lab. majority 4,139	

FALKIRK WEST
(Scotland Central region)
E. 53,404　*T.* 63.04%

D. Canavan, *Falkirk W.*	18,511
R. Martin, *Lab.*	6,319
M. Matheson, *SNP*	5,986
G. Miller, *C.*	1,897
A. Smith, *LD*	954
Falkirk W. majority 12,192	

FIFE CENTRAL
(Scotland Mid and Fife region)
E. 58,850　*T.* 55.82%

H. McLeish, *Lab.*	18,828
Ms P. Marwick, *SNP*	10,153
Ms J. A. Liston, *LD*	1,953
K. Harding, *C.*	1,918
Lab. majority 8,675	

FIFE NORTH EAST
(Scotland Mid and Fife region)
E. 60,886　*T.* 59.03%

I. Smith, *LD*	13,590
E. Brocklebank, *C.*	8,526
C. Welsh, *SNP*	6,373
C. Milne, *Lab.*	5,175
D. Macgregor, *Ind.*	1,540
R. Beveridge, *Ind.*	737
LD majority 5,064	

GALLOWAY AND UPPER NITHSDALE
(Scotland South region)
E. 53,057   T. 66.56%

A. Morgan, *SNP*	13,873
A. Fergusson, *C.*	10,672
J. Stevens, *Lab.*	7,209
Ms J. Mitchell, *LD*	3,562

SNP majority 3,201

GLASGOW ANNIESLAND
(Glasgow region)
E. 54,378   T. 52.37%

D. Dewar, *Lab.*	16,749
K. Stewart, *SNP*	5,756
W. Aitken, *C.*	3,032
I. Brown, *LD*	1,804
Ms A. Lynch, *SSP*	1,000
E. Boyd, *Soc. Lab.*	139

Lab. majority 10,993

GLASGOW BAILLIESTON
(Glasgow region)
E. 49,068   T. 48.32%

Ms M. Curran, *Lab.*	11,289
Ms D. Elder, *SNP*	8,217
J. McVicar, *SSP*	1,864
Ms K. Pickering, *C.*	1,526
Ms J. Fryer, *LD*	813

Lab. majority 3,072

GLASGOW CATHCART
(Glasgow region)
E. 51,338   T. 52.55%

M. Watson, *Lab.*	12,966
Ms M. Whitehead, *SNP*	7,592
Ms M. Leishman, *C.*	3,311
C. Dick, *LD*	2,187
R. Slorach, *SWP*	920

Lab. majority 5,374

GLASGOW GOVAN
(Glasgow region)
E. 53,257   T. 49.52%

G. Jackson, *Lab.*	11,421
Ms N. Sturgeon, *SNP*	9,665
Ms T. Ahmed-Sheikh, *C.*	2,343
M. Aslam Khan, *LD*	1,479
C. McCarthy, *SSP*	1,275
J. Foster, *Comm. Brit.*	190

Lab. majority 1,756

GLASGOW KELVIN
(Glasgow region)
E. 61,207   T. 46.34%

Ms P. McNeill, *Lab.*	12,711
Ms S. White, *SNP*	8,303
Ms M. Craig, *LD*	3,720
A. Rasul, *C.*	2,253
Ms H. Ritchie, *SSP*	1,375

Lab. majority 4,408

GLASGOW MARYHILL
(Glasgow region)
E. 56,469   T. 40.75%

Ms P. Ferguson, *Lab.*	11,455
W. Wilson, *SNP*	7,129
Ms C. Hamblen, *LD*	1,793
G. Scott, *SSP*	1,439
M. Fry, *C.*	1,194

Lab. majority 4,326

GLASGOW POLLOCK
(Glasgow region)
E. 47,970   T. 54.37%

J. Lamont, *Lab. Co-op.*	11,405
K. Gibson, *SNP*	6,763
T. Sheridan, *SSP*	5,611
R. O'Brien, *C.*	1,370
J. King, *LD*	931

Lab. Co-op. majority 4,642

GLASGOW RUTHERGLEN
(Glasgow region)
E. 51,012   T. 56.89%

Ms J. Hughes, *Lab.*	13,442
T. Chalmers, *SNP*	6,155
R. Brown, *LD*	5,798
I. Stewart, *C.*	2,315
W. Bonnar, *SSP*	832
J. Nisbet, *Soc. Lab.*	481

Lab. majority 7,287

GLASGOW SHETTLESTON
(Glasgow region)
E. 50,592   T. 40.58%

F. McAveety, *Lab. Co-op.*	11,078
J. Byrne, *SNP*	5,611
Ms R. Kane, *SSP*	1,640
C. Bain, *C.*	1,260
L. Clarke, *LD*	943

Lab. Co-op. majority 5,467

GLASGOW SPRINGBURN
(Glasgow region)
E. 55,670   T. 43.77%

P. Martin, *Lab.*	14,268
J. Brady, *SNP*	6,375
M. Roxburgh, *C.*	1,293
M. Dunnigan, *LD*	1,288
J. Friel, *SSP*	1,141

Lab. majority 7,893

GORDON
(Scotland North East region)
E. 59,497   T. 56.51%

Ms N. Radcliffe, *LD*	12,353
A. Stronach, *SNP*	8,158
A. Johnstone, *C.*	6,602
Ms G. Carlin-Kulwicki, *Lab.*	3,950
H. Watt, *Ind.*	2,559

LD majority 4,195

GREENOCK AND INVERCLYDE
(Scotland West region)
E. 48,584   T. 58.95%

D. McNeil, *Lab.*	11,817
R. Finnie, *LD*	7,504
I. Hamilton, *SNP*	6,762
R. Wilkinson, *C.*	1,699
D. Landels, *SSP*	857

Lab. majority 4,313

HAMILTON NORTH AND BELLSHILL
(Scotland Central region)
E. 53,992   T. 57.82%

M. McMahon, *Lab.*	15,227
Ms K. McAlorum, *SNP*	9,621
S. Thomson, *C.*	3,199
Ms J. Struthers, *LD*	2,105
Ms K. McGavigan, *Soc. Lab.*	1,064

Lab. majority 5,606

HAMILTON SOUTH
(Scotland Central region)
E. 46,765   T. 55.43%

T. McCabe, *Lab.*	14,098
A. Ardrey, *SNP*	6,922

Ms M. Mitchell, *C.*	2,918
J. Oswald, *LD*	1,982
Lab. majority 7,176	

INVERNESS EAST, NAIRN AND LOCHABER
(Highlands and Islands region)
E. 66,285   *T.* 63.10%

F. Ewing, *SNP*	13,825
Ms J. Aitken, *Lab.*	13,384
D. Fraser, *LD*	8,508
Ms M. Scanlon, *C.*	6,107
SNP majority 441	

KILMARNOCK AND LOUDOUN
(Scotland Central region)
E. 61,454   *T.* 64.03%

Ms M. Jamieson, *Lab.*	17,345
A. Neil, *SNP*	14,585
L. McIntosh, *C.*	4,589
J. Stewart, *LD*	2,830
Lab. majority 2,760	

KIRKCALDY
(Scotland Mid and Fife region)
E. 51,640   *T.* 54.88%

Ms M. Livingstone, *Lab. Co-op.*	13,645
S. Hosie, *SNP*	9,170
M. Scott-Hayward, *C.*	2,907
J. Mainland, *LD*	2,620
Lab. Co-op. majority 4,475	

LINLITHGOW
(Lothians region)
E. 54,262   *T.* 62.26%

Ms M. Mulligan, *Lab.*	15,247
S. Stevenson, *SNP*	12,319
G. Lindhurst, *C.*	3,158
J. Barrett, *LD*	2,643
Ms I. Ovenstone, *Ind.*	415
Lab. majority 2,928	

LIVINGSTON
(Lothians region)
E. 62,060   *T.* 58.93%

B. Muldoon, *Lab.*	17,313
G. McCarra, *SNP*	13,409
D. Younger, *C.*	3,014
M. Oliver, *LD*	2,834
Lab. majority 3,904	

MIDLOTHIAN
(Lothians region)
E. 48,374   *T.* 61.51%

Ms R. Brankin, *Lab. Co-op.*	14,467
A. Robertson, *SNP*	8,942
J. Elder, *LD*	3,184
G. Turnbull, *C.*	2,544
D. Pryde, *Ind.*	618
Lab. Co-op. majority 5,525	

MORAY
(Highlands and Islands region)
E. 58,388   *T.* 57.50%

Mrs M. Ewing, *SNP*	13,027
A. Farquharson, *Lab.*	8,898
A. Findlay, *C.*	8,595
Ms P. Kenton, *LD*	3,056
SNP majority 4,129	

MOTHERWELL AND WISHAW
(Scotland Central region)
E. 52,613   *T.* 57.71%

J. McConnell, *Lab.*	13,955
J. McGuigan, *SNP*	8,879

W. Gibson, *C.*	3,694
J. Milligan, *Soc. Lab.*	1,941
R. Spillane, *LD*	1,895
Lab. majority 5,076	

OCHIL
(Scotland Mid and Fife region)
E. 57,083   *T.* 64.58%

R. Simpson, *Lab.*	15,385
G. Reid, *SNP*	14,082
N. Johnston, *C.*	4,151
Earl of Mar and Kellie, *LD*	3,249
Lab. majority 1,303	

ORKNEY
(Highlands and Islands region)
E. 15,658   *T.* 56.95%

J. Wallace, *LD*	6,010
C. Zawadzki, *C.*	1,391
J. Mowat, *SNP*	917
A. Macleod, *Lab.*	600
LD majority 4,619	

PAISLEY NORTH
(Scotland West region)
E. 49,020   *T.* 56.61%

Ms W. Alexander, *Lab.*	13,492
I. Mackay, *SNP*	8,876
P. Ramsay, *C.*	2,242
Ms T. Mayberry, *LD*	2,133
Ms F. Macdonald, *SSP*	1,007
Lab. majority 4,616	

PAISLEY SOUTH
(Scotland West region)
E. 53,637   *T.* 57.15%

H. Henry, *Lab.*	13,899
W. Martin, *SNP*	9,404
S. Callison, *LD*	2,974
Ms S. Laidlaw, *C.*	2,433
P. Mack, *Ind.*	1,273
Ms J. Forrest, *SWP*	673
Lab. majority 4,495	

PERTH
(Scotland Mid and Fife region)
E. 61,034   *T.* 61.27%

Ms R. Cunningham, *SNP*	13,570
I. Stevenson, *C.*	11,543
Ms J. Richards, *Lab.*	8,725
C. Brodie, *LD*	3,558
SNP majority 2,027	

RENFREWSHIRE WEST
(Scotland West region)
E. 52,452   *T.* 64.89%

Ms P. Godman, *Lab.*	12,708
C. Campbell, *SNP*	9,815
Ms A. Goldie, *C.*	7,243
N. Ascherson, *LD*	2,659
A. McGraw, *Ind.*	1,136
P. Clark, *SWP*	476
Lab. majority 2,893	

ROSS, SKYE AND INVERNESS WEST
(Highlands and Islands region)
E. 55,845   *T.* 63.42%

J. Farquhar-Munro, *LD*	11,652
D. Munro, *Lab.*	10,113
J. Mather, *SNP*	7,997
J. Scott, *C.*	3,351
D. Briggs, *Ind.*	2,302
LD majority 1,539	

ROXBURGH AND BERWICKSHIRE
(Scotland South region)
E. 47,639   *T.* 58.52%

E. Robson, *LD*	11,320
A. Hutton, *C.*	7,735
S. Crawford, *SNP*	4,719
Ms S. McLeod, *Lab.*	4,102
LD majority 3,585	

SHETLAND
(Highlands and Islands region)
E. 16,978   *T.* 58.77%

T. Scott, *LD*	5,435
J. Wills, *Lab.*	2,241
W. Ross, *SNP*	1,430
G. Robinson, *C.*	872
LD majority 3,194	

STIRLING
(Scotland Mid and Fife region)
E. 52,904   *T.* 67.68%

Ms S. Jackson, *Lab.*	13,533
Ms A. Ewing, *SNP*	9,552
B. Monteith, *C.*	9,158
I. Macfarlane, *LD*	3,407
S. Kilgour, *Ind.*	155
Lab. majority 3,981	

STRATHKELVIN AND BEARSDEN
(Scotland West region)
E. 63,111   *T.* 67.17%

S. Galbraith, *Lab.*	21,505

Ms F. McLeod, *SNP*	9,384
C. Ferguson, *C.*	6,934
Ms A. Howarth, *LD*	4,144
Ms M. Richards, *Anti-Drug*	423
Lab. majority 12,121	

TAYSIDE NORTH
(Scotland Mid and Fife region)
E. 61,795   *T.* 61.58%

J. Swinney, *SNP*	16,786
M. Fraser, *C.*	12,594
Ms M. Dingwall, *Lab.*	5,727
P. Regent, *LD*	2,948
SNP majority 4,192	

TWEEDDALE, ETTRICK AND LAUDERDALE
(Scotland South region)
E. 51,577   *T.* 65.37%

I. Jenkins, *LD*	12,078
Ms C. Creech, *SNP*	7,600
G. McGregor, *Lab.*	7,546
J. Campbell, *C.*	6,491
LD majority 4,478	

WESTERN ISLES
(Highlands and Islands region)
E. 22,412   *T.* 62.26%

A. Morrison, *Lab.*	7,248
A. Nicholson, *SNP*	5,155
J. MacGrigor, *C.*	1,095
J. Horne, *LD*	456
Lab. majority 2,093	

REGIONS

GLASGOW
E. 531,956   *T.* 48.19%

Lab.	112,588 (43.92%)
SNP	65,360 (25.50%)
C.	20,239 (7.90%)
SSP	18,581 (7.25%)
LD	18,473 (7.21%)
Green	10,159 (3.96%)
Soc. Lab.	4,391 (1.71%)
ProLife	2,357 (0.92%)
SUP	2,283 (0.89%)
Comm. Brit.	521 (0.20%)
Humanist	447 (0.17%)
NLP	419 (0.16%)
SPGB	309 (0.12%)
Choice	221 (0.09%)

Lab. majority 47,228
(May 1997, Lab. maj. 166,061)
Additional Members: W. Aitken, *C.;* R. Brown, *LD;* Ms D. Elder, *SNP;* Ms S. White, *SNP;* Ms N. Sturgeon, *SNP;* K. Gibson, *SNP;* T. Sheridan, *SSP*

HIGHLANDS AND ISLANDS
E. 326,553   *T.* 61.76%

SNP	55,933 (27.73%)
Lab.	51,371 (25.47%)
LD	43,226 (21.43%)
C.	30,122 (14.94%)
Green	7,560 (3.75%)
Ind. Noble	3,522 (1.75%)
Soc. Lab.	2,808 (1.39%)
Highlands	2,607 (1.29%)
SSP	1,770 (0.88%)
Mission	1,151 (0.57%)
Int. Ind.	712 (0.35%)

NLP	536 (0.27%)
Ind. R.	354 (0.18%)

SNP majority 4,562
(May 1997, LD maj. 1,388)
Additional Members: J. MacGrigor, *C.;* Mrs M. Scanlon, *C.;* Ms M. MacMillan, *Lab.;* P. Peacock, *Lab.;* Ms R. Grant, *Lab.;* Mrs W. Ewing, *SNP;* D. Hamilton, *SNP*

LOTHIANS
E. 539,656   *T.* 61.25%

Lab.	99,908 (30.23%)
SNP	85,085 (25.74%)
C.	52,067 (15.75%)
LD	47,565 (14.39%)
Green	22,848 (6.91%)
Soc. Lab.	10,895 (3.30%)
SSP	5,237 (1.58%)
Lib.	2,056 (0.62%)
Witchery	1,184 (0.36%)
ProLife	898 (0.27%)
Rights	806 (0.24%)
NLP	564 (0.17%)
Braveheart	557 (0.17%)
SPGB	388 (0.12%)
Ind. Voice	256 (0.08%)
Ind. Ind.	145 (0.04%)
Anti-Corr.	54 (0.02%)

Lab. majority 14,823
(May 1997, Lab. maj. 101,991)
Additional Members: The Lord Selkirk of Douglas, *C.;* D. McLetchie, *C.;* Rt. Hon. Sir David Steel, *LD;* K. MacAskill, *SNP;* Ms M. MacDonald, *SNP;* Ms F. Hyslop, *SNP;* R. Harper, *Green*

SCOTLAND CENTRAL
E. 551,733   *T.* 59.90%

Lab.	129,822 (39.28%)

SNP	91,802 (27.78%)
C.	30,243 (9.15%)
Falkirk W.	27,700 (8.38%)
LD	20,505 (6.20%)
Soc. Lab.	10,956 (3.32%)
Green	5,926 (1.79%)
SSP	5,739 (1.74%)
SUP	2,886 (0.87%)
ProLife	2,567 (0.78%)
SFPP	1,373 (0.42%)
NLP	719 (0.22%)
Ind. Prog.	248 (0.08%)

Lab. majority 38,020
(May 1997, Lab. maj. 143,376)
Additional Members: Mrs L. McIntosh, *C.;* D. Gorrie, *LD;* A. Neil, *SNP;* M. Matheson, *SNP;* Ms L. Fabiani, *SNP;* A. Wilson, *SNP;* G. Paterson, *SNP*

SCOTLAND MID AND FIFE
E. 509,387   *T.* 60.01%

Lab.	101,964 (33.36%)
SNP	87,659 (28.68%)
C.	56,719 (18.56%)
LD	38,896 (12.73%)
Green	11,821 (3.87%)
Soc. Lab.	4,266 (1.40%)
SSP	3,044 (1.00%)
ProLife	735 (0.24%)
NLP	558 (0.18%)

Lab. majority 14,305
(May 1997, Lab. maj. 54,087)
Additional Members: N. Johnston, *C.;* B. Monteith, *C.;* K. Harding, *C.;* K. Raffan, *LD;* B. Crawford, *SNP;* G. Reid, *SNP;* Ms P. Marwick, *SNP*

SCOTLAND NORTH EAST
E. 518,521   *T.* 55.05%

SNP	92,329 (32.35%)
Lab.	72,666 (25.46%)
C.	52,149 (18.27%)
LD	49,843 (17.46%)
Green	8,067 (2.83%)
Soc. Lab.	3,557 (1.25%)
SSP	3,016 (1.06%)
Ind. Watt.	2,303 (0.81%)

Ind. SB	770 (0.27%)
NLP	746 (0.26%)

SNP majority 19,663
(May 1997, Lab. maj. 17,518)
Additional Members: D. Davidson, *C.;* A. Johnstone, *C.;* B. Wallace, *C.;* R. Lochhead, *SNP;* Ms S. Robison, *SNP;* B. Adam, *SNP;* Ms I. McGugan, *SNP*

SCOTLAND SOUTH
E. 510,634   *T.* 62.35%

Lab.	98,836 (31.04%)
SNP	80,059 (25.15%)
C.	68,904 (21.64%)
LD	38,157 (11.99%)
Soc. Lab.	13,887 (4.36%)
Green	9,468 (2.97%)
Lib.	3,478 (1.09%)
SSP	3,304 (1.04%)
UK Ind.	1,502 (0.47%)
NLP	775 (0.24%)

Lab. majority 18,777
(May 1997, Lab. maj. 79,585)
Additional Members: P. Gallie, *C.;* D. Mundell, *C.;* M. Tosh, *C.;* A. Fergusson, *C.;* M. Russell, *SNP;* A. Ingram, *SNP;* Ms C. Creech, *SNP*

SCOTLAND WEST
E. 498,466   *T.* 62.27%

Lab.	119,663 (38.55%)
SNP	80,417 (25.91%)
C.	48,666 (15.68%)
LD	34,095 (10.98%)
Green	8,175 (2.63%)
SSP	5,944 (1.91%)
Soc. Lab.	4,472 (1.44%)
ProLife	3,227 (1.04%)
Individual	2,761 (0.89%)
SUP	1,840 (0.59%)
NLP	589 (0.19%)
Ind. Water	565 (0.18%)

Lab. majority 39,246
(May 1997, Lab. maj. 115,995)
Additional Members: Miss A. Goldie, *C.;* J. Young, *C.;* R. Finnie, *LD;* L. Quinan, *SNP;* Ms F. McLeod, *SNP;* Ms K. Ullrich, *SNP;* C. Campbell, *SNP*

MEMBERS OF THE SCOTTISH PARLIAMENT

Adam, Brian, *SNP, Scotland North East region*
Aitken, William, *C., Glasgow region*
Alexander, Ms Wendy, *Lab., Paisley North*, maj. 4,616
Baillie, Ms Jackie, *Lab., Dumbarton*, maj. 4,758
Barrie, Scott, *Lab., Dunfermline West*, maj. 5,021
Boyack, Ms Sarah, *Lab., Edinburgh Central*, maj. 4,626
Brankin, Ms Rhona, *Lab. Co-op., Midlothian*, maj. 5,525
Brown, Robert, *LD, Glasgow region*
Campbell, Colin, *SNP, Scotland West region*
Canavan, Dennis A., MP, *Lab., Falkirk West*, maj. 12,192
Chisholm, Malcolm G. R., MP, *Lab., Edinburgh North and Leith*, maj. 7,736
Craigie, Ms Cathy, *Lab., Cumbernauld and Kilsyth*, maj. 4,259
Crawford, Bruce, *SNP, Scotland Mid and Fife region*
Creech, Ms Christine, *SNP, Scotland South region*
Cunningham, Ms Roseanna, MP, *SNP, Perth*, maj. 2,027
Curran, Ms Margaret, *Lab., Glasgow Baillieston*, maj. 3,072
Davidson, David, *C., Scotland North East region*
Deacon, Ms Susan, *Lab., Edinburgh East and Musselburgh*, maj. 6,714
Dewar, Rt. Hon. Donald C., MP, *Lab., Glasgow Anniesland*, maj. 10,993
Selkirk of Douglas, The Lord, PC, QC, *C., Lothians region*
Eadie, Ms Helen, *Lab. Co-op., Dunfermline East*, maj. 8,699
Elder, Ms Dorothy, *SNP, Glasgow region*
Ewing, Fergus, *SNP, Inverness East, Nairn and Lochaber*, maj. 441
Ewing, Mrs Margaret A., MP, *SNP, Moray*, maj. 4,129
Ewing, Mrs Winnifred, *SNP, Highlands and Islands region*
Fabiani, Ms Linda, *SNP, Scotland Central region*
Farquhar-Munro, John, *LD, Ross, Skye and Inverness West*, maj. 1,539
Ferguson, Ms Patricia, *Lab., Glasgow Maryhill*, maj. 4,326
Fergusson, Alex, *C., Scotland South region*
Finnie, Ross, *LD, Scotland West region*
Galbraith, Samuel L., MP, *Lab., Strathkelvin and Bearsden*, maj. 12,121
Gallie, Phil, *C., Scotland South region*
Gibson, Kenneth, *SNP, Glasgow region*
Godman, Ms Patricia, *Lab., Renfrewshire West*, maj. 2,893
Goldie, Miss Annabel, *C., Scotland West region*
Gorrie, Donald C. E., MP, *LD, Scotland Central region*
Grant, Ms Rhoda, *Lab., Highlands and Islands region*
Gray, Iain, *Lab., Edinburgh Pentlands*, maj. 2,885
Hamilton, Duncan, *SNP, Highlands and Islands region*
Harding, Keith, *C., Scotland Mid and Fife region*
Harper, Robin, *Green, Lothians region*
Henry, Hugh, *Lab., Paisley South*, maj. 4,495
Home Robertson, John D., MP, *Lab., East Lothian*, maj. 10,946
Hughes, Ms Janice, *Lab., Glasgow Rutherglen*, maj. 7,287
Hyslop, Ms Fiona, *SNP, Lothians region*
Ingram, Adam, *SNP, Scotland South region*
Jackson, Gordon, *Lab., Glasgow Govan*, maj. 1,756
Jackson, Ms Sylvia, *Lab., Stirling*, maj. 3,981
Jamieson, Ms Cathy, *Lab. Co-op., Carrick, Cumnock and Doon Valley*, maj. 8,803
Jamieson, Ms Margaret, *Lab., Kilmarnock and Loudoun*, maj. 2,760
Jenkins, Ian, *LD, Tweeddale, Ettrick and Lauderdale*, maj. 4,478
Johnston, Nicholas, *C., Scotland Mid and Fife region*
Johnstone, Alex, *C., Scotland North East region*
Kerr, Andy, *Lab., East Kilbride*, maj. 6,499
Lamont, Johann, *Lab. Co-op., Glasgow Pollock*, maj. 4,642
Livingstone, Ms Marilyn, *Lab. Co-op., Kirkcaldy*, maj. 4,475
Lochhead, Richard, *SNP, Scotland North East region*

Lyon, George, *LD, Argyll and Bute*, maj. 2,057
McAllion, John, MP, *Lab., Dundee East*, maj. 2,854
MacAskill, Kenny, *SNP, Lothians region*
McAveety, Frank, *Lab. Co-op., Glasgow Shettleston*, maj. 5,467
McCabe, Tom, *Lab., Hamilton South*, maj. 7,176
McConnell, Jack, *Lab., Motherwell and Wishaw*, maj. 5,076
Macdonald, Lewis, *Lab., Aberdeen Central*, maj. 2,696
MacDonald, Ms Margo, *SNP, Lothians region*
MacGrigor, Jamie, *C., Highlands and Islands region*
McGugan, Ms Irene, *SNP, Scotland North East region*
Macintosh, Ken, *Lab., Eastwood*, maj. 2,125
McIntosh, Mrs Lindsay, *C., Scotland Central region*
MacKay, Angus, *Lab., Edinburgh South*, maj. 5,424
MacLean, Ms Kate, *Lab., Dundee West*, maj. 121
McLeish, Henry B., MP, *Lab., Fife Central*, maj. 8,675
McLeod, Ms Fiona, *SNP, Scotland West region*
McLetchie, David, *C., Lothians region*
McMahon, Michael, *Lab., Hamilton North and Bellshill*, maj. 5,606
MacMillan, Ms Maureen, *Lab., Highlands and Islands region*
McNeil, Duncan, *Lab., Greenock and Inverclyde*, maj. 4,313
McNeill, Ms Pauline, *Lab., Glasgow Kelvin*, maj. 4,408
McNulty, Des, *Lab., Clydebank and Milngavie*, maj. 4,710
Martin, Paul, *Lab., Glasgow Springburn*, maj. 7,893
Marwick, Ms Tricia, *SNP, Scotland Mid and Fife region*
Matheson, Michael, *SNP, Scotland Central region*
Monteith, Brian, *C., Scotland Mid and Fife region*
Morgan, Alasdair N., MP, *SNP, Galloway and Upper Nithsdale*, maj. 3,201
Morrison, Alasdair, *Lab., Western Isles*, maj. 2,093
Muldoon, Bristow, *Lab., Livingston*, maj. 3,904
Mulligan, Ms Mary, *Lab., Linlithgow*, maj. 2,928
Mundell, David, *C., Scotland South region*
Murray, Ms Elaine, *Lab., Dumfries*, maj. 3,654
Neil, Alex, *SNP, Scotland Central region*
Oldfather, Ms Irene, *Lab., Cunninghame South*, maj. 6,541
Paterson, Gil, *SNP, Scotland Central region*
Peacock, Peter, *Lab., Highlands and Islands region*
Peattie, Ms Cathy, *Lab., Falkirk East*, maj. 4,139
Quinan, Lloyd, *SNP, Scotland West region*
Radcliffe, Ms Nora, *LD, Gordon*, maj. 4,195
Raffan, Keith, *LD, Scotland Mid and Fife region*
Reid, George, *SNP, Scotland Mid and Fife region*
Robison, Ms Shona, *SNP, Scotland North East region*
Robson, Euan, *LD, Roxburgh and Berwickshire*, maj. 3,585
Rumbles, Mike, *LD, Aberdeenshire West and Kincardine*, maj. 2,289
Russell, Michael, *SNP, Scotland South region*
Salmond, Alex E. A., MP, *SNP, Banff and Buchan*, maj. 11,292
Scanlon, Mrs Mary, *C., Highlands and Islands region*
Scott, Tavish, *LD, Shetland*, maj. 3,194
Sheridan, Tommy, *SSP, Glasgow region*
Simpson, Richard, *Lab., Ochil*, maj. 1,303
Smith, Ms Elaine, *Lab., Coatbridge and Chryston*, maj. 10,404
Smith, Iain, *LD, Fife North East*, maj. 5,064
Smith, Ms Margaret, *LD, Edinburgh West*, maj. 4,583
Steel, Rt. Hon. Sir David (The Lord Steel of Aikwood), KBE, PC, *LD, Lothians region*
Stephen, Nicol, *LD, Aberdeen South*, maj. 1,760
Stone, Jamie, *LD, Caithness, Sutherland and Easter Ross*, maj. 4,391
Sturgeon, Ms Nicola, *SNP, Glasgow region*
Swinney, John R., MP, *SNP, Tayside North*, maj. 4,192
Thomson, Ms Elaine, *Lab., Aberdeen North*, maj. 398
Tosh, Murray, *C., Scotland South region*

Turnbull, Ms Karen, *Lab., Clydesdale,* maj. 3,880
Ullrich, Ms Kay, *SNP, Scotland West region*
Wallace, Ben, *C., Scotland North East region*
Wallace, James R., MP, *LD, Orkney,* maj. 4,619
Watson, Mike (The Lord Watson of Invergowrie), *Lab., Glasgow Cathcart,* maj. 5,374
Welsh, Andrew P., MP, *SNP, Angus,* maj. 8,901
Welsh, Ian, *Lab., Ayr,* maj. 25
White, Ms Sandra, *SNP, Glasgow region*
Whitefield, Ms Karen, *Lab., Airdrie and Shotts,* maj. 8,985
Wilson, Allan, *Lab., Cunninghame North,* maj. 4,796
Wilson, Andrew, *SNP, Scotland Central region*
Young, John, *C., Scotland West region*

CONSTITUTENCIES - WALES

ABERAVON
(S. Wales West)
E. 49,786   *T.* 46.79%

B. Gibbons, *Lab.*	11,941
Ms J. Davies, *PC*	5,198
K. Davies, *LD*	3,165
Ms M. E. Davies, *C.*	1,624
Beany, *Bean*	849
D. Pudner, *United Soc.*	517

Lab. majority 6,743

ALYN AND DEESIDE
(Wales N.)
E. 59,386   *T.* 32.04%

T. Middlehurst, *Lab.*	9,772
N. Formstone, *C.*	3,413
Ms A. Owen, *PC*	2,304
J. Clarke, *LD*	1,879
J. Cooksey, *Ind.*	1,333
G. Davies, *Comm.*	329

Lab. majority 6,359

BLAENAU GWENT
(S. Wales East)
E. 53,919   *T.* 48.21%

P. Law, *Lab. Co-op.*	16,069
P. Williams, *PC*	5,501
K. Rogers, *LD*	2,980
D. Thomas, *C.*	1,444

Lab. Co-op. majority 10,568

BRECON AND RADNORSHIRE
(Wales Mid and W.)
E. 51,166   *T.* 57.10%

Ms K. Williams, *LD*	13,022
N. Bourne, *C.*	7,170
I. Janes, *Lab. Co-op.*	5,165
D. Patterson, *PC*	2,356
M. Shaw, *Ind.*	1,502

LD majority 5,852

BRIDGEND
(S. Wales West)
E. 60,234   *T.* 41.56%

C. Jones, *Lab.*	9,321
A. Cairns, *C.*	5,063
J. Canning, *PC*	4,919
R. Humphreys, *LD*	3,910
A. Jones, *Ind.*	1,819

Lab. majority 4,258

CAERNARFON
(Wales N.)
E. 47,213   *T.* 60.32%

D. Wigley, *PC*	18,748
T. Jones, *Lab.*	6,475

Ms B. Naish, *C.*	2,464
D. Shankland, *LD*	791

PC majority 12,273

CAERPHILLY
(S. Wales East)
E. 65,997   *T.* 43.20%

R. Davies, *Lab.*	12,602
R. Gough, *PC*	9,741
M. German, *LD*	3,543
Ms M. Taylor, *C.*	2,213
T. Richards, *United Soc.*	412

Lab. majority 2,861

CARDIFF CENTRAL
(S. Wales Central)
E. 57,815   *T.* 44.75%

Ms J. Randerson, *LD*	10,937
M. Drakeford, *Lab.*	7,769
O. J. Thomas, *PC*	3,795
S. Jones, *C.*	3,034
J. Goss, *United Soc.*	338

LD majority 3,168

CARDIFF NORTH
(S. Wales Central)
E. 61,398   *T.* 51.33%

Ms S. Essex, *Lab.*	12,198
J. Morgan, *C.*	9,894
A. Meikle, *LD*	5,088
C. Mann, *PC*	4,337

Lab. majority 2,304

CARDIFF SOUTH AND PENARTH
(S. Wales Central)
E. 61,149   *T.* 37.67%

Ms L. Barrett, *Lab. Co-op.*	11,057
Ms M. Davies, *C.*	4,254
J. Rowlands, *PC*	3,931
Ms J. Maw-Cornish, *LD*	2,890
D. Bartlett, *United Soc.*	355
J. Foreman, *Ind. Lab.*	339
T. Davies, *Celtic All.*	210

Lab. Co-op. majority 6,803

CARDIFF WEST
(S. Wales Central)
E. 57,717   *T.* 40.22%

R. Morgan, *Lab.*	14,305
Ms M. Boult, *C.*	3,446
Ms E. Bush, *PC*	3,402
D. Garrow-Smith, *LD*	2,063

Lab. majority 10,859

CARMARTHEN EAST AND DINEFWR
(Wales Mid and W.)
E. 53,634   *T.* 60.88%

R. Thomas, *PC*	17,328
C. Llewellyn, *Lab.*	10,348
Ms H. Stoddart, *C.*	2,776
Ms J. Hughes, *LD*	2,202

PC majority 6,980

CARMARTHEN WEST AND PEMBROKESHIRE SOUTH
(Wales Mid and W.)
E. 55,655   *T.* 50.58%

Ms C. Gwyther, *Lab.*	9,891
R. Llewellyn, *PC*	8,399
D. Edwards, *C.*	5,079
E. Davies, *Ind.*	2,090
R. Williams, *LD*	1,875
G. Fry, *TFPW*	815

Lab. majority 1,492

CEREDIGION
(Wales Mid and W.)
E. 55,311   *T.* 57.67%

E. Jones, *PC*	15,258
Ms M. Battle, *Lab.*	5,009
D. Lloyd Evans, *Ind.*	4,114
D. Evans, *LD*	3,571
H. Lloyd Davies, *C.*	2,944
D. Bradney, *Green*	1,002
PC majority 10,249	

CLWYD SOUTH
(Wales N.)
E. 53,843   *T.* 40.51%

Ms K. Sinclair, *Lab.*	9,196
H. Williams, *PC*	5,511
D. R. Jones, *C.*	4,167
D. Burnham, *LD*	2,432
M. Jones, *United Soc.*	508
Lab. majority 3,685	

CLWYD WEST
(Wales N.)
E. 53,952   *T.* 46.77%

A. Pugh, *Lab.*	7,824
R. Richards, *C.*	7,064
Ms E. Williams, *PC*	6,886
Ms R. Feeley, *LD*	3,462
Lab. majority 760	

CONWY
(Wales N.)
E. 55,189   *T.* 49.11%

G. Jones, *PC*	8,285
Ms C. Sherrington, *Lab.*	8,171
D. I. Jones, *C.*	5,006
Ms C. Humphreys, *LD*	4,480
G. Edwards, *Ind.*	1,160
PC majority 114	

CYNON VALLEY
(S. Wales Central)
E. 47,619   *T.* 45.50%

Ms C. Chapman, *Lab. Co-op.*	9,883
P. Richards, *PC*	9,206
Ms A. Willott, *LD*	1,531
E. Hayward, *C.*	1,046
Lab. Co-op. majority 677	

DELYN
(Wales N.)
E. 54,047   *T.* 44.13%

Ms A. Halford, *Lab.*	10,672
Ms K. Lumley, *C.*	5,255
Ms M. Ellis, *PC*	4,837
Ms E. Burnham, *LD*	3,089
Lab. majority 5,417	

GOWER
(S. Wales West)
E. 58,523   *T.* 47.33%

Ms E. Hart, *Lab.*	9,813
D. Jones, *PC*	6,653
A. Jones, *C.*	3,912
H. Evans, *LD*	3,260
R. Lewis, *Ind.*	2,307
I. Richard, *PRP*	1,755
Lab. majority 3,160	

ISLWYN
(S. Wales East)
E. 50,600   *T.* 47.29%

B. Hancock, *PC*	10,042

S. Williams, *Lab.*	9,438
Ms C. Bennett, *LD*	2,351
C. Stevens, *C.*	1,621
I. Thomas, *United Soc.*	475
PC majority 604	

LLANELLI
(Wales Mid and W.)
E. 58,371   *T.* 48.63%

Ms H. M. Jones, *PC*	11,973
Ms A. Garrard, *Lab. Co-op.*	11,285
T. Dumper, *LD*	2,920
B. Harding, *C.*	1,864
A. Popham, *Ind.*	345
PC majority 688	

MEIRIONNYDD NANT CONWY
(Wales Mid and W.)
E. 32,922   *T.* 57.33%

D. Elis Thomas, *PC*	12,034
Ms D. Jones, *Lab.*	3,292
O. J. Williams, *C.*	2,170
G. Worley, *LD*	1,378
PC majority 8,742	

MERTHYR TYDFIL AND RHYMNEY
(S. Wales East)
E. 55,858   *T.* 44.91%

H. Lewis, *Lab. Co-op.*	11,024
A. Cox, *PC*	6,810
A. Rogers, *Ind.*	3,746
E. Jones, *LD*	1,682
Ms C. Hyde, *C.*	1,246
M. Jenkins, *United Soc.*	580
Lab. Co-op. majority 4,214	

MONMOUTH
(S. Wales East)
E. 61,999   *T.* 51.13%

D. Davies, *C.*	12,950
Ms C. Short, *Lab.*	10,238
C. Lines, *LD*	4,639
M. Hubbard, *PC*	1,964
A. Carrington, *TFPW*	1,911
C. majority 2,712	

MONTGOMERYSHIRE
(Wales Mid and W.)
E. 43,386   *T.* 49.41%

M. Bates, *LD*	10,374
G. Davies, *C.*	4,870
D. Senior, *PC*	3,554
C. Hewitt, *Lab.*	2,638
LD majority 5,504	

NEATH
(S. Wales West)
E. 56,085   *T.* 47.95%

Ms G. Thomas, *Lab.*	12,234
T. Jones, *PC*	9,616
D. Davies, *LD*	2,631
Ms J. Chambers, *C.*	1,895
N. Duncan, *United Soc.*	519
Lab. majority 2,618	

NEWPORT EAST
(S. Wales East)
E. 54,196   *T.* 35.45%

J. Griffiths, *Lab. Co-op.*	9,497
M. Major, *C.*	4,386
A. Cameron, *LD*	2,684
C. Holland, *PC*	2,647
Lab. Co-op. majority 5,111	

NEWPORT WEST
(S. Wales East)
E. 57,243   *T.* 42.34%
Ms R. Butler, *Lab.*	11,538
W. Graham, *C.*	6,828
R. Vickery, *PC*	3,053
Ms V. Watkins, *LD*	2,820

Lab. majority 4,710

OGMORE
(S. Wales West)
E. 51,998   *T.* 41.54%
Ms J. Gregory, *Lab.*	10,407
J. Rogers, *PC*	5,842
R. Hughes, *Ind.*	2,439
Ms S. Waye, *LD*	1,496
C. Smart, *C.*	1,415

Lab. majority 4,565

PONTYPRIDD
(S. Wales Central)
E. 64,597   *T.* 45.71%
Ms J. Davidson, *Lab.*	11,330
B. Hancock, *PC*	9,755
G. Orsi, *LD*	5,240
Ms S. Ingerfield, *C.*	2,485
P. Phillips, *Ind.*	436
R. Griffiths, *Comm.*	280

Lab. majority 1,575

PRESELI PEMBROKESHIRE
(Wales Mid and W.)
E. 54,225   *T.* 53.63%
R. Edwards, *Lab.*	9,977
C. Bryant, *PC*	7,239
F. Aubel, *C.*	6,585
D. Lloyd, *LD*	3,338
A. Luke, *Ind.*	1,944

Lab. majority 2,738

RHONDDA
(S. Wales Central)
E. 55,398   *T.* 50.22%
G. Davies, *PC*	13,558
W. David, *Lab.*	11,273
M. Williams, *LD*	1,303
G. Summers, *Ind.*	913
P. Hobbins, *C.*	774

PC majority 2,285

SWANSEA EAST
(S. Wales West)
E. 57,766   *T.* 36.07%
Ms V. Feld, *Lab.*	9,495
J. Ball, *PC*	5,714
P. Black, *LD*	3,963
W.Hughes, *C.*	1,663

Lab. majority 3,781

SWANSEA WEST
(S. Wales West)
E. 59,369   *T.* 39.97%
A. Davies, *Lab.*	8,217
D. Lloyd, *PC*	6,291
P. Valerio, *C.*	3,643
J. Newbury, *LD*	3,543
D. Evans, *Ind.*	996
J. Harris, *PRP*	774
A. Thraves, *United Soc.*	263

Lab. majority 1,926

TORFAEN
(S. Wales East)
E. 61,037   *T.* 39.19%

Ms L. Neagle, *Lab.*	9,080
M. Gough, *Ind. Lab.*	3,795
Ms I. Nutt, *Ind.*	2,828
N. Turner, *PC*	2,614
Ms J. Gray, *LD*	2,614
Ms K. Thomas, *C.*	2,152
S. Smith, *Local Soc.*	839

Lab. majority 5,285

VALE OF CLWYD
(Wales N.)
E. 51,124   *T.* 43.43%
Ms A. Jones, *Lab.*	8,359
R. Salisbury, *C.*	5,018
Ms S. Brynach, *PC*	4,295
G. Clague, *Dem. All.*	1,908
P. Lloyd, *LD*	1,376
D. Roberts, *Ind.*	661
D. Pennant, *Ind.*	586

Lab. majority 3,341

VALE OF GLAMORGAN
(S. Wales Central)
E. 67,804   *T.* 48.31%
Ms J. Hutt, *Lab.*	11,448
D. Melding, *C.*	10,522
C. Franks, *PC*	7,848
F. Little, *LD*	2,938

Lab. majority 926

WREXHAM
(Wales N.)
E. 50,932   *T.* 34.19%
J. Marek, *Lab.*	9,239
Ms C. O'Toole, *LD*	2,767
Ms F. Elphick, *C.*	2,747
Ms J. Ryder, *PC*	2,659

Lab. majority 6,472

YNYS MON
(Wales N.)
E. 52,571   *T.* 59.56%
I. W. Jones, *PC*	16,469
A. Owen, *Lab.*	7,181
P. Rogers, *C.*	6,031
J. Clarke, *LD*	1,630

PC majority 9,288

REGIONS

SOUTH WALES CENTRAL
E. 473,494   *T.* 45.51%
Lab.	79,564 (36.92%)
PC	58,080 (26.95%)
C.	34,944 (16.22%)
LD	30,911 (14.35%)
Green	5,336 (2.48%)
Soc. Lab.	2,822 (1.31%)
Ind. Matt.	1,524 (0.71%)
NLP	665 (0.31%)
Comm.	652 (0.30%)
United Soc.	602 (0.28%)
Ind. Phill.	378 (0.18%)

Lab. majority 21,484
(May 1997, Lab. maj. 131,398)
Additional Members elected: J. Morgan, *C.*; D. Melding, *C.*;
Ms P. Jarman, *PC;* O. J. Thomas, *PC*

SOUTH WALES EAST
E. 460,846   *T.* 43.95%

Lab.	83,953 (41.45%)
PC	49,139 (24.26%)
C.	33,947 (16.76%)
LD	24,757 (12.22%)
Soc. Lab.	4,879 (2.41%)
Green	4,055 (2.00%)
United Soc.	903 (0.45%)
NLP	898 (0.44%)

Lab. majority 34,814
(May 1997, Lab. maj. 163,134)
Additional Members elected: W. Graham, *C.*; M. German, *LD*; Ms J. Davies, *PC*; Dr P. Williams, *PC*

SOUTH WALES WEST
E. 393,758   *T.* 42.44%

Lab.	70,625 (42.26%)
PC	50,757 (30.37%)
C.	20,993 (12.56%)
LD	18,527 (11.09%)
Green	4,082 (2.44%)
United Soc.	1,257 (0.75%)
NLP	676 (0.40%)
PRP	204 (0.12%)

Lab. majority 19,868
(May 1997, Lab. maj. 142,286)
Additional Members elected: A. Cairns, *C.*; P. Black, *LD*; Dr D. Lloyd, *PC*; Ms J. Davies, *PC*

WALES MID AND WEST
E. 404,667   *T.* 54.21%

PC	84,554 (38.55%)
Lab.	53,842 (24.55%)
C.	36,622 (16.70%)
LD	31,683 (14.44%)
Green	7,718 (3.52%)
Soc. Lab.	3,019 (1.38%)
Ind. Turner	1,214 (0.55%)
NLP	705 (0.32%)

PC majority 30,712
(May 1997, Lab. maj. 52,382)
Additional Members elected: G. Davies, *C.*; Prof. N. Bourne, *C.*; A. Michael, *Lab.*; C. Dafis, *PC*

WALES NORTH
E. 478,252   *T.* 45.06%

Lab.	73,673 (34.19%)
PC	69,518 (32.26%)
C.	41,700 (19.35%)
LD	22,130 (10.27%)
Green	4,667 (2.17%)
Rhuddlan	1,353 (0.63%)
NLP	917 (0.43%)
United Soc.	828 (0.38%)
Comm.	714 (0.33%)

Lab. majority 4,155
(May 1997, Lab. maj. 80,590)
Additional Members elected: P. Rogers, *C.*; R. Richards, *C.*; Ms C. Humphreys, *LD*; Ms J. Ryder, *PC*

MEMBERS OF THE WELSH ASSEMBLY

Barrett, Ms Lorraine, *Lab. Co-op., Cardiff South and Penarth*, maj. 6,803
Bates, Mick, *LD, Montgomeryshire*, maj. 5,504
Black, Peter, *LD, South Wales West region*
Bourne, Prof. Nicholas, *C., Wales Mid and West region*
Butler, Ms Rosemary, *Lab., Newport West*, maj. 4,710
Cairns, Alun, *C., South Wales West region*
Chapman, Ms Christine, *Lab. Co-op., Cynon Valley*, maj. 677
Dafis, Cynog G., MP, *PC, Wales Mid and West region*
Davidson, Ms Jane, *Lab., Pontypridd*, maj. 1,575
Davies, Andrew, *Lab., Swansea West*, maj. 1,926
Davies, David, *C., Monmouth*, maj. 2,712
Davies, Geraint, *PC, Rhondda*, maj. 2,285
Davies, Glyn, *C., Wales Mid and West region*
Davies, Ms Janet, *PC, South Wales West region*
Davies, Ms Jocelyn, *PC, South Wales East region*
Davies, Rt. Hon. Ronald, MP, *Lab., Caerphilly*, maj. 2,861
Edwards, Richard, *Lab., Preseli Pembrokeshire*, maj. 2,738
Elis Thomas, Dafydd, *PC, Meirionnydd Nant Conwy*, maj. 8,742
Essex, Ms Sue, *Lab., Cardiff North*, maj. 2,304
Feld, Ms Val, *Lab., Swansea East*, maj. 3,781
German, Michael, *LD, South Wales East region*
Gibbons, Brian, *Lab., Aberavon*, maj. 6,743
Graham, William, *C., South Wales East region*
Gregory, Ms Janice, *Lab., Ogmore*, maj. 4,565
Griffiths, John, *Lab. Co-op., Newport East*, maj. 5,111
Gwyther, Ms Christine, *Lab., Carmarthen West and Pembrokeshire South*, maj. 1,492
Halford, Ms Alison, *Lab., Delyn*, maj. 5,417
Hancock, Brian, *PC, Islwyn*, maj. 604
Hart, Ms Edwina, *Lab., Gower*, maj. 3,160
Humphreys, Ms Christine, *LD, Wales North region*
Hutt, Ms Jane, *Lab., Vale of Glamorgan*, maj. 926
Jarman, Ms Pauline, *PC, South Wales Central region*

Jones, Ms Ann, *Lab., Vale of Clwyd*, maj. 3,341
Jones, Carwyn, *Lab., Bridgend*, maj. 4,258
Jones, Elin, *PC, Ceredigion*, maj. 10,249
Jones, Gareth, *PC, Conwy*, maj. 114
Jones, Ms Helen Mary, *PC, Llanelli*, maj. 688
Jones, Ieuan W., MP, *PC, Ynys Môn*, maj. 9,288
Law, Peter, *Lab. Co-op., Blaenau Gwent*, maj. 10,568
Lewis, Huw, *Lab. Co-op., Merthyr Tydfil and Rhymney*, maj. 4,214
Lloyd, Dr David, *PC, South Wales West region*
Marek, John, MP, PH.D., *Lab., Wrexham*, maj. 6,472
Melding, David, *C., South Wales Central region*
Michael, Rt. Hon. Alun E., MP, *Lab., Wales Mid and West region*
Middlehurst, Tom, *Lab., Alyn and Deeside*, maj. 6,359
Morgan, H. Rhodri, MP, *Lab., Cardiff West*, maj. 10,859
Morgan, Jonathan, *C., South Wales Central region*
Neagle, Ms Lynne, *Lab., Torfaen*, maj. 5,285
Pugh, Alun, *Lab., Clwyd West*, maj. 760
Randerson, Ms Jenny, *LD, Cardiff Central*, maj. 3,168
Richards, Rod, *C., Wales North region*
Rogers, Peter, *C., Wales North region*
Ryder, Ms Janet, *PC, Wales North region*
Sinclair, Ms Karen, *Lab., Clwyd South*, maj. 3,685
Thomas, Ms Gwenda, *Lab., Neath*, maj. 2,618
Thomas, Owen John, *PC, South Wales Central region*
Thomas, Rhodri, *PC, Carmarthen East and Dinefwr*, maj. 6,980
Wigley, Rt. Hon. Dafydd, MP, *PC, Caernarfon*, maj. 12,273
Williams, Ms Kirsty, *LD, Brecon and Radnorshire*, maj. 5,852
Williams, Dr Phil, *PC, South Wales East region*